S0-DSP-525

PETERSON'S

GRADUATE & PROFESSIONAL PROGRAMS

AN OVERVIEW

2003

THIRTY-SEVENTH EDITION

BOOK 1

THOMSON
PETERSON'S™

AUSTRALIA • CANADA • MEXICO • SINGAPORE • SPAIN • UNITED KINGDOM • UNITED STATES

About The Thomson Corporation and Peterson's

With revenues of US$7.2 billion, The Thomson Corporation (www.thomson.com) is a leading global provider of integrated information solutions for business, education, and professional customers. Its Learning businesses and brands (www.thomsonlearning.com) serve the needs of individuals, learning institutions, and corporations with products and services for both traditional and distributed learning.

Peterson's, part of The Thomson Corporation, is one of the nation's most respected providers of lifelong learning online resources, software, reference guides, and books. The Education Supersite℠ at www.petersons.com—the Internet's most heavily traveled education resource—has searchable databases and interactive tools for contacting U.S.-accredited institutions and programs. In addition, Peterson's serves more than 105 million education consumers annually.

For more information, contact Peterson's, 2000 Lenox Drive, Lawrenceville, NJ 08648; 800-338-3282; or find us on the World Wide Web at www.petersons.com/about.

ISSN 1520-4359
ISBN 0-7689-0810-8

Printed in the United States of America

10 9 8 7 6 5 4 3 2 1 05 04 03

Contents

Introduction

How to Use These Guides

OVERVIEW

The six volumes of Peterson's Annual Guides to Graduate Study, the only annually updated reference work of its kind, provide wide-ranging information on the graduate and professional programs offered by accredited colleges and universities in the United States and U.S. territories and by those institutions in Canada, Mexico, Europe, and Africa that are accredited by U.S. accrediting bodies. More than 36,000 individual academic and professional programs at more than 1,800 institutions are listed. Peterson's Annual Guides to Graduate Study have been used for more than thirty-five years by prospective graduate and professional students, placement counselors, faculty advisers, and all others interested in postbaccalaureate education.

Book 1, *Graduate & Professional Programs: An Overview*, contains information on institutions as a whole. Books 2 through 6 are devoted to specific academic and professional fields:

- Book 2—*Graduate Programs in the Humanities, Arts & Social Sciences*
- Book 3—*Graduate Programs in the Biological Sciences*
- Book 4—*Graduate Programs in the Physical Sciences, Mathematics, Agricultural Sciences, the Environment & Natural Resources*
- Book 5—*Graduate Programs in Engineering & Applied Sciences*
- Book 6—*Graduate Programs in Business, Education, Health, Information Studies, Law & Social Work*

The books may be used individually or as a set. For example, if you have chosen a field of study but do not know what institution you want to attend or if you have a college or university in mind but have not chosen an academic field of study, the best place to begin is Book 1.

Book 1 presents several directories to help you identify programs of study that might interest you; you can then research those programs further in Books 2 through 6. The Directory of Graduate and Professional Programs by Field lists the 452 fields for which there are program directories in Books 2 through 6 and gives the names of those institutions that offer graduate degree programs in each. Degrees granted are also indicated.

For geographical or financial reasons, you may be interested in attending a particular institution and will want to know what it has to offer. You should turn to the Directory of Institutions and Their Offerings, which lists the degree programs available at each institution, again, in the 452 academic and professional fields for which Books 2 through 6 have program directories. As in the Graduate and Professional Programs by Field directory, the level of degrees offered is also indicated.

CLASSIFICATION OF PROGRAMS

After you identify the particular programs and institutions that interest you, use both Book 1 and the specialized volumes to obtain detailed information—Book 1 for information on the institutions overall and Books 2 through 6 for details about the individual graduate units and their degree programs.

Books 2 through 6 are divided into sections that contain one or more directories devoted to programs in a particular field. If you do not find a directory devoted to your field of interest in a specific book, consult the Index of Directories and Subject Areas in Books 2–6; this index appears at the end of each book. After you have identified the correct book, consult the Index of Directories and Subject Areas in This Book, which shows (as does the more general directory) what directories cover subjects not specifically named in a directory or section title. This index in Book 2, for example, will tell you that if you are interested in sculpture, you should see the directory entitled Art/Fine Arts. The Art/Fine Arts entry will direct you to the proper page.

Books 2 through 6 have a number of general directories. These directories have entries for the largest unit at an institution granting graduate degrees in that field. For example, the general Engineering and Applied Sciences directory in Book 5 consists of profiles for colleges, schools, and departments of engineering and applied sciences.

General directories are followed by other directories, or sections, in Books 3, 5, and 6, that give more detailed information about programs in particular areas of the general field that has been covered. The general Psychology directory, in the example above, is followed by fourteen directories in specific areas of psychology, such as Clinical Psychology, Health Psychology, and School Psychology.

Because of the broad nature of many fields, any system of organization is bound to involve a certain amount of overlap. Environmental studies, for example, is a field whose various aspects are studied in several types of departments and schools. Readers interested in such studies will find information on relevant programs in Book 3 under Ecology and Environmental Biology; in Book 4 under Environmental Management and Policy and Natural Resources; in Book 5 under Energy Management and Policy and Environmental Engineering; and in Book 6 under Environmental and Occupational Health. To help you find all of the programs of interest to you, the introduction to each section of Books 2 through 6 includes, if applicable, a paragraph suggesting other sections and directories with information on related areas of study to consult.

SCHOOL AND PROGRAM INFORMATION

In all of the books, information is presented in three forms: profiles (capsule summaries of basic information) and short announcements and In-Depth Descriptions, which are written by graduate school and program administrators. The format of the profiles is constant, making it easy to compare one institution with another and one program with another. The Book 1 profile description is found immediately preceding the profiles. A number of graduate school and program administrators have attached brief announcements to the end of their profile listings. In them you will find information that an institution or program wants to emphasize. The In-Depth Descriptions are by their very nature more expansive and flexible than the profiles, and the administrators who have written them may emphasize different aspects of their programs. All of these In-Depth Descriptions are organized in the same way (with the exception of a few that describe research and training opportunities instead of degree programs), and in each one you will find information on the same basic topics, such as programs of study, research facilities, tuition and fees, financial aid, and application procedures. If an institution or program has submitted an In-Depth Description, a boldface cross-reference appears below its profiles. As with the profile announcements, all of the In-Depth Descriptions in the guides have been submitted by choice; the absence of an announcement or In-Depth Description does not reflect any type of editorial judgment on the part of Peterson's.

Interdisciplinary Programs (Books 2–6)

In addition to the regular directories that present profiles of programs in each field of study, many sections in Books 2 through 6 contain special notices under the heading Cross-Discipline Announcements. Appearing at the end of the profiles in many sections, these Cross-Discipline Announcements inform you about programs that you may find of interest described in a different section. A biochemistry department, for example, may place a notice under Cross-Discipline Announcements in the Chemistry section (Book 4) to alert chemistry students to their current description in the Biochemistry section of Book 3. Cross-discipline announcements, also written by administrators to highlight their programs, will be helpful to you not only in finding out about programs in fields related to your own but also in locating departments that are actively recruiting students with a specific undergraduate major.

Data Collection and Editorial Procedures

DIRECTORIES AND PROFILES

The information published in the directories and profiles of all the books is collected through Peterson's Annual Survey of Graduate and Professional Institutions. The survey is sent each spring and summer to more than 1,800 institutions offering postbaccalaureate degree programs, including accredited institutions in the United States and U.S. territories and those institutions in Canada, Mexico, Europe, and Africa that are accredited by U.S. accrediting bodies. Deans and other administrators complete these surveys, providing information on programs in the 452 academic and professional fields covered in the guides as well as overall institutional information. Peterson's staff then goes over each returned survey carefully and verifies or revises responses after further research and discussion with administrators at the institutions. Extensive files on past responses are kept from year to year.

While every effort has been made to ensure the accuracy and completeness of the data, information is sometimes unavailable or changes occur after publication deadlines. All usable information received in time for publication has been included. The omission of any particular item from a directory or profile signifies either that the item is not applicable to the institution or program or that information was not available. Profiles of programs scheduled to begin during the 2002–03 academic year cannot, obviously, include statistics on enrollment or, in many cases, the number of faculty members. If no usable data were submitted by an institution, its name, address, and program name where appropriate nonetheless appear in order to indicate the availability of graduate work.

ANNOUNCEMENTS AND IN-DEPTH DESCRIPTIONS

The announcements and In-Depth Descriptions are supplementary insertions submitted by deans, chairs, and other administrators who wish to make an additional, more individualized statement to readers. Those who have chosen to write these insertions are responsible for the accuracy of the content, but Peterson's editors have reserved the right to delete irrelevant material or questionable self-appraisals and to edit for style. Statements regarding a university's objectives and accomplishments are a reflection of its own beliefs and are not the opinions of the editors. Since inclusion of announcements and descriptions is by choice, their presence or absence in the guides should not be taken as an indication of status, quality, or approval.

The Graduate Adviser

This section includes two essays and information about accreditation. The first essay, The Admissions Process, discusses general admission requirements, admission tests, factors to consider when selecting a graduate school or program, when and how to apply, and how admission decisions are made. Also included is special information for international students. The second essay, Financial Support, is an overview of the broad range of support available at the graduate level. Fellowships, scholarships, and grants; assistantships and internships; federal and private loan programs, as well as Federal Work-Study; and the GI bill are detailed. This essay concludes with advice on applying for need-based financial aid. Accreditation and Accrediting Agencies gives information on accreditation and its purpose and lists first institutional accrediting agencies and then specialized accrediting agencies.

This section is filled with crucial information for all students; it is addressed to the reader who is still in college but also contains information for anyone who is thinking about pursuing a graduate degree.

The Admissions Process

Generalizations about graduate admissions practices are not always helpful because each institution has its own set of guidelines and procedures. Nevertheless, some broad statements can be made about the admissions process that may help you plan your strategy.

General Requirements

All graduate schools and departments have some requirements that applicants for admission must meet. Typically, these requirements include undergraduate transcripts (which provide information about undergraduate grade point average and course work applied toward a major), admission test scores, and letters of recommendation. In some fields, such as art and music, portfolios or auditions may be required in addition to other evidence of talent. Some institutions require that the applicant have an undergraduate degree in the same subject as the intended graduate major.

Most institutions evaluate each applicant on the basis of the applicant's total record, and the weight accorded any given factor varies widely from institution to institution and from program to program.

Admission Tests

Two major testing programs are used in graduate admissions: the Graduate Record Examinations (GRE) testing program, sponsored by the GRE Board and administered by Educational Testing Service, Princeton, New Jersey, and the Miller Analogies Test, produced by The Psychological Corporation, San Antonio, Texas.

As of October 1, 2002, the Graduate Record Examinations testing program consists of a General Test and eight Subject Tests. The General Test measures verbal and quantitative skills and analytical writing skills. The verbal section takes 30 minutes, the quantitative section, 45. The analytical writing section measures proficiency in critical thinking and analytical writing ability. It consists of two analytical writing tasks: a 45-minute "Present Your Perspective on an Issue" task and a 30-minute "Analyze an Argument" task. The General Test is available on computer at test centers around the world.

The Subject Tests measure achievement and assume undergraduate majors or extensive background in the following eight disciplines:

- Biochemistry, Cell and Molecular Biology
- Biology
- Chemistry
- Computer Science
- Literature in English
- Mathematics
- Physics
- Psychology

Testing time is approximately 2 hours and 50 minutes. The Subject Tests are available at regularly scheduled paper-based administrations at test centers around the world.

You can obtain more information about the GRE tests by consulting the *GRE Information and Registration Bulletin* or visiting the GRE Web site at www.gre.org. The *Bulletin* can be obtained at many undergraduate colleges. You can also download it from the GRE Web site or obtain it by contacting Graduate Record Examinations, Educational Testing Service, P.O. Box 6000, Princeton, NJ 08541-6000, telephone 1-609-771-7670.

If you expect to apply for admission to a program that requires any of the GRE tests, you should select a test date well in advance of the application deadline. Score reporting for the computer-based tests takes approximately ten to fifteen days. Score reporting for the paper-based tests takes approximately six weeks.

The Miller Analogies Test is administered at more than 600 licensed testing centers in the United States and Canada. Testing time is 50 minutes. The test consists entirely of analogies. You can obtain a list of test centers and a Bulletin of Information, which contains instructions for taking the test, by writing to The Psychological Corporation, Controlled Test Center, 555 Academic Court, San Antonio, Texas 78204; 800-622-3231.

Factors Involved in Selecting a Graduate School or Program

Selecting a graduate school and a specific program of study is a complex matter. Program and course offerings; the nature, size, and location of the institution; admission requirements; cost; and the availability of financial assistance are among the many factors that affect one's choice of institution. Other considerations are the quality of the faculty, the job placement and achievements of the program's graduates, and the institution's resources, such as libraries, laboratories, and computer facilities. If you are to make the best possible choice, you need to learn as much as you can about the schools and programs you are considering before you apply.

The following steps may help you narrow your choices.

- Talk to alumni of the programs or institutions you are considering to get their impressions of how well they were prepared for work in their fields of study.
- Remember that graduate school requirements change, so be sure to get the most up-to-date information possible.
- Talk to department faculty and the graduate adviser at your undergraduate institution. They often have information about programs of study at other institutions.
- Visit the Web sites of the graduate schools in which you are interested to request a graduate catalog. Contact the department chair in your chosen field of study for additional information about the department and the field.
- Visit as many campuses as possible. Call ahead for an appointment with the graduate adviser in your field of interest and be sure to check out the facilities and talk to students.

When and How to Apply

You should begin the application process at least one year before you expect to begin your graduate study. Find out the application deadline for each institution (many are provided in the profile section of this volume). Go to the institution Web site and find out if you can apply online. If not, request a paper application form. Fill out this form thoroughly and neatly. Assume that the school needs all the information it is requesting and that the admissions officer will be sensitive to the neatness and overall quality of what you submit. Do not supply more information than the school requires.

The institution may ask at least one question that will require a three- or four-paragraph answer. Compose your response on the assumption that the admissions officer is interested in both what you think and how you express yourself. Keep your statement brief and to the point, but, at the same time, include all pertinent information about your past experiences and your educational goals. Individual statements vary greatly in style and content, which helps admissions officers to differentiate among applicants. Many graduate departments give considerable weight to the statement in making their admissions decisions, so be sure to take the time to prepare a thoughtful and concise statement.

If recommendations are a part of the admissions requirements, choose carefully the individuals you ask to write them. It is generally best to ask current or former professors to write the recommendations, provided they are able to attest to your intellectual ability and motivation for doing the work required of a graduate student. It is advisable to provide stamped, preaddressed envelopes to people being asked to submit recommendations on your behalf.

Completed applications, including references and transcripts and admission test scores, should be received at the institution by the specified date.

Be advised that institutions do not usually make admissions decisions until all materials have been received. Enclose a self-addressed postcard with your application, requesting confirmation of receipt. Allow at least 10 days for the return of the postcard before making further inquiries. In addition, if you plan to apply for financial support, it is imperative that you file your application early.

How Admission Decisions Are Made

The program you apply to is directly involved in the admissions process. Although the final decision is usually made by the graduate dean (or an associate) or by the faculty admissions committee, recommendations from faculty members in your intended field are important. At some institutions, an interview is incorporated into the decision process.

A Special Note for International Students

In addition to the steps already described, there are some special considerations for international students who intend to apply for graduate study in the United States. All graduate schools require an indication of competence in English. The purpose of the Test of English as a Foreign Language (TOEFL) is to evaluate the English proficiency of people who are nonnative speakers of English and want to study at colleges and universities where English is the language of instruction. The TOEFL is administered by Educational Testing Service (ETS) under the general direction of a policy board established by the College Board and the Graduate Record Examinations Board.

The TOEFL is administered as a computer-based test (CBT) throughout the world and is available year-round by appointment only. (However, over the next year, ETS is closing some CBT centers outside the U.S. and Canada. Visit www.ets.org to see the list.) It is not necessary to have previous computer experience to take the test. The test consists of four sections—listening, structure, reading, and writing. Total testing time is approximately 4 hours. The fee for the computer-based TOEFL is $110, which must be paid in U.S. dollars. The *Information Bulletin for Computer-Based Testing* contains information about the new testing format, registration procedures, and testing sites.

TOEFL will be offered in the paper-based format in the People's Republic of China and in low-volume testing areas. The paper-based TOEFL consists of three sections—listening comprehension, structure and written expression, and reading comprehension. Testing time is approximately 3 hours. The Test of Written English (TWE) is also given. TWE is a 30-minute essay that measures the examinee's ability to compose in English. Examinees receive a TWE score separate from their TOEFL score. The fee for the paper-based TOEFL is $110, which must be paid in U.S. dollars. There is no additional charge for TWE. The *Information Bulletin* contains information on local fees and registration procedures.

Additional information and registration materials are available from the TOEFL Program Office, P.O. Box 6151, Princeton, New Jersey 08541-6151. Telephone: 609-771-7100. E-mail: toefl@ets.org. World Wide Web: http://www.toefl.org.

International students should apply especially early because of the time lags associated with overseas mail. Furthermore, many United States graduate schools have a limited number of spaces for international students, and many more students apply than the schools can accommodate.

Most graduate schools in the United States require international applicants to submit a certification of support, which is a statement attesting to the applicant's financial resources for the period of graduate study. International students may find financial assistance from institutions so limited that they must be essentially self-supporting during graduate study.

Financial Support

The range of financial support at the graduate level is very broad. The following generalized descriptions will give you an idea of what you might expect and what will be expected of you as a financial support recipient.

Fellowships, Scholarships, and Grants

These are usually outright awards of a few hundred to many thousands of dollars with no service to the institution required in return. Fellowships and scholarships are usually awarded on the basis of merit and are highly competitive. Grants are made on the basis of financial need or special talent in a field of study. Many grants not only cover tuition, fees, and supplies but also include stipends for living expenses with allowances for dependents. However, the terms of each grant should be examined because some do not permit recipients to supplement their income with outside work. Fellowships, scholarships, and grants may vary in the number of years for which they are awarded.

Assistantships and Internships

TEACHING ASSISTANTSHIPS

These usually provide a salary and full or partial tuition remission, and they may also provide health benefits. Unlike fellowships, scholarships, and grants, which require no service to the institution, teaching assistantships require recipients to provide the institution with a specific amount of undergraduate teaching, ideally related to the student's field of study. Some teaching assistants are limited to grading papers, compiling bibliographies, or monitoring laboratories. At some graduate schools, teaching assistants must carry lighter course loads than regular full-time students.

RESEARCH ASSISTANTSHIPS

These are very similar to teaching assistantships in the manner in which financial assistance is provided. The difference is that recipients are given basic research assignments in their disciplines rather than teaching responsibilities. The work required is normally related to the student's field of study; in most instances, the assistantship supports the student's thesis or dissertation research.

ADMINISTRATIVE INTERNSHIPS

These are similar to assistantships in application of financial assistance funds, but the student is given an assignment on a part-time basis, usually as a special assistant to one of the university's administrative officers. The assignment may not necessarily be directly related to the recipient's discipline.

DORMITORY AND COUNSELING ASSISTANTSHIPS

These are frequently assigned to graduate students in psychology, counseling, and social work. Duties can vary from being available in a dean's office for a specific number of hours for consultation with undergraduates to living in campus residences and being responsible for both counseling and administrative tasks or advising student activity groups. Dormitory assistantships sometimes include room and board in addition to tuition and stipends.

The GI Bill

This provides financial assistance for students who are veterans of the United States armed forces. If you are a veteran, contact your local Veterans Administration office to determine your eligibility and to get full details about benefits.

Loans

Most graduate students, except those pursuing Ph.D.'s in certain fields, borrow to finance their graduate programs. There are basically two sources of student loans—the federal government and private loan programs. You should read and understand the terms of these loan programs before submitting your loan application.

FEDERAL LOANS

Federal Stafford Loans. The Federal Stafford Loan Program offers government-sponsored, low-interest loans to students through a private lender such as a bank, credit union, or savings and loan association.

There are two components of the Federal Stafford Loan program. Under the *subsidized* component of the program, the federal government pays the interest accruing on the loan while you are enrolled in graduate school on at least a half-time basis. Under the *unsubsidized* component of the program, you pay the interest on the loan from the day proceeds are issued. Eligibility for the federal subsidy is based on demonstrated financial need as determined by the financial aid office from the information you provide on the Free Application for Federal Student Aid (FAFSA). (See "Applying for Need-Based Financial Aid" for more information on the FAFSA.) A cosigner is not required, since the loan is not based on creditworthiness.

Although Unsubsidized Federal Stafford Loans may not be as desirable as Subsidized Federal Stafford Loans from the consumer's perspective, they are a useful source of support for those who may not qualify for the subsidized loans or who need additional financial assistance.

Graduate students may borrow up to $18,500 per year through the Stafford Loan Program, up to a maximum of $138,500, including undergraduate borrowing. This may include up to $8500 in Subsidized Stafford Loans, depending on eligibility, up to a maximum of $65,000, including undergraduate borrowing. The amount of the loan borrowed through the Unsubsidized Stafford Program equals the total amount of the loan (as much $18,500) minus your eligibility for a Subsidized Stafford Loan (as much as $8500). You may borrow up to a maximum of $18,500, minus estimated financial assistance from other federal, state, and private sources.

The interest rate for the Federal Stafford Loans varies annually and is set every July. The rate during in-school, grace, and deferment periods is based on the 91-Day U.S. Treasury Bill rate plus 1.7 percent, capped at 8.25 percent. The rate during repayment is based on the 91-Day U.S. Treasury Bill rate plus 2.3 percent, capped at 8.25 percent. The 2002–03 rate is 4.06 percent.

Two fees may be deducted from the loan proceeds upon disbursement: a guarantee fee of up to 1 percent, which is deposited in an insurance pool to ensure repayment to the lender if the borrower defaults, and a federally mandated 3 percent origination fee, which is used to offset the administrative cost of the Federal Stafford Loan Program.

Under the *subsidized* Federal Stafford Loan Program, repayment begins six months after your last enrollment on at least a half-time basis. Under the *unsubsidized* program, repayment of interest begins within thirty days from disbursement of the loan proceeds, and repayment of the principal begins six months after your last enrollment on at least a half-time basis. Some lenders may require that some payments be made even while you are in school, although most lenders will allow you to defer payments and will add the accrued interest to the loan balance. Under both components of the program repayment may extend over a maximum of ten years with no prepayment penalty.

Federal Direct Loans. Some schools participate in the Department of Education's Direct Lending Program instead of offering Federal Stafford Loans. The two programs are essentially the same except that with the Direct Loans, schools themselves generate the loans with funds provided from the federal government. Terms and interest rates are virtually the same except that there are a few more repayment options with Federal Direct Loans.

Federal Perkins Loans. The Federal Perkins Loan is a long-term loan available to students demonstrating financial need and is administered directly by the school. Not all schools have these funds, and some may award them to undergraduates only. Eligibility is determined from the information you provide on the FAFSA. The school will notify you of your eligibility.

Eligible graduate students may borrow up to $5000 per year, up to a maximum of $30,000, including undergraduate borrowing (even if your previous Perkins Loans have been repaid). The interest rate for Federal Perkins Loans is 5 percent, and no interest accrues while you remain in school at least half-time. There are no guarantee, loan, or disbursement fees. Repayment begins nine months after your last enrollment on at least a half-time basis and may extend over a maximum of ten years with no prepayment penalty.

Deferring Your Federal Loan Repayments. If you borrowed under the Federal Stafford Loan Program or the Federal Perkins Loan Program for previous undergraduate or graduate study, some of your repayments may be deferred (i.e., suspended) when you return to graduate school, depending on when you borrowed and under which program.

There are other deferment options available if you are temporarily unable to repay your loan. Information about these deferments is provided at your entrance and exit interviews. If you believe you are eligible for a deferment of your loan repayments, you must contact your lender to complete a deferment form. The deferment must be filed prior to the time your repayment is due, and it must be refiled when it expires if you remain eligible for deferment at that time.

SUPPLEMENTAL LOANS

Many lending institutions offer supplemental loan programs and other financing plans to students seeking assistance in meeting their expected contribution toward educational expenses.

If you are considering borrowing through a supplemental loan program, you should carefully consider the terms of the program and be sure to "read the fine print." Check with the program sponsor for the most current terms that will be applicable to the amounts you intend to borrow for graduate study. Most supplemental loan programs for graduate study offer unsubsidized, credit-based loans. In general, a credit-ready borrower is one who has a satisfactory credit history or no credit history at all. A creditworthy borrower generally must pass a credit test to be eligible to borrow or act as a cosigner for the loan funds.

Many supplemental loan programs have a minimum annual loan limit and a maximum annual loan limit. Some offer amounts equal to the cost of attendance minus any other aid you will receive for graduate study. If you are planning to borrow for several years of graduate study, consider whether there is a cumulative or aggregate limit on the amount you may borrow. Often this cumulative or aggregate limit will include any amounts you borrowed and have not repaid for undergraduate or previous graduate study.

The combination of the annual interest rate, loan fees, and the repayment terms you choose will determine how much you will repay over time. Compare these features in combination before you decide which loan program to use. Some loans offer interest rates that are adjusted monthly, some quarterly, some annually. Some offer interest rates that are lower during the in-school, grace, and deferment periods, and then increase when you begin repayment. Most programs include a loan "origination" fee, which is usually deducted from the principal amount you receive when the loan is disbursed and must be repaid along with the interest and other principal when you graduate, withdraw from school, or drop below half-time study. Sometimes the loan fees are reduced if you borrow with a qualified cosigner. Some programs allow you to defer interest and/or principal payments while you are enrolled in graduate school. Many programs allow you to capitalize your interest payments; the interest due on your loan is added to the outstanding balance of your loan, so you don't have to repay immediately, but this increases the amount you owe. Other programs allow you to pay the interest as you go, which will reduce the amount you later have to repay.

Federal Work-Study Program (FWS)

Employment is another way some students finance their graduate studies. The federally funded Federal Work-Study Program provides eligible students with employment opportunities, usually in public and private nonprofit organizations. Federal funds pay up to 75 percent of the wages, with the remainder paid by the employing agency. FWS is available to graduate students who demonstrate financial need. Not all schools have these funds, and some only award them to undergraduates. Each school sets its application deadline and work-study earnings limits. Wages vary and are related to the type of work done.

Private Student Loans

In addition to the federal loan programs, there are many private loan programs that can help graduate students. Most private loan programs disburse funds based on creditworthiness rather than financial need. Some loan programs target all types of graduate students; others are designed specifically for business, law, or medical students. In addition, you can use other types of private loans not specifically designed for education to help finance your graduate degree.

CitiAssist Loans. Offered by Citibank, these no-fee loans help graduate students fill the gap between the financial aid they receive and the money they need for school. Visit www.studentloan.com for more loan information from Citibank.

GradEXCEL Loan. This program, sponsored by Nellie Mae, is designed for students who are not ready to borrow on their own and wish to borrow with a creditworthy cosigner. Visit www.nelliemae.com for more information.

Key Alternative Loan. This loan can bridge the gap between education costs and traditional funding. Visit www.keybank.com for more information.

Graduate Access Loan. Sponsored by the Access Group, this is for graduate students enrolled at least half-time. The Web site is www.accessgroup.com.

Signature Student Loan. A loan program for students who are enrolled at least half-time, this is sponsored by Sallie Mae. Visit www.salliemae.com for more information.

Remember that these are generalized statements about financial assistance at the graduate level. Because each institution allots its aid differently, you should communicate directly with the school and the specific department of interest to you. It is not unusual, for example, to find that an endowment vested within a specific department supports one or more fellowships. You may fit its requirements and specifications.

Applying for Need-Based Financial Aid

Schools that award federal and institutional financial assistance based on need will require you to complete the FAFSA and, in some cases, an institutional financial aid application.

If you are applying for federal student assistance, you must complete the FAFSA. A service of the U.S. Department of Education, it is free to all applicants. You must send the FAFSA to the address listed in the FAFSA instructions or you can apply online at http://www.fafsa.ed.gov.

After your FAFSA information has been processed, you will receive a Student Aid Report (SAR). If you are an entering student, you may want to make copies of the SAR and send them to the school(s) to which you are applying. If you are a continuing student, you should make a copy of the SAR and forward the original document to the school you are attending.

Follow the instructions on the FAFSA if your situation changes and you need to correct information reported on your original application.

If you would like more information on federal student financial aid, visit the FAFSA Web site or request *The Student Guide 2002–2003* from the following address: Federal Student Aid Information Center, P.O. Box 84, Washington, DC 20044.

The U.S. Department of Education also has a toll-free number for questions concerning federal student aid programs. The number is 1-800-4-FED AID (1-800-433-3243). If you are hearing impaired, call toll-free, 1-800-730-8913.

Accreditation and Accrediting Agencies

Colleges and universities in the United States, and their individual academic and professional programs, are accredited by nongovernmental agencies concerned with monitoring the quality of education in this country. Agencies with both regional and national jurisdictions grant accreditation to institutions as a whole, while specialized bodies acting on a nationwide basis—often national professional associations—grant accreditation to departments and programs in specific fields.

Institutional and specialized accrediting agencies share the same basic concerns: the purpose an academic unit—whether university or program—has set for itself and how well it fulfills that purpose, the adequacy of its financial and other resources, the quality of its academic offerings, and the level of services it provides. Agencies that grant institutional accreditation take a broader view, of course, and examine university-wide or college-wide services that a specialized agency may not concern itself with.

Both types of agencies follow the same general procedures when considering an application for accreditation. The academic unit prepares a self-evaluation, focusing on the concerns mentioned above and usually including an assessment of both its strengths and weaknesses; a team of representatives of the accrediting body reviews this evaluation, visits the campus, and makes its own report; and finally, the accrediting body makes a decision on the application. Often, even when accreditation is granted, the agency makes a recommendation regarding how the institution or program can improve. All institutions and programs are also reviewed every few years to determine whether they continue to meet established standards; if they do not, they may lose their accreditation.

Accrediting agencies themselves are reviewed and evaluated periodically by the U.S. Department of Education and the Council for Higher Education Accreditation (CHEA). Agencies recognized adhere to certain standards and practices, and their authority in matters of accreditation is widely accepted in the educational community.

This does not mean, however, that accreditation is a simple matter, either for schools wishing to become accredited or for students deciding where to apply. Indeed, in certain fields the very meaning and methods of accreditation are the subject of a good deal of debate. For their part, those applying to graduate school should be aware of the safeguards provided by regional accreditation, especially in terms of degree acceptance and institutional longevity. Beyond this, applicants should understand the role that specialized accreditation plays in their field, as this varies considerably from one discipline to another. In certain professional fields, it is necessary to have graduated from a program that is accredited in order to be eligible for a license to practice, and in some fields the federal government also makes this a hiring requirement. In other disciplines, however, accreditation is not as essential, and there can be excellent programs that are not accredited. In fact, some programs choose not to seek accreditation, although most do.

Institutions and programs that present themselves for accreditation are sometimes granted the status of candidate for accreditation, or what is known as "preaccreditation." This may happen, for example, when an academic unit is too new to have met all the requirements for accreditation. Such status signifies initial recognition and indicates that the school or program in question is working to fulfill all requirements; it does not, however, guarantee that accreditation will be granted.

Readers are advised to contact agencies directly for answers to their questions about accreditation. The names and addresses of all agencies recognized by the U.S. Department of Education and the Council for Higher Education Accreditation are listed here.

Institutional Accrediting Agencies—Regional

MIDDLE STATES ASSOCIATION OF COLLEGES AND SCHOOLS
Accredits institutions in Delaware, District of Columbia, Maryland, New Jersey, New York, Pennsylvania, Puerto Rico, and the Virgin Islands.
Jean Avnet Morse, Executive Director
Commission on Higher Education
3624 Market Street
Philadelphia, Pennsylvania 19104-2680
Telephone: 215-662-5606
Fax: 215-662-5501
E-mail: jmorse@msache.org
World Wide Web: http://www.msache.org

NEW ENGLAND ASSOCIATION OF SCHOOLS AND COLLEGES
Accredits institutions in Connecticut, Maine, Massachusetts, New Hampshire, Rhode Island, and Vermont.
Charles M. Cook, Director
Commission on Institutions of Higher Education
209 Burlington Road
Bedford, Massachusetts 01730-1433
Telephone: 781-271-0022
Fax: 781-271-0950
E-mail: CIHE@neasc.org
World Wide Web: http://www.neasc.org

NORTH CENTRAL ASSOCIATION OF COLLEGES AND SCHOOLS
Accredits institutions in Arizona, Arkansas, Colorado, Illinois, Indiana, Iowa, Kansas, Michigan, Minnesota, Missouri, Nebraska, New Mexico, North Dakota, Ohio, Oklahoma, South Dakota, West Virginia, Wisconsin, and Wyoming.
Steven D. Crow, Executive Director
The Higher Learning Commission
30 North LaSalle Street, Suite 2400
Chicago, Illinois 60602-2504
Telephone: 312-263-0456
Fax: 312-263-7462
E-mail: scrow@hlcommission.org
World Wide Web: http://www.ncahigherlearningcommission.org

NORTHWEST ASSOCIATION OF SCHOOLS AND COLLEGES
Accredits institutions in Alaska, Idaho, Montana, Nevada, Oregon, Utah, and Washington.
Sandra E. Elman, Executive Director
Commission on Colleges and Universities
8060 165th Avenue, NE, Suite 100
Redmond, Washington 98052
Telephone: 425-558-4224
Fax: 425-376-0596
E-mail: pjarnold@nwccu.org
World Wide Web: http://www.nwccu.org

SOUTHERN ASSOCIATION OF COLLEGES AND SCHOOLS
Accredits institutions in Alabama, Florida, Georgia, Kentucky, Louisiana, Mississippi, North Carolina, South Carolina, Tennessee, Texas, and Virginia.
James T. Rogers, Executive Director
Commission on Colleges
1866 Southern Lane
Decatur, Georgia 30033
Telephone: 404-679-4500
Fax: 404-679-4528
E-mail: jrogers@sacscoc.org
World Wide Web: http://www.sacscoc.org

WESTERN ASSOCIATION OF SCHOOLS AND COLLEGES
Accredits institutions in California, Guam, and Hawaii.
Ralph A. Wolff, Executive Director
The Senior College Commission
985 Atlantic Avenue, Suite 100
Alameda, California 94501
Telephone: 510-748-9001
Fax: 510-748-9797
E-mail: rwolff@wascsenior.org
World Wide Web: http://www.wascweb.org

Institutional Accrediting Agencies—Other

ACCREDITING COUNCIL FOR INDEPENDENT COLLEGES AND SCHOOLS
Stephen A. Eggland, Executive Director
750 First Street, NE, Suite 980
Washington, D.C. 20002-4241
Telephone: 202-336-6780
Fax: 202-842-2593
E-mail: steve@acics.org
World Wide Web: http://www.acics.org

DISTANCE EDUCATION AND TRAINING COUNCIL
Accrediting Commission
Michael P. Lambert, Executive Secretary
1601 18th Street, NW
Washington, D.C. 20009
Telephone: 202-234-5100
Fax: 202-332-1386
E-mail: detc@detc.org
World Wide Web: http://www.detc.org

Specialized Accrediting Agencies

[Only Book 1 of Peterson's Annual Guides to Graduate Study includes the complete list of specialized accrediting groups recognized by the U.S. Department of Education and the Council on Higher Education Accreditation (CHEA). The lists in Books 2, 4, 5, and 6 are abridged, and there are no such recognized specialized accrediting bodies for the programs in Book 3.]

ACUPUNCTURE AND ORIENTAL MEDICINE
Dort S. Bigg, Executive Director
Accreditation Commission for Acupuncture and Oriental Medicine
7501 Greenway Center Drive, Suite 820
Greenbelt, Maryland 20770
Telephone: 301-313-0855
Fax: 301-313-0912
E-mail: 73352.2467@compuserve.com
World Wide Web: http://www.ccaom.org

ART AND DESIGN
Samuel Hope, Executive Director
National Association of Schools of Art and Design
11250 Roger Bacon Drive, Suite 21
Reston, Virginia 20190
Telephone: 703-437-0700
Fax: 703-437-6312
E-mail: shope@arts-accredit.org
World Wide Web: http://www.arts-accredit.org

BUSINESS
Milton R. Blood, Managing Director
AACSB International—The Association to Advance Collegiate Schools of Business
600 Emerson Road, Suite 300
St. Louis, Missouri 63141
Telephone: 314-872-8481
Fax: 314-872-8495
E-mail: accreditation@aacsb.edu
World Wide Web: http://www.aacsb.edu

CHIROPRACTIC
Paul D. Walker, Executive Vice President
The Council on Chiropractic Education
8049 North 85th Way
Scottsdale, Arizona 85258
Telephone: 480-443-8877
Fax: 480-483-7333
E-mail: cce@adata.com
World Wide Web: http://www.cce-usa.org

CLINICAL LABORATORY SCIENCES
Olive M. Kimball, Chief Executive Officer
National Accrediting Agency for Clinical Laboratory Sciences
8410 West Bryn Mawr Avenue, Suite 670
Chicago, Illinois 60631
Telephone: 773-714-8880
Fax: 773-714-8886
E-mail: naacls@naacls.org
World Wide Web: http://www.naacls.org

CLINICAL PASTORAL EDUCATION
Teresa E. Shorton, Executive Director
Accreditation Commission
Association for Clinical Pastoral Education, Inc.
1549 Claremont Road, Suite 103
Decatur, Georgia 30033-4611
Telephone: 404-320-1472
Fax: 404-320-0849
E-mail: acpe@acpe.edu
World Wide Web: http://www.acpe.edu

DANCE
Samuel Hope, Executive Director
National Association of Schools of Dance
11250 Roger Bacon Drive, Suite 21
Reston, Virginia 20190
Telephone: 703-437-0700
Fax: 703-437-6312
E-mail: shope@arts-accredit.org
World Wide Web: http://www.arts-accredit.org

DENTISTRY
Karen M. Hart, Director
American Dental Association
211 East Chicago Avenue, 18th Floor
Chicago, Illinois 60611
Telephone: 312-440-2500; 800-621-8099
Fax: 312-440-2915
E-mail: hartk@ada.org
World Wide Web: http://www.ada.org

EDUCATION
Arthur Wise, President
National Council for Accreditation of Teacher Education
2010 Massachusetts Avenue, NW, Suite 500
Washington, D.C. 20036
Telephone: 202-466-7496
Fax: 202-296-6620
E-mail: ncate@ncate.org
World Wide Web: http://www.ncate.org

Frank B. Murray, President
Teacher Education Accreditation Council (TEAC)
One Dupont Circle, NW, Suite 320
Washington, DC 20036
Telephone: 202-466-7236
Fax: 202-831-3013
E-mail: teac@teac.org
World Wide Web: http://www.teac.org

ENGINEERING
George D. Peterson, Executive Director
Accreditation Board for Engineering and Technology, Inc.
111 Market Place, Suite 1050
Baltimore, Maryland 21202

Telephone: 410-347-7700
Fax: 410-625-2238
E-mail: gpeterson@abet.org
World Wide Web: http://www.abet.org

FORESTRY
Michelle Harvey, Director, Science and Education
Committee on Education
Society of American Foresters
5400 Grosvenor Lane
Bethesda, Maryland 20814-2198
Telephone: 301-897-8720 Ext. 119
Fax: 301-897-3690
E-mail: harveym@safnet.org
World Wide Web: http://www.safnet.org

HEALTH SERVICES ADMINISTRATION
Accrediting Commission on Education for Health Services Administration
Pamela Jenness
Director of Accreditation Operations
730 11th Street, NW, Fourth Floor
Washington, DC 20001-4510
Telephone: 202-638-5131
Fax: 202-638-3429
E-mail: acehsa@aupha.com
World Wide Web: http://acehsa.org

INTERIOR DESIGN
Kayem Dunn, Executive Director
Foundation for Interior Design Education Research
146 Monroe Center, NW, Suite 1318
Grand Rapids, Michigan 49503
Telephone: 616-458-0400
Fax: 616-458-0460
E-mail: kayem@fider.org
World Wide Web: http://www.fider.org

JOURNALISM AND MASS COMMUNICATIONS
Susanne Shaw, Executive Director
Accrediting Council on Education in Journalism and Mass Communications
School of Journalism
Stauffer-Flint Hall
University of Kansas
1435 Jayhawk Boulevard
Lawrence, Kansas 66045-7575
Telephone: 785-864-3986
Fax: 785-864-5225
E-mail: sshaw@ukans.edu
World Wide Web: http://www.ukans.edu/~acejmc

LANDSCAPE ARCHITECTURE
Ronald C. Leighton, Accreditation Manager
Landscape Architectural Accreditation Board
American Society of Landscape Architects
636 Eye Street, NW
Washington, D.C. 20001
Telephone: 202-898-2444
Fax: 202-898-1185
E-mail: rleighton@asla.org
World Wide Web: http://www.asla.org

LAW
Carl Monk, Executive Director
Accreditation Committee
Association of American Law Schools
1201 Connecticut Avenue, NW, Suite 800
Washington, D.C. 20036
Telephone: 202-296-8851
Fax: 202-296-8869
E-mail: cmonk@aals.org
World Wide Web: http://www.aals.org

John A. Sebert, Consultant on Legal Education
American Bar Association
750 North Lake Shore Drive
Chicago, Illinois 60611
Telephone: 312-988-6738
Fax: 312-988-5681
E-mail: sebertj@staff.abanet.org
World Wide Web: http://www.abanet.org/legaled

LIBRARY
Ann L. O'Neill, Director
Office for Accreditation
American Library Association
50 East Huron Street
Chicago, Illinois 60611
Telephone: 800-545-2433 Ext.2435
Fax: 312-280-2433
E-mail: aoneill@ala.org
World Wide Web: http://www.ala.org/education

MARRIAGE AND FAMILY THERAPY
Donald B. Kaveny, Director
Commission on Accreditation
American Association for Marriage and Family Therapy
112 South Alfred Street
Alexandria, Virginia 22314
Telephone: 703-838-9808
Fax: 703-253-0508
E-mail: dkaveny@aamft.org
World Wide Web: http://www.aamft.org

MEDICAL ILLUSTRATION
Alice Katz, Chair
Accreditation Review Committee for the Medical Illustrator
St. Luke's Hospital
Instructional Resources
232 South Woods Mill Road
Chesterfield, Missouri 63017
Telephone: 314-205-6158
Fax: 314-205-6144
World Wide Web: http://www.caahep.org/accreditation/mi/mi_accreditation.htm

MEDICINE
Liaison Committee on Medical Education

The LCME is administered in even-numbered years, beginning each July 1, by:
David P. Stevens, M.D., Secretary
Association of American Medical Colleges
2450 N Street, NW
Washington, D.C. 20037
Telephone: 202-828-0596
Fax: 202-828-1125
E-mail: dstevens@aamc.org
World Wide Web: http://www.lcme.org

The LCME is administered in odd-numbered years, beginning each July 1, by:
Frank Simon, M.D.
American Medical Association
515 North State Street
Chicago, Illinois 60610
Telephone: 312-464-4933
Fax: 312-464-5830
E-mail: frank_simon@ama-assn.org
World Wide Web: http://www.lcme.org

MUSIC
Samuel Hope, Executive Director
National Association of Schools of Music
11250 Roger Bacon Drive, Suite 21
Reston, Virginia 20190
Telephone: 703-437-0700
Fax: 703-437-6312
E-mail: shope@arts-accredit.org

World Wide Web: http://www.arts-accredit.org

NATUROPATHIC MEDICINE
Robert Lofft, Executive Director
Council on Naturopathic Medical Education
P.O. Box 11426
Eugene, Oregon 97440-3626
Telephone: 541-484-6028
E-mail: dir@cnme.org
World Wide Web: http://www.cnme.org

NURSE ANESTHESIA
Francis Gerbasi, Director of Accreditation
Council on Accreditation of Nurse Anesthesia Educational Programs
222 South Prospect Avenue, Suite 304
Park Ridge, Illinois 60068
Telephone: 847-692-7050 Ext. 3154
Fax: 847-692-7137
E-mail: fgerbasi@aana.com
World Wide Web: http://www.aana.com

NURSE EDUCATION
Jennifer Butlin, Director
Commission on Collegiate Nursing Education (CCNE)
One Dupont Circle, NW, Suite 530
Washington, DC 20036
Telephone: 202-887-6791
Fax: 202-887-8476
E-mail: jbutlin@aacn.nche.edu
World Wide Web: http://www.aacn.nche.edu/accreditation

NURSE MIDWIFERY
Betty Watts Carrington, Chair
Division of Accreditation
American College of Nurse-Midwives
818 Connecticut Avenue, NW, Suite 900
Washington, D.C. 20006
Telephone: 202-728-9877
Fax: 202-728-9897
E-mail: bjwcarrington@netscape.net
World Wide Web: http://www.midwife.org

Mary Ann Baul, Executive Director
Midwifery Education Accreditation Council
220 West Birch
Flagstaff, Arizona 86001
Telephone: 928-214-0997
Fax: 928-773-9694
E-mail: meac@altavista.net
World Wide Web: http://www.meacschools.org

NURSING
Barbara R. Grumet, Executive Director
National League for Nursing
61 Broadway
New York, New York 10006
Telephone: 800-669-1656 Ext. 451
Fax: 212-812-0390
E-mail: bgrumet@nlnac.org
World Wide Web: http://www.nlnac.org

OCCUPATIONAL THERAPY
Sue Graves, Senior Program Administrator in Accreditation
American Occupational Therapy Association
4720 Montgomery Lane
P.O. Box 31220
Bethesda, Maryland 20824
Telephone: 301-652-2682
TDD: 800-377-8555
Fax: 301-652-7711
E-mail: accred@aota.org
World Wide Web: http://www.aota.org

OPTOMETRY
Joyce Urbeck, Administrative Director
Council on Optometric Education
American Optometric Association
243 North Lindbergh Boulevard
St. Louis, Missouri 63141
Telephone: 314-991-4100 Ext. 246
Fax: 314-991-4101
E-mail: jlurbeck@theaoa.org
World Wide Web: http://www.aoanet.org/accreditation.html

OSTEOPATHIC MEDICINE
Konrad C. Miskowicz-Retz, Director
Department of Education
Bureau of Professional Education
American Osteopathic Association
142 East Ontario Street
Chicago, Illinois 60611
Telephone: 312-202-8048
Fax: 312-202-8424
E-mail: kretz@aoa-net.org
World Wide Web: http://www.aoa-net.org

PHARMACY
Peter H. Vlasses, Executive Director
American Council on Pharmaceutical Education
20 North Clark Street, Suite 2500
Chicago, Illinois 60602-5109
Telephone: 312-664-3575
Fax: 312-664-4652
E-mail: pvlasses@acpe-accredit.org
World Wide Web: http://www.acpe-accredit.org

PHYSICAL THERAPY
Mary Jane Harris, Director
Commission on Accreditation
American Physical Therapy Association
1111 North Fairfax Street
Alexandria, Virginia 22314
Telephone: 703-706-3245
TDD: 703-683-6748
Fax: 703-838-8910
E-mail: maryjaneharris@apta.org
World Wide Web: http://www.apta.org

PLANNING
Beatrice Clupper, Executive Director
American Institute of Certified Planners/Association
of Collegiate Schools of Planning
Merle Hay Tower, Suite 302
3800 Merle Hay Road
Des Moines, Iowa 50310
Telephone: 515-252-0729/0733
Fax: 515-252-7404
E-mail: fi_pab@netins.net
World Wide Web: http://netins.net/showcase/pab_fi66

PODIATRIC MEDICINE
Alan R. Tinkleman, Director
Council on Podiatric Medical Education
American Podiatric Medical Association
9312 Old Georgetown Road
Bethesda, Maryland 20814
Telephone: 301-571-9200
Fax: 301-571-4903
E-mail: artinkleman@apma.org
World Wide Web: http://www.apma.org

PSYCHOLOGY AND COUNSELING
Susan F. Zlotlow, Director
Committee on Accreditation
American Psychological Association
750 First Street, NE

Washington, D.C. 20002
Telephone: 202-336-5979
Fax: 202-336-5978
E-mail: szotlow@apa.org
World Wide Web: http://www.apa.org

Carol L. Bobby, Executive Director
Council for Accreditation of Counseling and Related Educational Programs
American Counseling Association
5999 Stevenson Avenue
Alexandria, Virginia 22304
Telephone: 703-823-9800
Fax: 703-823-1581
E-mail: cacrep@aol.com
World Wide Web: http://www.counseling.org/cacrep

PUBLIC AFFAIRS AND ADMINISTRATION

Laurel L. McFarland, Managing Director
Commission on Peer Review and Accreditation
National Association of Schools of Public Affairs and Administration
1120 G Street, NW, Suite 730
Washington, D.C. 20005
Telephone: 202-628-8965
Fax: 202-626-4978
E-mail: naspaa@naspaa.org
World Wide Web: http://www.naspaa.org

PUBLIC HEALTH

Patricia Evans, Executive Director
Council on Education for Public Health
800 Eye Street, NW, Suite 202
Washington, D.C. 20001-3710
Telephone: 202-789-1050
Fax: 202-789-1895
E-mail: patevans@ceph.org
World Wide Web: http://www.ceph.org

RABBINICAL AND TALMUDIC EDUCATION

Bernard Fryshman, Executive Vice President
Association of Advanced Rabbinical and Talmudic Schools
11 Broadway, Suite 405
New York, New York 10004
Telephone: 212-363-1991
Fax: 212-533-5335

REHABILITATION EDUCATION

Donald C. Linkowski, Executive Director
Council on Rehabilitation Education
Commission on Standards and Accreditation
1835 Rohlwing Road, Suite E
Rolling Meadows, Illinois 60008
Telephone: 847-394-1785
Fax: 847-394-2108
E-mail: dclink@wans.net
World Wide Web: http://www.core-rehab.org

SOCIAL WORK

Ann Johnson, Interim Director
Division of Standards and Accreditation
Council on Social Work Education
1725 Duke Street, Suite 500
Alexandria, Virginia 22314
Telephone: 703-683-8080 Ext. 205
Fax: 703-739-9048
E-mail: ajohnson@cswe.org
World Wide Web: http://www.cswe.org

SPEECH-LANGUAGE PATHOLOGY AND AUDIOLOGY

Patrima Tice, Director of Credentialing
American Speech-Language-Hearing Association
10801 Rockville Pike
Rockville, Maryland 20852
Telephone: 301-897-5700 Ext. 4140
Fax: 301-571-0481
E-mail: ptice@asha.org
World Wide Web: http://www.asha.org/

TECHNOLOGY

Elise Scanlon, Executive Director
Accrediting Commission of Career Schools and Colleges of Technology
2101 Wilson Boulevard, Suite 302
Arlington, Virginia 22201
Telephone:703-247-4212
Fax: 703-247-4533
E-mail: info@accsct.org
World Wide Web: http://www.accsct.org

THEATER

Samuel Hope, Executive Director
National Association of Schools of Theatre
11250 Roger Bacon Drive, Suite 21
Reston, Virginia 20190
Telephone: 703-437-0700
Fax: 703-437-6312
E-mail: shope@arts-accredit.org
World Wide Web: http://www.arts-accredit.org

THEOLOGY

Daniel O. Aleshire, Executive Director
Association of Theological Schools in the United States and Canada
10 Summit Park Drive
Pittsburgh, Pennsylvania 15275
Telephone: 412-788-6505
Fax: 412-788-6510
E-mail: aleshire@ats.edu
World Wide Web: http://www.ats.edu

VETERINARY MEDICINE

Donald G. Simmons, Director of Education and Research
American Veterinary Medical Association
1931 North Meacham Road, Suite 100
Schaumburg, Illinois 60173
Telephone: 847-925-8070 Ext. 236
Fax: 847-925-1329
E-mail: dsimmons@avma.org
World Wide Web: http://www.avma.org

Directory of Graduate and Professional Programs by Field

The **Directory of Graduate and Professional Programs by Field,** beginning on the following page, lists the 452 fields covered in the Annual Guides to Graduate Study, with an alphabetical listing of each of the institutions offering graduate or professional work in that field. Institutions in the United States and U.S. territories and those in Canada, Mexico, Europe, and Africa that are accredited by U.S. accrediting bodies are included. The directory enables readers who are interested in a particular academic area to quickly identify the colleges and universities that they might wish to attend. In each field, degree levels are given if an institution provided the information in response to Peterson's Annual Survey of Graduate and Professional Institutions. An *M* indicates that a master's degree program is offered; a *D* indicates that a doctoral program is offered; a *P* indicates that the first professional degree is offered; and an *O* signifies that other advanced degrees (e.g., certificates and specialist degrees) are offered. If no degree is listed, the school offers a degree in a subdiscipline of the field, not in the field itself.

All of the programs listed in this directory are profiled, and many are described in detail in In-Depth Descriptions or outlined briefly in Announcements in Books 2–6. These Announcements and In-Depth Descriptions are indicated in the directory listings by an asterisk, and their page numbers may be found by consulting the indexes of Books 2–6. A dagger indicates that a general graduate school In-Depth Description is contained in this volume. For the page number of the description, the reader should refer to the index in the back of this book.

ACCOUNTING

Institution	Degrees
Abilene Christian University	M
Alabama State University	M
American University	M*†
Angelo State University	M†
Appalachian State University	M
Argosy University-Chicago Northwest	M,D*
Argosy University-Sarasota	M,D*†
Arizona State University	M,D*
Armstrong University	M
Auburn University	M*†
Baker College Center for Graduate Studies	M
Baldwin-Wallace College	M*
Ball State University	M*
Bayamón Central University	M
Baylor University	M*†
Bentley College	M,O*
Bernard M. Baruch College of the City University of New York	M,D*
Bloomsburg University of Pennsylvania	M
Boise State University	M*
Boston University	M,D,O*†
Bowling Green State University	M*†
Bradley University	M†
Brenau University	M
Bridgewater State College	M
Brigham Young University	M*
Brock University	M
Brooklyn College of the City University of New York	M†
Bryant College	M,O
Bucknell University	M
Caldwell College	M
California State University, Chico	M
California State University, Fullerton	M
California State University, Hayward	M
California State University, Los Angeles	M
California State University, Sacramento	M
Canisius College	M
Carnegie Mellon University	D*
Case Western Reserve University	M,D*†
The Catholic University of America	M*†
Centenary College	M
Central Michigan University	M†
Central Missouri State University	M†
Charleston Southern University	M
Clark University	M*†
Cleary University	M
Clemson University	M*
Cleveland State University	M*†
College of Charleston	M*†
The College of Saint Rose	M*†
The College of William and Mary	M*†
Colorado State University	M*
Columbia University	M,D*†
Concordia University (Canada)	M,D,O*†
Cornell University	D*
Dallas Baptist University	M
Davenport University	M
Davenport University	M
Delta State University	M
DePaul University	M*†
DeVry University-Keller Graduate School of Management	M
Dominican University	M*
Drexel University	M,D,O*†
Eastern Connecticut State University	M
Eastern Michigan University	M*
Eastern University	M*
East Tennessee State University	M†
École des Hautes Études Commerciales de Montréal	M,O*
Edinboro University of Pennsylvania	O
Elmhurst College	M
Fairfield University	M,O*
Fairleigh Dickinson University, College at Florham	M*†
Fairleigh Dickinson University, Metropolitan Campus	M*†
Florida Agricultural and Mechanical University	M*
Florida Atlantic University	M*
Florida Atlantic University, Ft. Lauderdale Campus	M
Florida Gulf Coast University	M
Florida International University	M*†
Florida Southern College	M
Florida State University	M,D*†
Fordham University	M*†
Fort Hays State University	M
Gannon University	O
The George Washington University	M,D*†
Georgia Southern University	M
Georgia State University	M,D*
Golden Gate University	M,D,O
Gonzaga University	M
Governors State University	M
Graduate School and University Center of the City University of New York	D*†
Hawai'i Pacific University	M*†
Hofstra University	M*
Houston Baptist University	M
Howard University	M*
Illinois State University	M*†
Indiana University Bloomington	M,D*
Indiana University Northwest	M,O
Indiana University South Bend	M
Indiana University Southeast	M,O
Inter American University of Puerto Rico, Metropolitan Campus	M
Inter American University of Puerto Rico, San Germán Campus	M
Iowa State University of Science and Technology	M*†
Jackson State University	M
James Madison University	M
Johnson & Wales University	M*†
Kansas State University	M*†
Kean University	M*†
Kennesaw State University	M
Kent State University	M,D*
King's College	M
Lamar University	M*†
Lehigh University	M,D,O*
Lehman College of the City University of New York	M
Lincoln University (MO)	M
Long Island University, Brooklyn Campus	M*
Long Island University, C.W. Post Campus	M*†
Louisiana State University and Agricultural and Mechanical College	M,D*
Louisiana Tech University	M,D*
Loyola University Chicago	M*†
Manchester College	M
Marquette University	M*†
Maryville University of Saint Louis	M,O
Miami University	M*†
Michigan State University	M,D*†
Middle Tennessee State University	M*
Millsaps College	M
Mississippi College	M
Mississippi State University	M,D*
Monmouth University	M,O*†
Montana State University–Bozeman	M*
Montclair State University	M†
Murray State University	M†
National University	M†
New Jersey City University	M
New Mexico State University	M
New York Institute of Technology	M,O*†
New York University	M,D,O*†
Nichols College	M
North Carolina State University	M*
Northeastern Illinois University	M
Northeastern University	M,O*†
Northern Illinois University	M,D*†
Northern Kentucky University	M
Northwestern University	D*
Northwest Missouri State University	M
Notre Dame College (OH)	M,O
Nova Southeastern University	M*
Oakland University	M,O†
The Ohio State University	M,D*
Oklahoma City University	M
Oklahoma State University	M,D*†
Old Dominion University	M*†
Oral Roberts University	M
Pace University	M*†
Pace University, White Plains Campus	M*
The Pennsylvania State University University Park Campus	M,D*†
Philadelphia University	M
Pittsburg State University	M
Pontifical Catholic University of Puerto Rico	M,D
Purdue University	M,D*
Purdue University Calumet	M
Queens College of the City University of New York	M†
Quinnipiac University	M*†
Regis University	M,O*†
Rhodes College	M
Rider University	M*
Robert Morris University	M†
Rochester Institute of Technology	M*†
Roosevelt University	M*†
Rowan University	M†
Rutgers, The State University of New Jersey, Newark	M,D*†
St. Ambrose University	M
St. Bonaventure University	M,O
St. Edward's University	M,O
St. John's University (NY)	M,O*†
Saint Joseph's University	M*†
Saint Louis University	M*†
St. Mary's University of San Antonio	M
Saint Peter's College	M,O†
St. Thomas University	M,O†
San Diego State University	M*
San Jose State University	M*
Seattle University	M*†
Seton Hall University	M,O*†
Slippery Rock University of Pennsylvania	M†
Southeastern University	M†
Southeast Missouri State University	M
Southern Adventist University	M
Southern Illinois University Carbondale	M,D*†
Southern Illinois University Edwardsville	M†
Southern Methodist University	M*†
Southern New Hampshire University	M,O*
Southern University and Agricultural and Mechanical College	M*
Southern Utah University	M
Southwestern Adventist University	M
Southwest Missouri State University	M*†
Southwest Texas State University	M*
State University of New York at Albany	M*†
State University of New York at Binghamton	M,D*†
State University of New York at New Paltz	M
State University of New York Institute of Technology at Utica/Rome	M*†
State University of West Georgia	M
Stephen F. Austin State University	M
Stetson University	M
Stonehill College	M
Suffolk University	M,O*
Syracuse University	M,D*
Temple University	M,D*†
Texas A&M International University	M
Texas A&M University	M,D*
Texas A&M University–Corpus Christi	M
Texas A&M University–Texarkana	M
Texas Christian University	M*
Texas Tech University	M,D*†
Trinity University	M*
Troy State University Dothan	M
Truman State University	M†
Universidad del Turabo	M
Universidad Metropolitana	M
Université de Sherbrooke	M
Université du Québec en Outaouais	O
Université du Québec à Montréal	M,O
Université du Québec à Trois-Rivières	O
Université Laval	M,O†
University at Buffalo, The State University of New York	M,D*†
The University of Akron	M†
The University of Alabama	M,D*
The University of Alabama in Huntsville	M,O*
University of Alberta	D*
The University of Arizona	M*
University of Arkansas	M*
University of Baltimore	M*
The University of British Columbia	D*
University of California, Berkeley	D*
University of Central Florida	M*†
University of Cincinnati	M,D*
University of Colorado at Boulder	M,D*
University of Colorado at Colorado Springs	M*
University of Colorado at Denver	M*
University of Connecticut	M,D*†
University of Delaware	M*†
University of Denver	M*†
University of Florida	M,D*†
University of Georgia	M*†
University of Hartford	M*
University of Hawaii at Manoa	M*
University of Houston	M,D*
University of Houston–Clear Lake	M*†
University of Idaho	M*†
University of Illinois at Chicago	M*
University of Illinois at Springfield	M†
University of Illinois at Urbana-Champaign	M,D*
University of Indianapolis	M
The University of Iowa	M,D*
University of Kansas	M,D*
University of Kentucky	M*
University of La Verne	M*
The University of Lethbridge	M,D,O
University of Louisville	M*†
University of Maine	M*
University of Manitoba	M*
University of Maryland University College	M*
The University of Memphis	M,D*†
University of Miami	M*†
University of Minnesota, Twin Cities Campus	M,D*
University of Mississippi	M,D*
University of Missouri–Columbia	M,D*
University of Missouri–Kansas City	M*†
University of Missouri–St. Louis	M,O†
The University of Montana–Missoula	M*†
University of Nebraska at Omaha	M
University of Nebraska–Lincoln	M,D*†
University of Nevada, Las Vegas	M*†
University of Nevada, Reno	M*
University of New Hampshire	M*†
University of New Haven	M*†
University of New Mexico	M*†
University of New Orleans	M*
The University of North Carolina at Chapel Hill	M,D*†
The University of North Carolina at Charlotte	M*
The University of North Carolina at Greensboro	M†
The University of North Carolina at Wilmington	M*
University of Northern Iowa	M
University of North Florida	M
University of North Texas	M,D*†
University of Notre Dame	M*†
University of Oklahoma	M*†
University of Oregon	M,D*
University of Pennsylvania	M,D*†
University of Rhode Island	M*
University of St. Thomas (MN)	M,O*†
University of Saskatchewan	M
The University of Scranton	M†
University of South Alabama	M*†
University of South Carolina	M,D*†
The University of South Dakota	M†
University of Southern California	M*†
University of Southern Indiana	M
University of Southern Maine	M
University of Southern Mississippi	M
University of South Florida	M*†
The University of Tampa	M
The University of Tennessee	M,D*†
The University of Tennessee at Chattanooga	M
The University of Tennessee at Martin	M
The University of Texas at Arlington	M,D*†
The University of Texas at Austin	M,D*
The University of Texas at Dallas	M*
The University of Texas at El Paso	M*†
The University of Texas at San Antonio	M*
The University of Texas of the Permian Basin	M
University of Toledo	M*†
University of Toronto	M,D*
University of Utah	M,D*
University of Virginia	M*
University of Waterloo	M,D
University of West Florida	M
University of Wisconsin–Madison	M,D*
University of Wisconsin–Whitewater	M*
University of Wyoming	M*†
Upper Iowa University	M
Utah State University	M*
Villanova University	M*†
Virginia Commonwealth University	M,D,O*†
Virginia Polytechnic Institute and State University	M,D*
Wake Forest University	M*†
Walsh College of Accountancy and Business Administration	M
Washington State University	M,D*
Weber State University	M
Western Carolina University	M†
Western Connecticut State University	M
Western Illinois University	M
Western Michigan University	M*†
Western New England College	M
West Texas A&M University	M†

West Virginia University M*
Wheeling Jesuit University M
Wichita State University M*†
Widener University M*†
Wilkes University M
William Woods University M
Wright State University M*
Xavier University M*
Yale University D*
York College of Pennsylvania M
Youngstown State University M

ACOUSTICS

The Catholic University of America M,D*†
Naval Postgraduate School M,D
The Pennsylvania State University University Park Campus M,D*†
Rensselaer Polytechnic Institute M*†

ACTUARIAL SCIENCE

Ball State University M*
Boston University M*†
Central Connecticut State University M*†
Georgia State University M*
Roosevelt University M*†
St. John's University (NY) M*†
Temple University M*†
Université du Québec à Montréal O
The University of Iowa M,D*
University of Manitoba M*
University of Nebraska–Lincoln M*†
University of Waterloo M,D
University of Wisconsin–Madison M,D*

ACUPUNCTURE AND ORIENTAL MEDICINE

Academy of Chinese Culture and Health Sciences M
Academy of Oriental Medicine at Austin M
American College of Acupuncture and Oriental Medicine M
American College of Traditional Chinese Medicine M*
Bastyr University M*
Dongguk Royal University M
Emperor's College of Traditional Oriental Medicine M
Five Branches Institute: College of Traditional Chinese Medicine M*
International Institute of Chinese Medicine M,O
Kyung San University USA M
Meiji College of Oriental Medicine M*
Mercy College M*
Midwest College of Oriental Medicine M,O*
National College of Naturopathic Medicine M*
National College of Oriental Medicine M*
New England School of Acupuncture M*
The New York College of Health Professions M
Northwestern Health Sciences University M*
Northwest Institute of Acupuncture and Oriental Medicine M
Oregon College of Oriental Medicine M*
Pacific College of Oriental Medicine M*
Pacific College of Oriental Medicine-Chicago M*
Pacific College of Oriental Medicine-New York M*
Samra University of Oriental Medicine M
Santa Barbara College of Oriental Medicine M
Seattle Institute of Oriental Medicine M
South Baylo University M
Southern California University of Health Sciences M
Southwest Acupuncture College M
Tai Hsuan Foundation: College of Acupuncture and Herbal Medicine M
Tai Sophia Institute M
Texas College of Traditional Chinese Medicine M
Tri State College of Acupuncture M,O*
University of Bridgeport M*†
Yo San University of Traditional Chinese Medicine M

ADDICTIONS/SUBSTANCE ABUSE COUNSELING

Adler School of Professional Psychology M,D,O*
Antioch New England Graduate School M*†
The College of New Jersey M,O†
The College of William and Mary M,D*†
Coppin State College M
D'Youville College M,O†
East Carolina University M*†
Eastern Kentucky University M
Georgian Court College M,O
Governors State University M
Indiana Wesleyan University M*
Johns Hopkins University M,D,O*†
Kean University M,O*†
Loyola College in Maryland M,O
Mercy College M,O*
Monmouth University M,O*†
National-Louis University M,O
New York University M,D,O*†
Notre Dame de Namur University M,O
Pace University, White Plains Campus M*
Sage Graduate School M†
St. Mary's University of San Antonio M,D,O
Springfield College M,O†
Thomas Edison State College M†
University of Alaska Anchorage O
University of Detroit Mercy O*
University of Great Falls M
University of Illinois at Springfield M†
University of Louisiana at Monroe M
University of North Florida M,O
University of Toronto M,D*
Wayne State University O*

ADULT EDUCATION

Alverno College M
Athabasca University M
Auburn University M,D,O*†
Ball State University M,D*
California State University, Los Angeles M
Central Missouri State University M,O†
Cheyney University of Pennsylvania M
Cleveland State University M*†
Concordia University (Canada) O*†
Coppin State College M
Cornell University M,D*
Curry College M,O
Drake University M,D,O*†
East Carolina University M,O*†
Eastern Washington University M†
Florida Agricultural and Mechanical University M,D*
Florida Atlantic University M,D,O*
Florida Atlantic University, Ft. Lauderdale Campus M,D,O
Florida International University M,D*†
Florida State University M,D,O*†
Fordham University M,D,O*†
Grand Valley State University M†
Harvard University M,D,O*†
Indiana University of Pennsylvania M*†
Kansas State University M,D*†
Marshall University M*†
Memorial University of Newfoundland M†
Michigan State University M,D,O*†
Morehead State University M,O
Mount Saint Vincent University M
National-Louis University M,D,O
Newman University M
North Carolina Agricultural and Technical State University M*
North Carolina State University M,D*
Northern Illinois University M,D*†
Northwestern State University of Louisiana M,O
Nova Southeastern University D*
Oregon State University M*
The Pennsylvania State University Harrisburg Campus of the Capital College D*†
The Pennsylvania State University University Park Campus M,D*†
Portland State University D*
Regis University M,O*†
Rutgers, The State University of New Jersey, New Brunswick M,D*
St. Francis Xavier University M
Saint Joseph's University M*†
Saint Michael's College M,O*
San Francisco State University M,O
Seattle University M,O*†
State University of New York College at Buffalo M
Suffolk University M,O*
Teachers College Columbia University M,D*
Texas A&M University–Kingsville M*†
Texas A&M University–Texarkana M
Troy State University Montgomery M
Tusculum College M
Université de Sherbrooke O
Université du Québec en Outaouais O
University of Alaska Anchorage M
University of Alberta M,D,O*
University of Arkansas M,D,O*
University of Arkansas at Little Rock M
The University of British Columbia M*
University of Calgary M,D*
University of Central Oklahoma M
University of Connecticut M,D*†
University of Denver M,D,O*†
University of Georgia M,D,O*†
University of Idaho M,D,O*†
The University of Memphis M,D,O*†
University of Michigan–Dearborn M*†
University of Minnesota, Twin Cities Campus M,D,O*
University of Missouri–Columbia M,D,O*
University of Missouri–St. Louis M,D†
University of New Brunswick Fredericton M
University of New Hampshire M,D,O*†
University of Oklahoma M,D*†
University of Rhode Island M*
University of Southern Maine M,O
University of Southern Mississippi M,D,O
University of South Florida M,D,O*†
The University of Tennessee M*†
The University of Texas at San Antonio M,D*
University of the Incarnate Word M†
The University of West Alabama M
University of Wisconsin–Madison M,D*
University of Wisconsin–Platteville M
University of Wyoming M,D,O*†
Valdosta State University M,D,O
Virginia Commonwealth University M*†
Virginia Polytechnic Institute and State University M,D,O*
Western Washington University M
Widener University M,D*†
Wright State University O*

ADVANCED PRACTICE NURSING

Allen College M
Athabasca University M,O
Barry University M*†
Baylor University M*†
Bowie State University M
Brenau University M
California State University, Fresno M
Carlow College M,O
Carson-Newman College M
Case Western Reserve University M*†
The Catholic University of America M,D*†
Clarke College M,O
Clarkson College M
College of Mount Saint Vincent M,O*†
The College of New Jersey M†
Columbia University M,O*†
Concordia University Wisconsin M
Coppin State College M
Daemen College M,O
DePaul University M*†
DeSales University M
Duke University M,O*†
Duquesne University M*†
D'Youville College M,O†
Eastern Kentucky University M
East Tennessee State University M,D,O†
Edinboro University of Pennsylvania M
Emory University M*†
Fairfield University M,O*
Felician College M
Florida Atlantic University M,D,O*
Florida State University M*†
Gannon University M,O
George Mason University M,D*†
Georgia Southern University M,O
Georgia State University M,D*
Graceland University M,O
Grambling State University M
Gwynedd-Mercy College M
Hardin-Simmons University M
Hawai'i Pacific University M*†
Holy Names College M
Houston Baptist University M
Howard University M,O*
Hunter College of the City University of New York M,O†
Husson College M
Indiana University–Purdue University Indianapolis M*
Jewish Hospital College of Nursing and Allied Health M
Johns Hopkins University M,O*†
Kennesaw State University M
La Roche College M
La Salle University M,O
Long Island University, Brooklyn Campus M,O*
Long Island University, C.W. Post Campus M,O*†
Louisiana State University Health Sciences Center M,D*
Loyola University Chicago M*†
Loyola University New Orleans M
Madonna University M
Marquette University M,O*†
Marymount University M,O†
Medical College of Georgia M,D*
Medical College of Ohio M,O*
Medical University of South Carolina M,O*
Mercy College M*
Midwestern State University M
Minnesota State University, Mankato M
Molloy College M,O
Monmouth University M,O*†
Mountain State University M†
Mount Saint Mary College M
New York University M,O*†
Niagara University M†
Northeastern University M,O*†
North Georgia College & State University M
Oakland University M,O†
Oregon Health & Science University M,O*
Otterbein College M,O
Pacific Lutheran University M†
Quinnipiac University M*†
Research College of Nursing M
Rush University M,D*
Rutgers, The State University of New Jersey, Newark M,D*†
Sacred Heart University M*†
Sage Graduate School M†
Saginaw Valley State University M
St. John Fisher College M,O
Saint Joseph College M,O
Saint Xavier University M,O*
Samuel Merritt College M,O
San Francisco State University M
San Jose State University M*
Seattle Pacific University O
Seton Hall University M*†
Shenandoah University M,O
Simmons College M,O*
Sonoma State University M
Southern Adventist University M
Southern Illinois University Edwardsville M†
Southern University and Agricultural and Mechanical College M,D,O*
Spalding University M†
State University of New York College at Brockport M,O*†
State University of New York Health Science Center at Brooklyn M,O*
State University of New York Institute of Technology at Utica/Rome M,O*†
Stony Brook University, State University of New York M,O*†
Texas Tech University Health Sciences Center M,O*
Texas Woman's University M,D*†
Uniformed Services University of the Health Sciences M*
University at Buffalo, The State University of New York M,D,O*†
University of Cincinnati M,D*
University of Colorado at Colorado Springs M*
University of Delaware M,O*†
University of Detroit Mercy M,O*
University of Hawaii at Manoa M,D,O*
University of Mary M
University of Massachusetts Worcester M,D,O*
University of Medicine and Dentistry of New Jersey M*

*P—first professional degree; M—master's degree; D—doctorate; O—other advanced degree; *full description and/or announcement in Book 2, 3, 4, 5, or 6; †full description in this book*

University of Miami M,D*†
University of Michigan M*
University of Minnesota, Twin Cities Campus M*
University of Missouri–Kansas City M,D*†
University of Nevada, Las Vegas M*†
University of Northern Colorado M†
University of North Florida M,O
University of Pennsylvania M,O*†
University of Phoenix–Hawaii Campus M
University of Phoenix–Phoenix Campus M
University of Phoenix–Sacramento Campus M
University of Phoenix–Southern California Campus M
University of Pittsburgh M*†
University of Portland M,O
University of San Diego M,D,O*†
University of San Francisco M*†
The University of Scranton M†
University of South Carolina O*†
University of Southern Maine M,O
University of Southern Mississippi M,D
The University of Tampa M
The University of Tennessee at Chattanooga M
The University of Texas at Arlington M*†
The University of Texas at El Paso M*†
The University of Texas at Tyler M
The University of Texas–Pan American M
University of Wisconsin–Oshkosh M*
Vanderbilt University M,D*
Villanova University M,O*†
Virginia Commonwealth University O*†
Wagner College O
Wayne State University M*
Western Connecticut State University M
Western University of Health Sciences M
Wilmington College M
Wright State University M*

ADVERTISING AND PUBLIC RELATIONS

Academy of Art College M†
Austin Peay State University M
Ball State University M*
Boston University M*†
California State University, Fullerton M
Carnegie Mellon University M*
Colorado State University M*
Emerson College M*†
Golden Gate University M,D,O
Marquette University M*†
Michigan State University M,D*†
Monmouth University M,O*†
Morehead State University M
Northwestern University M*
Rowan University M†
Royal Roads University M
San Diego State University M*
Syracuse University M*
Texas Christian University M*
Towson University O†
Université Laval O†
The University of Alabama M*
University of Denver M*†
University of Florida M,D*†
University of Houston M*
University of Illinois at Urbana–Champaign M*
University of Maryland, College Park M,D*
University of Miami M,D*†
University of New Haven M*†
University of Oklahoma M*†
University of St. Thomas (MN) M,O*†
University of Southern California M*†
University of Southern Mississippi M,D
The University of Tennessee M,D*†
The University of Texas at Austin M,D*
University of the Sacred Heart M
University of Wisconsin–Stevens Point M
Virginia Commonwealth University M*†
Wayne State University M,D*

AEROSPACE/AERONAUTICAL ENGINEERING

Air Force Institute of Technology M,D*
Arizona State University M,D*
Arizona State University East M
Auburn University M,D*†
Boston University M,D*†
Brown University M,D*
California Institute of Technology M,D,O*
California Polytechnic State University, San Luis Obispo M†
California State University, Long Beach M
California State University, Northridge M
Carleton University M,D
Case Western Reserve University M,D*†
Concordia University (Canada) M*†
Cornell University M,D*
École Polytechnique de Montréal M,D,O
Embry-Riddle Aeronautical University (FL) M*
Embry-Riddle Aeronautical University, Extended Campus M*
Florida Institute of Technology M,D*†
The George Washington University M,D,O*†
Georgia Institute of Technology M,D*
Illinois Institute of Technology M,D*†
Iowa State University of Science and Technology M,D*†
Massachusetts Institute of Technology M,D,O*
Middle Tennessee State University M*
Mississippi State University M*
Naval Postgraduate School M,D,O
North Carolina State University M,D*
The Ohio State University M,D*
Old Dominion University M,D*†
The Pennsylvania State University University Park Campus M,D*†
Polytechnic University, Brooklyn Campus M*
Polytechnic University, Long Island Graduate Center M
Princeton University M,D*
Purdue University M,D*
Rensselaer Polytechnic Institute M,D*†
Rutgers, The State University of New Jersey, New Brunswick M,D*
Saint Louis University M*†
San Diego State University M,D*
San Jose State University M*
Stanford University M,D,O*
Syracuse University M,D*
Texas A&M University M,D*
Université Laval M†
University at Buffalo, The State University of New York M,D*†
The University of Alabama M,D*
The University of Alabama in Huntsville M,D*
The University of Arizona M,D*
University of California, Davis M,D,O*†
University of California, Irvine M,D*
University of California, Los Angeles M,D*
University of California, San Diego M,D*
University of Central Florida M*†
University of Cincinnati M,D*
University of Colorado at Boulder M,D*
University of Colorado at Colorado Springs M*
University of Connecticut M,D*†
University of Dayton M,D*†
University of Florida M,D,O*†
University of Houston M,D*
University of Illinois at Urbana–Champaign M,D*
University of Kansas M,D*
University of Maryland, College Park M,D*
University of Michigan M,D,O*
University of Minnesota, Twin Cities Campus M,D*
University of Missouri–Columbia M,D*
University of Missouri–Rolla M,D*
University of Notre Dame M,D*†
University of Oklahoma M,D*†
University of Ottawa M,D*
University of Southern California M,D,O*†
The University of Tennessee M,D*†
The University of Tennessee Space Institute M,D*
The University of Texas at Arlington M,D*†
The University of Texas at Austin M,D*
University of Toronto M,D*
University of Virginia M,D*
University of Washington M,D*
Utah State University M,D*
Virginia Polytechnic Institute and State University M,D*
Webster University M
West Virginia University M,D*
Wichita State University M,D*†

AFRICAN-AMERICAN STUDIES

Boston University M*†
Clark Atlanta University M,D
Columbia University M*†
Cornell University M*
Indiana University Bloomington M*
Morgan State University M,D*
North Carolina Agricultural and Technical State University M*
The Ohio State University M*
Princeton University D*
State University of New York at Albany M*†
Temple University M,D*†
University of California, Berkeley D*
University of California, Los Angeles M*
The University of Iowa M*
University of Massachusetts Amherst M,D*†
University of Wisconsin–Madison M*
West Virginia University M,D*
Yale University M,D*

AFRICAN STUDIES

Boston University M,O*†
Columbia University O*†
Cornell University M*
Florida International University M*†
Howard University M,D*
Johns Hopkins University M,D,O*†
New York University M*†
Northwestern University O*
The Ohio State University M*
Ohio University M*
St. John's University (NY) M,O*†
State University of New York at Albany M*†
University of California, Los Angeles M*
University of Connecticut M*†
University of Florida O*†
University of Illinois at Urbana–Champaign M*
University of Louisville M*†
University of Wisconsin–Madison M,D*
West Virginia University M,D*
Yale University M*

AGRICULTURAL ECONOMICS AND AGRIBUSINESS

Alabama Agricultural and Mechanical University M
Alcorn State University M
Arizona State University East M
Auburn University M,D*†
California Polytechnic State University, San Luis Obispo M†
Clemson University M*
Colorado State University M,D*
Cornell University M,D*
Illinois State University M*†
Iowa State University of Science and Technology M,D*†
Kansas State University M,D*†
Louisiana State University and Agricultural and Mechanical College M,D*
McGill University M,D*
Michigan State University M,D*†
Mississippi State University M,D*
Montana State University–Bozeman M*
New Mexico State University M
North Carolina Agricultural and Technical State University M*
North Carolina State University M,D*
North Dakota State University M†
Northwest Missouri State University M
The Ohio State University M,D*
Oklahoma State University M,D*†
Oregon State University M,D*
The Pennsylvania State University University Park Campus M,D*†
Prairie View A&M University M
Purdue University M*
Rutgers, The State University of New Jersey, New Brunswick M*
Sam Houston State University M*
South Carolina State University M
Southern Illinois University Carbondale M*†
Texas A&M University M,D*
Texas A&M University–Kingsville M*†
Texas Tech University M,D*†
Tuskegee University M
Université Laval M†
University of Alberta M,D*
The University of Arizona M*
University of Arkansas M*
The University of British Columbia M*
University of California, Berkeley D*
University of California, Davis M,D*†
University of Connecticut M,D*†
University of Delaware M*†
University of Florida M,D*†
University of Georgia M,D*†
University of Guelph M,D
University of Hawaii at Manoa M,D*
University of Idaho M*†
University of Illinois at Urbana–Champaign M,D*
University of Kentucky M,D*
University of Maine M*
University of Manitoba M,D*
University of Maryland, College Park M,D*
University of Massachusetts Amherst M,D*†
University of Minnesota, Twin Cities Campus M,D*
University of Missouri–Columbia M,D*
University of Nebraska–Lincoln M,D*†
University of Nevada, Reno M*
University of Puerto Rico, Mayagüez Campus M*
University of Rhode Island M,D*
University of Saskatchewan M,D
The University of Tennessee M*†
University of Vermont M*†
University of Wisconsin–Madison M,D*
University of Wyoming M*†
Virginia Polytechnic Institute and State University M,D*
Washington State University M,D*
West Texas A&M University M†
West Virginia University M*

AGRICULTURAL EDUCATION

Alcorn State University M,O
Arkansas State University M,O
Clemson University M*
Cornell University M,D*
Eastern Kentucky University M
Florida Agricultural and Mechanical University M*
Iowa State University of Science and Technology M,D*†
Louisiana State University and Agricultural and Mechanical College M,D*
Michigan State University M,D*†
Mississippi State University M,D,O*
New Mexico State University M
North Carolina Agricultural and Technical State University M*
North Carolina State University M,D,O*
North Dakota State University M†
Northwest Missouri State University M
The Ohio State University M,D*
Oklahoma State University M,D*†
Oregon State University M*
The Pennsylvania State University University Park Campus M,D*†
Purdue University M,D,O*
Sam Houston State University M*
Southwest Texas State University M*
Stephen F. Austin State University M
Texas A&M University M,D*
Texas A&M University–Commerce M†
Texas A&M University–Kingsville M*†
Texas Tech University M,D*†
The University of Arizona M*
University of Arkansas M*
University of Florida M,D*†
University of Georgia M,D,O*†
University of Idaho M*†
University of Illinois at Urbana–Champaign M*
University of Maryland Eastern Shore M†
University of Minnesota, Twin Cities Campus M,D*
University of Nebraska–Lincoln M*†
University of Puerto Rico, Mayagüez Campus M*
The University of Tennessee M*†
University of Wisconsin–River Falls M
Utah State University M*
West Virginia University M*

AGRICULTURAL ENGINEERING

Colorado State University M,D*
Cornell University M,D*
Dalhousie University M,D*
Instituto Tecnológico y de Estudios Superiores de Monterrey, Campus Monterrey M,D

Iowa State University of Science and Technology M,D*†
Kansas State University M,D*†
Louisiana State University and Agricultural and Mechanical College M,D*
McGill University M,D*
Michigan State University M,D*†
North Carolina Agricultural and Technical State University M*
North Carolina State University M,D*
North Dakota State University M,D†
The Ohio State University M,D*
Oklahoma State University M,D*†
The Pennsylvania State University University Park Campus M,D*†
Purdue University M,D*
Rutgers, The State University of New Jersey, New Brunswick M*
South Dakota State University M,D*
Texas A&M University M,D*
Université Laval M†
The University of Arizona M,D*
University of Arkansas M,D*
University of California, Davis M,D*†
University of Dayton M*†
University of Florida M,D,O*†
University of Georgia M,D*†
University of Idaho M,D*†
University of Illinois at Urbana–Champaign M,D*
University of Kentucky M,D*
University of Manitoba M,D*
University of Maryland, College Park M,D*
University of Minnesota, Twin Cities Campus M,D*
University of Missouri–Columbia M,D*
University of Nebraska–Lincoln M*†
University of Saskatchewan M,D
The University of Tennessee M,D*†
University of Wisconsin–Madison M,D*
Utah State University M,D*
Virginia Polytechnic Institute and State University M,D*

AGRICULTURAL SCIENCES—GENERAL

Alabama Agricultural and Mechanical University M,D
Alcorn State University M
Arkansas State University M,O
Auburn University M,D*†
Brigham Young University M,D*
California Polytechnic State University, San Luis Obispo M†
California State Polytechnic University, Pomona M*
California State University, Fresno M
Clemson University M,D*
Colorado State University M,D*
Dalhousie University M*
Illinois State University M*†
Instituto Tecnológico y de Estudios Superiores de Monterrey, Campus Monterrey M,D
Iowa State University of Science and Technology M,D*†
Kansas State University M,D*†
Louisiana State University and Agricultural and Mechanical College M,D*
McGill University M,D,O*
Michigan State University M,D*†
Mississippi State University M,D,O*
Montana State University–Bozeman M,D*
Murray State University M†
New Mexico State University M,D
North Carolina Agricultural and Technical State University M*
North Carolina State University M,D*
North Dakota State University M,D†
Northwest Missouri State University M
Nova Scotia Agricultural College M
The Ohio State University M,D*
Oklahoma State University M,D*†
Oregon State University M,D*
The Pennsylvania State University University Park Campus M,D*†
Prairie View A&M University M
Purdue University M,D*
Sam Houston State University M*
South Dakota State University M,D*
Southern Illinois University Carbondale M*†
Southern University and Agricultural and Mechanical College M*
Southwest Missouri State University M*†
Tarleton State University M
Tennessee State University M*
Texas A&M University M,D*
Texas A&M University–Commerce M†
Texas A&M University–Kingsville M,D*†
Texas Tech University M,D*†
Tuskegee University M
Université Laval M,D,O†
University of Alberta M,D*
The University of Arizona M,D*
University of Arkansas M,D*
The University of British Columbia M,D*
University of California, Davis M*†
University of Connecticut M,D*†
University of Delaware M,D*†
University of Florida M,D*†
University of Georgia M,D*†
University of Guelph M,D
University of Hawaii at Manoa M,D*
University of Idaho M*†
University of Illinois at Urbana–Champaign M,D*
University of Kentucky M,D*
The University of Lethbridge M,D
University of Maine M,D*
University of Manitoba M,D*
University of Maryland, College Park P,M,D*
University of Maryland Eastern Shore M†
University of Minnesota, Twin Cities Campus M,D*
University of Missouri–Columbia M,D*
University of Nebraska–Lincoln M,D*†
University of Nevada, Reno M*
University of New Hampshire M,D*†
University of Puerto Rico, Mayagüez Campus M*
University of Saskatchewan M,D
The University of Tennessee M,D*†
University of Vermont M,D*†
University of Wisconsin–Madison M,D*
University of Wisconsin–River Falls M
University of Wyoming M,D*†
Utah State University M,D*
Virginia Polytechnic Institute and State University M,D*
Washington State University M,D*
Western Kentucky University M†
West Texas A&M University M†
West Virginia University M,D*

AGRONOMY AND SOIL SCIENCES

Alabama Agricultural and Mechanical University M,D
Alcorn State University M
Auburn University M,D*†
Brigham Young University M*
Colorado State University M,D*
Cornell University M,D*
Iowa State University of Science and Technology M,D*†
Kansas State University M,D*†
Louisiana State University and Agricultural and Mechanical College M,D*
McGill University M,D*
Michigan State University M,D*†
Mississippi State University M,D*
Montana State University–Bozeman M*
New Mexico State University M,D
North Carolina State University M,D*
North Dakota State University M,D†
Nova Scotia Agricultural College M
The Ohio State University M,D*
Oklahoma State University M,D*†
Oregon State University M,D*
The Pennsylvania State University University Park Campus M,D*†
Prairie View A&M University M
Purdue University M,D*
South Dakota State University M,D*
Southern Illinois University Carbondale M*†
Southwest Missouri State University M*†
Texas A&M University M,D*
Texas A&M University–Kingsville M*†
Texas Tech University M,D*†
Tuskegee University M
Université Laval M,D†
University of Alberta M,D*
The University of Arizona M,D*
University of Arkansas M,D*
The University of British Columbia M,D*
University of California, Davis M,D*†
University of California, Riverside M,D*
University of Connecticut M,D*†
University of Delaware M,D*†
University of Florida M,D*†
University of Georgia M,D*†
University of Guelph M,D
University of Hawaii at Manoa M,D*
University of Idaho M,D*†
University of Illinois at Urbana–Champaign M,D*
University of Kentucky M,D*
University of Maine M,D*
University of Manitoba M,D*
University of Maryland, College Park M,D*
University of Massachusetts Amherst M,D*†
University of Minnesota, Twin Cities Campus M,D*
University of Missouri–Columbia M,D*
University of Nebraska–Lincoln M,D*†
University of New Hampshire M*†
University of Puerto Rico, Mayagüez Campus M*
University of Saskatchewan M,D
University of Vermont M,D*†
University of Wisconsin–Madison M,D*
University of Wyoming M,D*†
Utah State University M,D*
Virginia Polytechnic Institute and State University M,D*
Washington State University M,D*
West Virginia University M,D*

ALLIED HEALTH—GENERAL

Alabama State University M
Alderson-Broaddus College M
Andrews University M
Athabasca University M,O
Baylor University M,D*†
Belmont University M,D
Boston University M,D*†
Chatham College M
College of Mount Saint Vincent M,O*†
Creighton University P,M,D*
Drexel University M,D,O*†
Duquesne University M,D*†
East Carolina University M,D*†
Eastern Kentucky University M
East Tennessee State University M,O†
Emory University M,D*†
Finch University of Health Sciences/The Chicago Medical School M,D*
Florida Gulf Coast University M
Georgia Southern University M,O
Georgia State University M,D*
Governors State University M
Grand Valley State University M†
Idaho State University M,D,O*
Indiana University–Purdue University Indianapolis M*
Ithaca College M†
Jackson State University M
Jewish Hospital College of Nursing and Allied Health M
Kirksville College of Osteopathic Medicine M,D,O
Loma Linda University M,D*
Long Island University, C.W. Post Campus M,O*†
Louisiana State University Health Sciences Center M*
Marymount University M,O†
Maryville University of Saint Louis M
Medical College of Georgia M,O*
Medical College of Ohio M,O*
Medical University of South Carolina M,D,O*
Mercy College M*
MGH Institute of Health Professions M,D,O*
Midwestern University, Downers Grove Campus M*
Midwestern University, Glendale Campus M,O*
Minnesota State University, Mankato M,O
Mountain State University M†
Northern Arizona University M,D,O
Nova Southeastern University M,D*
Oakland University M,D,O†
The Ohio State University M*
Old Dominion University M,D*†
Quinnipiac University M*†
Regis University M,D*†
Saint Louis University M*†
Seton Hall University M,D*†
Southwest Texas State University M*
State University of New York Upstate Medical University M*
Temple University M,D*†
Tennessee State University M*
Texas Christian University M*
Texas Tech University Health Sciences Center M,D*
Texas Woman's University M,D*†
Towson University M†
University at Buffalo, The State University of New York M,D,O*†
The University of Alabama at Birmingham M,D,O*†
University of Connecticut M*†
University of Detroit Mercy M,O*
University of Florida M,D*†
University of Illinois at Chicago M,D*
University of Kansas M,D*
University of Kentucky M,D*
University of Louisiana at Monroe M
University of Massachusetts Lowell M,D*†
University of Medicine and Dentistry of New Jersey M,D,O*
University of Mississippi Medical Center M,D*
University of Nebraska Medical Center M*
The University of North Carolina at Chapel Hill M,D*†
University of North Florida M,O
University of Oklahoma Health Sciences Center M,D,O*
University of Ottawa M*
University of Puerto Rico, Medical Sciences Campus M*
University of St. Francis (IL) M
University of Saint Francis (IN) M
University of South Alabama M,D*†
The University of South Dakota M†
University of Southern California M,D,O*†
The University of Tennessee Health Science Center M*
The University of Texas at El Paso M*†
The University of Texas Medical Branch M*
University of Vermont M*†
University of Wisconsin–Eau Claire M†
University of Wisconsin–Milwaukee M
Virginia Commonwealth University M,D,O*†
Washington University in St. Louis M,D,O*†
Wayne State University M,O*
Western University of Health Sciences M
Wichita State University M*†

ALLOPATHIC MEDICINE

Albany Medical College P*
Baylor College of Medicine P*
Boston University P*†
Brown University P*
Case Western Reserve University P*†
Charles R. Drew University of Medicine and Science P
Columbia University P*†
Creighton University P*
Dalhousie University P*
Dartmouth College P*†
Drexel University P*†
Duke University P*†
East Carolina University P*†
Eastern Virginia Medical School P
East Tennessee State University P†
Emory University P*†
Finch University of Health Sciences/The Chicago Medical School P*
Georgetown University P*
The George Washington University P*†
Harvard University P*†
Howard University P,D*
Indiana University–Purdue University Indianapolis P*
Joan and Sanford I. Weill Medical College and Graduate School of Medical Sciences of Cornell University P*
Johns Hopkins University P*†
Loma Linda University P*
Louisiana State University Health Sciences Center P,M*
Loyola University Chicago P*†
Marshall University P*†
Mayo Medical School P
McGill University P*
Medical College of Georgia P*
Medical College of Ohio P*
Medical College of Wisconsin P*
Medical University of South Carolina P*
Meharry Medical College P

*P—first professional degree; M—master's degree; D—doctorate; O—other advanced degree; *full description and/or announcement in Book 2, 3, 4, 5, or 6; †full description in this book*

Memorial University of Newfoundland P†
Mercer University P,M
Michigan State University P*†
Morehouse School of Medicine P*
Mount Sinai School of Medicine of New York University P*
New York Medical College P*
New York University P*†
Northeastern Ohio Universities College of Medicine P
Northwestern University P*
The Ohio State University P*
Oregon Health & Science University P*
The Pennsylvania State University Milton S. Hershey Medical Center P*
Ponce School of Medicine P
Queen's University at Kingston P
Rush University P*
Saint Louis University P,M,D*†
Southern Illinois University Carbondale P*†
Stanford University P*
State University of New York Health Science Center at Brooklyn P*
State University of New York Upstate Medical University P*
Stony Brook University, State University of New York P*†
Temple University P*†
Texas Tech University Health Sciences Center P*
Thomas Jefferson University P*
Tufts University P*†
Tulane University P*†
Uniformed Services University of the Health Sciences P*
Universidad Central del Caribe P
Université de Montréal P,O
Université de Sherbrooke P
Université Laval P,O†
University at Buffalo, The State University of New York P*†
The University of Alabama at Birmingham P,M,D*†
The University of Arizona P*
University of Arkansas for Medical Sciences P*
The University of British Columbia P,M*
University of Calgary P*
University of California, Davis P,M*†
University of California, Irvine P*
University of California, Los Angeles P*
University of California, San Diego P*
University of California, San Francisco P*
University of Chicago P*
University of Cincinnati P*
University of Colorado Health Sciences Center P*
University of Connecticut Health Center P*
University of Florida P*†
University of Hawaii at Manoa P*
University of Illinois at Chicago P*
University of Illinois at Urbana–Champaign *
The University of Iowa P*
University of Kansas P*
University of Kentucky P*
University of Louisville P*†
University of Maryland P*†
University of Massachusetts Worcester P*
University of Medicine and Dentistry of New Jersey P,M,D*
University of Miami P*†
University of Michigan P*
University of Minnesota, Duluth P*
University of Minnesota, Twin Cities Campus P*
University of Mississippi Medical Center P*
University of Missouri–Columbia P*
University of Missouri–Kansas City P*†
University of Nebraska Medical Center P*
University of Nevada, Reno P*
University of New Mexico P*†
The University of North Carolina at Chapel Hill P*†
University of North Dakota P*
University of Oklahoma Health Sciences Center P*
University of Ottawa M,D*
University of Pennsylvania P*†
University of Pittsburgh P*†
University of Puerto Rico, Medical Sciences Campus P*
University of Rochester P*
University of Saskatchewan P
University of South Alabama P*†
University of South Carolina P*†
The University of South Dakota P†
University of Southern California P*†
University of South Florida P*†
The University of Tennessee Health Science Center P*
The University of Texas Health Science Center at Houston P*
The University of Texas Health Science Center at San Antonio P*
The University of Texas Medical Branch P*
The University of Texas Southwestern Medical Center at Dallas P*
University of Toronto P*
University of Utah P*
University of Vermont P*†
University of Virginia P,M*
University of Washington P*
The University of Western Ontario P,M*
University of Wisconsin–Madison P*
Vanderbilt University P,M,D*
Virginia Commonwealth University P*†
Wake Forest University P*†
Washington University in St. Louis P*†
Wayne State University P*
West Virginia University P*
Wright State University P*
Yale University P*
Yeshiva University P*

AMERICAN STUDIES

Appalachian State University M
Baylor University M*†
Boston University D*†
Bowling Green State University M,D*†
Brandeis University M,D*†
Brigham Young University M*
Brown University M,D*
California State University, Fullerton M
Case Western Reserve University M,D*†
Claremont Graduate University M,D*
The College of William and Mary M,D*†
Columbia University M*†
East Carolina University M*†
Eastern Michigan University M*
Fairfield University M*
Florida State University M*†
Fordham University M,D*†
The George Washington University M,D*†
Harvard University D*†
Lehigh University M*
Michigan State University M,D*†
New Mexico Highlands University M
New York University M,D*†
Northeastern State University M
The Pennsylvania State University Harrisburg Campus of the Capital College M*†
Pepperdine University M*
Purdue University M,D*
Saint Louis University M,D*†
State University of New York College at Cortland O
Stony Brook University, State University of New York M,O*†
Trinity College (CT) M
Universidad de las Américas–Puebla M
University at Buffalo, The State University of New York M,D*†
The University of Alabama M*
University of Central Oklahoma M
University of Dallas M*
University of Delaware M*†
University of Hawaii at Manoa M,D*
The University of Iowa M,D*
University of Kansas M,D*
University of Louisiana at Lafayette D*
University of Maryland, College Park M,D*
University of Massachusetts Boston M*†
University of Michigan M,D*
University of Michigan–Flint M
University of Minnesota, Twin Cities Campus D*
University of Mississippi M*
University of New Brunswick Fredericton M
University of New Mexico M,D*†
University of Pennsylvania M,D*†
University of Southern Maine M
University of South Florida M*†
The University of Texas at Austin M,D*
University of Wyoming M*†
Utah State University M*
Washington State University M,D*
Western Carolina University M†
West Virginia University M,D*
Wheaton College M†
Yale University M,D*

ANALYTICAL CHEMISTRY

Brigham Young University M,D*
California State University, Fullerton M
California State University, Los Angeles M
Case Western Reserve University M,D*†
Clarkson University M,D*
Cleveland State University M,D*†
Cornell University D*
Florida State University M,D*†
Georgetown University M,D*
The George Washington University M,D*†
Governors State University M
Howard University M,D*
Illinois Institute of Technology M,D*†
Indiana University Bloomington M,D*
Kansas State University M,D*†
Kent State University M,D*
Marquette University M,D*†
McMaster University M,D
Miami University M,D*†
Michigan State University M,D*†
Northeastern University M,D*†
Old Dominion University M*†
Oregon State University M,D*
Purdue University M,D*
Rensselaer Polytechnic Institute M,D*†
Rutgers, The State University of New Jersey, Newark M,D*†
Rutgers, The State University of New Jersey, New Brunswick M,D*
San Jose State University M*
Seton Hall University M,D*†
South Dakota State University M,D*
Southern University and Agricultural and Mechanical College M*
State University of New York at Binghamton M,D*†
Stevens Institute of Technology M,D,O*†
Tufts University M,D*†
University of Calgary M,D*
University of Cincinnati M,D*
University of Georgia M,D*†
University of Louisville M,D*†
University of Maryland, College Park M,D*
University of Michigan D*
University of Missouri–Columbia M,D*
University of Missouri–Kansas City M,D*†
The University of Montana–Missoula M,D*†
University of Nebraska–Lincoln M,D*†
University of Regina M,D
University of Southern Mississippi M,D
University of South Florida M,D*†
The University of Tennessee M,D*†
The University of Texas at Austin M,D*
University of Toledo M,D*†
Wake Forest University M,D*†
Washington State University M,D*
West Virginia University M,D*

ANATOMY

Auburn University M*†
Boston University M,D*†
Case Western Reserve University M,D*†
Colorado State University M,D*
Columbia University M,D*†
Dalhousie University M,D*
Duke University D*†
East Carolina University D*†
East Tennessee State University M,D†
Finch University of Health Sciences/The Chicago Medical School M,D*
Howard University M,D*
Indiana University Bloomington M,D*
Indiana University–Purdue University Indianapolis M,D*
Iowa State University of Science and Technology M,D*†
Johns Hopkins University D*†
Kansas State University M,D*†
Loma Linda University M,D*
Louisiana State University Health Sciences Center M,D*
Loyola University Chicago M,D*†
McGill University M,D*
Medical College of Georgia M,D*
Medical College of Ohio M*
Medical University of South Carolina D*
Michigan State University M,D*†
New York Medical College M,D*
The Ohio State University M,D*
Palmer College of Chiropractic M
The Pennsylvania State University Milton S. Hershey Medical Center M,D*
Purdue University M,D*
Queen's University at Kingston M,D
Rush University M,D*
State University of New York Health Science Center at Brooklyn D*
State University of New York Upstate Medical University M,D*
Stony Brook University, State University of New York D*†
Temple University D*†
Texas A&M University M,D*
Texas A&M University System Health Science Center D*
Texas Tech University Health Sciences Center M,D*
Uniformed Services University of the Health Sciences M,D*
Université Laval M,D,O†
University at Buffalo, The State University of New York M,D*†
The University of Arizona D*
University of Arkansas for Medical Sciences M,D*
The University of British Columbia M,D*
University of California, Irvine M,D*
University of California, Los Angeles D*
University of California, San Francisco D*
University of Chicago D*
University of Cincinnati D*
University of Florida D*†
University of Georgia M*†
University of Guelph M,D
University of Illinois at Chicago M,D*
The University of Iowa D*
University of Kansas M,D*
University of Kentucky D*
University of Louisville M,D*†
University of Manitoba M,D*
University of Maryland M,D*†
University of Minnesota, Duluth M,D*
University of Mississippi Medical Center M,D*
University of Nebraska Medical Center M,D*
University of North Dakota M,D*
University of North Texas Health Science Center at Fort Worth M,D*
University of Prince Edward Island M,D
University of Puerto Rico, Medical Sciences Campus M,D*
University of Rochester M,D*
University of Saskatchewan M,D
University of Southern California M,D*†
University of South Florida D*†
The University of Tennessee M,D*†
The University of Tennessee Health Science Center D*
University of Toronto M,D*
University of Utah M,D*
University of Vermont D*†
The University of Western Ontario M,D*
University of Wisconsin–Madison M,D*
Virginia Commonwealth University M,D,O*†
Wake Forest University D*†
Wayne State University M,D*
West Virginia University M,D*
Wright State University M*
Yeshiva University D*

ANIMAL BEHAVIOR

Arizona State University M,D*
Bucknell University M
University of California, Davis M,D*†
University of Colorado at Boulder M,D*
University of Minnesota, Twin Cities Campus M,D*
University of Missouri–St. Louis M,D,O†
The University of Montana–Missoula D*†
The University of Tennessee M,D*†
The University of Texas at Austin M,D*

ANIMAL SCIENCES

Alabama Agricultural and Mechanical University M,D
Alcorn State University M
Angelo State University M†
Auburn University M,D*†
Brigham Young University M*
California State Polytechnic University, Pomona M*

California State University, Fresno	M
Clemson University	M*
Colorado State University	M,D*
Cornell University	M,D*
Iowa State University of Science and Technology	M,D*†
Kansas State University	M,D*†
Louisiana State University and Agricultural and Mechanical College	M,D*
McGill University	M,D*
Michigan State University	M,D*†
Mississippi State University	M*
Montana State University–Bozeman	M*
New Mexico State University	M,D
North Carolina State University	M,D*
North Dakota State University	M,D†
Nova Scotia Agricultural College	M
Oklahoma State University	M,D*†
Oregon State University	M,D*
The Pennsylvania State University University Park Campus	M,D*†
Prairie View A&M University	M
Purdue University	M,D*
Rutgers, The State University of New Jersey, New Brunswick	M,D*
South Dakota State University	M,D*
Southern Illinois University Carbondale	M*†
Sul Ross State University	M*
Texas A&M University	M,D*
Texas A&M University–Kingsville	M*†
Texas Tech University	M,D*†
Tuskegee University	M
Université Laval	M,D†
The University of Arizona	M,D*
University of Arkansas	M,D*
The University of British Columbia	M,D*
University of California, Davis	M*†
University of Connecticut	M,D*†
University of Florida	M,D*†
University of Georgia	M,D*†
University of Guelph	M,D
University of Hawaii at Manoa	M*
University of Idaho	M,D*†
University of Illinois at Urbana–Champaign	M,D*
University of Kentucky	M,D*
University of Maine	M*
University of Manitoba	M,D*
University of Maryland, College Park	M,D*
University of Massachusetts Amherst	M,D*†
University of Minnesota, Twin Cities Campus	M,D*
University of Missouri–Columbia	M,D*
University of Nebraska–Lincoln	M,D*†
University of Nevada, Reno	M*
University of New Hampshire	M*†
University of Puerto Rico, Mayagüez Campus	M*
University of Rhode Island	M*
University of Saskatchewan	M,D,O
The University of Tennessee	M,D*†
University of Vermont	M,D*†
University of Wisconsin–Madison	M,D*
University of Wyoming	M,D*†
Utah State University	M,D*
Virginia Polytechnic Institute and State University	M,D*
Washington State University	M,D*
West Texas A&M University	M†
West Virginia University	M,D*

ANTHROPOLOGY

American University	M,D*†
American University in Cairo	M
Arizona State University	M,D*
Ball State University	M*
Bethel College (MN)	M
Boston University	M,D*†
Brandeis University	M,D*†
Brigham Young University	M*
Brown University	M,D*
California Institute of Integral Studies	M,D*
California State University, Bakersfield	M
California State University, Chico	M
California State University, Fullerton	M
California State University, Hayward	M
California State University, Long Beach	M
California State University, Los Angeles	M
California State University, Northridge	M
California State University, Sacramento	M
Carleton University	M
Case Western Reserve University	M,D*†
The Catholic University of America	M,D*†
City College of the City University of New York	M*†
Claremont Graduate University	M,D*
The College of William and Mary	M,D*†
Colorado State University	M*
Columbia University	M,D*†
Concordia University (Canada)	M*†
Cornell University	D*
Dalhousie University	M,D*
Duke University	D*†
East Carolina University	M*†
Eastern New Mexico University	M
Emory University	D*†
Florida Atlantic University	M*
Florida State University	M,D*†
The George Washington University	M*†
Georgia State University	M*
Graduate School and University Center of the City University of New York	D*†
Harvard University	M,D*†
Hunter College of the City University of New York	M†
Idaho State University	M*
Indiana University Bloomington	M,D*
Iowa State University of Science and Technology	M*†
Johns Hopkins University	D*†
Kent State University	M,D*
Lehigh University	M*
Louisiana State University and Agricultural and Mechanical College	M,D*
Marshall University	M*†
McGill University	M,D*
McMaster University	M,D
Memorial University of Newfoundland	M,D†
Michigan State University	M,D*†
Minnesota State University, Mankato	M
Montclair State University	M†
New Mexico Highlands University	M
New Mexico State University	M
New School University	M,D*†
New York University	M,D*†
Northern Arizona University	M
Northern Illinois University	M*†
Northwestern University	D*
The Ohio State University	M,D*
Oregon State University	M*
The Pennsylvania State University University Park Campus	M,D*†
Portland State University	M,D*
Princeton University	D*
Purdue University	M,D*
Rice University	M,D*
Rutgers, The State University of New Jersey, New Brunswick	M,D*
San Diego State University	M*
San Francisco State University	M
Simon Fraser University	M,D
Southern Illinois University Carbondale	M,D*†
Southern Methodist University	M,D*†
Stanford University	M,D*
State University of New York at Albany	M,D*†
State University of New York at Binghamton	M,D*†
Stony Brook University, State University of New York	M,D*†
Syracuse University	M,D*
Teachers College Columbia University	M,D*
Temple University	M,D*†
Texas A&M University	M,D*
Texas Tech University	M*†
Trent University	M
Tulane University	M,D*†
Universidad de las Américas–Puebla	M
Université de Montréal	M,D
Université Laval	M,D†
University at Buffalo, The State University of New York	M,D*†
The University of Alabama	M*
The University of Alabama at Birmingham	M*†
University of Alaska Fairbanks	M,D*
University of Alberta	M,D*
The University of Arizona	M,D*
University of Arkansas	M,D*
The University of British Columbia	M,D*
University of Calgary	M,D*
University of California, Berkeley	D*
University of California, Davis	M,D*†
University of California, Irvine	M,D*
University of California, Los Angeles	M,D*
University of California, Riverside	M,D*
University of California, San Diego	D*
University of California, San Francisco	D*
University of California, Santa Barbara	M,D*
University of California, Santa Cruz	M,D*
University of Chicago	M,D*
University of Cincinnati	M*
University of Colorado at Boulder	M,D*
University of Colorado at Denver	M*
University of Connecticut	M,D*†
University of Denver	M*†
University of Florida	M,D*†
University of Georgia	M,D*†
University of Guelph	M
University of Hawaii at Manoa	M,D*
University of Houston	M*
University of Idaho	M*†
University of Illinois at Chicago	M,D*
University of Illinois at Urbana–Champaign	M,D*
The University of Iowa	M,D*
University of Kansas	M,D*
University of Kentucky	M,D*
The University of Lethbridge	M,D
University of Manitoba	M*
University of Maryland, College Park	M*
University of Massachusetts Amherst	M,D*†
The University of Memphis	M*†
University of Michigan	M,D*
University of Minnesota, Duluth	M*
University of Minnesota, Twin Cities Campus	M,D*
University of Mississippi	M*
University of Missouri–Columbia	M,D*
The University of Montana–Missoula	M*†
University of Nebraska–Lincoln	M*†
University of Nevada, Las Vegas	M,D*†
University of Nevada, Reno	M,D*
University of New Brunswick Fredericton	M
University of New Mexico	M,D*†
The University of North Carolina at Chapel Hill	M,D*†
University of Oklahoma	M,D*†
University of Oregon	M,D*
University of Pennsylvania	M,D*†
University of Pittsburgh	M,D*†
University of Regina	M,D
University of Saskatchewan	M,D
University of South Carolina	M*†
University of Southern California	M,D*†
University of Southern Mississippi	M
University of South Florida	M,D*†
The University of Tennessee	M,D*†
The University of Texas at Arlington	M*†
The University of Texas at Austin	M,D*
The University of Texas at San Antonio	M*
University of Toledo	M*†
University of Toronto	M,D*
University of Tulsa	M†
University of Utah	M,D*
University of Victoria	M
University of Virginia	M,D*
University of Washington	M,D*
The University of Western Ontario	M*
University of Wisconsin–Madison	M,D*
University of Wisconsin–Milwaukee	M,D
University of Wyoming	M,D*†
Vanderbilt University	M,D*
Washington State University	M,D*
Washington University in St. Louis	M,D*†
Wayne State University	M,D*
West Chester University of Pennsylvania	M,O*†
Western Michigan University	M*†
Western Washington University	M
West Virginia University	M*
Wichita State University	M*†
Yale University	M,D*
York University	M,D*

APPLIED ARTS AND DESIGN—GENERAL

Academy of Art College	M†
Alfred University	M*†
Arizona State University	M*
Art Center College of Design	M*
California College of Arts and Crafts	M*
California Institute of the Arts	M,O*
California State University, Fresno	M
California State University, Fullerton	M,O
California State University, Los Angeles	M
Cardinal Stritch University	M*
Carnegie Mellon University	M,D*
Concordia University (Canada)	O*†
Cranbrook Academy of Art	M*
Drexel University	M*†
Fashion Institute of Technology	M*
The George Washington University	M*†
Howard University	M*
Illinois Institute of Technology	M,D*†
Indiana University Bloomington	M*
Iowa State University of Science and Technology	M*†
Lamar University	M*†
Louisiana State University and Agricultural and Mechanical College	M*
Louisiana Tech University	M*
Massachusetts College of Art	M
Memphis College of Art	M*
Minneapolis College of Art and Design	M,O*
New School University	M*†
New York University	M*†
North Carolina State University	M,D*
Nova Scotia College of Art and Design	M
Oklahoma State University	M,D*†
Pratt Institute	M*
Purdue University	M*
Rhode Island School of Design	M
Rochester Institute of Technology	M*†
Rutgers, The State University of New Jersey, New Brunswick	M*
San Diego State University	M*
San Jose State University	M*
Savannah College of Art and Design	M*
School of Visual Arts	M†
Southern Illinois University Carbondale	M*†
Stephen F. Austin State University	M
Suffolk University	M*
Sul Ross State University	M*
Syracuse University	M*
University of Alberta	M*
University of California, Berkeley	M*
University of California, Los Angeles	M*
University of Central Oklahoma	M
University of Cincinnati	M*
University of Illinois at Urbana–Champaign	M,D*
University of Kansas	M*
University of Massachusetts Dartmouth	M*†
University of Michigan	M*
University of Minnesota, Twin Cities Campus	M,D*
University of Notre Dame	M*†
The University of Texas at Austin	M,D*
University of Wisconsin–Madison	M,D*
Virginia Commonwealth University	M*†
Wayne State University	M*
Western Michigan University	M*†
Yale University	M*

APPLIED ECONOMICS

American University	M,D,O*†
Clemson University	M,D*
Cornell University	D*
Eastern Michigan University	M*
École des Hautes Études Commerciales de Montréal	M*
Mississippi State University	M,D*
Montana State University–Bozeman	M*
North Carolina Agricultural and Technical State University	M*
Portland State University	M,D*
Roosevelt University	M*†
St. Cloud State University	M
San Jose State University	M*
Southern Methodist University	M,D*†
State University of New York College at Buffalo	M
Texas Tech University	M,D*†

*P—first professional degree; M—master's degree; D—doctorate; O—other advanced degree; *full description and/or announcement in Book 2, 3, 4, 5, or 6; †full description in this book*

University of California, Santa Cruz M*
University of Georgia M,D*†
University of Michigan M*
University of Minnesota, Twin Cities Campus M,D*
University of Nevada, Reno M*
The University of North Carolina at Greensboro M†
University of North Texas M*†
The University of Texas at Dallas M*
University of Vermont M*†
University of Wisconsin–Madison M,D*
University of Wyoming M*†
Utah State University M,D*
Virginia Polytechnic Institute and State University M,D*
Western Michigan University M,D*†
Wright State University M*

APPLIED MATHEMATICS

Air Force Institute of Technology M,D*
American University M*†
Arizona State University M,D*
Auburn University M,D*†
Brown University M,D*
California Institute of Technology M,D*
California State Polytechnic University, Pomona M*
California State University, Fullerton M
California State University, Long Beach M
California State University, Los Angeles M
Case Western Reserve University M,D*†
Central Missouri State University M†
Claremont Graduate University M,D*
Clark Atlanta University M
Clemson University M,D*
Cleveland State University M*†
Columbia University M,D,O*†
Cornell University M,D*
Dalhousie University M,D*
East Carolina University M*†
École Polytechnique de Montréal M,D
Florida Institute of Technology M,D*†
Florida State University M,D*†
The George Washington University M*†
Georgia Institute of Technology M,D*
Hampton University M*†
Harvard University M,D*†
Hofstra University M*
Howard University M,D*
Hunter College of the City University of New York M†
Illinois Institute of Technology M,D*†
Indiana University Bloomington M,D*
Indiana University of Pennsylvania M*†
Indiana University–Purdue University Fort Wayne M
Indiana University–Purdue University Indianapolis M,D*
Indiana University South Bend M
Iowa State University of Science and Technology M,D*†
Johns Hopkins University M,D*†
Kent State University M,D*
Lehigh University M,D*
Long Island University, C.W. Post Campus M*†
Michigan State University M,D*†
Montclair State University M,O†
New Jersey Institute of Technology M
Nicholls State University M
North Carolina State University M,D*
North Dakota State University M,D†
Northwestern University M,D*
Oakland University M†
Oklahoma State University M,D*†
The Pennsylvania State University University Park Campus M,D*†
Princeton University M,D*
Rensselaer Polytechnic Institute M*†
Rice University M,D*
Rochester Institute of Technology M*†
Rutgers, The State University of New Jersey, New Brunswick M,D*
St. John's University (NY) M*†
San Diego State University M*
Santa Clara University M*
Simon Fraser University M,D
Southern Methodist University M,D*†
Stevens Institute of Technology M,D*†
Stony Brook University, State University of New York M,D*†
Temple University M,D*†
Towson University M†
Tulane University M,D*†
The University of Akron M,D†
The University of Alabama M,D*
The University of Alabama at Birmingham M,D*†
The University of Alabama in Huntsville M,D*
University of Alberta M,D,O*
The University of Arizona M,D*
University of Arkansas at Little Rock M
The University of British Columbia M,D*
University of California, Berkeley D*
University of California, Davis M,D*†
University of California, San Diego M,D*
University of California, Santa Barbara M*
University of California, Santa Cruz M,D*
University of Central Oklahoma M
University of Chicago M,D*
University of Cincinnati M,D*
University of Colorado at Boulder M,D*
University of Colorado at Colorado Springs M*
University of Colorado at Denver M,D*
University of Dayton M*†
University of Delaware M,D*†
University of Denver M,D*†
University of Florida M,D*†
University of Georgia M,D*†
University of Guelph M,D
University of Houston M,D*
University of Illinois at Chicago M,D*
University of Illinois at Urbana–Champaign M,D*
The University of Iowa D*
University of Kansas M,D*
University of Manitoba M*
University of Maryland, Baltimore County M,D*†
University of Maryland, College Park M,D*
University of Massachusetts Amherst M*†
University of Massachusetts Lowell M,D*†
The University of Memphis M,D*†
University of Michigan–Dearborn M*†
University of Minnesota, Duluth M*
University of Missouri–Columbia M*
University of Missouri–Rolla M*
University of Missouri–St. Louis M,D,O†
University of Nevada, Las Vegas M*†
University of New Hampshire M,D*†
The University of North Carolina at Charlotte M,D*
University of Pittsburgh M*†
University of Puerto Rico, Mayagüez Campus M*
University of Rhode Island M,D*
University of Southern California M,D*†
University of South Florida M,D*†
The University of Tennessee M,D*†
The University of Tennessee Space Institute M*
The University of Texas at Austin M,D*
The University of Texas at Dallas M,D*
University of Toledo M,D*†
University of Victoria M,D
University of Washington M,D*
University of Waterloo M,D
The University of Western Ontario M,D*
Virginia Commonwealth University M*†
Virginia Polytechnic Institute and State University M,D*
Wayne State University M,D*
Western Michigan University M*†
West Virginia University M,D*
Wichita State University M,D*†
Worcester Polytechnic Institute M,D,O*†
Wright State University M*
Yale University M,D*

APPLIED PHYSICS

Air Force Institute of Technology M,D*
Alabama Agricultural and Mechanical University M,D
Appalachian State University M
Brooklyn College of the City University of New York M,D†
California Institute of Technology M,D*
Carnegie Mellon University M,D*
Christopher Newport University M†
Colorado School of Mines M,D†
Columbia University M,D,O*†
Cornell University M,D*
DePaul University M*†
George Mason University M*†
Georgia Institute of Technology M,D*
Harvard University M,D*†
Iowa State University of Science and Technology M,D*†
Laurentian University M
New Jersey Institute of Technology M,D
Northern Arizona University M
Pittsburg State University M
Princeton University M,D*
Rensselaer Polytechnic Institute M,D*†
Rice University M,D*
Rutgers, The State University of New Jersey, Newark M,D*†
Stanford University M,D*
State University of New York at Binghamton M*†
Texas A&M University M,D*
Texas Tech University M,D*†
The University of Arizona M*
University of Arkansas M*
University of California, San Diego M,D*
University of Central Oklahoma M
University of Louisiana at Lafayette M*
University of Maryland, Baltimore County M,D*†
University of Massachusetts Boston M*†
University of Massachusetts Lowell M,D*†
University of Michigan D*
University of Missouri–St. Louis M,D†
University of New Orleans M*
The University of North Carolina at Charlotte M*
University of Puerto Rico, Río Piedras M,D*
University of Washington M,D*
Virginia Commonwealth University M*†
Virginia Polytechnic Institute and State University M,D*
West Virginia University M,D*
Yale University M,D*

APPLIED SCIENCE AND TECHNOLOGY

Capella University M
The College of William and Mary M,D*†
Harvard University M,O*†
James Madison University M
Memorial University of Newfoundland M†
Oklahoma State University M*†
Rensselaer Polytechnic Institute M*†
Southern Methodist University M,D*†
Southwest Missouri State University M*†
University of Arkansas at Little Rock M,D
University of California, Berkeley D*
University of California, Davis M,D*†
University of Mississippi M,D*

AQUACULTURE

Auburn University M,D*†
Clemson University M,D*
Kentucky State University M
Memorial University of Newfoundland M†
Purdue University M,D*
University of Florida M,D*†
University of Guelph M
University of Rhode Island M*

ARCHAEOLOGY

Boston University M,D*†
Brown University M,D*
Bryn Mawr College M,D
Columbia University M,D*†
Cornell University M,D*
Florida State University M,D*†
George Mason University M*†
Graduate School and University Center of the City University of New York D*†
Harvard University M,D*†
Michigan Technological University M*†
New York University M,D*†
Northern Arizona University M
Princeton University D*
Simon Fraser University M,D
Southern Methodist University M,D*†
Tufts University M*†
Universidad de las Américas–Puebla M
Université Laval M,D†
University of Alberta M,D*
The University of British Columbia M,D*
University of Calgary M,D*
University of California, Berkeley M,D*
University of California, Los Angeles M,D*
University of Chicago M,D*
The University of Lethbridge M,D
University of Massachusetts Boston M*†
The University of Memphis M*†
University of Michigan D*
University of Minnesota, Twin Cities Campus M,D*
University of Missouri–Columbia M,D*
The University of North Carolina at Chapel Hill M,D*†
University of Pennsylvania M,D*†
The University of Tennessee M,D*†
The University of Texas at Austin M,D*
University of Virginia M,D*
Washington University in St. Louis M,D*†
Wheaton College M†
Yale University M*

ARCHITECTURAL ENGINEERING

Illinois Institute of Technology M,D*†
Kansas State University M*†
North Carolina Agricultural and Technical State University M*
Oklahoma State University M*†
The Pennsylvania State University University Park Campus M,D*†
Rensselaer Polytechnic Institute M*†
University of Colorado at Boulder M,D*
University of Detroit Mercy M*
University of Kansas M,D*
University of Louisiana at Lafayette M*
The University of Memphis M*†
University of Miami M,D*†
The University of Texas at Austin M*

ARCHITECTURAL HISTORY

Arizona State University D*
Cornell University M,D*
Graduate School and University Center of the City University of New York D*†
McGill University M,D,O*
Savannah College of Art and Design M*
Texas A&M University M,D*
University of California, Berkeley M,D*
University of Pittsburgh M,D*†
University of Virginia M,D*

ARCHITECTURE

Arizona State University M*
Ball State University M*
Boston Architectural Center M*
California Polytechnic State University, San Luis Obispo M†
California State Polytechnic University, Pomona M*
Carleton University M
Carnegie Mellon University M,D*
The Catholic University of America M*†
City College of the City University of New York M,O*†
Clemson University M*
Columbia College Chicago M†
Columbia University M,D*†
Cornell University M,D*
Cranbrook Academy of Art M*
Dalhousie University M*
Drexel University M*†
Florida Agricultural and Mechanical University M*
Florida International University M*†
Frank Lloyd Wright School of Architecture M*
Georgia Institute of Technology M,D*
Harvard University M,D*†
Illinois Institute of Technology M,D*†
Instituto Tecnológico y de Estudios Superiores de Monterrey, Campus Irapuato M,D
Iowa State University of Science and Technology M*†
Kansas State University M*†
Kent State University M*
Lawrence Technological University M
Louisiana State University and Agricultural and Mechanical College M*
Massachusetts Institute of Technology M,D*
McGill University M,D,O*

Institution	Degrees
Miami University	M*†
Mississippi State University	M*
Montana State University–Bozeman	M*
Morgan State University	M*
New Jersey Institute of Technology	M
Newschool of Architecture & Design	M
New School University	M*†
New York Institute of Technology	M*†
North Carolina State University	M*
The Ohio State University	M*
Oklahoma State University	M*†
The Pennsylvania State University University Park Campus	M*†
Pratt Institute	M*
Princeton University	M,D*
Rensselaer Polytechnic Institute	M*†
Rhode Island School of Design	M
Rice University	M,D*
Savannah College of Art and Design	M*
Southern California Institute of Architecture	M*
Syracuse University	M*
Texas A&M University	M,D*
Texas Tech University	M*†
Tulane University	M*†
Université Laval	M†
University at Buffalo, The State University of New York	M*†
The University of Arizona	M*
The University of British Columbia	M*
University of Calgary	M,D*
University of California, Berkeley	M,D*
University of California, Los Angeles	M,D*
University of Cincinnati	M*
University of Colorado at Denver	M,D*
University of Florida	M,D*†
University of Hawaii at Manoa	D*
University of Houston	M*
University of Idaho	M*†
University of Illinois at Chicago	M*
University of Illinois at Urbana–Champaign	M*
University of Kansas	M*
University of Kentucky	M*
University of Manitoba	M*
University of Maryland, College Park	M*
University of Miami	M*†
University of Michigan	M,D*
University of Minnesota, Twin Cities Campus	M*
University of Nebraska–Lincoln	M*†
University of Nevada, Las Vegas	M*†
University of New Mexico	M*†
The University of North Carolina at Charlotte	M*
University of Notre Dame	M*†
University of Oklahoma	M*†
University of Oregon	M*
University of Pennsylvania	M,D,O*†
University of Puerto Rico, Río Piedras	M*
University of Southern California	M*†
University of South Florida	M*†
The University of Tennessee	M*†
The University of Texas at Arlington	M*†
The University of Texas at Austin	M,D*
The University of Texas at San Antonio	M*
University of Toronto	M*
University of Utah	M*
University of Virginia	M*
University of Washington	M,O*
University of Waterloo	M
University of Wisconsin–Milwaukee	M,D
Virginia Polytechnic Institute and State University	M*
Washington State University	M*
Washington State University Spokane	M†
Washington University in St. Louis	M*†
Yale University	M*

ART/FINE ARTS

Institution	Degrees
Academy of Art College	M†
Adams State College	M
Adelphi University	M*
Alfred University	M*†
American University	M*†
Arizona State University	M*
Arkansas State University	M
Arkansas Tech University	M
Art Center College of Design	M*
The Art Institute of Boston at Lesley University	M
Auburn University	M,D*†
Ball State University	M*
Bard College	M*†
Barry University	M*†
Bennington College	M†
Bloomsburg University of Pennsylvania	M
Boise State University	M*
Boston University	M*†
Bowling Green State University	M*†
Bradley University	M†
Brandeis University	O*†
Brigham Young University	M*
Brooklyn College of the City University of New York	M,D†
California College of Arts and Crafts	M*
California Institute of the Arts	M,O*
California State University, Chico	M
California State University, Fresno	M
California State University, Fullerton	M,O
California State University, Long Beach	M
California State University, Los Angeles	M
California State University, Northridge	M
California State University, Sacramento	M
California State University, San Bernardino	M
Carnegie Mellon University	M*
Central Michigan University	M†
Central Washington University	M†
City College of the City University of New York	M*†
Claremont Graduate University	M*
Clemson University	M*
The College of New Rochelle	M†
Colorado State University	M*
Columbia University	M*†
Concordia University (Canada)	M*†
Cornell University	M*
Cranbrook Academy of Art	M*
East Carolina University	M*†
Eastern Illinois University	M†
Eastern Michigan University	M*
East Tennessee State University	M†
Edinboro University of Pennsylvania	M
Florida Atlantic University	M*
Florida Atlantic University, Ft. Lauderdale Campus	M
Florida International University	M*†
Florida State University	M*†
Fontbonne University	M
Fort Hays State University	M
Framingham State College	M*
The George Washington University	M*†
Georgia Southern University	M
Georgia State University	M*
Governors State University	M
Graduate School of Figurative Art of the New York Academy of Art	M†
Howard University	M*
Hunter College of the City University of New York	M†
Idaho State University	M*
Illinois State University	M*†
Indiana State University	M*†
Indiana University Bloomington	M*
Indiana University of Pennsylvania	M*†
Inter American University of Puerto Rico, San Germán Campus	M
James Madison University	M
John F. Kennedy University	M*†
Johnson State College	M
Kansas State University	M*†
Kent State University	M*
Lamar University	M*†
Lehman College of the City University of New York	M
Lesley University	M*†
Long Island University, C.W. Post Campus	M*†
Louisiana State University and Agricultural and Mechanical College	M*
Louisiana Tech University	M*
Maharishi University of Management	M
Maine College of Art	M
Mansfield University of Pennsylvania	M
Marshall University	M*†
Maryland Institute College of Art	M,O*
Marywood University	M*†
Massachusetts College of Art	M
Memphis College of Art	M*
Miami University	M*†
Michigan State University	M*†
Mills College	M*†
Minneapolis College of Art and Design	M,O*
Minnesota State University, Mankato	M
Mississippi College	M
Mississippi State University	M*
Montana State University–Bozeman	M*
Montclair State University	M†
Morehead State University	M
New Jersey City University	M
New Mexico State University	M
New School University	M*†
New York University	M,D*†
Norfolk State University	M†
Northern Illinois University	M*†
Northwestern State University of Louisiana	M
Northwestern University	M*
Nova Scotia College of Art and Design	M
The Ohio State University	M*
Ohio University	M*
Oklahoma City University	M
Old Dominion University	M*†
Otis College of Art and Design	M
Pennsylvania Academy of the Fine Arts	M,O*
The Pennsylvania State University University Park Campus	M*†
Pittsburg State University	M
Portland State University	M*
Pratt Institute	M*
Purchase College, State University of New York	M
Purdue University	M*
Queens College of the City University of New York	M†
Radford University	M†
Rensselaer Polytechnic Institute	M*†
Rhode Island College	M†
Rhode Island School of Design	M
Rochester Institute of Technology	M*†
Rutgers, The State University of New Jersey, New Brunswick	M*
St. Cloud State University	M
Sam Houston State University	M*
San Diego State University	M*
San Francisco Art Institute	M,O*
San Francisco State University	M
San Jose State University	M*
Savannah College of Art and Design	M*
School of the Art Institute of Chicago	M*
School of the Museum of Fine Arts	M,O
School of Visual Arts	M†
Southern Illinois University Carbondale	M*†
Southern Illinois University Edwardsville	M†
Southern Methodist University	M*†
Southern Utah University	M
Stanford University	M,D*
State University of New York at Albany	M*†
State University of New York at New Paltz	M
State University of New York at Oswego	M
State University of New York College at Brockport	M*†
Stephen F. Austin State University	M
Stony Brook University, State University of New York	M*†
Sul Ross State University	M*
Syracuse University	M*
Temple University	M*†
Texas A&M University–Commerce	M†
Texas A&M University–Kingsville	M*†
Texas Christian University	M*
Texas Tech University	M,D*†
Texas Woman's University	M*†
Towson University	M*†
Tufts University	M*†
Tulane University	M*†
Université du Québec à Chicoutimi	M
Université du Québec à Montréal	M
Université Laval	M†
University at Buffalo, The State University of New York	M*†
The University of Alabama	M*
University of Alaska Fairbanks	M*
University of Alberta	M*
The University of Arizona	M*
University of Arkansas	M*
University of Arkansas at Little Rock	M
The University of British Columbia	M,D*
University of Calgary	M*
University of California, Berkeley	M*
University of California, Davis	M*†
University of California, Irvine	M*
University of California, Los Angeles	M*
University of California, San Diego	M*
University of California, Santa Barbara	M*
University of Chicago	M,D*
University of Cincinnati	M*
University of Colorado at Boulder	M*
University of Connecticut	M*†
University of Dallas	M*
University of Delaware	M*†
University of Denver	M*†
University of Florida	M*†
University of Georgia	M,D*†
University of Guam	M*
University of Guelph	M
University of Hartford	M*
University of Hawaii at Manoa	M*
University of Houston	M*
University of Idaho	M*†
University of Illinois at Chicago	M*
University of Indianapolis	M
The University of Iowa	M*
University of Kansas	M*
University of Kentucky	M*
The University of Lethbridge	M,D
University of Louisville	M*†
University of Maryland, Baltimore County	M*†
University of Maryland, College Park	M*
University of Massachusetts Amherst	M*†
University of Massachusetts Dartmouth	M*†
The University of Memphis	M*†
University of Miami	M*†
University of Michigan	M*
University of Minnesota, Duluth	M*
University of Minnesota, Twin Cities Campus	M*
University of Mississippi	M*
University of Missouri–Columbia	M*
University of Missouri–Kansas City	M,D*†
The University of Montana–Missoula	M*†
University of Nebraska–Lincoln	M*†
University of Nevada, Las Vegas	M*†
University of New Hampshire	M*†
University of New Mexico	M*†
University of New Orleans	M*
The University of North Carolina at Chapel Hill	M*†
The University of North Carolina at Greensboro	M†
University of North Dakota	M*
University of Northern Colorado	M†
University of Northern Iowa	M
University of North Texas	M,D*†
University of Notre Dame	M*†
University of Oklahoma	M*†
University of Oregon	M*
University of Pennsylvania	M*†
University of Regina	M
University of Rochester	M,D*
University of Saint Francis (IN)	M
University of Saskatchewan	M
University of South Carolina	M*†
The University of South Dakota	M†
University of Southern California	M*†
University of South Florida	M*†
The University of Tennessee	M*†
The University of Texas at Austin	M*
The University of Texas at El Paso	M*†
The University of Texas at San Antonio	M*
The University of Texas at Tyler	M
The University of Texas–Pan American	M
The University of the Arts	M*
University of Tulsa	M†
University of Utah	M*
University of Victoria	M
University of Washington	M*
University of Waterloo	M
University of Windsor	M
University of Wisconsin–Madison	M*
University of Wisconsin–Milwaukee	M

P—first professional degree; M—master's degree; D—doctorate; O—other advanced degree;
**full description and/or announcement in Book 2, 3, 4, 5, or 6; †full description in this book*

University of Wisconsin–Superior M
Utah State University M*
Vanderbilt University M*
Vermont College M,O
Virginia Commonwealth University M*†
Washington State University M*
Washington University in St. Louis M*†
Wayne State University M*
Webster University M
Western Carolina University M†
Western Connecticut State University M
Western Washington University M
West Texas A&M University M†
West Virginia University M*
Wichita State University M*†
William Paterson University of New Jersey M*†
Winthrop University M
Yale University M*
York University M*

ART EDUCATION

Alfred University M*†
Arcadia University M,D,O†
Art Academy of Cincinnati M
Ball State University M*
Boise State University M*
Boston University M*†
Bridgewater State College M
Brigham Young University M*
Brooklyn College of the City University of New York M†
California State University, Long Beach M
California State University, Los Angeles M
Carlow College M
Carthage College M,O
Case Western Reserve University M*†
Central Connecticut State University M*†
College of Mount St. Joseph M†
The College of New Rochelle M†
The College of Saint Rose M*†
The Colorado College M
Columbus State University M
Concordia University (Canada) M,D*†
Eastern Kentucky University M
Eastern Michigan University M*
Eastern Washington University M†
East Tennessee State University M†
Endicott College M
Fitchburg State College M†
Florida Atlantic University M*
Florida International University M,D*†
Florida State University M,D,O*†
Georgia Southern University M,O
Georgia State University M,D,O*
Harvard University M,D,O*†
Henderson State University M
Hofstra University M*
Indiana University Bloomington M,D,O*
Indiana University–Purdue University Indianapolis M*
Iowa State University of Science and Technology M*†
Jacksonville University M
James Madison University M
Kean University M*†
Kent State University M*
Kutztown University of Pennsylvania M,O†
Lesley University M,D,O*†
Long Island University, C.W. Post Campus M*†
Manhattanville College M*†
Maryland Institute College of Art M*
Maryville University of Saint Louis M
Marywood University M*†
Massachusetts College of Art M
Miami University M*†
Millersville University of Pennsylvania M†
Minnesota State University, Mankato M
Mississippi College M
Montclair State University M†
Morehead State University M
Nazareth College of Rochester M
New Jersey City University M
New York University M,D*†
North Carolina Agricultural and Technical State University M*
North Georgia College & State University M,O
Nova Scotia College of Art and Design M
The Ohio State University M,D*
Ohio University M*
The Pennsylvania State University University Park Campus M,D*†
Pittsburg State University M
Pratt Institute M*
Purdue University M,D,O*
Queens College of the City University of New York M,O†
Radford University M†
Rhode Island College M†
Rhode Island School of Design M
Rochester Institute of Technology M*†
Rockford College M
Rowan University M†
Saint Michael's College M,O*
Salisbury University M
Sam Houston State University M*
San Jose State University M*
School of the Art Institute of Chicago M,O*
Southeast Missouri State University M
Southern Connecticut State University M†
Southwestern Oklahoma State University M
Stanford University M,D*
State University of New York at New Paltz M
State University of New York at Oswego M
State University of New York College at Buffalo M
State University of West Georgia M
Stony Brook University, State University of New York M,O*†
Sul Ross State University M*
Syracuse University M,O*
Teachers College Columbia University M,D*
Temple University M*†
Texas Tech University M,D*†
Towson University M†
The University of Alabama at Birmingham M*†
The University of Arizona M*
University of Arkansas at Little Rock M
The University of British Columbia M,D*
University of Central Florida M*†
University of Cincinnati M*
University of Dayton M*†
University of Florida M*†
University of Georgia M,D,O*†
University of Houston M,D*
University of Idaho M*†
University of Illinois at Urbana–Champaign M,D*
University of Indianapolis M
The University of Iowa M,D*
University of Kansas M*
University of Kentucky M*
University of Louisville M*†
University of Manitoba M*
University of Massachusetts Amherst M*†
University of Massachusetts Dartmouth M*†
University of Minnesota, Twin Cities Campus M,D*
University of Mississippi M*
University of Nebraska at Kearney M
University of New Mexico M*†
The University of North Carolina at Greensboro M†
The University of North Carolina at Pembroke M
University of Northern Iowa M
University of North Texas M,D*†
University of Rio Grande M
University of South Alabama M*†
University of South Carolina M,D*†
University of Southern Mississippi M
University of South Florida M*†
The University of Tennessee M,D,O*†
The University of Texas at Austin M*
The University of Texas at Tyler M
The University of the Arts M*
University of Victoria M
University of Wisconsin–Madison M,D*
University of Wisconsin–Milwaukee M
University of Wisconsin–Superior M
Virginia Commonwealth University M*†
Wayne State College M
Wayne State University M,D,O*
Western Carolina University M†
Western Kentucky University M†
West Virginia University M*
Wichita State University M*†
William Carey College M
Winthrop University M

ART HISTORY

American University M*†
Bard Graduate Center for Studies in the Decorative Arts, Design, and Culture M,D*
Bloomsburg University of Pennsylvania M
Boston University M,D,O*†
Bowling Green State University M*†
Brigham Young University M*
Brooklyn College of the City University of New York M†
Brown University M,D*
Bryn Mawr College M,D
California State University, Fullerton M,O
California State University, Long Beach M
California State University, Los Angeles M
California State University, Northridge M
Carleton University M
Case Western Reserve University M,D*†
City College of the City University of New York M*†
Cleveland State University M*†
Columbia University M,D*†
Concordia University (Canada) M,D*†
Cornell University D*
Duke University D*†
East Tennessee State University M†
Emory University D*†
Florida State University M,D,O*†
The George Washington University M*†
Georgia State University M*
Graduate School and University Center of the City University of New York D*†
Harvard University D*†
Howard University M*
Hunter College of the City University of New York M†
Illinois State University M*†
Indiana State University M*†
Indiana University Bloomington M,D*
James Madison University M
Johns Hopkins University M,D*†
Lamar University M*†
Louisiana State University and Agricultural and Mechanical College M*
McGill University M,D*
Michigan State University M*†
Montclair State University M†
New York University M,D*†
Northwestern University D*
The Ohio State University M,D*
Ohio University M*
The Pennsylvania State University University Park Campus M,D*†
Pratt Institute M*
Purchase College, State University of New York M
Queens College of the City University of New York M†
Queen's University at Kingston M,D
Richmond, The American International University in London M*
Rutgers, The State University of New Jersey, New Brunswick M,D*
San Diego State University M*
San Francisco State University M
San Jose State University M*
Savannah College of Art and Design M*
School of the Art Institute of Chicago M,O*
Southern Methodist University M*†
State University of New York at Binghamton M,D*†
Stony Brook University, State University of New York M,D*†
Sul Ross State University M*
Syracuse University M*
Temple University M,D*†
Texas A&M University–Commerce M†
Texas Christian University M*
Tufts University M*†
Tulane University M*†
Université de Montréal M,D
Université du Québec à Montréal M,D
Université Laval M,D†
University at Buffalo, The State University of New York M*†
The University of Alabama M*
The University of Alabama at Birmingham M*†
University of Alberta M*
The University of Arizona M,D*
University of Arkansas at Little Rock M
The University of British Columbia M,D*
University of California, Berkeley D*
University of California, Davis M*†
University of California, Irvine M,D*
University of California, Los Angeles M,D*
University of California, Riverside M*
University of California, Santa Barbara M,D*
University of Chicago M,D*
University of Cincinnati M*
University of Colorado at Boulder M*
University of Connecticut M*†
University of Delaware M,D*†
University of Denver M*†
University of Florida M*†
University of Georgia M*†
University of Hawaii at Manoa M*
University of Illinois at Chicago M,D*
University of Illinois at Urbana–Champaign M,D*
The University of Iowa M,D*
University of Kansas M,D*
University of Kentucky M*
University of Louisville M,D*†
University of Maryland, College Park M,D*
University of Massachusetts Amherst M*†
The University of Memphis M*†
University of Miami M*†
University of Michigan D*
University of Minnesota, Twin Cities Campus M,D*
University of Mississippi M*
University of Missouri–Columbia M,D*
University of Missouri–Kansas City M,D*†
University of Nebraska–Lincoln M*†
University of New Mexico M,D*†
The University of North Carolina at Chapel Hill M,D*†
University of North Texas M,D*†
University of Notre Dame M*†
University of Oklahoma M*†
University of Oregon M,D*
University of Pennsylvania M,D*†
University of Pittsburgh M,D*†
University of Rochester M,D*
University of St. Thomas (MN) M*†
University of South Carolina M*†
University of Southern California M,D,O*†
University of South Florida M*†
The University of Texas at Austin M,D*
The University of Texas at San Antonio M*
University of Toronto M,D*
University of Utah M*
University of Victoria M,D
University of Virginia M,D*
University of Washington M,D*
University of Wisconsin–Madison M,D*
University of Wisconsin–Milwaukee M,O
University of Wisconsin–Superior M
Virginia Commonwealth University M,D*†
Washington University in St. Louis M,D*†
Wayne State University M*
West Virginia University M*
Williams College M
Yale University D*
York University M*

ARTIFICIAL INTELLIGENCE/ROBOTICS

Carnegie Mellon University M,D*
The Catholic University of America M,D*†
Cornell University M,D*
Instituto Tecnológico y de Estudios Superiores de Monterrey, Campus Monterrey M,D
Ohio University D*
San Jose State University M*
Southern New Hampshire University M,O*
University of California, San Diego M,D*
University of Georgia M*†
University of Southern California M*†
The University of Tennessee M,D*†

ARTS ADMINISTRATION

American University M,O*†
Boston University M*†
Carnegie Mellon University M*
Columbia College Chicago M†
Drexel University M*†
Eastern Michigan University M*
École des Hautes Études Commerciales de Montréal O*
Fashion Institute of Technology M*
Florida State University M,D*†

Goucher College	M
Indiana University Bloomington	M*
New York University	M*†
The Ohio State University	M*
Oklahoma City University	M
Pratt Institute	M*
Saint Mary's University of Minnesota	M
School of the Art Institute of Chicago	M*
Seton Hall University	M*†
Shenandoah University	M,D,O
Southern Methodist University	*†
Teachers College Columbia University	M*
Temple University	M,D*†
The University of Akron	M†
University of Cincinnati	M*
University of New Orleans	M*
University of Oregon	M*
University of Southern California	M*†
University of Wisconsin–Madison	M*
Virginia Polytechnic Institute and State University	M*
Webster University	M

ART THERAPY

Adler School of Professional Psychology	M,D,O*
Albertus Magnus College	M
Caldwell College	M,O
California Institute of Integral Studies	M,D,O*
California State University, Los Angeles	M
The College of New Rochelle	M†
Drexel University	M*†
Eastern Virginia Medical School	M
Emporia State University	M*†
The George Washington University	M*†
Hofstra University	M,O*
Lesley University	M,D,O*†
Long Island University, C.W. Post Campus	M*†
Marylhurst University	M
Marywood University	M*†
Mount Mary College	M
Naropa University	P,M*
National University	M,O†
Nazareth College of Rochester	M
New York University	M*†
Notre Dame de Namur University	M
Pratt Institute	M*
Sage Graduate School	M†
Saint Mary-of-the-Woods College	M
School of the Art Institute of Chicago	M*
School of Visual Arts	M†
Seton Hill University	M,O†
Southern Illinois University Edwardsville	M†
Southwestern College (NM)	M,O†
Springfield College	M,O†
University of Illinois at Chicago	M*
University of Louisville	M*†
University of Wisconsin–Superior	M
Ursuline College	M
Vermont College	M,O

ASIAN-AMERICAN STUDIES

California State University, Long Beach	M,O
University of California, Los Angeles	M*

ASIAN LANGUAGES

Brigham Young University	M*
Columbia University	M,D*†
Cornell University	M,D*
Harvard University	M,D*†
Indiana University Bloomington	M,D*
Naropa University	M*
The Ohio State University	M,D*
St. John's College (NM)	M
San Francisco State University	M
Stanford University	M,D*
University of California, Berkeley	M,D*
University of California, Irvine	M,D*
University of California, Los Angeles	M,D*
University of Chicago	M,D*
University of Colorado at Boulder	M*
University of Hawaii at Manoa	M,D*
University of Illinois at Urbana–Champaign	M,D*
University of Kansas	M*
University of Massachusetts Amherst	M*†
University of Michigan	M,D*
University of Oregon	M,D*
University of Southern California	M,D*†
The University of Texas at Austin	M,D*
University of Washington	M,D*
University of Wisconsin–Madison	M,D*
Washington University in St. Louis	M,D*†
Yale University	D*

ASIAN STUDIES

Brigham Young University	M*
California Institute of Integral Studies	M,D*
California State University, Long Beach	M,O
Columbia University	M,D,O*†
Cornell University	M,D*
Duke University	M,O*†
Florida State University	M*†
The George Washington University	M*†
Harvard University	M,D*†
Indiana University Bloomington	M,D*
Johns Hopkins University	M,D,O*†
McGill University	M,D*
Ohio University	M*
Princeton University	D*
St. John's College (NM)	M
St. John's University (NY)	M,O*†
San Diego State University	M*
Seton Hall University	M*†
Stanford University	M*
University of Alberta	M*
The University of Arizona	M,D*
The University of British Columbia	M,D*
University of California, Berkeley	M,D*
University of California, Irvine	M,D*
University of California, Los Angeles	M,D*
University of California, Santa Barbara	M*
University of Chicago	M,D*
University of Hawaii at Manoa	M*
University of Illinois at Urbana–Champaign	M,D*
The University of Iowa	M*
University of Kansas	M*
University of Michigan	M,D*
University of Minnesota, Twin Cities Campus	M*
University of Oregon	M*
University of Pennsylvania	M,D*†
University of Pittsburgh	M*†
University of San Francisco	M*†
University of Southern California	M,D*†
The University of Texas at Austin	M,D*
University of Toronto	M,D*
University of Virginia	M*
University of Washington	M*
University of Wisconsin–Madison	M,D*
Washington University in St. Louis	M,D*†
West Virginia University	M,D*
Yale University	M*

ASTRONOMY

Arizona State University	M,D*
Boston University	M,D*†
Bowling Green State University	M*†
Brigham Young University	M,D*
California Institute of Technology	D*
Case Western Reserve University	M,D*†
Clemson University	M,D*
Columbia University	M,D*†
Cornell University	D*
Dartmouth College	M,D*†
Georgia State University	D*
Harvard University	M,D*†
Indiana University Bloomington	M,D*
Iowa State University of Science and Technology	M,D*†
Johns Hopkins University	D*†
Louisiana State University and Agricultural and Mechanical College	M,D*
Michigan State University	M,D*†
Minnesota State University, Mankato	M
New Mexico State University	M,D
Northwestern University	M,D*
The Ohio State University	M,D*
The Pennsylvania State University University Park Campus	M,D*†
Rice University	M,D*
Saint Mary's University	M
San Diego State University	M*
Université de Moncton	M
The University of Arizona	M,D*
University of Calgary	M,D*
University of California, Los Angeles	M,D*
University of California, Santa Cruz	D*
University of Chicago	M,D*
University of Delaware	M,D*†
University of Florida	M,D*†
University of Georgia	M,D*†
University of Hawaii at Manoa	M,D*
University of Illinois at Urbana–Champaign	M,D*
The University of Iowa	M*
University of Kansas	M,D*
University of Kentucky	M,D*
University of Maryland, College Park	M,D*
University of Massachusetts Amherst	M,D*†
University of Michigan	M,D*
University of Minnesota, Twin Cities Campus	M,D*
University of Nebraska–Lincoln	M,D*†
The University of North Carolina at Chapel Hill	M,D*†
University of Pittsburgh	M,D*†
University of Rochester	M,D*
University of South Carolina	M,D*†
University of Southern Mississippi	M
The University of Texas at Austin	M,D*
University of Toronto	M,D*
University of Victoria	M,D
University of Virginia	M,D*
University of Washington	M,D*
The University of Western Ontario	M,D*
University of Wisconsin–Madison	D*
Vanderbilt University	M*
Wesleyan University	M*
West Chester University of Pennsylvania	M*†
Yale University	M,D*
York University	M,D*

ASTROPHYSICS

Clemson University	M,D*
Cornell University	D*
Harvard University	M,D*†
ICR Graduate School	M
Indiana University Bloomington	D*
Iowa State University of Science and Technology	M,D*†
Louisiana State University and Agricultural and Mechanical College	M,D*
McMaster University	M,D
Michigan State University	M,D*†
New Mexico Institute of Mining and Technology	M,D†
Northwestern University	M,D*
The Pennsylvania State University University Park Campus	M,D*†
Princeton University	D*
Rensselaer Polytechnic Institute	M,D*†
San Francisco State University	M
University of Alaska Fairbanks	M,D*
University of Alberta	M,D*
University of California, Berkeley	D*
University of California, Los Angeles	M,D*
University of California, Santa Cruz	D*
University of Chicago	M,D*
University of Colorado at Boulder	M,D*
University of Minnesota, Twin Cities Campus	M,D*
University of Missouri–St. Louis	M,D†
The University of North Carolina at Chapel Hill	M,D*†
University of Oklahoma	M,D*†
University of Pennsylvania	D*†
University of Victoria	M,D

ATMOSPHERIC SCIENCES

City College of the City University of New York	M,D*†
Clemson University	M,D*
Colorado State University	M,D*
Columbia University	M,D*†
Cornell University	M,D*
Creighton University	M*
Georgia Institute of Technology	M,D*
Howard University	M,D*
Massachusetts Institute of Technology	M,D*
McGill University	M,D*
New Mexico Institute of Mining and Technology	M,D†
North Carolina State University	M,D*
The Ohio State University	M,D*
Oregon State University	M,D*
Princeton University	D*
Purdue University	M,D*
South Dakota School of Mines and Technology	M,D*†
South Dakota State University	D*
State University of New York at Albany	M,D*†
Stony Brook University, State University of New York	M,D*†
Texas Tech University	M,D*†
Université du Québec à Montréal	M,D,O
The University of Alabama in Huntsville	M,D*
University of Alaska Fairbanks	M,D*
The University of Arizona	M,D*
The University of British Columbia	M,D*
University of California, Davis	M,D*†
University of California, Los Angeles	M,D*
University of Chicago	M,D*
University of Colorado at Boulder	M,D*
University of Delaware	D*†
University of Guelph	M,D
University of Illinois at Urbana–Champaign	M,D*
University of Maryland, Baltimore County	M,D*†
University of Miami	M,D*†
University of Michigan	M,D*
University of Missouri–Columbia	M,D*
University of Nevada, Reno	M,D*
University of New Hampshire	*†
The University of North Carolina at Chapel Hill	M,D*†
University of North Dakota	M*
University of Washington	M,D*
University of Wisconsin–Madison	M,D*
University of Wyoming	M,D*†

AUTOMOTIVE ENGINEERING

Colorado State University	M,D*
Kettering University	M
Lawrence Technological University	M,D
University of Detroit Mercy	M,D*
University of Michigan	M*
University of Michigan–Dearborn	M*†

AVIATION

Central Missouri State University	M†
Middle Tennessee State University	M*
University of New Haven	M*†
University of North Dakota	M*
The University of Tennessee	M*†
The University of Tennessee Space Institute	M*

AVIATION MANAGEMENT

Delta State University	M
Dowling College	M,O
Embry-Riddle Aeronautical University (FL)	M*
Embry-Riddle Aeronautical University, Extended Campus	M*
University of Dubuque	M

BACTERIOLOGY

Purdue University	M,D*
The University of Iowa	M,D*
University of Prince Edward Island	M,D
The University of Tennessee Health Science Center	D*
The University of Texas Medical Branch	D*
University of Virginia	*
University of Wisconsin–Madison	M*
West Virginia University	M,D*

BIOCHEMICAL ENGINEERING

California Polytechnic State University, San Luis Obispo	M†
Cornell University	M,D*
Dartmouth College	M,D*†
Drexel University	M*†
Rutgers, The State University of New Jersey, New Brunswick	M,D*
University of California, Irvine	M,D*
The University of Iowa	M,D*
University of Maryland, Baltimore County	M,D*†

BIOCHEMISTRY

Arizona State University	M,D*
Baylor College of Medicine	D*

*P—first professional degree; M—master's degree; D—doctorate; O—other advanced degree; *full description and/or announcement in Book 2, 3, 4, 5, or 6; †full description in this book*

Boston College	M,D*†
Boston University	M,D*†
Brandeis University	M,D*†
Brigham Young University	M,D*
Brown University	M,D*
Bryn Mawr College	M,D
California Institute of Technology	D*
California State University, Fullerton	M
California State University, Hayward	M
California State University, Long Beach	M
California State University, Los Angeles	M
Carnegie Mellon University	M,D*
Case Western Reserve University	M,D*†
City College of the City University of New York	M,D*†
Clemson University	M,D*
Colorado State University	M,D*
Columbia University	M,D*†
Cornell University	D*
Dalhousie University	M,D*
Dartmouth College	D*†
DePaul University	M*†
Drexel University	M,D*†
Duke University	D,O*†
Duquesne University	M,D*†
East Carolina University	D*†
East Tennessee State University	M,D†
Emory University	D*†
Finch University of Health Sciences/The Chicago Medical School	M,D*
Florida Atlantic University	M,D*
Florida State University	M,D*†
Georgetown University	M,D*
The George Washington University	M,D*†
Georgia Institute of Technology	M,D*
Georgia State University	M,D*
Graduate School and University Center of the City University of New York	D*†
Harvard University	M,D*†
Howard University	M,D*
Hunter College of the City University of New York	M†
Illinois Institute of Technology	M,D*†
Indiana University Bloomington	M,D*
Indiana University–Purdue University Indianapolis	M,D*
Iowa State University of Science and Technology	M,D*†
Joan and Sanford I. Weill Medical College and Graduate School of Medical Sciences of Cornell University	D*
Johns Hopkins University	M,D*†
Kansas State University	M,D*†
Kent State University	M,D*
Laurentian University	M
Lehigh University	D*
Loma Linda University	M,D*
Louisiana State University and Agricultural and Mechanical College	M,D*
Louisiana State University Health Sciences Center	M,D*
Loyola University Chicago	M,D*†
Massachusetts Institute of Technology	D*
Mayo Graduate School	D*
McGill University	M,D*
McMaster University	M,D
Medical College of Georgia	M,D*
Medical College of Ohio	M*
Medical College of Wisconsin	M,D*
Medical University of South Carolina	M,D*
Meharry Medical College	D
Memorial University of Newfoundland	M,D†
Miami University	M,D*†
Michigan State University	M,D*†
Mississippi State University	M,D*
Montana State University–Bozeman	M,D*
Mount Sinai School of Medicine of New York University	D*
New Mexico Institute of Mining and Technology	M,D†
New Mexico State University	M,D
New York Medical College	M,D*
New York University	M,D*†
North Carolina State University	M,D*
North Dakota State University	M,D†
Northern Illinois University	M,D*†
Northern Michigan University	M
Northwestern University	D*
OGI School of Science & Engineering at Oregon Health & Science University	M,D*
The Ohio State University	M,D*
Ohio University	M,D*
Oklahoma State University	M,D*†
Old Dominion University	M*†
Oregon Health & Science University	D*
Oregon State University	M,D*
The Pennsylvania State University Milton S. Hershey Medical Center	M,D*
The Pennsylvania State University University Park Campus	M,D*†
Purdue University	M,D*
Queens College of the City University of New York	M†
Queen's University at Kingston	M,D
Rensselaer Polytechnic Institute	M,D*†
Rice University	M,D*
Rush University	D*
Rutgers, The State University of New Jersey, Newark	M,D*†
Rutgers, The State University of New Jersey, New Brunswick	M,D*
Saint Louis University	D*†
San Jose State University	M*
The Scripps Research Institute	D
Seton Hall University	M,D*†
Simon Fraser University	M,D
South Dakota State University	M,D*
Southern Illinois University Carbondale	M,D*†
Southern University and Agricultural and Mechanical College	M*
Southwest Texas State University	M*
Stanford University	D*
State University of New York at Albany	M,D*†
State University of New York College of Environmental Science and Forestry	M,D
State University of New York Upstate Medical University	M,D*
Stevens Institute of Technology	M,D,O*†
Stony Brook University, State University of New York	D*†
Syracuse University	D*
Temple University	M,D*†
Texas A&M University	M,D*
Texas A&M University System Health Science Center	D*
Texas Tech University Health Sciences Center	M,D*
Thomas Jefferson University	M,D*
Tufts University	D*†
Tulane University	M,D*†
Uniformed Services University of the Health Sciences	D*
Université de Moncton	M
Université de Montréal	M,D,O
Université de Sherbrooke	M,D
Université Laval	M,D,O†
University at Buffalo, The State University of New York	M,D*†
The University of Alabama at Birmingham	D*†
University of Alaska Fairbanks	M,D*
University of Alberta	M,D*
The University of Arizona	M,D*
University of Arkansas for Medical Sciences	M,D*
The University of British Columbia	M,D*
University of Calgary	M,D*
University of California, Berkeley	D*
University of California, Davis	M,D*†
University of California, Irvine	M,D*
University of California, Los Angeles	M,D*
University of California, Riverside	M,D*
University of California, San Diego	M,D*
University of California, San Francisco	D*
University of California, Santa Barbara	D*
University of Chicago	D*
University of Cincinnati	M,D*
University of Colorado at Boulder	M,D*
University of Colorado Health Sciences Center	D*
University of Connecticut	M,D*†
University of Connecticut Health Center	D*
University of Delaware	M,D*†
University of Detroit Mercy	M*
University of Florida	M,D*†
University of Georgia	M,D*†
University of Guelph	M,D
University of Hawaii at Manoa	M,D*
University of Houston	M,D*
University of Idaho	M,D*†
University of Illinois at Chicago	M,D*
University of Illinois at Urbana–Champaign	M,D*
The University of Iowa	M,D*
University of Kansas	M,D*
University of Kentucky	D*
The University of Lethbridge	M,D
University of Louisville	M,D*†
University of Maine	M,D*
University of Manitoba	M,D*
University of Maryland	D*†
University of Maryland, Baltimore County	D*†
University of Maryland, College Park	M,D*
University of Massachusetts Amherst	M,D*†
University of Massachusetts Lowell	M,D*†
University of Massachusetts Worcester	D*
University of Medicine and Dentistry of New Jersey	M,D*
University of Miami	D*†
University of Michigan	D*
University of Minnesota, Duluth	M,D*
University of Minnesota, Twin Cities Campus	D*
University of Mississippi Medical Center	M,D*
University of Missouri–Columbia	M,D*
University of Missouri–Kansas City	D*†
University of Missouri–St. Louis	M,D,O†
The University of Montana–Missoula	M,D*†
University of Nebraska–Lincoln	M,D*†
University of Nebraska Medical Center	M,D*
University of Nevada, Las Vegas	M*†
University of Nevada, Reno	M,D*
University of New Hampshire	M,D*†
University of New Mexico	M,D*†
The University of North Carolina at Chapel Hill	M,D*†
University of North Dakota	M,D*
University of North Texas	M,D*†
University of North Texas Health Science Center at Fort Worth	M,D*
University of Notre Dame	M,D*†
University of Oklahoma	M,D*†
University of Oklahoma Health Sciences Center	M,D*
University of Oregon	M,D*
University of Ottawa	M,D*
University of Pennsylvania	D*†
University of Pittsburgh	M,D*†
University of Puerto Rico, Medical Sciences Campus	M,D*
University of Regina	M,D
University of Rhode Island	M,D*
University of Rochester	M,D*
University of Saskatchewan	M,D,O
The University of Scranton	M†
University of South Alabama	D*†
University of South Carolina	M,D*†
University of Southern California	M,D*†
University of Southern Mississippi	M,D
University of South Florida	M,D*†
The University of Tennessee	M,D*†
The University of Tennessee Health Science Center	D*
The University of Texas at Austin	M,D*
The University of Texas Health Science Center at Houston	M,D*
The University of Texas Health Science Center at San Antonio	M,D*
The University of Texas Medical Branch	M,D*
The University of Texas Southwestern Medical Center at Dallas	D*
University of the Pacific	M,D*
University of the Sciences in Philadelphia	M,D*
University of Toledo	M,D*†
University of Toronto	M,D*
University of Utah	M,D*
University of Vermont	M,D*†
University of Victoria	M,D
University of Virginia	D*
University of Washington	D*
The University of Western Ontario	M,D*
University of Windsor	M,D
University of Wisconsin–Madison	M,D*
Utah State University	M,D*
Vanderbilt University	M,D*
Virginia Commonwealth University	M,D,O*†
Virginia Polytechnic Institute and State University	M,D*
Wake Forest University	D*†
Washington State University	M,D*
Washington University in St. Louis	D*†
Wayne State University	M,D*
Wesleyan University	M,D*
West Virginia University	M,D*
Wright State University	M*
Yale University	M,D*
Yeshiva University	D*

BIOENGINEERING

Alfred University	M,D*†
Arizona State University	M,D*
Auburn University	M,D*†
Baylor College of Medicine	*
California Institute of Technology	M,D*
California Polytechnic State University, San Luis Obispo	M†
Carnegie Mellon University	M,D*
Case Western Reserve University	M,D*†
Clemson University	M,D*
Colorado State University	M,D*
Cornell University	M,D*
Dalhousie University	M,D*
Georgia Institute of Technology	M,D,O*
Kansas State University	M,D*†
Louisiana State University and Agricultural and Mechanical College	M,D*
Massachusetts Institute of Technology	M,D*
McMaster University	M,D
Mississippi State University	M,D*
North Carolina State University	M,D*
The Ohio State University	M,D*
Oklahoma State University	M,D*†
Oregon State University	M,D*
The Pennsylvania State University Milton S. Hershey Medical Center	M,D*
The Pennsylvania State University University Park Campus	M,D*†
Purdue University	M,D*
Rice University	M,D*
Rutgers, The State University of New Jersey, New Brunswick	M*
Syracuse University	M,D*
Texas A&M University	M,D*
Tufts University	O*†
University of Arkansas	M,D*
University of California, Berkeley	D*
University of California, Davis	M,D*†
University of California, San Diego	M,D*
University of California, San Francisco	D*
University of Connecticut	M,D*†
University of Florida	M,D,O*†
University of Georgia	M,D*†
University of Guelph	M,D
University of Hawaii at Manoa	M,D*
University of Illinois at Chicago	M,D*
University of Illinois at Urbana–Champaign	*
University of Maine	M*
University of Maryland, College Park	M,D*
University of Missouri–Columbia	M,D*
University of Nebraska–Lincoln	M*†
University of Notre Dame	M,D*†
University of Pennsylvania	M,D*†
University of Pittsburgh	M,D*†
University of Toledo	M,D*†
University of Utah	M,D*
University of Washington	M,D*
Virginia Polytechnic Institute and State University	M,D*

BIOETHICS

Albany Medical College	M*
Augustana College	M
Case Western Reserve University	M*†
Drew University	M,D,O†
Duquesne University	M,D*†
Loma Linda University	M*
McGill University	M,D*
Medical College of Wisconsin	M*
Midwestern University, Glendale Campus	O*
Rush University	M*
Saint Louis University	D*†
Trinity International University	P,M,D,O
Union College (NY)	M*
Université de Montréal	M,O
University of Maryland	M*†
University of Pennsylvania	*†
University of Pittsburgh	M*†
The University of Tennessee	M,D*†
University of Toronto	M,D*
University of Virginia	M*

BIOINFORMATICS

Boston University	M,D*†
George Mason University	M*†
Indiana University Bloomington	M*
Iowa State University of Science and Technology	D*†
Marquette University	M*†
North Carolina State University	M,D*

Rensselaer Polytechnic Institute M*†
University of California, Riverside D*
University of California, San Diego D*
University of Medicine and Dentistry of New Jersey M,D*
University of Michigan M,D*
University of Pittsburgh M,D,O*†
The University of Texas at El Paso M*†
University of Washington M*
Vanderbilt University M,D*
Yale University D*

BIOLOGICAL AND BIOMEDICAL SCIENCES—GENERAL

Acadia University M
Adelphi University M*
Alabama Agricultural and Mechanical University M
Alabama State University O
Albany Medical College M,D*
Alcorn State University M
American University M*†
Andrews University M
Angelo State University M†
Appalachian State University M
Arizona State University M,D*
Arkansas State University M,D,O
Auburn University M,D*†
Austin Peay State University M
Ball State University M,D*
Barry University M*†
Baylor College of Medicine M,D*
Baylor University M,D*†
Bemidji State University M
Bennington College O†
Bloomsburg University of Pennsylvania M
Boise State University M*
Boston College M,D*†
Boston University M,D*†
Bowling Green State University M,D,O*†
Bradley University M†
Brandeis University M,D,O*†
Brigham Young University M,D*
Brock University M
Brooklyn College of the City University of New York M,D†
Brown University M,D*
Bryn Mawr College M,D
Bucknell University M
California Institute of Technology D*
California Polytechnic State University, San Luis Obispo M†
California State Polytechnic University, Pomona M*
California State University, Chico M
California State University, Dominguez Hills M,O†
California State University, Fresno M
California State University, Fullerton M
California State University, Hayward M
California State University, Long Beach M
California State University, Los Angeles M
California State University, Northridge M
California State University, Sacramento M
California State University, San Bernardino M
California State University, San Marcos M
California University of Pennsylvania M
Carleton University M,D
Carnegie Mellon University M,D*
Case Western Reserve University M,D*†
The Catholic University of America M,D*†
Central Connecticut State University M,O*†
Central Michigan University M†
Central Missouri State University M†
Central Washington University M†
Chatham College M
Chicago State University M
City College of the City University of New York M,D*†
City of Hope National Medical Center/Beckman Research Institute D*
Clarion University of Pennsylvania M†
Clark Atlanta University M,D
Clark University M,D*†
Clemson University M,D*
Cleveland State University M,D*†
Cold Spring Harbor Laboratory, Watson School of Biological Sciences D*
College of Staten Island of the City University of New York M†
The College of William and Mary M*†
Colorado State University M,D*
Columbia University M,D*†
Concordia University (Canada) M,D*†
Creighton University M,D*
Dalhousie University M,D*
Dartmouth College D*†
Delta State University M
DePaul University M*†
Drexel University M,D,O*†
Duke University D*†
Duquesne University M,D*†
East Carolina University M,D*†
Eastern Illinois University M†
Eastern Kentucky University M
Eastern Michigan University M*
Eastern New Mexico University M
Eastern Virginia Medical School M,D
Eastern Washington University M†
East Stroudsburg University of Pennsylvania M†
East Tennessee State University M,D†
Edinboro University of Pennsylvania M
Emory University D*†
Emporia State University M*†
Fairleigh Dickinson University, College at Florham M*†
Fairleigh Dickinson University, Metropolitan Campus M*†
Fayetteville State University M
Finch University of Health Sciences/The Chicago Medical School M,D*
Fisk University M
Florida Agricultural and Mechanical University M*
Florida Atlantic University M*
Florida Institute of Technology M,D*†
Florida International University M,D*†
Florida State University M,D*†
Fordham University M,D*†
Fort Hays State University M
Frostburg State University M
George Mason University M*†
Georgetown University M,D*
The George Washington University M,D*†
Georgia College & State University M
Georgia Institute of Technology M,D*
Georgian Court College M
Georgia Southern University M
Georgia State University M,D*
Goucher College O
Graduate School and University Center of the City University of New York D*†
Hampton University M*†
Harvard University M,D,O*†
Hofstra University M,O*
Hood College M,O
Howard University M,D*
Humboldt State University M
Hunter College of the City University of New York M,D†
ICR Graduate School M
Idaho State University M,D*
Illinois Institute of Technology M,D*†
Illinois State University M,D*†
Indiana State University M,D*†
Indiana University Bloomington M,D*
Indiana University of Pennsylvania M*†
Indiana University–Purdue University Fort Wayne M
Indiana University–Purdue University Indianapolis M,D*
Institute of Paper Science and Technology M,D*
Jackson State University M,D
Jacksonville State University M
James Madison University M
Joan and Sanford I. Weill Medical College and Graduate School of Medical Sciences of Cornell University M,D*
John Carroll University M
Johns Hopkins University M,D*†
Kansas State University M,D*†
Keck Graduate Institute of Applied Life Sciences M*
Kent State University M,D*
Kirksville College of Osteopathic Medicine M
Lakehead University M
Lamar University M*†
Laurentian University M
Lehigh University D*
Lehman College of the City University of New York M,D
Loma Linda University M,D*
Long Island University, Brooklyn Campus M*
Long Island University, C.W. Post Campus M*†
Louisiana State University and Agricultural and Mechanical College M,D*
Louisiana State University Health Sciences Center M,D*
Louisiana Tech University M*
Loyola University Chicago M*†
Marquette University M,D*†
Marshall University M,D*†
Massachusetts Institute of Technology P,D*
Mayo Graduate School D*
McGill University M,D*
McMaster University M,D
McNeese State University M
Medical College of Georgia M,D*
Medical College of Ohio M,D,O*
Medical College of Wisconsin M,D*
Medical University of South Carolina M,D*
Meharry Medical College D
Memorial University of Newfoundland M,D,O†
Miami University M,D*†
Michigan State University M,D*†
Michigan Technological University M,D*†
Middle Tennessee State University M*
Midwestern State University M
Midwestern University, Downers Grove Campus M*
Midwestern University, Glendale Campus M*
Millersville University of Pennsylvania M†
Mills College O*†
Minnesota State University, Mankato M
Mississippi College M
Mississippi State University M,D*
Montana State University–Bozeman M,D*
Montclair State University M,O†
Morehead State University M
Morehouse School of Medicine D*
Morgan State University M,D*
Mount Allison University M
Mount Sinai School of Medicine of New York University D*
Murray State University M,D†
New Jersey Institute of Technology M,D
New Mexico Highlands University M
New Mexico Institute of Mining and Technology M†
New Mexico State University M,D
New York Medical College M,D*
New York University M,D*†
North Carolina Agricultural and Technical State University M*
North Carolina Central University M
North Carolina State University M,D*
Northeastern Illinois University M
Northeastern University M,D*†
Northern Arizona University M,D
Northern Illinois University M,D*†
Northern Michigan University M
Northwestern University D*
Northwest Missouri State University M
Notre Dame de Namur University O
Nova Southeastern University M*
Oakland University M†
Occidental College M
The Ohio State University M,D*
Ohio University M,D*
Oklahoma State University Center for Health Sciences D
Old Dominion University M,D*†
Oregon Health & Science University M,D,O*
The Pennsylvania State University Milton S. Hershey Medical Center M,D*
The Pennsylvania State University University Park Campus M,D*†
Philadelphia College of Osteopathic Medicine M*
Pittsburg State University M
Ponce School of Medicine D
Portland State University M,D*
Prairie View A&M University M
Princeton University D*
Purdue University M,D*
Purdue University Calumet M
Queens College of the City University of New York M†
Queen's University at Kingston M,D
Quinnipiac University M*†
Rensselaer Polytechnic Institute M,D*†
Rhode Island College M†
The Rockefeller University D*
Rutgers, The State University of New Jersey, Camden M†
Rutgers, The State University of New Jersey, Newark M,D*†
St. Cloud State University M
Saint Francis University M*
St. Francis Xavier University M
St. John's University (NY) M,D*†
Saint Joseph College M
Saint Joseph's University M*†
Saint Louis University M,D*†
Salem International University M
Sam Houston State University M*
San Diego State University M,D*
San Francisco State University M
San Jose State University M*
Seton Hall University M*†
Shippensburg University of Pennsylvania M†
Simon Fraser University M,D,O
Smith College M,D*
Sonoma State University M
South Dakota State University M,D*
Southeastern Louisiana University M
Southeast Missouri State University M
Southern Connecticut State University M†
Southern Illinois University Carbondale M,D*†
Southern Illinois University Edwardsville M†
Southern Methodist University M,D*†
Southern University and Agricultural and Mechanical College M*
Southwest Missouri State University M*†
Southwest Texas State University M*
Stanford University M,D*
State University of New York at Albany M,D*†
State University of New York at Binghamton M,D*†
State University of New York at New Paltz M
State University of New York College at Brockport M*†
State University of New York College at Buffalo M
State University of New York College at Cortland M
State University of New York College at Fredonia M
State University of New York College at Oneonta M
State University of New York Health Science Center at Brooklyn D*
State University of New York Upstate Medical University M,D*
State University of West Georgia M
Stephen F. Austin State University M
Stony Brook University, State University of New York M,D*†
Sul Ross State University M*
Syracuse University M,D*
Tarleton State University M
Temple University M,D*†
Tennessee State University M,D*
Tennessee Technological University M*
Texas A&M International University M
Texas A&M University M,D*
Texas A&M University–Commerce M†
Texas A&M University–Corpus Christi M
Texas A&M University–Kingsville M*†
Texas A&M University System Health Science Center M,D*
Texas Christian University M*
Texas Southern University M†
Texas Tech University M,D*†
Texas Tech University Health Sciences Center M,D*
Texas Woman's University M,D*†
Thomas Jefferson University M,D,O*
Touro College M
Towson University M†
Trent University M,D
Truman State University M†
Tufts University M,D,O*†
Tulane University M,D,O*†
Tuskegee University M
Uniformed Services University of the Health Sciences M,D*
Université de Moncton M
Université de Montréal M,D,O
Université de Sherbrooke M,D

*P—first professional degree; M—master's degree; D—doctorate; O—other advanced degree; *full description and/or announcement in Book 2, 3, 4, 5, or 6; †full description in this book*

Université du Québec à Montréal M,D
Université du Québec, Institut National de la Recherche Scientifique M,D
Université Laval M,D,O†
University at Buffalo, The State University of New York M,D*†
The University of Akron M†
The University of Alabama M,D*
The University of Alabama at Birmingham M,D*†
The University of Alabama in Huntsville M*
University of Alaska Anchorage M
University of Alaska Fairbanks M,D*
University of Alberta M,D,O*
The University of Arizona M,D*
University of Arkansas M,D*
University of Arkansas for Medical Sciences M,D*
The University of British Columbia M,D*
University of Calgary M,D*
University of California, Berkeley D*
University of California, Irvine M,D*
University of California, Los Angeles M,D*
University of California, Riverside M,D*
University of California, San Diego M,D*
University of California, San Francisco D*
University of California, Santa Cruz M,D*
University of Central Arkansas M
University of Central Florida M,O*†
University of Central Oklahoma M
University of Chicago M,D*
University of Cincinnati M,D*
University of Colorado at Denver M*
University of Colorado Health Sciences Center M,D*
University of Connecticut M,D*†
University of Connecticut Health Center D*
University of Dayton M,D*†
University of Delaware M,D*†
University of Denver M,D*†
University of Florida M,D*†
University of Guam M
University of Guelph M,D
University of Hartford M*
University of Hawaii at Manoa M,D*
University of Houston M,D*
University of Houston–Clear Lake M*†
University of Idaho M,D*†
University of Illinois at Chicago M,D*
University of Illinois at Springfield M†
University of Illinois at Urbana–Champaign M,D*
University of Indianapolis M
The University of Iowa M,D*
University of Kansas M,D*
University of Kentucky M,D*
The University of Lethbridge M,D
University of Louisiana at Lafayette M,D*
University of Louisiana at Monroe M
University of Louisville M,D*†
University of Maine D*
University of Manitoba M,D*
University of Maryland M,D*†
University of Maryland, Baltimore County M,D*†
University of Maryland, College Park M,D*
University of Massachusetts Amherst M,D*†
University of Massachusetts Boston M*†
University of Massachusetts Dartmouth M*†
University of Massachusetts Lowell M,D*†
University of Massachusetts Worcester D*
University of Medicine and Dentistry of New Jersey M,D*
The University of Memphis M,D*†
University of Miami M,D*†
University of Michigan M,D*
University of Minnesota, Duluth M*
University of Minnesota, Twin Cities Campus M,D*
University of Mississippi M,D*
University of Mississippi Medical Center M,D*
University of Missouri–Columbia M,D*
University of Missouri–Kansas City M*†
University of Missouri–St. Louis M,D,O†
The University of Montana–Missoula M,D*†
University of Nebraska at Kearney M
University of Nebraska at Omaha M
University of Nebraska–Lincoln M,D*†
University of Nebraska Medical Center M,D*
University of Nevada, Las Vegas M,D*†
University of Nevada, Reno M,D*
University of New Brunswick Fredericton M,D
University of New Brunswick Saint John M,D
University of New Mexico M,D*†
University of New Orleans M,D*
The University of North Carolina at Chapel Hill M,D*†
The University of North Carolina at Charlotte M,D*
The University of North Carolina at Greensboro M†
The University of North Carolina at Wilmington M*
University of North Dakota M,D*
University of Northern Colorado M,D†
University of Northern Iowa M
University of North Texas M,D*†
University of North Texas Health Science Center at Fort Worth M,D*
University of Notre Dame M,D*†
University of Oklahoma Health Sciences Center M,D*
University of Oregon M,D*
University of Ottawa M,D*
University of Pennsylvania M,D*†
University of Pittsburgh M,D*†
University of Puerto Rico, Mayagüez Campus M*
University of Puerto Rico, Medical Sciences Campus M,D*
University of Puerto Rico, Río Piedras M,D*
University of Regina M,D
University of Richmond M*†
University of Rochester M,D,O*
University of San Francisco M*†
University of Saskatchewan M,D,O
University of South Alabama M,D*†
University of South Carolina M,D*†
The University of South Dakota M,D†
University of Southern California M,D*†
University of Southern Colorado M
University of Southern Mississippi M,D
University of South Florida M,D*†
The University of Tennessee M,D*†
The University of Tennessee Health Science Center M,D*
The University of Tennessee–Oak Ridge National Laboratory Graduate School of Genome Science and Technology M,D*
The University of Texas at Arlington M,D*†
The University of Texas at Austin M,D*
The University of Texas at Brownsville M
The University of Texas at El Paso M,D*†
The University of Texas at San Antonio M,D*
The University of Texas at Tyler M
The University of Texas Health Science Center at Houston M,D*
The University of Texas Health Science Center at San Antonio P,M,D,O*
The University of Texas Medical Branch M,D*
The University of Texas of the Permian Basin M
The University of Texas–Pan American M
The University of Texas Southwestern Medical Center at Dallas D*
University of the Incarnate Word M†
University of the Pacific M*
University of Toledo M,D*†
University of Toronto M,D*
University of Tulsa M,D†
University of Utah M,D*
University of Vermont M,D*†
University of Victoria M,D
University of Virginia M,D*
University of Washington M,D*
University of Waterloo M,D
The University of Western Ontario M,D*
University of West Florida M
University of Windsor M,D
University of Wisconsin–Eau Claire M†
University of Wisconsin–La Crosse M†
University of Wisconsin–Madison M,D*
University of Wisconsin–Milwaukee M,D
University of Wisconsin–Oshkosh M*
Utah State University M,D*
Vanderbilt University M,D*
Vassar College M
Villanova University M*†
Virginia Commonwealth University M,D,O*†
Virginia Polytechnic Institute and State University M,D*
Virginia State University M
Wagner College M
Wake Forest University M,D*†
Walla Walla College M
Washington State University M,D*
Washington University in St. Louis D*†
Wayne State University M,D,O*
Wesleyan University D*
West Chester University of Pennsylvania M*†
Western Carolina University M†
Western Connecticut State University M
Western Illinois University M,O
Western Kentucky University M†
Western Michigan University M,D*†
Western Washington University M
West Texas A&M University M†
West Virginia University M,D*
Wichita State University M*†
William Paterson University of New Jersey M*†
Winthrop University M
Wright State University M,D*
Yale University D*
Yeshiva University D*
York University M,D*
Youngstown State University M

BIOMEDICAL ENGINEERING

Arizona State University M,D*
Boston University M,D*†
Brown University M,D*
California Polytechnic State University, San Luis Obispo M†
California State University, Northridge M
Carnegie Mellon University M,D*
Case Western Reserve University M,D*†
The Catholic University of America M,D*†
Clemson University M,D*
Cleveland State University D*†
Colorado State University M,D*
Columbia University M,D*†
Cornell University M,D*
Dalhousie University M*
Dartmouth College M,D*†
Drexel University M,D*†
Duke University M,D*†
École Polytechnique de Montréal M,D,O
Florida International University M*†
Georgia Institute of Technology M,D,O*
Harvard University M,D*†
Illinois Institute of Technology D*†
Indiana University–Purdue University Indianapolis M,D*
Johns Hopkins University M*†
Louisiana Tech University M,D*
Marquette University M,D*†
Massachusetts Institute of Technology M,D*
Mayo Graduate School D*
McGill University M,D*
Mercer University M
Milwaukee School of Engineering M*
Mississippi State University M,D*
New Jersey Institute of Technology M
Northwestern University M,D*
The Ohio State University M,D*
The Pennsylvania State University University Park Campus M,D*†
Purdue University M,D*
Rensselaer Polytechnic Institute M,D*†
Rice University M,D*
Rose-Hulman Institute of Technology M*
Rutgers, The State University of New Jersey, New Brunswick M,D*
Stanford University M*
Stony Brook University, State University of New York M,D,O*†
Syracuse University M,D*
Texas A&M University M,D*
Thomas Jefferson University D*
Tulane University M,D*†
Université de Montréal M,D
The University of Akron M†
The University of Alabama at Birmingham M,D*†
University of Alberta M,D*
University of Calgary M,D*
University of California, Berkeley D*
University of California, Davis M,D*†
University of California, Irvine M,D*
University of California, Los Angeles M,D*
University of California, San Diego M,D*
University of California, San Francisco D*
University of Connecticut M,D*†
University of Florida M,D,O*†
University of Houston M,D*
University of Illinois at Chicago M,D*
University of Illinois at Urbana–Champaign *
The University of Iowa M,D*
University of Kentucky M,D*
University of Massachusetts Worcester D*
University of Medicine and Dentistry of New Jersey M,D*
The University of Memphis M,D*†
University of Miami M,D*†
University of Michigan M,D*
University of Minnesota, Twin Cities Campus M,D*
University of Nevada, Reno M,D*
The University of North Carolina at Chapel Hill M,D*†
University of Pennsylvania M,D*†
University of Pittsburgh M,D*†
University of Rochester M,D*
University of Saskatchewan M,D
University of Southern California M,D*†
University of South Florida M*†
The University of Tennessee M,D*†
The University of Tennessee Health Science Center M,D*
The University of Texas at Arlington M,D*†
The University of Texas at Austin M,D*
The University of Texas Southwestern Medical Center at Dallas M,D*
University of Toronto M,D*
University of Utah M,D*
University of Vermont M*†
University of Virginia M,D*
University of Washington M,D*
University of Wisconsin–Madison M,D*
Vanderbilt University M,D*
Virginia Commonwealth University M,D*†
Virginia Polytechnic Institute and State University M,D*
Wake Forest University D*†
Washington University in St. Louis M,D*†
Wayne State University M,D*
Worcester Polytechnic Institute M,D,O*†
Wright State University M,D*

BIOMETRICS

Cornell University M,D*
Louisiana State University Health Sciences Center M*
Medical University of South Carolina M,D*
Mount Sinai School of Medicine of New York University D*
North Carolina State University M,D*
Oregon State University M,D*
State University of New York at Albany M,D*†
The University of Alabama at Birmingham M,D*†
University of California, Los Angeles M,D*
University of Colorado Health Sciences Center M,D*
University of Nebraska–Lincoln M*†
University of Southern California M*†
The University of Texas Health Science Center at Houston M,D*
University of Wisconsin–Madison M*

BIOPHYSICS

Baylor College of Medicine D*
Boston University M,D*†
Brandeis University D*†
California Institute of Technology D*
Carnegie Mellon University M,D*
Case Western Reserve University M,D*†
Clemson University M,D*
Columbia University M,D*†

Cornell University D*
Dalhousie University M,D*
Duke University O*†
East Carolina University M,D*†
East Tennessee State University M,D†
Emory University D*†
Florida State University D*†
Georgetown University M,D*
Harvard University D*†
Howard University D*
Indiana University–Purdue University Indianapolis M,D*
Iowa State University of Science and Technology M,D*†
Joan and Sanford I. Weill Medical College and Graduate School of Medical Sciences of Cornell University D*
Johns Hopkins University M,D*†
Massachusetts Institute of Technology D*
Medical College of Wisconsin D*
Mount Sinai School of Medicine of New York University D*
Northwestern University D*
The Ohio State University M,D*
Oregon State University M,D*
Princeton University D*
Purdue University D*
Rensselaer Polytechnic Institute M,D*†
Simon Fraser University M,D
Stanford University D*
Stony Brook University, State University of New York D*†
Syracuse University M,D*
Texas A&M University M,D*
Université de Montréal M,D
Université de Sherbrooke M,D
Université du Québec à Trois-Rivières M,D
University at Buffalo, The State University of New York M,D*†
The University of Alabama at Birmingham D*†
University of Arkansas for Medical Sciences M,D*
University of California, Berkeley M,D*
University of California, Davis M,D*†
University of California, Irvine D*
University of California, San Diego M,D*
University of California, San Francisco D*
University of Cincinnati D*
University of Colorado Health Sciences Center M,D*
University of Connecticut M,D*†
University of Guelph M,D
University of Hawaii at Manoa M,D*
University of Illinois at Chicago M,D*
University of Illinois at Urbana–Champaign D*
The University of Iowa M,D*
University of Kansas M,D*
University of Louisville M,D*†
University of Maryland, College Park M,D*
University of Miami D*†
University of Michigan D*
University of Minnesota, Twin Cities Campus M,D*
University of Mississippi Medical Center M,D*
University of Missouri–Kansas City D*†
The University of North Carolina at Chapel Hill M,D*†
University of Pennsylvania D*†
University of Pittsburgh D*†
University of Rochester M,D*
University of Southern California M,D*†
University of South Florida D*†
The University of Tennessee Health Science Center M,D*
The University of Texas Health Science Center at Houston M,D*
The University of Texas Medical Branch M,D*
The University of Texas Southwestern Medical Center at Dallas D*
University of Toronto M,D*
University of Vermont M,D*†
University of Virginia D*
University of Washington D*
The University of Western Ontario M,D*
University of Wisconsin–Madison D*
Vanderbilt University D*
Virginia Commonwealth University M,D,O*†
Washington State University M,D*
Washington University in St. Louis D*†
Wright State University M*
Yale University M,D*
Yeshiva University D*

BIOPSYCHOLOGY

Alliant International University M*†
American University M,D*†
Boston University M*†
Bryn Mawr College D
Carnegie Mellon University D*
College of Staten Island of the City University of New York D†
Columbia University M,D*†
Cornell University D*
Drexel University D*†
Duke University D*†
Emory University D*†
Graduate School and University Center of the City University of New York D*†
Harvard University M,D*†
Howard University M,D*
Hunter College of the City University of New York M†
Louisiana State University and Agricultural and Mechanical College M,D*
Memorial University of Newfoundland M,D†
Northwestern University D*
The Ohio State University D*
Oregon Health & Science University M,D*
The Pennsylvania State University University Park Campus M,D*†
Rutgers, The State University of New Jersey, Newark D*†
Rutgers, The State University of New Jersey, New Brunswick D*
State University of New York at Albany M,D*†
State University of New York at Binghamton M,D*†
Stony Brook University, State University of New York D*†
University of Colorado at Boulder M,D*
University of Connecticut M,D*†
University of Illinois at Urbana–Champaign M,D*
University of Michigan D*
University of Minnesota, Twin Cities Campus D*
University of New Orleans M,D*
University of Oklahoma Health Sciences Center M,D*
University of Oregon M,D*
University of Wisconsin–Madison D*

BIOSTATISTICS

Arizona State University M,D*
Boston University M,D*†
Brown University M,D*
Case Western Reserve University M,D*†
Columbia University M,D*†
Drexel University M,D*†
Emory University M,D*†
Georgetown University M*
The George Washington University M,D*†
Harvard University M,D*†
Iowa State University of Science and Technology D*†
Johns Hopkins University M,D*†
Loma Linda University M*
McGill University M,D,O*
Medical College of Wisconsin D*
Medical University of South Carolina M,D*
Mount Sinai School of Medicine of New York University D*
New York Medical College M*
The Ohio State University D*
Oregon Health & Science University M*
Rice University M,D*
Saint Louis University M*†
San Diego State University M,D*
Tufts University M,D*†
Tulane University M,D*†
The University of Alabama at Birmingham M,D*†
University of California, Berkeley M,D*
University of California, Los Angeles M,D*
University of Cincinnati M,D*
University of Illinois at Chicago M,D*
The University of Iowa M,D*
University of Louisville M*†
University of Michigan M,D*
University of Minnesota, Twin Cities Campus M,D*
The University of North Carolina at Chapel Hill M,D*†
University of North Texas Health Science Center at Fort Worth M,D*
University of Oklahoma Health Sciences Center M,D*
University of Pennsylvania M,D*†
University of Pittsburgh M,D*†
University of Puerto Rico, Medical Sciences Campus M*
University of Rochester M,D*
University of South Carolina M,D*†
University of Southern California M,D*†
University of South Florida M,D*†
University of Utah M*
University of Vermont M*†
University of Washington M,D*
University of Waterloo M,D
The University of Western Ontario M,D*
Virginia Commonwealth University M,D*†
Western Michigan University M*†
Yale University M,D*

BIOTECHNOLOGY

Brock University M,D
Brown University M,D*
Dartmouth College M,D*†
East Carolina University M*†
Florida Institute of Technology M,D*†
Howard University M,D*
Illinois Institute of Technology M,D*†
Illinois State University M*†
Instituto Tecnológico y de Estudios Superiores de Monterrey, Campus Monterrey M,D
Kean University M*†
Keck Graduate Institute of Applied Life Sciences M*
Manhattan College M*†
McGill University M,D,O*
National University M†
North Carolina State University M*
Northwestern University D*
The Pennsylvania State University University Park Campus M,D*†
Salem International University M
Stephen F. Austin State University M
Texas A&M University M*
Texas Tech University M,D*†
Texas Tech University Health Sciences Center M*
Thomas Jefferson University D*
Tufts University O*†
Université du Québec, Institut National de la Recherche Scientifique M,D
The University of Alabama in Huntsville M,D*
University of Alberta M,D*
University of Calgary M*
University of Connecticut M,D*†
University of Delaware M,D*†
University of Guelph M,D
University of Maryland University College M*
University of Massachusetts Boston M*†
University of Massachusetts Lowell M,D*†
University of Minnesota, Twin Cities Campus M*
University of Missouri–St. Louis M,D,O†
University of North Texas Health Science Center at Fort Worth M,D*
University of Pennsylvania M*†
The University of Texas at San Antonio M,D*
University of the Sciences in Philadelphia M*
University of Virginia D*
University of Wisconsin–Madison *
William Paterson University of New Jersey M*†
Worcester Polytechnic Institute M,D*†
Worcester State College M

BOTANY

Auburn University M,D*†
Brigham Young University M,D*
California State University, Chico M
California State University, Fullerton M
Claremont Graduate University M,D*
Colorado State University M,D*
Connecticut College M
Eastern Illinois University M†
Emporia State University M*†
Illinois State University M,D*†
Iowa State University of Science and Technology M,D*†
Kent State University M,D*
Miami University M,D*†
North Carolina State University M,D*
North Dakota State University M,D†
Nova Scotia Agricultural College M
Oklahoma State University M,D*†
Oregon State University M,D*
Purdue University M,D*
Texas A&M University M,D*
University of Alaska Fairbanks M,D*
The University of British Columbia M,D*
University of California, Riverside M,D*
University of Connecticut M,D*†
University of Florida M,D*†
University of Georgia M,D*†
University of Guelph M,D
University of Hawaii at Manoa M,D*
University of Idaho M,D*†
University of Kansas M,D*
University of Maine M*
University of Manitoba M,D*
University of Missouri–St. Louis M,D,O†
The University of North Carolina at Chapel Hill M,D*†
University of North Dakota M,D*
University of Oklahoma M,D*†
University of Rhode Island M,D*
University of South Florida M*†
The University of Tennessee M,D*†
University of Toronto M,D*
University of Vermont M,D*†
University of Washington M,D*
University of Wisconsin–Madison M,D*
University of Wisconsin–Oshkosh M*
University of Wyoming M,D*†
Virginia Polytechnic Institute and State University M,D*
Washington State University M,D*

BUILDING SCIENCE

Arizona State University M*
Auburn University M*†
Carnegie Mellon University M,D*
Georgia Institute of Technology M,D*
Michigan State University M*†
Rensselaer Polytechnic Institute M*†
University of California, Berkeley M,D*
University of Florida M*†
University of Southern California M*†

BUSINESS ADMINISTRATION AND MANAGEMENT—GENERAL

Adelphi University M,O*
Air Force Institute of Technology M*
Alabama Agricultural and Mechanical University M
Alabama State University M
Alaska Pacific University M
Albany State University M
Albertus Magnus College M
Alcorn State University M
Alfred University M*†
Alliant International University M,D*†
Alliant International University–México City M
Alvernia College M
Amberton University M
American InterContinental University-London M
American InterContinental University Online M
American International College M*
American Military University M
American University M*†
American University in Cairo M,O
The American University in Dubai M
Andrew Jackson University M
Andrews University M
Angelo State University M†
Anna Maria College M,O
Antioch New England Graduate School M*†
Antioch University Los Angeles M
Antioch University McGregor M†
Antioch University Seattle M†
Appalachian State University M
Aquinas College M
Argosy University-Chicago M*
Argosy University-Chicago Northwest M,D*
Argosy University-Orange County M,D*
Argosy University-Sarasota M,D*†
Argosy University-Tampa M*

*P—first professional degree; M—master's degree; D—doctorate; O—other advanced degree; *full description and/or announcement in Book 2, 3, 4, 5, or 6; †full description in this book*

Institution	Degrees
Arizona State University	M,D*
Arizona State University West	M
Arkansas State University	M,O
Armstrong University	M
Arthur D. Little School of Management	M
Ashland University	M
Assumption College	M,O†
Athabasca University	M,O
Auburn University	M,D*†
Auburn University Montgomery	M
Audrey Cohen College	M†
Augsburg College	M
Augusta State University	M
Aurora University	M
Averett University	M
Avila University	M
Azusa Pacific University	M*†
Babson College	M
Baker College Center for Graduate Studies	M
Baker University	M
Baldwin-Wallace College	M*
Ball State University	M*
Barry University	M,O*†
Bayamón Central University	M
Baylor University	M*†
Belhaven College	M
Bellarmine University	M
Bellevue University	M*†
Belmont University	M
Benedictine College	M
Benedictine University	M†
Bentley College	M,O*
Bernard M. Baruch College of the City University of New York	M,D,O*
Berry College	M
Bethel College (IN)	M
Biola University	M
Birmingham-Southern College	M
Black Hills State University	M*
Bloomsburg University of Pennsylvania	M
Boise State University	M*
Boston College	M*†
Boston University	M*†
Bowie State University	M
Bowling Green State University	M*†
Bradley University	M†
Brandeis University	M*†
Brenau University	M
Brescia University	M
Bridgewater State College	M
Briercrest Biblical Seminary	M
Brigham Young University	M*
Bryant College	M,O
Bucknell University	M
Butler University	M
Caldwell College	M
California Baptist University	M
California Lutheran University	M
California National University for Advanced Studies	M
California Polytechnic State University, San Luis Obispo	M†
California State Polytechnic University, Pomona	M*
California State University, Bakersfield	M
California State University, Chico	M
California State University, Dominguez Hills	M†
California State University, Fresno	M
California State University, Fullerton	M
California State University, Hayward	M
California State University, Long Beach	M
California State University, Los Angeles	M
California State University, Northridge	M
California State University, Sacramento	M
California State University, San Bernardino	M
California State University, San Marcos	M
California State University, Stanislaus	M
California University of Pennsylvania	M
Cambridge College	M†
Cameron University	M
Campbellsville University	M
Campbell University	M
Canisius College	M
Capella University	M,D
Capital University	M
Cardean University	M†
Cardinal Stritch University	M*
Carleton University	M,D
Carlos Albizu University, Miami Campus	M,D
Carnegie Mellon University	M,D*
Case Western Reserve University	M,D,O*†
The Catholic University of America	M*†
Cedarville University	M
Centenary College	M
Centenary College of Louisiana	M
Central Connecticut State University	M*†
Central Michigan University	M†
Central Missouri State University	M†
Central Washington University	M†
Chadron State College	M
Chaminade University of Honolulu	M*
Chapman University	M*†
Charleston Southern University	M
Chatham College	M
Christian Brothers University	M
The Citadel, The Military College of South Carolina	M
City University	M,O†
Claremont Graduate University	M,D,O*
Clarion University of Pennsylvania	M†
Clark Atlanta University	M
Clarke College	M
Clarkson University	M*
Clark University	M*†
Cleary University	M
Clemson University	M,D*
Cleveland State University	M,D*†
College of Charleston	M*†
College of Notre Dame of Maryland	M
College of Saint Elizabeth	M
College of St. Joseph	M
The College of Saint Rose	M*†
The College of St. Scholastica	M
College of Santa Fe	M
The College of William and Mary	M*†
Colorado State University	M*
Colorado Technical University	M,D
Colorado Technical University Denver Campus	M
Colorado Technical University Sioux Falls Campus	M
Columbia College (MO)	M
Columbia Southern University	M
Columbia University	M,D*†
Concordia University (CA)	M
Concordia University (Canada)	M,D,O*†
Concordia University Wisconsin	M
Cornell University	M,D*
Creighton University	M*
Cumberland University	M
Daemen College	M
Dalhousie University	M*
Dallas Baptist University	M
Dartmouth College	M*†
Davenport University	M
Davenport University	M
Davenport University	M
Defiance College	M
Delaware State University	M
Delta State University	M
DePaul University	M*†
DeSales University	M
DeVry University-Keller Graduate School of Management	M
Doane College	M
Dominican University	M*
Dominican University of California	M
Dowling College	M,O
Drake University	M*†
Drexel University	M,D,O*†
Drury University	M
Duke University	M,D*†
Duquesne University	M*†
East Carolina University	M*†
Eastern Illinois University	M†
Eastern Kentucky University	M
Eastern Mennonite University	M
Eastern Michigan University	M*
Eastern New Mexico University	M
Eastern University	M*
Eastern Washington University	M†
East Tennessee State University	M,O†
École des Hautes Études Commerciales de Montréal	M,D,O*
Edgewood College	M
Elon University	M
Embry-Riddle Aeronautical University (FL)	M*
Emmanuel College	M*
Emory University	M,D*†
Emporia State University	M*†
Endicott College	M
Fairfield University	M,O*
Fairleigh Dickinson University, College at Florham	M*†
Fairleigh Dickinson University, Metropolitan Campus	M*†
Fayetteville State University	M
Ferris State University	M
Fitchburg State College	M†
Florida Agricultural and Mechanical University	M*
Florida Atlantic University	M,D*
Florida Atlantic University, Ft. Lauderdale Campus	M,D
Florida Gulf Coast University	M
Florida Institute of Technology	M*†
Florida International University	M,D*†
Florida Metropolitan University–Brandon Campus	M
Florida Metropolitan University–Fort Lauderdale Campus	M
Florida Metropolitan University–Melbourne Campus	M
Florida Metropolitan University–North Orlando Campus	M
Florida Metropolitan University–Pinellas Campus	M
Florida Metropolitan University–Tampa Campus	M
Florida Southern College	M
Florida State University	M,D*†
Fontbonne University	M
Fordham University	M*†
Fort Hays State University	M
Framingham State College	M*
Franciscan University of Steubenville	M
Francis Marion University	M
Franklin Pierce College	M
Franklin University	M
Fresno Pacific University	M
Friends University	M
Frostburg State University	M
Gannon University	M,O
Gardner-Webb University	M
Geneva College	M*
George Fox University	M†
George Mason University	M*†
Georgetown University	M*
The George Washington University	M,D*†
Georgia College & State University	M
Georgia Institute of Technology	M,D*
Georgian Court College	M
Georgia Southern University	M
Georgia Southwestern State University	M
Georgia State University	M,D*
Golden Gate University	M,D,O
Goldey-Beacom College	M
Gonzaga University	M
Governors State University	M
Graduate School and University Center of the City University of New York	D*†
Grand Canyon University	M
Grand Valley State University	M†
Hamline University	M*
Hampton University	M*†
Harding University	M
Hardin-Simmons University	M
Harvard University	M,D,O*†
Hawai'i Pacific University	M*†
Heidelberg College	M
Henderson State University	M
High Point University	M
Hofstra University	M*
Holy Family College	M
Holy Names College	M
Hood College	M
Hope International University	M
Houston Baptist University	M
Howard University	M*
Hsi Lai University	M*
Humboldt State University	M
Huron University USA in London	M
Husson College	M
Idaho State University	M*
Illinois Institute of Technology	M,D*†
Illinois State University	M*†
IMCA–International Management Centres Association	M,D
Indiana Institute of Technology	M
Indiana State University	M,D,O*†
Indiana University Bloomington	M,D*
Indiana University Kokomo	M
Indiana University Northwest	M,O
Indiana University of Pennsylvania	M*†
Indiana University–Purdue University Fort Wayne	M
Indiana University–Purdue University Indianapolis	M*
Indiana University South Bend	M*
Indiana University Southeast	M,O
Indiana Wesleyan University	M*
Instituto Centroamericano de Administración de Empresas	M
Instituto Tecnológico y de Estudios Superiores de Monterrey, Campus Central de Veracruz	M
Instituto Tecnológico y de Estudios Superiores de Monterrey, Campus Ciudad de México	M,D
Instituto Tecnológico y de Estudios Superiores de Monterrey, Campus Ciudad Juárez	M
Instituto Tecnológico y de Estudios Superiores de Monterrey, Campus Ciudad Obregón	M
Instituto Tecnológico y de Estudios Superiores de Monterrey, Campus Cuernavaca	M
Instituto Tecnológico y de Estudios Superiores de Monterrey, Campus Guadalajara	M
Instituto Tecnológico y de Estudios Superiores de Monterrey, Campus Irapuato	M,D
Instituto Tecnológico y de Estudios Superiores de Monterrey, Campus Laguna	M
Instituto Tecnológico y de Estudios Superiores de Monterrey, Campus León	M
Instituto Tecnológico y de Estudios Superiores de Monterrey, Campus Monterrey	M,D
Instituto Tecnológico y de Estudios Superiores de Monterrey, Campus Querétaro	M
Instituto Tecnológico y de Estudios Superiores de Monterrey, Campus Sonora Norte	M
Instituto Tecnológico y de Estudios Superiores de Monterrey, Campus Toluca	M
Inter American University of Puerto Rico, Metropolitan Campus	M,D
Inter American University of Puerto Rico, San Germán Campus	M,D
International College of the Cayman Islands	M
International Technological University	M
Iona College	M,O*†
Iowa State University of Science and Technology	M*†
ISIM University	M
Ithaca College	M†
ITI-Information Technology Institute	M
Jackson State University	M,D
Jacksonville State University	M
Jacksonville University	M
James Madison University	M
John Brown University	M
John Carroll University	M
John F. Kennedy University	M,O*†
Johns Hopkins University	M,O*†
Johnson & Wales University	M*†
Jones International University	M*†
Kansas State University	M*†
Kansas Wesleyan University	M
Kennesaw State University	M
Kent State University	M*
King's College	M
Kutztown University of Pennsylvania	M†
Lake Erie College	M
Lake Forest Graduate School of Management	M
Lakeland College	M
Lamar University	M*†
La Salle University	M,O
La Sierra University	M,O
Laurentian University	M
Lawrence Technological University	M
The Leadership Institute of Seattle	M*
Lebanese American University	M
Lebanon Valley College	M
Lehigh University	M,D,O*
Le Moyne College	M
Lenoir-Rhyne College	M
Lesley University	M*†
LeTourneau University	M
Lewis University	M
Liberty University	M†
Lincoln Memorial University	M
Lincoln University (CA)	M
Lincoln University (MO)	M
Lindenwood University	M
Lipscomb University	M
Long Island University, Brentwood Campus	M
Long Island University, Brooklyn Campus	M*
Long Island University, C.W. Post Campus	M,O*†
Long Island University, Rockland Graduate Campus	M

Institution	Degrees
Long Island University, Westchester Graduate Campus	M
Louisiana State University and Agricultural and Mechanical College	M,D*
Louisiana State University in Shreveport	M†
Louisiana Tech University	M,D*
Loyola College in Maryland	M
Loyola Marymount University	M†
Loyola University Chicago	M*†
Loyola University New Orleans	M
Lynchburg College	M
Lynn University	M†
Madonna University	M
Maharishi University of Management	M,D
Malone College	M†
Marian College of Fond du Lac	M
Marist College	M,O
Marquette University	M*†
Marshall University	M*†
Marylhurst University	M
Marymount University	M,O†
Maryville University of Saint Louis	M,O
Marywood University	M*†
Massachusetts Institute of Technology	M,D*
McGill University	M,D*
McMaster University	M,D
McNeese State University	M
Medaille College	M
Memorial University of Newfoundland	M†
Mercer University	M
Mercy College	M*
Meredith College	M
Mesa State College	M
Metropolitan State University	M
Miami University	M*†
Michigan State University	M,D*†
Michigan Technological University	M*†
MidAmerica Nazarene University	M
Middle Tennessee State University	M*
Midwestern State University	M
Millsaps College	M
Mills College	M*†
Minot State University	M
Mississippi College	M
Mississippi State University	M,D*
Monmouth University	M,O*†
Montclair State University	M†
Monterey Institute of International Studies	M*
Montreat College	M
Moravian College	M
Morgan State University	M,D*
Morrison University	M
Mount Saint Mary College	M
Mount Saint Mary's College and Seminary	M
Murray State University	M†
National American University	M
The National Graduate School of Quality Management	M*
National-Louis University	M*
National University	M†
Nazareth College of Rochester	M
New England College	M,O*
New Jersey Institute of Technology	M
New Mexico Highlands University	M
New Mexico State University	M,D
New School University	M,D,O*†
New York Institute of Technology	M,O*†
New York University	M,D,O*†
Niagara University	M†
Nicholls State University	M
Nichols College	M
North Carolina Central University	M
North Carolina State University	M*
North Central College	M
North Dakota State University	M†
Northeastern Illinois University	M
Northeastern State University	M
Northeastern University	M,O*†
Northern Arizona University	M
Northern Illinois University	M*†
Northern Kentucky University	M
North Park University	M
Northwest Christian College	M
Northwestern Polytechnic University	M
Northwestern University	M*
Northwest Missouri State University	M
Northwest Nazarene University	M
Northwood University	M
Norwich University	M
Notre Dame College (OH)	M,O
Notre Dame de Namur University	M
Nova Southeastern University	M,D*
Oakland City University	M
Oakland University	M,O†
OGI School of Science & Engineering at Oregon Health & Science University	M,O*
Oglala Lakota College	M
Oglethorpe University	M
The Ohio State University	M,D*
Ohio University	M*
Oklahoma City University	M
Oklahoma State University	M,D*†
Old Dominion University	M,D*†
Olivet Nazarene University	M
Oral Roberts University	M
Oregon State University	M,O*
Otterbein College	M
Our Lady of the Lake University of San Antonio	M
Pace University	M*†
Pace University, White Plains Campus	M*
Pacific Lutheran University	M†
Palm Beach Atlantic University	M
Park University	M
The Pennsylvania State University at Erie, The Behrend College	M
The Pennsylvania State University Great Valley Campus	M,O
The Pennsylvania State University Harrisburg Campus of the Capital College	M*†
The Pennsylvania State University University Park Campus	M,D*†
Pepperdine University	M*†
Pepperdine University	M*
Pfeiffer University	M
Philadelphia University	M
Piedmont College	M
Pittsburg State University	M
Plymouth State College	M*
Point Loma Nazarene University	M
Point Park College	M*
Polytechnic University, Brooklyn Campus	M*
Polytechnic University, Long Island Graduate Center	M
Polytechnic University of Puerto Rico	M
Polytechnic University, Westchester Graduate Center	M
Pontifical Catholic University of Puerto Rico	M,D
Portland State University	M,D*
Prairie View A&M University	M
Providence College	M*
Purdue University	M,D*
Purdue University Calumet	M
Queen's University at Kingston	M
Queens University of Charlotte	M
Quincy University	M
Quinnipiac University	M*†
Radford University	M†
Regent University	M†
Regis College (MA)	M
Regis University	M,O*†
Rensselaer Polytechnic Institute	M,D*†
Rice University	M*
The Richard Stockton College of New Jersey	M*
Richmond, The American International University in London	M*
Rider University	M*
Rivier College	M*†
Robert Morris University	M†
Roberts Wesleyan College	M*
Rochester Institute of Technology	M*†
Rockford College	M
Rockhurst University	M
Rollins College	M*
Roosevelt University	M*†
Rosemont College	M†
Rowan University	M†
Royal Military College of Canada	M
Royal Roads University	M
Rutgers, The State University of New Jersey, Camden	M†
Rutgers, The State University of New Jersey, Newark	M,D*†
Sacred Heart University	M*†
Sage Graduate School	M†
Saginaw Valley State University	M
St. Ambrose University	M,D
St. Bonaventure University	M,O
St. Cloud State University	M
St. Edward's University	M,O
Saint Francis University	M*
St. John Fisher College	M
St. John's University (NY)	M,O*†
Saint Joseph's University	M*†
Saint Leo University	M
Saint Louis University	M*†
Saint Martin's College	M
Saint Mary College	M
Saint Mary's College of California	M
Saint Mary's University	M,D
Saint Mary's University of Minnesota	M
St. Mary's University of San Antonio	M
Saint Michael's College	M,O*
Saint Peter's College	M†
St. Thomas Aquinas College	M
St. Thomas University	M,O†
Saint Xavier University	M,O*
Salem State College	M
Salisbury University	M
Salve Regina University	M†
Samford University	M
Sam Houston State University	M*
San Diego State University	M*
San Francisco State University	M
San Jose State University	M*
Santa Clara University	M*
Schiller International University (United States)	M
Schiller International University (Germany)	M
Schiller International University	M
Schiller International University (Spain)	M
Schiller International University	M
Schiller International University, American College of Switzerland	M
School for International Training	M,O†
Seattle Pacific University	M
Seattle University	M,O*†
Seton Hall University	O*†
Seton Hill University	M†
Shenandoah University	M,O
Shippensburg University of Pennsylvania	M†
Shorter College	M
Silver Lake College	M
Simmons College	M*
Simon Fraser University	M
Slippery Rock University of Pennsylvania	M†
Sonoma State University	M
South Carolina State University	M
Southeastern Louisiana University	M
Southeastern Oklahoma State University	M
Southeastern University	M†
Southeast Missouri State University	M
Southern Adventist University	M
Southern Connecticut State University	M†
Southern Illinois University Carbondale	M,D*†
Southern Illinois University Edwardsville	M†
Southern Methodist University	M*†
Southern Nazarene University	M
Southern New Hampshire University	M,O*
Southern Oregon University	M
Southern University and Agricultural and Mechanical College	M*
Southern Utah University	M
Southern Wesleyan University	M
Southwest Baptist University	M
Southwestern Adventist University	M
Southwestern Oklahoma State University	M
Southwest Missouri State University	M*†
Southwest State University	M
Southwest Texas State University	M*
Spring Arbor University	M
Spring Hill College	M
Stanford University	M,D*
State University of New York at Albany	M,D*†
State University of New York at Binghamton	M,D*†
State University of New York at New Paltz	M
State University of New York at Oswego	M
State University of New York Empire State College	M
State University of New York Institute of Technology at Utica/Rome	M*†
State University of West Georgia	M
Stephen F. Austin State University	M
Stephens College	M
Stetson University	M
Stevens Institute of Technology	M,D,O*†
Stony Brook University, State University of New York	M,O*†
Strayer University	M
Suffolk University	M,O*
Sullivan University	M
Sul Ross State University	M*
Syracuse University	M,D*
Tarleton State University	M
Temple University	M,D*†
Tennessee State University	M*
Tennessee Technological University	M*
Texas A&M International University	M
Texas A&M University	M,D*
Texas A&M University–Commerce	M†
Texas A&M University–Corpus Christi	M
Texas A&M University–Kingsville	M*†
Texas A&M University–Texarkana	M
Texas Christian University	M*
Texas Southern University	M†
Texas Tech University	D*†
Texas Wesleyan University	M
Texas Woman's University	M*†
Thomas College	M
Thomas Edison State College	M†
Thomas More College	M
Thomas University	M
Thunderbird, The American Graduate School of International Management	M
Tiffin University	M†
Trevecca Nazarene University	M
Trinity College (DC)	M†
Trinity International University	P,M,D,O
Trinity University	M*
Troy State University	M
Troy State University Dothan	M
Troy State University Montgomery	M
Tulane University	M,D*†
Tusculum College	M
Union College (NY)	M*
Union University	M
United States International University	M
Universidad de las Americas, A.C.	M
Universidad de las Américas–Puebla	M
Universidad del Turabo	M
Universidad Metropolitana	M
Université de Moncton	M
Université de Sherbrooke	M,D,O
Université du Québec à Chicoutimi	M
Université du Québec à Montréal	M,D,O
Université du Québec à Trois-Rivières	M,D
Université du Québec en Abitibi-Témiscamingue	M
Université Laval	M,D,O†
University at Buffalo, The State University of New York	M,D*†
University College of Cape Breton	M
The University of Akron	M†
The University of Alabama	M,D*
The University of Alabama at Birmingham	M,D*†
The University of Alabama in Huntsville	M*
University of Alaska Anchorage	M
University of Alaska Fairbanks	M*
University of Alberta	M,D*
The University of Arizona	M,D*
University of Arkansas	M,D*
University of Arkansas at Little Rock	M
University of Baltimore	M*
University of Bridgeport	M*†
The University of British Columbia	M,D*
University of Calgary	M,D*
University of California, Berkeley	M,D,O*
University of California, Davis	M*†
University of California, Irvine	M,D*
University of California, Los Angeles	M,D*
University of California, Riverside	M*
University of Central Arkansas	M
University of Central Florida	M,D*†
University of Central Oklahoma	M
University of Charleston	M
University of Chicago	M*
University of Cincinnati	M,D*
University of Colorado at Boulder	M,D*
University of Colorado at Colorado Springs	M*

*P—first professional degree; M—master's degree; D—doctorate; O—other advanced degree; *full description and/or announcement in Book 2, 3, 4, 5, or 6; †full description in this book*

University of Colorado at Denver M*
University of Connecticut M,D*†
University of Dallas M*
University of Dayton M*†
University of Delaware M,D*†
University of Denver M*†
University of Detroit Mercy M*
University of Dubuque M
The University of Findlay M
University of Florida M,D*†
University of Georgia M,D*†
University of Guam M
University of Hartford M*
University of Hawaii at Manoa M*
University of Houston M,D*
University of Houston–Clear Lake M*†
University of Houston–Victoria M
University of Idaho M*†
University of Illinois at Chicago M,D*
University of Illinois at Springfield M†
University of Illinois at Urbana–Champaign M,D*
University of Indianapolis M
The University of Iowa M,D*
University of Judaism M
University of Kansas M,D*
University of Kentucky M,D*
University of La Verne M*
The University of Lethbridge M,D
University of Louisiana at Lafayette M*
University of Louisiana at Monroe M
University of Louisville M*†
University of Maine M*
University of Manitoba M*
University of Mary M
University of Mary Hardin-Baylor M
University of Maryland, College Park M,D*
University of Maryland University College M,D*
University of Massachusetts Amherst M,D*†
University of Massachusetts Boston M*†
University of Massachusetts Dartmouth M*†
University of Massachusetts Lowell M*†
The University of Memphis M,D*†
University of Miami M,D*†
University of Michigan M,D*
University of Michigan–Dearborn M*†
University of Michigan–Flint M
University of Minnesota, Duluth M*
University of Minnesota, Twin Cities Campus M,D*
University of Mississippi M,D*
University of Missouri–Columbia M,D*
University of Missouri–Kansas City M*†
University of Missouri–St. Louis M,O†
University of Mobile M
The University of Montana–Missoula M*†
University of Nebraska at Kearney M
University of Nebraska at Omaha M
University of Nebraska–Lincoln M,D*†
University of Nevada, Las Vegas M*†
University of Nevada, Reno M*
University of New Brunswick Fredericton M
University of New Brunswick Saint John M
University of New Hampshire M*†
University of New Haven M*†
University of New Mexico M*†
University of New Orleans M*
University of North Alabama M
The University of North Carolina at Chapel Hill M,D*†
The University of North Carolina at Charlotte M*
The University of North Carolina at Greensboro M,O†
The University of North Carolina at Pembroke M
The University of North Carolina at Wilmington M*
University of North Dakota M*
University of Northern Iowa M
University of North Florida M
University of North Texas M,D*†
University of Notre Dame M*†
University of Oklahoma M,D*†
University of Oregon M,D*
University of Ottawa M,O*
University of Pennsylvania M,D*†
University of Phoenix–Boston Campus M
University of Phoenix-Chicago Campus M
University of Phoenix–Colorado Campus M
University of Phoenix–Dallas Campus M
University of Phoenix–Fort Lauderdale Campus M
University of Phoenix–Hawaii Campus M
University of Phoenix–Houston Campus M
University of Phoenix–Jacksonville Campus M
University of Phoenix-Kansas City Campus M
University of Phoenix–Louisiana Campus M
University of Phoenix–Maryland Campus M
University of Phoenix–Metro Detroit Campus M
University of Phoenix–Nevada Campus M
University of Phoenix–New Mexico Campus M
University of Phoenix–Northern California Campus M
University of Phoenix–Ohio Campus M
University of Phoenix–Oklahoma City Campus M
University of Phoenix–Oregon Campus M
University of Phoenix–Orlando Campus M
University of Phoenix–Philadelphia Campus M
University of Phoenix–Phoenix Campus M
University of Phoenix–Pittsburgh Campus M
University of Phoenix–Puerto Rico Campus M
University of Phoenix–Sacramento Campus M
University of Phoenix–St. Louis Campus M
University of Phoenix–San Diego Campus M
University of Phoenix–Southern Arizona Campus M
University of Phoenix–Southern California Campus M
University of Phoenix–Southern Colorado Campus M
University of Phoenix–Tampa Campus M
University of Phoenix–Tulsa Campus M
University of Phoenix–Utah Campus M
University of Phoenix-Vancouver Campus M
University of Phoenix–Washington Campus M
University of Phoenix–West Michigan Campus M
University of Pittsburgh M,D*†
University of Portland M
University of Puerto Rico, Mayagüez Campus M*
University of Puerto Rico, Río Piedras M,D*
University of Redlands M
University of Regina M
University of Rhode Island M,D*
University of Richmond M*†
University of Rochester M,D*
University of Saint Francis (IN) M
University of St. Thomas (MN) M,O*†
University of St. Thomas (TX) M
University of San Diego M*†
University of San Francisco M*†
University of Saskatchewan M,D,O
The University of Scranton M†
University of Sioux Falls M
University of South Alabama M*†
University of South Carolina M,D*†
The University of South Dakota M†
University of Southern California M,D*†
University of Southern Colorado M
University of Southern Indiana M
University of Southern Maine M
University of Southern Mississippi M
University of South Florida M,D*†
The University of Tampa M
The University of Tennessee M,D*†
The University of Tennessee at Chattanooga M
The University of Tennessee at Martin M
The University of Texas at Arlington M,D*†
The University of Texas at Austin M,D*
The University of Texas at Brownsville M
The University of Texas at Dallas M,D*
The University of Texas at El Paso M*†
The University of Texas at San Antonio M*
The University of Texas at Tyler M
The University of Texas of the Permian Basin M
The University of Texas–Pan American M,D
University of the District of Columbia M*
University of the Incarnate Word M,D†
University of the Pacific M*
University of the Sacred Heart M
University of the Virgin Islands M
University of Toledo M*†
University of Toronto M,D*
University of Tulsa M†
University of Utah M,D*
University of Vermont M*†
University of Victoria M
University of Virginia M,D*
University of Washington M,D*
The University of Western Ontario M,D*
University of West Florida M
University of Windsor M
University of Wisconsin–Eau Claire M†
University of Wisconsin–Green Bay M
University of Wisconsin–La Crosse M†
University of Wisconsin–Madison M,D*
University of Wisconsin–Milwaukee M,D
University of Wisconsin–Oshkosh M*
University of Wisconsin–Parkside M
University of Wisconsin–River Falls M
University of Wisconsin–Stevens Point M
University of Wisconsin–Whitewater M*
University of Wyoming M*†
Upper Iowa University M
Utah State University M*
Valdosta State University M
Valparaiso University M
Vanderbilt University M,D*
Villanova University M*†
Virginia Commonwealth University M,D,O*†
Virginia Polytechnic Institute and State University M,D*
Virginia State University M
Wagner College M
Wake Forest University M*†
Walsh College of Accountancy and Business Administration M
Walsh University M
Washburn University of Topeka M
Washington State University M,D*
Washington University in St. Louis M,D*†
Wayland Baptist University M
Waynesburg College M
Wayne State College M
Wayne State University M*
Webber International University M
Weber State University M
Webster University M,D
Wesley College M
West Chester University of Pennsylvania M*†
Western Carolina University M†
Western Connecticut State University M
Western Illinois University M
Western International University M
Western Kentucky University M†
Western Michigan University M*†
Western New England College M
Western New Mexico University M
Western Washington University M
Westminster College (UT) M,O
West Texas A&M University M†
West Virginia University M*
West Virginia Wesleyan College M
Wheeling Jesuit University M
Whitworth College M
Wichita State University M*†
Widener University M*†
Wilfrid Laurier University M
Wilkes University M
Willamette University M*
William Carey College M
William Paterson University of New Jersey M*†
William Woods University M
Wilmington College M
Wingate University M
Winthrop University M
Woodbury University M*
Worcester Polytechnic Institute M,O*†
Wright State University M*
Xavier University M*
Yale University M,D*
York College of Pennsylvania M
York University M,D*
Youngstown State University M

BUSINESS EDUCATION

Albany State University M
Alfred University M*†
Arkansas State University M,O
Armstrong Atlantic State University M†
Ashland University M
Auburn University M,D,O*†
Ball State University M*
Bloomsburg University of Pennsylvania M
Bowling Green State University M,O*†
California State University, Northridge M
Central Connecticut State University M*†
Central Michigan University M†
Central Washington University M†
Chadron State College M,O
College of Mount St. Joseph M†
Eastern Kentucky University M
Eastern Michigan University M*
Emporia State University M*†
Florida Agricultural and Mechanical University M*
Georgia Southern University M
Georgia Southwestern State University M,O
Hofstra University M*
Inter American University of Puerto Rico, Metropolitan Campus M
Inter American University of Puerto Rico, San Germán Campus M
Iona College M*†
Jackson State University M
Johnson & Wales University M*†
Lehman College of the City University of New York M
Louisiana State University and Agricultural and Mechanical College M,D*
Louisiana Tech University M,D,O*
Maryville University of Saint Louis M,O
McNeese State University M
Middle Tennessee State University M*
Mississippi College M
Montclair State University M†
Nazareth College of Rochester M
New York University M,D,O*†
Northwestern State University of Louisiana M,O
Old Dominion University M*†
Rider University O*
Robert Morris University M†
Salisbury University M
Shenandoah University M,D,O
South Carolina State University M
Southeast Missouri State University M
Southern New Hampshire University M*
State University of New York College at Buffalo M
State University of West Georgia M,O
Texas Southern University M†
Troy State University Dothan M
The University of British Columbia M,D*
University of Central Arkansas M
University of Georgia M,D,O*†
University of Idaho M,D,O*†
University of Manitoba M*
University of Minnesota, Twin Cities Campus M,D*
University of South Alabama M*†
University of South Carolina M,D*†
University of South Florida M*†
University of Toledo M,D,O*†
University of Wisconsin–Whitewater M*
Utah State University M,D*
Valdosta State University M,D,O
Wayne State College M
Western Kentucky University M†
Wright State University M*

CANADIAN STUDIES

Athabasca University M
Carleton University M,D
Collège universitaire de Saint-Boniface M
Johns Hopkins University M,D,O*†
Saint Mary's University M
Trent University M

Université de Sherbrooke M,D
Université du Québec à Chicoutimi M
Université du Québec à Trois-Rivières M,D
Université Laval M,D†
The University of Lethbridge M,D
University of Ottawa D*
University of Regina M,D
University of Saskatchewan M,D

CANCER BIOLOGY/ONCOLOGY

Brown University M,D*
Drexel University M,D*†
Duke University D*†
Emory University M,D*†
Georgetown University *
The George Washington University D*†
Harvard University D*†
Kansas State University M,D*†
Mayo Graduate School D*
McMaster University M,D
New York University D*†
Northwestern University D*
Stanford University D*
Thomas Jefferson University D*
Université Laval O†
University at Buffalo, The State University of New York D*†
University of Alberta M,D*
The University of Arizona D*
University of California, San Diego D*
University of Chicago D*
University of Medicine and Dentistry of New Jersey *
The University of North Carolina at Chapel Hill *†
University of Pennsylvania D*†
University of South Florida D*†
The University of Texas Health Science Center at Houston M,D*
University of Utah M,D*
University of Wisconsin–Madison D*
Vanderbilt University M,D*
Wake Forest University D*†
Wayne State University M,D*
West Virginia University M,D*

CARDIOVASCULAR SCIENCES

Albany Medical College M,D*
Baylor College of Medicine D*
Long Island University, C.W. Post Campus M,O*†
McMaster University M,D
Medical College of Georgia D*
Midwestern University, Glendale Campus M*
Northeastern University M*†
Université Laval O†
University of Calgary M,D*
University of Medicine and Dentistry of New Jersey M,D*
The University of South Dakota M,D†
University of Toronto M,D*
University of Virginia *

CELL BIOLOGY

Albany Medical College M,D*
Arizona State University M,D*
Baylor College of Medicine D*
Boston University M,D*†
Brandeis University M,D*†
Brock University M
Brown University M,D*
California Institute of Technology D*
Carnegie Mellon University M,D*
Case Western Reserve University M,D*†
The Catholic University of America M,D*†
Central Connecticut State University M,O*†
Colorado State University M,D*
Columbia University M,D*†
Cornell University D*
Drexel University M,D*†
Duke University D,O*†
East Carolina University D*†
Emory University D*†
Emporia State University M*†
Finch University of Health Sciences/The Chicago Medical School M,D*
Florida Institute of Technology D*†
Florida State University M,D*†
Fordham University M,D*†
George Mason University M*†
Georgetown University D*
Georgia State University M,D*
Harvard University D*†
Illinois Institute of Technology M,D*†
Indiana University Bloomington M,D*
Indiana University–Purdue University Indianapolis M,D*
Iowa State University of Science and Technology M,D*†
Joan and Sanford I. Weill Medical College and Graduate School of Medical Sciences of Cornell University D*
Johns Hopkins University D*†
Kansas State University M,D*†
Kent State University M,D*
Louisiana State University Health Sciences Center M,D*
Loyola University Chicago M,D*†
Maharishi University of Management M,D
Marquette University M,D*†
McMaster University M,D
Medical College of Georgia M,D*
Medical College of Ohio D*
Medical College of Wisconsin M,D*
Medical University of South Carolina D*
Michigan State University D*†
Montana State University–Bozeman D*
Mount Sinai School of Medicine of New York University D*
New York Medical College M,D*
New York University M,D*†
North Carolina State University M,D*
North Dakota State University D†
Northwestern University D*
Oakland University M†
The Ohio State University M,D*
Ohio University M,D*
Oregon Health & Science University D*
Oregon State University D*
The Pennsylvania State University Milton S. Hershey Medical Center M,D*
The Pennsylvania State University University Park Campus M,D*†
Princeton University D*
Purdue University D*
Queen's University at Kingston M,D
Quinnipiac University M*†
Rensselaer Polytechnic Institute M,D*†
Rice University M,D*
Rutgers, The State University of New Jersey, New Brunswick M,D*
Saint Joseph College M
San Diego State University M,D*
San Francisco State University M
The Scripps Research Institute D
Southwest Missouri State University M*†
State University of New York at Albany M,D*†
State University of New York Health Science Center at Brooklyn D*
State University of New York Upstate Medical University M,D*
Stony Brook University, State University of New York M,D*†
Temple University D*†
Texas A&M University D*
Texas Tech University Health Sciences Center M,D*
Thomas Jefferson University D*
Tufts University D*†
Tulane University M,D*†
Uniformed Services University of the Health Sciences D*
Université de Montréal M,D
Université de Sherbrooke M,D
Université Laval M,D†
University at Buffalo, The State University of New York D*†
The University of Alabama at Birmingham D*†
University of Alberta M,D*
The University of Arizona M,D*
University of Arkansas M,D*
University of California, Berkeley D*
University of California, Davis D*†
University of California, Irvine M,D*
University of California, Los Angeles M,D*
University of California, Riverside M,D*
University of California, San Diego D*
University of California, San Francisco D*
University of California, Santa Barbara M,D*
University of California, Santa Cruz M,D*
University of Chicago D*
University of Cincinnati D*
University of Colorado at Boulder M,D*
University of Colorado Health Sciences Center D*
University of Connecticut M,D*†
University of Connecticut Health Center D*
University of Delaware M,D*†
University of Florida M,D*†
University of Georgia M,D*†
University of Hawaii at Manoa M,D*
University of Illinois at Chicago M,D*
University of Illinois at Urbana–Champaign D*
The University of Iowa D*
University of Kansas M,D*
University of Maryland D*†
University of Maryland, Baltimore County D*†
University of Maryland, College Park M,D*
University of Massachusetts Amherst D*†
University of Massachusetts Boston *†
University of Massachusetts Worcester D*
University of Medicine and Dentistry of New Jersey M,D*
The University of Memphis M,D*†
University of Miami D*†
University of Michigan M,D*
University of Minnesota, Duluth M,D*
University of Minnesota, Twin Cities Campus M,D*
University of Missouri–Kansas City M,D*†
University of Missouri–St. Louis M,D,O†
University of Nebraska Medical Center M,D*
University of Nevada, Reno M,D*
University of New Haven M*†
University of New Mexico M,D*†
The University of North Carolina at Chapel Hill M,D*†
University of Notre Dame M,D*†
University of Oklahoma Health Sciences Center M,D*
University of Ottawa M,D*
University of Pennsylvania D*†
University of Pittsburgh M,D*†
University of Saskatchewan M,D
University of South Alabama D*†
University of South Carolina M,D*†
The University of South Dakota M,D†
University of Southern California M,D*†
University of South Florida D*†
The University of Tennessee Health Science Center D*
The University of Texas at Austin D*
The University of Texas at Dallas M,D*
The University of Texas Health Science Center at Houston M,D*
The University of Texas Health Science Center at San Antonio D*
The University of Texas Medical Branch M,D*
The University of Texas Southwestern Medical Center at Dallas D*
University of the Sciences in Philadelphia M*
University of Toronto M,D*
University of Utah *
University of Vermont M,D*†
University of Victoria M,D
University of Virginia D*
University of Washington D*
The University of Western Ontario M,D*
University of Wisconsin–Madison M,D*
Vanderbilt University M,D*
Virginia Polytechnic Institute and State University M,D*
Washington State University M,D*
Washington University in St. Louis D*†
Wayne State University M,D*
Wesleyan University D*
West Virginia University M,D*
Yale University D*
Yeshiva University D*

CELTIC LANGUAGES

Harvard University M,D*†

CERAMIC SCIENCES AND ENGINEERING

Alfred University M,D*†
Case Western Reserve University M,D*†
Clemson University M,D*
Georgia Institute of Technology M,D*
The Pennsylvania State University University Park Campus M,D*†
Rensselaer Polytechnic Institute M,D*†
Rutgers, The State University of New Jersey, New Brunswick M,D*
University of California, Berkeley M,D*
University of California, Los Angeles M,D*
University of Cincinnati M,D*
University of Florida M,D,O*†
University of Missouri–Rolla M,D*

CHEMICAL ENGINEERING

Arizona State University M,D*
Auburn University M,D*†
Brigham Young University M,D*
Brown University M,D*
Bucknell University M
California Institute of Technology M,D*
Carnegie Mellon University M,D*
Case Western Reserve University M,D*†
City College of the City University of New York M,D*†
Clarkson University M,D*
Clemson University M,D*
Cleveland State University M,D*†
Colorado School of Mines M,D†
Colorado State University M,D*
Columbia University M,D,O*†
Cornell University M,D*
Dalhousie University M,D*
Drexel University M,D*†
École Polytechnique de Montréal M,D,O
Florida Agricultural and Mechanical University M,D*
Florida Institute of Technology M,D*†
Florida State University M,D*†
Georgia Institute of Technology M,D,O*
Graduate School and University Center of the City University of New York D*†
Howard University M*
Illinois Institute of Technology M,D*†
Institute of Paper Science and Technology M,D*
Instituto Tecnológico y de Estudios Superiores de Monterrey, Campus Monterrey M,D
Iowa State University of Science and Technology M,D*†
Johns Hopkins University M,D*†
Kansas State University M,D*†
Lamar University M,D*†
Lehigh University M,D*
Louisiana State University and Agricultural and Mechanical College M,D*
Louisiana Tech University M,D*
Manhattan College M*†
Massachusetts Institute of Technology M,D*
McGill University M,D*
McMaster University M,D
McNeese State University M
Michigan State University M,D*†
Michigan Technological University M,D*†
Mississippi State University M,D*
Montana State University–Bozeman D*
National Technological University M
New Jersey Institute of Technology M,D
New Mexico State University M,D
North Carolina Agricultural and Technical State University M*
North Carolina State University M,D*
Northeastern University M,D*†
Northwestern University M,D*
The Ohio State University M,D*
Ohio University M,D*
Oklahoma State University M,D*†
Oregon State University M,D*
The Pennsylvania State University University Park Campus M,D*†
Polytechnic University, Brooklyn Campus M,D*
Polytechnic University, Long Island Graduate Center M,D
Polytechnic University, Westchester Graduate Center M
Princeton University M,D*
Purdue University M,D*
Queen's University at Kingston M,D
Rensselaer Polytechnic Institute M,D*†
Rice University M,D*

*P—first professional degree; M—master's degree; D—doctorate; O—other advanced degree; *full description and/or announcement in Book 2, 3, 4, 5, or 6; †full description in this book*

Institution	Degrees
Rose-Hulman Institute of Technology	M*
Royal Military College of Canada	M,D
Rutgers, The State University of New Jersey, New Brunswick	M,D*
San Jose State University	M*
South Dakota School of Mines and Technology	M,D*†
Stanford University	M,D,O*
Stevens Institute of Technology	M,D,O*†
Syracuse University	M,D*
Tennessee Technological University	M,D*
Texas A&M University	M,D*
Texas A&M University–Kingsville	M*†
Texas Tech University	M,D*†
Tufts University	M,D*†
Tulane University	M,D*†
Universidad de las Américas–Puebla	M
Université de Sherbrooke	M,D
Université Laval	M,D†
University at Buffalo, The State University of New York	M,D*†
The University of Akron	M,D†
The University of Alabama	M,D*
The University of Alabama in Huntsville	M,D*
University of Alberta	M,D*
The University of Arizona	M,D*
University of Arkansas	M,D*
The University of British Columbia	M,D*
University of Calgary	M,D*
University of California, Berkeley	M,D*
University of California, Davis	M,D,O*†
University of California, Irvine	M,D*
University of California, Los Angeles	M,D*
University of California, Riverside	M,D*
University of California, San Diego	M,D*
University of California, Santa Barbara	M,D*
University of Cincinnati	M,D*
University of Colorado at Boulder	M,D*
University of Connecticut	M,D*†
University of Dayton	M*†
University of Delaware	M,D*†
University of Detroit Mercy	M,D*
University of Florida	M,D,O*†
University of Houston	M,D*
University of Idaho	M,D*†
University of Illinois at Chicago	M,D*
University of Illinois at Urbana–Champaign	M,D*
The University of Iowa	M,D*
University of Kansas	M,D*
University of Kentucky	M,D*
University of Louisiana at Lafayette	M*
University of Louisville	M,D*†
University of Maine	M,D*
University of Maryland, Baltimore County	M,D*†
University of Maryland, College Park	M,D*
University of Massachusetts Amherst	M,D*†
University of Massachusetts Lowell	M*†
University of Michigan	M,D,O*
University of Minnesota, Twin Cities Campus	M,D*
University of Missouri–Columbia	M,D*
University of Missouri–Rolla	M,D*
University of Nebraska–Lincoln	M,D*†
University of Nevada, Reno	M,D*
University of New Brunswick Fredericton	M,D
University of New Hampshire	M,D*†
University of New Mexico	M*†
University of North Dakota	M*
University of Notre Dame	M,D*†
University of Oklahoma	M,D*†
University of Ottawa	M,D*
University of Pennsylvania	M,D*†
University of Pittsburgh	M,D*†
University of Puerto Rico, Mayagüez Campus	M*
University of Rhode Island	M,D*
University of Rochester	M,D*
University of Saskatchewan	M,D
University of South Alabama	M*†
University of South Carolina	M,D*†
University of Southern California	M,D,O*†
University of South Florida	M,D*†
The University of Tennessee	M,D*†
The University of Tennessee Space Institute	M*
The University of Texas at Austin	M,D*
University of Toledo	M,D*†
University of Toronto	M,D*
University of Tulsa	M,D†
University of Utah	M,D*
University of Virginia	M,D*
University of Washington	M,D*
University of Waterloo	M,D
University of Wisconsin–Madison	M,D*
University of Wyoming	M,D*†
Vanderbilt University	M,D*
Villanova University	M*†
Virginia Polytechnic Institute and State University	M,D*
Washington State University	M,D*
Washington University in St. Louis	M,D*†
Wayne State University	M,D*
Western Michigan University	M,D*†
West Virginia University	M,D*
Widener University	M*†
Worcester Polytechnic Institute	M,D*†
Yale University	M,D*
Youngstown State University	M

CHEMISTRY

Institution	Degrees
Acadia University	M
American University	M,D*†
Arizona State University	M,D*
Arkansas State University	M,O
Auburn University	M,D*†
Ball State University	M*
Baylor University	M,D*†
Boston College	M,D*†
Boston University	M,D*†
Bowling Green State University	M,D*†
Bradley University	M†
Brandeis University	M,D*†
Brigham Young University	M,D*
Brock University	M,D
Brooklyn College of the City University of New York	M,D†
Brown University	M,D*
Bryn Mawr College	M,D
Bucknell University	M
California Institute of Technology	M,D*
California State Polytechnic University, Pomona	M*
California State University, Fresno	M
California State University, Fullerton	M
California State University, Hayward	M
California State University, Long Beach	M
California State University, Los Angeles	M
California State University, Northridge	M
California State University, Sacramento	M
Carleton University	M,D
Carnegie Mellon University	M,D*
Case Western Reserve University	M,D*†
The Catholic University of America	M,D*†
Central Connecticut State University	M*†
Central Michigan University	M†
Central Washington University	M†
City College of the City University of New York	M,D*†
Clark Atlanta University	M,D
Clarkson University	M,D*
Clark University	M,D*†
Clemson University	M,D*
Cleveland State University	M,D*†
College of Staten Island of the City University of New York	D†
The College of William and Mary	M*†
Colorado School of Mines	M,D†
Colorado State University	M,D*
Columbia University	M,D*†
Concordia University (Canada)	M,D*†
Cornell University	D*
Dalhousie University	M,D*
Dartmouth College	D*†
DePaul University	M*†
Drexel University	M,D*†
Duke University	D*†
Duquesne University	M,D*†
East Carolina University	M*†
Eastern Illinois University	M†
Eastern Kentucky University	M
Eastern Michigan University	M*
Eastern New Mexico University	M
East Tennessee State University	M†
Emory University	D*†
Emporia State University	M*†
Fairleigh Dickinson University, College at Florham	M*†
Fisk University	M
Florida Agricultural and Mechanical University	M*
Florida Atlantic University	M,D*
Florida Institute of Technology	M,D*†
Florida International University	M,D*†
Florida State University	M,D*†
Furman University	M
George Mason University	M*†
Georgetown University	M,D*
The George Washington University	M,D*†
Georgia Institute of Technology	M,D*
Georgia State University	M,D*
Graduate School and University Center of the City University of New York	D*†
Hampton University	M*†
Harvard University	M,D*†
Howard University	M,D*
Hunter College of the City University of New York	M†
Idaho State University	M*
Illinois Institute of Technology	M,D*†
Illinois State University	M*†
Indiana State University	M*†
Indiana University Bloomington	M,D*
Indiana University of Pennsylvania	M*†
Indiana University–Purdue University Indianapolis	M,D*
Institute of Paper Science and Technology	M,D*
Instituto Tecnológico y de Estudios Superiores de Monterrey, Campus Monterrey	M,D
Iowa State University of Science and Technology	M,D*†
Jackson State University	M,D
John Carroll University	M
Johns Hopkins University	M,D*†
Kansas State University	M,D*†
Kent State University	M,D*
Lakehead University	M
Lamar University	M*†
Laurentian University	M
Lehigh University	M,D*
Long Island University, Brooklyn Campus	M*
Louisiana State University and Agricultural and Mechanical College	M,D*
Louisiana Tech University	M*
Loyola University Chicago	M,D*†
Marquette University	M,D*†
Marshall University	M*†
Massachusetts College of Pharmacy and Health Sciences	M,D*
Massachusetts Institute of Technology	D*
McGill University	M,D*
McMaster University	M,D
McNeese State University	M
Memorial University of Newfoundland	M,D†
Miami University	M,D*†
Michigan State University	M,D*†
Michigan Technological University	M,D*†
Middle Tennessee State University	M,D*
Minnesota State University, Mankato	M
Mississippi College	M
Mississippi State University	M,D*
Montana State University–Bozeman	M,D*
Montclair State University	M†
Morgan State University	M*
Mount Allison University	M
Murray State University	M†
New Jersey Institute of Technology	M,D
New Mexico Highlands University	M
New Mexico Institute of Mining and Technology	M,D†
New Mexico State University	M,D
New York University	M,D*†
North Carolina Agricultural and Technical State University	M*
North Carolina Central University	M
North Carolina State University	M,D*
North Dakota State University	M,D†
Northeastern Illinois University	M
Northeastern University	M,D*†
Northern Arizona University	M
Northern Illinois University	M,D*†
Northern Michigan University	M
Northwestern University	D*
Oakland University	M,D†
The Ohio State University	M,D*
Oklahoma State University	M,D*†
Old Dominion University	M*†
Oregon State University	M,D*
The Pennsylvania State University University Park Campus	M,D*†
Pittsburg State University	M
Polytechnic University, Brooklyn Campus	M,D*
Polytechnic University, Long Island Graduate Center	M,D
Polytechnic University, Westchester Graduate Center	M
Pontifical Catholic University of Puerto Rico	M
Portland State University	M,D*
Prairie View A&M University	M
Princeton University	M,D*†
Purdue University	M,D*
Queens College of the City University of New York	M†
Queen's University at Kingston	M,D
Rensselaer Polytechnic Institute	M,D*†
Rice University	M,D*
Rochester Institute of Technology	M*†
Roosevelt University	M*†
Royal Military College of Canada	M,D
Rutgers, The State University of New Jersey, Camden	M†
Rutgers, The State University of New Jersey, Newark	M,D*†
Rutgers, The State University of New Jersey, New Brunswick	M,D*
Sacred Heart University	M*†
St. Francis Xavier University	M
St. John's University (NY)	M*†
Saint Joseph College	M
Saint Joseph's University	M*†
Saint Louis University	M*†
Sam Houston State University	M*
San Diego State University	M,D*
San Francisco State University	M
San Jose State University	M*
The Scripps Research Institute	D
Seton Hall University	M,D*†
Simon Fraser University	M,D
Smith College	M*
South Dakota School of Mines and Technology	M,D*†
South Dakota State University	M,D*
Southeast Missouri State University	M
Southern Connecticut State University	M†
Southern Illinois University Carbondale	M,D*†
Southern Illinois University Edwardsville	M†
Southern Methodist University	M*†
Southern University and Agricultural and Mechanical College	M*
Southwest Missouri State University	M*†
Southwest Texas State University	M*
Stanford University	D*
State University of New York at Albany	M,D*†
State University of New York at Binghamton	M,D*†
State University of New York at New Paltz	M
State University of New York at Oswego	M
State University of New York College at Buffalo	M
State University of New York College at Fredonia	M
State University of New York College of Environmental Science and Forestry	M,D
Stephen F. Austin State University	M
Stevens Institute of Technology	M,D,O*†
Stony Brook University, State University of New York	M,D*†
Sul Ross State University	M*
Syracuse University	M,D*
Temple University	M,D*†
Tennessee State University	M*
Tennessee Technological University	M*
Texas A&M University	M,D*
Texas A&M University–Commerce	M†
Texas A&M University–Kingsville	M*†
Texas Christian University	M,D*
Texas Southern University	M†
Texas Tech University	M,D*†
Texas Woman's University	M*†
Trent University	M
Tufts University	M,D*†
Tulane University	M,D*†
Tuskegee University	M
Université de Moncton	M
Université de Montréal	M,D
Université de Sherbrooke	M,D
Université du Québec à Montréal	M
Université du Québec à Trois-Rivières	M
Université Laval	M,D†
University at Buffalo, The State University of New York	M,D*†
The University of Akron	M,D†
The University of Alabama	M,D*
The University of Alabama at Birmingham	M,D*†

The University of Alabama in Huntsville M*
University of Alaska Fairbanks M,D*
University of Alberta M,D*
The University of Arizona M,D*
University of Arkansas M,D*
University of Arkansas at Little Rock M
The University of British Columbia M,D*
University of Calgary M,D*
University of California, Berkeley M,D*
University of California, Davis M,D*†
University of California, Irvine M,D*
University of California, Los Angeles M,D*
University of California, Riverside M,D*
University of California, San Diego M,D*
University of California, San Francisco D*
University of California, Santa Barbara M,D*
University of California, Santa Cruz M,D*
University of Central Florida M*†
University of Central Oklahoma M
University of Chicago M,D*
University of Cincinnati M,D*
University of Colorado at Boulder M,D*
University of Colorado at Denver M*
University of Connecticut M,D*†
University of Dayton M*†
University of Delaware M,D*†
University of Denver M,D*†
University of Detroit Mercy M*
University of Florida M,D*†
University of Georgia M,D*†
University of Guelph M,D
University of Hawaii at Manoa M,D*
University of Houston M,D*
University of Houston–Clear Lake M*†
University of Idaho M,D*†
University of Illinois at Chicago M,D*
University of Illinois at Urbana–Champaign M,D*
The University of Iowa M,D*
University of Kansas M,D*
University of Kentucky M,D*
The University of Lethbridge M,D
University of Louisiana at Monroe M
University of Louisville M,D*†
University of Maine M,D*
University of Manitoba M,D*
University of Maryland, Baltimore County D*†
University of Maryland, College Park M,D*
University of Massachusetts Amherst M,D*†
University of Massachusetts Boston M*†
University of Massachusetts Dartmouth M*†
University of Massachusetts Lowell M,D*†
The University of Memphis M,D*†
University of Miami M,D*†
University of Michigan D*
University of Minnesota, Duluth M*
University of Minnesota, Twin Cities Campus M,D*
University of Mississippi M,D*
University of Missouri–Columbia M,D*
University of Missouri–Kansas City M,D*†
University of Missouri–Rolla M,D*
University of Missouri–St. Louis M,D†
The University of Montana–Missoula M,D*†
University of Nebraska–Lincoln M,D*†
University of Nevada, Las Vegas M*†
University of Nevada, Reno M,D*
University of New Brunswick Fredericton M,D
University of New Hampshire M,D*†
University of New Mexico M,D*†
University of New Orleans M,D*
The University of North Carolina at Chapel Hill M,D*†
The University of North Carolina at Charlotte M*
The University of North Carolina at Greensboro M†
The University of North Carolina at Wilmington M*
University of North Dakota M,D*
University of Northern Colorado M,D†
University of Northern Iowa M
University of North Texas M,D*†
University of Notre Dame M,D*†
University of Oklahoma M,D*†
University of Oregon M,D*
University of Ottawa M,D*
University of Pennsylvania M,D*†
University of Pittsburgh M,D*†
University of Puerto Rico, Mayagüez Campus M*
University of Puerto Rico, Río Piedras M,D*
University of Regina M,D
University of Rhode Island M,D*
University of Rochester M,D*
University of San Francisco M*†
University of Saskatchewan M,D
The University of Scranton M†
University of South Carolina M,D*†
The University of South Dakota M†
University of Southern California M,D*†
University of Southern Mississippi M,D
University of South Florida M,D*†
The University of Tennessee M,D*†
The University of Texas at Arlington M,D*†
The University of Texas at Austin M,D*
The University of Texas at Dallas M,D*
The University of Texas at El Paso M*†
The University of Texas at San Antonio M*
The University of Texas at Tyler M
University of the Pacific M,D*
University of the Sciences in Philadelphia M,D*
University of Toledo M,D*†
University of Toronto M,D*
University of Tulsa M†
University of Utah M,D*
University of Vermont M,D*†
University of Victoria M,D
University of Virginia M,D*
University of Washington M,D*
University of Waterloo M,D
The University of Western Ontario M,D*
University of Windsor M,D
University of Wisconsin–Madison M,D*
University of Wisconsin–Milwaukee M,D
University of Wyoming M,D*†
Utah State University M,D*
Vanderbilt University M,D*
Vassar College M
Villanova University M*†
Virginia Commonwealth University M,D,O*†
Virginia Polytechnic Institute and State University M,D*
Wake Forest University M,D*†
Washington State University M,D*
Washington University in St. Louis M,D*†
Wayne State University M,D*
Wesleyan University M,D*
West Chester University of Pennsylvania M*†
Western Carolina University M†
Western Illinois University M
Western Kentucky University M†
Western Michigan University M,D*†
Western Washington University M
West Texas A&M University M†
West Virginia University M,D*
Wichita State University M,D*†
Worcester Polytechnic Institute M,D*†
Wright State University M*
Yale University D*
York University M,D*
Youngstown State University M

CHILD AND FAMILY STUDIES

Antioch University Santa Barbara M
Arizona State University D*
Auburn University M,D*†
Bank Street College of Education M*
Bowling Green State University M,D*†
Brandeis University M*†
Brigham Young University M,D*
Brock University M
California State University, Los Angeles M
Central Michigan University M†
Central Washington University M†
College of Mount Saint Vincent M,O*†
Colorado State University M*
Concordia University (MN) M
Concordia University (NE) M
Concordia University (Canada) M*†
Concordia University Wisconsin M
Cornell University D*
East Carolina University M*†
Fitchburg State College M,O†
Florida State University M,D*†
Indiana State University M*†
Iowa State University of Science and Technology M,D*†
Kansas State University M,D*†
Kent State University M*
Loma Linda University M,O*
Miami University M*†
Michigan State University M,D*†
Middle Tennessee State University M*
Montclair State University M†
Mount Saint Vincent University M
North Dakota State University M,D†
Northern Illinois University M*†
Nova Southeastern University M,D*
The Ohio State University M,D*
Ohio University M*
Oklahoma State University M,D*†
Oregon State University M,D*
The Pennsylvania State University University Park Campus M,D*†
Purdue University M,D*
Roberts Wesleyan College M*
Sage Graduate School M†
St. Cloud State University M
Saint Joseph College M,O
San Jose State University M*
South Carolina State University M
Southwest Texas State University M*
Stanford University D*
Syracuse University M,D*
Tennessee State University M*
Texas Tech University M,D*†
Texas Woman's University M,D*†
Tufts University M,D,O*†
Université de Moncton M
The University of Akron M†
The University of Alabama M*
The University of Arizona M,D*
The University of British Columbia M*
University of California, Davis M*†
University of Connecticut M,D*†
University of Delaware M,D*†
University of Denver M,D,O*†
University of Georgia M,D*†
University of Great Falls M
University of Guelph M,D
University of Illinois at Springfield M†
University of Kentucky M,D*
University of La Verne M*
University of Manitoba M*
University of Maryland, College Park M,D*
University of Minnesota, Twin Cities Campus M,D*
University of Missouri–Columbia M,D*
University of Nebraska–Lincoln M,D*†
University of Nevada, Reno M*
University of New Hampshire M*†
University of New Mexico M,D*†
The University of North Carolina at Charlotte M,D*
The University of North Carolina at Greensboro M,D†
University of North Texas M*†
University of Pittsburgh M*†
University of Rhode Island M*
University of Southern Mississippi M,D
The University of Tennessee M,D*†
The University of Tennessee at Martin M
The University of Texas at Austin M,D*
The University of Texas at Dallas M*
University of Utah M*
University of Vermont M*†
University of Wisconsin–Madison M,D*
Utah State University M,D*
Virginia Polytechnic Institute and State University M,D*
Wayne State University O*
West Virginia University M*
Wheelock College M,O*

CHIROPRACTIC

Anglo-European College of Chiropractic M
Canadian Memorial Chiropractic College P,O*
Cleveland Chiropractic College-Kansas City Campus P*
Cleveland Chiropractic College-Los Angeles Campus P*
Institut Franco-European de Chiropratique P
Life Chiropractic College West P*
Life University P*
Logan University-College of Chiropractic P
National University of Health Sciences P*
New York Chiropractic College P*
Northwestern Health Sciences University P*
Palmer College of Chiropractic P
Palmer College of Chiropractic West P
Parker College of Chiropractic P*
Sherman College of Straight Chiropractic P*
Southern California University of Health Sciences P
Texas Chiropractic College P*
University of Bridgeport P,M*†
Western States Chiropractic College P*

CITY AND REGIONAL PLANNING

Alabama Agricultural and Mechanical University M
Arizona State University M*
Auburn University M*†
Ball State University M*
Boston University M*†
California Polytechnic State University, San Luis Obispo M†
California State Polytechnic University, Pomona M*
California State University, Chico M
The Catholic University of America M*†
Clark University M*†
Clemson University M*
Cleveland State University M*†
Columbia University M,D*†
Concordia University (Canada) O*†
Cornell University M,D*
Dalhousie University M*
Delta State University M
DePaul University M,O*†
Eastern Kentucky University M
Eastern Washington University M†
East Tennessee State University M†
Florida Atlantic University M*
Florida Atlantic University, Ft. Lauderdale Campus M
Florida State University M,D*†
George Mason University M*†
Georgia Institute of Technology M*
Harvard University M,D*†
Hunter College of the City University of New York M†
Indiana University–Purdue University Indianapolis M*
Iowa State University of Science and Technology M*†
Jackson State University M
Kansas State University M*†
Massachusetts Institute of Technology M,D*
McGill University M*
Michigan State University M,D*†
Morgan State University M*
New York University M,O*†
North Park University M
The Ohio State University M,D*
Old Dominion University M*†
The Pennsylvania State University University Park Campus M*†
Portland State University M,D*
Pratt Institute M*
Princeton University M,D*
Queen's University at Kingston M
Rutgers, The State University of New Jersey, New Brunswick M,D*
San Diego State University M*
San Jose State University M*
Southwest Missouri State University M*†
State University of New York at Albany M*†
State University of New York College of Environmental Science and Forestry M,D
Texas A&M University M,D*
Texas Southern University M†
Tufts University M*†
Université du Québec en Outaouais M
Université du Québec à Rimouski M
Université Laval M,D†
University at Buffalo, The State University of New York M*†
The University of Akron M†
The University of Arizona M*
The University of British Columbia M,D*
University of Calgary M,D*

*P—first professional degree; M—master's degree; D—doctorate; O—other advanced degree; *full description and/or announcement in Book 2, 3, 4, 5, or 6; †full description in this book*

University of California, Berkeley M,D*
University of California, Davis M*†
University of California, Irvine M,D*
University of California, Los Angeles M,D*
University of Cincinnati M*
University of Colorado at Denver M*
University of Florida M*†
University of Hawaii at Manoa M*
University of Illinois at Chicago M,D*
University of Illinois at Urbana–Champaign M,D*
The University of Iowa M*
University of Kansas M*
University of Louisville M*†
University of Manitoba M*
University of Maryland, College Park M*
University of Massachusetts Amherst M,D*†
The University of Memphis M*†
University of Michigan M,D,O*
University of Minnesota, Twin Cities Campus M*
University of Nebraska–Lincoln M*†
University of New Mexico M*†
University of New Orleans M*
The University of North Carolina at Chapel Hill M,D*†
University of Oklahoma M*†
University of Oregon M*
University of Pennsylvania M,D,O*†
University of Pittsburgh M*†
University of Puerto Rico, Río Piedras M*
University of Rhode Island M*
University of Southern California M,D*†
University of Southern Maine M,O
The University of Tennessee M*†
The University of Texas at Arlington M*†
The University of Texas at Austin M,D*
University of Toledo M*†
University of Toronto M*
University of Virginia M*
University of Washington M,D*
University of Waterloo M,D
University of Wisconsin–Madison M,D*
University of Wisconsin–Milwaukee M
Utah State University M*
Valdosta State University M
Virginia Commonwealth University M,O*†
Virginia Polytechnic Institute and State University M*
Washington State University M*
Wayne State University M*
West Chester University of Pennsylvania M*†
West Virginia University M,D*

CIVIL ENGINEERING

Arizona State University M,D*
Auburn University M,D*†
Boise State University M*
Bradley University M†
Brigham Young University M,D*
Bucknell University M
California Institute of Technology M,D*
California Polytechnic State University, San Luis Obispo M†
California State University, Fresno M
California State University, Fullerton M
California State University, Long Beach M,O
California State University, Los Angeles M
California State University, Northridge M
California State University, Sacramento M
Carleton University M,D
Carnegie Mellon University M,D*
Case Western Reserve University M,D*†
The Catholic University of America M,D*†
City College of the City University of New York M,D*†
Clarkson University M,D*
Clemson University M,D*
Cleveland State University M,D*†
Colorado State University M,D*
Columbia University M,D,O*†
Concordia University (Canada) M,D,O*†
Cornell University M,D*
Dalhousie University M,D*
Drexel University M,D*†
Duke University M,D*†
École Polytechnique de Montréal M,D,O
Florida Agricultural and Mechanical University M,D*
Florida Atlantic University M,D*
Florida Institute of Technology M,D*†
Florida International University M,D*†
Florida State University M,D*†
The George Washington University M,D,O*†
Georgia Institute of Technology M,D*
Graduate School and University Center of the City University of New York D*†
Howard University M*
Illinois Institute of Technology M,D*†
Instituto Tecnológico y de Estudios Superiores de Monterrey, Campus Monterrey M,D
Iowa State University of Science and Technology M,D*†
Johns Hopkins University M,D*†
Kansas State University M,D*†
Lamar University M,D*†
Lawrence Technological University M,D
Lehigh University M,D*
Louisiana State University and Agricultural and Mechanical College M,D*
Louisiana Tech University M,D*
Loyola Marymount University M†
Manhattan College M*†
Marquette University M,D*†
Massachusetts Institute of Technology M,D,O*
McGill University M,D*
McMaster University M,D
McNeese State University M
Memorial University of Newfoundland M,D†
Michigan State University M,D*†
Michigan Technological University M,D*†
Mississippi State University M,D*
Montana State University–Bozeman D*
New Jersey Institute of Technology M,D
New Mexico State University M,D
North Carolina Agricultural and Technical State University M*
North Carolina State University M,D*
North Dakota State University M†
Northeastern University M,D*†
Northwestern University M,D*
The Ohio State University M,D*
Ohio University M*
Oklahoma State University M,D*†
Old Dominion University M,D*†
Oregon State University M,D*
The Pennsylvania State University University Park Campus M,D*†
Polytechnic University, Brooklyn Campus M,D*
Polytechnic University, Long Island Graduate Center M,D
Polytechnic University of Puerto Rico M
Polytechnic University, Westchester Graduate Center M,D
Portland State University M,D*
Princeton University M,D*
Purdue University M,D*
Queen's University at Kingston M,D
Rensselaer Polytechnic Institute M,D*†
Rice University M,D*
Royal Military College of Canada M,D
Rutgers, The State University of New Jersey, New Brunswick M,D*
Saint Martin's College M
San Diego State University M*
San Jose State University M*
Santa Clara University M*
South Dakota School of Mines and Technology M,D*†
South Dakota State University M*
Southern Illinois University Carbondale M*†
Southern Illinois University Edwardsville M†
Southern Methodist University M,D*†
Stanford University M,D,O*
Stevens Institute of Technology M,D,O*†
Syracuse University M,D*
Temple University M*†
Tennessee Technological University M,D*
Texas A&M University M,D*
Texas A&M University–Kingsville M*†
Texas Tech University M,D*†
Tufts University M,D*†
Tulane University M,D*†
Université de Moncton M
Université de Sherbrooke M,D
Université Laval M,D,O†
University at Buffalo, The State University of New York M,D*†
The University of Akron M,D†
The University of Alabama M,D*
The University of Alabama at Birmingham M,D*†
The University of Alabama in Huntsville M*
University of Alaska Anchorage M
University of Alaska Fairbanks M*
University of Alberta M,D*
The University of Arizona M,D*
University of Arkansas M,D*
The University of British Columbia M,D*
University of Calgary M,D*
University of California, Berkeley M,D*
University of California, Davis M,D,O*†
University of California, Irvine M,D*
University of California, Los Angeles M,D*
University of Central Florida M,D,O*†
University of Cincinnati M,D*
University of Colorado at Boulder M,D*
University of Colorado at Denver M,D*
University of Connecticut M,D*†
University of Dayton M*†
University of Delaware M,D*†
University of Detroit Mercy M*
University of Florida M,D,O*†
University of Hawaii at Manoa M,D*
University of Houston M,D*
University of Idaho M,D*†
University of Illinois at Chicago M,D*
University of Illinois at Urbana–Champaign M,D*
The University of Iowa M,D*
University of Kansas M,D*
University of Kentucky M,D*
University of Louisiana at Lafayette M*
University of Louisville M,D*†
University of Maine M,D*
University of Manitoba M,D*
University of Maryland, College Park M,D*
University of Massachusetts Amherst M,D*†
University of Massachusetts Lowell M*†
The University of Memphis M,D*†
University of Miami M,D*†
University of Michigan M,D,O*
University of Minnesota, Twin Cities Campus M,D*
University of Missouri–Columbia M,D*
University of Missouri–Rolla M,D*
University of Nebraska–Lincoln M,D*†
University of Nevada, Las Vegas M,D*†
University of Nevada, Reno M,D*
University of New Brunswick Fredericton M,D
University of New Hampshire M,D*†
University of New Mexico M,D*†
University of New Orleans M*
The University of North Carolina at Charlotte M*
University of North Dakota M*
University of Notre Dame M,D*†
University of Oklahoma M,D*†
University of Ottawa M,D*
University of Pittsburgh M,D*†
University of Puerto Rico, Mayagüez Campus M,D*
University of Rhode Island M,D*
University of Saskatchewan M,D
University of South Carolina M,D*†
University of Southern California M,D,O*†
University of South Florida M,D*†
The University of Tennessee M,D*†
The University of Texas at Arlington M,D*†
The University of Texas at Austin M,D*
The University of Texas at El Paso M*†
The University of Texas at San Antonio M*
University of Toledo M,D*†
University of Toronto M,D*
University of Utah M,D*
University of Vermont M,D*†
University of Virginia M,D*
University of Washington M,D*
University of Waterloo M,D
University of Windsor M,D
University of Wisconsin–Madison M,D*
University of Wyoming M,D*†
Utah State University M,D,O*
Vanderbilt University M,D*
Villanova University M*†
Virginia Polytechnic Institute and State University M,D*
Washington State University M,D*
Washington University in St. Louis M,D*†
Wayne State University M,D*
West Virginia University M,D*
Widener University M*†
Worcester Polytechnic Institute M,D,O*†
Youngstown State University M

CLASSICS

Boston College M*†
Boston University M,D*†
Brandeis University M*†
Brown University M,D*
Bryn Mawr College M,D
The Catholic University of America M,D*†
Columbia University M,D*†
Connecticut College M
Cornell University D*
Dalhousie University M,D*
Duke University D*†
Florida State University M,D*†
Fordham University M,D*†
Graduate School and University Center of the City University of New York M,D*†
Harvard University M,D*†
Hunter College of the City University of New York M†
Indiana University Bloomington M,D*
Johns Hopkins University M,D*†
Kent State University M*
Loyola University Chicago M,D*†
McMaster University M,D
Memorial University of Newfoundland M†
New York University M,D,O*†
The Ohio State University M,D*
Princeton University D*
Queen's University at Kingston M
Rutgers, The State University of New Jersey, New Brunswick M,D*
San Francisco State University M
Stanford University M,D*
State University of New York at Albany M*†
Syracuse University M*
Texas Tech University M*†
Tufts University M*†
Tulane University M*†
University at Buffalo, The State University of New York M,D*†
University of Alberta M,D*
The University of Arizona M*
The University of British Columbia M,D*
University of Calgary M*
University of California, Berkeley M,D*
University of California, Irvine M,D*
University of California, Los Angeles M,D*
University of California, Riverside M,D*
University of California, Santa Barbara M,D*
University of Chicago M,D*
University of Cincinnati M,D*
University of Colorado at Boulder M,D*
University of Florida M,D*†
University of Georgia M*†
University of Hawaii at Manoa M*
University of Illinois at Urbana–Champaign M,D*
The University of Iowa M,D*
University of Kansas M*
University of Kentucky M*
University of Manitoba M*
University of Maryland, College Park M*
University of Massachusetts Amherst M*†
University of Michigan M,D*
University of Minnesota, Twin Cities Campus M,D*
University of Mississippi M*
University of Missouri–Columbia M,D*
University of Nebraska–Lincoln M*†
University of New Brunswick Fredericton M
The University of North Carolina at Chapel Hill M,D*†
The University of North Carolina at Greensboro M†
University of Oregon M*
University of Ottawa M,D*
University of Pennsylvania M,D*†
University of Pittsburgh M,D*†
University of Southern California M,D*†
The University of Texas at Austin M,D*
University of Toronto M,D*
University of Vermont M*†
University of Victoria M
University of Virginia M,D*
University of Washington M,D*

- The University of Western Ontario M*
- University of Wisconsin–Madison M,D*
- University of Wisconsin–Milwaukee M
- Vanderbilt University M,D*
- Villanova University M*†
- Washington University in St. Louis M*†
- Wayne State University M*
- West Chester University of Pennsylvania M*†
- Yale University D*

CLINICAL LABORATORY SCIENCES/ MEDICAL TECHNOLOGY

- Baylor College of Medicine M,D*
- California State University, Dominguez Hills M,O†
- California State University, Long Beach M
- The Catholic University of America M,D*†
- Fairleigh Dickinson University, Metropolitan Campus M*†
- Finch University of Health Sciences/The Chicago Medical School M*
- Indiana State University M,D*†
- Inter American University of Puerto Rico, Metropolitan Campus M
- Inter American University of Puerto Rico, San Germán Campus O
- Long Island University, C.W. Post Campus M*†
- Medical College of Georgia M*
- Medical College of Wisconsin D*
- Medical University of South Carolina M*
- Michigan State University M*†
- Northeastern University M,D*†
- Quinnipiac University M*†
- Rush University M*
- St. John's University (NY) M*†
- San Francisco State University M
- State University of New York Upstate Medical University M*
- Thomas Jefferson University M*
- Universidad de las Américas–Puebla M
- Université de Montréal O
- Université de Sherbrooke M,D
- University at Buffalo, The State University of New York M*†
- The University of Alabama at Birmingham M*†
- University of Alberta M,D*
- University of Colorado Health Sciences Center D*
- University of Guelph M,D,O
- University of Illinois at Chicago M*
- The University of Iowa M,D*
- University of Kentucky M,D*
- University of Maryland M*†
- University of Massachusetts Lowell M*†
- University of Medicine and Dentistry of New Jersey M,D*
- University of Minnesota, Twin Cities Campus M*
- University of Mississippi Medical Center M,D*
- University of North Dakota M*
- University of Puerto Rico, Medical Sciences Campus M*
- University of Rhode Island M*
- University of Southern Mississippi M
- University of the Sacred Heart O
- University of Utah M*
- University of Vermont M*†
- University of Washington M*
- University of Wisconsin–Milwaukee M
- Virginia Commonwealth University M*†
- Wayne State University M,O*
- West Virginia University M*

CLINICAL PSYCHOLOGY

- Abilene Christian University M
- Acadia University M
- Adelphi University D,O*
- Adler School of Professional Psychology M,D,O*
- Alabama Agricultural and Mechanical University M,O
- Alliant International University D*†
- Alliant International University D*†
- Alliant International University D*†
- Alliant International University D*†
- American International College M*
- American University D*†
- Antioch New England Graduate School D*†
- Antioch University Los Angeles M
- Antioch University Santa Barbara M
- Appalachian State University M
- Argosy University-Atlanta M,D*
- Argosy University-Chicago M*
- Argosy University-Chicago Northwest M,D*
- Argosy University-Dallas M,D*
- Argosy University-Honolulu D,O*
- Argosy University-Orange County D*
- Argosy University-Phoenix M,D,O*
- Argosy University-San Francisco Bay Area M,D*
- Argosy University-Seattle M,D*
- Argosy University-Tampa M,D*
- Argosy University-Twin Cities M,D*
- Argosy University-Washington D.C. M,D,O*
- Arizona State University D*
- Austin Peay State University M
- Azusa Pacific University M,D*†
- Ball State University M*
- Barry University M,O*†
- Baylor University M,D*†
- Bowling Green State University M,D*†
- Brigham Young University M,D*
- Bryn Mawr College D
- California Institute of Integral Studies M,D,O*
- California Lutheran University M
- California State University, Dominguez Hills M†
- California State University, Fullerton M
- California State University, San Bernardino M
- Cardinal Stritch University M*
- Carlos Albizu University M,D
- Carlos Albizu University, Miami Campus M,D
- Case Western Reserve University D*†
- The Catholic University of America D*†
- Center for Humanistic Studies M,D*
- Central Michigan University D†
- Chapman University M*†
- Chestnut Hill College M,D†
- Chicago School of Professional Psychology M,D*
- City College of the City University of New York M,D*†
- Clark University D*†
- Cleveland State University M*†
- College of St. Joseph M
- College of Staten Island of the City University of New York D†
- The College of William and Mary D*†
- Concordia University (Canada) M,D*†
- Dalhousie University M,D*
- DePaul University M,D*†
- Drexel University M,D*†
- Duke University D*†
- Duquesne University D*†
- East Carolina University M*†
- Eastern Illinois University M†
- Eastern Kentucky University M,O
- Eastern Michigan University M*
- East Tennessee State University M†
- Edinboro University of Pennsylvania M
- Emory University D*†
- Emporia State University M*†
- Evangel University M
- Fairleigh Dickinson University, College at Florham M*†
- Fairleigh Dickinson University, Metropolitan Campus D*†
- Fielding Graduate Institute M,D
- Finch University of Health Sciences/The Chicago Medical School M,D*
- Fisk University M
- Florida Institute of Technology D*†
- Florida State University D*†
- Fordham University D*†
- Forest Institute of Professional Psychology M,D
- Francis Marion University M
- Fuller Theological Seminary M,D
- Gallaudet University D
- George Fox University M,D†
- George Mason University D*†
- The George Washington University D*†
- Graduate School and University Center of the City University of New York D*†
- Hofstra University M,D,O*
- Howard University M,D*
- Idaho State University M,D*
- Illinois Institute of Technology M,D*†
- Illinois State University M,D,O*†
- Immaculata University M,D,O†
- Indiana State University M,D*†
- Indiana University of Pennsylvania D*†
- Indiana University–Purdue University Indianapolis M,D*
- Jackson State University D
- Kent State University M,D*
- Lakehead University M,D
- Lamar University M*†
- La Salle University M,D
- Lesley University M,D,O*†
- Loma Linda University D*
- Long Island University, Brooklyn Campus D*
- Long Island University, C.W. Post Campus D*†
- Louisiana State University and Agricultural and Mechanical College M,D*
- Loyola College in Maryland M,D,O
- Loyola University Chicago M,D*†
- Madonna University M
- Marquette University M,D*†
- Marshall University M,D*†
- Massachusetts School of Professional Psychology M,D,O*
- McGill University D*
- Miami University D*†
- Millersville University of Pennsylvania M†
- Minnesota State University, Mankato M
- Montclair State University M†
- Morehead State University M
- Murray State University M†
- Naropa University M*
- New College of California M*†
- New School University M,D*†
- New York University M,D,O*†
- Norfolk State University M†
- North Dakota State University M,D†
- Northwestern State University of Louisiana M
- Northwestern University D*
- Nova Southeastern University D,O*
- The Ohio State University D*
- Ohio University D*
- Oklahoma State University M,D*†
- Old Dominion University D*†
- Pace University M,D*†
- Pacifica Graduate Institute M,D*
- Pacific Graduate School of Psychology D
- The Pennsylvania State University Harrisburg Campus of the Capital College M*†
- The Pennsylvania State University University Park Campus M,D*†
- Pepperdine University M*†
- Philadelphia College of Osteopathic Medicine M,D*
- Ponce School of Medicine D
- Pontifical Catholic University of Puerto Rico M,D
- Queens College of the City University of New York M†
- Queen's University at Kingston M,D
- Radford University M,O†
- Roosevelt University M,D*†
- Rutgers, The State University of New Jersey, New Brunswick M,D*
- St. John's University (NY) M,D*†
- Saint Louis University M,D*†
- Saint Mary's University M
- St. Mary's University of San Antonio M
- Saint Michael's College M*
- Sam Houston State University M†
- San Diego State University M,D*
- San Jose State University M*
- Seattle Pacific University D
- Southern Illinois University Carbondale M,D*†
- Southern Illinois University Edwardsville M†
- Southern Methodist University M*†
- Spalding University M,D†
- State University of New York at Albany M,D*†
- State University of New York at Binghamton M,D*†
- Stony Brook University, State University of New York D*†
- Suffolk University D*
- Syracuse University M,D*
- Teachers College Columbia University M,D*
- Temple University D*†
- Texas A&M University M,D*
- Texas Tech University M,D*†
- Towson University M,O†
- Uniformed Services University of the Health Sciences D*
- Union Institute & University D
- Université Laval D†
- University at Buffalo, The State University of New York M,D*†
- The University of Alabama M,D*
- The University of Alabama at Birmingham M,D*†
- University of Alaska Anchorage M
- The University of British Columbia M,D*
- University of Calgary M,D*
- University of California, San Diego D*
- University of California, Santa Barbara M,D*
- University of Central Florida M,D*†
- University of Cincinnati D*
- University of Connecticut D*†
- University of Dayton M*†
- University of Delaware D*†
- University of Denver D*†
- University of Detroit Mercy M,D*
- University of Florida D*†
- University of Hartford M,D*
- University of Hawaii at Manoa M,D*
- University of Houston D*
- University of Houston–Clear Lake M*†
- University of Illinois at Urbana–Champaign M,D*
- University of Kansas D*
- University of La Verne M,D*
- University of Louisville D*†
- University of Maine M,D*
- University of Manitoba M,D*
- University of Maryland, College Park M,D*
- University of Massachusetts Amherst M,D*†
- University of Massachusetts Boston D*†
- University of Massachusetts Dartmouth M*†
- The University of Memphis M,D*†
- University of Miami M,D*†
- University of Michigan D*
- University of Minnesota, Twin Cities Campus D*
- University of Mississippi M,D*
- University of Missouri–St. Louis M,D,O†
- The University of Montana–Missoula D*†
- University of Nevada, Las Vegas M,D*†
- University of New Mexico M,D*†
- The University of North Carolina at Chapel Hill D*†
- The University of North Carolina at Charlotte M*
- The University of North Carolina at Greensboro M,D†
- University of North Dakota D*
- University of North Texas M,D*†
- University of Oregon D*
- University of Pennsylvania D*†
- University of Rhode Island D*
- University of Rochester M,D*
- University of South Carolina D*†
- University of South Carolina Aiken M
- The University of South Dakota M,D†
- University of Southern California M,D*†
- University of South Florida D*†
- The University of Tennessee M,D*†
- The University of Texas at El Paso M,D*†
- The University of Texas at Tyler M
- The University of Texas of the Permian Basin M
- The University of Texas–Pan American M
- The University of Texas Southwestern Medical Center at Dallas D*
- University of the District of Columbia M*
- University of Toledo M,D*†
- University of Tulsa M,D†
- University of Vermont D*†
- University of Virginia D*
- University of Washington M,D*
- University of Windsor M,D
- University of Wisconsin–Madison D*
- University of Wisconsin–Milwaukee M,D
- Utah State University M,D*
- Valdosta State University M,O
- Valparaiso University M
- Vanguard University of Southern California M
- Virginia Commonwealth University D*†
- Virginia Polytechnic Institute and State University M,D*
- Washburn University of Topeka M
- Washington State University M,D*
- Washington University in St. Louis M,D*†
- Wayne State University M,D*
- West Chester University of Pennsylvania M*†
- Western Carolina University M†

*P—first professional degree; M—master's degree; D—doctorate; O—other advanced degree; *full description and/or announcement in Book 2, 3, 4, 5, or 6; †full description in this book*

Western Illinois University M,O
Western Michigan University M,D,O*†
Westfield State College M
West Virginia University M,D*
Wheaton College M,D†
Wichita State University M,D*†
Widener University D*†
William Paterson University of New Jersey M*†
Wisconsin School of Professional Psychology M,D
Wright State University D*
Xavier University M,D*
Yeshiva University D*

CLINICAL RESEARCH

Boston University M*†
Duke University M*†
Johns Hopkins University M,D,O*†
McMaster University M,D
Medical University of South Carolina M,D*
MGH Institute of Health Professions M,O*
New York Medical College M*
New York University M*†
Northwestern University M,O*
Thomas Jefferson University O*
Tufts University M,D*†
University of California, Los Angeles M*
University of Florida M*†
University of Louisville O*†
University of Michigan M*
University of Minnesota, Twin Cities Campus M*
University of Pittsburgh M,O*†
University of Virginia M*
Vanderbilt University M*

CLOTHING AND TEXTILES

Auburn University M*†
Cornell University M,D*
Fashion Institute of Technology M*
Florida State University M,D*†
Indiana State University M*†
Indiana University Bloomington M*
Iowa State University of Science and Technology M,D*†
Kansas State University M,D*†
Michigan State University M,D*†
North Carolina State University M*
The Ohio State University M,D*
Oklahoma State University M,D*†
Oregon State University M,D*
Philadelphia University M
Purdue University M,D*
Syracuse University M*
The University of Akron M†
The University of Alabama M*
University of Alberta M,D*
University of California, Davis M*†
University of Georgia M,D*†
University of Kentucky M*
University of Manitoba M*
University of Missouri–Columbia M*
University of Nebraska–Lincoln M*†
University of North Texas M*†
University of Rhode Island M*
The University of Tennessee M,D*†
Virginia Polytechnic Institute and State University M,D*
Washington State University M*

COGNITIVE SCIENCES

Arizona State University D*
Ball State University M*
Boston University M,D*†
Brandeis University M,D*†
Brown University M,D*
Carleton University D
Carnegie Mellon University D*
Claremont Graduate University M,D*
College of Staten Island of the City University of New York D†
Colorado State University D*
Dartmouth College D*†
Duke University D*†
Emory University D*†
Florida State University D*†
The George Washington University D*†
Georgia Institute of Technology M*
Graduate School and University Center of the City University of New York D*†
Harvard University M,D,O*†
Hunter College of the City University of New York M†
Indiana University Bloomington D*
Iowa State University of Science and Technology M,D*†
Johns Hopkins University D*†
Louisiana State University and Agricultural and Mechanical College M,D*
Massachusetts Institute of Technology D*
New Mexico Highlands University M
New York University M,D,O*†
Northwestern University D*
The Ohio State University D*
The Pennsylvania State University University Park Campus M,D*†
Queen's University at Kingston M,D
Rutgers, The State University of New Jersey, Newark D*†
Rutgers, The State University of New Jersey, New Brunswick D*
State University of New York at Binghamton M,D*†
Temple University D*†
University at Buffalo, The State University of New York M,D*†
The University of Akron M,D†
The University of Alabama M,D*
The University of British Columbia M,D*
University of California, San Diego D*
University of Connecticut D*†
University of Delaware D*†
University of Illinois at Urbana–Champaign M,D*
University of Louisiana at Lafayette D*
University of Maryland M,D*†
University of Maryland, Baltimore County M,D*†
University of Maryland, College Park D*
University of Minnesota, Twin Cities Campus D*
The University of North Carolina at Greensboro M,D†
University of Notre Dame D*†
University of Oregon M,D*
University of Pittsburgh D*†
University of Rochester M,D*
The University of Texas at Austin M,D*
The University of Texas at Dallas M*
University of Wisconsin–Madison D*
Wayne State University M,D*

COMMUNICATION—GENERAL

Abilene Christian University M
American University M*†
American University in Cairo M,O
Andrews University M
Angelo State University M†
Arizona State University M,D*
Arizona State University West M
Arkansas State University M,O
Arkansas Tech University M
Auburn University M*†
Austin Peay State University M
Ball State University M*
Barry University M,O*†
Baylor University M*†
Bethel College (MN) M
Boise State University M*
Boston University M*†
Bowling Green State University M,D*†
Brigham Young University M*
California State University, Chico M
California State University, Fullerton M
California State University, Long Beach M
California State University, Los Angeles M
California State University, Northridge M
California State University, Sacramento M
California State University, San Bernardino M
California University of Pennsylvania M
Carleton University M,D
Carnegie Mellon University M*
Central Connecticut State University M*†
Central Michigan University M†
Central Missouri State University M†
Chatham College M
Clarion University of Pennsylvania M†
Clark University M*†
Clemson University M*
Cleveland State University M*†
The College of New Rochelle M,O†
College of Notre Dame of Maryland M
Colorado State University M*
Columbia University M,D*†
Concordia University (Canada) M,D,O*†
Cornell University M,D*
DePaul University M*†
Drexel University M*†
Drury University M
Duquesne University M,D*†
East Carolina University M*†
Eastern Michigan University M*
Eastern New Mexico University M
Eastern Washington University M†
East Tennessee State University M†
Edinboro University of Pennsylvania M
Emerson College M*†
Fairleigh Dickinson University, Metropolitan Campus M*†
Fitchburg State College M†
Florida Atlantic University M*
Florida Institute of Technology M*†
Florida State University M,D*†
Fordham University M*†
Fort Hays State University M
Georgetown University M*
Georgia State University M,D*
Governors State University M
Grand Valley State University M†
Harvard University M,O*†
Hawai'i Pacific University M*†
Howard University M,D*
Illinois Institute of Technology M*†
Illinois State University M*†
Indiana State University M*†
Indiana University Bloomington M,D*
Indiana University–Purdue University Fort Wayne M
Instituto Tecnológico y de Estudios Superiores de Monterrey, Campus Ciudad Obregón M
Instituto Tecnológico y de Estudios Superiores de Monterrey, Campus Monterrey M,D
Iona College M,O*†
Ithaca College M†
Kent State University M,D*
Loyola Marymount University M†
Loyola University New Orleans M
Mansfield University of Pennsylvania M
Marquette University M*†
Marshall University M*†
Marywood University M*†
McGill University M,D*
Miami University M*†
Michigan State University M,D*†
Michigan Technological University M,D*†
Mississippi College M
Monmouth University M,O*†
Montana State University–Billings M*
Morehead State University M
New Jersey Institute of Technology M
New Mexico State University M
New School University M*†
New York Institute of Technology M*†
New York University M,D,O*†
Norfolk State University M†
North Carolina State University M*
North Dakota State University M,D†
Northeastern State University M
Northern Illinois University M*†
Northwestern University M,D*
The Ohio State University M,D*
Ohio University M,D*
The Pennsylvania State University University Park Campus M,D*†
Pepperdine University M*
Pittsburg State University M
Point Park College M*
Purdue University M,D*
Purdue University Calumet M
Quinnipiac University M*†
Regent University M,D†
Regis University M,O*†
Rensselaer Polytechnic Institute M,D*†
Rochester Institute of Technology M*†
Roosevelt University M*†
Rutgers, The State University of New Jersey, New Brunswick M,D*
Sage Graduate School M†
Saginaw Valley State University M
Saint Louis University M*†
St. Mary's University of San Antonio M
San Diego State University M*
San Jose State University M*
Seton Hall University M*†
Shippensburg University of Pennsylvania M†
Simon Fraser University M,D
South Dakota State University M*
Southeastern Louisiana University M
Southern Illinois University Carbondale M,D*†
Southern Methodist University M*†
Southwest Missouri State University M*†
Southwest Texas State University M*
Stanford University M,D*
State University of New York at Albany M,D*†
State University of New York College at Brockport M*†
State University of New York College of Environmental Science and Forestry M,D
Stephen F. Austin State University M
Suffolk University M*
Syracuse University M,D*
Teachers College Columbia University M,D*
Temple University M,D*†
Texas Southern University M†
Texas Tech University M*†
Towson University M,O†
Trinity College (DC) M†
Université de Montréal M,D
Université du Québec à Montréal M,D
University at Buffalo, The State University of New York M,D*†
The University of Akron M†
The University of Alabama M,D,O*
The University of Arizona M,D*
University of Arkansas M*
University of Baltimore M,D*
University of Calgary M,D*
University of California, San Diego M,D*
University of California, Santa Barbara D*
University of California, Santa Cruz O*
University of Central Florida M*†
University of Cincinnati M*
University of Colorado at Boulder M,D*
University of Colorado at Colorado Springs M*
University of Colorado at Denver M*
University of Connecticut M*†
University of Dayton M*†
University of Delaware M*†
University of Denver M,D*†
University of Dubuque M
University of Florida M,D*†
University of Georgia M,D*†
University of Hartford M*
University of Hawaii at Manoa M*
University of Houston M*
University of Illinois at Chicago M*
University of Illinois at Springfield M†
University of Illinois at Urbana–Champaign D*
The University of Iowa M,D*
University of Kansas M,D*
University of Kentucky M,D*
University of Louisiana at Lafayette M*
University of Louisiana at Monroe M
University of Maine M*
University of Maryland, Baltimore County M*†
University of Maryland, College Park M,D*
University of Massachusetts Amherst M,D*†
The University of Memphis M,D*†
University of Miami M,D*†
University of Minnesota, Twin Cities Campus M,D*
University of Missouri–Columbia M,D*
University of Missouri–Kansas City M*†
University of Missouri–St. Louis M†
The University of Montana–Missoula M*†
University of Nebraska at Omaha M
University of Nebraska–Lincoln M,D*†
University of Nevada, Las Vegas M*†
University of New Mexico M,D*†
The University of North Carolina at Chapel Hill M,D*†
The University of North Carolina at Charlotte M*
The University of North Carolina at Greensboro M†
University of North Dakota M,D*
University of Northern Colorado M†
University of Northern Iowa M
University of North Texas M*†
University of Oklahoma M,D*†
University of Oregon M,D*
University of Pennsylvania M,D*†
University of Pittsburgh M,D*†
University of Portland M
University of South Alabama M*†

- University of Southern California M,D*†
- University of Southern Mississippi M,D
- University of South Florida M,D*†
- The University of Tennessee M,D*†
- The University of Texas at Austin M,D*
- The University of Texas at Dallas D*
- The University of Texas at El Paso M*†
- The University of Texas at Tyler M
- The University of Texas–Pan American M
- University of the Incarnate Word M†
- University of the Pacific M*
- University of the Sacred Heart M
- University of Utah M,D*
- University of Vermont M*†
- University of Washington M,D*
- University of West Florida M
- University of Wisconsin–Madison M,D*
- University of Wisconsin–Milwaukee M
- University of Wisconsin–Stevens Point M
- University of Wisconsin–Superior M
- University of Wisconsin–Whitewater M*
- University of Wyoming M*†
- Utah State University M*
- Wake Forest University M*†
- Washington State University M*
- Wayne State College M
- Wayne State University M,D*
- Webster University M
- West Chester University of Pennsylvania M*†
- Western Illinois University M
- Western Kentucky University M†
- Western Michigan University M*†
- Westminster College (UT) M
- West Texas A&M University M†
- West Virginia University M*
- Wichita State University M*†
- William Paterson University of New Jersey M*†
- York University M,D*

COMMUNICATION DISORDERS

- Abilene Christian University M
- Adelphi University M,D*
- Alabama Agricultural and Mechanical University M
- Appalachian State University M
- Arizona State University M,D*
- Arkansas State University M
- Armstrong Atlantic State University M†
- Auburn University M*†
- Ball State University M,D*
- Baylor University M*†
- Bloomsburg University of Pennsylvania M
- Boston University M,D,O*†
- Bowling Green State University M,D*†
- Brigham Young University M*
- Brooklyn College of the City University of New York M†
- California State University, Chico M
- California State University, Fresno M
- California State University, Fullerton M
- California State University, Hayward M
- California State University, Long Beach M
- California State University, Los Angeles M
- California State University, Northridge M
- California State University, Sacramento M
- California University of Pennsylvania M
- Case Western Reserve University M,D,O*†
- Central Michigan University M,D†
- Central Missouri State University M†
- Clarion University of Pennsylvania M†
- Cleveland State University M*†
- The College of New Jersey M†
- The College of New Rochelle M†
- The College of Saint Rose M*†
- Dalhousie University M*
- Duquesne University M,D*†
- East Carolina University M,D*†
- Eastern Illinois University M†
- Eastern Kentucky University M
- Eastern Michigan University M*
- Eastern New Mexico University M
- Eastern Washington University M†
- East Stroudsburg University of Pennsylvania M†
- East Tennessee State University M†
- Edinboro University of Pennsylvania M
- Emerson College M*†
- Florida Atlantic University M*
- Florida International University M*†
- Florida State University M,D*†
- Fontbonne University M
- Fort Hays State University M
- Gallaudet University M,D
- The George Washington University M*†
- Georgia State University M*
- Governors State University M
- Graduate School and University Center of the City University of New York D*†
- Hampton University M*†
- Harvard University D*†
- Hofstra University M*
- Howard University M,D*
- Hunter College of the City University of New York M†
- Idaho State University M*
- Illinois State University M*†
- Indiana State University M,D,O*†
- Indiana University Bloomington M,D*
- Indiana University of Pennsylvania M*†
- Ithaca College M†
- Jackson State University M
- James Madison University M
- Kean University M*†
- Kent State University M,D*
- Kirksville College of Osteopathic Medicine M,D
- Lamar University M,D*†
- Lehman College of the City University of New York M
- Lewis & Clark College M
- Loma Linda University M*
- Long Island University, Brooklyn Campus M*
- Long Island University, C.W. Post Campus M*†
- Louisiana State University and Agricultural and Mechanical College M,D*
- Louisiana State University Health Sciences Center M*
- Louisiana Tech University M*
- Loyola College in Maryland M,O
- Marquette University M*†
- Marshall University M*†
- Marywood University M*†
- Massachusetts Institute of Technology D*
- McGill University M,D*
- Medical University of South Carolina M*
- MGH Institute of Health Professions M*
- Miami University M*†
- Michigan State University M,D*†
- Minnesota State University, Mankato M
- Minnesota State University, Moorhead M
- Minot State University M
- Mississippi University for Women M
- Montclair State University M†
- Murray State University M†
- Nazareth College of Rochester M
- New Mexico State University M
- New York Medical College M*
- New York University M,D*†
- North Carolina Central University M
- Northeastern State University M
- Northeastern University M*†
- Northern Arizona University M
- Northern Illinois University M*†
- Northern Michigan University M
- Northwestern University M,D*
- Nova Southeastern University M,D*
- The Ohio State University M,D*
- Ohio University M,D*
- Oklahoma State University M*†
- Old Dominion University M*†
- Our Lady of the Lake University of San Antonio M
- Pennsylvania College of Optometry M,D,O
- The Pennsylvania State University University Park Campus M,D*†
- Plattsburgh State University of New York M
- Portland State University M*
- Purdue University M,D*
- Queens College of the City University of New York M†
- Radford University M†
- Rockhurst University M
- Rush University M,D*
- St. Cloud State University M
- St. John's University (NY) M*†
- Saint Louis University M*†
- Saint Xavier University M*
- San Diego State University M,D*
- San Francisco State University M
- San Jose State University M*
- Seton Hall University M,D*†
- South Carolina State University M
- Southeastern Louisiana University M
- Southeast Missouri State University M
- Southern Connecticut State University M†
- Southern Illinois University Carbondale M*†
- Southern Illinois University Edwardsville M†
- Southwest Missouri State University M*†
- Southwest Texas State University M*
- State University of New York at New Paltz M
- State University of New York College at Buffalo M
- State University of New York College at Fredonia M
- State University of New York College at Geneseo M
- State University of West Georgia M
- Stephen F. Austin State University M
- Syracuse University M,D*
- Teachers College Columbia University M,D*
- Temple University M*†
- Texas A&M University–Kingsville M*†
- Texas Christian University M*
- Texas Tech University Health Sciences Center M,D*
- Texas Woman's University M*†
- Towson University M,D†
- Truman State University M†
- Université de Montréal M
- Université Laval M†
- University at Buffalo, The State University of New York M,D*†
- The University of Akron M†
- The University of Alabama M*
- University of Alberta M*
- The University of Arizona M,D*
- University of Arkansas M*
- University of Arkansas for Medical Sciences M*
- The University of British Columbia M,D*
- University of California, San Diego D*
- University of Central Arkansas M
- University of Central Florida M*†
- University of Central Oklahoma M
- University of Cincinnati M,D*
- University of Colorado at Boulder M,D*
- University of Connecticut M,D*†
- University of Florida M,D*†
- University of Georgia M,D,O*†
- University of Hawaii at Manoa M*
- University of Houston M*
- University of Illinois at Urbana–Champaign M,D*
- The University of Iowa M,D*
- University of Kansas M,D*
- University of Kentucky M*
- University of Louisiana at Lafayette M,D*
- University of Louisiana at Monroe M
- University of Louisville M,D*†
- University of Maine M*
- University of Maryland, College Park M,D*
- University of Massachusetts Amherst M,D*†
- The University of Memphis M,D*†
- University of Minnesota, Duluth M*
- University of Minnesota, Twin Cities Campus M,D*
- University of Mississippi M*
- University of Missouri–Columbia M*
- University of Montevallo M
- University of Nebraska at Kearney M
- University of Nebraska at Omaha M
- University of Nebraska–Lincoln M*†
- University of Nevada, Reno M,D*
- University of New Hampshire M*†
- University of New Mexico M*†
- The University of North Carolina at Chapel Hill M,D*†
- The University of North Carolina at Greensboro M†
- University of North Dakota M,D*
- University of Northern Colorado M†
- University of Northern Iowa M
- University of North Texas M*†
- University of Oklahoma Health Sciences Center M,D,O*
- University of Ottawa M*
- University of Pittsburgh M,D*†
- University of Puerto Rico, Medical Sciences Campus M*
- University of Redlands M
- University of Rhode Island M*
- University of South Alabama M,D*†
- University of South Carolina M,D*†
- The University of South Dakota M†
- University of Southern Mississippi M,D
- University of South Florida M,D*†
- The University of Tennessee M,D,O*†
- The University of Texas at Austin M,D*
- The University of Texas at Dallas M,D*
- The University of Texas at El Paso M*†
- The University of Texas–Pan American M
- University of the District of Columbia M*
- University of the Pacific M*
- University of Toledo M*†
- University of Toronto M,D*
- University of Tulsa M†
- University of Utah M,D*
- University of Virginia M*
- University of Washington M,D*
- The University of Western Ontario M*
- University of Wisconsin–Eau Claire M†
- University of Wisconsin–Madison M,D*
- University of Wisconsin–Milwaukee M
- University of Wisconsin–Oshkosh M*
- University of Wisconsin–River Falls M
- University of Wisconsin–Stevens Point M
- University of Wisconsin–Whitewater M*
- University of Wyoming M*†
- Utah State University M,O*
- Valdosta State University M,O
- Vanderbilt University M,D*
- Washington State University M*
- Washington State University Spokane M†
- Washington University in St. Louis M,D*†
- Wayne State University M,D*
- West Chester University of Pennsylvania M*†
- Western Carolina University M†
- Western Illinois University M
- Western Kentucky University M†
- Western Michigan University M*†
- Western Washington University M
- West Texas A&M University M†
- West Virginia University M*
- Wichita State University M,D*†
- William Paterson University of New Jersey M*†
- Worcester State College M

COMMUNITY COLLEGE EDUCATION

- Eastern Washington University M†
- George Mason University D*†
- Michigan State University M,D*†
- North Carolina State University M,D*
- Northern Arizona University M,D
- Old Dominion University M*†
- Pittsburg State University O
- Princeton University D*
- University of South Florida M*†
- Western Carolina University M†

COMMUNITY HEALTH

- Arcadia University M†
- Brooklyn College of the City University of New York M†
- Brown University M,D*
- California College for Health Sciences M
- Columbia University M,D*†
- Dalhousie University M*
- Eastern Kentucky University M
- East Tennessee State University M,O†
- Emory University M*†
- The George Washington University M*†
- Harvard University M*†
- Johns Hopkins University M,D*†
- Long Island University, Brooklyn Campus M*

*P—first professional degree; M—master's degree; D—doctorate; O—other advanced degree; *full description and/or announcement in Book 2, 3, 4, 5, or 6; †full description in this book*

McGill University M,D,O*
Meharry Medical College M
Memorial University of Newfoundland M,D,O†
Minnesota State University, Mankato M
Mountain State University M†
New York Medical College M*
Old Dominion University M*†
Sage Graduate School M†
Saint Louis University M,D*†
Stony Brook University, State University of New York M,O*†
Temple University M*†
Trinity College (DC) M†
Université de Montréal M,D,O
Université Laval M,D,O†
University at Buffalo, The State University of New York M,D*†
The University of British Columbia M,D*
University of Calgary M,D*
University of California, Los Angeles M,D*
University of Illinois at Chicago M,D*
University of Illinois at Urbana–Champaign M,D*
University of Manitoba M,D*
University of Miami M,D*†
University of Minnesota, Twin Cities Campus M*
University of Missouri–Columbia M*
The University of North Carolina at Greensboro M†
University of Northern British Columbia M,D
University of Northern Colorado M†
University of North Florida M,O
University of North Texas M*†
University of North Texas Health Science Center at Fort Worth M,D*
University of Ottawa M*
University of Pittsburgh M,D,O*†
University of Saskatchewan M,D
University of South Florida M,D*†
The University of Tennessee M,D*†
The University of Texas Medical Branch M,D*
University of Toronto M,D*
University of Wisconsin–La Crosse M†
University of Wisconsin–Madison M,D*
Wayne State University M,O*
West Virginia University M*

COMMUNITY HEALTH NURSING

Augsburg College M
Augustana College M
Bellarmine University M
Boston College M,D*†
Capital University M
Case Western Reserve University M*†
Cleveland State University M*†
Georgia Southern University M,O
Hawai'i Pacific University M*†
Holy Names College M
Hunter College of the City University of New York M†
Indiana University–Purdue University Indianapolis M*
Indiana Wesleyan University M,O*
Johns Hopkins University M*†
La Roche College M
La Salle University M,O
Lewis University M,O
Louisiana State University Health Sciences Center M,D*
Medical College of Georgia M,D*
Northeastern University M,O*†
Oregon Health & Science University M,O*
Rush University M,D*
Rutgers, The State University of New Jersey, Newark M,D*†
Sage Graduate School M†
Saint Xavier University M,O*
San Jose State University M*
Southern Illinois University Edwardsville M†
Texas Tech University Health Sciences Center M,O*
Texas Woman's University M,D*†
University of Cincinnati M,D*
University of Colorado at Colorado Springs M*
University of Hartford M*
University of Hawaii at Manoa M,D,O*
University of Illinois at Chicago M*
University of Maryland M,D*†
University of Massachusetts Lowell M*†
University of Massachusetts Worcester M,D,O*
University of Michigan M*
University of Minnesota, Twin Cities Campus M*
The University of North Carolina at Chapel Hill M,D*†
The University of North Carolina at Charlotte M*
University of South Carolina M*†
University of Southern Mississippi M,D
The University of Texas at Brownsville M
The University of Texas at El Paso M*†
Valdosta State University M
Wayne State University M*
Worcester State College M
Wright State University M*

COMPARATIVE AND INTERDISCIPLINARY ARTS

Columbia College Chicago M†
Goddard College M
John F. Kennedy University M*†
Ohio University D*
San Francisco State University M
Simon Fraser University M

COMPARATIVE LITERATURE

American University M*†
American University in Cairo M
Antioch University McGregor M†
Arizona State University M,D*
Brigham Young University M*
Brown University M,D*
California State University, Fullerton M
Carleton University M,D
Carnegie Mellon University M,D*
Case Western Reserve University M,D*†
The Catholic University of America M,D*†
Columbia University M,D*†
Cornell University D*
Dartmouth College M*†
Duke University D*†
Emory University D,O*†
Fairleigh Dickinson University, Metropolitan Campus M*†
Florida Atlantic University M*
Graduate School and University Center of the City University of New York M,D*†
Harvard University D*†
Indiana University Bloomington M,D*
Johns Hopkins University D*†
Long Island University, Brooklyn Campus M*
Louisiana State University and Agricultural and Mechanical College M,D*
Michigan State University M*†
New York University M,D*†
Northwestern University M,D,O*
Ohio University M*
Oklahoma City University M
The Pennsylvania State University University Park Campus M,D*†
Princeton University D*
Purdue University M,D*
Rutgers, The State University of New Jersey, New Brunswick D*
San Francisco State University M
Stanford University D*
State University of New York at Binghamton M,D*†
Stony Brook University, State University of New York M,D*†
Université de Montréal M,D
Université de Sherbrooke M,D
Université du Québec à Chicoutimi M
Université du Québec à Montréal M,D
Université du Québec à Rimouski M
Université du Québec à Trois-Rivières M
University at Buffalo, The State University of New York M,D*†
The University of Arizona M,D*
University of Arkansas M,D*
The University of British Columbia M,D*
University of California, Berkeley M,D*
University of California, Davis D*†
University of California, Irvine M,D*
University of California, Los Angeles M,D*
University of California, Riverside M,D*
University of California, San Diego M,D*
University of California, Santa Barbara M,D*
University of California, Santa Cruz M,D*
University of Chicago M,D*
University of Colorado at Boulder M,D*
University of Connecticut M,D*†
University of Dallas D*
University of Georgia M,D*†
University of Illinois at Urbana–Champaign M,D*
The University of Iowa M,D*
University of Maryland, College Park M,D*
University of Massachusetts Amherst M,D*†
University of Michigan D*
University of Minnesota, Twin Cities Campus M,D*
University of Missouri–Columbia M,D*
University of New Hampshire M,D*†
University of New Mexico M,D*†
The University of North Carolina at Chapel Hill M,D*†
University of Notre Dame D*†
University of Oregon M,D*
University of Pennsylvania M,D*†
University of Puerto Rico, Río Piedras M*
University of Southern California M,D*†
The University of Texas at Austin M,D*
The University of Texas at Dallas M,D*
University of Toronto M,D*
University of Utah M,D*
University of Washington M,D*
The University of Western Ontario M*
University of Wisconsin–Madison M,D*
University of Wisconsin–Milwaukee M,D
Vanderbilt University M,D*
Washington University in St. Louis M,D*†
Wayne State University M*
Western Kentucky University M†
West Virginia University M*
Yale University D*

COMPUTATIONAL SCIENCES

Arizona State University M,D*
California Institute of Technology M,D*
Carnegie Mellon University M,D*
Chatham College M
Clemson University M,D*
The College of William and Mary M*†
Cornell University M,D*
George Mason University M,D,O*†
The George Washington University M*†
Iowa State University of Science and Technology D*†
Kean University M*†
Louisiana Tech University M,D*
Massachusetts Institute of Technology D*
Memorial University of Newfoundland M†
Michigan State University M,D*†
Michigan Technological University D*†
Mississippi State University M,D*
New Jersey Institute of Technology M
Princeton University D*
Rice University M,D*
Stanford University M,D*
State University of New York College at Brockport M*†
Temple University M,D*†
The University of Iowa D*
University of Massachusetts Lowell M,D*†
University of Michigan–Dearborn M*†
University of Minnesota, Duluth M*
University of Minnesota, Twin Cities Campus M,D*
University of Puerto Rico, Mayagüez Campus M*
The University of Texas at Austin M,D*
Washington University in St. Louis D*†
Western Michigan University M*†
Yale University D*

COMPUTER ART AND DESIGN

Academy of Art College M†
Alfred University M*†
Art Center College of Design M*
Carnegie Mellon University M,D*
Clemson University M*
Columbia University M*†
Concordia University (Canada) O*†
Cornell University M,D*
DePaul University M*†
Florida Atlantic University M*
Florida Atlantic University, Davie Campus M
Indiana University Bloomington M*
International Fine Arts College M
Long Island University, C.W. Post Campus M*†
Maryland Institute College of Art M*
Memphis College of Art M*
Mississippi State University M*
New Mexico Highlands University M
New School University M*†
New York University M*†
Rensselaer Polytechnic Institute M*†
Rochester Institute of Technology M*†
Savannah College of Art and Design M*
School of Visual Arts M†
Syracuse University M*
Universidad de las Américas–Puebla M

COMPUTER EDUCATION

Arcadia University M,D,O†
Ashland University M
California State University, Dominguez Hills M,O†
California State University, Los Angeles M
California University of Pennsylvania M
Cardinal Stritch University M*
Dalhousie University M*
DeSales University M
Eastern Washington University M†
Florida Institute of Technology M,D,O*†
Fontbonne University M
ITI-Information Technology Institute M
Jacksonville University M
Lesley University M,D,O*†
Long Island University, C.W. Post Campus M*†
Maple Springs Baptist Bible College and Seminary P,M,D,O
Marlboro College M,O*
Mississippi College M
Morningside College M
Nazareth College of Rochester M
Nova Southeastern University M,D,O*
Ohio University M,D*
Oklahoma State University M,D*†
Philadelphia University M
Providence College M*
Saint Martin's College M
Shenandoah University M,D,O
Stanford University M,D*
Stony Brook University, State University of New York M*†
Teachers College Columbia University M*
Thomas College M
Union College (NY) M*
University of Bridgeport M,O*†
University of Central Oklahoma M
University of Florida M,D,O*†
University of Georgia M*†
University of Michigan M,D*
The University of North Carolina at Wilmington M*
University of North Texas M*†
The University of Texas at Tyler M
Wilkes University M
Wright State University M*

COMPUTER ENGINEERING

Air Force Institute of Technology M,D*
Arizona State University East M
Auburn University M,D*†
Boise State University M*
Boston University M,D*†
California State University, Long Beach M
California State University, Northridge M
Carnegie Mellon University M,D*
Case Western Reserve University M,D*†
Clarkson University M,D*
Clemson University M,D*
Cleveland State University M,D*†
Colorado State University M,D*
Colorado Technical University M
Concordia University (Canada) M,D,O*†
Cornell University M,D*
Dalhousie University M,D*
Dartmouth College M,D*†
Drexel University M*†
Duke University M,D*†
École Polytechnique de Montréal M,D,O
Fairleigh Dickinson University, Metropolitan Campus M*†
Florida Atlantic University M,D*
Florida Institute of Technology M,D*†
Florida International University M*†
George Mason University M,D*†
The George Washington University M,D,O*†

Georgia Institute of Technology M,D*
Illinois Institute of Technology M,D*†
Indiana State University M*†
Instituto Tecnológico y de Estudios Superiores de Monterrey, Campus Chihuahua M,O
International Technological University M
Iowa State University of Science and Technology M,D*†
Johns Hopkins University M,D*†
Kansas State University M,D*†
Lawrence Technological University M,D
Lehigh University M*
Louisiana State University and Agricultural and Mechanical College M,D*
Manhattan College M*†
Marquette University M,D*†
McGill University M,D*
Michigan State University M,D*†
Michigan Technological University D*†
Mississippi State University M,D*
National Technological University M
Naval Postgraduate School M,D,O
New Jersey Institute of Technology M,D
New Mexico State University M,D
New York Institute of Technology M*†
North Carolina State University M,D*
North Dakota State University M†
Northeastern University M,D*†
Northwestern Polytechnic University M
Northwestern University M,D,O*
Oakland University M†
OGI School of Science & Engineering at Oregon Health & Science University M,D,O*
Oklahoma State University M,D*†
Old Dominion University M,D*†
Oregon State University M,D*
The Pennsylvania State University University Park Campus M,D*†
Polytechnic University, Brooklyn Campus M*
Polytechnic University, Long Island Graduate Center M
Polytechnic University, Westchester Graduate Center M
Portland State University M,D*
Princeton University M,D*
Purdue University M,D*
Queen's University at Kingston M,D
Rensselaer at Hartford M
Rensselaer Polytechnic Institute M,D*†
Rice University M,D*
Rochester Institute of Technology M*†
Royal Military College of Canada M,D
Rutgers, The State University of New Jersey, New Brunswick M,D*
St. Mary's University of San Antonio M
San Jose State University M*
Santa Clara University M,D,O*
Southern Methodist University M,D*†
Southern Polytechnic State University M†
State University of New York at New Paltz M
Stevens Institute of Technology M,D,O*†
Stony Brook University, State University of New York M,D*†
Syracuse University M,D,O*
Temple University M*†
Texas A&M University M,D*
Université de Sherbrooke M,D
The University of Alabama at Birmingham M,D*†
The University of Alabama in Huntsville M,D*
University of Alberta M,D*
The University of Arizona M,D*
University of Arkansas M,D*
University of Bridgeport M*†
The University of British Columbia M,D*
University of Calgary M,D*
University of California, Davis M,D*†
University of California, Irvine M,D*
University of California, San Diego M,D*
University of California, Santa Barbara M,D*
University of California, Santa Cruz M,D*
University of Central Florida M,D,O*†
University of Cincinnati M,D*
University of Colorado at Boulder M,D*
University of Colorado at Colorado Springs M,D*
University of Dayton M,D*†
University of Denver M,D*†
University of Florida M,D,O*†
University of Houston M,D*
University of Houston–Clear Lake M*†
University of Idaho M,D*†
University of Illinois at Chicago M,D*
University of Illinois at Urbana–Champaign M,D*
The University of Iowa M,D*
University of Kansas M*
University of Louisiana at Lafayette M,D*
University of Louisville M,D*†
University of Maine M,D*
University of Manitoba M,D*
University of Maryland, College Park M,D*
University of Massachusetts Amherst M,D*†
University of Massachusetts Dartmouth M,D,O*†
University of Massachusetts Lowell M,D*†
The University of Memphis M,D*†
University of Miami M,D*†
University of Michigan M,D*
University of Michigan–Dearborn M*†
University of Minnesota, Twin Cities Campus M,D*
University of Missouri–Columbia M,D*
University of Missouri–Rolla M,D*
University of Nebraska–Lincoln M,D*†
University of Nevada, Las Vegas M,D*†
University of Nevada, Reno M,D*
University of New Brunswick Fredericton M,D
University of New Mexico M,D*†
The University of North Carolina at Charlotte M,D*
University of Notre Dame M,D*†
University of Oklahoma M,D*†
University of Ottawa M,D,O*
University of Puerto Rico, Mayagüez Campus M*
University of Regina M,D
University of Rhode Island M,D*
University of Rochester M,D*
University of South Carolina M,D*†
University of Southern California M,D*†
University of South Florida M,D*†
The University of Texas at Arlington M,D*†
The University of Texas at Austin M,D*
The University of Texas at El Paso M,D*†
University of Toronto M,D*
University of Virginia M,D*
University of Waterloo M,D
Villanova University M*†
Virginia Polytechnic Institute and State University M,D*
Wayne State University M,D*
Western Michigan University M,D*†
Western New England College M
West Virginia University D*
Widener University M*†
Worcester Polytechnic Institute M,D,O*†
Wright State University M,D*

COMPUTER SCIENCE

Acadia University M
Adelphi University M,D*
Air Force Institute of Technology M,D*
Alabama Agricultural and Mechanical University M
Alcorn State University M
American College of Computer & Information Sciences M
American University M*†
American University in Cairo M
Appalachian State University M
Arizona State University M,D*
Arkansas State University M
Auburn University M,D*†
Azusa Pacific University M,O*†
Ball State University M*
Baylor University M*†
Boise State University M*
Boston University M,D*†
Bowie State University M
Bowling Green State University M*†
Bradley University M†
Brandeis University M,D*†
Bridgewater State College M
Brigham Young University M,D*
Brooklyn College of the City University of New York M,D†
Brown University M,D*
California Institute of Technology M,D*
California Polytechnic State University, San Luis Obispo M†
California State Polytechnic University, Pomona M*
California State University, Chico M
California State University, Fresno M
California State University, Fullerton M
California State University, Hayward M
California State University, Long Beach M
California State University, Northridge M
California State University, Sacramento M
California State University, San Bernardino M
California State University, San Marcos M
Capitol College M
Carleton University M,D
Carnegie Mellon University M,D*
Case Western Reserve University M,D*†
The Catholic University of America M,D*†
Central Connecticut State University M*†
Central Michigan University M†
Chicago State University M
Christopher Newport University M†
City College of the City University of New York M,D*†
City University M,O†
Claremont Graduate University M,D*
Clark Atlanta University M
Clarkson University M,D*
Clemson University M,D*
College of Charleston M*†
The College of Saint Rose M*†
College of Staten Island of the City University of New York M,D†
The College of William and Mary M,D*†
Colorado School of Mines M,D†
Colorado State University M,D*
Colorado Technical University M,D
Colorado Technical University Denver Campus M
Columbia University M,D,O*†
Columbus State University M
Concordia University (Canada) M,D,O*†
Cornell University M,D*
Creighton University M*
Dakota State University M*
Dalhousie University M,D*
Dartmouth College M,D*†
DePaul University M,D*†
Drexel University M,D*†
Duke University M,D*†
East Carolina University M*†
Eastern Michigan University M*
Eastern Washington University M†
East Stroudsburg University of Pennsylvania M†
East Tennessee State University M†
École Polytechnique de Montréal M,D,O
Edinboro University of Pennsylvania O
Elmhurst College M
Emory University M,D*†
Emporia State University M*†
Fairleigh Dickinson University, Metropolitan Campus M*†
Fitchburg State College M†
Florida Atlantic University M,D*
Florida Gulf Coast University M
Florida Institute of Technology M,D*†
Florida International University M,D*†
Florida State University M,D*†
Fordham University M*†
Franklin University M
Frostburg State University M
George Mason University M,D*†
The George Washington University M,D,O*†
Georgia Institute of Technology M,D*
Georgia Southwestern State University M
Georgia State University M,D*
Governors State University M
Graduate School and University Center of the City University of New York D*†
Hampton University M*†
Harvard University D*†
Hofstra University M*
Hollins University M,O
Hood College M
Howard University M*
Illinois Institute of Technology M,D*†
Illinois State University M*†
Indiana University Bloomington M,D*
Indiana University–Purdue University Fort Wayne M
Indiana University–Purdue University Indianapolis M*
Indiana University South Bend M
Instituto Tecnológico y de Estudios Superiores de Monterrey, Campus Central de Veracruz M
Instituto Tecnológico y de Estudios Superiores de Monterrey, Campus Ciudad de México M,D
Instituto Tecnológico y de Estudios Superiores de Monterrey, Campus Cuernavaca M,D
Instituto Tecnológico y de Estudios Superiores de Monterrey, Campus Irapuato M,D
Instituto Tecnológico y de Estudios Superiores de Monterrey, Campus Monterrey M,D
Inter American University of Puerto Rico, Metropolitan Campus M
Iona College M*†
Iowa State University of Science and Technology M,D*†
Jackson State University M
Jacksonville State University M
James Madison University M
Johns Hopkins University M,D*†
Kansas State University M,D*†
Kent State University M,D*
Knowledge Systems Institute M
Kutztown University of Pennsylvania M†
Lakehead University M
Lamar University M*†
La Salle University M
Lawrence Technological University M
Lebanese American University M
Lehigh University M,D*
Lehman College of the City University of New York M
Long Island University, Brooklyn Campus M*
Long Island University, C.W. Post Campus M*†
Louisiana State University and Agricultural and Mechanical College M,D*
Louisiana Tech University M*
Loyola Marymount University M†
Loyola University Chicago M*†
Maharishi University of Management M
Marist College M
Marlboro College M*
Marquette University M,D*†
Marymount University M,O†
Massachusetts Institute of Technology M,D,O*
McGill University M,D*
McMaster University M
McNeese State University M
Memorial University of Newfoundland M,D†
Michigan State University M,D*†
Michigan Technological University M,D*†
Middle Tennessee State University M*
Midwestern State University M
Mills College M,O*†
Minnesota State University, Mankato M
Mississippi College M
Mississippi State University M,D*
Monmouth University M*†
Montana State University–Bozeman M,D*
Montclair State University M,O†
National Technological University M
Naval Postgraduate School M,D
New Jersey Institute of Technology M,D
New Mexico Highlands University M
New Mexico Institute of Mining and Technology M,D†
New Mexico State University M,D
New York Institute of Technology M*†
New York University M,D*†
North Carolina Agricultural and Technical State University M*
North Carolina State University M,D*
North Central College M
North Dakota State University M,D†
Northeastern Illinois University M
Northeastern University M,D*†
Northern Illinois University M*†
Northern Kentucky University M

*P—first professional degree; M—master's degree; D—doctorate; O—other advanced degree; *full description and/or announcement in Book 2, 3, 4, 5, or 6; †full description in this book*

Northwestern Polytechnic University M
Northwestern University M,D*
Northwest Missouri State University M
Nova Southeastern University M,D*
Oakland University M†
OGI School of Science & Engineering at Oregon Health & Science University M,D,O*
The Ohio State University M,D*
Ohio University M,D*
Oklahoma City University M
Oklahoma State University M,D*†
Old Dominion University M,D*†
Oregon State University M,D*
Pace University M,D,O*†
Pace University, White Plains Campus M,D,O*
Pacific States University M
The Pennsylvania State University Harrisburg Campus of the Capital College M*†
The Pennsylvania State University University Park Campus M,D*†
Polytechnic University, Brooklyn Campus M,D*
Polytechnic University, Long Island Graduate Center M,D
Polytechnic University, Westchester Graduate Center M,D
Portland State University M*
Princeton University M,D*
Purdue University M,D*
Queens College of the City University of New York M†
Queen's University at Kingston M,D
Regis University M,O*†
Rensselaer at Hartford M
Rensselaer Polytechnic Institute M,D*†
Rice University M,D*
Rivier College M*†
Rochester Institute of Technology M*†
Roosevelt University M*†
Royal Military College of Canada M
Rutgers, The State University of New Jersey, New Brunswick M,D*
Sacred Heart University M,O*†
St. Cloud State University M
St. John's University (NY) M*†
Saint Joseph's University M*†
St. Mary's University of San Antonio M
Saint Xavier University M*
Sam Houston State University M*
San Diego State University M*
San Francisco State University M
San Jose State University M*
Santa Clara University M,D,O*
Shippensburg University of Pennsylvania M†
Simon Fraser University M,D
South Dakota School of Mines and Technology M*†
South Dakota State University M*
Southeastern University M†
Southern Illinois University Carbondale M*†
Southern Illinois University Edwardsville M†
Southern Methodist University M,D*†
Southern Oregon University M
Southern Polytechnic State University M†
Southern University and Agricultural and Mechanical College M*
Southwest Missouri State University M*†
Southwest Texas State University M*
Stanford University M,D*
State University of New York at Albany M,D*†
State University of New York at Binghamton M,D*†
State University of New York at New Paltz M
State University of New York Institute of Technology at Utica/Rome M*†
State University of West Georgia M
Stephen F. Austin State University M
Stevens Institute of Technology M,D,O*†
Stony Brook University, State University of New York M,D,O*†
Suffolk University M*
Syracuse University M,D*
Tarleton State University M
Technical University of British Columbia M
Temple University M,D*†
Texas A&M University M,D*
Texas A&M University–Commerce M†
Texas A&M University–Corpus Christi M
Texas A&M University–Kingsville M*†
Texas Tech University M,D*†
Towson University M†
Trent University M
Tufts University M,D,O*†
Tulane University M,D*†
Union College (NY) M*
Universidad de las Américas–Puebla M
Université de Moncton M,O
Université de Montréal M,D,O
Université du Québec en Outaouais M,O
Université du Québec à Trois-Rivières M
Université Laval M,D†
University at Buffalo, The State University of New York M,D*†
The University of Akron M†
The University of Alabama M,D*
The University of Alabama at Birmingham M,D*†
The University of Alabama in Huntsville M,D,O*
University of Alaska Fairbanks M,D*
University of Alberta M,D*
The University of Arizona M,D*
University of Arkansas M,D*
University of Arkansas at Little Rock M
University of Bridgeport M*†
The University of British Columbia M,D*
University of Calgary M,D*
University of California, Berkeley M,D*
University of California, Davis M,D*†
University of California, Irvine M,D*
University of California, Los Angeles M,D*
University of California, Riverside M,D*
University of California, San Diego M,D*
University of California, Santa Barbara M,D*
University of California, Santa Cruz M,D*
University of Central Florida M,D*†
University of Central Oklahoma M
University of Chicago M,D*
University of Cincinnati M,D*
University of Colorado at Boulder M,D*
University of Colorado at Colorado Springs M,D*
University of Colorado at Denver M*
University of Connecticut M,D*†
University of Dayton M*†
University of Delaware M,D*†
University of Denver M,D*†
University of Detroit Mercy M*
University of Florida M,D,O*†
University of Georgia M,D*†
University of Guelph M
University of Hawaii at Manoa M,D,O*
University of Houston M,D*
University of Houston–Clear Lake M*†
University of Idaho M,D*†
University of Illinois at Chicago M,D*
University of Illinois at Springfield M†
University of Illinois at Urbana–Champaign M,D*
The University of Iowa M,D*
University of Kansas M,D*
University of Kentucky M,D*
The University of Lethbridge M,D
University of Louisiana at Lafayette M,D*
University of Louisville M,D*†
University of Maine M,D*
University of Manitoba M,D*
University of Maryland, Baltimore County M,D*†
University of Maryland, College Park M,D*
University of Maryland Eastern Shore M†
University of Massachusetts Amherst M,D*†
University of Massachusetts Boston M,D*†
University of Massachusetts Dartmouth M,O*†
University of Massachusetts Lowell M,D*†
The University of Memphis M,D*†
University of Miami M*†
University of Michigan M,D*
University of Michigan–Dearborn M*†
University of Minnesota, Duluth M*
University of Minnesota, Twin Cities Campus M,D*
University of Missouri–Columbia M,D*
University of Missouri–Kansas City M,D*†
University of Missouri–Rolla M,D*
University of Missouri–St. Louis M,D,O†
The University of Montana–Missoula M*†
University of Nebraska at Omaha M
University of Nebraska–Lincoln M,D*†
University of Nevada, Las Vegas M,D*†
University of Nevada, Reno M*
University of New Brunswick Fredericton M,D
University of New Hampshire M,D*†
University of New Haven M*†
University of New Mexico M,D*†
University of New Orleans M*
The University of North Carolina at Chapel Hill M,D*†
The University of North Carolina at Charlotte M*
The University of North Carolina at Greensboro M†
University of North Dakota M*
University of Northern British Columbia M,D
University of Northern Iowa M
University of North Florida M
University of North Texas M,D*†
University of Notre Dame M,D*†
University of Oklahoma M,D*†
University of Oregon M,D*
University of Ottawa M,D,O*
University of Pennsylvania M,D*†
University of Phoenix–Phoenix Campus M
University of Pittsburgh M,D*†
University of Regina M,D
University of Rhode Island M,D*
University of Rochester M,D*
University of San Francisco M*†
University of Saskatchewan M,D
University of South Alabama M*†
University of South Carolina M,D*†
The University of South Dakota M†
University of Southern California M,D*†
University of Southern Maine M
University of Southern Mississippi M,D
University of South Florida M,D*†
The University of Tennessee M,D*†
The University of Tennessee at Chattanooga M
The University of Texas at Arlington M,D*†
The University of Texas at Austin M,D*
The University of Texas at Dallas M,D*
The University of Texas at El Paso M*†
The University of Texas at San Antonio M,D*
The University of Texas at Tyler M
The University of Texas–Pan American M
University of Toledo M,D*†
University of Toronto M,D*
University of Tulsa M,D†
University of Utah M,D*
University of Vermont M*†
University of Victoria M,D
University of Virginia M,D*
University of Washington M,D*
University of Waterloo M,D
The University of Western Ontario M,D*
University of West Florida M
University of Windsor M
University of Wisconsin–Madison M,D*
University of Wisconsin–Milwaukee M,D
University of Wisconsin–Parkside M
University of Wyoming M,D*†
Utah State University M,D*
Vanderbilt University M,D*
Villanova University M*†
Virginia Commonwealth University M*†
Virginia Polytechnic Institute and State University M,D*
Wake Forest University M*†
Washington State University M,D*
Washington State University Spokane M†
Washington University in St. Louis M,D*†
Wayne State University M,D,O*
Webster University M,O
West Chester University of Pennsylvania M,O*†
Western Carolina University M†
Western Connecticut State University M
Western Illinois University M
Western Kentucky University M†
Western Michigan University M,D*†
Western Washington University M
West Virginia University M,D*
Wichita State University M*†
Worcester Polytechnic Institute M,D,O*†
Wright State University M,D*
Yale University D*
York University M,D*

CONDENSED MATTER PHYSICS

Cleveland State University M*†
Iowa State University of Science and Technology M,D*†
Memorial University of Newfoundland M,D†
Rutgers, The State University of New Jersey, New Brunswick M,D*
University of Alberta M,D*
University of Victoria M,D
West Virginia University M,D*

CONFLICT RESOLUTION AND MEDIATION/PEACE STUDIES

American University M,D,O*†
Antioch University McGregor M†
Arcadia University M†
Associated Mennonite Biblical Seminary P,M,O
Bethany Theological Seminary P,M,O
California State University, Dominguez Hills M,O†
Chaminade University of Honolulu M*
Columbia College (SC) M,O
Cornell University M,D*
Dallas Baptist University M
Duquesne University M,O*†
Eastern Mennonite University M
Fresno Pacific University M
George Mason University M,D*†
Huron University USA in London M
John F. Kennedy University O*†
Johns Hopkins University M,D,O*†
Jones International University M*†
Kennesaw State University M
Lesley University M,O*†
Montclair State University M,O†
Nova Southeastern University M,D,O*
Pepperdine University M*
Royal Roads University M
St. Edward's University M,O
St. Mary's University of San Antonio M
Université de Sherbrooke M,D,O
University of Baltimore M*
University of Massachusetts Boston M,O*†
University of Missouri–Columbia M*
University of Missouri–St. Louis M†
University of Notre Dame M*†
University of Victoria M
Wayne State University M,O*

CONSERVATION BIOLOGY

Arizona State University M,D*
Central Michigan University M†
Columbia University M,D,O*†
Frostburg State University M
San Francisco State University M
State University of New York at Albany M*†
State University of New York College of Environmental Science and Forestry M,D
University of Alberta M,D*
University of Arkansas D*
University of Central Florida M,O*†
University of Hawaii at Manoa M,D*
University of Maryland, College Park M*
University of Minnesota, Twin Cities Campus M,D*
University of Missouri–St. Louis M,D,O†
University of Nevada, Reno D*
University of New Orleans M,D*
University of Wisconsin–Madison M*

CONSTRUCTION ENGINEERING AND MANAGEMENT

Arizona State University M*
Auburn University M,D*†
Bradley University M†
The Catholic University of America M*†
Central Connecticut State University M*†
Clemson University *
Colorado State University M,D*
Concordia University (Canada) M,D,O*†

Florida International University M*†
Georgia Institute of Technology M,D*
Iowa State University of Science and Technology M,D*†
Marquette University M,D*†
Michigan State University M*†
Oregon State University M,D*
Southern Polytechnic State University M†
State University of New York College of Environmental Science and Forestry M,D
Stevens Institute of Technology M*†
Texas A&M University M,D*
Universidad de las Américas–Puebla M
University of Alberta M,D*
University of California, Berkeley M,D*
University of Colorado at Boulder M,D*
University of Denver M*†
University of Florida M*†
University of Houston M*
University of Kansas M,D*
University of Michigan M,D,O*
University of Missouri–Rolla M,D*
University of New Brunswick Fredericton M,D
University of Southern California M*†
University of Washington M,D*
Washington University in St. Louis M*†
Western Michigan University M*†

CONSUMER ECONOMICS

Colorado State University M*
Cornell University M,D*
Florida State University M,D*†
Iowa State University of Science and Technology M,D*†
Michigan State University M,D*†
Minnesota State University, Mankato M
Montclair State University M†
The Ohio State University M,D*
Purdue University M,D*
Syracuse University M*
Texas Tech University D*†
Université Laval O†
The University of Alabama M*
The University of Arizona M,D*
University of Georgia M,D*†
University of Guelph M
University of Illinois at Urbana–Champaign M,D*
The University of Memphis M*†
University of Missouri–Columbia M*
University of Nebraska–Lincoln M,D*†
The University of Tennessee M,D*†
University of Utah M*
University of Vermont M*†
University of Wisconsin–Madison M,D*
University of Wyoming M*†
Virginia Polytechnic Institute and State University M,D*

CORPORATE AND ORGANIZATIONAL COMMUNICATION

Audrey Cohen College M†
Austin Peay State University M
Barry University M,O*†
Bentley College M,O*
Bernard M. Baruch College of the City University of New York M*
Bowie State University M,O
Canisius College M
Carnegie Mellon University M*
Central Connecticut State University M*†
Central Michigan University M†
Columbia University M*†
Concordia University Wisconsin M
DePaul University M*†
École des Hautes Études Commerciales de Montréal O*
Emerson College M*†
Fairleigh Dickinson University, College at Florham M*†
Florida State University M,D*†
Fordham University M*†
Franklin University M
Howard University M,D*
Illinois Institute of Technology M*†
Iowa State University of Science and Technology M,D*†
John Carroll University M
Jones International University M*†
La Salle University M
Lindenwood University M
Loyola University Chicago M*†
Manhattanville College M*†
Marylhurst University M
Monmouth University M,O*†
Murray State University M†
North Carolina State University M*
Northwestern University M*
Oklahoma City University M
Queens University of Charlotte M
Radford University M†
Rollins College M*
Roosevelt University M*†
Royal Roads University M
Sage Graduate School M†
Seton Hall University M*†
Simmons College M*
Syracuse University M*
Towson University M†
University of Arkansas at Little Rock M
University of Colorado at Boulder M,D*
University of Connecticut M,D*†
University of Denver M*†
University of Florida M,D*†
University of Portland M
University of St. Thomas (MN) M,O*†
University of Southern California M,D*†
University of Wisconsin–Stevens Point M
University of Wisconsin–Whitewater M*
Wayne State University M,D*
Western Kentucky University M†
Western Michigan University M*†
West Virginia University M*

COUNSELING PSYCHOLOGY

Abilene Christian University M
Adler School of Professional Psychology M,D,O*
Alabama Agricultural and Mechanical University M,O
Alaska Pacific University M
Alfred Adler Graduate School M,O
Alliant International University M*†
Amberton University M
Andrews University D
Angelo State University M†
Anna Maria College M,O
Antioch New England Graduate School M*†
Antioch University McGregor M†
Antioch University Santa Barbara M
Arcadia University M†
Argosy University-Atlanta M,D*
Argosy University-Chicago M*
Argosy University-Chicago Northwest M,D*
Argosy University-Dallas M,D*
Argosy University-Honolulu M*
Argosy University-Orange County M,D*
Argosy University-Phoenix M*
Argosy University-San Francisco Bay Area M,D*
Argosy University-Sarasota M,D,O*†
Argosy University-Seattle M*
Argosy University-Twin Cities M,D*
Argosy University-Washington D.C. M,D,O*
Arizona State University D*
Assumption College M,O†
Auburn University M,D,O*†
Avila University M
Ball State University M,D*
Benedictine University M†
Bethel College (IN) M
Boston College M,D*†
Boston University M,D*†
Bowie State University M
Brigham Young University M,D*
Caldwell College M
California Baptist University M
California Institute of Integral Studies M,D,O*
California State University, Bakersfield M
California State University, Chico M
California State University, Sacramento M
California State University, San Bernardino M
California State University, Stanislaus M
Cambridge College M†
Carlos Albizu University, Miami Campus M,D
Centenary College M
Central Washington University M†
Chaminade University of Honolulu M*
Chatham College M
Chestnut Hill College M,D†
City University M†
Cleveland State University M*†
College of Mount Saint Vincent M,O*†
The College of New Rochelle M†
College of Saint Elizabeth M
College of St. Joseph M
Colorado State University D*
Columbus State University M,O
Concordia University (IL) M,O
Dominican University of California M
Eastern Nazarene College M
Eastern University M*
Eastern Washington University M†
Fitchburg State College M,O†
Florida State University D*†
Fordham University M,D,O*†
Fort Valley State University M
Framingham State College M*
Franciscan University of Steubenville M
Frostburg State University M
Gallaudet University M
Gannon University M,D
Gardner-Webb University M
Geneva College M*
George Fox University M†
Georgian Court College M
Georgia State University M,D,O*
Goddard College M
Golden Gate University M,O
Gonzaga University M
Grace College M
Grace University M
Holy Family College M
Holy Names College M,O
Hope International University M
Houston Baptist University M
Howard University M,D,O*
Idaho State University M,O*
Illinois State University M,D,O*†
Immaculata University M,D,O†
Indiana State University M,D,O*†
Institute of Transpersonal Psychology M,D*
Inter American University of Puerto Rico, San Germán Campus M,D
Iowa State University of Science and Technology M,D*†
James Madison University M,O
John Carroll University M,O
John F. Kennedy University M*†
Kutztown University of Pennsylvania M†
La Salle University M
Lee University M
Lehigh University M,D,O*
Lesley University M,D,O*†
Lewis & Clark College M
Lewis University M
Liberty University M†
Lindenwood University M
Louisiana Tech University M,D,O*
Loyola College in Maryland M,O
Loyola Marymount University M†
Loyola University Chicago D*†
Marist College M,O
Marymount University M,O†
Marywood University M,D*†
McGill University M,D*
Michigan State University M,D,O*†
Michigan Theological Seminary P,M,D
MidAmerica Nazarene University M
Mississippi College M,O
Monmouth University M,O*†
Morehead State University M
Mount St. Mary's College M*
Naropa University M*
National University M,O†
New Jersey City University M
New Mexico State University M,D,O
New York Institute of Technology M*†
New York University M,D,O*†
Nicholls State University M,O
Northeastern State University M
Northeastern University M,D,O*†
Northern Arizona University D
Northwestern University M*
Northwest Missouri State University M
Notre Dame de Namur University M,O
Nova Southeastern University M*
The Ohio State University D*
Ottawa University M
Our Lady of the Lake University of San Antonio M,D
Pacifica Graduate Institute M,D*
Palm Beach Atlantic University M
The Pennsylvania State University University Park Campus D*†
Prescott College M†
Radford University M,O†
Regent University M,D†
Regis University M,O*†
Rivier College M*†
Rosemont College M†
Rutgers, The State University of New Jersey, New Brunswick M*
St. Edward's University M
Saint Martin's College M
Saint Mary's University of Minnesota M
St. Mary's University of San Antonio M,D,O
St. Thomas University M†
Saint Xavier University M,O*
Salve Regina University M,O†
Sam Houston State University M,D*
San Francisco State University M
San Jose State University M*
Santa Clara University M*
Seton Hall University D*†
Southern California Bible College & Seminary P,M
Southern Christian University P,M,D
Southern Illinois University Carbondale M,D*†
Southern Methodist University M*†
Southern Nazarene University M
Southwestern Assemblies of God University M
Southwestern College (NM) M,O†
Springfield College M,O†
Stanford University D*
State University of New York at Albany M,D,O*†
State University of New York at Oswego M,O
Tarleton State University M
Teachers College Columbia University M,D*
Temple University M,D*†
Tennessee State University M,D*
Texas A&M International University M
Texas A&M University D*
Texas A&M University–Commerce M,D†
Texas A&M University–Texarkana M
Texas Tech University M,D*†
Texas Woman's University M,D*†
Towson University M,O†
Trevecca Nazarene University M
Trinity International University P,M,D,O
Trinity International University, South Florida Campus M
Trinity Western University M
Truman State University M†
The University of Akron M,D†
University of Alberta M,D*
University of Baltimore M,D*
The University of British Columbia M,D,O*
University of Calgary M,D*
University of California, Santa Barbara M,D*
University of Central Arkansas M
University of Central Oklahoma M
University of Colorado at Denver M*
University of Connecticut M,D*†
University of Denver M,D,O*†
University of Georgia M,D*†
University of Great Falls M
University of Houston M,D*
University of Kansas M,D*
University of Kentucky M,D,O*
University of La Verne M,D*
The University of Lethbridge M,D
University of Louisville M,D*†
University of Mary Hardin-Baylor M
University of Maryland, College Park M,D,O*
The University of Memphis M,D*†
University of Miami D*†
University of Minnesota, Twin Cities Campus D*
University of Missouri–Columbia M,D,O*
University of Missouri–Kansas City M,D,O*†
University of Nevada, Las Vegas M*†
The University of North Carolina at Greensboro M,D,O†
University of North Dakota M,D*
University of Northern Colorado M,D†
University of North Florida M
University of North Texas M,D*†
University of Notre Dame D*†
University of Oklahoma D*†
University of Pennsylvania M*†
University of Phoenix–New Mexico Campus M
University of Phoenix–Phoenix Campus M
University of Rhode Island M*
University of Saint Francis (IN) M
University of St. Thomas (MN) M,D,O*†
University of San Francisco M,D*†
The University of Scranton M,O†
University of Southern California M,D,O*†
The University of Tennessee M,D,O*†
The University of Texas at Austin M,D*

*P—first professional degree; M—master's degree; D—doctorate; O—other advanced degree; *full description and/or announcement in Book 2, 3, 4, 5, or 6; †full description in this book*

The University of Texas at Tyler M
University of the Pacific M,D,O*
University of Vermont M*†
University of Victoria M,D
University of Wisconsin–Madison D*
University of Wisconsin–Stout M
Utah State University M,D*
Valdosta State University M,O
Valparaiso University M
Virginia Commonwealth University M,D,O*†
Walla Walla College M
Washington State University M,D*
Webster University M
Western Michigan University M,D*†
Western Washington University M
Westfield State College M
West Virginia University M,D*
William Carey College M

COUNSELOR EDUCATION

Abilene Christian University M
Acadia University M,O
Adams State College M
Alabama Agricultural and Mechanical University M,O
Alabama State University M,D,O
Albany State University M
Alcorn State University M,O
Alfred University M*†
Angelo State University M†
Appalachian State University M,O
Argosy University-Sarasota M,D,O*†
Arizona State University M*
Arkansas State University M,O
Arkansas Tech University M
Auburn University M,D,O*†
Auburn University Montgomery M,O
Augusta State University M,O
Austin Peay State University M,O
Baptist Bible College of Pennsylvania M
Barry University M,D,O*†
Bayamón Central University M
Boise State University M*
Boston University M,O*†
Bowie State University M
Bowling Green State University M*†
Bradley University M†
Brandon University M,O
Bridgewater State College M,O
Brigham Young University M,D*
Brooklyn College of the City University of New York M,O†
Bucknell University M
Buena Vista University M
Butler University M
California Lutheran University M
California Polytechnic State University, San Luis Obispo M†
California State University, Bakersfield M
California State University, Dominguez Hills M†
California State University, Fresno M
California State University, Fullerton M
California State University, Hayward M
California State University, Long Beach M,O
California State University, Los Angeles M
California State University, Northridge M,O
California State University, Sacramento M
California State University, San Bernardino M
California State University, Stanislaus M
California University of Pennsylvania M
Campbell University M
Canisius College M,O
Carson-Newman College M
Carthage College M,O
The Catholic University of America M,D*†
Central Connecticut State University M*†
Central Michigan University M†
Central Missouri State University M,O†
Central Washington University M†
Chadron State College M,O
Chapman University M*†
Chicago State University M
The Citadel, The Military College of South Carolina M
Clark Atlanta University M,D
Clemson University M*
Cleveland State University M,D,O*†
The College of New Jersey M†
College of St. Joseph M
The College of Saint Rose M,O*†
College of Santa Fe M
College of the Southwest M
The College of William and Mary M,D*†
Columbia International University M
Columbus State University M,O
Concordia University (IL) M,O
Concordia University Wisconsin M
Creighton University M*
Dallas Baptist University M
Delta State University M
DePaul University M*†
Doane College M
Drake University M*†
Duquesne University M,D*†
East Carolina University M,O*†
East Central University M
Eastern Illinois University M†
Eastern Kentucky University M
Eastern Michigan University M,O*
Eastern New Mexico University M
Eastern University M*
Eastern Washington University M†
East Tennessee State University M†
Edinboro University of Pennsylvania M,O
Emporia State University M*†
Evangel University M
Fairfield University M,O*
Fitchburg State College M,O†
Florida Agricultural and Mechanical University M,D*
Florida Atlantic University M,O*
Florida Atlantic University, Ft. Lauderdale Campus M,O
Florida Gulf Coast University M
Florida International University M*†
Florida State University M,O*†
Fordham University M,D,O*†
Fort Hays State University M
Fort Valley State University M,O
Freed-Hardeman University M
Fresno Pacific University M
Frostburg State University M
Gallaudet University M
Geneva College M*
George Mason University M*†
The George Washington University M,D,O*†
Georgia Southern University M,O
Georgia State University M,D,O*
Governors State University M
Gwynedd-Mercy College M
Hampton University M*†
Hardin-Simmons University M
Heidelberg College M
Henderson State University M
Heritage College M
Hofstra University M,O*
Houston Baptist University M
Howard University M,D,O*
Hunter College of the City University of New York M†
Idaho State University M,D,O*
Illinois State University M,D*†
Immaculata University M,D,O†
Indiana State University M,D,O*†
Indiana University Bloomington M,D,O*
Indiana University of Pennsylvania M*†
Indiana University–Purdue University Fort Wayne M
Indiana University–Purdue University Indianapolis M*
Indiana University South Bend M
Indiana University Southeast M
Indiana Wesleyan University M,O*
Inter American University of Puerto Rico, Arecibo Campus M
Inter American University of Puerto Rico, Metropolitan Campus M
Inter American University of Puerto Rico, San Germán Campus M
Iona College M*†
Iowa State University of Science and Technology M,D*†
Jackson State University M,O
Jacksonville State University M,O
John Brown University M
John Carroll University M,O
Johns Hopkins University M,D,O*†
Johnson State College M
Kansas State University M,D*†
Kean University M,O*†
Keene State College M,O
Kent State University M,D*
Kutztown University of Pennsylvania M†
Lamar University M,O*†
Lancaster Bible College M
La Sierra University M,O
Lehigh University M,D,O*
Lehman College of the City University of New York M
Lenoir-Rhyne College M
Lewis University M
Liberty University M,D†
Lincoln Memorial University M,O
Lincoln University (MO) M
Long Island University, Brentwood Campus M
Long Island University, Brooklyn Campus M,O*
Long Island University, C.W. Post Campus M,O*†
Long Island University, Rockland Graduate Campus M
Long Island University, Westchester Graduate Campus M
Longwood College M
Loras College M
Louisiana State University and Agricultural and Mechanical College M,D,O*
Louisiana Tech University M,D,O*
Loyola College in Maryland M,O
Loyola Marymount University M†
Loyola University Chicago M*†
Loyola University New Orleans M
Lynchburg College M
Lyndon State College M
Malone College M†
Manhattan College M,O*†
Marshall University M,O*†
Marymount University M,O†
Marywood University M*†
McDaniel College M
McNeese State University M
Mercy College M,O*
Michigan State University M,D,O*†
Middle Tennessee State University M,O*
Midwestern State University M
Millersville University of Pennsylvania M†
Minnesota State University, Mankato M
Minnesota State University, Moorhead M
Mississippi College M,O
Mississippi State University M,D,O*
Montana State University–Billings M*
Montana State University–Northern M
Montclair State University M†
Morehead State University M,O
Murray State University M,O†
National University M†
New Mexico Highlands University M
New Mexico State University M,D,O
New York Institute of Technology M*†
New York University M,D,O*†
Niagara University M,O†
Nicholls State University M,O
North Carolina Agricultural and Technical State University M*
North Carolina Central University M
North Carolina State University M,D,O*
North Dakota State University M†
Northeastern Illinois University M
Northeastern State University M
Northeastern University M*†
Northern Arizona University M
Northern Illinois University M,D*†
Northern State University M
Northwest Christian College M
Northwestern Oklahoma State University M
Northwestern State University of Louisiana M,O
Northwest Missouri State University M
Northwest Nazarene University M
Oakland University M,D†
Ohio University M,D*
Oklahoma State University M,D*†
Old Dominion University M,O*†
Oregon State University M,D*
Our Lady of Holy Cross College M
Our Lady of the Lake University of San Antonio M
Palm Beach Atlantic University M
The Pennsylvania State University University Park Campus M,D*†
Phillips Graduate Institute M
Pittsburg State University M
Plattsburgh State University of New York M,O
Plymouth State College M*
Portland State University M*
Prairie View A&M University M*
Providence College M*
Purdue University M,D,O*
Purdue University Calumet M
Queens College of the City University of New York M†
Radford University M†
Regent University M,D†
Rhode Island College M,O†
Rider University M,O*
Rivier College M*†
Rollins College M*
Roosevelt University M,D*†
Rosemont College M†
Sage Graduate School M,O†
St. Bonaventure University M,O
St. Cloud State University M
St. John's University (NY) M,O*†
St. Lawrence University M,O
Saint Louis University M,D,O*†
Saint Martin's College M
Saint Mary's College of California M
St. Mary's University of San Antonio M,D,O
St. Thomas University M,O†
Salem State College M
Sam Houston State University M,D*
San Diego State University M*
San Jose State University M*
Santa Clara University M*
Seattle Pacific University M
Seattle University M*†
Seton Hall University M*†
Shippensburg University of Pennsylvania M,O†
Siena Heights University M
Simon Fraser University M
Slippery Rock University of Pennsylvania M†
Sonoma State University M
South Carolina State University M,D,O
South Dakota State University M*
Southeastern Louisiana University M
Southeastern Oklahoma State University M
Southeast Missouri State University M,D,O
Southern Adventist University M
Southern Arkansas University–Magnolia M
Southern Connecticut State University M,O†
Southern Illinois University Carbondale M,D*†
Southern Oregon University M
Southern University and Agricultural and Mechanical College M*
Southwestern College (NM) M,O†
Southwestern Oklahoma State University M
Southwest Missouri State University M*†
Southwest Texas State University M*
Spalding University M†
Springfield College M,O†
State University of New York at Albany M,D,O*†
State University of New York College at Brockport M,O*†
State University of New York College at Oneonta M,O
State University of West Georgia M,O
Stephen F. Austin State University M
Stephens College M
Stetson University M
Suffolk University M,O*
Sul Ross State University M*
Syracuse University M,D,O*
Tarleton State University M
Tennessee State University M,D*
Texas A&M University M,D*
Texas A&M University–Commerce M,D†
Texas A&M University–Corpus Christi M
Texas A&M University–Kingsville M*†
Texas Christian University M*
Texas Southern University M,D†
Texas Tech University M,D,O*†
Texas Woman's University M,D*†
Trevecca Nazarene University M
Trinity College (DC) M†
Troy State University M
Troy State University Dothan M,O
Troy State University Montgomery M,O
Université de Moncton M
Université de Sherbrooke M
Université Laval M,D†
University at Buffalo, The State University of New York M,D,O*†
University College of Cape Breton O
The University of Akron M†
The University of Alabama at Birmingham M*†
University of Alaska Anchorage M
University of Alaska Fairbanks M,O*
University of Alberta M,D*
University of Arkansas M,D,O*
University of Arkansas at Little Rock M
University of Central Arkansas M
University of Central Florida M,D*†
University of Central Oklahoma M
University of Cincinnati M,D,O*

Institution	Degrees
University of Colorado at Colorado Springs	M*
University of Colorado at Denver	M*
University of Dayton	M*†
University of Delaware	M,D*†
University of Florida	M,D,O*†
University of Georgia	M,D*†
University of Great Falls	M
University of Guam	M
University of Hartford	M,O*
University of Hawaii at Manoa	M*
University of Houston–Clear Lake	M*†
University of Idaho	M,D,O*†
University of Illinois at Urbana–Champaign	M,D,O*
The University of Iowa	M,D*
University of La Verne	M,O*
University of Louisiana at Lafayette	M*
University of Louisiana at Monroe	M,O
University of Louisville	M,D*†
University of Maine	M,O*
University of Manitoba	M*
University of Maryland, College Park	M,D,O*
University of Maryland Eastern Shore	M†
University of Massachusetts Amherst	M,D,O*†
University of Massachusetts Boston	M,O*†
The University of Memphis	M,D*†
University of Miami	M,O*†
University of Minnesota, Twin Cities Campus	M,D,O*
University of Mississippi	M,D,O*
University of Missouri–Kansas City	M,D,O*†
University of Missouri–St. Louis	M,D†
The University of Montana–Missoula	M,D,O*†
University of Montevallo	M
University of Nebraska at Kearney	M,O
University of Nebraska at Omaha	M
University of Nevada, Reno	M,D,O*
University of New Brunswick Fredericton	M
University of New Hampshire	M*†
University of New Mexico	M,D*†
University of New Orleans	M,D,O*
University of North Alabama	M
The University of North Carolina at Chapel Hill	M*†
The University of North Carolina at Charlotte	M,D*
The University of North Carolina at Greensboro	M,D,O†
The University of North Carolina at Pembroke	M
University of Northern Colorado	M,D†
University of Northern Iowa	M,D
University of North Florida	M
University of North Texas	M,D*†
University of Phoenix–Hawaii Campus	M,O
University of Phoenix–Nevada Campus	M
University of Phoenix–Phoenix Campus	M
University of Puerto Rico, Río Piedras	M,D*
University of Puget Sound	M
University of Saint Francis (IN)	M
University of San Diego	M*†
University of San Francisco	M,D*†
The University of Scranton	M†
University of South Alabama	M,O*†
University of South Carolina	D,O*†
The University of South Dakota	M,D,O†
University of Southern Maine	M,O
University of South Florida	M*†
The University of Tennessee	M,D,O*†
The University of Tennessee at Chattanooga	M,O
The University of Tennessee at Martin	M
The University of Texas at Austin	M,D*
The University of Texas at Brownsville	M
The University of Texas at San Antonio	M,D*
The University of Texas of the Permian Basin	M
The University of Texas–Pan American	M,D
University of the District of Columbia	M*
University of the Pacific	M,D,O*
University of Toledo	M,D*†
University of Vermont	M*†
University of Victoria	M,D
University of Virginia	M,D,O*
University of Washington	M,D*
The University of West Alabama	M
The University of Western Ontario	M*
University of West Florida	M
University of Wisconsin–Madison	M*
University of Wisconsin–Oshkosh	M*
University of Wisconsin–Platteville	M
University of Wisconsin–River Falls	M,O
University of Wisconsin–Stevens Point	M
University of Wisconsin–Stout	M
University of Wisconsin–Superior	M
University of Wisconsin–Whitewater	M*
University of Wyoming	M,D*†
Utah State University	M,D*
Valdosta State University	M,O
Vanderbilt University	M*
Villanova University	M*†
Virginia Commonwealth University	M*†
Virginia Polytechnic Institute and State University	M,D,O*
Virginia State University	M
Wake Forest University	M*†
Walla Walla College	M
Walsh University	M
Wayne State College	M
Wayne State University	M,D,O*
West Chester University of Pennsylvania	M*†
Western Carolina University	M†
Western Connecticut State University	M
Western Illinois University	M,O
Western Kentucky University	M,O†
Western Michigan University	M,D*†
Western New Mexico University	M
Western Washington University	M
Westminster College (PA)	M,O
West Texas A&M University	M†
Whitworth College	M
Wichita State University	M,D,O*†
Widener University	M,D*†
William Paterson University of New Jersey	M*†
Wilmington College	M,D
Winona State University	M
Winthrop University	M
Wright State University	M*
Xavier University	M*
Xavier University of Louisiana	M
Youngstown State University	M

CRIMINAL JUSTICE AND CRIMINOLOGY

Institution	Degrees
Albany State University	M
American International College	M*
American Military University	M
American University	M,D*†
Andrew Jackson University	M
Anna Maria College	M
Arizona State University West	M
Armstrong Atlantic State University	M†
Auburn University Montgomery	M
Boise State University	M*
Boston University	M*†
Bowling Green State University	M,D*†
California State University, Fresno	M
California State University, Long Beach	M
California State University, Los Angeles	M
California State University, Sacramento	M
California State University, San Bernardino	M
California State University, Stanislaus	M
Central Connecticut State University	M*†
Central Michigan University	M†
Central Missouri State University	M,O†
Chaminade University of Honolulu	M*
Charleston Southern University	M
Chicago State University	M
Clark Atlanta University	M
Colorado Technical University Denver Campus	M
Columbia College (MO)	M
Concordia University (MN)	M
Coppin State College	M
Delta State University	M
Drury University	M
East Carolina University	M*†
East Central University	M
Eastern Kentucky University	M
Eastern Michigan University	M*
East Tennessee State University	M†
Ferris State University	M
Fitchburg State College	M†
Florida Atlantic University	M*
Florida Atlantic University, Ft. Lauderdale Campus	M
Florida Gulf Coast University	M
Florida International University	M*†
Florida Metropolitan University–Brandon Campus	M
Florida Metropolitan University–Pinellas Campus	M
Florida State University	M,D*†
Fordham University	M,D*†
The George Washington University	M*†
Georgia State University	M*
Graduate School and University Center of the City University of New York	D*†
Grambling State University	M
Grand Valley State University	M†
Illinois State University	M*†
Indiana State University	M*†
Indiana University Bloomington	M,D*
Indiana University Northwest	M,O
Indiana University of Pennsylvania	M,D*†
Inter American University of Puerto Rico, Metropolitan Campus	M
Iona College	M*†
Jackson State University	M
Jacksonville State University	M
John Jay College of Criminal Justice of the City University of New York	M,D*
Kent State University	M*
Lamar University	M*†
Lewis University	M
Lincoln University (MO)	M
Long Island University, Brentwood Campus	M
Long Island University, C.W. Post Campus	M*†
Longwood College	M
Loyola University Chicago	M*†
Loyola University New Orleans	M
Lynn University	M†
Madonna University	M
Marshall University	M*†
Marywood University	M*†
Mercyhurst College	M
Metropolitan State University	M
Michigan State University	M,D*†
Middle Tennessee State University	M*
Minot State University	M
Mississippi College	M
Mississippi Valley State University	M
Monmouth University	M,O*†
Morehead State University	M
Mountain State University	M†
National University	M†
New Jersey City University	M
New Mexico State University	M
Niagara University	M†
North Carolina Central University	M
North Dakota State University	M,D†
Northeastern State University	M
Northeastern University	M*†
Northern Arizona University	M,O
Northern Michigan University	M
Oklahoma City University	M
Oklahoma State University	M,D*†
The Pennsylvania State University University Park Campus	M,D*†
Pontifical Catholic University of Puerto Rico	M,D
Portland State University	M,D*
Radford University	M†
Rosemont College	M†
Rutgers, The State University of New Jersey, Camden	M†
Rutgers, The State University of New Jersey, Newark	M,D*†
St. Ambrose University	M
St. Cloud State University	M
Saint Joseph's University	M*†
Saint Mary's University	M
Saint Mary's University of Minnesota	M
St. Mary's University of San Antonio	M
St. Thomas University	M,O†
Salve Regina University	M†
Sam Houston State University	M,D*
San Diego State University	M*
San Jose State University	M*
Seton Hall University	M*†
Shippensburg University of Pennsylvania	M†
Simon Fraser University	M,D
Southeast Missouri State University	M
Southern Illinois University Carbondale	M*†
Southwest Texas State University	M*
State University of New York at Albany	M,D*†
State University of New York College at Buffalo	M
Suffolk University	*
Sul Ross State University	M*
Tarleton State University	M
Temple University	M,D*†
Tennessee State University	M*
Texas A&M International University	M
Tiffin University	M†
Troy State University	M
Universidad del Turabo	M
Université de Montréal	M,D
The University of Alabama	M*
The University of Alabama at Birmingham	M*†
University of Alaska Fairbanks	M*
University of Alberta	M,D*
University of Arkansas at Little Rock	M
University of Baltimore	M*
University of California, Irvine	D*
University of Central Florida	M,O*†
University of Central Oklahoma	M
University of Cincinnati	M,D*
University of Colorado at Colorado Springs	M*
University of Colorado at Denver	M*
University of Delaware	M,D*†
University of Detroit Mercy	M*
University of Great Falls	M
University of Illinois at Chicago	M*
University of Louisiana at Monroe	M
University of Louisville	M*†
University of Maryland, College Park	M,D*
University of Massachusetts Lowell	M*†
The University of Memphis	M*†
University of Missouri–Kansas City	M*†
University of Missouri–St. Louis	M,D†
The University of Montana–Missoula	M*†
University of Nebraska at Omaha	M,D
University of Nevada, Las Vegas	M*†
University of New Haven	M*†
University of North Alabama	M
The University of North Carolina at Charlotte	M*
University of North Florida	M
University of Ottawa	M*
University of Pittsburgh	M,D*†
University of South Carolina	M*†
University of Southern Mississippi	M,D
University of South Florida	M,D*†
The University of Tennessee	M,D*†
The University of Tennessee at Chattanooga	M
The University of Texas at Arlington	M*†
The University of Texas at San Antonio	M*
The University of Texas at Tyler	M
The University of Texas of the Permian Basin	M
The University of Texas–Pan American	M
University of Toronto	M,D*
University of Wisconsin–Milwaukee	M
University of Wisconsin–Platteville	M
Utica College	M
Valdosta State University	M
Villanova University	M*†
Virginia Commonwealth University	M,O*†
Washington State University	M*
Washington State University Spokane	M†
Wayne State University	M*
Webster University	M
West Chester University of Pennsylvania	M*†
Western Connecticut State University	M
Western Illinois University	M,O
Western New England College	M
Western Oregon University	M
Westfield State College	M
West Texas A&M University	M†
Wichita State University	M*†
Widener University	M*†
Wilmington College	M
Wright State University	M*
Xavier University	M*

*P—first professional degree; M—master's degree; D—doctorate; O—other advanced degree; *full description and/or announcement in Book 2, 3, 4, 5, or 6; †full description in this book*

- Youngstown State University M

CULTURAL STUDIES

- Athabasca University M
- Brock University M
- Claremont Graduate University M,D*
- Cornell University M,D*
- George Mason University D*†
- Graduate Theological Union M,D,O
- Simmons College M*
- Sonoma State University M
- Southern Illinois University Carbondale M*†
- Stony Brook University, State University of New York M,O*†
- Trinity International University P,M,D,O
- University of California, Davis M,D*†
- University of Chicago M,D*
- University of Minnesota, Twin Cities Campus M,D*
- University of Pittsburgh M,D*†
- The University of Texas at San Antonio M,D*
- University of the Sacred Heart M
- Valparaiso University M
- Wheaton College M,O†

CURRICULUM AND INSTRUCTION

- Acadia University M
- Alverno College M
- Andrews University M,D,O
- Angelo State University M†
- Appalachian State University M
- Argosy University-Orange County M,D,O*
- Argosy University-San Francisco Bay Area M,D*
- Argosy University-Sarasota M,D,O*†
- Argosy University-Tampa M*
- Argosy University-Twin Cities M*
- Arizona State University M,D*
- Arkansas State University M,D,O
- Arkansas Tech University M
- Ashland University M
- Auburn University M,D,O*†
- Aurora University M,D
- Austin Peay State University M,O
- Averett University M
- Azusa Pacific University M*†
- Ball State University M,O*
- Bank Street College of Education M*
- Baylor University M,D,O*†
- Benedictine University M†
- Berry College O
- Black Hills State University M*
- Bloomsburg University of Pennsylvania M
- Boise State University M,D*
- Boston College M,D,O*†
- Boston University M,D,O*†
- Bowling Green State University M*†
- Bradley University M†
- Brandon University M,O
- Brescia University M
- Brock University M
- Bucknell University M
- Caldwell College M
- California Baptist University M
- California Polytechnic State University, San Luis Obispo M†
- California State University, Bakersfield M
- California State University, Chico M
- California State University, Dominguez Hills M†
- California State University, Fresno M
- California State University, Sacramento M
- California State University, Stanislaus M
- Calvin College M
- Carson-Newman College M
- Castleton State College M
- The Catholic University of America M,D*†
- Centenary College of Louisiana M
- Central Missouri State University M,O†
- Central Washington University M†
- Chapman University M*†
- City University M,O†
- Clark Atlanta University M,O
- Clemson University D*
- Cleveland State University M*†
- College Misericordia M
- The College of St. Scholastica M
- College of the Southwest M
- The College of William and Mary M*†
- Colorado Christian University M
- Columbia International University M
- Concordia University (CA) M
- Concordia University (IL) M,O
- Concordia University (OR) M
- Concordia University Wisconsin M
- Converse College O
- Coppin State College M
- Cornell University M,D*
- Delaware State University M
- DePaul University M,D*†
- Doane College M
- Dominican University M*
- Dominican University of California M
- Drexel University M*†
- Duquesne University D*†
- East Carolina University M*†
- Eastern Kentucky University M
- Eastern Michigan University M*
- Eastern Washington University M†
- Emporia State University M*†
- Fairleigh Dickinson University, Metropolitan Campus M*†
- Ferris State University M
- Florida Atlantic University M,D,O*
- Florida Atlantic University, Ft. Lauderdale Campus M,D,O
- Florida Gulf Coast University M
- Florida International University M,D,O*†
- Fordham University M,D,O*†
- Framingham State College M*
- Franciscan University of Steubenville M
- Freed-Hardeman University M
- Fresno Pacific University M
- Frostburg State University M
- Gannon University M
- The George Washington University M,D,O*†
- Georgia Southern University D
- Gonzaga University M
- Grambling State University M,D
- Harvard University M,D,O*†
- Holy Names College M,O
- Hood College M
- Houston Baptist University M
- Idaho State University M,O*
- Illinois State University M,D*†
- Indiana State University M,D,O*†
- Indiana University Bloomington M,D,O*
- Indiana University of Pennsylvania M,D*†
- Indiana Wesleyan University M*
- Inter American University of Puerto Rico, San Germán Campus M
- Iowa State University of Science and Technology M,D*†
- Johns Hopkins University M*†
- Johnson State College M
- Kansas State University D*†
- Kean University M,O*†
- Keene State College M
- Kent State University M,D,O*
- Kutztown University of Pennsylvania M,O†
- Lakehead University M,D
- Lander University M
- La Sierra University M,D,O
- Lehigh University M,D,O*
- Lesley University M,D,O*†
- Lewis University M
- Lincoln Memorial University M,O
- Lock Haven University of Pennsylvania M
- Loras College M
- Louisiana State University and Agricultural and Mechanical College M,D,O*
- Louisiana Tech University M,D,O*
- Loyola College in Maryland M,O
- Loyola University Chicago M,D*†
- Lynchburg College M
- Lyndon State College M
- Malone College M†
- Massachusetts College of Liberal Arts M
- McGill University M,D,O*
- Miami University M*†
- Michigan State University M,D,O*†
- MidAmerica Nazarene University M
- Middle Tennessee State University M,O*
- Midwestern State University M
- Mills College M,D*†
- Minnesota State University, Mankato M,O
- Minnesota State University, Moorhead M
- Mississippi State University M,D,O*
- Montana State University–Billings M*
- Montclair State University M,D†
- Moravian College M
- Morehead State University O
- Mount Saint Vincent University M
- National-Louis University M,D,O
- New Mexico Highlands University M
- New Mexico State University M,D,O
- Nicholls State University M
- North Carolina State University M,D*
- Northeastern University M*†
- Northern Arizona University D
- Northern Illinois University M,D*†
- Northwest Nazarene University M
- Notre Dame de Namur University M
- Oakland University M,D,O†
- Ohio University M,D*
- Oklahoma City University M
- Oklahoma State University M,D*†
- Olivet Nazarene University M
- Oral Roberts University M,D
- Our Lady of Holy Cross College M
- Our Lady of the Lake University of San Antonio M,D
- Pace University M,O*†
- Pace University, White Plains Campus M,O*
- Pacific Lutheran University M†
- The Pennsylvania State University Great Valley Campus M
- The Pennsylvania State University Harrisburg Campus of the Capital College M*†
- The Pennsylvania State University University Park Campus M,D*†
- Philadelphia Biblical University M
- Piedmont College M,O
- Plattsburgh State University of New York M
- Point Park College M*
- Pontifical Catholic University of Puerto Rico M,D
- Portland State University M,D*
- Prairie View A&M University M
- Purdue University M,D,O*
- Purdue University Calumet M
- Radford University M†
- Rhode Island College O†
- Rider University M*
- Rosemont College M†
- Rowan University M†
- St. Cloud State University M
- Saint Louis University M,D*†
- Saint Martin's College M
- Saint Mary College M
- Saint Michael's College M,O*
- Saint Peter's College M,O†
- Saint Xavier University M,O*
- Sam Houston State University M,D,O*
- San Diego State University M*
- Seattle University M,O*†
- Shippensburg University of Pennsylvania M,O†
- Siena Heights University M
- Simon Fraser University M,D
- Simpson College and Graduate School M
- Sonoma State University M
- South Dakota State University M*
- Southeastern Louisiana University M
- Southern Adventist University M
- Southern Illinois University Carbondale M,D*†
- Southwestern Assemblies of God University M
- Stanford University M,D*
- State University of New York at Albany M,D,O*†
- Suffolk University M,O*
- Syracuse University M,D,O*
- Tarleton State University M
- Teachers College Columbia University M,D*
- Tennessee State University M,D*
- Tennessee Technological University M,O*
- Tennessee Temple University M
- Texas A&M International University M
- Texas A&M University M,D*
- Texas A&M University–Corpus Christi M
- Texas Southern University M,D†
- Texas Tech University M,D,O*†
- Trevecca Nazarene University M
- Trinity College (DC) M†
- Troy State University Dothan M,O
- Tuskegee University M
- Universidad Metropolitana M
- Université de Montréal M,D,O
- Université Laval M,D†
- University College of Cape Breton O
- The University of Alabama M,D,O*
- University of Alaska Fairbanks M,O*
- University of Arkansas D*
- The University of British Columbia M,D*
- University of Calgary M,D*
- University of California, Davis D*†
- University of Central Florida M,D*†
- University of Cincinnati M,D*
- University of Colorado at Boulder M,D*
- University of Colorado at Colorado Springs M*
- University of Colorado at Denver M*
- University of Connecticut M,D*†
- University of Delaware M,D*†
- University of Denver M,D,O*†
- University of Detroit Mercy M*
- University of Great Falls M
- University of Hawaii at Manoa D*
- University of Houston M,D*
- University of Houston–Clear Lake M*†
- University of Illinois at Chicago M,D*
- University of Illinois at Urbana–Champaign M,D,O*
- The University of Iowa M,D*
- University of Kansas M,D*
- University of Kentucky M,D*
- University of Louisiana at Lafayette M*
- University of Louisiana at Monroe D,O
- University of Manitoba M*
- University of Massachusetts Amherst M,D,O*†
- University of Massachusetts Boston M*†
- University of Massachusetts Lowell M,D,O*†
- The University of Memphis M,D*†
- University of Michigan M,D*
- University of Minnesota, Twin Cities Campus M,D*
- University of Mississippi M,D,O*
- University of Missouri–Kansas City M,D,O*†
- University of Missouri–St. Louis M,D†
- The University of Montana–Missoula M,D*†
- University of Nebraska at Kearney M
- University of Nebraska–Lincoln M,D,O*†
- University of Nevada, Las Vegas M,D,O*†
- University of Nevada, Reno M,D,O*
- University of New Brunswick Fredericton M
- University of New Orleans M,D,O*
- The University of North Carolina at Chapel Hill M,D*†
- The University of North Carolina at Charlotte M,D,O*
- The University of North Carolina at Greensboro D†
- The University of North Carolina at Wilmington M*
- University of Northern Iowa M,D
- University of North Texas D*†
- University of Oklahoma M,D,O*†
- University of Phoenix–Louisiana Campus M
- University of Phoenix–Northern California Campus M
- University of Phoenix–San Diego Campus M
- University of Phoenix–Southern California Campus M
- University of Phoenix-Vancouver Campus M
- University of Puerto Rico, Río Piedras M,D*
- University of Redlands M
- University of Regina M
- University of St. Thomas (MN) M,D,O*†
- University of San Diego M,D*†
- University of San Francisco M,D*†
- University of Saskatchewan M,D,O
- University of South Carolina M,D,O*†
- The University of South Dakota M,D,O†
- University of Southern California M,D*†
- University of Southern Mississippi M,D,O
- The University of Tennessee M,D,O*†
- The University of Tennessee at Chattanooga M,O
- The University of Tennessee at Martin M
- The University of Texas at Arlington M*†
- The University of Texas at Austin M,D*
- The University of Texas at Brownsville M
- The University of Texas at San Antonio M*
- The University of Texas at Tyler M
- University of the Pacific M,D*
- University of Toledo M,D,O*†
- University of Vermont M*†
- University of Victoria M,D
- University of Virginia M,D,O*
- University of Washington M,D*
- The University of Western Ontario M*
- University of West Florida M,D,O
- University of Wisconsin–Madison M,D*
- University of Wisconsin–Milwaukee M
- University of Wisconsin–Oshkosh M*
- University of Wisconsin–Superior M

University of Wisconsin–Whitewater M*
University of Wyoming M,D*†
Utah State University D*
Valparaiso University M
Vanderbilt University M,D*
Virginia Commonwealth University M,O*†
Virginia Polytechnic Institute and State University M,D,O*
Walla Walla College M
Washburn University of Topeka M
Washington State University M,D*
Wayne State College M
Wayne State University M,D,O*
Weber State University M
Western Connecticut State University M
Western Illinois University M,O
Westminster College (PA) M,O
West Texas A&M University M†
West Virginia University M,D*
Wichita State University M*†
William Woods University M
Wright State University O*
Xavier University of Louisiana M

DANCE

American University M*†
Arizona State University M*
Bennington College M†
Brigham Young University M*
California Institute of the Arts M,O*
California State University, Fullerton M
California State University, Long Beach M
California State University, Sacramento M
Case Western Reserve University M,D*†
Connecticut College M
Florida State University M*†
George Mason University M*†
Indiana University Bloomington M*
Mills College M*†
New York University M,D*†
Northern Illinois University M*†
The Ohio State University M*
Purchase College, State University of New York M
Sam Houston State University M*
San Diego State University M*
Sarah Lawrence College M*†
Shenandoah University M,D,O
Smith College M*
Southern Methodist University M*†
State University of New York College at Brockport M*†
Teachers College Columbia University M*
Temple University M,D*†
Texas Christian University M*
Texas Tech University D*†
Texas Woman's University M,D*†
Tufts University M,D*†
Université du Québec à Montréal M
University of California, Irvine M*
University of California, Los Angeles M,D*
University of California, Riverside M,D*
University of Colorado at Boulder M,D*
University of Hawaii at Manoa M,D*
University of Illinois at Urbana–Champaign M*
The University of Iowa M*
University of Maryland, College Park M*
University of Michigan M*
University of Minnesota, Twin Cities Campus M,D*
University of Nevada, Las Vegas M,D*†
University of New Mexico M*†
The University of North Carolina at Greensboro M†
University of Oklahoma M*†
University of Oregon M*
University of Utah M*
University of Washington M*
University of Wisconsin–Milwaukee M
York University M*

DECORATIVE ARTS

Bard Graduate Center for Studies in the Decorative Arts, Design, and Culture M,D*
New School University M*†

DEMOGRAPHY AND POPULATION STUDIES

Arizona State University M,D*
Bowling Green State University M,D*†
Brown University D*
Cornell University M,D*
Duke University D*†
Florida State University M,O*†
Fordham University M,D*†
Georgetown University M*
Harvard University M,D*†
Johns Hopkins University M*†
Princeton University D*
State University of New York at Albany M,D,O*†
Tulane University M*†
Université de Montréal M,D
University of Alberta M,D*
University of California, Berkeley M,D*
University of California, Irvine M*
University of Illinois at Urbana–Champaign M,D*
University of Pennsylvania M,D*†
University of Puerto Rico, Medical Sciences Campus M*
University of Southern California M*†

DENTAL HYGIENE

Boston University P,M,D,O*†
Medical College of Georgia M*
Old Dominion University M*†
Texas A&M University System Health Science Center M*
Université de Montréal M,O
University of Alberta O*
University of Maryland M*†
University of Missouri–Kansas City M*†

DENTISTRY

Boston University P*†
Case Western Reserve University P*†
Columbia University P*†
Creighton University P*
Dalhousie University P*
Harvard University P,M,D,O*†
Howard University P,O*
Idaho State University O*
Indiana University–Purdue University Indianapolis P*
Loma Linda University P,O*
Louisiana State University Health Sciences Center P*
Marquette University P*†
McGill University P*
Medical College of Georgia P*
Medical University of South Carolina P*
Meharry Medical College P
New York University P*†
Nova Southeastern University P*
The Ohio State University P*
Oregon Health & Science University P*
Southern Illinois University Edwardsville P†
Stony Brook University, State University of New York P,O*†
Temple University P*†
Texas A&M University System Health Science Center P*
Tufts University P*†
Université de Montréal P
Université Laval P†
University at Buffalo, The State University of New York P*†
The University of Alabama at Birmingham P*†
University of Alberta P*
The University of British Columbia P*
University of California, Los Angeles P,O*
University of California, San Francisco P*
University of Colorado Health Sciences Center P,M*
University of Connecticut Health Center P,O*
University of Detroit Mercy P*
University of Florida P,O*†
University of Illinois at Chicago P*
The University of Iowa P*
University of Kentucky P,M*
University of Louisville P*†
University of Manitoba P*
University of Maryland P*†
University of Medicine and Dentistry of New Jersey P,M,O*
University of Michigan P*
University of Minnesota, Twin Cities Campus P*
University of Mississippi Medical Center P*
University of Missouri–Kansas City P*†
University of Nebraska Medical Center P,O*
The University of North Carolina at Chapel Hill P*†
University of Oklahoma Health Sciences Center P*
University of Pennsylvania P*†
University of Pittsburgh P,O*†
University of Puerto Rico, Medical Sciences Campus P*
University of Saskatchewan P
University of Southern California P,O*†
The University of Tennessee Health Science Center P,M*
The University of Texas Health Science Center at Houston P*
The University of Texas Health Science Center at San Antonio P,M,O*
University of the Pacific P*
University of Toronto P*
University of Washington P*
The University of Western Ontario P*
Virginia Commonwealth University P*†
West Virginia University P*

DEVELOPMENTAL BIOLOGY

Arizona State University M,D*
Baylor College of Medicine D*
Brandeis University M,D*†
Brown University M,D*
California Institute of Technology D*
Carnegie Mellon University M,D*
Case Western Reserve University M,D*†
Columbia University M,D*†
Cornell University M,D*
Duke University O*†
Emory University D*†
Florida State University M,D*†
Indiana University Bloomington D*
Iowa State University of Science and Technology M,D*†
Johns Hopkins University D*†
Kansas State University M,D*†
Louisiana State University Health Sciences Center M,D*
Marquette University M,D*†
Massachusetts Institute of Technology D*
Medical College of Wisconsin M,D*
Mount Sinai School of Medicine of New York University D*
Northwestern University D*
The Ohio State University M,D*
Oregon Health & Science University D*
The Pennsylvania State University University Park Campus M,D*†
Princeton University D*
Purdue University D*
Rensselaer Polytechnic Institute M,D*†
Rutgers, The State University of New Jersey, New Brunswick M,D*
Stanford University D*
State University of New York at Albany M,D*†
State University of New York Upstate Medical University D*
Stony Brook University, State University of New York M,D*†
Thomas Jefferson University M,D*
Tufts University D*†
Uniformed Services University of the Health Sciences D*
University of California, Davis D*†
University of California, Irvine M,D*
University of California, Los Angeles M,D*
University of California, Riverside M,D*
University of California, San Diego D*
University of California, San Francisco D*
University of California, Santa Barbara M,D*
University of Chicago D*
University of Cincinnati M,D*
University of Colorado at Boulder M,D*
University of Colorado Health Sciences Center D*
University of Connecticut M,D*†
University of Connecticut Health Center D*
University of Illinois at Chicago M,D*
University of Kansas M,D*
University of Massachusetts Amherst D*†
University of Medicine and Dentistry of New Jersey M,D*
University of Miami D*†
University of Michigan M,D*
University of Minnesota, Twin Cities Campus M,D*
University of Missouri–St. Louis M,D,O†
The University of North Carolina at Chapel Hill M,D*†
University of Pennsylvania D*†
University of Pittsburgh D*†
University of South Carolina M,D*†
The University of Texas at Austin D*
The University of Texas Health Science Center at Houston M,D*
The University of Texas Southwestern Medical Center at Dallas D*
University of Toronto D*
University of Victoria M,D
University of Wisconsin–Madison D*
Virginia Polytechnic Institute and State University M,D*
Washington University in St. Louis D*†
Wesleyan University D*
West Virginia University M,D*
Yale University D*
Yeshiva University D*

DEVELOPMENTAL EDUCATION

Ferris State University M
Grambling State University M,D
Instituto Tecnológico y de Estudios Superiores de Monterrey, Campus Ciudad Obregón M
National-Louis University M,O
Rutgers, The State University of New Jersey, New Brunswick M*
Southwest Texas State University M*
University of California, Berkeley M*
The University of Iowa M,D*

DEVELOPMENTAL PSYCHOLOGY

Andrews University M
Arizona State University D*
Boston College M,D*†
Bowling Green State University M,D*†
Brandeis University M,D*†
Bryn Mawr College D
California State University, San Bernardino M
Carnegie Mellon University D*
Claremont Graduate University M,D*
Clark University D*†
College of Staten Island of the City University of New York D†
Cornell University D*
Duke University D*†
Duquesne University D*†
Eastern Washington University M†
Emory University D*†
Erikson Institute M,D
Florida International University M,D*†
Fordham University D*†
Gallaudet University M,O
George Mason University M,D*†
Graduate School and University Center of the City University of New York D*†
Harvard University M,D*†
Howard University M,D*
Illinois State University M,D,O*†
Indiana University Bloomington D*
Louisiana State University and Agricultural and Mechanical College M,D*
Loyola University Chicago D*†
McGill University D*†
Michigan State University M,D*†
New York University M,D,O*†
The Ohio State University D*
The Pennsylvania State University University Park Campus M,D*†
Queen's University at Kingston M,D
Rutgers, The State University of New Jersey, New Brunswick D*
Stanford University D*
Suffolk University D*
Teachers College Columbia University M,D*
Temple University D*†
Tufts University M;D,O*†
Université de Montréal M
The University of Alabama at Birmingham M,D*†
The University of British Columbia M,D*
University of California, Santa Cruz D*
University of Connecticut D*†
University of Guelph M,D
University of Illinois at Urbana–Champaign M,D*

*P—first professional degree; M—master's degree; D—doctorate; O—other advanced degree; *full description and/or announcement in Book 2, 3, 4, 5, or 6; †full description in this book*

University of Kansas M,D*
University of Maine M,D*
University of Maryland, Baltimore County D*†
University of Maryland, College Park M,D*
University of Miami M,D*†
University of Michigan D*
The University of Montana–Missoula D*†
University of Nebraska at Omaha M,D,O
University of New Orleans M,D*
The University of North Carolina at Chapel Hill D*†
The University of North Carolina at Greensboro M,D†
University of Notre Dame D*†
University of Oregon M,D*
University of Pittsburgh D*†
University of Rochester M,D*
University of Victoria M,D
University of Wisconsin–Madison D*
Virginia Polytechnic Institute and State University M,D*
Wayne State University M,D*
West Virginia University M,D*
Yeshiva University D*

DISABILITY STUDIES

Brandeis University M*†
Johns Hopkins University M,D,O*†
New York Medical College M,O*
Suffolk University M,O*
University of Illinois at Chicago M,D*
University of Northern British Columbia M,D

DISTANCE EDUCATION DEVELOPMENT

Athabasca University M,O
Florida State University M,D,O*†
Jones International University M*†
New York Institute of Technology M,O*†
Nova Southeastern University M,D*
Télé-université M,D
University of Maryland University College M*
Western Illinois University M,O

EARLY CHILDHOOD EDUCATION

Agnes Scott College M*
Alabama Agricultural and Mechanical University M,O
Alabama State University M,O
Albany State University M
Anna Maria College M
Appalachian State University M
Arcadia University M,D,O†
Arkansas State University M,O
Ashland University M
Auburn University M,D,O*†
Auburn University Montgomery M,O
Augusta State University M,O
Averett University M
Ball State University M,D*
Bank Street College of Education M*
Barry University M*†
Bayamón Central University M
Bellarmine University M
Belmont University M
Berry College M
Bloomsburg University of Pennsylvania M
Boise State University M*
Boston College M*†
Boston University M,D,O*†
Brenau University M,O
Bridgewater State College M
Brooklyn College of the City University of New York M†
California State University, Fresno M
California State University, Sacramento M
Carlow College M
Central Connecticut State University M*†
Central Michigan University M†
Chestnut Hill College M†
Cheyney University of Pennsylvania O
Chicago State University M
City College of the City University of New York M*†
Clarke College M
Cleveland State University M*†
Coastal Carolina University M
College of Charleston M*†
College of Mount St. Joseph M†
The College of New Jersey M†
The College of New Rochelle M†
The College of Saint Rose M*†
Columbus State University M,O
Concordia University (IL) M,D,O
Concordia University (MN) M
Concordia University (NE) M
Concordia University Wisconsin M
Cumberland College M
Dallas Baptist University M
Dominican University M*
Drake University M*†
Duquesne University M*†
Eastern Connecticut State University M
Eastern Michigan University M*
Eastern Nazarene College M,O
Eastern Washington University M†
East Tennessee State University M†
Edinboro University of Pennsylvania M
Elms College M,O
Emporia State University M*†
Erikson Institute M,O
Fairfield University M,O*
Fitchburg State College M†
Florida Agricultural and Mechanical University M*
Florida International University M*†
Florida State University M,D,O*†
Fordham University M,D,O*†
Fort Valley State University M
Francis Marion University M
Furman University M
Gallaudet University M,D,O
Gannon University M,O
George Mason University M*†
The George Washington University M*†
Georgia College & State University M,O
Georgia Southern University M,O
Georgia Southwestern State University M,O
Georgia State University M,D,O*
Golden Gate Baptist Theological Seminary P,M,D,O
Governors State University M
Grambling State University M
Grand Valley State University M†
Hebrew College M,O†
Henderson State University M
Heritage College M
Hofstra University M,O*
Hood College M
Howard University M,O*
Hunter College of the City University of New York M,O†
Idaho State University M,O*
Indiana State University M,D,O*†
Indiana University of Pennsylvania M*†
Indiana University–Purdue University Indianapolis M*
Jackson State University M,D,O
Jacksonville State University M,O
Jacksonville University M,O
James Madison University M
Johns Hopkins University M*†
Kean University M*†
Kennesaw State University M
Kent State University M*
Kutztown University of Pennsylvania M,O†
LaGrange College M
Lehman College of the City University of New York M
Lenoir-Rhyne College M
Lesley University M,D,O*†
Liberty University M,D†
Long Island University, C.W. Post Campus M*†
Loyola College in Maryland M,O
Lynchburg College M
Marshall University M*†
Marygrove College M
Maryville University of Saint Louis M
Marywood University M*†
McNeese State University M
Mercer University M,O
Miami University M*†
Middle Tennessee State University M,O*
Millersville University of Pennsylvania M†
Mills College M,D*†
Minnesota State University, Mankato M
Montana State University–Billings M*
Montclair State University M†
Mount Saint Mary College M
Murray State University M†
National-Louis University M,O
Nazareth College of Rochester M
New Jersey City University M
New York University M,D,O*†
Norfolk State University M†
North Carolina Agricultural and Technical State University M*
Northeastern State University M
Northern Arizona University M
Northern Illinois University M*†
North Georgia College & State University M,O
Northwestern State University of Louisiana M
Northwest Missouri State University M
Nova Southeastern University M,D,O*
Oakland University M,D,O†
Oglethorpe University M
Oklahoma City University M
Old Dominion University M*†
Oral Roberts University M,D
Pacific University M
The Pennsylvania State University University Park Campus M,D*†
Piedmont College M,O
Pittsburg State University M
Portland State University M*
Rhode Island College M†
Rivier College M*†
Roosevelt University M,D*†
Rutgers, The State University of New Jersey, New Brunswick M,D*
Saginaw Valley State University M
Saint Joseph College M
St. Joseph's College, Suffolk Campus M
Saint Mary's College of California M
Saint Xavier University M,O*
Salem College M
Salem State College M
Salisbury University M
Samford University M,D,O
Sam Houston State University M,O*
San Francisco State University M
Siena Heights University M
Slippery Rock University of Pennsylvania M†
Smith College M*
Sonoma State University M
South Carolina State University M
Southern Oregon University M
Southwestern Oklahoma State University M
Southwest Missouri State University M*†
Spring Hill College M
State University of New York at Binghamton M*†
State University of New York at New Paltz M
State University of New York College at Buffalo M
State University of New York College at Cortland M
State University of West Georgia M,O
Stephen F. Austin State University M
Sunbridge College M
Syracuse University M*
Teachers College Columbia University M,D*
Temple University M,D*†
Tennessee Technological University M,O*
Texas A&M International University M
Texas A&M University–Commerce M,D†
Texas A&M University–Kingsville M*†
Texas Southern University M,D†
Texas Tech University M,D,O*†
Texas Woman's University M,D*†
Towson University M†
Trinity College (DC) M†
Troy State University M,O
Tufts University M,D,O*†
Universidad Metropolitana M
The University of Alabama at Birmingham M,D*†
University of Alaska Southeast M
University of Arkansas M*
University of Arkansas at Little Rock M,O
University of Bridgeport M,O*†
The University of British Columbia M,D*
University of Central Arkansas M
University of Central Florida M*†
University of Central Oklahoma M
University of Cincinnati M*
University of Colorado at Denver M*
University of Dayton M*†
University of Detroit Mercy M*
The University of Findlay M
University of Florida M,D,O*†
University of Georgia M,D,O*†
University of Hartford M*
University of Houston M,D*
University of Houston–Clear Lake M*†
The University of Iowa M,D*
University of Kansas M,D*
University of Louisville M*†
University of Manitoba M*
University of Maryland, Baltimore County M,D*†
University of Maryland, College Park M,D,O*
University of Massachusetts Amherst M,D,O*†
The University of Memphis M,D*†
University of Miami M,O*†
University of Michigan M,D*
University of Michigan–Flint M
University of Minnesota, Twin Cities Campus M,D,O*
University of Missouri–Columbia M,D,O*
University of Montevallo M
University of Nebraska at Kearney M
University of New Hampshire M*†
University of North Alabama M
The University of North Carolina at Chapel Hill D*†
The University of North Carolina at Greensboro M†
University of North Dakota M*
University of Northern Colorado M†
University of Northern Iowa M
University of North Texas M,D*†
University of Oklahoma M,D,O*†
University of Pennsylvania M*†
University of Pittsburgh M*†
University of Portland M
University of Puerto Rico, Río Piedras M*
The University of Scranton M†
University of South Alabama M,O*†
University of South Carolina M,D*†
University of South Carolina Spartanburg M
University of Southern Mississippi M,D,O
University of South Florida M,D*†
The University of Tennessee M,D,O*†
The University of Tennessee at Chattanooga M,O
The University of Texas at Brownsville M
The University of Texas at San Antonio M*
The University of Texas at Tyler M
The University of Texas of the Permian Basin M
The University of Texas–Pan American M
University of the District of Columbia M*
University of the Incarnate Word M†
University of Toledo M,D,O*†
The University of West Alabama M
University of West Florida M
University of Wisconsin–Milwaukee M
University of Wisconsin–Oshkosh M*
Valdosta State University M,O
Vanderbilt University M,D*
Virginia Commonwealth University M,O*†
Wayne State University M,D,O*
Webster University M
Wesleyan College M
Western Illinois University M,O
Western Kentucky University M†
Western Michigan University M*†
Western Oregon University M
Westfield State College M
Wheelock College M*
Widener University M,D*†
Worcester State College M
Wright State University M*
Xavier University M*
Youngstown State University M

EAST EUROPEAN AND RUSSIAN STUDIES

Boston College M*†
Carleton University M
Columbia University M,O*†
Florida State University M*†
Georgetown University M*
The George Washington University M*†
Harvard University M*†
Indiana University Bloomington M,O*
Johns Hopkins University M,D,O*†
La Salle University M
The Ohio State University M,D,O*
Stanford University M*
University of Alberta M,D*
The University of British Columbia M,D*
University of Connecticut M*†
University of Illinois at Chicago M,D*
University of Illinois at Urbana–Champaign M*
University of Kansas M*
University of Michigan M,O*

University of Minnesota, Twin Cities Campus M*
The University of North Carolina at Chapel Hill M*†
University of Saskatchewan M
The University of Texas at Austin M*
University of Toronto M*
University of Washington M*
Yale University M*

ECOLOGY

Arizona State University M,D*
Brock University M
Brown University D*
Colorado State University M,D*
Columbia University D,O*†
Cornell University D*
Duke University M,D,O*†
Eastern Kentucky University M
Emory University D*†
Florida Institute of Technology M*†
Florida State University M,D*†
Fordham University M,D*†
Frostburg State University M
George Mason University M*†
Goddard College M
Illinois State University M,D*†
Indiana State University M,D*†
Indiana University Bloomington M,D*
Iowa State University of Science and Technology M,D*†
Kansas State University M,D*†
Kent State University M,D*
Lesley University M,D,O*†
Marquette University M,D*†
Michigan State University M,D*†
Minnesota State University, Mankato M
Montana State University–Bozeman M,D*
North Carolina State University M,D*
Northern Arizona University M,O
Nova Scotia Agricultural College M
The Ohio State University M,D*
Oklahoma State University M,D*†
Old Dominion University D*†
The Pennsylvania State University University Park Campus M,D*†
Princeton University D*
Purdue University M,D*
Rice University M,D*
Rutgers, The State University of New Jersey, New Brunswick M,D*
San Diego State University D*
San Francisco State University M
State University of New York at Albany M,D*†
State University of New York College of Environmental Science and Forestry M,D
Stony Brook University, State University of New York D*†
University of Alberta M,D*
The University of Arizona M,D*
University of California, Davis M,D*†
University of California, Irvine M,D*
University of California, San Diego D*
University of California, Santa Barbara M,D*
University of California, Santa Cruz M,D*
University of Chicago D*
University of Colorado at Boulder M,D*
University of Connecticut M,D*†
University of Delaware M,D*†
University of Florida M,D*†
University of Georgia M,D*†
University of Hawaii at Manoa M,D*
University of Illinois at Chicago M,D*
University of Illinois at Urbana–Champaign D*
University of Kansas M,D*
University of Maine M,D*
University of Maryland, College Park M,D*
University of Miami M,D*†
University of Michigan M,D*
University of Minnesota, Twin Cities Campus M,D*
University of Missouri–St. Louis M,D,O†
The University of Montana–Missoula M,D*†
University of Nevada, Reno D*
The University of North Carolina at Chapel Hill M,D*†
University of North Dakota M,D*
University of Notre Dame M,D*†
University of Oregon M,D*
University of Pennsylvania D*†
University of Pittsburgh M,D*†
University of South Carolina M,D*†
University of South Florida M,D*†
The University of Tennessee M,D*†
The University of Texas at Austin M,D*
University of Toledo M*†
University of Utah M,D*
University of Victoria M,D
University of Wisconsin–Madison M,D*
Utah State University M,D*
Virginia Polytechnic Institute and State University M,D*
Washington University in St. Louis D*†
William Paterson University of New Jersey M*†
Yale University D*

ECONOMICS

Alabama Agricultural and Mechanical University M
Albany State University M
American University M,D*†
American University in Cairo M
Arizona State University M,D*
Auburn University M,D*†
Baylor University M*†
Bentley College M,O*
Bernard M. Baruch College of the City University of New York M*
Boston College M,D*†
Boston University M,D*†
Bowling Green State University M*†
Brandeis University M,D*†
Brooklyn College of the City University of New York M†
Brown University M,D*
California Institute of Technology D*
California State Polytechnic University, Pomona M*
California State University, Fullerton M
California State University, Hayward M
California State University, Long Beach M
California State University, Los Angeles M
Carleton University M,D
Carnegie Mellon University M,D*
Case Western Reserve University M*†
The Catholic University of America M*†
Central Michigan University M†
Central Missouri State University M†
City College of the City University of New York M*†
Claremont Graduate University M,D*
Clark Atlanta University M
Clark University D*†
Clemson University M,D*
Cleveland State University M*†
Colorado State University M,D*
Columbia University M,D*†
Concordia University (Canada) M,D,O*†
Converse College M
Cornell University D*
Dalhousie University M,D*
DePaul University M*†
Drexel University M,D,O*†
Duke University M,D*†
East Carolina University M*†
Eastern Illinois University M†
Eastern Michigan University M*
Eastern University M*
East Tennessee State University M†
Emory University D*†
Emporia State University M*†
Florida Atlantic University M*
Florida International University M,D*†
Florida State University M,D*†
Fordham University M,D,O*†
George Mason University M,D*†
Georgetown University D*
The George Washington University M,D*†
Georgia Institute of Technology M*
Georgia State University M,D*
Golden Gate University M,D,O
Graduate School and University Center of the City University of New York D*†
Harvard University M,D*†
Howard University M,D*
Hunter College of the City University of New York M†
Illinois State University M*†
Indiana State University M*†
Indiana University Bloomington M,D*
Indiana University–Purdue University Indianapolis M*
Indiana University Southeast M,O
Instituto Centroamericano de Administración de Empresas M
Instituto Tecnológico y de Estudios Superiores de Monterrey, Campus Ciudad de México M,D
Iowa State University of Science and Technology M,D*†
Johns Hopkins University M,D,O*†
Kansas State University M,D*†
Kent State University M*
Lakehead University M
Lehigh University M,D*
Long Island University, Brooklyn Campus M*
Louisiana State University and Agricultural and Mechanical College M,D*
Louisiana Tech University M,D*
Loyola College in Maryland M
Marquette University M*†
Massachusetts Institute of Technology M,D*
McGill University M,D*
McMaster University M,D
Memorial University of Newfoundland M†
Miami University M*†
Michigan State University M,D*†
Middle Tennessee State University M,D*
Mississippi State University M,D*
Montclair State University M†
Morgan State University M*
Murray State University M†
New Mexico State University M
New School University M,D*†
New York University M,D,O*†
North Carolina State University M,D*
Northeastern University M*†
Northern Illinois University M,D*†
Northwestern University M,D*
The Ohio State University M,D*
Ohio University M*
Oklahoma State University M,D*†
Old Dominion University M*†
Oregon State University M,D*
Pace University M*†
Pace University, White Plains Campus M*
The Pennsylvania State University University Park Campus M,D*†
Portland State University M,D*
Princeton University D*
Purdue University M,D*
Queen's University at Kingston M,D
Quinnipiac University M*†
Rensselaer Polytechnic Institute M*†
Rice University M,D*
Roosevelt University M*†
Rutgers, The State University of New Jersey, Newark M*†
Rutgers, The State University of New Jersey, New Brunswick M,D*
St. Cloud State University M
St. John's University (NY) M,O*†
Saint Louis University M*†
St. Mary's University of San Antonio M
San Diego State University M*
San Francisco State University M
San Jose State University M*
Seattle Pacific University M
Simon Fraser University M,D
South Dakota State University M*
Southern Illinois University Carbondale M,D*†
Southern Illinois University Edwardsville M†
Southern Methodist University M,D*†
Southern New Hampshire University M,D*
Stanford University D*
State University of New York at Albany M,D,O*†
State University of New York at Binghamton M,D*†
State University of New York College at Buffalo M
Stony Brook University, State University of New York M,D*†
Suffolk University M*
Syracuse University M,D*
Teachers College Columbia University M,D*
Temple University M,D*†
Texas A&M University M,D*
Texas A&M University–Commerce M†
Texas Christian University M*
Texas Tech University M,D*†
Trinity College (CT) M
Tufts University M*†
Tulane University M,D*†
Universidad de las Américas–Puebla M
Université de Moncton M
Université de Montréal M,D
Université de Sherbrooke M
Université du Québec à Montréal M,D
Université Laval M,D†
University at Buffalo, The State University of New York M,D,O*†
The University of Akron M†
The University of Alabama M,D*
University of Alaska Fairbanks M*
University of Alberta M,D*
The University of Arizona M,D*
University of Arkansas M,D*
The University of British Columbia M,D*
University of Calgary M,D*
University of California, Berkeley D*
University of California, Davis M,D*†
University of California, Irvine M,D*
University of California, Los Angeles M,D*
University of California, Riverside M,D*
University of California, San Diego M,D*
University of California, Santa Barbara M,D*
University of California, Santa Cruz D*
University of Central Florida M*†
University of Chicago D*
University of Cincinnati M*
University of Colorado at Boulder M,D*
University of Colorado at Denver M*
University of Connecticut M,D*†
University of Delaware M,D*†
University of Denver M*†
University of Florida M,D*†
University of Georgia M,D*†
University of Guelph M,D
University of Hawaii at Manoa M,D*
University of Houston M,D*
University of Idaho M*†
University of Illinois at Chicago M,D*
University of Illinois at Springfield M†
University of Illinois at Urbana–Champaign M,D*
The University of Iowa D*
University of Kansas M,D*
University of Kentucky M,D*
The University of Lethbridge M,D
University of Maine M*
University of Manitoba M,D*
University of Maryland, Baltimore County M*†
University of Maryland, College Park M,D*
University of Massachusetts Amherst M,D*†
University of Massachusetts Lowell M*†
The University of Memphis M,D*†
University of Miami M,D*†
University of Michigan M,D*
University of Minnesota, Twin Cities Campus D*
University of Mississippi M,D*
University of Missouri–Columbia M,D*
University of Missouri–Kansas City M,D*†
University of Missouri–St. Louis M,O†
The University of Montana–Missoula M*†
University of Nebraska at Omaha M
University of Nebraska–Lincoln M,D*†
University of Nevada, Las Vegas M*†
University of Nevada, Reno M*
University of New Brunswick Fredericton M
University of New Hampshire M,D*†
University of New Mexico M,D*†
University of New Orleans D*
The University of North Carolina at Chapel Hill M,D*†
The University of North Carolina at Charlotte M*
The University of North Carolina at Greensboro M†
University of North Texas M*†
University of Notre Dame M,D*†
University of Oklahoma M,D*†
University of Oregon M,D*
University of Ottawa M,D*
University of Pennsylvania M,D*†
University of Pittsburgh M,D*†
University of Puerto Rico, Río Piedras M*
University of Regina M
University of Rhode Island M,D*
University of Rochester M,D*
University of San Francisco M*†
University of Saskatchewan M
University of South Carolina M,D*†

*P—first professional degree; M—master's degree; D—doctorate; O—other advanced degree; *full description and/or announcement in Book 2, 3, 4, 5, or 6; †full description in this book*

University of Southern California M,D*†
University of Southern Mississippi M,D
University of South Florida M*†
The University of Tennessee M,D*†
The University of Tennessee at Chattanooga M
The University of Texas at Arlington M,D*†
The University of Texas at Austin M,D*
The University of Texas at Dallas D*
The University of Texas at El Paso M*†
The University of Texas at San Antonio M*
The University of Texas at Tyler M
University of Toledo M*†
University of Toronto M,D*
University of Utah M,D*
University of Victoria M
University of Virginia M,D*
University of Washington M,D*
University of Waterloo M
The University of Western Ontario M,D*
University of Windsor M,D
University of Wisconsin–Madison D*
University of Wisconsin–Milwaukee M,D
University of Wyoming M,D*†
Utah State University M,D*
Vanderbilt University M,D*
Virginia Commonwealth University M*†
Virginia Polytechnic Institute and State University M,D*
Virginia State University M
Walsh College of Accountancy and Business Administration M
Washington State University M,D,O*
Washington University in St. Louis M,D*†
Wayne State University M,D,O*
West Chester University of Pennsylvania M*†
Western Illinois University M
Western Michigan University M,D*†
West Texas A&M University M†
West Virginia University M,D*
Wichita State University M*†
Wilfrid Laurier University M
Wright State University M*
Yale University M,D*
York University M,D*
Youngstown State University M

EDUCATION—GENERAL

Abilene Christian University M
Acadia University M,O
Adams State College M
Adelphi University M,D,O*
Alabama Agricultural and Mechanical University M,O
Alabama State University M,D,O
Alaska Pacific University M
Albany State University M,O
Alcorn State University M,O
Alfred University M*†
Alliant International University M,D,O*†
Alliant International University M,D,O*†
Alvernia College M
Alverno College M
American International College M,D,O*
American University M,D,O*†
Andrews University M,D,O
Angelo State University M†
Anna Maria College M
Antioch New England Graduate School M*†
Antioch University Los Angeles M
Antioch University McGregor M†
Antioch University Santa Barbara M
Antioch University Seattle M†
Appalachian State University M,D,O
Aquinas College M
Arcadia University M,D,O†
Argosy University-Chicago M,D,O*
Argosy University-Orange County M,D,O*
Argosy University-Phoenix D,O*
Argosy University-San Francisco Bay Area M,D*
Argosy University-Sarasota M,D,O*†
Argosy University-Seattle M*
Argosy University-Tampa M*
Argosy University-Twin Cities M*
Arizona State University M,D*
Arizona State University West M
Arkansas State University M,D,O
Arkansas Tech University M,O
Armstrong Atlantic State University M†
Ashland University M,D
Athabasca University M,O
Atlantic Union College M
Auburn University M,D,O*†
Auburn University Montgomery M,O
Augustana College M
Augusta State University M,O
Aurora University M,D
Austin College M
Austin Peay State University M,O
Averett University M
Avila University M
Azusa Pacific University M,D*†
Baker University M
Baldwin-Wallace College M*
Ball State University M,D,O*
Bank Street College of Education M*
Barry University M,D,O*†
Bayamón Central University M
Baylor University M,D,O*†
Bellarmine University M
Belmont University M
Bemidji State University M
Benedictine University M†
Bennington College M†
Berry College M,O
Bethany College of the Assemblies of God M
Bethel College (MN) M
Bethel College (TN) M
Biola University M
Bishop's University M,O
Black Hills State University M*
Bloomsburg University of Pennsylvania M
Bluffton College M
Boise State University M,D*
Boston College M,D,O*†
Boston University M,D,O*†
Bowie State University M
Bowling Green State University M,D,O*†
Bradley University M†
Brandon University M,O
Brenau University M,O
Bridgewater State College M,O
Brigham Young University M,D*
Brock University M
Brooklyn College of the City University of New York M,O†
Brown University M*
Bucknell University M
Buena Vista University M
Butler University M
Cabrini College M
California Baptist University M
California Lutheran University M,O
California Polytechnic State University, San Luis Obispo M†
California State Polytechnic University, Pomona M*
California State University, Bakersfield M
California State University, Chico M
California State University, Dominguez Hills M,O†
California State University, Fresno M,D
California State University, Fullerton M
California State University, Hayward M
California State University, Long Beach M,O
California State University, Los Angeles M,D
California State University, Monterey Bay M
California State University, Northridge M,O
California State University, Sacramento M
California State University, San Bernardino M
California State University, San Marcos M
California State University, Stanislaus M
California University of Pennsylvania M
Calvin College M
Cambridge College M†
Cameron University M
Campbellsville University M
Campbell University M
Canisius College M,O
Capella University M,D
Cardinal Stritch University M,D*
Carlow College M
Carnegie Mellon University M,D*
Carroll College M
Carson-Newman College M
Carthage College M,O
Castleton State College M,O
Catawba College M
The Catholic University of America M,D*†
Centenary College M
Centenary College of Louisiana M
Central Connecticut State University M,D,O*†
Central Methodist College M
Central Michigan University M,D,O†
Central Missouri State University M,O†
Central State University M
Central Washington University M†
Chadron State College M,O
Chaminade University of Honolulu M*
Chapman University M,O*†
Charleston Southern University M
Chatham College M
Chestnut Hill College M†
Cheyney University of Pennsylvania M,O
Chicago State University M
Christopher Newport University M†
The Citadel, The Military College of South Carolina M,O
City College of the City University of New York M,O*†
City University M,O†
Claremont Graduate University M,D*
Clarion University of Pennsylvania M,O†
Clark Atlanta University M,D,O
Clarke College M
Clark University M*†
Clemson University M,D,O*
Cleveland State University M,D,O*†
Coastal Carolina University M
Coe College M
Colgate University M
College Misericordia M
College of Charleston M*†
College of Mount St. Joseph M†
College of Mount Saint Vincent M,O*†
The College of New Jersey M,O†
The College of New Rochelle M,O†
College of Notre Dame of Maryland M
College of St. Catherine M†
College of Saint Elizabeth M,O
College of St. Joseph M
The College of Saint Rose M,O*†
The College of St. Scholastica M
College of Santa Fe M
College of Staten Island of the City University of New York M,O†
College of the Southwest M
The College of William and Mary M,D,O*†
Collège universitaire de Saint-Boniface M
Colorado Christian University M
The Colorado College M
Columbia College (MO) M
Columbia College Chicago M†
Columbia International University M
Columbus State University M,O
Concordia University (CA) M
Concordia University (IL) M,O
Concordia University (OR) M
Concordia University (NE) M
Concordia University (Canada) M,D,O*†
Concordia University at Austin M
Concordia University Wisconsin M
Connecticut College M
Converse College M,O
Coppin State College M
Cornell University M,D*
Covenant College M
Creighton University M*
Cumberland College M,O
Cumberland University M
Curry College M,O
Daemen College M
Dakota State University M*
Dallas Baptist University M
Defiance College M
Delta State University M,D,O
DePaul University M*†
DeSales University M
Doane College M
Dominican College M†
Dominican University M*
Dominican University of California M
Dordt College M
Dowling College M,D,O
Drake University M,D,O*†
Drexel University M,D*†
Drury University M
Duke University M*†
Duquesne University M,D,O*†
D'Youville College M,O†
East Carolina University M,D,O*†
East Central University M
Eastern Connecticut State University M
Eastern Illinois University M,O†
Eastern Kentucky University M
Eastern Mennonite University M
Eastern Michigan University M,D,O*
Eastern Nazarene College M,O
Eastern New Mexico University M
Eastern Oregon University M
Eastern University M,O*
Eastern Washington University M†
East Stroudsburg University of Pennsylvania M†
East Tennessee State University M†
Edgewood College M,O
Edinboro University of Pennsylvania M,O
Elms College M,O
Elon University M
Emmanuel College M*
Emory University M,D,O*†
Emporia State University M,O*†
Endicott College M
Evangel University M
The Evergreen State College M*
Fairfield University M,O*
Fairleigh Dickinson University, Metropolitan Campus M*†
Felician College M
Ferris State University M
Fitchburg State College M,O†
Florida Agricultural and Mechanical University M,D*
Florida Atlantic University M,D,O*
Florida Atlantic University, Ft. Lauderdale Campus M,D,O
Florida Gulf Coast University M
Florida International University M,D,O*†
Florida State University M,D,O*†
Fontbonne University M
Fordham University M,D,O*†
Fort Hays State University M,O
Franciscan University of Steubenville M
Francis Marion University M
Freed-Hardeman University M
Fresno Pacific University M
Friends University M
Frostburg State University M
Furman University M
Gallaudet University M,D,O
Gannon University M,D,O
Gardner-Webb University M
Geneva College M*
George Fox University M,D†
George Mason University M,D*†
Georgetown College M
The George Washington University M,D,O*†
Georgia College & State University M,O
Georgian Court College M,O
Georgia Southern University M,D,O
Georgia Southwestern State University M,O
Georgia State University M,D,O*
Goddard College M
Gonzaga University M,D
Gordon College M*
Goucher College M
Governors State University M
Graceland University M
Grambling State University M,D
Grand Canyon University M
Grand Valley State University M†
Gratz College M†
Gwynedd-Mercy College M
Hamline University M,D*
Hampton University M*†
Harding University M
Hardin-Simmons University M
Harvard University M,D,O*†
Hastings College M
Hebrew College M,O†
Hebrew Union College–Jewish Institute of Religion (CA) M,D
Hebrew Union College–Jewish Institute of Religion (NY) M
Heidelberg College M
Henderson State University M
Heritage College M
Hofstra University M,D,O*
Hollins University M
Holy Family College M
Holy Names College M,O
Hood College M
Hope International University M
Houston Baptist University M
Howard University M,D,O*
Hunter College of the City University of New York M,O†
Idaho State University M,D,O*
Illinois State University M,D*†
Indiana State University M,D,O*†
Indiana University Bloomington M,D,O*
Indiana University Kokomo M
Indiana University Northwest M
Indiana University of Pennsylvania M,D,O*†
Indiana University–Purdue University Fort Wayne M
Indiana University–Purdue University Indianapolis M*
Indiana University South Bend M
Indiana University Southeast M
Indiana Wesleyan University M*
Institute for Christian Studies M,D
Instituto Tecnológico y de Estudios Superiores de Monterrey, Campus Central de Veracruz M
Instituto Tecnológico y de Estudios Superiores de

Institution	Degrees
Monterrey, Campus Ciudad de México	M,D
Instituto Tecnológico y de Estudios Superiores de Monterrey, Campus Ciudad Juárez	M
Instituto Tecnológico y de Estudios Superiores de Monterrey, Campus Ciudad Obregón	M
Instituto Tecnológico y de Estudios Superiores de Monterrey, Campus Irapuato	M,D
Instituto Tecnológico y de Estudios Superiores de Monterrey, Campus Sonora Norte	M
Inter American University of Puerto Rico, Arecibo Campus	M
Inter American University of Puerto Rico, Metropolitan Campus	M,D
Inter American University of Puerto Rico, San Germán Campus	M
Iowa State University of Science and Technology	M,D*†
Jackson State University	M,D,O
Jacksonville State University	M,O
Jacksonville University	M,O
James Madison University	M
John Carroll University	M
John F. Kennedy University	M*†
Johns Hopkins University	M,D,O*†
Johnson & Wales University	M*†
Johnson Bible College	M
Johnson State College	M
Kansas State University	M,D*†
Kean University	M,O*†
Keene State College	M,O
Kennesaw State University	M
Kent State University	M,D,O*
Kutztown University of Pennsylvania	M,O†
LaGrange College	M
Lake Erie College	M
Lakehead University	M,D
Lakeland College	M
Lamar University	M,O*†
Lander University	M
Langston University	M
La Salle University	M
La Sierra University	M,D,O
Lawrence Technological University	M
Lee University	M
Lehigh University	M,D,O*
Lehman College of the City University of New York	M
Le Moyne College	M
Lenoir-Rhyne College	M
Lesley University	M,D,O*†
Lewis & Clark College	M,O
Lewis University	M,O
Liberty University	M,D†
Lincoln Memorial University	M,O
Lincoln University (MO)	M,O
Lindenwood University	M,O
Lipscomb University	M
Lock Haven University of Pennsylvania	M
Long Island University, Brentwood Campus	M
Long Island University, Brooklyn Campus	M,O*
Long Island University, C.W. Post Campus	M,O*†
Long Island University, Rockland Graduate Campus	M
Long Island University, Southampton College	M
Long Island University, Westchester Graduate Campus	M
Longwood College	M
Louisiana State University and Agricultural and Mechanical College	M,D,O*
Louisiana State University in Shreveport	M,O†
Louisiana Tech University	M,D,O*
Loyola College in Maryland	M,O
Loyola Marymount University	M†
Loyola University Chicago	M,D,O*†
Loyola University New Orleans	M
Lynchburg College	M
Lyndon State College	M
Lynn University	M,D†
Madonna University	M
Maharishi University of Management	M
Malone College	M†
Manhattan College	M,O*†
Manhattanville College	M*†
Mansfield University of Pennsylvania	M
Marian College of Fond du Lac	M
Marietta College	M
Marlboro College	M*
Marquette University	M,D,O*†
Marshall University	M,D,O*†
Mary Baldwin College	M
Marycrest International University	M
Marygrove College	M
Marymount University	M,O†
Maryville University of Saint Louis	M
Marywood University	M*†
Massachusetts College of Liberal Arts	M
McDaniel College	M
McGill University	M,D,O*
McNeese State University	M
Medaille College	M
Memorial University of Newfoundland	M†
Mercer University	M,O
Mercy College	M,O*
Meredith College	M
Merrimack College	M
Miami University	M,D,O*†
Michigan State University	M,D,O*†
MidAmerica Nazarene University	M
Middle Tennessee State University	M,D,O*
Midwestern State University	M
Millersville University of Pennsylvania	M†
Milligan College	M
Mills College	M,D*†
Minnesota State University, Mankato	M,O
Minnesota State University, Moorhead	M,O
Mississippi College	M,O
Mississippi State University	M,D,O*
Mississippi University for Women	M
Mississippi Valley State University	M
Monmouth University	M,O*†
Montana State University–Billings	M*
Montana State University–Bozeman	M,D*
Montana State University–Northern	M
Montclair State University	M,D†
Moravian College	M
Morehead State University	M,O
Morgan State University	M,D*
Morningside College	M
Mount Mary College	M
Mount Saint Mary College	M
Mount St. Mary's College	M*
Mount Saint Mary's College and Seminary	M
Mount Saint Vincent University	M
Mount Vernon Nazarene University	M
Murray State University	M,D,O†
Muskingum College	M
Naropa University	M*
National-Louis University	M,D,O
National University	M†
Nazareth College of Rochester	M
Neumann College	M
New England College	M*
New Jersey City University	M,O
Newman University	M
New Mexico Highlands University	M
New Mexico State University	M,D,O
New School University	M*†
New York Institute of Technology	M,O*†
New York University	M,D,O*†
Niagara University	M,O†
Nicholls State University	M
Nipissing University	M,O
Norfolk State University	M†
North Carolina Agricultural and Technical State University	M*
North Carolina Central University	M
North Carolina State University	M,D,O*
North Central College	M
North Dakota State University	M,O†
Northeastern Illinois University	M*
Northeastern State University	M
Northeastern University	M*†
Northern Arizona University	M,D,O
Northern Illinois University	M,D,O*†
Northern Kentucky University	M
Northern Michigan University	M,O
Northern State University	M
North Georgia College & State University	M,O
North Park University	M
Northwestern Oklahoma State University	M
Northwestern State University of Louisiana	M,O
Northwestern University	M,D*
Northwest Missouri State University	M,O
Northwest Nazarene University	M
Notre Dame College (OH)	M,O
Notre Dame de Namur University	M
Nova Southeastern University	M,D,O*
Oakland City University	M
Oakland University	M,D,O†
Occidental College	M
Oglethorpe University	M
The Ohio State University	M,D,O*
Ohio University	M,D*
Oklahoma City University	M
Oklahoma State University	M,D,O*†
Old Dominion University	M,D,O*†
Olivet College	M
Olivet Nazarene University	M
Oral Roberts University	M,D
Oregon State University	M,D*
Ottawa University	M
Otterbein College	M
Our Lady of Holy Cross College	M
Our Lady of the Lake University of San Antonio	M,D
Pace University	M,O*†
Pace University, White Plains Campus	M,O*
Pacific Lutheran University	M†
Pacific Union College	M
Pacific University	M
Palm Beach Atlantic University	M
Park University	M
The Pennsylvania State University Great Valley Campus	M
The Pennsylvania State University Harrisburg Campus of the Capital College	M,D*†
The Pennsylvania State University University Park Campus	M,D*†
Pepperdine University	M,D*†
Peru State College	M
Philadelphia Biblical University	M
Piedmont College	M,O
Pittsburg State University	M,O
Plymouth State College	M,O*
Point Loma Nazarene University	M,O
Point Park College	M*
Pontifical Catholic University of Puerto Rico	M,D
Portland State University	M,D*
Prairie View A&M University	M
Prescott College	M†
Providence College	M*
Purdue University	M,D,O*
Purdue University Calumet	M
Purdue University North Central	M
Queens College of the City University of New York	M,O†
Queen's University at Kingston	M,D
Queens University of Charlotte	M
Quincy University	M
Quinnipiac University	M*†
Radford University	M†
Regent University	M,D,O†
Regis College (MA)	M
Regis University	M,O*†
Rhode Island College	D†
Rice University	M*
Rider University	M,O*
Rivier College	M*†
Robert Morris University	M†
Roberts Wesleyan College	M,O*
Rockford College	M
Rockhurst University	M
Rollins College	M*
Roosevelt University	M,D*†
Rowan University	M,D,O†
Rutgers, The State University of New Jersey, New Brunswick	M,D,O*
Sacred Heart University	M,O*†
Sage Graduate School	M,O†
Saginaw Valley State University	M,O
St. Bonaventure University	M,O
St. Cloud State University	M,O
Saint Francis University	M*
St. Francis Xavier University	M,O
St. John's University (NY)	M,D,O*†
Saint Joseph College	M
Saint Joseph's College (ME)	M
St. Joseph's College, Suffolk Campus	M
Saint Joseph's University	M,D,O*†
St. Lawrence University	M,O
Saint Leo University	M
Saint Louis University	M,D*†
Saint Martin's College	M
Saint Mary College	M
Saint Mary's College of California	M
Saint Mary's University of Minnesota	M
St. Mary's University of San Antonio	M,O
Saint Michael's College	M,O*
St. Norbert College	M
Saint Peter's College	M,O†
St. Thomas Aquinas College	M,O
St. Thomas University	M,O†
Saint Xavier University	M,O*
Salem College	M
Salem International University	M
Salem State College	M,O
Salisbury University	M
Samford University	M,D,O
San Diego State University	M,D*
San Francisco State University	M,D,O
San Jose State University	M,O*
Santa Clara University	M,O*
Sarah Lawrence College	M*†
School for International Training	M†
Schreiner University	M
Seattle Pacific University	M,D,O
Seattle University	M,D,O*†
Seton Hall University	M,D,O*†
Shenandoah University	M,D,O
Shippensburg University of Pennsylvania	M,O†
Siena Heights University	M
Sierra Nevada College	O
Silver Lake College	M
Simmons College	M,O*
Simon Fraser University	M,D
Simpson College and Graduate School	M
Sinte Gleska University	M
Slippery Rock University of Pennsylvania	M†
Smith College	M*
Sonoma State University	M
South Carolina State University	M,D,O
South Dakota State University	M*
Southeastern Louisiana University	M
Southeastern Oklahoma State University	M
Southern Adventist University	M
Southern Arkansas University–Magnolia	M
Southern Connecticut State University	M,O†
Southern Illinois University Carbondale	M,D*†
Southern Illinois University Edwardsville	M,O†
Southern Nazarene University	M
Southern Oregon University	M
Southern University and Agricultural and Mechanical College	M*
Southern Utah University	M
Southwest Baptist University	M
Southwestern Adventist University	M
Southwestern Assemblies of God University	M
Southwestern College (KS)	M
Southwestern Oklahoma State University	M
Southwest Missouri State University	M*†
Southwest State University	M
Southwest Texas State University	M*
Spalding University	M,D†
Spring Arbor University	M
Springfield College	M†
Spring Hill College	M
Stanford University	M,D*
State University of New York at Albany	M,D,O*†
State University of New York at Binghamton	M,D*†
State University of New York at New Paltz	M,O
State University of New York at Oswego	M,O
State University of New York College at Brockport	M*†
State University of New York College at Cortland	M,O
State University of New York College at Fredonia	M,O
State University of New York College at Geneseo	M
State University of New York College at Oneonta	M,O
State University of New York College at Potsdam	M
State University of West Georgia	M,D,O
Stephen F. Austin State University	M,D
Stephens College	M
Stetson University	M
Suffolk University	M,O*
Sul Ross State University	M*
Sunbridge College	M
Syracuse University	M,D,O*
Tarleton State University	M,O
Teachers College Columbia University	M,D*
Temple University	M,D*†

*P—first professional degree; M—master's degree; D—doctorate; O—other advanced degree; *full description and/or announcement in Book 2, 3, 4, 5, or 6; †full description in this book*

Tennessee State University M,D*
Tennessee Technological University M,D,O*
Tennessee Temple University M
Texas A&M International University M
Texas A&M University M,D*
Texas A&M University–Commerce M,D†
Texas A&M University–Corpus Christi M,D
Texas A&M University–Kingsville M,D*†
Texas A&M University–Texarkana M
Texas Christian University M,D,O*
Texas Southern University M,D†
Texas Tech University M,D,O*†
Texas Wesleyan University M
Texas Woman's University M,D*†
Towson University M†
Trevecca Nazarene University M,D
Trinity University M*
Troy State University M,O
Troy State University Dothan M,O
Troy State University Montgomery M,O
Truman State University M†
Tufts University M,O*†
Tusculum College M
Tuskegee University M
Union College (KY) M
Union College (NY) M*
Union University M,O
Universidad de las Americas, A.C. M
Universidad de las Américas–Puebla M
Universidad del Turabo M
Universidad Metropolitana M
Université de Moncton M
Université de Montréal M,D,O
Université de Sherbrooke M,O
Université du Québec à Chicoutimi M,D
Université du Québec en Outaouais M,D,O
Université du Québec à Montréal M,D,O
Université du Québec à Rimouski M,D
Université du Québec à Trois-Rivières M,O
Université du Québec en Abitibi-Témiscamingue M,D
Université Laval M,D,O†
University at Buffalo, The State University of New York M,D,O*†
University College of Cape Breton O
The University of Akron M,D†
The University of Alabama at Birmingham M,D,O*†
University of Alaska Anchorage M
University of Alaska Fairbanks M,O*
University of Alaska Southeast M
The University of Arizona M,D,O*
University of Arkansas M,D,O*
University of Arkansas at Little Rock M,D,O
University of Arkansas at Monticello M
University of Arkansas at Pine Bluff M
University of Bridgeport M,D,O*†
The University of British Columbia M,D,O*
University of Calgary M,D*
University of California, Berkeley M,D,O*
University of California, Davis D*†
University of California, Irvine M,D*
University of California, Los Angeles M,D*
University of California, Riverside M,D*
University of California, San Diego M*
University of California, Santa Barbara M,D*
University of California, Santa Cruz M,O*
University of Central Arkansas M,D
University of Central Florida M,D,O*†
University of Central Oklahoma M
University of Cincinnati M,D,O*
University of Colorado at Boulder M,D*
University of Colorado at Colorado Springs M*
University of Colorado at Denver M,D,O*
University of Connecticut M,D*†
University of Dayton M,D,O*†
University of Delaware M,D*†
University of Denver M,D,O*†
University of Detroit Mercy M*
University of Evansville M
The University of Findlay M
University of Florida M,D,O*†
University of Georgia M,D,O*†
University of Great Falls M
University of Guam M
University of Hartford M,D,O*
University of Hawaii at Manoa M,D*
University of Houston M,D*
University of Houston–Clear Lake M*†
University of Houston–Victoria M
University of Idaho M,D,O*†
University of Illinois at Chicago M,D*
University of Illinois at Urbana–Champaign M,D,O*
University of Indianapolis M
The University of Iowa M,D,O*
University of Judaism M
University of Kansas M,D,O*
University of Kentucky M,D,O*
University of La Verne M,O*
The University of Lethbridge M,D,O
University of Louisiana at Lafayette M*
University of Louisiana at Monroe M,D,O
University of Louisville M,D,O*†
University of Maine M,D,O*
University of Manitoba M*
University of Mary M
University of Mary Hardin-Baylor M
University of Maryland, Baltimore County M,D*†
University of Maryland, College Park M,D,O*
University of Maryland Eastern Shore M†
University of Maryland University College M*
University of Massachusetts Amherst M,D,O*†
University of Massachusetts Boston M,D,O*†
University of Massachusetts Dartmouth M*†
University of Massachusetts Lowell M,D,O*†
The University of Memphis M,D,O*†
University of Miami M,D,O*†
University of Michigan M,D*
University of Michigan–Dearborn M*†
University of Michigan–Flint M
University of Minnesota, Twin Cities Campus M,D*
University of Mississippi M,D,O*
University of Missouri–Columbia M,D,O*
University of Missouri–Kansas City M,D,O*†
University of Missouri–St. Louis M,D†
University of Mobile M
The University of Montana–Missoula M,D,O*†
University of Montevallo M,O
University of Nebraska at Kearney M,O
University of Nebraska at Omaha M,D,O
University of Nebraska–Lincoln M,D,O*†
University of Nevada, Las Vegas M,D,O*†
University of Nevada, Reno M,D,O*
University of New Brunswick Fredericton M
University of New England M*
University of New Hampshire M,D,O*†
University of New Haven M*†
University of New Mexico M,D*†
University of New Orleans M,D,O*
University of North Alabama M,O
The University of North Carolina at Chapel Hill M,D*†
The University of North Carolina at Charlotte M,D,O*
The University of North Carolina at Greensboro M,D,O†
The University of North Carolina at Pembroke M
The University of North Carolina at Wilmington M*
University of North Dakota M,D,O*
University of Northern British Columbia M,D
University of Northern Colorado M,D,O†
University of Northern Iowa M,D,O
University of North Florida M,D
University of North Texas M,D,O*†
University of Notre Dame M*†
University of Oklahoma M,D,O*†
University of Oregon M,D*
University of Ottawa M,D*
University of Pennsylvania M,D*†
University of Phoenix–Colorado Campus M
University of Phoenix–Hawaii Campus M,O
University of Phoenix–Louisiana Campus M
University of Phoenix–Nevada Campus M
University of Phoenix–New Mexico Campus M
University of Phoenix–Northern California Campus M
University of Phoenix–Oregon Campus M
University of Phoenix–Phoenix Campus M
University of Phoenix–Puerto Rico Campus M
University of Phoenix–Sacramento Campus M
University of Phoenix–San Diego Campus M
University of Phoenix–Southern Arizona Campus M
University of Phoenix–Southern California Campus M
University of Phoenix–Southern Colorado Campus M
University of Phoenix–Utah Campus M
University of Phoenix-Vancouver Campus M
University of Pittsburgh M,D*†
University of Portland M
University of Puerto Rico, Río Piedras M,D*
University of Puget Sound M
University of Redlands M
University of Regina M,D,O
University of Rhode Island M*
University of Rio Grande M
University of Rochester M,D*
University of St. Francis (IL) M
University of Saint Francis (IN) M
University of St. Thomas (MN) M*†
University of St. Thomas (TX) M
University of San Diego M,D*†
University of San Francisco M,D*†
University of Saskatchewan M,D,O
The University of Scranton M†
University of Sioux Falls M
University of South Alabama M,D,O*†
University of South Carolina M,D,O*†
University of South Carolina Aiken M
University of South Carolina Spartanburg M
The University of South Dakota M,D,O†
University of Southern California M,D,O*†
University of Southern Colorado M
University of Southern Indiana M
University of Southern Maine M,O
University of Southern Mississippi M,D,O
University of South Florida M,D,O*†
The University of Tennessee M,D,O*†
The University of Tennessee at Chattanooga M,O
The University of Tennessee at Martin M
The University of Texas at Arlington M*†
The University of Texas at Austin M,D*
The University of Texas at Brownsville M
The University of Texas at El Paso M,D*†
The University of Texas at San Antonio M,D*
The University of Texas at Tyler M,O
The University of Texas of the Permian Basin M
The University of Texas–Pan American M,D
University of the District of Columbia M*
University of the Incarnate Word M†
University of the Pacific M,D,O*
University of the Sacred Heart M
University of the Virgin Islands M
University of Toledo M,D,O*†
University of Toronto M,D*
University of Tulsa M†
University of Utah M,D*
University of Vermont M,D*†
University of Victoria M,D
University of Virginia M,D,O*
University of Washington M,D,O*
The University of West Alabama M
The University of Western Ontario M*
University of West Florida M,D,O
University of Windsor M,D
University of Wisconsin–Eau Claire M†
University of Wisconsin–Green Bay M
University of Wisconsin–La Crosse M†
University of Wisconsin–Madison M,D*
University of Wisconsin–Milwaukee M,D
University of Wisconsin–Oshkosh M*
University of Wisconsin–Platteville M
University of Wisconsin–River Falls M
University of Wisconsin–Stevens Point M
University of Wisconsin–Stout M
University of Wisconsin–Superior M
University of Wisconsin–Whitewater M*
University of Wyoming M,D,O*†
Urbana University M
Ursuline College M
Utah State University M,D,O*
Valdosta State University M,D,O
Valparaiso University M
Vanderbilt University M,D*
Vanguard University of Southern California M
Vermont College M,O
Villanova University M*†
Virginia Commonwealth University M,D,O*†
Virginia State University M,O
Viterbo University M
Wagner College M
Wake Forest University M*†
Walden University D†
Walla Walla College M
Walsh University M
Washburn University of Topeka M
Washington State University M,D*
Washington State University Spokane M†
Washington University in St. Louis M,D*†
Wayland Baptist University M
Wayne State College M,O
Wayne State University M,D,O*
Weber State University M
Webster University M,O
Wesleyan College M
Wesley College M
West Chester University of Pennsylvania M,O*†
Western Carolina University M,D,O†
Western Connecticut State University M
Western Governors University M,O
Western Illinois University M,O
Western Kentucky University M,O†
Western Michigan University M,D,O*†
Western New Mexico University M
Western Oregon University M
Western Washington University M
Westfield State College M,O
Westminster College (PA) M,O
Westminster College (UT) M
West Texas A&M University M†
West Virginia University M,D*
Wheaton College M†
Wheelock College M,O*
Whittier College M
Whitworth College M
Wichita State University M,D,O*†
Widener University M,D*†
Wilkes University M
Willamette University M*
William Carey College M
William Paterson University of New Jersey M*†
William Woods University M
Wilmington College M,D
Winona State University M
Winthrop University M
Worcester State College M,O
Wright State University M,O*
Xavier University M*
Xavier University of Louisiana M
York University M,D*
Youngstown State University M,D

EDUCATIONAL ADMINISTRATION

Abilene Christian University M
Acadia University M
Adelphi University M,O*
Alabama Agricultural and Mechanical University M,O
Alabama State University M,D,O
Albany State University M,O
Alliant International University M,D,O*†
Alliant International University M,D,O*†
Alverno College M
American International College M,D,O*
American University M*†
Andrews University M,D,O
Angelo State University M†
Antioch New England Graduate School M*†
Appalachian State University M,D
Arcadia University M,D,O†
Argosy University-Orange County M,D,O*
Argosy University-Phoenix D,O*
Argosy University-San Francisco Bay Area M,D*
Argosy University-Sarasota M,D,O*†
Argosy University-Tampa M*
Arizona State University M,D*

Institution	Degrees
Arizona State University West	M
Arkansas State University	M,D,O
Arkansas Tech University	M
Ashland University	M,D
Auburn University	M,D,O*†
Auburn University Montgomery	M,O
Augusta State University	M,O
Aurora University	M,D
Austin Peay State University	M,O
Azusa Pacific University	M,D*†
Baldwin-Wallace College	M*
Ball State University	M,D,O*
Bank Street College of Education	M*
Barry University	M,D,O*†
Bayamón Central University	M
Baylor University	M,D,O*†
Benedictine College	M
Bernard M. Baruch College of the City University of New York	M,O*
Bethany College of the Assemblies of God	M
Bethel College (TN)	M
Boston College	M,D,O*†
Boston University	M,O*†
Bowie State University	M
Bowling Green State University	M,D,O*†
Bradley University	M†
Brandon University	M,O
Bridgewater State College	M,O
Brigham Young University	M,D*
Brock University	M
Brooklyn College of the City University of New York	O†
Bucknell University	M
Buena Vista University	M
Butler University	M
Caldwell College	M
California Baptist University	M
California Lutheran University	M
California Polytechnic State University, San Luis Obispo	M†
California State University, Bakersfield	M
California State University, Chico	M
California State University, Dominguez Hills	M†
California State University, Fresno	M,D
California State University, Fullerton	M
California State University, Hayward	M
California State University, Long Beach	M
California State University, Los Angeles	M
California State University, Northridge	M
California State University, Sacramento	M
California State University, San Bernardino	M
California State University, Stanislaus	M
California University of Pennsylvania	M
Campbell University	M
Canisius College	M,O
Cardinal Stritch University	M,D*
Carlow College	M
Carthage College	M,O
Castleton State College	M,O
The Catholic University of America	M,D*†
Centenary College	M
Centenary College of Louisiana	M
Central Connecticut State University	M,D,O*†
Central Michigan University	M,D,O†
Central Missouri State University	M,O†
Central State University	M
Central Washington University	M†
Chadron State College	M,O
Chapman University	M*†
Charleston Southern University	M
Chestnut Hill College	M†
Cheyney University of Pennsylvania	M,O
Chicago State University	M
The Citadel, The Military College of South Carolina	M,O
City College of the City University of New York	M,O*†
City University	M,O†
Claremont Graduate University	M,D*
Clark Atlanta University	M,D,O
Clarke College	M
Clemson University	M,D,O*
Cleveland State University	M,D,O*†
The College of New Jersey	M†
The College of New Rochelle	M,O†
College of Notre Dame of Maryland	M
College of Saint Elizabeth	O
The College of Saint Rose	M,O*†
College of Santa Fe	M
College of Staten Island of the City University of New York	O†
College of the Southwest	M
The College of William and Mary	M,D*†
Columbia International University	M
Columbus State University	M,O
Concordia University (CA)	M
Concordia University (IL)	M,D,O
Concordia University (OR)	M
Concordia University (NE)	M
Concordia University Wisconsin	M
Converse College	M,O
Creighton University	M*
Cumberland College	O
Dallas Baptist University	M
Delaware Valley College	M
Delta State University	M,O
DePaul University	M,D*†
Doane College	M
Dominican University	M*
Dowling College	D,O
Drake University	M,D,O*†
Drexel University	D*†
Duquesne University	M,D*†
East Carolina University	M,D,O*†
Eastern Illinois University	M,O†
Eastern Kentucky University	M
Eastern Michigan University	M,D,O*
Eastern Nazarene College	M,O
Eastern Washington University	M†
East Tennessee State University	M,D,O†
Edgewood College	M,O
Edinboro University of Pennsylvania	M,O
Emmanuel College	M*
Emporia State University	M*†
Erikson Institute	M,O
Fairleigh Dickinson University, Metropolitan Campus	M*†
Fayetteville State University	M,D
Ferris State University	M
Fielding Graduate Institute	D
Fitchburg State College	M,O†
Florida Agricultural and Mechanical University	M,D*
Florida Atlantic University	M,D,O*
Florida Atlantic University, Ft. Lauderdale Campus	M,D,O
Florida Gulf Coast University	M
Florida International University	M,D,O*†
Florida State University	M,D,O*†
Fordham University	M,D,O*†
Fort Hays State University	M,O
Framingham State College	M*
Franciscan University of Steubenville	M
Fresno Pacific University	M
Friends University	M
Frostburg State University	M
Furman University	M
Gallaudet University	M,D,O
Gardner-Webb University	M
Geneva College	M*
George Mason University	M*†
The George Washington University	M,D,O*†
Georgia College & State University	M,O
Georgian Court College	M,O
Georgia Southern University	M,D,O
Georgia State University	M,D,O*
Gonzaga University	M,D
Governors State University	M
Grambling State University	M,D
Grand Valley State University	M†
Gwynedd-Mercy College	M
Harding University	M
Harvard University	M,D,O*†
Henderson State University	M
Heritage College	M
Hofstra University	M,D,O*
Hood College	M
Houston Baptist University	M
Howard University	M,O*
Hunter College of the City University of New York	O†
Idaho State University	M,D,O*
Illinois State University	M,D*†
Immaculata University	M,D,O†
Indiana State University	M,D,O*†
Indiana University Bloomington	M,D,O*
Indiana University of Pennsylvania	M,D,O*†
Indiana University–Purdue University Fort Wayne	M
Indiana University–Purdue University Indianapolis	M*
Instituto Tecnológico y de Estudios Superiores de Monterrey, Campus Central de Veracruz	M
Instituto Tecnológico y de Estudios Superiores de Monterrey, Campus Irapuato	M,D
Inter American University of Puerto Rico, Arecibo Campus	M
Inter American University of Puerto Rico, Metropolitan Campus	M
Inter American University of Puerto Rico, San Germán Campus	M
Iona College	M*†
Iowa State University of Science and Technology	M,D*†
Jackson State University	M,D,O
Jacksonville State University	M,O
Jacksonville University	M
James Madison University	M
John Carroll University	M
Johns Hopkins University	M,D,O*†
Johnson & Wales University	D*†
Kansas State University	M,D*†
Kean University	M,O*†
Keene State College	M,O
Kent State University	M,D,O*
Kutztown University of Pennsylvania	M†
Lakehead University	M,D
Lamar University	M,O*†
La Sierra University	M,D,O
Lehigh University	M,D,O*
Lesley University	M,D,O*†
Lewis & Clark College	O
Lewis University	M
Liberty University	M,D†
Lincoln Memorial University	M,O
Lincoln University (MO)	M
Long Island University, Brentwood Campus	M
Long Island University, Brooklyn Campus	M*
Long Island University, C.W. Post Campus	M,O*†
Long Island University, Rockland Graduate Campus	M
Longwood College	M
Loras College	M
Louisiana State University and Agricultural and Mechanical College	M,D,O*
Louisiana Tech University	M,D,O*
Loyola College in Maryland	M,O
Loyola Marymount University	M†
Loyola University Chicago	M,D*†
Lynchburg College	M
Lynn University	M,D†
Madonna University	M
Manhattan College	M,O*†
Marian College of Fond du Lac	M
Marshall University	M,O*†
Marygrove College	M
Maryville University of Saint Louis	M
Marywood University	M*†
Massachusetts College of Liberal Arts	M
McDaniel College	M
McGill University	M,D,O*
McNeese State University	M,O
Memorial University of Newfoundland	M†
Mercy College	M,O*
Mercyhurst College	M,O
Miami University	M,D*†
Michigan State University	M,D,O*†
Middle Tennessee State University	M,O*
Midwestern State University	M
Mills College	M,D*†
Minnesota State University, Mankato	M,O
Minnesota State University, Moorhead	M,O
Mississippi College	M
Mississippi State University	M,D,O*
Monmouth University	M,O*†
Montclair State University	M†
Morehead State University	M,O
Morgan State University	M,D*
Mount St. Mary's College	M*
Murray State University	M,O†
National-Louis University	M,D,O
National University	M†
New England College	M*
New Jersey City University	M
Newman Theological College	M,O
Newman University	M
New Mexico Highlands University	M
New Mexico State University	M,D,O
New York Institute of Technology	M,O*†
New York University	M,D,O*†
Niagara University	M,O†
Nicholls State University	M
Norfolk State University	M†
North Carolina Agricultural and Technical State University	M*
North Carolina Central University	M
North Carolina State University	M,D*
North Central College	M
North Dakota State University	M,O†
Northeastern Illinois University	M
Northeastern State University	M
Northern Arizona University	M,D
Northern Illinois University	M,D,O*†
Northern Michigan University	M,O
Northern State University	M
North Georgia College & State University	M,O
Northwestern State University of Louisiana	M,O
Northwest Missouri State University	M,O
Northwest Nazarene University	M
Notre Dame de Namur University	M,O
Nova Southeastern University	M,D,O*
Oakland University	M,D,O†
Oglala Lakota College	M
The Ohio State University	M,D,O*
Ohio University	M,D*
Oklahoma State University	M,D,O*†
Old Dominion University	M,O*†
Oral Roberts University	M,D
Our Lady of Holy Cross College	M
Our Lady of the Lake University of San Antonio	M,D
Pace University	M,O*†
Pace University, White Plains Campus	M,O*
Pacific Lutheran University	M†
The Pennsylvania State University University Park Campus	M,D*†
Pepperdine University	M,D*†
Philadelphia Biblical University	M
Pittsburg State University	M
Plattsburgh State University of New York	O
Plymouth State College	M*
Portland State University	M,D*
Prairie View A&M University	M
Providence College	M*
Purdue University	M,D,O*
Purdue University Calumet	M
Queens College of the City University of New York	O†
Radford University	M†
Rhode Island College	M,O†
Rider University	M*
Rivier College	M*†
Robert Morris University	M†
Roosevelt University	M,D*†
Rowan University	M,D†
Royal Roads University	M
Rutgers, The State University of New Jersey, New Brunswick	M,D,O*
Sacred Heart University	M,O*†
Saginaw Valley State University	M,O
St. Bonaventure University	M,O
St. Cloud State University	M
Saint Francis University	M*
St. John Fisher College	M
St. John's University (NY)	M,D,O*†
Saint Joseph's University	D*†
St. Lawrence University	M,O
Saint Louis University	M,D,O*†
Saint Mary's College of California	M
Saint Mary's University of Minnesota	M,D
St. Mary's University of San Antonio	M,O
Saint Michael's College	M,O*
Saint Peter's College	M,O†
Saint Xavier University	M,O*
Salem State College	M
Salisbury University	M
Samford University	M,D,O
Sam Houston State University	M,D*
San Diego State University	M*
San Francisco State University	M,O
San Jose State University	M,O*
Santa Clara University	M*
Seattle Pacific University	M,D
Seattle University	M,D,O*†
Seton Hall University	M,D,O*†
Shenandoah University	M,D,O
Shippensburg University of Pennsylvania	M†
Silver Lake College	M
Simmons College	M,O*
Simon Fraser University	M
Sonoma State University	M
South Carolina State University	M,D,O
South Dakota State University	M*
Southeastern Louisiana University	M
Southeastern Oklahoma State University	M
Southeast Missouri State University	M,D,O
Southern Adventist University	M
Southern Arkansas University–Magnolia	M

*P—first professional degree; M—master's degree; D—doctorate; O—other advanced degree; *full description and/or announcement in Book 2, 3, 4, 5, or 6; †full description in this book*

Southern Connecticut State University O†
Southern Illinois University Carbondale M,D*†
Southern Illinois University Edwardsville M,O†
Southern Oregon University M
Southern University and Agricultural and Mechanical College M*
Southwest Baptist University M
Southwestern Assemblies of God University M
Southwestern Oklahoma State University M
Southwest Missouri State University M,D,O*†
Southwest Texas State University M*
Spalding University M,D†
Stanford University M,D*
State University of New York at Albany M,D,O*†
State University of New York at New Paltz M,O
State University of New York at Oswego M,O
State University of New York College at Brockport M,O*†
State University of New York College at Buffalo O
State University of New York College at Cortland O
State University of New York College at Fredonia O
State University of West Georgia M,O
Stephen F. Austin State University M,D
Stetson University M,O
Stony Brook University, State University of New York M,O*†
Suffolk University M,O*
Sul Ross State University M*
Syracuse University M,D,O*
Tarleton State University M,O
Teachers College Columbia University M,D*
Temple University M,D*†
Tennessee State University M,D*
Tennessee Technological University M,O*
Tennessee Temple University M
Texas A&M International University M
Texas A&M University M,D*
Texas A&M University–Commerce M,D†
Texas A&M University–Corpus Christi M,D
Texas A&M University–Kingsville M,D*†
Texas A&M University–Texarkana M
Texas Christian University M,D*
Texas Southern University M,D†
Texas Tech University M,D,O*†
Texas Woman's University M*†
Towson University O†
Trevecca Nazarene University M
Trinity College (DC) M†
Trinity International University P,M,D,O
Trinity University M*
Trinity Western University M
Troy State University M
Troy State University Dothan M,O
Troy State University Montgomery O
Union College (KY) M,O
Union University M,O
Universidad del Turabo M
Universidad Metropolitana M
Université de Moncton M
Université de Montréal M,D,O
Université de Sherbrooke M
Université du Québec à Trois-Rivières D
Université Laval M,D,O†
University at Buffalo, The State University of New York M,D,O*†
The University of Akron M,D†
The University of Alabama M,D,O*
The University of Alabama at Birmingham M,D,O*†
University of Alaska Anchorage M
University of Alaska Fairbanks M,O*
University of Alberta M,D,O*
The University of Arizona D,O*
University of Arkansas M,D,O*
University of Arkansas at Little Rock M,D,O
University of Bridgeport D,O*†
The University of British Columbia M,D*
University of Calgary M,D*
University of California, Berkeley M,D*
University of California, Irvine M,D*
University of California, Los Angeles D*
University of Central Arkansas M,D,O
University of Central Florida M,D,O*†
University of Central Oklahoma M
University of Cincinnati M,D,O*
University of Colorado at Colorado Springs M*
University of Colorado at Denver M,D,O*
University of Connecticut M,D*†
University of Dayton M,D*†
University of Delaware M,D*†
University of Denver M,D,O*†
University of Detroit Mercy M*
The University of Findlay M
University of Florida M,D,O*†
University of Georgia M,D,O*†
University of Great Falls M
University of Guam M
University of Hartford D,O*
University of Hawaii at Manoa M,D*
University of Houston M,D*
University of Houston–Clear Lake M*†
University of Idaho M,D,O*†
University of Illinois at Chicago M,D*
University of Illinois at Springfield M†
University of Illinois at Urbana–Champaign M,D,O*
The University of Iowa M,D,O*
University of Kansas M*
University of Kentucky M,D,O*
University of La Verne M,D*
University of Louisiana at Lafayette M*
University of Louisiana at Monroe M,D,O
University of Louisville M,D,O*†
University of Maine M,D,O*
University of Manitoba M*
University of Mary M
University of Mary Hardin-Baylor M
University of Maryland, College Park M,D,O*
University of Massachusetts Amherst M,D,O*†
University of Massachusetts Boston M,D,O*†
University of Massachusetts Lowell M,D,O*†
The University of Memphis M,D,O*†
University of Miami M*†
University of Michigan M,D*
University of Minnesota, Twin Cities Campus M,D,O*
University of Mississippi M,D,O*
University of Missouri–Columbia M,D,O*
University of Missouri–Kansas City M,D,O*†
University of Missouri–St. Louis M,D†
The University of Montana–Missoula M,D,O*†
University of Montevallo M,O
University of Nebraska at Kearney M,O
University of Nebraska at Omaha M,D,O
University of Nebraska–Lincoln M,D,O*†
University of Nevada, Las Vegas M,D,O*†
University of Nevada, Reno M,D,O*
University of New Brunswick Fredericton M
University of New Hampshire M,O*†
University of New Mexico M,D*†
University of New Orleans M,D,O*
University of North Alabama M,O
The University of North Carolina at Chapel Hill M,D*†
The University of North Carolina at Charlotte M,D,O*
The University of North Carolina at Greensboro M,D,O†
The University of North Carolina at Pembroke M
The University of North Carolina at Wilmington M*
University of North Dakota M,D,O*
University of Northern Colorado M,D,O†
University of Northern Iowa M,D
University of North Florida M,D
University of North Texas M,D*†
University of Oklahoma M,D*†
University of Pennsylvania M,D*†
University of Phoenix–Nevada Campus M
University of Phoenix–Phoenix Campus M
University of Pittsburgh M,D*†
University of Puerto Rico, Río Piedras M,D*
University of Puget Sound M
University of Redlands M
University of Regina M,O
University of St. Thomas (MN) M,D,O*†
University of San Diego M,D*†
University of San Francisco M,D*†
University of Saskatchewan M,D,O
The University of Scranton M†
University of Sioux Falls M
University of South Alabama M,O*†
University of South Carolina M,D,O*†
The University of South Dakota M,D,O†
University of Southern California M,D,O*†
University of Southern Maine M,O
University of Southern Mississippi M,D,O
University of South Florida M,D,O*†
The University of Tennessee M,D,O*†
The University of Tennessee at Chattanooga M,O
The University of Tennessee at Martin M
The University of Texas at Arlington M*†
The University of Texas at Austin M,D*
The University of Texas at Brownsville M
The University of Texas at El Paso M,D*†
The University of Texas at San Antonio M,D*
The University of Texas at Tyler M
The University of Texas of the Permian Basin M
The University of Texas–Pan American M
University of the Pacific M,D*
University of Toledo M,D,O*†
University of Utah M,D*
University of Vermont M,D*†
University of Victoria M,D
University of Virginia M,D,O*
University of Washington M,D,O*
The University of West Alabama M
The University of Western Ontario M*
University of West Florida M,O
University of Wisconsin–Madison M,D*
University of Wisconsin–Milwaukee M
University of Wisconsin–Oshkosh M*
University of Wisconsin–Stevens Point M
University of Wisconsin–Superior M,O
University of Wisconsin–Whitewater M*
University of Wyoming M,D,O*†
Ursuline College M
Valdosta State University M,D,O
Vanderbilt University M,D*
Villanova University M*†
Virginia Commonwealth University M*†
Virginia Polytechnic Institute and State University M,D,O*
Virginia State University M
Walla Walla College M
Washburn University of Topeka M
Washington State University M,D*
Wayne State College M,O
Wayne State University M,D,O*
Webster University M,O
Western Carolina University M,D,O†
Western Governors University M,O
Western Illinois University M,O
Western Kentucky University M,O†
Western Michigan University M,D,O*†
Western New Mexico University M
Western Washington University M
Westfield State College M,O
Westminster College (PA) M,O
West Texas A&M University M†
West Virginia University M,D*
Wheelock College M,O*
Whittier College M
Whitworth College M
Wichita State University M,D,O*†
Widener University M,D*†
Wilkes University M
William Carey College M
William Paterson University of New Jersey M*†
William Woods University M
Wilmington College M,D
Winona State University M
Winthrop University M
Worcester State College M
Wright State University M,O*
Xavier University M*
Xavier University of Louisiana M
Yeshiva University M,D,O*
Youngstown State University M,D

EDUCATIONAL MEASUREMENT AND EVALUATION

Abilene Christian University M
Angelo State University M†
Arkansas State University M,O
Boston College M,D,O*†
Bucknell University M
Claremont Graduate University M,D*
Cleveland State University M*†
College of the Southwest M
Florida Atlantic University, Ft. Lauderdale Campus M
Florida State University M,D,O*†
Gallaudet University O
George Mason University M*†
Georgia State University M,D*
Hofstra University M*
Houston Baptist University M
Iowa State University of Science and Technology M,D*†
Kent State University M,D*
Louisiana State University and Agricultural and Mechanical College M,D,O*
Loyola University Chicago M,D*†
Michigan State University M,D,O*†
Mississippi College M
New York University M,D,O*†
North Carolina State University D*
Northwestern Oklahoma State University M
Ohio University M,D*
Rutgers, The State University of New Jersey, New Brunswick M*
Seattle University O*†
Southern Connecticut State University M†
Southern Illinois University Carbondale M,D*†
Southwestern Oklahoma State University M
Stanford University M,D*
State University of New York at Albany M,D,O*†
State University of West Georgia D
Sul Ross State University M*
Syracuse University M,D,O*
Teachers College Columbia University M,D*
Texas A&M University M,D*
Texas Christian University M*
Texas Southern University M,D†
Université Laval M,D,O†
The University of British Columbia M,D,O*
University of California, Berkeley M,D*
University of Colorado at Boulder D*
University of Connecticut M,D*†
University of Delaware M,D*†
University of Denver M,D,O*†
University of Florida M,D,O*†
University of Hawaii at Manoa D*
The University of Iowa M,D,O*
University of Kansas M,D*
University of Kentucky M,D*
University of Louisville M*†
University of Manitoba M*
University of Maryland, College Park M,D*
University of Massachusetts Amherst M,D,O*†
The University of Memphis M,D*†
University of Miami M*†
University of Michigan M,D*
University of Minnesota, Twin Cities Campus M,D*
University of Missouri–St. Louis M,D†
University of Nevada, Las Vegas M,D,O*†
The University of North Carolina at Greensboro M,D†
University of North Dakota D*
University of Northern Colorado M,D†
University of North Texas D*†
University of Pennsylvania M,D*†
University of Pittsburgh M,D*†
University of Puerto Rico, Río Piedras M*
University of South Carolina M,D*†
University of South Florida M,D,O*†
The University of Tennessee M,D,O*†
The University of Texas–Pan American M,D
University of the Incarnate Word M†
University of the Pacific M,D,O*
University of Toledo M,D,O*†
University of Virginia M,D*
University of Washington M,D*
Utah State University M,D*
Vanderbilt University M,D*
Virginia Polytechnic Institute and State University D*
Washington University in St. Louis D*†
Wayne State University M,D,O*
West Chester University of Pennsylvania M*†
Western Michigan University M,D*†
West Texas A&M University M†

Wilkes University M

EDUCATIONAL MEDIA/INSTRUCTIONAL TECHNOLOGY

Acadia University M
Adelphi University M,O*
Alabama State University M,O
Alliant International University M,D*†
Alverno College M
American University M*†
Appalachian State University M,O
Arcadia University M,D,O†
Arizona State University M,D*
Arkansas Tech University M
Auburn University M,D,O*†
Azusa Pacific University M*†
Baldwin-Wallace College M*
Barry University M,D,O*†
Belmont University M
Bloomsburg University of Pennsylvania M
Boise State University M*
Boston University M,D,O*†
Bowling Green State University M*†
Bridgewater State College M
Brigham Young University M,D*
Cabrini College M
California State University, Chico M
California State University, Los Angeles M
California State University, San Bernardino M
California State University, Stanislaus M
Central Connecticut State University M,D,O*†
Central Michigan University M†
Central Missouri State University M†
Central State University M
Chestnut Hill College M†
Chicago State University M
City University M,O†
Clarke College M
Cleveland State University M*†
Coastal Carolina University M
College of Mount Saint Vincent M,O*†
The College of New Jersey M,O†
College of Saint Elizabeth M,O
The College of Saint Rose M,O*†
The College of St. Scholastica M
Concordia University (CA) M
Concordia University (Canada) M,D,O*†
Dakota State University M*
Dowling College D,O
Drexel University D*†
Duquesne University M*†
East Carolina University M,O*†
Eastern Washington University M†
East Stroudsburg University of Pennsylvania M†
East Tennessee State University M†
Emporia State University M*†
Fairfield University M,O*
Ferris State University M
Florida Atlantic University M*
Florida Atlantic University, Ft. Lauderdale Campus M
Florida Gulf Coast University M
Florida State University M,D,O*†
Fort Hays State University M
Framingham State College M*
Fresno Pacific University M
Frostburg State University M
Gallaudet University O
Gannon University M
George Mason University M*†
The George Washington University M*†
Georgia College & State University M,O
Georgian Court College M,O
Georgia Southern University M,O
Georgia State University M,D,O*
Governors State University M
Grand Valley State University M†
Harvard University M,D,O*†
Idaho State University M,D,O*
Indiana State University M,D,O*†
Indiana University Bloomington M,D,O*
Indiana University of Pennsylvania M*†
Indiana University–Purdue University Indianapolis M*
Instituto Tecnológico y de Estudios Superiores de Monterrey, Campus Central de Veracruz M
Instituto Tecnológico y de Estudios Superiores de Monterrey, Campus Ciudad de México M,D
Instituto Tecnológico y de Estudios Superiores de Monterrey, Campus Irapuato M,D
Inter American University of Puerto Rico, Metropolitan Campus M
Iona College M,O*†
Iowa State University of Science and Technology M,D*†
Jackson State University M,D,O
Jacksonville State University M
Jacksonville University M
Johns Hopkins University M,D,O*†
Johnson Bible College M
Kean University M*†
Kent State University M*
Lehigh University M,D*
Long Island University, Brooklyn Campus M*
Long Island University, C.W. Post Campus M,D,O*†
Longwood College M
Louisiana State University and Agricultural and Mechanical College M,D,O*
Loyola College in Maryland M
Malone College M†
Marywood University M*†
McDaniel College M
McNeese State University M
Memorial University of Newfoundland M†
Mercy College M,O*
Michigan State University M,D,O*†
MidAmerica Nazarene University M
Minnesota State University, Mankato M,O
Mississippi State University M,D,O*
Mississippi University for Women M
Montana State University–Billings M*
National-Louis University M,O
National University M†
Nazareth College of Rochester M
New Jersey City University M
New York Institute of Technology M,O*†
New York University M,D,O*†
North Carolina Agricultural and Technical State University M*
North Carolina Central University M
North Carolina State University D*
Northern Arizona University M
Northern Illinois University M,D*†
Northwestern State University of Louisiana M,O
Northwestern University M,D*
Northwest Missouri State University M
Notre Dame de Namur University M,O
Nova Southeastern University M,D,O*
Oakland University O†
Ohio University M,D*
Old Dominion University M*†
Our Lady of the Lake University of San Antonio M
Pacific Lutheran University M†
The Pennsylvania State University Great Valley Campus M
The Pennsylvania State University University Park Campus M,D*†
Pepperdine University M,D*†
Pittsburg State University M
Pontifical Catholic University of Puerto Rico M,D
Portland State University M*
Purdue University M,D,O*
Purdue University Calumet M
Radford University M†
The Richard Stockton College of New Jersey M*
Rochester Institute of Technology M*†
Rosemont College M†
Rowan University M†
Royal Roads University M
St. Cloud State University M
Saint Michael's College M,O*
Salem State College M
Salisbury University M
San Diego State University M*
San Francisco State University M,O
San Jose State University M,O*
Seton Hall University M,O*†
Seton Hill University M†
Simmons College M,O*
Southeastern Oklahoma State University M
Southeast Missouri State University M
Southern Connecticut State University M,O†
Southern Illinois University Edwardsville M†
Southern University and Agricultural and Mechanical College M*
Southwest Missouri State University M*†
State University of New York at Albany M,D,O*†
State University of New York College at Buffalo M
State University of New York College at Potsdam M
State University of West Georgia M,O
Stony Brook University, State University of New York M,O*†
Teachers College Columbia University M,D*
Texas A&M University M,D*
Texas A&M University–Commerce M,D†
Texas Southern University M†
Texas Tech University M,D,O*†
Towson University M†
Troy State University Dothan M,O
Université Laval M,D†
University College of Cape Breton O
The University of Alabama M,D,O*
University of Alaska Southeast M
University of Alberta M,D*
University of Arkansas M*
University of Arkansas at Little Rock M
University of Calgary M,D*
University of Central Arkansas M
University of Central Florida M,D*†
University of Central Oklahoma M
University of Colorado at Denver M,O*
University of Connecticut M,D*†
University of Dayton M*†
The University of Findlay M
University of Florida M,D,O*†
University of Georgia M,D,O*†
University of Hartford M*
University of Hawaii at Manoa M*
University of Houston–Clear Lake M*†
The University of Iowa M,D,O*
University of Louisville M*†
University of Maine M*
University of Manitoba M*
University of Maryland, Baltimore County M,D*†
University of Maryland, College Park M,D,O*
University of Massachusetts Amherst M,D,O*†
University of Medicine and Dentistry of New Jersey M*
The University of Memphis M,D*†
University of Michigan M,D*
University of Minnesota, Twin Cities Campus M,D*
University of Missouri–Columbia M,D,O*
University of Nebraska at Kearney M,O
University of Nebraska at Omaha M,O
University of Nevada, Las Vegas M,D,O*†
University of New Mexico M,D*†
The University of North Carolina at Charlotte M,D,O*
University of North Dakota M*
University of Northern Colorado M†
University of Northern Iowa M
University of Phoenix–Louisiana Campus M
University of Phoenix–Northern California Campus M
University of Phoenix–San Diego Campus M
University of Phoenix–Southern California Campus M
University of San Francisco M,D*†
University of Sioux Falls M
University of South Alabama M,D*†
University of South Carolina M*†
University of South Carolina Aiken M
The University of South Dakota M,O†
University of Southern California M,D*†
University of South Florida M,D*†
The University of Tennessee M,D,O*†
The University of Texas at Brownsville M
University of the Incarnate Word M†
University of the Sacred Heart M
University of Toledo M,D,O*†
University of Washington M,D*
The University of West Alabama M
University of Wyoming M,D,O*†
Utah State University M,D,O*
Vanderbilt University M,D*
Walden University M†
Wayne State College M
Wayne State University M,D,O*
Webster University M,O
West Chester University of Pennsylvania M,O*†
Western Connecticut State University M
Western Governors University M,O
Western Illinois University M,O
Western Kentucky University M†
Western Oregon University M
Westfield State College M
West Texas A&M University M†
Widener University M,D*†
Wilmington College M,D

EDUCATIONAL PSYCHOLOGY

American International College M,D,O*
Andrews University M,D
Arcadia University M,D,O†
Argosy University-Twin Cities M,D*
Arizona State University M,D*
Auburn University M,D,O*†
Austin Peay State University M,O
Ball State University M,D,O*
Baylor University M,D,O*†
Boston College M,D*†
Brigham Young University M,D*
California State University, Long Beach M
California State University, Northridge M,O
California State University, San Bernardino M
The Catholic University of America M,D*†
Center for Humanistic Studies M,D*
Chapman University M,O*†
Clark Atlanta University M,D
The College of Saint Rose M*†
Eastern Illinois University M†
Eastern Michigan University M*
Eastern University M*
Edinboro University of Pennsylvania M
Florida Atlantic University, Ft. Lauderdale Campus M,D,O
Florida State University M,D,O*†
Fordham University M,D,O*†
Georgia State University M,D*
Graduate School and University Center of the City University of New York D*†
Harvard University M,D,O*†
Holy Names College M,O
Howard University M,D,O*
Illinois State University M,D,O*†
Indiana State University M,D,O*†
Indiana University Bloomington M,D,O*
Indiana University of Pennsylvania M,O*†
John Carroll University M
Kansas State University M,D*†
Kean University M,O*†
Kent State University M,D*
La Sierra University M,O
Lindsey Wilson College M
Long Island University, Rockland Graduate Campus M
Loyola Marymount University M†
Loyola University Chicago M,D*†
Marist College M,O
McGill University M,D*
Memorial University of Newfoundland M†
Miami University M,O*†
Michigan State University M,D,O*†
Minot State University O
Mississippi State University M,D,O*
Montclair State University M†
Mount Saint Vincent University M
National-Louis University M,D,O
New Jersey City University M,O
New York University M,D,O*†
Northeastern University M*†
Northern Arizona University D
Northern Illinois University M,D*†
Oklahoma State University M,D*†
The Pennsylvania State University University Park Campus M,D*†
Purdue University M,D,O*
Rhode Island College M†
Rutgers, The State University of New Jersey, New Brunswick M,D*
Simon Fraser University M,D
Southern Illinois University Carbondale M,D*†
Southern Illinois University Edwardsville M†
Stanford University D*
State University of New York at Albany M,D,O*†

*P—first professional degree; M—master's degree; D—doctorate; O—other advanced degree; *full description and/or announcement in Book 2, 3, 4, 5, or 6; †full description in this book*

Teachers College Columbia University M,D*
Temple University M,D*†
Tennessee Technological University M,O*
Texas A&M University M,D*
Texas A&M University–Commerce M,D†
Texas Tech University M,D,O*†
Université de Moncton M
Université de Montréal M,D,O
Université du Québec en Outaouais M
Université du Québec à Trois-Rivières M
Université Laval M,D†
University at Buffalo, The State University of New York M,D,O*†
University of Alberta M,D*
The University of Arizona M,D*
The University of British Columbia M,D,O*
University of Calgary M,D*
University of California, Davis D*†
University of Colorado at Boulder M,D*
University of Colorado at Denver M*
University of Connecticut M,D*†
University of Denver M,D,O*†
University of Florida M,D,O*†
University of Georgia M,D,O*†
University of Hawaii at Manoa M,D*
University of Houston M,D*
University of Illinois at Urbana–Champaign M,D,O*
The University of Iowa M,D,O*
University of Kansas M,D*
University of Kentucky M,D,O*
University of Louisville M,D*†
University of Mary Hardin-Baylor M
University of Maryland, College Park M,D,O*
The University of Memphis M,D*†
University of Minnesota, Twin Cities Campus M,D,O*
University of Missouri–Columbia M,D,O*
University of Missouri–St. Louis M,D†
University of Nebraska at Omaha M,D,O
University of Nebraska–Lincoln M,O*†
University of Nevada, Las Vegas M,D*†
University of Nevada, Reno M,D,O*
University of New Brunswick Fredericton M
University of New Mexico M,D*†
The University of North Carolina at Chapel Hill M,D*†
University of Northern Colorado M,D†
University of Northern Iowa M,O
University of Oklahoma M,D*†
University of Pittsburgh D*†
University of Regina M,D,O
University of Saskatchewan M,D,O
University of South Carolina M,D*†
The University of South Dakota M,D,O†
University of Southern California M,D,O*†
The University of Tennessee M,D,O*†
The University of Texas at Austin M,D*
The University of Texas at El Paso M*†
The University of Texas at San Antonio M*
The University of Texas–Pan American M,D
University of the Pacific M,D,O*
University of Toledo M,D,O*†
University of Utah M,D*
University of Victoria M,D
University of Virginia M,D,O*
University of Washington M,D*
The University of Western Ontario M*
University of Wisconsin–Madison M,D*
University of Wisconsin–Milwaukee M
Wayne State University M,D,O*
West Virginia University M,D*
Wichita State University M,D,O*†
Widener University M,D*†

EDUCATION OF THE GIFTED

Arkansas State University M,D,O
Arkansas Tech University M
Ashland University M
Barry University M,D,O*†
Belmont University M
California State University, Los Angeles M,D
California State University, Northridge M
Carthage College M,O
Clark Atlanta University M,O
Cleveland State University M*†
The College of New Rochelle M,O†
The College of William and Mary M*†
Converse College M
Drury University M
Emporia State University M*†
Grand Valley State University M†
Hardin-Simmons University M
Indiana State University M,D,O*†
Jacksonville University M,O
Johns Hopkins University M,D,O*†
Johnson State College M
Kent State University M,D,O*
Liberty University M,D†
Maryville University of Saint Louis M
Millersville University of Pennsylvania M†
Minnesota State University, Mankato M
Mississippi University for Women M
Norfolk State University M†
Northeastern Illinois University M
Nova Southeastern University M,O*
Ohio University M,D*
Purdue University M,D,O*
Sierra Nevada College O
Teachers College Columbia University M,D*
Tennessee Technological University D*
Texas A&M University M,D*
University of Arkansas at Little Rock M
University of Central Arkansas M
University of Connecticut M,D*†
University of Georgia M,D,O*†
University of Houston M,D*
University of Louisiana at Lafayette M*
University of Minnesota, Twin Cities Campus M,D,O*
University of Nebraska at Kearney M
University of Northern Colorado M†
University of Northern Iowa M
University of South Alabama M*†
University of Southern Mississippi M,D,O
University of South Florida M*†
The University of Texas–Pan American M,D
West Virginia University M,D*
Whitworth College M
William Carey College M
Wright State University M*
Youngstown State University M

EDUCATION OF THE MULTIPLY HANDICAPPED

Boston College M,O*†
Cleveland State University M*†
Fresno Pacific University M
Gallaudet University M,D,O
Georgia State University M*
Hunter College of the City University of New York M†
Minnesota State University, Mankato M
Minot State University M
Montclair State University M†
Norfolk State University M†
University of Arkansas at Little Rock M
University of Illinois at Urbana–Champaign M,D,O*
University of South Alabama M*†
Western Oregon University M
West Virginia University M,D*

ELECTRICAL ENGINEERING

Air Force Institute of Technology M,D*
Alfred University M*†
Arizona State University M,D*
Arizona State University East M
Auburn University M,D*†
Boise State University M*
Boston University M,D*†
Bradley University M†
Brigham Young University M,D*
Brown University M,D*
Bucknell University M
California Institute of Technology M,D*
California Polytechnic State University, San Luis Obispo M†
California State Polytechnic University, Pomona M*
California State University, Chico M
California State University, Fresno M
California State University, Fullerton M
California State University, Long Beach M
California State University, Los Angeles M
California State University, Northridge M
California State University, Sacramento M
Capitol College M
Carleton University M,D
Carnegie Mellon University M,D*
Case Western Reserve University M,D*†
The Catholic University of America M,D*†
City College of the City University of New York M,D*†
Clarkson University M,D*
Clemson University M,D*
Cleveland State University M,D*†
Colorado State University M,D*
Colorado Technical University M
Columbia University M,D,O*†
Concordia University (Canada) M,D,O*†
Cornell University M,D*
Dalhousie University M,D*
Dartmouth College M,D*†
Drexel University M,D*†
Duke University M,D*†
École Polytechnique de Montréal M,D,O
Fairleigh Dickinson University, Metropolitan Campus M*†
Florida Agricultural and Mechanical University M,D*
Florida Atlantic University M,D*
Florida Institute of Technology M,D*†
Florida International University M,D*†
Florida State University M,D*†
Gannon University M
George Mason University M,D*†
The George Washington University M,D,O*†
Georgia Institute of Technology M,D*
Graduate School and University Center of the City University of New York D*†
Howard University M,D*
Illinois Institute of Technology M,D*†
Indiana University–Purdue University Indianapolis M,D*
Instituto Tecnológico y de Estudios Superiores de Monterrey, Campus Chihuahua M,O
Instituto Tecnológico y de Estudios Superiores de Monterrey, Campus Monterrey M,D
International Technological University M
Iowa State University of Science and Technology M,D*†
Johns Hopkins University M,D*†
Kansas State University M,D*†
Lamar University M,D*†
Lawrence Technological University M,D
Lehigh University M,D*
Louisiana State University and Agricultural and Mechanical College M,D*
Louisiana Tech University M,D*
Loyola Marymount University M†
Manhattan College M*†
Marquette University M,D*†
Massachusetts Institute of Technology M,D,O*
McGill University M,D*
McMaster University M,D
McNeese State University M
Memorial University of Newfoundland M,D†
Mercer University M
Michigan State University M,D*†
Michigan Technological University M,D*†
Minnesota State University, Mankato M
Mississippi State University M,D*
Montana State University–Bozeman M,D*
National Technological University M
Naval Postgraduate School M,D,O
New Jersey Institute of Technology M,D
New Mexico State University M,D
New York Institute of Technology M*†
North Carolina Agricultural and Technical State University M,D*
North Carolina State University M,D*
North Dakota State University M†
Northeastern University M,D*†
Northern Illinois University M*†
Northwestern Polytechnic University M
Northwestern University M,D,O*
Oakland University M†
OGI School of Science & Engineering at Oregon Health & Science University M,D*
The Ohio State University M,D*
Ohio University M,D*
Oklahoma State University M,D*†
Old Dominion University M,D*†
Oregon State University M,D*
The Pennsylvania State University Harrisburg Campus of the Capital College M*†
The Pennsylvania State University University Park Campus M,D*†
Polytechnic University, Brooklyn Campus M,D*
Polytechnic University, Long Island Graduate Center M,D
Polytechnic University, Westchester Graduate Center M,D
Portland State University M,D*
Princeton University M,D*
Purdue University M,D*
Queen's University at Kingston M,D
Rensselaer at Hartford M
Rensselaer Polytechnic Institute M,D*†
Rice University M,D*
Rochester Institute of Technology M*†
Rose-Hulman Institute of Technology M*
Royal Military College of Canada M,D
Rutgers, The State University of New Jersey, New Brunswick M,D*
St. Cloud State University M
St. Mary's University of San Antonio M
San Diego State University M*
San Jose State University M*
Santa Clara University M,D,O*
South Dakota School of Mines and Technology M,D*†
South Dakota State University M*
Southern Illinois University Carbondale M,D*†
Southern Illinois University Edwardsville M†
Southern Methodist University M,D*†
Southern Polytechnic State University M†
Stanford University M,D,O*
State University of New York at Binghamton M,D*†
State University of New York at New Paltz M
Stevens Institute of Technology M,D,O*†
Stony Brook University, State University of New York M,D*†
Syracuse University M,D,O*
Temple University M*†
Tennessee Technological University M,D*
Texas A&M University M,D*
Texas A&M University–Kingsville M*†
Texas Tech University M,D*†
Tufts University M,D,O*†
Tulane University M,D*†
Tuskegee University M
Union College (NY) M*
Universidad de las Américas–Puebla M
Université de Moncton M
Université du Québec à Trois-Rivières M,D
Université Laval M,D†
University at Buffalo, The State University of New York M,D*†
The University of Akron M,D†
The University of Alabama M,D*
The University of Alabama at Birmingham M,D*†
The University of Alabama in Huntsville M,D*
University of Alaska Fairbanks M*
University of Alberta M,D*
The University of Arizona M,D*
University of Arkansas M,D*
University of Bridgeport M*†
The University of British Columbia M,D*
University of Calgary M,D*
University of California, Berkeley M,D*
University of California, Davis M,D*†
University of California, Irvine M,D*
University of California, Los Angeles M,D*
University of California, Riverside M,D*
University of California, San Diego M,D*
University of California, Santa Barbara M,D*
University of California, Santa Cruz M,D*
University of Central Florida M,D,O*†
University of Cincinnati M,D*
University of Colorado at Boulder M,D*

University of Colorado at Colorado Springs M,D*
University of Colorado at Denver M*
University of Connecticut M,D*†
University of Dayton M,D*†
University of Delaware M,D*†
University of Denver M,D*†
University of Detroit Mercy M,D*
University of Florida M,D,O*†
University of Hawaii at Manoa M,D*
University of Houston M,D*
University of Idaho M,D*†
University of Illinois at Chicago M,D*
University of Illinois at Urbana–Champaign M,D*
The University of Iowa M,D*
University of Kansas M,D*
University of Kentucky M,D*
University of Louisville M*†
University of Maine M,D*
University of Manitoba M,D*
University of Maryland, Baltimore County M,D*†
University of Maryland, College Park M,D*
University of Massachusetts Amherst M,D*†
University of Massachusetts Dartmouth M,D,O*†
University of Massachusetts Lowell M,D*†
The University of Memphis M,D*†
University of Miami M,D*†
University of Michigan M,D*
University of Michigan–Dearborn M*†
University of Minnesota, Twin Cities Campus M,D*
University of Missouri–Columbia M,D*
University of Missouri–Rolla M,D*
University of Nebraska–Lincoln M,D*†
University of Nevada, Las Vegas M,D*†
University of Nevada, Reno M,D*
University of New Brunswick Fredericton M,D
University of New Hampshire M,D*†
University of New Haven M*†
University of New Mexico M,D*†
University of New Orleans M*
The University of North Carolina at Charlotte M,D*
University of North Dakota M*
University of Notre Dame M,D*†
University of Oklahoma M,D*†
University of Ottawa M,D,O*
University of Pennsylvania M,D*†
University of Pittsburgh M,D*†
University of Puerto Rico, Mayagüez Campus M*
University of Rhode Island M,D*
University of Rochester M,D*
University of Saskatchewan M,D
University of South Alabama M*†
University of South Carolina M,D*†
University of Southern California M,D,O*†
University of South Florida M,D*†
The University of Tennessee M,D*†
The University of Tennessee Space Institute M,D*
The University of Texas at Arlington M,D*†
The University of Texas at Austin M,D*
The University of Texas at Dallas M,D*
The University of Texas at El Paso M,D*†
The University of Texas at San Antonio M*
University of Toledo M,D*†
University of Toronto M,D*
University of Tulsa M†
University of Utah M,D,O*
University of Vermont M,D*†
University of Victoria M,D
University of Virginia M,D*
University of Washington M,D*
University of Waterloo M,D
University of Windsor M,D
University of Wisconsin–Madison M,D*
University of Wyoming M,D*†
Utah State University M,D,O*
Vanderbilt University M,D*
Villanova University M*†
Virginia Polytechnic Institute and State University M,D*
Washington State University M,D*
Washington State University Spokane M†
Washington University in St. Louis M,D*†
Wayne State University M,D*
Western Michigan University M,D*†
Western New England College M
West Virginia University M,D*
Wichita State University M,D*†
Widener University M*†
Wilkes University M
Worcester Polytechnic Institute M,D,O*†
Wright State University M*
Yale University M,D*
Youngstown State University M

ELECTRONIC COMMERCE

American University M*†
Audrey Cohen College M†
Bentley College M,O*
Boston University M*†
California State University, Hayward M
Cambridge College M†
Capitol College M
Carnegie Mellon University M*
City University M,O†
Claremont Graduate University M,D*
Clemson University M*
Columbia Southern University M
Concordia University (Canada) M,D,O*†
Creighton University M*
Dalhousie University M,D*
Dallas Baptist University M
Davenport University M
Davenport University M
DePaul University M*†
École des Hautes Études Commerciales de Montréal M,O*
Fairleigh Dickinson University, Metropolitan Campus M*†
Instituto Tecnológico y de Estudios Superiores de Monterrey, Campus Central de Veracruz M
Instituto Tecnológico y de Estudios Superiores de Monterrey, Campus Irapuato M,D
Johns Hopkins University M,O*†
Jones International University M*†
Marlboro College M*
Maryville University of Saint Louis M,O
Mercy College M*
Morehead State University M
The National Graduate School of Quality Management M*
National University M†
Northwestern University M*
Notre Dame de Namur University M
Old Dominion University M*†
Regis University M,O*†
Rensselaer Polytechnic Institute M,D*†
Sacred Heart University M,O*†
St. Edward's University M,O
Southern Illinois University Edwardsville M†
Stevens Institute of Technology M,O*†
Temple University M*†
Texas Tech University M*†
Université Laval M,O†
University at Buffalo, The State University of New York M,D,O*†
The University of Akron M†
University of Dallas M*
University of Denver M*†
University of Maryland University College M*
University of Minnesota, Twin Cities Campus M*
University of Missouri–St. Louis M,D,O†
University of New Brunswick Saint John M
University of Phoenix-Chicago Campus M
University of Phoenix–Colorado Campus M
University of Phoenix–Dallas Campus M
University of Phoenix–Hawaii Campus M
University of Phoenix–Houston Campus M
University of Phoenix-Kansas City Campus M
University of Phoenix–Louisiana Campus M
University of Phoenix–Ohio Campus M
University of Phoenix–Oklahoma City Campus M
University of Phoenix–Sacramento Campus M
University of Phoenix–St. Louis Campus M
University of Phoenix–Tulsa Campus M
University of Phoenix–West Michigan Campus M
University of St. Thomas (MN) M,O*†
University of San Diego M*†
Villa Julie College M
West Chester University of Pennsylvania M*†
Wright State University M*
Xavier University M*

ELECTRONIC MATERIALS

Colorado School of Mines M,D†
Northwestern University M,D,O*
Princeton University M,D*
University of Arkansas M,D*

ELEMENTARY EDUCATION

Abilene Christian University M
Adams State College M
Adelphi University M,O*
Alabama Agricultural and Mechanical University M,O
Alabama State University M,O
Alaska Pacific University M
Alcorn State University M,O
Alfred University M*†
American International College M,D,O*
American University M*†
Andrews University M
Anna Maria College M
Appalachian State University M
Arcadia University M,D,O†
Argosy University-Orange County M,D,O*
Arizona State University West M
Arkansas State University M,O
Arkansas Tech University M
Armstrong Atlantic State University M†
Auburn University M,D,O*†
Auburn University Montgomery M,O
Augustana College M
Austin College M
Austin Peay State University M,O
Ball State University M,D*
Bank Street College of Education M*
Barry University M,O*†
Bayamón Central University M
Bellarmine University M
Belmont University M
Benedictine University M†
Bethel College (TN) M
Bloomsburg University of Pennsylvania M
Boston College M*†
Boston University M*†
Bowie State University M
Bridgewater State College M
Brigham Young University M,D*
Brooklyn College of the City University of New York M†
Brown University M*
Butler University M
California State University, Fullerton M
California State University, Long Beach M
California State University, Los Angeles M
California State University, Northridge M
California State University, San Bernardino M
California State University, Stanislaus M
California University of Pennsylvania M
Campbell University M
Carson-Newman College M
Catawba College M
Centenary College of Louisiana M
Central Connecticut State University M*†
Central Michigan University M†
Central Missouri State University M,O†
Central Washington University M†
Chadron State College M,O
Charleston Southern University M
Chatham College M
Chestnut Hill College M†
Cheyney University of Pennsylvania M
Chicago State University M
City College of the City University of New York M*†
Clarion University of Pennsylvania M†
Clemson University M*
Cleveland State University M*†
Coastal Carolina University M
College of Charleston M*†
The College of New Jersey M†
The College of New Rochelle M†
College of St. Joseph M
The College of Saint Rose M*†
College of Staten Island of the City University of New York M†
The College of William and Mary M*†
The Colorado College M
Columbia College (SC) M
Columbia College Chicago M†
Concordia University (OR) M
Concordia University (NE) M
Connecticut College M
Converse College M
Cumberland College M,O
Dallas Baptist University M
Delta State University M,O
DePaul University M*†
Dowling College M
Drake University M*†
Drury University M
Duquesne University M*†
D'Youville College M,O†
East Carolina University M*†
Eastern Connecticut State University M
Eastern Illinois University M†
Eastern Kentucky University M
Eastern Michigan University M*
Eastern Nazarene College M,O
Eastern Oregon University M
Eastern Washington University M†
East Stroudsburg University of Pennsylvania M†
East Tennessee State University M†
Edinboro University of Pennsylvania M,O
Elms College M,O
Elon University M
Emmanuel College M*
Emporia State University M*†
Endicott College M
Evangel University M
Fairfield University M,O*
Fayetteville State University M
Ferris State University M
Fitchburg State College M†
Florida Agricultural and Mechanical University M*
Florida Atlantic University M*
Florida Atlantic University, Ft. Lauderdale Campus M,D,O
Florida Gulf Coast University M
Florida International University M*†
Florida State University M,D,O*†
Fordham University M,D,O*†
Fort Hays State University M
Francis Marion University M
Friends University M
Frostburg State University M
Furman University M
Gallaudet University M,D,O
Gardner-Webb University M
The George Washington University M*†
Grambling State University M
Grand Canyon University M
Grand Valley State University M†
Hampton University M*†
Harding University M
Harvard University M,D,O*†
Henderson State University M
Hofstra University M,O*
Holy Family College M
Hood College M
Houston Baptist University M
Howard University M*
Hunter College of the City University of New York M†
Immaculata University M,D,O†
Indiana State University M,D,O*†
Indiana University Bloomington M,D,O*
Indiana University Kokomo M
Indiana University Northwest M
Indiana University–Purdue University Fort Wayne M
Indiana University–Purdue University Indianapolis M*
Indiana University South Bend M
Indiana University Southeast M
Inter American University of Puerto Rico, Metropolitan Campus M
Iona College M*†
Iowa State University of Science and Technology M,D*†
Jackson State University M,D,O
Jacksonville State University M,O
Jacksonville University M
John Carroll University M
Johns Hopkins University M*†
Kansas State University M*†
Kutztown University of Pennsylvania M,O†
Lamar University M,O*†
Lander University M
Lehigh University M,D,O*
Lehman College of the City University of New York M
Lenoir-Rhyne College M
Lesley University M,D,O*†
Lewis & Clark College M
Liberty University M,D†
Lincoln University (MO) M
Long Island University, Brentwood Campus M
Long Island University, Brooklyn Campus M*
Long Island University, Rockland Graduate Campus M

*P—first professional degree; M—master's degree; D—doctorate; O—other advanced degree; *full description and/or announcement in Book 2, 3, 4, 5, or 6; †full description in this book*

Long Island University, Southampton College M
Long Island University, Westchester Graduate Campus M
Longwood College M
Louisiana State University and Agricultural and Mechanical College M,D,O*
Loyola Marymount University M†
Loyola University New Orleans M
Maharishi University of Management M
Manhattanville College M*†
Mansfield University of Pennsylvania M
Marshall University M*†
Mary Baldwin College M
Marymount University M,O†
Maryville University of Saint Louis M
Marywood University M*†
McDaniel College M
McNeese State University M
Mercy College M,O*
Miami University M*†
Middle Tennessee State University M,O*
Midwestern State University M
Millersville University of Pennsylvania M†
Mills College M,D*†
Minnesota State University, Mankato M,O
Minot State University M
Mississippi College M
Mississippi State University M,D,O*
Mississippi Valley State University M
Monmouth University M,O*†
Montana State University–Northern M
Morehead State University M
Morgan State University M*
Morningside College M
Mount Saint Mary College M
Mount St. Mary's College M*
Mount Saint Vincent University M
Murray State University M,O†
National-Louis University M
Nazareth College of Rochester M
Newman University M
New York Institute of Technology M,O*†
New York University M,D,O*†
Niagara University M†
North Carolina Agricultural and Technical State University M*
North Carolina Central University M
Northern Arizona University M
Northern Illinois University M,D*†
Northern Kentucky University M
Northern Michigan University M
Northern State University M
Northwestern Oklahoma State University M
Northwestern State University of Louisiana M,O
Northwestern University M*
Northwest Missouri State University M,O
Nova Southeastern University M,O*
Occidental College M
Ohio University M,D*
Oklahoma City University M
Old Dominion University M*†
Olivet Nazarene University M
Oregon State University M*
Pacific Lutheran University M†
Pacific University M
Palm Beach Atlantic University M
The Pennsylvania State University University Park Campus M,D*†
Pittsburg State University M
Plattsburgh State University of New York M
Plymouth State College M*
Portland State University M*
Purdue University M,D,O*
Purdue University Calumet M
Purdue University North Central M
Queens College of the City University of New York M,O†
Queens University of Charlotte M
Quinnipiac University M*†
Rhode Island College M†
Rider University O*
Rivier College M*†
Rockford College M
Rollins College M*
Roosevelt University M,D*†
Rosemont College M†
Rowan University M†
Rutgers, The State University of New Jersey, New Brunswick M,D*
Sacred Heart University M,O*†
Sage Graduate School M†
Saginaw Valley State University M
St. John Fisher College M
St. John's University (NY) M*†
Saint Peter's College M,O†
St. Thomas Aquinas College M
St. Thomas University M†
Saint Xavier University M,O*
Salem College M
Salem International University M
Salem State College M
Salisbury University M
Samford University M,D,O
Sam Houston State University M,D,O*
San Diego State University M*
San Francisco State University M
San Jose State University M*
Seton Hall University M*†
Seton Hill University M,O†
Shenandoah University M,D,O
Shippensburg University of Pennsylvania M,O†
Siena Heights University M
Sierra Nevada College O
Simmons College M,O*
Sinte Gleska University M
Slippery Rock University of Pennsylvania M†
Smith College M*
South Carolina State University M
Southeastern Oklahoma State University M
Southeast Missouri State University M
Southern Arkansas University–Magnolia M
Southern Connecticut State University M,O†
Southern Illinois University Edwardsville M†
Southern Oregon University M
Southern University and Agricultural and Mechanical College M*
Southwestern Adventist University M
Southwestern Oklahoma State University M
Southwest Missouri State University M,O*†
Southwest Texas State University M*
Spalding University M†
Spring Hill College M
State University of New York at Binghamton M*†
State University of New York at New Paltz M
State University of New York at Oswego M
State University of New York College at Brockport M*†
State University of New York College at Buffalo M,O
State University of New York College at Cortland M
State University of New York College at Fredonia M
State University of New York College at Geneseo M
State University of New York College at Oneonta M
State University of New York College at Potsdam M
Stephen F. Austin State University M
Stetson University M,O
Sul Ross State University M*
Sunbridge College M
Syracuse University M,O*
Teachers College Columbia University M*
Temple University M,D*†
Tennessee State University M,D*
Tennessee Technological University M,O*
Texas A&M University–Commerce M,D†
Texas A&M University–Corpus Christi M
Texas A&M University–Kingsville M*†
Texas A&M University–Texarkana M
Texas Christian University M,O*
Texas Southern University M,D†
Texas Tech University M,D,O*†
Texas Woman's University M,D*†
Towson University M†
Trinity College (DC) M†
Troy State University M,O
Troy State University Montgomery M
Tufts University M,O*†
Union College (KY) M
Université de Sherbrooke M,O
University at Buffalo, The State University of New York M,D,O*†
The University of Akron M,D†
The University of Alabama M,D,O*
The University of Alabama at Birmingham M*†
University of Alaska Southeast M
University of Alberta M,D*
The University of Arizona M,D*
University of Arkansas M,O*
University of Arkansas at Monticello M
University of Arkansas at Pine Bluff M
University of Bridgeport M,O*†
University of California, Irvine M,D*
University of Central Arkansas M
University of Central Florida M,D*†
University of Central Oklahoma M
University of Cincinnati M*
University of Connecticut M,D*†
The University of Findlay M
University of Florida M,D,O*†
University of Georgia M,D,O*†
University of Great Falls M
University of Hartford M*
University of Hawaii at Manoa M*
University of Houston M,D*
University of Idaho M,D,O*†
University of Illinois at Chicago M,D*
University of Indianapolis M
The University of Iowa M,D*
University of Louisiana at Monroe M,O
University of Louisville M*†
University of Maine M,O*
University of Mary M
University of Maryland, Baltimore County M,D*†
University of Massachusetts Amherst M,D,O*†
University of Massachusetts Boston M,D,O*†
The University of Memphis M,D*†
University of Miami M,O*†
University of Minnesota, Twin Cities Campus M,D*
University of Missouri–Columbia M,D,O*
University of Missouri–St. Louis M,D†
University of Montevallo M
University of Nebraska at Kearney M
University of Nebraska at Omaha M
University of Nevada, Las Vegas M,D,O*†
University of Nevada, Reno M,D,O*
University of New Hampshire M*†
University of New Mexico M*†
University of North Alabama M,O
The University of North Carolina at Chapel Hill M*†
The University of North Carolina at Charlotte M*
The University of North Carolina at Pembroke M
The University of North Carolina at Wilmington M*
University of North Dakota M,D*
University of Northern Colorado M,D†
University of Northern Iowa M
University of North Florida M
University of North Texas M*†
University of Oklahoma M,D,O*†
University of Pennsylvania M*†
University of Pittsburgh M*†
University of Puget Sound M
University of Rhode Island M*
The University of Scranton M†
University of South Alabama M,O*†
University of South Carolina M,D*†
University of South Carolina Aiken M
University of South Carolina Spartanburg M
The University of South Dakota M†
University of Southern Indiana M
University of Southern Mississippi M,D,O
University of South Florida M,D,O*†
The University of Tennessee M,D,O*†
The University of Texas at Brownsville M
The University of Texas at San Antonio M*
The University of Texas of the Permian Basin M
The University of Texas–Pan American M
University of the Incarnate Word M†
University of Toledo M,D,O*†
The University of West Alabama M
University of West Florida M
University of Wisconsin–Eau Claire M†
University of Wisconsin–La Crosse M†
University of Wisconsin–Milwaukee M
University of Wisconsin–Platteville M
University of Wisconsin–River Falls M
University of Wisconsin–Stevens Point M
Utah State University M*
Vanderbilt University M,D*
Villanova University M*†
Wagner College M
Washington State University M,D*
Washington University in St. Louis M*†
Wayne State College M
Wayne State University M,D,O*
West Chester University of Pennsylvania M*†
Western Carolina University M†
Western Illinois University M,O
Western Kentucky University M,O†
Western Michigan University M*†
Western New Mexico University M
Western Washington University M
Westfield State College M
Westminster College (PA) M,O
West Texas A&M University M†
West Virginia University M*
Wheelock College M*
Whittier College M
Widener University M,D*†
Wilkes University M
William Carey College M
William Paterson University of New Jersey M*†
Wilmington College M,D
Wingate University M
Winthrop University M
Worcester State College M
Wright State University M*
Xavier University M*
Youngstown State University M

EMERGENCY MEDICAL SERVICES

Alderson-Broaddus College M
Drexel University M*†
Mountain State University M†
New York Medical College M,O*
Uniformed Services University of the Health Sciences M,D*
Université de Montréal O
Université Laval O†

ENERGY AND POWER ENGINEERING

New York Institute of Technology M,O*†
Rensselaer Polytechnic Institute M,D*†
Southern Illinois University Carbondale D*†
University of Alberta M,D*
University of Massachusetts Lowell M,D*†
The University of Memphis M,D*†
University of North Dakota D*
Worcester Polytechnic Institute M,D,O*†

ENERGY MANAGEMENT AND POLICY

Boston University M*†
New York Institute of Technology M,O*†
Université du Québec à Trois-Rivières M,D
Université du Québec, Institut National de la Recherche Scientifique M,D
University of California, Berkeley M,D*

ENGINEERING AND APPLIED SCIENCES—GENERAL

Air Force Institute of Technology M,D*
Alabama Agricultural and Mechanical University M
American University in Cairo M,O
Andrews University M
Arizona State University M,D*
Arizona State University East M
Auburn University M,D*†
Boston University M,D*†
Bradley University M†
Brigham Young University M,D*
Brown University M,D*
Bucknell University M
California Institute of Technology M,D,O*
California National University for Advanced Studies M
California Polytechnic State University, San Luis Obispo M†
California State Polytechnic University, Pomona M*
California State University, Chico M
California State University, Fresno M
California State University, Fullerton M

Institution	Degrees
California State University, Long Beach	M,D,O
California State University, Los Angeles	M
California State University, Northridge	M
California State University, Sacramento	M
Carleton University	M,D
Carnegie Mellon University	M,D*
Case Western Reserve University	M,D*†
The Catholic University of America	M,D*†
Central Connecticut State University	M*†
Central Missouri State University	M,O†
Central Washington University	M†
Christian Brothers University	M
City College of the City University of New York	M,D*†
Clarkson University	M,D*
Clemson University	M,D*
Cleveland State University	M,D*†
Colorado School of Mines	M,D,O†
Colorado State University	M,D*
Columbia University	M,D,O*†
Concordia University (Canada)	M,D,O*†
Cornell University	M,D*
Dalhousie University	M,D*
Dartmouth College	M,D*†
Drexel University	M,D*†
Duke University	M,D*†
East Carolina University	M*†
Eastern Illinois University	M†
East Tennessee State University	M†
École Polytechnique de Montréal	M,D,O
Fairfield University	M*
Fairleigh Dickinson University, Metropolitan Campus	M*†
Florida Agricultural and Mechanical University	M,D*
Florida Atlantic University	M,D*
Florida Institute of Technology	M,D*†
Florida International University	M,D*†
Florida State University	M,D*†
Gannon University	M
George Mason University	M,D*†
The George Washington University	M,D,O*†
Georgia Institute of Technology	M,D,O*
Georgia Southern University	M
Golden Gate University	M,O
Graduate School and University Center of the City University of New York	D*†
Grand Valley State University	M†
Harvard University	M,D*†
Harvey Mudd College	M
Howard University	M,D*
Idaho State University	M,D*
Illinois Institute of Technology	M,D*†
Indiana State University	M,D*†
Indiana University–Purdue University Fort Wayne	M
Indiana University–Purdue University Indianapolis	M*
Instituto Tecnológico y de Estudios Superiores de Monterrey, Campus Ciudad Obregón	M
Instituto Tecnológico y de Estudios Superiores de Monterrey, Campus Monterrey	M,D
Iowa State University of Science and Technology	M,D*†
Johns Hopkins University	M,D*†
Kansas State University	M,D*†
Kent State University	M*
Kettering University	M
Lakehead University	M
Lamar University	M,D*†
Laurentian University	M
Lawrence Technological University	M,D
Lehigh University	M,D*
Louisiana State University and Agricultural and Mechanical College	M,D*
Louisiana Tech University	M,D*
Loyola College in Maryland	M
Loyola Marymount University	M†
Manhattan College	M*†
Marquette University	M,D*†
Marshall University	M*†
Massachusetts Institute of Technology	M,D,O*
McGill University	M,D,O*
McMaster University	M,D
McNeese State University	M
Memorial University of Newfoundland	M,D†
Mercer University	M
Miami University	M*†
Michigan State University	M,D*†
Michigan Technological University	M,D*†
Milwaukee School of Engineering	M*
Mississippi State University	M,D*
Montana State University–Bozeman	M,D*
Montana Tech of The University of Montana	M
Morgan State University	M,D*
National Technological University	M
National University	M†
New Jersey Institute of Technology	M,D,O
New Mexico State University	M,D
New York Institute of Technology	M,O*†
North Carolina Agricultural and Technical State University	M,D*
North Carolina State University	M*
North Dakota State University	M,D†
Northeastern University	M,D*†
Northern Arizona University	M
Northern Illinois University	M*†
Northwestern Polytechnic University	M
Northwestern University	M,D,O*
Oakland University	M,D†
The Ohio State University	M,D*
Ohio University	M,D*
Oklahoma State University	M,D*†
Old Dominion University	M,D*†
Oregon State University	M,D*
The Pennsylvania State University at Erie, The Behrend College	M
The Pennsylvania State University Harrisburg Campus of the Capital College	M*†
The Pennsylvania State University University Park Campus	M,D*†
Pittsburg State University	M
Portland State University	M,D,O*
Prairie View A&M University	M
Princeton University	M,D*
Purdue University	M,D*
Purdue University Calumet	M
Queen's University at Kingston	M,D
Rensselaer at Hartford	M
Rensselaer Polytechnic Institute	M,D*†
Rice University	M,D*
Robert Morris University	M†
Rochester Institute of Technology	M,O*†
Rose-Hulman Institute of Technology	M*
Rowan University	M†
Royal Military College of Canada	M,D
Rutgers, The State University of New Jersey, New Brunswick	M,D*
Saginaw Valley State University	M
St. Cloud State University	M
St. Mary's University of San Antonio	M
San Diego State University	M,D*
San Francisco State University	M
San Jose State University	M*
Santa Clara University	M,D,O*
Seattle University	M*†
Simon Fraser University	M,D
South Dakota State University	M,D*
Southern Illinois University Carbondale	M,D*†
Southern Illinois University Edwardsville	M†
Southern Methodist University	M,D*†
Southern Polytechnic State University	M†
Stanford University	M,D,O*
State University of New York at Binghamton	M,D*†
State University of New York Institute of Technology at Utica/Rome	M*†
Stevens Institute of Technology	M,D,O*†
Stony Brook University, State University of New York	M,D,O*†
Syracuse University	M,D,O*
Temple University	M,D*†
Tennessee State University	M*
Tennessee Technological University	M,D*
Texas A&M University	M,D*
Texas A&M University–Kingsville	M*†
Texas Tech University	M,D*†
Tufts University	M,D*†
Tulane University	M,D*†
Tuskegee University	M,D
Union College (NY)	M*
Universidad de las Américas–Puebla	M
Université de Moncton	M
Université de Sherbrooke	M,D
Université du Québec à Chicoutimi	M,D
Université du Québec, École de technologie supérieure	M,D,O
Université Laval	M,D,O†
University at Buffalo, The State University of New York	M,D*†
The University of Akron	M,D†
The University of Alabama	M,D*
The University of Alabama at Birmingham	M,D*†
The University of Alabama in Huntsville	M,D*
University of Alaska Anchorage	M
The University of Arizona	M,D*
University of Arkansas	M,D*
University of Bridgeport	M*†
The University of British Columbia	M,D*
University of Calgary	M,D*
University of California, Berkeley	M,D*
University of California, Davis	M,D,O*†
University of California, Irvine	M,D*
University of California, Los Angeles	M,D*
University of California, Santa Barbara	M,D*
University of Central Florida	M,D,O*†
University of Cincinnati	M,D*
University of Colorado at Boulder	M,D*
University of Colorado at Colorado Springs	M,D*
University of Colorado at Denver	M,D*
University of Connecticut	M,D*†
University of Dayton	M,D*†
University of Delaware	M,D*†
University of Denver	M,D*†
University of Detroit Mercy	M,D*
University of Florida	M,D,O*†
University of Guelph	M,D
University of Hartford	M*
University of Hawaii at Manoa	M,D*
University of Houston	M,D*
University of Idaho	M,D*†
University of Illinois at Chicago	M,D*
University of Illinois at Urbana–Champaign	M,D*
The University of Iowa	M,D*
University of Kansas	M,D*
University of Kentucky	M,D*
University of Louisiana at Lafayette	M,D*
University of Louisville	M,D*†
University of Maine	M,D*
University of Manitoba	M,D*
University of Maryland, Baltimore County	M,D*†
University of Maryland, College Park	M,D*
University of Massachusetts Amherst	M,D*†
University of Massachusetts Dartmouth	M,D,O*†
University of Massachusetts Lowell	M,D*†
The University of Memphis	M,D*†
University of Miami	M,D*†
University of Michigan	M,D,O*
University of Michigan–Dearborn	M,D*†
University of Minnesota, Twin Cities Campus	M,D*
University of Mississippi	M,D*
University of Missouri–Columbia	M,D*
University of Missouri–Rolla	M,D*
University of Nebraska–Lincoln	M,D*†
University of Nevada, Las Vegas	M,D*†
University of Nevada, Reno	M,D*
University of New Brunswick Fredericton	M,D,O
University of New Haven	M,O*†
University of New Mexico	M,D*†
University of New Orleans	M,D,O*
The University of North Carolina at Charlotte	M,D*
University of North Dakota	M,D*
University of North Texas	M*†
University of Notre Dame	M,D*†
University of Oklahoma	M,D*†
University of Ottawa	M,D,O*
University of Pennsylvania	M,D,O*†
University of Pittsburgh	M,D,O*†
University of Portland	M
University of Puerto Rico, Mayagüez Campus	M,D*
University of Regina	M,D
University of Rhode Island	M,D*
University of Rochester	M,D*
University of St. Thomas (MN)	M,O*†
University of Saskatchewan	M,D,O
University of South Alabama	M*†
University of South Carolina	M,D*†
University of Southern California	M,D,O*†
University of Southern Colorado	M
University of Southern Indiana	M
University of Southern Mississippi	M
University of South Florida	M,D*†
The University of Tennessee	M,D*†
The University of Tennessee at Chattanooga	M
The University of Tennessee Space Institute	M,D*
The University of Texas at Arlington	M,D*†
The University of Texas at Austin	M,D*
The University of Texas at Dallas	M,D*
The University of Texas at El Paso	M,D*†
The University of Texas at San Antonio	M*
The University of Texas at Tyler	M
University of Toledo	M*†
University of Toronto	M,D*
University of Tulsa	M,D†
University of Utah	M,D,O*
University of Vermont	M,D*†
University of Victoria	M,D
University of Virginia	M,D*
University of Washington	M,D*
University of Waterloo	M,D
The University of Western Ontario	M,D*
University of Windsor	M,D
University of Wisconsin–Madison	M,D,O*
University of Wisconsin–Milwaukee	M,D
University of Wisconsin–Platteville	M
University of Wyoming	M,D*†
Utah State University	M,D,O*
Vanderbilt University	M,D*
Villanova University	M,O*†
Virginia Commonwealth University	M,D*†
Virginia Polytechnic Institute and State University	M,D*
Washington State University	M,D*
Washington University in St. Louis	M,D*†
Wayne State University	M,D,O*
Western Michigan University	M,D*†
Western New England College	M
West Texas A&M University	M†
West Virginia University	M,D*
West Virginia University Institute of Technology	M
Wichita State University	M,D*†
Widener University	M*†
Worcester Polytechnic Institute	M,D,O*†
Wright State University	M,D*
Yale University	M,D*
Youngstown State University	M

ENGINEERING DESIGN

Institution	Degrees
The Catholic University of America	M,D*†
Kettering University	M
Rochester Institute of Technology	M*†
Stanford University	M*
University of Central Florida	M,D,O*†
University of Illinois at Urbana–Champaign	M*
University of New Haven	M,O*†

ENGINEERING MANAGEMENT

Institution	Degrees
Air Force Institute of Technology	M*
California Polytechnic State University, San Luis Obispo	M†
California State University, Northridge	M
The Catholic University of America	M*†
Clarkson University	M*
Colorado School of Mines	M,D†
Colorado State University	M,D*
Dallas Baptist University	M
Dartmouth College	M*†
Drexel University	M,D*†
Duke University	M*†
Florida Institute of Technology	M*†
The George Washington University	M,D,O*†
Instituto Tecnológico y de Estudios Superiores de Monterrey, Campus Chihuahua	M,O
Kansas State University	M,D*†
Lamar University	M*†
Long Island University, C.W. Post Campus	M*†
Loyola Marymount University	M†
Marquette University	M,D*†
Massachusetts Institute of Technology	M*

*P—first professional degree; M—master's degree; D—doctorate; O—other advanced degree; *full description and/or announcement in Book 2, 3, 4, 5, or 6; †full description in this book*

Mercer University M
Milwaukee School of Engineering M*
National Technological University M
New Jersey Institute of Technology M
Northeastern University M,D*†
Northwestern University M*
Oakland University M†
Ohio University M,D*
Old Dominion University M,D*†
The Pennsylvania State University University Park Campus M*†
Point Park College M*
Polytechnic University of Puerto Rico M
Portland State University M,D*
Rensselaer Polytechnic Institute M,D*†
Robert Morris University M†
Rochester Institute of Technology M*†
Rose-Hulman Institute of Technology M*
Saint Martin's College M
St. Mary's University of San Antonio M
Santa Clara University M*
Southern Methodist University M,D*†
Stanford University M,D*
Syracuse University M*
Texas Tech University M,D*†
Tufts University M*†
Université de Sherbrooke M
The University of Akron M†
University of Alaska Anchorage M
University of Alberta M,D*
University of Central Florida M,D,O*†
University of Colorado at Boulder M*
University of Colorado at Colorado Springs M*
University of Dayton M*†
University of Denver M*†
University of Detroit Mercy M*
University of Florida M,D,O*†
University of Kansas M*
University of Louisiana at Lafayette M*
University of Louisville M*†
University of Maryland, Baltimore County M*†
University of Massachusetts Amherst M*†
University of Michigan–Dearborn M*†
University of Minnesota, Duluth M*
University of Missouri–Rolla M,D*
University of New Orleans M,O*
The University of North Carolina at Charlotte M*
University of Oklahoma M*†
University of Ottawa M,O*
University of St. Thomas (MN) M,O*†
University of Southern California M*†
University of South Florida M,D*†
The University of Tennessee M*†
The University of Tennessee at Chattanooga M
The University of Tennessee Space Institute M*
University of Tulsa M†
University of Waterloo M,D
Virginia Polytechnic Institute and State University M*
Washington State University Spokane M†
Wayne State University M*
Western Michigan University M*†
Widener University M*†

ENGINEERING PHYSICS

Air Force Institute of Technology M,D*
Cornell University M,D*
École Polytechnique de Montréal M,D,O
George Mason University M*†
McMaster University M,D
Michigan Technological University D*†
Polytechnic University, Long Island Graduate Center M
Polytechnic University, Westchester Graduate Center M
Rensselaer Polytechnic Institute M,D*†
Stevens Institute of Technology M,D,O*†
The University of British Columbia M*
University of California, San Diego M,D*
University of Florida M,D,O*†
University of Maine M*
University of Oklahoma M,D*†
University of South Florida M,D*†
University of Vermont M*†
University of Virginia M,D*
University of Wisconsin–Madison M,D*
Yale University M,D*

ENGLISH

Abilene Christian University M
Acadia University M
Adelphi University M*
American University in Cairo M
Andrews University M
Angelo State University M†
Appalachian State University M
Arcadia University M†
Arizona State University M,D*
Arkansas State University M,O
Arkansas Tech University M
Auburn University M,D*†
Austin Peay State University M
Ball State University M,D*
Baylor University M,D*†
Belmont University M
Bemidji State University M
Bennington College M†
Boise State University M*
Boston College M,D,O*†
Boston University M,D*†
Bowling Green State University M,D*†
Bradley University M†
Brandeis University M,D*†
Bridgewater State College M
Brigham Young University M*
Brooklyn College of the City University of New York M,D†
Brown University M,D*
Bucknell University M
Butler University M
California Polytechnic State University, San Luis Obispo M†
California State Polytechnic University, Pomona M*
California State University, Bakersfield M
California State University, Chico M
California State University, Dominguez Hills M,O†
California State University, Fresno M
California State University, Fullerton M
California State University, Hayward M
California State University, Long Beach M
California State University, Los Angeles M
California State University, Northridge M
California State University, Sacramento M
California State University, San Bernardino M
California State University, San Marcos M
California State University, Stanislaus M
Carleton University M
Carnegie Mellon University M,D*
Case Western Reserve University M,D*†
The Catholic University of America M,D*†
Central Connecticut State University M*†
Central Michigan University M†
Central Missouri State University M†
Central Washington University M†
Chapman University M*†
Chicago State University M
The Citadel, The Military College of South Carolina M
City College of the City University of New York M*†
Claremont Graduate University M,D*
Clarion University of Pennsylvania M†
Clark Atlanta University M
Clark University M*†
Clemson University M*
Cleveland State University M*†
College of Charleston M*†
The College of New Jersey M†
The College of Saint Rose M*†
College of Staten Island of the City University of New York M†
Colorado State University M*
Columbia University M,D*†
Concordia University (Canada) M*†
Connecticut College M
Converse College M
Cornell University M,D*
Dalhousie University M,D*
DePaul University M*†
Drew University M,D†
Duke University D*†
Duquesne University M,D*†
East Carolina University M*†
Eastern Illinois University M†
Eastern Kentucky University M
Eastern Michigan University M*
Eastern New Mexico University M
Eastern Washington University M†
East Tennessee State University M†
Emory University D*†
Emporia State University M*†
Fairleigh Dickinson University, Metropolitan Campus M*†
Fayetteville State University M
Florida Atlantic University M*
Florida International University M*†
Florida State University M,D*†
Fordham University M,D*†
Fort Hays State University M
Gannon University M
Gardner-Webb University M
George Mason University M*†
Georgetown University M*
The George Washington University M,D*†
Georgia College & State University M
Georgia Southern University M
Georgia State University M,D*
Governors State University M
Graduate School and University Center of the City University of New York D*†
Hardin-Simmons University M
Harvard University M,D,O*†
Henderson State University M
Hofstra University M*
Hollins University M
Holy Names College M
Howard University M,D*
Humboldt State University M
Hunter College of the City University of New York M†
Idaho State University M,D*
Illinois State University M,D*†
Indiana State University M,O*†
Indiana University Bloomington M,D*
Indiana University of Pennsylvania M,D*†
Indiana University–Purdue University Fort Wayne M
Indiana University–Purdue University Indianapolis M*
Iona College M*†
Iowa State University of Science and Technology M,D*†
Jackson State University M
Jacksonville State University M
James Madison University M
John Carroll University M
Johns Hopkins University D*†
Kansas State University M*†
Kent State University M,D*
Kutztown University of Pennsylvania M†
Lakehead University M
Lamar University M*†
La Sierra University M
Lehigh University M,D*
Lehman College of the City University of New York M
Long Island University, Brooklyn Campus M*
Long Island University, C.W. Post Campus M*†
Long Island University, Southampton College M
Longwood College M
Loras College M
Louisiana State University and Agricultural and Mechanical College M,D*
Louisiana Tech University M*
Loyola Marymount University M†
Loyola University Chicago M,D*†
Madonna University M
Maharishi University of Management M
Marquette University M,D*†
Marshall University M*†
Marymount University M†
McGill University M,D*
McMaster University M,D
McNeese State University M
Memorial University of Newfoundland M,D†
Mercy College M*
Miami University M,D*†
Michigan State University M,D*†
Middlebury College M
Middle Tennessee State University M,D*
Midwestern State University M
Millersville University of Pennsylvania M†
Mills College M*†
Minnesota State University, Mankato M
Mississippi College M
Mississippi State University M*
Montana State University–Bozeman M*
Montclair State University M†
Morehead State University M
Morgan State University M,D*
Murray State University M†
New Mexico Highlands University M
New Mexico State University M,D
New York University M,D*†
North Carolina Agricultural and Technical State University M*
North Carolina Central University M
North Carolina State University M*
North Dakota State University M†
Northeastern Illinois University M
Northeastern State University M
Northeastern University M,D,O*†
Northern Arizona University M,D,O
Northern Illinois University M,D*†
Northern Michigan University M
Northwestern State University of Louisiana M
Northwestern University M,D*
Northwest Missouri State University M
Notre Dame de Namur University M
Oakland University M†
The Ohio State University M,D*
Ohio University M,D*
Oklahoma State University M,D*†
Old Dominion University M*†
Oregon State University M*
Our Lady of the Lake University of San Antonio M
The Pennsylvania State University University Park Campus M,D*†
Pittsburg State University M
Portland State University M*
Prairie View A&M University M
Princeton University D*
Purdue University M,D*
Purdue University Calumet M
Queens College of the City University of New York M†
Queen's University at Kingston M,D
Radford University M†
Rhode Island College M†
Rice University M,D*
Rivier College M*†
Roosevelt University M*†
Rosemont College M†
Rutgers, The State University of New Jersey, Camden M†
Rutgers, The State University of New Jersey, Newark M*†
Rutgers, The State University of New Jersey, New Brunswick D*
St. Bonaventure University M
St. Cloud State University M
St. Francis Xavier University M
St. John's University (NY) M,D*†
Saint Louis University M,D*†
St. Mary's University of San Antonio M
Saint Xavier University M,O*
Salem State College M
Salisbury University M
Sam Houston State University M*
San Diego State University M*
San Francisco State University M,O
San Jose State University M*
Seton Hall University M*†
Simmons College M*
Simon Fraser University M,D
Slippery Rock University of Pennsylvania M†
Sonoma State University M
South Dakota State University M*
Southeastern Louisiana University M
Southeast Missouri State University M
Southern Connecticut State University M†
Southern Illinois University Carbondale M,D*†
Southern Illinois University Edwardsville M†
Southern Methodist University M*†
Southwest Missouri State University M*†
Southwest Texas State University M*
Stanford University M,D*
State University of New York at Albany M,D*†
State University of New York at Binghamton M,D*†
State University of New York at New Paltz M
State University of New York at Oswego M
State University of New York College at Brockport M*†
State University of New York College at Buffalo M
State University of New York College at Cortland M
State University of New York College at Fredonia M
State University of New York College at Potsdam M

State University of West Georgia M
Stephen F. Austin State University M
Stetson University M
Stony Brook University, State University of New York M,D*†
Sul Ross State University M*
Syracuse University M,D*
Tarleton State University M
Temple University M,D*†
Tennessee State University M*
Tennessee Technological University M*
Texas A&M International University M
Texas A&M University M,D*
Texas A&M University–Commerce M,D†
Texas A&M University–Corpus Christi M
Texas A&M University–Kingsville M*†
Texas Christian University M,D*
Texas Southern University M†
Texas Tech University M,D*†
Texas Woman's University M,D*†
Trinity College (CT) M
Truman State University M†
Tufts University M,D*†
Tulane University M,D*†
Universidad de las Américas–Puebla M
Université de Montréal M,D
Université Laval M,D†
University at Buffalo, The State University of New York M,D*†
The University of Akron M†
The University of Alabama M,D*
The University of Alabama at Birmingham M*†
The University of Alabama in Huntsville M,O*
University of Alaska Anchorage M
University of Alaska Fairbanks M*
University of Alberta M,D*
The University of Arizona M,D*
University of Arkansas M,D*
The University of British Columbia M,D*
University of Calgary M,D*
University of California, Berkeley D*
University of California, Davis M,D*†
University of California, Irvine M,D*
University of California, Los Angeles M,D*
University of California, Riverside M,D*
University of California, San Diego M,D*
University of California, Santa Barbara D*
University of Central Arkansas M
University of Central Florida M,O*†
University of Central Oklahoma M
University of Chicago M,D*
University of Cincinnati M,D*
University of Colorado at Boulder M,D*
University of Colorado at Denver M*
University of Connecticut M,D*†
University of Dallas M*
University of Dayton M*†
University of Delaware M,D*†
University of Denver M,D*†
University of Florida M,D*†
University of Georgia M,D*†
University of Guelph M,D
University of Hawaii at Manoa M,D*
University of Houston M,D*
University of Houston–Clear Lake M*†
University of Idaho M*†
University of Illinois at Chicago M,D*
University of Illinois at Springfield M†
University of Illinois at Urbana–Champaign M,D*
University of Indianapolis M
The University of Iowa M,D*
University of Kansas M,D*
University of Kentucky M,D*
The University of Lethbridge M,D
University of Louisiana at Lafayette M,D*
University of Louisiana at Monroe M
University of Louisville M,D*†
University of Maine M*
University of Manitoba M,D*
University of Maryland, College Park M,D*
University of Massachusetts Amherst M,D*†
University of Massachusetts Boston M*†
The University of Memphis M,D*†
University of Miami M,D*†
University of Michigan M,D,O*
University of Minnesota, Duluth M*
University of Minnesota, Twin Cities Campus M,D*
University of Mississippi M,D*
University of Missouri–Columbia M,D*
University of Missouri–Kansas City M,D*†
University of Missouri–St. Louis M†
The University of Montana–Missoula M*†
University of Montevallo M
University of Nebraska at Kearney M
University of Nebraska at Omaha M,O
University of Nebraska–Lincoln M,D*†
University of Nevada, Las Vegas M,D*†
University of Nevada, Reno M,D*
University of New Brunswick Fredericton M,D
University of New Hampshire M,D*†
University of New Mexico M,D*†
University of New Orleans M*
University of North Alabama M
The University of North Carolina at Chapel Hill M,D*†
The University of North Carolina at Charlotte M*
The University of North Carolina at Greensboro M,D,O†
The University of North Carolina at Wilmington M*
University of North Dakota M,D*
University of Northern Colorado M†
University of Northern Iowa M
University of North Florida M
University of North Texas M,D*†
University of Notre Dame M,D*†
University of Oklahoma M,D*†
University of Oregon M,D*
University of Ottawa M,D*
University of Pennsylvania M,D*†
University of Pittsburgh M,D*†
University of Puerto Rico, Mayagüez Campus M*
University of Puerto Rico, Río Piedras M*
University of Regina M,D
University of Rhode Island M,D*
University of Richmond M*†
University of Rochester M,D*
University of St. Thomas (MN) M*†
University of Saskatchewan M,D
The University of Scranton M†
University of South Alabama M*†
University of South Carolina M,D*†
The University of South Dakota M,D†
University of Southern California M,D*†
University of Southern Mississippi M,D
University of South Florida M,D*†
The University of Tennessee M,D*†
The University of Tennessee at Chattanooga M
The University of Texas at Arlington M,D*†
The University of Texas at Austin M,D*
The University of Texas at Brownsville M
The University of Texas at El Paso M*†
The University of Texas at San Antonio M*
The University of Texas at Tyler M
The University of Texas of the Permian Basin M
The University of Texas–Pan American M
University of the Incarnate Word M†
University of Toledo M*†
University of Toronto M,D*
University of Tulsa M,D†
University of Utah M,D*
University of Vermont M*†
University of Victoria M,D
University of Virginia M,D*
University of Washington M,D*
University of Waterloo M,D
The University of Western Ontario M,D*
University of West Florida M
University of Windsor M
University of Wisconsin–Eau Claire M†
University of Wisconsin–Madison M,D*
University of Wisconsin–Milwaukee M,D
University of Wisconsin–Oshkosh M*
University of Wisconsin–Stevens Point M
University of Wyoming M*†
Utah State University M*
Valdosta State University M
Valparaiso University M
Vanderbilt University M,D*
Villanova University M*†
Virginia Commonwealth University M*†
Virginia Polytechnic Institute and State University M*
Virginia State University M
Wake Forest University M*†
Washington College M
Washington State University M,D*
Washington University in St. Louis M,D*†
Wayne State University M,D*
West Chester University of Pennsylvania M*†
Western Carolina University M†
Western Connecticut State University M
Western Illinois University M
Western Kentucky University M†
Western Michigan University M,D*†
Western Washington University M
Westfield State College M
West Texas A&M University M†
West Virginia University M,D*
Wichita State University M*†
Wilfrid Laurier University M,D
William Paterson University of New Jersey M*†
Winona State University M
Winthrop University M
Wright State University M*
Xavier University M*
Yale University M,D*
York University M,D*
Youngstown State University M

ENGLISH AS A SECOND LANGUAGE

Adelphi University M,O*
Alliant International University D*†
American University M,O*†
American University in Cairo M,O
Andrews University M
Arizona State University M*
Azusa Pacific University M*†
Ball State University M,D*
Biola University M,D,O
Bishop's University M,O
Boston University M,O*†
Bowling Green State University M,D*†
Brigham Young University M,D*
California State University, Dominguez Hills M,O†
California State University, Fresno M
California State University, Fullerton M
California State University, Los Angeles M
California State University, Sacramento M
California State University, San Bernardino M
California State University, Stanislaus M
Carson-Newman College M
The Catholic University of America M,D*†
Central Connecticut State University M*†
Central Michigan University M†
Central Missouri State University M†
Central Washington University M†
Cleveland State University M*†
The College of New Jersey M,O†
The College of New Rochelle M,O†
College of Notre Dame of Maryland M
Columbia International University P,M,D,O
Eastern Michigan University M*
Eastern Nazarene College M,O
Eastern University O*
Elms College M,O
Emporia State University M*†
Fairfield University M,O*
Florida Atlantic University, Ft. Lauderdale Campus M,D,O
Florida International University M*†
Fordham University M,D,O*†
Framingham State College M*
Fresno Pacific University M
George Mason University M*†
Georgetown University M,D,O*
Georgia State University M,O*
Gonzaga University M
Grand Canyon University M
Grand Valley State University M†
Hawai'i Pacific University M*†
Heritage College M
Hofstra University M*
Holy Names College M,O
Hunter College of the City University of New York M†
Indiana State University M*†
Indiana University Bloomington M,D,O*
Indiana University of Pennsylvania M,D*†
Inter American University of Puerto Rico, Metropolitan Campus M
Inter American University of Puerto Rico, San Germán Campus M
Kean University M,O*†
Lehman College of the City University of New York M
Long Island University, Brooklyn Campus M*
Long Island University, Westchester Graduate Campus M
Lynn University M,D†
Madonna University M
Manhattanville College M*†
Mercy College M,O*
Michigan State University M,D*†
Montclair State University M†
Monterey Institute of International Studies M*
Moody Bible Institute P,M,O
Mount Saint Vincent University M
Murray State University M†
Nazareth College of Rochester M
New Jersey City University M
Newman University M
New York University M,D,O*†
Northern Arizona University M,D,O
Nova Southeastern University M,O*
Ohio University M*
Oklahoma City University M
Oral Roberts University M,D
The Pennsylvania State University University Park Campus M*†
Pontifical Catholic University of Puerto Rico M,D
Portland State University M*
Prescott College M†
Providence College and Theological Seminary P,M,D,O
Queens College of the City University of New York M†
Rhode Island College M†
Rutgers, The State University of New Jersey, New Brunswick M,D*
St. Cloud State University M
St. John's University (NY) M*†
Saint Michael's College M,O*
Salem State College M
Salisbury University M
Sam Houston State University M,O*
San Francisco State University M
San Jose State University M,O*
School for International Training M†
Seattle Pacific University M
Seattle University M,O*†
Seton Hall University M,O*†
Shenandoah University M,D,O
Sierra Nevada College O
Simmons College M*
Southeast Missouri State University M
Southern Connecticut State University M†
Southern Illinois University Carbondale M*†
Southern Illinois University Edwardsville M†
State University of New York at New Paltz M
Stony Brook University, State University of New York M,D*†
Teachers College Columbia University M,D*
Texas A&M University–Kingsville M*†
Trinity College (DC) M†
Universidad del Turabo M
University at Buffalo, The State University of New York M,D,O*†
The University of Alabama in Huntsville M,O*
University of Alberta M,D*
The University of Arizona M,D*
The University of British Columbia M,D*
University of Calgary M,D*
University of California, Los Angeles M*
University of Central Florida M,O*†
University of Central Oklahoma M
University of Colorado at Denver M*
University of Delaware M,D*†
The University of Findlay M
University of Florida M,D,O*†
University of Guam M
University of Hawaii at Manoa M,D*
University of Houston M,D*

P—first professional degree; M—master's degree; D—doctorate; O—other advanced degree;
**full description and/or announcement in Book 2, 3, 4, 5, or 6; †full description in this book*

University of Idaho M*†
University of Illinois at Chicago M*
University of Illinois at Urbana–Champaign M*
University of Manitoba M*
University of Maryland, Baltimore County M*†
University of Maryland, College Park M,D,O*
University of Massachusetts Boston M*†
University of Miami M,D,O*†
University of Minnesota, Twin Cities Campus M,D*
University of Nevada, Las Vegas M,D,O*†
University of Nevada, Reno M,D,O*
University of Northern Iowa M
University of Pennsylvania M,D*†
University of Phoenix–Phoenix Campus M
University of Pittsburgh M,O*†
University of San Francisco M,D*†
University of South Carolina M,D,O*†
University of Southern California M,D*†
University of Southern Maine M,O
University of South Florida M*†
The University of Tennessee M,D,O*†
The University of Texas at Brownsville M
The University of Texas at San Antonio M,D*
The University of Texas–Pan American M
University of Toledo M*†
University of Washington M,D*
Wagner College M
Wayne State College M
West Chester University of Pennsylvania M*†
Western Kentucky University M†
West Virginia University M*
Wheaton College M,O†
Whitworth College M
Wright State University M*

ENGLISH EDUCATION

Agnes Scott College M*
Alabama State University M,O
Albany State University M
Alfred University M*†
Andrews University M
Appalachian State University M
Arcadia University M,D,O†
Arkansas State University M,O
Arkansas Tech University M
Armstrong Atlantic State University M†
Auburn University M,D,O*†
Austin Peay State University M
Belmont University M
Bethel College (TN) M
Boston College M*†
Boston University M,D,O*†
Brooklyn College of the City University of New York M†
Brown University M*
California Baptist University M
California State University, San Bernardino M
Campbell University M
Carthage College M,O
Central Missouri State University M†
Chadron State College M,O
Chapman University M*†
Charleston Southern University M
Chatham College M
Christopher Newport University M†
Clemson University M*
Coastal Carolina University M
The College of William and Mary M*†
The Colorado College M
Colorado State University M*
Columbia College Chicago M†
Columbus State University M,O
Connecticut College M
Delta State University M
DeSales University M
Eastern Kentucky University M
Edinboro University of Pennsylvania M
Elms College M,O
Emory & Henry College M
Fitchburg State College M†
Florida Atlantic University M*
Florida Atlantic University, Davie Campus M
Florida Gulf Coast University M
Florida International University M,D*†
Florida State University M,D,O*†
Framingham State College M*
Gardner-Webb University M
Georgia College & State University M,O
Georgia Southern University M,O
Georgia State University M,D,O*
Henderson State University M
Hofstra University M*
Hunter College of the City University of New York M†
Indiana University Bloomington M,D*
Indiana University of Pennsylvania M,D*†
Indiana University–Purdue University Fort Wayne M
Indiana University–Purdue University Indianapolis M*
Iona College M*†
Jackson State University M
Jacksonville University M
Kutztown University of Pennsylvania M,O†
Lehman College of the City University of New York M
Long Island University, Brooklyn Campus M*
Long Island University, C.W. Post Campus M*†
Longwood College M
Louisiana Tech University M,D,O*
Loyola Marymount University M†
Lynchburg College M
Manhattanville College M*†
McNeese State University M
Mercer University M,O
Miami University M,D*†
Michigan State University M,D*†
Millersville University of Pennsylvania M†
Mills College M,D*†
Minnesota State University, Mankato M
Minot State University M
Montclair State University M†
National-Louis University M,O
New York University M,D,O*†
North Carolina Agricultural and Technical State University M*
Northeastern Illinois University M
Northeastern University M*†
Northern State University M
North Georgia College & State University M,O
Northwestern State University of Louisiana M
Northwest Missouri State University M
Nova Southeastern University M,O*
Occidental College M
Plattsburgh State University of New York M
Plymouth State College M*
Portland State University M*
Purdue University M,D,O*
Queens College of the City University of New York M,O†
Quinnipiac University M*†
Rider University O*
Rockford College M
Rollins College M*
Rutgers, The State University of New Jersey, New Brunswick M*
Sage Graduate School M†
Salem State College M,O
Salisbury University M
San Francisco State University M,O
Smith College M*
Sonoma State University M
South Carolina State University M
Southern Illinois University Edwardsville M†
Stanford University M,D*
State University of New York at Binghamton M*†
State University of New York College at Brockport M*†
State University of New York College at Buffalo M
State University of New York College at Cortland M
State University of West Georgia M,O
Stony Brook University, State University of New York M,O*†
Syracuse University M,D,O*
Teachers College Columbia University M,D*
Texas A&M University–Commerce M,D†
Texas Tech University M,D,O*†
Union College (NY) M*
University at Buffalo, The State University of New York M,D,O*†
University of Alaska Fairbanks M,O*
The University of Arizona M,D*
University of Arkansas at Pine Bluff M
The University of British Columbia M,D*
University of California, Berkeley M,D,O*
University of Central Florida M*†
University of Colorado at Denver M*
University of Connecticut M,D*†
University of Delaware M,D*†
University of Florida M,D,O*†
University of Georgia M,D,O*†
University of Idaho M*†
University of Illinois at Chicago M,D*
University of Indianapolis M
The University of Iowa M,D*
University of Louisiana at Monroe M,D,O
University of Michigan M,D*
University of Minnesota, Twin Cities Campus M,D*
The University of Montana–Missoula M*†
University of Nevada, Las Vegas M,D,O*†
University of Nevada, Reno M,D*
University of New Hampshire M,D*†
The University of North Carolina at Chapel Hill M*†
The University of North Carolina at Greensboro M,D,O†
The University of North Carolina at Pembroke M
University of Oklahoma M,D,O*†
University of Pittsburgh M,D*†
University of Puerto Rico, Río Piedras M,D*
University of South Carolina M,D*†
University of South Florida M,D*†
The University of Tennessee M,D,O*†
The University of Texas at El Paso M*†
The University of Texas at Tyler M
University of the District of Columbia M*
University of Vermont M*†
University of Victoria M,D
University of Washington M,D*
The University of West Alabama M
University of Wisconsin–Eau Claire M†
University of Wisconsin–Madison M,D*
University of Wisconsin–River Falls M
Vanderbilt University M,D*
Washington State University M,D*
Wayne State College M
Wayne State University M,D,O*
Western Carolina University M†
Western Connecticut State University M
Western Kentucky University M†
Widener University M,D*†
Wilkes University M
William Carey College M
Worcester State College M,O

ENTOMOLOGY

Auburn University M,D*†
Clemson University M,D*
Colorado State University M,D*
Cornell University M,D*
Iowa State University of Science and Technology M,D*†
Kansas State University M,D*†
Louisiana State University and Agricultural and Mechanical College M,D*
McGill University M,D*
Michigan State University M,D*†
Mississippi State University M,D*
Montana State University–Bozeman M*
New Mexico State University M
North Carolina State University M,D*
North Dakota State University M,D†
The Ohio State University M,D*
Oklahoma State University M,D*†
Oregon State University M,D*
The Pennsylvania State University University Park Campus M,D*†
Purdue University M,D*
Rutgers, The State University of New Jersey, New Brunswick M,D*
Simon Fraser University M,D,O
South Dakota State University M*
State University of New York College of Environmental Science and Forestry M,D
Texas A&M University M,D*
Texas Tech University M,D*†
The University of Arizona M,D*
University of Arkansas M,D*
University of California, Davis M,D*†
University of California, Riverside M,D*
University of Connecticut M,D*†
University of Delaware M,D*†
University of Florida M,D*†
University of Georgia M,D*†
University of Hawaii at Manoa M,D*
University of Idaho M,D*†
University of Illinois at Urbana–Champaign M,D*
University of Kansas M,D*
University of Kentucky M,D*
University of Maine M*
University of Manitoba M,D*
University of Maryland, College Park M,D*
University of Massachusetts Amherst M,D*†
University of Minnesota, Twin Cities Campus M,D*
University of Missouri–Columbia M,D*
University of Nebraska–Lincoln M,D*†
University of North Dakota M,D*
University of Rhode Island M,D*
The University of Tennessee M*†
University of Wisconsin–Madison M,D*
University of Wyoming M,D*†
Virginia Polytechnic Institute and State University M,D*
Washington State University M,D*
West Virginia University M,D*

ENTREPRENEURSHIP

American University M*†
Baldwin-Wallace College M*
Bentley College M,O*
California Lutheran University M
California State University, Hayward M
Columbia University M*†
DePaul University M*†
Fairleigh Dickinson University, College at Florham M*†
Fairleigh Dickinson University, Metropolitan Campus M*†
Georgia State University M,D*
Huron University USA in London M
Indiana Institute of Technology M
Indiana University Bloomington M*
Jones International University M*†
Kennesaw State University M
Michigan State University M,D*†
Rensselaer Polytechnic Institute M,D*†
St. Edward's University M,O
Texas Tech University M*†
Université du Québec à Trois-Rivières M
The University of Akron M†
University of Colorado at Boulder M,D*
University of Dallas M*
University of Houston D*
University of Minnesota, Twin Cities Campus M*
The University of Tampa M
University of the Incarnate Word D†
University of Wisconsin–Madison M*
Xavier University M*

ENVIRONMENTAL AND OCCUPATIONAL HEALTH

Anna Maria College M
Boston University M,D*†
California State University, Fresno M
California State University, Northridge M
Central Missouri State University M,O†
Colorado State University M,D*
Columbia Southern University M
Columbia University M,D*†
East Carolina University M*†
Eastern Kentucky University M
East Tennessee State University M†
Emory University M*†
The George Washington University M*†
Harvard University M,D*†
Hunter College of the City University of New York M†
Illinois State University M*†
Indiana University of Pennsylvania M*†
Johns Hopkins University M,D*†
Loma Linda University M*
McGill University M,D,O*
Medical College of Ohio M,O*
Medical College of Wisconsin M*
Meharry Medical College M
Mississippi Valley State University M
Montclair State University M,O†
Murray State University M†
New Jersey Institute of Technology M
New York Medical College M*
New York University M,D*†
Old Dominion University M*†
Oregon State University M*
Polytechnic University, Brooklyn Campus M*
Purdue University M,D*
Saint Louis University M*†
San Diego State University M,D*
State University of New York at Albany M,D*†

- Stony Brook University, State University of New York M,O*†
- Temple University M*†
- Texas A&M University System Health Science Center M*
- Towson University D†
- Tufts University M,D*†
- Tulane University M,D*†
- Uniformed Services University of the Health Sciences M,D*
- Université de Montréal M,O
- Université du Québec à Montréal O
- Université Laval O†
- The University of Alabama at Birmingham D*†
- University of Alberta M,D,O*
- University of Arkansas for Medical Sciences M*
- The University of British Columbia M,D*
- University of California, Berkeley M,D*
- University of California, Los Angeles M,D*
- University of Cincinnati M,D*
- University of Georgia M,D*†
- University of Illinois at Chicago M,D*
- The University of Iowa M,D*
- University of Miami M*†
- University of Michigan M,D*
- University of Minnesota, Twin Cities Campus M,D*
- University of Nevada, Reno M,D*
- University of New Haven M*†
- The University of North Carolina at Chapel Hill M,D*†
- University of North Texas Health Science Center at Fort Worth M,D*
- University of Oklahoma M,D*†
- University of Oklahoma Health Sciences Center M,D*
- University of Pittsburgh M,D*†
- University of Puerto Rico, Medical Sciences Campus M,D*
- University of South Carolina M,D*†
- University of Southern Mississippi M
- University of South Florida M,D*†
- University of the Sacred Heart M
- University of Washington M,D*
- University of Wisconsin–Eau Claire M†
- University of Wisconsin–Whitewater M*
- Virginia Commonwealth University M*†
- Wayne State University M,O*
- West Chester University of Pennsylvania M*†
- Western Kentucky University M†
- Yale University M,D*

ENVIRONMENTAL BIOLOGY

- Antioch New England Graduate School M*†
- Baylor University M,D*†
- Eastern Illinois University M†
- Emporia State University M*†
- Georgia State University M,D*
- Governors State University M
- Hood College M
- Montana State University–Bozeman M,D*
- Morgan State University D*
- New York University M,D*†
- Nova Scotia Agricultural College M
- Ohio University M,D*
- Rutgers, The State University of New Jersey, New Brunswick M,D*
- Sonoma State University M
- State University of New York College of Environmental Science and Forestry M,D
- Tennessee Technological University M*
- University of Alberta M,D*
- University of California, Berkeley M*
- University of California, Santa Cruz M,D*
- University of Colorado at Boulder M,D*
- University of Guelph M,D
- University of Louisiana at Lafayette M,D*
- University of Louisville D*†
- University of Massachusetts Amherst M,D*†
- University of Massachusetts Boston D*†
- University of North Dakota M,D*
- University of Notre Dame M,D*†
- University of Southern Mississippi M,D
- University of Wisconsin–Madison M,D*
- Washington University in St. Louis D*†
- West Virginia University M,D*

ENVIRONMENTAL DESIGN

- Arizona State University D*
- Art Center College of Design M*
- Cornell University M*
- Michigan State University M,D*†
- San Diego State University M*
- San Jose State University M*
- State University of New York College of Environmental Science and Forestry M
- Texas Tech University D*†
- Université de Montréal M,D,O
- University of Calgary M,D*
- University of California, Berkeley M,D*
- University of California, Irvine D*
- University of Missouri–Columbia M*
- Virginia Polytechnic Institute and State University D*
- Yale University M*

ENVIRONMENTAL EDUCATION

- Antioch New England Graduate School M,D*†
- Arcadia University M,D,O†
- Brooklyn College of the City University of New York M†
- California State University, Fullerton M
- California State University, San Bernardino M
- Chatham College M
- City College of the City University of New York M*†
- Florida Institute of Technology M,D,O*†
- Gannon University M,O
- Indiana University Bloomington M,D,O*
- Lesley University M,D,O*†
- Maryville University of Saint Louis M
- New York University M*†
- Northern Illinois University M,D*†
- Prescott College M†
- Rowan University M†
- Slippery Rock University of Pennsylvania M†
- Southern Connecticut State University M,O†
- Southern Oregon University M
- State University of New York at New Paltz M
- Universidad Metropolitana M
- Université du Québec à Montréal M,D,O
- University of New Hampshire M*†
- West Virginia University M*

ENVIRONMENTAL ENGINEERING

- Air Force Institute of Technology M*
- Auburn University M,D*†
- California Institute of Technology M,D*
- California Polytechnic State University, San Luis Obispo M†
- Carleton University M,D
- Carnegie Mellon University M,D*
- The Catholic University of America M*†
- Clarkson University M,D*
- Clemson University M,D*
- Cleveland State University M,D*†
- Colorado School of Mines M,D†
- Colorado State University M,D*
- Columbia University M,D*†
- Concordia University (Canada) M,D,O*†
- Cornell University M,D*
- Dartmouth College M,D*†
- Drexel University M,D*†
- Duke University M,D*†
- École Polytechnique de Montréal M,D,O
- Florida Agricultural and Mechanical University M,D*
- Florida International University M*†
- Florida State University M,D*†
- The George Washington University M,D,O*†
- Georgia Institute of Technology M,D*
- Harvard University M,D*†
- Idaho State University M,D*
- Illinois Institute of Technology M,D*†
- Instituto Tecnológico y de Estudios Superiores de Monterrey, Campus Ciudad de México M,D
- Instituto Tecnológico y de Estudios Superiores de Monterrey, Campus Monterrey M,D
- Iowa State University of Science and Technology M,D*†
- Johns Hopkins University M,D*†
- Lamar University M*†
- Lehigh University M,D*
- Louisiana State University and Agricultural and Mechanical College M,D*
- Manhattan College M*†
- Marquette University M,D*†
- Massachusetts Institute of Technology M,D,O*
- McGill University M,D*
- Memorial University of Newfoundland M†
- Michigan State University M,D*†
- Michigan Technological University M,D*†
- Milwaukee School of Engineering M*
- Montana Tech of The University of Montana M
- New Jersey Institute of Technology M,D
- New Mexico Institute of Mining and Technology M†
- New Mexico State University M,D
- New York Institute of Technology M*†
- North Carolina Agricultural and Technical State University M*
- North Dakota State University M†
- Northeastern University M,D*†
- Northwestern University M,D*
- OGI School of Science & Engineering at Oregon Health & Science University M,D*
- Ohio University M,D*
- Oklahoma State University M,D*†
- Old Dominion University M,D*†
- Oregon State University M,D*
- The Pennsylvania State University Harrisburg Campus of the Capital College M*†
- The Pennsylvania State University University Park Campus M,D*†
- Polytechnic University, Brooklyn Campus M*
- Polytechnic University, Long Island Graduate Center M
- Polytechnic University, Westchester Graduate Center M
- Princeton University D*
- Rensselaer Polytechnic Institute M,D*†
- Rice University M,D*
- Rose-Hulman Institute of Technology M*
- Royal Military College of Canada M,D
- Rutgers, The State University of New Jersey, New Brunswick M,D*
- San Jose State University M*
- South Dakota State University M*
- Southern Methodist University M,D*†
- Stanford University M,D,O*
- State University of New York College of Environmental Science and Forestry M,D
- Stevens Institute of Technology M,D,O*†
- Syracuse University M,D*
- Temple University M*†
- Texas A&M University M,D*
- Texas A&M University–Kingsville M*†
- Texas Tech University M,D*†
- Tufts University M,D*†
- Tulane University M,D*†
- Université de Sherbrooke M
- University at Buffalo, The State University of New York M,D*†
- The University of Alabama M,D*
- The University of Alabama at Birmingham M,D*†
- The University of Alabama in Huntsville M*
- University of Alaska Fairbanks M*
- University of Alberta M,D*
- The University of Arizona M,D*
- University of Arkansas M*
- University of California, Berkeley M,D*
- University of California, Davis M,D,O*†
- University of California, Irvine M,D*
- University of California, Los Angeles M,D*
- University of California, Riverside M,D*
- University of California, Santa Barbara M,D*
- University of Central Florida M,D,O*†
- University of Cincinnati M,D*
- University of Colorado at Boulder M,D*
- University of Connecticut M,D*†
- University of Dayton M*†
- University of Delaware M,D*†
- University of Detroit Mercy M*
- University of Florida M,D,O*†
- University of Guelph M,D
- University of Houston M,D*
- University of Idaho M*†
- University of Illinois at Urbana–Champaign M,D*
- The University of Iowa M,D*
- University of Kansas M,D*
- University of Louisville M,D*†
- University of Maine M,D*
- University of Maryland, College Park M,D*
- University of Massachusetts Amherst M*†
- University of Massachusetts Lowell M*†
- The University of Memphis M,D*†
- University of Michigan M,D,O*
- University of Missouri–Columbia M,D*
- University of Missouri–Rolla M,D*
- University of Nebraska–Lincoln M,D*†
- University of Nevada, Las Vegas M,D*†
- University of New Brunswick Fredericton M,D
- University of New Haven M,O*†
- The University of North Carolina at Chapel Hill M,D*†
- University of Notre Dame M,D*†
- University of Oklahoma M,D*†
- University of Pennsylvania M,D*†
- University of Pittsburgh M,D*†
- University of Regina M,D
- University of Rhode Island M,D*
- University of Saskatchewan M,D,O
- University of Southern California M,D*†
- University of South Florida M,D*†
- The University of Tennessee M*†
- The University of Texas at Arlington M,D*†
- The University of Texas at Austin M*
- The University of Texas at El Paso M,D*†
- University of Toronto M,D*
- University of Utah M,D*
- University of Virginia M,D*
- University of Washington M,D*
- University of Windsor M,D
- University of Wisconsin–Madison M,D*
- University of Wyoming M,D*†
- Utah State University M,D,O*
- Vanderbilt University M,D*
- Villanova University M*†
- Virginia Polytechnic Institute and State University M*
- Washington State University M*
- Wayne State University M,D*
- West Virginia University M,D*
- Worcester Polytechnic Institute M,D,O*†
- Youngstown State University M

ENVIRONMENTAL MANAGEMENT AND POLICY

- Air Force Institute of Technology M*
- American University M,D,O*†
- Antioch New England Graduate School M,D*†
- Antioch University Seattle M†
- Arizona State University East M
- Bard College M,O*†
- Baylor University M*†
- Bemidji State University M
- Boise State University M*
- Boston University M,O*†
- Brown University M*
- California State University, Fullerton M
- Carleton University M,D
- Central Washington University M†
- Clark University M*†
- Clemson University M,D*
- College of the Atlantic M
- Colorado State University M,D*
- Columbia University M*†
- Concordia University (Canada) O*†
- Cornell University M,D*
- Dalhousie University M*
- Drexel University M*†
- Duke University M,D*†
- Duquesne University M,O*†
- East Carolina University D*†
- The Evergreen State College M*
- Florida Gulf Coast University M
- Florida Institute of Technology M,D*†
- Florida International University M*†
- Friends University M
- George Mason University M,D*†
- The George Washington University M*†
- Hardin-Simmons University M
- Harvard University M,O*†
- Illinois Institute of Technology P,M*†

*P—first professional degree; M—master's degree; D—doctorate; O—other advanced degree; *full description and/or announcement in Book 2, 3, 4, 5, or 6; †full description in this book*

Instituto Tecnológico y de Estudios Superiores de Monterrey, Campus Irapuato M,D
Johns Hopkins University M,D,O*†
Kansas State University M*†
Lamar University M*†
Long Island University, C.W. Post Campus M*†
Longwood College M
Louisiana State University and Agricultural and Mechanical College M*
Michigan State University M,D*†
Michigan Technological University M*†
Montana State University–Bozeman M*
Montclair State University M,O†
Monterey Institute of International Studies M*
Naropa University M*
National Technological University M
National University M†
New Jersey Institute of Technology M,D
New Mexico Highlands University M
New York Institute of Technology M,O*†
New York University M,D,O*†
North Carolina State University M*
North Dakota State University M,D†
Northeastern Illinois University M
Northern Arizona University M,O
Nova Scotia Agricultural College M
OGI School of Science & Engineering at Oregon Health & Science University M,D*
Ohio University M*
Oregon State University M,D*
The Pennsylvania State University University Park Campus M*†
Polytechnic University of Puerto Rico M
Portland State University M,D*
Prescott College M†
Princeton University M,D*
Purdue University M,D*
Rensselaer Polytechnic Institute M,D*†
Rice University M*
Rochester Institute of Technology M*†
Royal Roads University M
St. Cloud State University M
Saint Mary-of-the-Woods College M
Saint Mary's University of Minnesota M
San Francisco State University M
San Jose State University M*
Seton Hall University O*†
Shippensburg University of Pennsylvania M†
Simon Fraser University M,D
Slippery Rock University of Pennsylvania M†
Southwest Missouri State University M*†
Southwest Texas State University M*
Stanford University M*
State University of New York at Albany M*†
State University of New York College of Environmental Science and Forestry M,D
Stony Brook University, State University of New York M*†
Texas Tech University D*†
Trent University M,D
Troy State University M
Tufts University M,D,O*†
Universidad del Turabo M
Universidad Metropolitana M
Université de Montréal O
Université du Québec à Chicoutimi M
Université du Québec, Institut National de la Recherche Scientifique M,D
University of Alaska Fairbanks M*
University of Alberta M,D*
The University of Arizona M*
The University of British Columbia M,D*
University of Calgary M,D*
University of California, Berkeley M,D*
University of California, Irvine D*
University of California, Santa Barbara M,D*
University of California, Santa Cruz D*
University of Chicago M,D*
University of Connecticut M*†
University of Delaware M,D*†
University of Denver M*†
University of Guelph M,D
University of Hawaii at Manoa M*
University of Houston–Clear Lake M*†
University of Idaho M,D*†
University of Illinois at Springfield M†
University of Maine M,D*
University of Manitoba M*
University of Maryland University College M*
University of Michigan M,D*
University of Minnesota, Twin Cities Campus M*
University of Missouri–St. Louis M,D,O†
The University of Montana–Missoula M*†
University of Nevada, Reno M*
University of New Hampshire M*†
The University of North Carolina at Chapel Hill M,D*†
University of Northern British Columbia M,D
University of Oregon M*
University of Pittsburgh M*†
University of Rhode Island M,D*
University of St. Thomas (MN) M,O*†
University of San Francisco M*†
University of South Carolina M*†
University of Southern California M*†
University of South Florida M*†
The University of Tennessee M,D*†
The University of Texas at Austin M*
University of Toronto M*
University of Vermont M,D*†
University of Washington M,D*
University of Waterloo M
University of Wisconsin–Green Bay M
University of Wisconsin–Madison M,D*
Vermont Law School M
Virginia Commonwealth University M*†
Webster University M
West Virginia University M,D*
Wright State University M*
Yale University M,D*
York University M,D*
Youngstown State University M,O

ENVIRONMENTAL SCIENCES

Air Force Institute of Technology M,D*
Alabama Agricultural and Mechanical University M,D
Alaska Pacific University M
American University M*†
Antioch New England Graduate School M,D*†
Arkansas State University M,D,O
California State University, Chico M
California State University, Fullerton M
Christopher Newport University M†
City College of the City University of New York M,D*†
Clemson University M,D*
Cleveland State University M,D*†
College of Charleston M*†
College of Staten Island of the City University of New York M†
Colorado School of Mines M,D†
Columbus State University M
Drexel University M,D*†
Duke University M,D*†
Duquesne University M,D,O*†
Florida Atlantic University M*
Florida Institute of Technology M,D*†
Florida International University M*†
George Mason University M,D*†
Graduate School and University Center of the City University of New York D*†
Harvard University M,D*†
Howard University M,D*
Humboldt State University M
Hunter College of the City University of New York M,O†
Idaho State University M,D*
Indiana University Bloomington M,D*
Instituto Tecnológico y de Estudios Superiores de Monterrey, Campus Ciudad de México M,D
Inter American University of Puerto Rico, San Germán Campus M
Jackson State University M,D
Lehigh University M,D*
Long Island University, C.W. Post Campus M*†
Louisiana State University and Agricultural and Mechanical College M,D*
Loyola Marymount University M†
Marshall University M*†
McNeese State University M
Memorial University of Newfoundland M†
Miami University M*†
Michigan State University M,D*†
Minnesota State University, Mankato M
Montana State University–Bozeman M,D*
Montclair State University M,O†
New Jersey Institute of Technology M,D
New Mexico Highlands University M
New Mexico Institute of Mining and Technology M,D†
North Carolina Agricultural and Technical State University M*
Northern Arizona University M,O
Nova Southeastern University M,D*
Oakland University M,D†
OGI School of Science & Engineering at Oregon Health & Science University M,D*
The Ohio State University M,D*
Ohio University M*
Oklahoma State University M,D*†
Oregon State University M,D*
Pace University, White Plains Campus M*
The Pennsylvania State University Harrisburg Campus of the Capital College M*†
The Pennsylvania State University University Park Campus M*†
Polytechnic University, Brooklyn Campus M*
Portland State University M,D*
Queens College of the City University of New York M†
Rensselaer Polytechnic Institute M,D*†
Rice University M,D*
Royal Military College of Canada M,D
Rutgers, The State University of New Jersey, New Brunswick M,D*
South Dakota School of Mines and Technology D*†
South Dakota State University D*
Southern Illinois University Carbondale D*†
Southern Illinois University Edwardsville M†
Southern University and Agricultural and Mechanical College M*
Stanford University M,D,O*
State University of New York at Albany M*†
State University of New York College of Environmental Science and Forestry M,D
Stephen F. Austin State University M
Stony Brook University, State University of New York M*†
Tarleton State University M
Tennessee Technological University D*
Texas A&M University–Corpus Christi M
Texas Christian University M*
Texas Tech University M,D*†
Towson University M,O†
Tufts University M,D*†
Tuskegee University M
Université de Sherbrooke M,O
Université du Québec à Montréal M,D
Université du Québec à Trois-Rivières M,D
The University of Alabama in Huntsville M,D*
University of Alaska Anchorage M
University of Alaska Fairbanks M*
University of Alberta M,D*
The University of Arizona M,D*
University of California, Berkeley M,D*
University of California, Davis M,D*†
University of California, Los Angeles D*
University of California, Riverside M,D*
University of California, Santa Barbara M,D*
University of Chicago M,D*
University of Cincinnati M,D*
University of Colorado at Denver M*
University of Guam M
University of Houston–Clear Lake M*†
University of Idaho M*†
University of Illinois at Urbana–Champaign M,D*
University of Kansas M,D*
The University of Lethbridge M,D
University of Maine M,D*
University of Maryland M,D*†
University of Maryland, Baltimore County M,D*†
University of Maryland, College Park M,D*
University of Maryland Eastern Shore M,D†
University of Massachusetts Boston M,D*†
University of Massachusetts Lowell M,D*†
University of Medicine and Dentistry of New Jersey D*
University of Michigan–Dearborn M*†
The University of Montana–Missoula M*†
University of Nevada, Las Vegas M,D*†
University of Nevada, Reno M,D*
University of New Haven M*†
The University of North Carolina at Chapel Hill M,D*†
University of Northern Iowa M
University of North Texas M,D*†
University of Oklahoma M,D*†
University of South Carolina M,D*†
The University of Tennessee at Chattanooga M
The University of Texas at Arlington M,D*†
The University of Texas at El Paso D*†
The University of Texas at San Antonio M*
University of Toledo D*†
University of Toronto M*
University of Virginia M,D*
The University of Western Ontario M,D*
University of Wisconsin–Green Bay M
University of Wisconsin–Madison M,D*
Virginia Commonwealth University M*†
Virginia Polytechnic Institute and State University M*
Washington State University M,D*
Washington University in St. Louis M*†
Wesley College M
Western Connecticut State University M
Western Washington University M
West Texas A&M University M†
Wichita State University M*†
Wright State University M,D*
Yale University M,D*

EPIDEMIOLOGY

Boston University M,D*†
Brown University M,D*
California State University, Long Beach M
Case Western Reserve University M,D*†
Columbia University M,D*†
Cornell University M,D*
Dalhousie University M*
Emory University M,D*†
Georgetown University M*
The George Washington University M,D*†
Harvard University M,D*†
Joan and Sanford I. Weill Medical College and Graduate School of Medical Sciences of Cornell University M*
Johns Hopkins University M,D*†
Loma Linda University M,D*
McGill University M,D,O*
Medical College of Wisconsin M*
Medical University of South Carolina M,D*
Memorial University of Newfoundland M,D,O†
Michigan State University M*†
New York Medical College M*
North Carolina State University M,D*
Oregon Health & Science University M*
Purdue University M,D*
Queen's University at Kingston M
Saint Louis University M*†
San Diego State University M,D*
Stanford University M,D*
State University of New York at Albany M,D*†
Texas A&M University M,D*
Texas A&M University System Health Science Center M*
Tufts University M,D,O*†
Tulane University M,D*†
Université Laval M,D†
University at Buffalo, The State University of New York M,D*†
The University of Alabama at Birmingham D*†
University of Alberta M,D,O*

The University of Arizona M,D*
The University of British Columbia M,D*
University of Calgary M,D*
University of California, Berkeley M,D*
University of California, Davis M,D*†
University of California, Los Angeles M,D*
University of California, San Diego D*
University of Cincinnati M,D*
University of Guelph M,D,O
University of Hawaii at Manoa M*
University of Illinois at Chicago M,D*
The University of Iowa M,D*
University of Louisville M,D*†
University of Maryland M,D*†
University of Maryland, Baltimore County M*†
University of Miami D*†
University of Michigan M,D*
University of Minnesota, Twin Cities Campus M,D*
The University of North Carolina at Chapel Hill M,D*†
University of North Texas Health Science Center at Fort Worth M,D*
University of Oklahoma Health Sciences Center M,D*
University of Ottawa M*
University of Pennsylvania M,D*†
University of Pittsburgh M,D*†
University of Prince Edward Island M,D
University of Puerto Rico, Medical Sciences Campus M*
University of Saskatchewan M,D
University of South Carolina M,D*†
University of Southern California M,D*†
University of South Florida M,D*†
University of Virginia M*
University of Washington M,D*
The University of Western Ontario M,D*
Yale University M,D*

ERGONOMICS AND HUMAN FACTORS

Bentley College M*
The Catholic University of America M*†
Clemson University M,D*
Cornell University M*
Embry-Riddle Aeronautical University (FL) M*
Florida Institute of Technology M*†
New York University M,D*†
Purdue University M,D*
Rensselaer Polytechnic Institute M*†
San Jose State University M*
Tufts University M,D*†
Université de Montréal O
Université du Québec à Montréal O
University of Central Florida M,D,O*†
The University of Iowa M,D*
University of Miami M,D*†
Wright State University M,D*

ETHICS

Biola University P,M,D
Claremont Graduate University M,D*
Drew University M,D†
Graduate Theological Union M,D,O
Marquette University M,D*†
Northern Baptist Theological Seminary P,M,D
St. Edward's University M
Southeastern Baptist Theological Seminary P,M,D
Université de Sherbrooke M,D,O
Université du Québec à Chicoutimi O
Université du Québec à Rimouski M
Université Laval O†
University of Baltimore M*
University of Maryland, Baltimore County M,O*†
University of Nevada, Las Vegas M*†
Valparaiso University M
Wilfrid Laurier University P,M,D

ETHNIC STUDIES

Cornell University M,D*
San Francisco State University M
Université Laval M,D†
University of California, Berkeley D*
University of California, San Diego D*
University of Toronto M,D*

EVOLUTIONARY BIOLOGY

Arizona State University M,D*
Brown University D*
Columbia University D,O*†
Cornell University D*
Emory University D*†
Florida State University M,D*†
George Mason University M*†
Harvard University D*†
Indiana University Bloomington M,D*
Iowa State University of Science and Technology M,D*†
Johns Hopkins University D*†
Lehigh University D*
Marquette University M,D*†
Michigan State University M,D*†
New York University M,D*†
Northwestern University D*
The Ohio State University M,D*
The Pennsylvania State University University Park Campus M,D*†
Princeton University D*
Purdue University M,D*
Rice University M,D*
Rutgers, The State University of New Jersey, New Brunswick M,D*
State University of New York at Albany M,D*†
Stony Brook University, State University of New York D*†
University of Alberta M,D*
The University of Arizona M,D*
University of California, Davis D*†
University of California, Irvine M,D*
University of California, Riverside D*
University of California, San Diego D*
University of California, Santa Barbara M,D*
University of California, Santa Cruz M,D*
University of Chicago D*
University of Colorado at Boulder M,D*
University of Delaware M,D*†
University of Hawaii at Manoa M,D*
University of Illinois at Chicago M,D*
University of Illinois at Urbana–Champaign D*
University of Kansas M,D*
University of Louisiana at Lafayette M,D*
University of Maryland, College Park M,D*
University of Massachusetts Amherst M,D*†
University of Miami M,D*†
University of Michigan M,D*
University of Minnesota, Twin Cities Campus M,D*
University of Missouri–St. Louis M,D,O†
University of Nevada, Reno D*
The University of North Carolina at Chapel Hill M,D*†
University of Notre Dame M,D*†
University of Oregon M,D*
University of Pittsburgh M,D*†
University of South Carolina M,D*†
The University of Tennessee M,D*†
The University of Texas at Austin M,D*
University of Utah M,D*
Virginia Polytechnic Institute and State University M,D*
Washington University in St. Louis D*†
Wesleyan University D*
Yale University D*

EXERCISE AND SPORTS SCIENCE

American University M*†
Appalachian State University M
Arizona State University M,D*
Arizona State University East M
Armstrong Atlantic State University M†
Ashland University M,D
Austin Peay State University M
Ball State University D*
Barry University M*†
Benedictine University M†
Bloomsburg University of Pennsylvania M
Boise State University M*
Brigham Young University M,D*
Brooklyn College of the City University of New York M†
California Baptist University M
California State University, Fresno M
California University of Pennsylvania M
Case Western Reserve University M,D*†
Central Connecticut State University M*†
Central Michigan University M†
Central Missouri State University M†
Cleveland State University M*†
The College of St. Scholastica M
Colorado State University M*
East Carolina University M,D*†
East Stroudsburg University of Pennsylvania M†
East Tennessee State University M†
Florida Atlantic University M*
Florida Atlantic University, Ft. Lauderdale Campus M
Florida State University M,D*†
George Mason University M*†
The George Washington University M*†
Georgia State University M,D*
Howard University M*
Indiana State University M*†
Indiana University Bloomington M,D,O*
Indiana University of Pennsylvania M*†
Iowa State University of Science and Technology M,D*†
Ithaca College M†
Kean University M*†
Kent State University M,D*
Kirksville College of Osteopathic Medicine M,D
Lakehead University M
Long Island University, Brooklyn Campus M*
Long Island University, Westchester Graduate Campus M
Marshall University M*†
Miami University M*†
Michigan State University M,D*†
Mississippi State University M*
Montclair State University M†
Morehead State University M
New Mexico Highlands University M
Northeastern University M*†
Northern Michigan University M
Oakland University M,O†
Ohio University M*
Oregon State University M,D*
Purdue University M,D*
Queens College of the City University of New York M†
Queen's University at Kingston M,D
St. Cloud State University M
San Diego State University M*
Seton Hall University M*†
Shenandoah University M
Smith College M*
Southeast Missouri State University M
Southern Connecticut State University M†
Southern Illinois University Edwardsville M,O†
Springfield College M,D,O†
Syracuse University M,O*
Tennessee State University M*
Texas Tech University M,D*†
Texas Tech University Health Sciences Center M*
Texas Woman's University M*†
United States Sports Academy M*
University at Buffalo, The State University of New York M,D*†
The University of Akron M†
University of Alberta M,D*
University of Calgary M,D*
University of California, Davis M*†
University of Central Florida M*†
University of Connecticut M,D*†
University of Dayton M*†
University of Delaware M*†
University of Florida M,D*†
University of Georgia M,D,O*†
University of Houston M,D*
University of Houston–Clear Lake M*†
The University of Iowa M,D*
University of Kentucky M,D*
The University of Lethbridge M,D
University of Louisville M*†
University of Massachusetts Amherst M,D*†
The University of Memphis M*†
University of Miami M,D*†
University of Minnesota, Twin Cities Campus M,D,O*
University of Mississippi M,D*
University of Missouri–Columbia M,D*
The University of Montana–Missoula M*†
University of Nebraska at Kearney M
University of Nevada, Las Vegas M*†
University of New Brunswick Fredericton M
University of New Orleans M,O*
The University of North Carolina at Chapel Hill M*†
The University of North Carolina at Greensboro M,D†
University of North Florida M,O
University of Oklahoma M*†
University of Oregon M,D*
University of Pittsburgh M,D*†
University of South Alabama M*†
University of South Carolina M,D*†
The University of Tennessee M,D,O*†
The University of Texas at El Paso M*†
The University of Texas at Tyler M
University of the Pacific M*
University of Toledo M*†
University of Utah M,D*
University of Victoria M
University of West Florida M
University of Wisconsin–La Crosse M†
Virginia Polytechnic Institute and State University M,D*
Wake Forest University M*†
Wayne State College M
West Chester University of Pennsylvania M,O*†
Western Michigan University M*†
West Texas A&M University M†
West Virginia University M,D*
Wichita State University M*†

EXPERIMENTAL PSYCHOLOGY

American University M,D*†
Appalachian State University M
Bowling Green State University M,D*†
Brooklyn College of the City University of New York M,D†
California State University, San Bernardino M
Case Western Reserve University D*†
The Catholic University of America M,D*†
Central Michigan University M,D†
Central Washington University M†
City College of the City University of New York M,D*†
Cleveland State University M*†
College of Staten Island of the City University of New York D†
The College of William and Mary M*†
Columbia University M,D*†
Cornell University D*
DePaul University M,D*†
Duke University D*†
Fairleigh Dickinson University, College at Florham M*†
Fairleigh Dickinson University, Metropolitan Campus M*†
George Mason University M*†
Graduate School and University Center of the City University of New York D*†
Harvard University M,D*†
Howard University M,D*
Illinois State University M,D,O*†
Johns Hopkins University D*†
Kent State University M,D*
Lakehead University M,D
Lehigh University D*
Long Island University, C.W. Post Campus M*†
McGill University M,D*
Memorial University of Newfoundland M,D†
Miami University D*†
Morehead State University M
Northeastern University M,D*†
The Ohio State University D*
Ohio University D*
Oklahoma State University M,D*†
Queen's University at Kingston M,D
St. John's University (NY) M*†
Saint Louis University M,D*†
Southern Illinois University Carbondale M,D*†
State University of New York at Albany M,D*†
Stony Brook University, State University of New York D*†
Syracuse University M,D*
Temple University D*†
Texas Tech University M,D*†
Towson University M,O†
University of California, Santa Cruz D*
University of Cincinnati D*
University of Connecticut D*†

*P—first professional degree; M—master's degree; D—doctorate; O—other advanced degree; *full description and/or announcement in Book 2, 3, 4, 5, or 6; †full description in this book*

University of Dayton M*†
University of Guelph M,D
University of Hartford M*
University of Louisville D*†
University of Maine M,D*
University of Maryland, College Park M,D*
The University of Memphis M,D*†
University of Mississippi M,D*
University of Missouri–St. Louis M,D,O†
The University of Montana–Missoula D*†
University of Nebraska at Omaha M,D,O
University of Nevada, Las Vegas M,D*†
The University of North Carolina at Chapel Hill D*†
University of North Dakota M,D*
University of North Texas M,D*†
University of Rhode Island D*
University of South Carolina M,D*†
University of South Florida D*†
The University of Tennessee M,D*†
The University of Tennessee at Chattanooga M
The University of Texas at Arlington M,D*†
The University of Texas at El Paso M,D*†
The University of Texas–Pan American M
University of Toledo M,D*†
University of Victoria M,D
University of Wisconsin–Oshkosh M*
Washington University in St. Louis M,D*†
Western Michigan University M,D,O*†
Wilfrid Laurier University M

FACILITIES MANAGEMENT

Cornell University M*
Indiana State University M*†
Indiana University of Pennsylvania M*†
Michigan State University M,D*†
Pratt Institute M*
Université Laval M,O†
University of North Texas M,O*†

FAMILY AND CONSUMER SCIENCES-GENERAL

Alabama Agricultural and Mechanical University M,D
Appalachian State University M
Ball State University M*
Bowling Green State University M*†
California State University, Fresno M
California State University, Long Beach M
California State University, Los Angeles M
Central Michigan University M†
Central Washington University M†
College of the Atlantic M
Cornell University M,D*
East Carolina University M*†
Eastern Illinois University M†
Eastern Michigan University M*
Florida State University M,D*†
Illinois State University M*†
Indiana State University M*†
Iowa State University of Science and Technology M,D*†
Kansas State University M,D*†
Kent State University M*
Lamar University M*†
Louisiana State University and Agricultural and Mechanical College M,D*
Louisiana Tech University M*
Marshall University M*†
Michigan State University M,D*†
Montclair State University M†
New Mexico State University M
North Carolina Central University M
North Dakota State University M†
The Ohio State University M,D*
Ohio University M*
Oklahoma State University M,D*†
Oregon State University M,D*
Prairie View A&M University M
Purdue University M,D*
Queens College of the City University of New York M†
Sam Houston State University M*
San Francisco State University M
South Dakota State University M*
Southeast Missouri State University M
Stephen F. Austin State University M
Texas A&M University–Kingsville M*†
Texas Southern University M†
Texas Tech University M,D*†
The University of Akron M†
The University of Alabama M,D*
University of Alberta M,D*
The University of Arizona M,D*
University of Arkansas M*
University of Central Arkansas M
University of Central Oklahoma M
University of Georgia M,D*†
University of Idaho M*†
University of Kentucky M,D*
University of Louisiana at Lafayette M*
University of Manitoba M,D*
University of Minnesota, Twin Cities Campus M,D*
University of Missouri–Columbia M,D*
University of Nebraska–Lincoln M,D*†
The University of North Carolina at Greensboro M,D†
University of North Florida M,O
University of Puerto Rico, Río Piedras M*
University of Southern Mississippi M,D
The University of Tennessee D*†
The University of Tennessee at Martin M
The University of Texas at Austin M,D*
University of Wisconsin–Madison M,D*
University of Wisconsin–Stevens Point M
University of Wisconsin–Stout M
Utah State University M*
Western Michigan University M*†

FILM, TELEVISION, AND VIDEO PRODUCTION

Academy of Art College M†
American Film Institute Conservatory M
American University M*†
Antioch University McGregor M†
Art Center College of Design M*
Boston University M*†
Brigham Young University M*
Brooklyn College of the City University of New York M†
California College of Arts and Crafts M*
California Institute of the Arts M,O*
California State University, Fullerton M
Carleton University M
Carnegie Mellon University M*
Central Michigan University M†
Chapman University M*†
Claremont Graduate University M*
Columbia College Chicago M†
Columbia University M*†
Concordia University (Canada) M*†
Emerson College M*†
Florida State University M*†
George Mason University M*†
Hollins University M
Howard University M*
Loyola Marymount University M†
Massachusetts College of Art M
Minneapolis College of Art and Design M,O*
Montana State University–Bozeman M*
New Mexico Highlands University M
New York University M*†
Northwestern University M,D*
Ohio University M*
Rochester Institute of Technology M*†
San Diego State University M*
San Francisco Art Institute M,O*
San Francisco State University M
Savannah College of Art and Design M*
School of the Art Institute of Chicago M*
Stanford University M,D*
Syracuse University M*
Temple University M*†
The University of Alabama M*
The University of British Columbia M*
University of California, Los Angeles M,D*
University of Denver M*†
The University of Iowa M*
The University of Memphis M,D*†
University of Miami M,D*†
University of Michigan O*
The University of Montana–Missoula M*†
University of Nevada, Las Vegas M*†
University of New Orleans M*
The University of North Carolina at Greensboro M†
University of North Texas M*†
University of Oklahoma M*†
University of Southern California M*†
The University of Texas at Austin M,D*
University of Utah M*
University of Wisconsin–Milwaukee M
York University M*

FILM, TELEVISION, AND VIDEO THEORY AND CRITICISM

Boston University M*†
California College of Arts and Crafts M*
Chapman University M*†
Claremont Graduate University M,D*
College of Staten Island of the City University of New York M†
Columbia University M*†
Concordia University (Canada) M*†
Emory University M*†
Hollins University M
National University M†
New York University M,D*†
Ohio University M*
San Francisco State University M
Université de Montréal M,D
Université Laval M,D†
The University of British Columbia M*
University of Chicago M,D*
The University of Iowa M,D*
University of Kansas M,D*
University of Miami M,D*†
University of Southern California M,D*†

FINANCE AND BANKING

Adelphi University M*
Alabama Agricultural and Mechanical University M
Alliant International University M,D*†
The American College M
American University M,D,O*†
Argosy University-Chicago Northwest M,D*
Argosy University-Orange County M,D*
Argosy University-Sarasota M,D*†
Argosy University-Tampa M*
Arizona State University M,D*
Armstrong University M
Baker College Center for Graduate Studies M
Bentley College M,O*
Bernard M. Baruch College of the City University of New York M,D*
Boston College M,D*†
Boston University P,M,D,O*†
Brandeis University M,D*†
Bridgewater State College M
Bryant College M,O
California Lutheran University M
California State University, Fullerton M
California State University, Hayward M
California State University, Los Angeles M
California State University, Northridge M
Cardean University M†
Cardinal Stritch University M*
Carnegie Mellon University D*
Case Western Reserve University M,D*†
The Catholic University of America M*†
Central Michigan University M†
Charleston Southern University M
City University M,O†
Claremont Graduate University M*
Clark Atlanta University M
Clark University M*†
College for Financial Planning M
Columbia University M,D*†
Concordia University Wisconsin M
Cornell University D*
Dallas Baptist University M
Davenport University M
Davenport University M
DePaul University M,O*†
DeVry University-Keller Graduate School of Management M
Dowling College M,O
Drexel University M,D,O*†
Eastern Michigan University M*
Eastern University M*
East Tennessee State University M†
École des Hautes Études Commerciales de Montréal M*
Fairfield University M,O*
Fairleigh Dickinson University, College at Florham M*†
Fairleigh Dickinson University, Metropolitan Campus M*†
Florida Agricultural and Mechanical University M*
Florida International University M*†
Florida State University M,D*†
Fordham University M*†
Gannon University O
The George Washington University M,D*†
Georgia State University M,D*
Golden Gate University M,D,O
Goldey-Beacom College M
Graduate School and University Center of the City University of New York D*†
Hawai'i Pacific University M*†
Hofstra University M*
Houston Baptist University M
Howard University M*
Hsi Lai University M*
Huron University USA in London M
Illinois Institute of Technology P,M*†
Indiana University Bloomington M,D*
Indiana University Southeast M,O
Instituto Tecnológico y de Estudios Superiores de Monterrey, Campus Central de Veracruz M
Instituto Tecnológico y de Estudios Superiores de Monterrey, Campus Ciudad de México M,D
Instituto Tecnológico y de Estudios Superiores de Monterrey, Campus Ciudad Juárez M
Instituto Tecnológico y de Estudios Superiores de Monterrey, Campus Ciudad Obregón M
Instituto Tecnológico y de Estudios Superiores de Monterrey, Campus Cuernavaca M
Instituto Tecnológico y de Estudios Superiores de Monterrey, Campus Guadalajara M
Instituto Tecnológico y de Estudios Superiores de Monterrey, Campus Irapuato M,D
Instituto Tecnológico y de Estudios Superiores de Monterrey, Campus Monterrey M
Inter American University of Puerto Rico, Metropolitan Campus M
Inter American University of Puerto Rico, San Germán Campus M
Iona College M,O*†
Johns Hopkins University M,O*†
Kennesaw State University M
Kent State University D*
King's College M
Long Island University, C.W. Post Campus M,O*†
Louisiana State University and Agricultural and Mechanical College M,D*
Louisiana Tech University M,D*
Loyola College in Maryland M
Marywood University M*†
Mercy College M*
Metropolitan State University M
Miami University M*†
Michigan State University M,D*†
Middle Tennessee State University M,D*
Mississippi State University M,D*
Montclair State University M†
National University M†
New School University M*†
New York Institute of Technology M,O*†
New York University M,D,O*†
Nichols College M
Northeastern Illinois University M
Northeastern University M*†
Northwestern University D*
Notre Dame College (OH) M,O
Oklahoma City University M
Oklahoma State University M,D*†
Oral Roberts University M
Our Lady of the Lake University of San Antonio M
Pace University M*†
Pace University, White Plains Campus M*
Pacific States University M
The Pennsylvania State University University Park Campus M,D*†
Philadelphia University M
Pontifical Catholic University of Puerto Rico M,D
Portland State University M*
Purdue University M,D*
Quinnipiac University M*†
Regis University M,O*†
Rensselaer Polytechnic Institute M,D*†
Robert Morris University M†

Rochester Institute of Technology M*†
Rutgers, The State University of New Jersey, Newark M,D*†
Sage Graduate School M†
St. Bonaventure University M,O
St. Cloud State University M
St. Edward's University M,O
St. John's University (NY) M,O*†
Saint Joseph's University M*†
Saint Louis University M*†
St. Mary's University of San Antonio M
Saint Peter's College M†
St. Thomas Aquinas College M
Saint Xavier University M,O*
San Diego State University M*
Seattle University M,O*†
Seton Hall University M,O*†
Southeastern University M†
Southern Illinois University Edwardsville M†
Southern New Hampshire University M,O*
State University of New York at Albany M*†
State University of New York at Binghamton M,D*†
State University of New York at New Paltz M
Suffolk University M,O*
Syracuse University M,D*
Télé-université M,D
Temple University M,D*†
Texas A&M International University M
Texas A&M University M,D*
Texas Tech University M,D*†
United States International University M
Universidad de las Americas, A.C. M
Universidad de las Américas–Puebla M
Université de Sherbrooke M
Université du Québec à Montréal O
Université du Québec à Trois-Rivières O
Université Laval M,O†
The University of Akron M†
The University of Alabama M,D*
University of Alaska Fairbanks M*
University of Alberta M,D*
The University of Arizona M,D*
University of Baltimore M*
The University of British Columbia M,D*
University of California, Berkeley D*
University of Central Florida M,D*†
University of Cincinnati M,D*
University of Colorado at Boulder M,D*
University of Colorado at Colorado Springs M*
University of Colorado at Denver M*
University of Connecticut M,D*†
University of Dallas M*
University of Denver M*†
University of Dubuque M
The University of Findlay M
University of Florida M,D*†
University of Houston M,D*
University of Houston–Clear Lake M*†
University of Illinois at Chicago D*
University of Illinois at Urbana–Champaign M,D*
The University of Iowa D*
University of La Verne M*
The University of Lethbridge M,D
University of Manitoba M*
University of Maryland University College M*
The University of Memphis M,D*†
University of Minnesota, Twin Cities Campus M,D*
University of Missouri–St. Louis M,O†
University of Nebraska–Lincoln M,D*†
University of New Haven M*†
University of New Mexico M*†
The University of North Carolina at Chapel Hill D*†
University of North Texas M,D*†
University of Oregon D*
University of Pennsylvania M,D*†
University of Rhode Island M,D*
University of St. Thomas (MN) M,O*†
University of San Francisco M*†
University of Saskatchewan M
The University of Scranton M†
University of Southern California M*†
The University of Tennessee M,D*†
The University of Tennessee at Chattanooga M
The University of Texas at Arlington M,D*†
The University of Texas at Austin D*
The University of Texas at San Antonio M*
University of Toledo M*†
University of Tulsa M†
University of Utah M,D*
University of Victoria M
University of Waterloo M,D
University of Wisconsin–Madison M*
University of Wisconsin–Whitewater M*
University of Wyoming M*†
Vanderbilt University D*
Virginia Commonwealth University M*†
Virginia Polytechnic Institute and State University M,D*
Virginia State University M
Wagner College M
Walsh College of Accountancy and Business Administration M
Webster University M
West Chester University of Pennsylvania M*†
Western International University M
Western New England College M
West Texas A&M University M†
Wilkes University M
Wright State University M*
Xavier University M*
Yale University D*
York College of Pennsylvania M
Youngstown State University M

FINANCIAL ENGINEERING

Claremont Graduate University M,D,O*
Columbia University M,D,O*†
École des Hautes Études Commerciales de Montréal M*
Kent State University M*
Polytechnic University, Brooklyn Campus M*
Polytechnic University, Long Island Graduate Center M
Polytechnic University, Westchester Graduate Center M
Princeton University M,D*
University of California, Berkeley M,O*
University of Michigan M*
University of Tulsa M†

FIRE PROTECTION ENGINEERING

Anna Maria College M
University of Maryland, College Park M*
University of New Haven M*†
Worcester Polytechnic Institute M,D,O*†

FISH, GAME, AND WILDLIFE MANAGEMENT

Arkansas Tech University M
Auburn University M,D*†
Brigham Young University M,D*
Clemson University M,D*
Colorado State University M,D*
Cornell University M,D*
Frostburg State University M
Iowa State University of Science and Technology M,D*†
Louisiana State University and Agricultural and Mechanical College M,D*
McGill University M,D*
Memorial University of Newfoundland M†
Michigan State University M,D*†
Mississippi State University M*
Montana State University–Bozeman M,D*
New Mexico State University M
North Carolina State University M*
Oregon State University M,D*
The Pennsylvania State University University Park Campus M,D*†
Purdue University M,D*
South Dakota State University M,D*
State University of New York College of Environmental Science and Forestry M,D
Sul Ross State University M*
Tennessee Technological University M*
Texas A&M University M,D*
Texas A&M University–Kingsville M,D*†
Texas Tech University M,D*†
Université du Québec à Rimouski M,O
University of Alaska Fairbanks M,D*
The University of Arizona M,D*
University of Florida M,D*†
University of Idaho M,D*†
University of Maine M,D*
University of Massachusetts Amherst M,D*†
University of Miami M,D*†
University of Minnesota, Twin Cities Campus M,D*
University of Missouri–Columbia M,D*
The University of Montana–Missoula M,D*†
University of New Hampshire M*†
University of North Dakota M,D*
University of Rhode Island M,D*
The University of Tennessee M*†
University of Vermont M*†
University of Washington M,D*
Utah State University M,D*
Virginia Polytechnic Institute and State University M,D*
West Virginia University M*

FOLKLORE

The George Washington University M*†
Indiana University Bloomington M,D*
Memorial University of Newfoundland M,D†
University of Alberta M,D*
University of California, Berkeley M*
University of Louisiana at Lafayette M,D*
The University of North Carolina at Chapel Hill M*†
University of Oregon M*
University of Pennsylvania M,D*†
The University of Texas at Austin M,D*
Utah State University M*
Western Kentucky University M†

FOOD SCIENCE AND TECHNOLOGY

Alabama Agricultural and Mechanical University M,D
Auburn University M,D*†
Brigham Young University M*
California State Polytechnic University, Pomona M*
California State University, Fresno M
Chapman University M*†
Clemson University D*
Colorado State University M,D*
Cornell University M,D*
Dalhousie University M,D*
Drexel University M,D*†
Florida State University M,D*†
Framingham State College M*
Illinois Institute of Technology M*†
Iowa State University of Science and Technology M,D*†
Kansas State University M,D*†
Louisiana State University and Agricultural and Mechanical College M,D*
McGill University M,D*
Memorial University of Newfoundland M,D†
Michigan State University M,D*†
Mississippi State University M,D*
North Carolina State University M,D*
North Dakota State University M,D†
Nova Scotia Agricultural College M
The Ohio State University M,D*
Oklahoma State University M,D*†
Oregon State University M,D*
The Pennsylvania State University University Park Campus M,D*†
Purdue University M,D*
Rutgers, The State University of New Jersey, New Brunswick M,D*
Texas A&M University M,D*
Texas Tech University M,D*†
Texas Woman's University M,D*†
Tuskegee University M
Universidad de las Américas–Puebla M
Université de Moncton M
Université Laval M,D†
The University of Akron M†
University of Arkansas M,D*
The University of British Columbia M,D*
University of California, Davis M,D*†
University of Delaware M,D*†
University of Florida M,D*†
University of Georgia M,D*†
University of Guelph M,D
University of Hawaii at Manoa M*
University of Idaho M*†
University of Illinois at Urbana–Champaign M,D*
University of Kentucky M*
University of Maine M,D*
University of Manitoba M*
University of Maryland, College Park M,D*
University of Maryland Eastern Shore M†
University of Massachusetts Amherst M,D*†
University of Minnesota, Twin Cities Campus M,D*
University of Missouri–Columbia M,D*
University of Nebraska–Lincoln M,D*†
University of Puerto Rico, Mayagüez Campus M*
University of Rhode Island M,D*
University of Saskatchewan M,D
The University of Tennessee M,D*†
The University of Tennessee at Martin M
University of Wisconsin–Madison M,D*
University of Wisconsin–Stout M
University of Wyoming M*†
Utah State University M,D*
Virginia Polytechnic Institute and State University M,D*
Washington State University M,D*
Wayne State University M,D,O*
West Virginia University M,D*

FOREIGN LANGUAGES EDUCATION

American University in Cairo M
Andrews University M
Auburn University M,D,O*†
Boston College M*†
Boston University M*†
Bowling Green State University M*†
Brigham Young University M*
Brooklyn College of the City University of New York M†
California State University, Chico M
The College of William and Mary M*†
The Colorado College M
Connecticut College M
Eastern Washington University M†
Elms College M,O
Fairfield University M,O*
Florida Atlantic University M*
Florida International University M,D*†
Framingham State College M*
George Mason University M*†
Georgia Southern University M
Georgia State University M,D,O*
Hofstra University M*
Hunter College of the City University of New York M†
Indiana University Bloomington M,D*
Iona College M*†
Jacksonville University M,O
Long Island University, C.W. Post Campus M*†
Louisiana Tech University M,D,O*
Manhattanville College M*†
Marquette University M*†
Marygrove College M
McGill University M,D,O*
Michigan State University M,D*†
Middle Tennessee State University M*
Mississippi State University M*
Monterey Institute of International Studies M*
New York University M,D,O*†
North Georgia College & State University M,O
Occidental College M
The Pennsylvania State University University Park Campus M,D*†
Plattsburgh State University of New York M
Purdue University M,D,O*
Queens College of the City University of New York M,O†
Quinnipiac University M*†
Rhode Island College M†
Rider University O*
Rivier College M*†
Rutgers, The State University of New Jersey, New Brunswick M,D*
Salisbury University M
School for International Training M†
Smith College M*
Southwest Texas State University M*
Stanford University M*
State University of New York at Binghamton M*†
State University of New York College at Cortland M
State University of West Georgia M
Stony Brook University, State University of New York M,O*†

*P—first professional degree; M—master's degree; D—doctorate; O—other advanced degree; *full description and/or announcement in Book 2, 3, 4, 5, or 6; †full description in this book*

Teachers College Columbia University M,D*
Texas A&M University–Kingsville M*†
Union College (NY) M*
University at Buffalo, The State University of New York M,D,O*†
The University of Arizona M,D*
University of California, Irvine M,D*
University of Central Arkansas M
University of Connecticut M,D*†
University of Delaware M*†
University of Florida M,D,O*†
University of Georgia M,D,O*†
University of Hawaii at Manoa M,D*
University of Idaho M*†
University of Illinois at Urbana–Champaign M,D*
University of Indianapolis M
The University of Iowa M,D*
University of Louisville M*†
University of Maine M*
University of Manitoba M*
University of Massachusetts Amherst M*†
University of Massachusetts Boston M*†
University of Michigan M,D*
University of Minnesota, Twin Cities Campus M,D*
University of Missouri–Columbia M,D*
University of Nebraska at Kearney M
University of Nevada, Reno M*
The University of North Carolina at Chapel Hill M*†
University of Pittsburgh M,D*†
University of Puerto Rico, Río Piedras M,D*
University of South Carolina M,D*†
University of Southern Mississippi M
University of South Florida M*†
The University of Tennessee M,D,O*†
The University of Texas at Austin M,D*
University of Utah M,D*
University of Vermont M*†
University of Virginia M,D*
University of Wisconsin–Madison M,D*
Vanderbilt University M,D*
West Chester University of Pennsylvania M*†
Western Kentucky University M†

FORENSIC NURSING

Fitchburg State College M†
Quinnipiac University M*†
University of Colorado at Colorado Springs M*

FORENSIC PSYCHOLOGY

Alliant International University D*†
Argosy University-Chicago D*
Argosy University-Washington D.C. M,D,O*
Castleton State College M
Chicago School of Professional Psychology M,D*
Drexel University M,D*†
John Jay College of Criminal Justice of the City University of New York M,D*
Marymount University M,O†
Prairie View A&M University M,D
Sage Graduate School M†
Sam Houston State University M,D*
The University of British Columbia M,D*

FORENSIC SCIENCES

Argosy University-Chicago M,D,O*
Fitchburg State College M,O†
Florida International University M,D*†
The George Washington University M*†
John Jay College of Criminal Justice of the City University of New York M,D*
Marshall University M*†
National University M†
Pace University M*†
State University of New York at Albany M,D*†
The University of Alabama at Birmingham M*†
University of Central Florida M,O*†
University of Illinois at Chicago M*
University of New Haven M*†
University of North Texas Health Science Center at Fort Worth M,D*
Virginia Commonwealth University M,O*†

FORESTRY

Auburn University M,D*†
California Polytechnic State University, San Luis Obispo M†
Clemson University M,D*
Colorado State University M,D*
Cornell University M,D*
Duke University M,D*†
Harvard University M*†
Iowa State University of Science and Technology M,D*†
Lakehead University M
Louisiana State University and Agricultural and Mechanical College M,D*
McGill University M,D*
Michigan State University M,D*†
Michigan Technological University M,D*†
Mississippi State University M*
North Carolina State University M,D*
Northern Arizona University M,D
Oklahoma State University M*†
Oregon State University M,D*
The Pennsylvania State University University Park Campus M,D*†
Purdue University M,D*
Southern Illinois University Carbondale M*†
Southern University and Agricultural and Mechanical College M*
State University of New York College of Environmental Science and Forestry M,D
Stephen F. Austin State University M,D
Texas A&M University M,D*
Université Laval M,D†
The University of Arizona M,D*
University of Arkansas at Monticello M
The University of British Columbia M,D*
University of California, Berkeley M,D*
University of Florida M,D*†
University of Georgia M,D*†
University of Idaho M,D*†
University of Kentucky M*
University of Maine M,D*
University of Massachusetts Amherst M,D*†
University of Michigan M,D,O*
University of Minnesota, Twin Cities Campus M,D*
University of Missouri–Columbia M,D*
The University of Montana–Missoula M,D*†
University of New Brunswick Fredericton M,D
University of New Hampshire M*†
The University of Tennessee M*†
University of Toronto M,D*
University of Vermont M*†
University of Washington M,D*
University of Wisconsin–Madison M,D*
Utah State University M,D*
Virginia Polytechnic Institute and State University M,D*
West Virginia University M,D*
Yale University M,D*

FOUNDATIONS AND PHILOSOPHY OF EDUCATION

Antioch New England Graduate School M*†
Arizona State University M*
Bank Street College of Education M*
Brigham Young University M,D*
California State University, Long Beach M
California State University, Los Angeles M
California State University, Northridge M
Central Connecticut State University M*†
Clemson University M*
College of Mount St. Joseph M†
DePaul University M*†
Duquesne University M*†
Eastern Michigan University M*
Eastern Washington University M†
Fairfield University M,O*
Florida Atlantic University M,D,O*
Florida State University M,D,O*†
The George Washington University M*†
Georgia State University M,D*
Harvard University M,D,O*†
Hofstra University M,D,O*
Indiana University Bloomington M,D,O*
Iowa State University of Science and Technology M,D*†
Kansas State University M,D*†
Kent State University M,D*
Loyola College in Maryland M,O
Loyola University Chicago M,D*†
Maharishi University of Management M
Millersville University of Pennsylvania M†
Mount Saint Vincent University M
New York University M,D*†
Niagara University M†
Northern Illinois University M*†
The Pennsylvania State University University Park Campus M,D*†
Purdue University M,D,O*
Rutgers, The State University of New Jersey, New Brunswick M,D,O*
Saint Louis University M,D*†
Southeast Missouri State University M
Southern Connecticut State University O†
Stanford University M,D*
State University of New York at Binghamton D*†
Suffolk University M,O*
Syracuse University M,D,O*
Teachers College Columbia University M,D*
Texas A&M University M,D*
Troy State University M
Troy State University Dothan M,O
University of Alberta M,D,O*
The University of British Columbia M,D*
University of California, Berkeley M,D*
University of Cincinnati M,D*
University of Connecticut M,D*†
University of Florida M,D,O*†
University of Georgia M,D,O*†
University of Hawaii at Manoa M,D*
University of Houston M,D*
University of Illinois at Urbana–Champaign M,D,O*
The University of Iowa M,D*
University of Kansas D*
University of Kentucky M,D*
University of Manitoba M*
University of Maryland, College Park M,D,O*
University of Michigan M,D*
University of Minnesota, Twin Cities Campus M,D,O*
University of New Mexico M,D*†
University of New Orleans M,D,O*
University of Oklahoma M,D*†
University of Pennsylvania M,D*†
University of Pittsburgh M,D*†
University of Saskatchewan M,D,O
University of South Carolina D*†
The University of Tennessee M,D,O*†
The University of Texas at El Paso M,D*†
University of Toledo M,D,O*†
University of Utah M,D*
University of Washington M,D*
The University of West Alabama M
University of Wisconsin–Madison M,D*
University of Wisconsin–Milwaukee M
Western Illinois University M
Widener University M,D*†
Youngstown State University M,D

FRENCH

American University M,O*†
Arizona State University M*
Auburn University M*†
Boston College M,D*†
Boston University M,D*†
Bowling Green State University M*†
Brigham Young University M*
Brooklyn College of the City University of New York M†
Brown University M,D*
Bryn Mawr College M
California State University, Fullerton M
California State University, Long Beach M
California State University, Los Angeles M
California State University, Sacramento M
Carleton University M
Case Western Reserve University M,D*†
The Catholic University of America M,D*†
Central Connecticut State University M*†
Colorado State University M*
Columbia University M,D*†
Concordia University (Canada) M,O*†
Connecticut College M
Dalhousie University M,D*
Duke University D*†
Eastern Michigan University M*
Emory University D*†
Florida Atlantic University M*
Florida State University M,D*†
Georgia State University M*
Graduate School and University Center of the City University of New York D*†
Harvard University M,D*†
Howard University M*
Hunter College of the City University of New York M†
Illinois State University M*†
Indiana State University M*†
Indiana University Bloomington M,D*
Johns Hopkins University M,D*†
Kansas State University M*†
Kent State University M*
Long Island University, C.W. Post Campus M*†
Louisiana State University and Agricultural and Mechanical College M,D*
McGill University M,D*
McMaster University M
Memorial University of Newfoundland M†
Miami University M*†
Michigan State University M,D*†
Middlebury College M,D
Millersville University of Pennsylvania M†
Minnesota State University, Mankato M
Montclair State University M†
New York University M,D,O*†
Northern Illinois University M*†
Northwestern University D,O*
The Ohio State University M,D*
Ohio University M*
The Pennsylvania State University University Park Campus M,D*†
Portland State University M*
Princeton University D*
Purdue University M,D*
Queens College of the City University of New York M†
Queen's University at Kingston M,D
Rhode Island College M†
Rice University M,D*
Rutgers, The State University of New Jersey, New Brunswick M,D*
Saint Louis University M*†
San Diego State University M*
San Francisco State University M
San Jose State University M*
Seton Hall University M*†
Simon Fraser University M
Smith College M*
Southern Connecticut State University M†
Stanford University M,D*
State University of New York at Albany M,D*†
State University of New York at Binghamton M*†
Stony Brook University, State University of New York M,D*†
Syracuse University M*
Texas Tech University M*†
Tufts University M*†
Tulane University M,D*†
Université de Moncton M,D
Université de Montréal M,D
Université de Sherbrooke M,D
Université du Québec à Chicoutimi O
Université Laval M,D†
University at Buffalo, The State University of New York M,D*†
The University of Alabama M,D*
University of Alberta M,D*
The University of Arizona M,D*
University of Arkansas M*
The University of British Columbia M,D*
University of Calgary M,D*
University of California, Berkeley D*
University of California, Davis D*†
University of California, Irvine M,D*
University of California, Los Angeles M,D*
University of California, San Diego M,D*
University of California, Santa Barbara M,D*
University of Chicago M,D*
University of Cincinnati M,D*
University of Colorado at Boulder M,D*
University of Connecticut M,D*†
University of Delaware M*†
University of Denver M*†
University of Florida M,D*†
University of Georgia M*†
University of Hawaii at Manoa M*
University of Houston M,D*
University of Idaho M*†
University of Illinois at Chicago M*
University of Illinois at Urbana–Champaign M,D*
The University of Iowa M,D*

University of Kansas	M,D*
University of Kentucky	M*
The University of Lethbridge	M,D
University of Louisiana at Lafayette	M,D*
University of Louisville	M*†
University of Maine	M*
University of Manitoba	M,D*
University of Maryland, Baltimore County	M*†
University of Maryland, College Park	M,D*
University of Massachusetts Amherst	M*†
The University of Memphis	M*†
University of Miami	D*†
University of Michigan	D*
University of Minnesota, Twin Cities Campus	M,D*
University of Mississippi	M*
University of Missouri–Columbia	M,D*
The University of Montana–Missoula	M*†
University of Nebraska–Lincoln	M,D*†
University of Nevada, Las Vegas	M*†
University of Nevada, Reno	M*
University of New Brunswick Fredericton	M
University of New Mexico	M,D*†
The University of North Carolina at Chapel Hill	M,D*†
The University of North Carolina at Greensboro	M†
University of Northern Iowa	M
University of North Texas	M*†
University of Notre Dame	M*†
University of Oklahoma	M,D*†
University of Oregon	M*
University of Ottawa	M,D*
University of Pennsylvania	M,D*†
University of Pittsburgh	M,D*†
University of Regina	M
University of Rhode Island	M*
University of Saskatchewan	M
University of Southern California	M,D*†
University of South Florida	M*†
The University of Tennessee	M,D*†
The University of Texas at Arlington	M*†
The University of Texas at Austin	M,D*
University of Toledo	M*†
University of Toronto	M,D*
University of Utah	M*
University of Vermont	M*†
University of Victoria	M
University of Virginia	M,D*
University of Washington	M,D*
University of Waterloo	M
The University of Western Ontario	M,D*
University of Wisconsin–Madison	M,D,O*
University of Wisconsin–Milwaukee	M
University of Wyoming	M*†
Vanderbilt University	M,D*
Washington University in St. Louis	M,D*†
Wayne State University	M*
West Chester University of Pennsylvania	M*†
West Virginia University	M*
Yale University	M,D*
York University	M*

GENDER STUDIES

Cornell University	M,D*
Harvard University	M,D,O*†
Northwestern University	*
Rutgers, The State University of New Jersey, New Brunswick	M*
Simmons College	M*
University of Central Florida	M,O*†
University of Missouri–St. Louis	O†
University of Northern British Columbia	M,D
University of Saskatchewan	M,D

GENETIC COUNSELING

Arcadia University	M†
Brandeis University	M*†
California State University, Northridge	M,O
Case Western Reserve University	M,D*†
Johns Hopkins University	M,D*†
McGill University	M,D*
Northwestern University	M*
Sarah Lawrence College	M*†
University of California, Berkeley	M*
University of California, Irvine	M*
University of Cincinnati	M*
University of Colorado Health Sciences Center	M*
University of Minnesota, Twin Cities Campus	M,D*
The University of North Carolina at Greensboro	M†
University of Pittsburgh	M*†
University of South Carolina	M*†
The University of Texas Health Science Center at Houston	M*
University of Toronto	M,D*
Virginia Commonwealth University	M,D,O*†

GENETICS

Arizona State University	M,D*
Baylor College of Medicine	D*
Brandeis University	M,D*†
California Institute of Technology	D*
Carnegie Mellon University	M,D*
Case Western Reserve University	D*†
Clemson University	M,D*
Colorado State University	M,D*
Columbia University	M,D*†
Cornell University	D*
Dartmouth College	D*†
Drexel University	M,D*†
Duke University	D*†
Emory University	D*†
Florida State University	M,D*†
The George Washington University	M,D*†
Georgia State University	M,D*
Harvard University	D*†
Howard University	M,D*
Hunter College of the City University of New York	†
Illinois State University	M,D*†
Indiana University Bloomington	D*
Indiana University–Purdue University Indianapolis	M,D*
Iowa State University of Science and Technology	M,D*†
Joan and Sanford I. Weill Medical College and Graduate School of Medical Sciences of Cornell University	D*
Johns Hopkins University	M,D*†
Kansas State University	M,D*†
Marquette University	M,D*†
Massachusetts Institute of Technology	D*
McMaster University	M,D
Medical College of Ohio	M*
Medical College of Wisconsin	M,D*
Michigan State University	D*†
Mount Sinai School of Medicine of New York University	D*
New York University	M,D*†
North Carolina State University	M,D*
Northwestern University	D*
The Ohio State University	M,D*
Oklahoma State University	M,D*†
Oregon Health & Science University	D*
Oregon State University	M,D*
The Pennsylvania State University Milton S. Hershey Medical Center	M,D*
The Pennsylvania State University University Park Campus	M,D*†
Purdue University	M,D*
Rutgers, The State University of New Jersey, New Brunswick	M,D*
Stanford University	D*
State University of New York at Albany	M,D*†
Stony Brook University, State University of New York	D*†
Temple University	D*†
Texas A&M University	M,D*
Texas A&M University System Health Science Center	D*
Thomas Jefferson University	D*
Tufts University	D*†
Université du Québec à Chicoutimi	M
The University of Alabama at Birmingham	D*†
University of Alberta	M,D*
The University of Arizona	M,D*
The University of British Columbia	M,D*
University of California, Davis	M,D*†
University of California, Irvine	M,D*
University of California, Los Angeles	M,D*
University of California, Riverside	D*
University of California, San Diego	D*
University of California, San Francisco	D*
University of Chicago	D*
University of Cincinnati	M,D*
University of Colorado at Boulder	M,D*
University of Colorado Health Sciences Center	M,D*
University of Connecticut	M,D*†
University of Connecticut Health Center	D*
University of Delaware	M,D*†
University of Florida	M,D*†
University of Georgia	M,D*†
University of Guelph	M,D
University of Hawaii at Manoa	M,D*
University of Illinois at Chicago	M,D*
The University of Iowa	M,D*
University of Kansas	D*
University of Maryland, College Park	M,D*
University of Massachusetts Worcester	D*
University of Medicine and Dentistry of New Jersey	M,D*
University of Miami	M,D*†
University of Michigan	*
University of Minnesota, Twin Cities Campus	M,D*
University of Missouri–Columbia	D*
University of Missouri–St. Louis	M,D,O†
University of New Hampshire	M,D*†
University of New Mexico	M,D*†
The University of North Carolina at Chapel Hill	M,D*†
University of North Dakota	M,D*
University of North Texas Health Science Center at Fort Worth	M,D*
University of Notre Dame	M,D*†
University of Oregon	M,D*
University of Pennsylvania	D*†
University of Pittsburgh	M,D*†
University of Rhode Island	M,D*
University of Rochester	M,D*
The University of Tennessee	M,D*†
The University of Texas at Austin	D*
The University of Texas Health Science Center at Houston	M,D*
The University of Texas Medical Branch	M,D*
The University of Texas Southwestern Medical Center at Dallas	D*
University of Toronto	M,D*
University of Utah	M,D*
University of Vermont	M,D*†
University of Virginia	D*
University of Washington	M,D*
University of Wisconsin–Madison	M,D*
Virginia Commonwealth University	M,D,O*†
Virginia Polytechnic Institute and State University	M,D*
Wake Forest University	M*†
Washington State University	M,D*
Washington University in St. Louis	D*†
Wayne State University	M,D*
Wesleyan University	D*
West Virginia University	M,D*
Yale University	D*
Yeshiva University	D*

GENOMIC SCIENCES

Case Western Reserve University	D*†
Mount Sinai School of Medicine of New York University	D*
North Carolina State University	M,D*
University of California, Riverside	D*
University of California, San Francisco	D*
University of Florida	D*†
The University of Tennessee	M,D*†
The University of Tennessee–Oak Ridge National Laboratory Graduate School of Genome Science and Technology	M,D*
University of Washington	D*

GEOCHEMISTRY

California Institute of Technology	M,D*
California State University, Fullerton	M
Colorado School of Mines	M,D,O†
Columbia University	M,D*†
Cornell University	M,D*
The George Washington University	M*†
Georgia Institute of Technology	M,D*
Indiana University Bloomington	M,D*
Johns Hopkins University	M,D*†
Massachusetts Institute of Technology	M,D,O*
McMaster University	M,D
Montana Tech of The University of Montana	M
New Mexico Institute of Mining and Technology	M,D†
The Pennsylvania State University University Park Campus	M,D*†
Rensselaer Polytechnic Institute	M,D*†
University of California, Los Angeles	M,D*
University of Georgia	M,D*†
University of Hawaii at Manoa	M,D*
University of Illinois at Chicago	M,D*
University of Illinois at Urbana–Champaign	M,D*
University of Michigan	M,D*
University of Missouri–Rolla	M,D*
University of Nevada, Reno	M,D,O*
University of New Hampshire	M,D*†
University of Victoria	M,D
Washington University in St. Louis	M,D*†
Wright State University	M*
Yale University	D*

GEODETIC SCIENCES

Columbia University	M,D*†
The Ohio State University	M,D*
Université Laval	M,D†
University of New Brunswick Fredericton	M,D,O

GEOGRAPHIC INFORMATION SYSTEMS

Boston University	M*†
Clark University	M*†
George Mason University	M*†
Hunter College of the City University of New York	M,O†
North Carolina State University	M*
Northern Arizona University	M,O
Saint Mary's University of Minnesota	M
Southwest Texas State University	M*
State University of New York at Albany	M,O*†
Université du Québec à Montréal	O
University at Buffalo, The State University of New York	M,D,O*†
University of Minnesota, Twin Cities Campus	M*
The University of Montana–Missoula	M*†
University of Pittsburgh	M,D*†
The University of Texas at Dallas	M*
University of Wisconsin–Madison	M,D,O*
West Virginia University	M,D*

GEOGRAPHY

Appalachian State University	M
Arizona State University	M,D*
Auburn University	M*†
Boston University	M,D*†
Brigham Young University	M*
California State University, Chico	M
California State University, Fullerton	M
California State University, Hayward	M
California State University, Long Beach	M
California State University, Los Angeles	M
California State University, Northridge	M
California University of Pennsylvania	M
Carleton University	M,D
Central Connecticut State University	M*†
Chicago State University	M
Clark University	D*†
Concordia University (Canada)	M,O*†
East Carolina University	M*†
Eastern Michigan University	M*
Florida Atlantic University	M*
Florida State University	M,D*†
George Mason University	M*†
The George Washington University	M*†
Georgia State University	M*
Hunter College of the City University of New York	M,O†
Indiana State University	M,D*†
Indiana University Bloomington	M,D*
Indiana University of Pennsylvania	M*†
Johns Hopkins University	M,D*†
Kansas State University	M,D*†
Kent State University	M,D*

*P—first professional degree; M—master's degree; D—doctorate; O—other advanced degree; *full description and/or announcement in Book 2, 3, 4, 5, or 6; †full description in this book*

Louisiana State University and Agricultural and Mechanical College	M,D*
Marshall University	M*†
McGill University	M,D*
McMaster University	M,D
Memorial University of Newfoundland	M,D†
Miami University	M*†
Michigan State University	M,D*†
Minnesota State University, Mankato	M
New Mexico State University	M
Northeastern Illinois University	M
Northern Arizona University	M,O
Northern Illinois University	M*†
The Ohio State University	M,D*
Ohio University	M*
Oklahoma State University	M*†
Oregon State University	M,D*
The Pennsylvania State University University Park Campus	M,D*†
Portland State University	M,D*
Queen's University at Kingston	M,D
Rutgers, The State University of New Jersey, New Brunswick	M,D*
St. Cloud State University	M
Salem State College	M
San Diego State University	M,D*
San Francisco State University	M
San Jose State University	M*
Simon Fraser University	M,D
South Dakota State University	M*
Southern Illinois University Carbondale	M,D*†
Southern Illinois University Edwardsville	M†
Southwest Texas State University	M,D*
State University of New York at Albany	M,O*†
State University of New York at Binghamton	M*†
Syracuse University	M,D*
Temple University	M*†
Texas A&M University	M,D*
Towson University	M†
Trent University	M,D
Université de Montréal	M,D,O
Université de Sherbrooke	M,D
Université du Québec à Montréal	M
Université Laval	M,D†
University at Buffalo, The State University of New York	M,D,O*†
The University of Akron	M,D†
The University of Alabama	M*
The University of Arizona	M,D*
University of Arkansas	M,D*
The University of British Columbia	M,D*
University of Calgary	M,D*
University of California, Berkeley	D*
University of California, Davis	M,D*†
University of California, Los Angeles	M,D*
University of California, Santa Barbara	M,D*
University of Cincinnati	M,D*
University of Colorado at Boulder	M,D*
University of Connecticut	M,D*†
University of Delaware	M,D*†
University of Denver	M,D*†
University of Florida	M,D*†
University of Georgia	M,D*†
University of Guelph	M,D
University of Hawaii at Manoa	M,D*
University of Idaho	M,D*†
University of Illinois at Chicago	M*
University of Illinois at Urbana–Champaign	M,D*
The University of Iowa	M,D*
University of Kansas	M,D*
University of Kentucky	M,D*
The University of Lethbridge	M,D
University of Louisiana at Lafayette	M*
University of Manitoba	M,D*
University of Maryland, College Park	M,D*
University of Massachusetts Amherst	M*†
The University of Memphis	M*†
University of Minnesota, Twin Cities Campus	M,D*
University of Missouri–Columbia	M*
The University of Montana–Missoula	M*†
University of Nebraska at Omaha	M,O
University of Nebraska–Lincoln	M,D*†
University of Nevada, Reno	M*
University of New Mexico	M*†
University of New Orleans	M*
The University of North Carolina at Chapel Hill	M,D*†
The University of North Carolina at Charlotte	M*
The University of North Carolina at Greensboro	M†
University of North Dakota	M*
University of Northern Iowa	M
University of North Texas	M*†
University of Oklahoma	M,D*†
University of Oregon	M,D*
University of Ottawa	M,D*
University of Regina	M
University of Saskatchewan	M,D
University of South Carolina	M,D*†
University of Southern California	M,D*†
University of Southern Mississippi	M
University of South Florida	M*†
The University of Tennessee	M,D*†
The University of Texas at Austin	M,D*
The University of Texas at San Antonio	M*
University of Toledo	M*†
University of Toronto	M,D*
University of Utah	M,D*
University of Vermont	M*†
University of Victoria	M,D
University of Washington	M,D*
University of Waterloo	M,D
The University of Western Ontario	M,D*
University of Wisconsin–Madison	M,D,O*
University of Wisconsin–Milwaukee	M
University of Wyoming	M*†
Utah State University	M*
Virginia Polytechnic Institute and State University	M*
Wayne State University	M*
West Chester University of Pennsylvania	M*†
Western Illinois University	M,O
Western Kentucky University	M†
Western Michigan University	M*†
Western Washington University	M
West Virginia University	M,D*
Wilfrid Laurier University	M,D
York University	M,D*

GEOLOGICAL ENGINEERING

Arizona State University	M,D*
Colorado School of Mines	M,D,O†
Columbia University	M,D*†
Drexel University	M*†
École Polytechnique de Montréal	M,D,O
Michigan State University	M,D*†
Michigan Technological University	M,D*†
Montana Tech of The University of Montana	M
South Dakota School of Mines and Technology	M,D*†
University of Alaska Fairbanks	M,O*
The University of Arizona	M,D*
The University of British Columbia	M,D*
University of California, Berkeley	M,D*
University of Idaho	M*†
University of Minnesota, Twin Cities Campus	M,D*
University of Missouri–Rolla	M,D*
University of Nevada, Reno	M,D,O*
University of Oklahoma	M,D*†
University of Utah	M,D*
University of Wisconsin–Madison	M,D*

GEOLOGY

Acadia University	M
Auburn University	M*†
Ball State University	M*
Baylor University	M,D*†
Boise State University	M*
Boston College	M*†
Bowling Green State University	M*†
Brigham Young University	M*
Brooklyn College of the City University of New York	M,D†
Bryn Mawr College	M,D
California Institute of Technology	M,D*
California State University, Bakersfield	M
California State University, Fresno	M
California State University, Fullerton	M
California State University, Hayward	M
California State University, Long Beach	M
California State University, Los Angeles	M
California State University, Northridge	M
Case Western Reserve University	M,D*†
Central Washington University	M†
Cleveland State University	M,D*†
Colorado School of Mines	M,D,O†
Colorado State University	M,D*
Cornell University	M,D*
Duke University	M,D*†
East Carolina University	M*†
Eastern Kentucky University	M,D
Eastern Washington University	M†
Florida Atlantic University	M*
Florida State University	M,D*†
Fort Hays State University	M
The George Washington University	M,D*†
Georgia State University	M*
ICR Graduate School	M
Idaho State University	M,O*
Indiana University Bloomington	M,D*
Indiana University–Purdue University Indianapolis	M*
Iowa State University of Science and Technology	M,D*†
Johns Hopkins University	M,D*†
Kansas State University	M*†
Kent State University	M,D*
Lakehead University	M
Laurentian University	M
Lehigh University	M,D*
Loma Linda University	M*
Louisiana State University and Agricultural and Mechanical College	M,D*
Massachusetts Institute of Technology	M,D*
McMaster University	M,D
Memorial University of Newfoundland	M,D†
Miami University	M,D*†
Michigan State University	M,D*†
Michigan Technological University	M,D*†
Montana Tech of The University of Montana	M
New Mexico Institute of Mining and Technology	M,D†
New Mexico State University	M
North Carolina State University	M,D*
Northern Arizona University	M
Northern Illinois University	M,D*†
Northwestern University	M,D*
Nova Scotia Agricultural College	M
The Ohio State University	M,D*
Ohio University	M*
Oklahoma State University	M*†
Old Dominion University	M*†
Oregon State University	M,D*
The Pennsylvania State University University Park Campus	M,D*†
Portland State University	M,D*
Princeton University	D*
Queens College of the City University of New York	M†
Queen's University at Kingston	M,D
Rensselaer Polytechnic Institute	M,D*†
Rutgers, The State University of New Jersey, Newark	M*†
Rutgers, The State University of New Jersey, New Brunswick	M,D*
St. Francis Xavier University	M
San Diego State University	M*
San Jose State University	M*
South Dakota School of Mines and Technology	M,D*†
Southern Illinois University Carbondale	M,D*†
Southern Methodist University	M,D*†
State University of New York at Albany	M,D*†
State University of New York at Binghamton	M,D*†
State University of New York at New Paltz	M
Stephen F. Austin State University	M
Sul Ross State University	M*
Syracuse University	M,D*
Temple University	M*†
Texas A&M University	M,D*
Texas A&M University–Kingsville	M*†
Texas Christian University	M*
Tulane University	M,D*†
Université du Québec à Montréal	M,D,O
Université Laval	M,D†
University at Buffalo, The State University of New York	M,D*†
The University of Akron	M†
The University of Alabama	M,D*
University of Alaska Fairbanks	M,D*
University of Arkansas	M*
The University of British Columbia	M,D*
University of Calgary	M,D*
University of California, Berkeley	M,D*
University of California, Davis	M,D*†
University of California, Los Angeles	M,D*
University of California, Riverside	M,D*
University of California, San Diego	M,D*
University of California, Santa Barbara	M,D*
University of Chicago	M,D*
University of Cincinnati	M,D*
University of Colorado at Boulder	M,D*
University of Connecticut	M,D*†
University of Delaware	M,D*†
University of Florida	M,D*†
University of Hawaii at Manoa	M,D*
University of Houston	M,D*
University of Idaho	M,D*†
University of Illinois at Chicago	M,D*
University of Illinois at Urbana–Champaign	M,D*
University of Kansas	M,D*
University of Kentucky	M,D*
University of Louisiana at Lafayette	M*
University of Maine	M,D*
University of Manitoba	M,D*
University of Maryland, College Park	M,D*
University of Massachusetts Amherst	M,D*†
The University of Memphis	M,D*†
University of Miami	M,D*†
University of Michigan	M,D*
University of Minnesota, Duluth	M*
University of Minnesota, Twin Cities Campus	M,D*
University of Missouri–Columbia	M,D*
University of Missouri–Kansas City	M,D*†
University of Missouri–Rolla	M,D*
The University of Montana–Missoula	M,D*†
University of Nevada, Reno	M,D,O*
University of New Brunswick Fredericton	M,D
University of New Hampshire	M,D*†
University of New Orleans	M*
The University of North Carolina at Chapel Hill	M,D*†
The University of North Carolina at Wilmington	M*
University of North Dakota	M,D*
University of Oklahoma	M,D*†
University of Oregon	M,D*
University of Pennsylvania	M,D*†
University of Pittsburgh	M,D*†
University of Puerto Rico, Mayagüez Campus	M*
University of Regina	M
University of Rhode Island	M*
University of Saskatchewan	M,D,O
University of South Carolina	M,D*†
University of Southern Mississippi	M
University of South Florida	M,D*†
The University of Tennessee	M,D*†
The University of Texas at Arlington	M*†
The University of Texas at Austin	M,D*
The University of Texas at El Paso	M,D*†
The University of Texas at San Antonio	M*
The University of Texas of the Permian Basin	M
University of Toledo	M*†
University of Toronto	M,D*
University of Tulsa	M†
University of Utah	M,D*
University of Vermont	M*†
University of Victoria	M,D
University of Washington	M,D*
The University of Western Ontario	M,D*
University of Wisconsin–Madison	M,D*
University of Wisconsin–Milwaukee	M,D
University of Wyoming	M,D*†
Utah State University	M*
Vanderbilt University	M*
Virginia Polytechnic Institute and State University	M,D*
Washington State University	M,D*
Washington University in St. Louis	M,D*†
Wayne State University	M*
West Chester University of Pennsylvania	M*†
Western Kentucky University	M†
Western Michigan University	M,D*†
Western Washington University	M
West Virginia University	M,D*
Wichita State University	M*†
Wright State University	M*
Yale University	D*

GEOPHYSICS

Institution	Degrees
Boise State University	M,D*
Boston College	M*†
California Institute of Technology	M,D*
Colorado School of Mines	M,D,O†
Columbia University	M,D*†
Cornell University	M,D*
Florida State University	D*†
Georgia Institute of Technology	M,D*
ICR Graduate School	M
Idaho State University	M,O*
Indiana University Bloomington	M,D*
Johns Hopkins University	M,D*†
Louisiana State University and Agricultural and Mechanical College	M,D*
Massachusetts Institute of Technology	M,D,O*
Memorial University of Newfoundland	M,D†
Michigan Technological University	M*†
New Mexico Institute of Mining and Technology	M,D†
North Carolina State University	M,D*
Oregon State University	M,D*
The Pennsylvania State University University Park Campus	M,D*†
Princeton University	D*
Rensselaer Polytechnic Institute	M,D*†
Saint Louis University	M,D*†
Southern Methodist University	M,D*†
Stanford University	M,D*
Texas A&M University	M,D*
The University of Akron	M†
University of Alaska Fairbanks	M,D*
University of Alberta	M,D*
The University of British Columbia	M,D*
University of Calgary	M,D*
University of California, Berkeley	M,D*
University of California, Los Angeles	M,D*
University of California, Santa Barbara	M,D*
University of Chicago	M,D*
University of Colorado at Boulder	M,D*
University of Connecticut	M,D*†
University of Georgia	M,D*†
University of Hawaii at Manoa	M,D*
University of Houston	M,D*
University of Idaho	M*†
University of Illinois at Chicago	M,D*
University of Illinois at Urbana–Champaign	M,D*
University of Manitoba	M,D*
The University of Memphis	M,D*†
University of Miami	M,D*†
University of Minnesota, Twin Cities Campus	M,D*
University of Missouri–Rolla	M,D*
University of Nevada, Reno	M,D,O*
University of New Orleans	M*
University of Oklahoma	M*†
The University of Texas at El Paso	M*†
University of Utah	M,D*
University of Victoria	M,D
University of Washington	M,D*
The University of Western Ontario	M,D*
University of Wisconsin–Madison	M,D*
University of Wyoming	M,D*†
Virginia Polytechnic Institute and State University	M,D*
Washington University in St. Louis	M,D*†
West Virginia University	M,D*
Wright State University	M*
Yale University	D*

GEOSCIENCES

Institution	Degrees
Ball State University	M*
Baylor University	M,D*†
Boise State University	M*
Boston University	M,D*†
Brock University	M
Brown University	M,D*
California State University, Chico	M
California University of Pennsylvania	M
Carleton University	M,D
Case Western Reserve University	M,D*†
Central Connecticut State University	M*†
City College of the City University of New York	M,D*†
Colorado School of Mines	M,D,O†
Colorado State University	M,D*
Columbia University	M,D*†
Cornell University	M,D*
Dalhousie University	M,D*
Dartmouth College	M,D*†
Emporia State University	M*†
Florida International University	M,D*†
Georgia Institute of Technology	M,D*
Graduate School and University Center of the City University of New York	D*†
Harvard University	M,D*†
Hunter College of the City University of New York	M,O†
Idaho State University	M,O*
Indiana State University	M,D*†
Indiana University Bloomington	M,D*
Iowa State University of Science and Technology	M,D*†
Lehigh University	M,D*
Louisiana State University and Agricultural and Mechanical College	M*
Massachusetts Institute of Technology	M,D*
McGill University	M,D,O*
McMaster University	M,D
Memorial University of Newfoundland	M,D†
Michigan State University	M,D*†
Mississippi State University	M*
Montana State University–Bozeman	M*
Montana Tech of The University of Montana	M
Montclair State University	M,O†
Murray State University	M†
New Mexico Institute of Mining and Technology	M,D†
North Carolina Central University	M
North Carolina State University	M,D*
Northeastern Illinois University	M
Northern Arizona University	M
Northwestern University	M,D*
Oregon State University	M,D*
The Pennsylvania State University University Park Campus	M,D*†
Princeton University	D*
Purdue University	M,D*
Radford University	M†
Rensselaer Polytechnic Institute	M,D*†
Rice University	M,D*
Saint Louis University	M,D*†
San Francisco State University	M
Simon Fraser University	M
Southeast Missouri State University	M
Stanford University	M,D,O*
State University of New York at Albany	M,D*†
State University of New York College at Oneonta	M
Stony Brook University, State University of New York	M,D*†
Texas A&M University–Commerce	M†
Texas Tech University	M,D*†
Université du Québec à Chicoutimi	M
Université du Québec à Montréal	M,D,O
Université du Québec, Institut National de la Recherche Scientifique	M,D
Université Laval	M,D†
The University of Akron	M†
University of Alberta	M,D*
The University of Arizona	M,D*
University of California, Irvine	M,D*
University of California, Los Angeles	M,D*
University of California, Santa Cruz	M,D*
University of Chicago	M,D*
University of Florida	M,D*†
University of Illinois at Chicago	M,D*
University of Illinois at Urbana–Champaign	M,D*
The University of Iowa	M,D*
University of Louisiana at Monroe	M
University of Maine	M,D*
University of Massachusetts Amherst	D*†
The University of Memphis	M,D*†
University of Michigan	M,D*
University of Missouri–Kansas City	M,D*†
University of Nebraska–Lincoln	M,D*†
University of Nevada, Las Vegas	M,D*†
University of New Hampshire	M,D*†
University of New Mexico	M,D*†
The University of North Carolina at Charlotte	M*
University of Northern Colorado	M†
University of Notre Dame	M,D*†
University of Ottawa	M,D*
University of Rochester	M,D*
University of San Diego	M,D,O*†
University of South Carolina	M,D*†
University of Southern California	M,D*†
The University of Texas at Austin	M,D*
The University of Texas at Dallas	M,D*
University of Tulsa	M,D†
University of Victoria	M,D
University of Waterloo	M,D
The University of Western Ontario	M,D*
University of Windsor	M
Washington University in St. Louis	M,D*†
Wesleyan University	M*
Western Connecticut State University	M
Western Michigan University	M*†
Yale University	D*
York University	M,D*

GEOTECHNICAL ENGINEERING

Institution	Degrees
Auburn University	M,D*†
The Catholic University of America	M,D*†
Colorado State University	M,D*
Cornell University	M,D*
École Polytechnique de Montréal	M,D,O
Iowa State University of Science and Technology	M,D*†
Louisiana State University and Agricultural and Mechanical College	M,D*
Marquette University	M,D*†
McGill University	M,D*
Michigan Technological University	D*†
Northwestern University	M,D*
Ohio University	M,D*
The Pennsylvania State University University Park Campus	M,D*†
Rensselaer Polytechnic Institute	M,D*†
Texas A&M University	M,D*
Tufts University	M,D*†
University of Alberta	M,D*
University of Calgary	M,D*
University of California, Berkeley	M,D*
University of California, Los Angeles	M,D*
University of Central Florida	M,D,O*†
University of Colorado at Boulder	M,D*
University of Delaware	M,D*†
University of Illinois at Chicago	D*
University of Maine	M,D*
University of Missouri–Columbia	M,D*
University of Missouri–Rolla	M,D*
University of New Brunswick Fredericton	M,D
University of Oklahoma	M,D*†
University of Rhode Island	M,D*
University of Southern California	M*†
The University of Texas at Austin	M,D*
University of Washington	M,D*

GERMAN

Institution	Degrees
Arizona State University	M*
Bowling Green State University	M*†
Brigham Young University	M,D*
Brown University	M,D*
California State University, Fullerton	M
California State University, Long Beach	M
California State University, Sacramento	M
The Catholic University of America	M*†
Colorado State University	M*
Columbia University	M,D*†
Cornell University	M,D*
Dalhousie University	M*
Duke University	D*†
Eastern Michigan University	M*
Florida Atlantic University	M*
Florida State University	M*†
Georgetown University	M,D*
Georgia State University	M*
Graduate School and University Center of the City University of New York	M,D*†
Harvard University	M,D*†
Illinois State University	M*†
Indiana University Bloomington	M,D*
Johns Hopkins University	D*†
Kansas State University	M*†
Kent State University	M*
McGill University	M,D*
Memorial University of Newfoundland	M†
Michigan State University	M,D*†
Middlebury College	M,D
Millersville University of Pennsylvania	M†
Minnesota State University, Mankato	M
New York University	M,D*†
Northwestern University	D*
The Ohio State University	M,D*
The Pennsylvania State University University Park Campus	M,D*†
Portland State University	M*
Princeton University	D*
Purdue University	M,D*
Queen's University at Kingston	M,D
Rutgers, The State University of New Jersey, New Brunswick	M,D*
San Francisco State University	M
Stanford University	M,D*
Stony Brook University, State University of New York	M,D*†
Texas Tech University	M*†
Tufts University	M*†
Université de Montréal	M,D
The University of Alabama	M,D*
University of Alberta	M,D*
The University of Arizona	M*
University of Arkansas	M*
University of Calgary	M*
University of California, Berkeley	M,D*
University of California, Davis	M,D*†
University of California, Irvine	M,D*
University of California, Los Angeles	M,D*
University of California, San Diego	M,D*
University of California, Santa Barbara	M,D*
University of Chicago	M,D*
University of Cincinnati	M,D*
University of Colorado at Boulder	M*
University of Connecticut	M,D*†
University of Delaware	M*†
University of Denver	M*†
University of Florida	M,D*†
University of Georgia	M*†
University of Hawaii at Manoa	M*
University of Illinois at Chicago	M,D*
University of Illinois at Urbana–Champaign	M,D*
The University of Iowa	M,D*
University of Kansas	M,D*
University of Kentucky	M*
The University of Lethbridge	M,D
University of Manitoba	M*
University of Maryland, Baltimore County	M*†
University of Maryland, College Park	M,D*
University of Massachusetts Amherst	M,D*†
University of Michigan	M,D*
University of Minnesota, Twin Cities Campus	M,D*
University of Mississippi	M*
University of Missouri–Columbia	M*
The University of Montana–Missoula	M*†
University of Nebraska–Lincoln	M,D*†
University of Nevada, Reno	M*
University of New Brunswick Fredericton	M
University of New Mexico	M,D*†
The University of North Carolina at Chapel Hill	M,D*†
University of Northern Iowa	M
University of Notre Dame	M*†
University of Oklahoma	M*†
University of Oregon	M,D*
University of Pennsylvania	M,D*†
University of Pittsburgh	M,D*†
University of Saskatchewan	M
University of South Carolina	M*†
The University of Tennessee	M,D*†
The University of Texas at Arlington	M*†
The University of Texas at Austin	M,D*
University of Toledo	M*†
University of Toronto	M,D*
University of Utah	M,D*
University of Vermont	M*†
University of Victoria	M
University of Virginia	M,D*
University of Washington	M,D*
University of Waterloo	M,D
University of Wisconsin–Madison	M,D*
University of Wisconsin–Milwaukee	M
University of Wyoming	M*†
Vanderbilt University	M,D*
Washington University in St. Louis	M,D*†
Wayne State University	M,D*

*P—first professional degree; M—master's degree; D—doctorate; O—other advanced degree; *full description and/or announcement in Book 2, 3, 4, 5, or 6; †full description in this book*

West Chester University of Pennsylvania M*†
West Virginia University M*
Yale University M,D*

GERONTOLOGICAL NURSING

Arkansas State University M,O
Boston College M,D*†
Case Western Reserve University M*†
The Catholic University of America M,D*†
College of Mount Saint Vincent M,O*†
Columbia University M,O*†
Concordia University Wisconsin M
Duke University M,O*†
Emory University M*†
Gannon University M,O
Gwynedd-Mercy College M
Hunter College of the City University of New York M†
Jewish Hospital College of Nursing and Allied Health M
La Roche College M
Lehman College of the City University of New York M
Loma Linda University M*
Marquette University M,O*†
Medical University of South Carolina M,O*
Nazareth College of Rochester M
New York University M,O*†
Oregon Health & Science University M,D,O*
Rush University M,D*
Rutgers, The State University of New Jersey, Newark M,D*†
San Jose State University M*
Seton Hall University M*†
State University of New York at New Paltz M
Stony Brook University, State University of New York M*†
Texas Tech University Health Sciences Center M,O*
University at Buffalo, The State University of New York M,D,O*†
University of Delaware M,O*†
University of Maryland M,D*†
University of Massachusetts Lowell M*†
University of Michigan M*
University of Minnesota, Twin Cities Campus M*
University of Nevada, Las Vegas M*†
The University of North Carolina at Greensboro M,O†
University of Pennsylvania M*†
University of Utah M,O*
Vanderbilt University M,D*
Villanova University M,O*†

GERONTOLOGY

Abilene Christian University M
Adler School of Professional Psychology M,D,O*
Appalachian State University M
Arizona State University O*
Ball State University M*
Baylor University M*†
California State University, Dominguez Hills M,O†
California State University, Fullerton M
California State University, Long Beach M
Case Western Reserve University M,D,O*†
Central Missouri State University M†
The College of New Rochelle M,O†
College of Notre Dame of Maryland M
Concordia University (IL) M,O
Eastern Illinois University M†
East Tennessee State University M,O†
Florida State University M*†
Gannon University O
George Mason University M*†
Hofstra University M,O*
Kirksville College of Osteopathic Medicine M,O
Lakehead University M
Lindenwood University M
Long Island University, C.W. Post Campus M,O*†
Long Island University, Southampton College M,O
Lynn University M,O†
Marylhurst University M
Miami University M*†
Minnesota State University, Mankato M
Morehead State University M
Mountain State University M†
Mount Mary College M
Mount Saint Vincent University M
Naropa University M*
National-Louis University M,O
New York Medical College M,O*
North Dakota State University M,D†
Northeastern Illinois University M
Notre Dame de Namur University M,O
Oregon State University M*
Portland State University O*
Roosevelt University M*†
Sage Graduate School M†
St. Cloud State University M
Saint Joseph College M,O
Saint Joseph's University M*†
San Francisco State University M
San Jose State University M,O*
Simon Fraser University M
State University of West Georgia M
Texas A&M University–Kingsville M*†
Towson University M†
Université de Sherbrooke M
Université Laval O†
The University of Arizona M,O*
University of Arkansas at Little Rock M,O
University of Central Florida M,O*†
University of Central Oklahoma M
University of Illinois at Springfield M†
University of Kansas M,D*
University of Kentucky D*
University of La Verne M*
University of Louisiana at Monroe M,O
University of Maryland, Baltimore County M,D,O*†
University of Massachusetts Boston D*†
University of Missouri–St. Louis M,O†
University of Nebraska at Omaha M,O
University of New Orleans M,O*
The University of North Carolina at Charlotte M*
The University of North Carolina at Greensboro M†
University of Northern Colorado M†
University of North Florida M,O
University of North Texas M,O*†
University of Pittsburgh M,D,O*†
University of Puerto Rico, Medical Sciences Campus M,O*
University of South Alabama O*†
University of South Carolina O*†
University of Southern California M,D,O*†
University of South Florida M*†
The University of Tennessee M*†
University of Utah M,O*
Virginia Commonwealth University M,O*†
Virginia Polytechnic Institute and State University M,D*
Washington State University Spokane O†
Wayne State University O*
Webster University M
West Chester University of Pennsylvania M,O*†
Western Kentucky University M†
Wichita State University M*†
Wilmington College M

GRAPHIC DESIGN

Academy of Art College M†
Boston University M*†
California Institute of the Arts M,O*
California State University, Los Angeles M
Cardinal Stritch University M*
City College of the City University of New York M*†
The College of New Rochelle M†
Colorado State University M*
Cranbrook Academy of Art M*
Florida Atlantic University M*
Florida Atlantic University, Davie Campus M
George Mason University M*†
Illinois Institute of Technology M,D*†
Illinois State University M*†
Indiana State University M*†
Indiana University Bloomington M*
Iowa State University of Science and Technology M*†
Kean University M*†
Kent State University M*
Louisiana State University and Agricultural and Mechanical College M*
Louisiana Tech University M*
Michigan State University M*†
Minneapolis College of Art and Design M,O*
North Carolina State University M*
The Pennsylvania State University University Park Campus M*†
Pratt Institute M*
Rhode Island School of Design M
Rochester Institute of Technology M*†
San Diego State University M*
San Jose State University M*
Savannah College of Art and Design M*
School of the Art Institute of Chicago M*
Syracuse University M*
Temple University M*†
Université Laval M†
University of Baltimore M*
University of Cincinnati M*
University of Guam M
University of Houston M*
University of Illinois at Chicago M*
University of Illinois at Urbana–Champaign M*
The University of Memphis M*†
University of Miami M*†
University of Minnesota, Duluth M*
University of New Orleans M*
University of North Texas M,D*†
University of Notre Dame M*†
The University of Tennessee M*†
University of Utah M*
Western Illinois University M,O
Western Michigan University M*†
West Virginia University M*
Yale University M*

HAZARDOUS MATERIALS MANAGEMENT

Colorado State University M,D*
Idaho State University M,D*
New Mexico Institute of Mining and Technology M†
Rutgers, The State University of New Jersey, New Brunswick M,D*
Stony Brook University, State University of New York M,O*†
University of Central Florida M,D,O*†
University of Idaho M*†
University of Oklahoma M,D*†
University of South Carolina M,D*†
Wayne State University M,D,O*

HEALTH EDUCATION

Adams State College M
Adelphi University M,O*
Albany State University M
Alcorn State University M,O
Allen College M
Arcadia University M†
Auburn University M,D,O*†
Austin Peay State University M
Ball State University M*
Baylor University M*†
Boston University M,O*†
Brooklyn College of the City University of New York M†
California State University, Long Beach M
California State University, Los Angeles M
California State University, Northridge M
Central Washington University M†
The Citadel, The Military College of South Carolina M
Cleveland State University M*†
The College of New Jersey M†
Dalhousie University M*
East Carolina University M*†
Eastern Kentucky University M
Eastern University M*
East Stroudsburg University of Pennsylvania M†
Edinboro University of Pennsylvania O
Finch University of Health Sciences/The Chicago Medical School M*
Florida Agricultural and Mechanical University M*
Florida Atlantic University, Ft. Lauderdale Campus M
Florida International University M*†
Florida State University M,D*†
Fort Hays State University M
Frostburg State University M
Georgia College & State University M,O
Georgia Southern University M,O
Georgia Southwestern State University M,O
Hofstra University M*
Howard University M*
Idaho State University M*
Illinois State University M*†
Indiana State University M*†
Indiana University of Pennsylvania M*†
Indiana University–Purdue University Indianapolis M*
Inter American University of Puerto Rico, Metropolitan Campus M
Iowa State University of Science and Technology M,D*†
Jackson State University M
Jacksonville State University M,O
James Madison University M
John F. Kennedy University M*†
Johns Hopkins University M,D*†
Kent State University M,D*
Lehman College of the City University of New York M
Lesley University M,O*†
Loma Linda University M,D*
Long Island University, Brooklyn Campus M*
Louisiana Tech University M,D,O*
Marshall University M*†
McNeese State University M
Michigan State University M,D*†
Middle Tennessee State University M,D*
Midwestern University, Glendale Campus M*
Minnesota State University, Mankato M
Mississippi State University M*
Mississippi University for Women M
Montana State University–Bozeman M*
Montclair State University M†
Morehead State University M
Mountain State University M†
Mount Mary College M
New Jersey City University M
New York University M,D,O*†
North Carolina Agricultural and Technical State University M*
North Carolina State University M*
Northeastern State University M
Northern Arizona University M
Northern State University M
Northwestern State University of Louisiana M,O
Northwest Missouri State University M
Nova Southeastern University D*
Oklahoma State University M,D*†
Oregon State University M*
The Pennsylvania State University Harrisburg Campus of the Capital College M*†
Plymouth State College M*
Portland State University M*
Prairie View A&M University M
Rhode Island College M†
Sage Graduate School M†
Saint Joseph's University M*†
Saint Louis University M*†
Saint Mary's College of California M
South Dakota State University M*
Southeastern Louisiana University M
Southern Connecticut State University M†
Southern Illinois University Carbondale M,D*†
Southern Illinois University Edwardsville M,O†
Southwestern Oklahoma State University M
Southwest Texas State University M*
Springfield College M†
State University of New York College at Brockport M*†
State University of New York College at Cortland M
Stephen F. Austin State University M
Tarleton State University M,O
Teachers College Columbia University M,D*
Temple University M,D*†
Tennessee Technological University M*
Texas A&M University M,D*
Texas A&M University–Commerce M†
Texas A&M University–Kingsville M*†
Texas A&M University System Health Science Center M*
Texas Southern University M†
Texas Woman's University M,D*†
Tulane University M*†
Union College (KY) M
The University of Alabama M,D*
The University of Alabama at Birmingham M,D*†
University of Arkansas M,D*
University of Central Arkansas M
University of Central Oklahoma M
University of Cincinnati M*
University of Colorado at Denver D*
University of Florida M,D*†
University of Georgia M,D,O*†
University of Houston M,D*
University of Illinois at Chicago M*
University of Kansas M,D*

University of Louisiana at Monroe M
University of Manitoba M*
University of Maryland, Baltimore County M*†
University of Maryland, College Park M,D*
University of Medicine and Dentistry of New Jersey M*
University of Michigan–Flint M
The University of Montana–Missoula M*†
University of Nebraska at Omaha M
University of Nebraska–Lincoln M*†
University of New Mexico M*†
University of New Orleans M,O*
The University of North Carolina at Chapel Hill M,D*†
University of Northern Iowa M
University of Oklahoma Health Sciences Center D*
University of Pittsburgh M,O*†
University of Puerto Rico, Medical Sciences Campus M*
University of Rhode Island M*
University of South Alabama M*†
University of South Carolina M,D,O*†
The University of South Dakota M†
University of Southern Mississippi M
The University of Tennessee M*†
The University of Texas at Austin M,D*
The University of Texas at El Paso M*†
The University of Texas at Tyler M
University of Toledo D*†
University of Utah M,D*
University of Virginia M,D*
University of Waterloo M,D
University of West Florida M
University of Wisconsin–La Crosse M†
University of Wyoming M*†
Utah State University M*
Valdosta State University M
Virginia Polytechnic Institute and State University M,D,O*
Wayne State College M
Wayne State University M*
West Chester University of Pennsylvania M*†
Western Illinois University M
Western Oregon University M
Western University of Health Sciences M
West Virginia University M,D*
Widener University M,D*†
Worcester State College M
Wright State University M*

HEALTH INFORMATICS

The College of St. Scholastica M
Duke University M,O*†
La Salle University M,O
Loma Linda University M*
Medical University of South Carolina M*
New York Medical College M*
New York University M,O*†
Touro College M,O
The University of Alabama at Birmingham M*†
University of Central Florida M,O*†
University of La Verne M*
University of Medicine and Dentistry of New Jersey M*
University of Minnesota, Twin Cities Campus M,D*
University of Missouri–Columbia M*
University of Puerto Rico, Medical Sciences Campus M*
University of Virginia M*
University of Washington M*

HEALTH PHYSICS/RADIOLOGICAL HEALTH

Colorado State University M,D*
Drexel University M,D*†
Emory University M,D*†
Georgetown University M*
Georgia Institute of Technology M,D*
Illinois Institute of Technology M,D*†
Johns Hopkins University M,D*†
Massachusetts Institute of Technology M,D,O*
McGill University M,D*
McMaster University M
Medical College of Georgia M*
Medical College of Ohio M*
Midwestern State University M
Mountain State University M†
Oregon State University M,D*
Purdue University M,D*
San Diego State University M*
Texas A&M University M*
Université Laval O†
University of Alberta M,D*
University of Cincinnati M*
University of Florida M,D,O*†
University of Illinois at Urbana–Champaign M,D*
University of Kentucky M*
University of Massachusetts Lowell M,D*†
University of Michigan M,D,O*
University of Missouri–Columbia M,D*
University of Nevada, Las Vegas M*†
University of Oklahoma Health Sciences Center M,D*
University of Pittsburgh M,O*†
Wayne State University M,D*

HEALTH PROMOTION

Ball State University M*
Boston University M*†
Bridgewater State College M
Brigham Young University M,D*
California College for Health Sciences M
California State University, Fresno M
Central Michigan University M†
Emerson College M*†
The George Washington University M*†
Georgia State University M,D*
Goddard College M
Harvard University M,D*†
Jewish Hospital College of Nursing and Allied Health M
Lehman College of the City University of New York M
Loma Linda University M,D*
Marymount University M†
Michigan State University M,D*†
Nebraska Methodist College M
New York Medical College M*
Northern Arizona University M
Northwestern State University of Louisiana M
Old Dominion University M*†
Portland State University M*
Purdue University M,D*
San Diego State University M,D*
Simmons College M,O*
Southwest Missouri State University M*†
Springfield College M,O†
Université de Montréal M,D,O
The University of Alabama M,D*
The University of Alabama at Birmingham M,D*†
University of Alberta M,O*
University of Chicago M*
University of Delaware M*†
University of Georgia M,D,O*†
University of Kentucky M,D*
University of Massachusetts Lowell D*†
The University of Memphis M*†
University of Michigan M,D*
The University of Montana–Missoula M*†
University of Nevada, Las Vegas M*†
The University of North Carolina at Chapel Hill M,D*†
The University of North Carolina at Charlotte M*
University of North Texas M*†
University of Oklahoma Health Sciences Center M,D*
University of Pittsburgh M*†
University of South Carolina M,D,O*†
University of Southern California M*†
The University of Tennessee M*†
University of Utah M,D*
Western Illinois University M
West Virginia University M*

HEALTH PSYCHOLOGY

Alliant International University D*†
Appalachian State University M
Argosy University-Chicago D*
California Institute of Integral Studies M,D,O*
Drexel University M,D*†
Duke University D*†
Emporia State University M*†
National-Louis University M,O
Northern Arizona University M
Philadelphia College of Osteopathic Medicine M,D*
Ponce School of Medicine D
Rutgers, The State University of New Jersey, New Brunswick D*
Santa Clara University M*
Saybrook Graduate School and Research Center M,D
Southwest Texas State University M*
Stony Brook University, State University of New York D*†
University of California, Irvine D*
University of Florida D*†
University of Miami M,D*†
The University of Montana–Missoula M*†
University of North Texas M,D*†
University of the Sciences in Philadelphia M*
Yeshiva University D*

HEALTH SERVICES MANAGEMENT AND HOSPITAL ADMINISTRATION

Albany State University M
Aquinas Institute of Theology P,M,D,O
Argosy University-Chicago Northwest M,D*
Argosy University-Orange County M,D*
Argosy University-Sarasota M,D*†
Argosy University-Tampa M*
Arizona State University M*
Armstrong Atlantic State University M†
Baker College Center for Graduate Studies M
Baldwin-Wallace College M*
Barry University M*†
Baylor University M*†
Bellevue University M*†
Bernard M. Baruch College of the City University of New York M*
Boston University M*†
Brandeis University M*†
Brenau University M
Brooklyn College of the City University of New York M†
California College for Health Sciences M
California Lutheran University M
California State University, Bakersfield M
California State University, Chico M
California State University, Fresno M
California State University, Long Beach M,O
California State University, Los Angeles M
California State University, Northridge M
California State University, San Bernardino M
Cardinal Stritch University M*
Carlow College M
Carnegie Mellon University M*
Central Michigan University M,D,O†
Charleston Southern University M
Clark University M*†
Clemson University M*
Cleveland State University M,D*†
College of Mount Saint Vincent M,O*†
College of Saint Elizabeth M
Colorado Technical University Sioux Falls Campus M
Columbia Southern University M
Columbia University M,D*†
Concordia University (IL) M,O
Concordia University (Canada) M,D,O*†
Concordia University Wisconsin M
Cornell University M,D*
Dalhousie University M*
Dallas Baptist University M
Davenport University M
Davenport University M
DePaul University M*†
Des Moines University Osteopathic Medical Center M*
Duke University M*†
Duquesne University M,D*†
D'Youville College M,O†
Eastern Kentucky University M
East Tennessee State University M,D,O†
Emory University M*†
Fairfield University M,O*
Fairleigh Dickinson University, Metropolitan Campus M*†
Finch University of Health Sciences/The Chicago Medical School M*
Florida Institute of Technology M*†
Florida International University M*†
Framingham State College M*
Francis Marion University M
The George Washington University M,O*†
Georgia Institute of Technology M*
Georgia Southern University M
Georgia State University M,D*
Governors State University M
Harvard University M,D*†
Hofstra University M,O*
Houston Baptist University M
Indiana State University M*†
Indiana University Northwest M,O
Indiana University–Purdue University Indianapolis M*
Institute of Public Administration M,O
Iona College M,O*†
Jewish Hospital College of Nursing and Allied Health M
Johns Hopkins University M,D,O*†
Jones International University M*†
Kean University M*†
King's College M
Kirksville College of Osteopathic Medicine M,O
Lake Erie College M
Lasell College M*
Lesley University M*†
LeTourneau University M
Lindenwood University M
Loma Linda University M*
Long Island University, Brentwood Campus M
Long Island University, Brooklyn Campus M*
Long Island University, C.W. Post Campus M,O*†
Long Island University, Rockland Graduate Campus M
Loyola University Chicago M*†
Lynn University M,O†
Madonna University M
Marshall University M*†
Marymount University M†
Maryville University of Saint Louis M
Marywood University M*†
Massachusetts College of Pharmacy and Health Sciences M*
McGill University M,D,O*
Medical College of Georgia M*
Medical University of South Carolina M,D,O*
Meharry Medical College M
Mercer University M
Mercy College M,O*
Midwestern State University M
Mississippi College M
Monmouth University M,O*†
Montana State University–Billings M*
Mountain State University M†
National University M†
New England College M,O*
New Jersey City University M
New School University M,O*†
New York Medical College M*
New York University M,O*†
Northeastern University M*†
Nova Southeastern University M*
The Ohio State University M*
Ohio University M*
Oklahoma City University M
Old Dominion University M,D*†
Oregon State University M*
Our Lady of the Lake University of San Antonio M
Pace University M*†
Pace University, White Plains Campus M*
The Pennsylvania State University Harrisburg Campus of the Capital College M*†
The Pennsylvania State University University Park Campus M,D*†
Philadelphia University M
Portland State University M*
Quinnipiac University M*†
Rochester Institute of Technology M,O*†
Rush University M*
Rutgers, The State University of New Jersey, Camden M†
Rutgers, The State University of New Jersey, Newark M,D*†
Sacred Heart University M*†
Sage Graduate School M†
St. Ambrose University M
St. John Fisher College M
Saint Joseph's College (ME) M
Saint Joseph's University M*†
Saint Louis University M*†
Saint Mary's University of Minnesota M
St. Thomas University M,O†
Saint Xavier University M,O*
Salve Regina University M†
San Diego State University M,D*
San Jose State University M,O*
Seton Hall University M,O*†
Shenandoah University M,O
Simmons College M,O*
Southeastern University M†
Southern Adventist University M
Southern New Hampshire University M,O*

*P—first professional degree; M—master's degree; D—doctorate; O—other advanced degree; *full description and/or announcement in Book 2, 3, 4, 5, or 6; †full description in this book*

- Southwest Baptist University M
- Southwest Missouri State University M*†
- Southwest Texas State University M*
- Springfield College M†
- State University of New York at Albany M*†
- State University of New York at Binghamton M,D*†
- State University of New York Institute of Technology at Utica/Rome M*†
- Stony Brook University, State University of New York M,O*†
- Suffolk University M,O*
- Syracuse University O*
- Temple University M,D*†
- Texas A&M University System Health Science Center M*
- Texas Tech University M,O*†
- Texas Woman's University M*†
- Touro College O
- Towson University O†
- Trinity University M*
- Tulane University M,D*†
- Union College (NY) M*
- Université de Montréal M,O
- The University of Alabama at Birmingham M,D*†
- University of Alberta M,D,O*
- University of Arkansas at Little Rock M
- The University of British Columbia M,D*
- University of California, Berkeley M,D*
- University of California, Los Angeles M,D*
- University of Central Florida M,O*†
- University of Chicago M,O*
- University of Colorado at Denver M*
- University of Connecticut M,D*†
- University of Dallas M*
- University of Denver M*†
- University of Detroit Mercy M*
- University of Florida M,D*†
- University of Houston–Clear Lake M*†
- University of Illinois at Chicago M,D*
- The University of Iowa M,D*
- University of Kansas M*
- University of Kentucky M*
- University of La Verne M*
- University of Louisiana at Lafayette M*
- University of Mary Hardin-Baylor M
- University of Maryland, Baltimore County M*†
- University of Massachusetts Lowell M*†
- University of Medicine and Dentistry of New Jersey M,O*
- The University of Memphis M*†
- University of Michigan M,D*
- University of Minnesota, Twin Cities Campus M,D*
- University of Missouri–Columbia M*
- University of Missouri–St. Louis M,O†
- University of New Hampshire M*†
- University of New Haven M*†
- University of New Orleans M*
- The University of North Carolina at Chapel Hill M,D*†
- The University of North Carolina at Charlotte M*
- University of North Florida M,O
- University of North Texas M,O*†
- University of North Texas Health Science Center at Fort Worth M,D*
- University of Oklahoma Health Sciences Center M,D*
- University of Ottawa M*
- University of Pennsylvania M,D*†
- University of Phoenix–Fort Lauderdale Campus M
- University of Phoenix–Hawaii Campus M
- University of Phoenix–Jacksonville Campus M
- University of Phoenix–Louisiana Campus M
- University of Phoenix–Metro Detroit Campus M
- University of Phoenix–New Mexico Campus M
- University of Phoenix–Orlando Campus M
- University of Phoenix–Phoenix Campus M
- University of Phoenix–San Diego Campus M
- University of Phoenix–Southern Arizona Campus M
- University of Phoenix–Southern California Campus M
- University of Phoenix–Tampa Campus M
- University of Phoenix–Tulsa Campus M
- University of Phoenix–West Michigan Campus M
- University of Pittsburgh M,D,O*†
- University of Puerto Rico, Medical Sciences Campus M*
- University of St. Thomas (MN) M,O*†
- University of San Francisco M*†
- The University of Scranton M†
- University of South Carolina M,D*†
- University of Southern California M*†
- University of Southern Indiana M
- University of Southern Maine M,O
- University of Southern Mississippi M
- University of South Florida M,D*†
- The University of Texas at Arlington M*†
- The University of Texas at Tyler M
- University of the Sciences in Philadelphia M,D*
- University of Virginia M*
- University of Washington M*
- University of Wisconsin–Oshkosh M*
- University of Wisconsin–Whitewater M*
- Villanova University M,O*†
- Virginia Commonwealth University M,D*†
- Walden University D†
- Washington State University M*
- Washington State University Spokane M†
- Washington University in St. Louis M,D*†
- Webster University M
- West Chester University of Pennsylvania M*†
- Western Carolina University M†
- Western Connecticut State University M
- Western Kentucky University M†
- Western New England College M
- Widener University M*†
- Wilkes University M
- William Woods University M
- Wilmington College M
- Worcester State College M
- Xavier University M*
- Yale University M*
- York College of Pennsylvania M
- Youngstown State University M

HEALTH SERVICES RESEARCH

- Arizona State University M,D*
- Brown University M,D*
- Dartmouth College M,D*†
- Florida State University M*†
- Indiana University–Purdue University Indianapolis M*
- Joan and Sanford I. Weill Medical College and Graduate School of Medical Sciences of Cornell University M*
- Johns Hopkins University M,D*†
- McMaster University M,D
- The Pennsylvania State University Milton S. Hershey Medical Center M*
- Southwest Texas State University M*
- Stanford University M*
- Texas Tech University Health Sciences Center M*
- Thomas Jefferson University O*
- University of Alberta M,D,O*
- The University of British Columbia M,D*
- University of Florida M,D*†
- University of Minnesota, Twin Cities Campus M,D*
- University of Puerto Rico, Medical Sciences Campus M*
- University of Rochester D*
- University of Southern California M,D*†
- University of Virginia M*
- University of Washington M,D*
- Virginia Commonwealth University D*†
- Wake Forest University M*†

HIGHER EDUCATION

- Appalachian State University M,O
- Argosy University-Orange County M,D,O*
- Argosy University-San Francisco Bay Area M,D*
- Arizona State University M,D*
- Auburn University M,D,O*†
- Ball State University M,D*
- Barry University M,D*†
- Bernard M. Baruch College of the City University of New York M*
- Boston College M,D*†
- Bowling Green State University D*†
- Briercrest Biblical Seminary M
- Claremont Graduate University M,D*
- Dallas Baptist University M
- DePaul University M*†
- Eastern Kentucky University M
- Eastern Washington University M†
- Florida Atlantic University M,D,O*
- Florida International University M,D,O*†
- Florida State University M,D,O*†
- Geneva College M*
- The George Washington University M,D,O*†
- Georgia Southern University M
- Georgia State University D*
- Grand Valley State University M†
- Harvard University M,D,O*†
- Illinois State University M,D*†
- Indiana State University M,D,O*†
- Indiana University Bloomington M,D,O*
- Indiana University of Pennsylvania M*†
- Indiana University–Purdue University Indianapolis M*
- Inter American University of Puerto Rico, Metropolitan Campus M
- Inter American University of Puerto Rico, San Germán Campus M
- Iowa State University of Science and Technology M,D*†
- Johns Hopkins University M,D,O*†
- Kent State University M,D,O*
- Louisiana State University and Agricultural and Mechanical College M,D,O*
- Loyola University Chicago M,D*†
- Minnesota State University, Mankato M,O
- Morehead State University M,O
- New York University M,D,O*†
- North Carolina State University M,D*
- Northeastern State University M
- Northwestern University M*
- Nova Southeastern University D*
- Ohio University M,D*
- Oklahoma State University M,D,O*†
- Old Dominion University M,O*†
- The Pennsylvania State University University Park Campus M,D*†
- Pittsburg State University M,O
- Portland State University D*
- Purdue University M,D,O*
- Rowan University M†
- St. John's University (NY) M,O*†
- Saint Louis University M,D,O*†
- San Jose State University M,O*
- Seton Hall University D*†
- Southern Illinois University Carbondale M*†
- Spalding University M†
- Stanford University M,D*
- Syracuse University M,D,O*
- Teachers College Columbia University M,D*
- Texas A&M University–Commerce M,D†
- Texas A&M University–Kingsville D*†
- Texas Southern University M,D†
- Texas Tech University M,D,O*†
- Université de Sherbrooke M,O
- University at Buffalo, The State University of New York M,D*†
- The University of Akron M†
- The University of Arizona M,D*
- University of Arkansas M,D,O*
- University of Arkansas at Little Rock D
- The University of British Columbia M*
- University of Central Oklahoma M
- University of Connecticut M,D*†
- University of Delaware M*†
- University of Denver M,D,O*†
- University of Florida M,D,O*†
- University of Georgia D*†
- University of Houston M,D*
- University of Illinois at Urbana–Champaign M,D,O*
- The University of Iowa M,D,O*
- University of Kansas M,D*
- University of Kentucky M,D*
- University of Louisville M,O*†
- University of Maine M,D,O*
- University of Mary M
- University of Maryland, Baltimore County M,D*†
- University of Massachusetts Amherst M,D,O*†
- University of Massachusetts Boston M,D,O*†
- The University of Memphis M,D,O*†
- University of Miami M*†
- University of Michigan M,D*
- University of Minnesota, Twin Cities Campus M,D*
- University of Mississippi M*
- University of Missouri–Columbia M,D,O*
- University of Nevada, Las Vegas M,D,O*†
- University of New Hampshire M*†
- The University of North Carolina at Greensboro M,D,O†
- University of Northern Colorado D†
- University of Northern Iowa M
- University of North Texas D*†
- University of Oklahoma M,D*†
- University of Pennsylvania M,D*†
- University of Pittsburgh M,D*†
- University of South Carolina M*†
- University of South Florida D,O*†
- The University of Texas at San Antonio M,D*
- University of Toledo M,D,O*†
- University of Virginia D,O*
- University of Washington M,D*
- University of Wisconsin–Whitewater M*
- Vanderbilt University M,D*
- Wayne State University M,D,O*
- West Virginia University M,D*
- Wright State University M,O*

HISPANIC STUDIES

- Brown University M,D*
- California State University, Los Angeles M
- California State University, Northridge M
- Connecticut College M
- McGill University M,D*
- New Mexico Highlands University M
- Pontifical Catholic University of Puerto Rico M
- San Jose State University M*
- Stony Brook University, State University of New York M,D*†
- University of Alberta M,D*
- University of California, Los Angeles D*
- University of California, Santa Barbara M,D*
- University of Illinois at Chicago M,D*
- University of Pittsburgh M,D*†
- University of Puerto Rico, Mayagüez Campus M*
- University of Puerto Rico, Río Piedras M,D*
- University of Washington M*

HISTORIC PRESERVATION

- Ball State University M*
- Boston University M*†
- Colorado State University M,D*
- Columbia University M*†
- Cornell University M,D*
- Eastern Michigan University M*
- The George Washington University M*†
- Georgia State University M*
- Goucher College M
- Middle Tennessee State University M,D*
- New York University *†
- Queen's University at Kingston M
- Rensselaer Polytechnic Institute M*†
- Savannah College of Art and Design M*
- School of the Art Institute of Chicago M*
- State University of New York College at Buffalo M,O
- Texas A&M University M,D*
- Texas Tech University M*†
- University of California, Riverside M,D*
- University of Delaware M*†
- University of Georgia M*†
- University of Kentucky M*
- University of Oregon M*
- University of Pennsylvania M,O*†
- University of South Carolina M,O*†
- University of Vermont M*†
- University of Washington O*
- Western Kentucky University M†

HISTORY

- Abilene Christian University M
- American University M,D*†
- Andrews University M
- Angelo State University M†
- Appalachian State University M
- Arizona State University M,D*
- Arkansas State University M,D,O
- Arkansas Tech University M
- Armstrong Atlantic State University M†
- Athabasca University M
- Auburn University M,D*†
- Ball State University M*

Institution	Degrees
Baylor University	M*†
Boise State University	M*
Boston College	M,D*†
Boston University	M,D*†
Bowling Green State University	M,D*†
Brandeis University	M,D*†
Brigham Young University	M*
Brooklyn College of the City University of New York	M,D†
Brown University	M,D*
Butler University	M
California State Polytechnic University, Pomona	M*
California State University, Bakersfield	M
California State University, Chico	M
California State University, Fresno	M
California State University, Fullerton	M
California State University, Hayward	M
California State University, Long Beach	M
California State University, Los Angeles	M
California State University, Northridge	M
California State University, Stanislaus	M
Carleton University	M,D
Carnegie Mellon University	M,D*
Case Western Reserve University	M,D*†
The Catholic University of America	M,D*†
Central Connecticut State University	M*†
Central Michigan University	M,D†
Central Missouri State University	M†
Central Washington University	M†
Chicago State University	M
Christopher Newport University	M†
The Citadel, The Military College of South Carolina	M
City College of the City University of New York	M*†
Claremont Graduate University	M,D*
Clark Atlanta University	M
Clark University	M,D,O*†
Clemson University	M*
Cleveland State University	M*†
College of Charleston	M*†
The College of Saint Rose	M*†
College of Staten Island of the City University of New York	M†
The College of William and Mary	M,D*†
Colorado State University	M*
Columbia University	M,D*†
Concordia University (Canada)	M,D*†
Converse College	M
Cornell University	M,D*
Dalhousie University	M,D*
DePaul University	M*†
Drew University	M,D†
Duke University	D*†
Duquesne University	M*†
East Carolina University	M*†
Eastern Illinois University	M†
Eastern Kentucky University	M
Eastern Michigan University	M*
Eastern Washington University	M†
East Stroudsburg University of Pennsylvania	M†
East Tennessee State University	M†
Emory University	D*†
Emporia State University	M*†
Fairleigh Dickinson University, Metropolitan Campus	M*†
Fayetteville State University	M
Florida Atlantic University	M*
Florida International University	M,D*†
Florida State University	M,D*†
Fordham University	M,D*†
Fort Hays State University	M
George Mason University	M*†
Georgetown University	M,D*
The George Washington University	M,D*†
Georgia College & State University	M
Georgia Southern University	M
Georgia State University	M,D*
Graduate School and University Center of the City University of New York	D*†
Hardin-Simmons University	M
Harvard University	D*†
Howard University	M,D*
Hunter College of the City University of New York	M†
Illinois State University	M*†
Indiana State University	M*†
Indiana University Bloomington	M,D*
Indiana University of Pennsylvania	M*†

Institution	Degrees
Indiana University–Purdue University Indianapolis	M*
Iona College	M*†
Iowa State University of Science and Technology	M,D*†
Jackson State University	M
Jacksonville State University	M
James Madison University	M
John Carroll University	M
Johns Hopkins University	D*†
Kansas State University	M,D*†
Kent State University	M,D*
Lakehead University	M
Lamar University	M*†
Laurentian University	M
Lehigh University	M,D*
Lehman College of the City University of New York	M
Lincoln University (MO)	M
Long Island University, Brooklyn Campus	M,O*
Long Island University, C.W. Post Campus	M*†
Louisiana State University and Agricultural and Mechanical College	M,D*
Louisiana Tech University	M*
Loyola University Chicago	M,D*†
Marquette University	M,D*†
Marshall University	M*†
McGill University	M,D*
McMaster University	M,D
Memorial University of Newfoundland	M,D†
Miami University	M*†
Michigan State University	M,D*†
Middle Tennessee State University	M,D*
Midwestern State University	M
Millersville University of Pennsylvania	M†
Minnesota State University, Mankato	M
Mississippi College	M
Mississippi State University	M,D*
Monmouth University	M*†
Montana State University–Bozeman	M*
Montclair State University	M†
Morgan State University	M,D*
Murray State University	M†
New Jersey Institute of Technology	M
New Mexico Highlands University	M
New Mexico State University	M
New School University	M,D*†
New York University	M,D,O*†
North Carolina Central University	M
North Carolina State University	M*
North Dakota State University	M†
Northeastern Illinois University	M
Northeastern University	M,D*†
Northern Arizona University	M,D
Northern Illinois University	M,D*†
Northwestern State University of Louisiana	M
Northwestern University	D*
Northwest Missouri State University	M
Oakland University	M†
The Ohio State University	M,D,O*
Ohio University	M,D*
Oklahoma State University	M,D*†
Old Dominion University	M*†
The Pennsylvania State University University Park Campus	M,D*†
Pepperdine University	M*
Pittsburg State University	M
Pontifical Catholic University of Puerto Rico	M
Portland State University	M*
Prescott College	M†
Princeton University	D*
Providence College	M*
Purdue University	M,D*
Purdue University Calumet	M
Queens College of the City University of New York	M†
Queen's University at Kingston	M,D
Rhode Island College	M†
Rice University	M,D*
Roosevelt University	M*†
Rutgers, The State University of New Jersey, Camden	M†
Rutgers, The State University of New Jersey, Newark	M*†
Rutgers, The State University of New Jersey, New Brunswick	D*
St. Cloud State University	M
St. John's University (NY)	M,D*†
Saint Louis University	M,D*†
Saint Mary's University	M
St. Mary's University of San Antonio	M
Salem State College	M
Salisbury University	M

Institution	Degrees
Sam Houston State University	M*
San Diego State University	M*
San Francisco State University	M
San Jose State University	M*
Sarah Lawrence College	M*†
Shippensburg University of Pennsylvania	M†
Simon Fraser University	M,D
Slippery Rock University of Pennsylvania	M†
Smith College	M*
Sonoma State University	M
Southeastern Louisiana University	M
Southeast Missouri State University	M
Southern Connecticut State University	M†
Southern Illinois University Carbondale	M,D*†
Southern Illinois University Edwardsville	M†
Southern Methodist University	M,D*†
Southern University and Agricultural and Mechanical College	M*
Southwest Missouri State University	M*†
Southwest Texas State University	M*
Stanford University	M,D*
State University of New York at Albany	M,D,O*†
State University of New York at Binghamton	M,D*†
State University of New York at Oswego	M
State University of New York College at Brockport	M*†
State University of New York College at Buffalo	M
State University of New York College at Cortland	M
State University of West Georgia	M
Stephen F. Austin State University	M
Stony Brook University, State University of New York	M,D*†
Sul Ross State University	M*
Syracuse University	M,D*
Tarleton State University	M
Temple University	M,D*†
Texas A&M International University	M
Texas A&M University	M,D*
Texas A&M University–Commerce	M†
Texas A&M University–Kingsville	M*†
Texas Christian University	M,D*
Texas Southern University	M†
Texas Tech University	M,D*†
Texas Woman's University	M*†
Trent University	M
Trinity College (CT)	M
Troy State University Dothan	M
Truman State University	M†
Tufts University	M,D*†
Tulane University	M,D*†
Université de Moncton	M
Université de Montréal	M,D
Université de Sherbrooke	M
Université du Québec à Montréal	M,D
Université Laval	M,D†
University at Buffalo, The State University of New York	M,D*†
The University of Akron	M,D†
The University of Alabama	M,D*
The University of Alabama at Birmingham	M*†
The University of Alabama in Huntsville	M*
University of Alberta	M,D*
The University of Arizona	M,D*
University of Arkansas	M,D*
The University of British Columbia	M,D*
University of Calgary	M,D*
University of California, Berkeley	M,D,O*
University of California, Davis	M,D*†
University of California, Irvine	M,D*
University of California, Los Angeles	M,D*
University of California, Riverside	M,D*
University of California, San Diego	M,D*
University of California, Santa Barbara	M,D*
University of California, Santa Cruz	D*
University of Central Arkansas	M
University of Central Florida	M*†
University of Central Oklahoma	M
University of Chicago	M,D*
University of Cincinnati	M,D*

Institution	Degrees
University of Colorado at Boulder	M,D*
University of Colorado at Colorado Springs	M*
University of Colorado at Denver	M*
University of Connecticut	M,D*†
University of Delaware	M,D*†
University of Denver	M*†
University of Florida	M,D*†
University of Georgia	M,D*†
University of Guelph	M,D
University of Hawaii at Manoa	M,D*
University of Houston	M,D*
University of Houston–Clear Lake	M*†
University of Idaho	M,D*†
University of Illinois at Chicago	M,D*
University of Illinois at Urbana–Champaign	M,D*
University of Indianapolis	M
The University of Iowa	M,D*
University of Kansas	M,D*
University of Kentucky	M,D*
The University of Lethbridge	M,D
University of Louisiana at Lafayette	M*
University of Louisiana at Monroe	M
University of Louisville	M*†
University of Maine	M,D*
University of Manitoba	M,D*
University of Maryland, Baltimore County	M*†
University of Maryland, College Park	M,D*
University of Massachusetts Amherst	M,D*†
University of Massachusetts Boston	M*†
The University of Memphis	M,D*†
University of Miami	M,D*†
University of Michigan	D,O*
University of Minnesota, Twin Cities Campus	M,D*
University of Mississippi	M,D*
University of Missouri–Columbia	M,D*
University of Missouri–Kansas City	M,D*†
University of Missouri–St. Louis	M,O†
The University of Montana–Missoula	M*†
University of Nebraska at Kearney	M
University of Nebraska at Omaha	M
University of Nebraska–Lincoln	M,D*†
University of Nevada, Las Vegas	M,D*†
University of Nevada, Reno	M,D*
University of New Brunswick Fredericton	M,D
University of New Hampshire	M,D*†
University of New Mexico	M,D*†
University of New Orleans	M*
The University of North Carolina at Chapel Hill	M,D*†
The University of North Carolina at Charlotte	M*
The University of North Carolina at Greensboro	M,O†
The University of North Carolina at Wilmington	M*
University of North Dakota	M,D*
University of Northern British Columbia	M,D
University of Northern Colorado	M†
University of Northern Iowa	M
University of North Florida	M
University of North Texas	M,D*†
University of Notre Dame	M,D*†
University of Oklahoma	M,D*†
University of Oregon	M,D*
University of Ottawa	M,D*
University of Pennsylvania	M,D*†
University of Pittsburgh	M,D*†
University of Puerto Rico, Río Piedras	M,D*
University of Regina	M
University of Rhode Island	M*
University of Richmond	M*†
University of Rochester	M,D*
University of San Diego	M*†
University of Saskatchewan	M,D
The University of Scranton	M†
University of South Alabama	M*†
University of South Carolina	M,D,O*†
The University of South Dakota	M†
University of Southern California	M,D*†
University of Southern Mississippi	M,D
University of South Florida	M*†
The University of Tennessee	M,D*†
The University of Texas at Arlington	M,D*†

*P—first professional degree; M—master's degree; D—doctorate; O—other advanced degree; *full description and/or announcement in Book 2, 3, 4, 5, or 6; †full description in this book*

The University of Texas at Austin M,D*
The University of Texas at Brownsville M
The University of Texas at El Paso M,D*†
The University of Texas at San Antonio M*
The University of Texas at Tyler M
The University of Texas of the Permian Basin M
The University of Texas–Pan American M
University of Toledo M,D*†
University of Toronto M,D*
University of Tulsa M†
University of Utah M,D*
University of Vermont M*†
University of Victoria M,D
University of Virginia M,D*
University of Washington M,D*
University of Waterloo M,D
The University of Western Ontario M,D*
University of West Florida M
University of Windsor M
The University of Winnipeg M
University of Wisconsin–Eau Claire M†
University of Wisconsin–Madison M,D*
University of Wisconsin–Milwaukee M
University of Wisconsin–Stevens Point M
University of Wyoming M*†
Utah State University M*
Valdosta State University M
Valparaiso University M
Vanderbilt University M,D*
Villanova University M*†
Virginia Commonwealth University M*†
Virginia Polytechnic Institute and State University M*
Virginia State University M
Wake Forest University M*†
Washington College M
Washington State University M,D*
Washington University in St. Louis M,D*†
Wayne State University M,D,O*
West Chester University of Pennsylvania M*†
Western Carolina University M†
Western Connecticut State University M
Western Illinois University M
Western Kentucky University M†
Western Michigan University M,D*†
Western Washington University M
Westfield State College M
West Texas A&M University M†
West Virginia University M,D*
Wichita State University M*†
Wilfrid Laurier University M,D
William Paterson University of New Jersey M*†
Winthrop University M
Wright State University M*
Yale University M,D*
York University M,D*
Youngstown State University M

HISTORY OF MEDICINE

Duke University *†
McGill University M,D*
New Jersey Institute of Technology M
Rutgers, The State University of New Jersey, New Brunswick D*
Uniformed Services University of the Health Sciences M*
University of Minnesota, Twin Cities Campus M,D*
Yale University M,D*

HISTORY OF SCIENCE AND TECHNOLOGY

Arizona State University M,D*
Brown University M,D*
Cornell University M,D*
Drexel University M*†
Georgia Institute of Technology M,D*
Harvard University M,D*†
Indiana University Bloomington M,D*
Iowa State University of Science and Technology M,D*†
Johns Hopkins University D*†
Massachusetts Institute of Technology D*
New Jersey Institute of Technology M
Polytechnic University, Brooklyn Campus M*
Princeton University D*
Rensselaer Polytechnic Institute M,D*†
Rutgers, The State University of New Jersey, New Brunswick D*
Uniformed Services University of the Health Sciences M,D*
University of California, Berkeley D*
University of California, San Diego M,D*
University of California, San Francisco M,D*
University of Chicago M,D*
University of Massachusetts Amherst M,D*†
University of Minnesota, Twin Cities Campus M,D*
University of Notre Dame M,D*†
University of Oklahoma M,D*†
University of Pennsylvania M,D*†
University of Pittsburgh M,D*†
University of Toronto M,D*
University of Wisconsin–Madison M,D*
Virginia Polytechnic Institute and State University M,D*
West Virginia University M,D*
Yale University M,D*

HIV/AIDS NURSING

Columbia University M,O*†
Duke University M,O*†
University of Delaware M,O*†

HOLOCAUST STUDIES

Clark University D*†
The Richard Stockton College of New Jersey M*

HOME ECONOMICS EDUCATION

Brooklyn College of the City University of New York M†
Central Washington University M†
Eastern Kentucky University M
Florida International University M,D,O*†
Iowa State University of Science and Technology M,D*†
Louisiana State University and Agricultural and Mechanical College M,D*
Michigan State University M,D*†
Montclair State University M†
Northwestern State University of Louisiana M
The Ohio State University M*
Purdue University M,D,O*
Queens College of the City University of New York M†
South Carolina State University M
Texas Tech University M,D*†
The University of British Columbia M,D*
University of Central Oklahoma M
University of Georgia M,D,O*†
University of Manitoba M*
University of Rhode Island M*
Wayne State College M
Western Carolina University M†

HORTICULTURE

Auburn University M,D*†
Brigham Young University M*
Colorado State University M,D*
Cornell University M,D*
Iowa State University of Science and Technology M,D*†
Kansas State University M,D*†
Louisiana State University and Agricultural and Mechanical College M,D*
Michigan State University M,D*†
New Mexico State University M,D
North Carolina State University M,D*
The Ohio State University M,D*
Oklahoma State University M*†
Oregon State University M,D*
The Pennsylvania State University University Park Campus M,D*†
Purdue University M,D*
Rutgers, The State University of New Jersey, New Brunswick M,D*
Southern Illinois University Carbondale M*†
Texas A&M University M,D*
Texas Tech University M,D*†
University of Arkansas M*
University of California, Davis M*†
University of Delaware M*†
University of Florida M,D*†
University of Georgia M,D*†
University of Guelph M,D
University of Hawaii at Manoa M,D*
University of Maine M*
University of Manitoba M,D*
University of Maryland, College Park M,D*
University of Minnesota, Twin Cities Campus M,D*
University of Missouri–Columbia M,D*
University of Nebraska–Lincoln M,D*†
University of Puerto Rico, Mayagüez Campus M*
The University of Tennessee M*†
University of Washington M,D*
University of Wisconsin–Madison M,D*
Virginia Polytechnic Institute and State University M,D*
Washington State University M,D*
West Virginia University M,D*

HOSPICE NURSING

D'Youville College M,O†
Madonna University M

HOSPITALITY MANAGEMENT

Central Michigan University M,O†
Cornell University M,D*
Endicott College M
Fairleigh Dickinson University, College at Florham M*†
Fairleigh Dickinson University, Metropolitan Campus M*†
Florida International University M*†
Florida State University M,D*†
The George Washington University M*†
Golden Gate University M,O
Iowa State University of Science and Technology M,D*†
Johnson & Wales University M*†
Kansas State University M,D*†
Lynn University M†
Michigan State University M*†
New York University M,D*†
The Ohio State University M,D*
Oklahoma State University M,D*†
The Pennsylvania State University University Park Campus M,D*†
Purdue University M,D*
Rochester Institute of Technology M*†
Roosevelt University M*†
Schiller International University (United States) M
Schiller International University (United Kingdom) M
Temple University M*†
Texas Tech University M*†
Texas Woman's University M,D*†
The University of Alabama M*
University of Denver M*†
University of Guelph M
University of Hawaii at Manoa M*
University of Houston M*
University of Kentucky M*
University of Massachusetts Amherst M*†
University of Missouri–Columbia M,D*
University of Nevada, Las Vegas M,D*†
University of New Haven M*†
The University of North Carolina at Greensboro M,D†
University of North Texas M*†
University of South Carolina M*†
The University of Tennessee M*†
University of Wisconsin–Stout M
Virginia Polytechnic Institute and State University M,D*

HUMAN-COMPUTER INTERACTION

Carnegie Mellon University M,D*
Dalhousie University M*
DePaul University M*†
Georgia Institute of Technology M*
Indiana University Bloomington M*
Naval Postgraduate School M,D
Tufts University O*†
University of Baltimore M,D*
University of Michigan M,D*

HUMAN DEVELOPMENT

Appalachian State University M
Argosy University-Chicago D*
Arizona State University M,D*
Auburn University M,D*†
Boston University M,D,O*†
Bowling Green State University M*†
Bradley University M†
Brigham Young University M,D*
Brock University M
The Catholic University of America D*†
Central Michigan University M†
Claremont Graduate University M,D*
Colorado State University M*
Concordia University (MN) M
Cornell University D*
Duke University D*†
Erikson Institute M,O
Fielding Graduate Institute M,D
The George Washington University M*†
Harvard University M,D,O*†
Howard University M*
Iowa State University of Science and Technology M,D*†
Kent State University D*
Laurentian University M
Lindsey Wilson College M
Marywood University D*†
Montana State University–Bozeman M*
National-Louis University M,D,O
New York Institute of Technology M*†
Northwestern University D*
The Ohio State University M,D*
Oregon State University M,D*
Our Lady of the Lake University of San Antonio M
Pacific Oaks College M
The Pennsylvania State University University Park Campus M,D*†
Purdue University M,D*
Saint Joseph College M,O
St. Lawrence University M,O
Saint Louis University M,D,O*†
Saint Mary's University of Minnesota M
Sarah Lawrence College M*†
Southern Illinois University Carbondale M,D*†
Texas A&M University M,D*
Texas Southern University M†
Texas Tech University M,D*†
Troy State University M
Troy State University Montgomery M,O
The University of Alabama M*
The University of Arizona M,D*
University of Calgary M,D*
University of California, Berkeley M,D*
University of California, Davis D*†
University of California, Irvine D*
University of Central Oklahoma M
University of Chicago D*
University of Connecticut M,D*†
University of Dayton M*†
University of Delaware M,D*†
University of Guelph M,D
University of Illinois at Chicago M,D*
University of Illinois at Springfield M†
University of Illinois at Urbana–Champaign M,D*
University of Kansas M,D*
University of Maine M*
University of Maryland, College Park M,D,O*
University of Missouri–Columbia M,D*
University of Nevada, Reno M*
The University of North Carolina at Greensboro M,D†
University of North Texas M*†
University of Pennsylvania M,D*†
University of Pittsburgh M*†
University of St. Thomas (MN) M,D,O*†
The University of Texas at Austin M,D*
The University of Texas at Dallas M,D*
University of Toronto M,D*
University of Victoria M
University of Washington M,D*
University of Wisconsin–Madison M,D*
Utah State University M*
Vanderbilt University M,D*
Virginia Polytechnic Institute and State University M,D*
Walsh University M
Washington State University M*
Wayne State University M*

HUMAN GENETICS

Baylor College of Medicine D*
Case Western Reserve University D*†
Drexel University M,D*†
Hofstra University M,O*
Howard University M,D*
Johns Hopkins University D*†
Louisiana State University Health Sciences Center M,D*
McGill University M,D*
Memorial University of Newfoundland M,D†
Sarah Lawrence College M*†
Tulane University M,D*†
University of California, Los Angeles M,D*
University of Chicago D*
University of Manitoba M,D*
University of Maryland M,D*†
University of Michigan M,D*
University of Pittsburgh M,D*†
The University of Texas Health Science Center at Houston M,D*

University of Utah M,D*
Virginia Commonwealth University M,D,O*†
West Virginia University M,D*

HUMANITIES

Arcadia University M†
Arizona State University M*
Brigham Young University M*
California Institute of Integral Studies M,D*
California State University, Dominguez Hills M†
Central Michigan University M†
Claremont Graduate University M,D*
Clark Atlanta University D
Concordia University (Canada) D*†
Dominican University of California M
Drew University M,D,O†
Duke University M*†
Florida State University M,D*†
Frostburg State University M
Grambling State University M
Hofstra University M*
Hollins University M,O
Indiana State University M*†
Instituto Tecnológico y de Estudios Superiores de Monterrey, Campus Central de Veracruz M
Instituto Tecnológico y de Estudios Superiores de Monterrey, Campus Ciudad de México M,D
Instituto Tecnológico y de Estudios Superiores de Monterrey, Campus Irapuato M,D
John Carroll University M
Laurentian University M
Marshall University M*†
Marymount University M†
Memorial University of Newfoundland M†
Michigan State University M*†
New College of California M*†
New York University M,O*†
Old Dominion University M*†
The Pennsylvania State University Harrisburg Campus of the Capital College M*†
Prescott College M†
Salve Regina University M,D,O†
San Francisco State University M
Stanford University M*
State University of New York at Albany D*†
Texas Tech University M,D*†
Towson University M†
University at Buffalo, The State University of New York M*†
University of California, Santa Cruz D*
University of Chicago M*
University of Colorado at Denver M*
University of Dallas M*
University of Houston–Clear Lake M*†
University of Louisville P,M*†
The University of Texas at Arlington M*†
The University of Texas at Dallas M,D*
The University of Texas Medical Branch M,D*
University of West Florida M
Western Kentucky University M†
Wright State University M*
Xavier University M*

HUMAN RESOURCES DEVELOPMENT

Abilene Christian University M
Amberton University M
American International College M,O*
Antioch University Los Angeles M
Argosy University-Tampa M*
Azusa Pacific University M*†
Barry University M,D*†
Bowie State University M
California State University, Sacramento M
Carlow College M
Chapman University M*†
Clemson University M*
The College of New Rochelle M,O†
Florida International University M*†
Friends University M
The George Washington University M,D,O*†
Georgia State University M,D*
Heritage College M
Illinois Institute of Technology M,D*†
Indiana Institute of Technology M
Indiana State University M,D*†
Indiana University Bloomington M*
Indiana University of Pennsylvania M*†
Inter American University of Puerto Rico, Metropolitan Campus M
Inter American University of Puerto Rico, San Germán Campus M
Iowa State University of Science and Technology M,D*†
John F. Kennedy University M,O*†
Johns Hopkins University M,O*†
Kennesaw State University M
Lesley University M*†
Loyola University Chicago M*†
Manhattanville College M*†
Marquette University M*†
McDaniel College M
Midwestern State University M
Mississippi State University M,D,O*
National-Louis University M
New School University M,O*†
North Carolina Agricultural and Technical State University M*
Northeastern Illinois University M
Oakland University M†
Ottawa University M
Palm Beach Atlantic University M
The Pennsylvania State University University Park Campus M*†
Pittsburgh State University M,O
Rochester Institute of Technology M*†
Rollins College M*
St. John Fisher College M
Siena Heights University M
Suffolk University M,O*
Syracuse University D*
Texas A&M University M,D*
Towson University M†
Universidad del Turabo M
University of Bridgeport M*†
University of Georgia M,D,O*†
University of Illinois at Urbana–Champaign M,D,O*
University of Louisville M*†
University of Minnesota, Twin Cities Campus M,D,O*
University of Pittsburgh M*†
University of Regina M
University of San Francisco M*†
The University of Scranton M†
The University of Tennessee M,D*†
The University of Texas at Austin M*
University of Wisconsin–Milwaukee M
University of Wisconsin–Stout M
Vanderbilt University M,D*
Villanova University M*†
Virginia Polytechnic Institute and State University M,D*
Webster University M
Western Carolina University M†
Western Michigan University M,D,O*†
Western New England College M
Xavier University M*

HUMAN RESOURCES MANAGEMENT

Adelphi University O*
Alabama Agricultural and Mechanical University M,O
Albany State University M
Amberton University M
American University M*†
Argosy University-Chicago Northwest M,D*
Argosy University-Orange County M,D*
Argosy University-Sarasota M,D*†
Auburn University M,D*†
Baker College Center for Graduate Studies M
Baldwin-Wallace College M*
Bernard M. Baruch College of the City University of New York M,D*
Boston University M,O*†
California State University, Hayward M
California State University, Sacramento M
Case Western Reserve University M,D*†
The Catholic University of America M*†
Central Michigan University M,O†
Chapman University M*†
City University M,O†
Claremont Graduate University M*
Clarkson University M*
Cleveland State University M*†
Colorado Technical University M,D
Colorado Technical University Sioux Falls Campus M
Columbia Southern University M
Columbia University M*†
Concordia University (MN) M
Concordia University Wisconsin M
Cornell University M,D*
Cumberland University M
Dallas Baptist University M
Davenport University M
Davenport University M
DePaul University M*†
DeVry University-Keller Graduate School of Management M
East Central University M
Eastern Michigan University M*
École des Hautes Études Commerciales de Montréal M*
Emmanuel College M*
Fairfield University M,O*
Fairleigh Dickinson University, College at Florham M*†
Fairleigh Dickinson University, Metropolitan Campus M*†
Florida Institute of Technology M*†
Florida Metropolitan University–Tampa Campus M
Fordham University M,D,O*†
Framingham State College M*
Gannon University O
George Mason University M*†
The George Washington University M,D*†
Georgia State University M,D*
Golden Gate University M,D,O
Goldey-Beacom College M
Hawai'i Pacific University M*†
Hofstra University M*
Holy Family College M
Houston Baptist University M
Indiana Institute of Technology M
Indiana University Bloomington M*
Instituto Tecnológico y de Estudios Superiores de Monterrey, Campus Cuernavaca M
Inter American University of Puerto Rico, Metropolitan Campus M
Inter American University of Puerto Rico, San Germán Campus M
Iona College M,O*†
Kennesaw State University M
La Roche College M
Lesley University M,O*†
Lindenwood University M
Long Island University, Brooklyn Campus M*
Long Island University, C.W. Post Campus M,O*†
Loyola University Chicago M*†
Lynchburg College M
Manhattanville College M*†
Marquette University M*†
Marshall University M*†
Marygrove College M
Marymount University M,O†
McMaster University M,D
Mercy College M*
Metropolitan State University M
Michigan State University M,D*†
National-Louis University M
National University M†
New England College M,O*
New School University M,O*†
New York Institute of Technology M,O*†
New York University M,D,O*†
North Carolina Agricultural and Technical State University M*
Nova Southeastern University M*
The Ohio State University M,D*
Oral Roberts University M
Ottawa University M
Pontifical Catholic University of Puerto Rico M,D
Purdue University M,D*
Regis University M,O*†
Rivier College M*†
Rollins College M*
Royal Roads University M
Rutgers, The State University of New Jersey, Newark M,D*†
Rutgers, The State University of New Jersey, New Brunswick M,D*
Sage Graduate School M†
St. Edward's University M,O
Saint Francis University M*
Saint Joseph's University M*†
St. Thomas University M,O†
San Diego State University M*
Southeast Missouri State University M
Southern New Hampshire University M,O*
State University of New York at Albany M*†
Stony Brook University, State University of New York M,O*†
Suffolk University M,O*
Temple University M,D*†
Texas A&M University M*
Thomas College M
Trinity College (DC) M†
Troy State University M
Troy State University Dothan M
Troy State University Montgomery M
Universidad del Turabo M
The University of Akron M†
University of Charleston M
University of Connecticut M,D*†
University of Dallas M*
The University of Findlay M
University of Florida M,D*†
University of Houston–Clear Lake M*†
University of Illinois at Chicago D*
University of Illinois at Urbana–Champaign M,D*
The University of Lethbridge M,D
The University of Memphis M*†
University of Minnesota, Twin Cities Campus M,D*
University of Missouri–St. Louis M,O†
University of New Haven M*†
University of New Mexico M*†
University of North Florida M
University of Pittsburgh O*†
University of Redlands M
University of Regina M
University of St. Thomas (MN) M,O*†
The University of Scranton M†
University of South Carolina M*†
The University of Texas at Arlington M,D*†
University of the Sacred Heart M
University of Wisconsin–Madison M*
University of Wisconsin–Whitewater M*
Upper Iowa University M
Utah State University M*
Valdosta State University M
Virginia Commonwealth University M*†
Webster University M
Western New England College M
Widener University M*†
Wilkes University M
Wilmington College M
York College of Pennsylvania M

HUMAN SERVICES

Abilene Christian University M
Andrews University M
Antioch New England Graduate School M*†
Bellevue University M*†
Boricua College M
Brandeis University M*†
Brooklyn College of the City University of New York M†
California State University, Sacramento M
Capella University M,D
Chestnut Hill College M,D†
Concordia University (IL) M,O
Concordia University (MN) M
DePaul University M*†
Drury University M
Ferris State University M
Fielding Graduate Institute M,D
Framingham State College M*
Franklin University M
Georgia State University M*
Indiana University Northwest M,O
Kansas State University M,D*†
Lehigh University M,D,O*
Lesley University M,O*†
Lincoln University (PA) M
Lindenwood University M
Lindsey Wilson College M
Louisiana State University in Shreveport M†
Minnesota State University, Mankato M
Minnesota State University, Moorhead M
Montclair State University M†
Murray State University M†
National-Louis University M,O
New England College M,O*
Pontifical Catholic University of Puerto Rico M,D
Rider University M*
Roberts Wesleyan College M*
Rosemont College M†
Sage Graduate School M†
St. Edward's University M,O
St. Mary's University of San Antonio M,D,O
Southern Oregon University M
Spertus Institute of Jewish Studies M
Springfield College M†
State University of New York at Oswego M
Texas Southern University M†
Universidad del Turabo M
Université de Montréal D

*P—first professional degree; M—master's degree; D—doctorate; O—other advanced degree; *full description and/or announcement in Book 2, 3, 4, 5, or 6; †full description in this book*

University of Baltimore M*
University of Bridgeport M*†
University of Colorado at Colorado Springs M*
University of Great Falls M
University of Illinois at Springfield M†
University of Maryland, Baltimore County M,D*†
University of Massachusetts Boston M*†
University of Oklahoma M*†
University of Toledo M,D*†
Walden University D†
Wayne State University O*
West Virginia University M*
Wichita State University M*†
Youngstown State University M

HYDRAULICS

Auburn University M,D*†
Colorado State University M,D*
École Polytechnique de Montréal M,D,O
McGill University M,D*
Texas A&M University M,D*
University of Missouri–Rolla M,D*
University of Washington M,D*

HYDROLOGY

Auburn University M,D*†
California State University, Bakersfield M
Clemson University M*
Colorado School of Mines M,D,O†
Colorado State University M,D*
Cornell University M,D*
Idaho State University M,O*
Illinois State University M*†
Montana Tech of The University of Montana M
New Mexico Institute of Mining and Technology M,D†
Rensselaer Polytechnic Institute M*†
State University of New York College of Environmental Science and Forestry M,D
Syracuse University M,D*
Texas A&M University M,D*
The University of Arizona M,D*
University of California, Davis M,D*†
University of Hawaii at Manoa M,D*
University of Idaho M*†
University of Illinois at Chicago M,D*
University of Missouri–Rolla M,D*
University of Nevada, Reno M,D*
University of New Brunswick Fredericton M,D
University of New Hampshire M,D*†
University of Southern Mississippi M,D
University of South Florida M,D*†
University of Washington M,D*
West Virginia University M,D*
Wright State University M*

ILLUSTRATION

Academy of Art College M†
California State University, Long Beach M
Kent State University M*
Minneapolis College of Art and Design M,O*
Savannah College of Art and Design M*
School of Visual Arts M†
Syracuse University M*
University of Utah M*
Western Connecticut State University M

IMMUNOLOGY

Albany Medical College M,D*
Baylor College of Medicine D*
Boston University D*†
Brown University M,D*
California Institute of Technology D*
Case Western Reserve University M,D*†
Colorado State University M,D*
Cornell University M,D*
Creighton University M,D*
Dalhousie University M,D*
Dartmouth College *†
Drexel University M,D*†
Duke University D*†
East Carolina University D*†
Emory University D*†
Finch University of Health Sciences/The Chicago Medical School M,D*
Florida State University M,D*†
Georgetown University D*
The George Washington University D*†
Harvard University D*†
Indiana University–Purdue University Indianapolis M,D*
Iowa State University of Science and Technology M,D*†
Joan and Sanford I. Weill Medical College and Graduate School of Medical Sciences of Cornell University M,D*
Johns Hopkins University M,D*†
Kansas State University M,D*†
Long Island University, C.W. Post Campus M*†
Louisiana State University Health Sciences Center M,D*
Loyola University Chicago M,D*†
Massachusetts Institute of Technology D*
Mayo Graduate School D*
McGill University M,D*
McMaster University M,D
Medical University of South Carolina M,D*
New York Medical College M,D*
New York University D*†
North Carolina State University M,D*
Northwestern University D*
The Ohio State University M,D*
Oregon Health & Science University D*
The Pennsylvania State University Milton S. Hershey Medical Center M,D*
Purdue University M,D*
Queen's University at Kingston M,D
Rush University D*
Rutgers, The State University of New Jersey, New Brunswick M,D*
Saint Louis University D*†
Stanford University D*
State University of New York at Albany M,D*†
State University of New York Upstate Medical University M,D*
Stony Brook University, State University of New York M,D*†
Temple University M,D*†
Texas A&M University System Health Science Center D*
Thomas Jefferson University D*
Tufts University D*†
Tulane University M,D*†
Uniformed Services University of the Health Sciences D*
Université de Montréal M,D
Université de Sherbrooke M,D
Université du Québec, Institut National de la Recherche Scientifique M,D
Université Laval M,D†
University at Buffalo, The State University of New York D*†
University of Alberta M,D*
The University of Arizona M,D*
University of Arkansas for Medical Sciences M,D*
The University of British Columbia M,D*
University of California, Berkeley M,D*
University of California, Davis M,D*†
University of California, Los Angeles M,D*
University of California, San Diego D*
University of California, San Francisco D*
University of Chicago D*
University of Colorado Health Sciences Center D*
University of Connecticut Health Center D*
University of Florida M,D*†
University of Guelph M,D,O
University of Illinois at Chicago D*
The University of Iowa M,D*
University of Kansas D*
University of Kentucky D*
University of Louisville M,D*†
University of Manitoba M,D*
University of Maryland M,D*†
University of Massachusetts Worcester D*
University of Medicine and Dentistry of New Jersey M,D*
University of Miami D*†
University of Michigan D*
University of Minnesota, Duluth M,D*
University of Missouri–Columbia M,D*
The University of North Carolina at Chapel Hill M,D*†
University of North Dakota M,D*
University of North Texas Health Science Center at Fort Worth M,D*
University of Oklahoma Health Sciences Center M,D*
University of Ottawa M,D*
University of Pennsylvania D*†
University of Pittsburgh M,D*†
University of Prince Edward Island M,D
University of Rochester M,D*
University of South Alabama D*†
The University of South Dakota M,D†
University of Southern California M,D*†
University of Southern Maine M
University of South Florida D*†
The University of Tennessee Health Science Center D*
The University of Texas at Austin D*
The University of Texas Health Science Center at Houston M,D*
The University of Texas Medical Branch M,D*
The University of Texas Southwestern Medical Center at Dallas D*
University of Toronto M,D*
University of Utah *
University of Virginia D*
University of Washington D*
The University of Western Ontario M,D*
Vanderbilt University M,D*
Virginia Commonwealth University M,D,O*†
Wake Forest University D*†
Washington University in St. Louis D*†
Wayne State University M,D*
West Virginia University M,D*
Wright State University M*
Yale University D*
Yeshiva University D*

INDUSTRIAL/MANAGEMENT ENGINEERING

Arizona State University M,D*
Auburn University M,D*†
Bradley University M†
California Polytechnic State University, San Luis Obispo M†
California State University, Fresno M
California State University, Northridge M
Central Missouri State University M,O†
Central Washington University M†
Clemson University M,D*
Cleveland State University M,D*†
Colorado State University M,D*
Columbia University M,D,O*†
Cornell University M,D*
Dalhousie University M,D*
East Carolina University M*†
Eastern Kentucky University M
Eastern Michigan University M*
École Polytechnique de Montréal M,O
Florida Agricultural and Mechanical University M*
Florida International University M*†
Florida State University M,D*†
Georgia Institute of Technology M,D*
Illinois State University M*†
Indiana State University M*†
Instituto Tecnológico y de Estudios Superiores de Monterrey, Campus Chihuahua M,O
Instituto Tecnológico y de Estudios Superiores de Monterrey, Campus Ciudad de México M,D
Instituto Tecnológico y de Estudios Superiores de Monterrey, Campus Ciudad Juárez M
Instituto Tecnológico y de Estudios Superiores de Monterrey, Campus Laguna M
Instituto Tecnológico y de Estudios Superiores de Monterrey, Campus Monterrey M,D
Iowa State University of Science and Technology M,D*†
Kansas State University M,D*†
Lamar University M,D*†
Lehigh University M,D*
Louisiana State University and Agricultural and Mechanical College M,D*
Louisiana Tech University M,D*
Loyola Marymount University M†
Mississippi State University M,D*
Montana State University–Bozeman M,D*
Montana Tech of The University of Montana M
New Jersey Institute of Technology M,D
New Mexico State University M,D
North Carolina Agricultural and Technical State University M,D*
North Carolina State University M,D*
North Dakota State University M†
Northeastern University M,D*†
Northern Illinois University M*†
Northwestern University M,D*
The Ohio State University M,D*
Ohio University M*
Oklahoma State University M,D*†
Oregon State University M,D*
The Pennsylvania State University University Park Campus M,D*†
Polytechnic University, Brooklyn Campus M*
Polytechnic University, Long Island Graduate Center M
Polytechnic University, Westchester Graduate Center M
Purdue University M,D*
Rensselaer Polytechnic Institute M*†
Rochester Institute of Technology M*†
Rutgers, The State University of New Jersey, New Brunswick M,D*
St. Mary's University of San Antonio M
South Dakota State University M*
Southern Polytechnic State University M†
Southwest Texas State University M*
Stanford University M,D*
State University of New York at Binghamton M,D*†
State University of New York College at Buffalo M
Stony Brook University, State University of New York M*†
Tennessee Technological University M,D*
Texas A&M University M,D*
Texas A&M University–Commerce M†
Texas A&M University–Kingsville M*†
Texas Tech University M,D*†
Universidad de las Américas–Puebla M
Université de Moncton M
Université du Québec à Trois-Rivières M,O
Université Laval O†
University at Buffalo, The State University of New York M,D*†
The University of Alabama M*
The University of Alabama in Huntsville M,D*
The University of Arizona M,D*
University of Arkansas M,D*
University of California, Berkeley M,D*
University of Central Florida M,D,O*†
University of Cincinnati M,D*
University of Dayton M*†
University of Florida M,D,O*†
University of Houston M,D*
University of Illinois at Chicago D*
University of Illinois at Urbana–Champaign M,D*
The University of Iowa M,D*
University of Louisville M,D*†
University of Manitoba M,D*
University of Massachusetts Amherst M,D*†
University of Massachusetts Lowell M,D*†
The University of Memphis M*†
University of Miami M,D*†
University of Michigan M,D,O*
University of Michigan–Dearborn M*†
University of Minnesota, Twin Cities Campus M,D*
University of Missouri–Columbia M,D*
University of Nebraska–Lincoln M,D*†
University of New Haven M,O*†
University of Oklahoma M,D*†
University of Pittsburgh M,D*†
University of Puerto Rico, Mayagüez Campus M*
University of Regina M,D
University of Rhode Island M*
University of Southern California M,D,O*†
University of Southern Colorado M
University of South Florida M,D*†
The University of Tennessee M,D*†
The University of Texas at Arlington M,D*†
The University of Texas at Austin M,D*
The University of Texas at El Paso M*†
University of Toledo M,D*†
University of Toronto M,D*
University of Washington M,D*
University of Windsor M,D

University of Wisconsin–Madison M,D*
Virginia Polytechnic Institute and State University M,D*
Wayne State University M,D*
Western Carolina University M†
Western Michigan University M*†
Western New England College M
West Virginia University M,D*
Wichita State University M,D*†
Youngstown State University M

INDUSTRIAL AND LABOR RELATIONS

Bernard M. Baruch College of the City University of New York M*
Case Western Reserve University M,D*†
Cleveland State University M*†
Cornell University M,D*
Georgia State University M,D*
Indiana University of Pennsylvania M*†
Inter American University of Puerto Rico, Metropolitan Campus M
Inter American University of Puerto Rico, San Germán Campus M
Iowa State University of Science and Technology M*†
Loyola University Chicago M*†
Michigan State University M,D*†
Middle Tennessee State University M,D*
New York Institute of Technology M,O*†
The Ohio State University M,D*
The Pennsylvania State University University Park Campus M*†
Queen's University at Kingston M
Rutgers, The State University of New Jersey, New Brunswick M,D*
State University of New York Empire State College M
Stony Brook University, State University of New York M,O*†
Université de Montréal M,D
Université du Québec en Outaouais M
Université du Québec à Trois-Rivières O
Université Laval M,D†
The University of Akron M†
University of Alberta D*
University of California, Berkeley D*
University of Cincinnati M*
University of Illinois at Urbana–Champaign M,D*
University of Louisville M*†
University of Manitoba M*
University of Massachusetts Amherst M*†
University of Minnesota, Twin Cities Campus M,D*
University of New Haven M*†
University of North Texas M,D*†
University of Rhode Island M*
University of Saskatchewan M
University of Toronto M,D*
University of Victoria M
University of Wisconsin–Madison M,D*
University of Wisconsin–Milwaukee M
Virginia Commonwealth University M*†
Wayne State University M*
West Virginia University M*

INDUSTRIAL AND MANUFACTURING MANAGEMENT

Baker College Center for Graduate Studies M
Bentley College M,O*
Bernard M. Baruch College of the City University of New York M,D*
Boston University M,D,O*†
Bryant College M
California Polytechnic State University, San Luis Obispo M†
Carnegie Mellon University M,D*
Case Western Reserve University M,D*†
Central Michigan University M†
Central Missouri State University M†
Clarkson University M*
Clemson University M,D*
Columbia University D*†
DePaul University M*†
Eastern Michigan University M*
École des Hautes Études Commerciales de Montréal M*
Florida Institute of Technology M*†
The George Washington University M*†
Georgia State University M,D*
Golden Gate University M,D,O
Illinois Institute of Technology M*†
Indiana University Southeast M,O
Instituto Tecnológico y de Estudios Superiores de Monterrey, Campus Irapuato M,D
Inter American University of Puerto Rico, Metropolitan Campus M
Lawrence Technological University M
Lynchburg College M
Massachusetts Institute of Technology *
McGill University M*
Michigan State University M,D*†
Michigan Technological University M*†
New York University M*†
Northeastern State University M
Northern Illinois University M*†
Northwestern University M*
The Pennsylvania State University University Park Campus M,D*†
Polytechnic University, Brooklyn Campus M*
Polytechnic University, Long Island Graduate Center M
Polytechnic University of Puerto Rico M
Polytechnic University, Westchester Graduate Center M
Purdue University M,D*
Regis University M,O*†
Rensselaer Polytechnic Institute M,D*†
Rochester Institute of Technology M*†
San Diego State University M*
San Jose State University M*
Southeastern Oklahoma State University M
Southeast Missouri State University M
Stevens Institute of Technology M,O*†
Stony Brook University, State University of New York M,O*†
Syracuse University D*
Texas Tech University M,D*†
Universidad de las Américas–Puebla M
The University of Alabama M,D*
University of Arkansas M*
University of Cincinnati M,D*
University of Colorado at Boulder M,D*
University of Colorado at Colorado Springs M*
University of Massachusetts Lowell M*†
University of Minnesota, Twin Cities Campus M,D*
University of North Dakota M*
University of North Texas M,D*†
University of Rhode Island M,D*
University of St. Thomas (MN) M,O*†
University of Southern Indiana M
The University of Tennessee M,D*†
The University of Tennessee at Chattanooga M
University of Toledo M,D*†
University of Victoria M
University of Wisconsin–Madison M*
University of Wisconsin–Platteville M
Washington University in St. Louis M,D*†
Wright State University M*

INDUSTRIAL AND ORGANIZATIONAL PSYCHOLOGY

Adler School of Professional Psychology M,D,O*
Alliant International University M,D*†
Alliant International University M,D*†
Alliant International University M,D*†
Alliant International University M,D*†
Angelo State University M†
Appalachian State University M
Bernard M. Baruch College of the City University of New York M,D,O*
Bowling Green State University M,D*†
Brooklyn College of the City University of New York M,D†
California State University, San Bernardino M
Carlos Albizu University M,D
Carlos Albizu University, Miami Campus M,D
Central Michigan University M,D†
Central Washington University M†
Chicago School of Professional Psychology M,D*
Christopher Newport University M†
Claremont Graduate University M,D*
Clemson University D*
Cleveland State University M*†
Colorado State University D*
DePaul University M,D*†
Eastern Kentucky University M,O
Elmhurst College M
Emporia State University M*†
Fairleigh Dickinson University, College at Florham M*†
Florida Institute of Technology M,D*†
George Mason University M,D*†
The George Washington University D*†
Goddard College M
Golden Gate University M,O
Graduate School and University Center of the City University of New York D*†
Hofstra University M*
Illinois Institute of Technology M,D*†
Illinois State University M,D,O*†
Indiana University–Purdue University Indianapolis M,D*
John F. Kennedy University M,O*†
Kean University M,O*†
Lamar University M*†
Louisiana State University and Agricultural and Mechanical College M,D*
Louisiana Tech University M,D,O*
Marshall University M,D*†
Middle Tennessee State University M,O*
Minnesota State University, Mankato M
Montclair State University M†
National-Louis University M,O
New York University M,D,O*†
Ohio University D*
Old Dominion University D*†
The Pennsylvania State University University Park Campus M,D*†
Philadelphia College of Osteopathic Medicine M,D*
Pontifical Catholic University of Puerto Rico M,D
Radford University M,O†
Rensselaer Polytechnic Institute M*†
Rice University M,D*
Roosevelt University M,D*†
Rutgers, The State University of New Jersey, New Brunswick M,D*
Saint Mary's University M
St. Mary's University of San Antonio M
San Diego State University M,D*
San Jose State University M*
Southern Illinois University Edwardsville M†
Springfield College M,O†
State University of New York at Albany M,D*†
Teachers College Columbia University M,D*
Temple University M,D*†
Texas A&M University M,D*
The University of Akron M,D†
University of Baltimore M,D*
University of Central Florida M,D*†
University of Connecticut D*†
University of Detroit Mercy M*
University of Guelph M,D
University of Houston D*
University of Illinois at Urbana–Champaign M,D*
University of Maryland, College Park M,D*
University of Michigan D*
University of Minnesota, Twin Cities Campus D*
University of Missouri–St. Louis M,D,O†
University of Nebraska at Omaha M,D,O
University of New Haven M,O*†
The University of North Carolina at Charlotte M*
University of North Texas M,D*†
University of South Florida D*†
The University of Tennessee D*†
The University of Tennessee at Chattanooga M
University of Tulsa M,D†
University of Wisconsin–Oshkosh M*
Valdosta State University M,O
Virginia Polytechnic Institute and State University M,D*
Wayne State University M,D*
West Chester University of Pennsylvania M*†
Western Michigan University M,D,O*†
William Carey College M
Wright State University M,D*

INDUSTRIAL DESIGN

Academy of Art College M†
Art Center College of Design M*
Auburn University M*†
Illinois Institute of Technology M,D*†
North Carolina State University M*
The Ohio State University M*
Pratt Institute M*
Rhode Island School of Design M
Rochester Institute of Technology M*†
San Francisco State University M
San Jose State University M*
Savannah College of Art and Design M*
University of Calgary M,D*
University of Cincinnati M*
University of Illinois at Chicago M*
University of Illinois at Urbana–Champaign M*
University of Notre Dame M*†
The University of the Arts M*

INDUSTRIAL HYGIENE

Central Missouri State University M,O†
Montana Tech of The University of Montana M
New Jersey Institute of Technology M
Purdue University M,D*
San Diego State University M,D*
Texas A&M University M*
The University of Alabama at Birmingham D*†
University of Cincinnati M,D*
University of Michigan M,D*
University of Minnesota, Twin Cities Campus M,D*
University of New Haven M*†
The University of North Carolina at Chapel Hill M,D*†
University of Puerto Rico, Medical Sciences Campus M*
University of South Carolina M,D*†
University of Washington M,D*
Wayne State University M,O*

INFORMATION SCIENCE

Alcorn State University M
American InterContinental University M*
American InterContinental University Online M
American University M,O*†
Arizona State University East M
Arkansas Tech University M
Athabasca University M
Ball State University M*
Barry University M*†
Bellevue University M*†
Bentley College M*
Bradley University M†
Brooklyn College of the City University of New York M,D†
Bryant College M
California State University, Fullerton M
Capella University M
Capitol College M
Carleton University M
Carnegie Mellon University M,D*
Case Western Reserve University M,D*†
Central Washington University M†
Claremont Graduate University M,D*
Clark Atlanta University M
Clarkson University M*
Clark University M*†
Coleman College M
The College of Saint Rose M*†
Colorado Technical University M,D
Dakota State University M*
DePaul University M*†
DeSales University M
Drexel University D*†
East Carolina University M*†
East Tennessee State University M†
Edinboro University of Pennsylvania O
Florida Gulf Coast University M
Florida Institute of Technology M,D*†
George Mason University M*†
Georgia Southwestern State University M
Grand Valley State University M†
Harvard University M,O*†
Hood College M
Indiana University Bloomington M,D,O*

*P—first professional degree; M—master's degree; D—doctorate; O—other advanced degree; *full description and/or announcement in Book 2, 3, 4, 5, or 6; †full description in this book*

Instituto Tecnológico y de Estudios Superiores de Monterrey, Campus Cuernavaca M,D
Instituto Tecnológico y de Estudios Superiores de Monterrey, Campus Irapuato M,D
Instituto Tecnológico y de Estudios Superiores de Monterrey, Campus Monterrey M,D
Instituto Tecnológico y de Estudios Superiores de Monterrey, Campus Sonora Norte M
Iowa State University of Science and Technology M*†
ISIM University M
ITI-Information Technology Institute M
Kansas State University M,D*†
Kennesaw State University M
Knowledge Systems Institute M
Kutztown University of Pennsylvania M†
Lamar University M*†
Lehigh University M,D,O*
Long Island University, C.W. Post Campus M*†
Marist College M
Marshall University M*†
Montclair State University M,O†
Naval Postgraduate School M
New Jersey Institute of Technology M,D
New York University M,D*†
Northeastern University M*†
Northern Kentucky University M
Northwestern University M*
Nova Southeastern University M,D*
Oakland University M,O†
The Ohio State University M,D*
Pace University M,D,O*†
Pace University, White Plains Campus M,D,O*
The Pennsylvania State University Great Valley Campus M
The Pennsylvania State University University Park Campus D*†
Polytechnic University, Brooklyn Campus M*
Polytechnic University, Long Island Graduate Center M
Polytechnic University, Westchester Graduate Center M
Princeton University M,D*
Queen's University at Kingston M,D
Regis University M,O*†
Rensselaer Polytechnic Institute M*†
Rivier College M*†
Robert Morris University M,D†
Rochester Institute of Technology M*†
Sacred Heart University M,O*†
St. Mary's University of San Antonio M
Saint Xavier University M*
San Jose State University M*
Shippensburg University of Pennsylvania M†
Southern Methodist University M,D*†
Southern Polytechnic State University M†
State University of New York at Albany M,D,O*†
State University of New York Institute of Technology at Utica/Rome M*†
Stevens Institute of Technology M,O*†
Syracuse University M,D*
Tarleton State University M
Technical University of British Columbia M
Temple University M,D*†
Towson University O†
Université du Québec, Institut National de la Recherche Scientifique M,D,O
The University of Alabama at Birmingham M,D*†
University of Baltimore M,D*
University of California, Irvine M,D*
University of Colorado at Colorado Springs M*
University of Delaware M,D*†
University of Florida M,D,O*†
University of Great Falls M
University of Hawaii at Manoa D*
University of Houston M,D*
University of Houston–Clear Lake M*†
University of Maryland, Baltimore County M,D*†
University of Maryland University College M*
University of Michigan–Dearborn M*†
University of Minnesota, Twin Cities Campus M,D*
University of New Haven M*†
The University of North Carolina at Charlotte M,D*
University of North Florida M
University of North Texas M,D*†
University of Oregon M,D*
University of Pennsylvania M,D*†
University of Phoenix–Phoenix Campus M
University of Pittsburgh M,D,O*†
University of South Alabama M*†
The University of Tennessee M,D*†
The University of Texas at San Antonio M*
The University of Texas at Tyler M
University of Washington M,D*
University of Waterloo M,D
University of Wisconsin–Parkside M
Villa Julie College M
Virginia Polytechnic Institute and State University M*

INFORMATION STUDIES

The Catholic University of America M*†
Central Connecticut State University M*†
Central Missouri State University M,O†
Clark Atlanta University M,O
College of St. Catherine M†
Dalhousie University M*
Dominican University M,O*
Drexel University M*†
Emporia State University M,D*†
Florida State University M,D,O*†
Indiana University–Purdue University Indianapolis M*
Long Island University, C.W. Post Campus M,D,O*†
Louisiana State University and Agricultural and Mechanical College M,O*
Mansfield University of Pennsylvania M
McGill University M,D,O*
Metropolitan State University M
Montana State University–Billings M*
North Carolina Central University M
Pratt Institute M,O*
Queens College of the City University of New York M,O†
Rutgers, The State University of New Jersey, New Brunswick M,D*
St. John's University (NY) M,O*†
San Jose State University M*
Simmons College M,D,O*
Southern Connecticut State University M,O†
Syracuse University M,D*
Université de Montréal M,D
University at Buffalo, The State University of New York M,D,O*†
The University of Alabama M,D,O*
University of Alberta M*
The University of Arizona M,D*
The University of British Columbia M,O*
University of California, Berkeley M,D*
University of California, Los Angeles M,D,O*
University of Denver M*†
University of Hawaii at Manoa M,D,O*
University of Illinois at Urbana–Champaign M,D,O*
The University of Iowa M*
University of Maryland, College Park M,D*
University of Michigan M,D*
University of Missouri–Columbia M,D,O*
The University of North Carolina at Chapel Hill M,D,O*†
The University of North Carolina at Greensboro M†
University of North Texas M,D*†
University of Oklahoma M,O*†
University of Pittsburgh M,D,O*†
University of Puerto Rico, Río Piedras M,O*
University of Rhode Island M*
University of South Carolina M,O*†
University of South Florida M*†
The University of Tennessee M*†
The University of Texas at Austin M,D*
University of Toronto M,D*
The University of Western Ontario M,D*
University of Wisconsin–Madison M,D,O*
University of Wisconsin–Milwaukee M,O
Valdosta State University M
Wayne State University M,O*

INORGANIC CHEMISTRY

Boston College M,D*†
Brandeis University M,D*†
Brigham Young University M,D*
California State University, Fullerton M
California State University, Los Angeles M
Case Western Reserve University M,D*†
Clark Atlanta University M,D
Clarkson University M,D*
Cleveland State University M,D*†
Columbia University M,D*†
Cornell University D*
Florida State University M,D*†
Georgetown University M,D*
The George Washington University M,D*†
Harvard University M,D*†
Howard University M,D*
Illinois Institute of Technology M,D*†
Indiana University Bloomington M,D*
Kansas State University M,D*†
Kent State University M,D*
Marquette University M,D*†
Massachusetts Institute of Technology D*
McMaster University M,D
Miami University M,D*†
Michigan State University M,D*†
Northeastern University M,D*†
Oregon State University M,D*
Purdue University M,D*
Rensselaer Polytechnic Institute M,D*†
Rice University M,D*
Rutgers, The State University of New Jersey, Newark M,D*†
Rutgers, The State University of New Jersey, New Brunswick M,D*
San Jose State University M*
Seton Hall University M,D*†
South Dakota State University M,D*
Southern University and Agricultural and Mechanical College M*
State University of New York at Binghamton M,D*†
Tufts University M,D*†
University of Calgary M,D*
University of Cincinnati M,D*
University of Georgia M,D*†
University of Louisville M,D*†
University of Maryland, College Park M,D*
University of Miami M,D*†
University of Michigan D*
University of Missouri–Columbia M,D*
University of Missouri–Kansas City M,D*†
University of Missouri–St. Louis M,D†
The University of Montana–Missoula M,D*†
University of Nebraska–Lincoln M,D*†
University of Notre Dame M,D*†
University of Regina M,D
University of Southern Mississippi M,D
University of South Florida M,D*†
The University of Tennessee M,D*†
The University of Texas at Austin M,D*
University of Toledo M,D*†
Wake Forest University M,D*†
Washington State University M,D*
Wesleyan University M,D*
West Virginia University M,D*
Yale University D*

INSURANCE

California State University, Northridge M
Florida State University M,D*†
Georgia State University M,D*
The Pennsylvania State University University Park Campus M,D*†
St. John's University (NY) M*†
Temple University M,D*†
Thomas Edison State College M†
University of North Texas M,D*†
University of Pennsylvania M,D*†
University of St. Thomas (MN) M,O*†
University of Wisconsin–Madison M,D*
Virginia Commonwealth University M*†

INTERDISCIPLINARY STUDIES

Alaska Pacific University M
American University M,O*†
Angelo State University M†
Antioch New England Graduate School M*†
Arizona State University West M
Athabasca University M
Baylor University M,D*†
Boise State University M*
Boston University M,D*†
Bowling Green State University M,D*†
California State University, Bakersfield M
California State University, Chico M
California State University, Fullerton M
California State University, Hayward M,O
California State University, Long Beach M
California State University, Los Angeles M
California State University, Monterey Bay
California State University, Northridge M
California State University, Sacramento M
California State University, San Bernardino M
California State University, Stanislaus M
Central Washington University M†
Claremont Graduate University M*
Clarkson University M*
Columbia University M*†
Dalhousie University D*
Dallas Baptist University M
DePaul University M*†
Eastern Washington University M†
Emory University D*†
Fitchburg State College O†
Fresno Pacific University M
George Mason University M*†
Goddard College M
Graduate School and University Center of the City University of New York M,D*†
Hofstra University M*
Hollins University M,O
Idaho State University M*
Iowa State University of Science and Technology M*†
John F. Kennedy University M,O*†
Kent State University M*
Lesley University M,D,O*†
Long Island University, C.W. Post Campus M*†
Loyola College in Maryland M
Manchester College M
Marquette University D*†
Marylhurst University M
Minnesota State University, Mankato M
Mountain State University M†
New Mexico State University M,D
New York University M*†
The Ohio State University M*
Ohio University M,D*
Oregon State University M*
Rochester Institute of Technology M*†
San Diego State University M*
San Jose State University M*
Sarah Lawrence College M*†
Sonoma State University M
Southern Methodist University M*†
Southwest Texas State University M*
Stanford University M,D*
State University of New York College at Buffalo M
Stephen F. Austin State University M
Teachers College Columbia University M,D*
Technical University of British Columbia D
Texas A&M International University M
Texas A&M University–Corpus Christi M
Texas A&M University–Texarkana M
Texas Tech University M*†
Trinity International University P,M,D,O
Union Institute & University D
University of Alaska Anchorage M
The University of Arizona M,D,O*
University of Cincinnati D*
University of Houston–Victoria M
University of Idaho M*†
University of Illinois at Springfield M†
University of Louisville M*†
University of Maine D*
University of Medicine and Dentistry of New Jersey M,D*
University of Minnesota, Twin Cities Campus M,D*
University of Missouri–Kansas City D*†
The University of Montana–Missoula M,D*†

University of Northern British Columbia M,D
University of Northern Colorado M,D,O†
University of North Texas M,D*†
University of Oklahoma M,D*†
University of Oregon M*
The University of South Dakota M†
The University of Texas at Arlington M*†
The University of Texas at Brownsville M
The University of Texas at Dallas M*
The University of Texas at El Paso M*†
The University of Texas at San Antonio M*
The University of Texas at Tyler M
The University of Texas–Pan American M
University of the Incarnate Word M†
The University of Western Ontario M,D*
University of Wisconsin–Milwaukee D
Vermont College M,O
Virginia Commonwealth University M*†
Virginia State University M
Wayne State University M,D*
Western New Mexico University M
West Texas A&M University M†
Wheaton College M†
Wright State University M*
York University M*

INTERIOR DESIGN

Academy of Art College M†
Boston Architectural Center M*
Colorado State University M*
Columbia College Chicago M†
Cornell University M*
Drexel University M*†
Florida State University M*†
The George Washington University M*†
Indiana University Bloomington M*
Iowa State University of Science and Technology M*†
Louisiana Tech University M*
Marymount University M†
Michigan State University M,D*†
Minnesota State University, Mankato M
New School University M*†
New York School of Interior Design M*
The Ohio State University M*
Pratt Institute M*
Rhode Island School of Design M
Rochester Institute of Technology M*†
San Diego State University M*
San Jose State University M*
Savannah College of Art and Design M*
School of the Art Institute of Chicago M*
State University of New York at Albany M,D,O*†
Suffolk University M*
The University of Alabama M*
University of Central Oklahoma M
University of Cincinnati M*
University of Florida M*†
University of Georgia M,D*†
University of Houston M*
University of Kentucky M*
University of Massachusetts Amherst M*†
The University of Memphis M*†
University of Minnesota, Twin Cities Campus M,D*
The University of North Carolina at Greensboro M†
University of North Texas M,D*†
University of Oregon M*
Virginia Commonwealth University M*†
Virginia Polytechnic Institute and State University M,D*
Washington State University M*
Washington State University Spokane M†

INTERNATIONAL AFFAIRS

Alliant International University M*†
American University M,D,O*†
Angelo State University M†
Baylor University M*†
Boston University M,O*†
Brandeis University M,D*†
Brigham Young University M*
Brock University M
California State University, Fresno M
California State University, Sacramento M
California State University, Stanislaus M
Carleton University M
The Catholic University of America M*†
Central Connecticut State University M*†
Central Michigan University M,O†
City College of the City University of New York M*†
Claremont Graduate University M,D*
Clark Atlanta University M,D
Columbia University M*†
Cornell University D*
Creighton University M*
DePaul University M*†
East Carolina University M*†
Fairleigh Dickinson University, Metropolitan Campus M*†
Florida International University M,D*†
Florida State University M*†
George Mason University M*†
Georgetown University M,D*
The George Washington University M*†
Georgia Institute of Technology M*
Harvard University M,D*†
Huron University USA in London M
Instituto Tecnológico y de Estudios Superiores de Monterrey, Campus Ciudad Obregón M
Johns Hopkins University M,D,O*†
Kansas State University M*†
Kent State University M,D*
Lebanese American University M
Lesley University M,D,O*†
Long Island University, Brooklyn Campus M,O*
Long Island University, C.W. Post Campus M*†
Loyola University Chicago M,D*†
Marquette University M*†
Monterey Institute of International Studies M*
Morgan State University M*
New School University M*†
New York University M,D,O*†
North Carolina State University M*
Northeastern University M,D*†
Northwestern University O*
Ohio University M*
Oklahoma City University M
Oklahoma State University M*†
Old Dominion University M,D*†
Princeton University M,D*
Rutgers, The State University of New Jersey, Camden M†
Rutgers, The State University of New Jersey, Newark M,D*†
Rutgers, The State University of New Jersey, New Brunswick D*
St. John Fisher College M
Salve Regina University M†
San Francisco State University M
Schiller International University (United Kingdom) M
Schiller International University M
School for International Training M,O†
Seton Hall University M*†
Southwest Missouri State University M*†
Southwest Texas State University M*
Stanford University M*
Syracuse University M*
Texas A&M University M*
Troy State University M
Tufts University M,D*†
Universidad de las Americas, A.C. M
Université Laval M†
The University of British Columbia M*
University of California, Berkeley M*
University of California, San Diego M,D*
University of California, Santa Cruz D*
University of Central Oklahoma M
University of Chicago M*
University of Colorado at Boulder M,D*
University of Connecticut M*†
University of Delaware M,D*†
University of Denver M,D*†
University of Florida M,D*†
University of Kansas M*
University of Kentucky M*
University of Miami M,D*†
University of Missouri–St. Louis O†
University of New Orleans M,D*
University of Northern British Columbia M,D
University of Oklahoma M*†
University of Oregon M*
University of Pennsylvania M*†
University of Pittsburgh M,D*†
University of Rhode Island M,O*
University of San Diego M*†
University of South Carolina M,D*†
University of Southern California M,D*†
University of the Pacific P,M,D*
University of Toronto M*
University of Virginia M,D*
University of Washington M*
University of Wyoming M*†
Virginia Polytechnic Institute and State University M*
Webster University M
West Virginia University M,D*
Yale University M*

INTERNATIONAL AND COMPARATIVE EDUCATION

American University M*†
Boston University M*†
Claremont Graduate University M,D*
Concordia University (CA) M
Endicott College M
Florida International University M,D,O*†
Florida State University M,D,O*†
The George Washington University M*†
Harvard University M,D,O*†
Indiana University Bloomington M,D,O*
Lesley University M,O*†
Louisiana State University and Agricultural and Mechanical College M,D*
Loyola University Chicago M,D*†
Lynn University M,D†
New York University M,D*†
School for International Training M,O†
Stanford University M,D*
Teachers College Columbia University M,D*
Tufts University M,D*†
University of Alberta M,D,O*
University of Bridgeport M,O*†
University of Massachusetts Amherst M,D,O*†
University of Minnesota, Twin Cities Campus M,D*
University of Pittsburgh M,D*†
University of San Francisco M,D*†
University of Southern California M,D*†
University of the Incarnate Word M,D†
Wright State University M*

INTERNATIONAL BUSINESS

Alliant International University M,D*†
Alliant International University–México City M
American InterContinental University (CA) M
American InterContinental University M*
American InterContinental University-London M
American University M*†
The American University in Dubai M
Argosy University-Chicago Northwest M,D*
Argosy University-Orange County M,D*
Argosy University-Sarasota M,D*†
Argosy University-Tampa M*
Armstrong University M
Azusa Pacific University M*†
Babson College M
Baker College Center for Graduate Studies M
Baldwin-Wallace College M*
Baylor University M*†
Bentley College M,O*
Bernard M. Baruch College of the City University of New York M*
Boston University M*†
Brandeis University M,D*†
California Lutheran University M
California State University, Fullerton M
California State University, Hayward M
California State University, Los Angeles M
Central Connecticut State University M*†
Central Michigan University M†
City University M,O†
Claremont Graduate University M*
Clark Atlanta University M,D
Clark University M*†
Columbia Southern University M
Columbia University M*†
Concordia University Wisconsin M
Daemen College M
Dallas Baptist University M
Davenport University M
DePaul University M*†
Dominican University of California M
Drury University M
D'Youville College M†
Eastern Michigan University M*
École des Hautes Études Commerciales de Montréal M*
Fairfield University M,O*
Fairleigh Dickinson University, College at Florham M*†
Fairleigh Dickinson University, Metropolitan Campus M*†
Florida Atlantic University M*
Florida International University M*†
Florida Metropolitan University–Tampa Campus M
The George Washington University M,D*†
Georgia State University M,D*
Golden Gate University M,D,O
Hawai'i Pacific University M*†
High Point University M
Hofstra University M*
Hope International University M
Howard University M*
Hsi Lai University M*
Huron University USA in London M
Illinois Institute of Technology M*†
Indiana University Bloomington M*
Instituto Tecnológico y de Estudios Superiores de Monterrey, Campus Central de Veracruz M
Instituto Tecnológico y de Estudios Superiores de Monterrey, Campus Chihuahua M,O
Instituto Tecnológico y de Estudios Superiores de Monterrey, Campus Ciudad de México M,D
Instituto Tecnológico y de Estudios Superiores de Monterrey, Campus Cuernavaca M
Instituto Tecnológico y de Estudios Superiores de Monterrey, Campus Irapuato M,D
Instituto Tecnológico y de Estudios Superiores de Monterrey, Campus Monterrey M
Iona College M,O*†
John Marshall Law School P,M
Johns Hopkins University M,D,O*†
Johnson & Wales University M*†
Long Island University, C.W. Post Campus M,O*†
Loyola College in Maryland M
Lynn University M†
Madonna University M
Marymount University M,O†
Maryville University of Saint Louis M,O
Mercy College M*
Metropolitan State University M
Montclair State University M†
Monterey Institute of International Studies M*
National Technological University M
National University M†
New School University M*†
New York Institute of Technology M,O*†
New York University M,D,O*†
Nichols College M
Nova Southeastern University M,D*
Oklahoma City University M
Oral Roberts University M
Our Lady of the Lake University of San Antonio M
Pace University M*†
Pace University, White Plains Campus M*
Pacific States University M
Pepperdine University M*
Philadelphia University M
Portland State University M*
Quinnipiac University M*†
Regis University M,O*†
Rochester Institute of Technology M*†
Roosevelt University M*†
Rutgers, The State University of New Jersey, Newark M,D*†
St. Edward's University M,O
St. John's University (NY) M*†
Saint Joseph's University M*†
Saint Louis University D*†

*P—first professional degree; M—master's degree; D—doctorate; O—other advanced degree; *full description and/or announcement in Book 2, 3, 4, 5, or 6; †full description in this book*

St. Mary's University of San Antonio M
Saint Peter's College M†
St. Thomas University M,O†
San Diego State University M*
Schiller International University (United States) M
Schiller International University (Germany) M
Schiller International University (United Kingdom) M
Schiller International University M
Schiller International University (Spain) M
Schiller International University M
Schiller International University, American College of Switzerland M
School for International Training M,O†
Seattle University M,O*†
Seton Hall University M,O*†
Simon Fraser University M
Southeastern University M†
Southern New Hampshire University M,D,O*
State University of New York at New Paltz M
Suffolk University M*
Sul Ross State University M*
Temple University M,D*†
Texas A&M International University M
Texas Tech University M*†
Thunderbird, The American Graduate School of International Management M
Tufts University M,D*†
Université de Sherbrooke M
Université du Québec, École nationale d'administration publique M,O
Université Laval M,O†
The University of Akron M†
University of Alberta M*
University of Chicago M*
University of Cincinnati M*
University of Colorado at Denver M*
University of Connecticut *†
University of Denver M*†
The University of Findlay M
University of Florida M*†
University of Hawaii at Manoa D*
University of Kentucky M*
University of La Verne M*
The University of Lethbridge M,D
University of Maryland University College M*
The University of Memphis M*†
University of Minnesota, Twin Cities Campus M*
University of New Brunswick Saint John M
University of New Haven M*†
University of New Mexico M*†
The University of North Carolina at Greensboro M,O†
University of Oklahoma M*†
University of Ottawa M*
University of Pennsylvania M*†
University of Phoenix–Boston Campus M
University of Phoenix–Maryland Campus M
University of Phoenix–Metro Detroit Campus M
University of Phoenix–New Mexico Campus M
University of Phoenix–Northern California Campus M
University of Phoenix–Ohio Campus M
University of Phoenix–Philadelphia Campus M
University of Phoenix–Phoenix Campus M
University of Phoenix–San Diego Campus M
University of Phoenix–Southern Arizona Campus M
University of Phoenix–Utah Campus M
University of Pittsburgh M*†
University of Rhode Island M,D*
University of St. Thomas (MN) M,O*†
University of San Francisco M*†
The University of Scranton M†
University of South Carolina M*†
University of Southern California M*†
The University of Tampa M
The University of Texas at Dallas M,D*
University of the Incarnate Word M,D†
University of Toledo M*†
University of Tulsa M†
University of Washington O*
University of Wisconsin–Madison M*
University of Wisconsin–Whitewater M*
Wagner College M
Washington State University M,D,O*
Webster University M
Western International University M
Western New England College M
Whitworth College M
Wilkes University M
Wright State University M*
Xavier University M*

INTERNATIONAL DEVELOPMENT

American University M,D,O*†
Andrews University M
Athabasca University M
Brandeis University M*†
Brigham Young University M*
Clark Atlanta University M,D
Clark University M*†
Cornell University M*
Dalhousie University M*
Duke University M*†
Fordham University M,O*†
The George Washington University M*†
Harvard University M*†
Hope International University M
Johns Hopkins University M,D,O*†
New School University M*†
Ohio University M*
Old Dominion University M*†
Rutgers, The State University of New Jersey, Camden M†
Saint Mary's University M
Tufts University M,D*†
Tulane University M,D*†
University of Florida M,D,O*†
University of Guelph M
University of Pittsburgh M*†
University of Rhode Island M,O*

INTERNATIONAL HEALTH

Boston University M,O*†
Emory University M*†
The George Washington University M*†
Harvard University M,D*†
Johns Hopkins University M,D*†
Loma Linda University M*
New York Medical College M,O*
Tufts University M,D*†
Tulane University M,D*†
Uniformed Services University of the Health Sciences M,D*
The University of Alabama at Birmingham D*†
University of Michigan M,D*
University of Washington M,D*
Yale University M*

INTERNET AND INTERACTIVE MULTIMEDIA

Abilene Christian University M
Alfred University M*†
American University M*†
Chapman University M*†
City University M,O†
Duquesne University M*†
Florida State University M,D*†
Georgetown University M*
Georgia Institute of Technology M*
Georgia State University M,D*
Indiana University Bloomington M*
Indiana University–Purdue University Indianapolis M*
Long Island University, C.W. Post Campus M*†
Marlboro College M*
Michigan State University M,D*†
New Mexico Highlands University M
New York University M*†
Pratt Institute M*
Quinnipiac University M*†
Regis University M,O*†
Robert Morris University M†
Rochester Institute of Technology O*†
Sacred Heart University M,O*†
San Diego State University M*
Syracuse University M*
Technical University of British Columbia M
Towson University M,O†
University of Miami M*†
University of Southern California M,D*†
Virginia Commonwealth University M*†
Western Illinois University M,O

INVESTMENT MANAGEMENT

Boston University M*†
Concordia University (Canada) M,D,O*†
The George Washington University M,D*†
Johns Hopkins University M,O*†
Marywood University M*†
Pace University M*†
Pace University, White Plains Campus M*
University of Tulsa M†
University of Wisconsin–Madison M*

ITALIAN

Boston College M,D*†
Brown University M,D*
The Catholic University of America M*†
Columbia University M,D*†
Connecticut College M
Florida State University M*†
Graduate School and University Center of the City University of New York M,D*†
Harvard University M,D*†
Hunter College of the City University of New York M†
Indiana University Bloomington M,D*
Johns Hopkins University M,D*†
Long Island University, C.W. Post Campus M*†
McGill University M,D*
Middlebury College M,D
New York University M,D*†
Northwestern University D,O*
The Ohio State University M,D*
Queens College of the City University of New York M†
Rutgers, The State University of New Jersey, New Brunswick M,D*
San Francisco State University M
Smith College M*
Stanford University M,D*
State University of New York at Albany M*†
State University of New York at Binghamton M*†
Stony Brook University, State University of New York M,D*†
University of Alberta M,D*
University of California, Berkeley M,D*
University of California, Los Angeles M,D*
University of Chicago M,D*
University of Connecticut M,D*†
University of Illinois at Urbana–Champaign M,D*
University of Minnesota, Twin Cities Campus M,D*
The University of North Carolina at Chapel Hill M,D*†
University of Notre Dame M*†
University of Oregon M*
University of Pennsylvania M,D*†
University of Pittsburgh M*†
The University of Tennessee D*†
University of Toronto M,D*
University of Virginia M*
University of Washington M,D*
University of Wisconsin–Madison M,D*
University of Wisconsin–Milwaukee M
Wayne State University M*
Yale University D*

JEWISH STUDIES

Baltimore Hebrew University M,D
Brandeis University M,D*†
Brooklyn College of the City University of New York M†
Brown University M,D*
Chicago Theological Seminary P,M,D
Columbia University M,D*†
Concordia University (Canada) M*†
Cornell University M,D*
Emory University M*†
Graduate Theological Union M,D,O
Gratz College M†
Harvard University M,D*†
Hebrew College M,O†
Hebrew Union College–Jewish Institute of Religion (CA) M,D
Hebrew Union College–Jewish Institute of Religion (NY) M
Hebrew Union College–Jewish Institute of Religion (OH) P,M,D
Jewish Theological Seminary of America M,D*
Jewish University of America P,D
Laura and Alvin Siegal College of Judaic Studies M
McGill University M,D*
New York University M,D*†
Seton Hall University M*†
Spertus Institute of Jewish Studies M,D
Touro College M
University of California, San Diego M,D*
University of Chicago M,D*
University of Denver M*†
University of Judaism M
The University of Montana–Missoula M*†
University of Wisconsin–Madison M,D*
University of Wisconsin–Milwaukee M
Washington University in St. Louis M*†
Yeshiva University M,D*

JOURNALISM

American University M*†
American University in Cairo M,O
Angelo State University M†
Arizona State University M*
Arkansas State University M
Arkansas Tech University M
Auburn University M*†
Austin Peay State University M
Ball State University M*
Baylor University M*†
Bernard M. Baruch College of the City University of New York M*
Boston University M*†
California State University, Fullerton M
California State University, Northridge M
Carleton University M,D
Columbia College Chicago M†
Columbia University M,D*†
Concordia University (Canada) O*†
Emerson College M*†
Florida Agricultural and Mechanical University M*
Georgia College & State University M
Indiana University Bloomington M,D*
Iona College M,O*†
Iowa State University of Science and Technology M*†
Kent State University M*
Marquette University M*†
Marshall University M*†
Michigan State University M,D*†
Morehead State University M
New York University M,D,O*†
Northeastern University M*†
Northwestern University M*
The Ohio State University M*
Ohio University M,D*
Point Park College M*
Polytechnic University, Brooklyn Campus M*
Quinnipiac University M*†
Regent University M†
Roosevelt University M*†
South Dakota State University M*
Stanford University M,D*
Syracuse University M*
Temple University M*†
Texas A&M University M*
Texas Christian University M*
Texas Southern University M*
Université Laval O†
The University of Alabama M,D*
University of Alaska Fairbanks M*
The University of Arizona M*
University of Arkansas M*
University of Arkansas at Little Rock M
The University of British Columbia M*
University of California, Berkeley M*
University of Colorado at Boulder M,D*
University of Florida M,D*†
University of Georgia M,D*†
University of Illinois at Springfield M†
University of Illinois at Urbana–Champaign M*
The University of Iowa M*
University of Kansas M*
University of Maryland, College Park M,D*
The University of Memphis M*†
University of Miami M,D*†
University of Mississippi M*
University of Missouri–Columbia M,D*
The University of Montana–Missoula M*†
University of Nebraska–Lincoln M*†
University of Nevada, Reno M*
University of North Texas M*†
University of Oklahoma M*†
University of Oregon M,D*
University of South Carolina M,D*†
University of Southern California M*†
The University of Tennessee M,D*†
The University of Texas at Austin M,D*
University of the Sacred Heart M
The University of Western Ontario M*
University of Wisconsin–Madison M,D*

University of Wisconsin–Milwaukee M
West Virginia University M*

KINESIOLOGY AND MOVEMENT STUDIES

Angelo State University M†
Armstrong Atlantic State University M†
Barry University M*†
Boston University M,D,O*†
Bowling Green State University M*†
California Polytechnic State University, San Luis Obispo M†
California State Polytechnic University, Pomona M*
California State University, Fresno M
California State University, Long Beach M
California State University, Northridge M
Dalhousie University M*
Florida State University M,D*†
Georgia Southern University M
Indiana University Bloomington M,D,O*
Inter American University of Puerto Rico, San Germán Campus M
James Madison University M
Kansas State University M*†
Lamar University M*†
Louisiana State University and Agricultural and Mechanical College M,D*
McGill University M*
McMaster University M,D
Memorial University of Newfoundland M†
Michigan State University M,D*†
Midwestern State University M
New York University M,D*†
Oregon State University M*
The Pennsylvania State University University Park Campus M,D*†
San Jose State University M*
Simon Fraser University M,D
Sonoma State University M
Southeastern Louisiana University M
Southern Arkansas University–Magnolia M
Southern Illinois University Edwardsville M,O†
Springfield College M†
Teachers College Columbia University M,D*
Temple University M,D*†
Texas A&M University M,D*
Texas A&M University–Kingsville M*†
Texas Christian University M*
Texas Woman's University M,D*†
Université de Montréal M,D,O
Université de Sherbrooke M,O
Université du Québec à Montréal M
Université Laval M,D†
The University of Alabama M,D*
University of Arkansas M,D*
The University of British Columbia M,D*
University of Calgary M,D*
University of Central Arkansas M
University of Colorado at Boulder M,D*
University of Delaware M,D*†
University of Florida D*†
University of Hawaii at Manoa M*
University of Illinois at Chicago M*
University of Illinois at Urbana–Champaign M,D*
University of Kentucky M,D*
The University of Lethbridge M,D
University of Maine M*
University of Maryland, College Park M,D*
University of Medicine and Dentistry of New Jersey M,D*
University of Michigan M,D*
University of Minnesota, Twin Cities Campus M,D*
University of Nevada, Las Vegas M*†
University of New Hampshire M*†
The University of North Carolina at Chapel Hill M,D*†
University of North Dakota M*
University of Northern Colorado M,D†
University of North Texas M*†
University of Oregon M,D*
University of Ottawa M*
University of Pittsburgh M,D*†
University of Regina M
University of Saskatchewan M,D,O
University of Southern California M,D*†
The University of Texas at Austin M,D*
The University of Texas at El Paso M*†
The University of Texas at Tyler M
The University of Texas–Pan American M
University of Toledo M*†
University of Waterloo M,D
The University of Western Ontario M,D*
University of Windsor M
University of Wisconsin–Madison M,D*
University of Wisconsin–Milwaukee M
Virginia Polytechnic Institute and State University M,D*
Washington State University M*
Washington University in St. Louis D*†
West Chester University of Pennsylvania M,O*†
Western Washington University M
York University M,D*

LANDSCAPE ARCHITECTURE

Ball State University M*
California State Polytechnic University, Pomona M*
Chatham College M
Colorado State University M,D*
Conway School of Landscape Design M
Cornell University M*
Florida International University M*†
Harvard University M,D*†
Iowa State University of Science and Technology M*†
Kansas State University M*†
Louisiana State University and Agricultural and Mechanical College M*
Mississippi State University M*
Morgan State University M*
North Carolina State University M*
The Ohio State University M*
Oklahoma State University M*†
The Pennsylvania State University University Park Campus M*†
Rhode Island School of Design M
State University of New York College of Environmental Science and Forestry M
Texas A&M University M,D*
Texas Tech University M*†
The University of Arizona M*
The University of British Columbia M*
University of California, Berkeley M*
University of Colorado at Denver M*
University of Florida M*†
University of Georgia M*†
University of Guelph M,D
University of Idaho M*†
University of Illinois at Urbana–Champaign M*
University of Manitoba M*
University of Massachusetts Amherst M*†
University of Michigan M,D*
University of Minnesota, Twin Cities Campus M*
University of New Mexico M*†
University of Oklahoma M*†
University of Oregon M*
University of Pennsylvania M,O*†
University of Southern California M*†
The University of Texas at Arlington M*†
University of Virginia M*
University of Washington M*
University of Wisconsin–Madison M*
Utah State University M*
Virginia Polytechnic Institute and State University M*
Washington State University M,D*
Washington State University Spokane M†

LATIN AMERICAN STUDIES

American University M,O*†
Arizona State University M,D*
Brown University M,D*
California State University, Los Angeles M
Centro de Estudios Avanzados de Puerto Rico y el Caribe M,D
Columbia University O*†
Duke University D,O*†
Florida International University M*†
Georgetown University M*
The George Washington University M*†
Indiana University Bloomington M*
Johns Hopkins University M,D,O*†
La Salle University M
New York University M*†
The Ohio State University M,D,O*
Ohio University M*
Princeton University D*
San Diego State University M*
Simon Fraser University M
Southern Methodist University M*†
Stanford University M*
State University of New York at Albany M,O*†
Tulane University M,D*†
The University of Alabama M,O*
The University of Arizona M*
University of California, Berkeley M,D*
University of California, Los Angeles M*
University of California, San Diego M*
University of California, Santa Barbara M,D*
University of Central Florida M,O*†
University of Chicago M*
University of Connecticut M*†
University of Florida M,O*†
University of Illinois at Urbana–Champaign M*
University of Kansas M*
University of New Mexico M,D*†
The University of North Carolina at Chapel Hill M,D,O*†
University of Notre Dame M*†
University of Pittsburgh M,O*†
The University of Texas at Austin M,D*
University of Wisconsin–Madison M*
Vanderbilt University M*
West Virginia University M,D*

LAW

Albany Law School of Union University P,M
American University P,M*†
Appalachian School of Law P
Arizona State University P*
Barry University P*†
Baylor University P*†
Boston College P*†
Boston University P,M*†
Brigham Young University P,M*
Brooklyn Law School P
California Western School of Law P,M
Campbell University P
Capital University P,M
Case Western Reserve University P,M*†
The Catholic University of America P*†
Chapman University P*†
City University of New York School of Law at Queens College P
Cleveland State University P,M*†
The College of William and Mary P,M*†
Columbia University P,M,D*†
Cornell University P,M,D*
Creighton University P*
Dalhousie University M,D*
DePaul University P,M*†
The Dickinson School of Law of The Pennsylvania State University P,M
Drake University P*†
Duke University P,M,D*†
Duquesne University P*†
Emory University P,M,O*†
Faulkner University P
Florida Coastal School of Law P
Florida State University P*†
Fordham University P,M*†
Franklin Pierce Law Center P,M,O
George Mason University P*†
Georgetown University P,M,D*
The George Washington University P,M,D*†
Georgia State University P*
Golden Gate University P,M,D
Gonzaga University P
Hamline University P,M*
Harvard University P,M,D*†
Hofstra University P,M*
Howard University P,M*
Humphreys College P
Illinois Institute of Technology P,M*†
Indiana University Bloomington P,M,D*
Indiana University School of Law-Bloomington P,M,D,O
Indiana University School of Law-Indianapolis P
Instituto Tecnológico y de Estudios Superiores de Monterrey, Campus Ciudad de México P
Inter American University of Puerto Rico, Metropolitan Campus P
John F. Kennedy University P*†
John Marshall Law School P,M
The Judge Advocate General's School, U.S. Army M
Lewis & Clark College P,M
Louisiana State University and Agricultural and Mechanical College P,M*
Loyola Marymount University P,M†
Loyola University Chicago P,M,D*†
Loyola University New Orleans P
Marquette University P*†
Massachusetts School of Law at Andover P
McGill University M,D,O*
Mercer University P
Michigan State University-Detroit College of Law P
Mississippi College P
New College of California P*†
New England School of Law P
New York Law School P
New York University P,M,D*†
North Carolina Central University P
Northeastern University P*†
Northern Illinois University P*†
Northern Kentucky University P
Northwestern University P,M,O*
Nova Southeastern University P,M*
Ohio Northern University P*
The Ohio State University P*
Oklahoma City University P
Pace University, White Plains Campus P,M,D*
Pepperdine University P*
Pontifical Catholic University of Puerto Rico P
Queen's University at Kingston P,M
Quinnipiac University P*†
Regent University P,M†
Roger Williams University P
Rutgers, The State University of New Jersey, Camden P†
Rutgers, The State University of New Jersey, Newark P*†
St. John's University (NY) P,M*†
Saint Louis University P,M,O*†
St. Mary's University of San Antonio P
St. Thomas University P,M†
Samford University P,D
San Joaquin College of Law P
Santa Clara University P,M,O*
Seattle University P*†
Seton Hall University P,M*†
Southern Illinois University Carbondale P*†
Southern Methodist University P,M,D*†
Southern New England School of Law P
Southern University and Agricultural and Mechanical College P*
South Texas College of Law P
Southwestern University School of Law P,M
Stanford University P,M,D*
Stetson University P,M
Suffolk University P*
Syracuse University P*
Temple University P,M*†
Texas Southern University P†
Texas Tech University P*†
Texas Wesleyan University P
Thomas Jefferson School of Law P
Thomas M. Cooley Law School P
Touro College P,M
Trinity International University P
Tulane University P,M,D*†
Université de Moncton P,M,O
Université de Montréal P,M,D,O
Université de Sherbrooke M,D,O
Université du Québec à Montréal M
Université Laval M,D,O†
University at Buffalo, The State University of New York P,M*†
The University of Akron P†
The University of Alabama P,M*
University of Alberta P,M,O*
The University of Arizona P,M*
University of Arkansas P,M*
University of Arkansas at Little Rock P
University of Baltimore P,M*
The University of British Columbia M,D*
University of Calgary P,M*
University of California, Berkeley P,M,D*
University of California, Davis P,M*†

*P—first professional degree; M—master's degree; D—doctorate; O—other advanced degree; *full description and/or announcement in Book 2, 3, 4, 5, or 6; †full description in this book*

University of California, Hastings College of the Law P,M
University of California, Los Angeles P,M*
University of Chicago P,M,D*
University of Cincinnati P*
University of Colorado at Boulder P*
University of Connecticut P*†
University of Dayton P*†
University of Denver P,M*†
University of Detroit Mercy P*
University of Florida P,M,D*†
University of Georgia P,M*†
University of Hawaii at Manoa P*
University of Houston P,M*
University of Idaho P*†
University of Illinois at Urbana–Champaign P,M,D*
The University of Iowa P,M*
University of Kansas P*
University of Kentucky P*
University of La Verne P*
University of Louisville P*†
University of Manitoba M*
University of Maryland P*†
University of Maryland, College Park *
The University of Memphis P*†
University of Miami P,M*†
University of Michigan P,M,D*
University of Minnesota, Twin Cities Campus P,M*
University of Mississippi P*
University of Missouri–Columbia P,M*
University of Missouri–Kansas City P,M*†
The University of Montana–Missoula P*†
University of Nebraska–Lincoln P,M*†
University of Nevada, Las Vegas P*†
University of New Brunswick Fredericton P
University of New Mexico P*†
The University of North Carolina at Chapel Hill P*†
University of North Dakota P*
University of Notre Dame P,M,D*†
University of Oklahoma P*†
University of Oregon P*
University of Ottawa M,D,O*
University of Pennsylvania P,M,D*†
University of Pittsburgh P,M,O*†
University of Puerto Rico, Río Piedras P*
University of Richmond P*†
University of San Diego P,M,O*†
University of San Francisco P*†
University of Saskatchewan P,M
University of South Carolina P*†
The University of South Dakota P†
University of Southern California P*†
University of Southern Maine P
The University of Tennessee P*†
The University of Texas at Austin P,M*
University of the District of Columbia P*
University of the Pacific P,M,D*
University of Toledo P*†
University of Toronto P,M,D*
University of Tulsa P,M†
University of Utah P,M*
University of Victoria P
University of Virginia P,M,D*
University of Washington P,M,D*
The University of Western Ontario P,O*
University of West Los Angeles P*
University of Wisconsin–Madison P,M,D*
University of Wyoming P*†
Valparaiso University P,M
Vanderbilt University P,M*
Vermont Law School P
Villanova University P*†
Wake Forest University P,M*†
Washburn University of Topeka P
Washington and Lee University P
Washington University in St. Louis P,M,D*†
Wayne State University P,M*
Western New England College P
Western State University College of Law P*
West Virginia University P*
Whittier College P,M
Widener University P,M,D*†
Willamette University P*
William Mitchell College of Law P
Yale University P,M,D*
Yeshiva University P,M*
York University M,D*

LEGAL AND JUSTICE STUDIES

American University M*†
Arizona State University M,D*
Boston University M*†
Brock University M
Capital University M
Carleton University M
Case Western Reserve University P,M*†
The Catholic University of America D,O*†
College of Charleston M*†
Denver Career College O
DePaul University M*†
Golden Gate University P,M,D
Governors State University M
Hofstra University P,M*
Illinois Institute of Technology M*†
Indiana University Bloomington P,M,D*
John Jay College of Criminal Justice of the City University of New York M,D*
John Marshall Law School P,M
Marymount University M,O†
Montclair State University M,O†
New York University D*†
Northeastern University M,D*†
Pace University, White Plains Campus P,M,D*
Prairie View A&M University M,D
Rutgers, The State University of New Jersey, New Brunswick D*
St. John's University (NY) M*†
Southwest Texas State University M*
Université Laval O†
University of Baltimore M*
University of California, Berkeley D*
University of Denver M*†
University of Illinois at Springfield M†
University of Manitoba M*
University of Nebraska–Lincoln M*†
University of Nevada, Reno M*
University of Ottawa M,D,O*
University of Pittsburgh M,O*†
University of San Diego P,M,O*†
University of the Pacific P,M,D*
University of Washington P,M,D*
University of Wisconsin–Madison M*
Vermont Law School M
Weber State University M
Webster University M,O
West Virginia University M*
Whittier College P,M

LEISURE STUDIES

Aurora University M
Boston University M*†
Bowling Green State University M*†
California State University, Long Beach M
California State University, Northridge M
Central Michigan University M†
Dalhousie University M*
East Carolina University M*†
Eastern Kentucky University M
Gallaudet University M
Howard University M*
Indiana University Bloomington M,D,O*
Murray State University M†
New Mexico Highlands University M
Oklahoma State University M,D*†
The Pennsylvania State University University Park Campus M,D*†
San Francisco State University M
San Jose State University M*
Southern Connecticut State University M†
Southwest Texas State University M*
State University of New York College at Brockport M*†
Temple University M*†
Universidad Metropolitana M
Université du Québec à Trois-Rivières M,O
University of Connecticut M,D*†
University of Georgia M,D*†
University of Hawaii at Manoa M*
University of Illinois at Urbana–Champaign M,D*
The University of Iowa M,D*
The University of Memphis M*†
University of Minnesota, Twin Cities Campus M,D*
University of Mississippi M,D*
University of Nevada, Las Vegas M*†
The University of North Carolina at Chapel Hill M*†
University of Northern Iowa M
University of North Texas M,O*†
University of South Alabama M*†
University of Toledo M*†
University of Utah M,D*
University of Victoria M
University of Waterloo M,D
University of West Florida M
Washington State University M*

LIBERAL STUDIES

Abilene Christian University M
Albertus Magnus College M
Alvernia College M
Antioch University McGregor M†
Arkansas Tech University M
Auburn University Montgomery M
Baker University M
Benedictine University M†
Bennington College M†
Boricua College M
Boston University M*†
Bradley University M†
Brooklyn College of the City University of New York M†
Chatham College M
Christian Brothers University M
Clark University M*†
College of Notre Dame of Maryland M
College of Staten Island of the City University of New York M†
Columbia University M*†
Converse College M
Creighton University M*
Dallas Baptist University M
Dartmouth College M*†
DePaul University M*†
Drew University M,D†
Duke University M*†
Duquesne University M*†
East Tennessee State University M†
Elms College M
Excelsior College M
Florida Atlantic University M*
Florida Atlantic University, Davie Campus M
Florida Atlantic University, Ft. Lauderdale Campus M
Fordham University M*†
Fort Hays State University M
George Mason University M*†
Georgetown University M*
Graduate School and University Center of the City University of New York M*†
Hamline University M,O*
Harvard University M,O*†
Henderson State University M
Hollins University M,O
Houston Baptist University M
Indiana University–Purdue University Fort Wayne M
Indiana University South Bend M
Indiana University Southeast M
Jacksonville State University M
Johns Hopkins University M,O*†
Kean University M*†
Kent State University M*
Lake Forest College M
Lee University M
Lock Haven University of Pennsylvania M
Louisiana State University and Agricultural and Mechanical College M*
Louisiana State University in Shreveport M†
Manhattanville College M*†
Marietta College M
Marylhurst University M
Mary Washington College M
McDaniel College M
Minnesota State University, Moorhead M
Mississippi College M
Monmouth University M*†
Nazareth College of Rochester M
New School University M*†
North Carolina State University M*
North Central College M
Northern Arizona University M
Northwestern University M*
Oakland University M†
Oklahoma City University M
Plattsburgh State University of New York M
Queens College of the City University of New York M†
Ramapo College of New Jersey M
Reed College M
Regis University M,O*†
Rollins College M*
Roosevelt University M*†
Rutgers, The State University of New Jersey, Camden M†
Rutgers, The State University of New Jersey, Newark M*†
St. Edward's University M
St. John's College (MD) M
St. John's College (NM) M
Saint Mary's College of California M
San Diego State University M*
Simon Fraser University M
Skidmore College M
Southwest Texas State University M*
Spring Hill College M
State University of New York at Albany M*†
State University of New York College at Brockport M*†
State University of New York Empire State College M
Stony Brook University, State University of New York M,O*†
Temple University M*†
Texas Christian University M*
Thomas Edison State College M†
Towson University M†
Tulane University M*†
University of Arkansas at Little Rock M
University of Central Florida M*†
University of Delaware M*†
University of Denver M*†
University of Detroit Mercy M*
University of Maine M*
University of Miami M*†
University of Michigan–Dearborn M*†
University of Missouri–Kansas City M*†
University of New Hampshire M*†
The University of North Carolina at Asheville M
The University of North Carolina at Charlotte M*
The University of North Carolina at Greensboro M†
The University of North Carolina at Wilmington M*
University of Oklahoma M*†
University of Richmond M*†
University of St. Thomas (TX) M
University of Southern Indiana M
University of South Florida M*†
University of Toledo M*†
Ursuline College M
Valparaiso University M
Vanderbilt University M*
Villanova University M*†
Wake Forest University M*†
Washburn University of Topeka M
Wesleyan University M,O*
West Virginia University M*
Wichita State University M*†
Widener University M*†
Winthrop University M

LIBRARY SCIENCE

Appalachian State University M,O
The Catholic University of America M*†
Central Missouri State University M,O†
Chicago State University M
Clarion University of Pennsylvania M,O†
Clark Atlanta University M,O
College of St. Catherine M†
Dalhousie University M*
Dominican University M,O*
Drexel University M,D,O*†
East Carolina University M,O*†
Emporia State University M,D*†
Florida State University M,D,O*†
Gratz College O†
Indiana University Bloomington M,D,O*
Indiana University–Purdue University Indianapolis M*
Instituto Tecnológico y de Estudios Superiores de Monterrey, Campus Irapuato M,D
Inter American University of Puerto Rico, San Germán Campus M
Kent State University M*
Kutztown University of Pennsylvania M,O†
Long Island University, C.W. Post Campus M,D,O*†
Louisiana State University and Agricultural and Mechanical College M,O*
Mansfield University of Pennsylvania M
McDaniel College M
McGill University M,D,O*
North Carolina Central University M
Old Dominion University M*†
Pratt Institute M,O*
Queens College of the City University of New York M,O†
Rutgers, The State University of New Jersey, New Brunswick M*
St. John's University (NY) M,O*†
Sam Houston State University M*
San Jose State University M*
Simmons College M,D,O*
Southern Arkansas University–Magnolia M
Southern Connecticut State University M,O†

Spalding University M†
State University of New York at Albany M,D,O*†
Syracuse University M,O*
Tennessee Technological University M*
Texas Woman's University M,D*†
Université de Montréal M,D
University at Buffalo, The State University of New York M,D,O*†
The University of Alabama M,D,O*
University of Alberta M*
The University of Arizona M,D*
The University of British Columbia M,O*
University of California, Los Angeles M,D,O*
University of Central Arkansas M
University of Denver M*†
University of Hawaii at Manoa M,D,O*
University of Illinois at Urbana–Champaign M,D,O*
The University of Iowa M*
University of Kentucky M*
University of Maryland, College Park *
University of Michigan M,D*
University of Missouri–Columbia M,D,O*
The University of North Carolina at Chapel Hill M,D,O*†
The University of North Carolina at Greensboro M†
University of North Texas M,D*†
University of Oklahoma M,O*†
University of Pittsburgh M,D,O*†
University of Puerto Rico, Río Piedras M,O*
University of Rhode Island M*
University of South Carolina M,O*†
University of Southern Mississippi M,O
University of South Florida M*†
The University of Tennessee M*†
The University of Texas at Austin M,D*
University of Toronto M,D*
University of Washington M,D*
The University of Western Ontario M,D*
University of Wisconsin–Madison M,D,O*
University of Wisconsin–Milwaukee M,O
Valdosta State University M
Wayne State University M,O*
Wright State University M*

LIMNOLOGY

Baylor University M,D*†
Cornell University D*
University of Alaska Fairbanks M,D*
University of Florida M,D*†
University of Wisconsin–Madison M,D*
William Paterson University of New Jersey M*†

LINGUISTICS

Arizona State University M,D*
Ball State University D*
Biola University M,D,O
Boston College M*†
Boston University M,D*†
Brigham Young University M,D*
Brown University M,D*
California State University, Fresno M
California State University, Fullerton M
California State University, Long Beach M
California State University, Northridge M
Carleton University M
Carnegie Mellon University M,D*
Claremont Graduate University M,D*
Concordia University (Canada) M*†
Cornell University M,D*
Eastern Michigan University M*
Florida International University M*†
Gallaudet University M
George Mason University M*†
Georgetown University M,D,O*
Georgia State University M*
Graduate School and University Center of the City University of New York M,D*†
Harvard University M,D*†
Hofstra University M*
Indiana State University M*†
Indiana University Bloomington M,D,O*
Indiana University of Pennsylvania M,D*†
Louisiana State University and Agricultural and Mechanical College M,D*
Massachusetts Institute of Technology D*
McGill University M,D*
Memorial University of Newfoundland M,D†
Michigan State University M,D*†
Montclair State University M†
New York University M,D*†
Northeastern Illinois University M
Northern Arizona University M,D,O
Northwestern University M,D*
Oakland University M†
The Ohio State University M,D*
Ohio University M*
Old Dominion University M*†
The Pennsylvania State University University Park Campus M,D*†
Purdue University M,D*
Queens College of the City University of New York M†
Rice University M,D*
Rutgers, The State University of New Jersey, New Brunswick D*
San Diego State University M,O*
San Francisco State University M
San Jose State University M,O*
Simon Fraser University M,D
Southern Illinois University Carbondale M*†
Stanford University M,D*
Stony Brook University, State University of New York M,D*†
Syracuse University M*
Teachers College Columbia University M,D*
Temple University M*†
Texas Tech University M,D*†
Universidad de las Américas–Puebla M
Université de Montréal M,D
Université de Sherbrooke M,D
Université du Québec à Chicoutimi M
Université du Québec à Montréal M,D
Université Laval M,D†
University at Buffalo, The State University of New York M,D*†
The University of Alabama M,D*
University of Alberta M,D*
The University of Arizona M,D*
The University of British Columbia M,D*
University of Calgary M,D*
University of California, Berkeley M,D*
University of California, Davis M*†
University of California, Irvine M,D*
University of California, Los Angeles M,D*
University of California, San Diego D*
University of California, Santa Barbara D*
University of California, Santa Cruz M,D*
University of Chicago M,D*
University of Colorado at Boulder M,D*
University of Connecticut M,D*†
University of Delaware M,D*†
University of Florida M,D,O*†
University of Georgia M,D*†
University of Hawaii at Manoa M,D*
University of Houston M,D*
University of Illinois at Chicago M*
University of Illinois at Urbana–Champaign M,D*
The University of Iowa M,D*
University of Kansas M,D*
University of Manitoba M,D*
University of Maryland, Baltimore County M*†
University of Maryland, College Park M,D*
University of Massachusetts Amherst M,D*†
University of Massachusetts Boston M*†
University of Michigan M,D*
University of Minnesota, Twin Cities Campus M,D*
University of Missouri–St. Louis M†
The University of Montana–Missoula M*†
University of New Hampshire M,D*†
University of New Mexico M,D*†
The University of North Carolina at Chapel Hill M,D*†
University of North Dakota M*
University of Oregon M,D*
University of Ottawa M,D*
University of Pennsylvania M,D*†
University of Pittsburgh M,D*†
University of Puerto Rico, Río Piedras M*
University of Regina M
University of South Carolina M,D,O*†
University of Southern California M,D*†
University of South Florida M*†
The University of Tennessee D*†
The University of Texas at Arlington M,D*†
The University of Texas at Austin M,D*
The University of Texas at El Paso M*†
University of Toronto M,D*
University of Utah M*
University of Victoria M,D
University of Virginia M*
University of Washington M,D*
University of Wisconsin–Madison M,D*
Wayne State University M*
West Virginia University M*
Yale University D*

LOGISTICS

Air Force Institute of Technology M,D*
Arizona State University M,D*
California State University, Hayward M
Case Western Reserve University M,D*†
Colorado Technical University M,D
École des Hautes Études Commerciales de Montréal M*
Elmhurst College M
Florida Institute of Technology M*†
George Mason University M*†
The George Washington University M*†
Georgia College & State University M
Long Island University, C.W. Post Campus M,O*†
Maine Maritime Academy M,O
Massachusetts Institute of Technology M,D*
Michigan State University M,D*†
The Pennsylvania State University University Park Campus M,D*†
Syracuse University D*
Universidad del Turabo M
University at Buffalo, The State University of New York M,D*†
University of Arkansas M*
The University of British Columbia M*
University of Minnesota, Twin Cities Campus M,D*
University of New Hampshire M,D*†
University of New Haven M,O*†
The University of Tennessee M,D*†
The University of Texas at Arlington M*†
University of Washington O*
University of Wisconsin–Madison M*
Virginia Polytechnic Institute and State University M,D*
Wilmington College M
Wright State University M*

MANAGEMENT INFORMATION SYSTEMS

Air Force Institute of Technology M*
Alliant International University M,D*†
American InterContinental University (CA) M
American InterContinental University M*
American University M*†
Appalachian State University O
Argosy University-Chicago Northwest M,D*
Argosy University-Orange County M,D*
Argosy University-Sarasota M,D*†
Arizona State University M,D*
Arizona State University East M
Armstrong University M
Auburn University M,D*†
Baker College Center for Graduate Studies M
Barry University M,O*†
Baylor University M*†
Bay Path College M
Bellevue University M*†
Benedictine University M†
Bentley College M,O*
Bernard M. Baruch College of the City University of New York M,D*
Boise State University M*
Boston University M,D*†
Bowie State University M,O
Brigham Young University M*
Bryant College M,O
California Lutheran University M
California State University, Dominguez Hills M†
California State University, Fullerton M
California State University, Hayward M
California State University, Los Angeles M
California State University, Northridge M
California State University, Sacramento M
Capitol College M
Carnegie Mellon University M,D*
Case Western Reserve University M,D*†
Central Michigan University M,O†
Central Missouri State University M†
Charleston Southern University M
City University M,O†
Claremont Graduate University M,D*
Clarkson University M*
Clark University M*†
Cleveland State University M*†
Colorado State University M*
Colorado Technical University M,D
Colorado Technical University Denver Campus M
Colorado Technical University Sioux Falls Campus M
Columbus State University M
Concordia University Wisconsin M
Creighton University M*
Dakota State University M*
Dalhousie University M*
Dallas Baptist University M
DePaul University M*†
DeVry University-Keller Graduate School of Management M
Dominican University M*
Duquesne University M*†
Eastern Michigan University M*
École des Hautes Études Commerciales de Montréal M*
Fairfield University M,O*
Fairleigh Dickinson University, College at Florham M*†
Fairleigh Dickinson University, Metropolitan Campus M*†
Ferris State University M
Florida Agricultural and Mechanical University M*
Florida Institute of Technology M*†
Florida International University D*†
Florida State University M,D*†
Fordham University M*†
Friends University M
Georgia Southwestern State University M
Georgia State University M,D*
Golden Gate University M,D,O
Goldey-Beacom College M
Governors State University M
Graduate School and University Center of the City University of New York D*†
Harvard University D*†
Hawai'i Pacific University M*†
Hofstra University M*
Holy Family College M
Houston Baptist University M
Howard University M*
Hsi Lai University M*
Huron University USA in London M
Idaho State University M*
Illinois Institute of Technology M*†
Indiana University Bloomington M,D*
Indiana University South Bend M
Indiana University Southeast M,O
Instituto Tecnológico y de Estudios Superiores de Monterrey, Campus Central de Veracruz M
Instituto Tecnológico y de Estudios Superiores de Monterrey, Campus Ciudad de México M,D
Instituto Tecnológico y de Estudios Superiores de Monterrey, Campus Ciudad Juárez M
Instituto Tecnológico y de Estudios Superiores de Monterrey, Campus Ciudad Obregón M
Instituto Tecnológico y de Estudios Superiores de Monterrey, Campus Irapuato M,D
Instituto Tecnológico y de Estudios Superiores de Monterrey, Campus Laguna M
Iowa State University of Science and Technology M*†
ISIM University M
Jackson State University M
John Marshall Law School P,M
Johns Hopkins University M,O*†
Kean University M*†

*P—first professional degree; M—master's degree; D—doctorate; O—other advanced degree; *full description and/or announcement in Book 2, 3, 4, 5, or 6; †full description in this book*

Kennesaw State University M
Kent State University D*
Lawrence Technological University M
The Leadership Institute of Seattle M*
Lesley University M*†
Long Island University, C.W. Post Campus M,O*†
Louisiana State University and Agricultural and Mechanical College M,D*
Loyola University Chicago M*†
Marlboro College M*
Marymount University M,O†
Maryville University of Saint Louis M,O
Marywood University M*†
McMaster University D
Metropolitan State University M
Miami University M*†
Michigan State University M,D*†
Middle Tennessee State University M*
Mississippi State University M*
Montclair State University M†
New York Institute of Technology M,O*†
New York University M,D,O*†
North Carolina State University M*
North Central College M
Northeastern University M*†
Northern Arizona University M
Northern Illinois University M*†
Northwestern University M*
Northwest Missouri State University M
Notre Dame College (OH) M,O
Nova Southeastern University M,D*
Oakland University M,O†
The Ohio State University M,D*
Oklahoma City University M
Oklahoma State University M,D*†
Pace University M*†
Pace University, White Plains Campus M*
The Pennsylvania State University Harrisburg Campus of the Capital College M*†
The Pennsylvania State University University Park Campus M*†
Philadelphia University M
Purdue University M,D*
Quinnipiac University M*†
Regis University M,O*†
Rensselaer Polytechnic Institute M,D*†
Rivier College M*†
Robert Morris University M,D†
Rochester Institute of Technology O*†
Roosevelt University M*†
Rutgers, The State University of New Jersey, Newark M,D*†
Sacred Heart University M,O*†
St. Edward's University M,O
St. John's University (NY) M,O*†
Saint Joseph's University M*†
Saint Peter's College M†
San Diego State University M*
San Jose State University M*
Schiller International University (United Kingdom) M
Seattle Pacific University M
Seton Hall University M,O*†
Shenandoah University M,O
Simon Fraser University M
Southeastern University M†
Southern Illinois University Edwardsville M†
Southern New Hampshire University M,O*
Southwest Missouri State University M*†
State University of New York at Albany M*†
Stevens Institute of Technology M,D,O*†
Stony Brook University, State University of New York M,O*†
Syracuse University M,D*
Temple University M,D*†
Texas A&M International University M
Texas A&M University M,D*
Texas Tech University M,D,O*†
Towson University M,O†
Troy State University Dothan M
Troy State University Montgomery M
Université de Sherbrooke M
Université du Québec à Montréal M
Université Laval M,O†
University at Buffalo, The State University of New York M,D*†
The University of Akron M†
The University of Alabama in Huntsville M*
The University of Arizona M*
University of Arkansas M*
University of Baltimore M*
The University of British Columbia M,D*
University of Cincinnati M,D*
University of Colorado at Colorado Springs M*
University of Colorado at Denver M*
University of Dallas M*
University of Delaware M*†
University of Denver M*†
University of Detroit Mercy M*
University of Florida M,D*†
University of Illinois at Chicago M,D*
University of Illinois at Springfield M†
University of Kansas M,D*
University of La Verne M*
The University of Lethbridge M,D
University of Maine M*
University of Mary Hardin-Baylor M
University of Maryland University College M*
The University of Memphis M,D*†
University of Miami M,O*†
University of Minnesota, Twin Cities Campus M,D*
University of Mississippi M,D*
University of Missouri–St. Louis M,D,O†
University of Nebraska at Omaha M
University of New Haven M*†
University of New Mexico M*†
The University of North Carolina at Chapel Hill D*†
The University of North Carolina at Greensboro M†
University of North Texas M,D*†
University of Oklahoma M*†
University of Oregon M*
University of Pennsylvania M,D*†
University of Phoenix–Colorado Campus M
University of Phoenix–Fort Lauderdale Campus M
University of Phoenix–Hawaii Campus M
University of Phoenix–Jacksonville Campus M
University of Phoenix–Maryland Campus M
University of Phoenix–Metro Detroit Campus M
University of Phoenix–Nevada Campus M
University of Phoenix–New Mexico Campus M
University of Phoenix–Northern California Campus M
University of Phoenix–Ohio Campus M
University of Phoenix–Oklahoma City Campus M
University of Phoenix–Orlando Campus M
University of Phoenix–Sacramento Campus M
University of Phoenix–San Diego Campus M
University of Phoenix–Southern Arizona Campus M
University of Phoenix–Southern Colorado Campus M
University of Phoenix–Tampa Campus M
University of Phoenix–Tulsa Campus M
University of Phoenix–Utah Campus M
University of Pittsburgh M*†
University of Rhode Island M,D*
University of St. Thomas (MN) M,O*†
University of San Francisco M*†
The University of Scranton M†
University of Southern California M*†
University of Southern Mississippi M
University of South Florida M*†
The University of Tampa M
The University of Texas at Arlington M,D*†
The University of Texas at Austin D*
The University of Texas–Pan American M,D
University of the Sacred Heart M
University of Toledo M,D*†
University of Virginia M*
University of Wisconsin–Madison M*
University of Wisconsin–Oshkosh M*
University of Wisconsin–Whitewater M*
Utah State University M,D*
Villa Julie College M
Virginia Commonwealth University M,D*†
Virginia Polytechnic Institute and State University M,D*
Walsh College of Accountancy and Business Administration M
Washington State University M*
Webster University M
Western International University M
Western New England College M
Worcester Polytechnic Institute M,O*†
Wright State University M*
Xavier University M*
York College of Pennsylvania M

MANAGEMENT OF TECHNOLOGY

Air Force Institute of Technology M,D*
Alliant International University M,D*†
Athabasca University M,O
Bentley College M,O*
Boston University M*†
Brigham Young University M*
California Polytechnic State University, San Luis Obispo M†
Carlow College M
Carnegie Mellon University M,D*
Central Connecticut State University M*†
Champlain College M*
Colorado School of Mines M,D†
Colorado State University M,D*
Dallas Baptist University M
École Polytechnique de Montréal M,O
Embry-Riddle Aeronautical University, Extended Campus M*
Fairfield University M*
George Mason University M,D*†
The George Washington University M,D*†
Georgia Institute of Technology M*
Idaho State University M*
Illinois Institute of Technology M*†
Instituto Tecnológico y de Estudios Superiores de Monterrey, Campus Central de Veracruz M
Instituto Tecnológico y de Estudios Superiores de Monterrey, Campus Cuernavaca M,D
Instituto Tecnológico y de Estudios Superiores de Monterrey, Campus Irapuato M,D
Iona College M,O*†
Jones International University M*†
La Salle University M,O
Marquette University M,D*†
Marshall University M*†
Mercer University M
Murray State University M†
National Technological University M
National University M†
New Jersey Institute of Technology M,D
New York University M,D,O*†
North Carolina Agricultural and Technical State University M*
North Carolina State University D*
Northern Kentucky University M
OGI School of Science & Engineering at Oregon Health & Science University M,O*
Pacific Lutheran University M†
Pacific States University M
Pepperdine University M*†
Polytechnic University, Brooklyn Campus M*
Portland State University M,D*
Rensselaer Polytechnic Institute M,D*†
Rhode Island College M†
Saginaw Valley State University M
St. Ambrose University M,D
South Dakota School of Mines and Technology M*†
Southern Polytechnic State University M†
Southwest Texas State University M*
Stevens Institute of Technology M,D,O*†
Stony Brook University, State University of New York M,O*†
Technical University of British Columbia M
Texas A&M University–Commerce M†
Université Laval O†
University of Advancing Technology M
The University of Akron M†
University of Bridgeport M*†
University of Colorado at Boulder M,D*
University of Delaware M*†
University of Denver M*†
University of Maryland University College M*
University of Miami M,D*†
University of Minnesota, Twin Cities Campus M*
University of New Haven M*†
University of New Mexico M*†
University of Pennsylvania M,O*†
University of Phoenix–Boston Campus M
University of Phoenix–Colorado Campus M
University of Phoenix–Fort Lauderdale Campus M
University of Phoenix–Jacksonville Campus M
University of Phoenix–Louisiana Campus M
University of Phoenix–Maryland Campus M
University of Phoenix–Metro Detroit Campus M
University of Phoenix–New Mexico Campus M
University of Phoenix–Northern California Campus M
University of Phoenix–Oregon Campus M
University of Phoenix–Orlando Campus M
University of Phoenix–Philadelphia Campus M
University of Phoenix–Phoenix Campus M
University of Phoenix–Pittsburgh Campus M
University of Phoenix–San Diego Campus M
University of Phoenix–Southern Arizona Campus M
University of Phoenix–Southern California Campus M
University of Phoenix–Southern Colorado Campus M
University of Phoenix–Tampa Campus M
University of Phoenix–Washington Campus M
University of Phoenix–West Michigan Campus M
University of St. Thomas (MN) M,O*†
The University of Scranton M†
The University of Tampa M
The University of Texas at Arlington M*†
University of Tulsa M†
University of Waterloo M,D
University of Wisconsin–Stout M
Vanderbilt University M,D*
Villa Julie College M
Washington State University M,D*
Washington State University Spokane M†

MANAGEMENT STRATEGY AND POLICY

Alliant International University M,D*†
Azusa Pacific University M*†
Bernard M. Baruch College of the City University of New York M,D*
Brenau University M
Case Western Reserve University M,D*†
Claremont Graduate University M*
DePaul University M*†
Dominican University of California M
Drexel University M,D,O*†
École des Hautes Études Commerciales de Montréal M*
The George Washington University M,D*†
Illinois Institute of Technology M*†
Lamar University M*†
Manhattanville College M*†
Marymount University M,O†
Michigan State University M,D*†
Mountain State University M†
Northwestern University D*
Purdue University M,D*
Regent University M,D,O†
Simmons College M*
Stevens Institute of Technology M*†
Syracuse University D*
Temple University M,D*†
Towson University O†
The University of Arizona M*
The University of British Columbia D*
University of Dallas M*
University of Florida M,D*†
University of Minnesota, Twin Cities Campus M,D*
University of New Haven M*†
The University of North Carolina at Chapel Hill D*†
University of North Texas M,D*†
Walden University D†

MANUFACTURING ENGINEERING

Arizona State University East M
Boston University M,D*†
Bowling Green State University M*†

Institution	Degrees
Bradley University	M†
Brigham Young University	M*
California Polytechnic State University, San Luis Obispo	M†
Colorado State University	M,D*
Cornell University	M,D*
Drexel University	M,D*†
Eastern Kentucky University	M
East Tennessee State University	M†
Florida Atlantic University	M*
Grand Valley State University	M†
Illinois Institute of Technology	M,D*†
Instituto Tecnológico y de Estudios Superiores de Monterrey, Campus Monterrey	M,D
Kansas State University	M,D*†
Kettering University	M
Lawrence Technological University	M,D
Lehigh University	M*
Louisiana Tech University	M,D*
Marquette University	M,D*†
Massachusetts Institute of Technology	*
Michigan State University	M,D*†
Minnesota State University, Mankato	M
National Technological University	M
New Jersey Institute of Technology	M,D
North Carolina State University	M*
North Dakota State University	M†
Northeastern University	M,D*†
Northwestern University	M*
Ohio University	M,D*
Oklahoma State University	M*†
Old Dominion University	M,D*†
Oregon State University	M,D*
The Pennsylvania State University University Park Campus	M*†
Polytechnic University, Brooklyn Campus	M*
Polytechnic University, Long Island Graduate Center	M
Polytechnic University of Puerto Rico	M
Polytechnic University, Westchester Graduate Center	M
Portland State University	M*
Purdue University	M,D*
Rensselaer Polytechnic Institute	M*†
Rochester Institute of Technology	M*†
Southern Illinois University Carbondale	M*†
Southern Methodist University	M,D*†
Stanford University	M,D*
Syracuse University	M*
Tufts University	O*†
University of California, Los Angeles	M*
University of Central Florida	M,D,O*†
University of Colorado at Colorado Springs	M*
University of Detroit Mercy	M,D*
University of Florida	M,D,O*†
University of Houston	M*
The University of Iowa	M,D*
University of Kentucky	M*
University of Maryland, College Park	M,D*
University of Massachusetts Amherst	M*†
The University of Memphis	M*†
University of Michigan	M,D*
University of Michigan–Dearborn	M,D*†
University of Missouri–Columbia	M,D*
University of Missouri–Rolla	M*
University of Nebraska–Lincoln	M,D*†
University of New Mexico	M*†
University of Pittsburgh	M*†
University of Rhode Island	M*
University of St. Thomas (MN)	M,O*†
University of Southern California	M*†
University of Southern Maine	M
The University of Tennessee	M,D*†
The University of Texas at Austin	M,D*
The University of Texas at El Paso	M*†
University of Toronto	M*
University of Windsor	M,D
University of Wisconsin–Madison	M*
Villanova University	M,O*†
Wayne State University	M*
Western Michigan University	M*†
Western New England College	M
Wichita State University	M,D*†
Worcester Polytechnic Institute	M,D,O*†

MARINE AFFAIRS

Institution	Degrees
Dalhousie University	M*
Duke University	M,D*†
East Carolina University	D*†
Florida Institute of Technology	M,D*†
Louisiana State University and Agricultural and Mechanical College	M,D*
Memorial University of Newfoundland	M†
Nova Southeastern University	M,D*
Oregon State University	M*
Stevens Institute of Technology	M*†
Université du Québec à Rimouski	M
University of Delaware	M,D*†
University of Maine	M*
University of Miami	M*†
University of Rhode Island	M,D*
University of San Diego	M*†
University of Washington	M*
University of West Florida	M

MARINE BIOLOGY

Institution	Degrees
California State University, Stanislaus	M
College of Charleston	M*†
Florida Institute of Technology	M*†
Florida State University	M,D*†
Massachusetts Institute of Technology	M,D,O*
Memorial University of Newfoundland	M,D†
Murray State University	M†
Nova Southeastern University	M,D*
Rutgers, The State University of New Jersey, New Brunswick	M,D*
San Francisco State University	M
Southwest Texas State University	M*
University of Alaska Fairbanks	M,D*
University of California, San Diego	M,D*
University of California, Santa Barbara	M,D*
University of Colorado at Boulder	M,D*
University of Guam	M
University of Hawaii at Manoa	M,D*
University of Maine	M,D*
University of Massachusetts Dartmouth	M*†
University of Miami	M,D*†
The University of North Carolina at Wilmington	M*
University of Oregon	M,D*
University of Southern California	M,D*†
University of Southern Mississippi	M,D
University of South Florida	M,D*†
University of Victoria	M,D
Western Illinois University	M,O

MARINE SCIENCES

Institution	Degrees
California State University, Fresno	M
California State University, Hayward	M
California State University, Monterey Bay	
California State University, Sacramento	M
The College of William and Mary	M,D*†
Duke University	M,D*†
Florida Institute of Technology	M,D*†
Memorial University of Newfoundland	M†
Murray State University	M†
North Carolina State University	M,D*
Nova Southeastern University	M,D*
Oregon State University	M,D*
San Jose State University	M*
Stony Brook University, State University of New York	M*†
University of Alaska Fairbanks	M,D*
University of California, San Diego	M,D*
University of California, Santa Barbara	M,D*
University of California, Santa Cruz	M,D*
University of Connecticut	M,D*†
University of Delaware	M,D*†
University of Florida	M,D*†
University of Georgia	M,D*†
University of Maine	M,D*
University of Maryland	M,D*†
University of Maryland, Baltimore County	M,D*†
University of Maryland, College Park	M,D*
University of Maryland Eastern Shore	M,D†
University of Massachusetts Boston	D*†
University of Miami	M,D*†
The University of North Carolina at Chapel Hill	M,D*†
University of Puerto Rico, Mayagüez Campus	M,D*
University of San Diego	M*†
University of South Alabama	M,D*†
University of South Carolina	M,D*†
University of Southern California	M,D*†
University of Southern Mississippi	M,D
University of South Florida	M,D*†
The University of Texas at Austin	M,D*
University of Wisconsin–Madison	M,D*

MARKETING

Institution	Degrees
Alabama Agricultural and Mechanical University	M
Alliant International University	M,D*†
American University	M*†
Andrews University	M
Argosy University-Chicago Northwest	M,D*
Argosy University-Orange County	M,D*
Argosy University-Sarasota	M,D*†
Argosy University-Tampa	M*
Arizona State University	M,D*
Armstrong University	M
Baker College Center for Graduate Studies	M
Bayamón Central University	M
Bentley College	M,O*
Bernard M. Baruch College of the City University of New York	M,D*
Boston University	M,D,O*†
Bryant College	M,O
California Lutheran University	M
California State University, Fullerton	M
California State University, Hayward	M
California State University, Los Angeles	M
California State University, Northridge	M
Cardean University	M†
Carnegie Mellon University	D*
Case Western Reserve University	M,D*†
Central Michigan University	M†
City University	M,O†
Claremont Graduate University	M*
Clark Atlanta University	M
Clark University	M*†
Columbia Southern University	M
Columbia University	M,D*†
Concordia University Wisconsin	M
Cornell University	D*
Dallas Baptist University	M
Davenport University	M
Delta State University	M
DePaul University	M*†
Drexel University	M,D,O*†
Eastern Michigan University	M*
Eastern University	M*
École des Hautes Études Commerciales de Montréal	M*
Fairfield University	M,O*
Fairleigh Dickinson University, College at Florham	M*†
Fairleigh Dickinson University, Metropolitan Campus	M*†
Fashion Institute of Technology	M*
Florida Agricultural and Mechanical University	M*
Florida State University	M,D*†
Fordham University	M*†
Franklin University	M
The George Washington University	M,D*†
Georgia State University	M,D*
Golden Gate University	M,D,O
Goldey-Beacom College	M
Hawai'i Pacific University	M*†
Hofstra University	M*
Howard University	M*
Huron University USA in London	M
Illinois Institute of Technology	M*†
Indiana Institute of Technology	M
Indiana University Bloomington	M,D*
Indiana University Southeast	M,O
Instituto Tecnológico y de Estudios Superiores de Monterrey, Campus Central de Veracruz	M
Instituto Tecnológico y de Estudios Superiores de Monterrey, Campus Ciudad Obregón	M
Instituto Tecnológico y de Estudios Superiores de Monterrey, Campus Cuernavaca	M
Instituto Tecnológico y de Estudios Superiores de Monterrey, Campus Monterrey	M
Inter American University of Puerto Rico, Metropolitan Campus	M
Inter American University of Puerto Rico, San Germán Campus	M
Iona College	M,O*†
Johns Hopkins University	M,O*†
Kennesaw State University	M
Kent State University	D*
Lindenwood University	M
Long Island University, C.W. Post Campus	M,O*†
Louisiana State University and Agricultural and Mechanical College	M,D*
Louisiana Tech University	M,D*
Loyola College in Maryland	M
Loyola University Chicago	M*†
Maryville University of Saint Louis	M,O
Mercy College	M*
Metropolitan State University	M
Miami University	M*†
Michigan State University	M,D*†
Middle Tennessee State University	M*
Mississippi State University	M,D*
Montclair State University	M†
National University	M†
New Mexico State University	D
New York Institute of Technology	M,O*†
New York University	M,D,O*†
Nichols College	M
Northeastern Illinois University	M
Northwestern University	M,D*
Oklahoma City University	M
Oklahoma State University	M,D*†
Oral Roberts University	M
Pace University	M*†
Pace University, White Plains Campus	M*
The Pennsylvania State University University Park Campus	M,D*†
Philadelphia University	M
Pontifical Catholic University of Puerto Rico	M,D
Purdue University	M,D*
Quinnipiac University	M*†
Regis University	M,O*†
Rensselaer Polytechnic Institute	M,D*†
Rutgers, The State University of New Jersey, Newark	M,D*†
Sage Graduate School	M†
St. Bonaventure University	M,O
St. Cloud State University	M
St. Edward's University	M,O
St. John's University (NY)	M,O*†
Saint Joseph's University	M*†
Saint Peter's College	M†
St. Thomas Aquinas College	M
Saint Xavier University	M,O*
San Diego State University	M*
Seton Hall University	M,O*†
Simon Fraser University	M
Southeastern University	M†
Southern New Hampshire University	M,O*
State University of New York at Albany	M*†
State University of New York at New Paltz	M
Stephen F. Austin State University	M
Syracuse University	D*
Temple University	M,D*†
Texas A&M University	M,D*
Texas Tech University	M,D*†
United States International University	M
Universidad del Turabo	M
Universidad Metropolitana	M
Université de Sherbrooke	M
Université Laval	M,O†
The University of Akron	M†
The University of Alabama	M,D*
University of Alberta	D*
The University of Arizona	D*
University of Baltimore	M*
The University of British Columbia	D*
University of California, Berkeley	D*
University of Central Florida	D*†
University of Cincinnati	M,D*
University of Colorado at Boulder	M,D*
University of Colorado at Colorado Springs	M*
University of Colorado at Denver	M*

*P—first professional degree; M—master's degree; D—doctorate; O—other advanced degree; *full description and/or announcement in Book 2, 3, 4, 5, or 6; †full description in this book*

University of Connecticut M,D*†
University of Dallas M*
University of Denver M*†
The University of Findlay M
University of Florida M,D*†
University of Houston D*
University of Illinois at Chicago D*
The University of Iowa D*
University of La Verne M*
University of Manitoba M*
The University of Memphis M,D*†
University of Minnesota, Twin Cities Campus M,D*
University of Missouri–St. Louis M,O†
University of Nebraska–Lincoln M,D*†
University of New Haven M*†
University of New Mexico M*†
The University of North Carolina at Chapel Hill D*†
The University of North Carolina at Greensboro M,D†
University of North Texas M,D*†
University of Oregon D*
University of Pennsylvania M,D*†
University of Rhode Island M,D*
University of St. Thomas (MN) M,O*†
University of San Francisco M*†
University of Saskatchewan M
The University of Scranton M†
The University of Tennessee M,D*†
The University of Tennessee at Chattanooga M
The University of Texas at Arlington M,D*†
The University of Texas at Austin D*
University of the Sacred Heart M
University of Toledo M*†
University of Wisconsin–Madison M*
University of Wisconsin–Whitewater M*
Vanderbilt University D*
Virginia Commonwealth University M*†
Virginia Polytechnic Institute and State University M,D*
Wagner College M
Webster University M
Western International University M
Western New England College M
Wilkes University M
Worcester Polytechnic Institute M,O*†
Wright State University M*
Xavier University M*
Yale University D*
York College of Pennsylvania M
Youngstown State University M

MARKETING RESEARCH

Hofstra University M*
Instituto Tecnológico y de Estudios Superiores de Monterrey, Campus Irapuato M,D
Pace University M*†
Pace University, White Plains Campus M*
Southern Illinois University Edwardsville M†
Universidad de las Americas, A.C. M
University of Georgia M*†
The University of Texas at Arlington M*†
University of Wisconsin–Madison M*

MARRIAGE AND FAMILY THERAPY

Abilene Christian University M
Adler School of Professional Psychology M,D,O*
Alliant International University M,D*†
Antioch New England Graduate School M*†
Appalachian State University M
Argosy University-Chicago D*
Argosy University-Honolulu M*
Argosy University-Twin Cities M,D*
Azusa Pacific University M,D*†
Barry University M,O*†
Bethel College (IN) M
Bethel Seminary P,M,D,O
Briercrest Biblical Seminary P,M
Brigham Young University M,D*
California Baptist University M
California Lutheran University M
California State University, Bakersfield M,O
California State University, Dominguez Hills M†
California State University, Fresno M
California State University, Northridge M,O
Carlos Albizu University, Miami Campus M,D
Central Connecticut State University M*†
Chapman University M*†
Christian Theological Seminary P,M,D
The College of New Jersey O†
The College of William and Mary M,D*†
Converse College O
Denver Seminary P,M,D,O
Drexel University M,D*†
East Carolina University M*†
Eastern Baptist Theological Seminary D
Eastern Nazarene College M
East Tennessee State University M†
Edgewood College M
Evangelical School of Theology P,M,O
Fairfield University M*
Fitchburg State College M,O†
Florida State University D*†
Friends University M
Fuller Theological Seminary M
Geneva College M*
George Fox University M†
Golden Gate University M,O
Harding University M
Hardin-Simmons University M
Hofstra University M,O*
Hope International University M
Idaho State University M,O*
Indiana State University M,D,O*†
Indiana Wesleyan University M*
Iona College M,O*†
Iowa State University of Science and Technology M,D*†
John Brown University M
Johnson Bible College M
Kean University M,O*†
Kutztown University of Pennsylvania M†
La Salle University D
Loma Linda University M,D*
Long Island University, C.W. Post Campus M,O*†
Loyola Marymount University M†
Mennonite Brethren Biblical Seminary M,O
Mercy College M,O*
Michigan State University M,D*†
Montclair State University M†
North American Baptist Seminary M
Northwestern University M*
Notre Dame de Namur University M
Nova Southeastern University M,D,O*
Oklahoma Baptist University M
Our Lady of Holy Cross College M
Pacific Lutheran University M†
Pacific Oaks College M
Palm Beach Atlantic University M
Phillips Graduate Institute M,D
Prairie View A&M University M
Purdue University M,D*
Purdue University Calumet M
Reformed Theological Seminary (MS) P,M,D,O
Saint Joseph College M
Saint Louis University M,D,O*†
Saint Mary's College of California M
St. Mary's University of San Antonio M,D,O
Saint Paul University M,O
St. Thomas University M†
San Francisco State University M
Santa Clara University M*
Seattle Pacific University M
Seton Hall University M,D,O*†
Seton Hill University M†
Sonoma State University M
Southern Adventist University M
Southern Christian University P,M,D
Southern Connecticut State University M†
Southern Nazarene University M
Springfield College M,O†
State University of New York College at Oneonta M,O
Stetson University M
Syracuse University M,D*
Texas Tech University M,D*†
Texas Woman's University M,D*†
Universidad de las Americas, A.C. M
The University of Akron M†
The University of Alabama at Birmingham M*†
University of Florida M,D,O*†
University of Great Falls M
University of Guelph M,D
University of Houston–Clear Lake M*†
University of La Verne M*
University of Louisiana at Monroe M,D
University of Maryland, College Park M,D*
University of Miami M,O*†
University of Mobile M
University of Nevada, Las Vegas M*†
University of New Hampshire M*†
The University of North Carolina at Greensboro M,D,O†
University of Phoenix–Hawaii Campus M
University of Phoenix–New Mexico Campus M
University of Phoenix–Phoenix Campus M
University of Phoenix–Sacramento Campus M
University of Phoenix–San Diego Campus M
University of Pittsburgh O*†
University of Rochester M*
University of St. Thomas (MN) M,D,O*†
University of San Diego M*†
University of San Francisco M,D*†
University of Southern California M,D,O*†
University of Southern Mississippi M,D
The University of Winnipeg P,M,O
University of Wisconsin–Stout M
Utah State University M*
Valdosta State University M
Virginia Polytechnic Institute and State University M,D*
Western Illinois University M,O
Western Michigan University M,D*†
Western Seminary M

MASS COMMUNICATION

American University M*†
American University in Cairo M,O
Auburn University M*†
Boston University M*†
Brigham Young University M*
California State University, Chico M
California State University, Fresno M
California State University, Northridge M
Central Michigan University M†
The College of Saint Rose M*†
Emerson College M*†
Florida International University M*†
Florida State University M,D*†
Fordham University M*†
The George Washington University M*†
Grambling State University M
Howard University M,D*
Indiana University Bloomington M,D*
Iowa State University of Science and Technology M*†
Jackson State University M
Kansas State University M*†
Kent State University M*
Lindenwood University M
Louisiana State University and Agricultural and Mechanical College M*
Loyola University New Orleans M
Marquette University M*†
Marshall University M*†
Miami University M*†
Middle Tennessee State University M*
Murray State University M†
New School University M*†
North Dakota State University M,D†
Oklahoma State University M,D*†
The Pennsylvania State University University Park Campus M,D*†
Point Park College M*
St. Cloud State University M
San Diego State University M*
San Jose State University M*
Seton Hall University M*†
Southern Illinois University Edwardsville M†
Southern University and Agricultural and Mechanical College M*
Southwest Texas State University M*
Stephen F. Austin State University M
Syracuse University D*
Temple University D*†
Texas Christian University M*
Texas Tech University M*†
Université Laval M†
University of Colorado at Boulder M,D*
University of Connecticut M*†
University of Denver M*†
University of Florida M,D*†
University of Georgia M,D*†
University of Houston M*
University of Illinois at Chicago M*
The University of Iowa M,D*
University of Louisiana at Lafayette M*
University of Maryland, College Park D*
University of Michigan D*
University of Minnesota, Twin Cities Campus M,D*
University of Nebraska–Lincoln M*†
University of Nevada, Las Vegas M*†
The University of North Carolina at Chapel Hill M,D*†
University of Oklahoma M*†
University of Puerto Rico, Río Piedras M*
The University of South Dakota M†
University of Southern California M,D*†
University of South Florida M*†
University of the Sacred Heart M
University of Wisconsin–Madison M,D*
University of Wisconsin–Milwaukee M
University of Wisconsin–Stevens Point M
University of Wisconsin–Superior M
University of Wisconsin–Whitewater M*
Virginia Commonwealth University M*†

MATERIALS ENGINEERING

Arizona State University M,D*
Auburn University M,D*†
California State University, Northridge M
Carleton University M,D
Carnegie Mellon University M,D*
Case Western Reserve University M,D*†
Clemson University M,D*
Colorado School of Mines M,D†
Colorado State University M,D*
Columbia University M,D*†
Cornell University M,D*
Dartmouth College M,D*†
Drexel University M,D*†
École Polytechnique de Montréal M,D,O
Georgia Institute of Technology M,D*
Illinois Institute of Technology M,D*†
Iowa State University of Science and Technology M,D*†
Johns Hopkins University M,D*†
Lehigh University M,D*
Massachusetts Institute of Technology M,D,O*
McGill University M,D*
McMaster University M,D
Michigan State University M,D*†
Michigan Technological University M,D*†
National Technological University M
New Jersey Institute of Technology M,D
New Mexico Institute of Mining and Technology M,D†
North Carolina State University M,D*
Northwestern University M,D,O*
The Ohio State University M,D*
Old Dominion University M*†
The Pennsylvania State University University Park Campus M,D*†
Purdue University M,D*
Rensselaer Polytechnic Institute M,D*†
Rochester Institute of Technology M*†
San Jose State University M*
South Dakota School of Mines and Technology M,D*†
Stanford University M,D,O*
Stevens Institute of Technology M,D,O*†
Stony Brook University, State University of New York M,D*†
Texas A&M University M,D*
Tuskegee University D
The University of Alabama M,D*
The University of Alabama at Birmingham M,D*†
The University of Alabama in Huntsville M,D*
University of Alberta M,D*
The University of Arizona M,D*
The University of British Columbia M,D*
University of California, Berkeley M,D*
University of California, Irvine M,D*
University of California, Los Angeles M,D*
University of California, Santa Barbara M,D*
University of Central Florida M,D*†
University of Cincinnati M,D*
University of Dayton M,D*†
University of Delaware M,D*†
University of Florida M,D,O*†
University of Houston M,D*
University of Illinois at Chicago M,D*

University of Illinois at Urbana–Champaign M,D*
University of Maryland, College Park M,D*
University of Michigan M,D*
University of Minnesota, Twin Cities Campus M,D*
University of Nebraska–Lincoln M,D*†
University of Pennsylvania M,D*†
University of Pittsburgh M,D*†
University of Southern California M*†
The University of Tennessee M,D*†
The University of Texas at Arlington M,D*†
The University of Texas at Austin M,D*
The University of Texas at El Paso D*†
University of Utah M,D*
University of Washington M,D*
University of Windsor M,D
Virginia Polytechnic Institute and State University M,D*
Washington State University M,D*
Washington University in St. Louis M,D*†
Wayne State University M,D,O*
Western Michigan University M*†
Worcester Polytechnic Institute M,D,O*†
Wright State University M*

MATERIALS SCIENCES

Air Force Institute of Technology M,D*
Alabama Agricultural and Mechanical University M,D
Alfred University M,D*†
Arizona State University M,D*
Brown University M,D*
California Institute of Technology M,D*
California Polytechnic State University, San Luis Obispo M†
Carnegie Mellon University M,D*
Case Western Reserve University M,D*†
Clemson University M,D*
Colorado School of Mines M,D†
Columbia University M,D,O*†
Cornell University M,D*
Dartmouth College M,D*†
Duke University M,D*†
École Polytechnique de Montréal M,D,O
The George Washington University M,D*†
Iowa State University of Science and Technology M,D*†
Jackson State University M
Johns Hopkins University M,D*†
Lehigh University M,D*
Massachusetts Institute of Technology M,D,O*
McMaster University M,D
Michigan State University M,D*†
National Technological University M
New Jersey Institute of Technology M,D
Norfolk State University M†
North Carolina State University M,D*
Northwestern University M,D,O*
The Ohio State University M,D*
Ohio University D*
Old Dominion University M*†
Oregon State University M*
The Pennsylvania State University University Park Campus M,D*†
Polytechnic University, Brooklyn Campus M*
Polytechnic University, Westchester Graduate Center M
Princeton University *
Rensselaer Polytechnic Institute M,D*†
Rice University M,D*
Rochester Institute of Technology M*†
Royal Military College of Canada M,D
Rutgers, The State University of New Jersey, New Brunswick M,D*
South Dakota School of Mines and Technology M,D*†
Southwest Missouri State University M*†
Stanford University M,D,O*
Stevens Institute of Technology M,D,O*†
Stony Brook University, State University of New York M,D*†
Syracuse University M,D*
Université du Québec, Institut National de la Recherche Scientifique M,D
University at Buffalo, The State University of New York M*†
The University of Alabama D*
The University of Alabama at Birmingham D*†
The University of Alabama in Huntsville M,D*
The University of Arizona M,D*
The University of British Columbia M,D*
University of California, Berkeley M,D*
University of California, Davis M,D,O*†
University of California, Irvine M,D*
University of California, Los Angeles M,D*
University of California, San Diego M,D*
University of California, Santa Barbara M,D*
University of Central Florida M,D*†
University of Cincinnati M,D*
University of Connecticut M,D*†
University of Delaware M,D*†
University of Denver M,D*†
University of Florida M,D,O*†
University of Illinois at Urbana–Champaign M,D*
University of Kentucky M,D*
University of Maryland, College Park M,D*
University of Michigan M,D*
University of Minnesota, Twin Cities Campus M,D*
University of New Brunswick Fredericton M,D
University of New Hampshire M,D*†
The University of North Carolina at Chapel Hill M,D*†
University of North Texas M,D*†
University of Pennsylvania M,D*†
University of Pittsburgh M,D*†
University of Rochester M,D*
University of Southern California M,D,O*†
The University of Tennessee M,D*†
The University of Texas at Arlington M,D*†
The University of Texas at Austin M,D*
The University of Texas at El Paso D*†
University of Toronto M,D*
University of Utah M,D*
University of Vermont M,D*†
University of Virginia M,D*
University of Washington M,D*
University of Wisconsin–Madison M,D*
Vanderbilt University M,D*
Virginia Polytechnic Institute and State University M,D*
Washington State University M,D*
Washington University in St. Louis M,D*†
Wayne State University M,D,O*
Western Michigan University M*†
Worcester Polytechnic Institute M,D,O*†
Wright State University M*

MATERNAL/CHILD NURSING

Baylor University M*†
Boston College M,D*†
Columbia University M,O*†
Duke University M,O*†
Florida Atlantic University M,D,O*
Hardin-Simmons University M
Hunter College of the City University of New York M†
Indiana University–Purdue University Indianapolis M*
Jewish Hospital College of Nursing and Allied Health M
Lehman College of the City University of New York M
Marquette University M,O*†
Medical College of Georgia M,D*
Medical University of South Carolina M,O*
Pontifical Catholic University of Puerto Rico M
Rush University M,D*
Rutgers, The State University of New Jersey, Newark M,D*†
Saint Joseph College M,O
Stony Brook University, State University of New York M,O*†
University at Buffalo, The State University of New York M,D,O*†
The University of Alabama in Huntsville M,O*
University of Cincinnati M,D*
University of Colorado at Colorado Springs M*
University of Delaware M,O*†
University of Illinois at Chicago M*
University of Maryland M,D*†
University of Missouri–Kansas City M,D*†
University of Pennsylvania M,O*†
University of South Alabama M*†
University of Southern Mississippi M,D
The University of Texas at El Paso M*†
Vanderbilt University M,D*
Wayne State University M*
Wichita State University M*†

MATERNAL AND CHILD HEALTH

Bank Street College of Education M*
Boston University M,O*†
Columbia University M*†
The George Washington University M*†
Harvard University M,D*†
New York Medical College M,O*
Tulane University M,D*†
The University of Alabama at Birmingham M*†
University of California, Berkeley M*
University of Minnesota, Twin Cities Campus M*
The University of North Carolina at Chapel Hill M,D*†
University of Puerto Rico, Medical Sciences Campus M*
University of Washington M,D*
Wheelock College M*

MATHEMATICAL AND COMPUTATIONAL FINANCE

Boston University M,D*†
Carnegie Mellon University M,D*
Florida State University M,D*†
New York University M,D*†
OGI School of Science & Engineering at Oregon Health & Science University M,O*
Purdue University M,D*
Rice University M,D*
Stanford University M,D*
University of Alberta M,D,O*
University of Chicago M*

MATHEMATICAL PHYSICS

New Mexico Institute of Mining and Technology M,D†
Princeton University D*
University of Alberta M,D,O*
University of Colorado at Boulder M,D*
Virginia Polytechnic Institute and State University M,D*

MATHEMATICS

Adelphi University M,D*
Alabama State University O
American University M*†
Andrews University M
Appalachian State University M
Arizona State University M,D*
Arkansas State University M
Auburn University M,D*†
Ball State University M*
Baylor University M*†
Boston College M*†
Boston University M,D*†
Bowling Green State University M,D,O*†
Brandeis University D*†
Brigham Young University M,D*
Brooklyn College of the City University of New York M,D†
Brown University M,D*
Bryn Mawr College M,D
Bucknell University M
California Institute of Technology D*
California Polytechnic State University, San Luis Obispo M†
California State Polytechnic University, Pomona M*
California State University, Fresno M
California State University, Fullerton M
California State University, Hayward M
California State University, Long Beach M
California State University, Los Angeles M
California State University, Northridge M
California State University, Sacramento M
California State University, San Bernardino M
California State University, San Marcos M
Carleton University M,D
Carnegie Mellon University M,D*
Case Western Reserve University M,D*†
Central Connecticut State University M*†
Central Michigan University M,D†
Central Missouri State University M†
Central Washington University M†
Chicago State University M
City College of the City University of New York M*†
Claremont Graduate University M,D*
Clarkson University M,D*
Clemson University M,D*
Cleveland State University M*†
College of Charleston M*†
Colorado School of Mines M,D†
Colorado State University M,D*
Columbia University M,D*†
Concordia University (Canada) M,D*†
Cornell University D*
Dalhousie University M,D*
Dartmouth College D*†
Delaware State University M
Drexel University M,D*†
Duke University D*†
Duquesne University M*†
East Carolina University M*†
Eastern Illinois University M†
Eastern Kentucky University M
Eastern Michigan University M*
Eastern New Mexico University M
Eastern Washington University M†
East Tennessee State University M†
École Polytechnique de Montréal M,D
Edinboro University of Pennsylvania O
Emory University M,D*†
Emporia State University M*†
Fairfield University M*
Fairleigh Dickinson University, College at Florham M*†
Fayetteville State University M
Florida Atlantic University M,D*
Florida International University M*†
Florida State University M,D*†
George Mason University M*†
The George Washington University M,D*†
Georgia Institute of Technology M,D*
Georgian Court College M
Georgia Southern University M
Georgia State University M*
Graduate School and University Center of the City University of New York D*†
Harvard University M,D*†
Howard University M,D*
Hunter College of the City University of New York M†
Idaho State University M,D*
Illinois State University M*†
Indiana State University M*†
Indiana University Bloomington M,D*
Indiana University of Pennsylvania M*†
Indiana University–Purdue University Fort Wayne M
Indiana University–Purdue University Indianapolis M,D*
Institute of Paper Science and Technology M,D*
Iowa State University of Science and Technology M,D*†
Jackson State University M
Jacksonville State University M
John Carroll University M
Johns Hopkins University M,D*†
Kansas State University M,D*†
Kean University M*†
Kent State University M,D*
Lakehead University M
Lamar University M*†
Lehigh University M,D*
Lehman College of the City University of New York M
Long Island University, C.W. Post Campus M*†
Louisiana State University and Agricultural and Mechanical College M,D*
Louisiana Tech University M*
Loyola University Chicago M*†
Maharishi University of Management M
Marquette University M,D*†
Marshall University M*†
Massachusetts Institute of Technology D*
McGill University M,D*
McMaster University M,D
McNeese State University M
Memorial University of Newfoundland M,D†
Miami University M*†
Michigan State University M,D*†
Michigan Technological University M,D*†
Middle Tennessee State University M*

*P—first professional degree; M—master's degree; D—doctorate; O—other advanced degree; *full description and/or announcement in Book 2, 3, 4, 5, or 6; †full description in this book*

Institution	Degrees
Minnesota State University, Mankato	M
Mississippi College	M
Mississippi State University	M,D*
Montana State University–Bozeman	M,D*
Montclair State University	M†
Morgan State University	M*
Murray State University	M†
Naval Postgraduate School	M,D
New Jersey Institute of Technology	D
New Mexico Institute of Mining and Technology	M†
New Mexico State University	M,D
New York University	M,D*†
Nicholls State University	M
North Carolina Central University	M
North Carolina State University	M,D*
North Dakota State University	M,D†
Northeastern Illinois University	M
Northeastern University	M,D*†
Northern Arizona University	M
Northern Illinois University	M,D*†
Northwestern University	D*
Oakland University	M,D,O†
The Ohio State University	M,D*
Ohio University	M,D*
Oklahoma State University	M,D*†
Old Dominion University	M,D*†
Oregon State University	M,D*
The Pennsylvania State University University Park Campus	M,D*†
Pittsburg State University	M
Polytechnic University, Brooklyn Campus	M,D*
Polytechnic University, Long Island Graduate Center	M,D
Portland State University	M,D*
Prairie View A&M University	M
Princeton University	D*
Purdue University	M,D*
Purdue University Calumet	M
Queens College of the City University of New York	M†
Queen's University at Kingston	M,D
Rensselaer Polytechnic Institute	M,D*†
Rhode Island College	M,O†
Rice University	M,D*
Rivier College	M*†
Roosevelt University	M*†
Rowan University	M†
Royal Military College of Canada	M
Rutgers, The State University of New Jersey, Camden	M†
Rutgers, The State University of New Jersey, Newark	D*†
Rutgers, The State University of New Jersey, New Brunswick	M,D*
St. Cloud State University	M
St. John's University (NY)	M*†
Saint Louis University	M,D*†
Salem State College	M
Sam Houston State University	M*
San Diego State University	M,D*
San Francisco State University	M
San Jose State University	M*
Shippensburg University of Pennsylvania	M†
Simon Fraser University	M,D
South Dakota State University	M*
Southeast Missouri State University	M
Southern Connecticut State University	M†
Southern Illinois University Carbondale	M,D*†
Southern Illinois University Edwardsville	M†
Southern Methodist University	M,D*†
Southern Oregon University	M
Southern University and Agricultural and Mechanical College	M*
Southwest Missouri State University	M*†
Southwest Texas State University	M*
Stanford University	M,D*
State University of New York at Albany	M,D*†
State University of New York at Binghamton	M,D*†
State University of New York at New Paltz	M
State University of New York College at Brockport	M*†
State University of New York College at Potsdam	M
Stephen F. Austin State University	M
Stevens Institute of Technology	M,D*†
Stony Brook University, State University of New York	M,D*†
Syracuse University	M,D*
Tarleton State University	M
Temple University	M,D*†
Tennessee State University	M*
Tennessee Technological University	M*
Texas A&M International University	M
Texas A&M University	M,D*
Texas A&M University–Commerce	M†
Texas A&M University–Corpus Christi	M
Texas A&M University–Kingsville	M*†
Texas Christian University	M*
Texas Southern University	M†
Texas Tech University	M,D*†
Texas Woman's University	M*†
Tufts University	M,D*†
Tulane University	M,D*†
Université de Moncton	M
Université de Montréal	M,D
Université de Sherbrooke	M,D
Université du Québec à Montréal	M,D
Université du Québec à Trois-Rivières	M
Université Laval	M,D†
University at Buffalo, The State University of New York	M,D*†
The University of Akron	M†
The University of Alabama	M,D*
The University of Alabama at Birmingham	M,D*†
The University of Alabama in Huntsville	M,D*
University of Alaska Fairbanks	M,D*
University of Alberta	M,D,O*
The University of Arizona	M,D*
University of Arkansas	M,D*
The University of British Columbia	M,D*
University of Calgary	M,D*
University of California, Berkeley	M,D,O*
University of California, Davis	M,D*†
University of California, Irvine	M,D*
University of California, Los Angeles	M,D*
University of California, Riverside	M,D*
University of California, San Diego	M,D*
University of California, Santa Barbara	M,D*
University of California, Santa Cruz	M,D*
University of Central Arkansas	M
University of Central Florida	M,D*†
University of Central Oklahoma	M
University of Chicago	M,D*
University of Cincinnati	M,D*
University of Colorado at Boulder	M,D*
University of Connecticut	M,D*†
University of Delaware	M,D*†
University of Denver	M,D*†
University of Detroit Mercy	M*
University of Florida	M,D*†
University of Georgia	M,D*†
University of Guelph	M,D
University of Hawaii at Manoa	M,D*
University of Houston	M,D*
University of Houston–Clear Lake	M*†
University of Idaho	M,D*†
University of Illinois at Chicago	M,D*
University of Illinois at Urbana–Champaign	M,D*
The University of Iowa	M,D*
University of Kansas	M,D*
University of Kentucky	M,D*
The University of Lethbridge	M,D
University of Louisiana at Lafayette	M,D*
University of Louisville	M*†
University of Maine	M*
University of Manitoba	M,D*
University of Maryland, College Park	M,D*
University of Massachusetts Amherst	M,D*†
University of Massachusetts Lowell	M,D*†
The University of Memphis	M,D*†
University of Miami	M,D*†
University of Michigan	M,D*
University of Minnesota, Twin Cities Campus	M,D*
University of Mississippi	M,D*
University of Missouri–Columbia	M,D*
University of Missouri–Kansas City	M,D*†
University of Missouri–Rolla	M,D*
University of Missouri–St. Louis	M,D,O†
The University of Montana–Missoula	M,D*†
University of Nebraska at Omaha	M
University of Nebraska–Lincoln	M,D*†
University of Nevada, Las Vegas	M*†
University of Nevada, Reno	M*
University of New Brunswick Fredericton	M,D
University of New Hampshire	M,D*†
University of New Mexico	M,D*†
University of New Orleans	M*
The University of North Carolina at Chapel Hill	M,D*†
The University of North Carolina at Charlotte	M,D*
The University of North Carolina at Greensboro	M†
The University of North Carolina at Wilmington	M*
University of North Dakota	M*
University of Northern British Columbia	M,D
University of Northern Colorado	M,D†
University of Northern Iowa	M
University of North Florida	M
University of North Texas	M,D*†
University of Notre Dame	M,D*†
University of Oklahoma	M,D*†
University of Oregon	M,D*
University of Ottawa	M,D*
University of Pennsylvania	M,D*†
University of Pittsburgh	M,D*†
University of Puerto Rico, Mayagüez Campus	M*
University of Puerto Rico, Río Piedras	M*
University of Regina	M,D
University of Rhode Island	M,D*
University of Rochester	M,D*
University of Saskatchewan	M,D
University of South Alabama	M*†
University of South Carolina	M,D*†
The University of South Dakota	M†
University of Southern California	M,D*†
University of Southern Mississippi	M
University of South Florida	M,D*†
The University of Tennessee	M,D*†
The University of Texas at Arlington	M,D*†
The University of Texas at Austin	M,D*
The University of Texas at Dallas	M,D*
The University of Texas at El Paso	M*†
The University of Texas at San Antonio	M*
The University of Texas at Tyler	M
The University of Texas–Pan American	M
University of the District of Columbia	M*
University of the Incarnate Word	M,D†
University of Toledo	M,D*†
University of Toronto	M,D*
University of Tulsa	M†
University of Utah	M,D*
University of Vermont	M,D*†
University of Victoria	M,D
University of Virginia	M,D*
University of Washington	M,D*
University of Waterloo	M,D
The University of Western Ontario	M,D*
University of West Florida	M
University of Windsor	M,D
University of Wisconsin–Madison	M,D*
University of Wisconsin–Milwaukee	M,D
University of Wyoming	M,D*†
Utah State University	M,D*
Vanderbilt University	M,D*
Villanova University	M*†
Virginia Commonwealth University	M,O*†
Virginia Polytechnic Institute and State University	M,D*
Virginia State University	M
Wake Forest University	M*†
Washington State University	M,D*
Washington University in St. Louis	M,D*†
Wayne State University	M,D*
Wesleyan University	M,D*
West Chester University of Pennsylvania	M*†
Western Carolina University	M†
Western Connecticut State University	M
Western Illinois University	M
Western Kentucky University	M†
Western Michigan University	M,D*†
Western Washington University	M
West Texas A&M University	M†
West Virginia University	M,D*
Wichita State University	M,D*†
Wilkes University	M
Winthrop University	M
Worcester Polytechnic Institute	M,D,O*†
Wright State University	M*
Yale University	M,D*
York University	M,D*
Youngstown State University	M

MATHEMATICS EDUCATION

Institution	Degrees
Acadia University	M
Alabama State University	M,O
Albany State University	M
Alfred University	M*†
American University	D*†
Appalachian State University	M
Arcadia University	M,D,O†
Arkansas State University	M
Arkansas Tech University	M
Armstrong Atlantic State University	M†
Auburn University	M,D,O*†
Ball State University	M*
Bank Street College of Education	M*
Belmont University	M
Bemidji State University	M
Boise State University	M*
Boston College	M*†
Boston University	M,D,O*†
Bowling Green State University	M,D,O*†
Bridgewater State College	M
Brooklyn College of the City University of New York	M,D†
California State University, Bakersfield	M
California State University, Dominguez Hills	M†
California State University, Fresno	M
California State University, Fullerton	M
California University of Pennsylvania	M
Campbell University	M
Chatham College	M
Christopher Newport University	M†
The Citadel, The Military College of South Carolina	M
Clarion University of Pennsylvania	M†
Clemson University	M*
Coastal Carolina University	M
College of Charleston	M*†
The College of William and Mary	M*†
The Colorado College	M
Columbus State University	M,O
Concordia University (Canada)	M,D*†
Connecticut College	M
Cornell University	M,D*
Delta State University	M
DePaul University	M*†
DeSales University	M
East Carolina University	M*†
Eastern Illinois University	M†
Eastern Kentucky University	M
Eastern Washington University	M†
Edinboro University of Pennsylvania	M
Fitchburg State College	M†
Florida Gulf Coast University	M
Florida Institute of Technology	M,D,O*†
Florida International University	M*†
Florida State University	M,D,O*†
Fort Hays State University	M
Framingham State College	M*
Fresno Pacific University	M
Georgia College & State University	M,O
Georgia Southern University	M,O
Georgia State University	M,D,O*
Harvard University	M,D,O*†
Henderson State University	M
Hofstra University	M*
Hood College	M
Hunter College of the City University of New York	M†
Illinois State University	D*†
Indiana University Bloomington	M,D*
Indiana University of Pennsylvania	M*†
Indiana University–Purdue University Indianapolis	M*
Instituto Tecnológico y de Estudios Superiores de Monterrey, Campus Ciudad Obregón	M
Iona College	M*†
Iowa State University of Science and Technology	M,D*†
Jackson State University	M
Jacksonville University	M
Johns Hopkins University	M,D,O*†
Kean University	M,O*†
Kutztown University of Pennsylvania	M,O†
Lehman College of the City University of New York	M
Long Island University, Brooklyn Campus	M*
Long Island University, C.W. Post Campus	M*†
Louisiana Tech University	M,D,O*
Loyola Marymount University	M†
Manhattanville College	M*†

Institution	Degrees
Marquette University	M,D*†
McNeese State University	M
Mercer University	M,O
Miami University	M*†
Michigan State University	M,D*†
Middle Tennessee State University	M*
Millersville University of Pennsylvania	M†
Mills College	M,D*†
Minnesota State University, Mankato	M
Minot State University	M
Mississippi College	M
Montclair State University	M,D†
Morgan State University	D*
National-Louis University	M,O
New Jersey City University	M
New York University	M,D*†
North Carolina Agricultural and Technical State University	M*
North Carolina State University	M,D*
Northeastern Illinois University	M
Northeastern University	M*†
Northern Arizona University	M
Northern Michigan University	M
North Georgia College & State University	M,O
Northwestern State University of Louisiana	M,O
Northwest Missouri State University	M
Nova Southeastern University	M,O*
Occidental College	M
Ohio University	M,D*
Oregon State University	M,D*
Plattsburgh State University of New York	M
Plymouth State College	M*
Portland State University	M,D*
Providence College	M*
Purdue University	M,D,O*
Queens College of the City University of New York	M,O†
Quinnipiac University	M*†
Rider University	O*
Rollins College	M*
Rowan University	M†
Rutgers, The State University of New Jersey, New Brunswick	M,D*
Sage Graduate School	M†
St. John Fisher College	M
Saint Joseph's University	M*†
Salem State College	M,O
Salisbury University	M
San Diego State University	M,D*
San Francisco State University	M
Slippery Rock University of Pennsylvania	M†
Smith College	M*
South Carolina State University	M
Southern University and Agricultural and Mechanical College	D*
Southwestern Oklahoma State University	M
Southwest Texas State University	M*
Stanford University	M,D*
State University of New York at Albany	M,D*†
State University of New York at Binghamton	M*†
State University of New York College at Brockport	M*†
State University of New York College at Buffalo	M
State University of New York College at Cortland	M
State University of New York College at Fredonia	M
State University of West Georgia	M,O
Stephen F. Austin State University	M
Syracuse University	M,D,O*
Teachers College Columbia University	M,D*
Temple University	M,D*†
Texas A&M University	M,D*
Texas Woman's University	M*†
Towson University	M†
Union College (NY)	M*
University at Buffalo, The State University of New York	M,D,O*†
University of Alaska Fairbanks	M,D*
University of Arkansas	M*
University of Arkansas at Pine Bluff	M
The University of British Columbia	M,D*
University of California, Berkeley	M,D*
University of California, San Diego	D*
University of Central Florida	M,D*†
University of Central Oklahoma	M
University of Cincinnati	M,D*
University of Connecticut	M,D*†
University of Detroit Mercy	M*
University of Florida	M,D,O*†
University of Georgia	M,D,O*†
University of Houston	M,D*
University of Idaho	M,D*†
University of Illinois at Chicago	M*
University of Illinois at Urbana–Champaign	M,D*
University of Indianapolis	M
University of Manitoba	M*
University of Massachusetts Lowell	D*†
University of Miami	M,O*†
University of Michigan	M,D*
University of Minnesota, Twin Cities Campus	M,D*
University of Missouri–Columbia	M,D*
University of Missouri–Rolla	M,D*
The University of Montana–Missoula	M,D*†
University of Nevada, Las Vegas	M,D,O*†
University of Nevada, Reno	M*
University of New Hampshire	M,D*†
The University of North Carolina at Chapel Hill	M*†
The University of North Carolina at Charlotte	M,D*
The University of North Carolina at Greensboro	M†
The University of North Carolina at Pembroke	M
University of Northern Colorado	M,D†
University of Northern Iowa	M
University of North Florida	M
University of Oklahoma	M,D,O*†
University of Pittsburgh	M,D*†
University of Puerto Rico, Río Piedras	M,D*
University of Rio Grande	M
University of South Carolina	M,D*†
University of South Florida	M,D,O*†
The University of Tennessee	M,D,O*†
The University of Texas at Austin	M,D*
The University of Texas at Dallas	M*
The University of Texas at San Antonio	M*
The University of Texas at Tyler	M
University of the Incarnate Word	M,D†
University of Toledo	M,D*†
University of Tulsa	M†
University of Vermont	M,D*†
University of Victoria	M
University of Washington	M,D*
The University of West Alabama	M
University of West Florida	M
University of Wisconsin–Eau Claire	M†
University of Wisconsin–Madison	M*
University of Wisconsin–Oshkosh	M*
University of Wisconsin–River Falls	M
University of Wyoming	M,D*†
Vanderbilt University	M,D*
Virginia State University	M
Washington State University	M,D*
Washington University in St. Louis	M,D*†
Wayne State College	M
Wayne State University	M,D,O*
Webster University	M,O
Wesleyan College	M
Western Carolina University	M†
Western Connecticut State University	M
Western Illinois University	M,O
Western Michigan University	M,D*†
Western Oregon University	M
West Virginia University	M,D*
Wheeling Jesuit University	M
Widener University	M,D*†
Wilkes University	M
Wright State University	M*

MECHANICAL ENGINEERING

Institution	Degrees
Alfred University	M*†
Arizona State University	M,D*
Auburn University	M,D*†
Boise State University	M*
Boston University	M,D*†
Bradley University	M†
Brigham Young University	M,D*
Brown University	M,D*
Bucknell University	M
California Institute of Technology	M,D,O*
California State University, Chico	M
California State University, Fresno	M
California State University, Fullerton	M
California State University, Long Beach	M
California State University, Los Angeles	M
California State University, Northridge	M
California State University, Sacramento	M
Carleton University	M,D
Carnegie Mellon University	M,D*
Case Western Reserve University	M,D*†
The Catholic University of America	M,D*†
City College of the City University of New York	M,D*†
Clarkson University	M,D*
Clemson University	M,D*
Cleveland State University	M,D*†
Colorado State University	M,D*
Columbia University	M,D*†
Concordia University (Canada)	M,D,O*†
Cornell University	M,D*
Dalhousie University	M,D*
Dartmouth College	M,D*†
Drexel University	M,D*†
Duke University	M,D*†
École Polytechnique de Montréal	M,D,O
Florida Agricultural and Mechanical University	M,D*
Florida Atlantic University	M,D*
Florida Institute of Technology	M,D*†
Florida International University	M,D*†
Florida State University	M,D*†
Gannon University	M
The George Washington University	M,D,O*†
Georgia Institute of Technology	M,D*
Graduate School and University Center of the City University of New York	D*†
Grand Valley State University	M†
Howard University	M,D*
Illinois Institute of Technology	M,D*†
Indiana University–Purdue University Indianapolis	M*
Institute of Paper Science and Technology	M,D*
Instituto Tecnológico y de Estudios Superiores de Monterrey, Campus Chihuahua	M,O
Instituto Tecnológico y de Estudios Superiores de Monterrey, Campus Monterrey	M,D
Iowa State University of Science and Technology	M,D*†
Johns Hopkins University	M,D*†
Kansas State University	M,D*†
Kettering University	M
Lamar University	M,D*†
Lehigh University	M,D*
Louisiana State University and Agricultural and Mechanical College	M,D*
Louisiana Tech University	M,D*
Loyola Marymount University	M†
Manhattan College	M*†
Marquette University	M,D*†
Massachusetts Institute of Technology	M,D,O*
McGill University	M,D*
McMaster University	M,D
McNeese State University	M
Memorial University of Newfoundland	M,D†
Mercer University	M
Michigan State University	M,D*†
Michigan Technological University	M,D*†
Minnesota State University, Mankato	M
Mississippi State University	M,D*
Montana State University–Bozeman	M,D*
National Technological University	M
Naval Postgraduate School	M,D,O
New Jersey Institute of Technology	M,D,O
New Mexico State University	M,D
North Carolina Agricultural and Technical State University	M,D*
North Carolina State University	M,D*
North Dakota State University	M†
Northeastern University	M,D*†
Northern Illinois University	M*†
Northwestern University	M,D*
Oakland University	M†
The Ohio State University	M,D*
Ohio University	M,D*
Oklahoma State University	M,D*†
Old Dominion University	M,D*†
Oregon State University	M,D*
The Pennsylvania State University University Park Campus	M,D*†
Polytechnic University, Brooklyn Campus	M,D*
Polytechnic University, Long Island Graduate Center	M,D
Portland State University	M,D*
Princeton University	M,D*
Purdue University	M,D*
Queen's University at Kingston	M,D
Rensselaer at Hartford	M
Rensselaer Polytechnic Institute	M,D*†
Rice University	M,D*
Rochester Institute of Technology	M*†
Rose-Hulman Institute of Technology	M*
Royal Military College of Canada	M,D
Rutgers, The State University of New Jersey, New Brunswick	M,D*
St. Cloud State University	M
Saint Louis University	M*†
San Diego State University	M,D*
San Jose State University	M*
Santa Clara University	M,D,O*
South Dakota School of Mines and Technology	M,D*†
South Dakota State University	M*
Southern Illinois University Carbondale	M*†
Southern Illinois University Edwardsville	M†
Southern Methodist University	M,D*†
Stanford University	M,D,O*
State University of New York at Binghamton	M,D*†
Stevens Institute of Technology	M,D,O*†
Stony Brook University, State University of New York	M,D,O*†
Syracuse University	M*
Temple University	M*†
Tennessee Technological University	M,D*
Texas A&M University	M,D*
Texas A&M University–Kingsville	M*†
Texas Tech University	M,D*†
Tufts University	M,D*†
Tulane University	M,D*†
Tuskegee University	M
Union College (NY)	M*
Université de Moncton	M
Université de Sherbrooke	M,D
Université Laval	M,D†
University at Buffalo, The State University of New York	M,D*†
The University of Akron	M,D†
The University of Alabama	M,D*
The University of Alabama at Birmingham	M,D*†
The University of Alabama in Huntsville	M,D*
University of Alaska Fairbanks	M*
University of Alberta	M,D*
The University of Arizona	M,D*
University of Arkansas	M,D*
University of Bridgeport	M*†
The University of British Columbia	M,D*
University of Calgary	M,D*
University of California, Berkeley	M,D*
University of California, Davis	M,D,O*†
University of California, Irvine	M,D*
University of California, Los Angeles	M,D*
University of California, San Diego	M,D*
University of California, Santa Barbara	M,D*
University of Central Florida	M,D,O*†
University of Cincinnati	M,D*
University of Colorado at Boulder	M,D*
University of Colorado at Colorado Springs	M*
University of Colorado at Denver	M*
University of Connecticut	M,D*†
University of Dayton	M,D*†
University of Delaware	M,D*†
University of Denver	M,D*†
University of Detroit Mercy	M,D*
University of Florida	M,D,O*†
University of Hawaii at Manoa	M,D*
University of Houston	M,D*
University of Idaho	M,D*†
University of Illinois at Chicago	M,D*
University of Illinois at Urbana–Champaign	M,D*
The University of Iowa	M,D*
University of Kansas	M,D*
University of Kentucky	M,D*
University of Louisiana at Lafayette	M*
University of Louisville	M*†

*P—first professional degree; M—master's degree; D—doctorate; O—other advanced degree; *full description and/or announcement in Book 2, 3, 4, 5, or 6; †full description in this book*

University of Maine M,D*
University of Manitoba M,D*
University of Maryland, Baltimore County M,D*†
University of Maryland, College Park M,D*
University of Massachusetts Amherst M,D*†
University of Massachusetts Dartmouth M*†
University of Massachusetts Lowell M,D*†
The University of Memphis M,D*†
University of Miami M,D*†
University of Michigan M,D*
University of Michigan–Dearborn M*†
University of Minnesota, Twin Cities Campus M,D*
University of Missouri–Columbia M,D*
University of Missouri–Rolla M,D*
University of Nebraska–Lincoln M,D*†
University of Nevada, Las Vegas M,D*†
University of Nevada, Reno M,D*
University of New Brunswick Fredericton M,D
University of New Hampshire M,D*†
University of New Haven M*†
University of New Mexico M,D*†
University of New Orleans M*
The University of North Carolina at Charlotte M,D*
University of North Dakota M*
University of Notre Dame M,D*†
University of Oklahoma M,D*†
University of Ottawa M,D*
University of Pennsylvania M,D*†
University of Pittsburgh M,D*†
University of Puerto Rico, Mayagüez Campus M*
University of Rhode Island M,D*
University of Rochester M,D*
University of Saskatchewan M,D,O
University of South Alabama M*†
University of South Carolina M,D*†
University of Southern California M,D,O*†
University of South Florida M,D*†
The University of Tennessee M,D*†
The University of Tennessee Space Institute M,D*
The University of Texas at Arlington M,D*†
The University of Texas at Austin M,D*
The University of Texas at El Paso M*†
The University of Texas at San Antonio M*
University of Toledo M,D*†
University of Toronto M,D*
University of Tulsa M,D†
University of Utah M,D*
University of Vermont M,D*†
University of Victoria M,D
University of Virginia M,D*
University of Washington M,D*
University of Waterloo M,D
University of Windsor M,D
University of Wisconsin–Madison M,D*
University of Wyoming M,D*†
Utah State University M,D*
Vanderbilt University M,D*
Villanova University M,O*†
Virginia Polytechnic Institute and State University M,D*
Washington State University M,D*
Washington University in St. Louis M,D*†
Wayne State University M,D*
Western Michigan University M,D*†
Western New England College M
West Virginia University M,D*
Wichita State University M,D*†
Widener University M*†
Worcester Polytechnic Institute M,D,O*†
Wright State University M*
Yale University M,D*
Youngstown State University M

MECHANICS

Brown University M,D*
California Institute of Technology M,D*
California State University, Fullerton M
California State University, Northridge M
Case Western Reserve University M,D*†
The Catholic University of America M,D*†
Colorado State University M,D*
Columbia University M,D,O*†
Cornell University M,D*
Drexel University M,D*†
École Polytechnique de Montréal M,D,O
Georgia Institute of Technology M,D*
Idaho State University M,D*
Iowa State University of Science and Technology M,D*†
Johns Hopkins University M,D*†
Lehigh University M,D*
Louisiana State University and Agricultural and Mechanical College M,D*
McGill University M,D*
Michigan State University M,D*†
Michigan Technological University M*†
Mississippi State University M*
New Mexico Institute of Mining and Technology M†
North Dakota State University M†
Northwestern University M,D*
The Ohio State University M,D*
Old Dominion University M,D*†
The Pennsylvania State University University Park Campus M,D*†
Rensselaer Polytechnic Institute M,D*†
Rutgers, The State University of New Jersey, New Brunswick M,D*
San Diego State University M,D*
Southern Illinois University Carbondale M,D*†
The University of Alabama M,D*
The University of Arizona M,D*
University of California, Berkeley M,D*
University of California, San Diego M,D*
University of Connecticut D*†
University of Dayton M*†
University of Florida M,D,O*†
University of Illinois at Urbana–Champaign M,D*
University of Maryland, College Park M,D*
University of Massachusetts Lowell M,D*†
University of Minnesota, Twin Cities Campus M,D*
University of Missouri–Rolla M,D*
University of Nebraska–Lincoln M,D*†
University of New Brunswick Fredericton M,D
University of Pennsylvania M,D*†
University of Rhode Island M,D*
University of Southern California M*†
The University of Tennessee M,D*†
The University of Tennessee Space Institute M,D*
The University of Texas at Austin M,D*
University of Virginia M*
University of Wisconsin–Madison M,D*
Virginia Polytechnic Institute and State University M,D*
Yale University M,D*

MEDIA STUDIES

American University M*†
Arkansas State University M
Audrey Cohen College M†
Austin Peay State University M
Boston University M*†
California State University, Fullerton M
Carnegie Mellon University M*
Central Michigan University M†
City College of the City University of New York M*†
Columbia College Chicago M†
Concordia University (Canada) M,D,O*†
Dallas Theological Seminary M,D,O
Emerson College M*†
Governors State University M
Hunter College of the City University of New York M†
Indiana State University M*†
Kutztown University of Pennsylvania M†
Marquette University M*†
Massachusetts Institute of Technology M,D*
Michigan State University M,D*†
Monmouth University M,O*†
New College of California M*†
New School University M*†
New York University M,D*†
Norfolk State University M†
Northwestern University M,D*
Ohio University M,D*
The Pennsylvania State University University Park Campus M*†
Queens College of the City University of New York M†
Regent University M†
Rochester Institute of Technology M*†
Saginaw Valley State University M
San Diego State University M*
San Francisco State University M
Savannah College of Art and Design M*
Suffolk University M*
Syracuse University M*
Temple University M,D*†
Texas Christian University M*
Texas Southern University M†
University at Buffalo, The State University of New York M*†
The University of Alabama M*
The University of Arizona M*
University of Chicago M,D*
University of Colorado at Boulder D*
University of Denver M*†
University of Florida M,D*†
University of Oklahoma M*†
University of South Carolina M*†
University of Southern California M*†
The University of Tennessee M,D*†
The University of Texas at Austin M,D*
Wayne State University M,D*
Webster University M
William Paterson University of New Jersey M*†

MEDICAL/SURGICAL NURSING

Angelo State University M†
Case Western Reserve University M*†
The Catholic University of America M,D*†
College of Mount Saint Vincent M,O*†
College of Staten Island of the City University of New York M†
Columbia University M,O*†
Daemen College M,O
Duke University M,O*†
Emory University M*†
Florida Atlantic University, Ft. Lauderdale Campus M
Gannon University M,O
George Mason University M,D*†
Georgia State University M,D*
Gwynedd-Mercy College M
Hunter College of the City University of New York M†
Indiana University–Purdue University Indianapolis M*
Jewish Hospital College of Nursing and Allied Health M
Johns Hopkins University M,O*†
Kent State University M*
La Roche College M
La Salle University M,O
Lehman College of the City University of New York M
Louisiana State University Health Sciences Center M,D*
Loyola University Chicago M*†
Madonna University M
Marquette University M,O*†
Marymount University M,O†
Medical College of Georgia M,D*
Medical University of South Carolina M,O*
Molloy College M,O
Mount Saint Mary College M
New York University M,O*†
Oakland University M†
Oregon Health & Science University M,O*
Otterbein College M,O
Pontifical Catholic University of Puerto Rico M
Rush University M,D*
Rutgers, The State University of New Jersey, Newark M,D*†
Sage Graduate School M†
Saint Xavier University M,O*
Seton Hall University M*†
Southern Adventist University M
Southern Illinois University Edwardsville M†
Stony Brook University, State University of New York M,O*†
Texas Woman's University M,D*†
University at Buffalo, The State University of New York M,D,O*†
University of Central Florida M*†
University of Cincinnati M,D*
University of Colorado at Colorado Springs M*
University of Delaware M,O*†
University of Hawaii at Manoa M,D,O*
University of Illinois at Chicago M*
University of Maryland M,D*†
University of Massachusetts Worcester M,D,O*
University of Medicine and Dentistry of New Jersey M*
University of Miami M,D*†
University of Michigan M*
University of Minnesota, Twin Cities Campus M*
University of Missouri–Kansas City M,D*†
The University of North Carolina at Charlotte M*
University of Pennsylvania M*†
University of San Diego M,D,O*†
University of San Francisco M*†
The University of Scranton M†
University of South Alabama M*†
University of South Carolina M*†
University of Southern Maine M,O
University of Southern Mississippi M,D
The University of Tampa M
The University of Tennessee at Chattanooga M
The University of Texas at El Paso M*†
The University of Texas–Pan American M
Vanderbilt University M,D*
Villanova University M,O*†
Virginia Commonwealth University M,D,O*†
Wayne State University M*
Western Connecticut State University M
Wichita State University M*†
Wright State University M*

MEDICAL ILLUSTRATION

Johns Hopkins University M*†
Medical College of Georgia M*
Rochester Institute of Technology M*†
University of Illinois at Chicago M*
University of Michigan M*
The University of Texas Southwestern Medical Center at Dallas M*

MEDICAL INFORMATICS

Columbia University M,D*†
Emory University M*†
Harvard University P,M,D*†
Kirksville College of Osteopathic Medicine M,D
Massachusetts Institute of Technology M*
Medical College of Wisconsin M*
Milwaukee School of Engineering M*
Oregon Health & Science University M,O*
Stanford University M,D*
University of California, Davis M*†
University of California, San Francisco M,D*
University of Medicine and Dentistry of New Jersey M,D*
University of Utah M,D*
University of Washington M*

MEDICAL MICROBIOLOGY

Creighton University M,D*
Finch University of Health Sciences/The Chicago Medical School M,D*
The Ohio State University M,D*
Rutgers, The State University of New Jersey, New Brunswick M,D*
Texas A&M University System Health Science Center D*
Texas Tech University Health Sciences Center M,D*
University of Alberta M,D*
University of Georgia M,D*†
University of Hawaii at Manoa M,D*
University of Manitoba M,D*
University of Minnesota, Duluth M,D*
University of South Florida D*†
University of Washington M,D*
University of Wisconsin–Madison D*

MEDICAL PHYSICS

Cleveland State University M*†
Columbia University M,D,O*†
Drexel University M,D*†
East Carolina University M,D*†
Finch University of Health Sciences/The Chicago Medical School M,D*
Harvard University M,D*†
Massachusetts Institute of Technology D*
McGill University M,D*
Oakland University M,D†
Purdue University M,D*
Rush University M,D*
Stony Brook University, State University of New York D*†
University of Alberta M,D*
University of California, Los Angeles M,D*
University of Central Arkansas M
University of Chicago D*
University of Colorado at Boulder M,D*

Institution	Degrees
University of Colorado Health Sciences Center	M,D*
University of Florida	M,D,O*†
University of Kentucky	M*
University of Massachusetts Worcester	D*
University of Minnesota, Twin Cities Campus	M,D*
University of Missouri–Columbia	M,D*
University of Oklahoma Health Sciences Center	M,D*
The University of Texas Health Science Center at Houston	M,D*
The University of Texas Health Science Center at San Antonio	M,D*
University of Victoria	M,D
University of Wisconsin–Madison	M,D*
Vanderbilt University	M*
Wayne State University	M,D*
Wright State University	M*

MEDICINAL AND PHARMACEUTICAL CHEMISTRY

Institution	Degrees
Duquesne University	M,D*†
Florida Agricultural and Mechanical University	M,D*
Idaho State University	M,D*
Long Island University, Brooklyn Campus	M*
Long Island University, C.W. Post Campus	M*†
The Ohio State University	M,D*
Purdue University	M,D*
Rutgers, The State University of New Jersey, New Brunswick	M,D*
St. John's University (NY)	M,D*†
Temple University	M,D*†
University at Buffalo, The State University of New York	M,D*†
University of California, San Francisco	D*
University of Connecticut	M,D*†
University of Florida	M,D*†
University of Georgia	M,D*†
University of Kansas	M,D*
University of Minnesota, Twin Cities Campus	M,D*
University of Mississippi	M,D*
University of Puerto Rico, Medical Sciences Campus	P,M*
University of Rhode Island	M,D*
University of the Pacific	M,D*
University of the Sciences in Philadelphia	M,D*
University of Toledo	M,D*†
University of Utah	M,D*
University of Washington	D*
West Virginia University	M,D*

MEDIEVAL AND RENAISSANCE STUDIES

Institution	Degrees
Arizona State University	O*
The Catholic University of America	M,D,O*†
Columbia University	M*†
Cornell University	D*
Duke University	O*†
Fordham University	M,D*†
Graduate School and University Center of the City University of New York	M,D*†
Harvard University	M,D*†
Indiana University Bloomington	M,D*
Marquette University	M,D*†
Rutgers, The State University of New Jersey, New Brunswick	D*
Southern Methodist University	M*†
University of Connecticut	M,D*†
University of Minnesota, Twin Cities Campus	M,D*
University of Notre Dame	M,D*†
University of Toronto	M,D*
Western Michigan University	M*†
Yale University	M,D*

METALLURGICAL ENGINEERING AND METALLURGY

Institution	Degrees
Colorado School of Mines	M,D†
Dalhousie University	M,D*
École Polytechnique de Montréal	M,D,O
Georgia Institute of Technology	M,D*
Illinois Institute of Technology	M,D*†
Laurentian University	M
Massachusetts Institute of Technology	M,D,O*
McGill University	M,D*
Michigan State University	M,D*†
Michigan Technological University	M,D*†
Montana Tech of The University of Montana	M
The Ohio State University	M,D*
The Pennsylvania State University University Park Campus	M,D*†
Purdue University	M,D*
Rensselaer Polytechnic Institute	M,D*†
Rutgers, The State University of New Jersey, New Brunswick	M,D*
South Dakota School of Mines and Technology	M,D*†
Université Laval	M,D†
The University of Alabama	M,D*
The University of Alabama at Birmingham	M,D*†
The University of British Columbia	M,D*
University of California, Berkeley	M,D*
University of California, Los Angeles	M,D*
University of Cincinnati	M,D*
University of Connecticut	M,D*†
University of Florida	M,D,O*†
University of Idaho	M,D*†
University of Missouri–Rolla	M,D*
University of Nevada, Reno	M,D,O*
University of Pittsburgh	M,D*†
The University of Tennessee Space Institute	M,D*
The University of Texas at El Paso	M*†
University of Toronto	M,D*
University of Utah	M,D*
University of Wisconsin–Madison	M,D*

METEOROLOGY

Institution	Degrees
Air Force Institute of Technology	M,D*
Florida Institute of Technology	M,D*†
Florida State University	M,D*†
Iowa State University of Science and Technology	M,D*†
McGill University	M,D*
Naval Postgraduate School	M,D
North Carolina State University	M,D*
The Pennsylvania State University University Park Campus	M,D*†
Saint Louis University	M,D*†
San Jose State University	M*
Texas A&M University	M,D*
Université du Québec à Montréal	M,D,O
University of Hawaii at Manoa	M,D*
University of Maryland, College Park	M,D*
University of Miami	M,D*†
University of Oklahoma	M,D*†
University of Utah	M,D*
Utah State University	M,D*
Yale University	D*

MICROBIOLOGY

Institution	Degrees
Albany Medical College	M,D*
Arizona State University	M,D*
Auburn University	M,D*†
Baylor College of Medicine	D*
Boston University	M,D*†
Brandeis University	M,D*†
Brigham Young University	M,D*
Brown University	M,D*
California State University, Fullerton	M
California State University, Long Beach	M
California State University, Los Angeles	M
Case Western Reserve University	D*†
The Catholic University of America	M,D*†
Clemson University	M,D*
Colorado State University	M,D*
Columbia University	M,D*†
Cornell University	D*
Dalhousie University	M,D*
Dartmouth College	*†
Drexel University	M,D*†
Duke University	D*†
East Carolina University	D*†
East Tennessee State University	M,D†
Emory University	D*†
Emporia State University	M*†
Finch University of Health Sciences/The Chicago Medical School	M,D*
Florida State University	M,D*†
Georgetown University	D*
The George Washington University	D*†
Georgia State University	M,D*
Harvard University	D*†
Howard University	D*
Idaho State University	M,D*
Illinois Institute of Technology	M,D*†
Illinois State University	M,D*†
Indiana State University	M,D*†
Indiana University Bloomington	M,D*
Indiana University–Purdue University Indianapolis	M,D*
Iowa State University of Science and Technology	M,D*†
Johns Hopkins University	M,D*†
Kansas State University	M,D*†
Loma Linda University	M,D*
Long Island University, C.W. Post Campus	M*†
Louisiana State University and Agricultural and Mechanical College	M,D*
Louisiana State University Health Sciences Center	M,D*
Loyola University Chicago	M,D*†
Marquette University	M,D*†
Massachusetts Institute of Technology	D*
McGill University	M,D*
Medical College of Ohio	M*
Medical College of Wisconsin	M,D*
Medical University of South Carolina	M,D*
Meharry Medical College	D
Miami University	M,D*†
Michigan State University	D*†
Montana State University–Bozeman	M,D*
Mount Sinai School of Medicine of New York University	D*
New York Medical College	M,D*
New York University	M,D*†
North Carolina State University	M,D*
North Dakota State University	M,D†
Northwestern University	D*
The Ohio State University	M,D*
Ohio University	M,D*
Oklahoma State University	M,D*†
Oregon Health & Science University	D*
Oregon State University	M,D*
The Pennsylvania State University Milton S. Hershey Medical Center	M,D*
The Pennsylvania State University University Park Campus	M,D*†
Purdue University	M,D*
Queen's University at Kingston	M,D
Quinnipiac University	M*†
Rensselaer Polytechnic Institute	M,D*†
Rush University	D*
Rutgers, The State University of New Jersey, New Brunswick	M,D*
Saint Louis University	D*†
San Diego State University	M*
San Francisco State University	M
Seton Hall University	M*†
South Dakota State University	M*
Southern Illinois University Carbondale	M,D*†
Stanford University	D*
State University of New York Upstate Medical University	M,D*
Stony Brook University, State University of New York	D*†
Temple University	M,D*†
Texas A&M University	M,D*
Texas A&M University System Health Science Center	D*
Texas Tech University	M,D*†
Thomas Jefferson University	M,D*
Tufts University	D*†
Tulane University	M,D*†
Uniformed Services University of the Health Sciences	D*
Université de Montréal	M,D,O
Université de Sherbrooke	M,D
Université du Québec, Institut National de la Recherche Scientifique	M,D
Université Laval	M,D†
University at Buffalo, The State University of New York	M,D*†
The University of Alabama at Birmingham	D*†
University of Alberta	M,D*
The University of Arizona	M,D*
University of Arkansas for Medical Sciences	M,D*
The University of British Columbia	M,D*
University of Calgary	M,D*
University of California, Berkeley	D*
University of California, Davis	M,D*†
University of California, Irvine	M,D*
University of California, Los Angeles	M,D*
University of California, Riverside	M,D*
University of California, San Francisco	D*
University of Central Florida	M*†
University of Chicago	D*
University of Cincinnati	M,D*
University of Colorado at Boulder	M,D*
University of Colorado Health Sciences Center	D*
University of Connecticut	M,D*†
University of Delaware	M,D*†
University of Florida	M,D*†
University of Georgia	M,D*†
University of Guelph	M,D
University of Hawaii at Manoa	M,D*
University of Idaho	M,D*†
University of Illinois at Chicago	D*
University of Illinois at Urbana–Champaign	M,D*
The University of Iowa	M,D*
University of Kansas	M,D*
University of Kentucky	D*
University of Louisville	M,D*†
University of Maine	M,D*
University of Manitoba	M,D*
University of Maryland	M,D*†
University of Maryland, College Park	M,D*
University of Massachusetts Amherst	M,D*†
University of Massachusetts Worcester	D*
University of Medicine and Dentistry of New Jersey	M,D*
The University of Memphis	M,D*†
University of Miami	D*†
University of Michigan	D*
University of Minnesota, Twin Cities Campus	M,D*
University of Mississippi Medical Center	M,D*
University of Missouri–Columbia	M,D*
The University of Montana–Missoula	M,D*†
University of Nebraska Medical Center	M,D*
University of New Hampshire	M,D*†
University of New Mexico	M,D*†
The University of North Carolina at Chapel Hill	M,D*†
University of North Dakota	M,D*
University of North Texas Health Science Center at Fort Worth	M,D*
University of Oklahoma	M,D*†
University of Oklahoma Health Sciences Center	M,D*
University of Ottawa	M,D*
University of Pennsylvania	D*†
University of Pittsburgh	M,D*†
University of Puerto Rico, Medical Sciences Campus	M,D*
University of Rhode Island	M,D*
University of Rochester	M,D*
University of Saskatchewan	M,D
University of South Alabama	D*†
The University of South Dakota	M,D†
University of Southern California	M,D*†
University of Southern Mississippi	M,D
University of South Florida	M*†
The University of Tennessee	M,D*†
The University of Tennessee Health Science Center	D*
The University of Texas at Austin	M,D*
The University of Texas Health Science Center at Houston	M,D*
The University of Texas Health Science Center at San Antonio	M,D*
The University of Texas Medical Branch	M,D*
The University of Texas Southwestern Medical Center at Dallas	D*
University of Utah	*
University of Vermont	M,D*†
University of Victoria	M,D
University of Virginia	M,D*
University of Washington	D*
The University of Western Ontario	M,D*
University of Wisconsin–La Crosse	M†
University of Wisconsin–Madison	D*
University of Wisconsin–Oshkosh	M*
Utah State University	M,D*
Vanderbilt University	M,D*
Virginia Commonwealth University	M,D,O*†
Virginia Polytechnic Institute and State University	M,D*
Wagner College	M
Wake Forest University	D*†
Washington State University	M,D*
Washington University in St. Louis	D*†
Wayne State University	M,D*

*P—first professional degree; M—master's degree; D—doctorate; O—other advanced degree; *full description and/or announcement in Book 2, 3, 4, 5, or 6; †full description in this book*

West Virginia University M,D*
Wright State University M*
Yale University D*
Yeshiva University D*

MIDDLE SCHOOL EDUCATION

Alaska Pacific University M
Albany State University M
Armstrong Atlantic State University M†
Augusta State University M,O
Averett University M
Ball State University M*
Bank Street College of Education M*
Bellarmine University M
Belmont University M
Berry College M
Brenau University M,O
Campbell University M
Central Michigan University M†
College of Mount Saint Vincent M,O*†
Columbus State University M,O
Cumberland College M
Drury University M
East Carolina University M*†
Eastern Illinois University M†
Eastern Michigan University M*
Eastern Nazarene College M,O
Edinboro University of Pennsylvania M
Emory University M,D,O*†
Fayetteville State University M
Fitchburg State College M†
Fort Valley State University M
Gardner-Webb University M
George Mason University M*†
Georgia College & State University M,O
Georgia Southern University M,O
Georgia Southwestern State University M,O
Georgia State University M,D,O*
Grand Valley State University M†
Hebrew College M,O†
James Madison University M
Kennesaw State University M
Kent State University M*
LaGrange College M
Lesley University M,D,O*†
Lynchburg College M
Mary Baldwin College M
Maryville University of Saint Louis M
Mercer University M,O
Middle Tennessee State University M,O*
Morehead State University M
Morgan State University M*
Mount Saint Vincent University M
Murray State University M,O†
Newman University M
North Carolina Agricultural and Technical State University M*
North Carolina State University M*
Northern Kentucky University M
North Georgia College & State University M,O
Northwest Missouri State University M
Ohio University M,D*
Old Dominion University M*†
Pacific University M
Quinnipiac University M*†
Rosemont College M†
Saginaw Valley State University M
St. John Fisher College M
St. Thomas Aquinas College M,O
Salem State College M
Shenandoah University M,D,O
Siena Heights University M
Southeast Missouri State University M
Southwest Missouri State University M*†
Spalding University M†
State University of New York College at Oneonta M
State University of West Georgia M,O
Tufts University M,O*†
Union College (KY) M
University of Arkansas M,D,O*
University of Arkansas at Little Rock M,O
University of Dayton M*†
University of Florida M,D,O*†
University of Georgia M,D,O*†
University of Louisville M*†
University of Missouri–Columbia M,D,O*
University of Nebraska at Kearney M
University of Nevada, Las Vegas M,D,O*†
The University of North Carolina at Charlotte M*
The University of North Carolina at Pembroke M
The University of North Carolina at Wilmington M*
University of Northern Iowa M
University of Puget Sound M
University of South Florida M*†
University of West Florida M
University of Wisconsin–Milwaukee M
University of Wisconsin–Platteville M
Valdosta State University M,O
Virginia Commonwealth University M,O*†
Wesleyan College M
Western Carolina University M†
Western Kentucky University M†
Western Michigan University M*†
Westfield State College M
Widener University M,D*†
Winthrop University M
Worcester State College M,O
Youngstown State University M

MILITARY AND DEFENSE STUDIES

American Military University M
California State University, San Bernardino M
Florida State University M,D,O*†
Georgetown University M*
The George Washington University M*†
Hawai'i Pacific University M*†
Johns Hopkins University M,D,O*†
Joint Military Intelligence College M,O
The Judge Advocate General's School, U.S. Army M
Mercyhurst College M
National Defense University M
Naval Postgraduate School M,D
Naval War College M
Norwich University M,O
Royal Military College of Canada M
School of Advanced Airpower Studies M
Southwest Missouri State University M*†
United States Army Command and General Staff College M
University of Pittsburgh M*†

MINERAL/MINING ENGINEERING

Colorado School of Mines M,D†
Columbia University M,D,O*†
Dalhousie University M,D*
École Polytechnique de Montréal M,D,O
Laurentian University M
McGill University M,D,O*
Michigan Technological University M,D*†
Montana Tech of The University of Montana M
The Pennsylvania State University University Park Campus M,D*†
Queen's University at Kingston M,D
Southern Illinois University Carbondale M,D*†
Université Laval M,D†
University of Alaska Fairbanks M,O*
University of Alberta M,D*
The University of Arizona M,D*
The University of British Columbia M,D*
University of California, Berkeley M,D*
University of Idaho M,D*†
University of Kentucky M,D*
University of Missouri–Rolla M,D*
University of Nevada, Reno M,O*
University of North Dakota M*
The University of Texas at Austin M*
University of Utah M,D*
Virginia Polytechnic Institute and State University M,D*
West Virginia University M,D*

MINERAL ECONOMICS

Colorado School of Mines M,D†
Michigan Technological University M*†
Montana Tech of The University of Montana M
The University of Texas at Austin M*

MINERALOGY

Cornell University M,D*
Indiana University Bloomington M,D*
Université du Québec à Chicoutimi D
Université du Québec à Montréal M,D,O
University of Illinois at Chicago M,D*
University of Michigan M,D*
Yale University D*

MISSIONS AND MISSIOLOGY

Abilene Christian University M
Alliance Theological Seminary P,M
Asbury Theological Seminary P,M,D,O
Associated Mennonite Biblical Seminary P,M,O
Bethel Seminary P,M,D,O
Bethesda Christian University P,M
Biola University M,D,O
Calvin Theological Seminary P,M,D
Canadian Theological Seminary P,M,O
Catholic Theological Union at Chicago P,M,D,O
Church of God Theological Seminary P,M
Columbia International University P,M,D,O
Concordia University (CA) M
Dallas Theological Seminary M,D,O
Eastern Baptist Theological Seminary D
Fuller Theological Seminary M,D
Gardner-Webb University P,D
Global University of the Assemblies of God M
Gordon-Conwell Theological Seminary P,M,D
Grace Theological Seminary P,M,D,O
Grand Rapids Baptist Seminary of Cornerstone University P,M,D
Luther Rice Bible College and Seminary P,M,D
Nazarene Theological Seminary P,M
Oral Roberts University P,M,D
Providence College and Theological Seminary P,M,D,O
Reformed Theological Seminary (NC) P,M,D
Reformed Theological Seminary (MS) P,M,D,O
Regent University P,M,D†
Saint Paul University M,O
Simpson College and Graduate School M
Southeastern Baptist Theological Seminary P,M,D
Southern Adventist University M
Southern Baptist Theological Seminary P,M,D
Southern Evangelical Seminary P,M,O
Southwestern Assemblies of God University M
Trinity Episcopal School for Ministry P,M,D,O
Trinity International University P,M,D,O
Westminster Theological Seminary P,M,D,O
Wheaton College M,O†

MOLECULAR BIOLOGY

Albany Medical College M,D*
Arizona State University M,D*
Baylor College of Medicine D*
Boston University M,D*†
Brandeis University M,D*†
Brigham Young University M,D*
Brock University M
Brown University M,D*
California Institute of Technology D*
Carnegie Mellon University M,D*
Case Western Reserve University M,D*†
Central Connecticut State University M,O*†
Colorado State University M,D*
Columbia University M,D*†
Cornell University D*
Drexel University M,D*†
Duke University D,O*†
East Carolina University M*†
Emory University D*†
Florida Institute of Technology D*†
Florida State University M,D*†
Fordham University M,D*†
George Mason University M*†
Georgetown University D*
The George Washington University M,D*†
Harvard University D*†
Howard University M,D*
Indiana University Bloomington M,D*
Indiana University–Purdue University Indianapolis M,D*
Iowa State University of Science and Technology M,D*†
Joan and Sanford I. Weill Medical College and Graduate School of Medical Sciences of Cornell University M,D*
Johns Hopkins University M,D*†
Kansas State University M,D*†
Kent State University M,D*
Lehigh University D*
Louisiana State University Health Sciences Center M,D*
Loyola University Chicago M,D*†
Maharishi University of Management M,D
Marquette University M,D*†
Massachusetts Institute of Technology D*
Mayo Graduate School D*
McMaster University M,D
Medical College of Georgia M,D*
Medical College of Ohio M,D*
Medical University of South Carolina M,D*
Michigan State University M,D*†
Mississippi State University M,D*
Montana State University–Bozeman M,D*
Montclair State University M,O†
Mount Sinai School of Medicine of New York University D*
New Mexico State University M,D
New York Medical College M,D*
New York University D*†
North Dakota State University M,D†
Northwestern University D*
OGI School of Science & Engineering at Oregon Health & Science University M,D*
The Ohio State University M,D*
Ohio University M,D*
Oklahoma State University M,D*†
Oregon Health & Science University D*
Oregon State University D*
The Pennsylvania State University Milton S. Hershey Medical Center M,D*
The Pennsylvania State University University Park Campus M,D*†
Princeton University D*
Purdue University M,D*
Quinnipiac University M*†
Rensselaer Polytechnic Institute M,D*†
Rutgers, The State University of New Jersey, New Brunswick M,D*
Saint Joseph College M
Saint Louis University D*†
Salem International University M
San Diego State University M,D*
San Francisco State University M
The Scripps Research Institute D
Simon Fraser University M,D
Southern Illinois University Carbondale M,D*†
Southwest Missouri State University M*†
State University of New York at Albany M,D*†
State University of New York Health Science Center at Brooklyn D*
State University of New York Upstate Medical University M,D*
Stony Brook University, State University of New York M,D*†
Temple University D*†
Texas A&M University D*
Texas A&M University System Health Science Center D*
Texas Woman's University M,D*†
Thomas Jefferson University D*
Tufts University D*†
Tulane University M,D*†
Uniformed Services University of the Health Sciences D*
Université de Montréal M,D
Université Laval M,D†
University at Buffalo, The State University of New York D*†
The University of Alabama at Birmingham *†
University of Alberta M,D*
The University of Arizona M,D*
University of Arkansas M,D*
University of Arkansas for Medical Sciences M,D*
The University of British Columbia M,D*
University of Calgary M,D*
University of California, Berkeley D*
University of California, Davis M,D*†
University of California, Irvine M,D*
University of California, Los Angeles M,D*
University of California, Riverside M,D*
University of California, San Diego D*
University of California, San Francisco D*
University of California, Santa Barbara M,D*
University of California, Santa Cruz M,D*
University of Central Florida M*†
University of Chicago D*
University of Cincinnati M,D*

University of Colorado at Boulder M,D*
University of Colorado Health Sciences Center D*
University of Connecticut Health Center D*
University of Delaware M,D*†
University of Florida M,D*†
University of Georgia M,D*†
University of Guelph M,D
University of Hawaii at Manoa M,D*
University of Idaho M,D*†
University of Illinois at Chicago M,D*
University of Illinois at Urbana–Champaign *
The University of Iowa D*
University of Kansas M,D*
University of Louisville M,D*†
University of Maine M,D*
University of Maryland D*†
University of Maryland, Baltimore County M,D*†
University of Maryland, College Park D*
University of Massachusetts Amherst D*†
University of Massachusetts Boston *†
University of Medicine and Dentistry of New Jersey M,D*
The University of Memphis M,D*†
University of Miami D*†
University of Michigan M,D*
University of Minnesota, Duluth M,D*
University of Minnesota, Twin Cities Campus M,D*
University of Missouri–Kansas City M,D*†
University of Missouri–St. Louis M,D,O†
University of Nebraska Medical Center M,D*
University of Nevada, Reno M,D*
University of New Hampshire M,D*†
University of New Haven M*†
University of New Mexico M,D*†
The University of North Carolina at Chapel Hill M,D*†
University of North Texas M,D*†
University of North Texas Health Science Center at Fort Worth M,D*
University of Notre Dame M,D*†
University of Oklahoma Health Sciences Center M,D*
University of Oregon M,D*
University of Ottawa M,D*
University of Pennsylvania D*†
University of Pittsburgh D*†
University of South Alabama D*†
University of South Carolina M,D*†
The University of South Dakota M,D†
University of Southern California M,D*†
University of Southern Maine M
University of Southern Mississippi M,D
University of South Florida D*†
The University of Tennessee Health Science Center D*
The University of Texas at Austin D*
The University of Texas at Dallas M,D*
The University of Texas Health Science Center at Houston M,D*
The University of Texas Medical Branch M,D*
The University of Texas Southwestern Medical Center at Dallas D*
University of Toronto D*
University of Utah D*
University of Vermont M,D*†
University of Virginia D*
University of Washington D*
The University of Western Ontario M,D*
University of Wisconsin–Madison M,D*
University of Wisconsin–Parkside M
University of Wyoming M,D*†
Utah State University M,D*
Vanderbilt University D*
Virginia Commonwealth University M,D,O*†
Virginia Polytechnic Institute and State University M,D*
Wake Forest University D*†
Washington State University M,D*
Washington University in St. Louis D*†
Wayne State University M,D*
Wesleyan University D*
West Virginia University M,D*
William Paterson University of New Jersey M*†
Wright State University M*
Yale University D*
Yeshiva University D*

MOLECULAR MEDICINE

Boston University D*†
Cleveland State University D*†
Cornell University M,D*
Johns Hopkins University D*†
Medical College of Georgia D*
The Pennsylvania State University University Park Campus M,D*†
Picower Graduate School of Molecular Medicine D
University of Cincinnati D*
University of Medicine and Dentistry of New Jersey M,D*
University of Oklahoma Health Sciences Center M,D*
University of Rochester *
The University of Texas Health Science Center at San Antonio M,D*
University of Virginia D*
University of Washington M,D*
Wake Forest University D*†
Yale University D*

MULTILINGUAL AND MULTICULTURAL EDUCATION

Adelphi University M*
Alliant International University M,D,O*†
Alliant International University M,D,O*†
Azusa Pacific University M*†
Bennington College M†
Boston University M,O*†
Brooklyn College of the City University of New York M†
Brown University M,D*
California Baptist University M
California State University, Bakersfield M
California State University, Dominguez Hills M†
California State University, Fullerton M
California State University, Los Angeles M,D
California State University, Sacramento M
California State University, San Bernardino M
California State University, Stanislaus M
Chicago State University M
City College of the City University of New York M*†
College of Mount Saint Vincent M,O*†
The College of New Rochelle M,O†
College of Santa Fe M
Columbia College Chicago M†
Eastern Michigan University M*
Eastern University M*
Emmanuel College M*
Fairfield University M,O*
Fairleigh Dickinson University, Metropolitan Campus M*†
Florida Atlantic University, Ft. Lauderdale Campus M,D,O
Florida State University M,D,O*†
Fordham University M,D,O*†
Fresno Pacific University M
George Mason University M*†
Georgetown University M,D,O*
Heritage College M
Hofstra University M*
Houston Baptist University M
Hunter College of the City University of New York M†
Immaculata University M†
Iona College M*†
Kean University M,O*†
Lehman College of the City University of New York M
Lesley University M,O*†
Long Island University, Brooklyn Campus M*
Long Island University, C.W. Post Campus M*†
Long Island University, Westchester Graduate Campus M
Loyola Marymount University M†
Mercy College M,O*
Mercyhurst College M,O
Minnesota State University, Mankato M,O
National University M†
New Jersey City University M
New York University M,D,O*†
Northeastern Illinois University M
Northern Arizona University M,O
The Pennsylvania State University University Park Campus M,D*†
Prescott College M†
Queens College of the City University of New York M,O†
Rhode Island College M†
St. John's University (NY) M*†
Salem State College M
Sam Houston State University M,O*
San Diego State University M*
School for International Training M†
Seton Hall University M,O*†
Southern Connecticut State University M†
Southern Methodist University M*†
Southwest Texas State University M*
State University of New York College at Brockport M*†
State University of New York College at Buffalo M
Sul Ross State University M*
Teachers College Columbia University M*
Texas A&M International University M
Texas A&M University M,D*
Texas A&M University–Kingsville M,D*†
Texas Southern University M,D†
Texas Tech University M,D,O*†
Universidad del Turabo M
University of Alaska Fairbanks M,O*
University of Alberta M,D,O*
The University of Arizona M,D,O*
University of California, Berkeley M,D,O*
University of Colorado at Boulder M,D*
University of Connecticut M,D*†
University of Delaware M,D*†
The University of Findlay M
University of Florida M,D,O*†
University of Houston M,D*
University of Houston–Clear Lake M*†
University of La Verne O*
University of Maryland, Baltimore County M,D*†
University of Massachusetts Amherst M,D,O*†
University of Massachusetts Boston M*†
University of Minnesota, Twin Cities Campus M,D*
University of New Mexico D*†
University of Pennsylvania M,D*†
University of San Francisco M,D*†
The University of Tennessee M,D,O*†
The University of Texas at Brownsville M
The University of Texas at San Antonio M,D*
The University of Texas–Pan American M
University of Washington M,D*
Utah State University M*
Washington State University M,D*
Wayne State University M,D,O*
Western Oregon University M
Xavier University M*

MUSEUM EDUCATION

Bank Street College of Education M*
The College of New Rochelle O†
The George Washington University M*†
The University of Montana–Missoula M*†

MUSEUM STUDIES

Bard College M*†
Baylor University M*†
Boston University M,D,O*†
California State University, Chico M
California State University, Fullerton M,O
Case Western Reserve University M,D*†
City College of the City University of New York M*†
Colorado State University M*
Duquesne University M*†
Fashion Institute of Technology M*
Florida State University M,D,O*†
The George Washington University M,O*†
Hampton University M*†
Harvard University M,O*†
John F. Kennedy University M,O*†
New York University M,D,O*†
Rutgers, The State University of New Jersey, New Brunswick M,D*
San Francisco State University M
Seton Hall University M*†
State University of New York College at Oneonta M
Syracuse University M*
Texas Tech University M*†
Tufts University O*†
Université de Montréal M
Université du Québec à Montréal M
Université Laval O†
The University of British Columbia M*
University of California, Riverside M,D*
University of Central Oklahoma M
University of Colorado at Boulder M*
University of Delaware O*†
University of Denver M*†
University of Florida M*†
University of Kansas M*
University of Missouri–St. Louis M,O†
University of Nebraska–Lincoln M*†
University of New Hampshire M,D*†
The University of North Carolina at Greensboro M,O†
University of South Carolina M,O*†
The University of the Arts M*
University of Toronto M*
University of Washington M*
University of Wisconsin–Milwaukee M,O

MUSIC

Alabama Agricultural and Mechanical University M
Alabama State University M
Andrews University M
Appalachian State University M
Arizona State University M,D*
Arkansas State University M,O
Auburn University M*†
Austin Peay State University M
Azusa Pacific University M*†
Baptist Theological Seminary at Richmond P,D
Baylor University M*†
Belmont University M
Bennington College M†
Bethel College (MN) M
Boise State University M*
The Boston Conservatory M,O
Boston University M,D,O*†
Bowling Green State University M*†
Brandeis University M,D,O*†
Brandon University M
Brigham Young University M*
Brooklyn College of the City University of New York M,D†
Brown University M,D*
Butler University M
California Institute of the Arts M,O*
California State University, Chico M
California State University, Fresno M
California State University, Fullerton M
California State University, Hayward M
California State University, Long Beach M
California State University, Los Angeles M
California State University, Northridge M
California State University, Sacramento M
Campbellsville University M
Carnegie Mellon University M*
Case Western Reserve University M,D*†
The Catholic University of America M,D*†
Central Michigan University M†
Central Missouri State University M†
Central Washington University M†
Christian Theological Seminary P,M,D
City College of the City University of New York M*†
Claremont Graduate University M,D*
Cleveland Institute of Music M,D,O
Cleveland State University M*†
The College of Saint Rose M*†
Colorado State University M*
Columbia University M,D*†
Concordia University (IL) M,O
Concordia University (Canada) O*†
Concordia University Wisconsin M
Connecticut College M
Converse College M
Cornell University D*
The Curtis Institute of Music M
Dartmouth College M*†
DePaul University M,O*†
Duke University M,D*†
Duquesne University M,O*†
East Carolina University M*†
Eastern Illinois University M†
Eastern Kentucky University M
Eastern Michigan University M*
Eastern New Mexico University M
Eastern Washington University M†

P—*first professional degree;* M—*master's degree;* D—*doctorate;* O—*other advanced degree;* **full description and/or announcement in Book 2, 3, 4, 5, or 6; †full description in this book*

Emory University M*†
Emporia State University M*†
Five Towns College M
Florida Atlantic University M*
Florida Atlantic University, Davie Campus M
Florida Atlantic University, Ft. Lauderdale Campus M
Florida International University M*†
Florida State University M,D*†
Gardner-Webb University P,D
Garrett-Evangelical Theological Seminary P,M,D
George Mason University M*†
Georgia Southern University M
Georgia State University M*
Golden Gate Baptist Theological Seminary P,M,D,O
Graduate School and University Center of the City University of New York D*†
Gratz College M,O†
Hardin-Simmons University M
Harvard University M,D*†
Hebrew College M,O†
Hebrew Union College–Jewish Institute of Religion (NY) M
Holy Names College M,O
Hope International University M
Howard University M*
Hunter College of the City University of New York M†
Illinois State University M*†
Indiana State University M*†
Indiana University Bloomington M,D*
Indiana University of Pennsylvania M*†
Indiana University–Purdue University Indianapolis M*
Indiana University South Bend M
Ithaca College M†
Jacksonville State University M
James Madison University M
Jewish Theological Seminary of America M,D*
Johns Hopkins University M,D,O*†
The Juilliard School M,D,O
Kansas State University M*†
Kent State University M,D*
Lamar University M*†
Lee University M
Long Island University, C.W. Post Campus M*†
Longy School of Music M,O
Louisiana State University and Agricultural and Mechanical College M,D*
Loyola University New Orleans M
Lynn University O†
Manhattan School of Music M,D
Mannes College of Music, New School University M,O
Mansfield University of Pennsylvania M
Marshall University M*†
Marywood University M*†
McGill University M,D*
McMaster University M
Meredith College M
Miami University M*†
Michigan State University M,D*†
Middle Tennessee State University M*
Midwestern Baptist Theological Seminary P,M,D
Mills College M*†
Minnesota State University, Mankato M
Minnesota State University, Moorhead M
Mississippi College M
Montclair State University M†
Morehead State University M
Morgan State University M*
Murray State University M†
New England Conservatory of Music M,D,O
New Mexico State University M
New Orleans Baptist Theological Seminary M,D
New York University M,D,O*†
The Nigerian Baptist Theological Seminary P,M,O
Norfolk State University M†
North American Baptist Seminary M
North Carolina School of the Arts M
Northeastern Illinois University M
Northern Arizona University M
Northern Illinois University M,O*†
Northwestern State University of Louisiana M
Northwestern University M,D,O*
Notre Dame de Namur University M
Oakland University M†
Oberlin College M
The Ohio State University M,D*
Ohio University M*
Oklahoma City University M
Oklahoma State University M*†
The Pennsylvania State University University Park Campus M*†
Pittsburg State University M
Portland State University M*
Princeton University D*
Purchase College, State University of New York M
Queens College of the City University of New York M†
Radford University M†
Rhode Island College M†
Rice University M,D*
Rider University M*
Roosevelt University M,O*†
Rowan University M†
Rutgers, The State University of New Jersey, Newark M*†
Rutgers, The State University of New Jersey, New Brunswick M,D,O*
St. Cloud State University M
Saint John's University (MN) P,M
Saint Joseph's College (IN) M,O
St. Vladimir's Orthodox Theological Seminary P,M,D
Samford University M
Sam Houston State University M*
San Diego State University M*
San Francisco Conservatory of Music M
San Francisco State University M
San Jose State University M*
Santa Clara University M*
Savannah College of Art and Design M*
Shenandoah University M,D,O
Smith College M*
Southeastern Baptist Theological Seminary P,M,D
Southeastern Louisiana University M
Southern Baptist Theological Seminary P,M,D
Southern Illinois University Carbondale M*†
Southern Illinois University Edwardsville M†
Southern Methodist University M*†
Southern Oregon University M
Southern Utah University M
Southwestern Baptist Theological Seminary P,M,D
Southwestern Oklahoma State University M
Southwest Missouri State University M*†
Southwest Texas State University M*
Stanford University M,D*
State University of New York at Binghamton M*†
State University of New York at New Paltz M
State University of New York College at Fredonia M
State University of New York College at Potsdam M
State University of West Georgia M
Stephen F. Austin State University M
Stony Brook University, State University of New York M,D*†
Syracuse University M*
Temple University M,D*†
Texas A&M University–Commerce M†
Texas Christian University M*
Texas Southern University M†
Texas Tech University M,D*†
Texas Woman's University M*†
Towson University M†
Trinity Lutheran Seminary P,M
Truman State University M†
Tufts University M*†
Tulane University M*†
Université de Montréal M,D,O
Université Laval M,D†
University at Buffalo, The State University of New York M,D*†
The University of Akron M†
The University of Alabama M,D,O*
University of Alaska Fairbanks M*
University of Alberta M,D*
The University of Arizona M,D*
University of Arkansas M*
The University of British Columbia M,D*
University of Calgary M,D*
University of California, Berkeley M,D*
University of California, Davis M,D*†
University of California, Irvine M*
University of California, Los Angeles M,D*
University of California, Riverside M*
University of California, San Diego M,D*
University of California, Santa Barbara M,D*
University of California, Santa Cruz M*
University of Central Arkansas M
University of Central Oklahoma M
University of Chicago M,D*
University of Cincinnati M,D,O*
University of Colorado at Boulder M,D*
University of Connecticut M,D*†
University of Delaware M*†
University of Denver M*†
University of Florida M,D*†
University of Georgia M,D*†
University of Hartford M,D,O*
University of Hawaii at Manoa M,D*
University of Houston M,D*
University of Idaho M*†
University of Illinois at Urbana–Champaign M,D*
The University of Iowa M,D*
University of Kansas M,D*
University of Kentucky M,D*
The University of Lethbridge M,D
University of Louisiana at Lafayette M*
University of Louisiana at Monroe M
University of Louisville M,D*†
University of Maine M*
University of Manitoba M*
University of Maryland, College Park M,D*
University of Massachusetts Amherst M,D*†
University of Massachusetts Lowell M*†
The University of Memphis M,D*†
University of Miami M,D*†
University of Michigan M,D*
University of Minnesota, Duluth M*
University of Minnesota, Twin Cities Campus M,D*
University of Mississippi M,D*
University of Missouri–Columbia M*
University of Missouri–Kansas City M,D*†
The University of Montana–Missoula M*†
University of Montevallo M
University of Nebraska at Omaha M
University of Nebraska–Lincoln M,D*†
University of Nevada, Las Vegas M,D*†
University of Nevada, Reno M*
University of New Hampshire M*†
University of New Mexico M*†
University of New Orleans M*
The University of North Carolina at Chapel Hill M,D*†
The University of North Carolina at Greensboro M,D†
University of North Dakota M*
University of Northern Colorado M,D†
University of Northern Iowa M
University of North Texas M,D*†
University of Notre Dame M*†
University of Oklahoma M,D*†
University of Oregon M,D*
University of Ottawa M*
University of Pennsylvania M,D*†
University of Pittsburgh M,D*†
University of Portland M
University of Redlands M
University of Regina M
University of Rhode Island M*
University of Rochester M,D*
University of Saskatchewan M
University of South Carolina M,D,O*†
The University of South Dakota M†
University of Southern California M,D*†
University of Southern Mississippi M,D
University of South Florida M*†
The University of Tennessee M*†
The University of Tennessee at Chattanooga M
The University of Texas at Arlington M*†
The University of Texas at Austin M,D*
The University of Texas at El Paso M*†
The University of Texas at San Antonio M*
The University of Texas at Tyler M
The University of Texas–Pan American O
The University of the Arts M*
University of the Pacific M*
University of Toledo M*†
University of Toronto M,D*
University of Trinity College P,M,D,O
University of Utah M,D*
University of Victoria M,D
University of Virginia M*
University of Washington M,D*
The University of Western Ontario M,D*
University of Wisconsin–Madison M,D*
University of Wisconsin–Milwaukee M
University of Wyoming M*†
Valparaiso University M
Virginia Commonwealth University M*†
Washington State University M*
Washington University in St. Louis M,D*†
Wayne State University M,O*
Webster University M
Wesleyan University M,D*
West Chester University of Pennsylvania M*†
Western Carolina University M†
Western Illinois University M
Western Michigan University M*†
Western Washington University M
West Texas A&M University M†
West Virginia University M,D*
Wichita State University M*†
William Paterson University of New Jersey M*†
Winthrop University M
Yale University M,D,O*
York University M,D*
Youngstown State University M

MUSIC EDUCATION

Alabama Agricultural and Mechanical University M
Alabama State University M
Albany State University M
Appalachian State University M
Arcadia University M,D,O†
Arkansas State University M,O
Auburn University M,D,O*†
Austin Peay State University M
Azusa Pacific University M*†
Ball State University M,D*
Baylor University M*†
Belmont University M
Boise State University M*
The Boston Conservatory M,O
Boston University M,D*†
Bowling Green State University M*†
Brandon University M
Brigham Young University M*
Brooklyn College of the City University of New York M,D†
Butler University M
California State University, Fresno M
California State University, Fullerton M
California State University, Los Angeles M
California State University, Northridge M
Campbellsville University M
Carnegie Mellon University M*
Case Western Reserve University M,D*†
The Catholic University of America M,D*†
Central Connecticut State University M*†
Central Michigan University M†
Claremont Graduate University M,D*
Cleveland State University M*†
The College of Saint Rose M*†
The Colorado College M
Colorado State University M*
Columbus State University M
Connecticut College M
Converse College M
Delta State University M
DePaul University M*†
Duquesne University M,O*†
East Carolina University M*†
Eastern Kentucky University M
Eastern Washington University M†
East Tennessee State University M†
Emporia State University M*†
Five Towns College M
Florida International University M*†
Florida State University M,D*†
George Mason University M*†
Georgia Southern University O
Georgia State University M,D,O*
Hardin-Simmons University M
Hofstra University M*
Holy Names College M,O
Howard University M*
Hunter College of the City University of New York M†
Indiana State University M*†
Indiana University Bloomington M,D,O*
Indiana University of Pennsylvania M*†
Ithaca College M†
Jackson State University M
Jacksonville State University M
Jacksonville University M
James Madison University M
Kansas State University M*†

Kent State University M,D*
Lamar University M*†
Lebanon Valley College M
Lehman College of the City University of New York M
Lewis & Clark College M
Long Island University, C.W. Post Campus M*†
Louisiana State University and Agricultural and Mechanical College M,D*
Manhattanville College M*†
Marywood University M*†
McGill University M,D*
McNeese State University M
Miami University M*†
Michigan State University M,D*†
Minnesota State University, Moorhead M
Minot State University M
Mississippi College M
Montclair State University M†
Morehead State University M
Murray State University M†
Nazareth College of Rochester M
New Jersey City University M
New York University M,D,O*†
Norfolk State University M†
Northern Arizona University M
Northwestern University M,D*
Northwest Missouri State University M
Notre Dame de Namur University M
Oregon State University M*
The Pennsylvania State University University Park Campus M,D*†
Pittsburg State University M
Portland State University M*
Queens College of the City University of New York M,O†
Radford University M†
Rhode Island College M†
Rider University M*
Rollins College M*
Roosevelt University M,O*†
Rowan University M†
St. Cloud State University M
Salisbury University M
Samford University M,D,O
Sam Houston State University M*
Shenandoah University M,D,O
Silver Lake College M
Southeast Missouri State University M
Southern Illinois University Carbondale M*†
Southern Illinois University Edwardsville M†
Southern Methodist University M*†
Southwest Texas State University M*
State University of New York at New Paltz M
State University of New York College at Fredonia M
State University of New York College at Potsdam M
State University of West Georgia M
Syracuse University M*
Teachers College Columbia University M,D*
Temple University M,D*†
Tennessee State University M*
Texas A&M University–Commerce M†
Texas A&M University–Kingsville M*†
Texas Christian University M*
Texas Tech University M,D*†
Towson University M,O†
Union College (KY) M
Université Laval M,D†
University at Buffalo, The State University of New York M,D,O*†
The University of Akron M†
The University of Alabama M,D,O*
University of Alaska Fairbanks M*
University of Arizona M,D*
The University of British Columbia M,D*
University of Central Arkansas M
University of Central Florida M*†
University of Central Oklahoma M
University of Cincinnati M*
University of Colorado at Boulder M,D*
University of Connecticut M,D*†
University of Delaware M*†
University of Denver M*†
University of Florida M,D*†
University of Georgia M,D,O*†
University of Hartford M,D,O*
University of Houston M,D*
The University of Iowa M,D*
University of Kansas M,D*
University of Louisiana at Lafayette M*
University of Louisville M*†
University of Manitoba M*
University of Maryland, College Park M,D*
University of Massachusetts Lowell M*†
The University of Memphis M,D*†
University of Miami M,D,O*†
University of Michigan D*
University of Minnesota, Duluth M*
University of Missouri–Kansas City M,D*†
University of Missouri–St. Louis M†
The University of Montana–Missoula M*†
University of Nebraska at Kearney M
University of Nevada, Las Vegas M,D*†
University of New Hampshire M*†
The University of North Carolina at Chapel Hill M*†
The University of North Carolina at Greensboro M,D†
University of North Dakota M*
University of Northern Colorado M,D†
University of Northern Iowa M
University of North Florida M
University of North Texas M,D*†
University of Oklahoma M,D*†
University of Oregon M,D*
University of Rochester M,D*
University of St. Thomas (MN) M*†
University of South Alabama M*†
University of South Carolina M,D*†
University of Southern California M,D*†
University of Southern Mississippi M,D
University of South Florida M,D*†
The University of Tennessee M*†
The University of Texas at El Paso M*†
The University of Texas at Tyler M
The University of the Arts M*
University of the Pacific M*
University of Toledo M*†
University of Victoria M
University of Washington M,D*
University of Wisconsin–Madison M,D*
University of Wisconsin–Stevens Point M
University of Wyoming M*†
Valdosta State University M
VanderCook College of Music M
Virginia Commonwealth University M*†
Wayne State College M
Wayne State University M,O*
Webster University M
West Chester University of Pennsylvania M*†
Western Connecticut State University M
Western Kentucky University M†
West Virginia University M,D*
Wichita State University M*†
Winthrop University M
Wright State University M*
Youngstown State University M

NATIVE AMERICAN STUDIES

Montana State University–Bozeman M*
Trent University M,D
The University of Arizona M,D*
University of California, Davis M,D*†
University of California, Los Angeles M*
University of Kansas M*
The University of Lethbridge M,D
University of Regina M,D

NATURAL RESOURCES

Ball State University M*
Colorado State University D*
Cornell University M,D*
Duke University M,D*†
Humboldt State University M
McGill University M,D*
Montana State University–Bozeman M,D*
North Carolina State University M,D*
The Ohio State University M,D*
Oklahoma State University M,D*†
Purdue University M,D*
State University of New York College of Environmental Science and Forestry M,D
Texas A&M University M,D*
Université du Québec à Montréal M,D,O
University of Alberta M,D*
The University of Arizona M,D*
University of Arkansas at Monticello M
University of Connecticut M*†
University of Florida M,D*†
University of Georgia M,D*†
University of Illinois at Urbana–Champaign M,D*
University of Maine M,D*
University of Maryland, College Park M,D*
University of Michigan M,D,O*
The University of Montana–Missoula M*†
University of Nebraska–Lincoln M*†
University of New Hampshire D*†
University of Northern British Columbia M,D
University of Rhode Island M,D*
University of Wisconsin–Stevens Point M
University of Wyoming M,D*†
Utah State University M*
Virginia Polytechnic Institute and State University M,D*
Washington State University M,D*
West Virginia University D*

NATUROPATHIC MEDICINE

Bastyr University D*
Canadian College of Naturopathic Medicine D
National College of Naturopathic Medicine D*
Southwest College of Naturopathic Medicine and Health Sciences D*
University of Bridgeport D*†

NEAR AND MIDDLE EASTERN LANGUAGES

American University in Cairo M,O
Brandeis University M,D*†
Brigham Young University M*
The Catholic University of America M,D*†
Columbia University M,D*†
Georgetown University M,D*
Harvard University M,D*†
Hebrew Union College–Jewish Institute of Religion (NY) D
Indiana University Bloomington M,D*
The Ohio State University M*
University of California, Los Angeles M,D*
University of Chicago M,D*
University of Michigan M,D*
The University of Texas at Austin M,D*
University of Wisconsin–Madison M,D*
Yale University M,D*

NEAR AND MIDDLE EASTERN STUDIES

American University in Cairo M,O
Brandeis University M,D*†
Brigham Young University M*
Columbia University M,D,O*†
Cornell University M,D*
Georgetown University M,O*
Gratz College O†
Harvard University M,D*†
Hebrew Union College–Jewish Institute of Religion (OH) M,D
Johns Hopkins University M,D,O*†
McGill University M,D*
New York University M,D*†
Princeton University M,D*
The University of Arizona M,D*
University of California, Berkeley M,D,O*
University of California, Los Angeles M,D*
University of Chicago M,D*
University of Michigan M,D*
University of Pennsylvania M,D*†
The University of Texas at Austin M,D*
University of Toronto M,D*
University of Utah M,D*
University of Virginia M*
University of Washington M,D*
Washington University in St. Louis M*†
Wayne State University M*

NEUROBIOLOGY

Boston University M,D*†
Brandeis University M,D*†
Bryn Mawr College D
California Institute of Technology D*
Carnegie Mellon University M,D*
Case Western Reserve University D*†
Colorado State University M,D*
Columbia University M,D*†
Cornell University D*
Dalhousie University M,D*
Duke University D*†
Emory University D*†
Georgia State University M,D*
Harvard University D*†
Indiana University–Purdue University Indianapolis M,D*
Louisiana State University Health Sciences Center M,D*
Loyola University Chicago M,D*†
Marquette University M,D*†
Massachusetts Institute of Technology D*
Northwestern University M,D*
Purdue University M,D*
Rutgers, The State University of New Jersey, New Brunswick D*
State University of New York at Albany M,D*†
Stony Brook University, State University of New York D*†
Texas A&M University System Health Science Center D*
Université Laval M,D†
The University of Alabama at Birmingham D*†
University of Arkansas for Medical Sciences M,D*
University of California, Irvine M,D*
University of California, Los Angeles D*
University of California, San Diego D*
University of Chicago D*
University of Cincinnati D*
University of Colorado at Boulder M,D*
University of Connecticut M,D*†
University of Illinois at Chicago M,D*
The University of Iowa M,D*
University of Kentucky D*
University of Louisville M,D*†
University of Maryland M,D*†
University of Medicine and Dentistry of New Jersey M,D*
University of Michigan D*
The University of North Carolina at Chapel Hill D*†
University of Pennsylvania D*†
University of Pittsburgh M,D*†
University of Rochester M,D*
University of Southern California M,D*†
The University of Tennessee Health Science Center D*
The University of Texas at San Antonio D*
University of Utah M,D*
University of Vermont D*†
University of Washington D*
University of Wisconsin–Madison D*
Wake Forest University D*†
Wayne State University D*
Wesleyan University D*
Yale University D*
Yeshiva University D*

NEUROSCIENCE

Albany Medical College M,D*
Arizona State University M,D*
Baylor College of Medicine D*
Baylor University M,D*†
Boston University M,D*†
Brandeis University M,D*†
Brown University D*
California Institute of Technology M,D*
Carleton University M,D
Carnegie Mellon University *
Case Western Reserve University D*†
College of Staten Island of the City University of New York D†
Colorado State University D*
Dalhousie University M,D*
Dartmouth College D*†
Drexel University D*†
Finch University of Health Sciences/The Chicago Medical School D*
Florida State University D*†
Georgetown University D*
The George Washington University D*†
Graduate School and University Center of the City University of New York D*†
Harvard University D*†
Indiana University Bloomington D*
Iowa State University of Science and Technology M,D*†
Joan and Sanford I. Weill Medical College and Graduate School of Medical Sciences of Cornell University D*
Johns Hopkins University D*†

*P—first professional degree; M—master's degree; D—doctorate; O—other advanced degree; *full description and/or announcement in Book 2, 3, 4, 5, or 6; †full description in this book*

Kent State University	M,D*
Lehigh University	D*
Louisiana State University Health Sciences Center	D*
Loyola University Chicago	M,D*†
Maharishi University of Management	M,D
Massachusetts Institute of Technology	D*
Mayo Graduate School	D*
McGill University	M,D*
McMaster University	M,D
Medical College of Ohio	M,D*
Medical University of South Carolina	M,D*
Michigan State University	D*†
Montana State University–Bozeman	D*
Mount Sinai School of Medicine of New York University	D*
New York Medical College	M,D*
New York University	M,D*†
Northwestern University	D*
The Ohio State University	D*
Ohio University	M,D*
Oregon Health & Science University	M,D*
The Pennsylvania State University Milton S. Hershey Medical Center	M,D*
The Pennsylvania State University University Park Campus	M,D*†
Princeton University	D*
Purdue University	D*
Rutgers, The State University of New Jersey, Newark	D*†
Stanford University	D*
State University of New York at Albany	M,D*†
State University of New York Health Science Center at Brooklyn	D*
State University of New York Upstate Medical University	D*
Syracuse University	M,D*
Teachers College Columbia University	M*
Texas A&M University System Health Science Center	D*
Tufts University	D*†
Tulane University	M,D*†
Uniformed Services University of the Health Sciences	D*
Université de Montréal	M,D,O
University at Buffalo, The State University of New York	M,D*†
The University of Alabama at Birmingham	M,D*†
University of Alberta	M,D*
The University of Arizona	D*
The University of British Columbia	M,D*
University of Calgary	M,D*
University of California, Berkeley	D*
University of California, Davis	D*†
University of California, Los Angeles	D*
University of California, Riverside	D*
University of California, San Diego	D*
University of California, San Francisco	D*
University of Cincinnati	D*
University of Colorado Health Sciences Center	D*
University of Connecticut	D*†
University of Connecticut Health Center	D*
University of Delaware	D*†
University of Florida	M,D*†
University of Guelph	M,D,O
University of Hartford	M*
University of Hawaii at Manoa	M,D*
University of Illinois at Urbana–Champaign	D*
The University of Lethbridge	M,D
University of Maryland	M,D*†
University of Maryland, Baltimore County	M,D*†
University of Maryland, College Park	D*
University of Massachusetts Amherst	M,D*†
University of Massachusetts Worcester	D*
University of Medicine and Dentistry of New Jersey	M,D*
University of Miami	M,D*†
University of Minnesota, Twin Cities Campus	M,D*
University of New Mexico	M,D*†
University of Oklahoma Health Sciences Center	M,D*
University of Oregon	M,D*
University of Pennsylvania	D*†
University of Pittsburgh	D*†
University of Rochester	M,D*
University of South Alabama	D*†
The University of South Dakota	M,D†
University of Southern California	D*†
The University of Texas at Austin	M,D*
The University of Texas at Dallas	M*
The University of Texas Health Science Center at Houston	M,D*
The University of Texas Medical Branch	D*
The University of Texas Southwestern Medical Center at Dallas	D*
University of Toronto	M,D*
University of Utah	D*
University of Virginia	D*
The University of Western Ontario	M,D*
University of Wisconsin–Madison	M,D*
Vanderbilt University	D*
Virginia Commonwealth University	M,D,O*†
Wake Forest University	D*†
Washington State University	M,D*
Washington University in St. Louis	D*†
Yale University	D*

NONPROFIT MANAGEMENT

Boston University	M,D,O*†
Carlow College	M
Case Western Reserve University	M,O*†
College of Notre Dame of Maryland	M
The College of Saint Rose	O*†
DePaul University	M,O*†
Eastern University	M*
Hamline University	M*
Hebrew College	M,O†
High Point University	M
Hope International University	M
Hsi Lai University	M*
Indiana University Northwest	M,O
Indiana University–Purdue University Indianapolis	M*
Lesley University	M*†
Metropolitan State University	M
New School University	M*†
New York University	M,D,O*†
North Central College	M
Oral Roberts University	M
Pace University, White Plains Campus	M*
Park University	M
Regis University	M,O*†
Robert Morris University	M†
Rosemont College	M†
St. Cloud State University	M
St. Edward's University	M,O
San Francisco State University	M
Seattle University	M*†
Seton Hall University	M*†
Suffolk University	M,O*
Trinity College (DC)	M†
Tufts University	O*†
University of Central Florida	M,O*†
University of Judaism	M
The University of Memphis	M*†
University of Missouri–St. Louis	M,O†
The University of North Carolina at Greensboro	M,O†
University of Pittsburgh	M,O*†
University of St. Thomas (MN)	M,O*†
University of San Francisco	M*†
Willamette University	M*
Worcester State College	M

NORTHERN STUDIES

University of Alaska Fairbanks	M,D*
University of Manitoba	M*

NUCLEAR ENGINEERING

Air Force Institute of Technology	M,D*
Cornell University	M,D*
École Polytechnique de Montréal	M,D,O
Georgia Institute of Technology	M,D*
Idaho State University	M,D*
Kansas State University	M,D*†
Massachusetts Institute of Technology	M,D,O*
McMaster University	M,D
North Carolina State University	M,D*
The Ohio State University	M,D*
Oregon State University	M,D*
The Pennsylvania State University University Park Campus	M,D*†
Purdue University	M,D*
Rensselaer Polytechnic Institute	M,D*†
Royal Military College of Canada	M,D
Texas A&M University	M,D*
The University of Arizona	M,D*
University of California, Berkeley	M,D*
University of Cincinnati	M,D*
University of Florida	M,D,O*†
University of Idaho	M,D*†
University of Illinois at Urbana–Champaign	M,D*
University of Maryland, College Park	M,D*
University of Michigan	M,D,O*
University of Missouri–Columbia	M,D*
University of Missouri–Rolla	M,D*
University of New Mexico	M*†
The University of Tennessee	M,D*†
University of Utah	M,D*
University of Virginia	M,D*
University of Wisconsin–Madison	M,D*

NURSE ANESTHESIA

Albany Medical College	M*
Barry University	M*†
Baylor College of Medicine	M*
California State University, Long Beach	M
Case Western Reserve University	M*†
Columbia University	M,O*†
DePaul University	M*†
Drexel University	M*†
Duke University	M,O*†
Emory University	M*†
Gannon University	M,O
Gonzaga University	M
Gooding Institute of Nurse Anesthesia	M
Inter American University of Puerto Rico, Arecibo Campus	M
La Roche College	M
Mayo School of Health Sciences	M
Medical College of Georgia	M,D*
Medical University of South Carolina	M*
Middle Tennessee School of Anesthesia	M
Mount Marty College	M
Newman University	M
Northeastern University	M*†
Oakland University	M,O†
Rush University	M,D*
Saint Joseph's University	M*†
Saint Mary's University of Minnesota	M
Samuel Merritt College	M,O
Southern Illinois University Edwardsville	M†
Southwest Missouri State University	M*†
State University of New York Health Science Center at Brooklyn	M*
Texas Wesleyan University	M
Uniformed Services University of the Health Sciences	M*
Université de Montréal	O
University at Buffalo, The State University of New York	M,D,O*†
The University of Alabama at Birmingham	M*†
University of Cincinnati	M,D*
University of Detroit Mercy	M*
University of Kansas	M*
University of Medicine and Dentistry of New Jersey	M*
University of Michigan–Flint	M
University of New England	M*
The University of North Carolina at Greensboro	M,O†
University of Pittsburgh	M*†
University of Puerto Rico, Medical Sciences Campus	M*
The University of Scranton	M†
University of South Carolina	M*†
The University of Tennessee at Chattanooga	M
University of Wisconsin–La Crosse	M†
Villanova University	M,O*†
Virginia Commonwealth University	M*†
Wayne State University	M*
Webster University	M
Xavier University of Louisiana	M

NURSE MIDWIFERY

Baylor College of Medicine	M*
Boston University	M,O*†
Case Western Reserve University	M*†
Columbia University	M*†
Emory University	M*†
Illinois State University	M,O*†
Loyola University Chicago	M*†
Marquette University	M,O*†
Medical University of South Carolina	M*
New York University	M,O*†
Oregon Health & Science University	M,O*
Philadelphia University	M
Stony Brook University, State University of New York	M,O*†
University of Cincinnati	M,D*
University of Illinois at Chicago	M*
University of Medicine and Dentistry of New Jersey	O*
University of Miami	M,D*†
University of Michigan	M*
University of Minnesota, Twin Cities Campus	M*
University of Pennsylvania	M*†
University of Puerto Rico, Medical Sciences Campus	M,O*
The University of Texas at El Paso	M*†
Vanderbilt University	M,D*

NURSING—GENERAL

Abilene Christian University	M
Adelphi University	M,O*
Albany State University	M
Alcorn State University	M
Allen College	M
Andrews University	M
Arizona State University	M*
Arkansas State University	M
Armstrong Atlantic State University	M†
Augustana College	M
Azusa Pacific University	M*†
Ball State University	M*
Barry University	D*†
Baylor University	M*†
Bellarmine University	M
Belmont University	M
Bethel College (MN)	M
Bloomsburg University of Pennsylvania	M
Boston College	M,D*†
Bowie State University	M
Bradley University	M†
Brenau University	M
Brigham Young University	M*
California State University, Bakersfield	M
California State University, Chico	M
California State University, Dominguez Hills	M†
California State University, Fresno	M
California State University, Fullerton	M
California State University, Long Beach	M
California State University, Los Angeles	M
California State University, Sacramento	M
California State University, San Bernardino	M
Capital University	M
Cardinal Stritch University	M*
Carlow College	M,O
Carson-Newman College	M
Case Western Reserve University	M,D*†
The Catholic University of America	M,D*†
Central Missouri State University	M†
Clarion University of Pennsylvania	M†
Clarke College	M,O
Clarkson College	M
Clemson University	M*
Cleveland State University	M*†
College Misericordia	M
College of Mount Saint Vincent	M,O*†
The College of New Jersey	M†
The College of New Rochelle	M,O†
College of St. Catherine	M†
The College of St. Scholastica	M
Columbia University	M,D,O*†
Concordia University Wisconsin	M
Coppin State College	M
Creighton University	M*
Daemen College	M,O
Dalhousie University	M*
Delta State University	M
DePaul University	M*†
DeSales University	M
Dominican College	M†
Dominican University of California	M
Drexel University	M*†
Duke University	M,O*†
Duquesne University	M,D*†
D'Youville College	M,O†
East Carolina University	M,D*†
Eastern Kentucky University	M
Eastern Washington University	M†
East Tennessee State University	M,D,O†
Edgewood College	M
Edinboro University of Pennsylvania	M

Institution	Degrees
Emory University	M,D*†
Excelsior College	M
Fairfield University	M,O*
Fairleigh Dickinson University, Metropolitan Campus	M*†
Felician College	M
Florida Atlantic University	M,D,O*
Florida Gulf Coast University	M
Florida International University	M*†
Florida State University	M*†
Fort Hays State University	M
Franciscan University of Steubenville	M
Gannon University	M,O
George Mason University	M,D*†
Georgetown University	M*
Georgia College & State University	M
Georgia Southern University	M,O
Georgia State University	M,D*
Gonzaga University	M
Governors State University	M
Graceland University	M,O
Grambling State University	M
Grand Valley State University	M†
Gwynedd-Mercy College	M
Hampton University	M*†
Harding University	M
Hardin-Simmons University	M
Hawai'i Pacific University	M*†
Holy Family College	M
Holy Names College	M
Houston Baptist University	M
Howard University	M,O*
Hunter College of the City University of New York	M,O†
Husson College	M
Idaho State University	M,O*
Illinois State University	M,O*†
Indiana State University	M*†
Indiana University of Pennsylvania	M*†
Indiana University–Purdue University Fort Wayne	M
Indiana University–Purdue University Indianapolis	M,D*
Indiana Wesleyan University	M,O*
Jacksonville State University	M
Jewish Hospital College of Nursing and Allied Health	M
Johns Hopkins University	M,D,O*†
Kean University	M*†
Kennesaw State University	M
Kent State University	M*
Lamar University	M*†
La Roche College	M
La Salle University	M,O
Lehman College of the City University of New York	M
Lewis University	M,O
Liberty University	M†
Loma Linda University	M,O*
Long Island University, Brooklyn Campus	M,O*
Long Island University, C.W. Post Campus	M,O*†
Louisiana State University Health Sciences Center	M,D*
Loyola University Chicago	M,D*†
Loyola University New Orleans	M
Madonna University	M
Marquette University	M,O*†
Marshall University	M*†
Maryville University of Saint Louis	M
Marywood University	M*†
McGill University	M,D*
McMaster University	M,D
McNeese State University	M
Medical College of Georgia	M,D*
Medical College of Ohio	M,O*
Medical University of South Carolina	M,D,O*
Memorial University of Newfoundland	M†
Mercy College	M*
Metropolitan State University	M
MGH Institute of Health Professions	M,O*
Michigan State University	M,D*†
Midwestern State University	M
Millersville University of Pennsylvania	M†
Minnesota State University, Mankato	M
Minnesota State University, Moorhead	M,O
Mississippi University for Women	M,O
Molloy College	M,O
Monmouth University	M,O*†
Montana State University–Bozeman	M*
Mount Marty College	M
Mount Saint Mary College	M
Murray State University	M†
National University	M†
Nazareth College of Rochester	M
Nebraska Methodist College	M
Neumann College	M
New Jersey City University	M
Newman University	M
New Mexico State University	M
New York University	M,D,O*†
Niagara University	M†
North Dakota State University	M†
Northeastern University	M,O*†
Northern Arizona University	M,O
Northern Illinois University	M*†
Northern Kentucky University	M
Northern Michigan University	M
North Georgia College & State University	M
North Park University	M
Northwestern State University of Louisiana	M
Oakland University	M,O†
The Ohio State University	M,D*
Old Dominion University	M*†
Oregon Health & Science University	M,D,O*
Otterbein College	M,O
Pace University	M,O*†
Pace University, Pleasantville/Briarcliff Campus	M,O
Pacific Lutheran University	M†
The Pennsylvania State University University Park Campus	M,D*†
Pittsburg State University	M
Pontifical Catholic University of Puerto Rico	M
Prairie View A&M University	M
Purdue University Calumet	M
Queen's University at Kingston	M
Queens University of Charlotte	M
Quinnipiac University	M*†
Radford University	M†
Regis College (MA)	M,O
Regis University	M*†
Research College of Nursing	M
The Richard Stockton College of New Jersey	M*
Rivier College	M*†
Rush University	M,D*
Rutgers, The State University of New Jersey, Newark	M,D*†
Sacred Heart University	M*†
Sage Graduate School	M,O†
Saginaw Valley State University	M
Saint Joseph College	M,O
Saint Joseph's College (ME)	M
Saint Peter's College	M†
Saint Xavier University	M,O*
Salem State College	M
Salisbury University	M
Samford University	M
Samuel Merritt College	M,O
San Diego State University	M*
San Francisco State University	M
San Jose State University	M*
Seattle Pacific University	M,O
Seattle University	M,O*†
Seton Hall University	M*†
Shenandoah University	M,O
Simmons College	M,O*
Slippery Rock University of Pennsylvania	M†
South Dakota State University	M*
Southeastern Louisiana University	M
Southeast Missouri State University	M
Southern Adventist University	M
Southern Connecticut State University	M†
Southern Illinois University Edwardsville	M†
Southern University and Agricultural and Mechanical College	M,D,O*
Southwest Missouri State University	M*†
Spalding University	M†
State University of New York at Binghamton	M,D,O*†
State University of New York at New Paltz	M
State University of New York Health Science Center at Brooklyn	M,O*
State University of New York Institute of Technology at Utica/Rome	M,O*†
State University of New York Upstate Medical University	M*
Stony Brook University, State University of New York	M,O*†
Syracuse University	M*
Temple University	M*†
Tennessee State University	M*
Texas A&M University–Corpus Christi	M
Texas Christian University	M*
Texas Tech University Health Sciences Center	M,O*
Texas Woman's University	M,D*†
Thomas Jefferson University	M*
Towson University	M,O†
Troy State University	M
Uniformed Services University of the Health Sciences	M*
Union University	M
Université de Montréal	M,D,O
Université du Québec en Outaouais	M,O
Université du Québec à Trois-Rivières	M,O
Université Laval	M,O†
University at Buffalo, The State University of New York	M,D,O*†
The University of Akron	M,D†
The University of Alabama	M*
The University of Alabama at Birmingham	M,D*†
The University of Alabama in Huntsville	M,O*
University of Alaska Anchorage	M
University of Alberta	M,D*
The University of Arizona	M,D*
University of Arkansas for Medical Sciences	M,D*
The University of British Columbia	M,D*
University of Calgary	M,D*
University of California, Los Angeles	M,D*
University of California, San Francisco	M,D*
University of Central Arkansas	M
University of Central Florida	M*†
University of Cincinnati	M,D*
University of Colorado at Colorado Springs	M*
University of Colorado Health Sciences Center	M,D*
University of Connecticut	M,D*†
University of Delaware	M,O*†
University of Evansville	M
University of Florida	M,D*†
University of Hartford	M*
University of Hawaii at Manoa	M,D,O*
University of Illinois at Chicago	M,D*
The University of Iowa	M,D*
University of Kansas	M,D*
University of Kentucky	M,D*
The University of Lethbridge	M,D
University of Louisiana at Lafayette	M*
University of Louisville	M*†
University of Maine	M,O*
University of Manitoba	M*
University of Mary	M
University of Maryland	M,D*†
University of Massachusetts Amherst	M,D*†
University of Massachusetts Boston	M,D*†
University of Massachusetts Dartmouth	M,O*†
University of Massachusetts Lowell	M,D*†
University of Massachusetts Worcester	M,D,O*
University of Medicine and Dentistry of New Jersey	M,O*
University of Miami	M,D*†
University of Michigan	M,D,O*
University of Michigan–Flint	M
University of Minnesota, Twin Cities Campus	M,D*
University of Mississippi Medical Center	M,D*
University of Missouri–Columbia	M,D*
University of Missouri–Kansas City	M,D*†
University of Missouri–St. Louis	M,D†
University of Mobile	M
University of Nebraska Medical Center	M,D*
University of Nevada, Las Vegas	M*†
University of Nevada, Reno	M*
University of New Hampshire	M*†
University of New Mexico	M*†
The University of North Carolina at Chapel Hill	M,D*†
The University of North Carolina at Greensboro	M,O†
The University of North Carolina at Wilmington	M*
University of North Dakota	M*
University of Northern Colorado	M†
University of North Florida	M,O
University of Oklahoma Health Sciences Center	M*
University of Ottawa	M*
University of Pennsylvania	M,D,O*†
University of Phoenix–Colorado Campus	M
University of Phoenix–Fort Lauderdale Campus	M
University of Phoenix–Hawaii Campus	M
University of Phoenix–Jacksonville Campus	M
University of Phoenix–Louisiana Campus	M
University of Phoenix–Metro Detroit Campus	M
University of Phoenix–New Mexico Campus	M
University of Phoenix–Northern California Campus	M
University of Phoenix–Orlando Campus	M
University of Phoenix–Phoenix Campus	M
University of Phoenix–Sacramento Campus	M
University of Phoenix–San Diego Campus	M
University of Phoenix–Southern Arizona Campus	M
University of Phoenix–Southern California Campus	M
University of Phoenix–Southern Colorado Campus	M
University of Phoenix–Tampa Campus	M
University of Phoenix–Utah Campus	M
University of Phoenix–West Michigan Campus	M
University of Pittsburgh	M,D*†
University of Portland	M,O
University of Puerto Rico, Medical Sciences Campus	M*
University of Rhode Island	M,D*
University of Rochester	M,D,O*
University of St. Francis (IL)	M
University of Saint Francis (IN)	M
University of San Diego	M,D,O*†
University of San Francisco	M*†
University of Saskatchewan	M
The University of Scranton	M†
University of South Alabama	M*†
University of South Carolina	M,D,O*†
University of Southern California	M,O*†
University of Southern Indiana	M
University of Southern Maine	M,O
University of Southern Mississippi	M,D
University of South Florida	M,D*†
The University of Tampa	M
The University of Tennessee	M,D*†
The University of Tennessee at Chattanooga	M
The University of Tennessee Health Science Center	M,D*
The University of Texas at Arlington	M*†
The University of Texas at Austin	M,D*
The University of Texas at El Paso	M*†
The University of Texas at Tyler	M
The University of Texas Health Science Center at Houston	M,D*
The University of Texas Health Science Center at San Antonio	M,D*
The University of Texas Medical Branch	M,D*
The University of Texas–Pan American	M
University of the Incarnate Word	M†
University of Toronto	M,D*
University of Utah	M,D*
University of Vermont	M*†
University of Virginia	M,D*
University of Washington	M,D*
The University of Western Ontario	M*
University of Windsor	M
University of Wisconsin–Eau Claire	M†
University of Wisconsin–Madison	M,D*
University of Wisconsin–Milwaukee	M,D
University of Wisconsin–Oshkosh	M*
University of Wyoming	M*†
Ursuline College	M
Valdosta State University	M
Valparaiso University	M
Vanderbilt University	M,D*
Villanova University	M,O*†
Virginia Commonwealth University	M,D,O*†
Viterbo University	M
Wagner College	M
Washington State University	M*
Wayne State University	M,D,O*
Webster University	M
Wesley College	M
West Chester University of Pennsylvania	M*†
Western Carolina University	M†
Western Connecticut State University	M
Western Kentucky University	M†

*P—first professional degree; M—master's degree; D—doctorate; O—other advanced degree; *full description and/or announcement in Book 2, 3, 4, 5, or 6; †full description in this book*

Western University of Health Sciences M
Westminster College (UT) M
West Texas A&M University M†
West Virginia University M,D,O*
Wheeling Jesuit University M
Wichita State University M*†
Widener University M,D,O*†
Wilkes University M
William Paterson University of New Jersey M*†
Wilmington College M
Winona State University M
Wright State University M*
Xavier University M*
Yale University M,D,O*
Youngstown State University M

NURSING AND HEALTHCARE ADMINISTRATION

Allen College M
Barry University M,D*†
Baylor University M*†
Bellarmine University M
Bowie State University M
Capital University M
Carlow College M,O
The Catholic University of America M,D*†
Clarke College M,O
Clarkson College M
College of Mount Saint Vincent M,O*†
The College of New Rochelle M,O†
Duke University M,O*†
Duquesne University M*†
Excelsior College M
Florida Atlantic University M,D,O*
Gannon University M,O
George Mason University M,D*†
Graceland University M,O
Indiana University–Purdue University Fort Wayne M
Indiana University–Purdue University Indianapolis M*
Johns Hopkins University M*†
Kent State University M*
Lamar University M*†
La Roche College M
La Salle University M,O
Lewis University M,O
Loma Linda University M,O*
Long Island University, Brooklyn Campus M*
Louisiana State University Health Sciences Center M,D*
Loyola University Chicago M*†
Madonna University M
Marymount University M,O†
Medical University of South Carolina M,O*
Minnesota State University, Mankato M
Molloy College M,O
Mountain State University M†
Mount Saint Mary College M
Northeastern University M*†
Otterbein College M,O
Pacific Lutheran University M†
Queens University of Charlotte M
Rivier College M*†
Sacred Heart University M*†
Saginaw Valley State University M
Saint Xavier University M,O*
Samuel Merritt College M,O
San Francisco State University M
San Jose State University M*
Seattle Pacific University M
Seton Hall University M*†
Southern Adventist University M
Southern Connecticut State University M†
Southern University and Agricultural and Mechanical College M,D,O*
Spalding University M†
State University of New York Institute of Technology at Utica/Rome M,O*†
Texas A&M University–Corpus Christi M
Texas Tech University Health Sciences Center M,O*
University of Cincinnati M,D*
University of Connecticut M,D*†
University of Delaware M,O*†
University of Hawaii at Manoa M,D,O*
University of Illinois at Chicago M*
University of Maryland M,D*†
University of Massachusetts Lowell D*†
University of Michigan M*
University of Minnesota, Twin Cities Campus M*
University of Missouri–Kansas City M,D*†
The University of North Carolina at Greensboro M,O†
University of Pennsylvania M,D*†
University of Phoenix–Northern California Campus M
University of Phoenix–Phoenix Campus M
University of Pittsburgh M*†
University of Portland M,O
University of Puerto Rico, Medical Sciences Campus M*
University of Rhode Island M,D*
University of San Diego M,D,O*†
University of San Francisco M*†
University of South Carolina M*†
University of Southern Maine M,O
University of Southern Mississippi M,D
The University of Tampa M
The University of Tennessee at Chattanooga M
The University of Texas at Arlington M*†
The University of Texas at El Paso M*†
Valdosta State University M
Vanderbilt University M,D*
Villanova University M,O*†
Virginia Commonwealth University M,D,O*†
Wichita State University M*†
Wright State University M*
Xavier University M*

NURSING EDUCATION

Barry University M*†
Bellarmine University M
Bowie State University M
The Catholic University of America M,D*†
Clarke College M,O
Clarkson College M
The College of New Rochelle M,O†
Concordia University Wisconsin M
Duquesne University M*†
Eastern Michigan University M*
Eastern Washington University M†
Florida State University M*†
Graceland University M,O
Indiana Wesleyan University M,O*
Jewish Hospital College of Nursing and Allied Health M
Kent State University M*
La Salle University M,O
Lewis University M,O
Midwestern State University M
Minnesota State University, Mankato M
Minnesota State University, Moorhead M
Molloy College M,O
Mountain State University M†
Mount Saint Mary College M
New York University M,O*†
Rivier College M*†
Saginaw Valley State University M
San Francisco State University M
San Jose State University M*
Seton Hall University M*†
Southern Connecticut State University M†
Southern University and Agricultural and Mechanical College M,D,O*
Teachers College Columbia University M,D*
Texas Tech University Health Sciences Center M,O*
University of Central Florida M*†
University of Connecticut M,D*†
University of Hartford M*
University of Mary M
University of Maryland M,D*†
University of Minnesota, Twin Cities Campus M*
University of Missouri–Kansas City M,D*†
University of Northern Colorado M†
University of Pittsburgh M*†
University of Portland M,O
University of Puerto Rico, Medical Sciences Campus M*
University of Rhode Island M,D*
The University of Tampa M
The University of Tennessee at Chattanooga M
The University of Texas at Arlington M*†
Villanova University M,O*†
Wayne State University O*
West Chester University of Pennsylvania M*†
Wichita State University M*†

NUTRITION

Andrews University M
Arizona State University East M
Auburn University M,D*†
Bastyr University M*
Boston University P,M,D,O*†
Bowling Green State University M*†
Brigham Young University M*
Brooklyn College of the City University of New York M†
California State Polytechnic University, Pomona M*
California State University, Chico M
California State University, Long Beach M
California State University, Los Angeles M
Case Western Reserve University M,D*†
Central Michigan University M†
Central Washington University M†
Chapman University M*†
College of Saint Elizabeth M,O
Colorado State University M,D*
Columbia University M,D*†
Cornell University M,D*
Drexel University M,D*†
D'Youville College M†
East Carolina University M*†
Eastern Illinois University M†
Eastern Kentucky University M
East Tennessee State University M†
Emory University D*†
Finch University of Health Sciences/The Chicago Medical School M*
Florida International University M,D*†
Florida State University M,D*†
Framingham State College M*
Georgia State University M*
Harvard University D*†
Howard University M,D*
Hunter College of the City University of New York M†
Immaculata University M†
Indiana State University M*†
Indiana University of Pennsylvania M*†
Indiana University–Purdue University Indianapolis M*
Iowa State University of Science and Technology M,D*†
Johns Hopkins University M,D*†
Kansas State University M,D*†
Kent State University M*
Lehman College of the City University of New York M
Loma Linda University M,D*
Long Island University, C.W. Post Campus M,O*†
Louisiana Tech University M*
Marywood University M*†
McGill University M,D*
Meredith College M
Michigan State University M,D*†
Middle Tennessee State University M*
Montclair State University M†
Mount Mary College M
Mount Saint Vincent University M
New York Institute of Technology M*†
New York University M,D*†
North Carolina Agricultural and Technical State University M*
North Carolina State University M,D*
Northern Illinois University M*†
The Ohio State University M,D*
Ohio University M*
Oklahoma State University M,D*†
Oregon State University M,D*
The Pennsylvania State University University Park Campus M,D*†
Purdue University M,D*
Rush University M*
Rutgers, The State University of New Jersey, New Brunswick M,D*
Sage Graduate School M†
Saint Louis University M*†
San Diego State University M*
San Jose State University M*
Simmons College M,O*
South Carolina State University M
Southeast Missouri State University M
Southern Illinois University Carbondale M*†
Syracuse University M*
Texas A&M University M,D*
Texas Southern University M†
Texas Tech University M,D*†
Texas Woman's University M,D*†
Tufts University M,D*†
Tulane University M*†
Tuskegee University M
Université de Moncton M
Université de Montréal M,D
Université Laval M,D†
University at Buffalo, The State University of New York M*†
The University of Akron M†
The University of Alabama M*
The University of Alabama at Birmingham M,D,O*†
The University of Arizona M,D,O*
University of Arkansas for Medical Sciences M*
University of Bridgeport M*†
The University of British Columbia M,D*
University of California, Berkeley M,D*
University of California, Davis M,D*†
University of Central Oklahoma M
University of Chicago D*
University of Cincinnati M*
University of Connecticut M,D*†
University of Delaware M*†
University of Florida M,D*†
University of Georgia M,D*†
University of Guelph M,D
University of Hawaii at Manoa M*
University of Illinois at Chicago M,D*
University of Illinois at Urbana–Champaign M,D*
University of Kansas M*
University of Kentucky D*
University of Maine M,D*
University of Manitoba M,D*
University of Maryland, College Park M,D*
University of Massachusetts Amherst M*†
University of Medicine and Dentistry of New Jersey M,D,O*
The University of Memphis M*†
University of Michigan M*
University of Minnesota, Twin Cities Campus M,D*
University of Missouri–Columbia M,D*
University of Nebraska–Lincoln M,D*†
University of Nevada, Reno M*
University of New Hampshire M*†
University of New Haven M*†
University of New Mexico M*†
The University of North Carolina at Chapel Hill M,D*†
The University of North Carolina at Greensboro M,D†
University of North Florida M,O
University of Oklahoma Health Sciences Center M*
University of Puerto Rico, Medical Sciences Campus M,D*
University of Puerto Rico, Río Piedras M*
University of Rhode Island M,D*
University of Southern California M*†
University of Southern Mississippi M,D
The University of Tennessee M*†
The University of Tennessee at Martin M
The University of Texas at Austin M,D*
University of the Incarnate Word M†
University of Toronto M,D*
University of Utah M*
University of Vermont M*†
University of Washington M,D*
University of Wisconsin–Madison M,D*
University of Wisconsin–Stevens Point M
University of Wisconsin–Stout M
University of Wyoming M*†
Utah State University M,D*
Virginia Polytechnic Institute and State University M,D*
Washington State University M,D*
Washington State University Spokane M†
Wayne State University M,D,O*
West Virginia University M,D*
Winthrop University M

OCCUPATIONAL HEALTH NURSING

Capital University M
University of Cincinnati M,D*
University of Massachusetts Lowell M*†
University of Medicine and Dentistry of New Jersey M*
University of Michigan M*
University of Minnesota, Twin Cities Campus M,D*
The University of North Carolina at Chapel Hill M,D*†
University of Pennsylvania M*†
Vanderbilt University M,D*

OCCUPATIONAL THERAPY

Alvernia College M
Barry University M*†
Belmont University M
Boston University M,D,O*†
Chatham College M
Cleveland State University M*†
College Misericordia M
College of St. Catherine M†
The College of St. Scholastica M
Colorado State University M*
Columbia University M*†

Concordia University Wisconsin M
Creighton University D*
Dalhousie University M*
Dominican College M†
Duquesne University M,D*†
D'Youville College M†
East Carolina University M*†
Eastern Kentucky University M
Eastern Michigan University M*
Florida International University M*†
Gannon University M
Governors State University M
Grand Valley State University M†
Idaho State University M*
Ithaca College M†
Kean University M*†
Kirksville College of Osteopathic Medicine M,D
Maryville University of Saint Louis M
McMaster University M
Medical College of Georgia M*
Medical College of Ohio M*
Medical University of South Carolina M*
Mercy College M*
Midwestern University, Downers Grove Campus M*
Midwestern University, Glendale Campus M*
Milligan College M
Mount Mary College M
New York Institute of Technology M*†
New York University M,D*†
Nova Southeastern University M,D*
Pacific University M
Philadelphia University M
The Richard Stockton College of New Jersey M*
Rockhurst University M
Rush University M*
Sacred Heart University M*†
St. Ambrose University M
Saint Francis University M*
Samuel Merritt College M
San Jose State University M*
Seton Hall University M*†
Shenandoah University M
Springfield College M,O†
Temple University M*†
Texas Tech University Health Sciences Center M*
Texas Woman's University M,D*†
Thomas Jefferson University M*
Touro College M
Towson University M†
Tufts University M,O*†
University at Buffalo, The State University of New York M*†
The University of Alabama at Birmingham M*†
University of Alberta M*
University of Central Arkansas M
The University of Findlay M
University of Florida M*†
University of Illinois at Chicago M*
University of Indianapolis M
University of Kansas M*
University of Mary M
University of New England M*
University of New Hampshire M*†
University of New Mexico M*†
The University of North Carolina at Chapel Hill M,D*†
University of North Dakota M*
University of Puget Sound M
University of St. Augustine for Health Sciences M,D†
The University of Scranton M†
The University of South Dakota M†
University of Southern California M,D*†
University of Southern Indiana M
University of Southern Maine M
University of Utah M*
University of Washington M*
The University of Western Ontario M*
University of Wisconsin–Milwaukee M
Virginia Commonwealth University M*†
Washington University in St. Louis M,D*†
Wayne State University M*
Western Michigan University M*†
West Virginia University M*
Worcester State College M

OCEAN ENGINEERING

Florida Atlantic University M,D*
Florida Atlantic University, Ft. Lauderdale Campus M,D
Florida Institute of Technology M,D*†
Massachusetts Institute of Technology M,D,O*
Memorial University of Newfoundland M,D†
Oregon State University M*
Stevens Institute of Technology M,D*†
Texas A&M University M,D*
University of California, Berkeley M,D*
University of California, San Diego M,D*
University of Connecticut M,D*†
University of Delaware M,D*†
University of Florida M,D,O*†
University of Hawaii at Manoa M,D*
University of Miami M,D*†
University of Michigan M,D,O*
University of New Hampshire M,D*†
University of Rhode Island M,D*
University of Southern California M*†
Virginia Polytechnic Institute and State University M*

OCEANOGRAPHY

Columbia University M,D*†
Cornell University D*
Dalhousie University M,D*
Florida Institute of Technology M,D*†
Florida State University M,D*†
Johns Hopkins University M,D*†
Louisiana State University and Agricultural and Mechanical College M,D*
Massachusetts Institute of Technology M,D,O*
McGill University M,D*
Memorial University of Newfoundland M,D†
Naval Postgraduate School M,D
North Carolina State University M,D*
Nova Southeastern University M,D*
Old Dominion University M,D*†
Oregon State University M,D*
Princeton University D*
Rutgers, The State University of New Jersey, New Brunswick M,D*
Stony Brook University, State University of New York M,D,O*†
Texas A&M University M,D*
Université du Québec à Rimouski M,D
Université Laval D†
University of Alaska Fairbanks M,D*
The University of British Columbia M,D*
University of California, San Diego M,D*
University of Connecticut M,D*†
University of Delaware M,D*†
University of Georgia M,D*†
University of Hawaii at Manoa M,D*
University of Maine M,D*
University of Miami M,D*†
University of Michigan M,D*
University of New Hampshire M,D*†
University of Puerto Rico, Mayagüez Campus M,D*
University of Rhode Island M,D*
University of Southern California M,D*†
University of South Florida M,D*†
University of Victoria M,D
University of Washington M,D*
University of Wisconsin–Madison M,D*
Yale University D*

ONCOLOGY NURSING

Case Western Reserve University M*†
Columbia University M,O*†
Duke University M,O*†
Emory University M*†
Loyola University Chicago M*†
University of Delaware M,O*†
University of Minnesota, Twin Cities Campus M*
University of Pennsylvania M*†

OPERATIONS RESEARCH

Air Force Institute of Technology M,D*
Bernard M. Baruch College of the City University of New York M*
California State University, Fullerton M
California State University, Hayward M
Carnegie Mellon University D*
Case Western Reserve University M,D*†
Claremont Graduate University M,D*
Clemson University M,D*
The College of William and Mary M*†
Columbia University M,D,O*†
Cornell University M,D*
École Polytechnique de Montréal M,D,O
Florida Institute of Technology M,D*†
George Mason University M*†
Georgia Institute of Technology M*
Georgia State University M,D*
Idaho State University M,D*
Indiana University–Purdue University Fort Wayne M
Iowa State University of Science and Technology M,D*†
Johns Hopkins University M,D*†
Kansas State University M,D*†
Kettering University M
Louisiana Tech University M,D*
Massachusetts Institute of Technology M,D*
Miami University M*†
Michigan State University M,D*†
Naval Postgraduate School M,D
New Mexico Institute of Mining and Technology M†
New York University M,D,O*†
North Carolina State University M,D*
North Dakota State University M,D†
Northeastern University M,D*†
Northwestern University M,D*
Old Dominion University M*†
Oregon State University M,D*
Princeton University M,D*
Purdue University M,D*
Rensselaer Polytechnic Institute M,D*†
Rutgers, The State University of New Jersey, New Brunswick D*
St. Mary's University of San Antonio M
Southern Methodist University M,D*†
Temple University M,D*†
The University of Alabama in Huntsville M*
University of Arkansas M*
University of California, Berkeley M,D*
University of California, Los Angeles M,D*
University of Central Florida M,D,O*†
University of Delaware M,D*†
University of Florida M,D,O*†
University of Illinois at Chicago D*
The University of Iowa M,D*
University of Massachusetts Amherst M,D*†
University of Miami M,D*†
University of Michigan M,D,O*
University of New Haven M*†
The University of North Carolina at Chapel Hill M,D*†
University of Southern California M*†
The University of Texas at Austin M,D*
University of Waterloo M,D
Virginia Commonwealth University M*†
Virginia Polytechnic Institute and State University M,D*
Wayne State University M,D*
Western Michigan University M*†

OPTICAL SCIENCES

Air Force Institute of Technology M,D*
Alabama Agricultural and Mechanical University M,D
Cleveland State University M*†
Columbia University M,D,O*†
École Polytechnique de Montréal M,D,O
Indiana University Bloomington M,D*
The Ohio State University M,D*
Rochester Institute of Technology M,D*†
Rose-Hulman Institute of Technology M*
Tufts University O*†
The University of Alabama in Huntsville D*
The University of Arizona M,D*
University of Central Florida M,D,O*†
University of Colorado at Boulder M,D*
University of Dayton M,D*†
University of Maryland, Baltimore County M,D*†
University of Massachusetts Lowell M,D*†
University of New Mexico M,D*†
University of Rochester M,D*

OPTOMETRY

Ferris State University P
Illinois College of Optometry P
Indiana University Bloomington P*
Inter American University of Puerto Rico School of Optometry P
The New England College of Optometry P*
Northeastern State University P
Nova Southeastern University P*
The Ohio State University P*
Pacific University P
Pennsylvania College of Optometry P
Southern California College of Optometry P
Southern College of Optometry P
State University of New York College of Optometry P
Université de Montréal P
The University of Alabama at Birmingham P*†
University of California, Berkeley P*
University of Houston P*
University of Missouri–St. Louis P†
University of Waterloo P,M,D

ORAL AND DENTAL SCIENCES

Boston University M,D*†
Case Western Reserve University M,O*†
Columbia University M*†
Dalhousie University *
The George Washington University M*†
Harvard University M,D,O*†
Howard University P,O*
Idaho State University O*
Indiana University–Purdue University Indianapolis M,D*
Loma Linda University M,O*
Marquette University M*†
McGill University M,D*
Medical College of Georgia M,D*
Medical College of Ohio M*
Medical University of South Carolina M*
New York University M,D,O*†
The Ohio State University M,D*
Oregon Health & Science University M,O*
Saint Louis University M*†
Stony Brook University, State University of New York P,D,O*†
Temple University M,O*†
Texas A&M University System Health Science Center P,M,D,O*
Tufts University M,O*†
Université de Montréal M,O
Université Laval M,O†
University at Buffalo, The State University of New York M,D,O*†
The University of Alabama at Birmingham M*†
University of Alberta P,M,D,O*
The University of British Columbia M,D,O*
University of California, Los Angeles M,D*
University of California, San Francisco M,D*
University of Connecticut M*†
University of Connecticut Health Center M,D*
University of Detroit Mercy M,O*
University of Florida M,D,O*†
University of Illinois at Chicago M*
The University of Iowa M,D,O*
University of Kentucky M*
University of Louisville M*†
University of Manitoba M,D*
University of Maryland M,D*†
University of Medicine and Dentistry of New Jersey P,M,O*
University of Michigan M,D,O*
University of Minnesota, Twin Cities Campus M,D*
University of Missouri–Kansas City M,D*†
The University of North Carolina at Chapel Hill M,D*†
University of Oklahoma Health Sciences Center M*
University of Pittsburgh M,O*†
University of Puerto Rico, Medical Sciences Campus M,O*
University of Rochester M*
University of Southern California M,D*†
The University of Texas Health Science Center at Houston M*
The University of Texas Health Science Center at San Antonio M,O*
University of the Pacific M*
University of Toronto M,D*
University of Washington M,D*
The University of Western Ontario M*
West Virginia University M*

ORGANIC CHEMISTRY

Boston College M,D*†

*P—first professional degree; M—master's degree; D—doctorate; O—other advanced degree; *full description and/or announcement in Book 2, 3, 4, 5, or 6; †full description in this book*

Brandeis University M,D*†
Brigham Young University M,D*
California State University, Fullerton M
California State University, Los Angeles M
Case Western Reserve University M,D*†
Clark Atlanta University M,D
Clarkson University M,D*
Cleveland State University M,D*†
Columbia University M,D*†
Cornell University D*
Florida State University M,D*†
Georgetown University M,D*
The George Washington University M,D*†
Harvard University M,D*†
Howard University M,D*
Illinois Institute of Technology M,D*†
Instituto Tecnológico y de Estudios Superiores de Monterrey, Campus Monterrey M,D
Kansas State University M,D*†
Kent State University M,D*
Marquette University M,D*†
Massachusetts Institute of Technology D*
McMaster University M,D
Miami University M,D*†
Michigan State University M,D*†
Northeastern University M,D*†
Old Dominion University M*†
Oregon State University M,D*
Purdue University M,D*
Rensselaer Polytechnic Institute M,D*†
Rice University M,D*
Rutgers, The State University of New Jersey, Newark M,D*†
Rutgers, The State University of New Jersey, New Brunswick M,D*
San Jose State University M*
Seton Hall University M,D*†
South Dakota State University M,D*
Southern University and Agricultural and Mechanical College M*
State University of New York at Binghamton M,D*†
State University of New York College of Environmental Science and Forestry M,D
Stevens Institute of Technology M,D,O*†
Tufts University M,D*†
University of Calgary M,D*
University of Cincinnati M,D*
University of Georgia M,D*†
University of Louisville M,D*†
University of Maryland, College Park M,D*
University of Miami M,D*†
University of Michigan D*
University of Missouri–Columbia M,D*
University of Missouri–Kansas City M,D*†
University of Missouri–St. Louis M,D†
The University of Montana–Missoula M,D*†
University of Nebraska–Lincoln M,D*†
University of Notre Dame M,D*†
University of Regina M,D
University of Southern Mississippi M,D
University of South Florida M,D*†
The University of Tennessee M,D*†
The University of Texas at Austin M,D*
University of Toledo M,D*†
Wake Forest University M,D*†
Washington State University M,D*
Washington University in St. Louis D*†
Wesleyan University M,D*
West Virginia University M,D*
Yale University D*

ORGANIZATIONAL BEHAVIOR

Benedictine University M†
Bernard M. Baruch College of the City University of New York M,D*
Boston College D*†
Boston University M,D,O*†
Brigham Young University M*
California Lutheran University M
Carnegie Mellon University D*
Case Western Reserve University M,D*†
Columbia College (SC) M,O
Cornell University M,D*
Drexel University M,D,O*†
Fairleigh Dickinson University, College at Florham M*†
George Mason University M*†
The George Washington University M,D*†
Graduate School and University Center of the City University of New York D*†
Harvard University D*†
Indiana University Bloomington D*
John Jay College of Criminal Justice of the City University of New York M,D*
The Leadership Institute of Seattle M*
Michigan State University M,D*†
Northwestern University D*
Phillips Graduate Institute M
Polytechnic University, Brooklyn Campus M*
Polytechnic University, Long Island Graduate Center M
Polytechnic University, Westchester Graduate Center M
Purdue University M,D*
Saybrook Graduate School and Research Center M,D
Silver Lake College M
Syracuse University D*
Universidad de las Americas, A.C. M
Université de Sherbrooke M
The University of British Columbia D*
University of California, Berkeley D*
University of Hartford M*
The University of North Carolina at Chapel Hill D*†
University of Pennsylvania M*†
University of Saskatchewan M

ORGANIZATIONAL MANAGEMENT

American International College M*
American University M*†
Antioch University Los Angeles M
Antioch University Santa Barbara M
Antioch University Seattle M†
Athabasca University M
Azusa Pacific University M*†
Benedictine University D†
Bernard M. Baruch College of the City University of New York M,D*
Bethel College (MN) M
Biola University M
Boston College D*†
Bowling Green State University M*†
Briercrest Biblical Seminary M
Cabrini College M
Capella University M,D
Cardean University M†
Carnegie Mellon University D*
Charleston Southern University M
City University M,O†
College Misericordia M
College of Mount St. Joseph M†
College of St. Catherine M†
Colorado Technical University M,D
Colorado Technical University Sioux Falls Campus M
Dallas Baptist University M
Defiance College M
Dominican University M*
Eastern Connecticut State University M
Eastern Michigan University M*
Endicott College M
Fielding Graduate Institute M,D
Geneva College M*
George Fox University M†
George Mason University M*†
The George Washington University M*†
Gonzaga University M
Hawai'i Pacific University M*†
Immaculata University M†
John F. Kennedy University M,O*†
The Leadership Institute of Seattle M*
Lewis University M
Loyola University Chicago M*†
Manhattanville College M*†
Marian College of Fond du Lac M
Marymount University M,O†
Mercy College M*
Mercyhurst College M,O
Metropolitan State University M
Newman University M
New School University M*†
Northwestern University D*
Palm Beach Atlantic University M
Pepperdine University M*†
Pfeiffer University M
Philadelphia Biblical University M
Regent University M,D,O†
Regis College (MA) M
Regis University M,O*†
Royal Roads University M
Rutgers, The State University of New Jersey, Newark M*†
St. Ambrose University M
St. Edward's University M
Saybrook Graduate School and Research Center M,D
Spring Arbor University M
State University of New York at Albany D*†
Trevecca Nazarene University M
Université Laval M,O†
University of Alberta D*
University of Colorado at Boulder M,D*
University of Colorado at Colorado Springs M*
University of La Verne M,D,O*
University of Medicine and Dentistry of New Jersey M*
University of North Texas M,D*†
University of Pennsylvania M*†
University of Phoenix-Chicago Campus M
University of Phoenix–Colorado Campus M
University of Phoenix–Dallas Campus M
University of Phoenix–Fort Lauderdale Campus M
University of Phoenix–Hawaii Campus M
University of Phoenix–Houston Campus M
University of Phoenix–Jacksonville Campus M
University of Phoenix-Kansas City Campus M
University of Phoenix–Louisiana Campus M
University of Phoenix–Maryland Campus M
University of Phoenix–Metro Detroit Campus M
University of Phoenix–Nevada Campus M
University of Phoenix–New Mexico Campus M
University of Phoenix–Northern California Campus M
University of Phoenix–Oklahoma City Campus M
University of Phoenix–Oregon Campus M
University of Phoenix–Orlando Campus M
University of Phoenix–Phoenix Campus M
University of Phoenix–Pittsburgh Campus M
University of Phoenix–Sacramento Campus M
University of Phoenix–St. Louis Campus M
University of Phoenix–San Diego Campus M
University of Phoenix–Southern Arizona Campus M
University of Phoenix–Southern California Campus M
University of Phoenix–Southern Colorado Campus M
University of Phoenix–Tampa Campus M
University of Phoenix–Tulsa Campus M
University of Phoenix–Utah Campus M
University of Phoenix-Vancouver Campus M
University of Phoenix–Washington Campus M
University of Phoenix–West Michigan Campus M
University of St. Thomas (MN) M,D,O*†
University of San Francisco M*†
The University of Scranton M†
The University of Tennessee at Chattanooga M
University of the Incarnate Word M,D†
Upper Iowa University M
Vanderbilt University M,D*

OSTEOPATHIC MEDICINE

Des Moines University Osteopathic Medical Center P*
Kirksville College of Osteopathic Medicine P
Lake Erie College of Osteopathic Medicine P,O
Michigan State University P*†
Midwestern University, Downers Grove Campus P*
Midwestern University, Glendale Campus P*
New York Institute of Technology P*†
Nova Southeastern University P,M*
Ohio University P*
Oklahoma State University Center for Health Sciences P
Philadelphia College of Osteopathic Medicine P*
Pikeville College P
The University of Health Sciences P
University of Medicine and Dentistry of New Jersey P*
University of New England P*
University of North Texas Health Science Center at Fort Worth P,M*
Western University of Health Sciences P
West Virginia School of Osteopathic Medicine P

PAPER AND PULP ENGINEERING

Georgia Institute of Technology O*
Institute of Paper Science and Technology M,D*
Miami University M*†
North Carolina State University M,D*
Oregon State University M,D*
State University of New York College of Environmental Science and Forestry M,D
Université du Québec à Trois-Rivières M,D
The University of British Columbia M*
University of Washington M,D*
Western Michigan University M,D*†

PARASITOLOGY

Louisiana State University Health Sciences Center M,D*
McGill University M,D,O*
New York University M,D*†
Purdue University M,D*
Texas A&M University M,D*
Tulane University M,D,O*†
University of Georgia M,D*†
University of Notre Dame M,D*†
University of Pennsylvania D*†
University of Prince Edward Island M,D
University of Washington M,D*
West Virginia University M,D*
Yale University D*

PASTORAL MINISTRY AND COUNSELING

Abilene Christian University M,D
Acadia University P,M,D
Alliance Theological Seminary P,M
American Christian College and Seminary P,D
Aquinas Institute of Theology P,M,D,O
Argosy University-Sarasota M,D,O*†
Asbury Theological Seminary P,M,D,O
Ashland University P,M,D
Assemblies of God Theological Seminary P,M,D
Athenaeum of Ohio P,M,O
Austin Presbyterian Theological Seminary P,M,D
Azusa Pacific University P,M,D*†
Baptist Bible College P,M
Baptist Bible College of Pennsylvania P,M,D
Baptist Theological Seminary at Richmond P,D
Barry University M,D*†
Bayamón Central University P,M
Bethel College (IN) M
Bethel Seminary P,M,D,O
Bethesda Christian University P,M
Biblical Theological Seminary P,M,D
Boston College M,D*†
Briercrest Biblical Seminary P,M
Caldwell College M
Calvary Bible College and Theological Seminary P,M,D
Canadian Theological Seminary P,M,O
Catholic Theological Union at Chicago P,M,D,O
Chaminade University of Honolulu M*
Chicago Theological Seminary P,M,D
Christian Theological Seminary P,M,D
Christ the King Seminary P,M
Church of God Theological Seminary P,M
Cincinnati Bible College and Seminary M
Claremont School of Theology D
Collège Dominicain de Philosophie et de Théologie M
College of Mount St. Joseph M†
Columbia International University P,M,D,O
Concordia University (MN) M
The Criswell College P,M
Dallas Theological Seminary M,D,O
Denver Seminary P,M,D,O
Eastern Baptist Theological Seminary D
Eastern Mennonite University M
Ecumenical Theological Seminary D
Evangelical School of Theology P,M,O

Institution	Degrees
Faith Baptist Bible College and Theological Seminary	P,M,D
Fordham University	M,D,O*†
Franciscan School of Theology	P,M,O
Freed-Hardeman University	M
Gannon University	M,O
Gardner-Webb University	P,D
Garrett-Evangelical Theological Seminary	P,M,D
George Fox University	P,M,D†
Golden Gate Baptist Theological Seminary	P,M,D,O
Gonzaga University	P,M
Gordon-Conwell Theological Seminary	P,M,D
Grace Theological Seminary	P,M,D,O
Grace University	M
Grand Rapids Baptist Seminary of Cornerstone University	P,M,D
Greenville College	M
Harding University	M
Hardin-Simmons University	M
Hartford Seminary	M,D,O
Holy Names College	M,O
Hope International University	M
Houston Baptist University	M
Houston Graduate School of Theology	P,M,D
Huntington College	M
Iliff School of Theology	P,M,D
International Baptist College	M,D
International College and Graduate School	P,M,D
Iona College	M,O*†
Jewish University of America	M,D
Lancaster Bible College	M
La Salle University	M
Lincoln Christian Seminary	P,M
Loyola College in Maryland	M,D,O
Loyola Marymount University	M†
Loyola University Chicago	M*†
Lutheran School of Theology at Chicago	P,M,D
Lutheran Theological Seminary	P,M
The Lutheran Theological Seminary at Philadelphia	P,M,D,O
Luther Rice Bible College and Seminary	P,M,D
Malone College	M†
Maple Springs Baptist Bible College and Seminary	P,M,D,O
Martin University	M
Marygrove College	M
The Master's College and Seminary	P,M,D
McCormick Theological Seminary	P,M,D,O
Meadville Lombard Theological School	P,D
Mennonite Brethren Biblical Seminary	M
Midwestern Baptist Theological Seminary	P,M,D
Multnomah Bible College and Biblical Seminary	M
Neumann College	M,O
New Brunswick Theological Seminary	D
New Orleans Baptist Theological Seminary	P,M,D
North American Baptist Seminary	P,M
Northern Baptist Theological Seminary	P,M,D
Northwest Graduate School of the Ministry	M,D
Notre Dame College (OH)	M,O
Oblate School of Theology	P,M,D
Oklahoma Christian University	M
Olivet Nazarene University	M
Oral Roberts University	P,M,D
Philadelphia Biblical University	M
Phillips Theological Seminary	D
Piedmont Baptist College	M
Providence College	M*
Providence College and Theological Seminary	P,M,D,O
Reformed Theological Seminary (NC)	P,M,D
Reformed Theological Seminary (MS)	P,M,D,O
Reformed Theological Seminary (FL)	P,M,D
Regis College (Canada)	P,M,D,O
Sacred Heart Major Seminary	P,M
St. Ambrose University	M
Saint Francis Seminary	P,M
Saint John's University (MN)	P,M
St. John's University (NY)	P,M,O*†
Saint Joseph College	M,O
Saint Joseph's College (ME)	M
Saint Mary's University of Minnesota	M,O
St. Mary's University of San Antonio	M
Saint Paul University	M,D,O
Saints Cyril and Methodius Seminary	P,M
St. Stephen's College	M,D
St. Thomas University	M,O†
Santa Clara University	M*
Seattle University	M*†
Seton Hall University	P,M,O*†
Southern Baptist Theological Seminary	P,M,D
Southern Evangelical Seminary	P,M,O
Southern Wesleyan University	M
Southwestern Christian University	M
Spalding University	M†
Texas Christian University	P,M,D,O*
Trinity International University	P,M,D,O
Trinity Western University	P,M
United Theological Seminary of the Twin Cities	M,D,O
Université de Montréal	M,D,O
University of Dallas	M*
University of Dayton	M,D*†
University of Portland	M
University of Puget Sound	M
University of St. Thomas (MN)	M,D*†
University of San Diego	M*†
University of San Francisco	M*†
University of Trinity College	P,M,D,O
Wake Forest University	M*†
Western Seminary	P,M,D,O
Westminster Theological Seminary	P,M,D,O
Wilfrid Laurier University	P,M,D
Winebrenner Theological Seminary	P,M,D,O
Xavier University of Louisiana	M

PATHOBIOLOGY

Institution	Degrees
Auburn University	M*†
Brown University	M,D*
Columbia University	M,D*†
Drexel University	D*†
Johns Hopkins University	D*†
Kansas State University	M,D*†
Medical University of South Carolina	D*
The Ohio State University	M,D*
The Pennsylvania State University University Park Campus	M,D*†
Purdue University	M,D*
Texas A&M University	M,D*
Uniformed Services University of the Health Sciences	M,D*
The University of Arizona	M,D*
University of Cincinnati	D*
University of Connecticut	M,D*†
University of Guelph	M,D,O
University of Illinois at Urbana–Champaign	M,D*
University of Missouri–Columbia	M,D*
University of Rochester	*
University of Southern California	M,D*†
University of Toronto	M,D*
University of Washington	M,D*
University of Wyoming	M*†
Wake Forest University	M,D*†

PATHOLOGY

Institution	Degrees
Boston University	D*†
Brown University	M,D*
Case Western Reserve University	M,D*†
Colorado State University	M,D*
Columbia University	M,D*†
Dalhousie University	M*
Duke University	M,D*†
East Carolina University	D*†
Finch University of Health Sciences/The Chicago Medical School	M,D*
Georgetown University	M,D*
Harvard University	D*†
Indiana University–Purdue University Indianapolis	M,D*
Iowa State University of Science and Technology	M,D*†
Johns Hopkins University	D*†
Louisiana State University Health Sciences Center	M,D*
McGill University	M,D*
Medical College of Ohio	M*
Medical College of Wisconsin	M,D*
Medical University of South Carolina	M,D*
Michigan State University	M,D*†
Mount Sinai School of Medicine of New York University	D*
New York Medical College	M,D*
New York University	M,D*†
North Carolina State University	M,D*
The Ohio State University	M*
Oregon State University	M*
Purdue University	M,D*
Queen's University at Kingston	M,D
Quinnipiac University	M*†
Saint Louis University	D*†
State University of New York at Albany	M,D*†
Stony Brook University, State University of New York	M,D*†
Temple University	D*†
Texas A&M University	M,D*
Texas A&M University System Health Science Center	D*
Texas Tech University Health Sciences Center	M*
Thomas Jefferson University	D*
Uniformed Services University of the Health Sciences	M,D*
Université de Montréal	M,D,O
Université Laval	O†
University at Buffalo, The State University of New York	M,D*†
The University of Alabama at Birmingham	D*†
University of Alberta	M,D*
University of Arkansas for Medical Sciences	M*
The University of British Columbia	M,D*
University of California, Davis	M,D*†
University of California, Los Angeles	M,D*
University of California, San Diego	D*
University of California, San Francisco	D*
University of Chicago	D*
University of Cincinnati	D*
University of Colorado Health Sciences Center	D*
University of Florida	M,D*†
University of Georgia	M,D*†
University of Guelph	M,D,O
University of Illinois at Chicago	M,D*
The University of Iowa	M*
University of Kansas	M,D*
University of Manitoba	M*
University of Maryland	M,D*†
University of Medicine and Dentistry of New Jersey	M,D*
University of Michigan	D*
University of Mississippi Medical Center	M,D*
University of Nebraska Medical Center	M,D*
University of New Mexico	M,D*†
The University of North Carolina at Chapel Hill	D*†
University of Oklahoma Health Sciences Center	D*
University of Pittsburgh	M,D*†
University of Prince Edward Island	M,D
University of Rochester	M,D*
University of Saskatchewan	M,D
University of Southern California	M,D*†
University of South Florida	D*†
The University of Tennessee Health Science Center	M,D*
The University of Texas Health Science Center at Houston	M,D*
The University of Texas Medical Branch	D*
University of Utah	D*
University of Vermont	M*†
University of Washington	M,D*
The University of Western Ontario	M,D*
University of Wisconsin–Madison	D*
Vanderbilt University	D*
Virginia Commonwealth University	M,D*†
Washington State University	M,D*
Wayne State University	D*
Yale University	D*
Yeshiva University	D*

PEDIATRIC NURSING

Institution	Degrees
Bank Street College of Education	M*
Baylor University	M*†
Case Western Reserve University	M*†
The Catholic University of America	M,D*†
Columbia University	M,O*†
Duke University	M,O*†
Emory University	M*†
Georgia State University	M,D*
Gwynedd-Mercy College	M
Hunter College of the City University of New York	M,O†
Indiana University–Purdue University Indianapolis	M*
Johns Hopkins University	M,O*†
Kent State University	M*
Lehman College of the City University of New York	M
Loma Linda University	M*
Louisiana State University Health Sciences Center	M,D*
Loyola University Chicago	M*†
Marquette University	M,O*†
Medical University of South Carolina	M,O*
Molloy College	M,O
New York University	M,O*†
Northeastern University	M,O*†
Oregon Health & Science University	M,O*
Rush University	M,D*
Seton Hall University	M*†
Stony Brook University, State University of New York	M,O*†
Texas Tech University Health Sciences Center	M,O*
Texas Woman's University	M,D*†
University at Buffalo, The State University of New York	M,D,O*†
University of Central Florida	M*†
University of Delaware	M,O*†
University of Illinois at Chicago	M*
University of Maryland	M,D*†
University of Michigan	M*
University of Minnesota, Twin Cities Campus	M*
University of Missouri–Kansas City	M,D*†
University of Nevada, Las Vegas	M*†
University of Pennsylvania	M*†
University of Pittsburgh	M*†
University of San Diego	M,D,O*†
The University of Texas–Pan American	M
Vanderbilt University	M,D*
Villanova University	M,O*†
Virginia Commonwealth University	M,D,O*†
Wayne State University	M*
Wright State University	M*

PETROLEUM ENGINEERING

Institution	Degrees
Colorado School of Mines	M,D†
Louisiana State University and Agricultural and Mechanical College	M,D*
Montana Tech of The University of Montana	M
New Mexico Institute of Mining and Technology	M,D†
The Pennsylvania State University University Park Campus	M,D*†
Stanford University	M,D,O*
Texas A&M University	M,D*
Texas A&M University–Kingsville	M*†
Texas Tech University	M,D*†
University of Alaska Fairbanks	M*
University of Alberta	M,D*
University of Calgary	M,D*
University of California, Berkeley	M,D*
University of Houston	M,D*
University of Kansas	M,D*
University of Louisiana at Lafayette	M*
University of Missouri–Rolla	M,D*
University of Oklahoma	M,D*†
University of Pittsburgh	M,D*†
University of Regina	M,D
University of Southern California	M,D,O*†
The University of Texas at Austin	M,D*
University of Tulsa	M,D†
University of Utah	M,D*
University of Wyoming	M,D*†
West Virginia University	M,D*

PHARMACEUTICAL ADMINISTRATION

Institution	Degrees
Duquesne University	M*†
Fairleigh Dickinson University, Metropolitan Campus	M*†
Florida Agricultural and Mechanical University	M,D*
Idaho State University	P,M,D*
Long Island University, Brooklyn Campus	M*
The Ohio State University	M,D*
St. John's University (NY)	M*†
St. Louis College of Pharmacy	M
Seton Hall University	M,O*†
University of Florida	M,D*†
University of Georgia	M,D*†
University of Houston	P,M,D*
University of Illinois at Chicago	M,D*
University of Maryland	D*†
University of Michigan	M,D*
University of Minnesota, Twin Cities Campus	M,D*
University of Mississippi	M,D*
University of Rhode Island	M*
University of the Sciences in Philadelphia	M*
University of Toledo	M*†
University of Wisconsin–Madison	M,D*
West Virginia University	M,D*

*P—first professional degree; M—master's degree; D—doctorate; O—other advanced degree; *full description and/or announcement in Book 2, 3, 4, 5, or 6; †full description in this book*

PHARMACEUTICAL SCIENCES

Auburn University M,D*†
Butler University P,M
Campbell University P,M
Creighton University M,D*
Dalhousie University M,D*
Duquesne University M,D*†
Florida Agricultural and Mechanical University M,D*
Idaho State University M,D*
Long Island University, Brooklyn Campus M,D*
Long Island University, Westchester Graduate Campus M
Massachusetts College of Pharmacy and Health Sciences M,D*
Medical University of South Carolina D*
Memorial University of Newfoundland M,D†
Mercer University P,D
New Jersey Institute of Technology M
North Dakota State University M,D†
Northeastern University M,D*†
The Ohio State University M,D*
Oregon State University P,M,D*
Purdue University M,D*
Rush University M,D*
Rutgers, The State University of New Jersey, New Brunswick M,D*
St. John's University (NY) M,D*†
South Dakota State University M*
Temple University M,D*†
Texas Tech University Health Sciences Center M,D*
Université de Montréal M,D
Université Laval M,D,O†
University at Buffalo, The State University of New York M,D*†
University of Alberta M,D*
The University of Arizona M,D*
University of Arkansas for Medical Sciences P,M*
The University of British Columbia M,D*
University of California, San Francisco D*
University of Cincinnati M,D*
University of Colorado Health Sciences Center D*
University of Connecticut M,D*†
University of Georgia M,D*†
University of Houston P,M,D*
University of Illinois at Chicago M,D*
The University of Iowa M,D*
University of Kansas M*
University of Kentucky M,D*
University of Louisiana at Monroe P,M,D
University of Manitoba M,D*
University of Maryland D*†
University of Michigan M,D*
University of Minnesota, Twin Cities Campus M,D*
University of Mississippi M,D*
University of Missouri–Kansas City M*†
The University of Montana–Missoula M,D*†
University of Nebraska Medical Center M,D*
University of New Mexico M,D*†
The University of North Carolina at Chapel Hill M,D*†
University of Oklahoma Health Sciences Center M,D*
University of Pittsburgh M,D*†
University of Puerto Rico, Medical Sciences Campus P,M*
University of Rhode Island M,D*
University of Saskatchewan M,D
University of South Carolina M,D*†
University of Southern California M,D*†
The University of Tennessee Health Science Center M,D*
The University of Texas at Austin M,D*
University of the Pacific M,D*
University of the Sciences in Philadelphia M,D*
University of Toledo M*†
University of Toronto M,D*
University of Washington M,D*
University of Wisconsin–Madison M,D*
Virginia Commonwealth University P,M,D*†
Wayne State University M,D*
West Virginia University M,D*

PHARMACOLOGY

Albany Medical College M,D*
Alliant International University M*†
Auburn University M*†
Baylor College of Medicine D*
Boston University M,D*†
Brown University M,D*
Case Western Reserve University M,D*†
Columbia University M,D*†
Cornell University M,D*
Creighton University M,D*
Dalhousie University M,D*
Dartmouth College D*†
Drexel University M,D*†
Duke University D*†
Duquesne University M,D*†
East Carolina University D*†
East Tennessee State University M,D†
Emory University D*†
Finch University of Health Sciences/The Chicago Medical School M,D*
Florida Agricultural and Mechanical University M,D*
Georgetown University D*
The George Washington University D*†
Harvard University D*†
Howard University M,D*
Idaho State University M,D*
Indiana University Bloomington M,D*
Indiana University–Purdue University Indianapolis M,D*
Joan and Sanford I. Weill Medical College and Graduate School of Medical Sciences of Cornell University D*
Johns Hopkins University D*†
Kent State University M,D*
Loma Linda University M,D*
Long Island University, Brooklyn Campus M*
Louisiana State University Health Sciences Center M,D*
Loyola University Chicago M,D*†
Massachusetts College of Pharmacy and Health Sciences M,D*
Mayo Graduate School D*
McGill University M,D*
McMaster University M,D
Medical College of Georgia M,D*
Medical College of Ohio M*
Medical College of Wisconsin M,D*
Medical University of South Carolina M,D*
Meharry Medical College M,D
Michigan State University M,D*†
Mount Sinai School of Medicine of New York University D*
New York Medical College M,D*
New York University M,D*†
North Carolina State University M,D*
Northeastern University M,D*†
Northwestern University D*
Nova Southeastern University M*
The Ohio State University M,D*
Oregon Health & Science University D*
The Pennsylvania State University Milton S. Hershey Medical Center M,D*
Purdue University M,D*
Queen's University at Kingston M,D
Rush University M,D*
Rutgers, The State University of New Jersey, New Brunswick D*
St. John's University (NY) M,D*†
Saint Louis University D*†
Southern Illinois University Carbondale M,D*†
Stanford University D*
State University of New York Health Science Center at Brooklyn D*
State University of New York Upstate Medical University M,D*
Stony Brook University, State University of New York D*†
Temple University M,D*†
Texas A&M University System Health Science Center D*
Texas Tech University Health Sciences Center M,D*
Thomas Jefferson University M,D*
Tufts University D*†
Tulane University M,D*†
Uniformed Services University of the Health Sciences D*
Université de Montréal M,D
Université de Sherbrooke M,D
University at Buffalo, The State University of New York M,D*†
The University of Alabama at Birmingham D*†
University of Alberta M,D*
The University of Arizona M,D*
University of Arkansas for Medical Sciences M,D*
The University of British Columbia M,D*
University of California, Davis M,D*†
University of California, Irvine M,D*
University of California, Los Angeles M,D*
University of California, San Diego D*
University of California, San Francisco D*
University of Chicago D*
University of Cincinnati D*
University of Colorado Health Sciences Center D*
University of Connecticut M,D*†
University of Connecticut Health Center D*
University of Florida M,D*†
University of Georgia M,D*†
University of Guelph M,D
University of Hawaii at Manoa M,D*
University of Houston P,M,D*
University of Illinois at Chicago D*
The University of Iowa M,D*
University of Kansas M,D*
University of Kentucky D*
University of Louisville M,D*†
University of Manitoba M,D*
University of Maryland M,D*†
University of Massachusetts Worcester D*
University of Medicine and Dentistry of New Jersey M,D*
University of Miami D*†
University of Michigan D*
University of Minnesota, Duluth M,D*
University of Minnesota, Twin Cities Campus M,D*
University of Mississippi M,D*
University of Mississippi Medical Center M,D*
University of Missouri–Columbia M,D*
The University of Montana–Missoula M,D*†
University of Nebraska Medical Center M,D*
University of Nevada, Reno M,D*
The University of North Carolina at Chapel Hill D*†
University of North Dakota M,D*
University of North Texas Health Science Center at Fort Worth M,D*
University of Pennsylvania D*†
University of Pittsburgh D*†
University of Prince Edward Island M,D
University of Puerto Rico, Medical Sciences Campus M,D*
University of Rhode Island M,D*
University of Rochester M,D*
University of Saskatchewan M,D
University of South Alabama D*†
The University of South Dakota M,D†
University of Southern California M,D*†
University of South Florida D*†
The University of Tennessee Health Science Center M,D*
The University of Texas Health Science Center at Houston M,D*
The University of Texas Health Science Center at San Antonio D*
The University of Texas Medical Branch M,D*
The University of Texas Southwestern Medical Center at Dallas *
University of the Pacific M,D*
University of the Sciences in Philadelphia M,D*
University of Toledo M*†
University of Toronto M,D*
University of Utah M,D*
University of Vermont M,D*†
University of Virginia D*
University of Washington M,D*
The University of Western Ontario M,D*
University of Wisconsin–Madison M,D*
Vanderbilt University D*
Virginia Commonwealth University M,D,O*†
Wake Forest University D*†
Washington State University M,D*
Wayne State University M,D*
West Virginia University M,D*
Wright State University M*
Yale University D*
Yeshiva University D*

PHARMACY

Albany College of Pharmacy of Union University P
Auburn University P*†
Butler University P,M
Campbell University P,M
Creighton University P*
Drake University P*†
Duquesne University P*†
Ferris State University P
Florida Agricultural and Mechanical University P*
Howard University P*
Idaho State University P,M,D*
Lebanese American University P
Medical University of South Carolina P*
Mercer University P,D
Midwestern University, Downers Grove Campus P*
Midwestern University, Glendale Campus P*
Northeastern University P*†
Nova Southeastern University P*
Ohio Northern University P*
The Ohio State University P*
Oregon State University P,M,D*
Palm Beach Atlantic University P
Purdue University P*
Rutgers, The State University of New Jersey, New Brunswick P*
St. John's University (NY) P*†
St. Louis College of Pharmacy P
Samford University P
Shenandoah University P
South Dakota State University P*
Southwestern Oklahoma State University P
Temple University P*†
Texas Southern University P†
University at Buffalo, The State University of New York P*†
University of Alberta M,D*
The University of Arizona P,M,D*
University of Arkansas for Medical Sciences P,M*
The University of British Columbia P*
University of California, San Francisco P*
University of Cincinnati P*
University of Colorado Health Sciences Center P*
University of Florida P*†
University of Georgia P*†
University of Houston P,M,D*
University of Illinois at Chicago P*
The University of Iowa P*
University of Kentucky P*
University of Maryland P,D*†
University of Michigan P*
University of Minnesota, Twin Cities Campus P*
University of Mississippi P*
University of Missouri–Kansas City P*†
University of Nebraska Medical Center P*
University of New Mexico P*†
University of Oklahoma Health Sciences Center P*
University of Pittsburgh P*†
University of Puerto Rico, Medical Sciences Campus P,M*
University of Rhode Island P*
University of South Carolina P*†
University of Southern California P*†
The University of Tennessee Health Science Center P,M,D*
The University of Texas at Austin P*
University of the Pacific P*
University of the Sciences in Philadelphia P*
University of Toledo P*†
University of Utah P,M*
University of Washington P*
University of Wisconsin–Madison P*
Virginia Commonwealth University P*†
Washington State University P*
Washington State University Spokane P†
Wayne State University P,M*
Western University of Health Sciences P
West Virginia University P,M,D*
Wilkes University P
Xavier University of Louisiana P

PHILANTHROPIC STUDIES

Indiana University–Purdue University Indianapolis M*
Saint Mary's University of Minnesota M
Suffolk University M*

PHILOSOPHY

American University M*†
Arizona State University M*
Baylor University M*†
Boston College M,D*†
Boston University M,D*†
Bowling Green State University M,D*†
Brock University M
Brown University M,D*
California Institute of Integral Studies M,D*

- California State University, Long Beach M
- California State University, Los Angeles M
- Carleton University M
- Carnegie Mellon University M,D*
- The Catholic University of America M,D,O*†
- Claremont Graduate University M,D*
- Cleveland State University M*†
- Collège Dominicain de Philosophie et de Théologie M,D
- Colorado State University M*
- Columbia University M,D*†
- Concordia University (Canada) M*†
- Cornell University D*
- Dalhousie University M,D*
- DePaul University M,D*†
- Dominican School of Philosophy and Theology M
- Duke University D*†
- Duquesne University M,D*†
- Emory University D*†
- Florida State University M,D*†
- Fordham University M,D*†
- Franciscan University of Steubenville M
- Georgetown University M,D*
- The George Washington University M*†
- Georgia State University M*
- Gonzaga University M
- Graduate School and University Center of the City University of New York M,D*†
- Harvard University M,D*†
- Howard University M*
- Indiana University Bloomington M,D*
- Institute for Christian Studies M,D
- Johns Hopkins University M,D*†
- Kent State University M*
- Lakehead University M
- Lewis University M
- Louisiana State University and Agricultural and Mechanical College M*
- Loyola University Chicago M,D*†
- Marquette University M,D*†
- Massachusetts Institute of Technology D*
- McGill University M,D*
- McMaster University M,D
- Memorial University of Newfoundland M†
- Miami University M*†
- Michigan State University M,D*†
- Montclair State University M,D†
- New School University M,D*†
- New York University M,D*†
- Northern Illinois University M*†
- Northwestern University D*
- The Ohio State University M,D*
- Ohio University M*
- Oklahoma City University M
- Oklahoma State University M,D*†
- The Pennsylvania State University University Park Campus M,D*†
- Princeton University D*
- Purdue University M,D*
- Queen's University at Kingston M,D
- Rensselaer Polytechnic Institute M*†
- Rice University M,D*
- Rutgers, The State University of New Jersey, New Brunswick D*
- Saint Louis University M,D*†
- Saint Mary's University M
- San Diego State University M*
- San Francisco State University M,O
- San Jose State University M,O*
- Simon Fraser University M,D
- Southeastern Baptist Theological Seminary P,M,D
- Southern Illinois University Carbondale M,D*†
- Stanford University M,D*
- State University of New York at Albany M,D*†
- State University of New York at Binghamton M,D*†
- Stony Brook University, State University of New York M,D,O*†
- Syracuse University M,D*
- Temple University M,D*†
- Texas A&M University M,D*
- Texas Tech University M*†
- Tufts University M*†
- Tulane University M,D*†
- Université de Montréal M,D
- Université de Sherbrooke M,D,O
- Université du Québec à Montréal M,D
- Université du Québec à Trois-Rivières M,D
- Université Laval †
- University at Buffalo, The State University of New York M,D*†
- University of Alberta M,D*
- The University of Arizona M,D*
- University of Arkansas M,D*
- The University of British Columbia M,D*
- University of Calgary M,D*
- University of California, Berkeley D*
- University of California, Davis M,D*†
- University of California, Irvine M,D*
- University of California, Los Angeles M,D*
- University of California, Riverside M,D*
- University of California, San Diego D*
- University of California, Santa Barbara D*
- University of Chicago M,D*
- University of Cincinnati M,D*
- University of Colorado at Boulder M,D*
- University of Connecticut M,D*†
- University of Dallas M,D*
- University of Denver M*†
- University of Florida M,D*†
- University of Georgia M,D*†
- University of Guelph M,D
- University of Hawaii at Manoa M,D*
- University of Houston M*
- University of Illinois at Chicago M,D*
- University of Illinois at Urbana–Champaign M,D*
- The University of Iowa M,D*
- University of Kansas M,D*
- University of Kentucky M,D*
- The University of Lethbridge M,D
- University of Louisville M*†
- University of Manitoba M*
- University of Maryland, Baltimore County M,O*†
- University of Maryland, College Park M,D*
- University of Massachusetts Amherst M,D*†
- The University of Memphis M,D*†
- University of Miami M,D*†
- University of Michigan M,D*
- University of Minnesota, Twin Cities Campus M,D*
- University of Mississippi M*
- University of Missouri–Columbia M,D*
- University of Missouri–St. Louis M†
- The University of Montana–Missoula M*†
- University of Nebraska–Lincoln M,D*†
- University of Nevada, Reno M*
- University of New Brunswick Fredericton M
- University of New Mexico M,D*†
- The University of North Carolina at Chapel Hill M,D*†
- University of North Texas M*†
- University of Notre Dame D*†
- University of Oklahoma M,D*†
- University of Oregon M,D*
- University of Ottawa M,D*
- University of Pennsylvania M,D*†
- University of Pittsburgh M,D*†
- University of Puerto Rico, Río Piedras M*
- University of Regina M
- University of Rhode Island M*
- University of Rochester M,D*
- University of St. Thomas (TX) M,D
- University of Saskatchewan M
- University of South Carolina M,D*†
- University of Southern California M,D*†
- University of Southern Mississippi M
- University of South Florida M,D*†
- The University of Tennessee M,D*†
- The University of Texas at Austin M,D*
- University of Toledo M*†
- University of Toronto M,D*
- University of Utah M,D*
- University of Virginia M,D*
- University of Washington M,D*
- University of Waterloo M,D
- The University of Western Ontario M,D*
- University of Windsor M
- University of Wisconsin–Madison M,D*
- University of Wisconsin–Milwaukee M
- University of Wyoming M*†
- Vanderbilt University M,D*
- Villanova University M,D*†
- Virginia Polytechnic Institute and State University M*
- Washington University in St. Louis M,D*†
- Wayne State University M,D*
- West Chester University of Pennsylvania M*†
- Western Kentucky University M†
- Western Michigan University M*†
- Wilfrid Laurier University D
- Yale University D*
- York University M,D*

PHOTOGRAPHY

- Academy of Art College M†
- Barry University M*†
- Bradley University M†
- Brooklyn College of the City University of New York M,D†
- Brooks Institute of Photography M
- California College of Arts and Crafts M*
- California Institute of the Arts M,O*
- California State University, Fullerton M,O
- California State University, Los Angeles M
- Claremont Graduate University M*
- Columbia College Chicago M†
- Columbia University M*†
- Cornell University M*
- Cranbrook Academy of Art M*
- The George Washington University M*†
- Howard University M*
- Illinois Institute of Technology M,D*†
- Illinois State University M*†
- Indiana State University M*†
- Indiana University Bloomington M*
- James Madison University M
- Lamar University M*†
- Louisiana State University and Agricultural and Mechanical College M*
- Louisiana Tech University M*
- Maryland Institute College of Art M*
- Massachusetts College of Art M
- Memphis College of Art M*
- Mills College M*†
- Minneapolis College of Art and Design M,O*
- Ohio University M*
- Otis College of Art and Design M
- The Pennsylvania State University University Park Campus M*†
- Pratt Institute M*
- Rhode Island School of Design M
- Rochester Institute of Technology M*†
- San Francisco Art Institute M,O*
- San Jose State University M*
- Savannah College of Art and Design M*
- School of the Art Institute of Chicago M*
- School of Visual Arts M†
- Southern Methodist University M*†
- State University of New York at New Paltz M
- Syracuse University M*
- Temple University M*†
- The University of Alabama M*
- University of Colorado at Boulder M*
- University of Houston M*
- University of Illinois at Chicago M*
- The University of Memphis M*†
- University of Miami M*†
- The University of Montana–Missoula M*†
- University of New Orleans M*
- University of North Texas M,D*†
- University of Notre Dame M*†
- University of Oklahoma M*†
- The University of Tennessee M*†
- University of Utah M*
- University of Victoria M
- Virginia Commonwealth University M*†
- Washington State University M*
- Washington University in St. Louis M*†
- Yale University M*

PHOTONICS

- Lehigh University M,D*
- Oklahoma State University M,D*†
- Princeton University *
- University of Arkansas M,D*
- University of California, San Diego M,D*

PHYSICAL CHEMISTRY

- Boston College M,D*†
- Brandeis University M,D*†
- Brigham Young University M,D*
- California State University, Fullerton M
- California State University, Los Angeles M
- Case Western Reserve University M,D*†
- Clark Atlanta University M,D
- Clarkson University M,D*
- Cleveland State University M,D*†
- Columbia University M,D*†
- Cornell University D*
- Florida State University M,D*†
- Georgetown University M,D*
- The George Washington University M,D*†
- Harvard University M,D*†
- Howard University M,D*
- Illinois Institute of Technology M,D*†
- Indiana University Bloomington M,D*
- Kansas State University M,D*†
- Kent State University M,D*
- Marquette University M,D*†
- Massachusetts Institute of Technology D*
- McMaster University M,D
- Miami University M,D*†
- Michigan State University M,D*†
- Northeastern University M,D*†
- The Ohio State University M,D*
- Old Dominion University M*†
- Oregon State University M,D*
- Princeton University M,D*
- Purdue University M,D*
- Rensselaer Polytechnic Institute M,D*†
- Rice University M,D*
- Rutgers, The State University of New Jersey, Newark M,D*†
- Rutgers, The State University of New Jersey, New Brunswick M,D*
- San Jose State University M*
- Seton Hall University M,D*†
- Simon Fraser University M,D
- South Dakota State University M,D*
- Southern University and Agricultural and Mechanical College M*
- State University of New York at Binghamton M,D*†
- Stevens Institute of Technology M,D,O*†
- Tufts University M,D*†
- University of Calgary M,D*
- University of Cincinnati M,D*
- University of Colorado at Boulder M,D*
- University of Georgia M,D*†
- University of Louisville M,D*†
- University of Maryland, College Park M,D*
- University of Miami M,D*†
- University of Michigan D*
- University of Missouri–Columbia M,D*
- University of Missouri–Kansas City M,D*†
- University of Missouri–St. Louis M,D†
- The University of Montana–Missoula M,D*†
- University of Nebraska–Lincoln M,D*†
- University of Nevada, Reno D*
- University of Notre Dame M,D*†
- University of Puerto Rico, Río Piedras M,D*
- University of Regina M,D
- University of Southern California D*†
- University of Southern Mississippi M,D
- University of South Florida M,D*†
- The University of Tennessee M,D*†
- The University of Texas at Austin M,D*
- University of Toledo M,D*†
- University of Utah M,D*
- Wake Forest University M,D*†
- Washington State University M,D*
- Wesleyan University M,D*
- West Virginia University M,D*
- Yale University D*

PHYSICAL EDUCATION

- Adams State College M
- Adelphi University M,O*
- Alabama Agricultural and Mechanical University M
- Alabama State University M
- Albany State University M
- Alcorn State University M,O
- Appalachian State University M
- Arizona State University M*
- Arkansas State University M,O
- Arkansas Tech University M
- Ashland University M
- Auburn University M,D,O*†
- Auburn University Montgomery M,O
- Azusa Pacific University M*†
- Ball State University M,D*
- Barry University M*†
- Baylor University M*†
- Bemidji State University M
- Bethel College (TN) M
- Boston University M,D,O*†
- Bridgewater State College M
- Brigham Young University M,D*

*P—first professional degree; M—master's degree; D—doctorate; O—other advanced degree; *full description and/or announcement in Book 2, 3, 4, 5, or 6; †full description in this book*

Brooklyn College of the City University of New York M†
California Polytechnic State University, San Luis Obispo M†
California State University, Chico M
California State University, Dominguez Hills M†
California State University, Fullerton M
California State University, Hayward M
California State University, Long Beach M
California State University, Los Angeles M
California State University, Sacramento M
California State University, Stanislaus M
Campbell University M
Canisius College M
Central Connecticut State University M*†
Central Michigan University M†
Central Missouri State University M†
Central Washington University M†
Chicago State University M
The Citadel, The Military College of South Carolina M
Cleveland State University M*†
The College of New Jersey M†
Columbus State University M
Delta State University M
DePaul University M*†
Drury University M
Eastern Illinois University M†
Eastern Kentucky University M
Eastern Michigan University M*
Eastern New Mexico University M
Eastern Washington University M†
East Stroudsburg University of Pennsylvania M†
East Tennessee State University M†
Edinboro University of Pennsylvania O
Emporia State University M*†
Florida Agricultural and Mechanical University M*
Florida International University M*†
Florida State University M,D,O*†
Fort Hays State University M
Frostburg State University M
Gardner-Webb University M
Georgia College & State University M,O
Georgia Southern University M,O
Georgia Southwestern State University M,O
Georgia State University M*
Hardin-Simmons University M
Henderson State University M
Hofstra University M*
Humboldt State University M
Idaho State University M*
Illinois State University M*†
Indiana State University M*†
Indiana University Bloomington M,D,O*
Indiana University of Pennsylvania M*†
Inter American University of Puerto Rico, Metropolitan Campus M
Inter American University of Puerto Rico, San Germán Campus M
Iowa State University of Science and Technology M,D*†
Jackson State University M
Jacksonville State University M,O
Kent State University M,D*
Lakehead University M
Long Island University, Brooklyn Campus M*
Longwood College M
Loras College M
Louisiana Tech University M,D,O*
Marshall University M*†
McDaniel College M
McGill University M*
McNeese State University M
Memorial University of Newfoundland M†
Michigan State University M,D*†
Middle Tennessee State University M,D*
Minnesota State University, Mankato M,O
Mississippi State University M*
Montclair State University M†
Morehead State University M
Murray State University M†
New Mexico Highlands University M
North Carolina Agricultural and Technical State University M*
North Carolina Central University M
North Dakota State University M†
Northern Arizona University M
Northern Illinois University M*†
Northern State University M
North Georgia College & State University M,O
Northwestern State University of Louisiana M,O
Northwest Missouri State University M
The Ohio State University M,D*
Ohio University M*
Oklahoma State University M,D*†
Old Dominion University M*†
Oregon State University M*
Pittsburg State University M
Plymouth State College M*
Prairie View A&M University M
Purdue University M,D*
Queens College of the City University of New York M†
St. Cloud State University M
Saint Mary's College of California M
San Diego State University M*
San Francisco State University M
Seattle Pacific University M
Slippery Rock University of Pennsylvania M†
South Dakota State University M*
Southern Connecticut State University M†
Southern Illinois University Carbondale M*†
Southwestern Oklahoma State University M
Southwest Missouri State University M*†
Southwest Texas State University M*
Springfield College M,D,O†
State University of New York College at Brockport M*†
State University of New York College at Cortland M
State University of West Georgia M,O
Stephen F. Austin State University M
Stony Brook University, State University of New York M,O*†
Sul Ross State University M*
Tarleton State University M,O
Teachers College Columbia University M,D*
Temple University M,D*†
Tennessee State University M*
Tennessee Technological University M*
Texas A&M University M,D*
Texas A&M University–Commerce M†
Texas Southern University M†
Texas Tech University M,D*†
Union College (KY) M
United States Sports Academy M*
Universidad Metropolitana M
Université de Montréal M,D,O
Université de Sherbrooke M,O
Université du Québec à Trois-Rivières M
Université Laval M,D†
The University of Akron M†
The University of Alabama at Birmingham M*†
University of Alberta M,D*
University of Arkansas M*
University of Arkansas at Pine Bluff M
The University of British Columbia M,D*
University of Central Florida M*†
University of Colorado at Boulder M,D*
University of Dayton M*†
University of Florida D*†
University of Georgia M,D,O*†
University of Houston M,D*
University of Idaho M,D*†
University of Indianapolis M
The University of Iowa M,D*
University of Kansas M,D*
University of Louisiana at Monroe M
University of Louisville M*†
University of Maine M*
University of Manitoba M*
University of Massachusetts Amherst M,D,O*†
University of Minnesota, Twin Cities Campus M,D,O*
The University of Montana–Missoula M*†
University of Nebraska at Kearney M
University of Nebraska at Omaha M
University of Nebraska–Lincoln M*†
University of New Brunswick Fredericton M
University of New Orleans M,O*
The University of North Carolina at Chapel Hill M*†
The University of North Carolina at Pembroke M
University of Northern Colorado M,D†
University of Northern Iowa M
University of Rhode Island M*
University of South Alabama M,O*†
University of South Carolina M,D*†
The University of South Dakota M†
University of Southern Mississippi M,D
University of South Florida M*†
The University of Tennessee at Chattanooga M
The University of Texas at El Paso M*†
The University of Texas of the Permian Basin M
University of the Incarnate Word M†
University of Toledo M,D*†
University of Victoria M
University of Virginia M,D*
The University of West Alabama M
University of West Florida M
University of Wisconsin–La Crosse M†
University of Wyoming M*†
Utah State University M*
Valdosta State University M
Virginia Commonwealth University M*†
Virginia Polytechnic Institute and State University M,D,O*
Wayne State College M
Wayne State University M*
West Chester University of Pennsylvania M,O*†
Western Carolina University M†
Western Illinois University M
Western Kentucky University M†
Western Michigan University M*†
Western Washington University M
Westfield State College M
West Virginia University M,D*
Whitworth College M
Wichita State University M*†
Winthrop University M
Wright State University M*

PHYSICAL THERAPY

Alabama State University M
American International College M*
Andrews University M
Angelo State University M†
Arcadia University D†
Arkansas State University M
Armstrong Atlantic State University M†
Azusa Pacific University M*†
Baylor University M,D*†
Belmont University M,D
Boston University M,D*†
Bradley University M†
California State University, Fresno M
California State University, Long Beach M
California State University, Northridge M
Carroll College M
Central Michigan University M†
Chapman University D*†
Chatham College M,D
Clarke College M
Clarkson University M*
College Misericordia M
College of Mount St. Joseph M†
College of St. Catherine M†
The College of St. Scholastica M
College of Staten Island of the City University of New York M†
Columbia University M*†
Concordia University Wisconsin M
Creighton University D*
Daemen College M
Des Moines University Osteopathic Medical Center D*
Dominican College M†
Drexel University M,D,O*†
Duke University M*†
Duquesne University M,D*†
D'Youville College M,O†
East Carolina University M*†
Eastern Washington University M†
East Tennessee State University M†
Elon University D
Emory University D*†
Finch University of Health Sciences/The Chicago Medical School M,D*
Florida Gulf Coast University M
Florida International University M*†
Gannon University M
The George Washington University M*†
Georgia State University M*
Governors State University M
Grand Valley State University M†
Hampton University D*†
Hardin-Simmons University M
Hunter College of the City University of New York M†
Husson College M
Idaho State University M*
Indiana University–Purdue University Indianapolis M*
Ithaca College M†
Kirksville College of Osteopathic Medicine M,D
Loma Linda University M,D*
Long Island University, Brooklyn Campus M*
Louisiana State University Health Sciences Center M*
Marquette University M*†
Marymount University M†
Maryville University of Saint Louis M
Mayo School of Health Sciences M
McMaster University M
Medical College of Georgia M*
Medical University of South Carolina M*
Mercy College M*
MGH Institute of Health Professions M,D,O*
Midwestern University, Downers Grove Campus M*
Mount St. Mary's College D*
Neumann College M
New York Institute of Technology M*†
New York Medical College M,D*
New York University M,D*†
Northern Arizona University M,D
Northern Illinois University M*†
North Georgia College & State University M
Northwestern University D*
Nova Southeastern University M,D*
Oakland University M,D,O†
The Ohio State University M*
Ohio University M*
Old Dominion University D*†
Pacific University D
Quinnipiac University M*†
Regis University D*†
The Richard Stockton College of New Jersey M*
Rockhurst University M
Rutgers, The State University of New Jersey, Camden M†
Sacred Heart University M*†
Sage Graduate School M†
St. Ambrose University D
Saint Francis University M*
Saint Louis University M*†
Samuel Merritt College M
San Francisco State University M
Seton Hall University D*†
Shenandoah University D
Simmons College D*
Slippery Rock University of Pennsylvania D†
Southwest Baptist University M
Southwest Missouri State University M*†
Southwest Texas State University M*
Springfield College M†
State University of New York Upstate Medical University M*
Temple University M,D*†
Texas Tech University Health Sciences Center M*
Texas Woman's University M,D*†
Thomas Jefferson University M*
Touro College M
University at Buffalo, The State University of New York M,D*†
The University of Alabama at Birmingham M*†
University of Alberta M*
University of California, San Francisco M*
University of Central Arkansas M,D
University of Central Florida M*†
University of Colorado Health Sciences Center M*
University of Delaware M*†
The University of Findlay M
University of Florida M*†
University of Hartford M*
University of Illinois at Chicago M*
University of Indianapolis M,D
The University of Iowa M,D*
University of Kansas M*
University of Kentucky M*
University of Mary M
University of Maryland D*†
University of Maryland Eastern Shore M†
University of Massachusetts Lowell M*†
University of Medicine and Dentistry of New Jersey M,D*
University of Miami M,D*†

- University of Michigan–Flint M
- University of Minnesota, Twin Cities Campus M,D*
- University of Mississippi Medical Center M*
- University of Missouri–Columbia M*
- The University of Montana–Missoula M,D*†
- University of Nebraska Medical Center M*
- University of Nevada, Las Vegas M*†
- University of New England M*
- University of New Mexico M*†
- The University of North Carolina at Chapel Hill M*†
- University of North Dakota M,D*
- University of North Florida M
- University of Pittsburgh M*†
- University of Puget Sound D
- University of Rhode Island M*
- University of St. Augustine for Health Sciences M,D†
- The University of Scranton M†
- The University of South Dakota M†
- University of Southern California M,D*†
- University of South Florida M*†
- The University of Tennessee at Chattanooga M
- The University of Tennessee Health Science Center M*
- The University of Texas at El Paso M*†
- The University of Texas Medical Branch M*
- The University of Texas Southwestern Medical Center at Dallas M*
- University of the Pacific M*
- University of Utah M*
- University of Vermont M*†
- University of Washington M*
- The University of Western Ontario M*
- University of Wisconsin–La Crosse M†
- Virginia Commonwealth University M,D,O*†
- Walsh University M
- Washington University in St. Louis D,O*†
- Wayne State University M*
- Western Carolina University M†
- Western University of Health Sciences M
- West Virginia University M*
- Wheeling Jesuit University M
- Wichita State University M*†
- Widener University M*†
- Youngstown State University M

PHYSICIAN ASSISTANT STUDIES

- Augsburg College M
- Barry University M*†
- Baylor College of Medicine M*
- Central Michigan University M†
- Chatham College M
- Daemen College M
- DeSales University M
- Des Moines University Osteopathic Medical Center M*
- Drexel University M*†
- Duke University M*†
- Duquesne University M,D*†
- Eastern Virginia Medical School M
- Emory University M*†
- Finch University of Health Sciences/The Chicago Medical School M*
- Gannon University M
- The George Washington University M*†
- Grand Valley State University M†
- Hofstra University M,O*
- Idaho State University M*
- King's College M
- Kirksville College of Osteopathic Medicine M,D
- Lock Haven University of Pennsylvania M
- Loma Linda University M*
- Marquette University M*†
- Medical College of Georgia M*
- Medical College of Ohio M*
- Medical University of South Carolina M*
- Mercy College M*
- Midwestern University, Downers Grove Campus M*
- Midwestern University, Glendale Campus M*
- Mountain State University M†
- Northeastern University M*†
- Pacific University M
- Philadelphia College of Osteopathic Medicine M*
- Philadelphia University M
- Quinnipiac University M*†
- Saint Francis University M*
- Saint Louis University M*†
- Samuel Merritt College M
- Seton Hall University M*†
- Shenandoah University M
- Southwest Missouri State University M*†
- Texas Tech University Health Sciences Center M*
- Towson University M†
- Trevecca Nazarene University M
- University of Colorado Health Sciences Center M*
- University of Detroit Mercy M*
- University of Florida M*†
- The University of Iowa M*
- University of Kentucky M*
- University of Medicine and Dentistry of New Jersey M*
- University of Nebraska Medical Center M*
- University of New England M*
- University of North Dakota M*
- University of North Texas Health Science Center at Fort Worth M*
- University of Saint Francis (IN) M
- University of South Alabama M*†
- The University of Texas Southwestern Medical Center at Dallas M*
- Wayne State University M*
- Western Michigan University M*†
- Western University of Health Sciences M
- Yale University M*

PHYSICS

- Adelphi University M*
- Alabama Agricultural and Mechanical University M,D
- American University M*†
- Arizona State University M,D*
- Auburn University M,D*†
- Ball State University M*
- Baylor University M,D*†
- Boston College M,D*†
- Boston University M,D*†
- Bowling Green State University M*†
- Brandeis University M,D*†
- Brigham Young University M,D*
- Brock University M
- Brooklyn College of the City University of New York M,D†
- Brown University M,D*
- Bryn Mawr College M,D
- California Institute of Technology D*
- California State University, Fresno M
- California State University, Fullerton M
- California State University, Long Beach M
- California State University, Los Angeles M
- California State University, Northridge M
- Carleton University M,D
- Carnegie Mellon University M,D*
- Case Western Reserve University M,D*†
- The Catholic University of America M,D*†
- Central Connecticut State University M*†
- Central Michigan University M†
- City College of the City University of New York M,D*†
- Clark Atlanta University M
- Clarkson University M,D*
- Clark University M,D*†
- Clemson University M,D*
- Cleveland State University M*†
- The College of William and Mary M,D*†
- Colorado School of Mines M,D†
- Colorado State University M,D*
- Columbia University M,D*†
- Cornell University M,D*
- Creighton University M*
- Dalhousie University M,D*
- Dartmouth College M,D*†
- DePaul University M*†
- Drexel University M,D*†
- Duke University D*†
- East Carolina University M,D*†
- Eastern Michigan University M*
- Emory University D*†
- Emporia State University M*†
- Fisk University M
- Florida Agricultural and Mechanical University M*
- Florida Atlantic University M,D*
- Florida Institute of Technology M,D*†
- Florida International University M,D*†
- Florida State University M,D*†
- George Mason University M*†
- The George Washington University D*†
- Georgia Institute of Technology M,D*
- Georgia State University M,D*
- Graduate School and University Center of the City University of New York D*†
- Hampton University M,D*†
- Harvard University M,D*†
- Howard University M,D*
- Hunter College of the City University of New York M,D†
- Idaho State University M*
- Illinois Institute of Technology M,D*†
- Indiana State University M*†
- Indiana University Bloomington M,D*
- Indiana University of Pennsylvania M*†
- Indiana University–Purdue University Indianapolis M,D*
- Institute of Paper Science and Technology M,D*
- Iowa State University of Science and Technology M,D*†
- John Carroll University M
- Johns Hopkins University D*†
- Kansas State University M,D*†
- Kent State University M,D*
- Lakehead University M
- Lehigh University M,D*
- Louisiana State University and Agricultural and Mechanical College M,D*
- Louisiana Tech University M,D*
- Marshall University M*†
- Massachusetts Institute of Technology M,D*
- McGill University M,D*
- McMaster University M,D
- Memorial University of Newfoundland M,D†
- Miami University M*†
- Michigan State University M,D*†
- Michigan Technological University M,D*†
- Minnesota State University, Mankato M
- Mississippi State University M,D*
- Montana State University–Bozeman M,D*
- Morgan State University M*
- Naval Postgraduate School M,D
- New Mexico Institute of Mining and Technology M,D†
- New Mexico State University M,D
- New York University M,D*†
- North Carolina State University M,D*
- North Dakota State University M,D†
- Northeastern University M,D*†
- Northern Illinois University M,D*†
- Northwestern University M,D*
- Oakland University M,D†
- The Ohio State University M,D*
- Ohio University M,D*
- Oklahoma State University M,D*†
- Old Dominion University M,D*†
- Oregon State University M,D*
- The Pennsylvania State University University Park Campus M,D*†
- Pittsburg State University M
- Polytechnic University, Brooklyn Campus M,D*
- Polytechnic University, Long Island Graduate Center M,D
- Portland State University M,D*
- Princeton University D*
- Purdue University M,D*
- Queens College of the City University of New York M†
- Queen's University at Kingston M,D
- Rensselaer Polytechnic Institute M,D*†
- Rice University M,D*
- Royal Military College of Canada M
- Rutgers, The State University of New Jersey, New Brunswick M,D*
- St. Francis Xavier University M
- Sam Houston State University M*
- San Diego State University M*
- San Francisco State University M
- San Jose State University M*
- Simon Fraser University M,D
- South Dakota School of Mines and Technology M,D*†
- South Dakota State University M*
- Southern Illinois University Carbondale M*†
- Southern Illinois University Edwardsville M†
- Southern Methodist University M,D*†
- Southern University and Agricultural and Mechanical College M*
- Southwest Texas State University M*
- Stanford University D*
- State University of New York at Albany M,D*†
- State University of New York at Binghamton M*†
- State University of New York at New Paltz M
- Stephen F. Austin State University M
- Stevens Institute of Technology M,D,O*†
- Stony Brook University, State University of New York M,D*†
- Syracuse University M,D*
- Temple University M,D*†
- Texas A&M University M,D*
- Texas A&M University–Commerce M†
- Texas Christian University M,D*
- Texas Tech University M,D*†
- Trent University M
- Tufts University M,D*†
- Tulane University M,D*†
- Université de Moncton M
- Université de Montréal M,D
- Université de Sherbrooke M,D
- Université Laval M,D†
- University at Buffalo, The State University of New York M,D*†
- The University of Akron M†
- The University of Alabama M,D*
- The University of Alabama at Birmingham M,D*†
- The University of Alabama in Huntsville M,D*
- University of Alaska Fairbanks M,D*
- University of Alberta M,D*
- The University of Arizona M,D*
- University of Arkansas M,D*
- The University of British Columbia M,D*
- University of Calgary M,D*
- University of California, Berkeley D*
- University of California, Davis M,D*†
- University of California, Irvine M,D*
- University of California, Los Angeles M,D*
- University of California, Riverside M,D*
- University of California, San Diego M,D*
- University of California, Santa Barbara D*
- University of California, Santa Cruz M,D*
- University of Central Florida M,D*†
- University of Chicago M,D*
- University of Cincinnati M,D*
- University of Colorado at Boulder M,D*
- University of Colorado at Colorado Springs M*
- University of Connecticut M,D*†
- University of Delaware M,D*†
- University of Denver M,D*†
- University of Florida M,D*†
- University of Georgia M,D*†
- University of Guelph M,D
- University of Hawaii at Manoa M,D*
- University of Houston M,D*
- University of Idaho M,D*†
- University of Illinois at Chicago M,D*
- University of Illinois at Urbana–Champaign M,D*
- The University of Iowa M,D*
- University of Kansas M,D*
- University of Kentucky M,D*
- The University of Lethbridge M,D
- University of Louisiana at Lafayette M*
- University of Louisville M*†
- University of Maine M,D*
- University of Manitoba M,D*
- University of Maryland, Baltimore County M,D*†
- University of Maryland, College Park M,D*
- University of Massachusetts Amherst M,D*†
- University of Massachusetts Dartmouth M*†
- University of Massachusetts Lowell M,D*†
- The University of Memphis M*†
- University of Miami M,D*†
- University of Michigan M,D*
- University of Minnesota, Duluth M*
- University of Minnesota, Twin Cities Campus M,D*
- University of Mississippi M,D*
- University of Missouri–Columbia M,D*
- University of Missouri–Kansas City M,D*†
- University of Missouri–Rolla M,D*
- University of Missouri–St. Louis M,D†
- University of Nebraska–Lincoln M,D*†

*P—first professional degree; M—master's degree; D—doctorate; O—other advanced degree; *full description and/or announcement in Book 2, 3, 4, 5, or 6; †full description in this book*

University of Nevada, Las Vegas M,D*†
University of Nevada, Reno M,D*
University of New Brunswick Fredericton M,D
University of New Hampshire M,D*†
University of New Mexico M,D*†
University of New Orleans M*
The University of North Carolina at Chapel Hill M,D*†
University of North Dakota M,D*
University of North Texas M,D*†
University of Notre Dame D*†
University of Oklahoma M,D*†
University of Oregon M,D*
University of Ottawa M,D*
University of Pennsylvania D*†
University of Pittsburgh M,D*†
University of Puerto Rico, Mayagüez Campus M*
University of Puerto Rico, Río Piedras M,D*
University of Regina M,D
University of Rhode Island M,D*
University of Rochester M,D*
University of Saskatchewan M,D
University of South Carolina M,D*†
University of Southern California M,D*†
University of Southern Mississippi M
University of South Florida M,D*†
The University of Tennessee M,D*†
The University of Tennessee Space Institute M,D*
The University of Texas at Arlington M,D*†
The University of Texas at Austin M,D*
The University of Texas at Dallas M,D*
The University of Texas at El Paso M*†
University of Toledo M,D*†
University of Toronto M,D*
University of Utah M,D*
University of Vermont M*†
University of Victoria M,D
University of Virginia M,D*
University of Washington M,D*
University of Waterloo M,D
The University of Western Ontario M,D*
University of Windsor M,D
University of Wisconsin–Madison M,D*
University of Wisconsin–Milwaukee M,D
University of Wisconsin–Oshkosh M*
Utah State University M,D*
Vanderbilt University M,D*
Virginia Commonwealth University M*†
Virginia Polytechnic Institute and State University M,D*
Virginia State University M
Wake Forest University M,D*†
Washington State University M,D*
Washington University in St. Louis M,D*†
Wayne State University M,D*
Wesleyan University M,D*
Western Carolina University M†
Western Illinois University M
Western Michigan University M,D*†
West Virginia University M,D*
Wichita State University M*†
Wilkes University M
Worcester Polytechnic Institute M,D*†
Wright State University M*
Yale University D*
York University M,D*

PHYSIOLOGY

Arizona State University M,D*
Auburn University M*†
Ball State University M*
Baylor College of Medicine D*
Boston University M,D*†
Brown University M,D*
Case Western Reserve University M,D*†
Clemson University M,D*
Colorado State University M,D*
Columbia University M,D*†
Cornell University M,D*
Dalhousie University M,D*
Dartmouth College D*†
East Carolina University D*†
East Tennessee State University M,D†
Finch University of Health Sciences/The Chicago Medical School M,D*
Florida State University M,D*†
Georgetown University M,D*
Georgia State University M,D*
Harvard University M,D*†
Howard University D*
Illinois State University M,D*†
Indiana State University M,D*†
Indiana University Bloomington M,D*
Indiana University–Purdue University Indianapolis M,D*
Iowa State University of Science and Technology M,D*†
Joan and Sanford I. Weill Medical College and Graduate School of Medical Sciences of Cornell University D*
Johns Hopkins University M,D*†
Kansas State University M,D*†
Kent State University M,D*
Loma Linda University M,D*
Louisiana State University Health Sciences Center M,D*
Loyola University Chicago M,D*†
Maharishi University of Management M,D
Marquette University M,D*†
McGill University M,D*
McMaster University M,D
Medical College of Georgia M,D*
Medical College of Ohio M*
Medical College of Wisconsin M,D*
Medical University of South Carolina M,D*
Meharry Medical College D
Michigan State University M,D*†
Mount Sinai School of Medicine of New York University D*
New York Medical College M,D*
New York University M,D*†
North Carolina State University M,D*
Northwestern University M*
Nova Scotia Agricultural College M
The Ohio State University M,D*
Oregon Health & Science University D*
The Pennsylvania State University Milton S. Hershey Medical Center M,D*
The Pennsylvania State University University Park Campus M,D*†
Purdue University M,D*
Queen's University at Kingston M,D
Rush University D*
Rutgers, The State University of New Jersey, New Brunswick D*
Saint Louis University D*†
Salisbury University M
San Francisco State University M
Southern Illinois University Carbondale M,D*†
Southern Illinois University Edwardsville M,O†
Stanford University D*
State University of New York Upstate Medical University M,D*
Stony Brook University, State University of New York D*†
Teachers College Columbia University M,D*
Temple University M,D*†
Texas A&M University M,D*
Texas A&M University System Health Science Center D*
Texas Tech University Health Sciences Center M,D*
Thomas Jefferson University D*
Tufts University D*†
Tulane University M,D*†
Uniformed Services University of the Health Sciences M,D*
Université de Montréal M,D,O
Université Laval M,D†
University at Buffalo, The State University of New York M,D*†
The University of Alabama at Birmingham D*†
University of Alberta M,D*
The University of Arizona D*
University of Arkansas for Medical Sciences M,D*
The University of British Columbia M,D*
University of California, Berkeley M,D*
University of California, Davis M,D*†
University of California, Irvine D*
University of California, Los Angeles M,D*
University of California, San Diego D*
University of California, San Francisco D*
University of Chicago D*
University of Cincinnati D*
University of Colorado at Boulder M,D*
University of Colorado Health Sciences Center D*
University of Connecticut M,D*†
University of Delaware M,D*†
University of Florida D*†
University of Georgia M,D*†
University of Guelph M,D
University of Hawaii at Manoa M,D*
University of Illinois at Chicago M,D*
University of Illinois at Urbana–Champaign M,D*
The University of Iowa M,D*
University of Kansas M,D*
University of Kentucky D*
University of Louisville M,D*†
University of Manitoba M,D*
University of Maryland D*†
University of Massachusetts Worcester D*
University of Medicine and Dentistry of New Jersey M,D*
University of Miami D*†
University of Michigan D*
University of Minnesota, Duluth M,D*
University of Minnesota, Twin Cities Campus M,D*
University of Mississippi Medical Center M,D*
University of Missouri–Columbia M,D*
University of Missouri–St. Louis M,D,O†
University of Nebraska Medical Center D*
University of Nevada, Reno M,D*
University of New Mexico M,D*†
The University of North Carolina at Chapel Hill D*†
University of North Dakota M,D*
University of North Texas Health Science Center at Fort Worth M,D*
University of Notre Dame M,D*†
University of Oklahoma Health Sciences Center M,D*
University of Pennsylvania D*†
University of Pittsburgh M,D*†
University of Prince Edward Island M,D
University of Puerto Rico, Medical Sciences Campus M,D*
University of Rochester M,D*
University of Saskatchewan M,D
University of South Alabama D*†
The University of South Dakota M,D†
University of Southern California M,D*†
University of South Florida M,D*†
The University of Tennessee M,D*†
The University of Tennessee Health Science Center M,D*
The University of Texas Health Science Center at Houston M,D*
The University of Texas Health Science Center at San Antonio M,D*
The University of Texas Medical Branch M,D*
University of the Pacific M,D*
University of Toronto M,D*
University of Utah D*
University of Vermont M,D*†
University of Victoria M,D
University of Virginia D*
University of Washington D*
The University of Western Ontario M,D*
University of Wisconsin–Madison M,D*
University of Wyoming M,D*†
Vanderbilt University D*
Virginia Commonwealth University M,D,O*†
Wake Forest University D*†
Wayne State University M,D*
Wesleyan University D*
West Virginia University M,D*
William Paterson University of New Jersey M*†
Wright State University M*
Yale University D*
Yeshiva University D*

PLANETARY AND SPACE SCIENCES

Air Force Institute of Technology M,D*
California Institute of Technology M,D*
Columbia University M,D*†
Cornell University D*
Florida Institute of Technology M,D*†
Harvard University M,D*†
Johns Hopkins University M,D*†
Massachusetts Institute of Technology M,D*
McGill University M,D,O*
Rensselaer Polytechnic Institute M,D*†
Stony Brook University, State University of New York M,D*†
The University of Arizona M,D*
University of California, Los Angeles M,D*
University of Chicago M,D*
University of Hawaii at Manoa M,D*
University of Michigan M,D*
University of New Mexico M,D*†
University of North Dakota M*
University of Pittsburgh M,D*†
Washington University in St. Louis M,D*†
Western Connecticut State University M
York University M,D*

PLANT BIOLOGY

Arizona State University M,D*
Clemson University M,D*
Cornell University D*
Florida State University M,D*†
Indiana University Bloomington M,D*
Louisiana State University and Agricultural and Mechanical College M,D*
Michigan State University M,D*†
The Ohio State University M,D*
Ohio University M,D*
Purdue University D*
Rutgers, The State University of New Jersey, New Brunswick M,D*
Southern Illinois University Carbondale M,D*†
Texas A&M University M,D*
Université Laval M,D,O†
University of Alberta M,D*
University of California, Berkeley D*
University of California, Davis M,D*†
University of California, Riverside M,D*
University of Colorado at Boulder M,D*
University of Connecticut M,D*†
University of Delaware M,D*†
University of Florida M,D*†
University of Hawaii at Manoa M,D*
University of Illinois at Chicago M,D*
University of Illinois at Urbana–Champaign M,D*
The University of Iowa M,D*
University of Maine M,D*
University of Maryland, College Park M,D*
University of Massachusetts Amherst M,D*†
University of Michigan M,D*
University of Minnesota, Twin Cities Campus M,D*
University of Missouri–Columbia M,D*
University of New Hampshire M,D*†
University of Pennsylvania D*†
The University of Texas at Austin M,D*
The University of Western Ontario M,D*
Washington University in St. Louis D*†
West Virginia University M,D*
Yale University D*

PLANT MOLECULAR BIOLOGY

Cornell University D*
Michigan Technological University D*†
Rutgers, The State University of New Jersey, New Brunswick M,D*
University of California, Los Angeles M,D*
University of California, San Diego D*
University of Connecticut M,D*†
University of Florida M,D*†

PLANT PATHOLOGY

Auburn University M,D*†
Colorado State University M,D*
Cornell University M,D*
Iowa State University of Science and Technology M,D*†
Kansas State University M,D*†
Louisiana State University and Agricultural and Mechanical College M,D*
Michigan State University M,D*†
Mississippi State University M,D*
Montana State University–Bozeman M,D*
New Mexico State University M
North Carolina State University M,D*
North Dakota State University M,D†
Nova Scotia Agricultural College M
The Ohio State University M,D*
Oklahoma State University M,D*†
Oregon State University M,D*
The Pennsylvania State University University Park Campus M,D*†
Purdue University M,D*
Rutgers, The State University of New Jersey, New Brunswick M,D*
South Dakota State University M*

State University of New York College of Environmental Science and Forestry M,D
Texas A&M University M,D*
The University of Arizona M,D*
University of Arkansas M*
University of California, Davis M,D*†
University of California, Riverside M,D*
University of Florida M,D*†
University of Georgia M,D*†
University of Hawaii at Manoa M,D*
University of Idaho M,D*†
University of Kentucky M,D*
University of Maine M*
University of Minnesota, Twin Cities Campus M,D*
University of Missouri–Columbia M,D*
University of Rhode Island M,D*
The University of Tennessee M*†
University of Wisconsin–Madison M,D*
Virginia Polytechnic Institute and State University M,D*
Washington State University M,D*
West Virginia University M,D*

PLANT PHYSIOLOGY

Colorado State University M,D*
Cornell University D*
Iowa State University of Science and Technology M,D*†
Nova Scotia Agricultural College M
Oregon State University M,D*
The Pennsylvania State University University Park Campus M,D*†
Purdue University D*
Rutgers, The State University of New Jersey, New Brunswick M,D*
University of Colorado at Boulder M,D*
University of Kentucky D*
The University of Tennessee M,D*†
Virginia Polytechnic Institute and State University M,D*
Washington State University M,D*

PLANT SCIENCES

Alabama Agricultural and Mechanical University M,D
California State University, Fresno M
Colorado State University M,D*
Cornell University M,D*
Lehman College of the City University of New York D
McGill University M,D*
Michigan State University D*†
Mississippi State University M,D*
Montana State University–Bozeman M,D*
North Carolina Agricultural and Technical State University M*
North Dakota State University M,D†
Oklahoma State University D*†
Rutgers, The State University of New Jersey, New Brunswick M,D*
South Dakota State University M,D*
Southern Illinois University Carbondale M*†
Southwest Missouri State University M*†
State University of New York College of Environmental Science and Forestry M,D
Texas A&M University M,D*
Texas A&M University–Kingsville M*†
Texas Tech University M,D*†
Tuskegee University M
The University of Arizona M,D*
University of Arkansas D*
The University of British Columbia M,D*
University of California, Davis M*†
University of California, Riverside M,D*
University of Connecticut M,D*†
University of Delaware M,D*†
University of Guelph M,D
University of Hawaii at Manoa M,D*
University of Idaho M,D*†
University of Kentucky M*
University of Maine M,D*
University of Massachusetts Amherst M,D*†
University of Minnesota, Twin Cities Campus M,D*
University of Rhode Island M,D*
University of Saskatchewan M,D
University of Vermont M,D*†
The University of Western Ontario M,D*
University of Wisconsin–Madison M,D*
Utah State University M,D*
West Texas A&M University M†
West Virginia University M,D*

PLASMA PHYSICS

Columbia University M,D,O*†
Princeton University D*
University of Colorado at Boulder M,D*
West Virginia University M,D*

PODIATRIC MEDICINE

Barry University P*†
California College of Podiatric Medicine P
Des Moines University Osteopathic Medical Center P*
New York College of Podiatric Medicine P*
Ohio College of Podiatric Medicine P
The Scholl College of Podiatric Medicine at Finch University of Health Sciences/The Chicago Medical School P*
Temple University P*†

POLITICAL SCIENCE

Acadia University M
American Military University M
American University M,D,O*†
American University in Cairo M
Appalachian State University M
Arizona State University M,D*
Arkansas State University M,O
Auburn University M,D*†
Auburn University Montgomery M
Augusta State University M
Ball State University M*
Baylor University M,D*†
Boston College M,D*†
Boston University M,D*†
Bowling Green State University *†
Brandeis University M,D*†
Brock University M
Brooklyn College of the City University of New York M,D†
Brown University M,D*
California Institute of Technology D*
California State University, Chico M
California State University, Fullerton M
California State University, Long Beach M
California State University, Los Angeles M
California State University, Northridge M
California State University, Sacramento M
Carleton University M,D
Case Western Reserve University M,D*†
The Catholic University of America M,D*†
Central Michigan University M†
Claremont Graduate University M,D*
Clark Atlanta University M,D
The College of Saint Rose M*†
Colorado State University M,D*
Columbia University M,D*†
Converse College M
Cornell University D*
Dalhousie University M,D*
Duke University M,D*†
East Carolina University M*†
Eastern Illinois University M†
Eastern Kentucky University M
East Stroudsburg University of Pennsylvania M†
Emory University D*†
Fairleigh Dickinson University, Metropolitan Campus M*†
Fayetteville State University M
Florida Atlantic University M*
Florida International University M,D*†
Florida State University M,D*†
Fordham University M*†
Georgetown University M,D*
The George Washington University M,D*†
Georgia Southern University M
Georgia State University M,D*
Governors State University M
Graduate School and University Center of the City University of New York M,D*†
Harvard University M,D*†
Hawai'i Pacific University M*†
Howard University M,D*
Huron University USA in London M
Idaho State University M,D*
Illinois State University M*†
Indiana State University M*†
Indiana University Bloomington M,D*
Indiana University of Pennsylvania M*†
Institute for Christian Studies M,D
Iowa State University of Science and Technology M*†
Jackson State University M
Jacksonville State University M
Johns Hopkins University D*†
Kansas State University M*†
Kent State University M,D*
Lamar University M*†
Lehigh University M*
Long Island University, Brooklyn Campus M*
Long Island University, C.W. Post Campus M*†
Louisiana State University and Agricultural and Mechanical College M,D*
Loyola University Chicago M,D*†
Marquette University M*†
Marshall University M*†
Massachusetts Institute of Technology M,D*
McGill University M,D*
McMaster University M
Memorial University of Newfoundland M†
Miami University M,D*†
Michigan State University M,D*†
Midwestern State University M
Minnesota State University, Mankato M
Mississippi College M
Mississippi State University M,D*
New Mexico Highlands University M
New Mexico State University M
New School University M,D*†
New York University M,D*†
North Dakota State University M†
Northeastern Illinois University M
Northeastern University M,D*†
Northern Arizona University M,D,O
Northern Illinois University M,D*†
Northwestern University M,D*
The Ohio State University M,D,O*
Ohio University M*
Oklahoma State University M*†
The Pennsylvania State University University Park Campus M,D*†
Portland State University M,D*
Princeton University D*
Purdue University M,D*
Purdue University Calumet M
Queen's University at Kingston M,D
Rice University M,D*
Roosevelt University M*†
Rutgers, The State University of New Jersey, Newark M*†
Rutgers, The State University of New Jersey, New Brunswick M,D*
St. John's University (NY) M*†
St. Mary's University of San Antonio M
Sam Houston State University M*
San Diego State University M*
San Francisco State University M
Simon Fraser University M,D
Sonoma State University M
Southern Connecticut State University M†
Southern Illinois University Carbondale M,D*†
Southern University and Agricultural and Mechanical College M*
Southwest Texas State University M*
Stanford University M,D*
State University of New York at Albany M,D*†
State University of New York at Binghamton M,D*†
Stony Brook University, State University of New York M,D*†
Suffolk University M*
Sul Ross State University M*
Syracuse University M,D*
Tarleton State University M
Teachers College Columbia University M,D*
Temple University M,D*†
Texas A&M International University M
Texas A&M University M,D*
Texas A&M University–Kingsville M*†
Texas Tech University M,D*†
Texas Woman's University M*†
Troy State University Dothan M
Tulane University M,D*†
Université de Montréal M,D
Université du Québec à Montréal M,D
Université Laval M,D†
University at Buffalo, The State University of New York M,D*†
The University of Akron M†
The University of Alabama M,D*
University of Alberta M,D*
The University of Arizona M,D*
University of Arkansas M*
The University of British Columbia M,D*
University of Calgary M,D*
University of California, Berkeley D*
University of California, Davis M,D*†
University of California, Irvine D*
University of California, Los Angeles M,D*
University of California, Riverside M,D*
University of California, San Diego M,D*
University of California, Santa Barbara M,D*
University of California, Santa Cruz D*
University of Central Florida M*†
University of Central Oklahoma M
University of Chicago D*
University of Cincinnati M,D*
University of Colorado at Boulder M,D*
University of Colorado at Denver M*
University of Connecticut M,D*†
University of Dallas M,D*
University of Delaware M,D*†
University of Florida M,D,O*†
University of Georgia M,D*†
University of Guelph M
University of Hawaii at Manoa M,D*
University of Houston M,D*
University of Idaho M,D*†
University of Illinois at Chicago M,D*
University of Illinois at Springfield M†
University of Illinois at Urbana–Champaign M,D*
The University of Iowa M,D*
University of Kansas M,D*
University of Kentucky M,D*
The University of Lethbridge M,D
University of Louisville M*†
University of Manitoba M*
University of Maryland, College Park M,D*
University of Massachusetts Amherst M,D*†
University of Massachusetts Boston O*†
The University of Memphis M*†
University of Miami M*†
University of Michigan M,D*
University of Minnesota, Twin Cities Campus M,D*
University of Mississippi M,D*
University of Missouri–Columbia M,D*
University of Missouri–Kansas City M,D*†
University of Missouri–St. Louis M,D†
The University of Montana–Missoula M*†
University of Nebraska at Omaha M
University of Nebraska–Lincoln M,D*†
University of Nevada, Las Vegas M*†
University of Nevada, Reno M,D*
University of New Brunswick Fredericton M
University of New Hampshire M*†
University of New Mexico M,D*†
University of New Orleans M,D*
The University of North Carolina at Chapel Hill M,D*†
The University of North Carolina at Greensboro M†
University of Northern British Columbia M,D
University of Northern Iowa M
University of North Texas M,D*†
University of Notre Dame D*†
University of Oklahoma M,D*†
University of Oregon M,D*
University of Ottawa M,D*
University of Pennsylvania M,D*†
University of Pittsburgh M,D*†
University of Regina M
University of Rhode Island M,O*
University of Rochester M,D*
University of Saskatchewan M,D
University of South Carolina M,D*†
The University of South Dakota M†
University of Southern California M,D*†
University of Southern Mississippi M
University of South Florida M*†
The University of Tennessee M,D*†

*P—first professional degree; M—master's degree; D—doctorate; O—other advanced degree; *full description and/or announcement in Book 2, 3, 4, 5, or 6; †full description in this book*

The University of Texas at Arlington M*†
The University of Texas at Austin M,D*
The University of Texas at Brownsville M
The University of Texas at El Paso M*†
The University of Texas at San Antonio M*
The University of Texas at Tyler M
University of Toledo M*†
University of Toronto M,D*
University of Utah M,D*
University of Vermont M*†
University of Victoria M
University of Virginia M,D*
University of Washington M,D*
University of Waterloo M
The University of Western Ontario M,D*
University of West Florida M
University of Windsor M
University of Wisconsin–Madison M,D*
University of Wisconsin–Milwaukee M,D
University of Wyoming M*†
Utah State University M*
Vanderbilt University M,D*
Villanova University M*†
Virginia Polytechnic Institute and State University M*
Washington State University M,D*
Washington University in St. Louis M,D*†
Wayne State University M,D*
Western Illinois University M
Western Michigan University M,D*†
Western Washington University M
West Texas A&M University M†
West Virginia University M,D*
Wichita State University M*†
Wilfrid Laurier University M
Yale University D*
York University M,D*

POLYMER SCIENCE AND ENGINEERING

Carnegie Mellon University M,D*
Case Western Reserve University M,D*†
Clemson University M,D*
Cornell University M,D*
DePaul University M*†
Eastern Michigan University M*
Georgia Institute of Technology M*
Illinois Institute of Technology *†
Lehigh University M,D*
North Dakota State University M,D†
The Pennsylvania State University University Park Campus M,D*†
Polytechnic University, Brooklyn Campus M*
Princeton University M,D*
Rensselaer Polytechnic Institute M,D*†
Rutgers, The State University of New Jersey, New Brunswick M,D*
San Jose State University M*
The University of Akron M,D†
University of Cincinnati M,D*
University of Connecticut M,D*†
University of Detroit Mercy M,D*
University of Florida M,D,O*†
University of Massachusetts Amherst M,D*†
University of Massachusetts Lowell M,D*†
University of Michigan M*
University of Missouri–Kansas City M,D*†
University of Southern Mississippi M,D
The University of Tennessee M,D*†
University of Wisconsin–Madison M,D*
Wayne State University M,D,O*

PORTUGUESE

Brigham Young University M*
Harvard University M,D*†
Indiana University Bloomington M,D*
New York University M,D*†
The Ohio State University M,D*
Tulane University M,D*†
University of California, Los Angeles M*
University of California, Santa Barbara M,D*
University of Minnesota, Twin Cities Campus M,D*
University of New Mexico M,D*†
The University of North Carolina at Chapel Hill M,D*†
The University of Tennessee D*†
The University of Texas at Austin M,D*
University of Toronto M,D*
University of Washington M*
University of Wisconsin–Madison M,D*
Vanderbilt University M,D*
Yale University M,D*

PROJECT MANAGEMENT

American Graduate University M,O
Athabasca University M,O
Carnegie Mellon University M,D*
City University M,O†
Colorado Technical University M,D
Colorado Technical University Denver Campus M
DeVry University-Keller Graduate School of Management M
The George Washington University M,D*†
ISIM University M
Lesley University M,O*†
Mississippi State University M,D*
Montana Tech of The University of Montana M
Naval Postgraduate School M
Northwestern University M*
Regis University M,O*†
Rosemont College M†
Stevens Institute of Technology M,O*†
Texas A&M University M,D*
Thomas Edison State College M†
Université du Québec à Chicoutimi M
Université du Québec en Outaouais M,O
Université du Québec à Montréal M,O
Université du Québec à Rimouski M
Université du Québec à Trois-Rivières M,O
Université du Québec en Abitibi-Témiscamingue M
University of Wisconsin–Platteville M
Western Carolina University M†
Wright State University M*

PSYCHIATRIC NURSING

Boston College M,D*†
Case Western Reserve University M*†
The Catholic University of America M,D*†
Columbia University M,O*†
Fairfield University M,O*
Georgia State University M,D*
Hunter College of the City University of New York M†
Husson College M
Indiana University–Purdue University Indianapolis M*
Kent State University M*
Louisiana State University Health Sciences Center M,D*
Medical College of Georgia M,D*
Medical University of South Carolina M,O*
Molloy College M,O
New York University M,O*†
Northeastern University M,O*†
Oregon Health & Science University M,O*
Pontifical Catholic University of Puerto Rico M
Rush University M,D*
Rutgers, The State University of New Jersey, Newark M,D*†
Sage Graduate School M†
Saint Joseph College M,O
Saint Xavier University M,O*
Southern Illinois University Edwardsville M†
Stony Brook University, State University of New York M,O*†
Texas Woman's University M,D*†
University at Buffalo, The State University of New York M,D,O*†
University of Cincinnati M,D*
University of Delaware M,O*†
University of Illinois at Chicago M*
University of Maryland M,D*†
University of Massachusetts Lowell M*†
University of Miami M,D*†
University of Michigan M*
University of Minnesota, Twin Cities Campus M*
University of Pennsylvania M*†
University of Pittsburgh M*†
University of South Alabama M*†
University of South Carolina M,O*†
University of Southern Maine M,O
University of Southern Mississippi M,D
The University of Texas at El Paso M*†
Vanderbilt University M,D*
Virginia Commonwealth University M,D,O*†
Wayne State University M*
Wichita State University M*†

PSYCHOLOGY—GENERAL

Abilene Christian University M
Acadia University M
Adelphi University M,D,O*
Adler School of Professional Psychology M,D,O*
Alabama Agricultural and Mechanical University M,O
Alfred Adler Graduate School M,O
Alliant International University M,D*†
American International College M,D,O*
American University M,D*†
Andrews University M,D,O
Angelo State University M†
Anna Maria College M,O
Antioch New England Graduate School M*†
Antioch University Los Angeles M
Antioch University McGregor M†
Antioch University Santa Barbara M
Antioch University Seattle M†
Appalachian State University M,O
Arcadia University M,D,O†
Argosy University-Atlanta M,D*
Argosy University-Chicago M,D,O*
Argosy University-Chicago Northwest M,D*
Argosy University-Dallas M,D*
Argosy University-Honolulu M,D,O*
Argosy University-Orange County M,D*
Argosy University-Phoenix M,D,O*
Argosy University-San Francisco Bay Area M,D*
Argosy University-Sarasota M,D,O*†
Argosy University-Tampa M,D*
Argosy University-Twin Cities M,D*
Argosy University-Washington D.C. M,D,O*
Arizona State University D*
Assumption College M,O†
Auburn University M,D*†
Auburn University Montgomery M
Augusta State University M
Austin Peay State University M
Avila University M
Azusa Pacific University M,D*†
Ball State University M*
Barry University M,O*†
Bayamón Central University M
Baylor University M,D*†
Bethel College (MN) M
Biola University M,D
Boston College D*†
Boston Graduate School of Psychoanalysis M,D,O*
Boston University M,D*†
Bowling Green State University M,D*†
Brandeis University M,D*†
Bridgewater State College M
Brigham Young University M,D*
Brock University M
Brooklyn College of the City University of New York M,D†
Brown University M,D*
Bryn Mawr College D
Bucknell University M
California Institute of Integral Studies M,D,O*
California Lutheran University M
California Polytechnic State University, San Luis Obispo M†
California State Polytechnic University, Pomona M*
California State University, Bakersfield M,O
California State University, Chico M
California State University, Dominguez Hills M†
California State University, Fresno M
California State University, Fullerton M
California State University, Long Beach M
California State University, Los Angeles M
California State University, Northridge M
California State University, Sacramento M
California State University, San Bernardino M
California State University, San Marcos M
California State University, Stanislaus M
Cameron University M
Capella University M,D
Cardinal Stritch University M*
Carleton University M,D
Carlos Albizu University M,D
Carlos Albizu University, Miami Campus M,D
Carnegie Mellon University D*
Case Western Reserve University D*†
Castleton State College M
The Catholic University of America M,D*†
Center for Humanistic Studies M,D*
Central Connecticut State University M*†
Central Michigan University M,D,O†
Central Missouri State University M,O†
Central Washington University M†
Chapman University M*†
Chestnut Hill College M,D†
Chicago School of Professional Psychology M,D*
Christopher Newport University M†
The Citadel, The Military College of South Carolina M
City College of the City University of New York M,D*†
Claremont Graduate University M,D*
Clark University D*†
Clemson University M,D*
Cleveland State University M,O*†
College of Saint Elizabeth M
College of St. Joseph M
College of Staten Island of the City University of New York D†
The College of William and Mary M,D*†
Colorado State University D*
Columbia University M,D*†
Concordia University (IL) M,O
Concordia University (Canada) M,D*†
Connecticut College M
Coppin State College M
Cornell University D*
Dalhousie University M,D*
Dartmouth College D*†
DePaul University M,D*†
Drexel University D*†
Duke University D*†
Duquesne University D*†
East Carolina University M*†
East Central University M
Eastern Illinois University M,O†
Eastern Kentucky University M,O
Eastern Michigan University M,D*
Eastern New Mexico University M
Eastern Virginia Medical School D
Eastern Washington University M†
East Tennessee State University M†
Edinboro University of Pennsylvania M
Emory University D*†
Emporia State University M*†
Evangel University M
Fairfield University M,O*
Fairleigh Dickinson University, College at Florham M*†
Fairleigh Dickinson University, Metropolitan Campus M,D*†
Fayetteville State University M
Fielding Graduate Institute M,D
Fisk University M
Florida Agricultural and Mechanical University M*
Florida Atlantic University M,D*
Florida Institute of Technology M,D*†
Florida International University M,D*†
Florida State University M,D*†
Fordham University D*†
Forest Institute of Professional Psychology M,D
Fort Hays State University M,O
Framingham State College M*
Francis Marion University M
Frostburg State University M
Fuller Theological Seminary M,D
Gallaudet University M,D,O
Gardner-Webb University M
Geneva College M*
George Fox University M,D†
George Mason University M,D*†
Georgetown University D*
The George Washington University D*†
Georgia College & State University M
Georgia Institute of Technology M,D*
Georgia Southern University M
Georgia State University D*
Golden Gate University M,O
Governors State University M
Graduate School and University Center of the City University of New York D*†
Graduate Theological Union M,D,O
Hardin-Simmons University M
Harvard University M,D*†
Hofstra University M,D,O*
Hood College M
Hope International University M
Houston Baptist University M
Howard University M,D*
Humboldt State University M
Hunter College of the City University of New York M†
Idaho State University M,D*
Illinois Institute of Technology M,D*†
Illinois State University M,D,O*†

Institution	Degrees
Immaculata University	M,D,O†
Indiana State University	M,D*†
Indiana University Bloomington	D*
Indiana University of Pennsylvania	M,D*†
Indiana University–Purdue University Indianapolis	M,D*
Indiana University South Bend	M
Institute of Transpersonal Psychology	M,D,O*
Inter American University of Puerto Rico, Metropolitan Campus	M
Inter American University of Puerto Rico, San Germán Campus	M,D
Iona College	M*†
Iowa State University of Science and Technology	M,D*†
Jackson State University	D
Jacksonville State University	M
James Madison University	M,D,O
John F. Kennedy University	M,D,O*†
Johns Hopkins University	D*†
Kansas State University	M,D*†
Kean University	M,O*†
Kent State University	M,D*
Lakehead University	M,D
Lamar University	M*†
La Salle University	D
Lehigh University	D*
Lesley University	M,D,O*†
Long Island University, Brooklyn Campus	M,D*
Long Island University, C.W. Post Campus	M,D*†
Loras College	M
Louisiana State University and Agricultural and Mechanical College	M,D*
Louisiana Tech University	M,D,O*
Loyola College in Maryland	M,D,O
Loyola Marymount University	M†
Loyola University Chicago	M,D*†
Madonna University	M
Maharishi University of Management	M,D
Marist College	M,O
Marquette University	M,D*†
Marshall University	M,D*†
Martin University	M
Marymount University	M,O†
Marywood University	M,D*†
Massachusetts Institute of Technology	D*
Massachusetts School of Professional Psychology	M,D,O*
McGill University	M,D*
McMaster University	M,D
McNeese State University	M
Memorial University of Newfoundland	M,D†
Mercy College	M,O*
Miami University	D*†
Michigan State University	M,D*†
Middle Tennessee State University	M,O*
Midwestern State University	M
Millersville University of Pennsylvania	M†
Minnesota State University, Mankato	M
Minnesota State University, Moorhead	M,O
Mississippi College	M
Mississippi State University	M,D*
Monmouth University	M,O*†
Montana State University–Billings	M*
Montana State University–Bozeman	M*
Montclair State University	M,O†
Morehead State University	M
Murray State University	M†
Naropa University	P,M*
National-Louis University	M,O
National University	M,O†
New College of California	M*†
New Jersey City University	M,O
New Mexico Highlands University	M
New Mexico State University	M,D
New School University	M,D*†
New York University	M,D,O*†
Norfolk State University	M,D†
North Carolina Central University	M
North Carolina State University	M,D*
North Dakota State University	M,D†
Northeastern Illinois University	M
Northeastern State University	M
Northeastern University	M,D,O*†
Northern Arizona University	M
Northern Illinois University	M,D*†
Northern Michigan University	M
Northwestern Oklahoma State University	M
Northwestern State University of Louisiana	M
Northwestern University	D*
Northwest Missouri State University	M
Notre Dame de Namur University	M,O
Nova Southeastern University	M,D,O*
The Ohio State University	D*
Ohio University	D*
Oklahoma State University	M,D*†
Old Dominion University	M*†
Our Lady of the Lake University of San Antonio	M,D
Pace University	M,D*†
Pace University, White Plains Campus	M*
Pacifica Graduate Institute	M,D*
Pacific Graduate School of Psychology	M,D
Pacific University	M,D
The Pennsylvania State University Harrisburg Campus of the Capital College	M*†
The Pennsylvania State University University Park Campus	M,D*†
Pepperdine University	M,D*†
Philadelphia College of Osteopathic Medicine	M,D*
Pittsburg State University	M
Plattsburgh State University of New York	M,O
Ponce School of Medicine	D
Pontifical Catholic University of Puerto Rico	M,D
Portland State University	M,D*
Princeton University	D*
Purdue University	D*
Queens College of the City University of New York	M†
Queen's University at Kingston	M,D
Radford University	M,O†
Regis University	M,O*†
Rensselaer Polytechnic Institute	M*†
Rhode Island College	M†
Rice University	M,D*
Roosevelt University	M,D*†
Rowan University	M†
Rutgers, The State University of New Jersey, Newark	D*†
Rutgers, The State University of New Jersey, New Brunswick	M,D*
Sage Graduate School	M†
St. Cloud State University	M
St. John's University (NY)	M,D*†
Saint Joseph College	M,O
Saint Joseph's University	M*†
Saint Louis University	M,D*†
Saint Mary College	M
Saint Mary's University	M
St. Mary's University of San Antonio	M
Saint Xavier University	M,O*
Salem State College	M
Sam Houston State University	M,D*
San Diego State University	M,D*
San Francisco State University	M
San Jose State University	M*
Saybrook Graduate School and Research Center	M,D
Seattle University	M*†
Seton Hall University	M,D,O*†
Shippensburg University of Pennsylvania	M†
Simon Fraser University	M,D
Southeastern Baptist Theological Seminary	P,M,D
Southeastern Louisiana University	M
Southern Adventist University	M
Southern Connecticut State University	M†
Southern Illinois University Carbondale	M,D*†
Southern Illinois University Edwardsville	M†
Southern Methodist University	M,D*†
Southern Nazarene University	M
Southern Oregon University	M
Southern University and Agricultural and Mechanical College	M*
Southwestern College (NM)	O†
Southwest Missouri State University	M*†
Southwest Texas State University	M*
Spalding University	M,D†
Stanford University	D*
State University of New York at Albany	M,D*†
State University of New York at Binghamton	M,D*†
State University of New York at New Paltz	M
State University of New York College at Brockport	M*†
State University of West Georgia	M
Stephen F. Austin State University	M
Stony Brook University, State University of New York	M,D*†
Suffolk University	D*
Sul Ross State University	M*
Syracuse University	M,D*
Temple University	D*†
Tennessee State University	M,D*
Texas A&M International University	M
Texas A&M University	M,D*
Texas A&M University–Commerce	M,D†
Texas A&M University–Corpus Christi	M
Texas A&M University–Kingsville	M*†
Texas Christian University	M,D*
Texas Tech University	M,D*†
Texas Woman's University	M,D*†
Towson University	M,O†
Tufts University	M,D*†
Tulane University	M,D*†
Uniformed Services University of the Health Sciences	D*
Union Institute & University	D
Universidad de las Americas, A.C.	M
Universidad de las Américas–Puebla	M
Université de Moncton	M
Université de Montréal	M,D
Université de Sherbrooke	M
Université du Québec à Montréal	D
Université du Québec à Trois-Rivières	M,D
Université Laval	M,D†
University at Buffalo, The State University of New York	M,D*†
The University of Akron	M,D†
The University of Alabama	M,D*
The University of Alabama at Birmingham	M,D*†
The University of Alabama in Huntsville	M*
University of Alaska Anchorage	M
University of Alaska Fairbanks	M*
University of Alberta	M,D*
The University of Arizona	D*
University of Arkansas	M,D*
University of Arkansas at Little Rock	M
University of Baltimore	M,D*
The University of British Columbia	M,D*
University of Calgary	M,D*
University of California, Berkeley	D*
University of California, Davis	D*†
University of California, Irvine	D*
University of California, Los Angeles	M,D*
University of California, Riverside	D*
University of California, San Diego	D*
University of California, Santa Barbara	M,D*
University of California, Santa Cruz	D*
University of Central Arkansas	M,D
University of Central Florida	M,D*†
University of Central Oklahoma	M
University of Chicago	D*
University of Cincinnati	D*
University of Colorado at Boulder	M,D*
University of Colorado at Colorado Springs	M*
University of Colorado at Denver	M*
University of Connecticut	D*†
University of Dallas	M*
University of Dayton	M*†
University of Delaware	D*†
University of Denver	D*†
University of Detroit Mercy	M,D,O*
University of Florida	M,D*†
University of Georgia	M,D*†
University of Guelph	M,D
University of Hartford	M*
University of Hawaii at Manoa	M,D*
University of Houston	D*
University of Houston–Clear Lake	M*†
University of Houston–Victoria	M
University of Idaho	M*†
University of Illinois at Chicago	D*
University of Illinois at Urbana–Champaign	M,D*
University of Indianapolis	M,D
The University of Iowa	M,D*
University of Judaism	M
University of Kansas	M,D*
University of Kentucky	M,D*
University of La Verne	M,D*
The University of Lethbridge	M,D
University of Louisiana at Lafayette	M*
University of Louisiana at Monroe	M,O
University of Louisville	M,D*†
University of Maine	M,D*
University of Manitoba	M,D*
University of Mary Hardin-Baylor	M
University of Maryland, Baltimore County	M,D*†
University of Maryland, College Park	M,D*
University of Massachusetts Amherst	M,D*†
University of Massachusetts Dartmouth	M*†
University of Massachusetts Lowell	M*†
The University of Memphis	M,D*†
University of Miami	M,D*†
University of Michigan	D,O*
University of Minnesota, Twin Cities Campus	M,D*
University of Mississippi	M,D*
University of Missouri–Columbia	M,D*
University of Missouri–Kansas City	M,D*†
University of Missouri–St. Louis	M,D,O†
The University of Montana–Missoula	M,D,O*†
University of Nebraska at Omaha	M,D,O
University of Nebraska–Lincoln	M,D*†
University of Nevada, Las Vegas	M,D*†
University of Nevada, Reno	M,D*
University of New Brunswick Fredericton	D
University of New Brunswick Saint John	M
University of New Hampshire	D*†
University of New Mexico	M,D*†
University of New Orleans	M,D*
The University of North Carolina at Chapel Hill	D*†
The University of North Carolina at Charlotte	M*
The University of North Carolina at Greensboro	M,D†
The University of North Carolina at Wilmington	M*
University of North Dakota	M,D*
University of Northern British Columbia	M,D
University of Northern Colorado	M†
University of Northern Iowa	M
University of North Florida	M
University of North Texas	M,D*†
University of Notre Dame	D*†
University of Oklahoma	M,D*†
University of Oregon	M,D*
University of Ottawa	D*
University of Pennsylvania	D*†
University of Phoenix–Hawaii Campus	M
University of Phoenix–New Mexico Campus	M
University of Phoenix–Puerto Rico Campus	M
University of Phoenix–Sacramento Campus	M
University of Phoenix–San Diego Campus	M
University of Phoenix–Southern Arizona Campus	M
University of Phoenix–Utah Campus	M
University of Pittsburgh	M,D*†
University of Puerto Rico, Río Piedras	M,D*
University of Regina	M,D
University of Rhode Island	M,D*
University of Richmond	M*†
University of Rochester	M,D*
University of Saint Francis (IN)	M
University of St. Thomas (MN)	M,D,O*†
University of Saskatchewan	M,D
University of South Alabama	M*†
University of South Carolina	M,D*†
The University of South Dakota	M,D†
University of Southern California	M,D*†
University of Southern Mississippi	M,D,O
University of South Florida	D*†
The University of Tennessee	M,D*†
The University of Tennessee at Chattanooga	M
The University of Texas at Arlington	M,D*†
The University of Texas at Austin	D*
The University of Texas at Brownsville	M

*P—first professional degree; M—master's degree; D—doctorate; O—other advanced degree; *full description and/or announcement in Book 2, 3, 4, 5, or 6; †full description in this book*

The University of Texas at El Paso M,D*†
The University of Texas at San Antonio M*
The University of Texas at Tyler M
The University of Texas of the Permian Basin M
The University of Texas–Pan American M
University of the Pacific M*
University of Toledo M,D*†
University of Toronto M,D*
University of Tulsa M,D†
University of Utah M,D*
University of Vermont D*†
University of Victoria M,D
University of Virginia M,D*
University of Washington D*
University of Waterloo M,D
The University of Western Ontario M,D*
University of West Florida M
University of Windsor M,D
University of Wisconsin–Eau Claire M,O†
University of Wisconsin–La Crosse M,O†
University of Wisconsin–Madison D*
University of Wisconsin–Milwaukee M,D
University of Wisconsin–Oshkosh M*
University of Wisconsin–Stout M
University of Wisconsin–Whitewater M*
University of Wyoming M,D*†
Utah State University M,D*
Valdosta State University M,O
Valparaiso University M
Vanderbilt University M,D*
Villanova University M*†
Virginia Commonwealth University D*†
Virginia Polytechnic Institute and State University M,D*
Virginia State University M
Wake Forest University M*†
Walden University M,D†
Washburn University of Topeka M
Washington College M
Washington State University M,D*
Washington University in St. Louis M,D*†
Wayne State University M,D*
Wesleyan University M*
West Chester University of Pennsylvania M*†
Western Carolina University M†
Western Illinois University M,O
Western Kentucky University M,O†
Western Michigan University M,D,O*†
Western Washington University M
West Texas A&M University M†
West Virginia University M,D*
Wheaton College M,D†
Wichita State University M,D*†
Widener University *†
Wilfrid Laurier University M
William Carey College M
Wilmington College M
Winthrop University M,O
Wisconsin School of Professional Psychology M,D
Wright Institute D
Wright State University M,D*
Xavier University M,D*
Yale University M,D*
Yeshiva University M,D*
York University M,D*

PUBLIC HEALTH—GENERAL

American Military University M
Armstrong Atlantic State University M†
Benedictine University M†
Boise State University M*
Boston University P,M,D,O*†
Bowling Green State University M*†
Brooklyn College of the City University of New York M†
California College for Health Sciences M
California State University, Fresno M
California State University, Northridge M
Case Western Reserve University M*†
Cleveland State University M,D*†
Columbia University M,D*†
Drexel University M*†
Eastern Virginia Medical School M
East Stroudsburg University of Pennsylvania M†
East Tennessee State University M,O†
Emerson College M*†
Emory University M,D*†
Florida Agricultural and Mechanical University M,D*
Florida International University M*†
The George Washington University M,D*†
Georgia Southern University M
Harvard University M,D,O*†
Hunter College of the City University of New York M†
Idaho State University M,O*
Indiana University Bloomington M,D,O*
Johns Hopkins University M,D,O*†
Kent State University M*
Kirksville College of Osteopathic Medicine M,O
Loma Linda University M,D*
Louisiana State University Health Sciences Center M*
Medical College of Ohio M*
Medical College of Wisconsin M*
Morehouse School of Medicine M*
Morgan State University D*
New Jersey Institute of Technology M
New Mexico State University M
New York Medical College M,D,O*
New York University M,D,O*†
Northern Arizona University M
Northern Illinois University M*†
Northwestern University M*
Nova Southeastern University M*
The Ohio State University M,D*
Old Dominion University M*†
Oregon State University M*
Portland State University M*
Purdue University M,D*
Rutgers, The State University of New Jersey, New Brunswick M,D*
Saint Louis University M,D*†
Saint Xavier University M,O*
San Diego State University M,D*
San Francisco State University M
San Jose State University M,O*
Sarah Lawrence College M*†
Southern Connecticut State University M†
Southwest Missouri State University M*†
State University of New York at Albany M,D*†
Temple University M*†
Texas A&M University M,D*
Texas A&M University System Health Science Center M*
Tufts University M*†
Tulane University M,D,O*†
Uniformed Services University of the Health Sciences M,D*
University at Buffalo, The State University of New York M,D*†
The University of Akron M,D†
The University of Alabama at Birmingham M,D*†
University of Alberta M,D,O*
The University of Arizona M*
University of California, Berkeley M,D*
University of California, Los Angeles M,D*
University of California, San Diego D*
University of Colorado Health Sciences Center M*
University of Connecticut M*†
University of Connecticut Health Center M*
University of Denver M*†
University of Florida M*†
University of Hawaii at Manoa M*
University of Illinois at Chicago M,D*
University of Illinois at Springfield M†
The University of Iowa M,D*
University of Kansas M*
University of Kentucky M,D*
University of Maryland, College Park M,D*
University of Massachusetts Amherst M,D*†
University of Medicine and Dentistry of New Jersey M,D*
University of Miami M*†
University of Michigan M,D*
University of Minnesota, Twin Cities Campus M,O*
University of Nebraska Medical Center M*
University of Nevada, Reno M*
University of New Hampshire M*†
University of New Mexico M*†
The University of North Carolina at Chapel Hill M,D*†
University of Northern Colorado M†
University of North Florida M,O
University of North Texas Health Science Center at Fort Worth M,D*
University of Oklahoma Health Sciences Center M,D*
University of Ottawa D*
University of Pittsburgh M,D,O*†
University of Puerto Rico, Medical Sciences Campus M*
University of Rochester M*
University of South Carolina M*†
University of Southern California M*†
University of Southern Mississippi M
University of South Florida M,D*†
The University of Tennessee M*†
The University of Texas Health Science Center at Houston M,D*
University of Toledo M*†
University of Utah M*
University of Washington M,D*
University of Wisconsin–Eau Claire M†
University of Wisconsin–La Crosse M†
Vanderbilt University M*
Virginia Commonwealth University M*†
Walden University M†
West Chester University of Pennsylvania M*†
Western Kentucky University M†
West Virginia University M*
Wichita State University M*†
Yale University M,D*

PUBLIC HISTORY

Appalachian State University M
Arizona State University M,D*
California State University, Sacramento M
Eastern Illinois University M†
Florida State University M,D*†
Indiana University–Purdue University Indianapolis M*
New York University M,D,O*†
North Carolina State University M*
Northeastern University M,D*†
Rutgers, The State University of New Jersey, Camden M†
Shippensburg University of Pennsylvania M†
Simmons College M*
Sonoma State University M
State University of New York at Albany M,D,O*†
University of Arkansas at Little Rock M
The University of British Columbia M,O*
University of Houston M,D*
University of Illinois at Springfield M†
University of Kansas M*
University of Massachusetts Amherst M,D*†
University of Massachusetts Boston M*†
University of New Orleans M*
University of South Carolina M,O*†
The University of Texas at Austin M,D*
University of Waterloo M,D
Wayne State University M,D,O*

PUBLIC POLICY AND ADMINISTRATION

Albany State University M
Alfred University M*†
American International College M*
American Military University M
American University M*†
Andrew Jackson University M
Angelo State University M†
Anna Maria College M
Appalachian State University M
Arizona State University M,D*
Arkansas State University M,O
Auburn University M,D*†
Auburn University Montgomery M,D
Audrey Cohen College M†
Ball State University M*
Baylor University M*†
Bernard M. Baruch College of the City University of New York M*
Birmingham-Southern College M
Boise State University M*
Boston University M,D,O*†
Bowie State University M
Bowling Green State University M*†
Brandeis University D*†
Bridgewater State College M
Brigham Young University M*
Brock University M
Brooklyn College of the City University of New York M†
California Lutheran University M
California State Polytechnic University, Pomona M*
California State University, Bakersfield M
California State University, Chico M
California State University, Dominguez Hills M†
California State University, Fresno M
California State University, Fullerton M
California State University, Hayward M
California State University, Long Beach M,O
California State University, Los Angeles M
California State University, Northridge M
California State University, Sacramento M
California State University, San Bernardino M
California State University, Stanislaus M
Carleton University M,D
Carnegie Mellon University M,D*
Central Michigan University M,O†
Central Missouri State University M,O†
Chaminade University of Honolulu M*
Christopher Newport University M†
City University M,O†
Claremont Graduate University M,D*
Clark Atlanta University M
Clark University M,O*†
Clemson University M,D,O*
Cleveland State University M,D*†
College of Charleston M*†
The College of William and Mary M*†
Columbia University M*†
Columbus State University M
Concordia University (Canada) M*†
Concordia University Wisconsin M
Cornell University M,D*
Cumberland University M
Dalhousie University M*
DePaul University M*†
Drake University M*†
Duke University M*†
Duquesne University M,O*†
East Carolina University M*†
Eastern Kentucky University M
Eastern Michigan University M*
Eastern Washington University M†
The Evergreen State College M*
Fairleigh Dickinson University, Metropolitan Campus M*†
Florida Atlantic University M,D*
Florida Atlantic University, Ft. Lauderdale Campus M,D
Florida Gulf Coast University M
Florida Institute of Technology M*†
Florida International University M,D*†
Florida State University M,D,O*†
Framingham State College M*
Gannon University M,O
George Mason University M,D*†
Georgetown University M*
The George Washington University M,D*†
Georgia College & State University M
Georgia Institute of Technology M,D*
Georgia Southern University M
Georgia State University M,D*
Golden Gate University M
Governors State University M
Graduate School and University Center of the City University of New York M,D*†
Grambling State University M
Grand Valley State University M†
Hamline University M*
Harvard University M,D*†
Howard University M*
Idaho State University M*
Illinois Institute of Technology M*†
Indiana State University M*†
Indiana University Bloomington M,D*
Indiana University Northwest M,O
Indiana University of Pennsylvania M*†
Indiana University–Purdue University Fort Wayne M,O
Indiana University–Purdue University Indianapolis M,O*
Indiana University South Bend M
Institute of Public Administration M,O
Iowa State University of Science and Technology M*†
Jackson State University M,D
Jacksonville State University M
James Madison University M
John Jay College of Criminal Justice of the City University of New York M,D*
Johns Hopkins University M*†
Kansas State University M*†
Kean University M*†
Kennesaw State University M
Kent State University M*
Kentucky State University M
Kutztown University of Pennsylvania M†

Lamar University M*†
Long Island University, Brentwood Campus M
Long Island University, Brooklyn Campus M*
Long Island University, C.W. Post Campus M,O*†
Long Island University, Westchester Graduate Campus M
Louisiana State University and Agricultural and Mechanical College M*
Marist College M,O
Marywood University M*†
McMaster University M
Metropolitan State University M
Michigan State University M,D*†
Midwestern State University M
Minnesota State University, Mankato M
Minnesota State University, Moorhead M
Mississippi State University M,D*
Montana State University–Bozeman M*
Monterey Institute of International Studies M*
Murray State University M†
National University M†
New Mexico Highlands University M
New School University D*†
New York University M,D,O*†
North Carolina Central University M
North Carolina State University M,D*
Northeastern University M,D*†
Northern Arizona University M,D,O
Northern Illinois University M*†
Northern Kentucky University M
Northern Michigan University M
North Georgia College & State University M
Northwestern University D*
Notre Dame de Namur University M
Nova Southeastern University M,D*
Oakland University M†
The Ohio State University M,D*
Ohio University M*
Oklahoma City University M
Oklahoma State University M*†
Old Dominion University M*†
Pace University, White Plains Campus M*
Park University M
The Pennsylvania State University Harrisburg Campus of the Capital College M,D*†
Pepperdine University M*
Piedmont College M
Pontifical Catholic University of Puerto Rico M,D
Portland State University M,D*
Princeton University M,D*
Queen's University at Kingston M
RAND Graduate School of Policy Studies D*
Regent University M†
Rochester Institute of Technology M*†
Roosevelt University M*†
Rutgers, The State University of New Jersey, Camden M†
Rutgers, The State University of New Jersey, Newark M,D*†
Rutgers, The State University of New Jersey, New Brunswick M*
Sage Graduate School M†
Saginaw Valley State University M
St. Edward's University M,O
Saint Louis University M,D*†
Saint Mary's University of Minnesota M
St. Thomas University M,O†
San Diego State University M*
San Francisco State University M
San Jose State University M*
Savannah State University M
Seattle University M*†
Seton Hall University M*†
Shenandoah University M,O
Shippensburg University of Pennsylvania M†
Sonoma State University M
Southeastern University M†
Southeast Missouri State University M
Southern Illinois University Carbondale M*†
Southern Illinois University Edwardsville M†
Southern University and Agricultural and Mechanical College M,D*
Southwest Missouri State University M*†
Southwest Texas State University M*
State University of New York at Albany M,D,O*†
State University of New York at Binghamton M,D*†
State University of New York College at Brockport M*†
State University of New York Empire State College M
State University of West Georgia M
Stephen F. Austin State University M
Stony Brook University, State University of New York M,D,O*†
Suffolk University M,O*
Sul Ross State University M*
Syracuse University M,D*
Tennessee State University M,D*
Texas A&M International University M
Texas A&M University M*
Texas A&M University–Corpus Christi M
Texas Southern University M†
Texas Tech University M,D*†
Trinity College (CT) M
Troy State University M
Tufts University M*†
Tulane University M*†
Université de Moncton M
Université du Québec à Montréal M
Université du Québec à Rimouski O
Université du Québec, École nationale d'administration publique O
The University of Akron M†
The University of Alabama M,D*
The University of Alabama at Birmingham M*†
The University of Alabama in Huntsville M*
University of Alaska Anchorage M
University of Alaska Southeast M
The University of Arizona M,D*
University of Arkansas M,D*
University of Arkansas at Little Rock M
University of Baltimore M,D*
University of California, Berkeley M,D*
University of California, Los Angeles M*
University of Central Florida M,D,O*†
University of Chicago M,D*
University of Colorado at Boulder M,D*
University of Colorado at Colorado Springs M*
University of Colorado at Denver M,D*
University of Connecticut M*†
University of Dayton M*†
University of Delaware M,D*†
The University of Findlay M
University of Florida M,D,O*†
University of Georgia M,D*†
University of Guam M
University of Hawaii at Manoa M,O*
University of Houston–Clear Lake M*†
University of Idaho M*†
University of Illinois at Chicago M,D*
University of Illinois at Springfield M,D†
University of Kansas M*
University of Kentucky M,D*
University of La Verne M,D*
University of Louisville M*†
University of Maine M*
University of Manitoba M*
University of Maryland, Baltimore County M,D*†
University of Maryland, College Park M,D*
University of Massachusetts Amherst M*†
University of Massachusetts Boston M,D*†
The University of Memphis M*†
University of Michigan M,D*
University of Michigan–Dearborn M*†
University of Michigan–Flint M
University of Minnesota, Twin Cities Campus M*
University of Missouri–Columbia M*
University of Missouri–Kansas City M,D*†
University of Missouri–St. Louis M,D,O†
The University of Montana–Missoula M*†
University of Nebraska at Omaha M,D
University of Nevada, Las Vegas M*†
University of Nevada, Reno M*
University of New Brunswick Fredericton M
University of New Hampshire M*†
University of New Haven M*†
University of New Mexico M*†
University of New Orleans M*
The University of North Carolina at Chapel Hill M,D*†
The University of North Carolina at Charlotte M,D*
The University of North Carolina at Greensboro M,O†
The University of North Carolina at Pembroke M
University of North Dakota M*
University of Northern Iowa M
University of North Florida M
University of North Texas M*†
University of Oklahoma M*†
University of Oregon M*
University of Pennsylvania M,D*†
University of Pittsburgh M,D*†
University of Puerto Rico, Río Piedras M*
University of Regina M
University of Rhode Island M*
University of San Francisco M*†
University of South Alabama M*†
University of South Carolina M*†
The University of South Dakota M†
University of Southern California M,D,O*†
University of Southern Maine M,D
University of South Florida M*†
The University of Tennessee M*†
The University of Tennessee at Chattanooga M
The University of Texas at Arlington M,D*†
The University of Texas at Austin M,D*
The University of Texas at Dallas M*
The University of Texas at San Antonio M*
The University of Texas at Tyler M
The University of Texas–Pan American M
University of the District of Columbia M*
University of the Pacific P,M,D*
University of the Virgin Islands M
University of Toledo M*†
University of Utah M,O*
University of Vermont M*†
University of Victoria M
University of Washington M*
University of West Florida M
The University of Winnipeg M
University of Wisconsin–Madison M*
University of Wisconsin–Milwaukee M
University of Wisconsin–Oshkosh M*
University of Wisconsin–Whitewater M*
University of Wyoming M*†
Valdosta State University M
Villanova University M*†
Virginia Commonwealth University M,D,O*†
Virginia Polytechnic Institute and State University M,D,O*
Washington State University M*
Washington University in St. Louis M*†
Wayne State University M*
Webster University M
West Chester University of Pennsylvania M*†
Western Carolina University M†
Western International University M
Western Kentucky University M†
Western Michigan University M,D*†
West Virginia University M,D*
Wichita State University M*†
Widener University M*†
Willamette University M*
Wilmington College M
Wright State University M*

PUBLISHING

Drexel University M*†
Emerson College M*†
New York University M*†
Northwestern University M*
Pace University M*†
Rochester Institute of Technology M*†
Rosemont College M†
Simon Fraser University M
University of Baltimore M*

QUALITY MANAGEMENT

California State University, Dominguez Hills M†
Case Western Reserve University M,D*†
Dowling College M,O
Eastern Michigan University M*
Hawai'i Pacific University M*†
Instituto Tecnológico y de Estudios Superiores de Monterrey, Campus Ciudad de México M,D
Instituto Tecnológico y de Estudios Superiores de Monterrey, Campus Ciudad Juárez M
Instituto Tecnológico y de Estudios Superiores de Monterrey, Campus Irapuato M,D
Madonna University M
Marian College of Fond du Lac M
The National Graduate School of Quality Management M*
North Carolina State University M*
The Pennsylvania State University University Park Campus M*†
Rutgers, The State University of New Jersey, New Brunswick M,D*
San Jose State University M*
Universidad de las Americas, A.C. M
The University of Akron M†
University of Central Florida M,O*†
University of Dubuque M
Upper Iowa University M

QUANTITATIVE ANALYSIS

California State University, Hayward M
Clark Atlanta University M
Drexel University M,D,O*†
Hofstra University M*
Louisiana Tech University M,D*
Loyola College in Maryland M
New York University M,D,O*†
Purdue University M,D*
St. John's University (NY) M,O*†
Syracuse University D*
Texas Tech University M,D*†
University of Cincinnati M,D*
University of Missouri–St. Louis M,O†
University of Oregon M,D*
University of Rhode Island M,D*
The University of Texas at Arlington M,D*†
Virginia Commonwealth University M*†

RADIATION BIOLOGY

Auburn University M*†
Colorado State University M,D*
Florida State University M,D*†
Georgetown University M*
Université de Sherbrooke M,D
The University of Iowa M,D*
University of Oklahoma Health Sciences Center M,D*
The University of Texas Southwestern Medical Center at Dallas M,D*

RANGE SCIENCE

Brigham Young University M,D*
Colorado State University M,D*
Kansas State University M,D*†
Montana State University–Bozeman M*
New Mexico State University M,D
North Dakota State University M,D†
Oregon State University M,D*
Sul Ross State University M*
Texas A&M University M,D*
Texas A&M University–Kingsville M*†
Texas Tech University M,D*†
The University of Arizona M,D*
University of California, Berkeley M,D*
University of Idaho M,D*†
University of Wyoming M,D*†
Utah State University M,D*

READING EDUCATION

Abilene Christian University M
Adelphi University M,O*
Alabama State University M,O
Albany State University M
Alfred University M*†
Alverno College M
American International College M,D,O*
Andrews University M

*P—first professional degree; M—master's degree; D—doctorate; O—other advanced degree; *full description and/or announcement in Book 2, 3, 4, 5, or 6; †full description in this book*

Institution	Degrees
Angelo State University	M†
Anna Maria College	M
Appalachian State University	M
Arcadia University	M,D,O†
Arkansas State University	M,O
Ashland University	M
Auburn University	M,D,O*†
Auburn University Montgomery	M,O
Austin Peay State University	M,O
Averett University	M
Baldwin-Wallace College	M*
Ball State University	M,D*
Barry University	M,O*†
Berry College	M
Bloomsburg University of Pennsylvania	M
Boise State University	M*
Boston College	M,O*†
Boston University	M,D,O*†
Bowie State University	M
Bowling Green State University	M,O*†
Bridgewater State College	M,O
Brigham Young University	M,D*
Brooklyn College of the City University of New York	M†
Bucknell University	M
Butler University	M
California Baptist University	M
California Lutheran University	M
California Polytechnic State University, San Luis Obispo	M†
California State University, Bakersfield	M
California State University, Chico	M
California State University, Fresno	M
California State University, Fullerton	M
California State University, Los Angeles	M
California State University, Sacramento	M
California State University, San Bernardino	M
California State University, Stanislaus	M
California University of Pennsylvania	M
Canisius College	M
Cardinal Stritch University	M*
Carthage College	M,O
Castleton State College	M,O
Central Connecticut State University	M,O*†
Central Michigan University	M†
Central Missouri State University	M,O†
Central State University	M
Central Washington University	M†
Chapman University	M*†
Chicago State University	M
The Citadel, The Military College of South Carolina	M
City College of the City University of New York	M,O*†
City University	M,O†
Claremont Graduate University	M,D*
Clarion University of Pennsylvania	M†
Clarke College	M
Clemson University	M*
Cleveland State University	M*†
College of Mount St. Joseph	M†
The College of New Jersey	M†
The College of New Rochelle	M†
College of St. Joseph	M
The College of Saint Rose	M*†
The College of William and Mary	M*†
Concordia University (CA)	M
Concordia University (IL)	M,O
Concordia University (NE)	M
Concordia University Wisconsin	M
Cumberland College	M
Curry College	M,O
Dallas Baptist University	M
DePaul University	M*†
Dowling College	M
Duquesne University	M*†
East Carolina University	M*†
Eastern Connecticut State University	M
Eastern Kentucky University	M
Eastern Michigan University	M*
Eastern Nazarene College	M,O
Eastern Washington University	M†
East Stroudsburg University of Pennsylvania	M†
East Tennessee State University	M†
Edinboro University of Pennsylvania	M,O
Elms College	M,O
Emporia State University	M*†
Endicott College	M
Evangel University	M
Ferris State University	M
Florida Atlantic University	M*
Florida Atlantic University, Ft. Lauderdale Campus	M,D,O
Florida Gulf Coast University	M
Florida International University	M*†
Florida State University	M,D,O*†
Fordham University	M,D,O*†
Framingham State College	M*
Fresno Pacific University	M
Frostburg State University	M
Furman University	M
Gannon University	M,O
George Mason University	M*†
Georgian Court College	M,O
Georgia Southern University	M,O
Georgia Southwestern State University	M,O
Georgia State University	M,O*
Governors State University	M
Grand Canyon University	M
Grand Valley State University	M†
Gwynedd-Mercy College	M
Hardin-Simmons University	M
Harvard University	M,D,O*†
Henderson State University	M
Hofstra University	M,D,O*
Holy Family College	M
Hood College	M
Houston Baptist University	M
Howard University	M,O*
Hunter College of the City University of New York	M,O†
Idaho State University	M,O*
Illinois State University	M*†
Indiana State University	M,D,O*†
Indiana University Bloomington	M,D,O*
Indiana University of Pennsylvania	M*†
Indiana University–Purdue University Indianapolis	M*
Jacksonville University	M
James Madison University	M
Johns Hopkins University	M,D,O*†
Johnson State College	M
Kean University	M,O*†
Kent State University	M*
King's College	M
Kutztown University of Pennsylvania	M†
Lake Erie College	M
Lamar University	M,O*†
Lehman College of the City University of New York	M
Lesley University	M,D,O*†
Liberty University	M,D†
Long Island University, Brentwood Campus	M
Long Island University, Brooklyn Campus	M*
Long Island University, C.W. Post Campus	M,O*†
Long Island University, Rockland Graduate Campus	M
Long Island University, Southampton College	M
Long Island University, Westchester Graduate Campus	M
Longwood College	M
Louisiana Tech University	M,D,O*
Loyola College in Maryland	M,O
Loyola Marymount University	M†
Loyola University New Orleans	M
Lynchburg College	M
Lyndon State College	M
Madonna University	M
Malone College	M†
Manhattanville College	M*†
Marshall University	M,O*†
Marycrest International University	M
Marygrove College	M
Marywood University	M*†
Massachusetts College of Liberal Arts	M
McDaniel College	M
McNeese State University	M
Mercer University	M,O
Mercy College	M,O*
Miami University	M*†
Michigan State University	M*†
Middle Tennessee State University	M*
Midwestern State University	M
Millersville University of Pennsylvania	M†
Minnesota State University, Mankato	M
Minnesota State University, Moorhead	M
Monmouth University	M,O*†
Montana State University–Billings	M*
Montclair State University	M†
Morehead State University	M
Morningside College	M
Mount Saint Mary College	M
Mount Saint Vincent University	M
Murray State University	M†
National-Louis University	M,D,O
Nazareth College of Rochester	M
New Jersey City University	M
New Mexico State University	M,D,O
Niagara University	M†
North Carolina Agricultural and Technical State University	M*
Northeastern Illinois University	M
Northeastern State University	M
Northern Arizona University	M
Northern Illinois University	M,D*†
Northern State University	M
Northwestern Oklahoma State University	M
Northwestern State University of Louisiana	M,O
Northwest Missouri State University	M
Notre Dame College (OH)	M,O
Nova Southeastern University	M,O*
Oakland University	M,D,O†
Ohio University	M,D*
Old Dominion University	M*†
Pacific Lutheran University	M†
The Pennsylvania State University University Park Campus	M,D*†
Pittsburg State University	M
Plattsburgh State University of New York	M
Plymouth State College	M*
Portland State University	M*
Providence College	M*
Purdue University	M,D,O*
Queens College of the City University of New York	M†
Radford University	M†
Rhode Island College	M,O†
Rider University	M*
Rivier College	M*†
Rockford College	M
Roosevelt University	M,D*†
Rowan University	M†
Rutgers, The State University of New Jersey, New Brunswick	M,D*
Sage Graduate School	M†
Saginaw Valley State University	M
St. Bonaventure University	M
St. John Fisher College	M
St. John's University (NY)	M,O*†
Saint Joseph's University	M*†
Saint Martin's College	M
Saint Mary's College of California	M
St. Mary's University of San Antonio	M
Saint Michael's College	M,O*
Saint Peter's College	M†
St. Thomas Aquinas College	M,O
Saint Xavier University	M,O*
Salem College	M
Salem State College	M
Salisbury University	M
Sam Houston State University	M,O*
San Diego State University	M*
San Francisco State University	M,O
Seattle Pacific University	M
Shippensburg University of Pennsylvania	M,O†
Siena Heights University	M
Slippery Rock University of Pennsylvania	M†
Sonoma State University	M
Southern Connecticut State University	M,O†
Southern Oregon University	M
Southwest Missouri State University	M*†
Southwest Texas State University	M*
Spalding University	M†
State University of New York at Albany	M,D,O*†
State University of New York at Binghamton	M*†
State University of New York at New Paltz	M
State University of New York at Oswego	M
State University of New York College at Brockport	M*†
State University of New York College at Buffalo	M,O
State University of New York College at Cortland	M
State University of New York College at Fredonia	M
State University of New York College at Geneseo	M
State University of New York College at Oneonta	M
State University of New York College at Potsdam	M
State University of West Georgia	M
Sul Ross State University	M*
Syracuse University	M,D,O*
Tarleton State University	M,O
Teachers College Columbia University	M*
Temple University	M,D*†
Tennessee Technological University	M,O*
Texas A&M International University	M
Texas A&M University	M,D*
Texas A&M University–Commerce	M,D†
Texas A&M University–Kingsville	M*†
Texas Southern University	M,D†
Texas Tech University	M,D,O*†
Texas Woman's University	M,D*†
Towson University	M†
Union College (KY)	M
University at Buffalo, The State University of New York	M,D,O*†
The University of Arizona	M,D,O*
University of Arkansas at Little Rock	M,O
University of Bridgeport	M,O*†
The University of British Columbia	M,D*
University of California, Berkeley	M,D,O*
University of Central Arkansas	M
University of Central Florida	M*†
University of Central Oklahoma	M
University of Cincinnati	M,D*
University of Connecticut	M,D*†
University of Dayton	M*†
University of Florida	M,D,O*†
University of Georgia	M,D,O*†
University of Guam	M
University of Houston	M,D*
University of Houston–Clear Lake	M*†
University of Illinois at Chicago	M,D*
University of La Verne	M,O*
University of Louisiana at Monroe	M
University of Louisville	M*†
University of Maine	M,D,O*
University of Manitoba	M*
University of Mary Hardin-Baylor	M
University of Maryland, College Park	M,D,O*
University of Massachusetts Amherst	M,D,O*†
University of Massachusetts Lowell	M,D,O*†
The University of Memphis	M,D*†
University of Miami	M,D,O*†
University of Michigan	M,D*
University of Minnesota, Twin Cities Campus	M,D*
University of Missouri–Kansas City	M,D,O*†
University of Missouri–St. Louis	M,D†
University of Nebraska at Kearney	M
University of Nebraska at Omaha	M
University of New Hampshire	M,D*†
The University of North Carolina at Chapel Hill	D*†
The University of North Carolina at Charlotte	M*
The University of North Carolina at Pembroke	M
The University of North Carolina at Wilmington	M*
University of North Dakota	M*
University of Northern Colorado	M†
University of Northern Iowa	M
University of North Texas	M,D*†
University of Oklahoma	M,D,O*†
University of Pennsylvania	M,D*†
University of Pittsburgh	M,D*†
University of Rhode Island	M*
University of Rio Grande	M
University of St. Thomas (MN)	M,D,O*†
The University of Scranton	M†
University of Sioux Falls	M
University of South Alabama	M*†
University of South Carolina	M,D*†
University of Southern California	M,D*†
University of Southern Maine	M,O
University of Southern Mississippi	M,D,O
University of South Florida	M,D,O*†
The University of Tennessee	M,D,O*†
The University of Tennessee at Chattanooga	M,O
The University of Texas at Brownsville	M
The University of Texas at San Antonio	M*
The University of Texas at Tyler	M,O
The University of Texas of the Permian Basin	M
The University of Texas–Pan American	M
University of the Incarnate Word	M†
University of Vermont	M*†
University of Washington	M,D*
University of West Florida	M
University of Wisconsin–Eau Claire	M†
University of Wisconsin–La Crosse	M†

University of Wisconsin–Milwaukee M
University of Wisconsin–Oshkosh M*
University of Wisconsin–River Falls M
University of Wisconsin–Stevens Point M
University of Wisconsin–Superior M
Valdosta State University M,O
Vanderbilt University M,D*
Virginia Commonwealth University M*†
Walla Walla College M
Washburn University of Topeka M
Washington State University M,D*
Wayne State University M,D,O*
West Chester University of Pennsylvania M*†
Western Carolina University M†
Western Connecticut State University M
Western Illinois University M,O
Western Kentucky University M†
Western Michigan University M*†
Western New Mexico University M
Westfield State College M
Westminster College (PA) M,O
West Texas A&M University M†
West Virginia University M*
Wheelock College M*
Whitworth College M
Widener University M,D*†
William Paterson University of New Jersey M*†
Wilmington College M,D
Winthrop University M
Worcester State College M,O
Xavier University M*
Youngstown State University M

REAL ESTATE

American University M*†
California State University, Northridge M
California State University, Sacramento M
Columbia University M*†
Cornell University M*
The George Washington University M*†
Georgia State University M,D*
John Marshall Law School P,M
Johns Hopkins University M,O*†
Massachusetts Institute of Technology M*
New York University M,O*†
The Pennsylvania State University University Park Campus M,D*†
Texas A&M University M*
University of California, Berkeley D*
University of Cincinnati M*
University of Colorado at Boulder M,D*
University of Denver M*†
University of Florida M,D*†
The University of Memphis M,D*†
University of North Texas M,D*†
University of Pennsylvania M,D*†
University of St. Thomas (MN) M,O*†
University of Southern California M*†
The University of Texas at Arlington M,D*†
University of Wisconsin–Madison M*
Virginia Commonwealth University M,O*†
Webster University M

RECREATION AND PARK MANAGEMENT

Adams State College M
Arizona State University M*
Aurora University M
Baker College Center for Graduate Studies M
Baylor University M*†
Bowling Green State University M*†
Brigham Young University M*
California State University, Chico M
California State University, Long Beach M
California State University, Northridge M
California State University, Sacramento M
Central Michigan University M†
Central Washington University M†
Clemson University M,D*
Cleveland State University M*†
Colorado State University M,D*
Delta State University M
East Carolina University M*†
Florida Agricultural and Mechanical University M*
Florida International University M*†
Florida State University M,D,O*†
Fort Hays State University M
Frostburg State University M
Georgia Southern University M
Hardin-Simmons University M
Howard University M*
Indiana University Bloomington M,D,O*
Lehman College of the City University of New York M
Michigan State University M,D*†
Middle Tennessee State University M,D*
Morehead State University M
Murray State University M†
Naropa University P,M*
New York University M,D,O*†
North Carolina Central University M
North Carolina State University M*
Ohio University M*
Old Dominion University M*†
Purdue University M,D*
San Francisco State University M
San Jose State University M*
South Dakota State University M*
Southern Connecticut State University M†
Southern Illinois University Carbondale M*†
Southern University and Agricultural and Mechanical College M*
Southwestern Oklahoma State University M
Southwest Missouri State University M*†
Southwest Texas State University M*
Springfield College M†
State University of New York College at Brockport M*†
State University of New York College at Cortland M
State University of New York College of Environmental Science and Forestry M,D
Temple University M*†
Texas A&M University M,D*
United States Sports Academy M*
Universidad Metropolitana M
University of Alberta M,D*
University of Arkansas M,D*
University of Florida M,D*†
University of Georgia M,D*†
University of Idaho M,D*†
University of Manitoba M*
University of Minnesota, Twin Cities Campus M,D*
University of Missouri–Columbia M*
The University of Montana–Missoula M*†
University of Nebraska at Omaha M
University of Nebraska–Lincoln M*†
University of New Brunswick Fredericton M
University of New Mexico M*†
The University of North Carolina at Chapel Hill M*†
The University of North Carolina at Greensboro M†
University of North Texas M,O*†
University of Rhode Island M*
University of South Alabama M*†
University of Southern Mississippi M,D
The University of Tennessee M*†
University of Toledo M*†
University of Utah M,D*
University of Waterloo M,D
University of Wisconsin–La Crosse M†
Utah State University M,D*
Virginia Commonwealth University M*†
Virginia Polytechnic Institute and State University M,D*
Washington State University M*
Wayne State University M*
Western Illinois University M
Western Kentucky University M†
West Virginia University M*
Wright State University M*

REHABILITATION COUNSELING

Arkansas State University M,O
Assumption College M,O†
Barry University M,O*†
Boston University M,D,O*†
Bowling Green State University M*†
California State University, Fresno M
California State University, Los Angeles M
California State University, San Bernardino M
Central Connecticut State University M*†
Coppin State College M
East Central University M
Edinboro University of Pennsylvania M,O
Emporia State University M*†
Florida State University M,D,O*†
Fort Valley State University M
The George Washington University M,D*†
Georgia State University M,O*
Hofstra University M,O*
Hunter College of the City University of New York M†
Illinois Institute of Technology M,D*†
Indiana University–Purdue University Indianapolis M,D*
Jackson State University M,O
Kent State University M,O*
La Salle University D
Louisiana State University Health Sciences Center M*
Maryville University of Saint Louis M
Michigan State University M,D,O*†
Minnesota State University, Mankato M
Montana State University–Billings M*
New York University M,D*†
Northeastern University M*†
Ohio University M,D*
St. Cloud State University M
St. John's University (NY) M,O*†
San Diego State University M*
San Francisco State University M
South Carolina State University M
Southern Illinois University Carbondale M,D*†
Southern University and Agricultural and Mechanical College M*
Springfield College M,O†
State University of New York at Albany M*†
Syracuse University M,D*
Thomas University M
University at Buffalo, The State University of New York M,D,O*†
The University of Alabama at Birmingham M*†
The University of Arizona M,D,O*
University of Arkansas M,D*
University of Florida M*†
University of Illinois at Urbana–Champaign M*
The University of Iowa M,D*
University of Kentucky M*
University of Louisiana at Lafayette M*
University of Maryland, College Park M,D,O*
University of Medicine and Dentistry of New Jersey M,D*
The University of Memphis M,D*†
University of Nevada, Las Vegas M*†
The University of North Carolina at Chapel Hill M,D*†
University of Northern Colorado M,D†
University of North Texas M*†
University of Puerto Rico, Río Piedras M*
The University of Scranton M†
University of South Florida M*†
The University of Tennessee M*†
The University of Texas–Pan American M
The University of Texas Southwestern Medical Center at Dallas M*
University of Wisconsin–Madison M,D*
University of Wisconsin–Stout M
Utah State University M*
Virginia Commonwealth University M,O*†
Wayne State University M,D,O*
Western Michigan University M*†
Western Oregon University M
Western Washington University M
West Virginia University M*
Wright State University M*

REHABILITATION SCIENCES

Boston University M,D*†
Duquesne University M,D*†
East Carolina University M*†
East Stroudsburg University of Pennsylvania M†
McGill University M,D*
McMaster University M
Medical University of South Carolina M*
New York University M*†
Pennsylvania College of Optometry M,D,O
Queen's University at Kingston M,D
Texas Tech University Health Sciences Center M*
University at Buffalo, The State University of New York D*†
University of Alberta D*
The University of British Columbia M*
University of Cincinnati M*
University of Florida D*†
University of Illinois at Urbana–Champaign M*
University of Kentucky D*
University of Manitoba M*
University of Maryland D*†
University of Minnesota, Twin Cities Campus M,D*
University of North Texas M*†
University of Oklahoma Health Sciences Center M*
University of Pittsburgh M,D,O*†
University of South Carolina M,O*†
University of Toledo M*†
University of Toronto M*
University of Washington M*
University of Wisconsin–La Crosse M†
University of Wisconsin–Madison M*
Wayne State University M*

RELIABILITY ENGINEERING

The University of Arizona M*
University of Maryland, College Park M,D*

RELIGION

Arizona State University M*
Azusa Pacific University P,M,D*†
Bayamón Central University P,M
Baylor University M,D*†
Bethany Theological Seminary P,M,O
Biola University P,M,D
Boston University M,D*†
Brown University M,D*
Bryn Athyn College of the New Church P,M
California Institute of Integral Studies M,D*
Canadian Theological Seminary P,M,O
Cardinal Stritch University M*
The Catholic University of America M,D,O*†
Chestnut Hill College M†
Cincinnati Bible College and Seminary P,M
Claremont Graduate University M,D*
Claremont School of Theology M,D
Columbia International University P,M,D,O
Columbia University M,D*†
Concordia University (IL) M,O
Concordia University (Canada) M,D*†
Denver Seminary P,M,D,O
Drew University M,D†
Duke University M,D*†
Earlham School of Religion P,M
Eastern Mennonite University P,M
Edgewood College M
Elms College M
Emmanuel School of Religion P,M,D
Emory University D*†
Evangelical School of Theology P,M,O
Faith Baptist Bible College and Theological Seminary P,M,D
Florida International University M*†
Florida State University M,D*†
Fordham University M,D,O*†
George Fox University P,M,D†
The George Washington University M*†
Gonzaga University P,M
Gordon-Conwell Theological Seminary P,M,D
Graceland University M
Graduate Theological Union M,D,O
Grand Rapids Baptist Seminary of Cornerstone University P,M,D
Harding University Graduate School of Religion P,M,D
Hardin-Simmons University M
Hartford Seminary M,D,O
Harvard University M,D*†
Hebrew Union College–Jewish Institute of Religion (OH) M,D
Holy Names College M,O
Hsi Lai University M,D*
Iliff School of Theology P,M,D
Indiana State University M*†
Indiana University Bloomington M,D*
International College and Graduate School P,M,D

*P—first professional degree; M—master's degree; D—doctorate; O—other advanced degree; *full description and/or announcement in Book 2, 3, 4, 5, or 6; †full description in this book*

Jewish Theological Seminary of America M,D*
John Carroll University M
La Salle University M
La Sierra University M
Liberty University M†
Lipscomb University P,M
Loras College M
Louisville Presbyterian Theological Seminary P,M,D
Loyola University New Orleans M
The Lutheran Theological Seminary at Philadelphia P,M,D,O
McGill University M,D*
McMaster University M,D
Memorial University of Newfoundland M†
Miami University M*†
Mount St. Mary's College M*
Naropa University M*
New York University M,O*†
North American Baptist Seminary M
Northern Baptist Theological Seminary P,M,D
Northwest Nazarene University M
Oklahoma City University M
Olivet Nazarene University M
Pacific School of Religion P,M,D,O
Pepperdine University P,M*
Point Loma Nazarene University M
Princeton Theological Seminary P,M,D
Princeton University D*
Providence College M*
Queen's University at Kingston M
Reformed Theological Seminary (NC) P,M,D
Reformed Theological Seminary (MD) M
Reformed Theological Seminary (FL) P,M,D
Rice University M,D*
Sacred Heart University M*†
St. Charles Borromeo Seminary, Overbrook M
Saint John's Seminary (MA) P,M
Santa Clara University M*
Seton Hall University M*†
Smith College M*
Southern Adventist University M
Southern California Bible College & Seminary P,M
Southern Evangelical Seminary P,M,O
Southern Methodist University M,D*†
Southern Nazarene University M
Southwest Missouri State University M*†
Spalding University M†
Stanford University M,D*
Syracuse University M,D*
Temple University M,D*†
Trevecca Nazarene University M
Trinity Episcopal School for Ministry P,M,D,O
Trinity International University P,M,D,O
Trinity International University, South Florida Campus M
Trinity Western University M
Université de Montréal M,D
Université de Sherbrooke M,D,O
Université du Québec à Montréal M,D
Université Laval M,D†
The University of British Columbia M*
University of Calgary M,D*
University of California, Berkeley D*
University of California, Santa Barbara M,D*
University of Chicago P,M,D*
University of Colorado at Boulder M*
University of Denver M,D*†
University of Detroit Mercy M*
University of Florida M*†
University of Georgia M*†
University of Hawaii at Manoa M*
The University of Iowa M,D*
University of Kansas M*
The University of Lethbridge M,D
University of Manitoba M,D*
University of Missouri–Columbia M*
The University of North Carolina at Chapel Hill M,D*†
University of North Texas M*†
University of Notre Dame M*†
University of Ottawa M,D*
University of Pennsylvania D*†
University of Pittsburgh M,D*†
University of Regina M
University of St. Thomas (MN) M*†
University of South Carolina M*†
University of Southern California M,D*†
University of South Florida M*†
The University of Tennessee M,D*†
University of the Incarnate Word M†
University of Toronto M,D*
University of Virginia M,D*
University of Washington M*
The University of Winnipeg M
Vanderbilt University M,D*
Vanguard University of Southern California M
Wake Forest University M*†
Warner Pacific College M
Washington University in St. Louis M*†
Wayland Baptist University M
Western Kentucky University M†
Western Michigan University M,D*†
Western Seminary M,O
Westminster Theological Seminary P,M,D,O
Westminster Theological Seminary in California P,M
Wheaton College M†
Wilfrid Laurier University M
Wycliffe College P,M,D,O
Yale University D*

RELIGIOUS EDUCATION

Alliance Theological Seminary P,M
Andover Newton Theological School P,M,D*
Andrews University M,D,O
Asbury Theological Seminary P,M,D,O
Ashland University P,M,D
Azusa Pacific University P,M,D*†
Baptist Bible College of Pennsylvania M
Baptist Theological Seminary at Richmond P,D
Bethel Seminary P,M,D,O
Biola University P,M,D
Boston College M,D,O*†
Calvin Theological Seminary P,M,D
Campbell University P,M
Canadian Theological Seminary P,M,O
The Catholic University of America M,D*†
Chicago Theological Seminary P,M,D
Christian Theological Seminary P,M,D
Columbia International University P,M,D,O
Concordia University (MN) M
Concordia University (NE) M
Dallas Theological Seminary M,D,O
Denver Seminary P,M,D,O
Felician College M
Fordham University M,D,O*†
Gardner-Webb University P,D
Garrett-Evangelical Theological Seminary P,M,D
George Fox University P,M,D†
Global University of the Assemblies of God M
Golden Gate Baptist Theological Seminary P,M,D,O
Gordon-Conwell Theological Seminary P,M,D
Grand Rapids Baptist Seminary of Cornerstone University P,M,D
Gratz College M,O†
Hebrew College M,O†
Hebrew Union College–Jewish Institute of Religion (CA) M,D
Hebrew Union College–Jewish Institute of Religion (NY) M
Huntington College M
Jewish Theological Seminary of America M,D*
Jewish University of America M,D
La Sierra University M
Loyola University Chicago M*†
Luther Rice Bible College and Seminary P,M,D
Meadville Lombard Theological School P,D
Michigan Theological Seminary P,M,D
Midwestern Baptist Theological Seminary P,M,D
Nazarene Theological Seminary P,M,D
Newman Theological College M,O
New Orleans Baptist Theological Seminary P,M,D
North Park Theological Seminary M
Nova Southeastern University M,O*
Oklahoma City University M
Oral Roberts University P,M,D
Pfeiffer University M
Pontifical Catholic University of Puerto Rico M,D
Providence College and Theological Seminary P,M,D,O
Reformed Theological Seminary (NC) P,M,D
Reformed Theological Seminary (MS) P,M,D,O
Saints Cyril and Methodius Seminary P,M
St. Vladimir's Orthodox Theological Seminary P,M,D
Southeastern Baptist Theological Seminary P,M,D
Southern Adventist University M
Southern Baptist Theological Seminary P,M,D
Southwestern Assemblies of God University M
Southwestern Baptist Theological Seminary M,D
Spertus Institute of Jewish Studies M
Teachers College Columbia University M,D*
Trinity International University P,M,D,O
Union Theological Seminary and Presbyterian School of Christian Education M,D,O
University of Portland M
University of St. Thomas (MN) M,D*†
University of San Francisco M,D*†
Western Seminary M,D
Wheaton College M†
Yeshiva University M,D,O*

REPRODUCTIVE BIOLOGY

Cornell University M,D*
Johns Hopkins University M,D*†
Northwestern University D*
Texas A&M University M,D*
The University of British Columbia M,D*
University of Hawaii at Manoa M,D*
University of Saskatchewan M,D
The University of Texas Health Science Center at Houston M,D*
University of Wyoming M,D*†
West Virginia University M,D*

RHETORIC

Ball State University M*
California State University, Dominguez Hills M,O†
Carnegie Mellon University M*
The Catholic University of America M,D*†
Colorado State University M*
Duquesne University M,D*†
Florida State University M,D*†
Georgia State University M,D*
Indiana State University M,O*†
Indiana University of Pennsylvania M,D*†
Iowa State University of Science and Technology M,D*†
Miami University M,D*†
Michigan Technological University M,D*†
Northern Arizona University M
Rensselaer Polytechnic Institute M,D*†
Southern Illinois University Carbondale M,D*†
Syracuse University D*
Texas Tech University M,D*†
Texas Woman's University M,D*†
The University of Alabama M,D*
The University of Arizona M,D*
University of Arkansas at Little Rock M
University of California, Berkeley D*
University of Illinois at Chicago M,D*
The University of Iowa M,D*
University of Louisiana at Lafayette M,D*
University of Louisville D*†
University of Minnesota, Twin Cities Campus M,D*
The University of Texas at Arlington M,D*†
The University of Texas at El Paso M*†
Virginia Commonwealth University M*†
Wright State University M*

ROMANCE LANGUAGES

Appalachian State University M
The Catholic University of America M,D*†
Clark Atlanta University M
Columbia University M,D*†
Cornell University D*
Johns Hopkins University M,D*†
New York University M,D*†
Northern Illinois University M*†
Southern Connecticut State University M†
Stony Brook University, State University of New York M,D*†
Texas Tech University M,D*†
The University of Alabama M,D*
University of California, Los Angeles M,D*
University of Georgia M,D*†
University of Michigan D*
University of Missouri–Columbia M,D*
University of Missouri–Kansas City M*†
University of New Orleans M*
The University of North Carolina at Chapel Hill M,D*†
University of Notre Dame M*†
University of Oregon M,D*
University of Pennsylvania M,D*†
The University of Texas at Austin M,D*
University of Washington M,D*
Washington University in St. Louis M,D*†

RURAL PLANNING AND STUDIES

Brandon University M,O
California State University, Chico M
Concordia University (Canada) M,D,O*†
Cornell University M*
Dalhousie University M*
Iowa State University of Science and Technology M,D*†
State University of West Georgia M
Université Laval O†
University of Alaska Fairbanks M,D*
University of Guelph M,D,O
University of Wyoming M*†

RURAL SOCIOLOGY

Auburn University M,D*†
Cornell University M,D*
Iowa State University of Science and Technology M,D*†
North Carolina State University M,D*
The Ohio State University M,D*
The Pennsylvania State University University Park Campus M,D*†
South Dakota State University M,D*
University of Alberta M,D*
University of Missouri–Columbia M,D*
The University of Montana–Missoula M*†
The University of Tennessee M*†
University of Wisconsin–Madison M,D*

RUSSIAN

American University M,O*†
Boston College M*†
Brigham Young University M*
Brown University M,D*
Bryn Mawr College M,D
Columbia University M,D*†
Harvard University M,D*†
McGill University M,D*
Michigan State University M,D*†
Middlebury College M,D
New York University M*†
The Pennsylvania State University University Park Campus M*†
San Francisco State University M
Stanford University M,D*
State University of New York at Albany M,D,O*†
Stony Brook University, State University of New York M,D*†
The University of Arizona M*
University of California, Berkeley M,D*
University of Illinois at Urbana–Champaign M,D*
University of Maryland, Baltimore County M*†
University of Maryland, College Park M*
University of Michigan M,D*
University of New Brunswick Fredericton M
The University of North Carolina at Chapel Hill M,D*†
University of Oregon M*
The University of Tennessee D*†
University of Washington M,D*
University of Waterloo M,D

SAFETY ENGINEERING

Central Missouri State University M,O†
Embry-Riddle Aeronautical University (FL) M*
Murray State University M†
New Jersey Institute of Technology M
Texas A&M University M*
University of Minnesota, Duluth M*
University of Wisconsin–Stout M
West Virginia University M*

SCANDINAVIAN LANGUAGES

Brigham Young University M*
Harvard University M,D*†
University of California, Berkeley M,D*

Institution	Degrees
University of California, Los Angeles	M,D*
University of Minnesota, Twin Cities Campus	M,D*
University of Washington	M,D*
University of Wisconsin–Madison	M,D*

SCHOOL NURSING

Institution	Degrees
Capital University	M
The College of New Jersey	M†
Kutztown University of Pennsylvania	O†
La Salle University	M,O
Monmouth University	M,O*†
Seton Hall University	M*†
University of Minnesota, Twin Cities Campus	M*
Wright State University	M*

SCHOOL PSYCHOLOGY

Institution	Degrees
Abilene Christian University	M
Alabama Agricultural and Mechanical University	M,O
Alfred University	M,D,O*†
Alliant International University	M,D,O*†
Alliant International University	M,D,O*†
Alliant International University	M,D,O*†
American International College	M,O*
Andrews University	M,O
Appalachian State University	M,O
Arcadia University	M†
Argosy University-Sarasota	M,D,O*†
Auburn University	M,D,O*†
Austin Peay State University	M
Ball State University	M,D,O*
Barry University	M,O*†
Bowling Green State University	M,O*†
Brigham Young University	M,D*
Brooklyn College of the City University of New York	M,O†
Bucknell University	M
California State University, Los Angeles	M
California State University, Sacramento	M
California University of Pennsylvania	M
Carlos Albizu University, Miami Campus	M,D
Central Connecticut State University	M*†
Central Michigan University	D,O†
Central Washington University	M†
The Citadel, The Military College of South Carolina	O
City University	M,O†
Cleveland State University	O*†
The College of New Rochelle	M†
College of St. Joseph	M
The College of Saint Rose	M,O*†
The College of William and Mary	M,O*†
Duquesne University	M,O*†
East Carolina University	*†
Eastern Illinois University	O†
Eastern Kentucky University	M,O
Eastern Washington University	M†
Edinboro University of Pennsylvania	O
Emporia State University	M,O*†
Fairfield University	M,O*
Fairleigh Dickinson University, Metropolitan Campus	M,D*†
Florida Agricultural and Mechanical University	M*
Florida International University	O*†
Florida State University	M,O*†
Fordham University	M,D,O*†
Fort Hays State University	O
Francis Marion University	M
Fresno Pacific University	M
Gallaudet University	M,O
Gardner-Webb University	M
George Mason University	M*†
Georgia Southern University	M,O
Georgia State University	M,D,O*
Hofstra University	M,D,O*
Howard University	M,D,O*
Idaho State University	M,O*
Illinois State University	D,O*†
Immaculata University	M,D,O†
Indiana State University	M,D,O*†
Indiana University Bloomington	M,D,O*
Indiana University of Pennsylvania	D*†
Inter American University of Puerto Rico, San Germán Campus	M,D
Iona College	M*†
James Madison University	M,O
Kean University	M,O*†
Kent State University	M,D,O*
La Sierra University	M,O
Lehigh University	D,O*
Lenoir-Rhyne College	M
Lesley University	M,D,O*†
Lewis & Clark College	M
Long Island University, Brooklyn Campus	M*
Long Island University, Westchester Graduate Campus	M
Louisiana State University and Agricultural and Mechanical College	M,D*
Louisiana State University in Shreveport	O†
Loyola Marymount University	M†
Loyola University Chicago	M,D,O*†
Marist College	M,O
Marshall University	O*†
McGill University	M,D*
Mercy College	M,O*
Miami University	M,O*†
Michigan State University	M,D,O*†
Middle Tennessee State University	M,O*
Millersville University of Pennsylvania	M†
Minnesota State University, Moorhead	M,O
Mount Saint Vincent University	M
National-Louis University	M,D,O
National University	M†
New Jersey City University	O
New York University	M,D,O*†
Nicholls State University	M,O
Northeastern University	M,D,O*†
Northern Arizona University	M,D
Nova Southeastern University	M*
Pace University	M,D*†
The Pennsylvania State University University Park Campus	M,D*†
Pittsburg State University	O
Plattsburgh State University of New York	M,O
Pontifical Catholic University of Puerto Rico	M,D
Queens College of the City University of New York	M,O†
Radford University	O†
Rhode Island College	O†
Rochester Institute of Technology	M,O*†
Rowan University	M,O†
Rutgers, The State University of New Jersey, New Brunswick	M,D*
St. John's University (NY)	M,D*†
St. Mary's University of San Antonio	M
Sam Houston State University	M*
San Diego State University	M*
Seattle Pacific University	O
Seattle University	O*†
Seton Hall University	O*†
Southern Connecticut State University	M,O†
Southern Illinois University Edwardsville	O†
Southwest Texas State University	M*
State University of New York at Albany	M,D,O*†
State University of New York at Oswego	M,O
Stephen F. Austin State University	M
Syracuse University	D*
Tarleton State University	M
Teachers College Columbia University	M,D*
Temple University	M,D*†
Tennessee State University	M,D*
Texas A&M University	D*
Texas Woman's University	M,D*†
Towson University	M,O†
Trinity University	M*
Tufts University	M,O*†
University at Buffalo, The State University of New York	M,D,O*†
The University of Akron	M,D†
The University of Alabama at Birmingham	M*†
University of Alberta	M,D*
The University of British Columbia	M,D,O*
University of Calgary	M,D*
University of California, Berkeley	D*
University of California, Santa Barbara	M,D*
University of Central Arkansas	M,D
University of Central Florida	O*†
University of Cincinnati	M,D*
University of Connecticut	M,D*†
University of Dayton	M*†
University of Delaware	M,D*†
University of Denver	M,D,O*†
University of Detroit Mercy	O*
University of Florida	M,D,O*†
University of Georgia	M,D,O*†
University of Hartford	M*
University of Houston–Clear Lake	M*†
University of Idaho	M,D,O*†
University of Kansas	D,O*
University of Louisiana at Monroe	O
University of Maryland, College Park	M,D,O*
University of Massachusetts Amherst	D*†
University of Massachusetts Boston	M,O*†
The University of Memphis	M,D*†
University of Minnesota, Twin Cities Campus	M,D,O*
The University of Montana–Missoula	M,O*†
University of Nebraska at Kearney	M,O
University of Nebraska at Omaha	M,D,O
University of Nevada, Las Vegas	M,D,O*†
The University of North Carolina at Chapel Hill	M,D*†
The University of North Carolina at Greensboro	M,D,O†
University of Northern Colorado	D,O†
University of Northern Iowa	M,O
University of North Texas	M,D*†
University of Pennsylvania	D*†
University of Rhode Island	M,D*
University of South Carolina	D*†
University of Southern Maine	M
University of South Florida	D,O*†
The University of Tennessee	M,D,O*†
The University of Tennessee at Chattanooga	M
The University of Texas at Austin	M,D*
The University of Texas at Tyler	M
The University of Texas–Pan American	M,D
University of the Pacific	M,D,O*
University of Toledo	M,O*†
University of Washington	M,D*
University of Wisconsin–Eau Claire	M,O†
University of Wisconsin–La Crosse	M,O†
University of Wisconsin–River Falls	M,O
University of Wisconsin–Stout	M,O
University of Wisconsin–Whitewater	M,O*
Utah State University	M,D*
Valdosta State University	M,O
Valparaiso University	M
Wayne State University	M,D,O*
Western Carolina University	M†
Western Illinois University	M,O
Western Kentucky University	M,O†
Western Michigan University	M,D,O*†
Wichita State University	M,D,O*†
Wilmington College	M
Yeshiva University	D*

SCIENCE EDUCATION

Institution	Degrees
Acadia University	M
Alabama State University	M,O
Albany State University	M
Alfred University	M*†
Alverno College	M
Andrews University	M
Antioch New England Graduate School	M*†
Arcadia University	M,D,O†
Arizona State University	M,D*
Arkansas State University	M,D,O
Armstrong Atlantic State University	M†
Auburn University	M,D,O*†
Averett University	M
Ball State University	M,D*
Belmont University	M
Bemidji State University	M
Bethel College (TN)	M
Bloomsburg University of Pennsylvania	M
Boise State University	M,D*
Boston College	M,D*†
Boston University	M,D,O*†
Bowling Green State University	M,D,O*†
Bridgewater State College	M
Brigham Young University	M,D*
Brooklyn College of the City University of New York	M†
Brown University	M*
California State University, Fullerton	M
California State University, San Bernardino	M
California University of Pennsylvania	M
Carthage College	M,O
Central Connecticut State University	M*†
Central Michigan University	M†
Charleston Southern University	M
Chatham College	M
Christopher Newport University	M†
The Citadel, The Military College of South Carolina	M
City College of the City University of New York	M*†
Clarion University of Pennsylvania	M†
Clark Atlanta University	M,D
Clemson University	M*
Coastal Carolina University	M
College of Charleston	M*†
The College of William and Mary	M*†
The Colorado College	M
Columbus State University	M,O
Connecticut College	M
Cornell University	M,D*
Delaware State University	M
DePaul University	M*†
DeSales University	M
East Carolina University	M*†
Eastern Connecticut State University	M
Eastern Kentucky University	M
Eastern Michigan University	M*
Eastern Washington University	M†
East Stroudsburg University of Pennsylvania	M†
Edinboro University of Pennsylvania	M
Elms College	M,O
Fitchburg State College	M†
Florida Atlantic University, Ft. Lauderdale Campus	M,D,O
Florida Gulf Coast University	M
Florida Institute of Technology	M,D,O*†
Florida International University	M,D*†
Florida State University	M,D,O*†
Fresno Pacific University	M
Gannon University	M,O
Georgia College & State University	M,O
Georgia Southern University	M,O
Georgia State University	M,D,O*
Grambling State University	M
Harvard University	M,D,O*†
Henderson State University	M
Hofstra University	M*
Hood College	M
Hunter College of the City University of New York	M,O†
ICR Graduate School	M
Illinois Institute of Technology	M,D*†
Indiana State University	M*†
Indiana University Bloomington	M,D,O*
Indiana University–Purdue University Indianapolis	M*
Instituto Tecnológico y de Estudios Superiores de Monterrey, Campus Monterrey	M,D
Inter American University of Puerto Rico, Metropolitan Campus	M
Inter American University of Puerto Rico, San Germán Campus	M
Iona College	M*†
Jackson State University	M,D
Johns Hopkins University	M,D,O*†
Kean University	M,O*†
Kutztown University of Pennsylvania	M,O†
Lawrence Technological University	M
Lebanon Valley College	M
Lehman College of the City University of New York	M
Long Island University, C.W. Post Campus	M*†
Louisiana Tech University	M,D,O*
Loyola Marymount University	M†
Lyndon State College	M
Manhattanville College	M*†
McNeese State University	M
Mercer University	M,O
Michigan State University	M,D*†
Michigan Technological University	M*†
Middle Tennessee State University	M*
Mills College	M,D*†
Minot State University	M
Mississippi College	M
Montana State University–Bozeman	M,D*
Montana State University–Northern	M
Montclair State University	M,O†
Morgan State University	D*
National-Louis University	M,O
New Mexico Institute of Mining and Technology	M†
New York University	M*†
Niagara University	M,O†
North Carolina Agricultural and Technical State University	M*
North Carolina State University	M,D*
Northeastern University	M*†
Northern Arizona University	M,D

*P—first professional degree; M—master's degree; D—doctorate; O—other advanced degree; *full description and/or announcement in Book 2, 3, 4, 5, or 6; †full description in this book*

Institution	Degrees
Northern Michigan University	M
North Georgia College & State University	M,O
Northwestern State University of Louisiana	M,O
Northwest Missouri State University	M
Nova Southeastern University	M,O*
Occidental College	M
Oregon State University	M,D*
The Pennsylvania State University University Park Campus	M,D*†
Plattsburgh State University of New York	M
Portland State University	M,D*
Purdue University	M,D,O*
Purdue University Calumet	M
Queens College of the City University of New York	M,O†
Quinnipiac University	M*†
Rhode Island College	M†
Rider University	O*
Rowan University	M†
Rutgers, The State University of New Jersey, New Brunswick	M,D*
Sage Graduate School	M†
Saginaw Valley State University	M
St. John Fisher College	M
Saint Joseph's University	M*†
Salem State College	M,O
Salisbury University	M
San Diego State University	M,D*
Slippery Rock University of Pennsylvania	M†
Smith College	M*
South Carolina State University	M
Southeast Missouri State University	M
Southern Connecticut State University	M,O†
Southern University and Agricultural and Mechanical College	D*
Southwestern Oklahoma State University	M
Southwest Missouri State University	M*†
Southwest Texas State University	M*
Stanford University	M,D*
State University of New York at Albany	M,D*†
State University of New York at Binghamton	M*†
State University of New York College at Brockport	M*†
State University of New York College at Buffalo	M
State University of New York College at Cortland	M
State University of West Georgia	M,O
Stevens Institute of Technology	O*†
Stony Brook University, State University of New York	M,O*†
Syracuse University	M,D,O*
Teachers College Columbia University	M,D*
Temple University	M,D*†
Texas A&M University	M,D*
Texas Woman's University	M,D*†
Tuskegee University	M
Union College (NY)	M*
University at Buffalo, The State University of New York	M,D,O*†
University of Alaska Fairbanks	M,D*
University of Arkansas at Pine Bluff	M
The University of British Columbia	M,D*
University of California, Berkeley	M,D*
University of California, Los Angeles	M,D*
University of California, San Diego	D*
University of Central Florida	M*†
University of Connecticut	M,D*†
University of Florida	M,D,O*†
University of Georgia	M,D,O*†
University of Houston	M,D*
University of Idaho	M,D*†
University of Indianapolis	M
The University of Iowa	M,D*
University of Maine	M,O*
University of Manitoba	M*
University of Massachusetts Amherst	D*†
University of Massachusetts Lowell	D*†
University of Miami	M,O*†
University of Michigan	M,D*
University of Minnesota, Twin Cities Campus	M,D*
University of Missouri–Rolla	M,D*
The University of Montana–Missoula	M,D*†
University of Nebraska at Kearney	M
University of New Orleans	M*
The University of North Carolina at Chapel Hill	M*†
The University of North Carolina at Pembroke	M
University of Northern Colorado	M,D†
University of Northern Iowa	M,O
University of North Florida	M
University of North Texas Health Science Center at Fort Worth	M,D*
University of Oklahoma	M,D,O*†
University of Pittsburgh	M,D*†
University of Puerto Rico, Río Piedras	M,D*
University of South Alabama	M*†
University of South Carolina	M,D*†
University of Southern Mississippi	M,D
University of South Florida	M,D,O*†
The University of Tennessee	M,D,O*†
The University of Texas at Austin	M,D*
The University of Texas at Dallas	M*
The University of Texas at Tyler	M
University of Tulsa	M†
University of Utah	M,D*
University of Vermont	M,D*†
University of Victoria	M
University of Virginia	M,D*
University of Washington	M,D*
The University of West Alabama	M
University of West Florida	M
University of Wisconsin–Eau Claire	M†
University of Wisconsin–Madison	M*
University of Wisconsin–Oshkosh	M*
University of Wisconsin–River Falls	M
University of Wisconsin–Stevens Point	M
University of Wyoming	M*†
Vanderbilt University	M,D*
Wayne State College	M
Wayne State University	M,D,O*
Webster University	M,O
Wesleyan College	M
West Chester University of Pennsylvania	M*†
Western Carolina University	M†
Western Illinois University	M,O
Western Kentucky University	M†
Western Michigan University	M,D*†
Western Oregon University	M
Western Washington University	M
Wheeling Jesuit University	M
Widener University	M,D*†
Wilkes University	M
Wright State University	M*

SECONDARY EDUCATION

Institution	Degrees
Abilene Christian University	M
Adams State College	M
Adelphi University	M*
Alabama Agricultural and Mechanical University	M,O
Alabama State University	M,O
Alcorn State University	M,O
Alfred University	M*†
American International College	M,D,O*
American University	M,O*†
Andrews University	M
Appalachian State University	M
Arcadia University	M,D,O†
Argosy University-Orange County	M,D,O*
Arizona State University West	M
Armstrong Atlantic State University	M†
Auburn University	M,D,O*†
Auburn University Montgomery	M,O
Augustana College	M
Augusta State University	M,O
Austin College	M
Austin Peay State University	M,O
Ball State University	M*
Belmont University	M
Berry College	M
Boston College	M*†
Bowie State University	M
Bridgewater State College	M
Brooklyn College of the City University of New York	M†
Brown University	M*
Butler University	M
California State University, Bakersfield	M
California State University, Long Beach	M
California State University, Los Angeles	M
California State University, Northridge	M
California State University, San Bernardino	M
California State University, Stanislaus	M
Campbell University	M
Canisius College	M
Carson-Newman College	M
Centenary College of Louisiana	M
Central Connecticut State University	M*†
Central Michigan University	M†
Central Missouri State University	M,O†
Chadron State College	M,O
Charleston Southern University	M
Chatham College	M
Chicago State University	M
The Citadel, The Military College of South Carolina	M
Clemson University	M*
Cleveland State University	M*†
Coastal Carolina University	M
Colgate University	M
The College of New Jersey	M†
The College of Saint Rose	M*†
College of Staten Island of the City University of New York	M†
The College of William and Mary	M*†
The Colorado College	M
Columbus State University	M,O
Concordia University (OR)	M
Connecticut College	M
Converse College	M
Cumberland College	M,O
DePaul University	M*†
Dowling College	M
Drake University	M*†
Drury University	M
Duquesne University	M*†
D'Youville College	M,O†
Eastern Kentucky University	M
Eastern Michigan University	M*
Eastern Nazarene College	M,O
Eastern Oregon University	M
East Stroudsburg University of Pennsylvania	M†
East Tennessee State University	M†
Edinboro University of Pennsylvania	M
Elms College	M,O
Emmanuel College	M*
Emory University	M,D,O*†
Emporia State University	M*†
Fayetteville State University	M,D
Fitchburg State College	M†
Florida Agricultural and Mechanical University	M*
Florida Atlantic University, Ft. Lauderdale Campus	M,D,O
Florida Gulf Coast University	M
Fordham University	M,D,O*†
Fort Hays State University	M
Francis Marion University	M
Friends University	M
Frostburg State University	M
Gallaudet University	M,D,O
Gannon University	M
George Mason University	M*†
The George Washington University	M*†
Georgia College & State University	M,O
Georgia Southwestern State University	M,O
Grand Canyon University	M
Harding University	M
Harvard University	M,D,O*†
Henderson State University	M
Hofstra University	M*
Holy Family College	M
Hood College	M
Houston Baptist University	M
Howard University	M,O*
Hunter College of the City University of New York	M†
Immaculata University	M,D,O†
Indiana State University	M,D,O*†
Indiana University Bloomington	M,D,O*
Indiana University Kokomo	M
Indiana University Northwest	M
Indiana University–Purdue University Fort Wayne	M
Indiana University–Purdue University Indianapolis	M*
Indiana University South Bend	M
Indiana University Southeast	M
Iona College	M*†
Jackson State University	M,D,O
Jacksonville State University	M,O
Jacksonville University	O
James Madison University	M
John Carroll University	M
Johns Hopkins University	M*†
Kansas State University	M*†
Kent State University	M*
Kutztown University of Pennsylvania	M,O†
Lamar University	M,O*†
Lehigh University	M,D,O*
Lewis & Clark College	M
Liberty University	M,D†
Lincoln University (MO)	M
Long Island University, C.W. Post Campus	M*†
Longwood College	M
Louisiana State University and Agricultural and Mechanical College	M,D,O*
Louisiana Tech University	M,D,O*
Loyola Marymount University	M†
Loyola University New Orleans	M
Lynchburg College	M
Maharishi University of Management	M
Manhattanville College	M*†
Mansfield University of Pennsylvania	M
Marshall University	M*†
Maryville University of Saint Louis	M
McDaniel College	M
McNeese State University	M
Mercer University	M,O
Mercy College	M,O*
Miami University	M*†
Michigan State University	M,D*†
Middle Tennessee State University	M,O*
Mills College	M,D*†
Minnesota State University, Mankato	M,O
Mississippi College	M
Mississippi State University	M,D,O*
Montana State University–Billings	M*
Morehead State University	M
Mount Saint Mary College	M
Mount St. Mary's College	M*
Murray State University	M,O†
National-Louis University	M
Nazareth College of Rochester	M
New School University	M*†
Niagara University	M†
Norfolk State University	M†
Northern Arizona University	M
Northern Illinois University	M,D*†
Northern Kentucky University	M
Northern Michigan University	M
Northern State University	M
North Georgia College & State University	M,O
Northwestern Oklahoma State University	M
Northwestern State University of Louisiana	M,O
Northwestern University	M*
Northwest Missouri State University	M,O
Occidental College	M
Old Dominion University	M*†
Olivet Nazarene University	M
Pacific Lutheran University	M†
Pacific University	M
Piedmont College	M,O
Pittsburg State University	M
Plattsburgh State University of New York	M
Plymouth State College	M*
Portland State University	M*
Purdue University Calumet	M
Queens College of the City University of New York	M,O†
Quinnipiac University	M*†
Rhode Island College	M†
Rivier College	M*†
Rochester Institute of Technology	M*†
Rockford College	M
Rollins College	M*
Roosevelt University	M,D*†
Rowan University	M†
Sacred Heart University	M,O*†
Sage Graduate School	M†
Saginaw Valley State University	M
St. John's University (NY)	M*†
Saint Joseph's University	M*†
St. Thomas Aquinas College	M
Saint Xavier University	M,O*
Salem International University	M
Salem State College	M
Salisbury University	M
Sam Houston State University	M,D,O*
San Diego State University	M*
San Francisco State University	M,O
San Jose State University	M*
Seattle Pacific University	M
Seton Hall University	M*†
Shenandoah University	M,D,O
Siena Heights University	M
Sierra Nevada College	O
Simmons College	M,O*
Slippery Rock University of Pennsylvania	M†
Smith College	M*
South Carolina State University	M
Southeastern Oklahoma State University	M
Southeast Missouri State University	M

Institution	Degrees
Southern Arkansas University–Magnolia	M
Southern Illinois University Edwardsville	M†
Southern Oregon University	M
Southern University and Agricultural and Mechanical College	M*
Southwestern Oklahoma State University	M
Southwest Missouri State University	M,O*†
Southwest Texas State University	M*
Springfield College	M†
Spring Hill College	M
State University of New York at Binghamton	M*†
State University of New York at New Paltz	M
State University of New York at Oswego	M
State University of New York College at Brockport	M*†
State University of New York College at Cortland	M
State University of New York College at Fredonia	M
State University of New York College at Geneseo	M
State University of New York College at Oneonta	M
State University of New York College at Potsdam	M
State University of West Georgia	M,O
Stephen F. Austin State University	M,D
Suffolk University	M*
Sul Ross State University	M*
Tarleton State University	M,O
Temple University	M,D*†
Tennessee Technological University	M,O*
Texas A&M University–Commerce	M,D†
Texas A&M University–Corpus Christi	M
Texas A&M University–Kingsville	M*†
Texas A&M University–Texarkana	M
Texas Christian University	M,O*
Texas Southern University	M,D†
Texas Tech University	M,D,O*†
Towson University	M†
Trinity College (DC)	M†
Troy State University	M,O
Tufts University	M,O*†
Union College (KY)	M
University at Buffalo, The State University of New York	M,D,O*†
The University of Akron	M,D†
The University of Alabama	M,D,O*
The University of Alabama at Birmingham	M*†
University of Alaska Southeast	M
University of Alberta	M,D*
The University of Arizona	M,D,O*
University of Arkansas	M,O*
University of Arkansas at Little Rock	M
University of Arkansas at Monticello	M
University of Arkansas at Pine Bluff	M
University of Bridgeport	M,O*†
University of California, Irvine	M,D*
University of Central Arkansas	M
University of Central Oklahoma	M
University of Cincinnati	M*
University of Connecticut	M,D*†
University of Dayton	M*†
University of Delaware	M,D*†
University of Florida	M,D,O*†
University of Georgia	M,D,O*†
University of Great Falls	M
University of Guam	M
University of Hawaii at Manoa	M*
University of Houston	M,D*
University of Idaho	M,D,O*†
University of Illinois at Chicago	M,D*
University of Indianapolis	M
The University of Iowa	M,D*
University of Louisiana at Monroe	M,O
University of Louisville	M*†
University of Maine	M,O*
University of Mary	M
University of Maryland, Baltimore County	M,D*†
University of Maryland, College Park	M,D,O*
University of Massachusetts Amherst	M,D,O*†
University of Massachusetts Boston	M,D,O*†
The University of Memphis	M,D*†
University of Mississippi	M,D,O*
University of Missouri–Columbia	M,D,O*
University of Missouri–St. Louis	M,D†
University of Montevallo	M,O
University of Nebraska at Omaha	M
University of Nevada, Las Vegas	M,D,O*†
University of Nevada, Reno	M,D,O*
University of New Hampshire	M*†
University of New Mexico	M*†
University of North Alabama	M
The University of North Carolina at Chapel Hill	M*†
The University of North Carolina at Charlotte	M*
The University of North Carolina at Wilmington	M*
University of North Dakota	D*
University of North Florida	M
University of North Texas	M*†
University of Oklahoma	M,D,O*†
University of Pennsylvania	M*†
University of Phoenix–Hawaii Campus	M,O
University of Pittsburgh	M,D*†
University of Portland	M
University of Puerto Rico, Río Piedras	M,D*
University of Puget Sound	M
University of Rhode Island	M*
The University of Scranton	M†
University of South Alabama	M,O*†
University of South Carolina	M,D,O*†
The University of South Dakota	M†
University of Southern Indiana	M
University of Southern Mississippi	M,D,O
University of South Florida	D*†
The University of Tennessee	M,D,O*†
The University of Tennessee at Chattanooga	M,O
The University of Texas at Tyler	M
The University of Texas of the Permian Basin	M
The University of Texas–Pan American	M
University of the Incarnate Word	M†
University of Toledo	M,D,O*†
University of Utah	M*
The University of West Alabama	M
University of West Florida	M
University of Wisconsin–Eau Claire	M†
University of Wisconsin–La Crosse	M†
University of Wisconsin–Milwaukee	M
University of Wisconsin–Platteville	M
University of Wisconsin–Whitewater	M*
Utah State University	M*
Valdosta State University	M,O
Vanderbilt University	M,D*
Villanova University	M*†
Virginia Commonwealth University	M,O*†
Wagner College	M
Wake Forest University	M*†
Washington State University	M,D*
Washington University in St. Louis	M*†
Wayne State University	M,D,O*
West Chester University of Pennsylvania	M*†
Western Carolina University	M†
Western Illinois University	M
Western Kentucky University	M,O†
Western New Mexico University	M
Western Oregon University	M
Western Washington University	M
Westfield State College	M
West Texas A&M University	M†
West Virginia University	M,D*
Wheaton College	M†
Whittier College	M
Wilkes University	M
William Carey College	M
Winthrop University	M
Worcester State College	M,O
Wright State University	M*
Xavier University	M*
Youngstown State University	M

SLAVIC LANGUAGES

Institution	Degrees
Boston College	M*†
Brown University	M,D*
Columbia University	M,D*†
Duke University	M*†
Florida State University	M*†
Harvard University	M,D*†
Indiana University Bloomington	M,D*
New York University	M*†
Northwestern University	D*
The Ohio State University	M,D,O*
Princeton University	D*
Stanford University	M,D*
Stony Brook University, State University of New York	M*†
University of Alberta	M,D*
University of California, Berkeley	M,D*
University of California, Los Angeles	M,D*
University of Chicago	M,D*
University of Illinois at Chicago	M,D*
University of Illinois at Urbana–Champaign	M,D*
University of Kansas	M,D*
University of Manitoba	M*
University of Michigan	M,D*
The University of North Carolina at Chapel Hill	M,D*†
University of Pittsburgh	M,D*†
University of Southern California	M,D*†
The University of Texas at Austin	M,D*
University of Toronto	M,D*
University of Virginia	M,D*
University of Washington	M,D*
University of Wisconsin–Madison	M,D*
University of Wisconsin–Milwaukee	M
Yale University	M,D*

SOCIAL PSYCHOLOGY

Institution	Degrees
Alliant International University	D*†
American University	M,D*†
Andrews University	M
Appalachian State University	M
Arcadia University	M†
Arizona State University	D*
Auburn University	M,D,O*†
Ball State University	M*
Bowling Green State University	M,D*†
Brandeis University	M,D*†
Brock University	M
Brooklyn College of the City University of New York	M,D†
California State University, Fullerton	M
Carnegie Mellon University	D*
Central Connecticut State University	M*†
Claremont Graduate University	M,D*
Clark University	D*†
The College of New Rochelle	M†
College of St. Joseph	M
College of Staten Island of the City University of New York	D†
Colorado State University	D*
Columbia University	M,D*†
Cornell University	M,D*
DePaul University	M,D*†
Fairleigh Dickinson University, College at Florham	M*†
Florida Agricultural and Mechanical University	M*
Francis Marion University	M
The George Washington University	D*†
Graduate School and University Center of the City University of New York	D*†
Harvard University	M,D*†
Henderson State University	M
Hofstra University	M,D*
Howard University	M,D*
Hunter College of the City University of New York	M†
Indiana University Bloomington	D*
Indiana Wesleyan University	M*
Iowa State University of Science and Technology	M,D*†
Lamar University	M*†
Lesley University	M,D,O*†
Loyola University Chicago	M,D*†
Marist College	M,O
Martin University	M
Memorial University of Newfoundland	M,D†
Miami University	D*†
Montclair State University	M†
New College of California	M*†
New England College	M,O*
New York University	M,D,O*†
Norfolk State University	M†
North Georgia College & State University	M
Northwestern University	D*
The Ohio State University	D*
Pace University	M,D*†
The Pennsylvania State University Harrisburg Campus of the Capital College	M*†
The Pennsylvania State University University Park Campus	M,D*†
Queen's University at Kingston	M,D
Rutgers, The State University of New Jersey, Newark	D*†
Rutgers, The State University of New Jersey, New Brunswick	D*
Sage Graduate School	M†
St. Cloud State University	M
Saint Joseph College	M,O
Saint Martin's College	M
Southeast Missouri State University	M
Southern Illinois University Edwardsville	M†
State University of New York at Albany	M,D*†
State University of New York College at Oneonta	M,O
Stony Brook University, State University of New York	D*†
Syracuse University	D*
Teachers College Columbia University	M,D*
Temple University	D*†
University at Buffalo, The State University of New York	M,D*†
University of Alaska Fairbanks	M*
The University of British Columbia	M,D*
University of California, Santa Cruz	D*
University of Central Arkansas	M,D
University of Connecticut	D*†
University of Dayton	M*†
University of Delaware	D*†
University of Guelph	M,D
University of Hawaii at Manoa	M,D*
University of Houston	D*
University of Illinois at Urbana–Champaign	M,D*
University of La Verne	M,D*
University of Maine	M,D*
University of Maryland, College Park	M,D*
University of Massachusetts Lowell	M*†
University of Michigan	D*
University of Minnesota, Twin Cities Campus	D*
University of Missouri–Kansas City	D*†
University of Nevada, Reno	D*
University of New Haven	M,O*†
The University of North Carolina at Chapel Hill	D*†
The University of North Carolina at Charlotte	M*
The University of North Carolina at Greensboro	M,D†
University of Oklahoma	M*†
University of Oregon	M,D*
University of Pennsylvania	D*†
University of Phoenix–Hawaii Campus	M
University of Phoenix–Phoenix Campus	M
University of Rochester	M,D*
The University of Scranton	M†
University of South Carolina	D*†
University of Victoria	M,D
University of Wisconsin–Madison	D*
University of Wisconsin–Superior	M
University of Wisconsin–Whitewater	M*
Valparaiso University	M
Washington University in St. Louis	M,D*†
Wayne State University	M,D*
Western Illinois University	M,O
Wichita State University	M,D*†
Wilfrid Laurier University	M
Wilmington College	M

SOCIAL SCIENCES

Institution	Degrees
Appalachian State University	M
Arkansas Tech University	M
Ball State University	M*
California Institute of Technology	M,D*
California State University, Chico	M
California State University, Fullerton	M
California State University, San Bernardino	M
California University of Pennsylvania	M
Campbellsville University	M
Carnegie Mellon University	D*
Central Connecticut State University	M*†
Columbia University	M*†
Coppin State College	M
Eastern Michigan University	M*
Edinboro University of Pennsylvania	M

*P—first professional degree; M—master's degree; D—doctorate; O—other advanced degree; *full description and/or announcement in Book 2, 3, 4, 5, or 6; †full description in this book*

Institution	Degrees
Florida Agricultural and Mechanical University	M*
Florida State University	M*†
Henderson State University	M
Hollins University	M,O
Humboldt State University	M
Indiana University Bloomington	P,M,D*
Johns Hopkins University	M,D*†
Long Island University, Brooklyn Campus	M,O*
Long Island University, C.W. Post Campus	M*†
Massachusetts Institute of Technology	D*
Michigan State University	M,D*†
Mississippi College	M
Montclair State University	M†
New School University	M,D*†
North Dakota State University	M,D†
Northwestern University	M,O*
Ohio University	M*
Old Dominion University	M*†
Pittsburg State University	M
Queens College of the City University of New York	M†
Regis University	M,O*†
San Francisco State University	M
San Jose State University	M*
Southern Oregon University	M
State University of New York at Binghamton	M*†
State University of New York College at Fredonia	M
Stony Brook University, State University of New York	M,O*†
Syracuse University	M,D*
Texas A&M International University	M
Texas A&M University–Commerce	M†
Towson University	M†
University at Buffalo, The State University of New York	M*†
University of California, Irvine	M,D*
University of California, Santa Cruz	D*
University of Chicago	M,D*
University of Colorado at Denver	M*
University of Illinois at Springfield	M†
University of Michigan	D*
University of Regina	M
The University of Texas at Tyler	M

SOCIAL SCIENCES EDUCATION

Institution	Degrees
Acadia University	M
Alabama State University	M,O
Albany State University	M
Alfred University	M*†
Andrews University	M
Arcadia University	M,D,O†
Arkansas State University	M,D,O
Arkansas Tech University	M
Armstrong Atlantic State University	M†
Auburn University	M,D,O*†
Belmont University	M
Bethel College (TN)	M
Boston College	M*†
Boston University	M,D,O*†
Bridgewater State College	M
Brooklyn College of the City University of New York	M†
Brown University	M*
California State University, San Bernardino	M
California State University, Stanislaus	M
Campbell University	M
Carthage College	M,O
Central Missouri State University	M†
Chadron State College	M,O
Chaminade University of Honolulu	M*
Charleston Southern University	M
Chatham College	M
The Citadel, The Military College of South Carolina	M
Clemson University	M*
Coastal Carolina University	M
The College of William and Mary	M*†
The Colorado College	M
Columbus State University	M,O
Delta State University	M
East Carolina University	M*†
Eastern Kentucky University	M
Eastern Washington University	M†
East Stroudsburg University of Pennsylvania	M†
Edinboro University of Pennsylvania	M
Emporia State University	M*†
Fayetteville State University	M
Fitchburg State College	M†
Florida Atlantic University, Ft. Lauderdale Campus	M,D,O
Florida Gulf Coast University	M
Florida International University	M*†
Florida State University	M,D,O*†
Framingham State College	M*
Georgia College & State University	M,O
Georgia Southern University	M,O
Georgia State University	M,D,O*
Grambling State University	M
Henderson State University	M
Hofstra University	M*
Hunter College of the City University of New York	M†
Indiana University Bloomington	M,D,O*
Iona College	M*†
Kutztown University of Pennsylvania	M,O†
Lehman College of the City University of New York	M
Longwood College	M
Louisiana Tech University	M,D,O*
Loyola Marymount University	M†
Manhattanville College	M*†
McNeese State University	M
Mercer University	M,O
Miami University	M*†
Mills College	M,D*†
Minnesota State University, Mankato	M
Montclair State University	M†
New Jersey Institute of Technology	M
New York University	M,D,O*†
North Carolina Agricultural and Technical State University	M*
Northeastern University	M*†
North Georgia College & State University	M,O
Northwestern State University of Louisiana	M
Northwest Missouri State University	M
Nova Southeastern University	M,O*
Occidental College	M
Ohio University	M,D*
The Pennsylvania State University University Park Campus	M,D*†
Plattsburgh State University of New York	M
Portland State University	M*
Princeton University	D*
Purdue University	M,D,O*
Queens College of the City University of New York	M,O†
Quinnipiac University	M*†
Rider University	O*
Rivier College	M*†
Rockford College	M
Rutgers, The State University of New Jersey, New Brunswick	M,D,O*
Sage Graduate School	M†
Salem State College	M,O
Salisbury University	M
Smith College	M*
South Carolina State University	M
Southeast Missouri State University	M
Southwestern Oklahoma State University	M
Southwest Texas State University	M,D*
Stanford University	M,D*
State University of New York at Binghamton	M*†
State University of New York College at Brockport	M*†
State University of New York College at Buffalo	M
State University of New York College at Cortland	M
State University of West Georgia	M,O
Stony Brook University, State University of New York	M,O*†
Syracuse University	M,O*
Teachers College Columbia University	M,D*
Texas A&M University–Commerce	M†
Trinity College (DC)	M†
Union College (NY)	M*
University at Buffalo, The State University of New York	M,D,O*†
University of Arkansas at Pine Bluff	M
The University of British Columbia	M,D*
University of Central Florida	M*†
University of Cincinnati	M,D*
University of Connecticut	M,D*†
University of Florida	M,D,O*†
University of Georgia	M,D,O*†
University of Houston	M,D*
University of Idaho	M,D*†
University of Indianapolis	M
The University of Iowa	M,D*
University of Maine	M,O*
University of Manitoba	M*
University of Michigan	M,D*
University of Minnesota, Twin Cities Campus	M,D*
The University of North Carolina at Chapel Hill	M*†
The University of North Carolina at Pembroke	M
University of Oklahoma	M,D,O*†
University of Pittsburgh	M,D*†
University of Puerto Rico, Río Piedras	M,D*
University of South Carolina	M,D,O*†
University of Southern Mississippi	M,D,O
University of South Florida	M*†
The University of Tennessee	M,D,O*†
The University of Texas at Tyler	M
University of Vermont	M*†
University of Victoria	M
University of Washington	M,D*
The University of West Alabama	M
University of Wisconsin–Eau Claire	M†
University of Wisconsin–Madison	M,D*
University of Wisconsin–River Falls	M
Virginia Commonwealth University	M,O*†
Wayne State College	M
Wayne State University	M,D,O*
Webster University	M,O
Western Carolina University	M†
Western Illinois University	M,O
Western Kentucky University	M†
Western Oregon University	M
Widener University	M,D*†
Wilkes University	M

SOCIAL WORK

Institution	Degrees
Adelphi University	M,D*
Alabama Agricultural and Mechanical University	M
Andrews University	M
Arizona State University	M,D*
Arizona State University West	M
Augsburg College	M
Aurora University	M
Barry University	M,D*†
Baylor University	M*†
Boise State University	M*
Boston College	M,D*†
Boston University	M,D*†
Brigham Young University	M*
Bryn Mawr College	M,D
California State University, Bakersfield	M
California State University, Chico	M
California State University, Fresno	M
California State University, Long Beach	M
California State University, Los Angeles	M
California State University, Sacramento	M
California State University, San Bernardino	M
California State University, Stanislaus	M
California University of Pennsylvania	M
Carleton University	M
Case Western Reserve University	M,D,O*†
The Catholic University of America	M,D*†
Chicago State University	M
Clark Atlanta University	M,D
Cleveland State University	M*†
College of St. Catherine	M†
Colorado State University	M*
Columbia University	M,D*†
Cornell University	M,D*
Dalhousie University	M*
Delaware State University	M
Delta State University	M
Dominican University	M*
East Carolina University	M*†
Eastern Michigan University	M*
Eastern Washington University	M†
East Tennessee State University	M†
Edinboro University of Pennsylvania	M
Florida Atlantic University	M*
Florida Gulf Coast University	M
Florida International University	M,D*†
Florida State University	M,D*†
Fordham University	M,D*†
Gallaudet University	M
Georgia State University	M*
Governors State University	M
Graduate School and University Center of the City University of New York	D*†
Grambling State University	M
Grand Valley State University	M†
Gratz College	M,O†
Hebrew College	M,O†
Hebrew Union College–Jewish Institute of Religion (CA)	M,O
Howard University	M,D*
Hunter College of the City University of New York	M,D†
Illinois State University	M*†
Indiana University Northwest	M
Indiana University–Purdue University Indianapolis	M,D*
Indiana University South Bend	M
Institute for Clinical Social Work	D
Inter American University of Puerto Rico, Metropolitan Campus	M
Jackson State University	M,D
Kean University	M*†
Lakehead University	M
Laurentian University	M
Loma Linda University	M,D*
Louisiana State University and Agricultural and Mechanical College	M,D*
Loyola University Chicago	M,D*†
Marywood University	M*†
McGill University	M,D*
McMaster University	M
Memorial University of Newfoundland	M,D†
Miami University	M*†
Michigan State University	M,D*†
Monmouth University	M*†
Nazareth College of Rochester	M
Newman University	M
New Mexico Highlands University	M
New Mexico State University	M
New York University	M,D*†
Norfolk State University	M,D†
North Carolina Agricultural and Technical State University	M*
Northwest Nazarene University	M
The Ohio State University	M,D*
Ohio University	M*
Our Lady of the Lake University of San Antonio	M
Pontifical Catholic University of Puerto Rico	M,D
Portland State University	M,D*
Radford University	M†
Rhode Island College	M†
Roberts Wesleyan College	M*
Rutgers, The State University of New Jersey, New Brunswick	M,D*
St. Ambrose University	M
Saint Louis University	M*†
Salem State College	M
Salisbury University	M
San Diego State University	M*
San Francisco State University	M
San Jose State University	M*
Savannah State University	M
Simmons College	M,D*
Smith College	M,D*
Southern Connecticut State University	M†
Southern Illinois University Carbondale	M*†
Southern Illinois University Edwardsville	M†
Southern University at New Orleans	M
Southwest Missouri State University	M*†
Southwest Texas State University	M*
Spalding University	M†
Springfield College	M†
State University of New York at Albany	M,D*†
State University of New York College at Brockport	M*†
Stephen F. Austin State University	M
Stony Brook University, State University of New York	M,D*†
Syracuse University	M*
Temple University	M*†
Texas A&M University–Commerce	M†
Tulane University	M,D*†
Université de Moncton	M
Université de Montréal	M,D,O
Université de Sherbrooke	M
Université du Québec en Outaouais	M
Université du Québec à Montréal	M
Université Laval	M,D†
University at Buffalo, The State University of New York	M,D*†
The University of Akron	M†
The University of Alabama	M,D*
University of Alaska Anchorage	M
University of Arkansas at Little Rock	M
The University of British Columbia	M*
University of Calgary	M,D*

University of California, Berkeley M,D*
University of California, Los Angeles M,D*
University of Central Florida M,O*†
University of Chicago M,D*
University of Cincinnati M*
University of Connecticut M*†
University of Denver M,D*†
University of Georgia M,D*†
University of Hawaii at Manoa M,D*
University of Houston M,D*
University of Illinois at Chicago M,D*
University of Illinois at Urbana–Champaign M,D*
The University of Iowa M,D*
University of Kentucky M,D*
The University of Lethbridge M,D
University of Louisville M,D*†
University of Maine M*
University of Manitoba M*
University of Maryland M,D*†
University of Michigan M,D*
University of Minnesota, Duluth M*
University of Minnesota, Twin Cities Campus M,D*
University of Missouri–Columbia M*
University of Missouri–Kansas City M*†
University of Missouri–St. Louis M,O†
University of Nebraska at Omaha M
University of Nevada, Las Vegas M*†
University of Nevada, Reno M*
University of New England M*
University of New Hampshire M*†
The University of North Carolina at Chapel Hill M,D*†
The University of North Carolina at Charlotte M*
The University of North Carolina at Greensboro M†
University of North Dakota M*
University of Northern British Columbia M,D
University of Northern Iowa M
University of Oklahoma M*†
University of Ottawa M*
University of Pennsylvania M,D*†
University of Pittsburgh M,D,O*†
University of Puerto Rico, Río Piedras M*
University of Regina M
University of St. Thomas (MN) M*†
University of South Carolina M,D*†
University of Southern California M,D*†
University of Southern Indiana M
University of Southern Mississippi M
University of South Florida M*†
The University of Tennessee M,D*†
The University of Texas at Arlington M,D*†
The University of Texas at Austin M,D*
The University of Texas–Pan American M
University of Toronto M,D*
University of Utah M,D*
University of Vermont M*†
University of Victoria M
University of Washington M,D*
University of Wisconsin–Madison M,D*
University of Wisconsin–Milwaukee M
University of Wyoming M*†
Valdosta State University M
Virginia Commonwealth University M,D*†
Walla Walla College M
Washington University in St. Louis M,D*†
Wayne State University M,O*
West Chester University of Pennsylvania M*†
Western Michigan University M*†
West Virginia University M*
Wheelock College M*
Wichita State University M*†
Widener University M*†
Wilfrid Laurier University M,D
Yeshiva University M,D*
York University M*

SOCIOLOGY

Acadia University M
American University M,D*†
American University in Cairo M
Arizona State University M,D*
Arkansas State University M,O
Auburn University M*†
Ball State University M*
Baylor University M,D*†
Bethel College (MN) M
Boston College M,D*†
Boston University M,D*†
Bowling Green State University M,D*†
Brandeis University M,D*†
Bridgewater State College M
Brigham Young University M,D*
Brooklyn College of the City University of New York M,D†
Brown University M,D*
California State University, Bakersfield M
California State University, Dominguez Hills M,O†
California State University, Fullerton M
California State University, Hayward M
California State University, Los Angeles M
California State University, Northridge M
California State University, Sacramento M
California State University, San Marcos M
Carleton University M,D
Case Western Reserve University D*†
The Catholic University of America M,D*†
Central Michigan University M†
Central Missouri State University M†
City College of the City University of New York M*†
Clark Atlanta University M
Clemson University M*
Cleveland State University M*†
Colorado State University M,D*
Columbia University M,D*†
Concordia University (Canada) M*†
Converse College M
Cornell University M,D*
Dalhousie University M,D*
DePaul University M*†
Duke University M,D*†
East Carolina University M*†
Eastern Michigan University M*
East Tennessee State University M†
Emory University D*†
Fayetteville State University M
Fisk University M
Florida Atlantic University M*
Florida International University M,D*†
Florida State University M,D*†
Fordham University M,D*†
George Mason University M*†
The George Washington University M*†
Georgia Southern University M
Georgia State University M,D*
Graduate School and University Center of the City University of New York D*†
Harvard University M,D*†
Howard University M,D*
Humboldt State University M
Hunter College of the City University of New York M†
Idaho State University M*
Illinois State University M*†
Indiana State University M*†
Indiana University Bloomington M,D*
Indiana University of Pennsylvania M*†
Indiana University–Purdue University Fort Wayne M
Iowa State University of Science and Technology M,D*†
Jackson State University M
Johns Hopkins University D*†
Kansas State University M,D*†
Kent State University M,D*
Lakehead University M
Laurentian University M
Lehigh University M*
Lincoln University (MO) M
Louisiana State University and Agricultural and Mechanical College M,D*
Loyola University Chicago M,D*†
Marshall University M*†
McGill University M,D*
McMaster University M,D
Memorial University of Newfoundland M,D†
Michigan State University M,D*†
Middle Tennessee State University M*
Minnesota State University, Mankato M
Mississippi College M
Mississippi State University M,D*
Montclair State University M†
Morehead State University M
Morgan State University M*
New Mexico Highlands University M
New Mexico State University M
New School University M,D*†
New York University M,D*†
Norfolk State University M†
North Carolina Central University M
North Carolina State University M,D*
Northeastern University M,D*†
Northern Arizona University M
Northern Illinois University M*†
Northwestern University D*
The Ohio State University M,D*
Ohio University M*
Oklahoma State University M,D*†
Old Dominion University M*†
Our Lady of the Lake University of San Antonio M
The Pennsylvania State University University Park Campus M,D*†
Portland State University M,D*
Prairie View A&M University M
Princeton University D*
Purdue University M,D*
Queens College of the City University of New York M†
Queen's University at Kingston M,D
Roosevelt University M*†
Rutgers, The State University of New Jersey, New Brunswick M,D*
St. John's University (NY) M*†
Sam Houston State University M*
San Diego State University M*
San Jose State University M*
Simon Fraser University M,D
Southern Connecticut State University M†
Southern Illinois University Carbondale M,D*†
Southern Illinois University Edwardsville M†
Southern University and Agricultural and Mechanical College M*
Southwest Texas State University M*
Stanford University D*
State University of New York at Albany M,D,O*†
State University of New York at Binghamton M,D*†
State University of New York at New Paltz M
State University of New York Institute of Technology at Utica/Rome M*†
State University of West Georgia M
Stony Brook University, State University of New York M,D*†
Syracuse University M,D*
Teachers College Columbia University M,D*
Temple University M,D*†
Texas A&M International University M
Texas A&M University M,D*
Texas A&M University–Commerce M†
Texas A&M University–Kingsville M*†
Texas Southern University M†
Texas Tech University M*†
Texas Woman's University M,D*†
Tulane University M,D*†
Université de Montréal M,D
Université du Québec à Montréal M,D
Université Laval M,D†
University at Buffalo, The State University of New York M,D*†
The University of Akron M,D†
The University of Alabama at Birmingham M,D*†
University of Alberta M,D*
The University of Arizona M,D*
University of Arkansas M*
The University of British Columbia M,D*
University of Calgary M,D*
University of California, Berkeley M,D*
University of California, Davis M,D*†
University of California, Irvine M,D*
University of California, Los Angeles M,D*
University of California, Riverside D*
University of California, San Diego D*
University of California, San Francisco D*
University of California, Santa Barbara M,D*
University of California, Santa Cruz D*
University of Central Florida M,O*†
University of Chicago D*
University of Cincinnati M,D*
University of Colorado at Boulder M,D*
University of Colorado at Colorado Springs M*
University of Colorado at Denver M*
University of Connecticut M,D*†
University of Delaware M,D*†
University of Florida M,D*†
University of Georgia M,D*†
University of Guelph M
University of Hawaii at Manoa M,D*
University of Houston M*
University of Houston–Clear Lake M*†
University of Illinois at Chicago M,D*
University of Illinois at Urbana–Champaign M,D*
University of Indianapolis M
The University of Iowa M,D*
University of Kansas M,D*
University of Kentucky M,D*
The University of Lethbridge M,D
University of Louisville M*†
University of Manitoba M*
University of Maryland, Baltimore County M,O*†
University of Maryland, College Park M,D*
University of Massachusetts Amherst M,D*†
University of Massachusetts Boston M*†
University of Massachusetts Lowell M*†
The University of Memphis M*†
University of Miami M,D*†
University of Michigan D*
University of Minnesota, Duluth M*
University of Minnesota, Twin Cities Campus M,D*
University of Mississippi M*
University of Missouri–Columbia M,D*
University of Missouri–Kansas City M,D*†
University of Missouri–St. Louis M†
The University of Montana–Missoula M*†
University of Nebraska at Omaha M
University of Nebraska–Lincoln M,D*†
University of Nevada, Las Vegas M,D*†
University of Nevada, Reno M*
University of New Brunswick Fredericton M,D
University of New Hampshire M,D*†
University of New Mexico M,D*†
University of New Orleans M*
The University of North Carolina at Chapel Hill M,D*†
The University of North Carolina at Charlotte M*
The University of North Carolina at Greensboro M†
University of North Dakota M*
University of Northern Colorado M†
University of Northern Iowa M
University of North Texas M,D*†
University of Notre Dame D*†
University of Oklahoma M,D*†
University of Oregon M,D*
University of Ottawa M*
University of Pennsylvania M,D*†
University of Pittsburgh M,D*†
University of Puerto Rico, Río Piedras M*
University of Regina M
University of Saskatchewan M,D
University of South Alabama M*†
University of South Carolina M,D*†
The University of South Dakota M†
University of Southern California M,D*†
University of South Florida M*†
The University of Tennessee M,D*†
The University of Texas at Arlington M*†
The University of Texas at Austin M,D*
The University of Texas at Dallas M*
The University of Texas at El Paso M*†
The University of Texas at San Antonio M*
The University of Texas at Tyler M
The University of Texas–Pan American M
University of Toledo M*†
University of Toronto M,D*
University of Victoria M,D
University of Virginia M,D*
University of Washington M,D*
University of Waterloo M,D

*P—first professional degree; M—master's degree; D—doctorate; O—other advanced degree; *full description and/or announcement in Book 2, 3, 4, 5, or 6; †full description in this book*

The University of Western Ontario M,D*
University of Windsor M,D
University of Wisconsin–Madison M,D*
University of Wisconsin–Milwaukee M
University of Wyoming M*†
Utah State University M,D*
Valdosta State University M
Vanderbilt University M,D*
Virginia Commonwealth University M,O*†
Virginia Polytechnic Institute and State University M,D*
Washington State University M,D*
Wayne State University M,D*
West Chester University of Pennsylvania M,O*†
Western Illinois University M
Western Kentucky University M†
Western Michigan University M,D*†
Western Washington University M
West Virginia University M*
Wichita State University M*†
William Paterson University of New Jersey M*†
Yale University D*
York University M,D*

SOFTWARE ENGINEERING

Andrews University M
Auburn University M,D*†
Azusa Pacific University M,O*†
California State University, Sacramento M
Carnegie Mellon University M,D*
Carroll College M
Central Michigan University M,O†
Colorado Technical University M,D
Colorado Technical University Denver Campus M
Concordia University (Canada) M,D,O*†
DePaul University M*†
Drexel University M*†
East Tennessee State University M†
Embry-Riddle Aeronautical University (FL) M*
Fairfield University M*
Florida Institute of Technology M,D*†
Florida State University M,D*†
Gannon University M
George Mason University M*†
Grand Valley State University M†
Illinois Institute of Technology M,D*†
International Technological University M
Jacksonville State University M
Kansas State University M*†
Mercer University M
Monmouth University M,O*†
National Technological University M
National University M†
Oakland University M†
The Pennsylvania State University Great Valley Campus M
Rochester Institute of Technology M*†
Royal Military College of Canada M,D
St. Mary's University of San Antonio M
San Jose State University M*
Santa Clara University M,D,O*
Seattle University M*†
Southern Adventist University M
Southern Methodist University M,D*†
Southern Polytechnic State University M†
Southwest Texas State University M*
Stevens Institute of Technology O*†
Stony Brook University, State University of New York M,D,O*†
Technical University of British Columbia M
Texas Tech University M,D*†
Towson University M,O†
Université du Québec, Institut National de la Recherche Scientifique M,D,O
Université Laval O†
The University of Alabama in Huntsville M,D,O*
University of Calgary M,D*
University of Colorado at Colorado Springs M*
University of Connecticut M,D*†
University of Houston–Clear Lake M*†
University of Maryland, College Park M*
University of Maryland University College M*
University of Michigan–Dearborn M*†
University of Minnesota, Twin Cities Campus M*
University of Missouri–Kansas City M,D*†
University of New Haven M*†
University of St. Thomas (MN) M,O*†
The University of Scranton M†
University of South Carolina M,D*†
University of Southern California M*†
The University of Texas at Arlington M,D*†
University of Toronto M*
University of Waterloo M,D
Wayne State University M,D,O*
West Virginia University M*
Widener University M*†

SPANISH

American University M,O*†
Arizona State University M,D*
Arkansas Tech University M
Auburn University M*†
Baylor University M*†
Boston College M,D*†
Boston University M,D*†
Bowling Green State University M*†
Brigham Young University M*
Brooklyn College of the City University of New York M†
California State University, Bakersfield M
California State University, Fresno M
California State University, Fullerton M
California State University, Long Beach M
California State University, Los Angeles M
California State University, Northridge M
California State University, Sacramento M
California State University, San Marcos M
The Catholic University of America M,D*†
Central Connecticut State University M*†
Central Michigan University M†
City College of the City University of New York M*†
Cleveland State University M*†
Colorado State University M*
Columbia University M,D*†
Cornell University D*
Duke University D*†
Eastern Michigan University M*
Emory University D,O*†
Florida Atlantic University M*
Florida International University M,D*†
Florida State University M,D*†
Framingham State College M*
Georgetown University M,D*
Georgia State University M*
Graduate School and University Center of the City University of New York D*†
Harvard University M,D*†
Howard University M*
Hunter College of the City University of New York M†
Illinois State University M*†
Indiana State University M*†
Indiana University Bloomington M,D*
Inter American University of Puerto Rico, Metropolitan Campus M
Iona College M*†
Johns Hopkins University M,D*†
Kansas State University M*†
Kent State University M*
Lehman College of the City University of New York M
Long Island University, C.W. Post Campus M*†
Louisiana State University and Agricultural and Mechanical College M*
Loyola University Chicago M*†
Marquette University M*†
Miami University M*†
Michigan State University M,D*†
Middlebury College M,D
Millersville University of Pennsylvania M†
Minnesota State University, Mankato M
Mississippi State University M*
Montclair State University M†
New Mexico Highlands University M
New Mexico State University M
New York University M,D*†
Northern Illinois University M*†
Nova Southeastern University M,O*
The Ohio State University M,D*
Ohio University M*
The Pennsylvania State University University Park Campus M,D*†
Portland State University M*
Princeton University D*
Purdue University M,D*
Queens College of the City University of New York M†
Queen's University at Kingston M
Rice University M*
Roosevelt University M*†
Rutgers, The State University of New Jersey, New Brunswick M,D*
St. John's University (NY) M*†
Saint Louis University M*†
San Diego State University M*
San Francisco State University M
San Jose State University M*
Seton Hall University M*†
Simmons College M*
Southern Connecticut State University M†
Southwest Texas State University M*
Stanford University M,D*
State University of New York at Albany M,D*†
State University of New York at Binghamton M,O*†
Syracuse University M*
Temple University M,D*†
Texas A&M International University M
Texas A&M University M*
Texas A&M University–Commerce M,D†
Texas A&M University–Kingsville M*†
Texas Tech University M,D*†
Tulane University M,D*†
Université de Montréal M,D
Université Laval M,D†
University at Buffalo, The State University of New York M,D*†
The University of Akron M†
The University of Alabama M,D*
The University of Arizona M,D*
University of Arkansas M*
The University of British Columbia M,D*
University of Calgary M,D*
University of California, Berkeley M,D*
University of California, Davis M,D*†
University of California, Irvine M,D*
University of California, Los Angeles M*
University of California, Riverside M,D*
University of California, San Diego M,D*
University of California, Santa Barbara M,D*
University of Central Florida M*†
University of Chicago M,D*
University of Cincinnati M,D*
University of Colorado at Boulder M,D*
University of Connecticut M,D*†
University of Delaware M*†
University of Denver M*†
University of Florida M,D*†
University of Georgia M*†
University of Hawaii at Manoa M*
University of Houston M,D*
University of Idaho M*†
The University of Iowa M,D*
University of Kansas M,D*
University of Kentucky M,D*
The University of Lethbridge M,D
University of Louisville M*†
University of Manitoba M,D*
University of Maryland, Baltimore County M*†
University of Maryland, College Park M,D*
University of Massachusetts Amherst M,D*†
The University of Memphis M*†
University of Miami D*†
University of Michigan D*
University of Minnesota, Twin Cities Campus M,D*
University of Mississippi M*
University of Missouri–Columbia M,D*
The University of Montana–Missoula M*†
University of Nebraska–Lincoln M,D*†
University of Nevada, Las Vegas M*†
University of Nevada, Reno M*
University of New Brunswick Fredericton M
University of New Hampshire M*†
University of New Mexico M,D*†
The University of North Carolina at Chapel Hill M,D*†
The University of North Carolina at Charlotte M*
The University of North Carolina at Greensboro M†
University of Northern Colorado M†
University of Northern Iowa M
University of North Texas M*†
University of Notre Dame M*†
University of Oklahoma M,D*†
University of Oregon M*
University of Ottawa M,D,O*
University of Pennsylvania M,D*†
University of Pittsburgh M,D*†
University of Rhode Island M*
University of South Carolina M*†
University of South Florida M*†
The University of Tennessee M,D*†
The University of Texas at Arlington M*†
The University of Texas at Austin M,D*
The University of Texas at Brownsville M
The University of Texas at El Paso M*†
The University of Texas at San Antonio M*
The University of Texas–Pan American M
University of Toledo M*†
University of Toronto M,D*
University of Utah M,D*
University of Virginia M,D*
University of Washington M*
The University of Western Ontario M*
University of Wisconsin–Madison M,D*
University of Wisconsin–Milwaukee M
University of Wyoming M*†
Vanderbilt University M,D*
Villanova University M*†
Washington State University M*
Washington University in St. Louis M,D*†
Wayne State University M*
West Chester University of Pennsylvania M*†
Western Michigan University M*†
West Virginia University M*
Wichita State University M*†
Winthrop University M
Yale University M,D*

SPECIAL EDUCATION

Acadia University M
Adams State College M
Adelphi University M,O*
Alabama Agricultural and Mechanical University M,O
Alabama State University M
Albany State University M
Alcorn State University M,O
American International College M,D,O*
American University M*†
Appalachian State University M
Arcadia University M,D,O†
Arizona State University M*
Arizona State University West M
Arkansas State University M,D,O
Armstrong Atlantic State University M†
Ashland University M
Assumption College M†
Auburn University M,D,O*†
Auburn University Montgomery M,O
Augustana College M
Augusta State University M,O
Austin Peay State University M,O
Averett University M
Azusa Pacific University M*†
Baldwin-Wallace College M*
Ball State University M,D,O*
Bank Street College of Education M*
Barry University M,D,O*†
Bayamón Central University M
Bellarmine University M
Bemidji State University M
Benedictine University M†
Bethel College (TN) M
Bloomsburg University of Pennsylvania M
Boise State University M*
Boston College M,O*†
Boston University M,D,O*†
Bowie State University M
Bowling Green State University M*†
Brandon University M,O
Brenau University M,O
Bridgewater State College M
Brigham Young University M,D*
Brooklyn College of the City University of New York M†
Butler University M
California Baptist University M
California Lutheran University M
California Polytechnic State University, San Luis Obispo M†
California State University, Bakersfield M
California State University, Chico M
California State University, Dominguez Hills M,O†

Institution	Degrees
California State University, Fresno	M
California State University, Fullerton	M
California State University, Hayward	M
California State University, Long Beach	M
California State University, Los Angeles	M,D
California State University, Northridge	M
California State University, Sacramento	M
California State University, San Bernardino	M
California State University, Stanislaus	M
California University of Pennsylvania	M
Calvin College	M
Canisius College	M
Cardinal Stritch University	M*
Castleton State College	M,O
Centenary College	M
Central Connecticut State University	M*†
Central Michigan University	M†
Central Missouri State University	M,O†
Central Washington University	M†
Chapman University	M*†
Chatham College	M
Cheyney University of Pennsylvania	M
Chicago State University	M
City College of the City University of New York	M*†
Clarion University of Pennsylvania	M†
Clarke College	M
Clemson University	M*
Cleveland State University	M*†
College of Charleston	M*†
College of Mount St. Joseph	M†
The College of New Jersey	M†
The College of New Rochelle	M†
College of St. Joseph	M
The College of Saint Rose	M*†
College of Santa Fe	M
College of Staten Island of the City University of New York	M†
The College of William and Mary	M*†
Columbus State University	M,O
Converse College	M
Coppin State College	M
Cumberland College	M
Curry College	M,O
Delaware State University	M
Delta State University	M
DePaul University	M*†
Dominican College	M†
Dominican University	M*
Dowling College	M
Drake University	M*†
Duquesne University	M*†
D'Youville College	M,O†
East Carolina University	M*†
Eastern Illinois University	M†
Eastern Kentucky University	M
Eastern Michigan University	M,O*
Eastern Nazarene College	M,O
Eastern New Mexico University	M
Eastern Washington University	M†
East Stroudsburg University of Pennsylvania	M†
East Tennessee State University	M†
Edgewood College	M,O
Edinboro University of Pennsylvania	M
Elmhurst College	M
Elms College	M,O
Elon University	M
Emporia State University	M*†
Endicott College	M
Fairfield University	M,O*
Fairleigh Dickinson University, Metropolitan Campus	M*†
Fitchburg State College	M†
Florida Atlantic University	M,D*
Florida Atlantic University, Ft. Lauderdale Campus	M,D
Florida Gulf Coast University	M
Florida International University	M,D*†
Florida State University	M,D,O*†
Fontbonne University	M
Fordham University	M,D,O*†
Fort Hays State University	M
Framingham State College	M*
Francis Marion University	M
Fresno Pacific University	M
Frostburg State University	M
Furman University	M
Gallaudet University	M,D,O
Geneva College	M*
George Mason University	M*†
The George Washington University	M,D,O*†
Georgia College & State University	M
Georgian Court College	M,O
Georgia Southern University	M,O
Georgia State University	M,D,O*
Gonzaga University	M
Governors State University	M
Grand Valley State University	M†
Hampton University	M*†
Hebrew College	M,O†
Henderson State University	M
Heritage College	M
Hofstra University	M,D,O*
Holy Names College	M,O
Hood College	M
Houston Baptist University	M
Howard University	M,O*
Hunter College of the City University of New York	M†
Idaho State University	M,O*
Illinois State University	M,D*†
Immaculata University	M,D,O†
Indiana State University	M,D,O*†
Indiana University Bloomington	M,D,O*
Indiana University of Pennsylvania	M*†
Indiana University–Purdue University Indianapolis	M*
Indiana University South Bend	M
Inter American University of Puerto Rico, Metropolitan Campus	M
Inter American University of Puerto Rico, San Germán Campus	M
Iowa State University of Science and Technology	M,D*†
Jackson State University	M,O
Jacksonville State University	M,O
Jacksonville University	M,O
James Madison University	M
Johns Hopkins University	M,D,O*†
Johnson State College	M
Kean University	M*†
Keene State College	M,O
Kennesaw State University	M
Kent State University	M,D,O*
Kutztown University of Pennsylvania	M,O†
Lamar University	M,D,O*†
La Sierra University	M,D,O
Lehigh University	M,D,O*
Lehman College of the City University of New York	M
Lesley University	M,D,O*†
Lewis & Clark College	M
Lewis University	M
Liberty University	M,D†
Long Island University, Brentwood Campus	M
Long Island University, Brooklyn Campus	M*
Long Island University, C.W. Post Campus	M,O*†
Long Island University, Rockland Graduate Campus	M
Long Island University, Westchester Graduate Campus	M
Longwood College	M
Loras College	M
Louisiana Tech University	M,D,O*
Loyola College in Maryland	M,O
Loyola Marymount University	M†
Loyola University Chicago	M*†
Lynchburg College	M
Lyndon State College	M
Lynn University	M,D†
Madonna University	M
Malone College	M†
Manhattan College	M,O*†
Manhattanville College	M*†
Marshall University	M*†
Marygrove College	M
Marywood University	M*†
Massachusetts College of Liberal Arts	M
McDaniel College	M
McNeese State University	M
Mercy College	M,O*
Mercyhurst College	M,O
Miami University	M*†
Michigan State University	M,D,O*†
Middle Tennessee State University	M*
Midwestern State University	M
Millersville University of Pennsylvania	M†
Minnesota State University, Mankato	M
Minnesota State University, Moorhead	M
Minot State University	M
Mississippi State University	M,D,O*
Monmouth University	M,O*†
Montana State University–Billings	M*
Montclair State University	M†
Morehead State University	M
Morningside College	M
Mount Saint Mary College	M
Mount St. Mary's College	M*
Mount Saint Vincent University	M
Murray State University	M†
National-Louis University	M,O
National University	M†
Nazareth College of Rochester	M
New England College	M*
New Jersey City University	M
New Mexico Highlands University	M
New Mexico State University	M
New York University	M,D,O*†
North Carolina Central University	M
North Carolina State University	M*
Northeastern Illinois University	M
Northeastern State University	M
Northeastern University	M*†
Northern Arizona University	M
Northern Illinois University	M*†
Northern Michigan University	M
Northern State University	M
North Georgia College & State University	M,O
Northwestern State University of Louisiana	M,O
Northwestern University	M,D*
Northwest Missouri State University	M
Northwest Nazarene University	M
Notre Dame College (OH)	M,O
Notre Dame de Namur University	M,O
Oakland University	M†
Ohio University	M,D*
Old Dominion University	M*†
Our Lady of the Lake University of San Antonio	M
Pacific Lutheran University	M†
Pennsylvania College of Optometry	M,D,O
The Pennsylvania State University Great Valley Campus	M
The Pennsylvania State University University Park Campus	M,D*†
Pittsburg State University	M
Plattsburgh State University of New York	M
Plymouth State College	M,O*
Portland State University	M*
Prairie View A&M University	M
Pratt Institute	M*
Providence College	M*
Purdue University	M,D,O*
Queens College of the City University of New York	M†
Radford University	M†
Rhode Island College	M,O†
Rivier College	M*†
Rochester Institute of Technology	M,O*†
Rockford College	M
Rowan University	M†
Rutgers, The State University of New Jersey, New Brunswick	M*
Sage Graduate School	M†
Saginaw Valley State University	M
St. Ambrose University	M
St. Cloud State University	M
St. John Fisher College	M
St. John's University (NY)	M,O*†
Saint Joseph College	M
Saint Joseph's University	M*†
Saint Louis University	M,D*†
Saint Martin's College	M
Saint Mary's College of California	M
Saint Mary's University of Minnesota	M
Saint Michael's College	M,O*
St. Thomas Aquinas College	M,O
Saint Xavier University	M,O*
Salem College	M
Salem State College	M
Sam Houston State University	M,O*
San Diego State University	M*
San Francisco State University	M,D,O
San Jose State University	M*
Santa Clara University	M*
Seton Hill University	M,O†
Shippensburg University of Pennsylvania	M,O†
Simmons College	M,O*
Slippery Rock University of Pennsylvania	M†
Smith College	M*
Sonoma State University	M
South Carolina State University	M
Southeastern Louisiana University	M
Southeast Missouri State University	M
Southern Connecticut State University	M,O†
Southern Illinois University Carbondale	M*†
Southern Illinois University Edwardsville	M†
Southern Oregon University	M
Southern Polytechnic State University	M†
Southern University and Agricultural and Mechanical College	M,D*
Southwestern College (KS)	M
Southwestern Oklahoma State University	M
Southwest Missouri State University	M,O*†
Southwest Texas State University	M*
State University of New York at Albany	M*†
State University of New York at Binghamton	M*†
State University of New York at New Paltz	M
State University of New York at Oswego	M
State University of New York College at Brockport	M*†
State University of New York College at Buffalo	M
State University of New York College at Geneseo	M
State University of New York College at Potsdam	M
State University of West Georgia	M,O
Stephen F. Austin State University	M
Stephens College	M
Stetson University	M
Syracuse University	M,D*
Tarleton State University	M,O
Teachers College Columbia University	M,D*
Temple University	M,D*†
Tennessee State University	M,D*
Tennessee Technological University	M,O*
Texas A&M International University	M
Texas A&M University	M,D*
Texas A&M University–Commerce	M,D†
Texas A&M University–Corpus Christi	M
Texas A&M University–Kingsville	M*†
Texas A&M University–Texarkana	M
Texas Christian University	M*
Texas Southern University	M,D†
Texas Tech University	M,D,O*†
Texas Woman's University	M,D*†
Troy State University	M,O
Union College (KY)	M
Universidad del Turabo	M
Universidad Metropolitana	M
Université de Sherbrooke	M,O
University at Buffalo, The State University of New York	M,D,O*†
The University of Akron	M†
The University of Alabama at Birmingham	M*†
University of Alaska Anchorage	M
University of Alberta	M,D*
The University of Arizona	M,D,O*
University of Arkansas	M*
University of Arkansas at Little Rock	M
The University of British Columbia	M,D,O*
University of Calgary	M,D*
University of California, Berkeley	D*
University of California, Los Angeles	D*
University of Central Arkansas	M
University of Central Florida	M,D*†
University of Central Oklahoma	M
University of Cincinnati	M,D*
University of Colorado at Colorado Springs	M*
University of Connecticut	M,D*†
University of Dayton	M*†
University of Delaware	M,D*†
University of Detroit Mercy	M*
The University of Findlay	M
University of Florida	M,D,O*†
University of Georgia	M,D,O*†
University of Guam	M
University of Hawaii at Manoa	M,D*
University of Houston	M,D*
University of Idaho	M,O*†
University of Illinois at Chicago	M,D*
University of Illinois at Urbana–Champaign	M,D,O*
The University of Iowa	M,D*
University of Kansas	M,D*
University of Kentucky	M,D,O*
University of La Verne	M*

*P—first professional degree; M—master's degree; D—doctorate; O—other advanced degree; *full description and/or announcement in Book 2, 3, 4, 5, or 6; †full description in this book*

University of Louisiana at Monroe M
University of Louisville M*†
University of Maine M,O*
University of Manitoba M*
University of Mary M
University of Maryland, College Park M,D,O*
University of Maryland Eastern Shore M†
University of Massachusetts Amherst M,D,O*†
University of Massachusetts Boston M*†
The University of Memphis M,D*†
University of Miami M,D,O*†
University of Michigan–Dearborn M*†
University of Minnesota, Twin Cities Campus M,D,O*
University of Missouri–Kansas City M,D,O*†
University of Missouri–St. Louis M†
University of Nebraska at Kearney M
University of Nebraska at Omaha M
University of Nebraska–Lincoln M*†
University of Nevada, Las Vegas M,D,O*†
University of Nevada, Reno M,D,O*
University of New Brunswick Fredericton M
University of New Hampshire M*†
University of New Mexico M,D*†
University of New Orleans M,D,O*
University of North Alabama M
The University of North Carolina at Chapel Hill M*†
The University of North Carolina at Charlotte M,D*
The University of North Carolina at Greensboro M†
The University of North Carolina at Wilmington M*
University of North Dakota M,D*
University of Northern Colorado M,D†
University of Northern Iowa M
University of North Florida M
University of North Texas M,D*†
University of Oklahoma M,D*†
University of Oklahoma Health Sciences Center M,D,O*
University of Phoenix–Hawaii Campus M,O
University of Pittsburgh M,D*†
University of Portland M
University of Puerto Rico, Medical Sciences Campus O*
University of Puerto Rico, Río Piedras M*
University of Rio Grande M
University of Saint Francis (IN) M
University of St. Thomas (MN) M,O*†
University of Saskatchewan M,D,O
University of South Alabama M,O*†
University of South Carolina M,D*†
The University of South Dakota M†
University of Southern California M,D*†
University of Southern Maine M
University of Southern Mississippi M,D,O
University of South Florida M,D,O*†
The University of Tennessee M,D,O*†
The University of Tennessee at Chattanooga M,O
The University of Texas at Austin M,D*
The University of Texas at Brownsville M
The University of Texas at San Antonio M*
The University of Texas at Tyler M,O
The University of Texas of the Permian Basin M
The University of Texas–Pan American M,D
University of the District of Columbia M*
University of the Incarnate Word M†
University of the Pacific M,D*
University of Toledo M,D,O*†
University of Utah M,D*
University of Vermont M*†
University of Victoria M,D
University of Virginia M,D,O*
University of Washington M,D*
The University of West Alabama M
The University of Western Ontario M*
University of West Florida M
University of Wisconsin–Eau Claire M†
University of Wisconsin–La Crosse M†
University of Wisconsin–Madison M,D*
University of Wisconsin–Milwaukee M
University of Wisconsin–Oshkosh M*
University of Wisconsin–Superior M
University of Wisconsin–Whitewater M*
University of Wyoming M,O*†
Utah State University M,D,O*
Valdosta State University M,O
Valparaiso University M
Vanderbilt University M,D*
Virginia Commonwealth University M*†
Virginia Polytechnic Institute and State University D,O*
Wagner College M
Walla Walla College M
Washburn University of Topeka M
Washington University in St. Louis M,D*†
Wayne State College M
Wayne State University M,D,O*
Webster University M,O
West Chester University of Pennsylvania M*†
Western Carolina University M†
Western Connecticut State University M
Western Illinois University M
Western Kentucky University M†
Western Michigan University M,D*†
Western New Mexico University M
Western Oregon University M
Western Washington University M
Westfield State College M
West Virginia University M,D*
Wheelock College M*
Whitworth College M
Wichita State University M*†
Widener University M,D*†
William Carey College M
William Paterson University of New Jersey M*†
Wilmington College M,D
Winona State University M
Winthrop University M
Wright State University M*
Xavier University M*
Youngstown State University M

SPEECH AND INTERPERSONAL COMMUNICATION

Abilene Christian University M
Arizona State University M,D*
Arkansas State University M,O
Austin Peay State University M
Ball State University M*
Bowling Green State University M,D*†
Brooklyn College of the City University of New York M,D†
California State University, Chico M
California State University, Fresno M
California State University, Fullerton M
California State University, Hayward M
California State University, Los Angeles M
California State University, Northridge M
Central Michigan University M†
Central Missouri State University M†
Colorado State University M*
Eastern Illinois University M†
Eastern Michigan University M*
Florida State University M,D*†
Georgia College & State University M
Idaho State University M*
Indiana University Bloomington M,D*
Kansas State University M*†
Louisiana State University and Agricultural and Mechanical College M,D*
Louisiana Tech University M*
Marquette University M*†
Miami University M*†
Minnesota State University, Mankato M
Montclair State University M†
Morehead State University M
New York University M,O*†
Norfolk State University M†
North Dakota State University M,D†
Northeastern Illinois University M
Northwestern University M,D*
Ohio University M,D*
The Pennsylvania State University University Park Campus M,D*†
Portland State University M*
Rensselaer Polytechnic Institute M,D*†
St. Mary's University of San Antonio M
San Francisco State University M
San Jose State University M*
Southern Illinois University Carbondale M,D*†
Southern Illinois University Edwardsville M†
Southwest Texas State University M*
Syracuse University M*
Temple University M*†
Texas A&M University M,D*
Texas A&M University–Commerce M†
Texas Christian University M*
Texas Southern University M†
The University of Alabama M*
University of Arkansas at Little Rock M
University of Connecticut M*†
University of Denver M,D*†
University of Georgia M,D*†
University of Hawaii at Manoa M*
University of Houston M*
University of Illinois at Urbana–Champaign M,D*
University of Maryland, College Park M,D*
University of Nevada, Reno M*
The University of North Carolina at Greensboro M†
University of South Carolina M,D*†
The University of South Dakota M†
University of Southern California M,D*†
The University of Tennessee M,D*†
The University of Texas–Pan American M
University of Wisconsin–Stevens Point M
University of Wisconsin–Superior M
Wake Forest University M*†
Wayne State University M,D*
Western Kentucky University M†

SPORT PSYCHOLOGY

Argosy University-Phoenix M,D,O*
Cleveland State University M*†
Florida State University M,D,O*†
John F. Kennedy University M*†
Purdue University M,D*
Queen's University at Kingston M,D
Southern Connecticut State University M†
Springfield College M,D,O†
University of Florida D*†
West Virginia University M,D*

SPORTS MANAGEMENT

Appalachian State University M
Audrey Cohen College M†
Barry University M*†
Belmont University M
Boise State University M*
Bowling Green State University M*†
Brooklyn College of the City University of New York M†
Canisius College M
Central Michigan University M†
Cleveland State University M*†
Concordia University (Canada) M,D,O*†
Eastern Kentucky University M
East Stroudsburg University of Pennsylvania M†
East Tennessee State University M†
Florida Atlantic University M*
Florida State University M,D,O*†
The George Washington University M*†
Georgia Southern University M
Georgia State University M*
Gonzaga University M
Grambling State University M
Hardin-Simmons University M
Idaho State University M*
Indiana State University M*†
Indiana University Bloomington M,D,O*
Indiana University of Pennsylvania M*†
Lynn University M†
Millersville University of Pennsylvania M†
Mississippi State University M*
Montana State University–Billings M*
Montclair State University M†
Morehead State University M
Neumann College M
North Carolina State University M*
North Dakota State University M†
Northwestern State University of Louisiana M
Ohio University M*
Old Dominion University M*†
Robert Morris University M†
St. Cloud State University M
St. Edward's University M,O
St. Thomas University M†
Seton Hall University M,O*†
Southeast Missouri State University M
Springfield College M,D,O†
Temple University M*†
United States Sports Academy M,D*
Université de Montréal M,D,O
University of Alberta M*
University of Dallas M*
University of Denver M*†
University of Louisville M*†
University of Miami M*†
University of Minnesota, Twin Cities Campus M,D,O*
University of New Brunswick Fredericton M
University of New Haven M*†
University of New Orleans M,O*
The University of North Carolina at Chapel Hill M*†
University of Northern Iowa M
University of Oklahoma M*†
University of Rhode Island M,D*
University of St. Thomas (MN) M,O*†
University of San Francisco M*†
University of Southern Mississippi M,D
The University of Tennessee M*†
University of the Incarnate Word M,D†
University of Wisconsin–La Crosse M†
Wayne State College M
Wayne State University M*
West Chester University of Pennsylvania M,O*†
Western Illinois University M
Western Michigan University M*†
West Virginia University M,D*
Whitworth College M
Wichita State University M*†
Xavier University M*

STATISTICS

American University M,D,O*†
Arizona State University M,D*
Auburn University M,D*†
Ball State University M*
Baylor University M,D*†
Bernard M. Baruch College of the City University of New York M*
Bowling Green State University M,D,O*†
Brigham Young University M*
California State University, Fullerton M
California State University, Hayward M
California State University, Sacramento M
Carnegie Mellon University M,D*
Case Western Reserve University M,D*†
Central Connecticut State University M*†
Claremont Graduate University M,D*
Clemson University M,D*
Colorado State University M,D*
Columbia University M,D*†
Concordia University (Canada) M,D*†
Cornell University M,D*
Dalhousie University M,D*
DePaul University M*†
Duke University D*†
Florida International University M*†
Florida State University M,D*†
George Mason University M*†
The George Washington University M,D*†
Georgia Institute of Technology M,D*
Harvard University M,D*†
Indiana University Bloomington M,D*
Indiana University–Purdue University Indianapolis M,D*
Instituto Tecnológico y de Estudios Superiores de Monterrey, Campus Monterrey M,D
Iowa State University of Science and Technology M,D*†
Johns Hopkins University M,D*†
Kansas State University M,D*†
Kean University M*†
Lakehead University M
Lehigh University M*
Louisiana State University and Agricultural and Mechanical College M*
Louisiana Tech University M*
Marquette University M,D*†
McGill University M,D*
McMaster University M,D
McNeese State University M
Memorial University of Newfoundland M,D†
Miami University M*†
Michigan State University M,D*†
Minnesota State University, Mankato M
Mississippi State University M,D*

- Montana State University–Bozeman M,D*
- Montclair State University M,O†
- New Jersey Institute of Technology M
- New Mexico State University M
- New York University M,D,O*†
- North Carolina State University M,D*
- North Dakota State University M,D†
- Northern Arizona University M
- Northern Illinois University M*†
- Northwestern University M,D*
- Oakland University M,D,O†
- The Ohio State University M,D*
- Oklahoma State University M,D*†
- Oregon State University M,D*
- The Pennsylvania State University University Park Campus M,D*†
- Princeton University M,D*
- Purdue University M,D*
- Queen's University at Kingston M,D
- Rensselaer Polytechnic Institute M*†
- Rice University M,D*
- Rochester Institute of Technology M,O*†
- Rutgers, The State University of New Jersey, New Brunswick M,D*
- St. John's University (NY) M*†
- Sam Houston State University M*
- San Diego State University M*
- Simon Fraser University M,D
- Southern Illinois University Carbondale M,D*†
- Southern Illinois University Edwardsville M†
- Southern Methodist University M,D*†
- Stanford University M,D*
- State University of New York at Albany M,D,O*†
- State University of New York at Binghamton M,D*†
- Stephen F. Austin State University M
- Stevens Institute of Technology M,O*†
- Stony Brook University, State University of New York M,D*†
- Syracuse University M*
- Temple University M,D*†
- Texas A&M University M,D*
- Tulane University M,D*†
- Université de Montréal M,D
- Université Laval M†
- The University of Akron M†
- The University of Alabama M,D*
- University of Alberta M,D,O*
- The University of Arizona M,D*
- University of Arkansas M*
- University of Arkansas at Little Rock M
- The University of British Columbia M,D*
- University of Calgary M,D*
- University of California, Berkeley M,D*
- University of California, Davis M,D*†
- University of California, Los Angeles M,D*
- University of California, Riverside M,D*
- University of California, San Diego M,D*
- University of California, Santa Barbara M,D*
- University of Central Florida M*†
- University of Central Oklahoma M
- University of Chicago M,D*
- University of Cincinnati M,D*
- University of Connecticut M,D*†
- University of Delaware M*†
- University of Florida M,D*†
- University of Georgia M,D*†
- University of Guelph M,D
- University of Houston–Clear Lake M*†
- University of Idaho M*†
- University of Illinois at Chicago M,D*
- University of Illinois at Urbana–Champaign M,D*
- The University of Iowa M,D*
- University of Kansas M,D*
- University of Kentucky M,D*
- University of Manitoba M,D*
- University of Maryland, Baltimore County M,D*†
- University of Maryland, College Park M,D*
- University of Massachusetts Amherst M,D*†
- The University of Memphis M,D*†
- University of Miami M,D*†
- University of Michigan M,D*
- University of Minnesota, Twin Cities Campus M,D*
- University of Missouri–Columbia M,D*
- University of Missouri–Kansas City M,D*†
- University of Nebraska–Lincoln M,D*†
- University of Nevada, Las Vegas M*†
- University of New Brunswick Fredericton M,D
- University of New Hampshire M,D*†
- University of New Mexico M,D*†
- The University of North Carolina at Chapel Hill M,D*†
- The University of North Carolina at Charlotte M,D*
- University of North Florida M
- University of Ottawa M,D*
- University of Pennsylvania M,D*†
- University of Pittsburgh M,D*†
- University of Puerto Rico, Mayagüez Campus M*
- University of Regina M,D
- University of Rhode Island M,D*
- University of Rochester M,D*
- University of Saskatchewan M,D
- University of South Carolina M,D,O*†
- University of Southern California M*†
- The University of Tennessee M,D*†
- The University of Texas at Austin M*
- The University of Texas at Dallas M,D*
- The University of Texas at El Paso M*†
- The University of Texas at San Antonio M*
- University of Toledo M,D*†
- University of Toronto M,D*
- University of Utah M*
- University of Vermont M*†
- University of Victoria M,D
- University of Virginia M,D*
- University of Washington M,D*
- University of Waterloo M,D
- The University of Western Ontario M,D*
- University of West Florida M
- University of Windsor M,D
- University of Wisconsin–Madison M,D*
- University of Wyoming M,D*†
- Utah State University M*
- Villanova University M*†
- Virginia Commonwealth University M,O*†
- Virginia Polytechnic Institute and State University M,D*
- Washington University in St. Louis M,D*†
- Wayne State University M,D*
- Western Michigan University M,D*†
- West Virginia University M,D*
- Wichita State University M,D*†
- Worcester Polytechnic Institute M,D,O*†
- Wright State University M*
- Yale University M,D*
- York University M,D*

STRUCTURAL BIOLOGY

- Baylor College of Medicine D*
- Brandeis University D*†
- Cornell University M,D*
- Iowa State University of Science and Technology D*†
- Joan and Sanford I. Weill Medical College and Graduate School of Medical Sciences of Cornell University D*
- Mount Sinai School of Medicine of New York University D*
- Northwestern University D*
- Stanford University D*
- State University of New York at Albany M,D*†
- Stony Brook University, State University of New York D*†
- Syracuse University D*
- Thomas Jefferson University D*
- Tulane University M,D*†
- University of Illinois at Urbana–Champaign D*
- University of Pennsylvania D*†
- The University of Tennessee Health Science Center D*
- The University of Texas Health Science Center at San Antonio D*
- The University of Texas Medical Branch M,D*
- University of Toronto D*
- University of Washington D*

STRUCTURAL ENGINEERING

- Auburn University M,D*†
- California State University, Northridge M
- The Catholic University of America M,D*†
- Cleveland State University M,D*†
- Colorado State University M,D*
- Cornell University M,D*
- École Polytechnique de Montréal M,D,O
- Iowa State University of Science and Technology M,D*†
- Louisiana State University and Agricultural and Mechanical College M,D*
- Marquette University M,D*†
- McGill University M,D*
- Michigan Technological University D*†
- Milwaukee School of Engineering M*
- Northwestern University M,D*
- Ohio University M*
- The Pennsylvania State University University Park Campus M,D*†
- Princeton University M,D*
- Rensselaer Polytechnic Institute M,D*†
- Texas A&M University M,D*
- Tufts University M,D*†
- University at Buffalo, The State University of New York M,D*†
- University of Alberta M,D*
- University of California, Berkeley M,D*
- University of California, Los Angeles M,D*
- University of California, San Diego M,D*
- University of Central Florida M,D,O*†
- University of Colorado at Boulder M,D*
- University of Dayton M*†
- University of Delaware M,D*†
- University of Maine M,D*
- The University of Memphis M,D*†
- University of Missouri–Columbia M,D*
- University of Missouri–Rolla M,D*
- University of New Brunswick Fredericton M,D
- University of North Dakota M*
- University of Oklahoma M,D*†
- University of Rhode Island M,D*
- University of Southern California M*†
- University of Virginia M,D*
- University of Washington M,D*
- Washington University in St. Louis M,D*†

STUDENT PERSONNEL SERVICES

- Azusa Pacific University M*†
- Bowling Green State University M*†
- Canisius College M
- Central Missouri State University M,O†
- The College of Saint Rose M*†
- Concordia University Wisconsin M
- Emporia State University M*†
- Hampton University M*†
- Kansas State University M,D*†
- Kent State University M,D,O*
- Miami University M*†
- Minnesota State University, Mankato M
- New York University M,D*†
- Northeastern University M*†
- Northwestern State University of Louisiana M,O
- Ohio University M,D*
- Oklahoma State University M,D*†
- Oregon State University M*
- Rowan University M†
- Slippery Rock University of Pennsylvania M†
- Springfield College M,O†
- State University of New York College at Buffalo M
- Teachers College Columbia University M,D*
- Tennessee Technological University M,O*
- University of Central Arkansas M
- University of Dayton M*†
- University of Florida M,D,O*†
- University of Georgia M,D*†
- University of Louisville M,D*†
- University of Maryland, College Park M,D,O*
- University of Minnesota, Twin Cities Campus M,D,O*
- University of Mississippi M*
- University of Northern Colorado D†
- University of Northern Iowa M
- University of South Carolina M*†
- University of Southern California M,D,O*†
- University of South Florida M*†
- The University of Tennessee M*†
- University of Wisconsin–La Crosse M†
- Western Illinois University M
- Western Washington University M

SURVEYING SCIENCE AND ENGINEERING

- The Ohio State University M,D*
- University of New Brunswick Fredericton M,D,O

SURVEY METHODOLOGY

- University of Maryland, College Park M,D*
- University of Michigan M,D,O*
- University of Nebraska–Lincoln M*†

SUSTAINABLE DEVELOPMENT

- Brandeis University M*†
- Carnegie Mellon University M*
- Clark University M*†
- Instituto Centroamericano de Administración de Empresas M
- New College of California M*†
- Prescott College M†
- School for International Training M,O†
- Slippery Rock University of Pennsylvania M†
- University of Georgia M,D*†
- University of Maryland, College Park M*
- University of Washington P,M,D*
- University of Wisconsin–Madison M*
- Western Illinois University M,O

SYSTEMS ENGINEERING

- Air Force Institute of Technology M,D*
- Auburn University M,D*†
- Boston University M,D*†
- California Institute of Technology M,D*
- California State University, Fullerton M
- Capitol College M
- Carleton University M
- Case Western Reserve University M,D*†
- Colorado School of Mines M,D†
- Cornell University M*
- Embry-Riddle Aeronautical University (FL) M*
- Florida Atlantic University M*
- George Mason University M*†
- The George Washington University M,D,O*†
- Georgia Institute of Technology M,D*
- Instituto Tecnológico y de Estudios Superiores de Monterrey, Campus Chihuahua M,O
- Instituto Tecnológico y de Estudios Superiores de Monterrey, Campus Monterrey M,D
- Iowa State University of Science and Technology M*†
- Lehigh University M*
- Louisiana State University in Shreveport M†
- Massachusetts Institute of Technology M*
- National Technological University M
- Naval Postgraduate School M
- North Carolina Agricultural and Technical State University M,D*
- Northeastern University M*†
- Oakland University M,D†
- The Ohio State University M,D*
- Ohio University M*
- Oklahoma State University M*†
- The Pennsylvania State University Great Valley Campus M
- Polytechnic University, Brooklyn Campus M*
- Polytechnic University, Long Island Graduate Center M
- Polytechnic University, Westchester Graduate Center M
- Portland State University M,O*
- Purdue University M,D*
- Rensselaer Polytechnic Institute M,D*†
- Rochester Institute of Technology M*†
- Rutgers, The State University of New Jersey, New Brunswick M,D*
- San Jose State University M*
- Southern Methodist University M,D*†
- Stanford University M*
- Texas Tech University M,D*†
- University of Alberta M,D*
- The University of Arizona M,D*
- University of Central Florida M,D,O*†

*P—first professional degree; M—master's degree; D—doctorate; O—other advanced degree; *full description and/or announcement in Book 2, 3, 4, 5, or 6; †full description in this book*

University of Connecticut M,D*†
University of Florida M,D,O*†
University of Houston M,D*
University of Idaho M*†
University of Illinois at Urbana–Champaign M*
University of Maryland, College Park M*
University of Massachusetts Lowell M,D*†
The University of Memphis M*†
University of Michigan M,D*
University of Michigan–Dearborn M*†
University of Minnesota, Twin Cities Campus M*
University of Missouri–Rolla M*
University of Pennsylvania M,D*†
University of Pittsburgh M*†
University of Regina M,D
University of Rhode Island M,D*
University of St. Thomas (MN) M,O*†
University of Southern California M,D,O*†
University of Southern Colorado M
University of Virginia M,D*
University of Waterloo M,D
University of West Florida M
Virginia Polytechnic Institute and State University M*
Washington University in St. Louis D*†
West Virginia University Institute of Technology M

SYSTEMS SCIENCE

Carleton University M
Colorado Technical University M,D
Colorado Technical University Denver Campus M
Fairleigh Dickinson University, Metropolitan Campus M*†
Florida Institute of Technology M*†
Hood College M
Louisiana State University and Agricultural and Mechanical College M,D*
Louisiana State University in Shreveport M†
Miami University M*†
Northern Kentucky University M
Oakland University M†
Old Dominion University M*†
Portland State University D*
Rensselaer at Hartford M
Southern Methodist University M,D*†
State University of New York at Binghamton M,D*†
Syracuse University M*
University of Michigan–Dearborn M*†
University of Ottawa M,O*
Washington University in St. Louis M,D*†

TAXATION

American University M*†
Arizona State University M*
Bentley College M,O*
Bernard M. Baruch College of the City University of New York M*
Boston University P,M*†
Bryant College M,O
California State University, Fullerton M
California State University, Hayward M
California State University, Los Angeles M
Capital University M
Case Western Reserve University P,M*†
DePaul University M*†
Drexel University M*†
Duquesne University M*†
École des Hautes Études Commerciales de Montréal M,O*
Fairfield University M,O*
Fairleigh Dickinson University, College at Florham M*†
Fairleigh Dickinson University, Metropolitan Campus M*†
Florida Atlantic University M*
Florida Atlantic University, Ft. Lauderdale Campus M
Florida Gulf Coast University M
Florida International University M*†
Fontbonne University M
Fordham University M*†
Georgetown University P,M,D*
Georgia State University M*
Golden Gate University P,M,D,O
Grand Valley State University M†
Hofstra University M*
Illinois Institute of Technology P,M*†
John Marshall Law School P,M
King's College M
Long Island University, Brooklyn Campus M*
Long Island University, C.W. Post Campus M*†
Loyola Marymount University P,M†
Mississippi State University M,D*
Northeastern University M,O*†
Northern Illinois University M*†
Old Dominion University M*†
Pace University M*†
Pace University, White Plains Campus M*
Philadelphia University M
Regent University P,M†
Robert Morris University M†
St. John Fisher College M
St. John's University (NY) M,O*†
St. Mary's University of San Antonio M
St. Thomas University P,M†
Saint Xavier University M,O*
San Francisco State University M
San Jose State University M*
Seton Hall University M*†
Southeastern University M†
Southern Methodist University P,M,D*†
Southern New Hampshire University M,O*
State University of New York at Albany M*†
Suffolk University M,O*
Temple University P,M*†
Texas Tech University M,D*†
Thomas College M
Université de Sherbrooke M,O
The University of Akron M†
The University of Alabama M,D*
University of Baltimore P,M*
University of Central Florida M*†
University of Colorado at Boulder M,D*
University of Denver M*†
University of Florida M*†
University of Hartford M*
University of Houston M,D*
The University of Memphis M*†
University of Miami M*†
University of Minnesota, Twin Cities Campus M*
University of Mississippi M,D*
University of Missouri–Kansas City M*†
University of Missouri–St. Louis M,O†
University of New Haven M*†
University of New Mexico M*†
University of New Orleans M*
University of San Diego P,M,O*†
University of South Carolina M*†
University of Southern California M*†
The University of Texas at Arlington M,D*†
The University of Texas at San Antonio M*
University of the Sacred Heart M
University of Tulsa M†
University of Washington P,M,D*
University of Waterloo M,D
Villanova University M*†
Virginia Commonwealth University M,D*†
Walsh College of Accountancy and Business Administration M
Wayne State University M*
Widener University M*†

TECHNICAL WRITING

Boise State University M*
Bowling Green State University M*†
Carnegie Mellon University M*
Colorado State University M*
Drexel University M*†
Florida Institute of Technology M*†
Georgia State University M,D*
Illinois Institute of Technology M*†
James Madison University M
Metropolitan State University M
Miami University M*†
Michigan Technological University M,D*†
Montana Tech of The University of Montana M
New Jersey Institute of Technology M
North Carolina State University M*
Northeastern University M,O*†
Polytechnic University, Brooklyn Campus M*
Regis University M,O*†
Rensselaer Polytechnic Institute M*†
San Jose State University M*
Southern Polytechnic State University M†
Southwest Texas State University M*
Texas Tech University M,D*†
The University of Alabama in Huntsville M,O*
University of Arkansas at Little Rock M
University of Central Florida M,O*†
University of Colorado at Denver M*
University of Minnesota, Twin Cities Campus M,D*
The University of North Carolina at Greensboro M,D,O†
University of the Sciences in Philadelphia M*
University of Washington M*
University of Waterloo M,D

TECHNOLOGY AND PUBLIC POLICY

California State University, Los Angeles M
Carnegie Mellon University M,D*
Colorado State University M,D*
Eastern Michigan University M*
George Mason University M*†
The George Washington University M*†
Massachusetts Institute of Technology M,D*
Northwestern University O*
Rensselaer Polytechnic Institute M,D*†
St. Cloud State University M
University of Minnesota, Twin Cities Campus M*
University of Pennsylvania M,D*†
The University of Texas at Austin M*
Western Illinois University M

TELECOMMUNICATIONS

Azusa Pacific University M,O*†
Boston University M*†
Columbia University M,D,O*†
DePaul University M*†
Drexel University M*†
George Mason University M*†
The George Washington University M*†
Illinois Institute of Technology M,D*†
Instituto Tecnológico y de Estudios Superiores de Monterrey, Campus Ciudad Juárez M
Iona College M,O*†
Michigan State University M,D*†
New Jersey Institute of Technology M,D
North Carolina State University M*
Northwestern University O*
Pace University M,D,O*†
Pace University, White Plains Campus M,D,O*
The Pennsylvania State University University Park Campus M*†
Polytechnic University, Brooklyn Campus M*
Polytechnic University, Long Island Graduate Center M
Polytechnic University, Westchester Graduate Center M
Regis University M,O*†
Roosevelt University M*†
Saint Mary's University of Minnesota M
Southern Methodist University M,D*†
State University of New York Institute of Technology at Utica/Rome M*†
Syracuse University M*
Texas Tech University M,D*†
Université du Québec, Institut National de la Recherche Scientifique M,D,O
University of Alberta M,D*
University of Arkansas M*
University of California, San Diego M,D*
University of Colorado at Boulder M*
University of Denver M*†
University of Louisiana at Lafayette M*
University of Maryland, College Park M*
University of Missouri–Kansas City M,D*†
University of Pennsylvania M*†
University of Pittsburgh M,O*†
The University of Texas at Dallas M,D*
Western Illinois University M,O
Widener University M*†

TELECOMMUNICATIONS MANAGEMENT

Alaska Pacific University M
Canisius College M
Capitol College M
Carleton University M
DeVry University-Keller Graduate School of Management M
Golden Gate University M,D,O
Hofstra University M*
Illinois Institute of Technology M*†
Instituto Tecnológico y de Estudios Superiores de Monterrey, Campus Ciudad de México M
Instituto Tecnológico y de Estudios Superiores de Monterrey, Campus Ciudad Obregón M
Instituto Tecnológico y de Estudios Superiores de Monterrey, Campus Irapuato M,D
Michigan State University M,D*†
Morgan State University M*
Murray State University M†
National University M†
Northwestern University O*
Oklahoma State University M*†
Polytechnic University, Brooklyn Campus M*
Regis University M,O*†
San Diego State University M*
Southern New Hampshire University M,O*
Stevens Institute of Technology M,D,O*†
Syracuse University M*
University of Colorado at Boulder M*
University of Denver M*†
University of Maryland University College M*
University of Miami M,O*†
University of Missouri–St. Louis M,D,O†
University of Pennsylvania M*†
University of San Francisco M*†
Webster University M

TEXTILE DESIGN

Academy of Art College M†
California College of Arts and Crafts M*
California State University, Los Angeles M
Central Washington University M†
Colorado State University M*
Cornell University M,D*
Cranbrook Academy of Art M*
Drexel University M*†
Illinois State University M*†
Indiana University Bloomington M*
James Madison University M
Kent State University M*
Massachusetts College of Art M
Memphis College of Art M*
New School University M*†
Philadelphia University M
Rhode Island School of Design M
Rochester Institute of Technology M*†
San Jose State University M*
Savannah College of Art and Design M*
Southern Illinois University Edwardsville M†
Sul Ross State University M*
Syracuse University M*
Temple University M*†
University of California, Davis M*†
University of Cincinnati M*
University of Minnesota, Twin Cities Campus M,D*
The University of North Carolina at Greensboro M,D†
University of North Texas M,D*†
Western Michigan University M*†

TEXTILE SCIENCES AND ENGINEERING

Auburn University M,D*†
Clemson University M,D*
Cornell University M,D*
Georgia Institute of Technology M,D*
Institute of Textile Technology M
North Carolina State University M,D*
Philadelphia University M
University of Massachusetts Dartmouth M*†

THANATOLOGY

Brooklyn College of the City University of New York M†
The College of New Rochelle O†
Hood College M

THEATER

American Conservatory Theater M,O*
Antioch University McGregor M†
Arcadia University M,D,O†
Arizona State University M,D*
Arkansas State University M,O
Austin Peay State University M
Baylor University M*†
Bennington College M†
The Boston Conservatory M
Boston University M,O*†
Bowling Green State University M,D*†
Brandeis University M*†
Brigham Young University M*

Institution	Degrees
Brooklyn College of the City University of New York	M†
Brown University	M*
California Institute of the Arts	M,O*
California State University, Fullerton	M
California State University, Long Beach	M
California State University, Los Angeles	M
California State University, Northridge	M
California State University, Sacramento	M
Carnegie Mellon University	M*
Case Western Reserve University	M,D*†
The Catholic University of America	M*†
Central Michigan University	M†
Central Missouri State University	M†
Central Washington University	M†
Claremont Graduate University	M,D*
Columbia University	M,D*†
Cornell University	D*
DePaul University	M,O*†
Eastern Kentucky University	M
Eastern Michigan University	M*
Emerson College	M*†
Florida Atlantic University	M*
Florida State University	M,D*†
The George Washington University	M*†
Graduate School and University Center of the City University of New York	D*†
Humboldt State University	M
Hunter College of the City University of New York	M†
Idaho State University	M*
Illinois State University	M*†
Indiana State University	M*†
Indiana University Bloomington	M,D*
Kent State University	M*
Lamar University	M*†
Lesley University	M,D,O*†
Long Island University, C.W. Post Campus	M*†
Louisiana State University and Agricultural and Mechanical College	M,D*
Massachusetts College of Art	M
Miami University	M*†
Michigan State University	M,D*†
Minnesota State University, Mankato	M
Montana State University–Billings	M*
Montclair State University	M†
Morehead State University	M
National Theatre Conservatory	M,O
New School University	M*†
New York University	M,D,O*†
North Carolina School of the Arts	M
Northern Illinois University	M*†
Northwestern University	M,D*
The Ohio State University	M,D*
Ohio University	M*
Oklahoma City University	M
Oklahoma State University	M*†
The Pennsylvania State University University Park Campus	M*†
Pittsburg State University	M
Portland State University	M*
Purchase College, State University of New York	M
Purdue University	M*
Regent University	M†
Rhode Island College	M†
Roosevelt University	M*†
Rowan University	M†
Rutgers, The State University of New Jersey, New Brunswick	M*
San Diego State University	M*
San Francisco State University	M
San Jose State University	M*
Sarah Lawrence College	M*†
Smith College	M*
South Dakota State University	M*
Southern Illinois University Carbondale	M,D*†
Southern Methodist University	M*†
Southwest Missouri State University	M*†
Southwest Texas State University	M*
Stanford University	D*
State University of New York at Albany	M*†
State University of New York at Binghamton	M*†
Stony Brook University, State University of New York	M*†
Syracuse University	M*
Temple University	M*†
Texas A&M University–Commerce	M†
Texas Tech University	M,D*†
Texas Woman's University	M*†
Towson University	M,O†
Tufts University	M,D*†
Tulane University	M*†
Université de Sherbrooke	M,D
Université du Québec à Montréal	M
Université Laval	M,D†
The University of Akron	M,D†
The University of Alabama	M*
University of Alberta	M*
The University of Arizona	M*
University of Arkansas	M*
The University of British Columbia	M,D*
University of Calgary	M,D*
University of California, Berkeley	D,O*
University of California, Davis	M,D*†
University of California, Irvine	M,D*
University of California, Los Angeles	M,D*
University of California, San Diego	M,D*
University of California, Santa Barbara	M,D*
University of California, Santa Cruz	O*
University of Central Florida	M*†
University of Cincinnati	M*
University of Colorado at Boulder	M,D*
University of Colorado at Denver	M*
University of Connecticut	M*†
University of Delaware	M*†
University of Florida	M*†
University of Georgia	M,D*†
University of Guelph	M
University of Hawaii at Manoa	M,D*
University of Houston	M*
University of Idaho	M*†
University of Illinois at Chicago	M*
University of Illinois at Urbana–Champaign	M,D*
The University of Iowa	M*
University of Kansas	M,D*
University of Kentucky	M*
University of Louisville	M*†
University of Maine	M*
University of Maryland, College Park	M,D*
University of Massachusetts Amherst	M*†
The University of Memphis	M*†
University of Michigan	M,D*
University of Minnesota, Twin Cities Campus	M,D*
University of Mississippi	M*
University of Missouri–Columbia	M,D*
University of Missouri–Kansas City	M*†
The University of Montana–Missoula	M*†
University of Nebraska at Omaha	M
University of Nebraska–Lincoln	M,D*†
University of Nevada, Las Vegas	M*†
University of New Mexico	M*†
University of New Orleans	M*
The University of North Carolina at Chapel Hill	M*†
The University of North Carolina at Greensboro	M†
University of North Dakota	M*
University of Northern Iowa	M
University of North Texas	M*†
University of Oklahoma	M*†
University of Oregon	M,D*
University of Pittsburgh	M,D*†
University of Portland	M
University of San Diego	M*†
University of Saskatchewan	M
University of South Carolina	M,D*†
The University of South Dakota	M†
University of Southern California	M*†
University of Southern Mississippi	M
University of South Florida	M*†
The University of Tennessee	M*†
The University of Texas at Austin	M,D*
The University of Texas at El Paso	M*†
The University of Texas–Pan American	M
University of Toronto	M,D*
University of Utah	M,D*
University of Virginia	M*
University of Washington	M,D*
University of Wisconsin–Madison	M,D*
University of Wisconsin–Milwaukee	M
University of Wisconsin–Superior	M
Utah State University	M*
Villanova University	M*†
Virginia Commonwealth University	M*†
Virginia Polytechnic Institute and State University	M*
Washington University in St. Louis	M*†
Wayne State University	M,D*
Western Illinois University	M
Western Washington University	M
West Virginia University	M*
Yale University	M,D,O*
York University	M*

THEOLOGY

Institution	Degrees
Abilene Christian University	P,M
Acadia University	P,M,D
Alliance Theological Seminary	P,M
American Baptist Seminary of the West	P,M
American Christian College and Seminary	P,M
Anderson University	P,M,D
Andover Newton Theological School	P,M,D*
Andrews University	P,M,D
Aquinas Institute of Theology	P,M,D,O
Asbury Theological Seminary	P,M,D,O
Ashland University	P,M,D
Assemblies of God Theological Seminary	P,M,D
Associated Mennonite Biblical Seminary	P,M,O
Athenaeum of Ohio	P,M,O
Atlantic School of Theology	P,M
Austin Presbyterian Theological Seminary	P,M,D
Azusa Pacific University	P,M,D*†
Bangor Theological Seminary	P,M,D
Baptist Bible College	P,M
Baptist Bible College of Pennsylvania	P,M,D
Baptist Missionary Association Theological Seminary	P,M
Baptist Theological Seminary at Richmond	P,D
Barry University	M,D*†
Bayamón Central University	P,M
Baylor University	P,D*†
Bethany Theological Seminary	P,M,O
Beth Benjamin Academy of Connecticut	
Bethel College (IN)	M
Bethel Seminary	P,M,D,O
Bethesda Christian University	P,M
Beth HaMedrash Shaarei Yosher Institute	
Beth Hatalmud Rabbinical College	
Beth Medrash Govoha	
Biblical Theological Seminary	P,M,D
Biola University	P,M,D
Blessed John XXIII National Seminary	P
Boston College	M,D*†
Boston University	P,M,D*†
Briercrest Biblical Seminary	P
Bryn Athyn College of the New Church	P,M
Calvary Bible College and Theological Seminary	P,M,D
Calvin Theological Seminary	P,M,D
Campbellsville University	M
Campbell University	P,M
Canadian Theological Seminary	P,M,O
Capital Bible Seminary	P,M
The Catholic Distance University	M
Catholic Theological Union at Chicago	P,M,D,O
The Catholic University of America	P,M,D,O*†
Central Baptist Theological Seminary	P,M,O
Central Yeshiva Tomchei Tmimim-Lubavitch	
Chicago Theological Seminary	P,M,D
Christendom College	M
Christian Theological Seminary	P,M,D
Christ the King Seminary	P,M
Church Divinity School of the Pacific	P,M,D,O
Church of God Theological Seminary	P,M
Cincinnati Bible College and Seminary	P,M
Claremont Graduate University	M,D*
Claremont School of Theology	P,M,D
Colegio Pentecostal Mizpa	M
Colgate Rochester Crozer Divinity School	P,M,D,O
Collège Dominicain de Philosophie et de Théologie	M,D,O
College of Emmanuel and St. Chad	P,M
College of Mount St. Joseph	M†
College of St. Catherine	M†
College of Saint Elizabeth	M
Columbia International University	P,M,D,O
Columbia Theological Seminary	P,M,D
Concordia Lutheran Seminary	P,M
Concordia Seminary	P,M,D,O
Concordia Theological Seminary	P,M,D
Concordia University (CA)	M
Concordia University (Canada)	M*†
Covenant Theological Seminary	P,M,D,O
Creighton University	M*
The Criswell College	P,M
Crown College	M
Dallas Theological Seminary	M,D,O
Darkei Noam Rabbinical College	
Denver Seminary	P,M,D,O
Dominican House of Studies	P,M,O
Dominican School of Philosophy and Theology	P,M,O
Drew University	P,M,D,O†
Duke University	P,M*†
Duquesne University	M,D*†
Earlham School of Religion	P,M
Eastern Baptist Theological Seminary	P,M,D
Eastern Mennonite University	P,M
Ecumenical Theological Seminary	P
Eden Theological Seminary	P,M,D
Emmanuel School of Religion	P,M,D
Emory University	P,M,D*†
Episcopal Divinity School	P,M,D,O*
Episcopal Theological Seminary of the Southwest	P,M,O
Erskine Theological Seminary	P,M,D
Evangelical School of Theology	P,M,O
Evangelical Seminary of Puerto Rico	P,M
Faith Baptist Bible College and Theological Seminary	P,M,D
Faith Evangelical Lutheran Seminary	P,M
Fordham University	M,D*†
Franciscan School of Theology	P,M,O
Franciscan University of Steubenville	M
Freed-Hardeman University	M
Friends University	M
Fuller Theological Seminary	P,M,D
Gardner-Webb University	P,D
Garrett-Evangelical Theological Seminary	P,M,D
General Theological Seminary	P,M,D
George Fox University	P,M,D†
Georgian Court College	M
Global University of the Assemblies of God	M
Golden Gate Baptist Theological Seminary	P,M,D,O
Gonzaga University	P,M
Gordon-Conwell Theological Seminary	P,M,D
Grace Theological Seminary	P,M,D,O
Grace University	M
Graduate Theological Union	M,D,O
Grand Rapids Baptist Seminary of Cornerstone University	P,M,D
Harding University Graduate School of Religion	P,M,D
Hardin-Simmons University	P
Hartford Seminary	M,D,O
Harvard University	P,M,D*†
Hebrew Theological College	O
Hebrew Union College–Jewish Institute of Religion (CA)	P
Hebrew Union College–Jewish Institute of Religion (NY)	P,D
Hebrew Union College–Jewish Institute of Religion (OH)	P
Heritage Baptist College and Heritage Theological Seminary	M,O
Holy Apostles College and Seminary	P,M,O
Holy Cross Greek Orthodox School of Theology	P,M
Hood Theological Seminary	P,M,D
Houston Baptist University	M
Houston Graduate School of Theology	P,M,D
Howard University	P,M,D*
Iliff School of Theology	P,M,D
Indiana Wesleyan University	M*
Institute for Christian Studies	M,D
Interdenominational Theological Center	P,M,D
International Baptist College	M
International College and Graduate School	P,M,D

*P—first professional degree; M—master's degree; D—doctorate; O—other advanced degree; *full description and/or announcement in Book 2, 3, 4, 5, or 6; †full description in this book*

Institution	Degrees
International School of Theology	P,M
Jesuit School of Theology at Berkeley	P,M,D,O
Jewish Theological Seminary of America	M,D,O*
Johnson Bible College	M
Kehilath Yakov Rabbinical Seminary	
Kenrick-Glennon Seminary	P,M,O
Knox College	P,M,D
Kol Yaakov Torah Center	O
Lakeland College	M
Lancaster Bible College	M
Lancaster Theological Seminary	P,M,D
La Salle University	M
Lexington Theological Seminary	P,M,D
Liberty University	P,M,D†
Lincoln Christian Seminary	P,M
Lipscomb University	P,M
Louisville Presbyterian Theological Seminary	P,M,D
Loyola Marymount University	M†
Loyola University Chicago	P,M,D*†
Loyola University New Orleans	M
Lubbock Christian University	M
Lutheran School of Theology at Chicago	P,M,D
Lutheran Theological Seminary	P,M
Lutheran Theological Seminary at Gettysburg	P,M
The Lutheran Theological Seminary at Philadelphia	P,M,D,O
Lutheran Theological Southern Seminary	P,M,D
Luther Rice Bible College and Seminary	P,M,D
Luther Seminary	P,M,D
Machzikei Hadath Rabbinical College	O
Maple Springs Baptist Bible College and Seminary	P,M,D,O
Maranatha Baptist Bible College	M
Marquette University	M,D*†
Marylhurst University	M
The Master's College and Seminary	P,M,D
McCormick Theological Seminary	P,M,D,O
McGill University	M,D*
McMaster University	P,M,D
Meadville Lombard Theological School	P,D
Memphis Theological Seminary	P,M,D
Mennonite Brethren Biblical Seminary	P,M
Mercer University	P
Mesivta of Eastern Parkway Rabbinical Seminary	
Mesivta Tifereth Jerusalem of America	
Mesivta Torah Vodaath Rabbinical Seminary	
Methodist Theological School in Ohio	P,M
Michigan Theological Seminary	P,M,D
Mid-America Baptist Theological Seminary	P,M,D
Mid-America Baptist Theological Seminary Northeast Branch	P
Midwestern Baptist Theological Seminary	P,M,D
Mirrer Yeshiva	
Moody Bible Institute	P,M,O
Moravian Theological Seminary	P,M
Mount Angel Seminary	P,M
Mount Saint Mary's College and Seminary	P,M
Mount Vernon Nazarene University	M
Multnomah Bible College and Biblical Seminary	P,M,O
Naropa University	P*
Nashotah House	P,M,O
Nazarene Theological Seminary	P,M,D
Ner Israel Rabbinical College	M,D
Ner Israel Yeshiva College of Toronto	
New Brunswick Theological Seminary	P,M,D
Newman Theological College	P,M
New Orleans Baptist Theological Seminary	P,D
New York Theological Seminary	P,M,D
The Nigerian Baptist Theological Seminary	P,M,O
North American Baptist Seminary	M,D,O
Northeastern Seminary at Roberts Wesleyan College	P,M
Northern Baptist Theological Seminary	P,M,D
North Park Theological Seminary	P,M,D,O
Northwest Baptist Seminary	P,M
Notre Dame Seminary	P,M
Oakland City University	P,D
Oblate School of Theology	P,M,D
Ohr Hameir Theological Seminary	
Oklahoma Christian University	M
Olivet Nazarene University	M
Oral Roberts University	P,M,D
Pacific Lutheran Theological Seminary	P,M,O
Pacific School of Religion	P,M,D,O
Palm Beach Atlantic University	M
Payne Theological Seminary	P
Philadelphia Biblical University	M
Phillips Theological Seminary	P,M,D
Piedmont Baptist College	M
Pittsburgh Theological Seminary	P,M,D
Pontifical Catholic University of Puerto Rico	M
Pontifical College Josephinum	P,M
Princeton Theological Seminary	P,M,D
The Protestant Episcopal Theological Seminary in Virginia	P,M,D
Providence College	M*
Providence College and Theological Seminary	P,M,D,O
Queen's University at Kingston	P,M
Rabbi Isaac Elchanan Theological Seminary	O
Rabbinical Academy Mesivta Rabbi Chaim Berlin	O
Rabbinical College Beth Shraga	
Rabbinical College Bobover Yeshiva B'nei Zion	
Rabbinical College Ch'san Sofer	
Rabbinical College of Long Island	
Rabbinical Seminary M'kor Chaim	
Rabbinical Seminary of America	
Reconstructionist Rabbinical College	P,M,D,O
Reformed Presbyterian Theological Seminary	P,M
Reformed Theological Seminary (NC)	P,M,D
Reformed Theological Seminary (MS)	P,M,D,O
Reformed Theological Seminary (FL)	P,M,D
Regent College	P,M,O
Regent University	P,M,D†
Regis College (Canada)	P,M,D,O
Sacred Heart Major Seminary	P,M
Sacred Heart School of Theology	P,M
St. Andrew's College in Winnipeg	P
St. Augustine's Seminary of Toronto	P,M
Saint Bernard's School of Theology and Ministry	P,M,O
St. Bonaventure University	M,O
St. Charles Borromeo Seminary, Overbrook	P,M
Saint Francis Seminary	P,M
St. John's Seminary (CA)	P,M
Saint John's Seminary (MA)	P,M
Saint John's University (MN)	P,M
St. John's University (NY)	P,M,O*†
St. Joseph's Seminary	P,M
Saint Louis University	M,D*†
Saint Mary-of-the-Woods College	M
Saint Mary Seminary and Graduate School of Theology	P,M,D
St. Mary's Seminary and University	P,M,D,O*
St. Mary's University of San Antonio	M
Saint Meinrad School of Theology	P,M
Saint Michael's College	M,O*
St. Norbert College	M
St. Patrick's Seminary	P,M
Saint Paul School of Theology	P,M,D
Saint Paul University	M,D,O
St. Peter's Seminary	P
Saints Cyril and Methodius Seminary	P,M
St. Stephen's College	M,D
Saint Vincent de Paul Regional Seminary	P,M
Saint Vincent Seminary	P,M
St. Vladimir's Orthodox Theological Seminary	P,M,D
Samford University	P,M,D
San Francisco Theological Seminary	P,M,D
Seabury-Western Theological Seminary	P,M,D,O
Seattle University	P,M,O*†
Seminary of the Immaculate Conception	P,M,D,O
Seton Hall University	P,M,O*†
Shaw University	P
Sh'or Yoshuv Rabbinical College	
Simpson College and Graduate School	M
Southeastern Baptist Theological Seminary	P,M,D
Southern Baptist Theological Seminary	P,M,D
Southern California Bible College & Seminary	P,M
Southern Christian University	P,M,D
Southern Evangelical Seminary	P,M,O
Southern Methodist University	P,M,D*†
Southern Nazarene University	M
Southwestern Assemblies of God University	M
Southwestern Baptist Theological Seminary	P,M,D
Spring Hill College	M
Starr King School for the Ministry	P
Talmudic College of Florida	M,D
Taylor University College and Seminary	P,M
Temple Baptist Seminary	P,M,D
Texas Christian University	P,M,D,O*
Toronto School of Theology	P,M,D
Trinity Episcopal School for Ministry	P,M,D,O
Trinity International University	P,M,D,O
Trinity Lutheran Seminary	P,M
Trinity Western University	P,M
Tyndale College & Seminary	P,M
Unification Theological Seminary	P,M
Union Theological Seminary and Presbyterian School of Christian Education	P,M,D
Union Theological Seminary in the City of New York	P,M,D
United Talmudical Seminary	
United Theological Seminary	P,M,D
United Theological Seminary of the Twin Cities	P,O
Université de Montréal	M,D,O
Université de Sherbrooke	M,D,O
Université du Québec à Chicoutimi	M,D
Université Laval	M,D†
University of Chicago	P,M,D*
University of Dallas	M*
University of Dayton	M,D*†
University of Dubuque	P,M,D
University of Judaism	M
University of Manitoba	P*
University of Mary Hardin-Baylor	M
University of Mobile	M
University of Notre Dame	P,M,D*†
University of Saint Mary of the Lake–Mundelein Seminary	P,D,O
University of St. Michael's College	P,M,D
University of St. Thomas (MN)	P,M,D*†
University of St. Thomas (TX)	P,M
University of San Diego	M*†
University of San Francisco	M*†
The University of Scranton	M†
University of the South	P,M,D
University of Trinity College	P,M,D,O
The University of Winnipeg	P,M,O
Ursuline College	M
Valparaiso University	M
Vancouver School of Theology	P,M,D,O
Vanderbilt University	P,M*
Vanguard University of Southern California	M
Victoria University	P,M,D
Villanova University	M*†
Virginia Union University	P,D
Wartburg Theological Seminary	P,M
Washington Theological Union	P,M
Wesley Biblical Seminary	P,M
Wesley Theological Seminary	P,M,D
Western Seminary	M,O
Western Theological Seminary	P,M,D
Westminster Theological Seminary	P,M,D,O
Westminster Theological Seminary in California	P,M
Weston Jesuit School of Theology	P,M,D,O
Wheaton College	M,O†
Wheeling Jesuit University	M
Wilfrid Laurier University	P,M,D
Winebrenner Theological Seminary	P,M,D,O
Wycliffe College	P,M,D,O
Xavier University	M*
Xavier University of Louisiana	M
Yale University	P,M*
Yeshiva Beth Moshe	O
Yeshiva Karlin Stolin Rabbinical Institute	O
Yeshiva of Nitra Rabbinical College	
Yeshiva Shaar Hatorah Talmudic Research Institute	
Yeshivath Zichron Moshe	O
Yeshiva Toras Chaim Talmudical Seminary	

THEORETICAL CHEMISTRY

Institution	Degrees
Cornell University	D*
Georgetown University	M,D*
Illinois Institute of Technology	M,D*†
University of Calgary	M,D*
The University of Tennessee	M,D*†
Wesleyan University	M,D*
West Virginia University	M,D*

THEORETICAL PHYSICS

Institution	Degrees
Cornell University	M,D*
Harvard University	M,D*†
Rutgers, The State University of New Jersey, New Brunswick	M,D*
St. John's University (NY)	M,O*†
University of Victoria	M,D
West Virginia University	M,D*

THERAPIES—DANCE, DRAMA, AND MUSIC

Institution	Degrees
Antioch New England Graduate School	M*†
California Institute of Integral Studies	M,D,O*
Colorado State University	M*
Columbia College Chicago	M†
Drexel University	M*†
East Carolina University	M*†
Florida State University	M,D*†
Immaculata University	M†
Lesley University	M,D,O*†
Michigan State University	M,D*†
Montclair State University	M†
Naropa University	M*
New York University	M,D*†
Ohio University	M*
Pratt Institute	M*
Saint Mary-of-the-Woods College	M
Shenandoah University	M,D,O
Southern Methodist University	M*†
Temple University	M,D*†
University of Kansas	M,D*
University of Miami	M,D,O*†
University of the Pacific	M*

TOXICOLOGY

Institution	Degrees
American University	M,O*†
Brown University	M,D*
Case Western Reserve University	M,D*†
Columbia University	M,D*†
Cornell University	M,D*
Dartmouth College	D*†
Duke University	O*†
Duquesne University	M,D*†
Florida Agricultural and Mechanical University	M,D*
The George Washington University	M*†
Indiana University–Purdue University Indianapolis	M,D*
Iowa State University of Science and Technology	M,D*†
Johns Hopkins University	D*†
Long Island University, Brooklyn Campus	M*
Louisiana State University and Agricultural and Mechanical College	M*
Massachusetts Institute of Technology	M,D*
Medical College of Georgia	M,D*
Medical College of Wisconsin	M,D*
Michigan State University	M,D*†
North Carolina State University	M,D*
Northeastern University	M,D*†
Northwestern University	D*
The Ohio State University	M,D*
Oregon State University	M,D*
Purdue University	M,D*
Queen's University at Kingston	M,D
Rutgers, The State University of New Jersey, New Brunswick	M,D*
St. John's University (NY)	M,D*†
San Diego State University	M,D*
Simon Fraser University	M,D,O
State University of New York at Albany	M,D*†
Texas A&M University	M,D*
Texas A&M University System Health Science Center	D*
Texas Southern University	M,D†
Texas Tech University	M,D*†
Université de Montréal	O
University at Buffalo, The State University of New York	M,D*†
The University of Alabama at Birmingham	D*†
The University of Arizona	M,D*
University of Arkansas for Medical Sciences	M,D*
University of California, Davis	M,D*†
University of California, Irvine	M,D*

University of California, Los Angeles D*
University of California, Riverside M,D*
University of California, Santa Cruz M,D*
University of Cincinnati M,D*
University of Colorado Health Sciences Center D*
University of Connecticut M,D*†
University of Florida M,D,O*†
University of Georgia M,D*†
University of Guelph M,D
University of Kansas M,D*
University of Kentucky M,D*
University of Louisville M,D*†
University of Maryland M,D*†
University of Maryland, College Park M,D*
University of Maryland Eastern Shore M,D†
University of Medicine and Dentistry of New Jersey M,D*
University of Michigan M,D*
University of Minnesota, Duluth M,D*
University of Minnesota, Twin Cities Campus M,D*
University of Mississippi M,D*
University of Mississippi Medical Center M,D*
University of Nebraska–Lincoln M,D*†
University of Nebraska Medical Center M,D*
University of New Mexico M,D*†
The University of North Carolina at Chapel Hill M,D*†
University of Prince Edward Island M,D
University of Puerto Rico, Medical Sciences Campus M,D*
University of Rhode Island M,D*
University of Rochester M,D*
University of Saskatchewan M,D,O
University of Southern California M,D*†
The University of Texas Health Science Center at Houston M,D*
The University of Texas Medical Branch D*
University of the Sciences in Philadelphia M,D*
University of Toronto M,D*
University of Utah M,D*
University of Washington M,D*
The University of Western Ontario M,D*
University of Wisconsin–Madison M,D*
Utah State University M,D*
Vanderbilt University *
Virginia Commonwealth University M,D,O*†
Washington State University M,D*
Wayne State University M,D,O*
West Virginia University M,D*
Wright State University M*

TRANSCULTURAL NURSING

Augsburg College M
Capital University M
New Jersey City University M
Wayne State University O*

TRANSLATION AND INTERPRETATION

American University M,O*†
Concordia University (Canada) M,O*†
Gallaudet University M
Georgia State University O*
Monterey Institute of International Studies M*
New York University M*†
Rutgers, The State University of New Jersey, New Brunswick M,D*
State University of New York at Albany M,O*†
State University of New York at Binghamton M,O*†
Université Laval M,O†
University of Arkansas M*
The University of Iowa M*
University of Ottawa M,D,O*
University of Puerto Rico, Río Piedras M,O*
York University M*

TRANSPERSONAL AND HUMANISTIC PSYCHOLOGY

Atlantic University M
Brock University M
Center for Humanistic Studies M,D*
Institute of Transpersonal Psychology M,D,O*
John F. Kennedy University M*†
Naropa University M*
Saybrook Graduate School and Research Center M,D
Seattle University M*†

TRANSPORTATION AND HIGHWAY ENGINEERING

Auburn University M,D*†
Cornell University M,D*
École Polytechnique de Montréal M,D,O
Iowa State University of Science and Technology M,D*†
Louisiana State University and Agricultural and Mechanical College M,D*
Marquette University M,D*†
Massachusetts Institute of Technology M,D*
New Jersey Institute of Technology M,D
Northwestern University M,D*
The Pennsylvania State University University Park Campus M,D*†
Polytechnic University, Brooklyn Campus M*
Polytechnic University, Long Island Graduate Center M
Princeton University M,D*
Rensselaer Polytechnic Institute M,D*†
Texas A&M University M,D*
Texas Southern University M†
University of Arkansas M*
University of California, Berkeley M,D*
University of California, Davis M,D*†
University of California, Irvine M,D*
University of Central Florida M,D,O*†
University of Dayton M*†
University of Delaware M,D*†
The University of Memphis M,D*†
University of Missouri–Columbia M,D*
University of New Brunswick Fredericton M,D
University of Oklahoma M,D*†
University of Pennsylvania M,D*†
University of Rhode Island M,D*
University of Southern California M*†
University of Virginia M,D*
University of Washington M,D*
Villanova University M*†
Washington University in St. Louis D*†

TRANSPORTATION MANAGEMENT

Arizona State University O*
Arizona State University East M
Central Missouri State University M,O†
Concordia University (Canada) M,D,O*†
Florida Institute of Technology M*†
George Mason University M*†
Iowa State University of Science and Technology M*†
Maine Maritime Academy M,O
Massachusetts Institute of Technology M,D*
McGill University M*
Middle Tennessee State University M*
Morgan State University M*
New Jersey Institute of Technology M,D
Polytechnic University, Brooklyn Campus M*
Polytechnic University, Westchester Graduate Center M
San Jose State University M*
State University of New York Maritime College M
University of Arkansas M*
The University of British Columbia M*
University of California, Davis M,D*†
The University of Tennessee M,D*†
University of Virginia M,D*
University of Washington O*

TRAVEL AND TOURISM

Central Michigan University M,O†
Clemson University M,D*
The George Washington University M*†
Golden Gate University M,O
Jones International University M*†
Michigan State University M,D*†
New York University M*†
North Carolina State University M*
Purdue University M,D*
Rochester Institute of Technology M*†
Schiller International University (United States) M
Schiller International University (United Kingdom) M
Temple University M,D*†
Université du Québec à Trois-Rivières M,O

University of Denver M*†
University of Hawaii at Manoa M*
University of Massachusetts Amherst M*†
University of New Haven M*†
University of South Carolina M*†
The University of Tennessee M*†
University of Wisconsin–Stout M
Virginia Polytechnic Institute and State University M,D*
Western Illinois University M

URBAN DESIGN

City College of the City University of New York M*†
Columbia University M*†
Cornell University M,D*
Harvard University M*†
New York Institute of Technology M*†
Prairie View A&M University M
Pratt Institute M*
Rice University M,D*
State University of New York College of Environmental Science and Forestry M
University at Buffalo, The State University of New York M*†
University of California, Berkeley M,D*
University of California, Los Angeles M,D*
University of Colorado at Denver M*
University of Miami M*†
University of Michigan M*
University of Washington M,D,O*
Washington University in St. Louis M*†

URBAN EDUCATION

Claremont Graduate University M,D*
Cleveland State University D*†
College of Mount Saint Vincent M,O*†
Columbia College Chicago M†
Concordia University (IL) M,O
DePaul University M*†
Florida International University M*†
Georgia State University M*
Graduate School and University Center of the City University of New York D*†
Harvard University M,D,O*†
Holy Names College M,O
Mercy College M,O*
Morgan State University D*
New Jersey City University M
Norfolk State University M†
Northeastern Illinois University M
Old Dominion University D*†
Saint Peter's College M†
Temple University M,D*†
Texas Southern University M,D†
University of Massachusetts Boston M,D,O*†
University of Nebraska at Omaha M,O
University of Wisconsin–Milwaukee M,D
Virginia Commonwealth University D*†

URBAN STUDIES

Boston University M*†
Brooklyn College of the City University of New York M†
Cleveland State University M,D*†
East Tennessee State University M†
Georgia State University M*
Graduate School and University Center of the City University of New York M,D*†
Hunter College of the City University of New York M†
Long Island University, Brooklyn Campus M*
Massachusetts Institute of Technology M,D*
McMaster University M,D
Michigan State University M,D*†
Minnesota State University, Mankato M
New Jersey City University M
New Jersey Institute of Technology D
New School University M*†
Norfolk State University M†
Old Dominion University M,D*†
Portland State University M,D*
Queens College of the City University of New York M†
Rutgers, The State University of New Jersey, Newark M,D*†
Saint Louis University M,D*†
Savannah State University M
Southern Connecticut State University M†

State University of New York at Albany M,D,O*†
Temple University M*†
Tufts University M*†
Université du Québec à Montréal M,D
Université du Québec, École nationale d'administration publique M
Université du Québec, Institut National de la Recherche Scientifique M,D,O
The University of Akron M,D†
University of Central Oklahoma M
University of Delaware M,D*†
The University of Lethbridge M,D
University of Louisville D*†
University of New Orleans M,D*
University of Wisconsin–Milwaukee M,D
Wright State University M*

VETERINARY MEDICINE

Auburn University P*†
Colorado State University P*
Cornell University P*
Iowa State University of Science and Technology P,M*†
Kansas State University P*†
Louisiana State University and Agricultural and Mechanical College P*
Michigan State University P*†
Mississippi State University P*
North Carolina State University P*
The Ohio State University P*
Oklahoma State University P*†
Oregon State University P*
Purdue University P*
Texas A&M University P,M,D*
Tufts University P*†
Tuskegee University P
Université de Montréal P
University of California, Davis P*†
University of Florida P*†
University of Georgia P*†
University of Guelph M,D,O
University of Illinois at Urbana–Champaign P*
University of Maryland, College Park P*
University of Minnesota, Twin Cities Campus P*
University of Missouri–Columbia P*
University of Pennsylvania P*†
University of Prince Edward Island P
University of Saskatchewan P,M,D,O
The University of Tennessee P*†
University of Wisconsin–Madison P*
Virginia Polytechnic Institute and State University P*
Washington State University P*

VETERINARY SCIENCES

Auburn University M,D*†
Colorado State University M,D*
Cornell University M,D*
Drexel University M*†
Iowa State University of Science and Technology M,D*†
Kansas State University M*†
Louisiana State University and Agricultural and Mechanical College M,D*
Michigan State University M,D*†
Mississippi State University M,D*
Montana State University–Bozeman M,D*
North Carolina State University M,D*
North Dakota State University M,D†
The Ohio State University M,D*
Oklahoma State University M,D*†
Oregon State University M,D*
The Pennsylvania State University Milton S. Hershey Medical Center M*
The Pennsylvania State University University Park Campus M,D*†
Purdue University M,D*
Texas A&M University M,D*
Tufts University M,D*†
Tuskegee University M
Université de Montréal M,D,O
University of California, Davis M,O*†
University of Florida M,D,O*†
University of Georgia M,D*†
University of Guelph M,D,O
University of Idaho M,D*†
University of Illinois at Urbana–Champaign M,D*
University of Kentucky M,D*
University of Maryland, College Park D*
University of Massachusetts Amherst M,D*†

*P—first professional degree; M—master's degree; D—doctorate; O—other advanced degree; *full description and/or announcement in Book 2, 3, 4, 5, or 6; †full description in this book*

University of Minnesota, Twin Cities Campus M,D*
University of Missouri–Columbia M,D*
University of Nebraska–Lincoln M,D*†
University of Prince Edward Island M,D
University of Saskatchewan M,D,O
University of Washington M*
University of Wisconsin–Madison M,D*
Utah State University M,D*
Virginia Polytechnic Institute and State University M,D*
Washington State University M,D*
West Virginia University M*

VIROLOGY

Baylor College of Medicine D*
Cornell University M,D*
Harvard University D*†
Kansas State University M,D*†
Loyola University Chicago M,D*†
McMaster University M,D
The Pennsylvania State University Milton S. Hershey Medical Center M,D*
Purdue University M,D*
Rush University D*
Rutgers, The State University of New Jersey, New Brunswick M,D*
Texas A&M University System Health Science Center D*
Thomas Jefferson University D*
Université de Montréal D
Université du Québec, Institut National de la Recherche Scientifique M,D
University of California, San Diego D*
The University of Iowa M,D*
University of Massachusetts Worcester D*
University of Pennsylvania D*†
University of Pittsburgh M,D*†
University of Prince Edward Island M,D
The University of Tennessee Health Science Center D*
The University of Texas Health Science Center at Houston M,D*
The University of Texas Medical Branch D*
University of Virginia *
West Virginia University M,D*

VISION SCIENCES

Emory University M*†
Indiana University Bloomington M,D*
Pacific University M
Pennsylvania College of Optometry M,D,O
State University of New York College of Optometry M,D
Université de Montréal M
The University of Alabama at Birmingham M,D*†
The University of Alabama in Huntsville M,D*
University of Alberta M,D*
University of California, Berkeley M,D*
University of Chicago D*
University of Guelph M,D,O
University of Houston M,D*
University of Louisville D*†
University of Missouri–St. Louis M,D†
University of Waterloo P,M,D

VOCATIONAL AND TECHNICAL EDUCATION

Alabama Agricultural and Mechanical University M
Alcorn State University M,O
Appalachian State University M
Ball State University M*
Bemidji State University M
Bowling Green State University M*†
Brigham Young University M*
California Baptist University M
California State University, Long Beach M
California State University, Sacramento M
California State University, San Bernardino M
California University of Pennsylvania M
Central Connecticut State University M*†
Central Michigan University M†
Central Missouri State University M,O†
Chicago State University M
Clemson University M,D*
Colorado State University M,D*
Drake University M*†
East Carolina University M*†
Eastern Kentucky University M
Eastern Michigan University M*
East Tennessee State University M†
Fitchburg State College M†
Florida Agricultural and Mechanical University M*
Florida International University M*†
Florida State University D,O*†
Georgia Southern University M,O
Georgia State University M,D,O*
Idaho State University M*
Indiana State University M,D,O*†
Inter American University of Puerto Rico, Metropolitan Campus M
Iowa State University of Science and Technology M,D*†
Jackson State University M
James Madison University M
Kent State University M,O*
Louisiana State University and Agricultural and Mechanical College M,D*
Marshall University M*†
Middle Tennessee State University M*
Millersville University of Pennsylvania M†
Mississippi State University M,D,O*
Montana State University–Northern M
Montclair State University M†
Morehead State University M
Murray State University M†
North Carolina Agricultural and Technical State University M*
North Carolina State University M,D,O*
Northern Arizona University M
Nova Southeastern University D*
The Ohio State University D*
Oklahoma State University M,D,O*†
Oregon State University M*
The Pennsylvania State University University Park Campus M,D*†
Pittsburg State University M,O
Purdue University M,D,O*
Rhode Island College M†
Rutgers, The State University of New Jersey, New Brunswick M,D,O*
Sam Houston State University M*
South Carolina State University M
Southern Illinois University Carbondale M,D*†
Southwestern Oklahoma State University M
Southwest Missouri State University M,O*†
Southwest Texas State University M*
State University of New York at Oswego M
State University of New York College at Buffalo M
Sul Ross State University M*
Temple University M,D*†
Texas A&M University–Commerce M,D†
Texas A&M University–Corpus Christi M
The University of Akron M†
University of Alaska Anchorage M
University of Arkansas M,D,O*
The University of British Columbia M,D*
University of Central Florida M*†
University of Connecticut M,D*†
University of Georgia M,D,O*†
University of Idaho M,D,O*†
University of Illinois at Urbana–Champaign M,D,O*
University of Kentucky M,D,O*
University of Manitoba M*
University of Maryland Eastern Shore M†
University of Minnesota, Twin Cities Campus M,D,O*
University of Nevada, Las Vegas M,D,O*†
University of New Brunswick Fredericton M
University of New Hampshire M*†
University of Northern Iowa M,D
University of North Texas M,D,O*†
University of Regina M,O
University of South Carolina M*†
University of Southern Maine M
University of Southern Mississippi M
University of South Florida M,D,O*†
The University of Texas at Tyler M
University of Toledo M,D,O*†
University of West Florida M
University of Wisconsin–Madison M,D*
University of Wisconsin–Platteville M
University of Wisconsin–Stout M,O
Utah State University M*
Valdosta State University M,D,O
Virginia Polytechnic Institute and State University M,D,O*
Virginia State University M,O
Wayne State College M
Wayne State University M,D,O*
Western Michigan University M*†
Western Washington University M
Westfield State College M
West Virginia University M,D*
Wright State University M*

WATER RESOURCES

Albany State University M
Colorado State University M,D*
Duke University M,D*†
Iowa State University of Science and Technology M,D*†
Johns Hopkins University M,D*†
Montclair State University M,O†
Rutgers, The State University of New Jersey, New Brunswick M,D*
South Dakota School of Mines and Technology D*†
South Dakota State University D*
State University of New York College of Environmental Science and Forestry M,D
Université du Québec, Institut National de la Recherche Scientifique M,D
The University of Arizona M,D*
University of Florida M,D*†
University of Illinois at Chicago M,D*
University of Kansas M,D*
University of Minnesota, Twin Cities Campus M,D*
University of Missouri–Rolla M,D*
University of Nevada, Las Vegas M*†
University of New Brunswick Fredericton M,D
University of New Hampshire M*†
University of New Mexico M*†
University of Oklahoma M,D*†
University of Vermont M*†
University of Wisconsin–Madison M*
University of Wyoming M,D*†
Utah State University M,D*

WATER RESOURCES ENGINEERING

California Polytechnic State University, San Luis Obispo M†
Cornell University M,D*
Louisiana State University and Agricultural and Mechanical College M,D*
Marquette University M,D*†
McGill University M,D*
New Mexico Institute of Mining and Technology M†
Ohio University M*
Oregon State University M,D*
The Pennsylvania State University University Park Campus M,D*†
Princeton University D*
Texas A&M University M,D*
Tufts University M,D*†
University of Alberta M,D*
University of California, Berkeley M,D*
University of California, Los Angeles M,D*
University of Central Florida M,D,O*†
University of Colorado at Boulder M,D*
University of Delaware M,D*†
University of Guelph M,D
University of Kansas M,D*
University of Maryland, College Park M,D*
The University of Memphis M,D*†
University of Missouri–Columbia M,D*
University of Southern California M*†
The University of Texas at Austin M*
University of Virginia M,D*
Utah State University M,D*
Villanova University M*†
Virginia Polytechnic Institute and State University M,D*

WESTERN EUROPEAN STUDIES

Boston College M,D*†
Brown University M,D*
The Catholic University of America M*†
Claremont Graduate University M,D*
Columbia University M,O*†
East Carolina University M*†
Georgetown University M*
The George Washington University M*†
Indiana University Bloomington M,D,O*
Johns Hopkins University M,D,O*†
New York University M*†
University of California, Santa Barbara M*
University of Connecticut M*†
University of Guelph M,D
University of Nevada, Reno D*
Washington University in St. Louis M*†

WOMEN'S HEALTH NURSING

Case Western Reserve University M*†
Columbia University M,O*†
Emory University M*†
Georgia Southern University M,O
Georgia State University M,D*
Indiana University–Purdue University Indianapolis M*
Loyola University Chicago M,D*†
Oregon Health & Science University M,O*
Rush University M,D*
Seton Hall University M*†
Stony Brook University, State University of New York M,O*†
Texas Woman's University M,D*†
University at Buffalo, The State University of New York M,D,O*†
University of Cincinnati M,D*
University of Delaware M,O*†
University of Medicine and Dentistry of New Jersey M*
University of Missouri–Kansas City M,D*†
University of Pennsylvania M*†
University of Phoenix–Phoenix Campus M
University of South Carolina O*†
The University of Texas at El Paso M*†
Vanderbilt University M,D*
Virginia Commonwealth University M,D,O*†

WOMEN'S STUDIES

Brandeis University M*†
California Institute of Integral Studies M,D*
Claremont Graduate University M,D*
Clark Atlanta University M,D
Clark University D*†
Dalhousie University M*
DePaul University O*†
Drew University M†
Duke University O*†
Eastern Michigan University M*
Emory University D,O*†
Fairleigh Dickinson University, College at Florham M*†
Florida Atlantic University M,O*
The George Washington University M,D*†
Georgia State University M*
Graduate School and University Center of the City University of New York M,D*†
Lakehead University M
Memorial University of Newfoundland M†
Minnesota State University, Mankato M
Mount Saint Vincent University M
New College of California M*†
The Ohio State University M*
Roosevelt University M*†
Rutgers, The State University of New Jersey, New Brunswick M,D*
Saint Mary's University M
San Diego State University M*
San Francisco State University M
Sarah Lawrence College M*†
Simon Fraser University M
Southeastern Baptist Theological Seminary P,M,D
Southern Connecticut State University M†
State University of New York at Albany M*†
Stony Brook University, State University of New York M,O*†
Syracuse University O*
Texas Woman's University M*†
Towson University M†
Université Laval O†
The University of Alabama M*
The University of Arizona M*
University of California, Los Angeles M,D*
University of Cincinnati M,O*
The University of Iowa D*
University of Maryland, College Park M,D*
University of Massachusetts Boston O*†
University of Michigan D,O*
University of Missouri–St. Louis O†
The University of North Carolina at Greensboro M,D,O†

University of Northern Iowa M
University of Ottawa M*
University of Pittsburgh O*†
University of Saskatchewan M,D
University of South Carolina O*†
University of South Florida M*†
University of Toronto M,D*
University of Washington M,D*
York University M,D*

WRITING

Abilene Christian University M
American University M*†
Antioch University Los Angeles M,O
Antioch University McGregor M†
Arizona State University M*
Ball State University M,D*
Belmont University M
Bennington College M†
Boise State University M*
Boston University M,D*†
Bowling Green State University M*†
Brooklyn College of the City University of New York M†
Brown University M*
California College of Arts and Crafts M*
California Institute of the Arts M,O*
California State University, Chico M
California State University, Fresno M
California State University, Long Beach M
California State University, Sacramento M
California State University, San Marcos M
Carnegie Mellon University M*
Central Michigan University M†
Chapman University M*†
Chatham College M
City College of the City University of New York M*†
Claremont Graduate University M,D*
Clemson University M*
Colorado State University M*
Columbia College Chicago M†
Columbia University M*†
Concordia University (Canada) M*†
Cornell University M,D*
DePaul University M*†
Eastern Michigan University M*
Eastern Washington University M†
Elmhurst College M
Emerson College M*†
Fairleigh Dickinson University, College at Florham M*†
Florida Atlantic University, Ft. Lauderdale Campus M
Florida International University M*†
Florida State University M,D*†
George Mason University M*†
Georgia State University M,D*
Goddard College M
Goucher College M
Hofstra University M*
Hollins University M
Hunter College of the City University of New York M†
Illinois State University M*†
Indiana University Bloomington M,D*
Indiana University of Pennsylvania M,D*†
Johns Hopkins University M*†
Kennesaw State University M
Lesley University M*†
Long Island University, Brooklyn Campus M*
Long Island University, Southampton College M
Longwood College M
Louisiana State University and Agricultural and Mechanical College M,D*
Loyola Marymount University M†
Maharishi University of Management M
Manhattanville College M*†
McNeese State University M
Miami University M,D*†
Michigan State University M,D*†
Mills College M*†
Minnesota State University, Mankato M
Minnesota State University, Moorhead M
Naropa University M*
National-Louis University M
New College of California M*†
New England College M*
New Mexico Highlands University M
New Mexico State University M,D
New School University M*†
New York University M*†
Northeastern Illinois University M
Northeastern University M,D,O*†
Northern Arizona University M
Northern Michigan University M
Northwestern University M*
Oklahoma City University M
Old Dominion University M*†
Otis College of Art and Design M
The Pennsylvania State University University Park Campus M,D*†
Purdue University M,D*
Queens College of the City University of New York M†
Queens University of Charlotte M
Rivier College M*†
Roosevelt University M*†
Rowan University M†
Rutgers, The State University of New Jersey, New Brunswick M*
Saint Mary's College of California M
Saint Xavier University M,O*
Salisbury University M
San Diego State University M*
San Francisco State University M
Sarah Lawrence College M*†
School of the Art Institute of Chicago M*
Seton Hill University M†
Sonoma State University M
Southern Illinois University Carbondale M*†
Southwest Texas State University M*
Spalding University M†
Syracuse University M,D*
Temple University M*†
Towson University M†
The University of Alabama M,D*
University of Alaska Anchorage M
University of Alaska Fairbanks M*
The University of Arizona M*
University of Arkansas M*
University of Arkansas at Little Rock M
University of Baltimore M*
The University of British Columbia M*
University of California, Davis M,D*†
University of California, Irvine M*
University of Central Florida M,O*†
University of Central Oklahoma M
University of Colorado at Boulder M,D*
University of Houston M,D*
University of Idaho M*†
University of Illinois at Chicago M,D*
The University of Iowa M,D*
University of Louisiana at Lafayette M,D*
University of Maryland, College Park M,D*
University of Massachusetts Amherst M,D*†
University of Massachusetts Dartmouth M*†
The University of Memphis M,D*†
University of Michigan M*
University of Missouri–St. Louis M†
The University of Montana–Missoula M*†
University of Nevada, Las Vegas M,D*†
University of New Hampshire M,D*†
University of New Mexico M*†
University of New Orleans M*
The University of North Carolina at Greensboro M†
The University of North Carolina at Wilmington M*
University of Notre Dame M*†
University of Oregon M*
University of Pennsylvania M,D*†
University of Pittsburgh M,D*†
University of St. Thomas (MN) M,O*†
University of San Francisco M*†
University of South Carolina M,D*†
University of Southern California M*†
The University of Texas at Austin M*
The University of Texas at El Paso M*†
University of Utah M,D*
University of Virginia M*
University of Windsor M
Utah State University M*
Vermont College M,O
Virginia Commonwealth University M*†
Warren Wilson College M
Washington University in St. Louis M*†
Wayne State University M,D*
Western Illinois University M
Western Kentucky University M†
Western Michigan University M,D*†
Westminster College (UT) M
West Virginia University M,D*
Wichita State University M*†
Wright State University M*

ZOOLOGY

Auburn University M,D*†
Brigham Young University M,D*
Clemson University M,D*
Colorado State University M,D*
Connecticut College M
Cornell University D*
Eastern Illinois University M†
Emporia State University M*†
Illinois State University M,D*†
Indiana University Bloomington M,D*
Iowa State University of Science and Technology M,D*†
Kent State University M,D*
Louisiana State University and Agricultural and Mechanical College M,D*
Miami University M,D*†
Michigan State University M,D*†
Montana State University–Bozeman M,D*
North Carolina State University M,D*
North Dakota State University M,D†
Ohio University M,D*
Oklahoma State University M,D*†
Oregon State University M,D*
Southern Illinois University Carbondale M,D*†
Texas A&M University M,D*
Texas Tech University M,D*†
Uniformed Services University of the Health Sciences M,D*
University of Alaska Fairbanks M,D*
The University of British Columbia M,D*
University of California, Davis M*†
University of Chicago D*
University of Colorado at Boulder M,D*
University of Connecticut M,D*†
University of Florida M,D*†
University of Guelph M,D
University of Hawaii at Manoa M,D*
University of Idaho M,D*†
University of Illinois at Urbana–Champaign D*
University of Maine M,D*
University of Manitoba M,D*
University of Maryland, College Park M,D*
University of New Hampshire M,D*†
University of North Dakota M,D*
University of Oklahoma M,D*†
University of Puerto Rico, Medical Sciences Campus M,D*
University of Rhode Island M,D*
University of South Florida M*†
University of Toronto M,D*
University of Washington D*
The University of Western Ontario M,D*
University of Wisconsin–Madison M,D*
University of Wisconsin–Oshkosh M*
University of Wyoming M,D*†
Virginia Polytechnic Institute and State University M,D*
Washington State University M,D*
Western Illinois University M,O

*P—first professional degree; M—master's degree; D—doctorate; O—other advanced degree; *full description and/or announcement in Book 2, 3, 4, 5, or 6; †full description in this book*

Directory of Institutions and Their Offerings

This directory contains information identical to that in the previous directory, Graduate and Professional Programs by Field, but conversely presented. Accredited institutions in the United States and U.S. territories and those in Canada, Mexico, Europe, and Africa that are accredited by U.S. accrediting bodies are given here, with an alphabetical listing of which programs they offer out of the 452 selected fields that are covered in the guides. The directory will be of value to readers who are interested in the range of programs at particular institutions, as well as those who wish to compare programs and degree levels. The degree levels are shown if the institution provided information in response to Peterson's Annual Survey of Graduate and Professional Institutions; the degree levels included are master's, doctorate, first professional, and other advanced degrees (e.g., certificates and specialist degrees), included as *M, D, P,* and *O,* respectively.

All of the programs listed in this directory are profiled, and many are described in detail in In-Depth Descriptions or outlined briefly in Announcements in Books 2–6. A note at the end of each institution's listing refers the reader to the specific page number if an Announcement or In-Depth Description appears in this book. If there is such information in Books 2–6, an asterisk appears in the column that lists the degree level offered. The reader should then refer to the index of the appropriate volume.

ABILENE CHRISTIAN UNIVERSITY

Program	Degrees
Accounting	M
Clinical Psychology	M
Communication Disorders	M
Communication—General	M
Counseling Psychology	M
Counselor Education	M
Education—General	M
Educational Administration	M
Educational Measurement and Evaluation	M
Elementary Education	M
English	M
Gerontology	M
History	M
Human Resources Development	M
Human Services	M
Internet and Interactive Multimedia	M
Liberal Studies	M
Marriage and Family Therapy	M
Missions and Missiology	M
Nursing—General	M
Pastoral Ministry and Counseling	M,D
Psychology—General	M
Reading Education	M
School Psychology	M
Secondary Education	M
Speech and Interpersonal Communication	M
Theology	P,M
Writing	M

ACADEMY OF ART COLLEGE

Program	Degrees
Advertising and Public Relations	M
Applied Arts and Design—General	M
Art/Fine Arts	M
Computer Art and Design	M
Film, Television, and Video Production	M
Graphic Design	M
Illustration	M
Industrial Design	M
Interior Design	M
Photography	M
Textile Design	M

In-depth description on page 721.

ACADEMY OF CHINESE CULTURE AND HEALTH SCIENCES

Program	Degrees
Acupuncture and Oriental Medicine	M

ACADEMY OF ORIENTAL MEDICINE AT AUSTIN

Program	Degrees
Acupuncture and Oriental Medicine	M

ACADIA UNIVERSITY

Program	Degrees
Biological and Biomedical Sciences—General	M
Chemistry	M
Clinical Psychology	M
Computer Science	M
Counselor Education	M,O
Curriculum and Instruction	M
Education—General	M,O
Educational Administration	M
Educational Media/Instructional Technology	M
English	M
Geology	M
Mathematics Education	M
Pastoral Ministry and Counseling	P,M,D
Political Science	M
Psychology—General	M
Science Education	M
Social Sciences Education	M
Sociology	M
Special Education	M
Theology	P,M,D

ADAMS STATE COLLEGE

Program	Degrees
Art/Fine Arts	M
Counselor Education	M
Education—General	M
Elementary Education	M
Health Education	M
Physical Education	M
Recreation and Park Management	M
Secondary Education	M
Special Education	M

ADELPHI UNIVERSITY

Program	Degrees
Art/Fine Arts	M
Biological and Biomedical Sciences—General	M
Business Administration and Management—General	M,O
Clinical Psychology	D,O
Communication Disorders	M,D
Computer Science	M,D
Education—General	M,D,O
Educational Administration	M,O
Educational Media/Instructional Technology	M,O
Elementary Education	M,O
English as a Second Language	M,O
English	M
Finance and Banking	M
Health Education	M,O
Human Resources Management	O
Mathematics	M,D
Multilingual and Multicultural Education	M
Nursing—General	M,O
Physical Education	M,O
Physics	M
Psychology—General	M,D,O*
Reading Education	M,O
Secondary Education	M
Social Work	M,D
Special Education	M,O

ADLER SCHOOL OF PROFESSIONAL PSYCHOLOGY

Program	Degrees
Addictions/Substance Abuse Counseling	M,D,O
Art Therapy	M,D,O
Clinical Psychology	M,D,O
Counseling Psychology	M,D,O
Gerontology	M,D,O
Industrial and Organizational Psychology	M,D,O
Marriage and Family Therapy	M,D,O
Psychology—General	M,D,O*

AGNES SCOTT COLLEGE

Program	Degrees
Early Childhood Education	M
English Education	M*

AIR FORCE INSTITUTE OF TECHNOLOGY

Program	Degrees
Aerospace/Aeronautical Engineering	M,D
Applied Mathematics	M,D
Applied Physics	M,D*
Business Administration and Management—General	M
Computer Engineering	M,D
Computer Science	M,D
Electrical Engineering	M,D
Engineering and Applied Sciences—General	M,D
Engineering Management	M
Engineering Physics	M,D
Environmental Engineering	M
Environmental Management and Policy	M
Environmental Sciences	M,D
Logistics	M,D
Management Information Systems	M
Management of Technology	M,D
Materials Sciences	M,D
Meteorology	M,D
Nuclear Engineering	M,D
Operations Research	M,D
Optical Sciences	M,D
Planetary and Space Sciences	M,D
Systems Engineering	M,D

ALABAMA AGRICULTURAL AND MECHANICAL UNIVERSITY

Program	Degrees
Agricultural Economics and Agribusiness	M
Agricultural Sciences—General	M,D
Agronomy and Soil Sciences	M,D
Animal Sciences	M,D
Applied Physics	M,D
Biological and Biomedical Sciences—General	M
Business Administration and Management—General	M
City and Regional Planning	M
Clinical Psychology	M,O
Communication Disorders	M
Computer Science	M
Counseling Psychology	M,O
Counselor Education	M,O
Early Childhood Education	M,O
Economics	M
Education—General	M,O
Educational Administration	M,O
Elementary Education	M,O
Engineering and Applied Sciences—General	M
Environmental Sciences	M,D
Family and Consumer Sciences-General	M,D
Finance and Banking	M
Food Science and Technology	M,D
Human Resources Management	M,O
Marketing	M
Materials Sciences	M,D
Music Education	M
Music	M
Optical Sciences	M,D
Physical Education	M
Physics	M,D
Plant Sciences	M,D
Psychology—General	M,O
School Psychology	M,O
Secondary Education	M,O
Social Work	M
Special Education	M,O
Vocational and Technical Education	M

ALABAMA STATE UNIVERSITY

Program	Degrees
Accounting	M
Allied Health—General	M
Biological and Biomedical Sciences—General	O
Business Administration and Management—General	M
Counselor Education	M,D,O
Early Childhood Education	M,O
Education—General	M,D,O
Educational Administration	M,D,O
Educational Media/Instructional Technology	M,O
Elementary Education	M,O
English Education	M,O
Mathematics Education	M,O
Mathematics	O
Music Education	M
Music	M
Physical Education	M
Physical Therapy	M
Reading Education	M,O
Science Education	M,O
Secondary Education	M,O
Social Sciences Education	M,O
Special Education	M

ALASKA PACIFIC UNIVERSITY

Program	Degrees
Business Administration and Management—General	M
Counseling Psychology	M
Education—General	M
Elementary Education	M
Environmental Sciences	M
Interdisciplinary Studies	M
Middle School Education	M
Telecommunications Management	M

ALBANY COLLEGE OF PHARMACY OF UNION UNIVERSITY

Program	Degrees
Pharmacy	P

ALBANY LAW SCHOOL OF UNION UNIVERSITY

Program	Degrees
Law	P,M

ALBANY MEDICAL COLLEGE

Program	Degrees
Allopathic Medicine	P
Bioethics	M*
Biological and Biomedical Sciences—General	M,D*
Cardiovascular Sciences	M,D*
Cell Biology	M,D*
Immunology	M,D*
Microbiology	M,D
Molecular Biology	M,D
Neuroscience	M,D
Nurse Anesthesia	M*
Pharmacology	M,D*

ALBANY STATE UNIVERSITY

Program	Degrees
Business Administration and Management—General	M
Business Education	M
Counselor Education	M
Criminal Justice and Criminology	M
Early Childhood Education	M
Economics	M
Education—General	M,O
Educational Administration	M,O
English Education	M
Health Education	M
Health Services Management and Hospital Administration	M
Human Resources Management	M
Mathematics Education	M
Middle School Education	M
Music Education	M
Nursing—General	M
Physical Education	M
Public Policy and Administration	M
Reading Education	M
Science Education	M
Social Sciences Education	M
Special Education	M
Water Resources	M

ALBERTUS MAGNUS COLLEGE

Program	Degrees
Art Therapy	M
Business Administration and Management—General	M
Liberal Studies	M

ALCORN STATE UNIVERSITY

Program	Degrees
Agricultural Economics and Agribusiness	M
Agricultural Education	M,O
Agricultural Sciences—General	M
Agronomy and Soil Sciences	M
Animal Sciences	M
Biological and Biomedical Sciences—General	M
Business Administration and Management—General	M
Computer Science	M
Counselor Education	M,O
Education—General	M,O
Elementary Education	M,O
Health Education	M,O
Information Science	M
Nursing—General	M
Physical Education	M,O
Secondary Education	M,O
Special Education	M,O
Vocational and Technical Education	M,O

ALDERSON-BROADDUS COLLEGE

Program	Degrees
Allied Health—General	M
Emergency Medical Services	M

ALFRED ADLER GRADUATE SCHOOL

Program	Degrees
Counseling Psychology	M,O
Psychology—General	M,O

ALFRED UNIVERSITY

Program	Degrees
Applied Arts and Design—General	M
Art Education	M
Art/Fine Arts	M
Bioengineering	M,D
Business Administration and Management—General	M
Business Education	M
Ceramic Sciences and Engineering	M,D*
Computer Art and Design	M
Counselor Education	M
Education—General	M
Electrical Engineering	M
Elementary Education	M
English Education	M
Internet and Interactive Multimedia	M
Materials Sciences	M,D
Mathematics Education	M
Mechanical Engineering	M
Public Policy and Administration	M
Reading Education	M
School Psychology	M,D,O*
Science Education	M
Secondary Education	M
Social Sciences Education	M

In-depth description on page 723.

ALLEN COLLEGE

Program	Degrees
Advanced Practice Nursing	M
Health Education	M
Nursing and Healthcare Administration	M
Nursing—General	M

ALLIANCE THEOLOGICAL SEMINARY

Program	Degrees
Missions and Missiology	P,M
Pastoral Ministry and Counseling	P,M
Religious Education	P,M
Theology	P,M

ALLIANT INTERNATIONAL UNIVERSITY

Program	Degrees
Biopsychology	M
Business Administration and Management—General	M,D
Clinical Psychology	D
Counseling Psychology	M
Education—General	M,D,O
Educational Administration	M,D,O
Educational Media/Instructional Technology	M,D
English as a Second Language	D
Finance and Banking	M,D
Forensic Psychology	D
Health Psychology	D
Industrial and Organizational Psychology	M,D
International Affairs	M
International Business	M,D
Management Information Systems	M,D
Management of Technology	M,D
Management Strategy and Policy	M,D
Marketing	M,D
Marriage and Family Therapy	M,D
Multilingual and Multicultural Education	M,D,O

Pharmacology M
Psychology—General M,D*
School Psychology M,D,O
Social Psychology D

In-depth description on page 725.

ALLIANT INTERNATIONAL UNIVERSITY–MÉXICO CITY

Business Administration and Management—General M
International Business M

ALVERNIA COLLEGE

Business Administration and Management—General M
Education—General M
Liberal Studies M
Occupational Therapy M

ALVERNO COLLEGE

Adult Education M
Curriculum and Instruction M
Education—General M
Educational Administration M
Educational Media/Instructional Technology M
Reading Education M
Science Education M

AMBERTON UNIVERSITY

Business Administration and Management—General M
Counseling Psychology M
Human Resources Development M
Human Resources Management M

AMERICAN BAPTIST SEMINARY OF THE WEST

Theology P,M

AMERICAN CHRISTIAN COLLEGE AND SEMINARY

Pastoral Ministry and Counseling P,D
Theology P,M

THE AMERICAN COLLEGE

Finance and Banking M

AMERICAN COLLEGE OF ACUPUNCTURE AND ORIENTAL MEDICINE

Acupuncture and Oriental Medicine M

AMERICAN COLLEGE OF COMPUTER & INFORMATION SCIENCES

Computer Science M

AMERICAN COLLEGE OF TRADITIONAL CHINESE MEDICINE

Acupuncture and Oriental Medicine M*

AMERICAN CONSERVATORY THEATER

Theater M,O*

AMERICAN FILM INSTITUTE CONSERVATORY

Film, Television, and Video Production M

AMERICAN GRADUATE UNIVERSITY

Project Management M,O

AMERICAN INTERCONTINENTAL UNIVERSITY

Information Science M*
International Business M
Management Information Systems M

AMERICAN INTERCONTINENTAL UNIVERSITY (CA)

International Business M
Management Information Systems M

AMERICAN INTERCONTINENTAL UNIVERSITY-LONDON

Business Administration and Management—General M
International Business M

AMERICAN INTERCONTINENTAL UNIVERSITY ONLINE

Business Administration and Management—General M
Information Science M

AMERICAN INTERNATIONAL COLLEGE

Business Administration and Management—General M*
Clinical Psychology M
Criminal Justice and Criminology M
Education—General M,D,O
Educational Administration M,D,O
Educational Psychology M,D,O
Elementary Education M,D,O
Human Resources Development M,O
Organizational Management M
Physical Therapy M
Psychology—General M,D,O
Public Policy and Administration M
Reading Education M,D,O
School Psychology M,O
Secondary Education M,D,O
Special Education M,D,O

AMERICAN MILITARY UNIVERSITY

Business Administration and Management—General M
Criminal Justice and Criminology M
Military and Defense Studies M
Political Science M
Public Health—General M
Public Policy and Administration M

AMERICAN UNIVERSITY

Accounting M
Anthropology M,D
Applied Economics M,D,O
Applied Mathematics M
Art History M
Art/Fine Arts M
Arts Administration M,O
Biological and Biomedical Sciences—General M*
Biopsychology M,D
Business Administration and Management—General M*
Chemistry M,D*
Clinical Psychology D
Communication—General M*
Comparative Literature M
Computer Science M
Conflict Resolution and Mediation/Peace Studies M,D,O
Criminal Justice and Criminology M,D
Dance M
Economics M,D*
Education—General M,D,O
Educational Administration M
Educational Media/Instructional Technology M
Electronic Commerce M
Elementary Education M
English as a Second Language M,O
Entrepreneurship M
Environmental Management and Policy M,D,O
Environmental Sciences M
Exercise and Sports Science M*
Experimental Psychology M,D
Film, Television, and Video Production M
Finance and Banking M,D,O
French M,O*
History M,D
Human Resources Management M
Information Science M,O
Interdisciplinary Studies M,O
International Affairs M,D,O
International and Comparative Education M
International Business M
International Development M,D,O
Internet and Interactive Multimedia M
Journalism M
Latin American Studies M,O
Law P,M
Legal and Justice Studies M
Management Information Systems M
Marketing M
Mass Communication M
Mathematics Education D
Mathematics M*
Media Studies M
Organizational Management M
Philosophy M*
Physics M
Political Science M,D,O*
Psychology—General M,D
Public Policy and Administration M
Real Estate M
Russian M,O
Secondary Education M,O
Social Psychology M,D
Sociology M,D
Spanish M,O*
Special Education M
Statistics M,D,O
Taxation M
Toxicology M,O
Translation and Interpretation M,O
Writing M

In-depth description on page 727.

AMERICAN UNIVERSITY IN CAIRO

Anthropology M
Business Administration and Management—General M,O
Communication—General M,O
Comparative Literature M
Computer Science M
Economics M
Engineering and Applied Sciences—General M,O
English as a Second Language M,O
English M
Foreign Languages Education M
Journalism M,O
Mass Communication M,O
Near and Middle Eastern Languages M,O
Near and Middle Eastern Studies M,O
Political Science M
Sociology M

THE AMERICAN UNIVERSITY IN DUBAI

Business Administration and Management—General M
International Business M

ANDERSON UNIVERSITY

Theology P,M,D

ANDOVER NEWTON THEOLOGICAL SCHOOL

Religious Education P,M,D
Theology P,M,D*

ANDREW JACKSON UNIVERSITY

Business Administration and Management—General M
Criminal Justice and Criminology M
Public Policy and Administration M

ANDREWS UNIVERSITY

Allied Health—General M
Biological and Biomedical Sciences—General M
Business Administration and Management—General M
Communication—General M
Counseling Psychology D
Curriculum and Instruction M,D,O
Developmental Psychology M
Education—General M,D,O
Educational Administration M,D,O
Educational Psychology M,D
Elementary Education M
Engineering and Applied Sciences—General M
English as a Second Language M
English Education M
English M
Foreign Languages Education M
History M
Human Services M
International Development M
Marketing M
Mathematics M
Music M
Nursing—General M
Nutrition M
Physical Therapy M
Psychology—General M,D,O
Reading Education M
Religious Education M,D,O
School Psychology M,O
Science Education M
Secondary Education M
Social Psychology M
Social Sciences Education M
Social Work M
Software Engineering M
Theology P,M,D

ANGELO STATE UNIVERSITY

Accounting M
Animal Sciences M
Biological and Biomedical Sciences—General M
Business Administration and Management—General M
Communication—General M
Counseling Psychology M
Counselor Education M
Curriculum and Instruction M
Education—General M
Educational Administration M
Educational Measurement and Evaluation M
English M
History M
Industrial and Organizational Psychology M
Interdisciplinary Studies M
International Affairs M
Journalism M
Kinesiology and Movement Studies M
Medical/Surgical Nursing M
Physical Therapy M
Psychology—General M
Public Policy and Administration M
Reading Education M

In-depth description on page 729.

ANGLO-EUROPEAN COLLEGE OF CHIROPRACTIC

Chiropractic M

ANNA MARIA COLLEGE

Business Administration and Management—General M,O
Counseling Psychology M,O
Criminal Justice and Criminology M
Early Childhood Education M
Education—General M
Elementary Education M
Environmental and Occupational Health M
Fire Protection Engineering M
Psychology—General M,O
Public Policy and Administration M
Reading Education M

ANTIOCH NEW ENGLAND GRADUATE SCHOOL

Addictions/Substance Abuse Counseling M
Business Administration and Management—General M*
Clinical Psychology D
Counseling Psychology M
Education—General M*
Educational Administration M
Environmental Biology M*
Environmental Education M,D
Environmental Management and Policy M,D*
Environmental Sciences M,D*
Foundations and Philosophy of Education M
Human Services M
Interdisciplinary Studies M
Marriage and Family Therapy M
Psychology—General M*
Science Education M*
Therapies—Dance, Drama, and Music M

In-depth description on page 731 and announcement on page 252.

ANTIOCH UNIVERSITY LOS ANGELES

Business Administration and Management—General M
Clinical Psychology M
Education—General M
Human Resources Development M
Organizational Management M
Psychology—General M
Writing M,O

ANTIOCH UNIVERSITY MCGREGOR

Business Administration and Management—General M
Comparative Literature M
Conflict Resolution and Mediation/Peace Studies M
Counseling Psychology M
Education—General M

Antioch University McGregor (continued)

Film, Television, and Video Production M
Liberal Studies M
Psychology—General M
Theater M
Writing M

In-depth description on page 733 and announcement on page 252.

ANTIOCH UNIVERSITY SANTA BARBARA

Child and Family Studies M
Clinical Psychology M
Counseling Psychology M
Education—General M
Organizational Management M
Psychology—General M

ANTIOCH UNIVERSITY SEATTLE

Business Administration and Management—General M
Education—General M
Environmental Management and Policy M
Organizational Management M
Psychology—General M

In-depth description on page 735.

APPALACHIAN SCHOOL OF LAW

Law P

APPALACHIAN STATE UNIVERSITY

Accounting M
American Studies M
Applied Physics M
Biological and Biomedical Sciences—General M
Business Administration and Management—General M
Clinical Psychology M
Communication Disorders M
Computer Science M
Counselor Education M,O
Curriculum and Instruction M
Early Childhood Education M
Education—General M,D,O
Educational Administration M,D
Educational Media/Instructional Technology M,O
Elementary Education M
English Education M
English M
Exercise and Sports Science M
Experimental Psychology M
Family and Consumer Sciences-General M
Geography M
Gerontology M
Health Psychology M
Higher Education M,O
History M
Human Development M
Industrial and Organizational Psychology M
Library Science M,O
Management Information Systems O
Marriage and Family Therapy M
Mathematics Education M
Mathematics M
Music Education M
Music M
Physical Education M
Political Science M
Psychology—General M,O
Public History M
Public Policy and Administration M
Reading Education M
Romance Languages M
School Psychology M,O
Secondary Education M
Social Psychology M
Social Sciences M
Special Education M
Sports Management M
Vocational and Technical Education M

AQUINAS COLLEGE

Business Administration and Management—General M
Education—General M

AQUINAS INSTITUTE OF THEOLOGY

Health Services Management and Hospital Administration P,M,D,O
Pastoral Ministry and Counseling P,M,D,O
Theology P,M,D,O

ARCADIA UNIVERSITY

Art Education M,D,O
Community Health M
Computer Education M,D,O
Conflict Resolution and Mediation/Peace Studies M
Counseling Psychology M
Early Childhood Education M,D,O
Education—General M,D,O
Educational Administration M,D,O
Educational Media/Instructional Technology M,D,O
Educational Psychology M,D,O
Elementary Education M,D,O
English Education M,D,O
English M
Environmental Education M,D,O
Genetic Counseling M
Health Education M
Humanities M
Mathematics Education M,D,O
Music Education M,D,O
Physical Therapy D
Psychology—General M,D,O
Reading Education M,D,O
School Psychology M
Science Education M,D,O
Secondary Education M,D,O
Social Psychology M
Social Sciences Education M,D,O
Special Education M,D,O
Theater M,D,O

In-depth description on page 737.

ARGOSY UNIVERSITY-ATLANTA

Clinical Psychology M,D
Counseling Psychology M,D
Psychology—General M,D*

ARGOSY UNIVERSITY-CHICAGO

Business Administration and Management—General M
Clinical Psychology M*
Counseling Psychology M
Education—General M,D,O*
Forensic Psychology D
Forensic Sciences M,D,O
Health Psychology D
Human Development D
Marriage and Family Therapy D
Psychology—General M,D,O

ARGOSY UNIVERSITY-CHICAGO NORTHWEST

Accounting M,D
Business Administration and Management—General M,D*
Clinical Psychology M,D
Counseling Psychology M,D
Finance and Banking M,D
Health Services Management and Hospital Administration M,D
Human Resources Management M,D
International Business M,D
Management Information Systems M,D
Marketing M,D
Psychology—General M,D*

ARGOSY UNIVERSITY-DALLAS

Clinical Psychology M,D*
Counseling Psychology M,D
Psychology—General M,D

ARGOSY UNIVERSITY-HONOLULU

Clinical Psychology D,O
Counseling Psychology M
Marriage and Family Therapy M
Psychology—General M,D,O*

ARGOSY UNIVERSITY-ORANGE COUNTY

Business Administration and Management—General M,D*
Clinical Psychology D
Counseling Psychology M,D
Curriculum and Instruction M,D,O
Education—General M,D,O*
Educational Administration M,D,O
Elementary Education M,D,O
Finance and Banking M,D
Health Services Management and Hospital Administration M,D
Higher Education M,D,O
Human Resources Management M,D
International Business M,D
Management Information Systems M,D
Marketing M,D
Psychology—General M,D*
Secondary Education M,D,O

ARGOSY UNIVERSITY-PHOENIX

Clinical Psychology M,D,O
Counseling Psychology M
Education—General D,O*
Educational Administration D,O
Psychology—General M,D,O*
Sport Psychology M,D,O

ARGOSY UNIVERSITY-SAN FRANCISCO BAY AREA

Clinical Psychology M,D
Counseling Psychology M,D
Curriculum and Instruction M,D
Education—General M,D*
Educational Administration M,D
Higher Education M,D
Psychology—General M,D*

ARGOSY UNIVERSITY-SARASOTA

Accounting M,D
Business Administration and Management—General M,D*
Counseling Psychology M,D,O
Counselor Education M,D,O
Curriculum and Instruction M,D,O
Education—General M,D,O*
Educational Administration M,D,O
Finance and Banking M,D
Health Services Management and Hospital Administration M,D
Human Resources Management M,D
International Business M,D
Management Information Systems M,D
Marketing M,D
Pastoral Ministry and Counseling M,D,O
Psychology—General M,D,O
School Psychology M,D,O

In-depth description on page 739.

ARGOSY UNIVERSITY-SEATTLE

Clinical Psychology M,D
Counseling Psychology M
Education—General M*

ARGOSY UNIVERSITY-TAMPA

Business Administration and Management—General M*
Clinical Psychology M,D
Curriculum and Instruction M
Education—General M*
Educational Administration M
Finance and Banking M
Health Services Management and Hospital Administration M
Human Resources Development M
International Business M
Marketing M
Psychology—General M,D*

ARGOSY UNIVERSITY-TWIN CITIES

Clinical Psychology M,D
Counseling Psychology M,D
Curriculum and Instruction M
Education—General M*
Educational Psychology M,D
Marriage and Family Therapy M,D
Psychology—General M,D*

ARGOSY UNIVERSITY-WASHINGTON D.C.

Clinical Psychology M,D,O*
Counseling Psychology M,D,O
Forensic Psychology M,D,O
Psychology—General M,D,O

ARIZONA STATE UNIVERSITY

Accounting M,D
Aerospace/Aeronautical Engineering M,D
Animal Behavior M,D
Anthropology M,D
Applied Arts and Design—General M
Applied Mathematics M,D
Architectural History D
Architecture M
Art/Fine Arts M
Astronomy M,D
Biochemistry M,D
Bioengineering M,D*
Biological and Biomedical Sciences—General M,D*
Biomedical Engineering M,D
Biostatistics M,D
Building Science M
Business Administration and Management—General M,D
Cell Biology M,D
Chemical Engineering M,D*
Chemistry M,D
Child and Family Studies D
City and Regional Planning M
Civil Engineering M,D
Clinical Psychology D
Cognitive Sciences D
Communication Disorders M,D
Communication—General M,D
Comparative Literature M,D
Computational Sciences M,D
Computer Science M,D*
Conservation Biology M,D
Construction Engineering and Management M
Counseling Psychology D
Counselor Education M
Curriculum and Instruction M,D
Dance M
Demography and Population Studies M,D
Developmental Biology M,D
Developmental Psychology D
Ecology M,D
Economics M,D
Education—General M,D*
Educational Administration M,D
Educational Media/Instructional Technology M,D
Educational Psychology M,D
Electrical Engineering M,D*
Engineering and Applied Sciences—General M,D*
English as a Second Language M
English M,D
Environmental Design D
Evolutionary Biology M,D
Exercise and Sports Science M,D
Finance and Banking M,D
Foundations and Philosophy of Education M
French M
Genetics M,D
Geography M,D
Geological Engineering M,D
German M
Gerontology O
Health Services Management and Hospital Administration M
Health Services Research M,D
Higher Education M,D
History of Science and Technology M,D
History M,D
Human Development M,D
Humanities M
Industrial/Management Engineering M,D
Journalism M
Latin American Studies M,D
Law P
Legal and Justice Studies M,D
Linguistics M,D
Logistics M,D
Management Information Systems M,D
Marketing M,D
Materials Engineering M,D
Materials Sciences M,D*
Mathematics M,D*
Mechanical Engineering M,D
Medieval and Renaissance Studies O
Microbiology M,D
Molecular Biology M,D
Music M,D
Neuroscience M,D
Nursing—General M
Philosophy M
Physical Education M
Physics M,D
Physiology M,D
Plant Biology M,D
Political Science M,D
Psychology—General D
Public History M,D
Public Policy and Administration M,D
Recreation and Park Management M
Religion M
Science Education M,D
Social Psychology D
Social Work M,D
Sociology M,D
Spanish M,D
Special Education M
Speech and Interpersonal Communication M,D
Statistics M,D
Taxation M
Theater M,D
Transportation Management O
Writing M

ARIZONA STATE UNIVERSITY EAST

Aerospace/Aeronautical Engineering M
Agricultural Economics and Agribusiness M
Computer Engineering M
Electrical Engineering M
Engineering and Applied Sciences—General M
Environmental Management and Policy M
Exercise and Sports Science M
Information Science M
Management Information Systems M
Manufacturing Engineering M

Nutrition M
Transportation Management M

ARIZONA STATE UNIVERSITY WEST

Business Administration and Management—General M
Communication—General M
Criminal Justice and Criminology M
Education—General M
Educational Administration M
Elementary Education M
Interdisciplinary Studies M
Secondary Education M
Social Work M
Special Education M

ARKANSAS STATE UNIVERSITY

Agricultural Education M,O
Agricultural Sciences—General M,O
Art/Fine Arts M
Biological and Biomedical Sciences—General M,D,O
Business Administration and Management—General M,O
Business Education M,O
Chemistry M,O
Communication Disorders M
Communication—General M,O
Computer Science M
Counselor Education M,O
Curriculum and Instruction M,D,O
Early Childhood Education M,O
Education of the Gifted M,D,O
Education—General M,D,O
Educational Administration M,D,O
Educational Measurement and Evaluation M,O
Elementary Education M,O
English Education M,O
English M,O
Environmental Sciences M,D,O
Gerontological Nursing M,O
History M,D,O
Journalism M
Mathematics Education M
Mathematics M
Media Studies M
Music Education M,O
Music M,O
Nursing—General M
Physical Education M,O
Physical Therapy M
Political Science M,O
Public Policy and Administration M,O
Reading Education M,O
Rehabilitation Counseling M,O
Science Education M,D,O
Social Sciences Education M,D,O
Sociology M,O
Special Education M,D,O
Speech and Interpersonal Communication M,O
Theater M,O

ARKANSAS TECH UNIVERSITY

Art/Fine Arts M
Communication—General M
Counselor Education M
Curriculum and Instruction M
Education of the Gifted M
Education—General M,O
Educational Administration M
Educational Media/Instructional Technology M
Elementary Education M
English Education M
English M
Fish, Game, and Wildlife Management M
History M
Information Science M
Journalism M
Liberal Studies M
Mathematics Education M
Physical Education M
Social Sciences Education M
Social Sciences M
Spanish M

ARMSTRONG ATLANTIC STATE UNIVERSITY

Business Education M
Communication Disorders M
Criminal Justice and Criminology M
Education—General M
Elementary Education M
English Education M
Exercise and Sports Science M
Health Services Management and Hospital Administration M
History M
Kinesiology and Movement Studies M
Mathematics Education M
Middle School Education M
Nursing—General M
Physical Therapy M
Public Health—General M
Science Education M
Secondary Education M
Social Sciences Education M
Special Education M

In-depth description on page 741.

ARMSTRONG UNIVERSITY

Accounting M
Business Administration and Management—General M
Finance and Banking M
International Business M
Management Information Systems M
Marketing M

ART ACADEMY OF CINCINNATI

Art Education M

ART CENTER COLLEGE OF DESIGN

Applied Arts and Design—General M*
Art/Fine Arts M
Computer Art and Design M
Environmental Design M
Film, Television, and Video Production M
Industrial Design M

ARTHUR D. LITTLE SCHOOL OF MANAGEMENT

Business Administration and Management—General M

THE ART INSTITUTE OF BOSTON AT LESLEY UNIVERSITY

Art/Fine Arts M

ASBURY THEOLOGICAL SEMINARY

Missions and Missiology P,M,D,O
Pastoral Ministry and Counseling P,M,D,O
Religious Education P,M,D,O
Theology P,M,D,O

ASHLAND UNIVERSITY

Business Administration and Management—General M
Business Education M
Computer Education M
Curriculum and Instruction M
Early Childhood Education M
Education of the Gifted M
Education—General M,D
Educational Administration M,D
Exercise and Sports Science M,D
Pastoral Ministry and Counseling P,M,D
Physical Education M
Reading Education M
Religious Education P,M,D
Special Education M
Theology P,M,D

ASSEMBLIES OF GOD THEOLOGICAL SEMINARY

Pastoral Ministry and Counseling P,M,D
Theology P,M,D

ASSOCIATED MENNONITE BIBLICAL SEMINARY

Conflict Resolution and Mediation/Peace Studies P,M,O
Missions and Missiology P,M,O
Theology P,M,O

ASSUMPTION COLLEGE

Business Administration and Management—General M,O
Counseling Psychology M,O
Psychology—General M,O
Rehabilitation Counseling M,O
Special Education M

In-depth description on page 743.

ATHABASCA UNIVERSITY

Adult Education M
Advanced Practice Nursing M,O
Allied Health—General M,O
Business Administration and Management—General M,O
Canadian Studies M
Cultural Studies M
Distance Education Development M,O
Education—General M,O
History M
Information Science M
Interdisciplinary Studies M
International Development M
Management of Technology M,O
Organizational Management M
Project Management M,O

ATHENAEUM OF OHIO

Pastoral Ministry and Counseling P,M,O
Theology P,M,O

ATLANTIC SCHOOL OF THEOLOGY

Theology P,M

ATLANTIC UNION COLLEGE

Education—General M

ATLANTIC UNIVERSITY

Transpersonal and Humanistic Psychology M

AUBURN UNIVERSITY

Accounting M
Adult Education M,D,O
Aerospace/Aeronautical Engineering M,D*
Agricultural Economics and Agribusiness M,D
Agricultural Sciences—General M,D
Agronomy and Soil Sciences M,D
Anatomy M
Animal Sciences M,D
Applied Mathematics M,D
Aquaculture M,D
Art/Fine Arts M,D
Bioengineering M,D
Biological and Biomedical Sciences—General M,D
Botany M,D
Building Science M
Business Administration and Management—General M,D*
Business Education M,D,O
Chemical Engineering M,D
Chemistry M,D
Child and Family Studies M,D
City and Regional Planning M
Civil Engineering M,D*
Clothing and Textiles M
Communication Disorders M
Communication—General M
Computer Engineering M,D
Computer Science M,D
Construction Engineering and Management M,D
Counseling Psychology M,D,O
Counselor Education M,D,O
Curriculum and Instruction M,D,O
Early Childhood Education M,D,O
Economics M,D
Education—General M,D,O*
Educational Administration M,D,O
Educational Media/Instructional Technology M,D,O
Educational Psychology M,D,O
Electrical Engineering M,D
Elementary Education M,D,O
Engineering and Applied Sciences—General M,D
English Education M,D,O
English M,D*
Entomology M,D
Environmental Engineering M,D
Fish, Game, and Wildlife Management M,D
Food Science and Technology M,D
Foreign Languages Education M,D,O
Forestry M,D
French M
Geography M
Geology M*
Geotechnical Engineering M,D
Health Education M,D,O
Higher Education M,D,O
History M,D
Horticulture M,D
Human Development M,D
Human Resources Management M,D
Hydraulics M,D
Hydrology M,D
Industrial Design M
Industrial/Management Engineering M,D
Journalism M
Management Information Systems M,D
Mass Communication M
Materials Engineering M,D
Mathematics Education M,D,O
Mathematics M,D
Mechanical Engineering M,D
Microbiology M,D
Music Education M,D,O
Music M
Nutrition M,D*
Pathobiology M
Pharmaceutical Sciences M,D
Pharmacology M
Pharmacy P
Physical Education M,D,O
Physics M,D
Physiology M
Plant Pathology M,D
Political Science M,D
Psychology—General M,D
Public Policy and Administration M,D*
Radiation Biology M
Reading Education M,D,O
Rural Sociology M,D
School Psychology M,D,O
Science Education M,D,O
Secondary Education M,D,O
Social Psychology M,D,O
Social Sciences Education M,D,O
Sociology M
Software Engineering M,D
Spanish M
Special Education M,D,O
Statistics M,D
Structural Engineering M,D
Systems Engineering M,D
Textile Sciences and Engineering M,D
Transportation and Highway Engineering M,D
Veterinary Medicine P
Veterinary Sciences M,D
Zoology M,D

In-depth description on page 745.

AUBURN UNIVERSITY MONTGOMERY

Business Administration and Management—General M
Counselor Education M,O
Criminal Justice and Criminology M
Early Childhood Education M,O
Education—General M,O
Educational Administration M,O
Elementary Education M,O
Liberal Studies M
Physical Education M,O
Political Science M
Psychology—General M
Public Policy and Administration M,D
Reading Education M,O
Secondary Education M,O
Special Education M,O

AUDREY COHEN COLLEGE

Business Administration and Management—General M
Corporate and Organizational Communication M
Electronic Commerce M
Media Studies M
Public Policy and Administration M
Sports Management M

In-depth description on page 747.

AUGSBURG COLLEGE

Business Administration and Management—General M
Community Health Nursing M
Physician Assistant Studies M
Social Work M
Transcultural Nursing M

AUGUSTANA COLLEGE

Bioethics M
Community Health Nursing M
Education—General M
Elementary Education M
Nursing—General M
Secondary Education M
Special Education M

AUGUSTA STATE UNIVERSITY

Business Administration and Management—General M
Counselor Education M,O
Early Childhood Education M,O
Education—General M,O
Educational Administration M,O
Middle School Education M,O
Political Science M
Psychology—General M
Secondary Education M,O
Special Education M,O

AURORA UNIVERSITY

Business Administration and Management—General M
Curriculum and Instruction M,D
Education—General M,D
Educational Administration M,D
Leisure Studies M

Aurora University (continued)

Recreation and Park Management M
Social Work M

AUSTIN COLLEGE

Education—General M
Elementary Education M
Secondary Education M

AUSTIN PEAY STATE UNIVERSITY

Advertising and Public Relations M
Biological and Biomedical Sciences—General M
Clinical Psychology M
Communication—General M
Corporate and Organizational Communication M
Counselor Education M,O
Curriculum and Instruction M,O
Education—General M,O
Educational Administration M,O
Educational Psychology M,O
Elementary Education M,O
English Education M
English M
Exercise and Sports Science M
Health Education M
Journalism M
Media Studies M
Music Education M
Music M
Psychology—General M
Reading Education M,O
School Psychology M
Secondary Education M,O
Special Education M,O
Speech and Interpersonal Communication M
Theater M

AUSTIN PRESBYTERIAN THEOLOGICAL SEMINARY

Pastoral Ministry and Counseling P,M,D
Theology P,M,D

AVERETT UNIVERSITY

Business Administration and Management—General M
Curriculum and Instruction M
Early Childhood Education M
Education—General M
Middle School Education M
Reading Education M
Science Education M
Special Education M

AVILA UNIVERSITY

Business Administration and Management—General M
Counseling Psychology M
Education—General M
Psychology—General M

AZUSA PACIFIC UNIVERSITY

Business Administration and Management—General M*
Clinical Psychology M,D
Computer Science M,O*
Curriculum and Instruction M
Education—General M,D*
Educational Administration M,D
Educational Media/Instructional Technology M
English as a Second Language M
Human Resources Development M
International Business M
Management Strategy and Policy M
Marriage and Family Therapy M,D
Multilingual and Multicultural Education M
Music Education M
Music M
Nursing—General M*
Organizational Management M
Pastoral Ministry and Counseling P,M,D
Physical Education M
Physical Therapy M*
Psychology—General M,D*
Religion P,M,D
Religious Education P,M,D
Software Engineering M,O
Special Education M
Student Personnel Services M
Telecommunications M,O
Theology P,M,D

In-depth description on page 749.

BABSON COLLEGE

Business Administration and Management—General M
International Business M

BAKER COLLEGE CENTER FOR GRADUATE STUDIES

Accounting M
Business Administration and Management—General M
Finance and Banking M
Health Services Management and Hospital Administration M
Human Resources Management M
Industrial and Manufacturing Management M
International Business M
Management Information Systems M
Marketing M
Recreation and Park Management M

BAKER UNIVERSITY

Business Administration and Management—General M
Education—General M
Liberal Studies M

BALDWIN-WALLACE COLLEGE

Accounting M
Business Administration and Management—General M
Education—General M
Educational Administration M
Educational Media/Instructional Technology M
Entrepreneurship M
Health Services Management and Hospital Administration M
Human Resources Management M
International Business M*
Reading Education M
Special Education M

BALL STATE UNIVERSITY

Accounting M
Actuarial Science M
Adult Education M,D
Advertising and Public Relations M
Anthropology M
Architecture M
Art Education M
Art/Fine Arts M
Biological and Biomedical Sciences—General M,D
Business Administration and Management—General M
Business Education M
Chemistry M
City and Regional Planning M*
Clinical Psychology M
Cognitive Sciences M
Communication Disorders M,D
Communication—General M*
Computer Science M
Counseling Psychology M,D
Curriculum and Instruction M,O
Early Childhood Education M,D
Education—General M,D,O
Educational Administration M,D,O
Educational Psychology M,D,O
Elementary Education M,D
English as a Second Language M,D
English M,D
Exercise and Sports Science D
Family and Consumer Sciences-General M
Geology M
Geosciences M
Gerontology M
Health Education M
Health Promotion M
Higher Education M,D
Historic Preservation M*
History M
Information Science M
Journalism M
Landscape Architecture M*
Linguistics D
Mathematics Education M
Mathematics M
Middle School Education M
Music Education M,D
Natural Resources M
Nursing—General M
Physical Education M,D
Physics M
Physiology M
Political Science M
Psychology—General M
Public Policy and Administration M
Reading Education M,D
Rhetoric M

School Psychology M,D,O
Science Education M,D
Secondary Education M
Social Psychology M
Social Sciences M
Sociology M
Special Education M,D,O
Speech and Interpersonal Communication M
Statistics M
Vocational and Technical Education M
Writing M,D

BALTIMORE HEBREW UNIVERSITY

Jewish Studies M,D

BANGOR THEOLOGICAL SEMINARY

Theology P,M,D

BANK STREET COLLEGE OF EDUCATION

Child and Family Studies M
Curriculum and Instruction M
Early Childhood Education M
Education—General M*
Educational Administration M
Elementary Education M
Foundations and Philosophy of Education M
Maternal and Child Health M
Mathematics Education M
Middle School Education M
Museum Education M
Pediatric Nursing M
Special Education M

BAPTIST BIBLE COLLEGE

Pastoral Ministry and Counseling P,M
Theology P,M

BAPTIST BIBLE COLLEGE OF PENNSYLVANIA

Counselor Education M
Pastoral Ministry and Counseling P,M,D
Religious Education M
Theology P,M,D

BAPTIST MISSIONARY ASSOCIATION THEOLOGICAL SEMINARY

Theology P,M

BAPTIST THEOLOGICAL SEMINARY AT RICHMOND

Music P,D
Pastoral Ministry and Counseling P,D
Religious Education P,D
Theology P,D

BARD COLLEGE

Art/Fine Arts M*
Environmental Management and Policy M,O*
Museum Studies M

In-depth description on page 751.

BARD GRADUATE CENTER FOR STUDIES IN THE DECORATIVE ARTS, DESIGN, AND CULTURE

Art History M,D*
Decorative Arts M,D*

Announcement on page 266.

BARRY UNIVERSITY

Advanced Practice Nursing M
Art/Fine Arts M
Biological and Biomedical Sciences—General M
Business Administration and Management—General M,O
Clinical Psychology M,O
Communication—General M,O
Corporate and Organizational Communication M,O
Counselor Education M,D,O
Early Childhood Education M
Education of the Gifted M,D,O
Education—General M,D,O
Educational Administration M,D,O
Educational Media/Instructional Technology M,D,O
Elementary Education M,O
Exercise and Sports Science M
Health Services Management and Hospital Administration M
Higher Education M,D
Human Resources Development M,D
Information Science M
Kinesiology and Movement Studies M

Law P
Management Information Systems M,O
Marriage and Family Therapy M,O
Nurse Anesthesia M
Nursing and Healthcare Administration M,D
Nursing Education M
Nursing—General D
Occupational Therapy M
Pastoral Ministry and Counseling M,D
Photography M
Physical Education M
Physician Assistant Studies M
Podiatric Medicine P*
Psychology—General M,O
Reading Education M,O
Rehabilitation Counseling M,O
School Psychology M,O
Social Work M,D*
Special Education M,D,O
Sports Management M
Theology M,D

In-depth description on page 753.

BASTYR UNIVERSITY

Acupuncture and Oriental Medicine M*
Naturopathic Medicine D*
Nutrition M*

BAYAMÓN CENTRAL UNIVERSITY

Accounting M
Business Administration and Management—General M
Counselor Education M
Early Childhood Education M
Education—General M
Educational Administration M
Elementary Education M
Marketing M
Pastoral Ministry and Counseling P,M
Psychology—General M
Religion P,M
Special Education M
Theology P,M

BAYLOR COLLEGE OF MEDICINE

Allopathic Medicine P
Biochemistry D*
Bioengineering
Biological and Biomedical Sciences—General M,D*
Biophysics D*
Cardiovascular Sciences D*
Cell Biology D*
Clinical Laboratory Sciences/Medical Technology M,D
Developmental Biology D*
Genetics D*
Human Genetics D
Immunology D*
Microbiology D
Molecular Biology D*
Neuroscience D*
Nurse Anesthesia M
Nurse Midwifery M
Pharmacology D
Physician Assistant Studies M
Physiology D*
Structural Biology D
Virology D*

BAYLOR UNIVERSITY

Accounting M
Advanced Practice Nursing M
Allied Health—General M,D
American Studies M
Biological and Biomedical Sciences—General M,D
Business Administration and Management—General M
Chemistry M,D*
Clinical Psychology M,D
Communication Disorders M
Communication—General M
Computer Science M
Curriculum and Instruction M,D,O
Economics M*
Education—General M,D,O
Educational Administration M,D,O
Educational Psychology M,D,O
English M,D
Environmental Biology M,D
Environmental Management and Policy M
Geology M,D
Geosciences M,D
Gerontology M
Health Education M
Health Services Management and Hospital Administration M
History M
Interdisciplinary Studies M,D
International Affairs M*
International Business M
Journalism M

Law P
Limnology M,D
Management Information Systems M
Maternal/Child Nursing M
Mathematics M
Museum Studies M
Music Education M
Music M
Neuroscience M,D
Nursing and Healthcare Administration M
Nursing—General M
Pediatric Nursing M
Philosophy M
Physical Education M
Physical Therapy M,D
Physics M,D
Political Science M,D
Psychology—General M,D
Public Policy and Administration M
Recreation and Park Management M
Religion M,D*
Social Work M
Sociology M,D
Spanish M
Statistics M,D
Theater M
Theology P,D

In-depth description on page 755.

BAY PATH COLLEGE

Management Information Systems M

BELHAVEN COLLEGE

Business Administration and Management—General M

BELLARMINE UNIVERSITY

Business Administration and Management—General M
Community Health Nursing M
Early Childhood Education M
Education—General M
Elementary Education M
Middle School Education M
Nursing and Healthcare Administration M
Nursing Education M
Nursing—General M
Special Education M

BELLEVUE UNIVERSITY

Business Administration and Management—General M
Health Services Management and Hospital Administration M*
Human Services M
Information Science M*
Management Information Systems M

In-depth description on page 757.

BELMONT UNIVERSITY

Allied Health—General M,D
Business Administration and Management—General M
Early Childhood Education M
Education of the Gifted M
Education—General M
Educational Media/Instructional Technology M
Elementary Education M
English Education M
English M
Mathematics Education M
Middle School Education M
Music Education M
Music M
Nursing—General M
Occupational Therapy M
Physical Therapy M,D
Science Education M
Secondary Education M
Social Sciences Education M
Sports Management M
Writing M

BEMIDJI STATE UNIVERSITY

Biological and Biomedical Sciences—General M
Education—General M
English M
Environmental Management and Policy M
Mathematics Education M
Physical Education M
Science Education M
Special Education M
Vocational and Technical Education M

BENEDICTINE COLLEGE

Business Administration and Management—General M
Educational Administration M

BENEDICTINE UNIVERSITY

Business Administration and Management—General M
Counseling Psychology M
Curriculum and Instruction M
Education—General M
Elementary Education M
Exercise and Sports Science M
Liberal Studies M
Management Information Systems M
Organizational Behavior M
Organizational Management D
Public Health—General M
Special Education M

In-depth description on page 759.

BENNINGTON COLLEGE

Art/Fine Arts M
Biological and Biomedical Sciences—General O
Dance M
Education—General M
English M
Liberal Studies M
Multilingual and Multicultural Education M
Music M
Theater M
Writing M

In-depth description on page 761.

BENTLEY COLLEGE

Accounting M,O*
Business Administration and Management—General M,O*
Corporate and Organizational Communication M,O
Economics M,O
Electronic Commerce M,O*
Entrepreneurship M,O
Ergonomics and Human Factors M*
Finance and Banking M,O*
Industrial and Manufacturing Management M,O
Information Science M*
International Business M,O
Management Information Systems M,O
Management of Technology M,O
Marketing M,O*
Taxation M,O*

BERNARD M. BARUCH COLLEGE OF THE CITY UNIVERSITY OF NEW YORK

Accounting M,D
Business Administration and Management—General M,D,O*
Corporate and Organizational Communication M*
Economics M
Educational Administration M,O
Finance and Banking M,D
Health Services Management and Hospital Administration M
Higher Education M
Human Resources Management M,D
Industrial and Labor Relations M
Industrial and Manufacturing Management M,D
Industrial and Organizational Psychology M,D,O*
International Business M
Journalism M*
Management Information Systems M,D
Management Strategy and Policy M,D
Marketing M,D
Operations Research M
Organizational Behavior M,D
Organizational Management M,D
Public Policy and Administration M*
Statistics M
Taxation M

BERRY COLLEGE

Business Administration and Management—General M
Curriculum and Instruction O
Early Childhood Education M
Education—General M,O
Middle School Education M
Reading Education M
Secondary Education M

BETHANY COLLEGE OF THE ASSEMBLIES OF GOD

Education—General M
Educational Administration M

BETHANY THEOLOGICAL SEMINARY

Conflict Resolution and Mediation/Peace Studies P,M,O
Religion P,M,O
Theology P,M,O

BETH BENJAMIN ACADEMY OF CONNECTICUT

Theology

BETHEL COLLEGE (IN)

Business Administration and Management—General M
Counseling Psychology M
Marriage and Family Therapy M
Pastoral Ministry and Counseling M
Theology M

BETHEL COLLEGE (MN)

Anthropology M
Communication—General M
Education—General M
Music M
Nursing—General M
Organizational Management M
Psychology—General M
Sociology M

BETHEL COLLEGE (TN)

Education—General M
Educational Administration M
Elementary Education M
English Education M
Physical Education M
Science Education M
Social Sciences Education M
Special Education M

BETHEL SEMINARY

Marriage and Family Therapy P,M,D,O
Missions and Missiology P,M,D,O
Pastoral Ministry and Counseling P,M,D,O
Religious Education P,M,D,O
Theology P,M,D,O

BETHESDA CHRISTIAN UNIVERSITY

Missions and Missiology P,M
Pastoral Ministry and Counseling P,M
Theology P,M

BETH HAMEDRASH SHAAREI YOSHER INSTITUTE

Theology

BETH HATALMUD RABBINICAL COLLEGE

Theology

BETH MEDRASH GOVOHA

Theology

BIBLICAL THEOLOGICAL SEMINARY

Pastoral Ministry and Counseling P,M,D
Theology P,M,D

BIOLA UNIVERSITY

Business Administration and Management—General M
Education—General M
English as a Second Language M,D,O
Ethics P,M,D
Linguistics M,D,O
Missions and Missiology M,D,O
Organizational Management M
Psychology—General M,D
Religion P,M,D
Religious Education P,M,D
Theology P,M,D

BIRMINGHAM-SOUTHERN COLLEGE

Business Administration and Management—General M
Public Policy and Administration M

BISHOP'S UNIVERSITY

Education—General M,O
English as a Second Language M,O

BLACK HILLS STATE UNIVERSITY

Business Administration and Management—General M
Curriculum and Instruction M
Education—General M*

BLESSED JOHN XXIII NATIONAL SEMINARY

Theology P

BLOOMSBURG UNIVERSITY OF PENNSYLVANIA

Accounting M
Art History M
Art/Fine Arts M
Biological and Biomedical Sciences—General M
Business Administration and Management—General M
Business Education M
Communication Disorders M
Curriculum and Instruction M
Early Childhood Education M
Education—General M
Educational Media/Instructional Technology M
Elementary Education M
Exercise and Sports Science M
Nursing—General M
Reading Education M
Science Education M
Special Education M

BLUFFTON COLLEGE

Education—General M

BOISE STATE UNIVERSITY

Accounting M
Art Education M
Art/Fine Arts M
Biological and Biomedical Sciences—General M
Business Administration and Management—General M*
Civil Engineering M
Communication—General M
Computer Engineering M
Computer Science M
Counselor Education M
Criminal Justice and Criminology M
Curriculum and Instruction M,D
Early Childhood Education M
Education—General M,D
Educational Media/Instructional Technology M
Electrical Engineering M
English M
Environmental Management and Policy M
Exercise and Sports Science M
Geology M
Geophysics M,D
Geosciences M
History M
Interdisciplinary Studies M
Management Information Systems M
Mathematics Education M
Mechanical Engineering M
Music Education M
Music M
Public Health—General M
Public Policy and Administration M
Reading Education M
Science Education M,D
Social Work M
Special Education M
Sports Management M
Technical Writing M
Writing M

BORICUA COLLEGE

Human Services M
Liberal Studies M

BOSTON ARCHITECTURAL CENTER

Architecture M*
Interior Design M

BOSTON COLLEGE

Biochemistry M,D*
Biological and Biomedical Sciences—General M,D*
Business Administration and Management—General M
Chemistry M,D*
Classics M
Community Health Nursing M,D
Counseling Psychology M,D
Curriculum and Instruction M,D,O
Developmental Psychology M,D
Early Childhood Education M

Boston College (continued)

East European and Russian Studies	M
Economics	M,D
Education of the Multiply Handicapped	M,O
Education—General	M,D,O*
Educational Administration	M,D,O
Educational Measurement and Evaluation	M,D,O
Educational Psychology	M,D
Elementary Education	M
English Education	M
English	M,D,O
Finance and Banking	M,D
Foreign Languages Education	M
French	M,D
Geology	M
Geophysics	M
Gerontological Nursing	M,D
Higher Education	M,D
History	M,D
Inorganic Chemistry	M,D
Italian	M,D
Law	P
Linguistics	M
Maternal/Child Nursing	M,D
Mathematics Education	M
Mathematics	M
Nursing—General	M,D
Organic Chemistry	M,D
Organizational Behavior	D
Organizational Management	D
Pastoral Ministry and Counseling	M,D
Philosophy	M,D
Physical Chemistry	M,D
Physics	M,D
Political Science	M,D
Psychiatric Nursing	M,D
Psychology—General	D
Reading Education	M,O
Religious Education	M,D,O
Russian	M
Science Education	M,D
Secondary Education	M
Slavic Languages	M
Social Sciences Education	M
Social Work	M,D*
Sociology	M,D
Spanish	M,D
Special Education	M,O
Theology	M,D
Western European Studies	M,D

In-depth description on page 763.

THE BOSTON CONSERVATORY

Music Education	M,O
Music	M,O
Theater	M

BOSTON GRADUATE SCHOOL OF PSYCHOANALYSIS

Psychology—General	M,D,O*

BOSTON UNIVERSITY

Accounting	M,D,O
Actuarial Science	M
Advertising and Public Relations	M
Aerospace/Aeronautical Engineering	M,D*
African Studies	M,O
African-American Studies	M
Allied Health—General	M,D
Allopathic Medicine	P
American Studies	D
Anatomy	M,D
Anthropology	M,D
Archaeology	M,D
Art Education	M
Art History	M,D,O
Art/Fine Arts	M
Arts Administration	M*
Astronomy	M,D
Biochemistry	M,D*
Bioinformatics	M,D*
Biological and Biomedical Sciences—General	M,D*
Biomedical Engineering	M,D*
Biophysics	M,D*
Biopsychology	M
Biostatistics	M,D
Business Administration and Management—General	M
Cell Biology	M,D*
Chemistry	M,D
City and Regional Planning	M
Classics	M,D
Clinical Research	M
Cognitive Sciences	M,D
Communication Disorders	M,D,O
Communication—General	M*
Computer Engineering	M,D
Computer Science	M,D
Counseling Psychology	M,D
Counselor Education	M,O
Criminal Justice and Criminology	M
Curriculum and Instruction	M,D,O
Dental Hygiene	P,M,D,O
Dentistry	P
Early Childhood Education	M,D,O
Economics	M,D
Education—General	M,D,O*
Educational Administration	M,O
Educational Media/Instructional Technology	M,D,O
Electrical Engineering	M,D*
Electronic Commerce	M
Elementary Education	M
Energy Management and Policy	M
Engineering and Applied Sciences—General	M,D*
English as a Second Language	M,O
English Education	M,D,O
English	M,D
Environmental and Occupational Health	M,D
Environmental Management and Policy	M,O
Epidemiology	M,D
Film, Television, and Video Production	M
Film, Television, and Video Theory and Criticism	M
Finance and Banking	P,M,D,O
Foreign Languages Education	M
French	M,D
Geographic Information Systems	M
Geography	M,D
Geosciences	M,D
Graphic Design	M
Health Education	M,O
Health Promotion	M
Health Services Management and Hospital Administration	M
Historic Preservation	M
History	M,D
Human Development	M,D,O
Human Resources Management	M,O
Immunology	D*
Industrial and Manufacturing Management	M,D,O
Interdisciplinary Studies	M,D
International Affairs	M,O
International and Comparative Education	M
International Business	M*
International Health	M,O
Investment Management	M
Journalism	M
Kinesiology and Movement Studies	M,D,O
Law	P,M
Legal and Justice Studies	M
Leisure Studies	M
Liberal Studies	M
Linguistics	M,D
Management Information Systems	M,D*
Management of Technology	M
Manufacturing Engineering	M,D*
Marketing	M,D,O
Mass Communication	M
Maternal and Child Health	M,O
Mathematical and Computational Finance	M,D
Mathematics Education	M,D,O
Mathematics	M,D
Mechanical Engineering	M,D
Media Studies	M
Microbiology	M,D*
Molecular Biology	M,D*
Molecular Medicine	D*
Multilingual and Multicultural Education	M,O
Museum Studies	M,D,O
Music Education	M,D
Music	M,D,O*
Neurobiology	M,D
Neuroscience	M,D*
Nonprofit Management	M,D,O*
Nurse Midwifery	M,O
Nutrition	P,M,D,O
Occupational Therapy	M,D,O
Oral and Dental Sciences	M,D*
Organizational Behavior	M,D,O
Pathology	D
Pharmacology	M,D*
Philosophy	M,D
Physical Education	M,D,O
Physical Therapy	M,D
Physics	M,D*
Physiology	M,D
Political Science	M,D
Psychology—General	M,D
Public Health—General	P,M,D,O*
Public Policy and Administration	M,D,O
Reading Education	M,D,O
Rehabilitation Counseling	M,D,O
Rehabilitation Sciences	M,D
Religion	M,D
Science Education	M,D,O
Social Sciences Education	M,D,O
Social Work	M,D*
Sociology	M,D
Spanish	M,D
Special Education	M,D,O
Systems Engineering	M,D
Taxation	P,M
Telecommunications	M
Theater	M,O
Theology	P,M,D
Urban Studies	M
Writing	M,D

In-depth description on page 765.

BOWIE STATE UNIVERSITY

Advanced Practice Nursing	M
Business Administration and Management—General	M
Computer Science	M
Corporate and Organizational Communication	M,O
Counseling Psychology	M
Counselor Education	M
Education—General	M
Educational Administration	M
Elementary Education	M
Human Resources Development	M
Management Information Systems	M,O
Nursing and Healthcare Administration	M
Nursing Education	M
Nursing—General	M
Public Policy and Administration	M
Reading Education	M
Secondary Education	M
Special Education	M

BOWLING GREEN STATE UNIVERSITY

Accounting	M
American Studies	M,D
Art History	M
Art/Fine Arts	M
Astronomy	M
Biological and Biomedical Sciences—General	M,D,O*
Business Administration and Management—General	M
Business Education	M,O
Chemistry	M,D*
Child and Family Studies	M,D
Clinical Psychology	M,D
Communication Disorders	M,D
Communication—General	M,D
Computer Science	M
Counselor Education	M
Criminal Justice and Criminology	M,D
Curriculum and Instruction	M
Demography and Population Studies	M,D
Developmental Psychology	M,D
Economics	M
Education—General	M,D,O
Educational Administration	M,D,O
Educational Media/Instructional Technology	M
English as a Second Language	M,D
English	M,D
Experimental Psychology	M,D
Family and Consumer Sciences-General	M
Foreign Languages Education	M
French	M
Geology	M
German	M
Higher Education	D
History	M,D
Human Development	M
Industrial and Organizational Psychology	M,D
Interdisciplinary Studies	M,D
Kinesiology and Movement Studies	M
Leisure Studies	M
Manufacturing Engineering	M
Mathematics Education	M,D,O
Mathematics	M,D,O*
Music Education	M
Music	M
Nutrition	M
Organizational Management	M
Philosophy	M,D
Physics	M
Political Science	
Psychology—General	M,D
Public Health—General	M
Public Policy and Administration	M
Reading Education	M,O
Recreation and Park Management	M
Rehabilitation Counseling	M
School Psychology	M,O
Science Education	M,D,O
Social Psychology	M,D
Sociology	M,D
Spanish	M
Special Education	M
Speech and Interpersonal Communication	M,D
Sports Management	M
Statistics	M,D,O
Student Personnel Services	M
Technical Writing	M
Theater	M,D
Vocational and Technical Education	M
Writing	M

In-depth description on page 767.

BRADLEY UNIVERSITY

Accounting	M
Art/Fine Arts	M
Biological and Biomedical Sciences—General	M
Business Administration and Management—General	M
Chemistry	M
Civil Engineering	M
Computer Science	M
Construction Engineering and Management	M
Counselor Education	M
Curriculum and Instruction	M
Education—General	M
Educational Administration	M
Electrical Engineering	M
Engineering and Applied Sciences—General	M
English	M
Human Development	M
Industrial/Management Engineering	M
Information Science	M
Liberal Studies	M
Manufacturing Engineering	M
Mechanical Engineering	M
Nursing—General	M
Photography	M
Physical Therapy	M

In-depth description on page 769.

BRANDEIS UNIVERSITY

American Studies	M,D
Anthropology	M,D
Art/Fine Arts	O
Biochemistry	M,D
Biological and Biomedical Sciences—General	M,D,O*
Biophysics	D
Business Administration and Management—General	M*
Cell Biology	M,D
Chemistry	M,D
Child and Family Studies	M
Classics	M
Cognitive Sciences	M,D
Computer Science	M,D
Developmental Biology	M,D
Developmental Psychology	M,D
Disability Studies	M
Economics	M,D*
English	M,D
Finance and Banking	M,D
Genetic Counseling	M
Genetics	M,D
Health Services Management and Hospital Administration	M
History	M,D
Human Services	M
Inorganic Chemistry	M,D
International Affairs	M,D*
International Business	M,D*
International Development	M
Jewish Studies	M,D
Mathematics	D*
Microbiology	M,D
Molecular Biology	M,D
Music	M,D,O
Near and Middle Eastern Languages	M,D
Near and Middle Eastern Studies	M,D
Neurobiology	M,D
Neuroscience	M,D
Organic Chemistry	M,D
Physical Chemistry	M,D
Physics	M,D
Political Science	M,D
Psychology—General	M,D
Public Policy and Administration	D*
Social Psychology	M,D
Sociology	M,D
Structural Biology	D
Sustainable Development	M
Theater	M
Women's Studies	M

In-depth description on page 771.

BRANDON UNIVERSITY

Counselor Education	M,O
Curriculum and Instruction	M,O
Education—General	M,O
Educational Administration	M,O
Music Education	M

- Music M
- Rural Planning and Studies M,O
- Special Education M,O

BRENAU UNIVERSITY

- Accounting M
- Advanced Practice Nursing M
- Business Administration and Management—General M
- Early Childhood Education M,O
- Education—General M,O
- Health Services Management and Hospital Administration M
- Management Strategy and Policy M
- Middle School Education M,O
- Nursing—General M
- Special Education M,O

BRESCIA UNIVERSITY

- Business Administration and Management—General M
- Curriculum and Instruction M

BRIDGEWATER STATE COLLEGE

- Accounting M
- Art Education M
- Business Administration and Management—General M
- Computer Science M
- Counselor Education M,O
- Early Childhood Education M
- Education—General M,O
- Educational Administration M,O
- Educational Media/Instructional Technology M
- Elementary Education M
- English M
- Finance and Banking M
- Health Promotion M
- Mathematics Education M
- Physical Education M
- Psychology—General M
- Public Policy and Administration M
- Reading Education M,O
- Science Education M
- Secondary Education M
- Social Sciences Education M
- Sociology M
- Special Education M

BRIERCREST BIBLICAL SEMINARY

- Business Administration and Management—General M
- Higher Education M
- Marriage and Family Therapy P,M
- Organizational Management M
- Pastoral Ministry and Counseling P,M
- Theology P

BRIGHAM YOUNG UNIVERSITY

- Accounting M
- Agricultural Sciences—General M,D
- Agronomy and Soil Sciences M
- American Studies M
- Analytical Chemistry M,D
- Animal Sciences M
- Anthropology M
- Art Education M
- Art History M
- Art/Fine Arts M
- Asian Languages M
- Asian Studies M
- Astronomy M,D
- Biochemistry M,D
- Biological and Biomedical Sciences—General M,D
- Botany M,D
- Business Administration and Management—General M
- Chemical Engineering M,D
- Chemistry M,D*
- Child and Family Studies M,D
- Civil Engineering M,D
- Clinical Psychology M,D
- Communication Disorders M
- Communication—General M
- Comparative Literature M
- Computer Science M,D
- Counseling Psychology M,D
- Counselor Education M,D
- Dance M
- Education—General M,D
- Educational Administration M,D
- Educational Media/Instructional Technology M,D
- Educational Psychology M,D
- Electrical Engineering M,D
- Elementary Education M,D
- Engineering and Applied Sciences—General M,D
- English as a Second Language M,D
- English M
- Exercise and Sports Science M,D
- Film, Television, and Video Production M
- Fish, Game, and Wildlife Management M,D
- Food Science and Technology M
- Foreign Languages Education M
- Foundations and Philosophy of Education M,D
- French M
- Geography M
- Geology M
- German M,D
- Health Promotion M,D
- History M
- Horticulture M
- Human Development M,D
- Humanities M
- Inorganic Chemistry M,D
- International Affairs M
- International Development M
- Law P,M
- Linguistics M,D
- Management Information Systems M
- Management of Technology M
- Manufacturing Engineering M
- Marriage and Family Therapy M,D
- Mass Communication M
- Mathematics M,D
- Mechanical Engineering M,D
- Microbiology M,D
- Molecular Biology M,D
- Music Education M
- Music M
- Near and Middle Eastern Languages M
- Near and Middle Eastern Studies M
- Nursing—General M*
- Nutrition M
- Organic Chemistry M,D
- Organizational Behavior M
- Physical Chemistry M,D
- Physical Education M,D
- Physics M,D
- Portuguese M
- Psychology—General M,D
- Public Policy and Administration M
- Range Science M,D
- Reading Education M,D
- Recreation and Park Management M
- Russian M
- Scandinavian Languages M
- School Psychology M,D
- Science Education M,D
- Social Work M
- Sociology M,D
- Spanish M
- Special Education M,D
- Statistics M
- Theater M
- Vocational and Technical Education M
- Zoology M,D

BROCK UNIVERSITY

- Accounting M
- Biological and Biomedical Sciences—General M
- Biotechnology M,D
- Cell Biology M
- Chemistry M,D
- Child and Family Studies M
- Cultural Studies M
- Curriculum and Instruction M
- Ecology M
- Education—General M
- Educational Administration M
- Geosciences M
- Human Development M
- International Affairs M
- Legal and Justice Studies M
- Molecular Biology M
- Philosophy M
- Physics M
- Political Science M
- Psychology—General M
- Public Policy and Administration M
- Social Psychology M
- Transpersonal and Humanistic Psychology M

BROOKLYN COLLEGE OF THE CITY UNIVERSITY OF NEW YORK

- Accounting M
- Applied Physics M,D
- Art Education M
- Art History M
- Art/Fine Arts M,D
- Biological and Biomedical Sciences—General M,D
- Chemistry M,D
- Communication Disorders M
- Community Health M
- Computer Science M,D
- Counselor Education M,O
- Early Childhood Education M
- Economics M
- Education—General M,O
- Educational Administration O
- Elementary Education M
- English Education M
- English M,D
- Environmental Education M
- Exercise and Sports Science M
- Experimental Psychology M,D
- Film, Television, and Video Production M
- Foreign Languages Education M
- French M
- Geology M,D
- Health Education M
- Health Services Management and Hospital Administration M
- History M,D
- Home Economics Education M
- Human Services M
- Industrial and Organizational Psychology M,D
- Information Science M,D
- Jewish Studies M
- Liberal Studies M
- Mathematics Education M,D
- Mathematics M,D
- Multilingual and Multicultural Education M
- Music Education M,D
- Music M,D
- Nutrition M
- Photography M,D
- Physical Education M
- Physics M,D
- Political Science M,D
- Psychology—General M,D
- Public Health—General M
- Public Policy and Administration M
- Reading Education M
- School Psychology M,O
- Science Education M
- Secondary Education M
- Social Psychology M,D
- Social Sciences Education M
- Sociology M,D
- Spanish M
- Special Education M
- Speech and Interpersonal Communication M,D
- Sports Management M
- Thanatology M
- Theater M
- Urban Studies M
- Writing M

In-depth description on page 773.

BROOKLYN LAW SCHOOL

- Law P

BROOKS INSTITUTE OF PHOTOGRAPHY

- Photography M

BROWN UNIVERSITY

- Aerospace/Aeronautical Engineering M,D
- Allopathic Medicine P
- American Studies M,D
- Anthropology M,D
- Applied Mathematics M,D*
- Archaeology M,D
- Art History M,D
- Biochemistry M,D
- Biological and Biomedical Sciences—General M,D
- Biomedical Engineering M,D
- Biostatistics M,D*
- Biotechnology M,D
- Cancer Biology/Oncology M,D
- Cell Biology M,D
- Chemical Engineering M,D
- Chemistry M,D
- Classics M,D
- Cognitive Sciences M,D
- Community Health M,D
- Comparative Literature M,D
- Computer Science M,D
- Demography and Population Studies D
- Developmental Biology M,D
- Ecology D
- Economics M,D
- Education—General M
- Electrical Engineering M,D
- Elementary Education M
- Engineering and Applied Sciences—General M,D*
- English Education M
- English M,D
- Environmental Management and Policy M
- Epidemiology M,D*
- Evolutionary Biology D
- French M,D
- Geosciences M,D
- German M,D
- Health Services Research M,D*
- Hispanic Studies M,D
- History of Science and Technology M,D
- History M,D
- Immunology M,D
- Italian M,D
- Jewish Studies M,D
- Latin American Studies M,D
- Linguistics M,D
- Materials Sciences M,D
- Mathematics M,D
- Mechanical Engineering M,D
- Mechanics M,D
- Microbiology M,D
- Molecular Biology M,D*
- Multilingual and Multicultural Education M,D
- Music M,D
- Neuroscience D*
- Pathobiology M,D*
- Pathology M,D
- Pharmacology M,D*
- Philosophy M,D
- Physics M,D
- Physiology M,D*
- Political Science M,D
- Psychology—General M,D
- Religion M,D
- Russian M,D
- Science Education M
- Secondary Education M
- Slavic Languages M,D
- Social Sciences Education M
- Sociology M,D
- Theater M
- Toxicology M,D
- Western European Studies M,D
- Writing M

BRYANT COLLEGE

- Accounting M,O
- Business Administration and Management—General M,O
- Finance and Banking M,O
- Industrial and Manufacturing Management M
- Information Science M
- Management Information Systems M,O
- Marketing M,O
- Taxation M,O

BRYN ATHYN COLLEGE OF THE NEW CHURCH

- Religion P,M
- Theology P,M

BRYN MAWR COLLEGE

- Archaeology M,D
- Art History M,D
- Biochemistry M,D
- Biological and Biomedical Sciences—General M,D
- Biopsychology D
- Chemistry M,D
- Classics M,D
- Clinical Psychology D
- Developmental Psychology D
- French M
- Geology M,D
- Mathematics M,D
- Neurobiology D
- Physics M,D
- Psychology—General D
- Russian M,D
- Social Work M,D

BUCKNELL UNIVERSITY

- Accounting M
- Animal Behavior M
- Biological and Biomedical Sciences—General M
- Business Administration and Management—General M
- Chemical Engineering M
- Chemistry M
- Civil Engineering M
- Counselor Education M
- Curriculum and Instruction M
- Education—General M
- Educational Administration M
- Educational Measurement and Evaluation M
- Electrical Engineering M
- Engineering and Applied Sciences—General M
- English M
- Mathematics M
- Mechanical Engineering M
- Psychology—General M
- Reading Education M
- School Psychology M

BUENA VISTA UNIVERSITY

- Counselor Education M

Buena Vista University (continued)
Education—General M
Educational Administration M

BUTLER UNIVERSITY
Business Administration and Management—General M
Counselor Education M
Education—General M
Educational Administration M
Elementary Education M
English M
History M
Music Education M
Music M
Pharmaceutical Sciences P,M
Pharmacy P,M
Reading Education M
Secondary Education M
Special Education M

CABRINI COLLEGE
Education—General M
Educational Media/Instructional Technology M
Organizational Management M

CALDWELL COLLEGE
Accounting M
Art Therapy M,O
Business Administration and Management—General M
Counseling Psychology M
Curriculum and Instruction M
Educational Administration M
Pastoral Ministry and Counseling M

CALIFORNIA BAPTIST UNIVERSITY
Business Administration and Management—General M
Counseling Psychology M
Curriculum and Instruction M
Education—General M
Educational Administration M
English Education M
Exercise and Sports Science M
Marriage and Family Therapy M
Multilingual and Multicultural Education M
Reading Education M
Special Education M
Vocational and Technical Education M

CALIFORNIA COLLEGE FOR HEALTH SCIENCES
Community Health M
Health Promotion M
Health Services Management and Hospital Administration M
Public Health—General M

CALIFORNIA COLLEGE OF ARTS AND CRAFTS
Applied Arts and Design—General M
Art/Fine Arts M*
Film, Television, and Video Production M
Film, Television, and Video Theory and Criticism M
Photography M
Textile Design M
Writing M

CALIFORNIA COLLEGE OF PODIATRIC MEDICINE
Podiatric Medicine P

CALIFORNIA INSTITUTE OF INTEGRAL STUDIES
Anthropology M,D
Art Therapy M,D,O
Asian Studies M,D
Clinical Psychology M,D,O
Counseling Psychology M,D,O
Health Psychology M,D,O
Humanities M,D*
Philosophy M,D
Psychology—General M,D,O*
Religion M,D
Therapies—Dance, Drama, and Music M,D,O
Women's Studies M,D

CALIFORNIA INSTITUTE OF TECHNOLOGY
Aerospace/Aeronautical Engineering M,D,O
Applied Mathematics M,D
Applied Physics M,D
Astronomy D
Biochemistry D
Bioengineering M,D
Biological and Biomedical Sciences—General D*
Biophysics D
Cell Biology D
Chemical Engineering M,D
Chemistry M,D
Civil Engineering M,D
Computational Sciences M,D
Computer Science M,D
Developmental Biology D
Economics D
Electrical Engineering M,D
Engineering and Applied Sciences—General M,D,O
Environmental Engineering M,D
Genetics D
Geochemistry M,D
Geology M,D
Geophysics M,D
Immunology D
Materials Sciences M,D
Mathematics D
Mechanical Engineering M,D,O
Mechanics M,D
Molecular Biology D
Neurobiology D
Neuroscience M,D
Physics D
Planetary and Space Sciences M,D
Political Science D
Social Sciences M,D
Systems Engineering M,D

CALIFORNIA INSTITUTE OF THE ARTS
Applied Arts and Design—General M,O
Art/Fine Arts M,O
Dance M,O
Film, Television, and Video Production M,O
Graphic Design M,O
Music M,O
Photography M,O
Theater M,O
Writing M,O*

CALIFORNIA LUTHERAN UNIVERSITY
Business Administration and Management—General M
Clinical Psychology M
Counselor Education M
Education—General M,O
Educational Administration M
Entrepreneurship M
Finance and Banking M
Health Services Management and Hospital Administration M
International Business M
Management Information Systems M
Marketing M
Marriage and Family Therapy M
Organizational Behavior M
Psychology—General M
Public Policy and Administration M
Reading Education M
Special Education M

CALIFORNIA NATIONAL UNIVERSITY FOR ADVANCED STUDIES
Business Administration and Management—General M
Engineering and Applied Sciences—General M

CALIFORNIA POLYTECHNIC STATE UNIVERSITY, SAN LUIS OBISPO
Aerospace/Aeronautical Engineering M
Agricultural Economics and Agribusiness M
Agricultural Sciences—General M
Architecture M
Biochemical Engineering M
Bioengineering M
Biological and Biomedical Sciences—General M
Biomedical Engineering M
Business Administration and Management—General M
City and Regional Planning M
Civil Engineering M
Computer Science M
Counselor Education M
Curriculum and Instruction M
Education—General M
Educational Administration M
Electrical Engineering M
Engineering and Applied Sciences—General M
Engineering Management M
English M
Environmental Engineering M
Forestry M
Industrial and Manufacturing Management M
Industrial/Management Engineering M
Kinesiology and Movement Studies M
Management of Technology M
Manufacturing Engineering M
Materials Sciences M
Mathematics M
Physical Education M
Psychology—General M
Reading Education M
Special Education M
Water Resources Engineering M

In-depth description on page 775.

CALIFORNIA STATE POLYTECHNIC UNIVERSITY, POMONA
Agricultural Sciences—General M
Animal Sciences M
Applied Mathematics M
Architecture M
Biological and Biomedical Sciences—General M
Business Administration and Management—General M
Chemistry M
City and Regional Planning M
Computer Science M
Economics M
Education—General M
Electrical Engineering M
Engineering and Applied Sciences—General M
English M
Food Science and Technology M
History M
Kinesiology and Movement Studies M
Landscape Architecture M*
Mathematics M
Nutrition M
Psychology—General M
Public Policy and Administration M

CALIFORNIA STATE UNIVERSITY, BAKERSFIELD
Anthropology M
Business Administration and Management—General M
Counseling Psychology M
Counselor Education M
Curriculum and Instruction M
Education—General M
Educational Administration M
English M
Geology M
Health Services Management and Hospital Administration M
History M
Hydrology M
Interdisciplinary Studies M
Marriage and Family Therapy M,O
Mathematics Education M
Multilingual and Multicultural Education M
Nursing—General M
Psychology—General M,O
Public Policy and Administration M
Reading Education M
Secondary Education M
Social Work M
Sociology M
Spanish M
Special Education M

CALIFORNIA STATE UNIVERSITY, CHICO
Accounting M
Anthropology M
Art/Fine Arts M
Biological and Biomedical Sciences—General M
Botany M
Business Administration and Management—General M
City and Regional Planning M
Communication Disorders M
Communication—General M
Computer Science M
Counseling Psychology M
Curriculum and Instruction M
Education—General M
Educational Administration M
Educational Media/Instructional Technology M
Electrical Engineering M
Engineering and Applied Sciences—General M
English M
Environmental Sciences M
Foreign Languages Education M
Geography M
Geosciences M
Health Services Management and Hospital Administration M
History M
Interdisciplinary Studies M
Mass Communication M
Mechanical Engineering M
Museum Studies M
Music M
Nursing—General M
Nutrition M
Physical Education M
Political Science M
Psychology—General M
Public Policy and Administration M
Reading Education M
Recreation and Park Management M
Rural Planning and Studies M
Social Sciences M
Social Work M
Special Education M
Speech and Interpersonal Communication M
Writing M

CALIFORNIA STATE UNIVERSITY, DOMINGUEZ HILLS
Biological and Biomedical Sciences—General M,O
Business Administration and Management—General M
Clinical Laboratory Sciences/Medical Technology M,O
Clinical Psychology M
Computer Education M,O
Conflict Resolution and Mediation/Peace Studies M,O
Counselor Education M
Curriculum and Instruction M
Education—General M,O
Educational Administration M
English as a Second Language M,O
English M,O
Gerontology M,O
Humanities M
Management Information Systems M
Marriage and Family Therapy M
Mathematics Education M
Multilingual and Multicultural Education M
Nursing—General M
Physical Education M
Psychology—General M
Public Policy and Administration M
Quality Management M
Rhetoric M,O
Sociology M,O
Special Education M,O

In-depth description on page 777.

CALIFORNIA STATE UNIVERSITY, FRESNO
Advanced Practice Nursing M
Agricultural Sciences—General M
Animal Sciences M
Applied Arts and Design—General M
Art/Fine Arts M
Biological and Biomedical Sciences—General M
Business Administration and Management—General M
Chemistry M
Civil Engineering M
Communication Disorders M
Computer Science M
Counselor Education M
Criminal Justice and Criminology M
Curriculum and Instruction M
Early Childhood Education M
Education—General M,D
Educational Administration M,D
Electrical Engineering M
Engineering and Applied Sciences—General M
English as a Second Language M
English M
Environmental and Occupational Health M
Exercise and Sports Science M
Family and Consumer Sciences-General M
Food Science and Technology M
Geology M
Health Promotion M
Health Services Management and Hospital Administration M
History M
Industrial/Management Engineering M
International Affairs M
Kinesiology and Movement Studies M
Linguistics M
Marine Sciences M
Marriage and Family Therapy M
Mass Communication M
Mathematics Education M
Mathematics M
Mechanical Engineering M
Music Education M

Music M
Nursing—General M
Physical Therapy M
Physics M
Plant Sciences M
Psychology—General M
Public Health—General M
Public Policy and Administration M
Reading Education M
Rehabilitation Counseling M
Social Work M
Spanish M
Special Education M
Speech and Interpersonal Communication M
Writing M

CALIFORNIA STATE UNIVERSITY, FULLERTON

Accounting M
Advertising and Public Relations M
American Studies M
Analytical Chemistry M
Anthropology M
Applied Arts and Design—General M,O
Applied Mathematics M
Art History M,O
Art/Fine Arts M,O
Biochemistry M
Biological and Biomedical Sciences—General M
Botany M
Business Administration and Management—General M
Chemistry M
Civil Engineering M
Clinical Psychology M
Communication Disorders M
Communication—General M
Comparative Literature M
Computer Science M
Counselor Education M
Dance M
Economics M
Education—General M
Educational Administration M
Electrical Engineering M
Elementary Education M
Engineering and Applied Sciences—General M
English as a Second Language M
English M
Environmental Education M
Environmental Management and Policy M
Environmental Sciences M
Film, Television, and Video Production M
Finance and Banking M
French M
Geochemistry M
Geography M
Geology M
German M
Gerontology M
History M
Information Science M
Inorganic Chemistry M
Interdisciplinary Studies M
International Business M
Journalism M
Linguistics M
Management Information Systems M
Marketing M
Mathematics Education M
Mathematics M
Mechanical Engineering M
Mechanics M
Media Studies M
Microbiology M
Multilingual and Multicultural Education M
Museum Studies M,O
Music Education M
Music M
Nursing—General M
Operations Research M
Organic Chemistry M
Photography M,O
Physical Chemistry M
Physical Education M
Physics M
Political Science M
Psychology—General M
Public Policy and Administration M
Reading Education M
Science Education M
Social Psychology M
Social Sciences M
Sociology M
Spanish M
Special Education M
Speech and Interpersonal Communication M
Statistics M
Systems Engineering M
Taxation M
Theater M

CALIFORNIA STATE UNIVERSITY, HAYWARD

Accounting M
Anthropology M
Biochemistry M
Biological and Biomedical Sciences—General M
Business Administration and Management—General M
Chemistry M
Communication Disorders M
Computer Science M
Counselor Education M
Economics M
Education—General M
Educational Administration M
Electronic Commerce M
English M
Entrepreneurship M
Finance and Banking M
Geography M
Geology M
History M
Human Resources Management M
Interdisciplinary Studies M,O
International Business M
Logistics M
Management Information Systems M
Marine Sciences M
Marketing M
Mathematics M
Music M
Operations Research M
Physical Education M
Public Policy and Administration M
Quantitative Analysis M
Sociology M
Special Education M
Speech and Interpersonal Communication M
Statistics M
Taxation M

Announcement on page 287.

CALIFORNIA STATE UNIVERSITY, LONG BEACH

Aerospace/Aeronautical Engineering M
Anthropology M
Applied Mathematics M
Art Education M
Art History M
Art/Fine Arts M
Asian Studies M,O
Asian-American Studies M,O
Biochemistry M
Biological and Biomedical Sciences—General M
Business Administration and Management—General M
Chemistry M
Civil Engineering M,O
Clinical Laboratory Sciences/Medical Technology M
Communication Disorders M
Communication—General M
Computer Engineering M
Computer Science M
Counselor Education M,O
Criminal Justice and Criminology M
Dance M
Economics M
Education—General M,O
Educational Administration M
Educational Psychology M
Electrical Engineering M
Elementary Education M
Engineering and Applied Sciences—General M,D,O
English M
Epidemiology M
Family and Consumer Sciences-General M
Foundations and Philosophy of Education M
French M
Geography M
Geology M
German M
Gerontology M
Health Education M
Health Services Management and Hospital Administration M,O
History M
Illustration M
Interdisciplinary Studies M
Kinesiology and Movement Studies M
Leisure Studies M
Linguistics M
Mathematics M
Mechanical Engineering M
Microbiology M
Music M
Nurse Anesthesia M
Nursing—General M
Nutrition M
Philosophy M
Physical Education M
Physical Therapy M
Physics M
Political Science M
Psychology—General M
Public Policy and Administration M,O
Recreation and Park Management M
Secondary Education M
Social Work M
Spanish M
Special Education M
Theater M
Vocational and Technical Education M
Writing M

CALIFORNIA STATE UNIVERSITY, LOS ANGELES

Accounting M
Adult Education M
Analytical Chemistry M
Anthropology M
Applied Arts and Design—General M
Applied Mathematics M
Art Education M
Art History M
Art Therapy M
Art/Fine Arts M
Biochemistry M
Biological and Biomedical Sciences—General M
Business Administration and Management—General M
Chemistry M
Child and Family Studies M
Civil Engineering M
Communication Disorders M
Communication—General M
Computer Education M
Counselor Education M
Criminal Justice and Criminology M
Economics M
Education of the Gifted M,D
Education—General M,D
Educational Administration M
Educational Media/Instructional Technology M
Electrical Engineering M
Elementary Education M
Engineering and Applied Sciences—General M
English as a Second Language M
English M
Family and Consumer Sciences-General M
Finance and Banking M
Foundations and Philosophy of Education M
French M
Geography M
Geology M
Graphic Design M
Health Education M
Health Services Management and Hospital Administration M
Hispanic Studies M
History M
Inorganic Chemistry M
Interdisciplinary Studies M
International Business M
Latin American Studies M
Management Information Systems M
Marketing M
Mathematics M
Mechanical Engineering M
Microbiology M
Multilingual and Multicultural Education M,D
Music Education M
Music M
Nursing—General M
Nutrition M
Organic Chemistry M
Philosophy M
Photography M
Physical Chemistry M
Physical Education M
Physics M
Political Science M
Psychology—General M
Public Policy and Administration M
Reading Education M
Rehabilitation Counseling M
School Psychology M
Secondary Education M
Social Work M
Sociology M
Spanish M
Special Education M,D
Speech and Interpersonal Communication M
Taxation M
Technology and Public Policy M
Textile Design M
Theater M

CALIFORNIA STATE UNIVERSITY, MONTEREY BAY

Education—General
Interdisciplinary Studies
Marine Sciences

CALIFORNIA STATE UNIVERSITY, NORTHRIDGE

Aerospace/Aeronautical Engineering M
Anthropology M
Art History M
Art/Fine Arts M
Biological and Biomedical Sciences—General M
Biomedical Engineering M
Business Administration and Management—General M
Business Education M
Chemistry M
Civil Engineering M
Communication Disorders M
Communication—General M
Computer Engineering M
Computer Science M
Counselor Education M,O
Education of the Gifted M
Education—General M,O
Educational Administration M
Educational Psychology M,O
Electrical Engineering M
Elementary Education M
Engineering and Applied Sciences—General M
Engineering Management M
English M
Environmental and Occupational Health M
Finance and Banking M
Foundations and Philosophy of Education M
Genetic Counseling M,O
Geography M
Geology M
Health Education M
Health Services Management and Hospital Administration M
Hispanic Studies M
History M
Industrial/Management Engineering M
Insurance M
Interdisciplinary Studies M
Journalism M
Kinesiology and Movement Studies M
Leisure Studies M
Linguistics M
Management Information Systems M
Marketing M
Marriage and Family Therapy M,O
Mass Communication M
Materials Engineering M
Mathematics M
Mechanical Engineering M
Mechanics M
Music Education M
Music M
Physical Therapy M
Physics M
Political Science M
Psychology—General M
Public Health—General M
Public Policy and Administration M
Real Estate M
Recreation and Park Management M
Secondary Education M
Sociology M
Spanish M
Special Education M
Speech and Interpersonal Communication M
Structural Engineering M
Theater M

CALIFORNIA STATE UNIVERSITY, SACRAMENTO

Accounting M

California State University, Sacramento (continued)

Anthropology M
Art/Fine Arts M
Biological and Biomedical Sciences—General M
Business Administration and Management—General M
Chemistry M
Civil Engineering M
Communication Disorders M
Communication—General M
Computer Science M
Counseling Psychology M
Counselor Education M
Criminal Justice and Criminology M
Curriculum and Instruction M
Dance M
Early Childhood Education M
Education—General M
Educational Administration M
Electrical Engineering M
Engineering and Applied Sciences—General M
English as a Second Language M
English M
French M
German M
Human Resources Development M
Human Resources Management M
Human Services M
Interdisciplinary Studies M
International Affairs M
Management Information Systems M
Marine Sciences M
Mathematics M
Mechanical Engineering M
Multilingual and Multicultural Education M
Music M
Nursing—General M
Physical Education M
Political Science M
Psychology—General M
Public History M
Public Policy and Administration M
Reading Education M
Real Estate M
Recreation and Park Management M
School Psychology M
Social Work M
Sociology M
Software Engineering M
Spanish M
Special Education M
Statistics M
Theater M
Vocational and Technical Education M
Writing M

CALIFORNIA STATE UNIVERSITY, SAN BERNARDINO

Art/Fine Arts M
Biological and Biomedical Sciences—General M
Business Administration and Management—General M
Clinical Psychology M
Communication—General M
Computer Science M
Counseling Psychology M
Counselor Education M
Criminal Justice and Criminology M
Developmental Psychology M
Education—General M
Educational Administration M
Educational Media/Instructional Technology M
Educational Psychology M
Elementary Education M
English as a Second Language M
English Education M
English M
Environmental Education M
Experimental Psychology M
Health Services Management and Hospital Administration M
Industrial and Organizational Psychology M
Interdisciplinary Studies M
Mathematics M
Military and Defense Studies M
Multilingual and Multicultural Education M
Nursing—General M
Psychology—General M
Public Policy and Administration M
Reading Education M
Rehabilitation Counseling M
Science Education M
Secondary Education M
Social Sciences Education M
Social Sciences M
Social Work M
Special Education M
Vocational and Technical Education M

CALIFORNIA STATE UNIVERSITY, SAN MARCOS

Biological and Biomedical Sciences—General M
Business Administration and Management—General M
Computer Science M
Education—General M
English M
Mathematics M
Psychology—General M
Sociology M
Spanish M
Writing M

CALIFORNIA STATE UNIVERSITY, STANISLAUS

Business Administration and Management—General M
Counseling Psychology M
Counselor Education M
Criminal Justice and Criminology M
Curriculum and Instruction M
Education—General M
Educational Administration M
Educational Media/Instructional Technology M
Elementary Education M
English as a Second Language M
English M
History M
Interdisciplinary Studies M
International Affairs M
Marine Biology M
Multilingual and Multicultural Education M
Physical Education M
Psychology—General M
Public Policy and Administration M
Reading Education M
Secondary Education M
Social Sciences Education M
Social Work M
Special Education M

CALIFORNIA UNIVERSITY OF PENNSYLVANIA

Biological and Biomedical Sciences—General M
Business Administration and Management—General M
Communication Disorders M
Communication—General M
Computer Education M
Counselor Education M
Education—General M
Educational Administration M
Elementary Education M
Exercise and Sports Science M
Geography M
Geosciences M
Mathematics Education M
Reading Education M
School Psychology M
Science Education M
Social Sciences M
Social Work M
Special Education M
Vocational and Technical Education M

CALIFORNIA WESTERN SCHOOL OF LAW

Law P,M

CALVARY BIBLE COLLEGE AND THEOLOGICAL SEMINARY

Pastoral Ministry and Counseling P,M,D
Theology P,M,D

CALVIN COLLEGE

Curriculum and Instruction M
Education—General M
Special Education M

CALVIN THEOLOGICAL SEMINARY

Missions and Missiology P,M,D
Religious Education P,M,D
Theology P,M,D

CAMBRIDGE COLLEGE

Business Administration and Management—General M
Counseling Psychology M
Education—General M
Electronic Commerce M

In-depth description on page 779.

CAMERON UNIVERSITY

Business Administration and Management—General M
Education—General M
Psychology—General M

CAMPBELLSVILLE UNIVERSITY

Business Administration and Management—General M
Education—General M
Music Education M
Music M
Social Sciences M
Theology M

CAMPBELL UNIVERSITY

Business Administration and Management—General M
Counselor Education M
Education—General M
Educational Administration M
Elementary Education M
English Education M
Law P
Mathematics Education M
Middle School Education M
Pharmaceutical Sciences P,M
Pharmacy P,M
Physical Education M
Religious Education P,M
Secondary Education M
Social Sciences Education M
Theology P,M

CANADIAN COLLEGE OF NATUROPATHIC MEDICINE

Naturopathic Medicine D

CANADIAN MEMORIAL CHIROPRACTIC COLLEGE

Chiropractic P,O*

CANADIAN THEOLOGICAL SEMINARY

Missions and Missiology P,M,O
Pastoral Ministry and Counseling P,M,O
Religion P,M,O
Religious Education P,M,O
Theology P,M,O

CANISIUS COLLEGE

Accounting M
Business Administration and Management—General M
Corporate and Organizational Communication M
Counselor Education M,O
Education—General M,O
Educational Administration M,O
Physical Education M
Reading Education M
Secondary Education M
Special Education M
Sports Management M
Student Personnel Services M
Telecommunications Management M

CAPELLA UNIVERSITY

Applied Science and Technology M
Business Administration and Management—General M,D
Education—General M,D
Human Services M,D
Information Science M
Organizational Management M,D
Psychology—General M,D

CAPITAL BIBLE SEMINARY

Theology P,M

CAPITAL UNIVERSITY

Business Administration and Management—General M
Community Health Nursing M
Law P,M
Legal and Justice Studies M
Nursing and Healthcare Administration M
Nursing—General M
Occupational Health Nursing M
School Nursing M
Taxation M
Transcultural Nursing M

CAPITOL COLLEGE

Computer Science M
Electrical Engineering M
Electronic Commerce M
Information Science M
Management Information Systems M
Systems Engineering M
Telecommunications Management M

CARDEAN UNIVERSITY

Business Administration and Management—General M
Finance and Banking M
Marketing M
Organizational Management M

In-depth description on page 781.

CARDINAL STRITCH UNIVERSITY

Applied Arts and Design—General M
Business Administration and Management—General M*
Clinical Psychology M
Computer Education M
Education—General M,D*
Educational Administration M,D
Finance and Banking M
Graphic Design M
Health Services Management and Hospital Administration M
Nursing—General M
Psychology—General M
Reading Education M
Religion M
Special Education M

CARLETON UNIVERSITY

Aerospace/Aeronautical Engineering M,D
Anthropology M
Architecture M
Art History M
Biological and Biomedical Sciences—General M,D
Business Administration and Management—General M,D
Canadian Studies M,D
Chemistry M,D
Civil Engineering M,D
Cognitive Sciences D
Communication—General M,D
Comparative Literature M,D
Computer Science M,D
East European and Russian Studies M
Economics M,D
Electrical Engineering M,D
Engineering and Applied Sciences—General M,D
English M
Environmental Engineering M,D
Environmental Management and Policy M,D
Film, Television, and Video Production M
French M
Geography M,D
Geosciences M,D
History M,D
Information Science M
International Affairs M
Journalism M,D
Legal and Justice Studies M
Linguistics M
Materials Engineering M,D
Mathematics M,D
Mechanical Engineering M,D
Neuroscience M,D
Philosophy M
Physics M,D
Political Science M,D
Psychology—General M,D
Public Policy and Administration M,D
Social Work M
Sociology M,D
Systems Engineering M
Systems Science M
Telecommunications Management M

CARLOS ALBIZU UNIVERSITY

Clinical Psychology M,D
Industrial and Organizational Psychology M,D
Psychology—General M,D

CARLOS ALBIZU UNIVERSITY, MIAMI CAMPUS

Business Administration and Management—General M,D
Clinical Psychology M,D
Counseling Psychology M,D
Industrial and Organizational Psychology M,D
Marriage and Family Therapy M,D
Psychology—General M,D
School Psychology M,D

CARLOW COLLEGE
Advanced Practice Nursing M,O
Art Education M
Early Childhood Education M
Education—General M
Educational Administration M
Health Services Management and Hospital Administration M
Human Resources Development M
Management of Technology M
Nonprofit Management M
Nursing and Healthcare Administration M,O
Nursing—General M,O

CARNEGIE MELLON UNIVERSITY
Accounting D
Advertising and Public Relations M
Applied Arts and Design—General M,D
Applied Physics M,D
Architecture M,D*
Art/Fine Arts M
Artificial Intelligence/Robotics M,D*
Arts Administration M
Biochemistry M,D
Bioengineering M,D
Biological and Biomedical Sciences—General M,D*
Biomedical Engineering M,D*
Biophysics M,D
Biopsychology D
Building Science M,D
Business Administration and Management—General M,D
Cell Biology M,D
Chemical Engineering M,D
Chemistry M,D*
Civil Engineering M,D*
Cognitive Sciences D
Communication—General M
Comparative Literature M,D
Computational Sciences M,D
Computer Art and Design M,D
Computer Engineering M,D*
Computer Science M,D*
Corporate and Organizational Communication M
Developmental Biology M,D
Developmental Psychology D
Economics M,D
Education—General M,D
Electrical Engineering M,D
Electronic Commerce M*
Engineering and Applied Sciences—General M,D
English M,D*
Environmental Engineering M,D
Film, Television, and Video Production M
Finance and Banking D
Genetics M,D
Health Services Management and Hospital Administration M
History M,D*
Human-Computer Interaction M,D
Industrial and Manufacturing Management M,D
Information Science M,D*
Linguistics M,D
Management Information Systems M,D
Management of Technology M,D
Marketing D
Materials Engineering M,D
Materials Sciences M,D*
Mathematical and Computational Finance M,D
Mathematics M,D*
Mechanical Engineering M,D
Media Studies M
Molecular Biology M,D
Music Education M
Music M
Neurobiology M,D
Neuroscience *
Operations Research D
Organizational Behavior D
Organizational Management D
Philosophy M,D
Physics M,D*
Polymer Science and Engineering M,D
Project Management M,D
Psychology—General D*
Public Policy and Administration M,D
Rhetoric M
Social Psychology D
Social Sciences D
Software Engineering M,D*
Statistics M,D*
Sustainable Development M
Technical Writing M
Technology and Public Policy M,D*
Theater M
Writing M*

CARROLL COLLEGE
Education—General M
Physical Therapy M
Software Engineering M

CARSON-NEWMAN COLLEGE
Advanced Practice Nursing M
Counselor Education M
Curriculum and Instruction M
Education—General M
Elementary Education M
English as a Second Language M
Nursing—General M
Secondary Education M

CARTHAGE COLLEGE
Art Education M,O
Counselor Education M,O
Education of the Gifted M,O
Education—General M,O
Educational Administration M,O
English Education M,O
Reading Education M,O
Science Education M,O
Social Sciences Education M,O

CASE WESTERN RESERVE UNIVERSITY
Accounting M,D
Advanced Practice Nursing M
Aerospace/Aeronautical Engineering M,D
Allopathic Medicine P
American Studies M,D
Analytical Chemistry M,D
Anatomy M,D
Anthropology M,D
Applied Mathematics M,D
Art Education M
Art History M,D
Astronomy M,D
Biochemistry M,D*
Bioengineering M,D
Bioethics M
Biological and Biomedical Sciences—General M,D*
Biomedical Engineering M,D*
Biophysics M,D
Biostatistics M,D
Business Administration and Management—General M,D,O
Cell Biology M,D
Ceramic Sciences and Engineering M,D
Chemical Engineering M,D
Chemistry M,D
Civil Engineering M,D
Clinical Psychology D
Communication Disorders M,D,O
Community Health Nursing M
Comparative Literature M,D
Computer Engineering M,D
Computer Science M,D
Dance M,D
Dentistry P
Developmental Biology M,D
Economics M
Electrical Engineering M,D
Engineering and Applied Sciences—General M,D*
English M,D*
Epidemiology M,D
Exercise and Sports Science M,D
Experimental Psychology D
Finance and Banking M,D
French M,D
Genetic Counseling M,D
Genetics D*
Genomic Sciences D*
Geology M,D
Geosciences M,D
Gerontological Nursing M
Gerontology M,D,O
History M,D
Human Genetics D
Human Resources Management M,D
Immunology M,D
Industrial and Labor Relations M,D
Industrial and Manufacturing Management M,D
Information Science M,D
Inorganic Chemistry M,D
Law P,M
Legal and Justice Studies P,M
Logistics M,D
Management Information Systems M,D*
Management Strategy and Policy M,D
Marketing M,D
Materials Engineering M,D
Materials Sciences M,D
Mathematics M,D
Mechanical Engineering M,D
Mechanics M,D
Medical/Surgical Nursing M
Microbiology D
Molecular Biology M,D*
Museum Studies M,D
Music Education M,D
Music M,D
Neurobiology D*
Neuroscience D*
Nonprofit Management M,O*
Nurse Anesthesia M
Nurse Midwifery M
Nursing—General M,D*
Nutrition M,D*
Oncology Nursing M
Operations Research M,D*
Oral and Dental Sciences M,O
Organic Chemistry M,D
Organizational Behavior M,D
Pathology M,D*
Pediatric Nursing M
Pharmacology M,D*
Physical Chemistry M,D
Physics M,D
Physiology M,D*
Political Science M,D
Polymer Science and Engineering M,D*
Psychiatric Nursing M
Psychology—General D
Public Health—General M
Quality Management M,D
Social Work M,D,O*
Sociology D*
Statistics M,D
Systems Engineering M,D
Taxation P,M
Theater M,D
Toxicology M,D*
Women's Health Nursing M

In-depth description on page 783.

CASTLETON STATE COLLEGE
Curriculum and Instruction M
Education—General M,O
Educational Administration M,O
Forensic Psychology M
Psychology—General M
Reading Education M,O
Special Education M,O

CATAWBA COLLEGE
Education—General M
Elementary Education M

THE CATHOLIC DISTANCE UNIVERSITY
Theology M

CATHOLIC THEOLOGICAL UNION AT CHICAGO
Missions and Missiology P,M,D,O
Pastoral Ministry and Counseling P,M,D,O
Theology P,M,D,O

THE CATHOLIC UNIVERSITY OF AMERICA
Accounting M
Acoustics M,D
Advanced Practice Nursing M,D
Anthropology M,D
Architecture M
Artificial Intelligence/Robotics M,D
Biological and Biomedical Sciences—General M,D
Biomedical Engineering M,D
Business Administration and Management—General M
Cell Biology M,D
Chemistry M,D
City and Regional Planning M
Civil Engineering M,D
Classics M,D
Clinical Laboratory Sciences/Medical Technology M,D
Clinical Psychology D
Comparative Literature M,D
Computer Science M,D
Construction Engineering and Management M
Counselor Education M,D
Curriculum and Instruction M,D
Economics M
Education—General M,D
Educational Administration M,D
Educational Psychology M,D
Electrical Engineering M,D
Engineering and Applied Sciences—General M,D*
Engineering Design M,D
Engineering Management M
English as a Second Language M,D
English M,D
Environmental Engineering M
Ergonomics and Human Factors M
Experimental Psychology M,D
Finance and Banking M
French M,D
Geotechnical Engineering M,D
German M
Gerontological Nursing M,D
History M,D
Human Development D
Human Resources Management M
Information Studies M
International Affairs M
Italian M
Law P
Legal and Justice Studies D,O
Library Science M
Mechanical Engineering M,D
Mechanics M,D
Medical/Surgical Nursing M,D
Medieval and Renaissance Studies M,D,O
Microbiology M,D
Music Education M,D
Music M,D
Near and Middle Eastern Languages M,D
Nursing and Healthcare Administration M,D
Nursing Education M,D
Nursing—General M,D
Pediatric Nursing M,D
Philosophy M,D,O
Physics M,D
Political Science M,D
Psychiatric Nursing M,D
Psychology—General M,D
Religion M,D,O
Religious Education M,D
Rhetoric M,D
Romance Languages M,D
Social Work M,D
Sociology M,D
Spanish M,D
Structural Engineering M,D
Theater M
Theology P,M,D,O
Western European Studies M

In-depth description on page 785.

CEDARVILLE UNIVERSITY
Business Administration and Management—General M

CENTENARY COLLEGE
Accounting M
Business Administration and Management—General M
Counseling Psychology M
Education—General M
Educational Administration M
Special Education M

CENTENARY COLLEGE OF LOUISIANA
Business Administration and Management—General M
Curriculum and Instruction M
Education—General M
Educational Administration M
Elementary Education M
Secondary Education M

CENTER FOR HUMANISTIC STUDIES
Clinical Psychology M,D
Educational Psychology M,D
Psychology—General M,D*
Transpersonal and Humanistic Psychology M,D

CENTRAL BAPTIST THEOLOGICAL SEMINARY
Theology P,M,O

CENTRAL CONNECTICUT STATE UNIVERSITY
Actuarial Science M
Art Education M
Biological and Biomedical Sciences—General M,O*
Business Administration and Management—General M
Business Education M
Cell Biology M,O
Chemistry M
Communication—General M
Computer Science M
Construction Engineering and Management M
Corporate and Organizational Communication M
Counselor Education M
Criminal Justice and Criminology M
Early Childhood Education M
Education—General M,D,O
Educational Administration M,D,O
Educational Media/Instructional Technology M,D,O

Central Connecticut State University (continued)

Elementary Education M
Engineering and Applied Sciences—General M
English as a Second Language M
English M
Exercise and Sports Science M
Foundations and Philosophy of Education M
French M
Geography M
Geosciences M
History M
Information Studies M
International Affairs M
International Business M
Management of Technology M
Marriage and Family Therapy M
Mathematics M
Molecular Biology M,O
Music Education M
Physical Education M
Physics M
Psychology—General M
Reading Education M,O
Rehabilitation Counseling M
School Psychology M
Science Education M
Secondary Education M
Social Psychology M
Social Sciences M
Spanish M
Special Education M
Statistics M
Vocational and Technical Education M

In-depth description on page 787.

CENTRAL METHODIST COLLEGE

Education—General M

CENTRAL MICHIGAN UNIVERSITY

Accounting M
Art/Fine Arts M
Biological and Biomedical Sciences—General M
Business Administration and Management—General M
Business Education M
Chemistry M
Child and Family Studies M
Clinical Psychology D
Communication Disorders M,D
Communication—General M
Computer Science M
Conservation Biology M
Corporate and Organizational Communication M
Counselor Education M
Criminal Justice and Criminology M
Early Childhood Education M
Economics M
Education—General M,D,O
Educational Administration M,D,O
Educational Media/Instructional Technology M
Elementary Education M
English as a Second Language M
English M
Exercise and Sports Science M
Experimental Psychology M,D
Family and Consumer Sciences-General M
Film, Television, and Video Production M
Finance and Banking M
Health Promotion M
Health Services Management and Hospital Administration M,D,O
History M,D
Hospitality Management M,O
Human Development M
Human Resources Management M,O
Humanities M
Industrial and Manufacturing Management M
Industrial and Organizational Psychology M,D
International Affairs M,O
International Business M
Leisure Studies M
Management Information Systems M,O
Marketing M
Mass Communication M
Mathematics M,D
Media Studies M
Middle School Education M
Music Education M
Music M
Nutrition M
Physical Education M
Physical Therapy M
Physician Assistant Studies M
Physics M
Political Science M
Psychology—General M,D,O
Public Policy and Administration M,O
Reading Education M
Recreation and Park Management M
School Psychology D,O
Science Education M
Secondary Education M
Sociology M
Software Engineering M,O
Spanish M
Special Education M
Speech and Interpersonal Communication M
Sports Management M
Theater M
Travel and Tourism M,O
Vocational and Technical Education M
Writing M

In-depth description on page 789.

CENTRAL MISSOURI STATE UNIVERSITY

Accounting M
Adult Education M,O
Applied Mathematics M
Aviation M
Biological and Biomedical Sciences—General M
Business Administration and Management—General M
Communication Disorders M
Communication—General M
Counselor Education M,O
Criminal Justice and Criminology M,O
Curriculum and Instruction M,O
Economics M
Education—General M,O
Educational Administration M,O
Educational Media/Instructional Technology M
Elementary Education M,O
Engineering and Applied Sciences—General M,O
English as a Second Language M
English Education M
English M
Environmental and Occupational Health M,O
Exercise and Sports Science M
Gerontology M
History M
Industrial and Manufacturing Management M
Industrial Hygiene M,O
Industrial/Management Engineering M,O
Information Studies M,O
Library Science M,O
Management Information Systems M
Mathematics M
Music M
Nursing—General M
Physical Education M
Psychology—General M,O
Public Policy and Administration M,O
Reading Education M,O
Safety Engineering M,O
Secondary Education M,O
Social Sciences Education M
Sociology M
Special Education M,O
Speech and Interpersonal Communication M
Student Personnel Services M,O
Theater M
Transportation Management M,O
Vocational and Technical Education M,O

In-depth description on page 791.

CENTRAL STATE UNIVERSITY

Education—General M
Educational Administration M
Educational Media/Instructional Technology M
Reading Education M

CENTRAL WASHINGTON UNIVERSITY

Art/Fine Arts M
Biological and Biomedical Sciences—General M
Business Administration and Management—General M
Business Education M
Chemistry M
Child and Family Studies M
Counseling Psychology M
Counselor Education M
Curriculum and Instruction M
Education—General M
Educational Administration M
Elementary Education M
Engineering and Applied Sciences—General M
English as a Second Language M
English M
Environmental Management and Policy M
Experimental Psychology M
Family and Consumer Sciences-General M
Geology M
Health Education M
History M
Home Economics Education M
Industrial and Organizational Psychology M
Industrial/Management Engineering M
Information Science M
Interdisciplinary Studies M
Mathematics M
Music M
Nutrition M
Physical Education M
Psychology—General M
Reading Education M
Recreation and Park Management M
School Psychology M
Special Education M
Textile Design M
Theater M

In-depth description on page 793 and announcement on page 300.

CENTRAL YESHIVA TOMCHEI TMIMIM-LUBAVITCH

Theology

CENTRO DE ESTUDIOS AVANZADOS DE PUERTO RICO Y EL CARIBE

Latin American Studies M,D

CHADRON STATE COLLEGE

Business Administration and Management—General M
Business Education M,O
Counselor Education M,O
Education—General M,O
Educational Administration M,O
Elementary Education M,O
English Education M,O
Secondary Education M,O
Social Sciences Education M,O

CHAMINADE UNIVERSITY OF HONOLULU

Business Administration and Management—General M*
Conflict Resolution and Mediation/Peace Studies M
Counseling Psychology M
Criminal Justice and Criminology M*
Education—General M
Pastoral Ministry and Counseling M
Public Policy and Administration M
Social Sciences Education M

CHAMPLAIN COLLEGE

Management of Technology M*

CHAPMAN UNIVERSITY

Business Administration and Management—General M
Clinical Psychology M
Counselor Education M
Curriculum and Instruction M
Education—General M,O
Educational Administration M
Educational Psychology M,O
English Education M
English M
Film, Television, and Video Production M
Film, Television, and Video Theory and Criticism M
Food Science and Technology M
Human Resources Development M
Human Resources Management M
Internet and Interactive Multimedia M
Law P*
Marriage and Family Therapy M
Nutrition M
Physical Therapy D
Psychology—General M
Reading Education M
Special Education M
Writing M

In-depth description on page 795.

CHARLES R. DREW UNIVERSITY OF MEDICINE AND SCIENCE

Allopathic Medicine P

CHARLESTON SOUTHERN UNIVERSITY

Accounting M
Business Administration and Management—General M
Criminal Justice and Criminology M
Education—General M
Educational Administration M
Elementary Education M
English Education M
Finance and Banking M
Health Services Management and Hospital Administration M
Management Information Systems M
Organizational Management M
Science Education M
Secondary Education M
Social Sciences Education M

CHATHAM COLLEGE

Allied Health—General M
Biological and Biomedical Sciences—General M
Business Administration and Management—General M
Communication—General M
Computational Sciences M
Counseling Psychology M
Education—General M
Elementary Education M
English Education M
Environmental Education M
Landscape Architecture M
Liberal Studies M
Mathematics Education M
Occupational Therapy M
Physical Therapy M,D
Physician Assistant Studies M
Science Education M
Secondary Education M
Social Sciences Education M
Special Education M
Writing M

CHESTNUT HILL COLLEGE

Clinical Psychology M,D
Counseling Psychology M,D
Early Childhood Education M
Education—General M
Educational Administration M
Educational Media/Instructional Technology M
Elementary Education M
Human Services M,D
Psychology—General M,D
Religion M

In-depth description on page 797.

CHEYNEY UNIVERSITY OF PENNSYLVANIA

Adult Education M
Early Childhood Education O
Education—General M,O
Educational Administration M,O
Elementary Education M
Special Education M

CHICAGO SCHOOL OF PROFESSIONAL PSYCHOLOGY

Clinical Psychology M,D
Forensic Psychology M,D
Industrial and Organizational Psychology M,D
Psychology—General M,D*

CHICAGO STATE UNIVERSITY

Biological and Biomedical Sciences—General M
Computer Science M
Counselor Education M
Criminal Justice and Criminology M
Early Childhood Education M
Education—General M
Educational Administration M
Educational Media/Instructional Technology M
Elementary Education M
English M
Geography M
History M
Library Science M
Mathematics M
Multilingual and Multicultural Education M
Physical Education M
Reading Education M
Secondary Education M
Social Work M
Special Education M
Vocational and Technical Education M

CHICAGO THEOLOGICAL SEMINARY

Jewish Studies P,M,D
Pastoral Ministry and Counseling P,M,D
Religious Education P,M,D
Theology P,M,D

CHRISTENDOM COLLEGE

Theology M

CHRISTIAN BROTHERS UNIVERSITY

Business Administration and Management—General M
Engineering and Applied Sciences—General M
Liberal Studies M

CHRISTIAN THEOLOGICAL SEMINARY

Marriage and Family Therapy P,M,D
Music P,M,D
Pastoral Ministry and Counseling P,M,D
Religious Education P,M,D
Theology P,M,D

CHRISTOPHER NEWPORT UNIVERSITY

Applied Physics M
Computer Science M
Education—General M
English Education M
Environmental Sciences M
History M
Industrial and Organizational Psychology M
Mathematics Education M
Psychology—General M
Public Policy and Administration M
Science Education M

In-depth description on page 799.

CHRIST THE KING SEMINARY

Pastoral Ministry and Counseling P,M
Theology P,M

CHURCH DIVINITY SCHOOL OF THE PACIFIC

Theology P,M,D,O

CHURCH OF GOD THEOLOGICAL SEMINARY

Missions and Missiology P,M
Pastoral Ministry and Counseling P,M
Theology P,M

CINCINNATI BIBLE COLLEGE AND SEMINARY

Pastoral Ministry and Counseling M
Religion P,M
Theology P,M

THE CITADEL, THE MILITARY COLLEGE OF SOUTH CAROLINA

Business Administration and Management—General M
Counselor Education M
Education—General M,O
Educational Administration M,O
English M
Health Education M
History M
Mathematics Education M
Physical Education M
Psychology—General M
Reading Education M
School Psychology O
Science Education M
Secondary Education M
Social Sciences Education M

CITY COLLEGE OF THE CITY UNIVERSITY OF NEW YORK

Anthropology M
Architecture M,O
Art History M
Art/Fine Arts M
Atmospheric Sciences M,D
Biochemistry M,D
Biological and Biomedical Sciences—General M,D
Chemical Engineering M,D
Chemistry M,D
Civil Engineering M,D
Clinical Psychology M,D
Computer Science M,D
Early Childhood Education M
Economics M
Education—General M,O
Educational Administration M,O
Electrical Engineering M,D
Elementary Education M
Engineering and Applied Sciences—General M,D*
English M
Environmental Education M
Environmental Sciences M,D
Experimental Psychology M,D
Geosciences M,D
Graphic Design M
History M
International Affairs M
Mathematics M
Mechanical Engineering M,D
Media Studies M
Multilingual and Multicultural Education M
Museum Studies M
Music M
Physics M,D*
Psychology—General M,D
Reading Education M,O
Science Education M
Sociology M
Spanish M
Special Education M
Urban Design M
Writing M

In-depth description on page 801.

CITY OF HOPE NATIONAL MEDICAL CENTER/BECKMAN RESEARCH INSTITUTE

Biological and Biomedical Sciences—General D*

CITY UNIVERSITY

Business Administration and Management—General M,O
Computer Science M,O
Counseling Psychology M
Curriculum and Instruction M,O
Education—General M,O
Educational Administration M,O
Educational Media/Instructional Technology M,O
Electronic Commerce M,O
Finance and Banking M,O
Human Resources Management M,O
International Business M,O
Internet and Interactive Multimedia M,O
Management Information Systems M,O
Marketing M,O
Organizational Management M,O
Project Management M,O
Public Policy and Administration M,O
Reading Education M,O
School Psychology M,O

In-depth description on page 803.

CITY UNIVERSITY OF NEW YORK SCHOOL OF LAW AT QUEENS COLLEGE

Law P

CLAREMONT GRADUATE UNIVERSITY

American Studies M,D
Anthropology M,D
Applied Mathematics M,D
Art/Fine Arts M
Botany M,D
Business Administration and Management—General M,D,O*
Cognitive Sciences M,D
Computer Science M,D
Cultural Studies M,D
Developmental Psychology M,D
Economics M,D
Education—General M,D*
Educational Administration M,D
Educational Measurement and Evaluation M,D
Electronic Commerce M,D
English M,D
Ethics M,D
Film, Television, and Video Production M
Film, Television, and Video Theory and Criticism M,D
Finance and Banking M
Financial Engineering M,D,O
Higher Education M,D
History M,D
Human Development M,D
Human Resources Management M
Humanities M,D*
Industrial and Organizational Psychology M,D
Information Science M,D*
Interdisciplinary Studies M
International Affairs M,D
International and Comparative Education M,D
International Business M
Linguistics M,D
Management Information Systems M,D
Management Strategy and Policy M
Marketing M
Mathematics M,D
Music Education M,D
Music M,D
Operations Research M,D
Philosophy M,D
Photography M
Political Science M,D*
Psychology—General M,D*
Public Policy and Administration M,D
Reading Education M,D
Religion M,D
Social Psychology M,D
Statistics M,D
Theater M,D
Theology M,D
Urban Education M,D
Western European Studies M,D
Women's Studies M,D
Writing M,D

CLAREMONT SCHOOL OF THEOLOGY

Pastoral Ministry and Counseling D
Religion M,D
Theology P,M,D

CLARION UNIVERSITY OF PENNSYLVANIA

Biological and Biomedical Sciences—General M
Business Administration and Management—General M
Communication Disorders M
Communication—General M
Education—General M,O
Elementary Education M
English M
Library Science M,O
Mathematics Education M
Nursing—General M
Reading Education M
Science Education M
Special Education M

In-depth description on page 805.

CLARK ATLANTA UNIVERSITY

African-American Studies M,D
Applied Mathematics M
Biological and Biomedical Sciences—General M,D
Business Administration and Management—General M
Chemistry M,D
Computer Science M
Counselor Education M,D
Criminal Justice and Criminology M
Curriculum and Instruction M,O
Economics M
Education of the Gifted M,O
Education—General M,D,O
Educational Administration M,D,O
Educational Psychology M,D
English M
Finance and Banking M
History M
Humanities D
Information Science M
Information Studies M,O
Inorganic Chemistry M,D
International Affairs M,D
International Business M,D
International Development M,D
Library Science M,O
Marketing M
Organic Chemistry M,D
Physical Chemistry M,D
Physics M
Political Science M,D
Public Policy and Administration M
Quantitative Analysis M
Romance Languages M
Science Education M,D
Social Work M,D
Sociology M
Women's Studies M,D

CLARKE COLLEGE

Advanced Practice Nursing M,O
Business Administration and Management—General M
Early Childhood Education M
Education—General M
Educational Administration M
Educational Media/Instructional Technology M
Nursing and Healthcare Administration M,O
Nursing Education M,O
Nursing—General M,O
Physical Therapy M
Reading Education M
Special Education M

CLARKSON COLLEGE

Advanced Practice Nursing M
Nursing and Healthcare Administration M
Nursing Education M
Nursing—General M

CLARKSON UNIVERSITY

Analytical Chemistry M,D
Business Administration and Management—General M
Chemical Engineering M,D
Chemistry M,D
Civil Engineering M,D
Computer Engineering M,D
Computer Science M,D*
Electrical Engineering M,D
Engineering and Applied Sciences—General M,D*
Engineering Management M
Environmental Engineering M,D
Human Resources Management M
Industrial and Manufacturing Management M
Information Science M*
Inorganic Chemistry M,D
Interdisciplinary Studies M
Management Information Systems M
Mathematics M,D*
Mechanical Engineering M,D
Organic Chemistry M,D
Physical Chemistry M,D
Physical Therapy M
Physics M,D

CLARK UNIVERSITY

Accounting M
Biological and Biomedical Sciences—General M,D
Business Administration and Management—General M*
Chemistry M,D
City and Regional Planning M
Clinical Psychology D
Communication—General M
Developmental Psychology D
Economics D
Education—General M
English M
Environmental Management and Policy M
Finance and Banking M
Geographic Information Systems M
Geography D
Health Services Management and Hospital Administration M
History M,D,O
Holocaust Studies D
Information Science M
International Business M
International Development M
Liberal Studies M
Management Information Systems M
Marketing M
Physics M,D
Psychology—General D
Public Policy and Administration M,O
Social Psychology D
Sustainable Development M*
Women's Studies D

In-depth description on page 807.

CLEARY UNIVERSITY

Accounting M
Business Administration and Management—General M

CLEMSON UNIVERSITY

Accounting M
Agricultural Economics and Agribusiness M
Agricultural Education M
Agricultural Sciences—General M,D*
Animal Sciences M
Applied Economics M,D
Applied Mathematics M,D
Aquaculture M,D
Architecture M
Art/Fine Arts M
Astronomy M,D
Astrophysics M,D
Atmospheric Sciences M,D
Biochemistry M,D

Clemson University (continued)

Bioengineering M,D*
Biological and Biomedical Sciences—General M,D
Biomedical Engineering M,D
Biophysics M,D
Business Administration and Management—General M,D
Ceramic Sciences and Engineering M,D
Chemical Engineering M,D
Chemistry M,D
City and Regional Planning M
Civil Engineering M,D
Communication—General M
Computational Sciences M,D
Computer Art and Design M
Computer Engineering M,D
Computer Science M,D*
Construction Engineering and Management
Counselor Education M
Curriculum and Instruction D
Economics M,D*
Education—General M,D,O
Educational Administration M,D,O
Electrical Engineering M,D
Electronic Commerce M
Elementary Education M
Engineering and Applied Sciences—General M,D*
English Education M
English M
Entomology M,D
Environmental Engineering M,D
Environmental Management and Policy M,D
Environmental Sciences M,D
Ergonomics and Human Factors M,D
Fish, Game, and Wildlife Management M,D
Food Science and Technology D
Forestry M,D
Foundations and Philosophy of Education M
Genetics M,D
Health Services Management and Hospital Administration M
History M
Human Resources Development M
Hydrology M
Industrial and Manufacturing Management M,D*
Industrial and Organizational Psychology D
Industrial/Management Engineering M,D
Materials Engineering M,D
Materials Sciences M,D*
Mathematics Education M
Mathematics M,D
Mechanical Engineering M,D
Microbiology M,D
Nursing—General M
Operations Research M,D
Physics M,D*
Physiology M,D
Plant Biology M,D
Polymer Science and Engineering M,D
Psychology—General M,D
Public Policy and Administration M,D,O
Reading Education M
Recreation and Park Management M,D
Science Education M
Secondary Education M
Social Sciences Education M
Sociology M
Special Education M
Statistics M,D
Textile Sciences and Engineering M,D
Travel and Tourism M,D
Vocational and Technical Education M,D
Writing M
Zoology M,D

CLEVELAND CHIROPRACTIC COLLEGE-KANSAS CITY CAMPUS

Chiropractic P*

CLEVELAND CHIROPRACTIC COLLEGE-LOS ANGELES CAMPUS

Chiropractic P*

CLEVELAND INSTITUTE OF MUSIC

Music M,D,O

CLEVELAND STATE UNIVERSITY

Accounting M
Adult Education M
Analytical Chemistry M,D
Applied Mathematics M
Art History M
Biological and Biomedical Sciences—General M,D
Biomedical Engineering D
Business Administration and Management—General M,D
Chemical Engineering M,D
Chemistry M,D
City and Regional Planning M
Civil Engineering M,D
Clinical Psychology M
Communication Disorders M
Communication—General M
Community Health Nursing M
Computer Engineering M,D
Condensed Matter Physics M
Counseling Psychology M
Counselor Education M,D,O
Curriculum and Instruction M
Early Childhood Education M
Economics M
Education of the Gifted M
Education of the Multiply Handicapped M
Education—General M,D,O
Educational Administration M,D,O
Educational Measurement and Evaluation M
Educational Media/Instructional Technology M
Electrical Engineering M,D
Elementary Education M
Engineering and Applied Sciences—General M,D*
English as a Second Language M
English M
Environmental Engineering M,D
Environmental Sciences M,D
Exercise and Sports Science M
Experimental Psychology M
Geology M,D
Health Education M
Health Services Management and Hospital Administration M,D
History M
Human Resources Management M
Industrial and Labor Relations M
Industrial and Organizational Psychology M
Industrial/Management Engineering M,D
Inorganic Chemistry M,D
Law P,M
Management Information Systems M
Mathematics M
Mechanical Engineering M,D
Medical Physics M
Molecular Medicine D
Music Education M
Music M
Nursing—General M
Occupational Therapy M
Optical Sciences M
Organic Chemistry M,D
Philosophy M
Physical Chemistry M,D
Physical Education M
Physics M
Psychology—General M,O
Public Health—General M,D
Public Policy and Administration M,D
Reading Education M
Recreation and Park Management M
School Psychology O
Secondary Education M
Social Work M
Sociology M
Spanish M
Special Education M
Sport Psychology M
Sports Management M
Structural Engineering M,D
Urban Education D
Urban Studies M,D

In-depth description on page 809.

COASTAL CAROLINA UNIVERSITY

Early Childhood Education M
Education—General M
Educational Media/Instructional Technology M
Elementary Education M
English Education M
Mathematics Education M
Science Education M
Secondary Education M
Social Sciences Education M

COE COLLEGE

Education—General M

COLD SPRING HARBOR LABORATORY, WATSON SCHOOL OF BIOLOGICAL SCIENCES

Biological and Biomedical Sciences—General D*

COLEGIO PENTECOSTAL MIZPA

Theology M

COLEMAN COLLEGE

Information Science M

COLGATE ROCHESTER CROZER DIVINITY SCHOOL

Theology P,M,D,O

COLGATE UNIVERSITY

Education—General M
Secondary Education M

COLLÈGE DOMINICAIN DE PHILOSOPHIE ET DE THÉOLOGIE

Pastoral Ministry and Counseling M
Philosophy M,D
Theology M,D,O

COLLEGE FOR FINANCIAL PLANNING

Finance and Banking M

COLLEGE MISERICORDIA

Curriculum and Instruction M
Education—General M
Nursing—General M
Occupational Therapy M
Organizational Management M
Physical Therapy M

COLLEGE OF CHARLESTON

Accounting M
Business Administration and Management—General M
Computer Science M
Early Childhood Education M
Education—General M
Elementary Education M
English M
Environmental Sciences M
History M
Legal and Justice Studies M
Marine Biology M*
Mathematics Education M
Mathematics M
Public Policy and Administration M
Science Education M
Special Education M

In-depth description on page 811.

COLLEGE OF EMMANUEL AND ST. CHAD

Theology P,M

COLLEGE OF MOUNT ST. JOSEPH

Art Education M
Business Education M
Early Childhood Education M
Education—General M
Foundations and Philosophy of Education M
Organizational Management M
Pastoral Ministry and Counseling M
Physical Therapy M
Reading Education M
Special Education M
Theology M

In-depth description on page 813.

COLLEGE OF MOUNT SAINT VINCENT

Advanced Practice Nursing M,O
Allied Health—General M,O*
Child and Family Studies M,O
Counseling Psychology M,O
Education—General M,O
Educational Media/Instructional Technology M,O
Gerontological Nursing M,O
Health Services Management and Hospital Administration M,O
Medical/Surgical Nursing M,O
Middle School Education M,O
Multilingual and Multicultural Education M,O
Nursing and Healthcare Administration M,O
Nursing—General M,O
Urban Education M,O

In-depth description on page 815.

THE COLLEGE OF NEW JERSEY

Addictions/Substance Abuse Counseling M,O
Advanced Practice Nursing M
Communication Disorders M
Counselor Education M
Early Childhood Education M
Education—General M,O
Educational Administration M
Educational Media/Instructional Technology M,O
Elementary Education M
English as a Second Language M,O
English M
Health Education M
Marriage and Family Therapy O
Nursing—General M
Physical Education M
Reading Education M
School Nursing M
Secondary Education M
Special Education M

In-depth description on page 817.

THE COLLEGE OF NEW ROCHELLE

Art Education M
Art Therapy M
Art/Fine Arts M
Communication Disorders M
Communication—General M,O
Counseling Psychology M
Early Childhood Education M
Education of the Gifted M,O
Education—General M,O
Educational Administration M,O
Elementary Education M
English as a Second Language M,O
Gerontology M,O
Graphic Design M
Human Resources Development M,O
Multilingual and Multicultural Education M,O
Museum Education O
Nursing and Healthcare Administration M,O
Nursing Education M,O
Nursing—General M,O
Reading Education M
School Psychology M
Social Psychology M
Special Education M
Thanatology O

In-depth description on page 819.

COLLEGE OF NOTRE DAME OF MARYLAND

Business Administration and Management—General M
Communication—General M
Education—General M
Educational Administration M
English as a Second Language M
Gerontology M
Liberal Studies M
Nonprofit Management M

COLLEGE OF ST. CATHERINE

Education—General M
Information Studies M
Library Science M
Nursing—General M
Occupational Therapy M
Organizational Management M
Physical Therapy M
Social Work M
Theology M

In-depth description on page 821.

COLLEGE OF SAINT ELIZABETH

Business Administration and Management—General M
Counseling Psychology M
Education—General M,O
Educational Administration O
Educational Media/Instructional Technology M,O
Health Services Management and Hospital Administration M
Nutrition M,O
Psychology—General M
Theology M

COLLEGE OF ST. JOSEPH

Business Administration and Management—General M
Clinical Psychology M
Counseling Psychology M
Counselor Education M
Education—General M
Elementary Education M
Psychology—General M
Reading Education M
School Psychology M

Social Psychology M
Special Education M

THE COLLEGE OF SAINT ROSE

Accounting M
Art Education M
Business Administration and Management—General M
Communication Disorders M
Computer Science M
Counselor Education M,O
Early Childhood Education M
Education—General M,O*
Educational Administration M,O
Educational Media/Instructional Technology M,O
Educational Psychology M
Elementary Education M
English M
History M
Information Science M
Mass Communication M
Music Education M
Music M
Nonprofit Management O
Political Science M
Reading Education M
School Psychology M,O
Secondary Education M
Special Education M
Student Personnel Services M

In-depth description on page 823.

THE COLLEGE OF ST. SCHOLASTICA

Business Administration and Management—General M
Curriculum and Instruction M
Education—General M
Educational Media/Instructional Technology M
Exercise and Sports Science M
Health Informatics M
Nursing—General M
Occupational Therapy M
Physical Therapy M

COLLEGE OF SANTA FE

Business Administration and Management—General M
Counselor Education M
Education—General M
Educational Administration M
Multilingual and Multicultural Education M
Special Education M

COLLEGE OF STATEN ISLAND OF THE CITY UNIVERSITY OF NEW YORK

Biological and Biomedical Sciences—General M
Biopsychology D
Chemistry D
Clinical Psychology D
Cognitive Sciences D
Computer Science M,D
Developmental Psychology D
Education—General M,O
Educational Administration O
Elementary Education M
English M
Environmental Sciences M
Experimental Psychology D
Film, Television, and Video Theory and Criticism M
History M
Liberal Studies M
Medical/Surgical Nursing M
Neuroscience D
Physical Therapy M
Psychology—General D
Secondary Education M
Social Psychology D
Special Education M

In-depth description on page 825.

COLLEGE OF THE ATLANTIC

Environmental Management and Policy M
Family and Consumer Sciences-General M

COLLEGE OF THE SOUTHWEST

Counselor Education M
Curriculum and Instruction M
Education—General M
Educational Administration M
Educational Measurement and Evaluation M

THE COLLEGE OF WILLIAM AND MARY

Accounting M
Addictions/Substance Abuse Counseling M,D
American Studies M,D
Anthropology M,D
Applied Science and Technology M,D*
Biological and Biomedical Sciences—General M
Business Administration and Management—General M
Chemistry M
Clinical Psychology D
Computational Sciences M
Computer Science M,D
Counselor Education M,D
Curriculum and Instruction M
Education of the Gifted M
Education—General M,D,O*
Educational Administration M,D
Elementary Education M
English Education M
Experimental Psychology M
Foreign Languages Education M
History M,D
Law P,M
Marine Sciences M,D*
Marriage and Family Therapy M,D
Mathematics Education M
Operations Research M
Physics M,D
Psychology—General M,D
Public Policy and Administration M*
Reading Education M
School Psychology M,O
Science Education M
Secondary Education M
Social Sciences Education M
Special Education M

In-depth description on page 827.

COLLÈGE UNIVERSITAIRE DE SAINT-BONIFACE

Canadian Studies M
Education—General M

COLORADO CHRISTIAN UNIVERSITY

Curriculum and Instruction M
Education—General M

THE COLORADO COLLEGE

Art Education M
Education—General M
Elementary Education M
English Education M
Foreign Languages Education M
Mathematics Education M
Music Education M
Science Education M
Secondary Education M
Social Sciences Education M

COLORADO SCHOOL OF MINES

Applied Physics M,D
Chemical Engineering M,D
Chemistry M,D
Computer Science M,D
Electronic Materials M,D
Engineering and Applied Sciences—General M,D,O
Engineering Management M,D
Environmental Engineering M,D
Environmental Sciences M,D
Geochemistry M,D,O
Geological Engineering M,D,O
Geology M,D,O
Geophysics M,D,O
Geosciences M,D,O
Hydrology M,D,O
Management of Technology M,D
Materials Engineering M,D
Materials Sciences M,D
Mathematics M,D
Metallurgical Engineering and Metallurgy M,D
Mineral Economics M,D
Mineral/Mining Engineering M,D
Petroleum Engineering M,D
Physics M,D
Systems Engineering M,D

In-depth description on page 829.

COLORADO STATE UNIVERSITY

Accounting M
Advertising and Public Relations M
Agricultural Economics and Agribusiness M,D
Agricultural Engineering M,D
Agricultural Sciences—General M,D
Agronomy and Soil Sciences M,D
Anatomy M,D
Animal Sciences M,D
Anthropology M
Art/Fine Arts M
Atmospheric Sciences M,D
Automotive Engineering M,D
Biochemistry M,D
Bioengineering M,D
Biological and Biomedical Sciences—General M,D
Biomedical Engineering M,D
Botany M,D
Business Administration and Management—General M*
Cell Biology M,D*
Chemical Engineering M,D
Chemistry M,D
Child and Family Studies M
Civil Engineering M,D
Cognitive Sciences D
Communication—General M
Computer Engineering M,D
Computer Science M,D*
Construction Engineering and Management M,D
Consumer Economics M
Counseling Psychology D
Ecology M,D
Economics M,D
Electrical Engineering M,D
Engineering and Applied Sciences—General M,D
Engineering Management M,D
English Education M
English M
Entomology M,D
Environmental and Occupational Health M,D
Environmental Engineering M,D
Environmental Management and Policy M,D
Exercise and Sports Science M
Fish, Game, and Wildlife Management M,D
Food Science and Technology M,D
Forestry M,D
French M
Genetics M,D
Geology M,D
Geosciences M,D
Geotechnical Engineering M,D
German M
Graphic Design M
Hazardous Materials Management M,D
Health Physics/Radiological Health M,D
Historic Preservation M,D
History M
Horticulture M,D
Human Development M
Hydraulics M,D
Hydrology M,D
Immunology M,D
Industrial and Organizational Psychology D
Industrial/Management Engineering M,D
Interior Design M
Landscape Architecture M,D
Management Information Systems M
Management of Technology M,D
Manufacturing Engineering M,D
Materials Engineering M,D
Mathematics M,D
Mechanical Engineering M,D
Mechanics M,D
Microbiology M,D*
Molecular Biology M,D
Museum Studies M
Music Education M
Music M
Natural Resources D
Neurobiology M,D
Neuroscience D*
Nutrition M,D
Occupational Therapy M
Pathology M,D
Philosophy M
Physics M,D
Physiology M,D
Plant Pathology M,D
Plant Physiology M,D
Plant Sciences M,D
Political Science M,D
Psychology—General D
Radiation Biology M,D
Range Science M,D
Recreation and Park Management M,D
Rhetoric M
Social Psychology D
Social Work M
Sociology M,D
Spanish M
Speech and Interpersonal Communication M
Statistics M,D
Structural Engineering M,D
Technical Writing M
Technology and Public Policy M,D
Textile Design M
Therapies—Dance, Drama, and Music M
Veterinary Medicine P
Veterinary Sciences M,D
Vocational and Technical Education M,D
Water Resources M,D
Writing M
Zoology M,D

COLORADO TECHNICAL UNIVERSITY

Business Administration and Management—General M,D
Computer Engineering M
Computer Science M,D
Electrical Engineering M
Human Resources Management M,D
Information Science M,D
Logistics M,D
Management Information Systems M,D
Organizational Management M,D
Project Management M,D
Software Engineering M,D
Systems Science M,D

COLORADO TECHNICAL UNIVERSITY DENVER CAMPUS

Business Administration and Management—General M
Computer Science M
Criminal Justice and Criminology M
Management Information Systems M
Project Management M
Software Engineering M
Systems Science M

COLORADO TECHNICAL UNIVERSITY SIOUX FALLS CAMPUS

Business Administration and Management—General M
Health Services Management and Hospital Administration M
Human Resources Management M
Management Information Systems M
Organizational Management M

COLUMBIA COLLEGE (MO)

Business Administration and Management—General M
Criminal Justice and Criminology M
Education—General M

COLUMBIA COLLEGE (SC)

Conflict Resolution and Mediation/Peace Studies M,O
Elementary Education M
Organizational Behavior M,O

COLUMBIA COLLEGE CHICAGO

Architecture M
Arts Administration M
Comparative and Interdisciplinary Arts M
Education—General M
Elementary Education M
English Education M
Film, Television, and Video Production M
Interior Design M
Journalism M
Media Studies M
Multilingual and Multicultural Education M
Photography M
Therapies—Dance, Drama, and Music M
Urban Education M
Writing M

In-depth description on page 831 and announcement on page 316.

COLUMBIA INTERNATIONAL UNIVERSITY

Counselor Education M
Curriculum and Instruction M
Education—General M
Educational Administration M
English as a Second Language P,M,D,O
Missions and Missiology P,M,D,O
Pastoral Ministry and Counseling P,M,D,O
Religion P,M,D,O
Religious Education P,M,D,O
Theology P,M,D,O

COLUMBIA SOUTHERN UNIVERSITY

Business Administration and Management—General M
Electronic Commerce M

Columbia Southern University (continued)

Environmental and Occupational Health M
Health Services Management and Hospital Administration M
Human Resources Management M
International Business M
Marketing M

COLUMBIA THEOLOGICAL SEMINARY

Theology P,M,D

COLUMBIA UNIVERSITY

Accounting M,D
Advanced Practice Nursing M,O
African Studies O
African-American Studies M
Allopathic Medicine P
American Studies M
Anatomy M,D
Anthropology M,D
Applied Mathematics M,D,O
Applied Physics M,D,O*
Archaeology M,D
Architecture M,D*
Art History M,D
Art/Fine Arts M
Asian Languages M,D
Asian Studies M,D,O
Astronomy M,D
Atmospheric Sciences M,D*
Biochemistry M,D
Biological and Biomedical Sciences—General M,D*
Biomedical Engineering M,D*
Biophysics M,D
Biopsychology M,D
Biostatistics M,D
Business Administration and Management—General M,D
Cell Biology M,D*
Chemical Engineering M,D,O
Chemistry M,D
City and Regional Planning M,D
Civil Engineering M,D,O
Classics M,D
Communication—General M,D
Community Health M,D
Comparative Literature M,D
Computer Art and Design M
Computer Science M,D,O*
Conservation Biology M,D,O
Corporate and Organizational Communication M
Dentistry P
Developmental Biology M,D
East European and Russian Studies M,O
Ecology D,O*
Economics M,D
Electrical Engineering M,D,O*
Engineering and Applied Sciences—General M,D,O*
English M,D
Entrepreneurship M
Environmental and Occupational Health M,D
Environmental Engineering M,D
Environmental Management and Policy M*
Epidemiology M,D
Evolutionary Biology D,O
Experimental Psychology M,D
Film, Television, and Video Production M
Film, Television, and Video Theory and Criticism M
Finance and Banking M,D
Financial Engineering M,D,O
French M,D
Genetics M,D
Geochemistry M,D
Geodetic Sciences M,D
Geological Engineering M,D
Geophysics M,D
Geosciences M,D
German M,D
Gerontological Nursing M,O
Health Services Management and Hospital Administration M,D
Historic Preservation M
History M,D
HIV/AIDS Nursing M,O
Human Resources Management M
Industrial and Manufacturing Management D
Industrial/Management Engineering M,D,O*
Inorganic Chemistry M,D
Interdisciplinary Studies M*
International Affairs M*
International Business M
Italian M,D
Jewish Studies M,D
Journalism M,D*
Latin American Studies O
Law P,M,D
Liberal Studies M
Marketing M,D
Materials Engineering M,D
Materials Sciences M,D,O
Maternal and Child Health M
Maternal/Child Nursing M,O
Mathematics M,D*
Mechanical Engineering M,D
Mechanics M,D,O
Medical Informatics M,D*
Medical Physics M,D,O
Medical/Surgical Nursing M,O
Medieval and Renaissance Studies M
Microbiology M,D*
Mineral/Mining Engineering M,D,O
Molecular Biology M,D
Music M,D
Near and Middle Eastern Languages M,D
Near and Middle Eastern Studies M,D,O
Neurobiology M,D
Nurse Anesthesia M,O
Nurse Midwifery M
Nursing—General M,D,O*
Nutrition M,D*
Occupational Therapy M
Oceanography M,D
Oncology Nursing M,O
Operations Research M,D,O
Optical Sciences M,D,O
Oral and Dental Sciences M
Organic Chemistry M,D
Pathobiology M,D
Pathology M,D
Pediatric Nursing M,O
Pharmacology M,D
Philosophy M,D
Photography M
Physical Chemistry M,D
Physical Therapy M
Physics M,D
Physiology M,D
Planetary and Space Sciences M,D
Plasma Physics M,D,O
Political Science M,D
Psychiatric Nursing M,O
Psychology—General M,D
Public Health—General M,D*
Public Policy and Administration M*
Real Estate M
Religion M,D
Romance Languages M,D
Russian M,D
Slavic Languages M,D
Social Psychology M,D
Social Sciences M
Social Work M,D*
Sociology M,D
Spanish M,D
Statistics M,D
Telecommunications M,D,O
Theater M,D*
Toxicology M,D
Urban Design M
Western European Studies M,O
Women's Health Nursing M,O
Writing M

In-depth description on page 833.

COLUMBUS STATE UNIVERSITY

Art Education M
Computer Science M
Counseling Psychology M,O
Counselor Education M,O
Early Childhood Education M,O
Education—General M,O
Educational Administration M,O
English Education M,O
Environmental Sciences M
Management Information Systems M
Mathematics Education M,O
Middle School Education M,O
Music Education M
Physical Education M
Public Policy and Administration M
Science Education M,O
Secondary Education M,O
Social Sciences Education M,O
Special Education M,O

CONCORDIA LUTHERAN SEMINARY

Theology P,M

CONCORDIA SEMINARY

Theology P,M,D,O

CONCORDIA THEOLOGICAL SEMINARY

Theology P,M,D

CONCORDIA UNIVERSITY (CA)

Business Administration and Management—General M
Curriculum and Instruction M
Education—General M
Educational Administration M
Educational Media/Instructional Technology M
International and Comparative Education M
Missions and Missiology M
Reading Education M
Theology M

CONCORDIA UNIVERSITY (CANADA)

Accounting M,D,O
Adult Education O
Aerospace/Aeronautical Engineering M
Anthropology M
Applied Arts and Design—General O
Art Education M,D
Art History M,D
Art/Fine Arts M
Biological and Biomedical Sciences—General M,D
Business Administration and Management—General M,D,O
Chemistry M,D
Child and Family Studies M
City and Regional Planning O
Civil Engineering M,D,O
Clinical Psychology M,D
Communication—General M,D,O
Computer Art and Design O
Computer Engineering M,D,O
Computer Science M,D,O
Construction Engineering and Management M,D,O
Economics M,D,O
Education—General M,D,O
Educational Media/Instructional Technology M,D,O
Electrical Engineering M,D,O
Electronic Commerce M,D,O
Engineering and Applied Sciences—General M,D,O*
English M
Environmental Engineering M,D,O
Environmental Management and Policy O
Film, Television, and Video Production M
Film, Television, and Video Theory and Criticism M
French M,O
Geography M,O
Health Services Management and Hospital Administration M,D,O
History M,D
Humanities D
Investment Management M,D,O
Jewish Studies M
Journalism O
Linguistics M
Mathematics Education M,D
Mathematics M,D
Mechanical Engineering M,D,O
Media Studies M,D,O
Music O
Philosophy M
Psychology—General M,D
Public Policy and Administration M
Religion M,D
Rural Planning and Studies M,D,O
Sociology M
Software Engineering M,D,O
Sports Management M,D,O
Statistics M,D
Theology M
Translation and Interpretation M,O
Transportation Management M,D,O
Writing M

In-depth description on page 835.

CONCORDIA UNIVERSITY (IL)

Counseling Psychology M,O
Counselor Education M,O
Curriculum and Instruction M,O
Early Childhood Education M,D,O
Education—General M,O
Educational Administration M,D,O
Gerontology M,O
Health Services Management and Hospital Administration M,O
Human Services M,O
Music M,O
Psychology—General M,O
Reading Education M,O
Religion M,O
Urban Education M,O

CONCORDIA UNIVERSITY (MN)

Child and Family Studies M
Criminal Justice and Criminology M
Early Childhood Education M
Human Development M
Human Resources Management M
Human Services M
Pastoral Ministry and Counseling M
Religious Education M

CONCORDIA UNIVERSITY (NE)

Child and Family Studies M
Early Childhood Education M
Education—General M
Educational Administration M
Elementary Education M
Reading Education M
Religious Education M

CONCORDIA UNIVERSITY (OR)

Curriculum and Instruction M
Education—General M
Educational Administration M
Elementary Education M
Secondary Education M

CONCORDIA UNIVERSITY AT AUSTIN

Education—General M

CONCORDIA UNIVERSITY WISCONSIN

Advanced Practice Nursing M
Business Administration and Management—General M
Child and Family Studies M
Corporate and Organizational Communication M
Counselor Education M
Curriculum and Instruction M
Early Childhood Education M
Education—General M
Educational Administration M
Finance and Banking M
Gerontological Nursing M
Health Services Management and Hospital Administration M
Human Resources Management M
International Business M
Management Information Systems M
Marketing M
Music M
Nursing Education M
Nursing—General M
Occupational Therapy M
Physical Therapy M
Public Policy and Administration M
Reading Education M
Student Personnel Services M

CONNECTICUT COLLEGE

Botany M
Classics M
Dance M
Education—General M
Elementary Education M
English Education M
English M
Foreign Languages Education M
French M
Hispanic Studies M
Italian M
Mathematics Education M
Music Education M
Music M
Psychology—General M
Science Education M
Secondary Education M
Zoology M

CONVERSE COLLEGE

Curriculum and Instruction O
Economics M
Education of the Gifted M
Education—General M,O
Educational Administration M,O
Elementary Education M
English M
History M
Liberal Studies M
Marriage and Family Therapy O
Music Education M
Music M
Political Science M
Secondary Education M
Sociology M
Special Education M

CONWAY SCHOOL OF LANDSCAPE DESIGN

Landscape Architecture M

COPPIN STATE COLLEGE

Addictions/Substance Abuse Counseling M
Adult Education M
Advanced Practice Nursing M
Criminal Justice and Criminology M
Curriculum and Instruction M
Education—General M
Nursing—General M

- Psychology—General M
- Rehabilitation Counseling M
- Social Sciences M
- Special Education M

CORNELL UNIVERSITY

- Accounting D
- Adult Education M,D
- Aerospace/Aeronautical Engineering M,D
- African Studies M
- African-American Studies M
- Agricultural Economics and Agribusiness M,D
- Agricultural Education M,D
- Agricultural Engineering M,D
- Agronomy and Soil Sciences M,D*
- Analytical Chemistry D
- Animal Sciences M,D
- Anthropology D
- Applied Economics D
- Applied Mathematics M,D*
- Applied Physics M,D
- Archaeology M,D
- Architectural History M,D
- Architecture M,D
- Art History D
- Art/Fine Arts M
- Artificial Intelligence/Robotics M,D
- Asian Languages M,D
- Asian Studies M,D
- Astronomy D
- Astrophysics D
- Atmospheric Sciences M,D
- Biochemical Engineering M,D
- Biochemistry D*
- Bioengineering M,D
- Biomedical Engineering M,D
- Biometrics M,D
- Biophysics D
- Biopsychology D
- Business Administration and Management—General M,D
- Cell Biology D
- Chemical Engineering M,D
- Chemistry D*
- Child and Family Studies D
- City and Regional Planning M,D
- Civil Engineering M,D*
- Classics D
- Clothing and Textiles M,D
- Communication—General M,D*
- Comparative Literature D
- Computational Sciences M,D
- Computer Art and Design M,D
- Computer Engineering M,D
- Computer Science M,D*
- Conflict Resolution and Mediation/Peace Studies M,D
- Consumer Economics M,D
- Cultural Studies M,D
- Curriculum and Instruction M,D
- Demography and Population Studies M,D
- Developmental Biology M,D
- Developmental Psychology D
- Ecology D
- Economics D
- Education—General M,D
- Electrical Engineering M,D*
- Engineering and Applied Sciences—General M,D
- Engineering Physics M,D
- English M,D
- Entomology M,D
- Environmental Design M
- Environmental Engineering M,D
- Environmental Management and Policy M,D
- Epidemiology M,D
- Ergonomics and Human Factors M
- Ethnic Studies M,D
- Evolutionary Biology D
- Experimental Psychology D
- Facilities Management M
- Family and Consumer Sciences-General M,D
- Finance and Banking D
- Fish, Game, and Wildlife Management M,D
- Food Science and Technology M,D
- Forestry M,D
- Gender Studies M,D
- Genetics D*
- Geochemistry M,D
- Geology M,D*
- Geophysics M,D
- Geosciences M,D
- Geotechnical Engineering M,D
- German M,D
- Health Services Management and Hospital Administration M,D
- Historic Preservation M,D
- History of Science and Technology M,D
- History M,D
- Horticulture M,D
- Hospitality Management M,D*
- Human Development D
- Human Resources Management M,D
- Hydrology M,D
- Immunology M,D
- Industrial and Labor Relations M,D*
- Industrial/Management Engineering M,D
- Inorganic Chemistry D
- Interior Design M
- International Affairs D
- International Development M
- Jewish Studies M,D
- Landscape Architecture M
- Law P,M,D
- Limnology D
- Linguistics M,D
- Manufacturing Engineering M,D
- Marketing D
- Materials Engineering M,D
- Materials Sciences M,D
- Mathematics Education M,D
- Mathematics D
- Mechanical Engineering M,D
- Mechanics M,D
- Medieval and Renaissance Studies D
- Microbiology D
- Mineralogy M,D
- Molecular Biology D
- Molecular Medicine M,D
- Music D
- Natural Resources M,D
- Near and Middle Eastern Studies M,D
- Neurobiology D
- Nuclear Engineering M,D
- Nutrition M,D*
- Oceanography D
- Operations Research M,D*
- Organic Chemistry D
- Organizational Behavior M,D
- Pharmacology M,D*
- Philosophy D
- Photography M
- Physical Chemistry D
- Physics M,D
- Physiology M,D
- Planetary and Space Sciences D
- Plant Biology D
- Plant Molecular Biology D
- Plant Pathology M,D
- Plant Physiology D
- Plant Sciences M,D
- Political Science D
- Polymer Science and Engineering M,D
- Psychology—General D
- Public Policy and Administration M,D*
- Real Estate M*
- Reproductive Biology M,D
- Romance Languages D
- Rural Planning and Studies M
- Rural Sociology M,D
- Science Education M,D
- Social Psychology M,D
- Social Work M,D
- Sociology M,D
- Spanish D
- Statistics M,D
- Structural Biology M,D
- Structural Engineering M,D
- Systems Engineering M
- Textile Design M,D
- Textile Sciences and Engineering M,D
- Theater D
- Theoretical Chemistry D
- Theoretical Physics M,D
- Toxicology M,D*
- Transportation and Highway Engineering M,D
- Urban Design M,D
- Veterinary Medicine P
- Veterinary Sciences M,D
- Virology M,D
- Water Resources Engineering M,D
- Writing M,D
- Zoology D

COVENANT COLLEGE

- Education—General M

COVENANT THEOLOGICAL SEMINARY

- Theology P,M,D,O

CRANBROOK ACADEMY OF ART

- Applied Arts and Design—General M
- Architecture M
- Art/Fine Arts M*
- Graphic Design M
- Photography M
- Textile Design M

CREIGHTON UNIVERSITY

- Allied Health—General P,M,D
- Allopathic Medicine P
- Atmospheric Sciences M
- Biological and Biomedical Sciences—General M,D
- Business Administration and Management—General M
- Computer Science M
- Counselor Education M
- Dentistry P
- Education—General M
- Educational Administration M
- Electronic Commerce M
- Immunology M,D
- International Affairs M
- Law P
- Liberal Studies M
- Management Information Systems M
- Medical Microbiology M,D*
- Nursing—General M
- Occupational Therapy D
- Pharmaceutical Sciences M,D
- Pharmacology M,D
- Pharmacy P
- Physical Therapy D
- Physics M
- Theology M

THE CRISWELL COLLEGE

- Pastoral Ministry and Counseling P,M
- Theology P,M

CROWN COLLEGE

- Theology M

CUMBERLAND COLLEGE

- Early Childhood Education M
- Education—General M,O
- Educational Administration O
- Elementary Education M,O
- Middle School Education M
- Reading Education M
- Secondary Education M,O
- Special Education M

CUMBERLAND UNIVERSITY

- Business Administration and Management—General M
- Education—General M
- Human Resources Management M
- Public Policy and Administration M

CURRY COLLEGE

- Adult Education M,O
- Education—General M,O
- Reading Education M,O
- Special Education M,O

THE CURTIS INSTITUTE OF MUSIC

- Music M

DAEMEN COLLEGE

- Advanced Practice Nursing M,O
- Business Administration and Management—General M
- Education—General M
- International Business M
- Medical/Surgical Nursing M,O
- Nursing—General M,O
- Physical Therapy M
- Physician Assistant Studies M

DAKOTA STATE UNIVERSITY

- Computer Science M
- Education—General M
- Educational Media/Instructional Technology M
- Information Science M
- Management Information Systems M*

DALHOUSIE UNIVERSITY

- Agricultural Engineering M,D
- Agricultural Sciences—General M
- Allopathic Medicine P
- Anatomy M,D
- Anthropology M,D
- Applied Mathematics M,D
- Architecture M
- Biochemistry M,D
- Bioengineering M,D
- Biological and Biomedical Sciences—General M,D
- Biomedical Engineering M
- Biophysics M,D
- Business Administration and Management—General M
- Chemical Engineering M,D
- Chemistry M,D
- City and Regional Planning M
- Civil Engineering M,D
- Classics M,D
- Clinical Psychology M,D
- Communication Disorders M
- Community Health M
- Computer Education M
- Computer Engineering M,D
- Computer Science M,D
- Dentistry P
- Economics M,D
- Electrical Engineering M,D
- Electronic Commerce M,D
- Engineering and Applied Sciences—General M,D*
- English M,D
- Environmental Management and Policy M
- Epidemiology M
- Food Science and Technology M,D
- French M,D
- Geosciences M,D
- German M
- Health Education M
- Health Services Management and Hospital Administration M
- History M,D
- Human-Computer Interaction M
- Immunology M,D
- Industrial/Management Engineering M,D
- Information Studies M
- Interdisciplinary Studies D
- International Development M
- Kinesiology and Movement Studies M
- Law M,D
- Leisure Studies M
- Library Science M
- Management Information Systems M
- Marine Affairs M
- Mathematics M,D
- Mechanical Engineering M,D
- Metallurgical Engineering and Metallurgy M,D
- Microbiology M,D
- Mineral/Mining Engineering M,D
- Neurobiology M,D
- Neuroscience M,D
- Nursing—General M
- Occupational Therapy M
- Oceanography M,D
- Oral and Dental Sciences
- Pathology M
- Pharmaceutical Sciences M,D
- Pharmacology M,D
- Philosophy M,D
- Physics M,D
- Physiology M,D
- Political Science M,D
- Psychology—General M,D
- Public Policy and Administration M
- Rural Planning and Studies M
- Social Work M
- Sociology M,D
- Statistics M,D
- Women's Studies M

DALLAS BAPTIST UNIVERSITY

- Accounting M
- Business Administration and Management—General M
- Conflict Resolution and Mediation/Peace Studies M
- Counselor Education M
- Early Childhood Education M
- Education—General M
- Educational Administration M
- Electronic Commerce M
- Elementary Education M
- Engineering Management M
- Finance and Banking M
- Health Services Management and Hospital Administration M
- Higher Education M
- Human Resources Management M
- Interdisciplinary Studies M
- International Business M
- Liberal Studies M
- Management Information Systems M
- Management of Technology M
- Marketing M
- Organizational Management M
- Reading Education M

DALLAS THEOLOGICAL SEMINARY

- Media Studies M,D,O
- Missions and Missiology M,D,O

Dallas Theological Seminary (continued)

Pastoral Ministry and Counseling M,D,O
Religious Education M,D,O
Theology M,D,O

DARKEI NOAM RABBINICAL COLLEGE

Theology

DARTMOUTH COLLEGE

Allopathic Medicine P
Astronomy M,D
Biochemical Engineering M,D
Biochemistry D*
Biological and Biomedical Sciences—General D*
Biomedical Engineering M,D
Biotechnology M,D
Business Administration and Management—General M
Chemistry D
Cognitive Sciences D
Comparative Literature M
Computer Engineering M,D
Computer Science M,D*
Electrical Engineering M,D
Engineering and Applied Sciences—General M,D*
Engineering Management M
Environmental Engineering M,D
Genetics D*
Geosciences M,D
Health Services Research M,D
Immunology *
Liberal Studies M*
Materials Engineering M,D
Materials Sciences M,D
Mathematics D*
Mechanical Engineering M,D
Microbiology *
Music M
Neuroscience D
Pharmacology D*
Physics M,D
Physiology D*
Psychology—General D
Toxicology D

In-depth description on page 837.

DAVENPORT UNIVERSITY

Accounting M
Business Administration and Management—General M
Electronic Commerce M
Finance and Banking M
Health Services Management and Hospital Administration M
Human Resources Management M
International Business M
Marketing M

DAVENPORT UNIVERSITY

Business Administration and Management—General M

DAVENPORT UNIVERSITY

Accounting M
Business Administration and Management—General M
Electronic Commerce M
Finance and Banking M
Health Services Management and Hospital Administration M
Human Resources Management M

DEFIANCE COLLEGE

Business Administration and Management—General M
Education—General M
Organizational Management M

DELAWARE STATE UNIVERSITY

Business Administration and Management—General M
Curriculum and Instruction M
Mathematics M
Science Education M
Social Work M
Special Education M

DELAWARE VALLEY COLLEGE

Educational Administration M

DELTA STATE UNIVERSITY

Accounting M
Aviation Management M
Biological and Biomedical Sciences—General M
Business Administration and Management—General M
City and Regional Planning M
Counselor Education M
Criminal Justice and Criminology M
Education—General M,D,O
Educational Administration M,O
Elementary Education M,O
English Education M
Marketing M
Mathematics Education M
Music Education M
Nursing—General M
Physical Education M
Recreation and Park Management M
Social Sciences Education M
Social Work M
Special Education M

DENVER CAREER COLLEGE

Legal and Justice Studies O

DENVER SEMINARY

Marriage and Family Therapy P,M,D,O
Pastoral Ministry and Counseling P,M,D,O
Religion P,M,D,O
Religious Education P,M,D,O
Theology P,M,D,O

DEPAUL UNIVERSITY

Accounting M
Advanced Practice Nursing M
Applied Physics M
Biochemistry M
Biological and Biomedical Sciences—General M*
Business Administration and Management—General M
Chemistry M
City and Regional Planning M,O
Clinical Psychology M,D
Communication—General M
Computer Art and Design M
Computer Science M,D
Corporate and Organizational Communication M
Counselor Education M
Curriculum and Instruction M,D
Economics M
Education—General M
Educational Administration M,D
Electronic Commerce M
Elementary Education M
English M
Entrepreneurship M
Experimental Psychology M,D
Finance and Banking M,O
Foundations and Philosophy of Education M
Health Services Management and Hospital Administration M
Higher Education M
History M
Human Resources Management M
Human Services M
Human-Computer Interaction M
Industrial and Manufacturing Management M
Industrial and Organizational Psychology M,D
Information Science M
Interdisciplinary Studies M
International Affairs M
International Business M
Law P,M
Legal and Justice Studies M
Liberal Studies M
Management Information Systems M
Management Strategy and Policy M
Marketing M
Mathematics Education M
Music Education M
Music M,O
Nonprofit Management M,O
Nurse Anesthesia M
Nursing—General M
Philosophy M,D
Physical Education M
Physics M
Polymer Science and Engineering M
Psychology—General M,D
Public Policy and Administration M
Reading Education M
Science Education M
Secondary Education M
Social Psychology M,D
Sociology M
Software Engineering M
Special Education M
Statistics M
Taxation M
Telecommunications M
Theater M,O*
Urban Education M
Women's Studies O
Writing M

In-depth description on page 839.

DESALES UNIVERSITY

Advanced Practice Nursing M
Business Administration and Management—General M
Computer Education M
Education—General M
English Education M
Information Science M
Mathematics Education M
Nursing—General M
Physician Assistant Studies M
Science Education M

DES MOINES UNIVERSITY OSTEOPATHIC MEDICAL CENTER

Health Services Management and Hospital Administration M
Osteopathic Medicine P
Physical Therapy D*
Physician Assistant Studies M
Podiatric Medicine P

DEVRY UNIVERSITY-KELLER GRADUATE SCHOOL OF MANAGEMENT

Accounting M
Business Administration and Management—General M
Finance and Banking M
Human Resources Management M
Management Information Systems M
Project Management M
Telecommunications Management M

THE DICKINSON SCHOOL OF LAW OF THE PENNSYLVANIA STATE UNIVERSITY

Law P,M

DOANE COLLEGE

Business Administration and Management—General M
Counselor Education M
Curriculum and Instruction M
Education—General M
Educational Administration M

DOMINICAN COLLEGE

Education—General M
Nursing—General M
Occupational Therapy M
Physical Therapy M
Special Education M

In-depth description on page 841.

DOMINICAN HOUSE OF STUDIES

Theology P,M,O

DOMINICAN SCHOOL OF PHILOSOPHY AND THEOLOGY

Philosophy M
Theology P,M,O

DOMINICAN UNIVERSITY

Accounting M
Business Administration and Management—General M
Curriculum and Instruction M
Early Childhood Education M
Education—General M
Educational Administration M
Information Studies M,O
Library Science M,O
Management Information Systems M
Organizational Management M
Social Work M*
Special Education M

DOMINICAN UNIVERSITY OF CALIFORNIA

Business Administration and Management—General M
Counseling Psychology M
Curriculum and Instruction M
Education—General M
Humanities M
International Business M
Management Strategy and Policy M
Nursing—General M

DONGGUK ROYAL UNIVERSITY

Acupuncture and Oriental Medicine M

DORDT COLLEGE

Education—General M

DOWLING COLLEGE

Aviation Management M,O
Business Administration and Management—General M,O
Education—General M,D,O
Educational Administration D,O
Educational Media/Instructional Technology D,O
Elementary Education M
Finance and Banking M,O
Quality Management M,O
Reading Education M
Secondary Education M
Special Education M

DRAKE UNIVERSITY

Adult Education M,D,O
Business Administration and Management—General M
Counselor Education M
Early Childhood Education M
Education—General M,D,O
Educational Administration M,D,O
Elementary Education M
Law P*
Pharmacy P
Public Policy and Administration M
Secondary Education M
Special Education M
Vocational and Technical Education M

In-depth description on page 843.

DREW UNIVERSITY

Bioethics M,D,O
English M,D
Ethics M,D
History M,D
Humanities M,D,O
Liberal Studies M,D
Religion M,D
Theology P,M,D,O
Women's Studies M

In-depth description on page 845.

DREXEL UNIVERSITY

Accounting M,D,O
Allied Health—General M,D,O*
Allopathic Medicine P
Applied Arts and Design—General M*
Architecture M
Art Therapy M
Arts Administration M
Biochemical Engineering M
Biochemistry M,D*
Biological and Biomedical Sciences—General M,D,O*
Biomedical Engineering M,D*
Biopsychology D
Biostatistics M,D
Business Administration and Management—General M,D,O*
Cancer Biology/Oncology M,D
Cell Biology M,D
Chemical Engineering M,D
Chemistry M,D*
Civil Engineering M,D
Clinical Psychology M,D*
Communication—General M*
Computer Engineering M
Computer Science M,D*
Curriculum and Instruction M
Economics M,D,O
Education—General M,D*
Educational Administration D
Educational Media/Instructional Technology D
Electrical Engineering M,D*
Emergency Medical Services M
Engineering and Applied Sciences—General M,D*
Engineering Management M,D
Environmental Engineering M,D*
Environmental Management and Policy M
Environmental Sciences M,D
Finance and Banking M,D,O
Food Science and Technology M,D
Forensic Psychology M,D
Genetics M,D
Geological Engineering M
Health Physics/Radiological Health M,D*
Health Psychology M,D
History of Science and Technology M
Human Genetics M,D
Immunology M,D
Information Science D*
Information Studies M*
Interior Design M
Library Science M,D,O
Management Strategy and Policy M,D,O
Manufacturing Engineering M,D
Marketing M,D,O
Marriage and Family Therapy M,D

Materials Engineering M,D
Mathematics M,D*
Mechanical Engineering M,D
Mechanics M,D*
Medical Physics M,D
Microbiology M,D*
Molecular Biology M,D*
Neuroscience D*
Nurse Anesthesia M
Nursing—General M
Nutrition M,D
Organizational Behavior M,D,O
Pathobiology D*
Pharmacology M,D*
Physical Therapy M,D,O*
Physician Assistant Studies M
Physics M,D*
Psychology—General D*
Public Health—General M*
Publishing M
Quantitative Analysis M,D,O
Software Engineering M*
Taxation M
Technical Writing M
Telecommunications M
Textile Design M
Therapies—Dance, Drama, and Music M
Veterinary Sciences M*

In-depth description on page 847.

DRURY UNIVERSITY

Business Administration and Management—General M
Communication—General M
Criminal Justice and Criminology M
Education of the Gifted M
Education—General M
Elementary Education M
Human Services M
International Business M
Middle School Education M
Physical Education M
Secondary Education M

DUKE UNIVERSITY

Advanced Practice Nursing M,O
Allopathic Medicine P
Anatomy D
Anthropology D
Art History D
Asian Studies M,O
Biochemistry D,O*
Biological and Biomedical Sciences—General D
Biomedical Engineering M,D*
Biophysics O*
Biopsychology D
Business Administration and Management—General M,D
Cancer Biology/Oncology D
Cell Biology D,O*
Chemistry D
Civil Engineering M,D*
Classics D
Clinical Psychology D
Clinical Research M
Cognitive Sciences D
Comparative Literature D
Computer Engineering M,D
Computer Science M,D*
Demography and Population Studies D
Developmental Biology O
Developmental Psychology D
Ecology M,D,O
Economics M,D
Education—General M
Electrical Engineering M,D*
Engineering and Applied Sciences—General M,D
Engineering Management M*
English D
Environmental Engineering M,D
Environmental Management and Policy M,D*
Environmental Sciences M,D
Experimental Psychology D
Forestry M,D
French D
Genetics D*
Geology M,D
German D
Gerontological Nursing M,O
Health Informatics M,O
Health Psychology D
Health Services Management and Hospital Administration M
History of Medicine
History D
HIV/AIDS Nursing M,O
Human Development D
Humanities M
Immunology D*
International Development M
Latin American Studies D,O
Law P,M,D
Liberal Studies M
Marine Affairs M,D
Marine Sciences M,D*
Materials Sciences M,D
Maternal/Child Nursing M,O
Mathematics D
Mechanical Engineering M,D*
Medical/Surgical Nursing M,O
Medieval and Renaissance Studies O
Microbiology D
Molecular Biology D,O
Music M,D
Natural Resources M,D*
Neurobiology D
Nurse Anesthesia M,O
Nursing and Healthcare Administration M,O
Nursing—General M,O
Oncology Nursing M,O
Pathology M,D*
Pediatric Nursing M,O
Pharmacology D*
Philosophy D
Physical Therapy M
Physician Assistant Studies M
Physics D*
Political Science M,D
Psychology—General D
Public Policy and Administration M*
Religion M,D
Slavic Languages M
Sociology M,D
Spanish D
Statistics D
Theology P,M
Toxicology O*
Water Resources M,D*
Women's Studies O

In-depth description on page 849.

DUQUESNE UNIVERSITY

Advanced Practice Nursing M
Allied Health—General M,D
Biochemistry M,D
Bioethics M,D
Biological and Biomedical Sciences—General M,D*
Business Administration and Management—General M*
Chemistry M,D*
Clinical Psychology D
Communication Disorders M,D
Communication—General M,D
Conflict Resolution and Mediation/Peace Studies M,O
Counselor Education M,D
Curriculum and Instruction D
Developmental Psychology D
Early Childhood Education M
Education—General M,D,O
Educational Administration M,D
Educational Media/Instructional Technology M
Elementary Education M
English M,D
Environmental Management and Policy M,O
Environmental Sciences M,D,O
Foundations and Philosophy of Education M
Health Services Management and Hospital Administration M,D
History M
Internet and Interactive Multimedia M
Law P
Liberal Studies M
Management Information Systems M
Mathematics M
Medicinal and Pharmaceutical Chemistry M,D
Museum Studies M
Music Education M,O
Music M,O
Nursing and Healthcare Administration M
Nursing Education M
Nursing—General M,D
Occupational Therapy M,D
Pharmaceutical Administration M
Pharmaceutical Sciences M,D*
Pharmacology M,D
Pharmacy P
Philosophy M,D
Physical Therapy M,D
Physician Assistant Studies M,D
Psychology—General D*
Public Policy and Administration M,O
Reading Education M
Rehabilitation Sciences M,D
Rhetoric M,D
School Psychology M,O
Secondary Education M
Special Education M
Taxation M
Theology M,D
Toxicology M,D

In-depth description on page 851.

D'YOUVILLE COLLEGE

Addictions/Substance Abuse Counseling M,O
Advanced Practice Nursing M,O
Education—General M,O
Elementary Education M,O
Health Services Management and Hospital Administration M,O
Hospice Nursing M,O
International Business M
Nursing—General M,O
Nutrition M
Occupational Therapy M
Physical Therapy M,O
Secondary Education M,O
Special Education M,O

In-depth description on page 853.

EARLHAM SCHOOL OF RELIGION

Religion P,M
Theology P,M

EAST CAROLINA UNIVERSITY

Addictions/Substance Abuse Counseling M
Adult Education M,O
Allied Health—General M,D
Allopathic Medicine P
American Studies M
Anatomy D
Anthropology M
Applied Mathematics M
Art/Fine Arts M
Biochemistry D
Biological and Biomedical Sciences—General M,D*
Biophysics M,D
Biotechnology M
Business Administration and Management—General M
Cell Biology D
Chemistry M
Child and Family Studies M
Clinical Psychology M
Communication Disorders M,D
Communication—General M
Computer Science M
Counselor Education M,O
Criminal Justice and Criminology M
Curriculum and Instruction M
Economics M
Education—General M,D,O
Educational Administration M,D,O
Educational Media/Instructional Technology M,O
Elementary Education M
Engineering and Applied Sciences—General M
English M
Environmental and Occupational Health M
Environmental Management and Policy D
Exercise and Sports Science M,D
Family and Consumer Sciences-General M
Geography M
Geology M
Health Education M
History M
Immunology D
Industrial/Management Engineering M
Information Science M
International Affairs M
Leisure Studies M
Library Science M,O
Marine Affairs D
Marriage and Family Therapy M
Mathematics Education M
Mathematics M
Medical Physics M,D
Microbiology D
Middle School Education M
Molecular Biology M
Music Education M
Music M
Nursing—General M,D
Nutrition M
Occupational Therapy M
Pathology D
Pharmacology D
Physical Therapy M
Physics M,D
Physiology D
Political Science M
Psychology—General M
Public Policy and Administration M
Reading Education M
Recreation and Park Management M
Rehabilitation Sciences M
School Psychology M
Science Education M
Social Sciences Education M
Social Work M
Sociology M
Special Education M
Therapies—Dance, Drama, and Music M
Vocational and Technical Education M
Western European Studies M

In-depth description on page 855.

EAST CENTRAL UNIVERSITY

Counselor Education M
Criminal Justice and Criminology M
Education—General M
Human Resources Management M
Psychology—General M
Rehabilitation Counseling M

EASTERN BAPTIST THEOLOGICAL SEMINARY

Marriage and Family Therapy D
Missions and Missiology D
Pastoral Ministry and Counseling D
Theology P,M,D

EASTERN CONNECTICUT STATE UNIVERSITY

Accounting M
Early Childhood Education M
Education—General M
Elementary Education M
Organizational Management M
Reading Education M
Science Education M

Announcement on page 333.

EASTERN ILLINOIS UNIVERSITY

Art/Fine Arts M
Biological and Biomedical Sciences—General M
Botany M
Business Administration and Management—General M
Chemistry M
Clinical Psychology M
Communication Disorders M
Counselor Education M
Economics M
Education—General M,O
Educational Administration M,O
Educational Psychology M
Elementary Education M
Engineering and Applied Sciences—General M
English M
Environmental Biology M
Family and Consumer Sciences-General M
Gerontology M
History M
Mathematics Education M
Mathematics M
Middle School Education M
Music M
Nutrition M
Physical Education M
Political Science M
Psychology—General M,O
Public History M
School Psychology O
Special Education M
Speech and Interpersonal Communication M
Zoology M

In-depth description on page 857.

EASTERN KENTUCKY UNIVERSITY

Addictions/Substance Abuse Counseling M
Advanced Practice Nursing M
Agricultural Education M
Allied Health—General M
Art Education M
Biological and Biomedical Sciences—General M
Business Administration and Management—General M
Business Education M
Chemistry M
City and Regional Planning M
Clinical Psychology M,O
Communication Disorders M
Community Health M
Counselor Education M
Criminal Justice and Criminology M
Curriculum and Instruction M
Ecology M

Eastern Kentucky University (continued)

Education—General M
Educational Administration M
Elementary Education M
English Education M
English M
Environmental and Occupational Health M
Geology M,D
Health Education M
Health Services Management and Hospital Administration M
Higher Education M
History M
Home Economics Education M
Industrial and Organizational Psychology M,O
Industrial/Management Engineering M
Leisure Studies M
Manufacturing Engineering M
Mathematics Education M
Mathematics M
Music Education M
Music M
Nursing—General M
Nutrition M
Occupational Therapy M
Physical Education M
Political Science M
Psychology—General M,O
Public Policy and Administration M
Reading Education M
School Psychology M,O
Science Education M
Secondary Education M
Social Sciences Education M
Special Education M
Sports Management M
Theater M
Vocational and Technical Education M

EASTERN MENNONITE UNIVERSITY

Business Administration and Management—General M
Conflict Resolution and Mediation/Peace Studies M
Education—General M
Pastoral Ministry and Counseling M
Religion P,M
Theology P,M

EASTERN MICHIGAN UNIVERSITY

Accounting M
American Studies M
Applied Economics M
Art Education M
Art/Fine Arts M
Arts Administration M
Biological and Biomedical Sciences—General M
Business Administration and Management—General M
Business Education M
Chemistry M*
Clinical Psychology M*
Communication Disorders M
Communication—General M
Computer Science M
Counselor Education M,O
Criminal Justice and Criminology M*
Curriculum and Instruction M
Early Childhood Education M
Economics M
Education—General M,D,O
Educational Administration M,D,O
Educational Psychology M
Elementary Education M
English as a Second Language M
English M
Family and Consumer Sciences-General M
Finance and Banking M
Foundations and Philosophy of Education M
French M
Geography M
German M
Historic Preservation M
History M
Human Resources Management M
Industrial and Manufacturing Management M
Industrial/Management Engineering M
International Business M
Linguistics M
Management Information Systems M
Marketing M
Mathematics M
Middle School Education M
Multilingual and Multicultural Education M
Music M
Nursing Education M
Occupational Therapy M
Organizational Management M
Physical Education M
Physics M
Polymer Science and Engineering M
Psychology—General M,D
Public Policy and Administration M
Quality Management M
Reading Education M
Science Education M
Secondary Education M
Social Sciences M
Social Work M
Sociology M
Spanish M
Special Education M,O
Speech and Interpersonal Communication M
Technology and Public Policy M
Theater M
Vocational and Technical Education M
Women's Studies M
Writing M

EASTERN NAZARENE COLLEGE

Counseling Psychology M
Early Childhood Education M,O
Education—General M,O
Educational Administration M,O
Elementary Education M,O
English as a Second Language M,O
Marriage and Family Therapy M
Middle School Education M,O
Reading Education M,O
Secondary Education M,O
Special Education M,O

EASTERN NEW MEXICO UNIVERSITY

Anthropology M
Biological and Biomedical Sciences—General M
Business Administration and Management—General M
Chemistry M
Communication Disorders M
Communication—General M
Counselor Education M
Education—General M
English M
Mathematics M
Music M
Physical Education M
Psychology—General M
Special Education M

EASTERN OREGON UNIVERSITY

Education—General M
Elementary Education M
Secondary Education M

EASTERN UNIVERSITY

Accounting M
Business Administration and Management—General M*
Counseling Psychology M*
Counselor Education M
Economics M
Education—General M,O*
Educational Psychology M
English as a Second Language O
Finance and Banking M
Health Education M
Marketing M
Multilingual and Multicultural Education M
Nonprofit Management M*

EASTERN VIRGINIA MEDICAL SCHOOL

Allopathic Medicine P
Art Therapy M
Biological and Biomedical Sciences—General M,D
Physician Assistant Studies M
Psychology—General D
Public Health—General M

EASTERN WASHINGTON UNIVERSITY

Adult Education M
Art Education M
Biological and Biomedical Sciences—General M
Business Administration and Management—General M
City and Regional Planning M
Communication Disorders M
Communication—General M
Community College Education M
Computer Education M
Computer Science M
Counseling Psychology M
Counselor Education M
Curriculum and Instruction M
Developmental Psychology M
Early Childhood Education M
Education—General M
Educational Administration M
Educational Media/Instructional Technology M
Elementary Education M
English M
Foreign Languages Education M
Foundations and Philosophy of Education M
Geology M
Higher Education M
History M
Interdisciplinary Studies M
Mathematics Education M
Mathematics M
Music Education M
Music M
Nursing Education M
Nursing—General M
Physical Education M
Physical Therapy M
Psychology—General M
Public Policy and Administration M
Reading Education M
School Psychology M
Science Education M
Social Sciences Education M
Social Work M
Special Education M
Writing M

In-depth description on page 859.

EAST STROUDSBURG UNIVERSITY OF PENNSYLVANIA

Biological and Biomedical Sciences—General M
Communication Disorders M
Computer Science M
Education—General M
Educational Media/Instructional Technology M
Elementary Education M
Exercise and Sports Science M
Health Education M
History M
Physical Education M
Political Science M
Public Health—General M
Reading Education M
Rehabilitation Sciences M
Science Education M
Secondary Education M
Social Sciences Education M
Special Education M
Sports Management M

In-depth description on page 861.

EAST TENNESSEE STATE UNIVERSITY

Accounting M
Advanced Practice Nursing M,D,O
Allied Health—General M,O
Allopathic Medicine P
Anatomy M,D
Art Education M
Art History M
Art/Fine Arts M
Biochemistry M,D
Biological and Biomedical Sciences—General M,D
Biophysics M,D
Business Administration and Management—General M,O
Chemistry M
City and Regional Planning M
Clinical Psychology M
Communication Disorders M
Communication—General M
Community Health M,O
Computer Science M
Counselor Education M
Criminal Justice and Criminology M
Early Childhood Education M
Economics M
Education—General M
Educational Administration M,D,O
Educational Media/Instructional Technology M
Elementary Education M
Engineering and Applied Sciences—General M
English M
Environmental and Occupational Health M
Exercise and Sports Science M
Finance and Banking M
Gerontology M,O
Health Services Management and Hospital Administration M,D,O
History M
Information Science M
Liberal Studies M
Manufacturing Engineering M
Marriage and Family Therapy M
Mathematics M
Microbiology M,D
Music Education M
Nursing—General M,D,O
Nutrition M
Pharmacology M,D
Physical Education M
Physical Therapy M
Physiology M,D
Psychology—General M
Public Health—General M,O
Reading Education M
Secondary Education M
Social Work M
Sociology M
Software Engineering M
Special Education M
Sports Management M
Urban Studies M
Vocational and Technical Education M

In-depth description on page 863.

ÉCOLE DES HAUTES ÉTUDES COMMERCIALES DE MONTRÉAL

Accounting M,O
Applied Economics M
Arts Administration O
Business Administration and Management—General M,D,O*
Corporate and Organizational Communication O
Electronic Commerce M,O
Finance and Banking M
Financial Engineering M
Human Resources Management M
Industrial and Manufacturing Management M
International Business M
Logistics M
Management Information Systems M
Management Strategy and Policy M
Marketing M
Taxation M,O

ÉCOLE POLYTECHNIQUE DE MONTRÉAL

Aerospace/Aeronautical Engineering M,D,O
Applied Mathematics M,D
Biomedical Engineering M,D,O
Chemical Engineering M,D,O
Civil Engineering M,D,O
Computer Engineering M,D,O
Computer Science M,D,O
Electrical Engineering M,D,O
Engineering and Applied Sciences—General M,D,O
Engineering Physics M,D,O
Environmental Engineering M,D,O
Geological Engineering M,D,O
Geotechnical Engineering M,D,O
Hydraulics M,D,O
Industrial/Management Engineering M,O
Management of Technology M,O
Materials Engineering M,D,O
Materials Sciences M,D,O
Mathematics M,D
Mechanical Engineering M,D,O
Mechanics M,D,O
Metallurgical Engineering and Metallurgy M,D,O
Mineral/Mining Engineering M,D,O
Nuclear Engineering M,D,O
Operations Research M,D,O
Optical Sciences M,D,O
Structural Engineering M,D,O
Transportation and Highway Engineering M,D,O

ECUMENICAL THEOLOGICAL SEMINARY

Pastoral Ministry and Counseling D
Theology P

EDEN THEOLOGICAL SEMINARY

Theology P,M,D

EDGEWOOD COLLEGE

Business Administration and Management—General M
Education—General M,O
Educational Administration M,O
Marriage and Family Therapy M
Nursing—General M
Religion M
Special Education M,O

EDINBORO UNIVERSITY OF PENNSYLVANIA

Accounting O
Advanced Practice Nursing M
Art/Fine Arts M

Program	Degrees
Biological and Biomedical Sciences—General	M
Clinical Psychology	M
Communication Disorders	M
Communication—General	M
Computer Science	O
Counselor Education	M,O
Early Childhood Education	M
Education—General	M,O
Educational Administration	M,O
Educational Psychology	M
Elementary Education	M,O
English Education	M
Health Education	O
Information Science	O
Mathematics Education	M
Mathematics	O
Middle School Education	M
Nursing—General	M
Physical Education	O
Psychology—General	M
Reading Education	M,O
Rehabilitation Counseling	M,O
School Psychology	O
Science Education	M
Secondary Education	M
Social Sciences Education	M
Social Sciences	M
Social Work	M
Special Education	M

ELMHURST COLLEGE

Program	Degrees
Accounting	M
Computer Science	M
Industrial and Organizational Psychology	M
Logistics	M
Special Education	M
Writing	M

ELMS COLLEGE

Program	Degrees
Early Childhood Education	M,O
Education—General	M,O
Elementary Education	M,O
English as a Second Language	M,O
English Education	M,O
Foreign Languages Education	M,O
Liberal Studies	M
Reading Education	M,O
Religion	M
Science Education	M,O
Secondary Education	M,O
Special Education	M,O

ELON UNIVERSITY

Program	Degrees
Business Administration and Management—General	M
Education—General	M
Elementary Education	M
Physical Therapy	D
Special Education	M

EMBRY-RIDDLE AERONAUTICAL UNIVERSITY (FL)

Program	Degrees
Aerospace/Aeronautical Engineering	M*
Aviation Management	M
Business Administration and Management—General	M
Ergonomics and Human Factors	M*
Safety Engineering	M*
Software Engineering	M*
Systems Engineering	M

EMBRY-RIDDLE AERONAUTICAL UNIVERSITY, EXTENDED CAMPUS

Program	Degrees
Aerospace/Aeronautical Engineering	M
Aviation Management	M
Management of Technology	M*

EMERSON COLLEGE

Program	Degrees
Advertising and Public Relations	M
Communication Disorders	M
Communication—General	M*
Corporate and Organizational Communication	M
Film, Television, and Video Production	M
Health Promotion	M
Journalism	M
Mass Communication	M
Media Studies	M
Public Health—General	M*
Publishing	M
Theater	M
Writing	M

In-depth description on page 865.

EMMANUEL COLLEGE

Program	Degrees
Business Administration and Management—General	M*
Education—General	M*
Educational Administration	M
Elementary Education	M
Human Resources Management	M
Multilingual and Multicultural Education	M
Secondary Education	M

EMMANUEL SCHOOL OF RELIGION

Program	Degrees
Religion	P,M,D
Theology	P,M,D

EMORY & HENRY COLLEGE

Program	Degrees
English Education	M

EMORY UNIVERSITY

Program	Degrees
Advanced Practice Nursing	M
Allied Health—General	M,D
Allopathic Medicine	P
Anthropology	D
Art History	D
Biochemistry	D*
Biological and Biomedical Sciences—General	D*
Biophysics	D
Biopsychology	D
Biostatistics	M,D*
Business Administration and Management—General	M,D
Cancer Biology/Oncology	M,D
Cell Biology	D*
Chemistry	D
Clinical Psychology	D
Cognitive Sciences	D
Community Health	M
Comparative Literature	D,O
Computer Science	M,D*
Developmental Biology	D
Developmental Psychology	D
Ecology	D*
Economics	D
Education—General	M,D,O
English	D
Environmental and Occupational Health	M
Epidemiology	M,D
Evolutionary Biology	D*
Film, Television, and Video Theory and Criticism	M*
French	D
Genetics	D*
Gerontological Nursing	M
Health Physics/Radiological Health	M,D
Health Services Management and Hospital Administration	M
History	D
Immunology	D*
Interdisciplinary Studies	D*
International Health	M
Jewish Studies	M
Law	P,M,O
Mathematics	M,D*
Medical Informatics	M*
Medical/Surgical Nursing	M
Microbiology	D*
Middle School Education	M,D,O
Molecular Biology	D*
Music	M
Neurobiology	D
Nurse Anesthesia	M
Nurse Midwifery	M
Nursing—General	M,D*
Nutrition	D*
Oncology Nursing	M
Pediatric Nursing	M
Pharmacology	D*
Philosophy	D
Physical Therapy	D
Physician Assistant Studies	M
Physics	D*
Political Science	D
Psychology—General	D
Public Health—General	M,D*
Religion	D
Secondary Education	M,D,O
Sociology	D*
Spanish	D,O
Theology	P,M,D
Vision Sciences	M
Women's Health Nursing	M
Women's Studies	D,O

In-depth description on page 867.

EMPEROR'S COLLEGE OF TRADITIONAL ORIENTAL MEDICINE

Program	Degrees
Acupuncture and Oriental Medicine	M

EMPORIA STATE UNIVERSITY

Program	Degrees
Art Therapy	M
Biological and Biomedical Sciences—General	M
Botany	M
Business Administration and Management—General	M*
Business Education	M
Cell Biology	M
Chemistry	M
Clinical Psychology	M
Computer Science	M
Counselor Education	M
Curriculum and Instruction	M
Early Childhood Education	M
Economics	M
Education of the Gifted	M
Education—General	M,O
Educational Administration	M
Educational Media/Instructional Technology	M
Elementary Education	M
English as a Second Language	M
English	M
Environmental Biology	M
Geosciences	M
Health Psychology	M
History	M
Industrial and Organizational Psychology	M
Information Studies	M,D
Library Science	M,D*
Mathematics	M
Microbiology	M
Music Education	M
Music	M
Physical Education	M
Physics	M
Psychology—General	M
Reading Education	M
Rehabilitation Counseling	M
School Psychology	M,O
Secondary Education	M
Social Sciences Education	M
Special Education	M
Student Personnel Services	M
Zoology	M

In-depth description on page 869.

ENDICOTT COLLEGE

Program	Degrees
Art Education	M
Business Administration and Management—General	M
Education—General	M
Elementary Education	M
Hospitality Management	M
International and Comparative Education	M
Organizational Management	M
Reading Education	M
Special Education	M

EPISCOPAL DIVINITY SCHOOL

Program	Degrees
Theology	P,M,D,O*

EPISCOPAL THEOLOGICAL SEMINARY OF THE SOUTHWEST

Program	Degrees
Theology	P,M,O

ERIKSON INSTITUTE

Program	Degrees
Developmental Psychology	M,D
Early Childhood Education	M,O
Educational Administration	M,O
Human Development	M,O

ERSKINE THEOLOGICAL SEMINARY

Program	Degrees
Theology	P,M,D

EVANGELICAL SCHOOL OF THEOLOGY

Program	Degrees
Marriage and Family Therapy	P,M,O
Pastoral Ministry and Counseling	P,M,O
Religion	P,M,O
Theology	P,M,O

EVANGELICAL SEMINARY OF PUERTO RICO

Program	Degrees
Theology	P,M

EVANGEL UNIVERSITY

Program	Degrees
Clinical Psychology	M
Counselor Education	M
Education—General	M
Elementary Education	M
Psychology—General	M
Reading Education	M

THE EVERGREEN STATE COLLEGE

Program	Degrees
Education—General	M
Environmental Management and Policy	M*
Public Policy and Administration	M*

EXCELSIOR COLLEGE

Program	Degrees
Liberal Studies	M
Nursing and Healthcare Administration	M
Nursing—General	M

FAIRFIELD UNIVERSITY

Program	Degrees
Accounting	M,O
Advanced Practice Nursing	M,O
American Studies	M
Business Administration and Management—General	M,O
Counselor Education	M,O
Early Childhood Education	M,O
Education—General	M,O*
Educational Media/Instructional Technology	M,O
Elementary Education	M,O
Engineering and Applied Sciences—General	M*
English as a Second Language	M,O
Finance and Banking	M,O
Foreign Languages Education	M,O
Foundations and Philosophy of Education	M,O
Health Services Management and Hospital Administration	M,O
Human Resources Management	M,O
International Business	M,O
Management Information Systems	M,O
Management of Technology	M
Marketing	M,O
Marriage and Family Therapy	M
Mathematics	M
Multilingual and Multicultural Education	M,O
Nursing—General	M,O
Psychiatric Nursing	M,O
Psychology—General	M,O
School Psychology	M,O
Software Engineering	M
Special Education	M,O
Taxation	M,O

FAIRLEIGH DICKINSON UNIVERSITY, COLLEGE AT FLORHAM

Program	Degrees
Accounting	M
Biological and Biomedical Sciences—General	M
Business Administration and Management—General	M*
Chemistry	M
Clinical Psychology	M*
Corporate and Organizational Communication	M
Entrepreneurship	M
Experimental Psychology	M
Finance and Banking	M
Hospitality Management	M*
Human Resources Management	M*
Industrial and Organizational Psychology	M
International Business	M
Management Information Systems	M
Marketing	M
Mathematics	M
Organizational Behavior	M
Psychology—General	M
Social Psychology	M
Taxation	M
Women's Studies	M
Writing	M

In-depth description on page 871.

FAIRLEIGH DICKINSON UNIVERSITY, METROPOLITAN CAMPUS

Program	Degrees
Accounting	M
Biological and Biomedical Sciences—General	M
Business Administration and Management—General	M*
Clinical Laboratory Sciences/Medical Technology	M
Clinical Psychology	D*
Communication—General	M
Comparative Literature	M
Computer Engineering	M
Computer Science	M*
Curriculum and Instruction	M
Education—General	M*
Educational Administration	M
Electrical Engineering	M
Electronic Commerce	M
Engineering and Applied Sciences—General	M*
English	M
Entrepreneurship	M
Experimental Psychology	M
Finance and Banking	M
Health Services Management and Hospital Administration	M
History	M
Hospitality Management	M*

Fairleigh Dickinson University, Metropolitan Campus (continued)

Human Resources Management M
International Affairs M
International Business M
Management Information Systems M
Marketing M
Multilingual and Multicultural Education M
Nursing—General M
Pharmaceutical Administration M
Political Science M
Psychology—General M,D
Public Policy and Administration M
School Psychology M,D
Special Education M
Systems Science M
Taxation M

In-depth description on page 871.

FAITH BAPTIST BIBLE COLLEGE AND THEOLOGICAL SEMINARY

Pastoral Ministry and Counseling P,M,D
Religion P,M,D
Theology P,M,D

FAITH EVANGELICAL LUTHERAN SEMINARY

Theology P,M

FASHION INSTITUTE OF TECHNOLOGY

Applied Arts and Design—General M*
Arts Administration M
Clothing and Textiles M
Marketing M
Museum Studies M

FAULKNER UNIVERSITY

Law P

FAYETTEVILLE STATE UNIVERSITY

Biological and Biomedical Sciences—General M
Business Administration and Management—General M
Educational Administration M,D
Elementary Education M
English M
History M
Mathematics M
Middle School Education M
Political Science M
Psychology—General M
Secondary Education M,D
Social Sciences Education M
Sociology M

FELICIAN COLLEGE

Advanced Practice Nursing M
Education—General M
Nursing—General M
Religious Education M

FERRIS STATE UNIVERSITY

Business Administration and Management—General M
Criminal Justice and Criminology M
Curriculum and Instruction M
Developmental Education M
Education—General M
Educational Administration M
Educational Media/Instructional Technology M
Elementary Education M
Human Services M
Management Information Systems M
Optometry P
Pharmacy P
Reading Education M

FIELDING GRADUATE INSTITUTE

Clinical Psychology M,D
Educational Administration D
Human Development M,D
Human Services M,D
Organizational Management M,D
Psychology—General M,D

FINCH UNIVERSITY OF HEALTH SCIENCES/THE CHICAGO MEDICAL SCHOOL

Allied Health—General M,D*
Allopathic Medicine P
Anatomy M,D
Biochemistry M,D*
Biological and Biomedical Sciences—General M,D*
Cell Biology M,D
Clinical Laboratory Sciences/Medical Technology M
Clinical Psychology M,D
Health Education M
Health Services Management and Hospital Administration M
Immunology M,D
Medical Microbiology M,D
Medical Physics M,D
Microbiology M,D*
Neuroscience D*
Nutrition M
Pathology M,D
Pharmacology M,D
Physical Therapy M,D
Physician Assistant Studies M
Physiology M,D*

FISK UNIVERSITY

Biological and Biomedical Sciences—General M
Chemistry M
Clinical Psychology M
Physics M
Psychology—General M
Sociology M

FITCHBURG STATE COLLEGE

Art Education M
Business Administration and Management—General M
Child and Family Studies M,O
Communication—General M
Computer Science M
Counseling Psychology M,O
Counselor Education M,O
Criminal Justice and Criminology M
Early Childhood Education M
Education—General M,O
Educational Administration M,O
Elementary Education M
English Education M
Forensic Nursing M
Forensic Sciences M,O
Interdisciplinary Studies O
Marriage and Family Therapy M,O
Mathematics Education M
Middle School Education M
Science Education M
Secondary Education M
Social Sciences Education M
Special Education M
Vocational and Technical Education M

In-depth description on page 873.

FIVE BRANCHES INSTITUTE: COLLEGE OF TRADITIONAL CHINESE MEDICINE

Acupuncture and Oriental Medicine M*

FIVE TOWNS COLLEGE

Music Education M
Music M

FLORIDA AGRICULTURAL AND MECHANICAL UNIVERSITY

Accounting M
Adult Education M,D
Agricultural Education M
Architecture M
Biological and Biomedical Sciences—General M
Business Administration and Management—General M
Business Education M
Chemical Engineering M,D
Chemistry M
Civil Engineering M,D*
Counselor Education M,D
Early Childhood Education M
Education—General M,D
Educational Administration M,D
Electrical Engineering M,D
Elementary Education M
Engineering and Applied Sciences—General M,D
Environmental Engineering M,D
Finance and Banking M
Health Education M
Industrial/Management Engineering M
Journalism M
Management Information Systems M
Marketing M
Mechanical Engineering M,D*
Medicinal and Pharmaceutical Chemistry M,D
Pharmaceutical Administration M,D
Pharmaceutical Sciences M,D*
Pharmacology M,D
Pharmacy P
Physical Education M
Physics M
Psychology—General M
Public Health—General M,D
Recreation and Park Management M
School Psychology M
Secondary Education M
Social Psychology M
Social Sciences M
Toxicology M,D
Vocational and Technical Education M

FLORIDA ATLANTIC UNIVERSITY

Accounting M
Adult Education M,D,O
Advanced Practice Nursing M,D,O
Anthropology M
Art Education M
Art/Fine Arts M
Biochemistry M,D
Biological and Biomedical Sciences—General M
Business Administration and Management—General M,D
Chemistry M,D
City and Regional Planning M
Civil Engineering M,D
Communication Disorders M
Communication—General M
Comparative Literature M
Computer Art and Design M
Computer Engineering M,D
Computer Science M,D
Counselor Education M,O
Criminal Justice and Criminology M
Curriculum and Instruction M,D,O
Economics M
Education—General M,D,O
Educational Administration M,D,O
Educational Media/Instructional Technology M
Electrical Engineering M,D
Elementary Education M
Engineering and Applied Sciences—General M,D
English Education M
English M
Environmental Sciences M
Exercise and Sports Science M
Foreign Languages Education M
Foundations and Philosophy of Education M,D,O
French M
Geography M
Geology M
German M
Graphic Design M
Higher Education M,D,O
History M
International Business M
Liberal Studies M
Manufacturing Engineering M
Maternal/Child Nursing M,D,O
Mathematics M,D
Mechanical Engineering M,D
Music M
Nursing and Healthcare Administration M,D,O
Nursing—General M,D,O
Ocean Engineering M,D
Physics M,D
Political Science M
Psychology—General M,D
Public Policy and Administration M,D
Reading Education M
Social Work M
Sociology M
Spanish M
Special Education M,D
Sports Management M
Systems Engineering M
Taxation M*
Theater M
Women's Studies M,O

FLORIDA ATLANTIC UNIVERSITY, DAVIE CAMPUS

Computer Art and Design M
English Education M
Graphic Design M
Liberal Studies M
Music M

FLORIDA ATLANTIC UNIVERSITY, FT. LAUDERDALE CAMPUS

Accounting M
Adult Education M,D,O
Art/Fine Arts M
Business Administration and Management—General M,D
City and Regional Planning M
Counselor Education M,O
Criminal Justice and Criminology M
Curriculum and Instruction M,D,O
Education—General M,D,O
Educational Administration M,D,O
Educational Measurement and Evaluation M
Educational Media/Instructional Technology M
Educational Psychology M,D,O
Elementary Education M,D,O
English as a Second Language M,D,O
Exercise and Sports Science M
Health Education M
Liberal Studies M
Medical/Surgical Nursing M
Multilingual and Multicultural Education M,D,O
Music M
Ocean Engineering M,D
Public Policy and Administration M,D
Reading Education M,D,O
Science Education M,D,O
Secondary Education M,D,O
Social Sciences Education M,D,O
Special Education M,D
Taxation M
Writing M

FLORIDA COASTAL SCHOOL OF LAW

Law P

FLORIDA GULF COAST UNIVERSITY

Accounting M
Allied Health—General M
Business Administration and Management—General M
Computer Science M
Counselor Education M
Criminal Justice and Criminology M
Curriculum and Instruction M
Education—General M
Educational Administration M
Educational Media/Instructional Technology M
Elementary Education M
English Education M
Environmental Management and Policy M
Information Science M
Mathematics Education M
Nursing—General M
Physical Therapy M
Public Policy and Administration M
Reading Education M
Science Education M
Secondary Education M
Social Sciences Education M
Social Work M
Special Education M
Taxation M

FLORIDA INSTITUTE OF TECHNOLOGY

Aerospace/Aeronautical Engineering M,D*
Applied Mathematics M,D
Biological and Biomedical Sciences—General M,D
Biotechnology M,D
Business Administration and Management—General M
Cell Biology D*
Chemical Engineering M,D
Chemistry M,D
Civil Engineering M,D*
Clinical Psychology D
Communication—General M
Computer Education M,D,O
Computer Engineering M,D
Computer Science M,D*
Ecology M
Electrical Engineering M,D*
Engineering and Applied Sciences—General M,D
Engineering Management M*
Environmental Education M,D,O
Environmental Management and Policy M,D
Environmental Sciences M,D*
Ergonomics and Human Factors M
Health Services Management and Hospital Administration M
Human Resources Management M
Industrial and Manufacturing Management M
Industrial and Organizational Psychology M,D
Information Science M,D
Logistics M
Management Information Systems M
Marine Affairs M,D
Marine Biology M*
Marine Sciences M,D
Mathematics Education M,D,O
Mechanical Engineering M,D*
Meteorology M,D
Molecular Biology D
Ocean Engineering M,D*
Oceanography M,D*
Operations Research M,D

Program	Degrees
Physics	M,D
Planetary and Space Sciences	M,D
Psychology—General	M,D*
Public Policy and Administration	M
Science Education	M,D,O
Software Engineering	M,D
Systems Science	M
Technical Writing	M
Transportation Management	M

In-depth description on page 875.

FLORIDA INTERNATIONAL UNIVERSITY

Program	Degrees
Accounting	M
Adult Education	M,D
African Studies	M
Architecture	M
Art Education	M,D
Art/Fine Arts	M
Biological and Biomedical Sciences—General	M,D
Biomedical Engineering	M
Business Administration and Management—General	M,D
Chemistry	M,D
Civil Engineering	M,D
Communication Disorders	M
Computer Engineering	M
Computer Science	M,D*
Construction Engineering and Management	M
Counselor Education	M
Criminal Justice and Criminology	M
Curriculum and Instruction	M,D,O
Developmental Psychology	M,D
Early Childhood Education	M
Economics	M,D
Education—General	M,D,O
Educational Administration	M,D,O
Electrical Engineering	M,D
Elementary Education	M
Engineering and Applied Sciences—General	M,D
English as a Second Language	M
English Education	M,D
English	M
Environmental Engineering	M
Environmental Management and Policy	M
Environmental Sciences	M
Finance and Banking	M
Foreign Languages Education	M,D
Forensic Sciences	M,D
Geosciences	M,D
Health Education	M
Health Services Management and Hospital Administration	M
Higher Education	M,D,O
History	M,D
Home Economics Education	M,D,O
Hospitality Management	M
Human Resources Development	M
Industrial/Management Engineering	M
International Affairs	M,D
International and Comparative Education	M,D,O
International Business	M
Landscape Architecture	M
Latin American Studies	M
Linguistics	M
Management Information Systems	D
Mass Communication	M
Mathematics Education	M
Mathematics	M
Mechanical Engineering	M,D
Music Education	M
Music	M
Nursing—General	M
Nutrition	M,D*
Occupational Therapy	M
Physical Education	M
Physical Therapy	M
Physics	M,D
Political Science	M,D
Psychology—General	M,D
Public Health—General	M
Public Policy and Administration	M,D
Reading Education	M
Recreation and Park Management	M
Religion	M
School Psychology	O
Science Education	M,D
Social Sciences Education	M
Social Work	M,D
Sociology	M,D
Spanish	M,D
Special Education	M,D
Statistics	M
Taxation	M
Urban Education	M
Vocational and Technical Education	M
Writing	M

In-depth description on page 877.

FLORIDA METROPOLITAN UNIVERSITY–BRANDON CAMPUS

Program	Degrees
Business Administration and Management—General	M
Criminal Justice and Criminology	M

FLORIDA METROPOLITAN UNIVERSITY–FORT LAUDERDALE CAMPUS

Program	Degrees
Business Administration and Management—General	M

FLORIDA METROPOLITAN UNIVERSITY–MELBOURNE CAMPUS

Program	Degrees
Business Administration and Management—General	M

FLORIDA METROPOLITAN UNIVERSITY–NORTH ORLANDO CAMPUS

Program	Degrees
Business Administration and Management—General	M

FLORIDA METROPOLITAN UNIVERSITY–PINELLAS CAMPUS

Program	Degrees
Business Administration and Management—General	M
Criminal Justice and Criminology	M

FLORIDA METROPOLITAN UNIVERSITY–TAMPA CAMPUS

Program	Degrees
Business Administration and Management—General	M
Human Resources Management	M
International Business	M

FLORIDA SOUTHERN COLLEGE

Program	Degrees
Accounting	M
Business Administration and Management—General	M

FLORIDA STATE UNIVERSITY

Program	Degrees
Accounting	M,D
Adult Education	M,D,O
Advanced Practice Nursing	M
American Studies	M
Analytical Chemistry	M,D
Anthropology	M,D
Applied Mathematics	M,D
Archaeology	M,D
Art Education	M,D,O
Art History	M,D,O
Art/Fine Arts	M
Arts Administration	M,D
Asian Studies	M
Biochemistry	M,D
Biological and Biomedical Sciences—General	M,D*
Biophysics	D*
Business Administration and Management—General	M,D
Cell Biology	M,D
Chemical Engineering	M,D
Chemistry	M,D*
Child and Family Studies	M,D
City and Regional Planning	M,D
Civil Engineering	M,D*
Classics	M,D
Clinical Psychology	D
Clothing and Textiles	M,D
Cognitive Sciences	D
Communication Disorders	M,D
Communication—General	M,D
Computer Science	M,D
Consumer Economics	M,D
Corporate and Organizational Communication	M,D
Counseling Psychology	D
Counselor Education	M,O
Criminal Justice and Criminology	M,D
Dance	M
Demography and Population Studies	M,O
Developmental Biology	M,D
Distance Education Development	M,D,O
Early Childhood Education	M,D,O
East European and Russian Studies	M
Ecology	M,D
Economics	M,D
Education—General	M,D,O
Educational Administration	M,D,O
Educational Measurement and Evaluation	M,D,O
Educational Media/Instructional Technology	M,D,O
Educational Psychology	M,D,O
Electrical Engineering	M,D
Elementary Education	M,D,O
Engineering and Applied Sciences—General	M,D
English Education	M,D,O
English	M,D
Environmental Engineering	M,D
Evolutionary Biology	M,D
Exercise and Sports Science	M,D
Family and Consumer Sciences-General	M,D*
Film, Television, and Video Production	M
Finance and Banking	M,D
Food Science and Technology	M,D
Foundations and Philosophy of Education	M,D,O
French	M,D
Genetics	M,D
Geography	M,D
Geology	M,D
Geophysics	D
German	M
Gerontology	M
Health Education	M,D
Health Services Research	M
Higher Education	M,D,O
History	M,D
Hospitality Management	M,D
Humanities	M,D
Immunology	M,D
Industrial/Management Engineering	M,D
Information Studies	M,D,O*
Inorganic Chemistry	M,D
Insurance	M,D
Interior Design	M
International Affairs	M*
International and Comparative Education	M,D,O
Internet and Interactive Multimedia	M,D
Italian	M
Kinesiology and Movement Studies	M,D
Law	P
Library Science	M,D,O
Management Information Systems	M,D
Marine Biology	M,D
Marketing	M,D
Marriage and Family Therapy	D
Mass Communication	M,D
Mathematical and Computational Finance	M,D
Mathematics Education	M,D,O
Mathematics	M,D
Mechanical Engineering	M,D*
Meteorology	M,D
Microbiology	M,D
Military and Defense Studies	M,D,O
Molecular Biology	M,D
Multilingual and Multicultural Education	M,D,O
Museum Studies	M,D,O
Music Education	M,D
Music	M,D
Neuroscience	D
Nursing Education	M
Nursing—General	M
Nutrition	M,D
Oceanography	M,D*
Organic Chemistry	M,D
Philosophy	M,D
Physical Chemistry	M,D
Physical Education	M,D,O
Physics	M,D*
Physiology	M,D
Plant Biology	M,D
Political Science	M,D
Psychology—General	M,D
Public History	M,D
Public Policy and Administration	M,D,O*
Radiation Biology	M,D
Reading Education	M,D,O
Recreation and Park Management	M,D,O
Rehabilitation Counseling	M,D,O
Religion	M,D
Rhetoric	M,D
School Psychology	M,O
Science Education	M,D,O
Slavic Languages	M
Social Sciences Education	M,D,O
Social Sciences	M
Social Work	M,D
Sociology	M,D
Software Engineering	M,D
Spanish	M,D
Special Education	M,D,O
Speech and Interpersonal Communication	M,D
Sport Psychology	M,D,O
Sports Management	M,D,O
Statistics	M,D
Theater	M,D
Therapies—Dance, Drama, and Music	M,D
Vocational and Technical Education	D,O
Writing	M,D

In-depth description on page 879.

FONTBONNE UNIVERSITY

Program	Degrees
Art/Fine Arts	M
Business Administration and Management—General	M
Communication Disorders	M
Computer Education	M
Education—General	M
Special Education	M
Taxation	M

FORDHAM UNIVERSITY

Program	Degrees
Accounting	M
Adult Education	M,D,O
American Studies	M,D
Biological and Biomedical Sciences—General	M,D*
Business Administration and Management—General	M*
Cell Biology	M,D
Classics	M,D
Clinical Psychology	D
Communication—General	M
Computer Science	M
Corporate and Organizational Communication	M
Counseling Psychology	M,D,O
Counselor Education	M,D,O
Criminal Justice and Criminology	M,D
Curriculum and Instruction	M,D,O
Demography and Population Studies	M,D
Developmental Psychology	D
Early Childhood Education	M,D,O
Ecology	M,D
Economics	M,D,O
Education—General	M,D,O*
Educational Administration	M,D,O
Educational Psychology	M,D,O
Elementary Education	M,D,O
English as a Second Language	M,D,O
English	M,D
Finance and Banking	M
History	M,D
Human Resources Management	M,D,O
International Development	M,O
Law	P,M
Liberal Studies	M
Management Information Systems	M
Marketing	M
Mass Communication	M
Medieval and Renaissance Studies	M,D
Molecular Biology	M,D
Multilingual and Multicultural Education	M,D,O
Pastoral Ministry and Counseling	M,D,O
Philosophy	M,D
Political Science	M
Psychology—General	D
Reading Education	M,D,O
Religion	M,D,O
Religious Education	M,D,O
School Psychology	M,D,O
Secondary Education	M,D,O
Social Work	M,D
Sociology	M,D
Special Education	M,D,O
Taxation	M
Theology	M,D

In-depth description on page 881.

FOREST INSTITUTE OF PROFESSIONAL PSYCHOLOGY

Program	Degrees
Clinical Psychology	M,D
Psychology—General	M,D

FORT HAYS STATE UNIVERSITY

Program	Degrees
Accounting	M
Art/Fine Arts	M
Biological and Biomedical Sciences—General	M
Business Administration and Management—General	M
Communication Disorders	M
Communication—General	M
Counselor Education	M
Education—General	M,O
Educational Administration	M,O
Educational Media/Instructional Technology	M
Elementary Education	M
English	M
Geology	M
Health Education	M
History	M
Liberal Studies	M
Mathematics Education	M
Nursing—General	M

Fort Hays State University (continued)

Physical Education M
Psychology—General M,O
Recreation and Park Management M
School Psychology O
Secondary Education M
Special Education M

FORT VALLEY STATE UNIVERSITY

Counseling Psychology M
Counselor Education M,O
Early Childhood Education M
Middle School Education M
Rehabilitation Counseling M

FRAMINGHAM STATE COLLEGE

Art/Fine Arts M
Business Administration and Management—General M
Counseling Psychology M
Curriculum and Instruction M
Educational Administration M
Educational Media/Instructional Technology M
English as a Second Language M
English Education M
Food Science and Technology M*
Foreign Languages Education M
Health Services Management and Hospital Administration M
Human Resources Management M
Human Services M
Mathematics Education M
Nutrition M
Psychology—General M
Public Policy and Administration M
Reading Education M
Social Sciences Education M
Spanish M
Special Education M

FRANCISCAN SCHOOL OF THEOLOGY

Pastoral Ministry and Counseling P,M,O
Theology P,M,O

FRANCISCAN UNIVERSITY OF STEUBENVILLE

Business Administration and Management—General M
Counseling Psychology M
Curriculum and Instruction M
Education—General M
Educational Administration M
Nursing—General M
Philosophy M
Theology M

FRANCIS MARION UNIVERSITY

Business Administration and Management—General M
Clinical Psychology M
Early Childhood Education M
Education—General M
Elementary Education M
Health Services Management and Hospital Administration M
Psychology—General M
School Psychology M
Secondary Education M
Social Psychology M
Special Education M

FRANKLIN PIERCE COLLEGE

Business Administration and Management—General M

FRANKLIN PIERCE LAW CENTER

Law P,M,O

FRANKLIN UNIVERSITY

Business Administration and Management—General M
Computer Science M
Corporate and Organizational Communication M
Human Services M
Marketing M

FRANK LLOYD WRIGHT SCHOOL OF ARCHITECTURE

Architecture M*

FREED-HARDEMAN UNIVERSITY

Counselor Education M
Curriculum and Instruction M
Education—General M
Pastoral Ministry and Counseling M
Theology M

FRESNO PACIFIC UNIVERSITY

Business Administration and Management—General M
Conflict Resolution and Mediation/Peace Studies M
Counselor Education M
Curriculum and Instruction M
Education of the Multiply Handicapped M
Education—General M
Educational Administration M
Educational Media/Instructional Technology M
English as a Second Language M
Interdisciplinary Studies M
Mathematics Education M
Multilingual and Multicultural Education M
Reading Education M
School Psychology M
Science Education M
Special Education M

FRIENDS UNIVERSITY

Business Administration and Management—General M
Education—General M
Educational Administration M
Elementary Education M
Environmental Management and Policy M
Human Resources Development M
Management Information Systems M
Marriage and Family Therapy M
Secondary Education M
Theology M

FROSTBURG STATE UNIVERSITY

Biological and Biomedical Sciences—General M
Business Administration and Management—General M
Computer Science M
Conservation Biology M
Counseling Psychology M
Counselor Education M
Curriculum and Instruction M
Ecology M
Education—General M
Educational Administration M
Educational Media/Instructional Technology M
Elementary Education M
Fish, Game, and Wildlife Management M
Health Education M
Humanities M
Physical Education M
Psychology—General M
Reading Education M
Recreation and Park Management M
Secondary Education M
Special Education M

FULLER THEOLOGICAL SEMINARY

Clinical Psychology M,D
Marriage and Family Therapy M
Missions and Missiology M,D
Psychology—General M,D
Theology P,M,D

FURMAN UNIVERSITY

Chemistry M
Early Childhood Education M
Education—General M
Educational Administration M
Elementary Education M
Reading Education M
Special Education M

GALLAUDET UNIVERSITY

Clinical Psychology D
Communication Disorders M,D
Counseling Psychology M
Counselor Education M
Developmental Psychology M,O
Early Childhood Education M,D,O
Education of the Multiply Handicapped M,D,O
Education—General M,D,O
Educational Administration M,D,O
Educational Measurement and Evaluation O
Educational Media/Instructional Technology O
Elementary Education M,D,O
Leisure Studies M
Linguistics M
Psychology—General M,D,O
School Psychology M,O
Secondary Education M,D,O
Social Work M
Special Education M,D,O
Translation and Interpretation M

GANNON UNIVERSITY

Accounting O
Advanced Practice Nursing M,O
Business Administration and Management—General M,O
Counseling Psychology M,D
Curriculum and Instruction M
Early Childhood Education M,O
Education—General M,D,O
Educational Media/Instructional Technology M
Electrical Engineering M
Engineering and Applied Sciences—General M
English M
Environmental Education M,O
Finance and Banking O
Gerontological Nursing M,O
Gerontology O
Human Resources Management O
Mechanical Engineering M
Medical/Surgical Nursing M,O
Nurse Anesthesia M,O
Nursing and Healthcare Administration M,O
Nursing—General M,O
Occupational Therapy M
Pastoral Ministry and Counseling M,O
Physical Therapy M
Physician Assistant Studies M
Public Policy and Administration M,O
Reading Education M,O
Science Education M,O
Secondary Education M
Software Engineering M

GARDNER-WEBB UNIVERSITY

Business Administration and Management—General M
Counseling Psychology M
Education—General M
Educational Administration M
Elementary Education M
English Education M
English M
Middle School Education M
Missions and Missiology P,D
Music P,D
Pastoral Ministry and Counseling P,D
Physical Education M
Psychology—General M
Religious Education P,D
School Psychology M
Theology P,D

GARRETT-EVANGELICAL THEOLOGICAL SEMINARY

Music P,M,D
Pastoral Ministry and Counseling P,M,D
Religious Education P,M,D
Theology P,M,D

GENERAL THEOLOGICAL SEMINARY

Theology P,M,D

GENEVA COLLEGE

Business Administration and Management—General M*
Counseling Psychology M*
Counselor Education M
Education—General M
Educational Administration M
Higher Education M
Marriage and Family Therapy M
Organizational Management M
Psychology—General M
Special Education M

GEORGE FOX UNIVERSITY

Business Administration and Management—General M
Clinical Psychology M,D
Counseling Psychology M
Education—General M,D
Marriage and Family Therapy M
Organizational Management M
Pastoral Ministry and Counseling P,M,D
Psychology—General M,D
Religion P,M,D
Religious Education P,M,D
Theology P,M,D

In-depth description on page 883.

GEORGE MASON UNIVERSITY

Advanced Practice Nursing M,D
Applied Physics M
Archaeology M
Bioinformatics M
Biological and Biomedical Sciences—General M
Business Administration and Management—General M
Cell Biology M
Chemistry M
City and Regional Planning M
Clinical Psychology D
Community College Education D
Computational Sciences M,D,O*
Computer Engineering M,D
Computer Science M,D
Conflict Resolution and Mediation/Peace Studies M,D*
Counselor Education M
Cultural Studies D*
Dance M
Developmental Psychology M,D
Early Childhood Education M
Ecology M
Economics M,D*
Education—General M,D
Educational Administration M
Educational Measurement and Evaluation M
Educational Media/Instructional Technology M
Electrical Engineering M,D
Engineering and Applied Sciences—General M,D*
Engineering Physics M
English as a Second Language M
English M
Environmental Management and Policy M,D
Environmental Sciences M,D
Evolutionary Biology M
Exercise and Sports Science M
Experimental Psychology M
Film, Television, and Video Production M
Foreign Languages Education M
Geographic Information Systems M
Geography M
Gerontology M
Graphic Design M
History M
Human Resources Management M
Industrial and Organizational Psychology M,D
Information Science M
Interdisciplinary Studies M
International Affairs M
Law P
Liberal Studies M
Linguistics M
Logistics M
Management of Technology M,D
Mathematics M
Medical/Surgical Nursing M,D
Middle School Education M
Molecular Biology M
Multilingual and Multicultural Education M
Music Education M
Music M
Nursing and Healthcare Administration M,D
Nursing—General M,D
Operations Research M
Organizational Behavior M
Organizational Management M
Physics M
Psychology—General M,D
Public Policy and Administration M,D*
Reading Education M
School Psychology M
Secondary Education M
Sociology M
Software Engineering M
Special Education M
Statistics M
Systems Engineering M
Technology and Public Policy M
Telecommunications M
Transportation Management M
Writing M

In-depth description on page 885.

GEORGETOWN COLLEGE

Education—General M

GEORGETOWN UNIVERSITY

Allopathic Medicine P
Analytical Chemistry M,D
Biochemistry M,D
Biological and Biomedical Sciences—General M,D*
Biophysics M,D
Biostatistics M
Business Administration and Management—General M
Cancer Biology/Oncology
Cell Biology D
Chemistry M,D
Communication—General M
Demography and Population Studies M

East European and Russian Studies	M
Economics	D
English as a Second Language	M,D,O
English	M
Epidemiology	M
German	M,D
Health Physics/Radiological Health	M
History	M,D
Immunology	D
Inorganic Chemistry	M,D
International Affairs	M,D*
Internet and Interactive Multimedia	M
Latin American Studies	M*
Law	P,M,D
Liberal Studies	M
Linguistics	M,D,O
Microbiology	D
Military and Defense Studies	M*
Molecular Biology	D
Multilingual and Multicultural Education	M,D,O
Near and Middle Eastern Languages	M,D*
Near and Middle Eastern Studies	M,O
Neuroscience	D
Nursing—General	M*
Organic Chemistry	M,D
Pathology	M,D
Pharmacology	D*
Philosophy	M,D
Physical Chemistry	M,D
Physiology	M,D
Political Science	M,D*
Psychology—General	D
Public Policy and Administration	M*
Radiation Biology	M
Spanish	M,D
Taxation	P,M,D
Theoretical Chemistry	M,D
Western European Studies	M

THE GEORGE WASHINGTON UNIVERSITY

Accounting	M,D
Aerospace/Aeronautical Engineering	M,D,O
Allopathic Medicine	P
American Studies	M,D
Analytical Chemistry	M,D
Anthropology	M
Applied Arts and Design—General	M
Applied Mathematics	M
Art History	M
Art Therapy	M
Art/Fine Arts	M
Asian Studies	M
Biochemistry	M,D*
Biological and Biomedical Sciences—General	M,D*
Biostatistics	M,D
Business Administration and Management—General	M,D
Cancer Biology/Oncology	D*
Chemistry	M,D
Civil Engineering	M,D,O*
Clinical Psychology	D
Cognitive Sciences	D
Communication Disorders	M
Community Health	M
Computational Sciences	M
Computer Engineering	M,D,O
Computer Science	M,D,O*
Counselor Education	M,D,O
Criminal Justice and Criminology	M
Curriculum and Instruction	M,D,O
Early Childhood Education	M
East European and Russian Studies	M
Economics	M,D
Education—General	M,D,O*
Educational Administration	M,D,O
Educational Media/Instructional Technology	M
Electrical Engineering	M,D,O*
Elementary Education	M
Engineering and Applied Sciences—General	M,D,O*
Engineering Management	M,D,O*
English	M,D
Environmental and Occupational Health	M*
Environmental Engineering	M,D,O
Environmental Management and Policy	M
Epidemiology	M,D*
Exercise and Sports Science	M*
Finance and Banking	M,D*
Folklore	M
Forensic Sciences	M
Foundations and Philosophy of Education	M
Genetics	M,D*
Geochemistry	M
Geography	M
Geology	M,D
Health Promotion	M
Health Services Management and Hospital Administration	M,O
Higher Education	M,D,O
Historic Preservation	M
History	M,D
Hospitality Management	M
Human Development	M
Human Resources Development	M,D,O
Human Resources Management	M,D
Immunology	D*
Industrial and Manufacturing Management	M
Industrial and Organizational Psychology	D
Inorganic Chemistry	M,D
Interior Design	M
International Affairs	M*
International and Comparative Education	M
International Business	M,D
International Development	M
International Health	M*
Investment Management	M,D
Latin American Studies	M
Law	P,M,D
Logistics	M
Management of Technology	M,D
Management Strategy and Policy	M,D
Marketing	M,D
Mass Communication	M
Materials Sciences	M,D
Maternal and Child Health	M
Mathematics	M,D
Mechanical Engineering	M,D,O*
Microbiology	D
Military and Defense Studies	M
Molecular Biology	M,D
Museum Education	M
Museum Studies	M,O
Neuroscience	D*
Oral and Dental Sciences	M
Organic Chemistry	M,D
Organizational Behavior	M,D
Organizational Management	M
Pharmacology	D*
Philosophy	M
Photography	M
Physical Chemistry	M,D
Physical Therapy	M
Physician Assistant Studies	M
Physics	D
Political Science	M,D
Project Management	M,D
Psychology—General	D
Public Health—General	M,D*
Public Policy and Administration	M,D*
Real Estate	M
Rehabilitation Counseling	M,D
Religion	M
Secondary Education	M
Social Psychology	D
Sociology	M
Special Education	M,D,O
Sports Management	M
Statistics	M,D*
Systems Engineering	M,D,O
Technology and Public Policy	M
Telecommunications	M
Theater	M
Toxicology	M
Travel and Tourism	M
Western European Studies	M
Women's Studies	M,D

In-depth description on page 887.

GEORGIA COLLEGE & STATE UNIVERSITY

Biological and Biomedical Sciences—General	M
Business Administration and Management—General	M
Early Childhood Education	M,O
Education—General	M,O
Educational Administration	M,O
Educational Media/Instructional Technology	M,O
English Education	M,O
English	M
Health Education	M,O
History	M
Journalism	M
Logistics	M
Mathematics Education	M,O
Middle School Education	M,O
Nursing—General	M
Physical Education	M,O
Psychology—General	M
Public Policy and Administration	M
Science Education	M,O
Secondary Education	M,O
Social Sciences Education	M,O
Special Education	M
Speech and Interpersonal Communication	M

GEORGIA INSTITUTE OF TECHNOLOGY

Aerospace/Aeronautical Engineering	M,D*
Applied Mathematics	M,D
Applied Physics	M,D
Architecture	M,D*
Atmospheric Sciences	M,D
Biochemistry	M,D
Bioengineering	M,D,O*
Biological and Biomedical Sciences—General	M,D*
Biomedical Engineering	M,D,O
Building Science	M,D
Business Administration and Management—General	M,D
Ceramic Sciences and Engineering	M,D
Chemical Engineering	M,D,O
Chemistry	M,D
City and Regional Planning	M
Civil Engineering	M,D
Cognitive Sciences	M
Computer Engineering	M,D*
Computer Science	M,D*
Construction Engineering and Management	M,D
Economics	M
Electrical Engineering	M,D
Engineering and Applied Sciences—General	M,D,O
Environmental Engineering	M,D
Geochemistry	M,D
Geophysics	M,D
Geosciences	M,D*
Health Physics/Radiological Health	M,D
Health Services Management and Hospital Administration	M
History of Science and Technology	M,D
Human-Computer Interaction	M
Industrial/Management Engineering	M,D*
International Affairs	M*
Internet and Interactive Multimedia	M
Management of Technology	M
Materials Engineering	M,D
Mathematics	M,D
Mechanical Engineering	M,D
Mechanics	M,D
Metallurgical Engineering and Metallurgy	M,D
Nuclear Engineering	M,D
Operations Research	M
Paper and Pulp Engineering	O
Physics	M,D*
Polymer Science and Engineering	M
Psychology—General	M,D
Public Policy and Administration	M,D*
Statistics	M,D
Systems Engineering	M,D
Textile Sciences and Engineering	M,D

GEORGIAN COURT COLLEGE

Addictions/Substance Abuse Counseling	M,O
Biological and Biomedical Sciences—General	M
Business Administration and Management—General	M
Counseling Psychology	M
Education—General	M,O
Educational Administration	M,O
Educational Media/Instructional Technology	M,O
Mathematics	M
Reading Education	M,O
Special Education	M,O
Theology	M

GEORGIA SOUTHERN UNIVERSITY

Accounting	M
Advanced Practice Nursing	M,O
Allied Health—General	M,O
Art Education	M,O
Art/Fine Arts	M
Biological and Biomedical Sciences—General	M
Business Administration and Management—General	M
Business Education	M
Community Health Nursing	M,O
Counselor Education	M,O
Curriculum and Instruction	D
Early Childhood Education	M,O
Education—General	M,D,O
Educational Administration	M,D,O
Educational Media/Instructional Technology	M,O
Engineering and Applied Sciences—General	M
English Education	M,O
English	M
Foreign Languages Education	M
Health Education	M,O
Health Services Management and Hospital Administration	M
Higher Education	M
History	M
Kinesiology and Movement Studies	M
Mathematics Education	M,O
Mathematics	M
Middle School Education	M,O
Music Education	O
Music	M
Nursing—General	M,O
Physical Education	M,O
Political Science	M
Psychology—General	M
Public Health—General	M
Public Policy and Administration	M
Reading Education	M,O
Recreation and Park Management	M
School Psychology	M,O
Science Education	M,O
Social Sciences Education	M,O
Sociology	M
Special Education	M,O
Sports Management	M
Vocational and Technical Education	M,O
Women's Health Nursing	M,O

GEORGIA SOUTHWESTERN STATE UNIVERSITY

Business Administration and Management—General	M
Business Education	M,O
Computer Science	M
Early Childhood Education	M,O
Education—General	M,O
Health Education	M,O
Information Science	M
Management Information Systems	M
Middle School Education	M,O
Physical Education	M,O
Reading Education	M,O
Secondary Education	M,O

GEORGIA STATE UNIVERSITY

Accounting	M,D
Actuarial Science	M
Advanced Practice Nursing	M,D
Allied Health—General	M,D
Anthropology	M*
Art Education	M,D,O
Art History	M
Art/Fine Arts	M*
Astronomy	D*
Biochemistry	M,D
Biological and Biomedical Sciences—General	M,D*
Business Administration and Management—General	M,D
Cell Biology	M,D
Chemistry	M,D*
Communication Disorders	M
Communication—General	M,D*
Computer Science	M,D*
Counseling Psychology	M,D,O
Counselor Education	M,D,O
Criminal Justice and Criminology	M
Early Childhood Education	M,D,O
Economics	M,D
Education of the Multiply Handicapped	M
Education—General	M,D,O*
Educational Administration	M,D,O
Educational Measurement and Evaluation	M,D
Educational Media/Instructional Technology	M,D,O
Educational Psychology	M,D
English as a Second Language	M,O*
English Education	M,D,O
English	M,D*
Entrepreneurship	M,D
Environmental Biology	M,D
Exercise and Sports Science	M,D
Finance and Banking	M,D
Foreign Languages Education	M,D,O
Foundations and Philosophy of Education	M,D
French	M
Genetics	M,D*
Geography	M*
Geology	M
German	M
Health Promotion	M,D

Georgia State University (continued)

Health Services Management and Hospital Administration M,D
Higher Education D
Historic Preservation M
History M,D*
Human Resources Development M,D
Human Resources Management M,D
Human Services M
Industrial and Labor Relations M,D
Industrial and Manufacturing Management M,D
Insurance M,D
International Business M,D
Internet and Interactive Multimedia M,D
Law P*
Linguistics M
Management Information Systems M,D
Marketing M,D
Mathematics Education M,D,O
Mathematics M
Medical/Surgical Nursing M,D
Microbiology M,D*
Middle School Education M,D,O
Music Education M,D,O
Music M
Neurobiology M,D
Nursing—General M,D
Nutrition M
Operations Research M,D
Pediatric Nursing M,D
Philosophy M*
Physical Education M
Physical Therapy M
Physics M,D*
Physiology M,D
Political Science M,D*
Psychiatric Nursing M,D
Psychology—General D*
Public Policy and Administration M,D
Reading Education M,O
Real Estate M,D
Rehabilitation Counseling M,O
Rhetoric M,D
School Psychology M,D,O
Science Education M,D,O
Social Sciences Education M,D,O
Social Work M
Sociology M,D*
Spanish M
Special Education M,D,O
Sports Management M
Taxation M
Technical Writing M,D
Translation and Interpretation O
Urban Education M
Urban Studies M
Vocational and Technical Education M,D,O
Women's Health Nursing M,D
Women's Studies M*
Writing M,D

GLOBAL UNIVERSITY OF THE ASSEMBLIES OF GOD

Missions and Missiology M
Religious Education M
Theology M

GODDARD COLLEGE

Comparative and Interdisciplinary Arts M
Counseling Psychology M
Ecology M
Education—General M
Health Promotion M
Industrial and Organizational Psychology M
Interdisciplinary Studies M
Writing M

GOLDEN GATE BAPTIST THEOLOGICAL SEMINARY

Early Childhood Education P,M,D,O
Music P,M,D,O
Pastoral Ministry and Counseling P,M,D,O
Religious Education P,M,D,O
Theology P,M,D,O

GOLDEN GATE UNIVERSITY

Accounting M,D,O
Advertising and Public Relations M,D,O
Business Administration and Management—General M,D,O
Counseling Psychology M,O
Economics M,D,O
Engineering and Applied Sciences—General M,O
Finance and Banking M,D,O
Hospitality Management M,O
Human Resources Management M,D,O
Industrial and Manufacturing Management M,D,O
Industrial and Organizational Psychology M,O
International Business M,D,O
Law P,M,D
Legal and Justice Studies P,M,D
Management Information Systems M,D,O
Marketing M,D,O
Marriage and Family Therapy M,O
Psychology—General M,O
Public Policy and Administration M
Taxation P,M,D,O
Telecommunications Management M,D,O
Travel and Tourism M,O

GOLDEY-BEACOM COLLEGE

Business Administration and Management—General M
Finance and Banking M
Human Resources Management M
Management Information Systems M
Marketing M

GONZAGA UNIVERSITY

Accounting M
Business Administration and Management—General M
Counseling Psychology M
Curriculum and Instruction M
Education—General M,D
Educational Administration M,D
English as a Second Language M
Law P
Nurse Anesthesia M
Nursing—General M
Organizational Management M
Pastoral Ministry and Counseling P,M
Philosophy M
Religion P,M
Special Education M
Sports Management M
Theology P,M

GOODING INSTITUTE OF NURSE ANESTHESIA

Nurse Anesthesia M

GORDON COLLEGE

Education—General M*

GORDON-CONWELL THEOLOGICAL SEMINARY

Missions and Missiology P,M,D
Pastoral Ministry and Counseling P,M,D
Religion P,M,D
Religious Education P,M,D
Theology P,M,D

GOUCHER COLLEGE

Arts Administration M
Biological and Biomedical Sciences—General O
Education—General M
Historic Preservation M
Writing M

GOVERNORS STATE UNIVERSITY

Accounting M
Addictions/Substance Abuse Counseling M
Allied Health—General M
Analytical Chemistry M
Art/Fine Arts M
Business Administration and Management—General M
Communication Disorders M
Communication—General M
Computer Science M
Counselor Education M
Early Childhood Education M
Education—General M
Educational Administration M
Educational Media/Instructional Technology M
English M
Environmental Biology M
Health Services Management and Hospital Administration M
Legal and Justice Studies M
Management Information Systems M
Media Studies M
Nursing—General M
Occupational Therapy M
Physical Therapy M
Political Science M
Psychology—General M
Public Policy and Administration M
Reading Education M
Social Work M
Special Education M

GRACE COLLEGE

Counseling Psychology M

GRACELAND UNIVERSITY

Advanced Practice Nursing M,O
Education—General M
Nursing and Healthcare Administration M,O
Nursing Education M,O
Nursing—General M,O
Religion M

GRACE THEOLOGICAL SEMINARY

Missions and Missiology P,M,D,O
Pastoral Ministry and Counseling P,M,D,O
Theology P,M,D,O

GRACE UNIVERSITY

Counseling Psychology M
Pastoral Ministry and Counseling M
Theology M

GRADUATE SCHOOL AND UNIVERSITY CENTER OF THE CITY UNIVERSITY OF NEW YORK

Accounting D
Anthropology D
Archaeology D
Architectural History D
Art History D
Biochemistry D
Biological and Biomedical Sciences—General D*
Biopsychology D
Business Administration and Management—General D
Chemical Engineering D
Chemistry D
Civil Engineering D
Classics M,D
Clinical Psychology D
Cognitive Sciences D
Communication Disorders D
Comparative Literature M,D
Computer Science D
Criminal Justice and Criminology D
Developmental Psychology D
Economics D
Educational Psychology D
Electrical Engineering D
Engineering and Applied Sciences—General D*
English D
Environmental Sciences D
Experimental Psychology D
Finance and Banking D
French D
Geosciences D
German M,D
History D
Industrial and Organizational Psychology D
Interdisciplinary Studies M,D
Italian M,D
Liberal Studies M
Linguistics M,D
Management Information Systems D
Mathematics D
Mechanical Engineering D
Medieval and Renaissance Studies M,D
Music D
Neuroscience D
Organizational Behavior D
Philosophy M,D
Physics D
Political Science M,D
Psychology—General D
Public Policy and Administration M,D
Social Psychology D
Social Work D
Sociology D
Spanish D
Theater D
Urban Education D
Urban Studies M,D
Women's Studies M,D

In-depth description on page 889.

GRADUATE SCHOOL OF FIGURATIVE ART OF THE NEW YORK ACADEMY OF ART

Art/Fine Arts M

In-depth description on page 891.

GRADUATE THEOLOGICAL UNION

Cultural Studies M,D,O
Ethics M,D,O
Jewish Studies M,D,O
Psychology—General M,D,O
Religion M,D,O
Theology M,D,O

GRAMBLING STATE UNIVERSITY

Advanced Practice Nursing M
Criminal Justice and Criminology M
Curriculum and Instruction M,D
Developmental Education M,D
Early Childhood Education M
Education—General M,D
Educational Administration M,D
Elementary Education M
Humanities M
Mass Communication M
Nursing—General M
Public Policy and Administration M
Science Education M
Social Sciences Education M
Social Work M
Sports Management M

GRAND CANYON UNIVERSITY

Business Administration and Management—General M
Education—General M
Elementary Education M
English as a Second Language M
Reading Education M
Secondary Education M

GRAND RAPIDS BAPTIST SEMINARY OF CORNERSTONE UNIVERSITY

Missions and Missiology P,M,D
Pastoral Ministry and Counseling P,M,D
Religion P,M,D
Religious Education P,M,D
Theology P,M,D

GRAND VALLEY STATE UNIVERSITY

Adult Education M
Allied Health—General M
Business Administration and Management—General M
Communication—General M
Criminal Justice and Criminology M
Early Childhood Education M
Education of the Gifted M
Education—General M
Educational Administration M
Educational Media/Instructional Technology M
Elementary Education M
Engineering and Applied Sciences—General M
English as a Second Language M
Higher Education M
Information Science M
Manufacturing Engineering M
Mechanical Engineering M
Middle School Education M
Nursing—General M
Occupational Therapy M
Physical Therapy M
Physician Assistant Studies M
Public Policy and Administration M
Reading Education M
Social Work M
Software Engineering M
Special Education M
Taxation M

In-depth description on page 893.

GRATZ COLLEGE

Education—General M
Jewish Studies M
Library Science O
Music M,O
Near and Middle Eastern Studies O
Religious Education M,O
Social Work M,O

In-depth description on page 895.

GREENVILLE COLLEGE

Pastoral Ministry and Counseling M

GWYNEDD-MERCY COLLEGE

Advanced Practice Nursing M
Counselor Education M
Education—General M
Educational Administration M
Gerontological Nursing M
Medical/Surgical Nursing M

Nursing—General M
Pediatric Nursing M
Reading Education M

HAMLINE UNIVERSITY

Business Administration and Management—General M
Education—General M,D
Law P,M*
Liberal Studies M,O
Nonprofit Management M
Public Policy and Administration M

HAMPTON UNIVERSITY

Applied Mathematics M
Biological and Biomedical Sciences—General M
Business Administration and Management—General M
Chemistry M
Communication Disorders M*
Computer Science M
Counselor Education M
Education—General M
Elementary Education M
Museum Studies M
Nursing—General M
Physical Therapy D
Physics M,D
Special Education M
Student Personnel Services M

In-depth description on page 897.

HARDING UNIVERSITY

Business Administration and Management—General M
Education—General M
Educational Administration M
Elementary Education M
Marriage and Family Therapy M
Nursing—General M
Pastoral Ministry and Counseling M
Secondary Education M

HARDING UNIVERSITY GRADUATE SCHOOL OF RELIGION

Religion P,M,D
Theology P,M,D

HARDIN-SIMMONS UNIVERSITY

Advanced Practice Nursing M
Business Administration and Management—General M
Counselor Education M
Education of the Gifted M
Education—General M
English M
Environmental Management and Policy M
History M
Marriage and Family Therapy M
Maternal/Child Nursing M
Music Education M
Music M
Nursing—General M
Pastoral Ministry and Counseling M
Physical Education M
Physical Therapy M
Psychology—General M
Reading Education M
Recreation and Park Management M
Religion M
Sports Management M
Theology P

HARTFORD SEMINARY

Pastoral Ministry and Counseling M,D,O
Religion M,D,O
Theology M,D,O

HARVARD UNIVERSITY

Adult Education M,D,O
Allopathic Medicine P
American Studies D
Anthropology M,D
Applied Mathematics M,D
Applied Physics M,D
Applied Science and Technology M,O
Archaeology M,D
Architecture M,D*
Art Education M,D,O
Art History D
Asian Languages M,D
Asian Studies M,D
Astronomy M,D*
Astrophysics M,D
Biochemistry M,D
Biological and Biomedical Sciences—General M,D,O*
Biomedical Engineering M,D*
Biophysics D*
Biopsychology M,D
Biostatistics M,D
Business Administration and Management—General M,D,O
Cancer Biology/Oncology D
Cell Biology D
Celtic Languages M,D
Chemistry M,D*
City and Regional Planning M,D
Classics M,D
Cognitive Sciences M,D,O
Communication Disorders D*
Communication—General M,O
Community Health M
Comparative Literature D
Computer Science D
Curriculum and Instruction M,D,O
Demography and Population Studies M,D
Dentistry P,M,D,O
Developmental Psychology M,D
East European and Russian Studies M
Economics M,D
Education—General M,D,O*
Educational Administration M,D,O
Educational Media/Instructional Technology M,D,O
Educational Psychology M,D,O
Elementary Education M,D,O
Engineering and Applied Sciences—General M,D*
English M,D,O
Environmental and Occupational Health M,D
Environmental Engineering M,D
Environmental Management and Policy M,O
Environmental Sciences M,D
Epidemiology M,D
Evolutionary Biology D*
Experimental Psychology M,D
Forestry M
Foundations and Philosophy of Education M,D,O
French M,D
Gender Studies M,D,O
Genetics D
Geosciences M,D*
German M,D
Health Promotion M,D
Health Services Management and Hospital Administration M,D
Higher Education M,D,O
History of Science and Technology M,D
History D
Human Development M,D,O
Immunology D*
Information Science M,O
Inorganic Chemistry M,D
International Affairs M,D
International and Comparative Education M,D,O
International Development M
International Health M,D
Italian M,D
Jewish Studies M,D
Landscape Architecture M,D
Law P,M,D
Liberal Studies M,O
Linguistics M,D
Management Information Systems D
Maternal and Child Health M,D
Mathematics Education M,D,O
Mathematics M,D
Medical Informatics P,M,D
Medical Physics M,D
Medieval and Renaissance Studies M,D
Microbiology D
Molecular Biology D*
Museum Studies M,O
Music M,D
Near and Middle Eastern Languages M,D
Near and Middle Eastern Studies M,D
Neurobiology D
Neuroscience D*
Nutrition D*
Oral and Dental Sciences M,D,O
Organic Chemistry M,D
Organizational Behavior D
Pathology D
Pharmacology D
Philosophy M,D
Physical Chemistry M,D
Physics M,D*
Physiology M,D
Planetary and Space Sciences M,D
Political Science M,D
Portuguese M,D
Psychology—General M,D
Public Health—General M,D,O*
Public Policy and Administration M,D*
Reading Education M,D,O
Religion M,D
Russian M,D
Scandinavian Languages M,D
Science Education M,D,O
Secondary Education M,D,O
Slavic Languages M,D
Social Psychology M,D
Sociology M,D
Spanish M,D
Statistics M,D*
Theology P,M,D
Theoretical Physics M,D
Urban Design M
Urban Education M,D,O
Virology D

In-depth description on page 899.

HARVEY MUDD COLLEGE

Engineering and Applied Sciences—General M

HASTINGS COLLEGE

Education—General M

HAWAI'I PACIFIC UNIVERSITY

Accounting M
Advanced Practice Nursing M
Business Administration and Management—General M*
Communication—General M*
Community Health Nursing M
English as a Second Language M*
Finance and Banking M
Human Resources Management M
International Business M
Management Information Systems M
Marketing M
Military and Defense Studies M*
Nursing—General M*
Organizational Management M
Political Science M*
Quality Management M

In-depth description on page 901.

HEBREW COLLEGE

Early Childhood Education M,O
Education—General M,O
Jewish Studies M,O
Middle School Education M,O
Music M,O
Nonprofit Management M,O
Religious Education M,O
Social Work M,O
Special Education M,O

In-depth description on page 903.

HEBREW THEOLOGICAL COLLEGE

Theology O

HEBREW UNION COLLEGE–JEWISH INSTITUTE OF RELIGION (CA)

Education—General M,D
Jewish Studies M,D
Religious Education M,D
Social Work M,O
Theology P

HEBREW UNION COLLEGE–JEWISH INSTITUTE OF RELIGION (NY)

Education—General M
Jewish Studies M
Music M
Near and Middle Eastern Languages D
Religious Education M
Theology P,D

HEBREW UNION COLLEGE–JEWISH INSTITUTE OF RELIGION (OH)

Jewish Studies P,M,D
Near and Middle Eastern Studies M,D
Religion M,D
Theology P

HEIDELBERG COLLEGE

Business Administration and Management—General M
Counselor Education M
Education—General M

HENDERSON STATE UNIVERSITY

Art Education M
Business Administration and Management—General M
Counselor Education M
Early Childhood Education M
Education—General M
Educational Administration M
Elementary Education M
English Education M
English M
Liberal Studies M
Mathematics Education M
Physical Education M
Reading Education M
Science Education M
Secondary Education M
Social Psychology M
Social Sciences Education M
Social Sciences M
Special Education M

HERITAGE BAPTIST COLLEGE AND HERITAGE THEOLOGICAL SEMINARY

Theology M,O

HERITAGE COLLEGE

Counselor Education M
Early Childhood Education M
Education—General M
Educational Administration M
English as a Second Language M
Human Resources Development M
Multilingual and Multicultural Education M
Special Education M

HIGH POINT UNIVERSITY

Business Administration and Management—General M
International Business M
Nonprofit Management M

HOFSTRA UNIVERSITY

Accounting M
Applied Mathematics M
Art Education M
Art Therapy M,O
Biological and Biomedical Sciences—General M,O*
Business Administration and Management—General M
Business Education M
Clinical Psychology M,D,O
Communication Disorders M
Computer Science M
Counselor Education M,O
Early Childhood Education M,O
Education—General M,D,O
Educational Administration M,D,O
Educational Measurement and Evaluation M
Elementary Education M,O
English as a Second Language M
English Education M
English M
Finance and Banking M
Foreign Languages Education M
Foundations and Philosophy of Education M,D,O
Gerontology M,O
Health Education M
Health Services Management and Hospital Administration M,O
Human Genetics M,O
Human Resources Management M
Humanities M
Industrial and Organizational Psychology M
Interdisciplinary Studies M
International Business M
Law P,M
Legal and Justice Studies P,M
Linguistics M
Management Information Systems M
Marketing Research M
Marketing M
Marriage and Family Therapy M,O
Mathematics Education M
Multilingual and Multicultural Education M
Music Education M
Physical Education M
Physician Assistant Studies M,O
Psychology—General M,D,O
Quantitative Analysis M
Reading Education M,D,O
Rehabilitation Counseling M,O
School Psychology M,D,O
Science Education M
Secondary Education M
Social Psychology M,D
Social Sciences Education M
Special Education M,D,O
Taxation M
Telecommunications Management M
Writing M

HOLLINS UNIVERSITY

Computer Science M,O
Education—General M
English M
Film, Television, and Video Production M
Film, Television, and Video Theory and Criticism M
Humanities M,O
Interdisciplinary Studies M,O
Liberal Studies M,O
Social Sciences M,O
Writing M

HOLY APOSTLES COLLEGE AND SEMINARY

Theology P,M,O

HOLY CROSS GREEK ORTHODOX SCHOOL OF THEOLOGY

Theology P,M

HOLY FAMILY COLLEGE

Business Administration and Management—General M
Counseling Psychology M
Education—General M
Elementary Education M
Human Resources Management M
Management Information Systems M
Nursing—General M
Reading Education M
Secondary Education M

HOLY NAMES COLLEGE

Advanced Practice Nursing M
Business Administration and Management—General M
Community Health Nursing M
Counseling Psychology M,O
Curriculum and Instruction M,O
Education—General M,O
Educational Psychology M,O
English as a Second Language M,O
English M
Music Education M,O
Music M,O
Nursing—General M
Pastoral Ministry and Counseling M,O
Religion M,O
Special Education M,O
Urban Education M,O

HOOD COLLEGE

Biological and Biomedical Sciences—General M,O
Business Administration and Management—General M
Computer Science M
Curriculum and Instruction M
Early Childhood Education M
Education—General M
Educational Administration M
Elementary Education M
Environmental Biology M
Information Science M
Mathematics Education M
Psychology—General M
Reading Education M
Science Education M
Secondary Education M
Special Education M
Systems Science M
Thanatology M

HOOD THEOLOGICAL SEMINARY

Theology P,M,D

HOPE INTERNATIONAL UNIVERSITY

Business Administration and Management—General M
Counseling Psychology M
Education—General M
International Business M
International Development M
Marriage and Family Therapy M
Music M
Nonprofit Management M
Pastoral Ministry and Counseling M
Psychology—General M

HOUSTON BAPTIST UNIVERSITY

Accounting M
Advanced Practice Nursing M
Business Administration and Management—General M
Counseling Psychology M
Counselor Education M
Curriculum and Instruction M
Education—General M
Educational Administration M
Educational Measurement and Evaluation M
Elementary Education M
Finance and Banking M
Health Services Management and Hospital Administration M
Human Resources Management M
Liberal Studies M
Management Information Systems M
Multilingual and Multicultural Education M
Nursing—General M
Pastoral Ministry and Counseling M
Psychology—General M
Reading Education M
Secondary Education M
Special Education M
Theology M

HOUSTON GRADUATE SCHOOL OF THEOLOGY

Pastoral Ministry and Counseling P,M,D
Theology P,M,D

HOWARD UNIVERSITY

Accounting M
Advanced Practice Nursing M,O
African Studies M,D
Allopathic Medicine P,D
Analytical Chemistry M,D
Anatomy M,D
Applied Arts and Design—General M
Applied Mathematics M,D
Art History M
Art/Fine Arts M
Atmospheric Sciences M,D
Biochemistry M,D*
Biological and Biomedical Sciences—General M,D*
Biophysics D
Biopsychology M,D
Biotechnology M,D
Business Administration and Management—General M
Chemical Engineering M
Chemistry M,D
Civil Engineering M
Clinical Psychology M,D
Communication Disorders M,D
Communication—General M,D
Computer Science M
Corporate and Organizational Communication M,D
Counseling Psychology M,D,O
Counselor Education M,D,O
Dentistry P,O
Developmental Psychology M,D
Early Childhood Education M,O
Economics M,D
Education—General M,D,O
Educational Administration M,O
Educational Psychology M,D,O
Electrical Engineering M,D*
Elementary Education M
Engineering and Applied Sciences—General M,D
English M,D
Environmental Sciences M,D
Exercise and Sports Science M
Experimental Psychology M,D
Film, Television, and Video Production M
Finance and Banking M
French M
Genetics M,D*
Health Education M
History M,D
Human Development M
Human Genetics M,D
Inorganic Chemistry M,D
International Business M
Law P,M
Leisure Studies M
Management Information Systems M
Marketing M
Mass Communication M,D
Mathematics M,D
Mechanical Engineering M,D*
Microbiology D*
Molecular Biology M,D
Music Education M
Music M
Nursing—General M,O
Nutrition M,D
Oral and Dental Sciences P,O
Organic Chemistry M,D
Pharmacology M,D
Pharmacy P
Philosophy M
Photography M
Physical Chemistry M,D
Physics M,D
Physiology D
Political Science M,D
Psychology—General M,D
Public Policy and Administration M
Reading Education M,O
Recreation and Park Management M
School Psychology M,D,O
Secondary Education M,O
Social Psychology M,D
Social Work M,D*
Sociology M,D
Spanish M
Special Education M,O
Theology P,M,D

HSI LAI UNIVERSITY

Business Administration and Management—General M
Finance and Banking M
International Business M
Management Information Systems M
Nonprofit Management M
Religion M,D*

HUMBOLDT STATE UNIVERSITY

Biological and Biomedical Sciences—General M
Business Administration and Management—General M
English M
Environmental Sciences M
Natural Resources M
Physical Education M
Psychology—General M
Social Sciences M
Sociology M
Theater M

HUMPHREYS COLLEGE

Law P

HUNTER COLLEGE OF THE CITY UNIVERSITY OF NEW YORK

Advanced Practice Nursing M,O
Anthropology M
Applied Mathematics M
Art History M
Art/Fine Arts M
Biochemistry M
Biological and Biomedical Sciences—General M,D
Biopsychology M
Chemistry M
City and Regional Planning M
Classics M
Cognitive Sciences M
Communication Disorders M
Community Health Nursing M
Counselor Education M
Early Childhood Education M,O
Economics M
Education of the Multiply Handicapped M
Education—General M,O
Educational Administration O
Elementary Education M
English as a Second Language M
English Education M
English M
Environmental and Occupational Health M
Environmental Sciences M,O
Foreign Languages Education M
French M
Genetics
Geographic Information Systems M,O
Geography M,O
Geosciences M,O
Gerontological Nursing M
History M
Italian M
Maternal/Child Nursing M
Mathematics Education M
Mathematics M
Media Studies M
Medical/Surgical Nursing M
Multilingual and Multicultural Education M
Music Education M
Music M
Nursing—General M,O
Nutrition M
Pediatric Nursing M,O
Physical Therapy M
Physics M,D
Psychiatric Nursing M
Psychology—General M
Public Health—General M
Reading Education M,O
Rehabilitation Counseling M
Science Education M,O
Secondary Education M
Social Psychology M
Social Sciences Education M
Social Work M,D
Sociology M
Spanish M
Special Education M
Theater M
Urban Studies M
Writing M

In-depth description on page 905.

HUNTINGTON COLLEGE

Pastoral Ministry and Counseling M
Religious Education M

HURON UNIVERSITY USA IN LONDON

Business Administration and Management—General M
Conflict Resolution and Mediation/Peace Studies M
Entrepreneurship M
Finance and Banking M
International Affairs M
International Business M
Management Information Systems M
Marketing M
Political Science M

HUSSON COLLEGE

Advanced Practice Nursing M
Business Administration and Management—General M
Nursing—General M
Physical Therapy M
Psychiatric Nursing M

ICR GRADUATE SCHOOL

Astrophysics M
Biological and Biomedical Sciences—General M
Geology M
Geophysics M
Science Education M

IDAHO STATE UNIVERSITY

Allied Health—General M,D,O
Anthropology M
Art/Fine Arts M
Biological and Biomedical Sciences—General M,D*
Business Administration and Management—General M
Chemistry M
Clinical Psychology M,D
Communication Disorders M
Counseling Psychology M,O
Counselor Education M,D,O
Curriculum and Instruction M,O
Dentistry O
Early Childhood Education M,O
Education—General M,D,O
Educational Administration M,D,O
Educational Media/Instructional Technology M,D,O
Engineering and Applied Sciences—General M,D
English M,D*
Environmental Engineering M,D
Environmental Sciences M,D
Geology M,O
Geophysics M,O
Geosciences M,O
Hazardous Materials Management M,D
Health Education M
Hydrology M,O
Interdisciplinary Studies M
Management Information Systems M
Management of Technology M
Marriage and Family Therapy M,O
Mathematics M,D*
Mechanics M,D
Medicinal and Pharmaceutical Chemistry M,D
Microbiology M,D
Nuclear Engineering M,D
Nursing—General M,O
Occupational Therapy M
Operations Research M,D
Oral and Dental Sciences O
Pharmaceutical Administration P,M,D
Pharmaceutical Sciences M,D
Pharmacology M,D
Pharmacy P,M,D
Physical Education M
Physical Therapy M
Physician Assistant Studies M
Physics M*
Political Science M,D*
Psychology—General M,D
Public Health—General M,O
Public Policy and Administration M
Reading Education M,O
School Psychology M,O
Sociology M
Special Education M,O
Speech and Interpersonal Communication M
Sports Management M

Program	Degrees
Theater	M
Vocational and Technical Education	M

ILIFF SCHOOL OF THEOLOGY

Program	Degrees
Pastoral Ministry and Counseling	P,M,D
Religion	P,M,D
Theology	P,M,D

ILLINOIS COLLEGE OF OPTOMETRY

Program	Degrees
Optometry	P

ILLINOIS INSTITUTE OF TECHNOLOGY

Program	Degrees
Aerospace/Aeronautical Engineering	M,D
Analytical Chemistry	M,D
Applied Arts and Design—General	M,D*
Applied Mathematics	M,D
Architectural Engineering	M,D
Architecture	M,D
Biochemistry	M,D
Biological and Biomedical Sciences—General	M,D
Biomedical Engineering	D*
Biotechnology	M,D
Business Administration and Management—General	M,D*
Cell Biology	M,D
Chemical Engineering	M,D
Chemistry	M,D
Civil Engineering	M,D
Clinical Psychology	M,D
Communication—General	M
Computer Engineering	M,D
Computer Science	M,D
Corporate and Organizational Communication	M
Electrical Engineering	M,D
Engineering and Applied Sciences—General	M,D
Environmental Engineering	M,D
Environmental Management and Policy	P,M
Finance and Banking	P,M*
Food Science and Technology	M
Graphic Design	M,D
Health Physics/Radiological Health	M,D
Human Resources Development	M,D
Industrial and Manufacturing Management	M
Industrial and Organizational Psychology	M,D
Industrial Design	M,D
Inorganic Chemistry	M,D
International Business	M
Law	P,M
Legal and Justice Studies	M
Management Information Systems	M
Management of Technology	M
Management Strategy and Policy	M
Manufacturing Engineering	M,D
Marketing	M
Materials Engineering	M,D
Mechanical Engineering	M,D
Metallurgical Engineering and Metallurgy	M,D
Microbiology	M,D
Organic Chemistry	M,D
Photography	M,D
Physical Chemistry	M,D
Physics	M,D
Polymer Science and Engineering	
Psychology—General	M,D
Public Policy and Administration	M
Rehabilitation Counseling	M,D
Science Education	M,D
Software Engineering	M,D
Taxation	P,M
Technical Writing	M
Telecommunications Management	M
Telecommunications	M,D
Theoretical Chemistry	M,D

In-depth description on page 907.

ILLINOIS STATE UNIVERSITY

Program	Degrees
Accounting	M
Agricultural Economics and Agribusiness	M
Agricultural Sciences—General	M
Art History	M
Art/Fine Arts	M
Biological and Biomedical Sciences—General	M,D*
Biotechnology	M
Botany	M,D
Business Administration and Management—General	M
Chemistry	M
Clinical Psychology	M,D,O
Communication Disorders	M
Communication—General	M*
Computer Science	M
Counseling Psychology	M,D,O
Counselor Education	M,D
Criminal Justice and Criminology	M
Curriculum and Instruction	M,D
Developmental Psychology	M,D,O
Ecology	M,D
Economics	M
Education—General	M,D
Educational Administration	M,D
Educational Psychology	M,D,O
English	M,D
Environmental and Occupational Health	M
Experimental Psychology	M,D,O
Family and Consumer Sciences-General	M
French	M
Genetics	M,D
German	M
Graphic Design	M
Health Education	M
Higher Education	M,D
History	M
Hydrology	M
Industrial and Organizational Psychology	M,D,O
Industrial/Management Engineering	M
Mathematics Education	D
Mathematics	M
Microbiology	M,D
Music	M
Nurse Midwifery	M,O
Nursing—General	M,O
Photography	M
Physical Education	M
Physiology	M,D
Political Science	M
Psychology—General	M,D,O
Reading Education	M
School Psychology	D,O
Social Work	M
Sociology	M
Spanish	M
Special Education	M,D
Textile Design	M
Theater	M
Writing	M
Zoology	M,D

In-depth description on page 909.

IMCA–INTERNATIONAL MANAGEMENT CENTRES ASSOCIATION

Program	Degrees
Business Administration and Management—General	M,D

IMMACULATA UNIVERSITY

Program	Degrees
Clinical Psychology	M,D,O
Counseling Psychology	M,D,O
Counselor Education	M,D,O
Educational Administration	M,D,O
Elementary Education	M,D,O
Multilingual and Multicultural Education	M
Nutrition	M
Organizational Management	M
Psychology—General	M,D,O
School Psychology	M,D,O
Secondary Education	M,D,O
Special Education	M,D,O
Therapies—Dance, Drama, and Music	M

In-depth description on page 911.

INDIANA INSTITUTE OF TECHNOLOGY

Program	Degrees
Business Administration and Management—General	M
Entrepreneurship	M
Human Resources Development	M
Human Resources Management	M
Marketing	M

INDIANA STATE UNIVERSITY

Program	Degrees
Art History	M
Art/Fine Arts	M
Biological and Biomedical Sciences—General	M,D*
Business Administration and Management—General	M,D,O
Chemistry	M
Child and Family Studies	M
Clinical Laboratory Sciences/Medical Technology	M,D
Clinical Psychology	M,D
Clothing and Textiles	M
Communication Disorders	M,D,O
Communication—General	M
Computer Engineering	M
Counseling Psychology	M,D,O
Counselor Education	M,D,O
Criminal Justice and Criminology	M
Curriculum and Instruction	M,D,O
Early Childhood Education	M,D,O
Ecology	M,D
Economics	M
Education of the Gifted	M,D,O
Education—General	M,D,O
Educational Administration	M,D,O
Educational Media/Instructional Technology	M,D,O
Educational Psychology	M,D,O
Elementary Education	M,D,O
Engineering and Applied Sciences—General	M,D
English as a Second Language	M
English	M,O
Exercise and Sports Science	M
Facilities Management	M
Family and Consumer Sciences-General	M
French	M
Geography	M,D*
Geosciences	M,D
Graphic Design	M
Health Education	M
Health Services Management and Hospital Administration	M
Higher Education	M,D,O
History	M
Human Resources Development	M,D
Humanities	M
Industrial/Management Engineering	M
Linguistics	M
Marriage and Family Therapy	M,D,O
Mathematics	M
Media Studies	M
Microbiology	M,D
Music Education	M
Music	M
Nursing—General	M
Nutrition	M
Photography	M
Physical Education	M
Physics	M
Physiology	M,D
Political Science	M
Psychology—General	M,D
Public Policy and Administration	M
Reading Education	M,D,O
Religion	M
Rhetoric	M,O
School Psychology	M,D,O
Science Education	M
Secondary Education	M,D,O
Sociology	M
Spanish	M
Special Education	M,D,O
Sports Management	M
Theater	M
Vocational and Technical Education	M,D,O

In-depth description on page 913.

INDIANA UNIVERSITY BLOOMINGTON

Program	Degrees
Accounting	M,D
African-American Studies	M
Analytical Chemistry	M,D
Anatomy	M,D
Anthropology	M,D
Applied Arts and Design—General	M
Applied Mathematics	M,D
Art Education	M,D,O
Art History	M,D
Art/Fine Arts	M
Arts Administration	M
Asian Languages	M,D
Asian Studies	M,D
Astronomy	M,D
Astrophysics	D
Biochemistry	M,D
Bioinformatics	M
Biological and Biomedical Sciences—General	M,D*
Business Administration and Management—General	M,D*
Cell Biology	M,D
Chemistry	M,D
Classics	M,D
Clothing and Textiles	M
Cognitive Sciences	D
Communication Disorders	M,D
Communication—General	M,D*
Comparative Literature	M,D
Computer Art and Design	M
Computer Science	M,D*
Counselor Education	M,D,O
Criminal Justice and Criminology	M,D*
Curriculum and Instruction	M,D,O
Dance	M
Developmental Biology	D
Developmental Psychology	D
East European and Russian Studies	M,O
Ecology	M,D
Economics	M,D
Education—General	M,D,O*
Educational Administration	M,D,O
Educational Media/Instructional Technology	M,D,O
Educational Psychology	M,D,O
Elementary Education	M,D,O
English as a Second Language	M,D,O
English Education	M,D
English	M,D
Entrepreneurship	M
Environmental Education	M,D,O
Environmental Sciences	M,D*
Evolutionary Biology	M,D
Exercise and Sports Science	M,D,O
Finance and Banking	M,D
Folklore	M,D
Foreign Languages Education	M,D
Foundations and Philosophy of Education	M,D,O
French	M,D
Genetics	D
Geochemistry	M,D
Geography	M,D
Geology	M,D
Geophysics	M,D
Geosciences	M,D
German	M,D
Graphic Design	M
Higher Education	M,D,O
History of Science and Technology	M,D
History	M,D
Human Resources Development	M
Human Resources Management	M
Human-Computer Interaction	M
Information Science	M,D,O
Inorganic Chemistry	M,D
Interior Design	M
International and Comparative Education	M,D,O
International Business	M
Internet and Interactive Multimedia	M
Italian	M,D
Journalism	M,D
Kinesiology and Movement Studies	M,D,O
Latin American Studies	M
Law	P,M,D
Legal and Justice Studies	P,M,D
Leisure Studies	M,D,O
Library Science	M,D,O*
Linguistics	M,D,O
Management Information Systems	M,D
Marketing	M,D
Mass Communication	M,D
Mathematics Education	M,D
Mathematics	M,D
Medieval and Renaissance Studies	M,D
Microbiology	M,D
Mineralogy	M,D
Molecular Biology	M,D
Music Education	M,D,O
Music	M,D
Near and Middle Eastern Languages	M,D
Neuroscience	D
Optical Sciences	M,D
Optometry	P
Organizational Behavior	D
Pharmacology	M,D
Philosophy	M,D
Photography	M
Physical Chemistry	M,D
Physical Education	M,D,O
Physics	M,D*
Physiology	M,D
Plant Biology	M,D
Political Science	M,D
Portuguese	M,D
Psychology—General	D
Public Health—General	M,D,O
Public Policy and Administration	M,D*
Reading Education	M,D,O
Recreation and Park Management	M,D,O
Religion	M,D
School Psychology	M,D,O
Science Education	M,D,O
Secondary Education	M,D,O
Slavic Languages	M,D
Social Psychology	D
Social Sciences Education	M,D,O
Social Sciences	P,M,D
Sociology	M,D
Spanish	M,D
Special Education	M,D,O
Speech and Interpersonal Communication	M,D
Sports Management	M,D,O

Indiana University Bloomington (continued)

Statistics	M,D
Textile Design	M
Theater	M,D*
Vision Sciences	M,D
Western European Studies	M,D,O
Writing	M,D
Zoology	M,D

INDIANA UNIVERSITY KOKOMO

Business Administration and Management—General	M
Education—General	M
Elementary Education	M
Secondary Education	M

INDIANA UNIVERSITY NORTHWEST

Accounting	M,O
Business Administration and Management—General	M,O
Criminal Justice and Criminology	M,O
Education—General	M
Elementary Education	M
Health Services Management and Hospital Administration	M,O
Human Services	M,O
Nonprofit Management	M,O
Public Policy and Administration	M,O
Secondary Education	M
Social Work	M

INDIANA UNIVERSITY OF PENNSYLVANIA

Adult Education	M
Applied Mathematics	M
Art/Fine Arts	M
Biological and Biomedical Sciences—General	M
Business Administration and Management—General	M
Chemistry	M
Clinical Psychology	D
Communication Disorders	M
Counselor Education	M
Criminal Justice and Criminology	M,D
Curriculum and Instruction	M,D
Early Childhood Education	M
Education—General	M,D,O
Educational Administration	M,D,O
Educational Media/Instructional Technology	M
Educational Psychology	M,O
English as a Second Language	M,D
English Education	M,D
English	M,D*
Environmental and Occupational Health	M
Exercise and Sports Science	M
Facilities Management	M
Geography	M
Health Education	M
Higher Education	M
History	M
Human Resources Development	M
Industrial and Labor Relations	M
Linguistics	M,D
Mathematics Education	M
Mathematics	M
Music Education	M
Music	M
Nursing—General	M
Nutrition	M
Physical Education	M
Physics	M
Political Science	M
Psychology—General	M,D
Public Policy and Administration	M
Reading Education	M
Rhetoric	M,D
School Psychology	D
Sociology	M
Special Education	M
Sports Management	M
Writing	M,D

In-depth description on page 915.

INDIANA UNIVERSITY–PURDUE UNIVERSITY FORT WAYNE

Applied Mathematics	M
Biological and Biomedical Sciences—General	M
Business Administration and Management—General	M
Communication—General	M
Computer Science	M
Counselor Education	M
Education—General	M
Educational Administration	M
Elementary Education	M
Engineering and Applied Sciences—General	M
English Education	M
English	M
Liberal Studies	M
Mathematics	M
Nursing and Healthcare Administration	M
Nursing—General	M
Operations Research	M
Public Policy and Administration	M,O
Secondary Education	M
Sociology	M

INDIANA UNIVERSITY–PURDUE UNIVERSITY INDIANAPOLIS

Advanced Practice Nursing	M
Allied Health—General	M
Allopathic Medicine	P
Anatomy	M,D
Applied Mathematics	M,D
Art Education	M
Biochemistry	M,D*
Biological and Biomedical Sciences—General	M,D
Biomedical Engineering	M,D
Biophysics	M,D
Business Administration and Management—General	M
Cell Biology	M,D
Chemistry	M,D
City and Regional Planning	M
Clinical Psychology	M,D
Community Health Nursing	M
Computer Science	M
Counselor Education	M
Dentistry	P
Early Childhood Education	M
Economics	M
Education—General	M
Educational Administration	M
Educational Media/Instructional Technology	M
Electrical Engineering	M,D
Elementary Education	M
Engineering and Applied Sciences—General	M
English Education	M
English	M
Genetics	M,D*
Geology	M
Health Education	M
Health Services Management and Hospital Administration	M
Health Services Research	M
Higher Education	M
History	M
Immunology	M,D
Industrial and Organizational Psychology	M,D
Information Studies	M
Internet and Interactive Multimedia	M
Library Science	M
Maternal/Child Nursing	M
Mathematics Education	M
Mathematics	M,D
Mechanical Engineering	M
Medical/Surgical Nursing	M
Microbiology	M,D*
Molecular Biology	M,D
Music	M
Neurobiology	M,D*
Nonprofit Management	M
Nursing and Healthcare Administration	M
Nursing—General	M,D*
Nutrition	M
Oral and Dental Sciences	M,D
Pathology	M,D
Pediatric Nursing	M
Pharmacology	M,D*
Philanthropic Studies	M
Physical Therapy	M
Physics	M,D
Physiology	M,D*
Psychiatric Nursing	M
Psychology—General	M,D*
Public History	M
Public Policy and Administration	M,O*
Reading Education	M
Rehabilitation Counseling	M,D
Science Education	M
Secondary Education	M
Social Work	M,D
Special Education	M
Statistics	M,D
Toxicology	M,D
Women's Health Nursing	M

INDIANA UNIVERSITY SCHOOL OF LAW-BLOOMINGTON

Law	P,M,D,O

INDIANA UNIVERSITY SCHOOL OF LAW-INDIANAPOLIS

Law	P

INDIANA UNIVERSITY SOUTH BEND

Accounting	M
Applied Mathematics	M
Business Administration and Management—General	M
Computer Science	M
Counselor Education	M
Education—General	M
Elementary Education	M
Liberal Studies	M
Management Information Systems	M
Music	M
Psychology—General	M
Public Policy and Administration	M
Secondary Education	M
Social Work	M
Special Education	M

INDIANA UNIVERSITY SOUTHEAST

Accounting	M,O
Business Administration and Management—General	M,O
Counselor Education	M
Economics	M,O
Education—General	M
Elementary Education	M
Finance and Banking	M,O
Industrial and Manufacturing Management	M,O
Liberal Studies	M
Management Information Systems	M,O
Marketing	M,O
Secondary Education	M

INDIANA WESLEYAN UNIVERSITY

Addictions/Substance Abuse Counseling	M
Business Administration and Management—General	M
Community Health Nursing	M,O
Counselor Education	M,O*
Curriculum and Instruction	M
Education—General	M
Marriage and Family Therapy	M
Nursing Education	M,O
Nursing—General	M,O*
Social Psychology	M
Theology	M*

INSTITUTE FOR CHRISTIAN STUDIES

Education—General	M,D
Philosophy	M,D
Political Science	M,D
Theology	M,D

INSTITUTE FOR CLINICAL SOCIAL WORK

Social Work	D

INSTITUTE OF PAPER SCIENCE AND TECHNOLOGY

Biological and Biomedical Sciences—General	M,D
Chemical Engineering	M,D
Chemistry	M,D*
Mathematics	M,D
Mechanical Engineering	M,D
Paper and Pulp Engineering	M,D
Physics	M,D

INSTITUTE OF PUBLIC ADMINISTRATION

Health Services Management and Hospital Administration	M,O
Public Policy and Administration	M,O

INSTITUTE OF TEXTILE TECHNOLOGY

Textile Sciences and Engineering	M

INSTITUTE OF TRANSPERSONAL PSYCHOLOGY

Counseling Psychology	M,D
Psychology—General	M,D,O
Transpersonal and Humanistic Psychology	M,D,O*

INSTITUT FRANCO-EUROPEAN DE CHIROPRATIQUE

Chiropractic	P

INSTITUTO CENTROAMERICANO DE ADMINISTRACIÓN DE EMPRESAS

Business Administration and Management—General	M
Economics	M
Sustainable Development	M

INSTITUTO TECNOLÓGICO Y DE ESTUDIOS SUPERIORES DE MONTERREY, CAMPUS CENTRAL DE VERACRUZ

Business Administration and Management—General	M
Computer Science	M
Education—General	M
Educational Administration	M
Educational Media/Instructional Technology	M
Electronic Commerce	M
Finance and Banking	M
Humanities	M
International Business	M
Management Information Systems	M
Management of Technology	M
Marketing	M

INSTITUTO TECNOLÓGICO Y DE ESTUDIOS SUPERIORES DE MONTERREY, CAMPUS CHIHUAHUA

Computer Engineering	M,O
Electrical Engineering	M,O
Engineering Management	M,O
Industrial/Management Engineering	M,O
International Business	M,O
Mechanical Engineering	M,O
Systems Engineering	M,O

INSTITUTO TECNOLÓGICO Y DE ESTUDIOS SUPERIORES DE MONTERREY, CAMPUS CIUDAD DE MÉXICO

Business Administration and Management—General	M,D
Computer Science	M,D
Economics	M,D
Education—General	M,D
Educational Media/Instructional Technology	M,D
Environmental Engineering	M,D
Environmental Sciences	M,D
Finance and Banking	M,D
Humanities	M,D
Industrial/Management Engineering	M,D
International Business	M,D
Law	P
Management Information Systems	M,D
Quality Management	M,D
Telecommunications Management	M

INSTITUTO TECNOLÓGICO Y DE ESTUDIOS SUPERIORES DE MONTERREY, CAMPUS CIUDAD JUÁREZ

Business Administration and Management—General	M
Education—General	M
Finance and Banking	M
Industrial/Management Engineering	M
Management Information Systems	M
Quality Management	M
Telecommunications	M

INSTITUTO TECNOLÓGICO Y DE ESTUDIOS SUPERIORES DE MONTERREY, CAMPUS CIUDAD OBREGÓN

Business Administration and Management—General	M
Communication—General	M
Developmental Education	M
Education—General	M
Engineering and Applied Sciences—General	M
Finance and Banking	M
International Affairs	M
Management Information Systems	M
Marketing	M
Mathematics Education	M
Telecommunications Management	M

INSTITUTO TECNOLÓGICO Y DE ESTUDIOS SUPERIORES DE MONTERREY, CAMPUS CUERNAVACA

Business Administration and Management—General	M
Computer Science	M,D
Finance and Banking	M
Human Resources Management	M
Information Science	M,D
International Business	M

Management of Technology M,D
Marketing M

INSTITUTO TECNOLÓGICO Y DE ESTUDIOS SUPERIORES DE MONTERREY, CAMPUS GUADALAJARA

Business Administration and Management—General M
Finance and Banking M

INSTITUTO TECNOLÓGICO Y DE ESTUDIOS SUPERIORES DE MONTERREY, CAMPUS IRAPUATO

Architecture M,D
Business Administration and Management—General M,D
Computer Science M,D
Education—General M,D
Educational Administration M,D
Educational Media/Instructional Technology M,D
Electronic Commerce M,D
Environmental Management and Policy M,D
Finance and Banking M,D
Humanities M,D
Industrial and Manufacturing Management M,D
Information Science M,D
International Business M,D
Library Science M,D
Management Information Systems M,D
Management of Technology M,D
Marketing Research M,D
Quality Management M,D
Telecommunications Management M,D

INSTITUTO TECNOLÓGICO Y DE ESTUDIOS SUPERIORES DE MONTERREY, CAMPUS LAGUNA

Business Administration and Management—General M
Industrial/Management Engineering M
Management Information Systems M

INSTITUTO TECNOLÓGICO Y DE ESTUDIOS SUPERIORES DE MONTERREY, CAMPUS LEÓN

Business Administration and Management—General M

INSTITUTO TECNOLÓGICO Y DE ESTUDIOS SUPERIORES DE MONTERREY, CAMPUS MONTERREY

Agricultural Engineering M,D
Agricultural Sciences—General M,D
Artificial Intelligence/Robotics M,D
Biotechnology M,D
Business Administration and Management—General M,D
Chemical Engineering M,D
Chemistry M,D
Civil Engineering M,D
Communication—General M,D
Computer Science M,D
Electrical Engineering M,D
Engineering and Applied Sciences—General M,D
Environmental Engineering M,D
Finance and Banking M
Industrial/Management Engineering M,D
Information Science M,D
International Business M
Manufacturing Engineering M,D
Marketing M
Mechanical Engineering M,D
Organic Chemistry M,D
Science Education M,D
Statistics M,D
Systems Engineering M,D

INSTITUTO TECNOLÓGICO Y DE ESTUDIOS SUPERIORES DE MONTERREY, CAMPUS QUERÉTARO

Business Administration and Management—General M

INSTITUTO TECNOLÓGICO Y DE ESTUDIOS SUPERIORES DE MONTERREY, CAMPUS SONORA NORTE

Business Administration and Management—General M
Education—General M
Information Science M

INSTITUTO TECNOLÓGICO Y DE ESTUDIOS SUPERIORES DE MONTERREY, CAMPUS TOLUCA

Business Administration and Management—General M

INTER AMERICAN UNIVERSITY OF PUERTO RICO, ARECIBO CAMPUS

Counselor Education M
Education—General M
Educational Administration M
Nurse Anesthesia M

INTER AMERICAN UNIVERSITY OF PUERTO RICO, METROPOLITAN CAMPUS

Accounting M
Business Administration and Management—General M,D
Business Education M
Clinical Laboratory Sciences/Medical Technology M
Computer Science M
Counselor Education M
Criminal Justice and Criminology M
Education—General M,D
Educational Administration M
Educational Media/Instructional Technology M
Elementary Education M
English as a Second Language M
Finance and Banking M
Health Education M
Higher Education M
Human Resources Development M
Human Resources Management M
Industrial and Labor Relations M
Industrial and Manufacturing Management M
Law P
Marketing M
Physical Education M
Psychology—General M
Science Education M
Social Work M
Spanish M
Special Education M
Vocational and Technical Education M

INTER AMERICAN UNIVERSITY OF PUERTO RICO, SAN GERMÁN CAMPUS

Accounting M
Art/Fine Arts M
Business Administration and Management—General M,D
Business Education M
Clinical Laboratory Sciences/Medical Technology O
Counseling Psychology M,D
Counselor Education M
Curriculum and Instruction M
Education—General M
Educational Administration M
English as a Second Language M
Environmental Sciences M
Finance and Banking M
Higher Education M
Human Resources Development M
Human Resources Management M
Industrial and Labor Relations M
Kinesiology and Movement Studies M
Library Science M
Marketing M
Physical Education M
Psychology—General M,D
School Psychology M,D
Science Education M
Special Education M

INTER AMERICAN UNIVERSITY OF PUERTO RICO SCHOOL OF OPTOMETRY

Optometry P

INTERDENOMINATIONAL THEOLOGICAL CENTER

Theology P,M,D

INTERNATIONAL BAPTIST COLLEGE

Pastoral Ministry and Counseling M,D
Theology M

INTERNATIONAL COLLEGE AND GRADUATE SCHOOL

Pastoral Ministry and Counseling P,M,D
Religion P,M,D
Theology P,M,D

INTERNATIONAL COLLEGE OF THE CAYMAN ISLANDS

Business Administration and Management—General M

INTERNATIONAL FINE ARTS COLLEGE

Computer Art and Design M

INTERNATIONAL INSTITUTE OF CHINESE MEDICINE

Acupuncture and Oriental Medicine M,O

INTERNATIONAL SCHOOL OF THEOLOGY

Theology P,M

INTERNATIONAL TECHNOLOGICAL UNIVERSITY

Business Administration and Management—General M
Computer Engineering M
Electrical Engineering M
Software Engineering M

IONA COLLEGE

Business Administration and Management—General M,O*
Business Education M
Communication—General M,O
Computer Science M
Counselor Education M
Criminal Justice and Criminology M
Educational Administration M
Educational Media/Instructional Technology M,O
Elementary Education M
English Education M
English M
Finance and Banking M,O
Foreign Languages Education M
Health Services Management and Hospital Administration M,O
History M
Human Resources Management M,O
International Business M,O
Journalism M,O
Management of Technology M,O
Marketing M,O
Marriage and Family Therapy M,O
Mathematics Education M
Multilingual and Multicultural Education M
Pastoral Ministry and Counseling M,O
Psychology—General M
School Psychology M
Science Education M
Secondary Education M
Social Sciences Education M
Spanish M
Telecommunications M,O

In-depth description on page 917.

IOWA STATE UNIVERSITY OF SCIENCE AND TECHNOLOGY

Accounting M
Aerospace/Aeronautical Engineering M,D
Agricultural Economics and Agribusiness M,D
Agricultural Education M,D
Agricultural Engineering M,D
Agricultural Sciences—General M,D
Agronomy and Soil Sciences M,D
Anatomy M,D
Animal Sciences M,D
Anthropology M
Applied Arts and Design—General M
Applied Mathematics M,D
Applied Physics M,D
Architecture M
Art Education M
Astronomy M,D
Astrophysics M,D
Biochemistry M,D*
Bioinformatics D*
Biophysics M,D
Biostatistics D
Botany M,D
Business Administration and Management—General M
Cell Biology M,D
Chemical Engineering M,D
Chemistry M,D
Child and Family Studies M,D
City and Regional Planning M
Civil Engineering M,D
Clothing and Textiles M,D
Cognitive Sciences M,D
Computational Sciences D
Computer Engineering M,D
Computer Science M,D*
Condensed Matter Physics M,D
Construction Engineering and Management M,D
Consumer Economics M,D
Corporate and Organizational Communication M,D
Counseling Psychology M,D
Counselor Education M,D
Curriculum and Instruction M,D
Developmental Biology M,D
Ecology M,D
Economics M,D*
Education—General M,D
Educational Administration M,D
Educational Measurement and Evaluation M,D
Educational Media/Instructional Technology M,D
Electrical Engineering M,D
Elementary Education M,D
Engineering and Applied Sciences—General M,D*
English M,D
Entomology M,D
Environmental Engineering M,D
Evolutionary Biology M,D
Exercise and Sports Science M,D
Family and Consumer Sciences-General M,D
Fish, Game, and Wildlife Management M,D
Food Science and Technology M,D*
Forestry M,D
Foundations and Philosophy of Education M,D
Genetics M,D*
Geology M,D
Geosciences M,D
Geotechnical Engineering M,D
Graphic Design M
Health Education M,D
Higher Education M,D
History of Science and Technology M,D
History M,D
Home Economics Education M,D
Horticulture M,D
Hospitality Management M,D
Human Development M,D
Human Resources Development M,D
Immunology M,D
Industrial and Labor Relations M
Industrial/Management Engineering M,D
Information Science M
Interdisciplinary Studies M
Interior Design M
Journalism M
Landscape Architecture M
Management Information Systems M
Marriage and Family Therapy M,D
Mass Communication M
Materials Engineering M,D
Materials Sciences M,D
Mathematics Education M,D
Mathematics M,D
Mechanical Engineering M,D
Mechanics M,D
Meteorology M,D
Microbiology M,D*
Molecular Biology M,D*
Neuroscience M,D*
Nutrition M,D*
Operations Research M,D
Pathology M,D
Physical Education M,D
Physics M,D
Physiology M,D
Plant Pathology M,D
Plant Physiology M,D*
Political Science M
Psychology—General M,D
Public Policy and Administration M
Rhetoric M,D
Rural Planning and Studies M,D
Rural Sociology M,D
Social Psychology M,D
Sociology M,D
Special Education M,D
Statistics M,D
Structural Biology D
Structural Engineering M,D
Systems Engineering M
Toxicology M,D

Iowa State University of Science and Technology (continued)

Transportation and Highway Engineering	M,D
Transportation Management	M
Veterinary Medicine	P,M
Veterinary Sciences	M,D
Vocational and Technical Education	M,D
Water Resources	M,D
Zoology	M,D*

In-depth description on page 919.

ISIM UNIVERSITY

Business Administration and Management—General	M
Information Science	M
Management Information Systems	M
Project Management	M

ITHACA COLLEGE

Allied Health—General	M
Business Administration and Management—General	M
Communication Disorders	M
Communication—General	M
Exercise and Sports Science	M
Music Education	M
Music	M
Occupational Therapy	M
Physical Therapy	M

In-depth description on page 921.

ITI-INFORMATION TECHNOLOGY INSTITUTE

Business Administration and Management—General	M
Computer Education	M
Information Science	M

JACKSON STATE UNIVERSITY

Accounting	M
Allied Health—General	M
Biological and Biomedical Sciences—General	M,D
Business Administration and Management—General	M,D
Business Education	M
Chemistry	M,D
City and Regional Planning	M
Clinical Psychology	D
Communication Disorders	M
Computer Science	M
Counselor Education	M,O
Criminal Justice and Criminology	M
Early Childhood Education	M,D,O
Education—General	M,D,O
Educational Administration	M,D,O
Educational Media/Instructional Technology	M,D,O
Elementary Education	M,D,O
English Education	M
English	M
Environmental Sciences	M,D
Health Education	M
History	M
Management Information Systems	M
Mass Communication	M
Materials Sciences	M
Mathematics Education	M
Mathematics	M
Music Education	M
Physical Education	M
Political Science	M
Psychology—General	D
Public Policy and Administration	M,D
Rehabilitation Counseling	M,O
Science Education	M,D
Secondary Education	M,D,O
Social Work	M,D
Sociology	M
Special Education	M,O
Vocational and Technical Education	M

JACKSONVILLE STATE UNIVERSITY

Biological and Biomedical Sciences—General	M
Business Administration and Management—General	M
Computer Science	M
Counselor Education	M,O
Criminal Justice and Criminology	M
Early Childhood Education	M,O
Education—General	M,O
Educational Administration	M,O
Educational Media/Instructional Technology	M
Elementary Education	M,O
English	M
Health Education	M,O
History	M
Liberal Studies	M
Mathematics	M
Music Education	M
Music	M
Nursing—General	M
Physical Education	M,O
Political Science	M
Psychology—General	M
Public Policy and Administration	M
Secondary Education	M,O
Software Engineering	M
Special Education	M,O

Announcement on page 387.

JACKSONVILLE UNIVERSITY

Art Education	M
Business Administration and Management—General	M
Computer Education	M
Early Childhood Education	M,O
Education of the Gifted	M,O
Education—General	M,O
Educational Administration	M
Educational Media/Instructional Technology	M
Elementary Education	M
English Education	M
Foreign Languages Education	M,O
Mathematics Education	M
Music Education	M
Reading Education	M
Secondary Education	O
Special Education	M,O

JAMES MADISON UNIVERSITY

Accounting	M
Applied Science and Technology	M
Art Education	M
Art History	M
Art/Fine Arts	M
Biological and Biomedical Sciences—General	M
Business Administration and Management—General	M
Communication Disorders	M
Computer Science	M
Counseling Psychology	M,O
Early Childhood Education	M
Education—General	M
Educational Administration	M
English	M
Health Education	M
History	M
Kinesiology and Movement Studies	M
Middle School Education	M
Music Education	M
Music	M
Photography	M
Psychology—General	M,D,O
Public Policy and Administration	M
Reading Education	M
School Psychology	M,O
Secondary Education	M
Special Education	M
Technical Writing	M
Textile Design	M
Vocational and Technical Education	M

JESUIT SCHOOL OF THEOLOGY AT BERKELEY

Theology	P,M,D,O

JEWISH HOSPITAL COLLEGE OF NURSING AND ALLIED HEALTH

Advanced Practice Nursing	M
Allied Health—General	M
Gerontological Nursing	M
Health Promotion	M
Health Services Management and Hospital Administration	M
Maternal/Child Nursing	M
Medical/Surgical Nursing	M
Nursing Education	M
Nursing—General	M

JEWISH THEOLOGICAL SEMINARY OF AMERICA

Jewish Studies	M,D
Music	M,D
Religion	M,D*
Religious Education	M,D*
Theology	M,D,O

JEWISH UNIVERSITY OF AMERICA

Jewish Studies	P,D
Pastoral Ministry and Counseling	M,D
Religious Education	M,D

JOAN AND SANFORD I. WEILL MEDICAL COLLEGE AND GRADUATE SCHOOL OF MEDICAL SCIENCES OF CORNELL UNIVERSITY

Allopathic Medicine	P
Biochemistry	D
Biological and Biomedical Sciences—General	M,D*
Biophysics	D
Cell Biology	D
Epidemiology	M
Genetics	D
Health Services Research	M
Immunology	M,D
Molecular Biology	M,D
Neuroscience	D
Pharmacology	D
Physiology	D
Structural Biology	D

JOHN BROWN UNIVERSITY

Business Administration and Management—General	M
Counselor Education	M
Marriage and Family Therapy	M

JOHN CARROLL UNIVERSITY

Biological and Biomedical Sciences—General	M
Business Administration and Management—General	M
Chemistry	M
Corporate and Organizational Communication	M
Counseling Psychology	M,O
Counselor Education	M,O
Education—General	M
Educational Administration	M
Educational Psychology	M
Elementary Education	M
English	M
History	M
Humanities	M
Mathematics	M
Physics	M
Religion	M
Secondary Education	M

JOHN F. KENNEDY UNIVERSITY

Art/Fine Arts	M
Business Administration and Management—General	M,O
Comparative and Interdisciplinary Arts	M
Conflict Resolution and Mediation/Peace Studies	O
Counseling Psychology	M
Education—General	M
Health Education	M
Human Resources Development	M,O
Industrial and Organizational Psychology	M,O
Interdisciplinary Studies	M,O
Law	P
Museum Studies	M,O*
Organizational Management	M,O
Psychology—General	M,D,O
Sport Psychology	M
Transpersonal and Humanistic Psychology	M

In-depth description on page 923.

JOHN JAY COLLEGE OF CRIMINAL JUSTICE OF THE CITY UNIVERSITY OF NEW YORK

Criminal Justice and Criminology	M,D*
Forensic Psychology	M,D
Forensic Sciences	M,D
Legal and Justice Studies	M,D
Organizational Behavior	M,D
Public Policy and Administration	M,D

JOHN MARSHALL LAW SCHOOL

International Business	P,M
Law	P,M
Legal and Justice Studies	P,M
Management Information Systems	P,M
Real Estate	P,M
Taxation	P,M

JOHNS HOPKINS UNIVERSITY

Addictions/Substance Abuse Counseling	M,D,O
Advanced Practice Nursing	M,O
African Studies	M,D,O
Allopathic Medicine	P
Anatomy	D
Anthropology	D
Applied Mathematics	M,D
Art History	M,D
Asian Studies	M,D,O
Astronomy	D
Biochemistry	M,D*
Biological and Biomedical Sciences—General	M,D*
Biomedical Engineering	M*
Biophysics	M,D
Biostatistics	M,D
Business Administration and Management—General	M,O
Canadian Studies	M,D,O
Cell Biology	D*
Chemical Engineering	M,D
Chemistry	M,D
Civil Engineering	M,D*
Classics	M,D
Clinical Research	M,D,O
Cognitive Sciences	D
Community Health Nursing	M
Community Health	M,D
Comparative Literature	D
Computer Engineering	M,D
Computer Science	M,D*
Conflict Resolution and Mediation/Peace Studies	M,D,O
Counselor Education	M,D,O
Curriculum and Instruction	M
Demography and Population Studies	M
Developmental Biology	D
Disability Studies	M,D,O
Early Childhood Education	M
East European and Russian Studies	M,D,O
Economics	M,D,O
Education of the Gifted	M,D,O
Education—General	M,D,O*
Educational Administration	M,D,O
Educational Media/Instructional Technology	M,D,O
Electrical Engineering	M,D*
Electronic Commerce	M,O
Elementary Education	M
Engineering and Applied Sciences—General	M,D*
English	D
Environmental and Occupational Health	M,D
Environmental Engineering	M,D
Environmental Management and Policy	M,D,O
Epidemiology	M,D
Evolutionary Biology	D
Experimental Psychology	D
Finance and Banking	M,O
French	M,D
Genetic Counseling	M,D
Genetics	M,D
Geochemistry	M,D
Geography	M,D
Geology	M,D
Geophysics	M,D
German	D
Health Education	M,D
Health Physics/Radiological Health	M,D
Health Services Management and Hospital Administration	M,D,O*
Health Services Research	M,D
Higher Education	M,D,O
History of Science and Technology	D
History	D
Human Genetics	D*
Human Resources Development	M,O
Immunology	M,D*
International Affairs	M,D,O*
International Business	M,D,O
International Development	M,D,O
International Health	M,D
Investment Management	M,O
Italian	M,D
Latin American Studies	M,D,O
Liberal Studies	M,O
Management Information Systems	M,O
Marketing	M,O
Materials Engineering	M,D
Materials Sciences	M,D*
Mathematics Education	M,D,O
Mathematics	M,D
Mechanical Engineering	M,D*
Mechanics	M,D
Medical Illustration	M
Medical/Surgical Nursing	M,O
Microbiology	M,D
Military and Defense Studies	M,D,O
Molecular Biology	M,D*
Molecular Medicine	D
Music	M,D,O
Near and Middle Eastern Studies	M,D,O
Neuroscience	D*
Nursing and Healthcare Administration	M
Nursing—General	M,D,O*
Nutrition	M,D
Oceanography	M,D
Operations Research	M,D
Pathobiology	D*
Pathology	D

Pediatric Nursing M,O
Pharmacology D*
Philosophy M,D
Physics D*
Physiology M,D*
Planetary and Space Sciences M,D
Political Science D
Psychology—General D
Public Health—General M,D,O*
Public Policy and Administration M*
Reading Education M,D,O
Real Estate M,O
Reproductive Biology M,D
Romance Languages M,D
Science Education M,D,O
Secondary Education M
Social Sciences M,D
Sociology D
Spanish M,D
Special Education M,D,O
Statistics M,D
Toxicology D
Water Resources M,D
Western European Studies M,D,O
Writing M

In-depth description on page 925.

JOHNSON & WALES UNIVERSITY

Accounting M
Business Administration and Management—General M
Business Education M
Education—General M
Educational Administration D
Hospitality Management M
International Business M

In-depth description on page 927.

JOHNSON BIBLE COLLEGE

Education—General M
Educational Media/Instructional Technology M
Marriage and Family Therapy M
Theology M

JOHNSON STATE COLLEGE

Art/Fine Arts M
Counselor Education M
Curriculum and Instruction M
Education of the Gifted M
Education—General M
Reading Education M
Special Education M

JOINT MILITARY INTELLIGENCE COLLEGE

Military and Defense Studies M,O

JONES INTERNATIONAL UNIVERSITY

Business Administration and Management—General M*
Conflict Resolution and Mediation/Peace Studies M
Corporate and Organizational Communication M
Distance Education Development M
Electronic Commerce M
Entrepreneurship M
Health Services Management and Hospital Administration M
Management of Technology M
Travel and Tourism M

In-depth description on page 929.

THE JUDGE ADVOCATE GENERAL'S SCHOOL, U.S. ARMY

Law M
Military and Defense Studies M

THE JUILLIARD SCHOOL

Music M,D,O

KANSAS STATE UNIVERSITY

Accounting M
Adult Education M,D
Agricultural Economics and Agribusiness M,D
Agricultural Engineering M,D
Agricultural Sciences—General M,D
Agronomy and Soil Sciences M,D
Analytical Chemistry M,D
Anatomy M,D
Animal Sciences M,D
Architectural Engineering M
Architecture M
Art/Fine Arts M
Biochemistry M,D
Bioengineering M,D
Biological and Biomedical Sciences—General M,D
Business Administration and Management—General M
Cancer Biology/Oncology M,D
Cell Biology M,D
Chemical Engineering M,D
Chemistry M,D
Child and Family Studies M,D
City and Regional Planning M
Civil Engineering M,D
Clothing and Textiles M,D
Computer Engineering M,D
Computer Science M,D*
Counselor Education M,D
Curriculum and Instruction D
Developmental Biology M,D
Ecology M,D
Economics M,D
Education—General M,D
Educational Administration M,D
Educational Psychology M,D
Electrical Engineering M,D
Elementary Education M
Engineering and Applied Sciences—General M,D*
Engineering Management M,D
English M
Entomology M,D
Environmental Management and Policy M
Family and Consumer Sciences-General M,D
Food Science and Technology M,D
Foundations and Philosophy of Education M,D
French M
Genetics M,D
Geography M,D
Geology M
German M
History M,D
Horticulture M,D
Hospitality Management M,D
Human Services M,D
Immunology M,D
Industrial/Management Engineering M,D
Information Science M,D
Inorganic Chemistry M,D
International Affairs M
Kinesiology and Movement Studies M
Landscape Architecture M
Manufacturing Engineering M,D
Mass Communication M
Mathematics M,D
Mechanical Engineering M,D
Microbiology M,D
Molecular Biology M,D
Music Education M
Music M
Nuclear Engineering M,D
Nutrition M,D
Operations Research M,D
Organic Chemistry M,D
Pathobiology M,D
Physical Chemistry M,D
Physics M,D
Physiology M,D
Plant Pathology M,D
Political Science M
Psychology—General M,D
Public Policy and Administration M
Range Science M,D
Secondary Education M
Sociology M,D
Software Engineering M
Spanish M
Speech and Interpersonal Communication M
Statistics M,D
Student Personnel Services M,D
Veterinary Medicine P
Veterinary Sciences M
Virology M,D

In-depth description on page 931 and announcement on page 392.

KANSAS WESLEYAN UNIVERSITY

Business Administration and Management—General M

KEAN UNIVERSITY

Accounting M
Addictions/Substance Abuse Counseling M,O
Art Education M
Biotechnology M*
Communication Disorders M
Computational Sciences M
Counselor Education M,O
Curriculum and Instruction M,O
Early Childhood Education M
Education—General M,O
Educational Administration M,O
Educational Media/Instructional Technology M
Educational Psychology M,O
English as a Second Language M,O
Exercise and Sports Science M
Graphic Design M
Health Services Management and Hospital Administration M
Industrial and Organizational Psychology M,O
Liberal Studies M
Management Information Systems M
Marriage and Family Therapy M,O
Mathematics Education M,O
Mathematics M
Multilingual and Multicultural Education M,O
Nursing—General M
Occupational Therapy M
Psychology—General M,O
Public Policy and Administration M
Reading Education M,O
School Psychology M,O
Science Education M,O
Social Work M
Special Education M
Statistics M

In-depth description on page 933.

KECK GRADUATE INSTITUTE OF APPLIED LIFE SCIENCES

Biological and Biomedical Sciences—General M*
Biotechnology M

KEENE STATE COLLEGE

Counselor Education M,O
Curriculum and Instruction M
Education—General M,O
Educational Administration M,O
Special Education M,O

KEHILATH YAKOV RABBINICAL SEMINARY

Theology

KENNESAW STATE UNIVERSITY

Accounting M
Advanced Practice Nursing M
Business Administration and Management—General M
Conflict Resolution and Mediation/Peace Studies M
Early Childhood Education M
Education—General M
Entrepreneurship M
Finance and Banking M
Human Resources Development M
Human Resources Management M
Information Science M
Management Information Systems M
Marketing M
Middle School Education M
Nursing—General M
Public Policy and Administration M
Special Education M
Writing M

KENRICK-GLENNON SEMINARY

Theology P,M,O

KENT STATE UNIVERSITY

Accounting M,D
Analytical Chemistry M,D
Anthropology M,D
Applied Mathematics M,D
Architecture M
Art Education M
Art/Fine Arts M*
Biochemistry M,D
Biological and Biomedical Sciences—General M,D*
Botany M,D
Business Administration and Management—General M*
Cell Biology M,D
Chemistry M,D*
Child and Family Studies M
Classics M
Clinical Psychology M,D
Communication Disorders M,D
Communication—General M,D
Computer Science M,D*
Counselor Education M,D
Criminal Justice and Criminology M
Curriculum and Instruction M,D,O
Early Childhood Education M
Ecology M,D*
Economics M
Education of the Gifted M,D,O
Education—General M,D,O
Educational Administration M,D,O
Educational Measurement and Evaluation M,D
Educational Media/Instructional Technology M
Educational Psychology M,D
Engineering and Applied Sciences—General M
English M,D
Exercise and Sports Science M,D
Experimental Psychology M,D
Family and Consumer Sciences-General M
Finance and Banking D
Financial Engineering M
Foundations and Philosophy of Education M,D
French M
Geography M,D
Geology M,D
German M
Graphic Design M
Health Education M,D
Higher Education M,D,O
History M,D
Human Development D
Illustration M
Inorganic Chemistry M,D
Interdisciplinary Studies M
International Affairs M,D
Journalism M
Liberal Studies M
Library Science M
Management Information Systems D
Marketing D
Mass Communication M
Mathematics M,D
Medical/Surgical Nursing M
Middle School Education M
Molecular Biology M,D
Music Education M,D
Music M,D*
Neuroscience M,D
Nursing and Healthcare Administration M
Nursing Education M
Nursing—General M
Nutrition M
Organic Chemistry M,D
Pediatric Nursing M
Pharmacology M,D
Philosophy M
Physical Chemistry M,D
Physical Education M,D
Physics M,D*
Physiology M,D*
Political Science M,D
Psychiatric Nursing M
Psychology—General M,D
Public Health—General M
Public Policy and Administration M
Reading Education M
Rehabilitation Counseling M,O
School Psychology M,D,O
Secondary Education M
Sociology M,D
Spanish M
Special Education M,D,O
Student Personnel Services M,D,O
Textile Design M
Theater M*
Vocational and Technical Education M,O
Zoology M,D

KENTUCKY STATE UNIVERSITY

Aquaculture M
Public Policy and Administration M

KETTERING UNIVERSITY

Automotive Engineering M
Engineering and Applied Sciences—General M
Engineering Design M
Manufacturing Engineering M
Mechanical Engineering M
Operations Research M

KING'S COLLEGE

Accounting M
Business Administration and Management—General M
Finance and Banking M
Health Services Management and Hospital Administration M
Physician Assistant Studies M
Reading Education M
Taxation M

KIRKSVILLE COLLEGE OF OSTEOPATHIC MEDICINE

Allied Health—General M,D,O

Kirksville College of Osteopathic Medicine (continued)

Biological and Biomedical Sciences—General M
Communication Disorders M,D
Exercise and Sports Science M,D
Gerontology M,O
Health Services Management and Hospital Administration M,O
Medical Informatics M,D
Occupational Therapy M,D
Osteopathic Medicine P
Physical Therapy M,D
Physician Assistant Studies M,D
Public Health—General M,O

KNOWLEDGE SYSTEMS INSTITUTE

Computer Science M
Information Science M

KNOX COLLEGE

Theology P,M,D

KOL YAAKOV TORAH CENTER

Theology O

KUTZTOWN UNIVERSITY OF PENNSYLVANIA

Art Education M,O
Business Administration and Management—General M
Computer Science M
Counseling Psychology M
Counselor Education M
Curriculum and Instruction M,O
Early Childhood Education M,O
Education—General M,O
Educational Administration M
Elementary Education M,O
English Education M,O
English M
Information Science M
Library Science M,O
Marriage and Family Therapy M
Mathematics Education M,O
Media Studies M
Public Policy and Administration M
Reading Education M
School Nursing O
Science Education M,O
Secondary Education M,O
Social Sciences Education M,O
Special Education M,O

In-depth description on page 935.

KYUNG SAN UNIVERSITY USA

Acupuncture and Oriental Medicine M

LAGRANGE COLLEGE

Early Childhood Education M
Education—General M
Middle School Education M

LAKE ERIE COLLEGE

Business Administration and Management—General M
Education—General M
Health Services Management and Hospital Administration M
Reading Education M

LAKE ERIE COLLEGE OF OSTEOPATHIC MEDICINE

Osteopathic Medicine P,O

LAKE FOREST COLLEGE

Liberal Studies M

LAKE FOREST GRADUATE SCHOOL OF MANAGEMENT

Business Administration and Management—General M

LAKEHEAD UNIVERSITY

Biological and Biomedical Sciences—General M
Chemistry M
Clinical Psychology M,D
Computer Science M
Curriculum and Instruction M,D
Economics M
Education—General M,D
Educational Administration M,D
Engineering and Applied Sciences—General M
English M
Exercise and Sports Science M
Experimental Psychology M,D
Forestry M
Geology M
Gerontology M
History M
Mathematics M
Philosophy M
Physical Education M
Physics M
Psychology—General M,D
Social Work M
Sociology M
Statistics M
Women's Studies M

LAKELAND COLLEGE

Business Administration and Management—General M
Education—General M
Theology M

LAMAR UNIVERSITY

Accounting M
Applied Arts and Design—General M
Art History M
Art/Fine Arts M
Biological and Biomedical Sciences—General M
Business Administration and Management—General M
Chemical Engineering M,D
Chemistry M
Civil Engineering M,D
Clinical Psychology M
Communication Disorders M,D
Computer Science M*
Counselor Education M,O
Criminal Justice and Criminology M
Education—General M,O
Educational Administration M,O
Electrical Engineering M,D
Elementary Education M,O
Engineering and Applied Sciences—General M,D
Engineering Management M
English M
Environmental Engineering M
Environmental Management and Policy M
Family and Consumer Sciences-General M
History M
Industrial and Organizational Psychology M
Industrial/Management Engineering M,D
Information Science M
Kinesiology and Movement Studies M
Management Strategy and Policy M
Mathematics M
Mechanical Engineering M,D
Music Education M
Music M
Nursing and Healthcare Administration M
Nursing—General M
Photography M
Political Science M
Psychology—General M
Public Policy and Administration M
Reading Education M,O
Secondary Education M,O
Social Psychology M
Special Education M,D,O
Theater M

In-depth description on page 937.

LANCASTER BIBLE COLLEGE

Counselor Education M
Pastoral Ministry and Counseling M
Theology M

LANCASTER THEOLOGICAL SEMINARY

Theology P,M,D

LANDER UNIVERSITY

Curriculum and Instruction M
Education—General M
Elementary Education M

LANGSTON UNIVERSITY

Education—General M

LA ROCHE COLLEGE

Advanced Practice Nursing M
Community Health Nursing M
Gerontological Nursing M
Human Resources Management M
Medical/Surgical Nursing M
Nurse Anesthesia M
Nursing and Healthcare Administration M
Nursing—General M

LA SALLE UNIVERSITY

Advanced Practice Nursing M,O
Business Administration and Management—General M,O
Clinical Psychology M,D
Community Health Nursing M,O
Computer Science M
Corporate and Organizational Communication M
Counseling Psychology M
East European and Russian Studies M
Education—General M
Health Informatics M,O
Latin American Studies M
Management of Technology M,O
Marriage and Family Therapy D
Medical/Surgical Nursing M,O
Nursing and Healthcare Administration M,O
Nursing Education M,O
Nursing—General M,O
Pastoral Ministry and Counseling M
Psychology—General D
Rehabilitation Counseling D
Religion M
School Nursing M,O
Theology M

LASELL COLLEGE

Health Services Management and Hospital Administration M*

LA SIERRA UNIVERSITY

Business Administration and Management—General M,O
Counselor Education M,O
Curriculum and Instruction M,D,O
Education—General M,D,O
Educational Administration M,D,O
Educational Psychology M,O
English M
Religion M
Religious Education M
School Psychology M,O
Special Education M,D,O

LAURA AND ALVIN SIEGAL COLLEGE OF JUDAIC STUDIES

Jewish Studies M

LAURENTIAN UNIVERSITY

Applied Physics M
Biochemistry M
Biological and Biomedical Sciences—General M
Business Administration and Management—General M
Chemistry M
Engineering and Applied Sciences—General M
Geology M
History M
Human Development M
Humanities M
Metallurgical Engineering and Metallurgy M
Mineral/Mining Engineering M
Social Work M
Sociology M

LAWRENCE TECHNOLOGICAL UNIVERSITY

Architecture M
Automotive Engineering M,D
Business Administration and Management—General M
Civil Engineering M,D
Computer Engineering M,D
Computer Science M
Education—General M
Electrical Engineering M,D
Engineering and Applied Sciences—General M,D
Industrial and Manufacturing Management M
Management Information Systems M
Manufacturing Engineering M,D
Science Education M

THE LEADERSHIP INSTITUTE OF SEATTLE

Business Administration and Management—General M
Management Information Systems M
Organizational Behavior M*
Organizational Management M

LEBANESE AMERICAN UNIVERSITY

Business Administration and Management—General M
Computer Science M
International Affairs M
Pharmacy P

LEBANON VALLEY COLLEGE

Business Administration and Management—General M
Music Education M
Science Education M

LEE UNIVERSITY

Counseling Psychology M
Education—General M
Liberal Studies M
Music M

LEHIGH UNIVERSITY

Accounting M,D,O*
American Studies M*
Anthropology M
Applied Mathematics M,D
Biochemistry D
Biological and Biomedical Sciences—General D*
Business Administration and Management—General M,D,O*
Chemical Engineering M,D*
Chemistry M,D*
Civil Engineering M,D*
Computer Engineering M
Computer Science M,D*
Counseling Psychology M,D,O
Counselor Education M,D,O
Curriculum and Instruction M,D,O
Economics M,D
Education—General M,D,O
Educational Administration M,D,O
Educational Media/Instructional Technology M,D
Electrical Engineering M,D*
Elementary Education M,D,O
Engineering and Applied Sciences—General M,D*
English M,D*
Environmental Engineering M,D
Environmental Sciences M,D*
Evolutionary Biology D
Experimental Psychology D
Geology M,D
Geosciences M,D
History M,D*
Human Services M,D,O
Industrial/Management Engineering M,D*
Information Science M,D,O
Manufacturing Engineering M
Materials Engineering M,D
Materials Sciences M,D*
Mathematics M,D*
Mechanical Engineering M,D*
Mechanics M,D
Molecular Biology D
Neuroscience D
Photonics M,D
Physics M,D*
Political Science M*
Polymer Science and Engineering M,D*
Psychology—General D*
School Psychology D,O
Secondary Education M,D,O
Sociology M*
Special Education M,D,O
Statistics M
Systems Engineering M

LEHMAN COLLEGE OF THE CITY UNIVERSITY OF NEW YORK

Accounting M
Art/Fine Arts M
Biological and Biomedical Sciences—General M,D
Business Education M
Communication Disorders M
Computer Science M
Counselor Education M
Early Childhood Education M
Education—General M
Elementary Education M
English as a Second Language M
English Education M
English M
Gerontological Nursing M
Health Education M
Health Promotion M
History M
Maternal/Child Nursing M
Mathematics Education M
Mathematics M
Medical/Surgical Nursing M
Multilingual and Multicultural Education M
Music Education M
Nursing—General M
Nutrition M
Pediatric Nursing M
Plant Sciences D
Reading Education M
Recreation and Park Management M
Science Education M
Social Sciences Education M
Spanish M

Special Education M

LE MOYNE COLLEGE

Business Administration and Management—General M
Education—General M

LENOIR-RHYNE COLLEGE

Business Administration and Management—General M
Counselor Education M
Early Childhood Education M
Education—General M
Elementary Education M
School Psychology M

LESLEY UNIVERSITY

Art Education M,D,O
Art Therapy M,D,O
Art/Fine Arts M*
Business Administration and Management—General M*
Clinical Psychology M,D,O
Computer Education M,D,O
Conflict Resolution and Mediation/Peace Studies M,O
Counseling Psychology M,D,O
Curriculum and Instruction M,D,O
Early Childhood Education M,D,O
Ecology M,D,O
Education—General M,D,O*
Educational Administration M,D,O
Elementary Education M,D,O
Environmental Education M,D,O
Health Education M,O
Health Services Management and Hospital Administration M
Human Resources Development M
Human Resources Management M,O
Human Services M,O
Interdisciplinary Studies M,D,O
International Affairs M,D,O
International and Comparative Education M,O
Management Information Systems M
Middle School Education M,D,O
Multilingual and Multicultural Education M,O
Nonprofit Management M
Project Management M,O
Psychology—General M,D,O
Reading Education M,D,O
School Psychology M,D,O
Social Psychology M,D,O
Special Education M,D,O
Theater M,D,O
Therapies—Dance, Drama, and Music M,D,O
Writing M

In-depth description on page 939.

LETOURNEAU UNIVERSITY

Business Administration and Management—General M
Health Services Management and Hospital Administration M

LEWIS & CLARK COLLEGE

Communication Disorders M
Counseling Psychology M
Education—General M,O
Educational Administration O
Elementary Education M
Law P,M
Music Education M
School Psychology M
Secondary Education M
Special Education M

LEWIS UNIVERSITY

Business Administration and Management—General M
Community Health Nursing M,O
Counseling Psychology M
Counselor Education M
Criminal Justice and Criminology M
Curriculum and Instruction M
Education—General M,O
Educational Administration M
Nursing and Healthcare Administration M,O
Nursing Education M,O
Nursing—General M,O
Organizational Management M
Philosophy M
Special Education M

LEXINGTON THEOLOGICAL SEMINARY

Theology P,M,D

LIBERTY UNIVERSITY

Business Administration and Management—General M
Counseling Psychology M
Counselor Education M,D
Early Childhood Education M,D
Education of the Gifted M,D
Education—General M,D
Educational Administration M,D
Elementary Education M,D
Nursing—General M
Reading Education M,D
Religion M
Secondary Education M,D
Special Education M,D
Theology P,M,D

In-depth description on page 941.

LIFE CHIROPRACTIC COLLEGE WEST

Chiropractic P*

LIFE UNIVERSITY

Chiropractic P*

LINCOLN CHRISTIAN SEMINARY

Pastoral Ministry and Counseling P,M
Theology P,M

LINCOLN MEMORIAL UNIVERSITY

Business Administration and Management—General M
Counselor Education M,O
Curriculum and Instruction M,O
Education—General M,O
Educational Administration M,O

LINCOLN UNIVERSITY (CA)

Business Administration and Management—General M

LINCOLN UNIVERSITY (MO)

Accounting M
Business Administration and Management—General M
Counselor Education M
Criminal Justice and Criminology M
Education—General M
Educational Administration M
Elementary Education M
History M
Secondary Education M
Sociology M

LINCOLN UNIVERSITY (PA)

Human Services M

LINDENWOOD UNIVERSITY

Business Administration and Management—General M
Corporate and Organizational Communication M
Counseling Psychology M
Education—General M,O
Gerontology M
Health Services Management and Hospital Administration M
Human Resources Management M
Human Services M
Marketing M
Mass Communication M

LINDSEY WILSON COLLEGE

Educational Psychology M
Human Development M
Human Services M

LIPSCOMB UNIVERSITY

Business Administration and Management—General M
Education—General M
Religion P,M
Theology P,M

LOCK HAVEN UNIVERSITY OF PENNSYLVANIA

Curriculum and Instruction M
Education—General M
Liberal Studies M
Physician Assistant Studies M

LOGAN UNIVERSITY-COLLEGE OF CHIROPRACTIC

Chiropractic P

LOMA LINDA UNIVERSITY

Allied Health—General M,D
Allopathic Medicine P
Anatomy M,D
Biochemistry M,D
Bioethics M
Biological and Biomedical Sciences—General M,D
Biostatistics M
Child and Family Studies M,O
Clinical Psychology D
Communication Disorders M
Dentistry P,O
Environmental and Occupational Health M
Epidemiology M,D*
Geology M
Gerontological Nursing M
Health Education M,D
Health Informatics M
Health Promotion M,D
Health Services Management and Hospital Administration M
International Health M
Marriage and Family Therapy M,D
Microbiology M,D*
Nursing and Healthcare Administration M,O
Nursing—General M,O
Nutrition M,D*
Oral and Dental Sciences M,O
Pediatric Nursing M
Pharmacology M,D
Physical Therapy M,D
Physician Assistant Studies M
Physiology M,D
Public Health—General M,D
Social Work M,D

LONG ISLAND UNIVERSITY, BRENTWOOD CAMPUS

Business Administration and Management—General M
Counselor Education M
Criminal Justice and Criminology M
Education—General M
Educational Administration M
Elementary Education M
Health Services Management and Hospital Administration M
Public Policy and Administration M
Reading Education M
Special Education M

LONG ISLAND UNIVERSITY, BROOKLYN CAMPUS

Accounting M
Advanced Practice Nursing M,O
Biological and Biomedical Sciences—General M
Business Administration and Management—General M
Chemistry M
Clinical Psychology D
Communication Disorders M
Community Health M
Comparative Literature M
Computer Science M
Counselor Education M,O
Economics M
Education—General M,O
Educational Administration M
Educational Media/Instructional Technology M
Elementary Education M
English as a Second Language M
English Education M
English M*
Exercise and Sports Science M
Health Education M
Health Services Management and Hospital Administration M
History M,O
Human Resources Management M
International Affairs M,O
Mathematics Education M
Medicinal and Pharmaceutical Chemistry M
Multilingual and Multicultural Education M
Nursing and Healthcare Administration M
Nursing—General M,O
Pharmaceutical Administration M
Pharmaceutical Sciences M,D
Pharmacology M
Physical Education M
Physical Therapy M
Political Science M
Psychology—General M,D
Public Policy and Administration M
Reading Education M
School Psychology M
Social Sciences M,O
Special Education M
Taxation M
Toxicology M
Urban Studies M
Writing M

LONG ISLAND UNIVERSITY, C.W. POST CAMPUS

Accounting M
Advanced Practice Nursing M,O
Allied Health—General M,O
Applied Mathematics M
Art Education M
Art Therapy M
Art/Fine Arts M
Biological and Biomedical Sciences—General M
Business Administration and Management—General M,O*
Cardiovascular Sciences M,O
Clinical Laboratory Sciences/Medical Technology M
Clinical Psychology D
Communication Disorders M
Computer Art and Design M
Computer Education M
Computer Science M
Counselor Education M,O
Criminal Justice and Criminology M
Early Childhood Education M
Education—General M,O
Educational Administration M,O
Educational Media/Instructional Technology M,D,O
Engineering Management M
English Education M
English M
Environmental Management and Policy M
Environmental Sciences M
Experimental Psychology M
Finance and Banking M,O
Foreign Languages Education M
French M
Gerontology M,O
Health Services Management and Hospital Administration M,O
History M
Human Resources Management M,O
Immunology M
Information Science M
Information Studies M,D,O
Interdisciplinary Studies M
International Affairs M
International Business M,O
Internet and Interactive Multimedia M
Italian M
Library Science M,D,O*
Logistics M,O
Management Information Systems M,O
Marketing M,O
Marriage and Family Therapy M,O
Mathematics Education M
Mathematics M
Medicinal and Pharmaceutical Chemistry M
Microbiology M
Multilingual and Multicultural Education M
Music Education M
Music M
Nursing—General M,O
Nutrition M,O
Political Science M
Psychology—General M,D
Public Policy and Administration M,O
Reading Education M,O
Science Education M
Secondary Education M
Social Sciences M
Spanish M
Special Education M,O
Taxation M
Theater M

In-depth description on page 943.

LONG ISLAND UNIVERSITY, ROCKLAND GRADUATE CAMPUS

Business Administration and Management—General M
Counselor Education M
Education—General M
Educational Administration M
Educational Psychology M
Elementary Education M
Health Services Management and Hospital Administration M
Reading Education M
Special Education M

LONG ISLAND UNIVERSITY, SOUTHAMPTON COLLEGE

Education—General M
Elementary Education M
English M
Gerontology M,O
Reading Education M
Writing M

LONG ISLAND UNIVERSITY, WESTCHESTER GRADUATE CAMPUS

Business Administration and Management—General M
Counselor Education M
Education—General M
Elementary Education M
English as a Second Language M
Exercise and Sports Science M
Multilingual and Multicultural Education M
Pharmaceutical Sciences M
Public Policy and Administration M
Reading Education M
School Psychology M
Special Education M

LONGWOOD COLLEGE

Counselor Education M
Criminal Justice and Criminology M
Education—General M
Educational Administration M
Educational Media/Instructional Technology M
Elementary Education M
English Education M
English M
Environmental Management and Policy M
Physical Education M
Reading Education M
Secondary Education M
Social Sciences Education M
Special Education M
Writing M

LONGY SCHOOL OF MUSIC

Music M,O

LORAS COLLEGE

Counselor Education M
Curriculum and Instruction M
Educational Administration M
English M
Physical Education M
Psychology—General M
Religion M
Special Education M

LOUISIANA STATE UNIVERSITY AND AGRICULTURAL AND MECHANICAL COLLEGE

Accounting M,D
Agricultural Economics and Agribusiness M,D
Agricultural Education M,D
Agricultural Engineering M,D
Agricultural Sciences—General M,D
Agronomy and Soil Sciences M,D
Animal Sciences M,D
Anthropology M,D
Applied Arts and Design—General M
Architecture M
Art History M
Art/Fine Arts M
Astronomy M,D
Astrophysics M,D
Biochemistry M,D
Bioengineering M,D
Biological and Biomedical Sciences—General M,D*
Biopsychology M,D
Business Administration and Management—General M,D
Business Education M,D
Chemical Engineering M,D*
Chemistry M,D
Civil Engineering M,D
Clinical Psychology M,D
Cognitive Sciences M,D
Communication Disorders M,D
Comparative Literature M,D
Computer Engineering M,D
Computer Science M,D
Counselor Education M,D,O
Curriculum and Instruction M,D,O
Developmental Psychology M,D
Economics M,D
Education—General M,D,O
Educational Administration M,D,O
Educational Measurement and Evaluation M,D,O
Educational Media/Instructional Technology M,D,O
Electrical Engineering M,D*
Elementary Education M,D,O
Engineering and Applied Sciences—General M,D
English M,D
Entomology M,D
Environmental Engineering M,D
Environmental Management and Policy M
Environmental Sciences M,D
Family and Consumer Sciences-General M,D
Finance and Banking M,D
Fish, Game, and Wildlife Management M,D
Food Science and Technology M,D
Forestry M,D
French M,D
Geography M,D
Geology M,D
Geophysics M,D
Geosciences M
Geotechnical Engineering M,D
Graphic Design M
Higher Education M,D,O
History M,D
Home Economics Education M,D
Horticulture M,D
Industrial and Organizational Psychology M,D
Industrial/Management Engineering M,D
Information Studies M,O
International and Comparative Education M,D
Kinesiology and Movement Studies M,D
Landscape Architecture M
Law P,M
Liberal Studies M
Library Science M,O
Linguistics M,D
Management Information Systems M,D
Marine Affairs M,D
Marketing M,D
Mass Communication M
Mathematics M,D
Mechanical Engineering M,D
Mechanics M,D
Microbiology M,D
Music Education M,D
Music M,D
Oceanography M,D
Petroleum Engineering M,D
Philosophy M
Photography M
Physics M,D*
Plant Biology M,D
Plant Pathology M,D
Political Science M,D
Psychology—General M,D
Public Policy and Administration M
School Psychology M,D
Secondary Education M,D,O
Social Work M,D
Sociology M,D
Spanish M
Speech and Interpersonal Communication M,D
Statistics M
Structural Engineering M,D
Systems Science M,D
Theater M,D
Toxicology M
Transportation and Highway Engineering M,D
Veterinary Medicine P
Veterinary Sciences M,D
Vocational and Technical Education M,D
Water Resources Engineering M,D
Writing M,D
Zoology M,D

LOUISIANA STATE UNIVERSITY HEALTH SCIENCES CENTER

Advanced Practice Nursing M,D
Allied Health—General M
Allopathic Medicine P,M
Anatomy M,D*
Biochemistry M,D*
Biological and Biomedical Sciences—General M,D*
Biometrics M
Cell Biology M,D*
Communication Disorders M
Community Health Nursing M,D
Dentistry P
Developmental Biology M,D
Human Genetics M,D
Immunology M,D
Medical/Surgical Nursing M,D
Microbiology M,D*
Molecular Biology M,D
Neurobiology M,D
Neuroscience D*
Nursing and Healthcare Administration M,D
Nursing—General M,D
Parasitology M,D
Pathology M,D
Pediatric Nursing M,D
Pharmacology M,D*
Physical Therapy M
Physiology M,D*
Psychiatric Nursing M,D
Public Health—General M
Rehabilitation Counseling M

LOUISIANA STATE UNIVERSITY IN SHREVEPORT

Business Administration and Management—General M
Education—General M,O
Human Services M
Liberal Studies M
School Psychology O
Systems Engineering M
Systems Science M

In-depth description on page 945.

LOUISIANA TECH UNIVERSITY

Accounting M,D
Applied Arts and Design—General M
Art/Fine Arts M*
Biological and Biomedical Sciences—General M
Biomedical Engineering M,D
Business Administration and Management—General M,D
Business Education M,D,O
Chemical Engineering M,D
Chemistry M
Civil Engineering M,D
Communication Disorders M
Computational Sciences M,D
Computer Science M
Counseling Psychology M,D,O
Counselor Education M,D,O
Curriculum and Instruction M,D,O
Economics M,D
Education—General M,D,O
Educational Administration M,D,O
Electrical Engineering M,D
Engineering and Applied Sciences—General M,D
English Education M,D,O
English M
Family and Consumer Sciences-General M
Finance and Banking M,D
Foreign Languages Education M,D,O
Graphic Design M
Health Education M,D,O
History M
Industrial and Organizational Psychology M,D,O
Industrial/Management Engineering M,D
Interior Design M
Manufacturing Engineering M,D
Marketing M,D
Mathematics Education M,D,O
Mathematics M
Mechanical Engineering M,D
Nutrition M
Operations Research M,D
Photography M
Physical Education M,D,O
Physics M,D
Psychology—General M,D,O
Quantitative Analysis M,D
Reading Education M,D,O
Science Education M,D,O
Secondary Education M,D,O
Social Sciences Education M,D,O
Special Education M,D,O
Speech and Interpersonal Communication M
Statistics M

LOUISVILLE PRESBYTERIAN THEOLOGICAL SEMINARY

Religion P,M,D
Theology P,M,D

LOYOLA COLLEGE IN MARYLAND

Addictions/Substance Abuse Counseling M,O
Business Administration and Management—General M
Clinical Psychology M,D,O
Communication Disorders M,O
Counseling Psychology M,O
Counselor Education M,O
Curriculum and Instruction M,O
Early Childhood Education M,O
Economics M
Education—General M,O
Educational Administration M,O
Educational Media/Instructional Technology M
Engineering and Applied Sciences—General M
Finance and Banking M
Foundations and Philosophy of Education M,O
Interdisciplinary Studies M
International Business M
Marketing M
Pastoral Ministry and Counseling M,D,O
Psychology—General M,D,O
Quantitative Analysis M
Reading Education M,O
Special Education M,O

LOYOLA MARYMOUNT UNIVERSITY

Business Administration and Management—General M
Civil Engineering M
Communication—General M
Computer Science M
Counseling Psychology M
Counselor Education M
Education—General M
Educational Administration M
Educational Psychology M
Electrical Engineering M
Elementary Education M
Engineering and Applied Sciences—General M
Engineering Management M
English Education M
English M
Environmental Sciences M
Film, Television, and Video Production M
Industrial/Management Engineering M
Law P,M
Marriage and Family Therapy M
Mathematics Education M
Mechanical Engineering M
Multilingual and Multicultural Education M
Pastoral Ministry and Counseling M
Psychology—General M
Reading Education M
School Psychology M
Science Education M
Secondary Education M
Social Sciences Education M
Special Education M
Taxation P,M
Theology M
Writing M

In-depth description on page 947.

LOYOLA UNIVERSITY CHICAGO

Accounting M
Advanced Practice Nursing M
Allopathic Medicine P
Anatomy M,D
Biochemistry M,D*
Biological and Biomedical Sciences—General M
Business Administration and Management—General M*
Cell Biology M,D*
Chemistry M,D
Classics M,D
Clinical Psychology M,D
Computer Science M*
Corporate and Organizational Communication M
Counseling Psychology D
Counselor Education M
Criminal Justice and Criminology M
Curriculum and Instruction M,D
Developmental Psychology D
Education—General M,D,O*
Educational Administration M,D
Educational Measurement and Evaluation M,D
Educational Psychology M,D
English M,D
Foundations and Philosophy of Education M,D
Health Services Management and Hospital Administration M
Higher Education M,D
History M,D
Human Resources Development M
Human Resources Management M
Immunology M,D
Industrial and Labor Relations M*
International Affairs M,D
International and Comparative Education M,D
Law P,M,D
Management Information Systems M*
Marketing M
Mathematics M*
Medical/Surgical Nursing M
Microbiology M,D*
Molecular Biology M,D*
Neurobiology M,D
Neuroscience M,D*
Nurse Midwifery M
Nursing and Healthcare Administration M
Nursing—General M,D

Oncology Nursing M
Organizational Management M
Pastoral Ministry and Counseling M
Pediatric Nursing M
Pharmacology M,D*
Philosophy M,D
Physiology M,D*
Political Science M,D
Psychology—General M,D*
Religious Education M
School Psychology M,D,O
Social Psychology M,D
Social Work M,D
Sociology M,D
Spanish M
Special Education M
Theology P,M,D
Virology M,D
Women's Health Nursing M,D*
In-depth description on page 949.

LOYOLA UNIVERSITY NEW ORLEANS

Advanced Practice Nursing M
Business Administration and Management—General M
Communication—General M
Counselor Education M
Criminal Justice and Criminology M
Education—General M
Elementary Education M
Law P
Mass Communication M
Music M
Nursing—General M
Reading Education M
Religion M
Secondary Education M
Theology M

LUBBOCK CHRISTIAN UNIVERSITY

Theology M

LUTHERAN SCHOOL OF THEOLOGY AT CHICAGO

Pastoral Ministry and Counseling P,M,D
Theology P,M,D

LUTHERAN THEOLOGICAL SEMINARY

Pastoral Ministry and Counseling P,M
Theology P,M

LUTHERAN THEOLOGICAL SEMINARY AT GETTYSBURG

Theology P,M

THE LUTHERAN THEOLOGICAL SEMINARY AT PHILADELPHIA

Pastoral Ministry and Counseling P,M,D,O
Religion P,M,D,O
Theology P,M,D,O

LUTHERAN THEOLOGICAL SOUTHERN SEMINARY

Theology P,M,D

LUTHER RICE BIBLE COLLEGE AND SEMINARY

Missions and Missiology P,M,D
Pastoral Ministry and Counseling P,M,D
Religious Education P,M,D
Theology P,M,D

LUTHER SEMINARY

Theology P,M,D

LYNCHBURG COLLEGE

Business Administration and Management—General M
Counselor Education M
Curriculum and Instruction M
Early Childhood Education M
Education—General M
Educational Administration M
English Education M
Human Resources Management M
Industrial and Manufacturing Management M
Middle School Education M
Reading Education M
Secondary Education M
Special Education M

LYNDON STATE COLLEGE

Counselor Education M
Curriculum and Instruction M
Education—General M
Reading Education M
Science Education M
Special Education M

LYNN UNIVERSITY

Business Administration and Management—General M
Criminal Justice and Criminology M
Education—General M,D
Educational Administration M,D
English as a Second Language M,D
Gerontology M,O
Health Services Management and Hospital Administration M,O
Hospitality Management M
International and Comparative Education M,D
International Business M
Music O
Special Education M,D
Sports Management M
In-depth description on page 951.

MACHZIKEI HADATH RABBINICAL COLLEGE

Theology O

MADONNA UNIVERSITY

Advanced Practice Nursing M
Business Administration and Management—General M
Clinical Psychology M
Criminal Justice and Criminology M
Education—General M
Educational Administration M
English as a Second Language M
English M
Health Services Management and Hospital Administration M
Hospice Nursing M
International Business M
Medical/Surgical Nursing M
Nursing and Healthcare Administration M
Nursing—General M
Psychology—General M
Quality Management M
Reading Education M
Special Education M

MAHARISHI UNIVERSITY OF MANAGEMENT

Art/Fine Arts M
Business Administration and Management—General M,D
Cell Biology M,D
Computer Science M
Education—General M
Elementary Education M
English M
Foundations and Philosophy of Education M
Mathematics M
Molecular Biology M,D
Neuroscience M,D
Physiology M,D
Psychology—General M,D
Secondary Education M
Writing M

MAINE COLLEGE OF ART

Art/Fine Arts M

MAINE MARITIME ACADEMY

Logistics M,O
Transportation Management M,O

MALONE COLLEGE

Business Administration and Management—General M
Counselor Education M
Curriculum and Instruction M
Education—General M
Educational Media/Instructional Technology M
Pastoral Ministry and Counseling M
Reading Education M
Special Education M
In-depth description on page 953.

MANCHESTER COLLEGE

Accounting M
Interdisciplinary Studies M

MANHATTAN COLLEGE

Biotechnology M
Chemical Engineering M
Civil Engineering M
Computer Engineering M
Counselor Education M,O
Education—General M,O*
Educational Administration M,O
Electrical Engineering M
Engineering and Applied Sciences—General M*
Environmental Engineering M
Mechanical Engineering M
Special Education M,O
In-depth description on page 955.

MANHATTAN SCHOOL OF MUSIC

Music M,D

MANHATTANVILLE COLLEGE

Art Education M
Corporate and Organizational Communication M
Education—General M*
Elementary Education M
English as a Second Language M
English Education M
Foreign Languages Education M
Human Resources Development M
Human Resources Management M
Liberal Studies M
Management Strategy and Policy M
Mathematics Education M
Music Education M
Organizational Management M
Reading Education M
Science Education M
Secondary Education M
Social Sciences Education M
Special Education M
Writing M
In-depth description on page 957.

MANNES COLLEGE OF MUSIC, NEW SCHOOL UNIVERSITY

Music M,O

MANSFIELD UNIVERSITY OF PENNSYLVANIA

Art/Fine Arts M
Communication—General M
Education—General M
Elementary Education M
Information Studies M
Library Science M
Music M
Secondary Education M
Announcement on page 413.

MAPLE SPRINGS BAPTIST BIBLE COLLEGE AND SEMINARY

Computer Education P,M,D,O
Pastoral Ministry and Counseling P,M,D,O
Theology P,M,D,O

MARANATHA BAPTIST BIBLE COLLEGE

Theology M

MARIAN COLLEGE OF FOND DU LAC

Business Administration and Management—General M
Education—General M
Educational Administration M
Organizational Management M
Quality Management M

MARIETTA COLLEGE

Education—General M
Liberal Studies M

MARIST COLLEGE

Business Administration and Management—General M,O
Computer Science M
Counseling Psychology M,O
Educational Psychology M,O
Information Science M
Psychology—General M,O
Public Policy and Administration M,O
School Psychology M,O
Social Psychology M,O

MARLBORO COLLEGE

Computer Education M,O
Computer Science M
Education—General M
Electronic Commerce M*
Internet and Interactive Multimedia M
Management Information Systems M

MARQUETTE UNIVERSITY

Accounting M
Advanced Practice Nursing M,O
Advertising and Public Relations M
Analytical Chemistry M,D
Bioinformatics M
Biological and Biomedical Sciences—General M,D
Biomedical Engineering M,D*
Business Administration and Management—General M
Cell Biology M,D
Chemistry M,D
Civil Engineering M,D*
Clinical Psychology M,D
Communication Disorders M
Communication—General M
Computer Engineering M,D*
Computer Science M,D
Construction Engineering and Management M,D
Dentistry P
Developmental Biology M,D
Ecology M,D
Economics M
Education—General M,D,O
Electrical Engineering M,D
Engineering and Applied Sciences—General M,D
Engineering Management M,D
English M,D
Environmental Engineering M,D
Ethics M,D
Evolutionary Biology M,D
Foreign Languages Education M
Genetics M,D
Geotechnical Engineering M,D
Gerontological Nursing M,O
History M,D
Human Resources Development M
Human Resources Management M
Inorganic Chemistry M,D
Interdisciplinary Studies D
International Affairs M
Journalism M
Law P
Management of Technology M,D
Manufacturing Engineering M,D
Mass Communication M
Maternal/Child Nursing M,O
Mathematics Education M,D
Mathematics M,D
Mechanical Engineering M,D*
Media Studies M
Medical/Surgical Nursing M,O
Medieval and Renaissance Studies M,D
Microbiology M,D
Molecular Biology M,D
Neurobiology M,D
Nurse Midwifery M,O
Nursing—General M,O
Oral and Dental Sciences M
Organic Chemistry M,D
Pediatric Nursing M,O
Philosophy M,D
Physical Chemistry M,D
Physical Therapy M
Physician Assistant Studies M
Physiology M,D
Political Science M
Psychology—General M,D
Spanish M
Speech and Interpersonal Communication M
Statistics M,D
Structural Engineering M,D
Theology M,D
Transportation and Highway Engineering M,D
Water Resources Engineering M,D
In-depth description on page 959.

MARSHALL UNIVERSITY

Adult Education M
Allopathic Medicine P
Anthropology M
Art/Fine Arts M
Biological and Biomedical Sciences—General M,D*
Business Administration and Management—General M
Chemistry M
Clinical Psychology M,D
Communication Disorders M
Communication—General M
Counselor Education M,O
Criminal Justice and Criminology M
Early Childhood Education M
Education—General M,D,O
Educational Administration M,O

Marshall University (continued)

Elementary Education M
Engineering and Applied Sciences—General M
English M
Environmental Sciences M
Exercise and Sports Science M
Family and Consumer Sciences-General M
Forensic Sciences M
Geography M
Health Education M
Health Services Management and Hospital Administration M
History M
Human Resources Management M
Humanities M
Industrial and Organizational Psychology M,D
Information Science M
Journalism M
Management of Technology M
Mass Communication M
Mathematics M
Music M
Nursing—General M
Physical Education M
Physics M
Political Science M
Psychology—General M,D
Reading Education M,O
School Psychology O
Secondary Education M
Sociology M
Special Education M
Vocational and Technical Education M

In-depth description on page 961.

MARTIN UNIVERSITY

Pastoral Ministry and Counseling M
Psychology—General M
Social Psychology M

MARY BALDWIN COLLEGE

Education—General M
Elementary Education M
Middle School Education M

MARYCREST INTERNATIONAL UNIVERSITY

Education—General M
Reading Education M

MARYGROVE COLLEGE

Early Childhood Education M
Education—General M
Educational Administration M
Foreign Languages Education M
Human Resources Management M
Pastoral Ministry and Counseling M
Reading Education M
Special Education M

MARYLAND INSTITUTE COLLEGE OF ART

Art Education M
Art/Fine Arts M,O*
Computer Art and Design M
Photography M

MARYLHURST UNIVERSITY

Art Therapy M
Business Administration and Management—General M
Corporate and Organizational Communication M
Gerontology M
Interdisciplinary Studies M
Liberal Studies M
Theology M

MARYMOUNT UNIVERSITY

Advanced Practice Nursing M,O
Allied Health—General M,O
Business Administration and Management—General M,O
Computer Science M,O
Counseling Psychology M,O
Counselor Education M,O
Education—General M,O
Elementary Education M,O
English M
Forensic Psychology M,O
Health Promotion M
Health Services Management and Hospital Administration M
Human Resources Management M,O
Humanities M
Interior Design M
International Business M,O
Legal and Justice Studies M,O
Management Information Systems M,O
Management Strategy and Policy M,O
Medical/Surgical Nursing M,O
Nursing and Healthcare Administration M,O
Organizational Management M,O
Physical Therapy M
Psychology—General M,O

In-depth description on page 963.

MARYVILLE UNIVERSITY OF SAINT LOUIS

Accounting M,O
Allied Health—General M
Art Education M
Business Administration and Management—General M,O
Business Education M,O
Early Childhood Education M
Education of the Gifted M
Education—General M
Educational Administration M
Electronic Commerce M,O
Elementary Education M
Environmental Education M
Health Services Management and Hospital Administration M
International Business M,O
Management Information Systems M,O
Marketing M,O
Middle School Education M
Nursing—General M
Occupational Therapy M
Physical Therapy M
Rehabilitation Counseling M
Secondary Education M

MARY WASHINGTON COLLEGE

Liberal Studies M

MARYWOOD UNIVERSITY

Art Education M
Art Therapy M
Art/Fine Arts M
Business Administration and Management—General M
Communication Disorders M
Communication—General M
Counseling Psychology M,D
Counselor Education M
Criminal Justice and Criminology M
Early Childhood Education M
Education—General M
Educational Administration M
Educational Media/Instructional Technology M
Elementary Education M
Finance and Banking M
Health Services Management and Hospital Administration M
Human Development D
Investment Management M
Management Information Systems M
Music Education M
Music M
Nursing—General M
Nutrition M
Psychology—General M,D*
Public Policy and Administration M
Reading Education M
Social Work M*
Special Education M

In-depth description on page 965.

MASSACHUSETTS COLLEGE OF ART

Applied Arts and Design—General M
Art Education M
Art/Fine Arts M
Film, Television, and Video Production M
Photography M
Textile Design M
Theater M

MASSACHUSETTS COLLEGE OF LIBERAL ARTS

Curriculum and Instruction M
Education—General M
Educational Administration M
Reading Education M
Special Education M

MASSACHUSETTS COLLEGE OF PHARMACY AND HEALTH SCIENCES

Chemistry M,D
Health Services Management and Hospital Administration M
Pharmaceutical Sciences M,D*
Pharmacology M,D

MASSACHUSETTS INSTITUTE OF TECHNOLOGY

Aerospace/Aeronautical Engineering M,D,O
Architecture M,D*
Atmospheric Sciences M,D
Biochemistry D
Bioengineering M,D*
Biological and Biomedical Sciences—General P,D*
Biomedical Engineering M,D*
Biophysics D
Business Administration and Management—General M,D
Chemical Engineering M,D
Chemistry D
City and Regional Planning M,D
Civil Engineering M,D,O
Cognitive Sciences D*
Communication Disorders D*
Computational Sciences D
Computer Science M,D,O
Developmental Biology D
Economics M,D
Electrical Engineering M,D,O
Engineering and Applied Sciences—General M,D,O
Engineering Management M
Environmental Engineering M,D,O
Genetics D
Geochemistry M,D,O
Geology M,D
Geophysics M,D,O
Geosciences M,D
Health Physics/Radiological Health M,D,O
History of Science and Technology D
Immunology D
Industrial and Manufacturing Management
Inorganic Chemistry D
Linguistics D
Logistics M,D
Manufacturing Engineering
Marine Biology M,D,O
Materials Engineering M,D,O
Materials Sciences M,D,O
Mathematics D
Mechanical Engineering M,D,O
Media Studies M,D
Medical Informatics M
Medical Physics D
Metallurgical Engineering and Metallurgy M,D,O
Microbiology D
Molecular Biology D
Neurobiology D
Neuroscience D*
Nuclear Engineering M,D,O*
Ocean Engineering M,D,O*
Oceanography M,D,O*
Operations Research M,D*
Organic Chemistry D
Philosophy D
Physical Chemistry D
Physics M,D
Planetary and Space Sciences M,D
Political Science M,D
Psychology—General D
Real Estate M*
Social Sciences D
Systems Engineering M
Technology and Public Policy M,D
Toxicology M,D*
Transportation and Highway Engineering M,D*
Transportation Management M,D
Urban Studies M,D

MASSACHUSETTS SCHOOL OF LAW AT ANDOVER

Law P

MASSACHUSETTS SCHOOL OF PROFESSIONAL PSYCHOLOGY

Clinical Psychology M,D,O
Psychology—General M,D,O*

THE MASTER'S COLLEGE AND SEMINARY

Pastoral Ministry and Counseling P,M,D
Theology P,M,D

MAYO GRADUATE SCHOOL

Biochemistry D
Biological and Biomedical Sciences—General D*
Biomedical Engineering D*
Cancer Biology/Oncology D*
Immunology D*
Molecular Biology D
Neuroscience D*
Pharmacology D*

MAYO MEDICAL SCHOOL

Allopathic Medicine P

MAYO SCHOOL OF HEALTH SCIENCES

Nurse Anesthesia M
Physical Therapy M

MCCORMICK THEOLOGICAL SEMINARY

Pastoral Ministry and Counseling P,M,D,O
Theology P,M,D,O

MCDANIEL COLLEGE

Counselor Education M
Education—General M
Educational Administration M
Educational Media/Instructional Technology M
Elementary Education M
Human Resources Development M
Liberal Studies M
Library Science M
Physical Education M
Reading Education M
Secondary Education M
Special Education M

MCGILL UNIVERSITY

Agricultural Economics and Agribusiness M,D
Agricultural Engineering M,D
Agricultural Sciences—General M,D,O
Agronomy and Soil Sciences M,D
Allopathic Medicine P
Anatomy M,D
Animal Sciences M,D
Anthropology M,D
Architectural History M,D,O
Architecture M,D,O
Art History M,D
Asian Studies M,D
Atmospheric Sciences M,D
Biochemistry M,D
Bioethics M,D
Biological and Biomedical Sciences—General M,D*
Biomedical Engineering M,D
Biostatistics M,D,O
Biotechnology M,D,O
Business Administration and Management—General M,D*
Chemical Engineering M,D
Chemistry M,D
City and Regional Planning M
Civil Engineering M,D
Clinical Psychology D
Communication Disorders M,D
Communication—General M,D
Community Health M,D,O
Computer Engineering M,D
Computer Science M,D
Counseling Psychology M,D
Curriculum and Instruction M,D,O
Dentistry P
Developmental Psychology M,D
Economics M,D
Education—General M,D,O
Educational Administration M,D,O
Educational Psychology M,D
Electrical Engineering M,D*
Engineering and Applied Sciences—General M,D,O
English M,D
Entomology M,D
Environmental and Occupational Health M,D,O
Environmental Engineering M,D
Epidemiology M,D,O
Experimental Psychology M,D
Fish, Game, and Wildlife Management M,D
Food Science and Technology M,D
Foreign Languages Education M,D,O
Forestry M,D
French M,D
Genetic Counseling M,D
Geography M,D
Geosciences M,D,O
Geotechnical Engineering M,D
German M,D
Health Physics/Radiological Health M,D
Health Services Management and Hospital Administration M,D,O
Hispanic Studies M,D
History of Medicine M,D
History M,D
Human Genetics M,D
Hydraulics M,D
Immunology M,D
Industrial and Manufacturing Management M*
Information Studies M,D,O
Italian M,D
Jewish Studies M,D
Kinesiology and Movement Studies M
Law M,D,O
Library Science M,D,O
Linguistics M,D
Materials Engineering M,D
Mathematics M,D

Mechanical Engineering M,D
Mechanics M,D
Medical Physics M,D
Metallurgical Engineering and Metallurgy M,D
Meteorology M,D
Microbiology M,D
Mineral/Mining Engineering M,D,O
Music Education M,D
Music M,D
Natural Resources M,D
Near and Middle Eastern Studies M,D
Neuroscience M,D
Nursing—General M,D
Nutrition M,D
Oceanography M,D
Oral and Dental Sciences M,D
Parasitology M,D,O
Pathology M,D
Pharmacology M,D
Philosophy M,D
Physical Education M
Physics M,D
Physiology M,D
Planetary and Space Sciences M,D,O
Plant Sciences M,D
Political Science M,D
Psychology—General M,D
Rehabilitation Sciences M,D
Religion M,D
Russian M,D
School Psychology M,D
Social Work M,D
Sociology M,D
Statistics M,D
Structural Engineering M,D
Theology M,D
Transportation Management M
Water Resources Engineering M,D

MCMASTER UNIVERSITY

Analytical Chemistry M,D
Anthropology M,D
Astrophysics M,D
Biochemistry M,D
Bioengineering M,D
Biological and Biomedical Sciences—General M,D
Business Administration and Management—General M,D
Cancer Biology/Oncology M,D
Cardiovascular Sciences M,D
Cell Biology M,D
Chemical Engineering M,D
Chemistry M,D
Civil Engineering M,D
Classics M,D
Clinical Research M,D
Computer Science M
Economics M,D
Electrical Engineering M,D
Engineering and Applied Sciences—General M,D
Engineering Physics M,D
English M,D
French M
Genetics M,D
Geochemistry M,D
Geography M,D
Geology M,D
Geosciences M,D
Health Physics/Radiological Health M
Health Services Research M,D
History M,D
Human Resources Management M,D
Immunology M,D
Inorganic Chemistry M,D
Kinesiology and Movement Studies M,D
Management Information Systems D
Materials Engineering M,D
Materials Sciences M,D
Mathematics M,D
Mechanical Engineering M,D
Molecular Biology M,D
Music M
Neuroscience M,D
Nuclear Engineering M,D
Nursing—General M,D
Occupational Therapy M
Organic Chemistry M,D
Pharmacology M,D
Philosophy M,D
Physical Chemistry M,D
Physical Therapy M
Physics M,D
Physiology M,D
Political Science M
Psychology—General M,D
Public Policy and Administration M
Rehabilitation Sciences M
Religion M,D
Social Work M
Sociology M,D
Statistics M,D
Theology P,M,D
Urban Studies M,D
Virology M,D

MCNEESE STATE UNIVERSITY

Biological and Biomedical Sciences—General M
Business Administration and Management—General M
Business Education M
Chemical Engineering M
Chemistry M
Civil Engineering M
Computer Science M
Counselor Education M
Early Childhood Education M
Education—General M
Educational Administration M,O
Educational Media/Instructional Technology M
Electrical Engineering M
Elementary Education M
Engineering and Applied Sciences—General M
English Education M
English M
Environmental Sciences M
Health Education M
Mathematics Education M
Mathematics M
Mechanical Engineering M
Music Education M
Nursing—General M
Physical Education M
Psychology—General M
Reading Education M
Science Education M
Secondary Education M
Social Sciences Education M
Special Education M
Statistics M
Writing M

MEADVILLE LOMBARD THEOLOGICAL SCHOOL

Pastoral Ministry and Counseling P,D
Religious Education P,D
Theology P,D

MEDAILLE COLLEGE

Business Administration and Management—General M
Education—General M

Announcement on page 422.

MEDICAL COLLEGE OF GEORGIA

Advanced Practice Nursing M,D
Allied Health—General M,O
Allopathic Medicine P
Anatomy M,D
Biochemistry M,D
Biological and Biomedical Sciences—General M,D*
Cardiovascular Sciences D
Cell Biology M,D
Clinical Laboratory Sciences/Medical Technology M
Community Health Nursing M,D
Dental Hygiene M
Dentistry P
Health Physics/Radiological Health M
Health Services Management and Hospital Administration M
Maternal/Child Nursing M,D
Medical Illustration M
Medical/Surgical Nursing M,D
Molecular Biology M,D
Molecular Medicine D
Nurse Anesthesia M,D
Nursing—General M,D
Occupational Therapy M
Oral and Dental Sciences M,D
Pharmacology M,D
Physical Therapy M
Physician Assistant Studies M
Physiology M,D
Psychiatric Nursing M,D
Toxicology M,D

MEDICAL COLLEGE OF OHIO

Advanced Practice Nursing M,O
Allied Health—General M,O
Allopathic Medicine P
Anatomy M
Biochemistry M
Biological and Biomedical Sciences—General M,D,O*
Cell Biology D
Environmental and Occupational Health M,O
Genetics M
Health Physics/Radiological Health M
Microbiology M
Molecular Biology M,D
Neuroscience M,D
Nursing—General M,O
Occupational Therapy M
Oral and Dental Sciences M
Pathology M
Pharmacology M
Physician Assistant Studies M
Physiology M
Public Health—General M

MEDICAL COLLEGE OF WISCONSIN

Allopathic Medicine P
Biochemistry M,D
Bioethics M
Biological and Biomedical Sciences—General M,D*
Biophysics D*
Biostatistics D*
Cell Biology M,D
Clinical Laboratory Sciences/Medical Technology D
Developmental Biology M,D
Environmental and Occupational Health M
Epidemiology M
Genetics M,D
Medical Informatics M
Microbiology M,D
Pathology M,D
Pharmacology M,D
Physiology M,D*
Public Health—General M
Toxicology M,D

MEDICAL UNIVERSITY OF SOUTH CAROLINA

Advanced Practice Nursing M,O
Allied Health—General M,D,O
Allopathic Medicine P
Anatomy D
Biochemistry M,D
Biological and Biomedical Sciences—General M,D*
Biometrics M,D
Biostatistics M,D
Cell Biology D
Clinical Laboratory Sciences/Medical Technology M
Clinical Research M,D
Communication Disorders M
Dentistry P
Epidemiology M,D
Gerontological Nursing M,O
Health Informatics M
Health Services Management and Hospital Administration M,D,O
Immunology M,D
Maternal/Child Nursing M,O
Medical/Surgical Nursing M,O
Microbiology M,D
Molecular Biology M,D
Neuroscience M,D
Nurse Anesthesia M
Nurse Midwifery M
Nursing and Healthcare Administration M,O
Nursing—General M,D,O
Occupational Therapy M
Oral and Dental Sciences M
Pathobiology D
Pathology M,D
Pediatric Nursing M,O
Pharmaceutical Sciences D
Pharmacology M,D
Pharmacy P
Physical Therapy M
Physician Assistant Studies M
Physiology M,D
Psychiatric Nursing M,O
Rehabilitation Sciences M

MEHARRY MEDICAL COLLEGE

Allopathic Medicine P
Biochemistry D
Biological and Biomedical Sciences—General D
Community Health M
Dentistry P
Environmental and Occupational Health M
Health Services Management and Hospital Administration M
Microbiology D
Pharmacology M,D
Physiology D

MEIJI COLLEGE OF ORIENTAL MEDICINE

Acupuncture and Oriental Medicine M*

MEMORIAL UNIVERSITY OF NEWFOUNDLAND

Adult Education M
Allopathic Medicine P
Anthropology M,D
Applied Science and Technology M
Aquaculture M
Biochemistry M,D
Biological and Biomedical Sciences—General M,D,O
Biopsychology M,D
Business Administration and Management—General M
Chemistry M,D
Civil Engineering M,D
Classics M
Community Health M,D,O
Computational Sciences M
Computer Science M,D
Condensed Matter Physics M,D
Economics M
Education—General M
Educational Administration M
Educational Media/Instructional Technology M
Educational Psychology M
Electrical Engineering M,D
Engineering and Applied Sciences—General M,D
English M,D
Environmental Engineering M
Environmental Sciences M
Epidemiology M,D,O
Experimental Psychology M,D
Fish, Game, and Wildlife Management M
Folklore M,D
Food Science and Technology M,D
French M
Geography M,D
Geology M,D
Geophysics M,D
Geosciences M,D
German M
History M,D
Human Genetics M,D
Humanities M
Kinesiology and Movement Studies M
Linguistics M,D
Marine Affairs M
Marine Biology M,D
Marine Sciences M
Mathematics M,D
Mechanical Engineering M,D
Nursing—General M
Ocean Engineering M,D
Oceanography M,D
Pharmaceutical Sciences M,D
Philosophy M
Physical Education M
Physics M,D
Political Science M
Psychology—General M,D
Religion M
Social Psychology M,D
Social Work M,D
Sociology M,D
Statistics M,D
Women's Studies M

In-depth description on page 967.

MEMPHIS COLLEGE OF ART

Applied Arts and Design—General M
Art/Fine Arts M*
Computer Art and Design M
Photography M
Textile Design M

MEMPHIS THEOLOGICAL SEMINARY

Theology P,M,D

MENNONITE BRETHREN BIBLICAL SEMINARY

Marriage and Family Therapy M,O
Pastoral Ministry and Counseling M
Theology P,M

MERCER UNIVERSITY

Allopathic Medicine P,M
Biomedical Engineering M
Business Administration and Management—General M
Early Childhood Education M,O
Education—General M,O
Electrical Engineering M
Engineering and Applied Sciences—General M
Engineering Management M
English Education M,O
Health Services Management and Hospital Administration M
Law P
Management of Technology M
Mathematics Education M,O
Mechanical Engineering M
Middle School Education M,O
Pharmaceutical Sciences P,D

Mercer University (continued)

Pharmacy	P,D
Reading Education	M,O
Science Education	M,O
Secondary Education	M,O
Social Sciences Education	M,O
Software Engineering	M
Theology	P

MERCY COLLEGE

Acupuncture and Oriental Medicine	M*
Addictions/Substance Abuse Counseling	M,O
Advanced Practice Nursing	M
Allied Health—General	M*
Business Administration and Management—General	M*
Counselor Education	M,O
Education—General	M,O*
Educational Administration	M,O
Educational Media/Instructional Technology	M,O
Electronic Commerce	M
Elementary Education	M,O
English as a Second Language	M,O
English	M
Finance and Banking	M
Health Services Management and Hospital Administration	M,O
Human Resources Management	M
International Business	M
Marketing	M
Marriage and Family Therapy	M,O
Multilingual and Multicultural Education	M,O
Nursing—General	M
Occupational Therapy	M
Organizational Management	M
Physical Therapy	M
Physician Assistant Studies	M
Psychology—General	M,O*
Reading Education	M,O
School Psychology	M,O
Secondary Education	M,O
Special Education	M,O
Urban Education	M,O

MERCYHURST COLLEGE

Criminal Justice and Criminology	M
Educational Administration	M,O
Military and Defense Studies	M
Multilingual and Multicultural Education	M,O
Organizational Management	M,O
Special Education	M,O

MEREDITH COLLEGE

Business Administration and Management—General	M
Education—General	M
Music	M
Nutrition	M

MERRIMACK COLLEGE

Education—General	M

MESA STATE COLLEGE

Business Administration and Management—General	M

MESIVTA OF EASTERN PARKWAY RABBINICAL SEMINARY

Theology	

MESIVTA TIFERETH JERUSALEM OF AMERICA

Theology	

MESIVTA TORAH VODAATH RABBINICAL SEMINARY

Theology	

METHODIST THEOLOGICAL SCHOOL IN OHIO

Theology	P,M

METROPOLITAN STATE UNIVERSITY

Business Administration and Management—General	M
Criminal Justice and Criminology	M
Finance and Banking	M
Human Resources Management	M
Information Studies	M
International Business	M
Management Information Systems	M
Marketing	M
Nonprofit Management	M
Nursing—General	M
Organizational Management	M
Public Policy and Administration	M
Technical Writing	M

MGH INSTITUTE OF HEALTH PROFESSIONS

Allied Health—General	M,D,O
Clinical Research	M,O
Communication Disorders	M
Nursing—General	M,O*
Physical Therapy	M,D,O

MIAMI UNIVERSITY

Accounting	M
Analytical Chemistry	M,D
Architecture	M*
Art Education	M
Art/Fine Arts	M*
Biochemistry	M,D
Biological and Biomedical Sciences—General	M,D
Botany	M,D*
Business Administration and Management—General	M*
Chemistry	M,D
Child and Family Studies	M
Clinical Psychology	D
Communication Disorders	M
Communication—General	M
Curriculum and Instruction	M
Early Childhood Education	M
Economics	M*
Education—General	M,D,O
Educational Administration	M,D
Educational Psychology	M,O
Elementary Education	M
Engineering and Applied Sciences—General	M
English Education	M,D
English	M,D
Environmental Sciences	M
Exercise and Sports Science	M
Experimental Psychology	D
Finance and Banking	M
French	M
Geography	M
Geology	M,D
Gerontology	M
History	M
Inorganic Chemistry	M,D
Management Information Systems	M
Marketing	M
Mass Communication	M
Mathematics Education	M
Mathematics	M
Microbiology	M,D
Music Education	M
Music	M
Operations Research	M
Organic Chemistry	M,D
Paper and Pulp Engineering	M*
Philosophy	M
Physical Chemistry	M,D
Physics	M
Political Science	M,D
Psychology—General	D
Reading Education	M
Religion	M
Rhetoric	M,D
School Psychology	M,O
Secondary Education	M
Social Psychology	D
Social Sciences Education	M
Social Work	M
Spanish	M
Special Education	M
Speech and Interpersonal Communication	M
Statistics	M
Student Personnel Services	M
Systems Science	M
Technical Writing	M
Theater	M
Writing	M,D
Zoology	M,D*

In-depth description on page 969.

MICHIGAN STATE UNIVERSITY

Accounting	M,D
Adult Education	M,D,O
Advertising and Public Relations	M,D
Agricultural Economics and Agribusiness	M,D*
Agricultural Education	M,D
Agricultural Engineering	M,D
Agricultural Sciences—General	M,D
Agronomy and Soil Sciences	M,D
Allopathic Medicine	P
American Studies	M,D
Analytical Chemistry	M,D
Anatomy	M,D
Animal Sciences	M,D
Anthropology	M,D
Applied Mathematics	M,D
Art History	M
Art/Fine Arts	M*
Astronomy	M,D
Astrophysics	M,D
Biochemistry	M,D*
Biological and Biomedical Sciences—General	M,D
Building Science	M
Business Administration and Management—General	M,D
Cell Biology	D*
Chemical Engineering	M,D
Chemistry	M,D
Child and Family Studies	M,D
City and Regional Planning	M,D
Civil Engineering	M,D
Clinical Laboratory Sciences/Medical Technology	M
Clothing and Textiles	M,D
Communication Disorders	M,D
Communication—General	M,D
Community College Education	M,D
Comparative Literature	M
Computational Sciences	M,D
Computer Engineering	M,D
Computer Science	M,D*
Construction Engineering and Management	M
Consumer Economics	M,D
Counseling Psychology	M,D,O
Counselor Education	M,D,O
Criminal Justice and Criminology	M,D*
Curriculum and Instruction	M,D,O
Developmental Psychology	M,D
Ecology	M,D*
Economics	M,D
Education—General	M,D,O
Educational Administration	M,D,O
Educational Measurement and Evaluation	M,D,O
Educational Media/Instructional Technology	M,D,O
Educational Psychology	M,D,O
Electrical Engineering	M,D
Engineering and Applied Sciences—General	M,D
English as a Second Language	M,D
English Education	M,D
English	M,D
Entomology	M,D
Entrepreneurship	M,D
Environmental Design	M,D
Environmental Engineering	M,D
Environmental Management and Policy	M,D
Environmental Sciences	M,D
Epidemiology	M
Evolutionary Biology	M,D
Exercise and Sports Science	M,D
Facilities Management	M,D
Family and Consumer Sciences-General	M,D
Finance and Banking	M,D
Fish, Game, and Wildlife Management	M,D
Food Science and Technology	M,D
Foreign Languages Education	M,D
Forestry	M,D
French	M,D
Genetics	D*
Geography	M,D
Geological Engineering	M,D
Geology	M,D
Geosciences	M,D
German	M,D
Graphic Design	M
Health Education	M,D
Health Promotion	M,D
History	M,D
Home Economics Education	M,D
Horticulture	M,D
Hospitality Management	M*
Human Resources Management	M,D
Humanities	M
Industrial and Labor Relations	M,D*
Industrial and Manufacturing Management	M,D
Inorganic Chemistry	M,D
Interior Design	M,D
Internet and Interactive Multimedia	M,D
Journalism	M,D
Kinesiology and Movement Studies	M,D
Linguistics	M,D
Logistics	M,D
Management Information Systems	M,D
Management Strategy and Policy	M,D
Manufacturing Engineering	M,D
Marketing	M,D
Marriage and Family Therapy	M,D
Materials Engineering	M,D
Materials Sciences	M,D
Mathematics Education	M,D
Mathematics	M,D
Mechanical Engineering	M,D
Mechanics	M,D
Media Studies	M,D
Metallurgical Engineering and Metallurgy	M,D
Microbiology	D*
Molecular Biology	M,D
Music Education	M,D
Music	M,D
Neuroscience	D*
Nursing—General	M,D
Nutrition	M,D
Operations Research	M,D
Organic Chemistry	M,D
Organizational Behavior	M,D
Osteopathic Medicine	P
Pathology	M,D
Pharmacology	M,D
Philosophy	M,D
Physical Chemistry	M,D
Physical Education	M,D
Physics	M,D*
Physiology	M,D*
Plant Biology	M,D*
Plant Pathology	M,D
Plant Sciences	D
Political Science	M,D
Psychology—General	M,D
Public Policy and Administration	M,D
Reading Education	M
Recreation and Park Management	M,D
Rehabilitation Counseling	M,D,O
Russian	M,D
School Psychology	M,D,O
Science Education	M,D
Secondary Education	M,D
Social Sciences	M,D
Social Work	M,D
Sociology	M,D
Spanish	M,D
Special Education	M,D,O
Statistics	M,D*
Telecommunications Management	M,D
Telecommunications	M,D
Theater	M,D
Therapies—Dance, Drama, and Music	M,D
Toxicology	M,D*
Travel and Tourism	M,D
Urban Studies	M,D
Veterinary Medicine	P
Veterinary Sciences	M,D
Writing	M,D
Zoology	M,D*

In-depth description on page 971.

MICHIGAN STATE UNIVERSITY-DETROIT COLLEGE OF LAW

Law	P

MICHIGAN TECHNOLOGICAL UNIVERSITY

Archaeology	M*
Biological and Biomedical Sciences—General	M,D*
Business Administration and Management—General	M
Chemical Engineering	M,D*
Chemistry	M,D*
Civil Engineering	M,D*
Communication—General	M,D
Computational Sciences	D*
Computer Engineering	D*
Computer Science	M,D*
Electrical Engineering	M,D*
Engineering and Applied Sciences—General	M,D*
Engineering Physics	D*
Environmental Engineering	M,D*
Environmental Management and Policy	M*
Forestry	M,D*
Geological Engineering	M,D*
Geology	M,D*
Geophysics	M*
Geotechnical Engineering	D
Industrial and Manufacturing Management	M
Materials Engineering	M,D*
Mathematics	M,D*
Mechanical Engineering	M,D*
Mechanics	M*
Metallurgical Engineering and Metallurgy	M,D
Mineral Economics	M*
Mineral/Mining Engineering	M,D*
Physics	M,D*
Plant Molecular Biology	D*
Rhetoric	M,D
Science Education	M*
Structural Engineering	D
Technical Writing	M,D*

In-depth description on page 973 and announcement on page 429.

MICHIGAN THEOLOGICAL SEMINARY

Counseling Psychology	P,M,D
Religious Education	P,M,D
Theology	P,M,D

MID-AMERICA BAPTIST THEOLOGICAL SEMINARY
Theology P,M,D

MID-AMERICA BAPTIST THEOLOGICAL SEMINARY NORTHEAST BRANCH
Theology P

MIDAMERICA NAZARENE UNIVERSITY
Business Administration and Management—General M
Counseling Psychology M
Curriculum and Instruction M
Education—General M
Educational Media/Instructional Technology M
Announcement on page 429.

MIDDLEBURY COLLEGE
English M
French M,D
German M,D
Italian M,D
Russian M,D
Spanish M,D

MIDDLE TENNESSEE SCHOOL OF ANESTHESIA
Nurse Anesthesia M

MIDDLE TENNESSEE STATE UNIVERSITY
Accounting M
Aerospace/Aeronautical Engineering M
Aviation M
Biological and Biomedical Sciences—General M
Business Administration and Management—General M
Business Education M
Chemistry M,D
Child and Family Studies M
Computer Science M
Counselor Education M,O
Criminal Justice and Criminology M
Curriculum and Instruction M,O
Early Childhood Education M,O
Economics M,D*
Education—General M,D,O
Educational Administration M,O
Elementary Education M,O
English M,D
Finance and Banking M,D
Foreign Languages Education M
Health Education M,D
Historic Preservation M,D
History M,D
Industrial and Labor Relations M,D
Industrial and Organizational Psychology M,O
Management Information Systems M
Marketing M
Mass Communication M
Mathematics Education M
Mathematics M
Middle School Education M,O
Music M
Nutrition M
Physical Education M,D
Psychology—General M,O
Reading Education M
Recreation and Park Management M,D
School Psychology M,O
Science Education M
Secondary Education M,O
Sociology M
Special Education M
Transportation Management M
Vocational and Technical Education M

MIDWEST COLLEGE OF ORIENTAL MEDICINE
Acupuncture and Oriental Medicine M,O*

MIDWESTERN BAPTIST THEOLOGICAL SEMINARY
Music P,M,D
Pastoral Ministry and Counseling P,M,D
Religious Education P,M,D
Theology P,M,D

MIDWESTERN STATE UNIVERSITY
Advanced Practice Nursing M
Biological and Biomedical Sciences—General M
Business Administration and Management—General M
Computer Science M
Counselor Education M
Curriculum and Instruction M
Education—General M
Educational Administration M
Elementary Education M
English M
Health Physics/Radiological Health M
Health Services Management and Hospital Administration M
History M
Human Resources Development M
Kinesiology and Movement Studies M
Nursing Education M
Nursing—General M
Political Science M
Psychology—General M
Public Policy and Administration M
Reading Education M
Special Education M

MIDWESTERN UNIVERSITY, DOWNERS GROVE CAMPUS
Allied Health—General M
Biological and Biomedical Sciences—General M*
Occupational Therapy M*
Osteopathic Medicine P*
Pharmacy P*
Physical Therapy M*
Physician Assistant Studies M*

MIDWESTERN UNIVERSITY, GLENDALE CAMPUS
Allied Health—General M,O
Bioethics O
Biological and Biomedical Sciences—General M
Cardiovascular Sciences M
Health Education M
Occupational Therapy M
Osteopathic Medicine P*
Pharmacy P
Physician Assistant Studies M

MILLERSVILLE UNIVERSITY OF PENNSYLVANIA
Art Education M
Biological and Biomedical Sciences—General M
Clinical Psychology M
Counselor Education M
Early Childhood Education M
Education of the Gifted M
Education—General M
Elementary Education M
English Education M
English M
Foundations and Philosophy of Education M
French M
German M
History M
Mathematics Education M
Nursing—General M
Psychology—General M
Reading Education M
School Psychology M
Spanish M
Special Education M
Sports Management M
Vocational and Technical Education M
In-depth description on page 975.

MILLIGAN COLLEGE
Education—General M
Occupational Therapy M

MILLSAPS COLLEGE
Accounting M
Business Administration and Management—General M

MILLS COLLEGE
Art/Fine Arts M
Biological and Biomedical Sciences—General O
Business Administration and Management—General M
Computer Science M,O*
Curriculum and Instruction M,D
Dance M
Early Childhood Education M,D
Education—General M,D
Educational Administration M,D
Elementary Education M,D
English Education M,D
English M
Mathematics Education M,D
Music M
Photography M
Science Education M,D
Secondary Education M,D
Social Sciences Education M,D
Writing M
In-depth description on page 977.

MILWAUKEE SCHOOL OF ENGINEERING
Biomedical Engineering M
Engineering and Applied Sciences—General M*
Engineering Management M
Environmental Engineering M
Medical Informatics M
Structural Engineering M

MINNEAPOLIS COLLEGE OF ART AND DESIGN
Applied Arts and Design—General M,O
Art/Fine Arts M,O*
Film, Television, and Video Production M,O
Graphic Design M,O
Illustration M,O
Photography M,O

MINNESOTA STATE UNIVERSITY, MANKATO
Advanced Practice Nursing M
Allied Health—General M,O
Anthropology M
Art Education M
Art/Fine Arts M
Astronomy M
Biological and Biomedical Sciences—General M
Chemistry M
Clinical Psychology M
Communication Disorders M
Community Health M
Computer Science M
Consumer Economics M
Counselor Education M
Curriculum and Instruction M,O
Early Childhood Education M
Ecology M
Education of the Gifted M
Education of the Multiply Handicapped M
Education—General M,O
Educational Administration M,O
Educational Media/Instructional Technology M,O
Electrical Engineering M
Elementary Education M,O
English Education M
English M
Environmental Sciences M
French M
Geography M
German M
Gerontology M
Health Education M
Higher Education M,O
History M
Human Services M
Industrial and Organizational Psychology M
Interdisciplinary Studies M
Interior Design M
Manufacturing Engineering M
Mathematics Education M
Mathematics M
Mechanical Engineering M
Multilingual and Multicultural Education M,O
Music M
Nursing and Healthcare Administration M
Nursing Education M
Nursing—General M
Physical Education M,O
Physics M
Political Science M
Psychology—General M
Public Policy and Administration M
Reading Education M
Rehabilitation Counseling M
Secondary Education M,O
Social Sciences Education M
Sociology M
Spanish M
Special Education M
Speech and Interpersonal Communication M
Statistics M
Student Personnel Services M
Theater M
Urban Studies M
Women's Studies M
Writing M

MINNESOTA STATE UNIVERSITY, MOORHEAD
Communication Disorders M
Counselor Education M
Curriculum and Instruction M
Education—General M,O
Educational Administration M,O
Human Services M
Liberal Studies M
Music Education M
Music M
Nursing Education M
Nursing—General M,O
Psychology—General M,O
Public Policy and Administration M
Reading Education M
School Psychology M,O
Special Education M
Writing M

MINOT STATE UNIVERSITY
Business Administration and Management—General M
Communication Disorders M
Criminal Justice and Criminology M
Education of the Multiply Handicapped M
Educational Psychology O
Elementary Education M
English Education M
Mathematics Education M
Music Education M
Science Education M
Special Education M

MIRRER YESHIVA
Theology

MISSISSIPPI COLLEGE
Accounting M
Art Education M
Art/Fine Arts M
Biological and Biomedical Sciences—General M
Business Administration and Management—General M
Business Education M
Chemistry M
Communication—General M
Computer Education M
Computer Science M
Counseling Psychology M,O
Counselor Education M,O
Criminal Justice and Criminology M
Education—General M,O
Educational Administration M
Educational Measurement and Evaluation M
Elementary Education M
English M
Health Services Management and Hospital Administration M
History M
Law P
Liberal Studies M
Mathematics Education M
Mathematics M
Music Education M
Music M
Political Science M
Psychology—General M
Science Education M
Secondary Education M
Social Sciences M
Sociology M

MISSISSIPPI STATE UNIVERSITY
Accounting M,D
Aerospace/Aeronautical Engineering M
Agricultural Economics and Agribusiness M,D
Agricultural Education M,D,O
Agricultural Sciences—General M,D,O
Agronomy and Soil Sciences M,D
Animal Sciences M
Applied Economics M,D
Architecture M
Art/Fine Arts M
Biochemistry M,D
Bioengineering M,D
Biological and Biomedical Sciences—General M,D
Biomedical Engineering M,D
Business Administration and Management—General M,D
Chemical Engineering M,D
Chemistry M,D
Civil Engineering M,D
Computational Sciences M,D
Computer Art and Design M
Computer Engineering M,D*
Computer Science M,D*
Counselor Education M,D,O
Curriculum and Instruction M,D,O
Economics M,D
Education—General M,D,O

Mississippi State University (continued)

Educational Administration M,D,O
Educational Media/Instructional Technology M,D,O
Educational Psychology M,D,O
Electrical Engineering M,D
Elementary Education M,D,O
Engineering and Applied Sciences—General M,D
English M
Entomology M,D
Exercise and Sports Science M
Finance and Banking M,D
Fish, Game, and Wildlife Management M
Food Science and Technology M,D
Foreign Languages Education M
Forestry M
Geosciences M
Health Education M
History M,D
Human Resources Development M,D,O
Industrial/Management Engineering M,D
Landscape Architecture M
Management Information Systems M
Marketing M,D
Mathematics M,D
Mechanical Engineering M,D
Mechanics M
Molecular Biology M,D
Physical Education M
Physics M,D
Plant Pathology M,D
Plant Sciences M,D
Political Science M,D
Project Management M,D
Psychology—General M,D
Public Policy and Administration M,D
Secondary Education M,D,O
Sociology M,D
Spanish M
Special Education M,D,O
Sports Management M
Statistics M,D
Taxation M,D
Veterinary Medicine P
Veterinary Sciences M,D
Vocational and Technical Education M,D,O

MISSISSIPPI UNIVERSITY FOR WOMEN

Communication Disorders M
Education of the Gifted M
Education—General M
Educational Media/Instructional Technology M
Health Education M
Nursing—General M,O

MISSISSIPPI VALLEY STATE UNIVERSITY

Criminal Justice and Criminology M
Education—General M
Elementary Education M
Environmental and Occupational Health M

MOLLOY COLLEGE

Advanced Practice Nursing M,O
Medical/Surgical Nursing M,O
Nursing and Healthcare Administration M,O
Nursing Education M,O
Nursing—General M,O
Pediatric Nursing M,O
Psychiatric Nursing M,O

MONMOUTH UNIVERSITY

Accounting M,O
Addictions/Substance Abuse Counseling M,O
Advanced Practice Nursing M,O
Advertising and Public Relations M,O
Business Administration and Management—General M,O*
Communication—General M,O*
Computer Science M*
Corporate and Organizational Communication M,O
Counseling Psychology M,O*
Criminal Justice and Criminology M,O*
Education—General M,O*
Educational Administration M,O
Elementary Education M,O
Health Services Management and Hospital Administration M,O
History M*
Liberal Studies M*
Media Studies M,O
Nursing—General M,O*
Psychology—General M,O
Reading Education M,O
School Nursing M,O
Social Work M*
Software Engineering M,O*
Special Education M,O

In-depth description on page 979.

MONTANA STATE UNIVERSITY–BILLINGS

Communication—General M
Counselor Education M
Curriculum and Instruction M
Early Childhood Education M
Education—General M
Educational Media/Instructional Technology M
Health Services Management and Hospital Administration M*
Information Studies M
Psychology—General M
Reading Education M
Rehabilitation Counseling M
Secondary Education M
Special Education M
Sports Management M
Theater M

MONTANA STATE UNIVERSITY–BOZEMAN

Accounting M
Agricultural Economics and Agribusiness M
Agricultural Sciences—General M,D
Agronomy and Soil Sciences M
Animal Sciences M
Applied Economics M
Architecture M
Art/Fine Arts M
Biochemistry M,D
Biological and Biomedical Sciences—General M,D
Cell Biology D
Chemical Engineering D
Chemistry M,D
Civil Engineering D
Computer Science M,D
Ecology M,D
Education—General M,D
Electrical Engineering M,D
Engineering and Applied Sciences—General M,D
English M
Entomology M
Environmental Biology M,D
Environmental Management and Policy M
Environmental Sciences M,D
Film, Television, and Video Production M
Fish, Game, and Wildlife Management M,D
Geosciences M
Health Education M
History M
Human Development M
Industrial/Management Engineering M,D
Mathematics M,D
Mechanical Engineering M,D
Microbiology M,D
Molecular Biology M,D
Native American Studies M
Natural Resources M,D
Neuroscience D*
Nursing—General M
Physics M,D
Plant Pathology M,D
Plant Sciences M,D
Psychology—General M
Public Policy and Administration M
Range Science M
Science Education M,D
Statistics M,D
Veterinary Sciences M,D
Zoology M,D

MONTANA STATE UNIVERSITY–NORTHERN

Counselor Education M
Education—General M
Elementary Education M
Science Education M
Vocational and Technical Education M

MONTANA TECH OF THE UNIVERSITY OF MONTANA

Engineering and Applied Sciences—General M
Environmental Engineering M
Geochemistry M
Geological Engineering M
Geology M
Geosciences M
Hydrology M
Industrial Hygiene M
Industrial/Management Engineering M
Metallurgical Engineering and Metallurgy M
Mineral Economics M
Mineral/Mining Engineering M
Petroleum Engineering M
Project Management M
Technical Writing M

MONTCLAIR STATE UNIVERSITY

Accounting M
Anthropology M
Applied Mathematics M,O
Art Education M
Art History M
Art/Fine Arts M
Biological and Biomedical Sciences—General M,O
Business Administration and Management—General M
Business Education M
Chemistry M
Child and Family Studies M
Clinical Psychology M
Communication Disorders M
Computer Science M,O
Conflict Resolution and Mediation/Peace Studies M,O
Consumer Economics M
Counselor Education M
Curriculum and Instruction M,D
Early Childhood Education M
Economics M
Education of the Multiply Handicapped M
Education—General M,D
Educational Administration M
Educational Psychology M
English as a Second Language M
English Education M
English M
Environmental and Occupational Health M,O
Environmental Management and Policy M,O
Environmental Sciences M,O
Exercise and Sports Science M
Family and Consumer Sciences-General M
Finance and Banking M
French M
Geosciences M,O
Health Education M
History M
Home Economics Education M
Human Services M
Industrial and Organizational Psychology M
Information Science M,O
International Business M
Legal and Justice Studies M,O
Linguistics M
Management Information Systems M
Marketing M
Marriage and Family Therapy M
Mathematics Education M,D
Mathematics M
Molecular Biology M,O
Music Education M
Music M
Nutrition M
Philosophy M,D
Physical Education M
Psychology—General M,O
Reading Education M
Science Education M,O
Social Psychology M
Social Sciences Education M
Social Sciences M
Sociology M
Spanish M
Special Education M
Speech and Interpersonal Communication M
Sports Management M
Statistics M,O
Theater M
Therapies—Dance, Drama, and Music M
Vocational and Technical Education M
Water Resources M,O

In-depth description on page 981.

MONTEREY INSTITUTE OF INTERNATIONAL STUDIES

Business Administration and Management—General M
English as a Second Language M*
Environmental Management and Policy M
Foreign Languages Education M
International Affairs M*
International Business M
Public Policy and Administration M
Translation and Interpretation M*

MONTREAT COLLEGE

Business Administration and Management—General M

MOODY BIBLE INSTITUTE

English as a Second Language P,M,O
Theology P,M,O

MORAVIAN COLLEGE

Business Administration and Management—General M
Curriculum and Instruction M
Education—General M

MORAVIAN THEOLOGICAL SEMINARY

Theology P,M

MOREHEAD STATE UNIVERSITY

Adult Education M,O
Advertising and Public Relations M
Art Education M
Art/Fine Arts M
Biological and Biomedical Sciences—General M
Clinical Psychology M
Communication—General M
Counseling Psychology M
Counselor Education M,O
Criminal Justice and Criminology M
Curriculum and Instruction O
Education—General M,O
Educational Administration M,O
Electronic Commerce M
Elementary Education M
English M
Exercise and Sports Science M
Experimental Psychology M
Gerontology M
Health Education M
Higher Education M,O
Journalism M
Middle School Education M
Music Education M
Music M
Physical Education M
Psychology—General M
Reading Education M
Recreation and Park Management M
Secondary Education M
Sociology M
Special Education M
Speech and Interpersonal Communication M
Sports Management M
Theater M
Vocational and Technical Education M

MOREHOUSE SCHOOL OF MEDICINE

Allopathic Medicine P
Biological and Biomedical Sciences—General D*
Public Health—General M

MORGAN STATE UNIVERSITY

African-American Studies M,D
Architecture M*
Biological and Biomedical Sciences—General M,D
Business Administration and Management—General M,D
Chemistry M
City and Regional Planning M
Economics M
Education—General M,D*
Educational Administration M,D
Elementary Education M
Engineering and Applied Sciences—General M,D
English M,D
Environmental Biology D*
History M,D
International Affairs M
Landscape Architecture M
Mathematics Education D
Mathematics M
Middle School Education M
Music M
Physics M
Public Health—General D
Science Education D
Sociology M
Telecommunications Management M
Transportation Management M
Urban Education D

MORNINGSIDE COLLEGE

Computer Education M
Education—General M
Elementary Education M
Reading Education M
Special Education M

MORRISON UNIVERSITY

Business Administration and Management—General M

MOUNTAIN STATE UNIVERSITY

Advanced Practice Nursing M
Allied Health—General M
Community Health M
Criminal Justice and Criminology M
Emergency Medical Services M
Gerontology M
Health Education M
Health Physics/Radiological Health M
Health Services Management and Hospital Administration M
Interdisciplinary Studies M
Management Strategy and Policy M
Nursing and Healthcare Administration M
Nursing Education M
Physician Assistant Studies M

In-depth description on page 983.

MOUNT ALLISON UNIVERSITY

Biological and Biomedical Sciences—General M
Chemistry M

MOUNT ANGEL SEMINARY

Theology P,M

MOUNT MARTY COLLEGE

Nurse Anesthesia M
Nursing—General M

MOUNT MARY COLLEGE

Art Therapy M
Education—General M
Gerontology M
Health Education M
Nutrition M
Occupational Therapy M

MOUNT SAINT MARY COLLEGE

Advanced Practice Nursing M
Business Administration and Management—General M
Early Childhood Education M
Education—General M
Elementary Education M
Medical/Surgical Nursing M
Nursing and Healthcare Administration M
Nursing Education M
Nursing—General M
Reading Education M
Secondary Education M
Special Education M

MOUNT ST. MARY'S COLLEGE

Counseling Psychology M
Education—General M
Educational Administration M
Elementary Education M
Physical Therapy D*
Religion M
Secondary Education M
Special Education M

MOUNT SAINT MARY'S COLLEGE AND SEMINARY

Business Administration and Management—General M
Education—General M
Theology P,M

MOUNT SAINT VINCENT UNIVERSITY

Adult Education M
Child and Family Studies M
Curriculum and Instruction M
Education—General M
Educational Psychology M
Elementary Education M
English as a Second Language M
Foundations and Philosophy of Education M
Gerontology M
Middle School Education M
Nutrition M
Reading Education M
School Psychology M
Special Education M
Women's Studies M

MOUNT SINAI SCHOOL OF MEDICINE OF NEW YORK UNIVERSITY

Allopathic Medicine P
Biochemistry D
Biological and Biomedical Sciences—General D*
Biometrics D
Biophysics D
Biostatistics D
Cell Biology D
Developmental Biology D
Genetics D
Genomic Sciences D
Microbiology D*
Molecular Biology D
Neuroscience D
Pathology D
Pharmacology D
Physiology D
Structural Biology D

MOUNT VERNON NAZARENE UNIVERSITY

Education—General M
Theology M

MULTNOMAH BIBLE COLLEGE AND BIBLICAL SEMINARY

Pastoral Ministry and Counseling M
Theology P,M,O

MURRAY STATE UNIVERSITY

Accounting M
Agricultural Sciences—General M
Biological and Biomedical Sciences—General M,D
Business Administration and Management—General M
Chemistry M
Clinical Psychology M
Communication Disorders M
Corporate and Organizational Communication M
Counselor Education M,O
Early Childhood Education M
Economics M
Education—General M,D,O
Educational Administration M,O
Elementary Education M,O
English as a Second Language M
English M
Environmental and Occupational Health M
Geosciences M
History M
Human Services M
Leisure Studies M
Management of Technology M
Marine Biology M
Marine Sciences M
Mass Communication M
Mathematics M
Middle School Education M,O
Music Education M
Music M
Nursing—General M
Physical Education M
Psychology—General M
Public Policy and Administration M
Reading Education M
Recreation and Park Management M
Safety Engineering M
Secondary Education M,O
Special Education M
Telecommunications Management M
Vocational and Technical Education M

In-depth description on page 985.

MUSKINGUM COLLEGE

Education—General M

NAROPA UNIVERSITY

Art Therapy P,M
Asian Languages M
Clinical Psychology M
Counseling Psychology M
Education—General M
Environmental Management and Policy M
Gerontology M
Psychology—General P,M*
Recreation and Park Management P,M
Religion M
Theology P
Therapies—Dance, Drama, and Music M
Transpersonal and Humanistic Psychology M
Writing M

NASHOTAH HOUSE

Theology P,M,O

NATIONAL AMERICAN UNIVERSITY

Business Administration and Management—General M

NATIONAL COLLEGE OF NATUROPATHIC MEDICINE

Acupuncture and Oriental Medicine M
Naturopathic Medicine D*

NATIONAL COLLEGE OF ORIENTAL MEDICINE

Acupuncture and Oriental Medicine M*

NATIONAL DEFENSE UNIVERSITY

Military and Defense Studies M

THE NATIONAL GRADUATE SCHOOL OF QUALITY MANAGEMENT

Business Administration and Management—General M
Electronic Commerce M
Quality Management M*

NATIONAL-LOUIS UNIVERSITY

Addictions/Substance Abuse Counseling M,O
Adult Education M,D,O
Business Administration and Management—General M
Curriculum and Instruction M,D,O
Developmental Education M,O
Early Childhood Education M,O
Education—General M,D,O
Educational Administration M,D,O
Educational Media/Instructional Technology M,O
Educational Psychology M,D,O
Elementary Education M
English Education M,O
Gerontology M,O
Health Psychology M,O
Human Development M,D,O
Human Resources Development M
Human Resources Management M
Human Services M,O
Industrial and Organizational Psychology M,O
Mathematics Education M,O
Psychology—General M,O
Reading Education M,D,O
School Psychology M,D,O
Science Education M,O
Secondary Education M
Special Education M,O
Writing M

NATIONAL TECHNOLOGICAL UNIVERSITY

Chemical Engineering M
Computer Engineering M
Computer Science M
Electrical Engineering M
Engineering and Applied Sciences—General M
Engineering Management M
Environmental Management and Policy M
International Business M
Management of Technology M
Manufacturing Engineering M
Materials Engineering M
Materials Sciences M
Mechanical Engineering M
Software Engineering M
Systems Engineering M

NATIONAL THEATRE CONSERVATORY

Theater M,O

NATIONAL UNIVERSITY

Accounting M
Art Therapy M,O
Biotechnology M
Business Administration and Management—General M
Counseling Psychology M,O
Counselor Education M
Criminal Justice and Criminology M
Education—General M
Educational Administration M
Educational Media/Instructional Technology M
Electronic Commerce M
Engineering and Applied Sciences—General M
Environmental Management and Policy M
Film, Television, and Video Theory and Criticism M
Finance and Banking M
Forensic Sciences M
Health Services Management and Hospital Administration M
Human Resources Management M
International Business M
Management of Technology M
Marketing M
Multilingual and Multicultural Education M
Nursing—General M
Psychology—General M,O
Public Policy and Administration M
School Psychology M
Software Engineering M
Special Education M
Telecommunications Management M

In-depth description on page 987.

NATIONAL UNIVERSITY OF HEALTH SCIENCES

Chiropractic P*

NAVAL POSTGRADUATE SCHOOL

Acoustics M,D
Aerospace/Aeronautical Engineering M,D,O
Computer Engineering M,D,O
Computer Science M,D
Electrical Engineering M,D,O
Human-Computer Interaction M,D
Information Science M
Mathematics M,D
Mechanical Engineering M,D,O
Meteorology M,D
Military and Defense Studies M,D
Oceanography M,D
Operations Research M,D
Physics M,D
Project Management M
Systems Engineering M

NAVAL WAR COLLEGE

Military and Defense Studies M

NAZARENE THEOLOGICAL SEMINARY

Missions and Missiology P,M
Religious Education P,M,D
Theology P,M,D

NAZARETH COLLEGE OF ROCHESTER

Art Education M
Art Therapy M
Business Administration and Management—General M
Business Education M
Communication Disorders M
Computer Education M
Early Childhood Education M
Education—General M
Educational Media/Instructional Technology M
Elementary Education M
English as a Second Language M
Gerontological Nursing M
Liberal Studies M
Music Education M
Nursing—General M
Reading Education M
Secondary Education M
Social Work M
Special Education M

NEBRASKA METHODIST COLLEGE

Health Promotion M
Nursing—General M

NER ISRAEL RABBINICAL COLLEGE

Theology M,D

NER ISRAEL YESHIVA COLLEGE OF TORONTO

Theology

NEUMANN COLLEGE

Education—General M
Nursing—General M
Pastoral Ministry and Counseling M,O
Physical Therapy M
Sports Management M

NEW BRUNSWICK THEOLOGICAL SEMINARY
Pastoral Ministry and Counseling D
Theology P,M,D

NEW COLLEGE OF CALIFORNIA
Clinical Psychology M
Humanities M
Law P*
Media Studies M
Psychology—General M
Social Psychology M
Sustainable Development M
Women's Studies M
Writing M
In-depth description on page 989.

NEW ENGLAND COLLEGE
Business Administration and Management—General M,O*
Education—General M
Educational Administration M
Health Services Management and Hospital Administration M,O
Human Resources Management M,O
Human Services M,O
Social Psychology M,O
Special Education M
Writing M*

THE NEW ENGLAND COLLEGE OF OPTOMETRY
Optometry P*

NEW ENGLAND CONSERVATORY OF MUSIC
Music M,D,O

NEW ENGLAND SCHOOL OF ACUPUNCTURE
Acupuncture and Oriental Medicine M*

NEW ENGLAND SCHOOL OF LAW
Law P

NEW JERSEY CITY UNIVERSITY
Accounting M
Art Education M
Art/Fine Arts M
Counseling Psychology M
Criminal Justice and Criminology M
Early Childhood Education M
Education—General M,O
Educational Administration M
Educational Media/Instructional Technology M
Educational Psychology M,O
English as a Second Language M
Health Education M
Health Services Management and Hospital Administration M
Mathematics Education M
Multilingual and Multicultural Education M
Music Education M
Nursing—General M
Psychology—General M,O
Reading Education M
School Psychology O
Special Education M
Transcultural Nursing M
Urban Education M
Urban Studies M

NEW JERSEY INSTITUTE OF TECHNOLOGY
Applied Mathematics M
Applied Physics M,D
Architecture M
Biological and Biomedical Sciences—General M,D
Biomedical Engineering M
Business Administration and Management—General M
Chemical Engineering M,D
Chemistry M,D
Civil Engineering M,D
Communication—General M
Computational Sciences M
Computer Engineering M,D
Computer Science M,D
Electrical Engineering M,D
Engineering and Applied Sciences—General M,D,O
Engineering Management M
Environmental and Occupational Health M
Environmental Engineering M,D
Environmental Management and Policy M,D
Environmental Sciences M,D
History of Medicine M
History of Science and Technology M
History M
Industrial Hygiene M
Industrial/Management Engineering M,D
Information Science M,D
Management of Technology M,D
Manufacturing Engineering M,D
Materials Engineering M,D
Materials Sciences M,D
Mathematics D
Mechanical Engineering M,D,O
Pharmaceutical Sciences M
Public Health—General M
Safety Engineering M
Social Sciences Education M
Statistics M
Technical Writing M
Telecommunications M,D
Transportation and Highway Engineering M,D
Transportation Management M,D
Urban Studies D

NEWMAN THEOLOGICAL COLLEGE
Educational Administration M,O
Religious Education M,O
Theology P,M

NEWMAN UNIVERSITY
Adult Education M
Education—General M
Educational Administration M
Elementary Education M
English as a Second Language M
Middle School Education M
Nurse Anesthesia M
Nursing—General M
Organizational Management M
Social Work M

NEW MEXICO HIGHLANDS UNIVERSITY
American Studies M
Anthropology M
Biological and Biomedical Sciences—General M
Business Administration and Management—General M
Chemistry M
Cognitive Sciences M
Computer Art and Design M
Computer Science M
Counselor Education M
Curriculum and Instruction M
Education—General M
Educational Administration M
English M
Environmental Management and Policy M
Environmental Sciences M
Exercise and Sports Science M
Film, Television, and Video Production M
Hispanic Studies M
History M
Internet and Interactive Multimedia M
Leisure Studies M
Physical Education M
Political Science M
Psychology—General M
Public Policy and Administration M
Social Work M
Sociology M
Spanish M
Special Education M
Writing M

NEW MEXICO INSTITUTE OF MINING AND TECHNOLOGY
Astrophysics M,D
Atmospheric Sciences M,D
Biochemistry M,D
Biological and Biomedical Sciences—General M
Chemistry M,D
Computer Science M,D
Environmental Engineering M
Environmental Sciences M,D
Geochemistry M,D
Geology M,D
Geophysics M,D
Geosciences M,D
Hazardous Materials Management M
Hydrology M,D
Materials Engineering M,D
Mathematical Physics M,D
Mathematics M
Mechanics M
Operations Research M
Petroleum Engineering M,D
Physics M,D
Science Education M
Water Resources Engineering M
In-depth description on page 991.

NEW MEXICO STATE UNIVERSITY
Accounting M
Agricultural Economics and Agribusiness M
Agricultural Education M
Agricultural Sciences—General M,D
Agronomy and Soil Sciences M,D
Animal Sciences M,D
Anthropology M
Art/Fine Arts M
Astronomy M,D
Biochemistry M,D
Biological and Biomedical Sciences—General M,D
Business Administration and Management—General M,D
Chemical Engineering M,D
Chemistry M,D
Civil Engineering M,D
Communication Disorders M
Communication—General M
Computer Engineering M,D
Computer Science M,D
Counseling Psychology M,D,O
Counselor Education M,D,O
Criminal Justice and Criminology M
Curriculum and Instruction M,D,O
Economics M
Education—General M,D,O
Educational Administration M,D,O
Electrical Engineering M,D
Engineering and Applied Sciences—General M,D
English M,D
Entomology M
Environmental Engineering M,D
Family and Consumer Sciences-General M
Fish, Game, and Wildlife Management M
Geography M
Geology M
History M
Horticulture M,D
Industrial/Management Engineering M,D
Interdisciplinary Studies M,D
Marketing D
Mathematics M,D
Mechanical Engineering M,D
Molecular Biology M,D
Music M
Nursing—General M
Physics M,D
Plant Pathology M
Political Science M
Psychology—General M,D
Public Health—General M
Range Science M,D
Reading Education M,D,O
Social Work M
Sociology M
Spanish M
Special Education M
Statistics M
Writing M,D

NEW ORLEANS BAPTIST THEOLOGICAL SEMINARY
Music M,D
Pastoral Ministry and Counseling P,M,D
Religious Education P,M,D
Theology P,D

NEWSCHOOL OF ARCHITECTURE & DESIGN
Architecture M

NEW SCHOOL UNIVERSITY
Anthropology M,D
Applied Arts and Design—General M
Architecture M
Art/Fine Arts M
Business Administration and Management—General M,D,O*
Clinical Psychology M,D
Communication—General M*
Computer Art and Design M
Decorative Arts M
Economics M,D
Education—General M
Finance and Banking M
Health Services Management and Hospital Administration M,O
History M,D
Human Resources Development M,O
Human Resources Management M,O
Interior Design M
International Affairs M*
International Business M
International Development M
Liberal Studies M
Mass Communication M
Media Studies M
Nonprofit Management M
Organizational Management M
Philosophy M,D
Political Science M,D
Psychology—General M,D
Public Policy and Administration D
Secondary Education M
Social Sciences M,D*
Sociology M,D
Textile Design M
Theater M
Urban Studies M
Writing M*
In-depth description on page 993.

NEW YORK CHIROPRACTIC COLLEGE
Chiropractic P*

THE NEW YORK COLLEGE OF HEALTH PROFESSIONS
Acupuncture and Oriental Medicine M

NEW YORK COLLEGE OF PODIATRIC MEDICINE
Podiatric Medicine P*

NEW YORK INSTITUTE OF TECHNOLOGY
Accounting M,O
Architecture M*
Business Administration and Management—General M,O
Communication—General M
Computer Engineering M
Computer Science M
Counseling Psychology M
Counselor Education M
Distance Education Development M,O
Education—General M,O
Educational Administration M,O
Educational Media/Instructional Technology M,O
Electrical Engineering M
Elementary Education M,O
Energy and Power Engineering M,O
Energy Management and Policy M,O
Engineering and Applied Sciences—General M,O
Environmental Engineering M
Environmental Management and Policy M,O
Finance and Banking M,O
Human Development M
Human Resources Management M,O
Industrial and Labor Relations M,O
International Business M,O
Management Information Systems M,O
Marketing M,O
Nutrition M
Occupational Therapy M
Osteopathic Medicine P*
Physical Therapy M
Urban Design M
In-depth description on page 995.

NEW YORK LAW SCHOOL
Law P

NEW YORK MEDICAL COLLEGE
Allopathic Medicine P
Anatomy M,D
Biochemistry M,D
Biological and Biomedical Sciences—General M,D*
Biostatistics M
Cell Biology M,D*
Clinical Research M
Communication Disorders M*
Community Health M
Disability Studies M,O
Emergency Medical Services M,O
Environmental and Occupational Health M
Epidemiology M
Gerontology M,O
Health Informatics M
Health Promotion M
Health Services Management and Hospital Administration M
Immunology M,D
International Health M,O
Maternal and Child Health M,O
Microbiology M,D
Molecular Biology M,D
Neuroscience M,D
Pathology M,D*
Pharmacology M,D
Physical Therapy M,D*
Physiology M,D*

Public Health—General M,D,O*

NEW YORK SCHOOL OF INTERIOR DESIGN

Interior Design M*

NEW YORK THEOLOGICAL SEMINARY

Theology P,M,D

NEW YORK UNIVERSITY

Accounting M,D,O
Addictions/Substance Abuse Counseling M,D,O
Advanced Practice Nursing M,O
African Studies M
Allopathic Medicine P
American Studies M,D
Anthropology M,D
Applied Arts and Design—General M
Archaeology M,D
Art Education M,D
Art History M,D
Art Therapy M
Art/Fine Arts M,D
Arts Administration M
Biochemistry M,D
Biological and Biomedical Sciences—General M,D*
Business Administration and Management—General M,D,O
Business Education M,D,O
Cancer Biology/Oncology D
Cell Biology M,D
Chemistry M,D*
City and Regional Planning M,O
Classics M,D,O
Clinical Psychology M,D,O
Clinical Research M
Cognitive Sciences M,D,O
Communication Disorders M,D
Communication—General M,D,O
Comparative Literature M,D
Computer Art and Design M*
Computer Science M,D*
Counseling Psychology M,D,O
Counselor Education M,D,O
Dance M,D
Dentistry P
Developmental Psychology M,D,O
Early Childhood Education M,D,O
Economics M,D,O
Education—General M,D,O*
Educational Administration M,D,O
Educational Measurement and Evaluation M,D,O
Educational Media/Instructional Technology M,D,O
Educational Psychology M,D,O
Elementary Education M,D,O
English as a Second Language M,D,O
English Education M,D,O
English M,D
Environmental and Occupational Health M,D
Environmental Biology M,D
Environmental Education M
Environmental Management and Policy M,D,O
Ergonomics and Human Factors M,D
Evolutionary Biology M,D
Film, Television, and Video Production M
Film, Television, and Video Theory and Criticism M,D
Finance and Banking M,D,O
Foreign Languages Education M,D,O
Foundations and Philosophy of Education M,D
French M,D,O
Genetics M,D
German M,D
Gerontological Nursing M,O
Health Education M,D,O
Health Informatics M,O
Health Services Management and Hospital Administration M,O
Higher Education M,D,O
Historic Preservation
History M,D,O
Hospitality Management M,D*
Human Resources Management M,D,O
Humanities M,O
Immunology D*
Industrial and Manufacturing Management M
Industrial and Organizational Psychology M,D,O
Information Science M,D
Interdisciplinary Studies M*
International Affairs M,D,O
International and Comparative Education M,D
International Business M,D,O
Internet and Interactive Multimedia M
Italian M,D
Jewish Studies M,D
Journalism M,D,O*
Kinesiology and Movement Studies M,D
Latin American Studies M
Law P,M,D
Legal and Justice Studies D
Linguistics M,D
Management Information Systems M,D,O*
Management of Technology M,D,O
Marketing M,D,O*
Mathematical and Computational Finance M,D
Mathematics Education M,D
Mathematics M,D*
Media Studies M,D
Medical/Surgical Nursing M,O
Microbiology M,D*
Molecular Biology D
Multilingual and Multicultural Education M,D,O
Museum Studies M,D,O*
Music Education M,D,O
Music M,D,O
Near and Middle Eastern Studies M,D
Neuroscience M,D*
Nonprofit Management M,D,O
Nurse Midwifery M,O
Nursing Education M,O
Nursing—General M,D,O
Nutrition M,D
Occupational Therapy M,D
Operations Research M,D,O
Oral and Dental Sciences M,D,O
Parasitology M,D
Pathology M,D
Pediatric Nursing M,O
Pharmacology M,D
Philosophy M,D
Physical Therapy M,D
Physics M,D
Physiology M,D
Political Science M,D
Portuguese M,D
Psychiatric Nursing M,O
Psychology—General M,D,O
Public Health—General M,D,O
Public History M,D,O
Public Policy and Administration M,D,O*
Publishing M*
Quantitative Analysis M,D,O
Real Estate M,O*
Recreation and Park Management M,D,O
Rehabilitation Counseling M,D
Rehabilitation Sciences M
Religion M,O
Romance Languages M,D
Russian M
School Psychology M,D,O
Science Education M
Slavic Languages M
Social Psychology M,D,O
Social Sciences Education M,D,O
Social Work M,D*
Sociology M,D
Spanish M,D
Special Education M,D,O
Speech and Interpersonal Communication M,O
Statistics M,D,O
Student Personnel Services M,D
Theater M,D,O*
Therapies—Dance, Drama, and Music M,D
Translation and Interpretation M
Travel and Tourism M
Western European Studies M
Writing M

In-depth descriptions on pages 997 and 999.

NIAGARA UNIVERSITY

Advanced Practice Nursing M
Business Administration and Management—General M
Counselor Education M,O
Criminal Justice and Criminology M
Education—General M,O
Educational Administration M,O
Elementary Education M
Foundations and Philosophy of Education M
Nursing—General M
Reading Education M
Science Education M,O
Secondary Education M

In-depth description on page 1001.

NICHOLLS STATE UNIVERSITY

Applied Mathematics M
Business Administration and Management—General M
Counseling Psychology M,O
Counselor Education M,O
Curriculum and Instruction M
Education—General M
Educational Administration M
Mathematics M
School Psychology M,O

NICHOLS COLLEGE

Accounting M
Business Administration and Management—General M
Finance and Banking M
International Business M
Marketing M

THE NIGERIAN BAPTIST THEOLOGICAL SEMINARY

Music P,M,O
Theology P,M,O

NIPISSING UNIVERSITY

Education—General M,O

NORFOLK STATE UNIVERSITY

Art/Fine Arts M
Clinical Psychology M
Communication—General M
Early Childhood Education M
Education of the Gifted M
Education of the Multiply Handicapped M
Education—General M
Educational Administration M
Materials Sciences M
Media Studies M
Music Education M
Music M
Psychology—General M,D
Secondary Education M
Social Psychology M
Social Work M,D
Sociology M
Speech and Interpersonal Communication M
Urban Education M
Urban Studies M

In-depth description on page 1003.

NORTH AMERICAN BAPTIST SEMINARY

Marriage and Family Therapy M
Music M
Pastoral Ministry and Counseling P,M
Religion M
Theology M,D,O

NORTH CAROLINA AGRICULTURAL AND TECHNICAL STATE UNIVERSITY

Adult Education M
African-American Studies M
Agricultural Economics and Agribusiness M
Agricultural Education M
Agricultural Engineering M
Agricultural Sciences—General M
Applied Economics M
Architectural Engineering M
Art Education M
Biological and Biomedical Sciences—General M
Chemical Engineering M
Chemistry M
Civil Engineering M
Computer Science M
Counselor Education M
Early Childhood Education M
Education—General M
Educational Administration M
Educational Media/Instructional Technology M
Electrical Engineering M,D
Elementary Education M
Engineering and Applied Sciences—General M,D*
English Education M
English M
Environmental Engineering M
Environmental Sciences M
Health Education M
Human Resources Development M
Human Resources Management M
Industrial/Management Engineering M,D
Management of Technology M
Mathematics Education M
Mechanical Engineering M,D
Middle School Education M
Nutrition M
Physical Education M
Plant Sciences M
Reading Education M
Science Education M
Social Sciences Education M
Social Work M
Systems Engineering M,D
Vocational and Technical Education M

NORTH CAROLINA CENTRAL UNIVERSITY

Biological and Biomedical Sciences—General M
Business Administration and Management—General M
Chemistry M
Communication Disorders M
Counselor Education M
Criminal Justice and Criminology M
Education—General M
Educational Administration M
Educational Media/Instructional Technology M
Elementary Education M
English M
Family and Consumer Sciences-General M
Geosciences M
History M
Information Studies M
Law P
Library Science M
Mathematics M
Physical Education M
Psychology—General M
Public Policy and Administration M
Recreation and Park Management M
Sociology M
Special Education M

NORTH CAROLINA SCHOOL OF THE ARTS

Music M
Theater M

NORTH CAROLINA STATE UNIVERSITY

Accounting M
Adult Education M,D
Aerospace/Aeronautical Engineering M,D
Agricultural Economics and Agribusiness M,D
Agricultural Education M,D,O
Agricultural Engineering M,D
Agricultural Sciences—General M,D*
Agronomy and Soil Sciences M,D
Animal Sciences M,D
Applied Arts and Design—General M,D
Applied Mathematics M,D
Architecture M
Atmospheric Sciences M,D
Biochemistry M,D*
Bioengineering M,D
Bioinformatics M,D
Biological and Biomedical Sciences—General M,D*
Biometrics M,D*
Biotechnology M
Botany M,D
Business Administration and Management—General M
Cell Biology M,D
Chemical Engineering M,D
Chemistry M,D
Civil Engineering M,D
Clothing and Textiles M
Communication—General M
Community College Education M,D
Computer Engineering M,D
Computer Science M,D
Corporate and Organizational Communication M
Counselor Education M,D,O
Curriculum and Instruction M,D
Ecology M,D
Economics M,D
Education—General M,D,O
Educational Administration M,D
Educational Measurement and Evaluation D
Educational Media/Instructional Technology D
Electrical Engineering M,D
Engineering and Applied Sciences—General M*
English M
Entomology M,D
Environmental Management and Policy M
Epidemiology M,D
Fish, Game, and Wildlife Management M
Food Science and Technology M,D

North Carolina State University (continued)

Forestry M,D
Genetics M,D*
Genomic Sciences M,D*
Geographic Information Systems M
Geology M,D
Geophysics M,D
Geosciences M,D*
Graphic Design M
Health Education M
Higher Education M,D
History M
Horticulture M,D
Immunology M,D
Industrial Design M
Industrial/Management Engineering M,D
International Affairs M
Landscape Architecture M
Liberal Studies M
Management Information Systems M
Management of Technology D
Manufacturing Engineering M
Marine Sciences M,D
Materials Engineering M,D
Materials Sciences M,D
Mathematics Education M,D
Mathematics M,D
Mechanical Engineering M,D*
Meteorology M,D
Microbiology M,D
Middle School Education M
Natural Resources M,D
Nuclear Engineering M,D*
Nutrition M,D
Oceanography M,D
Operations Research M,D
Paper and Pulp Engineering M,D
Pathology M,D
Pharmacology M,D
Physics M,D
Physiology M,D
Plant Pathology M,D
Psychology—General M,D
Public History M
Public Policy and Administration M,D
Quality Management M
Recreation and Park Management M
Rural Sociology M,D
Science Education M,D
Sociology M,D
Special Education M
Sports Management M
Statistics M,D*
Technical Writing M
Telecommunications M
Textile Sciences and Engineering M,D
Toxicology M,D
Travel and Tourism M
Veterinary Medicine P
Veterinary Sciences M,D
Vocational and Technical Education M,D,O
Zoology M,D

NORTH CENTRAL COLLEGE

Business Administration and Management—General M
Computer Science M
Education—General M
Educational Administration M
Liberal Studies M
Management Information Systems M
Nonprofit Management M

NORTH DAKOTA STATE UNIVERSITY

Agricultural Economics and Agribusiness M
Agricultural Education M
Agricultural Engineering M,D
Agricultural Sciences—General M,D
Agronomy and Soil Sciences M,D
Animal Sciences M,D
Applied Mathematics M,D
Biochemistry M,D
Botany M,D
Business Administration and Management—General M
Cell Biology D
Chemistry M,D
Child and Family Studies M,D
Civil Engineering M
Clinical Psychology M,D
Communication—General M,D
Computer Engineering M
Computer Science M,D
Counselor Education M
Criminal Justice and Criminology M,D
Education—General M,O
Educational Administration M,O
Electrical Engineering M
Engineering and Applied Sciences—General M,D
English M
Entomology M,D
Environmental Engineering M
Environmental Management and Policy M,D
Family and Consumer Sciences-General M
Food Science and Technology M,D
Gerontology M,D
History M
Industrial/Management Engineering M
Manufacturing Engineering M
Mass Communication M,D
Mathematics M,D
Mechanical Engineering M
Mechanics M
Microbiology M,D
Molecular Biology M,D
Nursing—General M
Operations Research M,D
Pharmaceutical Sciences M,D
Physical Education M
Physics M,D
Plant Pathology M,D
Plant Sciences M,D
Political Science M
Polymer Science and Engineering M,D
Psychology—General M,D
Range Science M,D
Social Sciences M,D
Speech and Interpersonal Communication M,D
Sports Management M
Statistics M,D
Veterinary Sciences M,D
Zoology M,D

In-depth description on page 1005.

NORTHEASTERN ILLINOIS UNIVERSITY

Accounting M
Biological and Biomedical Sciences—General M
Business Administration and Management—General M
Chemistry M
Computer Science M
Counselor Education M
Education of the Gifted M
Education—General M
Educational Administration M
English Education M
English M
Environmental Management and Policy M
Finance and Banking M
Geography M
Geosciences M
Gerontology M
History M
Human Resources Development M
Linguistics M
Marketing M
Mathematics Education M
Mathematics M
Multilingual and Multicultural Education M
Music M
Political Science M
Psychology—General M
Reading Education M
Special Education M
Speech and Interpersonal Communication M
Urban Education M
Writing M

NORTHEASTERN OHIO UNIVERSITIES COLLEGE OF MEDICINE

Allopathic Medicine P

NORTHEASTERN SEMINARY AT ROBERTS WESLEYAN COLLEGE

Theology P,M

NORTHEASTERN STATE UNIVERSITY

American Studies M
Business Administration and Management—General M
Communication Disorders M
Communication—General M
Counseling Psychology M
Counselor Education M
Criminal Justice and Criminology M
Early Childhood Education M
Education—General M
Educational Administration M
English M
Health Education M
Higher Education M
Industrial and Manufacturing Management M
Optometry P
Psychology—General M
Reading Education M
Special Education M

NORTHEASTERN UNIVERSITY

Accounting M,O
Advanced Practice Nursing M,O
Analytical Chemistry M,D
Biological and Biomedical Sciences—General M,D*
Business Administration and Management—General M,O*
Cardiovascular Sciences M
Chemical Engineering M,D
Chemistry M,D
Civil Engineering M,D
Clinical Laboratory Sciences/Medical Technology M,D
Communication Disorders M*
Community Health Nursing M,O
Computer Engineering M,D
Computer Science M,D*
Counseling Psychology M,D,O*
Counselor Education M
Criminal Justice and Criminology M*
Curriculum and Instruction M
Economics M*
Education—General M
Educational Psychology M
Electrical Engineering M,D*
Engineering and Applied Sciences—General M,D*
Engineering Management M,D
English Education M
English M,D,O
Environmental Engineering M,D
Exercise and Sports Science M*
Experimental Psychology M,D
Finance and Banking M
Health Services Management and Hospital Administration M
History M,D*
Industrial/Management Engineering M,D
Information Science M
Inorganic Chemistry M,D
International Affairs M,D
Journalism M*
Law P
Legal and Justice Studies M,D
Management Information Systems M
Manufacturing Engineering M,D
Mathematics Education M
Mathematics M,D
Mechanical Engineering M,D*
Nurse Anesthesia M
Nursing and Healthcare Administration M
Nursing—General M,O*
Operations Research M,D
Organic Chemistry M,D
Pediatric Nursing M,O
Pharmaceutical Sciences M,D
Pharmacology M,D*
Pharmacy P*
Physical Chemistry M,D
Physician Assistant Studies M
Physics M,D*
Political Science M,D*
Psychiatric Nursing M,O
Psychology—General M,D,O
Public History M,D
Public Policy and Administration M,D
Rehabilitation Counseling M
School Psychology M,D,O
Science Education M
Social Sciences Education M
Sociology M,D
Special Education M
Student Personnel Services M
Systems Engineering M
Taxation M,O
Technical Writing M,O*
Toxicology M,D
Writing M,D,O

In-depth descriptions on pages 1007 and 1009.

NORTHERN ARIZONA UNIVERSITY

Allied Health—General M,D,O
Anthropology M
Applied Physics M
Archaeology M
Biological and Biomedical Sciences—General M,D
Business Administration and Management—General M
Chemistry M
Communication Disorders M
Community College Education M,D
Counseling Psychology D
Counselor Education M
Criminal Justice and Criminology M,O
Curriculum and Instruction D
Early Childhood Education M
Ecology M,O
Education—General M,D,O
Educational Administration M,D
Educational Media/Instructional Technology M
Educational Psychology D
Elementary Education M
Engineering and Applied Sciences—General M
English as a Second Language M,D,O
English M,D,O
Environmental Management and Policy M,O
Environmental Sciences M,O
Forestry M,D
Geographic Information Systems M,O
Geography M,O
Geology M
Geosciences M
Health Education M
Health Promotion M
Health Psychology M
History M,D
Liberal Studies M
Linguistics M,D,O
Management Information Systems M
Mathematics Education M
Mathematics M
Multilingual and Multicultural Education M,O
Music Education M
Music M
Nursing—General M,O
Physical Education M
Physical Therapy M,D
Political Science M,D,O
Psychology—General M
Public Health—General M
Public Policy and Administration M,D,O
Reading Education M
Rhetoric M
School Psychology M,D
Science Education M,D
Secondary Education M
Sociology M
Special Education M
Statistics M
Vocational and Technical Education M
Writing M

NORTHERN BAPTIST THEOLOGICAL SEMINARY

Ethics P,M,D
Pastoral Ministry and Counseling P,M,D
Religion P,M,D
Theology P,M,D

NORTHERN ILLINOIS UNIVERSITY

Accounting M,D
Adult Education M,D
Anthropology M
Art/Fine Arts M
Biochemistry M,D
Biological and Biomedical Sciences—General M,D
Business Administration and Management—General M
Chemistry M,D
Child and Family Studies M
Communication Disorders M
Communication—General M
Computer Science M
Counselor Education M,D
Curriculum and Instruction M,D
Dance M
Early Childhood Education M
Economics M,D
Education—General M,D,O
Educational Administration M,D,O
Educational Media/Instructional Technology M,D
Educational Psychology M,D
Electrical Engineering M
Elementary Education M,D
Engineering and Applied Sciences—General M*
English M,D
Environmental Education M,D
Foundations and Philosophy of Education M
French M
Geography M
Geology M,D
History M,D
Industrial and Manufacturing Management M
Industrial/Management Engineering M
Law P
Management Information Systems M
Mathematics M,D
Mechanical Engineering M
Music M,O
Nursing—General M
Nutrition M
Philosophy M

Physical Education M
Physical Therapy M
Physics M,D
Political Science M,D
Psychology—General M,D
Public Health—General M
Public Policy and Administration M
Reading Education M,D
Romance Languages M
Secondary Education M,D
Sociology M
Spanish M
Special Education M
Statistics M
Taxation M
Theater M

In-depth description on page 1011.

NORTHERN KENTUCKY UNIVERSITY

Accounting M
Business Administration and Management—General M
Computer Science M
Education—General M
Elementary Education M
Information Science M
Law P
Management of Technology M
Middle School Education M
Nursing—General M
Public Policy and Administration M
Secondary Education M
Systems Science M

NORTHERN MICHIGAN UNIVERSITY

Biochemistry M
Biological and Biomedical Sciences—General M
Chemistry M
Communication Disorders M
Criminal Justice and Criminology M
Education—General M,O
Educational Administration M,O
Elementary Education M
English M
Exercise and Sports Science M
Mathematics Education M
Nursing—General M
Psychology—General M
Public Policy and Administration M
Science Education M
Secondary Education M
Special Education M
Writing M

NORTHERN STATE UNIVERSITY

Counselor Education M
Education—General M
Educational Administration M
Elementary Education M
English Education M
Health Education M
Physical Education M
Reading Education M
Secondary Education M
Special Education M

NORTH GEORGIA COLLEGE & STATE UNIVERSITY

Advanced Practice Nursing M
Art Education M,O
Early Childhood Education M,O
Education—General M,O
Educational Administration M,O
English Education M,O
Foreign Languages Education M,O
Mathematics Education M,O
Middle School Education M,O
Nursing—General M
Physical Education M,O
Physical Therapy M
Public Policy and Administration M
Science Education M,O
Secondary Education M,O
Social Psychology M
Social Sciences Education M,O
Special Education M,O

NORTH PARK THEOLOGICAL SEMINARY

Religious Education M
Theology P,M,D,O

NORTH PARK UNIVERSITY

Business Administration and Management—General M
City and Regional Planning M
Education—General M
Nursing—General M

NORTHWEST BAPTIST SEMINARY

Theology P,M

NORTHWEST CHRISTIAN COLLEGE

Business Administration and Management—General M
Counselor Education M

NORTHWESTERN HEALTH SCIENCES UNIVERSITY

Acupuncture and Oriental Medicine M
Chiropractic P*

NORTHWESTERN OKLAHOMA STATE UNIVERSITY

Counselor Education M
Education—General M
Educational Measurement and Evaluation M
Elementary Education M
Psychology—General M
Reading Education M
Secondary Education M

NORTHWESTERN POLYTECHNIC UNIVERSITY

Business Administration and Management—General M
Computer Engineering M
Computer Science M
Electrical Engineering M
Engineering and Applied Sciences—General M

NORTHWESTERN STATE UNIVERSITY OF LOUISIANA

Adult Education M,O
Art/Fine Arts M
Business Education M,O
Clinical Psychology M
Counselor Education M,O
Early Childhood Education M
Education—General M,O
Educational Administration M,O
Educational Media/Instructional Technology M,O
Elementary Education M,O
English Education M
English M
Health Education M,O
Health Promotion M
History M
Home Economics Education M
Mathematics Education M,O
Music M
Nursing—General M
Physical Education M,O
Psychology—General M
Reading Education M,O
Science Education M,O
Secondary Education M,O
Social Sciences Education M
Special Education M,O
Sports Management M
Student Personnel Services M,O

NORTHWESTERN UNIVERSITY

Accounting D
Advertising and Public Relations M
African Studies O
Allopathic Medicine P
Anthropology D
Applied Mathematics M,D*
Art History D
Art/Fine Arts M*
Astronomy M,D
Astrophysics M,D
Biochemistry D*
Biological and Biomedical Sciences—General D*
Biomedical Engineering M,D*
Biophysics D
Biopsychology D
Biotechnology D
Business Administration and Management—General M
Cancer Biology/Oncology D
Cell Biology D
Chemical Engineering M,D
Chemistry D
Civil Engineering M,D*
Clinical Psychology D
Clinical Research M,O
Cognitive Sciences D
Communication Disorders M,D*
Communication—General M,D
Comparative Literature M,D,O
Computer Engineering M,D,O
Computer Science M,D*
Corporate and Organizational Communication M
Counseling Psychology M*
Developmental Biology D
Economics M,D
Education—General M,D*
Educational Media/Instructional Technology M,D
Electrical Engineering M,D,O*
Electronic Commerce M
Electronic Materials M,D,O
Elementary Education M
Engineering and Applied Sciences—General M,D,O*
Engineering Management M
English M,D*
Environmental Engineering M,D
Evolutionary Biology D
Film, Television, and Video Production M,D
Finance and Banking D
French D,O
Gender Studies
Genetic Counseling M
Genetics D
Geology M,D
Geosciences M,D
Geotechnical Engineering M,D
German D
Higher Education M
History D
Human Development D
Immunology D
Industrial and Manufacturing Management M
Industrial/Management Engineering M,D*
Information Science M
International Affairs O
Italian D,O
Journalism M*
Law P,M,O
Liberal Studies M
Linguistics M,D
Management Information Systems M
Management Strategy and Policy D
Manufacturing Engineering M
Marketing M,D*
Marriage and Family Therapy M
Materials Engineering M,D,O
Materials Sciences M,D,O
Mathematics D
Mechanical Engineering M,D*
Mechanics M,D
Media Studies M,D
Microbiology D
Molecular Biology D
Music Education M,D
Music M,D,O
Neurobiology M,D
Neuroscience D*
Operations Research M,D
Organizational Behavior D
Organizational Management D
Pharmacology D
Philosophy D
Physical Therapy D
Physics M,D
Physiology M
Political Science M,D
Project Management M
Psychology—General D*
Public Health—General M
Public Policy and Administration D*
Publishing M
Reproductive Biology D
Secondary Education M
Slavic Languages D
Social Psychology D
Social Sciences M,O
Sociology D
Special Education M,D
Speech and Interpersonal Communication M,D
Statistics M,D
Structural Biology D
Structural Engineering M,D
Technology and Public Policy O
Telecommunications Management O
Telecommunications O
Theater M,D
Toxicology D
Transportation and Highway Engineering M,D
Writing M

NORTHWEST GRADUATE SCHOOL OF THE MINISTRY

Pastoral Ministry and Counseling M,D

NORTHWEST INSTITUTE OF ACUPUNCTURE AND ORIENTAL MEDICINE

Acupuncture and Oriental Medicine M

NORTHWEST MISSOURI STATE UNIVERSITY

Accounting M
Agricultural Economics and Agribusiness M
Agricultural Education M
Agricultural Sciences—General M
Biological and Biomedical Sciences—General M
Business Administration and Management—General M
Computer Science M
Counseling Psychology M
Counselor Education M
Early Childhood Education M
Education—General M,O
Educational Administration M,O
Educational Media/Instructional Technology M
Elementary Education M,O
English Education M
English M
Health Education M
History M
Management Information Systems M
Mathematics Education M
Middle School Education M
Music Education M
Physical Education M
Psychology—General M
Reading Education M
Science Education M
Secondary Education M,O
Social Sciences Education M
Special Education M

NORTHWEST NAZARENE UNIVERSITY

Business Administration and Management—General M
Counselor Education M
Curriculum and Instruction M
Education—General M
Educational Administration M
Religion M
Social Work M
Special Education M

NORTHWOOD UNIVERSITY

Business Administration and Management—General M

NORWICH UNIVERSITY

Business Administration and Management—General M
Military and Defense Studies M,O

NOTRE DAME COLLEGE (OH)

Accounting M,O
Business Administration and Management—General M,O
Education—General M,O
Finance and Banking M,O
Management Information Systems M,O
Pastoral Ministry and Counseling M,O
Reading Education M,O
Special Education M,O

NOTRE DAME DE NAMUR UNIVERSITY

Addictions/Substance Abuse Counseling M,O
Art Therapy M
Biological and Biomedical Sciences—General O
Business Administration and Management—General M
Counseling Psychology M,O
Curriculum and Instruction M
Education—General M
Educational Administration M,O
Educational Media/Instructional Technology M,O
Electronic Commerce M
English M
Gerontology M,O
Marriage and Family Therapy M
Music Education M
Music M
Psychology—General M,O
Public Policy and Administration M
Special Education M,O

NOTRE DAME SEMINARY

Theology P,M

NOVA SCOTIA AGRICULTURAL COLLEGE

Agricultural Sciences—General M
Agronomy and Soil Sciences M
Animal Sciences M

Nova Scotia Agricultural College (continued)

Botany M
Ecology M
Environmental Biology M
Environmental Management and Policy M
Food Science and Technology M
Geology M
Physiology M
Plant Pathology M
Plant Physiology M

NOVA SCOTIA COLLEGE OF ART AND DESIGN

Applied Arts and Design—General M
Art Education M
Art/Fine Arts M

NOVA SOUTHEASTERN UNIVERSITY

Accounting M
Adult Education D
Allied Health—General M,D
Biological and Biomedical Sciences—General M
Business Administration and Management—General M,D*
Child and Family Studies M,D
Clinical Psychology D,O
Communication Disorders M,D
Computer Education M,D,O
Computer Science M,D*
Conflict Resolution and Mediation/Peace Studies M,D,O
Counseling Psychology M
Dentistry P
Distance Education Development M,D
Early Childhood Education M,D,O
Education of the Gifted M,O
Education—General M,D,O*
Educational Administration M,D,O
Educational Media/Instructional Technology M,D,O*
Elementary Education M,O
English as a Second Language M,O
English Education M,O
Environmental Sciences M,D
Health Education D
Health Services Management and Hospital Administration M
Higher Education D
Human Resources Management M
Information Science M,D
International Business M,D
Law P,M
Management Information Systems M,D*
Marine Affairs M,D
Marine Biology M,D
Marine Sciences M,D
Marriage and Family Therapy M,D,O
Mathematics Education M,O
Occupational Therapy M,D
Oceanography M,D*
Optometry P
Osteopathic Medicine P,M
Pharmacology M
Pharmacy P
Physical Therapy M,D
Psychology—General M,D,O
Public Health—General M
Public Policy and Administration M,D
Reading Education M,O
Religious Education M,O
School Psychology M
Science Education M,O
Social Sciences Education M,O
Spanish M,O
Vocational and Technical Education D

OAKLAND CITY UNIVERSITY

Business Administration and Management—General M
Education—General M
Theology P,D

OAKLAND UNIVERSITY

Accounting M,O
Advanced Practice Nursing M,O
Allied Health—General M,D,O
Applied Mathematics M
Biological and Biomedical Sciences—General M
Business Administration and Management—General M,O
Cell Biology M
Chemistry M,D
Computer Engineering M
Computer Science M
Counselor Education M,D
Curriculum and Instruction M,D,O
Early Childhood Education M,D,O
Education—General M,D,O
Educational Administration M,D,O
Educational Media/Instructional Technology O
Electrical Engineering M
Engineering and Applied Sciences—General M,D
Engineering Management M
English M
Environmental Sciences M,D
Exercise and Sports Science M,O
History M
Human Resources Development M
Information Science M,O
Liberal Studies M
Linguistics M
Management Information Systems M,O
Mathematics M,D,O
Mechanical Engineering M
Medical Physics M,D
Medical/Surgical Nursing M
Music M
Nurse Anesthesia M,O
Nursing—General M,O
Physical Therapy M,D,O
Physics M,D
Public Policy and Administration M
Reading Education M,D,O
Software Engineering M
Special Education M
Statistics M,D,O
Systems Engineering M,D
Systems Science M

In-depth description on page 1013.

OBERLIN COLLEGE

Music M

OBLATE SCHOOL OF THEOLOGY

Pastoral Ministry and Counseling P,M,D
Theology P,M,D

OCCIDENTAL COLLEGE

Biological and Biomedical Sciences—General M
Education—General M
Elementary Education M
English Education M
Foreign Languages Education M
Mathematics Education M
Science Education M
Secondary Education M
Social Sciences Education M

OGI SCHOOL OF SCIENCE & ENGINEERING AT OREGON HEALTH & SCIENCE UNIVERSITY

Biochemistry M,D*
Business Administration and Management—General M,O*
Computer Engineering M,D,O
Computer Science M,D,O*
Electrical Engineering M,D*
Environmental Engineering M,D
Environmental Management and Policy M,D
Environmental Sciences M,D*
Management of Technology M,O
Mathematical and Computational Finance M,O*
Molecular Biology M,D

OGLALA LAKOTA COLLEGE

Business Administration and Management—General M
Educational Administration M

OGLETHORPE UNIVERSITY

Business Administration and Management—General M
Early Childhood Education M
Education—General M

OHIO COLLEGE OF PODIATRIC MEDICINE

Podiatric Medicine P

OHIO NORTHERN UNIVERSITY

Law P*
Pharmacy P

THE OHIO STATE UNIVERSITY

Accounting M,D
Aerospace/Aeronautical Engineering M,D
African Studies M
African-American Studies M
Agricultural Economics and Agribusiness M,D
Agricultural Education M,D
Agricultural Engineering M,D
Agricultural Sciences—General M,D
Agronomy and Soil Sciences M,D
Allied Health—General M
Allopathic Medicine P
Anatomy M,D
Anthropology M,D
Architecture M*
Art Education M,D
Art History M,D
Art/Fine Arts M
Arts Administration M
Asian Languages M,D
Astronomy M,D
Atmospheric Sciences M,D
Biochemistry M,D
Bioengineering M,D
Biological and Biomedical Sciences—General M,D
Biomedical Engineering M,D*
Biophysics M,D*
Biopsychology D
Biostatistics D
Business Administration and Management—General M,D
Cell Biology M,D
Chemical Engineering M,D
Chemistry M,D
Child and Family Studies M,D
City and Regional Planning M,D
Civil Engineering M,D
Classics M,D
Clinical Psychology D
Clothing and Textiles M,D
Cognitive Sciences D
Communication Disorders M,D
Communication—General M,D*
Computer Science M,D
Consumer Economics M,D
Counseling Psychology D
Dance M
Dentistry P
Developmental Biology M,D
Developmental Psychology D
East European and Russian Studies M,D,O
Ecology M,D
Economics M,D
Education—General M,D,O*
Educational Administration M,D,O
Electrical Engineering M,D*
Engineering and Applied Sciences—General M,D
English M,D
Entomology M,D
Environmental Sciences M,D
Evolutionary Biology M,D
Experimental Psychology D
Family and Consumer Sciences-General M,D
Food Science and Technology M,D
French M,D
Genetics M,D*
Geodetic Sciences M,D
Geography M,D
Geology M,D
German M,D
Health Services Management and Hospital Administration M
History M,D,O
Home Economics Education M
Horticulture M,D
Hospitality Management M,D
Human Development M,D
Human Resources Management M,D
Immunology M,D
Industrial and Labor Relations M,D
Industrial Design M
Industrial/Management Engineering M,D
Information Science M,D
Interdisciplinary Studies M
Interior Design M
Italian M,D
Journalism M
Landscape Architecture M
Latin American Studies M,D,O
Law P
Linguistics M,D
Management Information Systems M,D
Materials Engineering M,D
Materials Sciences M,D*
Mathematics M,D*
Mechanical Engineering M,D
Mechanics M,D
Medical Microbiology M,D
Medicinal and Pharmaceutical Chemistry M,D
Metallurgical Engineering and Metallurgy M,D
Microbiology M,D*
Molecular Biology M,D*
Music M,D
Natural Resources M,D
Near and Middle Eastern Languages M
Neuroscience D
Nuclear Engineering M,D
Nursing—General M,D*
Nutrition M,D
Optical Sciences M,D
Optometry P
Oral and Dental Sciences M,D
Pathobiology M,D
Pathology M
Pharmaceutical Administration M,D
Pharmaceutical Sciences M,D*
Pharmacology M,D
Pharmacy P
Philosophy M,D
Physical Chemistry M,D
Physical Education M,D
Physical Therapy M
Physics M,D
Physiology M,D
Plant Biology M,D
Plant Pathology M,D
Political Science M,D,O
Portuguese M,D
Psychology—General D
Public Health—General M,D
Public Policy and Administration M,D*
Rural Sociology M,D
Slavic Languages M,D,O
Social Psychology D
Social Work M,D
Sociology M,D
Spanish M,D
Statistics M,D*
Surveying Science and Engineering M,D
Systems Engineering M,D
Theater M,D
Toxicology M,D
Veterinary Medicine P
Veterinary Sciences M,D
Vocational and Technical Education D
Women's Studies M

OHIO UNIVERSITY

African Studies M
Art Education M
Art History M
Art/Fine Arts M
Artificial Intelligence/Robotics D
Asian Studies M
Biochemistry M,D
Biological and Biomedical Sciences—General M,D*
Business Administration and Management—General M*
Cell Biology M,D
Chemical Engineering M,D
Child and Family Studies M
Civil Engineering M
Clinical Psychology D
Communication Disorders M,D
Communication—General M,D
Comparative and Interdisciplinary Arts D*
Comparative Literature M
Computer Education M,D
Computer Science M,D
Counselor Education M,D
Curriculum and Instruction M,D
Economics M
Education of the Gifted M,D
Education—General M,D
Educational Administration M,D
Educational Measurement and Evaluation M,D
Educational Media/Instructional Technology M,D
Electrical Engineering M,D*
Elementary Education M,D
Engineering and Applied Sciences—General M,D
Engineering Management M,D
English as a Second Language M
English M,D
Environmental Biology M,D
Environmental Engineering M,D
Environmental Management and Policy M
Environmental Sciences M
Exercise and Sports Science M
Experimental Psychology D
Family and Consumer Sciences-General M
Film, Television, and Video Production M
Film, Television, and Video Theory and Criticism M
French M
Geography M
Geology M
Geotechnical Engineering M,D
Health Services Management and Hospital Administration M
Higher Education M,D
History M,D
Industrial and Organizational Psychology D
Industrial/Management Engineering M
Interdisciplinary Studies M,D
International Affairs M
International Development M
Journalism M,D
Latin American Studies M

- Linguistics M
- Manufacturing Engineering M,D
- Materials Sciences D
- Mathematics Education M,D
- Mathematics M,D*
- Mechanical Engineering M,D
- Media Studies M,D
- Microbiology M,D
- Middle School Education M,D
- Molecular Biology M,D*
- Music M
- Neuroscience M,D*
- Nutrition M
- Osteopathic Medicine P
- Philosophy M
- Photography M
- Physical Education M
- Physical Therapy M
- Physics M,D*
- Plant Biology M,D
- Political Science M
- Psychology—General D
- Public Policy and Administration M
- Reading Education M,D
- Recreation and Park Management M
- Rehabilitation Counseling M,D
- Social Sciences Education M,D
- Social Sciences M
- Social Work M
- Sociology M
- Spanish M
- Special Education M,D
- Speech and Interpersonal Communication M,D
- Sports Management M
- Structural Engineering M
- Student Personnel Services M,D
- Systems Engineering M
- Theater M
- Therapies—Dance, Drama, and Music M
- Water Resources Engineering M
- Zoology M,D

OHR HAMEIR THEOLOGICAL SEMINARY

- Theology

OKLAHOMA BAPTIST UNIVERSITY

- Marriage and Family Therapy M

OKLAHOMA CHRISTIAN UNIVERSITY

- Pastoral Ministry and Counseling M
- Theology M

OKLAHOMA CITY UNIVERSITY

- Accounting M
- Art/Fine Arts M
- Arts Administration M
- Business Administration and Management—General M
- Comparative Literature M
- Computer Science M
- Corporate and Organizational Communication M
- Criminal Justice and Criminology M
- Curriculum and Instruction M
- Early Childhood Education M
- Education—General M
- Elementary Education M
- English as a Second Language M
- Finance and Banking M
- Health Services Management and Hospital Administration M
- International Affairs M
- International Business M
- Law P
- Liberal Studies M
- Management Information Systems M
- Marketing M
- Music M
- Philosophy M
- Public Policy and Administration M
- Religion M
- Religious Education M
- Theater M
- Writing M

OKLAHOMA STATE UNIVERSITY

- Accounting M,D
- Agricultural Economics and Agribusiness M,D
- Agricultural Education M,D
- Agricultural Engineering M,D
- Agricultural Sciences—General M,D
- Agronomy and Soil Sciences M,D
- Animal Sciences M,D
- Applied Arts and Design—General M,D
- Applied Mathematics M,D
- Applied Science and Technology M
- Architectural Engineering M
- Architecture M
- Biochemistry M,D*
- Bioengineering M,D
- Botany M,D
- Business Administration and Management—General M,D*
- Chemical Engineering M,D
- Chemistry M,D
- Child and Family Studies M,D
- Civil Engineering M,D
- Clinical Psychology M,D
- Clothing and Textiles M,D
- Communication Disorders M
- Computer Education M,D
- Computer Engineering M,D
- Computer Science M,D*
- Counselor Education M,D
- Criminal Justice and Criminology M,D
- Curriculum and Instruction M,D
- Ecology M,D
- Economics M,D
- Education—General M,D,O
- Educational Administration M,D,O
- Educational Psychology M,D
- Electrical Engineering M,D*
- Engineering and Applied Sciences—General M,D*
- English M,D
- Entomology M,D
- Environmental Engineering M,D
- Environmental Sciences M,D
- Experimental Psychology M,D
- Family and Consumer Sciences-General M,D
- Finance and Banking M,D
- Food Science and Technology M,D
- Forestry M
- Genetics M,D
- Geography M
- Geology M
- Health Education M,D
- Higher Education M,D,O
- History M,D
- Horticulture M
- Hospitality Management M,D
- Industrial/Management Engineering M,D
- International Affairs M
- Landscape Architecture M
- Leisure Studies M,D
- Management Information Systems M,D
- Manufacturing Engineering M
- Marketing M,D
- Mass Communication M,D
- Mathematics M,D*
- Mechanical Engineering M,D
- Microbiology M,D
- Molecular Biology M,D
- Music M
- Natural Resources M,D
- Nutrition M,D
- Philosophy M,D
- Photonics M,D*
- Physical Education M,D
- Physics M,D*
- Plant Pathology M,D
- Plant Sciences D
- Political Science M
- Psychology—General M,D
- Public Policy and Administration M
- Sociology M,D
- Statistics M,D
- Student Personnel Services M,D
- Systems Engineering M
- Telecommunications Management M
- Theater M
- Veterinary Medicine P
- Veterinary Sciences M,D
- Vocational and Technical Education M,D,O
- Zoology M,D

In-depth description on page 1015.

OKLAHOMA STATE UNIVERSITY CENTER FOR HEALTH SCIENCES

- Biological and Biomedical Sciences—General D
- Osteopathic Medicine P

OLD DOMINION UNIVERSITY

- Accounting M
- Aerospace/Aeronautical Engineering M,D
- Allied Health—General M,D
- Analytical Chemistry M
- Art/Fine Arts M
- Biochemistry M
- Biological and Biomedical Sciences—General M,D
- Business Administration and Management—General M,D*
- Business Education M
- Chemistry M
- City and Regional Planning M
- Civil Engineering M,D
- Clinical Psychology D
- Communication Disorders M
- Community College Education M
- Community Health M
- Computer Engineering M,D
- Computer Science M,D
- Counselor Education M,O
- Dental Hygiene M
- Early Childhood Education M
- Ecology D
- Economics M
- Education—General M,D,O
- Educational Administration M,O
- Educational Media/Instructional Technology M
- Electrical Engineering M,D
- Electronic Commerce M
- Elementary Education M
- Engineering and Applied Sciences—General M,D*
- Engineering Management M,D
- English M
- Environmental and Occupational Health M
- Environmental Engineering M,D
- Geology M
- Health Promotion M
- Health Services Management and Hospital Administration M,D
- Higher Education M,O
- History M
- Humanities M
- Industrial and Organizational Psychology D
- International Affairs M,D
- International Development M
- Library Science M
- Linguistics M
- Manufacturing Engineering M,D
- Materials Engineering M
- Materials Sciences M
- Mathematics M,D*
- Mechanical Engineering M,D
- Mechanics M,D
- Middle School Education M
- Nursing—General M
- Oceanography M,D
- Operations Research M
- Organic Chemistry M
- Physical Chemistry M
- Physical Education M
- Physical Therapy D
- Physics M,D
- Psychology—General M
- Public Health—General M
- Public Policy and Administration M
- Reading Education M
- Recreation and Park Management M
- Secondary Education M
- Social Sciences M
- Sociology M
- Special Education M
- Sports Management M
- Systems Science M
- Taxation M
- Urban Education D
- Urban Studies M,D
- Writing M

In-depth description on page 1017.

OLIVET COLLEGE

- Education—General M

OLIVET NAZARENE UNIVERSITY

- Business Administration and Management—General M
- Curriculum and Instruction M
- Education—General M
- Elementary Education M
- Pastoral Ministry and Counseling M
- Religion M
- Secondary Education M
- Theology M

ORAL ROBERTS UNIVERSITY

- Accounting M
- Business Administration and Management—General M
- Curriculum and Instruction M,D
- Early Childhood Education M,D
- Education—General M,D
- Educational Administration M,D
- English as a Second Language M,D
- Finance and Banking M
- Human Resources Management M
- International Business M
- Marketing M
- Missions and Missiology P,M,D
- Nonprofit Management M
- Pastoral Ministry and Counseling P,M,D
- Religious Education P,M,D
- Theology P,M,D

OREGON COLLEGE OF ORIENTAL MEDICINE

- Acupuncture and Oriental Medicine M*

OREGON HEALTH & SCIENCE UNIVERSITY

- Advanced Practice Nursing M,O
- Allopathic Medicine P
- Biochemistry D*
- Biological and Biomedical Sciences—General M,D,O*
- Biopsychology M,D
- Biostatistics M
- Cell Biology D
- Community Health Nursing M,O
- Dentistry P
- Developmental Biology D
- Epidemiology M
- Genetics D*
- Gerontological Nursing M,D,O
- Immunology D
- Medical Informatics M,O*
- Medical/Surgical Nursing M,O
- Microbiology D*
- Molecular Biology D
- Neuroscience M,D*
- Nurse Midwifery M,O
- Nursing—General M,D,O
- Oral and Dental Sciences M,O
- Pediatric Nursing M,O
- Pharmacology D*
- Physiology D*
- Psychiatric Nursing M,O
- Women's Health Nursing M,O

OREGON STATE UNIVERSITY

- Adult Education M
- Agricultural Economics and Agribusiness M,D
- Agricultural Education M
- Agricultural Sciences—General M,D
- Agronomy and Soil Sciences M,D
- Analytical Chemistry M,D
- Animal Sciences M,D
- Anthropology M
- Atmospheric Sciences M,D
- Biochemistry M,D
- Bioengineering M,D
- Biometrics M,D
- Biophysics M,D*
- Botany M,D
- Business Administration and Management—General M,O
- Cell Biology D
- Chemical Engineering M,D
- Chemistry M,D
- Child and Family Studies M,D
- Civil Engineering M,D
- Clothing and Textiles M,D
- Computer Engineering M,D
- Computer Science M,D*
- Construction Engineering and Management M,D
- Counselor Education M,D
- Economics M,D*
- Education—General M,D
- Electrical Engineering M,D
- Elementary Education M
- Engineering and Applied Sciences—General M,D*
- English M
- Entomology M,D
- Environmental and Occupational Health M
- Environmental Engineering M,D
- Environmental Management and Policy M,D
- Environmental Sciences M,D
- Exercise and Sports Science M,D
- Family and Consumer Sciences-General M,D
- Fish, Game, and Wildlife Management M,D
- Food Science and Technology M,D
- Forestry M,D
- Genetics M,D
- Geography M,D
- Geology M,D
- Geophysics M,D
- Geosciences M,D
- Gerontology M
- Health Education M
- Health Physics/Radiological Health M,D
- Health Services Management and Hospital Administration M
- Horticulture M,D
- Human Development M,D
- Industrial/Management Engineering M,D
- Inorganic Chemistry M,D

Oregon State University (continued)

- Interdisciplinary Studies M
- Kinesiology and Movement Studies M
- Manufacturing Engineering M,D
- Marine Affairs M
- Marine Sciences M,D
- Materials Sciences M
- Mathematics Education M,D
- Mathematics M,D
- Mechanical Engineering M,D
- Microbiology M,D
- Molecular Biology D
- Music Education M
- Nuclear Engineering M,D*
- Nutrition M,D
- Ocean Engineering M
- Oceanography M,D
- Operations Research M,D
- Organic Chemistry M,D
- Paper and Pulp Engineering M,D
- Pathology M
- Pharmaceutical Sciences P,M,D
- Pharmacy P,M,D
- Physical Chemistry M,D
- Physical Education M
- Physics M,D*
- Plant Pathology M,D
- Plant Physiology M,D
- Public Health—General M
- Range Science M,D
- Science Education M,D
- Statistics M,D*
- Student Personnel Services M
- Toxicology M,D
- Veterinary Medicine P
- Veterinary Sciences M,D
- Vocational and Technical Education M
- Water Resources Engineering M,D
- Zoology M,D

OTIS COLLEGE OF ART AND DESIGN

- Art/Fine Arts M
- Photography M
- Writing M

OTTAWA UNIVERSITY

- Counseling Psychology M
- Education—General M
- Human Resources Development M
- Human Resources Management M

OTTERBEIN COLLEGE

- Advanced Practice Nursing M,O
- Business Administration and Management—General M
- Education—General M
- Medical/Surgical Nursing M,O
- Nursing and Healthcare Administration M,O
- Nursing—General M,O

OUR LADY OF HOLY CROSS COLLEGE

- Counselor Education M
- Curriculum and Instruction M
- Education—General M
- Educational Administration M
- Marriage and Family Therapy M

OUR LADY OF THE LAKE UNIVERSITY OF SAN ANTONIO

- Business Administration and Management—General M
- Communication Disorders M
- Counseling Psychology M,D
- Counselor Education M
- Curriculum and Instruction M,D
- Education—General M,D
- Educational Administration M,D
- Educational Media/Instructional Technology M
- English M
- Finance and Banking M
- Health Services Management and Hospital Administration M
- Human Development M
- International Business M
- Psychology—General M,D
- Social Work M
- Sociology M
- Special Education M

PACE UNIVERSITY

- Accounting M
- Business Administration and Management—General M*
- Clinical Psychology M,D
- Computer Science M,D,O*
- Curriculum and Instruction M,O
- Economics M
- Education—General M,O*
- Educational Administration M,O
- Finance and Banking M
- Forensic Sciences M
- Health Services Management and Hospital Administration M
- Information Science M,D,O
- International Business M
- Investment Management M
- Management Information Systems M
- Marketing Research M
- Marketing M
- Nursing—General M,O*
- Psychology—General M,D*
- Publishing M*
- School Psychology M,D
- Social Psychology M,D
- Taxation M
- Telecommunications M,D,O

In-depth description on page 1019 and announcement on page 472.

PACE UNIVERSITY, PLEASANTVILLE/ BRIARCLIFF CAMPUS

- Nursing—General M,O

PACE UNIVERSITY, WHITE PLAINS CAMPUS

- Accounting M
- Addictions/Substance Abuse Counseling M*
- Business Administration and Management—General M
- Computer Science M,D,O
- Curriculum and Instruction M,O
- Economics M
- Education—General M,O
- Educational Administration M,O
- Environmental Sciences M*
- Finance and Banking M
- Health Services Management and Hospital Administration M
- Information Science M,D,O
- International Business M
- Investment Management M
- Law P,M,D
- Legal and Justice Studies P,M,D
- Management Information Systems M
- Marketing Research M
- Marketing M
- Nonprofit Management M
- Psychology—General M
- Public Policy and Administration M*
- Taxation M
- Telecommunications M,D,O

PACIFICA GRADUATE INSTITUTE

- Clinical Psychology M,D
- Counseling Psychology M,D
- Psychology—General M,D*

PACIFIC COLLEGE OF ORIENTAL MEDICINE

- Acupuncture and Oriental Medicine M*

PACIFIC COLLEGE OF ORIENTAL MEDICINE-CHICAGO

- Acupuncture and Oriental Medicine M*

PACIFIC COLLEGE OF ORIENTAL MEDICINE-NEW YORK

- Acupuncture and Oriental Medicine M*

PACIFIC GRADUATE SCHOOL OF PSYCHOLOGY

- Clinical Psychology D
- Psychology—General M,D

PACIFIC LUTHERAN THEOLOGICAL SEMINARY

- Theology P,M,O

PACIFIC LUTHERAN UNIVERSITY

- Advanced Practice Nursing M
- Business Administration and Management—General M
- Curriculum and Instruction M
- Education—General M
- Educational Administration M
- Educational Media/Instructional Technology M
- Elementary Education M
- Management of Technology M
- Marriage and Family Therapy M
- Nursing and Healthcare Administration M
- Nursing—General M
- Reading Education M
- Secondary Education M
- Special Education M

In-depth description on page 1021.

PACIFIC OAKS COLLEGE

- Human Development M
- Marriage and Family Therapy M

PACIFIC SCHOOL OF RELIGION

- Religion P,M,D,O
- Theology P,M,D,O

PACIFIC STATES UNIVERSITY

- Computer Science M
- Finance and Banking M
- International Business M
- Management of Technology M

PACIFIC UNION COLLEGE

- Education—General M

PACIFIC UNIVERSITY

- Early Childhood Education M
- Education—General M
- Elementary Education M
- Middle School Education M
- Occupational Therapy M
- Optometry P
- Physical Therapy D
- Physician Assistant Studies M
- Psychology—General M,D
- Secondary Education M
- Vision Sciences M

PALM BEACH ATLANTIC UNIVERSITY

- Business Administration and Management—General M
- Counseling Psychology M
- Counselor Education M
- Education—General M
- Elementary Education M
- Human Resources Development M
- Marriage and Family Therapy M
- Organizational Management M
- Pharmacy P
- Theology M

PALMER COLLEGE OF CHIROPRACTIC

- Anatomy M
- Chiropractic P

PALMER COLLEGE OF CHIROPRACTIC WEST

- Chiropractic P

PARKER COLLEGE OF CHIROPRACTIC

- Chiropractic P*

PARK UNIVERSITY

- Business Administration and Management—General M
- Education—General M
- Nonprofit Management M
- Public Policy and Administration M

PAYNE THEOLOGICAL SEMINARY

- Theology P

PENNSYLVANIA ACADEMY OF THE FINE ARTS

- Art/Fine Arts M,O*

PENNSYLVANIA COLLEGE OF OPTOMETRY

- Communication Disorders M,D,O
- Optometry P
- Rehabilitation Sciences M,D,O
- Special Education M,D,O
- Vision Sciences M,D,O

THE PENNSYLVANIA STATE UNIVERSITY AT ERIE, THE BEHREND COLLEGE

- Business Administration and Management—General M
- Engineering and Applied Sciences—General M

THE PENNSYLVANIA STATE UNIVERSITY GREAT VALLEY CAMPUS

- Business Administration and Management—General M,O
- Curriculum and Instruction M
- Education—General M
- Educational Media/Instructional Technology M
- Information Science M
- Software Engineering M
- Special Education M
- Systems Engineering M

THE PENNSYLVANIA STATE UNIVERSITY HARRISBURG CAMPUS OF THE CAPITAL COLLEGE

- Adult Education D
- American Studies M
- Business Administration and Management—General M*
- Clinical Psychology M
- Computer Science M
- Curriculum and Instruction M
- Education—General M,D
- Electrical Engineering M
- Engineering and Applied Sciences—General M
- Environmental Engineering M
- Environmental Sciences M
- Health Education M
- Health Services Management and Hospital Administration M
- Humanities M
- Management Information Systems M
- Psychology—General M
- Public Policy and Administration M,D
- Social Psychology M

In-depth description on page 1023.

THE PENNSYLVANIA STATE UNIVERSITY MILTON S. HERSHEY MEDICAL CENTER

- Allopathic Medicine P
- Anatomy M,D
- Biochemistry M,D
- Bioengineering M,D
- Biological and Biomedical Sciences—General M,D*
- Cell Biology M,D
- Genetics M,D
- Health Services Research M
- Immunology M,D
- Microbiology M,D
- Molecular Biology M,D
- Neuroscience M,D
- Pharmacology M,D
- Physiology M,D
- Veterinary Sciences M
- Virology M,D

THE PENNSYLVANIA STATE UNIVERSITY UNIVERSITY PARK CAMPUS

- Accounting M,D
- Acoustics M,D
- Adult Education M,D
- Aerospace/Aeronautical Engineering M,D*
- Agricultural Economics and Agribusiness M,D
- Agricultural Education M,D
- Agricultural Engineering M,D
- Agricultural Sciences—General M,D*
- Agronomy and Soil Sciences M,D
- Animal Sciences M,D
- Anthropology M,D
- Applied Mathematics M,D
- Architectural Engineering M,D*
- Architecture M
- Art Education M,D
- Art History M,D
- Art/Fine Arts M
- Astronomy M,D
- Astrophysics M,D
- Biochemistry M,D*
- Bioengineering M,D*
- Biological and Biomedical Sciences—General M,D*
- Biomedical Engineering M,D
- Biopsychology M,D*
- Biotechnology M,D
- Business Administration and Management—General M,D
- Cell Biology M,D*
- Ceramic Sciences and Engineering M,D
- Chemical Engineering M,D
- Chemistry M,D
- Child and Family Studies M,D
- City and Regional Planning M
- Civil Engineering M,D
- Clinical Psychology M,D
- Cognitive Sciences M,D
- Communication Disorders M,D
- Communication—General M,D*
- Comparative Literature M,D
- Computer Engineering M,D
- Computer Science M,D*
- Counseling Psychology D
- Counselor Education M,D
- Criminal Justice and Criminology M,D
- Curriculum and Instruction M,D
- Developmental Biology M,D
- Developmental Psychology M,D
- Early Childhood Education M,D
- Ecology M,D*
- Economics M,D
- Education—General M,D
- Educational Administration M,D

Educational Media/Instructional Technology M,D
Educational Psychology M,D
Electrical Engineering M,D
Elementary Education M,D
Engineering and Applied Sciences—General M,D*
Engineering Management M
English as a Second Language M
English M,D
Entomology M,D
Environmental Engineering M,D
Environmental Management and Policy M
Environmental Sciences M
Evolutionary Biology M,D
Finance and Banking M,D
Fish, Game, and Wildlife Management M,D
Food Science and Technology M,D
Foreign Languages Education M,D
Forestry M,D
Foundations and Philosophy of Education M,D
French M,D
Genetics M,D*
Geochemistry M,D
Geography M,D
Geology M,D
Geophysics M,D
Geosciences M,D*
Geotechnical Engineering M,D
German M,D
Graphic Design M
Health Services Management and Hospital Administration M,D*
Higher Education M,D
History M,D
Horticulture M,D
Hospitality Management M,D
Human Development M,D*
Human Resources Development M
Industrial and Labor Relations M
Industrial and Manufacturing Management M,D
Industrial and Organizational Psychology M,D
Industrial/Management Engineering M,D
Information Science D
Insurance M,D
Kinesiology and Movement Studies M,D
Landscape Architecture M
Leisure Studies M,D
Linguistics M,D
Logistics M,D
Management Information Systems M
Manufacturing Engineering M
Marketing M,D
Mass Communication M,D
Materials Engineering M,D
Materials Sciences M,D
Mathematics M,D*
Mechanical Engineering M,D
Mechanics M,D
Media Studies M
Metallurgical Engineering and Metallurgy M,D
Meteorology M,D
Microbiology M,D
Mineral/Mining Engineering M,D
Molecular Biology M,D
Molecular Medicine M,D
Multilingual and Multicultural Education M,D
Music Education M,D
Music M
Neuroscience M,D
Nuclear Engineering M,D
Nursing—General M,D
Nutrition M,D
Pathobiology M,D*
Petroleum Engineering M,D
Philosophy M,D
Photography M
Physics M,D*
Physiology M,D
Plant Pathology M,D
Plant Physiology M,D*
Political Science M,D
Polymer Science and Engineering M,D
Psychology—General M,D
Quality Management M
Reading Education M,D
Real Estate M,D
Rural Sociology M,D
Russian M
School Psychology M,D
Science Education M,D
Social Psychology M,D
Social Sciences Education M,D
Sociology M,D
Spanish M,D
Special Education M,D
Speech and Interpersonal Communication M,D
Statistics M,D
Structural Engineering M,D
Telecommunications M
Theater M
Transportation and Highway Engineering M,D
Veterinary Sciences M,D
Vocational and Technical Education M,D
Water Resources Engineering M,D
Writing M,D

In-depth description on page 1025.

PEPPERDINE UNIVERSITY

Business Administration and Management—General M
Clinical Psychology M
Education—General M,D*
Educational Administration M,D
Educational Media/Instructional Technology M,D
Management of Technology M
Organizational Management M
Psychology—General M,D*

In-depth description on page 1027.

PEPPERDINE UNIVERSITY

American Studies M
Business Administration and Management—General M*
Communication—General M
Conflict Resolution and Mediation/Peace Studies M
History M
International Business M
Law P
Public Policy and Administration M*
Religion P,M

PERU STATE COLLEGE

Education—General M

PFEIFFER UNIVERSITY

Business Administration and Management—General M
Organizational Management M
Religious Education M

PHILADELPHIA BIBLICAL UNIVERSITY

Curriculum and Instruction M
Education—General M
Educational Administration M
Organizational Management M
Pastoral Ministry and Counseling M
Theology M

PHILADELPHIA COLLEGE OF OSTEOPATHIC MEDICINE

Biological and Biomedical Sciences—General M
Clinical Psychology M,D
Health Psychology M,D
Industrial and Organizational Psychology M,D
Osteopathic Medicine P
Physician Assistant Studies M*
Psychology—General M,D*

PHILADELPHIA UNIVERSITY

Accounting M
Business Administration and Management—General M
Clothing and Textiles M
Computer Education M
Finance and Banking M
Health Services Management and Hospital Administration M
International Business M
Management Information Systems M
Marketing M
Nurse Midwifery M
Occupational Therapy M
Physician Assistant Studies M
Taxation M
Textile Design M
Textile Sciences and Engineering M

PHILLIPS GRADUATE INSTITUTE

Counselor Education M
Marriage and Family Therapy M,D
Organizational Behavior M

PHILLIPS THEOLOGICAL SEMINARY

Pastoral Ministry and Counseling D
Theology P,M,D

PICOWER GRADUATE SCHOOL OF MOLECULAR MEDICINE

Molecular Medicine D

PIEDMONT BAPTIST COLLEGE

Pastoral Ministry and Counseling M
Theology M

PIEDMONT COLLEGE

Business Administration and Management—General M
Curriculum and Instruction M,O
Early Childhood Education M,O
Education—General M,O
Public Policy and Administration M
Secondary Education M,O

PIKEVILLE COLLEGE

Osteopathic Medicine P

PITTSBURGH THEOLOGICAL SEMINARY

Theology P,M,D

PITTSBURG STATE UNIVERSITY

Accounting M
Applied Physics M
Art Education M
Art/Fine Arts M
Biological and Biomedical Sciences—General M
Business Administration and Management—General M
Chemistry M
Communication—General M
Community College Education O
Counselor Education M
Early Childhood Education M
Education—General M,O
Educational Administration M
Educational Media/Instructional Technology M
Elementary Education M
Engineering and Applied Sciences—General M
English M
Higher Education M,O
History M
Human Resources Development M,O
Mathematics M
Music Education M
Music M
Nursing—General M
Physical Education M
Physics M
Psychology—General M
Reading Education M
School Psychology O
Secondary Education M
Social Sciences M
Special Education M
Theater M
Vocational and Technical Education M,O

PLATTSBURGH STATE UNIVERSITY OF NEW YORK

Communication Disorders M
Counselor Education M,O
Curriculum and Instruction M
Educational Administration O
Elementary Education M
English Education M
Foreign Languages Education M
Liberal Studies M
Mathematics Education M
Psychology—General M,O
Reading Education M
School Psychology M,O
Science Education M
Secondary Education M
Social Sciences Education M
Special Education M

PLYMOUTH STATE COLLEGE

Business Administration and Management—General M*
Counselor Education M
Education—General M,O*
Educational Administration M
Elementary Education M
English Education M
Health Education M
Mathematics Education M
Physical Education M
Reading Education M
Secondary Education M
Special Education M,O

POINT LOMA NAZARENE UNIVERSITY

Business Administration and Management—General M
Education—General M,O
Religion M

POINT PARK COLLEGE

Business Administration and Management—General M
Communication—General M*
Curriculum and Instruction M
Education—General M
Engineering Management M
Journalism M
Mass Communication M

POLYTECHNIC UNIVERSITY, BROOKLYN CAMPUS

Aerospace/Aeronautical Engineering M
Business Administration and Management—General M
Chemical Engineering M,D
Chemistry M,D
Civil Engineering M,D
Computer Engineering M
Computer Science M,D*
Electrical Engineering M,D*
Environmental and Occupational Health M
Environmental Engineering M
Environmental Sciences M
Financial Engineering M
History of Science and Technology M
Industrial and Manufacturing Management M
Industrial/Management Engineering M
Information Science M
Journalism M
Management of Technology M
Manufacturing Engineering M
Materials Sciences M
Mathematics M,D
Mechanical Engineering M,D
Organizational Behavior M
Physics M,D
Polymer Science and Engineering M
Systems Engineering M
Technical Writing M
Telecommunications Management M
Telecommunications M
Transportation and Highway Engineering M
Transportation Management M

POLYTECHNIC UNIVERSITY, LONG ISLAND GRADUATE CENTER

Aerospace/Aeronautical Engineering M
Business Administration and Management—General M
Chemical Engineering M,D
Chemistry M,D
Civil Engineering M,D
Computer Engineering M
Computer Science M,D
Electrical Engineering M,D
Engineering Physics M
Environmental Engineering M
Financial Engineering M
Industrial and Manufacturing Management M
Industrial/Management Engineering M
Information Science M
Manufacturing Engineering M
Mathematics M,D
Mechanical Engineering M,D
Organizational Behavior M
Physics M,D
Systems Engineering M
Telecommunications M
Transportation and Highway Engineering M

POLYTECHNIC UNIVERSITY OF PUERTO RICO

Business Administration and Management—General M
Civil Engineering M
Engineering Management M
Environmental Management and Policy M
Industrial and Manufacturing Management M
Manufacturing Engineering M

POLYTECHNIC UNIVERSITY, WESTCHESTER GRADUATE CENTER

Business Administration and Management—General M
Chemical Engineering M
Chemistry M
Civil Engineering M,D
Computer Engineering M
Computer Science M,D

Polytechnic University, Westchester Graduate Center (continued)

Electrical Engineering M,D
Engineering Physics M
Environmental Engineering M
Financial Engineering M
Industrial and Manufacturing Management M
Industrial/Management Engineering M
Information Science M
Manufacturing Engineering M
Materials Sciences M
Organizational Behavior M
Systems Engineering M
Telecommunications M
Transportation Management M

PONCE SCHOOL OF MEDICINE

Allopathic Medicine P
Biological and Biomedical Sciences—General D
Clinical Psychology D
Health Psychology D
Psychology—General D

PONTIFICAL CATHOLIC UNIVERSITY OF PUERTO RICO

Accounting M,D
Business Administration and Management—General M,D
Chemistry M
Clinical Psychology M,D
Criminal Justice and Criminology M,D
Curriculum and Instruction M,D
Education—General M,D
Educational Media/Instructional Technology M,D
English as a Second Language M,D
Finance and Banking M,D
Hispanic Studies M
History M
Human Resources Management M,D
Human Services M,D
Industrial and Organizational Psychology M,D
Law P
Marketing M,D
Maternal/Child Nursing M
Medical/Surgical Nursing M
Nursing—General M
Psychiatric Nursing M
Psychology—General M,D
Public Policy and Administration M,D
Religious Education M,D
School Psychology M,D
Social Work M,D
Theology M

PONTIFICAL COLLEGE JOSEPHINUM

Theology P,M

PORTLAND STATE UNIVERSITY

Adult Education D
Anthropology M,D
Applied Economics M,D
Art/Fine Arts M
Biological and Biomedical Sciences—General M,D
Business Administration and Management—General M,D
Chemistry M,D
City and Regional Planning M,D
Civil Engineering M,D*
Communication Disorders M
Computer Engineering M,D*
Computer Science M*
Counselor Education M
Criminal Justice and Criminology M,D
Curriculum and Instruction M,D
Early Childhood Education M
Economics M,D
Education—General M,D
Educational Administration M,D
Educational Media/Instructional Technology M
Electrical Engineering M,D
Elementary Education M
Engineering and Applied Sciences—General M,D,O*
Engineering Management M,D*
English as a Second Language M
English Education M
English M
Environmental Management and Policy M,D
Environmental Sciences M,D
Finance and Banking M
French M
Geography M,D
Geology M,D
German M
Gerontology O
Health Education M
Health Promotion M
Health Services Management and Hospital Administration M
Higher Education D
History M
International Business M
Management of Technology M,D
Manufacturing Engineering M
Mathematics Education M,D
Mathematics M,D
Mechanical Engineering M,D*
Music Education M
Music M
Physics M,D
Political Science M,D
Psychology—General M,D
Public Health—General M
Public Policy and Administration M,D
Reading Education M
Science Education M,D
Secondary Education M
Social Sciences Education M
Social Work M,D
Sociology M,D
Spanish M
Special Education M
Speech and Interpersonal Communication M
Systems Engineering M,O*
Systems Science D
Theater M
Urban Studies M,D

PRAIRIE VIEW A&M UNIVERSITY

Agricultural Economics and Agribusiness M
Agricultural Sciences—General M
Agronomy and Soil Sciences M
Animal Sciences M
Biological and Biomedical Sciences—General M
Business Administration and Management—General M
Chemistry M
Counselor Education M
Curriculum and Instruction M
Education—General M
Educational Administration M
Engineering and Applied Sciences—General M
English M
Family and Consumer Sciences-General M
Forensic Psychology M,D
Health Education M
Legal and Justice Studies M,D
Marriage and Family Therapy M
Mathematics M
Nursing—General M
Physical Education M
Sociology M
Special Education M
Urban Design M

PRATT INSTITUTE

Applied Arts and Design—General M
Architecture M*
Art Education M
Art History M
Art Therapy M
Art/Fine Arts M*
Arts Administration M
City and Regional Planning M
Facilities Management M
Graphic Design M
Industrial Design M
Information Studies M,O*
Interior Design M
Internet and Interactive Multimedia M
Library Science M,O
Photography M
Special Education M
Therapies—Dance, Drama, and Music M
Urban Design M

PRESCOTT COLLEGE

Counseling Psychology M
Education—General M
English as a Second Language M
Environmental Education M
Environmental Management and Policy M
History M
Humanities M
Multilingual and Multicultural Education M
Sustainable Development M

In-depth description on page 1029.

PRINCETON THEOLOGICAL SEMINARY

Religion P,M,D
Theology P,M,D

PRINCETON UNIVERSITY

Aerospace/Aeronautical Engineering M,D*
African-American Studies D
Anthropology D
Applied Mathematics M,D*
Applied Physics M,D
Archaeology D
Architecture M,D*
Asian Studies D
Astrophysics D
Atmospheric Sciences D
Biological and Biomedical Sciences—General D
Biophysics D*
Cell Biology D
Chemical Engineering M,D
Chemistry M,D*
City and Regional Planning M,D
Civil Engineering M,D*
Classics D
Community College Education D
Comparative Literature D
Computational Sciences D
Computer Engineering M,D
Computer Science M,D*
Demography and Population Studies D
Developmental Biology D
Ecology D*
Economics D
Electrical Engineering M,D
Electronic Materials M,D*
Engineering and Applied Sciences—General M,D
English D
Environmental Engineering D
Environmental Management and Policy M,D
Evolutionary Biology D
Financial Engineering M,D
French D
Geology D
Geophysics D
Geosciences D
German D
History of Science and Technology D
History D
Information Science M,D
International Affairs M,D
Latin American Studies D
Materials Sciences
Mathematical Physics D
Mathematics D
Mechanical Engineering M,D
Molecular Biology D*
Music D
Near and Middle Eastern Studies M,D
Neuroscience D
Oceanography D
Operations Research M,D
Philosophy D
Photonics
Physical Chemistry M,D
Physics D
Plasma Physics D
Political Science D
Polymer Science and Engineering M,D
Psychology—General D
Public Policy and Administration M,D
Religion D
Slavic Languages D
Social Sciences Education D
Sociology D
Spanish D
Statistics M,D
Structural Engineering M,D
Transportation and Highway Engineering M,D
Water Resources Engineering D

THE PROTESTANT EPISCOPAL THEOLOGICAL SEMINARY IN VIRGINIA

Theology P,M,D

PROVIDENCE COLLEGE

Business Administration and Management—General M*
Computer Education M
Counselor Education M
Education—General M
Educational Administration M
History M
Mathematics Education M
Pastoral Ministry and Counseling M
Reading Education M
Religion M
Special Education M
Theology M

PROVIDENCE COLLEGE AND THEOLOGICAL SEMINARY

English as a Second Language P,M,D,O
Missions and Missiology P,M,D,O
Pastoral Ministry and Counseling P,M,D,O
Religious Education P,M,D,O
Theology P,M,D,O

PURCHASE COLLEGE, STATE UNIVERSITY OF NEW YORK

Art History M
Art/Fine Arts M
Dance M
Music M
Theater M

PURDUE UNIVERSITY

Accounting M,D
Aerospace/Aeronautical Engineering M,D*
Agricultural Economics and Agribusiness M*
Agricultural Education M,D,O
Agricultural Engineering M,D
Agricultural Sciences—General M,D
Agronomy and Soil Sciences M,D
American Studies M,D
Analytical Chemistry M,D
Anatomy M,D
Animal Sciences M,D
Anthropology M,D
Applied Arts and Design—General M
Aquaculture M,D
Art Education M,D,O
Art/Fine Arts M
Atmospheric Sciences M,D
Bacteriology M,D
Biochemistry M,D*
Bioengineering M,D
Biological and Biomedical Sciences—General M,D
Biomedical Engineering M,D*
Biophysics D
Botany M,D*
Business Administration and Management—General M,D
Cell Biology D
Chemical Engineering M,D
Chemistry M,D
Child and Family Studies M,D
Civil Engineering M,D
Clothing and Textiles M,D
Communication Disorders M,D*
Communication—General M,D
Comparative Literature M,D
Computer Engineering M,D*
Computer Science M,D*
Consumer Economics M,D
Counselor Education M,D,O
Curriculum and Instruction M,D,O
Developmental Biology D
Ecology M,D
Economics M,D
Education of the Gifted M,D,O
Education—General M,D,O
Educational Administration M,D,O
Educational Media/Instructional Technology M,D,O
Educational Psychology M,D,O
Electrical Engineering M,D*
Elementary Education M,D,O
Engineering and Applied Sciences—General M,D*
English Education M,D,O
English M,D
Entomology M,D
Environmental and Occupational Health M,D
Environmental Management and Policy M,D
Epidemiology M,D
Ergonomics and Human Factors M,D
Evolutionary Biology M,D
Exercise and Sports Science M,D
Family and Consumer Sciences-General M,D
Finance and Banking M,D
Fish, Game, and Wildlife Management M,D
Food Science and Technology M,D
Foreign Languages Education M,D,O
Forestry M,D*
Foundations and Philosophy of Education M,D,O
French M,D
Genetics M,D*
Geosciences M,D
German M,D
Health Physics/Radiological Health M,D
Health Promotion M,D
Higher Education M,D,O
History M,D
Home Economics Education M,D,O
Horticulture M,D
Hospitality Management M,D*
Human Development M,D
Human Resources Management M,D
Immunology M,D
Industrial and Manufacturing Management M,D

Industrial Hygiene M,D
Industrial/Management Engineering M,D
Inorganic Chemistry M,D
Linguistics M,D
Management Information Systems M,D
Management Strategy and Policy M,D
Manufacturing Engineering M,D
Marketing M,D
Marriage and Family Therapy M,D
Materials Engineering M,D
Mathematical and Computational Finance M,D
Mathematics Education M,D,O
Mathematics M,D
Mechanical Engineering M,D*
Medical Physics M,D
Medicinal and Pharmaceutical Chemistry M,D
Metallurgical Engineering and Metallurgy M,D
Microbiology M,D
Molecular Biology M,D*
Natural Resources M,D
Neurobiology M,D
Neuroscience D
Nuclear Engineering M,D
Nutrition M,D*
Operations Research M,D
Organic Chemistry M,D
Organizational Behavior M,D
Parasitology M,D
Pathobiology M,D
Pathology M,D
Pharmaceutical Sciences M,D
Pharmacology M,D
Pharmacy P
Philosophy M,D
Physical Chemistry M,D
Physical Education M,D
Physics M,D
Physiology M,D
Plant Biology D
Plant Pathology M,D
Plant Physiology D
Political Science M,D
Psychology—General D
Public Health—General M,D
Quantitative Analysis M,D
Reading Education M,D,O
Recreation and Park Management M,D
Science Education M,D,O
Social Sciences Education M,D,O
Sociology M,D
Spanish M,D
Special Education M,D,O
Sport Psychology M,D
Statistics M,D*
Systems Engineering M,D
Theater M
Toxicology M,D
Travel and Tourism M,D
Veterinary Medicine P
Veterinary Sciences M,D
Virology M,D
Vocational and Technical Education M,D,O
Writing M,D

PURDUE UNIVERSITY CALUMET

Accounting M
Biological and Biomedical Sciences—General M
Business Administration and Management—General M
Communication—General M
Counselor Education M
Curriculum and Instruction M
Education—General M
Educational Administration M
Educational Media/Instructional Technology M
Elementary Education M
Engineering and Applied Sciences—General M
English M
History M
Marriage and Family Therapy M
Mathematics M
Nursing—General M
Political Science M
Science Education M
Secondary Education M

PURDUE UNIVERSITY NORTH CENTRAL

Education—General M
Elementary Education M

QUEENS COLLEGE OF THE CITY UNIVERSITY OF NEW YORK

Accounting M
Art Education M,O
Art History M
Art/Fine Arts M
Biochemistry M
Biological and Biomedical Sciences—General M
Chemistry M
Clinical Psychology M
Communication Disorders M
Computer Science M
Counselor Education M
Education—General M,O
Educational Administration O
Elementary Education M,O
English as a Second Language M
English Education M,O
English M
Environmental Sciences M
Exercise and Sports Science M
Family and Consumer Sciences-General M
Foreign Languages Education M,O
French M
Geology M
History M
Home Economics Education M
Information Studies M,O
Italian M
Liberal Studies M
Library Science M,O
Linguistics M
Mathematics Education M,O
Mathematics M
Media Studies M
Multilingual and Multicultural Education M,O
Music Education M,O
Music M
Physical Education M
Physics M
Psychology—General M
Reading Education M
School Psychology M,O
Science Education M,O
Secondary Education M,O
Social Sciences Education M,O
Social Sciences M
Sociology M
Spanish M
Special Education M
Urban Studies M
Writing M

In-depth description on page 1031.

QUEEN'S UNIVERSITY AT KINGSTON

Allopathic Medicine P
Anatomy M,D
Art History M,D
Biochemistry M,D
Biological and Biomedical Sciences—General M,D
Business Administration and Management—General M
Cell Biology M,D
Chemical Engineering M,D
Chemistry M,D
City and Regional Planning M
Civil Engineering M,D
Classics M
Clinical Psychology M,D
Cognitive Sciences M,D
Computer Engineering M,D
Computer Science M,D
Developmental Psychology M,D
Economics M,D
Education—General M,D
Electrical Engineering M,D
Engineering and Applied Sciences—General M,D
English M,D
Epidemiology M
Exercise and Sports Science M,D
Experimental Psychology M,D
French M,D
Geography M,D
Geology M,D
German M,D
Historic Preservation M
History M,D
Immunology M,D
Industrial and Labor Relations M
Information Science M,D
Law P,M
Mathematics M,D
Mechanical Engineering M,D
Microbiology M,D
Mineral/Mining Engineering M,D
Nursing—General M
Pathology M,D
Pharmacology M,D
Philosophy M,D
Physics M,D
Physiology M,D
Political Science M,D
Psychology—General M,D
Public Policy and Administration M
Rehabilitation Sciences M,D
Religion M
Social Psychology M,D
Sociology M,D
Spanish M
Sport Psychology M,D
Statistics M,D
Theology P,M
Toxicology M,D

QUEENS UNIVERSITY OF CHARLOTTE

Business Administration and Management—General M
Corporate and Organizational Communication M
Education—General M
Elementary Education M
Nursing and Healthcare Administration M
Nursing—General M
Writing M

QUINCY UNIVERSITY

Business Administration and Management—General M
Education—General M

QUINNIPIAC UNIVERSITY

Accounting M*
Advanced Practice Nursing M
Allied Health—General M
Biological and Biomedical Sciences—General M
Business Administration and Management—General M*
Cell Biology M
Clinical Laboratory Sciences/Medical Technology M*
Communication—General M
Economics M
Education—General M*
Elementary Education M
English Education M
Finance and Banking M
Foreign Languages Education M
Forensic Nursing M*
Health Services Management and Hospital Administration M*
International Business M
Internet and Interactive Multimedia M*
Journalism M*
Law P*
Management Information Systems M*
Marketing M
Mathematics Education M
Microbiology M
Middle School Education M
Molecular Biology M*
Nursing—General M*
Pathology M
Physical Therapy M*
Physician Assistant Studies M*
Science Education M
Secondary Education M
Social Sciences Education M

In-depth description on page 1033.

RABBI ISAAC ELCHANAN THEOLOGICAL SEMINARY

Theology O

RABBINICAL ACADEMY MESIVTA RABBI CHAIM BERLIN

Theology O

RABBINICAL COLLEGE BETH SHRAGA

Theology

RABBINICAL COLLEGE BOBOVER YESHIVA B'NEI ZION

Theology

RABBINICAL COLLEGE CH'SAN SOFER

Theology

RABBINICAL COLLEGE OF LONG ISLAND

Theology

RABBINICAL SEMINARY M'KOR CHAIM

Theology

RABBINICAL SEMINARY OF AMERICA

Theology

RADFORD UNIVERSITY

Art Education M
Art/Fine Arts M
Business Administration and Management—General M
Clinical Psychology M,O
Communication Disorders M
Corporate and Organizational Communication M
Counseling Psychology M,O
Counselor Education M
Criminal Justice and Criminology M
Curriculum and Instruction M
Education—General M
Educational Administration M
Educational Media/Instructional Technology M
English M
Geosciences M
Industrial and Organizational Psychology M,O
Music Education M
Music M
Nursing—General M
Psychology—General M,O
Reading Education M
School Psychology O
Social Work M
Special Education M

In-depth description on page 1035.

RAMAPO COLLEGE OF NEW JERSEY

Liberal Studies M

RAND GRADUATE SCHOOL OF POLICY STUDIES

Public Policy and Administration D*

RECONSTRUCTIONIST RABBINICAL COLLEGE

Theology P,M,D,O

REED COLLEGE

Liberal Studies M

REFORMED PRESBYTERIAN THEOLOGICAL SEMINARY

Theology P,M

REFORMED THEOLOGICAL SEMINARY (FL)

Pastoral Ministry and Counseling P,M,D
Religion P,M,D
Theology P,M,D

REFORMED THEOLOGICAL SEMINARY (MD)

Religion M

REFORMED THEOLOGICAL SEMINARY (MS)

Marriage and Family Therapy P,M,D,O
Missions and Missiology P,M,D,O
Pastoral Ministry and Counseling P,M,D,O
Religious Education P,M,D,O
Theology P,M,D,O

REFORMED THEOLOGICAL SEMINARY (NC)

Missions and Missiology P,M,D
Pastoral Ministry and Counseling P,M,D
Religion P,M,D
Religious Education P,M,D
Theology P,M,D

REGENT COLLEGE

Theology P,M,O

REGENT UNIVERSITY

Business Administration and Management—General M
Communication—General M,D
Counseling Psychology M,D
Counselor Education M,D
Education—General M,D,O
Journalism M
Law P,M
Management Strategy and Policy M,D,O
Media Studies M
Missions and Missiology P,M,D
Organizational Management M,D,O
Public Policy and Administration M
Taxation P,M
Theater M
Theology P,M,D

In-depth description on page 1037 and announcement on page 490.

REGIS COLLEGE (CANADA)

Pastoral Ministry and Counseling P,M,D,O
Theology P,M,D,O

REGIS COLLEGE (MA)
- Business Administration and Management—General M
- Education—General M
- Nursing—General M,O
- Organizational Management M

REGIS UNIVERSITY
- Accounting M,O
- Adult Education M,O
- Allied Health—General M,D
- Business Administration and Management—General M,O
- Communication—General M,O
- Computer Science M,O
- Counseling Psychology M,O
- Education—General M,O
- Electronic Commerce M,O
- Finance and Banking M,O
- Human Resources Management M,O
- Industrial and Manufacturing Management M,O
- Information Science M,O
- International Business M,O
- Internet and Interactive Multimedia M,O
- Liberal Studies M,O
- Management Information Systems M,O
- Marketing M,O
- Nonprofit Management M,O
- Nursing—General M
- Organizational Management M,O
- Physical Therapy D*
- Project Management M,O
- Psychology—General M,O
- Social Sciences M,O
- Technical Writing M,O
- Telecommunications Management M,O
- Telecommunications M,O

In-depth description on page 1039 and announcement on page 491.

RENSSELAER AT HARTFORD
- Computer Engineering M
- Computer Science M
- Electrical Engineering M
- Engineering and Applied Sciences—General M
- Mechanical Engineering M
- Systems Science M

RENSSELAER POLYTECHNIC INSTITUTE
- Acoustics M
- Aerospace/Aeronautical Engineering M,D*
- Analytical Chemistry M,D
- Applied Mathematics M*
- Applied Physics M,D
- Applied Science and Technology M
- Architectural Engineering M
- Architecture M*
- Art/Fine Arts M*
- Astrophysics M,D
- Biochemistry M,D
- Bioinformatics M*
- Biological and Biomedical Sciences—General M,D*
- Biomedical Engineering M,D*
- Biophysics M,D
- Building Science M
- Business Administration and Management—General M,D*
- Cell Biology M,D
- Ceramic Sciences and Engineering M,D
- Chemical Engineering M,D*
- Chemistry M,D*
- Civil Engineering M,D*
- Communication—General M,D*
- Computer Art and Design M
- Computer Engineering M,D
- Computer Science M,D*
- Developmental Biology M,D
- Economics M*
- Electrical Engineering M,D*
- Electronic Commerce M,D*
- Energy and Power Engineering M,D*
- Engineering and Applied Sciences—General M,D*
- Engineering Management M,D*
- Engineering Physics M,D
- Entrepreneurship M,D
- Environmental Engineering M,D*
- Environmental Management and Policy M,D*
- Environmental Sciences M,D
- Ergonomics and Human Factors M
- Finance and Banking M,D
- Geochemistry M,D
- Geology M,D
- Geophysics M,D
- Geosciences M,D*
- Geotechnical Engineering M,D
- Historic Preservation M
- History of Science and Technology M,D
- Hydrology M
- Industrial and Manufacturing Management M,D
- Industrial and Organizational Psychology M
- Industrial/Management Engineering M*
- Information Science M*
- Inorganic Chemistry M,D
- Management Information Systems M,D
- Management of Technology M,D
- Manufacturing Engineering M
- Marketing M,D
- Materials Engineering M,D
- Materials Sciences M,D*
- Mathematics M,D*
- Mechanical Engineering M,D
- Mechanics M,D
- Metallurgical Engineering and Metallurgy M,D
- Microbiology M,D
- Molecular Biology M,D
- Nuclear Engineering M,D
- Operations Research M,D
- Organic Chemistry M,D
- Philosophy M*
- Physical Chemistry M,D
- Physics M,D*
- Planetary and Space Sciences M,D
- Polymer Science and Engineering M,D
- Psychology—General M*
- Rhetoric M,D
- Speech and Interpersonal Communication M,D
- Statistics M*
- Structural Engineering M,D
- Systems Engineering M,D
- Technical Writing M
- Technology and Public Policy M,D*
- Transportation and Highway Engineering M,D

In-depth description on page 1041.

RESEARCH COLLEGE OF NURSING
- Advanced Practice Nursing M
- Nursing—General M

RHODE ISLAND COLLEGE
- Art Education M
- Art/Fine Arts M
- Biological and Biomedical Sciences—General M
- Counselor Education M,O
- Curriculum and Instruction O
- Early Childhood Education M
- Education—General D
- Educational Administration M,O
- Educational Psychology M
- Elementary Education M
- English as a Second Language M
- English M
- Foreign Languages Education M
- French M
- Health Education M
- History M
- Management of Technology M
- Mathematics M,O
- Multilingual and Multicultural Education M
- Music Education M
- Music M
- Psychology—General M
- Reading Education M,O
- School Psychology O
- Science Education M
- Secondary Education M
- Social Work M
- Special Education M,O
- Theater M
- Vocational and Technical Education M

In-depth description on page 1043.

RHODE ISLAND SCHOOL OF DESIGN
- Applied Arts and Design—General M
- Architecture M
- Art Education M
- Art/Fine Arts M
- Graphic Design M
- Industrial Design M
- Interior Design M
- Landscape Architecture M
- Photography M
- Textile Design M

RHODES COLLEGE
- Accounting M

RICE UNIVERSITY
- Anthropology M,D
- Applied Mathematics M,D
- Applied Physics M,D
- Architecture M,D
- Astronomy M,D
- Biochemistry M,D*
- Bioengineering M,D
- Biomedical Engineering M,D
- Biostatistics M,D
- Business Administration and Management—General M*
- Cell Biology M,D
- Chemical Engineering M,D*
- Chemistry M,D
- Civil Engineering M,D
- Computational Sciences M,D
- Computer Engineering M,D
- Computer Science M,D*
- Ecology M,D
- Economics M,D
- Education—General M
- Electrical Engineering M,D
- Engineering and Applied Sciences—General M,D
- English M,D
- Environmental Engineering M,D
- Environmental Management and Policy M*
- Environmental Sciences M,D
- Evolutionary Biology M,D
- French M,D*
- Geosciences M,D*
- History M,D
- Industrial and Organizational Psychology M,D
- Inorganic Chemistry M,D
- Linguistics M,D
- Materials Sciences M,D
- Mathematical and Computational Finance M,D
- Mathematics M,D
- Mechanical Engineering M,D
- Music M,D
- Organic Chemistry M,D
- Philosophy M,D
- Physical Chemistry M,D
- Physics M,D*
- Political Science M,D
- Psychology—General M,D
- Religion M,D
- Spanish M
- Statistics M,D
- Urban Design M,D

THE RICHARD STOCKTON COLLEGE OF NEW JERSEY
- Business Administration and Management—General M*
- Educational Media/Instructional Technology M*
- Holocaust Studies M*
- Nursing—General M*
- Occupational Therapy M*
- Physical Therapy M*

RICHMOND, THE AMERICAN INTERNATIONAL UNIVERSITY IN LONDON
- Art History M*
- Business Administration and Management—General M

RIDER UNIVERSITY
- Accounting M*
- Business Administration and Management—General M*
- Business Education O
- Counselor Education M,O
- Curriculum and Instruction M
- Education—General M,O*
- Educational Administration M
- Elementary Education O
- English Education O
- Foreign Languages Education O
- Human Services M
- Mathematics Education O
- Music Education M
- Music M
- Reading Education M
- Science Education O
- Social Sciences Education O

RIVIER COLLEGE
- Business Administration and Management—General M*
- Computer Science M
- Counseling Psychology M
- Counselor Education M
- Early Childhood Education M
- Education—General M
- Educational Administration M
- Elementary Education M
- English M
- Foreign Languages Education M
- Human Resources Management M
- Information Science M
- Management Information Systems M
- Mathematics M
- Nursing and Healthcare Administration M
- Nursing Education M
- Nursing—General M
- Reading Education M
- Secondary Education M
- Social Sciences Education M
- Special Education M
- Writing M

In-depth description on page 1045.

ROBERT MORRIS UNIVERSITY
- Accounting M
- Business Administration and Management—General M
- Business Education M
- Education—General M
- Educational Administration M
- Engineering and Applied Sciences—General M
- Engineering Management M
- Finance and Banking M
- Information Science M,D
- Internet and Interactive Multimedia M
- Management Information Systems M,D
- Nonprofit Management M
- Sports Management M
- Taxation M

In-depth description on page 1047.

ROBERTS WESLEYAN COLLEGE
- Business Administration and Management—General M
- Child and Family Studies M
- Education—General M,O
- Human Services M
- Social Work M*

ROCHESTER INSTITUTE OF TECHNOLOGY
- Accounting M
- Applied Arts and Design—General M
- Applied Mathematics M
- Art Education M
- Art/Fine Arts M
- Business Administration and Management—General M
- Chemistry M
- Communication—General M
- Computer Art and Design M
- Computer Engineering M
- Computer Science M
- Educational Media/Instructional Technology M
- Electrical Engineering M
- Engineering and Applied Sciences—General M,O
- Engineering Design M
- Engineering Management M*
- Environmental Management and Policy M
- Film, Television, and Video Production M
- Finance and Banking M
- Graphic Design M
- Health Services Management and Hospital Administration M,O
- Hospitality Management M
- Human Resources Development M
- Industrial and Manufacturing Management M
- Industrial Design M
- Industrial/Management Engineering M
- Information Science M
- Interdisciplinary Studies M
- Interior Design M
- International Business M
- Internet and Interactive Multimedia O
- Management Information Systems O
- Manufacturing Engineering M
- Materials Engineering M
- Materials Sciences M
- Mechanical Engineering M
- Media Studies M
- Medical Illustration M
- Optical Sciences M,D
- Photography M
- Public Policy and Administration M
- Publishing M
- School Psychology M,O
- Secondary Education M
- Software Engineering M
- Special Education M,O
- Statistics M,O
- Systems Engineering M
- Textile Design M
- Travel and Tourism M

In-depth description on page 1049.

THE ROCKEFELLER UNIVERSITY
- Biological and Biomedical Sciences—General D*

ROCKFORD COLLEGE

- Art Education M
- Business Administration and Management—General M
- Education—General M
- Elementary Education M
- English Education M
- Reading Education M
- Secondary Education M
- Social Sciences Education M
- Special Education M

ROCKHURST UNIVERSITY

- Business Administration and Management—General M
- Communication Disorders M
- Education—General M
- Occupational Therapy M
- Physical Therapy M

ROGER WILLIAMS UNIVERSITY

- Law P

ROLLINS COLLEGE

- Business Administration and Management—General M*
- Corporate and Organizational Communication M
- Counselor Education M
- Education—General M
- Elementary Education M
- English Education M
- Human Resources Development M
- Human Resources Management M
- Liberal Studies M
- Mathematics Education M
- Music Education M
- Secondary Education M

ROOSEVELT UNIVERSITY

- Accounting M
- Actuarial Science M
- Applied Economics M
- Business Administration and Management—General M
- Chemistry M
- Clinical Psychology M,D
- Communication—General M
- Computer Science M
- Corporate and Organizational Communication M
- Counselor Education M,D
- Early Childhood Education M,D
- Economics M
- Education—General M,D*
- Educational Administration M,D
- Elementary Education M,D
- English M
- Gerontology M
- History M
- Hospitality Management M
- Industrial and Organizational Psychology M,D
- International Business M
- Journalism M
- Liberal Studies M
- Management Information Systems M
- Mathematics M
- Music Education M,O
- Music M,O
- Political Science M
- Psychology—General M,D
- Public Policy and Administration M
- Reading Education M,D
- Secondary Education M,D
- Sociology M
- Spanish M
- Telecommunications M
- Theater M
- Women's Studies M
- Writing M

In-depth description on page 1051.

ROSE-HULMAN INSTITUTE OF TECHNOLOGY

- Biomedical Engineering M
- Chemical Engineering M
- Electrical Engineering M
- Engineering and Applied Sciences—General M*
- Engineering Management M
- Environmental Engineering M
- Mechanical Engineering M
- Optical Sciences M

ROSEMONT COLLEGE

- Business Administration and Management—General M
- Counseling Psychology M
- Counselor Education M
- Criminal Justice and Criminology M
- Curriculum and Instruction M
- Educational Media/Instructional Technology M
- Elementary Education M
- English M
- Human Services M
- Middle School Education M
- Nonprofit Management M
- Project Management M
- Publishing M

In-depth description on page 1053.

ROWAN UNIVERSITY

- Accounting M
- Advertising and Public Relations M
- Art Education M
- Business Administration and Management—General M
- Curriculum and Instruction M
- Education—General M,D,O
- Educational Administration M,D
- Educational Media/Instructional Technology M
- Elementary Education M
- Engineering and Applied Sciences—General M
- Environmental Education M
- Higher Education M
- Mathematics Education M
- Mathematics M
- Music Education M
- Music M
- Psychology—General M
- Reading Education M
- School Psychology M,O
- Science Education M
- Secondary Education M
- Special Education M
- Student Personnel Services M
- Theater M
- Writing M

In-depth description on page 1055.

ROYAL MILITARY COLLEGE OF CANADA

- Business Administration and Management—General M
- Chemical Engineering M,D
- Chemistry M,D
- Civil Engineering M,D
- Computer Engineering M,D
- Computer Science M
- Electrical Engineering M,D
- Engineering and Applied Sciences—General M,D
- Environmental Engineering M,D
- Environmental Sciences M,D
- Materials Sciences M,D
- Mathematics M
- Mechanical Engineering M,D
- Military and Defense Studies M
- Nuclear Engineering M,D
- Physics M
- Software Engineering M,D

ROYAL ROADS UNIVERSITY

- Advertising and Public Relations M
- Business Administration and Management—General M
- Conflict Resolution and Mediation/Peace Studies M
- Corporate and Organizational Communication M
- Educational Administration M
- Educational Media/Instructional Technology M
- Environmental Management and Policy M
- Human Resources Management M
- Organizational Management M

RUSH UNIVERSITY

- Advanced Practice Nursing M,D
- Allopathic Medicine P
- Anatomy M,D
- Biochemistry D
- Bioethics M*
- Clinical Laboratory Sciences/Medical Technology M*
- Communication Disorders M,D*
- Community Health Nursing M,D
- Gerontological Nursing M,D
- Health Services Management and Hospital Administration M*
- Immunology D*
- Maternal/Child Nursing M,D
- Medical Physics M,D
- Medical/Surgical Nursing M,D
- Microbiology D
- Nurse Anesthesia M,D
- Nursing—General M,D*
- Nutrition M
- Occupational Therapy M*
- Pediatric Nursing M,D
- Pharmaceutical Sciences M,D
- Pharmacology M,D
- Physiology D
- Psychiatric Nursing M,D
- Virology D
- Women's Health Nursing M,D

RUTGERS, THE STATE UNIVERSITY OF NEW JERSEY, CAMDEN

- Biological and Biomedical Sciences—General M
- Business Administration and Management—General M
- Chemistry M
- Criminal Justice and Criminology M
- English M
- Health Services Management and Hospital Administration M
- History M
- International Affairs M
- International Development M
- Law P
- Liberal Studies M
- Mathematics M
- Physical Therapy M
- Public History M
- Public Policy and Administration M

In-depth description on page 1057.

RUTGERS, THE STATE UNIVERSITY OF NEW JERSEY, NEWARK

- Accounting M,D
- Advanced Practice Nursing M,D
- Analytical Chemistry M,D
- Applied Physics M,D
- Biochemistry M,D
- Biological and Biomedical Sciences—General M,D
- Biopsychology D
- Business Administration and Management—General M,D
- Chemistry M,D*
- Cognitive Sciences D*
- Community Health Nursing M,D
- Criminal Justice and Criminology M,D
- Economics M
- English M
- Finance and Banking M,D
- Geology M
- Gerontological Nursing M,D
- Health Services Management and Hospital Administration M,D
- History M
- Human Resources Management M,D
- Inorganic Chemistry M,D
- International Affairs M,D*
- International Business M,D
- Law P
- Liberal Studies M
- Management Information Systems M,D
- Marketing M,D
- Maternal/Child Nursing M,D
- Mathematics D
- Medical/Surgical Nursing M,D
- Music M
- Neuroscience D
- Nursing—General M,D
- Organic Chemistry M,D
- Organizational Management M
- Physical Chemistry M,D
- Political Science M
- Psychiatric Nursing M,D
- Psychology—General D
- Public Policy and Administration M,D
- Social Psychology D
- Urban Studies M,D

In-depth description on page 1059.

RUTGERS, THE STATE UNIVERSITY OF NEW JERSEY, NEW BRUNSWICK

- Adult Education M,D
- Aerospace/Aeronautical Engineering M,D
- Agricultural Economics and Agribusiness M
- Agricultural Engineering M
- Analytical Chemistry M,D
- Animal Sciences M,D
- Anthropology M,D
- Applied Arts and Design—General M
- Applied Mathematics M,D
- Art History M,D
- Art/Fine Arts M
- Biochemical Engineering M,D
- Biochemistry M,D
- Bioengineering M
- Biomedical Engineering M,D
- Biopsychology D
- Cell Biology M,D
- Ceramic Sciences and Engineering M,D
- Chemical Engineering M,D
- Chemistry M,D*
- City and Regional Planning M,D
- Civil Engineering M,D
- Classics M,D
- Clinical Psychology M,D
- Cognitive Sciences D
- Communication—General M,D
- Comparative Literature D
- Computer Engineering M,D
- Computer Science M,D*
- Condensed Matter Physics M,D
- Counseling Psychology M
- Developmental Biology M,D
- Developmental Education M
- Developmental Psychology D
- Early Childhood Education M,D
- Ecology M,D
- Economics M,D
- Education—General M,D,O
- Educational Administration M,D,O
- Educational Measurement and Evaluation M
- Educational Psychology M,D
- Electrical Engineering M,D*
- Elementary Education M,D
- Engineering and Applied Sciences—General M,D
- English as a Second Language M,D
- English Education M
- English D
- Entomology M,D
- Environmental Biology M,D
- Environmental Engineering M,D
- Environmental Sciences M,D
- Evolutionary Biology M,D
- Food Science and Technology M,D
- Foreign Languages Education M,D
- Foundations and Philosophy of Education M,D,O
- French M,D
- Gender Studies M
- Genetics M,D
- Geography M,D
- Geology M,D
- German M,D
- Hazardous Materials Management M,D
- Health Psychology D
- History of Medicine D
- History of Science and Technology D
- History D
- Horticulture M,D
- Human Resources Management M,D*
- Immunology M,D
- Industrial and Labor Relations M,D*
- Industrial and Organizational Psychology M,D
- Industrial/Management Engineering M,D
- Information Studies M,D
- Inorganic Chemistry M,D
- International Affairs D
- Italian M,D
- Legal and Justice Studies D
- Library Science M
- Linguistics D
- Marine Biology M,D
- Materials Sciences M,D
- Mathematics Education M,D
- Mathematics M,D
- Mechanical Engineering M,D
- Mechanics M,D
- Medical Microbiology M,D
- Medicinal and Pharmaceutical Chemistry M,D
- Medieval and Renaissance Studies D
- Metallurgical Engineering and Metallurgy M,D
- Microbiology M,D
- Molecular Biology M,D*
- Museum Studies M,D
- Music M,D,O
- Neurobiology D
- Nutrition M,D
- Oceanography M,D*
- Operations Research D
- Organic Chemistry M,D
- Pharmaceutical Sciences M,D
- Pharmacology D
- Pharmacy P
- Philosophy D
- Physical Chemistry M,D
- Physics M,D*
- Physiology D
- Plant Biology M,D
- Plant Molecular Biology M,D
- Plant Pathology M,D
- Plant Physiology M,D
- Plant Sciences M,D
- Political Science M,D

Rutgers, The State University of New Jersey, New Brunswick (continued)

Polymer Science and Engineering	M,D
Psychology—General	M,D
Public Health—General	M,D
Public Policy and Administration	M
Quality Management	M,D
Reading Education	M,D
School Psychology	M,D
Science Education	M,D
Social Psychology	D
Social Sciences Education	M,D,O
Social Work	M,D
Sociology	M,D
Spanish	M,D
Special Education	M
Statistics	M,D
Systems Engineering	M,D
Theater	M
Theoretical Physics	M,D
Toxicology	M,D
Translation and Interpretation	M,D
Virology	M,D
Vocational and Technical Education	M,D,O
Water Resources	M,D
Women's Studies	M,D
Writing	M

SACRED HEART MAJOR SEMINARY

Pastoral Ministry and Counseling	P,M
Theology	P,M

SACRED HEART SCHOOL OF THEOLOGY

Theology	P,M

SACRED HEART UNIVERSITY

Advanced Practice Nursing	M
Business Administration and Management—General	M
Chemistry	M
Computer Science	M,O
Education—General	M,O
Educational Administration	M,O
Electronic Commerce	M,O
Elementary Education	M,O
Health Services Management and Hospital Administration	M
Information Science	M,O
Internet and Interactive Multimedia	M,O
Management Information Systems	M,O
Nursing and Healthcare Administration	M
Nursing—General	M
Occupational Therapy	M*
Physical Therapy	M
Religion	M
Secondary Education	M,O

In-depth description on page 1061.

SAGE GRADUATE SCHOOL

Addictions/Substance Abuse Counseling	M
Advanced Practice Nursing	M
Art Therapy	M
Business Administration and Management—General	M
Child and Family Studies	M
Communication—General	M
Community Health Nursing	M
Community Health	M
Corporate and Organizational Communication	M
Counselor Education	M,O
Education—General	M,O
Elementary Education	M
English Education	M
Finance and Banking	M
Forensic Psychology	M
Gerontology	M
Health Education	M
Health Services Management and Hospital Administration	M
Human Resources Management	M
Human Services	M
Marketing	M
Mathematics Education	M
Medical/Surgical Nursing	M
Nursing—General	M,O
Nutrition	M
Physical Therapy	M
Psychiatric Nursing	M
Psychology—General	M
Public Policy and Administration	M
Reading Education	M
Science Education	M
Secondary Education	M
Social Psychology	M
Social Sciences Education	M
Special Education	M

In-depth description on page 1063.

SAGINAW VALLEY STATE UNIVERSITY

Advanced Practice Nursing	M
Business Administration and Management—General	M
Communication—General	M
Early Childhood Education	M
Education—General	M,O
Educational Administration	M,O
Elementary Education	M
Engineering and Applied Sciences—General	M
Management of Technology	M
Media Studies	M
Middle School Education	M
Nursing and Healthcare Administration	M
Nursing Education	M
Nursing—General	M
Public Policy and Administration	M
Reading Education	M
Science Education	M
Secondary Education	M
Special Education	M

ST. AMBROSE UNIVERSITY

Accounting	M
Business Administration and Management—General	M,D
Criminal Justice and Criminology	M
Health Services Management and Hospital Administration	M
Management of Technology	M,D
Occupational Therapy	M
Organizational Management	M
Pastoral Ministry and Counseling	M
Physical Therapy	D
Social Work	M
Special Education	M

ST. ANDREW'S COLLEGE IN WINNIPEG

Theology	P

ST. AUGUSTINE'S SEMINARY OF TORONTO

Theology	P,M

SAINT BERNARD'S SCHOOL OF THEOLOGY AND MINISTRY

Theology	P,M,O

ST. BONAVENTURE UNIVERSITY

Accounting	M,O
Business Administration and Management—General	M,O
Counselor Education	M,O
Education—General	M,O
Educational Administration	M,O
English	M
Finance and Banking	M,O
Marketing	M,O
Reading Education	M
Theology	M,O

ST. CHARLES BORROMEO SEMINARY, OVERBROOK

Religion	M
Theology	P,M

ST. CLOUD STATE UNIVERSITY

Applied Economics	M
Art/Fine Arts	M
Biological and Biomedical Sciences—General	M
Business Administration and Management—General	M
Child and Family Studies	M
Communication Disorders	M
Computer Science	M
Counselor Education	M
Criminal Justice and Criminology	M
Curriculum and Instruction	M
Economics	M
Education—General	M,O
Educational Administration	M
Educational Media/Instructional Technology	M
Electrical Engineering	M
Engineering and Applied Sciences—General	M
English as a Second Language	M
English	M
Environmental Management and Policy	M
Exercise and Sports Science	M
Finance and Banking	M
Geography	M
Gerontology	M
History	M
Marketing	M
Mass Communication	M
Mathematics	M
Mechanical Engineering	M
Music Education	M
Music	M
Nonprofit Management	M
Physical Education	M
Psychology—General	M
Rehabilitation Counseling	M
Social Psychology	M
Special Education	M
Sports Management	M
Technology and Public Policy	M

ST. EDWARD'S UNIVERSITY

Accounting	M,O
Business Administration and Management—General	M,O
Conflict Resolution and Mediation/Peace Studies	M,O
Counseling Psychology	M
Electronic Commerce	M,O
Entrepreneurship	M,O
Ethics	M
Finance and Banking	M,O
Human Resources Management	M,O
Human Services	M,O
International Business	M,O
Liberal Studies	M
Management Information Systems	M,O
Marketing	M,O
Nonprofit Management	M,O
Organizational Management	M
Public Policy and Administration	M,O
Sports Management	M,O

SAINT FRANCIS SEMINARY

Pastoral Ministry and Counseling	P,M
Theology	P,M

SAINT FRANCIS UNIVERSITY

Biological and Biomedical Sciences—General	M
Business Administration and Management—General	M
Education—General	M
Educational Administration	M
Human Resources Management	M*
Occupational Therapy	M
Physical Therapy	M
Physician Assistant Studies	M

ST. FRANCIS XAVIER UNIVERSITY

Adult Education	M
Biological and Biomedical Sciences—General	M
Chemistry	M
Education—General	M,O
English	M
Geology	M
Physics	M

ST. JOHN FISHER COLLEGE

Advanced Practice Nursing	M,O
Business Administration and Management—General	M
Educational Administration	M
Elementary Education	M
Health Services Management and Hospital Administration	M
Human Resources Development	M
International Affairs	M
Mathematics Education	M
Middle School Education	M
Reading Education	M
Science Education	M
Special Education	M
Taxation	M

ST. JOHN'S COLLEGE (MD)

Liberal Studies	M

ST. JOHN'S COLLEGE (NM)

Asian Languages	M
Asian Studies	M
Liberal Studies	M

ST. JOHN'S SEMINARY (CA)

Theology	P,M

SAINT JOHN'S SEMINARY (MA)

Religion	P,M
Theology	P,M

SAINT JOHN'S UNIVERSITY (MN)

Music	P,M
Pastoral Ministry and Counseling	P,M
Theology	P,M

ST. JOHN'S UNIVERSITY (NY)

Accounting	M,O
Actuarial Science	M
African Studies	M,O
Applied Mathematics	M
Asian Studies	M,O
Biological and Biomedical Sciences—General	M,D*
Business Administration and Management—General	M,O
Chemistry	M
Clinical Laboratory Sciences/Medical Technology	M
Clinical Psychology	M,D
Communication Disorders	M
Computer Science	M
Counselor Education	M,O
Economics	M,O
Education—General	M,D,O
Educational Administration	M,D,O
Elementary Education	M
English as a Second Language	M
English	M,D
Experimental Psychology	M
Finance and Banking	M,O
Higher Education	M,O
History	M,D
Information Studies	M,O
Insurance	M
International Business	M
Law	P,M
Legal and Justice Studies	M
Library Science	M,O
Management Information Systems	M,O
Marketing	M,O
Mathematics	M
Medicinal and Pharmaceutical Chemistry	M,D
Multilingual and Multicultural Education	M
Pastoral Ministry and Counseling	P,M,O
Pharmaceutical Administration	M
Pharmaceutical Sciences	M,D
Pharmacology	M,D
Pharmacy	P
Political Science	M
Psychology—General	M,D
Quantitative Analysis	M,O
Reading Education	M,O
Rehabilitation Counseling	M,O
School Psychology	M,D
Secondary Education	M
Sociology	M
Spanish	M
Special Education	M,O
Statistics	M
Taxation	M,O
Theology	P,M,O
Theoretical Physics	M,O
Toxicology	M,D

In-depth description on page 1065.

SAINT JOSEPH COLLEGE

Advanced Practice Nursing	M,O
Biological and Biomedical Sciences—General	M
Cell Biology	M
Chemistry	M
Child and Family Studies	M,O
Early Childhood Education	M
Education—General	M
Gerontology	M,O
Human Development	M,O
Marriage and Family Therapy	M
Maternal/Child Nursing	M,O
Molecular Biology	M
Nursing—General	M,O
Pastoral Ministry and Counseling	M,O
Psychiatric Nursing	M,O
Psychology—General	M,O
Social Psychology	M,O
Special Education	M

SAINT JOSEPH'S COLLEGE (IN)

Music	M,O

SAINT JOSEPH'S COLLEGE (ME)

Education—General	M
Health Services Management and Hospital Administration	M
Nursing—General	M
Pastoral Ministry and Counseling	M

ST. JOSEPH'S COLLEGE, SUFFOLK CAMPUS

Early Childhood Education	M
Education—General	M

ST. JOSEPH'S SEMINARY

Theology	P,M

SAINT JOSEPH'S UNIVERSITY

Program	Degrees
Accounting	M
Adult Education	M
Biological and Biomedical Sciences—General	M
Business Administration and Management—General	M
Chemistry	M
Computer Science	M
Criminal Justice and Criminology	M
Education—General	M,D,O
Educational Administration	D
Finance and Banking	M*
Gerontology	M
Health Education	M
Health Services Management and Hospital Administration	M
Human Resources Management	M
International Business	M
Management Information Systems	M
Marketing	M*
Mathematics Education	M
Nurse Anesthesia	M
Psychology—General	M*
Reading Education	M
Science Education	M
Secondary Education	M
Special Education	M

In-depth description on page 1067.

ST. LAWRENCE UNIVERSITY

Program	Degrees
Counselor Education	M,O
Education—General	M,O
Educational Administration	M,O
Human Development	M,O

SAINT LEO UNIVERSITY

Program	Degrees
Business Administration and Management—General	M
Education—General	M

ST. LOUIS COLLEGE OF PHARMACY

Program	Degrees
Pharmaceutical Administration	M
Pharmacy	P

SAINT LOUIS UNIVERSITY

Program	Degrees
Accounting	M
Aerospace/Aeronautical Engineering	M
Allied Health—General	M
Allopathic Medicine	P,M,D
American Studies	M,D
Biochemistry	D*
Bioethics	D
Biological and Biomedical Sciences—General	M,D*
Biostatistics	M
Business Administration and Management—General	M
Chemistry	M
Clinical Psychology	M,D
Communication Disorders	M
Communication—General	M
Community Health	M,D
Counselor Education	M,D,O
Curriculum and Instruction	M,D
Economics	M
Education—General	M,D
Educational Administration	M,D,O
English	M,D
Environmental and Occupational Health	M
Epidemiology	M
Experimental Psychology	M,D
Finance and Banking	M
Foundations and Philosophy of Education	M,D
French	M
Geophysics	M,D
Geosciences	M,D
Health Education	M
Health Services Management and Hospital Administration	M
Higher Education	M,D,O
History	M,D
Human Development	M,D,O
Immunology	D
International Business	D
Law	P,M,O
Marriage and Family Therapy	M,D,O
Mathematics	M,D
Mechanical Engineering	M
Meteorology	M,D
Microbiology	D*
Molecular Biology	D
Nutrition	M
Oral and Dental Sciences	M
Pathology	D
Pharmacology	D*
Philosophy	M,D
Physical Therapy	M
Physician Assistant Studies	M
Physiology	D*
Psychology—General	M,D
Public Health—General	M,D
Public Policy and Administration	M,D
Social Work	M
Spanish	M
Special Education	M,D
Theology	M,D
Urban Studies	M,D

In-depth description on page 1069.

SAINT MARTIN'S COLLEGE

Program	Degrees
Business Administration and Management—General	M
Civil Engineering	M
Computer Education	M
Counseling Psychology	M
Counselor Education	M
Curriculum and Instruction	M
Education—General	M
Engineering Management	M
Reading Education	M
Social Psychology	M
Special Education	M

SAINT MARY COLLEGE

Program	Degrees
Business Administration and Management—General	M
Curriculum and Instruction	M
Education—General	M
Psychology—General	M

SAINT MARY-OF-THE-WOODS COLLEGE

Program	Degrees
Art Therapy	M
Environmental Management and Policy	M
Theology	M
Therapies—Dance, Drama, and Music	M

SAINT MARY'S COLLEGE OF CALIFORNIA

Program	Degrees
Business Administration and Management—General	M
Counselor Education	M
Early Childhood Education	M
Education—General	M
Educational Administration	M
Health Education	M
Liberal Studies	M
Marriage and Family Therapy	M
Physical Education	M
Reading Education	M
Special Education	M
Writing	M

SAINT MARY SEMINARY AND GRADUATE SCHOOL OF THEOLOGY

Program	Degrees
Theology	P,M,D

ST. MARY'S SEMINARY AND UNIVERSITY

Program	Degrees
Theology	P,M,D,O*

SAINT MARY'S UNIVERSITY

Program	Degrees
Astronomy	M
Business Administration and Management—General	M,D
Canadian Studies	M
Clinical Psychology	M
Criminal Justice and Criminology	M
History	M
Industrial and Organizational Psychology	M
International Development	M
Philosophy	M
Psychology—General	M
Women's Studies	M

SAINT MARY'S UNIVERSITY OF MINNESOTA

Program	Degrees
Arts Administration	M
Business Administration and Management—General	M
Counseling Psychology	M
Criminal Justice and Criminology	M
Education—General	M
Educational Administration	M,D
Environmental Management and Policy	M
Geographic Information Systems	M
Health Services Management and Hospital Administration	M
Human Development	M
Nurse Anesthesia	M
Pastoral Ministry and Counseling	M,O
Philanthropic Studies	M
Public Policy and Administration	M
Special Education	M
Telecommunications	M

ST. MARY'S UNIVERSITY OF SAN ANTONIO

Program	Degrees
Accounting	M
Addictions/Substance Abuse Counseling	M,D,O
Business Administration and Management—General	M
Clinical Psychology	M
Communication—General	M
Computer Engineering	M
Computer Science	M
Conflict Resolution and Mediation/Peace Studies	M
Counseling Psychology	M,D,O
Counselor Education	M,D,O
Criminal Justice and Criminology	M
Economics	M
Education—General	M,O
Educational Administration	M,O
Electrical Engineering	M
Engineering and Applied Sciences—General	M
Engineering Management	M
English	M
Finance and Banking	M
History	M
Human Services	M,D,O
Industrial and Organizational Psychology	M
Industrial/Management Engineering	M
Information Science	M
International Business	M
Law	P
Marriage and Family Therapy	M,D,O
Operations Research	M
Pastoral Ministry and Counseling	M
Political Science	M
Psychology—General	M
Reading Education	M
School Psychology	M
Software Engineering	M
Speech and Interpersonal Communication	M
Taxation	M
Theology	M

SAINT MEINRAD SCHOOL OF THEOLOGY

Program	Degrees
Theology	P,M

SAINT MICHAEL'S COLLEGE

Program	Degrees
Adult Education	M,O
Art Education	M,O
Business Administration and Management—General	M,O
Clinical Psychology	M
Curriculum and Instruction	M,O
Education—General	M,O
Educational Administration	M,O
Educational Media/Instructional Technology	M,O
English as a Second Language	M,O*
Reading Education	M,O
Special Education	M,O
Theology	M,O

ST. NORBERT COLLEGE

Program	Degrees
Education—General	M
Theology	M

ST. PATRICK'S SEMINARY

Program	Degrees
Theology	P,M

SAINT PAUL SCHOOL OF THEOLOGY

Program	Degrees
Theology	P,M,D

SAINT PAUL UNIVERSITY

Program	Degrees
Marriage and Family Therapy	M,O
Missions and Missiology	M,O
Pastoral Ministry and Counseling	M,D,O
Theology	M,D,O

SAINT PETER'S COLLEGE

Program	Degrees
Accounting	M,O
Business Administration and Management—General	M
Curriculum and Instruction	M,O
Education—General	M,O
Educational Administration	M,O
Elementary Education	M,O
Finance and Banking	M
International Business	M
Management Information Systems	M
Marketing	M
Nursing—General	M
Reading Education	M
Urban Education	M

In-depth description on page 1071.

ST. PETER'S SEMINARY

Program	Degrees
Theology	P

SAINTS CYRIL AND METHODIUS SEMINARY

Program	Degrees
Pastoral Ministry and Counseling	P,M
Religious Education	P,M
Theology	P,M

ST. STEPHEN'S COLLEGE

Program	Degrees
Pastoral Ministry and Counseling	M,D
Theology	M,D

ST. THOMAS AQUINAS COLLEGE

Program	Degrees
Business Administration and Management—General	M
Education—General	M,O
Elementary Education	M
Finance and Banking	M
Marketing	M
Middle School Education	M,O
Reading Education	M,O
Secondary Education	M
Special Education	M,O

Announcement on page 510.

ST. THOMAS UNIVERSITY

Program	Degrees
Accounting	M,O
Business Administration and Management—General	M,O
Counseling Psychology	M
Counselor Education	M,O
Criminal Justice and Criminology	M,O
Education—General	M,O
Elementary Education	M
Health Services Management and Hospital Administration	M,O
Human Resources Management	M,O
International Business	M,O
Law	P,M
Marriage and Family Therapy	M
Pastoral Ministry and Counseling	M,O
Public Policy and Administration	M,O
Sports Management	M
Taxation	P,M

In-depth description on page 1073.

SAINT VINCENT DE PAUL REGIONAL SEMINARY

Program	Degrees
Theology	P,M

SAINT VINCENT SEMINARY

Program	Degrees
Theology	P,M

ST. VLADIMIR'S ORTHODOX THEOLOGICAL SEMINARY

Program	Degrees
Music	P,M,D
Religious Education	P,M,D
Theology	P,M,D

SAINT XAVIER UNIVERSITY

Program	Degrees
Advanced Practice Nursing	M,O
Business Administration and Management—General	M,O*
Communication Disorders	M*
Community Health Nursing	M,O
Computer Science	M*
Counseling Psychology	M,O
Curriculum and Instruction	M,O
Early Childhood Education	M,O
Education—General	M,O*
Educational Administration	M,O
Elementary Education	M,O
English	M,O
Finance and Banking	M,O
Health Services Management and Hospital Administration	M,O
Information Science	M
Marketing	M,O
Medical/Surgical Nursing	M,O
Nursing and Healthcare Administration	M,O
Nursing—General	M,O*
Psychiatric Nursing	M,O
Psychology—General	M,O*
Public Health—General	M,O
Reading Education	M,O

Saint Xavier University (continued)

Secondary Education M,O
Special Education M,O
Taxation M,O
Writing M,O

SALEM COLLEGE

Early Childhood Education M
Education—General M
Elementary Education M
Reading Education M
Special Education M

SALEM INTERNATIONAL UNIVERSITY

Biological and Biomedical Sciences—General M
Biotechnology M
Education—General M
Elementary Education M
Molecular Biology M
Secondary Education M

SALEM STATE COLLEGE

Business Administration and Management—General M
Counselor Education M
Early Childhood Education M
Education—General M,O
Educational Administration M
Educational Media/Instructional Technology M
Elementary Education M
English as a Second Language M
English Education M,O
English M
Geography M
History M
Mathematics Education M,O
Mathematics M
Middle School Education M
Multilingual and Multicultural Education M
Nursing—General M
Psychology—General M
Reading Education M
Science Education M,O
Secondary Education M
Social Sciences Education M,O
Social Work M
Special Education M

SALISBURY UNIVERSITY

Art Education M
Business Administration and Management—General M
Business Education M
Early Childhood Education M
Education—General M
Educational Administration M
Educational Media/Instructional Technology M
Elementary Education M
English as a Second Language M
English Education M
English M
Foreign Languages Education M
History M
Mathematics Education M
Music Education M
Nursing—General M
Physiology M
Reading Education M
Science Education M
Secondary Education M
Social Sciences Education M
Social Work M
Writing M

SALVE REGINA UNIVERSITY

Business Administration and Management—General M
Counseling Psychology M,O
Criminal Justice and Criminology M
Health Services Management and Hospital Administration M
Humanities M,D,O
International Affairs M

In-depth description on page 1075.

SAMFORD UNIVERSITY

Business Administration and Management—General M
Early Childhood Education M,D,O
Education—General M,D,O
Educational Administration M,D,O
Elementary Education M,D,O
Law P,D
Music Education M,D,O
Music M
Nursing—General M
Pharmacy P
Theology P,M,D

SAM HOUSTON STATE UNIVERSITY

Agricultural Economics and Agribusiness M
Agricultural Education M
Agricultural Sciences—General M
Art Education M
Art/Fine Arts M
Biological and Biomedical Sciences—General M
Business Administration and Management—General M
Chemistry M
Clinical Psychology M
Computer Science M
Counseling Psychology M,D
Counselor Education M,D
Criminal Justice and Criminology M,D*
Curriculum and Instruction M,D,O
Dance M
Early Childhood Education M,O
Educational Administration M,D
Elementary Education M,D,O
English as a Second Language M,O
English M
Family and Consumer Sciences-General M
Forensic Psychology M,D
History M
Library Science M
Mathematics M
Multilingual and Multicultural Education M,O
Music Education M
Music M
Physics M
Political Science M
Psychology—General M,D
Reading Education M,O
School Psychology M
Secondary Education M,D,O
Sociology M
Special Education M,O
Statistics M
Vocational and Technical Education M

SAMRA UNIVERSITY OF ORIENTAL MEDICINE

Acupuncture and Oriental Medicine M

SAMUEL MERRITT COLLEGE

Advanced Practice Nursing M,O
Nurse Anesthesia M,O
Nursing and Healthcare Administration M,O
Nursing—General M,O
Occupational Therapy M
Physical Therapy M
Physician Assistant Studies M

SAN DIEGO STATE UNIVERSITY

Accounting M
Advertising and Public Relations M
Aerospace/Aeronautical Engineering M,D
Anthropology M
Applied Arts and Design—General M
Applied Mathematics M
Art History M
Art/Fine Arts M
Asian Studies M
Astronomy M
Biological and Biomedical Sciences—General M,D*
Biostatistics M,D
Business Administration and Management—General M
Cell Biology M,D
Chemistry M,D
City and Regional Planning M
Civil Engineering M
Clinical Psychology M,D
Communication Disorders M,D
Communication—General M
Computer Science M
Counselor Education M
Criminal Justice and Criminology M
Curriculum and Instruction M
Dance M
Ecology D
Economics M
Education—General M,D
Educational Administration M
Educational Media/Instructional Technology M
Electrical Engineering M
Elementary Education M
Engineering and Applied Sciences—General M,D
English M
Environmental and Occupational Health M,D
Environmental Design M
Epidemiology M,D
Exercise and Sports Science M
Film, Television, and Video Production M
Finance and Banking M
French M
Geography M,D
Geology M
Graphic Design M
Health Physics/Radiological Health M
Health Promotion M,D
Health Services Management and Hospital Administration M,D
History M
Human Resources Management M
Industrial and Manufacturing Management M
Industrial and Organizational Psychology M,D
Industrial Hygiene M,D
Interdisciplinary Studies M
Interior Design M
International Business M
Internet and Interactive Multimedia M
Latin American Studies M
Liberal Studies M
Linguistics M,O
Management Information Systems M
Marketing M
Mass Communication M
Mathematics Education M,D
Mathematics M,D
Mechanical Engineering M,D
Mechanics M,D
Media Studies M
Microbiology M
Molecular Biology M,D*
Multilingual and Multicultural Education M
Music M
Nursing—General M
Nutrition M
Philosophy M
Physical Education M
Physics M
Political Science M
Psychology—General M,D
Public Health—General M,D
Public Policy and Administration M
Reading Education M
Rehabilitation Counseling M
School Psychology M
Science Education M,D
Secondary Education M
Social Work M
Sociology M
Spanish M
Special Education M
Statistics M
Telecommunications Management M
Theater M
Toxicology M,D
Women's Studies M
Writing M

SAN FRANCISCO ART INSTITUTE

Art/Fine Arts M,O*
Film, Television, and Video Production M,O
Photography M,O

SAN FRANCISCO CONSERVATORY OF MUSIC

Music M

SAN FRANCISCO STATE UNIVERSITY

Adult Education M,O
Advanced Practice Nursing M
Anthropology M
Art History M
Art/Fine Arts M
Asian Languages M
Astrophysics M
Biological and Biomedical Sciences—General M
Business Administration and Management—General M
Cell Biology M
Chemistry M
Classics M
Clinical Laboratory Sciences/Medical Technology M
Communication Disorders M
Comparative and Interdisciplinary Arts M
Comparative Literature M
Computer Science M
Conservation Biology M
Counseling Psychology M
Early Childhood Education M
Ecology M
Economics M
Education—General M,D,O
Educational Administration M,O
Educational Media/Instructional Technology M,O
Elementary Education M
Engineering and Applied Sciences—General M
English as a Second Language M
English Education M,O
English M,O
Environmental Management and Policy M
Ethnic Studies M
Family and Consumer Sciences-General M
Film, Television, and Video Production M
Film, Television, and Video Theory and Criticism M
French M
Geography M
Geosciences M
German M
Gerontology M
History M
Humanities M
Industrial Design M
International Affairs M
Italian M
Leisure Studies M
Linguistics M
Marine Biology M
Marriage and Family Therapy M
Mathematics Education M
Mathematics M
Media Studies M
Microbiology M
Molecular Biology M
Museum Studies M
Music M
Nonprofit Management M
Nursing and Healthcare Administration M
Nursing Education M
Nursing—General M
Philosophy M,O
Physical Education M
Physical Therapy M
Physics M
Physiology M
Political Science M
Psychology—General M
Public Health—General M
Public Policy and Administration M
Reading Education M,O
Recreation and Park Management M
Rehabilitation Counseling M
Russian M
Secondary Education M,O
Social Sciences M
Social Work M
Spanish M
Special Education M,D,O
Speech and Interpersonal Communication M
Taxation M
Theater M
Women's Studies M
Writing M

SAN FRANCISCO THEOLOGICAL SEMINARY

Theology P,M,D

SAN JOAQUIN COLLEGE OF LAW

Law P

SAN JOSE STATE UNIVERSITY

Accounting M
Advanced Practice Nursing M
Aerospace/Aeronautical Engineering M
Analytical Chemistry M
Applied Arts and Design—General M
Applied Economics M
Art Education M
Art History M
Art/Fine Arts M
Artificial Intelligence/Robotics M
Biochemistry M
Biological and Biomedical Sciences—General M
Business Administration and Management—General M*
Chemical Engineering M
Chemistry M
Child and Family Studies M
City and Regional Planning M
Civil Engineering M
Clinical Psychology M
Communication Disorders M
Communication—General M
Community Health Nursing M
Computer Engineering M
Computer Science M

Counseling Psychology M
Counselor Education M
Criminal Justice and Criminology M
Economics M
Education—General M,O
Educational Administration M,O
Educational Media/Instructional Technology M,O
Electrical Engineering M
Elementary Education M
Engineering and Applied Sciences—General M
English as a Second Language M,O
English M
Environmental Design M
Environmental Engineering M
Environmental Management and Policy M
Ergonomics and Human Factors M
French M
Geography M
Geology M
Gerontological Nursing M
Gerontology M,O
Graphic Design M
Health Services Management and Hospital Administration M,O
Higher Education M,O
Hispanic Studies M
History M
Industrial and Manufacturing Management M
Industrial and Organizational Psychology M
Industrial Design M
Information Science M
Information Studies M
Inorganic Chemistry M
Interdisciplinary Studies M
Interior Design M
Kinesiology and Movement Studies M
Leisure Studies M
Library Science M
Linguistics M,O
Management Information Systems M
Marine Sciences M
Mass Communication M
Materials Engineering M
Mathematics M
Mechanical Engineering M
Meteorology M
Music M
Nursing and Healthcare Administration M
Nursing Education M
Nursing—General M
Nutrition M
Occupational Therapy M
Organic Chemistry M
Philosophy M,O
Photography M
Physical Chemistry M
Physics M
Polymer Science and Engineering M
Psychology—General M
Public Health—General M,O
Public Policy and Administration M
Quality Management M
Recreation and Park Management M
Secondary Education M
Social Sciences M
Social Work M
Sociology M
Software Engineering M
Spanish M
Special Education M
Speech and Interpersonal Communication M
Systems Engineering M
Taxation M
Technical Writing M
Textile Design M
Theater M
Transportation Management M

SANTA BARBARA COLLEGE OF ORIENTAL MEDICINE

Acupuncture and Oriental Medicine M

SANTA CLARA UNIVERSITY

Applied Mathematics M
Business Administration and Management—General M
Civil Engineering M
Computer Engineering M,D,O
Computer Science M,D,O
Counseling Psychology M*
Counselor Education M
Education—General M,O
Educational Administration M
Electrical Engineering M,D,O
Engineering and Applied Sciences—General M,D,O*
Engineering Management M
Health Psychology M
Law P,M,O
Marriage and Family Therapy M
Mechanical Engineering M,D,O
Music M
Pastoral Ministry and Counseling M
Religion M
Software Engineering M,D,O
Special Education M

SARAH LAWRENCE COLLEGE

Dance M*
Education—General M
Genetic Counseling M
History M
Human Development M
Human Genetics M*
Interdisciplinary Studies M
Public Health—General M*
Theater M
Women's Studies M*
Writing M

In-depth description on page 1077.

SAVANNAH COLLEGE OF ART AND DESIGN

Applied Arts and Design—General M
Architectural History M
Architecture M
Art History M
Art/Fine Arts M*
Computer Art and Design M
Film, Television, and Video Production M
Graphic Design M
Historic Preservation M
Illustration M
Industrial Design M
Interior Design M
Media Studies M
Music M
Photography M
Textile Design M

SAVANNAH STATE UNIVERSITY

Public Policy and Administration M
Social Work M
Urban Studies M

SAYBROOK GRADUATE SCHOOL AND RESEARCH CENTER

Health Psychology M,D
Organizational Behavior M,D
Organizational Management M,D
Psychology—General M,D
Transpersonal and Humanistic Psychology M,D

SCHILLER INTERNATIONAL UNIVERSITY (GERMANY)

Business Administration and Management—General M
International Business M

SCHILLER INTERNATIONAL UNIVERSITY

Business Administration and Management—General M
International Affairs M
International Business M

SCHILLER INTERNATIONAL UNIVERSITY (SPAIN)

Business Administration and Management—General M
International Business M

SCHILLER INTERNATIONAL UNIVERSITY

Business Administration and Management—General M
International Business M

SCHILLER INTERNATIONAL UNIVERSITY (UNITED KINGDOM)

Hospitality Management M
International Affairs M
International Business M
Management Information Systems M
Travel and Tourism M

SCHILLER INTERNATIONAL UNIVERSITY (UNITED STATES)

Business Administration and Management—General M
Hospitality Management M
International Business M
Travel and Tourism M

SCHILLER INTERNATIONAL UNIVERSITY, AMERICAN COLLEGE OF SWITZERLAND

Business Administration and Management—General M
International Business M

THE SCHOLL COLLEGE OF PODIATRIC MEDICINE AT FINCH UNIVERSITY OF HEALTH SCIENCES/THE CHICAGO MEDICAL SCHOOL

Podiatric Medicine P*

SCHOOL FOR INTERNATIONAL TRAINING

Business Administration and Management—General M,O
Education—General M
English as a Second Language M
Foreign Languages Education M
International Affairs M,O
International and Comparative Education M,O
International Business M,O
Multilingual and Multicultural Education M
Sustainable Development M,O

In-depth description on page 1079.

SCHOOL OF ADVANCED AIRPOWER STUDIES

Military and Defense Studies M

SCHOOL OF THE ART INSTITUTE OF CHICAGO

Art Education M,O
Art History M,O
Art Therapy M
Art/Fine Arts M*
Arts Administration M
Film, Television, and Video Production M
Graphic Design M
Historic Preservation M
Interior Design M
Photography M
Writing M

SCHOOL OF THE MUSEUM OF FINE ARTS

Art/Fine Arts M,O

SCHOOL OF VISUAL ARTS

Applied Arts and Design—General M
Art Therapy M
Art/Fine Arts M
Computer Art and Design M
Illustration M
Photography M

In-depth description on page 1081.

SCHREINER UNIVERSITY

Education—General M

THE SCRIPPS RESEARCH INSTITUTE

Biochemistry D
Cell Biology D
Chemistry D
Molecular Biology D

SEABURY-WESTERN THEOLOGICAL SEMINARY

Theology P,M,D,O

SEATTLE INSTITUTE OF ORIENTAL MEDICINE

Acupuncture and Oriental Medicine M

SEATTLE PACIFIC UNIVERSITY

Advanced Practice Nursing O
Business Administration and Management—General M
Clinical Psychology D
Counselor Education M
Economics M
Education—General M,D,O
Educational Administration M,D
English as a Second Language M
Management Information Systems M
Marriage and Family Therapy M
Nursing and Healthcare Administration M
Nursing—General M,O
Physical Education M
Reading Education M
School Psychology O
Secondary Education M

SEATTLE UNIVERSITY

Accounting M
Adult Education M,O
Business Administration and Management—General M,O
Counselor Education M
Curriculum and Instruction M,O
Education—General M,D,O
Educational Administration M,D,O
Educational Measurement and Evaluation O
Engineering and Applied Sciences—General M
English as a Second Language M,O
Finance and Banking M,O
International Business M,O
Law P
Nonprofit Management M*
Nursing—General M,O
Pastoral Ministry and Counseling M
Psychology—General M
Public Policy and Administration M
School Psychology O
Software Engineering M
Theology P,M,O
Transpersonal and Humanistic Psychology M

In-depth description on page 1083.

SEMINARY OF THE IMMACULATE CONCEPTION

Theology P,M,D,O

SETON HALL UNIVERSITY

Accounting M,O
Advanced Practice Nursing M
Allied Health—General M,D
Analytical Chemistry M,D
Arts Administration M*
Asian Studies M
Biochemistry M,D
Biological and Biomedical Sciences—General M
Business Administration and Management—General O*
Chemistry M,D*
Communication Disorders M,D
Communication—General M
Corporate and Organizational Communication M
Counseling Psychology D
Counselor Education M
Criminal Justice and Criminology M
Education—General M,D,O
Educational Administration M,D,O
Educational Media/Instructional Technology M,O
Elementary Education M
English as a Second Language M,O
English M*
Environmental Management and Policy O
Exercise and Sports Science M
Finance and Banking M,O
French M
Gerontological Nursing M
Health Services Management and Hospital Administration M,O*
Higher Education D
Inorganic Chemistry M,D
International Affairs M*
International Business M,O
Jewish Studies M
Law P,M
Management Information Systems M,O
Marketing M,O
Marriage and Family Therapy M,D,O
Mass Communication M
Medical/Surgical Nursing M
Microbiology M
Multilingual and Multicultural Education M,O
Museum Studies M*
Nonprofit Management M*
Nursing and Healthcare Administration M
Nursing Education M
Nursing—General M
Occupational Therapy M
Organic Chemistry M,D
Pastoral Ministry and Counseling P,M,O
Pediatric Nursing M
Pharmaceutical Administration M,O
Physical Chemistry M,D
Physical Therapy D
Physician Assistant Studies M

Seton Hall University (continued)
Psychology—General M,D,O
Public Policy and Administration M*
Religion M
School Nursing M
School Psychology O
Secondary Education M
Spanish M
Sports Management M,O
Taxation M
Theology P,M,O
Women's Health Nursing M
In-depth description on page 1085.

SETON HILL UNIVERSITY
Art Therapy M,O
Business Administration and Management—General M
Educational Media/Instructional Technology M
Elementary Education M,O
Marriage and Family Therapy M
Special Education M,O
Writing M
In-depth description on page 1087.

SHAW UNIVERSITY
Theology P

SHENANDOAH UNIVERSITY
Advanced Practice Nursing M,O
Arts Administration M,D,O
Business Administration and Management—General M,O
Business Education M,D,O
Computer Education M,D,O
Dance M,D,O
Education—General M,D,O
Educational Administration M,D,O
Elementary Education M,D,O
English as a Second Language M,D,O
Exercise and Sports Science M
Health Services Management and Hospital Administration M,O
Management Information Systems M,O
Middle School Education M,D,O
Music Education M,D,O
Music M,D,O
Nursing—General M,O
Occupational Therapy M
Pharmacy P
Physical Therapy D
Physician Assistant Studies M
Public Policy and Administration M,O
Secondary Education M,D,O
Therapies—Dance, Drama, and Music M,D,O

SHERMAN COLLEGE OF STRAIGHT CHIROPRACTIC
Chiropractic P*

SHIPPENSBURG UNIVERSITY OF PENNSYLVANIA
Biological and Biomedical Sciences—General M
Business Administration and Management—General M
Communication—General M
Computer Science M
Counselor Education M,O
Criminal Justice and Criminology M
Curriculum and Instruction M,O
Education—General M,O
Educational Administration M
Elementary Education M,O
Environmental Management and Policy M
History M
Information Science M
Mathematics M
Psychology—General M
Public History M
Public Policy and Administration M
Reading Education M,O
Special Education M,O
In-depth description on page 1089.

SHORTER COLLEGE
Business Administration and Management—General M

SH'OR YOSHUV RABBINICAL COLLEGE
Theology

SIENA HEIGHTS UNIVERSITY
Counselor Education M
Curriculum and Instruction M
Early Childhood Education M
Education—General M
Elementary Education M
Human Resources Development M
Middle School Education M
Reading Education M
Secondary Education M

SIERRA NEVADA COLLEGE
Education of the Gifted O
Education—General O
Elementary Education O
English as a Second Language O
Secondary Education O

SILVER LAKE COLLEGE
Business Administration and Management—General M
Education—General M
Educational Administration M
Music Education M
Organizational Behavior M

SIMMONS COLLEGE
Advanced Practice Nursing M,O
Business Administration and Management—General M*
Corporate and Organizational Communication M
Cultural Studies M
Education—General M,O
Educational Administration M,O
Educational Media/Instructional Technology M,O
Elementary Education M,O
English as a Second Language M
English M
Gender Studies M
Health Promotion M,O
Health Services Management and Hospital Administration M,O*
Information Studies M,D,O
Library Science M,D,O*
Management Strategy and Policy M*
Nursing—General M,O
Nutrition M,O
Physical Therapy D
Public History M
Secondary Education M,O
Social Work M,D*
Spanish M
Special Education M,O

SIMON FRASER UNIVERSITY
Anthropology M,D
Applied Mathematics M,D
Archaeology M,D
Biochemistry M,D
Biological and Biomedical Sciences—General M,D,O
Biophysics M,D
Business Administration and Management—General M
Chemistry M,D
Communication—General M,D
Comparative and Interdisciplinary Arts M
Computer Science M,D
Counselor Education M
Criminal Justice and Criminology M,D
Curriculum and Instruction M,D
Economics M,D
Education—General M,D
Educational Administration M
Educational Psychology M,D
Engineering and Applied Sciences—General M,D
English M,D
Entomology M,D,O
Environmental Management and Policy M,D
French M
Geography M,D
Geosciences M
Gerontology M
History M,D
International Business M
Kinesiology and Movement Studies M,D
Latin American Studies M
Liberal Studies M
Linguistics M,D
Management Information Systems M
Marketing M
Mathematics M,D
Molecular Biology M,D
Philosophy M,D
Physical Chemistry M,D
Physics M,D
Political Science M,D
Psychology—General M,D
Publishing M
Sociology M,D
Statistics M,D
Toxicology M,D,O
Women's Studies M

SIMPSON COLLEGE AND GRADUATE SCHOOL
Curriculum and Instruction M
Education—General M
Missions and Missiology M
Theology M

SINTE GLESKA UNIVERSITY
Education—General M
Elementary Education M

SKIDMORE COLLEGE
Liberal Studies M

SLIPPERY ROCK UNIVERSITY OF PENNSYLVANIA
Accounting M
Business Administration and Management—General M
Counselor Education M
Early Childhood Education M
Education—General M
Elementary Education M
English M
Environmental Education M
Environmental Management and Policy M
History M
Mathematics Education M
Nursing—General M
Physical Education M
Physical Therapy D
Reading Education M
Science Education M
Secondary Education M
Special Education M
Student Personnel Services M
Sustainable Development M
In-depth description on page 1091.

SMITH COLLEGE
Biological and Biomedical Sciences—General M,D*
Chemistry M
Dance M
Early Childhood Education M
Education—General M
Elementary Education M
English Education M
Exercise and Sports Science M
Foreign Languages Education M
French M
History M
Italian M
Mathematics Education M
Music M
Religion M
Science Education M
Secondary Education M
Social Sciences Education M
Social Work M,D*
Special Education M
Theater M

SONOMA STATE UNIVERSITY
Advanced Practice Nursing M
Biological and Biomedical Sciences—General M
Business Administration and Management—General M
Counselor Education M
Cultural Studies M
Curriculum and Instruction M
Early Childhood Education M
Education—General M
Educational Administration M
English Education M
English M
Environmental Biology M
History M
Interdisciplinary Studies M
Kinesiology and Movement Studies M
Marriage and Family Therapy M
Political Science M
Public History M
Public Policy and Administration M
Reading Education M
Special Education M
Writing M

SOUTH BAYLO UNIVERSITY
Acupuncture and Oriental Medicine M

SOUTH CAROLINA STATE UNIVERSITY
Agricultural Economics and Agribusiness M
Business Administration and Management—General M
Business Education M
Child and Family Studies M
Communication Disorders M
Counselor Education M,D,O
Early Childhood Education M
Education—General M,D,O
Educational Administration M,D,O
Elementary Education M
English Education M
Home Economics Education M
Mathematics Education M
Nutrition M
Rehabilitation Counseling M
Science Education M
Secondary Education M
Social Sciences Education M
Special Education M
Vocational and Technical Education M

SOUTH DAKOTA SCHOOL OF MINES AND TECHNOLOGY
Atmospheric Sciences M,D*
Chemical Engineering M,D
Chemistry M,D
Civil Engineering M,D
Computer Science M
Electrical Engineering M,D
Environmental Sciences D
Geological Engineering M,D
Geology M,D
Management of Technology M
Materials Engineering M,D*
Materials Sciences M,D
Mechanical Engineering M,D
Metallurgical Engineering and Metallurgy M,D
Physics M,D
Water Resources D
In-depth description on page 1093.

SOUTH DAKOTA STATE UNIVERSITY
Agricultural Engineering M,D
Agricultural Sciences—General M,D
Agronomy and Soil Sciences M,D
Analytical Chemistry M,D
Animal Sciences M,D
Atmospheric Sciences D*
Biochemistry M,D
Biological and Biomedical Sciences—General M,D
Chemistry M,D
Civil Engineering M
Communication—General M
Computer Science M
Counselor Education M
Curriculum and Instruction M
Economics M
Education—General M
Educational Administration M
Electrical Engineering M
Engineering and Applied Sciences—General M,D
English M
Entomology M
Environmental Engineering M
Environmental Sciences D
Family and Consumer Sciences-General M
Fish, Game, and Wildlife Management M,D
Geography M
Health Education M
Industrial/Management Engineering M
Inorganic Chemistry M,D
Journalism M
Mathematics M
Mechanical Engineering M
Microbiology M
Nursing—General M
Organic Chemistry M,D
Pharmaceutical Sciences M
Pharmacy P
Physical Chemistry M,D
Physical Education M
Physics M
Plant Pathology M
Plant Sciences M,D
Recreation and Park Management M
Rural Sociology M,D
Theater M
Water Resources D

SOUTHEASTERN BAPTIST THEOLOGICAL SEMINARY
Ethics P,M,D
Missions and Missiology P,M,D
Music P,M,D
Philosophy P,M,D
Psychology—General P,M,D
Religious Education P,M,D
Theology P,M,D
Women's Studies P,M,D

SOUTHEASTERN LOUISIANA UNIVERSITY
Biological and Biomedical Sciences—General M

Business Administration and Management—General M
Communication Disorders M
Communication—General M
Counselor Education M
Curriculum and Instruction M
Education—General M
Educational Administration M
English M
Health Education M
History M
Kinesiology and Movement Studies M
Music M
Nursing—General M
Psychology—General M
Special Education M

SOUTHEASTERN OKLAHOMA STATE UNIVERSITY

Business Administration and Management—General M
Counselor Education M
Education—General M
Educational Administration M
Educational Media/Instructional Technology M
Elementary Education M
Industrial and Manufacturing Management M
Secondary Education M

SOUTHEASTERN UNIVERSITY

Accounting M
Business Administration and Management—General M
Computer Science M
Finance and Banking M
Health Services Management and Hospital Administration M
International Business M
Management Information Systems M
Marketing M
Public Policy and Administration M
Taxation M

In-depth description on page 1095.

SOUTHEAST MISSOURI STATE UNIVERSITY

Accounting M
Art Education M
Biological and Biomedical Sciences—General M
Business Administration and Management—General M
Business Education M
Chemistry M
Communication Disorders M
Counselor Education M,D,O
Criminal Justice and Criminology M
Educational Administration M,D,O
Educational Media/Instructional Technology M
Elementary Education M
English as a Second Language M
English M
Exercise and Sports Science M
Family and Consumer Sciences-General M
Foundations and Philosophy of Education M
Geosciences M
History M
Human Resources Management M
Industrial and Manufacturing Management M
Mathematics M
Middle School Education M
Music Education M
Nursing—General M
Nutrition M
Public Policy and Administration M
Science Education M
Secondary Education M
Social Psychology M
Social Sciences Education M
Special Education M
Sports Management M

SOUTHERN ADVENTIST UNIVERSITY

Accounting M
Advanced Practice Nursing M
Business Administration and Management—General M
Counselor Education M
Curriculum and Instruction M
Education—General M
Educational Administration M
Health Services Management and Hospital Administration M
Marriage and Family Therapy M
Medical/Surgical Nursing M
Missions and Missiology M
Nursing and Healthcare Administration M
Nursing—General M
Psychology—General M
Religion M
Religious Education M
Software Engineering M

SOUTHERN ARKANSAS UNIVERSITY–MAGNOLIA

Counselor Education M
Education—General M
Educational Administration M
Elementary Education M
Kinesiology and Movement Studies M
Library Science M
Secondary Education M

SOUTHERN BAPTIST THEOLOGICAL SEMINARY

Missions and Missiology P,M,D
Music P,M,D
Pastoral Ministry and Counseling P,M,D
Religious Education P,M,D
Theology P,M,D

SOUTHERN CALIFORNIA BIBLE COLLEGE & SEMINARY

Counseling Psychology P,M
Religion P,M
Theology P,M

SOUTHERN CALIFORNIA COLLEGE OF OPTOMETRY

Optometry P

SOUTHERN CALIFORNIA INSTITUTE OF ARCHITECTURE

Architecture M*

SOUTHERN CALIFORNIA UNIVERSITY OF HEALTH SCIENCES

Acupuncture and Oriental Medicine M
Chiropractic P

SOUTHERN CHRISTIAN UNIVERSITY

Counseling Psychology P,M,D
Marriage and Family Therapy P,M,D
Theology P,M,D

SOUTHERN COLLEGE OF OPTOMETRY

Optometry P

SOUTHERN CONNECTICUT STATE UNIVERSITY

Art Education M
Biological and Biomedical Sciences—General M
Business Administration and Management—General M
Chemistry M
Communication Disorders M
Counselor Education M,O
Education—General M,O
Educational Administration O
Educational Measurement and Evaluation M
Educational Media/Instructional Technology M,O
Elementary Education M,O
English as a Second Language M
English M
Environmental Education M,O
Exercise and Sports Science M
Foundations and Philosophy of Education O
French M
Health Education M
History M
Information Studies M,O
Leisure Studies M
Library Science M,O
Marriage and Family Therapy M
Mathematics M
Multilingual and Multicultural Education M
Nursing and Healthcare Administration M
Nursing Education M
Nursing—General M
Physical Education M
Political Science M
Psychology—General M
Public Health—General M
Reading Education M,O
Recreation and Park Management M
Romance Languages M
School Psychology M,O
Science Education M,O
Social Work M
Sociology M
Spanish M
Special Education M,O
Sport Psychology M
Urban Studies M
Women's Studies M

In-depth description on page 1097 and announcement on page 525.

SOUTHERN EVANGELICAL SEMINARY

Missions and Missiology P,M,O
Pastoral Ministry and Counseling P,M,O
Religion P,M,O
Theology P,M,O

SOUTHERN ILLINOIS UNIVERSITY CARBONDALE

Accounting M,D*
Agricultural Economics and Agribusiness M*
Agricultural Sciences—General M
Agronomy and Soil Sciences M*
Allopathic Medicine P
Animal Sciences M*
Anthropology M,D*
Applied Arts and Design—General M*
Art/Fine Arts M
Biochemistry M,D
Biological and Biomedical Sciences—General M,D*
Business Administration and Management—General M,D*
Chemistry M,D*
Civil Engineering M*
Clinical Psychology M,D
Communication Disorders M*
Communication—General M,D*
Computer Science M*
Counseling Psychology M,D
Counselor Education M,D
Criminal Justice and Criminology M*
Cultural Studies M*
Curriculum and Instruction M,D*
Economics M,D*
Education—General M,D
Educational Administration M,D*
Educational Measurement and Evaluation M,D
Educational Psychology M,D*
Electrical Engineering M,D*
Energy and Power Engineering D
Engineering and Applied Sciences—General M,D*
English as a Second Language M
English M,D*
Environmental Sciences D*
Experimental Psychology M,D
Forestry M*
Geography M,D*
Geology M,D*
Health Education M,D*
Higher Education M*
History M,D*
Horticulture M
Human Development M,D
Law P
Linguistics M*
Manufacturing Engineering M*
Mathematics M,D*
Mechanical Engineering M*
Mechanics M,D
Microbiology M,D
Mineral/Mining Engineering M,D*
Molecular Biology M,D*
Music Education M
Music M*
Nutrition M*
Pharmacology M,D*
Philosophy M,D*
Physical Education M*
Physics M*
Physiology M,D*
Plant Biology M,D*
Plant Sciences M
Political Science M,D*
Psychology—General M,D*
Public Policy and Administration M*
Recreation and Park Management M*
Rehabilitation Counseling M,D*
Rhetoric M,D
Social Work M*
Sociology M,D*
Special Education M*
Speech and Interpersonal Communication M,D*
Statistics M,D
Theater M,D*
Vocational and Technical Education M,D*
Writing M*
Zoology M,D*

In-depth description on page 1099 and announcement on page 526.

SOUTHERN ILLINOIS UNIVERSITY EDWARDSVILLE

Accounting M
Advanced Practice Nursing M
Art Therapy M
Art/Fine Arts M
Biological and Biomedical Sciences—General M
Business Administration and Management—General M
Chemistry M
Civil Engineering M
Clinical Psychology M
Communication Disorders M
Community Health Nursing M
Computer Science M
Dentistry P
Economics M
Education—General M,O
Educational Administration M,O
Educational Media/Instructional Technology M
Educational Psychology M
Electrical Engineering M
Electronic Commerce M
Elementary Education M
Engineering and Applied Sciences—General M
English as a Second Language M
English Education M
English M
Environmental Sciences M
Exercise and Sports Science M,O
Finance and Banking M
Geography M
Health Education M,O
History M
Industrial and Organizational Psychology M
Kinesiology and Movement Studies M,O
Management Information Systems M
Marketing Research M
Mass Communication M
Mathematics M
Mechanical Engineering M
Medical/Surgical Nursing M
Music Education M
Music M
Nurse Anesthesia M
Nursing—General M
Physics M
Physiology M,O
Psychiatric Nursing M
Psychology—General M
Public Policy and Administration M
School Psychology O
Secondary Education M
Social Psychology M
Social Work M
Sociology M
Special Education M
Speech and Interpersonal Communication M
Statistics M
Textile Design M

In-depth description on page 1101.

SOUTHERN METHODIST UNIVERSITY

Accounting M
Anthropology M,D
Applied Economics M,D
Applied Mathematics M,D
Applied Science and Technology M,D
Archaeology M,D
Art History M
Art/Fine Arts M
Arts Administration
Biological and Biomedical Sciences—General M,D*
Business Administration and Management—General M
Chemistry M
Civil Engineering M,D
Clinical Psychology M
Communication—General M
Computer Engineering M,D
Computer Science M,D*
Counseling Psychology M
Dance M
Economics M,D
Electrical Engineering M,D*
Engineering and Applied Sciences—General M,D
Engineering Management M,D*
English M
Environmental Engineering M,D*
Geology M,D

Southern Methodist University (continued)

Geophysics M,D
History M,D*
Information Science M,D
Interdisciplinary Studies M
Latin American Studies M
Law P,M,D
Manufacturing Engineering M,D
Mathematics M,D
Mechanical Engineering M,D*
Medieval and Renaissance Studies M
Multilingual and Multicultural Education M
Music Education M
Music M
Operations Research M,D
Photography M
Physics M,D
Psychology—General M,D
Religion M,D
Software Engineering M,D
Statistics M,D
Systems Engineering M,D
Systems Science M,D
Taxation P,M,D
Telecommunications M,D
Theater M
Theology P,M,D
Therapies—Dance, Drama, and Music M

In-depth description on page 1103.

SOUTHERN NAZARENE UNIVERSITY

Business Administration and Management—General M
Counseling Psychology M
Education—General M
Marriage and Family Therapy M
Psychology—General M
Religion M
Theology M

SOUTHERN NEW ENGLAND SCHOOL OF LAW

Law P

SOUTHERN NEW HAMPSHIRE UNIVERSITY

Accounting M,O
Artificial Intelligence/Robotics M,O
Business Administration and Management—General M,O*
Business Education M
Economics M,D*
Finance and Banking M,O
Health Services Management and Hospital Administration M,O
Human Resources Management M,O
International Business M,D,O
Management Information Systems M,O
Marketing M,O
Taxation M,O
Telecommunications Management M,O

SOUTHERN OREGON UNIVERSITY

Business Administration and Management—General M
Computer Science M
Counselor Education M
Early Childhood Education M
Education—General M
Educational Administration M
Elementary Education M
Environmental Education M
Human Services M
Mathematics M
Music M
Psychology—General M
Reading Education M
Secondary Education M
Social Sciences M
Special Education M

SOUTHERN POLYTECHNIC STATE UNIVERSITY

Computer Engineering M
Computer Science M
Construction Engineering and Management M
Electrical Engineering M
Engineering and Applied Sciences—General M
Industrial/Management Engineering M
Information Science M
Management of Technology M
Software Engineering M
Special Education M
Technical Writing M

In-depth description on page 1105.

SOUTHERN UNIVERSITY AND AGRICULTURAL AND MECHANICAL COLLEGE

Accounting M
Advanced Practice Nursing M,D,O
Agricultural Sciences—General M
Analytical Chemistry M
Biochemistry M
Biological and Biomedical Sciences—General M
Business Administration and Management—General M
Chemistry M
Computer Science M
Counselor Education M
Education—General M
Educational Administration M
Educational Media/Instructional Technology M
Elementary Education M
Environmental Sciences M
Forestry M
History M
Inorganic Chemistry M
Law P*
Mass Communication M
Mathematics Education D
Mathematics M
Nursing and Healthcare Administration M,D,O
Nursing Education M,D,O
Nursing—General M,D,O
Organic Chemistry M
Physical Chemistry M
Physics M
Political Science M
Psychology—General M
Public Policy and Administration M,D
Recreation and Park Management M
Rehabilitation Counseling M*
Science Education D
Secondary Education M
Sociology M
Special Education M,D

SOUTHERN UNIVERSITY AT NEW ORLEANS

Social Work M

SOUTHERN UTAH UNIVERSITY

Accounting M
Art/Fine Arts M
Business Administration and Management—General M
Education—General M
Music M

SOUTHERN WESLEYAN UNIVERSITY

Business Administration and Management—General M
Pastoral Ministry and Counseling M

SOUTH TEXAS COLLEGE OF LAW

Law P

SOUTHWEST ACUPUNCTURE COLLEGE

Acupuncture and Oriental Medicine M

SOUTHWEST BAPTIST UNIVERSITY

Business Administration and Management—General M
Education—General M
Educational Administration M
Health Services Management and Hospital Administration M
Physical Therapy M

SOUTHWEST COLLEGE OF NATUROPATHIC MEDICINE AND HEALTH SCIENCES

Naturopathic Medicine D*

SOUTHWESTERN ADVENTIST UNIVERSITY

Accounting M
Business Administration and Management—General M
Education—General M
Elementary Education M

SOUTHWESTERN ASSEMBLIES OF GOD UNIVERSITY

Counseling Psychology M
Curriculum and Instruction M
Education—General M
Educational Administration M
Missions and Missiology M
Religious Education M
Theology M

SOUTHWESTERN BAPTIST THEOLOGICAL SEMINARY

Music P,M,D
Religious Education M,D
Theology P,M,D

SOUTHWESTERN CHRISTIAN UNIVERSITY

Pastoral Ministry and Counseling M

SOUTHWESTERN COLLEGE (KS)

Education—General M
Special Education M

SOUTHWESTERN COLLEGE (NM)

Art Therapy M,O
Counseling Psychology M,O
Counselor Education M,O
Psychology—General O

In-depth description on page 1107.

SOUTHWESTERN OKLAHOMA STATE UNIVERSITY

Art Education M
Business Administration and Management—General M
Counselor Education M
Early Childhood Education M
Education—General M
Educational Administration M
Educational Measurement and Evaluation M
Elementary Education M
Health Education M
Mathematics Education M
Music M
Pharmacy P
Physical Education M
Recreation and Park Management M
Science Education M
Secondary Education M
Social Sciences Education M
Special Education M
Vocational and Technical Education M

SOUTHWESTERN UNIVERSITY SCHOOL OF LAW

Law P,M

SOUTHWEST MISSOURI STATE UNIVERSITY

Accounting M
Agricultural Sciences—General M
Agronomy and Soil Sciences M
Applied Science and Technology M
Biological and Biomedical Sciences—General M
Business Administration and Management—General M
Cell Biology M
Chemistry M
City and Regional Planning M
Communication Disorders M
Communication—General M
Computer Science M
Counselor Education M
Early Childhood Education M
Education—General M
Educational Administration M,D,O
Educational Media/Instructional Technology M
Elementary Education M,O
English M
Environmental Management and Policy M
Health Promotion M
Health Services Management and Hospital Administration M
History M
International Affairs M
Management Information Systems M
Materials Sciences M
Mathematics M
Middle School Education M
Military and Defense Studies M*
Molecular Biology M
Music M
Nurse Anesthesia M
Nursing—General M
Physical Education M
Physical Therapy M
Physician Assistant Studies M
Plant Sciences M
Psychology—General M
Public Health—General M
Public Policy and Administration M
Reading Education M
Recreation and Park Management M

Religion M
Science Education M
Secondary Education M,O
Social Work M
Special Education M,O
Theater M
Vocational and Technical Education M,O

In-depth description on page 1109.

SOUTHWEST STATE UNIVERSITY

Business Administration and Management—General M
Education—General M

SOUTHWEST TEXAS STATE UNIVERSITY

Accounting M
Agricultural Education M
Allied Health—General M
Biochemistry M
Biological and Biomedical Sciences—General M
Business Administration and Management—General M
Chemistry M
Child and Family Studies M
Communication Disorders M
Communication—General M
Computer Science M*
Counselor Education M
Criminal Justice and Criminology M
Developmental Education M
Education—General M
Educational Administration M
Elementary Education M
English M
Environmental Management and Policy M
Foreign Languages Education M
Geographic Information Systems M
Geography M,D
Health Education M
Health Psychology M
Health Services Management and Hospital Administration M
Health Services Research M
History M
Industrial/Management Engineering M
Interdisciplinary Studies M
International Affairs M
Legal and Justice Studies M
Leisure Studies M
Liberal Studies M
Management of Technology M
Marine Biology M
Mass Communication M
Mathematics Education M
Mathematics M
Multilingual and Multicultural Education M
Music Education M
Music M
Physical Education M
Physical Therapy M
Physics M
Political Science M
Psychology—General M
Public Policy and Administration M
Reading Education M
Recreation and Park Management M
School Psychology M
Science Education M
Secondary Education M
Social Sciences Education M,D
Social Work M
Sociology M
Software Engineering M
Spanish M
Special Education M
Speech and Interpersonal Communication M
Technical Writing M
Theater M
Vocational and Technical Education M
Writing M

SPALDING UNIVERSITY

Advanced Practice Nursing M
Clinical Psychology M,D
Counselor Education M
Education—General M,D
Educational Administration M,D
Elementary Education M
Higher Education M
Library Science M
Middle School Education M
Nursing and Healthcare Administration M
Nursing—General M
Pastoral Ministry and Counseling M
Psychology—General M,D

Reading Education M
Religion M
Social Work M
Writing M

In-depth description on page 1111.

SPERTUS INSTITUTE OF JEWISH STUDIES

Human Services M
Jewish Studies M,D
Religious Education M

SPRING ARBOR UNIVERSITY

Business Administration and Management—General M
Education—General M
Organizational Management M

SPRINGFIELD COLLEGE

Addictions/Substance Abuse Counseling M,O
Art Therapy M,O
Counseling Psychology M,O
Counselor Education M,O
Education—General M
Exercise and Sports Science M,D,O
Health Education M
Health Promotion M,O
Health Services Management and Hospital Administration M
Human Services M
Industrial and Organizational Psychology M,O
Kinesiology and Movement Studies M
Marriage and Family Therapy M,O
Occupational Therapy M,O
Physical Education M,D,O
Physical Therapy M
Recreation and Park Management M
Rehabilitation Counseling M,O
Secondary Education M
Social Work M
Sport Psychology M,D,O
Sports Management M,D,O
Student Personnel Services M,O

In-depth description on page 1113.

SPRING HILL COLLEGE

Business Administration and Management—General M
Early Childhood Education M
Education—General M
Elementary Education M
Liberal Studies M
Secondary Education M
Theology M

STANFORD UNIVERSITY

Aerospace/Aeronautical Engineering M,D,O*
Allopathic Medicine P
Anthropology M,D
Applied Physics M,D
Art Education M,D
Art/Fine Arts M,D
Asian Languages M,D
Asian Studies M
Biochemistry D*
Biological and Biomedical Sciences—General M,D
Biomedical Engineering M
Biophysics D
Business Administration and Management—General M,D
Cancer Biology/Oncology D
Chemical Engineering M,D,O
Chemistry D*
Child and Family Studies D
Civil Engineering M,D,O
Classics M,D
Communication—General M,D
Comparative Literature D
Computational Sciences M,D
Computer Education M,D
Computer Science M,D
Counseling Psychology D
Curriculum and Instruction M,D
Developmental Biology D
Developmental Psychology D
East European and Russian Studies M
Economics D
Education—General M,D*
Educational Administration M,D
Educational Measurement and Evaluation M,D
Educational Psychology D
Electrical Engineering M,D,O
Engineering and Applied Sciences—General M,D,O
Engineering Design M
Engineering Management M,D*
English Education M,D
English M,D
Environmental Engineering M,D,O
Environmental Management and Policy M
Environmental Sciences M,D,O
Epidemiology M,D
Film, Television, and Video Production M,D
Foreign Languages Education M
Foundations and Philosophy of Education M,D
French M,D
Genetics D*
Geophysics M,D
Geosciences M,D,O
German M,D
Health Services Research M
Higher Education M,D
History M,D
Humanities M
Immunology D*
Industrial/Management Engineering M,D
Interdisciplinary Studies M,D
International Affairs M
International and Comparative Education M,D
Italian M,D
Journalism M,D
Latin American Studies M
Law P,M,D
Linguistics M,D
Manufacturing Engineering M,D
Materials Engineering M,D,O
Materials Sciences M,D,O
Mathematical and Computational Finance M,D
Mathematics Education M,D
Mathematics M,D
Mechanical Engineering M,D,O*
Medical Informatics M,D*
Microbiology D*
Music M,D*
Neuroscience D
Petroleum Engineering M,D,O
Pharmacology D
Philosophy M,D
Physics D
Physiology D
Political Science M,D
Psychology—General D
Religion M,D
Russian M,D
Science Education M,D
Slavic Languages M,D
Social Sciences Education M,D
Sociology D
Spanish M,D
Statistics M,D
Structural Biology D
Systems Engineering M
Theater D

STARR KING SCHOOL FOR THE MINISTRY

Theology P

STATE UNIVERSITY OF NEW YORK AT ALBANY

Accounting M
African Studies M
African-American Studies M
Anthropology M,D
Art/Fine Arts M
Atmospheric Sciences M,D*
Biochemistry M,D
Biological and Biomedical Sciences—General M,D*
Biometrics M,D
Biopsychology M,D
Business Administration and Management—General M,D
Cell Biology M,D
Chemistry M,D
City and Regional Planning M
Classics M
Clinical Psychology M,D
Communication—General M,D
Computer Science M,D
Conservation Biology M
Counseling Psychology M,D,O
Counselor Education M,D,O
Criminal Justice and Criminology M,D
Curriculum and Instruction M,D,O
Demography and Population Studies M,D,O
Developmental Biology M,D
Ecology M,D
Economics M,D,O
Education—General M,D,O
Educational Administration M,D,O
Educational Measurement and Evaluation M,D,O
Educational Media/Instructional Technology M,D,O
Educational Psychology M,D,O
English M,D*
Environmental and Occupational Health M,D
Environmental Management and Policy M
Environmental Sciences M
Epidemiology M,D
Evolutionary Biology M,D
Experimental Psychology M,D
Finance and Banking M
Forensic Sciences M,D
French M,D
Genetics M,D
Geographic Information Systems M,O
Geography M,O
Geology M,D
Geosciences M,D
Health Services Management and Hospital Administration M
History M,D,O
Human Resources Management M
Humanities D
Immunology M,D
Industrial and Organizational Psychology M,D
Information Science M,D,O
Interior Design M,D,O
Italian M
Latin American Studies M,O
Liberal Studies M
Library Science M,D,O
Management Information Systems M
Marketing M
Mathematics Education M,D
Mathematics M,D
Molecular Biology M,D
Neurobiology M,D
Neuroscience M,D
Organizational Management D
Pathology M,D
Philosophy M,D
Physics M,D
Political Science M,D
Psychology—General M,D
Public Health—General M,D
Public History M,D,O
Public Policy and Administration M,D,O
Reading Education M,D,O
Rehabilitation Counseling M
Russian M,D,O
School Psychology M,D,O
Science Education M,D
Social Psychology M,D
Social Work M,D
Sociology M,D,O
Spanish M,D
Special Education M
Statistics M,D,O
Structural Biology M,D
Taxation M
Theater M
Toxicology M,D*
Translation and Interpretation M,O
Urban Studies M,D,O
Women's Studies M

In-depth description on page 1115.

STATE UNIVERSITY OF NEW YORK AT BINGHAMTON

Accounting M,D
Analytical Chemistry M,D
Anthropology M,D
Applied Physics M
Art History M,D*
Biological and Biomedical Sciences—General M,D
Biopsychology M,D
Business Administration and Management—General M,D
Chemistry M,D
Clinical Psychology M,D
Cognitive Sciences M,D
Comparative Literature M,D
Computer Science M,D
Early Childhood Education M
Economics M,D
Education—General M,D
Electrical Engineering M,D
Elementary Education M
Engineering and Applied Sciences—General M,D*
English Education M
English M,D
Finance and Banking M,D
Foreign Languages Education M
Foundations and Philosophy of Education D
French M
Geography M
Geology M,D
Health Services Management and Hospital Administration M,D
History M,D
Industrial/Management Engineering M,D
Inorganic Chemistry M,D
Italian M
Mathematics Education M
Mathematics M,D
Mechanical Engineering M,D
Music M
Nursing—General M,D,O
Organic Chemistry M,D
Philosophy M,D
Physical Chemistry M,D
Physics M
Political Science M,D
Psychology—General M,D
Public Policy and Administration M,D
Reading Education M
Science Education M
Secondary Education M
Social Sciences Education M
Social Sciences M
Sociology M,D
Spanish M,O
Special Education M
Statistics M,D
Systems Science M,D
Theater M
Translation and Interpretation M,O

In-depth description on page 1117.

STATE UNIVERSITY OF NEW YORK AT NEW PALTZ

Accounting M
Art Education M
Art/Fine Arts M
Biological and Biomedical Sciences—General M
Business Administration and Management—General M
Chemistry M
Communication Disorders M
Computer Engineering M
Computer Science M
Early Childhood Education M
Education—General M,O
Educational Administration M,O
Electrical Engineering M
Elementary Education M
English as a Second Language M
English M
Environmental Education M
Finance and Banking M
Geology M
Gerontological Nursing M
International Business M
Marketing M
Mathematics M
Music Education M
Music M
Nursing—General M
Photography M
Physics M
Psychology—General M
Reading Education M
Secondary Education M
Sociology M
Special Education M

STATE UNIVERSITY OF NEW YORK AT OSWEGO

Art Education M
Art/Fine Arts M
Business Administration and Management—General M
Chemistry M
Counseling Psychology M,O
Education—General M,O
Educational Administration M,O
Elementary Education M
English M
History M
Human Services M
Reading Education M
School Psychology M,O
Secondary Education M
Special Education M
Vocational and Technical Education M

STATE UNIVERSITY OF NEW YORK COLLEGE AT BROCKPORT

Advanced Practice Nursing M,O
Art/Fine Arts M
Biological and Biomedical Sciences—General M
Communication—General M
Computational Sciences M
Counselor Education M,O
Dance M
Education—General M
Educational Administration M,O
Elementary Education M
English Education M
English M
Health Education M
History M
Leisure Studies M
Liberal Studies M
Mathematics Education M
Mathematics M*

State University of New York College at Brockport (continued)

Multilingual and Multicultural Education M
Physical Education M
Psychology—General M
Public Policy and Administration M
Reading Education M
Recreation and Park Management M
Science Education M
Secondary Education M
Social Sciences Education M
Social Work M
Special Education M

In-depth description on page 1119.

STATE UNIVERSITY OF NEW YORK COLLEGE AT BUFFALO

Adult Education M
Applied Economics M
Art Education M
Biological and Biomedical Sciences—General M
Business Education M
Chemistry M
Communication Disorders M
Criminal Justice and Criminology M
Early Childhood Education M
Economics M
Educational Administration O
Educational Media/Instructional Technology M
Elementary Education M,O
English Education M
English M
Historic Preservation M,O
History M
Industrial/Management Engineering M
Interdisciplinary Studies M
Mathematics Education M
Multilingual and Multicultural Education M
Reading Education M,O
Science Education M
Social Sciences Education M
Special Education M
Student Personnel Services M
Vocational and Technical Education M

STATE UNIVERSITY OF NEW YORK COLLEGE AT CORTLAND

American Studies O
Biological and Biomedical Sciences—General M
Early Childhood Education M
Education—General M,O
Educational Administration O
Elementary Education M
English Education M
English M
Foreign Languages Education M
Health Education M
History M
Mathematics Education M
Physical Education M
Reading Education M
Recreation and Park Management M
Science Education M
Secondary Education M
Social Sciences Education M

STATE UNIVERSITY OF NEW YORK COLLEGE AT FREDONIA

Biological and Biomedical Sciences—General M
Chemistry M
Communication Disorders M
Education—General M,O
Educational Administration O
Elementary Education M
English M
Mathematics Education M
Music Education M
Music M
Reading Education M
Secondary Education M
Social Sciences M

STATE UNIVERSITY OF NEW YORK COLLEGE AT GENESEO

Communication Disorders M
Education—General M
Elementary Education M
Reading Education M
Secondary Education M
Special Education M

STATE UNIVERSITY OF NEW YORK COLLEGE AT ONEONTA

Biological and Biomedical Sciences—General M
Counselor Education M,O
Education—General M,O
Elementary Education M
Geosciences M
Marriage and Family Therapy M,O
Middle School Education M
Museum Studies M
Reading Education M
Secondary Education M
Social Psychology M,O

STATE UNIVERSITY OF NEW YORK COLLEGE AT POTSDAM

Education—General M
Educational Media/Instructional Technology M
Elementary Education M
English M
Mathematics M
Music Education M
Music M
Reading Education M
Secondary Education M
Special Education M

STATE UNIVERSITY OF NEW YORK COLLEGE OF ENVIRONMENTAL SCIENCE AND FORESTRY

Biochemistry M,D
Chemistry M,D
City and Regional Planning M,D
Communication—General M,D
Conservation Biology M,D
Construction Engineering and Management M,D
Ecology M,D
Entomology M,D
Environmental Biology M,D
Environmental Design M
Environmental Engineering M,D
Environmental Management and Policy M,D
Environmental Sciences M,D
Fish, Game, and Wildlife Management M,D
Forestry M,D
Hydrology M,D
Landscape Architecture M
Natural Resources M,D
Organic Chemistry M,D
Paper and Pulp Engineering M,D
Plant Pathology M,D
Plant Sciences M,D
Recreation and Park Management M,D
Urban Design M
Water Resources M,D

STATE UNIVERSITY OF NEW YORK COLLEGE OF OPTOMETRY

Optometry P
Vision Sciences M,D

STATE UNIVERSITY OF NEW YORK EMPIRE STATE COLLEGE

Business Administration and Management—General M
Industrial and Labor Relations M
Liberal Studies M
Public Policy and Administration M

STATE UNIVERSITY OF NEW YORK HEALTH SCIENCE CENTER AT BROOKLYN

Advanced Practice Nursing M,O
Allopathic Medicine P
Anatomy D
Biological and Biomedical Sciences—General D*
Cell Biology D
Molecular Biology D
Neuroscience D
Nurse Anesthesia M
Nursing—General M,O
Pharmacology D

STATE UNIVERSITY OF NEW YORK INSTITUTE OF TECHNOLOGY AT UTICA/ROME

Accounting M*
Advanced Practice Nursing M,O
Business Administration and Management—General M
Computer Science M*
Engineering and Applied Sciences—General M
Health Services Management and Hospital Administration M
Information Science M
Nursing and Healthcare Administration M,O
Nursing—General M,O
Sociology M
Telecommunications M*

In-depth description on page 1121.

STATE UNIVERSITY OF NEW YORK MARITIME COLLEGE

Transportation Management M

STATE UNIVERSITY OF NEW YORK UPSTATE MEDICAL UNIVERSITY

Allied Health—General M
Allopathic Medicine P
Anatomy M,D
Biochemistry M,D*
Biological and Biomedical Sciences—General M,D*
Cell Biology M,D*
Clinical Laboratory Sciences/Medical Technology M
Developmental Biology D
Immunology M,D
Microbiology M,D
Molecular Biology M,D
Neuroscience D
Nursing—General M
Pharmacology M,D
Physical Therapy M
Physiology M,D

STATE UNIVERSITY OF WEST GEORGIA

Accounting M
Art Education M
Biological and Biomedical Sciences—General M
Business Administration and Management—General M
Business Education M,O
Communication Disorders M
Computer Science M
Counselor Education M,O
Early Childhood Education M,O
Education—General M,D,O
Educational Administration M,O
Educational Measurement and Evaluation D
Educational Media/Instructional Technology M,O
English Education M,O
English M
Foreign Languages Education M
Gerontology M
History M
Mathematics Education M,O
Middle School Education M,O
Music Education M
Music M
Physical Education M,O
Psychology—General M
Public Policy and Administration M
Reading Education M
Rural Planning and Studies M
Science Education M,O
Secondary Education M,O
Social Sciences Education M,O
Sociology M
Special Education M,O

STEPHEN F. AUSTIN STATE UNIVERSITY

Accounting M
Agricultural Education M
Applied Arts and Design—General M
Art/Fine Arts M
Biological and Biomedical Sciences—General M
Biotechnology M
Business Administration and Management—General M
Chemistry M
Communication Disorders M
Communication—General M
Computer Science M
Counselor Education M
Early Childhood Education M
Education—General M,D
Educational Administration M,D
Elementary Education M
English M
Environmental Sciences M
Family and Consumer Sciences-General M
Forestry M,D
Geology M
Health Education M
History M
Interdisciplinary Studies M
Marketing M
Mass Communication M
Mathematics Education M
Mathematics M
Music M
Physical Education M
Physics M
Psychology—General M
Public Policy and Administration M
School Psychology M
Secondary Education M,D
Social Work M
Special Education M
Statistics M

STEPHENS COLLEGE

Business Administration and Management—General M
Counselor Education M
Education—General M
Special Education M

STETSON UNIVERSITY

Accounting M
Business Administration and Management—General M
Counselor Education M
Education—General M,O
Educational Administration M,O
Elementary Education M,O
English M
Law P,M
Marriage and Family Therapy M
Special Education M

STEVENS INSTITUTE OF TECHNOLOGY

Analytical Chemistry M,D,O
Applied Mathematics M,D
Biochemistry M,D,O
Business Administration and Management—General M,D,O
Chemical Engineering M,D,O
Chemistry M,D,O
Civil Engineering M,D,O
Computer Engineering M,D,O
Computer Science M,D,O*
Construction Engineering and Management M
Electrical Engineering M,D,O
Electronic Commerce M,O
Engineering and Applied Sciences—General M,D,O*
Engineering Physics M,D,O
Environmental Engineering M,D,O
Industrial and Manufacturing Management M,O
Information Science M,O
Management Information Systems M,D,O
Management of Technology M,D,O
Management Strategy and Policy M
Marine Affairs M
Materials Engineering M,D,O
Materials Sciences M,D,O
Mathematics M,D
Mechanical Engineering M,D,O*
Ocean Engineering M,D
Organic Chemistry M,D,O
Physical Chemistry M,D,O
Physics M,D,O
Project Management M,O
Science Education O
Software Engineering O
Statistics M,O
Telecommunications Management M,D,O

In-depth description on page 1123.

STONEHILL COLLEGE

Accounting M

STONY BROOK UNIVERSITY, STATE UNIVERSITY OF NEW YORK

Advanced Practice Nursing M,O
Allopathic Medicine P
American Studies M,O
Anatomy D*
Anthropology M,D*
Applied Mathematics M,D*
Art Education M,O
Art History M,D*
Art/Fine Arts M*
Atmospheric Sciences M,D*
Biochemistry D*
Biological and Biomedical Sciences—General M,D*
Biomedical Engineering M,D,O*
Biophysics D*
Biopsychology D*
Business Administration and Management—General M,O*
Cell Biology M,D
Chemistry M,D*
Clinical Psychology D
Community Health M,O
Comparative Literature M,D*
Computer Education M*
Computer Engineering M,D
Computer Science M,D,O*
Cultural Studies M,O
Dentistry P,O
Developmental Biology M,D*
Ecology D*
Economics M,D*
Educational Administration M,O
Educational Media/Instructional Technology M,O
Electrical Engineering M,D*
Engineering and Applied Sciences—General M,D,O
English as a Second Language M,D

English Education M,O
English M,D*
Environmental and Occupational Health M,O
Environmental Management and Policy M*
Environmental Sciences M
Evolutionary Biology D
Experimental Psychology D*
Foreign Languages Education M,O
French M,D
Genetics D*
Geosciences M,D*
German M,D
Gerontological Nursing M
Hazardous Materials Management M,O
Health Psychology D
Health Services Management and Hospital Administration M,O
Hispanic Studies M,D*
History M,D*
Human Resources Management M,O
Immunology M,D
Industrial and Labor Relations M,O
Industrial and Manufacturing Management M,O
Industrial/Management Engineering M
Italian M,D
Liberal Studies M,O
Linguistics M,D*
Management Information Systems M,O
Management of Technology M,O*
Marine Sciences M*
Materials Engineering M,D
Materials Sciences M,D*
Maternal/Child Nursing M,O
Mathematics M,D*
Mechanical Engineering M,D,O*
Medical Physics D
Medical/Surgical Nursing M,O
Microbiology D*
Molecular Biology M,D*
Music M,D*
Neurobiology D*
Nurse Midwifery M,O
Nursing—General M,O
Oceanography M,D,O
Oral and Dental Sciences P,D,O*
Pathology M,D
Pediatric Nursing M,O
Pharmacology D*
Philosophy M,D,O*
Physical Education M,O
Physics M,D
Physiology D*
Planetary and Space Sciences M,D
Political Science M,D*
Psychiatric Nursing M,O
Psychology—General M,D*
Public Policy and Administration M,D,O*
Romance Languages M,D
Russian M,D
Science Education M,O
Slavic Languages M
Social Psychology D*
Social Sciences Education M,O
Social Sciences M,O
Social Work M,D*
Sociology M,D*
Software Engineering M,D,O
Statistics M,D
Structural Biology D
Theater M
Women's Health Nursing M,O
Women's Studies M,O

In-depth description on page 1125.

STRAYER UNIVERSITY

Business Administration and Management—General M

SUFFOLK UNIVERSITY

Accounting M,O
Adult Education M,O
Applied Arts and Design—General M
Business Administration and Management—General M,O*
Clinical Psychology D*
Communication—General M*
Computer Science M
Counselor Education M,O
Criminal Justice and Criminology
Curriculum and Instruction M,O
Developmental Psychology D
Disability Studies M,O
Economics M
Education—General M,O*
Educational Administration M,O
Finance and Banking M,O
Foundations and Philosophy of Education M,O
Health Services Management and Hospital Administration M,O
Human Resources Development M,O
Human Resources Management M,O
Interior Design M*
International Business M
Law P
Media Studies M
Nonprofit Management M,O
Philanthropic Studies M
Political Science M*
Psychology—General D
Public Policy and Administration M,O
Secondary Education M
Taxation M,O

SULLIVAN UNIVERSITY

Business Administration and Management—General M

SUL ROSS STATE UNIVERSITY

Animal Sciences M
Applied Arts and Design—General M
Art Education M
Art History M
Art/Fine Arts M
Biological and Biomedical Sciences—General M
Business Administration and Management—General M
Chemistry M
Counselor Education M
Criminal Justice and Criminology M
Education—General M
Educational Administration M
Educational Measurement and Evaluation M
Elementary Education M
English M
Fish, Game, and Wildlife Management M
Geology M*
History M
International Business M
Multilingual and Multicultural Education M
Physical Education M
Political Science M
Psychology—General M
Public Policy and Administration M
Range Science M
Reading Education M
Secondary Education M
Textile Design M
Vocational and Technical Education M

SUNBRIDGE COLLEGE

Early Childhood Education M
Education—General M
Elementary Education M

SYRACUSE UNIVERSITY

Accounting M,D
Advertising and Public Relations M
Aerospace/Aeronautical Engineering M,D
Anthropology M,D
Applied Arts and Design—General M
Architecture M
Art Education M,O
Art History M*
Art/Fine Arts M
Biochemistry D
Bioengineering M,D*
Biological and Biomedical Sciences—General M,D*
Biomedical Engineering M,D
Biophysics M,D
Business Administration and Management—General M,D*
Chemical Engineering M,D*
Chemistry M,D
Child and Family Studies M,D
Civil Engineering M,D*
Classics M
Clinical Psychology M,D
Clothing and Textiles M
Communication Disorders M,D
Communication—General M,D*
Computer Art and Design M
Computer Engineering M,D,O
Computer Science M,D
Consumer Economics M
Corporate and Organizational Communication M
Counselor Education M,D,O
Curriculum and Instruction M,D,O
Early Childhood Education M
Economics M,D
Education—General M,D,O*
Educational Administration M,D,O
Educational Measurement and Evaluation M,D,O
Electrical Engineering M,D,O*
Elementary Education M,O
Engineering and Applied Sciences—General M,D,O*
Engineering Management M
English Education M,D,O
English M,D
Environmental Engineering M,D
Exercise and Sports Science M,O
Experimental Psychology M,D
Film, Television, and Video Production M
Finance and Banking M,D
Foundations and Philosophy of Education M,D,O
French M
Geography M,D
Geology M,D
Graphic Design M
Health Services Management and Hospital Administration O
Higher Education M,D,O
History M,D
Human Resources Development D
Hydrology M,D
Illustration M
Industrial and Manufacturing Management D
Information Science M,D
Information Studies M,D*
International Affairs M
Internet and Interactive Multimedia M
Journalism M
Law P
Library Science M,O
Linguistics M
Logistics D
Management Information Systems M,D*
Management Strategy and Policy D
Manufacturing Engineering M
Marketing D
Marriage and Family Therapy M,D
Mass Communication D
Materials Sciences M,D
Mathematics Education M,D,O
Mathematics M,D
Mechanical Engineering M*
Media Studies M
Museum Studies M
Music Education M
Music M
Neuroscience M,D
Nursing—General M
Nutrition M
Organizational Behavior D
Philosophy M,D
Photography M
Physics M,D
Political Science M,D
Psychology—General M,D
Public Policy and Administration M,D*
Quantitative Analysis D
Reading Education M,D,O
Rehabilitation Counseling M,D
Religion M,D
Rhetoric D
School Psychology D
Science Education M,D,O
Social Psychology D
Social Sciences Education M,O
Social Sciences M,D
Social Work M
Sociology M,D
Spanish M
Special Education M,D
Speech and Interpersonal Communication M
Statistics M
Structural Biology D
Systems Science M
Telecommunications Management M
Telecommunications M*
Textile Design M
Theater M
Women's Studies O
Writing M,D

TAI HSUAN FOUNDATION: COLLEGE OF ACUPUNCTURE AND HERBAL MEDICINE

Acupuncture and Oriental Medicine M

TAI SOPHIA INSTITUTE

Acupuncture and Oriental Medicine M

TALMUDIC COLLEGE OF FLORIDA

Theology M,D

TARLETON STATE UNIVERSITY

Agricultural Sciences—General M
Biological and Biomedical Sciences—General M
Business Administration and Management—General M
Computer Science M
Counseling Psychology M
Counselor Education M
Criminal Justice and Criminology M
Curriculum and Instruction M
Education—General M,O
Educational Administration M,O
English M
Environmental Sciences M
Health Education M,O
History M
Information Science M
Mathematics M
Physical Education M,O
Political Science M
Reading Education M,O
School Psychology M
Secondary Education M,O
Special Education M,O

TAYLOR UNIVERSITY COLLEGE AND SEMINARY

Theology P,M

TEACHERS COLLEGE COLUMBIA UNIVERSITY

Adult Education M,D
Anthropology M,D
Art Education M,D
Arts Administration M
Clinical Psychology M,D
Communication Disorders M,D
Communication—General M,D
Computer Education M
Counseling Psychology M,D
Curriculum and Instruction M,D
Dance M
Developmental Psychology M,D
Early Childhood Education M,D
Economics M,D
Education of the Gifted M,D
Education—General M,D*
Educational Administration M,D
Educational Measurement and Evaluation M,D
Educational Media/Instructional Technology M,D
Educational Psychology M,D
Elementary Education M
English as a Second Language M,D
English Education M,D
Foreign Languages Education M,D
Foundations and Philosophy of Education M,D
Health Education M,D
Higher Education M,D
Industrial and Organizational Psychology M,D
Interdisciplinary Studies M,D
International and Comparative Education M,D
Kinesiology and Movement Studies M,D
Linguistics M,D
Mathematics Education M,D
Multilingual and Multicultural Education M
Music Education M,D
Neuroscience M
Nursing Education M,D
Physical Education M,D
Physiology M,D
Political Science M,D
Reading Education M
Religious Education M,D
School Psychology M,D
Science Education M,D
Social Psychology M,D
Social Sciences Education M,D
Sociology M,D
Special Education M,D
Student Personnel Services M,D

TECHNICAL UNIVERSITY OF BRITISH COLUMBIA

Computer Science M
Information Science M
Interdisciplinary Studies D

Technical University of British Columbia (continued)

Internet and Interactive Multimedia M
Management of Technology M
Software Engineering M

TÉLÉ-UNIVERSITÉ

Distance Education Development M,D
Finance and Banking M,D

TEMPLE BAPTIST SEMINARY

Theology P,M,D

TEMPLE UNIVERSITY

Accounting M,D
Actuarial Science M
African-American Studies M,D
Allied Health—General M,D*
Allopathic Medicine P
Anatomy D
Anthropology M,D
Applied Mathematics M,D
Art Education M
Art History M,D*
Art/Fine Arts M
Arts Administration M,D
Biochemistry M,D
Biological and Biomedical Sciences—General M,D*
Business Administration and Management—General M,D*
Cell Biology D
Chemistry M,D
Civil Engineering M
Clinical Psychology D
Cognitive Sciences D
Communication Disorders M
Communication—General M,D*
Community Health M
Computational Sciences M,D
Computer Engineering M
Computer Science M,D
Counseling Psychology M,D
Criminal Justice and Criminology M,D
Dance M,D
Dentistry P
Developmental Psychology D
Early Childhood Education M,D
Economics M,D
Education—General M,D
Educational Administration M,D
Educational Psychology M,D
Electrical Engineering M
Electronic Commerce M*
Elementary Education M,D
Engineering and Applied Sciences—General M,D*
English M,D*
Environmental and Occupational Health M
Environmental Engineering M
Experimental Psychology D
Film, Television, and Video Production M
Finance and Banking M,D
Genetics D
Geography M
Geology M
Graphic Design M
Health Education M,D
Health Services Management and Hospital Administration M,D
History M,D
Hospitality Management M
Human Resources Management M,D
Immunology M,D
Industrial and Organizational Psychology M,D
Information Science M,D
Insurance M,D
International Business M,D
Journalism M
Kinesiology and Movement Studies M,D
Law P,M
Leisure Studies M
Liberal Studies M
Linguistics M
Management Information Systems M,D
Management Strategy and Policy M,D
Marketing M,D
Mass Communication D
Mathematics Education M,D
Mathematics M,D*
Mechanical Engineering M
Media Studies M,D
Medicinal and Pharmaceutical Chemistry M,D
Microbiology M,D*
Molecular Biology D*
Music Education M,D
Music M,D
Nursing—General M
Occupational Therapy M
Operations Research M,D
Oral and Dental Sciences M,O
Pathology D*
Pharmaceutical Sciences M,D
Pharmacology M,D
Pharmacy P
Philosophy M,D
Photography M
Physical Education M,D
Physical Therapy M,D
Physics M,D*
Physiology M,D
Podiatric Medicine P
Political Science M,D
Psychology—General D*
Public Health—General M*
Reading Education M,D
Recreation and Park Management M
Religion M,D
School Psychology M,D
Science Education M,D
Secondary Education M,D
Social Psychology D
Social Work M
Sociology M,D
Spanish M,D
Special Education M,D
Speech and Interpersonal Communication M
Sports Management M
Statistics M,D
Taxation P,M
Textile Design M
Theater M
Therapies—Dance, Drama, and Music M,D
Travel and Tourism M,D*
Urban Education M,D
Urban Studies M
Vocational and Technical Education M,D
Writing M

In-depth description on page 1127 and announcement on page 547.

TENNESSEE STATE UNIVERSITY

Agricultural Sciences—General M
Allied Health—General M
Biological and Biomedical Sciences—General M,D*
Business Administration and Management—General M
Chemistry M
Child and Family Studies M
Counseling Psychology M,D
Counselor Education M,D
Criminal Justice and Criminology M
Curriculum and Instruction M,D
Education—General M,D
Educational Administration M,D
Elementary Education M,D
Engineering and Applied Sciences—General M
English M
Exercise and Sports Science M
Mathematics M
Music Education M
Nursing—General M
Physical Education M
Psychology—General M,D
Public Policy and Administration M,D
School Psychology M,D
Special Education M,D

TENNESSEE TECHNOLOGICAL UNIVERSITY

Biological and Biomedical Sciences—General M
Business Administration and Management—General M*
Chemical Engineering M,D
Chemistry M
Civil Engineering M,D
Curriculum and Instruction M,O
Early Childhood Education M,O
Education of the Gifted D
Education—General M,D,O
Educational Administration M,O
Educational Psychology M,O
Electrical Engineering M,D
Elementary Education M,O
Engineering and Applied Sciences—General M,D*
English M
Environmental Biology M
Environmental Sciences D*
Fish, Game, and Wildlife Management M
Health Education M
Industrial/Management Engineering M,D
Library Science M
Mathematics M
Mechanical Engineering M,D
Physical Education M
Reading Education M,O
Secondary Education M,O
Special Education M,O*
Student Personnel Services M,O

TENNESSEE TEMPLE UNIVERSITY

Curriculum and Instruction M
Education—General M
Educational Administration M

TEXAS A&M INTERNATIONAL UNIVERSITY

Accounting M
Biological and Biomedical Sciences—General M
Business Administration and Management—General M
Counseling Psychology M
Criminal Justice and Criminology M
Curriculum and Instruction M
Early Childhood Education M
Education—General M
Educational Administration M
English M
Finance and Banking M
History M
Interdisciplinary Studies M
International Business M
Management Information Systems M
Mathematics M
Multilingual and Multicultural Education M
Political Science M
Psychology—General M
Public Policy and Administration M
Reading Education M
Social Sciences M
Sociology M
Spanish M
Special Education M

TEXAS A&M UNIVERSITY

Accounting M,D
Aerospace/Aeronautical Engineering M,D
Agricultural Economics and Agribusiness M,D
Agricultural Education M,D
Agricultural Engineering M,D
Agricultural Sciences—General M,D
Agronomy and Soil Sciences M,D
Anatomy M,D
Animal Sciences M,D
Anthropology M,D
Applied Physics M,D
Architectural History M,D
Architecture M,D
Biochemistry M,D*
Bioengineering M,D
Biological and Biomedical Sciences—General M,D*
Biomedical Engineering M,D
Biophysics M,D
Biotechnology M
Botany M,D*
Business Administration and Management—General M,D
Cell Biology D
Chemical Engineering M,D
Chemistry M,D*
City and Regional Planning M,D
Civil Engineering M,D*
Clinical Psychology M,D
Computer Engineering M,D
Computer Science M,D*
Construction Engineering and Management M,D
Counseling Psychology D
Counselor Education M,D
Curriculum and Instruction M,D
Economics M,D
Education of the Gifted M,D
Education—General M,D
Educational Administration M,D
Educational Measurement and Evaluation M,D
Educational Media/Instructional Technology M,D
Educational Psychology M,D
Electrical Engineering M,D*
Engineering and Applied Sciences—General M,D
English M,D
Entomology M,D*
Environmental Engineering M,D
Epidemiology M,D
Finance and Banking M,D
Fish, Game, and Wildlife Management M,D
Food Science and Technology M,D
Forestry M,D
Foundations and Philosophy of Education M,D
Genetics M,D*
Geography M,D
Geology M,D
Geophysics M,D
Geotechnical Engineering M,D
Health Education M,D
Health Physics/Radiological Health M*
Historic Preservation M,D
History M,D
Horticulture M,D
Human Development M,D
Human Resources Development M,D
Human Resources Management M*
Hydraulics M,D
Hydrology M,D
Industrial and Organizational Psychology M,D
Industrial Hygiene M
Industrial/Management Engineering M,D
International Affairs M
Journalism M
Kinesiology and Movement Studies M,D
Landscape Architecture M,D
Management Information Systems M,D
Marketing M,D
Materials Engineering M,D
Mathematics Education M,D
Mathematics M,D
Mechanical Engineering M,D*
Meteorology M,D
Microbiology M,D
Molecular Biology D
Multilingual and Multicultural Education M,D
Natural Resources M,D
Nuclear Engineering M,D*
Nutrition M,D
Ocean Engineering M,D
Oceanography M,D
Parasitology M,D
Pathobiology M,D
Pathology M,D
Petroleum Engineering M,D*
Philosophy M,D
Physical Education M,D
Physics M,D
Physiology M,D
Plant Biology M,D
Plant Pathology M,D
Plant Sciences M,D
Political Science M,D
Project Management M,D
Psychology—General M,D
Public Health—General M,D
Public Policy and Administration M*
Range Science M,D
Reading Education M,D
Real Estate M
Recreation and Park Management M,D
Reproductive Biology M,D
Safety Engineering M
School Psychology D
Science Education M,D
Sociology M,D*
Spanish M
Special Education M,D
Speech and Interpersonal Communication M,D
Statistics M,D
Structural Engineering M,D
Toxicology M,D
Transportation and Highway Engineering M,D
Veterinary Medicine P,M,D
Veterinary Sciences M,D
Water Resources Engineering M,D
Zoology M,D

TEXAS A&M UNIVERSITY–COMMERCE

Agricultural Education M
Agricultural Sciences—General M
Art History M
Art/Fine Arts M
Biological and Biomedical Sciences—General M
Business Administration and Management—General M
Chemistry M
Computer Science M
Counseling Psychology M,D
Counselor Education M,D
Early Childhood Education M,D
Economics M
Education—General M,D
Educational Administration M,D
Educational Media/Instructional Technology M,D
Educational Psychology M,D
Elementary Education M,D
English Education M,D
English M,D
Geosciences M
Health Education M
Higher Education M,D
History M
Industrial/Management Engineering M
Management of Technology M

Program	Degrees
Mathematics	M
Music Education	M
Music	M
Physical Education	M
Physics	M
Psychology—General	M,D
Reading Education	M,D
Secondary Education	M,D
Social Sciences Education	M
Social Sciences	M
Social Work	M
Sociology	M
Spanish	M,D
Special Education	M,D
Speech and Interpersonal Communication	M
Theater	M
Vocational and Technical Education	M,D

In-depth description on page 1129.

TEXAS A&M UNIVERSITY–CORPUS CHRISTI

Program	Degrees
Accounting	M
Biological and Biomedical Sciences—General	M
Business Administration and Management—General	M
Computer Science	M
Counselor Education	M
Curriculum and Instruction	M
Education—General	M,D
Educational Administration	M,D
Elementary Education	M
English	M
Environmental Sciences	M
Interdisciplinary Studies	M
Mathematics	M
Nursing and Healthcare Administration	M
Nursing—General	M
Psychology—General	M
Public Policy and Administration	M
Secondary Education	M
Special Education	M
Vocational and Technical Education	M

TEXAS A&M UNIVERSITY–KINGSVILLE

Program	Degrees
Adult Education	M
Agricultural Economics and Agribusiness	M
Agricultural Education	M
Agricultural Sciences—General	M,D
Agronomy and Soil Sciences	M
Animal Sciences	M
Art/Fine Arts	M
Biological and Biomedical Sciences—General	M
Business Administration and Management—General	M
Chemical Engineering	M
Chemistry	M
Civil Engineering	M
Communication Disorders	M
Computer Science	M
Counselor Education	M
Early Childhood Education	M
Education—General	M,D
Educational Administration	M,D
Electrical Engineering	M
Elementary Education	M
Engineering and Applied Sciences—General	M*
English as a Second Language	M
English	M
Environmental Engineering	M*
Family and Consumer Sciences-General	M
Fish, Game, and Wildlife Management	M,D
Foreign Languages Education	M
Geology	M
Gerontology	M
Health Education	M
Higher Education	D
History	M
Industrial/Management Engineering	M
Kinesiology and Movement Studies	M
Mathematics	M
Mechanical Engineering	M
Multilingual and Multicultural Education	M,D
Music Education	M
Petroleum Engineering	M
Plant Sciences	M
Political Science	M
Psychology—General	M
Range Science	M
Reading Education	M
Secondary Education	M
Sociology	M
Spanish	M
Special Education	M

In-depth description on page 1131.

TEXAS A&M UNIVERSITY SYSTEM HEALTH SCIENCE CENTER

Program	Degrees
Anatomy	D*
Biochemistry	D*
Biological and Biomedical Sciences—General	M,D*
Dental Hygiene	M
Dentistry	P
Environmental and Occupational Health	M
Epidemiology	M
Genetics	D*
Health Education	M
Health Services Management and Hospital Administration	M
Immunology	D
Medical Microbiology	D*
Microbiology	D
Molecular Biology	D*
Neurobiology	D
Neuroscience	D*
Oral and Dental Sciences	P,M,D,O
Pathology	D*
Pharmacology	D*
Physiology	D*
Public Health—General	M
Toxicology	D
Virology	D

TEXAS A&M UNIVERSITY–TEXARKANA

Program	Degrees
Accounting	M
Adult Education	M
Business Administration and Management—General	M
Counseling Psychology	M
Education—General	M
Educational Administration	M
Elementary Education	M
Interdisciplinary Studies	M
Secondary Education	M
Special Education	M

TEXAS CHIROPRACTIC COLLEGE

Program	Degrees
Chiropractic	P*

TEXAS CHRISTIAN UNIVERSITY

Program	Degrees
Accounting	M
Advertising and Public Relations	M
Allied Health—General	M
Art History	M
Art/Fine Arts	M*
Biological and Biomedical Sciences—General	M
Business Administration and Management—General	M
Chemistry	M,D
Communication Disorders	M
Counselor Education	M
Dance	M
Economics	M
Education—General	M,D,O
Educational Administration	M,D
Educational Measurement and Evaluation	M
Elementary Education	M,O
English	M,D
Environmental Sciences	M
Geology	M
History	M,D
Journalism	M
Kinesiology and Movement Studies	M
Liberal Studies	M
Mass Communication	M
Mathematics	M
Media Studies	M
Music Education	M
Music	M
Nursing—General	M
Pastoral Ministry and Counseling	P,M,D,O
Physics	M,D
Psychology—General	M,D
Secondary Education	M,O
Special Education	M
Speech and Interpersonal Communication	M
Theology	P,M,D,O

TEXAS COLLEGE OF TRADITIONAL CHINESE MEDICINE

Program	Degrees
Acupuncture and Oriental Medicine	M

TEXAS SOUTHERN UNIVERSITY

Program	Degrees
Biological and Biomedical Sciences—General	M
Business Administration and Management—General	M
Business Education	M
Chemistry	M
City and Regional Planning	M
Communication—General	M
Counselor Education	M,D
Curriculum and Instruction	M,D
Early Childhood Education	M,D
Education—General	M,D
Educational Administration	M,D
Educational Measurement and Evaluation	M,D
Educational Media/Instructional Technology	M
Elementary Education	M,D
English	M
Family and Consumer Sciences-General	M
Health Education	M
Higher Education	M,D
History	M
Human Development	M
Human Services	M
Journalism	M
Law	P
Mathematics	M
Media Studies	M
Multilingual and Multicultural Education	M,D
Music	M
Nutrition	M
Pharmacy	P
Physical Education	M
Public Policy and Administration	M
Reading Education	M,D
Secondary Education	M,D
Sociology	M
Special Education	M,D
Speech and Interpersonal Communication	M
Toxicology	M,D
Transportation and Highway Engineering	M
Urban Education	M,D

In-depth description on page 1133.

TEXAS TECH UNIVERSITY

Program	Degrees
Accounting	M,D
Agricultural Economics and Agribusiness	M,D
Agricultural Education	M,D
Agricultural Sciences—General	M,D
Agronomy and Soil Sciences	M,D
Animal Sciences	M,D
Anthropology	M
Applied Economics	M,D
Applied Physics	M,D
Architecture	M
Art Education	M,D
Art/Fine Arts	M,D
Atmospheric Sciences	M,D
Biological and Biomedical Sciences—General	M,D
Biotechnology	M,D
Business Administration and Management—General	D*
Chemical Engineering	M,D
Chemistry	M,D
Child and Family Studies	M,D
Civil Engineering	M,D*
Classics	M
Clinical Psychology	M,D
Communication—General	M
Computer Science	M,D
Consumer Economics	D
Counseling Psychology	M,D
Counselor Education	M,D,O
Curriculum and Instruction	M,D,O
Dance	D
Early Childhood Education	M,D,O
Economics	M,D
Education—General	M,D,O
Educational Administration	M,D,O
Educational Media/Instructional Technology	M,D,O
Educational Psychology	M,D,O
Electrical Engineering	M,D
Electronic Commerce	M
Elementary Education	M,D,O
Engineering and Applied Sciences—General	M,D
Engineering Management	M,D
English Education	M,D,O
English	M,D
Entomology	M,D
Entrepreneurship	M
Environmental Design	D
Environmental Engineering	M,D
Environmental Management and Policy	D
Environmental Sciences	M,D
Exercise and Sports Science	M,D
Experimental Psychology	M,D
Family and Consumer Sciences-General	M,D
Finance and Banking	M,D
Fish, Game, and Wildlife Management	M,D
Food Science and Technology	M,D
French	M
Geosciences	M,D
German	M
Health Services Management and Hospital Administration	M,O
Higher Education	M,D,O
Historic Preservation	M
History	M,D
Home Economics Education	M,D
Horticulture	M,D
Hospitality Management	M*
Human Development	M,D
Humanities	M,D
Industrial and Manufacturing Management	M,D
Industrial/Management Engineering	M,D
Interdisciplinary Studies	M
International Business	M
Landscape Architecture	M
Law	P
Linguistics	M,D
Management Information Systems	M,D,O
Marketing	M,D
Marriage and Family Therapy	M,D
Mass Communication	M
Mathematics	M,D
Mechanical Engineering	M,D
Microbiology	M,D
Multilingual and Multicultural Education	M,D,O
Museum Studies	M
Music Education	M,D
Music	M,D
Nutrition	M,D
Petroleum Engineering	M,D
Philosophy	M
Physical Education	M,D
Physics	M,D
Plant Sciences	M,D
Political Science	M,D
Psychology—General	M,D
Public Policy and Administration	M,D
Quantitative Analysis	M,D
Range Science	M,D
Reading Education	M,D,O
Rhetoric	M,D
Romance Languages	M,D
Secondary Education	M,D,O
Sociology	M
Software Engineering	M,D
Spanish	M,D
Special Education	M,D,O
Systems Engineering	M,D
Taxation	M,D
Technical Writing	M,D
Telecommunications	M,D
Theater	M,D
Toxicology	M,D*
Zoology	M,D

In-depth description on page 1135.

TEXAS TECH UNIVERSITY HEALTH SCIENCES CENTER

Program	Degrees
Advanced Practice Nursing	M,O
Allied Health—General	M,D
Allopathic Medicine	P
Anatomy	M,D
Biochemistry	M,D
Biological and Biomedical Sciences—General	M,D*
Biotechnology	M*
Cell Biology	M,D*
Communication Disorders	M,D
Community Health Nursing	M,O
Exercise and Sports Science	M
Gerontological Nursing	M,O
Health Services Research	M
Medical Microbiology	M,D
Nursing and Healthcare Administration	M,O
Nursing Education	M,O
Nursing—General	M,O
Occupational Therapy	M
Pathology	M
Pediatric Nursing	M,O
Pharmaceutical Sciences	M,D
Pharmacology	M,D
Physical Therapy	M
Physician Assistant Studies	M
Physiology	M,D
Rehabilitation Sciences	M

TEXAS WESLEYAN UNIVERSITY

Program	Degrees
Business Administration and Management—General	M
Education—General	M
Law	P
Nurse Anesthesia	M

TEXAS WOMAN'S UNIVERSITY

Program	Degrees
Advanced Practice Nursing	M,D
Allied Health—General	M,D
Art/Fine Arts	M

Texas Woman's University (continued)

- Biological and Biomedical Sciences—General M,D*
- Business Administration and Management—General M
- Chemistry M
- Child and Family Studies M,D
- Communication Disorders M
- Community Health Nursing M,D
- Counseling Psychology M,D
- Counselor Education M,D
- Dance M,D
- Early Childhood Education M,D
- Education—General M,D
- Educational Administration M
- Elementary Education M,D
- English M,D
- Exercise and Sports Science M
- Food Science and Technology M,D
- Health Education M,D
- Health Services Management and Hospital Administration M
- History M
- Hospitality Management M,D
- Kinesiology and Movement Studies M,D
- Library Science M,D
- Marriage and Family Therapy M,D
- Mathematics Education M
- Mathematics M
- Medical/Surgical Nursing M,D
- Molecular Biology M,D
- Music M
- Nursing—General M,D
- Nutrition M,D
- Occupational Therapy M,D
- Pediatric Nursing M,D
- Physical Therapy M,D
- Political Science M
- Psychiatric Nursing M,D
- Psychology—General M,D
- Reading Education M,D
- Rhetoric M,D
- School Psychology M,D
- Science Education M,D
- Sociology M,D
- Special Education M,D
- Theater M
- Women's Health Nursing M,D
- Women's Studies M

In-depth description on page 1137.

THOMAS COLLEGE

- Business Administration and Management—General M
- Computer Education M
- Human Resources Management M
- Taxation M

THOMAS EDISON STATE COLLEGE

- Addictions/Substance Abuse Counseling M
- Business Administration and Management—General M
- Insurance M
- Liberal Studies M
- Project Management M

In-depth description on page 1139.

THOMAS JEFFERSON SCHOOL OF LAW

- Law P

THOMAS JEFFERSON UNIVERSITY

- Allopathic Medicine P
- Biochemistry M,D*
- Biological and Biomedical Sciences—General M,D,O*
- Biomedical Engineering D
- Biotechnology D*
- Cancer Biology/Oncology D
- Cell Biology D
- Clinical Laboratory Sciences/Medical Technology M
- Clinical Research O
- Developmental Biology M,D*
- Genetics D*
- Health Services Research O
- Immunology D*
- Microbiology M,D*
- Molecular Biology D*
- Nursing—General M*
- Occupational Therapy M
- Pathology D*
- Pharmacology M,D*
- Physical Therapy M
- Physiology D
- Structural Biology D*
- Virology D

THOMAS M. COOLEY LAW SCHOOL

- Law P

THOMAS MORE COLLEGE

- Business Administration and Management—General M

THOMAS UNIVERSITY

- Business Administration and Management—General M
- Rehabilitation Counseling M

THUNDERBIRD, THE AMERICAN GRADUATE SCHOOL OF INTERNATIONAL MANAGEMENT

- Business Administration and Management—General M
- International Business M

TIFFIN UNIVERSITY

- Business Administration and Management—General M
- Criminal Justice and Criminology M

In-depth description on page 1141.

TORONTO SCHOOL OF THEOLOGY

- Theology P,M,D

TOURO COLLEGE

- Biological and Biomedical Sciences—General M
- Health Informatics M,O
- Health Services Management and Hospital Administration O
- Jewish Studies M
- Law P,M
- Occupational Therapy M
- Physical Therapy M

TOWSON UNIVERSITY

- Advertising and Public Relations O
- Allied Health—General M
- Applied Mathematics M
- Art Education M
- Art/Fine Arts M
- Biological and Biomedical Sciences—General M
- Clinical Psychology M,O
- Communication Disorders M,D
- Communication—General M,O
- Computer Science M
- Corporate and Organizational Communication M
- Counseling Psychology M,O
- Early Childhood Education M
- Education—General M
- Educational Administration O
- Educational Media/Instructional Technology M
- Elementary Education M
- Environmental and Occupational Health D
- Environmental Sciences M,O
- Experimental Psychology M,O
- Geography M
- Gerontology M
- Health Services Management and Hospital Administration O
- Human Resources Development M
- Humanities M
- Information Science O
- Internet and Interactive Multimedia M,O
- Liberal Studies M
- Management Information Systems M,O
- Management Strategy and Policy O
- Mathematics Education M
- Music Education M,O
- Music M
- Nursing—General M,O
- Occupational Therapy M
- Physician Assistant Studies M
- Psychology—General M,O
- Reading Education M
- School Psychology M,O
- Secondary Education M
- Social Sciences M
- Software Engineering M,O
- Theater M,O
- Women's Studies M
- Writing M

In-depth description on page 1143.

TRENT UNIVERSITY

- Anthropology M
- Biological and Biomedical Sciences—General M,D
- Canadian Studies M
- Chemistry M
- Computer Science M
- Environmental Management and Policy M,D
- Geography M,D
- History M
- Native American Studies M,D
- Physics M

TREVECCA NAZARENE UNIVERSITY

- Business Administration and Management—General M
- Counseling Psychology M
- Counselor Education M
- Curriculum and Instruction M
- Education—General M,D
- Educational Administration M
- Organizational Management M
- Physician Assistant Studies M
- Religion M

TRINITY COLLEGE (CT)

- American Studies M
- Economics M
- English M
- History M
- Public Policy and Administration M

TRINITY COLLEGE (DC)

- Business Administration and Management—General M
- Communication—General M
- Community Health M
- Counselor Education M
- Curriculum and Instruction M
- Early Childhood Education M
- Educational Administration M
- Elementary Education M
- English as a Second Language M
- Human Resources Management M
- Nonprofit Management M
- Secondary Education M
- Social Sciences Education M

In-depth description on page 1145.

TRINITY EPISCOPAL SCHOOL FOR MINISTRY

- Missions and Missiology P,M,D,O
- Religion P,M,D,O
- Theology P,M,D,O

TRINITY INTERNATIONAL UNIVERSITY

- Bioethics P,M,D,O
- Business Administration and Management—General P,M,D,O
- Counseling Psychology P,M,D,O
- Cultural Studies P,M,D,O
- Educational Administration P,M,D,O
- Interdisciplinary Studies P,M,D,O
- Law P
- Missions and Missiology P,M,D,O
- Pastoral Ministry and Counseling P,M,D,O
- Religion P,M,D,O
- Religious Education P,M,D,O
- Theology P,M,D,O

TRINITY INTERNATIONAL UNIVERSITY, SOUTH FLORIDA CAMPUS

- Counseling Psychology M
- Religion M

TRINITY LUTHERAN SEMINARY

- Music P,M
- Theology P,M

TRINITY UNIVERSITY

- Accounting M
- Business Administration and Management—General M
- Education—General M
- Educational Administration M
- Health Services Management and Hospital Administration M*
- School Psychology M

TRINITY WESTERN UNIVERSITY

- Counseling Psychology M
- Educational Administration M
- Pastoral Ministry and Counseling P,M
- Religion M
- Theology P,M

TRI STATE COLLEGE OF ACUPUNCTURE

- Acupuncture and Oriental Medicine M,O*

TROY STATE UNIVERSITY

- Business Administration and Management—General M
- Counselor Education M
- Criminal Justice and Criminology M
- Early Childhood Education M,O
- Education—General M,O
- Educational Administration M
- Elementary Education M,O
- Environmental Management and Policy M
- Foundations and Philosophy of Education M
- Human Development M
- Human Resources Management M
- International Affairs M
- Nursing—General M
- Public Policy and Administration M
- Secondary Education M,O
- Special Education M,O

TROY STATE UNIVERSITY DOTHAN

- Accounting M
- Business Administration and Management—General M
- Business Education M
- Counselor Education M,O
- Curriculum and Instruction M,O
- Education—General M,O
- Educational Administration M,O
- Educational Media/Instructional Technology M,O
- Foundations and Philosophy of Education M,O
- History M
- Human Resources Management M
- Management Information Systems M
- Political Science M

TROY STATE UNIVERSITY MONTGOMERY

- Adult Education M
- Business Administration and Management—General M
- Counselor Education M,O
- Education—General M,O
- Educational Administration O
- Elementary Education M
- Human Development M,O
- Human Resources Management M
- Management Information Systems M

TRUMAN STATE UNIVERSITY

- Accounting M
- Biological and Biomedical Sciences—General M
- Communication Disorders M
- Counseling Psychology M
- Education—General M
- English M
- History M
- Music M

In-depth description on page 1147.

TUFTS UNIVERSITY

- Allopathic Medicine P
- Analytical Chemistry M,D
- Archaeology M
- Art History M
- Art/Fine Arts M
- Biochemistry D
- Bioengineering O
- Biological and Biomedical Sciences—General M,D,O*
- Biostatistics M,D
- Biotechnology O
- Cell Biology D
- Chemical Engineering M,D
- Chemistry M,D*
- Child and Family Studies M,D,O*
- City and Regional Planning M
- Civil Engineering M,D
- Classics M
- Clinical Research M,D
- Computer Science M,D,O
- Dance M,D
- Dentistry P
- Developmental Biology D
- Developmental Psychology M,D,O
- Early Childhood Education M,D,O
- Economics M
- Education—General M,O*
- Electrical Engineering M,D,O
- Elementary Education M,O
- Engineering and Applied Sciences—General M,D*
- Engineering Management M
- English M,D
- Environmental and Occupational Health M,D
- Environmental Engineering M,D
- Environmental Management and Policy M,D,O
- Environmental Sciences M,D
- Epidemiology M,D,O
- Ergonomics and Human Factors M,D
- French M
- Genetics D
- Geotechnical Engineering M,D

- German M
- History M,D
- Human-Computer Interaction O
- Immunology D
- Inorganic Chemistry M,D
- International Affairs M,D*
- International and Comparative Education M,D
- International Business M,D
- International Development M,D
- International Health M,D
- Manufacturing Engineering O
- Mathematics M,D
- Mechanical Engineering M,D
- Microbiology D
- Middle School Education M,O
- Molecular Biology D
- Museum Studies O
- Music M
- Neuroscience D
- Nonprofit Management O
- Nutrition M,D*
- Occupational Therapy M,O
- Optical Sciences O
- Oral and Dental Sciences M,O
- Organic Chemistry M,D
- Pharmacology D
- Philosophy M
- Physical Chemistry M,D
- Physics M,D*
- Physiology D
- Psychology—General M,D
- Public Health—General M*
- Public Policy and Administration M*
- School Psychology M,O
- Secondary Education M,O
- Structural Engineering M,D
- Theater M,D*
- Urban Studies M
- Veterinary Medicine P
- Veterinary Sciences M,D
- Water Resources Engineering M,D

In-depth description on page 1149.

TULANE UNIVERSITY

- Allopathic Medicine P
- Anthropology M,D
- Applied Mathematics M,D
- Architecture M*
- Art History M
- Art/Fine Arts M
- Biochemistry M,D*
- Biological and Biomedical Sciences—General M,D,O
- Biomedical Engineering M,D*
- Biostatistics M,D
- Business Administration and Management—General M,D
- Cell Biology M,D
- Chemical Engineering M,D
- Chemistry M,D*
- Civil Engineering M,D
- Classics M
- Computer Science M,D
- Demography and Population Studies M
- Economics M,D
- Electrical Engineering M,D
- Engineering and Applied Sciences—General M,D
- English M,D
- Environmental and Occupational Health M,D
- Environmental Engineering M,D
- Epidemiology M,D
- French M,D
- Geology M,D*
- Health Education M
- Health Services Management and Hospital Administration M,D*
- History M,D
- Human Genetics M,D
- Immunology M,D
- International Development M,D
- International Health M,D
- Latin American Studies M,D*
- Law P,M,D
- Liberal Studies M
- Maternal and Child Health M,D
- Mathematics M,D
- Mechanical Engineering M,D*
- Microbiology M,D*
- Molecular Biology M,D
- Music M
- Neuroscience M,D
- Nutrition M
- Parasitology M,D,O
- Pharmacology M,D*
- Philosophy M,D
- Physics M,D
- Physiology M,D*
- Political Science M,D
- Portuguese M,D
- Psychology—General M,D
- Public Health—General M,D,O*
- Public Policy and Administration M
- Social Work M,D
- Sociology M,D
- Spanish M,D
- Statistics M,D
- Structural Biology M,D
- Theater M

In-depth description on page 1151.

TUSCULUM COLLEGE

- Adult Education M
- Business Administration and Management—General M
- Education—General M

TUSKEGEE UNIVERSITY

- Agricultural Economics and Agribusiness M
- Agricultural Sciences—General M
- Agronomy and Soil Sciences M
- Animal Sciences M
- Biological and Biomedical Sciences—General M
- Chemistry M
- Curriculum and Instruction M
- Education—General M
- Electrical Engineering M
- Engineering and Applied Sciences—General M,D
- Environmental Sciences M
- Food Science and Technology M
- Materials Engineering D
- Mechanical Engineering M
- Nutrition M
- Plant Sciences M
- Science Education M
- Veterinary Medicine P
- Veterinary Sciences M

TYNDALE COLLEGE & SEMINARY

- Theology P,M

UNIFICATION THEOLOGICAL SEMINARY

- Theology P,M

UNIFORMED SERVICES UNIVERSITY OF THE HEALTH SCIENCES

- Advanced Practice Nursing M
- Allopathic Medicine P
- Anatomy M,D
- Biochemistry D
- Biological and Biomedical Sciences—General M,D*
- Cell Biology D*
- Clinical Psychology D
- Developmental Biology D
- Emergency Medical Services M,D
- Environmental and Occupational Health M,D
- History of Medicine M
- History of Science and Technology M,D
- Immunology D*
- International Health M,D
- Microbiology D*
- Molecular Biology D*
- Neuroscience D*
- Nurse Anesthesia M
- Nursing—General M
- Pathobiology M,D
- Pathology M,D
- Pharmacology D
- Physiology M,D
- Psychology—General D
- Public Health—General M,D
- Zoology M,D

UNION COLLEGE (KY)

- Education—General M
- Educational Administration M,O
- Elementary Education M
- Health Education M
- Middle School Education M
- Music Education M
- Physical Education M
- Reading Education M
- Secondary Education M
- Special Education M

UNION COLLEGE (NY)

- Bioethics M*
- Business Administration and Management—General M*
- Computer Education M
- Computer Science M
- Education—General M
- Electrical Engineering M
- Engineering and Applied Sciences—General M
- English Education M
- Foreign Languages Education M
- Health Services Management and Hospital Administration M
- Mathematics Education M
- Mechanical Engineering M
- Science Education M
- Social Sciences Education M

UNION INSTITUTE & UNIVERSITY

- Clinical Psychology D
- Interdisciplinary Studies D
- Psychology—General D

UNION THEOLOGICAL SEMINARY AND PRESBYTERIAN SCHOOL OF CHRISTIAN EDUCATION

- Religious Education M,D,O
- Theology P,M,D

UNION THEOLOGICAL SEMINARY IN THE CITY OF NEW YORK

- Theology P,M,D

UNION UNIVERSITY

- Business Administration and Management—General M
- Education—General M,O
- Educational Administration M,O
- Nursing—General M

UNITED STATES ARMY COMMAND AND GENERAL STAFF COLLEGE

- Military and Defense Studies M

UNITED STATES INTERNATIONAL UNIVERSITY

- Business Administration and Management—General M
- Finance and Banking M
- Marketing M

UNITED STATES SPORTS ACADEMY

- Exercise and Sports Science M
- Physical Education M
- Recreation and Park Management M
- Sports Management M,D*

UNITED TALMUDICAL SEMINARY

- Theology

UNITED THEOLOGICAL SEMINARY

- Theology P,M,D

UNITED THEOLOGICAL SEMINARY OF THE TWIN CITIES

- Pastoral Ministry and Counseling M,D,O
- Theology P,O

UNIVERSIDAD CENTRAL DEL CARIBE

- Allopathic Medicine P

UNIVERSIDAD DE LAS AMERICAS, A.C.

- Business Administration and Management—General M
- Education—General M
- Finance and Banking M
- International Affairs M
- Marketing Research M
- Marriage and Family Therapy M
- Organizational Behavior M
- Psychology—General M
- Quality Management M

UNIVERSIDAD DE LAS AMÉRICAS–PUEBLA

- American Studies M
- Anthropology M
- Archaeology M
- Business Administration and Management—General M
- Chemical Engineering M
- Clinical Laboratory Sciences/Medical Technology M
- Computer Art and Design M
- Computer Science M
- Construction Engineering and Management M
- Economics M
- Education—General M
- Electrical Engineering M
- Engineering and Applied Sciences—General M
- English M
- Finance and Banking M
- Food Science and Technology M
- Industrial and Manufacturing Management M
- Industrial/Management Engineering M
- Linguistics M
- Psychology—General M

UNIVERSIDAD DEL TURABO

- Accounting M
- Business Administration and Management—General M
- Criminal Justice and Criminology M
- Education—General M
- Educational Administration M
- English as a Second Language M
- Environmental Management and Policy M
- Human Resources Development M
- Human Resources Management M
- Human Services M
- Logistics M
- Marketing M
- Multilingual and Multicultural Education M
- Special Education M

UNIVERSIDAD METROPOLITANA

- Accounting M
- Business Administration and Management—General M
- Curriculum and Instruction M
- Early Childhood Education M
- Education—General M
- Educational Administration M
- Environmental Education M
- Environmental Management and Policy M
- Leisure Studies M
- Marketing M
- Physical Education M
- Recreation and Park Management M
- Special Education M

UNIVERSITÉ DE MONCTON

- Astronomy M
- Biochemistry M
- Biological and Biomedical Sciences—General M
- Business Administration and Management—General M
- Chemistry M
- Child and Family Studies M
- Civil Engineering M
- Computer Science M,O
- Counselor Education M
- Economics M
- Education—General M
- Educational Administration M
- Educational Psychology M
- Electrical Engineering M
- Engineering and Applied Sciences—General M
- Food Science and Technology M
- French M,D
- History M
- Industrial/Management Engineering M
- Law P,M,O
- Mathematics M
- Mechanical Engineering M
- Nutrition M
- Physics M
- Psychology—General M
- Public Policy and Administration M
- Social Work M

UNIVERSITÉ DE MONTRÉAL

- Allopathic Medicine P,O
- Anthropology M,D
- Art History M,D
- Biochemistry M,D,O
- Bioethics M,O
- Biological and Biomedical Sciences—General M,D,O
- Biomedical Engineering M,D
- Biophysics M,D
- Cell Biology M,D
- Chemistry M,D
- Clinical Laboratory Sciences/Medical Technology O
- Communication Disorders M
- Communication—General M,D
- Community Health M,D,O
- Comparative Literature M,D
- Computer Science M,D,O
- Criminal Justice and Criminology M,D
- Curriculum and Instruction M,D,O
- Demography and Population Studies M,D
- Dental Hygiene M,O
- Dentistry P
- Developmental Psychology M
- Economics M,D
- Education—General M,D,O
- Educational Administration M,D,O
- Educational Psychology M,D,O
- Emergency Medical Services O
- English M,D
- Environmental and Occupational Health M,O
- Environmental Design M,D,O

Université de Montréal (continued)

Program	Degrees
Environmental Management and Policy	O
Ergonomics and Human Factors	O
Film, Television, and Video Theory and Criticism	M,D
French	M,D
Geography	M,D,O
German	M,D
Health Promotion	M,D,O
Health Services Management and Hospital Administration	M,O
History	M,D
Human Services	D
Immunology	M,D
Industrial and Labor Relations	M,D
Information Studies	M,D
Kinesiology and Movement Studies	M,D,O
Law	P,M,D,O
Library Science	M,D
Linguistics	M,D
Mathematics	M,D
Microbiology	M,D,O
Molecular Biology	M,D
Museum Studies	M
Music	M,D,O
Neuroscience	M,D,O
Nurse Anesthesia	O
Nursing—General	M,D,O
Nutrition	M,D
Optometry	P
Oral and Dental Sciences	M,O
Pastoral Ministry and Counseling	M,D,O
Pathology	M,D,O
Pharmaceutical Sciences	M,D
Pharmacology	M,D
Philosophy	M,D
Physical Education	M,D,O
Physics	M,D
Physiology	M,D,O
Political Science	M,D
Psychology—General	M,D
Religion	M,D
Social Work	M,D,O
Sociology	M,D
Spanish	M,D
Sports Management	M,D,O
Statistics	M,D
Theology	M,D,O
Toxicology	O
Veterinary Medicine	P
Veterinary Sciences	M,D,O
Virology	D
Vision Sciences	M

UNIVERSITÉ DE SHERBROOKE

Program	Degrees
Accounting	M
Adult Education	O
Allopathic Medicine	P
Biochemistry	M,D
Biological and Biomedical Sciences—General	M,D
Biophysics	M,D
Business Administration and Management—General	M,D,O
Canadian Studies	M,D
Cell Biology	M,D
Chemical Engineering	M,D
Chemistry	M,D
Civil Engineering	M,D
Clinical Laboratory Sciences/Medical Technology	M,D
Comparative Literature	M,D
Computer Engineering	M,D
Conflict Resolution and Mediation/Peace Studies	M,D,O
Counselor Education	M
Economics	M
Education—General	M,O
Educational Administration	M
Elementary Education	M,O
Engineering and Applied Sciences—General	M,D
Engineering Management	M
Environmental Engineering	M
Environmental Sciences	M,O
Ethics	M,D,O
Finance and Banking	M
French	M,D
Geography	M,D
Gerontology	M
Higher Education	M,O
History	M
Immunology	M,D
International Business	M
Kinesiology and Movement Studies	M,O
Law	M,D,O
Linguistics	M,D
Management Information Systems	M
Marketing	M
Mathematics	M,D
Mechanical Engineering	M,D
Microbiology	M,D
Organizational Behavior	M
Pharmacology	M,D
Philosophy	M,D,O
Physical Education	M,O
Physics	M,D
Psychology—General	M
Radiation Biology	M,D
Religion	M,D,O
Social Work	M
Special Education	M,O
Taxation	M,O
Theater	M,D
Theology	M,D,O

UNIVERSITÉ DU QUÉBEC À CHICOUTIMI

Program	Degrees
Art/Fine Arts	M
Business Administration and Management—General	M
Canadian Studies	M
Comparative Literature	M
Education—General	M,D
Engineering and Applied Sciences—General	M,D
Environmental Management and Policy	M
Ethics	O
French	O
Genetics	M
Geosciences	M
Linguistics	M
Mineralogy	D
Project Management	M
Theology	M,D

UNIVERSITÉ DU QUÉBEC EN OUTAOUAIS

Program	Degrees
Accounting	O
Adult Education	O
City and Regional Planning	M
Computer Science	M,O
Education—General	M,D,O
Educational Psychology	M
Industrial and Labor Relations	M
Nursing—General	M,O
Project Management	M,O
Social Work	M

UNIVERSITÉ DU QUÉBEC À MONTRÉAL

Program	Degrees
Accounting	M,O
Actuarial Science	O
Art History	M,D
Art/Fine Arts	M
Atmospheric Sciences	M,D,O
Biological and Biomedical Sciences—General	M,D
Business Administration and Management—General	M,D,O
Chemistry	M
Communication—General	M,D
Comparative Literature	M,D
Dance	M
Economics	M,D
Education—General	M,D,O
Environmental and Occupational Health	O
Environmental Education	M,D,O
Environmental Sciences	M,D
Ergonomics and Human Factors	O
Finance and Banking	O
Geographic Information Systems	O
Geography	M
Geology	M,D,O
Geosciences	M,D,O
History	M,D
Kinesiology and Movement Studies	M
Law	M
Linguistics	M,D
Management Information Systems	M
Mathematics	M,D
Meteorology	M,D,O
Mineralogy	M,D,O
Museum Studies	M
Natural Resources	M,D,O
Philosophy	M,D
Political Science	M,D
Project Management	M,O
Psychology—General	D
Public Policy and Administration	M
Religion	M,D
Social Work	M
Sociology	M,D
Theater	M
Urban Studies	M,D

UNIVERSITÉ DU QUÉBEC À RIMOUSKI

Program	Degrees
City and Regional Planning	M
Comparative Literature	M
Education—General	M,D
Ethics	M
Fish, Game, and Wildlife Management	M,O
Marine Affairs	M
Oceanography	M,D
Project Management	M
Public Policy and Administration	O

UNIVERSITÉ DU QUÉBEC À TROIS-RIVIÈRES

Program	Degrees
Accounting	O
Biophysics	M,D
Business Administration and Management—General	M,D
Canadian Studies	M,D
Chemistry	M
Comparative Literature	M
Computer Science	M
Education—General	M,O
Educational Administration	D
Educational Psychology	M
Electrical Engineering	M,D
Energy Management and Policy	M,D
Entrepreneurship	M
Environmental Sciences	M,D
Finance and Banking	O
Industrial and Labor Relations	O
Industrial/Management Engineering	M,O
Leisure Studies	M,O
Mathematics	M
Nursing—General	M,O
Paper and Pulp Engineering	M,D
Philosophy	M,D
Physical Education	M
Project Management	M,O
Psychology—General	M,D
Travel and Tourism	M,O

UNIVERSITÉ DU QUÉBEC, ÉCOLE DE TECHNOLOGIE SUPÉRIEURE

Program	Degrees
Engineering and Applied Sciences—General	M,D,O

UNIVERSITÉ DU QUÉBEC, ÉCOLE NATIONALE D'ADMINISTRATION PUBLIQUE

Program	Degrees
International Business	M,O
Public Policy and Administration	O
Urban Studies	M

UNIVERSITÉ DU QUÉBEC EN ABITIBI-TÉMISCAMINGUE

Program	Degrees
Business Administration and Management—General	M
Education—General	M,D
Project Management	M

UNIVERSITÉ DU QUÉBEC, INSTITUT NATIONAL DE LA RECHERCHE SCIENTIFIQUE

Program	Degrees
Biological and Biomedical Sciences—General	M,D
Biotechnology	M,D
Energy Management and Policy	M,D
Environmental Management and Policy	M,D
Geosciences	M,D
Immunology	M,D
Information Science	M,D,O
Materials Sciences	M,D
Microbiology	M,D
Software Engineering	M,D,O
Telecommunications	M,D,O
Urban Studies	M,D,O
Virology	M,D
Water Resources	M,D

UNIVERSITÉ LAVAL

Program	Degrees
Accounting	M,O
Advertising and Public Relations	O
Aerospace/Aeronautical Engineering	M
Agricultural Economics and Agribusiness	M
Agricultural Engineering	M
Agricultural Sciences—General	M,D,O
Agronomy and Soil Sciences	M,D
Allopathic Medicine	P,O
Anatomy	M,D,O
Animal Sciences	M,D
Anthropology	M,D
Archaeology	M,D
Architecture	M
Art History	M,D
Art/Fine Arts	M
Biochemistry	M,D,O
Biological and Biomedical Sciences—General	M,D,O
Business Administration and Management—General	M,D,O
Canadian Studies	M,D
Cancer Biology/Oncology	O
Cardiovascular Sciences	O
Cell Biology	M,D
Chemical Engineering	M,D
Chemistry	M,D
City and Regional Planning	M,D
Civil Engineering	M,D,O
Clinical Psychology	D
Communication Disorders	M
Community Health	M,D,O
Computer Science	M,D
Consumer Economics	O
Counselor Education	M,D
Curriculum and Instruction	M,D
Dentistry	P
Economics	M,D
Education—General	M,D,O
Educational Administration	M,D,O
Educational Measurement and Evaluation	M,D,O
Educational Media/Instructional Technology	M,D
Educational Psychology	M,D
Electrical Engineering	M,D
Electronic Commerce	M,O
Emergency Medical Services	O
Engineering and Applied Sciences—General	M,D,O
English	M,D
Environmental and Occupational Health	O
Epidemiology	M,D
Ethics	O
Ethnic Studies	M,D
Facilities Management	M,O
Film, Television, and Video Theory and Criticism	M,D
Finance and Banking	M,D
Food Science and Technology	M,D
Forestry	M,D
French	M,D
Geodetic Sciences	M,D
Geography	M,D
Geology	M,D
Geosciences	M,D
Gerontology	O
Graphic Design	M
Health Physics/Radiological Health	O
History	M,D
Immunology	M,D
Industrial and Labor Relations	M,D
Industrial/Management Engineering	O
International Affairs	M
International Business	M,O
Journalism	O
Kinesiology and Movement Studies	M,D
Law	M,D,O
Legal and Justice Studies	O
Linguistics	M,D
Management Information Systems	M,O
Management of Technology	O
Marketing	M,O
Mass Communication	M
Mathematics	M,D
Mechanical Engineering	M,D
Metallurgical Engineering and Metallurgy	M,D
Microbiology	M,D
Mineral/Mining Engineering	M,D
Molecular Biology	M,D
Museum Studies	O
Music Education	M,D
Music	M,D
Neurobiology	M,D
Nursing—General	M,O
Nutrition	M,D
Oceanography	D
Oral and Dental Sciences	M,O
Organizational Management	M,O
Pathology	O
Pharmaceutical Sciences	M,D,O
Philosophy	
Physical Education	M,D
Physics	M,D
Physiology	M,D
Plant Biology	M,D,O
Political Science	M,D
Psychology—General	M,D
Religion	M,D
Rural Planning and Studies	O
Social Work	M,D
Sociology	M,D
Software Engineering	O
Spanish	M,D
Statistics	M
Theater	M,D
Theology	M,D
Translation and Interpretation	M,O
Women's Studies	O

In-depth description on page 1153.

UNIVERSITY AT BUFFALO, THE STATE UNIVERSITY OF NEW YORK

Program	Degrees
Accounting	M,D
Advanced Practice Nursing	M,D,O
Aerospace/Aeronautical Engineering	M,D
Allied Health—General	M,D,O
Allopathic Medicine	P
American Studies	M,D
Anatomy	M,D
Anthropology	M,D
Architecture	M
Art History	M
Art/Fine Arts	M
Biochemistry	M,D

Biological and Biomedical Sciences—General M,D*
Biophysics M,D
Business Administration and Management—General M,D
Cancer Biology/Oncology D
Cell Biology D
Chemical Engineering M,D*
Chemistry M,D
City and Regional Planning M
Civil Engineering M,D*
Classics M,D
Clinical Laboratory Sciences/Medical Technology M
Clinical Psychology M,D
Cognitive Sciences M,D
Communication Disorders M,D
Communication—General M,D
Community Health M,D
Comparative Literature M,D
Computer Science M,D*
Counselor Education M,D,O
Dentistry P
Economics M,D,O
Education—General M,D,O*
Educational Administration M,D,O
Educational Psychology M,D,O
Electrical Engineering M,D*
Electronic Commerce M,D,O
Elementary Education M,D,O
Engineering and Applied Sciences—General M,D
English as a Second Language M,D,O
English Education M,D,O
English M,D
Environmental Engineering M,D
Epidemiology M,D
Exercise and Sports Science M,D
Foreign Languages Education M,D,O
French M,D
Geographic Information Systems M,D,O
Geography M,D,O
Geology M,D
Gerontological Nursing M,D,O
Higher Education M,D
History M,D
Humanities M
Immunology D*
Industrial/Management Engineering M,D*
Information Studies M,D,O
Law P,M
Library Science M,D,O
Linguistics M,D
Logistics M,D
Management Information Systems M,D
Materials Sciences M
Maternal/Child Nursing M,D,O
Mathematics Education M,D,O
Mathematics M,D
Mechanical Engineering M,D*
Media Studies M*
Medical/Surgical Nursing M,D,O
Medicinal and Pharmaceutical Chemistry M,D
Microbiology M,D*
Molecular Biology D
Music Education M,D,O
Music M,D
Neuroscience M,D
Nurse Anesthesia M,D,O
Nursing—General M,D,O
Nutrition M*
Occupational Therapy M
Oral and Dental Sciences M,D,O
Pathology M,D
Pediatric Nursing M,D,O
Pharmaceutical Sciences M,D
Pharmacology M,D*
Pharmacy P
Philosophy M,D
Physical Therapy M,D
Physics M,D*
Physiology M,D
Political Science M,D
Psychiatric Nursing M,D,O
Psychology—General M,D
Public Health—General M,D
Reading Education M,D,O
Rehabilitation Counseling M,D,O
Rehabilitation Sciences D
School Psychology M,D,O
Science Education M,D,O
Secondary Education M,D,O
Social Psychology M,D
Social Sciences Education M,D,O
Social Sciences M
Social Work M,D
Sociology M,D
Spanish M,D
Special Education M,D,O
Structural Engineering M,D
Toxicology M,D
Urban Design M
Women's Health Nursing M,D,O

In-depth description on page 1155.

UNIVERSITY COLLEGE OF CAPE BRETON

Business Administration and Management—General M
Counselor Education O
Curriculum and Instruction O
Education—General O
Educational Media/Instructional Technology O

UNIVERSITY OF ADVANCING TECHNOLOGY

Management of Technology M

THE UNIVERSITY OF AKRON

Accounting M
Applied Mathematics M,D
Arts Administration M
Biological and Biomedical Sciences—General M
Biomedical Engineering M
Business Administration and Management—General M
Chemical Engineering M,D
Chemistry M,D
Child and Family Studies M
City and Regional Planning M
Civil Engineering M,D
Clothing and Textiles M
Cognitive Sciences M,D
Communication Disorders M
Communication—General M
Computer Science M
Counseling Psychology M,D
Counselor Education M
Economics M
Education—General M,D
Educational Administration M,D
Electrical Engineering M,D
Electronic Commerce M
Elementary Education M,D
Engineering and Applied Sciences—General M,D
Engineering Management M
English M
Entrepreneurship M
Exercise and Sports Science M
Family and Consumer Sciences-General M
Finance and Banking M
Food Science and Technology M
Geography M,D
Geology M
Geophysics M
Geosciences M
Higher Education M
History M,D
Human Resources Management M
Industrial and Labor Relations M
Industrial and Organizational Psychology M,D
International Business M
Law P
Management Information Systems M
Management of Technology M
Marketing M
Marriage and Family Therapy M
Mathematics M
Mechanical Engineering M,D
Music Education M
Music M
Nursing—General M,D
Nutrition M
Physical Education M
Physics M
Political Science M
Polymer Science and Engineering M,D
Psychology—General M,D
Public Health—General M,D
Public Policy and Administration M
Quality Management M
School Psychology M,D
Secondary Education M,D
Social Work M
Sociology M,D
Spanish M
Special Education M
Statistics M
Taxation M
Theater M,D
Urban Studies M,D
Vocational and Technical Education M

In-depth description on page 1157.

THE UNIVERSITY OF ALABAMA

Accounting M,D
Advertising and Public Relations M
Aerospace/Aeronautical Engineering M,D
American Studies M
Anthropology M
Applied Mathematics M,D
Art History M
Art/Fine Arts M
Biological and Biomedical Sciences—General M,D
Business Administration and Management—General M,D
Chemical Engineering M,D
Chemistry M,D*
Child and Family Studies M
Civil Engineering M,D
Clinical Psychology M,D
Clothing and Textiles M
Cognitive Sciences M,D
Communication Disorders M
Communication—General M,D,O
Computer Science M,D
Consumer Economics M
Criminal Justice and Criminology M
Curriculum and Instruction M,D,O
Economics M,D
Educational Administration M,D,O
Educational Media/Instructional Technology M,D,O
Electrical Engineering M,D
Elementary Education M,D,O
Engineering and Applied Sciences—General M,D*
English M,D
Environmental Engineering M,D
Family and Consumer Sciences-General M,D
Film, Television, and Video Production M
Finance and Banking M,D
French M,D
Geography M
Geology M,D
German M,D
Health Education M,D
Health Promotion M,D
History M,D
Hospitality Management M
Human Development M
Industrial and Manufacturing Management M,D
Industrial/Management Engineering M
Information Studies M,D,O
Interior Design M
Journalism M,D
Kinesiology and Movement Studies M,D
Latin American Studies M,O
Law P,M
Library Science M,D,O
Linguistics M,D
Marketing M,D
Materials Engineering M,D
Materials Sciences D
Mathematics M,D
Mechanical Engineering M,D
Mechanics M,D
Media Studies M
Metallurgical Engineering and Metallurgy M,D
Music Education M,D,O
Music M,D,O
Nursing—General M
Nutrition M
Photography M
Physics M,D
Political Science M,D
Psychology—General M,D
Public Policy and Administration M,D
Rhetoric M,D
Romance Languages M,D
Secondary Education M,D,O
Social Work M,D
Spanish M,D
Speech and Interpersonal Communication M
Statistics M,D
Taxation M,D
Theater M
Women's Studies M
Writing M,D

THE UNIVERSITY OF ALABAMA AT BIRMINGHAM

Allied Health—General M,D,O
Allopathic Medicine P,M,D
Anthropology M
Applied Mathematics M,D
Art Education M
Art History M
Biochemistry D*
Biological and Biomedical Sciences—General M,D*
Biomedical Engineering M,D
Biometrics M,D
Biophysics D
Biostatistics M,D*
Business Administration and Management—General M,D
Cell Biology D*
Chemistry M,D
Civil Engineering M,D
Clinical Laboratory Sciences/Medical Technology M
Clinical Psychology M,D
Computer Engineering M,D
Computer Science M,D*
Counselor Education M
Criminal Justice and Criminology M
Dentistry P
Developmental Psychology M,D
Early Childhood Education M,D
Education—General M,D,O
Educational Administration M,D,O
Electrical Engineering M,D
Elementary Education M
Engineering and Applied Sciences—General M,D
English M
Environmental and Occupational Health D
Environmental Engineering M,D
Epidemiology D
Forensic Sciences M
Genetics D*
Health Education M,D
Health Informatics M
Health Promotion M,D
Health Services Management and Hospital Administration M,D*
History M
Industrial Hygiene D
Information Science M,D
International Health D
Marriage and Family Therapy M
Materials Engineering M,D
Materials Sciences D
Maternal and Child Health M
Mathematics M,D
Mechanical Engineering M,D
Metallurgical Engineering and Metallurgy M,D
Microbiology D*
Molecular Biology
Neurobiology D
Neuroscience M,D*
Nurse Anesthesia M
Nursing—General M,D*
Nutrition M,D,O
Occupational Therapy M
Optometry P
Oral and Dental Sciences M
Pathology D
Pharmacology D*
Physical Education M
Physical Therapy M
Physics M,D
Physiology D*
Psychology—General M,D
Public Health—General M,D*
Public Policy and Administration M
Rehabilitation Counseling M
School Psychology M
Secondary Education M
Sociology M,D
Special Education M
Toxicology D*
Vision Sciences M,D

In-depth description on page 1159.

THE UNIVERSITY OF ALABAMA IN HUNTSVILLE

Accounting M,O
Aerospace/Aeronautical Engineering M,D
Applied Mathematics M,D
Atmospheric Sciences M,D
Biological and Biomedical Sciences—General M
Biotechnology M,D
Business Administration and Management—General M
Chemical Engineering M,D
Chemistry M
Civil Engineering M
Computer Engineering M,D
Computer Science M,D,O
Electrical Engineering M,D*
Engineering and Applied Sciences—General M,D
English as a Second Language M,O
English M,O
Environmental Engineering M
Environmental Sciences M,D
History M
Industrial/Management Engineering M,D
Management Information Systems M
Materials Engineering M,D
Materials Sciences M,D
Maternal/Child Nursing M,O
Mathematics M,D
Mechanical Engineering M,D
Nursing—General M,O
Operations Research M
Optical Sciences D

The University of Alabama in Huntsville (continued)
Physics M,D
Psychology—General M
Public Policy and Administration M
Software Engineering M,D,O
Technical Writing M,O
Vision Sciences M,D

UNIVERSITY OF ALASKA ANCHORAGE
Addictions/Substance Abuse Counseling O
Adult Education M
Biological and Biomedical Sciences—General M
Business Administration and Management—General M
Civil Engineering M
Clinical Psychology M
Counselor Education M
Education—General M
Educational Administration M
Engineering and Applied Sciences—General M
Engineering Management M
English M
Environmental Sciences M
Interdisciplinary Studies M
Nursing—General M
Psychology—General M
Public Policy and Administration M
Social Work M
Special Education M
Vocational and Technical Education M
Writing M

UNIVERSITY OF ALASKA FAIRBANKS
Anthropology M,D
Art/Fine Arts M
Astrophysics M,D
Atmospheric Sciences M,D
Biochemistry M,D
Biological and Biomedical Sciences—General M,D
Botany M,D
Business Administration and Management—General M
Chemistry M,D
Civil Engineering M
Computer Science M,D
Counselor Education M,O
Criminal Justice and Criminology M
Curriculum and Instruction M,O
Economics M
Education—General M,O
Educational Administration M,O
Electrical Engineering M
English Education M,O
English M
Environmental Engineering M
Environmental Management and Policy M
Environmental Sciences M
Finance and Banking M
Fish, Game, and Wildlife Management M,D
Geological Engineering M,O
Geology M,D
Geophysics M,D
Journalism M
Limnology M,D
Marine Biology M,D
Marine Sciences M,D*
Mathematics Education M,D
Mathematics M,D
Mechanical Engineering M
Mineral/Mining Engineering M,O
Multilingual and Multicultural Education M,O
Music Education M
Music M
Northern Studies M,D
Oceanography M,D
Petroleum Engineering M
Physics M,D
Psychology—General M
Rural Planning and Studies M,D
Science Education M,D
Social Psychology M
Writing M
Zoology M,D

UNIVERSITY OF ALASKA SOUTHEAST
Early Childhood Education M
Education—General M
Educational Media/Instructional Technology M
Elementary Education M
Public Policy and Administration M
Secondary Education M

UNIVERSITY OF ALBERTA
Accounting D
Adult Education M,D,O
Agricultural Economics and Agribusiness M,D
Agricultural Sciences—General M,D
Agronomy and Soil Sciences M,D
Anthropology M,D
Applied Arts and Design—General M
Applied Mathematics M,D,O
Archaeology M,D
Art History M
Art/Fine Arts M
Asian Studies M
Astrophysics M,D
Biochemistry M,D
Biological and Biomedical Sciences—General M,D,O
Biomedical Engineering M,D
Biotechnology M,D
Business Administration and Management—General M,D*
Cancer Biology/Oncology M,D
Cell Biology M,D
Chemical Engineering M,D
Chemistry M,D
Civil Engineering M,D
Classics M,D
Clinical Laboratory Sciences/Medical Technology M,D
Clothing and Textiles M,D
Communication Disorders M
Computer Engineering M,D
Computer Science M,D*
Condensed Matter Physics M,D
Conservation Biology M,D
Construction Engineering and Management M,D
Counseling Psychology M,D
Counselor Education M,D
Criminal Justice and Criminology M,D
Demography and Population Studies M,D
Dental Hygiene O
Dentistry P
East European and Russian Studies M,D
Ecology M,D
Economics M,D
Educational Administration M,D,O
Educational Media/Instructional Technology M,D
Educational Psychology M,D
Electrical Engineering M,D
Elementary Education M,D
Energy and Power Engineering M,D
Engineering Management M,D
English as a Second Language M,D
English M,D
Environmental and Occupational Health M,D,O
Environmental Biology M,D
Environmental Engineering M,D
Environmental Management and Policy M,D
Environmental Sciences M,D
Epidemiology M,D,O
Evolutionary Biology M,D
Exercise and Sports Science M,D
Family and Consumer Sciences-General M,D
Finance and Banking M,D
Folklore M,D
Foundations and Philosophy of Education M,D,O
French M,D
Genetics M,D
Geophysics M,D
Geosciences M,D
Geotechnical Engineering M,D
German M,D
Health Physics/Radiological Health M,D
Health Promotion M,O
Health Services Management and Hospital Administration M,D,O
Health Services Research M,D,O
Hispanic Studies M,D
History M,D
Immunology M,D
Industrial and Labor Relations D
Information Studies M
International and Comparative Education M,D,O
International Business M
Italian M,D
Law P,M,O
Library Science M
Linguistics M,D
Marketing D
Materials Engineering M,D
Mathematical and Computational Finance M,D,O
Mathematical Physics M,D,O
Mathematics M,D,O
Mechanical Engineering M,D
Medical Microbiology M,D
Medical Physics M,D
Microbiology M,D
Mineral/Mining Engineering M,D
Molecular Biology M,D
Multilingual and Multicultural Education M,D,O
Music M,D
Natural Resources M,D
Neuroscience M,D
Nursing—General M,D
Occupational Therapy M
Oral and Dental Sciences P,M,D,O
Organizational Management D
Pathology M,D
Petroleum Engineering M,D
Pharmaceutical Sciences M,D
Pharmacology M,D
Pharmacy M,D
Philosophy M,D
Physical Education M,D
Physical Therapy M
Physics M,D
Physiology M,D
Plant Biology M,D
Political Science M,D
Psychology—General M,D
Public Health—General M,D,O
Recreation and Park Management M,D
Rehabilitation Sciences D
Rural Sociology M,D
School Psychology M,D
Secondary Education M,D
Slavic Languages M,D
Sociology M,D
Special Education M,D
Sports Management M
Statistics M,D,O
Structural Engineering M,D
Systems Engineering M,D
Telecommunications M,D
Theater M
Vision Sciences M,D
Water Resources Engineering M,D

THE UNIVERSITY OF ARIZONA
Accounting M
Aerospace/Aeronautical Engineering M,D*
Agricultural Economics and Agribusiness M
Agricultural Education M
Agricultural Engineering M,D
Agricultural Sciences—General M,D*
Agronomy and Soil Sciences M,D
Allopathic Medicine P
Anatomy D
Animal Sciences M,D
Anthropology M,D
Applied Mathematics M,D*
Applied Physics M
Architecture M
Art Education M
Art History M,D
Art/Fine Arts M
Asian Studies M,D
Astronomy M,D
Atmospheric Sciences M,D
Biochemistry M,D
Biological and Biomedical Sciences—General M,D
Business Administration and Management—General M,D
Cancer Biology/Oncology D
Cell Biology M,D*
Chemical Engineering M,D
Chemistry M,D
Child and Family Studies M,D
City and Regional Planning M
Civil Engineering M,D
Classics M
Communication Disorders M,D
Communication—General M,D
Comparative Literature M,D
Computer Engineering M,D
Computer Science M,D
Consumer Economics M,D
Ecology M,D
Economics M,D
Education—General M,D,O*
Educational Administration D,O
Educational Psychology M,D
Electrical Engineering M,D*
Elementary Education M,D
Engineering and Applied Sciences—General M,D
English as a Second Language M,D
English Education M,D
English M,D
Entomology M,D
Environmental Engineering M,D
Environmental Management and Policy M
Environmental Sciences M,D
Epidemiology M,D
Evolutionary Biology M,D
Family and Consumer Sciences-General M,D
Finance and Banking M,D
Fish, Game, and Wildlife Management M,D
Foreign Languages Education M,D
Forestry M,D
French M,D
Genetics M,D
Geography M,D
Geological Engineering M,D
Geosciences M,D
German M
Gerontology M,O
Higher Education M,D
History M,D
Human Development M,D
Hydrology M,D
Immunology M,D
Industrial/Management Engineering M,D
Information Studies M,D
Interdisciplinary Studies M,D,O
Journalism M
Landscape Architecture M
Latin American Studies M
Law P,M
Library Science M,D
Linguistics M,D
Management Information Systems M
Management Strategy and Policy M
Marketing D
Materials Engineering M,D
Materials Sciences M,D
Mathematics M,D
Mechanical Engineering M,D
Mechanics M,D
Media Studies M
Microbiology M,D*
Mineral/Mining Engineering M,D*
Molecular Biology M,D*
Multilingual and Multicultural Education M,D,O
Music Education M,D
Music M,D
Native American Studies M,D
Natural Resources M,D
Near and Middle Eastern Studies M,D
Neuroscience D
Nuclear Engineering M,D
Nursing—General M,D
Nutrition M,D,O
Optical Sciences M,D
Pathobiology M,D
Pharmaceutical Sciences M,D
Pharmacology M,D
Pharmacy P,M,D
Philosophy M,D
Physics M,D
Physiology D*
Planetary and Space Sciences M,D*
Plant Pathology M,D
Plant Sciences M,D
Political Science M,D
Psychology—General D*
Public Health—General M
Public Policy and Administration M,D
Range Science M,D
Reading Education M,D,O
Rehabilitation Counseling M,D,O
Reliability Engineering M
Rhetoric M,D
Russian M
Secondary Education M,D,O
Sociology M,D
Spanish M,D
Special Education M,D,O
Statistics M,D
Systems Engineering M,D
Theater M
Toxicology M,D
Water Resources M,D
Women's Studies M*
Writing M

UNIVERSITY OF ARKANSAS
Accounting M
Adult Education M,D,O
Agricultural Economics and Agribusiness M
Agricultural Education M
Agricultural Engineering M,D
Agricultural Sciences—General M,D
Agronomy and Soil Sciences M,D
Animal Sciences M,D
Anthropology M,D
Applied Physics M
Art/Fine Arts M
Bioengineering M,D
Biological and Biomedical Sciences—General M,D
Business Administration and Management—General M,D*
Cell Biology M,D
Chemical Engineering M,D
Chemistry M,D
Civil Engineering M,D
Communication Disorders M
Communication—General M
Comparative Literature M,D
Computer Engineering M,D
Computer Science M,D
Conservation Biology D
Counselor Education M,D,O
Curriculum and Instruction D

Early Childhood Education M
Economics M,D
Education—General M,D,O
Educational Administration M,D,O
Educational Media/Instructional Technology M
Electrical Engineering M,D
Electronic Materials M,D
Elementary Education M,O
Engineering and Applied Sciences—General M,D
English M,D
Entomology M,D
Environmental Engineering M
Family and Consumer Sciences-General M
Food Science and Technology M,D
French M
Geography M,D
Geology M
German M
Health Education M,D
Higher Education M,D,O
History M,D
Horticulture M
Industrial and Manufacturing Management M
Industrial/Management Engineering M,D
Journalism M
Kinesiology and Movement Studies M,D
Law P,M
Logistics M
Management Information Systems M
Mathematics Education M
Mathematics M,D
Mechanical Engineering M,D
Middle School Education M,D,O
Molecular Biology M,D
Music M
Operations Research M
Philosophy M,D
Photonics M,D
Physical Education M
Physics M,D
Plant Pathology M
Plant Sciences D
Political Science M
Psychology—General M,D
Public Policy and Administration M,D
Recreation and Park Management M,D
Rehabilitation Counseling M,D
Secondary Education M,O
Sociology M
Spanish M
Special Education M
Statistics M
Telecommunications M
Theater M
Translation and Interpretation M
Transportation and Highway Engineering M
Transportation Management M
Vocational and Technical Education M,D,O
Writing M

UNIVERSITY OF ARKANSAS AT LITTLE ROCK

Adult Education M
Applied Mathematics M
Applied Science and Technology M,D
Art Education M
Art History M
Art/Fine Arts M
Business Administration and Management—General M
Chemistry M
Computer Science M
Corporate and Organizational Communication M
Counselor Education M
Criminal Justice and Criminology M
Early Childhood Education M,O
Education of the Gifted M
Education of the Multiply Handicapped M
Education—General M,D,O
Educational Administration M,D,O
Educational Media/Instructional Technology M
Gerontology M,O
Health Services Management and Hospital Administration M
Higher Education D
Journalism M
Law P
Liberal Studies M
Middle School Education M,O
Psychology—General M
Public History M
Public Policy and Administration M

Reading Education M,O
Rhetoric M
Secondary Education M
Social Work M
Special Education M
Speech and Interpersonal Communication M
Statistics M
Technical Writing M
Writing M

UNIVERSITY OF ARKANSAS AT MONTICELLO

Education—General M
Elementary Education M
Forestry M
Natural Resources M
Secondary Education M

UNIVERSITY OF ARKANSAS AT PINE BLUFF

Education—General M
Elementary Education M
English Education M
Mathematics Education M
Physical Education M
Science Education M
Secondary Education M
Social Sciences Education M

UNIVERSITY OF ARKANSAS FOR MEDICAL SCIENCES

Allopathic Medicine P
Anatomy M,D*
Biochemistry M,D
Biological and Biomedical Sciences—General M,D*
Biophysics M,D
Communication Disorders M
Environmental and Occupational Health M
Immunology M,D
Microbiology M,D*
Molecular Biology M,D
Neurobiology M,D
Nursing—General M,D*
Nutrition M
Pathology M
Pharmaceutical Sciences P,M
Pharmacology M,D*
Pharmacy P,M
Physiology M,D*
Toxicology M,D

UNIVERSITY OF BALTIMORE

Accounting M
Business Administration and Management—General M
Communication—General M,D*
Conflict Resolution and Mediation/Peace Studies M
Counseling Psychology M,D
Criminal Justice and Criminology M*
Ethics M
Finance and Banking M
Graphic Design M*
Human Services M
Human-Computer Interaction M,D
Industrial and Organizational Psychology M,D
Information Science M,D
Law P,M
Legal and Justice Studies M
Management Information Systems M
Marketing M
Psychology—General M,D*
Public Policy and Administration M,D
Publishing M
Taxation P,M
Writing M

UNIVERSITY OF BRIDGEPORT

Acupuncture and Oriental Medicine M
Business Administration and Management—General M
Chiropractic P,M*
Computer Education M,O
Computer Engineering M
Computer Science M*
Early Childhood Education M,O
Education—General M,D,O*
Educational Administration D,O
Electrical Engineering M
Elementary Education M,O
Engineering and Applied Sciences—General M*
Human Resources Development M*
Human Services M
International and Comparative Education M,O
Management of Technology M
Mechanical Engineering M

Naturopathic Medicine D*
Nutrition M*
Reading Education M,O
Secondary Education M,O

In-depth description on page 1161.

THE UNIVERSITY OF BRITISH COLUMBIA

Accounting D
Adult Education M
Agricultural Economics and Agribusiness M
Agricultural Sciences—General M,D
Agronomy and Soil Sciences M,D
Allopathic Medicine P,M
Anatomy M,D
Animal Sciences M,D
Anthropology M,D
Applied Mathematics M,D
Archaeology M,D
Architecture M
Art Education M,D
Art History M,D
Art/Fine Arts M,D
Asian Studies M,D
Atmospheric Sciences M,D
Biochemistry M,D
Biological and Biomedical Sciences—General M,D
Botany M,D
Business Administration and Management—General M,D
Business Education M,D
Chemical Engineering M,D
Chemistry M,D
Child and Family Studies M
City and Regional Planning M,D
Civil Engineering M,D
Classics M,D
Clinical Psychology M,D
Cognitive Sciences M,D
Communication Disorders M,D
Community Health M,D
Comparative Literature M,D
Computer Engineering M,D
Computer Science M,D*
Counseling Psychology M,D,O
Curriculum and Instruction M,D
Dentistry P
Developmental Psychology M,D
Early Childhood Education M,D
East European and Russian Studies M,D
Economics M,D
Education—General M,D,O
Educational Administration M,D
Educational Measurement and Evaluation M,D,O
Educational Psychology M,D,O
Electrical Engineering M,D
Engineering and Applied Sciences—General M,D
Engineering Physics M
English as a Second Language M,D
English Education M,D
English M,D
Environmental and Occupational Health M,D
Environmental Management and Policy M,D
Epidemiology M,D
Film, Television, and Video Production M
Film, Television, and Video Theory and Criticism M
Finance and Banking M,D
Food Science and Technology M,D
Forensic Psychology M,D
Forestry M,D
Foundations and Philosophy of Education M,D
French M,D
Genetics M,D
Geography M,D
Geological Engineering M,D
Geology M,D
Geophysics M,D
Health Services Management and Hospital Administration M,D
Health Services Research M,D
Higher Education M
History M,D
Home Economics Education M,D
Immunology M,D
Information Studies M,O
International Affairs M
Journalism M
Kinesiology and Movement Studies M,D
Landscape Architecture M
Law M,D
Library Science M,O
Linguistics M,D
Logistics M
Management Information Systems M,D
Management Strategy and Policy D

Marketing D
Materials Engineering M,D
Materials Sciences M,D
Mathematics Education M,D
Mathematics M,D
Mechanical Engineering M,D
Metallurgical Engineering and Metallurgy M,D
Microbiology M,D
Mineral/Mining Engineering M,D
Molecular Biology M,D
Museum Studies M
Music Education M,D
Music M,D
Neuroscience M,D
Nursing—General M,D
Nutrition M,D
Oceanography M,D
Oral and Dental Sciences M,D,O
Organizational Behavior D
Paper and Pulp Engineering M
Pathology M,D
Pharmaceutical Sciences M,D
Pharmacology M,D
Pharmacy P
Philosophy M,D
Physical Education M,D
Physics M,D
Physiology M,D
Plant Sciences M,D
Political Science M,D
Psychology—General M,D
Public History M,O
Reading Education M,D
Rehabilitation Sciences M
Religion M
Reproductive Biology M,D
School Psychology M,D,O
Science Education M,D
Social Psychology M,D
Social Sciences Education M,D
Social Work M
Sociology M,D
Spanish M,D
Special Education M,D,O
Statistics M,D
Theater M,D
Transportation Management M
Vocational and Technical Education M,D
Writing M
Zoology M,D

UNIVERSITY OF CALGARY

Adult Education M,D
Allopathic Medicine P
Analytical Chemistry M,D
Anthropology M,D
Archaeology M,D
Architecture M,D
Art/Fine Arts M
Astronomy M,D
Biochemistry M,D
Biological and Biomedical Sciences—General M,D
Biomedical Engineering M,D
Biotechnology M
Business Administration and Management—General M,D*
Cardiovascular Sciences M,D
Chemical Engineering M,D
Chemistry M,D
City and Regional Planning M,D
Civil Engineering M,D
Classics M
Clinical Psychology M,D
Communication—General M,D
Community Health M,D
Computer Engineering M,D
Computer Science M,D
Counseling Psychology M,D
Curriculum and Instruction M,D
Economics M,D
Education—General M,D
Educational Administration M,D
Educational Media/Instructional Technology M,D
Educational Psychology M,D
Electrical Engineering M,D
Engineering and Applied Sciences—General M,D
English as a Second Language M,D
English M,D
Environmental Design M,D
Environmental Management and Policy M,D
Epidemiology M,D
Exercise and Sports Science M,D
French M,D
Geography M,D
Geology M,D
Geophysics M,D
Geotechnical Engineering M,D
German M
History M,D
Human Development M,D
Industrial Design M,D
Inorganic Chemistry M,D

University of Calgary (continued)

Program	Degrees
Kinesiology and Movement Studies	M,D
Law	P,M
Linguistics	M,D
Mathematics	M,D
Mechanical Engineering	M,D
Microbiology	M,D
Molecular Biology	M,D
Music	M,D
Neuroscience	M,D
Nursing—General	M,D
Organic Chemistry	M,D
Petroleum Engineering	M,D
Philosophy	M,D
Physical Chemistry	M,D
Physics	M,D
Political Science	M,D
Psychology—General	M,D
Religion	M,D
School Psychology	M,D
Social Work	M,D
Sociology	M,D
Software Engineering	M,D
Spanish	M,D
Special Education	M,D
Statistics	M,D
Theater	M,D
Theoretical Chemistry	M,D

UNIVERSITY OF CALIFORNIA, BERKELEY

Program	Degrees
Accounting	D
African-American Studies	D
Agricultural Economics and Agribusiness	D
Anthropology	D
Applied Arts and Design—General	M
Applied Mathematics	D
Applied Science and Technology	D
Archaeology	M,D
Architectural History	M,D
Architecture	M,D*
Art History	D
Art/Fine Arts	M
Asian Languages	M,D
Asian Studies	M,D
Astrophysics	D
Biochemistry	D
Bioengineering	D
Biological and Biomedical Sciences—General	D
Biomedical Engineering	D
Biophysics	M,D*
Biostatistics	M,D
Building Science	M,D
Business Administration and Management—General	M,D,O*
Cell Biology	D
Ceramic Sciences and Engineering	M,D
Chemical Engineering	M,D
Chemistry	M,D
City and Regional Planning	M,D
Civil Engineering	M,D*
Classics	M,D
Comparative Literature	M,D
Computer Science	M,D
Construction Engineering and Management	M,D
Demography and Population Studies	M,D
Developmental Education	M
Economics	D
Education—General	M,D,O
Educational Administration	M,D
Educational Measurement and Evaluation	M,D
Electrical Engineering	M,D
Energy Management and Policy	M,D
Engineering and Applied Sciences—General	M,D
English Education	M,D,O
English	D
Environmental and Occupational Health	M,D
Environmental Biology	M
Environmental Design	M,D
Environmental Engineering	M,D
Environmental Management and Policy	M,D*
Environmental Sciences	M,D
Epidemiology	M,D
Ethnic Studies	D
Finance and Banking	D
Financial Engineering	M,O
Folklore	M
Forestry	M,D
Foundations and Philosophy of Education	M,D
French	D
Genetic Counseling	M
Geography	D
Geological Engineering	M,D
Geology	M,D
Geophysics	M,D
Geotechnical Engineering	M,D
German	M,D
Health Services Management and Hospital Administration	M,D
History of Science and Technology	D
History	M,D,O
Human Development	M,D
Immunology	M,D
Industrial and Labor Relations	D
Industrial/Management Engineering	M,D*
Information Studies	M,D
International Affairs	M
Italian	M,D
Journalism	M
Landscape Architecture	M
Latin American Studies	M,D
Law	P,M,D
Legal and Justice Studies	D
Linguistics	M,D
Marketing	D
Materials Engineering	M,D
Materials Sciences	M,D
Maternal and Child Health	M
Mathematics Education	M,D
Mathematics	M,D,O
Mechanical Engineering	M,D*
Mechanics	M,D
Metallurgical Engineering and Metallurgy	M,D
Microbiology	D
Mineral/Mining Engineering	M,D
Molecular Biology	D*
Multilingual and Multicultural Education	M,D,O
Music	M,D
Near and Middle Eastern Studies	M,D,O
Neuroscience	D*
Nuclear Engineering	M,D
Nutrition	M,D*
Ocean Engineering	M,D
Operations Research	M,D
Optometry	P
Organizational Behavior	D
Petroleum Engineering	M,D
Philosophy	D
Physics	D
Physiology	M,D
Plant Biology	D
Political Science	D
Psychology—General	D
Public Health—General	M,D
Public Policy and Administration	M,D
Range Science	M,D
Reading Education	M,D,O
Real Estate	D
Religion	D
Rhetoric	D
Russian	M,D
Scandinavian Languages	M,D
School Psychology	D
Science Education	M,D
Slavic Languages	M,D
Social Work	M,D
Sociology	M,D
Spanish	M,D
Special Education	D
Statistics	M,D
Structural Engineering	M,D
Theater	D,O
Transportation and Highway Engineering	M,D
Urban Design	M,D
Vision Sciences	M,D
Water Resources Engineering	M,D

UNIVERSITY OF CALIFORNIA, DAVIS

Program	Degrees
Aerospace/Aeronautical Engineering	M,D,O
Agricultural Economics and Agribusiness	M,D
Agricultural Engineering	M,D
Agricultural Sciences—General	M
Agronomy and Soil Sciences	M,D
Allopathic Medicine	P,M
Animal Behavior	M,D
Animal Sciences	M
Anthropology	M,D
Applied Mathematics	M,D
Applied Science and Technology	M,D
Art History	M*
Art/Fine Arts	M
Atmospheric Sciences	M,D
Biochemistry	M,D
Bioengineering	M,D
Biomedical Engineering	M,D
Biophysics	M,D
Business Administration and Management—General	M
Cell Biology	D
Chemical Engineering	M,D,O
Chemistry	M,D*
Child and Family Studies	M
City and Regional Planning	M
Civil Engineering	M,D,O
Clothing and Textiles	M
Comparative Literature	D
Computer Engineering	M,D
Computer Science	M,D
Cultural Studies	M,D
Curriculum and Instruction	D
Developmental Biology	D
Ecology	M,D
Economics	M,D
Education—General	D
Educational Psychology	D
Electrical Engineering	M,D
Engineering and Applied Sciences—General	M,D,O
English	M,D
Entomology	M,D
Environmental Engineering	M,D,O
Environmental Sciences	M,D
Epidemiology	M,D
Evolutionary Biology	D
Exercise and Sports Science	M
Food Science and Technology	M,D
French	D
Genetics	M,D
Geography	M,D
Geology	M,D
German	M,D
History	M,D
Horticulture	M
Human Development	D
Hydrology	M,D
Immunology	M,D
Law	P,M
Linguistics	M
Materials Sciences	M,D,O
Mathematics	M,D
Mechanical Engineering	M,D,O
Medical Informatics	M
Microbiology	M,D*
Molecular Biology	M,D
Music	M,D
Native American Studies	M,D
Neuroscience	D*
Nutrition	M,D
Pathology	M,D
Pharmacology	M,D
Philosophy	M,D
Physics	M,D
Physiology	M,D*
Plant Biology	M,D
Plant Pathology	M,D
Plant Sciences	M
Political Science	M,D
Psychology—General	D
Sociology	M,D
Spanish	M,D
Statistics	M,D
Textile Design	M
Theater	M,D
Toxicology	M,D
Transportation and Highway Engineering	M,D*
Transportation Management	M,D
Veterinary Medicine	P
Veterinary Sciences	M,O
Writing	M,D
Zoology	M

In-depth description on page 1163.

UNIVERSITY OF CALIFORNIA, HASTINGS COLLEGE OF THE LAW

Program	Degrees
Law	P,M

UNIVERSITY OF CALIFORNIA, IRVINE

Program	Degrees
Aerospace/Aeronautical Engineering	M,D
Allopathic Medicine	P
Anatomy	M,D
Anthropology	M,D
Art History	M,D
Art/Fine Arts	M
Asian Languages	M,D
Asian Studies	M,D
Biochemical Engineering	M,D
Biochemistry	M,D
Biological and Biomedical Sciences—General	M,D
Biomedical Engineering	M,D
Biophysics	D
Business Administration and Management—General	M,D*
Cell Biology	M,D
Chemical Engineering	M,D*
Chemistry	M,D
City and Regional Planning	M,D*
Civil Engineering	M,D*
Classics	M,D
Comparative Literature	M,D
Computer Engineering	M,D
Computer Science	M,D*
Criminal Justice and Criminology	D
Dance	M
Demography and Population Studies	M
Developmental Biology	M,D
Ecology	M,D
Economics	M,D
Education—General	M,D
Educational Administration	M,D
Electrical Engineering	M,D*
Elementary Education	M,D
Engineering and Applied Sciences—General	M,D*
English	M,D
Environmental Design	D
Environmental Engineering	M,D
Environmental Management and Policy	D
Evolutionary Biology	M,D
Foreign Languages Education	M,D
French	M,D
Genetic Counseling	M
Genetics	M,D
Geosciences	M,D
German	M,D
Health Psychology	D
History	M,D
Human Development	D
Information Science	M,D
Linguistics	M,D
Materials Engineering	M,D
Materials Sciences	M,D
Mathematics	M,D
Mechanical Engineering	M,D*
Microbiology	M,D
Molecular Biology	M,D*
Music	M
Neurobiology	M,D
Pharmacology	M,D*
Philosophy	M,D
Physics	M,D
Physiology	D
Political Science	D
Psychology—General	D
Secondary Education	M,D
Social Sciences	M,D
Sociology	M,D
Spanish	M,D
Theater	M,D
Toxicology	M,D
Transportation and Highway Engineering	M,D
Writing	M

UNIVERSITY OF CALIFORNIA, LOS ANGELES

Program	Degrees
Aerospace/Aeronautical Engineering	M,D
African Studies	M
African-American Studies	M
Allopathic Medicine	P
Anatomy	D
Anthropology	M,D
Applied Arts and Design—General	M
Archaeology	M,D
Architecture	M,D
Art History	M,D
Art/Fine Arts	M
Asian Languages	M,D
Asian Studies	M,D
Asian-American Studies	M
Astronomy	M,D
Astrophysics	M,D
Atmospheric Sciences	M,D
Biochemistry	M,D
Biological and Biomedical Sciences—General	M,D
Biomedical Engineering	M,D
Biometrics	M,D*
Biostatistics	M,D
Business Administration and Management—General	M,D*
Cell Biology	M,D*
Ceramic Sciences and Engineering	M,D
Chemical Engineering	M,D
Chemistry	M,D
City and Regional Planning	M,D*
Civil Engineering	M,D*
Classics	M,D
Clinical Research	M
Community Health	M,D
Comparative Literature	M,D
Computer Science	M,D
Dance	M,D
Dentistry	P,O
Developmental Biology	M,D
Economics	M,D
Education—General	M,D
Educational Administration	D
Electrical Engineering	M,D
Engineering and Applied Sciences—General	M,D*
English as a Second Language	M
English	M,D
Environmental and Occupational Health	M,D
Environmental Engineering	M,D
Environmental Sciences	D*
Epidemiology	M,D
Film, Television, and Video Production	M,D
French	M,D
Genetics	M,D*
Geochemistry	M,D
Geography	M,D
Geology	M,D
Geophysics	M,D
Geosciences	M,D
Geotechnical Engineering	M,D
German	M,D

Health Services Management and Hospital Administration M,D
Hispanic Studies D
History M,D
Human Genetics M,D*
Immunology M,D
Information Studies M,D,O
Italian M,D
Latin American Studies M
Law P,M
Library Science M,D,O
Linguistics M,D
Manufacturing Engineering M
Materials Engineering M,D
Materials Sciences M,D
Mathematics M,D
Mechanical Engineering M,D
Medical Physics M,D
Metallurgical Engineering and Metallurgy M,D
Microbiology M,D*
Molecular Biology M,D*
Music M,D
Native American Studies M
Near and Middle Eastern Languages M,D
Near and Middle Eastern Studies M,D
Neurobiology D
Neuroscience D
Nursing—General M,D
Operations Research M,D
Oral and Dental Sciences M,D
Pathology M,D
Pharmacology M,D*
Philosophy M,D
Physics M,D*
Physiology M,D
Planetary and Space Sciences M,D
Plant Molecular Biology M,D
Political Science M,D
Portuguese M
Psychology—General M,D
Public Health—General M,D
Public Policy and Administration M
Romance Languages M,D
Scandinavian Languages M,D
Science Education M,D
Slavic Languages M,D
Social Work M,D
Sociology M,D
Spanish M
Special Education D
Statistics M,D
Structural Engineering M,D
Theater M,D*
Toxicology D*
Urban Design M,D
Water Resources Engineering M,D
Women's Studies M,D

UNIVERSITY OF CALIFORNIA, RIVERSIDE

Agronomy and Soil Sciences M,D
Anthropology M,D
Art History M
Biochemistry M,D*
Bioinformatics D
Biological and Biomedical Sciences—General M,D*
Botany M,D*
Business Administration and Management—General M
Cell Biology M,D
Chemical Engineering M,D*
Chemistry M,D*
Classics M,D
Comparative Literature M,D
Computer Science M,D
Dance M,D
Developmental Biology M,D
Economics M,D*
Education—General M,D
Electrical Engineering M,D*
English M,D
Entomology M,D
Environmental Engineering M,D
Environmental Sciences M,D
Evolutionary Biology D
Genetics D*
Genomic Sciences D
Geology M,D*
Historic Preservation M,D
History M,D
Mathematics M,D
Microbiology M,D*
Molecular Biology M,D
Museum Studies M,D
Music M
Neuroscience D*
Philosophy M,D
Physics M,D
Plant Biology M,D
Plant Pathology M,D*
Plant Sciences M,D
Political Science M,D
Psychology—General D
Sociology D

Spanish M,D
Statistics M,D
Toxicology M,D

UNIVERSITY OF CALIFORNIA, SAN DIEGO

Aerospace/Aeronautical Engineering M,D
Allopathic Medicine P
Anthropology D
Applied Mathematics M,D
Applied Physics M,D
Art/Fine Arts M
Artificial Intelligence/Robotics M,D
Biochemistry M,D*
Bioengineering M,D*
Bioinformatics D*
Biological and Biomedical Sciences—General M,D*
Biomedical Engineering M,D
Biophysics M,D
Cancer Biology/Oncology D
Cell Biology D*
Chemical Engineering M,D*
Chemistry M,D*
Clinical Psychology D
Cognitive Sciences D
Communication Disorders D
Communication—General M,D
Comparative Literature M,D
Computer Engineering M,D
Computer Science M,D*
Developmental Biology D
Ecology D*
Economics M,D
Education—General M
Electrical Engineering M,D*
Engineering Physics M,D
English M,D
Epidemiology D
Ethnic Studies D
Evolutionary Biology D
French M,D
Genetics D*
Geology M,D
German M,D
History of Science and Technology M,D
History M,D
Immunology D
International Affairs M,D*
Jewish Studies M,D
Latin American Studies M
Linguistics D
Marine Biology M,D
Marine Sciences M,D
Materials Sciences M,D
Mathematics Education D
Mathematics M,D
Mechanical Engineering M,D*
Mechanics M,D
Molecular Biology D
Music M,D*
Neurobiology D*
Neuroscience D*
Ocean Engineering M,D
Oceanography M,D
Pathology D*
Pharmacology D*
Philosophy D
Photonics M,D
Physics M,D*
Physiology D
Plant Molecular Biology D
Political Science M,D
Psychology—General D
Public Health—General D
Science Education D
Sociology D
Spanish M,D
Statistics M,D
Structural Engineering M,D*
Telecommunications M,D
Theater M,D
Virology D

UNIVERSITY OF CALIFORNIA, SAN FRANCISCO

Allopathic Medicine P
Anatomy D
Anthropology D
Biochemistry D*
Bioengineering D
Biological and Biomedical Sciences—General D
Biomedical Engineering D
Biophysics D*
Cell Biology D
Chemistry D*
Dentistry P
Developmental Biology D
Genetics D
Genomic Sciences D
History of Science and Technology M,D
Immunology D
Medical Informatics M,D
Medicinal and Pharmaceutical Chemistry D

Microbiology D
Molecular Biology D
Neuroscience D
Nursing—General M,D
Oral and Dental Sciences M,D
Pathology D
Pharmaceutical Sciences D
Pharmacology D
Pharmacy P
Physical Therapy M
Physiology D
Sociology D*

UNIVERSITY OF CALIFORNIA, SANTA BARBARA

Anthropology M,D
Applied Mathematics M
Art History M,D
Art/Fine Arts M
Asian Studies M
Biochemistry D
Cell Biology M,D
Chemical Engineering M,D
Chemistry M,D
Classics M,D
Clinical Psychology M,D
Communication—General D
Comparative Literature M,D
Computer Engineering M,D
Computer Science M,D
Counseling Psychology M,D
Developmental Biology M,D
Ecology M,D
Economics M,D
Education—General M,D
Electrical Engineering M,D
Engineering and Applied Sciences—General M,D
English D
Environmental Engineering M,D
Environmental Management and Policy M,D
Environmental Sciences M,D*
Evolutionary Biology M,D
French M,D
Geography M,D
Geology M,D
Geophysics M,D
German M,D
Hispanic Studies M,D
History M,D
Latin American Studies M,D
Linguistics D
Marine Biology M,D
Marine Sciences M,D
Materials Engineering M,D*
Materials Sciences M,D
Mathematics M,D
Mechanical Engineering M,D
Molecular Biology M,D
Music M,D
Philosophy D
Physics D
Political Science M,D
Portuguese M,D
Psychology—General M,D
Religion M,D
School Psychology M,D
Sociology M,D
Spanish M,D
Statistics M,D
Theater M,D
Western European Studies M

UNIVERSITY OF CALIFORNIA, SANTA CRUZ

Anthropology M,D
Applied Economics M
Applied Mathematics M,D
Astronomy D
Astrophysics D
Biological and Biomedical Sciences—General M,D
Cell Biology M,D
Chemistry M,D
Communication—General O
Comparative Literature M,D
Computer Engineering M,D*
Computer Science M,D*
Developmental Psychology D
Ecology M,D
Economics D
Education—General M,O
Electrical Engineering M,D*
Environmental Biology M,D
Environmental Management and Policy D
Evolutionary Biology M,D
Experimental Psychology D
Geosciences M,D
History D
Humanities D
International Affairs D
Linguistics M,D
Marine Sciences M,D
Mathematics M,D
Molecular Biology M,D
Music M
Physics M,D

Political Science D
Psychology—General D
Social Psychology D
Social Sciences D
Sociology D
Theater O
Toxicology M,D

UNIVERSITY OF CENTRAL ARKANSAS

Biological and Biomedical Sciences—General M
Business Administration and Management—General M
Business Education M
Communication Disorders M
Counseling Psychology M
Counselor Education M
Early Childhood Education M
Education of the Gifted M
Education—General M,D
Educational Administration M,D,O
Educational Media/Instructional Technology M
Elementary Education M
English M
Family and Consumer Sciences-General M
Foreign Languages Education M
Health Education M
History M
Kinesiology and Movement Studies M
Library Science M
Mathematics M
Medical Physics M
Music Education M
Music M
Nursing—General M
Occupational Therapy M
Physical Therapy M,D
Psychology—General M,D
Reading Education M
School Psychology M,D
Secondary Education M
Social Psychology M,D
Special Education M
Student Personnel Services M

UNIVERSITY OF CENTRAL FLORIDA

Accounting M
Aerospace/Aeronautical Engineering M
Art Education M
Biological and Biomedical Sciences—General M,O
Business Administration and Management—General M,D*
Chemistry M
Civil Engineering M,D,O
Clinical Psychology M,D
Communication Disorders M
Communication—General M
Computer Engineering M,D,O
Computer Science M,D
Conservation Biology M,O
Counselor Education M,D
Criminal Justice and Criminology M,O
Curriculum and Instruction M,D
Early Childhood Education M
Economics M
Education—General M,D,O
Educational Administration M,D,O
Educational Media/Instructional Technology M,D
Electrical Engineering M,D,O
Elementary Education M,D
Engineering and Applied Sciences—General M,D,O*
Engineering Design M,D,O
Engineering Management M,D,O
English as a Second Language M,O
English Education M
English M,O
Environmental Engineering M,D,O
Ergonomics and Human Factors M,D,O
Exercise and Sports Science M
Finance and Banking M,D
Forensic Sciences M,O
Gender Studies M,O
Geotechnical Engineering M,D,O
Gerontology M,O
Hazardous Materials Management M,D,O
Health Informatics M,O
Health Services Management and Hospital Administration M,O
History M
Industrial and Organizational Psychology M,D
Industrial/Management Engineering M,D,O*
Latin American Studies M,O
Liberal Studies M
Manufacturing Engineering M,D,O
Marketing D
Materials Engineering M,D

University of Central Florida (continued)

Materials Sciences M,D
Mathematics Education M,D
Mathematics M,D
Mechanical Engineering M,D,O*
Medical/Surgical Nursing M
Microbiology M
Molecular Biology M
Music Education M
Nonprofit Management M,O
Nursing Education M
Nursing—General M
Operations Research M,D,O
Optical Sciences M,D,O
Pediatric Nursing M
Physical Education M
Physical Therapy M
Physics M,D
Political Science M
Psychology—General M,D
Public Policy and Administration M,D,O
Quality Management M,O
Reading Education M
School Psychology O
Science Education M
Social Sciences Education M
Social Work M,O
Sociology M,O
Spanish M
Special Education M,D
Statistics M
Structural Engineering M,D,O
Systems Engineering M,D,O
Taxation M
Technical Writing M,O
Theater M
Transportation and Highway Engineering M,D,O
Vocational and Technical Education M
Water Resources Engineering M,D,O
Writing M,O

In-depth description on page 1165.

UNIVERSITY OF CENTRAL OKLAHOMA

Adult Education M
American Studies M
Applied Arts and Design—General M
Applied Mathematics M
Applied Physics M
Biological and Biomedical Sciences—General M
Business Administration and Management—General M
Chemistry M
Communication Disorders M
Computer Education M
Computer Science M
Counseling Psychology M
Counselor Education M
Criminal Justice and Criminology M
Early Childhood Education M
Education—General M
Educational Administration M
Educational Media/Instructional Technology M
Elementary Education M
English as a Second Language M
English M
Family and Consumer Sciences-General M
Gerontology M
Health Education M
Higher Education M
History M
Home Economics Education M
Human Development M
Interior Design M
International Affairs M
Mathematics Education M
Mathematics M
Museum Studies M
Music Education M
Music M
Nutrition M
Political Science M
Psychology—General M
Reading Education M
Secondary Education M
Special Education M
Statistics M
Urban Studies M
Writing M

UNIVERSITY OF CHARLESTON

Business Administration and Management—General M
Human Resources Management M

UNIVERSITY OF CHICAGO

Allopathic Medicine P
Anatomy D
Anthropology M,D
Applied Mathematics M,D
Archaeology M,D
Art History M,D
Art/Fine Arts M,D
Asian Languages M,D
Asian Studies M,D
Astronomy M,D
Astrophysics M,D
Atmospheric Sciences M,D
Biochemistry D
Biological and Biomedical Sciences—General M,D
Business Administration and Management—General M
Cancer Biology/Oncology D
Cell Biology D
Chemistry M,D
Classics M,D
Comparative Literature M,D
Computer Science M,D
Cultural Studies M,D
Developmental Biology D
Ecology D
Economics D
English M,D
Environmental Management and Policy M,D
Environmental Sciences M,D
Evolutionary Biology D
Film, Television, and Video Theory and Criticism M,D
French M,D
Genetics D
Geology M,D
Geophysics M,D
Geosciences M,D
German M,D
Health Promotion M
Health Services Management and Hospital Administration M,O*
History of Science and Technology M,D
History M,D
Human Development D
Human Genetics D
Humanities M*
Immunology D
International Affairs M
International Business M
Italian M,D
Jewish Studies M,D
Latin American Studies M
Law P,M,D
Linguistics M,D
Mathematical and Computational Finance M
Mathematics M,D
Media Studies M,D
Medical Physics D*
Microbiology D
Molecular Biology D
Music M,D
Near and Middle Eastern Languages M,D
Near and Middle Eastern Studies M,D
Neurobiology D
Nutrition D
Pathology D
Pharmacology D
Philosophy M,D
Physics M,D
Physiology D
Planetary and Space Sciences M,D
Political Science D
Psychology—General D
Public Policy and Administration M,D*
Religion P,M,D
Slavic Languages M,D
Social Sciences M,D*
Social Work M,D*
Sociology D
Spanish M,D
Statistics M,D
Theology P,M,D
Vision Sciences D
Zoology D

UNIVERSITY OF CINCINNATI

Accounting M,D
Advanced Practice Nursing M,D
Aerospace/Aeronautical Engineering M,D
Allopathic Medicine P
Analytical Chemistry M,D
Anatomy D
Anthropology M
Applied Arts and Design—General M
Applied Mathematics M,D
Architecture M*
Art Education M
Art History M
Art/Fine Arts M
Arts Administration M
Biochemistry M,D
Biological and Biomedical Sciences—General M,D*
Biophysics D
Biostatistics M,D
Business Administration and Management—General M,D
Cell Biology D
Ceramic Sciences and Engineering M,D
Chemical Engineering M,D
Chemistry M,D
City and Regional Planning M
Civil Engineering M,D
Classics M,D
Clinical Psychology D
Communication Disorders M,D
Communication—General M
Community Health Nursing M,D
Computer Engineering M,D
Computer Science M,D
Counselor Education M,D,O
Criminal Justice and Criminology M,D
Curriculum and Instruction M,D
Developmental Biology M,D*
Early Childhood Education M
Economics M
Education—General M,D,O*
Educational Administration M,D,O
Electrical Engineering M,D*
Elementary Education M
Engineering and Applied Sciences—General M,D
English M,D
Environmental and Occupational Health M,D*
Environmental Engineering M,D
Environmental Sciences M,D
Epidemiology M,D
Experimental Psychology D
Finance and Banking M,D
Foundations and Philosophy of Education M,D
French M,D
Genetic Counseling M
Genetics M,D
Geography M,D
Geology M,D
German M,D
Graphic Design M
Health Education M
Health Physics/Radiological Health M
History M,D
Industrial and Labor Relations M
Industrial and Manufacturing Management M,D
Industrial Design M
Industrial Hygiene M,D
Industrial/Management Engineering M,D
Inorganic Chemistry M,D
Interdisciplinary Studies D
Interior Design M
International Business M
Law P
Management Information Systems M,D
Marketing M,D
Materials Engineering M,D
Materials Sciences M,D
Maternal/Child Nursing M,D
Mathematics Education M,D
Mathematics M,D
Mechanical Engineering M,D
Medical/Surgical Nursing M,D
Metallurgical Engineering and Metallurgy M,D
Microbiology M,D
Molecular Biology M,D
Molecular Medicine D
Music Education M
Music M,D,O
Neurobiology D
Neuroscience D*
Nuclear Engineering M,D
Nurse Anesthesia M,D
Nurse Midwifery M,D
Nursing and Healthcare Administration M,D
Nursing—General M,D
Nutrition M
Occupational Health Nursing M,D
Organic Chemistry M,D
Pathobiology D*
Pathology D
Pharmaceutical Sciences M,D*
Pharmacology D*
Pharmacy P
Philosophy M,D
Physical Chemistry M,D
Physics M,D
Physiology D
Political Science M,D
Polymer Science and Engineering M,D
Psychiatric Nursing M,D
Psychology—General D
Quantitative Analysis M,D
Reading Education M,D
Real Estate M
Rehabilitation Sciences M
School Psychology M,D
Secondary Education M
Social Sciences Education M,D
Social Work M
Sociology M,D
Spanish M,D
Special Education M,D
Statistics M,D
Textile Design M
Theater M
Toxicology M,D*
Women's Health Nursing M,D
Women's Studies M,O

UNIVERSITY OF COLORADO AT BOULDER

Accounting M,D
Aerospace/Aeronautical Engineering M,D
Animal Behavior M,D
Anthropology M,D
Applied Mathematics M,D
Architectural Engineering M,D
Art History M
Art/Fine Arts M
Asian Languages M
Astrophysics M,D
Atmospheric Sciences M,D
Biochemistry M,D
Biopsychology M,D
Business Administration and Management—General M,D*
Cell Biology M,D
Chemical Engineering M,D
Chemistry M,D
Civil Engineering M,D
Classics M,D
Communication Disorders M,D
Communication—General M,D
Comparative Literature M,D
Computer Engineering M,D
Computer Science M,D
Construction Engineering and Management M,D
Corporate and Organizational Communication M,D
Curriculum and Instruction M,D
Dance M,D
Developmental Biology M,D
Ecology M,D
Economics M,D
Education—General M,D
Educational Measurement and Evaluation D
Educational Psychology M,D
Electrical Engineering M,D
Engineering and Applied Sciences—General M,D*
Engineering Management M
English M,D
Entrepreneurship M,D
Environmental Biology M,D
Environmental Engineering M,D
Evolutionary Biology M,D
Finance and Banking M,D
French M,D
Genetics M,D
Geography M,D
Geology M,D
Geophysics M,D
Geotechnical Engineering M,D
German M
History M,D
Industrial and Manufacturing Management M,D
International Affairs M,D
Journalism M,D
Kinesiology and Movement Studies M,D
Law P
Linguistics M,D
Management of Technology M,D
Marine Biology M,D
Marketing M,D
Mass Communication M,D*
Mathematical Physics M,D
Mathematics M,D
Mechanical Engineering M,D
Media Studies D*
Medical Physics M,D
Microbiology M,D
Molecular Biology M,D*
Multilingual and Multicultural Education M,D
Museum Studies M
Music Education M,D
Music M,D
Neurobiology M,D
Optical Sciences M,D
Organizational Management M,D
Philosophy M,D
Photography M
Physical Chemistry M,D
Physical Education M,D
Physics M,D
Physiology M,D
Plant Biology M,D
Plant Physiology M,D
Plasma Physics M,D
Political Science M,D
Psychology—General M,D
Public Policy and Administration M,D
Real Estate M,D
Religion M

- Sociology M,D
- Spanish M,D
- Structural Engineering M,D
- Taxation M,D
- Telecommunications Management M
- Telecommunications M*
- Theater M,D
- Water Resources Engineering M,D
- Writing M,D
- Zoology M,D

UNIVERSITY OF COLORADO AT COLORADO SPRINGS

- Accounting M
- Advanced Practice Nursing M
- Aerospace/Aeronautical Engineering M
- Applied Mathematics M
- Business Administration and Management—General M*
- Communication—General M
- Community Health Nursing M
- Computer Engineering M,D
- Computer Science M,D
- Counselor Education M
- Criminal Justice and Criminology M
- Curriculum and Instruction M
- Education—General M
- Educational Administration M
- Electrical Engineering M,D
- Engineering and Applied Sciences—General M,D
- Engineering Management M
- Finance and Banking M
- Forensic Nursing M
- History M
- Human Services M
- Industrial and Manufacturing Management M
- Information Science M
- Management Information Systems M
- Manufacturing Engineering M
- Marketing M
- Maternal/Child Nursing M
- Mechanical Engineering M
- Medical/Surgical Nursing M
- Nursing—General M
- Organizational Management M
- Physics M
- Psychology—General M
- Public Policy and Administration M
- Sociology M
- Software Engineering M
- Special Education M

UNIVERSITY OF COLORADO AT DENVER

- Accounting M
- Anthropology M
- Applied Mathematics M,D
- Architecture M,D
- Biological and Biomedical Sciences—General M
- Business Administration and Management—General M
- Chemistry M
- City and Regional Planning M
- Civil Engineering M,D
- Communication—General M
- Computer Science M
- Counseling Psychology M
- Counselor Education M
- Criminal Justice and Criminology M*
- Curriculum and Instruction M
- Early Childhood Education M
- Economics M
- Education—General M,D,O
- Educational Administration M,D,O
- Educational Media/Instructional Technology M,O
- Educational Psychology M
- Electrical Engineering M
- Engineering and Applied Sciences—General M,D
- English as a Second Language M
- English Education M
- English M
- Environmental Sciences M
- Finance and Banking M
- Health Education D
- Health Services Management and Hospital Administration M
- History M
- Humanities M
- International Business M
- Landscape Architecture M
- Management Information Systems M
- Marketing M
- Mechanical Engineering M
- Political Science M
- Psychology—General M
- Public Policy and Administration M,D*
- Social Sciences M
- Sociology M
- Technical Writing M
- Theater M
- Urban Design M

UNIVERSITY OF COLORADO HEALTH SCIENCES CENTER

- Allopathic Medicine P
- Biochemistry D*
- Biological and Biomedical Sciences—General M,D
- Biometrics M,D
- Biophysics M,D
- Cell Biology D*
- Clinical Laboratory Sciences/Medical Technology D
- Dentistry P,M
- Developmental Biology D
- Genetic Counseling M
- Genetics M,D
- Immunology D*
- Medical Physics M,D
- Microbiology D*
- Molecular Biology D*
- Neuroscience D*
- Nursing—General M,D*
- Pathology D
- Pharmaceutical Sciences D*
- Pharmacology D
- Pharmacy P
- Physical Therapy M
- Physician Assistant Studies M
- Physiology D*
- Public Health—General M*
- Toxicology D

UNIVERSITY OF CONNECTICUT

- Accounting M,D
- Adult Education M,D
- Aerospace/Aeronautical Engineering M,D
- African Studies M
- Agricultural Economics and Agribusiness M,D
- Agricultural Sciences—General M,D
- Agronomy and Soil Sciences M,D
- Allied Health—General M
- Animal Sciences M,D
- Anthropology M,D
- Art History M
- Art/Fine Arts M*
- Biochemistry M,D
- Bioengineering M,D
- Biological and Biomedical Sciences—General M,D
- Biomedical Engineering M,D
- Biophysics M,D
- Biopsychology M,D
- Biotechnology M,D*
- Botany M,D
- Business Administration and Management—General M,D*
- Cell Biology M,D*
- Chemical Engineering M,D
- Chemistry M,D
- Child and Family Studies M,D
- Civil Engineering M,D
- Clinical Psychology D
- Cognitive Sciences D
- Communication Disorders M,D
- Communication—General M
- Comparative Literature M,D
- Computer Science M,D
- Corporate and Organizational Communication M,D
- Counseling Psychology M,D
- Curriculum and Instruction M,D
- Developmental Biology M,D
- Developmental Psychology D
- East European and Russian Studies M
- Ecology M,D*
- Economics M,D*
- Education of the Gifted M,D
- Education—General M,D
- Educational Administration M,D
- Educational Measurement and Evaluation M,D
- Educational Media/Instructional Technology M,D
- Educational Psychology M,D
- Electrical Engineering M,D
- Elementary Education M,D
- Engineering and Applied Sciences—General M,D
- English Education M,D
- English M,D*
- Entomology M,D
- Environmental Engineering M,D
- Environmental Management and Policy M
- Exercise and Sports Science M,D
- Experimental Psychology D
- Finance and Banking M,D
- Foreign Languages Education M,D
- Foundations and Philosophy of Education M,D
- French M,D
- Genetics M,D
- Geography M,D
- Geology M,D
- Geophysics M,D
- German M,D
- Health Services Management and Hospital Administration M,D
- Higher Education M,D
- History M,D
- Human Development M,D
- Human Resources Management M,D
- Industrial and Organizational Psychology D
- International Affairs M
- International Business
- Italian M,D
- Latin American Studies M
- Law P
- Leisure Studies M,D
- Linguistics M,D
- Marine Sciences M,D
- Marketing M,D
- Mass Communication M
- Materials Sciences M,D
- Mathematics Education M,D
- Mathematics M,D
- Mechanical Engineering M,D
- Mechanics D
- Medicinal and Pharmaceutical Chemistry M,D
- Medieval and Renaissance Studies M,D
- Metallurgical Engineering and Metallurgy M,D
- Microbiology M,D
- Multilingual and Multicultural Education M,D
- Music Education M,D
- Music M,D
- Natural Resources M
- Neurobiology M,D
- Neuroscience D
- Nursing and Healthcare Administration M,D
- Nursing Education M,D
- Nursing—General M,D
- Nutrition M,D
- Ocean Engineering M,D
- Oceanography M,D
- Oral and Dental Sciences M
- Pathobiology M,D
- Pharmaceutical Sciences M,D*
- Pharmacology M,D*
- Philosophy M,D
- Physics M,D*
- Physiology M,D*
- Plant Biology M,D
- Plant Molecular Biology M,D
- Plant Sciences M,D
- Political Science M,D
- Polymer Science and Engineering M,D*
- Psychology—General D
- Public Health—General M
- Public Policy and Administration M
- Reading Education M,D
- School Psychology M,D
- Science Education M,D
- Secondary Education M,D
- Social Psychology D
- Social Sciences Education M,D
- Social Work M
- Sociology M,D
- Software Engineering M,D
- Spanish M,D
- Special Education M,D
- Speech and Interpersonal Communication M
- Statistics M,D
- Systems Engineering M,D
- Theater M
- Toxicology M,D
- Vocational and Technical Education M,D
- Western European Studies M
- Zoology M,D

In-depth description on page 1167.

UNIVERSITY OF CONNECTICUT HEALTH CENTER

- Allopathic Medicine P
- Biochemistry D
- Biological and Biomedical Sciences—General D*
- Cell Biology D*
- Dentistry P,O
- Developmental Biology D*
- Genetics D
- Immunology D*
- Molecular Biology D*
- Neuroscience D*
- Oral and Dental Sciences M,D*
- Pharmacology D*
- Public Health—General M

UNIVERSITY OF DALLAS

- American Studies M
- Art/Fine Arts M
- Business Administration and Management—General M*
- Comparative Literature D
- Electronic Commerce M
- English M
- Entrepreneurship M
- Finance and Banking M
- Health Services Management and Hospital Administration M
- Human Resources Management M
- Humanities M
- Management Information Systems M
- Management Strategy and Policy M
- Marketing M
- Pastoral Ministry and Counseling M
- Philosophy M,D
- Political Science M,D
- Psychology—General M
- Sports Management M
- Theology M

UNIVERSITY OF DAYTON

- Aerospace/Aeronautical Engineering M,D
- Agricultural Engineering M
- Applied Mathematics M
- Art Education M
- Biological and Biomedical Sciences—General M,D*
- Business Administration and Management—General M
- Chemical Engineering M
- Chemistry M
- Civil Engineering M
- Clinical Psychology M
- Communication—General M
- Computer Engineering M,D
- Computer Science M
- Counselor Education M
- Early Childhood Education M
- Education—General M,D,O
- Educational Administration M,D
- Educational Media/Instructional Technology M
- Electrical Engineering M,D
- Engineering and Applied Sciences—General M,D*
- Engineering Management M
- English M
- Environmental Engineering M
- Exercise and Sports Science M
- Experimental Psychology M
- Human Development M
- Industrial/Management Engineering M
- Law P
- Materials Engineering M,D
- Mechanical Engineering M,D
- Mechanics M
- Middle School Education M
- Optical Sciences M,D
- Pastoral Ministry and Counseling M,D
- Physical Education M
- Psychology—General M
- Public Policy and Administration M
- Reading Education M
- School Psychology M
- Secondary Education M
- Social Psychology M
- Special Education M
- Structural Engineering M
- Student Personnel Services M
- Theology M,D
- Transportation and Highway Engineering M

In-depth description on page 1169.

UNIVERSITY OF DELAWARE

- Accounting M
- Advanced Practice Nursing M,O
- Agricultural Economics and Agribusiness M
- Agricultural Sciences—General M,D
- Agronomy and Soil Sciences M,D
- American Studies M
- Applied Mathematics M,D
- Art History M,D
- Art/Fine Arts M*
- Astronomy M,D
- Atmospheric Sciences D
- Biochemistry M,D
- Biological and Biomedical Sciences—General M,D*
- Biotechnology M,D
- Business Administration and Management—General M,D*
- Cell Biology M,D
- Chemical Engineering M,D
- Chemistry M,D

University of Delaware (continued)

- Child and Family Studies M,D
- Civil Engineering M,D*
- Clinical Psychology D
- Cognitive Sciences D
- Communication—General M
- Computer Science M,D*
- Counselor Education M,D
- Criminal Justice and Criminology M,D
- Curriculum and Instruction M,D
- Ecology M,D
- Economics M,D
- Education—General M,D
- Educational Administration M,D
- Educational Measurement and Evaluation M,D
- Electrical Engineering M,D
- Engineering and Applied Sciences—General M,D*
- English as a Second Language M,D
- English Education M,D
- English M,D*
- Entomology M,D
- Environmental Engineering M,D
- Environmental Management and Policy M,D*
- Evolutionary Biology M,D
- Exercise and Sports Science M
- Food Science and Technology M,D
- Foreign Languages Education M
- French M
- Genetics M,D
- Geography M,D
- Geology M,D*
- Geotechnical Engineering M,D
- German M
- Gerontological Nursing M,O
- Health Promotion M
- Higher Education M
- Historic Preservation M
- History M,D
- HIV/AIDS Nursing M,O
- Horticulture M
- Human Development M,D
- Information Science M,D
- International Affairs M,D
- Kinesiology and Movement Studies M,D
- Liberal Studies M
- Linguistics M,D
- Management Information Systems M
- Management of Technology M
- Marine Affairs M,D
- Marine Sciences M,D
- Materials Engineering M,D
- Materials Sciences M,D
- Maternal/Child Nursing M,O
- Mathematics M,D*
- Mechanical Engineering M,D*
- Medical/Surgical Nursing M,O
- Microbiology M,D
- Molecular Biology M,D
- Multilingual and Multicultural Education M,D
- Museum Studies O
- Music Education M
- Music M
- Neuroscience D
- Nursing and Healthcare Administration M,O
- Nursing—General M,O
- Nutrition M
- Ocean Engineering M,D
- Oceanography M,D
- Oncology Nursing M,O
- Operations Research M,D*
- Pediatric Nursing M,O
- Physical Therapy M
- Physics M,D
- Physiology M,D
- Plant Biology M,D
- Plant Sciences M,D
- Political Science M,D*
- Psychiatric Nursing M,O
- Psychology—General D
- Public Policy and Administration M,D*
- School Psychology M,D
- Secondary Education M,D
- Social Psychology D
- Sociology M,D
- Spanish M
- Special Education M,D
- Statistics M
- Structural Engineering M,D
- Theater M*
- Transportation and Highway Engineering M,D
- Urban Studies M,D
- Water Resources Engineering M,D
- Women's Health Nursing M,O

In-depth description on page 1171.

UNIVERSITY OF DENVER

- Accounting M
- Adult Education M,D,O
- Advertising and Public Relations M
- Anthropology M
- Applied Mathematics M,D
- Art History M
- Art/Fine Arts M
- Biological and Biomedical Sciences—General M,D
- Business Administration and Management—General M*
- Chemistry M,D
- Child and Family Studies M,D,O
- Clinical Psychology D
- Communication—General M,D*
- Computer Engineering M,D
- Computer Science M,D
- Construction Engineering and Management M
- Corporate and Organizational Communication M
- Counseling Psychology M,D,O
- Curriculum and Instruction M,D,O
- Economics M
- Education—General M,D,O
- Educational Administration M,D,O
- Educational Measurement and Evaluation M,D,O
- Educational Psychology M,D,O
- Electrical Engineering M,D
- Electronic Commerce M
- Engineering and Applied Sciences—General M,D
- Engineering Management M
- English M,D
- Environmental Management and Policy M
- Film, Television, and Video Production M
- Finance and Banking M
- French M
- Geography M,D
- German M
- Health Services Management and Hospital Administration M
- Higher Education M,D,O
- History M
- Hospitality Management M
- Information Studies M
- International Affairs M,D
- International Business M
- Jewish Studies M
- Law P,M
- Legal and Justice Studies M
- Liberal Studies M
- Library Science M
- Management Information Systems M
- Management of Technology M
- Marketing M
- Mass Communication M
- Materials Sciences M,D
- Mathematics M,D
- Mechanical Engineering M,D
- Media Studies M
- Museum Studies M
- Music Education M
- Music M
- Philosophy M
- Physics M,D
- Psychology—General D
- Public Health—General M
- Real Estate M
- Religion M,D
- School Psychology M,D,O
- Social Work M,D*
- Spanish M
- Speech and Interpersonal Communication M,D
- Sports Management M
- Taxation M*
- Telecommunications Management M
- Telecommunications M
- Travel and Tourism M

In-depth descriptions on pages 1173 and 1175.

UNIVERSITY OF DETROIT MERCY

- Addictions/Substance Abuse Counseling O
- Advanced Practice Nursing M,O
- Allied Health—General M,O
- Architectural Engineering M
- Automotive Engineering M,D
- Biochemistry M
- Business Administration and Management—General M*
- Chemical Engineering M,D
- Chemistry M
- Civil Engineering M
- Clinical Psychology M,D
- Computer Science M
- Criminal Justice and Criminology M
- Curriculum and Instruction M
- Dentistry P
- Early Childhood Education M
- Education—General M
- Educational Administration M
- Electrical Engineering M,D
- Engineering and Applied Sciences—General M,D
- Engineering Management M
- Environmental Engineering M
- Health Services Management and Hospital Administration M
- Industrial and Organizational Psychology M
- Law P
- Liberal Studies M
- Management Information Systems M
- Manufacturing Engineering M,D
- Mathematics Education M
- Mathematics M
- Mechanical Engineering M,D
- Nurse Anesthesia M
- Oral and Dental Sciences M,O
- Physician Assistant Studies M
- Polymer Science and Engineering M,D
- Psychology—General M,D,O
- Religion M
- School Psychology O
- Special Education M

UNIVERSITY OF DUBUQUE

- Aviation Management M
- Business Administration and Management—General M
- Communication—General M
- Finance and Banking M
- Quality Management M
- Theology P,M,D

UNIVERSITY OF EVANSVILLE

- Education—General M
- Nursing—General M

THE UNIVERSITY OF FINDLAY

- Business Administration and Management—General M
- Early Childhood Education M
- Education—General M
- Educational Administration M
- Educational Media/Instructional Technology M
- Elementary Education M
- English as a Second Language M
- Finance and Banking M
- Human Resources Management M
- International Business M
- Marketing M
- Multilingual and Multicultural Education M
- Occupational Therapy M
- Physical Therapy M
- Public Policy and Administration M
- Special Education M

UNIVERSITY OF FLORIDA

- Accounting M,D
- Advertising and Public Relations M,D
- Aerospace/Aeronautical Engineering M,D,O
- African Studies O
- Agricultural Economics and Agribusiness M,D
- Agricultural Education M,D
- Agricultural Engineering M,D,O
- Agricultural Sciences—General M,D
- Agronomy and Soil Sciences M,D
- Allied Health—General M,D
- Allopathic Medicine P
- Anatomy D
- Animal Sciences M,D
- Anthropology M,D
- Applied Mathematics M,D
- Aquaculture M,D
- Architecture M,D
- Art Education M
- Art History M
- Art/Fine Arts M
- Astronomy M,D
- Biochemistry M,D
- Bioengineering M,D,O
- Biological and Biomedical Sciences—General M,D*
- Biomedical Engineering M,D,O
- Botany M,D
- Building Science M
- Business Administration and Management—General M,D
- Cell Biology M,D*
- Ceramic Sciences and Engineering M,D,O
- Chemical Engineering M,D,O*
- Chemistry M,D
- City and Regional Planning M
- Civil Engineering M,D,O
- Classics M,D
- Clinical Psychology D
- Clinical Research M
- Communication Disorders M,D
- Communication—General M,D
- Computer Education M,D,O
- Computer Engineering M,D,O
- Computer Science M,D,O*
- Construction Engineering and Management M
- Corporate and Organizational Communication M,D
- Counselor Education M,D,O
- Dentistry P,O
- Early Childhood Education M,D,O
- Ecology M,D
- Economics M,D
- Education—General M,D,O*
- Educational Administration M,D,O
- Educational Measurement and Evaluation M,D,O
- Educational Media/Instructional Technology M,D,O
- Educational Psychology M,D,O
- Electrical Engineering M,D,O*
- Elementary Education M,D,O
- Engineering and Applied Sciences—General M,D,O*
- Engineering Management M,D,O
- Engineering Physics M,D,O
- English as a Second Language M,D,O
- English Education M,D,O
- English M,D
- Entomology M,D
- Environmental Engineering M,D,O
- Exercise and Sports Science M,D
- Finance and Banking M,D
- Fish, Game, and Wildlife Management M,D
- Food Science and Technology M,D*
- Foreign Languages Education M,D,O
- Forestry M,D
- Foundations and Philosophy of Education M,D,O
- French M,D
- Genetics M,D*
- Genomic Sciences D
- Geography M,D
- Geology M,D
- Geosciences M,D
- German M,D
- Health Education M,D
- Health Physics/Radiological Health M,D,O
- Health Psychology D
- Health Services Management and Hospital Administration M,D*
- Health Services Research M,D
- Higher Education M,D,O
- History M,D
- Horticulture M,D
- Human Resources Management M,D
- Immunology M,D*
- Industrial/Management Engineering M,D,O*
- Information Science M,D,O
- Interior Design M
- International Affairs M,D
- International Business M
- International Development M,D,O
- Journalism M,D*
- Kinesiology and Movement Studies D
- Landscape Architecture M
- Latin American Studies M,O*
- Law P,M,D
- Limnology M,D
- Linguistics M,D,O
- Management Information Systems M,D
- Management Strategy and Policy M,D
- Manufacturing Engineering M,D,O
- Marine Sciences M,D
- Marketing M,D
- Marriage and Family Therapy M,D,O
- Mass Communication M,D
- Materials Engineering M,D,O
- Materials Sciences M,D,O*
- Mathematics Education M,D,O
- Mathematics M,D
- Mechanical Engineering M,D,O*
- Mechanics M,D,O
- Media Studies M,D
- Medical Physics M,D,O
- Medicinal and Pharmaceutical Chemistry M,D
- Metallurgical Engineering and Metallurgy M,D,O
- Microbiology M,D
- Middle School Education M,D,O
- Molecular Biology M,D*
- Multilingual and Multicultural Education M,D,O
- Museum Studies M
- Music Education M,D
- Music M,D
- Natural Resources M,D
- Neuroscience M,D*
- Nuclear Engineering M,D,O
- Nursing—General M,D
- Nutrition M,D
- Occupational Therapy M
- Ocean Engineering M,D,O
- Operations Research M,D,O

Oral and Dental Sciences	M,D,O
Pathology	M,D
Pharmaceutical Administration	M,D
Pharmacology	M,D*
Pharmacy	P
Philosophy	M,D
Physical Education	D
Physical Therapy	M
Physician Assistant Studies	M
Physics	M,D*
Physiology	D
Plant Biology	M,D
Plant Molecular Biology	M,D*
Plant Pathology	M,D
Political Science	M,D,O
Polymer Science and Engineering	M,D,O
Psychology—General	M,D
Public Health—General	M
Public Policy and Administration	M,D,O
Reading Education	M,D,O
Real Estate	M,D
Recreation and Park Management	M,D
Rehabilitation Counseling	M
Rehabilitation Sciences	D
Religion	M
School Psychology	M,D,O
Science Education	M,D,O
Secondary Education	M,D,O
Social Sciences Education	M,D,O
Sociology	M,D
Spanish	M,D
Special Education	M,D,O
Sport Psychology	D
Statistics	M,D
Student Personnel Services	M,D,O
Systems Engineering	M,D,O
Taxation	M
Theater	M
Toxicology	M,D,O
Veterinary Medicine	P
Veterinary Sciences	M,D,O
Water Resources	M,D
Zoology	M,D

In-depth description on page 1177.

UNIVERSITY OF GEORGIA

Accounting	M
Adult Education	M,D,O*
Agricultural Economics and Agribusiness	M,D*
Agricultural Education	M,D,O
Agricultural Engineering	M,D
Agricultural Sciences—General	M,D
Agronomy and Soil Sciences	M,D
Analytical Chemistry	M,D
Anatomy	M
Animal Sciences	M,D
Anthropology	M,D
Applied Economics	M,D
Applied Mathematics	M,D
Art Education	M,D,O
Art History	M
Art/Fine Arts	M,D
Artificial Intelligence/Robotics	M
Astronomy	M,D
Biochemistry	M,D
Bioengineering	M,D*
Botany	M,D
Business Administration and Management—General	M,D
Business Education	M,D,O
Cell Biology	M,D*
Chemistry	M,D
Child and Family Studies	M,D
Classics	M
Clothing and Textiles	M,D
Communication Disorders	M,D,O
Communication—General	M,D*
Comparative Literature	M,D
Computer Education	M
Computer Science	M,D
Consumer Economics	M,D
Counseling Psychology	M,D
Counselor Education	M,D
Early Childhood Education	M,D,O
Ecology	M,D
Economics	M,D
Education of the Gifted	M,D,O
Education—General	M,D,O
Educational Administration	M,D,O
Educational Media/Instructional Technology	M,D,O
Educational Psychology	M,D,O
Elementary Education	M,D,O
English Education	M,D,O
English	M,D
Entomology	M,D
Environmental and Occupational Health	M,D
Exercise and Sports Science	M,D,O
Family and Consumer Sciences-General	M,D
Food Science and Technology	M,D
Foreign Languages Education	M,D,O
Forestry	M,D
Foundations and Philosophy of Education	M,D,O
French	M
Genetics	M,D*
Geochemistry	M,D
Geography	M,D
Geophysics	M,D
German	M
Health Education	M,D,O
Health Promotion	M,D,O
Higher Education	D
Historic Preservation	M
History	M,D
Home Economics Education	M,D,O
Horticulture	M,D
Human Resources Development	M,D,O*
Inorganic Chemistry	M,D
Interior Design	M,D
Journalism	M,D
Landscape Architecture	M
Law	P,M
Leisure Studies	M,D
Linguistics	M,D
Marine Sciences	M,D*
Marketing Research	M
Mass Communication	M,D
Mathematics Education	M,D,O
Mathematics	M,D
Medical Microbiology	M,D
Medicinal and Pharmaceutical Chemistry	M,D
Microbiology	M,D*
Middle School Education	M,D,O
Molecular Biology	M,D
Music Education	M,D,O
Music	M,D
Natural Resources	M,D
Nutrition	M,D
Oceanography	M,D
Organic Chemistry	M,D
Parasitology	M,D
Pathology	M,D
Pharmaceutical Administration	M,D
Pharmaceutical Sciences	M,D*
Pharmacology	M,D
Pharmacy	P
Philosophy	M,D
Physical Chemistry	M,D
Physical Education	M,D,O
Physics	M,D*
Physiology	M,D
Plant Pathology	M,D
Political Science	M,D
Psychology—General	M,D
Public Policy and Administration	M,D
Reading Education	M,D,O
Recreation and Park Management	M,D
Religion	M
Romance Languages	M,D
School Psychology	M,D,O
Science Education	M,D,O
Secondary Education	M,D,O
Social Sciences Education	M,D,O
Social Work	M,D
Sociology	M,D
Spanish	M
Special Education	M,D,O
Speech and Interpersonal Communication	M,D
Statistics	M,D*
Student Personnel Services	M,D
Sustainable Development	M,D
Theater	M,D
Toxicology	M,D
Veterinary Medicine	P
Veterinary Sciences	M,D
Vocational and Technical Education	M,D,O

In-depth description on page 1179.

UNIVERSITY OF GREAT FALLS

Addictions/Substance Abuse Counseling	M
Child and Family Studies	M
Counseling Psychology	M
Counselor Education	M
Criminal Justice and Criminology	M
Curriculum and Instruction	M
Education—General	M
Educational Administration	M
Elementary Education	M
Human Services	M
Information Science	M
Marriage and Family Therapy	M
Secondary Education	M

UNIVERSITY OF GUAM

Art/Fine Arts	M
Biological and Biomedical Sciences—General	M
Business Administration and Management—General	M
Counselor Education	M
Education—General	M
Educational Administration	M
English as a Second Language	M
Environmental Sciences	M
Graphic Design	M
Marine Biology	M
Public Policy and Administration	M
Reading Education	M
Secondary Education	M
Special Education	M

UNIVERSITY OF GUELPH

Agricultural Economics and Agribusiness	M,D
Agricultural Sciences—General	M,D
Agronomy and Soil Sciences	M,D
Anatomy	M,D
Animal Sciences	M,D
Anthropology	M
Applied Mathematics	M,D
Aquaculture	M
Art/Fine Arts	M
Atmospheric Sciences	M,D
Biochemistry	M,D
Bioengineering	M,D
Biological and Biomedical Sciences—General	M,D
Biophysics	M,D
Biotechnology	M,D
Botany	M,D
Chemistry	M,D
Child and Family Studies	M,D
Clinical Laboratory Sciences/Medical Technology	M,D,O
Computer Science	M
Consumer Economics	M
Developmental Psychology	M,D
Economics	M,D
Engineering and Applied Sciences—General	M,D
English	M,D
Environmental Biology	M,D
Environmental Engineering	M,D
Environmental Management and Policy	M,D
Epidemiology	M,D,O
Experimental Psychology	M,D
Food Science and Technology	M,D
Genetics	M,D
Geography	M,D
History	M,D
Horticulture	M,D
Hospitality Management	M
Human Development	M,D
Immunology	M,D,O
Industrial and Organizational Psychology	M,D
International Development	M
Landscape Architecture	M,D
Marriage and Family Therapy	M,D
Mathematics	M,D
Microbiology	M,D
Molecular Biology	M,D
Neuroscience	M,D,O
Nutrition	M,D
Pathobiology	M,D,O
Pathology	M,D,O
Pharmacology	M,D
Philosophy	M,D
Physics	M,D
Physiology	M,D
Plant Sciences	M,D
Political Science	M
Psychology—General	M,D
Rural Planning and Studies	M,D,O
Social Psychology	M,D
Sociology	M
Statistics	M,D
Theater	M
Toxicology	M,D
Veterinary Medicine	M,D,O
Veterinary Sciences	M,D,O
Vision Sciences	M,D,O
Water Resources Engineering	M,D
Western European Studies	M,D
Zoology	M,D

UNIVERSITY OF HARTFORD

Accounting	M
Art/Fine Arts	M
Biological and Biomedical Sciences—General	M
Business Administration and Management—General	M
Clinical Psychology	M,D
Communication—General	M
Community Health Nursing	M
Counselor Education	M,O
Early Childhood Education	M
Education—General	M,D,O
Educational Administration	D,O
Educational Media/Instructional Technology	M
Elementary Education	M
Engineering and Applied Sciences—General	M
Experimental Psychology	M
Music Education	M,D,O
Music	M,D,O
Neuroscience	M*
Nursing Education	M
Nursing—General	M
Organizational Behavior	M
Physical Therapy	M
Psychology—General	M
School Psychology	M
Taxation	M

UNIVERSITY OF HAWAII AT MANOA

Accounting	M
Advanced Practice Nursing	M,D,O
Agricultural Economics and Agribusiness	M,D
Agricultural Sciences—General	M,D*
Agronomy and Soil Sciences	M,D
Allopathic Medicine	P
American Studies	M,D
Animal Sciences	M
Anthropology	M,D
Architecture	D*
Art History	M
Art/Fine Arts	M
Asian Languages	M,D
Asian Studies	M
Astronomy	M,D
Biochemistry	M,D
Bioengineering	M,D
Biological and Biomedical Sciences—General	M,D
Biophysics	M,D
Botany	M,D
Business Administration and Management—General	M
Cell Biology	M,D
Chemistry	M,D
City and Regional Planning	M*
Civil Engineering	M,D
Classics	M
Clinical Psychology	M,D
Communication Disorders	M
Communication—General	M
Community Health Nursing	M,D,O
Computer Science	M,D,O
Conservation Biology	M,D
Counselor Education	M
Curriculum and Instruction	D
Dance	M,D
Ecology	M,D
Economics	M,D
Education—General	M,D
Educational Administration	M,D
Educational Measurement and Evaluation	D
Educational Media/Instructional Technology	M
Educational Psychology	M,D
Electrical Engineering	M,D
Elementary Education	M
Engineering and Applied Sciences—General	M,D
English as a Second Language	M,D
English	M,D
Entomology	M,D
Environmental Management and Policy	M
Epidemiology	M
Evolutionary Biology	M,D
Food Science and Technology	M
Foreign Languages Education	M,D
Foundations and Philosophy of Education	M,D
French	M
Genetics	M,D
Geochemistry	M,D
Geography	M,D
Geology	M,D
Geophysics	M,D
German	M
History	M,D
Horticulture	M,D
Hospitality Management	M
Hydrology	M,D
Information Science	D
Information Studies	M,D,O
International Business	D
Kinesiology and Movement Studies	M
Law	P
Leisure Studies	M
Library Science	M,D,O*
Linguistics	M,D
Marine Biology	M,D
Mathematics	M,D
Mechanical Engineering	M,D
Medical Microbiology	M,D
Medical/Surgical Nursing	M,D,O
Meteorology	M,D
Microbiology	M,D
Molecular Biology	M,D
Music	M,D
Neuroscience	M,D
Nursing and Healthcare Administration	M,D,O
Nursing—General	M,D,O
Nutrition	M
Ocean Engineering	M,D

University of Hawaii at Manoa (continued)

Program	Degrees
Oceanography	M,D
Pharmacology	M,D
Philosophy	M,D
Physics	M,D
Physiology	M,D*
Planetary and Space Sciences	M,D
Plant Biology	M,D
Plant Pathology	M,D
Plant Sciences	M,D
Political Science	M,D
Psychology—General	M,D
Public Health—General	M
Public Policy and Administration	M,O
Religion	M
Reproductive Biology	M,D
Secondary Education	M
Social Psychology	M,D
Social Work	M,D
Sociology	M,D
Spanish	M
Special Education	M,D
Speech and Interpersonal Communication	M
Theater	M,D*
Travel and Tourism	M
Zoology	M,D

THE UNIVERSITY OF HEALTH SCIENCES

Program	Degrees
Osteopathic Medicine	P

UNIVERSITY OF HOUSTON

Program	Degrees
Accounting	M,D
Advertising and Public Relations	M
Aerospace/Aeronautical Engineering	M,D
Anthropology	M
Applied Mathematics	M,D
Architecture	M*
Art Education	M,D
Art/Fine Arts	M
Biochemistry	M,D*
Biological and Biomedical Sciences—General	M,D
Biomedical Engineering	M,D
Business Administration and Management—General	M,D
Chemical Engineering	M,D
Chemistry	M,D*
Civil Engineering	M,D*
Clinical Psychology	D
Communication Disorders	M
Communication—General	M
Computer Engineering	M,D
Computer Science	M,D*
Construction Engineering and Management	M
Counseling Psychology	M,D
Curriculum and Instruction	M,D
Early Childhood Education	M,D
Economics	M,D
Education of the Gifted	M,D
Education—General	M,D
Educational Administration	M,D
Educational Psychology	M,D
Electrical Engineering	M,D
Elementary Education	M,D
Engineering and Applied Sciences—General	M,D
English as a Second Language	M,D
English	M,D
Entrepreneurship	D
Environmental Engineering	M,D
Exercise and Sports Science	M,D
Finance and Banking	M,D
Foundations and Philosophy of Education	M,D
French	M,D
Geology	M,D
Geophysics	M,D
Graphic Design	M
Health Education	M,D
Higher Education	M,D
History	M,D
Hospitality Management	M
Industrial and Organizational Psychology	D
Industrial/Management Engineering	M,D
Information Science	M,D
Interior Design	M
Law	P,M
Linguistics	M,D
Manufacturing Engineering	M
Marketing	D
Mass Communication	M
Materials Engineering	M,D
Mathematics Education	M,D
Mathematics	M,D*
Mechanical Engineering	M,D*
Multilingual and Multicultural Education	M,D
Music Education	M,D
Music	M,D
Optometry	P
Petroleum Engineering	M,D
Pharmaceutical Administration	P,M,D
Pharmaceutical Sciences	P,M,D
Pharmacology	P,M,D
Pharmacy	P,M,D
Philosophy	M
Photography	M
Physical Education	M,D
Physics	M,D
Political Science	M,D
Psychology—General	D
Public History	M,D
Reading Education	M,D
Science Education	M,D
Secondary Education	M,D
Social Psychology	D
Social Sciences Education	M,D
Social Work	M,D
Sociology	M
Spanish	M,D
Special Education	M,D
Speech and Interpersonal Communication	M
Systems Engineering	M,D
Taxation	M,D
Theater	M
Vision Sciences	M,D*
Writing	M,D

UNIVERSITY OF HOUSTON–CLEAR LAKE

Program	Degrees
Accounting	M
Biological and Biomedical Sciences—General	M
Business Administration and Management—General	M
Chemistry	M
Clinical Psychology	M
Computer Engineering	M
Computer Science	M
Counselor Education	M
Curriculum and Instruction	M
Early Childhood Education	M
Education—General	M*
Educational Administration	M
Educational Media/Instructional Technology	M
English	M
Environmental Management and Policy	M
Environmental Sciences	M
Exercise and Sports Science	M
Finance and Banking	M
Health Services Management and Hospital Administration	M
History	M
Human Resources Management	M
Humanities	M
Information Science	M
Marriage and Family Therapy	M
Mathematics	M
Multilingual and Multicultural Education	M
Psychology—General	M
Public Policy and Administration	M
Reading Education	M
School Psychology	M
Sociology	M
Software Engineering	M
Statistics	M

In-depth description on page 1181.

UNIVERSITY OF HOUSTON–VICTORIA

Program	Degrees
Business Administration and Management—General	M
Education—General	M
Interdisciplinary Studies	M
Psychology—General	M

UNIVERSITY OF IDAHO

Program	Degrees
Accounting	M*
Adult Education	M,D,O
Agricultural Economics and Agribusiness	M*
Agricultural Education	M
Agricultural Engineering	M,D*
Agricultural Sciences—General	M*
Agronomy and Soil Sciences	M,D*
Animal Sciences	M,D*
Anthropology	M*
Architecture	M*
Art Education	M
Art/Fine Arts	M*
Biochemistry	M,D
Biological and Biomedical Sciences—General	M,D*
Botany	M,D
Business Administration and Management—General	M
Business Education	M,D,O
Chemical Engineering	M,D*
Chemistry	M,D*
Civil Engineering	M,D*
Computer Engineering	M,D
Computer Science	M,D*
Counselor Education	M,D,O*
Economics	M*
Education—General	M,D,O
Educational Administration	M,D,O*
Electrical Engineering	M,D*
Elementary Education	M,D,O
Engineering and Applied Sciences—General	M,D
English as a Second Language	M
English Education	M
English	M*
Entomology	M,D
Environmental Engineering	M
Environmental Management and Policy	M,D*
Environmental Sciences	M*
Family and Consumer Sciences-General	M*
Fish, Game, and Wildlife Management	M,D*
Food Science and Technology	M*
Foreign Languages Education	M
Forestry	M,D*
French	M
Geography	M,D*
Geological Engineering	M
Geology	M,D*
Geophysics	M
Hazardous Materials Management	M
History	M,D*
Hydrology	M
Interdisciplinary Studies	M
Landscape Architecture	M*
Law	P*
Mathematics Education	M,D
Mathematics	M,D*
Mechanical Engineering	M,D*
Metallurgical Engineering and Metallurgy	M,D
Microbiology	M,D
Mineral/Mining Engineering	M,D
Molecular Biology	M,D
Music	M*
Nuclear Engineering	M,D
Physical Education	M,D*
Physics	M,D*
Plant Pathology	M,D
Plant Sciences	M,D
Political Science	M,D
Psychology—General	M*
Public Policy and Administration	M
Range Science	M,D*
Recreation and Park Management	M,D*
School Psychology	M,D,O
Science Education	M,D
Secondary Education	M,D,O
Social Sciences Education	M,D
Spanish	M
Special Education	M,O
Statistics	M*
Systems Engineering	M
Theater	M*
Veterinary Sciences	M,D
Vocational and Technical Education	M,D,O
Writing	M
Zoology	M,D

In-depth description on page 1183.

UNIVERSITY OF ILLINOIS AT CHICAGO

Program	Degrees
Accounting	M
Allied Health—General	M,D*
Allopathic Medicine	P
Anatomy	M,D*
Anthropology	M,D
Applied Mathematics	M,D
Architecture	M
Art History	M,D
Art Therapy	M
Art/Fine Arts	M
Biochemistry	M,D*
Bioengineering	M,D*
Biological and Biomedical Sciences—General	M,D*
Biomedical Engineering	M,D
Biophysics	M,D
Biostatistics	M,D
Business Administration and Management—General	M,D
Cell Biology	M,D
Chemical Engineering	M,D*
Chemistry	M,D
City and Regional Planning	M,D
Civil Engineering	M,D*
Clinical Laboratory Sciences/Medical Technology	M
Communication—General	M
Community Health Nursing	M
Community Health	M,D
Computer Engineering	M,D
Computer Science	M,D*
Criminal Justice and Criminology	M*
Curriculum and Instruction	M,D
Dentistry	P
Developmental Biology	M,D
Disability Studies	M,D
East European and Russian Studies	M,D
Ecology	M,D
Economics	M,D
Education—General	M,D
Educational Administration	M,D
Electrical Engineering	M,D*
Elementary Education	M,D
Engineering and Applied Sciences—General	M,D*
English as a Second Language	M
English Education	M,D
English	M,D
Environmental and Occupational Health	M,D
Epidemiology	M,D
Evolutionary Biology	M,D
Finance and Banking	D
Forensic Sciences	M
French	M
Genetics	M,D*
Geochemistry	M,D
Geography	M
Geology	M,D
Geophysics	M,D
Geosciences	M,D
Geotechnical Engineering	D
German	M,D
Graphic Design	M
Health Education	M
Health Services Management and Hospital Administration	M,D
Hispanic Studies	M,D
History	M,D
Human Development	M,D
Human Resources Management	D
Hydrology	M,D
Immunology	D
Industrial Design	M
Industrial/Management Engineering	D
Kinesiology and Movement Studies	M
Linguistics	M
Management Information Systems	M,D
Marketing	D
Mass Communication	M
Materials Engineering	M,D
Maternal/Child Nursing	M
Mathematics Education	M
Mathematics	M,D*
Mechanical Engineering	M,D*
Medical Illustration	M
Medical/Surgical Nursing	M
Microbiology	D*
Mineralogy	M,D
Molecular Biology	M,D*
Neurobiology	M,D
Nurse Midwifery	M
Nursing and Healthcare Administration	M
Nursing—General	M,D
Nutrition	M,D
Occupational Therapy	M
Operations Research	D
Oral and Dental Sciences	M
Pathology	M,D
Pediatric Nursing	M
Pharmaceutical Administration	M,D
Pharmaceutical Sciences	M,D
Pharmacology	D*
Pharmacy	P
Philosophy	M,D
Photography	M
Physical Therapy	M
Physics	M,D
Physiology	M,D*
Plant Biology	M,D
Political Science	M,D
Psychiatric Nursing	M
Psychology—General	D
Public Health—General	M,D
Public Policy and Administration	M,D*
Reading Education	M,D
Rhetoric	M,D
Secondary Education	M,D
Slavic Languages	M,D
Social Work	M,D
Sociology	M,D
Special Education	M,D
Statistics	M,D
Theater	M
Water Resources	M,D
Writing	M,D

UNIVERSITY OF ILLINOIS AT SPRINGFIELD

Program	Degrees
Accounting	M
Addictions/Substance Abuse Counseling	M
Biological and Biomedical Sciences—General	M
Business Administration and Management—General	M
Child and Family Studies	M
Communication—General	M
Computer Science	M
Economics	M
Educational Administration	M
English	M

Environmental Management and Policy M
Gerontology M
Human Development M
Human Services M
Interdisciplinary Studies M
Journalism M
Legal and Justice Studies M
Management Information Systems M
Political Science M
Public Health—General M
Public History M
Public Policy and Administration M,D
Social Sciences M

In-depth description on page 1185.

UNIVERSITY OF ILLINOIS AT URBANA-CHAMPAIGN

Accounting M,D*
Advertising and Public Relations M
Aerospace/Aeronautical Engineering M,D*
African Studies M
Agricultural Economics and Agribusiness M,D
Agricultural Education M
Agricultural Engineering M,D
Agricultural Sciences—General M,D
Agronomy and Soil Sciences M,D
Allopathic Medicine
Animal Sciences M,D
Anthropology M,D
Applied Arts and Design—General M,D
Applied Mathematics M,D
Architecture M
Art Education M,D
Art History M,D
Asian Languages M,D
Asian Studies M,D
Astronomy M,D
Atmospheric Sciences M,D
Biochemistry M,D*
Bioengineering *
Biological and Biomedical Sciences—General M,D
Biomedical Engineering
Biophysics D*
Biopsychology M,D
Business Administration and Management—General M,D*
Cell Biology D*
Chemical Engineering M,D
Chemistry M,D
City and Regional Planning M,D
Civil Engineering M,D*
Classics M,D
Clinical Psychology M,D
Cognitive Sciences M,D
Communication Disorders M,D
Communication—General D*
Community Health M,D
Comparative Literature M,D
Computer Engineering M,D
Computer Science M,D*
Consumer Economics M,D
Counselor Education M,D,O
Curriculum and Instruction M,D,O
Dance M
Demography and Population Studies M,D
Developmental Psychology M,D
East European and Russian Studies M
Ecology D
Economics M,D*
Education of the Multiply Handicapped M,D,O
Education—General M,D,O*
Educational Administration M,D,O
Educational Psychology M,D,O
Electrical Engineering M,D*
Engineering and Applied Sciences—General M,D*
Engineering Design M
English as a Second Language M
English M,D
Entomology M,D*
Environmental Engineering M,D
Environmental Sciences M,D
Evolutionary Biology D
Finance and Banking M,D*
Food Science and Technology M,D
Foreign Languages Education M,D
Foundations and Philosophy of Education M,D,O
French M,D
Geochemistry M,D
Geography M,D
Geology M,D
Geophysics M,D
Geosciences M,D
German M,D
Graphic Design M
Health Physics/Radiological Health M,D
Higher Education M,D,O
History M,D
Human Development M,D
Human Resources Development M,D,O
Human Resources Management M,D
Industrial and Labor Relations M,D
Industrial and Organizational Psychology M,D
Industrial Design M
Industrial/Management Engineering M,D
Information Studies M,D,O
Italian M,D
Journalism M
Kinesiology and Movement Studies M,D*
Landscape Architecture M
Latin American Studies M
Law P,M,D
Leisure Studies M,D
Library Science M,D,O*
Linguistics M,D
Materials Engineering M,D
Materials Sciences M,D
Mathematics Education M,D
Mathematics M,D*
Mechanical Engineering M,D*
Mechanics M,D*
Microbiology M,D*
Molecular Biology
Music M,D
Natural Resources M,D
Neuroscience D
Nuclear Engineering M,D*
Nutrition M,D*
Pathobiology M,D
Philosophy M,D
Physics M,D
Physiology M,D*
Plant Biology M,D
Political Science M,D
Psychology—General M,D
Rehabilitation Counseling M
Rehabilitation Sciences M
Russian M,D
Slavic Languages M,D
Social Psychology M,D
Social Work M,D
Sociology M,D
Special Education M,D,O
Speech and Interpersonal Communication M,D
Statistics M,D
Structural Biology D
Systems Engineering M*
Theater M,D
Veterinary Medicine P
Veterinary Sciences M,D
Vocational and Technical Education M,D,O
Zoology D

UNIVERSITY OF INDIANAPOLIS

Accounting M
Art Education M
Art/Fine Arts M
Biological and Biomedical Sciences—General M
Business Administration and Management—General M
Education—General M
Elementary Education M
English Education M
English M
Foreign Languages Education M
History M
Mathematics Education M
Occupational Therapy M
Physical Education M
Physical Therapy M,D
Psychology—General M,D
Science Education M
Secondary Education M
Social Sciences Education M
Sociology M

THE UNIVERSITY OF IOWA

Accounting M,D
Actuarial Science M,D
African-American Studies M
Allopathic Medicine P
American Studies M,D
Anatomy D
Anthropology M,D
Applied Mathematics D
Art Education M,D
Art History M,D
Art/Fine Arts M
Asian Studies M
Astronomy M
Bacteriology M,D
Biochemical Engineering M,D
Biochemistry M,D*
Biological and Biomedical Sciences—General M,D*
Biomedical Engineering M,D*
Biophysics M,D
Biostatistics M,D
Business Administration and Management—General M,D*
Cell Biology D
Chemical Engineering M,D
Chemistry M,D
City and Regional Planning M
Civil Engineering M,D
Classics M,D
Clinical Laboratory Sciences/Medical Technology M,D
Communication Disorders M,D
Communication—General M,D
Comparative Literature M,D
Computational Sciences D
Computer Engineering M,D
Computer Science M,D*
Counselor Education M,D
Curriculum and Instruction M,D
Dance M
Dentistry P
Developmental Education M,D
Early Childhood Education M,D
Economics D
Education—General M,D,O
Educational Administration M,D,O
Educational Measurement and Evaluation M,D,O
Educational Media/Instructional Technology M,D,O
Educational Psychology M,D,O
Electrical Engineering M,D
Elementary Education M,D
Engineering and Applied Sciences—General M,D*
English Education M,D
English M,D
Environmental and Occupational Health M,D
Environmental Engineering M,D
Epidemiology M,D
Ergonomics and Human Factors M,D
Exercise and Sports Science M,D
Film, Television, and Video Production M
Film, Television, and Video Theory and Criticism M,D
Finance and Banking D
Foreign Languages Education M,D
Foundations and Philosophy of Education M,D
French M,D
Genetics M,D*
Geography M,D
Geosciences M,D
German M,D
Health Services Management and Hospital Administration M,D
Higher Education M,D,O
History M,D
Immunology M,D*
Industrial/Management Engineering M,D
Information Studies M
Journalism M
Law P,M
Leisure Studies M,D
Library Science M
Linguistics M,D
Manufacturing Engineering M,D
Marketing D
Mass Communication M,D
Mathematics M,D
Mechanical Engineering M,D*
Microbiology M,D*
Molecular Biology D*
Music Education M,D
Music M,D
Neurobiology M,D
Nursing—General M,D
Operations Research M,D
Oral and Dental Sciences M,D,O
Pathology M
Pharmaceutical Sciences M,D
Pharmacology M,D*
Pharmacy P
Philosophy M,D
Physical Education M,D
Physical Therapy M,D
Physician Assistant Studies M
Physics M,D*
Physiology M,D*
Plant Biology M,D
Political Science M,D
Psychology—General M,D
Public Health—General M,D
Radiation Biology M,D*
Rehabilitation Counseling M,D
Religion M,D
Rhetoric M,D
Science Education M,D
Secondary Education M,D
Social Sciences Education M,D
Social Work M,D
Sociology M,D
Spanish M,D
Special Education M,D
Statistics M,D*
Theater M
Translation and Interpretation M
Virology M,D
Women's Studies D
Writing M,D

UNIVERSITY OF JUDAISM

Business Administration and Management—General M
Education—General M
Jewish Studies M
Nonprofit Management M
Psychology—General M
Theology M

UNIVERSITY OF KANSAS

Accounting M,D
Aerospace/Aeronautical Engineering M,D
Allied Health—General M,D
Allopathic Medicine P
American Studies M,D
Anatomy M,D
Anthropology M,D
Applied Arts and Design—General M
Applied Mathematics M,D
Architectural Engineering M,D
Architecture M
Art Education M
Art History M,D
Art/Fine Arts M
Asian Languages M
Asian Studies M
Astronomy M,D
Biochemistry M,D
Biological and Biomedical Sciences—General M,D*
Biophysics M,D
Botany M,D
Business Administration and Management—General M,D
Cell Biology M,D
Chemical Engineering M,D
Chemistry M,D
City and Regional Planning M
Civil Engineering M,D
Classics M
Clinical Psychology D
Communication Disorders M,D
Communication—General M,D
Computer Engineering M
Computer Science M,D
Construction Engineering and Management M,D
Counseling Psychology M,D
Curriculum and Instruction M,D
Developmental Biology M,D
Developmental Psychology M,D
Early Childhood Education M,D
East European and Russian Studies M
Ecology M,D
Economics M,D
Education—General M,D,O
Educational Administration M
Educational Measurement and Evaluation M,D
Educational Psychology M,D
Electrical Engineering M,D
Engineering and Applied Sciences—General M,D*
Engineering Management M
English M,D
Entomology M,D
Environmental Engineering M,D
Environmental Sciences M,D
Evolutionary Biology M,D
Film, Television, and Video Theory and Criticism M,D
Foundations and Philosophy of Education D
French M,D
Genetics D
Geography M,D
Geology M,D
German M,D
Gerontology M,D
Health Education M,D
Health Services Management and Hospital Administration M
Higher Education M,D
History M,D
Human Development M,D
Immunology D
International Affairs M
Journalism M
Latin American Studies M
Law P
Linguistics M,D
Management Information Systems M,D
Mathematics M,D
Mechanical Engineering M,D
Medicinal and Pharmaceutical Chemistry M,D
Microbiology M,D
Molecular Biology M,D

University of Kansas (continued)

Program	Degrees
Museum Studies	M
Music Education	M,D
Music	M,D
Native American Studies	M
Nurse Anesthesia	M
Nursing—General	M,D
Nutrition	M
Occupational Therapy	M
Pathology	M,D
Petroleum Engineering	M,D
Pharmaceutical Sciences	M*
Pharmacology	M,D
Philosophy	M,D
Physical Education	M,D
Physical Therapy	M
Physics	M,D*
Physiology	M,D
Political Science	M,D
Psychology—General	M,D
Public Health—General	M
Public History	M
Public Policy and Administration	M
Religion	M
School Psychology	D,O
Slavic Languages	M,D
Sociology	M,D
Spanish	M,D
Special Education	M,D
Statistics	M,D
Theater	M,D
Therapies—Dance, Drama, and Music	M,D
Toxicology	M,D
Water Resources Engineering	M,D
Water Resources	M,D

UNIVERSITY OF KENTUCKY

Program	Degrees
Accounting	M
Agricultural Economics and Agribusiness	M,D*
Agricultural Engineering	M,D
Agricultural Sciences—General	M,D
Agronomy and Soil Sciences	M,D
Allied Health—General	M,D*
Allopathic Medicine	P
Anatomy	D
Animal Sciences	M,D
Anthropology	M,D
Architecture	M
Art Education	M
Art History	M
Art/Fine Arts	M
Astronomy	M,D
Biochemistry	D
Biological and Biomedical Sciences—General	M,D*
Biomedical Engineering	M,D
Business Administration and Management—General	M,D*
Chemical Engineering	M,D
Chemistry	M,D
Child and Family Studies	M,D
Civil Engineering	M,D
Classics	M
Clinical Laboratory Sciences/ Medical Technology	M,D
Clothing and Textiles	M
Communication Disorders	M
Communication—General	M,D
Computer Science	M,D*
Counseling Psychology	M,D,O
Curriculum and Instruction	M,D
Dentistry	P,M
Economics	M,D
Education—General	M,D,O
Educational Administration	M,D,O
Educational Measurement and Evaluation	M,D
Educational Psychology	M,D,O
Electrical Engineering	M,D
Engineering and Applied Sciences—General	M,D
English	M,D
Entomology	M,D
Exercise and Sports Science	M,D
Family and Consumer Sciences-General	M,D
Food Science and Technology	M
Forestry	M
Foundations and Philosophy of Education	M,D
French	M
Geography	M,D
Geology	M,D
German	M
Gerontology	D
Health Physics/Radiological Health	M
Health Promotion	M,D
Health Services Management and Hospital Administration	M
Higher Education	M,D
Historic Preservation	M
History	M,D
Hospitality Management	M
Immunology	D
Interior Design	M
International Affairs	M*
International Business	M
Kinesiology and Movement Studies	M,D
Law	P
Library Science	M
Manufacturing Engineering	M
Materials Sciences	M,D
Mathematics	M,D
Mechanical Engineering	M,D
Medical Physics	M*
Microbiology	D*
Mineral/Mining Engineering	M,D
Music	M,D
Neurobiology	D
Nursing—General	M,D
Nutrition	D*
Oral and Dental Sciences	M
Pharmaceutical Sciences	M,D
Pharmacology	D
Pharmacy	P
Philosophy	M,D
Physical Therapy	M
Physician Assistant Studies	M
Physics	M,D
Physiology	D
Plant Pathology	M,D
Plant Physiology	D
Plant Sciences	M
Political Science	M,D
Psychology—General	M,D
Public Health—General	M,D
Public Policy and Administration	M,D
Rehabilitation Counseling	M
Rehabilitation Sciences	D
Social Work	M,D
Sociology	M,D
Spanish	M,D
Special Education	M,D,O
Statistics	M,D
Theater	M
Toxicology	M,D*
Veterinary Sciences	M,D
Vocational and Technical Education	M,D,O

UNIVERSITY OF LA VERNE

Program	Degrees
Accounting	M
Business Administration and Management—General	M
Child and Family Studies	M
Clinical Psychology	M,D
Counseling Psychology	M,D
Counselor Education	M,O
Education—General	M,O
Educational Administration	M,D
Finance and Banking	M
Gerontology	M
Health Informatics	M
Health Services Management and Hospital Administration	M
International Business	M
Law	P
Management Information Systems	M
Marketing	M
Marriage and Family Therapy	M
Multilingual and Multicultural Education	O
Organizational Management	M,D,O
Psychology—General	M,D
Public Policy and Administration	M,D*
Reading Education	M,O
Social Psychology	M,D
Special Education	M

THE UNIVERSITY OF LETHBRIDGE

Program	Degrees
Accounting	M,D,O
Agricultural Sciences—General	M,D
Anthropology	M,D
Archaeology	M,D
Art/Fine Arts	M,D
Biochemistry	M,D
Biological and Biomedical Sciences—General	M,D
Business Administration and Management—General	M,D
Canadian Studies	M,D
Chemistry	M,D
Computer Science	M,D
Counseling Psychology	M,D
Economics	M,D
Education—General	M,D,O
English	M,D
Environmental Sciences	M,D
Exercise and Sports Science	M,D
Finance and Banking	M,D
French	M,D
Geography	M,D
German	M,D
History	M,D
Human Resources Management	M,D
International Business	M,D
Kinesiology and Movement Studies	M,D
Management Information Systems	M,D
Mathematics	M,D
Music	M,D
Native American Studies	M,D
Neuroscience	M,D
Nursing—General	M,D
Philosophy	M,D
Physics	M,D
Political Science	M,D
Psychology—General	M,D
Religion	M,D
Social Work	M,D
Sociology	M,D
Spanish	M,D
Urban Studies	M,D

UNIVERSITY OF LOUISIANA AT LAFAYETTE

Program	Degrees
American Studies	D
Applied Physics	M
Architectural Engineering	M
Biological and Biomedical Sciences—General	M,D*
Business Administration and Management—General	M
Chemical Engineering	M
Civil Engineering	M
Cognitive Sciences	D
Communication Disorders	M,D*
Communication—General	M
Computer Engineering	M,D
Computer Science	M,D*
Counselor Education	M
Curriculum and Instruction	M
Education of the Gifted	M
Education—General	M
Educational Administration	M
Engineering and Applied Sciences—General	M,D
Engineering Management	M
English	M,D
Environmental Biology	M,D
Evolutionary Biology	M,D
Family and Consumer Sciences-General	M
Folklore	M,D
French	M,D
Geography	M
Geology	M
Health Services Management and Hospital Administration	M
History	M
Mass Communication	M
Mathematics	M,D
Mechanical Engineering	M
Music Education	M
Music	M
Nursing—General	M
Petroleum Engineering	M
Physics	M
Psychology—General	M
Rehabilitation Counseling	M
Rhetoric	M,D
Telecommunications	M
Writing	M,D

UNIVERSITY OF LOUISIANA AT MONROE

Program	Degrees
Addictions/Substance Abuse Counseling	M
Allied Health—General	M
Biological and Biomedical Sciences—General	M
Business Administration and Management—General	M
Chemistry	M
Communication Disorders	M
Communication—General	M
Counselor Education	M,O
Criminal Justice and Criminology	M
Curriculum and Instruction	D,O
Education—General	M,D,O
Educational Administration	M,D,O
Elementary Education	M,O
English Education	M,D,O
English	M
Geosciences	M
Gerontology	M,O
Health Education	M
History	M
Marriage and Family Therapy	M,D
Music	M
Pharmaceutical Sciences	P,M,D
Physical Education	M
Psychology—General	M,O
Reading Education	M
School Psychology	O
Secondary Education	M,O
Special Education	M

UNIVERSITY OF LOUISVILLE

Program	Degrees
Accounting	M
African Studies	M
Allopathic Medicine	P
Analytical Chemistry	M,D
Anatomy	M,D
Art Education	M
Art History	M,D
Art Therapy	M
Art/Fine Arts	M
Biochemistry	M,D
Biological and Biomedical Sciences—General	M,D*
Biophysics	M,D
Biostatistics	M
Business Administration and Management—General	M
Chemical Engineering	M,D
Chemistry	M,D
City and Regional Planning	M
Civil Engineering	M,D
Clinical Psychology	D
Clinical Research	O
Communication Disorders	M,D
Computer Engineering	M,D
Computer Science	M,D
Counseling Psychology	M,D
Counselor Education	M,D
Criminal Justice and Criminology	M
Dentistry	P
Early Childhood Education	M
Education—General	M,D,O
Educational Administration	M,D,O
Educational Measurement and Evaluation	M
Educational Media/Instructional Technology	M
Educational Psychology	M,D
Electrical Engineering	M
Elementary Education	M
Engineering and Applied Sciences—General	M,D*
Engineering Management	M
English	M,D
Environmental Biology	D
Environmental Engineering	M,D
Epidemiology	M,D
Exercise and Sports Science	M
Experimental Psychology	D
Foreign Languages Education	M
French	M
Higher Education	M,O
History	M
Human Resources Development	M
Humanities	P,M
Immunology	M,D
Industrial and Labor Relations	M
Industrial/Management Engineering	M,D
Inorganic Chemistry	M,D
Interdisciplinary Studies	M
Law	P
Mathematics	M
Mechanical Engineering	M
Microbiology	M,D
Middle School Education	M
Molecular Biology	M,D
Music Education	M
Music	M,D
Neurobiology	M,D
Nursing—General	M
Oral and Dental Sciences	M
Organic Chemistry	M,D
Pharmacology	M,D
Philosophy	M
Physical Chemistry	M,D
Physical Education	M
Physics	M
Physiology	M,D
Political Science	M
Psychology—General	M,D
Public Policy and Administration	M*
Reading Education	M
Rhetoric	D
Secondary Education	M
Social Work	M,D
Sociology	M
Spanish	M
Special Education	M
Sports Management	M
Student Personnel Services	M,D
Theater	M
Toxicology	M,D
Urban Studies	D
Vision Sciences	D

In-depth description on page 1187.

UNIVERSITY OF MAINE

Program	Degrees
Accounting	M
Agricultural Economics and Agribusiness	M
Agricultural Sciences—General	M,D
Agronomy and Soil Sciences	M,D
Animal Sciences	M
Biochemistry	M,D
Bioengineering	M
Biological and Biomedical Sciences—General	D
Botany	M
Business Administration and Management—General	M
Chemical Engineering	M,D
Chemistry	M,D
Civil Engineering	M,D
Clinical Psychology	M,D
Communication Disorders	M
Communication—General	M
Computer Engineering	M,D
Computer Science	M,D
Counselor Education	M,O
Developmental Psychology	M,D

Program	Degrees
Ecology	M,D*
Economics	M
Education—General	M,D,O*
Educational Administration	M,D,O
Educational Media/Instructional Technology	M
Electrical Engineering	M,D
Elementary Education	M,O
Engineering and Applied Sciences—General	M,D
Engineering Physics	M
English	M
Entomology	M
Environmental Engineering	M,D
Environmental Management and Policy	M,D
Environmental Sciences	M,D
Experimental Psychology	M,D
Fish, Game, and Wildlife Management	M,D
Food Science and Technology	M,D
Foreign Languages Education	M
Forestry	M,D
French	M
Geology	M,D
Geosciences	M,D
Geotechnical Engineering	M,D
Higher Education	M,D,O
History	M,D
Horticulture	M
Human Development	M
Interdisciplinary Studies	D
Kinesiology and Movement Studies	M
Liberal Studies	M
Management Information Systems	M
Marine Affairs	M
Marine Biology	M,D
Marine Sciences	M,D
Mathematics	M
Mechanical Engineering	M,D
Microbiology	M,D
Molecular Biology	M,D
Music	M
Natural Resources	M,D
Nursing—General	M,O
Nutrition	M,D
Oceanography	M,D
Physical Education	M
Physics	M,D
Plant Biology	M,D
Plant Pathology	M
Plant Sciences	M,D
Psychology—General	M,D
Public Policy and Administration	M*
Reading Education	M,D,O
Science Education	M,O
Secondary Education	M,O
Social Psychology	M,D
Social Sciences Education	M,O
Social Work	M
Special Education	M,O
Structural Engineering	M,D
Theater	M
Zoology	M,D

UNIVERSITY OF MANITOBA

Program	Degrees
Accounting	M
Actuarial Science	M
Agricultural Economics and Agribusiness	M,D
Agricultural Engineering	M,D
Agricultural Sciences—General	M,D
Agronomy and Soil Sciences	M,D
Anatomy	M,D
Animal Sciences	M,D
Anthropology	M
Applied Mathematics	M
Architecture	M
Art Education	M
Biochemistry	M,D
Biological and Biomedical Sciences—General	M,D
Botany	M,D
Business Administration and Management—General	M
Business Education	M
Chemistry	M,D
Child and Family Studies	M
City and Regional Planning	M
Civil Engineering	M,D
Classics	M
Clinical Psychology	M,D
Clothing and Textiles	M
Community Health	M,D
Computer Engineering	M,D
Computer Science	M,D
Counselor Education	M
Curriculum and Instruction	M
Dentistry	P
Early Childhood Education	M
Economics	M,D
Education—General	M
Educational Administration	M
Educational Measurement and Evaluation	M
Educational Media/Instructional Technology	M
Electrical Engineering	M,D
Engineering and Applied Sciences—General	M,D
English as a Second Language	M
English	M,D
Entomology	M,D
Environmental Management and Policy	M
Family and Consumer Sciences-General	M,D
Finance and Banking	M
Food Science and Technology	M
Foreign Languages Education	M
Foundations and Philosophy of Education	M
French	M,D
Geography	M,D
Geology	M,D
Geophysics	M,D
German	M
Health Education	M
History	M,D
Home Economics Education	M
Horticulture	M,D
Human Genetics	M,D
Immunology	M,D
Industrial and Labor Relations	M
Industrial/Management Engineering	M,D
Landscape Architecture	M
Law	M
Legal and Justice Studies	M
Linguistics	M,D
Marketing	M
Mathematics Education	M
Mathematics	M,D
Mechanical Engineering	M,D
Medical Microbiology	M,D*
Microbiology	M,D
Music Education	M
Music	M
Northern Studies	M
Nursing—General	M
Nutrition	M,D
Oral and Dental Sciences	M,D
Pathology	M
Pharmaceutical Sciences	M,D
Pharmacology	M,D
Philosophy	M
Physical Education	M
Physics	M,D
Physiology	M,D
Political Science	M
Psychology—General	M,D
Public Policy and Administration	M
Reading Education	M
Recreation and Park Management	M
Rehabilitation Sciences	M
Religion	M,D
Science Education	M
Slavic Languages	M
Social Sciences Education	M
Social Work	M
Sociology	M
Spanish	M,D
Special Education	M
Statistics	M,D
Theology	P
Vocational and Technical Education	M
Zoology	M,D

UNIVERSITY OF MARY

Program	Degrees
Advanced Practice Nursing	M
Business Administration and Management—General	M
Education—General	M
Educational Administration	M
Elementary Education	M
Higher Education	M
Nursing Education	M
Nursing—General	M
Occupational Therapy	M
Physical Therapy	M
Secondary Education	M
Special Education	M

UNIVERSITY OF MARY HARDIN-BAYLOR

Program	Degrees
Business Administration and Management—General	M
Counseling Psychology	M
Education—General	M
Educational Administration	M
Educational Psychology	M
Health Services Management and Hospital Administration	M
Management Information Systems	M
Psychology—General	M
Reading Education	M
Theology	M

UNIVERSITY OF MARYLAND

Program	Degrees
Allopathic Medicine	P
Anatomy	M,D
Biochemistry	D*
Bioethics	M
Biological and Biomedical Sciences—General	M,D
Cell Biology	D
Clinical Laboratory Sciences/Medical Technology	M*
Cognitive Sciences	M,D
Community Health Nursing	M,D
Dental Hygiene	M
Dentistry	P
Environmental Sciences	M,D
Epidemiology	M,D
Gerontological Nursing	M,D
Human Genetics	M,D
Immunology	M,D
Law	P
Marine Sciences	M,D
Maternal/Child Nursing	M,D
Medical/Surgical Nursing	M,D
Microbiology	M,D*
Molecular Biology	D*
Neurobiology	M,D
Neuroscience	M,D
Nursing and Healthcare Administration	M,D
Nursing Education	M,D
Nursing—General	M,D*
Oral and Dental Sciences	M,D
Pathology	M,D*
Pediatric Nursing	M,D
Pharmaceutical Administration	D
Pharmaceutical Sciences	D
Pharmacology	M,D*
Pharmacy	P,D
Physical Therapy	D
Physiology	D
Psychiatric Nursing	M,D
Rehabilitation Sciences	D
Social Work	M,D*
Toxicology	M,D

In-depth description on page 1189.

UNIVERSITY OF MARYLAND, BALTIMORE COUNTY

Program	Degrees
Applied Mathematics	M,D
Applied Physics	M,D
Art/Fine Arts	M
Atmospheric Sciences	M,D
Biochemical Engineering	M,D
Biochemistry	D*
Biological and Biomedical Sciences—General	M,D*
Cell Biology	D
Chemical Engineering	M,D*
Chemistry	D*
Cognitive Sciences	M,D
Communication—General	M*
Computer Science	M,D
Developmental Psychology	D
Early Childhood Education	M,D
Economics	M
Education—General	M,D
Educational Media/Instructional Technology	M,D
Electrical Engineering	M,D
Elementary Education	M,D
Engineering and Applied Sciences—General	M,D*
Engineering Management	M
English as a Second Language	M*
Environmental Sciences	M,D
Epidemiology	M
Ethics	M,O
French	M
German	M
Gerontology	M,D,O*
Health Education	M
Health Services Management and Hospital Administration	M
Higher Education	M,D
History	M
Human Services	M,D
Information Science	M,D*
Linguistics	M
Marine Sciences	M,D
Mechanical Engineering	M,D
Molecular Biology	M,D*
Multilingual and Multicultural Education	M,D
Neuroscience	M,D*
Optical Sciences	M,D
Philosophy	M,O*
Physics	M,D
Psychology—General	M,D
Public Policy and Administration	M,D*
Russian	M
Secondary Education	M,D
Sociology	M,O*
Spanish	M
Statistics	M,D

In-depth description on page 1191.

UNIVERSITY OF MARYLAND, COLLEGE PARK

Program	Degrees
Advertising and Public Relations	M,D
Aerospace/Aeronautical Engineering	M,D
Agricultural Economics and Agribusiness	M,D
Agricultural Engineering	M,D*
Agricultural Sciences—General	P,M,D
Agronomy and Soil Sciences	M,D
American Studies	M,D
Analytical Chemistry	M,D
Animal Sciences	M,D
Anthropology	M
Applied Mathematics	M,D
Architecture	M
Art History	M,D
Art/Fine Arts	M
Astronomy	M,D
Biochemistry	M,D
Bioengineering	M,D*
Biological and Biomedical Sciences—General	M,D
Biophysics	M,D*
Business Administration and Management—General	M,D
Cell Biology	M,D
Chemical Engineering	M,D
Chemistry	M,D
Child and Family Studies	M,D*
City and Regional Planning	M
Civil Engineering	M,D*
Classics	M
Clinical Psychology	M,D
Cognitive Sciences	D
Communication Disorders	M,D*
Communication—General	M,D
Comparative Literature	M,D
Computer Engineering	M,D
Computer Science	M,D
Conservation Biology	M
Counseling Psychology	M,D,O
Counselor Education	M,D,O
Criminal Justice and Criminology	M,D
Dance	M
Developmental Psychology	M,D
Early Childhood Education	M,D,O
Ecology	M,D
Economics	M,D
Education—General	M,D,O*
Educational Administration	M,D,O
Educational Measurement and Evaluation	M,D
Educational Media/Instructional Technology	M,D,O
Educational Psychology	M,D,O
Electrical Engineering	M,D*
Engineering and Applied Sciences—General	M,D
English as a Second Language	M,D,O
English	M,D
Entomology	M,D
Environmental Engineering	M,D*
Environmental Sciences	M,D
Evolutionary Biology	M,D
Experimental Psychology	M,D
Fire Protection Engineering	M
Food Science and Technology	M,D
Foundations and Philosophy of Education	M,D,O
French	M,D
Genetics	M,D
Geography	M,D
Geology	M,D*
German	M,D
Health Education	M,D
History	M,D
Horticulture	M,D
Human Development	M,D,O
Industrial and Organizational Psychology	M,D
Information Studies	M,D
Inorganic Chemistry	M,D
Journalism	M,D*
Kinesiology and Movement Studies	M,D
Law	
Library Science	*
Linguistics	M,D
Manufacturing Engineering	M,D
Marine Sciences	M,D*
Marriage and Family Therapy	M,D
Mass Communication	D
Materials Engineering	M,D
Materials Sciences	M,D
Mathematics	M,D
Mechanical Engineering	M,D
Mechanics	M,D
Meteorology	M,D*
Microbiology	M,D
Molecular Biology	D
Music Education	M,D
Music	M,D
Natural Resources	M,D
Neuroscience	D
Nuclear Engineering	M,D
Nutrition	M,D

University of Maryland, College Park (continued)

- Organic Chemistry M,D
- Philosophy M,D
- Physical Chemistry M,D*
- Physics M,D*
- Plant Biology M,D
- Political Science M,D
- Psychology—General M,D
- Public Health—General M,D
- Public Policy and Administration M,D*
- Reading Education M,D,O
- Rehabilitation Counseling M,D,O
- Reliability Engineering M,D*
- Russian M
- School Psychology M,D,O
- Secondary Education M,D,O
- Social Psychology M,D
- Sociology M,D
- Software Engineering M
- Spanish M,D
- Special Education M,D,O
- Speech and Interpersonal Communication M,D
- Statistics M,D
- Student Personnel Services M,D,O
- Survey Methodology M,D
- Sustainable Development M
- Systems Engineering M
- Telecommunications M*
- Theater M,D
- Toxicology M,D
- Veterinary Medicine P
- Veterinary Sciences D
- Water Resources Engineering M,D
- Women's Studies M,D
- Writing M,D
- Zoology M,D

UNIVERSITY OF MARYLAND EASTERN SHORE

- Agricultural Education M
- Agricultural Sciences—General M
- Computer Science M
- Counselor Education M
- Education—General M
- Environmental Sciences M,D
- Food Science and Technology M
- Marine Sciences M,D
- Physical Therapy M
- Special Education M
- Toxicology M,D
- Vocational and Technical Education M

In-depth description on page 1193.

UNIVERSITY OF MARYLAND UNIVERSITY COLLEGE

- Accounting M
- Biotechnology M
- Business Administration and Management—General M,D*
- Distance Education Development M
- Education—General M
- Electronic Commerce M
- Environmental Management and Policy M
- Finance and Banking M
- Information Science M
- International Business M
- Management Information Systems M
- Management of Technology M
- Software Engineering M
- Telecommunications Management M

UNIVERSITY OF MASSACHUSETTS AMHERST

- African-American Studies M,D
- Agricultural Economics and Agribusiness M,D
- Agronomy and Soil Sciences M,D
- Animal Sciences M,D
- Anthropology M,D
- Applied Mathematics M
- Art Education M
- Art History M
- Art/Fine Arts M
- Asian Languages M*
- Astronomy M,D
- Biochemistry M,D*
- Biological and Biomedical Sciences—General M,D
- Business Administration and Management—General M,D
- Cell Biology D
- Chemical Engineering M,D
- Chemistry M,D
- City and Regional Planning M,D
- Civil Engineering M,D
- Classics M
- Clinical Psychology M,D
- Communication Disorders M,D
- Communication—General M,D
- Comparative Literature M,D
- Computer Engineering M,D
- Computer Science M,D*
- Counselor Education M,D,O
- Curriculum and Instruction M,D,O
- Developmental Biology D
- Early Childhood Education M,D,O
- Economics M,D
- Education—General M,D,O*
- Educational Administration M,D,O
- Educational Measurement and Evaluation M,D,O
- Educational Media/Instructional Technology M,D,O
- Electrical Engineering M,D
- Elementary Education M,D,O
- Engineering and Applied Sciences—General M,D*
- Engineering Management M
- English M,D
- Entomology M,D
- Environmental Biology M,D
- Environmental Engineering M
- Evolutionary Biology M,D
- Exercise and Sports Science M,D
- Fish, Game, and Wildlife Management M,D
- Food Science and Technology M,D
- Foreign Languages Education M
- Forestry M,D
- French M
- Geography M
- Geology M,D
- Geosciences D
- German M,D
- Higher Education M,D,O
- History of Science and Technology M,D
- History M,D*
- Hospitality Management M
- Industrial and Labor Relations M
- Industrial/Management Engineering M,D
- Interior Design M
- International and Comparative Education M,D,O
- Landscape Architecture M
- Linguistics M,D
- Manufacturing Engineering M
- Mathematics M,D
- Mechanical Engineering M,D
- Microbiology M,D*
- Molecular Biology D*
- Multilingual and Multicultural Education M,D,O
- Music M,D
- Neuroscience M,D*
- Nursing—General M,D
- Nutrition M
- Operations Research M,D
- Philosophy M,D
- Physical Education M,D,O
- Physics M,D
- Plant Biology M,D
- Plant Sciences M,D
- Political Science M,D
- Polymer Science and Engineering M,D*
- Psychology—General M,D
- Public Health—General M,D
- Public History M,D
- Public Policy and Administration M
- Reading Education M,D,O
- School Psychology D
- Science Education D
- Secondary Education M,D,O
- Sociology M,D
- Spanish M,D
- Special Education M,D,O
- Statistics M,D
- Theater M
- Travel and Tourism M
- Veterinary Sciences M,D
- Writing M,D

In-depth description on page 1195.

UNIVERSITY OF MASSACHUSETTS BOSTON

- American Studies M
- Applied Physics M
- Archaeology M
- Biological and Biomedical Sciences—General M
- Biotechnology M
- Business Administration and Management—General M
- Cell Biology
- Chemistry M
- Clinical Psychology D
- Computer Science M,D
- Conflict Resolution and Mediation/Peace Studies M,O
- Counselor Education M,O
- Curriculum and Instruction M
- Education—General M,D,O
- Educational Administration M,D,O
- Elementary Education M,D,O
- English as a Second Language M
- English M
- Environmental Biology D
- Environmental Sciences M,D
- Foreign Languages Education M
- Gerontology D*
- Higher Education M,D,O
- History M
- Human Services M
- Linguistics M
- Marine Sciences D
- Molecular Biology
- Multilingual and Multicultural Education M
- Nursing—General M,D
- Political Science O
- Public History M
- Public Policy and Administration M,D*
- School Psychology M,O
- Secondary Education M,D,O
- Sociology M
- Special Education M
- Urban Education M,D,O
- Women's Studies O

In-depth description on page 1197.

UNIVERSITY OF MASSACHUSETTS DARTMOUTH

- Applied Arts and Design—General M
- Art Education M
- Art/Fine Arts M
- Biological and Biomedical Sciences—General M
- Business Administration and Management—General M
- Chemistry M
- Clinical Psychology M
- Computer Engineering M,D,O
- Computer Science M,O
- Education—General M
- Electrical Engineering M,D,O
- Engineering and Applied Sciences—General M,D,O*
- Marine Biology M
- Mechanical Engineering M
- Nursing—General M,O
- Physics M
- Psychology—General M
- Textile Sciences and Engineering M
- Writing M

In-depth description on page 1199.

UNIVERSITY OF MASSACHUSETTS LOWELL

- Allied Health—General M,D
- Applied Mathematics M,D
- Applied Physics M,D
- Biochemistry M,D
- Biological and Biomedical Sciences—General M,D
- Biotechnology M,D
- Business Administration and Management—General M
- Chemical Engineering M
- Chemistry M,D
- Civil Engineering M
- Clinical Laboratory Sciences/Medical Technology M
- Community Health Nursing M
- Computational Sciences M,D
- Computer Engineering M,D
- Computer Science M,D
- Criminal Justice and Criminology M
- Curriculum and Instruction M,D,O
- Economics M
- Education—General M,D,O*
- Educational Administration M,D,O
- Electrical Engineering M,D
- Energy and Power Engineering M,D
- Engineering and Applied Sciences—General M,D*
- Environmental Engineering M
- Environmental Sciences M,D
- Gerontological Nursing M
- Health Physics/Radiological Health M,D
- Health Promotion D
- Health Services Management and Hospital Administration M
- Industrial and Manufacturing Management M
- Industrial/Management Engineering M,D
- Mathematics Education D
- Mathematics M,D
- Mechanical Engineering M,D
- Mechanics M,D
- Music Education M
- Music M
- Nursing and Healthcare Administration D
- Nursing—General M,D
- Occupational Health Nursing M
- Optical Sciences M,D
- Physical Therapy M
- Physics M,D*
- Polymer Science and Engineering M,D
- Psychiatric Nursing M
- Psychology—General M
- Reading Education M,D,O
- Science Education D
- Social Psychology M
- Sociology M
- Systems Engineering M,D

In-depth description on page 1201.

UNIVERSITY OF MASSACHUSETTS WORCESTER

- Advanced Practice Nursing M,D,O
- Allopathic Medicine P
- Biochemistry D*
- Biological and Biomedical Sciences—General D*
- Biomedical Engineering D*
- Cell Biology D*
- Community Health Nursing M,D,O
- Genetics D*
- Immunology D*
- Medical Physics D
- Medical/Surgical Nursing M,D,O
- Microbiology D
- Neuroscience D*
- Nursing—General M,D,O
- Pharmacology D
- Physiology D*
- Virology D

UNIVERSITY OF MEDICINE AND DENTISTRY OF NEW JERSEY

- Advanced Practice Nursing M
- Allied Health—General M,D,O*
- Allopathic Medicine P,M,D
- Biochemistry M,D*
- Bioinformatics M,D
- Biological and Biomedical Sciences—General M,D*
- Biomedical Engineering M,D*
- Cancer Biology/Oncology
- Cardiovascular Sciences M,D
- Cell Biology M,D*
- Clinical Laboratory Sciences/Medical Technology M,D
- Dentistry P,M,O
- Developmental Biology M,D
- Educational Media/Instructional Technology M
- Environmental Sciences D
- Genetics M,D
- Health Education M
- Health Informatics M
- Health Services Management and Hospital Administration M,O
- Immunology M,D
- Interdisciplinary Studies M,D
- Kinesiology and Movement Studies M,D
- Medical Informatics M,D
- Medical/Surgical Nursing M
- Microbiology M,D*
- Molecular Biology M,D*
- Molecular Medicine M,D
- Neurobiology M,D
- Neuroscience M,D*
- Nurse Anesthesia M
- Nurse Midwifery O
- Nursing—General M,O
- Nutrition M,D,O
- Occupational Health Nursing M
- Oral and Dental Sciences P,M,O
- Organizational Management M
- Osteopathic Medicine P
- Pathology M,D*
- Pharmacology M,D
- Physical Therapy M,D
- Physician Assistant Studies M
- Physiology M,D*
- Public Health—General M,D*
- Rehabilitation Counseling M,D
- Toxicology M,D
- Women's Health Nursing M

THE UNIVERSITY OF MEMPHIS

- Accounting M,D
- Adult Education M,D,O
- Anthropology M
- Applied Mathematics M,D
- Archaeology M
- Architectural Engineering M
- Art History M
- Art/Fine Arts M
- Biological and Biomedical Sciences—General M,D
- Biomedical Engineering M,D*
- Business Administration and Management—General M,D
- Cell Biology M,D
- Chemistry M,D
- City and Regional Planning M
- Civil Engineering M,D
- Clinical Psychology M,D
- Communication Disorders M,D
- Communication—General M,D
- Computer Engineering M,D
- Computer Science M,D
- Consumer Economics M
- Counseling Psychology M,D
- Counselor Education M,D

Criminal Justice and Criminology M
Curriculum and Instruction M,D
Early Childhood Education M,D
Economics M,D
Education—General M,D,O
Educational Administration M,D,O
Educational Measurement and Evaluation M,D
Educational Media/Instructional Technology M,D
Educational Psychology M,D
Electrical Engineering M,D
Elementary Education M,D
Energy and Power Engineering M,D
Engineering and Applied Sciences—General M,D
English M,D
Environmental Engineering M,D
Exercise and Sports Science M
Experimental Psychology M,D
Film, Television, and Video Production M,D
Finance and Banking M,D
French M
Geography M
Geology M,D
Geophysics M,D
Geosciences M,D
Graphic Design M
Health Promotion M
Health Services Management and Hospital Administration M
Higher Education M,D,O
History M,D
Human Resources Management M
Industrial/Management Engineering M
Interior Design M
International Business M
Journalism M
Law P
Leisure Studies M
Management Information Systems M,D
Manufacturing Engineering M
Marketing M,D
Mathematics M,D
Mechanical Engineering M,D
Microbiology M,D*
Molecular Biology M,D
Music Education M,D
Music M,D
Nonprofit Management M
Nutrition M
Philosophy M,D
Photography M
Physics M
Political Science M
Psychology—General M,D
Public Policy and Administration M
Reading Education M,D
Real Estate M,D
Rehabilitation Counseling M,D
School Psychology M,D
Secondary Education M,D
Sociology M
Spanish M
Special Education M,D
Statistics M,D
Structural Engineering M,D
Systems Engineering M
Taxation M
Theater M
Transportation and Highway Engineering M,D
Water Resources Engineering M,D
Writing M,D

In-depth description on page 1203.

UNIVERSITY OF MIAMI

Accounting M
Advanced Practice Nursing M,D
Advertising and Public Relations M,D
Allopathic Medicine P
Architectural Engineering M,D
Architecture M*
Art History M
Art/Fine Arts M
Atmospheric Sciences M,D
Biochemistry D
Biological and Biomedical Sciences—General M,D*
Biomedical Engineering M,D
Biophysics D
Business Administration and Management—General M,D*
Cell Biology D
Chemistry M,D
Civil Engineering M,D
Clinical Psychology M,D
Communication—General M,D*
Community Health M,D
Computer Engineering M,D
Computer Science M
Counseling Psychology D
Counselor Education M,O
Developmental Biology D
Developmental Psychology M,D
Early Childhood Education M,O
Ecology M,D
Economics M,D
Education—General M,D,O*
Educational Administration M
Educational Measurement and Evaluation M
Electrical Engineering M,D
Elementary Education M,O
Engineering and Applied Sciences—General M,D*
English as a Second Language M,D,O
English M,D
Environmental and Occupational Health M
Epidemiology D
Ergonomics and Human Factors M,D
Evolutionary Biology M,D
Exercise and Sports Science M,D*
Film, Television, and Video Production M,D
Film, Television, and Video Theory and Criticism M,D
Fish, Game, and Wildlife Management M,D
French D
Genetics M,D
Geology M,D
Geophysics M,D
Graphic Design M
Health Psychology M,D
Higher Education M
History M,D
Immunology D
Industrial/Management Engineering M,D
Inorganic Chemistry M,D
International Affairs M,D
Internet and Interactive Multimedia M
Journalism M,D
Law P,M
Liberal Studies M
Management Information Systems M,O
Management of Technology M,D
Marine Affairs M
Marine Biology M,D
Marine Sciences M,D
Marriage and Family Therapy M,O
Mathematics Education M,O
Mathematics M,D
Mechanical Engineering M,D
Medical/Surgical Nursing M,D
Meteorology M,D*
Microbiology D*
Molecular Biology D*
Music Education M,D,O
Music M,D
Neuroscience M,D*
Nurse Midwifery M,D
Nursing—General M,D
Ocean Engineering M,D
Oceanography M,D
Operations Research M,D
Organic Chemistry M,D
Pharmacology D*
Philosophy M,D
Photography M
Physical Chemistry M,D
Physical Therapy M,D
Physics M,D*
Physiology D*
Political Science M
Psychiatric Nursing M,D
Psychology—General M,D
Public Health—General M*
Reading Education M,D,O
Science Education M,O
Sociology M,D
Spanish D
Special Education M,D,O
Sports Management M*
Statistics M,D
Taxation M
Telecommunications Management M,O
Therapies—Dance, Drama, and Music M,D,O
Urban Design M

In-depth description on page 1205.

UNIVERSITY OF MICHIGAN

Advanced Practice Nursing M
Aerospace/Aeronautical Engineering M,D,O
Allopathic Medicine P
American Studies M,D
Analytical Chemistry D
Anthropology M,D
Applied Arts and Design—General M*
Applied Economics M
Applied Physics D
Archaeology D
Architecture M,D*
Art History D
Art/Fine Arts M
Asian Languages M,D
Asian Studies M,D
Astronomy M,D
Atmospheric Sciences M,D
Automotive Engineering M
Biochemistry D*
Bioinformatics M,D
Biological and Biomedical Sciences—General M,D*
Biomedical Engineering M,D*
Biophysics D
Biopsychology D
Biostatistics M,D
Business Administration and Management—General M,D
Cell Biology M,D*
Chemical Engineering M,D,O*
Chemistry D
City and Regional Planning M,D,O*
Civil Engineering M,D,O
Classics M,D
Clinical Psychology D
Clinical Research M
Community Health Nursing M
Comparative Literature D
Computer Education M,D
Computer Engineering M,D
Computer Science M,D
Construction Engineering and Management M,D,O
Curriculum and Instruction M,D
Dance M
Dentistry P
Developmental Biology M,D
Developmental Psychology D
Early Childhood Education M,D
East European and Russian Studies M,O
Ecology M,D*
Economics M,D
Education—General M,D*
Educational Administration M,D
Educational Measurement and Evaluation M,D
Educational Media/Instructional Technology M,D
Electrical Engineering M,D*
Engineering and Applied Sciences—General M,D,O*
English Education M,D
English M,D,O
Environmental and Occupational Health M,D
Environmental Engineering M,D,O
Environmental Management and Policy M,D
Epidemiology M,D
Evolutionary Biology M,D
Film, Television, and Video Production O
Financial Engineering M*
Foreign Languages Education M,D
Forestry M,D,O
Foundations and Philosophy of Education M,D
French D
Genetics
Geochemistry M,D
Geology M,D
Geosciences M,D
German M,D
Gerontological Nursing M
Health Physics/Radiological Health M,D,O
Health Promotion M,D
Health Services Management and Hospital Administration M,D
Higher Education M,D
History D,O
Human Genetics M,D*
Human-Computer Interaction M,D
Immunology D*
Industrial and Organizational Psychology D
Industrial Hygiene M,D
Industrial/Management Engineering M,D,O
Information Studies M,D*
Inorganic Chemistry D
International Health M,D
Kinesiology and Movement Studies M,D
Landscape Architecture M,D
Law P,M,D
Library Science M,D
Linguistics M,D
Manufacturing Engineering M,D
Mass Communication D*
Materials Engineering M,D
Materials Sciences M,D*
Mathematics Education M,D
Mathematics M,D
Mechanical Engineering M,D
Medical Illustration M
Medical/Surgical Nursing M
Microbiology D*
Mineralogy M,D
Molecular Biology M,D
Music Education D
Music M,D*
Natural Resources M,D,O
Near and Middle Eastern Languages M,D
Near and Middle Eastern Studies M,D
Neurobiology D
Nuclear Engineering M,D,O*
Nurse Midwifery M
Nursing and Healthcare Administration M
Nursing—General M,D,O
Nutrition M
Occupational Health Nursing M
Ocean Engineering M,D,O
Oceanography M,D
Operations Research M,D,O
Oral and Dental Sciences M,D,O
Organic Chemistry D
Pathology D*
Pediatric Nursing M
Pharmaceutical Administration M,D
Pharmaceutical Sciences M,D*
Pharmacology D*
Pharmacy P
Philosophy M,D
Physical Chemistry D
Physics M,D*
Physiology D*
Planetary and Space Sciences M,D
Plant Biology M,D
Political Science M,D
Polymer Science and Engineering M
Psychiatric Nursing M
Psychology—General D,O*
Public Health—General M,D*
Public Policy and Administration M,D*
Reading Education M,D
Romance Languages D
Russian M,D
Science Education M,D
Slavic Languages M,D
Social Psychology D
Social Sciences Education M,D
Social Sciences D
Social Work M,D*
Sociology D
Spanish D
Statistics M,D
Survey Methodology M,D,O
Systems Engineering M,D
Theater M,D
Toxicology M,D*
Urban Design M*
Women's Studies D,O
Writing M

UNIVERSITY OF MICHIGAN–DEARBORN

Adult Education M
Applied Mathematics M
Automotive Engineering M
Business Administration and Management—General M
Computational Sciences M
Computer Engineering M
Computer Science M
Education—General M
Electrical Engineering M
Engineering and Applied Sciences—General M,D*
Engineering Management M
Environmental Sciences M
Industrial/Management Engineering M
Information Science M
Liberal Studies M
Manufacturing Engineering M,D
Mechanical Engineering M
Public Policy and Administration M
Software Engineering M
Special Education M
Systems Engineering M
Systems Science M

In-depth description on page 1207.

UNIVERSITY OF MICHIGAN–FLINT

American Studies M
Business Administration and Management—General M
Early Childhood Education M
Education—General M
Health Education M
Nurse Anesthesia M
Nursing—General M
Physical Therapy M
Public Policy and Administration M

UNIVERSITY OF MINNESOTA, DULUTH

Allopathic Medicine P
Anatomy M,D

University of Minnesota, Duluth (continued)
Anthropology M
Applied Mathematics M*
Art/Fine Arts M
Biochemistry M,D
Biological and Biomedical Sciences—General M
Business Administration and Management—General M
Cell Biology M,D
Chemistry M
Communication Disorders M
Computational Sciences M
Computer Science M
Engineering Management M
English M
Geology M*
Graphic Design M
Immunology M,D
Medical Microbiology M,D
Molecular Biology M,D
Music Education M
Music M
Pharmacology M,D
Physics M*
Physiology M,D
Safety Engineering M
Social Work M
Sociology M
Toxicology M,D

UNIVERSITY OF MINNESOTA, TWIN CITIES CAMPUS
Accounting M,D
Adult Education M,D,O
Advanced Practice Nursing M
Aerospace/Aeronautical Engineering M,D*
Agricultural Economics and Agribusiness M,D
Agricultural Education M,D
Agricultural Engineering M,D
Agricultural Sciences—General M,D
Agronomy and Soil Sciences M,D
Allopathic Medicine P
American Studies D
Animal Behavior M,D
Animal Sciences M,D
Anthropology M,D
Applied Arts and Design—General M,D
Applied Economics M,D
Archaeology M,D
Architecture M
Art Education M,D
Art History M,D
Art/Fine Arts M
Asian Studies M
Astronomy M,D
Astrophysics M,D
Biochemistry D*
Biological and Biomedical Sciences—General M,D
Biomedical Engineering M,D
Biophysics M,D
Biopsychology D
Biostatistics M,D
Biotechnology M*
Business Administration and Management—General M,D*
Business Education M,D
Cell Biology M,D
Chemical Engineering M,D
Chemistry M,D*
Child and Family Studies M,D
City and Regional Planning M
Civil Engineering M,D
Classics M,D
Clinical Laboratory Sciences/Medical Technology M*
Clinical Psychology D
Clinical Research M
Cognitive Sciences D
Communication Disorders M,D
Communication—General M,D*
Community Health Nursing M
Community Health M
Comparative Literature M,D
Computational Sciences M,D
Computer Engineering M,D*
Computer Science M,D
Conservation Biology M,D
Counseling Psychology D
Counselor Education M,D,O
Cultural Studies M,D*
Curriculum and Instruction M,D
Dance M,D
Dentistry P
Developmental Biology M,D*
Early Childhood Education M,D,O
East European and Russian Studies M
Ecology M,D
Economics D
Education of the Gifted M,D,O
Education—General M,D
Educational Administration M,D,O
Educational Measurement and Evaluation M,D
Educational Media/Instructional Technology M,D
Educational Psychology M,D,O
Electrical Engineering M,D*
Electronic Commerce M
Elementary Education M,D
Engineering and Applied Sciences—General M,D
English as a Second Language M,D
English Education M,D
English M,D
Entomology M,D
Entrepreneurship M
Environmental and Occupational Health M,D
Environmental Management and Policy M
Epidemiology M,D
Evolutionary Biology M,D
Exercise and Sports Science M,D,O
Family and Consumer Sciences-General M,D
Finance and Banking M,D
Fish, Game, and Wildlife Management M,D
Food Science and Technology M,D
Foreign Languages Education M,D
Forestry M,D*
Foundations and Philosophy of Education M,D,O
French M,D
Genetic Counseling M,D
Genetics M,D
Geographic Information Systems M
Geography M,D
Geological Engineering M,D
Geology M,D
Geophysics M,D
German M,D
Gerontological Nursing M
Health Informatics M,D*
Health Services Management and Hospital Administration M,D*
Health Services Research M,D
Higher Education M,D
History of Medicine M,D
History of Science and Technology M,D
History M,D
Horticulture M,D
Human Resources Development M,D,O
Human Resources Management M,D
Industrial and Labor Relations M,D*
Industrial and Manufacturing Management M,D
Industrial and Organizational Psychology D
Industrial Hygiene M,D
Industrial/Management Engineering M,D*
Information Science M,D
Interdisciplinary Studies M,D
Interior Design M,D
International and Comparative Education M,D
International Business M
Italian M,D
Kinesiology and Movement Studies M,D
Landscape Architecture M
Law P,M
Leisure Studies M,D
Linguistics M,D
Logistics M,D
Management Information Systems M,D
Management of Technology M
Management Strategy and Policy M,D
Marketing M,D
Mass Communication M,D
Materials Engineering M,D
Materials Sciences M,D
Maternal and Child Health M
Mathematics Education M,D
Mathematics M,D
Mechanical Engineering M,D*
Mechanics M,D
Medical Physics M,D*
Medical/Surgical Nursing M
Medicinal and Pharmaceutical Chemistry M,D
Medieval and Renaissance Studies M,D
Microbiology M,D*
Molecular Biology M,D
Multilingual and Multicultural Education M,D
Music M,D
Neuroscience M,D*
Nurse Midwifery M
Nursing and Healthcare Administration M
Nursing Education M
Nursing—General M,D
Nutrition M,D*
Occupational Health Nursing M,D
Oncology Nursing M
Oral and Dental Sciences M,D
Pediatric Nursing M
Pharmaceutical Administration M,D
Pharmaceutical Sciences M,D
Pharmacology M,D
Pharmacy P
Philosophy M,D
Physical Education M,D,O
Physical Therapy M,D
Physics M,D
Physiology M,D
Plant Biology M,D*
Plant Pathology M,D
Plant Sciences M,D
Political Science M,D
Portuguese M,D
Psychiatric Nursing M
Psychology—General M,D
Public Health—General M,O
Public Policy and Administration M*
Reading Education M,D
Recreation and Park Management M,D
Rehabilitation Sciences M,D
Rhetoric M,D
Scandinavian Languages M,D
School Nursing M
School Psychology M,D,O
Science Education M,D
Social Psychology D
Social Sciences Education M,D
Social Work M,D
Sociology M,D
Software Engineering M
Spanish M,D
Special Education M,D,O
Sports Management M,D,O
Statistics M,D
Student Personnel Services M,D,O
Systems Engineering M
Taxation M
Technical Writing M,D
Technology and Public Policy M
Textile Design M,D
Theater M,D
Toxicology M,D
Veterinary Medicine P
Veterinary Sciences M,D
Vocational and Technical Education M,D,O
Water Resources M,D

UNIVERSITY OF MISSISSIPPI
Accounting M,D
American Studies M
Anthropology M
Applied Science and Technology M,D
Art Education M
Art History M
Art/Fine Arts M
Biological and Biomedical Sciences—General M,D
Business Administration and Management—General M,D*
Chemistry M,D
Classics M
Clinical Psychology M,D
Communication Disorders M
Counselor Education M,D,O
Curriculum and Instruction M,D,O
Economics M,D
Education—General M,D,O
Educational Administration M,D,O
Engineering and Applied Sciences—General M,D*
English M,D
Exercise and Sports Science M,D
Experimental Psychology M,D
French M
German M
Higher Education M
History M,D
Journalism M
Law P
Leisure Studies M,D
Management Information Systems M,D
Mathematics M,D
Medicinal and Pharmaceutical Chemistry M,D
Music M,D
Pharmaceutical Administration M,D
Pharmaceutical Sciences M,D
Pharmacology M,D
Pharmacy P
Philosophy M
Physics M,D
Political Science M,D
Psychology—General M,D
Secondary Education M,D,O
Sociology M
Spanish M
Student Personnel Services M
Taxation M,D
Theater M
Toxicology M,D

UNIVERSITY OF MISSISSIPPI MEDICAL CENTER
Allied Health—General M,D
Allopathic Medicine P
Anatomy M,D
Biochemistry M,D*
Biological and Biomedical Sciences—General M,D*
Biophysics M,D
Clinical Laboratory Sciences/Medical Technology M,D
Dentistry P
Microbiology M,D
Nursing—General M,D
Pathology M,D
Pharmacology M,D*
Physical Therapy M
Physiology M,D
Toxicology M,D

UNIVERSITY OF MISSOURI–COLUMBIA
Accounting M,D
Adult Education M,D,O
Aerospace/Aeronautical Engineering M,D
Agricultural Economics and Agribusiness M,D
Agricultural Engineering M,D
Agricultural Sciences—General M,D
Agronomy and Soil Sciences M,D
Allopathic Medicine P
Analytical Chemistry M,D
Animal Sciences M,D
Anthropology M,D
Applied Mathematics M
Archaeology M,D
Art History M,D
Art/Fine Arts M
Atmospheric Sciences M,D
Biochemistry M,D
Bioengineering M,D
Biological and Biomedical Sciences—General M,D
Business Administration and Management—General M,D*
Chemical Engineering M,D
Chemistry M,D
Child and Family Studies M,D
Civil Engineering M,D
Classics M,D
Clothing and Textiles M
Communication Disorders M
Communication—General M,D
Community Health M
Comparative Literature M,D
Computer Engineering M,D
Computer Science M,D*
Conflict Resolution and Mediation/Peace Studies M
Consumer Economics M
Counseling Psychology M,D,O
Early Childhood Education M,D,O
Economics M,D
Education—General M,D,O
Educational Administration M,D,O
Educational Media/Instructional Technology M,D,O
Educational Psychology M,D,O
Electrical Engineering M,D*
Elementary Education M,D,O
Engineering and Applied Sciences—General M,D
English M,D
Entomology M,D
Environmental Design M
Environmental Engineering M,D
Exercise and Sports Science M,D
Family and Consumer Sciences-General M,D
Fish, Game, and Wildlife Management M,D
Food Science and Technology M,D
Foreign Languages Education M,D
Forestry M,D
French M,D
Genetics D
Geography M
Geology M,D
Geotechnical Engineering M,D
German M
Health Informatics M
Health Physics/Radiological Health M,D
Health Services Management and Hospital Administration M
Higher Education M,D,O
History M,D
Horticulture M,D
Hospitality Management M,D
Human Development M,D
Immunology M,D*
Industrial/Management Engineering M,D
Information Studies M,D,O
Inorganic Chemistry M,D
Journalism M,D
Law P,M

Library Science M,D,O
Manufacturing Engineering M,D
Mathematics Education M,D
Mathematics M,D
Mechanical Engineering M,D
Medical Physics M,D
Microbiology M,D
Middle School Education M,D,O
Music M
Nuclear Engineering M,D*
Nursing—General M,D*
Nutrition M,D*
Organic Chemistry M,D
Pathobiology M,D
Pharmacology M,D
Philosophy M,D*
Physical Chemistry M,D
Physical Therapy M
Physics M,D
Physiology M,D
Plant Biology M,D
Plant Pathology M,D
Political Science M,D
Psychology—General M,D
Public Policy and Administration M
Recreation and Park Management M
Religion M
Romance Languages M,D*
Rural Sociology M,D
Secondary Education M,D,O
Social Work M
Sociology M,D
Spanish M,D
Statistics M,D
Structural Engineering M,D
Theater M,D
Transportation and Highway Engineering M,D
Veterinary Medicine P
Veterinary Sciences M,D
Water Resources Engineering M,D

UNIVERSITY OF MISSOURI–KANSAS CITY

Accounting M
Advanced Practice Nursing M,D
Allopathic Medicine P
Analytical Chemistry M,D
Art History M,D
Art/Fine Arts M,D
Biochemistry D
Biological and Biomedical Sciences—General M
Biophysics D
Business Administration and Management—General M
Cell Biology M,D*
Chemistry M,D*
Communication—General M
Computer Science M,D
Counseling Psychology M,D,O
Counselor Education M,D,O
Criminal Justice and Criminology M
Curriculum and Instruction M,D,O
Dental Hygiene M
Dentistry P
Economics M,D
Education—General M,D,O
Educational Administration M,D,O
English M,D
Geology M,D
Geosciences M,D
History M,D
Inorganic Chemistry M,D
Interdisciplinary Studies D
Law P,M
Liberal Studies M
Maternal/Child Nursing M,D
Mathematics M,D
Medical/Surgical Nursing M,D
Molecular Biology M,D*
Music Education M,D
Music M,D
Nursing and Healthcare Administration M,D
Nursing Education M,D
Nursing—General M,D
Oral and Dental Sciences M,D
Organic Chemistry M,D
Pediatric Nursing M,D
Pharmaceutical Sciences M
Pharmacy P
Physical Chemistry M,D
Physics M,D
Political Science M,D
Polymer Science and Engineering M,D
Psychology—General M,D
Public Policy and Administration M,D
Reading Education M,D,O
Romance Languages M
Social Psychology D
Social Work M
Sociology M,D
Software Engineering M,D
Special Education M,D,O
Statistics M,D
Taxation M
Telecommunications M,D*
Theater M
Women's Health Nursing M,D

In-depth description on page 1209.

UNIVERSITY OF MISSOURI–ROLLA

Aerospace/Aeronautical Engineering M,D
Applied Mathematics M
Ceramic Sciences and Engineering M,D
Chemical Engineering M,D
Chemistry M,D
Civil Engineering M,D
Computer Engineering M,D
Computer Science M,D
Construction Engineering and Management M,D
Electrical Engineering M,D
Engineering and Applied Sciences—General M,D*
Engineering Management M,D
Environmental Engineering M,D
Geochemistry M,D
Geological Engineering M,D
Geology M,D
Geophysics M,D
Geotechnical Engineering M,D
Hydraulics M,D
Hydrology M,D
Manufacturing Engineering M
Mathematics Education M,D
Mathematics M,D
Mechanical Engineering M,D
Mechanics M,D
Metallurgical Engineering and Metallurgy M,D
Mineral/Mining Engineering M,D
Nuclear Engineering M,D
Petroleum Engineering M,D
Physics M,D
Science Education M,D
Structural Engineering M,D
Systems Engineering M
Water Resources M,D

UNIVERSITY OF MISSOURI–ST. LOUIS

Accounting M,O
Adult Education M,D
Animal Behavior M,D,O
Applied Mathematics M,D,O
Applied Physics M,D
Astrophysics M,D
Biochemistry M,D,O
Biological and Biomedical Sciences—General M,D,O
Biotechnology M,D,O
Botany M,D,O
Business Administration and Management—General M,O
Cell Biology M,D,O
Chemistry M,D
Clinical Psychology M,D,O
Communication—General M
Computer Science M,D,O
Conflict Resolution and Mediation/Peace Studies M
Conservation Biology M,D,O
Counselor Education M,D
Criminal Justice and Criminology M,D
Curriculum and Instruction M,D
Developmental Biology M,D,O
Ecology M,D,O
Economics M,O
Education—General M,D
Educational Administration M,D
Educational Measurement and Evaluation M,D
Educational Psychology M,D
Electronic Commerce M,D,O
Elementary Education M,D
English M
Environmental Management and Policy M,D,O
Evolutionary Biology M,D,O
Experimental Psychology M,D,O
Finance and Banking M,O
Gender Studies O
Genetics M,D,O
Gerontology M,O
Health Services Management and Hospital Administration M,O
History M,O
Human Resources Management M,O
Industrial and Organizational Psychology M,D,O
Inorganic Chemistry M,D
International Affairs O
Linguistics M
Management Information Systems M,D,O
Marketing M,O
Mathematics M,D,O
Molecular Biology M,D,O
Museum Studies M,O
Music Education M
Nonprofit Management M,O
Nursing—General M,D
Optometry P
Organic Chemistry M,D
Philosophy M
Physical Chemistry M,D
Physics M,D
Physiology M,D,O
Political Science M,D
Psychology—General M,D,O
Public Policy and Administration M,D,O
Quantitative Analysis M,O
Reading Education M,D
Secondary Education M,D
Social Work M,O
Sociology M
Special Education M
Taxation M,O
Telecommunications Management M,D,O
Vision Sciences M,D
Women's Studies O
Writing M

In-depth description on page 1211.

UNIVERSITY OF MOBILE

Business Administration and Management—General M
Education—General M
Marriage and Family Therapy M
Nursing—General M
Theology M

THE UNIVERSITY OF MONTANA–MISSOULA

Accounting M
Analytical Chemistry M,D
Animal Behavior D
Anthropology M
Art/Fine Arts M
Biochemistry M,D
Biological and Biomedical Sciences—General M,D
Business Administration and Management—General M*
Chemistry M,D
Clinical Psychology D
Communication—General M
Computer Science M
Counselor Education M,D,O
Criminal Justice and Criminology M
Curriculum and Instruction M,D
Developmental Psychology D
Ecology M,D
Economics M
Education—General M,D,O
Educational Administration M,D,O
English Education M
English M
Environmental Management and Policy M
Environmental Sciences M*
Exercise and Sports Science M
Experimental Psychology D
Film, Television, and Video Production M
Fish, Game, and Wildlife Management M,D
Forestry M,D
French M
Geographic Information Systems M
Geography M
Geology M,D
German M
Health Education M
Health Promotion M
Health Psychology M
History M
Inorganic Chemistry M,D
Interdisciplinary Studies M,D
Jewish Studies M
Journalism M
Law P
Linguistics M
Mathematics Education M,D
Mathematics M,D
Microbiology M,D
Museum Education M
Music Education M
Music M
Natural Resources M
Organic Chemistry M,D
Pharmaceutical Sciences M,D*
Pharmacology M,D
Philosophy M*
Photography M
Physical Chemistry M,D
Physical Education M
Physical Therapy M,D
Political Science M
Psychology—General M,D,O
Public Policy and Administration M
Recreation and Park Management M
Rural Sociology M
School Psychology M,O
Science Education M,D
Sociology M
Spanish M
Theater M
Writing M

In-depth description on page 1213.

UNIVERSITY OF MONTEVALLO

Communication Disorders M
Counselor Education M
Early Childhood Education M
Education—General M,O
Educational Administration M,O
Elementary Education M
English M
Music M
Secondary Education M,O

UNIVERSITY OF NEBRASKA AT KEARNEY

Art Education M
Biological and Biomedical Sciences—General M
Business Administration and Management—General M
Communication Disorders M
Counselor Education M,O
Curriculum and Instruction M
Early Childhood Education M
Education of the Gifted M
Education—General M,O
Educational Administration M,O
Educational Media/Instructional Technology M,O
Elementary Education M
English M
Exercise and Sports Science M
Foreign Languages Education M
History M
Middle School Education M
Music Education M
Physical Education M
Reading Education M
School Psychology M,O
Science Education M
Special Education M

Announcement on page 625.

UNIVERSITY OF NEBRASKA AT OMAHA

Accounting M
Biological and Biomedical Sciences—General M
Business Administration and Management—General M
Communication Disorders M
Communication—General M
Computer Science M
Counselor Education M
Criminal Justice and Criminology M,D
Developmental Psychology M,D,O
Economics M
Education—General M,D,O
Educational Administration M,D,O
Educational Media/Instructional Technology M,O
Educational Psychology M,D,O
Elementary Education M
English M,O
Experimental Psychology M,D,O
Geography M,O
Gerontology M,O
Health Education M
History M
Industrial and Organizational Psychology M,D,O
Management Information Systems M
Mathematics M
Music M
Physical Education M
Political Science M
Psychology—General M,D,O
Public Policy and Administration M,D
Reading Education M
Recreation and Park Management M
School Psychology M,D,O
Secondary Education M
Social Work M
Sociology M
Special Education M
Theater M
Urban Education M,O

UNIVERSITY OF NEBRASKA–LINCOLN

Accounting M,D
Actuarial Science M

University of Nebraska–Lincoln (continued)

Agricultural Economics and Agribusiness M,D
Agricultural Education M
Agricultural Engineering M
Agricultural Sciences—General M,D
Agronomy and Soil Sciences M,D
Analytical Chemistry M,D
Animal Sciences M,D
Anthropology M
Architecture M
Art History M
Art/Fine Arts M
Astronomy M,D
Biochemistry M,D*
Bioengineering M
Biological and Biomedical Sciences—General M,D*
Biometrics M
Business Administration and Management—General M,D
Chemical Engineering M,D
Chemistry M,D
Child and Family Studies M,D
City and Regional Planning M
Civil Engineering M,D
Classics M
Clothing and Textiles M
Communication Disorders M
Communication—General M,D
Computer Engineering M,D*
Computer Science M,D*
Consumer Economics M,D
Curriculum and Instruction M,D,O
Economics M,D
Education—General M,D,O
Educational Administration M,D,O
Educational Psychology M,O
Electrical Engineering M,D*
Engineering and Applied Sciences—General M,D*
English M,D
Entomology M,D
Environmental Engineering M,D
Family and Consumer Sciences-General M,D
Finance and Banking M,D
Food Science and Technology M,D
French M,D
Geography M,D
Geosciences M,D
German M,D
Health Education M
History M,D
Horticulture M,D
Industrial/Management Engineering M,D
Inorganic Chemistry M,D
Journalism M
Law P,M
Legal and Justice Studies M
Manufacturing Engineering M,D
Marketing M,D
Mass Communication M
Materials Engineering M,D
Mathematics M,D
Mechanical Engineering M,D*
Mechanics M,D*
Museum Studies M
Music M,D
Natural Resources M
Nutrition M,D
Organic Chemistry M,D
Philosophy M,D
Physical Chemistry M,D
Physical Education M
Physics M,D
Political Science M,D
Psychology—General M,D
Recreation and Park Management M
Sociology M,D
Spanish M,D
Special Education M
Statistics M,D
Survey Methodology M
Theater M,D
Toxicology M,D
Veterinary Sciences M,D

In-depth description on page 1215.

UNIVERSITY OF NEBRASKA MEDICAL CENTER

Allied Health—General M
Allopathic Medicine P
Anatomy M,D
Biochemistry M,D
Biological and Biomedical Sciences—General M,D*
Cell Biology M,D
Dentistry P,O
Microbiology M,D
Molecular Biology M,D
Nursing—General M,D
Pathology M,D
Pharmaceutical Sciences M,D
Pharmacology M,D
Pharmacy P
Physical Therapy M
Physician Assistant Studies M
Physiology D
Public Health—General M
Toxicology M,D

UNIVERSITY OF NEVADA, LAS VEGAS

Accounting M
Advanced Practice Nursing M
Anthropology M,D
Applied Mathematics M
Architecture M
Art/Fine Arts M
Biochemistry M
Biological and Biomedical Sciences—General M,D
Business Administration and Management—General M
Chemistry M
Civil Engineering M,D
Clinical Psychology M,D
Communication—General M
Computer Engineering M,D
Computer Science M,D
Counseling Psychology M
Criminal Justice and Criminology M
Curriculum and Instruction M,D,O
Dance M,D
Economics M
Education—General M,D,O
Educational Administration M,D,O
Educational Measurement and Evaluation M,D,O
Educational Media/Instructional Technology M,D,O
Educational Psychology M,D
Electrical Engineering M,D
Elementary Education M,D,O
Engineering and Applied Sciences—General M,D*
English as a Second Language M,D,O
English Education M,D,O
English M,D
Environmental Engineering M,D
Environmental Sciences M,D
Ethics M
Exercise and Sports Science M
Experimental Psychology M,D
Film, Television, and Video Production M
French M
Geosciences M,D
Gerontological Nursing M
Health Physics/Radiological Health M
Health Promotion M
Higher Education M,D,O
History M,D
Hospitality Management M,D
Kinesiology and Movement Studies M
Law P
Leisure Studies M
Marriage and Family Therapy M
Mass Communication M
Mathematics Education M,D,O
Mathematics M
Mechanical Engineering M,D
Middle School Education M,D,O
Music Education M,D
Music M,D
Nursing—General M
Pediatric Nursing M
Physical Therapy M
Physics M,D
Political Science M
Psychology—General M,D
Public Policy and Administration M
Rehabilitation Counseling M
School Psychology M,D,O
Secondary Education M,D,O
Social Work M
Sociology M,D
Spanish M
Special Education M,D,O
Statistics M
Theater M
Vocational and Technical Education M,D,O
Water Resources M
Writing M,D

In-depth description on page 1217.

UNIVERSITY OF NEVADA, RENO

Accounting M
Agricultural Economics and Agribusiness M
Agricultural Sciences—General M
Allopathic Medicine P
Animal Sciences M
Anthropology M,D
Applied Economics M
Atmospheric Sciences M,D
Biochemistry M,D
Biological and Biomedical Sciences—General M,D
Biomedical Engineering M,D
Business Administration and Management—General M
Cell Biology M,D*
Chemical Engineering M,D
Chemistry M,D
Child and Family Studies M
Civil Engineering M,D
Communication Disorders M,D
Computer Engineering M,D
Computer Science M
Conservation Biology D
Counselor Education M,D,O
Curriculum and Instruction M,D,O
Ecology D
Economics M
Education—General M,D,O
Educational Administration M,D,O
Educational Psychology M,D,O
Electrical Engineering M,D
Elementary Education M,D,O
Engineering and Applied Sciences—General M,D
English as a Second Language M,D,O
English Education M,D
English M,D
Environmental and Occupational Health M,D
Environmental Management and Policy M
Environmental Sciences M,D
Evolutionary Biology D
Foreign Languages Education M
French M
Geochemistry M,D,O
Geography M
Geological Engineering M,D,O
Geology M,D,O
Geophysics M,D,O
German M
History M,D
Human Development M
Hydrology M,D
Journalism M
Legal and Justice Studies M
Mathematics Education M
Mathematics M
Mechanical Engineering M,D
Metallurgical Engineering and Metallurgy M,D,O
Mineral/Mining Engineering M,O
Molecular Biology M,D
Music M
Nursing—General M
Nutrition M
Pharmacology M,D*
Philosophy M
Physical Chemistry D
Physics M,D
Physiology M,D
Political Science M,D
Psychology—General M,D
Public Health—General M
Public Policy and Administration M
Secondary Education M,D,O
Social Psychology D
Social Work M
Sociology M
Spanish M
Special Education M,D,O
Speech and Interpersonal Communication M
Western European Studies D

UNIVERSITY OF NEW BRUNSWICK FREDERICTON

Adult Education M
American Studies M
Anthropology M
Biological and Biomedical Sciences—General M,D
Business Administration and Management—General M
Chemical Engineering M,D
Chemistry M,D
Civil Engineering M,D
Classics M
Computer Engineering M,D
Computer Science M,D
Construction Engineering and Management M,D
Counselor Education M
Curriculum and Instruction M
Economics M
Education—General M
Educational Administration M
Educational Psychology M
Electrical Engineering M,D
Engineering and Applied Sciences—General M,D,O
English M,D
Environmental Engineering M,D
Exercise and Sports Science M
Forestry M,D
French M
Geodetic Sciences M,D,O
Geology M,D
Geotechnical Engineering M,D
German M
History M,D
Hydrology M,D
Law P
Materials Sciences M,D
Mathematics M,D
Mechanical Engineering M,D
Mechanics M,D
Philosophy M
Physical Education M
Physics M,D
Political Science M
Psychology—General D
Public Policy and Administration M
Recreation and Park Management M
Russian M
Sociology M,D
Spanish M
Special Education M
Sports Management M
Statistics M,D
Structural Engineering M,D
Surveying Science and Engineering M,D,O
Transportation and Highway Engineering M,D
Vocational and Technical Education M
Water Resources M,D

UNIVERSITY OF NEW BRUNSWICK SAINT JOHN

Biological and Biomedical Sciences—General M,D
Business Administration and Management—General M
Electronic Commerce M
International Business M
Psychology—General M

UNIVERSITY OF NEW ENGLAND

Education—General M
Nurse Anesthesia M
Occupational Therapy M
Osteopathic Medicine P
Physical Therapy M
Physician Assistant Studies M
Social Work M*

UNIVERSITY OF NEW HAMPSHIRE

Accounting M*
Adult Education M,D,O
Agricultural Sciences—General M,D
Agronomy and Soil Sciences M
Animal Sciences M
Applied Mathematics M,D
Art/Fine Arts M
Atmospheric Sciences
Biochemistry M,D
Business Administration and Management—General M
Chemical Engineering M,D
Chemistry M,D
Child and Family Studies M
Civil Engineering M,D
Communication Disorders M
Comparative Literature M,D
Computer Science M,D
Counselor Education M
Early Childhood Education M
Economics M,D*
Education—General M,D,O
Educational Administration M,O
Electrical Engineering M,D
Elementary Education M
English Education M,D
English M,D
Environmental Education M
Environmental Management and Policy M
Fish, Game, and Wildlife Management M
Forestry M
Genetics M,D
Geochemistry M,D
Geology M,D
Geosciences M,D
Health Services Management and Hospital Administration M
Higher Education M
History M,D
Hydrology M,D
Kinesiology and Movement Studies M
Liberal Studies M
Linguistics M,D
Logistics M,D
Marriage and Family Therapy M
Materials Sciences M,D
Mathematics Education M,D
Mathematics M,D*
Mechanical Engineering M,D
Microbiology M,D
Molecular Biology M,D*
Museum Studies M,D
Music Education M
Music M
Natural Resources D
Nursing—General M
Nutrition M

Program	Degrees
Occupational Therapy	M
Ocean Engineering	M,D
Oceanography	M,D
Physics	M,D
Plant Biology	M,D
Political Science	M
Psychology—General	D
Public Health—General	M
Public Policy and Administration	M
Reading Education	M,D
Secondary Education	M
Social Work	M
Sociology	M,D
Spanish	M
Special Education	M
Statistics	M,D
Vocational and Technical Education	M
Water Resources	M
Writing	M,D
Zoology	M,D

In-depth description on page 1219.

UNIVERSITY OF NEW HAVEN

Program	Degrees
Accounting	M
Advertising and Public Relations	M
Aviation	M
Business Administration and Management—General	M
Cell Biology	M
Computer Science	M
Criminal Justice and Criminology	M
Education—General	M
Electrical Engineering	M
Engineering and Applied Sciences—General	M,O*
Engineering Design	M,O
Environmental and Occupational Health	M
Environmental Engineering	M,O
Environmental Sciences	M
Finance and Banking	M
Fire Protection Engineering	M
Forensic Sciences	M
Health Services Management and Hospital Administration	M
Hospitality Management	M
Human Resources Management	M
Industrial and Labor Relations	M
Industrial and Organizational Psychology	M,O
Industrial Hygiene	M
Industrial/Management Engineering	M,O
Information Science	M
International Business	M
Logistics	M,O
Management Information Systems	M
Management of Technology	M
Management Strategy and Policy	M
Marketing	M
Mechanical Engineering	M
Molecular Biology	M
Nutrition	M
Operations Research	M
Public Policy and Administration	M
Social Psychology	M,O
Software Engineering	M
Sports Management	M
Taxation	M
Travel and Tourism	M

In-depth description on page 1221.

UNIVERSITY OF NEW MEXICO

Program	Degrees
Accounting	M
Allopathic Medicine	P
American Studies	M,D
Anthropology	M,D
Architecture	M
Art Education	M
Art History	M,D
Art/Fine Arts	M
Biochemistry	M,D
Biological and Biomedical Sciences—General	M,D
Business Administration and Management—General	M
Cell Biology	M,D
Chemical Engineering	M
Chemistry	M,D
Child and Family Studies	M,D
City and Regional Planning	M
Civil Engineering	M,D
Clinical Psychology	M,D
Communication Disorders	M
Communication—General	M,D
Comparative Literature	M,D
Computer Engineering	M,D
Computer Science	M,D
Counselor Education	M,D
Dance	M
Economics	M,D
Education—General	M,D
Educational Administration	M,D
Educational Media/Instructional Technology	M,D
Educational Psychology	M,D
Electrical Engineering	M,D*
Elementary Education	M
Engineering and Applied Sciences—General	M,D*
English	M,D
Finance and Banking	M
Foundations and Philosophy of Education	M,D
French	M,D
Genetics	M,D
Geography	M
Geosciences	M,D
German	M,D
Health Education	M
History	M,D
Human Resources Management	M
International Business	M
Landscape Architecture	M
Latin American Studies	M,D
Law	P
Linguistics	M,D
Management Information Systems	M
Management of Technology	M
Manufacturing Engineering	M*
Marketing	M
Mathematics	M,D
Mechanical Engineering	M,D*
Microbiology	M,D
Molecular Biology	M,D
Multilingual and Multicultural Education	D
Music	M
Neuroscience	M,D
Nuclear Engineering	M
Nursing—General	M
Nutrition	M
Occupational Therapy	M
Optical Sciences	M,D
Pathology	M,D
Pharmaceutical Sciences	M,D
Pharmacy	P
Philosophy	M,D
Physical Therapy	M
Physics	M,D
Physiology	M,D
Planetary and Space Sciences	M,D
Political Science	M,D
Portuguese	M,D
Psychology—General	M,D
Public Health—General	M
Public Policy and Administration	M
Recreation and Park Management	M
Secondary Education	M
Sociology	M,D*
Spanish	M,D
Special Education	M,D
Statistics	M,D
Taxation	M
Theater	M
Toxicology	M,D
Water Resources	M
Writing	M

In-depth description on page 1223.

UNIVERSITY OF NEW ORLEANS

Program	Degrees
Accounting	M
Applied Physics	M
Art/Fine Arts	M
Arts Administration	M
Biological and Biomedical Sciences—General	M,D*
Biopsychology	M,D
Business Administration and Management—General	M
Chemistry	M,D
City and Regional Planning	M
Civil Engineering	M
Computer Science	M
Conservation Biology	M,D
Counselor Education	M,D,O
Curriculum and Instruction	M,D,O
Developmental Psychology	M,D
Economics	D
Education—General	M,D,O
Educational Administration	M,D,O
Electrical Engineering	M
Engineering and Applied Sciences—General	M,D,O*
Engineering Management	M,O
English	M
Exercise and Sports Science	M,O
Film, Television, and Video Production	M
Foundations and Philosophy of Education	M,D,O
Geography	M
Geology	M
Geophysics	M
Gerontology	M,O
Graphic Design	M
Health Education	M,O
Health Services Management and Hospital Administration	M
History	M
International Affairs	M,D
Mathematics	M
Mechanical Engineering	M
Music	M
Photography	M
Physical Education	M,O
Physics	M
Political Science	M,D
Psychology—General	M,D
Public History	M
Public Policy and Administration	M
Romance Languages	M
Science Education	M
Sociology	M
Special Education	M,D,O
Sports Management	M,O
Taxation	M
Theater	M
Urban Studies	M,D
Writing	M

UNIVERSITY OF NORTH ALABAMA

Program	Degrees
Business Administration and Management—General	M
Counselor Education	M
Criminal Justice and Criminology	M
Early Childhood Education	M
Education—General	M,O
Educational Administration	M,O
Elementary Education	M,O
English	M
Secondary Education	M
Special Education	M

THE UNIVERSITY OF NORTH CAROLINA AT ASHEVILLE

Program	Degrees
Liberal Studies	M

THE UNIVERSITY OF NORTH CAROLINA AT CHAPEL HILL

Program	Degrees
Accounting	M,D
Allied Health—General	M,D
Allopathic Medicine	P
Anthropology	M,D
Archaeology	M,D
Art History	M,D
Art/Fine Arts	M
Astronomy	M,D
Astrophysics	M,D
Atmospheric Sciences	M,D
Biochemistry	M,D
Biological and Biomedical Sciences—General	M,D*
Biomedical Engineering	M,D*
Biophysics	M,D
Biostatistics	M,D
Botany	M,D*
Business Administration and Management—General	M,D
Cancer Biology/Oncology	
Cell Biology	M,D
Chemistry	M,D
City and Regional Planning	M,D
Classics	M,D
Clinical Psychology	D
Communication Disorders	M,D
Communication—General	M,D
Community Health Nursing	M,D
Comparative Literature	M,D
Computer Science	M,D*
Counselor Education	M
Curriculum and Instruction	M,D
Dentistry	P
Developmental Biology	M,D
Developmental Psychology	D
Early Childhood Education	D
East European and Russian Studies	M
Ecology	M,D
Economics	M,D
Education—General	M,D
Educational Administration	M,D
Educational Psychology	M,D
Elementary Education	M
English Education	M
English	M,D
Environmental and Occupational Health	M,D
Environmental Engineering	M,D
Environmental Management and Policy	M,D
Environmental Sciences	M,D
Epidemiology	M,D
Evolutionary Biology	M,D
Exercise and Sports Science	M
Experimental Psychology	D
Finance and Banking	D
Folklore	M
Foreign Languages Education	M
French	M,D
Genetics	M,D*
Geography	M,D
Geology	M,D
German	M,D
Health Education	M,D
Health Promotion	M,D
Health Services Management and Hospital Administration	M,D
History	M,D
Immunology	M,D
Industrial Hygiene	M,D
Information Studies	M,D,O
Italian	M,D
Kinesiology and Movement Studies	M,D
Latin American Studies	M,D,O
Law	P
Leisure Studies	M
Library Science	M,D,O
Linguistics	M,D
Management Information Systems	D
Management Strategy and Policy	D
Marine Sciences	M,D
Marketing	D
Mass Communication	M,D
Materials Sciences	M,D
Maternal and Child Health	M,D
Mathematics Education	M
Mathematics	M,D*
Microbiology	M,D*
Molecular Biology	M,D
Music Education	M
Music	M,D
Neurobiology	D
Nursing—General	M,D
Nutrition	M,D
Occupational Health Nursing	M,D
Occupational Therapy	M,D
Operations Research	M,D
Oral and Dental Sciences	M,D*
Organizational Behavior	D
Pathology	D*
Pharmaceutical Sciences	M,D
Pharmacology	D*
Philosophy	M,D
Physical Education	M
Physical Therapy	M
Physics	M,D
Physiology	D*
Political Science	M,D
Portuguese	M,D
Psychology—General	D
Public Health—General	M,D*
Public Policy and Administration	M,D
Reading Education	D
Recreation and Park Management	M
Rehabilitation Counseling	M,D
Religion	M,D
Romance Languages	M,D
Russian	M,D
School Psychology	M,D
Science Education	M
Secondary Education	M
Slavic Languages	M,D
Social Psychology	D
Social Sciences Education	M
Social Work	M,D
Sociology	M,D
Spanish	M,D
Special Education	M
Sports Management	M
Statistics	M,D
Theater	M
Toxicology	M,D*

In-depth description on page 1225.

THE UNIVERSITY OF NORTH CAROLINA AT CHARLOTTE

Program	Degrees
Accounting	M
Applied Mathematics	M,D
Applied Physics	M
Architecture	M
Biological and Biomedical Sciences—General	M,D
Business Administration and Management—General	M*
Chemistry	M
Child and Family Studies	M,D
Civil Engineering	M
Clinical Psychology	M
Communication—General	M
Community Health Nursing	M
Computer Engineering	M,D
Computer Science	M
Counselor Education	M,D
Criminal Justice and Criminology	M
Curriculum and Instruction	M,D,O
Economics	M
Education—General	M,D,O
Educational Administration	M,D,O
Educational Media/Instructional Technology	M,D,O
Electrical Engineering	M,D
Elementary Education	M

The University of North Carolina at Charlotte (continued)

Engineering and Applied Sciences—General M,D*
Engineering Management M
English M
Geography M
Geosciences M
Gerontology M
Health Promotion M
Health Services Management and Hospital Administration M
History M
Industrial and Organizational Psychology M
Information Science M,D
Liberal Studies M
Mathematics Education M,D
Mathematics M,D*
Mechanical Engineering M,D
Medical/Surgical Nursing M
Middle School Education M
Psychology—General M
Public Policy and Administration M,D
Reading Education M
Secondary Education M
Social Psychology M
Social Work M
Sociology M
Spanish M
Special Education M,D
Statistics M,D

THE UNIVERSITY OF NORTH CAROLINA AT GREENSBORO

Accounting M
Applied Economics M
Art Education M
Art/Fine Arts M
Biological and Biomedical Sciences—General M
Business Administration and Management—General M,O
Chemistry M
Child and Family Studies M,D
Classics M
Clinical Psychology M,D
Cognitive Sciences M,D
Communication Disorders M
Communication—General M
Community Health M
Computer Science M
Counseling Psychology M,D,O
Counselor Education M,D,O
Curriculum and Instruction D
Dance M
Developmental Psychology M,D
Early Childhood Education M
Economics M
Education—General M,D,O
Educational Administration M,D,O
Educational Measurement and Evaluation M,D
English Education M,D,O
English M,D,O
Exercise and Sports Science M,D
Family and Consumer Sciences-General M,D
Film, Television, and Video Production M
French M
Genetic Counseling M
Geography M
Gerontological Nursing M,O
Gerontology M
Higher Education M,D,O
History M,O
Hospitality Management M,D
Human Development M,D
Information Studies M
Interior Design M
International Business M,O
Liberal Studies M
Library Science M
Management Information Systems M
Marketing M,D
Marriage and Family Therapy M,D,O
Mathematics Education M
Mathematics M
Museum Studies M,O
Music Education M,D
Music M,D
Nonprofit Management M,O
Nurse Anesthesia M,O
Nursing and Healthcare Administration M,O
Nursing—General M,O
Nutrition M,D
Political Science M
Psychology—General M,D
Public Policy and Administration M,O
Recreation and Park Management M
School Psychology M,D,O
Social Psychology M,D
Social Work M
Sociology M
Spanish M
Special Education M
Speech and Interpersonal Communication M
Technical Writing M,D,O
Textile Design M,D
Theater M
Women's Studies M,D,O
Writing M

In-depth description on page 1227.

THE UNIVERSITY OF NORTH CAROLINA AT PEMBROKE

Art Education M
Business Administration and Management—General M
Counselor Education M
Education—General M
Educational Administration M
Elementary Education M
English Education M
Mathematics Education M
Middle School Education M
Physical Education M
Public Policy and Administration M
Reading Education M
Science Education M
Social Sciences Education M

THE UNIVERSITY OF NORTH CAROLINA AT WILMINGTON

Accounting M
Biological and Biomedical Sciences—General M
Business Administration and Management—General M
Chemistry M
Computer Education M
Curriculum and Instruction M
Education—General M
Educational Administration M
Elementary Education M
English M
Geology M
History M
Liberal Studies M
Marine Biology M*
Mathematics M
Middle School Education M
Nursing—General M
Psychology—General M
Reading Education M
Secondary Education M
Special Education M
Writing M*

UNIVERSITY OF NORTH DAKOTA

Allopathic Medicine P
Anatomy M,D
Art/Fine Arts M
Atmospheric Sciences M
Aviation M
Biochemistry M,D
Biological and Biomedical Sciences—General M,D
Botany M,D
Business Administration and Management—General M
Chemical Engineering M
Chemistry M,D
Civil Engineering M
Clinical Laboratory Sciences/Medical Technology M
Clinical Psychology D
Communication Disorders M,D
Communication—General M,D
Computer Science M
Counseling Psychology M,D
Early Childhood Education M
Ecology M,D
Education—General M,D,O
Educational Administration M,D,O
Educational Measurement and Evaluation D
Educational Media/Instructional Technology M
Electrical Engineering M
Elementary Education M,D
Energy and Power Engineering D
Engineering and Applied Sciences—General M,D
English M,D
Entomology M,D
Environmental Biology M,D
Experimental Psychology M,D
Fish, Game, and Wildlife Management M,D
Genetics M,D
Geography M
Geology M,D
History M,D
Immunology M,D
Industrial and Manufacturing Management M
Kinesiology and Movement Studies M
Law P
Linguistics M
Mathematics M
Mechanical Engineering M
Microbiology M,D*
Mineral/Mining Engineering M
Music Education M
Music M
Nursing—General M
Occupational Therapy M
Pharmacology M,D
Physical Therapy M,D
Physician Assistant Studies M
Physics M,D
Physiology M,D
Planetary and Space Sciences M
Psychology—General M,D
Public Policy and Administration M
Reading Education M
Secondary Education D
Social Work M
Sociology M
Special Education M,D
Structural Engineering M
Theater M
Zoology M,D

UNIVERSITY OF NORTHERN BRITISH COLUMBIA

Community Health M,D
Computer Science M,D
Disability Studies M,D
Education—General M,D
Environmental Management and Policy M,D
Gender Studies M,D
History M,D
Interdisciplinary Studies M,D
International Affairs M,D
Mathematics M,D
Natural Resources M,D
Political Science M,D
Psychology—General M,D
Social Work M,D

UNIVERSITY OF NORTHERN COLORADO

Advanced Practice Nursing M
Art/Fine Arts M
Biological and Biomedical Sciences—General M,D
Chemistry M,D
Communication Disorders M
Communication—General M
Community Health M
Counseling Psychology M,D
Counselor Education M,D
Early Childhood Education M
Education of the Gifted M
Education—General M,D,O
Educational Administration M,D,O
Educational Measurement and Evaluation M,D
Educational Media/Instructional Technology M
Educational Psychology M,D
Elementary Education M,D
English M
Geosciences M
Gerontology M
Higher Education D
History M
Interdisciplinary Studies M,D,O
Kinesiology and Movement Studies M,D
Mathematics Education M,D
Mathematics M,D
Music Education M,D
Music M,D
Nursing Education M
Nursing—General M
Physical Education M,D
Psychology—General M
Public Health—General M
Reading Education M
Rehabilitation Counseling M,D
School Psychology D,O
Science Education M,D
Sociology M
Spanish M
Special Education M,D
Student Personnel Services D

In-depth description on page 1229.

UNIVERSITY OF NORTHERN IOWA

Accounting M
Art Education M
Art/Fine Arts M
Biological and Biomedical Sciences—General M
Business Administration and Management—General M
Chemistry M
Communication Disorders M
Communication—General M
Computer Science M
Counselor Education M,D
Curriculum and Instruction M,D
Early Childhood Education M
Education of the Gifted M
Education—General M,D,O
Educational Administration M,D
Educational Media/Instructional Technology M
Educational Psychology M,O
Elementary Education M
English as a Second Language M
English M
Environmental Sciences M
French M
Geography M
German M
Health Education M
Higher Education M
History M
Leisure Studies M
Mathematics Education M
Mathematics M
Middle School Education M
Music Education M
Music M
Physical Education M
Political Science M
Psychology—General M
Public Policy and Administration M
Reading Education M
School Psychology M,O
Science Education M,O
Social Work M
Sociology M
Spanish M
Special Education M
Sports Management M
Student Personnel Services M
Theater M
Vocational and Technical Education M,D
Women's Studies M

UNIVERSITY OF NORTH FLORIDA

Accounting M
Addictions/Substance Abuse Counseling M,O
Advanced Practice Nursing M,O
Allied Health—General M,O
Business Administration and Management—General M
Community Health M,O
Computer Science M
Counseling Psychology M
Counselor Education M
Criminal Justice and Criminology M
Education—General M,D
Educational Administration M,D
Elementary Education M
English M
Exercise and Sports Science M,O
Family and Consumer Sciences-General M,O
Gerontology M,O
Health Services Management and Hospital Administration M,O
History M
Human Resources Management M
Information Science M
Mathematics Education M
Mathematics M
Music Education M
Nursing—General M,O
Nutrition M,O
Physical Therapy M
Psychology—General M
Public Health—General M,O
Public Policy and Administration M
Science Education M
Secondary Education M
Special Education M
Statistics M

UNIVERSITY OF NORTH TEXAS

Accounting M,D
Applied Economics M
Art Education M,D
Art History M,D
Art/Fine Arts M,D
Biochemistry M,D
Biological and Biomedical Sciences—General M,D
Business Administration and Management—General M,D
Chemistry M,D
Child and Family Studies M
Clinical Psychology M,D
Clothing and Textiles M
Communication Disorders M
Communication—General M
Community Health M
Computer Education M
Computer Science M,D*
Counseling Psychology M,D
Counselor Education M,D
Curriculum and Instruction D
Early Childhood Education M,D
Economics M
Education—General M,D,O
Educational Administration M,D
Educational Measurement and Evaluation D

Elementary Education M
Engineering and Applied Sciences—General M
English M,D
Environmental Sciences M,D
Experimental Psychology M,D
Facilities Management M,O
Film, Television, and Video Production M
Finance and Banking M,D
French M
Geography M
Gerontology M,O
Graphic Design M,D
Health Promotion M
Health Psychology M,D
Health Services Management and Hospital Administration M,O
Higher Education D
History M,D
Hospitality Management M
Human Development M
Industrial and Labor Relations M,D
Industrial and Manufacturing Management M,D
Industrial and Organizational Psychology M,D
Information Science M,D
Information Studies M,D
Insurance M,D
Interdisciplinary Studies M,D
Interior Design M,D
Journalism M
Kinesiology and Movement Studies M
Leisure Studies M,O
Library Science M,D
Management Information Systems M,D
Management Strategy and Policy M,D
Marketing M,D
Materials Sciences M,D
Mathematics M,D
Molecular Biology M,D
Music Education M,D
Music M,D
Organizational Management M,D
Philosophy M
Photography M,D
Physics M,D
Political Science M,D
Psychology—General M,D
Public Policy and Administration M
Reading Education M,D
Real Estate M,D
Recreation and Park Management M,O
Rehabilitation Counseling M
Rehabilitation Sciences M
Religion M
School Psychology M,D
Secondary Education M
Sociology M,D
Spanish M
Special Education M,D
Textile Design M,D
Theater M
Vocational and Technical Education M,D,O

In-depth description on page 1231.

UNIVERSITY OF NORTH TEXAS HEALTH SCIENCE CENTER AT FORT WORTH

Anatomy M,D
Biochemistry M,D
Biological and Biomedical Sciences—General M,D*
Biostatistics M,D
Biotechnology M,D
Community Health M,D
Environmental and Occupational Health M,D
Epidemiology M,D
Forensic Sciences M,D
Genetics M,D
Health Services Management and Hospital Administration M,D
Immunology M,D
Microbiology M,D
Molecular Biology M,D
Osteopathic Medicine P,M
Pharmacology M,D
Physician Assistant Studies M
Physiology M,D
Public Health—General M,D*
Science Education M,D

UNIVERSITY OF NOTRE DAME

Accounting M
Aerospace/Aeronautical Engineering M,D*
Applied Arts and Design—General M
Architecture M*
Art History M
Art/Fine Arts M
Biochemistry M,D
Bioengineering M,D
Biological and Biomedical Sciences—General M,D*
Business Administration and Management—General M
Cell Biology M,D
Chemical Engineering M,D
Chemistry M,D
Civil Engineering M,D
Cognitive Sciences D
Comparative Literature D
Computer Engineering M,D
Computer Science M,D*
Conflict Resolution and Mediation/Peace Studies M
Counseling Psychology D
Developmental Psychology D
Ecology M,D
Economics M,D
Education—General M
Electrical Engineering M,D*
Engineering and Applied Sciences—General M,D
English M,D
Environmental Biology M,D
Environmental Engineering M,D
Evolutionary Biology M,D
French M
Genetics M,D
Geosciences M,D
German M
Graphic Design M
History of Science and Technology M,D
History M,D
Industrial Design M
Inorganic Chemistry M,D
Italian M
Latin American Studies M
Law P,M,D
Mathematics M,D*
Mechanical Engineering M,D
Medieval and Renaissance Studies M,D
Molecular Biology M,D
Music M
Organic Chemistry M,D
Parasitology M,D
Philosophy D
Photography M
Physical Chemistry M,D
Physics D*
Physiology M,D
Political Science D
Psychology—General D
Religion M
Romance Languages M
Sociology D
Spanish M
Theology P,M,D
Writing M

In-depth description on page 1233.

UNIVERSITY OF OKLAHOMA

Accounting M
Adult Education M,D
Advertising and Public Relations M
Aerospace/Aeronautical Engineering M,D*
Anthropology M,D
Architecture M
Art History M
Art/Fine Arts M*
Astrophysics M,D
Biochemistry M,D
Botany M,D
Business Administration and Management—General M,D*
Chemical Engineering M,D
Chemistry M,D
City and Regional Planning M
Civil Engineering M,D
Communication—General M,D
Computer Engineering M,D
Computer Science M,D
Counseling Psychology D
Curriculum and Instruction M,D,O
Dance M
Early Childhood Education M,D,O
Economics M,D
Education—General M,D,O
Educational Administration M,D
Educational Psychology M,D
Electrical Engineering M,D
Elementary Education M,D,O
Engineering and Applied Sciences—General M,D
Engineering Management M
Engineering Physics M,D
English Education M,D,O
English M,D
Environmental and Occupational Health M,D
Environmental Engineering M,D
Environmental Sciences M,D
Exercise and Sports Science M
Film, Television, and Video Production M
Foundations and Philosophy of Education M,D
French M,D
Geography M,D
Geological Engineering M,D
Geology M,D
Geophysics M
Geotechnical Engineering M,D
German M
Hazardous Materials Management M,D
Higher Education M,D
History of Science and Technology M,D
History M,D
Human Services M
Industrial/Management Engineering M,D
Information Studies M,O
Interdisciplinary Studies M,D
International Affairs M
International Business M
Journalism M
Landscape Architecture M
Law P
Liberal Studies M
Library Science M,O
Management Information Systems M
Mass Communication M
Mathematics Education M,D,O
Mathematics M,D*
Mechanical Engineering M,D
Media Studies M
Meteorology M,D
Microbiology M,D
Music Education M,D
Music M,D
Petroleum Engineering M,D
Philosophy M,D
Photography M
Physics M,D
Political Science M,D
Psychology—General M,D
Public Policy and Administration M
Reading Education M,D,O
Science Education M,D,O
Secondary Education M,D,O
Social Psychology M
Social Sciences Education M,D,O
Social Work M
Sociology M,D
Spanish M,D
Special Education M,D
Sports Management M
Structural Engineering M,D
Theater M
Transportation and Highway Engineering M,D
Water Resources M,D
Zoology M,D*

In-depth description on page 1235.

UNIVERSITY OF OKLAHOMA HEALTH SCIENCES CENTER

Allied Health—General M,D,O
Allopathic Medicine P
Biochemistry M,D*
Biological and Biomedical Sciences—General M,D*
Biopsychology M,D
Biostatistics M,D
Cell Biology M,D
Communication Disorders M,D,O
Dentistry P
Environmental and Occupational Health M,D
Epidemiology M,D
Health Education D
Health Physics/Radiological Health M,D
Health Promotion M,D
Health Services Management and Hospital Administration M,D
Immunology M,D
Medical Physics M,D
Microbiology M,D
Molecular Biology M,D
Molecular Medicine M,D
Neuroscience M,D
Nursing—General M
Nutrition M
Oral and Dental Sciences M
Pathology D
Pharmaceutical Sciences M,D
Pharmacy P
Physiology M,D
Public Health—General M,D
Radiation Biology M,D
Rehabilitation Sciences M
Special Education M,D,O

UNIVERSITY OF OREGON

Accounting M,D
Anthropology M,D
Architecture M
Art History M,D
Art/Fine Arts M
Arts Administration M*
Asian Languages M,D
Asian Studies M
Biochemistry M,D
Biological and Biomedical Sciences—General M,D*
Biopsychology M,D
Business Administration and Management—General M,D
Chemistry M,D
City and Regional Planning M
Classics M
Clinical Psychology D
Cognitive Sciences M,D
Communication—General M,D
Comparative Literature M,D
Computer Science M,D*
Dance M
Developmental Psychology M,D
Ecology M,D
Economics M,D
Education—General M,D
English M,D
Environmental Management and Policy M*
Evolutionary Biology M,D
Exercise and Sports Science M,D
Finance and Banking D
Folklore M
French M
Genetics M,D
Geography M,D
Geology M,D
German M,D
Historic Preservation M
History M,D
Information Science M,D
Interdisciplinary Studies M
Interior Design M
International Affairs M
Italian M
Journalism M,D
Kinesiology and Movement Studies M,D
Landscape Architecture M
Law P
Linguistics M,D
Management Information Systems M
Marine Biology M,D
Marketing D
Mathematics M,D
Molecular Biology M,D
Music Education M,D
Music M,D
Neuroscience M,D
Philosophy M,D
Physics M,D
Political Science M,D
Psychology—General M,D
Public Policy and Administration M
Quantitative Analysis M,D
Romance Languages M,D
Russian M
Social Psychology M,D
Sociology M,D
Spanish M
Theater M,D
Writing M

UNIVERSITY OF OTTAWA

Aerospace/Aeronautical Engineering M,D
Allied Health—General M
Allopathic Medicine M,D
Biochemistry M,D
Biological and Biomedical Sciences—General M,D
Business Administration and Management—General M,O*
Canadian Studies D
Cell Biology M,D
Chemical Engineering M,D
Chemistry M,D
Civil Engineering M,D
Classics M,D
Communication Disorders M
Community Health M
Computer Engineering M,D,O
Computer Science M,D,O
Criminal Justice and Criminology M
Economics M,D
Education—General M,D
Electrical Engineering M,D,O
Engineering and Applied Sciences—General M,D,O
Engineering Management M,O
English M,D
Epidemiology M
French M,D
Geography M,D
Geosciences M,D
Health Services Management and Hospital Administration M

University of Ottawa (continued)

History M,D
Immunology M,D
International Business M
Kinesiology and Movement Studies M
Law M,D,O
Legal and Justice Studies M,D,O
Linguistics M,D
Mathematics M,D
Mechanical Engineering M,D
Microbiology M,D
Molecular Biology M,D
Music M
Nursing—General M
Philosophy M,D
Physics M,D
Political Science M,D
Psychology—General D
Public Health—General D
Religion M,D
Social Work M
Sociology M
Spanish M,D,O
Statistics M,D
Systems Science M,O
Translation and Interpretation M,D,O
Women's Studies M

UNIVERSITY OF PENNSYLVANIA

Accounting M,D
Advanced Practice Nursing M,O
Allopathic Medicine P
American Studies M,D
Anthropology M,D
Archaeology M,D
Architecture M,D,O*
Art History M,D
Art/Fine Arts M
Asian Studies M,D
Astrophysics D
Biochemistry D*
Bioengineering M,D
Bioethics
Biological and Biomedical Sciences—General M,D*
Biomedical Engineering M,D
Biophysics D
Biostatistics M,D
Biotechnology M*
Business Administration and Management—General M,D
Cancer Biology/Oncology D*
Cell Biology D*
Chemical Engineering M,D
Chemistry M,D
City and Regional Planning M,D,O*
Classics M,D
Clinical Psychology D
Communication—General M,D
Comparative Literature M,D
Computer Science M,D*
Counseling Psychology M
Demography and Population Studies M,D
Dentistry P
Developmental Biology D*
Early Childhood Education M
Ecology D*
Economics M,D
Education—General M,D*
Educational Administration M,D
Educational Measurement and Evaluation M,D
Electrical Engineering M,D*
Elementary Education M
Engineering and Applied Sciences—General M,D,O*
English as a Second Language M,D
English M,D
Environmental Engineering M,D
Epidemiology M,D
Finance and Banking M,D
Folklore M,D
Foundations and Philosophy of Education M,D
French M,D
Genetics D*
Geology M,D
German M,D
Gerontological Nursing M
Health Services Management and Hospital Administration M,D
Higher Education M,D
Historic Preservation M,O
History of Science and Technology M,D
History M,D
Human Development M,D
Immunology D*
Information Science M,D
Insurance M,D
International Affairs M
International Business M
Italian M,D
Landscape Architecture M,O
Law P,M,D
Linguistics M,D
Management Information Systems M,D
Management of Technology M,O
Marketing M,D
Materials Engineering M,D
Materials Sciences M,D*
Maternal/Child Nursing M,O
Mathematics M,D
Mechanical Engineering M,D
Mechanics M,D
Medical/Surgical Nursing M
Microbiology D*
Molecular Biology D
Multilingual and Multicultural Education M,D
Music M,D
Near and Middle Eastern Studies M,D
Neurobiology D
Neuroscience D*
Nurse Midwifery M
Nursing and Healthcare Administration M,D
Nursing—General M,D,O
Occupational Health Nursing M
Oncology Nursing M
Organizational Behavior M
Organizational Management M
Parasitology D*
Pediatric Nursing M
Pharmacology D*
Philosophy M,D
Physics D
Physiology D*
Plant Biology D
Political Science M,D*
Psychiatric Nursing M
Psychology—General D
Public Policy and Administration M,D*
Reading Education M,D
Real Estate M,D
Religion D
Romance Languages M,D
School Psychology D
Secondary Education M
Social Psychology D
Social Work M,D*
Sociology M,D
Spanish M,D
Statistics M,D
Structural Biology D
Systems Engineering M,D*
Technology and Public Policy M,D
Telecommunications Management M
Telecommunications M*
Transportation and Highway Engineering M,D
Veterinary Medicine P
Virology D
Women's Health Nursing M
Writing M,D

In-depth description on page 1237.

UNIVERSITY OF PHOENIX–BOSTON CAMPUS

Business Administration and Management—General M
International Business M
Management of Technology M

UNIVERSITY OF PHOENIX–CHICAGO CAMPUS

Business Administration and Management—General M
Electronic Commerce M
Organizational Management M

UNIVERSITY OF PHOENIX–COLORADO CAMPUS

Business Administration and Management—General M
Education—General M
Electronic Commerce M
Management Information Systems M
Management of Technology M
Nursing—General M
Organizational Management M

UNIVERSITY OF PHOENIX–DALLAS CAMPUS

Business Administration and Management—General M
Electronic Commerce M
Organizational Management M

UNIVERSITY OF PHOENIX–FORT LAUDERDALE CAMPUS

Business Administration and Management—General M
Health Services Management and Hospital Administration M
Management Information Systems M
Management of Technology M
Nursing—General M
Organizational Management M

UNIVERSITY OF PHOENIX–HAWAII CAMPUS

Advanced Practice Nursing M
Business Administration and Management—General M
Counselor Education M,O
Education—General M,O
Electronic Commerce M
Health Services Management and Hospital Administration M
Management Information Systems M
Marriage and Family Therapy M
Nursing—General M
Organizational Management M
Psychology—General M
Secondary Education M,O
Social Psychology M
Special Education M,O

UNIVERSITY OF PHOENIX–HOUSTON CAMPUS

Business Administration and Management—General M
Electronic Commerce M
Organizational Management M

UNIVERSITY OF PHOENIX–JACKSONVILLE CAMPUS

Business Administration and Management—General M
Health Services Management and Hospital Administration M
Management Information Systems M
Management of Technology M
Nursing—General M
Organizational Management M

UNIVERSITY OF PHOENIX–KANSAS CITY CAMPUS

Business Administration and Management—General M
Electronic Commerce M
Organizational Management M

UNIVERSITY OF PHOENIX–LOUISIANA CAMPUS

Business Administration and Management—General M
Curriculum and Instruction M
Education—General M
Educational Media/Instructional Technology M
Electronic Commerce M
Health Services Management and Hospital Administration M
Management of Technology M
Nursing—General M
Organizational Management M

UNIVERSITY OF PHOENIX–MARYLAND CAMPUS

Business Administration and Management—General M
International Business M
Management Information Systems M
Management of Technology M
Organizational Management M

UNIVERSITY OF PHOENIX–METRO DETROIT CAMPUS

Business Administration and Management—General M
Health Services Management and Hospital Administration M
International Business M
Management Information Systems M
Management of Technology M
Nursing—General M
Organizational Management M

UNIVERSITY OF PHOENIX–NEVADA CAMPUS

Business Administration and Management—General M
Counselor Education M
Education—General M
Educational Administration M
Management Information Systems M
Organizational Management M

UNIVERSITY OF PHOENIX–NEW MEXICO CAMPUS

Business Administration and Management—General M
Counseling Psychology M
Education—General M
Health Services Management and Hospital Administration M
International Business M
Management Information Systems M
Management of Technology M
Marriage and Family Therapy M
Nursing—General M
Organizational Management M
Psychology—General M

UNIVERSITY OF PHOENIX–NORTHERN CALIFORNIA CAMPUS

Business Administration and Management—General M
Curriculum and Instruction M
Education—General M
Educational Media/Instructional Technology M
International Business M
Management Information Systems M
Management of Technology M
Nursing and Healthcare Administration M
Nursing—General M
Organizational Management M

UNIVERSITY OF PHOENIX–OHIO CAMPUS

Business Administration and Management—General M
Electronic Commerce M
International Business M
Management Information Systems M

UNIVERSITY OF PHOENIX–OKLAHOMA CITY CAMPUS

Business Administration and Management—General M
Electronic Commerce M
Management Information Systems M
Organizational Management M

UNIVERSITY OF PHOENIX–OREGON CAMPUS

Business Administration and Management—General M
Education—General M
Management of Technology M
Organizational Management M

UNIVERSITY OF PHOENIX–ORLANDO CAMPUS

Business Administration and Management—General M
Health Services Management and Hospital Administration M
Management Information Systems M
Management of Technology M
Nursing—General M
Organizational Management M

UNIVERSITY OF PHOENIX–PHILADELPHIA CAMPUS

Business Administration and Management—General M
International Business M
Management of Technology M

UNIVERSITY OF PHOENIX–PHOENIX CAMPUS

Advanced Practice Nursing M
Business Administration and Management—General M
Computer Science M
Counseling Psychology M
Counselor Education M
Education—General M
Educational Administration M
English as a Second Language M
Health Services Management and Hospital Administration M
Information Science M
International Business M
Management of Technology M
Marriage and Family Therapy M
Nursing and Healthcare Administration M
Nursing—General M
Organizational Management M
Social Psychology M
Women's Health Nursing M

UNIVERSITY OF PHOENIX–PITTSBURGH CAMPUS

Business Administration and Management—General M
Management of Technology M
Organizational Management M

UNIVERSITY OF PHOENIX–PUERTO RICO CAMPUS

Business Administration and Management—General M
Education—General M
Psychology—General M

UNIVERSITY OF PHOENIX–SACRAMENTO CAMPUS

Advanced Practice Nursing M
Business Administration and Management—General M
Education—General M
Electronic Commerce M
Management Information Systems M
Marriage and Family Therapy M
Nursing—General M
Organizational Management M
Psychology—General M

UNIVERSITY OF PHOENIX–ST. LOUIS CAMPUS

Business Administration and Management—General M
Electronic Commerce M
Organizational Management M

UNIVERSITY OF PHOENIX–SAN DIEGO CAMPUS

Business Administration and Management—General M
Curriculum and Instruction M
Education—General M
Educational Media/Instructional Technology M
Health Services Management and Hospital Administration M
International Business M
Management Information Systems M
Management of Technology M
Marriage and Family Therapy M
Nursing—General M
Organizational Management M
Psychology—General M

UNIVERSITY OF PHOENIX–SOUTHERN ARIZONA CAMPUS

Business Administration and Management—General M
Education—General M
Health Services Management and Hospital Administration M
International Business M
Management Information Systems M
Management of Technology M
Nursing—General M
Organizational Management M
Psychology—General M

UNIVERSITY OF PHOENIX–SOUTHERN CALIFORNIA CAMPUS

Advanced Practice Nursing M
Business Administration and Management—General M
Curriculum and Instruction M
Education—General M
Educational Media/Instructional Technology M
Health Services Management and Hospital Administration M
Management of Technology M
Nursing—General M
Organizational Management M

UNIVERSITY OF PHOENIX–SOUTHERN COLORADO CAMPUS

Business Administration and Management—General M
Education—General M
Management Information Systems M
Management of Technology M
Nursing—General M
Organizational Management M

UNIVERSITY OF PHOENIX–TAMPA CAMPUS

Business Administration and Management—General M
Health Services Management and Hospital Administration M
Management Information Systems M
Management of Technology M
Nursing—General M
Organizational Management M

UNIVERSITY OF PHOENIX–TULSA CAMPUS

Business Administration and Management—General M
Electronic Commerce M
Health Services Management and Hospital Administration M
Management Information Systems M
Organizational Management M

UNIVERSITY OF PHOENIX–UTAH CAMPUS

Business Administration and Management—General M
Education—General M
International Business M
Management Information Systems M
Nursing—General M
Organizational Management M
Psychology—General M

UNIVERSITY OF PHOENIX-VANCOUVER CAMPUS

Business Administration and Management—General M
Curriculum and Instruction M
Education—General M
Organizational Management M

UNIVERSITY OF PHOENIX–WASHINGTON CAMPUS

Business Administration and Management—General M
Management of Technology M
Organizational Management M

UNIVERSITY OF PHOENIX–WEST MICHIGAN CAMPUS

Business Administration and Management—General M
Electronic Commerce M
Health Services Management and Hospital Administration M
Management of Technology M
Nursing—General M
Organizational Management M

UNIVERSITY OF PITTSBURGH

Advanced Practice Nursing M
Allopathic Medicine P
Anthropology M,D
Applied Mathematics M
Architectural History M,D
Art History M,D
Asian Studies M
Astronomy M,D
Biochemistry M,D*
Bioengineering M,D*
Bioethics M
Bioinformatics M,D,O
Biological and Biomedical Sciences—General M,D*
Biomedical Engineering M,D
Biophysics D*
Biostatistics M,D
Business Administration and Management—General M,D*
Cell Biology M,D*
Chemical Engineering M,D
Chemistry M,D*
Child and Family Studies M
City and Regional Planning M
Civil Engineering M,D
Classics M,D
Clinical Research M,O
Cognitive Sciences D
Communication Disorders M,D
Communication—General M,D
Community Health M,D,O
Computer Science M,D
Criminal Justice and Criminology M,D
Cultural Studies M,D
Dentistry P,O
Developmental Biology D*
Developmental Psychology D
Early Childhood Education M
Ecology M,D*
Economics M,D
Education—General M,D
Educational Administration M,D
Educational Measurement and Evaluation M,D
Educational Psychology D
Electrical Engineering M,D*
Elementary Education M
Engineering and Applied Sciences—General M,D,O
English as a Second Language M,O
English Education M,D
English M,D*
Environmental and Occupational Health M,D
Environmental Engineering M,D
Environmental Management and Policy M
Epidemiology M,D
Evolutionary Biology M,D
Exercise and Sports Science M,D
Foreign Languages Education M,D
Foundations and Philosophy of Education M,D
French M,D
Genetic Counseling M
Genetics M,D
Geographic Information Systems M,D
Geology M,D
German M,D
Gerontology M,D,O
Health Education M,O
Health Physics/Radiological Health M,O
Health Promotion M
Health Services Management and Hospital Administration M,D,O
Higher Education M,D
Hispanic Studies M,D
History of Science and Technology M,D
History M,D
Human Development M
Human Genetics M,D
Human Resources Development M
Human Resources Management O
Immunology M,D*
Industrial/Management Engineering M,D
Information Science M,D,O*
Information Studies M,D,O
International Affairs M,D
International and Comparative Education M,D
International Business M
International Development M
Italian M
Kinesiology and Movement Studies M,D
Latin American Studies M,O
Law P,M,O
Legal and Justice Studies M,O
Library Science M,D,O
Linguistics M,D
Management Information Systems M
Manufacturing Engineering M
Marriage and Family Therapy O
Materials Engineering M,D
Materials Sciences M,D
Mathematics Education M,D
Mathematics M,D
Mechanical Engineering M,D
Metallurgical Engineering and Metallurgy M,D
Microbiology M,D*
Military and Defense Studies M
Molecular Biology D*
Music M,D
Neurobiology M,D
Neuroscience D*
Nonprofit Management M,O
Nurse Anesthesia M
Nursing and Healthcare Administration M
Nursing Education M
Nursing—General M,D
Oral and Dental Sciences M,O
Pathology M,D*
Pediatric Nursing M
Petroleum Engineering M,D
Pharmaceutical Sciences M,D
Pharmacology D*
Pharmacy P
Philosophy M,D
Physical Therapy M
Physics M,D*
Physiology M,D*
Planetary and Space Sciences M,D
Political Science M,D
Psychiatric Nursing M
Psychology—General M,D
Public Health—General M,D,O*
Public Policy and Administration M,D*
Reading Education M,D
Rehabilitation Sciences M,D,O*
Religion M,D
Science Education M,D
Secondary Education M,D
Slavic Languages M,D
Social Sciences Education M,D
Social Work M,D,O
Sociology M,D
Spanish M,D
Special Education M,D
Statistics M,D
Systems Engineering M
Telecommunications M,O
Theater M,D
Virology M,D
Women's Studies O
Writing M,D

In-depth description on page 1239.

UNIVERSITY OF PORTLAND

Advanced Practice Nursing M,O
Business Administration and Management—General M
Communication—General M
Corporate and Organizational Communication M
Early Childhood Education M
Education—General M
Engineering and Applied Sciences—General M
Music M
Nursing and Healthcare Administration M,O
Nursing Education M,O
Nursing—General M,O
Pastoral Ministry and Counseling M
Religious Education M
Secondary Education M
Special Education M
Theater M

UNIVERSITY OF PRINCE EDWARD ISLAND

Anatomy M,D
Bacteriology M,D
Epidemiology M,D
Immunology M,D
Parasitology M,D
Pathology M,D
Pharmacology M,D
Physiology M,D
Toxicology M,D
Veterinary Medicine P
Veterinary Sciences M,D
Virology M,D

UNIVERSITY OF PUERTO RICO, MAYAGÜEZ CAMPUS

Agricultural Economics and Agribusiness M
Agricultural Education M
Agricultural Sciences—General M
Agronomy and Soil Sciences M
Animal Sciences M
Applied Mathematics M
Biological and Biomedical Sciences—General M
Business Administration and Management—General M
Chemical Engineering M
Chemistry M
Civil Engineering M,D
Computational Sciences M
Computer Engineering M
Electrical Engineering M
Engineering and Applied Sciences—General M,D
English M
Food Science and Technology M
Geology M*
Hispanic Studies M
Horticulture M
Industrial/Management Engineering M
Marine Sciences M,D*
Mathematics M
Mechanical Engineering M
Oceanography M,D
Physics M
Statistics M

UNIVERSITY OF PUERTO RICO, MEDICAL SCIENCES CAMPUS

Allied Health—General M
Allopathic Medicine P
Anatomy M,D
Biochemistry M,D
Biological and Biomedical Sciences—General M,D*
Biostatistics M
Clinical Laboratory Sciences/Medical Technology M
Communication Disorders M
Demography and Population Studies M
Dentistry P
Environmental and Occupational Health M,D
Epidemiology M
Gerontology M,O
Health Education M
Health Informatics M
Health Services Management and Hospital Administration M
Health Services Research M
Industrial Hygiene M
Maternal and Child Health M
Medicinal and Pharmaceutical Chemistry P,M
Microbiology M,D
Nurse Anesthesia M
Nurse Midwifery M,O
Nursing and Healthcare Administration M
Nursing Education M
Nursing—General M
Nutrition M,D
Oral and Dental Sciences M,O
Pharmaceutical Sciences P,M
Pharmacology M,D
Pharmacy P,M
Physiology M,D
Public Health—General M
Special Education O

University of Puerto Rico, Medical Sciences Campus (continued)

Toxicology M,D
Zoology M,D

UNIVERSITY OF PUERTO RICO, RÍO PIEDRAS

Applied Physics M,D
Architecture M
Biological and Biomedical Sciences—General M,D
Business Administration and Management—General M,D
Chemistry M,D*
City and Regional Planning M
Comparative Literature M
Counselor Education M,D
Curriculum and Instruction M,D
Early Childhood Education M
Economics M
Education—General M,D
Educational Administration M,D
Educational Measurement and Evaluation M
English Education M,D
English M
Family and Consumer Sciences-General M
Foreign Languages Education M,D
Hispanic Studies M,D
History M,D
Information Studies M,O
Law P
Library Science M,O
Linguistics M
Mass Communication M
Mathematics Education M,D
Mathematics M
Nutrition M
Philosophy M
Physical Chemistry M,D
Physics M,D
Psychology—General M,D
Public Policy and Administration M
Rehabilitation Counseling M
Science Education M,D
Secondary Education M,D
Social Sciences Education M,D
Social Work M
Sociology M
Special Education M
Translation and Interpretation M,O

UNIVERSITY OF PUGET SOUND

Counselor Education M
Education—General M
Educational Administration M
Elementary Education M
Middle School Education M
Occupational Therapy M
Pastoral Ministry and Counseling M
Physical Therapy D
Secondary Education M

UNIVERSITY OF REDLANDS

Business Administration and Management—General M
Communication Disorders M
Curriculum and Instruction M
Education—General M
Educational Administration M
Human Resources Management M
Music M

UNIVERSITY OF REGINA

Analytical Chemistry M,D
Anthropology M,D
Art/Fine Arts M
Biochemistry M,D
Biological and Biomedical Sciences—General M,D
Business Administration and Management—General M
Canadian Studies M,D
Chemistry M,D
Computer Engineering M,D
Computer Science M,D
Curriculum and Instruction M
Economics M
Education—General M,D,O
Educational Administration M,O
Educational Psychology M,D,O
Engineering and Applied Sciences—General M,D
English M,D
Environmental Engineering M,D
French M
Geography M
Geology M
History M
Human Resources Development M
Human Resources Management M
Industrial/Management Engineering M,D
Inorganic Chemistry M,D
Kinesiology and Movement Studies M
Linguistics M
Mathematics M,D
Music M
Native American Studies M,D
Organic Chemistry M,D
Petroleum Engineering M,D
Philosophy M
Physical Chemistry M,D
Physics M,D
Political Science M
Psychology—General M,D
Public Policy and Administration M
Religion M
Social Sciences M
Social Work M
Sociology M
Statistics M,D
Systems Engineering M,D
Vocational and Technical Education M,O

UNIVERSITY OF RHODE ISLAND

Accounting M
Adult Education M
Agricultural Economics and Agribusiness M,D
Animal Sciences M
Applied Mathematics M,D
Aquaculture M
Biochemistry M,D
Botany M,D
Business Administration and Management—General M,D
Chemical Engineering M,D
Chemistry M,D
Child and Family Studies M
City and Regional Planning M
Civil Engineering M,D
Clinical Laboratory Sciences/ Medical Technology M
Clinical Psychology D
Clothing and Textiles M
Communication Disorders M
Computer Engineering M,D
Computer Science M,D
Counseling Psychology M
Economics M,D*
Education—General M
Electrical Engineering M,D*
Elementary Education M
Engineering and Applied Sciences—General M,D
English M,D
Entomology M,D
Environmental Engineering M,D
Environmental Management and Policy M,D
Experimental Psychology D
Finance and Banking M,D
Fish, Game, and Wildlife Management M,D
Food Science and Technology M,D
French M
Genetics M,D
Geology M
Geotechnical Engineering M,D
Health Education M
History M
Home Economics Education M
Industrial and Labor Relations M
Industrial and Manufacturing Management M,D
Industrial/Management Engineering M
Information Studies M
International Affairs M,O
International Business M,D
International Development M,O
Library Science M
Management Information Systems M,D
Manufacturing Engineering M
Marine Affairs M,D*
Marketing M,D
Mathematics M,D
Mechanical Engineering M,D
Mechanics M,D
Medicinal and Pharmaceutical Chemistry M,D
Microbiology M,D
Music M
Natural Resources M,D
Nursing and Healthcare Administration M,D
Nursing Education M,D
Nursing—General M,D
Nutrition M,D
Ocean Engineering M,D
Oceanography M,D
Pharmaceutical Administration M
Pharmaceutical Sciences M,D
Pharmacology M,D
Pharmacy P
Philosophy M
Physical Education M
Physical Therapy M
Physics M,D
Plant Pathology M,D
Plant Sciences M,D
Political Science M,O
Psychology—General M,D
Public Policy and Administration M
Quantitative Analysis M,D
Reading Education M
Recreation and Park Management M
School Psychology M,D
Secondary Education M
Spanish M
Sports Management M,D
Statistics M,D
Structural Engineering M,D
Systems Engineering M,D
Toxicology M,D
Transportation and Highway Engineering M,D
Zoology M,D

UNIVERSITY OF RICHMOND

Biological and Biomedical Sciences—General M*
Business Administration and Management—General M
English M
History M
Law P
Liberal Studies M
Psychology—General M

In-depth description on page 1241.

UNIVERSITY OF RIO GRANDE

Art Education M
Education—General M
Mathematics Education M
Reading Education M
Special Education M

UNIVERSITY OF ROCHESTER

Allopathic Medicine P
Anatomy M,D
Art History M,D
Art/Fine Arts M,D*
Astronomy M,D
Biochemistry M,D*
Biological and Biomedical Sciences—General M,D,O*
Biomedical Engineering M,D
Biophysics M,D*
Biostatistics M,D
Business Administration and Management—General M,D
Chemical Engineering M,D
Chemistry M,D
Clinical Psychology M,D
Cognitive Sciences M,D
Computer Engineering M,D
Computer Science M,D*
Developmental Psychology M,D
Economics M,D
Education—General M,D
Electrical Engineering M,D*
Engineering and Applied Sciences—General M,D*
English M,D
Genetics M,D*
Geosciences M,D
Health Services Research D
History M,D
Immunology M,D
Marriage and Family Therapy M*
Materials Sciences M,D
Mathematics M,D
Mechanical Engineering M,D
Microbiology M,D*
Molecular Medicine
Music Education M,D
Music M,D
Neurobiology M,D
Neuroscience M,D*
Nursing—General M,D,O
Optical Sciences M,D*
Oral and Dental Sciences M
Pathobiology
Pathology M,D*
Pharmacology M,D*
Philosophy M,D
Physics M,D*
Physiology M,D
Political Science M,D
Psychology—General M,D
Public Health—General M*
Social Psychology M,D
Statistics M,D*
Toxicology M,D*

Announcement on page 653.

UNIVERSITY OF ST. AUGUSTINE FOR HEALTH SCIENCES

Occupational Therapy M,D
Physical Therapy M,D

In-depth description on page 1243.

UNIVERSITY OF ST. FRANCIS (IL)

Allied Health—General M
Education—General M
Nursing—General M

UNIVERSITY OF SAINT FRANCIS (IN)

Allied Health—General M
Art/Fine Arts M
Business Administration and Management—General M
Counseling Psychology M
Counselor Education M
Education—General M
Nursing—General M
Physician Assistant Studies M
Psychology—General M
Special Education M

UNIVERSITY OF SAINT MARY OF THE LAKE–MUNDELEIN SEMINARY

Theology P,D,O

UNIVERSITY OF ST. MICHAEL'S COLLEGE

Theology P,M,D

UNIVERSITY OF ST. THOMAS (MN)

Accounting M,O
Advertising and Public Relations M,O
Art History M*
Business Administration and Management—General M,O*
Corporate and Organizational Communication M,O
Counseling Psychology M,D,O
Curriculum and Instruction M,D,O
Education—General M
Educational Administration M,D,O
Electronic Commerce M,O
Engineering and Applied Sciences—General M,O
Engineering Management M,O
English M*
Environmental Management and Policy M,O
Finance and Banking M,O
Health Services Management and Hospital Administration M,O
Human Development M,D,O
Human Resources Management M,O
Industrial and Manufacturing Management M,O
Insurance M,O
International Business M,O
Management Information Systems M,O
Management of Technology M,O
Manufacturing Engineering M,O
Marketing M,O
Marriage and Family Therapy M,D,O
Music Education M
Nonprofit Management M,O
Organizational Management M,D,O
Pastoral Ministry and Counseling M,D
Psychology—General M,D,O
Reading Education M,D,O
Real Estate M,O
Religion M
Religious Education M,D
Social Work M
Software Engineering M,O*
Special Education M,O
Sports Management M,O
Systems Engineering M,O
Theology P,M,D
Writing M,O

In-depth description on page 1245.

UNIVERSITY OF ST. THOMAS (TX)

Business Administration and Management—General M
Education—General M
Liberal Studies M
Philosophy M,D
Theology P,M

UNIVERSITY OF SAN DIEGO

Advanced Practice Nursing M,D,O
Business Administration and Management—General M*
Counselor Education M
Curriculum and Instruction M,D
Education—General M,D
Educational Administration M,D
Electronic Commerce M
Geosciences M,D,O
History M
International Affairs M
Law P,M,O

Program	Degrees
Legal and Justice Studies	P,M,O
Marine Affairs	M
Marine Sciences	M
Marriage and Family Therapy	M
Medical/Surgical Nursing	M,D,O
Nursing and Healthcare Administration	M,D,O
Nursing—General	M,D,O
Pastoral Ministry and Counseling	M
Pediatric Nursing	M,D,O
Taxation	P,M,O
Theater	M
Theology	M

In-depth description on page 1247.

UNIVERSITY OF SAN FRANCISCO

Program	Degrees
Advanced Practice Nursing	M
Asian Studies	M*
Biological and Biomedical Sciences—General	M
Business Administration and Management—General	M
Chemistry	M*
Computer Science	M
Counseling Psychology	M,D
Counselor Education	M,D
Curriculum and Instruction	M,D
Economics	M
Education—General	M,D*
Educational Administration	M,D
Educational Media/Instructional Technology	M,D
English as a Second Language	M,D
Environmental Management and Policy	M
Finance and Banking	M
Health Services Management and Hospital Administration	M
Human Resources Development	M
International and Comparative Education	M,D
International Business	M
Law	P
Management Information Systems	M
Marketing	M
Marriage and Family Therapy	M,D
Medical/Surgical Nursing	M
Multilingual and Multicultural Education	M,D
Nonprofit Management	M
Nursing and Healthcare Administration	M
Nursing—General	M*
Organizational Management	M
Pastoral Ministry and Counseling	M
Public Policy and Administration	M
Religious Education	M,D
Sports Management	M
Telecommunications Management	M
Theology	M
Writing	M*

In-depth description on page 1249.

UNIVERSITY OF SASKATCHEWAN

Program	Degrees
Accounting	M
Agricultural Economics and Agribusiness	M,D
Agricultural Engineering	M,D
Agricultural Sciences—General	M,D
Agronomy and Soil Sciences	M,D
Allopathic Medicine	P
Anatomy	M,D
Animal Sciences	M,D,O
Anthropology	M,D
Art/Fine Arts	M
Biochemistry	M,D,O
Biological and Biomedical Sciences—General	M,D,O
Biomedical Engineering	M,D
Business Administration and Management—General	M,D,O
Canadian Studies	M,D
Cell Biology	M,D
Chemical Engineering	M,D
Chemistry	M,D
Civil Engineering	M,D
Community Health	M,D
Computer Science	M,D
Curriculum and Instruction	M,D,O
Dentistry	P
East European and Russian Studies	M
Economics	M
Education—General	M,D,O
Educational Administration	M,D,O
Educational Psychology	M,D,O
Electrical Engineering	M,D
Engineering and Applied Sciences—General	M,D,O
English	M,D
Environmental Engineering	M,D,O
Epidemiology	M,D
Finance and Banking	M
Food Science and Technology	M,D
Foundations and Philosophy of Education	M,D,O
French	M
Gender Studies	M,D
Geography	M,D
Geology	M,D,O
German	M
History	M,D
Industrial and Labor Relations	M
Kinesiology and Movement Studies	M,D,O
Law	P,M
Marketing	M
Mathematics	M,D
Mechanical Engineering	M,D,O
Microbiology	M,D
Music	M
Nursing—General	M
Organizational Behavior	M
Pathology	M,D
Pharmaceutical Sciences	M,D
Pharmacology	M,D
Philosophy	M
Physics	M,D
Physiology	M,D
Plant Sciences	M,D
Political Science	M,D
Psychology—General	M,D
Reproductive Biology	M,D
Sociology	M,D
Special Education	M,D,O
Statistics	M,D
Theater	M
Toxicology	M,D,O
Veterinary Medicine	P,M,D,O
Veterinary Sciences	M,D,O
Women's Studies	M,D

Announcement on page 657.

THE UNIVERSITY OF SCRANTON

Program	Degrees
Accounting	M
Advanced Practice Nursing	M
Biochemistry	M
Business Administration and Management—General	M
Chemistry	M
Counseling Psychology	M,O
Counselor Education	M
Early Childhood Education	M
Education—General	M
Educational Administration	M
Elementary Education	M
English	M
Finance and Banking	M
Health Services Management and Hospital Administration	M
History	M
Human Resources Development	M
Human Resources Management	M
International Business	M
Management Information Systems	M
Management of Technology	M
Marketing	M
Medical/Surgical Nursing	M
Nurse Anesthesia	M
Nursing—General	M
Occupational Therapy	M
Organizational Management	M
Physical Therapy	M
Reading Education	M
Rehabilitation Counseling	M
Secondary Education	M
Social Psychology	M
Software Engineering	M
Theology	M

In-depth description on page 1251.

UNIVERSITY OF SIOUX FALLS

Program	Degrees
Business Administration and Management—General	M
Education—General	M
Educational Administration	M
Educational Media/Instructional Technology	M
Reading Education	M

UNIVERSITY OF SOUTH ALABAMA

Program	Degrees
Accounting	M
Allied Health—General	M,D
Allopathic Medicine	P
Art Education	M
Biochemistry	D
Biological and Biomedical Sciences—General	M,D*
Business Administration and Management—General	M
Business Education	M
Cell Biology	D
Chemical Engineering	M
Communication Disorders	M,D
Communication—General	M
Computer Science	M
Counselor Education	M,O
Early Childhood Education	M,O
Education of the Gifted	M
Education of the Multiply Handicapped	M
Education—General	M,D,O
Educational Administration	M,O
Educational Media/Instructional Technology	M,D
Electrical Engineering	M
Elementary Education	M,O
Engineering and Applied Sciences—General	M
English	M
Exercise and Sports Science	M
Gerontology	O
Health Education	M
History	M
Immunology	D
Information Science	M
Leisure Studies	M
Marine Sciences	M,D
Maternal/Child Nursing	M
Mathematics	M
Mechanical Engineering	M
Medical/Surgical Nursing	M
Microbiology	D
Molecular Biology	D
Music Education	M
Neuroscience	D
Nursing—General	M
Pharmacology	D
Physical Education	M,O
Physician Assistant Studies	M
Physiology	D
Psychiatric Nursing	M
Psychology—General	M
Public Policy and Administration	M
Reading Education	M
Recreation and Park Management	M
Science Education	M
Secondary Education	M,O
Sociology	M
Special Education	M,O

In-depth description on page 1253.

UNIVERSITY OF SOUTH CAROLINA

Program	Degrees
Accounting	M,D
Advanced Practice Nursing	O
Allopathic Medicine	P
Anthropology	M
Art Education	M,D
Art History	M
Art/Fine Arts	M
Astronomy	M,D
Biochemistry	M,D
Biological and Biomedical Sciences—General	M,D*
Biostatistics	M,D
Business Administration and Management—General	M,D*
Business Education	M,D
Cell Biology	M,D
Chemical Engineering	M,D
Chemistry	M,D
Civil Engineering	M,D
Clinical Psychology	D
Communication Disorders	M,D
Community Health Nursing	M
Computer Engineering	M,D
Computer Science	M,D
Counselor Education	D,O
Criminal Justice and Criminology	M
Curriculum and Instruction	M,D,O
Developmental Biology	M,D
Early Childhood Education	M,D
Ecology	M,D*
Economics	M,D
Education—General	M,D,O
Educational Administration	M,D,O
Educational Measurement and Evaluation	M,D
Educational Media/Instructional Technology	M
Educational Psychology	M,D
Electrical Engineering	M,D
Elementary Education	M,D
Engineering and Applied Sciences—General	M,D
English as a Second Language	M,D,O
English Education	M,D
English	M,D
Environmental and Occupational Health	M,D
Environmental Management and Policy	M
Environmental Sciences	M,D
Epidemiology	M,D
Evolutionary Biology	M,D
Exercise and Sports Science	M,D
Experimental Psychology	M,D
Foreign Languages Education	M,D
Foundations and Philosophy of Education	D
Genetic Counseling	M
Geography	M,D
Geology	M,D*
Geosciences	M,D
German	M
Gerontology	O
Hazardous Materials Management	M,D
Health Education	M,D,O
Health Promotion	M,D,O
Health Services Management and Hospital Administration	M,D
Higher Education	M
Historic Preservation	M,O
History	M,D,O
Hospitality Management	M
Human Resources Management	M
Industrial Hygiene	M,D
Information Studies	M,O
International Affairs	M,D
International Business	M
Journalism	M,D
Law	P
Library Science	M,O
Linguistics	M,D,O
Marine Sciences	M,D
Mathematics Education	M,D
Mathematics	M,D
Mechanical Engineering	M,D*
Media Studies	M
Medical/Surgical Nursing	M
Molecular Biology	M,D*
Museum Studies	M,O
Music Education	M,D
Music	M,D,O
Nurse Anesthesia	M
Nursing and Healthcare Administration	M
Nursing—General	M,D,O
Pharmaceutical Sciences	M,D
Pharmacy	P
Philosophy	M,D
Physical Education	M,D
Physics	M,D*
Political Science	M,D
Psychiatric Nursing	M,O
Psychology—General	M,D
Public Health—General	M
Public History	M,O
Public Policy and Administration	M
Reading Education	M,D
Rehabilitation Sciences	M,O
Religion	M
School Psychology	D
Science Education	M,D
Secondary Education	M,D,O
Social Psychology	D
Social Sciences Education	M,D,O
Social Work	M,D
Sociology	M,D
Software Engineering	M,D
Spanish	M
Special Education	M,D
Speech and Interpersonal Communication	M,D
Statistics	M,D,O
Student Personnel Services	M
Taxation	M
Theater	M,D
Travel and Tourism	M
Vocational and Technical Education	M
Women's Health Nursing	O
Women's Studies	O
Writing	M,D

In-depth description on page 1255.

UNIVERSITY OF SOUTH CAROLINA AIKEN

Program	Degrees
Clinical Psychology	M
Education—General	M
Educational Media/Instructional Technology	M
Elementary Education	M

UNIVERSITY OF SOUTH CAROLINA SPARTANBURG

Program	Degrees
Early Childhood Education	M
Education—General	M
Elementary Education	M

THE UNIVERSITY OF SOUTH DAKOTA

Program	Degrees
Accounting	M
Allied Health—General	M
Allopathic Medicine	P
Art/Fine Arts	M
Biological and Biomedical Sciences—General	M,D
Business Administration and Management—General	M
Cardiovascular Sciences	M,D
Cell Biology	M,D
Chemistry	M
Clinical Psychology	M,D
Communication Disorders	M

The University of South Dakota (continued)

- Computer Science M
- Counselor Education M,D,O
- Curriculum and Instruction M,D,O
- Education—General M,D,O
- Educational Administration M,D,O
- Educational Media/Instructional Technology M,O
- Educational Psychology M,D,O
- Elementary Education M
- English M,D
- Health Education M
- History M
- Immunology M,D
- Interdisciplinary Studies M
- Law P
- Mass Communication M
- Mathematics M
- Microbiology M,D
- Molecular Biology M,D
- Music M
- Neuroscience M,D
- Occupational Therapy M
- Pharmacology M,D
- Physical Education M
- Physical Therapy M
- Physiology M,D
- Political Science M
- Psychology—General M,D
- Public Policy and Administration M
- Secondary Education M
- Sociology M
- Special Education M
- Speech and Interpersonal Communication M
- Theater M

In-depth description on page 1257.

UNIVERSITY OF SOUTHERN CALIFORNIA

- Accounting M
- Advertising and Public Relations M
- Aerospace/Aeronautical Engineering M,D,O*
- Allied Health—General M,D,O
- Allopathic Medicine P
- Anatomy M,D
- Anthropology M,D
- Applied Mathematics M,D
- Architecture M*
- Art History M,D,O
- Art/Fine Arts M
- Artificial Intelligence/Robotics M
- Arts Administration M
- Asian Languages M,D
- Asian Studies M,D
- Biochemistry M,D
- Biological and Biomedical Sciences—General M,D*
- Biomedical Engineering M,D
- Biometrics M
- Biophysics M,D
- Biostatistics M,D*
- Building Science M
- Business Administration and Management—General M,D
- Cell Biology M,D
- Chemical Engineering M,D,O
- Chemistry M,D
- City and Regional Planning M,D*
- Civil Engineering M,D,O*
- Classics M,D
- Clinical Psychology M,D
- Communication—General M,D*
- Comparative Literature M,D
- Computer Engineering M,D
- Computer Science M,D*
- Construction Engineering and Management M*
- Corporate and Organizational Communication M,D
- Counseling Psychology M,D,O
- Curriculum and Instruction M,D
- Demography and Population Studies M
- Dentistry P,O
- Economics M,D*
- Education—General M,D,O*
- Educational Administration M,D,O
- Educational Media/Instructional Technology M,D
- Educational Psychology M,D,O
- Electrical Engineering M,D,O*
- Engineering and Applied Sciences—General M,D,O*
- Engineering Management M
- English as a Second Language M,D
- English M,D
- Environmental Engineering M,D*
- Environmental Management and Policy M
- Epidemiology M,D
- Film, Television, and Video Production M
- Film, Television, and Video Theory and Criticism M,D
- Finance and Banking M
- French M,D
- Geography M,D
- Geosciences M,D
- Geotechnical Engineering M
- Gerontology M,D,O*
- Health Promotion M
- Health Services Management and Hospital Administration M*
- Health Services Research M,D
- History M,D
- Immunology M,D
- Industrial/Management Engineering M,D,O
- International Affairs M,D
- International and Comparative Education M,D
- International Business M
- Internet and Interactive Multimedia M,D
- Journalism M*
- Kinesiology and Movement Studies M,D
- Landscape Architecture M
- Law P
- Linguistics M,D
- Management Information Systems M
- Manufacturing Engineering M
- Marine Biology M,D*
- Marine Sciences M,D
- Marriage and Family Therapy M,D,O
- Mass Communication M,D
- Materials Engineering M
- Materials Sciences M,D,O
- Mathematics M,D*
- Mechanical Engineering M,D,O*
- Mechanics M
- Media Studies M
- Microbiology M,D
- Molecular Biology M,D*
- Music Education M,D
- Music M,D
- Neurobiology M,D
- Neuroscience D*
- Nursing—General M,O*
- Nutrition M
- Occupational Therapy M,D
- Ocean Engineering M
- Oceanography M,D
- Operations Research M
- Oral and Dental Sciences M,D
- Pathobiology M,D*
- Pathology M,D
- Petroleum Engineering M,D,O
- Pharmaceutical Sciences M,D*
- Pharmacology M,D*
- Pharmacy P
- Philosophy M,D
- Physical Chemistry D
- Physical Therapy M,D
- Physics M,D
- Physiology M,D
- Political Science M,D
- Psychology—General M,D
- Public Health—General M*
- Public Policy and Administration M,D,O
- Reading Education M,D
- Real Estate M*
- Religion M,D
- Slavic Languages M,D
- Social Work M,D
- Sociology M,D
- Software Engineering M
- Special Education M,D
- Speech and Interpersonal Communication M,D
- Statistics M
- Structural Engineering M
- Student Personnel Services M,D,O
- Systems Engineering M,D,O
- Taxation M
- Theater M*
- Toxicology M,D
- Transportation and Highway Engineering M
- Water Resources Engineering M
- Writing M

In-depth description on page 1259.

UNIVERSITY OF SOUTHERN COLORADO

- Biological and Biomedical Sciences—General M
- Business Administration and Management—General M
- Education—General M
- Engineering and Applied Sciences—General M
- Industrial/Management Engineering M
- Systems Engineering M

UNIVERSITY OF SOUTHERN INDIANA

- Accounting M
- Business Administration and Management—General M
- Education—General M
- Elementary Education M
- Engineering and Applied Sciences—General M
- Health Services Management and Hospital Administration M
- Industrial and Manufacturing Management M
- Liberal Studies M
- Nursing—General M
- Occupational Therapy M
- Secondary Education M
- Social Work M

UNIVERSITY OF SOUTHERN MAINE

- Accounting M
- Adult Education M,O
- Advanced Practice Nursing M,O
- American Studies M
- Business Administration and Management—General M
- City and Regional Planning M,O
- Computer Science M
- Counselor Education M,O
- Education—General M,O
- Educational Administration M,O
- English as a Second Language M,O
- Health Services Management and Hospital Administration M,O
- Immunology M
- Law P
- Manufacturing Engineering M
- Medical/Surgical Nursing M,O
- Molecular Biology M
- Nursing and Healthcare Administration M,O
- Nursing—General M,O
- Occupational Therapy M
- Psychiatric Nursing M,O
- Public Policy and Administration M,D
- Reading Education M,O
- School Psychology M
- Special Education M
- Vocational and Technical Education M

UNIVERSITY OF SOUTHERN MISSISSIPPI

- Accounting M
- Adult Education M,D,O
- Advanced Practice Nursing M,D
- Advertising and Public Relations M,D
- Analytical Chemistry M,D
- Anthropology M
- Art Education M
- Astronomy M
- Biochemistry M,D
- Biological and Biomedical Sciences—General M,D
- Business Administration and Management—General M
- Chemistry M,D
- Child and Family Studies M,D
- Clinical Laboratory Sciences/Medical Technology M
- Communication Disorders M,D
- Communication—General M,D
- Community Health Nursing M,D
- Computer Science M,D
- Criminal Justice and Criminology M,D
- Curriculum and Instruction M,D,O
- Early Childhood Education M,D,O
- Economics M,D
- Education of the Gifted M,D,O
- Education—General M,D,O
- Educational Administration M,D,O
- Elementary Education M,D,O
- Engineering and Applied Sciences—General M
- English M,D
- Environmental and Occupational Health M
- Environmental Biology M,D
- Family and Consumer Sciences-General M,D
- Foreign Languages Education M
- Geography M
- Geology M
- Health Education M
- Health Services Management and Hospital Administration M
- History M,D
- Hydrology M,D
- Inorganic Chemistry M,D
- Library Science M,O
- Management Information Systems M
- Marine Biology M,D
- Marine Sciences M,D
- Marriage and Family Therapy M,D
- Maternal/Child Nursing M,D
- Mathematics M
- Medical/Surgical Nursing M,D
- Microbiology M,D
- Molecular Biology M,D
- Music Education M,D
- Music M,D
- Nursing and Healthcare Administration M,D
- Nursing—General M,D
- Nutrition M,D
- Organic Chemistry M,D
- Philosophy M
- Physical Chemistry M,D
- Physical Education M,D
- Physics M
- Political Science M
- Polymer Science and Engineering M,D
- Psychiatric Nursing M,D
- Psychology—General M,D,O
- Public Health—General M
- Reading Education M,D,O
- Recreation and Park Management M,D
- Science Education M,D
- Secondary Education M,D,O
- Social Sciences Education M,D,O
- Social Work M
- Special Education M,D,O
- Sports Management M,D
- Theater M
- Vocational and Technical Education M

UNIVERSITY OF SOUTH FLORIDA

- Accounting M
- Adult Education M,D,O
- Allopathic Medicine P
- American Studies M
- Analytical Chemistry M,D
- Anatomy D
- Anthropology M,D
- Applied Mathematics M,D
- Architecture M
- Art Education M
- Art History M
- Art/Fine Arts M
- Biochemistry M,D*
- Biological and Biomedical Sciences—General M,D*
- Biomedical Engineering M
- Biophysics D
- Biostatistics M,D
- Botany M
- Business Administration and Management—General M,D
- Business Education M
- Cancer Biology/Oncology D*
- Cell Biology D
- Chemical Engineering M,D
- Chemistry M,D
- Civil Engineering M,D
- Clinical Psychology D
- Communication Disorders M,D
- Communication—General M,D
- Community College Education M
- Community Health M,D
- Computer Engineering M,D
- Computer Science M,D*
- Counselor Education M
- Criminal Justice and Criminology M,D
- Early Childhood Education M,D
- Ecology M,D
- Economics M
- Education of the Gifted M
- Education—General M,D,O*
- Educational Administration M,D,O
- Educational Measurement and Evaluation M,D,O
- Educational Media/Instructional Technology M,D
- Electrical Engineering M,D*
- Elementary Education M,D,O
- Engineering and Applied Sciences—General M,D*
- Engineering Management M,D
- Engineering Physics M,D
- English as a Second Language M
- English Education M,D
- English M,D
- Environmental and Occupational Health M,D
- Environmental Engineering M,D
- Environmental Management and Policy M
- Epidemiology M,D
- Experimental Psychology D
- Foreign Languages Education M
- French M
- Geography M
- Geology M,D
- Gerontology M
- Health Services Management and Hospital Administration M,D
- Higher Education D,O
- History M
- Hydrology M,D
- Immunology D
- Industrial and Organizational Psychology D
- Industrial/Management Engineering M,D
- Information Studies M
- Inorganic Chemistry M,D
- Liberal Studies M
- Library Science M
- Linguistics M

- Management Information Systems M
- Marine Biology M,D
- Marine Sciences M,D*
- Mass Communication M
- Mathematics Education M,D,O
- Mathematics M,D
- Mechanical Engineering M,D
- Medical Microbiology D
- Microbiology M
- Middle School Education M
- Molecular Biology D
- Music Education M,D
- Music M
- Nursing—General M,D*
- Oceanography M,D
- Organic Chemistry M,D
- Pathology D
- Pharmacology D
- Philosophy M,D
- Physical Chemistry M,D
- Physical Education M
- Physical Therapy M
- Physics M,D
- Physiology M,D
- Political Science M
- Psychology—General D
- Public Health—General M,D
- Public Policy and Administration M
- Reading Education M,D,O
- Rehabilitation Counseling M
- Religion M
- School Psychology D,O
- Science Education M,D,O
- Secondary Education D
- Social Sciences Education M
- Social Work M
- Sociology M
- Spanish M
- Special Education M,D,O
- Student Personnel Services M
- Theater M
- Vocational and Technical Education M,D,O
- Women's Studies M
- Zoology M

In-depth description on page 1261.

THE UNIVERSITY OF TAMPA

- Accounting M
- Advanced Practice Nursing M
- Business Administration and Management—General M
- Entrepreneurship M
- International Business M
- Management Information Systems M
- Management of Technology M
- Medical/Surgical Nursing M
- Nursing and Healthcare Administration M
- Nursing Education M
- Nursing—General M

THE UNIVERSITY OF TENNESSEE

- Accounting M,D
- Adult Education M
- Advertising and Public Relations M,D
- Aerospace/Aeronautical Engineering M,D
- Agricultural Economics and Agribusiness M
- Agricultural Education M
- Agricultural Engineering M,D
- Agricultural Sciences—General M,D
- Analytical Chemistry M,D
- Anatomy M,D
- Animal Behavior M,D
- Animal Sciences M,D
- Anthropology M,D
- Applied Mathematics M,D
- Archaeology M,D
- Architecture M*
- Art Education M,D,O
- Art/Fine Arts M
- Artificial Intelligence/Robotics M,D
- Aviation M
- Biochemistry M,D
- Bioethics M,D
- Biological and Biomedical Sciences—General M,D
- Biomedical Engineering M,D
- Botany M,D
- Business Administration and Management—General M,D
- Chemical Engineering M,D
- Chemistry M,D*
- Child and Family Studies M,D
- City and Regional Planning M
- Civil Engineering M,D
- Clinical Psychology M,D
- Clothing and Textiles M,D
- Communication Disorders M,D,O
- Communication—General M,D*
- Community Health M,D
- Computer Science M,D*
- Consumer Economics M,D
- Counseling Psychology M,D,O
- Counselor Education M,D,O
- Criminal Justice and Criminology M,D
- Curriculum and Instruction M,D,O
- Early Childhood Education M,D,O
- Ecology M,D
- Economics M,D*
- Education—General M,D,O
- Educational Administration M,D,O
- Educational Measurement and Evaluation M,D,O
- Educational Media/Instructional Technology M,D,O
- Educational Psychology M,D,O
- Electrical Engineering M,D
- Elementary Education M,D,O
- Engineering and Applied Sciences—General M,D*
- Engineering Management M
- English as a Second Language M,D,O
- English Education M,D,O
- English M,D
- Entomology M
- Environmental Engineering M
- Environmental Management and Policy M,D
- Evolutionary Biology M,D
- Exercise and Sports Science M,D,O
- Experimental Psychology M,D
- Family and Consumer Sciences-General D*
- Finance and Banking M,D
- Fish, Game, and Wildlife Management M
- Food Science and Technology M,D
- Foreign Languages Education M,D,O
- Forestry M
- Foundations and Philosophy of Education M,D,O
- French M,D
- Genetics M,D
- Genomic Sciences M,D
- Geography M,D
- Geology M,D
- German M,D
- Gerontology M
- Graphic Design M
- Health Education M
- Health Promotion M
- History M,D
- Horticulture M
- Hospitality Management M
- Human Resources Development M,D
- Industrial and Manufacturing Management M,D
- Industrial and Organizational Psychology D
- Industrial/Management Engineering M,D
- Information Science M,D
- Information Studies M*
- Inorganic Chemistry M,D
- Italian D
- Journalism M,D
- Law P
- Library Science M
- Linguistics D
- Logistics M,D
- Manufacturing Engineering M,D
- Marketing M,D
- Materials Engineering M,D
- Materials Sciences M,D
- Mathematics Education M,D,O
- Mathematics M,D
- Mechanical Engineering M,D
- Mechanics M,D
- Media Studies M,D
- Microbiology M,D*
- Multilingual and Multicultural Education M,D,O
- Music Education M
- Music M
- Nuclear Engineering M,D
- Nursing—General M,D
- Nutrition M*
- Organic Chemistry M,D
- Philosophy M,D
- Photography M
- Physical Chemistry M,D
- Physics M,D*
- Physiology M,D
- Plant Pathology M
- Plant Physiology M,D
- Political Science M,D
- Polymer Science and Engineering M,D
- Portuguese D
- Psychology—General M,D
- Public Health—General M
- Public Policy and Administration M
- Reading Education M,D,O
- Recreation and Park Management M
- Rehabilitation Counseling M
- Religion M,D
- Rural Sociology M
- Russian D
- School Psychology M,D,O
- Science Education M,D,O
- Secondary Education M,D,O
- Social Sciences Education M,D,O
- Social Work M,D
- Sociology M,D*
- Spanish M,D
- Special Education M,D,O
- Speech and Interpersonal Communication M,D
- Sports Management M
- Statistics M,D
- Student Personnel Services M
- Theater M
- Theoretical Chemistry M,D
- Transportation Management M,D
- Travel and Tourism M
- Veterinary Medicine P

In-depth description on page 1263.

THE UNIVERSITY OF TENNESSEE AT CHATTANOOGA

- Accounting M
- Advanced Practice Nursing M
- Business Administration and Management—General M
- Computer Science M
- Counselor Education M,O
- Criminal Justice and Criminology M
- Curriculum and Instruction M,O
- Early Childhood Education M,O
- Economics M
- Education—General M,O
- Educational Administration M,O
- Engineering and Applied Sciences—General M
- Engineering Management M
- English M
- Environmental Sciences M
- Experimental Psychology M
- Finance and Banking M
- Industrial and Manufacturing Management M
- Industrial and Organizational Psychology M
- Marketing M
- Medical/Surgical Nursing M
- Music M
- Nurse Anesthesia M
- Nursing and Healthcare Administration M
- Nursing Education M
- Nursing—General M
- Organizational Management M
- Physical Education M
- Physical Therapy M
- Psychology—General M
- Public Policy and Administration M
- Reading Education M,O
- School Psychology M
- Secondary Education M,O
- Special Education M,O

Announcement on page 666.

THE UNIVERSITY OF TENNESSEE AT MARTIN

- Accounting M
- Business Administration and Management—General M
- Child and Family Studies M
- Counselor Education M
- Curriculum and Instruction M
- Education—General M
- Educational Administration M
- Family and Consumer Sciences-General M
- Food Science and Technology M
- Nutrition M

THE UNIVERSITY OF TENNESSEE HEALTH SCIENCE CENTER

- Allied Health—General M
- Allopathic Medicine P
- Anatomy D
- Bacteriology D
- Biochemistry D
- Biological and Biomedical Sciences—General M,D
- Biomedical Engineering M,D*
- Biophysics M,D
- Cell Biology D
- Dentistry P,M
- Immunology D
- Microbiology D
- Molecular Biology D*
- Neurobiology D
- Nursing—General M,D
- Pathology M,D*
- Pharmaceutical Sciences M,D
- Pharmacology M,D
- Pharmacy P,M,D
- Physical Therapy M
- Physiology M,D*
- Structural Biology D
- Virology D

THE UNIVERSITY OF TENNESSEE–OAK RIDGE NATIONAL LABORATORY GRADUATE SCHOOL OF GENOME SCIENCE AND TECHNOLOGY

- Biological and Biomedical Sciences—General M,D
- Genomic Sciences M,D*

THE UNIVERSITY OF TENNESSEE SPACE INSTITUTE

- Aerospace/Aeronautical Engineering M,D
- Applied Mathematics M
- Aviation M
- Chemical Engineering M
- Electrical Engineering M,D
- Engineering and Applied Sciences—General M,D*
- Engineering Management M
- Mechanical Engineering M,D
- Mechanics M,D
- Metallurgical Engineering and Metallurgy M,D
- Physics M,D

THE UNIVERSITY OF TEXAS AT ARLINGTON

- Accounting M,D
- Advanced Practice Nursing M
- Aerospace/Aeronautical Engineering M,D
- Anthropology M
- Architecture M
- Biological and Biomedical Sciences—General M,D
- Biomedical Engineering M,D*
- Business Administration and Management—General M,D*
- Chemistry M,D*
- City and Regional Planning M
- Civil Engineering M,D
- Computer Engineering M,D
- Computer Science M,D*
- Criminal Justice and Criminology M
- Curriculum and Instruction M
- Economics M,D
- Education—General M
- Educational Administration M
- Electrical Engineering M,D*
- Engineering and Applied Sciences—General M,D*
- English M,D
- Environmental Engineering M,D
- Environmental Sciences M,D
- Experimental Psychology M,D
- Finance and Banking M,D
- French M
- Geology M
- German M
- Health Services Management and Hospital Administration M
- History M,D
- Human Resources Management M,D
- Humanities M
- Industrial/Management Engineering M,D
- Interdisciplinary Studies M
- Landscape Architecture M
- Linguistics M,D
- Logistics M
- Management Information Systems M,D
- Management of Technology M
- Marketing Research M
- Marketing M,D
- Materials Engineering M,D
- Materials Sciences M,D*
- Mathematics M,D
- Mechanical Engineering M,D*
- Music M
- Nursing and Healthcare Administration M
- Nursing Education M
- Nursing—General M
- Physics M,D
- Political Science M
- Psychology—General M,D
- Public Policy and Administration M,D
- Quantitative Analysis M,D
- Real Estate M,D
- Rhetoric M,D
- Social Work M,D
- Sociology M
- Software Engineering M,D
- Spanish M
- Taxation M,D

In-depth description on page 1265.

THE UNIVERSITY OF TEXAS AT AUSTIN

- Accounting M,D

The University of Texas at Austin (continued)

Program	Degrees
Advertising and Public Relations	M,D
Aerospace/Aeronautical Engineering	M,D*
American Studies	M,D
Analytical Chemistry	M,D
Animal Behavior	M,D
Anthropology	M,D
Applied Arts and Design—General	M,D
Applied Mathematics	M,D
Archaeology	M,D
Architectural Engineering	M
Architecture	M,D
Art Education	M
Art History	M,D
Art/Fine Arts	M
Asian Languages	M,D
Asian Studies	M,D
Astronomy	M,D
Biochemistry	M,D
Biological and Biomedical Sciences—General	M,D*
Biomedical Engineering	M,D*
Business Administration and Management—General	M,D
Cell Biology	D
Chemical Engineering	M,D
Chemistry	M,D
Child and Family Studies	M,D
City and Regional Planning	M,D
Civil Engineering	M,D*
Classics	M,D
Cognitive Sciences	M,D
Communication Disorders	M,D
Communication—General	M,D
Comparative Literature	M,D
Computational Sciences	M,D
Computer Engineering	M,D
Computer Science	M,D*
Counseling Psychology	M,D
Counselor Education	M,D
Curriculum and Instruction	M,D
Developmental Biology	D
East European and Russian Studies	M
Ecology	M,D
Economics	M,D
Education—General	M,D
Educational Administration	M,D
Educational Psychology	M,D
Electrical Engineering	M,D*
Engineering and Applied Sciences—General	M,D*
English	M,D
Environmental Engineering	M
Environmental Management and Policy	M
Evolutionary Biology	M,D
Family and Consumer Sciences-General	M,D
Film, Television, and Video Production	M,D
Finance and Banking	D
Folklore	M,D
Foreign Languages Education	M,D
French	M,D
Genetics	D
Geography	M,D
Geology	M,D
Geosciences	M,D
Geotechnical Engineering	M,D
German	M,D
Health Education	M,D
History	M,D
Human Development	M,D
Human Resources Development	M
Immunology	D
Industrial/Management Engineering	M,D
Information Studies	M,D
Inorganic Chemistry	M,D
Journalism	M,D
Kinesiology and Movement Studies	M,D
Latin American Studies	M,D
Law	P,M
Library Science	M,D
Linguistics	M,D
Management Information Systems	D
Manufacturing Engineering	M,D
Marine Sciences	M,D*
Marketing	D
Materials Engineering	M,D
Materials Sciences	M,D
Mathematics Education	M,D
Mathematics	M,D
Mechanical Engineering	M,D
Mechanics	M,D
Media Studies	M,D
Microbiology	M,D*
Mineral Economics	M
Mineral/Mining Engineering	M
Molecular Biology	D*
Music	M,D
Near and Middle Eastern Languages	M,D
Near and Middle Eastern Studies	M,D
Neuroscience	M,D
Nursing—General	M,D
Nutrition	M,D
Operations Research	M,D
Organic Chemistry	M,D
Petroleum Engineering	M,D
Pharmaceutical Sciences	M,D
Pharmacy	P
Philosophy	M,D
Physical Chemistry	M,D
Physics	M,D*
Plant Biology	M,D
Political Science	M,D
Portuguese	M,D
Psychology—General	D
Public History	M,D
Public Policy and Administration	M,D*
Romance Languages	M,D
School Psychology	M,D
Science Education	M,D
Slavic Languages	M,D
Social Work	M,D
Sociology	M,D
Spanish	M,D
Special Education	M,D
Statistics	M
Technology and Public Policy	M
Theater	M,D
Water Resources Engineering	M
Writing	M

Announcement on page 669.

THE UNIVERSITY OF TEXAS AT BROWNSVILLE

Program	Degrees
Biological and Biomedical Sciences—General	M
Business Administration and Management—General	M
Community Health Nursing	M
Counselor Education	M
Curriculum and Instruction	M
Early Childhood Education	M
Education—General	M
Educational Administration	M
Educational Media/Instructional Technology	M
Elementary Education	M
English as a Second Language	M
English	M
History	M
Interdisciplinary Studies	M
Multilingual and Multicultural Education	M
Political Science	M
Psychology—General	M
Reading Education	M
Spanish	M
Special Education	M

THE UNIVERSITY OF TEXAS AT DALLAS

Program	Degrees
Accounting	M
Applied Economics	M
Applied Mathematics	M,D
Business Administration and Management—General	M,D*
Cell Biology	M,D
Chemistry	M,D
Child and Family Studies	M
Cognitive Sciences	M
Communication Disorders	M,D
Communication—General	D
Comparative Literature	M,D
Computer Science	M,D*
Economics	D
Electrical Engineering	M,D
Engineering and Applied Sciences—General	M,D
Geographic Information Systems	M
Geosciences	M,D
Human Development	M,D
Humanities	M,D
Interdisciplinary Studies	M
International Business	M,D
Mathematics Education	M
Mathematics	M,D*
Molecular Biology	M,D
Neuroscience	M
Physics	M,D
Public Policy and Administration	M*
Science Education	M
Sociology	M
Statistics	M,D
Telecommunications	M,D

THE UNIVERSITY OF TEXAS AT EL PASO

Program	Degrees
Accounting	M
Advanced Practice Nursing	M
Allied Health—General	M
Art/Fine Arts	M
Bioinformatics	M
Biological and Biomedical Sciences—General	M,D*
Business Administration and Management—General	M
Chemistry	M
Civil Engineering	M
Clinical Psychology	M,D
Communication Disorders	M
Communication—General	M
Community Health Nursing	M
Computer Engineering	M,D
Computer Science	M
Economics	M
Education—General	M,D
Educational Administration	M,D
Educational Psychology	M
Electrical Engineering	M,D
Engineering and Applied Sciences—General	M,D
English Education	M
English	M
Environmental Engineering	M,D
Environmental Sciences	D
Exercise and Sports Science	M
Experimental Psychology	M,D
Foundations and Philosophy of Education	M,D
Geology	M,D
Geophysics	M
Health Education	M
History	M,D
Industrial/Management Engineering	M
Interdisciplinary Studies	M
Kinesiology and Movement Studies	M
Linguistics	M
Manufacturing Engineering	M
Materials Engineering	D
Materials Sciences	D
Maternal/Child Nursing	M
Mathematics	M
Mechanical Engineering	M
Medical/Surgical Nursing	M
Metallurgical Engineering and Metallurgy	M
Music Education	M
Music	M
Nurse Midwifery	M
Nursing and Healthcare Administration	M
Nursing—General	M
Physical Education	M
Physical Therapy	M
Physics	M
Political Science	M
Psychiatric Nursing	M
Psychology—General	M,D
Rhetoric	M
Sociology	M
Spanish	M
Statistics	M
Theater	M
Women's Health Nursing	M
Writing	M

In-depth description on page 1267.

THE UNIVERSITY OF TEXAS AT SAN ANTONIO

Program	Degrees
Accounting	M
Adult Education	M,D
Anthropology	M
Architecture	M
Art History	M
Art/Fine Arts	M
Biological and Biomedical Sciences—General	M,D*
Biotechnology	M,D
Business Administration and Management—General	M
Chemistry	M
Civil Engineering	M
Computer Science	M,D
Counselor Education	M,D
Criminal Justice and Criminology	M
Cultural Studies	M,D
Curriculum and Instruction	M
Early Childhood Education	M
Economics	M
Education—General	M,D
Educational Administration	M,D
Educational Psychology	M
Electrical Engineering	M
Elementary Education	M
Engineering and Applied Sciences—General	M
English as a Second Language	M,D
English	M
Environmental Sciences	M
Finance and Banking	M
Geography	M
Geology	M
Higher Education	M,D
History	M
Information Science	M
Interdisciplinary Studies	M
Mathematics Education	M
Mathematics	M
Mechanical Engineering	M
Multilingual and Multicultural Education	M,D
Music	M
Neurobiology	D
Political Science	M
Psychology—General	M
Public Policy and Administration	M
Reading Education	M
Sociology	M
Spanish	M
Special Education	M
Statistics	M
Taxation	M

THE UNIVERSITY OF TEXAS AT TYLER

Program	Degrees
Advanced Practice Nursing	M
Art Education	M
Art/Fine Arts	M
Biological and Biomedical Sciences—General	M
Business Administration and Management—General	M
Chemistry	M
Clinical Psychology	M
Communication—General	M
Computer Education	M
Computer Science	M
Counseling Psychology	M
Criminal Justice and Criminology	M
Curriculum and Instruction	M
Early Childhood Education	M
Economics	M
Education—General	M,O
Educational Administration	M
Engineering and Applied Sciences—General	M
English Education	M
English	M
Exercise and Sports Science	M
Health Education	M
Health Services Management and Hospital Administration	M
History	M
Information Science	M
Interdisciplinary Studies	M
Kinesiology and Movement Studies	M
Mathematics Education	M
Mathematics	M
Music Education	M
Music	M
Nursing—General	M
Political Science	M
Psychology—General	M
Public Policy and Administration	M
Reading Education	M,O
School Psychology	M
Science Education	M
Secondary Education	M
Social Sciences Education	M
Social Sciences	M
Sociology	M
Special Education	M,O
Vocational and Technical Education	M

THE UNIVERSITY OF TEXAS HEALTH SCIENCE CENTER AT HOUSTON

Program	Degrees
Allopathic Medicine	P
Biochemistry	M,D*
Biological and Biomedical Sciences—General	M,D*
Biometrics	M,D
Biophysics	M,D*
Cancer Biology/Oncology	M,D*
Cell Biology	M,D*
Dentistry	P
Developmental Biology	M,D
Genetic Counseling	M
Genetics	M,D*
Human Genetics	M,D
Immunology	M,D*
Medical Physics	M,D
Microbiology	M,D*
Molecular Biology	M,D
Neuroscience	M,D*
Nursing—General	M,D
Oral and Dental Sciences	M
Pathology	M,D*
Pharmacology	M,D*
Physiology	M,D*
Public Health—General	M,D
Reproductive Biology	M,D*
Toxicology	M,D*
Virology	M,D*

THE UNIVERSITY OF TEXAS HEALTH SCIENCE CENTER AT SAN ANTONIO

Program	Degrees
Allopathic Medicine	P
Biochemistry	M,D
Biological and Biomedical Sciences—General	P,M,D,O
Cell Biology	D
Dentistry	P,M,O
Medical Physics	M,D*
Microbiology	M,D*
Molecular Medicine	M,D*
Nursing—General	M,D
Oral and Dental Sciences	M,O

Program	Degrees
Pharmacology	D
Physiology	M,D*
Structural Biology	D

THE UNIVERSITY OF TEXAS MEDICAL BRANCH

Program	Degrees
Allied Health—General	M
Allopathic Medicine	P
Bacteriology	D*
Biochemistry	M,D*
Biological and Biomedical Sciences—General	M,D
Biophysics	M,D
Cell Biology	M,D*
Community Health	M,D
Genetics	M,D
Humanities	M,D
Immunology	M,D
Microbiology	M,D*
Molecular Biology	M,D
Neuroscience	D*
Nursing—General	M,D
Pathology	D*
Pharmacology	M,D*
Physical Therapy	M
Physiology	M,D
Structural Biology	M,D
Toxicology	D*
Virology	D

THE UNIVERSITY OF TEXAS OF THE PERMIAN BASIN

Program	Degrees
Accounting	M
Biological and Biomedical Sciences—General	M
Business Administration and Management—General	M
Clinical Psychology	M
Counselor Education	M
Criminal Justice and Criminology	M
Early Childhood Education	M
Education—General	M
Educational Administration	M
Elementary Education	M
English	M
Geology	M
History	M
Physical Education	M
Psychology—General	M
Reading Education	M
Secondary Education	M
Special Education	M

THE UNIVERSITY OF TEXAS–PAN AMERICAN

Program	Degrees
Advanced Practice Nursing	M
Art/Fine Arts	M
Biological and Biomedical Sciences—General	M
Business Administration and Management—General	M,D
Clinical Psychology	M
Communication Disorders	M
Communication—General	M
Computer Science	M
Counselor Education	M,D
Criminal Justice and Criminology	M
Early Childhood Education	M
Education of the Gifted	M,D
Education—General	M,D
Educational Administration	M
Educational Measurement and Evaluation	M,D
Educational Psychology	M,D
Elementary Education	M
English as a Second Language	M
English	M
Experimental Psychology	M
History	M
Interdisciplinary Studies	M
Kinesiology and Movement Studies	M
Management Information Systems	M,D
Mathematics	M
Medical/Surgical Nursing	M
Multilingual and Multicultural Education	M
Music	O
Nursing—General	M
Pediatric Nursing	M
Psychology—General	M
Public Policy and Administration	M
Reading Education	M
Rehabilitation Counseling	M
School Psychology	M,D
Secondary Education	M
Social Work	M
Sociology	M
Spanish	M
Special Education	M,D
Speech and Interpersonal Communication	M
Theater	M

THE UNIVERSITY OF TEXAS SOUTHWESTERN MEDICAL CENTER AT DALLAS

Program	Degrees
Allopathic Medicine	P
Biochemistry	D*
Biological and Biomedical Sciences—General	D*
Biomedical Engineering	M,D*
Biophysics	D*
Cell Biology	D*
Clinical Psychology	D
Developmental Biology	D*
Genetics	D
Immunology	D*
Medical Illustration	M
Microbiology	D*
Molecular Biology	D
Neuroscience	D*
Pharmacology	*
Physical Therapy	M
Physician Assistant Studies	M
Radiation Biology	M,D*
Rehabilitation Counseling	M

THE UNIVERSITY OF THE ARTS

Program	Degrees
Art Education	M
Art/Fine Arts	M*
Industrial Design	M
Museum Studies	M
Music Education	M
Music	M

UNIVERSITY OF THE DISTRICT OF COLUMBIA

Program	Degrees
Business Administration and Management—General	M
Clinical Psychology	M
Communication Disorders	M
Counselor Education	M
Early Childhood Education	M
Education—General	M
English Education	M
Law	P*
Mathematics	M
Public Policy and Administration	M
Special Education	M

UNIVERSITY OF THE INCARNATE WORD

Program	Degrees
Adult Education	M
Biological and Biomedical Sciences—General	M
Business Administration and Management—General	M,D
Communication—General	M
Early Childhood Education	M
Education—General	M
Educational Measurement and Evaluation	M
Educational Media/Instructional Technology	M
Elementary Education	M
English	M
Entrepreneurship	D
Interdisciplinary Studies	M
International and Comparative Education	M,D
International Business	M,D
Mathematics Education	M,D
Mathematics	M,D
Nursing—General	M
Nutrition	M
Organizational Management	M,D
Physical Education	M
Reading Education	M
Religion	M
Secondary Education	M
Special Education	M
Sports Management	M,D

In-depth description on page 1269.

UNIVERSITY OF THE PACIFIC

Program	Degrees
Biochemistry	M,D
Biological and Biomedical Sciences—General	M
Business Administration and Management—General	M
Chemistry	M,D
Communication Disorders	M
Communication—General	M
Counseling Psychology	M,D,O
Counselor Education	M,D,O
Curriculum and Instruction	M,D
Dentistry	P
Education—General	M,D,O
Educational Administration	M,D
Educational Measurement and Evaluation	M,D,O
Educational Psychology	M,D,O
Exercise and Sports Science	M
International Affairs	P,M,D
Law	P,M,D
Legal and Justice Studies	P,M,D
Medicinal and Pharmaceutical Chemistry	M,D
Music Education	M
Music	M
Oral and Dental Sciences	M
Pharmaceutical Sciences	M,D*
Pharmacology	M,D
Pharmacy	P
Physical Therapy	M
Physiology	M,D
Psychology—General	M
Public Policy and Administration	P,M,D
School Psychology	M,D,O
Special Education	M,D
Therapies—Dance, Drama, and Music	M

UNIVERSITY OF THE SACRED HEART

Program	Degrees
Advertising and Public Relations	M
Business Administration and Management—General	M
Clinical Laboratory Sciences/Medical Technology	O
Communication—General	M
Cultural Studies	M
Education—General	M
Educational Media/Instructional Technology	M
Environmental and Occupational Health	M
Human Resources Management	M
Journalism	M
Management Information Systems	M
Marketing	M
Mass Communication	M
Taxation	M

UNIVERSITY OF THE SCIENCES IN PHILADELPHIA

Program	Degrees
Biochemistry	M,D
Biotechnology	M
Cell Biology	M
Chemistry	M,D
Health Psychology	M
Health Services Management and Hospital Administration	M,D
Medicinal and Pharmaceutical Chemistry	M,D
Pharmaceutical Administration	M
Pharmaceutical Sciences	M,D*
Pharmacology	M,D
Pharmacy	P
Technical Writing	M
Toxicology	M,D

UNIVERSITY OF THE SOUTH

Program	Degrees
Theology	P,M,D

UNIVERSITY OF THE VIRGIN ISLANDS

Program	Degrees
Business Administration and Management—General	M
Education—General	M
Public Policy and Administration	M

UNIVERSITY OF TOLEDO

Program	Degrees
Accounting	M
Analytical Chemistry	M,D
Anthropology	M
Applied Mathematics	M,D
Biochemistry	M,D
Bioengineering	M,D*
Biological and Biomedical Sciences—General	M,D*
Business Administration and Management—General	M
Business Education	M,D,O
Chemical Engineering	M,D*
Chemistry	M,D*
City and Regional Planning	M
Civil Engineering	M,D*
Clinical Psychology	M,D
Communication Disorders	M
Computer Science	M,D
Counselor Education	M,D
Curriculum and Instruction	M,D,O
Early Childhood Education	M,D,O
Ecology	M*
Economics	M
Education—General	M,D,O
Educational Administration	M,D,O
Educational Measurement and Evaluation	M,D,O
Educational Media/Instructional Technology	M,D,O
Educational Psychology	M,D,O
Electrical Engineering	M,D*
Elementary Education	M,D,O
Engineering and Applied Sciences—General	M
English as a Second Language	M
English	M
Environmental Sciences	D*
Exercise and Sports Science	M
Experimental Psychology	M,D
Finance and Banking	M
Foundations and Philosophy of Education	M,D,O
French	M
Geography	M
Geology	M
German	M
Health Education	D
Higher Education	M,D,O
History	M,D
Human Services	M,D
Industrial and Manufacturing Management	M,D
Industrial/Management Engineering	M,D
Inorganic Chemistry	M,D
International Business	M
Kinesiology and Movement Studies	M
Law	P*
Leisure Studies	M
Liberal Studies	M
Management Information Systems	M,D
Marketing	M
Mathematics Education	M,D
Mathematics	M,D
Mechanical Engineering	M,D*
Medicinal and Pharmaceutical Chemistry	M,D
Music Education	M
Music	M
Organic Chemistry	M,D
Pharmaceutical Administration	M
Pharmaceutical Sciences	M
Pharmacology	M
Pharmacy	P
Philosophy	M
Physical Chemistry	M,D
Physical Education	M,D
Physics	M,D*
Political Science	M
Psychology—General	M,D*
Public Health—General	M
Public Policy and Administration	M
Recreation and Park Management	M
Rehabilitation Sciences	M
School Psychology	M,O
Secondary Education	M,D,O
Sociology	M
Spanish	M
Special Education	M,D,O
Statistics	M,D
Vocational and Technical Education	M,D,O

In-depth description on page 1271.

UNIVERSITY OF TORONTO

Program	Degrees
Accounting	M,D
Addictions/Substance Abuse Counseling	M,D
Aerospace/Aeronautical Engineering	M,D
Allopathic Medicine	P
Anatomy	M,D
Anthropology	M,D
Architecture	M
Art History	M,D
Asian Studies	M,D
Astronomy	M,D
Biochemistry	M,D
Bioethics	M,D
Biological and Biomedical Sciences—General	M,D
Biomedical Engineering	M,D
Biophysics	M,D
Botany	M,D
Business Administration and Management—General	M,D
Cardiovascular Sciences	M,D
Cell Biology	M,D
Chemical Engineering	M,D
Chemistry	M,D
City and Regional Planning	M
Civil Engineering	M,D
Classics	M,D
Communication Disorders	M,D
Community Health	M,D
Comparative Literature	M,D
Computer Engineering	M,D
Computer Science	M,D
Criminal Justice and Criminology	M,D
Dentistry	P
Developmental Biology	D
East European and Russian Studies	M
Economics	M,D
Education—General	M,D
Electrical Engineering	M,D
Engineering and Applied Sciences—General	M,D*
English	M,D
Environmental Engineering	M,D
Environmental Management and Policy	M
Environmental Sciences	M

University of Toronto (continued)

Ethnic Studies M,D
Forestry M,D
French M,D
Genetic Counseling M,D
Genetics M,D
Geography M,D
Geology M,D
German M,D
History of Science and Technology M,D
History M,D
Human Development M,D
Immunology M,D
Industrial and Labor Relations M,D
Industrial/Management Engineering M,D
Information Studies M,D
International Affairs M
Italian M,D
Law P,M,D
Library Science M,D
Linguistics M,D
Manufacturing Engineering M
Materials Sciences M,D
Mathematics M,D
Mechanical Engineering M,D
Medieval and Renaissance Studies M,D
Metallurgical Engineering and Metallurgy M,D
Molecular Biology D
Museum Studies M
Music M,D
Near and Middle Eastern Studies M,D
Neuroscience M,D
Nursing—General M,D
Nutrition M,D
Oral and Dental Sciences M,D
Pathobiology M,D
Pharmaceutical Sciences M,D
Pharmacology M,D
Philosophy M,D
Physics M,D
Physiology M,D
Political Science M,D
Portuguese M,D
Psychology—General M,D
Rehabilitation Sciences M
Religion M,D
Slavic Languages M,D
Social Work M,D
Sociology M,D
Software Engineering M
Spanish M,D
Statistics M,D
Structural Biology D
Theater M,D
Toxicology M,D
Women's Studies M,D
Zoology M,D

UNIVERSITY OF TRINITY COLLEGE

Music P,M,D,O
Pastoral Ministry and Counseling P,M,D,O
Theology P,M,D,O

UNIVERSITY OF TULSA

Anthropology M
Art/Fine Arts M
Biological and Biomedical Sciences—General M,D
Business Administration and Management—General M
Chemical Engineering M,D
Chemistry M
Clinical Psychology M,D
Communication Disorders M
Computer Science M,D
Education—General M
Electrical Engineering M
Engineering and Applied Sciences—General M,D
Engineering Management M
English M,D
Finance and Banking M
Financial Engineering M
Geology M
Geosciences M,D
History M
Industrial and Organizational Psychology M,D
International Business M
Investment Management M
Law P,M
Management of Technology M
Mathematics Education M
Mathematics M
Mechanical Engineering M,D
Petroleum Engineering M,D
Psychology—General M,D
Science Education M
Taxation M

In-depth description on page 1273.

UNIVERSITY OF UTAH

Accounting M,D
Allopathic Medicine P
Anatomy M,D
Anthropology M,D
Architecture M
Art History M
Art/Fine Arts M
Biochemistry M,D*
Bioengineering M,D*
Biological and Biomedical Sciences—General M,D*
Biomedical Engineering M,D
Biostatistics M
Business Administration and Management—General M,D
Cancer Biology/Oncology M,D
Cell Biology
Chemical Engineering M,D
Chemistry M,D
Child and Family Studies M
Civil Engineering M,D
Clinical Laboratory Sciences/Medical Technology M
Communication Disorders M,D
Communication—General M,D
Comparative Literature M,D*
Computer Science M,D*
Consumer Economics M
Dance M
Ecology M,D
Economics M,D
Education—General M,D
Educational Administration M,D
Educational Psychology M,D
Electrical Engineering M,D,O
Engineering and Applied Sciences—General M,D,O
English M,D
Environmental Engineering M,D
Evolutionary Biology M,D
Exercise and Sports Science M,D
Film, Television, and Video Production M
Finance and Banking M,D
Foreign Languages Education M,D
Foundations and Philosophy of Education M,D
French M
Genetics M,D
Geography M,D
Geological Engineering M,D
Geology M,D
Geophysics M,D
German M,D
Gerontological Nursing M,O
Gerontology M,O
Graphic Design M
Health Education M,D
Health Promotion M,D
History M,D
Human Genetics M,D
Illustration M
Immunology
Law P,M
Leisure Studies M,D
Linguistics M
Materials Engineering M,D
Materials Sciences M,D
Mathematics M,D*
Mechanical Engineering M,D
Medical Informatics M,D
Medicinal and Pharmaceutical Chemistry M,D
Metallurgical Engineering and Metallurgy M,D
Meteorology M,D
Microbiology
Mineral/Mining Engineering M,D
Molecular Biology D*
Music M,D
Near and Middle Eastern Studies M,D
Neurobiology M,D
Neuroscience D*
Nuclear Engineering M,D
Nursing—General M,D
Nutrition M
Occupational Therapy M
Pathology D
Petroleum Engineering M,D
Pharmacology M,D
Pharmacy P,M
Philosophy M,D
Photography M
Physical Chemistry M,D
Physical Therapy M
Physics M,D
Physiology D
Political Science M,D
Psychology—General M,D
Public Health—General M
Public Policy and Administration M,O
Recreation and Park Management M,D
Science Education M,D
Secondary Education M
Social Work M,D
Spanish M,D
Special Education M,D
Statistics M
Theater M,D
Toxicology M,D
Writing M,D

UNIVERSITY OF VERMONT

Agricultural Economics and Agribusiness M
Agricultural Sciences—General M,D
Agronomy and Soil Sciences M,D*
Allied Health—General M
Allopathic Medicine P
Anatomy D
Animal Sciences M,D*
Applied Economics M
Biochemistry M,D*
Biological and Biomedical Sciences—General M,D*
Biomedical Engineering M
Biophysics M,D
Biostatistics M
Botany M,D*
Business Administration and Management—General M
Cell Biology M,D*
Chemistry M,D*
Child and Family Studies M
Civil Engineering M,D*
Classics M
Clinical Laboratory Sciences/Medical Technology M
Clinical Psychology D
Communication—General M*
Computer Science M
Consumer Economics M
Counseling Psychology M*
Counselor Education M
Curriculum and Instruction M
Education—General M,D
Educational Administration M,D*
Electrical Engineering M,D*
Engineering and Applied Sciences—General M,D*
Engineering Physics M
English Education M
English M
Environmental Management and Policy M,D*
Fish, Game, and Wildlife Management M
Foreign Languages Education M
Forestry M
French M
Genetics M,D
Geography M
Geology M
German M
Historic Preservation M
History M
Materials Sciences M,D*
Mathematics Education M,D
Mathematics M,D*
Mechanical Engineering M,D*
Microbiology M,D*
Molecular Biology M,D
Neurobiology D
Nursing—General M
Nutrition M
Pathology M
Pharmacology M,D*
Physical Therapy M*
Physics M
Physiology M,D*
Plant Sciences M,D
Political Science M
Psychology—General D*
Public Policy and Administration M
Reading Education M
Science Education M,D
Social Sciences Education M
Social Work M*
Special Education M
Statistics M
Water Resources M

In-depth description on page 1275.

UNIVERSITY OF VICTORIA

Anthropology M
Applied Mathematics M,D
Art Education M
Art History M,D
Art/Fine Arts M
Astronomy M,D
Astrophysics M,D
Biochemistry M,D
Biological and Biomedical Sciences—General M,D
Business Administration and Management—General M
Cell Biology M,D
Chemistry M,D
Classics M
Computer Science M,D
Condensed Matter Physics M,D
Conflict Resolution and Mediation/Peace Studies M
Counseling Psychology M,D
Counselor Education M,D
Curriculum and Instruction M,D
Developmental Biology M,D
Developmental Psychology M,D
Ecology M,D
Economics M
Education—General M,D
Educational Administration M,D
Educational Psychology M,D
Electrical Engineering M,D
Engineering and Applied Sciences—General M,D
English Education M,D
English M,D
Exercise and Sports Science M
Experimental Psychology M,D
Finance and Banking M
French M
Geochemistry M,D
Geography M,D
Geology M,D
Geophysics M,D
Geosciences M,D
German M
History M,D
Human Development M
Industrial and Labor Relations M
Industrial and Manufacturing Management M
Law P
Leisure Studies M
Linguistics M,D
Marine Biology M,D
Mathematics Education M
Mathematics M,D
Mechanical Engineering M,D
Medical Physics M,D
Microbiology M,D
Music Education M
Music M,D
Oceanography M,D
Photography M
Physical Education M
Physics M,D
Physiology M,D
Political Science M
Psychology—General M,D
Public Policy and Administration M
Science Education M
Social Psychology M,D
Social Sciences Education M
Social Work M
Sociology M,D
Special Education M,D
Statistics M,D
Theoretical Physics M,D

UNIVERSITY OF VIRGINIA

Accounting M
Aerospace/Aeronautical Engineering M,D
Allopathic Medicine P,M
Anthropology M,D
Archaeology M,D
Architectural History M,D
Architecture M*
Art History M,D
Asian Studies M
Astronomy M,D
Bacteriology *
Biochemistry D*
Bioethics M
Biological and Biomedical Sciences—General M,D
Biomedical Engineering M,D*
Biophysics D*
Biotechnology D*
Business Administration and Management—General M,D
Cardiovascular Sciences
Cell Biology D*
Chemical Engineering M,D
Chemistry M,D
City and Regional Planning M
Civil Engineering M,D
Classics M,D
Clinical Psychology D
Clinical Research M
Communication Disorders M
Computer Engineering M,D
Computer Science M,D*
Counselor Education M,D,O
Curriculum and Instruction M,D,O
Economics M,D
Education—General M,D,O
Educational Administration M,D,O
Educational Measurement and Evaluation M,D
Educational Psychology M,D,O
Electrical Engineering M,D*
Engineering and Applied Sciences—General M,D
Engineering Physics M,D
English M,D
Environmental Engineering M,D
Environmental Sciences M,D
Epidemiology M
Foreign Languages Education M,D
French M,D
Genetics D
German M,D
Health Education M,D
Health Informatics M
Health Services Management and Hospital Administration M

Health Services Research	M
Higher Education	D,O
History	M,D
Immunology	D*
International Affairs	M,D
Italian	M
Landscape Architecture	M
Law	P,M,D
Linguistics	M
Management Information Systems	M
Materials Sciences	M,D
Mathematics	M,D
Mechanical Engineering	M,D*
Mechanics	M
Microbiology	M,D*
Molecular Biology	D
Molecular Medicine	D*
Music	M
Near and Middle Eastern Studies	M
Neuroscience	D
Nuclear Engineering	M,D
Nursing—General	M,D*
Pharmacology	D*
Philosophy	M,D
Physical Education	M,D
Physics	M,D*
Physiology	D*
Political Science	M,D
Psychology—General	M,D
Religion	M,D
Science Education	M,D
Slavic Languages	M,D
Sociology	M,D
Spanish	M,D
Special Education	M,D,O
Statistics	M,D
Structural Engineering	M,D
Systems Engineering	M,D*
Theater	M*
Transportation and Highway Engineering	M,D
Transportation Management	M,D
Virology	*
Water Resources Engineering	M,D
Writing	M

UNIVERSITY OF WASHINGTON

Aerospace/Aeronautical Engineering	M,D
Allopathic Medicine	P
Anthropology	M,D
Applied Mathematics	M,D
Applied Physics	M,D
Architecture	M,O
Art History	M,D
Art/Fine Arts	M
Asian Languages	M,D
Asian Studies	M
Astronomy	M,D
Atmospheric Sciences	M,D*
Biochemistry	D
Bioengineering	M,D
Bioinformatics	M
Biological and Biomedical Sciences—General	M,D
Biomedical Engineering	M,D
Biophysics	D
Biostatistics	M,D
Botany	M,D
Business Administration and Management—General	M,D
Cell Biology	D*
Chemical Engineering	M,D*
Chemistry	M,D
City and Regional Planning	M,D
Civil Engineering	M,D
Classics	M,D
Clinical Laboratory Sciences/Medical Technology	M
Clinical Psychology	M,D
Communication Disorders	M,D
Communication—General	M,D
Comparative Literature	M,D
Computer Science	M,D*
Construction Engineering and Management	M,D
Counselor Education	M,D
Curriculum and Instruction	M,D
Dance	M
Dentistry	P
East European and Russian Studies	M
Economics	M,D
Education—General	M,D,O
Educational Administration	M,D,O
Educational Measurement and Evaluation	M,D
Educational Media/Instructional Technology	M,D
Educational Psychology	M,D
Electrical Engineering	M,D*
Engineering and Applied Sciences—General	M,D
English as a Second Language	M,D
English Education	M,D
English	M,D
Environmental and Occupational Health	M,D*
Environmental Engineering	M,D
Environmental Management and Policy	M,D*
Epidemiology	M,D
Fish, Game, and Wildlife Management	M,D
Forestry	M,D*
Foundations and Philosophy of Education	M,D
French	M,D
Genetics	M,D
Genomic Sciences	D*
Geography	M,D
Geology	M,D
Geophysics	M,D*
Geotechnical Engineering	M,D
German	M,D
Health Informatics	M
Health Services Management and Hospital Administration	M
Health Services Research	M,D
Higher Education	M,D
Hispanic Studies	M
Historic Preservation	O
History	M,D
Horticulture	M,D
Human Development	M,D
Hydraulics	M,D
Hydrology	M,D
Immunology	D*
Industrial Hygiene	M,D
Industrial/Management Engineering	M,D
Information Science	M,D
International Affairs	M*
International Business	O
International Health	M,D
Italian	M,D
Landscape Architecture	M
Law	P,M,D
Legal and Justice Studies	P,M,D
Library Science	M,D
Linguistics	M,D
Logistics	O
Marine Affairs	M
Materials Engineering	M,D
Materials Sciences	M,D*
Maternal and Child Health	M,D
Mathematics Education	M,D
Mathematics	M,D
Mechanical Engineering	M,D
Medical Informatics	M
Medical Microbiology	M,D
Medicinal and Pharmaceutical Chemistry	D
Microbiology	D*
Molecular Biology	D
Molecular Medicine	M,D
Multilingual and Multicultural Education	M,D
Museum Studies	M
Music Education	M,D
Music	M,D
Near and Middle Eastern Studies	M,D
Neurobiology	D*
Nursing—General	M,D
Nutrition	M,D
Occupational Therapy	M
Oceanography	M,D
Oral and Dental Sciences	M,D
Paper and Pulp Engineering	M,D
Parasitology	M,D
Pathobiology	M,D*
Pathology	M,D
Pharmaceutical Sciences	M,D
Pharmacology	M,D*
Pharmacy	P
Philosophy	M,D
Physical Therapy	M
Physics	M,D
Physiology	D
Political Science	M,D
Portuguese	M
Psychology—General	D
Public Health—General	M,D*
Public Policy and Administration	M*
Reading Education	M,D
Rehabilitation Sciences	M
Religion	M
Romance Languages	M,D
Russian	M,D
Scandinavian Languages	M,D
School Psychology	M,D
Science Education	M,D
Slavic Languages	M,D
Social Sciences Education	M,D
Social Work	M,D
Sociology	M,D
Spanish	M
Special Education	M,D
Statistics	M,D
Structural Biology	D
Structural Engineering	M,D
Sustainable Development	P,M,D
Taxation	P,M,D
Technical Writing	M
Theater	M,D
Toxicology	M,D
Transportation and Highway Engineering	M,D
Transportation Management	O
Urban Design	M,D,O
Veterinary Sciences	M
Women's Studies	M,D
Zoology	D

UNIVERSITY OF WATERLOO

Accounting	M,D
Actuarial Science	M,D
Applied Mathematics	M,D
Architecture	M
Art/Fine Arts	M
Biological and Biomedical Sciences—General	M,D
Biostatistics	M,D
Chemical Engineering	M,D
Chemistry	M,D
City and Regional Planning	M,D
Civil Engineering	M,D
Computer Engineering	M,D
Computer Science	M,D
Economics	M
Electrical Engineering	M,D
Engineering and Applied Sciences—General	M,D
Engineering Management	M,D
English	M,D
Environmental Management and Policy	M
Finance and Banking	M,D
French	M
Geography	M,D
Geosciences	M,D
German	M,D
Health Education	M,D
History	M,D
Information Science	M,D
Kinesiology and Movement Studies	M,D
Leisure Studies	M,D
Management of Technology	M,D
Mathematics	M,D
Mechanical Engineering	M,D
Operations Research	M,D
Optometry	P,M,D
Philosophy	M,D
Physics	M,D
Political Science	M
Psychology—General	M,D
Public History	M,D
Recreation and Park Management	M,D
Russian	M,D
Sociology	M,D
Software Engineering	M,D
Statistics	M,D
Systems Engineering	M,D
Taxation	M,D
Technical Writing	M,D
Vision Sciences	P,M,D

THE UNIVERSITY OF WEST ALABAMA

Adult Education	M
Counselor Education	M
Early Childhood Education	M
Education—General	M
Educational Administration	M
Educational Media/Instructional Technology	M
Elementary Education	M
English Education	M
Foundations and Philosophy of Education	M
Mathematics Education	M
Physical Education	M
Science Education	M
Secondary Education	M
Social Sciences Education	M
Special Education	M

THE UNIVERSITY OF WESTERN ONTARIO

Allopathic Medicine	P,M
Anatomy	M,D
Anthropology	M
Applied Mathematics	M,D
Astronomy	M,D
Biochemistry	M,D
Biological and Biomedical Sciences—General	M,D
Biophysics	M,D
Biostatistics	M,D
Business Administration and Management—General	M,D
Cell Biology	M,D
Chemistry	M,D
Classics	M
Communication Disorders	M
Comparative Literature	M
Computer Science	M,D
Counselor Education	M
Curriculum and Instruction	M
Dentistry	P
Economics	M,D
Education—General	M
Educational Administration	M
Educational Psychology	M
Engineering and Applied Sciences—General	M,D
English	M,D
Environmental Sciences	M,D
Epidemiology	M,D
French	M,D
Geography	M,D
Geology	M,D
Geophysics	M,D
Geosciences	M,D
History	M,D
Immunology	M,D
Information Studies	M,D*
Interdisciplinary Studies	M,D
Journalism	M*
Kinesiology and Movement Studies	M,D
Law	P,O
Library Science	M,D
Mathematics	M,D
Microbiology	M,D
Molecular Biology	M,D
Music	M,D
Neuroscience	M,D
Nursing—General	M
Occupational Therapy	M
Oral and Dental Sciences	M
Pathology	M,D
Pharmacology	M,D
Philosophy	M,D
Physical Therapy	M
Physics	M,D
Physiology	M,D
Plant Biology	M,D
Plant Sciences	M,D
Political Science	M,D
Psychology—General	M,D
Sociology	M,D
Spanish	M
Special Education	M
Statistics	M,D
Toxicology	M,D
Zoology	M,D

UNIVERSITY OF WEST FLORIDA

Accounting	M
Biological and Biomedical Sciences—General	M
Business Administration and Management—General	M
Communication—General	M
Computer Science	M
Counselor Education	M
Curriculum and Instruction	M,D,O
Early Childhood Education	M
Education—General	M,D,O
Educational Administration	M,O
Elementary Education	M
English	M
Exercise and Sports Science	M
Health Education	M
History	M
Humanities	M
Leisure Studies	M
Marine Affairs	M
Mathematics Education	M
Mathematics	M
Middle School Education	M
Physical Education	M
Political Science	M
Psychology—General	M
Public Policy and Administration	M
Reading Education	M
Science Education	M
Secondary Education	M
Special Education	M
Statistics	M
Systems Engineering	M
Vocational and Technical Education	M

UNIVERSITY OF WEST LOS ANGELES

Law	P*

UNIVERSITY OF WINDSOR

Art/Fine Arts	M
Biochemistry	M,D
Biological and Biomedical Sciences—General	M,D
Business Administration and Management—General	M
Chemistry	M,D
Civil Engineering	M,D
Clinical Psychology	M,D
Computer Science	M
Economics	M,D
Education—General	M,D
Electrical Engineering	M,D
Engineering and Applied Sciences—General	M,D
English	M
Environmental Engineering	M,D
Geosciences	M
History	M

University of Windsor (continued)

Industrial/Management Engineering M,D
Kinesiology and Movement Studies M
Manufacturing Engineering M,D
Materials Engineering M,D
Mathematics M,D
Mechanical Engineering M,D
Nursing—General M
Philosophy M
Physics M,D
Political Science M
Psychology—General M,D
Sociology M,D
Statistics M,D
Writing M

THE UNIVERSITY OF WINNIPEG

History M
Marriage and Family Therapy P,M,O
Public Policy and Administration M
Religion M
Theology P,M,O

UNIVERSITY OF WISCONSIN–EAU CLAIRE

Allied Health—General M
Biological and Biomedical Sciences—General M
Business Administration and Management—General M
Communication Disorders M
Education—General M
Elementary Education M
English Education M
English M
Environmental and Occupational Health M
History M
Mathematics Education M
Nursing—General M
Psychology—General M,O
Public Health—General M
Reading Education M
School Psychology M,O
Science Education M
Secondary Education M
Social Sciences Education M
Special Education M

In-depth description on page 1277.

UNIVERSITY OF WISCONSIN–GREEN BAY

Business Administration and Management—General M
Education—General M
Environmental Management and Policy M
Environmental Sciences M

UNIVERSITY OF WISCONSIN–LA CROSSE

Biological and Biomedical Sciences—General M
Business Administration and Management—General M
Community Health M
Education—General M
Elementary Education M
Exercise and Sports Science M
Health Education M
Microbiology M
Nurse Anesthesia M
Physical Education M
Physical Therapy M
Psychology—General M,O
Public Health—General M
Reading Education M
Recreation and Park Management M
Rehabilitation Sciences M
School Psychology M,O
Secondary Education M
Special Education M
Sports Management M
Student Personnel Services M

In-depth description on page 1279.

UNIVERSITY OF WISCONSIN–MADISON

Accounting M,D
Actuarial Science M,D
Adult Education M,D
African Studies M,D
African-American Studies M
Agricultural Economics and Agribusiness M,D
Agricultural Engineering M,D
Agricultural Sciences—General M,D
Agronomy and Soil Sciences M,D
Allopathic Medicine P
Anatomy M,D
Animal Sciences M,D
Anthropology M,D
Applied Arts and Design—General M,D
Applied Economics M,D
Art Education M,D
Art History M,D
Art/Fine Arts M
Arts Administration M
Asian Languages M,D
Asian Studies M,D
Astronomy D
Atmospheric Sciences M,D
Bacteriology M
Biochemistry M,D*
Biological and Biomedical Sciences—General M,D
Biomedical Engineering M,D
Biometrics M
Biophysics D
Biopsychology D
Biotechnology *
Botany M,D
Business Administration and Management—General M,D*
Cancer Biology/Oncology D*
Cell Biology M,D*
Chemical Engineering M,D
Chemistry M,D
Child and Family Studies M,D
City and Regional Planning M,D
Civil Engineering M,D
Classics M,D
Clinical Psychology D
Cognitive Sciences D
Communication Disorders M,D
Communication—General M,D
Community Health M,D
Comparative Literature M,D
Computer Science M,D
Conservation Biology M
Consumer Economics M,D
Counseling Psychology D
Counselor Education M
Curriculum and Instruction M,D
Developmental Biology D
Developmental Psychology D
Ecology M,D
Economics D
Education—General M,D*
Educational Administration M,D
Educational Psychology M,D
Electrical Engineering M,D
Engineering and Applied Sciences—General M,D,O*
Engineering Physics M,D
English Education M,D
English M,D
Entomology M,D
Entrepreneurship M
Environmental Biology M,D
Environmental Engineering M,D
Environmental Management and Policy M,D
Environmental Sciences M,D
Family and Consumer Sciences-General M,D
Finance and Banking M
Food Science and Technology M,D
Foreign Languages Education M,D
Forestry M,D
Foundations and Philosophy of Education M,D
French M,D,O
Genetics M,D*
Geographic Information Systems M,D,O
Geography M,D,O
Geological Engineering M,D
Geology M,D
Geophysics M,D
German M,D
History of Science and Technology M,D
History M,D
Horticulture M,D
Human Development M,D
Human Resources Management M
Industrial and Labor Relations M,D
Industrial and Manufacturing Management M
Industrial/Management Engineering M,D
Information Studies M,D,O
Insurance M,D
International Business M
Investment Management M
Italian M,D
Jewish Studies M,D
Journalism M,D
Kinesiology and Movement Studies M,D
Landscape Architecture M
Latin American Studies M
Law P,M,D
Legal and Justice Studies M
Library Science M,D,O
Limnology M,D
Linguistics M,D
Logistics M
Management Information Systems M
Manufacturing Engineering M*
Marine Sciences M,D
Marketing Research M
Marketing M
Mass Communication M,D
Materials Sciences M,D
Mathematics Education M
Mathematics M,D
Mechanical Engineering M,D*
Mechanics M,D
Medical Microbiology D
Medical Physics M,D
Metallurgical Engineering and Metallurgy M,D
Microbiology D*
Molecular Biology M,D
Music Education M,D
Music M,D
Near and Middle Eastern Languages M,D
Neurobiology D
Neuroscience M,D*
Nuclear Engineering M,D*
Nursing—General M,D
Nutrition M,D*
Oceanography M,D
Pathology D*
Pharmaceutical Administration M,D
Pharmaceutical Sciences M,D
Pharmacology M,D*
Pharmacy P
Philosophy M,D
Physics M,D
Physiology M,D
Plant Pathology M,D
Plant Sciences M,D
Political Science M,D
Polymer Science and Engineering M,D
Portuguese M,D
Psychology—General D
Public Policy and Administration M*
Real Estate M
Rehabilitation Counseling M,D
Rehabilitation Sciences M
Rural Sociology M,D
Scandinavian Languages M,D
Science Education M
Slavic Languages M,D
Social Psychology D
Social Sciences Education M,D
Social Work M,D
Sociology M,D
Spanish M,D
Special Education M,D
Statistics M,D
Sustainable Development M
Theater M,D
Toxicology M,D*
Veterinary Medicine P
Veterinary Sciences M,D
Vocational and Technical Education M,D
Water Resources M
Zoology M,D*

UNIVERSITY OF WISCONSIN–MILWAUKEE

Allied Health—General M
Anthropology M,D
Architecture M,D
Art Education M
Art History M,O
Art/Fine Arts M
Biological and Biomedical Sciences—General M,D
Business Administration and Management—General M,D
Chemistry M,D
City and Regional Planning M
Classics M
Clinical Laboratory Sciences/Medical Technology M
Clinical Psychology M,D
Communication Disorders M
Communication—General M
Comparative Literature M,D
Computer Science M,D
Criminal Justice and Criminology M
Curriculum and Instruction M
Dance M
Early Childhood Education M
Economics M,D
Education—General M,D
Educational Administration M
Educational Psychology M
Elementary Education M
Engineering and Applied Sciences—General M,D
English M,D
Film, Television, and Video Production M
Foundations and Philosophy of Education M
French M
Geography M
Geology M,D
German M
History M
Human Resources Development M
Industrial and Labor Relations M
Information Studies M,O
Interdisciplinary Studies D
Italian M
Jewish Studies M
Journalism M
Kinesiology and Movement Studies M
Library Science M,O
Mass Communication M
Mathematics M,D
Middle School Education M
Museum Studies M,O
Music M
Nursing—General M,D
Occupational Therapy M
Philosophy M
Physics M,D
Political Science M,D
Psychology—General M,D
Public Policy and Administration M
Reading Education M
Secondary Education M
Slavic Languages M
Social Work M
Sociology M
Spanish M
Special Education M
Theater M
Urban Education M,D
Urban Studies M,D

UNIVERSITY OF WISCONSIN–OSHKOSH

Advanced Practice Nursing M
Biological and Biomedical Sciences—General M*
Botany M
Business Administration and Management—General M
Communication Disorders M
Counselor Education M
Curriculum and Instruction M
Early Childhood Education M
Education—General M
Educational Administration M
English M
Experimental Psychology M
Health Services Management and Hospital Administration M
Industrial and Organizational Psychology M
Management Information Systems M
Mathematics Education M
Microbiology M
Nursing—General M
Physics M
Psychology—General M
Public Policy and Administration M
Reading Education M
Science Education M
Special Education M
Zoology M

UNIVERSITY OF WISCONSIN–PARKSIDE

Business Administration and Management—General M
Computer Science M
Information Science M
Molecular Biology M

UNIVERSITY OF WISCONSIN–PLATTEVILLE

Adult Education M
Counselor Education M
Criminal Justice and Criminology M
Education—General M
Elementary Education M
Engineering and Applied Sciences—General M
Industrial and Manufacturing Management M
Middle School Education M
Project Management M
Secondary Education M
Vocational and Technical Education M

UNIVERSITY OF WISCONSIN–RIVER FALLS

Agricultural Education M
Agricultural Sciences—General M
Business Administration and Management—General M
Communication Disorders M
Counselor Education M,O
Education—General M
Elementary Education M
English Education M
Mathematics Education M
Reading Education M
School Psychology M,O

Science Education M
Social Sciences Education M

UNIVERSITY OF WISCONSIN–STEVENS POINT

Advertising and Public Relations M
Business Administration and Management—General M
Communication Disorders M
Communication—General M
Corporate and Organizational Communication M
Counselor Education M
Education—General M
Educational Administration M
Elementary Education M
English M
Family and Consumer Sciences-General M
History M
Mass Communication M
Music Education M
Natural Resources M
Nutrition M
Reading Education M
Science Education M
Speech and Interpersonal Communication M

UNIVERSITY OF WISCONSIN–STOUT

Counseling Psychology M
Counselor Education M
Education—General M
Family and Consumer Sciences-General M
Food Science and Technology M
Hospitality Management M
Human Resources Development M
Management of Technology M
Marriage and Family Therapy M
Nutrition M
Psychology—General M
Rehabilitation Counseling M
Safety Engineering M
School Psychology M,O
Travel and Tourism M
Vocational and Technical Education M,O

UNIVERSITY OF WISCONSIN–SUPERIOR

Art Education M
Art History M
Art Therapy M
Art/Fine Arts M
Communication—General M
Counselor Education M
Curriculum and Instruction M
Education—General M
Educational Administration M,O
Mass Communication M
Reading Education M
Social Psychology M
Special Education M
Speech and Interpersonal Communication M
Theater M

UNIVERSITY OF WISCONSIN–WHITEWATER

Accounting M
Business Administration and Management—General M*
Business Education M
Communication Disorders M
Communication—General M
Corporate and Organizational Communication M
Counselor Education M
Curriculum and Instruction M
Education—General M
Educational Administration M
Environmental and Occupational Health M
Finance and Banking M
Health Services Management and Hospital Administration M
Higher Education M
Human Resources Management M
International Business M
Management Information Systems M
Marketing M
Mass Communication M
Psychology—General M
Public Policy and Administration M
School Psychology M,O
Secondary Education M
Social Psychology M
Special Education M

UNIVERSITY OF WYOMING

Accounting M
Adult Education M,D,O
Agricultural Economics and Agribusiness M
Agricultural Sciences—General M,D
Agronomy and Soil Sciences M,D
American Studies M
Animal Sciences M,D
Anthropology M,D
Applied Economics M
Atmospheric Sciences M,D
Botany M,D
Business Administration and Management—General M
Chemical Engineering M,D
Chemistry M,D
Civil Engineering M,D
Communication Disorders M
Communication—General M
Computer Science M,D
Consumer Economics M
Counselor Education M,D
Curriculum and Instruction M,D
Economics M,D
Education—General M,D,O
Educational Administration M,D,O
Educational Media/Instructional Technology M,D,O
Electrical Engineering M,D
Engineering and Applied Sciences—General M,D
English M
Entomology M,D
Environmental Engineering M,D
Finance and Banking M
Food Science and Technology M
French M
Geography M
Geology M,D
Geophysics M,D
German M
Health Education M
History M
International Affairs M
Law P
Mathematics Education M,D
Mathematics M,D
Mechanical Engineering M,D
Molecular Biology M,D
Music Education M
Music M
Natural Resources M,D
Nursing—General M
Nutrition M
Pathobiology M
Petroleum Engineering M,D
Philosophy M
Physical Education M
Physiology M,D
Political Science M
Psychology—General M,D
Public Policy and Administration M
Range Science M,D
Reproductive Biology M,D
Rural Planning and Studies M
Science Education M
Social Work M
Sociology M
Spanish M
Special Education M,O
Statistics M,D
Water Resources M,D
Zoology M,D*

In-depth description on page 1281.

UPPER IOWA UNIVERSITY

Accounting M
Business Administration and Management—General M
Human Resources Management M
Organizational Management M
Quality Management M

URBANA UNIVERSITY

Education—General M

URSULINE COLLEGE

Art Therapy M
Education—General M
Educational Administration M
Liberal Studies M
Nursing—General M
Theology M

UTAH STATE UNIVERSITY

Accounting M
Aerospace/Aeronautical Engineering M,D
Agricultural Education M
Agricultural Engineering M,D
Agricultural Sciences—General M,D
Agronomy and Soil Sciences M,D
American Studies M
Animal Sciences M,D
Applied Economics M,D
Art/Fine Arts M
Biochemistry M,D
Biological and Biomedical Sciences—General M,D
Business Administration and Management—General M
Business Education M,D
Chemistry M,D*
Child and Family Studies M,D
City and Regional Planning M
Civil Engineering M,D,O
Clinical Psychology M,D
Communication Disorders M,O
Communication—General M
Computer Science M,D
Counseling Psychology M,D
Counselor Education M,D
Curriculum and Instruction D
Ecology M,D
Economics M,D
Education—General M,D,O
Educational Measurement and Evaluation M,D
Educational Media/Instructional Technology M,D,O
Electrical Engineering M,D,O
Elementary Education M
Engineering and Applied Sciences—General M,D,O*
English M
Environmental Engineering M,D,O
Family and Consumer Sciences-General M
Fish, Game, and Wildlife Management M,D
Folklore M
Food Science and Technology M,D
Forestry M,D
Geography M
Geology M
Health Education M
History M
Human Development M
Human Resources Management M
Landscape Architecture M
Management Information Systems M,D
Marriage and Family Therapy M
Mathematics M,D
Mechanical Engineering M,D
Meteorology M,D
Microbiology M,D
Molecular Biology M,D
Multilingual and Multicultural Education M
Natural Resources M
Nutrition M,D
Physical Education M
Physics M,D
Plant Sciences M,D
Political Science M
Psychology—General M,D
Range Science M,D
Recreation and Park Management M,D
Rehabilitation Counseling M
School Psychology M,D
Secondary Education M
Sociology M,D
Special Education M,D,O
Statistics M
Theater M
Toxicology M,D
Veterinary Sciences M,D
Vocational and Technical Education M
Water Resources Engineering M,D
Water Resources M,D
Writing M

UTICA COLLEGE

Criminal Justice and Criminology M

VALDOSTA STATE UNIVERSITY

Adult Education M,D,O
Business Administration and Management—General M
Business Education M,D,O
City and Regional Planning M
Clinical Psychology M,O
Communication Disorders M,O
Community Health Nursing M
Counseling Psychology M,O
Counselor Education M,O
Criminal Justice and Criminology M
Early Childhood Education M,O
Education—General M,D,O
Educational Administration M,D,O
English M
Health Education M
History M
Human Resources Management M
Industrial and Organizational Psychology M,O
Information Studies M
Library Science M
Marriage and Family Therapy M
Middle School Education M,O
Music Education M
Nursing and Healthcare Administration M
Nursing—General M
Physical Education M
Psychology—General M,O
Public Policy and Administration M
Reading Education M,O
School Psychology M,O
Secondary Education M,O
Social Work M
Sociology M
Special Education M,O
Vocational and Technical Education M,D,O

VALPARAISO UNIVERSITY

Business Administration and Management—General M
Clinical Psychology M
Counseling Psychology M
Cultural Studies M
Curriculum and Instruction M
Education—General M
English M
Ethics M
History M
Law P,M
Liberal Studies M
Music M
Nursing—General M
Psychology—General M
School Psychology M
Social Psychology M
Special Education M
Theology M

VANCOUVER SCHOOL OF THEOLOGY

Theology P,M,D,O

VANDERBILT UNIVERSITY

Advanced Practice Nursing M,D
Allopathic Medicine P,M,D
Anthropology M,D
Art/Fine Arts M
Astronomy M
Biochemistry M,D*
Bioinformatics M,D
Biological and Biomedical Sciences—General M,D*
Biomedical Engineering M,D*
Biophysics D*
Business Administration and Management—General M,D
Cancer Biology/Oncology M,D
Cell Biology M,D
Chemical Engineering M,D
Chemistry M,D
Civil Engineering M,D
Classics M,D
Clinical Research M
Communication Disorders M,D
Comparative Literature M,D
Computer Science M,D
Counselor Education M
Curriculum and Instruction M,D
Early Childhood Education M,D
Economics M,D
Education—General M,D*
Educational Administration M,D
Educational Measurement and Evaluation M,D
Educational Media/Instructional Technology M,D
Electrical Engineering M,D
Elementary Education M,D
Engineering and Applied Sciences—General M,D*
English Education M,D
English M,D
Environmental Engineering M,D
Finance and Banking D
Foreign Languages Education M,D
French M,D
Geology M
German M,D
Gerontological Nursing M,D
Higher Education M,D
History M,D
Human Development M,D
Human Resources Development M,D
Immunology M,D
Latin American Studies M
Law P,M
Liberal Studies M
Management of Technology M,D
Marketing D
Materials Sciences M,D
Maternal/Child Nursing M,D
Mathematics Education M,D
Mathematics M,D
Mechanical Engineering M,D
Medical Physics M
Medical/Surgical Nursing M,D
Microbiology M,D*

Vanderbilt University (continued)

Program	Degrees
Molecular Biology	D
Neuroscience	D*
Nurse Midwifery	M,D
Nursing and Healthcare Administration	M,D
Nursing—General	M,D
Occupational Health Nursing	M,D
Organizational Management	M,D
Pathology	D*
Pediatric Nursing	M,D
Pharmacology	D*
Philosophy	M,D
Physics	M,D
Physiology	D
Political Science	M,D
Portuguese	M,D
Psychiatric Nursing	M,D
Psychology—General	M,D
Public Health—General	M
Reading Education	M,D
Religion	M,D
Science Education	M,D
Secondary Education	M,D
Sociology	M,D
Spanish	M,D
Special Education	M,D
Theology	P,M
Toxicology	*
Women's Health Nursing	M,D

VANDERCOOK COLLEGE OF MUSIC

Program	Degrees
Music Education	M

VANGUARD UNIVERSITY OF SOUTHERN CALIFORNIA

Program	Degrees
Clinical Psychology	M
Education—General	M
Religion	M
Theology	M

VASSAR COLLEGE

Program	Degrees
Biological and Biomedical Sciences—General	M
Chemistry	M

VERMONT COLLEGE

Program	Degrees
Art Therapy	M,O
Art/Fine Arts	M,O
Education—General	M,O
Interdisciplinary Studies	M,O
Writing	M,O

VERMONT LAW SCHOOL

Program	Degrees
Environmental Management and Policy	M
Law	P
Legal and Justice Studies	M

VICTORIA UNIVERSITY

Program	Degrees
Theology	P,M,D

VILLA JULIE COLLEGE

Program	Degrees
Electronic Commerce	M
Information Science	M
Management Information Systems	M
Management of Technology	M

VILLANOVA UNIVERSITY

Program	Degrees
Accounting	M
Advanced Practice Nursing	M,O
Biological and Biomedical Sciences—General	M*
Business Administration and Management—General	M
Chemical Engineering	M
Chemistry	M*
Civil Engineering	M
Classics	M
Computer Engineering	M
Computer Science	M
Counselor Education	M*
Criminal Justice and Criminology	M
Education—General	M*
Educational Administration	M
Electrical Engineering	M*
Elementary Education	M
Engineering and Applied Sciences—General	M,O*
English	M*
Environmental Engineering	M
Gerontological Nursing	M,O
Health Services Management and Hospital Administration	M,O
History	M*
Human Resources Development	M
Law	P
Liberal Studies	M
Manufacturing Engineering	M,O
Mathematics	M
Mechanical Engineering	M,O*
Medical/Surgical Nursing	M,O
Nurse Anesthesia	M,O
Nursing and Healthcare Administration	M,O
Nursing Education	M,O
Nursing—General	M,O*
Pediatric Nursing	M,O
Philosophy	M,D
Political Science	M*
Psychology—General	M*
Public Policy and Administration	M
Secondary Education	M
Spanish	M
Statistics	M
Taxation	M
Theater	M*
Theology	M
Transportation and Highway Engineering	M
Water Resources Engineering	M

In-depth description on page 1283.

VIRGINIA COMMONWEALTH UNIVERSITY

Program	Degrees
Accounting	M,D,O
Adult Education	M
Advanced Practice Nursing	O
Advertising and Public Relations	M
Allied Health—General	M,D,O
Allopathic Medicine	P
Anatomy	M,D,O
Applied Arts and Design—General	M
Applied Mathematics	M
Applied Physics	M
Art Education	M
Art History	M,D
Art/Fine Arts	M
Biochemistry	M,D,O*
Biological and Biomedical Sciences—General	M,D,O*
Biomedical Engineering	M,D*
Biophysics	M,D,O
Biostatistics	M,D
Business Administration and Management—General	M,D,O
Chemistry	M,D,O
City and Regional Planning	M,O
Clinical Laboratory Sciences/Medical Technology	M
Clinical Psychology	D
Computer Science	M
Counseling Psychology	M,D,O
Counselor Education	M
Criminal Justice and Criminology	M,O
Curriculum and Instruction	M,O
Dentistry	P
Early Childhood Education	M,O
Economics	M
Education—General	M,D,O
Educational Administration	M
Engineering and Applied Sciences—General	M,D*
English	M
Environmental and Occupational Health	M
Environmental Management and Policy	M
Environmental Sciences	M
Finance and Banking	M
Forensic Sciences	M,O
Genetic Counseling	M,D,O
Genetics	M,D,O
Gerontology	M,O
Health Services Management and Hospital Administration	M,D*
Health Services Research	D
History	M
Human Genetics	M,D,O*
Human Resources Management	M
Immunology	M,D,O
Industrial and Labor Relations	M
Insurance	M
Interdisciplinary Studies	M*
Interior Design	M
Internet and Interactive Multimedia	M
Management Information Systems	M,D
Marketing	M
Mass Communication	M
Mathematics	M,O
Medical/Surgical Nursing	M,D,O
Microbiology	M,D,O*
Middle School Education	M,O
Molecular Biology	M,D,O
Music Education	M
Music	M
Neuroscience	M,D,O*
Nurse Anesthesia	M
Nursing and Healthcare Administration	M,D,O
Nursing—General	M,D,O
Occupational Therapy	M
Operations Research	M
Pathology	M,D*
Pediatric Nursing	M,D,O
Pharmaceutical Sciences	P,M,D*
Pharmacology	M,D,O*
Pharmacy	P
Photography	M
Physical Education	M
Physical Therapy	M,D,O
Physics	M
Physiology	M,D,O*
Psychiatric Nursing	M,D,O
Psychology—General	D
Public Health—General	M
Public Policy and Administration	M,D,O
Quantitative Analysis	M
Reading Education	M
Real Estate	M,O
Recreation and Park Management	M
Rehabilitation Counseling	M,O
Rhetoric	M
Secondary Education	M,O
Social Sciences Education	M,O
Social Work	M,D
Sociology	M,O
Special Education	M
Statistics	M,O
Taxation	M,D
Theater	M
Toxicology	M,D,O
Urban Education	D
Women's Health Nursing	M,D,O
Writing	M

In-depth description on page 1285.

VIRGINIA POLYTECHNIC INSTITUTE AND STATE UNIVERSITY

Program	Degrees
Accounting	M,D*
Adult Education	M,D,O
Aerospace/Aeronautical Engineering	M,D
Agricultural Economics and Agribusiness	M,D
Agricultural Engineering	M,D
Agricultural Sciences—General	M,D
Agronomy and Soil Sciences	M,D
Animal Sciences	M,D
Applied Economics	M,D
Applied Mathematics	M,D
Applied Physics	M,D
Architecture	M*
Arts Administration	M
Biochemistry	M,D*
Bioengineering	M,D
Biological and Biomedical Sciences—General	M,D
Biomedical Engineering	M,D
Botany	M,D
Business Administration and Management—General	M,D*
Cell Biology	M,D
Chemical Engineering	M,D
Chemistry	M,D
Child and Family Studies	M,D
City and Regional Planning	M
Civil Engineering	M,D*
Clinical Psychology	M,D
Clothing and Textiles	M,D
Computer Engineering	M,D
Computer Science	M,D*
Consumer Economics	M,D
Counselor Education	M,D,O
Curriculum and Instruction	M,D,O
Developmental Biology	M,D
Developmental Psychology	M,D
Ecology	M,D
Economics	M,D
Educational Administration	M,D,O
Educational Measurement and Evaluation	D
Electrical Engineering	M,D*
Engineering and Applied Sciences—General	M,D*
Engineering Management	M
English	M
Entomology	M,D
Environmental Design	D
Environmental Engineering	M
Environmental Sciences	M
Evolutionary Biology	M,D
Exercise and Sports Science	M,D
Finance and Banking	M,D
Fish, Game, and Wildlife Management	M,D
Food Science and Technology	M,D*
Forestry	M,D
Genetics	M,D
Geography	M
Geology	M,D
Geophysics	M,D
Gerontology	M,D
Health Education	M,D,O
History of Science and Technology	M,D
History	M
Horticulture	M,D
Hospitality Management	M,D
Human Development	M,D
Human Resources Development	M,D
Industrial and Organizational Psychology	M,D
Industrial/Management Engineering	M,D
Information Science	M
Interior Design	M,D
International Affairs	M
Kinesiology and Movement Studies	M,D
Landscape Architecture	M
Logistics	M,D
Management Information Systems	M,D
Marketing	M,D
Marriage and Family Therapy	M,D
Materials Engineering	M,D
Materials Sciences	M,D
Mathematical Physics	M,D
Mathematics	M,D
Mechanical Engineering	M,D
Mechanics	M,D*
Microbiology	M,D
Mineral/Mining Engineering	M,D
Molecular Biology	M,D
Natural Resources	M,D*
Nutrition	M,D
Ocean Engineering	M
Operations Research	M,D
Philosophy	M
Physical Education	M,D,O
Physics	M,D
Plant Pathology	M,D
Plant Physiology	M,D
Political Science	M
Psychology—General	M,D
Public Policy and Administration	M,D,O
Recreation and Park Management	M,D
Sociology	M,D
Special Education	D,O
Statistics	M,D
Systems Engineering	M
Theater	M
Travel and Tourism	M,D
Veterinary Medicine	P
Veterinary Sciences	M,D
Vocational and Technical Education	M,D,O
Water Resources Engineering	M,D
Zoology	M,D

VIRGINIA STATE UNIVERSITY

Program	Degrees
Biological and Biomedical Sciences—General	M
Business Administration and Management—General	M
Counselor Education	M
Economics	M
Education—General	M,O
Educational Administration	M
English	M
Finance and Banking	M
History	M
Interdisciplinary Studies	M
Mathematics Education	M
Mathematics	M
Physics	M
Psychology—General	M
Vocational and Technical Education	M,O

VIRGINIA UNION UNIVERSITY

Program	Degrees
Theology	P,D

VITERBO UNIVERSITY

Program	Degrees
Education—General	M
Nursing—General	M

WAGNER COLLEGE

Program	Degrees
Advanced Practice Nursing	O
Biological and Biomedical Sciences—General	M
Business Administration and Management—General	M
Education—General	M
Elementary Education	M
English as a Second Language	M
Finance and Banking	M
International Business	M
Marketing	M
Microbiology	M
Nursing—General	M
Secondary Education	M
Special Education	M

WAKE FOREST UNIVERSITY

Program	Degrees
Accounting	M
Allopathic Medicine	P
Analytical Chemistry	M,D
Anatomy	D
Biochemistry	D*
Biological and Biomedical Sciences—General	M,D
Biomedical Engineering	D
Business Administration and Management—General	M
Cancer Biology/Oncology	D*
Chemistry	M,D
Communication—General	M
Computer Science	M
Counselor Education	M

- Education—General M
- English M
- Exercise and Sports Science M
- Genetics M
- Health Services Research M
- History M
- Immunology D
- Inorganic Chemistry M,D
- Law P,M
- Liberal Studies M
- Mathematics M
- Microbiology D*
- Molecular Biology D*
- Molecular Medicine D*
- Neurobiology D
- Neuroscience D*
- Organic Chemistry M,D
- Pastoral Ministry and Counseling M
- Pathobiology M,D*
- Pharmacology D*
- Physical Chemistry M,D
- Physics M,D*
- Physiology D
- Psychology—General M
- Religion M
- Secondary Education M
- Speech and Interpersonal Communication M

In-depth description on page 1287.

WALDEN UNIVERSITY

- Education—General D
- Educational Media/Instructional Technology M
- Health Services Management and Hospital Administration D
- Human Services D
- Management Strategy and Policy D
- Psychology—General M,D
- Public Health—General M

In-depth description on page 1289.

WALLA WALLA COLLEGE

- Biological and Biomedical Sciences—General M
- Counseling Psychology M
- Counselor Education M
- Curriculum and Instruction M
- Education—General M
- Educational Administration M
- Reading Education M
- Social Work M
- Special Education M

WALSH COLLEGE OF ACCOUNTANCY AND BUSINESS ADMINISTRATION

- Accounting M
- Business Administration and Management—General M
- Economics M
- Finance and Banking M
- Management Information Systems M
- Taxation M

WALSH UNIVERSITY

- Business Administration and Management—General M
- Counselor Education M
- Education—General M
- Human Development M
- Physical Therapy M

WARNER PACIFIC COLLEGE

- Religion M

WARREN WILSON COLLEGE

- Writing M

WARTBURG THEOLOGICAL SEMINARY

- Theology P,M

WASHBURN UNIVERSITY OF TOPEKA

- Business Administration and Management—General M
- Clinical Psychology M
- Curriculum and Instruction M
- Education—General M
- Educational Administration M
- Law P
- Liberal Studies M
- Psychology—General M
- Reading Education M
- Special Education M

WASHINGTON AND LEE UNIVERSITY

- Law P

WASHINGTON COLLEGE

- English M
- History M
- Psychology—General M

WASHINGTON STATE UNIVERSITY

- Accounting M,D
- Agricultural Economics and Agribusiness M,D
- Agricultural Sciences—General M,D
- Agronomy and Soil Sciences M,D
- American Studies M,D
- Analytical Chemistry M,D
- Animal Sciences M,D
- Anthropology M,D
- Architecture M
- Art/Fine Arts M
- Biochemistry M,D
- Biological and Biomedical Sciences—General M,D
- Biophysics M,D
- Botany M,D
- Business Administration and Management—General M,D*
- Cell Biology M,D
- Chemical Engineering M,D
- Chemistry M,D
- City and Regional Planning M
- Civil Engineering M,D
- Clinical Psychology M,D
- Clothing and Textiles M
- Communication Disorders M
- Communication—General M
- Computer Science M,D
- Counseling Psychology M,D
- Criminal Justice and Criminology M
- Curriculum and Instruction M,D
- Economics M,D,O
- Education—General M,D
- Educational Administration M,D
- Electrical Engineering M,D
- Elementary Education M,D
- Engineering and Applied Sciences—General M,D
- English Education M,D
- English M,D
- Entomology M,D
- Environmental Engineering M
- Environmental Sciences M,D*
- Food Science and Technology M,D
- Genetics M,D
- Geology M,D*
- Health Services Management and Hospital Administration M
- History M,D
- Horticulture M,D
- Human Development M
- Inorganic Chemistry M,D
- Interior Design M
- International Business M,D,O
- Kinesiology and Movement Studies M
- Landscape Architecture M,D
- Leisure Studies M
- Management Information Systems M
- Management of Technology M,D
- Materials Engineering M,D
- Materials Sciences M,D
- Mathematics Education M,D
- Mathematics M,D*
- Mechanical Engineering M,D
- Microbiology M,D
- Molecular Biology M,D*
- Multilingual and Multicultural Education M,D
- Music M
- Natural Resources M,D
- Neuroscience M,D
- Nursing—General M
- Nutrition M,D
- Organic Chemistry M,D
- Pathology M,D
- Pharmacology M,D
- Pharmacy P
- Photography M
- Physical Chemistry M,D
- Physics M,D
- Plant Pathology M,D
- Plant Physiology M,D
- Political Science M,D
- Psychology—General M,D
- Public Policy and Administration M
- Reading Education M,D
- Recreation and Park Management M
- Secondary Education M,D
- Sociology M,D
- Spanish M
- Toxicology M,D
- Veterinary Medicine P
- Veterinary Sciences M,D
- Zoology M,D

WASHINGTON STATE UNIVERSITY SPOKANE

- Architecture M
- Communication Disorders M
- Computer Science M
- Criminal Justice and Criminology M
- Education—General M
- Electrical Engineering M
- Engineering Management M
- Gerontology O
- Health Services Management and Hospital Administration M
- Interior Design M
- Landscape Architecture M
- Management of Technology M
- Nutrition M
- Pharmacy P

In-depth description on page 1291.

WASHINGTON THEOLOGICAL UNION

- Theology P,M

WASHINGTON UNIVERSITY IN ST. LOUIS

- Allied Health—General M,D,O
- Allopathic Medicine P
- Anthropology M,D
- Archaeology M,D
- Architecture M*
- Art History M,D*
- Art/Fine Arts M
- Asian Languages M,D
- Asian Studies M,D
- Biochemistry D
- Biological and Biomedical Sciences—General D*
- Biomedical Engineering M,D*
- Biophysics D
- Business Administration and Management—General M,D
- Cell Biology D
- Chemical Engineering M,D
- Chemistry M,D
- Civil Engineering M,D
- Classics M
- Clinical Psychology M,D
- Communication Disorders M,D*
- Comparative Literature M,D
- Computational Sciences D
- Computer Science M,D*
- Construction Engineering and Management M
- Developmental Biology D
- Ecology D
- Economics M,D*
- Education—General M,D*
- Educational Measurement and Evaluation D
- Electrical Engineering M,D
- Elementary Education M
- Engineering and Applied Sciences—General M,D
- English M,D
- Environmental Biology D
- Environmental Sciences M
- Evolutionary Biology D
- Experimental Psychology M,D
- French M,D
- Genetics D
- Geochemistry M,D
- Geology M,D
- Geophysics M,D
- Geosciences M,D
- German M,D
- Health Services Management and Hospital Administration M,D*
- History M,D*
- Immunology D
- Industrial and Manufacturing Management M,D
- Jewish Studies M
- Kinesiology and Movement Studies D
- Law P,M,D
- Materials Engineering M,D
- Materials Sciences M,D
- Mathematics Education M,D
- Mathematics M,D
- Mechanical Engineering M,D*
- Microbiology D
- Molecular Biology D
- Music M,D
- Near and Middle Eastern Studies M
- Neuroscience D
- Occupational Therapy M,D*
- Organic Chemistry D
- Philosophy M,D
- Photography M
- Physical Therapy D,O
- Physics M,D*
- Planetary and Space Sciences M,D
- Plant Biology D
- Political Science M,D
- Psychology—General M,D
- Public Policy and Administration M
- Religion M
- Romance Languages M,D
- Secondary Education M
- Social Psychology M,D
- Social Work M,D*
- Spanish M,D
- Special Education M,D
- Statistics M,D
- Structural Engineering M,D
- Systems Engineering D
- Systems Science M,D*
- Theater M*
- Transportation and Highway Engineering D
- Urban Design M
- Western European Studies M
- Writing M

In-depth description on page 1293.

WAYLAND BAPTIST UNIVERSITY

- Business Administration and Management—General M
- Education—General M
- Religion M

WAYNESBURG COLLEGE

- Business Administration and Management—General M

WAYNE STATE COLLEGE

- Art Education M
- Business Administration and Management—General M
- Business Education M
- Communication—General M
- Counselor Education M
- Curriculum and Instruction M
- Education—General M,O
- Educational Administration M,O
- Educational Media/Instructional Technology M
- Elementary Education M
- English as a Second Language M
- English Education M
- Exercise and Sports Science M
- Health Education M
- Home Economics Education M
- Mathematics Education M
- Music Education M
- Physical Education M
- Science Education M
- Social Sciences Education M
- Special Education M
- Sports Management M
- Vocational and Technical Education M

WAYNE STATE UNIVERSITY

- Addictions/Substance Abuse Counseling O
- Advanced Practice Nursing M
- Advertising and Public Relations M,D
- Allied Health—General M,O
- Allopathic Medicine P
- Anatomy M,D
- Anthropology M,D
- Applied Arts and Design—General M
- Applied Mathematics M,D
- Art Education M,D,O
- Art History M
- Art/Fine Arts M
- Biochemistry M,D
- Biological and Biomedical Sciences—General M,D,O
- Biomedical Engineering M,D
- Business Administration and Management—General M*
- Cancer Biology/Oncology M,D*
- Cell Biology M,D
- Chemical Engineering M,D
- Chemistry M,D
- Child and Family Studies O
- City and Regional Planning M
- Civil Engineering M,D
- Classics M
- Clinical Laboratory Sciences/Medical Technology M,O
- Clinical Psychology M,D
- Cognitive Sciences M,D
- Communication Disorders M,D
- Communication—General M,D
- Community Health Nursing M
- Community Health M,O
- Comparative Literature M
- Computer Engineering M,D
- Computer Science M,D,O
- Conflict Resolution and Mediation/Peace Studies M,O
- Corporate and Organizational Communication M,D
- Counselor Education M,D,O
- Criminal Justice and Criminology M
- Curriculum and Instruction M,D,O
- Developmental Psychology M,D
- Early Childhood Education M,D,O
- Economics M,D,O
- Education—General M,D,O*
- Educational Administration M,D,O

Wayne State University (continued)

Program	Degrees
Educational Measurement and Evaluation	M,D,O
Educational Media/Instructional Technology	M,D,O
Educational Psychology	M,D,O
Electrical Engineering	M,D
Elementary Education	M,D,O
Engineering and Applied Sciences—General	M,D,O*
Engineering Management	M
English Education	M,D,O
English	M,D*
Environmental and Occupational Health	M,O
Environmental Engineering	M,D
Food Science and Technology	M,D,O
French	M
Genetics	M,D*
Geography	M
Geology	M
German	M,D
Gerontology	O
Hazardous Materials Management	M,D,O
Health Education	M
Health Physics/Radiological Health	M,D*
Higher Education	M,D,O
History	M,D,O
Human Development	M
Human Services	O
Immunology	M,D*
Industrial and Labor Relations	M
Industrial and Organizational Psychology	M,D
Industrial Hygiene	M,O
Industrial/Management Engineering	M,D
Information Studies	M,O
Interdisciplinary Studies	M,D
Italian	M
Law	P,M
Library Science	M,O
Linguistics	M
Manufacturing Engineering	M
Materials Engineering	M,D,O
Materials Sciences	M,D,O
Maternal/Child Nursing	M
Mathematics Education	M,D,O
Mathematics	M,D
Mechanical Engineering	M,D
Media Studies	M,D
Medical Physics	M,D
Medical/Surgical Nursing	M
Microbiology	M,D
Molecular Biology	M,D*
Multilingual and Multicultural Education	M,D,O
Music Education	M,O
Music	M,O
Near and Middle Eastern Studies	M
Neurobiology	D
Nurse Anesthesia	M
Nursing Education	O
Nursing—General	M,D,O
Nutrition	M,D,O
Occupational Therapy	M
Operations Research	M,D
Pathology	D
Pediatric Nursing	M
Pharmaceutical Sciences	M,D
Pharmacology	M,D
Pharmacy	P,M
Philosophy	M,D
Physical Education	M
Physical Therapy	M
Physician Assistant Studies	M
Physics	M,D
Physiology	M,D
Political Science	M,D
Polymer Science and Engineering	M,D,O
Psychiatric Nursing	M
Psychology—General	M,D*
Public History	M,D,O
Public Policy and Administration	M
Reading Education	M,D,O
Recreation and Park Management	M
Rehabilitation Counseling	M,D,O
Rehabilitation Sciences	M
School Psychology	M,D,O
Science Education	M,D,O
Secondary Education	M,D,O
Social Psychology	M,D
Social Sciences Education	M,D,O
Social Work	M,O
Sociology	M,D
Software Engineering	M,D,O
Spanish	M
Special Education	M,D,O
Speech and Interpersonal Communication	M,D
Sports Management	M
Statistics	M,D
Taxation	M
Theater	M,D
Toxicology	M,D,O*
Transcultural Nursing	O
Vocational and Technical Education	M,D,O
Writing	M,D

WEBBER INTERNATIONAL UNIVERSITY

Program	Degrees
Business Administration and Management—General	M

WEBER STATE UNIVERSITY

Program	Degrees
Accounting	M
Business Administration and Management—General	M
Curriculum and Instruction	M
Education—General	M
Legal and Justice Studies	M

WEBSTER UNIVERSITY

Program	Degrees
Aerospace/Aeronautical Engineering	M
Art/Fine Arts	M
Arts Administration	M
Business Administration and Management—General	M,D
Communication—General	M
Computer Science	M,O
Counseling Psychology	M
Criminal Justice and Criminology	M
Early Childhood Education	M
Education—General	M,O
Educational Administration	M,O
Educational Media/Instructional Technology	M,O
Environmental Management and Policy	M
Finance and Banking	M
Gerontology	M
Health Services Management and Hospital Administration	M
Human Resources Development	M
Human Resources Management	M
International Affairs	M
International Business	M
Legal and Justice Studies	M,O
Management Information Systems	M
Marketing	M
Mathematics Education	M,O
Media Studies	M
Music Education	M
Music	M
Nurse Anesthesia	M
Nursing—General	M
Public Policy and Administration	M
Real Estate	M
Science Education	M,O
Social Sciences Education	M,O
Special Education	M,O
Telecommunications Management	M

WESLEYAN COLLEGE

Program	Degrees
Early Childhood Education	M
Education—General	M
Mathematics Education	M
Middle School Education	M
Science Education	M

WESLEYAN UNIVERSITY

Program	Degrees
Astronomy	M
Biochemistry	M,D*
Biological and Biomedical Sciences—General	D*
Cell Biology	D
Chemistry	M,D*
Developmental Biology	D
Evolutionary Biology	D
Genetics	D
Geosciences	M
Inorganic Chemistry	M,D
Liberal Studies	M,O
Mathematics	M,D*
Molecular Biology	D*
Music	M,D
Neurobiology	D
Organic Chemistry	M,D
Physical Chemistry	M,D
Physics	M,D*
Physiology	D
Psychology—General	M
Theoretical Chemistry	M,D

WESLEY BIBLICAL SEMINARY

Program	Degrees
Theology	P,M

WESLEY COLLEGE

Program	Degrees
Business Administration and Management—General	M
Education—General	M
Environmental Sciences	M
Nursing—General	M

WESLEY THEOLOGICAL SEMINARY

Program	Degrees
Theology	P,M,D

WEST CHESTER UNIVERSITY OF PENNSYLVANIA

Program	Degrees
Anthropology	M,O
Astronomy	M
Biological and Biomedical Sciences—General	M
Business Administration and Management—General	M
Chemistry	M*
City and Regional Planning	M
Classics	M
Clinical Psychology	M
Communication Disorders	M
Communication—General	M
Computer Science	M,O
Counselor Education	M
Criminal Justice and Criminology	M
Economics	M
Education—General	M,O
Educational Measurement and Evaluation	M
Educational Media/Instructional Technology	M,O
Electronic Commerce	M
Elementary Education	M
English as a Second Language	M
English	M
Environmental and Occupational Health	M
Exercise and Sports Science	M,O
Finance and Banking	M
Foreign Languages Education	M
French	M
Geography	M
Geology	M
German	M
Gerontology	M,O
Health Education	M
Health Services Management and Hospital Administration	M
History	M
Industrial and Organizational Psychology	M
Kinesiology and Movement Studies	M,O
Mathematics	M
Music Education	M
Music	M*
Nursing Education	M
Nursing—General	M
Philosophy	M
Physical Education	M,O
Psychology—General	M
Public Health—General	M
Public Policy and Administration	M
Reading Education	M
Science Education	M
Secondary Education	M
Social Work	M
Sociology	M,O
Spanish	M
Special Education	M
Sports Management	M,O

In-depth description on page 1295.

WESTERN CAROLINA UNIVERSITY

Program	Degrees
Accounting	M
American Studies	M
Art Education	M
Art/Fine Arts	M
Biological and Biomedical Sciences—General	M
Business Administration and Management—General	M
Chemistry	M
Clinical Psychology	M
Communication Disorders	M
Community College Education	M
Computer Science	M
Counselor Education	M
Education—General	M,D,O
Educational Administration	M,D,O
Elementary Education	M
English Education	M
English	M
Health Services Management and Hospital Administration	M
History	M
Home Economics Education	M
Human Resources Development	M
Industrial/Management Engineering	M
Mathematics Education	M
Mathematics	M
Middle School Education	M
Music	M
Nursing—General	M
Physical Education	M
Physical Therapy	M
Physics	M
Project Management	M
Psychology—General	M
Public Policy and Administration	M
Reading Education	M
School Psychology	M
Science Education	M
Secondary Education	M
Social Sciences Education	M
Special Education	M

In-depth description on page 1297.

WESTERN CONNECTICUT STATE UNIVERSITY

Program	Degrees
Accounting	M
Advanced Practice Nursing	M
Art/Fine Arts	M
Biological and Biomedical Sciences—General	M
Business Administration and Management—General	M
Computer Science	M
Counselor Education	M
Criminal Justice and Criminology	M
Curriculum and Instruction	M
Education—General	M
Educational Media/Instructional Technology	M
English Education	M
English	M
Environmental Sciences	M
Geosciences	M
Health Services Management and Hospital Administration	M
History	M
Illustration	M
Mathematics Education	M
Mathematics	M
Medical/Surgical Nursing	M
Music Education	M
Nursing—General	M
Planetary and Space Sciences	M
Reading Education	M
Special Education	M

WESTERN GOVERNORS UNIVERSITY

Program	Degrees
Education—General	M,O
Educational Administration	M,O
Educational Media/Instructional Technology	M,O

WESTERN ILLINOIS UNIVERSITY

Program	Degrees
Accounting	M
Biological and Biomedical Sciences—General	M,O
Business Administration and Management—General	M
Chemistry	M
Clinical Psychology	M,O
Communication Disorders	M
Communication—General	M
Computer Science	M
Counselor Education	M,O
Criminal Justice and Criminology	M,O
Curriculum and Instruction	M,O
Distance Education Development	M,O
Early Childhood Education	M,O
Economics	M
Education—General	M,O
Educational Administration	M,O
Educational Media/Instructional Technology	M,O
Elementary Education	M,O
English	M
Foundations and Philosophy of Education	M
Geography	M,O
Graphic Design	M,O
Health Education	M
Health Promotion	M
History	M
Internet and Interactive Multimedia	M,O
Marine Biology	M,O
Marriage and Family Therapy	M,O
Mathematics Education	M,O
Mathematics	M
Music	M
Physical Education	M
Physics	M
Political Science	M
Psychology—General	M,O
Reading Education	M,O
Recreation and Park Management	M
School Psychology	M,O
Science Education	M,O
Secondary Education	M
Social Psychology	M,O
Social Sciences Education	M,O
Sociology	M
Special Education	M
Sports Management	M
Student Personnel Services	M
Sustainable Development	M,O
Technology and Public Policy	M

Telecommunications M,O
Theater M
Travel and Tourism M
Writing M
Zoology M,O

WESTERN INTERNATIONAL UNIVERSITY

Business Administration and Management—General M
Finance and Banking M
International Business M
Management Information Systems M
Marketing M
Public Policy and Administration M

WESTERN KENTUCKY UNIVERSITY

Agricultural Sciences—General M
Art Education M
Biological and Biomedical Sciences—General M
Business Administration and Management—General M
Business Education M
Chemistry M
Communication Disorders M
Communication—General M
Comparative Literature M
Computer Science M
Corporate and Organizational Communication M
Counselor Education M,O
Early Childhood Education M
Education—General M,O
Educational Administration M,O
Educational Media/Instructional Technology M
Elementary Education M,O
English as a Second Language M
English Education M
English M
Environmental and Occupational Health M
Folklore M
Foreign Languages Education M
Geography M
Geology M
Gerontology M
Health Services Management and Hospital Administration M
Historic Preservation M
History M
Humanities M
Mathematics M
Middle School Education M
Music Education M
Nursing—General M
Philosophy M
Physical Education M
Psychology—General M,O
Public Health—General M
Public Policy and Administration M
Reading Education M
Recreation and Park Management M
Religion M
School Psychology M,O
Science Education M
Secondary Education M,O
Social Sciences Education M
Sociology M
Special Education M
Speech and Interpersonal Communication M
Writing M

In-depth description on page 1299 and announcement on page 704.

WESTERN MICHIGAN UNIVERSITY

Accounting M
Anthropology M
Applied Arts and Design—General M
Applied Economics M,D
Applied Mathematics M
Biological and Biomedical Sciences—General M,D
Biostatistics M
Business Administration and Management—General M
Chemical Engineering M,D
Chemistry M,D
Clinical Psychology M,D,O
Communication Disorders M
Communication—General M
Computational Sciences M
Computer Engineering M,D
Computer Science M,D
Construction Engineering and Management M
Corporate and Organizational Communication M
Counseling Psychology M,D
Counselor Education M,D
Early Childhood Education M
Economics M,D
Education—General M,D,O
Educational Administration M,D,O
Educational Measurement and Evaluation M,D
Electrical Engineering M,D
Elementary Education M
Engineering and Applied Sciences—General M,D*
Engineering Management M
English M,D
Exercise and Sports Science M
Experimental Psychology M,D,O
Family and Consumer Sciences-General M
Geography M
Geology M,D
Geosciences M
Graphic Design M
History M,D
Human Resources Development M,D,O
Industrial and Organizational Psychology M,D,O
Industrial/Management Engineering M
Manufacturing Engineering M
Marriage and Family Therapy M,D
Materials Engineering M
Materials Sciences M
Mathematics Education M,D
Mathematics M,D
Mechanical Engineering M,D
Medieval and Renaissance Studies M
Middle School Education M
Music M
Occupational Therapy M
Operations Research M
Paper and Pulp Engineering M,D
Philosophy M
Physical Education M
Physician Assistant Studies M
Physics M,D
Political Science M,D
Psychology—General M,D,O
Public Policy and Administration M,D
Reading Education M
Rehabilitation Counseling M
Religion M,D
School Psychology M,D,O
Science Education M,D
Social Work M
Sociology M,D
Spanish M
Special Education M,D
Sports Management M
Statistics M,D
Textile Design M
Vocational and Technical Education M
Writing M,D

In-depth description on page 1301.

WESTERN NEW ENGLAND COLLEGE

Accounting M
Business Administration and Management—General M
Computer Engineering M
Criminal Justice and Criminology M
Electrical Engineering M
Engineering and Applied Sciences—General M
Finance and Banking M
Health Services Management and Hospital Administration M
Human Resources Development M
Human Resources Management M
Industrial/Management Engineering M
International Business M
Law P
Management Information Systems M
Manufacturing Engineering M
Marketing M
Mechanical Engineering M

WESTERN NEW MEXICO UNIVERSITY

Business Administration and Management—General M
Counselor Education M
Education—General M
Educational Administration M
Elementary Education M
Interdisciplinary Studies M
Reading Education M
Secondary Education M
Special Education M

WESTERN OREGON UNIVERSITY

Criminal Justice and Criminology M
Early Childhood Education M
Education of the Multiply Handicapped M
Education—General M
Educational Media/Instructional Technology M
Health Education M
Mathematics Education M
Multilingual and Multicultural Education M
Rehabilitation Counseling M
Science Education M
Secondary Education M
Social Sciences Education M
Special Education M

WESTERN SEMINARY

Marriage and Family Therapy M
Pastoral Ministry and Counseling P,M,D,O
Religion M,O
Religious Education M,D
Theology M,O

WESTERN STATES CHIROPRACTIC COLLEGE

Chiropractic P*

WESTERN STATE UNIVERSITY COLLEGE OF LAW

Law P*

WESTERN THEOLOGICAL SEMINARY

Theology P,M,D

WESTERN UNIVERSITY OF HEALTH SCIENCES

Advanced Practice Nursing M
Allied Health—General M
Health Education M
Nursing—General M
Osteopathic Medicine P
Pharmacy P
Physical Therapy M
Physician Assistant Studies M

WESTERN WASHINGTON UNIVERSITY

Adult Education M
Anthropology M
Art/Fine Arts M
Biological and Biomedical Sciences—General M
Business Administration and Management—General M
Chemistry M
Communication Disorders M
Computer Science M
Counseling Psychology M
Counselor Education M
Education—General M
Educational Administration M
Elementary Education M
English M
Environmental Sciences M
Geography M
Geology M
History M
Kinesiology and Movement Studies M
Mathematics M
Music M
Physical Education M
Political Science M
Psychology—General M
Rehabilitation Counseling M
Science Education M
Secondary Education M
Sociology M
Special Education M
Student Personnel Services M
Theater M
Vocational and Technical Education M

WESTFIELD STATE COLLEGE

Clinical Psychology M
Counseling Psychology M
Criminal Justice and Criminology M
Early Childhood Education M
Education—General M,O
Educational Administration M,O
Educational Media/Instructional Technology M
Elementary Education M
English M
History M
Middle School Education M
Physical Education M
Reading Education M
Secondary Education M
Special Education M
Vocational and Technical Education M

WESTMINSTER COLLEGE (PA)

Counselor Education M,O
Curriculum and Instruction M,O
Education—General M,O
Educational Administration M,O
Elementary Education M,O
Reading Education M,O

WESTMINSTER COLLEGE (UT)

Business Administration and Management—General M,O
Communication—General M
Education—General M
Nursing—General M
Writing M

WESTMINSTER THEOLOGICAL SEMINARY

Missions and Missiology P,M,D,O
Pastoral Ministry and Counseling P,M,D,O
Religion P,M,D,O
Theology P,M,D,O

WESTMINSTER THEOLOGICAL SEMINARY IN CALIFORNIA

Religion P,M
Theology P,M

WESTON JESUIT SCHOOL OF THEOLOGY

Theology P,M,D,O

WEST TEXAS A&M UNIVERSITY

Accounting M
Agricultural Economics and Agribusiness M
Agricultural Sciences—General M
Animal Sciences M
Art/Fine Arts M
Biological and Biomedical Sciences—General M
Business Administration and Management—General M
Chemistry M
Communication Disorders M
Communication—General M
Counselor Education M
Criminal Justice and Criminology M
Curriculum and Instruction M
Economics M
Education—General M
Educational Administration M
Educational Measurement and Evaluation M
Educational Media/Instructional Technology M
Elementary Education M
Engineering and Applied Sciences—General M
English M
Environmental Sciences M
Exercise and Sports Science M
Finance and Banking M
History M
Interdisciplinary Studies M
Mathematics M
Music M
Nursing—General M
Plant Sciences M
Political Science M
Psychology—General M
Reading Education M
Secondary Education M

In-depth description on page 1303.

WEST VIRGINIA SCHOOL OF OSTEOPATHIC MEDICINE

Osteopathic Medicine P

WEST VIRGINIA UNIVERSITY

Accounting M
Aerospace/Aeronautical Engineering M,D
African Studies M,D
African-American Studies M,D
Agricultural Economics and Agribusiness M
Agricultural Education M
Agricultural Sciences—General M,D
Agronomy and Soil Sciences M,D
Allopathic Medicine P
American Studies M,D
Analytical Chemistry M,D
Anatomy M,D
Animal Sciences M,D
Anthropology M

West Virginia University (continued)

Applied Mathematics M,D
Applied Physics M,D
Art Education M
Art History M
Art/Fine Arts M
Asian Studies M,D
Bacteriology M,D
Biochemistry M,D
Biological and Biomedical Sciences—General M,D*
Business Administration and Management—General M
Cancer Biology/Oncology M,D
Cell Biology M,D
Chemical Engineering M,D
Chemistry M,D
Child and Family Studies M
City and Regional Planning M,D
Civil Engineering M,D
Clinical Laboratory Sciences/Medical Technology M
Clinical Psychology M,D
Communication Disorders M
Communication—General M
Community Health M
Comparative Literature M
Computer Engineering D
Computer Science M,D
Condensed Matter Physics M,D
Corporate and Organizational Communication M
Counseling Psychology M,D
Curriculum and Instruction M,D
Dentistry P
Developmental Biology M,D
Developmental Psychology M,D
Economics M,D
Education of the Gifted M,D
Education of the Multiply Handicapped M,D
Education—General M,D
Educational Administration M,D
Educational Psychology M,D
Electrical Engineering M,D
Elementary Education M
Engineering and Applied Sciences—General M,D*
English as a Second Language M
English M,D
Entomology M,D
Environmental Biology M,D
Environmental Education M
Environmental Engineering M,D
Environmental Management and Policy M,D
Exercise and Sports Science M,D
Fish, Game, and Wildlife Management M
Food Science and Technology M,D
Forestry M,D
French M
Genetics M,D*
Geographic Information Systems M,D
Geography M,D
Geology M,D
Geophysics M,D
German M
Graphic Design M
Health Education M,D
Health Promotion M
Higher Education M,D
History of Science and Technology M,D
History M,D
Horticulture M,D
Human Genetics M,D
Human Services M
Hydrology M,D
Immunology M,D
Industrial and Labor Relations M
Industrial/Management Engineering M,D
Inorganic Chemistry M,D
International Affairs M,D
Journalism M
Latin American Studies M,D
Law P*
Legal and Justice Studies M
Liberal Studies M
Linguistics M
Mathematics Education M
Mathematics M,D
Mechanical Engineering M,D
Medicinal and Pharmaceutical Chemistry M,D
Microbiology M,D
Mineral/Mining Engineering M,D
Molecular Biology M,D
Music Education M,D
Music M,D
Natural Resources D
Nursing—General M,D,O
Nutrition M,D
Occupational Therapy M
Oral and Dental Sciences M
Organic Chemistry M,D
Parasitology M,D
Petroleum Engineering M,D
Pharmaceutical Administration M,D
Pharmaceutical Sciences M,D
Pharmacology M,D
Pharmacy P,M,D
Physical Chemistry M,D
Physical Education M,D
Physical Therapy M
Physics M,D
Physiology M,D
Plant Biology M,D
Plant Pathology M,D
Plant Sciences M,D
Plasma Physics M,D
Political Science M,D
Psychology—General M,D
Public Health—General M
Public Policy and Administration M,D
Reading Education M
Recreation and Park Management M
Rehabilitation Counseling M
Reproductive Biology M,D
Safety Engineering M
Secondary Education M,D
Social Work M
Sociology M
Software Engineering M
Spanish M
Special Education M,D
Sport Psychology M,D
Sports Management M,D
Statistics M,D
Theater M
Theoretical Chemistry M,D
Theoretical Physics M,D
Toxicology M,D
Veterinary Sciences M
Virology M,D
Vocational and Technical Education M,D
Writing M,D

WEST VIRGINIA UNIVERSITY INSTITUTE OF TECHNOLOGY

Engineering and Applied Sciences—General M
Systems Engineering M

WEST VIRGINIA WESLEYAN COLLEGE

Business Administration and Management—General M

WHEATON COLLEGE

American Studies M
Archaeology M
Clinical Psychology M,D
Cultural Studies M,O
Education—General M
English as a Second Language M,O
Interdisciplinary Studies M
Missions and Missiology M,O
Psychology—General M,D
Religion M
Religious Education M
Secondary Education M
Theology M,O

In-depth description on page 1305.

WHEELING JESUIT UNIVERSITY

Accounting M
Business Administration and Management—General M
Mathematics Education M
Nursing—General M
Physical Therapy M
Science Education M
Theology M

WHEELOCK COLLEGE

Child and Family Studies M,O
Early Childhood Education M
Education—General M,O*
Educational Administration M,O
Elementary Education M
Maternal and Child Health M
Reading Education M
Social Work M
Special Education M

WHITTIER COLLEGE

Education—General M
Educational Administration M
Elementary Education M
Law P,M
Legal and Justice Studies P,M
Secondary Education M

WHITWORTH COLLEGE

Business Administration and Management—General M
Counselor Education M
Education of the Gifted M
Education—General M
Educational Administration M
English as a Second Language M
International Business M
Physical Education M
Reading Education M
Special Education M
Sports Management M

WICHITA STATE UNIVERSITY

Accounting M
Aerospace/Aeronautical Engineering M,D
Allied Health—General M
Anthropology M
Applied Mathematics M,D
Art Education M
Art/Fine Arts M
Biological and Biomedical Sciences—General M*
Business Administration and Management—General M
Chemistry M,D
Clinical Psychology M,D
Communication Disorders M,D
Communication—General M
Computer Science M
Counselor Education M,D,O
Criminal Justice and Criminology M
Curriculum and Instruction M
Economics M
Education—General M,D,O
Educational Administration M,D,O
Educational Psychology M,D,O
Electrical Engineering M,D
Engineering and Applied Sciences—General M,D
English M
Environmental Sciences M
Exercise and Sports Science M
Geology M
Gerontology M
History M
Human Services M
Industrial/Management Engineering M,D
Liberal Studies M
Manufacturing Engineering M,D
Maternal/Child Nursing M
Mathematics M,D
Mechanical Engineering M,D
Medical/Surgical Nursing M
Music Education M
Music M
Nursing and Healthcare Administration M
Nursing Education M
Nursing—General M
Physical Education M
Physical Therapy M
Physics M
Political Science M
Psychiatric Nursing M
Psychology—General M,D
Public Health—General M
Public Policy and Administration M
School Psychology M,D,O
Social Psychology M,D
Social Work M
Sociology M
Spanish M
Special Education M
Sports Management M
Statistics M,D
Writing M

In-depth description on page 1307.

WIDENER UNIVERSITY

Accounting M
Adult Education M,D
Business Administration and Management—General M
Chemical Engineering M
Civil Engineering M
Clinical Psychology D*
Computer Engineering M
Counselor Education M,D
Criminal Justice and Criminology M
Early Childhood Education M,D
Education—General M,D
Educational Administration M,D
Educational Media/Instructional Technology M,D
Educational Psychology M,D
Electrical Engineering M
Elementary Education M,D
Engineering and Applied Sciences—General M*
Engineering Management M
English Education M,D
Foundations and Philosophy of Education M,D
Health Education M,D
Health Services Management and Hospital Administration M
Human Resources Management M
Law P,M,D*
Liberal Studies M
Mathematics Education M,D
Mechanical Engineering M
Middle School Education M,D
Nursing—General M,D,O
Physical Therapy M
Psychology—General
Public Policy and Administration M
Reading Education M,D
Science Education M,D
Social Sciences Education M,D
Social Work M*
Software Engineering M
Special Education M,D
Taxation M
Telecommunications M

In-depth description on page 1309 and announcement on page 711.

WILFRID LAURIER UNIVERSITY

Business Administration and Management—General M
Economics M
English M,D
Ethics P,M,D
Experimental Psychology M
Geography M,D
History M,D
Pastoral Ministry and Counseling P,M,D
Philosophy D
Political Science M
Psychology—General M
Religion M
Social Psychology M
Social Work M,D
Theology P,M,D

WILKES UNIVERSITY

Accounting M
Business Administration and Management—General M
Computer Education M
Education—General M
Educational Administration M
Educational Measurement and Evaluation M
Electrical Engineering M
Elementary Education M
English Education M
Finance and Banking M
Health Services Management and Hospital Administration M
Human Resources Management M
International Business M
Marketing M
Mathematics Education M
Mathematics M
Nursing—General M
Pharmacy P
Physics M
Science Education M
Secondary Education M
Social Sciences Education M

WILLAMETTE UNIVERSITY

Business Administration and Management—General M*
Education—General M
Law P
Nonprofit Management M
Public Policy and Administration M*

WILLIAM CAREY COLLEGE

Art Education M
Business Administration and Management—General M
Counseling Psychology M
Education of the Gifted M
Education—General M
Educational Administration M
Elementary Education M
English Education M
Industrial and Organizational Psychology M
Psychology—General M
Secondary Education M
Special Education M

WILLIAM MITCHELL COLLEGE OF LAW

Law P

WILLIAM PATERSON UNIVERSITY OF NEW JERSEY

Art/Fine Arts M
Biological and Biomedical Sciences—General M*
Biotechnology M
Business Administration and Management—General M
Clinical Psychology M
Communication Disorders M
Communication—General M
Counselor Education M

Ecology M
Education—General M
Educational Administration M
Elementary Education M
English M
History M
Limnology M
Media Studies M
Molecular Biology M
Music M
Nursing—General M
Physiology M
Reading Education M
Sociology M
Special Education M

In-depth description on page 1311.

WILLIAMS COLLEGE

Art History M

WILLIAM WOODS UNIVERSITY

Accounting M
Business Administration and Management—General M
Curriculum and Instruction M
Education—General M
Educational Administration M
Health Services Management and Hospital Administration M

WILMINGTON COLLEGE

Advanced Practice Nursing M
Business Administration and Management—General M
Counselor Education M,D
Criminal Justice and Criminology M
Education—General M,D
Educational Administration M,D
Educational Media/Instructional Technology M,D
Elementary Education M,D
Gerontology M
Health Services Management and Hospital Administration M
Human Resources Management M
Logistics M
Nursing—General M
Psychology—General M
Public Policy and Administration M
Reading Education M,D
School Psychology M
Social Psychology M
Special Education M,D

WINEBRENNER THEOLOGICAL SEMINARY

Pastoral Ministry and Counseling P,M,D,O
Theology P,M,D,O

WINGATE UNIVERSITY

Business Administration and Management—General M
Elementary Education M

WINONA STATE UNIVERSITY

Counselor Education M
Education—General M
Educational Administration M
English M
Nursing—General M
Special Education M

WINTHROP UNIVERSITY

Art Education M
Art/Fine Arts M
Biological and Biomedical Sciences—General M
Business Administration and Management—General M
Counselor Education M
Education—General M
Educational Administration M
Elementary Education M
English M
History M
Liberal Studies M
Mathematics M
Middle School Education M
Music Education M
Music M
Nutrition M
Physical Education M
Psychology—General M,O
Reading Education M
Secondary Education M
Spanish M
Special Education M

WISCONSIN SCHOOL OF PROFESSIONAL PSYCHOLOGY

Clinical Psychology M,D
Psychology—General M,D

WOODBURY UNIVERSITY

Business Administration and Management—General M*

WORCESTER POLYTECHNIC INSTITUTE

Applied Mathematics M,D,O
Biomedical Engineering M,D,O*
Biotechnology M,D
Business Administration and Management—General M,O
Chemical Engineering M,D*
Chemistry M,D
Civil Engineering M,D,O
Computer Engineering M,D,O
Computer Science M,D,O*
Electrical Engineering M,D,O
Energy and Power Engineering M,D,O
Engineering and Applied Sciences—General M,D,O*
Environmental Engineering M,D,O
Fire Protection Engineering M,D,O
Management Information Systems M,O
Manufacturing Engineering M,D,O
Marketing M,O
Materials Engineering M,D,O
Materials Sciences M,D,O
Mathematics M,D,O
Mechanical Engineering M,D,O*
Physics M,D
Statistics M,D,O

In-depth description on page 1313.

WORCESTER STATE COLLEGE

Biotechnology M
Communication Disorders M
Community Health Nursing M
Early Childhood Education M
Education—General M,O
Educational Administration M
Elementary Education M
English Education M,O
Health Education M
Health Services Management and Hospital Administration M
Middle School Education M,O
Nonprofit Management M
Occupational Therapy M
Reading Education M,O
Secondary Education M,O

WRIGHT INSTITUTE

Psychology—General D

WRIGHT STATE UNIVERSITY

Accounting M
Adult Education O
Advanced Practice Nursing M
Allopathic Medicine P
Anatomy M
Applied Economics M
Applied Mathematics M
Biochemistry M*
Biological and Biomedical Sciences—General M,D*
Biomedical Engineering M,D
Biophysics M
Business Administration and Management—General M*
Business Education M
Chemistry M
Clinical Psychology D
Community Health Nursing M
Computer Education M
Computer Engineering M,D*
Computer Science M,D*
Counselor Education M
Criminal Justice and Criminology M
Curriculum and Instruction O
Early Childhood Education M
Economics M
Education of the Gifted M
Education—General M,O
Educational Administration M,O
Electrical Engineering M
Electronic Commerce M
Elementary Education M
Engineering and Applied Sciences—General M,D*
English as a Second Language M
English M
Environmental Management and Policy M
Environmental Sciences M,D
Ergonomics and Human Factors M,D
Finance and Banking M
Geochemistry M
Geology M
Geophysics M
Health Education M
Higher Education M,O
History M
Humanities M
Hydrology M
Immunology M
Industrial and Manufacturing Management M
Industrial and Organizational Psychology M,D
Interdisciplinary Studies M
International and Comparative Education M
International Business M
Library Science M
Logistics M
Management Information Systems M
Marketing M
Materials Engineering M
Materials Sciences M
Mathematics Education M
Mathematics M
Mechanical Engineering M
Medical Physics M
Medical/Surgical Nursing M
Microbiology M
Molecular Biology M
Music Education M
Nursing and Healthcare Administration M
Nursing—General M
Pediatric Nursing M
Pharmacology M
Physical Education M
Physics M*
Physiology M
Project Management M
Psychology—General M,D
Public Policy and Administration M
Recreation and Park Management M
Rehabilitation Counseling M
Rhetoric M
School Nursing M
Science Education M
Secondary Education M
Special Education M
Statistics M
Toxicology M
Urban Studies M
Vocational and Technical Education M
Writing M

WYCLIFFE COLLEGE

Religion P,M,D,O
Theology P,M,D,O

XAVIER UNIVERSITY

Accounting M
Business Administration and Management—General M
Clinical Psychology M,D
Counselor Education M
Criminal Justice and Criminology M
Early Childhood Education M
Education—General M
Educational Administration M
Electronic Commerce M
Elementary Education M
English M
Entrepreneurship M
Finance and Banking M
Health Services Management and Hospital Administration M*
Human Resources Development M
Humanities M
International Business M
Management Information Systems M
Marketing M
Multilingual and Multicultural Education M
Nursing and Healthcare Administration M
Nursing—General M
Psychology—General M,D*
Reading Education M
Secondary Education M
Special Education M
Sports Management M
Theology M

XAVIER UNIVERSITY OF LOUISIANA

Counselor Education M
Curriculum and Instruction M
Education—General M
Educational Administration M
Nurse Anesthesia M
Pastoral Ministry and Counseling M
Pharmacy P
Theology M

YALE UNIVERSITY

Accounting D
African Studies M
African-American Studies M,D
Allopathic Medicine P
American Studies M,D
Anthropology M,D
Applied Arts and Design—General M
Applied Mathematics M,D
Applied Physics M,D
Archaeology M
Architecture M
Art History D
Art/Fine Arts M
Asian Languages D
Asian Studies M
Astronomy M,D
Biochemistry M,D*
Bioinformatics D*
Biological and Biomedical Sciences—General D*
Biophysics M,D
Biostatistics M,D
Business Administration and Management—General M,D*
Cell Biology D
Chemical Engineering M,D*
Chemistry D*
Classics D
Comparative Literature D
Computational Sciences D
Computer Science D*
Developmental Biology D
East European and Russian Studies M
Ecology D*
Economics M,D
Electrical Engineering M,D*
Engineering and Applied Sciences—General M,D*
Engineering Physics M,D
English M,D
Environmental and Occupational Health M,D
Environmental Design M
Environmental Management and Policy M,D
Environmental Sciences M,D
Epidemiology M,D
Evolutionary Biology D
Finance and Banking D
Forestry M,D*
French M,D
Genetics D
Geochemistry D
Geology D*
Geophysics D
Geosciences D
German M,D
Graphic Design M
Health Services Management and Hospital Administration M
History of Medicine M,D
History of Science and Technology M,D
History M,D
Immunology D*
Inorganic Chemistry D
International Affairs M*
International Health M
Italian D
Law P,M,D
Linguistics D
Marketing D
Mathematics M,D
Mechanical Engineering M,D
Mechanics M,D
Medieval and Renaissance Studies M,D
Meteorology D
Microbiology D*
Mineralogy D
Molecular Biology D
Molecular Medicine D
Music M,D,O
Near and Middle Eastern Languages M,D
Neurobiology D
Neuroscience D*
Nursing—General M,D,O*
Oceanography D
Organic Chemistry D
Parasitology D*
Pathology D
Pharmacology D*
Philosophy D
Photography M
Physical Chemistry D
Physician Assistant Studies M
Physics D*
Physiology D*
Plant Biology D

Yale University (continued)

Political Science	D
Portuguese	M,D
Psychology—General	M,D
Public Health—General	M,D*
Religion	D
Slavic Languages	M,D
Sociology	D
Spanish	M,D
Statistics	M,D
Theater	M,D,O
Theology	P,M

YESHIVA BETH MOSHE

Theology	O

YESHIVA KARLIN STOLIN RABBINICAL INSTITUTE

Theology	O

YESHIVA OF NITRA RABBINICAL COLLEGE

Theology

YESHIVA SHAAR HATORAH TALMUDIC RESEARCH INSTITUTE

Theology

YESHIVATH ZICHRON MOSHE

Theology	O

YESHIVA TORAS CHAIM TALMUDICAL SEMINARY

Theology

YESHIVA UNIVERSITY

Allopathic Medicine	P
Anatomy	D
Biochemistry	D*
Biological and Biomedical Sciences—General	D*
Biophysics	D
Cell Biology	D
Clinical Psychology	D
Developmental Biology	D
Developmental Psychology	D
Educational Administration	M,D,O
Genetics	D
Health Psychology	D
Immunology	D
Jewish Studies	M,D
Law	P,M
Microbiology	D*
Molecular Biology	D
Neurobiology	D
Pathology	D
Pharmacology	D*
Physiology	D*
Psychology—General	M,D
Religious Education	M,D,O
School Psychology	D
Social Work	M,D

YORK COLLEGE OF PENNSYLVANIA

Accounting	M
Business Administration and Management—General	M
Finance and Banking	M
Health Services Management and Hospital Administration	M
Human Resources Management	M
Management Information Systems	M
Marketing	M

YORK UNIVERSITY

Anthropology	M,D
Art History	M
Art/Fine Arts	M
Astronomy	M,D
Biological and Biomedical Sciences—General	M,D
Business Administration and Management—General	M,D*
Chemistry	M,D
Communication—General	M,D
Computer Science	M,D
Dance	M
Economics	M,D
Education—General	M,D
English	M,D
Environmental Management and Policy	M,D
Film, Television, and Video Production	M
French	M
Geography	M,D
Geosciences	M,D
History	M,D
Interdisciplinary Studies	M
Kinesiology and Movement Studies	M,D
Law	M,D
Mathematics	M,D
Music	M,D
Philosophy	M,D
Physics	M,D
Planetary and Space Sciences	M,D
Political Science	M,D
Psychology—General	M,D
Social Work	M
Sociology	M,D
Statistics	M,D
Theater	M
Translation and Interpretation	M
Women's Studies	M,D

YO SAN UNIVERSITY OF TRADITIONAL CHINESE MEDICINE

Acupuncture and Oriental Medicine	M

YOUNGSTOWN STATE UNIVERSITY

Accounting	M
Biological and Biomedical Sciences—General	M
Business Administration and Management—General	M
Chemical Engineering	M
Chemistry	M
Civil Engineering	M
Counselor Education	M
Criminal Justice and Criminology	M
Early Childhood Education	M
Economics	M
Education of the Gifted	M
Education—General	M,D
Educational Administration	M,D
Electrical Engineering	M
Elementary Education	M
Engineering and Applied Sciences—General	M
English	M
Environmental Engineering	M
Environmental Management and Policy	M,O
Finance and Banking	M
Foundations and Philosophy of Education	M,D
Health Services Management and Hospital Administration	M
History	M
Human Services	M
Industrial/Management Engineering	M
Marketing	M
Mathematics	M
Mechanical Engineering	M
Middle School Education	M
Music Education	M
Music	M
Nursing—General	M
Physical Therapy	M
Reading Education	M
Secondary Education	M
Special Education	M

Profiles of Institutions Offering Graduate and Professional Work

This section presents profiles of accredited colleges and universities in the United States and U.S. territories and those in Canada, Mexico, Europe, and Africa that are accredited by U.S. accrediting bodies offering graduate and professional degree programs. Together with the other sections of Book 1, it is both a basic reference source and a foundation for the other five volumes of the Annual Guides to Graduate Study. (Books 2–6 provide descriptions of graduate programs in the humanities, arts, and social sciences; the biological sciences; the physical sciences, mathematics, agricultural sciences, the environment, and natural resources; engineering and applied sciences; and business, education, health, information studies, law, and social work, respectively.) The profiles in this section include the data on graduate and professional units that were submitted in 2002 by each institution in response to Peterson's Annual Survey of Graduate and Professional Institutions, supplemented by information taken from college catalogs and over the telephone. If an institution provided all of the information requested, the profile includes all of the items listed below. A number of graduate school administrators have written brief Announcements, which follow their profiles. In these, readers will find information an institution wants to emphasize. In addition, bolded reference lines at the end of a profile indicate the page number on which the reader will find an In-Depth Description, if the institution has chosen to submit one. The absence of an Announcement or In-Depth Description does not reflect any type of editorial judgment on the part of Peterson's.

General Information

Type. An institution's control is indicated as independent (private nonprofit), independent with religious affiliation, proprietary (private profit-making), or public. Whether an institution is coeducational or primarily for men or women is indicated. Institutional type is given as university, comprehensive, graduate only, or upper level.

CGS Membership. Membership in the Council of Graduate Schools in the United States and in Canada is indicated here.

Enrollment. Enrollment figures include total matriculated students (graduate, professional, and undergraduate), total full- and part-time matriculated graduate and professional students, and the number of women in each category.

Enrollment by Degree Level. Figures include the total number of students enrolled at each degree level—master's, doctoral, first-professional, and other advanced degrees.

Graduate Faculty. The numbers of full-time and part-time/adjunct faculty members actively involved with graduate students through teaching or research are given, followed by numbers of women and minority-group members. The last figure is further broken down into numbers of Asian-American, Hispanic-American, African-American, and Native American faculty members.

Graduate Expenses. Tuition and fees for the overall institution for 2001–02 are indicated on a full-time (per academic year, semester, quarter, etc.) and/or a part-time (per credit, semester hour, quarter hour, course, etc.) basis. In-state and out-of-state figures are supplied where applicable. For exact costs at any given time, contact the schools and programs directly. Keep in mind that the tuition of Canadian institutions is usually given in Canadian dollars.

Graduate Housing. Institutions were asked to indicate whether housing for single and married students is guaranteed or available on a first-come, first-served basis and whether that includes board and to indicate the typical cost per year.

Student Services. Each institution was asked which of the following services are available to graduate and professional students: campus employment opportunities, campus safety program, career counseling, child day-care facilities, disabled student services, exercise/wellness program, free psychological counseling, grant writing training, international student services, low-cost health insurance, multicultural affairs office, teacher training, and writing training.

Library Facilities. The main library name and the number of additional on-campus libraries, if any, are provided. Also provided are online resources, such as library catalog, Web page, and other libraries' catalogs, and numbers of titles, current serial subscriptions, and audiovisual materials.

Research Affiliations. Institutions were asked to name up to six independent research centers, laboratories, or institutes with which they maintain formal arrangements providing extra research or study opportunities for graduate students.

Computer Facilities

Institutions were asked to provide the total number of PCs and/or terminals available for student use, whether a campuswide network is available, and whether Internet access and/or online class registration is available. The institution's Web site also appears here if that information was supplied.

General Application Contact

The name, title, telephone number, fax number, and e-mail address of the person to contact for further information about applying to graduate and professional programs appear here.

Graduate Units

Each major graduate and professional unit within the institution (school, college, institute, center, etc.) is listed below the general information. These units are arranged to show the hierarchical structure of the institution. Those units offering advanced degree programs through the graduate school are listed immediately beneath it. Professional schools not connected with the graduate school are listed separately.

Enrollment. The number of full- and part-time matriculated students and the number of women, minority-group members, and international students are given. Average age is indicated, followed by the number of applicants, percentage accepted, and the number enrolled.

Faculty. Full-time and part-time/adjunct figures are given, and the number of women is indicated.

Expenses. For individual program expenses, readers are advised to contact the institution.

Financial Support. Information is given on the number of fellowships and assistantships awarded in 2001–02 and the availability of other types of aid. The financial aid application deadline is also indicated.

Degree Program Information. The number of degrees awarded in calendar year 2001 is given, broken down by degree level, followed by the availability of part-time and evening/weekend programs. Degree programs offered through the subunits and the specific degrees awarded are listed. Special degree information is also included, such as that a degree is offered jointly with another university.

Applying. The application deadline and application fee are given, followed by a person to contact and a telephone number, fax number, and e-mail address (if provided).

Head. The head of the unit and his or her title are indicated, along with a telephone number, fax number, and e-mail address (if provided).

ABILENE CHRISTIAN UNIVERSITY, Abilene, TX 79699-9100

General Information Independent-religious, coed, comprehensive institution. *Enrollment:* 198 full-time matriculated graduate/professional students (89 women), 155 part-time matriculated graduate/professional students (63 women). *Graduate faculty:* 12 full-time (0 women), 92 part-time/adjunct (20 women). *Tuition:* Full-time $8,904; part-time $371 per hour. *Required fees:* $520; $17 per hour. $5. *Graduate housing:* Rooms and/or apartments available on a first-come, first-served basis to single and married students. Typical cost: $4,230 per year ($6,930 including board) for married students. Housing application deadline: 5/11. *Student services:* Campus employment opportunities, campus safety program, career counseling, disabled student services, exercise/wellness program, grant writing training, international student services, low-cost health insurance, multicultural affairs office, teacher training, writing training. *Library facilities:* Brown Library. *Online resources:* library catalog, web page, access to other libraries' catalogs. *Collection:* 478,831 titles, 2,387 serial subscriptions, 57,395 audiovisual materials. *Research affiliation:* Los Alamos National Laboratory (particle physics), Fermilab (peanut toxins).

Computer facilities: 650 computers available on campus for general student use. A campuswide network can be accessed from student residence rooms and from off campus. Internet access and online class registration are available. *Web address:* http://www.acu.edu/.

General Application Contact: Dr. Roger Gee, Graduate Dean, 915-674-2122, Fax: 915-674-2123, E-mail: gradinfo@education.acu.edu.

GRADUATE UNITS

Graduate School Students: 198 full-time (89 women), 155 part-time (63 women); includes 27 minority (12 African Americans, 3 Asian Americans or Pacific Islanders, 10 Hispanic Americans, 2 Native Americans), 29 international. Average age 30. 261 applicants, 76% accepted, 165 enrolled. *Faculty:* 12 full-time (0 women), 92 part-time/adjunct (20 women). Expenses: Contact institution. *Financial support:* In 2001–02, 353 students received support, including 30 research assistantships with partial tuition reimbursements available, 30 teaching assistantships with partial tuition reimbursements available (averaging $4,600 per year); career-related internships or fieldwork, Federal Work-Study, institutionally sponsored loans, and scholarships/grants also available. Support available to part-time students. Financial award application deadline: 4/1; financial award applicants required to submit FAFSA. In 2001, 12 first professional degrees, 166 master's, 4 doctorates awarded. *Degree program information:* Part-time and evening/weekend programs available. Postbaccalaureate distance learning degree programs offered. Offers organizational and human resource development (MS). *Application deadline:* For fall admission, 4/1 (priority date); for spring admission, 11/1 (priority date). Applications are processed on a rolling basis. *Application fee:* $25 ($45 for international students). *Graduate Dean*, Dr. Roger Gee, 915-674-2122, Fax: 915-674-2123, E-mail: gradinfo@education.acu.edu.

College of Arts and Sciences Students: 68 full-time (48 women), 64 part-time (40 women); includes 13 minority (5 African Americans, 1 Asian American or Pacific Islander, 6 Hispanic Americans, 1 Native American), 7 international. 119 applicants, 74% accepted, 70 enrolled. *Faculty:* 60 part-time/adjunct (13 women). Expenses: Contact institution. *Financial support:* Research assistantships, teaching assistantships, career-related internships or fieldwork and Federal Work-Study available. Support available to part-time students. Financial award application deadline: 4/1. In 2001, 101 degrees awarded. *Degree program information:* Part-time programs available. Offers arts and sciences (M Ed, MA, MLA, MS); clinical psychology (MS); communication sciences and disorders (MS); counseling psychology (MS); digital media (MS); educational diagnosis (M Ed); elementary teaching (M Ed); general psychology (MS); gerontology (MS); history (MA); human communication (MA); liberal arts (MLA); literature (MA); reading specialist (M Ed); school administrator (M Ed); school counselor (M Ed); school psychology (MS); secondary teaching (M Ed); social services administration (MS); writing (MA). *Application deadline:* For fall admission, 4/1 (priority date); for spring admission, 11/1. Applications are processed on a rolling basis. *Application fee:* $25 ($45 for international students). *Application Contact:* Dr. Roger Gee, Graduate Dean, 915-674-2122, Fax: 915-674-2123, E-mail: gradinfo@education.acu.edu. *Dean*, Dr. Colleen Durrington, 915-674-2209.

College of Biblical Studies Students: 114 full-time (30 women), 72 part-time (14 women); includes 10 minority (5 African Americans, 2 Asian Americans or Pacific Islanders, 2 Hispanic Americans, 1 Native American), 18 international. 109 applicants, 79% accepted, 71 enrolled. *Faculty:* 12 full-time (0 women), 13 part-time/adjunct (3 women). Expenses: Contact institution. *Financial support:* Teaching assistantships, career-related internships or fieldwork and Federal Work-Study available. Support available to part-time students. Financial award application deadline: 4/1. In 2001, 12 first professional degrees, 28 master's, 4 doctorates awarded. *Degree program information:* Part-time and evening/weekend programs available. Offers biblical studies (MA); Christian ministry (MAR); divinity (M Div); history and theology (MA); marriage and family therapy (MMFT); ministry (D Min); missions (MA, MS); New Testament (MA); Old Testament (MA). *Application deadline:* For fall admission, 4/1 (priority date); for spring admission, 11/1. Applications are processed on a rolling basis. *Application fee:* $25 ($45 for international students). *Application Contact:* Dr. Roger Gee, Graduate Dean, 915-674-2122, Fax: 915-674-2123, E-mail: gradinfo@education.acu.edu. *Dean*, Dr. Jack Reese, 915-674-3700.

College of Business Administration Students: 6 full-time (4 women), 2 part-time (both women). 9 applicants, 100% accepted, 8 enrolled. *Faculty:* 6 part-time/adjunct (0 women). Expenses: Contact institution. *Financial support:* Teaching assistantships, Federal Work-Study available. Support available to part-time students. Financial award application deadline: 4/1. In 2001, 13 degrees awarded. *Degree program information:* Part-time programs available. Offers business administration (M Acc). *Application deadline:* For fall admission, 4/1 (priority date); for spring admission, 11/1. Applications are processed on a rolling basis. *Application fee:* $25 ($45 for international students). *Application Contact:* Dr. Roger Gee, Graduate Dean, 915-674-2122, Fax: 915-674-2123, E-mail: gradinfo@education.acu.edu. *Department Chair*, Bill Fowler, 915-674-2080, Fax: 915-674-2564, E-mail: bill.fowler@coba.acu.edu.

School of Nursing 3 applicants, 100% accepted, 3 enrolled. *Faculty:* 4 part-time/adjunct (3 women). Expenses: Contact institution. *Financial support:* Application deadline: 4/1. In 2001, 4 degrees awarded. Offers nursing (MSN). *Application deadline:* For fall admission, 4/1 (priority date); for spring admission, 11/1. Applications are processed on a rolling basis. *Application fee:* $25 ($45 for international students). *Application Contact:* Dr. Roger Gee, Graduate Dean, 915-674-2122, Fax: 915-674-2123, E-mail: gradinfo@education.acu.edu. *Dean*, Dr. Cecilia Tiller, 915-672-2441.

ACADEMY FOR FIVE ELEMENT ACUPUNCTURE, Hallandale, FL 33009

General Information Independent, coed, graduate-only institution.

ACADEMY OF ART COLLEGE, San Francisco, CA 94105-3410

General Information Proprietary, coed, comprehensive institution. *Enrollment:* 248 full-time matriculated graduate/professional students (123 women), 435 part-time matriculated graduate/professional students (209 women). *Enrollment by degree level:* 683 master's. *Graduate faculty:* 16 full-time (4 women), 109 part-time/adjunct (36 women). *Tuition:* Full-time $14,400; part-time $600 per unit. *Graduate housing:* Rooms and/or apartments guaranteed to single students and available to married students. *Student services:* Campus employment opportunities, campus safety program, career counseling, disabled student services, international student services, low-cost health insurance, teacher training, writing training. *Library facilities:* Academy of Art College Library. *Online resources:* library catalog. *Collection:* 19,500 titles, 285 serial subscriptions, 90,000 audiovisual materials.

Computer facilities: 600 computers available on campus for general student use. Internet access is available. *Web address:* http://www.academyart.edu/.

General Application Contact: Sandra Webber, Vice President of Graduate Admissions, 800-544-ARTS, Fax: 415-263-4130, E-mail: info@academyart.edu.

GRADUATE UNITS

Graduate Program Students: 248 full-time (123 women), 435 part-time (209 women); includes 91 minority (14 African Americans, 59 Asian Americans or Pacific Islanders, 15 Hispanic Americans, 3 Native Americans), 411 international. Average age 27. 280 applicants, 89% accepted, 182 enrolled. *Faculty:* 16 full-time (4 women), 109 part-time/adjunct (36 women). Expenses: Contact institution. *Financial support:* Fellowships, teaching assistantships, career-related internships or fieldwork, Federal Work-Study, and institutionally sponsored loans available. Support available to part-time students. Financial award application deadline: 7/31; financial award applicants required to submit FAFSA. In 2001, 50 degrees awarded. *Degree program information:* Part-time and evening/weekend programs available. Offers advertising (MFA); computer graphics (MFA); drawing/painting (MFA); fashion design (MFA); fashion merchandising (MFA); fashion textiles (MFA); graphic design (MFA); illustration (MFA); interior architecture and design (MFA); motion pictures and television (MFA); new media (MFA); photography (MFA); printmaking (MFA); sculpture (MFA); transportation design (MFA). *Application deadline:* For fall admission, 9/7; for spring admission, 2/2. Applications are processed on a rolling basis. *Application fee:* $100 ($500 for international students). Electronic applications accepted. *Application Contact:* 800-544-ARTS, Fax: 415-263-4130, E-mail: info@academyarts.edu. *Executive Vice President of Education*, Sue Rowley, 800-544-ARTS, E-mail: info@academyart.edu.

See in-depth description on page 721.

ACADEMY OF CHINESE CULTURE AND HEALTH SCIENCES, Oakland, CA 94612

General Information Private, coed, graduate-only institution. *Enrollment by degree level:* 161 master's. *Graduate faculty:* 6 full-time (3 women), 31 part-time/adjunct (17 women). *Tuition:* Part-time $156 per unit. *Graduate housing:* On-campus housing not available.

Computer facilities: 5 computers available on campus for general student use. A campuswide network can be accessed. Internet access is available. *Web address:* http://www.acchs.edu/.

General Application Contact: Wei Tsuei, President/Founder, 510-763-7787, Fax: 510-834-8646.

GRADUATE UNITS

Program in Traditional Chinese Medicine Students: 155 full-time (93 women), 23 part-time (14 women); includes 100 minority (4 African Americans, 89 Asian Americans or Pacific Islanders, 6 Hispanic Americans, 1 Native American), 16 international. Average age 36. 73 applicants, 81% accepted, 51 enrolled. *Faculty:* 6 full-time (3 women), 31 part-time/adjunct (17 women). Expenses: Contact institution. In 2001, 19 degrees awarded. *Degree program information:* Part-time and evening/weekend programs available. Offers traditional Chinese medicine (MS). *Application deadline:* For fall admission, 9/3 (priority date); for spring admission, 1/8. Applications are processed on a rolling basis. *Application fee:* $50 ($100 for international students). *Application Contact:* Y. Chun Hsieh, Admissions Administrator, 510-763-7787, Fax: 510-834-8646, E-mail: ychun@acchs.edu. *Director of Administration*, Jane Zhang, 510-763-7787, Fax: 510-834-8646, E-mail: jane@acchs.edu.

ACADEMY OF ORIENTAL MEDICINE AT AUSTIN, Austin, TX 78757

General Information Proprietary, coed, graduate-only institution.

GRADUATE UNITS

Program in Oriental Medicine Offers Oriental medicine (MS).

ACADIA UNIVERSITY, Wolfville, NS B0P 1X0, Canada

General Information Province-supported, coed, comprehensive institution. *Enrollment:* 76 full-time matriculated graduate/professional students (48 women), 141 part-time matriculated graduate/professional students (91 women). *Enrollment by degree level:* 217 master's. *Graduate tuition:* Tuition charges are reported in Canadian dollars. *Tuition:* Full-time $4,947 Canadian dollars; part-time $574 Canadian dollars per course. *Graduate housing:* Room and/or apartments available on a first-come, first-served basis to single students; on-campus housing not available to married students. Typical cost: $3,180 Canadian dollars per year ($5,410 Canadian dollars including board). Room and board charges vary according to board plan, campus/location and housing facility selected. *Student services:* Campus employment opportunities, campus safety program, career counseling, disabled student services, exercise/wellness program, free psychological counseling, international student services, low-cost health insurance. *Library facilities:* Vaughan Memorial Library. *Online resources:* library catalog, web page, access to other libraries' catalogs. *Collection:* 822,030 titles, 4,106 serial subscriptions, 4,406 audiovisual materials. *Research affiliation:* Atlantic Research Laboratory.

Computer facilities: 3,700 computers available on campus for general student use. A campuswide network can be accessed from student residence rooms and from off campus. Internet access and online class registration, online course and grade information are available. *Web address:* http://www.acadiau.ca/.

General Application Contact: Anne Scott, Manager, Admissions, 902-585-1222, Fax: 902-585-1081, E-mail: admissions@acadiau.ca.

GRADUATE UNITS

Divinity College Students: 76 full-time (21 women), 11 part-time (6 women). Average age 33. 39 applicants, 87% accepted. *Faculty:* 8 full-time (1 woman), 8 part-time/adjunct (2 women). Expenses: Contact institution. *Financial support:* In 2001–02, 7 research assistantships, 6 teaching assistantships were awarded. Career-related internships or fieldwork, scholarships/grants, and tuition waivers (partial) also available. Financial award application deadline: 7/1. In 2001, 9 first professional degrees, 1 master's, 2 doctorates awarded. *Degree program information:* Part-time programs available. Offers clinical pastoral education (M Th); divinity (M Div); theology (MA, D Min). *Application deadline:* For fall admission, 5/31 (priority date); for spring admission, 4/15. Applications are processed on a rolling basis. *Application fee:* $25. *Application Contact:* Rev. Maxine Ashley, Dean of Students, 902-585-2216, Fax: 902-542-7527, E-mail: maxine.ashley@acadiau.ca. *Principal*, Dr. Lee M. McDonald, 902-585-2212, Fax: 902-542-7527.

Faculty of Arts Students: 7 full-time (5 women), 7 part-time (3 women). *Faculty:* 28 full-time (14 women). Expenses: Contact institution. *Financial support:* Research assistantships, teaching assistantships, career-related internships or fieldwork, scholarships/grants, and unspecified assistantships available. Financial award application deadline: 2/1. In 2001, 8 degrees awarded. Offers arts (MA); English (MA); political science (MA); sociology (MA). *Application deadline:* For fall admission, 2/1. *Application fee:* $50. Electronic applications accepted. *Dean*, Dr. Bruce Matthews, 902-585-1485, Fax: 902-585-1070, E-mail: bruce.matthews@acadiau.ca.

Faculty of Professional Studies Students: 23 full-time, 221 part-time. 175 applicants, 75% accepted. *Faculty:* 13 full-time (6 women). Expenses: Contact institution. *Financial support:* Research assistantships, teaching assistantships available. Financial award application deadline: 2/1. *Degree program information:* Part-time and evening/weekend programs available. Offers professional studies (M Ed, Certificate). *Application fee:* $50. *Dean*, Dr. William McLeod, 902-585-1198, Fax: 902-585-1086.

School of Education Students: 23 full-time, 221 part-time. Average age 35. 175 applicants, 75% accepted. *Faculty:* 13 full-time (6 women). Expenses: Contact institution. *Financial support:* In 2001–02, 7 teaching assistantships (averaging $4,000 per year) were awarded. Financial award application deadline: 2/1. In 2001, 31 degrees awarded. *Degree program information:* Part-time and evening/weekend programs available. Offers counseling (M Ed, Certificate); cultural and media studies (M Ed); curriculum studies (M Ed); inclusive education (M Ed, Certificate); leadership and school development (M Ed); learning and technology (M Ed); science, math and technology (M Ed); special education (M Ed). *Application fee:* $50. *Application Contact:* Sheila Langille, Secretary, 902-585-1229, Fax: 902-585-

Acadia University (continued)

1071, E-mail: sheila.langille@acadiau.ca. *Director,* Dr. Heather Hemming, 902-585-1229, Fax: 902-585-1071, E-mail: heather.hemming@acadiau.ca.

Faculty of Pure and Applied Science Students: 59 full-time (31 women). *Faculty:* 73. Expenses: Contact institution. *Financial support:* Fellowships, research assistantships, teaching assistantships, career-related internships or fieldwork and scholarships/grants available. Financial award application deadline: 2/1. In 2001, 16 degrees awarded. Offers biology (M Sc); chemistry (M Sc); clinical psychology (M Sc); geology (M Sc); pure and applied science (M Sc). *Application deadline:* For fall admission, 2/1. *Application fee:* $50. *Application Contact:* Anne Mercer-Hall, Office Manager, 902-585-1472, Fax: 902-585-1637, E-mail: anne.mercer—hall@acadiau.ca. *Dean,* Dr. Cyrus MacLatchy, 902-585-1472, Fax: 902-585-1637.

School of Computer Science Students: 19 full-time (4 women), 10 international. Average age 22. *Faculty:* 9 full-time (2 women). Expenses: Contact institution. *Financial support:* Teaching assistantships, career-related internships or fieldwork available. Financial award application deadline: 2/1. Offers computer science (M Sc). *Application deadline:* For fall admission, 2/1. *Application fee:* $50. *Application Contact:* Secretary, 902-585-1585, Fax: 902-585-1067, E-mail: cs@acadiau.ca. *Director,* Dr. A. Trudel, 902-585-1331, Fax: 902-585-1067, E-mail: cs@acadiau.ca.

ADAMS STATE COLLEGE, Alamosa, CO 81102

General Information State-supported, coed, comprehensive institution. *Enrollment:* 44 full-time matriculated graduate/professional students (26 women), 266 part-time matriculated graduate/professional students (206 women). *Enrollment by degree level:* 310 master's. *Graduate faculty:* 42 full-time (15 women). Tuition, state resident: full-time $856. Tuition, nonresident: full-time $3,376. One-time fee: $284 full-time. *Graduate housing:* Rooms and/or apartments available to single and married students. Typical cost: $2,720 (including board) for married students. Housing application deadline: 5/15. *Student services:* Campus employment opportunities, career counseling, child daycare facilities, exercise/wellness program, free psychological counseling, low-cost health insurance. *Library facilities:* Nielsen Library. *Online resources:* library catalog, web page, access to other libraries' catalogs. *Collection:* 472,594 titles, 1,646 serial subscriptions, 1,954 audiovisual materials. *Research affiliation:* Sandia National Laboratories (science education).

Computer facilities: 261 computers available on campus for general student use. A campuswide network can be accessed from student residence rooms and from off campus. Internet access and online class registration are available. *Web address:* http://www.adams.edu/.

General Application Contact: Dr. Don Basse, Dean of Graduate Studies, 719-587-7936, Fax: 719-587-7873, E-mail: dtbasse@adams.edu.

GRADUATE UNITS

Graduate Studies *Degree program information:* Part-time programs available. Postbaccalaureate distance learning degree programs offered.

School of Arts and Letters *Degree program information:* Part-time programs available. Offers art (MA); arts and letters (MA).

School of Education and Graduate Studies *Degree program information:* Part-time programs available. Postbaccalaureate distance learning degree programs offered. Offers counseling (MA); education and graduate studies (MA); elementary education (MA); health, physical education, and recreation (MA); secondary education (MA); special education (MA).

ADELPHI UNIVERSITY, Garden City, NY 11530

General Information Independent, coed, university. CGS member. *Enrollment:* 750 full-time matriculated graduate/professional students (630 women), 2,228 part-time matriculated graduate/professional students (1,771 women). *Enrollment by degree level:* 2,668 master's, 241 doctoral, 69 other advanced degrees. *Tuition:* Full-time $12,960; part-time $540 per credit. One-time fee: $400 part-time. Tuition and fees vary according to course load, degree level and program. *Graduate housing:* Room and/or apartments available on a first-come, first-served basis to single students; on-campus housing not available to married students. Typical cost: $8,050 (including board). *Student services:* Campus employment opportunities, career counseling, child daycare facilities, disabled student services, free psychological counseling, international student services, low-cost health insurance, multicultural affairs office. *Library facilities:* Swirbul Library plus 1 other. *Online resources:* library catalog, web page. *Collection:* 630,090 titles, 1,762 serial subscriptions, 43,298 audiovisual materials. *Research affiliation:* Mill Neck Manor School for Deaf Children, Brookhaven National Laboratory, North Shore Hospital, Long Island Jewish Medical Center (social work).

Computer facilities: 450 computers available on campus for general student use. A campuswide network can be accessed from student residence rooms. Internet access is available. *Web address:* http://www.adelphi.edu/.

General Application Contact: Ernie Shepelsky, Associate Director of Admissions, 516-877-3050, Fax: 516-877-3244.

GRADUATE UNITS

Derner Institute of Advanced Psychological Studies Students: 123 full-time (100 women), 207 part-time (166 women); includes 47 minority (23 African Americans, 11 Asian Americans or Pacific Islanders, 13 Hispanic Americans), 16 international. Average age 34. 301 applicants, 57% accepted, 72 enrolled. Expenses: Contact institution. *Financial support:* Research assistantships, teaching assistantships, career-related internships or fieldwork, institutionally sponsored loans, and clinical placements available. Financial award application deadline: 2/15; financial award applicants required to submit FAFSA. In 2001, 85 master's, 25 doctorates, 4 other advanced degrees awarded. Offers clinical psychology (PhD, Post-Doctoral Certificate); general psychology (MA). *Application deadline:* For fall admission, 1/15 (priority date). *Application fee:* $50. *Dean,* Dr. Louis Primavera, 516-877-4800.

Graduate School of Arts and Sciences Students: 2 full-time (1 woman), 37 part-time (26 women); includes 8 minority (4 African Americans, 1 Asian American or Pacific Islander, 3 Hispanic Americans), 3 international. Average age 33. 39 applicants, 69% accepted, 13 enrolled. Expenses: Contact institution. *Financial support:* Fellowships, research assistantships, teaching assistantships, career-related internships or fieldwork, Federal Work-Study, and tuition waivers (full and partial) available. Support available to part-time students. Financial award application deadline: 2/15; financial award applicants required to submit FAFSA. In 2001, 14 degrees awarded. *Degree program information:* Part-time and evening/weekend programs available. Offers art and art history (MA); arts and sciences (MA, MS, DA); biology (MS); English (MA); mathematics and computer science (MS, DA); physics (MS). *Application deadline:* Applications are processed on a rolling basis. *Application fee:* $50. *Application Contact:* Associate Director of Admissions, 516-877-3050, Fax: 516-877-3244. *Dean,* Gail Insler, 516-877-4120, Fax: 516-877-4191.

School of Business Students: 28 full-time (16 women), 223 part-time (99 women). Average age 28. 200 applicants, 57% accepted, 84 enrolled. *Faculty:* 23 full-time (3 women), 23 part-time/adjunct (2 women). Expenses: Contact institution. *Financial support:* In 2001–02, 12 research assistantships with partial tuition reimbursements were awarded; career-related internships or fieldwork and scholarships/grants also available. Financial award application deadline: 3/1. In 2001, 75 master's, 5 other advanced degrees awarded. *Degree program information:* Part-time and evening/weekend programs available. Offers administrative sciences (MBA); business (MBA, MS, Certificate); finance (MS); human resource management (Certificate); management for non-business majors (Certificate); management for women (Certificate). *Application deadline:* For fall admission, 8/15 (priority date); for spring admission, 12/15. Applications are processed on a rolling basis. *Application fee:* $50. *Application Contact:* Rory Shaffer-Walsh, Associate Director of Admissions, 516-877-3050, Fax: 516-877-3244, E-mail: shaffer@adelphi.edu. *Dean,* Dr. Anthony F. Libertella, 516-877-4690, Fax: 516-877-4607, E-mail: libertel@adelphi.edu.

School of Education Students: 424 full-time (374 women), 1,154 part-time (943 women); includes 189 minority (82 African Americans, 10 Asian Americans or Pacific Islanders, 96 Hispanic Americans, 1 Native American), 8 international. Average age 31. 1,183 applicants, 49% accepted. Expenses: Contact institution. *Financial support:* Fellowships, research assistantships, teaching assistantships, career-related internships or fieldwork, Federal Work-Study, institutionally sponsored loans, and tuition waivers (full) available. Support available to part-time students. Financial award application deadline: 2/15; financial award applicants required to submit FAFSA. In 2001, 637 master's, 4 other advanced degrees awarded. *Degree program information:* Part-time and evening/weekend programs available. Offers bilingual education (MA, MS); communication sciences and disorders (MS, DA); education (MA, MS, DA, Certificate); educational leadership and technology (MA, Certificate); elementary education (MA, Certificate); health studies (MA, Certificate); physical education and human performance science (MA, Certificate); reading (MS, Certificate); secondary education (MA); special education (MS, Certificate); teaching English to speakers of other languages (MA, Certificate). *Application deadline:* For fall admission, 5/1 (priority date); for spring admission, 11/1 (priority date). Applications are processed on a rolling basis. *Application fee:* $50. *Dean,* Dr. Elaine Sands, 516-877-4065.

School of Nursing Average age 39. 37 applicants, 59% accepted, 21 enrolled. Expenses: Contact institution. *Financial support:* Research assistantships, teaching assistantships, career-related internships or fieldwork and graduate achievement awards available. Support available to part-time students. Financial award application deadline: 2/15; financial award applicants required to submit FAFSA. In 2001, 22 master's, 14 other advanced degrees awarded. *Degree program information:* Part-time and evening/weekend programs available. Offers nursing (MS, Certificate). *Application deadline:* For fall admission, 8/15 (priority date); for spring admission, 1/15 (priority date). Applications are processed on a rolling basis. *Application fee:* $50. *Acting Dean,* Dr. Kathleen Bond, 516-877-4545.

School of Social Work Students: 173 full-time (145 women), 501 part-time (432 women); includes 153 minority (109 African Americans, 5 Asian Americans or Pacific Islanders, 39 Hispanic Americans), 4 international. Average age 37. 548 applicants, 65% accepted, 214 enrolled. Expenses: Contact institution. *Financial support:* Research assistantships, career-related internships or fieldwork, Federal Work-Study, tuition waivers (full and partial), and unspecified assistantships available. Financial award application deadline: 2/15; financial award applicants required to submit FAFSA. In 2001, 239 master's, 6 doctorates awarded. *Degree program information:* Part-time and evening/weekend programs available. Offers social welfare (DSW); social work (MSW). *Application deadline:* For fall admission, 4/1 (priority date). Applications are processed on a rolling basis. *Application fee:* $50. *Application Contact:* Muriel Levin, Admissions Coordinator, 516-877-4384. *Acting Dean,* Dr. Brooke Spiro, 516-877-4341.

ADLER SCHOOL OF PROFESSIONAL PSYCHOLOGY, Chicago, IL 60601-7203

General Information Independent, coed, graduate-only institution. *Enrollment by degree level:* 162 master's, 246 doctoral. *Graduate faculty:* 19 full-time (9 women), 48 part-time/adjunct (21 women). *Tuition:* Full-time $13,680; part-time $380 per credit. *Required fees:* $100; $15 per credit. *Graduate housing:* On-campus housing not available. *Student services:* Campus employment opportunities, career counseling, international student services. *Library facilities:* Sol and Elaine Mosak Library. *Online resources:* library catalog, web page, access to other libraries' catalogs. *Collection:* 15,000 titles, 170 serial subscriptions, 1,800 audiovisual materials.

Computer facilities: 10 computers available on campus for general student use. A campuswide network can be accessed. Internet access is available. *Web address:* http://www.adler.edu/.

General Application Contact: Holly Hart, Admissions Coordinator, 312-201-5900 Ext. 233, Fax: 312-201-5917, E-mail: hlh@adler.edu.

GRADUATE UNITS

Programs in Psychology Students: 124 full-time (78 women), 284 part-time (208 women); includes 77 minority (43 African Americans, 20 Asian Americans or Pacific Islanders, 13 Hispanic Americans, 1 Native American), 8 international. Average age 39. 253 applicants, 59% accepted, 121 enrolled. *Faculty:* 19 full-time (9 women), 48 part-time/adjunct (21 women). Expenses: Contact institution. *Financial support:* In 2001–02, 180 students received support. Career-related internships or fieldwork, Federal Work-Study, scholarships/grants, and tuition waivers (full and partial) available. Support available to part-time students. Financial award application deadline: 5/15; financial award applicants required to submit FAFSA. In 2001, 101 master's, 29 doctorates, 5 other advanced degrees awarded. *Degree program information:* Part-time and evening/weekend programs available. Offers art therapy (Certificate); clinical hypnosis (Certificate); clinical psychology (Psy D); counseling psychology (MACP); counseling psychology/art therapy (MACAT); gerontology (MAGP, Certificate); marriage and family counseling (MAMFC); marriage and family therapy (Certificate); organizational psychology (MAO); substance abuse counseling (MASAC, Certificate). *Application deadline:* For fall admission, 1/1 (priority date). Applications are processed on a rolling basis. *Application fee:* $50. *Application Contact:* Erene Soliman, Admissions Counselor, 312-201-5900, Fax: 312-201-5917. *Dean of Academic Affairs,* Dr. Frank Gruba-McCallister, 312-201-5900, Fax: 312-201-5917.

AGNES SCOTT COLLEGE, Decatur, GA 30030-3797

General Information Independent-religious, women only, comprehensive institution. *Graduate housing:* On-campus housing not available.

GRADUATE UNITS

Program in Early Childhood Education Offers early childhood education (MAT).

Secondary English Program *Degree program information:* Part-time programs available. Offers secondary English (MAT).

AIR FORCE INSTITUTE OF TECHNOLOGY, Dayton, OH 45433-7765

General Information Federally supported, coed, primarily men, graduate-only institution. CGS member. *Graduate housing:* On-campus housing not available. *Research affiliation:* U.S. Air Force Office of Scientific Research, U.S. Air Force Research Laboratory, Dayton Area Graduate Studies Institute (aerospace), Defense Advanced Research Projects Agency, U.S. Air Force Air Education and Training Command (applied research), Arnold Engineering and Development Center.

GRADUATE UNITS

School of Engineering and Management *Degree program information:* Part-time programs available. Offers aeronautical engineering (MS, PhD); applied mathematics (MS, PhD); applied physics (MS, PhD); astronautical engineering (MS, PhD); computer engineering (MS, PhD); computer systems/science (MS); electrical engineering (MS, PhD); electro-optics (MS, PhD); engineering and management (MS, PhD); environmental and engineering management (MS); environmental science (MS, PhD); information resource management (MS); logistics management (MS); materials science (MS, PhD); meteorology (MS); nuclear engineering (MS, PhD); operations research (MS, PhD); space operations (MS); systems acquisition management (MS); systems engineering (MS).

ALABAMA AGRICULTURAL AND MECHANICAL UNIVERSITY, Huntsville, AL 35811

General Information State-supported, coed, university. *Enrollment:* 531 full-time matriculated graduate/professional students (361 women), 647 part-time matriculated graduate/professional students (454 women). *Enrollment by degree level:* 1,127 master's, 38 doctoral. *Graduate faculty:* 138 full-time (39 women), 14 part-time/adjunct (2 women). Tuition, state resident: full-time $1,380. Tuition, nonresident: full-time $2,500. *Graduate housing:* Rooms and/or apartments available on a first-come, first-served basis to single students and available to married students. Housing application deadline: 5/1. *Student services:* Campus employment opportunities, career counseling, child daycare facilities, disabled student services, international student services, low-cost health insurance. *Library facilities:* J. F. Drake Learning

Resources Center. *Online resources:* library catalog, access to other libraries' catalogs. *Collection:* 507,500 titles, 2,500 serial subscriptions, 33,000 audiovisual materials. *Research affiliation:* Hughes Aircraft Corporation (physics), Nichols Research Corporation (computer science), Alabama Supercomputer Network, Lawrence Livermore National Laboratory (chemistry, physics), Boeing Defense and Space Group (plant science), NASA (utilization of space resources).

Computer facilities: 1,000 computers available on campus for general student use. A campuswide network can be accessed from student residence rooms and from off campus. Internet access is available. *Web address:* http://www.aamu.edu/.

General Application Contact: Dr. Chandra Reddy, Dean, School of Graduate Studies, 256-851-5266, Fax: 256-851-5269, E-mail: reddyc@aamu.edu.

GRADUATE UNITS

School of Graduate Studies Students: 452 full-time (298 women), 713 part-time (499 women). Average age 29. 151 applicants, 56% accepted. *Faculty:* 138 full-time (39 women), 14 part-time/adjunct (2 women). Expenses: Contact institution. *Financial support:* In 2001–02, fellowships with tuition reimbursements (averaging $18,000 per year), research assistantships with tuition reimbursements (averaging $13,500 per year), teaching assistantships with tuition reimbursements (averaging $9,000 per year) were awarded. Career-related internships or fieldwork, Federal Work-Study, and institutionally sponsored loans also available. Support available to part-time students. Financial award application deadline: 4/1. In 2001, 336 master's, 16 doctorates, 5 other advanced degrees awarded. *Application deadline:* For fall admission, 5/1 (priority date). Applications are processed on a rolling basis. *Application fee:* $25. Electronic applications accepted. *Dean, School of Graduate Studies,* Dr. Chandra Reddy, 256-851-5266, Fax: 256-851-5269, E-mail: reddyc@aamu.edu.

School of Agricultural and Environmental Sciences Students: 15 full-time (0 women), 25 part-time (4 women); includes 31 minority (all African Americans), 1 international. *Faculty:* 30 full-time (6 women). Expenses: Contact institution. *Financial support:* Fellowships, research assistantships, teaching assistantships, career-related internships or fieldwork and Federal Work-Study available. Support available to part-time students. Financial award application deadline: 4/1. *Degree program information:* Part-time and evening/weekend programs available. Offers agribusiness (MS); agricultural and environmental sciences (MS, MURP, PhD); animal sciences (MS); environmental science (MS); family and consumer sciences (MS); food science (MS, PhD); plant and soil science (PhD); urban and regional planning (MURP). *Application deadline:* For fall admission, 5/1. *Application fee:* $15 ($20 for international students). *Dean,* Dr. James W. Shuford, 256-851-5783, Fax: 256-851-5906.

School of Arts and Sciences Students: 29 full-time (16 women), 94 part-time (61 women); includes 58 minority (55 African Americans, 3 Asian Americans or Pacific Islanders), 36 international. *Faculty:* 31 full-time (3 women), 5 part-time/adjunct (0 women). Expenses: Contact institution. *Financial support:* In 2001–02, 2 fellowships with tuition reimbursements (averaging $15,000 per year), 15 research assistantships with tuition reimbursements (averaging $9,000 per year), 6 teaching assistantships with tuition reimbursements (averaging $9,000 per year) were awarded. Career-related internships or fieldwork and Federal Work-Study also available. Financial award application deadline: 4/1. In 2001, 36 master's, 4 doctorates awarded. *Degree program information:* Part-time and evening/weekend programs available. Offers arts and sciences (MS, MSW, PhD); biology (MS); computer science (MS); physics (MS, PhD); social work (MSW). *Application deadline:* For fall admission, 5/1 (priority date). Applications are processed on a rolling basis. *Application fee:* $15 ($20 for international students). *Dean,* Dr. Jerry Shipman, 256-851-5300.

School of Business Students: 16 full-time (8 women), 98 part-time (63 women); includes 80 minority (all African Americans), 17 international. Average age 26. *Faculty:* 24 full-time (2 women). Expenses: Contact institution. *Financial support:* Research assistantships, teaching assistantships, career-related internships or fieldwork, Federal Work-Study, and institutionally sponsored loans available. Financial award application deadline: 4/1. In 2001, 39 degrees awarded. *Degree program information:* Part-time and evening/weekend programs available. Offers business (MBA, MS); economics and finance (MS); management and marketing (MBA). *Application deadline:* For fall admission, 5/1. Applications are processed on a rolling basis. *Application fee:* $15 ($20 for international students). *Dean,* Dr. Barbara A. P. Jones, 256-851-5485, Fax: 256-851-5081.

School of Education Students: 35 full-time (33 women), 306 part-time (243 women). *Faculty:* 36 full-time (18 women), 4 part-time/adjunct (1 woman). Expenses: Contact institution. *Financial support:* Fellowships, research assistantships, career-related internships or fieldwork, Federal Work-Study, institutionally sponsored loans, and traineeships available. Support available to part-time students. Financial award application deadline: 4/1. In 2001, 147 master's, 2 other advanced degrees awarded. *Degree program information:* Part-time and evening/weekend programs available. Offers communicative disorders (M Ed, MS); early childhood education (M Ed, MS, Ed S); education (M Ed, Ed S); elementary and early childhood education (M Ed, MS, Ed S); elementary education (M Ed, MS, Ed S); health and physical education (M Ed, MS); higher administration (MS); music (MS); music education (M Ed, MS); physical education (M Ed, MS); psychology and counseling (MS, Ed S); secondary education (M Ed, MS, Ed S); special education (M Ed, MS). *Application deadline:* For fall admission, 5/1. *Application fee:* $15 ($20 for international students). *Interim Dean,* Dr. John Vickers, 256-851-5500.

School of Engineering and Technology *Faculty:* 4 full-time (1 woman). Expenses: Contact institution. *Financial support:* Research assistantships with tuition reimbursements, career-related internships or fieldwork available. Financial award application deadline: 4/1. In 2001, 8 degrees awarded. *Degree program information:* Part-time and evening/weekend programs available. Offers engineering and technology (M Ed, MS); industry and education (MS); trade and industrial education (M Ed). *Application deadline:* For fall admission, 5/1. *Application fee:* $15 ($20 for international students). *Dean,* Dr. Arthur Bond, 256-851-5560.

ALABAMA STATE UNIVERSITY, Montgomery, AL 36101-0271

General Information State-supported, coed, comprehensive institution. *Enrollment:* 186 full-time matriculated graduate/professional students (121 women), 693 part-time matriculated graduate/professional students (545 women). *Enrollment by degree level:* 757 master's, 122 other advanced degrees. *Graduate faculty:* 57 full-time (23 women), 20 part-time/adjunct (11 women). Tuition, state resident: part-time $138 per credit. Tuition, nonresident: part-time $276 per credit. *Graduate housing:* Room and/or apartments available on a first-come, first-served basis to single students; on-campus housing not available to married students. Typical cost: $3,500 (including board). Housing application deadline: 7/15. *Student services:* Campus employment opportunities, career counseling, child daycare facilities, disabled student services, free psychological counseling, international student services, low-cost health insurance. *Library facilities:* Levi Watkins Learning Center. *Online resources:* library catalog, web page, access to other libraries' catalogs. *Collection:* 395,321 titles, 1,299 serial subscriptions, 42,304 audiovisual materials.

Computer facilities: 380 computers available on campus for general student use. A campuswide network can be accessed from off campus. Internet access and online class registration, e-mail are available. *Web address:* http://www.alasu.edu/.

General Application Contact: Dr. Annette Marie Allen, Dean of Graduate Studies, 334-229-4275, Fax: 334-229-4928, E-mail: aallen@asunet.alasu.edu.

GRADUATE UNITS

School of Graduate Studies Students: 186 full-time (121 women), 693 part-time (545 women); includes 622 minority (614 African Americans, 4 Asian Americans or Pacific Islanders, 3 Hispanic Americans, 1 Native American) Average age 33. 231 applicants, 87% accepted. *Faculty:* 57 full-time (23 women), 20 part-time/adjunct (11 women). Expenses: Contact institution. *Financial support:* In 2001–02, 17 research assistantships (averaging $9,000 per year) were awarded; Federal Work-Study, scholarships/grants, and unspecified assistantships also available. Support available to part-time students. In 2001, 256 master's, 12 other advanced degrees awarded. *Degree program information:* Part-time and evening/weekend programs available. Offers health sciences (MS); physical therapy (MS). *Application deadline:* For fall admission, 7/15; for spring admission, 12/15. Applications are processed on a rolling basis. *Application fee:* $10. *Dean,* Dr. Annette Marie Allen, 334-229-4276, Fax: 334-229-4928, E-mail: aallen@asunet.alasu.edu.

College of Arts and Sciences Students: 8 full-time (6 women), 25 part-time (15 women); includes 25 minority (all African Americans) 10 applicants, 70% accepted. *Faculty:* 13 full-time (3 women). Expenses: Contact institution. *Financial support:* In 2001–02, 2 research assistantships (averaging $9,000 per year) were awarded In 2001, 10 degrees awarded. *Degree program information:* Part-time programs available. Offers arts and sciences (MS, Ed S); biology education (Ed S); mathematics (Ed S). *Application deadline:* For fall admission, 7/15; for spring admission, 12/15. Applications are processed on a rolling basis. *Application fee:* $10. *Application Contact:* Dr. Annette Marie Allen, Dean of Graduate Studies, 334-229-4275, Fax: 334-229-4928, E-mail: aallen@asunet.alasu.edu. *Acting Dean,* Dr. Thelma Ivery, 334-229-4316, Fax: 334-229-4916, E-mail: tivery@asunet.alasu.edu.

College of Business Administration 12 applicants, 83% accepted. *Faculty:* 11 full-time (2 women). Expenses: Contact institution. *Financial support:* In 2001–02, 2 research assistantships (averaging $9,000 per year) were awarded In 2001, 2 degrees awarded. *Degree program information:* Part-time programs available. Offers accountancy (M Acc, MS); business administration (M Acc, MS). *Application deadline:* For fall admission, 7/15; for spring admission, 12/15. Applications are processed on a rolling basis. *Application fee:* $10. *Application Contact:* Dr. Annette Marie Allen, Dean of Graduate Studies, 334-229-4275, Fax: 334-229-4928, E-mail: aallen@asunet.alasu.edu. *Dean,* Dr. Percy Vaughn, 334-229-4124, Fax: 334-229-4870, E-mail: pvaughn@asunet.alasu.edu.

College of Education Students: 161 full-time (118 women), 573 part-time (474 women); includes 513 minority (508 African Americans, 2 Asian Americans or Pacific Islanders, 2 Hispanic Americans, 1 Native American) *Faculty:* 24 full-time (14 women), 20 part-time/adjunct (11 women). Expenses: Contact institution. *Financial support:* In 2001–02, 2 research assistantships (averaging $9,000 per year) were awarded In 2001, 250 master's, 12 other advanced degrees awarded. *Degree program information:* Part-time programs available. Offers biology education (M Ed); early childhood education (M Ed, Ed S); education (M Ed, MS, Ed D, Ed S); educational administration (M Ed, Ed S); educational leadership (Ed D); elementary education (M Ed, Ed S); English education (M Ed); general counseling (MS); guidance and counseling (M Ed, MS, Ed S); health, physical education, recreation, and safety (M Ed); history education (M Ed); library educational media (M Ed, Ed S); mathematics education (M Ed); physical education (M Ed); reading education (M Ed); school counseling (M Ed, Ed S); secondary education (M Ed, Ed S); special education (M Ed). *Application deadline:* For fall admission, 7/15; for spring admission, 12/15. Applications are processed on a rolling basis. *Application fee:* $10. *Application Contact:* Dr. Annette Marie Allen, Dean of Graduate Studies, 334-229-4275, Fax: 334-229-4928, E-mail: aallen@asunet.alasu.edu. *Dean,* Dr. Daniel Vertrees, 334-229-4252, Fax: 334-229-4904, E-mail: dvertrees@asunet.alasu.edu.

School of Music Students: 4 full-time (2 women), 2 part-time; all minorities (all African Americans) 5 applicants, 100% accepted. *Faculty:* 2 full-time (0 women). Expenses: Contact institution. *Financial support:* In 2001–02, research assistantships (averaging $9,000 per year) In 2001, 6 degrees awarded. *Degree program information:* Part-time programs available. Offers music education (MME). *Application deadline:* For fall admission, 7/15; for spring admission, 12/15. Applications are processed on a rolling basis. *Application fee:* $10. *Application Contact:* Dr. Annette Marie Allen, Dean of Graduate Studies, 334-229-4275, Fax: 334-229-4928, E-mail: aallen@asunet.alasu.edu. *Dean,* Dr. Horace B. Lamar, 334-229-4341, Fax: 334-229-4901.

ALASKA PACIFIC UNIVERSITY, Anchorage, AK 99508-4672

General Information Independent, coed, comprehensive institution. *Enrollment:* 96 full-time matriculated graduate/professional students (64 women), 77 part-time matriculated graduate/professional students (41 women). *Enrollment by degree level:* 173 master's. *Graduate faculty:* 15 full-time (6 women), 11 part-time/adjunct (6 women). *Tuition:* Full-time $9,600; part-time $400 per semester hour. *Required fees:* $80; $40 per semester. Tuition and fees vary according to program. *Graduate housing:* Rooms and/or apartments available to single and married students. Typical cost: $5,550 (including board) for single students. Room and board charges vary according to board plan. Housing application deadline: 8/15. *Student services:* Campus employment opportunities, career counseling, exercise/wellness program, free psychological counseling, international student services, low-cost health insurance, multicultural affairs office. *Library facilities:* Consortium Library. *Online resources:* library catalog, web page, access to other libraries' catalogs. *Collection:* 676,745 titles, 3,842 serial subscriptions.

Computer facilities: 35 computers available on campus for general student use. A campuswide network can be accessed. Internet access is available. *Web address:* http://www.alaskapacific.edu/.

General Application Contact: Ernie Norton, Director of Admissions, 907-564-8248, Fax: 907-564-8317, E-mail: ernien@alaskapacific.edu.

GRADUATE UNITS

Graduate Programs Students: 96 full-time (64 women), 77 part-time (41 women); includes 38 minority (9 African Americans, 9 Asian Americans or Pacific Islanders, 4 Hispanic Americans, 16 Native Americans), 7 international. Average age 37. 136 applicants, 74% accepted. *Faculty:* 15 full-time (6 women), 11 part-time/adjunct (6 women). Expenses: Contact institution. *Financial support:* Career-related internships or fieldwork, Federal Work-Study, scholarships/grants, and unspecified assistantships available. Support available to part-time students. Financial award application deadline: 3/15; financial award applicants required to submit FAFSA. In 2001, 78 degrees awarded. *Degree program information:* Part-time and evening/weekend programs available. Offers business administration (MBA); environmental science (MSES); psychology (MSCP); self designed programs (MA); teaching (K-8) (MAT); telecommunication management (MBATM). *Application deadline:* For fall admission, 4/1 (priority date). Applications are processed on a rolling basis. *Application fee:* $25. *Application Contact:* Ernie Norton, Director of Admissions, 907-564-8248, Fax: 907-564-8317, E-mail: ernien@alaskapacific.edu. *Academic Dean,* Dr. Charles B. Fahl, 907-564-8242, Fax: 907-562-4276, E-mail: cfahl@alaskapacific.edu.

ALBANY COLLEGE OF PHARMACY OF UNION UNIVERSITY, Albany, NY 12208-3425

General Information Independent, coed, comprehensive institution. *Enrollment:* 124 full-time matriculated graduate/professional students (76 women). *Enrollment by degree level:* 124 first professional. *Graduate faculty:* 47 full-time (22 women), 13 part-time/adjunct (10 women). *Tuition:* Full-time $13,550. *Required fees:* $800. *Graduate housing:* On-campus housing not available. *Student services:* Campus employment opportunities, career counseling, free psychological counseling, international student services, low-cost health insurance, writing training. *Library facilities:* George and Leona Lewis Library. *Online resources:* library catalog, web page, access to other libraries' catalogs. *Collection:* 12,314 titles, 1,399 serial subscriptions, 2,676 audiovisual materials. *Research affiliation:* Renal Research Institute, Interstitial Cystitis Association, Ni Cox SA, Naval Research Institute, Langeloth Foundation, F. Hoffman- La Roche Limited.

Computer facilities: 100 computers available on campus for general student use. A campuswide network can be accessed from student residence rooms and from off campus. Internet access is available. *Web address:* http://www.acp.edu/.

General Application Contact: Jacqueline Harris, Senior Assistant to Director of Admissions, 518-445-7221, Fax: 518-445-7202.

GRADUATE UNITS

Program in Pharmacy Students: 124 full-time (76 women); includes 23 minority (2 African Americans, 18 Asian Americans or Pacific Islanders, 3 Hispanic Americans), 1 international. Average age 26. 403 applicants, 67% accepted, 147 enrolled. *Faculty:* 47 full-time (22 women), 13 part-time/adjunct (10 women). Expenses: Contact institution. *Financial support:* Federal Work-Study available. Support available to part-time students. Financial award application deadline: 2/1; financial award applicants required to submit FAFSA. In 2001, 57 degrees awarded. *Degree program information:* Part-time programs available. Post-baccalaureate distance learning degree programs offered (minimal on-campus study). Offers

Albany College of Pharmacy of Union University (continued)
pharmacy (Pharm D). *Application deadline:* For fall admission, 2/1 (priority date). Applications are processed on a rolling basis. *Application fee:* $50. Electronic applications accepted. *Application Contact:* Jacqueline Harris, Senior Assistant to Director of Admissions, 518-445-7221, Fax: 518-445-7202. *Dean,* Dr. Mary H. Andritz, 518-445-7200, Fax: 518-445-7202.

ALBANY LAW SCHOOL OF UNION UNIVERSITY, Albany, NY 12208-3494

General Information Independent, coed, graduate-only institution. *Enrollment by degree level:* 771 first professional. *Graduate faculty:* 47 full-time (19 women), 28 part-time/adjunct (10 women). *Tuition:* Full-time $22,250; part-time $16,688 per year. *Required fees:* $130; $130 per year. Part-time tuition and fees vary according to course load. *Graduate housing:* On-campus housing not available. *Student services:* Campus employment opportunities, campus safety program, career counseling, disabled student services, free psychological counseling, low-cost health insurance, writing training. *Library facilities:* Schaffer Law Library. *Online resources:* library catalog, web page. *Collection:* 68,323 titles, 5,038 serial subscriptions, 447 audiovisual materials.

Computer facilities: 35 computers available on campus for general student use. A campuswide network can be accessed from student residence rooms and from off campus. Internet access is available. *Web address:* http://www.als.edu/.

General Application Contact: Dawn M. Chamberlaine, Assistant Dean of Admissions and Financial Aid, 518-445-2326, Fax: 518-445-2369, E-mail: admissions@mail.als.edu.

GRADUATE UNITS

Professional Program Students: 711 full-time (380 women), 60 part-time (31 women); includes 130 minority (58 African Americans, 31 Asian Americans or Pacific Islanders, 38 Hispanic Americans, 3 Native Americans), 25 international. Average age 27. 1,543 applicants, 61% accepted. *Faculty:* 47 full-time (19 women), 28 part-time/adjunct (10 women). Expenses: Contact institution. *Financial support:* In 2001–02, 676 students received support, including 50 research assistantships (averaging $1,500 per year); career-related internships or fieldwork, Federal Work-Study, institutionally sponsored loans, scholarships/grants, and tuition waivers (full and partial) also available. Support available to part-time students. Financial award applicants required to submit FAFSA. In 2001, 194 degrees awarded. *Degree program information:* Part-time programs available. Offers law (JD, MSLS). *Application deadline:* For fall admission, 3/15 (priority date). Applications are processed on a rolling basis. *Application fee:* $50. *Application Contact:* Dawn M. Chamberlaine, Assistant Dean of Admissions and Financial Aid, 518-445-2326, Fax: 518-445-2369, E-mail: admissions@mail.als.edu. *Dean,* Thomas H. Sponsler, 518-445-2321, Fax: 518-472-5865.

ALBANY MEDICAL COLLEGE, Albany, NY 12208-3479

General Information Independent, coed, graduate-only institution. *Graduate faculty:* 54 full-time (13 women), 35 part-time/adjunct (6 women). *Tuition:* Full-time $14,737; part-time $491 per credit hour. *Graduate housing:* On-campus housing not available. *Student services:* Campus employment opportunities, campus safety program, child daycare facilities, exercise/wellness program, free psychological counseling, international student services, low-cost health insurance. *Library facilities:* Schaffer Library of the Health Sciences. *Online resources:* library catalog, web page, access to other libraries' catalogs. *Collection:* 140,434 titles, 1,060 serial subscriptions, 1,724 audiovisual materials. *Research affiliation:* Stratton Veterans' Affairs Medical Center, Wadsworth Center for Laboratories and Research, Trudeau Institute (immunology), General Electric Corporation (imaging), State University of New York at Albany (behavioral science).

Computer facilities: 50 computers available on campus for general student use. A campuswide network can be accessed. Internet access is available. *Web address:* http://www.amc.edu/.

General Application Contact: Jean M. Cornwell, Admissions Coordinator, 518-262-5253, Fax: 518-262-5183, E-mail: graduate-studies@mail.amc.edu.

GRADUATE UNITS

Graduate Programs in the Biological Sciences Students: 71 full-time (46 women), 1 part-time; includes 20 minority (4 African Americans, 16 Asian Americans or Pacific Islanders), 10 international. Average age 27. 116 applicants, 53% accepted, 32 enrolled. *Faculty:* 54 full-time (13 women), 35 part-time/adjunct (6 women). Expenses: Contact institution. *Financial support:* In 2001–02, 70 research assistantships with full tuition reimbursements (averaging $18,000 per year) were awarded; Federal Work-Study, scholarships/grants, and tuition waivers (full) also available. Financial award applicants required to submit FAFSA. In 2001, 20 master's, 9 doctorates awarded. *Degree program information:* Part-time programs available. Offers biological sciences (MS, PhD); cardiovascular sciences (MS, PhD); cell biology and cancer research (MS, PhD); immunology and microbial disease (MS, PhD); neuropharmacology and neuroscience (MS, PhD). *Application deadline:* For fall admission, 3/15 (priority date). Applications are processed on a rolling basis. *Application fee:* $0 ($60 for international students). *Application Contact:* Jean M. Cornwell, Admissions Coordinator, 518-262-5253, Fax: 518-262-5183, E-mail: graduate-studies@mail.amc.edu. *Senior Associate Dean for Education Programs,* Dr. Henry S. Pohl, 518-262-5253, Fax: 518-262-5183.

Professional Program Students: 624 full-time (325 women), 1 part-time; includes 183 minority (22 African Americans, 143 Asian Americans or Pacific Islanders, 16 Hispanic Americans, 2 Native Americans), 41 international. Average age 27. 6,079 applicants, 6% accepted, 107 enrolled. *Faculty:* 54 full-time (13 women), 35 part-time/adjunct (6 women). Expenses: Contact institution. *Financial support:* In 2001–02, 223 students received support. Federal Work-Study and institutionally sponsored loans available. Financial award application deadline: 4/15. In 2001, 126 degrees awarded. Offers medicine (MD). *Application deadline:* For fall admission, 11/15. Applications are processed on a rolling basis. *Application fee:* $75. Electronic applications accepted. *Application Contact:* Sara J. Kremer, Assistant Dean for Admissions and Student Records, 518-262-5521, Fax: 518-262-5887. *Dean,* Dr. Vincent Verdile, 518-262-6008.

Program in Nurse Anesthesiology Students: 29 full-time (14 women); includes 2 minority (1 African American, 1 Asian American or Pacific Islander) Average age 33. 29 applicants, 72% accepted, 15 enrolled. *Faculty:* 12 full-time (4 women). Expenses: Contact institution. *Financial support:* Tuition waivers (partial) available. Financial award applicants required to submit FAFSA. In 2001, 10 degrees awarded. Offers nurse anesthesiology (MS). *Application deadline:* For fall admission, 3/15 (priority date). Applications are processed on a rolling basis. *Application fee:* $60. *Application Contact:* Jean M. Cornwell, Admissions Coordinator, 518-262-5253, Fax: 518-262-5183, E-mail: graduate-studies@mail.amc.edu. *Graduate Director,* Dr. Kathleen M. O'Donnell, 518-262-4303, E-mail: nurseanesthprog@mail.amc.edu.

ALBANY STATE UNIVERSITY, Albany, GA 31705-2717

General Information State-supported, coed, comprehensive institution. CGS member. *Graduate housing:* On-campus housing not available.

GRADUATE UNITS

College of Arts and Sciences *Degree program information:* Part-time programs available. Offers arts and sciences (MPA, MS); community and economic development (MPA); criminal justice (MPA, MS); fiscal management (MPA); general management (MPA); health administration and policy (MPA); human resources management (MPA); public policy (MPA); water resource management and policy (MPA). Electronic applications accepted.

College of Education *Degree program information:* Part-time programs available. Offers biology (M Ed); business education (M Ed); chemistry (M Ed); early childhood education (M Ed); education (M Ed, Certificate, Ed S); educational administration and supervision (M Ed, Certificate, Ed S); English education (M Ed); health and physical education (M Ed); mathematics education (M Ed); middle grades education (M Ed); music education (M Ed); reading education (M Ed); school counseling (M Ed); social science education (M Ed); special education (M Ed). Electronic applications accepted.

College of Health Professions *Degree program information:* Part-time programs available. Offers nursing (MS). Electronic applications accepted.

School of Business *Degree program information:* Part-time and evening/weekend programs available. Postbaccalaureate distance learning degree programs offered (no on-campus study). Offers water policy (MBA). Electronic applications accepted.

ALBERTUS MAGNUS COLLEGE, New Haven, CT 06511-1189

General Information Independent-religious, coed, comprehensive institution. *Enrollment:* 300 full-time matriculated graduate/professional students (128 women), 97 part-time matriculated graduate/professional students (45 women). *Enrollment by degree level:* 397 master's. *Graduate faculty:* 17 full-time (5 women), 33 part-time/adjunct (11 women). *Tuition:* Full-time $6,420; part-time $350 per credit. *Required fees:* $1,500; $83 per credit. One-time fee: $400 full-time. Tuition and fees vary according to program. *Graduate housing:* On-campus housing not available. *Student services:* Campus employment opportunities, career counseling, free psychological counseling, international student services. *Library facilities:* Rosary Hall. *Online resources:* web page. *Collection:* 538 serial subscriptions, 817 audiovisual materials.

Computer facilities: 75 computers available on campus for general student use. A campuswide network can be accessed from student residence rooms and from off campus. Internet access is available.

General Application Contact: Sr. Charles Marie Brantl, Director of Assessment and Reseach, 203-772-0116, Fax: 203-401-4072, E-mail: brantl@albertus.edu.

GRADUATE UNITS

Liberal Studies Program Average age 39. 15 applicants, 80% accepted. *Faculty:* 6 full-time (2 women), 3 part-time/adjunct (2 women). Expenses: Contact institution. *Financial support:* Available to part-time students. Application deadline: 8/17. In 2001, 2 degrees awarded. *Degree program information:* Part-time and evening/weekend programs available. Offers liberal studies (MALS). *Application deadline:* For fall admission, 8/31 (priority date); for spring admission, 1/10. Applications are processed on a rolling basis. *Application fee:* $25. *Director,* Dr. Mary Jo Fox, 203-773-8556, Fax: 203-773-3117, E-mail: mjfox@albertus.edu.

Program in Art Therapy Students: 14 full-time (12 women), 21 part-time (20 women); includes 4 minority (2 African Americans, 2 Hispanic Americans) 8 applicants, 88% accepted. *Faculty:* 5 full-time (3 women), 6 part-time/adjunct (3 women). Expenses: Contact institution. *Financial support:* Available to part-time students. Application deadline: 8/17. *Degree program information:* Part-time and evening/weekend programs available. Offers art therapy (MAAT). *Application deadline:* For fall admission, 8/30; for spring admission, 12/30. *Application fee:* $35. *Director,* Dr. Ragaa Mazen, 203-773-8594, Fax: 203-773-3117, E-mail: cmazen@albertus.edu.

Program in Management Students: 286 full-time (116 women); includes 67 minority (43 African Americans, 7 Asian Americans or Pacific Islanders, 16 Hispanic Americans, 1 Native American) Average age 35. 120 applicants, 89% accepted. *Faculty:* 6 full-time (0 women), 24 part-time/adjunct (6 women). Expenses: Contact institution. *Financial support:* Available to part-time students. In 2001, 106 degrees awarded. *Degree program information:* Evening/weekend programs available. Offers management (MBA, MSM). *Application deadline:* Applications are processed on a rolling basis. *Application fee:* $75. *Application Contact:* Joe Chadwick, Director of Program Marketing, 203-777-0800 Ext. 213, Fax: 203-777-2112, E-mail: joe.chadwick@apollogrg.edu. *Dean,* Dr. Phyllis DeLeo, 203-773-0800, Fax: 203-777-2112, E-mail: pdeleo@albertus.edu.

ALCORN STATE UNIVERSITY, Alcorn State, MS 39096-7500

General Information State-supported, coed, comprehensive institution. CGS member. *Enrollment:* 156 full-time matriculated graduate/professional students (87 women), 397 part-time matriculated graduate/professional students (296 women). *Enrollment by degree level:* 553 master's. *Graduate faculty:* 64 full-time (21 women), 12 part-time/adjunct (4 women). Tuition, state resident: full-time $6,418; part-time $924 per credit. Tuition, nonresident: full-time $12,497; part-time $1,656 per credit. *Graduate housing:* Room and/or apartments available on a first-come, first-served basis to single students; on-campus housing not available to married students. *Student services:* Campus employment opportunities, career counseling, child daycare facilities. *Library facilities:* John Dewey Boyd Library. *Online resources:* library catalog, access to other libraries' catalogs. *Collection:* 195,433 titles, 1,046 serial subscriptions, 9,908 audiovisual materials.

Computer facilities: 400 computers available on campus for general student use. A campuswide network can be accessed from student residence rooms and from off campus. Online class registration is available. *Web address:* http://www.alcorn.edu/.

General Application Contact: Lula Russell, Administrative Assistant to the Dean, School of Graduate Studies, 601-877-6122, Fax: 601-877-6995, E-mail: lulagr@lorman.alcorn.edu.

GRADUATE UNITS

School of Graduate Studies Students: 156 full-time (87 women), 397 part-time (296 women); includes 462 minority (453 African Americans, 7 Asian Americans or Pacific Islanders, 1 Hispanic American, 1 Native American), 23 international. *Faculty:* 64 full-time (21 women), 12 part-time/adjunct (4 women). Expenses: Contact institution. *Financial support:* Career-related internships or fieldwork available. Support available to part-time students. In 2001, 123 degrees awarded. *Degree program information:* Part-time programs available. *Application deadline:* For fall admission, 7/15 (priority date); for spring admission, 11/25. Applications are processed on a rolling basis. *Application fee:* $0 ($10 for international students). Electronic applications accepted. *Application Contact:* Lula Russell, Administrative Assistant to the Dean, School of Graduate Studies, 601-877-6122, Fax: 601-877-6995, E-mail: lulagr@lorman.alcorn.edu. *Interim Dean,* Dr. Irene Harris Johnson, 601-877-6122, Fax: 601-877-6995, E-mail: ijohnson@lorman.alcorn.edu.

School of Agriculture and Applied Science *Faculty:* 11 full-time (2 women). Expenses: Contact institution. *Financial support:* Career-related internships or fieldwork available. Support available to part-time students. Offers agricultural economics (MS Ag); agronomy (MS Ag); animal science (MS Ag). *Application deadline:* For fall admission, 7/15 (priority date); for spring admission, 11/25. Applications are processed on a rolling basis. *Application fee:* $0 ($10 for international students). *Dean,* Napoleon Moses, 601-877-6137, Fax: 601-877-6219.

School of Arts and Sciences *Faculty:* 30 full-time (7 women). Expenses: Contact institution. *Financial support:* Career-related internships or fieldwork available. Support available to part-time students. Offers arts and sciences (MS); biology (MS); computer and information sciences (MS). *Application deadline:* For fall admission, 7/15 (priority date); for spring admission, 11/25. Applications are processed on a rolling basis. *Application fee:* $0 ($10 for international students). *Dean,* Dr. Bernard Cotton, 601-877-6120, E-mail: asugsl@aol.com.

School of Business *Faculty:* 7 full-time (1 woman). Expenses: Contact institution. Offers business (MBA). *Application deadline:* For fall admission, 7/15; for spring admission, 11/25. *Application fee:* $10 for international students. *Dean,* Dr. John Gill, 601-304-4300 Ext. 4309.

School of Nursing *Faculty:* 3 full-time (all women), 2 part-time/adjunct (both women). Expenses: Contact institution. Offers rural nursing (MSN). *Application deadline:* For fall admission, 7/15 (priority date); for spring admission, 11/25. Applications are processed on a rolling basis. *Application fee:* $0 ($10 for international students). *Dean,* Dr. Frances C. Henderson, 601-304-4304.

School of Psychology and Education *Faculty:* 11 full-time (7 women), 12 part-time/adjunct (4 women). Expenses: Contact institution. *Financial support:* Career-related internships or fieldwork available. Support available to part-time students. Offers agricultural education (MS Ed); elementary education (MS Ed, Ed S); guidance and counseling (MS Ed); industrial education (MS Ed); secondary education (MS Ed); special education (MS Ed). *Application deadline:* For fall admission, 7/15 (priority date); for spring admission, 11/25. Applications are processed on a rolling basis. *Application fee:* $0 ($10 for international students). *Dean,* Dr. Josephine M. Posey, 601-877-6141, Fax: 601-877-3867.

ALDERSON-BROADDUS COLLEGE, Philippi, WV 26416

General Information Independent-religious, coed, comprehensive institution. *Enrollment:* 55 full-time matriculated graduate/professional students (27 women). *Enrollment by degree*

level: 55 master's. *Graduate faculty:* 17 part-time/adjunct (3 women). Tuition, state resident: full-time $8,000. Tuition, nonresident: full-time $8,000. Full-time tuition and fees vary according to degree level. *Graduate housing:* Rooms and/or apartments available on a first-come, first-served basis to single and married students. Housing application deadline: 8/21. *Student services:* Career counseling, low-cost health insurance. *Library facilities:* Pickett Library. *Online resources:* library catalog, web page, access to other libraries' catalogs. *Collection:* 82,685 titles, 270 serial subscriptions.

Computer facilities: 92 computers available on campus for general student use. A campuswide network can be accessed from student residence rooms and from off campus. Internet access is available. *Web address:* http://www.ab.edu/.

General Application Contact: Carl D. Mercer, Director, Master's Program, 304-457-6356, Fax: 304-457-6308, E-mail: mercer@ab.edu.

GRADUATE UNITS

Medical Science Department Students: 55 full-time (30 women); includes 5 minority (4 African Americans, 1 Hispanic American) Average age 35. 40 applicants, 78% accepted, 24 enrolled. *Faculty:* 17 part-time/adjunct (3 women). Expenses: Contact institution. *Financial support:* Fellowships, research assistantships, teaching assistantships, career-related internships or fieldwork and institutionally sponsored loans available. Support available to part-time students. Financial award application deadline: 6/1. In 2001, 21 degrees awarded. Post-baccalaureate distance learning degree programs offered (minimal on-campus study). Offers emergency medical care (MS); rural primary care (MS); surgery (MS). *Application deadline:* For fall admission, 7/1 (priority date). Applications are processed on a rolling basis. *Application fee:* $35. *Director, Master's Program,* Carl D. Mercer, 304-457-6356, Fax: 304-457-6308, E-mail: mercer@ab.edu.

ALFRED ADLER GRADUATE SCHOOL, Hopkins, MN 55305

General Information Independent, coed, graduate-only institution. *Enrollment by degree level:* 162 master's. *Graduate faculty:* 1 full-time (0 women), 30 part-time/adjunct (18 women). *Tuition:* Full-time $10,620; part-time $295 per credit. *Required fees:* $40 per quarter. Tuition and fees vary according to course load. *Graduate housing:* On-campus housing not available. *Student services:* Career counseling. *Collection:* 2,000 titles, 8 serial subscriptions, 100 audiovisual materials.

Computer facilities: 2 computers available on campus for general student use. A campuswide network can be accessed. Internet access is available. *Web address:* http://www.alfredadler.edu/.

General Application Contact: Evelyn B. Haas, Director of Academic Affairs, 952-988-4327 Ext. 5723, Fax: 952-988-4171, E-mail: ev@alfredadler.edu.

GRADUATE UNITS

Program in Counseling and Psychotherapy Average age 37. 30 applicants, 90% accepted. *Faculty:* 1 full-time (0 women), 30 part-time/adjunct (18 women). Expenses: Contact institution. *Financial support:* Career-related internships or fieldwork and tuition waivers (partial) available. Support available to part-time students. Financial award applicants required to submit FAFSA. In 2001, 32 degrees awarded. *Degree program information:* Part-time and evening/weekend programs available. Offers Adlerian psychotherapy (Diploma); counseling and psychotherapy (MA). *Application deadline:* For fall admission, 10/1 (priority date); for winter admission, 1/1 (priority date); for spring admission, 4/1 (priority date). Applications are processed on a rolling basis. *Application fee:* $50. *Application Contact:* Evelyn B. Haas, Director of Academic Affairs, 952-988-4327 Ext. 5723, Fax: 952-988-4171, E-mail: ev@alfredadler.edu. *President,* Dennis Rislove, 952-988-4185, Fax: 952-988-4171, E-mail: rislove@alfredadler.edu.

ALFRED UNIVERSITY, Alfred, NY 14802-1205

General Information Independent, coed, university. CGS member. *Enrollment:* 181 full-time matriculated graduate/professional students (95 women), 147 part-time matriculated graduate/professional students (100 women). *Enrollment by degree level:* 270 master's, 57 doctoral, 1 other advanced degree. *Graduate faculty:* 128. *Tuition:* Full-time $23,554. *Required fees:* $698. One-time fee: $116 part-time. Full-time tuition and fees vary according to program. *Graduate housing:* Room and/or apartments available on a first-come, first-served basis to single students; on-campus housing not available to married students. Housing application deadline: 7/1. *Student services:* Campus employment opportunities, campus safety program, career counseling, free psychological counseling, international student services, low-cost health insurance, multicultural affairs office, writing training. *Library facilities:* Herrick Memorial Library plus 1 other. *Online resources:* library catalog, web page. *Collection:* 317,832 titles, 1,507 serial subscriptions, 162,547 audiovisual materials. *Research affiliation:* Laboratory for Electronic Ceramics, Polymer-Assisted Ceramics Manufacturing Center, New York State Center for Advanced Ceramic Technology, National Science Foundation Industry-University Center for Glass Research, Whitewares Research Center Industry University Center (whitewares processing, traditional ceramics), National Science Foundation Industry-University Center for Biosurfaces (bioceramics).

Computer facilities: 390 computers available on campus for general student use. A campuswide network can be accessed from student residence rooms and from off campus. Internet access is available. *Web address:* http://www.alfred.edu/.

General Application Contact: Cathleen R. Johnson, Coordinator of Graduate Admissions, 607-871-2141, Fax: 607-871-2198, E-mail: johnsonc@alfred.edu.

GRADUATE UNITS

Graduate School Students: 181 full-time (95 women), 147 part-time (100 women). Average age 25. 610 applicants, 29% accepted. *Faculty:* 128. Expenses: Contact institution. *Financial support:* Fellowships, research assistantships, teaching assistantships, career-related internships or fieldwork, tuition waivers (full and partial), and unspecified assistantships available. Financial award applicants required to submit FAFSA. In 2001, 136 master's, 12 doctorates awarded. *Degree program information:* Part-time programs available. Offers community services administration (MPS); electrical engineering (MS); mechanical engineering (MS); school psychology (MA, Psy D, CAS). *Application deadline:* Applications are processed on a rolling basis. *Application fee:* $50. Electronic applications accepted. *Application Contact:* Cathleen R. Johnson, Coordinator of Graduate Admissions, 607-871-2141, Fax: 607-871-2198, E-mail: johnsonc@alfred.edu. *Provost, Vice President for Academic and Statutory Affairs, Director of Graduate Studies,* Dr. David Szcerbacki, 607-871-2141, Fax: 607-871-2339, E-mail: fszcerbacki@alfred.edu.

College of Business Students: 8 full-time (4 women), 9 part-time (2 women). Average age 25. 82 applicants, 20% accepted. Expenses: Contact institution. *Financial support:* Research assistantships, tuition waivers (partial) and unspecified assistantships available. Financial award applicants required to submit FAFSA. In 2001, 18 degrees awarded. *Degree program information:* Part-time programs available. Offers business (MBA). *Application deadline:* Applications are processed on a rolling basis. *Application fee:* $50. Electronic applications accepted. *Application Contact:* Cathleen R. Johnson, Coordinator of Graduate Admissions, 607-871-2141, Fax: 607-871-2198, E-mail: johnsonc@alfred.edu. *Director of MBA Program,* Lori Hollenbeck, 607-871-2630, E-mail: hollenl@alfred.edu.

Division of Education Students: 35 full-time (25 women), 42 part-time (34 women). Average age 24. 66 applicants, 56% accepted. Expenses: Contact institution. *Financial support:* Research assistantships, tuition waivers (partial) and unspecified assistantships available. Financial award applicants required to submit FAFSA. In 2001, 51 degrees awarded. *Degree program information:* Part-time programs available. Offers counseling (MS Ed); elementary education (MS Ed); literacy teacher (MS Ed); secondary education (MS Ed). *Application deadline:* Applications are processed on a rolling basis. *Application fee:* $50. Electronic applications accepted. *Application Contact:* Cathleen R. Johnson, Coordinator of Graduate Admissions, 607-871-2141, Fax: 607-871-2198, E-mail: johnsonc@alfred.edu. *Chair,* Dr. Katherine D. Wiesendanger, 607-871-2219, E-mail: fwiesendange@bigvax.alfred.edu.

New York State College of Ceramics Students: 85 full-time (31 women), 12 part-time (2 women). 341 applicants, 15% accepted. Expenses: Contact institution. *Financial support:* Fellowships, research assistantships, teaching assistantships, tuition waivers (full and partial) available. Financial award applicants required to submit FAFSA. In 2001, 29 master's, 3 doctorates awarded. Offers biomedical materials engineering science (MS); ceramic engineering (MS); ceramics (MFA, PhD); electronic integrated arts (MFA); glass art (MFA); glass science (MS, PhD); materials science (MS); sculpture (MFA). *Application deadline:* Applications are processed on a rolling basis. *Application fee:* $50. Electronic applications accepted. *Application Contact:* Cathleen R. Johnson, Coordinator of Graduate Admissions, 607-871-2141, Fax: 607-871-2198, E-mail: johnsonc@alfred.edu. *Provost, Vice President for Academic and Statutory Affairs, Director of Graduate Studies,* Dr. David Szcerbacki, 607-871-2141, Fax: 607-871-2339, E-mail: fszcerbacki@alfred.edu.

See in-depth description on page 723.

ALLEN COLLEGE, Waterloo, IA 50703

General Information Independent, coed, primarily women, comprehensive institution. *Enrollment:* 13 full-time matriculated graduate/professional students (all women), 11 part-time matriculated graduate/professional students (10 women). *Enrollment by degree level:* 24 master's. *Graduate faculty:* 6 full-time (all women), 4 part-time/adjunct (3 women). *Tuition:* Full-time $18,257; part-time $466 per credit. *Required fees:* $331; $140 per year. Tuition and fees vary according to course load. *Student services:* Career counseling, child daycare facilities, exercise/wellness program, free psychological counseling, low-cost health insurance. *Library facilities:* Barrett Library. *Online resources:* web page. *Collection:* 2,951 titles, 188 serial subscriptions, 478 audiovisual materials.

Computer facilities: 14 computers available on campus for general student use. Internet access is available. *Web address:* http://www.allencollege.edu/.

General Application Contact: Barb J. Seible, Director of Admissions, 319-226-2002, Fax: 319-226-2051, E-mail: seiblebj@lhs.org.

GRADUATE UNITS

Program in Nursing Students: 13 full-time (all women), 8 part-time (7 women); includes 4 minority (3 African Americans, 1 Native American) Average age 39. 18 applicants, 67% accepted, 12 enrolled. *Faculty:* 6 full-time (all women), 4 part-time/adjunct (3 women). Expenses: Contact institution. *Financial support:* In 2001–02, 21 students received support. Federal Work-Study, institutionally sponsored loans, scholarships/grants, and traineeships available. Support available to part-time students. Financial award application deadline: 3/1; financial award applicants required to submit FAFSA. In 2001, 7 degrees awarded. *Degree program information:* Part-time and evening/weekend programs available. Offers family nurse practitioner (MSN); health education (MSN); leadership in heatlh care delivery (MSN). *Application deadline:* For fall admission, 8/1 (priority date); for spring admission, 12/1 (priority date). Applications are processed on a rolling basis. *Application fee:* $20. Electronic applications accepted. *Application Contact:* Barb J. Seible, Director of Admissions, 319-226-2002, Fax: 319-226-2051, E-mail: seiblebj@lhs.org. *Chair,* Diane Marie Young, 319-226-2047, Fax: 319-226-2070, E-mail: youngdm@lhs.org.

ALLIANCE THEOLOGICAL SEMINARY, Nyack, NY 10960

General Information Independent-religious, coed, graduate-only institution. *Enrollment by degree level:* 217 first professional, 270 master's. *Graduate faculty:* 14 full-time (2 women), 26 part-time/adjunct (7 women). *Tuition:* Full-time $7,680; part-time $320 per credit. *Required fees:* $20 per semester. Tuition and fees vary according to course load and program. *Graduate housing:* Rooms and/or apartments available on a first-come, first-served basis to single and married students. Typical cost: $3,060 per year for single students. Room charges vary according to housing facility selected. *Student services:* Campus employment opportunities, career counseling, international student services, low-cost health insurance. *Library facilities:* Main library plus 1 other. *Online resources:* library catalog, web page, access to other libraries' catalogs. *Collection:* 48,600 titles, 332 serial subscriptions, 1,100 audiovisual materials.

Computer facilities: 5 computers available on campus for general student use. A campuswide network can be accessed. Internet access is available. *Web address:* http://www.alliance.edu/.

General Application Contact: Eric Bennett, Director of Enrollment Services, 845-353-2020, Fax: 845-348-3912, E-mail: admissions@alliance.edu.

GRADUATE UNITS

Graduate Programs *Degree program information:* Part-time programs available. Offers Chinese pastoral ministries (M Div); Christian education (M Div); Christian ministry (MPS); church ministries (M Div); counseling (M Div, MA); intercultural studies (MA); missions (M Div, MPS); New Testament (MA); Old Testament (MA); theology (M Div); urban ministries (M Div); urban ministry (MPS); youth ministries (M Div). Electronic applications accepted.

ALLIANT INTERNATIONAL UNIVERSITY, San Francisco, CA 94109

General Information Independent, coed, graduate-only institution. *Enrollment by degree level:* 486 master's, 2,526 doctoral, 132 other advanced degrees. *Graduate faculty:* 191 full-time (84 women), 301 part-time/adjunct (141 women). *Tuition:* Part-time $397 per credit hour. Tuition and fees vary according to degree level, campus/location and program. *Graduate housing:* On-campus housing not available. *Student services:* Campus employment opportunities, campus safety program, career counseling, disabled student services, exercise/wellness program, free psychological counseling, international student services, low-cost health insurance, teacher training, writing training. *Online resources:* library catalog. *Collection:* 140,000 titles, 1,320 serial subscriptions.

Computer facilities: 55 computers available on campus for general student use. A campuswide network can be accessed from off campus. Internet access is available. *Web address:* http://www.alliant.edu/.

General Application Contact: Patricia J. Mullen, Vice President, Enrollment and Student Services, 800-457-1273 Ext. 303, Fax: 415-931-8322, E-mail: admissions@alliant.edu.

GRADUATE UNITS

California School of Organizational Studies Students: 250 full-time (162 women), 146 part-time (86 women); includes 141 minority (31 African Americans, 71 Asian Americans or Pacific Islanders, 36 Hispanic Americans, 3 Native Americans) Average age 34. *Faculty:* 15 full-time (4 women), 38 part-time/adjunct (14 women). Expenses: Contact institution. *Financial support:* In 2001–02, 228 students received support; research assistantships, teaching assistantships, career-related internships or fieldwork, Federal Work-Study, institutionally sponsored loans, and scholarships/grants available. Financial award application deadline: 2/15; financial award applicants required to submit FAFSA. In 2001, 19 master's, 37 doctorates awarded. *Degree program information:* Part-time and evening/weekend programs available. Offers change leadership (MA); consulting psychology (PhD); executive management (Psy D); industrial-organizational psychology (PhD); organizational behavior (MA, MOB); organizational consulting (Psy D); organizational development (MA, Psy D); organizational psychology (MA, PhD); organizational studies (MA, MOB, PhD, Psy D). Programs available at Fresno, Los Angeles, San Diego, and San Francisco. *Application deadline:* Applications are processed on a rolling basis. *Application Contact:* Patricia J. Mullen, Vice President, Enrollment and Student Services, 800-457-1273 Ext. 303, Fax: 415-931-8322, E-mail: admissions@alliant.edu. *Dean,* Dr. Rodney Lowman, 626-284-2777, Fax: 626-284-0550, E-mail: rlowman@alliant.edu.

California School of Professional Psychology Students: 1,878 (1,449 women); includes 471 minority (106 African Americans, 180 Asian Americans or Pacific Islanders, 162 Hispanic Americans, 23 Native Americans) Average age 32. Expenses: Contact institution. *Financial support:* Research assistantships, teaching assistantships, career-related internships or fieldwork, Federal Work-Study, institutionally sponsored loans, and scholarships/grants available. Financial award application deadline: 2/15; financial award applicants required to submit FAFSA. In 2001, 8 master's, 340 doctorates awarded. Offers clinical psychology (PhD, Psy D); clinical psychophysiology and biofeedback (MS); health psychology (PhD); Indian family and child mental health (MA); marital and family therapy (MA, Psy D); psychology (MA, MS, PhD, Psy D); psychopharmacology (MS). Programs available at Fresno, Los Angeles, San Diego, and San Francisco. *Application deadline:* For fall admission, 1/2 (prior-

Alliant International University (continued)

ity date). *Application Contact:* Patricia J. Mullen, Vice President, Enrollment and Student Services, 800-457-1273 Ext. 303, Fax: 415-931-8322, E-mail: admissions@alliant.edu. *Dean,* Dr. Adele Rabin, 858-635-4801, Fax: 858-635-4585, E-mail: arabin@alliant.edu.

Graduate School of Education Students: 7 full-time (all women), 13 part-time (7 women); includes 6 minority (3 African Americans, 2 Asian Americans or Pacific Islanders, 1 Hispanic American) *Faculty:* 1 (woman) full-time, 6 part-time/adjunct (5 women). Expenses: Contact institution. Offers BCLAD (Credential); CLAD (Credential); cross-cultural studies (MA, Ed D); education (MA, Ed D, Psy D, Credential); educational leadership (Ed D); school psychology (MA, Ed D); teaching English to speakers of other languages (Ed D); technology and learning (MA, Ed D). Programs available at Fresno, Los Angeles, and San Francisco. *Application Contact:* Patricia J. Mullen, Vice President, Enrollment and Student Services, 800-457-1273 Ext. 303, Fax: 415-931-8322, E-mail: admissions@alliant.edu. *Dean,* Dr. Karen Schuster Webb, 510-523-2300 Ext. 194, Fax: 510-521-3678, E-mail: kwebb@alliant.edu.

Programs in Education–Fresno Expenses: Contact institution. Offers BCLAD (Credential); CLAD (Credential); educational leadership (Ed D); school psychology (MA, Ed D). *Application deadline:* For fall admission, 8/1. *Application fee:* $20. *Application Contact:* Patricia J. Mullen, Vice President, Enrollment and Student Services, 800-457-1273 Ext. 303, Fax: 415-931-8322, E-mail: admissions@alliant.edu.

School of Social and Policy Studies Students: 79 full-time (60 women), 23 part-time (18 women); includes 35 minority (15 African Americans, 8 Asian Americans or Pacific Islanders, 7 Hispanic Americans, 5 Native Americans) Average age 38. *Faculty:* 11 full-time (1 woman), 11 part-time/adjunct (4 women). Expenses: Contact institution. *Financial support:* Research assistantships, teaching assistantships, career-related internships or fieldwork and Federal Work-Study available. Financial award application deadline: 2/15; financial award applicants required to submit FAFSA. In 2001, 4 degrees awarded. Offers culture and human behavior (Psy D); forensic psychology (PhD, Psy D); social and policy studies (PhD, Psy D). Programs available at Fresno and San Diego. *Application fee:* $65. *Application Contact:* Patricia J. Mullen, Vice President, Enrollment and Student Services, 800-457-1273 Ext. 303, Fax: 415-931-8322, E-mail: admissions@alliant.edu. *Interim Dean,* Dr. Ramona Kunard, 858-635-4505, Fax: 858-635-4843, E-mail: rkunard@alliant.edu.

United States International College of Business Students: 205. *Faculty:* 14 full-time (5 women), 14 part-time/adjunct (6 women). Expenses: Contact institution. *Financial support:* Research assistantships, teaching assistantships, career-related internships or fieldwork, Federal Work-Study, institutionally sponsored loans, scholarships/grants, and tuition waivers (partial) available. Support available to part-time students. Financial award applicants required to submit FAFSA. *Degree program information:* Part-time and evening/weekend programs available. Offers business administration (MBA); information and technology management (DBA); international business (MIBA, DBA); strategic business (DBA). *Application deadline:* For fall admission, 8/1 (priority date); for winter admission, 12/1 (priority date); for spring admission, 3/1 (priority date). Applications are processed on a rolling basis. *Application fee:* $40. Electronic applications accepted. *Dean,* Dr. Mink H. Stavenga, 858-635-4695, Fax: 858-635-4528, E-mail: mstaveng@alliant.edu.

See in-depth description on page 725.

ALLIANT INTERNATIONAL UNIVERSITY–MÉXICO CITY, CP06700 Mexico City, Mexico

General Information Independent, coed, comprehensive institution. *Graduate housing:* On-campus housing not available.

GRADUATE UNITS

Programs in Business *Degree program information:* Part-time programs available. Offers business administration (MBA); international business administration (MIBA); management and organizational development (MS).

ALVERNIA COLLEGE, Reading, PA 19607-1799

General Information Independent-religious, coed, comprehensive institution. *Enrollment:* 19 full-time matriculated graduate/professional students (14 women), 214 part-time matriculated graduate/professional students (140 women). *Enrollment by degree level:* 233 master's. *Graduate faculty:* 4 full-time (1 woman), 14 part-time/adjunct (7 women). *Tuition:* Part-time $390 per credit. *Graduate housing:* On-campus housing not available. *Student services:* Campus employment opportunities, career counseling, disabled student services, free psychological counseling, grant writing training, teacher training, writing training. *Library facilities:* Franco Library. *Online resources:* library catalog, web page. *Collection:* 86,000 titles, 400 serial subscriptions, 7,600 audiovisual materials.

Computer facilities: 60 computers available on campus for general student use. A campuswide network can be accessed from student residence rooms. *Web address:* http://www.alvernia.edu/.

General Application Contact: Carmela Baruck, Coordinator of Graduate Admissions and Program Service, 610-796-8296, Fax: 610-796-8480, E-mail: carmela.baruck@alvernia.edu.

GRADUATE UNITS

Graduate and Continuing Studies Students: 19 full-time (14 women), 214 part-time (140 women); includes 14 minority (11 African Americans, 3 Hispanic Americans) *Faculty:* 4 full-time (1 woman), 14 part-time/adjunct (7 women). Expenses: Contact institution. *Financial support:* Unspecified assistantships and alumni and partnership discounts available. Support available to part-time students. In 2001, 36 degrees awarded. *Degree program information:* Part-time and evening/weekend programs available. Offers business (MBA); education (M Ed); liberal studies (MALS). *Application deadline:* Applications are processed on a rolling basis. *Application fee:* $50. Electronic applications accepted. *Application Contact:* Carmela Baruck, Coordinator of Graduate Admissions and Program Service, 610-796-8296, Fax: 610-796-8480, E-mail: carmela.baruck@alvernia.edu. *Dean of Graduate and Continuing Studies,* Joan Lewis, 610-796-8264, E-mail: joan.lewis@alvernia.edu.

ALVERNO COLLEGE, Milwaukee, WI 53234-3922

General Information Independent-religious, women only, comprehensive institution. *Enrollment:* 6 full-time matriculated graduate/professional students (all women), 167 part-time matriculated graduate/professional students (144 women). *Enrollment by degree level:* 173 master's. *Graduate faculty:* 96 full-time (74 women), 95 part-time/adjunct (71 women). *Tuition:* Full-time $8,976; part-time $374 per credit hour. *Required fees:* $150; $150 per year. *Graduate housing:* On-campus housing not available. *Student services:* Campus employment opportunities, campus safety program, career counseling, child daycare facilities, exercise/wellness program, multicultural affairs office. *Library facilities:* Library Media Center. *Online resources:* library catalog, web page, access to other libraries' catalogs. *Collection:* 89,683 titles, 1,197 serial subscriptions, 20,409 audiovisual materials.

Computer facilities: 250 computers available on campus for general student use. A campuswide network can be accessed from student residence rooms and from off campus. Internet access, email are available. *Web address:* http://www.alverno.edu/.

General Application Contact: Sarajane Kennedy, Assistant Director of Admissions, 414-382-6104, Fax: 414-382-6332, E-mail: sarajane.kennedy@alverno.edu.

GRADUATE UNITS

School of Education Students: 6 full-time (all women), 167 part-time (144 women); includes 70 minority (62 African Americans, 3 Asian Americans or Pacific Islanders, 4 Hispanic Americans, 1 Native American), 2 international. 33 applicants, 94% accepted. *Faculty:* 96 full-time (74 women), 95 part-time/adjunct (71 women). Expenses: Contact institution. *Financial support:* In 2001–02, 67 students received support. Federal Work-Study available. Support available to part-time students. Financial award application deadline: 6/1; financial award applicants required to submit FAFSA. In 2001, 23 degrees awarded. *Degree program information:* Part-time and evening/weekend programs available. Offers adaptive education (MA); administrative leadership (MA); adult education and organizational development (MA); adult educational in structural design (MA); adult educational instructional design (MA); constructing technology for K-12 settings (MA); director of instruction (MA); instructional design (MA); professional development (MA); reading education (MA); reading education with adaptive education (MA); science education (MA); teaching in alternative schools (MA). *Application deadline:* For fall admission, 8/1 (priority date); for spring admission, 12/15 (priority date). Applications are processed on a rolling basis. *Application fee:* $20. Electronic applications accepted. *Application Contact:* Sarajane Kennedy, Assistant Director of Admissions, 414-382-6104, Fax: 414-382-6332, E-mail: sarajane.kennedy@alverno.edu. *Graduate Dean,* Dr. Mary Diez, 414-382-6214, Fax: 414-382-6332, E-mail: mary.diez@alverno.edu.

AMBERTON UNIVERSITY, Garland, TX 75041-5595

General Information Independent-religious, coed, upper-level institution. *Graduate housing:* On-campus housing not available.

GRADUATE UNITS

Graduate School *Degree program information:* Part-time and evening/weekend programs available. Offers counseling (MA); general business (MBA); human relations and business (MA, MS); management (MBA); professional development (MA).

AMERICAN BAPTIST SEMINARY OF THE WEST, Berkeley, CA 94704-3029

General Information Independent-religious, coed, graduate-only institution. *Graduate housing:* Rooms and/or apartments available to single and married students. Housing application deadline: 6/1.

GRADUATE UNITS

Graduate and Professional Programs *Degree program information:* Part-time programs available. Offers theology (M Div, MA).

AMERICAN CHRISTIAN COLLEGE AND SEMINARY, Oklahoma City, OK 73108

General Information Independent-religious, coed, comprehensive institution. *Enrollment:* 119 full-time matriculated graduate/professional students (56 women), 107 part-time matriculated graduate/professional students (34 women). *Enrollment by degree level:* 35 first professional, 139 master's, 52 doctoral. *Graduate faculty:* 5 full-time (1 woman), 9 part-time/adjunct (2 women). *Tuition:* Full-time $2,880; part-time $160 per hour. *Required fees:* $82; $4 per hour. $10 per term. One-time fee: $50. Full-time tuition and fees vary according to degree level. *Graduate housing:* On-campus housing not available. *Student services:* Campus employment opportunities, career counseling, free psychological counseling, international student services, teacher training. *Library facilities:* Corvin Library. *Collection:* 14,652 titles, 47 serial subscriptions, 554 audiovisual materials.

Computer facilities: 1 computer available on campus for general student use. *Web address:* http://www.accs.edu/.

General Application Contact: Dr. Mitchel Beville, Director of Admissions, 405-945-0100, Fax: 405-945-0311, E-mail: mbeville@accs.edu.

GRADUATE UNITS

Graduate and Professional Programs Students: 119 full-time (56 women), 107 part-time (34 women); includes 106 minority (66 African Americans, 20 Asian Americans or Pacific Islanders, 15 Hispanic Americans, 5 Native Americans) Average age 38. *Faculty:* 5 full-time (1 woman), 9 part-time/adjunct (2 women). Expenses: Contact institution. *Financial support:* Career-related internships or fieldwork and Federal Work-Study available. Support available to part-time students. Financial award application deadline: 5/5; financial award applicants required to submit FAFSA. In 2001, 7 first professional degrees, 31 master's, 22 doctorates awarded. *Degree program information:* Part-time and evening/weekend programs available. Postbaccalaureate distance learning degree programs offered (no on-campus study). Offers biblical studies (MA); Christian counseling (M Div, MA, D Min); divinity (M Div); ministry (MA, D Min). *Application deadline:* Applications are processed on a rolling basis. *Application fee:* $50. Electronic applications accepted. *Application Contact:* Dr. Mitchel Beville, Director of Admissions, 405-945-0100, Fax: 405-945-0311, E-mail: mbeville@accs.edu. *Vice President of Academic Affairs,* Dr. A. Fred Hambrick, 405-945-0100, Fax: 405-945-0311, E-mail: info@abcs.edu.

THE AMERICAN COLLEGE, Bryn Mawr, PA 19010-2105

General Information Independent, coed, graduate-only institution. *Graduate faculty:* 21 full-time (2 women), 5 part-time/adjunct (0 women). *Tuition:* Part-time $525 per course. *Graduate housing:* On-campus housing not available. *Student services:* Career counseling, international student services. *Library facilities:* Lucas Memorial Library plus 1 other. *Collection:* 12,500 titles, 620 serial subscriptions. *Web address:* http://www.amercoll.edu/.

General Application Contact: Joanne F. Patterson, Associate Director of Graduate Administration, 610-526-1366, Fax: 610-526-1310, E-mail: joannep@amercoll.edu.

GRADUATE UNITS

Richard D. Irwin Graduate School *Faculty:* 21 full-time (2 women), 5 part-time/adjunct (0 women). Expenses: Contact institution. In 2001, 147 degrees awarded. *Degree program information:* Part-time and evening/weekend programs available. Postbaccalaureate distance learning degree programs offered (minimal on-campus study). Offers financial sciences (MSFS). *Application deadline:* Applications are processed on a rolling basis. *Application fee:* $275. Electronic applications accepted. *Application Contact:* Joanne F. Patterson, Associate Director of Graduate Administration, 610-526-1366, Fax: 610-526-1310, E-mail: joannep@amercoll.edu. *Vice President and Dean,* Dr. Walter J. Woerheide, 610-526-1398, Fax: 610-526-1310, E-mail: waltw@amercoll.edu.

AMERICAN COLLEGE OF ACUPUNCTURE AND ORIENTAL MEDICINE, Houston, TX 77063

General Information Proprietary, coed, graduate-only institution. *Enrollment by degree level:* 147 master's. *Graduate faculty:* 6 full-time (3 women), 15 part-time/adjunct (6 women). *Tuition:* Part-time $180 per credit. Part-time tuition and fees vary according to class time. *Student services:* Campus safety program, international student services. *Library facilities:* American College of Acupuncture and Oriental Medicine Library plus 1 other. *Collection:* 1,500 titles, 12 serial subscriptions, 205 audiovisual materials.

Computer facilities: 2 computers available on campus for general student use. Internet access and online class registration are available. *Web address:* http://www.acaom.edu/.

General Application Contact: Minmay J. Liang, Executive Director, 713-780-9777 Ext. 101, Fax: 713-781-5781, E-mail: acaom@compuserve.com.

GRADUATE UNITS

Graduate Studies Students: 77 full-time (47 women), 70 part-time (48 women); includes 56 minority (6 African Americans, 41 Asian Americans or Pacific Islanders, 9 Hispanic Americans), 7 international. Average age 37. 27 applicants, 85% accepted. *Faculty:* 6 full-time (3 women), 15 part-time/adjunct (6 women). Expenses: Contact institution. In 2001, 16 degrees awarded. *Degree program information:* Part-time programs available. *Application deadline:* For fall admission, 8/23 (priority date); for spring admission, 12/21 (priority date). Applications are processed on a rolling basis. *Application fee:* $50 ($100 for international students). *Application Contact:* Minmay J. Liang, Executive Director, 713-780-9777 Ext. 101, Fax: 713-781-5781, E-mail: acaom@compuserve.com. *Dean of Academic Affairs,* Wen Huang, 713-780-9777, Fax: 713-781-5781, E-mail: acaom@compuserve.com.

AMERICAN COLLEGE OF COMPUTER & INFORMATION SCIENCES, Birmingham, AL 35205

General Information Proprietary, coed, comprehensive institution. *Enrollment:* 880 part-time matriculated graduate/professional students (80 women). *Enrollment by degree level:* 880 master's. *Graduate faculty:* 1 (woman) full-time. *Tuition:* Full-time $5,580. *Graduate housing:* On-campus housing not available. *Web address:* http://www.accis.edu/.

General Application Contact: Natalie Nixon, Director of Admissions, 800-767-2427, Fax: 205-328-2229, E-mail: admiss@accis.edu.

GRADUATE UNITS

Department of Computer Science Average age 35. 244 applicants, 28% accepted. *Faculty:* 1 (woman) full-time. Expenses: Contact institution. In 2001, 10 degrees awarded. *Degree program information:* Part-time and evening/weekend programs available. Postbaccalaureate distance learning degree programs offered (no on-campus study). Offers computer science (MSCS). *Application deadline:* Applications are processed on a rolling basis. *Application fee:* $20. Electronic applications accepted. *Application Contact:* Natalie Nixon, Director of Admissions, 800-767-2427, Fax: 205-328-2229, E-mail: admiss@accis.edu. *Program Director,* Cheryl Mills, 800-767-2427, Fax: 205-326-3822, E-mail: faculty@accis.edu.

AMERICAN COLLEGE OF TRADITIONAL CHINESE MEDICINE, San Francisco, CA 94107

General Information Independent, coed, graduate-only institution. *Enrollment by degree level:* 236 master's. *Graduate faculty:* 8 full-time (2 women), 25 part-time/adjunct (14 women). *Tuition:* Full-time $7,680; part-time $160 per credit. *Required fees:* $100; $160 per credit. $25 per term. *Graduate housing:* On-campus housing not available. *Student services:* Campus employment opportunities, campus safety program, career counseling, disabled student services, free psychological counseling, international student services. *Library facilities:* American College of Traditional Chinese Medicine Library. *Online resources:* library catalog. *Collection:* 4,590 titles, 65 serial subscriptions, 583 audiovisual materials. *Research affiliation:* California Pacific Medical Center and The Institute for Health and Healing (acupuncture and stroke recovery), University of California San Francisco Medical Center (evaluation of health and vitality through herbal formulas).

Computer facilities: 4 computers available on campus for general student use. A campuswide network can be accessed. Internet access is available. *Web address:* http://www.actcm.edu/.

General Application Contact: Yu-Wen Chiu, Admissions Officer, 415-282-7600 Ext. 14, Fax: 415-282-0856, E-mail: admissions@actcm.edu.

GRADUATE UNITS

Graduate Program Students: 141 full-time (104 women), 95 part-time (74 women); includes 68 minority (7 African Americans, 55 Asian Americans or Pacific Islanders, 5 Hispanic Americans, 1 Native American) Average age 33. 62 applicants, 95% accepted, 40 enrolled. *Faculty:* 8 full-time (2 women), 25 part-time/adjunct (14 women). Expenses: Contact institution. *Financial support:* In 2001–02, 175 students received support, including 36 teaching assistantships (averaging $1,665 per year); career-related internships or fieldwork, Federal Work-Study, institutionally sponsored loans, and scholarships/grants also available. Support available to part-time students. Financial award applicants required to submit FAFSA. In 2001, 73 degrees awarded. *Degree program information:* Part-time programs available. Offers traditional Chinese medicine (MS). *Application deadline:* For fall admission, 9/1; for winter admission, 12/1; for spring admission, 3/1. Applications are processed on a rolling basis. *Application fee:* $125 ($150 for international students). *Application Contact:* Yu-Wen Chiu, Admissions Officer, 415-282-7600 Ext. 14, Fax: 415-282-0856, E-mail: admissions@actcm.edu. *President,* Lixin Huang, 415-282-7600 Ext. 12, Fax: 415-282-0856, E-mail: lixinhuang@actcm.edu.

AMERICAN CONSERVATORY THEATER, San Francisco, CA 94108-5800

General Information Independent, coed, graduate-only institution. *Enrollment by degree level:* 44 master's, 8 other advanced degrees. *Graduate faculty:* 7 full-time (2 women), 17 part-time/adjunct (9 women). *Tuition:* Full-time $12,510. *Graduate housing:* On-campus housing not available. *Student services:* Campus employment opportunities, campus safety program, career counseling, multicultural affairs office. *Library facilities:* Allen Fletcher Theater Collection. *Online resources:* library catalog, access to other libraries' catalogs. *Collection:* 14,500 titles, 20 serial subscriptions, 450 audiovisual materials.

Computer facilities: 2 computers available on campus for general student use. A campuswide network can be accessed. Internet access is available. *Web address:* http://www.act-sfbay.org/.

General Application Contact: Dr. Jack F. Sharrar, Director of Academic Affairs, 415-439-2350, Fax: 415-834-3300, E-mail: jsharrar@act-sfbay.org.

GRADUATE UNITS

Graduate Program in Acting Students: 52 full-time (25 women). Average age 24. 383 applicants, 4% accepted. *Faculty:* 7 full-time (2 women), 17 part-time/adjunct (9 women). Expenses: Contact institution. *Financial support:* In 2001–02, 36 students received support. Federal Work-Study, scholarships/grants, and tuition waivers (full and partial) available. Financial award application deadline: 3/1; financial award applicants required to submit FAFSA. In 2001, 18 degrees awarded. Offers acting (MFA, Certificate). Certificate open only to applicants with undergraduate degree from a non-accredited institution. *Application deadline:* For fall admission, 2/1. *Application fee:* $65. Electronic applications accepted. *Application Contact:* Dr. Jack F. Sharrar, Director of Academic Affairs, 415-439-2350, Fax: 415-834-3300, E-mail: jsharrar@act-sfbay.org. *Conservatory Director,* Melissa Smith, 415-439-2350.

AMERICAN FILM INSTITUTE CONSERVATORY, Los Angeles, CA 90027-1657

General Information Independent, coed, graduate-only institution. *Enrollment by degree level:* 288 master's. *Graduate faculty:* 9 full-time (2 women), 53 part-time/adjunct (15 women). *Tuition:* Full-time $22,000. *Required fees:* $1,590. *Graduate housing:* On-campus housing not available. *Student services:* Campus safety program, career counseling, international student services. *Library facilities:* Louis B. Mayer Library. *Online resources:* library catalog, web page, access to other libraries' catalogs. *Collection:* 14,000 titles, 100 serial subscriptions, 6,000 audiovisual materials.

Computer facilities: 25 computers available on campus for general student use. A campuswide network can be accessed from off campus. Internet access, online class schedule are available. *Web address:* http://www.afionline.org/.

General Application Contact: Scott Hardman, Admissions Counselor, 323-856-7714, Fax: 323-856-7720, E-mail: shardman@afi.com.

GRADUATE UNITS

Graduate Program Students: 288 full-time (99 women); includes 43 minority (14 African Americans, 17 Asian Americans or Pacific Islanders, 12 Hispanic Americans), 83 international. Average age 27. 499 applicants, 36% accepted, 125 enrolled. *Faculty:* 9 full-time (2 women), 53 part-time/adjunct (15 women). Expenses: Contact institution. *Financial support:* In 2001–02, 130 students received support, including 12 teaching assistantships with partial tuition reimbursements available (averaging $3,000 per year); scholarships/grants and unspecified assistantships also available. Financial award application deadline: 6/1; financial award applicants required to submit FAFSA. In 2001, 94 degrees awarded. Offers cinematography (MFA); directing (MFA); editing (MFA); producing (MFA); production design (MFA); screenwriting (MFA). *Application deadline:* For fall admission, 1/5. *Application fee:* $75. *Application Contact:* Scott Hardman, Admissions Counselor, 323-856-7714, Fax: 323-856-7720, E-mail: shardman@afi.com/. *Provost,* James Hindman, 323-856-7600, Fax: 323-467-4578, E-mail: education@afi.com.

AMERICAN GRADUATE UNIVERSITY, Covina, CA 91724

General Information Proprietary, coed, graduate-only institution. *Enrollment by degree level:* 70 master's, 7 other advanced degrees. *Graduate faculty:* 2 full-time (1 woman), 5 part-time/adjunct (3 women). *Tuition:* Part-time $600 per course. Part-time tuition and fees vary according to campus/location. *Library facilities:* American Graduate University Library. *Collection:* 11,000 titles, 33 serial subscriptions.

Computer facilities: Internet access and online class registration are available. *Web address:* http://www.agu.edu/.

General Application Contact: Linda Olsen, Registrar, 626-966-4576, Fax: 626-915-1709, E-mail: lindaolsen@agu.edu.

GRADUATE UNITS

Program in Acquisition Management *Faculty:* 2 full-time (1 woman), 5 part-time/adjunct (3 women). Expenses: Contact institution. In 2001, 7 degrees awarded. Postbaccalaureate distance learning degree programs offered. Offers acquisition management (MAM, Certificate). *Application deadline:* Applications are processed on a rolling basis. *Application fee:* $0. *Head,* 626-966-4576.

Program in Project Management *Faculty:* 2 full-time (1 woman), 5 part-time/adjunct (3 women). Expenses: Contact institution. In 2001, 4 degrees awarded. Postbaccalaureate distance learning degree programs offered. Offers project management (MPM, Certificate). *Application deadline:* Applications are processed on a rolling basis. *Application fee:* $0. *Head,* 626-966-4576.

AMERICAN INTERCONTINENTAL UNIVERSITY, Atlanta, GA 30328

General Information Proprietary, coed, comprehensive institution. *Enrollment:* 71 full-time matriculated graduate/professional students (36 women), 316 part-time matriculated graduate/professional students (166 women). *Enrollment by degree level:* 387 master's. *Graduate faculty:* 44 full-time (12 women), 33 part-time/adjunct (13 women). *Tuition:* Part-time $3,485 per term. *Required fees:* $300 per term. Tuition and fees vary according to program. *Graduate housing:* On-campus housing not available. *Student services:* Campus employment opportunities, career counseling, international student services. *Web address:* http://www.aiuniv.edu/.

General Application Contact: Information Contact, 888-754-4422 Ext. 8072, Fax: 404-965-6502.

GRADUATE UNITS

Program in Global Technology Management Students: 37 full-time (23 women), 140 part-time (75 women); includes 81 minority (75 African Americans, 3 Asian Americans or Pacific Islanders, 3 Hispanic Americans) Average age 30. 147 applicants, 44% accepted, 64 enrolled. *Faculty:* 4 full-time (2 women), 27 part-time/adjunct (11 women). Expenses: Contact institution. *Financial support:* Institutionally sponsored loans available. Support available to part-time students. Financial award application deadline: 4/30; financial award applicants required to submit FAFSA. In 2001, 26 degrees awarded. *Degree program information:* Part-time and evening/weekend programs available. Offers global technology management (MBA). *Application deadline:* For fall admission, 11/27 (priority date); for winter admission, 1/28 (priority date); for spring admission, 4/8 (priority date). Applications are processed on a rolling basis. *Application fee:* $50. Electronic applications accepted. *Application Contact:* Karen Thurgood, Director of Admissions, 404-965-6500 Ext. 8072, Fax: 404-965-6502, E-mail: kthurgood@aiuniv.edu. *Dean,* Dr. Carla Bryan, 404-965-6500 Ext. 8118, Fax: 404-965-6502.

Program in Information Technology Students: 34 full-time (13 women), 190 part-time (91 women); includes 124 minority (106 African Americans, 13 Asian Americans or Pacific Islanders, 5 Hispanic Americans) 189 applicants, 46% accepted, 86 enrolled. *Faculty:* 40 full-time (10 women), 6 part-time/adjunct (2 women). Expenses: Contact institution. *Financial support:* Institutionally sponsored loans available. Support available to part-time students. Financial award application deadline: 4/30; financial award applicants required to submit FAFSA. *Degree program information:* Part-time and evening/weekend programs available. Offers information technology (MIT). *Application deadline:* For fall admission, 11/27 (priority date); for winter admission, 1/28 (priority date); for spring admission, 4/8 (priority date). Applications are processed on a rolling basis. *Application fee:* $50. Electronic applications accepted. *Application Contact:* Karen Thurgood, Director of Admissions, 404-965-6500 Ext. 8072, Fax: 404-965-6502, E-mail: kthurgood@aiuniv.edu. *Dean,* Ed Malin, 404-965-6500 Ext. 6536, Fax: 404-965-6502, E-mail: emalin@aiuniv.edu.

AMERICAN INTERCONTINENTAL UNIVERSITY, Los Angeles, CA 90066

General Information Proprietary, coed, comprehensive institution. *Graduate housing:* Room and/or apartments available on a first-come, first-served basis to single students; on-campus housing not available to married students.

GRADUATE UNITS

Graduate School of Information Technology *Degree program information:* Part-time and evening/weekend programs available. Offers information technology (MIT).

Program in International Business *Degree program information:* Part-time and evening/weekend programs available. Offers international business (MBA).

AMERICAN INTERCONTINENTAL UNIVERSITY, Plantation, FL 33324

General Information Proprietary, coed, comprehensive institution.

GRADUATE UNITS

Program in Information Technology Offers information technology (MIT).

Program in International Business Offers international business (MIB).

AMERICAN INTERCONTINENTAL UNIVERSITY-LONDON, London, W1U 4RY, United Kingdom

General Information Proprietary, coed, comprehensive institution. *Graduate housing:* Room and/or apartments available to single students; on-campus housing not available to married students.

GRADUATE UNITS

Program in Business Administration Offers international business (MBA).

AMERICAN INTERCONTINENTAL UNIVERSITY ONLINE, Hoffman Estates, IL 60192

General Information Proprietary, coed, comprehensive institution. *Tuition:* Full-time $18,000. *Required fees:* $2,300. One-time fee: $175 full-time. Full-time tuition and fees vary according to program. *Student services:* Career counseling. *Web address:* http://www.aiu-online.com/.

General Application Contact: Stephen Fireng, Vice President of Admissions, 877-701-3800, Fax: 847-585-2695, E-mail: sfireng@careered.com.

GRADUATE UNITS

Program in Business Administration Expenses: Contact institution. *Degree program information:* Evening/weekend programs available. Postbaccalaureate distance learning degree programs offered. Offers business administration (MBA). *Application deadline:* Applications are processed on a rolling basis. *Application fee:* $50. *Application Contact:* Stephen Fireng, Vice President of Admissions, 877-701-3800, Fax: 847-585-2695, E-mail: sfireng@careered.com. *Chief Academic Officer,* Dr. Robin Throne, 847-585-2002, Fax: 847-585-2042, E-mail: rthrone@aiu-online.com.

Program in Information Technology Expenses: Contact institution. Offers information technology (MIT). *Application deadline:* Applications are processed on a rolling basis. *Application fee:* $50. *Application Contact:* Stephen Fireng, Vice President of Admissions, 877-701-3800, Fax: 847-585-2695, E-mail: sfireng@careered.com. *Chief Academic Officer,* Dr. Robin Throne, 847-585-2002, Fax: 847-585-2042, E-mail: rthrone@aiu-online.com.

AMERICAN INTERNATIONAL COLLEGE, Springfield, MA 01109-3189

General Information Independent, coed, comprehensive institution. *Graduate housing:* Room and/or apartments available to single students; on-campus housing not available to married students.

GRADUATE UNITS

School of Continuing Education and Graduate Studies *Degree program information:* Part-time and evening/weekend programs available. Offers organization development (MSOD); physical therapy (MPT); public administration (MPA). Electronic applications accepted.

School of Business Administration Offers business administration (MBA).

School of Psychology and Education *Degree program information:* Part-time and evening/weekend programs available. Offers administration (M Ed, CAGS); child development (MA, Ed D); clinical psychology (MS); criminal justice studies (MS); educational psychology (MA, Ed D); elementary education (M Ed, CAGS); human resource development (MA, CAGS); psychology and education (M Ed, MA, MS, Ed D, CAGS); reading (M Ed, CAGS); school psychology (MA, CAGS); secondary education (M Ed, CAGS); special education (M Ed, CAGS). Electronic applications accepted.

AMERICAN MILITARY UNIVERSITY, Manassas, VA 20110

General Information Proprietary, coed, primarily men, comprehensive institution. *Enrollment by degree level:* 933 master's. *Graduate faculty:* 2 full-time (1 woman), 100 part-time/adjunct (8 women). *Tuition:* Part-time $750 per course. *Graduate housing:* On-campus housing not available. *Student services:* International student services, writing training. *Web address:* http://www.amunet.edu/.

General Application Contact: Cathi Bauer, Office of Student Services, 703-330-5398 Ext. 894, Fax: 703-330-5109, E-mail: info@amunet.edu.

GRADUATE UNITS

Graduate School of Military Studies Average age 35. 830 applicants, 100% accepted, 550 enrolled. *Faculty:* 2 full-time (1 woman), 100 part-time/adjunct (8 women). Expenses: Contact institution. In 2001, 87 degrees awarded. *Degree program information:* Part-time and evening/weekend programs available. Postbaccalaureate distance learning degree programs offered (no on-campus study). Offers air warfare (MA Military Studies); American revolution studies (MA Military Studies); business administration (MBA); civil war studies (MA Military Studies); criminal justice (MA); defense management (MA Military Studies); emergency and disaster management (MA); intelligence (MA Strategic Intelligence); land warfare (MA Military Studies); management (MA); national security studies (MA); naval warfare (MA Military Studies); political science (MA); public administration (MA); public health (MA); security management (MA); space studies (MA Military Studies); special operations (MA Military Studies); transportation management (MA); unconventional warfare (MA Military Studies). Program offered via distance learning only. *Application deadline:* For fall admission, 9/1 (priority date); for winter admission, 1/1; for spring admission, 5/1 (priority date). Applications are processed on a rolling basis. Electronic applications accepted. *Application Contact:* Cathi Bauer, Office of Student Services, 703-330-5398 Ext. 894, Fax: 703-330-5109, E-mail: info@amunet.edu. *Provost,* Dr. Michael J. Hillyard, 703-330-5398 Ext. 862, Fax: 703-330-5109, E-mail: mhillyard@amunet.edu.

AMERICAN UNIVERSITY, Washington, DC 20016-8001

General Information Independent-religious, coed, university. CGS member. *Enrollment:* 2,506 full-time matriculated graduate/professional students (1,551 women), 2,310 part-time matriculated graduate/professional students (1,375 women). *Enrollment by degree level:* 1,306 first professional, 2,820 master's, 557 doctoral, 133 other advanced degrees. *Graduate faculty:* 487 full-time (194 women), 528 part-time/adjunct (223 women). *Tuition:* Full-time $14,274; part-time $793 per credit. *Required fees:* $290; $793 per credit. Tuition and fees vary according to program. *Graduate housing:* Room and/or apartments available on a first-come, first-served basis to single students; on-campus housing not available to married students. Typical cost: $7,790 per year ($10,704 including board). Room and board charges vary according to housing facility selected. *Student services:* Campus employment opportunities, campus safety program, career counseling, child daycare facilities, disabled student services, free psychological counseling, international student services, low-cost health insurance, multicultural affairs office, teacher training. *Library facilities:* Bender Library plus 1 other. *Online resources:* library catalog, web page, access to other libraries' catalogs. *Collection:* 725,000 titles, 3,600 serial subscriptions, 40,700 audiovisual materials.

Computer facilities: 600 computers available on campus for general student use. A campuswide network can be accessed from student residence rooms and from off campus. Internet access, online course support are available. *Web address:* http://www.american.edu/.

General Application Contact: Office of Graduate Affairs and Admissions, 202-885-6000.

GRADUATE UNITS

College of Arts and Sciences Students: 494 full-time (327 women), 873 part-time (543 women); includes 262 minority (165 African Americans, 52 Asian Americans or Pacific Islanders, 41 Hispanic Americans, 4 Native Americans), 285 international. Average age 31. 1,740 applicants, 65% accepted, 351 enrolled. *Faculty:* 227 full-time (98 women), 215 part-time/adjunct (123 women). Expenses: Contact institution. *Financial support:* Fellowships, research assistantships, teaching assistantships, career-related internships or fieldwork, Federal Work-Study, institutionally sponsored loans, scholarships/grants, traineeships, tuition waivers (full and partial), unspecified assistantships, and administrative fellowships available. Support available to part-time students. Financial award applicants required to submit FAFSA. In 2001, 320 master's, 44 doctorates awarded. *Degree program information:* Part-time and evening/weekend programs available. Offers anthropology (MA, PhD); applied anthropology (MA); applied economics (Certificate); applied mathematics (MA); applied sociology (MA); applied statistics (Certificate); art history (MA); arts and sciences (MA, MAT, MFA, MS, PhD, Certificate); arts management (MA, Certificate); biology (MA, MS); chemistry (MS, PhD); clinical psychology (PhD); computer science (MS); creative writing (MFA); dance (MA); development banking (MA); economics (MA, PhD); environmental science (MS); environmental studies (MA); experimental psychology (PhD); experimental/biological psychology (MA); financial economics for public policy (MA); French studies (MA, Certificate); general psychology (MA, PhD); health fitness management (MS); history (MA, PhD); information systems (MS, Certificate); interdisciplinary studies (MA); international training and education (MA); literature (MA); mathematics (MA); mathematics education (PhD); painting, sculpture and printmaking (MFA); personality/social psychology (MA); philosophy (MA); philosophy and social policy (MA); physics (MS); professinoal development (Certificate); psychology (MA); Russian studies (MA, Certificate); social research (Certificate); sociology (MA, PhD); sociology/justice (PhD); Spanish: Latin American studies (MA, Certificate); statistical computing (MS); statistics (MA, MS, PhD, Certificate); statistics for policy analysis (MS); teaching English to speakers of other languages (MA, Certificate); toxicology (MS, Certificate); translation (Certificate). *Application deadline:* For fall admission, 2/1; for spring admission, 10/1. *Application fee:* $50. Electronic applications accepted. *Application Contact:* Jo-Anne Saxe, Director, Graduate Admissions, 202-885-3621, Fax: 202-885-1505. *Dean,* Dr. Kay Mussell, 202-885-2446, Fax: 202-885-2429.

School of Education Students: 42 full-time (34 women), 152 part-time (108 women); includes 39 minority (31 African Americans, 3 Asian Americans or Pacific Islanders, 4 Hispanic Americans, 1 Native American), 6 international. Average age 34. 147 applicants, 80% accepted, 45 enrolled. *Faculty:* 9 full-time (6 women), 17 part-time/adjunct (15 women). Expenses: Contact institution. *Financial support:* Fellowships with full tuition reimbursements, research assistantships with partial tuition reimbursements, teaching assistantships, career-related internships or fieldwork, Federal Work-Study, and institutionally sponsored loans available. Support available to part-time students. Financial award application deadline: 2/1; financial award applicants required to submit FAFSA. In 2001, 52 master's, 6 doctorates awarded. *Degree program information:* Part-time and evening/weekend programs available. Offers education (MA, MAT, PhD, Certificate); educational leadership (MA); educational technology (MA); elementary education (MAT); English for speakers of other languages (MAT); learning disabilities (MA); secondary teaching (MAT, Certificate); specialized studies (MA). *Application deadline:* For fall admission, 2/1 (priority date); for spring admission, 10/1 (priority date). Applications are processed on a rolling basis. *Application fee:* $50. *Dean,* Dr. Lynn Fox, 202-885-3730, Fax: 202-885-1187, E-mail: educate@american.edu.

Kogod School of Business Students: 278 full-time (120 women), 241 part-time (113 women); includes 96 minority (46 African Americans, 33 Asian Americans or Pacific Islanders, 16 Hispanic Americans, 1 Native American), 159 international. Average age 29. 686 applicants, 67% accepted, 117 enrolled. *Faculty:* 54 full-time (11 women), 39 part-time/adjunct (9 women). Expenses: Contact institution. *Financial support:* In 2001–02, 28 students received support; fellowships, research assistantships with partial tuition reimbursements available, career-related internships or fieldwork, Federal Work-Study, institutionally sponsored loans, tuition waivers (partial), and administrative fellowships available. Support available to part-time students. Financial award application deadline: 2/1; financial award applicants required to submit FAFSA. In 2001, 291 degrees awarded. *Degree program information:* Part-time and evening/weekend programs available. Postbaccalaureate distance learning degree programs offered. Offers accounting (MBA, MS); business (MBA, MS); business administration (MBA); business management information systems (MS); entrepreneurship and management (MBA); finance (MBA, MS); human resource management (MBA); international business (MBA); management of global information technology (MBA); marketing information and technology (MBA); marketing management (MBA); real estate (MBA); taxation (MS). *Application deadline:* For fall admission, 2/1 (priority date). Applications are processed on a rolling basis. *Application fee:* $50. *Application Contact:* Dr. August Schomburg, Director of Graduate Programs, 202-885-1988, Fax: 202-885-1078. *Dean,* Dr. Myron Roomkin, 202-885-1900, Fax: 202-885-1955.

School of Communication Students: 280. 411 applicants, 74% accepted, 128 enrolled. *Faculty:* 37 full-time, 40 part-time/adjunct. Expenses: Contact institution. *Financial support:* In 2001–02, 33 students received support, including 4 research assistantships, 19 teaching assistantships; career-related internships or fieldwork, institutionally sponsored loans, and scholarships/grants also available. In 2001, 137 degrees awarded. *Degree program information:* Part-time and evening/weekend programs available. Offers broadcast journalism (MA); communication (MA, MFA); film and video production (MA, MFA); interactive journalism (MA); journalism and public affairs (MA); multimedia development (MA, MFA); print journalism (MA); producing for film and video (MA); public communication (MA); screenwriting (MFA). *Application deadline:* For fall admission, 2/1 (priority date). Applications are processed on a rolling basis. *Application fee:* $50. Electronic applications accepted. *Application Contact:* Ezra Krumhansl, Director, Graduate Recruitment and Admissions, 202-885-3940. *Dean,* Prof. Larry Kirkman, 202-885-2058, Fax: 202-885-2099, E-mail: larry@american.edu.

School of International Service Students: 347 full-time (214 women), 300 part-time (176 women); includes 87 minority (30 African Americans, 20 Asian Americans or Pacific Islanders, 35 Hispanic Americans, 2 Native Americans), 152 international. Average age 27. 1,254 applicants, 74% accepted, 215 enrolled. *Faculty:* 59 full-time (21 women), 35 part-time/adjunct (11 women). Expenses: Contact institution. *Financial support:* In 2001–02, 13 fellowships with tuition reimbursements, 62 research assistantships with tuition reimbursements were awarded. Teaching assistantships, career-related internships or fieldwork, Federal Work-Study, and institutionally sponsored loans also available. Financial award application deadline: 1/15. In 2001, 193 master's, 1 doctorate awarded. *Degree program information:* Part-time and evening/weekend programs available. Offers comparative and regional studies (MA); development management (MS); environmental policy (MA); international communication (MA); international development (MA); international development management (Certificate); international economic policy (MA); international economic relations (Certificate); international peace and conflict resolution (MA); international politics (MA); international relations (PhD); U.S. foreign policy (MA). *Application deadline:* For fall admission, 1/15 (priority date); for spring admission, 10/1 (priority date). Applications are processed on a rolling basis. *Application fee:* $50. *Application Contact:* Christopher Derickson, Director of Graduate Admissions and Financial Aid, 202-885-1599, Fax: 202-885-2494. *Dean,* Dr. Louis W. Goodman, 202-885-1600, Fax: 202-885-2494.

School of Public Affairs Students: 246 full-time (169 women), 235 part-time (153 women); includes 130 minority (92 African Americans, 15 Asian Americans or Pacific Islanders, 23 Hispanic Americans), 51 international. Average age 32. 556 applicants, 80% accepted, 179 enrolled. *Faculty:* 56 full-time (26 women), 84 part-time/adjunct (28 women). Expenses: Contact institution. *Financial support:* In 2001–02, 50 teaching assistantships were awarded; fellowships, research assistantships, career-related internships or fieldwork, Federal Work-Study, institutionally sponsored loans, and tuition waivers (full and partial) also available. Financial award application deadline: 2/1. In 2001, 181 master's, 6 doctorates awarded. *Degree program information:* Part-time and evening/weekend programs available. Offers justice, law and society (MS); organization development (MSOD); organizational development (Certificate); personnel and human resource management (MS); political science (MA, PhD); public administration (MPA, PhD, Certificate); public affairs (MA, MPA, MPP, MS, MSOD, PhD, Certificate); public financial management (Certificate); public management (Certificate); public policy (MPP); sociology/justice (PhD). *Application deadline:* For fall admission, 2/1; for spring admission, 10/1. *Application fee:* $50. *Application Contact:* Brenda Manley, Admissions and Financial Aid Manager, 202-885-6202, Fax: 202-885-2355, E-mail: bmanley@american.edu. *Dean,* Dr. Walter Broadmax, 202-885-2940, Fax: 202-885-1008.

Washington College of Law Students: 1,044 full-time (642 women), 478 part-time (265 women); includes 330 minority (109 African Americans, 129 Asian Americans or Pacific Islanders, 87 Hispanic Americans, 5 Native Americans), 204 international. Average age 27. 6,340 applicants, 36% accepted. *Faculty:* 56 full-time (22 women), 111 part-time/adjunct (35 women). Expenses: Contact institution. *Financial support:* In 2001–02, 379 students received support; fellowships with full tuition reimbursements available, career-related internships or fieldwork, Federal Work-Study, institutionally sponsored loans, tuition waivers (full and partial), and dean's fellowships available. Support available to part-time students. Financial award application deadline: 2/15; financial award applicants required to submit FAFSA. In 2001, 349 first professional degrees, 150 master's awarded. *Degree program information:* Part-time and evening/weekend programs available. Offers international legal studies (LL M); judicial sciences (JSD); law (JD); law and government (LL M). *Application deadline:* Applications are processed on a rolling basis. *Application fee:* $55. *Application Contact:* Sandra J. Oakman, Director of Admissions, 202-274-4101, Fax: 202-274-4107, E-mail: wcladmit@american.edu. *Dean,* Claudio Grossman, 202-274-4004, Fax: 202-274-4005, E-mail: grossman@wcl.american.edu.

See in-depth description on page 727.

AMERICAN UNIVERSITY IN CAIRO, 11511 Cairo, Egypt

General Information Independent, coed, comprehensive institution. CGS member. *Graduate housing:* Room and/or apartments available to single students; on-campus housing not available to married students.

GRADUATE UNITS

Graduate Studies and Research *Degree program information:* Part-time programs available. Electronic applications accepted.

School of Business, Economics and Communication *Degree program information:* Part-time programs available. Offers business, economics and communication (MA, MBA, MPA, Diploma); economics (MA); journalism/mass communication (MA); management (MBA, MPA, Diploma); television journalism (MA, Diploma). Electronic applications accepted.

School of Humanities and Social Sciences *Degree program information:* Part-time programs available. Offers Arab language and literature (MA); English and comparative literature (MA); humanities and social sciences (MA, Diploma); Islamic art and architecture (MA); Islamic studies (Diploma); Middle East studies (MA, Diploma); Middle Eastern history (MA); political science (MA); sociology and anthropology (MA); teaching Arabic as a foreign language (MA); teaching English as a foreign language (MA, Diploma). Electronic applications accepted.

School of Sciences and Engineering Offers computer science (MS); engineering (MS, Diploma); sciences and engineering (MS, Diploma). Electronic applications accepted.

THE AMERICAN UNIVERSITY IN DUBAI, Dubai, United Arab Emirates

General Information Proprietary, coed, comprehensive institution. *Graduate housing:* Room and/or apartments available on a first-come, first-served basis to single students. Housing application deadline: 7/31.

GRADUATE UNITS

Program in International Business *Degree program information:* Part-time programs available. Offers international business (MBA). Electronic applications accepted.

ANDERSON UNIVERSITY, Anderson, IN 46012-3495

General Information Independent-religious, coed, comprehensive institution. *Graduate housing:* Rooms and/or apartments available to single and married students. Housing application deadline: 6/1.

GRADUATE UNITS

School of Education

School of Theology *Degree program information:* Part-time programs available. Offers theology (M Div, MA, MRE, D Min).

ANDOVER NEWTON THEOLOGICAL SCHOOL, Newton Centre, MA 02459-2243

General Information Independent-religious, coed, graduate-only institution. *Enrollment by degree level:* 258 first professional, 48 master's, 70 doctoral, 8 other advanced degrees. *Graduate faculty:* 16 full-time (7 women), 83 part-time/adjunct (34 women). *Tuition:* Part-time $354 per credit hour. *Required fees:* $614. Tuition and fees vary according to degree level and program. *Graduate housing:* Rooms and/or apartments available on a first-come, first-served basis to single and married students. Typical cost: $1,698 per year ($3,635 including board) for single students; $6,777 per year ($9,897 including board) for married students. Room and board charges vary according to board plan, campus/location and housing facility selected. Housing application deadline: 7/1. *Student services:* Campus employment opportunities, career counseling, international student services, low-cost health insurance. *Library facilities:* Franklin Trask Library. *Online resources:* library catalog, web page. *Collection:* 232,555 titles, 556 serial subscriptions, 67 audiovisual materials.

Computer facilities: 7 computers available on campus for general student use. A campuswide network can be accessed. Internet access is available. *Web address:* http://www.ants.edu/.

GRADUATE UNITS

Graduate and Professional Programs Students: 44 full-time (27 women), 340 part-time (230 women); includes 47 minority (30 African Americans, 5 Asian Americans or Pacific Islanders, 8 Hispanic Americans, 4 Native Americans), 13 international. Average age 40. 128 applicants, 91% accepted, 80 enrolled. *Faculty:* 16 full-time (7 women), 83 part-time/adjunct (34 women). Expenses: Contact institution. *Financial support:* In 2001–02, 143 students received support; fellowships, teaching assistantships with partial tuition reimbursements available, career-related internships or fieldwork, Federal Work-Study, scholarships/grants, and tuition waivers (full) available. Support available to part-time students. Financial award application deadline: 4/1; financial award applicants required to submit FAFSA. In 2001, 33 first professional degrees, 21 master's, 11 doctorates awarded. *Degree program information:* Part-time programs available. Offers divinity (M Div); general research (MA); religious education (MA); sacred theology (STM); theology (MA, D Min). *Application deadline:* For fall admission, 8/1 (priority date); for winter admission, 11/1; for spring admission, 12/1 (priority date). Applications are processed on a rolling basis. *Application fee:* $15 ($50 for international students). Electronic applications accepted. *Application Contact:* Margaret L. Carroll, Director of Enrollment, 800-964-2687 Ext. 272, Fax: 617-558-9785, E-mail: admissions@ants.edu. *President,* Dr. Benjamin Griffin, 617-964-1100 Ext. 211, Fax: 617-965-9756, E-mail: bgriffin@ants.edu.

ANDREW JACKSON UNIVERSITY, Birmingham, AL 35209

General Information Private, coed, comprehensive institution. *Enrollment:* 250 part-time matriculated graduate/professional students. *Enrollment by degree level:* 250 master's. *Graduate faculty:* 46 part-time/adjunct. *Tuition:* Part-time $475 per course. *Graduate housing:* On-campus housing not available. *Web address:* http://www.aju.edu/.

General Application Contact: Bell N. Woods, Director of Admissions, 205-871-9288, Fax: 205-871-9294, E-mail: bnw@aju.edu.

GRADUATE UNITS

School of Business Average age 40. *Faculty:* 12 part-time/adjunct. Expenses: Contact institution. *Degree program information:* Part-time and evening/weekend programs available. Postbaccalaureate distance learning degree programs offered (no on-campus study). Offers business (MBA). *Application deadline:* Applications are processed on a rolling basis. *Application fee:* $75. Electronic applications accepted. *Application Contact:* Bell N. Woods, Director of Admissions, 205-871-9288, Fax: 205-871-9294, E-mail: bnw@aju.edu. *Dean,* Robert McKim Norris, 205-871-9288, Fax: 205-871-9294, E-mail: rmn@aju.edu.

School of Civil Sciences *Faculty:* 13 part-time/adjunct. Expenses: Contact institution. *Degree program information:* Part-time and evening/weekend programs available. Postbaccalaureate distance learning degree programs offered (no on-campus study). Offers civil sciences (MPA, MS); criminal justice (MS); public administration (MPA). *Application deadline:* Applications are processed on a rolling basis. *Application fee:* $75. Electronic applications accepted. *Application Contact:* Bell N. Woods, Director of Admissions, 205-871-9288, Fax: 205-871-9294, E-mail: bnw@aju.edu. *Dean,* Dr. James E. Bridges, 205-871-9288, Fax: 205-871-9294.

ANDREWS UNIVERSITY, Berrien Springs, MI 49104

General Information Independent-religious, coed, university. CGS member. *Enrollment:* 497 full-time matriculated graduate/professional students (170 women), 442 part-time matriculated graduate/professional students (191 women). *Enrollment by degree level:* 295 first professional, 339 master's, 291 doctoral, 14 other advanced degrees. *Graduate faculty:* 162 full-time (49 women), 20 part-time/adjunct (13 women). *Tuition:* Full-time $12,600; part-time $525 per semester. *Required fees:* $268. Tuition and fees vary according to degree level. *Graduate housing:* Rooms and/or apartments available to single and married students. Typical cost: $2,360 per year ($4,420 including board) for single students; $4,500 per year ($8,400 including board) for married students. *Student services:* Campus employment opportunities, campus safety program, career counseling, child daycare facilities, free psychological counseling, international student services, low-cost health insurance. *Library facilities:* James White Library plus 2 others. *Online resources:* library catalog, web page, access to other libraries' catalogs. *Collection:* 684,686 titles, 3,060 serial subscriptions, 79,225 audiovisual materials. *Research affiliation:* Deutches Electronen Synchroton (physics), Argonne National Laboratory (physics), RAND Corporation (drug abuse).

Computer facilities: 130 computers available on campus for general student use. A campuswide network can be accessed from student residence rooms and from off campus. Internet access is available. *Web address:* http://www.andrews.edu/.

General Application Contact: Carolyn Hurst, Supervisor of Graduate Admission, 800-253-2874, Fax: 616-471-3228, E-mail: enroll@andrews.edu.

GRADUATE UNITS

School of Graduate Studies Students: 497 full-time (170 women), 442 part-time (191 women); includes 305 minority (179 African Americans, 45 Asian Americans or Pacific Islanders, 81 Hispanic Americans), 303 international. Average age 35. 817 applicants, 65% accepted. *Faculty:* 162 full-time (49 women), 20 part-time/adjunct (13 women). Expenses: Contact institution. *Financial support:* Fellowships, research assistantships, teaching assistantships, career-related internships or fieldwork, Federal Work-Study, institutionally sponsored loans, and tuition waivers (partial) available. Support available to part-time students. Financial award applicants required to submit FAFSA. In 2001, 77 first professional degrees, 149 master's, 36 doctorates, 10 other advanced degrees awarded. *Degree program information:* Part-time and evening/weekend programs available. Offers international development (MSA). *Application deadline:* Applications are processed on a rolling basis. *Application fee:* $40. *Application Contact:* Carolyn Hurst, Supervisor of Graduate Admission, 800-253-2874, Fax: 616-471-3228, E-mail: enroll@andrews.edu. *Dean,* Dr. Lyndon G. Furst, 616-471-3405.

College of Arts and Sciences Students: 60 full-time (48 women), 51 part-time (43 women); includes 41 minority (29 African Americans, 3 Asian Americans or Pacific Islanders, 9 Hispanic Americans), 26 international. Average age 33. *Faculty:* 80 full-time (33 women), 14 part-time/adjunct (10 women). Expenses: Contact institution. *Financial support:* Fellowships, research assistantships, teaching assistantships, career-related internships or fieldwork, Federal Work-Study, and institutionally sponsored loans available. Financial award applicants required to submit FAFSA. In 2001, 61 degrees awarded. *Degree program information:* Part-time and evening/weekend programs available. Offers allied health (MSMT); arts and sciences (M Mus, MA, MAT, MPT, MS, MSA, MSMT, MSPT, MSW); biology (MAT, MS); communication (MA); community services management (MSA); English (MA, MAT); history (MA, MAT); mathematics and physical science (MS); modern languages (MAT); music (M Mus, MA); nursing (MS); nutrition (MS); physical therapy (MPT, MSPT); social work (MSW). *Application deadline:* Applications are processed on a rolling basis. *Application fee:* $40. *Application Contact:* Carolyn Hurst, Supervisor of Graduate Admission, 800-253-2874, Fax: 616-471-3228, E-mail: enroll@andrews.edu. *Dean,* Dr. William Richardson, 616-471-3411.

College of Technology Students: 19 full-time (5 women), 20 part-time (8 women); includes 5 minority (2 African Americans, 2 Asian Americans or Pacific Islanders, 1 Hispanic American), 32 international. Average age 30. *Faculty:* 6 full-time. Expenses: Contact institution. In 2001, 2 degrees awarded. Offers software engineering (MS); technology (MS). *Application deadline:* Applications are processed on a rolling basis. *Application fee:* $40. *Application Contact:* Carolyn Hurst, Supervisor of Graduate Admission, 800-253-2874, Fax: 616-471-3228, E-mail: enroll@andrews.edu. *Head,* Dr. M. Wesley Schultz, 616-471-3413.

School of Business Students: 26 full-time (15 women), 11 part-time (6 women); includes 12 minority (4 African Americans, 2 Asian Americans or Pacific Islanders, 6 Hispanic Americans), 22 international. Average age 30. *Faculty:* 18 full-time (5 women). Expenses: Contact institution. *Financial support:* Fellowships, research assistantships, teaching assistantships, Federal Work-Study available. In 2001, 16 degrees awarded. *Degree program information:* Part-time programs available. Offers business (MBA, MSA); management and marketing (MBA, MSA). *Application deadline:* For fall admission, 8/15. Applications are processed on a rolling basis. *Application fee:* $40. *Application Contact:* Carolyn Hurst, Supervisor of Graduate Admission, 800-253-2874, Fax: 616-471-3228, E-mail: enroll@andrews.edu. *Dean,* Dr. Ann Gibson, 616-471-3102.

School of Education Students: 96 full-time (67 women), 206 part-time (122 women); includes 85 minority (57 African Americans, 5 Asian Americans or Pacific Islanders, 23 Hispanic Americans), 70 international. Average age 40. *Faculty:* 22 full-time (8 women). Expenses: Contact institution. *Financial support:* Fellowships, research assistantships, teaching assistantships, career-related internships or fieldwork, Federal Work-Study, institutionally sponsored loans, and tuition waivers (partial) available. Support available to part-time students. In 2001, 45 master's, 18 doctorates, 10 other advanced degrees awarded. *Degree program information:* Part-time programs available. Offers community counseling (MA); counseling psychology (PhD); curriculum and instruction (MA, Ed D, PhD, Ed S); education (MA, MAT, Ed D, PhD, Ed S); educational administration and leadership (MA, Ed D, PhD, Ed S); educational and developmental psychology (MA); educational psychology (Ed D, PhD); elementary education (MAT); leadership (Ed D, PhD); reading (MA); religious education (MA, Ed D, PhD, Ed S); school counseling (MA); school psychology (Ed D, Ed S); secondary education (MAT); teacher education (MAT). *Application deadline:* Applications are processed on a rolling basis. *Application fee:* $40. *Application Contact:* Carolyn Hurst, Supervisor of Graduate Admission, 800-253-2874, Fax: 616-471-3228, E-mail: enroll@andrews.edu. *Dean,* Dr. Karen R. Graham, 616-471-3109.

Seventh-day Adventist Theological Seminary Students: 286 full-time (25 women), 154 part-time (12 women); includes 162 minority (87 African Americans, 33 Asian Americans or Pacific Islanders, 42 Hispanic Americans), 153 international. Average age 34. *Faculty:* 42 full-time (3 women), 6 part-time/adjunct (3 women). Expenses: Contact institution. *Financial support:* Fellowships, research assistantships, teaching assistantships, career-related internships or fieldwork, Federal Work-Study, and institutionally sponsored loans available. In 2001, 77 first professional degrees, 25 master's, 18 doctorates awarded. Offers theology (M Div, M Th, MA, D Min, PhD, Th D). *Application deadline:* Applications are processed on a rolling basis. *Application fee:* $40. *Application Contact:* Dr. J. Bjornar Storfjell, Director, 616-471-3205. *Dean,* Dr. John K. McVay, 616-471-3537.

ANGELO STATE UNIVERSITY, San Angelo, TX 76909

General Information State-supported, coed, comprehensive institution. CGS member. *Enrollment:* 148 full-time matriculated graduate/professional students (98 women), 281 part-time matriculated graduate/professional students (184 women). *Enrollment by degree level:* 429 master's. *Graduate faculty:* 111 full-time (40 women). *Tuition, area resident:* Full-time $960; part-time $40 per credit hour. Tuition, nonresident: full-time $6,120; part-time $255 per credit hour. *Required fees:* $1,336; $56 per credit hour. *Graduate housing:* Room and/or apartments available on a first-come, first-served basis to single students; on-campus housing not available to married students. Typical cost: $2,552 per year ($4,028 including board). Housing application deadline: 7/15. *Student services:* Campus employment opportunities, campus safety program, career counseling, low-cost health insurance. *Library facilities:* Portor Henderson Library plus 1 other. *Online resources:* library catalog, web page. *Collection:* 452,232 titles, 1,850 serial subscriptions, 28,781 audiovisual materials.

Computer facilities: 325 computers available on campus for general student use. A campuswide network can be accessed from student residence rooms and from off campus. Internet access and online class registration are available. *Web address:* http://www.angelo.edu/.

General Application Contact: Jackie Droll, Coordinator of Graduate Admissions, 915-942-2169, Fax: 915-942-2194, E-mail: jackie.droll@angelo.edu.

GRADUATE UNITS

Graduate School Students: 148 full-time (98 women), 281 part-time (184 women); includes 56 minority (7 African Americans, 2 Asian Americans or Pacific Islanders, 45 Hispanic Americans, 2 Native Americans), 14 international. Average age 35. 189 applicants, 72% accepted, 98 enrolled. *Faculty:* 111 full-time (40 women). Expenses: Contact institution. *Financial support:* In 2001–02, 197 students received support, including 136 fellowships with full and partial tuition reimbursements available, 16 teaching assistantships; research assistantships, career-related internships or fieldwork, Federal Work-Study, tuition waivers (partial), and unspecified assistantships also available. Support available to part-time students. Financial award application deadline: 8/1. In 2001, 121 degrees awarded. *Degree program information:* Part-time and evening/weekend programs available. Offers interdisciplinary studies (MA, MS). *Application deadline:* For fall admission, 7/15 (priority date); for spring admission, 11/15 (priority date). Applications are processed on a rolling basis. *Application fee:* $25 ($50 for international students). Electronic applications accepted. *Application Contact:* Jackie Droll, Coordinator of Graduate Admissions, 915-942-2169, Fax: 915-942-2194, E-mail: jackie.droll@angelo.edu. *Dean of Graduate School,* Dr. Carol Diminnie, 915-942-2169.

College of Business and Professional Studies Students: 28 full-time (16 women), 59 part-time (29 women); includes 12 minority (all Hispanic Americans), 8 international. Average age 35. 40 applicants, 70% accepted, 19 enrolled. *Faculty:* 23 full-time (7 women). Expenses: Contact institution. *Financial support:* In 2001–02, 37 students received support, including 28 fellowships with full and partial tuition reimbursements available, 2 teaching assistantships; career-related internships or fieldwork, Federal Work-Study, tuition waivers (partial), and unspecified assistantships also available. Support available to part-time students. Financial award application deadline: 8/1. In 2001, 38 degrees awarded. *Degree program information:* Part-time and evening/weekend programs available. Offers accounting (MBA); business and professional studies (MBA, MS); kinesiology (MS); management (MBA). *Application deadline:* For fall admission, 8/7 (priority date); for spring admis-

Angelo State University (continued)

sion, 1/2. Applications are processed on a rolling basis. *Application fee:* $25 ($50 for international students). *Dean,* Dr. Michael Butler, 915-942-2337, E-mail: michael.butler@angelo.edu.

College of Liberal and Fine Arts Students: 53 full-time (42 women), 75 part-time (57 women); includes 24 minority (5 African Americans, 1 Asian American or Pacific Islander, 17 Hispanic Americans, 1 Native American), 6 international. Average age 34. 79 applicants, 59% accepted, 30 enrolled. *Faculty:* 43 full-time (13 women). Expenses: Contact institution. *Financial support:* In 2001–02, 74 students received support, including 49 fellowships with full and partial tuition reimbursements available, 10 teaching assistantships; career-related internships or fieldwork, Federal Work-Study, tuition waivers (partial), and unspecified assistantships also available. Support available to part-time students. Financial award application deadline: 8/1. In 2001, 32 degrees awarded. *Degree program information:* Part-time and evening/weekend programs available. Offers communications systems management (MA); English (MA); history (MA); international studies (MA); liberal and fine arts (MA, MPA, MS); psychology (MS); public administration (MPA). *Application deadline:* For fall admission, 8/7 (priority date); for spring admission, 1/2. Applications are processed on a rolling basis. *Application fee:* $25 ($50 for international students). Electronic applications accepted. *Dean,* Dr. E. James Holland, 915-942-2110.

College of Sciences Students: 48 full-time (28 women), 36 part-time (16 women); includes 7 minority (1 Asian American or Pacific Islander, 5 Hispanic Americans, 1 Native American) Average age 30. 33 applicants, 88% accepted, 27 enrolled. *Faculty:* 33 full-time (14 women). Expenses: Contact institution. *Financial support:* In 2001–02, 54 students received support, including 30 fellowships with full and partial tuition reimbursements available, 1 research assistantship, 4 teaching assistantships; career-related internships or fieldwork, Federal Work-Study, tuition waivers (partial), and unspecified assistantships also available. Support available to part-time students. Financial award application deadline: 8/1. In 2001, 15 degrees awarded. *Degree program information:* Part-time and evening/weekend programs available. Offers animal science (MS); biology (MS); medical-surgical nursing (MSN); physical therapy (MPT); sciences (MPT, MS, MSN). *Application deadline:* Applications are processed on a rolling basis. *Application fee:* $25 ($50 for international students). *Dean,* Dr. David Loyd, 915-942-2024.

School of Education Students: 18 full-time (12 women), 111 part-time (82 women); includes 13 minority (2 African Americans, 11 Hispanic Americans) Average age 39. 36 applicants, 89% accepted, 22 enrolled. *Faculty:* 11 full-time (5 women). Expenses: Contact institution. *Financial support:* In 2001–02, 32 students received support, including 29 fellowships with full and partial tuition reimbursements available; teaching assistantships, career-related internships or fieldwork, Federal Work-Study, tuition waivers (partial), and unspecified assistantships also available. Support available to part-time students. Financial award application deadline: 8/1. In 2001, 36 degrees awarded. *Degree program information:* Part-time and evening/weekend programs available. Offers education (M Ed, MA); educational diagnostics (M Ed); guidance and counseling (M Ed); instructional technology (MA); reading specialist (M Ed); school administration (M Ed). *Application deadline:* For fall admission, 8/7 (priority date); for spring admission, 1/2. Applications are processed on a rolling basis. *Application fee:* $25 ($50 for international students). *Dean of the School of Education,* Dr. John J. Miazga, 915-942-2052 Ext. 255, E-mail: john.miazga@angelo.edu.

See in-depth description on page 729.

ANGLO-EUROPEAN COLLEGE OF CHIROPRACTIC, Bournemouth, Dorset BH5 2DF, United Kingdom

General Information Independent, coed, graduate-only institution. *Graduate housing:* On-campus housing not available.

GRADUATE UNITS

Program in Chiropractic Postbaccalaureate distance learning degree programs offered. Offers chiropractic (M Sc).

ANNA MARIA COLLEGE, Paxton, MA 01612

General Information Independent-religious, coed, comprehensive institution. *Enrollment:* 78 full-time matriculated graduate/professional students (32 women), 269 part-time matriculated graduate/professional students (149 women). *Enrollment by degree level:* 345 master's, 2 other advanced degrees. *Graduate faculty:* 9 full-time (4 women), 38 part-time/adjunct (16 women). *Tuition:* Part-time $900 per course. *Graduate housing:* On-campus housing not available. *Student services:* Campus safety program, career counseling, free psychological counseling, international student services. *Library facilities:* Mondor-Eagen Library. *Online resources:* library catalog, web page, access to other libraries' catalogs. *Collection:* 65,794 titles, 364 serial subscriptions, 1,247 audiovisual materials.

Computer facilities: 57 computers available on campus for general student use. A campuswide network can be accessed from student residence rooms and from off campus. Internet access, on-line class schedules, student account information are available. *Web address:* http://www.annamaria.edu/.

General Application Contact: Eva Eaton, Director of Admissions for Graduate Programs and the Department of Professional Studies, 508-849-3488, Fax: 508-849-3362, E-mail: eveaton@annamaria.edu.

GRADUATE UNITS

Graduate Division Students: 78 full-time (32 women), 269 part-time (149 women); includes 9 minority (5 African Americans, 2 Asian Americans or Pacific Islanders, 2 Hispanic Americans), 5 international. Average age 36. *Faculty:* 9 full-time (4 women), 38 part-time/adjunct (16 women). Expenses: Contact institution. *Financial support:* Institutionally sponsored loans available. Financial award applicants required to submit FAFSA. In 2001, 203 master's, 2 other advanced degrees awarded. *Degree program information:* Part-time and evening/weekend programs available. Offers business administration (MBA, AC); counseling psychology (MA, CAGS); criminal justice (MA); early childhood development (M Ed); elementary education (M Ed); emergency response planning (MS); fire science (MA); occupational and environmental health and safety (MS); psychology (MA, CAGS); reading (M Ed). *Application deadline:* For fall admission, 3/1 (priority date); for spring admission, 11/1 (priority date). Applications are processed on a rolling basis. *Application fee:* $30. Electronic applications accepted. *Application Contact:* Eva Eaton, Director of Admissions for Graduate Programs and the Department of Professional Studies, 508-849-3488, Fax: 508-849-3362, E-mail: eveaton@annamaria.edu. *Dean,* Dr. Cynthia Patterson, 508-849-3335, Fax: 508-849-3339, E-mail: cpatterson@annamaria.edu.

ANTIOCH NEW ENGLAND GRADUATE SCHOOL, Keene, NH 03431-3552

General Information Independent, coed, graduate-only institution. *Enrollment by degree level:* 582 master's, 220 doctoral. *Graduate faculty:* 33 full-time (15 women), 80 part-time/adjunct (40 women). *Tuition:* Full-time $15,150. *Graduate housing:* On-campus housing not available. *Student services:* Campus employment opportunities, disabled student services, international student services, multicultural affairs office, teacher training, writing training. *Library facilities:* Antioch New England Graduate School Library. *Online resources:* library catalog, web page. *Collection:* 38,320 titles, 1,625 serial subscriptions, 1,122 audiovisual materials. *Research affiliation:* Harris Center for Conservation Education (environmental studies), Cheshire Medical Center Cardiac Rehabilitation Program (clinical psychology), Northeast Foundation for Children (education), Pine Hill Waldorf School (education).

Computer facilities: 12 computers available on campus for general student use. A campuswide network can be accessed. Internet access, e-mail, intranet services are available. *Web address:* http://www.antiochne.edu/.

General Application Contact: Robbie P. Hertneky, Director of Admissions, 603-357-6265 Ext. 287, Fax: 603-357-0718, E-mail: rhertneky@antoichne.edu.

GRADUATE UNITS

Graduate School Students: 675 full-time (506 women), 127 part-time (103 women); includes 25 minority (7 African Americans, 3 Asian Americans or Pacific Islanders, 13 Hispanic Americans, 2 Native Americans), 20 international. Average age 37. 539 applicants, 85% accepted. *Faculty:* 33 full-time (15 women), 80 part-time/adjunct (40 women). Expenses: Contact institution. *Financial support:* In 2001–02, 580 students received support, including 21 fellowships (averaging $925 per year), 4 research assistantships (averaging $1,350 per year), 6 teaching assistantships (averaging $650 per year); career-related internships or fieldwork, Federal Work-Study, and scholarships/grants also available. Financial award applicants required to submit FAFSA. In 2001, 220 master's, 33 doctorates awarded. *Degree program information:* Evening/weekend programs available. Offers clinical psychology (Psy D); conservation biology (MS); counseling psychology (MA); dance/movement therapy (M Ed, MA); educational administration and supervision (M Ed); environmental advocacy (MS); environmental education (MS); environmental studies (MS, PhD); experienced educators (M Ed); human services administration (MHSA); integrated learning (M Ed); management (MS); marriage and family therapy (MA); resource management and administration (MS); substance abuse counseling (M Ed); substance abuse/addictions counseling (M Ed, MA); teacher certification in biology (7th-12th grade) (MS); teacher certification in general science (5th-9th grade) (MS); Waldorf teacher training (M Ed). *Application deadline:* Applications are processed on a rolling basis. *Application fee:* $40. *Application Contact:* Robbie P. Hertneky, Director of Admissions, 603-357-6265, Fax: 603-357-0718, E-mail: rhertneky@antiochne.edu. *Chancellor,* James H. Craiglow, 603-357-3122 Ext. 256, Fax: 603-357-0718, E-mail: jcraiglow@antiochne.edu.

Interdisciplinary Studies *Faculty:* 1 full-time (0 women), 10 part-time/adjunct (4 women). Expenses: Contact institution. *Financial support:* Fellowships, career-related internships or fieldwork and Federal Work-Study available. Financial award applicants required to submit FAFSA. Offers interdisciplinary studies (MA). *Application deadline:* Applications are processed on a rolling basis. *Application fee:* $40. *Application Contact:* Robbie P. Hertneky, Director of Admissions, 603-357-6265, Fax: 603-357-0718, E-mail: rhertneky@antiochne.edu. *Chancellor,* James H. Craiglow, 603-357-3122 Ext. 256, Fax: 603-357-0718, E-mail: jcraiglow@antiochne.edu.

Announcement: Blending theory, practice, and research through learning experiences in scholarly, practice-oriented, values-based study is the core of Antioch New England's master's and doctoral programs for the adult learner. Faculty members are practicing professionals with exceptional experience and skill in teaching adult learners. Internships and a practicum are fundamental aspects of all programs.

See in-depth description on page 731.

ANTIOCH UNIVERSITY LOS ANGELES, Marina del Rey, CA 90292-7008

General Information Independent, coed, upper-level institution. *Graduate housing:* On-campus housing not available.

GRADUATE UNITS

Graduate Programs *Degree program information:* Part-time and evening/weekend programs available. Postbaccalaureate distance learning degree programs offered. Offers clinical psychology (MA); creative writing (MFA); education (MA); human resource development (MA); leadership (MA); organizational development (MA); pedagogy of creative writing (Certificate); psychology (MA).

ANTIOCH UNIVERSITY MCGREGOR, Yellow Springs, OH 45387-1609

General Information Independent, coed, upper-level institution. *Enrollment:* 222 full-time matriculated graduate/professional students (138 women), 309 part-time matriculated graduate/professional students (212 women). *Graduate faculty:* 15 full-time (9 women), 31 part-time/adjunct (12 women). *Tuition:* Part-time $317 per credit hour. *Required fees:* $75 per quarter. *Graduate housing:* On-campus housing not available. *Library facilities:* Olive Kettering Library. *Online resources:* web page. *Collection:* 285,000 titles, 1,000 serial subscriptions.

Computer facilities: 49 computers available on campus for general student use. A campuswide network can be accessed from off campus. Internet access is available. *Web address:* http://www.mcgregor.edu/.

General Application Contact: Karen E. Crist, Enrollment Services Officer, 937-769-1818, Fax: 937-769-1804, E-mail: kcrist@mcgregor.edu.

GRADUATE UNITS

Graduate Programs Students: 222 full-time (138 women), 309 part-time (212 women); includes 115 minority (95 African Americans, 12 Asian Americans or Pacific Islanders, 5 Hispanic Americans, 3 Native Americans) 189 applicants, 89% accepted, 157 enrolled. *Faculty:* 15 full-time (9 women), 31 part-time/adjunct (12 women). Expenses: Contact institution. *Financial support:* Federal Work-Study available. Financial award applicants required to submit FAFSA. In 2001, 119 degrees awarded. *Degree program information:* Part-time and evening/weekend programs available. Postbaccalaureate distance learning degree programs offered (minimal on-campus study). Offers conflict resolution (MA); liberal and professional studies (MA); management (MA); teacher education (M Ed). *Application deadline:* Applications are processed on a rolling basis. *Application fee:* $50. Electronic applications accepted. *Application Contact:* Karen E. Crist, Enrollment Services Officer, 937-769-1818, Fax: 937-769-1804, E-mail: kcrist@mcgregor.edu. *Academic Dean,* Dr. Steven Brzezinski, 937-769-1860, Fax: 937-769-1804.

Announcement: Offers high-quality academic programs responsive to emerging societal needs and provides an innovative education. Flexible programs promote the integration of life and work experience with academic knowledge. Antioch McGregor seeks to pass on to its students a passion for lifelong learning and a commitment to the betterment of the workplace, the community, and the wider society.

See in-depth description on page 733.

ANTIOCH UNIVERSITY SANTA BARBARA, Santa Barbara, CA 93101-1581

General Information Independent, coed, upper-level institution. *Enrollment:* 124 full-time matriculated graduate/professional students (103 women), 42 part-time matriculated graduate/professional students (30 women). *Enrollment by degree level:* 166 master's. *Graduate faculty:* 14 full-time (8 women), 43 part-time/adjunct (29 women). *Tuition:* Part-time $375 per unit. *Required fees:* $426 per year. $10 per quarter. Tuition and fees vary according to class time and program. *Graduate housing:* On-campus housing not available. *Student services:* Campus employment opportunities, international student services, low-cost health insurance.

Computer facilities: 12 computers available on campus for general student use. A campuswide network can be accessed from off campus. *Web address:* http://www.antiochsb.edu/.

General Application Contact: Carol Flores, Admissions Director, 805-962-8179 Ext. 113, Fax: 805-962-4786, E-mail: cflores@antiochsb.edu.

GRADUATE UNITS

Clinical Psychology Program Students: 62 full-time, 17 part-time. *Faculty:* 14 full-time (8 women), 43 part-time/adjunct (29 women). Expenses: Contact institution. *Financial support:* Federal Work-Study available. Support available to part-time students. Financial award application deadline: 8/5; financial award applicants required to submit FAFSA. In 2001, 40 degrees awarded. *Degree program information:* Part-time and evening/weekend programs available. Offers clinical psychology (MA). *Application deadline:* For fall admission, 8/5 (priority date); for winter admission, 11/11 (priority date). Applications are processed on a rolling basis. *Application fee:* $60. *Application Contact:* Carol Flores, Admissions Director, 805-962-8179

Ext. 113, Fax: 805-962-4786, E-mail: cflores@antiochsb.edu. *Chair,* Dr. Catherine Radecki-Bush, 805-962-8179 Ext. 229, Fax: 805-962-4786, E-mail: cradecki-bush@antiochsb.edu.

Program in Education/Teacher Credentialing Students: 14 full-time, 7 part-time. *Faculty:* 14 full-time (8 women), 43 part-time/adjunct (29 women). Expenses: Contact institution. *Financial support:* Application deadline: 8/5; Offers education/teacher credentialing (MA). *Application deadline:* For fall admission, 8/5 (priority date); for winter admission, 11/11 (priority date). *Application fee:* $60. *Application Contact:* Carol Flores, Admissions Director, 805-962-8179 Ext. 113, Fax: 805-962-4786, E-mail: cflores@antiochsb.edu. *Chair,* Dr. Michele Britton Bass, 805-962-8179 Ext. 114, Fax: 805-962-4786, E-mail: britbass@antiochsb.edu.

Program in Organizational Management Students: 23 full-time, 9 part-time. *Faculty:* 14 full-time (8 women), 43 part-time/adjunct (29 women). Expenses: Contact institution. *Financial support:* Federal Work-Study available. Support available to part-time students. Financial award application deadline: 8/5; financial award applicants required to submit FAFSA. In 2001, 12 degrees awarded. *Degree program information:* Part-time and evening/weekend programs available. Offers organizational management (MA). *Application deadline:* For fall admission, 8/5 (priority date); for winter admission, 11/11 (priority date). Applications are processed on a rolling basis. *Application fee:* $60. *Application Contact:* Carol Flores, Admissions Director, 805-962-8179 Ext. 113, Fax: 805-962-4786, E-mail: cflores@antiochsb.edu. *Chair,* Donna Starr, 805-962-8179 Ext. 111, Fax: 805-962-4786, E-mail: dstarr@antiochsb.edu.

Psychology Program Students: 13 full-time, 8 part-time. *Faculty:* 14 full-time (8 women), 43 part-time/adjunct (29 women). Expenses: Contact institution. *Financial support:* Federal Work-Study available. Support available to part-time students. Financial award application deadline: 8/5; financial award applicants required to submit FAFSA. In 2001, 12 degrees awarded. *Degree program information:* Part-time and evening/weekend programs available. Offers family and child studies (MA); professional development and career counseling (MA). *Application deadline:* For fall admission, 8/5 (priority date); for winter admission, 11/11 (priority date). Applications are processed on a rolling basis. *Application fee:* $60. *Application Contact:* Carol Flores, Admissions Director, 805-962-8179 Ext. 113, Fax: 805-962-4786, E-mail: cflores@antiochsb.edu. *Chair,* Dr. Catherine Radecki-Bush, 805-962-8179 Ext. 229, Fax: 805-962-4786, E-mail: cradecki-bush@antiochsb.edu.

ANTIOCH UNIVERSITY SEATTLE, Seattle, WA 98121-1814

General Information Independent, coed, upper-level institution. *Enrollment:* 402 full-time matriculated graduate/professional students (254 women), 465 part-time matriculated graduate/professional students (292 women). *Enrollment by degree level:* 867 master's. *Graduate faculty:* 40 full-time, 56 part-time/adjunct. *Tuition:* Part-time $395 per credit. *Required fees:* $45 per year. Tuition and fees vary according to program. *Graduate housing:* On-campus housing not available. *Student services:* Campus employment opportunities, international student services, low-cost health insurance. *Library facilities:* Antioch Seattle Library. *Online resources:* library catalog, web page. *Collection:* 4,750 titles, 85 serial subscriptions.

Computer facilities: 8 computers available on campus for general student use. *Web address:* http://www.antiochsea.edu/.

General Application Contact: Rita Hunter, Director of Admissions and Enrollment Services, 206-441-5352 Ext. 5200.

GRADUATE UNITS

Graduate Programs Students: 402 full-time (254 women), 464 part-time (292 women). Average age 36. 267 applicants, 96% accepted. *Faculty:* 40 full-time, 56 part-time/adjunct. Expenses: Contact institution. *Financial support:* Federal Work-Study and institutionally sponsored loans available. Financial award application deadline: 6/15. In 2001, 290 degrees awarded. *Degree program information:* Part-time and evening/weekend programs available. Offers education (MA); environment and community (MS); individualized design (MA); management (MS); organizational systems renewal (MA); psychology (MA). *Application deadline:* Applications are processed on a rolling basis. *Application fee:* $50. *Application Contact:* Rita Hunter, Director of Admissions and Enrollment Services, 206-441-5352 Ext. 5200. *President,* Toni Murdock, 206-441-5352.

See in-depth description on page 735.

APPALACHIAN SCHOOL OF LAW, Grundy, VA 24614

General Information Independent, coed, graduate-only institution. *Enrollment by degree level:* 241 first professional. *Graduate faculty:* 15 full-time (4 women), 5 part-time/adjunct (2 women). *Tuition:* Full-time $16,000; part-time $525 per credit. *Required fees:* $200; $100 per semester. Part-time tuition and fees vary according to course load. *Student services:* Campus employment opportunities, career counseling, disabled student services, writing training. *Library facilities:* ASL Library. *Online resources:* library catalog, web page, access to other libraries' catalogs. *Collection:* 76,275 titles, 2,940 serial subscriptions, 295 audiovisual materials.

Computer facilities: 12 computers available on campus for general student use. A campuswide network can be accessed. Internet access, printing access are available. *Web address:* http://www.asl.edu/.

General Application Contact: Veronica Keene, Director of Admissions, 276-935-4349 Ext. 229, Fax: 276-935-8261, E-mail: vkeene@asl.edu.

GRADUATE UNITS

Professional Program in Law Students: 234 full-time (100 women), 7 part-time (3 women); includes 24 minority (15 African Americans, 4 Asian Americans or Pacific Islanders, 3 Hispanic Americans, 2 Native Americans), 1 international. Average age 29. 546 applicants, 59% accepted. *Faculty:* 15 full-time (4 women), 5 part-time/adjunct (2 women). Expenses: Contact institution. *Financial support:* In 2001–02, 153 students received support, including 12 research assistantships (averaging $1,000 per year); career-related internships or fieldwork, Federal Work-Study, institutionally sponsored loans, scholarships/grants, and tuition waivers (full and partial) also available. Financial award application deadline: 7/1; financial award applicants required to submit FAFSA. In 2001, 34 degrees awarded. *Degree program information:* Part-time programs available. Offers law (JD). *Application deadline:* For spring admission, 4/15 (priority date). Applications are processed on a rolling basis. *Application fee:* $40. Electronic applications accepted. *Application Contact:* Veronica Keene, Director of Admissions, 276-935-4349 Ext. 229, Fax: 276-935-8261, E-mail: vkeene@asl.edu. *Interim Dean and Associate Professor,* Paul E. Lund, 276-935-4349 Ext. 210.

APPALACHIAN STATE UNIVERSITY, Boone, NC 28608

General Information State-supported, coed, comprehensive institution. CGS member. *Enrollment:* 783 full-time matriculated graduate/professional students (512 women), 407 part-time matriculated graduate/professional students (337 women). *Graduate faculty:* 437 full-time (128 women). Tuition, state resident: full-time $1,286. Tuition, nonresident: full-time $9,354. *Required fees:* $1,116. *Graduate housing:* Rooms and/or apartments available on a first-come, first-served basis to single and married students. *Student services:* Campus employment opportunities, campus safety program, career counseling, child daycare facilities, exercise/wellness program, free psychological counseling, grant writing training, international student services, low-cost health insurance, multicultural affairs office, teacher training, writing training. *Library facilities:* Carol Grotnes Belk Library plus 1 other. *Online resources:* library catalog, web page, access to other libraries' catalogs. *Collection:* 780,111 titles, 4,998 serial subscriptions, 36,228 audiovisual materials.

Computer facilities: 500 computers available on campus for general student use. A campuswide network can be accessed from student residence rooms. Internet access is available. *Web address:* http://www.appstate.edu/.

General Application Contact: Dr. E. D. Huntley, Senior Associate Dean for Graduate Studies, 828-262-2130, Fax: 828-262-2709, E-mail: huntleyed@appstate.edu.

GRADUATE UNITS

Cratis D. Williams Graduate School Students: 783 full-time (512 women), 407 part-time (337 women); includes 73 minority (53 African Americans, 7 Asian Americans or Pacific Islanders, 8 Hispanic Americans, 5 Native Americans), 28 international. 1,113 applicants, 72% accepted, 551 enrolled. *Faculty:* 437 full-time (128 women). Expenses: Contact institution. *Financial support:* In 2001–02, 45 fellowships (averaging $1,000 per year), 282 research assistantships (averaging $6,500 per year), 120 teaching assistantships (averaging $8,000 per year) were awarded. Career-related internships or fieldwork, Federal Work-Study, institutionally sponsored loans, scholarships/grants, tuition waivers (partial), and unspecified assistantships also available. Support available to part-time students. Financial award application deadline: 7/1; financial award applicants required to submit FAFSA. In 2001, 412 master's, 3 doctorates, 16 other advanced degrees awarded. *Degree program information:* Part-time and evening/weekend programs available. Postbaccalaureate distance learning degree programs offered (minimal on-campus study). Offers information systems (Certificate). *Application deadline:* For fall admission, 7/1; for spring admission, 11/1. Applications are processed on a rolling basis. *Application fee:* $35. *Application Contact:* Dr. E. D. Huntley, Senior Associate Dean for Graduate Studies, 828-262-2130, Fax: 828-262-2709, E-mail: huntleyed@appstate.edu. *Dean of Graduate Studies and Research,* Dr. Judith E. Domer, 828-262-2130.

College of Arts and Sciences Students: 257 full-time (148 women), 41 part-time (23 women); includes 20 minority (13 African Americans, 3 Asian Americans or Pacific Islanders, 2 Hispanic Americans, 2 Native Americans), 15 international. 333 applicants, 60% accepted, 139 enrolled. *Faculty:* 233 full-time (65 women). Expenses: Contact institution. *Financial support:* In 2001–02, 97 research assistantships (averaging $7,000 per year), 64 teaching assistantships (averaging $8,000 per year) were awarded. Fellowships, career-related internships or fieldwork, Federal Work-Study, scholarships/grants, and unspecified assistantships also available. Support available to part-time students. Financial award application deadline: 7/1; financial award applicants required to submit FAFSA. In 2001, 78 degrees awarded. *Degree program information:* Part-time programs available. Offers Appalachian studies (MA); applied physics (MS); arts and sciences (MA, MPA, MS, CAS); biology (MA, MS); clinical psychology (MA); computer science (MS); English (MA); English education (MA); general experimental psychology (MA); geography (MA); gerontology (MA); health psychology (MA); history (MA); industrial and organizational psychology (MA); mathematics (MA); mathematics education (MA); political science (MA); public administration (MPA); public history (MA); romance languages (MA); school psychology (MA, CAS); social sciences (MA). *Application deadline:* For fall admission, 7/1; for spring admission, 11/1. Applications are processed on a rolling basis. *Application fee:* $35. *Dean,* Linda Bennett, 828-262-3078.

College of Education Students: 387 full-time (297 women), 349 part-time (305 women); includes 49 minority (38 African Americans, 3 Asian Americans or Pacific Islanders, 6 Hispanic Americans, 2 Native Americans), 1 international. 575 applicants, 78% accepted, 298 enrolled. *Faculty:* 85 full-time (35 women). Expenses: Contact institution. *Financial support:* In 2001–02, fellowships (averaging $1,000 per year), 74 research assistantships (averaging $6,250 per year), 11 teaching assistantships (averaging $6,250 per year) were awarded. Career-related internships or fieldwork, Federal Work-Study, scholarships/grants, and unspecified assistantships also available. Support available to part-time students. Financial award application deadline: 7/1; financial award applicants required to submit FAFSA. In 2001, 227 master's, 3 doctorates, 12 other advanced degrees awarded. *Degree program information:* Part-time and evening/weekend programs available. Postbaccalaureate distance learning degree programs offered (minimal on-campus study). Offers communication disorders (MA); community counseling (MA); curriculum specialist (MA); early childhood education (MA); education (MA, MLS, MSA, Ed D, Ed S); educational leadership (Ed D); educational media (MA, Ed S); elementary education (MA); higher education (MA, Ed S); instructional technology (MA, Ed S); library science (MA, MLS, Ed S); marriage and family therapy (MA); reading education (MA); school administration (MSA); school counseling (MA, Ed S); secondary education (MA); special education (MA); speech pathology (MA); student development (Ed S). *Application deadline:* For fall admission, 7/1; for spring admission, 11/1. *Application fee:* $35. *Dean,* Dr. Charles Duke, 828-262-2232.

College of Fine and Applied Arts Students: 57 full-time (27 women), 4 part-time (3 women); includes 1 minority (Native American), 2 international. 71 applicants, 68% accepted, 26 enrolled. *Faculty:* 34 full-time (13 women). Expenses: Contact institution. *Financial support:* In 2001–02, 19 research assistantships, 44 teaching assistantships were awarded. Fellowships, career-related internships or fieldwork, Federal Work-Study, institutionally sponsored loans, scholarships/grants, and unspecified assistantships also available. Support available to part-time students. Financial award application deadline: 7/1; financial award applicants required to submit FAFSA. In 2001, 32 degrees awarded. *Degree program information:* Part-time programs available. Offers child development (MA); exercise science (MS); family and consumer science (MA); fine and applied arts (MA, MS); industrial education (MA); industrial technology (MA); master teacher (MA); physical education (MA); sport management (MA); sports management (MA). *Application deadline:* For fall admission, 7/1 (priority date). *Application fee:* $35. *Dean,* Dr. Ming Land, 828-262-3036.

John A. Walker College of Business Students: 65 full-time (35 women), 13 part-time (6 women); includes 2 minority (1 African American, 1 Asian American or Pacific Islander), 9 international. 91 applicants, 76% accepted, 57 enrolled. *Faculty:* 61 full-time (11 women). Expenses: Contact institution. *Financial support:* In 2001–02, fellowships (averaging $2,000 per year), 43 research assistantships (averaging $3,000 per year) were awarded. Teaching assistantships, career-related internships or fieldwork, Federal Work-Study, scholarships/grants, and unspecified assistantships also available. Support available to part-time students. Financial award application deadline: 7/1; financial award applicants required to submit FAFSA. In 2001, 66 degrees awarded. *Degree program information:* Part-time programs available. Postbaccalaureate distance learning degree programs offered (minimal on-campus study). Offers accounting (MS); business (MBA, MS); business administration (MBA). *Application fee:* $35. *Application Contact:* Dr. Rickey C. Kirkpatrick, Assistant Dean for Graduate and External Programs, 828-262-6127, Fax: 828-262-2925, E-mail: kirkprc@appstate.edu. *Dean,* Dr. Kenneth Peacock, 828-262-2058.

School of Music Students: 17 full-time (5 women); includes 1 minority (African American), 1 international. 18 applicants, 89% accepted, 11 enrolled. *Faculty:* 24 full-time (4 women). Expenses: Contact institution. *Financial support:* In 2001–02, 11 research assistantships (averaging $6,250 per year) were awarded; fellowships, teaching assistantships, career-related internships or fieldwork, tuition waivers (partial), and unspecified assistantships also available. Support available to part-time students. Financial award application deadline: 7/1. In 2001, 9 degrees awarded. Offers music education (MM); music performance (MM). *Application deadline:* For fall admission, 7/1 (priority date); for spring admission, 11/1. *Application fee:* $35. *Application Contact:* Dr. Douglas James, Graduate Program Director, 828-262-6463. *Dean,* Dr. William Harbinson, 828-262-3020, Fax: 828-262-6446, E-mail: harbinsonwg@appstate.edu.

AQUINAS COLLEGE, Grand Rapids, MI 49506-1799

General Information Independent-religious, coed, comprehensive institution. *Enrollment:* 194 full-time matriculated graduate/professional students (137 women), 361 part-time matriculated graduate/professional students (243 women). *Enrollment by degree level:* 555 master's. *Graduate faculty:* 42 full-time (22 women), 41 part-time/adjunct (28 women). *Tuition:* Full-time $6,300; part-time $350 per credit. *Graduate housing:* Room and/or apartments available on a first-come, first-served basis to single students; on-campus housing not available to married students. Typical cost: $2,630 per year ($5,416 including board). *Student services:* Campus employment opportunities, campus safety program, career counseling, child daycare facilities, disabled student services, exercise/wellness program, free psychological counseling, multicultural affairs office, teacher training. *Library facilities:* Woodhouse Library. *Online resources:* library catalog, web page, access to other libraries' catalogs. *Collection:* 104,564 titles, 843 serial subscriptions, 6,170 audiovisual materials.

Computer facilities: 85 computers available on campus for general student use. A campuswide network can be accessed. *Web address:* http://www.aquinas.edu/.

General Application Contact: Lynn Atkins-Rykert, Executive Assistant, School of Management, 616-459-8281 Ext. 8000, Fax: 616-732-4489, E-mail: atkinlyn@aquinas.edu.

GRADUATE UNITS

Graduate School of Management Students: 168; includes 16 minority (9 African Americans, 3 Asian Americans or Pacific Islanders, 4 Hispanic Americans), 2 international. Average age 34. 30 applicants, 97% accepted, 29 enrolled. *Faculty:* 16 full-time (4 women), 6 part-time/

Aquinas College (continued)

adjunct (2 women). Expenses: Contact institution. *Financial support:* Available to part-time students. Application deadline: 3/15. In 2001, 73 degrees awarded. *Degree program information:* Part-time and evening/weekend programs available. Offers management (M Mgt). *Application deadline:* Applications are processed on a rolling basis. *Application fee:* $35. *Application Contact:* Lynn Atkins-Rykert, Executive Assistant, School of Management, 616-459-8281 Ext. 8000, Fax: 616-732-4489, E-mail: atkinlyn@aquinas.edu. *Dean,* Cynthia VanGelderen, 616-732-4488, Fax: 616-732-4489, E-mail: vangecyn@aquinas.edu.

School of Education Students: 175 full-time (126 women), 212 part-time (165 women); includes 23 minority (7 African Americans, 6 Asian Americans or Pacific Islanders, 10 Hispanic Americans) Average age 32. 73 applicants, 92% accepted. *Faculty:* 26 full-time (18 women), 35 part-time/adjunct (26 women). Expenses: Contact institution. *Financial support:* Available to part-time students. Application deadline: 3/15. In 2001, 61 degrees awarded. *Degree program information:* Part-time and evening/weekend programs available. Offers education (MAT, ME, MS). *Application deadline:* Applications are processed on a rolling basis. *Application fee:* $35. *Application Contact:* Sandy Rademaker, Coordinator of Graduate Education Programs, 616-459-8281 Ext. 5400, E-mail: rademsan@aquinas.edu. *Dean,* Dr. V. James Garofalo, 616-732-4464, Fax: 616-732-4465, E-mail: garofv@aquinas.edu.

AQUINAS INSTITUTE OF THEOLOGY, St. Louis, MO 63108-3396

General Information Independent-religious, coed, graduate-only institution. *Enrollment by degree level:* 132 first professional, 33 master's, 33 doctoral, 54 other advanced degrees. *Graduate faculty:* 18 full-time (9 women), 10 part-time/adjunct (6 women). *Tuition:* Part-time $470 per credit. *Student services:* Campus employment opportunities, campus safety program, career counseling, exercise/wellness program, free psychological counseling, international student services, low-cost health insurance, writing training. *Library facilities:* Pius XII Memorial Library plus 3 others. *Online resources:* library catalog, web page, access to other libraries' catalogs. *Collection:* 900,000 titles, 5,700 serial subscriptions.

Computer facilities: 166 computers available on campus for general student use. A campuswide network can be accessed from student residence rooms and from off campus. Internet access is available. *Web address:* http://www.ai.edu/.

General Application Contact: Ronald L. Knapp, Director of Admissions, 314-977-3869, Fax: 314-977-7225, E-mail: aquinas@slu.edu.

GRADUATE UNITS

Graduate and Professional Programs Students: 72 full-time (27 women), 180 part-time (124 women); includes 28 minority (13 African Americans, 6 Asian Americans or Pacific Islanders, 9 Hispanic Americans), 11 international. Average age 41. 66 applicants, 88% accepted, 48 enrolled. *Faculty:* 18 full-time (9 women), 10 part-time/adjunct (6 women). Expenses: Contact institution. *Financial support:* In 2001–02, 48 students received support, including 7 research assistantships with full tuition reimbursements available (averaging $1,000 per year); scholarships/grants and tuition waivers (partial) also available. Support available to part-time students. Financial award application deadline: 3/30; financial award applicants required to submit CSS PROFILE or FAFSA. In 2001, 27 first professional degrees, 4 master's, 3 doctorates, 17 other advanced degrees awarded. *Degree program information:* Part-time and evening/weekend programs available. Postbaccalaureate distance learning degree programs offered (minimal on-campus study). Offers health care mission (MAHCM); ministry (M Div); pastoral care (Certificate); pastoral ministry (MAPM); pastoral studies (MAPS); preaching (D Min); spiritual direction (Certificate); theology (M Div, MA). *Application deadline:* For fall admission, 3/15 (priority date); for spring admission, 11/15 (priority date). Applications are processed on a rolling basis. *Application fee:* $40. *Application Contact:* Ronald L. Knapp, Director of Admissions, 314-977-3869, Fax: 314-977-7225, E-mail: aquinas@slu.edu. *Academic Dean,* Sr. Diane Kennedy, OP, 314-977-3882, Fax: 314-977-7225, E-mail: kennedd@slu.edu.

ARCADIA UNIVERSITY, Glenside, PA 19038-3295

General Information Independent-religious, coed, comprehensive institution. *Enrollment:* 379 full-time matriculated graduate/professional students (286 women), 938 part-time matriculated graduate/professional students (703 women). *Enrollment by degree level:* 1,179 master's, 138 doctoral. *Graduate faculty:* 71 full-time, 135 part-time/adjunct. *Tuition:* Part-time $420 per credit. Tuition and fees vary according to degree level and program. *Graduate housing:* On-campus housing not available. *Student services:* Campus safety program, career counseling, international student services, low-cost health insurance, multicultural affairs office, writing training. *Library facilities:* Eugenia Fuller Atwood Library. *Online resources:* library catalog, web page. *Collection:* 139,903 titles, 798 serial subscriptions, 2,861 audiovisual materials.

Computer facilities: 110 computers available on campus for general student use. A campuswide network can be accessed from student residence rooms and from off campus. Internet access is available. *Web address:* http://www.arcadia.edu.

General Application Contact: 215-572-2910, Fax: 215-572-4049, E-mail: admiss@arcadia.edu.

GRADUATE UNITS

Graduate Studies Students: 379 full-time (286 women), 938 part-time (703 women); includes 173 minority (137 African Americans, 20 Asian Americans or Pacific Islanders, 13 Hispanic Americans, 3 Native Americans), 8 international. Average age 31. *Faculty:* 71 full-time, 135 part-time/adjunct. Expenses: Contact institution. *Financial support:* Research assistantships, teaching assistantships, career-related internships or fieldwork, scholarships/grants, tuition waivers (partial), and unspecified assistantships available. Support available to part-time students. In 2001, 332 degrees awarded. *Degree program information:* Part-time and evening/weekend programs available. Offers allied health (MSHE, MSPH); art education (M Ed, MA Ed); biology education (MA Ed); chemistry education (MA Ed); child development (CAS); computer education (M Ed, CAS); computer education 7–12 (MA Ed); counseling (MAC); early childhood education (M Ed, CAS); educational leadership (M Ed, CAS); educational psychology (CAS); elementary education (M Ed, CAS); English (MAE); English education (MA Ed); environmental education (MA Ed, CAS); fine arts, theater, and music (MAH); genetic counseling (MSGC); history education (MA Ed); history, philosophy, and religion (MAH); international peace and conflict management (MAIPCR); language arts (M Ed, CAS); literature and language (MAH); mathematics education (M Ed, MA Ed, CAS); medical science and community health (MM Sc, MSHE, MSPH); music education (MA Ed); physical therapy (DPT); psychology (MA Ed); pupil personnel services (CAS); reading (M Ed, CAS); school library science (M Ed); science education (M Ed, CAS); secondary education (M Ed, CAS); special education (M Ed, Ed D, CAS); theater arts (MA Ed); written communication (MA Ed). Electronic applications accepted. *Application Contact:* 215-572-2910, Fax: 215-572-4049, E-mail: admiss@arcadia.edu. *Dean of Graduate and Professional Studies,* Mark Curchack, 215-572-2928, Fax: 215-572-2126, E-mail: curchack@arcadia.edu.

See in-depth description on page 737.

ARGOSY UNIVERSITY-ATLANTA, Atlanta, GA 30328-5505

General Information Proprietary, coed, primarily women, graduate-only institution. *Enrollment by degree level:* 198 master's, 200 doctoral. *Graduate faculty:* 11 full-time (6 women), 16 part-time/adjunct (6 women). *Tuition:* Part-time $374 per credit. *Graduate housing:* On-campus housing not available. *Student services:* Campus employment opportunities. *Library facilities:* Main library plus 1 other. *Online resources:* library catalog, web page, access to other libraries' catalogs. *Collection:* 1,100 titles, 88 serial subscriptions.

Computer facilities: 8 computers available on campus for general student use. Internet access is available. *Web address:* http://www.argosyu.edu/.

General Application Contact: Nick Colletti, Director of Enrollment Services, 770-671-1200, Fax: 770-671-0476, E-mail: ncolletti@argosyu.edu.

GRADUATE UNITS

Graduate Programs Students: 398; includes 70 minority (52 African Americans, 8 Asian Americans or Pacific Islanders, 8 Hispanic Americans, 2 Native Americans), 2 international. Average age 26. 272 applicants, 46% accepted. *Faculty:* 11 full-time (6 women), 16 part-time/adjunct (6 women). Expenses: Contact institution. *Financial support:* In 2001–02, 280 students received support, including 40 teaching assistantships (averaging $700 per year); career-related internships or fieldwork and Federal Work-Study also available. Support available to part-time students. Financial award application deadline: 6/30; financial award applicants required to submit FAFSA. In 2001, 40 degrees awarded. *Degree program information:* Part-time and evening/weekend programs available. Offers clinical psychology (MA, Psy D); professional counseling (MA); psychology (MA). *Application deadline:* For fall admission, 1/15 (priority date); for spring admission, 10/15 (priority date). Applications are processed on a rolling basis. *Application fee:* $55. Electronic applications accepted. *Application Contact:* Nick Colletti, Director of Enrollment Services, 770-671-1200, Fax: 770-671-0476, E-mail: ncolletti@argosyu.edu. *Dean,* Dr. Joseph Bascuas, 770-671-1200, Fax: 770-671-0476.

ARGOSY UNIVERSITY-CHICAGO, Chicago, IL 60603

General Information Proprietary, coed, graduate-only institution. *Enrollment by degree level:* 173 master's, 382 doctoral, 3 other advanced degrees. *Graduate faculty:* 28 full-time (15 women), 58 part-time/adjunct (35 women). *Tuition:* Part-time $332 per credit hour. *Required fees:* $75 per year. $35 per term. *Graduate housing:* On-campus housing not available. *Student services:* Campus employment opportunities, career counseling, disabled student services, international student services, writing training. *Library facilities:* Illinois School of Professional Psychology Library plus 1 other. *Online resources:* library catalog. *Collection:* 17,808 titles, 96 serial subscriptions, 731 audiovisual materials.

Computer facilities: 15 computers available on campus for general student use. A campuswide network can be accessed from off campus. Internet access and online class registration are available. *Web address:* http://www.argosyu.edu/.

General Application Contact: Ashley Delaney, Director of Admissions, 312-279-3906, Fax: 312-201-1907, E-mail: adelaney@argosyu.edu.

GRADUATE UNITS

Illinois School of Professional Psychology Students: 403 full-time (304 women), 155 part-time (120 women); includes 115 minority (64 African Americans, 28 Asian Americans or Pacific Islanders, 23 Hispanic Americans) Average age 39. 374 applicants, 67% accepted. *Faculty:* 28 full-time (15 women), 58 part-time/adjunct (35 women). Expenses: Contact institution. *Financial support:* In 2001–02, 200 students received support, including 25 fellowships with partial tuition reimbursements available (averaging $2,000 per year), 150 teaching assistantships with partial tuition reimbursements available (averaging $600 per year); research assistantships with partial tuition reimbursements available, career-related internships or fieldwork, Federal Work-Study, scholarships/grants, tuition waivers (partial), and unspecified assistantships also available. Support available to part-time students. Financial award application deadline: 5/29; financial award applicants required to submit FAFSA. In 2001, 58 master's, 92 doctorates, 43 other advanced degrees awarded. *Degree program information:* Part-time programs available. Offers child and adolescent psychology (Psy D); clinical psychology (MA, Psy D); clinical respecialization (Certificate); ethnic and racial psychology (Psy D); family psychology (Psy D); forensic psychology (Psy D); health psychology (Psy D); health sciences (MA); maltreatment and trauma (Psy D); professional counseling (MA); psychoanalytic psychotherapy (Psy D); psychology and spirituality (Psy D). *Application deadline:* For fall admission, 5/15; for winter admission, 10/15. *Application fee:* $55. Electronic applications accepted. *Application Contact:* Ashley Delaney, Director of Admissions, 312-279-3906, Fax: 312-201-1907, E-mail: adelaney@argosyu.edu. *President,* Dr. David Harpool, 312-279-3902, Fax: 312-201-1907, E-mail: dharpool@argosyu.edu.

ARGOSY UNIVERSITY-CHICAGO NORTHWEST, Rolling Meadows, IL 60008

General Information Proprietary, coed, graduate-only institution. *Graduate faculty:* 7 full-time (3 women), 16 part-time/adjunct (8 women). *Tuition:* Part-time $416 per credit hour. *Graduate housing:* On-campus housing not available. *Student services:* Campus employment opportunities, campus safety program, career counseling. *Library facilities:* Learning Resource Center. *Collection:* 7,900 titles, 83 serial subscriptions.

Computer facilities: 5 computers available on campus for general student use. A campuswide network can be accessed. Internet access is available. *Web address:* http://www.argosyu.edu/.

General Application Contact: Tim Florer, Director of Admissions, 847-290-7400, Fax: 847-290-9977, E-mail: tflorer@argosyu.edu.

GRADUATE UNITS

Graduate Programs *Degree program information:* Evening/weekend programs available. Offers clinical psychology (MA, Psy D); professional counseling (MA).

ARGOSY UNIVERSITY-DALLAS, Dallas, TX 75231

General Information Proprietary, coed, upper-level institution. *Tuition:* Part-time $345 per credit hour. *Required fees:* $150 per semester. *Student services:* Campus employment opportunities, career counseling, disabled student services. *Web address:* http://www.argosyu.edu/.

General Application Contact: Dee Pinkston, Director of Admissions, 214-890-9900, Fax: 214-696-3500, E-mail: dpinkston@argosyu.edu.

GRADUATE UNITS

Program in Clinical Psychology Expenses: Contact institution. Offers clinical psychology (MA); professional counseling (MA); psychology (Psy D). *Application fee:* $50. *Application Contact:* Dee Pinkston, Director of Admissions, 214-890-9900, Fax: 214-696-3500, E-mail: dpinkston@argosyu.edu. *Head,* Dr. Abby Calish, 214-890-9900, Fax: 214-696-3500.

ARGOSY UNIVERSITY-HONOLULU, Honolulu, HI 96813

General Information Proprietary, coed, graduate-only institution. *Enrollment by degree level:* 100 master's, 124 doctoral, 12 other advanced degrees. *Graduate faculty:* 8 full-time, 40 part-time/adjunct. *Tuition:* Part-time $530 per credit. Tuition and fees vary according to program. *Graduate housing:* On-campus housing not available. *Student services:* Campus employment opportunities, career counseling, international student services, writing training. *Library facilities:* Resource Materials Collection. *Online resources:* web page. *Collection:* 2,800 titles, 39 serial subscriptions, 106 audiovisual materials.

Computer facilities: 7 computers available on campus for general student use. Internet access is available. *Web address:* http://www.argosyu.edu/.

General Application Contact: Eric C. Carlson, Director of Admissions, 808-536-5555, Fax: 808-536-5505, E-mail: ecarlson@argosyu.edu.

GRADUATE UNITS

Graduate Studies Students: 186 full-time (142 women), 48 part-time (34 women); includes 86 minority (4 African Americans, 77 Asian Americans or Pacific Islanders, 5 Hispanic Americans) Average age 35. 43 applicants, 74% accepted. *Faculty:* 8 full-time, 40 part-time/adjunct. Expenses: Contact institution. *Financial support:* In 2001–02, 232 students received support, including 9 teaching assistantships; career-related internships or fieldwork, Federal Work-Study, and scholarships/grants also available. Support available to part-time students. Financial award application deadline: 5/1; financial award applicants required to submit FAFSA. *Degree program information:* Part-time and evening/weekend programs available. Offers clinical psychology (MA, Psy D); clinical psychopharmacology (Certificate); marriage and family specialty (MA); professional counseling (MA). *Application fee:* $50. Electronic applications accepted. *Application Contact:* Eric C. Carlson, Director of Admissions, 808-536-5555, Fax: 808-536-5505, E-mail: ecarlson@argosyu.edu. *President,* Dr. Ray Crossman, 808-536-5555, Fax: 808-536-5505, E-mail: rcrossman@argosyu.edu.

ARGOSY UNIVERSITY-ORANGE COUNTY, Orange, CA 92868

General Information Proprietary, coed, comprehensive institution. *Enrollment by degree level:* 57 master's, 145 doctoral. *Graduate faculty:* 6 full-time (4 women), 57 part-time/adjunct (13 women). *Tuition:* Part-time $437 per credit hour. *Required fees:* $10 per credit hour.

Tuition and fees vary according to degree level and program. *Student services:* Campus employment opportunities, disabled student services, free psychological counseling, teacher training, writing training. *Web address:* http://www.argosyu.edu/.

General Application Contact: Joe Buechner, Director of Admissions, 800-716-9598, Fax: 714-940-0767, E-mail: jbuechner@argosyu.edu.

GRADUATE UNITS

School of Business Students: 79 full-time (25 women), 30 part-time (7 women); includes 47 minority (13 African Americans, 19 Asian Americans or Pacific Islanders, 13 Hispanic Americans, 2 Native Americans) Average age 45. 88 applicants, 63% accepted, 45 enrolled. *Faculty:* 1 (woman) full-time, 33 part-time/adjunct (5 women). Expenses: Contact institution. *Financial support:* In 2001–02, 60 students received support, including 15 fellowships (averaging $1,500 per year); Federal Work-Study, institutionally sponsored loans, scholarships/grants, traineeships, and unspecified assistantships also available. Support available to part-time students. Financial award applicants required to submit FAFSA. *Degree program information:* Part-time and evening/weekend programs available. Offers accounting (DBA); finance (MBA); healthcare administration (MBA); human resources (MBA); information systems (DBA); international business (DBA); international trade (MBA); management (DBA); marketing (MBA, DBA); organizational leadership (Ed D). *Application deadline:* Applications are processed on a rolling basis. *Application fee:* $50. *Application Contact:* Joe Buechner, Director of Admissions, 800-716-9598, Fax: 714-940-0767, E-mail: jbuechner@argosyu.edu. *Director of Academic Programs and Administration,* Diana Siganoff, 714-940-0025 Ext. 105, Fax: 714-940-0630, E-mail: dsiganoff@argosyu.edu.

School of Education Students: 33 full-time (22 women), 22 part-time (18 women); includes 20 minority (11 African Americans, 6 Asian Americans or Pacific Islanders, 2 Hispanic Americans, 1 Native American) Average age 42. 24 applicants, 75% accepted, 18 enrolled. *Faculty:* 2 full-time (both women), 13 part-time/adjunct (5 women). Expenses: Contact institution. *Financial support:* Fellowships, Federal Work-Study available. Financial award applicants required to submit FAFSA. In 2001, 2 degrees awarded. *Degree program information:* Part-time and evening/weekend programs available. Offers California community college leadership (Certificate); community college leadership (MA Ed); curriculum and instruction (MA Ed, D Ed); educational leadership (MA Ed, D Ed); multiple and single subject credentials (MA Ed). *Application deadline:* Applications are processed on a rolling basis. *Application fee:* $50. *Application Contact:* Joe Buechner, Director of Admissions, 800-716-9598, Fax: 714-940-0767, E-mail: jbuechner@argosyu.edu. *Dean, School of Education,* Dr. Joy R. Kliewer, 714-940-0025 Ext. 104, Fax: 714-940-0630, E-mail: jkliewer@argosyu.edu.

School of Psychology Students: 28 full-time (20 women), 10 part-time (7 women); includes 15 minority (6 African Americans, 3 Asian Americans or Pacific Islanders, 5 Hispanic Americans, 1 Native American) Average age 42. 29 applicants, 90% accepted, 15 enrolled. *Faculty:* 3 full-time (1 woman), 11 part-time/adjunct (3 women). Expenses: Contact institution. *Financial support:* In 2001–02, 15 students received support. Career-related internships or fieldwork, Federal Work-Study, institutionally sponsored loans, scholarships/grants, traineeships, and unspecified assistantships available. Support available to part-time students. Financial award applicants required to submit FAFSA. *Degree program information:* Part-time and evening/weekend programs available. Offers clinical psychology (Psy D); counseling psychology (Ed D); counseling psychology with MFT licensure (MA); psychology (MA, Ed D, Psy D). *Application deadline:* Applications are processed on a rolling basis. *Application fee:* $50. *Application Contact:* Joe Buechner, Director of Admissions, 800-716-9598, Fax: 714-940-0767, E-mail: jbuechner@argosyu.edu. *Associate Dean, School of Psychology,* Dr. Gary Bruss, 714-940-0025 Ext. 110, Fax: 714-940-0630, E-mail: gbruss@argosyu.edu.

ARGOSY UNIVERSITY-PHOENIX, Phoenix, AZ 85021

General Information Proprietary, coed, graduate-only institution. *Enrollment by degree level:* 63 master's, 152 doctoral, 1 other advanced degree. *Graduate faculty:* 13 full-time (5 women), 10 part-time/adjunct (4 women). *Tuition:* Full-time $16,000; part-time $640 per credit. *Required fees:* $500; $250 per term. Full-time tuition and fees vary according to program. *Graduate housing:* On-campus housing not available. *Student services:* Campus employment opportunities, career counseling, disabled student services, international student services, writing training. *Library facilities:* Library Services. *Online resources:* library catalog. *Collection:* 1,000 titles, 57 serial subscriptions, 129 audiovisual materials.

Computer facilities: 10 computers available on campus for general student use. A campuswide network can be accessed from off campus. Internet access is available. *Web address:* http://www.argosyu.edu/.

General Application Contact: Gail L. Bartkovich, Director of Admissions, 866-216-2777 Ext. 209, Fax: 602-216-2601, E-mail: gbartkovich@argosyu.edu.

GRADUATE UNITS

Program in Clinical Psychology Students: 124 full-time (98 women), 49 part-time (43 women); includes 29 minority (14 African Americans, 7 Asian Americans or Pacific Islanders, 7 Hispanic Americans, 1 Native American) Average age 30. 150 applicants, 47% accepted, 45 enrolled. *Faculty:* 10 full-time (5 women), 8 part-time/adjunct (3 women). Expenses: Contact institution. *Financial support:* In 2001–02, 36 students received support, including 36 teaching assistantships with partial tuition reimbursements available; career-related internships or fieldwork, Federal Work-Study, and institutionally sponsored loans also available. Support available to part-time students. Financial award application deadline: 3/20; financial award applicants required to submit FAFSA. In 2001, 46 degrees awarded. Offers clinical psychology (MA, Psy D, Post-Doctoral Certificate). *Application deadline:* For fall admission, 1/15 (priority date); for winter admission, 10/15 (priority date). Applications are processed on a rolling basis. *Application fee:* $50. Electronic applications accepted. *Application Contact:* Gail L. Bartkovich, Director of Admissions, 866-216-2777 Ext. 209, Fax: 602-216-2601, E-mail: gbartkovich@argosyu.edu. *Director,* Dr. Philinda Smith Hutchings, 602-216-2600, Fax: 602-216-2601, E-mail: phutchings@argosyu.edu.

Program in Professional Counseling Average age 33. 25 applicants, 60% accepted, 12 enrolled. *Faculty:* 12 part-time/adjunct (6 women). Expenses: Contact institution. In 2001, 6 degrees awarded. *Degree program information:* Part-time and evening/weekend programs available. Offers professional counseling (MA). *Application deadline:* For fall admission, 7/15 (priority date); for spring admission, 11/15 (priority date). Applications are processed on a rolling basis. *Application fee:* $50. Electronic applications accepted. *Application Contact:* Gail L. Bartkovich, Director of Admissions, 866-216-2777 Ext. 209, Fax: 602-216-2601, E-mail: gbartkovich@argosyu.edu. *Director,* Dr. Bart Lerner, 602-216-2600, Fax: 602-216-2601, E-mail: blerner@argosyu.edu.

Program in Sport–Exercise Psychology Students: 20 full-time (10 women), 1 (woman) part-time. Average age 24. 25 applicants, 60% accepted, 10 enrolled. *Faculty:* 3 full-time (0 women), 2 part-time/adjunct (1 woman). Expenses: Contact institution. *Financial support:* Career-related internships or fieldwork, Federal Work-Study, and institutionally sponsored loans available. Support available to part-time students. In 2001, 18 degrees awarded. Offers clinical psychology (Psy D); sport–exercise psychology (MA, Post-Doctoral Certificate). *Application deadline:* For fall admission, 1/15 (priority date); for winter admission, 10/15 (priority date). Applications are processed on a rolling basis. *Application fee:* $50. Electronic applications accepted. *Application Contact:* Gail L. Bartkovich, Director of Admissions, 866-216-2777 Ext. 209, Fax: 602-216-2601, E-mail: gbartkovich@argosyu.edu. *Director,* Dr. Douglas Jowdy, 602-216-2600, Fax: 602-216-2601, E-mail: djowdy@argosyu.edu.

ARGOSY UNIVERSITY-SAN FRANCISCO BAY AREA, Point Richmond, CA 94804-3547

General Information Proprietary, coed, primarily women, graduate-only institution. *Enrollment by degree level:* 28 master's, 107 doctoral. *Graduate faculty:* 8 full-time (3 women), 7 part-time/adjunct (4 women). *Tuition:* Part-time $640 per credit. *Graduate housing:* On-campus housing not available. *Student services:* Campus employment opportunities, disabled student services, low-cost health insurance. *Library facilities:* Argosy University/San Francisco Bay Area. *Collection:* 4,000 titles, 65 serial subscriptions, 100 audiovisual materials.

Computer facilities: 10 computers available on campus for general student use. A campuswide network can be accessed. Internet access is available. *Web address:* http://www.argosyu.edu/.

General Application Contact: Cynthia R. Sirkin, Director of Outreach Services, 510-215-0277 Ext. 202, Fax: 510-215-0299, E-mail: csirkin@argosy.edu.

GRADUATE UNITS

School of Behavioral Sciences Students: 94 full-time (71 women), 41 part-time (33 women); includes 38 minority (14 African Americans, 15 Asian Americans or Pacific Islanders, 6 Hispanic Americans, 3 Native Americans) Average age 30. 185 applicants, 37% accepted. *Faculty:* 8 full-time (3 women), 7 part-time/adjunct (4 women). Expenses: Contact institution. *Financial support:* In 2001–02, 36 students received support, including teaching assistantships (averaging $1,200 per year); Federal Work-Study and scholarships/grants also available. Support available to part-time students. Financial award application deadline: 3/1. In 2001, 2 master's, 1 doctorate awarded. *Degree program information:* Part-time programs available. Offers clinical psychology (MA, Psy D); counseling psychology (MA). *Application deadline:* For fall admission, 1/15 (priority date); for winter admission, 8/15 (priority date). Applications are processed on a rolling basis. *Application fee:* $50. Electronic applications accepted. *Application Contact:* Cynthia R. Sirkin, Director of Outreach Services, 510-215-0277 Ext. 202, Fax: 510-215-0299, E-mail: csirkin@argosy.edu. *Clinical Psychology Department Head,* Dr. Anarea Morrison, 510-215-0277, Fax: 510-215-0299.

ARGOSY UNIVERSITY-SARASOTA, Sarasota, FL 34235-8246

General Information Proprietary, coed, university. *Enrollment by degree level:* 165 master's, 1,289 doctoral, 54 other advanced degrees. *Graduate faculty:* 29 full-time (12 women), 58 part-time/adjunct (24 women). *Tuition:* Part-time $397 per credit hour. *Required fees:* $10 per credit hour. *Graduate housing:* On-campus housing not available. *Student services:* Campus employment opportunities, campus safety program, international student services. *Web address:* http://www.argosyu.edu/.

General Application Contact: Elmina Taylor, Admissions Representative, 800-331-5995 Ext. 221, Fax: 941-371-8910.

GRADUATE UNITS

School of Business Students: 195 full-time (85 women), 134 part-time (59 women); includes 114 minority (50 African Americans, 39 Asian Americans or Pacific Islanders, 23 Hispanic Americans, 2 Native Americans) Average age 45. *Faculty:* 6 full-time (2 women), 10 part-time/adjunct (1 woman). Expenses: Contact institution. *Financial support:* Available to part-time students. Applicants required to submit FAFSA. In 2001, 21 master's, 13 doctorates awarded. *Degree program information:* Part-time and evening/weekend programs available. Postbaccalaureate distance learning degree programs offered (minimal on-campus study). Offers accounting (DBA); finance (MBA); health services management (MS); healthcare administration (MBA); human resources (MBA); information systems (DBA); international business (DBA); international trade (MBA); management (MBA, DBA); marketing (MBA, DBA). *Application deadline:* Applications are processed on a rolling basis. *Application fee:* $50. *Application Contact:* Admissions Representative, 800-331-5995 Ext. 221, Fax: 941-371-8910. *Dean,* Dr. Kathleen Cornett, 800-331-5995, Fax: 941-379-9464, E-mail: kcornett@argosy.edu.

School of Education Students: 382 full-time (267 women), 312 part-time (217 women); includes 323 minority (297 African Americans, 3 Asian Americans or Pacific Islanders, 22 Hispanic Americans, 1 Native American) Average age 45. *Faculty:* 10 full-time (7 women), 28 part-time/adjunct (12 women). Expenses: Contact institution. *Financial support:* Available to part-time students. Applicants required to submit FAFSA. In 2001, 1 master's, 53 doctorates, 11 other advanced degrees awarded. *Degree program information:* Part-time and evening/weekend programs available. Postbaccalaureate distance learning degree programs offered (minimal on-campus study). Offers curriculum and instruction (MA Ed, Ed D, Ed S); educational leadership (MA Ed, Ed D, Ed S). *Application deadline:* Applications are processed on a rolling basis. *Application fee:* $50. *Application Contact:* Admissions Representative, 800-331-5995 Ext. 221, Fax: 941-371-8910. *Dean,* Dr. Nancy Hoover, 800-331-5995, Fax: 941-379-9464, E-mail: nancy_hoover@embanet.com.

School of Psychology and Behavioral Sciences Students: 265 full-time (180 women), 220 part-time (149 women); includes 163 minority (138 African Americans, 9 Asian Americans or Pacific Islanders, 12 Hispanic Americans, 4 Native Americans) Average age 45. *Faculty:* 13 full-time (4 women), 19 part-time/adjunct (9 women). Expenses: Contact institution. *Financial support:* Federal Work-Study available. Support available to part-time students. Financial award applicants required to submit FAFSA. In 2001, 25 master's, 24 doctorates, 5 other advanced degrees awarded. *Degree program information:* Part-time and evening/weekend programs available. Postbaccalaureate distance learning degree programs offered (minimal on-campus study). Offers counseling psychology (Ed D); guidance counseling (MA); mental health counseling (MA); organizational leadership (Ed D); pastoral community counseling (Ed D); school counseling (Ed S). *Application deadline:* Applications are processed on a rolling basis. *Application fee:* $50. *Application Contact:* Admissions Representative, 800-331-5995 Ext. 221, Fax: 941-371-8910. *Dean,* Dr. Douglas G. Riedmiller, 800-331-5995, Fax: 941-379-9464, E-mail: douglas_griedmiller@embanet.com.

See in-depth description on page 739.

ARGOSY UNIVERSITY-SEATTLE, Seattle, WA 98109

General Information Proprietary, coed, graduate-only institution. *Enrollment by degree level:* 45 master's, 76 doctoral. *Graduate faculty:* 6 full-time (4 women), 12 part-time/adjunct (7 women). *Tuition:* Part-time $510 per credit hour. *Required fees:* $35 per term. Part-time tuition and fees vary according to program. *Graduate housing:* On-campus housing not available. *Student services:* Disabled student services. *Library facilities:* Argosy University–Seattle Library plus 1 other. *Online resources:* web page.

Computer facilities: 6 computers available on campus for general student use. A campuswide network can be accessed. Internet access is available. *Web address:* http://www.argosyu.edu/.

General Application Contact: Heather Simpson, Director of Admissions, 206-283-4500 Ext. 206, Fax: 206-283-5777, E-mail: hsimpson@argosyu.edu.

GRADUATE UNITS

Program in Clinical Psychology Students: 58 full-time (38 women), 36 part-time (25 women); includes 5 minority (2 African Americans, 1 Asian American or Pacific Islander, 2 Hispanic Americans) Average age 32. 85 applicants, 75% accepted, 28 enrolled. *Faculty:* 6 full-time (4 women), 12 part-time/adjunct (7 women). Expenses: Contact institution. *Financial support:* In 2001–02, 66 students received support. Federal Work-Study, scholarships/grants, and unspecified assistantships available. Support available to part-time students. Financial award applicants required to submit FAFSA. In 2001, 7 master's, 2 doctorates awarded. *Degree program information:* Part-time and evening/weekend programs available. Offers clinical psychology (MA, Psy D). *Application deadline:* For fall admission, 8/11 (priority date). Applications are processed on a rolling basis. *Application fee:* $50. Electronic applications accepted. *Application Contact:* Heather Simpson, Director of Admissions, 206-283-4500 Ext. 206, Fax: 206-283-5777, E-mail: hsimpson@argosyu.edu. *Interim Director of Psychology and Counseling Program,* Dr. F. Jeri Carter, 206-283-4500 Ext. 213, Fax: 206-283-5777, E-mail: jcarter@argosyu.edu.

ARGOSY UNIVERSITY-TAMPA, Tampa, FL 33619

General Information Proprietary, coed, graduate-only institution.

GRADUATE UNITS

Program in Clinical Psychology *Degree program information:* Part-time programs available. Offers clinical psychology (MA, Psy D).

ARGOSY UNIVERSITY-TWIN CITIES, Bloomington, MN 55437-9761

General Information Proprietary, coed, graduate-only institution. *Enrollment by degree level:* 104 master's, 251 doctoral. *Graduate faculty:* 13 full-time (6 women), 33 part-time/

Argosy University-Twin Cities (continued)

adjunct (13 women). *Tuition:* Part-time $424 per credit hour. *Required fees:* $31 per year. Tuition and fees vary according to program and student level. *Graduate housing:* On-campus housing not available. *Student services:* Campus employment opportunities, campus safety program, disabled student services, free psychological counseling, international student services, low-cost health insurance, writing training. *Library facilities:* Argosy University/Twin Cities. *Online resources:* library catalog, web page, access to other libraries' catalogs. *Collection:* 12,000 titles, 150 serial subscriptions, 300 audiovisual materials.

Computer facilities: 35 computers available on campus for general student use. Internet access is available. *Web address:* http://www.argosyu.edu/.

General Application Contact: Jennifer Radke, Graduate Admissions Representative, 952-921-9500 Ext. 353, Fax: 952-921-9574, E-mail: tcadmissions@argosyu.edu.

GRADUATE UNITS

College of Education Expenses: Contact institution. Offers curriculum and instruction (MA Ed).

Graduate Programs Students: 233 full-time (192 women), 122 part-time (83 women); includes 9 minority (3 African Americans, 4 Asian Americans or Pacific Islanders, 1 Hispanic American, 1 Native American), 1 international. Average age 31. 224 applicants, 62% accepted, 95 enrolled. *Faculty:* 13 full-time (6 women), 33 part-time/adjunct (13 women). Expenses: Contact institution. *Financial support:* In 2001–02, 12 fellowships with partial tuition reimbursements, 12 teaching assistantships with partial tuition reimbursements were awarded. Career-related internships or fieldwork and Federal Work-Study also available. Support available to part-time students. Financial award application deadline: 3/14; financial award applicants required to submit FAFSA. In 2001, 27 master's, 41 doctorates awarded. *Degree program information:* Part-time programs available. Offers clinical psychology (MA, Psy D); education (MA); professional counseling/marriage and family therapy (MA). *Application deadline:* For fall admission, 5/15 (priority date); for winter admission, 1/15 (priority date). Applications are processed on a rolling basis. *Application fee:* $50. Electronic applications accepted. *Application Contact:* Jennifer Radke, Graduate Admissions Representative, 952-921-9500 Ext. 353, Fax: 952-921-9574, E-mail: tcadmissions@argosyu.edu. *Vice President Academic Affairs,* Dr. Jack T. O'Regan, 952-252-7575, Fax: 952-921-9574, E-mail: joregan@argosyu.edu.

ARGOSY UNIVERSITY-WASHINGTON D.C., Arlington, VA 22209

General Information Proprietary, coed, graduate-only institution. *Enrollment by degree level:* 161 master's, 262 doctoral. *Graduate faculty:* 12 full-time (7 women), 43 part-time/adjunct (26 women). *Tuition:* Full-time $6,732; part-time $374 per credit. *Required fees:* $22; $90 per term. Tuition and fees vary according to course load, degree level and program. *Graduate housing:* On-campus housing not available. *Student services:* Campus employment opportunities, writing training. *Library facilities:* Library. *Online resources:* library catalog. *Collection:* 3,290 titles, 63 serial subscriptions, 210 audiovisual materials.

Computer facilities: 15 computers available on campus for general student use. A campuswide network can be accessed. Internet access and online class registration are available. *Web address:* http://www.argosyu.edu/.

General Application Contact: Debbie Jacobs, Director of Admissions, 703-243-5300 Ext. 118, Fax: 703-243-8973, E-mail: ddmjacobs@argosyu.edu.

GRADUATE UNITS

Professional Programs in Psychology Students: 304 full-time (237 women), 119 part-time (96 women); includes 112 minority (83 African Americans, 15 Asian Americans or Pacific Islanders, 11 Hispanic Americans, 3 Native Americans), 1 international. Average age 33. 341 applicants, 59% accepted. *Faculty:* 12 full-time (7 women), 43 part-time/adjunct (26 women). Expenses: Contact institution. *Financial support:* In 2001–02, 347 students received support, including 2 fellowships with tuition reimbursements available (averaging $3,600 per year), 55 teaching assistantships with full and partial tuition reimbursements available (averaging $1,530 per year); research assistantships, career-related internships or fieldwork, Federal Work-Study, and scholarships/grants also available. Support available to part-time students. Financial award application deadline: 6/30; financial award applicants required to submit FAFSA. In 2001, 26 master's, 20 doctorates awarded. *Degree program information:* Part-time and evening/weekend programs available. Offers clinical psychology (MA, Psy D, Certificate); counseling psychology (MA); forensic psychology (MA). *Application deadline:* For fall admission, 1/15 (priority date); for spring admission, 10/15. Applications are processed on a rolling basis. *Application fee:* $55. Electronic applications accepted. *Application Contact:* Debbie Jacobs, Director of Admissions, 703-243-5300 Ext. 118, Fax: 703-243-8973, E-mail: ddmjacobs@argosyu.edu. *Campus President,* Dr. Cynthia G. Baum, 703-243-5300, Fax: 703-243-8973, E-mail: cbaum@argosyu.edu.

ARIZONA STATE UNIVERSITY, Tempe, AZ 85287

General Information State-supported, coed, university. CGS member. *Graduate housing:* Room and/or apartments available to single students; on-campus housing not available to married students. *Research affiliation:* Semiconductor Industries, Aerospace Industries, Arizona State University Research Park Facilities and Partnerships with Industry, Architecture Research Centers Consortium, Southwest Center for Environmental Research and Policy, Industrial University Cooperative Center for Health Management Research.

GRADUATE UNITS

College of Law Students: 534 full-time (268 women); includes 151 minority (25 African Americans, 21 Asian Americans or Pacific Islanders, 70 Hispanic Americans, 35 Native Americans), 5 international. Average age 28. 2,003 applicants, 24% accepted, 182 enrolled. *Faculty:* 39 full-time (9 women), 19 part-time/adjunct (0 women). Expenses: Contact institution. *Financial support:* In 2001–02, 459 students received support, including 25 research assistantships with partial tuition reimbursements available (averaging $1,825 per year), 12 teaching assistantships with partial tuition reimbursements available (averaging $1,275 per year); career-related internships or fieldwork, Federal Work-Study, institutionally sponsored loans, scholarships/grants, tuition waivers (full and partial), and legal writing internships also available. Financial award application deadline: 3/1; financial award applicants required to submit FAFSA. In 2001, 153 degrees awarded. Offers law (JD). *Application deadline:* For fall admission, 3/1. Applications are processed on a rolling basis. *Application fee:* $45. *Application Contact:* Brenda Brock, Assistant Dean and Director of Admissions, 480-965-1474, Fax: 480-727-7930, E-mail: law.admissions@asu.edu. *Dean,* Patricia D. White, 480-965-6188, Fax: 480-965-6521, E-mail: patricia.white@asu.edu.

Graduate College *Degree program information:* Part-time programs available. Offers creative writing (MFA); curriculum and instruction (PhD); exercise science (PhD); gerontology (Certificate); justice studies (PhD); public administration (DPA); science and engineering of materials (PhD); speech and hearing science (PhD); statistics (MS); transportation systems (Certificate).

College of Architecture and Environmental Design Offers architecture (M Arch); architecture and environmental design (M Arch, MEP, MS, MSD, PhD); building design (MS); design (MSD, PhD); history, theory, and criticism (PhD); planning (MEP, PhD).

College of Business *Degree program information:* Part-time programs available. Offers accountancy (M Accy, PhD); business (M Accy, M Tax, MBA, MHSA, MS, PhD); business administration (MBA); economics (MS, PhD); finance (PhD); health administration and policy (MHSA); health services research (PhD); information management (MS, PhD); management (PhD); marketing (PhD); supply chain management (PhD); taxation (M Tax).

College of Education *Degree program information:* Part-time programs available. Offers counseling (M Ed, MC); counseling psychology (PhD); curriculum and instruction (M Ed, MA, Ed D); education (M Ed, MA, MC, Ed D, PhD); educational administration and supervision (M Ed, Ed D); educational leadership and policy studies (M Ed, MA, Ed D, PhD); educational psychology (M Ed, MA, PhD); higher and post-secondary education (M Ed, Ed D); learning and instructional technology (M Ed, MA, PhD); psychology in education (M Ed, MA, MC, PhD); social and philosophical foundations of education (MA); special education (M Ed, MA).

College of Engineering and Applied Sciences *Degree program information:* Part-time programs available. Offers aerospace engineering (MS, MSE, PhD); bioengineering (MS, PhD); chemical engineering (MS, MSE, PhD); civil engineering (MS, MSE, PhD); computer science (MCS, MS, PhD); construction (MS); electrical engineering (MS, MSE, PhD); engineering and applied sciences (M Eng, MCS, MS, MSE, PhD); engineering science (MS, MSE, PhD); industrial engineering (MS, MSE, PhD); materials science and engineering (MS, MSE, PhD); mechanical engineering (MS, MSE, PhD).

College of Fine Arts Offers art (MA, MFA); dance (MFA); fine arts (MA, MFA, MM, DMA, PhD); music (MA, MM, DMA); theater (MA, MFA, PhD).

College of Liberal Arts and Sciences Offers anthropology (MA, PhD); applied mathematics (MA, PhD); Asian history (MA, PhD); behavior (MS, PhD); behavioral neuroscience (PhD); biology (MNS); biology education (MS, PhD); British history (MA, PhD); cell and developmental biology (MS, PhD); chemistry and biochemistry (MNS, MS, PhD); clinical psychology (PhD); cognitive/behavioral systems (PhD); communication disorders (MS); computational, statistical, and mathematical biology (MS, PhD); conservation (MS, PhD); demography and population studies (MA, PhD); developmental psychology (PhD); ecology (MS, PhD); English (MA, PhD); environmental psychology (PhD); European history (MA, PhD); evolution (MS, PhD); exercise science and physical education (MPE, MS); family resources and human development (MS); family science (PhD); French (MA); genetics (MS, PhD); geography (MA, PhD); geological engineering (MS, PhD); German (MA); history and philosophy of biology (MS, PhD); humanities (MA); Latin American studies (MA, PhD); liberal arts and sciences (MA, MNS, MPE, MS, MTESL, PhD, Certificate); mathematics (MA, MNS, PhD); medieval studies (Certificate); microbiology (MNS, MS, PhD); molecular and cellular biology (MS, PhD); natural science (MNS); neuroscience (MS, PhD); philosophy (MA); physics and astronomy (MNS, MS, PhD); physiology (MS, PhD); plant biology (MNS, MS, PhD); political science (MA, PhD); public history (MA); quantitative research methods (PhD); religious studies (MA); Renaissance studies (Certificate); social psychology (PhD); sociology (MA, PhD); Spanish (MA, PhD); statistics (MA, PhD); teaching English as a second language (MTESL); U.S. history (PhD); U.S. western history (MA).

College of Nursing Offers nursing (MS).

College of Public Programs Offers communication (PhD); journalism and telecommunication (MMC); justice studies (MS); public affairs (MPA, DPA); public programs (MA, MMC, MPA, MS, MSW, DPA, PhD); recreation (MS); social work (MSW, PhD); speech and interpersonal communication (MA).

ARIZONA STATE UNIVERSITY EAST, Mesa, AZ 85212

General Information State-supported, coed, comprehensive institution. *Enrollment:* 135 full-time matriculated graduate/professional students (60 women), 194 part-time matriculated graduate/professional students (85 women). *Enrollment by degree level:* 329 master's. *Graduate faculty:* 59 full-time (12 women), 4 part-time/adjunct (0 women). Tuition, state resident: full-time $2,412; part-time $126 per credit hour. Tuition, nonresident: full-time $10,278; part-time $428 per credit hour. *Required fees:* $26. Tuition and fees vary according to course load. *Graduate housing:* Rooms and/or apartments available on a first-come, first-served basis to single and married students. Typical cost: $3,090 per year ($5,090 including board) for single students; $4,415 per year ($9,015 including board) for married students. Room and board charges vary according to board plan and housing facility selected. *Student services:* Campus employment opportunities, career counseling, child daycare facilities, disabled student services, exercise/wellness program, free psychological counseling, grant writing training, international student services, low-cost health insurance, multicultural affairs office, teacher training, writing training. *Library facilities:* ASU East Library. *Online resources:* library catalog, web page, access to other libraries' catalogs. *Collection:* 4.3 million titles, 144 serial subscriptions, 57 audiovisual materials.

Computer facilities: 216 computers available on campus for general student use. A campuswide network can be accessed from off campus. Internet access and online class registration, specialized software applications are available. *Web address:* http://www.east.asu.edu/.

General Application Contact: Dr. C. Vinette Williams, Director of Academic Services, 480-727-1028, Fax: 480-727-1876, E-mail: asueast@asu.edu.

GRADUATE UNITS

College of Technology and Applied Sciences Students: 107 full-time (43 women), 167 part-time (71 women); includes 35 minority (5 African Americans, 18 Asian Americans or Pacific Islanders, 12 Hispanic Americans), 129 international. Average age 32. 185 applicants, 62% accepted, 68 enrolled. *Faculty:* 32 full-time (5 women), 2 part-time/adjunct (0 women). Expenses: Contact institution. *Financial support:* In 2001–02, 91 students received support, including 27 research assistantships with partial tuition reimbursements available (averaging $5,472 per year), 11 teaching assistantships with partial tuition reimbursements available (averaging $4,534 per year); career-related internships or fieldwork, Federal Work-Study, scholarships/grants, tuition waivers (full and partial), and unspecified assistantships also available. Support available to part-time students. Financial award application deadline: 3/1; financial award applicants required to submit FAFSA. In 2001, 58 degrees awarded. *Degree program information:* Part-time and evening/weekend programs available. Offers aeronautical management technology (MS); electronics and computer engineering technology (MS); information and management technology (MS); manufacturing and aeronautical engineering technology (MS); technology and applied sciences (MS). *Application deadline:* Applications are processed on a rolling basis. *Application fee:* $45. Electronic applications accepted. *Dean,* Dr. Albert L. McHenry, 480-727-1093, Fax: 480-727-1089, E-mail: iacaxm@asuvm.inre.asu.edu.

Department of Nutrition Students: 9 full-time (8 women), 12 part-time (10 women); includes 1 minority (Hispanic American) Average age 33. 19 applicants, 47% accepted, 6 enrolled. *Faculty:* 4 full-time (3 women), 1 part-time/adjunct (0 women). Expenses: Contact institution. *Financial support:* In 2001–02, 14 research assistantships with partial tuition reimbursements (averaging $5,000 per year) were awarded; health care benefits and unspecified assistantships also available. Financial award application deadline: 3/1; financial award applicants required to submit FAFSA. In 2001, 6 degrees awarded. *Degree program information:* Part-time and evening/weekend programs available. Offers nutrition (MS). *Application deadline:* Applications are processed on a rolling basis. *Application fee:* $45. Electronic applications accepted. *Application Contact:* Christina Shepard, Administrative Associate/Adviser, 480-727-1748, Fax: 480-727-1064, E-mail: tina.shepard@asu.edu. *Chair,* Linda Vaughn.

Morrison School of Agribusiness and Resource Management Students: 30 full-time (19 women), 38 part-time (17 women); includes 4 minority (all Hispanic Americans), 17 international. Average age 32. 64 applicants, 59% accepted, 1 enrolled. *Faculty:* 17 full-time (1 woman), 1 part-time/adjunct (0 women). Expenses: Contact institution. *Financial support:* In 2001–02, 30 students received support, including 18 research assistantships with partial tuition reimbursements available (averaging $4,202 per year), 3 teaching assistantships with partial tuition reimbursements available (averaging $4,202 per year); fellowships, career-related internships or fieldwork, Federal Work-Study, institutionally sponsored loans, scholarships/grants, and tuition waivers (full and partial) also available. Support available to part-time students. Financial award application deadline: 3/1; financial award applicants required to submit CSS PROFILE or FAFSA. In 2001, 18 degrees awarded. *Degree program information:* Part-time and evening/weekend programs available. Offers agribusiness (MS); environmental resources (MS). *Application deadline:* Applications are processed on a rolling basis. *Application fee:* $45. Electronic applications accepted. *Dean,* Dr. Raymond Marquardt, 480-727-1585, Fax: 480-727-1961, E-mail: ray.marquardt@asu.edu.

ARIZONA STATE UNIVERSITY WEST, Phoenix, AZ 85069-7100

General Information State-supported, coed, upper-level institution. *Enrollment:* 183 full-time matriculated graduate/professional students (124 women), 583 part-time matriculated graduate/professional students (331 women). *Enrollment by degree level:* 766 master's. *Graduate faculty:* 86 full-time (39 women), 40 part-time/adjunct (25 women). Tuition, state resident: full-time $2,412; part-time $126 per credit hour. Tuition, nonresident: full-time $10,352; part-time $428 per credit hour. Tuition and fees vary according to program. *Graduate housing:* On-campus housing not available. *Student services:* Campus employment opportunities, campus safety program, career counseling, child daycare facilities, disabled student services, exercise/wellness program, free psychological counseling, international student services, low-cost health insurance, multicultural affairs office, writing training. *Library facilities:* ASU West Library. *Online resources:* library catalog, web page, access to other libraries' catalogs. *Collection:* 314,760 titles, 3,429 serial subscriptions, 25,534 audiovisual materials.

Computer facilities: 391 computers available on campus for general student use. A campuswide network can be accessed from off campus. Internet access is available. *Web address:* http://www.west.asu.edu/.

General Application Contact: Marge A. Runyan, Coordinator, Graduate College, 602-543-4567, Fax: 602-543-4561, E-mail: mrunyan@asu.edu.

GRADUATE UNITS

College of Arts and Sciences Students: 5 full-time (3 women), 21 part-time (15 women); includes 3 minority (1 Asian American or Pacific Islander, 2 Native Americans), 3 international. Average age 41. 73 applicants, 86% accepted, 46 enrolled. *Faculty:* 16 full-time (7 women), 4 part-time/adjunct (1 woman). Expenses: Contact institution. *Financial support:* Scholarships/grants available. *Degree program information:* Part-time and evening/weekend programs available. Offers interdisciplinary studies (MA). *Application deadline:* For fall admission, 6/1; for spring admission, 11/1. Applications are processed on a rolling basis. *Application fee:* $45. *Application Contact:* Brian Richardson, Program Coordinator, 602-543-6089, Fax: 602-543-6004, E-mail: b.richardson@asu.edu. *Director,* Dr. Andrew Kirby, 602-543-6122, Fax: 602-543-6004, E-mail: andrew.kirby@asu.edu.

College of Education Students: 22 full-time (17 women), 232 part-time (186 women); includes 33 minority (5 African Americans, 4 Asian Americans or Pacific Islanders, 23 Hispanic Americans, 1 Native American), 4 international. Average age 36. 318 applicants, 91% accepted, 229 enrolled. *Faculty:* 23 full-time (16 women), 30 part-time/adjunct (21 women). Expenses: Contact institution. *Financial support:* Fellowships with tuition reimbursements, career-related internships or fieldwork, institutionally sponsored loans, and tuition waivers (full and partial) available. Support available to part-time students. Financial award application deadline: 4/1; financial award applicants required to submit FAFSA. In 2001, 60 degrees awarded. *Degree program information:* Part-time and evening/weekend programs available. Offers educational administration and supervision (M Ed); elementary education (M Ed); secondary education (M Ed); special education (M Ed). *Application deadline:* Applications are processed on a rolling basis. *Application fee:* $45. *Application Contact:* Ray Buss, Assistant Dean, 602-543-6300, Fax: 602-543-6350. *Dean,* Dr. Michael Awender, 602-543-6300, Fax: 602-543-6350, E-mail: michael.awender@asu.edu.

College of Human Services Students: 95 full-time (79 women), 68 part-time (52 women); includes 31 minority (11 African Americans, 5 Asian Americans or Pacific Islanders, 12 Hispanic Americans, 3 Native Americans), 3 international. Average age 35. 136 applicants, 45% accepted, 47 enrolled. *Faculty:* 28 full-time (12 women), 3 part-time/adjunct (all women). Expenses: Contact institution. *Financial support:* Career-related internships or fieldwork, Federal Work-Study, scholarships/grants, and traineeships available. Support available to part-time students. *Degree program information:* Part-time and evening/weekend programs available. Offers communication studies (MA); criminal justice (MA); human services (MA, MSW); social work (MSW). *Application fee:* $45. *Application Contact:* Information Contact, 602-543-6600, E-mail: cohs@asu.edu. *Dean,* Dr. Mark Searle.

School of Management Students: 61 full-time (25 women), 262 part-time (78 women); includes 30 minority (4 African Americans, 10 Asian Americans or Pacific Islanders, 15 Hispanic Americans, 1 Native American), 31 international. Average age 34. 262 applicants, 66% accepted, 138 enrolled. *Faculty:* 19 full-time (4 women), 3 part-time/adjunct (0 women). Expenses: Contact institution. *Financial support:* In 2001–02, 15 research assistantships with partial tuition reimbursements (averaging $2,778 per year) were awarded; fellowships, career-related internships or fieldwork and tuition waivers (full and partial) also available. Financial award applicants required to submit FAFSA. In 2001, 116 degrees awarded. *Degree program information:* Part-time and evening/weekend programs available. Offers management (MBA). *Application deadline:* For fall admission, 6/1 (priority date); for spring admission, 11/1. *Application fee:* $45. *Application Contact:* Jon Delany, Academic Advising Coordinator, 602-543-6201, Fax: 602-543-6221, E-mail: delaney@asu.edu. *Director,* Dr. David Van Fleet, 602-543-6201, Fax: 602-543-6221, E-mail: david.vanfleet@asu.edu.

ARKANSAS STATE UNIVERSITY, Jonesboro, State University, AR 72467

General Information State-supported, coed, comprehensive institution. CGS member. *Enrollment:* 232 full-time matriculated graduate/professional students (147 women), 668 part-time matriculated graduate/professional students (440 women). *Graduate faculty:* 234 full-time (62 women), 7 part-time/adjunct (6 women). Tuition, state resident: full-time $3,384; part-time $141 per hour. Tuition, nonresident: full-time $8,520; part-time $355 per hour. *Required fees:* $742; $28 per hour. $25 per semester. One-time fee: $15 full-time. Tuition and fees vary according to degree level. *Graduate housing:* Rooms and/or apartments available on a first-come, first-served basis to single and married students. Typical cost: $3,210 (including board) for single students; $3,060 per year for married students. Room and board charges vary according to board plan and housing facility selected. *Student services:* Campus employment opportunities, campus safety program, career counseling, disabled student services, exercise/wellness program, free psychological counseling, international student services, low-cost health insurance. *Library facilities:* Dean B. Ellis Library. *Online resources:* library catalog, web page. *Collection:* 557,643 titles, 1,773 serial subscriptions, 8,377 audiovisual materials. *Research affiliation:* National Center for Toxicological Research, Associated Universities for Toxicology Research and Education.

Computer facilities: 556 computers available on campus for general student use. A campuswide network can be accessed from student residence rooms and from off campus. Internet access and online class registration are available. *Web address:* http://www.astate.edu/.

General Application Contact: Dr. Thomas G. Wheeler, Dean of the Graduate School, 870-972-3029, Fax: 870-972-3857, E-mail: twheeler@astate.edu.

GRADUATE UNITS

Graduate School Students: 232 full-time (147 women), 668 part-time (440 women); includes 105 minority (94 African Americans, 5 Asian Americans or Pacific Islanders, 4 Hispanic Americans, 2 Native Americans), 49 international. Average age 35. 763 applicants, 80% accepted, 399 enrolled. *Faculty:* 234 full-time (62 women), 6 part-time/adjunct (5 women). Expenses: Contact institution. *Financial support:* Fellowships, research assistantships, teaching assistantships, career-related internships or fieldwork, Federal Work-Study, and scholarships/grants available. Support available to part-time students. Financial award application deadline: 7/1; financial award applicants required to submit FAFSA. In 2001, 328 master's, 6 doctorates, 32 other advanced degrees awarded. *Degree program information:* Part-time programs available. *Application deadline:* For fall admission, 7/1 (priority date); for spring admission, 11/15 (priority date). Applications are processed on a rolling basis. *Application fee:* $15 ($25 for international students). Electronic applications accepted. *Dean of the Graduate School,* Dr. Thomas G. Wheeler, 870-972-3029, Fax: 870-972-3857, E-mail: twheeler@astate.edu.

College of Agriculture Students: 8 full-time (2 women), 26 part-time (13 women); includes 1 minority (Native American) Average age 32. *Faculty:* 12 full-time (2 women). Expenses: Contact institution. *Financial support:* Teaching assistantships, Federal Work-Study and scholarships/grants available. Support available to part-time students. Financial award application deadline: 7/1; financial award applicants required to submit FAFSA. In 2001, 15 degrees awarded. *Degree program information:* Part-time programs available. Offers agricultural education (MSA, SCCT); agriculture (MSA); vocational-technical administration (MS, SCCT). *Application deadline:* For fall admission, 7/1 (priority date); for spring admission, 11/15 (priority date). Applications are processed on a rolling basis. *Application fee:* $15 ($25 for international students). Electronic applications accepted. *Interim Dean,* Dr. Calvin Shumway, 870-972-2085, Fax: 870-972-3885, E-mail: cshumway@astate.edu.

College of Arts and Sciences Students: 56 full-time (29 women), 103 part-time (57 women); includes 18 minority (12 African Americans, 4 Asian Americans or Pacific Islanders, 2 Hispanic Americans), 21 international. Average age 30. *Faculty:* 89 full-time (22 women), 1 (woman) part-time/adjunct. Expenses: Contact institution. *Financial support:* Fellowships, teaching assistantships, career-related internships or fieldwork, Federal Work-Study, and scholarships/grants available. Support available to part-time students. Financial award application deadline: 7/1; financial award applicants required to submit FAFSA. In 2001, 58 master's, 5 other advanced degrees awarded. *Degree program information:* Part-time programs available. Offers arts and sciences (MA, MPA, MS, MSE, PhD, SCCT); biology (MS); biology education (MSE, SCCT); chemistry (MS); chemistry education (MSE, SCCT); computer science (MS); English (MA); English education (MSE, SCCT); environmental sciences (PhD); heritage studies (PhD); history (MA, SCCT); mathematics (MS, MSE); political science (MA, SCCT); public administration (MPA); social science (MSE); sociology (MA, SCCT). *Application deadline:* For fall admission, 7/1 (priority date); for spring admission, 11/15 (priority date). Applications are processed on a rolling basis. *Application fee:* $15 ($25 for international students). Electronic applications accepted. *Dean,* Dr. Linda Pritchard, 870-972-3079, Fax: 870-972-3827, E-mail: lpritcha@astate.edu.

College of Business Students: 35 full-time (15 women), 66 part-time (36 women); includes 6 minority (5 African Americans, 1 Hispanic American), 19 international. Average age 31. *Faculty:* 32 full-time (7 women). Expenses: Contact institution. *Financial support:* Teaching assistantships, career-related internships or fieldwork, Federal Work-Study, and scholarships/grants available. Support available to part-time students. Financial award application deadline: 7/1; financial award applicants required to submit FAFSA. In 2001, 48 master's, 4 other advanced degrees awarded. *Degree program information:* Part-time programs available. Offers business (EMBA, MBA, MSE, SCCT); business administration (EMBA, MBA, SCCT); business education (MSE, SCCT). *Application deadline:* For fall admission, 7/1 (priority date); for spring admission, 11/15 (priority date). Applications are processed on a rolling basis. *Application fee:* $15 ($25 for international students). Electronic applications accepted. *Dean,* Dr. Jan Duggar, 870-972-3035, Fax: 870-972-3744, E-mail: jduggar@astate.edu.

College of Communications Students: 17 full-time (11 women), 7 part-time (5 women); includes 2 minority (both African Americans) Average age 27. *Faculty:* 14 full-time (3 women). Expenses: Contact institution. *Financial support:* Teaching assistantships, Federal Work-Study and scholarships/grants available. Support available to part-time students. Financial award application deadline: 7/1; financial award applicants required to submit FAFSA. In 2001, 15 master's, 1 other advanced degree awarded. *Degree program information:* Part-time programs available. Offers communications (MA, MSMC, SCCT); journalism (MSMC); radio-television (MSMC); speech communications and theater (MA, SCCT). *Application deadline:* For fall admission, 7/1 (priority date); for spring admission, 11/15 (priority date). Applications are processed on a rolling basis. *Application fee:* $15 ($25 for international students). Electronic applications accepted. *Dean,* Dr. Russell Shain, 870-972-2468, Fax: 870-972-3856, E-mail: rshain@astate.edu.

College of Education Students: 44 full-time (30 women), 399 part-time (270 women); includes 65 minority (63 African Americans, 1 Hispanic American, 1 Native American), 4 international. Average age 36. *Faculty:* 42 full-time (12 women), 3 part-time/adjunct (all women). Expenses: Contact institution. *Financial support:* Teaching assistantships, career-related internships or fieldwork, Federal Work-Study, and scholarships/grants available. Support available to part-time students. Financial award application deadline: 7/1; financial award applicants required to submit FAFSA. In 2001, 153 master's, 6 doctorates, 22 other advanced degrees awarded. *Degree program information:* Part-time programs available. Offers counselor education (MSE, Ed S); early childhood education (MSE); early childhood services (MS); education (MRC, MS, MSE, Ed D, Ed S, SCCT); educational administration (MSE, Ed S); educational leadership (Ed D); elementary education (MSE); emotionally disturbed (MSE); gifted, talented, and creative (MSE); instructional specialist (4-12) (MSE); instructional specialist (P-4) (MSE); physical education (MS, MSE, SCCT); reading (MSE, SCCT); rehabilitation counseling (MRC); special education (MSE). *Application deadline:* For fall admission, 7/1 (priority date); for spring admission, 11/15 (priority date). Applications are processed on a rolling basis. *Application fee:* $15 ($25 for international students). Electronic applications accepted. *Dean,* Dr. John Beineke, 870-972-3057, Fax: 870-972-3828, E-mail: jbeineke@astate.edu.

College of Fine Arts Students: 6 full-time (2 women), 10 part-time (8 women), 2 international. Average age 35. *Faculty:* 28 full-time (6 women), 2 part-time/adjunct (1 woman). Expenses: Contact institution. *Financial support:* Teaching assistantships, Federal Work-Study and scholarships/grants available. Support available to part-time students. Financial award application deadline: 7/1; financial award applicants required to submit FAFSA. In 2001, 5 degrees awarded. *Degree program information:* Part-time programs available. Offers art (MA); fine arts (MA, MM, MME, SCCT); music education (MME, SCCT); performance (MM); speech communication and theater (MA, SCCT). *Application deadline:* For fall admission, 7/1 (priority date); for spring admission, 11/15 (priority date). Applications are processed on a rolling basis. *Application fee:* $15 ($25 for international students). Electronic applications accepted. *Dean,* Dr. Daniel Reeves, 870-972-3053, Fax: 870-972-3932, E-mail: dreeves@astate.edu.

College of Nursing and Health Professions Students: 66 full-time (58 women), 57 part-time (51 women); includes 13 minority (12 African Americans, 1 Asian American or Pacific Islander), 3 international. Average age 31. *Faculty:* 17 full-time (10 women). Expenses: Contact institution. *Financial support:* Fellowships, teaching assistantships, career-related internships or fieldwork, Federal Work-Study, scholarships/grants, and tuition waivers (partial) available. Support available to part-time students. Financial award application deadline: 7/1; financial award applicants required to submit FAFSA. In 2001, 34 degrees awarded. *Degree program information:* Part-time programs available. Offers aging studies (Certificate); communication disorders (MCD); nursing (MSN); physical therapy (MPT). *Application deadline:* For fall admission, 7/1 (priority date); for spring admission, 11/15 (priority date). Applications are processed on a rolling basis. *Application fee:* $15 ($25 for international students). Electronic applications accepted. *Dean,* Dr. Susan Hanrahan, 870-972-3112, Fax: 870-972-2040, E-mail: hanrahan@astate.edu.

ARKANSAS TECH UNIVERSITY, Russellville, AR 72801-2222

General Information State-supported, coed, comprehensive institution. *Enrollment:* 249 full-time matriculated graduate/professional students (148 women), 143 part-time matriculated graduate/professional students (93 women). *Enrollment by degree level:* 392 master's. *Graduate faculty:* 99 full-time (33 women), 26 part-time/adjunct (11 women). *Tuition:* Part-time $125 per hour. *Graduate housing:* Room and/or apartments available on a first-come, first-served basis to single students; on-campus housing not available to married students. Typical cost: $810 per year ($1,634 including board). Room and board charges vary according to board plan and housing facility selected. Housing application deadline: 8/1. *Student services:* Campus employment opportunities, campus safety program, career counseling, child daycare facilities, disabled student services, exercise/wellness program, free psychological counseling, international student services, low-cost health insurance. *Library facilities:* Ross Pendergraft Library and Technology Center. *Online resources:* library catalog, web page. *Collection:* 229,450 titles, 1,245 serial subscriptions, 3,991 audiovisual materials.

Computer facilities: 258 computers available on campus for general student use. A campuswide network can be accessed from student residence rooms and from off campus. Internet access and online class registration are available. *Web address:* http://www.atu.edu/.

General Application Contact: Dr. Eldon G. Clary, Dean of Graduate Studies, 479-968-0398, Fax: 479-964-0542, E-mail: graduate.school@mail.atu.edu.

GRADUATE UNITS

Graduate Studies Students: 249 full-time (148 women), 143 part-time (93 women); includes 26 minority (9 African Americans, 5 Asian Americans or Pacific Islanders, 6 Hispanic Americans, 6 Native Americans), 87 international. Average age 36. 190 applicants, 89% accepted, 160 enrolled. *Faculty:* 99 full-time (33 women), 26 part-time/adjunct (11 women). Expenses: Contact institution. *Financial support:* In 2001–02, 128 students received support, including teaching assistantships (averaging $4,000 per year); research assistantships, Federal Work-Study also available. Support available to part-time students. Financial award application deadline: 4/15; financial award applicants required to submit FAFSA. In 2001, 51 degrees awarded. *Degree program information:* Part-time and evening/weekend programs available. *Applica-*

Arkansas Tech University (continued)

tion deadline: For fall admission, 3/1 (priority date); for spring admission, 10/1 (priority date). Applications are processed on a rolling basis. *Application fee:* $0 ($30 for international students). Electronic applications accepted. *Dean,* Dr. Eldon G. Clary, 479-968-0398, Fax: 479-964-0542, E-mail: graduate.school@mail.atu.edu.

School of Education Students: 203 full-time (140 women); includes 13 minority (6 African Americans, 1 Asian American or Pacific Islander, 1 Hispanic American, 5 Native Americans) Average age 38. 83 applicants, 88% accepted, 73 enrolled. *Faculty:* 21 full-time (11 women), 18 part-time/adjunct (9 women). Expenses: Contact institution. *Financial support:* In 2001–02, 15 students received support, including teaching assistantships with full tuition reimbursements available (averaging $4,000 per year); Federal Work-Study, scholarships/grants, health care benefits, and unspecified assistantships also available. Support available to part-time students. Financial award application deadline: 4/15; financial award applicants required to submit FAFSA. In 2001, 38 degrees awarded. *Degree program information:* Part-time and evening/weekend programs available. Offers education (M Ed, MSE, Ed S); educational leadership (M Ed); elementary education (M Ed); English (M Ed); gifted education (MSE); instructional improvement (M Ed); instructional technology (M Ed); mathematics (M Ed); physical education (M Ed); school counseling and leadership (M Ed); social studies (M Ed); teaching, learning and leadership (M Ed). *Application deadline:* For fall admission, 3/1 (priority date); for spring admission, 10/1 (priority date). Applications are processed on a rolling basis. *Application fee:* $0 ($30 for international students). Electronic applications accepted. *Application Contact:* Dr. Eldon G. Clary, Dean, 479-968-0398, Fax: 479-964-0542, E-mail: graduate.school@mail.atu.edu. *Dean,* Dr. Dennis W. Fleniken, 479-968-0350, E-mail: dennis.fleniken@mail.atu.edu.

School of Liberal Arts Students: 32 (25 women); includes 3 minority (1 African American, 1 Hispanic American, 1 Native American) Average age 38. 18 applicants, 72% accepted, 13 enrolled. *Faculty:* 26 full-time (6 women), 2 part-time/adjunct (1 woman). Expenses: Contact institution. *Financial support:* In 2001–02, 17 students received support, including 8 teaching assistantships (averaging $4,000 per year); Federal Work-Study, health care benefits, and unspecified assistantships also available. Support available to part-time students. Financial award application deadline: 4/15; financial award applicants required to submit FAFSA. In 2001, 5 degrees awarded. *Degree program information:* Part-time and evening/weekend programs available. Offers communications (MLA); English (MA); fine arts (MLA); history (MA); multi-media journalism (MA); social sciences (MLA); Spanish (MLA). *Application deadline:* For fall admission, 3/1 (priority date); for spring admission, 10/1. Applications are processed on a rolling basis. *Application fee:* $0 ($30 for international students). Electronic applications accepted. *Application Contact:* Dr. Eldon G. Clary, Dean, 479-968-0398, Fax: 479-964-0542, E-mail: graduate.school@mail.atu.edu. *Dean,* Dr. Georgena Duncan, 479-968-0266, E-mail: georgena.duncan@mail.atu.edu.

School of Physical and Life Sciences Students: 7 full-time (4 women), 1 (woman) part-time; includes 1 minority (Hispanic American) 5 applicants, 60% accepted, 3 enrolled. *Faculty:* 5 full-time (0 women). Expenses: Contact institution. *Financial support:* In 2001–02, 4 research assistantships with full tuition reimbursements (averaging $4,000 per year) were awarded; Federal Work-Study and health care benefits also available. Support available to part-time students. Financial award application deadline: 4/15; financial award applicants required to submit FAFSA. Offers fisheries and wildlife biology (MS); physical and life sciences (MS). *Application deadline:* For fall admission, 3/1 (priority date); for spring admission, 10/1 (priority date). Applications are processed on a rolling basis. *Application fee:* $0 ($70 for international students). Electronic applications accepted. *Application Contact:* Dr. Eldon G. Clary, Dean, 479-968-0398, Fax: 479-964-0542, E-mail: graduate.school@mail.atu.edu. *Dean,* Dr. Richard Cohoon, 479-968-0498, E-mail: richard.cohoon@mail.atu.edu.

School of System Science Students: 89 (32 women); includes 6 minority (4 Asian Americans or Pacific Islanders, 2 Hispanic Americans) 51 international. 27 applicants, 96% accepted, 17 enrolled. *Faculty:* 7 full-time (2 women). Expenses: Contact institution. *Financial support:* In 2001–02, 5 students received support, including 2 teaching assistantships (averaging $4,000 per year); Federal Work-Study also available. Support available to part-time students. Financial award application deadline: 4/15; financial award applicants required to submit FAFSA. In 2001, 9 degrees awarded. Offers information technology (MS); system science (MS). *Application deadline:* For fall admission, 3/1 (priority date); for spring admission, 10/1 (priority date). Applications are processed on a rolling basis. *Application fee:* $0 ($30 for international students). Electronic applications accepted. *Application Contact:* Dr. Eldon G. Clary, Dean, 479-968-0398, Fax: 479-964-0542, E-mail: graduate.school@mail.atu.edu. *Dean,* Dr. Jack Namm, 479-968-0353 Ext. 501, E-mail: jack.namm@mail.atu.edu.

ARMSTRONG ATLANTIC STATE UNIVERSITY, Savannah, GA 31419-1997

General Information State-supported, coed, comprehensive institution. CGS member. *Graduate housing:* Room and/or apartments available on a first-come, first-served basis to single students; on-campus housing not available to married students.

GRADUATE UNITS

School of Graduate Studies *Degree program information:* Part-time and evening/weekend programs available. Offers athletic training (MS); criminal justice (MS); education (M Ed); elementary education (M Ed); health services administration (MHSA); history (MA); middle grades education (M Ed); nursing (MSN); physical therapy (MSPT); public health (MPH); secondary education (M Ed); special education (M Ed); sports health sciences (MS). Electronic applications accepted.

See in-depth description on page 741.

ARMSTRONG UNIVERSITY, Oakland, CA 94612

General Information Independent, coed, comprehensive institution. *Graduate housing:* On-campus housing not available.

GRADUATE UNITS

Graduate School of Business Administration *Degree program information:* Part-time and evening/weekend programs available. Offers accounting (MBA); finance (MBA); finance and accounting (MBA); international business (MBA); management (MBA); management information systems (MBA); marketing (MBA); marketing and management (MBA).

ART ACADEMY OF CINCINNATI, Cincinnati, OH 45202-1799

General Information Independent, coed, comprehensive institution. *Enrollment:* 19 part-time matriculated graduate/professional students (18 women). *Enrollment by degree level:* 19 master's. *Graduate faculty:* 3 full-time (1 woman), 6 part-time/adjunct (5 women). *Tuition:* Part-time $680 per credit. One-time fee: $50 part-time. *Graduate housing:* On-campus housing not available. *Student services:* Career counseling, free psychological counseling, international student services, low-cost health insurance. *Library facilities:* Mary Schiff Library. *Collection:* 50,000 titles, 75 serial subscriptions.

Computer facilities: 40 computers available on campus for general student use. Internet access is available. *Web address:* http://www.artacademy.edu/.

General Application Contact: Mary Jane Zumwalde, Director of Admissions, 513-562-8744, Fax: 513-562-8778, E-mail: zumwalde@artacademy.edu.

GRADUATE UNITS

Program in Art Education Average age 37. 15 applicants, 80% accepted. *Faculty:* 3 full-time (1 woman), 6 part-time/adjunct (5 women). Expenses: Contact institution. *Financial support:* In 2001–02, 12 students received support. Institutionally sponsored loans and scholarships/grants available. Support available to part-time students. Financial award applicants required to submit FAFSA. *Degree program information:* Part-time programs available. Offers art education (MA). Offered during summer only. *Application deadline:* Applications are processed on a rolling basis. *Application fee:* $25. *Application Contact:* Jack McCullough, Admissions Counselor, 513-562-8758, Fax: 513-562-8778, E-mail: jmccullough@artacademy.edu. *Chair,* Paige Williams, 513-562-8768.

ART CENTER COLLEGE OF DESIGN, Pasadena, CA 91103-1999

General Information Independent, coed, comprehensive institution. *Enrollment:* 88 full-time matriculated graduate/professional students (39 women). *Enrollment by degree level:* 88 master's. *Graduate faculty:* 26 part-time/adjunct (8 women). *Tuition:* Full-time $22,310. *Graduate housing:* On-campus housing not available. *Student services:* Campus employment opportunities, career counseling, free psychological counseling, international student services, low-cost health insurance. *Library facilities:* James LeMont Fogg Library. *Online resources:* library catalog. *Collection:* 73,595 titles, 385 serial subscriptions, 5,265 audiovisual materials.

Computer facilities: 225 computers available on campus for general student use. A campuswide network can be accessed. Internet access is available. *Web address:* http://www.artcenter.edu/.

General Application Contact: Kit Baron, Vice President, Student Services, 626-396-2373, Fax: 626-795-0578.

GRADUATE UNITS

Graduate Division Students: 88 full-time (39 women). Average age 29. *Faculty:* 26 part-time/adjunct (8 women). Expenses: Contact institution. *Financial support:* In 2001–02, 63 students received support, including 26 teaching assistantships; career-related internships or fieldwork, Federal Work-Study, and scholarships/grants also available. Financial award application deadline: 3/1. In 2001, 31 degrees awarded. Offers art theory and criticism (MA); environmental design (MS); film (MFA); fine arts (MFA); media design (MFA); product design (MS); transportation design (MS). *Application deadline:* For fall admission, 3/1 (priority date). Applications are processed on a rolling basis. *Application fee:* $45 ($65 for international students). *Application Contact:* Kit Baron, Vice-President, Student Services, 626-396-2373, Fax: 626-795-0578.

ARTHUR D. LITTLE SCHOOL OF MANAGEMENT, Chestnut Hill, MA 02467-3853

General Information Independent, coed, graduate-only institution. *Enrollment by degree level:* 51 master's. *Graduate faculty:* 6 full-time (2 women), 18 part-time/adjunct (3 women). *Tuition:* Full-time $36,000. *Graduate housing:* On-campus housing not available. *Student services:* Campus employment opportunities, career counseling, international student services, low-cost health insurance. *Library facilities:* O'Neill Library plus 5 others. *Online resources:* library catalog, web page, access to other libraries' catalogs. *Collection:* 1.6 million titles, 17,500 serial subscriptions.

Computer facilities: 200 computers available on campus for general student use. A campuswide network can be accessed from student residence rooms and from off campus. Internet access is available. *Web address:* http://www.adlsom.edu/.

General Application Contact: Holly Chase, Director of Recruiting and Admissions, 617-552-2681, Fax: 617-552-2051, E-mail: chase.holly@adlittle.com.

GRADUATE UNITS

Graduate Program Students: 51 full-time (11 women). Average age 34. 103 applicants, 94% accepted. *Faculty:* 6 full-time (2 women), 18 part-time/adjunct (3 women). Expenses: Contact institution. *Financial support:* In 2001–02, 1 student received support. Tuition waivers (partial) available. Financial award application deadline: 6/1; financial award applicants required to submit FAFSA. In 2001, 62 degrees awarded. Offers management (MSM). *Application deadline:* Applications are processed on a rolling basis. *Application fee:* $75. Electronic applications accepted. *Application Contact:* William G. Makris, Information Contact, 617-552-2835, Fax: 617-552-2141, E-mail: makris.will@adlittle.com. *President,* Dr. William K. Harper, 617-552-2838, Fax: 617-552-2141, E-mail: harper.william@adlittle.com.

THE ART INSTITUTE OF BOSTON AT LESLEY UNIVERSITY, Boston, MA 02215-2598

General Information Independent, coed, comprehensive institution.

GRADUATE UNITS

Program in Visual Arts Offers visual arts (MFA).

ASBURY THEOLOGICAL SEMINARY, Wilmore, KY 40390-1199

General Information Independent-religious, coed, primarily men, graduate-only institution. *Enrollment by degree level:* 858 first professional, 283 master's, 252 doctoral, 21 other advanced degrees. *Graduate faculty:* 61 full-time (9 women), 22 part-time/adjunct (4 women). *Tuition:* Part-time $256 per credit hour. *Required fees:* $150; $45 per semester. Tuition and fees vary according to course load and program. *Graduate housing:* Rooms and/or apartments available on a first-come, first-served basis to single and married students. Typical cost: $1,420 per year ($3,040 including board) for single students; $2,790 per year for married students. Room and board charges vary according to board plan and housing facility selected. Housing application deadline: 3/1. *Student services:* Campus employment opportunities, free psychological counseling, international student services, low-cost health insurance, writing training. *Library facilities:* B. L. Fisher Library. *Online resources:* library catalog, web page, access to other libraries' catalogs. *Collection:* 357,400 titles, 1,500 serial subscriptions, 13,257 audiovisual materials.

Computer facilities: 67 computers available on campus for general student use. A campuswide network can be accessed from student residence rooms and from off campus. Internet access and online class registration are available. *Web address:* http://www.ats.wilmore.ky.us/.

General Application Contact: Janelle Vernon, Director: Admissions, 859-858-2210, Fax: 859-858-2287, E-mail: admissions_office@ats.wilmore.ky.us.

GRADUATE UNITS

Graduate and Professional Programs Students: 761 full-time (229 women), 653 part-time (198 women). 648 applicants, 65% accepted, 313 enrolled. *Faculty:* 61 full-time (9 women), 22 part-time/adjunct (4 women). Expenses: Contact institution. *Financial support:* In 2001–02, 1,103 students received support. Career-related internships or fieldwork, Federal Work-Study, institutionally sponsored loans, and scholarships/grants available. Support available to part-time students. Financial award application deadline: 4/15; financial award applicants required to submit FAFSA. In 2001, 132 first professional degrees, 70 master's, 28 doctorates awarded. *Degree program information:* Part-time programs available. Postbaccalaureate distance learning degree programs offered (minimal on-campus study). *Application deadline:* For fall admission, 5/1 (priority date). Applications are processed on a rolling basis. *Application fee:* $25. Electronic applications accepted. *Application Contact:* Janelle Vernon, Director: Admissions, 859-858-2210, Fax: 859-858-2287, E-mail: admissions_office@ats.wilmore.ky.us. *Chief Academic Officer,* Dr. M. Robert Mulholland, 859-858-2206, Fax: 859-858-2258, E-mail: robert_mulholland@asburyseminary.edu.

E. Stanley Jones School of World Mission and Evangelism Students: 14 full-time (5 women), 39 part-time (6 women); includes 1 minority (Asian American or Pacific Islander), 16 international. 35 applicants, 43% accepted, 13 enrolled. *Faculty:* 6 full-time (1 woman), 4 part-time/adjunct (0 women). Expenses: Contact institution. *Financial support:* In 2001–02, 37 students received support. Federal Work-Study and scholarships/grants available. Support available to part-time students. Financial award application deadline: 4/15; financial award applicants required to submit FAFSA. In 2001, 5 master's, 4 doctorates awarded. *Degree program information:* Part-time programs available. Offers intercultural studies (PhD); mission and evangelism (M Th, D Miss). *Application deadline:* For fall admission, 5/1 (priority date). Applications are processed on a rolling basis. *Application fee:* $25. Electronic applications accepted. *Application Contact:* Janelle Vernon, Director: Admissions, 859-858-2210, Fax: 859-858-2287, E-mail: admissions_office@ats.wilmore.ky.us. *Dean,* Dr. Darrell L. Whiteman, 859-858-2215, Fax: 859-858-2375, E-mail: darrell_whiteman@asburyseminary.edu.

School of Theology Students: 1,360. 613 applicants, 66% accepted, 300 enrolled. *Faculty:* 55 full-time (8 women), 18 part-time/adjunct (4 women). Expenses: Contact institution. *Financial support:* In 2001–02, 1,013 students received support. Career-related internships or fieldwork, Federal Work-Study, institutionally sponsored loans, and scholarships/grants available. Support available to part-time students. Financial award application deadline: 4/15; financial award applicants required to submit FAFSA. In 2001, 132 first professional degrees, 65 master's, 24 doctorates awarded. *Degree program information:* Part-time programs available. Postbaccalaureate distance learning degree programs offered (minimal on-campus study). Offers biblical studies (MA); Christian education (MA); Christian studies (Certificate); counseling (MA); parish counseling (MA); theological studies (MA); theology (M Div, D Min); world mission and evangelism (MA); youth ministry (MA). *Application deadline:* For fall admission, 7/1 (priority date); for spring admission, 12/1 (priority date). Applications are processed on a rolling basis. *Application fee:* $25. Electronic applications accepted. *Application Contact:* Janelle Vernon, Director of Admissions, 859-858-2210, Fax: 859-858-2287, E-mail: admissions_office@asburyseminary.edu. *Dean,* Dr. Joel B. Green, 859-858-2147, Fax: 859-858-2371, E-mail: joel_green@asburyseminary.edu.

ASHLAND UNIVERSITY, Ashland, OH 44805-3702

General Information Independent-religious, coed, comprehensive institution. CGS member. *Enrollment:* 1,032 full-time matriculated graduate/professional students (572 women), 1,551 part-time matriculated graduate/professional students (939 women). *Enrollment by degree level:* 242 first professional, 2,206 master's, 135 doctoral. *Graduate faculty:* 96 full-time (45 women), 136 part-time/adjunct (61 women). *Tuition:* Part-time $315 per credit hour. Tuition and fees vary according to degree level and program. *Graduate housing:* Room and/or apartments guaranteed to single students; on-campus housing not available to married students. *Student services:* Campus employment opportunities, campus safety program, career counseling, disabled student services, free psychological counseling, international student services, low-cost health insurance, multicultural affairs office, teacher training, writing training. *Library facilities:* Ashland Library plus 2 others. *Online resources:* library catalog, web page. *Collection:* 265,229 titles, 950 serial subscriptions.

Computer facilities: 90 computers available on campus for general student use. A campuswide network can be accessed from student residence rooms and from off campus. *Web address:* http://www.ashland.edu/.

General Application Contact: Dr. John P. Sikula, Associate Provost, 419-289-5751, Fax: 419-289-5738, E-mail: jsikula@ashland.edu.

GRADUATE UNITS

College of Business Administration and Economics Students: 231 full-time (92 women), 376 part-time (142 women); includes 61 minority (54 African Americans, 6 Asian Americans or Pacific Islanders, 1 Hispanic American), 15 international. Average age 34. *Faculty:* 17 full-time (4 women), 10 part-time/adjunct (3 women). Expenses: Contact institution. In 2001, 147 degrees awarded. *Degree program information:* Part-time and evening/weekend programs available. Offers business administration and economics (MBA). *Application deadline:* For fall admission, 8/1 (priority date); for spring admission, 12/1 (priority date). Applications are processed on a rolling basis. *Application fee:* $25. Electronic applications accepted. *Application Contact:* Stephen W. Krispinsky, Executive Director of MBA Program, 419-289-5236, Fax: 419-289-5910, E-mail: skrispin@ashland.edu. *Dean,* Dr. Paul A. Sears, 419-289-5212, Fax: 419-289-5910, E-mail: psears@ashland.edu.

College of Education Students: 310 full-time (233 women), 979 part-time (716 women); includes 62 minority (53 African Americans, 1 Asian American or Pacific Islander, 5 Hispanic Americans, 3 Native Americans), 17 international. Average age 35. *Faculty:* 44 full-time (24 women), 104 part-time/adjunct (55 women). Expenses: Contact institution. *Financial support:* In 2001–02, 5 teaching assistantships with partial tuition reimbursements (averaging $3,500 per year) were awarded; scholarships/grants also available. In 2001, 618 degrees awarded. *Degree program information:* Part-time and evening/weekend programs available. Offers education (M Ed, Ed D). *Application deadline:* For fall admission, 8/27; for spring admission, 1/14. Applications are processed on a rolling basis. *Application fee:* $25. *Application Contact:* Dr. James Van Keuren, Director and Chair, Graduate Studies in Education, 419-289-5377, Fax: 419-207-6702, E-mail: jvankeu1@ashland.edu. *Dean,* Frank Pettigrew, 419-289-5365, E-mail: fpettig@ashland.edu.

Doctoral Studies in Educational Leadership Students: 42 full-time (29 women), 7 part-time (4 women); includes 6 minority (5 African Americans, 1 Native American) Average age 43. 18 applicants, 72% accepted, 13 enrolled. *Faculty:* 4 full-time (2 women), 10 part-time/adjunct (5 women). Expenses: Contact institution. *Financial support:* In 2001–02, 4 teaching assistantships (averaging $2,800 per year) were awarded *Degree program information:* Evening/weekend programs available. Offers educational leadership (Ed D). *Application deadline:* For spring admission, 3/1. Applications are processed on a rolling basis. *Application fee:* $25. *Director,* Dr. W. Gregory Gerrick, 419-289-5343, Fax: 419-289-5097, E-mail: ggerrick@ashland.edu.

Graduate Studies in Education Students: 293 full-time (221 women), 956 part-time (701 women); includes 59 minority (51 African Americans, 1 Asian American or Pacific Islander, 5 Hispanic Americans, 2 Native Americans), 17 international. Average age 35. *Faculty:* 43 full-time (24 women), 103 part-time/adjunct (54 women). Expenses: Contact institution. *Financial support:* In 2001–02, 5 teaching assistantships with partial tuition reimbursements (averaging $3,500 per year) were awarded; institutionally sponsored loans and scholarships/grants also available. In 2001, 618 degrees awarded. *Degree program information:* Part-time and evening/weekend programs available. Offers administration (M Ed); business manager (M Ed); classroom instruction (M Ed); curriculum and instruction (M Ed); early childhood education (M Ed); early childhood intervention specialist (M Ed); economics education (M Ed); education (Ed D); intervention specialist-mild/moderate (M Ed); intervention specialist-moderate/intensive (M Ed); literacy (M Ed); school treasurer (M Ed); school treasurer or business manager (M Ed); sport education (M Ed); talent development education (M Ed); technology education (M Ed). *Application deadline:* For fall admission, 8/27; for spring admission, 1/14. Applications are processed on a rolling basis. *Application fee:* $25. *Director and Chair,* Dr. James Van Keuren, 419-289-5377, Fax: 419-207-6702, E-mail: jvankeu1@ashland.edu.

Theological Seminary Students: 491 full-time (247 women), 196 part-time (81 women); includes 201 minority (185 African Americans, 6 Asian Americans or Pacific Islanders, 8 Hispanic Americans, 2 Native Americans), 28 international. Average age 41. *Faculty:* 27 full-time (4 women), 22 part-time/adjunct (3 women). Expenses: Contact institution. *Financial support:* In 2001–02, 17 teaching assistantships were awarded; research assistantships, career-related internships or fieldwork and institutionally sponsored loans also available. Support available to part-time students. Financial award application deadline: 8/1. In 2001, 37 first professional degrees, 103 master's, 11 doctorates awarded. *Degree program information:* Part-time programs available. Offers biblical and theological studies (MA); Christian education (MACE); Christian ministry (MACM); ministry (D Min); ministry management (MAMM); pastoral counseling (MAPC); theological studies (MA); theology (M Div). *Application deadline:* For fall admission, 8/8. Applications are processed on a rolling basis. *Application fee:* $30. *Application Contact:* Mario Guerreiro, Director of Admissions, 419-289-5704, Fax: 419-289-5969, E-mail: mario@ashland.edu. *President,* Dr. Frederick J. Finks, 419-289-5160, Fax: 419-289-5969, E-mail: ffinks@ashland.edu.

ASSEMBLIES OF GOD THEOLOGICAL SEMINARY, Springfield, MO 65802

General Information Independent-religious, coed, graduate-only institution. *Enrollment by degree level:* 133 first professional, 204 master's, 58 doctoral. *Graduate faculty:* 15 full-time (1 woman), 113 part-time/adjunct (9 women). *Tuition:* Full-time $9,207; part-time $279 per credit hour. *Graduate housing:* On-campus housing not available. *Student services:* Career counseling, free psychological counseling, international student services. *Library facilities:* Cordas C. Burnett Library. *Collection:* 84,910 titles, 500 serial subscriptions, 4,382 audiovisual materials.

Computer facilities: 15 computers available on campus for general student use. A campuswide network can be accessed. Internet access is available. *Web address:* http://www.agts.edu/.

General Application Contact: Dorothea J. Lotter, Director of Admissions and Records, 417-268-1000, Fax: 417-268-1001, E-mail: dlotter@agseminary.edu.

GRADUATE UNITS

Graduate and Professional Programs Students: 196 full-time (78 women), 199 part-time (50 women); includes 46 minority (17 African Americans, 7 Asian Americans or Pacific Islanders, 21 Hispanic Americans, 1 Native American), 19 international. Average age 36. 190 applicants, 71% accepted. *Faculty:* 15 full-time (1 woman), 113 part-time/adjunct (9 women). Expenses: Contact institution. *Financial support:* Career-related internships or fieldwork and Federal Work-Study available. Support available to part-time students. Financial award application deadline: 7/15; financial award applicants required to submit FAFSA. In 2001, 28 first professional degrees, 63 master's, 9 doctorates awarded. *Degree program information:* Part-time and evening/weekend programs available. Postbaccalaureate distance learning degree programs offered (minimal on-campus study). Offers Christian ministries (MA); counseling (MA); divinity (M Div); intercultural ministries (MA); theological studies (MA); vocational ministry (D Min). *Application deadline:* Applications are processed on a rolling basis. *Application fee:* $35. Electronic applications accepted. *Director of Admissions and Records,* Dorothea J. Lotter, 417-268-1000, Fax: 417-268-1001, E-mail: dlotter@agseminary.edu.

ASSOCIATED MENNONITE BIBLICAL SEMINARY, Elkhart, IN 46517-1999

General Information Independent-religious, coed, graduate-only institution. *Enrollment by degree level:* 76 first professional, 86 master's. *Graduate faculty:* 11 full-time (2 women), 20 part-time/adjunct (6 women). *Tuition:* Part-time $270 per credit hour. *Required fees:* $7 per semester. *Graduate housing:* Rooms and/or apartments available on a first-come, first-served basis to single and married students. Housing application deadline: 5/1. *Student services:* Campus employment opportunities, child daycare facilities, free psychological counseling, international student services. *Library facilities:* Associated Mennonite Biblical Seminary Library. *Online resources:* library catalog, web page, access to other libraries' catalogs. *Collection:* 105,000 titles, 543 serial subscriptions.

Computer facilities: 13 computers available on campus for general student use. A campuswide network can be accessed from off campus. Internet access is available. *Web address:* http://www.ambs.edu/.

General Application Contact: Randall C. Miller, Director of Admissions, 574-295-3726, Fax: 574-295-0092, E-mail: admissions@ambs.edu.

GRADUATE UNITS

Graduate and Professional Programs Students: 56 full-time (29 women), 106 part-time (63 women); includes 8 minority (3 African Americans, 1 Asian American or Pacific Islander, 3 Hispanic Americans, 1 Native American), 22 international. Average age 36. 44 applicants, 57% accepted. *Faculty:* 11 full-time (2 women), 20 part-time/adjunct (6 women). Expenses: Contact institution. *Financial support:* Career-related internships or fieldwork and scholarships/grants available. Support available to part-time students. Financial award application deadline: 5/1; financial award applicants required to submit FAFSA. In 2001, 12 first professional degrees, 20 master's, 1 other advanced degree awarded. *Degree program information:* Part-time programs available. Offers Christian formation (MA); divinity (M Div); mission and evangelism (MA); peace studies (MA); theological studies (MA, Certificate). *Application deadline:* For fall admission, 5/1 (priority date). Applications are processed on a rolling basis. *Application fee:* $30. *Application Contact:* Randall C. Miller, Director of Admissions, 574-295-3726, Fax: 574-295-0092, E-mail: admissions@ambs.edu. *President,* J. Nelson Kraybill, 574-295-3726, Fax: 574-295-0092.

ASSUMPTION COLLEGE, Worcester, MA 01609-1296

General Information Independent-religious, coed, comprehensive institution. *Enrollment:* 114 full-time matriculated graduate/professional students (90 women), 159 part-time matriculated graduate/professional students (106 women). *Enrollment by degree level:* 273 master's. *Graduate faculty:* 32 full-time (11 women), 37 part-time/adjunct (16 women). *Tuition:* Part-time $1,005 per credit. *Graduate housing:* On-campus housing not available. *Student services:* Campus safety program, career counseling, disabled student services, exercise/wellness program, free psychological counseling, international student services, low-cost health insurance. *Library facilities:* Emmanuel d'Alzon Library. *Online resources:* library catalog, web page, access to other libraries' catalogs. *Collection:* 104,586 titles, 1,119 serial subscriptions, 1,450 audiovisual materials.

Computer facilities: 190 computers available on campus for general student use. A campuswide network can be accessed from student residence rooms and from off campus. Internet access is available. *Web address:* http://www.assumption.edu/.

General Application Contact: Adrian O. Dumas, Director of Graduate Enrollment Management and Services, 508-767-7365, Fax: 508-767-7030, E-mail: adumas@assumption.edu.

GRADUATE UNITS

Graduate School Students: 114 full-time (90 women), 159 part-time (106 women). 77 applicants, 97% accepted. *Faculty:* 32 full-time (11 women), 37 part-time/adjunct (16 women). Expenses: Contact institution. *Financial support:* In 2001–02, 107 students received support, including 9 fellowships with partial tuition reimbursements available, 14 research assistantships with full and partial tuition reimbursements available; career-related internships or fieldwork, scholarships/grants, and traineeships also available. Support available to part-time students. Financial award application deadline: 7/1; financial award applicants required to submit FAFSA. In 2001, 102 master's, 15 other advanced degrees awarded. *Degree program information:* Part-time and evening/weekend programs available. Offers business studies (MBA, CPS); counseling psychology (MA, CAGS); special education (MA). *Application deadline:* Applications are processed on a rolling basis. *Application fee:* $30. *Application Contact:* Adrian O. Dumas, Director of Graduate Enrollment Management and Services, 508-767-7365, Fax: 508-767-7030, E-mail: adumas@assumption.edu. *Dean of the College,* Dr. MaryLou Anderson, 508-767-7276, Fax: 508-767-7053.

Institute for Social and Rehabilitation Services Students: 99 (76 women); includes 21 minority (6 African Americans, 7 Asian Americans or Pacific Islanders, 8 Hispanic Americans) 21 applicants, 100% accepted. *Faculty:* 13 full-time (4 women), 13 part-time/adjunct (7 women). Expenses: Contact institution. *Financial support:* In 2001–02, 14 research assistantships with full tuition reimbursements (averaging $11,232 per year) were awarded; career-related internships or fieldwork and traineeships also available. Support available to part-time students. Financial award applicants required to submit FAFSA. In 2001, 38 master's, 15 other advanced degrees awarded. *Degree program information:* Part-time and evening/weekend programs available. Offers rehabilitation counseling (MA, CAGS). *Application deadline:* Applications are processed on a rolling basis. *Application fee:* $30. *Application Contact:* Prof. Lee Pearson, Coordinator of Graduate Program, 508-767-7063, E-mail: lpearson@assumption.edu. *Acting Director,* Dr. David St. John, 508-767-7228, Fax: 508-798-2872, E-mail: dstjohn@assumption.edu.

See in-depth description on page 743.

ATHABASCA UNIVERSITY, Athabasca, AB T9S 3A3, Canada

General Information Province-supported, coed, comprehensive institution. *Enrollment:* 2,109 part-time matriculated graduate/professional students (1,067 women). *Enrollment by degree level:* 2,109 master's. *Graduate faculty:* 33 full-time (11 women), 157 part-time/adjunct (67 women). *Graduate tuition:* Tuition charges are reported in Canadian dollars. *Tuition:* Part-time $850 Canadian dollars per course. Tuition and fees vary according to degree level and program. *Student services:* Disabled student services. *Library facilities:* Athabasca University Library plus 1 other. *Collection:* 130,000 titles, 4,000 serial subscriptions, 3,345 audiovisual materials. *Research affiliation:* IBM (software), SAP (software).

Computer facilities: 28 computers available on campus for general student use. A campuswide network can be accessed from off campus. Internet access and online class registration, computing services help desk are available. *Web address:* http://www.athabascau.ca/.

General Application Contact: 800-788-9041, Fax: 780-675-6437.

Athabasca University (continued)

GRADUATE UNITS

Centre for Computing and Information Systems *Faculty:* 8 full-time (0 women), 2 part-time/adjunct (0 women). Expenses: Contact institution. *Degree program information:* Part-time programs available. Postbaccalaureate distance learning degree programs offered (no on-campus study). Offers information systems (M Sc). *Application deadline:* For fall admission, 7/15; for winter admission, 11/15; for spring admission, 3/15. *Application fee:* $250. Electronic applications accepted. *Application Contact:* Claire Gemmell, Administration and Production Coordinator, 780-675-6777, Fax: 780-675-6148, E-mail: claire@athabascau.ca. *Professor*, Dr. Peter Holt, 780-675-6225, Fax: 780-675-6148, E-mail: holt@athabarcau.ca.

Centre for Distance Education Students: 334. Average age 41. 139 applicants, 94% accepted. *Faculty:* 8 full-time (3 women), 17 part-time/adjunct (4 women). Expenses: Contact institution. In 2001, 37 degrees awarded. *Degree program information:* Part-time programs available. Postbaccalaureate distance learning degree programs offered (no on-campus study). Offers distance education (MDE); distance education technology (Advanced Diploma). *Application deadline:* For fall admission, 3/1. *Application fee:* $50. *Application Contact:* Glenda Hawryluk, Administrative Assistant, 780-675-6179, E-mail: glendah@athabascau.ca. *Head*, Dr. Bob Spencer, 780-675-6238, E-mail: bobs@athabascau.edu.

Centre for Innovative Management Average age 40. 501 applicants, 71% accepted. *Faculty:* 11 full-time (5 women), 61 part-time/adjunct. Expenses: Contact institution. *Financial support:* Scholarships/grants available. In 2001, 262 degrees awarded. *Degree program information:* Part-time programs available. Offers business administration (MBA); information technology management (MBA, Advanced Diploma); management (Diploma); project management (MBA, Advanced Diploma). *Application deadline:* For fall admission, 6/15; for winter admission, 10/15; for spring admission, 2/15. Applications are processed on a rolling basis. *Application fee:* $165. Electronic applications accepted. *Application Contact:* Shelley Lynes, Manager, Registrations, Records, and Graduate Student Services, 800-561-4650, Fax: 800-561-4660, E-mail: shelleyl@athabascau.ca. *Executive Director*, Dr. Lindsay Redpath, 780-459-1144, Fax: 780-459-2093, E-mail: lindsayr@cs.athabascau.ca.

Centre for Integrated Studies Average age 40. 35 applicants, 100% accepted, 34 enrolled. *Faculty:* 2 full-time (0 women), 62 part-time/adjunct (41 women). Expenses: Contact institution. *Degree program information:* Part-time programs available. Postbaccalaureate distance learning degree programs offered (no on-campus study). Offers adult education (MA); Canadian studies (MA); cultural studies (MA); educational studies (MA); global change (MA); historical studies (MA); work, organizations, and leadership (MA). *Application deadline:* For fall admission, 3/1; for winter admission, 10/1. Applications are processed on a rolling basis. *Application fee:* $55. Electronic applications accepted. *Application Contact:* Rebecca A. Heartt, Program Administrator, 780-675-6792, Fax: 780-675-6186, E-mail: mais@athabascau.ca. *Program Director*, Dr. Mike Gismondi, 780-675-6218, Fax: 780-675-6186, E-mail: mikeg@athabascou.ca.

Centre for Nursing and Health Studies Students: 369. 190 applicants, 95% accepted. *Faculty:* 2 full-time, 24 part-time/adjunct. Expenses: Contact institution. In 2001, 1 degree awarded. *Degree program information:* Part-time programs available. Postbaccalaureate distance learning degree programs offered. Offers advanced nursing practice (Advanced Diploma); health studies (MHS). *Application deadline:* For fall admission, 3/1. *Application fee:* $50. Electronic applications accepted. *Director*, Dr. Donna Romyn, 780-675-6381, Fax: 780-675-6468, E-mail: mhs@athabascau.ca.

ATHENAEUM OF OHIO, Cincinnati, OH 45230-5900

General Information Independent-religious, coed, graduate-only institution. *Enrollment by degree level:* 35 first professional, 56 master's. *Graduate faculty:* 18 full-time (4 women), 40 part-time/adjunct (15 women). *Tuition:* Full-time $10,890; part-time $190 per credit. *Graduate housing:* Room and/or apartments guaranteed to single students; on-campus housing not available to married students. Typical cost: $3,200 per year ($6,000 including board). *Student services:* Campus employment opportunities, career counseling, free psychological counseling, international student services, low-cost health insurance. *Library facilities:* Eugene H. Maly Memorial Library. *Online resources:* library catalog, web page, access to other libraries' catalogs. *Collection:* 76,578 titles, 414 serial subscriptions, 2,501 audiovisual materials.

Computer facilities: 3 computers available on campus for general student use. A campuswide network can be accessed. Internet access is available. *Web address:* http://www.mtsm.org/.

General Application Contact: Michael E. Sweeney, Registrar, 513-231-2223, Fax: 513-231-3254, E-mail: msweeney@mtsm.org.

GRADUATE UNITS

Graduate Programs Students: 78 full-time (30 women), 13 part-time (8 women); includes 4 minority (2 African Americans, 2 Asian Americans or Pacific Islanders) Average age 42. 33 applicants, 94% accepted, 30 enrolled. *Faculty:* 18 full-time (4 women), 40 part-time/adjunct (15 women). Expenses: Contact institution. *Financial support:* In 2001–02, 8 students received support. Career-related internships or fieldwork, institutionally sponsored loans, and scholarships/grants available. Support available to part-time students. Financial award application deadline: 8/1. In 2001, 2 first professional degrees, 14 master's awarded. *Degree program information:* Part-time and evening/weekend programs available. Offers biblical studies (MABS); divinity (M Div); pastoral counseling (MAPC); religion (MAR); theology (MA Th). *Application deadline:* For fall admission, 4/15 (priority date); for winter admission, 11/1 (priority date). *Application fee:* $30. *Application Contact:* Michael E. Sweeney, Registrar, 513-231-2223, Fax: 513-231-3254, E-mail: msweeney@mtsm.org. *Dean*, Dr. Terrance D. Callan, 513-231-2223, Fax: 513-231-3254, E-mail: tcallan@mtsm.org.

ATLANTIC INSTITUTE OF ORIENTAL MEDICINE, Fort Lauderdale, FL 33316-2116

General Information Independent, coed, graduate-only institution.

ATLANTIC SCHOOL OF THEOLOGY, Halifax, NS B3H 3B5, Canada

General Information Independent, coed, graduate-only institution. *Graduate faculty:* 5 full-time, 9 part-time/adjunct. *Graduate housing:* Rooms and/or apartments available on a first-come, first-served basis to single and married students. Housing application deadline:6/1. *Student services:* Campus employment opportunities, international student services, low-cost health insurance. *Library facilities:* Atlantic School of Theology Library. *Online resources:* library catalog, access to other libraries' catalogs. *Collection:* 71,910 titles, 365 serial subscriptions.

Computer facilities: 3 computers available on campus for general student use. A campuswide network can be accessed. Internet access is available. *Web address:* http://www.astheology.ns.ca/.

General Application Contact: Rev. Dr. David MacLachlan, Academic Dean/Registrar, 902-496-7941, Fax: 902-492-4048, E-mail: dmaclachlan@astheology.ns.ca.

GRADUATE UNITS

Graduate and Professional Programs Students: 60 full-time (33 women), 97 part-time (58 women). Average age 38. Expenses: Contact institution. *Financial support:* In 2001–02, 27 students received support. Career-related internships or fieldwork available. Support available to part-time students. Financial award application deadline: 9/30. In 2001, 14 M Divs, 4 master's awarded. *Degree program information:* Part-time programs available. Offers theology (M Div, MTS). *Application deadline:* For fall admission, 7/31 (priority date). Applications are processed on a rolling basis. *Application fee:* $0. *Application Contact:* Patricia Munt, Academic Secretary, 902-423-5592, Fax: 902-492-4048, E-mail: pmunt@astheology.ns.ca. *Academic Dean/Registrar*, Rev. Dr. David MacLachlan, 902-496-7941, Fax: 902-492-4048, E-mail: dmaclachlan@astheology.ns.ca.

ATLANTIC UNION COLLEGE, South Lancaster, MA 01561-1000

General Information Independent-religious, coed, comprehensive institution. *Graduate housing:* Room and/or apartments available to single students; on-campus housing not available to married students.

GRADUATE UNITS

Graduate Education Program *Degree program information:* Part-time programs available. Postbaccalaureate distance learning degree programs offered (minimal on-campus study). Offers education (M Ed). Offered during summer only.

ATLANTIC UNIVERSITY, Virginia Beach, VA 23451-2061

General Information Independent, coed, primarily women, graduate-only institution. *Enrollment by degree level:* 223 master's. *Graduate faculty:* 11 part-time/adjunct (5 women). *Graduate housing:* On-campus housing not available. *Web address:* http://www.atlanticuniv.edu/.

General Application Contact: Dr. Robert Danner, Director of Admissions, 757-631-8101 Ext. 210, Fax: 757-631-8096, E-mail: registrar@atlanticuniv.edu.

GRADUATE UNITS

Program in Transpersonal Studies Students: 233. 52 applicants, 69% accepted. *Faculty:* 11 part-time/adjunct (5 women). Expenses: Contact institution. In 2001, 20 degrees awarded. *Degree program information:* Part-time and evening/weekend programs available. Postbaccalaureate distance learning degree programs offered (no on-campus study). Offers transpersonal studies (MA). *Application deadline:* Applications are processed on a rolling basis. *Application fee:* $25. Electronic applications accepted. *Application Contact:* Dr. Robert Danner, Director of Admissions, 757-631-8101 Ext. 210, Fax: 757-631-8096, E-mail: info@atlanticuniv.edu. *Chief Executive Officer*, H. A. Stokely, 757-631-8101, Fax: 757-631-8096, E-mail: info@atlanticuniv.edu.

AUBURN UNIVERSITY, Auburn University, AL 36849

General Information State-supported, coed, university. CGS member. *Enrollment:* 2,097 full-time matriculated graduate/professional students (1,136 women), 1,437 part-time matriculated graduate/professional students (617 women). *Enrollment by degree level:* 724 first professional, 1,850 master's, 944 doctoral, 16 other advanced degrees. *Graduate faculty:* 993 full-time (208 women). *Graduate housing:* Rooms and/or apartments available to single and married students. Housing application deadline: 7/1. *Student services:* Campus employment opportunities, campus safety program, career counseling, disabled student services, international student services, low-cost health insurance, teacher training. *Library facilities:* R. B. Draughon Library plus 2 others. *Online resources:* library catalog, web page, access to other libraries' catalogs. *Collection:* 2.5 million titles, 18,919 serial subscriptions, 629,038 audiovisual materials. *Research affiliation:* National Asphalt Pavement Association (asphalt technology), National Textile Center.

Computer facilities: 600 computers available on campus for general student use. A campuswide network can be accessed from student residence rooms and from off campus. Online class registration is available. *Web address:* http://www.auburn.edu/.

General Application Contact: Dr. Stephen L. McFarland, Interim Dean of the Graduate School, 334-844-4700.

GRADUATE UNITS

College of Veterinary Medicine Students: 363 full-time (236 women), 40 part-time (21 women); includes 9 minority (5 African Americans, 1 Asian American or Pacific Islander, 3 Hispanic Americans), 9 international. 31 applicants, 61% accepted. *Faculty:* 84 full-time (20 women). Expenses: Contact institution. *Financial support:* Fellowships, research assistantships, teaching assistantships, Federal Work-Study available. Support available to part-time students. Financial award application deadline: 3/15. In 2001, 90 first professional degrees, 7 master's, 6 doctorates awarded. *Degree program information:* Part-time programs available. Offers veterinary medicine (DVM, MS, PhD). *Application deadline:* For fall admission, 7/7. Applications are processed on a rolling basis. *Application fee:* $25. *Dean*, Dr. Timothy R. Boosinger, 334-844-4546.

Graduate Programs in Veterinary Medicine Students: 4 full-time (1 woman), 40 part-time (21 women); includes 3 minority (1 African American, 2 Hispanic Americans), 8 international. 27 applicants, 52% accepted. *Faculty:* 84 full-time (20 women). Expenses: Contact institution. *Financial support:* Research assistantships, teaching assistantships, Federal Work-Study available. Support available to part-time students. Financial award application deadline: 3/15. In 2001, 7 master's, 6 doctorates awarded. *Degree program information:* Part-time programs available. Offers anatomy and histology (MS); anatomy, physiology and pharmacology (MS); biomedical sciences (PhD); clinical sciences (MS); large animal surgery and medicine (MS); pathobiology (MS); physiology and pharmacology (MS); radiology (MS); small animal surgery and medicine (MS); veterinary medicine (MS, PhD). *Application deadline:* For fall admission, 7/7; for spring admission, 11/24. Applications are processed on a rolling basis. *Application fee:* $25 ($50 for international students). Electronic applications accepted. *Application Contact:* Dr. John F. Pritchett, Dean of the Graduate School, 334-844-4700, E-mail: hatchlb@mail.auburn.edu.

Graduate School Students: 1,384 full-time (653 women), 1,426 part-time (611 women); includes 262 minority (195 African Americans, 22 Asian Americans or Pacific Islanders, 36 Hispanic Americans, 9 Native Americans), 500 international. Average age 25. 2,840 applicants, 51% accepted. *Faculty:* 993 full-time (208 women). Expenses: Contact institution. *Financial support:* Fellowships, research assistantships, teaching assistantships, career-related internships or fieldwork and Federal Work-Study available. Support available to part-time students. In 2001, 720 master's, 186 doctorates, 4 other advanced degrees awarded. *Degree program information:* Part-time and evening/weekend programs available. Offers integrated textile and apparel sciences (MS, PhD); sociology (MA, MS); textile science (MS). *Application deadline:* For fall admission, 7/7; for spring admission, 11/24. *Application fee:* $25 ($50 for international students). *Interim Dean*, Dr. Stephen McFarland, 334-844-4700.

College of Agriculture Students: 124 full-time (47 women), 109 part-time (31 women); includes 10 minority (7 African Americans, 1 Asian American or Pacific Islander, 1 Hispanic American, 1 Native American), 69 international. 116 applicants, 59% accepted. *Faculty:* 154 full-time (13 women). Expenses: Contact institution. *Financial support:* Fellowships, research assistantships, teaching assistantships, Federal Work-Study available. Support available to part-time students. Financial award application deadline: 3/15. In 2001, 50 master's, 23 doctorates awarded. *Degree program information:* Part-time programs available. Offers agricultural economics and rural sociology (M Ag, MS, PhD); agriculture (M Ag, M Aq, MS, PhD); agronomy and soils (M Ag, MS, PhD); animal and dairy sciences (M Ag, MS, PhD); biosystems engineering (MS, PhD); entomology (M Ag, MS, PhD); fisheries and allied aquacultures (M Aq, MS, PhD); horticulture (M Ag, MS, PhD); plant pathology (M Ag, MS, PhD); poultry science (M Ag, MS, PhD). *Application deadline:* For fall admission, 7/7; for spring admission, 11/24. Applications are processed on a rolling basis. *Application fee:* $25 ($50 for international students). Electronic applications accepted. *Application Contact:* Dr. John F. Pritchett, Dean of the Graduate School, 334-844-4700, E-mail: hatchlb@mail.auburn.edu. *Interim Dean*, Dr. John W. Jensen, 334-844-2345.

College of Architecture, Design, and Construction Students: 29 full-time (3 women), 5 part-time (1 woman), 2 international. 37 applicants, 73% accepted. *Faculty:* 38 full-time (8 women). Expenses: Contact institution. *Financial support:* Fellowships, Federal Work-Study available. Support available to part-time students. Financial award application deadline: 3/15. In 2001, 15 degrees awarded. *Degree program information:* Part-time programs available. Offers architecture, design, and construction (MBS, MCP, MID, MLA); building science (MBS); community planning (MCP); construction management (MBS); industrial design (MID). *Application deadline:* For fall admission, 7/7; for spring admission, 11/24. Applications are processed on a rolling basis. *Application fee:* $25 ($50 for international students). Electronic applications accepted. *Application Contact:* Dr. John F. Pritchett, Dean of the Graduate School, 334-844-4700, E-mail: hatchlb@mail.auburn.edu. *Dean*, Dan D. Bennett, 334-844-4524.

College of Business Students: 195 full-time (65 women), 368 part-time (84 women); includes 44 minority (24 African Americans, 8 Asian Americans or Pacific Islanders, 10 Hispanic

Americans, 2 Native Americans), 30 international. 466 applicants, 60% accepted. *Faculty:* 62 full-time (6 women). Expenses: Contact institution. *Financial support:* Fellowships, research assistantships, teaching assistantships, career-related internships or fieldwork and Federal Work-Study available. Support available to part-time students. Financial award application deadline: 3/15. In 2001, 218 master's, 7 doctorates awarded. *Degree program information:* Part-time programs available. Offers accountancy (M Acc); business (M Acc, MBA, MMIS, MS, PhD); business administration (MBA); economics (MS, PhD); human relations management (PhD); management (MS); management information systems (MMIS, PhD). *Application deadline:* For fall admission, 7/7; for spring admission, 11/24. Applications are processed on a rolling basis. *Application fee:* $25 ($50 for international students). Electronic applications accepted. *Application Contact:* Dr. John F. Pritchett, Dean of the Graduate School, 334-844-4700, E-mail: hatchlb@mail.auburn.edu. *Interim Dean,* Dr. John S. Jahera, 334-844-4832.

College of Education Students: 266 full-time (189 women), 318 part-time (209 women); includes 98 minority (87 African Americans, 1 Asian American or Pacific Islander, 8 Hispanic Americans, 2 Native Americans), 13 international. 411 applicants, 68% accepted. *Faculty:* 70 full-time (33 women). Expenses: Contact institution. *Financial support:* Fellowships, research assistantships, teaching assistantships, career-related internships or fieldwork and Federal Work-Study available. Support available to part-time students. Financial award application deadline: 3/15. In 2001, 185 master's, 48 doctorates, 4 other advanced degrees awarded. *Degree program information:* Part-time programs available. Offers adult education (M Ed, MS, Ed D); business education (M Ed, MS, PhD); community agency counseling (M Ed, MS, Ed D, PhD, Ed S); counseling psychology (PhD); counselor education (Ed D, PhD); curriculum and instruction (M Ed, MS, Ed D, Ed S); curriculum supervision (M Ed, MS, Ed D, Ed S); early childhood education (M Ed, MS, PhD, Ed S); education (M Ed, MS, Ed D, PhD, Ed S); educational psychology (PhD); elementary education (M Ed, MS, PhD, Ed S); foreign languages (M Ed, MS); health and human performance (M Ed, MS, Ed D, PhD, Ed S); higher education administration (M Ed, MS, Ed D, Ed S); media instructional design (MS); media specialist (M Ed); music education (M Ed, MS, PhD, Ed S); postsecondary education (PhD); reading education (PhD, Ed S); rehabilitation and special education (M Ed, MS, PhD, Ed S); school administration (M Ed, MS, Ed D, Ed S); school counseling (M Ed, MS, Ed D, PhD, Ed S); school psychometry (M Ed, MS, Ed D, PhD, Ed S); secondary education (M Ed, MS, PhD, Ed S). *Application fee:* $25 ($50 for international students). Electronic applications accepted. *Application Contact:* Dr. John F. Pritchett, Dean of the Graduate School, 334-844-4700, E-mail: hatchlb@mail.auburn.edu. *Interim Dean,* Dr. Frances Kochan, 334-844-4446.

College of Engineering Students: 244 full-time (57 women), 203 part-time (53 women); includes 29 minority (19 African Americans, 5 Asian Americans or Pacific Islanders, 4 Hispanic Americans, 1 Native American), 210 international. 699 applicants, 39% accepted. *Faculty:* 118 full-time (5 women). Expenses: Contact institution. *Financial support:* Fellowships, research assistantships, teaching assistantships, Federal Work-Study available. Support available to part-time students. Financial award application deadline: 3/15. In 2001, 102 master's, 51 doctorates awarded. *Degree program information:* Part-time programs available. Offers aerospace engineering (MAE, MS, PhD); chemical engineering (M Ch E, MS, PhD); computer science and software engineering (MS, MSWE, PhD); construction engineering and management (MCE, MS, PhD); electrical and computer engineering (MEE, MS, PhD); engineering (M Ch E, M Mtl E, MAE, MCE, MEE, MIE, MME, MS, MSWE, PhD); environmental engineering (MCE, MS, PhD); geotechnical/materials engineering (MCE, MS, PhD); hydraulics/hydrology (MCE, MS, PhD); industrial and systems engineering (MIE, MS, PhD); materials engineering (M Mtl E, MS, PhD); mechanical engineering (MME, MS, PhD); structural engineering (MCE, MS, PhD); transportation engineering (MCE, MS, PhD). *Application deadline:* For fall admission, 7/7; for spring admission, 11/24. Applications are processed on a rolling basis. *Application fee:* $25 ($50 for international students). Electronic applications accepted. *Application Contact:* Dr. John F. Pritchett, Dean of the Graduate School, 334-844-4700, E-mail: hatchlb@mail.auburn.edu. *Dean,* Dr. Larry Benefield, 334-844-2308.

College of Human Sciences Students: 50 full-time (38 women), 42 part-time (27 women); includes 12 minority (11 African Americans, 1 Native American), 21 international. 119 applicants, 55% accepted. *Faculty:* 43 full-time (28 women). Expenses: Contact institution. *Financial support:* Fellowships, research assistantships, teaching assistantships, career-related internships or fieldwork and Federal Work-Study available. Support available to part-time students. Financial award application deadline: 3/15. In 2001, 24 master's, 6 doctorates awarded. *Degree program information:* Part-time programs available. Offers apparel and textiles (MS); human development and family studies (MS, PhD); human sciences (MS, PhD); nutrition and food science (MS, PhD). *Application deadline:* For fall admission, 7/7; for spring admission, 11/24. Applications are processed on a rolling basis. *Application fee:* $25 ($50 for international students). Electronic applications accepted. *Application Contact:* Dr. John F. Pritchett, Dean of the Graduate School, 334-844-4700, E-mail: hatchlb@mail.auburn.edu. *Dean,* Dr. June Henton, 334-844-3790, E-mail: jhenton@humsci.auburn.edu.

College of Liberal Arts Students: 209 full-time (146 women), 193 part-time (117 women); includes 41 minority (28 African Americans, 3 Asian Americans or Pacific Islanders, 8 Hispanic Americans, 2 Native Americans), 13 international. 496 applicants, 43% accepted. *Faculty:* 166 full-time (51 women). Expenses: Contact institution. *Financial support:* Fellowships, research assistantships, teaching assistantships, career-related internships or fieldwork and Federal Work-Study available. Support available to part-time students. Financial award application deadline: 3/15. In 2001, 81 master's, 35 doctorates awarded. *Degree program information:* Part-time programs available. Offers art (MFA, PhD); audiology (MCD, MS); communication (MA, MSC); English (MA, PhD); French (MA, MFS); history (MA, PhD); liberal arts (MA, MCD, MFA, MFS, MHS, MM, MPA, MS, MSC, PhD); mass communications (MA, MSC); music (MM); psychology (MS, PhD); public administration (MPA, PhD); Spanish (MA, MHS); speech pathology (MCD, MS). *Application deadline:* For fall admission, 7/7; for spring admission, 11/24. Applications are processed on a rolling basis. *Application fee:* $25 ($50 for international students). Electronic applications accepted. *Application Contact:* Dr. John F. Pritchett, Dean of the Graduate School, 334-844-4700, E-mail: hatchlb@mail.auburn.edu. *Interim Dean,* Dr. Rebekah Pindzola, 334-844-2185.

College of Sciences and Mathematics Students: 180 full-time (76 women), 61 part-time (19 women); includes 13 minority (10 African Americans, 1 Asian American or Pacific Islander, 2 Hispanic Americans), 80 international. 228 applicants, 61% accepted. *Faculty:* 137 full-time (11 women). Expenses: Contact institution. *Financial support:* Fellowships, research assistantships, teaching assistantships, career-related internships or fieldwork and Federal Work-Study available. Support available to part-time students. In 2001, 35 master's, 30 doctorates awarded. *Degree program information:* Part-time programs available. Offers botany (MS, PhD); chemistry (MS, PhD); discrete and statistical sciences (M Prob S, MAM, MS, PhD); geology and geography (MS); mathematics (MAM, MS, PhD); microbiology (MS, PhD); physics (MS, PhD); sciences and mathematics (M Prob S, MAM, MS, PhD); zoology (MS, PhD). *Application deadline:* For fall admission, 7/7; for spring admission, 11/24. Applications are processed on a rolling basis. *Application fee:* $25 ($50 for international students). *Application Contact:* Dr. John F. Pritchett, Dean of the Graduate School, 334-844-4700, E-mail: hatchlb@mail.auburn.edu. *Dean,* Dr. Stewart W. Schneller, 334-844-4555.

School of Forestry and Wildlife Sciences Students: 21 full-time (3 women), 27 part-time (8 women); includes 1 minority (Asian American or Pacific Islander), 8 international. 40 applicants, 40% accepted. *Faculty:* 29 full-time (3 women). Expenses: Contact institution. *Financial support:* Fellowships, research assistantships, teaching assistantships, Federal Work-Study available. Support available to part-time students. Financial award application deadline: 3/15. In 2001, 5 master's, 4 doctorates awarded. *Degree program information:* Part-time programs available. Offers forestry and wildlife sciences (MF, MS, PhD). *Application deadline:* For fall admission, 7/7; for spring admission, 11/24. Applications are processed on a rolling basis. *Application fee:* $25 ($50 for international students). Electronic applications accepted. *Application Contact:* Dr. John F. Pritchett, Dean of the Graduate School, 334-844-4700, E-mail: hatchlb@mail.auburn.edu. *Dean,* Richard W. Brinker, 334-844-1007, Fax: 334-844-1084, E-mail: brinker@forestry.auburn.edu.

School of Pharmacy Students: 365 full-time (249 women), 25 part-time (16 women); includes 50 minority (24 African Americans, 19 Asian Americans or Pacific Islanders, 1 Hispanic American, 6 Native Americans), 16 international. *Faculty:* 32 full-time (9 women). Expenses: Contact institution. *Financial support:* Fellowships, research assistantships, teaching assistantships, Federal Work-Study available. Support available to part-time students. In 2001, 38 first professional degrees, 3 doctorates awarded. *Degree program information:* Part-time programs available. Offers pharmacy (Pharm D, MS, PhD). *Application deadline:* For fall admission, 7/7; for spring admission, 11/24. Applications are processed on a rolling basis. *Application fee:* $25. Electronic applications accepted. *Application Contact:* Dr. John F. Pritchett, Dean of the Graduate School, 334-844-4700, E-mail: hatchlb@mail.auburn.edu. *Dean,* Dr. R. Lee Evans, 334-844-8348.

See in-depth description on page 745.

AUBURN UNIVERSITY MONTGOMERY, Montgomery, AL 36124-4023

General Information State-supported, coed, comprehensive institution. *Enrollment:* 244 full-time matriculated graduate/professional students (155 women), 573 part-time matriculated graduate/professional students (390 women). *Graduate faculty:* 128 full-time (49 women), 21 part-time/adjunct (8 women). Tuition, state resident: full-time $3,072; part-time $128 per credit hour. Tuition, nonresident: full-time $9,216; part-time $384 per credit hour. *Graduate housing:* Rooms and/or apartments available to single and married students. Typical cost: $2,120 per year for single students; $4,240 per year for married students. *Student services:* Campus employment opportunities, campus safety program, career counseling, disabled student services, free psychological counseling, international student services, low-cost health insurance. *Library facilities:* Auburn University Montgomery Library. *Online resources:* library catalog, web page, access to other libraries' catalogs. *Collection:* 292,586 titles, 5,820 serial subscriptions, 24,158 audiovisual materials.

Computer facilities: 300 computers available on campus for general student use. A campuswide network can be accessed from student residence rooms and from off campus. Internet access and online class registration are available. *Web address:* http://www.aum.edu/.

General Application Contact: Michele M. Moore, Associate Director of Enrollment Services, 334-244-3614, Fax: 334-244-3762, E-mail: mmoore@mickey.aum.edu.

GRADUATE UNITS

School of Business Students: 50 full-time (25 women), 131 part-time (53 women); includes 41 minority (36 African Americans, 3 Asian Americans or Pacific Islanders, 2 Hispanic Americans), 7 international. Average age 30. *Faculty:* 29 full-time (8 women). Expenses: Contact institution. *Financial support:* In 2001–02, 5 research assistantships were awarded; career-related internships or fieldwork and scholarships/grants also available. Support available to part-time students. Financial award application deadline: 3/1; financial award applicants required to submit FAFSA. In 2001, 82 degrees awarded. *Degree program information:* Part-time and evening/weekend programs available. Offers business (MBA). *Application deadline:* Applications are processed on a rolling basis. *Application fee:* $25. Electronic applications accepted. *Dean,* Dr. Jane Goodson, 334-244-3565, E-mail: jgoodson@monk.aum.edu.

School of Education Students: 104 full-time (88 women), 181 part-time (158 women); includes 113 minority (108 African Americans, 3 Asian Americans or Pacific Islanders, 2 Hispanic Americans), 1 international. Average age 33. *Faculty:* 27 full-time (19 women), 1 (woman) part-time/adjunct. Expenses: Contact institution. *Financial support:* In 2001–02, 5 teaching assistantships were awarded; career-related internships or fieldwork and scholarships/grants also available. Support available to part-time students. Financial award application deadline: 3/1; financial award applicants required to submit FAFSA. In 2001, 93 master's, 18 other advanced degrees awarded. *Degree program information:* Part-time and evening/weekend programs available. Offers counseling (M Ed, Ed S); early childhood education (M Ed, Ed S); education (M Ed, Ed S); education administration (M Ed, Ed S); elementary education (M Ed, Ed S); physical education (M Ed); reading education (M Ed, Ed S); secondary education (M Ed, Ed S); special education (M Ed, Ed S). *Application deadline:* Applications are processed on a rolling basis. *Application fee:* $25. Electronic applications accepted. *Application Contact:* Dr. Jennifer A. Brown, Associate Graduate Coordinator, 334-244-3545, E-mail: jbrown@edla.aum.edu. *Dean,* Dr. Janet S. Warren, 334-244-3413, E-mail: jwarren@edla.aum.edu.

School of Liberal Arts Students: 2 full-time (0 women), 26 part-time (15 women); includes 2 minority (both African Americans) Average age 38. *Faculty:* 34 full-time (12 women), 1 part-time/adjunct (0 women). Expenses: Contact institution. *Financial support:* Teaching assistantships, career-related internships or fieldwork and scholarships/grants available. Support available to part-time students. Financial award application deadline: 3/1; financial award applicants required to submit FAFSA. In 2001, 5 degrees awarded. *Degree program information:* Part-time and evening/weekend programs available. Offers liberal arts (MLA). *Application deadline:* Applications are processed on a rolling basis. *Application fee:* $25. Electronic applications accepted. *Application Contact:* Dr. Susan L. Willis, Graduate Coordinator, 334-244-3406. *Dean,* Dr. Larry C. Mullins, 334-244-3382, E-mail: lmullins@mickey.aum.edu.

School of Sciences Students: 71 full-time (30 women), 146 part-time (102 women); includes 79 minority (67 African Americans, 3 Asian Americans or Pacific Islanders, 7 Hispanic Americans, 2 Native Americans), 1 international. Average age 33. *Faculty:* 38 full-time (10 women), 18 part-time/adjunct (6 women). Expenses: Contact institution. *Financial support:* In 2001–02, 8 teaching assistantships were awarded; career-related internships or fieldwork and scholarships/grants also available. Support available to part-time students. Financial award application deadline: 3/1; financial award applicants required to submit FAFSA. In 2001, 79 degrees awarded. *Degree program information:* Part-time and evening/weekend programs available. Offers justice and public safety (MSJPS); political science (MPS); psychology (MSPG); public administration (MPA, PhD); sciences (MPA, MPS, MSJPS, MSPG, PhD). *Application deadline:* Applications are processed on a rolling basis. *Application fee:* $25. Electronic applications accepted. *Application Contact:* Dr. Cyril J. Sadowski, Acting Graduate Coordinator, 334-244-3589, E-mail: sadowski@sciences.aum.edu. *Dean,* Dr. Robert H. Elliott, 334-224-3678, E-mail: belliott@strudel.aum.edu.

AUDREY COHEN COLLEGE, New York, NY 10013-1919

General Information Independent, coed, primarily women, comprehensive institution. *Enrollment:* 227 full-time matriculated graduate/professional students (189 women), 8 part-time matriculated graduate/professional students (5 women). *Graduate faculty:* 21 full-time (11 women), 25 part-time/adjunct (11 women). *Tuition:* Full-time $17,210; part-time $380 per credit. *Graduate housing:* On-campus housing not available. *Student services:* Career counseling, free psychological counseling, grant writing training, international student services. *Library facilities:* Main Library. *Online resources:* library catalog, web page, access to other libraries' catalogs. *Collection:* 26,800 titles, 3,414 serial subscriptions, 45 audiovisual materials.

Computer facilities: 130 computers available on campus for general student use. A campuswide network can be accessed from off campus. Internet access is available. *Web address:* http://www.audreycohen.edu/.

General Application Contact: Steven K. Lenhart, Director of Graduate Admissions, 212-343-1234 Ext. 2700, Fax: 212-343-8470, E-mail: slenhart@audreycohen.edu.

GRADUATE UNITS

Program in Media Management Students: 23 full-time (16 women), 1 (woman) part-time; includes 11 minority (6 African Americans, 4 Asian Americans or Pacific Islanders, 1 Hispanic American) Average age 28. 57 applicants, 46% accepted, 24 enrolled. *Faculty:* 2 full-time (1 woman), 14 part-time/adjunct (6 women). Expenses: Contact institution. *Financial support:* In 2001–02, fellowships with tuition reimbursements (averaging $21,538 per year), research assistantships with partial tuition reimbursements (averaging $7,438 per year) were awarded. Career-related internships or fieldwork, scholarships/grants, tuition waivers (partial), and unspecified assistantships also available. Financial award application deadline: 8/15; financial award applicants required to submit FAFSA. In 2001, 15 degrees awarded. *Degree program information:* Evening/weekend programs available. Offers media management (MBA). *Applica-*

Audrey Cohen College (continued)

tion deadline: For fall admission, 7/15 (priority date); for winter admission, 11/10; for spring admission, 3/30. Applications are processed on a rolling basis. *Application fee:* $45. Electronic applications accepted. *Director of Graduate Admissions,* Steven K. Lenhart, 212-343-1234 Ext. 2700, Fax: 212-343-8470, E-mail: slenhart@audreycohen.edu.

Program in Public Administration Students: 85 full-time (59 women), 6 part-time (4 women); includes 116 African Americans, 7 Asian Americans or Pacific Islanders, 35 Hispanic Americans Average age 32. 122 applicants, 79% accepted, 87 enrolled. *Faculty:* 13 full-time (5 women), 11 part-time/adjunct (4 women). Expenses: Contact institution. *Financial support:* In 2001–02, 3 fellowships with tuition reimbursements (averaging $5,700 per year) were awarded; career-related internships or fieldwork, scholarships/grants, and tuition waivers (partial) also available. Financial award application deadline: 8/15; financial award applicants required to submit FAFSA. In 2001, 129 degrees awarded. *Degree program information:* Evening/weekend programs available. Offers public administration (MPA). *Application deadline:* For fall admission, 7/30 (priority date); for winter admission, 11/30 (priority date); for spring admission, 3/30 (priority date). Applications are processed on a rolling basis. *Application fee:* $45. Electronic applications accepted. *Director of Graduate Admissions,* Steven K. Lenhart, 212-343-1234 Ext. 2700, Fax: 212-343-8470, E-mail: slenhart@audreycohen.edu.

See in-depth description on page 747.

AUGSBURG COLLEGE, Minneapolis, MN 55454-1351

General Information Independent-religious, coed, comprehensive institution. *Enrollment:* 72 full-time matriculated graduate/professional students (63 women), 59 part-time matriculated graduate/professional students (51 women). *Enrollment by degree level:* 131 master's. *Graduate faculty:* 18 full-time (17 women), 19 part-time/adjunct (10 women). *Tuition:* Part-time $1,370 per course. *Graduate housing:* On-campus housing not available. *Student services:* Career counseling, free psychological counseling. *Library facilities:* James G. Lindell Library. *Online resources:* library catalog, web page, access to other libraries' catalogs. *Collection:* 142,739 titles, 1,007 serial subscriptions, 2,355 audiovisual materials.

Computer facilities: 224 computers available on campus for general student use. A campuswide network can be accessed from student residence rooms and from off campus. Internet access and online class registration are available. *Web address:* http://www.augsburg.edu/.

General Application Contact: Terry Cook, Coordinator, 612-330-1787, Fax: 612-330-1350, E-mail: cookt@augsburg.edu.

GRADUATE UNITS

Program in Leadership Students: 4 full-time (3 women), 32 part-time (26 women); includes 8 minority (4 African Americans, 3 Asian Americans or Pacific Islanders, 1 Native American) Average age 38. 13 applicants, 100% accepted, 8 enrolled. *Faculty:* 12 part-time/adjunct (6 women). Expenses: Contact institution. *Financial support:* In 2001–02, 9 students received support. Available to part-time students. Application deadline: 8/1; In 2001, 11 degrees awarded. *Degree program information:* Part-time and evening/weekend programs available. Offers leadership (MA). *Application deadline:* For fall admission, 8/9 (priority date); for winter admission, 12/15; for spring admission, 3/7. Applications are processed on a rolling basis. *Application fee:* $35. *Application Contact:* Barb Pappenfus, Coordinator, 612-330-1150, Fax: 612-330-1350, E-mail: pappen@augsburg.edu. *Director,* Dr. Norma Noonan, 612-330-1198, Fax: 612-330-1355, E-mail: noonan@augsburg.edu.

Program in Physicians Assistant Studies Students: 27 full-time (20 women); includes 3 minority (1 Asian American or Pacific Islander, 2 Hispanic Americans) Average age 27. 124 applicants, 23% accepted, 28 enrolled. *Faculty:* 5 full-time (4 women), 4 part-time/adjunct (2 women). Expenses: Contact institution. *Financial support:* In 2001–02, 26 students received support. Application deadline: 8/1; Offers physicians assistant studies (MS). *Application deadline:* For spring admission, 10/1. *Application fee:* $20. *Application Contact:* Information Contact, 612-330-1039, Fax: 612-330-1757, E-mail: paprog@augsburg.edu. *Director,* Dawn B. Ludwig, 612-330-1331, Fax: 612-330-1757, E-mail: ludwig@augsburg.edu.

Program in Social Work Students: 40 full-time (39 women), 8 part-time (7 women); includes 2 minority (1 African American, 1 Asian American or Pacific Islander), 2 international. Average age 32. 45 applicants, 98% accepted, 17 enrolled. *Faculty:* 10 full-time (all women), 1 part-time/adjunct (0 women). Expenses: Contact institution. *Financial support:* In 2001–02, 38 students received support. Career-related internships or fieldwork, institutionally sponsored loans, and tuition waivers (partial) available. Support available to part-time students. Financial award application deadline: 4/15. In 2001, 52 degrees awarded. *Degree program information:* Part-time and evening/weekend programs available. Offers social work (MSW). *Application deadline:* For fall admission, 1/15; for spring admission, 10/1. *Application fee:* $25. *Application Contact:* Janna Caywood, Program Assistant, 612-330-1763, Fax: 612-330-1493, E-mail: caywood@augsburg.edu. *Director,* Dr. Tony Bibus, 612-330-1746, Fax: 612-330-1493, E-mail: bibus@augsburg.edu.

Program in Transcultural Community Health Nursing Students: 1 (woman) full-time, 19 part-time (18 women); includes 2 minority (1 African American, 1 Asian American or Pacific Islander) Average age 47. 7 applicants, 71% accepted, 4 enrolled. *Faculty:* 3 full-time (all women), 2 part-time/adjunct (both women). Expenses: Contact institution. *Financial support:* In 2001–02, 5 students received support. Application deadline: 8/1; Offers transcultural community health nursing (MA). *Application deadline:* For fall admission, 8/1; for winter admission, 12/4; for spring admission, 3/9. *Application fee:* $25. *Application Contact:* Lu Ann Watson, Coordinator, 612-330-1204, E-mail: watson@augsberg.edu. *Director,* Dr. Ruth C. Enestvedt, 612-330-1209, E-mail: enestved@augsburg.edu.

AUGUSTANA COLLEGE, Sioux Falls, SD 57197

General Information Independent-religious, coed, comprehensive institution. *Enrollment:* 1 (woman) full-time matriculated graduate/professional student, 32 part-time matriculated graduate/professional students (29 women). *Enrollment by degree level:* 33 master's. *Graduate faculty:* 26 full-time, 2 part-time/adjunct. *Tuition:* Full-time $16,696; part-time $270 per credit. *Graduate housing:* Rooms and/or apartments available to single and married students. *Student services:* Campus safety program, career counseling, child daycare facilities, disabled student services, exercise/wellness program, free psychological counseling, international student services, low-cost health insurance, writing training. *Library facilities:* Mikkelsen Library plus 1 other. *Online resources:* library catalog, web page, access to other libraries' catalogs. *Collection:* 234,515 titles, 1,085 serial subscriptions, 6,147 audiovisual materials. *Research affiliation:* Midwest Research Institute (field research).

Computer facilities: 360 computers available on campus for general student use. A campuswide network can be accessed from student residence rooms and from off campus. Internet access is available. *Web address:* http://www.augie.edu/.

General Application Contact: Dr. Mary Brendtro, Director of Graduate Education, 605-274-4725, Fax: 605-274-4450, E-mail: graduate@augie.edu.

GRADUATE UNITS

Department of Education Expenses: Contact institution. *Financial support:* Career-related internships or fieldwork, Federal Work-Study, institutionally sponsored loans, scholarships/grants, tuition waivers (partial), and unspecified assistantships available. Financial award application deadline: 3/1; financial award applicants required to submit FAFSA. In 2001, 16 degrees awarded. *Degree program information:* Part-time programs available. Offers education (MA); educator/child and youth services (MA); elementary (MA); secondary (MA); special education (MA). *Application deadline:* For fall admission, 6/1 (priority date). Applications are processed on a rolling basis. *Application fee:* $50. *Application Contact:* Graduate Coordinator, 274-274-4043, Fax: 274-274-4450, E-mail: graduate@augie.edu. *Chair,* Dr. Robert Kiner, 605-274-4628, Fax: 605-274-4616, E-mail: kiner@wise.augie.edu.

Program in Advanced Nursing Practice in Emerging Health Systems Expenses: Contact institution. *Financial support:* Career-related internships or fieldwork, Federal Work-Study, institutionally sponsored loans, and scholarships/grants available. *Degree program information:* Part-time programs available. Postbaccalaureate distance learning degree programs offered (minimal on-campus study). Offers community health nursing (MA). *Application deadline:* For fall admission, 6/1 (priority date). Applications are processed on a rolling basis. *Application fee:* $50. *Application Contact:* Graduate Coordinator, 274-274-4043, Fax: 274-274-4450, E-mail: graduate@augie.edu. *Chair,* Dr. Margot Nelson, 605-274-4729, Fax: 605-274-4723, E-mail: mnelson@wise.augie.edu.

Program in Bioethics Expenses: Contact institution. *Financial support:* Career-related internships or fieldwork, Federal Work-Study, institutionally sponsored loans, and scholarships/grants available. *Degree program information:* Part-time programs available. Offers bioethics (MA). *Application fee:* $50. *Application Contact:* Graduate Coordinator, 274-274-4043, Fax: 274-274-4450, E-mail: graduate@augie.edu. *Chair,* Dr. Ann Pederson, 605-274-5489, E-mail: pederson@wise.augie.edu.

AUGUSTA STATE UNIVERSITY, Augusta, GA 30904-2200

General Information State-supported, coed, comprehensive institution. *Enrollment:* 72 full-time matriculated graduate/professional students, 251 part-time matriculated graduate/professional students. *Graduate faculty:* 57 full-time (33 women), 6 part-time/adjunct (2 women). *Tuition, area resident:* Full-time $2,320; part-time $97 per credit hour. *Required fees:* $175. *Graduate housing:* On-campus housing not available. *Student services:* Campus employment opportunities, career counseling, child daycare facilities, disabled student services, low-cost health insurance, teacher training. *Library facilities:* Reese Library plus 1 other. *Online resources:* library catalog, web page, access to other libraries' catalogs. *Collection:* 275,052 titles, 1,866 serial subscriptions, 7,185 audiovisual materials. *Research affiliation:* Veterans Administration Hospital (psychology).

Computer facilities: 160 computers available on campus for general student use. A campuswide network can be accessed from off campus. Internet access and online class registration are available. *Web address:* http://www.aug.edu/.

General Application Contact: Katherine Sweeney, Director of Admissions and Registrar, 706-737-1405, Fax: 706-667-4355, E-mail: ksweeney@aug.edu.

GRADUATE UNITS

Graduate Studies Students: 72 full-time, 251 part-time; includes 66 minority (52 African Americans, 9 Asian Americans or Pacific Islanders, 5 Hispanic Americans), 8 international. 240 applicants, 42% accepted, 86 enrolled. *Faculty:* 57 full-time (33 women), 6 part-time/adjunct (2 women). Expenses: Contact institution. *Financial support:* In 2001–02, 17 research assistantships with partial tuition reimbursements (averaging $2,400 per year) were awarded; career-related internships or fieldwork, Federal Work-Study, institutionally sponsored loans, and unspecified assistantships also available. Support available to part-time students. Financial award application deadline: 4/15; financial award applicants required to submit FAFSA. In 2001, 86 master's, 10 other advanced degrees awarded. *Degree program information:* Part-time and evening/weekend programs available. *Application deadline:* Applications are processed on a rolling basis. *Application fee:* $20. *Vice President for Academic Affairs,* Dr. Bill E. Bompart, 706-737-1422, Fax: 706-737-1585, E-mail: bbompart@aug.edu.

College of Arts and Sciences Students: 25 full-time (22 women), 20 part-time (12 women); includes 12 minority (8 African Americans, 2 Asian Americans or Pacific Islanders, 2 Hispanic Americans) Average age 27. 43 applicants, 77% accepted, 22 enrolled. *Faculty:* 8 full-time (4 women), 4 part-time/adjunct (2 women). Expenses: Contact institution. *Financial support:* In 2001–02, 17 research assistantships with partial tuition reimbursements (averaging $2,400 per year) were awarded; career-related internships or fieldwork, Federal Work-Study, and institutionally sponsored loans also available. Financial award application deadline: 4/15; financial award applicants required to submit FAFSA. In 2001, 9 degrees awarded. *Degree program information:* Part-time and evening/weekend programs available. Offers arts and sciences (MPA, MS); political science (MPA); psychology (MS). *Application deadline:* Applications are processed on a rolling basis. *Application fee:* $20. *Dean,* Dr. Elizabeth B. House, 706-737-1738, Fax: 706-737-1773, E-mail: ehouse@aug.edu.

College of Business Administration Students: 41 full-time (18 women), 94 part-time (45 women); includes 21 minority (12 African Americans, 6 Asian Americans or Pacific Islanders, 3 Hispanic Americans), 8 international. Average age 31. 57 applicants, 61% accepted, 31 enrolled. *Faculty:* 16 full-time (7 women). Expenses: Contact institution. *Financial support:* In 2001–02, research assistantships with partial tuition reimbursements (averaging $1,800 per year); Federal Work-Study and institutionally sponsored loans also available. Support available to part-time students. Financial award application deadline: 4/15; financial award applicants required to submit FAFSA. In 2001, 36 degrees awarded. *Degree program information:* Part-time and evening/weekend programs available. Offers business administration (MBA). *Application deadline:* For fall admission, 7/15 (priority date); for spring admission, 12/1 (priority date). Applications are processed on a rolling basis. *Application fee:* $20. *Application Contact:* Dr. Richard Bramblett, Director, MBA Office, 706-737-1562, Fax: 706-667-4064, E-mail: rbramble@aug.edu. *Dean,* Jackson K. Widener, 706-737-1418, Fax: 706-667-4064, E-mail: jwidener@aug.edu.

College of Education Students: 6 full-time, 137 part-time; includes 33 minority (32 African Americans, 1 Asian American or Pacific Islander) Average age 35. 140 applicants, 24% accepted, 33 enrolled. *Faculty:* 33 full-time (22 women), 2 part-time/adjunct (0 women). Expenses: Contact institution. *Financial support:* Career-related internships or fieldwork, Federal Work-Study, institutionally sponsored loans, and unspecified assistantships available. Support available to part-time students. Financial award application deadline: 4/15; financial award applicants required to submit FAFSA. In 2001, 41 master's, 10 other advanced degrees awarded. *Degree program information:* Part-time and evening/weekend programs available. Offers counseling/guidance (M Ed, Ed S); early childhood education (M Ed, Ed S); education (M Ed, Ed S); educational leadership (M Ed, Ed S); middle grades education (M Ed, Ed S); secondary education (M Ed, Ed S); special education (M Ed, Ed S). *Application deadline:* For fall admission, 7/16 (priority date). Applications are processed on a rolling basis. *Application fee:* $20. *Application Contact:* Alison S. Lindley, Secretary to the Dean, 706-737-1499, Fax: 706-667-4706, E-mail: alindley@aug.edu. *Dean,* Dr. Ronald Weber, 706-737-1499, Fax: 706-667-4706, E-mail: rweber@aug.edu.

AURORA UNIVERSITY, Aurora, IL 60506-4892

General Information Independent, coed, comprehensive institution. *Graduate housing:* Room and/or apartments available on a first-come, first-served basis to single students; on-campus housing not available to married students.

GRADUATE UNITS

College of Education *Degree program information:* Part-time and evening/weekend programs available. Offers curriculum and instruction (Ed D); education (MAT); education and administration (Ed D); educational leadership (MEL). Electronic applications accepted.

George Williams College *Degree program information:* Part-time and evening/weekend programs available.

School of Professional Studies *Degree program information:* Part-time and evening/weekend programs available. Offers administration of leisure services (MS); outdoor pursuits recreation administration (MS); outdoor therapeutic recreation administration (MS); therapeutic recreation administration (MS).

School of Social Work *Degree program information:* Part-time and evening/weekend programs available. Offers social work (MSW).

John and Judy Dunham School of Business *Degree program information:* Part-time and evening/weekend programs available. Offers business (MBA).

AUSTIN COLLEGE, Sherman, TX 75090-4400

General Information Independent-religious, coed, comprehensive institution. *Enrollment:* 34 full-time matriculated graduate/professional students (27 women). *Enrollment by degree level:* 34 master's. *Graduate faculty:* 5 full-time (3 women), 1 (woman) part-time/adjunct. *Tuition:* Full-time $18,845; part-time $2,375 per course. *Required fees:* $125. *Graduate housing:* Room and/or apartments available on a first-come, first-served basis to single students; on-campus housing not available to married students. Typical cost: $2,811 per year ($6,187 including board). Housing application deadline: 5/1. *Student services:* Campus employment opportunities, career counseling, free psychological counseling, teacher training. *Library* *facilities:* Abell Library. *Online resources:* library catalog, web page, access to other libraries' catalogs. *Collection:* 201,354 titles, 1,364 serial subscriptions, 6,913 audiovisual materials.

Computer facilities: 165 computers available on campus for general student use. A campuswide network can be accessed from student residence rooms and from off campus. Internet access is available. *Web address:* http://www.austinc.edu/.

General Application Contact: Dr. Barbara Sylvester, Director of Teaching Program, 903-813-2498, Fax: 903-813-2326, E-mail: bsylvester@austinc.edu.

GRADUATE UNITS

Program in Education Students: 34 full-time (27 women); includes 1 minority (Hispanic American) Average age 23. *Faculty:* 5 full-time (3 women), 1 (woman) part-time/adjunct. Expenses: Contact institution. *Financial support:* In 2001–02, 26 students received support. Career-related internships or fieldwork, Federal Work-Study, scholarships/grants, and unspecified assistantships available. Support available to part-time students. Financial award application deadline: 4/1; financial award applicants required to submit FAFSA. In 2001, 26 degrees awarded. *Degree program information:* Part-time programs available. Offers teacher education (MA). Applicants must meet Austin College's undergraduate curriculum requirements. *Application deadline:* For fall admission, 5/1 (priority date); for spring admission, 1/15 (priority date). Applications are processed on a rolling basis. *Application fee:* $35. Electronic applications accepted. *Director of Teaching Program,* Dr. Barbara Sylvester, 903-813-2498, Fax: 903-813-2326, E-mail: bsylvester@austinc.edu.

AUSTIN PEAY STATE UNIVERSITY, Clarksville, TN 37044-0001

General Information State-supported, coed, comprehensive institution. CGS member. *Graduate housing:* Rooms and/or apartments available on a first-come, first-served basis to single and married students. Housing application deadline: 5/1.

GRADUATE UNITS

Graduate School *Degree program information:* Part-time and evening/weekend programs available.

College of Arts and Sciences *Degree program information:* Part-time programs available. Offers arts and sciences (M Mu, MA, MA Ed, MS); biology (MS); clinical psychology (MA); communication arts (MA); English (MA, MA Ed); guidance and counseling (MS); music (M Mu); music education (M Mu); psychological science (MA); school psychology (MA).

College of Education *Degree program information:* Part-time and evening/weekend programs available. Offers administration and supervision (MA Ed, Ed S); counseling and guidance (Ed S); curriculum and instruction (MA Ed); education (MA, MA Ed, Ed S); elementary education (MA Ed, Ed S); reading (MA Ed); school psychology (Ed S); secondary education (Ed S); special education (MA).

College of Human Services and Nursing *Degree program information:* Part-time and evening/weekend programs available. Offers health and human performance (MA Ed, MS); human services and nursing (MA Ed, MS).

AUSTIN PRESBYTERIAN THEOLOGICAL SEMINARY, Austin, TX 78705-5797

General Information Independent-religious, coed, graduate-only institution. *Enrollment by degree level:* 77 first professional, 185 master's. *Graduate faculty:* 15 full-time (5 women), 9 part-time/adjunct (2 women). *Graduate housing:* Rooms and/or apartments available on a first-come, first-served basis to single students and available to married students. Housing application deadline: 7/31. *Student services:* Campus employment opportunities, career counseling, international student services. *Library facilities:* David and Jane Stitt Library. *Online resources:* library catalog, web page, access to other libraries' catalogs. *Collection:* 155,500 titles, 504 serial subscriptions, 5,921 audiovisual materials.

Computer facilities: 8 computers available on campus for general student use. A campuswide network can be accessed. Internet access and online class registration, Biblical Theological Research are available.

General Application Contact: Dr. E. Quinn Fox, Director of Vocations and Admissions, 512-472-6736, Fax: 512-479-0738.

GRADUATE UNITS

Graduate and Professional Programs Students: 159 full-time (74 women), 103 part-time (34 women). Average age 35. 82 applicants, 79% accepted. *Faculty:* 15 full-time (5 women), 9 part-time/adjunct (2 women). Expenses: Contact institution. *Financial support:* Fellowships, research assistantships, teaching assistantships, career-related internships or fieldwork, institutionally sponsored loans, and tutorships available. Support available to part-time students. Financial award application deadline: 6/15; financial award applicants required to submit FAFSA. *Degree program information:* Part-time programs available. Offers divinity (M Div); ministry (D Min); religious studies (MA). *Application deadline:* For fall admission, 7/15 (priority date); for spring admission, 12/15. Applications are processed on a rolling basis. *Application fee:* $25. *Application Contact:* Dr. E. Quinn Fox, Director of Vocations and Admissions, 512-472-6736, Fax: 512-479-0738. *Academic Dean,* Dr. J. Andrew Dearman, 512-472-6736.

AVE MARIA SCHOOL OF LAW, Ann Arbor, MI 48105-2550

General Information Independent-religious, coed, graduate-only institution.

AVERETT UNIVERSITY, Danville, VA 24541-3692

General Information Independent-religious, coed, comprehensive institution. *Enrollment:* 313 full-time matriculated graduate/professional students (196 women), 275 part-time matriculated graduate/professional students (119 women). *Enrollment by degree level:* 588 master's. *Graduate faculty:* 10 full-time (4 women), 31 part-time/adjunct (7 women). *Tuition:* Part-time $358 per credit. Tuition and fees vary according to campus/location and program. *Graduate housing:* On-campus housing not available. *Student services:* Campus employment opportunities, campus safety program, career counseling, disabled student services, exercise/wellness program, free psychological counseling, international student services, teacher training, writing training. *Library facilities:* Mary B. Blount Library. *Online resources:* library catalog, web page, access to other libraries' catalogs. *Collection:* 202,044 titles, 502 serial subscriptions, 19 audiovisual materials.

Computer facilities: 100 computers available on campus for general student use. A campuswide network can be accessed. Internet access is available. *Web address:* http://www.averett.edu/.

General Application Contact: Katherine Pappas-Smith, Marketing Manager, 434-791-5844, Fax: 434-791-5850, E-mail: kapappas@averett.edu.

GRADUATE UNITS

Division of Education Students: 11 full-time (8 women), 27 part-time (19 women); includes 7 minority (5 African Americans, 1 Asian American or Pacific Islander, 1 Native American) Average age 32. 16 applicants, 100% accepted, 13 enrolled. *Faculty:* 2 full-time (1 woman), 3 part-time/adjunct (all women). Expenses: Contact institution. *Financial support:* In 2001–02, 9 students received support. Career-related internships or fieldwork, Federal Work-Study, and scholarships/grants available. Support available to part-time students. Financial award application deadline: 8/25; financial award applicants required to submit FAFSA. In 2001, 6 degrees awarded. *Degree program information:* Part-time and evening/weekend programs available. Offers curriculum and instruction (M Ed); early childhood (M Ed); middle grades (M Ed); reading (M Ed); science (M Ed); special education (M Ed); teaching (MAT). *Application deadline:* For fall admission, 8/25 (priority date); for spring admission, 1/7. Applications are processed on a rolling basis. *Application fee:* $20. *Chair,* Dr. Pam Riedel, 434-791-5744, E-mail: priedel@averett.edu.

Program in Business Administration Students: 302 full-time (188 women), 248 part-time (100 women); includes 186 minority (159 African Americans, 14 Asian Americans or Pacific Islanders, 13 Hispanic Americans) Average age 36. 206 applicants, 67% accepted, 137 enrolled. *Faculty:* 6 full-time (2 women), 24 part-time/adjunct (2 women). Expenses: Contact institution. *Financial support:* In 2001–02, 94 students received support. Career-related internships or fieldwork, Federal Work-Study, and scholarships/grants available. Support available to part-time students. Financial award application deadline: 8/25; financial award applicants required to submit FAFSA. In 2001, 239 degrees awarded. *Degree program information:* Part-time and evening/weekend programs available. Postbaccalaureate distance learning degree programs offered (no on-campus study). Offers business administration (MBA). *Application deadline:* For fall admission, 8/25 (priority date); for spring admission, 1/7. Applications are processed on a rolling basis. *Application fee:* $20. *Application Contact:* Katherine Pappas-Smith, Marketing Manager, 434-791-5844, Fax: 434-791-5850, E-mail: kapappas@averett.edu. *Dean,* Dr. Peggy Wright, 434-791-5651, Fax: 434-799-0658, E-mail: pwright@averett.edu.

AVILA UNIVERSITY, Kansas City, MO 64145-1698

General Information Independent-religious, coed, comprehensive institution. *Enrollment:* 29 full-time matriculated graduate/professional students (21 women), 135 part-time matriculated graduate/professional students (87 women). *Enrollment by degree level:* 164 master's. *Graduate faculty:* 14 full-time (8 women), 20 part-time/adjunct (12 women). *Tuition:* Part-time $335 per credit hour. *Required fees:* $5 per credit hour. *Graduate housing:* Room and/or apartments available on a first-come, first-served basis to single students; on-campus housing not available to married students. Housing application deadline: 7/31. *Student services:* Campus employment opportunities, campus safety program, career counseling, child daycare facilities, disabled student services, exercise/wellness program, free psychological counseling, international student services, low-cost health insurance, multicultural affairs office. *Library facilities:* Hooley Bundshu Library. *Online resources:* library catalog, web page, access to other libraries' catalogs. *Collection:* 75,505 titles, 7,179 serial subscriptions, 3,094 audiovisual materials.

Computer facilities: 68 computers available on campus for general student use. A campuswide network can be accessed from student residence rooms and from off campus. Internet access is available. *Web address:* http://www.avila.edu/.

General Application Contact: Sr. Marie Joan Harris, Vice President for Academic Affairs, 816-501-3758, Fax: 816-501-2455, E-mail: harrismj@mail.avila.edu.

GRADUATE UNITS

Graduate Programs Students: 29 full-time (21 women), 135 part-time (87 women); includes 20 minority (13 African Americans, 1 Asian American or Pacific Islander, 6 Hispanic Americans) Average age 35. 100 applicants, 80% accepted. *Faculty:* 14 full-time (8 women), 20 part-time/adjunct (12 women). Expenses: Contact institution. *Financial support:* In 2001–02, 1 research assistantship was awarded; career-related internships or fieldwork also available. Support available to part-time students. Financial award applicants required to submit FAFSA. In 2001, 65 degrees awarded. *Degree program information:* Part-time and evening/weekend programs available. Offers business and economics (MBA); counseling psychology (MS); education (MS); psychology (MS). *Application deadline:* For fall admission, 4/30 (priority date); for spring admission, 11/30. Applications are processed on a rolling basis. Electronic applications accepted. *Application Contact:* Susan Randolph, Admissions Office, 816-501-3792, Fax: 816-501-2455, E-mail: randolphs@mail.avila.edu. *Vice President for Academic Affairs,* Sr. Marie Joan Harris, 816-501-3758, Fax: 816-501-2455, E-mail: harrismj@mail.avila.edu.

AZUSA PACIFIC UNIVERSITY, Azusa, CA 91702-7000

General Information Independent-religious, coed, comprehensive institution. CGS member. *Enrollment:* 1,302 full-time matriculated graduate/professional students (799 women), 1,879 part-time matriculated graduate/professional students (1,146 women). *Tuition:* Part-time $265 per unit. *Required fees:* $175 per semester. Tuition and fees vary according to degree level and program. *Graduate housing:* On-campus housing not available. *Student services:* Campus employment opportunities, campus safety program, career counseling, disabled student services, exercise/wellness program, free psychological counseling, international student services, low-cost health insurance, multicultural affairs office, teacher training. *Library facilities:* Marshburn Memorial Library plus 2 others. *Online resources:* library catalog, web page. *Collection:* 147,377 titles, 1,411 serial subscriptions.

Computer facilities: 300 computers available on campus for general student use. A campuswide network can be accessed from off campus. Internet access is available. *Web address:* http://www.apu.edu/.

General Application Contact: Norma Mocabee, Graduate Registrar, 626-812-3016, Fax: 626-815-4545, E-mail: nmocabee@apu.edu.

GRADUATE UNITS

College of Liberal Arts and Sciences Students: 96 full-time (40 women), 151 part-time (52 women); includes 66 minority (5 African Americans, 43 Asian Americans or Pacific Islanders, 16 Hispanic Americans, 2 Native Americans), 48 international. *Faculty:* 16 full-time (3 women), 20 part-time/adjunct (8 women). Expenses: Contact institution. *Financial support:* Teaching assistantships, career-related internships or fieldwork available. Support available to part-time students. In 2001, 203 degrees awarded. *Degree program information:* Part-time and evening/weekend programs available. Postbaccalaureate distance learning degree programs offered. Offers applied computer science and technology (MS); client/server technology (Certificate); computer information systems (Certificate); computer science (Certificate); end-user training and support (Certificate); liberal arts and sciences (MPT, MS, MSE, Certificate); physical therapy (MPT); software engineering (MSE); technical programming (Certificate); telecommunications (Certificate). *Application deadline:* Applications are processed on a rolling basis. *Application fee:* $45 ($65 for international students). *Application Contact:* Ann Grave, Director of Graduate Admissions, 626-812-3037, Fax: 626-969-7180. *Dean,* Dr. David Weeks, 626-969-3434 Ext. 3500, E-mail: dweeks@apu.edu.

Graduate School of Theology Students: 127 full-time (28 women), 172 part-time (61 women); includes 118 minority (16 African Americans, 42 Asian Americans or Pacific Islanders, 59 Hispanic Americans, 1 Native American), 28 international. Expenses: Contact institution. *Financial support:* Teaching assistantships, career-related internships or fieldwork available. Support available to part-time students. *Degree program information:* Part-time and evening/weekend programs available. Offers Christian education (MA); Christian nonprofit leadership (MA); pastoral studies (MAPS); religion (MA); theology (M Div, D Min). *Application fee:* $45 ($65 for international students). *Application Contact:* Deana Porterfield, Acting Director of Graduate Admissions, 626-812-3037, Fax: 626-969-7180, E-mail: dporterfield@apu.edu. *Interim Dean,* Dr. Lane Scott, 626-812-3049, E-mail: lscott@apu.edu.

School of Business and Management Students: 75 full-time (41 women), 96 part-time (41 women); includes 55 minority (16 African Americans, 13 Asian Americans or Pacific Islanders, 25 Hispanic Americans, 1 Native American), 31 international. Average age 32. Expenses: Contact institution. *Financial support:* Scholarships/grants available. *Degree program information:* Part-time and evening/weekend programs available. Offers business administration (MBA); human and organizational development (MA); human resource development (MHRD); international business (MBA); organizational management (MAOM); strategic management (MBA). *Application deadline:* For fall admission, 8/15 (priority date). Applications are processed on a rolling basis. *Application fee:* $45 ($65 for international students). *Dean,* Dr. Ilene Bezjian, 626-815-3090, Fax: 626-815-3802.

School of Education and Behavioral Studies Students: 558 full-time (351 women), 737 part-time (438 women). Expenses: Contact institution. *Financial support:* Career-related internships or fieldwork available. Support available to part-time students. Financial award applicants required to submit FAFSA. *Degree program information:* Part-time and evening/weekend programs available. Offers clinical psychology (MA, Psy D); college student affairs (M Ed); curriculum and instruction in a multicultural setting (MA); education and behavioral studies (M Ed, MA, MFT, Ed D, Psy D); educational leadership and administration (Ed D); educational technology (M Ed); family therapy (MFT); language development (MA); physical education (M Ed); pupil personnel services (MA); school administration (MA); social science leadership studies (MA); special education (MA); teaching (MA). *Application fee:* $45 ($65 for international students). *Dean,* Dr. Alice Watkins, 626-815-5348.

School of Music Students: 10 full-time (8 women), 13 part-time (9 women); includes 2 minority (1 African American, 1 Asian American or Pacific Islander), 9 international. Expenses:

Azusa Pacific University (continued)

Contact institution. *Financial support:* Career-related internships or fieldwork available. Support available to part-time students. Financial award applicants required to submit FAFSA. In 2001, 6 degrees awarded. *Degree program information:* Part-time and evening/weekend programs available. Postbaccalaureate distance learning degree programs offered (no on-campus study). Offers conducting (M Mus); education (M Mus). *Application fee:* $45 ($65 for international students). *Application Contact:* Graduate Admissions, 626-815-5470, Fax: 626-815-3867, E-mail: dfunderburk@apu.edu. *Dean,* Dr. Duane Funderburk, 626-812-3020, E-mail: dfunderburk@apu.edu.

School of Nursing Students: 14 full-time (7 women), 12 part-time (6 women). 47 applicants, 81% accepted. Expenses: Contact institution. *Financial support:* Teaching assistantships, scholarships/grants, traineeships, and unspecified assistantships available. Support available to part-time students. Financial award application deadline: 10/15. *Degree program information:* Part-time and evening/weekend programs available. Offers nursing (MSN). *Application deadline:* Applications are processed on a rolling basis. *Application fee:* $45 ($65 for international students). *Application Contact:* Barb Barthelmess, Graduate Program Secretary, 626-815-5391, Fax: 626-815-5414. *Dean,* Dr. Rose Liegler, 626-815-5384.

See in-depth description on page 749.

BABSON COLLEGE, Wellesley, Babson Park, MA 02457-0310

General Information Independent, coed, comprehensive institution. *Enrollment:* 463 full-time matriculated graduate/professional students, 1,146 part-time matriculated graduate/professional students. *Graduate faculty:* 161 full-time (53 women), 65 part-time/adjunct (21 women). *Tuition:* Full-time $25,710; part-time $776 per credit. *Graduate housing:* Rooms and/or apartments available on a first-come, first-served basis to single and married students. Typical cost: $11,150 per year ($15,730 including board) for single students. Housing application deadline: 6/20. *Student services:* Campus employment opportunities, campus safety program, career counseling, disabled student services, free psychological counseling, international student services, low-cost health insurance, writing training. *Library facilities:* Horn Library plus 1 other. *Online resources:* library catalog, web page, access to other libraries' catalogs. *Collection:* 129,401 titles, 1,224 serial subscriptions, 4,053 audiovisual materials.

Computer facilities: 350 computers available on campus for general student use. A campuswide network can be accessed from student residence rooms and from off campus. Internet access and online class registration are available. *Web address:* http://www.babson.edu/.

General Application Contact: Martha Snelling, Admissions Services Team, 781-239-4317, Fax: 781-239-4194, E-mail: mbaadmissions@babson.edu.

GRADUATE UNITS

F. W. Olin Graduate School of Business Students: 463 full-time, 1,146 part-time. Average age 28. 707 applicants, 41% accepted, 137 enrolled. *Faculty:* 161 full-time (53 women), 65 part-time/adjunct (21 women). Expenses: Contact institution. *Financial support:* In 2001–02, 238 students received support, including 40 fellowships with full tuition reimbursements available, 14 research assistantships with partial tuition reimbursements available; career-related internships or fieldwork, Federal Work-Study, scholarships/grants, tuition waivers (partial), and unspecified assistantships also available. Financial award application deadline: 4/15; financial award applicants required to submit FAFSA. In 2001, 436 degrees awarded. *Degree program information:* Part-time and evening/weekend programs available. Offers business administration (MBA); international business (MBA). *Application deadline:* For fall admission, 4/15 (priority date). Applications are processed on a rolling basis. *Application fee:* $50. Electronic applications accepted. *Application Contact:* Martha Snelling, Admission Services Team, 781-239-4317, Fax: 781-239-4194, E-mail: mbaadmission@babson.edu. *Dean,* Mark Rice, 781-239-4542, Fax: 781-239-4194.

BAKER COLLEGE CENTER FOR GRADUATE STUDIES, Flint, MI 48507-9843

General Information Independent, coed, graduate-only institution. *Enrollment by degree level:* 775 master's. *Graduate faculty:* 12 full-time, 97 part-time/adjunct. *Tuition:* Full-time $3,760; part-time $235 per quarter hour. *Required fees:* $235 per quarter hour. *Graduate housing:* On-campus housing not available. *Student services:* Campus employment opportunities, disabled student services, international student services. *Online resources:* library catalog, web page, access to other libraries' catalogs.

Computer facilities: A campuswide network can be accessed. Internet access and online class registration are available. *Web address:* http://online.baker.edu/.

General Application Contact: Chuck J. Gurden, Director of Graduate and On Line Admissions, 800-469-3165, Fax: 810-766-4399, E-mail: chuck@baker.edu.

GRADUATE UNITS

Programs in Business Students: 775 full-time (465 women); includes 99 minority (58 African Americans, 29 Asian Americans or Pacific Islanders, 10 Hispanic Americans, 2 Native Americans) Average age 38. 252 applicants, 73% accepted. *Faculty:* 12 full-time, 97 part-time/adjunct. Expenses: Contact institution. *Financial support:* In 2001–02, 201 students received support. Scholarships/grants available. Support available to part-time students. Financial award applicants required to submit FAFSA. In 2001, 172 degrees awarded. *Degree program information:* Part-time and evening/weekend programs available. Offers accounting (MBA); computer information systems (MBA); finance (MBA); general business (MBA); health and recreation services management (MBA); health care management (MBA); human resource management (MBA); industrial management (MBA); international business (MBA); leadership (MBA); marketing (MBA). MBA (health and recreation services management) enrollment limited to international students. *Application deadline:* For fall admission, 8/6 (priority date); for winter admission, 12/15 (priority date); for spring admission, 2/15 (priority date). Applications are processed on a rolling basis. *Application fee:* $25. *Application Contact:* Chuck J. Gurden, Director of Graduate and On Line Admissions, 800-469-3165, Fax: 810-766-4399, E-mail: chuck@baker.edu. *President,* Dr. Michael Heberling, 800-469-3165, Fax: 810-766-4399, E-mail: heberling@baker.edu.

BAKER UNIVERSITY, Baldwin City, KS 66006-0065

General Information Independent-religious, coed, comprehensive institution. *Enrollment:* 817 full-time matriculated graduate/professional students (396 women), 164 part-time matriculated graduate/professional students (108 women). *Enrollment by degree level:* 981 master's. *Graduate faculty:* 18 full-time (7 women), 276 part-time/adjunct (101 women). *Tuition:* Full-time $8,400; part-time $350 per credit hour. One-time fee: $105. Full-time tuition and fees vary according to program. *Graduate housing:* On-campus housing not available. *Student services:* Campus safety program, disabled student services, international student services. *Library facilities:* Collins Library. *Online resources:* library catalog, web page, access to other libraries' catalogs. *Collection:* 84,114 titles, 507 serial subscriptions, 1,139 audiovisual materials.

Computer facilities: 151 computers available on campus for general student use. A campuswide network can be accessed from student residence rooms and from off campus. Internet access is available. *Web address:* http://www.bakeru.edu/.

General Application Contact: Dr. Donald B. Clardy, Dean, School of Professional and Graduate Studies, 913-491-4432, Fax: 913-491-0470.

GRADUATE UNITS

School of Professional and Graduate Studies Students: 817 full-time (396 women), 164 part-time (108 women); includes 147 minority (79 African Americans, 30 Asian Americans or Pacific Islanders, 30 Hispanic Americans, 8 Native Americans), 1 international. Average age 33. 290 applicants, 98% accepted, 239 enrolled. *Faculty:* 18 full-time (7 women), 276 part-time/adjunct (101 women). Expenses: Contact institution. *Financial support:* In 2001–02, 559 students received support. Applicants required to submit FAFSA. In 2001, 463 degrees awarded. *Degree program information:* Part-time and evening/weekend programs available. Offers business (MBA, MSM); education (MA Ed, MASL); liberal arts (MLA). *Application deadline:* Applications are processed on a rolling basis. *Application fee:* $20. *Application Contact:* Kelly Belk, Director of Marketing, 913-491-432, Fax: 913-491-0470. *Dean,* Dr. Donald B. Clardy, 913-491-4432, Fax: 913-491-0470.

BALDWIN-WALLACE COLLEGE, Berea, OH 44017-2088

General Information Independent-religious, coed, comprehensive institution. *Enrollment:* 214 full-time matriculated graduate/professional students (125 women), 677 part-time matriculated graduate/professional students (476 women). *Enrollment by degree level:* 891 master's. *Graduate faculty:* 48 full-time (12 women), 43 part-time/adjunct (14 women). *Tuition:* Full-time $9,960; part-time $415 per semester hour. *Graduate housing:* Room and/or apartments available to single students; on-campus housing not available to married students. *Student services:* Campus employment opportunities, career counseling, child daycare facilities, disabled student services, exercise/wellness program, free psychological counseling, international student services, low-cost health insurance, multicultural affairs office, teacher training, writing training. *Library facilities:* Ritter Library plus 2 others. *Online resources:* library catalog, web page, access to other libraries' catalogs. *Collection:* 200,000 titles, 12,960 serial subscriptions.

Computer facilities: 386 computers available on campus for general student use. A campuswide network can be accessed from student residence rooms. Internet access is available. *Web address:* http://www.bw.edu/.

General Application Contact: Winifred W. Gerhardt, Director of Admission for the Evening and Weekend College, 440-826-2222, Fax: 440-826-3830, E-mail: admit@bw.edu.

GRADUATE UNITS

Graduate Programs Students: 214 full-time (125 women), 677 part-time (476 women); includes 55 minority (37 African Americans, 9 Asian Americans or Pacific Islanders, 9 Hispanic Americans), 72 international. Average age 33. 351 applicants, 85% accepted, 229 enrolled. *Faculty:* 48 full-time (12 women), 43 part-time/adjunct (14 women). Expenses: Contact institution. *Financial support:* Career-related internships or fieldwork available. Support available to part-time students. Financial award applicants required to submit FAFSA. In 2001, 191 degrees awarded. *Degree program information:* Part-time and evening/weekend programs available. *Application deadline:* Applications are processed on a rolling basis. *Application fee:* $15. Electronic applications accepted. *Application Contact:* Winifred W. Gerhardt, Director of Admission for the Evening and Weekend College, 440-826-2222, Fax: 440-826-3830, E-mail: admit@bw.edu.

Division of Business Administration Students: 155 full-time (75 women), 265 part-time (138 women); includes 29 minority (18 African Americans, 6 Asian Americans or Pacific Islanders, 5 Hispanic Americans), 71 international. Average age 32. 199 applicants, 82% accepted, 116 enrolled. *Faculty:* 30 full-time (7 women), 25 part-time/adjunct (7 women). Expenses: Contact institution. *Financial support:* Career-related internships or fieldwork available. Support available to part-time students. Financial award applicants required to submit FAFSA. In 2001, 148 degrees awarded. *Degree program information:* Part-time and evening/weekend programs available. Offers accounting (MBA); business administration (MBA); entrepreneurship (MBA); executive management (MBA); health care executive management (MBA); human resources (MBA); international management (MBA). *Application deadline:* For fall admission, 7/25 (priority date); for spring admission, 12/15 (priority date). Applications are processed on a rolling basis. *Application fee:* $15. Electronic applications accepted. *Application Contact:* Winifred W. Gerhardt, Director of Admission for the Evening and Weekend College, 440-826-2222, Fax: 440-826-3830, E-mail: admit@bw.edu. *Chairperson, Business Administration,* Dr. Peter Rea, 440-826-3559, Fax: 440-826-3868, E-mail: prea@bw.edu.

Division of Education Students: 59 full-time (50 women), 410 part-time (338 women); includes 26 minority (19 African Americans, 3 Asian Americans or Pacific Islanders, 4 Hispanic Americans) Average age 34. 152 applicants, 88% accepted, 113 enrolled. *Faculty:* 18 full-time (5 women), 18 part-time/adjunct (7 women). Expenses: Contact institution. *Financial support:* Career-related internships or fieldwork available. Financial award applicants required to submit FAFSA. In 2001, 43 degrees awarded. *Degree program information:* Part-time and evening/weekend programs available. Offers educational technology (MA Ed); mild/moderate educational needs (MA Ed); pre-administration (MA Ed); reading (MA Ed). *Application deadline:* For fall admission, 8/15 (priority date); for winter admission, 12/15 (priority date). Applications are processed on a rolling basis. *Application fee:* $15. *Application Contact:* Winifred W. Gerhardt, Director of Admission for the Evening and Weekend College, 440-826-2222, Fax: 440-826-3830, E-mail: admit@bw.edu. *Chairperson and Director of MA Ed,* Dr. Patrick F. Cosiano, 440-826-2168, Fax: 440-826-3779, E-mail: pcosiano@bw.edu.

BALL STATE UNIVERSITY, Muncie, IN 47306-1099

General Information State-supported, coed, university. CGS member. *Enrollment:* 881 full-time matriculated graduate/professional students (491 women), 1,234 part-time matriculated graduate/professional students (760 women). *Enrollment by degree level:* 1,822 master's, 271 doctoral, 22 other advanced degrees. *Graduate faculty:* 703. Tuition, state resident: full-time $4,068; part-time $2,542. Tuition, nonresident: full-time $10,944; part-time $6,462. *Required fees:* $1,000; $500 per term. *Graduate housing:* Rooms and/or apartments available on a first-come, first-served basis to single and married students. Typical cost: $6,678 (including board) for single students. Room and board charges vary according to board plan and housing facility selected. Housing application deadline: 3/1. *Student services:* Campus employment opportunities, campus safety program, career counseling, child daycare facilities, disabled student services, exercise/wellness program, free psychological counseling, international student services, low-cost health insurance, multicultural affairs office, teacher training. *Library facilities:* Bracken Library plus 3 others. *Online resources:* library catalog, web page, access to other libraries' catalogs. *Collection:* 1.1 million titles, 4,091 serial subscriptions, 501,621 audiovisual materials.

Computer facilities: 1,500 computers available on campus for general student use. A campuswide network can be accessed from student residence rooms and from off campus. *Web address:* http://www.bsu.edu/.

General Application Contact: Dr. Deborah W. Balogh, Dean, 765-285-1300, Fax: 765-285-1328, E-mail: dbalogh@bsu.edu.

GRADUATE UNITS

Graduate School Students: 881 full-time (491 women), 1,234 part-time (760 women); includes 119 minority (82 African Americans, 12 Asian Americans or Pacific Islanders, 18 Hispanic Americans, 7 Native Americans), 251 international. 1,553 applicants, 74% accepted, 637 enrolled. *Faculty:* 703. Expenses: Contact institution. *Financial support:* In 2001–02, 8 fellowships with full tuition reimbursements, 792 teaching assistantships with full tuition reimbursements were awarded. Research assistantships with full tuition reimbursements, career-related internships or fieldwork, Federal Work-Study, tuition waivers (partial), and unspecified assistantships also available. Support available to part-time students. Financial award application deadline: 3/1. In 2001, 797 master's, 45 doctorates, 8 other advanced degrees awarded. *Degree program information:* Part-time and evening/weekend programs available. Postbaccalaureate distance learning degree programs offered. *Application deadline:* Applications are processed on a rolling basis. *Application fee:* $25 ($35 for international students). Electronic applications accepted. *Dean,* Dr. Deborah W. Balogh, 765-285-1300, Fax: 765-285-1328, E-mail: dbalogh@bsu.edu.

College of Applied Science and Technology Students: 105 full-time (68 women), 290 part-time (225 women); includes 20 minority (11 African Americans, 3 Asian Americans or Pacific Islanders, 5 Hispanic Americans, 1 Native American) Average age 29. 219 applicants, 69% accepted. *Faculty:* 85. Expenses: Contact institution. *Financial support:* In 2001–02, 87 teaching assistantships with full tuition reimbursements were awarded; fellowships with full tuition reimbursements, research assistantships with full tuition reimbursements, career-related internships or fieldwork and tuition waivers (full) also available. Financial award application deadline: 3/1. In 2001, 100 master's, 2 doctorates awarded. *Degree program information:* Part-time programs available. Offers applied gerontology (MA); applied science and technology (MA, MAE, MS, PhD); family and consumer sciences (MA, MAE, MS); human bioenergetics (PhD); industry and technology (MA, MAE); nursing (MS);

physical education (MA, MAE, PhD); wellness management (MA, MS). *Application fee:* $25 ($35 for international students). *Dean,* Dr. Donald Smith, 765-285-5818, Fax: 765-285-1071, E-mail: dsmith@bsu.edu.

College of Architecture and Planning Students: 67 full-time (32 women), 15 part-time (8 women); includes 3 African Americans, 1 Asian American or Pacific Islander Average age 28. 75 applicants, 76% accepted. *Faculty:* 45. Expenses: Contact institution. *Financial support:* In 2001–02, 51 teaching assistantships with full tuition reimbursements were awarded; fellowships with full tuition reimbursements, research assistantships with full tuition reimbursements, career-related internships or fieldwork also available. Support available to part-time students. Financial award application deadline: 3/1. In 2001, 23 degrees awarded. *Degree program information:* Part-time programs available. Offers architecture (M Arch); architecture and planning (M Arch, MLA, MS, MURP); historic preservation (M Arch, MS); landscape architecture (MLA); urban planning (MURP). *Application fee:* $25 ($35 for international students). *Dean,* Dr. Joseph Bilello, 765-285-5861, Fax: 765-285-3726.

College of Business Students: 41 full-time (22 women), 149 part-time (51 women). Average age 29. 113 applicants, 75% accepted. *Faculty:* 66. Expenses: Contact institution. *Financial support:* In 2001–02, 39 teaching assistantships with full tuition reimbursements (averaging $7,031 per year) were awarded; unspecified assistantships also available. Support available to part-time students. Financial award application deadline: 3/1. In 2001, 65 degrees awarded. *Degree program information:* Part-time and evening/weekend programs available. Offers accounting (MS); business (MA, MAE, MBA, MS); business administration (MBA); business information technology (MAE). *Application fee:* $25 ($35 for international students). *Application Contact:* Tamara Estep, Graduate Coordinator, 765-285-1931, Fax: 765-285-8818, E-mail: testep@bsu.edu. *Dean,* Dr. Lynne D. Richardson, 765-285-8192, Fax: 765-285-5117.

College of Communication, Information, and Media Students: 146 full-time (57 women), 110 part-time (54 women); includes 14 minority (8 African Americans, 2 Asian Americans or Pacific Islanders, 3 Hispanic Americans, 1 Native American), 27 international. Average age 27. 205 applicants, 80% accepted. *Faculty:* 19. Expenses: Contact institution. *Financial support:* In 2001–02, 65 research assistantships with full tuition reimbursements (averaging $6,727 per year) were awarded; teaching assistantships with full tuition reimbursements, career-related internships or fieldwork also available. Financial award application deadline: 3/1. In 2001, 127 degrees awarded. Offers communication, information, and media (MA, MS); information and communication sciences (MS); journalism (MA); public relations (MA); speech, public address, forensics, and rhetoric (MA). *Application fee:* $25 ($35 for international students). *Dean,* Dr. Scott Olson, 765-285-6000, Fax: 765-285-6002, E-mail: solson@bsu.edu.

College of Fine Arts Students: 38 full-time (16 women), 42 part-time (24 women); includes 3 minority (2 African Americans, 1 Native American), 15 international. Average age 27. 55 applicants, 80% accepted. *Faculty:* 76. Expenses: Contact institution. *Financial support:* In 2001–02, 51 teaching assistantships with full tuition reimbursements were awarded; fellowships with full tuition reimbursements Support available to part-time students. Financial award application deadline: 3/1. In 2001, 21 master's, 5 doctorates awarded. *Degree program information:* Part-time programs available. Offers art (MA); art education (MA, MAE); fine arts (MA, MAE, MM, DA); music education (MA, MM, DA). *Application fee:* $25 ($35 for international students). *Interim Dean,* Dr. Robert Kvam, 765-285-5495, Fax: 765-285-3790, E-mail: rkvam@bsu.edu.

College of Sciences and Humanities Students: 276 full-time (155 women), 233 part-time (119 women); includes 28 minority (19 African Americans, 4 Asian Americans or Pacific Islanders, 3 Hispanic Americans, 2 Native Americans), 120 international. Average age 27. 518 applicants, 55% accepted. *Faculty:* 279. Expenses: Contact institution. *Financial support:* In 2001–02, 215 teaching assistantships with full tuition reimbursements were awarded; research assistantships with full tuition reimbursements, career-related internships or fieldwork and Federal Work-Study also available. Support available to part-time students. Financial award application deadline: 3/1. In 2001, 185 master's, 8 doctorates awarded. *Degree program information:* Part-time programs available. Offers actuarial science (MA); anthropology (MA); applied linguistics (PhD); biology (MA, MAE, MS); biology education (Ed D); chemistry (MA, MS); clinical psychology (MA); cognitive and social processes (MA); computer science (MA, MS); earth sciences (MA); English (MA, PhD); geology (MA, MS); health education (MA, MAE); history (MA); linguistics (MA, PhD); linguistics and teaching English to speakers of other languages (MA); mathematical statistics (MA); mathematics (MA, MAE, MS); mathematics education (MAE); natural resources (MA, MS); physics (MA, MS); physiology (MA, MS); political science (MA); public administration (MPA); sciences and humanities (MA, MAE, MPA, MS, Au D, Ed D, PhD); social sciences (MA); sociology (MA); speech pathology and audiology (MA, Au D); teaching English to speakers of other languages (MA). *Application fee:* $25 ($35 for international students). *Dean,* Dr. Ronald L. Johnstone, 765-285-1042, Fax: 765-285-8980, E-mail: rjohnstone@bsu.edu.

Teachers College Students: 208 full-time (141 women), 395 part-time (279 women); includes 36 minority (29 African Americans, 1 Asian American or Pacific Islander, 5 Hispanic Americans, 1 Native American), 54 international. 479 applicants, 62% accepted. *Faculty:* 106. Expenses: Contact institution. *Financial support:* In 2001–02, 144 teaching assistantships with full tuition reimbursements were awarded; research assistantships with full tuition reimbursements, career-related internships or fieldwork and Federal Work-Study also available. Support available to part-time students. Financial award application deadline: 3/1. In 2001, 276 master's, 32 doctorates, 8 other advanced degrees awarded. *Degree program information:* Part-time and evening/weekend programs available. Offers adult and community education (MA); adult education (MA, Ed D); adult, community, and higher education (Ed D); counseling psychology (MA, PhD); curriculum (MAE, Ed S); curriculum and instruction (MAE, Ed S); early childhood education (MAE, Ed D); education (MA, MAE, Ed D, PhD, Ed S); educational administration (MAE, Ed D); educational psychology (MA, PhD, Ed S); educational studies (MAE); elementary education (MAE, Ed D, PhD); executive development (MA); junior high/middle school education (MAE); reading education (MAE, Ed D); school psychology (MA, PhD, Ed S); school superintendency (Ed S); secondary education (MA); social psychology (MA); special education (MA, MAE, Ed D, Ed S); student affairs administration in higher education (MA); teaching in elementary education (MAE). *Application fee:* $25 ($35 for international students). *Dean,* Dr. Roy Weaver, 765-285-5251, Fax: 765-285-5455, E-mail: rweaver@bsu.edu.

BALTIMORE HEBREW UNIVERSITY, Baltimore, MD 21215-3996

General Information Independent, coed, comprehensive institution. *Enrollment:* 11 full-time matriculated graduate/professional students (9 women), 53 part-time matriculated graduate/professional students (37 women). *Enrollment by degree level:* 50 master's, 14 doctoral. *Graduate faculty:* 8 full-time (2 women), 3 part-time/adjunct (2 women). *Tuition:* Part-time $900 per course. *Graduate housing:* On-campus housing not available. *Student services:* Disabled student services, teacher training. *Library facilities:* Joseph Meyerhoff Library. *Collection:* 100,000 titles, 250 serial subscriptions, 30,000 audiovisual materials. *Research affiliation:* American Schools of Oriental Research (archaeology).

Computer facilities: 15 computers available on campus for general student use. Internet access is available. *Web address:* http://www.bhu.edu/.

General Application Contact: Essie Keyser, Director of Admissions, 410-578-6967, Fax: 410-578-6940, E-mail: keyser@bhu.edu.

GRADUATE UNITS

Peggy Meyerhoff Pearlstone School of Graduate Studies Students: 11 full-time (9 women), 53 part-time (37 women). Average age 35. 19 applicants, 95% accepted, 12 enrolled. *Faculty:* 8 full-time (2 women), 3 part-time/adjunct (2 women). Expenses: Contact institution. *Financial support:* In 2001–02, 5 students received support; fellowships with partial tuition reimbursements available, career-related internships or fieldwork, scholarships/grants, and tuition waivers (partial) available. Support available to part-time students. Financial award application deadline: 9/15; financial award applicants required to submit FAFSA. In 2001, 15 master's awarded. *Degree program information:* Part-time programs available. Offers Jewish communal service (MAJCS); Jewish education (MAJE); Jewish studies (MA, PhD). *Application deadline:* For fall admission, 7/15; for spring admission, 11/15. Applications are processed on a rolling basis. *Application fee:* $50. *Application Contact:* Essie Keyser, Director of Admissions, 410-578-6967, Fax: 410-578-6940, E-mail: keyser@bhu.edu. *Dean,* Dr. Barry M. Gittlen, 410-578-6900, Fax: 410-578-6940, E-mail: gittlen@bhu.edu.

BANGOR THEOLOGICAL SEMINARY, Bangor, ME 04401-4699

General Information Independent-religious, coed, graduate-only institution. *Graduate housing:* Rooms and/or apartments available on a first-come, first-served basis to single and married students. Housing application deadline: 5/1.

GRADUATE UNITS

Professional Program *Degree program information:* Part-time programs available. Offers theology (M Div, MA, MTS, D Min). M Div not offered at Portland, ME campus.

BANK STREET COLLEGE OF EDUCATION, New York, NY 10025-1120

General Information Independent, coed, primarily women, graduate-only institution. *Enrollment by degree level:* 923 master's. *Graduate faculty:* 75 full-time (66 women), 42 part-time/adjunct (36 women). *Tuition:* Part-time $690 per credit. One-time fee: $250 full-time. *Graduate housing:* On-campus housing not available. *Student services:* Campus employment opportunities, campus safety program, career counseling, child daycare facilities, international student services, teacher training, writing training. *Library facilities:* Bank Street College Library. *Online resources:* library catalog, web page, access to other libraries' catalogs. *Collection:* 123,215 titles, 79,510 serial subscriptions, 823 audiovisual materials. *Research affiliation:* Educational Development Corporation (education).

Computer facilities: 52 computers available on campus for general student use. A campuswide network can be accessed from off campus. Internet access is available. *Web address:* http://www.bankstreet.edu/.

General Application Contact: Ann K. Morgan, Director of Graduate Admissions, 212-875-4404, Fax: 212-875-4678, E-mail: gradcourses@bankstreet.edu.

GRADUATE UNITS

Graduate School Students: 358 full-time (318 women), 565 part-time (485 women); includes 250 minority (139 African Americans, 30 Asian Americans or Pacific Islanders, 78 Hispanic Americans, 3 Native Americans), 12 international. Average age 31. 670 applicants, 77% accepted, 400 enrolled. *Faculty:* 75 full-time (66 women), 42 part-time/adjunct (36 women). Expenses: Contact institution. *Financial support:* In 2001–02, 460 students received support. Career-related internships or fieldwork, Federal Work-Study, scholarships/grants, and unspecified assistantships available. Support available to part-time students. Financial award application deadline: 4/15; financial award applicants required to submit FAFSA. In 2001, 268 degrees awarded. Offers advanced literacy specialization (Ed M); child life (MS); curriculum and instruction (Ed M, MS Ed); early child leadership (MS Ed); early childhood and elementary education (MS Ed); early childhood bilingual education (MS Ed); early childhood bilingual general and special education (MS Ed); early childhood education (MS Ed); early childhood general and special education (MS Ed); early childhood special professional education (Ed M, MS Ed); education (Ed M, MS, MS Ed); educational leadership (Ed M, MS Ed); elementary bilingual general education (MS Ed); elementary education (MS Ed); elementary general and special education (MS Ed); elementary special education professional certification (Ed M, MS Ed); elementary, bilingual and special education (MS Ed); infant and parent development and early intervention (MS Ed); leadership in mathematics education (MS Ed); leadership in museum education (MS Ed); middle school bilingual general and special education (MS Ed); middle school bilingual general education (MS Ed); middle school education (MS Ed); middle school general and special education (MS Ed); middle school special education professional certificate (Ed M); middle school special education professional certification (MS Ed); museum education (MS Ed); museum education: elementary education certification (MS Ed); museum education: middle school certification (MS Ed); reading and literacy (MS Ed); supervision and administration in the visual arts (MS Ed); teaching literacy (MS Ed); teaching literacy and elementary education dual certification (MS Ed). *Application deadline:* For fall admission, 3/1 (priority date); for spring admission, 11/1 (priority date). Applications are processed on a rolling basis. *Application fee:* $50. *Application Contact:* Ann K. Morgan, Director of Graduate Admissions, 212-875-4404, Fax: 212-875-4678, E-mail: gradcourses@bankstreet.edu. *Dean,* Dr. Jon Snyder, 212-875-4466, Fax: 212-875-4753, E-mail: jsnyder@bankstreet.edu.

BAPTIST BIBLE COLLEGE, Springfield, MO 65803-3498

General Information Independent-religious, coed, comprehensive institution. *Enrollment:* 21 full-time matriculated graduate/professional students (2 women), 32 part-time matriculated graduate/professional students (7 women). *Graduate faculty:* 5 full-time (0 women), 4 part-time/adjunct (0 women). *Tuition:* Part-time $165 per credit hour. *Required fees:* $150 per semester. *Graduate housing:* Rooms and/or apartments available to single and married students. *Student services:* Campus employment opportunities, campus safety program, career counseling, child daycare facilities, free psychological counseling, international student services, low-cost health insurance. *Collection:* 36,844 titles, 226 serial subscriptions.

Computer facilities: 50 computers available on campus for general student use. *Web address:* http://www.bbcnet.edu/bbgst.html.

General Application Contact: Linda McElroy, Graduate School Secretary, 417-268-6054, Fax: 417-268-6694, E-mail: lmcelroy@bbcnet.edu.

GRADUATE UNITS

Graduate School of Theology Students: 21 full-time (2 women), 32 part-time (7 women), 3 international. 32 applicants, 91% accepted. *Faculty:* 5 full-time (0 women), 4 part-time/adjunct (0 women). Expenses: Contact institution. *Financial support:* In 2001–02, 5 students received support, including 1 research assistantship with full tuition reimbursement available (averaging $3,250 per year); career-related internships or fieldwork also available. Financial award application deadline: 3/6. In 2001, 8 degrees awarded. *Degree program information:* Part-time programs available. Offers biblical counseling (MA); biblical studies (MA); church ministries (MA); intercultural studies (MA); theology (M Div). *Application deadline:* For fall admission, 8/1 (priority date); for spring admission, 1/14. *Application fee:* $40. Electronic applications accepted. *Application Contact:* Linda McElroy, Graduate School Secretary, 417-268-6054, Fax: 417-268-6694, E-mail: lmcelroy@bbcnet.edu. *Dean,* Dr. Gregory T. Christopher, 417-268-6054, Fax: 417-268-6694, E-mail: gchristopher@bbcnet.edu.

BAPTIST BIBLE COLLEGE OF PENNSYLVANIA, Clarks Summit, PA 18411-1297

General Information Independent-religious, coed, comprehensive institution. *Enrollment:* 240 matriculated graduate/professional students. *Graduate faculty:* 11 full-time, 16 part-time/adjunct. *Tuition:* Full-time $2,680; part-time $1,608 per year. *Graduate housing:* Rooms and/or apartments guaranteed to single and married students. *Student services:* Campus employment opportunities, campus safety program, career counseling, free psychological counseling, international student services. *Library facilities:* Murphy Memorial Library plus 1 other. *Collection:* 104,534 titles, 502 serial subscriptions, 27,088 audiovisual materials.

Computer facilities: 25 computers available on campus for general student use. A campuswide network can be accessed from student residence rooms. Internet access is available. *Web address:* http://www.bbc.edu/.

General Application Contact: Steve Bowers, Director of Admissions, 570-586-2400 Ext. 9345, Fax: 570-586-1753, E-mail: gradadmissions@bbc.edu.

GRADUATE UNITS

Baptist Bible Seminary Students: 170. *Faculty:* 9 full-time (0 women), 5 part-time/adjunct (0 women). Expenses: Contact institution. *Financial support:* Career-related internships or fieldwork available. Support available to part-time students. In 2001, 22 master's, 3 doctorates awarded. *Degree program information:* Part-time programs available. Postbaccalaureate distance learning degree programs offered (minimal on-campus study). Offers ministry (M Min, D Min); theology (M Div, Th M, PhD). *Application deadline:* Applications are processed on a rolling basis. *Application fee:* $25. Electronic applications accepted. *Application Contact:* Paul

Baptist Bible College of Pennsylvania (continued)
Golden, Director of Admissions and Recruitment, 570-586-9396, Fax: 570-585-4057, E-mail: pgolden@bbc.edu. *Seminary Dean,* Dr. Howard Bixby, 570-586-2400 Ext. 9230, E-mail: hbixby@bbc.edu.

Graduate School Students: 70 full-time (58 women); includes 6 minority (3 African Americans, 2 Asian Americans or Pacific Islanders, 1 Hispanic American) Average age 33. 78 applicants, 100% accepted, 70 enrolled. *Faculty:* 2 full-time, 11 part-time/adjunct. Expenses: Contact institution. *Financial support:* In 2001–02, 43 students received support. Scholarships/grants available. In 2001, 13 degrees awarded. *Degree program information:* Part-time and evening/weekend programs available. Offers Christian school education (MS); counseling (MS). *Application deadline:* Applications are processed on a rolling basis. *Application fee:* $30. *Application Contact:* Steve Bowers, Director of Admissions, 570-586-2400 Ext. 9345, Fax: 570-586-1753, E-mail: gradadmissions@bbc.edu. *Director of Graduate Studies,* Dr. Hubert Hartzler, 570-586-2400 Ext. 9226.

BAPTIST MISSIONARY ASSOCIATION THEOLOGICAL SEMINARY, Jacksonville, TX 75766-5407

General Information Independent-religious, coed, primarily men, comprehensive institution. *Graduate housing:* Rooms and/or apartments available on a first-come, first-served basis to single students and available to married students. Housing application deadline: 6/1.

GRADUATE UNITS

Graduate and Professional Programs *Degree program information:* Part-time programs available. Offers theology (M Div, MAR).

BAPTIST THEOLOGICAL SEMINARY AT RICHMOND, Richmond, VA 23227

General Information Independent-religious, coed, graduate-only institution. *Enrollment by degree level:* 159 first professional, 43 doctoral. *Graduate faculty:* 14 full-time (3 women), 14 part-time/adjunct (2 women). *Tuition:* Full-time $5,800. Full-time tuition and fees vary according to degree level and program. *Graduate housing:* Rooms and/or apartments available on a first-come, first-served basis to single and married students. Typical cost: $1,980 per year ($4,680 including board) for single students; $3,960 per year ($6,910 including board) for married students. Room and board charges vary according to board plan, campus/location and housing facility selected. Housing application deadline: 6/1. *Student services:* Campus employment opportunities, campus safety program, career counseling, exercise/wellness program, international student services, low-cost health insurance. *Library facilities:* Morton at Union Theological Seminary-PSCE. *Online resources:* library catalog, web page, access to other libraries' catalogs. *Collection:* 309,610 titles, 1,358 serial subscriptions, 34,252 audiovisual materials.

Computer facilities: 9 computers available on campus for general student use. *Web address:* http://www.btsr.edu/.

General Application Contact: Rob Fox, Director of Prospective Student Services, 804-355-8135, Fax: 804-355-8182, E-mail: rfox@btsr.edu.

GRADUATE UNITS

Graduate and Professional Program Students: 159 full-time (65 women), 43 part-time (22 women); includes 6 African Americans, 1 Asian American or Pacific Islander, 3 Hispanic Americans, 4 international. Average age 39. 100 applicants, 60% accepted, 50 enrolled. *Faculty:* 14 full-time (3 women), 14 part-time/adjunct (2 women). Expenses: Contact institution. *Financial support:* In 2001–02, 83 students received support, including 15 teaching assistantships (averaging $1,000 per year); scholarships/grants also available. Financial award application deadline: 2/1. In 2001, 35 first professional degrees, 10 doctorates awarded. *Degree program information:* Part-time programs available. Postbaccalaureate distance learning degree programs offered (minimal on-campus study). Offers Christian education (M Div); church music (M Div); ministry (M Div); theology (M Div). *Application deadline:* For fall admission, 8/1 (priority date); for winter admission, 12/1 (priority date); for spring admission, 1/1 (priority date). Applications are processed on a rolling basis. *Application fee:* $35. *Application Contact:* Rob Fox, Director of Prospective Student Services, 804-355-8135, Fax: 804-355-8182, E-mail: rfox@btsr.edu.

BARD COLLEGE, Annandale-on-Hudson, NY 12504

General Information Independent, coed, comprehensive institution. *Enrollment:* 117 full-time matriculated graduate/professional students (58 women). *Enrollment by degree level:* 117 master's. *Graduate faculty:* 12 full-time (6 women), 31 part-time/adjunct (12 women). *Tuition:* Full-time $11,648. Full-time tuition and fees vary according to program. *Graduate housing:* Room and/or apartments available on a first-come, first-served basis to single students; on-campus housing not available to married students. *Student services:* Low-cost health insurance. *Library facilities:* Stevenson Library plus 3 others. *Online resources:* library catalog, web page. *Collection:* 275,000 titles, 1,400 serial subscriptions, 5,800 audiovisual materials.

Computer facilities: 150 computers available on campus for general student use. A campuswide network can be accessed from student residence rooms and from off campus. Internet access is available. *Web address:* http://www.bard.edu/.

General Application Contact: Robert L. Martin, Dean of Graduate Studies and Associate Dean of the College, 845-758-7419, Fax: 845-758-7043, E-mail: martin@bard.edu.

GRADUATE UNITS

Bard Center for Environmental Policy Students: 10 full-time. Average age 26. *Faculty:* 3 full-time (1 woman), 19 part-time/adjunct (10 women). Expenses: Contact institution. *Financial support:* In 2001–02, 10 students received support, including 6 fellowships (averaging $8,000 per year); scholarships/grants also available. Financial award application deadline: 2/15; financial award applicants required to submit FAFSA. *Degree program information:* Part-time programs available. Offers environmental policy (MS, Professional Certificate). *Application deadline:* For fall admission, 2/15 (priority date). Applications are processed on a rolling basis. *Application fee:* $50. *Application Contact:* Marie Beichert, Assistant Director for Admissions and Administration, 845-758-7073, Fax: 845-758-7636, E-mail: cep@bard.edu. *Director,* Dr. Joanne Fox-Przeworski, 845-758-7071, Fax: 845-758-7636, E-mail: jfp@bard.edu.

Center for Curatorial Studies Students: 24 full-time (19 women). Average age 28. 56 applicants, 39% accepted. *Faculty:* 1 full-time (0 women), 13 part-time/adjunct (7 women). Expenses: Contact institution. *Financial support:* Fellowships, research assistantships, career-related internships or fieldwork, scholarships/grants, tuition waivers (partial), and unspecified assistantships available. Financial award application deadline: 2/15; financial award applicants required to submit FAFSA. In 2001, 7 degrees awarded. Offers curatorial studies (MA). *Application deadline:* For fall admission, 2/15. *Application fee:* $50. *Application Contact:* Letitia Smith, Assistant to the Director, 845-758-7598, Fax: 845-758-2442, E-mail: lsmith@bard.edu. *Director,* Dr. Norton Batkin, 845-758-7598, Fax: 845-758-2442, E-mail: batkin@bard.edu.

Milton Avery Graduate School of the Arts Students: 72 full-time (37 women); includes 12 minority (3 African Americans, 5 Asian Americans or Pacific Islanders, 3 Hispanic Americans, 1 Native American), 3 international. Average age 34. 173 applicants, 14% accepted. *Faculty:* 7 full-time (4 women), 22 part-time/adjunct (11 women). Expenses: Contact institution. *Financial support:* In 2001–02, 43 fellowships were awarded; scholarships/grants also available. Financial award application deadline: 2/15; financial award applicants required to submit FAFSA. In 2001, 22 degrees awarded. Offers arts (MFA). *Application deadline:* For fall admission, 2/1. *Application fee:* $45. *Application Contact:* Heidi Simmons, Coordinator, 845-758-7483, Fax: 845-758-7507, E-mail: hsimmons@bard.edu. *Director,* Arthur Gibbons, 845-758-7442, Fax: 845-758-7507, E-mail: gibbons@bard.edu.

See in-depth description on page 751.

BARD GRADUATE CENTER FOR STUDIES IN THE DECORATIVE ARTS, DESIGN, AND CULTURE, New York, NY 10024-3602

General Information Independent, coed, primarily women, graduate-only institution. *Enrollment by degree level:* 31 master's, 15 doctoral. *Graduate faculty:* 10 full-time (6 women), 41 part-time/adjunct (28 women). *Tuition:* Full-time $20,309; part-time $764 per credit. *Required fees:* $75. *Graduate housing:* Room and/or apartments guaranteed to single students; on-campus housing not available to married students. Housing application deadline: 5/1. *Student services:* Campus employment opportunities, career counseling, grant writing training, low-cost health insurance, writing training. *Online resources:* library catalog, web page. *Collection:* 33,000 titles, 195 serial subscriptions. *Research affiliation:* Brooklyn Museum of Art, Metropolitan Museum of Art.

Computer facilities: 8 computers available on campus for general student use. A campuswide network can be accessed from off campus. Internet access is available. *Web address:* http://www.bgc.bard.edu/.

General Application Contact: Elena Pinto Simon, Associate Dean, 212-501-3019, Fax: 212-501-3079, E-mail: simon@bgc.bard.edu.

GRADUATE UNITS

Program in History of the Decorative Arts, Design and Culture Students: 38 full-time (35 women), 8 part-time (all women). Average age 31. 79 applicants, 51% accepted. *Faculty:* 10 full-time (6 women), 41 part-time/adjunct (28 women). Expenses: Contact institution. *Financial support:* In 2001–02, 25 students received support, including 15 fellowships; career-related internships or fieldwork and scholarships/grants also available. Financial award application deadline: 2/1; financial award applicants required to submit FAFSA. *Degree program information:* Part-time programs available. Offers history of the decorative arts, design and culture (MA, PhD). Bard Graduate Center for Studies in the Decorative Arts is a unit of Bard College. *Application deadline:* For fall admission, 2/1. *Application fee:* $50. *Application Contact:* Elena Pinto Simon, Associate Dean, 212-501-3019, Fax: 212-501-3079, E-mail: simon@bgc.bard.edu. *Director,* Susan Weber Soros, 212-501-3000, Fax: 212-501-3079.

Announcement: The Bard Graduate Center's (BGC) MA and PhD programs offer advanced training in the history of the decorative arts, design, and culture; museum studies; and garden history and landscape studies. Interdisciplinary curriculum focuses on the roles objects and places play in people's lives. Hands-on study is integral to the program. Internship and thesis required for MA; qualifying examinations and dissertation required for PhD.

BARRY UNIVERSITY, Miami Shores, FL 33161-6695

General Information Independent-religious, coed, university. *Enrollment:* 1,184 full-time matriculated graduate/professional students (781 women), 1,600 part-time matriculated graduate/professional students (1,150 women). *Graduate faculty:* 128 full-time, 76 part-time/adjunct. *Tuition:* Full-time $12,480. Tuition and fees vary according to degree level and program. *Graduate housing:* Room and/or apartments available to single students; on-campus housing not available to married students. Typical cost: $6,600 (including board). *Student services:* Campus employment opportunities, campus safety program, career counseling, disabled student services, free psychological counseling, international student services, low-cost health insurance, multicultural affairs office. *Library facilities:* Monsignor William Barry Memorial Library plus 1 other. *Online resources:* library catalog, web page. *Collection:* 233,938 titles, 2,880 serial subscriptions, 4,247 audiovisual materials. *Research affiliation:* Baxter Corporation (immunology, diagnostics), Coulter Corporation (immunology, cytology), Cordis Corporation (cardiac product development), Diamedix (immunological diagnostics), Noven Pharmaceutical, Sano Pharmaceuticals.

Computer facilities: 250 computers available on campus for general student use. A campuswide network can be accessed from student residence rooms and from off campus. Internet access is available. *Web address:* http://www.barry.edu/.

General Application Contact: Marcia Nance, Dean, Enrollment Services, 305-899-3112, Fax: 305-899-3149.

GRADUATE UNITS

Andreas School of Business Students: 78. Average age 30. 105 applicants, 16% accepted, 12 enrolled. Expenses: Contact institution. *Financial support:* In 2001–02, 57 students received support, including 2 research assistantships with tuition reimbursements available; career-related internships or fieldwork and scholarships/grants also available. Support available to part-time students. Financial award application deadline: 5/1; financial award applicants required to submit FAFSA. In 2001, 36 degrees awarded. *Degree program information:* Part-time and evening/weekend programs available. Offers business (MBA); e-commerce (MS); management information systems (Certificate). *Application deadline:* Applications are processed on a rolling basis. *Application fee:* $30. Electronic applications accepted. *Application Contact:* José Poza, Director of Marketing, 800-892-1111, Fax: 305-892-6412, E-mail: poza@mail.barry.edu. *Dean,* Dr. Jack Scarborough, 800-892-1111, Fax: 305-892-6412, E-mail: jscarborough@mail.barry.edu.

School of Adult and Continuing Education Average age 37. Expenses: Contact institution. Offers adult and continuing education (MS); information technology (MS). *Application Contact:* Mary Hernandez, Information Contact, 305-899-3300, Fax: 305-899-3346, E-mail: mhernandez@mail.barry.edu. *Dean,* Carol Rae Sodano, 305-899-3300.

School of Arts and Sciences Students: 166. Average age 39. 96 applicants, 70% accepted, 25 enrolled. *Faculty:* 8 full-time (5 women), 9 part-time/adjunct (3 women). Expenses: Contact institution. *Financial support:* Research assistantships, tuition waivers (partial) available. *Degree program information:* Part-time and evening/weekend programs available. Offers arts and sciences (EMS, MA, MFA, MS, D Min, Certificate, SSP); broadcasting (Certificate); clinical psychology (MS); communication (EMS, MA); organizational communication (MS); pastoral ministry for Hispanics (MA); pastoral theology (MA); photography (MA, MFA); school psychology (MS, SSP); theology (MA, D Min). *Application deadline:* Applications are processed on a rolling basis. *Application fee:* $30. Electronic applications accepted. *Application Contact:* Dave Fletcher, Director of Graduate Admissions, 305-899-3113, Fax: 305-899-2971, E-mail: dfletcher@mail.barry.edu. *Dean,* Dr. Laura Armesto, 305-899-3401, Fax: 305-899-3466, E-mail: larmesto@mail.barry.edu.

School of Education Students: 863. Average age 38. 361 applicants, 68% accepted, 140 enrolled. Expenses: Contact institution. *Financial support:* In 2001–02, 342 students received support. In 2001, 180 master's, 5 doctorates, 23 other advanced degrees awarded. *Degree program information:* Part-time and evening/weekend programs available. Postbaccalaureate distance learning degree programs offered. Offers counseling (MS, PhD, Ed S); education (MAT, MS, PhD, Ed S, PMC); educational computing and technology (MS, PhD, Ed S); educational leadership (MS, Ed S); elementary education (MS, PMC); exceptional student education (MS, PhD, Ed S); guidance and counseling (MS, Ed S); higher education administration (MS, PhD); human resource development (MS, PhD); leadership (PhD); marriage and family counseling (MS, Ed S); mental health counseling (MS, Ed S); Montessori education (MS, Ed S); pre-kindergarten and primary education (MS); reading (MS, Ed S); rehabilitation counseling (MS, Ed S); teaching (MAT). *Application deadline:* For fall admission, 5/1 (priority date). Applications are processed on a rolling basis. *Application fee:* $30. Electronic applications accepted. *Application Contact:* Angela Scott, Assistant Dean, Enrollment Services, 305-899-3112, Fax: 305-899-3149, E-mail: ascott@mail.barry.edu. *Dean,* Sr. Evelyn Piche, OP, 305-899-3700, Fax: 305-899-3630, E-mail: epiche@mail.barry.edu.

School of Graduate Medical Sciences Students: 340. Average age 28. 251 applicants, 63% accepted, 96 enrolled. Expenses: Contact institution. In 2001, 54 first professional degrees, 12 master's awarded. Offers medical sciences (DPM, MCMS); physician assistant (MCMS); podiatric medicine (DPM). *Application deadline:* For fall admission, 6/1. Applications are processed on a rolling basis. *Application Contact:* Alex Collins, Director of Graduate Medical Sciences Admissions, 305-899-3130, Fax: 305-899-3253, E-mail: acollins@mail.barry.edu. *Academic Dean,* Dr. Chet Evans, 305-899-3250, Fax: 305-899-3253, E-mail: cevans@mail.barry.edu.

School of Human Performance and Leisure Sciences Students: 43. Average age 28. 32 applicants, 91% accepted, 15 enrolled. *Faculty:* 9 full-time (6 women), 7 part-time/adjunct (3 women). Expenses: Contact institution. *Financial support:* Career-related internships or fieldwork available. In 2001, 5 degrees awarded. *Degree program information:* Part-time and evening/weekend programs available. Offers athletic training (MS); biomechanics (MS); exercise science (MS); human performance and leisure sciences (MS); sport management (MS). *Application deadline:* Applications are processed on a rolling basis. *Application fee:* $30. Electronic applications accepted. *Application Contact:* Desh Sherman-Moeller, Administrative Assistant for Graduate Programs, 305-899-3490, Fax: 305-899-3556, E-mail: dsherman@mail.barry.edu. *Vice Provost, Academic Services*, Dr. G. Jean Cerra, 305-899-3554, Fax: 305-899-3556, E-mail: jcerra@mall.barry.edu.

School of Law Students: 206. Average age 34. 153 applicants, 40% accepted, 24 enrolled. Expenses: Contact institution. In 2001, 48 degrees awarded. Offers law (JD). *Application Contact:* John Agett, Contact, 400-275-2000 Ext. 237, E-mail: lawinfo@mail.barry.edu. *Dean*, Stanley Talcott, 407-275-2000 Ext. 232, E-mail: stalcott@mail.barry.edu.

School of Natural and Health Sciences Students: 251. Average age 30. 158 applicants, 73% accepted, 78 enrolled. *Faculty:* 20. Expenses: Contact institution. *Financial support:* Teaching assistantships, tuition waivers (partial) available. Financial award application deadline: 5/1; financial award applicants required to submit FAFSA. In 2001, 102 degrees awarded. *Degree program information:* Part-time and evening/weekend programs available. Offers anesthesiology (MS); biology (MS); biomedical sciences (MS); health services administration (MS); natural and health sciences (MS); occupational therapy (MS). *Application fee:* $30. *Application Contact:* Dr. Jocelyn Goulet, Director, Health Services Admissions Operation, 305-899-3541, Fax: 305-899-3232, E-mail: jgoulet@mail.barry.edu. *Dean*, Sr. John Karen Frei, 305-899-3200, Fax: 305-899-3225.

School of Nursing Students: 107. Average age 43. 41 applicants, 39% accepted, 12 enrolled. *Faculty:* 15 full-time (14 women), 8 part-time/adjunct (all women). Expenses: Contact institution. *Financial support:* In 2001–02, 3 research assistantships (averaging $5,000 per year), 3 teaching assistantships (averaging $5,000 per year) were awarded. Tuition waivers (full) also available. Financial award application deadline: 5/1; financial award applicants required to submit FAFSA. In 2001, 43 master's, 3 doctorates awarded. *Degree program information:* Part-time and evening/weekend programs available. Offers advanced nursing completion (MSN); nurse practitioner (MSN); nursing (MSN, PhD); nursing administration (MSN, PhD); nursing education (MSN). *Application deadline:* For fall admission, 5/1 (priority date). Applications are processed on a rolling basis. *Application fee:* $30. *Application Contact:* Dr. Claudia M. Hauri, Director, 305-899-3813, Fax: 305-899-2971, E-mail: chauri@barry.edu. *Dean*, Dr. Judith Ann Balcerski, 305-899-3840, Fax: 305-899-3831, E-mail: jbalcerski@mail.barry.edu.

School of Social Work Students: 381. Average age 36. 286 applicants, 69% accepted, 139 enrolled. *Faculty:* 20 full-time (12 women). Expenses: Contact institution. *Financial support:* Available to part-time students. Applicants required to submit FAFSA. In 2001, 149 master's, 2 doctorates awarded. *Degree program information:* Part-time and evening/weekend programs available. Offers social work (MSW, PhD). *Application fee:* $30. Electronic applications accepted. *Application Contact:* Philip Mack, Director of Admissions, 305-899-3900, Fax: 305-899-3934, E-mail: sswadm@mail.barry.edu. *Dean*, Dr. Stephen Holloway, 305-899-3900, Fax: 305-899-3934.

See in-depth description on page 753.

BASTYR UNIVERSITY, Kenmore, WA 98028-4966

General Information Independent, coed, upper-level institution. *Enrollment:* 627 full-time matriculated graduate/professional students (482 women), 148 part-time matriculated graduate/professional students (113 women). *Enrollment by degree level:* 586 first professional, 159 master's. *Graduate faculty:* 21 full-time, 74 part-time/adjunct. *Tuition, area resident:* Part-time $230 per credit. Tuition and fees vary according to program. *Graduate housing:* Rooms and/or apartments available on a first-come, first-served basis to single and married students. *Student services:* Campus employment opportunities, child daycare facilities, free psychological counseling, low-cost health insurance. *Library facilities:* Bastyr University Library. *Online resources:* library catalog, web page. *Collection:* 11,000 titles, 250 serial subscriptions, 2,000 audiovisual materials.

Computer facilities: 16 computers available on campus for general student use. Internet access is available. *Web address:* http://www.bastyr.edu/.

General Application Contact: Richard Dent, Director, Enrollment Services, 425-602-3080, Fax: 425-602-3090.

GRADUATE UNITS

Graduate and Professional Programs Students: 627 full-time (482 women), 148 part-time (113 women). Average age 28. 455 applicants, 75% accepted, 215 enrolled. *Faculty:* 21 full-time, 74 part-time/adjunct. Expenses: Contact institution. *Financial support:* Teaching assistantships, career-related internships or fieldwork, Federal Work-Study, and scholarships/grants available. Support available to part-time students. Financial award application deadline: 4/15; financial award applicants required to submit FAFSA. In 2001, 50 master's, 90 doctorates awarded. *Degree program information:* Part-time programs available. Offers acupuncture and Oriental medicine (MS); midwifery (Certificate); naturopathic medicine (ND); nutrition (MS). *Application deadline:* Applications are processed on a rolling basis. *Application fee:* $60. *Application Contact:* Richard Dent, Director, Enrollment Services, 425-602-3080, Fax: 425-602-3090. *Vice President, Academics and Research*, Dr. Joseph Chu, 425-823-1300, Fax: 425-823-6222.

BAYAMÓN CENTRAL UNIVERSITY, Bayamón, PR 00960-1725

General Information Independent-religious, coed, comprehensive institution. *Enrollment:* 196 full-time matriculated graduate/professional students (119 women), 177 part-time matriculated graduate/professional students (123 women). *Enrollment by degree level:* 328 master's. *Graduate faculty:* 1 (woman) full-time, 30 part-time/adjunct (13 women). *Tuition:* Full-time $5,400; part-time $150 per credit. *Required fees:* $320. *Student services:* Career counseling, disabled student services. *Library facilities:* BCU Library plus 1 other. *Online resources:* library catalog. *Collection:* 51,011 titles, 3,027 serial subscriptions, 900 audiovisual materials.

Computer facilities: 130 computers available on campus for general student use. A campuswide network can be accessed. Internet access is available. *Web address:* http://www.ucb.edu.pr/.

General Application Contact: Christine Hernández, Director of Admissions, 787-786-3030 Ext. 2100, Fax: 787-740-2200, E-mail: chernandez@ucb.edu.pr.

GRADUATE UNITS

Graduate Programs Students: 196 full-time (119 women), 177 part-time (123 women); all minorities (all Hispanic Americans) Average age 35. 37 applicants, 86% accepted. *Faculty:* 1 (woman) full-time, 30 part-time/adjunct (13 women). Expenses: Contact institution. *Financial support:* Institutionally sponsored loans available. In 2001, 52 degrees awarded. *Degree program information:* Part-time and evening/weekend programs available. Offers accounting (MBA); administration and supervision (MA Ed); biblical studies (MA); divinity (M Div); education of the autistic (MA Ed); elementary education (K–3) (MA Ed); elementary education (K–6) (MA Ed); general business (MBA); guidance and counseling (MA Ed); management (MBA); marketing (MBA); pastoral theology (MA); pre-elementary teacher (MA Ed); psychology (MA); religious studies (MA); special education (MA Ed); specific learning disabled (MA Ed); theological studies (MA); theology (MA). *Application deadline:* For fall admission, 10/3; for winter admission, 12/20; for spring admission, 4/3. Applications are processed on a rolling basis. *Application fee:* $25. *Application Contact:* Christine Hernández, Director of Admissions, 787-786-3030 Ext. 2100, Fax: 787-740-2200, E-mail: chernandez@ucb.edu.pr. *Director*, Dr. Carmen Ortiz, 787-786-3030 Ext. 2200, Fax: 787-740-2200.

BAYLOR COLLEGE OF MEDICINE, Houston, TX 77030-3498

General Information Independent, coed, graduate-only institution. CGS member. *Graduate faculty:* 1,710 full-time, 143 part-time/adjunct. Tuition, state resident: full-time $6,550. Tuition, nonresident: full-time $19,650. *Required fees:* $933. Full-time tuition and fees vary according to program and student level. *Graduate housing:* On-campus housing not available. *Student services:* Campus employment opportunities, campus safety program, career counseling, child daycare facilities, disabled student services, exercise/wellness program, free psychological counseling, international student services, low-cost health insurance. *Library facilities:* Houston Academy of Medicine–Texas Medical Center Library. *Online resources:* library catalog, web page, access to other libraries' catalogs. *Collection:* 333,115 titles, 5,019 serial subscriptions, 713 audiovisual materials. *Research affiliation:* Children's Nutrition Research Center (pediatric nutrition), Harris County Hospital District (biomedical research), National Space Biomedical Research Institute, The Methodist Hospital (biomedical research), Texas Children's Hospital (pediatric biomedical research), Veterans Affairs Medical Center (biomedical research).

Computer facilities: 100 computers available on campus for general student use. A campuswide network can be accessed from off campus. Internet access is available. *Web address:* http://www.bcm.tmc.edu/.

General Application Contact: Dr. L. Leighton Hill, Associate Dean of the Medical School, 713-798-4842, Fax: 713-798-5563, E-mail: melodym@bcm.tmc.edu.

GRADUATE UNITS

Graduate School of Biomedical Sciences Students: 421 full-time (176 women); includes 65 minority (12 African Americans, 30 Asian Americans or Pacific Islanders, 23 Hispanic Americans), 152 international. Average age 28. 1,068 applicants, 19% accepted, 102 enrolled. *Faculty:* 333 full-time (81 women). Expenses: Contact institution. *Financial support:* In 2001–02, 421 students received support, including 207 fellowships (averaging $20,000 per year), 211 research assistantships (averaging $20,000 per year), 3 teaching assistantships (averaging $20,000 per year); career-related internships or fieldwork, Federal Work-Study, institutionally sponsored loans, and tuition waivers (full and partial) also available. Financial award applicants required to submit FAFSA. In 2001, 4 master's, 46 doctorates awarded. Offers biochemistry and molecular biology (PhD); biomedical sciences (MS, PhD); cardiovascular sciences (PhD); cell and molecular biology (PhD); clinical scientist training (MS, PhD); developmental biology (PhD); immunology (PhD); molecular and cellular biology (PhD); molecular and human genetics (PhD); molecular physiology and biophysics (PhD); molecular virology and microbiology (PhD); neuroscience (PhD); pharmacology (PhD); structural and computational biology and molecular biophysics (PhD). *Application deadline:* For fall admission, 2/1 (priority date). Applications are processed on a rolling basis. *Application fee:* $30. Electronic applications accepted. *Application Contact:* Donna Otwell, Administrative Associate, 713-798-4029, Fax: 713-798-6325, E-mail: dotwell@bcm.tmc.edu. *Dean of Graduate Sciences*, Dr. William R. Brinkley, 713-798-5263, Fax: 713-798-6325, E-mail: brinkley@bcm.tmc.edu.

Medical School Students: 790 full-time (403 women), 7 part-time; includes 351 minority (54 African Americans, 207 Asian Americans or Pacific Islanders, 83 Hispanic Americans, 7 Native Americans), 2 international. Average age 25. 3,650 applicants, 10% accepted. Expenses: Contact institution. *Financial support:* Career-related internships or fieldwork, Federal Work-Study, institutionally sponsored loans, scholarships/grants, traineeships, and tuition waivers (full and partial) available. Financial award applicants required to submit FAFSA. In 2001, 167 first professional degrees, 42 master's awarded. Offers medicine (MD, MS); nurse anesthesia (MS); nurse midwifery (MS); physician assistant (MS). *Application deadline:* Applications are processed on a rolling basis. *Application Contact:* Dr. L. Leighton Hill, Senior Associate Dean, 713-798-4842, Fax: 713-798-5563, E-mail: melodym@bcm.tmc.edu. *President*, Dr. Ralph D. Feigin, 713-798-4433, Fax: 713-798-8811, E-mail: rfeigin@bcm.tmc.edu.

BAYLOR UNIVERSITY, Waco, TX 76798

General Information Independent-religious, coed, university. CGS member. *Enrollment:* 1,620 full-time matriculated graduate/professional students (699 women), 398 part-time matriculated graduate/professional students (220 women). *Enrollment by degree level:* 673 first professional, 914 master's, 431 doctoral. *Graduate faculty:* 350. *Tuition:* Part-time $379 per semester hour. *Required fees:* $42 per semester hour. $101 per semester. Tuition and fees vary according to program. *Graduate housing:* Rooms and/or apartments available to single and married students. Typical cost: $1,203 per year ($2,655 including board) for single students. Room and board charges vary according to board plan and housing facility selected. *Student services:* Campus safety program, career counseling, exercise/wellness program, free psychological counseling, international student services, low-cost health insurance, multicultural affairs office. *Library facilities:* Moody Memorial Library plus 8 others. *Online resources:* library catalog, web page, access to other libraries' catalogs. *Collection:* 1.1 million titles, 9,106 serial subscriptions, 71,076 audiovisual materials. *Research affiliation:* Oak Ridge National Laboratory, National Center for Supercomputing Applications (physics), Royal Institute of Technology, Stockholm, Sweden (aviation sciences).

Computer facilities: 1,300 computers available on campus for general student use. A campuswide network can be accessed from student residence rooms and from off campus. Internet access and online class registration are available. *Web address:* http://www.baylor.edu/.

General Application Contact: Suzanne Keener, Administrative Assistant, 254-710-3588, Fax: 254-710-3870, E-mail: graduate_school@baylor.edu.

GRADUATE UNITS

George W. Truett Seminary Students: 234 full-time (81 women), 60 part-time (18 women); includes 35 minority (10 African Americans, 4 Asian Americans or Pacific Islanders, 20 Hispanic Americans, 1 Native American), 8 international. *Faculty:* 14 full-time (3 women), 7 part-time/adjunct (1 woman). Expenses: Contact institution. *Financial support:* In 2001–02, 207 students received support, including 1 research assistantship, 12 teaching assistantships; career-related internships or fieldwork, Federal Work-Study, institutionally sponsored loans, scholarships/grants, and tuition waivers (partial) also available. Support available to part-time students. Financial award application deadline: 8/1; financial award applicants required to submit FAFSA. In 2001, 24 degrees awarded. Offers theology (M Div, D Min). *Application deadline:* For fall admission, 8/1 (priority date); for spring admission, 11/1 (priority date). Applications are processed on a rolling basis. *Application fee:* $25. Electronic applications accepted. *Application Contact:* Dr. Grear Howard, Director of Student Services, 254-710-3755, Fax: 254-710-7233, E-mail: grear_howard@baylor.edu. *Dean*, Dr. Paul W. Powell, 254-710-3755, Fax: 254-710-3753.

Graduate School Students: 977 full-time (454 women), 334 part-time (202 women); includes 153 minority (59 African Americans, 39 Asian Americans or Pacific Islanders, 54 Hispanic Americans, 1 Native American), 159 international. 1,135 applicants, 60% accepted. *Faculty:* 350. Expenses: Contact institution. *Financial support:* Fellowships, research assistantships with full and partial tuition reimbursements, teaching assistantships with full and partial tuition reimbursements, career-related internships or fieldwork, Federal Work-Study, institutionally sponsored loans, scholarships/grants, tuition waivers (full and partial), and unspecified assistantships available. Support available to part-time students. In 2001, 503 master's, 62 doctorates awarded. *Degree program information:* Part-time and evening/weekend programs available. Postbaccalaureate distance learning degree programs offered (minimal on-campus study). *Application deadline:* Applications are processed on a rolling basis. *Application fee:* $25. *Application Contact:* Suzanne Keener, Administrative Assistant, 254-710-3588, Fax: 254-710-3870, E-mail: graduate_school@baylor.edu. *Dean*, Dr. Larry Lyon, 254-710-3588, Fax: 254-710-3870, E-mail: larry_lyon@baylor.edu.

Academy of Health Sciences Students: 95 full-time (22 women), 8 part-time (1 woman); includes 13 minority (3 African Americans, 6 Asian Americans or Pacific Islanders, 4 Hispanic Americans) Expenses: Contact institution. In 2001, 60 master's, 10 doctorates awarded. Offers health care administration (MHA); health sciences (MHA, MPT, Dr Sc PT); physical therapy (MPT, Dr Sc PT). *Application deadline:* Applications are processed on a rolling basis. *Application fee:* $25. *Dean*, Col. Richard Shipley, 210-221-8715, Fax: 210-221-7306.

College of Arts and Sciences Students: 466 full-time (241 women), 83 part-time (43 women); includes 49 minority (16 African Americans, 11 Asian Americans or Pacific Islanders, 21 Hispanic Americans, 1 Native American), 61 international. Expenses: Contact institution. *Financial support:* Fellowships, research assistantships with partial tuition reimbursements, teaching assistantships, career-related internships or fieldwork, Federal Work-Study, institutionally sponsored loans, scholarships/grants, tuition waivers (full and

Baylor University (continued)

partial), unspecified assistantships, and laboratory assistantships, practicum stipends available. Support available to part-time students. In 2001, 148 master's, 27 doctorates awarded. *Degree program information:* Part-time and evening/weekend programs available. Offers American studies (MA); applied sociology (PhD); arts and sciences (MA, MCG, MES, MFA, MIJ, MPPA, MS, MSCP, MSCSD, MSG, MSL, MSW, PhD, Psy D); biology (MA, MS, PhD); chemistry (MS, PhD); clinical gerontology (MCG); clinical psychology (MSCP, Psy D); communication sciences and disorders (MA, MSCSD); communication studies (MA); directing (MFA); earth science (MA); English (MA, PhD); environmental biology (MS); environmental studies (MES, MS); geology (MS, PhD); gerontology (MSG); history (MA); international journalism (MIJ); international studies (MA); journalism (MA); limnology (MSL); mathematics (MS); museum studies (MA); neuroscience (MA, PhD); philosophy (MA); physics (MA, MS, PhD); political science (MA); public policy and administration (MPPA); religion (MA, PhD); social work (MCG, MSG, MSW); sociology (MA); Spanish (MA); theater arts (MA). *Application deadline:* Applications are processed on a rolling basis. *Application fee:* $25. Electronic applications accepted. *Dean,* Dr. Wallace Daniel, 254-710-3361, Fax: 254-710-3639.

Hankamer School of Business Students: 211 full-time (68 women), 13 part-time (5 women); includes 28 minority (5 African Americans, 16 Asian Americans or Pacific Islanders, 7 Hispanic Americans), 54 international. Expenses: Contact institution. *Financial support:* Research assistantships, teaching assistantships, career-related internships or fieldwork, Federal Work-Study, and institutionally sponsored loans available. In 2001, 243 degrees awarded. *Degree program information:* Part-time programs available. Offers accounting (M Acc, MT); business (M Acc, MA, MBA, MBAIM, MIM, MS, MS Eco, MSIS, MT); business administration (MBA); economics (MS Eco); information systems (MSIS); information systems management (MBA); international economics (MA, MS); international management (MBA, MBAIM, MIM). *Application deadline:* For fall admission, 8/1; for spring admission, 12/1. Applications are processed on a rolling basis. *Application fee:* $25. *Application Contact:* Vicky Todd, Administrative Assistant, 254-710-3718, Fax: 254-710-1066, E-mail: mba@hsb.baylor.edu. *Director of Graduate Programs,* Dr. Linda Livingstone, 254-710-3718, Fax: 254-710-1092.

Institute of Biomedical Studies Students: 21 full-time (10 women), 1 part-time; includes 2 minority (both Asian Americans or Pacific Islanders), 9 international. Expenses: Contact institution. *Financial support:* Research assistantships, teaching assistantships available. In 2001, 8 master's, 2 doctorates awarded. Offers biomedical studies (MS, PhD). *Application deadline:* Applications are processed on a rolling basis. *Application fee:* $25. *Application Contact:* Suzanne Keener, Administrative Assistant, 254-710-3588, Fax: 254-710-3870, E-mail: graduate_school@baylor.edu. *Director,* Dr. Darden Powers, 254-710-2514, Fax: 254-710-3878, E-mail: darden_powers@baylor.edu.

Institute of Statistics Students: 11 full-time (5 women), 4 part-time (3 women), 2 international. Average age 24. 38 applicants, 16% accepted. *Faculty:* 7 full-time (1 woman), 4 part-time/adjunct (1 woman). Expenses: Contact institution. *Financial support:* In 2001–02, 1 fellowship, 5 research assistantships, 7 teaching assistantships were awarded. Institutionally sponsored loans also available. In 2001, 5 master's, 5 doctorates awarded. Offers statistics (MA, PhD). *Application deadline:* Applications are processed on a rolling basis. *Application fee:* $25. *Application Contact:* Suzanne Keener, Administrative Assistant, 254-710-3588, Fax: 254-710-3870, E-mail: graduate_school@baylor.edu. *Director,* Dr. Tom Bratcher, 254-710-1699, Fax: 254-710-3033, E-mail: tom_bratcher@baylor.edu.

J. M. Dawson Institute of Church-State Studies Students: 24 full-time (4 women), 1 (woman) part-time; includes 1 minority (Asian American or Pacific Islander), 3 international. Expenses: Contact institution. *Financial support:* Fellowships, research assistantships, teaching assistantships, Federal Work-Study and institutionally sponsored loans available. Financial award application deadline: 3/1. In 2001, 3 master's, 3 doctorates awarded. Offers church-state studies (MA, PhD). *Application deadline:* For fall admission, 3/1. Applications are processed on a rolling basis. *Application fee:* $25. *Application Contact:* Suzanne Keener, Administrative Assistant, 254-710-3588, Fax: 254-710-3870, E-mail: graduate_school@baylor.edu. *Director,* Dr. Derek H. Davis, 254-710-1510, Fax: 254-710-1571, E-mail: derek_davis@baylor.edu.

Louise Herrington School of Nursing of Baylor University Students: 23 full-time (all women), 17 part-time (14 women); includes 5 minority (2 African Americans, 1 Asian American or Pacific Islander, 2 Hispanic Americans) Expenses: Contact institution. In 2001, 11 degrees awarded. Offers family nurse practitioner (MSN); neonatal nurse practitioner (MSN); nursing administration and management (MSN). *Application deadline:* For fall admission, 8/1; for spring admission, 12/1. Applications are processed on a rolling basis. *Application fee:* $25. *Application Contact:* Suzanne Keener, Administrative Assistant, 254-710-3588, Fax: 254-710-3870, E-mail: graduate_school@baylor.edu. *Dean,* Dr. Phyllis S. Karns, 214-820-3361, Fax: 214-818-8692, E-mail: phyllis_karns@baylor.edu.

School of Education Students: 130 full-time (82 women), 163 part-time (112 women); includes 55 minority (32 African Americans, 3 Asian Americans or Pacific Islanders, 20 Hispanic Americans), 9 international. Expenses: Contact institution. *Financial support:* Research assistantships, teaching assistantships, career-related internships or fieldwork, Federal Work-Study, institutionally sponsored loans, scholarships/grants, and tuition waivers (partial) available. In 2001, 68 master's, 25 doctorates awarded. *Degree program information:* Part-time programs available. Postbaccalaureate distance learning degree programs offered (minimal on-campus study). Offers curriculum and instruction (MA, MS Ed, Ed D, Ed S); education (MA, MS Ed, Ed D, PhD, Ed S); educational administration (MS Ed, Ed D, Ed S); educational psychology (MA, MS Ed, PhD, Ed S); health, human performance and recreation (MS Ed). *Application deadline:* Applications are processed on a rolling basis. *Application fee:* $25. Electronic applications accepted. *Application Contact:* Suzanne Keener, Administrative Assistant, 254-710-3588, Fax: 254-710-3870, E-mail: graduate_school@baylor.edu. *Dean,* Dr. Robert Yinger, 254-710-3111, Fax: 254-710-3987.

School of Engineering and Computer Science Students: 14 full-time (1 woman), 5 part-time (1 woman), 13 international. Expenses: Contact institution. *Financial support:* Teaching assistantships available. Financial award application deadline: 3/15. In 2001, 3 degrees awarded. *Degree program information:* Part-time programs available. Offers computer science (MS). *Application deadline:* For fall admission, 8/1; for spring admission, 12/1. Applications are processed on a rolling basis. *Application fee:* $25. *Application Contact:* Suzanne Keener, Administrative Assistant, 254-710-3588, Fax: 254-710-3870, E-mail: graduate_school@baylor.edu. *Director of Graduate Studies,* Dr. Greg Speegle, 254-710-3876, Fax: 254-710-3839, E-mail: greg_speegle@baylor.edu.

School of Music Students: 6 full-time (2 women), 40 part-time (23 women); includes 1 minority (African American), 11 international. Expenses: Contact institution. *Financial support:* Federal Work-Study and institutionally sponsored loans available. In 2001, 24 degrees awarded. Offers church music (MM); composition (MM); conducting (MM); music education (MM); music history and literature (MM); music theory (MM); performance (MM); piano accompanying (MM); piano pedagogy and performance (MM). *Application deadline:* For fall admission, 8/1; for spring admission, 12/1. Applications are processed on a rolling basis. *Application fee:* $25. *Application Contact:* Suzanne Keener, Administrative Assistant, 254-710-3588, Fax: 254-710-3870, E-mail: graduate_school@baylor.edu. *Director of Graduate Studies,* Dr. Harry Elzinga, 254-710-1161, Fax: 254-710-1191, E-mail: harry_elzinga@baylor.edu.

School of Law Students: 409 full-time (164 women), 4 part-time; includes 48 minority (2 African Americans, 10 Asian Americans or Pacific Islanders, 35 Hispanic Americans, 1 Native American), 2 international. Average age 24. 1,259 applicants, 37% accepted. *Faculty:* 20 full-time (5 women), 38 part-time/adjunct (4 women). Expenses: Contact institution. *Financial support:* In 2001–02, 379 students received support. Career-related internships or fieldwork, Federal Work-Study, institutionally sponsored loans, and scholarships/grants available. Financial award applicants required to submit FAFSA. In 2001, 125 degrees awarded. Offers law (JD). *Application deadline:* For fall admission, 3/1; for spring admission, 11/1. Applications are processed on a rolling basis. *Application fee:* $40. Electronic applications accepted. *Application Contact:* Becky Beck, Admissions Director, 254-710-1911, Fax: 254-710-2316, E-mail: becky_beck@baylor.edu. *Dean,* Dr. Bradley J. B. Toben, 254-710-1911, Fax: 254-710-2316.

See in-depth description on page 755.

BAY PATH COLLEGE, Longmeadow, MA 01106-2292

General Information Independent, women only, comprehensive institution. *Enrollment:* 33 full-time matriculated graduate/professional students (29 women), 15 part-time matriculated graduate/professional students (10 women). *Enrollment by degree level:* 48 master's. *Graduate faculty:* 7 full-time (4 women). *Tuition:* Full-time $15,408. *Graduate housing:* Room and/or apartments available on a first-come, first-served basis to single students; on-campus housing not available to married students. Typical cost: $7,554 (including board). Room and board charges vary according to board plan and campus/location. Housing application deadline: 7/2. *Student services:* Campus safety program, career counseling, disabled student services, exercise/wellness program, international student services, low-cost health insurance, teacher training, writing training. *Library facilities:* Frank and Marion Hatch Library. *Online resources:* library catalog, access to other libraries' catalogs. *Collection:* 43,997 titles, 317 serial subscriptions, 2,153 audiovisual materials.

Computer facilities: 114 computers available on campus for general student use. A campuswide network can be accessed from student residence rooms and from off campus. *Web address:* http://www.baypath.edu/.

General Application Contact: Diane M. Ranaldi, M.Ed., Director, Continuing Education and Graduate Admissions, 413-565-1332, Fax: 413-565-1105, E-mail: dranaldi@baypath.edu.

GRADUATE UNITS

Program in Communications and Information Management Students: 33 full-time (29 women), 15 part-time (10 women). *Faculty:* 7 full-time (4 women). Expenses: Contact institution. Offers information management (MS); information systems (MS). *Application Contact:* Diane M. Ranaldi, M.Ed., Director, Continuing Education and Graduate Admissions, 413-565-1332, Fax: 413-565-1105, E-mail: dranaldi@baypath.edu.

BELHAVEN COLLEGE, Jackson, MS 39202-1789

General Information Independent-religious, coed, comprehensive institution. *Graduate housing:* On-campus housing not available.

GRADUATE UNITS

Program in Business *Degree program information:* Evening/weekend programs available. Postbaccalaureate distance learning degree programs offered (minimal on-campus study). Offers business (MBA).

BELLARMINE UNIVERSITY, Louisville, KY 40205-0671

General Information Independent-religious, coed, comprehensive institution. *Graduate housing:* Room and/or apartments available to single students; on-campus housing not available to married students. Housing application deadline: 7/15.

GRADUATE UNITS

Allan and Donna Lansing School of Nursing and Health Sciences *Degree program information:* Part-time and evening/weekend programs available. Offers advanced community health nursing (MSN); nursing administration (MSN); nursing and health sciences (MSN); nursing education (MSN). Electronic applications accepted.

Annsley Frazier Thornton School of Education *Degree program information:* Part-time and evening/weekend programs available. Offers early elementary education (MA, MAT); elementary education (MA); learning and behavior disorders (MA); middle school education (MA, MAT). Electronic applications accepted.

W. Fielding Rubel School of Business *Degree program information:* Part-time and evening/weekend programs available. Offers business (EMBA, MBA). Electronic applications accepted.

BELLEVUE UNIVERSITY, Bellevue, NE 68005-3098

General Information Independent, coed, comprehensive institution. *Enrollment:* 460 full-time matriculated graduate/professional students (229 women), 260 part-time matriculated graduate/professional students (105 women). *Enrollment by degree level:* 720 master's. *Graduate faculty:* 62 full-time (24 women), 36 part-time/adjunct (10 women). Tuition, state resident: part-time $265 per credit. One-time fee: $50 part-time. *Graduate housing:* Room and/or apartments available to single students; on-campus housing not available to married students. *Student services:* Campus employment opportunities, career counseling, disabled student services, international student services. *Library facilities:* Freeman/Lozier Library plus 1 other. *Online resources:* library catalog, web page, access to other libraries' catalogs. *Collection:* 131,400 titles, 2,858 serial subscriptions, 3,314 audiovisual materials.

Computer facilities: 377 computers available on campus for general student use. A campuswide network can be accessed from off campus. Internet access and online class registration are available. *Web address:* http://www.bellevue.edu/.

General Application Contact: Elizabeth A. Wall, Director of Marketing and Enrollment, 402-293-3702, Fax: 402-293-3730, E-mail: eaw@scholars.bellevue.edu.

GRADUATE UNITS

Graduate School Students: 460 full-time (229 women), 260 part-time (105 women); includes 113 minority (70 African Americans, 24 Asian Americans or Pacific Islanders, 18 Hispanic Americans, 1 Native American), 73 international. Average age 33. 190 applicants, 95% accepted. *Faculty:* 62 full-time (24 women), 36 part-time/adjunct (10 women). Expenses: Contact institution. *Financial support:* In 2001–02, 324 students received support. Federal Work-Study and scholarships/grants available. Financial award applicants required to submit FAFSA. In 2001, 205 degrees awarded. *Degree program information:* Part-time and evening/weekend programs available. Postbaccalaureate distance learning degree programs offered (no on-campus study). Offers business (MBA); computer information systems (MS); health care administration (MS); human services (MS); leadership (MA); management (MA). MA is delivered in an accelerated executive format. *Application deadline:* For fall admission, 7/15 (priority date); for winter admission, 9/30 (priority date); for spring admission, 11/15 (priority date). Applications are processed on a rolling basis. *Application fee:* $50. *Application Contact:* Elizabeth A. Wall, Director of Marketing and Enrollment, 402-293-3702, Fax: 402-293-3730, E-mail: eaw@scholars.bellevue.edu. *Provost,* Dr. Mary Hawkins, 402-293-2021, Fax: 402-293-2035, E-mail: mhawkins@bellevue.edu.

See in-depth description on page 757.

BELMONT UNIVERSITY, Nashville, TN 37212-3757

General Information Independent-religious, coed, comprehensive institution. *Enrollment:* 196 full-time matriculated graduate/professional students (144 women), 316 part-time matriculated graduate/professional students (171 women). *Enrollment by degree level:* 433 master's, 79 doctoral. *Graduate faculty:* 84 full-time (42 women), 38 part-time/adjunct (25 women). *Tuition:* Part-time $535 per credit hour. Tuition and fees vary according to program. *Graduate housing:* Room and/or apartments available on a first-come, first-served basis to single students; on-campus housing not available to married students. Typical cost: $4,344 per year ($7,757 including board). Housing application deadline: 7/1. *Student services:* Campus employment opportunities, career counseling, exercise/wellness program, free psychological counseling, international student services, low-cost health insurance, multicultural affairs office. *Library facilities:* Lila D. Bunch Library. *Online resources:* library catalog, web page, access to other libraries' catalogs. *Collection:* 178,660 titles, 1,476 serial subscriptions, 23,922 audiovisual materials.

Computer facilities: 250 computers available on campus for general student use. A campuswide network can be accessed from student residence rooms and from off campus. Internet access and online class registration are available. *Web address:* http://www.belmont.edu/.

General Application Contact: Dr. Kathryn Baugher, Dean of Enrollment Services, 615-460-6785, Fax: 615-460-5434, E-mail: baugherk@mail.belmont.edu.

GRADUATE UNITS

College of Arts and Sciences Students: 33 full-time (19 women), 63 part-time (48 women); includes 7 minority (4 African Americans, 2 Hispanic Americans, 1 Native American) Average

age 32. 49 applicants, 61% accepted. *Faculty:* 25 full-time (14 women), 1 part-time/adjunct (0 women). Expenses: Contact institution. *Financial support:* Fellowships with tuition reimbursements available. In 2001, 19 degrees awarded. Offers arts and sciences (M Ed, MA); literature (MA); writing (MA). *Application deadline:* Applications are processed on a rolling basis. *Application fee:* $50. *Dean,* Dr. Larry M. Hall, 615-460-6437, Fax: 615-385-5084, E-mail: hall@mail.belmont.edu.

School of Education Students: 33 full-time (19 women), 46 part-time (35 women); includes 4 African Americans, 2 Hispanic Americans, 1 Native American Average age 30. 24 applicants, 79% accepted. *Faculty:* 14 full-time (9 women), 1 part-time/adjunct (0 women). Expenses: Contact institution. *Financial support:* In 2001–02, 17 students received support; fellowships with partial tuition reimbursements available, institutionally sponsored loans and tuition waivers (partial) available. Financial award application deadline: 4/15; financial award applicants required to submit FAFSA. In 2001, 16 degrees awarded. *Degree program information:* Part-time and evening/weekend programs available. Offers elementary education (M Ed); English (M Ed); history (M Ed); mathematics (M Ed); middle grade education (M Ed); science (M Ed); secondary education (M Ed); sports administration (M Ed); technology (M Ed). *Application deadline:* For fall admission, 7/15 (priority date); for spring admission, 11/15 (priority date). Applications are processed on a rolling basis. *Application fee:* $50. *Application Contact:* Tammi Newton, Admission Licensure Officer, 615-460-6879, Fax: 615-385-5483, E-mail: newtont@email.belmont.edu. *Associate Dean,* Dr. Trevor F. Hutchins, 615-460-6232, Fax: 615-460-6414.

College of Health Sciences Students: 152 full-time (117 women), 19 part-time (18 women); includes 14 minority (10 African Americans, 3 Asian Americans or Pacific Islanders, 1 Hispanic American), 1 international. Average age 28. 107 applicants, 83% accepted. *Faculty:* 17 full-time (11 women), 24 part-time/adjunct (19 women). Expenses: Contact institution. *Financial support:* Research assistantships, teaching assistantships, career-related internships or fieldwork, scholarships/grants, and traineeships available. Financial award applicants required to submit FAFSA. In 2001, 55 degrees awarded. *Degree program information:* Part-time programs available. Postbaccalaureate distance learning degree programs offered (minimal on-campus study). Offers health sciences (MPT, MSN, MSOT, DPT). *Application deadline:* Applications are processed on a rolling basis. *Application fee:* $50. *Application Contact:* Dr. Kathryn Baugher, Dean of Enrollment Services, 615-460-6785, Fax: 615-460-5434, E-mail: baugherk@mail.belmont.edu. *Dean,* Dr. Debra B. Wollaber, 615-460-6106, Fax: 615-460-5644, E-mail: wollaberd@mail.belmont.edu.

School of Nursing Students: 8 full-time (all women), 6 part-time (all women); includes 1 minority (African American) Average age 36. 8 applicants, 88% accepted. *Faculty:* 2 full-time (both women), 7 part-time/adjunct (all women). Expenses: Contact institution. *Financial support:* In 2001–02, 14 students received support; research assistantships, teaching assistantships, scholarships/grants and traineeships available. In 2001, 7 degrees awarded. *Degree program information:* Part-time programs available. Offers nursing (MSN). *Application deadline:* For fall admission, 2/15 (priority date); for spring admission, 10/15 (priority date). Applications are processed on a rolling basis. *Application fee:* $50. *Application Contact:* Cathy Hendon, Admissions Coordinator, 615-460-6027, Fax: 615-460-5644, E-mail: hendonc@mail.belmont.edu. *Director, Graduate Program,* Dr. Leslie J. Higgins, 615-460-6027, Fax: 615-460-5644, E-mail: higginsl@mail.belmont.edu.

School of Occupational Therapy Students: 65 full-time (56 women), 13 part-time (12 women); includes 9 minority (6 African Americans, 3 Asian Americans or Pacific Islanders), 1 international. Average age 29. 59 applicants, 93% accepted, 40 enrolled. *Faculty:* 6 full-time (5 women), 6 part-time/adjunct (5 women). Expenses: Contact institution. *Financial support:* In 2001–02, 41 students received support, including 1 teaching assistantship with full tuition reimbursement available (averaging $24,000 per year) Financial award application deadline: 3/1; financial award applicants required to submit FAFSA. In 2001, 26 degrees awarded. Postbaccalaureate distance learning degree programs offered (minimal on-campus study). Offers occupational therapy (MSOT). *Application deadline:* For fall admission, 2/1 (priority date). Applications are processed on a rolling basis. *Application fee:* $50. *Associate Dean,* Dr. Scott Douglas McPhee, 615-460-6700, Fax: 615-460-6475, E-mail: mcphees@mail.belmont.edu.

School of Physical Therapy Students: 75 full-time (49 women); includes 4 minority (3 African Americans, 1 Hispanic American) Average age 25. 55 applicants, 78% accepted. *Faculty:* 8 full-time (4 women), 14 part-time/adjunct (9 women). Expenses: Contact institution. *Financial support:* Applicants required to submit FAFSA. In 2001, 55 degrees awarded. Offers physical therapy (MPT, DPT). *Application deadline:* For fall admission, 2/1 (priority date). Applications are processed on a rolling basis. *Application fee:* $50. *Application Contact:* Bridget M. Jacobs, Program Assistant, 615-460-6726, Fax: 615-460-6729, E-mail: jacobsbm@mail.belmont.edu. *Chairman,* Dr. David G. Greathouse, 615-460-6727, Fax: 615-460-6729, E-mail: greathoused@mail.belmont.edu.

College of Visual and Performing Arts Students: 10 full-time (8 women), 34 part-time (20 women); includes 2 minority (both African Americans) Average age 28. 22 applicants, 91% accepted. *Faculty:* 18 full-time (7 women), 11 part-time/adjunct (5 women). Expenses: Contact institution. *Financial support:* In 2001–02, 33 fellowships (averaging $1,000 per year), 5 teaching assistantships (averaging $1,000 per year) were awarded. Career-related internships or fieldwork, scholarships/grants, and unspecified assistantships also available. Financial award application deadline: 3/1; financial award applicants required to submit FAFSA. In 2001, 10 degrees awarded. *Degree program information:* Part-time programs available. Offers visual and performing arts (MM). *Application deadline:* Applications are processed on a rolling basis. *Application fee:* $50. *Application Contact:* Linda Boyte, Graduate Secretary, 615-460-8117, Fax: 615-386-0239, E-mail: boytel@mail.belmont.edu. *Dean,* Dr. Cynthia R. Curtis.

School of Music Students: 10 full-time (8 women), 34 part-time (20 women); includes 2 minority (both African Americans) Average age 28. 22 applicants, 91% accepted. *Faculty:* 18 full-time (7 women), 11 part-time/adjunct (5 women). Expenses: Contact institution. *Financial support:* In 2001–02, 33 fellowships (averaging $1,000 per year), 5 teaching assistantships (averaging $1,000 per year) were awarded. Career-related internships or fieldwork, scholarships/grants, and unspecified assistantships also available. Financial award application deadline: 3/1; financial award applicants required to submit FAFSA. In 2001, 10 degrees awarded. *Degree program information:* Part-time programs available. Offers church music (MM); composition (MM); music education (MM); pedagogy (MM); performance (MM). *Application fee:* $50. *Application Contact:* Linda Boyte, Graduate Secretary, 615-460-8117, Fax: 615-386-0239, E-mail: boytel@mail.belmont.edu. *Director,* Dr. Robert Gregg, 615-460-8106, Fax: 615-386-0239, E-mail: greggr@mail.belmont.edu.

Jack C. Massey Graduate School of Business Students: 1 full-time (0 women), 200 part-time (85 women); includes 21 minority (14 African Americans, 4 Asian Americans or Pacific Islanders, 2 Hispanic Americans, 1 Native American), 2 international. Average age 30. 95 applicants, 60% accepted. *Faculty:* 24 full-time (10 women), 2 part-time/adjunct (1 woman). Expenses: Contact institution. *Financial support:* In 2001–02, 90 students received support, including 3 research assistantships with full tuition reimbursements available; career-related internships or fieldwork and scholarships/grants also available. Support available to part-time students. Financial award application deadline: 7/1; financial award applicants required to submit FAFSA. In 2001, 79 degrees awarded. *Degree program information:* Part-time and evening/weekend programs available. Offers business (M Acc, MBA). *Application deadline:* For fall admission, 7/1; for spring admission, 11/1. Applications are processed on a rolling basis. *Application fee:* $50. Electronic applications accepted. *Application Contact:* Randy Raggio, Director of Graduate Business Program, 615-460-6480, Fax: 615-460-6455, E-mail: masseygrad@mail.belmont.edu. *Dean,* Dr. James Clapper, 615-460-6784, Fax: 615-460-6455, E-mail: clapperj@mail.belmont.edu.

BEMIDJI STATE UNIVERSITY, Bemidji, MN 56601-2699

General Information State-supported, coed, comprehensive institution. *Enrollment:* 36 full-time matriculated graduate/professional students (24 women), 204 part-time matriculated graduate/professional students (145 women). *Enrollment by degree level:* 240 master's. *Graduate faculty:* 62 part-time/adjunct (22 women). *Tuition:* Part-time $174 per credit. *Required fees:* $31 per credit. *Graduate housing:* Rooms and/or apartments available on a first-come, first-served basis to single and married students. Housing application deadline: 4/25. *Student services:* Campus employment opportunities, campus safety program, career counseling, child daycare facilities, disabled student services, exercise/wellness program, free psychological counseling, international student services, multicultural affairs office, teacher training. *Library facilities:* A. C. Clark Library. *Online resources:* library catalog, web page, access to other libraries' catalogs. *Collection:* 554,087 titles, 991 serial subscriptions, 4,673 audiovisual materials.

Computer facilities: 400 computers available on campus for general student use. A campuswide network can be accessed from student residence rooms and from off campus. Internet access and online class registration are available. *Web address:* http://www.bemidjistate.edu/.

General Application Contact: Dr. Martin K. Tadlock, Dean, 218-755-3732, Fax: 218-755-3788, E-mail: mtadlock@bemidjistate.edu.

GRADUATE UNITS

Graduate Studies Students: 240. Average age 34. *Faculty:* 62 part-time/adjunct (22 women). Expenses: Contact institution. *Financial support:* In 2001–02, 14 research assistantships with partial tuition reimbursements (averaging $5,500 per year), 20 teaching assistantships with partial tuition reimbursements (averaging $5,500 per year) were awarded. Career-related internships or fieldwork, Federal Work-Study, and institutionally sponsored loans also available. Support available to part-time students. Financial award application deadline: 5/1. In 2001, 23 degrees awarded. *Degree program information:* Part-time programs available. *Application deadline:* For fall admission, 5/1. Applications are processed on a rolling basis. *Application fee:* $20. *Dean,* Dr. Martin K. Tadlock, 218-755-3732, Fax: 218-755-3788, E-mail: mtadlock@bemidjistate.edu.

College of Professional Studies Average age 35. *Faculty:* 24 part-time/adjunct (13 women). Expenses: Contact institution. *Financial support:* In 2001–02, research assistantships with partial tuition reimbursements (averaging $8,000 per year), 15 teaching assistantships with partial tuition reimbursements (averaging $8,000 per year) were awarded. Career-related internships or fieldwork and Federal Work-Study also available. Support available to part-time students. Financial award application deadline: 5/1. In 2001, 9 degrees awarded. *Degree program information:* Part-time programs available. Postbaccalaureate distance learning degree programs offered (minimal on-campus study). Offers industrial education (MS); physical education (MS); professional studies (MS); special education (MS); teacher education (MS). *Application deadline:* For fall admission, 5/1. *Application fee:* $20. *Interim Dean,* Dr. Martin K. Tadlock, 218-755-2027, Fax: 218-755-3788, E-mail: dlarkin@vax1.bemidji.msus.edu.

College of Social and Natural Sciences Students: 9 full-time (4 women), 16 part-time (2 women). Average age 31. *Faculty:* 29 part-time/adjunct (6 women). Expenses: Contact institution. *Financial support:* In 2001–02, 5 research assistantships with partial tuition reimbursements (averaging $8,000 per year), 4 teaching assistantships with partial tuition reimbursements (averaging $8,000 per year) were awarded. Career-related internships or fieldwork and Federal Work-Study also available. Support available to part-time students. Financial award application deadline: 5/1. In 2001, 9 degrees awarded. *Degree program information:* Part-time programs available. Offers biology (MA); environmental studies (MS); mathematics (MS); science (MS); social and natural sciences (MA, MS). *Application deadline:* For fall admission, 5/1. *Application fee:* $20. *Dean,* Dr. Ranae Womack, 218-755-2965, Fax: 218-755-2822, E-mail: rwomack@bemidjistate.edu.

Division of Arts and Letters Average age 32. *Faculty:* 8 part-time/adjunct (3 women). Expenses: Contact institution. *Financial support:* In 2001–02, research assistantships with partial tuition reimbursements (averaging $8,000 per year), 7 teaching assistantships with partial tuition reimbursements (averaging $8,000 per year) were awarded. Career-related internships or fieldwork and Federal Work-Study also available. Support available to part-time students. Financial award application deadline: 5/1. In 2001, 2 degrees awarded. *Degree program information:* Part-time programs available. Offers arts and letters (MA, MS); English (MA, MS). *Application deadline:* For fall admission, 5/1 (priority date). Applications are processed on a rolling basis. *Application fee:* $20. *Dean,* Dr. Nancy Erickson, 218-755-2988, E-mail: nerickson@bemidjistate.edu.

BENEDICTINE COLLEGE, Atchison, KS 66002-1499

General Information Independent-religious, coed, comprehensive institution. *Enrollment:* 29 full-time matriculated graduate/professional students (9 women), 48 part-time matriculated graduate/professional students (25 women). *Enrollment by degree level:* 77 master's. *Graduate faculty:* 4 full-time (0 women), 9 part-time/adjunct (3 women). *Tuition:* Full-time $16,000; part-time $210 per credit hour. One-time fee: $100 part-time. Full-time tuition and fees vary according to course load and program. *Graduate housing:* On-campus housing not available. *Student services:* Campus employment opportunities, career counseling, disabled student services, free psychological counseling. *Library facilities:* Benedictine College Library. *Online resources:* library catalog, web page, access to other libraries' catalogs. *Collection:* 366,212 titles, 501 serial subscriptions, 831 audiovisual materials.

Computer facilities: 80 computers available on campus for general student use. A campuswide network can be accessed from student residence rooms and from off campus. Internet access is available. *Web address:* http://www.benedictine.edu/.

General Application Contact: Kelly Vowels, Dean of Enrollment Management, 913-367-5340 Ext. 2476, Fax: 913-367-5462, E-mail: bcadmiss@benedictine.edu.

GRADUATE UNITS

Executive Master of Business Administration Program Students: 29 full-time (9 women), 9 part-time (3 women); includes 9 minority (7 African Americans, 1 Asian American or Pacific Islander, 1 Hispanic American), 1 international. Average age 35. 25 applicants, 100% accepted. *Faculty:* 4 full-time (0 women), 4 part-time/adjunct (0 women). Expenses: Contact institution. *Financial support:* Federal Work-Study and scholarships/grants available. Support available to part-time students. Financial award application deadline: 3/1; financial award applicants required to submit FAFSA. In 2001, 19 degrees awarded. *Degree program information:* Evening/weekend programs available. Offers executive business administration (EMBA). *Application deadline:* For fall admission, 7/1 (priority date). *Application fee:* $100. Electronic applications accepted. *Chair,* Carol Shomin, 913-367-5340 Ext. 2589, Fax: 913-367-1049, E-mail: cshomin@benedictine.edu.

Program in Educational Administration Average age 35. 16 applicants, 100% accepted. *Faculty:* 5 part-time/adjunct (3 women). Expenses: Contact institution. *Financial support:* Career-related internships or fieldwork and Federal Work-Study available. Support available to part-time students. Financial award application deadline: 3/1; financial award applicants required to submit FAFSA. *Degree program information:* Part-time and evening/weekend programs available. Offers educational administration (MA). *Application deadline:* Applications are processed on a rolling basis. *Application fee:* $25. *Director,* Dr. Dianna Henderson, 913-367-5340 Ext. 2386, E-mail: diannah@benedictine.edu.

BENEDICTINE UNIVERSITY, Lisle, IL 60532-0900

General Information Independent-religious, coed, comprehensive institution. *Graduate housing:* On-campus housing not available.

GRADUATE UNITS

Graduate Programs *Degree program information:* Part-time and evening/weekend programs available. Offers business (EMBA); business administration (MBA); counseling psychology (MS); curriculum and instruction and collaborative teaching (M Ed); elementary education (MA Ed); exercise physiology (MS); fitness management (MS); liberal studies (MA); management and organizational behavior (MS); management information systems (MS); organizational development (PhD); public health (MPH); special education (MA Ed). Electronic applications accepted.

See in-depth description on page 759.

BENNINGTON COLLEGE, Bennington, VT 05201

General Information Independent, coed, comprehensive institution. *Enrollment:* 130 full-time matriculated graduate/professional students (88 women), 7 part-time matriculated graduate/professional students (5 women). *Enrollment by degree level:* 136 master's, 1 other

Bennington College (continued)

advanced degree. *Graduate faculty:* 53 full-time, 47 part-time/adjunct. *Tuition:* Full-time $15,400. *Required fees:* $550. Full-time tuition and fees vary according to program. *Graduate housing:* On-campus housing not available. *Student services:* Campus employment opportunities, campus safety program, career counseling, child daycare facilities, exercise/wellness program, free psychological counseling, international student services, low-cost health insurance, teacher training, writing training. *Library facilities:* Crossett Library plus 2 others. *Online resources:* library catalog, web page, access to other libraries' catalogs. *Collection:* 121,000 titles, 500 serial subscriptions, 27,500 audiovisual materials.

Computer facilities: 60 computers available on campus for general student use. A campuswide network can be accessed from student residence rooms and from off campus. Internet access is available. *Web address:* http://www.bennington.edu/.

General Application Contact: Deane Bogardus, Director, Admissions and The First Year, 802-440-4312, Fax: 802-440-4320, E-mail: admissions@bennington.edu.

GRADUATE UNITS

Graduate Programs Students: 130 full-time (88 women), 7 part-time (5 women); includes 7 minority (2 African Americans, 5 Hispanic Americans), 7 international. Average age 32. 110 applicants, 39% accepted. *Faculty:* 53 full-time, 47 part-time/adjunct. Expenses: Contact institution. *Financial support:* In 2001–02, 23 students received support, including 11 fellowships (averaging $7,622 per year), 12 teaching assistantships with full and partial tuition reimbursements available (averaging $9,370 per year); career-related internships or fieldwork, scholarships/grants, and unspecified assistantships also available. Financial award application deadline: 3/1; financial award applicants required to submit FAFSA. In 2001, 62 master's, 5 other advanced degrees awarded. *Degree program information:* Part-time programs available. Postbaccalaureate distance learning degree programs offered (minimal on-campus study). Offers biological sciences (Certificate); creative writing (MFA); dance (MFA); drama (MFA); liberal studies (MALS); music (MFA); teaching (MAT); teaching a second language (MATSL); visual arts (MFA). *Application deadline:* Applications are processed on a rolling basis. *Application fee:* $50. *Application Contact:* Deane Bogardus, Director, Admissions and The First Year, 802-440-4312, Fax: 802-440-4320, E-mail: admissions@bennington.edu. *Dean of Studies,* Wendy Hirsch, 802-440-4400, Fax: 802-440-4320, E-mail: thedean@bennington.edu.

See in-depth description on page 761.

BENTLEY COLLEGE, Waltham, MA 02452-4705

General Information Independent, coed, comprehensive institution. CGS member. *Enrollment:* 302 full-time matriculated graduate/professional students (132 women), 1,029 part-time matriculated graduate/professional students (478 women). *Enrollment by degree level:* 1,298 master's, 33 other advanced degrees. *Graduate faculty:* 243 full-time (82 women), 179 part-time/adjunct (79 women). *Tuition:* Full-time $18,640; part-time $777 per credit. *Required fees:* $100. *Graduate housing:* Rooms and/or apartments available on a first-come, first-served basis to single and married students. Housing application deadline: 6/15. *Student services:* Campus employment opportunities, campus safety program, career counseling, free psychological counseling, international student services, low-cost health insurance, multicultural affairs office. *Library facilities:* Soloman R. Baker Library. *Online resources:* library catalog, web page, access to other libraries' catalogs. *Collection:* 208,986 titles, 9,319 serial subscriptions.

Computer facilities: 3,349 computers available on campus for general student use. A campuswide network can be accessed from student residence rooms and from off campus. Internet access and online class registration are available. *Web address:* http://www.bentley.edu/.

General Application Contact: Paul Vaccaro, Director of Graduate Admissions, 781-891-2108, Fax: 781-891-2464, E-mail: pvaccaro@bentley.edu.

GRADUATE UNITS

The Elkin B. McCallum Graduate School of Business Students: 302 full-time (132 women), 1,029 part-time (478 women); includes 90 minority (20 African Americans, 52 Asian Americans or Pacific Islanders, 16 Hispanic Americans, 2 Native Americans), 224 international. Average age 30. *Faculty:* 243 full-time (82 women), 179 part-time/adjunct (79 women). Expenses: Contact institution. *Financial support:* In 2001–02, 302 students received support, including 54 research assistantships; career-related internships or fieldwork, Federal Work-Study, and unspecified assistantships also available. Support available to part-time students. Financial award application deadline: 4/15; financial award applicants required to submit CSS PROFILE or FAFSA. In 2001, 556 degrees awarded. *Degree program information:* Part-time and evening/weekend programs available. Offers accountancy (MBA); accounting (MSA, Certificate); accounting information systems (MSAIS, Certificate); advanced accountancy (MBA); business (IAMBA, MBA, MSA, MSAIS, MSCIS, MSF, MSFP, MSGFA, MSHFID, MSIAM, MSIT, MSPFP, MST, Advanced Certificate, Certificate); business administration (Advanced Certificate); business communication (MBA); business data analysis (MBA, Certificate); business economics (MBA); business ethics (MBA, Certificate); computer information systems (MSCIS); corporate finance (MSF); e-business (MBA, Certificate); entrepreneurial studies (MBA); finance (MBA); financial planning (MSFP, Advanced Certificate, Certificate); global financial analysis (MSGFA); human factors in information design (MSHFID); information age marketing (MSIAM, Certificate); information technology (MSIT); international business (MBA); management (MBA); management information systems (MBA); management of technology (MBA); marketing (MBA); operations management (MBA); taxation (MBA, MST, Advanced Certificate, Certificate). *Application deadline:* For fall admission, 6/1 (priority date); for spring admission, 11/1. Applications are processed on a rolling basis. *Application fee:* $50. Electronic applications accepted. *Application Contact:* Paul Vaccaro, Director of Graduate Admissions, 781-891-2108, Fax: 781-891-2464, E-mail: pvaccaro@bentley.edu. *Dean,* Dr. Patricia M. Flynn, 781-891-2921, Fax: 781-891-2464.

BERNARD M. BARUCH COLLEGE OF THE CITY UNIVERSITY OF NEW YORK, New York, NY 10010-5585

General Information State and locally supported, coed, comprehensive institution. *Enrollment:* 1,058 full-time matriculated graduate/professional students (524 women), 1,748 part-time matriculated graduate/professional students (868 women). *Enrollment by degree level:* 2,735 master's, 71 doctoral. *Graduate faculty:* 261 full-time (59 women), 72 part-time/adjunct (23 women). Tuition, state resident: full-time $4,350; part-time $185 per credit. Tuition, nonresident: full-time $7,600; part-time $320 per credit. Tuition and fees vary according to program. *Graduate housing:* On-campus housing not available. *Student services:* Campus employment opportunities, campus safety program, career counseling, child daycare facilities, disabled student services, exercise/wellness program, free psychological counseling, international student services, low-cost health insurance, multicultural affairs office, teacher training, writing training. *Library facilities:* The William and Anita Newman Library plus 1 other. *Collection:* 248,909 titles, 4,167 serial subscriptions, 951 audiovisual materials.

Computer facilities: 1,500 computers available on campus for general student use. A campuswide network can be accessed from off campus. Internet access is available. *Web address:* http://www.baruch.cuny.edu/.

General Application Contact: Frances Murphy, Office of Graduate Admissions, 646-312-1300, Fax: 646-312-1301, E-mail: zicklingradadmissions@baruch.cuny.edu.

GRADUATE UNITS

School of Public Affairs Students: 148 full-time (77 women), 463 part-time (311 women); includes 303 minority (166 African Americans, 39 Asian Americans or Pacific Islanders, 98 Hispanic Americans), 13 international. Average age 33. 434 applicants, 52% accepted, 210 enrolled. *Faculty:* 31 full-time (8 women), 26 part-time/adjunct (17 women). Expenses: Contact institution. *Financial support:* In 2001–02, 21 research assistantships with tuition reimbursements (averaging $9,000 per year), 1 teaching assistantship (averaging $6,000 per year) were awarded. Fellowships, career-related internships or fieldwork, Federal Work-Study, scholarships/grants, tuition waivers (full), and unspecified assistantships also available. Support available to part-time students. Financial award application deadline: 5/30; financial award applicants required to submit FAFSA. In 2001, 127 master's, 6 other advanced degrees awarded. *Degree program information:* Part-time and evening/weekend programs available. Offers educational administration and supervision (MS Ed, SAS); higher education administration (MS Ed); public administration (MPA); public affairs (MPA, MS Ed, SAS). *Application deadline:* For fall admission, 7/15; for spring admission, 12/3. Applications are processed on a rolling basis. *Application fee:* $40. *Application Contact:* Pamela S. Ferner, Director of Admissions, 212-802-5912, Fax: 212-802-5928, E-mail: spa_admissions@baruch.cuny.edu. *Dean,* Stan Altman, 212-802-5900, Fax: 212-802-5903, E-mail: stan_altman@baruch.uny.edu.

Weissman School of Arts and Sciences Offers arts and sciences (MA); business journalism (MA); corporate communication (MA).

Zicklin School of Business Students: 866 full-time (396 women), 1,136 part-time (488 women); includes 395 minority (96 African Americans, 225 Asian Americans or Pacific Islanders, 72 Hispanic Americans, 2 Native Americans), 702 international. Average age 28. 2,076 applicants, 52% accepted, 634 enrolled. *Faculty:* 198 full-time (48 women), 39 part-time/adjunct (6 women). Expenses: Contact institution. *Financial support:* In 2001–02, 34 fellowships (averaging $2,500 per year), 28 research assistantships (averaging $5,000 per year) were awarded. Career-related internships or fieldwork, Federal Work-Study, institutionally sponsored loans, and scholarships/grants also available. Financial award application deadline: 5/1; financial award applicants required to submit FAFSA. In 2001, 766 master's, 9 doctorates awarded. *Degree program information:* Part-time and evening/weekend programs available. Offers accounting (MBA, MS, PhD); business (EMBA, EMSF, MBA, MS, PhD, Certificate); business administration (EMBA); computer information systems (MBA, MS, PhD); economics (MBA); finance (EMSF, MBA, MS, PhD); general business (MBA); general management and policy (MBA); health care administration (MBA); human resources management (MBA); industrial and labor relations (MS); industrial and organizational psychology (MBA, MS, PhD, Certificate); industrial and service management (MBA); international business (MBA); management planning systems (PhD); management science (MBA); marketing (MBA, MS, PhD); operations research (MBA, MS); organization and policy studies (PhD); organizational behavior (MBA); statistics (MBA, MS); taxation (MBA, MS). *Application deadline:* For fall admission, 4/30; for spring admission, 10/31. Applications are processed on a rolling basis. *Application fee:* $40. Electronic applications accepted. *Application Contact:* Frances Murphy, Office of Graduate Admissions, 646-312-1300, Fax: 646-312-1301, E-mail: zicklingradadmissions@baruch.cuny.edu. *Director of Graduate Studies,* Sidney Lirtzman, 646-312-3065, Fax: 646-312-3131, E-mail: andreas_grein@baruch.cuny.edu.

BERRY COLLEGE, Mount Berry, GA 30149-0159

General Information Independent-religious, coed, comprehensive institution. *Enrollment:* 25 full-time matriculated graduate/professional students (18 women), 121 part-time matriculated graduate/professional students (87 women). *Enrollment by degree level:* 120 master's, 26 other advanced degrees. *Graduate faculty:* 2 full-time (1 woman), 20 part-time/adjunct (11 women). *Tuition:* Full-time $8,064; part-time $448 per credit hour. *Graduate housing:* On-campus housing not available. *Student services:* Campus employment opportunities, campus safety program, career counseling, child daycare facilities, exercise/wellness program, free psychological counseling, international student services, low-cost health insurance. *Library facilities:* Memorial Library plus 1 other. *Online resources:* library catalog, web page. *Collection:* 264,714 titles, 1,364 serial subscriptions. *Research affiliation:* Gulf Coast Research Laboratory (marine science).

Computer facilities: 100 computers available on campus for general student use. A campuswide network can be accessed from student residence rooms. Internet access is available. *Web address:* http://www.berry.edu/.

General Application Contact: George Gaddie, Dean of Admissions, 706-236-2215, Fax: 706-290-2178, E-mail: ggaddie@berry.edu.

GRADUATE UNITS

Graduate Programs Students: 25 full-time (18 women), 121 part-time (87 women); includes 5 minority (4 African Americans, 1 Native American), 2 international. Average age 34. 51 applicants, 75% accepted, 28 enrolled. *Faculty:* 2 full-time (1 woman), 20 part-time/adjunct (11 women). Expenses: Contact institution. *Financial support:* In 2001–02, 90 students received support, including 7 research assistantships with full tuition reimbursements available (averaging $4,500 per year); scholarships/grants and unspecified assistantships also available. Support available to part-time students. Financial award application deadline: 4/1; financial award applicants required to submit FAFSA. In 2001, 42 master's awarded. *Degree program information:* Part-time and evening/weekend programs available. Offers curriculum and instruction (Ed S); early childhood education (M Ed); middle-grades education and reading (M Ed); secondary education (M Ed). *Application deadline:* For fall admission, 7/26; for spring admission, 12/9. Applications are processed on a rolling basis. *Application fee:* $25 ($30 for international students). *Application Contact:* George Gaddie, Dean of Admissions, 706-236-2215, Fax: 706-290-2178, E-mail: ggaddie@berry.edu. *Provost,* Dr. Thomas E. Dasher, 706-236-2216, Fax: 706-290-2179, E-mail: tdasher@berry.edu.

Campbell School of Business Students: 1 full-time (0 women), 15 part-time (5 women); includes 1 minority (African American), 1 international. Average age 29. 12 applicants, 75% accepted, 6 enrolled. *Faculty:* 4 part-time/adjunct (2 women). Expenses: Contact institution. *Financial support:* In 2001–02, 8 students received support, including 3 research assistantships with full tuition reimbursements available (averaging $4,500 per year); scholarships/grants and unspecified assistantships also available. Support available to part-time students. Financial award application deadline: 4/1; financial award applicants required to submit FAFSA. In 2001, 8 degrees awarded. *Degree program information:* Part-time and evening/weekend programs available. Offers business (MBA). *Application deadline:* For fall admission, 7/26; for spring admission, 12/9. Applications are processed on a rolling basis. *Application fee:* $25 ($30 for international students). *Application Contact:* George Gaddie, Dean of Admissions, 706-236-2215, Fax: 706-290-2178, E-mail: ggaddie@berry.edu. *Dean,* Dr. Krishna Dhir, 706-236-2233, Fax: 706-802-6728, E-mail: kdhir@campbell.berry.edu.

BETHANY COLLEGE OF THE ASSEMBLIES OF GOD, Scotts Valley, CA 95066-2820

General Information Independent-religious, coed, comprehensive institution. *Graduate housing:* Rooms and/or apartments available to single and married students. Housing application deadline: 7/31.

GRADUATE UNITS

Program in Teacher Education *Degree program information:* Part-time and evening/weekend programs available. Offers education (MA); educational leadership (MA).

BETHANY THEOLOGICAL SEMINARY, Richmond, IN 47374-4019

General Information Independent-religious, coed, graduate-only institution. *Graduate faculty:* 9 full-time (3 women), 12 part-time/adjunct (5 women). *Graduate housing:* On-campus housing not available. *Student services:* Campus employment opportunities, career counseling, exercise/wellness program, free psychological counseling, international student services, low-cost health insurance. *Library facilities:* Lilly Library plus 1 other. *Online resources:* library catalog, web page, access to other libraries' catalogs. *Collection:* 350,000 titles, 1,400 serial subscriptions.

Computer facilities: 135 computers available on campus for general student use. A campuswide network can be accessed from off campus. Internet access is available. *Web address:* http://www.brethren.org/bethany/.

General Application Contact: David Shetler, Director of Admissions and Student Development, 800-BTS-8822 Ext. 1806, Fax: 765-983-1840, E-mail: bethanysem@aol.com.

GRADUATE UNITS

Graduate and Professional Programs Students: 32 full-time (17 women), 44 part-time (19 women), 2 international. Average age 34. 30 applicants, 93% accepted. *Faculty:* 9 full-time (3 women), 12 part-time/adjunct (5 women). Expenses: Contact institution. *Financial support:* Career-related internships or fieldwork and scholarships/grants available. Support available to part-time students. Financial award application deadline: 4/1; financial award applicants required to submit FAFSA. In 2001, 9 first professional degrees, 4 master's awarded. *Degree program information:* Part-time programs available. Offers biblical studies (MA Th); ministry studies (M Div); peace studies (M Div, MA Th); theological studies (MA Th, CATS). *Application deadline:* For fall admission, 7/31; for spring admission, 12/1. Applications are processed on a rolling basis. *Application fee:* $25. *Application Contact:* David Shetler, Director of Admissions and Student Development, 800-BTS-8822 Ext. 1806, Fax: 765-983-1840, E-mail: bethanysem@aol.com. *Academic Dean*, Richard B. Gardner, 765-983-1800, Fax: 765-983-1840, E-mail: gardnri@earlham.edu.

BETH BENJAMIN ACADEMY OF CONNECTICUT, Stamford, CT 06901-1202

General Information Independent-religious, men only, comprehensive institution. *Graduate housing:* Rooms and/or apartments available to single and married students.

GRADUATE UNITS

Graduate and Professional Programs

BETHEL COLLEGE, Mishawaka, IN 46545-5591

General Information Independent-religious, coed, comprehensive institution. *Enrollment:* 5 full-time matriculated graduate/professional students (1 woman), 114 part-time matriculated graduate/professional students (55 women). *Enrollment by degree level:* 119 master's. *Graduate faculty:* 10 part-time/adjunct (2 women). *Tuition:* Full-time $5,940; part-time $330 per semester hour. *Graduate housing:* On-campus housing not available. *Student services:* Campus employment opportunities, career counseling. *Library facilities:* Otis and Elizabeth Bowen Library. *Online resources:* library catalog, web page, access to other libraries' catalogs. *Collection:* 99,381 titles, 3,450 serial subscriptions, 3,740 audiovisual materials.

Computer facilities: 110 computers available on campus for general student use. A campuswide network can be accessed from student residence rooms and from off campus. Internet access is available. *Web address:* http://www.bethelcollege.edu.

General Application Contact: Dr. Robert Laurent, Dean, Division of Graduate Studies, 219-257-3353, Fax: 219-257-3357.

GRADUATE UNITS

Division of Graduate Studies Students: 5 full-time (1 woman), 114 part-time (55 women); includes 9 minority (6 African Americans, 1 Asian American or Pacific Islander, 1 Hispanic American, 1 Native American), 6 international. 15 applicants, 100% accepted. *Faculty:* 10 part-time/adjunct (2 women). Expenses: Contact institution. *Financial support:* Career-related internships or fieldwork and unspecified assistantships available. Financial award applicants required to submit FAFSA. In 2001, 24 degrees awarded. *Degree program information:* Part-time programs available. Offers business administration (MBA); Christian ministries (M Min); marriage and family counseling/therapy (MA); mental health counseling (MA); theological studies (MA). *Application deadline:* Applications are processed on a rolling basis. *Application fee:* $25. Electronic applications accepted. *Dean*, Dr. Robert Laurent, 219-257-3353, Fax: 219-257-3357.

BETHEL COLLEGE, St. Paul, MN 55112-6999

General Information Independent-religious, coed, comprehensive institution. *Enrollment:* 274 full-time matriculated graduate/professional students (197 women). *Enrollment by degree level:* 274 master's. *Graduate faculty:* 62 full-time (30 women), 27 part-time/adjunct (13 women). *Tuition:* Part-time $325 per credit. One-time fee: $125 full-time. *Graduate housing:* On-campus housing not available. *Student services:* Campus employment opportunities, campus safety program, career counseling, free psychological counseling, low-cost health insurance, multicultural affairs office, writing training. *Library facilities:* Bethel College Library plus 1 other. *Online resources:* library catalog, web page, access to other libraries' catalogs. *Collection:* 156,000 titles, 4,045 serial subscriptions, 6,970 audiovisual materials.

Computer facilities: 367 computers available on campus for general student use. A campuswide network can be accessed from student residence rooms and from off campus. Internet access is available. *Web address:* http://www.bethel.edu/.

General Application Contact: Vanessa Beaudry, Senior Admissions Coordinator, 651-635-8000, Fax: 651-635-1464, E-mail: v_beaudry@bethel.edu.

GRADUATE UNITS

Center for Graduate and Continuing Studies Students: 274 full-time (197 women). Average age 35. *Faculty:* 62 full-time (30 women), 27 part-time/adjunct (13 women). Expenses: Contact institution. *Financial support:* Institutionally sponsored loans and scholarships/grants available. Financial award applicants required to submit FAFSA. *Degree program information:* Evening/weekend programs available. Offers anthropology and sociology (MA); communication (MA); education (M Ed, MAT); music (MA); nursing (MA); organizational studies (MA); psychology (MA). *Application deadline:* Applications are processed on a rolling basis. *Application fee:* $25. *Application Contact:* Vanessa Beaudry, Senior Admissions Coordinator, 651-635-8000, Fax: 651-635-1464, E-mail: m-washenberger@bethel.edu. *Dean*, Dr. Carl Polding, 651-635-8000, Fax: 651-635-1464, E-mail: cgcs@bethel.edu.

BETHEL COLLEGE, McKenzie, TN 38201

General Information Independent-religious, coed, comprehensive institution. *Enrollment:* 37 full-time matriculated graduate/professional students (27 women), 53 part-time matriculated graduate/professional students (31 women). *Enrollment by degree level:* 90 master's. *Graduate faculty:* 6 full-time (4 women), 2 part-time/adjunct (1 woman). *Tuition:* Part-time $230 per semester hour. *Graduate housing:* Room and/or apartments available on a first-come, first-served basis to single students; on-campus housing not available to married students. Typical cost: $965 per year ($2,370 including board). Housing application deadline: 7/31. *Student services:* Career counseling, free psychological counseling. *Library facilities:* Burroughs Learning Center. *Collection:* 73,288 titles, 254 serial subscriptions.

Computer facilities: 35 computers available on campus for general student use. A campuswide network can be accessed. Internet access is available. *Web address:* http://www.bethel-college.edu/.

General Application Contact: Dr. Ben G. McClure, Associate Dean for Graduate Studies, 731-352-4025, Fax: 731-352-4069, E-mail: graduate@bethel-college.edu.

GRADUATE UNITS

Program in Education Students: 37 full-time (27 women), 53 part-time (31 women). Average age 32. 14 applicants, 100% accepted. *Faculty:* 6 full-time (4 women), 2 part-time/adjunct (1 woman). Expenses: Contact institution. *Financial support:* In 2001–02, 15 students received support. Career-related internships or fieldwork available. Support available to part-time students. Financial award application deadline: 6/1; financial award applicants required to submit FAFSA. In 2001, 26 degrees awarded. *Degree program information:* Part-time and evening/weekend programs available. Offers Administration and Supervision (MA Ed); biology education 78-12 (MAT); elementary education (MAT); english education 78-12 (MAT); history education 78-12 (MAT); physical education K8-12 (MAT); special education K8-12 (MAT). *Application deadline:* For fall admission, 8/24 (priority date); for spring admission, 1/7 (priority date). Applications are processed on a rolling basis. *Application fee:* $10. *Associate Dean for Graduate Studies*, Dr. Ben G. McClure, 731-352-4025, Fax: 731-352-4069, E-mail: graduate@bethel-college.edu.

BETHEL SEMINARY, St. Paul, MN 55112-6998

General Information Independent-religious, coed, graduate-only institution. *Enrollment by degree level:* 430 first professional, 449 master's, 109 doctoral, 11 other advanced degrees. *Graduate faculty:* 24 full-time (4 women), 108 part-time/adjunct (15 women). *Tuition:* Full-time $9,420; part-time $196 per quarter hour. *Required fees:* $15; $5 per quarter. *Graduate housing:* Rooms and/or apartments available on a first-come, first-served basis to single and married students. Typical cost: $2,295 per year for single students; $4,590 per year for married students. Room charges vary according to housing facility selected. Housing application deadline: 6/1. *Student services:* Campus employment opportunities, campus safety program, career counseling, child daycare facilities, free psychological counseling, multicultural affairs office. *Library facilities:* Carl H. Lundquist Library plus 1 other. *Online resources:* library catalog, web page, access to other libraries' catalogs. *Collection:* 221,888 titles, 628 serial subscriptions, 7,875 audiovisual materials.

Computer facilities: 19 computers available on campus for general student use. A campuswide network can be accessed from student residence rooms and from off campus. Internet access is available. *Web address:* http://www.bethel.edu/seminary/btshome.htm.

General Application Contact: Morris Anderson, Director of Admissions, 651-638-6288, Fax: 651-638-6002.

GRADUATE UNITS

Graduate and Professional Programs Students: 480 full-time (127 women), 519 part-time (218 women); includes 129 minority (61 African Americans, 51 Asian Americans or Pacific Islanders, 15 Hispanic Americans, 2 Native Americans), 19 international. Average age 36. 275 applicants, 89% accepted. *Faculty:* 24 full-time (4 women), 108 part-time/adjunct (15 women). Expenses: Contact institution. *Financial support:* In 2001–02, 375 students received support, including 20 teaching assistantships; career-related internships or fieldwork, Federal Work-Study, institutionally sponsored loans, and scholarships/grants also available. Financial award application deadline: 7/15; financial award applicants required to submit FAFSA. In 2001, 47 first professional degrees, 62 master's, 18 doctorates awarded. *Degree program information:* Part-time and evening/weekend programs available. Postbaccalaureate distance learning degree programs offered (minimal on-campus study). Offers biblical studies (M Div, MATS); children's and family ministry (MACFM); Christian education (M Div, MACE); Christian thought (MACT); church leadership (D Min); evangelism (M Div); global missions (Certificate); historical studies (M Div, MATS); marriage and family studies (M Div, MAMFT, D Min); missions (M Div, MATS); New Testament (M Div); Old Testament (M Div); pastoral care (M Div, MATS); pastoral ministries (M Div); preaching (M Div); theological studies (M Div, MATS); transformational leadership (MATL); youth ministry (M Div, MACE). *Application deadline:* For fall admission, 8/1 (priority date); for winter admission, 12/1 (priority date); for spring admission, 1/1 (priority date). Applications are processed on a rolling basis. *Application fee:* $20. *Application Contact:* Morris Anderson, Director of Admissions, 651-638-6288, Fax: 651-638-6002. *Executive Vice President and Provost*, Dr. Leland Eliason, 651-638-6182.

BETHESDA CHRISTIAN UNIVERSITY, Anaheim, CA 92801

General Information Independent-religious, comprehensive institution.

GRADUATE UNITS

Graduate and Professional Programs Offers ministerial studies (MA); missionary ministry (M Div); missionary studies (MA); pastoral ministry (M Div). Electronic applications accepted.

BETH HAMEDRASH SHAAREI YOSHER INSTITUTE, Brooklyn, NY 11204

General Information Independent-religious, men only, comprehensive institution.

BETH HATALMUD RABBINICAL COLLEGE, Brooklyn, NY 11214

General Information Independent-religious, men only, comprehensive institution.

BETH MEDRASH GOVOHA, Lakewood, NJ 08701-2797

General Information Independent-religious, men only, upper-level institution.

BIBLICAL THEOLOGICAL SEMINARY, Hatfield, PA 19440-2499

General Information Independent-religious, coed, graduate-only institution. *Enrollment by degree level:* 152 first professional, 113 master's, 14 doctoral. *Graduate faculty:* 10 full-time (1 woman), 5 part-time/adjunct (0 women). *Tuition:* Full-time $7,200; part-time $300 per credit. One-time fee: $30 full-time. *Graduate housing:* Rooms and/or apartments available to single students and available on a first-come, first-served basis to married students. Typical cost: $1,980 per year for single students; $1,980 per year for married students. *Student services:* Campus employment opportunities, career counseling, free psychological counseling. *Library facilities:* Biblical Theological Library. *Collection:* 52,000 titles, 210 serial subscriptions. *Research affiliation:* Institute of Holy Land Studies (Israel, Hebrew, archaeology), Christian Counseling and Education Foundation (psychology).

Computer facilities: 20 computers available on campus for general student use. A campuswide network can be accessed. Internet access and online class registration are available. *Web address:* http://www.biblical.edu/.

General Application Contact: Rev. Darryl John Lang, Assistant Director of Admissions, 215-368-5000, Fax: 215-368-7002, E-mail: dlang@biblical.edu.

GRADUATE UNITS

Graduate and Professional Programs Students: 124 full-time (26 women), 155 part-time (41 women); includes 106 minority (29 African Americans, 76 Asian Americans or Pacific Islanders, 1 Hispanic American), 23 international. *Faculty:* 10 full-time (1 woman), 5 part-time/adjunct (all women). Expenses: Contact institution. *Financial support:* Career-related internships or fieldwork, institutionally sponsored loans, and scholarships/grants available. Support available to part-time students. Financial award application deadline: 5/15. In 2001, 13 first professional degrees, 45 master's, 1 doctorate awarded. *Degree program information:* Part-time and evening/weekend programs available. Offers counseling (MA); ministry (MA); theology (M Div, Th M, D Min). *Application deadline:* Applications are processed on a rolling basis. *Application fee:* $30. *Application Contact:* Rev. Darryl John Lang, Assistant Director of Admissions, 215-368-5000, Fax: 215-368-7002, E-mail: dlang@biblical.edu. *Acting Academic Dean*, Dr. David G. Dunbar, 215-368-5000, Fax: 215-368-7002.

BIOLA UNIVERSITY, La Mirada, CA 90639-0001

General Information Independent-religious, coed, university. *Enrollment:* 487 full-time matriculated graduate/professional students (161 women), 750 part-time matriculated graduate/professional students (292 women). *Enrollment by degree level:* 127 first professional, 696 master's, 399 doctoral, 15 other advanced degrees. *Graduate faculty:* 69 full-time (18 women), 71 part-time/adjunct (27 women). *Tuition:* Part-time $327 per unit. Full-time tuition and fees vary according to degree level and program. *Graduate housing:* Room and/or apartments available on a first-come, first-served basis to single students; on-campus housing not available to married students. Typical cost: $3,400 per year ($5,298 including board). Room and board charges vary according to board plan. Housing application deadline: 6/1. *Student services:* Campus employment opportunities, campus safety program, career counseling, disabled student services, international student services, low-cost health insurance, multicultural affairs office, teacher training, writing training. *Library facilities:* Rose Memorial Library. *Online resources:* library catalog, web page. *Collection:* 259,285 titles, 1,188 serial subscriptions, 10,343 audiovisual materials.

Computer facilities: 115 computers available on campus for general student use. A campuswide network can be accessed from student residence rooms and from off campus. Internet access and online class registration are available. *Web address:* http://www.biola.edu/.

General Application Contact: Roy M. Allinson, Director of Graduate Admissions, 562-903-4752, Fax: 562-903-4709, E-mail: admissions@biola.edu.

GRADUATE UNITS

Rosemead School of Psychology Students: 130 full-time (77 women); includes 24 minority (1 African American, 19 Asian Americans or Pacific Islanders, 4 Hispanic Americans), 13

Biola University (continued)

international. Average age 29. 116 applicants, 30% accepted, 23 enrolled. *Faculty:* 14 full-time (5 women), 8 part-time/adjunct (3 women). Expenses: Contact institution. *Financial support:* Research assistantships, teaching assistantships, career-related internships or fieldwork, institutionally sponsored loans, and scholarships/grants available. Support available to part-time students. Financial award application deadline: 3/2; financial award applicants required to submit FAFSA. In 2001, 17 master's, 30 doctorates awarded. Offers psychology (MA, PhD, Psy D). *Application deadline:* For fall admission, 1/15. *Application fee:* $45. *Application Contact:* Roy M. Allinson, Director of Graduate Admissions, 562-903-4752, Fax: 562-903-4709, E-mail: admissions@biola.edu. *Administrative Dean,* Dr. Patricia Pike, 562-903-4867, Fax: 562-903-4864.

School of Arts and Sciences Students: 45 full-time (30 women), 105 part-time (84 women); includes 50 minority (10 African Americans, 26 Asian Americans or Pacific Islanders, 14 Hispanic Americans), 9 international. 138 applicants, 74% accepted. *Faculty:* 7 full-time (6 women), 17 part-time/adjunct (12 women). Expenses: Contact institution. *Financial support:* Career-related internships or fieldwork, institutionally sponsored loans, and scholarships/grants available. Support available to part-time students. Financial award application deadline: 3/2; financial award applicants required to submit FAFSA. In 2001, 48 degrees awarded. *Degree program information:* Part-time and evening/weekend programs available. Offers arts and sciences (MA Ed). *Application deadline:* For fall admission, 7/1; for spring admission, 12/1. Applications are processed on a rolling basis. *Application fee:* $45. *Application Contact:* Roy M. Allinson, Director of Graduate Admissions, 562-903-4752, Fax: 562-903-4709, E-mail: admissions@biola.edu. *Chair of Education Department,* Dr. June Hetzel, 562-903-4843, Fax: 562-903-4709, E-mail: june_hetzel@peter.biola.edu.

School of Business Students: 5 full-time (1 woman), 1 part-time; includes 1 minority (Hispanic American), 1 international. 12 applicants, 50% accepted, 6 enrolled. *Faculty:* 4. Expenses: Contact institution. *Financial support:* Institutionally sponsored loans and scholarships/grants available. Support available to part-time students. *Degree program information:* Part-time and evening/weekend programs available. Offers business (MBA). *Application deadline:* For fall admission, 4/30 (priority date). *Application fee:* $45. *Application Contact:* Kathliene Pedrick, Program Administrator, 562-777-4015, Fax: 562-906-4545, E-mail: mba@biola.edu. *Dean,* Larry D. Strand, 562-777-4015, Fax: 562-906-4545, E-mail: mba@biola.edu.

School of Intercultural Studies Students: 99 full-time (48 women), 53 part-time (26 women); includes 36 minority (4 African Americans, 28 Asian Americans or Pacific Islanders, 3 Hispanic Americans, 1 Native American), 47 international. Average age 26. 115 applicants, 55 enrolled. *Faculty:* 12 full-time (4 women), 2 part-time/adjunct (0 women). Expenses: Contact institution. *Financial support:* Teaching assistantships, career-related internships or fieldwork, institutionally sponsored loans, and scholarships/grants available. Support available to part-time students. Financial award application deadline: 3/2; financial award applicants required to submit FAFSA. In 2001, 27 master's, 7 doctorates awarded. *Degree program information:* Part-time and evening/weekend programs available. Offers applied linguistics (MA); intercultural education (PhD); intercultural studies (MAICS); missiology (D Miss); missions (MA); teaching English to speakers of other languages (MA, Certificate). *Application deadline:* For fall admission, 8/1; for spring admission, 1/1. Applications are processed on a rolling basis. *Application fee:* $45. Electronic applications accepted. *Application Contact:* Roy M. Allinson, Director of Graduate Admissions, 562-903-4752, Fax: 562-903-4709, E-mail: admissions@biola.edu. *Dean,* Dr. Douglas Pennoyer, 562-903-4844, Fax: 562-903-4748, E-mail: douglas_pennoyer@peter.biola.edu.

School of Professional Studies Students: 12 full-time (2 women), 130 part-time (35 women); includes 36 minority (9 African Americans, 20 Asian Americans or Pacific Islanders, 6 Hispanic Americans, 1 Native American), 6 international. *Faculty:* 1 full-time (0 women), 15 part-time/adjunct (3 women). Expenses: Contact institution. *Financial support:* Institutionally sponsored loans and scholarships/grants available. Support available to part-time students. Financial award application deadline: 3/2; financial award applicants required to submit FAFSA. In 2001, 43 degrees awarded. *Degree program information:* Part-time and evening/weekend programs available. Offers Christian apologetics (MA); organizational leadership (MA). *Application deadline:* For fall admission, 7/1; for spring admission, 12/1. Applications are processed on a rolling basis. *Application fee:* $45. *Application Contact:* Roy M. Allinson, Director of Graduate Admissions, 562-903-4752, Fax: 562-903-4709, E-mail: admissions@biola.edu. *Dean,* Dr. Ed Norman, 562-903-4715, E-mail: ed_norman@peter.biola.edu.

Talbot School of Theology Students: 300 full-time (55 women), 358 part-time (93 women); includes 253 minority (30 African Americans, 196 Asian Americans or Pacific Islanders, 26 Hispanic Americans, 1 Native American), 95 international. Average age 33. 327 applicants, 188 enrolled. *Faculty:* 36 full-time (3 women), 29 part-time/adjunct (9 women). Expenses: Contact institution. *Financial support:* Research assistantships, teaching assistantships, career-related internships or fieldwork, institutionally sponsored loans, and scholarships/grants available. Support available to part-time students. Financial award application deadline: 3/2; financial award applicants required to submit FAFSA. In 2001, 34 first professional degrees, 92 master's, 5 doctorates awarded. *Degree program information:* Part-time and evening/weekend programs available. Offers Bible exposition (MA); biblical and theological studies (MA); Christian education (MACE); Christian ministry and leadership (MA); divinity (M Div); education (PhD); ministry (MA Min); New Testament (MA); Old Testament (MA); philosophy of religion and ethics (MA); theology (Th M, D Min). *Application deadline:* For fall admission, 7/1; for spring admission, 1/1. Applications are processed on a rolling basis. *Application fee:* $45. *Application Contact:* Roy M. Allinson, Director of Graduate Admissions, 562-903-4752, Fax: 562-903-4709, E-mail: admissions@biola.edu. *Dean,* Dr. Dennis Dirks, 562-903-4816, Fax: 562-903-4748, E-mail: dennis_dirks@peter.biola.edu.

BIRMINGHAM-SOUTHERN COLLEGE, Birmingham, AL 35254

General Information Independent-religious, coed, comprehensive institution. *Enrollment:* 41 full-time matriculated graduate/professional students (23 women), 34 part-time matriculated graduate/professional students (12 women). *Enrollment by degree level:* 75 master's. *Graduate faculty:* 8 full-time (1 woman), 1 part-time/adjunct (0 women). *Tuition:* Full-time $11,360; part-time $1,420 per term. *Required fees:* $144; $18 per term. *Graduate housing:* On-campus housing not available. *Student services:* Campus employment opportunities, campus safety program, career counseling, disabled student services, exercise/wellness program, free psychological counseling, international student services, low-cost health insurance, multicultural affairs office, writing training. *Library facilities:* Charles Andrew Rush Learning Center/N. E. Miles Library. *Online resources:* library catalog, web page, access to other libraries' catalogs. *Collection:* 170,103 titles, 1,155 serial subscriptions, 23,801 audiovisual materials.

Computer facilities: 156 computers available on campus for general student use. A campuswide network can be accessed from student residence rooms and from off campus. *Web address:* http://www.bsc.edu/.

General Application Contact: Patricia Redmond, Director of Admissions and Marketing, 205-226-4803, Fax: 205-226-4843, E-mail: graduate@bsc.edu.

GRADUATE UNITS

Program in Public and Private Management Students: 41 full-time (23 women), 34 part-time (12 women); includes 13 minority (12 African Americans, 1 Hispanic American) Average age 36. 21 applicants, 71% accepted. *Faculty:* 8 full-time (1 woman), 1 part-time/adjunct (0 women). Expenses: Contact institution. *Financial support:* Scholarships/grants available. Support available to part-time students. In 2001, 24 degrees awarded. *Degree program information:* Part-time and evening/weekend programs available. Offers public and private management (MPPM). *Application deadline:* For fall admission, 7/27; for spring admission, 12/14. Applications are processed on a rolling basis. *Application fee:* $25. *Application Contact:* Patricia Redmond, Director of Admissions and Marketing, 205-226-4803, Fax: 205-226-4843, E-mail: graduate@bsc.edu. *Dean-Partner,* Dr. Cecilia McInnis-Bowers, 205-226-4985, Fax: 205-226-4843, E-mail: cmcinnis@bsc.edu.

BISHOP'S UNIVERSITY, Lennoxville, QC J1M 1Z7, Canada

General Information Province-supported, coed, comprehensive institution. *Graduate housing:* Room and/or apartments available on a first-come, first-served basis to single students; on-campus housing not available to married students. Housing application deadline: 7/1.

GRADUATE UNITS

School of Education *Degree program information:* Part-time programs available. Post-baccalaureate distance learning degree programs offered (minimal on-campus study). Offers advanced studies in education (Diploma); education (M Ed, MA); teaching English as a second language (Certificate).

BLACK HILLS STATE UNIVERSITY, Spearfish, SD 57799

General Information State-supported, coed, comprehensive institution. *Enrollment:* 10 full-time matriculated graduate/professional students (5 women), 118 part-time matriculated graduate/professional students (103 women). *Enrollment by degree level:* 128 master's. *Graduate faculty:* 21 full-time (8 women). Tuition, state resident: full-time $2,367; part-time $91 per credit hour. Tuition, nonresident: full-time $6,978; part-time $291 per credit hour. *Required fees:* $66 per credit hour. Tuition and fees vary according to course load and reciprocity agreements. *Graduate housing:* Rooms and/or apartments available on a first-come, first-served basis to single and married students. Typical cost: $3,582 per year ($1,524 including board) for single students; $5,821 per year for married students. Room and board charges vary according to board plan and housing facility selected. Housing application deadline: 3/1. *Student services:* Campus employment opportunities, career counseling, child daycare facilities, disabled student services, low-cost health insurance. *Library facilities:* E. Y. Berry Library-Learning Center. *Online resources:* library catalog, access to other libraries' catalogs. *Collection:* 209,738 titles, 4,481 serial subscriptions, 23,901 audiovisual materials.

Computer facilities: 220 computers available on campus for general student use. A campuswide network can be accessed from student residence rooms and from off campus. Internet access is available. *Web address:* http://www.bhsu.edu/.

General Application Contact: Dr. George Earley, Director of Graduate Studies, 605-642-6270, Fax: 605-642-6273, E-mail: GeorgeEarly@bhsu.edu.

GRADUATE UNITS

College of Business and Technology Students: 7 full-time (4 women), 7 part-time (4 women); includes 2 minority (both Asian Americans or Pacific Islanders) Average age 32. 10 applicants, 100% accepted, 10 enrolled. *Faculty:* 6 full-time (1 woman). Expenses: Contact institution. *Financial support:* In 2001–02, 1 research assistantship (averaging $6,000 per year) was awarded; career-related internships or fieldwork, Federal Work-Study, and tuition waivers (partial) also available. Support available to part-time students. Financial award application deadline: 3/1; financial award applicants required to submit FAFSA. In 2001, 3 degrees awarded. *Degree program information:* Part-time programs available. Offers business services management (MS). *Application deadline:* For fall admission, 8/1 (priority date). Applications are processed on a rolling basis. *Application fee:* $35 ($103 for international students). *Dean,* Gary Meek, 605-642-6212.

College of Education Students: 4 full-time (2 women), 112 part-time (99 women); includes 4 minority (1 Asian American or Pacific Islander, 3 Native Americans) Average age 39. 26 applicants, 100% accepted. *Faculty:* 15 full-time (7 women). Expenses: Contact institution. *Financial support:* In 2001–02, 2 students received support, including 2 research assistantships (averaging $6,000 per year), 1 teaching assistantship (averaging $6,000 per year); career-related internships or fieldwork, Federal Work-Study, and tuition waivers (partial) also available. Support available to part-time students. Financial award application deadline: 2/1. In 2001, 14 degrees awarded. *Degree program information:* Part-time programs available. Offers curriculum and instruction (MS). *Application deadline:* For fall admission, 4/1 (priority date); for spring admission, 10/1. Applications are processed on a rolling basis. *Application fee:* $35 ($103 for international students). *Application Contact:* Dr. George Earley, Director of Graduate Studies, 605-642-6270, Fax: 605-642-6273, E-mail: GeorgeEarly@bhsu.edu. *Dean,* Dr. Dean Myers, 605-642-6550, Fax: 605-642-6273.

BLESSED JOHN XXIII NATIONAL SEMINARY, Weston, MA 02493-2618

General Information Independent-religious, men only, graduate-only institution. *Enrollment by degree level:* 73 first professional. *Graduate faculty:* 12 full-time (1 woman), 11 part-time/adjunct (4 women). *Tuition:* Full-time $15,500. *Graduate housing:* Room and/or apartments available to single students; on-campus housing not available to married students. Typical cost: $15,500 (including board). *Student services:* Campus safety program, career counseling. *Collection:* 48,482 titles, 262 serial subscriptions.

Computer facilities: 3 computers available on campus for general student use. Internet access is available. *Web address:* http://www.blessedjohnxxiii.org/.

General Application Contact: Msgr. Francis D. Kelly, President and Rector, 781-899-5500, Fax: 781-899-9057.

GRADUATE UNITS

School of Theology Students: 73; includes 7 minority (2 African Americans, 2 Asian Americans or Pacific Islanders, 3 Hispanic Americans), 3 international. Average age 45. *Faculty:* 12 full-time (1 woman), 11 part-time/adjunct (4 women). Expenses: Contact institution. *Financial support:* Career-related internships or fieldwork available. Offers theology (M Div). *Application deadline:* For fall admission, 7/15 (priority date). Applications are processed on a rolling basis. *Application fee:* $0. *President and Rector,* Msgr. Francis D. Kelly, 781-899-5500, Fax: 781-899-9057.

BLOOMSBURG UNIVERSITY OF PENNSYLVANIA, Bloomsburg, PA 17815-1301

General Information State-supported, coed, comprehensive institution. CGS member. *Enrollment:* 193 full-time matriculated graduate/professional students (134 women), 356 part-time matriculated graduate/professional students (257 women). *Enrollment by degree level:* 549 master's. *Graduate faculty:* 203 full-time (75 women), 1 part-time/adjunct (0 women). Tuition, state resident: full-time $4,600; part-time $256 per credit. Tuition, nonresident: full-time $7,554; part-time $420 per credit. *Required fees:* $834. Part-time tuition and fees vary according to course load. *Graduate housing:* Room and/or apartments available to single students; on-campus housing not available to married students. *Student services:* Campus employment opportunities, campus safety program, career counseling, child daycare facilities, disabled student services, free psychological counseling, international student services, low-cost health insurance, multicultural affairs office. *Library facilities:* Andruss Library. *Online resources:* library catalog. *Collection:* 278,835 titles, 2,372 serial subscriptions, 6,118 audiovisual materials. *Research affiliation:* Marine Science Consortium.

Computer facilities: 700 computers available on campus for general student use. A campuswide network can be accessed from student residence rooms and from off campus. Internet access and online class registration are available. *Web address:* http://www.bloomu.edu/.

General Application Contact: Carol Arnold, Administrative Assistant, 570-389-4015, Fax: 570-389-3054, E-mail: carnold@bloomu.edu.

GRADUATE UNITS

School of Graduate Studies Students: 193 full-time (134 women), 356 part-time (257 women); includes 17 minority (6 African Americans, 7 Asian Americans or Pacific Islanders, 3 Hispanic Americans, 1 Native American), 32 international. 257 applicants, 100% accepted. *Faculty:* 203 full-time (75 women), 1 part-time/adjunct (0 women). Expenses: Contact institution. *Financial support:* In 2001–02, 218 research assistantships were awarded; teaching assistantships with partial tuition reimbursements, career-related internships or fieldwork, Federal Work-Study, institutionally sponsored loans, and minority assistantships also available. Support available to part-time students. In 2001, 227 degrees awarded. *Degree program information:* Part-time and evening/weekend programs available. Offers biology (MS); biology education (M Ed); instructional technology (MS); science and technology (M Ed, MS). *Application fee:* $30. Electronic applications accepted. *Application Contact:* Carol Arnold, Administrative Assistant, 570-389-4015, Fax: 570-389-3054, E-mail: carnold@bloomu.edu. *Dean of Graduate Studies*, Dr. James F. Matta, 570-389-4015, Fax: 570-389-3054.

College of Business Students: 15 full-time (5 women), 64 part-time (20 women); includes 2 minority (both Asian Americans or Pacific Islanders), 9 international. 23 applicants, 100% accepted. *Faculty:* 34 full-time (8 women). Expenses: Contact institution. *Financial support:* Unspecified assistantships available. In 2001, 38 degrees awarded. Offers accounting (MAC); business (M Ed, MAC, MBA, MS); business administration (MBA); business education (M Ed). *Application deadline:* Applications are processed on a rolling basis. *Application fee:* $30. *Dean*, Dr. David Long, 570-389-4745, Fax: 570-389-3892, E-mail: dlong@bloomu.edu.

College of Liberal Arts Students: 22 full-time (13 women), 8 part-time (6 women); includes 4 minority (2 African Americans, 1 Asian American or Pacific Islander, 1 Hispanic American), 3 international. 20 applicants, 100% accepted. *Faculty:* 75 full-time (26 women). Expenses: Contact institution. *Financial support:* Unspecified assistantships available. In 2001, 13 degrees awarded. *Degree program information:* Part-time programs available. Offers art history (MA); arts and sciences (MA, MS); exercise science and adult fitness (MS); studio art (MA). *Application deadline:* Applications are processed on a rolling basis. *Application fee:* $30. *Dean*, Dr. Hsien-Tung Liu, 570-389-4410, Fax: 570-389-3026, E-mail: liu@bloomu.edu.

College of Professional Studies Students: 131 full-time (109 women), 199 part-time (177 women); includes 8 minority (4 African Americans, 1 Asian American or Pacific Islander, 2 Hispanic Americans, 1 Native American), 11 international. 173 applicants, 100% accepted. *Faculty:* 56 full-time (30 women). Expenses: Contact institution. *Financial support:* Unspecified assistantships available. In 2001, 144 degrees awarded. Offers audiology (MS); curriculum and instruction (M Ed); early childhood education (MS); education (M Ed, MS); education of deaf/hard of hearing (MS); elementary education (M Ed); health sciences (MS, MSN); nursing (MSN); professional studies (M Ed, MS, MSN); reading (M Ed); special education (MS); speech language pathology (MS). *Application fee:* $30. *Dean*, Dr. Ann L. Lee, 570-389-4005, Fax: 570-389-5049, E-mail: alee@bloomu.edu.

BLUFFTON COLLEGE, Bluffton, OH 45817-1196

General Information Independent-religious, coed, comprehensive institution.

GRADUATE UNITS

Program in Education *Degree program information:* Part-time programs available. Offers education (MA Ed).

BOISE STATE UNIVERSITY, Boise, ID 83725-0399

General Information State-supported, coed, comprehensive institution. *Graduate housing:* Rooms and/or apartments available on a first-come, first-served basis to single and married students. Housing application deadline: 8/1. *Research affiliation:* U.S. Department of Interior, Idaho Water Resources Research Institute, World Center for Birds of Prey, U.S. Department of Energy–Interuniversity Research Consortium, U.S. Army Research Institute, U.S. Department of Agriculture.

GRADUATE UNITS

Graduate College *Degree program information:* Part-time programs available. Post-baccalaureate distance learning degree programs offered (no on-campus study). Electronic applications accepted.

College of Arts and Sciences *Degree program information:* Part-time programs available. Offers applied geophysics (MS); art (MA); arts and sciences (MA, MFA, MM, MS, PhD); biology (MA, MS); computer science (MS); creative writing (MFA); earth science (MS); English (MA); fine arts, creative writing (MFA); fine arts, visual arts (MFA); geology (MS); geophysics (PhD); interdisciplinary studies (MA, MS); music (MM); music education (MM); pedagogy (MM); performance (MM); raptor biology (MS); technical communication (MA); visual arts (MFA). Electronic applications accepted.

College of Business and Economics *Degree program information:* Part-time programs available. Offers accountancy (MS); business administration (MBA); business and economics (MBA, MS); management information systems (MS). Electronic applications accepted.

College of Education *Degree program information:* Part-time programs available. Offers athletic administration (MPE); curriculum and instruction (MA, Ed D); early childhood education (MA); education (MA, MPE, MS, Ed D); educational technology (MS); exercise and sport studies (MS); mathematics education (MS); physical education (MPE); reading (MA); school counseling (MA); special education (MA). Electronic applications accepted.

College of Engineering *Degree program information:* Part-time programs available. Post-baccalaureate distance learning degree programs offered (no on-campus study). Offers civil engineering (MS); computer engineering (MS); electrical engineering (MS); engineering (MS); instructional and performance technology (MS); mechanical engineering (MS). Electronic applications accepted.

College of Health Science *Degree program information:* Part-time programs available. Offers health science (MHS); health studies (MHS). Electronic applications accepted.

College of Social Science and Public Affairs *Degree program information:* Part-time programs available. Offers communication (MA); criminal justice administration (MA); environmental and natural resources policy and administration (MPA); general public administration (MPA); history (MA); social science and public affairs (MA, MPA, MSW); social work (MSW); state and local government policy and administration (MPA). Electronic applications accepted.

BORICUA COLLEGE, New York, NY 10032-1560

General Information Independent, coed, comprehensive institution.

GRADUATE UNITS

Program in Human Services Offers human services (MS).

Program in Liberal Studies Offers liberal studies (MA).

BOSTON ARCHITECTURAL CENTER, Boston, MA 02115-2795

General Information Independent, coed, comprehensive institution.

GRADUATE UNITS

Graduate Programs Offers architecture (M Arch); interior design (MID). Electronic applications accepted.

BOSTON COLLEGE, Chestnut Hill, MA 02467-3800

General Information Independent-religious, coed, university. CGS member. *Enrollment:* 2,132 full-time matriculated graduate/professional students (1,295 women), 2,378 part-time matriculated graduate/professional students (1,291 women). *Graduate faculty:* 647. *Tuition:* Full-time $17,664; part-time $8,832 per semester. *Graduate housing:* On-campus housing not available. *Student services:* Campus employment opportunities, campus safety program, career counseling, child daycare facilities, disabled student services, exercise/wellness program, free psychological counseling, grant writing training, international student services, low-cost health insurance, multicultural affairs office, teacher training, writing training. *Library facilities:* Thomas P. O'Neill Library plus 6 others. *Online resources:* library catalog, web page. *Collection:* 2 million titles, 21,121 serial subscriptions, 121,969 audiovisual materials.

Computer facilities: 200 computers available on campus for general student use. A campuswide network can be accessed from student residence rooms and from off campus. *Web address:* http://www.bc.edu/.

General Application Contact: Stephanie Autenrieth, Assistant Dean, 617-552-3265, Fax: 617-552-3700, E-mail: autenri@bc.edu.

GRADUATE UNITS

Graduate School of Arts and Sciences Students: 326 full-time (163 women), 689 part-time (334 women). 1,737 applicants, 42% accepted, 264 enrolled. *Faculty:* 387. Expenses: Contact institution. *Financial support:* Fellowships with tuition reimbursements, research assistantships with tuition reimbursements, teaching assistantships with tuition reimbursements, career-related internships or fieldwork, Federal Work-Study, scholarships/grants, and tuition waivers (full and partial) available. Support available to part-time students. Financial award application deadline: 3/1; financial award applicants required to submit FAFSA. In 2001, 166 master's, 69 doctorates awarded. *Degree program information:* Part-time programs available. Offers arts and sciences (MA, MS, MST, PhD, CAGS); biochemistry (MS, PhD); biology (MS, PhD); classics (MA); economics (MA, PhD); English (MA, PhD, CAGS); European national studies (MA); French (MA, PhD); geology and geophysics (MS); Greek (MA); history (MA, PhD); inorganic chemistry (PhD); Italian (MA); Latin (MA); linguistics (MA); mathematics (MA); medieval language (PhD); medieval studies (MA); organic chemistry (PhD); philosophy (MA, PhD); physical chemistry (PhD); physics (MS, PhD); political science (MA, PhD); psychology (PhD); Russian and Slavic languages and literature (MA); science education (MST); Slavic studies (MA); sociology (MA, PhD); Spanish (MA, PhD); theology (MA, PhD). *Application fee:* $50. *Application Contact:* Stephanie Autenrieth, Assistant Dean, 617-552-3265, Fax: 617-552-3700, E-mail: autenri@bc.edu. *Dean*, Dr. Michael A. Smyer, 617-552-3265, Fax: 617-552-3700.

Institute of Religious Education and Pastoral Ministry Expenses: Contact institution. *Financial support:* Fellowships, career-related internships or fieldwork, Federal Work-Study, and tuition waivers (full and partial) available. Support available to part-time students. Financial award application deadline: 3/1; financial award applicants required to submit FAFSA. *Degree program information:* Part-time programs available. Offers church leadership (MA); pastoral ministry (MA); religious education (MA, PhD); social justice/social ministry (MA); youth ministry (MA). *Application deadline:* For fall admission, 3/1 (priority date). *Application fee:* $50. *Application Contact:* Dr. Harold Horell, Assistant Director, Academic Affairs, 617-552-8440, Fax: 617-552-0811, E-mail: horell@bc.edu. *Chairperson*, Dr. Mary Anne Hinsdale, 617-552-8603, Fax: 617-552-0811, E-mail: maryane.hinsdale@bc.edu.

Graduate School of Social Work *Degree program information:* Part-time programs available. Offers social work (MSW, PhD).

Law School Offers law (JD).

Lynch Graduate School of Education Students: 430 full-time (322 women), 552 part-time (416 women); includes 127 minority (53 African Americans, 39 Asian Americans or Pacific Islanders, 32 Hispanic Americans, 3 Native Americans), 76 international. 1,421 applicants, 64% accepted. *Faculty:* 61 full-time (30 women), 39 part-time/adjunct (22 women). Expenses: Contact institution. *Financial support:* In 2001–02, 689 fellowships with full and partial tuition reimbursements, 210 research assistantships with full and partial tuition reimbursements, 100 teaching assistantships with full and partial tuition reimbursements were awarded. Career-related internships or fieldwork, Federal Work-Study, institutionally sponsored loans, scholarships/grants, traineeships, tuition waivers (full and partial), and unspecified assistantships also available. Support available to part-time students. Financial award applicants required to submit FAFSA. In 2001, 372 master's, 28 doctorates, 11 other advanced degrees awarded. Offers biology (MST); Catholic school leadership (M Ed, CAES); chemistry (MST); counseling psychology (MA, PhD); curriculum and instruction (M Ed, PhD, CAES); developmental and educational psychology (MA, PhD); early childhood education/teacher option (M Ed); early childhood/specialist option (MA); education (M Ed, MA, MAT, MST, Ed D, PhD, CAES); educational administration (M Ed, Ed D, PhD, CAES); educational research, measurement, and evaluation (M Ed, PhD, CAES); elementary teaching (M Ed); English (MAT); geology (MST); higher education administration (MA, PhD); history (MAT); Latin and classics (MAT); mathematics (MST); moderate special needs (M Ed, CAES); multiple disabilities and deaf/blindness (M Ed, CAES); physics (MST); professional school administrator (PhD); reading specialist (M Ed, CAES); religious education (M Ed, CAES); Romance languages (MAT); secondary education (M Ed, MAT, MST); secondary teaching (M Ed); severe special needs (M Ed); visual impairment studies (M Ed, CAES). *Application fee:* $40. *Application Contact:* Arline Riordan, Graduate Admissions Director, 617-552-4214, Fax: 617-552-0812, E-mail: grad.ed.info@bc.edu. *Dean*, Dr. Mary Brabeck, 617-552-4200, Fax: 617-552-0812.

School of Nursing Students: 85 full-time (82 women), 55 part-time (52 women); includes 6 minority (1 African American, 3 Asian Americans or Pacific Islanders, 2 Hispanic Americans), 2 international. 193 applicants, 52% accepted, 53 enrolled. *Faculty:* 31 full-time (30 women). Expenses: Contact institution. *Financial support:* In 2001–02, 95 students received support, including 15 fellowships with full tuition reimbursements available (averaging $8,600 per year), 4 research assistantships, 4 teaching assistantships (averaging $10,500 per year); Federal Work-Study, institutionally sponsored loans, scholarships/grants, traineeships, and tuition waivers (partial) also available. Support available to part-time students. Financial award application deadline: 3/2; financial award applicants required to submit FAFSA. In 2001, 46 master's, 7 doctorates awarded. *Degree program information:* Part-time programs available. Offers adult health nursing (MS); community health nursing (MS); family health (MS); gerontology (MS); maternal/child health nursing (MS); nursing (PhD); psychiatric-mental health nursing (MS). *Application deadline:* For fall admission, 10/15; for winter admission, 3/1; for spring admission, 4/15. *Application fee:* $40. *Application Contact:* Andrea Alexander, Administrative Secretary, 617-552-4059, Fax: 617-552-0745, E-mail: alexanan@bc.edu. *Dean*, Dr. Barbara Munro, 617-552-4251, Fax: 617-552-0931, E-mail: barbara.munro@bc.edu.

The Wallace E. Carroll School of Management Students: 384 full-time (135 women), 599 part-time (180 women); includes 65 minority (11 African Americans, 37 Asian Americans or Pacific Islanders, 16 Hispanic Americans, 1 Native American), 146 international. Average age 28. *Faculty:* 57 full-time (12 women), 11 part-time/adjunct (2 women). Expenses: Contact institution. *Financial support:* Fellowships with full tuition reimbursements, research assistantships with full and partial tuition reimbursements, teaching assistantships, career-related internships or fieldwork, Federal Work-Study, institutionally sponsored loans, scholarships/grants, tuition waivers (full and partial), and unspecified assistantships available. Support available to part-time students. Financial award application deadline: 3/1; financial award applicants required to submit FAFSA. In 2001, 529 master's, 3 doctorates awarded. *Degree program information:* Part-time and evening/weekend programs available. Offers business administration (MBA); finance (MSF, PhD); management (MBA, MSF, PhD); organization studies (PhD). *Application Contact:* Shelley B. Conley, Director of Graduate Enrollment and MBA Admissions, 617-552-3920, Fax: 617-552-8078, E-mail: bcmba@bc.edu. *Associate Dean for Graduate Programs*, Dr. Robert A. Taggart, 617-552-3073, Fax: 617-552-0564, E-mail: robert.taggart@bc.edu.

See in-depth description on page 763.

THE BOSTON CONSERVATORY, Boston, MA 02215

General Information Independent, coed, comprehensive institution. *Enrollment:* 117 full-time matriculated graduate/professional students (82 women), 20 part-time matriculated graduate/professional students (11 women). *Enrollment by degree level:* 118 master's, 19 other advanced degrees. *Graduate faculty:* 24 full-time (13 women), 61 part-time/adjunct (35 women). *Tuition:* Full-time $19,250; part-time $790 per credit. *Required fees:* $950; $225 per term. Full-time tuition and fees vary according to course load and program. *Graduate housing:* Room and/or apartments available on a first-come, first-served basis to single students; on-campus housing not available to married students. Typical cost: $7,120 per year ($9,280 including board) ; $7,120 per year ($9,280 including board) for married students. Housing application deadline: 4/1. *Student services:* Campus employment opportunities, campus safety program, career counseling, exercise/wellness program, international student services, low-cost health insurance, multicultural affairs office, teacher training. *Library facilities:* The Albert Alphin Music Library. *Collection:* 40,000 titles, 92 serial subscriptions.

Computer facilities: 16 computers available on campus for general student use. A campuswide network can be accessed. Internet access is available. *Web address:* http://www.bostonconservatory.edu/.

General Application Contact: Halley Shefler, Dean of Enrollment Services, 617-912-9116, Fax: 617-536-6340.

GRADUATE UNITS

Graduate Division Students: 117 full-time (82 women), 20 part-time (11 women); includes 43 minority (2 African Americans, 36 Asian Americans or Pacific Islanders, 4 Hispanic Americans,

The Boston Conservatory (continued)

1 Native American), 5 international. 239 applicants, 67% accepted. *Faculty:* 24 full-time (13 women), 61 part-time/adjunct (35 women). Expenses: Contact institution. *Financial support:* In 2001–02, fellowships (averaging $6,500 per year), teaching assistantships (averaging $2,000 per year) were awarded. Federal Work-Study, institutionally sponsored loans, scholarships/grants, tuition waivers (full and partial), and work assistantships also available. Support available to part-time students. Financial award application deadline: 3/1; financial award applicants required to submit FAFSA. In 2001, 44 master's, 19 Certificates awarded. *Degree program information:* Part-time programs available. Offers choral conducting (MM); composition (MM); jazz studies (MM); music (MM, ADP, Certificate); music education (MM); music performance (MM, ADP, Certificate); opera (MM, ADP, Certificate); theater (MM). *Application deadline:* For fall admission, 2/1 (priority date); for spring admission, 12/1. Applications are processed on a rolling basis. *Application fee:* $75. *Application Contact:* Halley Shefler, Dean of Enrollment Services, 617-912-9116, Fax: 617-536-6340. *Dean of the Conservatory,* Dr. Michael Nash, 617-912-9166, Fax: 617-536-3176, E-mail: mnash@bostonconservatory.edu.

BOSTON GRADUATE SCHOOL OF PSYCHOANALYSIS, Brookline, MA 02446-4602

General Information Independent, coed, graduate-only institution. *Enrollment by degree level:* 33 master's, 53 doctoral, 48 other advanced degrees. *Graduate faculty:* 15 full-time (11 women), 35 part-time/adjunct (14 women). *Tuition:* Full-time $16,870. Tuition and fees vary according to degree level, program and student level. *Student services:* Campus employment opportunities, career counseling, low-cost health insurance, teacher training, writing training. *Library facilities:* Boston Graduate School of Psycohanalysis Library. *Collection:* 10,766 titles, 15 serial subscriptions, 732 audiovisual materials.

Computer facilities: 4 computers available on campus for general student use. A campuswide network can be accessed from off campus. Internet access and online class registration are available. *Web address:* http://www.bgsp.edu/.

General Application Contact: Dr. Mara Wagner, Director of Admissions, 617-277-3915, Fax: 617-277-0312, E-mail: bgsp@bgsp.edu.

GRADUATE UNITS

Cyril Z. Meadow Institute of Psychoanalysis Students: 10 full-time (8 women), 30 part-time (19 women). 18 applicants, 78% accepted. *Faculty:* 2 full-time (1 woman), 6 part-time/adjunct (5 women). Expenses: Contact institution. *Financial support:* In 2001–02, 5 students received support. Unspecified assistantships available. Financial award applicants required to submit FAFSA. *Degree program information:* Evening/weekend programs available. Offers psychoanalysis (Psya D). *Application deadline:* Applications are processed on a rolling basis. *Application fee:* $100. Electronic applications accepted. *Application Contact:* Robert Welber, Registrar, 802-257-0919. *Head,* Dr. Dena Reed.

Master's, Certificate, and Doctoral Programs Students: 27 full-time (17 women), 49 part-time (39 women). 19 applicants, 53% accepted. *Faculty:* 10 full-time (9 women), 10 part-time/adjunct (4 women). Expenses: Contact institution. *Financial support:* In 2001–02, 6 students received support. Career-related internships or fieldwork and unspecified assistantships available. Financial award applicants required to submit FAFSA. In 2001, 7 master's, 5 other advanced degrees awarded. *Degree program information:* Part-time programs available. *Application deadline:* Applications are processed on a rolling basis. *Application fee:* $100. Electronic applications accepted. *Application Contact:* Sherry Ceridan, Registrar, 617-277-3915, Fax: 617-277-0312, E-mail: bgsp@bgsp.edu. *Dean,* Dr. Jane Snyder, 617-277-3915, Fax: 617-277-0312, E-mail: bgsp@bgsp.edu.

Program in Psychoanalysis in the Study of Violence Students: 13 full-time (9 women). 4 applicants, 100% accepted, 2 enrolled. *Faculty:* 2 full-time (1 woman), 20 part-time/adjunct (6 women). Expenses: Contact institution. *Financial support:* In 2001–02, 1 student received support. Unspecified assistantships available. Financial award applicants required to submit FAFSA. *Degree program information:* Evening/weekend programs available. Offers psychoanalysis in the study of violence (Psya D). *Application deadline:* Applications are processed on a rolling basis. *Application fee:* $100. Electronic applications accepted. *Application Contact:* Dr. Jane Snyder, Co-Director, Institute for the Study of Violence, 617-277-3915, Fax: 617-277-0312, E-mail: bgsp@bgsp.edu. *Director, Institute for the Study of Violence,* Dr. Phyllis W. Meadow, 617-277-3915, E-mail: bgsp@bgsp.edu.

BOSTON UNIVERSITY, Boston, MA 02215

General Information Independent, coed, university. CGS member. *Enrollment:* 7,229 full-time matriculated graduate/professional students (3,747 women), 2,677 part-time matriculated graduate/professional students (1,425 women). *Enrollment by degree level:* 2,120 first professional, 5,970 master's, 1,655 doctoral, 161 other advanced degrees. *Graduate faculty:* 3,222. *Tuition:* Full-time $25,872; part-time $340 per credit. *Required fees:* $40 per semester. Part-time tuition and fees vary according to class time, course level and program. *Graduate housing:* Rooms and/or apartments available on a first-come, first-served basis to single students and available to married students. Typical cost: $8,978 (including board) for single students. *Student services:* Campus employment opportunities, campus safety program, career counseling, child daycare facilities, free psychological counseling, international student services, low-cost health insurance. *Library facilities:* Mugar Memorial Library plus 18 others. *Online resources:* library catalog, web page, access to other libraries' catalogs. *Collection:* 2.3 million titles, 30,689 serial subscriptions, 71,678 audiovisual materials. *Research affiliation:* Woods Hole Oceanographic Institution–Marine Biological Laboratory, Massachusetts Historical Society, Society for the Preservation of New England Antiquities, NASA–Ames Research Center.

Computer facilities: 750 computers available on campus for general student use. A campuswide network can be accessed from student residence rooms and from off campus. Internet access, research and educational networks are available. *Web address:* http://www.bu.edu/.

GRADUATE UNITS

College of Communication Students: 262 full-time (180 women), 74 part-time (57 women); includes 27 minority (7 African Americans, 12 Asian Americans or Pacific Islanders, 7 Hispanic Americans, 1 Native American), 84 international. Average age 27. 612 applicants, 58% accepted. *Faculty:* 57 full-time, 81 part-time/adjunct. Expenses: Contact institution. *Financial support:* In 2001–02, 290 students received support, including 18 teaching assistantships with partial tuition reimbursements available; career-related internships or fieldwork, Federal Work-Study, institutionally sponsored loans, scholarships/grants, tuition waivers (full and partial), and unspecified assistantships also available. Support available to part-time students. Financial award application deadline: 4/30; financial award applicants required to submit FAFSA. In 2001, 165 degrees awarded. *Degree program information:* Part-time programs available. Offers advertising (MS); broadcast journalism (MS); business and economics journalism (MS); communication (MFA, MS); film production (MFA); film studies (MFA); health communication (MS); mass communication (MS); photo journalism (MS); print journalism (MS); public relations (MS); science journalism (MS); screenwriting (MFA); television (MS); television management (MS). *Application deadline:* For fall admission, 2/15. *Application fee:* $60. Electronic applications accepted. *Application Contact:* Micha Sabovik, Assistant Director of Graduate Services and Financial Aid, 617-353-4658, Fax: 617-358-0399, E-mail: mabbott@bu.edu. *Dean,* Brent Baker, 617-353-3450, Fax: 617-358-0399, E-mail: com@bu.edu.

College of Engineering Students: 315 full-time (77 women), 53 part-time (14 women); includes 24 minority (5 African Americans, 13 Asian Americans or Pacific Islanders, 6 Hispanic Americans), 176 international. Average age 28. 1,205 applicants, 25% accepted, 120 enrolled. *Faculty:* 114 full-time (11 women), 30 part-time/adjunct (1 woman). Expenses: Contact institution. *Financial support:* In 2001–02, 244 students received support, including 18 fellowships with full tuition reimbursements available (averaging $15,500 per year), 131 research assistantships with full tuition reimbursements available (averaging $13,500 per year), 48 teaching assistantships with full tuition reimbursements available (averaging $13,500 per year); career-related internships or fieldwork, Federal Work-Study, institutionally sponsored loans, scholarships/grants, and tuition waivers (full and partial) also available. Financial award application deadline: 1/15; financial award applicants required to submit FAFSA. In 2001, 83 master's, 25 doctorates awarded. *Degree program information:* Part-time programs available. Postbaccalaureate distance learning degree programs offered (no on-campus study). Offers aerospace engineering (MS, PhD); biomedical engineering (MS, PhD); computer engineering (PhD); computer systems engineering (MS); electrical engineering (MS, PhD); engineering (MS, PhD); general engineering (MS); manufacturing engineering (MS, PhD); mechanical engineering (MS, PhD); systems engineering (PhD). *Application deadline:* For fall admission, 4/1; for spring admission, 10/1. Applications are processed on a rolling basis. *Application fee:* $60. Electronic applications accepted. *Application Contact:* Cheryl Kelley, Director of Graduate Programs, 617-353-9760, Fax: 617-353-0259, E-mail: enggrad@bu.edu. *Dean,* Dr. David Campbell, 617-353-2800, Fax: 617-353-6322.

College of Fine Arts Students: 332 full-time (202 women), 12 part-time (7 women); includes 13 minority (2 African Americans, 8 Asian Americans or Pacific Islanders, 3 Hispanic Americans), 122 international. Average age 29. 866 applicants, 40% accepted. *Faculty:* 68 full-time, 34 part-time/adjunct. Expenses: Contact institution. *Financial support:* Fellowships, teaching assistantships, Federal Work-Study and scholarships/grants available. Support available to part-time students. Financial award application deadline: 3/1. In 2001, 104 master's, 14 doctorates, 6 other advanced degrees awarded. *Degree program information:* Part-time programs available. Offers art education (MFA); arts (MFA, MM, DMA, Artist Diploma, Certificate, Performance Diploma); collaborative piano (MM, DMA); composition (MM, DMA); conducting (MM, Artist Diploma, Performance Diploma); costume design (MFA); costume production (MFA); directing (MFA); graphic design (MFA); historical performance (MM, DMA, Artist Diploma, Performance Diploma); lighting design (MFA); music education (MM, DMA); music history and literature (MM); music theory (MM); opera performance (Certificate); painting (MFA); performance (MM, DMA, Artist Diploma, Performance Diploma); scene design (MFA); sculpture (MFA); studio teaching (MFA); technical production (MFA, Certificate); theatre crafts (Certificate); theatre education (MFA). *Application deadline:* For fall admission, 3/1 (priority date). *Application fee:* $60. Electronic applications accepted. *Application Contact:* Mark Krone, Manager, Graduate Admissions, 617-353-3350, E-mail: arts@bu.edu. *Dean,* Jeffrey N. Babcock, 617-353-3350.

Graduate School of Arts and Sciences Students: 1,461 full-time (737 women), 221 part-time (127 women); includes 101 minority (26 African Americans, 45 Asian Americans or Pacific Islanders, 29 Hispanic Americans, 1 Native American), 607 international. Average age 30. 5,808 applicants, 27% accepted, 503 enrolled. Expenses: Contact institution. *Financial support:* In 2001–02, 989 students received support, including 90 fellowships, 421 research assistantships, 359 teaching assistantships; career-related internships or fieldwork, Federal Work-Study, scholarships/grants, traineeships, and unspecified assistantships also available. Support available to part-time students. Financial award application deadline: 1/15; financial award applicants required to submit FAFSA. In 2001, 355 master's, 157 doctorates awarded. Offers African American studies (MA); African studies (Certificate); American and New England studies (PhD); anthropology (MA, PhD); applied linguistics (MA, PhD); archaeology (MA, PhD); art history (MA, PhD); arts and sciences (MA, MAEP, MAPE, MS, PhD, Certificate); astronomy (MA, PhD); bioinformatics (MS, PhD); biology (MA, PhD); biostatistics (MA, PhD); cellular biophysics (PhD); chemistry (MA, PhD); classical studies (MA, PhD); cognitive and neural systems (MA, PhD); composition (MA); computer science (MA, PhD); creative writing (MA); earth sciences (MA, PhD); economic policy (MAEP); economics (MA, PhD); energy and environmental analysis (MA); English (MA, PhD); environmental remote sensing and geographic information systems (MA); French language and literature (MA, PhD); geography (MA, PhD); Hispanic language and literatures (MA, PhD); history (MA, PhD); international relations (MA); international relations and enivronmental policy (MA); international relations and environmental policy management (MA); international relations and international communication (MA); mathematical finance (MA); mathematics (MA, PhD); molecular biology, cell biology, and biochemistry (MA, PhD); museum studies (Certificate); music education (MA); music history/theory (PhD); musicology (MA, PhD); neuroscience (MA, PhD); philosophy (MA, PhD); physics (MA, PhD); political economy (MAPE); political science (MA, PhD); preservation studies (MA); psychology (MA, PhD); religious and theological studies (MA, PhD); sociology (MA, PhD); sociology and social work (PhD). *Application fee:* $60. *Application Contact:* Patricia A. Schiavoni, Admissions Officer, 617-353-2696, Fax: 617-358-0540. *Associate Dean,* J. Scott Whittaker, 617-353-2690, Fax: 617-358-0540.

Editorial Institute Students: 6 full-time (3 women), 1 international. Average age 30. 15 applicants, 47% accepted, 4 enrolled. Expenses: Contact institution. *Financial support:* In 2001–02, 4 teaching assistantships with full tuition reimbursements (averaging $12,500 per year) were awarded; Federal Work-Study, scholarships/grants, and unspecified assistantships also available. Support available to part-time students. Financial award application deadline: 1/15. Offers editorial studies (MA, PhD). *Application deadline:* For fall admission, 4/1. *Application fee:* $60. *Application Contact:* Ellen O'Reilly Wrigley, Administrative Assistant, 617-353-6631, Fax: 617-353-6917, E-mail: editinst@bu.edu. *Co-Director,* Christopher Ricks, 617-353-5404, E-mail: cricks@bu.edu.

Henry M. Goldman School of Dental Medicine Students: 684 full-time (284 women); includes 230 minority (2 African Americans, 207 Asian Americans or Pacific Islanders, 19 Hispanic Americans, 2 Native Americans), 231 international. Average age 28. *Faculty:* 100 full-time (38 women), 212 part-time/adjunct (35 women). Expenses: Contact institution. *Financial support:* In 2001–02, 480 students received support. Career-related internships or fieldwork and institutionally sponsored loans available. Financial award application deadline: 4/15; financial award applicants required to submit CSS PROFILE or FAFSA. In 2001, 165 first professional degrees, 14 master's, 8 doctorates, 55 other advanced degrees awarded. Offers advanced general dentistry (CAGS); dental medicine (DMD, MS, MSD, D Sc, D Sc D, PhD, CAGS); dental public health (MS, MSD, D Sc D, CAGS); dentistry (DMD); endodontics (MSD, D Sc D, CAGS); implantology (CAGS); nutritional science (MS, D Sc); operative dentistry (MSD, D Sc D, CAGS); oral and maxillofacial surgery (MSD, D Sc D, CAGS); oral biology (MSD, D Sc, D Sc D, PhD); orthodontics (MSD, D Sc D, CAGS); pediatric dentistry (MSD, D Sc D, CAGS); periodontology (MSD, D Sc D, CAGS); prosthodontics (MSD, D Sc D, CAGS). *Application deadline:* For fall admission, 3/1. Applications are processed on a rolling basis. *Application fee:* $60. *Application Contact:* Office of Admissions and Student Services, 617-638-4787, Fax: 617-638-4798. *Dean,* Dr. Spencer Frankl, 617-638-4780.

Metropolitan College Students: 194 full-time (87 women), 686 part-time (237 women); includes 125 minority (23 African Americans, 88 Asian Americans or Pacific Islanders, 14 Hispanic Americans), 227 international. Average age 32. *Faculty:* 22 full-time (3 women), 221 part-time/adjunct. Expenses: Contact institution. *Financial support:* Fellowships, research assistantships, teaching assistantships, career-related internships or fieldwork, Federal Work-Study, institutionally sponsored loans, and tuition waivers (full and partial) available. Support available to part-time students. In 2001, 407 degrees awarded. *Degree program information:* Part-time and evening/weekend programs available. Offers actuarial science (MS); arts administration (MS); city planning (MCP); computer information systems (MS); computer science (MS); criminal justice (MCJ); electronic commerce (MSAS); financial economics (MSAS); innovation and technology (MSAS); liberal arts (MLA); multinational commerce (MSAS); telecommunications (MS); urban affairs (MUA). *Application deadline:* Applications are processed on a rolling basis. *Dean,* Dr. Jay Halford, 617-353-6776, Fax: 617-353-6066, E-mail: jhalford@bu.edu.

Sargent College of Health and Rehabilitation Sciences Students: 400 full-time (340 women), 60 part-time (46 women); includes 44 minority (5 African Americans, 30 Asian Americans or Pacific Islanders, 9 Hispanic Americans), 21 international. Average age 27. 475 applicants, 52% accepted. *Faculty:* 42 full-time (30 women), 50 part-time/adjunct (35 women). Expenses: Contact institution. *Financial support:* In 2001–02, 450 students received support; fellowships with full tuition reimbursements available, research assistantships with full tuition reimbursements available, teaching assistantships with full tuition reimbursements available, career-related internships or fieldwork, Federal Work-Study, institutionally sponsored loans, and scholarships/grants available. Support available to part-time students. Financial award application deadline: 4/15; financial award applicants required to submit FAFSA. In 2001, 241 master's, 3 doctorates awarded. *Degree program information:* Part-time programs available. Offers applied anatomy and physiology (MS, PhD); audiology (D Sc); health and rehabilitation sciences (MS, MSOT, MSPT, D Sc, DPT, PhD, CAGS); movement and rehabilitation sciences

(MS, D Sc); nutrition (MS); occupational therapy (MS, MSOT, CAGS); physical therapy (MSPT, DPT); rehabilitation counseling (MS, D Sc, CAGS); speech-language pathology (MS, D Sc, CAGS); therapeutic studies (D Sc). *Application deadline:* For fall admission, 2/1 (priority date). Applications are processed on a rolling basis. *Application fee:* $60. Electronic applications accepted. *Application Contact:* Judy Skeffington, Director, Graduate Admissions and Financial Aid, 617-353-2713, Fax: 617-353-7500, E-mail: jaskeff@bu.edu. *Dean,* Dr. Alan M. Jette, 617-353-2704, Fax: 617-353-7500, E-mail: ajette@bu.edu.

School of Education Students: 523 (389 women); includes 35 minority (9 African Americans, 13 Asian Americans or Pacific Islanders, 13 Hispanic Americans) 89 international. Average age 33. 941 applicants, 70% accepted. *Faculty:* 31 full-time, 57 part-time/adjunct. Expenses: Contact institution. *Financial support:* In 2001–02, 325 students received support, including 7 fellowships, 9 research assistantships, 32 teaching assistantships with partial tuition reimbursements available; career-related internships or fieldwork, Federal Work-Study, and scholarships/grants also available. Support available to part-time students. Financial award application deadline: 2/15; financial award applicants required to submit FAFSA. In 2001, 272 master's, 26 doctorates, 16 other advanced degrees awarded. *Degree program information:* Part-time programs available. Offers administration, training, and policy studies (Ed D); bilingual education (Ed M, CAGS); counseling (Ed M, CAGS); counseling psychology (Ed D); curriculum and teaching (Ed M, MAT, Ed D, CAGS); developmental studies (Ed M, Ed D, CAGS); early childhood education (Ed M, Ed D, CAGS); education (Ed M, MAT, Ed D, CAGS); education of the deaf (Ed M, CAGS); educational administration (Ed M); educational media and technology (Ed M, Ed D, CAGS); elementary education (Ed M); English and language arts education (Ed M, Ed D, CAGS); health education (Ed M, CAGS); human movement (Ed M, Ed D, CAGS); human resource education (Ed M, CAGS); international educational development (Ed M); Latin and classical studies (MAT); leisure education (Ed M); mathematics education (Ed M, MAT, Ed D, CAGS); modern foreign language education (Ed M, MAT); policy, planning, and administration (Ed M, CAGS); reading education (Ed M, Ed D, CAGS); science education (Ed M, MAT, Ed D, CAGS); social studies education (Ed M, MAT, Ed D, CAGS); special education (Ed M, Ed D, CAGS); teaching of English to speakers of other languages (Ed M, CAGS). *Application deadline:* For fall admission, 2/15 (priority date); for winter admission, 10/1 (priority date). Applications are processed on a rolling basis. *Application fee:* $60. Electronic applications accepted. *Application Contact:* Margaret Sullivan, Graduate Admissions Office, 617-353-4237, Fax: 617-353-8937, E-mail: sedgrad@bu.edu. *Interim Dean,* Dr. Douglas Sears, 617-353-3212.

School of Law Students: 1,015 full-time (518 women), 157 part-time (70 women); includes 197 minority (33 African Americans, 93 Asian Americans or Pacific Islanders, 69 Hispanic Americans, 2 Native Americans), 157 international. Average age 27. 5,171 applicants, 25% accepted, 246 enrolled. *Faculty:* 75 full-time (22 women), 123 part-time/adjunct (29 women). Expenses: Contact institution. *Financial support:* In 2001–02, 772 students received support, including 1 fellowship; career-related internships or fieldwork, Federal Work-Study, institutionally sponsored loans, and scholarships/grants also available. Financial award application deadline: 3/1; financial award applicants required to submit CSS PROFILE or FAFSA. In 2001, 292 first professional degrees, 191 master's awarded. *Degree program information:* Part-time and evening/weekend programs available. Offers American law (LL M); banking law (LL M); law (JD); taxation (LL M). *Application deadline:* For fall admission, 3/1. Applications are processed on a rolling basis. *Application fee:* $60. Electronic applications accepted. *Application Contact:* Joan Horgan, Director of Admissions and Financial Aid, 617-353-3100, Fax: 617-353-0578, E-mail: bulawadm@bu.edu. *Dean,* Ronald A. Cass, 617-353-3112, Fax: 617-353-7400.

School of Management Students: 690 full-time (219 women), 542 part-time (195 women); includes 129 minority (21 African Americans, 81 Asian Americans or Pacific Islanders, 26 Hispanic Americans, 1 Native American), 379 international. Average age 31. 1,365 applicants, 43% accepted, 287 enrolled. *Faculty:* 116 full-time. Expenses: Contact institution. *Financial support:* Career-related internships or fieldwork, Federal Work-Study, institutionally sponsored loans, and tuition waivers (partial) available. Support available to part-time students. Financial award applicants required to submit FAFSA. In 2001, 502 master's, 10 doctorates awarded. *Degree program information:* Part-time and evening/weekend programs available. Offers accounting (DBA); advanced accounting (Certificate); business administration (Exec MBA); business and information management); finance (DBA); general management (MBA); health-care management (MBA); information systems (MSIS, DBA); investment management (MSIM); management policy (DBA); marketing (DBA); nonprofit management (MBA); operations management (DBA); organizational behavior (DBA); public and nonprofit management (MBA); public management (MBA). *Application deadline:* For fall admission, 5/1. Applications are processed on a rolling basis. *Application fee:* $60. Electronic applications accepted. *Application Contact:* Evelyn Tate, Director, Admissions and Financial Aid, 617-353-2670, Fax: 617-353-7368, E-mail: mba@bu.edu. *Assistant Dean,* Katherine Nolan, 617-353-9827, Fax: 617-353-7368, E-mail: knolan@bu.edu.

School of Medicine Students: 969 full-time (423 women), 40 part-time (26 women); includes 270 minority (39 African Americans, 202 Asian Americans or Pacific Islanders, 27 Hispanic Americans, 2 Native Americans), 106 international. Average age 27. *Faculty:* 886 full-time, 180 part-time/adjunct. Expenses: Contact institution. *Financial support:* Fellowships, research assistantships, teaching assistantships, career-related internships or fieldwork, Federal Work-Study, and institutionally sponsored loans available. Support available to part-time students. In 2001, 145 first professional degrees, 92 master's, 36 doctorates awarded. *Degree program information:* Part-time and evening/weekend programs available. Offers medicine (MD, MA, PhD). *Application Contact:* Dr. John F. O'Connor, Associate Dean for Admissions, 617-638-4630. *Dean,* Dr. Aram V. Chobanian, 617-638-5300.

Division of Graduate Medical Sciences Students: 303 full-time (147 women), 27 part-time (17 women); includes 71 minority (9 African Americans, 52 Asian Americans or Pacific Islanders, 9 Hispanic Americans, 1 Native American), 66 international. Average age 27. *Faculty:* 80 full-time (20 women), 134 part-time/adjunct (19 women). Expenses: Contact institution. *Financial support:* In 2001–02, 38 fellowships with tuition reimbursements, 121 research assistantships with tuition reimbursements, 6 teaching assistantships with tuition reimbursements were awarded. Federal Work-Study, scholarships/grants, and traineeships also available. In 2001, 89 master's, 45 doctorates awarded. *Degree program information:* Part-time programs available. Offers anatomy and neurobiology (MA, PhD); behavioral neurosciences (PhD); biochemistry (MA, PhD); cell and molecular biology (PhD); clinical investigation (MA); experimental pathology (PhD); immunology (PhD); medical sciences (MA, PhD); mental health counseling and behavioral medicine (MA); microbiology (MA, PhD); molecular medicine (PhD); pharmacology and experimental therapeutics (MA, PhD); physiology (MA, PhD); physiology and biophysics (MA, PhD). *Application deadline:* For spring admission, 10/15 (priority date). Electronic applications accepted. *Application Contact:* Michelle Hall, Assistant Director of Admissions, 617-638-5121, Fax: 617-638-5740, E-mail: natashah@bu.edu. *Associate Dean,* Dr. Carl Franzblau, 617-638-5120, Fax: 617-638-4842, E-mail: medsci@bu.edu.

School of Public Health Students: 270 full-time (213 women), 351 part-time (281 women); includes 114 minority (27 African Americans, 62 Asian Americans or Pacific Islanders, 23 Hispanic Americans, 2 Native Americans), 93 international. Average age 30. *Faculty:* 90 full-time (45 women), 223 part-time/adjunct (98 women). Expenses: Contact institution. *Financial support:* Career-related internships or fieldwork, institutionally sponsored loans, and scholarships/grants available. Support available to part-time students. In 2001, 271 master's, 5 doctorates awarded. *Degree program information:* Part-time and evening/weekend programs available. Offers biostatistics (MA, MPH, PhD); environmental health (MPH, D Sc); epidemiology (M Sc, MPH, D Sc); health behavior, health promotion, and disease prevention (MPH); health law (MPH); health services (MPH); international health (MPH, Certificate); maternal and child health (MPH); nurse midwifery education (Certificate); public health (M Sc, MA, MPH, D Sc, PhD, Certificate). *Application deadline:* For fall admission, 4/15; for spring admission, 10/25. Applications are processed on a rolling basis. *Application fee:* $60. Electronic applications accepted. *Application Contact:* Barbara J. St. Onge, Director of Admissions, 617-638-4640, Fax: 617-638-5299, E-mail: bso@bu.edu. *Dean,* Dr. Robert F. Meenan, 617-638-4640, Fax: 617-638-5299.

School of Social Work Students: 159 full-time (149 women), 164 part-time (144 women); includes 36 minority (14 African Americans, 11 Asian Americans or Pacific Islanders, 10 Hispanic Americans, 1 Native American), 6 international. Average age 30. 400 applicants, 68% accepted, 130 enrolled. *Faculty:* 26 full-time (18 women), 93 part-time/adjunct (74 women). Expenses: Contact institution. *Financial support:* In 2001–02, 90 students received support, including 3 research assistantships with tuition reimbursements available (averaging $4,000 per year); fellowships, career-related internships or fieldwork, Federal Work-Study, institutionally sponsored loans, and scholarships/grants also available. Support available to part-time students. Financial award application deadline: 3/1; financial award applicants required to submit FAFSA. In 2001, 177 master's, 3 doctorates awarded. *Degree program information:* Part-time programs available. Offers clinical practice with groups (MSW); clinical practice with individuals and families (MSW); macro social work practice (MSW); social work and sociology (PhD); special education and social work). *Application deadline:* For fall admission, 3/2. *Application fee:* $60. *Application Contact:* Edward M. Greene, Director of Admissions, 617-353-3765, Fax: 617-353-5612, E-mail: busswad@bu.edu. *Dean,* Wilma Peebles-Wilkins, 617-353-3760, Fax: 617-353-5612.

School of Theology Students: 218 full-time (103 women), 49 part-time (24 women); includes 37 minority (19 African Americans, 10 Asian Americans or Pacific Islanders, 6 Hispanic Americans, 2 Native Americans), 80 international. Average age 37. 229 applicants, 70% accepted. *Faculty:* 21 full-time (7 women), 14 part-time/adjunct (1 woman). Expenses: Contact institution. *Financial support:* In 2001–02, 266 students received support, including 7 fellowships (averaging $4,000 per year), 9 research assistantships (averaging $3,000 per year), 27 teaching assistantships (averaging $5,500 per year); Federal Work-Study, institutionally sponsored loans, and scholarships/grants also available. Support available to part-time students. Financial award application deadline: 7/15; financial award applicants required to submit FAFSA. In 2001, 46 first professional degrees, 11 master's, 13 doctorates awarded. *Degree program information:* Part-time programs available. Offers theology (M Div, MSM, MTS, STM, D Min, Th D). *Application deadline:* For fall admission, 2/15 (priority date); for spring admission, 10/15 (priority date). Applications are processed on a rolling basis. *Application fee:* $50. Electronic applications accepted. *Application Contact:* Rev. Earl R. Beane, Director of Admissions, 617-353-3036, Fax: 617-358-0140, E-mail: sthadmis@bu.edu. *Dean,* Dr. Robert Neville, 617-353-3050, Fax: 617-353-3061.

University Professors Program Students: 22 full-time (12 women), 4 part-time (3 women), 7 international. Average age 35. 19 applicants, 68% accepted. *Faculty:* 24 full-time (3 women), 4 part-time/adjunct (0 women). Expenses: Contact institution. *Financial support:* In 2001–02, 24 students received support, including 5 fellowships with tuition reimbursements available, 6 teaching assistantships with tuition reimbursements available; research assistantships, Federal Work-Study, institutionally sponsored loans, scholarships/grants, and tuition waivers (partial) also available. Support available to part-time students. Financial award application deadline: 4/1. In 2001, 3 master's, 7 doctorates awarded. *Degree program information:* Part-time programs available. Offers interdisciplinary studies (MA, PhD). *Application deadline:* For fall admission, 1/15 (priority date); for spring admission, 10/15 (priority date). Applications are processed on a rolling basis. *Application fee:* $60. *Application Contact:* Edna Newmark, Coordinator, 617-353-4020, Fax: 617-353-5084, E-mail: enewmark@bu.edu. *Director,* Claudio Véliz, 617-353-4020, Fax: 617-353-5084.

See in-depth description on page 765.

BOWIE STATE UNIVERSITY, Bowie, MD 20715-9465

General Information State-supported, coed, comprehensive institution. CGS member. *Graduate housing:* Room and/or apartments available to single students; on-campus housing not available to married students.

GRADUATE UNITS

Graduate Programs *Degree program information:* Part-time and evening/weekend programs available. Offers administration of nursing services (MS); business administration (M Adm Mgt); computer science (MS); counseling psychology (MA); elementary education (M Ed); family nurse practitioner (MS); guidance and counseling (M Ed); human resource development (MA); information systems analyst (Certificate); management information systems (MS); nursing education (MS); organizational communication (MA, Certificate); public administration (M Adm Mgt); reading education (M Ed); school administration and supervision (M Ed); secondary education (M Ed); special education (M Ed); teaching (MAT).

BOWLING GREEN STATE UNIVERSITY, Bowling Green, OH 43403

General Information State-supported, coed, university. CGS member. *Enrollment:* 1,398 full-time matriculated graduate/professional students (804 women), 975 part-time matriculated graduate/professional students (622 women). *Enrollment by degree level:* 1,694 master's, 550 doctoral. *Graduate faculty:* 587. Tuition, state resident: full-time $7,376; part-time $342 per credit hour. Tuition, nonresident: full-time $13,628; part-time $640 per credit hour. *Graduate housing:* On-campus housing not available. *Student services:* Campus employment opportunities, campus safety program, career counseling, child daycare facilities, disabled student services, exercise/wellness program, free psychological counseling, grant writing training, international student services, low-cost health insurance, multicultural affairs office, teacher training, writing training. *Library facilities:* Jerome Library plus 7 others. *Online resources:* library catalog, web page, access to other libraries' catalogs. *Collection:* 2.3 million titles, 4,520 serial subscriptions, 672,745 audiovisual materials. *Research affiliation:* Edison Industrial Systems Center (manufacturing).

Computer facilities: 1,800 computers available on campus for general student use. A campuswide network can be accessed from student residence rooms and from off campus. Internet access and online class registration are available. *Web address:* http://www.bgsu.edu/.

General Application Contact: Terry L. Lawrence, Assistant Dean for Graduate Admissions and Studies, 419-372-7710, Fax: 419-372-8569, E-mail: tlawren@bgnet.bgsu.edu.

GRADUATE UNITS

Graduate College Students: 1,398 full-time (804 women), 975 part-time (622 women); includes 224 minority (137 African Americans, 33 Asian Americans or Pacific Islanders, 51 Hispanic Americans, 3 Native Americans), 396 international. Average age 31. 2,326 applicants, 57% accepted, 655 enrolled. Expenses: Contact institution. *Financial support:* In 2001–02, 306 research assistantships with full and partial tuition reimbursements (averaging $8,150 per year), 744 teaching assistantships with full and partial tuition reimbursements (averaging $7,637 per year) were awarded. Fellowships with full tuition reimbursements, career-related internships or fieldwork, Federal Work-Study, institutionally sponsored loans, tuition waivers (full and partial), and unspecified assistantships also available. Support available to part-time students. Financial award applicants required to submit FAFSA. In 2001, 808 master's, 99 doctorates awarded. *Degree program information:* Part-time and evening/weekend programs available. *Application fee:* $30. Electronic applications accepted. *Application Contact:* Terry L. Lawrence, Assistant Dean for Graduate Admissions and Studies, 419-372-7710, Fax: 419-372-8569, E-mail: tlawren@bgnet.bgsu.edu. *Interim Vice Provost for Research and Dean,* Dr. Heinz Bulmahn, 419-372-7714, Fax: 419-372-8569, E-mail: bulmahn@bgnet.bgsu.edu.

College of Arts and Sciences Students: 715 full-time (381 women), 154 part-time (86 women); includes 80 minority (32 African Americans, 21 Asian Americans or Pacific Islanders, 22 Hispanic Americans, 5 Native Americans), 226 international. Average age 29. 1,231 applicants, 49% accepted, 258 enrolled. *Faculty:* 295. Expenses: Contact institution. *Financial support:* In 2001–02, 134 research assistantships with full and partial tuition reimbursements (averaging $10,057 per year), 524 teaching assistantships with full and partial tuition reimbursements (averaging $8,684 per year) were awarded. Career-related internships or fieldwork, Federal Work-Study, institutionally sponsored loans, tuition waivers (full and partial), and unspecified assistantships also available. Support available to part-time students. Financial award applicants required to submit FAFSA. In 2001, 219 master's, 84 doctorates awarded. *Degree program information:* Part-time programs available. Offers American culture studies (MA, MAT, PhD); applied biology (Specialist); applied philosophy (PhD); applied statistics (MS); art (MA); arts and sciences (MA, MAT, MFA, MPA, MS, PhD, Ed S, Specialist); biological sciences (MAT, MS, PhD); chemistry (MAT, MS); clinical psychology (MA, PhD); communication studies (MA, MAT, PhD); computer science (MS); creative

Bowling Green State University (continued)

writing (MFA); criminology/deviant behavior (MA, PhD); demography and population studies (MA, PhD); developmental psychology (MA, PhD); English (MA, PhD); experimental psychology (MA, PhD); family studies (MA, PhD); French (MA, MAT); French education (MAT); geology (MAT, MS); German (MA, MAT); history (MA, MAT, PhD); industrial/organizational psychology (MA, PhD); interpersonal communication (MA, PhD); mathematics (MA, MAT, PhD); mathematics supervision (Ed S); philosophy (MA); photochemical sciences (PhD); physics (MAT, MS); physics and astronomy (MAT); popular culture (MA); public administration (MPA); quantitative psychology (MA, PhD); scientific and technical communication (MA); social psychology (MA, PhD); Spanish (MA, MAT); Spanish education (MAT); statistics (MA, MAT, PhD); studio art (MFA); teaching English as a second language (MA); theatre (MA, PhD). *Application fee:* $30. Electronic applications accepted. *Dean,* Dr. Donald Nieman, 419-372-2340.

College of Business Administration Students: 147 full-time (69 women), 138 part-time (47 women); includes 25 minority (9 African Americans, 3 Asian Americans or Pacific Islanders, 13 Hispanic Americans), 83 international. Average age 30. 255 applicants, 67% accepted, 94 enrolled. *Faculty:* 61. Expenses: Contact institution. *Financial support:* In 2001–02, 56 research assistantships with full tuition reimbursements (averaging $5,405 per year), 51 teaching assistantships with full tuition reimbursements (averaging $4,797 per year) were awarded. Career-related internships or fieldwork, Federal Work-Study, institutionally sponsored loans, and unspecified assistantships also available. Financial award applicants required to submit FAFSA. In 2001, 124 degrees awarded. *Degree program information:* Part-time and evening/weekend programs available. Offers accountancy (M Acc); applied statistics (MS); business (MBA); business administration (M Acc, MA, MBA, MOD, MS); economics (MA); organization development (MOD). *Application deadline:* Applications are processed on a rolling basis. *Application fee:* $30. Electronic applications accepted. *Dean,* Dr. James Sullivan, 419-372-8795.

College of Education and Human Development Students: 333 full-time (230 women), 562 part-time (429 women); includes 91 minority (73 African Americans, 6 Asian Americans or Pacific Islanders, 12 Hispanic Americans), 29 international. Average age 33. 526 applicants, 63% accepted, 186 enrolled. *Faculty:* 107. Expenses: Contact institution. *Financial support:* In 2001–02, 96 research assistantships with full tuition reimbursements (averaging $6,428 per year), 61 teaching assistantships with full tuition reimbursements (averaging $4,897 per year) were awarded. Career-related internships or fieldwork, Federal Work-Study, institutionally sponsored loans, tuition waivers (full and partial), and unspecified assistantships also available. Support available to part-time students. Financial award applicants required to submit FAFSA. In 2001, 356 master's, 15 doctorates awarded. *Degree program information:* Part-time and evening/weekend programs available. Offers business education (M Ed); classroom technology (M Ed); college student personnel (MA); curriculum and teaching (M Ed); development kinesiology (M Ed); education and human development (M Ed, MA, MFCS, MRC, Ed D, PhD, Ed S, SP); education and intervention services (M Ed, MA, MRC, Ed S, SP); educational administration and supervision (M Ed, Ed S); food and nutrition (MFCS); guidance and counseling (M Ed, MA); higher education administration (PhD); human development and family studies (MFCS); leadership and policy studies (M Ed, MA, Ed D, PhD, Ed S); leadership studies (Ed D); mathematics supervision (Ed S); reading (M Ed, Ed S); recreation and leisure (M Ed); rehabilitation counseling (MRC); school psychology (M Ed, SP); special education (M Ed); sport administration (M Ed). *Application deadline:* Applications are processed on a rolling basis. *Application fee:* $30. Electronic applications accepted. *Interim Dean,* Dr. Ellen Williams, 419-372-7403.

College of Health and Human Services Students: 56 full-time (49 women), 31 part-time (17 women); includes 9 minority (5 African Americans, 2 Asian Americans or Pacific Islanders, 1 Hispanic American, 1 Native American), 17 international. Average age 25. 128 applicants, 64% accepted, 45 enrolled. *Faculty:* 22. Expenses: Contact institution. *Financial support:* In 2001–02, 11 research assistantships with full tuition reimbursements (averaging $9,520 per year), 20 teaching assistantships with full tuition reimbursements (averaging $5,401 per year) were awarded. Career-related internships or fieldwork, Federal Work-Study, institutionally sponsored loans, and unspecified assistantships also available. Financial award applicants required to submit FAFSA. In 2001, 23 degrees awarded. *Degree program information:* Part-time and evening/weekend programs available. Offers communication disorders (MS, PhD); criminal justice (MSCJ); health and human services (MPH, MS, MSCJ, PhD); public health (MPH). *Application fee:* $30. Electronic applications accepted. *Dean,* Dr. Clyde Willis, 419-372-8243.

College of Musical Arts Students: 85 full-time (42 women), 20 part-time (12 women); includes 8 African Americans, 1 Asian American or Pacific Islander, 17 international. Average age 27. 101 applicants, 65% accepted, 37 enrolled. *Faculty:* 52. Expenses: Contact institution. *Financial support:* In 2001–02, 1 research assistantship with full tuition reimbursement (averaging $7,300 per year), 73 teaching assistantships with full tuition reimbursements (averaging $5,348 per year) were awarded. Career-related internships or fieldwork, Federal Work-Study, and unspecified assistantships also available. Financial award applicants required to submit FAFSA. In 2001, 53 degrees awarded. *Degree program information:* Part-time programs available. Offers composition (MM); music education (MM); music history (MM); music theory (MM); performance (MM). *Application deadline:* For fall admission, 3/2 (priority date). *Application fee:* $30. Electronic applications accepted. *Application Contact:* Dr. Penny Kruse, Graduate Coordinator, 419-372-2757. *Interim Dean,* Dr. Richard Kennell, 419-372-2188.

College of Technology Students: 29 full-time (11 women), 52 part-time (18 women); includes 6 minority (5 African Americans, 1 Hispanic American), 16 international. Average age 31. 33 applicants, 88% accepted, 19 enrolled. *Faculty:* 30. Expenses: Contact institution. *Financial support:* In 2001–02, 6 research assistantships with full tuition reimbursements (averaging $8,365 per year), 17 teaching assistantships with full tuition reimbursements (averaging $7,754 per year) were awarded. Career-related internships or fieldwork, Federal Work-Study, institutionally sponsored loans, tuition waivers (full and partial), and unspecified assistantships also available. Financial award applicants required to submit FAFSA. In 2001, 18 degrees awarded. *Degree program information:* Part-time programs available. Offers career and technology education (M Ed); manufacturing technology (MIT); technology (M Ed, MIT). *Application deadline:* For fall admission, 3/1. *Application fee:* $30. Electronic applications accepted. *Dean,* Dr. Ernie Savage, 419-372-2438.

Interdisciplinary Studies Expenses: Contact institution. *Financial support:* Fellowships with full tuition reimbursements, research assistantships with full tuition reimbursements, teaching assistantships with full tuition reimbursements, Federal Work-Study and unspecified assistantships available. Financial award applicants required to submit FAFSA. *Degree program information:* Part-time programs available. Offers interdisciplinary studies (MA, MS, PhD). *Application fee:* $30. Electronic applications accepted. *Application Contact:* Terry L. Lawrence, Assistant Dean for Graduate Admissions and Studies, 419-372-7710, Fax: 419-372-8569, E-mail: tlawren@bgnet.bgsu.edu.

See in-depth description on page 767.

BRADLEY UNIVERSITY, Peoria, IL 61625-0002

General Information Independent, coed, comprehensive institution. CGS member. *Enrollment:* 188 full-time matriculated graduate/professional students, 641 part-time matriculated graduate/professional students. *Enrollment by degree level:* 829 master's. *Graduate faculty:* 246. *Tuition:* Part-time $7,615 per semester. Tuition and fees vary according to course load. *Graduate housing:* Room and/or apartments available to single students; on-campus housing not available to married students. Typical cost: $3,293 (including board). *Student services:* Campus employment opportunities, campus safety program, career counseling, child daycare facilities, free psychological counseling, international student services, low-cost health insurance, multicultural affairs office, teacher training. *Library facilities:* Cullom-Davis Library. *Online resources:* library catalog, web page, access to other libraries' catalogs. *Collection:* 524,945 titles, 1,965 serial subscriptions, 12,225 audiovisual materials. *Research affiliation:* Northern Research Laboratory, Peoria School of Medicine, Caterpillar, Inc., Ford Motor Credit/Visteon, Illinois Manufacturing Extension Center.

Computer facilities: 2,000 computers available on campus for general student use. A campuswide network can be accessed from student residence rooms and from off campus. Internet access is available. *Web address:* http://www.bradley.edu/.

General Application Contact: Sarah E. Vance, Assistant Director, Graduate Enrollment Management, 309-677-2375, Fax: 309-677-3343, E-mail: bugrad@bradley.edu.

GRADUATE UNITS

Graduate School Students: 188 full-time, 641 part-time; includes 53 minority (29 African Americans, 11 Asian Americans or Pacific Islanders, 10 Hispanic Americans, 3 Native Americans), 230 international. Average age 33. 987 applicants, 73% accepted, 275 enrolled. *Faculty:* 246. Expenses: Contact institution. *Financial support:* In 2001–02, 300 students received support, including 13 fellowships with full and partial tuition reimbursements available (averaging $8,000 per year), 97 research assistantships with full and partial tuition reimbursements available (averaging $5,000 per year), 20 teaching assistantships with full and partial tuition reimbursements available (averaging $5,000 per year); career-related internships or fieldwork, institutionally sponsored loans, scholarships/grants, and tuition waivers (partial) also available. Support available to part-time students. Financial award application deadline: 3/1. In 2001, 246 degrees awarded. *Degree program information:* Part-time and evening/weekend programs available. *Application deadline:* For fall admission, 7/1 (priority date); for spring admission, 11/1 (priority date). Applications are processed on a rolling basis. *Application fee:* $40 ($50 for international students). *Application Contact:* Sarah E. Vance, Assistant Director, Graduate Enrollment Management, 309-677-2375, Fax: 309-677-3343, E-mail: bugrad@bradley.edu. *Dean of the Graduate School,* 309-677-2264, Fax: 309-677-3343.

College of Communications and Fine Arts Students: 4 full-time, 1 part-time. 7 applicants, 29% accepted. *Faculty:* 19. Expenses: Contact institution. *Financial support:* In 2001–02, 5 research assistantships with full and partial tuition reimbursements (averaging $4,600 per year) were awarded; scholarships/grants and tuition waivers (partial) also available. Support available to part-time students. Financial award application deadline: 3/1. In 2001, 3 degrees awarded. *Degree program information:* Part-time and evening/weekend programs available. Offers ceramics (MA, MFA); communications and fine arts (MA, MFA); painting (MA, MFA); photography (MA, MFA); printmaking (MA, MFA); sculpture (MA, MFA). *Application deadline:* For fall admission, 7/1 (priority date); for spring admission, 11/1 (priority date). Applications are processed on a rolling basis. *Application fee:* $40 ($50 for international students). *Dean,* Dr. Jeffrey Huberman, 309-677-2360.

College of Education and Health Sciences Students: 57 full-time, 171 part-time. 72 applicants, 69% accepted. *Faculty:* 81. Expenses: Contact institution. *Financial support:* In 2001–02, 18 research assistantships with full and partial tuition reimbursements (averaging $4,600 per year) were awarded; teaching assistantships, career-related internships or fieldwork, institutionally sponsored loans, scholarships/grants, and tuition waivers (partial) also available. Support available to part-time students. Financial award application deadline: 3/1. In 2001, 68 degrees awarded. *Degree program information:* Part-time and evening/weekend programs available. Offers curriculum and instruction (MA); education and health sciences (MA, MPT, MSN); human development counseling (MA); leadership in educational administration (MA); leadership in human services administration (MA); nursing (MSN); physical therapy (MPT). *Application deadline:* For fall admission, 7/1 (priority date); for spring admission, 11/1 (priority date). Applications are processed on a rolling basis. *Application fee:* $40 ($50 for international students). *Dean,* Dr. Joan Sattler, 309-677-3180.

College of Engineering and Technology Students: 44 full-time, 112 part-time. 534 applicants, 68% accepted. *Faculty:* 45. Expenses: Contact institution. *Financial support:* In 2001–02, 29 research assistantships with full and partial tuition reimbursements (averaging $1,405 per year) were awarded; teaching assistantships, institutionally sponsored loans, scholarships/grants, and tuition waivers (partial) also available. Support available to part-time students. Financial award application deadline: 3/1. In 2001, 69 degrees awarded. *Degree program information:* Part-time and evening/weekend programs available. Offers civil engineering and construction (MSCE); electrical engineering (MSEE); engineering and technology (MSCE, MSEE, MSIE, MSME, MSMFE); industrial and manufacturing engineering and technology (MSIE, MSMFE); mechanical engineering (MSME). *Application deadline:* For fall admission, 7/1 (priority date); for spring admission, 11/1. Applications are processed on a rolling basis. *Application fee:* $40 ($50 for international students). *Dean,* Dr. Richard Johnson, 309-677-2721.

College of Liberal Arts and Sciences Students: 54 full-time, 80 part-time. 264 applicants, 56% accepted. *Faculty:* 67. Expenses: Contact institution. *Financial support:* In 2001–02, 19 research assistantships with full and partial tuition reimbursements were awarded; teaching assistantships, career-related internships or fieldwork, institutionally sponsored loans, and tuition waivers (partial) also available. Support available to part-time students. Financial award application deadline: 3/1. In 2001, 48 degrees awarded. *Degree program information:* Part-time and evening/weekend programs available. Offers biology (MS); chemistry (MS); computer information systems (MS); computer science (MS); English (MA); liberal arts and sciences (MA, MLS, MS); liberal studies (MLS). *Application deadline:* For fall admission, 7/1 (priority date); for spring admission, 11/1. Applications are processed on a rolling basis. *Application fee:* $40 ($50 for international students). *Dean,* Dr. Claire Etaugh, 309-677-2380.

Foster College of Business Administration Students: 24 full-time, 143 part-time. 115 applicants, 79% accepted. *Faculty:* 34. Expenses: Contact institution. *Financial support:* In 2001–02, 20 teaching assistantships with full and partial tuition reimbursements were awarded; fellowships, research assistantships with full and partial tuition reimbursements, career-related internships or fieldwork, institutionally sponsored loans, scholarships/grants, and tuition waivers (partial) also available. Support available to part-time students. Financial award application deadline: 3/1. In 2001, 58 degrees awarded. *Degree program information:* Part-time and evening/weekend programs available. Offers accounting (MS); business administration (MBA, MS, MSA); executive leadership in business administration (MBA). *Application deadline:* For fall admission, 7/1 (priority date); for spring admission, 11/1. Applications are processed on a rolling basis. *Application fee:* $40 ($50 for international students). *Application Contact:* Lisa Stufflebeam, Assistant Director of Graduate Programs, 309-677-2256, Fax: 309-677-3374. *Dean,* Dr. Rob Baer, 309-677-2255, Fax: 309-677-3374.

See in-depth description on page 769.

BRANDEIS UNIVERSITY, Waltham, MA 02454-9110

General Information Independent, coed, university. CGS member. *Enrollment:* 737 full-time matriculated graduate/professional students (373 women), 39 part-time matriculated graduate/professional students (24 women). *Graduate faculty:* 360 full-time (117 women), 181 part-time/adjunct (91 women). *Tuition:* Full-time $27,392. *Required fees:* $35. *Graduate housing:* Room and/or apartments available on a first-come, first-served basis to single students; on-campus housing not available to married students. Housing application deadline: 6/15. *Student services:* Campus employment opportunities, campus safety program, career counseling, child daycare facilities, disabled student services, exercise/wellness program, free psychological counseling, grant writing training, international student services, low-cost health insurance, multicultural affairs office, teacher training, writing training. *Library facilities:* Goldfarb Library plus 2 others. *Online resources:* library catalog, web page, access to other libraries' catalogs. *Collection:* 1.1 million titles, 16,119 serial subscriptions, 32,996 audiovisual materials.

Computer facilities: 104 computers available on campus for general student use. A campuswide network can be accessed from student residence rooms and from off campus. Internet access and online class registration, educational software are available. *Web address:* http://www.brandeis.edu/.

General Application Contact: Margaret Haley, Assistant Dean, Graduate Admissions, 781-736-3406, Fax: 781-736-3412, E-mail: haley@brandeis.edu.

GRADUATE UNITS

Graduate School of Arts and Sciences Students: 737 full-time (373 women), 39 part-time (24 women). Average age 30. 1,400 applicants, 17% accepted. *Faculty:* 360 full-time (117 women), 181 part-time/adjunct (91 women). Expenses: Contact institution. *Financial* *support:* Fellowships, research assistantships, teaching assistantships, career-related internships or fieldwork, institutionally sponsored loans, scholarships/grants, and tuition waivers (full and partial) available. Support available to part-time students. Financial award application deadline: 4/15; financial award applicants required to submit CSS PROFILE or FAFSA. In 2001, 261 master's, 102 doctorates awarded. *Degree program information:* Part-time programs available. Offers American history (MA, PhD); anthropology (MA, PhD); anthropology and women's studies (MA); arts and sciences (MA, MAMM, MFA, MS, PhD, AD, Certificate); biochemistry (MS, PhD); biophysics and structural biology (PhD); classical studies (MA); cognitive neuroscience (PhD); comparative history (MA, PhD); composition and theory (MA, MFA, PhD); developmental biology (PhD); English and American literature (PhD); English and women's studies (MA); general psychology (MA); genetic counseling (MS); genetics (PhD); inorganic chemistry (MS, PhD); Jewish communal service (MA, MAMM); mathematics (PhD); microbiology (PhD); molecular and cell biology (MS, PhD); molecular biology (PhD); music and women's studies (MA, MFA); musicology (MA, MFA, PhD); Near Eastern and Judaic studies (MA, PhD); Near Eastern and Judaic studies and sociology (PhD); near Eastern and Judaic studies and sociology (MA, PhD); Near Eastern and Judaic studies and women's studies (MA); Near Eastern and Judiac studies and sociology (MA); neurobiology (PhD); neuroscience (MS, PhD); organic chemistry (MS, PhD); physical chemistry (MS, PhD); physics (MS, PhD); politics (MA, PhD); postbaccalaureate premedical (Certificate); social policy and sociology (PhD); social/developmental psychology (PhD); sociology (MA, PhD); sociology and women's studies (MA); studio art (Certificate); teaching of Hebrew (MA); theater arts (MFA). *Application fee:* $60. Electronic applications accepted. *Application Contact:* Margaret Haley, Assistant Dean, Graduate Admissions, 781-736-3406, Fax: 781-736-3412, E-mail: haley@brandeis.edu. *Associate Dean of Arts and Sciences for Graduate Education,* Dr. Milton Kornfeld, 781-736-3410, Fax: 781-736-3412, E-mail: kornfeld@brandeis.edu.

Michtom School of Computer Science Students: 53 full-time (9 women); includes 5 minority (all Asian Americans or Pacific Islanders), 25 international. 120 applicants, 38% accepted. *Faculty:* 10 full-time (1 woman). Expenses: Contact institution. *Financial support:* In 2001–02, 40 students received support, including research assistantships with tuition reimbursements available (averaging $18,000 per year), teaching assistantships with tuition reimbursements available (averaging $18,000 per year); institutionally sponsored loans and tuition waivers (full and partial) also available. Financial award application deadline: 4/15; financial award applicants required to submit CSS PROFILE or FAFSA. In 2001, 5 master's, 4 doctorates awarded. *Degree program information:* Part-time programs available. Offers computer science (MA, PhD). *Application deadline:* For fall admission, 2/15. *Application fee:* $60. Electronic applications accepted. *Application Contact:* Myrna Fox, Department Administrator, 781-736-2701, E-mail: maf@cs.brandeis.edu. *Director of Graduate Studies,* Dr. James Pustejovsky, 781-736-2709, Fax: 781-736-2741.

Graduate School of International Economics and Finance Students: 165 full-time (63 women), 57 part-time (14 women). Average age 28. 450 applicants, 50% accepted, 114 enrolled. *Faculty:* 25 full-time (4 women), 10 part-time/adjunct (0 women). Expenses: Contact institution. *Financial support:* In 2001–02, 166 students received support, including research assistantships (averaging $4,000 per year), teaching assistantships (averaging $4,000 per year); career-related internships or fieldwork, Federal Work-Study, institutionally sponsored loans, scholarships/grants, and unspecified assistantships also available. Financial award application deadline: 2/15; financial award applicants required to submit FAFSA. In 2001, 58 master's, 1 doctorate awarded. *Degree program information:* Part-time and evening/weekend programs available. Offers finance (MSF); international business (MBAi); international economics and finance (MA, PhD). *Application deadline:* For fall admission, 2/15 (priority date). *Application fee:* $50. Electronic applications accepted. *Application Contact:* Geraldine F. Koch, Assistant Dean for Admission, 781-736-2252, Fax: 781-736-2263, E-mail: admission@lemberg.brandeis.edu. *Dean,* Dr. Peter Petri, 781-736-4817, Fax: 781-736-2267, E-mail: ppetri@brandeis.edu.

The Heller School for Social Policy and Management Students: 125 full-time (72 women), 54 part-time (33 women). Average age 30. 159 applicants, 58% accepted. *Faculty:* 44 full-time (17 women), 16 part-time/adjunct (6 women). Expenses: Contact institution. *Financial support:* Fellowships with full and partial tuition reimbursements, research assistantships, teaching assistantships, institutionally sponsored loans, scholarships/grants, traineeships, tuition waivers (full and partial), and unspecified assistantships available. Financial award application deadline: 2/15; financial award applicants required to submit CSS PROFILE or FAFSA. In 2001, 59 master's, 14 doctorates awarded. *Degree program information:* Part-time and evening/weekend programs available. Offers child, youth, and family services (MBA, MM); elder and disabled services (MBA, MM); health care administration (MBA, MM); human services (MBA, MM); social policy (PhD); social policy and management (MA, MAMM, MBA, MM, PhD); sustainable international development (MA). *Application deadline:* For fall admission, 12/15; for winter admission, 2/15; for spring admission, 6/1. Applications are processed on a rolling basis. *Application fee:* $50. *Application Contact:* Lisa Hamlin Sherry, Assistant Director for Admissions and Financial Aid, 781-736-3835, Fax: 781-736-3881, E-mail: sherry@brandeis.edu. *Dean,* Dr. Jack Shonkoff, 781-736-3883, Fax: 781-736-3881, E-mail: shonkoff@brandeis.edu.

See in-depth description on page 771.

BRANDON UNIVERSITY, Brandon, MB R7A 6A9, Canada

General Information Province-supported, coed, comprehensive institution. *Enrollment:* 300 matriculated graduate/professional students. *Enrollment by degree level:* 89 master's, 211 other advanced degrees. *Graduate faculty:* 36 full-time (5 women), 1 part-time/adjunct (0 women). *Tuition:* Part-time $500 per course. *Graduate housing:* Room and/or apartments available to single students; on-campus housing not available to married students. *Student services:* Campus employment opportunities, career counseling, disabled student services, free psychological counseling, international student services, writing training. *Library facilities:* John E. Robbins Library. *Online resources:* library catalog, web page, access to other libraries' catalogs. *Collection:* 238,816 titles, 1,699 serial subscriptions, 12,233 audiovisual materials.

Computer facilities: 160 computers available on campus for general student use. A campuswide network can be accessed from student residence rooms and from off campus. Internet access is available. *Web address:* http://www.brandonu.ca/.

General Application Contact: Faye Douglas, Admissions Director, 204-727-7352, Fax: 204-725-2143, E-mail: douglas@brandonu.ca.

GRADUATE UNITS

Department of Rural Development Students: 6 full-time (1 woman), 29 part-time (15 women); includes 4 minority (1 Asian American or Pacific Islander, 3 Native Americans) Average age 35. *Faculty:* 4 full-time (0 women), 3 part-time/adjunct (1 woman). Expenses: Contact institution. *Financial support:* In 2001–02, 3 students received support, including 2 fellowships (averaging $3,000 per year), 2 research assistantships (averaging $5,000 per year); scholarships/grants and unspecified assistantships also available. *Degree program information:* Part-time and evening/weekend programs available. Postbaccalaureate distance learning degree programs offered (minimal on-campus study). Offers rural development (MRD, Diploma). *Application deadline:* For fall admission, 7/1 (priority date); for winter admission, 10/1 (priority date); for spring admission, 3/1 (priority date). Applications are processed on a rolling basis. *Application fee:* $35 Canadian dollars. Electronic applications accepted. *Director,* Dr. Robert Annis, 204-571-8513 Ext. 513, Fax: 204-725-0364, E-mail: annis@brandonu.ca.

Faculty of Education Offers curriculum (Diploma); curriculum studies (M Ed); education administration (M Ed, Diploma); guidance and counseling (M Ed, Diploma); special education (M Ed, Diploma).

School of Music Students: 12 full-time (8 women), 5 part-time, 12 international. Average age 27. 5 applicants, 100% accepted. *Faculty:* 6 full-time (2 women), 1 part-time/adjunct. Expenses: Contact institution. *Financial support:* In 2001–02, 12 students received support, including 8 teaching assistantships (averaging $3,250 per year) Financial award application deadline:5/1. In 2001, 1 degree awarded. *Degree program information:* Part-time programs available. Offers music education (M Mus); performance and literature (M Mus). *Application deadline:* For spring admission, 5/1 (priority date). Applications are processed on a rolling basis. *Application fee:* $35. Electronic applications accepted. *Application Contact:* Robert Richardson, Chair of Graduate Music Department, 204-727-7343, Fax: 204-728-6839, E-mail: richardsonr@brandonu.ca. *Dean,* Dr. Glen Carruthers, 204-727-9633, Fax: 204-728-6839, E-mail: carruthers@brandonu.ca.

BRENAU UNIVERSITY, Gainesville, GA 30501-3697

General Information Independent, women only, comprehensive institution. *Enrollment:* 212 full-time matriculated graduate/professional students (171 women), 588 part-time matriculated graduate/professional students (441 women). *Enrollment by degree level:* 614 master's, 186 other advanced degrees. *Graduate faculty:* 37 full-time (22 women), 32 part-time/adjunct (12 women). *Tuition:* Part-time $212 per hour. Tuition and fees vary according to degree level and program. *Graduate housing:* Room and/or apartments available to single students; on-campus housing not available to married students. Typical cost: $7,320 (including board). Room and board charges vary according to housing facility selected. *Student services:* Campus employment opportunities, career counseling. *Library facilities:* Trustee Library. *Online resources:* library catalog, web page. *Collection:* 99,678 titles, 527 serial subscriptions, 16,023 audiovisual materials.

Computer facilities: 120 computers available on campus for general student use. A campuswide network can be accessed from student residence rooms and from off campus. Internet access is available. *Web address:* http://www.brenau.edu/.

General Application Contact: Michelle Leavell, Graduate Admissions Coordinator, 770-534-6162, Fax: 770-538-4701, E-mail: mleavell@lib.brenau.edu.

GRADUATE UNITS

Graduate Programs Students: 212 full-time (171 women), 588 part-time (441 women); includes 129 minority (111 African Americans, 8 Asian Americans or Pacific Islanders, 8 Hispanic Americans, 2 Native Americans), 3 international. Average age 36. 431 applicants, 58% accepted. *Faculty:* 37 full-time (22 women), 32 part-time/adjunct (12 women). Expenses: Contact institution. *Financial support:* In 2001–02, 249 students received support. Career-related internships or fieldwork and scholarships/grants available. Financial award applicants required to submit FAFSA. In 2001, 304 master's, 44 other advanced degrees awarded. *Degree program information:* Part-time and evening/weekend programs available. Postbaccalaureate distance learning degree programs offered (no on-campus study). *Application deadline:* Applications are processed on a rolling basis. *Application Contact:* Michelle Leavell, Graduate Admissions Coordinator, 770-534-6162, Fax: 770-538-4701, E-mail: mleavell@lib.brenau.edu. *Dean,* Dr. Helen Ray, 770-534-6119.

School of Business and Mass Communication Students: 68 full-time (34 women), 229 part-time (117 women); includes 53 minority (45 African Americans, 3 Asian Americans or Pacific Islanders, 3 Hispanic Americans, 2 Native Americans), 1 international. Average age 34. 135 applicants, 56% accepted. *Faculty:* 11 full-time (2 women), 14 part-time/adjunct (2 women). Expenses: Contact institution. *Financial support:* Career-related internships or fieldwork available. In 2001, 129 degrees awarded. *Degree program information:* Part-time and evening/weekend programs available. Postbaccalaureate distance learning degree programs offered (no on-campus study). Offers accounting (MBA); healthcare management (MBA); leadership development (MBA); management (MBA). *Application deadline:* Applications are processed on a rolling basis. *Application fee:* $30. Electronic applications accepted. *Application Contact:* Michelle Leavell, Graduate Admissions Coordinator, 770-534-6162, Fax: 770-538-4701, E-mail: mleavell@lib.brenau.edu. *Dean,* Dr. Diane Garsombke, 770-538-4707, Fax: 770-538-4701, E-mail: dgarsombke@lib.brenau.edu.

School of Education and Human Development Students: 122 full-time (115 women), 322 part-time (291 women); includes 63 minority (59 African Americans, 2 Asian Americans or Pacific Islanders, 2 Hispanic Americans) Average age 37. 284 applicants, 58% accepted. *Faculty:* 12 full-time (8 women), 16 part-time/adjunct (8 women). Expenses: Contact institution. *Financial support:* Career-related internships or fieldwork available. In 2001, 138 master's, 44 other advanced degrees awarded. *Degree program information:* Part-time and evening/weekend programs available. Offers early childhood education (M Ed, Ed S); learning disabilities (M Ed); middle grades education (M Ed, Ed S). *Application deadline:* Applications are processed on a rolling basis. *Application Contact:* Michelle Leavell, Graduate Admissions Coordinator, 770-534-6162, Fax: 770-538-4701, E-mail: mleavell@lib.brenau.edu. *Dean,* Dr. William B. Ware, 770-534-6220.

School of Health and Science Students: 22 full-time (all women), 37 part-time (33 women); includes 13 minority (7 African Americans, 3 Asian Americans or Pacific Islanders, 3 Hispanic Americans), 2 international. Average age 33. 12 applicants, 67% accepted. *Faculty:* 14 full-time (12 women), 2 part-time/adjunct (both women). Expenses: Contact institution. *Financial support:* Career-related internships or fieldwork available. In 2001, 37 degrees awarded. *Degree program information:* Part-time programs available. Offers family nurse practitioner (MSN); occupational therapy (MS). *Application deadline:* Applications are processed on a rolling basis. *Application fee:* $30. *Application Contact:* Michelle Leavell, Graduate Admissions Coordinator, 770-534-6162, Fax: 770-538-4701, E-mail: mleavell@lib.brenau.edu. *Head.*

BRESCIA UNIVERSITY, Owensboro, KY 42301-3023

General Information Independent-religious, coed, comprehensive institution. *Enrollment:* 35 part-time matriculated graduate/professional students (21 women). *Enrollment by degree level:* 35 master's. *Graduate faculty:* 8 full-time (5 women), 1 part-time/adjunct (0 women). *Tuition:* Part-time $200 per credit hour. Part-time tuition and fees vary according to program. *Student services:* Free psychological counseling. *Library facilities:* Brescia University Library. *Online resources:* library catalog, web page, access to other libraries' catalogs. *Collection:* 62,607 titles, 2,466 serial subscriptions, 6,717 audiovisual materials.

Computer facilities: 41 computers available on campus for general student use. A campuswide network can be accessed from student residence rooms and from off campus. Internet access is available. *Web address:* http://www.brescia.edu/.

General Application Contact: Sr. Mary Austin Blank, Director of Admissions, 270-686-4241, Fax: 270-686-4201, E-mail: admissions@brescia.edu.

GRADUATE UNITS

Program in Curriculum and Instruction Average age 39. 4 applicants, 100% accepted, 4 enrolled. *Faculty:* 4 full-time (3 women). Expenses: Contact institution. *Financial support:* In 2001–02, 6 students received support. Institutionally sponsored loans available. Support available to part-time students. Financial award application deadline: 3/1; financial award applicants required to submit FAFSA. *Degree program information:* Part-time and evening/weekend programs available. Offers curriculum and instruction (MSCI). *Application deadline:* Applications are processed on a rolling basis. *Application fee:* $50. Electronic applications accepted. *Application Contact:* Sr. Mary Austin Blank, Director of Admissions, 270-686-4241, Fax: 270-686-4201, E-mail: admissions@brescia.edu. *Coordinator,* Kathleen Filkins, 270-686-4271, Fax: 270-686-4230, E-mail: kathleenf@brescia.edu.

Program in Management Average age 36. 13 applicants, 85% accepted, 11 enrolled. *Faculty:* 4 full-time (2 women), 1 part-time/adjunct (0 women). Expenses: Contact institution. *Financial support:* In 2001–02, 9 students received support. Institutionally sponsored loans available. Support available to part-time students. Financial award application deadline: 3/1; financial award applicants required to submit FAFSA. In 2001, 15 degrees awarded. *Degree program information:* Part-time and evening/weekend programs available. Offers management (MSM). *Application deadline:* Applications are processed on a rolling basis. *Application fee:* $50. *Application Contact:* Sr. Mary Austin Blank, Director of Admissions, 270-686-4241, Fax: 270-686-4201, E-mail: admissions@brescia.edu. *Director,* Dr. Dorn Fowler, 270-686-4274, Fax: 270-686-4266, E-mail: dornf@brescia.edu.

BRIDGEWATER STATE COLLEGE, Bridgewater, MA 02325-0001

General Information State-supported, coed, comprehensive institution. CGS member. *Enrollment:* 1,800 matriculated graduate/professional students. *Graduate faculty:* 140 full-time. Tuition, state resident: part-time $135 per credit. Tuition, nonresident: part-time $294 per credit. Tuition and fees vary according to class time. *Graduate housing:* On-campus housing not available. *Student services:* Career counseling, child daycare facilities, low-cost health insurance. *Library facilities:* Clement Maxwell Library. *Online resources:* library catalog, web page,

Bridgewater State College (continued)

access to other libraries' catalogs. *Collection:* 280,000 titles, 1,600 serial subscriptions, 9,700 audiovisual materials.

Computer facilities: 534 computers available on campus for general student use. A campuswide network can be accessed from student residence rooms and from off campus. Internet access and online class registration, student account information, application software are available. *Web address:* http://www.bridgew.edu/.

General Application Contact: James Plotner, Assistant Dean, Graduate Admissions, 508-531-1300, Fax: 508-531-6162, E-mail: jplotner@bridgew.edu.

GRADUATE UNITS

School of Graduate and Continuing Education Students: 1,800. *Faculty:* 140 full-time. Expenses: Contact institution. *Financial support:* Career-related internships or fieldwork available. Support available to part-time students. *Degree program information:* Part-time and evening/weekend programs available. *Application deadline:* For fall admission, 3/1 (priority date); for spring admission, 10/1 (priority date). *Application fee:* $50. *Application Contact:* James Plotner, Assistant Dean, Graduate Admissions, 508-531-1300, Fax: 508-531-6162, E-mail: jplotner@bridgew.edu. *Dean,* Dr. Edward Minnock, 508-531-1300, Fax: 508-531-6162, E-mail: eminnock@bridgew.edu.

School of Arts and Sciences Students: 250. Expenses: Contact institution. *Financial support:* Career-related internships or fieldwork available. *Degree program information:* Part-time and evening/weekend programs available. Offers art (MAT); arts and sciences (MA, MAT, MPA, MS); biological sciences (MAT); chemical sciences (MAT); computer science (MS); criminal justice (MS); earth sciences (MAT); English (MA, MAT); history (MAT); mathematics (MAT); physical sciences (MAT); physics (MAT); political science (MPA); psychology (MA); public administration (MPA); sociology (MS). *Application deadline:* For fall admission, 3/1 (priority date); for spring admission, 10/1 (priority date). *Application fee:* $50. *Application Contact:* James Plotner, Assistant Dean, Graduate Admissions, 508-531-1300, Fax: 508-531-6162, E-mail: jplotner@bridgew.edu. *Dean,* Dr. Howard London, 508-531-1218.

School of Education and Allied Science Students: 1,525. Expenses: Contact institution. *Financial support:* Career-related internships or fieldwork available. *Degree program information:* Part-time and evening/weekend programs available. Offers counseling (M Ed, CAGS); early childhood education (M Ed); education (M Ed, MAT, MS, CAGS); educational leadership (M Ed, CAGS); elementary education (M Ed); health promotion (M Ed, MAT); instructional technology (M Ed); library media (M Ed); physical education (MAT, MS); reading (M Ed, CAGS); secondary education (MAT); special education (M Ed). *Application deadline:* For fall admission, 3/1 (priority date); for spring admission, 10/1 (priority date). *Application fee:* $50. *Application Contact:* James Plotner, Assistant Dean, Graduate Admissions, 508-531-1300, Fax: 508-531-6162, E-mail: jplotner@bridgew.edu. *Dean,* Dr. Ronald Cromwell, 508-697-1347.

School of Management Students: 25. Expenses: Contact institution. *Degree program information:* Part-time and evening/weekend programs available. Offers accounting and finance (MSM); management (MSM). *Application deadline:* For fall admission, 3/1 (priority date); for spring admission, 10/1 (priority date). *Application fee:* $50. *Application Contact:* James Plotner, Assistant Dean, Graduate Admissions, 508-531-1300, Fax: 508-531-6162, E-mail: jplotner@bridgew.edu. *Acting Dean,* Dr. Dorothy Oppenheim, 508-531-1395.

BRIERCREST BIBLICAL SEMINARY, Caronport, SK S0H 0S0, Canada

General Information Independent-religious, coed, graduate-only institution. *Enrollment by degree level:* 280 master's. *Graduate faculty:* 7 full-time (0 women), 22 part-time/adjunct (1 woman). *Graduate tuition:* Tuition charges are reported in Canadian dollars. *Tuition:* Full-time $6,720 Canadian dollars; part-time $210 Canadian dollars per credit. *Graduate housing:* Rooms and/or apartments guaranteed to single students and available on a first-come, first-served basis to married students. Typical cost: $2,000 Canadian dollars per year ($4,000 Canadian dollars including board) for single students; $4,000 Canadian dollars per year for married students. *Student services:* Campus employment opportunities, career counseling, exercise/wellness program, free psychological counseling. *Library facilities:* Archibald Library plus 1 other. *Online resources:* library catalog, web page, access to other libraries' catalogs. *Collection:* 59,298 titles, 6,457 serial subscriptions.

Computer facilities: 24 computers available on campus for general student use. A campuswide network can be accessed from off campus. Internet access is available. *Web address:* http://www.briercrest.ca/.

General Application Contact: Paul Wilder, Enrollment Management Officer, 306-756-3221, Fax: 306-756-7366, E-mail: pwilder@briercrest.ca.

GRADUATE UNITS

Graduate Programs Students: 86 full-time (18 women), 194 part-time (58 women). Average age 38. 90 applicants, 70% accepted. *Faculty:* 7 full-time (0 women), 22 part-time/adjunct (1 woman). Expenses: Contact institution. *Financial support:* Teaching assistantships, career-related internships or fieldwork available. In 2001, 48 degrees awarded. *Degree program information:* Part-time programs available. Offers biblical studies (M Div); higher education (MA); leadership management (M Div); marriage and family counseling (M Div, MA); New Testament (M Div); Old Testament (M Div); organizational leadership (MA); pastoral ministry (M Div); theological studies (M Div); youth and family ministry (M Div, MA). *Application deadline:* Applications are processed on a rolling basis. *Application fee:* $25. *Application Contact:* Paul Wilder, Enrollment Management Officer, 306-756-3221, Fax: 306-756-7366, E-mail: pwilder@briercrest.ca. *Dean,* Dr. Dwayne Uglem, 306-756-3212, Fax: 306-756-3366.

BRIGHAM YOUNG UNIVERSITY, Provo, UT 84602-1001

General Information Independent-religious, coed, university. CGS member. *Enrollment:* 1,872 full-time matriculated graduate/professional students (673 women), 982 part-time matriculated graduate/professional students (460 women). *Enrollment by degree level:* 492 first professional, 1,963 master's, 399 doctoral. *Graduate faculty:* 931 full-time (187 women), 156 part-time/adjunct (75 women). *Tuition:* Full-time $3,860; part-time $214 per hour. *Graduate housing:* Rooms and/or apartments available on a first-come, first-served basis to single and married students. *Student services:* Campus employment opportunities, campus safety program, career counseling, disabled student services, exercise/wellness program, free psychological counseling, international student services, low-cost health insurance, multicultural affairs office, teacher training, writing training. *Library facilities:* Harold B. Lee Library plus 2 others. *Online resources:* library catalog, web page, access to other libraries' catalogs. *Collection:* 2.6 million titles, 16,201 serial subscriptions, 56,353 audiovisual materials.

Computer facilities: 1,800 computers available on campus for general student use. A campuswide network can be accessed from student residence rooms and from off campus. Internet access and online class registration are available. *Web address:* http://www.byu.edu/.

General Application Contact: Adviser, 801-378-4541, Fax: 801-378-5238.

GRADUATE UNITS

The David M. Kennedy Center for International and Area Studies Students: 16 full-time (8 women), 13 part-time (9 women); includes 1 minority (Hispanic American), 4 international. Average age 25. 62 applicants, 31% accepted. *Faculty:* 21 full-time (2 women), 2 part-time/adjunct (0 women). Expenses: Contact institution. *Financial support:* In 2001–02, 18 research assistantships (averaging $3,500 per year), 2 teaching assistantships (averaging $3,500 per year) were awarded. Fellowships with full tuition reimbursements, career-related internships or fieldwork and tuition waivers (full) also available. Financial award application deadline: 2/1. In 2001, 17 degrees awarded. Offers American studies (MA); ancient Near Eastern studies (MA); Asian studies (MA); international development (MA); international relations (MA). *Application deadline:* For fall admission, 2/1. *Application fee:* $50. Electronic applications accepted. *Application Contact:* Dr. Phillip J. Bryson, Director of Graduate Studies, Associate Director, 801-422-7402, Fax: 801-378-8748, E-mail: phillip_bryson@byu.edu. *Director,* Dr. Donald B. Holsinger, 801-422-3378, Fax: 801-378-8748, E-mail: donald_holsinger@byu.edu.

Graduate Studies Students: 1,872 full-time (673 women), 982 part-time (460 women). Average age 30. 2,587 applicants, 45% accepted. *Faculty:* 931 full-time (187 women), 156 part-time/adjunct (75 women). Expenses: Contact institution. *Financial support:* Fellowships, research assistantships, teaching assistantships, career-related internships or fieldwork, institutionally sponsored loans, and tuition waivers (full and partial) available. Support available to part-time students. Financial award applicants required to submit FAFSA. In 2001, 158 first professional degrees, 1,360 master's, 98 doctorates awarded. *Degree program information:* Part-time and evening/weekend programs available. *Application deadline:* For fall admission, 1/10 (priority date); for winter and spring admission, 2/1 (priority date). Applications are processed on a rolling basis. *Application fee:* $50. Electronic applications accepted. *Application Contact:* Adviser, 801-422-4541, Fax: 801-378-5238, E-mail: gradstudies@byu.edu. *Dean,* Bonnie Brinton, 801-422-4465, Fax: 801-378-5238.

College of Biological and Agricultural Sciences Students: 84 full-time (39 women), 35 part-time (13 women); includes 4 minority (2 Asian Americans or Pacific Islanders, 2 Hispanic Americans), 12 international. Average age 27. 98 applicants, 58% accepted. *Faculty:* 95 full-time (8 women), 4 part-time/adjunct (3 women). Expenses: Contact institution. *Financial support:* Fellowships, research assistantships, teaching assistantships, career-related internships or fieldwork, institutionally sponsored loans, scholarships/grants, tuition waivers (partial), and tuition awards available. Support available to part-time students. In 2001, 35 master's, 3 doctorates awarded. *Degree program information:* Part-time programs available. Offers agronomy (MS); animal and veterinary sciences (MS); biological and agricultural sciences (MS, PhD); biological science education (MS); botany (MS, PhD); food science (MS); horticulture (MS); microbiology (MS, PhD); molecular biology (MS, PhD); nutrition (MS); range science (MS); wildlife and range resources (MS, PhD); zoology (MS, PhD). *Application deadline:* Applications are processed on a rolling basis. *Application fee:* $50. Electronic applications accepted. *Dean,* Dr. R. Kent Crookston, 801-422-2007, Fax: 801-378-7499.

College of Engineering and Technology Students: 314 full-time (28 women). Average age 26. 369 applicants, 51% accepted, 125 enrolled. *Faculty:* 94 full-time (0 women). Expenses: Contact institution. *Financial support:* In 2001–02, 11 fellowships with full tuition reimbursements (averaging $13,000 per year), 73 research assistantships with partial tuition reimbursements (averaging $5,000 per year), 93 teaching assistantships with partial tuition reimbursements (averaging $6,300 per year) were awarded. Career-related internships or fieldwork, institutionally sponsored loans, and scholarships/grants also available. Support available to part-time students. Financial award application deadline: 3/15; financial award applicants required to submit FAFSA. In 2001, 113 master's, 11 doctorates awarded. *Degree program information:* Part-time programs available. Offers chemical (PhD); chemical engineering (MS); civil engineering (MS, PhD); electrical engineering (MS); engineering (PhD); engineering and technology (MS, PhD); engineering technology (MS); mechanical engineering (MS, PhD); technology teacher education (MS). *Application deadline:* For fall admission, 2/15. Applications are processed on a rolling basis. *Application fee:* $50. Electronic applications accepted. *Dean,* Dr. Douglas M. Chabries, 801-422-4327, Fax: 801-422-0218, E-mail: college@et.byu.edu.

College of Family, Home, and Social Sciences Students: 281 full-time (150 women), 74 part-time (38 women); includes 39 minority (1 African American, 24 Asian Americans or Pacific Islanders, 9 Hispanic Americans, 5 Native Americans), 24 international. Average age 29. 528 applicants, 25% accepted, 33 enrolled. *Faculty:* 132 full-time (30 women), 36 part-time/adjunct (18 women). Expenses: Contact institution. *Financial support:* In 2001–02, 163 students received support, including 9 fellowships, 81 research assistantships with partial tuition reimbursements available, 70 teaching assistantships with partial tuition reimbursements available; career-related internships or fieldwork, institutionally sponsored loans, tuition waivers (full and partial), and administrative aides, paid field practicums also available. Support available to part-time students. Financial award applicants required to submit FAFSA. In 2001, 83 master's, 22 doctorates awarded. Offers anthropology (MA); clinical psychology (PhD); family, home, and social sciences (MA, MS, MSW, PhD); general psychology (MS); geography (MS); history (MA); marriage and family therapy (MS, PhD); marriage, family and human development (MS, PhD); psychology (PhD); social work (MSW); sociology (MS, PhD). *Application fee:* $50. Electronic applications accepted. *Dean,* Dr. David B. Magleby, 801-422-2083, Fax: 801-378-5978, E-mail: david_magleby@byu.edu.

College of Fine Arts and Communications Students: 119 full-time (83 women), 36 part-time (24 women). Average age 30. 99 applicants, 56% accepted. *Faculty:* 99 full-time (24 women), 1 (woman) part-time/adjunct. Expenses: Contact institution. *Financial support:* In 2001–02, 119 students received support, including 25 research assistantships, 85 teaching assistantships; career-related internships or fieldwork, institutionally sponsored loans, tuition waivers (partial), and administrative aides, supplementary awards also available. Support available to part-time students. Financial award applicants required to submit FAFSA. In 2001, 44 master's, 2 doctorates awarded. Offers art education (MA); art history (MA); ceramics (MFA); child drama (MA); composition (MM); conducting (MM); fine arts and communications (MA, MFA, MM, PhD); mass communication (MA); music education (MA, MM); musicology (MA); painting-drawing (MFA); performance (MM); printmaking-drawing (MFA); sculpture (MFA); theatre history, theory, and criticism (MA). *Application fee:* $50. Electronic applications accepted. *Dean,* Dr. K. Newell Dayley, 801-422-2818, Fax: 801-378-4730, E-mail: cfac@byu.edu.

College of Health and Human Performance Students: 35 full-time (24 women), 5 part-time (3 women); includes 2 Asian Americans or Pacific Islanders, 1 Hispanic American, 4 international. Average age 28. 62 applicants, 74% accepted, 40 enrolled. *Faculty:* 60 full-time (28 women). Expenses: Contact institution. *Financial support:* In 2001–02, research assistantships (averaging $3,850 per year), teaching assistantships (averaging $4,000 per year) were awarded. Fellowships, career-related internships or fieldwork, institutionally sponsored loans, scholarships/grants, tuition waivers (full and partial), and administrative aides also available. Support available to part-time students. Financial award application deadline: 3/1. In 2001, 28 master's, 4 doctorates awarded. Offers athletic training (MS); curriculum and instruction in physical education (PhD); dance (MS); exercise physiology (MS); health and human performance (MS, PhD); health promotion (MS); health promotion (physical medicine and rehabilitation) (PhD); sports pedagogy (MS); youth and family recreation (MS). *Application deadline:* For fall admission, 2/1. Applications are processed on a rolling basis. *Application fee:* $50. Electronic applications accepted. *Application Contact:* Dr. Thomas S. Catherall, Chair, 801-422-4991, Fax: 801-378-7461, E-mail: catherall@byu.edu. *Dean,* Dr. Robert K. Conlee, 801-422-2645, Fax: 801-378-6585, E-mail: robert_conlee@byu.edu.

College of Humanities Students: 144 full-time (104 women), 106 part-time (73 women); includes 14 minority (3 Asian Americans or Pacific Islanders, 11 Hispanic Americans), 30 international. Average age 26. 146 applicants, 65% accepted. *Faculty:* 157 full-time (38 women), 48 part-time/adjunct (33 women). Expenses: Contact institution. *Financial support:* In 2001–02, 199 students received support, including 6 fellowships, 24 research assistantships, 87 teaching assistantships; career-related internships or fieldwork, institutionally sponsored loans, tuition waivers (full and partial), and student instructorships also available. Support available to part-time students. In 2001, 78 degrees awarded. *Degree program information:* Part-time programs available. Offers Arabic (MA); Chinese (MA); comparative literature (MA); English (MA); Finnish (MA); French (MA); French studies (MA); general linguistics (MA); German (MA); Germanic and Slavic languages (PhD); humanities (MA); Japanese (MA); Korean (MA); Portuguese (MA); Portuguese linguistics (MA); Portuguese literature (MA); Russian (MA); Scandinavian (MA); Spanish linguistics (MA); Spanish literature (MA); Spanish teaching (MA); Spanish/Latin American Literature (MA); teaching English as a second language (MA, PhD). *Application fee:* $50. Electronic applications accepted. *Dean,* Dr. Van C. Gessel, 801-422-2775, Fax: 801-378-5317, E-mail: van_gessel@byu.edu.

College of Nursing Students: 13 full-time (10 women), 8 part-time (5 women). Average age 32. 15 applicants, 60% accepted. *Faculty:* 26 full-time (24 women). Expenses: Contact institution. *Financial support:* In 2001–02, research assistantships with full and partial tuition reimbursements (averaging $10,000 per year), teaching assistantships with full and partial tuition reimbursements (averaging $10,000 per year) were awarded. Career-related internships or fieldwork and institutionally sponsored loans also available. Support available to part-time students. Financial award application deadline: 2/1; financial award applicants required to submit FAFSA. In 2001, 11 degrees awarded. Offers family nurse practitioner (MS). *Application deadline:* For spring admission, 12/1. Applications are processed on a rolling basis. *Application fee:* $50. Electronic applications accepted. *Application Contact:* Dr. Mary Williams, Associate Dean, 801-422-5626, Fax: 801-422-0536, E-mail: mary_williams@byu.edu. *Dean,* Dr. Elaine S. Marshall, 801-422-2747, Fax: 801-378-3198, E-mail: elaine_marshall@byu.edu.

College of Physical and Mathematical Sciences Students: 199 full-time (61 women), 87 part-time (18 women); includes 21 minority (18 Asian Americans or Pacific Islanders, 3 Hispanic Americans), 82 international. Average age 26. 361 applicants, 31% accepted. *Faculty:* 143 full-time (3 women), 5 part-time/adjunct (2 women). Expenses: Contact institution. *Financial support:* In 2001–02, 18 fellowships (averaging $15,309 per year), 96 research assistantships (averaging $14,000 per year), 113 teaching assistantships (averaging $12,500 per year) were awarded. Career-related internships or fieldwork, institutionally sponsored loans, scholarships/grants, and tuition waivers (full and partial) also available. Support available to part-time students. In 2001, 60 master's, 15 doctorates awarded. *Degree program information:* Part-time programs available. Offers analytical chemistry (MS, PhD); applied statistics (MS); biochemistry (MS, PhD); computer science (MS, PhD); geology (MS); inorganic chemistry (MS, PhD); mathematics (MS, PhD); organic chemistry (MS, PhD); physical and mathematical sciences (MS, PhD); physical chemistry (MS, PhD); physics (MS, PhD); physics and astronomy (PhD). *Application fee:* $50. *Dean,* Earl M. Woolley, 801-422-2674, Fax: 801-378-2575, E-mail: emwoolle@chemdept.byu.edu.

David O. McKay School of Education Students: 152 full-time (89 women), 147 part-time (83 women); includes 16 minority (3 African Americans, 9 Asian Americans or Pacific Islanders, 4 Hispanic Americans), 39 international. Average age 32. 311 applicants, 38% accepted. *Faculty:* 65 full-time (21 women), 28 part-time/adjunct (9 women). Expenses: Contact institution. *Financial support:* In 2001–02, 50 research assistantships, 26 teaching assistantships were awarded. Fellowships, career-related internships or fieldwork, institutionally sponsored loans, scholarships/grants, and tuition waivers (partial) also available. Support available to part-time students. Financial award applicants required to submit FAFSA. In 2001, 77 master's, 13 doctorates awarded. *Degree program information:* Part-time programs available. Offers audiology (MS); counseling and school psychology (MS); counseling psychology (PhD); education (M Ed, MA, MS, Ed D, PhD); educational leadership and foundations (M Ed, Ed D, PhD); instructional psychology and technology (MS, PhD); reading (Ed D); special education (MS); speech-language pathology (MS); teaching and learning (M Ed, MA). *Application deadline:* For fall admission, 2/1. *Application fee:* $50. Electronic applications accepted. *Dean,* Dr. Robert S. Patterson, 801-422-3695, Fax: 801-378-4017, E-mail: bob_patterson@byu.edu.

J. Reuben Clark Law School Students: 489 full-time (150 women); includes 58 minority (2 African Americans, 24 Asian Americans or Pacific Islanders, 26 Hispanic Americans, 6 Native Americans), 17 international. Average age 26. 677 applicants, 35% accepted, 153 enrolled. *Faculty:* 38 full-time (9 women), 32 part-time/adjunct (9 women). Expenses: Contact institution. *Financial support:* In 2001–02, 326 students received support; research assistantships, teaching assistantships, career-related internships or fieldwork, institutionally sponsored loans, and scholarships/grants available. Financial award application deadline: 6/1; financial award applicants required to submit FAFSA. In 2001, 156 degrees awarded. Offers law (JD, LL M). *Application deadline:* For fall admission, 2/1. Applications are processed on a rolling basis. *Application fee:* $50. *Application Contact:* Lola Wilcock, Admissions Director, 801-422-4277, Fax: 801-378-5897, E-mail: wilcockl@lawgate.byu.edu. *Dean,* H. Reese Hansen, 801-422-6383, Fax: 801-378-5897, E-mail: hansenr@lawgate.byu.edu.

Marriott School of Management *Degree program information:* Part-time and evening/weekend programs available. Offers accountancy and information systems (M Acc, MISM); business administration (MBA); executive business administration (MBA); management (M Acc, MBA, MISM, MOB, MPA); organizational behavior (MOB); public management (MPA). Electronic applications accepted.

BROCK UNIVERSITY, St. Catharines, ON L2S 3A1, Canada

General Information Province-supported, coed, comprehensive institution. *Enrollment:* 200 full-time matriculated graduate/professional students (103 women), 640 part-time matriculated graduate/professional students (457 women). *Enrollment by degree level:* 825 master's, 15 doctoral. *Graduate faculty:* 265 full-time (106 women), 81 part-time/adjunct (43 women). *Graduate housing:* Room and/or apartments available on a first-come, first-served basis to single students; on-campus housing not available to married students. Housing application deadline: 6/30. *Student services:* Campus employment opportunities, campus safety program, career counseling, child daycare facilities, disabled student services, exercise/wellness program, free psychological counseling, grant writing training, international student services, low-cost health insurance, teacher training, writing training. *Library facilities:* James A-Gibson Library plus 1 other. *Online resources:* library catalog, web page, access to other libraries' catalogs. *Collection:* 1.4 million titles, 2,900 serial subscriptions, 19,500 audiovisual materials. *Research affiliation:* Imaging Research, Inc. (software and integrated systems for image analysis), Collective of Canadian Grape Growers and Wineries (oenology, viticulture), Norgen Biotek Corporation (biotechnology).

Computer facilities: 275 computers available on campus for general student use. A campuswide network can be accessed from student residence rooms and from off campus. Internet access and online class registration are available. *Web address:* http://www.brocku.ca/.

General Application Contact: Charlotte Sheridan, Assistant Director, Graduate Studies Office, 905-688-5550 Ext. 4390, Fax: 905-688-0748, E-mail: csherida@brucku.ca.

GRADUATE UNITS

Graduate Studies and Research Students: 200 full-time (103 women), 640 part-time (457 women), 20 international. Average age 27. 610 applicants, 53% accepted, 273 enrolled. *Faculty:* 265 full-time (106 women), 81 part-time/adjunct (43 women). Expenses: Contact institution. *Financial support:* Fellowships, research assistantships, teaching assistantships, career-related internships or fieldwork, scholarships/grants, unspecified assistantships, and bursaries available. Support available to part-time students. In 2001, 167 degrees awarded. *Degree program information:* Part-time and evening/weekend programs available. *Application deadline:* Applications are processed on a rolling basis. *Application fee:* $35. *Application Contact:* Charlotte Sheridan, Assistant Director, Graduate Studies Office, 905-688-5550 Ext. 4390, Fax: 905-688-0748, E-mail: csherida@brucku.ca. *Associate Vice President, Research and Dean,* Dr. Jack M. Miller, 905-688-5550 Ext. 3789, Fax: 905-684-2277, E-mail: jmiller@brocku.ca.

Faculty of Applied Health Sciences Students: 17 full-time (11 women). 30 applicants, 63% accepted, 18 enrolled. *Faculty:* 35 full-time (23 women). Expenses: Contact institution. *Financial support:* Fellowships, research assistantships, teaching assistantships, career-related internships or fieldwork, scholarships/grants, and unspecified assistantships available. Support available to part-time students. Offers applied health sciences (M Sc, MA). *Application deadline:* For fall admission, 3/15. *Application fee:* $35. *Application Contact:* Mike I. Plyley, Assistant Dean, Research and Graduate Studies, 905-688-5550 Ext. 3383, E-mail: mplyley@brocku.ca. *Dean,* Dr. Robert Kerr, 905-688-5550 Ext. 3385, Fax: 905-688-8364, E-mail: rkerr@arnie.pec.brocku.ca.

Faculty of Business Students: 13 full-time (5 women). 98 applicants, 23% accepted, 20 enrolled. *Faculty:* 18 full-time (5 women). Expenses: Contact institution. In 2001, 22 degrees awarded. Offers business (M Acc). *Application deadline:* For fall admission, 3/30 (priority date); for winter admission, 9/30 (priority date). Applications are processed on a rolling basis. *Application fee:* $35. *Application Contact:* Dr. Barbara Sainty, Director of M Acc, 905-688-5550 Ext. 3182, Fax: 905-984-4188, E-mail: linda@peregrine.bus.brocku.ca. *Dean,* Dr. Martin Kusey, 905-688-5550 Ext. 4006, Fax: 905-984-4188, E-mail: mkusey@spartan.ac.brocku.ca.

Faculty of Education Students: 65 full-time (45 women), 604 part-time (439 women). Average age 35. 243 applicants, 77% accepted, 171 enrolled. *Faculty:* 49 full-time (25 women), 29 part-time/adjunct (17 women). Expenses: Contact institution. *Financial support:* Fellowships, research assistantships, teaching assistantships, career-related internships or fieldwork, scholarships/grants, and unspecified assistantships available. Support available to part-time students. In 2001, 120 degrees awarded. *Degree program information:* Part-time and evening/weekend programs available. Offers curriculum (M Ed); education (M Ed); organization and administrative studies (M Ed); teaching and learning (M Ed). *Application deadline:* For fall admission, 4/15. Applications are processed on a rolling basis. *Application fee:* $35. *Application Contact:* Charlotte Sheridan, Assistant Director, Graduate Studies Office, 905-688-5550 Ext. 4390, Fax: 905-688-0748, E-mail: csherida@brucku.ca. *Dean,* Michael Manley-Casimer, 905-688-5550 Ext. 3710, Fax: 905-685-4131, E-mail: manleyc@ed.brocku.ca.

Faculty of Humanities Students: 18 full-time (9 women), 7 part-time (4 women). Average age 23. 28 applicants, 50% accepted, 13 enrolled. *Faculty:* 27 full-time (11 women). Expenses: Contact institution. *Financial support:* Fellowships, research assistantships, teaching assistantships, scholarships/grants and unspecified assistantships available. Support available to part-time students. In 2001, 2 degrees awarded. *Degree program information:* Part-time programs available. Offers philosophy (MA); popular culture (MA). *Application deadline:* For fall admission, 3/1 (priority date). Applications are processed on a rolling basis. *Application fee:* $35. *Application Contact:* Charlotte Sheridan, Assistant Director, Graduate Studies Office, 905-688-5550 Ext. 4390, Fax: 905-688-0748, E-mail: csherida@brucku.ca. *Dean,* Dr. Rosemary Drage Hale, 905-688-5550 Ext. 3427, Fax: 905-688-0748, E-mail: rhale@spartan.ac.brocku.ca.

Faculty of Mathematics and Science Students: 40 full-time (18 women), 8 part-time (4 women). Average age 24. 92 applicants, 24% accepted, 20 enrolled. *Faculty:* 66 full-time (13 women), 11 part-time/adjunct (1 woman). Expenses: Contact institution. *Financial support:* Fellowships, research assistantships, teaching assistantships, career-related internships or fieldwork, scholarships/grants, and unspecified assistantships available. Support available to part-time students. In 2001, 10 degrees awarded. *Degree program information:* Part-time programs available. Offers biotechnology (M Sc, PhD); cell and molecular biology (M Sc); chemistry (M Sc, PhD); earth sciences (M Sc); ecological/behavioral studies (M Sc); mathematics and science (M Sc, PhD); physics (M Sc). *Application deadline:* Applications are processed on a rolling basis. *Application fee:* $35. *Application Contact:* Charlotte Sheridan, Assistant Director, Graduate Studies Office, 905-688-5550 Ext. 4390, Fax: 905-688-0748, E-mail: csherida@brucku.ca. *Interim Dean,* Dr. Ian Brindle, 905-688-5550 Ext. 3421, Fax: 905-641-0406, E-mail: ibrindle@spartan.ac.brocku.ca.

Faculty of Social Sciences Students: 47 full-time (15 women), 21 part-time (10 women), 7 international. Average age 24. 119 applicants, 48% accepted, 31 enrolled. *Faculty:* 70 full-time (29 women), 6 part-time/adjunct (2 women). Expenses: Contact institution. *Financial support:* Fellowships, research assistantships, teaching assistantships, career-related internships or fieldwork, scholarships/grants, and unspecified assistantships available. Support available to part-time students. In 2001, 13 degrees awarded. *Degree program information:* Part-time programs available. Offers behavioral neuroscience (MA); Canadian politics (MA); child and youth studies (MA); international and comparative politics (MA); life span development (MA); political philosophy (MA); political science (MA); psychology (MA); public administration (MA); social justice and equity studies (MA); social personality (MA). *Application deadline:* For fall admission, 3/1 (priority date). *Application fee:* $35. *Application Contact:* Charlotte Sheridan, Assistant Director, Graduate Studies Office, 905-688-5550 Ext. 4390, Fax: 905-688-0748, E-mail: csherida@brucku.ca. *Dean,* Dr. David Siegel, 905-688-5550 Ext. 3425, Fax: 905-688-2789, E-mail: dsiegel@spartan.ac.brocku.ca.

BROOKLYN COLLEGE OF THE CITY UNIVERSITY OF NEW YORK, Brooklyn, NY 11210-2889

General Information State and locally supported, coed, comprehensive institution. *Enrollment:* 321 full-time matriculated graduate/professional students (207 women), 3,102 part-time matriculated graduate/professional students (2,114 women). *Enrollment by degree level:* 3,423 master's. Tuition, state resident: full-time $4,350; part-time $185 per credit. Tuition, nonresident: full-time $7,600; part-time $320 per credit. *Graduate housing:* On-campus housing not available. *Student services:* Campus employment opportunities, career counseling, child daycare facilities, disabled student services, exercise/wellness program, free psychological counseling, international student services, low-cost health insurance, multicultural affairs office, writing training. *Library facilities:* Brooklyn College Library plus 1 other. *Online resources:* library catalog, web page, access to other libraries' catalogs. *Collection:* 1.3 million titles, 13,500 serial subscriptions, 21,731 audiovisual materials. *Research affiliation:* Consolidated Edison, Walt Disney Imagineering (computer graphics), Pennie and Edmonds (chemistry), Semiconductor Characterization Instruments, Inc. (physics).

Computer facilities: 600 computers available on campus for general student use. A campuswide network can be accessed from off campus. Internet access and online class registration are available. *Web address:* http://www.brooklyn.cuny.edu/.

General Application Contact: Michael Lovaglio, Assistant Director of Graduate Admissions, 718-951-5914, E-mail: adminqry@brooklyn.cuny.edu.

GRADUATE UNITS

Division of Graduate Studies Students: 321 full-time (207 women), 3,102 part-time (2,114 women); includes 1,494 minority (940 African Americans, 264 Asian Americans or Pacific Islanders, 288 Hispanic Americans, 2 Native Americans), 269 international. Expenses: Contact institution. *Financial support:* Fellowships, research assistantships, teaching assistantships, career-related internships or fieldwork, Federal Work-Study, institutionally sponsored loans, scholarships/grants, and tuition waivers (full and partial) available. Support available to part-time students. Financial award application deadline: 5/1; financial award applicants required to submit FAFSA. In 2001, 995 master's, 118 other advanced degrees awarded. *Degree program information:* Part-time and evening/weekend programs available. Offers accounting (MA); acting (MFA); applied biology (MA); applied chemistry (MA); applied geology (MA); applied physics (MA); art (PhD); art history (MA); audiology (MS); biology (MA, PhD); chemistry (MA, PhD); community health (MA, MPH, MS); computer and information science (MA, PhD); computer science and health science (MS); creative writing (MFA); criticism (MA); design and technical production (MFA); directing (MFA); dramaturgy (MFA); drawing and painting (MFA); economics (MA); economics and computer and information science (MPS); English (MA, PhD); exercise science and rehabilitation (MS); experimental psychology (MA); fiction (MFA); French (MA); geology (MA, PhD); health care management (MA, MPH); health care policy and administration (MA, MPH); history (MA, PhD); industrial and organizational psychology (MA); information systems (MS); Judaic studies (MA); liberal studies (MA); management and programming (MS); mathematics (MA, PhD); nutrition (MS); nutrition sciences (MS); pathology (MS); performing arts management (MFA); photography (MFA); physical education (MS, MS Ed); physics (MA, PhD); playwriting (MFA); poetry (MFA); political science (MA, PhD); political science, urban policy and administration (MA); printmaking (MFA); psychology (PhD); sculpture (MFA); secondary mathematics education (MA); sociology (MA, PhD); Spanish (MA); speech (MA, MS Ed, PhD); speech-language pathology and audiology (MS); television and radio (MS); television production (MFA); thanatology (MA); theater history (MA). *Application deadline:* For fall admission, 3/1; for spring admission, 11/1. *Application fee:* $40. *Application Contact:* Michael Lovaglio, Assistant Director of Graduate Admissions, 718-951-5914, E-mail: adminqry@brooklyn.cuny.edu. *Dean,* Dr. Richard Pizer, 718-951-5252, Fax: 718-951-4727, E-mail: rdpizer@brooklyn.cuny.edu.

Conservatory of Music Students: 2 full-time (1 woman), 76 part-time (58 women); includes 13 minority (5 African Americans, 3 Asian Americans or Pacific Islanders, 5 Hispanic Americans), 38 international. 61 applicants, 59% accepted. Expenses: Contact institution. *Financial support:* In 2001–02, 9 teaching assistantships were awarded; career-related internships or fieldwork, Federal Work-Study, institutionally sponsored loans, scholarships/grants, and tuition waivers (partial) also available. Support available to part-time students. Financial award application deadline: 5/1; financial award applicants required to submit FAFSA. In 2001, 20 degrees awarded. *Degree program information:* Part-time programs available. Offers composition (MM); music (PhD); music education (MA); musicology (MA); performance (MM); performance practice (MA). *Application deadline:* For fall admission, 3/1; for spring admission, 11/1. *Application fee:* $40. *Application Contact:* Dr. Bruce MacIntyre, Graduate Deputy Chairperson, 718-921-5954, Fax: 718-951-4502, E-mail: brucem@brooklyn.cuny.edu. *Chairperson,* Dr. Nancy Hager, 718-951-5286, Fax: 718-951-4502, E-mail: nhager@brooklyn.cuny.edu.

Brooklyn College of the City University of New York (continued)

School of Education Students: 129 full-time (95 women), 1,737 part-time (1,329 women); includes 877 minority (609 African Americans, 70 Asian Americans or Pacific Islanders, 198 Hispanic Americans), 10 international. 998 applicants, 73% accepted. Expenses: Contact institution. *Financial support:* Fellowships, career-related internships or fieldwork, Federal Work-Study, institutionally sponsored loans, scholarships/grants, and tuition waivers (full and partial) available. Support available to part-time students. Financial award application deadline: 5/1; financial award applicants required to submit FAFSA. In 2001, 558 master's, 118 other advanced degrees awarded. *Degree program information:* Part-time and evening/weekend programs available. Offers art education (MS Ed); art teacher (MA); bilingual education (MS Ed); bilingual special education (MS Ed); biology teacher (MA); chemistry teacher (MA); children with emotional handicaps (MS Ed); children with neuropsychological learning disabilities (MS Ed); children with retarded mental development (MS Ed); early childhood education (MS Ed); education (MA, MS Ed, CAS); education of speech and hearing handicapped (MS Ed); elementary education teacher (MS Ed); elementary mathematics education (MS Ed); English teacher (MA); general science teacher (MA); guidance and counseling (MS Ed, CAS); health and nutrition sciences: health teacher (MS Ed); home economics education (MS Ed); humanities education (MS Ed); liberal arts (MS Ed); mathematics teacher (MA); music education (MS Ed); music teacher (MS Ed); physical education teacher (MS Ed); physics teacher (MA); school administration and supervision (CAS); school psychology (MS Ed, CAS); school psychology-bilingual (CAS); science and environmental education (MS Ed); social science education (MS Ed); social studies teacher (MA); Spanish teacher (MA); speech teacher (MA); teaching reading (MS Ed). *Application deadline:* For fall admission, 3/1; for spring admission, 11/1. Applications are processed on a rolling basis. *Application fee:* $40. *Application Contact:* Michael Lovaglio, Assistant Director of Graduate Admissions, 718-951-5914, E-mail: adminqry@brooklyn.cuny.edu. *Dean,* Dr. Deborah Shanley, 718-951-5214, Fax: 718-951-4816.

See in-depth description on page 773.

BROOKLYN LAW SCHOOL, Brooklyn, NY 11201-3798

General Information Independent, coed, graduate-only institution. *Enrollment by degree level:* 1,515 first professional. *Graduate faculty:* 57 full-time (24 women), 62 part-time/adjunct (17 women). *Tuition:* Full-time $26,720; part-time $20,075. *Required fees:* $155. One-time fee: $155 part-time. Tuition and fees vary according to program. *Graduate housing:* Rooms and/or apartments available to single and married students. Housing application deadline: 5/1. *Student services:* Campus employment opportunities, campus safety program, career counseling, disabled student services, free psychological counseling, international student services, writing training. *Library facilities:* Brooklyn Law School Library plus 2 others. *Online resources:* library catalog, web page, access to other libraries' catalogs. *Collection:* 242,209 titles, 2,615 serial subscriptions, 1,356 audiovisual materials.

Computer facilities: 83 computers available on campus for general student use. A campuswide network can be accessed from off campus. Internet access is available. *Web address:* http://www.brooklaw.edu/.

General Application Contact: Henry W. Haverstick, Dean of Admissions and Financial Aid, 718-780-7906, Fax: 718-780-0395, E-mail: admitq@brooklaw.edu.

GRADUATE UNITS

Professional Program Students: 1,072 full-time (563 women), 443 part-time (212 women); includes 313 minority (76 African Americans, 166 Asian Americans or Pacific Islanders, 67 Hispanic Americans, 4 Native Americans), 13 international. Average age 28. 3,600 applicants, 39% accepted, 487 enrolled. *Faculty:* 57 full-time (24 women), 62 part-time/adjunct (17 women). Expenses: Contact institution. *Financial support:* In 2001–02, 1,327 students received support, including 43 fellowships with partial tuition reimbursements available (averaging $2,950 per year), 113 research assistantships with partial tuition reimbursements available (averaging $3,014 per year); career-related internships or fieldwork, Federal Work-Study, institutionally sponsored loans, scholarships/grants, and tuition waivers (partial) also available. Support available to part-time students. Financial award application deadline: 4/15; financial award applicants required to submit FAFSA. In 2001, 454 degrees awarded. *Degree program information:* Part-time and evening/weekend programs available. Offers law (JD). *Application deadline:* For fall admission, 2/1 (priority date). Applications are processed on a rolling basis. *Application fee:* $65. Electronic applications accepted. *Application Contact:* Henry W. Haverstick, Dean of Admissions and Financial Aid, 718-780-7906, Fax: 718-780-0395, E-mail: admitq@brooklaw.edu. *Dean,* Joan G. Wexler, 718-780-7900, Fax: 718-780-0393.

BROOKS INSTITUTE OF PHOTOGRAPHY, Santa Barbara, CA 93108-2399

General Information Proprietary, coed, comprehensive institution. *Enrollment:* 30 full-time matriculated graduate/professional students (13 women). *Enrollment by degree level:* 30 master's. *Graduate faculty:* 1 full-time (0 women), 8 part-time/adjunct (3 women). *Tuition:* Full-time $17,100. *Required fees:* $600. *Graduate housing:* On-campus housing not available. *Student services:* Campus employment opportunities, career counseling, free psychological counseling, international student services. *Library facilities:* Brooks Institute of Photography Library. *Collection:* 6,500 titles, 128 serial subscriptions.

Computer facilities: 15 computers available on campus for general student use. Internet access is available. *Web address:* http://www.brooks.edu/.

General Application Contact: Erick R. Anderson, 1, 805-966-3888, Fax: 805-565-3386, E-mail: admissions@brooks.edu.

GRADUATE UNITS

Graduate Program in Professional Photography *Degree program information:* Evening/weekend programs available. Offers still photography (MS).

BROWN UNIVERSITY, Providence, RI 02912

General Information Independent, coed, university. CGS member. *Graduate housing:* Room and/or apartments available to single students; on-campus housing not available to married students. *Research affiliation:* Woods Hole Oceanographic Institution–Marine Biological Laboratory, Rhode Island Reactor, International Center for Numismatic Studies, Meeting Street School.

GRADUATE UNITS

Graduate School *Degree program information:* Part-time programs available. Offers American civilization (AM, PhD); anthropology (AM, PhD); art history (AM, PhD); biochemistry (PhD); chemistry (Sc M, PhD); classics (AM, PhD); cognitive science (Sc M, PhD); comparative literature (AM, PhD); comparative study of development (AM); computer science (Sc M, PhD); economics (AM, PhD); Egyptology (AM, PhD); elementary education K–6 (MAT); English literature and language (AM, PhD); French studies (AM, PhD); geological sciences (MA, Sc M, PhD); German (AM, PhD); Hispanic studies (AM, PhD); history (AM, PhD); history of mathematics (AM, PhD); Italian studies (AM, PhD); Judaic studies (AM, PhD); linguistics (AM, PhD); mathematics (M Sc, MA, PhD); music (AM, PhD); old world archaeology and art (AM, PhD); philosophy (AM, PhD); physics (Sc M, PhD); political science (AM, PhD); population studies (PhD); psychology (AM, Sc M, PhD); religious studies (AM, PhD); Russian (AM, PhD); secondary biology (MAT); secondary English (MAT); secondary social studies (MAT); Slavic languages (AM, PhD); sociology (AM, PhD); theatre arts (AM); writing (MFA).

Center for Environmental Studies Students: 17 full-time (9 women), 7 part-time (3 women); includes 6 minority (1 African American, 5 Asian Americans or Pacific Islanders), 2 international. Average age 25. 33 applicants, 61% accepted, 11 enrolled. *Faculty:* 4 full-time (1 woman), 2 part-time/adjunct (1 woman). Expenses: Contact institution. *Financial support:* In 2001–02, 17 students received support, including 2 teaching assistantships with full tuition reimbursements available (averaging $12,800 per year); career-related internships or fieldwork, Federal Work-Study, health care benefits, and tuition waivers (partial) also available. Financial award application deadline: 1/2; financial award applicants required to submit FAFSA. In 2001, 7 degrees awarded. *Degree program information:* Part-time programs available. Offers environmental studies (AM). *Application deadline:* For fall admission, 1/2 (priority date). Applications are processed on a rolling basis. *Application fee:* $60. Electronic applications accepted. *Application Contact:* Patricia-Ann Caton, Administrative Manager, 401-863-3449, Fax: 401-863-3503, E-mail: patti_caton@brown.edu. *Director,* Harold Ward, 401-863-3449, Fax: 401-863-3503, E-mail: harold_ward@brown.edu.

Center for Old World Archaeology and Art Offers old world archaeology and art (AM, PhD).

Center for Portuguese and Brazilian Studies Offers Brazilian studies (AM); Luso-Brazilian studies (PhD); Portuguese studies and bilingual education (AM).

Division of Applied Mathematics Offers applied mathematics (Sc M, PhD).

Division of Biology and Medicine Students: 154 full-time (84 women); includes 20 minority (6 African Americans, 12 Asian Americans or Pacific Islanders, 2 Hispanic Americans), 31 international. Average age 24. 327 applicants, 17% accepted. *Faculty:* 152 full-time (50 women), 6 part-time/adjunct (3 women). Expenses: Contact institution. *Financial support:* Fellowships with full tuition reimbursements, research assistantships with full tuition reimbursements, teaching assistantships with full tuition reimbursements, institutionally sponsored loans, traineeships, and tuition waivers (full) available. Financial award application deadline: 1/2. In 2001, 4 master's, 19 doctorates awarded. *Degree program information:* Part-time programs available. Offers artificial organs/biomaterials/cellular technology (MA, Sc M, PhD); biochemistry (M Med Sc, Sc M, PhD); biology (MA, PhD); biology and medicine (M Med Sc, MA, MS, Sc M, PhD); biostatistics (MS, PhD); cancer biology (PhD); cell biology (M Med Sc, Sc M, PhD); developmental biology (M Med Sc, Sc M, PhD); ecology and evolutionary biology (PhD); epidemiology (MS, PhD); health services research (MS, PhD); immunology (M Med Sc, Sc M, PhD); immunology and infection (PhD); medical science (PhD); molecular microbiology (M Med Sc, Sc M, PhD); molecular pharmacology and physiology (MA, Sc M, PhD); neuroscience (PhD); pathobiology (Sc M); toxicology and environmental pathology (PhD). *Application deadline:* For fall admission, 1/2 (priority date). Applications are processed on a rolling basis. *Application fee:* $60. Electronic applications accepted. *Application Contact:* Dr. Peter Shank, Associate Dean, 401-863-3281, Fax: 401-863-7411, E-mail: peter_shank@brown.edu. *Dean,* Dr. Donald Marsh, 401-863-3330.

Division of Engineering Offers aerospace engineering (Sc M, PhD); biomedical engineering (Sc M); electrical sciences (Sc M, PhD); fluid mechanics, thermodynamics, and chemical processes (Sc M, PhD); materials science (Sc M, PhD); mechanics of solids and structures (Sc M, PhD).

Program in Medicine Offers medicine (MD).

BRYANT COLLEGE, Smithfield, RI 02917-1284

General Information Independent, coed, comprehensive institution. *Enrollment:* 60 full-time matriculated graduate/professional students (24 women), 416 part-time matriculated graduate/professional students (145 women). *Enrollment by degree level:* 465 master's, 11 other advanced degrees. *Graduate faculty:* 32 full-time (8 women), 6 part-time/adjunct (0 women). *Tuition:* Part-time $433 per credit. Tuition and fees vary according to program. *Graduate housing:* Room and/or apartments available on a first-come, first-served basis to single students; on-campus housing not available to married students. Typical cost: $5,800 per year ($8,900 including board). Room and board charges vary according to board plan. *Student services:* Campus safety program, career counseling, disabled student services, exercise/wellness program, free psychological counseling, low-cost health insurance, multicultural affairs office, writing training. *Library facilities:* Edith M. Hodgson Memorial Library. *Online resources:* library catalog, web page, access to other libraries' catalogs. *Collection:* 127,000 titles, 4,000 serial subscriptions, 810 audiovisual materials. *Research affiliation:* Department of Education (curriculum development in international trade education for secondary schools), General Electric Foundation (field study of accelerating mathematics skills in secondary and middle schools), Human Resource Investment Council (product design and commercialization research assistance, international market research, international video streaming education), National Institutes of Health/Biomedical Research Infrastructure Network (biomedical research in computational neuroscience and bioinformatics), Northern Rhode Island Business Education Alliance (developing and conducting technology education for K-12 teachers), Rhode Island Economic Development Corporation/State of Rhode Island (international market research and trade assistance).

Computer facilities: 365 computers available on campus for general student use. A campuswide network can be accessed from student residence rooms and from off campus. Internet access, e-mail are available. *Web address:* http://www.bryant.edu/.

General Application Contact: Kristopher T. Sullivan, Director of Graduate Programs, 401-232-6230, Fax: 401-232-6494, E-mail: gradprog@bryant.edu.

GRADUATE UNITS

Graduate School Students: 60 full-time (24 women), 416 part-time (145 women); includes 7 minority (3 Asian Americans or Pacific Islanders, 3 Hispanic Americans, 1 Native American), 33 international. Average age 32. 190 applicants, 54% accepted, 96 enrolled. *Faculty:* 32 full-time (8 women), 6 part-time/adjunct (0 women). Expenses: Contact institution. *Financial support:* In 2001–02, 10 students received support, including 10 research assistantships with full tuition reimbursements available; unspecified assistantships also available. Support available to part-time students. Financial award applicants required to submit FAFSA. In 2001, 107 master's, 5 other advanced degrees awarded. *Degree program information:* Part-time and evening/weekend programs available. *Application deadline:* For fall admission, 7/15 (priority date); for spring admission, 11/15. Applications are processed on a rolling basis. *Application fee:* $60 ($80 for international students). Electronic applications accepted. *Director of Graduate Programs,* Kristopher T. Sullivan, 401-232-6230, Fax: 401-232-6494, E-mail: gradprog@bryant.edu.

College of Business Administration Students: 60 full-time (24 women), 416 part-time (145 women); includes 7 minority (3 Asian Americans or Pacific Islanders, 3 Hispanic Americans, 1 Native American), 33 international. Average age 32. 190 applicants, 54% accepted, 96 enrolled. *Faculty:* 32 full-time (8 women), 6 part-time/adjunct (0 women). Expenses: Contact institution. *Financial support:* In 2001–02, 10 students received support, including 10 research assistantships with full tuition reimbursements available; unspecified assistantships also available. Support available to part-time students. Financial award applicants required to submit FAFSA. In 2001, 107 master's, 5 other advanced degrees awarded. *Degree program information:* Part-time and evening/weekend programs available. Offers accounting (MBA, MSA, CAGS); computer information systems (MBA, CAGS); finance (MBA, CAGS); general business (MBA); information systems (MSIS); management (MBA, CAGS); marketing (MBA, CAGS); operations management (MBA); taxation (MST, CAGS). *Application deadline:* For fall admission, 7/15 (priority date); for spring admission, 11/15. Applications are processed on a rolling basis. *Application fee:* $60 ($80 for international students). Electronic applications accepted. *Application Contact:* Kristopher T. Sullivan, Director of Graduate Programs, 401-232-6230, Fax: 401-232-6494, E-mail: gradprog@bryant.edu.

BRYN ATHYN COLLEGE OF THE NEW CHURCH, Bryn Athyn, PA 19009-0717

General Information Independent-religious, coed, comprehensive institution. *Enrollment:* 7 full-time matriculated graduate/professional students, 19 part-time matriculated graduate/professional students (13 women). *Enrollment by degree level:* 8 first professional, 17 master's. *Graduate faculty:* 12. *Graduate housing:* Room and/or apartments available to single students; on-campus housing not available to married students. Typical cost: $4,764 (including board). Housing application deadline: 1/31. *Student services:* Campus employment opportunities, career counseling, free psychological counseling, international student services, low-cost health insurance, teacher training. *Library facilities:* Swedenborg Library plus 2 others. *Online resources:* library catalog. *Collection:* 91,591 titles, 180 serial subscriptions, 559 audiovisual materials.

Computer facilities: 40 computers available on campus for general student use. A campuswide network can be accessed from student residence rooms. Internet access is available. *Web address:* http://www.newchurch.edu/college/.

General Application Contact: Rev. Brian W. Keith, Dean of the Theological School, 215-938-2525, Fax: 215-938-2658, E-mail: bwkeith@newchurch.edu.

GRADUATE UNITS

Academy of the New Church Theological School Students: 7 full-time (0 women), 19 part-time (13 women), 10 international. Average age 37. 26 applicants, 100% accepted. *Faculty:* 12. Expenses: Contact institution. *Financial support:* In 2001–02, 7 students received support. Career-related internships or fieldwork, Federal Work-Study, and institutionally sponsored loans available. Financial award application deadline: 1/31. In 2001, 4 first professional degrees, 2 master's awarded. *Degree program information:* Part-time programs available. Postbaccalaureate distance learning degree programs offered (minimal on-campus study). Offers divinity (M Div); religious studies (MA). *Application deadline:* For fall admission, 1/31. Applications are processed on a rolling basis. *Dean*, Rev. Brian W. Keith, 215-938-2525, Fax: 215-938-2658, E-mail: bwkeith@newchurch.edu.

BRYN MAWR COLLEGE, Bryn Mawr, PA 19010-2899

General Information Independent, women only, university. CGS member. *Enrollment:* 236 full-time matriculated graduate/professional students (186 women), 178 part-time matriculated graduate/professional students (152 women). *Graduate faculty:* 125 full-time, 89 part-time/adjunct. *Tuition:* Full-time $22,260. *Graduate housing:* Rooms and/or apartments available to single and married students. Typical cost: $4,960 per year ($8,590 including board) for single students; $4,960 per year ($8,590 including board) for married students. Housing application deadline: 1/15. *Student services:* Campus employment opportunities, campus safety program, career counseling, international student services, low-cost health insurance. *Library facilities:* Miriam Coffin Canaday Library plus 2 others. *Online resources:* library catalog, web page, access to other libraries' catalogs. *Collection:* 932,423 titles, 4,045 serial subscriptions, 1,380 audiovisual materials.

Computer facilities: 200 computers available on campus for general student use. A campuswide network can be accessed from student residence rooms and from off campus. Internet access is available. *Web address:* http://www.brynmawr.edu/.

General Application Contact: Graduate School, 610-526-5072.

GRADUATE UNITS

Graduate School of Arts and Sciences Students: 78 full-time (48 women), 114 part-time (98 women); includes 12 minority (4 African Americans, 6 Asian Americans or Pacific Islanders, 1 Hispanic American, 1 Native American), 30 international. *Faculty:* 110 full-time, 70 part-time/adjunct. Expenses: Contact institution. *Financial support:* Fellowships, research assistantships, teaching assistantships, career-related internships or fieldwork, Federal Work-Study, institutionally sponsored loans, unspecified assistantships, and tuition awards available. Support available to part-time students. *Degree program information:* Part-time programs available. Offers arts and sciences (MA, PhD); biochemistry (MA, PhD); biology (MA, PhD); chemistry (MA, PhD); classical and Near Eastern archaeology (MA, PhD); clinical developmental psychology (PhD); French (MA); geology (MA, PhD); Greek and Latin (MA, PhD); history of art (MA, PhD); mathematics (MA, PhD); neural and behavioral science (PhD); physics (MA, PhD); Russian (MA, PhD). *Application deadline:* Applications are processed on a rolling basis. *Application fee:* $25. *Application Contact:* Graduate School of Arts and Sciences, 610-526-5072. *Dean*, Dr. Dale Kinney, 610-526-5073, Fax: 610-526-5076, E-mail: dkinney@brynmawr.edu.

Graduate School of Social Work and Social Research Students: 158 full-time (138 women), 64 part-time (54 women); includes 47 minority (38 African Americans, 5 Asian Americans or Pacific Islanders, 4 Hispanic Americans), 5 international. Average age 34. 172 applicants, 85% accepted, 82 enrolled. *Faculty:* 15 full-time (8 women), 19 part-time/adjunct (18 women). Expenses: Contact institution. *Financial support:* In 2001–02, 194 students received support, including 12 fellowships with full and partial tuition reimbursements available (averaging $3,517 per year), 4 research assistantships with full and partial tuition reimbursements available (averaging $9,382 per year), 8 teaching assistantships with full and partial tuition reimbursements available (averaging $9,121 per year); career-related internships or fieldwork, Federal Work-Study, institutionally sponsored loans, scholarships/grants, tuition waivers (full and partial), and PhD dissertation award also available. Support available to part-time students. Financial award application deadline: 3/1; financial award applicants required to submit FAFSA. In 2001, 67 master's, 4 doctorates awarded. *Degree program information:* Part-time programs available. Offers social work and social research (MLSP, MSS, PhD). *Application deadline:* For fall admission, 3/1 (priority date). Applications are processed on a rolling basis. *Application fee:* $50. *Application Contact:* Nancy J. Kirby, Assistant Dean and Director of Admissions, 610-520-2601, Fax: 610-520-2655, E-mail: swadmiss@brynmawr.edu. *Dean*, Ruth W. Mayden, 610-520-2600.

BUCKNELL UNIVERSITY, Lewisburg, PA 17837

General Information Independent, coed, comprehensive institution. *Enrollment:* 85 full-time matriculated graduate/professional students (47 women), 19 part-time matriculated graduate/professional students (10 women). *Enrollment by degree level:* 104 master's. *Graduate faculty:* 146 full-time (37 women). *Tuition:* Part-time $2,875 per course. *Graduate housing:* On-campus housing not available. *Student services:* Campus employment opportunities, campus safety program, career counseling, disabled student services, free psychological counseling, international student services, low-cost health insurance, multicultural affairs office, teacher training, writing training. *Library facilities:* Ellen Clarke Bertrand Library. *Online resources:* library catalog, web page, access to other libraries' catalogs. *Collection:* 432,730 titles, 2,789 serial subscriptions, 5,946 audiovisual materials.

Computer facilities: 350 computers available on campus for general student use. A campuswide network can be accessed from student residence rooms and from off campus. Internet access is available. *Web address:* http://www.bucknell.edu/.

General Application Contact: Dr. Marion Lois Huffines, Director of Graduate Studies, 570-577-1304, Fax: 570-577-3760, E-mail: gradstds@bucknell.edu.

GRADUATE UNITS

Graduate Studies Students: 85 full-time (47 women), 19 part-time (10 women); includes 1 minority (Hispanic American), 12 international. *Faculty:* 146 full-time (37 women). Expenses: Contact institution. *Financial support:* In 2001–02, 74 students received support, including 52 teaching assistantships with tuition reimbursements available; fellowships, research assistantships, scholarships/grants, tuition waivers (partial), and unspecified assistantships also available. Financial award application deadline: 3/1. In 2001, 52 degrees awarded. *Degree program information:* Part-time programs available. *Application deadline:* For fall admission, 6/1 (priority date); for spring admission, 12/1 (priority date). Applications are processed on a rolling basis. *Application fee:* $25. *Director*, Dr. Marion Lois Huffines, 570-577-1304, Fax: 570-577-3760, E-mail: gradstds@bucknell.edu.

College of Arts and Sciences Students: 66 full-time (43 women), 18 part-time (10 women); includes 1 minority (Hispanic American), 2 international. *Faculty:* 109 full-time (34 women). Expenses: Contact institution. *Financial support:* In 2001–02, 53 students received support; fellowships, scholarships/grants and unspecified assistantships available. Financial award application deadline: 3/1. *Degree program information:* Part-time programs available. Offers accounting (MSBA); animal behavior (MA, MS); arts and sciences (MA, MS, MS Ed, MSBA); biology (MA, MS); chemistry (MA, MS); classroom teaching (MS Ed); educational research (MS Ed); elementary and secondary counseling (MA, MS Ed); elementary and secondary principalship (MA, MS Ed); English (MA); mathematics (MA, MS); psychology (MA, MS); reading (MA, MS Ed); school psychology (MS Ed); supervision of curriculum and instruction (MA, MS Ed). *Application deadline:* For fall admission, 6/1 (priority date); for spring admission, 12/1 (priority date). Applications are processed on a rolling basis. *Application fee:* $25. *Interim Dean*, Dr. Mark Padilla, 570-577-3292.

College of Engineering Students: 19 full-time (4 women), 1 part-time, 10 international. *Faculty:* 37 full-time (3 women). Expenses: Contact institution. *Financial support:* Fellowships, research assistantships, teaching assistantships, unspecified assistantships available. Financial award application deadline: 3/1. *Degree program information:* Part-time programs available. Offers chemical engineering (MS, MS Ch E); civil and environmental engineering (MS, MSCE); electrical engineering (MS, MSEE); engineering (MS, MS Ch E, MSCE, MSEE, MSME); mechanical engineering (MS, MSME). *Application deadline:* For fall admission, 6/1 (priority date); for spring admission, 12/1 (priority date). Applications are processed on a rolling basis. *Application fee:* $25. *Interim Dean*, Dr. James Orbison, 570-577-3711.

BUENA VISTA UNIVERSITY, Storm Lake, IA 50588

General Information Independent-religious, coed, comprehensive institution. *Graduate housing:* Room and/or apartments available on a first-come, first-served basis to single students; on-campus housing not available to married students. Housing application deadline: 5/1.

GRADUATE UNITS

School of Education *Degree program information:* Part-time and evening/weekend programs available. Postbaccalaureate distance learning degree programs offered (minimal on-campus study). Offers education administration (MS Ed); school guidance and counseling (MS Ed). Offered in summer only. Electronic applications accepted.

BUTLER UNIVERSITY, Indianapolis, IN 46208-3485

General Information Independent, coed, comprehensive institution. *Enrollment:* 382 full-time matriculated graduate/professional students (264 women), 618 part-time matriculated graduate/professional students (304 women). *Enrollment by degree level:* 309 first professional, 691 master's. *Graduate faculty:* 68 full-time (17 women), 43 part-time/adjunct (22 women). *Tuition:* Part-time $250 per credit. Part-time tuition and fees vary according to program and student level. *Graduate housing:* Room and/or apartments guaranteed to single students; on-campus housing not available to married students. Typical cost: $6,450 (including board). Room and board charges vary according to board plan and campus/location. Housing application deadline: 8/1. *Student services:* Campus employment opportunities, campus safety program, career counseling, child daycare facilities, free psychological counseling, international student services, low-cost health insurance, multicultural affairs office. *Library facilities:* Irwin Library System plus 1 other. *Online resources:* library catalog, web page, access to other libraries' catalogs. *Collection:* 845,415 titles, 2,202 serial subscriptions, 13,316 audiovisual materials.

Computer facilities: 250 computers available on campus for general student use. A campuswide network can be accessed from student residence rooms and from off campus. Internet access, e-mail are available. *Web address:* http://www.butler.edu/.

General Application Contact: Lindsay Lamar, Assistant Director Student Services, 317-940-8100, Fax: 317-940-8250, E-mail: llamar@butler.edu.

GRADUATE UNITS

College of Business Administration Students: 27 full-time (9 women), 337 part-time (102 women); includes 27 minority (10 African Americans, 10 Asian Americans or Pacific Islanders, 6 Hispanic Americans, 1 Native American), 29 international. Average age 32. 155 applicants, 63% accepted, 96 enrolled. *Faculty:* 12 full-time (3 women), 2 part-time/adjunct (0 women). Expenses: Contact institution. *Financial support:* Career-related internships or fieldwork and institutionally sponsored loans available. Support available to part-time students. Financial award application deadline: 7/15; financial award applicants required to submit FAFSA. In 2001, 94 degrees awarded. *Degree program information:* Part-time and evening/weekend programs available. Offers business administration (MBA). *Application deadline:* For fall admission, 8/15 (priority date). Applications are processed on a rolling basis. *Application fee:* $25. Electronic applications accepted. *Application Contact:* Dr. William Rieber, Director of Graduate Studies, 317-940-9846, Fax: 317-940-9455, E-mail: wrieber@butler.edu. *Dean*, Dr. Richard Fetter, 317-940-9221, Fax: 317-940-9455, E-mail: rfetter@butler.edu.

College of Education Students: 23 full-time (16 women), 209 part-time (156 women); includes 13 minority (all African Americans), 2 international. Average age 33. 78 applicants, 63% accepted, 49 enrolled. *Faculty:* 10 full-time (2 women), 14 part-time/adjunct (11 women). Expenses: Contact institution. *Financial support:* Institutionally sponsored loans available. Support available to part-time students. Financial award application deadline: 7/15; financial award applicants required to submit FAFSA. In 2001, 70 master's awarded. *Degree program information:* Part-time and evening/weekend programs available. Offers administration (MS); elementary education (MS); reading (MS); school counseling (MS); secondary education (MS); special education (MS). *Application deadline:* For fall admission, 8/15 (priority date). Applications are processed on a rolling basis. *Application fee:* $25. Electronic applications accepted. *Dean*, Dr. Robert Rider, 317-940-9752, Fax: 317-940-6481.

College of Liberal Arts and Sciences Students: 5 full-time (4 women), 29 part-time (20 women); includes 2 minority (1 African American, 1 Native American) Average age 35. 13 applicants, 77% accepted, 10 enrolled. *Faculty:* 15 full-time (5 women), 1 (woman) part-time/adjunct. Expenses: Contact institution. *Financial support:* Career-related internships or fieldwork, institutionally sponsored loans, and tuition waivers (full and partial) available. Support available to part-time students. Financial award applicants required to submit FAFSA. In 2001, 10 degrees awarded. *Degree program information:* Part-time and evening/weekend programs available. Offers English (MA); history (MA); liberal arts and sciences (MA, MS). *Application deadline:* For fall admission, 8/15 (priority date). Applications are processed on a rolling basis. *Application fee:* $25. Electronic applications accepted. *Interim Dean*, Dr. Joseph Kirsch, 317-940-9874, E-mail: jkirsch@butler.edu.

College of Pharmacy Students: 307 full-time (224 women), 15 part-time (10 women); includes 33 minority (10 African Americans, 23 Asian Americans or Pacific Islanders), 9 international. Average age 23. 3 applicants, 33% accepted, 1 enrolled. *Faculty:* 7 full-time (3 women), 3 part-time/adjunct (2 women). Expenses: Contact institution. *Financial support:* Applicants required to submit FAFSA. In 2001, 58 first professional degrees, 4 master's awarded. *Degree program information:* Part-time and evening/weekend programs available. Offers pharmaceutical science (Pharm D, MS). *Application deadline:* For fall admission, 8/1 (priority date); for spring admission, 12/15. Applications are processed on a rolling basis. *Application fee:* $25. Electronic applications accepted. *Application Contact:* Dr. Beverly Sandmann, Principal Graduate Adviser, 317-940-9553, E-mail: bsandman@butler.edu. *Dean*, Dr. Patricia Chase, 317-940-9735, Fax: 317-940-6172, E-mail: pchase@butler.edu.

Jordan College of Fine Arts Students: 20 full-time (11 women), 28 part-time (16 women); includes 1 minority (Asian American or Pacific Islander), 4 international. Average age 30. 44 applicants, 84% accepted, 19 enrolled. *Faculty:* 24 full-time (4 women), 23 part-time/adjunct (8 women). Expenses: Contact institution. *Financial support:* In 2001–02, 11 teaching assistantships with full tuition reimbursements (averaging $2,500 per year) were awarded; fellowships, career-related internships or fieldwork, institutionally sponsored loans, and scholarships/grants also available. Support available to part-time students. Financial award application deadline: 7/15; financial award applicants required to submit FAFSA. In 2001, 10 degrees awarded. *Degree program information:* Part-time and evening/weekend programs available. Offers composition (MM); conducting (MM); fine arts (MM); music (MM); music education (MM); music history (MM); organ (MM); performance (MM). *Application deadline:* For fall admission, 8/15 (priority date). Applications are processed on a rolling basis. *Application fee:* $25. Electronic applications accepted. *Application Contact:* Sherry Gillespie, Admission Secretary, 317-940-9656, Fax: 317-940-9658, E-mail: sgillesp@butler.edu. *Dean*, Dr. Peter Alexander, 317-940-9231, Fax: 317-940-9658, E-mail: palexand@butler.edu.

CABRINI COLLEGE, Radnor, PA 19087-3698

General Information Independent-religious, coed, comprehensive institution. *Enrollment:* 41 full-time matriculated graduate/professional students (30 women), 420 part-time matriculated graduate/professional students (327 women). *Enrollment by degree level:* 461 master's. *Graduate faculty:* 1 (woman) full-time, 30 part-time/adjunct (13 women). *Tuition:* Part-time $395 per credit. *Required fees:* $45 per term. Tuition and fees vary according to course load. *Graduate housing:* On-campus housing not available. *Student services:* Campus safety program, career counseling, disabled student services, free psychological counseling, international student services, low-cost health insurance, multicultural affairs office. *Library facilities:* Holy Spirit Library. *Online resources:* library catalog, web page, access to other libraries' catalogs. *Collection:* 178,499 titles, 545 serial subscriptions, 991 audiovisual materials.

Cabrini College (continued)

Computer facilities: 195 computers available on campus for general student use. A campuswide network can be accessed from student residence rooms. Internet access is available. *Web address:* http://www.cabrini.edu/.

General Application Contact: Jennifer Hubbard, Assistant Director of Marketing and Recruitment, 610-902-8600, Fax: 610-902-8522, E-mail: gpsadmit@cabrini.edu.

GRADUATE UNITS

Graduate and Professional Studies Students: 41 full-time (30 women), 420 part-time (327 women); includes 23 minority (18 African Americans, 2 Asian Americans or Pacific Islanders, 3 Hispanic Americans), 6 international. 158 applicants, 75% accepted, 93 enrolled. *Faculty:* 1 (woman) full-time, 26 part-time/adjunct (13 women). Expenses: Contact institution. *Financial support:* Career-related internships or fieldwork and unspecified assistantships available. Support available to part-time students. Financial award applicants required to submit FAFSA. In 2001, 122 degrees awarded. *Degree program information:* Part-time and evening/weekend programs available. Offers education (M Ed); instructional systems technology (MS); organization leadership (MS). *Application deadline:* For fall admission, 7/29 (priority date); for spring admission, 12/9. Applications are processed on a rolling basis. *Application fee:* $35. Electronic applications accepted. *Application Contact:* Jennifer Hubbard, Assistant Director of Marketing and Recruitment, 610-902-8552, Fax: 610-902-8508, E-mail: admit@cabrini.edu. *Executive Director of Graduate and Professional Studies,* Leslie Petty, 610-902-8519, Fax: 610-902-9522, E-mail: lpetty@cabrini.edu.

CALDWELL COLLEGE, Caldwell, NJ 07006-6195

General Information Independent-religious, coed, comprehensive institution. *Enrollment:* 18 full-time matriculated graduate/professional students (16 women), 159 part-time matriculated graduate/professional students (125 women). *Enrollment by degree level:* 172 master's, 5 other advanced degrees. *Graduate faculty:* 17 full-time (10 women), 20 part-time/adjunct (5 women). *Tuition:* Part-time $437 per credit. *Graduate housing:* On-campus housing not available. *Student services:* Career counseling, child daycare facilities, disabled student services, free psychological counseling, international student services. *Library facilities:* Jennings Library. *Online resources:* library catalog, web page. *Collection:* 132,204 titles, 765 serial subscriptions, 4,088 audiovisual materials.

Computer facilities: 166 computers available on campus for general student use. A campuswide network can be accessed from student residence rooms. Internet access is available. *Web address:* http://www.caldwell.edu/.

General Application Contact: Bette Jo Ho'Aire, Administrative Assistant, 973-618-3408, Fax: 973-618-3640, E-mail: ehoaire@caldwell.edu.

GRADUATE UNITS

Graduate Studies Students: 18 full-time (16 women), 159 part-time (125 women); includes 13 minority (10 African Americans, 3 Hispanic Americans), 2 international. Average age 40. 48 applicants, 81% accepted, 34 enrolled. *Faculty:* 17 full-time (10 women), 20 part-time/adjunct (5 women). Expenses: Contact institution. *Financial support:* Available to part-time students. Applicants required to submit FAFSA. In 2001, 28 degrees awarded. *Degree program information:* Part-time and evening/weekend programs available. Offers accounting (MS); art therapy (MA); contemporary management (MS); counseling psychology (MA); curriculum and instruction (MA); education administration (MA); educational administration for catholic school leadership (MA); pastoral ministry (MA). *Application deadline:* Applications are processed on a rolling basis. *Application fee:* $40. *Application Contact:* Bette Jo Ho'Aire, Administrative Assistant, 973-618-3408, Fax: 973-618-3640, E-mail: ehoaire@caldwell.edu. *Associate Dean of Graduate Studies,* Dr. Rina Gangemi Spano, 973-618-3408, Fax: 973-618-3640, E-mail: rspano@caldwell.edu.

CALIFORNIA BAPTIST UNIVERSITY, Riverside, CA 92504-3206

General Information Independent-religious, coed, comprehensive institution. *Enrollment:* 125 full-time matriculated graduate/professional students (88 women), 385 part-time matriculated graduate/professional students (288 women). *Enrollment by degree level:* 510 master's. *Graduate faculty:* 19 full-time (9 women), 12 part-time/adjunct (4 women). *Tuition:* Full-time $8,736; part-time $364 per semester hour. *Required fees:* $420; $210 per term. Tuition and fees vary according to program. *Graduate housing:* Rooms and/or apartments available on a first-come, first-served basis to single and married students. Typical cost: $2,250 per year ($5,046 including board) for single students. Room and board charges vary according to board plan. Housing application deadline: 4/1. *Student services:* Campus employment opportunities, career counseling, exercise/wellness program, free psychological counseling, international student services, low-cost health insurance, teacher training. *Library facilities:* Annie Gabriel Library. *Online resources:* library catalog, web page, access to other libraries' catalogs. *Collection:* 87,688 titles, 428 serial subscriptions, 4,242 audiovisual materials.

Computer facilities: 132 computers available on campus for general student use. A campuswide network can be accessed from student residence rooms and from off campus. Internet access, intranet are available. *Web address:* http://www.calbaptist.edu/.

General Application Contact: Gail Ronveaux, Associate Dean, Enrollment Services, 909-343-5045, Fax: 909-343-5095, E-mail: gradservices@calbaptist.edu.

GRADUATE UNITS

Graduate Program in Business Administration Students: 30. 19 applicants, 95% accepted, 10 enrolled. *Faculty:* 3 full-time (0 women), 3 part-time/adjunct (1 woman). Expenses: Contact institution. *Financial support:* In 2001–02, 22 students received support. Federal Work-Study available. Support available to part-time students. Financial award applicants required to submit FAFSA. In 2001, 20 degrees awarded. *Degree program information:* Part-time programs available. Offers business administration (MBA). *Application deadline:* For fall admission, 7/15; for spring admission, 11/1. Applications are processed on a rolling basis. *Application fee:* $45. Electronic applications accepted. *Application Contact:* Gail Ronveaux, Associate Dean, Enrollment Services, 909-343-5045, Fax: 909-343-5095, E-mail: gradservices@calbaptist.edu. *Director,* Dr. Gary Barfoot, 909-343-4427, Fax: 909-343-4533, E-mail: gbarfoot@calbaptist.edu.

Graduate Program in Education Students: 400. 252 applicants, 94% accepted, 182 enrolled. *Faculty:* 7 full-time (5 women), 6 part-time/adjunct (4 women). Expenses: Contact institution. *Financial support:* In 2001–02, 39 students received support. Career-related internships or fieldwork and Federal Work-Study available. Support available to part-time students. Financial award applicants required to submit FAFSA. In 2001, 44 degrees awarded. *Degree program information:* Part-time programs available. Offers cross-cultural language academic development (MA Ed); educational leadership (MS Ed); educational technology (MS Ed); English education (MA Ed); reading (MS Ed); special education (MS Ed); sport leadership (MS Ed); teaching and curriculum (MS Ed). *Application deadline:* For fall admission, 7/15; for spring admission, 11/1. Applications are processed on a rolling basis. *Application fee:* $45. *Application Contact:* Gail Ronveaux, Associate Dean, Enrollment Services, 909-343-5045, Fax: 909-343-5095, E-mail: gradservices@calbaptist.edu. *Dean, School of Education,* Dr. Mary Crist, 909-343-4313, Fax: 909-343-4516, E-mail: mcrist@calbaptist.edu.

Graduate Program in Marriage and Family Therapy Students: 75. 40 applicants, 78% accepted, 23 enrolled. *Faculty:* 4 full-time (1 woman), 3 part-time/adjunct (1 woman). Expenses: Contact institution. *Financial support:* In 2001–02, 59 students received support. Career-related internships or fieldwork and Federal Work-Study available. Support available to part-time students. Financial award applicants required to submit FAFSA. In 2001, 18 degrees awarded. *Degree program information:* Part-time programs available. Offers counseling psychology (MS). *Application deadline:* For fall admission, 7/15; for spring admission, 11/1. Applications are processed on a rolling basis. *Application fee:* $45. *Application Contact:* Gail Ronveaux, Associate Dean, Enrollment Services, 909-343-5045, Fax: 909-343-5095, E-mail: gradservices@calbaptist.edu. *Director,* Dr. Gary Collins, 909-343-4304, Fax: 909-343-4569, E-mail: gcollins@calbaptist.edu.

CALIFORNIA COLLEGE FOR HEALTH SCIENCES, National City, CA 91950-6605

General Information Proprietary, coed, comprehensive institution. *Graduate housing:* On-campus housing not available.

GRADUATE UNITS

Program in Business Administration in Healthcare *Degree program information:* Part-time and evening/weekend programs available. Postbaccalaureate distance learning degree programs offered (no on-campus study). Offers healthcare administration (MBA).

Program in Healthcare Administration *Degree program information:* Part-time and evening/weekend programs available. Postbaccalaureate distance learning degree programs offered (no on-campus study). Offers healthcare administration (MSHCA).

Program in Health Services *Degree program information:* Part-time and evening/weekend programs available. Postbaccalaureate distance learning degree programs offered (no on-campus study). Offers community health (MSHS); wellness promotion (MSHS).

Program in Public Health *Degree program information:* Part-time and evening/weekend programs available. Postbaccalaureate distance learning degree programs offered (no on-campus study). Offers public health (MPH).

CALIFORNIA COLLEGE OF ARTS AND CRAFTS, San Francisco, CA 94107

General Information Independent, coed, comprehensive institution. *Enrollment:* 122 full-time matriculated graduate/professional students (82 women), 5 part-time matriculated graduate/professional students (4 women). *Enrollment by degree level:* 127 master's. *Graduate faculty:* 39 part-time/adjunct (18 women). *Tuition:* Full-time $21,670. *Required fees:* $250; $125. *Graduate housing:* Rooms and/or apartments available on a first-come, first-served basis to single students and available to married students. Typical cost: $5,733 per year for single students. Housing application deadline: 4/1. *Student services:* Campus employment opportunities, career counseling, free psychological counseling, international student services, low-cost health insurance. *Library facilities:* Meyer Library plus 1 other. *Online resources:* library catalog, web page, access to other libraries' catalogs. *Collection:* 57,800 titles, 320 serial subscriptions, 800 audiovisual materials.

Computer facilities: 160 computers available on campus for general student use. A campuswide network can be accessed from student residence rooms and from off campus. Internet access is available. *Web address:* http://www.ccac-art.edu/.

General Application Contact: Geoff Chadsey, Assistant Director for Graduate Admissions, 415-551-9243, Fax: 415-703-9539, E-mail: graduateprograms@ccac-art.edu.

GRADUATE UNITS

Graduate Programs in Fine Art Students: 122 full-time (82 women), 5 part-time (4 women); includes 12 minority (3 African Americans, 2 Asian Americans or Pacific Islanders, 6 Hispanic Americans, 1 Native American), 3 international. Average age 30. *Faculty:* 22 part-time/adjunct (9 women). Expenses: Contact institution. *Financial support:* In 2001–02, 5 fellowships (averaging $10,000 per year), 20 teaching assistantships (averaging $1,200 per year) were awarded. Career-related internships or fieldwork, Federal Work-Study, and scholarships/grants also available. Support available to part-time students. Financial award application deadline: 3/2; financial award applicants required to submit FAFSA. In 2001, 21 degrees awarded. Offers ceramics (MFA); design (MFA); film/video/performance (MFA); fine art (MA, MFA); glass (MFA); jewelry/metal arts (MFA); painting/drawing (MFA); photography (MFA); printmaking (MFA); sculpture (MFA); textiles (MFA); visual criticism (MA); wood/furniture (MFA); writing (MFA). *Application deadline:* For fall admission, 2/1. *Application fee:* $50. *Application Contact:* Geoff Chadsey, Assistant Director for Graduate Admissions, 415-551-9243, Fax: 415-703-9539, E-mail: graduateprograms@ccac-art.edu. *Director,* Steven Goldstine, 415-551-9212.

CALIFORNIA COLLEGE OF PODIATRIC MEDICINE, Vallejo, CA 94590

General Information Independent, coed, graduate-only institution. *Graduate housing:* Rooms and/or apartments available to single and married students. *Research affiliation:* University of Southern California–Los Angeles County Medical Center, University of California, San Francisco Health Sciences Center, University of Texas Health Science Center–San Antonio.

GRADUATE UNITS

Graduate and Professional Programs Offers podiatric medicine (DPM).

CALIFORNIA INSTITUTE OF INTEGRAL STUDIES, San Francisco, CA 94103

General Information Independent, coed, upper-level institution. *Graduate faculty:* 47 full-time (19 women), 100 part-time/adjunct (50 women). *Tuition:* Full-time $10,890; part-time $605 per unit. Tuition and fees vary according to degree level. *Graduate housing:* On-campus housing not available. *Student services:* Campus employment opportunities, career counseling, disabled student services, international student services. *Library facilities:* The Laurance S. Rockefeller. *Collection:* 4,000 titles. *Research affiliation:* Bay Area Reference Service.

Computer facilities: A campuswide network can be accessed from off campus. Internet access is available. *Web address:* http://www.ciis.edu/.

General Application Contact: Gregory E. Canada, Director of Admissions, 415-575-6155, Fax: 415-575-1268, E-mail: gregc@ciis.edu.

GRADUATE UNITS

Graduate Programs Students: 265 full-time, 379 part-time. Average age 35. 491 applicants, 70% accepted, 218 enrolled. *Faculty:* 47 full-time (19 women), 100 part-time/adjunct (50 women). Expenses: Contact institution. *Financial support:* Career-related internships or fieldwork, Federal Work-Study, institutionally sponsored loans, and scholarships/grants available. Support available to part-time students. Financial award application deadline: 6/15; financial award applicants required to submit FAFSA. In 2001, 93 master's, 19 doctorates awarded. *Degree program information:* Part-time and evening/weekend programs available. Postbaccalaureate distance learning degree programs offered (minimal on-campus study). *Application deadline:* For fall admission, 10/15 (priority date); for spring admission, 3/15 (priority date). Applications are processed on a rolling basis. *Application fee:* $65. *Application Contact:* Gregory E. Canada, Director of Admissions, 415-575-6156, Fax: 415-575-1268, E-mail: gregc@ciis.edu. *President,* Dr. Joseph Subbiondo, 415-575-6105, Fax: 415-575-1264, E-mail: josephs@ciis.edu.

School of Consciousness and Transformation Students: 60 full-time, 143 part-time. 157 applicants, 78% accepted, 85 enrolled. *Faculty:* 20 full-time (9 women), 72 part-time/adjunct (35 women). Expenses: Contact institution. *Financial support:* Career-related internships or fieldwork, Federal Work-Study, institutionally sponsored loans, and scholarships/grants available. Support available to part-time students. Financial award application deadline: 6/15; financial award applicants required to submit FAFSA. In 2001, 58 master's, 21 doctorates awarded. *Degree program information:* Part-time and evening/weekend programs available. Postbaccalaureate distance learning degree programs offered (minimal on-campus study). Offers cultural anthropology and social transformation (MA); East-West psychology (MA, PhD); philosophy and religion (MA, PhD); social and cultural anthropology (PhD); transformative learning and change (PhD). *Application deadline:* For fall admission, 3/15 (priority date); for spring admission, 10/15 (priority date). Applications are processed on a rolling basis. *Application fee:* $65. *Application Contact:* Gregory E. Canada, Director of Admissions, 415-575-6155, Fax: 415-575-1268, E-mail: gregc@ciis.edu. *Director,* Daniel Deslaurier, 415-575-6260, Fax: 415-575-1264, E-mail: danield@ciis.edu.

School of Professional Psychology Students: 205 full-time, 236 part-time. 298 applicants, 65% accepted, 115 enrolled. Expenses: Contact institution. *Financial support:* Career-related internships or fieldwork, Federal Work-Study, institutionally sponsored loans, and scholarships/grants available. Support available to part-time students. Financial award application deadline: 6/15; financial award applicants required to submit FAFSA. *Degree* *program information:* Part-time and evening/weekend programs available. Offers drama therapy (MA); expressive arts therapy (MA, Certificate); integral counseling psychology (MA); psychology (Psy D); somatics (MA, Certificate). *Application deadline:* Applications are processed on a rolling basis. *Application fee:* $65. *Application Contact:* David Towner, Admissions Officer, 415-575-6152, Fax: 415-575-1268, E-mail: dtowner@ciis.edu. *Head,* Dr. Harrison Voigt, 415-575-6218.

CALIFORNIA INSTITUTE OF TECHNOLOGY, Pasadena, CA 91125-0001

General Information Independent, coed, university. CGS member. *Graduate housing:* Rooms and/or apartments available on a first-come, first-served basis to single students and available to married students. Housing application deadline: 5/1. *Research affiliation:* Scripps Institute of Oceanography, Stanford Linear Accelerator Center (high-energy physics), European Center for Nuclear Research (high-energy physics), National Science Foundation Center for Research in Parallel Computing, Cosmic Gravitational Waves Observatory (laser interferometer gravitational waves).

GRADUATE UNITS

Division of Biology Students: 82 full-time (29 women). 299 applicants, 16% accepted, 15 enrolled. *Faculty:* 40 full-time (7 women). Expenses: Contact institution. *Financial support:* In 2001–02, fellowships with full tuition reimbursements (averaging $16,500 per year), teaching assistantships with full tuition reimbursements (averaging $3,840 per year) were awarded. Research assistantships with full tuition reimbursements, institutionally sponsored loans also available. Financial award application deadline: 1/1. In 2001, 11 degrees awarded. Offers biochemistry and molecular biophysics (PhD); cell biology and biophysics (PhD); developmental biology (PhD); genetics (PhD); immunology (PhD); molecular biology (PhD); neurobiology (PhD). *Application deadline:* For fall admission, 1/1. *Application fee:* $50. Electronic applications accepted. *Application Contact:* Elizabeth Ayala, Chairman, 626-395-4497, Fax: 626-449-0756, E-mail: biograd@cco.caltech.edu. *Chairman,* Elizabeth Ayala, 626-395-4497, Fax: 626-449-0756, E-mail: biograd@cco.caltech.edu.

Division of Chemistry and Chemical Engineering Students: 259 full-time (76 women). Average age 24. 646 applicants, 22% accepted, 54 enrolled. *Faculty:* 37 full-time (5 women). Expenses: Contact institution. *Financial support:* In 2001–02, 259 students received support, including 104 fellowships, 89 research assistantships, 145 teaching assistantships; Federal Work-Study, institutionally sponsored loans, scholarships/grants, traineeships, health care benefits, and unspecified assistantships also available. Financial award application deadline: 1/1. In 2001, 13 master's, 38 doctorates awarded. Offers chemical engineering (MS, PhD); chemistry (MS, PhD). *Application deadline:* For fall admission, 1/1. *Application fee:* $0. Electronic applications accepted. *Chairman,* Dr. David A. Tirrell, 626-395-3646, Fax: 626-568-8824, E-mail: tirell@caltech.edu.

Division of Engineering and Applied Science Students: 458 full-time (93 women). 1,884 applicants, 14% accepted, 138 enrolled. *Faculty:* 88 full-time (4 women). Expenses: Contact institution. *Financial support:* Fellowships, research assistantships, teaching assistantships, Federal Work-Study and institutionally sponsored loans available. Support available to part-time students. In 2001, 87 master's, 81 doctorates awarded. Offers aeronautics (MS, PhD, Engr); applied and computational mathematics (MS, PhD); applied mechanics (MS, PhD); applied physics (MS, PhD); bioengineering (MS, PhD); civil engineering (MS, PhD); computation and neural systems (MS, PhD); computer science (MS, PhD); control and dynamical systems (MS, PhD); electrical engineering (MS, PhD); engineering science (PhD); environmental science and engineering (MS, PhD); materials science (MS, PhD); mechanical engineering (MS, PhD, Engr). *Application deadline:* For fall admission, 1/15. *Application fee:* $50. Electronic applications accepted. *Chair,* Dr. Richard M. Murray, 626-395-4101, Fax: 626-585-1729, E-mail: murray@caltech.edu.

Division of Geological and Planetary Sciences Students: 63 full-time (30 women); includes 31 minority (2 African Americans, 28 Asian Americans or Pacific Islanders, 1 Hispanic American) Average age 27. 99 applicants, 21% accepted. *Faculty:* 32 full-time (2 women). Expenses: Contact institution. *Financial support:* In 2001–02, 18 fellowships with full tuition reimbursements (averaging $19,949 per year), 46 research assistantships with full tuition reimbursements (averaging $19,949 per year) were awarded. Teaching assistantships with full tuition reimbursements, institutionally sponsored loans, scholarships/grants, health care benefits, and unspecified assistantships also available. Financial award applicants required to submit FAFSA. In 2001, 8 master's, 12 doctorates awarded. Offers cosmochemistry (PhD); geobiology (PhD); geochemistry (MS, PhD); geology (MS, PhD); geophysics (MS, PhD); planetary science (MS, PhD). *Application deadline:* For fall admission, 1/15. *Application fee:* $50. *Application Contact:* Dr. George R. Rossman, Division Academic Officer, 626-395-6125, Fax: 626-568-0935, E-mail: divgps@gps.caltech.edu. *Chair,* Dr. Edward M. Stolper, 626-395-6108, Fax: 626-795-6028, E-mail: divgps@gps.caltech.edu.

Division of Physics, Mathematics and Astronomy Offers astronomy (PhD); mathematics (PhD); physics (PhD).

Division of the Humanities and Social Sciences Students: 21 full-time (9 women); includes 3 minority (2 Asian Americans or Pacific Islanders, 1 Hispanic American), 6 international. Average age 22. 157 applicants, 10% accepted, 8 enrolled. *Faculty:* 22 full-time (2 women). Expenses: Contact institution. *Financial support:* In 2001–02, 21 students received support, including 5 fellowships (averaging $21,000 per year), 9 research assistantships (averaging $21,000 per year), 8 teaching assistantships (averaging $21,000 per year); Federal Work-Study, institutionally sponsored loans, and scholarships/grants also available. In 2001, 7 master's, 6 doctorates awarded. Offers economics (PhD); humanities and social sciences (MS, PhD); political science (PhD); social science (MS). *Application deadline:* For fall admission, 1/1. *Application fee:* $50. Electronic applications accepted. *Application Contact:* Laurel Auchampaugh, Graduate Secretary, 626-395-4206, Fax: 626-405-9841, E-mail: gradsec@hss.caltech.edu. *Chair,* Jean Ensminger, Fax: 626-405-9841, E-mail: jkatz@hss.caltech.edu.

CALIFORNIA INSTITUTE OF THE ARTS, Valencia, CA 91355-2340

General Information Independent, coed, comprehensive institution. *Enrollment:* 415 full-time matriculated graduate/professional students (214 women), 4 part-time matriculated graduate/professional students (all women). *Enrollment by degree level:* 419 master's. *Graduate faculty:* 138 full-time (55 women), 129 part-time/adjunct (47 women). *Tuition:* Full-time $20,930. *Required fees:* $345. *Graduate housing:* Room and/or apartments available on a first-come, first-served basis to single students; on-campus housing not available to married students. Typical cost: $2,600 per year ($3,000 including board). Housing application deadline: 7/1. *Student services:* Campus employment opportunities, career counseling, free psychological counseling, low-cost health insurance. *Library facilities:* Main library plus 1 other. *Online resources:* library catalog, web page, access to other libraries' catalogs. *Collection:* 95,973 titles, 613 serial subscriptions, 20,611 audiovisual materials.

Computer facilities: 87 computers available on campus for general student use. A campuswide network can be accessed from student residence rooms and from off campus. Internet access is available. *Web address:* http://www.calarts.edu/.

General Application Contact: Kenneth Young, Director of Admissions, 661-253-7863, Fax: 661-253-8352, E-mail: vfye@calarts.edu.

GRADUATE UNITS

School of Art Students: 81 full-time (46 women); includes 17 minority (3 African Americans, 8 Asian Americans or Pacific Islanders, 4 Hispanic Americans, 2 Native Americans), 15 international. Average age 28. *Faculty:* 50. Expenses: Contact institution. *Financial support:* Teaching assistantships, career-related internships or fieldwork, Federal Work-Study, institutionally sponsored loans, scholarships/grants, and tuition waivers (partial) available. Support available to part-time students. Financial award application deadline: 3/1; financial award applicants required to submit FAFSA. In 2001, 34 degrees awarded. *Degree program information:* Part-time programs available. Offers art (MFA, Adv C); graphic design (MFA); graphics design (Adv C); photography (MFA, Adv C). *Application deadline:* For fall admission, 1/11 (priority date); for spring admission, 11/15 (priority date). Applications are processed on a rolling basis. *Application fee:* $60. *Application Contact:* Dwayne Moser, Admissions Counselor, 661-255-1050, Fax: 661-253-8352, E-mail: admiss@calarts.edu. *Dean,* Thomas Lawson, 661-253-7801, Fax: 661-259-5871, E-mail: tlawson@calarts.edu.

School of Critical Studies Students: 29 full-time (17 women); includes 8 minority (2 African Americans, 2 Asian Americans or Pacific Islanders, 4 Hispanic Americans), 4 international. Average age 30. 39 applicants, 85% accepted. *Faculty:* 29. Expenses: Contact institution. *Financial support:* Research assistantships, teaching assistantships, career-related internships or fieldwork, Federal Work-Study, scholarships/grants, and tuition waivers (partial) available. Support available to part-time students. Financial award application deadline: 3/1; financial award applicants required to submit FAFSA. In 2001, 8 degrees awarded. Offers writing (MFA, Adv C). *Application deadline:* For fall admission, 1/11 (priority date); for spring admission, 11/15. Applications are processed on a rolling basis. *Application fee:* $60. *Application Contact:* Dwayne Moser, Admissions Counselor, 661-255-1050, Fax: 661-253-8352, E-mail: admiss@calarts.edu. *Dean,* Richard Hebdidge, 661-253-7802.

School of Dance Students: 11 full-time (all women); includes 1 minority (Asian American or Pacific Islander), 8 international. Average age 25. 22 applicants, 59% accepted. *Faculty:* 16. Expenses: Contact institution. *Financial support:* Fellowships, teaching assistantships, career-related internships or fieldwork and Federal Work-Study available. Financial award application deadline: 3/1; financial award applicants required to submit FAFSA. In 2001, 4 degrees awarded. Offers dance (MFA, Adv C). *Application deadline:* For fall admission, 1/15 (priority date). Applications are processed on a rolling basis. *Application fee:* $60. *Application Contact:* Clyde Howell, Admissions Counselor, 661-255-1050, E-mail: chowell@calarts.edu. *Dean,* Cristyne Lawson, 661-253-7899.

School of Film/Video Students: 125 full-time (63 women); includes 21 minority (6 African Americans, 9 Asian Americans or Pacific Islanders, 5 Hispanic Americans, 1 Native American), 35 international. Average age 27. *Faculty:* 58. Expenses: Contact institution. *Financial support:* Career-related internships or fieldwork and Federal Work-Study available. Financial award application deadline: 3/1; financial award applicants required to submit FAFSA. In 2001, 54 degrees awarded. Offers experimental animation (MFA); film directing (MFA); film/video (Adv C); live-action film/video (MFA). *Application deadline:* For fall admission, 1/15 (priority date). Applications are processed on a rolling basis. *Application fee:* $60. *Application Contact:* Admissions Officer, 661-255-1050. *Dean,* Hartmut Bitomsky, 661-253-7825.

School of Music Students: 81 full-time (29 women); includes 11 minority (3 African Americans, 5 Asian Americans or Pacific Islanders, 3 Hispanic Americans), 15 international. Average age 25. 101 applicants, 79% accepted. *Faculty:* 57. Expenses: Contact institution. *Financial support:* In 2001–02, 64 students received support, including 20 teaching assistantships; career-related internships or fieldwork, Federal Work-Study, institutionally sponsored loans, and scholarships/grants also available. Support available to part-time students. Financial award application deadline: 3/1; financial award applicants required to submit FAFSA. In 2001, 24 degrees awarded. *Degree program information:* Part-time programs available. Offers African music (MFA); composition (MFA); composition/new media (MFA); Indonesian music (MFA); jazz (MFA); music (MFA, Adv C); North Indian music (MFA); performance (MFA); performer/composer (MFA); voice (MFA). *Application deadline:* For fall admission, 1/15 (priority date); for spring admission, 11/15 (priority date). Applications are processed on a rolling basis. *Application fee:* $60. *Application Contact:* Eric Barber, Assistant Director of Admissions, 661-255-1050, Fax: 661-253-7710, E-mail: admiss@calarts.edu. *Dean,* David Rosenboom, 661-253-7816, Fax: 661-255-0938.

School of Theatre Students: 90 full-time (50 women); includes 26 minority (10 African Americans, 6 Asian Americans or Pacific Islanders, 10 Hispanic Americans), 6 international. Average age 25. *Faculty:* 24 full-time (9 women), 23 part-time/adjunct (10 women). Expenses: Contact institution. *Financial support:* Teaching assistantships, career-related internships or fieldwork, Federal Work-Study, institutionally sponsored loans, and scholarships/grants available. Support available to part-time students. Financial award application deadline: 3/1; financial award applicants required to submit FAFSA. In 2001, 21 degrees awarded. Offers acting (MFA); directing (MFA); performing arts design and technology (MFA); theater (Adv C); theatre management (MFA); writing for performance (MFA). *Application deadline:* For fall admission, 1/15 (priority date). *Application fee:* $60. *Application Contact:* Geralyn Flood, Director of Admissions, 661-255-1050, Fax: 661-253-7710, E-mail: admiss@calarts.edu. *Dean,* Susan Solt, 661-253-7861, E-mail: ssolt@calarts.edu.

CALIFORNIA LUTHERAN UNIVERSITY, Thousand Oaks, CA 91360-2787

General Information Independent-religious, coed, comprehensive institution. *Graduate housing:* On-campus housing not available.

GRADUATE UNITS

Graduate Studies *Degree program information:* Part-time and evening/weekend programs available. Offers clinical psychology (MS); marital and family therapy (MS); public policy and administration (MPPA).

School of Business *Degree program information:* Evening/weekend programs available. Offers finance (MBA); healthcare management (MBA); international business (MBA); management information systems (MBA); marketing (MBA); organizational behavior (MBA); small business/entrepreneurship (MBA).

School of Education *Degree program information:* Part-time and evening/weekend programs available. Offers counseling and guidance (MS); curriculum and instruction (MA); education (M Ed); educational administration (MA); reading education (MA); special education (MS); teacher preparation (Certificate).

CALIFORNIA NATIONAL UNIVERSITY FOR ADVANCED STUDIES, North Hills, CA 91343

General Information Private, comprehensive institution.

GRADUATE UNITS

College of Business Administration *Degree program information:* Part-time programs available. Postbaccalaureate distance learning degree programs offered (no on-campus study). Offers business administration (MBA, MHRM).

College of Engineering *Degree program information:* Part-time programs available. Postbaccalaureate distance learning degree programs offered (no on-campus study). Offers engineering (MS Eng).

CALIFORNIA POLYTECHNIC STATE UNIVERSITY, SAN LUIS OBISPO, San Luis Obispo, CA 93407

General Information State-supported, coed, comprehensive institution. *Enrollment:* 602 full-time matriculated graduate/professional students (328 women), 411 part-time matriculated graduate/professional students (238 women). *Enrollment by degree level:* 1,013 master's. *Graduate faculty:* 344 full-time, 291 part-time/adjunct. Tuition, nonresident: part-time $164 per unit. One-time fee: $2,153 part-time. *Graduate housing:* Room and/or apartments available on a first-come, first-served basis to single students; on-campus housing not available to married students. Housing application deadline: 6/15. *Student services:* Campus employment opportunities, campus safety program, career counseling, child daycare facilities, disabled student services, exercise/wellness program, free psychological counseling, grant writing training, international student services, low-cost health insurance, multicultural affairs office, teacher training, writing training. *Library facilities:* Kennedy Library. *Online resources:* library catalog, web page, access to other libraries' catalogs. *Collection:* 1.2 million titles, 2,617 serial subscriptions, 48,300 audiovisual materials. *Research affiliation:* NASA–Ames Research Center (aeroengineering), IBM (engineering), Associated Western Universities, Inc. (energy).

Computer facilities: 1,880 computers available on campus for general student use. A campuswide network can be accessed from student residence rooms and from off campus. *Web address:* http://www.calpoly.edu/.

General Application Contact: Jim Maraviglia, Admissions Office, 805-756-2311, Fax: 805-756-5400, E-mail: admprosp@calpoly.edu.

California Polytechnic State University, San Luis Obispo (continued)

GRADUATE UNITS

College of Agriculture Students: 50 full-time (32 women), 41 part-time (24 women); includes 7 Hispanic Americans 79 applicants, 67% accepted, 30 enrolled. *Faculty:* 5 full-time (1 woman), 2 part-time/adjunct (1 woman). Expenses: Contact institution. *Financial support:* In 2001–02, 40 students received support, including 6 fellowships (averaging $2,000 per year), 20 research assistantships (averaging $10,000 per year), 10 teaching assistantships (averaging $2,000 per year); career-related internships or fieldwork, Federal Work-Study, institutionally sponsored loans, and scholarships/grants also available. Support available to part-time students. Financial award application deadline: 3/2; financial award applicants required to submit FAFSA. In 2001, 34 degrees awarded. *Degree program information:* Part-time programs available. Offers agriculture (MS); forestry sciences (MS). *Application deadline:* For fall admission, 7/1; for winter admission, 11/1; for spring admission, 3/1. Applications are processed on a rolling basis. *Application fee:* $55. Electronic applications accepted. *Application Contact:* Admissions Office, 805-756-2311, E-mail: admprosp@polymail.calpoly.edu. *Graduate Coordinator,* Dr. Mark Shelton, 805-756-2161, Fax: 805-756-6577, E-mail: mshelton@calpoly.edu.

College of Architecture and Environmental Design Students: 44 full-time (15 women), 9 part-time (5 women), 7 international. 51 applicants, 76% accepted, 23 enrolled. *Faculty:* 61 full-time (10 women), 27 part-time/adjunct (7 women). Expenses: Contact institution. *Financial support:* Research assistantships, teaching assistantships, career-related internships or fieldwork, Federal Work-Study, and institutionally sponsored loans available. Support available to part-time students. Financial award application deadline: 3/2; financial award applicants required to submit FAFSA. In 2001, 21 degrees awarded. *Degree program information:* Evening/weekend programs available. Offers architecture (MS Arch); architecture and environmental design (MCRP, MS Arch); city and regional planning (MCRP). *Application deadline:* Applications are processed on a rolling basis. *Application fee:* $55. *Dean,* Martin Harms, 805-756-1311, Fax: 805-756-2765, E-mail: mharms@calpoly.edu.

College of Engineering Students: 91 full-time (14 women), 72 part-time (15 women); includes 21 Asian Americans or Pacific Islanders, 19 international. 135 applicants, 59% accepted, 56 enrolled. *Faculty:* 98 full-time (8 women), 82 part-time/adjunct (14 women). Expenses: Contact institution. *Financial support:* Fellowships, research assistantships, teaching assistantships, career-related internships or fieldwork, Federal Work-Study, and institutionally sponsored loans available. Financial award application deadline: 3/2; financial award applicants required to submit FAFSA. In 2001, 42 degrees awarded. *Degree program information:* Part-time programs available. Offers aeronautical engineering (MSAE); biochemical engineering (MS); civil and environmental engineering (MS); computer science (MSCS); electrical engineering (MS); engineering (MS, MSAE, MSCS); industrial engineering (MS); integrated technology management (MS); materials engineering (MS); water engineering (MS). *Application deadline:* For fall admission, 5/31 (priority date). Applications are processed on a rolling basis. *Application fee:* $55. Electronic applications accepted. *Application Contact:* Dr. Daniel W. Walsh, Associate Dean, 805-756-2131, Fax: 805-756-6503, E-mail: dwalsh@calpoly.edu. *Dean,* Dr. Peter Y. Lee, 805-756-2131, Fax: 805-756-6503, E-mail: plee@calpoly.edu.

College of Liberal Arts Students: 42 full-time (32 women), 44 part-time (36 women); includes 6 Hispanic Americans 75 applicants, 57% accepted, 27 enrolled. *Faculty:* 44 full-time (19 women), 49 part-time/adjunct (29 women). Expenses: Contact institution. *Financial support:* Teaching assistantships, career-related internships or fieldwork, Federal Work-Study, institutionally sponsored loans, and tutorships, writing laboratory assistantships available. Support available to part-time students. Financial award application deadline: 3/2; financial award applicants required to submit FAFSA. In 2001, 31 degrees awarded. *Degree program information:* Part-time programs available. Offers English (MA); liberal arts (MA, MS); psychology (MS). *Application fee:* $55. *Dean,* Harold Hellenbrand, 805-756-2706, Fax: 805-756-5748, E-mail: hhellenb@calpoly.edu.

College of Science and Mathematics Students: 36 full-time (18 women), 38 part-time (21 women); includes 6 Asian Americans or Pacific Islanders, 7 Hispanic Americans 51 applicants, 67% accepted, 16 enrolled. *Faculty:* 77 full-time (12 women), 71 part-time/adjunct (34 women). Expenses: Contact institution. *Financial support:* Teaching assistantships, career-related internships or fieldwork and Federal Work-Study available. Support available to part-time students. Financial award application deadline: 3/2; financial award applicants required to submit FAFSA. In 2001, 22 degrees awarded. *Degree program information:* Part-time programs available. Offers biological sciences (MS); kinesiology (MS); mathematics (MS); science and mathematics (MS). *Application deadline:* For fall admission, 7/1; for spring admission, 3/1. *Application fee:* $55. Electronic applications accepted. *Dean,* Philip S. Bailey, 805-756-2226, Fax: 805-756-1670, E-mail: pbailey@calpoly.edu.

Orfalea College of Business Students: 99 full-time (29 women), 16 part-time (4 women); includes 18 minority (11 Asian Americans or Pacific Islanders, 7 Hispanic Americans) 123 applicants, 73% accepted, 65 enrolled. *Faculty:* 60 full-time (13 women). Expenses: Contact institution. *Financial support:* Career-related internships or fieldwork, Federal Work-Study, and institutionally sponsored loans available. Support available to part-time students. Financial award application deadline: 3/2; financial award applicants required to submit FAFSA. In 2001, 43 degrees awarded. Offers agribusiness management (MBA); architectural management (MBA); engineering management (MA, MBA); industrial and technical studies (MA); industrial technology (MA). *Application deadline:* For fall admission, 7/1. Applications are processed on a rolling basis. *Application fee:* $55. *Application Contact:* Dr. Earl Keller, Director, Graduate Programs, 805-756-2588, Fax: 805-756-0110, E-mail: eckeller@calpoly.edu. *Dean,* Dr. Terry Swartz, 805-756-2705, Fax: 805-756-5452.

University Center for Teacher Education Students: 210 full-time (168 women), 154 part-time (116 women); includes 17 Asian Americans or Pacific Islanders, 46 Hispanic Americans 254 applicants, 60% accepted, 101 enrolled. *Faculty:* 14 full-time (9 women), 16 part-time/adjunct (10 women). Expenses: Contact institution. *Financial support:* Career-related internships or fieldwork, Federal Work-Study, and institutionally sponsored loans available. Financial award application deadline: 3/2; financial award applicants required to submit FAFSA. In 2001, 57 degrees awarded. *Degree program information:* Part-time and evening/weekend programs available. Offers counseling (MA); curriculum and instruction (MA); education (MA); educational administration (MA); reading (MA); special education (MA). *Application deadline:* For fall admission, 3/15 (priority date); for spring admission, 12/1 (priority date). *Application fee:* $55. *Director,* Dr. Bonnie Konopak, 805-756-2584, Fax: 805-756-5682, E-mail: bkonopak@calpoly.edu.

See in-depth description on page 775.

CALIFORNIA STATE POLYTECHNIC UNIVERSITY, POMONA, Pomona, CA 91768-2557

General Information State-supported, coed, comprehensive institution. CGS member. *Enrollment:* 533 full-time matriculated graduate/professional students (264 women), 534 part-time matriculated graduate/professional students (255 women). *Enrollment by degree level:* 1,067 master's. *Graduate faculty:* 663 full-time (207 women), 542 part-time/adjunct (229 women). Tuition, nonresident: part-time $164 per unit. *Required fees:* $1,850. *Graduate housing:* Room and/or apartments available on a first-come, first-served basis to single students; on-campus housing not available to married students. Typical cost: $6,843 (including board). Room and board charges vary according to board plan and housing facility selected. Housing application deadline: 5/1. *Student services:* Campus employment opportunities, campus safety program, career counseling, child daycare facilities, disabled student services, free psychological counseling, international student services, low-cost health insurance. *Library facilities:* University Library. *Online resources:* library catalog, web page, access to other libraries' catalogs. *Collection:* 433,342 titles, 5,863 serial subscriptions, 10,799 audiovisual materials.

Computer facilities: 1,864 computers available on campus for general student use. A campuswide network can be accessed from student residence rooms and from off campus. Internet access is available. *Web address:* http://www.csupomona.edu/.

General Application Contact: Dan Aseltine, Coordinator, Graduate and International Programs, 909-869-3252, Fax: 909-869-4529, E-mail: daseltine@csupomona.edu.

GRADUATE UNITS

Academic Affairs Students: 533 full-time (264 women), 534 part-time (255 women); includes 384 minority (28 African Americans, 218 Asian Americans or Pacific Islanders, 134 Hispanic Americans, 4 Native Americans), 152 international. Average age 31. 869 applicants, 46% accepted. *Faculty:* 663 full-time (207 women), 542 part-time/adjunct (229 women). Expenses: Contact institution. *Financial support:* In 2001–02, 4 fellowships, 5 research assistantships, 3 teaching assistantships were awarded. Career-related internships or fieldwork, Federal Work-Study, institutionally sponsored loans, and unspecified assistantships also available. Support available to part-time students. Financial award application deadline: 3/2; financial award applicants required to submit FAFSA. In 2001, 322 degrees awarded. *Degree program information:* Part-time and evening/weekend programs available. *Application deadline:* Applications are processed on a rolling basis. *Application fee:* $55. Electronic applications accepted. *Vice President for Academic Affairs,* Dr. Jane Ollenburger, 909-869-3405, E-mail: jollenburger@csupomona.edu.

College of Agriculture Students: 32 full-time (22 women), 24 part-time (12 women); includes 11 minority (4 Asian Americans or Pacific Islanders, 6 Hispanic Americans, 1 Native American), 9 international. Average age 30. 50 applicants, 72% accepted. *Faculty:* 47 full-time (13 women), 20 part-time/adjunct (12 women). Expenses: Contact institution. *Financial support:* Career-related internships or fieldwork, Federal Work-Study, and institutionally sponsored loans available. Support available to part-time students. Financial award application deadline: 3/2; financial award applicants required to submit FAFSA. In 2001, 20 degrees awarded. *Degree program information:* Part-time programs available. Offers agricultural science (MS); animal science (MS); foods and nutrition (MS). *Application deadline:* For fall admission, 5/1 (priority date); for winter admission, 10/15 (priority date); for spring admission, 1/2 (priority date). Applications are processed on a rolling basis. *Application fee:* $55. Electronic applications accepted. *Dean,* Dr. Wayne R. Bidlack, 909-869-2200, E-mail: wrbidlack@csupomona.edu.

College of Business Administration Students: 130 full-time (61 women), 92 part-time (32 women); includes 81 minority (3 African Americans, 64 Asian Americans or Pacific Islanders, 14 Hispanic Americans), 58 international. Average age 30. 188 applicants, 34% accepted. *Faculty:* 113 full-time (41 women), 49 part-time/adjunct (17 women). Expenses: Contact institution. *Financial support:* In 2001–02, 5 research assistantships, 3 teaching assistantships were awarded. Career-related internships or fieldwork, Federal Work-Study, and institutionally sponsored loans also available. Support available to part-time students. Financial award application deadline: 3/2; financial award applicants required to submit FAFSA. In 2001, 103 degrees awarded. *Degree program information:* Part-time programs available. Offers business administration (MBA, MSBA). *Application deadline:* For fall admission, 5/1 (priority date); for winter admission, 10/15 (priority date); for spring admission, 1/2 (priority date). Applications are processed on a rolling basis. *Application fee:* $55. Electronic applications accepted. *Application Contact:* Dr. Eric J. McLaughlin, Director, Graduate Program, 909-869-2362, E-mail: ejmclaughlin@csupomona.edu. *Dean,* Dr. Eduardo M. Ochoa, 909-869-2400, E-mail: emochoa@csupomona.edu.

College of Engineering Students: 48 full-time (10 women), 101 part-time (11 women); includes 66 minority (57 Asian Americans or Pacific Islanders, 9 Hispanic Americans), 34 international. Average age 28. 133 applicants, 68% accepted. *Faculty:* 106 full-time (15 women), 34 part-time/adjunct (1 woman). Expenses: Contact institution. *Financial support:* In 2001–02, 1 fellowship, 6 research assistantships, 5 teaching assistantships were awarded. Career-related internships or fieldwork, Federal Work-Study, institutionally sponsored loans, and unspecified assistantships also available. Support available to part-time students. Financial award application deadline: 3/2; financial award applicants required to submit FAFSA. In 2001, 49 degrees awarded. *Degree program information:* Part-time programs available. Offers electrical engineering (MSEE); engineering (MSE). *Application deadline:* For fall admission, 5/1 (priority date); for winter admission, 10/15 (priority date); for spring admission, 1/2 (priority date). Applications are processed on a rolling basis. *Application fee:* $55. Electronic applications accepted. *Application Contact:* Dr. Rajan Chandra, Director, 909-869-2476, Fax: 909-869-4687, E-mail: rmchandra@csupomona.edu. *Dean,* Dr. Ed Hohmann, 909-869-2472, Fax: 909-869-4370, E-mail: echohmann@csupomona.edu.

College of Environmental Design Students: 130 full-time (58 women), 22 part-time (12 women); includes 45 minority (7 African Americans, 17 Asian Americans or Pacific Islanders, 20 Hispanic Americans, 1 Native American), 14 international. Average age 31. 160 applicants, 30% accepted. *Faculty:* 50 full-time (17 women), 36 part-time/adjunct (14 women). Expenses: Contact institution. *Financial support:* Career-related internships or fieldwork, Federal Work-Study, and institutionally sponsored loans available. Support available to part-time students. Financial award application deadline: 3/2; financial award applicants required to submit FAFSA. In 2001, 36 degrees awarded. *Degree program information:* Part-time programs available. Offers architecture (M Arch); environmental design (M Arch, M Land Arch, MURP); landscape architecture (M Land Arch); urban and regional planning (MURP). *Application deadline:* For fall admission, 5/1 (priority date); for winter admission, 10/15 (priority date); for spring admission, 1/20 (priority date). Applications are processed on a rolling basis. *Application fee:* $55. Electronic applications accepted. *Dean,* Linda Sanders, 909-869-2661, E-mail: lwsanders@csupomona.edu.

College of Letters, Arts, and Social Sciences Students: 72 full-time (45 women), 96 part-time (55 women); includes 58 minority (5 African Americans, 17 Asian Americans or Pacific Islanders, 36 Hispanic Americans), 7 international. Average age 32. 133 applicants, 56% accepted. *Faculty:* 132 full-time (57 women), 179 part-time/adjunct (80 women). Expenses: Contact institution. *Financial support:* In 2001–02, 2 fellowships were awarded; Federal Work-Study and institutionally sponsored loans also available. Support available to part-time students. Financial award application deadline: 3/2; financial award applicants required to submit FAFSA. In 2001, 45 degrees awarded. *Degree program information:* Part-time and evening/weekend programs available. Offers economics (MS); English (MA); history (MA); kinesiology (MS); letters, arts, and social sciences (MA, MPA, MS); psychology (MS); public administration (MPA). *Application deadline:* Applications are processed on a rolling basis. *Application fee:* $55. Electronic applications accepted. *Dean,* Dr. Barbara J. Way, 909-869-3943, E-mail: bjburtway@csupomona.edu.

College of Science Students: 68 full-time (30 women), 82 part-time (37 women); includes 60 minority (3 African Americans, 37 Asian Americans or Pacific Islanders, 19 Hispanic Americans, 1 Native American), 28 international. Average age 28. 143 applicants, 39% accepted. *Faculty:* 131 full-time (31 women), 130 part-time/adjunct (56 women). Expenses: Contact institution. *Financial support:* Career-related internships or fieldwork, Federal Work-Study, and institutionally sponsored loans available. Support available to part-time students. Financial award application deadline: 3/2; financial award applicants required to submit FAFSA. In 2001, 25 degrees awarded. *Degree program information:* Part-time and evening/weekend programs available. Offers applied mathematics (MS); biological sciences (MS); chemistry (MS); computer science (MS); pure mathematics (MS); science (MS). *Application deadline:* For fall admission, 5/1 (priority date); for winter admission, 10/15 (priority date); for spring admission, 1/20 (priority date). Applications are processed on a rolling basis. *Application fee:* $55. Electronic applications accepted. *Dean,* Dr. Simon J. Bernau, 909-869-3600, E-mail: sjbernau@csupomona.edu.

School of Education and Integrative Studies Students: 42 full-time (30 women), 103 part-time (87 women); includes 51 minority (8 African Americans, 16 Asian Americans or Pacific Islanders, 26 Hispanic Americans, 1 Native American), 2 international. Average age 35. 40 applicants, 65% accepted. *Faculty:* 32 full-time (19 women), 58 part-time/adjunct (35 women). Expenses: Contact institution. *Financial support:* Career-related internships or fieldwork, Federal Work-Study, and institutionally sponsored loans available. Support available to part-time students. Financial award application deadline: 3/2; financial award applicants required to submit FAFSA. In 2001, 44 degrees awarded. *Degree program information:* Part-time programs available. Offers education and integrative studies (MA). *Application deadline:* For fall admission, 5/1 (priority date); for winter admission, 10/15 (priority date); for spring admission, 1/20 (priority date). Applications are processed on a rolling basis. *Application fee:* $55. Electronic applications accepted. *Application Contact:* Dr. Richard L. DeNovellis, Graduate Program Coordinator/Professor, 909-869-2316, Fax: 909-869-4963, E-mail: rdenovellis@csupomona.edu. *Dean,* Dr. Richard A. Navarro, 909-869-2307, E-mail: ranavarro@csupomona.edu.

CALIFORNIA STATE UNIVERSITY, BAKERSFIELD, Bakersfield, CA 93311-1099

General Information State-supported, coed, comprehensive institution. CGS member. *Enrollment:* 834 full-time matriculated graduate/professional students (579 women), 988 part-time matriculated graduate/professional students (677 women). *Graduate faculty:* 165 full-time (96 women), 103 part-time/adjunct (63 women). Tuition, state resident: full-time $876; part-time $292. Tuition, nonresident: full-time $1,122; part-time $456. *Graduate housing:* Room and/or apartments available on a first-come, first-served basis to single students; on-campus housing not available to married students. Typical cost: $4,662 (including board). Housing application deadline: 8/1. *Student services:* Campus employment opportunities, campus safety program, career counseling, child daycare facilities, disabled student services, free psychological counseling, grant writing training, international student services, teacher training. *Library facilities:* Walter W. Stiern Library. *Online resources:* web page. *Collection:* 354,016 titles, 2,260 serial subscriptions.

Computer facilities: 600 computers available on campus for general student use. A campuswide network can be accessed from student residence rooms and from off campus. Internet access is available. *Web address:* http://www.csubak.edu/.

General Application Contact: Dr. George Hibbard, Dean of Students, 661-664-2161.

GRADUATE UNITS

Division of Graduate Studies and Research *Degree program information:* Part-time and evening/weekend programs available. Postbaccalaureate distance learning degree programs offered (no on-campus study). Offers administration (MS); counseling psychology (MS); interdisciplinary studies (MA).

School of Business and Public Administration Offers business administration (MBA); business and public administration (MBA, MPA, MSA); health care management (MSA); public administration (MPA).

School of Education Offers bilingual/bicultural education (MA); counseling (MS); counseling and personnel services (MA); curriculum and instruction (MA); education administration (MA); elementary curriculum and instruction (MA); reading education (MA); secondary curriculum and instruction (MA); special education (MA).

School of Humanities and Social Sciences *Degree program information:* Part-time and evening/weekend programs available. Offers anthropology (MA); English (MA); family and child counseling (MFCC); history (MA); humanities and social sciences (MA, MS, MSW, MFCC); psychology (MS); social work (MSW); sociology (MA); Spanish (MA).

School of Natural Sciences, Mathematics, and Engineering Offers geology (MS); hydrology (MS); natural sciences, mathematics, and engineering (MA, MS); nursing (MS); secondary school mathematics teaching (MA).

CALIFORNIA STATE UNIVERSITY, CHICO, Chico, CA 95929-0722

General Information State-supported, coed, comprehensive institution. CGS member. *Enrollment:* 1,199 full-time matriculated graduate/professional students, 775 part-time matriculated graduate/professional students. *Graduate faculty:* 231. Tuition, state resident: full-time $2,148. Tuition, nonresident: full-time $6,576. *Graduate housing:* Room and/or apartments available to single students; on-campus housing not available to married students. Typical cost: $4,692 per year ($6,973 including board). Room and board charges vary according to board plan and housing facility selected. Housing application deadline: 3/22. *Student services:* Campus employment opportunities, campus safety program, career counseling, child daycare facilities, disabled student services, free psychological counseling, international student services, low-cost health insurance. *Library facilities:* Meriam Library. *Online resources:* library catalog, web page, access to other libraries' catalogs. *Collection:* 928,450 titles, 13,390 serial subscriptions, 20,215 audiovisual materials. *Research affiliation:* Hewlett-Packard Company (computer science).

Computer facilities: 1,000 computers available on campus for general student use. A campuswide network can be accessed from student residence rooms and from off campus. Internet access, student account information are available. *Web address:* http://www.csuchico.edu/.

General Application Contact: Dr. Robert M. Jackson, Dean, Graduate and International Programs, 530-898-6880, Fax: 530-898-6889, E-mail: bmjackson@csuchico.edu.

GRADUATE UNITS

Graduate School Students: 1,199 full-time, 775 part-time. Expenses: Contact institution. *Financial support:* Fellowships, research assistantships, teaching assistantships, career-related internships or fieldwork, Federal Work-Study, and stipends available. Support available to part-time students. In 2001, 259 degrees awarded. *Degree program information:* Part-time programs available. Offers applied mechanical engineering (MS); interdisciplinary studies (MS); interdispinary studies (MA); simulation science (MS). *Application deadline:* Applications are processed on a rolling basis. *Dean, Graduate and International Programs,* Dr. Robert M. Jackson, 530-898-6880, Fax: 530-898-6889, E-mail: bmjackson@csuchico.edu.

College of Behavioral and Social Sciences Students: 137 full-time, 73 part-time; includes 35 minority (4 African Americans, 11 Asian Americans or Pacific Islanders, 17 Hispanic Americans, 3 Native Americans) 151 applicants, 83% accepted, 88 enrolled. *Faculty:* 45. Expenses: Contact institution. *Financial support:* Fellowships, teaching assistantships, career-related internships or fieldwork and Federal Work-Study available. Support available to part-time students. In 2001, 60 degrees awarded. *Degree program information:* Part-time programs available. Offers behavioral and social sciences (MA, MPA, MRTP, MS, MSW); counseling (MS); geography (MA); health administration (MPA); museum studies (MA); political science (MA); psychology (MA); public administration (MPA); rural and town planning (MRTP); social science (MA); social work (MSW). *Application deadline:* For fall admission, 4/1. Applications are processed on a rolling basis. *Application fee:* $55. Electronic applications accepted. *Dean,* Dr. Jeanne L. Thomas, 530-898-6171.

College of Business Students: 42 full-time, 22 part-time; includes 18 minority (all Asian Americans or Pacific Islanders) 73 applicants, 58% accepted, 24 enrolled. *Faculty:* 15. Expenses: Contact institution. In 2001, 32 degrees awarded. Offers accountancy (MSA); business (MBA, MSA); business administration (MBA). *Application deadline:* For fall admission, 4/1; for spring admission, 10/1. Applications are processed on a rolling basis. *Application fee:* $55. Electronic applications accepted. *Application Contact:* Steve Adams, Graduate Coordinator, 530-898-6359. *Dean,* Dr. Dalen Chiang, 520-898-6271.

College of Communication and Education Students: 730 full-time, 414 part-time; includes 146 minority (13 African Americans, 42 Asian Americans or Pacific Islanders, 74 Hispanic Americans, 17 Native Americans) 199 applicants, 84% accepted, 123 enrolled. *Faculty:* 70. Expenses: Contact institution. *Financial support:* Fellowships, teaching assistantships, career-related internships or fieldwork, Federal Work-Study, and stipends available. Support available to part-time students. In 2001, 81 degrees awarded. *Degree program information:* Part-time programs available. Offers communication and education (MA, MS); education (MA); human communication (MA); information and communication studies (MA); instructional technology (MS); physical education (MA); public communication (MA); recreation administration (MA); speech pathology and audiology (MA); teaching international languages (MA). *Application deadline:* For fall admission, 4/1. Applications are processed on a rolling basis. *Application fee:* $55. Electronic applications accepted. *Dean,* Dr. Stephen King, 530-898-4015.

College of Engineering, Computer Science, and Technology Students: 122 full-time, 53 part-time; includes 89 minority (2 African Americans, 84 Asian Americans or Pacific Islanders, 3 Hispanic Americans) Average age 31. 215 applicants, 65% accepted, 48 enrolled. *Faculty:* 20. Expenses: Contact institution. *Financial support:* Fellowships, research assistantships, teaching assistantships, career-related internships or fieldwork and Federal Work-Study available. Support available to part-time students. In 2001, 34 degrees awarded. *Degree program information:* Part-time programs available. Offers computer science (MS); electrical engineering (MS); engineering, computer science, and technology (MS). *Application deadline:* For fall admission, 4/1; for spring admission, 10/1. Applications are processed on a rolling basis. *Application fee:* $55. Electronic applications accepted. *Dean,* Dr. Kenneth Derucher, 530-898-5963.

College of Humanities and Fine Arts Students: 42 full-time, 48 part-time; includes 14 minority (7 Asian Americans or Pacific Islanders, 6 Hispanic Americans, 1 Native American) 38 applicants, 89% accepted, 22 enrolled. *Faculty:* 37. Expenses: Contact institution. *Financial support:* Teaching assistantships, career-related internships or fieldwork and Federal Work-Study available. Support available to part-time students. In 2001, 23 degrees awarded. *Degree program information:* Part-time programs available. Offers art (MA); creative writing (MFA); English (MA); history (MA); humanities and fine arts (MA, MFA); music (MA). *Application deadline:* For fall admission, 4/1. Applications are processed on a rolling basis. *Application fee:* $55. Electronic applications accepted. *Acting Dean,* Dr. Sarah Blackstone, 530-898-5351.

College of Natural Sciences Students: 26 full-time, 49 part-time; includes 7 minority (1 Asian American or Pacific Islander, 6 Hispanic Americans) 34 applicants, 88% accepted, 22 enrolled. *Faculty:* 44. Expenses: Contact institution. *Financial support:* Fellowships, research assistantships, teaching assistantships, career-related internships or fieldwork and Federal Work-Study available. Support available to part-time students. In 2001, 16 degrees awarded. *Degree program information:* Part-time programs available. Offers biological sciences (MS); botany (MS); earth sciences (MS); environmental science (MS); geosciences (MS); natural sciences (MS); nursing (MS); nutrition education (MS); nutritional science (MS). *Application deadline:* For fall admission, 4/1; for spring admission, 10/1. Applications are processed on a rolling basis. *Application fee:* $55. Electronic applications accepted. *Dean,* Dr. James Houpis, 530-898-6121.

CALIFORNIA STATE UNIVERSITY, DOMINGUEZ HILLS, Carson, CA 90747-0001

General Information State-supported, coed, comprehensive institution. CGS member. *Enrollment:* 2,771 full-time matriculated graduate/professional students (2,004 women), 5,970 part-time matriculated graduate/professional students (4,384 women). *Graduate faculty:* 292 full-time, 243 part-time/adjunct. Tuition, nonresident: full-time $1,508; part-time $438 per semester. *Required fees:* $442; $246 per unit. $227 per semester. *Graduate housing:* Rooms and/or apartments available to single and married students. Housing application deadline: 4/15. *Student services:* Career counseling, child daycare facilities, free psychological counseling, low-cost health insurance. *Library facilities:* Leo F. Cain Educational Resource Center. *Online resources:* library catalog, web page. *Collection:* 440,181 titles. *Research affiliation:* Drew Medical School.

Computer facilities: 200 computers available on campus for general student use. *Web address:* http://www.csudh.edu/.

General Application Contact: Linda Wise, Associate Director, 310-243-3613, E-mail: lwise@research.csudh.edu.

GRADUATE UNITS

College of Arts and Sciences Students: 160 full-time (132 women), 249 part-time (179 women); includes 229 minority (140 African Americans, 28 Asian Americans or Pacific Islanders, 58 Hispanic Americans, 3 Native Americans), 12 international. Average age 36. 360 applicants, 86% accepted, 83 enrolled. *Faculty:* 110. Expenses: Contact institution. *Financial support:* Institutionally sponsored loans available. Support available to part-time students. In 2001, 342 degrees awarded. *Degree program information:* Part-time and evening/weekend programs available. Offers applied behavioral science (MA); arts and sciences (MA, MS, Certificate); biology (MA); clinical psychology (MA); English (MA); general psychology (MA); gerontology (MA); human cytogenic technology (Certificate); humanities (MA); marriage, family, and child counseling (MS); negotiation and conflict resolution (MA, Certificate); quality assurance (MS); rhetoric and composition (Certificate); social research (Certificate); sociology (MA); teaching English as a second language (Certificate). *Application deadline:* For fall admission, 6/1. *Application fee:* $55. *Dean,* Dr. Selase Williams, 310-243-3389, E-mail: swilliams@cas.csudh.edu.

School of Business and Public Administration Students: 191 full-time (140 women), 241 part-time (161 women); includes 260 minority (101 African Americans, 39 Asian Americans or Pacific Islanders, 120 Hispanic Americans), 52 international. Average age 34. 273 applicants, 83% accepted, 67 enrolled. *Faculty:* 27 full-time (5 women), 5 part-time/adjunct (3 women). Expenses: Contact institution. In 2001, 125 degrees awarded. *Degree program information:* Part-time and evening/weekend programs available. Offers business and public administration (MBA, MPA); computer information systems (MBA); public administration (MPA). *Application deadline:* For fall admission, 6/1. *Application fee:* $55. *Dean,* Dr. Donald Bates, 310-243-3548, E-mail: dbates@soma.csudh.edu.

School of Education Students: 2,349 full-time (1,674 women), 5,183 part-time (3,777 women); includes 4,524 minority (2,031 African Americans, 605 Asian Americans or Pacific Islanders, 1,857 Hispanic Americans, 31 Native Americans), 192 international. Average age 37. 95 applicants, 93% accepted, 42 enrolled. *Faculty:* 15 full-time (5 women), 6 part-time/adjunct (3 women). Expenses: Contact institution. *Degree program information:* Part-time and evening/weekend programs available. Offers computer-based education (MA, Certificate); counseling (MA); education (MA, Certificate); educational administration (MA); individualized education (MA); learning handicapped (MA); multicultural education (MA); physical education (MA); severely handicapped (MA); special education (MA); teaching mathematics (MA); teaching/curriculum (MA). *Application deadline:* For fall admission, 6/1. *Application fee:* $55. *Application Contact:* 310-243-3600. *Dean,* Dr. Billie Blair, 310-243-3519, E-mail: bblair@research.csudh.edu.

School of Health Students: 71 full-time (58 women), 297 part-time (267 women); includes 149 minority (51 African Americans, 56 Asian Americans or Pacific Islanders, 38 Hispanic Americans, 4 Native Americans), 7 international. Average age 37. Expenses: Contact institution. In 2001, 102 degrees awarded. Offers health (MS, MSN, Certificate); nursing (MSN). *Application deadline:* For fall admission, 6/1. *Application fee:* $55. *Dean,* Abel Whittemore, 301-243-2046, E-mail: aawhittemore@son.csudh.edu.

Division of Clinical Sciences Students: 26 full-time (19 women), 14 part-time (7 women); includes 25 minority (3 African Americans, 17 Asian Americans or Pacific Islanders, 5 Hispanic Americans), 7 international. Average age 31. 21 applicants, 95% accepted, 13 enrolled. *Faculty:* 8 full-time (5 women), 7 part-time/adjunct (2 women). Expenses: Contact institution. In 2001, 12 degrees awarded. Offers clinical sciences (MS, Certificate). *Application deadline:* For fall admission, 6/1. *Application fee:* $55. *Chair,* Dr. Kathleen McEnerney, 310-243-3748.

See in-depth description on page 777.

CALIFORNIA STATE UNIVERSITY, FRESNO, Fresno, CA 93740-8027

General Information State-supported, coed, comprehensive institution. CGS member. *Enrollment:* 1,032 full-time matriculated graduate/professional students (661 women), 962 part-time matriculated graduate/professional students (559 women). *Enrollment by degree level:* 1,958 master's, 36 doctoral. *Graduate faculty:* 424 full-time (148 women), 34 part-time/adjunct (12 women). Tuition, nonresident: part-time $246 per unit. *Required fees:* $605 per semester. Tuition and fees vary according to course load. *Graduate housing:* Room and/or apartments available on a first-come, first-served basis to single students; on-campus housing not available to married students. Typical cost: $4,287 per year ($7,066 including board). Room and board charges vary according to board plan. Housing application deadline: 6/1. *Student services:* Campus employment opportunities, campus safety program, career counseling, child daycare facilities, disabled student services, exercise/wellness program, free psychological counseling, international student services, low-cost health insurance, multicultural affairs office. *Library facilities:* Henry Madden Library. *Online resources:* library catalog, web page, access to other libraries' catalogs. *Collection:* 977,198 titles, 2,500 serial subscriptions, 71,482 audiovisual materials. *Research affiliation:* Autoline, Inc. (engineering), Ford Foundation (business), California Wellness Foundation (health and human services), Irvine Foundation (administration).

California State University, Fresno (continued)

Computer facilities: 853 computers available on campus for general student use. A campuswide network can be accessed from off campus. Internet access, common applications are available. *Web address:* http://www.csufresno.edu/.

General Application Contact: Shirlee C. Fulton, Administrative Analyst/Specialist, 559-278-2448, Fax: 559-278-4658, E-mail: shirlee_fulton@csufresno.edu.

GRADUATE UNITS

Division of Graduate Studies Students: 1,032 full-time (661 women), 962 part-time (559 women). Average age 31. 1,135 applicants, 78% accepted, 499 enrolled. *Faculty:* 424 full-time (148 women), 34 part-time/adjunct (12 women). Expenses: Contact institution. *Financial support:* In 2001–02, 121 teaching assistantships (averaging $7,617 per year) were awarded; career-related internships or fieldwork, Federal Work-Study, scholarships/grants, traineeships, tuition waivers (partial), unspecified assistantships, and research awards, travel grants also available. Support available to part-time students. Financial award application deadline: 3/1; financial award applicants required to submit FAFSA. In 2001, 543 master's, 12 doctorates awarded. *Degree program information:* Part-time and evening/weekend programs available. Postbaccalaureate distance learning degree programs offered. Offers animal science (MA). *Application deadline:* Applications are processed on a rolling basis. *Application fee:* $55. Electronic applications accepted. *Application Contact:* Shirlee C. Fulton, Administrative Analyst/Specialist, 559-278-2448, Fax: 559-278-4658, E-mail: shirlee_fulton@csufresno.edu. *Dean,* Dr. Vivian A. Vidoli, 559-278-2448, Fax: 559-278-4658, E-mail: vivian_vidoli@csufresno.edu.

College of Agricultural Sciences and Technology Students: 29 full-time (13 women), 38 part-time (20 women); includes 17 minority (1 African American, 6 Asian Americans or Pacific Islanders, 9 Hispanic Americans, 1 Native American), 12 international. Average age 31. 46 applicants, 63% accepted, 16 enrolled. *Faculty:* 31 full-time (9 women). Expenses: Contact institution. *Financial support:* In 2001–02, 2 teaching assistantships (averaging $2,500 per year) were awarded; career-related internships or fieldwork, Federal Work-Study, and scholarships/grants also available. Support available to part-time students. Financial award application deadline: 3/1; financial award applicants required to submit FAFSA. In 2001, 10 degrees awarded. *Degree program information:* Part-time and evening/weekend programs available. Offers agricultural sciences and technology (MS); family and consumer sciences (MS); food science and nutritional sciences (MS); industrial technology (MS); plant science (MS). *Application deadline:* For fall admission, 6/1 (priority date); for spring admission, 11/1. Applications are processed on a rolling basis. *Application fee:* $55. Electronic applications accepted. *Dean,* Dr. Daniel P. Bartell, 559-278-2061, Fax: 559-278-4496, E-mail: daniel_bartell@csufresno.edu.

College of Arts and Humanities Students: 113 full-time (70 women), 116 part-time (72 women); includes 71 minority (4 African Americans, 9 Asian Americans or Pacific Islanders, 56 Hispanic Americans, 2 Native Americans), 23 international. Average age 31. 147 applicants, 75% accepted, 67 enrolled. *Faculty:* 99 full-time (42 women). Expenses: Contact institution. *Financial support:* In 2001–02, 50 teaching assistantships were awarded; career-related internships or fieldwork, Federal Work-Study, scholarships/grants, and unspecified assistantships also available. Support available to part-time students. Financial award application deadline: 3/1; financial award applicants required to submit FAFSA. In 2001, 63 degrees awarded. *Degree program information:* Part-time and evening/weekend programs available. Offers art (MA); arts and humanities (MA, MFA); communication (MA); composition theory (MA); creative writing (MFA); linguistics (MA); literature (MA); mass communication (MA); music (MA); music education (MA); nonfiction prose (MA); performance (MA); Spanish (MA). *Application deadline:* For fall admission, 8/1 (priority date); for spring admission, 12/1. Applications are processed on a rolling basis. *Application fee:* $55. Electronic applications accepted. *Dean,* Dr. Luis F. Costa, 559-278-3056, Fax: 559-278-6758, E-mail: luis_costa@csufresno.edu.

College of Engineering and Computer Science Students: 50 full-time (12 women), 76 part-time (10 women); includes 21 minority (2 African Americans, 15 Asian Americans or Pacific Islanders, 4 Hispanic Americans), 79 international. Average age 31. 194 applicants, 72% accepted, 52 enrolled. *Faculty:* 26 full-time (2 women). Expenses: Contact institution. *Financial support:* In 2001–02, 12 teaching assistantships were awarded; career-related internships or fieldwork, Federal Work-Study, scholarships/grants, and unspecified assistantships also available. Financial award application deadline: 3/1; financial award applicants required to submit FAFSA. In 2001, 24 degrees awarded. *Degree program information:* Part-time and evening/weekend programs available. Offers civil engineering (MS); computer science (MS); electrical engineering (MS); engineering and computer science (MS); mechanical engineering (MS). *Application deadline:* For fall admission, 8/1 (priority date); for spring admission, 12/1. Applications are processed on a rolling basis. *Application fee:* $55. Electronic applications accepted. *Application Contact:* Dr. Jesus Larralde-Muro, Graduate Program Coordinator, 559-278-2566, E-mail: jesus_larralde-muro@csufresno.edu. *Dean,* Dr. Karl Longley, 559-278-2500, Fax: 559-278-7071, E-mail: karl_longley@csufresno.edu.

College of Health and Human Services Students: 371 full-time (273 women), 175 part-time (119 women); includes 224 minority (25 African Americans, 55 Asian Americans or Pacific Islanders, 138 Hispanic Americans, 6 Native Americans), 9 international. Average age 31. 279 applicants, 81% accepted, 173 enrolled. *Faculty:* 65 full-time (30 women). Expenses: Contact institution. *Financial support:* In 2001–02, 14 teaching assistantships were awarded; career-related internships or fieldwork, Federal Work-Study, scholarships/grants, traineeships, and unspecified assistantships also available. Financial award application deadline: 3/1; financial award applicants required to submit FAFSA. In 2001, 193 degrees awarded. *Degree program information:* Part-time and evening/weekend programs available. Offers communicative disorders (MA); environmental/occupational health (MPH); exercise science (MA); health administration (MPH); health and human services (MA, MPH, MPT, MS, MSW); health promotion (MPH); nursing (MS); physical therapy (MPT); social work education (MSW). *Application deadline:* Applications are processed on a rolling basis. *Application fee:* $55. Electronic applications accepted. *Dean,* Benjamin Cuellar, 559-278-4004, Fax: 559-278-4437, E-mail: benjamin_cuellar@csufresno.edu.

College of Science and Mathematics Students: 64 full-time (43 women), 66 part-time (25 women); includes 34 minority (3 African Americans, 9 Asian Americans or Pacific Islanders, 19 Hispanic Americans, 3 Native Americans), 9 international. Average age 31. 58 applicants, 86% accepted, 23 enrolled. *Faculty:* 81 full-time (20 women). Expenses: Contact institution. *Financial support:* In 2001–02, 58 teaching assistantships were awarded; career-related internships or fieldwork, Federal Work-Study, scholarships/grants, and unspecified assistantships also available. Support available to part-time students. Financial award application deadline: 3/1; financial award applicants required to submit FAFSA. In 2001, 27 degrees awarded. *Degree program information:* Part-time and evening/weekend programs available. Offers biology (MA); chemistry (MS); geology (MS); marine sciences (MS); mathematics (MA); physics (MS); psychology (MA, MS); science and mathematics (MA, MS); teaching (MA). *Application deadline:* Applications are processed on a rolling basis. *Application fee:* $55. Electronic applications accepted. *Dean,* Dr. Kin-Ping Wong, 559-278-3936, Fax: 559-278-7139.

College of Social Sciences Students: 51 full-time (24 women), 77 part-time (32 women); includes 45 minority (7 African Americans, 3 Asian Americans or Pacific Islanders, 35 Hispanic Americans), 10 international. Average age 31. 62 applicants, 77% accepted, 28 enrolled. *Faculty:* 39 full-time (10 women). Expenses: Contact institution. *Financial support:* In 2001–02, 1 teaching assistantship (averaging $1,000 per year) was awarded; career-related internships or fieldwork, Federal Work-Study, scholarships/grants, and unspecified assistantships also available. Support available to part-time students. Financial award application deadline: 3/1; financial award applicants required to submit FAFSA. In 2001, 39 degrees awarded. *Degree program information:* Part-time and evening/weekend programs available. Offers criminology (MS); history (MA); international relations (MA); public administration (MPA); social sciences (MA, MPA, MS). *Application deadline:* For fall admission, 8/1 (priority date); for spring admission, 12/1. Applications are processed on a rolling basis. *Application fee:* $55. Electronic applications accepted. *Dean,* Dr. Ellen Gruenbaum, 559-278-3013, Fax: 559-278-7664, E-mail: ellen_gruenbaum@csufresno.edu.

School of Education and Human Development Students: 295 full-time (197 women), 341 part-time (255 women); includes 310 minority (29 African Americans, 67 Asian Americans or Pacific Islanders, 208 Hispanic Americans, 6 Native Americans), 8 international. Average age 31. 213 applicants, 87% accepted, 88 enrolled. *Faculty:* 57 full-time (28 women), 34 part-time/adjunct (12 women). Expenses: Contact institution. *Financial support:* Career-related internships or fieldwork, Federal Work-Study, scholarships/grants, and research awards, travel grants available. Support available to part-time students. Financial award application deadline: 3/1; financial award applicants required to submit FAFSA. In 2001, 179 master's, 9 doctorates awarded. *Degree program information:* Part-time and evening/weekend programs available. Offers counseling and student services (MS); education (MA); education and human development (MA, MS, Ed D); educational leadership (Ed D); marriage and family therapy (MS); rehabilitation counseling (MS); special education (MA). *Application deadline:* Applications are processed on a rolling basis. *Application fee:* $55. Electronic applications accepted. *Application Contact:* Dr. Robert Monke, Associate Dean, 559-278-0205, Fax: 559-278-6203, E-mail: robert_monke@csufresno.edu. *Dean,* Dr. Paul Shaker, 559-278-0210, Fax: 559-278-6203, E-mail: paul_shaker@csufresno.edu.

Sid Craig School of Business Students: 59 full-time (29 women), 73 part-time (26 women); includes 19 minority (5 Asian Americans or Pacific Islanders, 14 Hispanic Americans), 34 international. 137 applicants, 61% accepted, 37 enrolled. *Faculty:* 26 full-time (7 women). Expenses: Contact institution. *Financial support:* In 2001–02, 4 teaching assistantships were awarded; career-related internships or fieldwork, Federal Work-Study, scholarships/grants, and unspecified assistantships also available. Support available to part-time students. Financial award application deadline: 3/1; financial award applicants required to submit FAFSA. In 2001, 44 degrees awarded. *Degree program information:* Part-time programs available. Offers business (MBA); business administration (MBA). *Application deadline:* For fall admission, 6/1 (priority date); for spring admission, 10/1. Applications are processed on a rolling basis. *Application fee:* $55. Electronic applications accepted. *Application Contact:* Dr. Mark Keppler, Director, 559-278-2107, Fax: 559-278-4911, E-mail: mark_keppler@csufresno.edu. *Dean,* Dr. Fred Evans, 559-278-2485, Fax: 559-278-6931, E-mail: fred_evans@csufresno.edu.

CALIFORNIA STATE UNIVERSITY, FULLERTON, Fullerton, CA 92834-9480

General Information State-supported, coed, comprehensive institution. CGS member. *Enrollment:* 1,410 full-time matriculated graduate/professional students (842 women), 2,472 part-time matriculated graduate/professional students (1,566 women). *Enrollment by degree level:* 3,882 master's. *Graduate faculty:* 752 full-time, 1,136 part-time/adjunct. Tuition, nonresident: part-time $246 per unit. *Required fees:* $964. *Graduate housing:* Room and/or apartments available on a first-come, first-served basis to single students; on-campus housing not available to married students. Typical cost: $3,993 per year. *Student services:* Campus employment opportunities, campus safety program, career counseling, child daycare facilities, disabled student services, exercise/wellness program, free psychological counseling, international student services, low-cost health insurance, multicultural affairs office, teacher training, writing training. *Library facilities:* California State University, Fullerton Library. *Online resources:* library catalog, access to other libraries' catalogs. *Collection:* 654,790 titles, 2,455 serial subscriptions.

Computer facilities: 1,000 computers available on campus for general student use. A campuswide network can be accessed from student residence rooms and from off campus. Internet access is available. *Web address:* http://www.fullerton.edu/.

General Application Contact: Gladys M. Fleckles, Director, Graduate Studies, 714-278-2618.

GRADUATE UNITS

Graduate Studies Students: 1,410 full-time (842 women), 2,472 part-time (1,566 women); includes 1,218 minority (91 African Americans, 608 Asian Americans or Pacific Islanders, 494 Hispanic Americans, 25 Native Americans), 459 international. Average age 32. 3,178 applicants, 57% accepted, 1168 enrolled. *Faculty:* 752 full-time (293 women), 1,136 part-time/adjunct. Expenses: Contact institution. *Financial support:* Research assistantships, teaching assistantships, career-related internships or fieldwork, Federal Work-Study, institutionally sponsored loans, and scholarships/grants available. Support available to part-time students. Financial award application deadline: 3/1. In 2001, 1011 degrees awarded. *Degree program information:* Part-time and evening/weekend programs available. Offers interdisciplinary studies (MA). *Application deadline:* Applications are processed on a rolling basis. *Application fee:* $55. *Application Contact:* Gladys M. Fleckles, Director, 714-278-2618. *Acting Associate Vice President, Academic Programs,* Dr. Keith Boyum, 714-278-3602.

College of Business and Economics Students: 240 full-time (119 women), 277 part-time (112 women); includes 161 minority (8 African Americans, 123 Asian Americans or Pacific Islanders, 28 Hispanic Americans, 2 Native Americans), 166 international. Average age 30. 756 applicants, 40% accepted, 158 enrolled. *Faculty:* 139 full-time (31 women), 105 part-time/adjunct. Expenses: Contact institution. *Financial support:* Teaching assistantships, career-related internships or fieldwork, Federal Work-Study, institutionally sponsored loans, and scholarships/grants available. Support available to part-time students. Financial award application deadline: 3/1. In 2001, 221 degrees awarded. *Degree program information:* Part-time and evening/weekend programs available. Offers accounting (MBA, MS); business administration (MBA); business and economics (MA, MBA, MS); business economics (MBA); economics (MA); finance (MBA); international business (MBA); management (MBA); management information systems (MS); management science (MBA, MS); marketing (MBA); operations research (MS); statistics (MS); taxation (MS). *Application fee:* $55. *Application Contact:* Robert Miyake, Assistant Dean, 714-278-2211. *Dean,* Dr. Anil Puri, 714-773-2592.

College of Communications Students: 94 full-time (78 women), 86 part-time (57 women); includes 50 minority (5 African Americans, 20 Asian Americans or Pacific Islanders, 25 Hispanic Americans), 28 international. Average age 31. 279 applicants, 40% accepted, 57 enrolled. *Faculty:* 50 full-time (22 women), 91 part-time/adjunct. Expenses: Contact institution. *Financial support:* Teaching assistantships, career-related internships or fieldwork, Federal Work-Study, institutionally sponsored loans, and scholarships/grants available. Support available to part-time students. Financial award application deadline: 3/1. In 2001, 51 degrees awarded. *Degree program information:* Part-time programs available. Offers advertising (MA); communications (MA); communicative disorders (MA); journalism education (MA); news editorial (MA); photo communication (MA); public relations (MA); radio, television and film (MA); speech communication (MA); technical communication (MA); theory and process (MA). *Application fee:* $55. *Dean,* Dr. Rick Pullen, 714-278-3355.

College of Engineering and Computer Science Students: 211 full-time (57 women), 238 part-time (54 women); includes 195 minority (6 African Americans, 170 Asian Americans or Pacific Islanders, 19 Hispanic Americans), 166 international. Average age 31. 508 applicants, 59% accepted, 140 enrolled. *Faculty:* 45 full-time (7 women), 62 part-time/adjunct. Expenses: Contact institution. *Financial support:* Career-related internships or fieldwork, Federal Work-Study, institutionally sponsored loans, and scholarships/grants available. Support available to part-time students. Financial award application deadline: 3/1. In 2001, 73 degrees awarded. *Degree program information:* Part-time programs available. Offers applications administrative information systems (MS); applications mathematical methods (MS); civil engineering and engineering mechanics (MS); computer science (MS); electrical engineering (MS); engineering and computer science (MS); engineering science (MS); information processing systems (MS); mechanical engineering (MS); systems engineering (MS). *Application fee:* $55. *Application Contact:* Dr. David Falconer, Associate Dean, 714-278-3362. *Dean,* Dr. Raman Unnikrishnan, 714-278-3362.

College of Human Development and Community Service Students: 324 full-time (246 women), 961 part-time (815 women); includes 355 minority (26 African Americans, 104 Asian Americans or Pacific Islanders, 208 Hispanic Americans, 17 Native Americans), 11 international. Average age 34. 766 applicants, 67% accepted, 420 enrolled. *Faculty:* 136 full-time (101 women), 313 part-time/adjunct. Expenses: Contact institution. *Financial support:* Teaching assistantships, career-related internships or fieldwork, Federal Work-Study, institutionally sponsored loans, and scholarships/grants available. Support available to part-time students. Financial award application deadline: 3/1. In 2001, 328 degrees awarded. *Degree program information:* Part-time programs available. Offers bilingual/bicultural education (MS); counseling (MS); educational leadership (MS); elementary curriculum and instruction (MS); human development and community service (MS); nursing (MS); physical education (MS); reading (MS); special education (MS). *Application fee:* $55. *Acting Dean,* Dr. Roberta Rikli, 714-278-3311.

College of Humanities and Social Sciences Students: 299 full-time (194 women), 448 part-time (260 women); includes 222 minority (25 African Americans, 75 Asian Americans or Pacific Islanders, 121 Hispanic Americans, 1 Native American), 57 international. Average age 33. 578 applicants, 72% accepted, 269 enrolled. *Faculty:* 193 full-time (77 women), 246 part-time/adjunct. Expenses: Contact institution. *Financial support:* Teaching assistantships, career-related internships or fieldwork, Federal Work-Study, institutionally sponsored loans, and scholarships/grants available. Support available to part-time students. Financial award application deadline: 3/1. In 2001, 225 degrees awarded. *Degree program information:* Part-time programs available. Offers American studies (MA); analysis of specific language structures (MA); anthropological linguistics (MA); anthropology (MA); applied linguistics (MA); clinical/community psychology (MS); communication and semantics (MA); comparative literature (MA); disorders of communication (MA); English (MA); environmental education and communication (MS); environmental policy and planning (MS); environmental sciences (MS); experimental phonetics (MA); French (MA); geography (MA); German (MA); gerontology (MS); history (MA); humanities and social sciences (MA, MPA, MS); political science (MA); psychology (MA); public administration (MPA); social sciences (MA); sociology (MA); Spanish (MA); teaching English to speakers of other languages (MS); technological studies (MS). *Application fee:* $55. *Dean,* Dr. Thomas Klammer, 714-278-3256.

College of Natural Science and Mathematics Students: 52 full-time (29 women), 162 part-time (83 women); includes 71 minority (4 African Americans, 34 Asian Americans or Pacific Islanders, 33 Hispanic Americans), 11 international. Average age 31. 164 applicants, 69% accepted, 77 enrolled. *Faculty:* 85 full-time (20 women), 152 part-time/adjunct. Expenses: Contact institution. *Financial support:* Research assistantships, teaching assistantships, career-related internships or fieldwork, Federal Work-Study, institutionally sponsored loans, and scholarships/grants available. Support available to part-time students. Financial award application deadline: 3/1. In 2001, 62 degrees awarded. *Degree program information:* Part-time programs available. Offers analytical chemistry (MS); applied mathematics (MA); biochemistry (MS); biological science (MA); botany (MA); geochemistry (MS); geological sciences (MS); inorganic chemistry (MS); mathematics (MA); mathematics for secondary school teachers (MA); microbiology (MA); natural science and mathematics (MA, MS); organic chemistry (MS); physical chemistry (MS); physics (MA); teaching science (MA). *Application fee:* $55. *Dean,* Dr. Kolf Jayaweera, 714-278-2638.

College of the Arts Students: 88 full-time (46 women), 94 part-time (54 women); includes 45 minority (2 African Americans, 26 Asian Americans or Pacific Islanders, 15 Hispanic Americans, 2 Native Americans), 13 international. Average age 34. 127 applicants, 57% accepted, 47 enrolled. *Faculty:* 74 full-time (24 women), 160 part-time/adjunct. Expenses: Contact institution. *Financial support:* Teaching assistantships, career-related internships or fieldwork, Federal Work-Study, institutionally sponsored loans, and scholarships/grants available. Support available to part-time students. Financial award application deadline:3/1. In 2001, 49 degrees awarded. *Degree program information:* Part-time programs available. Offers acting (MFA); acting and directing (MA); art (MA, MFA); art history (MA); arts (MA, MFA, MM, Certificate); dance (MA); design (MA); directing (MFA); dramatic literature/criticism (MA); museum studies (Certificate); music education (MA); music history and literature (MA); oral interpretation (MA); performance (MM); playwriting (MA); technical theater (MA); technical theater and design (MFA); television (MA); theatre for children (MA); theatre history (MA); theory-composition (MM). *Application fee:* $55. *Dean,* Jerry Samuelson, 714-278-3256.

CALIFORNIA STATE UNIVERSITY, HAYWARD, Hayward, CA 94542-3000

General Information State-supported, coed, comprehensive institution. CGS member. *Enrollment:* 1,509 full-time matriculated graduate/professional students (1,012 women), 2,203 part-time matriculated graduate/professional students (1,353 women). *Enrollment by degree level:* 3,712 master's. *Graduate faculty:* 368. Tuition, nonresident: part-time $164 per unit. *Required fees:* $405 per semester. *Graduate housing:* Room and/or apartments available on a first-come, first-served basis to single students; on-campus housing not available to married students. Housing application deadline: 3/1. *Student services:* Campus employment opportunities, campus safety program, career counseling, child daycare facilities, disabled student services, free psychological counseling, international student services, low-cost health insurance. *Library facilities:* California State University, Hayward Library plus 1 other. *Online resources:* library catalog, web page, access to other libraries' catalogs. *Collection:* 908,577 titles, 2,210 serial subscriptions, 28,416 audiovisual materials. *Research affiliation:* Pacific Telesis (urban education), Academy of Economy, Moscow (business management training), NASA–Ames Research Center, Lawrence Livermore National Laboratory (technology transfer), Stanford University (complex learning), Sandia National Laboratories (technology marketing assessment).

Computer facilities: 700 computers available on campus for general student use. A campuswide network can be accessed from student residence rooms and from off campus. Internet access and online class registration are available. *Web address:* http://www.csuhayward.edu/.

General Application Contact: Jennifer Cason, Graduate Program Coordinator/Operations Analyst, 510-885-3286, Fax: 510-885-4777, E-mail: jcason@csuhayward.edu.

GRADUATE UNITS

Academic Programs and Graduate Studies Students: 1,509 full-time (1,012 women), 2,203 part-time (1,353 women); includes 1,085 minority (325 African Americans, 521 Asian Americans or Pacific Islanders, 222 Hispanic Americans, 17 Native Americans), 753 international. Average age 34. 2,242 applicants, 82% accepted. Expenses: Contact institution. *Financial support:* Fellowships, teaching assistantships, career-related internships or fieldwork, Federal Work-Study, institutionally sponsored loans, and scholarships/grants available. Support available to part-time students. Financial award application deadline: 3/1; financial award applicants required to submit FAFSA. In 2001, 1002 degrees awarded. *Degree program information:* Part-time and evening/weekend programs available. Offers interdisciplinary studies (MA, MS, Certificate). *Application deadline:* For fall admission, 6/15; for winter admission, 10/27; for spring admission, 1/7. Applications are processed on a rolling basis. *Application fee:* $55. Electronic applications accepted. *Application Contact:* Jennifer Cason, Graduate Program Coordinator/Operations Analyst, 510-885-3286, Fax: 510-885-4777, E-mail: jcason@csuhayward.edu. *Associate Vice President,* Dr. Carl Bellone, 510-885-3286, Fax: 510-885-4795, E-mail: cbellone@csuhayward.edu.

School of Arts, Letters, and Social Sciences Students: 143 full-time (111 women), 337 part-time (231 women); includes 156 minority (83 African Americans, 34 Asian Americans or Pacific Islanders, 36 Hispanic Americans, 3 Native Americans), 15 international. 296 applicants, 61% accepted. Expenses: Contact institution. *Financial support:* Fellowships, teaching assistantships, career-related internships or fieldwork, Federal Work-Study, institutionally sponsored loans, and scholarships/grants available. Support available to part-time students. Financial award application deadline: 3/1. In 2001, 159 degrees awarded. *Degree program information:* Part-time and evening/weekend programs available. Offers anthropology (MA); arts, letters, and social sciences (MA, MPA, MS); English (MA); geography (MA); history (MA); music (MA); public administration (MPA); sociology (MA); speech communication (MA); speech pathology (MS). *Application deadline:* For fall admission, 6/15; for winter admission, 10/27; for spring admission, 1/5. Applications are processed on a rolling basis. *Application fee:* $55. Electronic applications accepted. *Application Contact:* Jennifer Cason, Graduate Program Coordinator/Operations Analyst, 510-885-3286, Fax: 510-885-4777, E-mail: jcason@csuhayward.edu. *Interim Dean,* Dr. David Larson, 510-885-3161.

School of Business and Economics Students: 241 full-time (144 women), 493 part-time (234 women); includes 99 minority (31 African Americans, 46 Asian Americans or Pacific Islanders, 21 Hispanic Americans, 1 Native American), 279 international. 682 applicants, 54% accepted. Expenses: Contact institution. *Financial support:* Career-related internships or fieldwork, Federal Work-Study, and institutionally sponsored loans available. Support available to part-time students. Financial award application deadline: 3/1. In 2001, 401 degrees awarded. *Degree program information:* Part-time and evening/weekend programs available. Offers accounting (MBA); business and economics (MA, MBA, MS); computer information systems (MBA); e-business (MBA); economics (MA, MBA); finance (MBA); human resources management (MBA); international business (MBA); management sciences (MBA); marketing management (MBA); new ventures/small business management (MBA); operations research (MBA); quantitative business methods (MS); supply chain management (MBA); taxation (MBA, MS). *Application deadline:* For fall admission, 6/15; for winter admission, 10/27; for spring admission, 1/5. Applications are processed on a rolling basis. *Application fee:* $55. Electronic applications accepted. *Application Contact:* Dr. Donna L. Wiley, Director of Graduate Programs, 510-885-3964. *Dean,* Dr. Jay Tontz, 510-885-3291.

School of Education Students: 223 full-time (171 women), 322 part-time (260 women); includes 154 minority (47 African Americans, 44 Asian Americans or Pacific Islanders, 54 Hispanic Americans, 9 Native Americans), 9 international. 360 applicants, 70% accepted. Expenses: Contact institution. *Financial support:* Career-related internships or fieldwork, Federal Work-Study, and institutionally sponsored loans available. Support available to part-time students. Financial award application deadline: 3/1. In 2001, 257 degrees awarded. *Degree program information:* Part-time and evening/weekend programs available. Offers counseling (MS); education (MS); educational leadership (MS); physical education (MS); special education (MS); teacher education (MS). *Application deadline:* For fall admission, 6/15; for winter admission, 10/27; for spring admission, 1/5. *Application fee:* $55. Electronic applications accepted. *Application Contact:* Jennifer Cason, Graduate Program Coordinator/Operations Analyst, 510-885-3286, Fax: 510-885-4777, E-mail: jcason@csuhayward.edu. *Dean,* Dr. Arthurlene Towner, 510-885-3942.

School of Science Students: 222 full-time (133 women), 333 part-time (168 women); includes 132 minority (7 African Americans, 110 Asian Americans or Pacific Islanders, 14 Hispanic Americans, 1 Native American), 307 international. 393 applicants, 38% accepted. Expenses: Contact institution. *Financial support:* Career-related internships or fieldwork, Federal Work-Study, and institutionally sponsored loans available. Support available to part-time students. Financial award application deadline: 3/1. In 2001, 161 degrees awarded. *Degree program information:* Part-time and evening/weekend programs available. Offers biochemistry (MS); biological sciences (MS); chemistry (MS); computer science (MS); geology (MS); marine sciences (MS); mathematics (MS); science (MS); statistics (MS). *Application deadline:* For fall admission, 6/15; for winter admission, 10/27; for spring admission, 1/5. *Application fee:* $55. Electronic applications accepted. *Application Contact:* Jennifer Cason, Graduate Program Coordinator/Operations Analyst, 510-885-3286, Fax: 510-885-4777, E-mail: jcason@csuhayward.edu. *Dean,* Dr. Michael Leung, 510-885-3441.

Announcement: California State University, Hayward, has 37 professional and research-oriented master's degree programs that have strong contacts with industry, government, and education. These programs have a proven track record for placing graduates in new and better careers. Most programs are designed for working students and offer evening courses. Cal State, Hayward, is located in the center of the culturally rich San Francisco Bay Area. The campus has modern research facilities, including electronic library services and well-equipped science and computer labs. World Wide Web: http://www.csuhayward.edu/grad/grad.html.

CALIFORNIA STATE UNIVERSITY, LONG BEACH, Long Beach, CA 90840

General Information State-supported, coed, comprehensive institution. CGS member. *Enrollment:* 1,483 full-time matriculated graduate/professional students (968 women), 2,327 part-time matriculated graduate/professional students (1,319 women). *Enrollment by degree level:* 3,795 master's, 15 doctoral. *Graduate faculty:* 773 full-time (265 women), 894 part-time/adjunct (466 women). *Graduate housing:* Room and/or apartments available on a first-come, first-served basis to single students; on-campus housing not available to married students. Housing application deadline: 4/1. *Student services:* Campus employment opportunities, campus safety program, career counseling, child daycare facilities, disabled student services, exercise/wellness program, free psychological counseling, grant writing training, international student services, low-cost health insurance, multicultural affairs office, teacher training, writing training. *Library facilities:* University Library. *Online resources:* library catalog, web page, access to other libraries' catalogs. *Collection:* 781,111 titles, 5,424 serial subscriptions, 68,354 audiovisual materials. *Research affiliation:* Boeing Company (aerospace engineering and manufacturing).

Computer facilities: 2,000 computers available on campus for general student use. A campuswide network can be accessed from off campus. Internet access is available. *Web address:* http://www.csulb.edu/.

General Application Contact: Dr. Henry C. Fung, Associate Vice President for Academic Affairs for Graduate Studies, Research, and Community Service Outreach, 562-985-4128, Fax: 562-985-1680, E-mail: hcfung@csulb.edu.

GRADUATE UNITS

Graduate Studies Students: 1,483 full-time (968 women), 2,327 part-time (1,319 women); includes 1,416 minority (236 African Americans, 580 Asian Americans or Pacific Islanders, 571 Hispanic Americans, 29 Native Americans), 362 international. Average age 33. 3,299 applicants, 50% accepted. *Faculty:* 773 full-time (265 women), 894 part-time/adjunct (466 women). Expenses: Contact institution. *Financial support:* Fellowships, research assistantships, teaching assistantships, career-related internships or fieldwork, Federal Work-Study, institutionally sponsored loans, scholarships/grants, traineeships, tuition waivers (partial), and unspecified assistantships available. Financial award application deadline: 3/2; financial award applicants required to submit FAFSA. In 2001, 1,099 master's awarded. *Degree program information:* Part-time and evening/weekend programs available. Postbaccalaureate distance learning degree programs offered (no on-campus study). Offers interdisciplinary studies (MA, MS). *Application deadline:* Applications are processed on a rolling basis. *Application fee:* $55. Electronic applications accepted. *Dean,* Dr. Henry C. Fung, 562-985-4128, Fax: 562-985-1680, E-mail: hcfung@csulb.edu.

College of Business Administration Students: 67 full-time (34 women), 269 part-time (108 women); includes 87 minority (13 African Americans, 53 Asian Americans or Pacific Islanders, 18 Hispanic Americans, 3 Native Americans), 68 international. Average age 32. 446 applicants, 30% accepted. Expenses: Contact institution. *Financial support:* Career-related internships or fieldwork and scholarships/grants available. Financial award application deadline: 3/2; financial award applicants required to submit FAFSA. In 2001, 134 degrees awarded. *Degree program information:* Part-time and evening/weekend programs available. Offers business administration (MBA). *Application deadline:* For fall admission, 8/1; for spring admission, 12/1. Applications are processed on a rolling basis. *Application fee:* $55. Electronic applications accepted. *Application Contact:* Dr. Jack Gregg, Director, MBA Program, 562-985-1797, Fax: 562-985-5543, E-mail: jrgregg@csulb.edu. *Dean,* Dr. Luis Ma. R. Calingo, 562-985-5306, Fax: 562-985-5742, E-mail: lcalingo@csulb.edu.

College of Education Students: 160 full-time (120 women), 338 part-time (277 women); includes 200 minority (37 African Americans, 54 Asian Americans or Pacific Islanders, 106 Hispanic Americans, 3 Native Americans), 7 international. Average age 33. 434 applicants, 48% accepted. *Faculty:* 53 full-time, 63 part-time/adjunct. Expenses: Contact institution. *Financial support:* Federal Work-Study, institutionally sponsored loans, and scholarships/grants available. Financial award application deadline: 3/2. In 2001, 177 degrees awarded. *Degree program information:* Part-time and evening/weekend programs available. Offers counseling (MS, Certificate); education (MA, MS, Certificate); educational administration (MA); educational psychology (MA); elementary education (MA); secondary education (MA); social and multicultural foundations of education (MA); special education (MS). *Application deadline:* For fall admission, 8/1; for spring admission, 12/1. Applications are processed on a rolling basis. *Application fee:* $55. Electronic applications accepted. *Application Contact:* Dr. Kathleen Cohn, Associate Dean, 562-985-8477, Fax: 562-985-4951, E-mail: kcohn@csulb.edu. *Dean,* Dr. Jean Houck, 562-985-4513, Fax: 562-985-1774, E-mail: jhouck@csulb.edu.

College of Engineering Students: 153 full-time (36 women), 394 part-time (78 women); includes 227 minority (18 African Americans, 172 Asian Americans or Pacific Islanders, 37

California State University, Long Beach (continued)

Hispanic Americans), 150 international. Average age 32. 523 applicants, 37% accepted. *Faculty:* 83 full-time (7 women), 44 part-time/adjunct (3 women). Expenses: Contact institution. *Financial support:* Research assistantships, teaching assistantships, career-related internships or fieldwork, Federal Work-Study, institutionally sponsored loans, scholarships/grants, and unspecified assistantships available. Financial award application deadline: 3/2. In 2001, 135 degrees awarded. *Degree program information:* Part-time and evening/weekend programs available. Offers aerospace engineering (MSAE); civil engineering (MSCE, MSE, CE); computer engineering (MS); computer science (MS); electrical engineering (MSE, MSEE); engineering (MS, MSAE, MSCE, MSE, MSEE, MSME, PhD, CE); mechanical engineering (MSE, MSME). *Application deadline:* For fall admission, 8/1; for spring admission, 12/1. *Application fee:* $55. Electronic applications accepted. *Application Contact:* Dr. Mihir K. Das, Associate Dean for Instruction, 562-985-5257, Fax: 562-985-7561, E-mail: mdas@engr.csulb.edu. *Interim Dean,* Dr. Michael Mahoney, 562-985-5190, Fax: 562-985-7561, E-mail: mahoney@csulb.edu.

College of Health and Human Services Students: 754 full-time (569 women), 763 part-time (550 women); includes 655 minority (135 African Americans, 210 Asian Americans or Pacific Islanders, 296 Hispanic Americans, 14 Native Americans), 47 international. Average age 33. 1,130 applicants, 62% accepted. *Faculty:* 154 full-time, 115 part-time/adjunct. Expenses: Contact institution. *Financial support:* Fellowships, research assistantships, teaching assistantships, career-related internships or fieldwork, Federal Work-Study, institutionally sponsored loans, and scholarships/grants available. Financial award application deadline: 3/2; financial award applicants required to submit FAFSA. In 2001, 389 degrees awarded. *Degree program information:* Part-time and evening/weekend programs available. Postbaccalaureate distance learning degree programs offered (no on-campus study). Offers audiology (MA); community health education (MPH); criminal justice (MS); gerontology (MS); health and human services (MA, MPA, MPH, MPT, MS, MSW, Certificate); health care administration (MS, Certificate); health science (MS); home economics (MA); kinesiology and physical education (MA); nurse anesthesiology (MS); nursing (MS); nutritional sciences (MS); occupational studies (MA); physical therapy (MPT); public policy and administration (MPA, Certificate); recreation and leisure studies (MS); social work (MSW); speech pathology (MA). *Application deadline:* For fall admission, 8/1; for spring admission, 12/1. Applications are processed on a rolling basis. *Application fee:* $55. Electronic applications accepted. *Application Contact:* Dr. William A. Sinclair, Associate Dean, 562-985-4067, Fax: 562-985-7581, E-mail: sinclair@csulb.edu. *Dean,* Dr. Donald Lauda, 562-985-4691, Fax: 562-985-7581, E-mail: dlauda@csulb.edu.

College of Liberal Arts Students: 179 full-time (112 women), 309 part-time (190 women); includes 136 minority (13 African Americans, 37 Asian Americans or Pacific Islanders, 82 Hispanic Americans, 4 Native Americans), 45 international. Average age 33. 461 applicants, 55% accepted. *Faculty:* 167 full-time, 122 part-time/adjunct. Expenses: Contact institution. *Financial support:* Research assistantships, teaching assistantships, career-related internships or fieldwork, Federal Work-Study, institutionally sponsored loans, and scholarships/grants available. Financial award application deadline: 3/2. In 2001, 155 degrees awarded. *Degree program information:* Part-time and evening/weekend programs available. Offers anthropology (MA); Asian American studies (Certificate); Asian studies (MA); communication studies (MA); creative writing (MFA); economics (MA); English (MA); French (MA); geography (MA); German (MA); history (MA); liberal arts (MA, MFA, MS, Certificate); linguistics (MA); philosophy (MA); political science (MA); psychology (MA, MS); Spanish (MA). *Application deadline:* Applications are processed on a rolling basis. *Application fee:* $55. Electronic applications accepted. *Application Contact:* Dr. Frank Fata, Associate Dean, 562-985-5381, Fax: 562-985-2463, E-mail: ffata@csulb.edu. *Dean,* Dr. Dorothy Abrahamse, 562-985-5381, Fax: 562-985-2463, E-mail: dabraham@csulb.edu.

College of Natural Sciences Students: 49 full-time (26 women), 99 part-time (31 women); includes 48 minority (7 African Americans, 30 Asian Americans or Pacific Islanders, 9 Hispanic Americans, 2 Native Americans), 16 international. Average age 31. 153 applicants, 49% accepted. *Faculty:* 118 full-time, 94 part-time/adjunct. Expenses: Contact institution. *Financial support:* Research assistantships, teaching assistantships, Federal Work-Study, institutionally sponsored loans, scholarships/grants, traineeships, and unspecified assistantships available. Financial award application deadline: 3/2. In 2001, 47 degrees awarded. *Degree program information:* Part-time programs available. Offers applied mathematics (MA); biochemistry (MS); biological sciences (MS); chemistry (MS); geological sciences (MS); mathematics (MA); medical technology (MPH); metals physics (MS); microbiology (MPH, MS); natural sciences (MA, MPH, MS, Certificate); nurse epidemiology (MPH); physics (MS). *Application deadline:* For fall admission, 8/1; for spring admission, 12/1. Applications are processed on a rolling basis. *Application fee:* $55. Electronic applications accepted. *Application Contact:* Dr. Elizabeth Ambos, Associate Dean, 562-985-7898, Fax: 562-985-2315, E-mail: bambos@csulb.edu. *Dean,* Dr. Glenn Nagel, 562-985-4707, Fax: 562-985-2315, E-mail: gnagel@csulb.edu.

College of the Arts Students: 100 full-time (58 women), 94 part-time (60 women); includes 44 minority (6 African Americans, 20 Asian Americans or Pacific Islanders, 17 Hispanic Americans, 1 Native American), 21 international. Average age 36. 124 applicants, 41% accepted. *Faculty:* 94 full-time, 96 part-time/adjunct. Expenses: Contact institution. *Financial support:* Research assistantships, teaching assistantships, Federal Work-Study, institutionally sponsored loans, scholarships/grants, and traineeships available. Financial award application deadline: 3/2. In 2001, 45 degrees awarded. *Degree program information:* Part-time programs available. Offers art education (MA); art history (MA); arts (MA, MFA, MM); crafts (MA, MFA); dance (MFA); illustration (MA, MFA); music (MA, MM); pictorial arts (MA, MFA); theatre arts (MA, MFA). *Application deadline:* For fall admission, 8/1; for spring admission, 12/1. Applications are processed on a rolling basis. *Application fee:* $55. Electronic applications accepted. *Application Contact:* Dr. Donald Para, Interim Associate Dean, 562-985-4781, Fax: 562-985-2490, E-mail: dpara@csulb.edu. *Interim Dean,* Kristi Jones, 562-985-7885, Fax: 562-985-7883, E-mail: kjones@csulb.edu.

CALIFORNIA STATE UNIVERSITY, LOS ANGELES, Los Angeles, CA 90032-8530

General Information State-supported, coed, comprehensive institution. CGS member. *Enrollment:* 1,375 full-time matriculated graduate/professional students (936 women), 2,842 part-time matriculated graduate/professional students (1,807 women). *Graduate faculty:* 598 full-time (261 women), 557 part-time/adjunct (255 women). Tuition, nonresident: part-time $164 per unit. *Graduate housing:* Room and/or apartments available to single students; on-campus housing not available to married students. Typical cost: $3,268 per year. Housing application deadline: 7/19. *Student services:* Campus employment opportunities, career counseling, child daycare facilities, free psychological counseling, international student services. *Library facilities:* John K. Kennedy Memorial Library. *Online resources:* library catalog, web page. *Collection:* 1.7 million titles, 2,438 serial subscriptions, 4,309 audiovisual materials.

Computer facilities: 1,500 computers available on campus for general student use. A campuswide network can be accessed from off campus. Internet access is available. *Web address:* http://www.calstatela.edu/.

General Application Contact: Dr. Theodore Crovello, Dean of Graduate Studies, 323-343-3820.

GRADUATE UNITS

Graduate Studies Students: 1,375 full-time (936 women), 2,842 part-time (1,807 women); includes 2,534 minority (328 African Americans, 698 Asian Americans or Pacific Islanders, 1,487 Hispanic Americans, 21 Native Americans), 358 international. Average age 34. *Faculty:* 598 full-time (261 women), 557 part-time/adjunct (255 women). Expenses: Contact institution. *Financial support:* Fellowships, teaching assistantships, career-related internships or fieldwork and Federal Work-Study available. Support available to part-time students. Financial award application deadline: 3/1. In 2001, 860 degrees awarded. *Degree program information:* Part-time and evening/weekend programs available. Offers interdisciplinary studies (MA, MS). *Application deadline:* For fall admission, 6/30. Applications are processed on a rolling basis. *Application fee:* $55. *Dean,* Dr. Theodore Crovello, 323-343-3820.

Charter College of Education Students: 585 full-time (434 women), 1,169 part-time (851 women); includes 1,147 minority (133 African Americans, 252 Asian Americans or Pacific Islanders, 754 Hispanic Americans, 8 Native Americans), 55 international. *Faculty:* 74 full-time, 119 part-time/adjunct. Expenses: Contact institution. *Financial support:* Career-related internships or fieldwork and Federal Work-Study available. Support available to part-time students. Financial award application deadline: 3/1. In 2001, 327 degrees awarded. *Degree program information:* Part-time and evening/weekend programs available. Offers adult and continuing education (MA); applied behavior analysis (MS); community college counseling (MS); computer education (MA); counseling (MS); early childhood education for the handicapped (MA); education (MA, MS, PhD); education of handicapped adolescents and young adults (MA); education of the communication handicapped (MA); education of the learning handicapped (MA); education of the physically handicapped (MA); education of the severely handicapped (MA); education of the visually handicapped (MA); educational administration (MA); educational foundations and interdivisional studies (MA); elementary teaching (MA); gifted education (MA); instructional technology (MA); multicultural and multilingual special education (MA); orientation and mobility specialist for the blind (MA); psychological foundations (MA); reading (MA); rehabilitation counseling (MS); resource specialist (MA); school counseling and school psychology (MS); secondary teaching (MA); social foundations (MA); special education (PhD); special interests (MA); teaching English to speakers of other languages (MA). *Application deadline:* For fall admission, 6/30; for spring admission, 2/1. Applications are processed on a rolling basis. *Application fee:* $55. *Dean,* Dr. Allen Mori, 323-343-4300.

College of Arts and Letters Students: 174 full-time (106 women), 370 part-time (209 women); includes 263 minority (46 African Americans, 55 Asian Americans or Pacific Islanders, 161 Hispanic Americans, 1 Native American), 56 international. *Faculty:* 86 full-time, 190 part-time/adjunct. Expenses: Contact institution. *Financial support:* Career-related internships or fieldwork and Federal Work-Study available. Support available to part-time students. Financial award application deadline: 3/1. In 2001, 80 degrees awarded. *Degree program information:* Part-time and evening/weekend programs available. Offers art (MA); arts and letters (MA, MFA, MM); English (MA); fine arts (MFA); French (MA); music composition (MM); music education (MA); musicology (MA); performance (MM); philosophy (MA); Spanish (MA); speech communication (MA); theater arts (MA). *Application deadline:* For fall admission, 6/30; for spring admission, 2/1. Applications are processed on a rolling basis. *Application fee:* $55. *Dean,* Carl Selkin, 323-343-4001.

College of Business and Economics Students: 107 full-time (57 women), 296 part-time (161 women); includes 210 minority (26 African Americans, 125 Asian Americans or Pacific Islanders, 59 Hispanic Americans), 119 international. *Faculty:* 61 full-time, 71 part-time/adjunct. Expenses: Contact institution. *Financial support:* Fellowships, career-related internships or fieldwork and Federal Work-Study available. Support available to part-time students. Financial award application deadline: 3/1. In 2001, 172 degrees awarded. *Degree program information:* Part-time and evening/weekend programs available. Offers accountancy (MS); accounting (MBA); analytical quantitative economics (MA); business and economics (MA, MBA, MS); business economics (MA, MBA, MS); business information systems (MBA); economics (MA); finance and banking (MBA, MS); finance and law (MBA, MS); health care management (MS); information systems (MBA, MS); international business (MBA, MS); management (MBA, MS); management information systems (MS); marketing (MBA, MS); office management (MBA). *Application deadline:* For fall admission, 6/30; for spring admission, 11/30. Applications are processed on a rolling basis. *Application fee:* $55. *Dean,* Dr. Timothy Haight, 323-343-2800.

College of Engineering, Computer Science, and Technology Students: 53 full-time (13 women), 158 part-time (24 women); includes 101 minority (8 African Americans, 57 Asian Americans or Pacific Islanders, 35 Hispanic Americans, 1 Native American), 63 international. *Faculty:* 30 full-time, 28 part-time/adjunct. Expenses: Contact institution. *Financial support:* Federal Work-Study available. Support available to part-time students. Financial award application deadline: 3/1. In 2001, 57 degrees awarded. *Degree program information:* Part-time and evening/weekend programs available. Offers civil engineering (MS); electrical engineering (MS); engineering, computer science and technology (MA, MS); industrial and technical studies (MA); mechanical engineering (MS). *Application deadline:* For fall admission, 6/30; for spring admission, 2/1. Applications are processed on a rolling basis. *Application fee:* $55. *Dean,* Dr. Kuei-wu Tsai, 323-343-4500.

College of Health and Human Services Students: 265 full-time (223 women), 342 part-time (278 women); includes 373 minority (67 African Americans, 108 Asian Americans or Pacific Islanders, 193 Hispanic Americans, 5 Native Americans), 23 international. *Faculty:* 65 full-time, 116 part-time/adjunct. Expenses: Contact institution. *Financial support:* Career-related internships or fieldwork and Federal Work-Study available. Support available to part-time students. Financial award application deadline: 3/1. In 2001, 111 degrees awarded. *Degree program information:* Part-time and evening/weekend programs available. Offers child development (MA); communicative disorders (MA); criminal justice (MS); criminalistics (MS); health and human services (MA, MS, MSW); health science (MA); hearing (MA); home economics (MA); nursing (MS); nutritional science (MS); physical education (MA); social work (MSW); speech (MA). *Application deadline:* For fall admission, 6/30; for spring admission, 2/1. Applications are processed on a rolling basis. *Application fee:* $55. *Acting Dean,* Dr. Alfredo Gonzalez, 323-343-4600.

College of Natural and Social Sciences Students: 191 full-time (103 women), 505 part-time (282 women); includes 439 minority (47 African Americans, 101 Asian Americans or Pacific Islanders, 285 Hispanic Americans, 6 Native Americans), 42 international. *Faculty:* 141 full-time, 192 part-time/adjunct. Expenses: Contact institution. *Financial support:* Teaching assistantships, career-related internships or fieldwork and Federal Work-Study available. Support available to part-time students. Financial award application deadline: 3/1. In 2001, 113 degrees awarded. *Degree program information:* Part-time and evening/weekend programs available. Offers analytical chemistry (MS); anthropology (MA); biochemistry (MS); biology (MS); chemistry (MS); geography (MA); geological sciences (MS); history (MA); inorganic chemistry (MS); Latin American studies (MA); mathematics (MS); Mexican-American studies (MA); natural and social sciences (MA, MS); organic chemistry (MS); physical chemistry (MS); physics (MS); political science (MA); psychology (MA, MS); public administration (MS); sociology (MA). *Application deadline:* For fall admission, 6/30; for spring admission, 2/1. Applications are processed on a rolling basis. *Application fee:* $55. *Dean,* Dr. Desdemona Cardoza, 323-343-2000.

CALIFORNIA STATE UNIVERSITY, MONTEREY BAY, Seaside, CA 93955-8001

General Information State-supported, coed, comprehensive institution.

CALIFORNIA STATE UNIVERSITY, NORTHRIDGE, Northridge, CA 91330

General Information State-supported, coed, comprehensive institution. CGS member. *Enrollment:* 1,218 full-time matriculated graduate/professional students (845 women), 2,038 part-time matriculated graduate/professional students (1,303 women). *Enrollment by degree level:* 3,256 master's. *Graduate faculty:* 841 full-time, 905 part-time/adjunct. Tuition, nonresident: part-time $631 per semester. *Required fees:* $246 per unit. *Graduate housing:* Room and/or apartments available to single students; on-campus housing not available to married students. *Student services:* Campus employment opportunities, campus safety program, career counseling, child daycare facilities, disabled student services, free psychological counseling, international student services, low-cost health insurance. *Library facilities:* Oviatt Library. *Online resources:* library catalog. *Collection:* 1.2 million titles, 2,754 serial subscriptions. *Research affiliation:* Hughes Aircraft Corporation (engineering), Jet Propulsion Laboratory (engineering), Warner Center Institute (child care), Northridge Hospital (biology), Haagen Company (archaeology), California Institute of Technology (science).

Computer facilities: A campuswide network can be accessed from off campus. Internet access and online class registration are available. *Web address:* http://www.csun.edu/.

General Application Contact: Dr. Mack Johnson, Associate Vice President, 818-677-2138.

GRADUATE UNITS

Graduate Studies Students: 1,218 full-time (845 women), 2,038 part-time (1,303 women); includes 994 minority (189 African Americans, 308 Asian Americans or Pacific Islanders, 473 Hispanic Americans, 24 Native Americans), 202 international. Average age 35. 4,072 applicants, 86% accepted, 751 enrolled. *Faculty:* 841 full-time, 905 part-time/adjunct. Expenses: Contact institution. *Financial support:* Fellowships, research assistantships, teaching assistantships, career-related internships or fieldwork, Federal Work-Study, institutionally sponsored loans, scholarships/grants, tuition waivers (partial), and unspecified assistantships available. Support available to part-time students. Financial award applicants required to submit FAFSA. In 2001, 798 degrees awarded. *Degree program information:* Part-time and evening/weekend programs available. Offers interdisciplinary studies (MA, MS). *Application fee:* $55. *Application Contact:* 818-677-3755. *Associate Vice President,* Dr. Mack Johnson, 818-677-2138.

College of Arts, Media, and Communications Students: 84 full-time (54 women), 163 part-time (110 women); includes 59 minority (17 African Americans, 19 Asian Americans or Pacific Islanders, 21 Hispanic Americans, 2 Native Americans), 21 international. Average age 35. 244 applicants, 75% accepted, 71 enrolled. *Faculty:* 103 full-time, 163 part-time/adjunct. Expenses: Contact institution. *Financial support:* Teaching assistantships, career-related internships or fieldwork, Federal Work-Study, and unspecified assistantships available. Support available to part-time students. Financial award application deadline: 3/1. In 2001, 47 degrees awarded. *Degree program information:* Part-time and evening/weekend programs available. Offers art (MA, MFA); art history (MA); arts (MA, MFA); arts, media, and communications (MA, MFA, MM); composition (MM); mass communication (MA); music education (MA); music theory (MA); musicology (MA); news communication (MA); performance (MM); speech communication (MA); theater (MA). *Application deadline:* For fall admission, 11/30. *Application fee:* $55. *Interim Dean,* William P. Toutant, 818-677-2246.

College of Business Administration and Economics Students: 57 full-time (25 women), 171 part-time (62 women); includes 56 minority (8 African Americans, 34 Asian Americans or Pacific Islanders, 12 Hispanic Americans, 2 Native Americans), 20 international. Average age 33. 274 applicants, 50% accepted, 47 enrolled. *Faculty:* 119 full-time, 34 part-time/adjunct. Expenses: Contact institution. *Financial support:* Teaching assistantships, Federal Work-Study available. Support available to part-time students. Financial award application deadline: 3/1. In 2001, 70 degrees awarded. *Degree program information:* Part-time programs available. Offers administrative/office management (MBA); business administration (MBA); business administration and economics (MBA, MS); business education (MBA, MS); finance, real estate and insurance (MBA); management (MBA); management of information systems (MBA); management science (MBA); marketing (MBA); production and management systems analysis (MS). *Application deadline:* For fall admission, 11/30. *Application fee:* $55. *Application Contact:* Dr. Richard Moore, Director of Graduate Programs, 818-677-2467. *Dean,* Dr. William Hosek, 818-677-2455.

College of Education Students: 471 full-time (395 women), 967 part-time (771 women); includes 452 minority (82 African Americans, 83 Asian Americans or Pacific Islanders, 279 Hispanic Americans, 8 Native Americans), 21 international. Average age 37. 376 applicants, 85% accepted, 301 enrolled. *Faculty:* 86 full-time, 192 part-time/adjunct. Expenses: Contact institution. *Financial support:* Fellowships, career-related internships or fieldwork, Federal Work-Study, institutionally sponsored loans, scholarships/grants, and tuition waivers (partial) available. Support available to part-time students. Financial award application deadline:3/1. In 2001, 301 degrees awarded. *Degree program information:* Part-time and evening/weekend programs available. Offers administration and supervision (MA); counseling (MS); counseling and guidance (MS, MFCC); early childhood special education (MA); education (MA, MS, MFCC); education of the deaf and hard of hearing (MA); education of the gifted (MA); education of the learning handicapped (MA); education of the severely handicapped (MA); educational psychology and counseling (MA); educational therapy (MA); elementary education (MA); foundations (MA); genetic counseling (MS); marriage, family and child counseling (MFCC); secondary education (MA). *Application deadline:* For fall admission, 11/30. *Application fee:* $55. *Head,* Dr. Philip J. Rusche.

College of Engineering and Computer Science Students: 108 full-time (31 women), 207 part-time (30 women); includes 84 minority (3 African Americans, 58 Asian Americans or Pacific Islanders, 22 Hispanic Americans, 1 Native American), 100 international. Average age 33. 538 applicants, 42% accepted, 68 enrolled. *Faculty:* 59 full-time, 34 part-time/adjunct. Expenses: Contact institution. *Financial support:* Teaching assistantships, career-related internships or fieldwork and Federal Work-Study available. Support available to part-time students. Financial award application deadline: 3/1. In 2001, 72 degrees awarded. *Degree program information:* Part-time and evening/weekend programs available. Offers aerospace engineering (MS); applied engineering (MS); applied mechanics (MSE); biomedical engineering (MS); civil engineering (MS); communications/radar engineering (MS); computer science (MS); control engineering (MS); digital/computer engineering (MS); electronics engineering (MS); engineering and computer science (MS); engineering management (MS); industrial engineering (MS); machine design (MS); materials engineering (MS); mechanical engineering (MS); mechanics (MS); microwave/antenna engineering (MS); structural engineering (MS); thermofluids (MS). *Application deadline:* For fall admission, 11/30. *Application fee:* $55. *Interim Dean,* Dr. Laurence Caretto, 818-677-4501.

College of Health and Human Development Students: 290 full-time (211 women), 179 part-time (133 women); includes 149 minority (18 African Americans, 68 Asian Americans or Pacific Islanders, 56 Hispanic Americans, 7 Native Americans), 16 international. Average age 31. 316 applicants, 80% accepted, 128 enrolled. *Faculty:* 88 full-time, 118 part-time/adjunct. Expenses: Contact institution. *Financial support:* Teaching assistantships, career-related internships or fieldwork, Federal Work-Study, and institutionally sponsored loans available. Support available to part-time students. Financial award application deadline:3/1. In 2001, 154 degrees awarded. *Degree program information:* Part-time and evening/weekend programs available. Offers communicative disorders and sciences (MA); environmental health (MS); family environmental sciences (MS); health administration (MS); health and human development (MA, MPH, MS); health education (MPH, MS); health science (MS); kinesiology (MA); leisure studies and recreation (MS); physical therapy (MS); public health (MPH). *Application deadline:* For fall admission, 11/30. *Application fee:* $55. *Dean,* Dr. Ann Stutts, 818-677-3001.

College of Humanities Students: 47 full-time (32 women), 141 part-time (96 women); includes 61 minority (7 African Americans, 12 Asian Americans or Pacific Islanders, 40 Hispanic Americans, 2 Native Americans), 6 international. Average age 36. 114 applicants, 86% accepted, 39 enrolled. *Faculty:* 119 full-time, 137 part-time/adjunct. Expenses: Contact institution. *Financial support:* Teaching assistantships, Federal Work-Study available. Support available to part-time students. Financial award application deadline: 3/1. In 2001, 39 degrees awarded. *Degree program information:* Part-time and evening/weekend programs available. Offers Chicano studies (MA); English (MA); humanities (MA); linguistics (MA); Spanish (MA). *Application deadline:* For fall admission, 11/30. *Application fee:* $55. *Dean,* Dr. Jorge Garcia, 818-677-3301.

College of Science and Mathematics Students: 59 full-time (42 women), 91 part-time (36 women); includes 43 minority (5 African Americans, 21 Asian Americans or Pacific Islanders, 17 Hispanic Americans), 12 international. Average age 31. 138 applicants, 73% accepted, 36 enrolled. *Faculty:* 115 full-time, 74 part-time/adjunct. Expenses: Contact institution. *Financial support:* Research assistantships, teaching assistantships, Federal Work-Study, institutionally sponsored loans, tuition waivers (partial), and unspecified assistantships available. Support available to part-time students. Financial award applicants required to submit FAFSA. In 2001, 23 degrees awarded. *Degree program information:* Part-time and evening/weekend programs available. Offers biology (MS); chemistry (MS); genetic counseling (MS); geological sciences (MS); mathematics (MS); physics (MS); science and mathematics (MS). *Application fee:* $55. *Interim Dean,* Dr. Edward J. Carroll, 818-677-2004.

College of Social and Behavioral Sciences Students: 97 full-time (51 women), 109 part-time (58 women); includes 47 minority (8 African Americans, 12 Asian Americans or Pacific Islanders, 25 Hispanic Americans, 2 Native Americans), 6 international. Average age 34. 261 applicants, 74% accepted, 53 enrolled. *Faculty:* 124 full-time, 114 part-time/adjunct. Expenses: Contact institution. *Financial support:* Teaching assistantships, career-related internships or fieldwork, Federal Work-Study, and institutionally sponsored loans available. Support available to part-time students. Financial award application deadline: 3/1. In 2001, 130 degrees awarded. *Degree program information:* Part-time and evening/weekend programs available. Offers anthropology (MA); geography (MA); history (MA); political science (MA); psychology (MA); public administration (MPA); social and behavioral sciences (MA, MPA); sociology (MA). *Application deadline:* For fall admission, 11/30. *Application fee:* $55. *Interim Dean,* Dr. Stella Z. Theodoulou, 818-677-3317.

CALIFORNIA STATE UNIVERSITY, SACRAMENTO, Sacramento, CA 95819-6048

General Information State-supported, coed, comprehensive institution. CGS member. *Enrollment:* 2,209 full-time matriculated graduate/professional students (1,567 women), 2,316 part-time matriculated graduate/professional students (1,506 women). *Enrollment by degree level:* 4,522 master's, 3 doctoral. *Graduate faculty:* 399 full-time, 222 part-time/adjunct. Tuition, state resident: full-time $1,965; part-time $668 per semester. Tuition, nonresident: part-time $246 per unit. *Graduate housing:* Room and/or apartments available on a first-come, first-served basis to single students; on-campus housing not available to married students. *Student services:* Campus employment opportunities, career counseling, child daycare facilities, disabled student services, free psychological counseling, grant writing training, international student services, low-cost health insurance, multicultural affairs office, teacher training, writing training. *Library facilities:* California State University, Sacramento Library. *Online resources:* library catalog, web page, access to other libraries' catalogs. *Collection:* 770,779 titles, 4,040 serial subscriptions, 152,128 audiovisual materials.

Computer facilities: 700 computers available on campus for general student use. A campuswide network can be accessed from student residence rooms and from off campus. Internet access and online class registration are available. *Web address:* http://www.csus.edu/.

General Application Contact: Vivian Llamas-Green, Coordinator of Graduate Admissions, 916-278-6470, Fax: 916-278-5669.

GRADUATE UNITS

Graduate Studies Students: 2,209 full-time (1,567 women), 2,316 part-time (1,506 women); includes 1,098 minority (208 African Americans, 374 Asian Americans or Pacific Islanders, 475 Hispanic Americans, 41 Native Americans), 289 international. Average age 34. *Faculty:* 399 full-time, 222 part-time/adjunct. Expenses: Contact institution. *Financial support:* Research assistantships, teaching assistantships, career-related internships or fieldwork and Federal Work-Study available. Support available to part-time students. Financial award application deadline: 3/1. *Degree program information:* Part-time and evening/weekend programs available. Offers special majors (MA, MS). *Application deadline:* For fall admission, 4/15; for spring admission, 11/1. *Application fee:* $55. *Application Contact:* Vivian Llamas-Green, Coordinator of Graduate Admissions, 916-278-6470, Fax: 916-278-5669. *Associate Dean,* Dr. Miki Vohryzek-Bolden, 916-248-6402.

College of Arts and Letters Students: 140 full-time (91 women), 271 part-time (175 women); includes 81 minority (15 African Americans, 20 Asian Americans or Pacific Islanders, 45 Hispanic Americans, 1 Native American), 5 international. Expenses: Contact institution. *Financial support:* Research assistantships, teaching assistantships, career-related internships or fieldwork and Federal Work-Study available. Support available to part-time students. Financial award application deadline: 3/1. *Degree program information:* Part-time and evening/weekend programs available. Offers arts and letters (MA, MM); communication studies (MA); creative writing (MA); foreign languages (MA); French (MA); German (MA); music (MM); public history (MA); Spanish (MA); studio art (MA); teaching English to speakers of other languages (MA); theater arts (MA); theatre and dance (MA). *Application deadline:* For fall admission, 4/15; for spring admission, 11/1. *Application fee:* $55. *Dean,* Dr. William J. Sullivan, 916-278-6502, Fax: 916-278-4588.

College of Business Administration Students: 106 full-time (51 women), 223 part-time (97 women); includes 66 minority (5 African Americans, 44 Asian Americans or Pacific Islanders, 17 Hispanic Americans), 64 international. Expenses: Contact institution. *Financial support:* Research assistantships, teaching assistantships, career-related internships or fieldwork and Federal Work-Study available. Support available to part-time students. Financial award application deadline: 3/1. *Degree program information:* Part-time and evening/weekend programs available. Offers accountancy (MS); business administration (MBA); human resources (MBA); management information science (MS); urban land development (MBA). *Application deadline:* For fall admission, 4/15; for spring admission, 11/1. *Application fee:* $55. *Application Contact:* Dr. Herbert Blake, Graduate Coordinator, 916-278-6772. *Dean,* Dr. Fel Ramey, 916-278-6578.

College of Education Students: 1,226 full-time (959 women), 1,061 part-time (817 women); includes 577 minority (100 African Americans, 185 Asian Americans or Pacific Islanders, 265 Hispanic Americans, 27 Native Americans), 12 international. Expenses: Contact institution. *Financial support:* Research assistantships, teaching assistantships, career-related internships or fieldwork and Federal Work-Study available. Support available to part-time students. Financial award application deadline: 3/1. *Degree program information:* Part-time programs available. Offers bilingual/cross-cultural education (MA); career counseling (MS); curriculum and instruction (MA); early childhood education (MA); education (MA, MS); educational administration (MA); generic counseling (MS); guidance (MA); reading education (MA); school counseling (MS); school psychology (MS); special education (MA); vocational rehabilitation (MS). *Application deadline:* For fall admission, 4/15; for spring admission, 11/1. *Application fee:* $55. *Dean,* Dr. Catherine Emihovich, 916-278-6639.

College of Engineering and Computer Science Students: 178 full-time (32 women), 183 part-time (33 women); includes 64 minority (3 African Americans, 51 Asian Americans or Pacific Islanders, 9 Hispanic Americans, 1 Native American), 184 international. Expenses: Contact institution. *Financial support:* Research assistantships, teaching assistantships, career-related internships or fieldwork and Federal Work-Study available. Support available to part-time students. Financial award application deadline: 3/1. *Degree program information:* Part-time and evening/weekend programs available. Offers civil engineering (MS); computer systems (MS); electrical engineering (MS); engineering and computer science (MS); mechanical engineering (MS); software engineering (MS). *Application deadline:* For fall admission, 4/15; for spring admission, 11/1. *Application fee:* $55. *Dean,* Dr. Braja Das, 916-278-6366.

College of Health and Human Services Students: 437 full-time (355 women), 320 part-time (240 women); includes 222 minority (65 African Americans, 45 Asian Americans or Pacific Islanders, 102 Hispanic Americans, 10 Native Americans), 6 international. Expenses: Contact institution. *Financial support:* Research assistantships, teaching assistantships, career-related internships or fieldwork and Federal Work-Study available. Support available to part-time students. Financial award application deadline: 3/1. *Degree program information:* Part-time programs available. Offers audiology (MS); criminal justice (MS); family and children's services (MSW); health and human services (MS, MSW); health care (MSW); mental health (MSW); nursing (MS); physical education (MS); recreation administration (MS); social justice and corrections (MSW); speech pathology (MS). *Application deadline:* For fall admission, 4/15; for spring admission, 11/1. *Application fee:* $55. *Dean,* Dr. Marilyn Hopkins, 916-278-7255.

College of Natural Sciences and Mathematics Students: 24 full-time (11 women), 60 part-time (24 women); includes 20 minority (1 African American, 10 Asian Americans or Pacific Islanders, 9 Hispanic Americans), 7 international. Expenses: Contact institution. *Financial support:* Research assistantships, teaching assistantships, career-related internships or fieldwork and Federal Work-Study available. Support available to part-time students. Financial award application deadline: 3/1. *Degree program information:* Part-time programs available. Offers biological sciences (MA, MS); chemistry (MS); immunohematology (MS); marine science (MS); mathematics and statistics (MA); natural sciences and mathematics (MA, MS). *Application deadline:* For fall admission, 4/15; for spring admission, 11/1. *Application fee:* $55. *Dean,* Marion O'Leary, 916-278-4655, Fax: 916-278-5787.

College of Social Sciences and Interdisciplinary Studies Students: 95 full-time (66 women), 183 part-time (110 women); includes 66 minority (19 African Americans, 19 Asian Americans or Pacific Islanders, 26 Hispanic Americans, 2 Native Americans), 11 international. Expenses:

California State University, Sacramento (continued)

Contact institution. *Financial support:* Teaching assistantships, career-related internships or fieldwork and Federal Work-Study available. Support available to part-time students. Financial award application deadline: 3/1. *Degree program information:* Part-time programs available. Offers anthropology (MA); counseling psychology (MA); government (MA); international affairs (MA); public policy and administration (MPPA); social sciences (MA, MPPA); sociology (MA). *Application deadline:* For fall admission, 4/15; for spring admission, 11/1. *Application fee:* $55. *Dean,* Joseph F. Sheley, 916-278-6504, Fax: 916-278-4678.

CALIFORNIA STATE UNIVERSITY, SAN BERNARDINO, San Bernardino, CA 92407-2397

General Information State-supported, coed, comprehensive institution. CGS member. *Enrollment:* 1,552 full-time matriculated graduate/professional students (1,004 women), 895 part-time matriculated graduate/professional students (557 women). *Enrollment by degree level:* 2,447 master's. *Graduate faculty:* 341. Tuition, nonresident: full-time $4,428. *Required fees:* $1,733. *Graduate housing:* Room and/or apartments available on a first-come, first-served basis to single students; on-campus housing not available to married students. Typical cost: $3,555 per year ($4,783 including board). Housing application deadline: 8/1. *Student services:* Campus employment opportunities, campus safety program, career counseling, child daycare facilities, disabled student services, free psychological counseling, international student services, multicultural affairs office. *Library facilities:* Pfau Library. *Collection:* 466,000 titles, 2,350 serial subscriptions.

Computer facilities: 1,300 computers available on campus for general student use. A campuswide network can be accessed from student residence rooms and from off campus. Internet access is available. *Web address:* http://www.csusb.edu/.

General Application Contact: Alan Liebrecht, Director of Admissions, 909-880-5188, Fax: 909-880-7034, E-mail: aliebrec@csusb.edu.

GRADUATE UNITS

Graduate Studies Students: 1,552 full-time (1,004 women), 895 part-time (557 women); includes 760 minority (200 African Americans, 110 Asian Americans or Pacific Islanders, 421 Hispanic Americans, 29 Native Americans), 298 international. Average age 35. 1,533 applicants, 69% accepted. *Faculty:* 341. Expenses: Contact institution. *Financial support:* Fellowships, research assistantships, teaching assistantships, career-related internships or fieldwork, Federal Work-Study, and institutionally sponsored loans available. Support available to part-time students. In 2001, 748 degrees awarded. *Degree program information:* Part-time and evening/weekend programs available. Offers interdisciplinary studies (MA). *Application fee:* $55. *Application Contact:* Alan Liebrecht, Director of Admissions, 909-880-5188, Fax: 909-880-7034, E-mail: aliebrec@csusb.edu. *Chair,* Dr. Sandra Kamusikiri, 909-880-5058, Fax: 909-880-7028, E-mail: skamusik@csusb.edu.

College of Arts and Letters Students: 64 full-time (41 women), 66 part-time (48 women); includes 41 minority (11 African Americans, 5 Asian Americans or Pacific Islanders, 24 Hispanic Americans, 1 Native American), 5 international. Average age 37. 113 applicants, 82% accepted. *Faculty:* 14 full-time (6 women), 1 (woman) part-time/adjunct. Expenses: Contact institution. *Financial support:* Research assistantships, teaching assistantships, career-related internships or fieldwork, Federal Work-Study, institutionally sponsored loans, and writing center tutorships available. Support available to part-time students. Financial award application deadline: 3/1. In 2001, 15 degrees awarded. *Degree program information:* Part-time and evening/weekend programs available. Offers art (MA); arts and letters (MA); communication studies (MA); English composition (MA). *Application deadline:* For fall admission, 8/31 (priority date). *Application fee:* $55. *Dean,* Dr. Eri F. Yasuhara, 909-880-5800, Fax: 909-880-5926, E-mail: eyasuha@csusb.edu.

College of Business and Public Administration Students: 317 full-time (152 women), 124 part-time (53 women); includes 100 minority (30 African Americans, 24 Asian Americans or Pacific Islanders, 43 Hispanic Americans, 3 Native Americans), 168 international. Average age 32. 418 applicants, 62% accepted. *Faculty:* 31 full-time (3 women), 5 part-time/adjunct (0 women). Expenses: Contact institution. *Financial support:* Career-related internships or fieldwork, Federal Work-Study, and institutionally sponsored loans available. Support available to part-time students. Financial award application deadline: 3/1. In 2001, 136 degrees awarded. *Degree program information:* Part-time and evening/weekend programs available. Offers business administration (MBA); business and public administration (MBA, MPA); public administration (MPA). *Application deadline:* For fall admission, 8/31 (priority date). Applications are processed on a rolling basis. *Application fee:* $55. *Dean,* Dr. Gordon Patzer, 909-880-5700, Fax: 909-880-7026, E-mail: gpatzer@csusb.edu.

College of Education Students: 742 full-time (525 women), 510 part-time (353 women); includes 390 minority (97 African Americans, 27 Asian Americans or Pacific Islanders, 247 Hispanic Americans, 19 Native Americans), 20 international. Average age 36. 537 applicants, 86% accepted. *Faculty:* 77 full-time (38 women). Expenses: Contact institution. *Financial support:* Career-related internships or fieldwork and Federal Work-Study available. Support available to part-time students. In 2001, 434 degrees awarded. *Degree program information:* Part-time and evening/weekend programs available. Offers bilingual/cross-cultural education (MA); educational administration (MA); educational psychology and counseling (MA, MS); elementary education (MA); English as a second language (MA); environmental education (MA); history and English for secondary teachers (MA); instructional technology (MA); reading (MA); rehabilitation counseling (MA); secondary education (MA); special education (MA); special education and rehabilitation counseling (MA); vocational education (MA). *Application deadline:* For fall admission, 8/31 (priority date). *Application fee:* $55. *Dean,* Dr. Patricia Arlin, 909-880-5600, Fax: 909-880-7011, E-mail: parlin@csusb.edu.

College of Natural Sciences Students: 132 full-time (69 women), 96 part-time (38 women); includes 70 minority (16 African Americans, 33 Asian Americans or Pacific Islanders, 17 Hispanic Americans, 4 Native Americans), 79 international. Average age 33. 169 applicants, 62% accepted. Expenses: Contact institution. *Financial support:* Fellowships, research assistantships, teaching assistantships, career-related internships or fieldwork and Federal Work-Study available. In 2001, 29 degrees awarded. *Degree program information:* Part-time programs available. Offers biology (MS); computer science (MS); health services administration (MS); mathematics (MA); natural sciences (MA, MAT, MS); nursing (MS); teaching of science (MAT). *Application fee:* $55. *Dean,* Dr. B. Robert Carlson, 909-880-5300, Fax: 909-880-7005, E-mail: carlson@csusb.edu.

College of Social and Behavioral Sciences Students: 266 full-time (199 women), 72 part-time (49 women); includes 138 minority (39 African Americans, 16 Asian Americans or Pacific Islanders, 81 Hispanic Americans, 2 Native Americans), 11 international. Average age 34. 296 applicants, 48% accepted. *Faculty:* 91 full-time (46 women), 4 part-time/adjunct (1 woman). Expenses: Contact institution. *Financial support:* Fellowships, research assistantships, teaching assistantships, career-related internships or fieldwork, Federal Work-Study, institutionally sponsored loans, and unspecified assistantships available. Support available to part-time students. In 2001, 117 degrees awarded. *Degree program information:* Part-time and evening/weekend programs available. Offers child development (MA); clinical/counseling psychology (MS); criminal justice (MA); general/experimental psychology (MA); industrial organizational psychology (MS); national security studies (MA); social and behavioral sciences (MA, MS, MSW); social sciences (MA); social work (MSW). *Application fee:* $55. *Chair,* Dr. John Conley, 909-880-5500, Fax: 909-880-7107, E-mail: jconley@csubs.edu.

CALIFORNIA STATE UNIVERSITY, SAN MARCOS, San Marcos, CA 92096-0001

General Information State-supported, coed, comprehensive institution. *Enrollment:* 156 full-time matriculated graduate/professional students (87 women), 303 part-time matriculated graduate/professional students (217 women). *Graduate faculty:* 194 full-time, 204 part-time/adjunct. Tuition, state resident: part-time $567 per semester. Tuition, nonresident: part-time $813 per semester. *Graduate housing:* On-campus housing not available. *Student services:* Campus employment opportunities, campus safety program, career counseling, disabled student services, free psychological counseling, international student services, low-cost health insurance, writing training. *Library facilities:* Library and Information Services. *Online resources:* library catalog, web page, access to other libraries' catalogs. *Collection:* 147,784 titles, 2,138 serial subscriptions, 7,888 audiovisual materials.

Computer facilities: 487 computers available on campus for general student use. A campuswide network can be accessed from student residence rooms and from off campus. Internet access and online class registration are available. *Web address:* http://ww2.csusm.edu/.

General Application Contact: Admissions, 760-750-4848, Fax: 760-750-3248.

GRADUATE UNITS

College of Arts and Sciences Students: 50 full-time (37 women), 81 part-time (52 women); includes 34 minority (2 African Americans, 12 Asian Americans or Pacific Islanders, 19 Hispanic Americans, 1 Native American), 15 international. 119 applicants, 41% accepted. *Faculty:* 64 full-time (31 women), 2 part-time/adjunct (1 woman). Expenses: Contact institution. *Financial support:* In 2001–02, 1 fellowship, 11 research assistantships, 8 teaching assistantships with tuition reimbursements were awarded. Career-related internships or fieldwork, Federal Work-Study, institutionally sponsored loans, scholarships/grants, traineeships, and unspecified assistantships also available. Support available to part-time students. *Degree program information:* Part-time and evening/weekend programs available. Offers arts and sciences (MA, MS); biological sciences (MS); computer science (MS); literature and writing studies (MA); mathematics (MS); psychology (MA); sociological practice (MA); Spanish (MA). *Application fee:* $55. *Acting Dean,* Miriam Schustack, 760-750-4200.

College of Business Administration Students: 103 full-time (39 women), 21 part-time (7 women); includes 27 minority (1 African American, 14 Asian Americans or Pacific Islanders, 12 Hispanic Americans), 5 international. Average age 33. 132 applicants, 53% accepted. *Faculty:* 21 full-time (5 women), 7 part-time/adjunct (3 women). Expenses: Contact institution. *Financial support:* In 2001–02, 35 students received support, including 1 research assistantship; teaching assistantships, Federal Work-Study also available. Support available to part-time students. Financial award applicants required to submit FAFSA. In 2001, 51 degrees awarded. *Degree program information:* Evening/weekend programs available. Offers business management (MBA); government management (MBA). *Application deadline:* For fall admission, 5/15 (priority date). Applications are processed on a rolling basis. *Application fee:* $55. *Dean, City of Business Administration,* Mohamed Moustafa, 760-750-4241.

College of Education Students: 11 full-time (6 women), 187 part-time (148 women); includes 46 minority (4 African Americans, 6 Asian Americans or Pacific Islanders, 34 Hispanic Americans, 2 Native Americans), 1 international. Average age 37. 120 applicants, 69% accepted. *Faculty:* 9 full-time (4 women), 9 part-time/adjunct (4 women). Expenses: Contact institution. *Financial support:* Fellowships, teaching assistantships, career-related internships or fieldwork and Federal Work-Study available. Support available to part-time students. Financial award applicants required to submit FAFSA. In 2001, 15 degrees awarded. *Degree program information:* Part-time and evening/weekend programs available. Offers education (MA). *Application deadline:* For spring admission, 4/1 (priority date). Applications are processed on a rolling basis. *Application fee:* $55. *Application Contact:* Beverly Mahdavi, Graduate Admissions Coordinator, 760-750-4281, Fax: 760-750-3538, E-mail: bmahdavi@csusm.edu. *Dean,* Dr. Steve Lilly, 760-750-4311, Fax: 760-750-4323, E-mail: steve_lilly@csusm.edu.

CALIFORNIA STATE UNIVERSITY, STANISLAUS, Turlock, CA 95382

General Information State-supported, coed, comprehensive institution. CGS member. *Enrollment:* 576 matriculated graduate/professional students (386 women). *Enrollment by degree level:* 576 master's. *Graduate faculty:* 78. Tuition, nonresident: part-time $246 per unit. *Required fees:* $1,919. Tuition and fees vary according to campus/location and program. *Graduate housing:* Room and/or apartments available to single students; on-campus housing not available to married students. Typical cost: $5,000 per year ($7,500 including board). Room and board charges vary according to board plan and housing facility selected. *Student services:* Campus employment opportunities, campus safety program, career counseling, child daycare facilities, disabled student services, exercise/wellness program, free psychological counseling, international student services, low-cost health insurance, teacher training. *Library facilities:* Vasche Library. *Online resources:* library catalog, web page, access to other libraries' catalogs. *Collection:* 338,736 titles, 1,984 serial subscriptions, 4,077 audiovisual materials.

Computer facilities: 150 computers available on campus for general student use. A campuswide network can be accessed from student residence rooms and from off campus. Internet access is available. *Web address:* http://www.csustan.edu/.

General Application Contact: Dr. James Burns, Director, The Graduate School, 209-667-3129, Fax: 209-664-7025, E-mail: jburns@csustan.edu.

GRADUATE UNITS

Graduate Programs Students: 576 (386 women); includes 156 minority (21 African Americans, 41 Asian Americans or Pacific Islanders, 85 Hispanic Americans, 9 Native Americans) Average age 35. 405 applicants, 91% accepted. *Faculty:* 78. Expenses: Contact institution. *Financial support:* In 2001–02, 19 fellowships (averaging $2,500 per year) were awarded; career-related internships or fieldwork, Federal Work-Study, and scholarships/grants also available. Support available to part-time students. Financial award application deadline: 3/2; financial award applicants required to submit FAFSA. In 2001, 188 degrees awarded. *Degree program information:* Part-time and evening/weekend programs available. Offers interdisciplinary studies (MA, MS). *Application fee:* $55. Electronic applications accepted. *Application Contact:* Dr. James Burns, Director, The Graduate School, 209-667-3129, Fax: 209-664-7025, E-mail: jburns@csustan.edu. *Dean, The Graduate School,* Dr. Diana Demetrulias, 209-667-3082, E-mail: ddemetrulias@csustan.edu.

College of Arts, Letters, and Sciences Students: 288 (189 women); includes 83 minority (14 African Americans, 18 Asian Americans or Pacific Islanders, 45 Hispanic Americans, 6 Native Americans) 233 applicants, 92% accepted. Expenses: Contact institution. *Financial support:* In 2001–02, 19 fellowships (averaging $2,500 per year) were awarded; research assistantships, teaching assistantships, career-related internships or fieldwork, Federal Work-Study, and scholarships/grants also available. Support available to part-time students. Financial award application deadline: 3/2. In 2001, 115 degrees awarded. *Degree program information:* Part-time and evening/weekend programs available. Offers arts, letters, and sciences (MA, MPA, MS, MSW); behavior analysis psychology (MS); counseling psychology (MS); criminal justice (MA); English (MA); general psychology (MA); history (MA); international relations (MA); marine science (MS); public administration (MPA); secondary school history teaching (MA); social work (MSW); teaching English to speakers of other languages (MA). *Application fee:* $55. Electronic applications accepted. *Dean,* Dr. Mary P. Cullinan, 209-667-3531.

College of Business Administration Students: 104 (44 women); includes 17 minority (3 African Americans, 10 Asian Americans or Pacific Islanders, 3 Hispanic Americans, 1 Native American) 65 applicants, 78% accepted. Expenses: Contact institution. *Financial support:* In 2001–02, 2 fellowships (averaging $2,800 per year) were awarded; Federal Work-Study also available. Financial award application deadline: 3/2; financial award applicants required to submit FAFSA. In 2001, 30 degrees awarded. *Degree program information:* Part-time and evening/weekend programs available. Offers business administration (MBA). *Application fee:* $55. *Application Contact:* Dr. Randall Brown, Director, 209-667-3064, Fax: 209-667-3080. *Dean,* Dr. Amin Elmallah, 209-667-3936, Fax: 209-667-3080, E-mail: AElmallah@csustan.edu.

College of Education Students: 226 (185 women); includes 64 minority (2 African Americans, 19 Asian Americans or Pacific Islanders, 42 Hispanic Americans, 1 Native American) 107 applicants, 94% accepted. *Faculty:* 34 full-time (18 women), 3 part-time/adjunct (2 women). Expenses: Contact institution. *Financial support:* In 2001–02, 7 fellowships (averaging $2,000 per year) were awarded; career-related internships or fieldwork and Federal Work-Study also available. Financial award application deadline: 3/2; financial award applicants required to submit FAFSA. In 2001, 43 degrees awarded. *Degree program information:* Part-time and evening/weekend programs available. Offers curriculum and instruction

(MA Ed); education (MA Ed); educational administration (MA Ed); educational technology (MA Ed); elementary education (MA Ed); multilingual education (MA Ed); physical education (MA Ed); reading education (MA Ed); school counseling (MA Ed); secondary education (MA Ed); special education (MA Ed). *Application fee:* $55. *Dean,* Dr. Irma Guzman Wagner, 209-667-3145, Fax: 209-664-7062.

CALIFORNIA UNIVERSITY OF PENNSYLVANIA, California, PA 15419-1394

General Information State-supported, coed, comprehensive institution. CGS member. *Enrollment:* 324 full-time matriculated graduate/professional students (206 women), 548 part-time matriculated graduate/professional students (357 women). *Enrollment by degree level:* 872 master's. *Graduate faculty:* 12 full-time (6 women), 77 part-time/adjunct (28 women). Tuition, state resident: full-time $4,600. Tuition, nonresident: full-time $7,554. *Graduate housing:* Room and/or apartments available to single students; on-campus housing not available to married students. *Student services:* Campus employment opportunities, campus safety program, career counseling, child daycare facilities, disabled student services, exercise/wellness program, free psychological counseling, grant writing training, international student services, low-cost health insurance, teacher training, writing training. *Library facilities:* Manderino Library. *Online resources:* library catalog, web page, access to other libraries' catalogs. *Collection:* 437,160 titles, 881 serial subscriptions, 59,703 audiovisual materials.

Computer facilities: 720 computers available on campus for general student use. A campuswide network can be accessed from student residence rooms and from off campus. Internet access is available. *Web address:* http://www.cup.edu/.

General Application Contact: Dr. Thomas G. Kinsey, Dean of Graduate Studies, 724-938-4187, Fax: 724-938-5712, E-mail: kinsey@cup.edu.

GRADUATE UNITS

School of Graduate Studies Students: 324 full-time (206 women), 548 part-time (357 women); includes 42 minority (21 African Americans, 18 Asian Americans or Pacific Islanders, 3 Hispanic Americans) *Faculty:* 12 full-time (6 women), 77 part-time/adjunct (28 women). Expenses: Contact institution. *Financial support:* Career-related internships or fieldwork, tuition waivers (full), and unspecified assistantships available. Financial award applicants required to submit FAFSA. In 2001, 270 degrees awarded. *Degree program information:* Part-time and evening/weekend programs available. Offers technology management (MSBA). *Application deadline:* Applications are processed on a rolling basis. *Application fee:* $25. *Dean,* Dr. Thomas G. Kinsey, 724-938-4187, Fax: 724-938-5712, E-mail: kinsey@cup.edu.

School of Education Students: 192 full-time (134 women), 402 part-time (285 women); includes 13 minority (11 African Americans, 1 Asian American or Pacific Islander, 1 Hispanic American) *Faculty:* 10 full-time (6 women), 38 part-time/adjunct (18 women). Expenses: Contact institution. *Financial support:* Career-related internships or fieldwork, tuition waivers (full), and unspecified assistantships available. *Degree program information:* Part-time and evening/weekend programs available. Offers athletic training (MS); communication disorders (MS); education (M Ed, MAT, MS, MSW); educational administration (M Ed); educational studies (MAT); elementary education (M Ed); guidance and counseling (M Ed, MS); mentally and/or physically handicapped education (M Ed); reading specialist (M Ed); reading specialist and reading supervision (M Ed); school psychology (MS); social work (MSW); technology education (M Ed). *Application deadline:* Applications are processed on a rolling basis. *Application fee:* $25. *Dean,* Geraldine Jones, 724-938-4125, E-mail: jones_gm@cup.edu.

School of Liberal Arts Students: 60 full-time (40 women), 33 part-time (16 women); includes 5 minority (4 African Americans, 1 Hispanic American) *Faculty:* 14 part-time/adjunct (5 women). Expenses: Contact institution. *Financial support:* Tuition waivers (full) and unspecified assistantships available. *Degree program information:* Part-time and evening/weekend programs available. Offers communication (MA); earth science (MS); geography (M Ed, MA); liberal arts (M Ed, MA, MS); social science (MA). *Application deadline:* Applications are processed on a rolling basis. *Application fee:* $25. *Acting Dean,* Dr. Richard Helldobler, 724-938-4240, E-mail: helldobler@cup.edu.

School of Science and Technology Students: 88 full-time (39 women), 66 part-time (28 women); includes 23 minority (5 African Americans, 17 Asian Americans or Pacific Islanders, 1 Hispanic American) *Faculty:* 26 part-time/adjunct (6 women). Expenses: Contact institution. *Financial support:* Career-related internships or fieldwork, tuition waivers (full), and unspecified assistantships available. *Degree program information:* Part-time and evening/weekend programs available. Offers biology (M Ed, MS); business administration (MS); computer science (M Ed); mathematics (M Ed); multimedia technology (MS); science and technology (M Ed, MS). *Application deadline:* Applications are processed on a rolling basis. *Application fee:* $25. *Dean,* Dr. Leonard Colelli, 724-938-4169, E-mail: colelli@cup.edu.

CALIFORNIA WESTERN SCHOOL OF LAW, San Diego, CA 92101-3090

General Information Independent, coed, graduate-only institution. *Enrollment by degree level:* 763 first professional. *Graduate faculty:* 33 full-time (13 women), 25 part-time/adjunct (9 women). *Tuition:* Full-time $24,750; part-time $870 per credit hour. *Required fees:* $70; $70 per year. *Graduate housing:* On-campus housing not available. *Student services:* Campus employment opportunities, career counseling, low-cost health insurance. *Library facilities:* California Western School of Law Library plus 1 other. *Online resources:* library catalog, web page. *Collection:* 287,445 titles, 3,867 serial subscriptions, 1,753 audiovisual materials.

Computer facilities: 69 computers available on campus for general student use. A campuswide network can be accessed from off campus. Internet access is available. *Web address:* http://www.californiawestern.edu/.

General Application Contact: Traci D. Howard, Director of Admissions, 619-525-1401, Fax: 619-615-1404, E-mail: tdh@cwsl.edu.

GRADUATE UNITS

Graduate and Professional Programs Students: 657 full-time (358 women), 106 part-time (58 women); includes 182 minority (25 African Americans, 70 Asian Americans or Pacific Islanders, 75 Hispanic Americans, 12 Native Americans), 16 international. Average age 30. 1,650 applicants, 66% accepted, 301 enrolled. *Faculty:* 33 full-time (13 women), 25 part-time/adjunct (9 women). Expenses: Contact institution. *Financial support:* Career-related internships or fieldwork, Federal Work-Study, institutionally sponsored loans, and scholarships/grants available. Support available to part-time students. Financial award application deadline: 3/16; financial award applicants required to submit FAFSA. In 2001, 214 degrees awarded. *Degree program information:* Part-time programs available. Offers law (JD, LL M). *Application deadline:* For fall admission, 4/1; for spring admission, 11/1. Applications are processed on a rolling basis. *Application fee:* $45. Electronic applications accepted. *Application Contact:* Traci D. Howard, Director of Admissions, 619-525-1401, Fax: 619-615-1404, E-mail: tdh@cwsl.edu. *Dean,* Steven R. Smith, 619-239-0391, Fax: 619-685-2916.

CALVARY BIBLE COLLEGE AND THEOLOGICAL SEMINARY, Kansas City, MO 64147-1341

General Information Independent-religious, coed, comprehensive institution. *Graduate housing:* Rooms and/or apartments available to single and married students.

GRADUATE UNITS

Graduate Studies *Degree program information:* Part-time and evening/weekend programs available. Offers Bible (MS); biblical and theological studies (MA, Th D); biblical counseling (MS, D Min); pastoral studies (M Div, D Min); theology (M Div).

CALVIN COLLEGE, Grand Rapids, MI 49546-4388

General Information Independent-religious, coed, comprehensive institution. *Enrollment:* 8 full-time matriculated graduate/professional students (6 women), 60 part-time matriculated graduate/professional students (48 women). *Enrollment by degree level:* 68 master's. *Graduate faculty:* 2 full-time (both women), 3 part-time/adjunct (2 women). *Tuition:* Full-time $7,140; part-time $340 per semester hour. *Graduate housing:* Room and/or apartments available on a first-come, first-served basis to single students; on-campus housing not available to married students. Typical cost: $5,485 (including board). Housing application deadline: 6/1. *Student services:* Campus employment opportunities, campus safety program, career counseling, disabled student services, exercise/wellness program, free psychological counseling, international student services, low-cost health insurance, multicultural affairs office. *Library facilities:* Hekman Library. *Online resources:* library catalog, web page. *Collection:* 700,000 titles, 2,660 serial subscriptions, 21,260 audiovisual materials.

Computer facilities: 659 computers available on campus for general student use. A campuswide network can be accessed from student residence rooms and from off campus. Internet access and online class registration are available. *Web address:* http://www.calvin.edu/.

General Application Contact: Karen Mahoney, Administrative Assistant, 616-957-6105, Fax: 616-957-6505, E-mail: kmahny@calvin.edu.

GRADUATE UNITS

Graduate Programs in Education Students: 8 full-time (6 women), 60 part-time (48 women); includes 2 minority (1 African American, 1 Asian American or Pacific Islander), 8 international. 9 applicants, 100% accepted, 6 enrolled. *Faculty:* 2 full-time (both women), 3 part-time/adjunct (2 women). Expenses: Contact institution. *Financial support:* In 2001–02, 9 students received support. Federal Work-Study, scholarships/grants, and tuition waivers (full and partial) available. Support available to part-time students. Financial award application deadline: 3/15. In 2001, 14 degrees awarded. *Degree program information:* Part-time programs available. Offers curriculum and instruction (M Ed); learning disabilities (M Ed). *Application deadline:* For fall admission, 8/1 (priority date); for spring admission, 1/1 (priority date). Applications are processed on a rolling basis. *Application fee:* $0. Electronic applications accepted. *Application Contact:* Karen Mahoney, Administrative Assistant, 616-957-6105, Fax: 616-957-6505, E-mail: kmahny@calvin.edu. *Director of Graduate Studies,* Dr. Shirley J. Roels, 616-957-6557, Fax: 616-957-6756, E-mail: roel@calvin.edu.

CALVIN THEOLOGICAL SEMINARY, Grand Rapids, MI 49546-4387

General Information Independent-religious, coed, graduate-only institution. *Enrollment by degree level:* 30 doctoral. *Graduate faculty:* 21 full-time (1 woman), 25 part-time/adjunct (0 women). *Tuition:* Full-time $9,020; part-time $170 per quarter hour. Tuition and fees vary according to degree level and program. *Graduate housing:* Rooms and/or apartments available on a first-come, first-served basis to single and married students. Housing application deadline: 4/1. *Student services:* Campus employment opportunities, campus safety program, career counseling, free psychological counseling, international student services, low-cost health insurance. *Library facilities:* Hekman Library. *Online resources:* library catalog, web page, access to other libraries' catalogs. *Collection:* 704,650 titles, 2,674 serial subscriptions, 20,113 audiovisual materials.

Computer facilities: 30 computers available on campus for general student use. A campuswide network can be accessed. Internet access is available. *Web address:* http://www.calvin.edu/seminary/.

General Application Contact: David DeBoer, Director of Recruitment and Financial Aid, 616-957-7035, Fax: 616-957-8621, E-mail: ddeboer@calvin.edu.

GRADUATE UNITS

Graduate and Professional Programs Students: 200 full-time (37 women), 74 part-time (25 women); includes 14 minority (2 African Americans, 9 Asian Americans or Pacific Islanders, 3 Hispanic Americans), 96 international. Average age 30. 150 applicants, 86% accepted, 88 enrolled. *Faculty:* 21 full-time (1 woman), 25 part-time/adjunct (0 women). Expenses: Contact institution. *Financial support:* In 2001–02, 5 fellowships with full tuition reimbursements (averaging $7,100 per year), 6 teaching assistantships with full tuition reimbursements (averaging $4,600 per year) were awarded. Career-related internships or fieldwork, institutionally sponsored loans, and tuition waivers (full and partial) also available. Financial award application deadline: 6/1. In 2001, 26 first professional degrees, 20 master's, 1 doctorate awarded. *Degree program information:* Part-time programs available. Offers divinity (M Div); educational ministry (MA); historical theology (PhD); missions: church growth (MA); philosophical and moral theology (PhD); systematic theology (PhD); theological studies (MTS); theology (Th M). *Application deadline:* For fall admission, 3/1 (priority date). Applications are processed on a rolling basis. *Application fee:* $25. *Application Contact:* David DeBoer, Director of Recruitment and Financial Aid, 616-957-7035, Fax: 616-957-8621, E-mail: ddeboer@calvin.edu. *Head,* Dr. Cornelius Plantinga, 616-957-6024, Fax: 616-957-8621, E-mail: plan@calvin.edu.

CAMBRIDGE COLLEGE, Cambridge, MA 02138-5304

General Information Independent, coed, comprehensive institution. *Graduate housing:* On-campus housing not available.

GRADUATE UNITS

Graduate Studies *Degree program information:* Part-time and evening/weekend programs available. Offers counseling psychology (M Ed); e-commerce (M Mgt); education/integrated studies (M Ed); management (M Mgt).

See in-depth description on page 779.

CAMERON UNIVERSITY, Lawton, OK 73505-6377

General Information State-supported, coed, comprehensive institution. CGS member. *Enrollment:* 128 full-time matriculated graduate/professional students (82 women), 358 part-time matriculated graduate/professional students (227 women). *Enrollment by degree level:* 486 master's. *Graduate faculty:* 51 full-time (23 women), 33 part-time/adjunct (14 women). Tuition, state resident: full-time $1,512; part-time $84 per credit hour. Tuition, nonresident: full-time $3,474; part-time $193 per credit hour. One-time fee: $15 part-time. Tuition and fees vary according to course load. *Graduate housing:* Room and/or apartments available on a first-come, first-served basis to single students; on-campus housing not available to married students. Typical cost: $4,050 (including board). Room and board charges vary according to board plan. *Student services:* Campus employment opportunities, campus safety program, child daycare facilities, disabled student services, exercise/wellness program, grant writing training, international student services, multicultural affairs office, teacher training, writing training. *Library facilities:* Cameron University Library. *Collection:* 258,000 titles, 3,840 serial subscriptions, 7,053 audiovisual materials. *Research affiliation:* U.S. Army–Field Artillery School (simulations).

Computer facilities: 350 computers available on campus for general student use. A campuswide network can be accessed. *Web address:* http://www.cameron.edu/.

General Application Contact: Suzanne Cartwright, School of Graduate Studies Admissions Coordinator, 580-581-2987, Fax: 580-581-5532, E-mail: suzannec@cameron.edu.

GRADUATE UNITS

School of Graduate Studies Students: 128 full-time (82 women), 358 part-time (227 women); includes 139 minority (73 African Americans, 14 Asian Americans or Pacific Islanders, 27 Hispanic Americans, 25 Native Americans), 15 international. Average age 36. 208 applicants, 90% accepted. *Faculty:* 51 full-time (23 women), 33 part-time/adjunct (14 women). Expenses: Contact institution. *Financial support:* In 2001–02, 6 research assistantships (averaging $3,600 per year) were awarded; career-related internships or fieldwork, Federal Work-Study, scholarships/grants, and tuition waivers (partial) also available. Support available to part-time students. Financial award application deadline: 4/15; financial award applicants required to submit FAFSA. In 2001, 168 degrees awarded. *Degree program information:* Part-time and evening/weekend programs available. Offers behavioral sciences (MS); business administration (MBA); education (M Ed); teaching (MAT). *Application deadline:* Applications are processed on a rolling basis. *Application fee:* $15. Electronic applications accepted. *Application Contact:* Suzanne Cartwright, School of Graduate Studies Admissions Coordinator, 580-581-2987, Fax: 580-581-5532, E-mail: suzannec@cameron.edu. *Dean,* Dr. Lloyd Dawe, 580-581-2987, Fax: 580-581-5532, E-mail: lloydd@cameron.edu.

CAMPBELLSVILLE UNIVERSITY, Campbellsville, KY 42718-2799

General Information Independent-religious, coed, comprehensive institution. *Enrollment:* 17 full-time matriculated graduate/professional students (6 women), 130 part-time matriculated graduate/professional students (70 women). *Enrollment by degree level:* 147 master's. *Graduate faculty:* 25 full-time (5 women), 9 part-time/adjunct (0 women). *Tuition:* Full-time $5,520; part-time $345 per credit. *Required fees:* $90. *Graduate housing:* Rooms and/or apartments available on a first-come, first-served basis to single and married students. Typical cost: $4,740 (including board) for single students. Housing application deadline: 6/30. *Student services:* Campus safety program, career counseling, exercise/wellness program, international student services, teacher training. *Library facilities:* Montgomery Library plus 2 others. *Online resources:* web page. *Collection:* 110,000 titles, 25,000 serial subscriptions, 8,000 audiovisual materials.

Computer facilities: 120 computers available on campus for general student use. Internet access is available. *Web address:* http://www.campbellsvil.edu/.

General Application Contact: Trent Argo, Director of Admissions, 270-789-5220, Fax: 270-789-5071, E-mail: targo@cambellsvil.edu.

GRADUATE UNITS

College of Arts and Sciences Students: 2 full-time (1 woman), 9 part-time (8 women). 7 applicants, 100% accepted, 7 enrolled. *Faculty:* 7 full-time (3 women), 1 part-time/adjunct (0 women). Expenses: Contact institution. *Financial support:* In 2001–02, fellowships with full tuition reimbursements (averaging $1,500 per year); unspecified assistantships also available. Financial award applicants required to submit FAFSA. *Degree program information:* Part-time programs available. *Application deadline:* Applications are processed on a rolling basis. *Application fee:* $25. Electronic applications accepted. *Application Contact:* Trent Argo, Director of Admissions, 270-789-5220, Fax: 270-789-5071, E-mail: targo@cambellsvil.edu. *Head,* Dr. Mary Wilgus.

School of Business Administration Students: 8 full-time (2 women), 28 part-time (16 women); includes 1 minority (African American), 10 international. 9 applicants, 89% accepted, 6 enrolled. *Faculty:* 6 full-time (1 woman). Expenses: Contact institution. *Financial support:* Unspecified assistantships available. *Degree program information:* Part-time and evening/weekend programs available. Offers business administration (MBA). *Application deadline:* For fall admission, 9/15 (priority date); for winter admission, 1/8 (priority date); for spring admission, 3/26 (priority date). Applications are processed on a rolling basis. *Application fee:* $25. *Application Contact:* Jay Barnett, Associate Director of Admissions, 270-789-5251, Fax: 270-789-5050, E-mail: jbarnett@campbellsvil.edu. *MBA Director,* Dr. Barry Griffin, 270-789-5317, Fax: 270-789-5050, E-mail: bgriffin@admin.campbellsvil.edu.

School of Education 5 applicants, 100% accepted, 5 enrolled. *Faculty:* 3 full-time (1 woman), 1 part-time/adjunct (0 women). Expenses: Contact institution. *Financial support:* Institutionally sponsored loans available. Support available to part-time students. In 2001, 15 degrees awarded. *Degree program information:* Part-time programs available. Offers education (MA Ed). *Application deadline:* Applications are processed on a rolling basis. *Application fee:* $0. *Application Contact:* Trent Argo, Director of Admissions, 270-789-5220, Fax: 270-789-5071, E-mail: targo@cambellsvil.edu. *Dean,* Dr. James E. Pirkle, 270-789-5344, Fax: 270-789-5550, E-mail: jprikle@campbellsvil.edu.

School of Music Students: 3 full-time (2 women), 47 part-time (26 women); includes 35 minority (all Hispanic Americans), 6 international. 42 applicants, 100% accepted, 38 enrolled. *Faculty:* 7 full-time (1 woman), 1 part-time/adjunct (0 women). Expenses: Contact institution. *Financial support:* In 2001–02, 8 students received support, including 1 teaching assistantship with full tuition reimbursement available (averaging $4,000 per year); institutionally sponsored loans and scholarships/grants also available. Support available to part-time students. Financial award applicants required to submit FAFSA. In 2001, 4 degrees awarded. *Degree program information:* Part-time programs available. Offers church music (MM); music (MA, MM Ed); music education (MM). *Application deadline:* Applications are processed on a rolling basis. *Application fee:* $0. Electronic applications accepted. *Application Contact:* Trent Argo, Director of Admissions, 270-789-5220, Fax: 270-789-5071, E-mail: targo@cambellsvil.edu. *Dean,* Dr. J. Robert Gaddis, 270-789-5269, Fax: 270-789-5524, E-mail: gaddisjr@campbellsvil.edu.

School of Theology Students: 4 full-time (1 woman), 29 part-time (5 women); includes 1 minority (Asian American or Pacific Islander), 4 international. Average age 37. 14 applicants, 100% accepted, 11 enrolled. *Faculty:* 5 full-time (0 women), 7 part-time/adjunct (0 women). Expenses: Contact institution. *Financial support:* In 2001–02, 16 students received support. Scholarships/grants available. In 2001, 4 degrees awarded. *Degree program information:* Part-time programs available. Offers Christian studies (MA); theology (M Th). *Application deadline:* For fall admission, 8/25 (priority date); for spring admission, 1/25. Applications are processed on a rolling basis. *Application fee:* $25 ($0 for international students). Electronic applications accepted. *Application Contact:* Trent Argo, Director of Admissions, 270-789-5220, Fax: 270-789-5071, E-mail: targo@cambellsvil.edu. *Dean,* Dr. Walter C. Jackson, 270-789-5541, E-mail: wjackson@campbellsvil.edu.

CAMPBELL UNIVERSITY, Buies Creek, NC 27506

General Information Independent-religious, coed, university. *Enrollment:* 867 full-time matriculated graduate/professional students (493 women), 542 part-time matriculated graduate/professional students (330 women). *Enrollment by degree level:* 881 first professional, 528 master's. *Graduate faculty:* 97 full-time (26 women), 28 part-time/adjunct (8 women). *Tuition:* Part-time $290 per semester hour. *Graduate housing:* Rooms and/or apartments available on a first-come, first-served basis to single students and available to married students. Typical cost: $2,500 per year for single students; $3,900 per year for married students. Housing application deadline: 6/2. *Student services:* Campus employment opportunities, campus safety program, career counseling, disabled student services, exercise/wellness program, international student services, low-cost health insurance. *Library facilities:* Carrie Rich Memorial Library plus 3 others. *Online resources:* library catalog, web page, access to other libraries' catalogs. *Collection:* 196,000 titles, 6,700 serial subscriptions, 3,500 audiovisual materials.

Computer facilities: 250 computers available on campus for general student use. A campuswide network can be accessed. Internet access is available. *Web address:* http://www.campbell.edu/.

General Application Contact: James S. Farthing, Director of Graduate Admissions, 910-893-1200 Ext. 1318, Fax: 910-893-1288, E-mail: farthing@mailcenter.campbell.edu.

GRADUATE UNITS

Graduate and Professional Programs Students: 867 full-time (493 women), 542 part-time (330 women); includes 114 minority (87 African Americans, 17 Hispanic Americans, 10 Native Americans), 52 international. Average age 28. 232 applicants, 71% accepted, 135 enrolled. *Faculty:* 97 full-time (26 women), 28 part-time/adjunct (8 women). Expenses: Contact institution. *Financial support:* In 2001–02, 430 students received support, including 5 fellowships (averaging $400 per year), 5 teaching assistantships (averaging $2,000 per year); research assistantships, career-related internships or fieldwork, Federal Work-Study, institutionally sponsored loans, and tuition waivers (partial) also available. Support available to part-time students. Financial award application deadline: 4/15; financial award applicants required to submit FAFSA. In 2001, 200 first professional degrees, 130 master's awarded. *Degree program information:* Part-time and evening/weekend programs available. *Application deadline:* Applications are processed on a rolling basis. *Application fee:* $25. *Application Contact:* James S. Farthing, Director of Graduate Admissions, 910-893-1200 Ext. 1318, Fax: 910-893-1306, E-mail: farthing@mailcenter.campbell.edu. *Vice President for Academic Affairs and Provost,* Dr. M. Dwaine Greene, 910-893-1211.

Divinity School Students: 129 full-time (53 women), 38 part-time (22 women); includes 15 minority (10 African Americans, 1 Asian American or Pacific Islander, 2 Hispanic Americans, 2 Native Americans), 2 international. Average age 34. 55 applicants, 78% accepted, 34 enrolled. *Faculty:* 6 full-time (1 woman), 14 part-time/adjunct (3 women). Expenses: Contact institution. *Financial support:* In 2001–02, 164 students received support, including 70 fellowships (averaging $800 per year); scholarships/grants also available. Support available to part-time students. Financial award application deadline: 5/1. In 2001, 25 degrees awarded. Offers Christian education (MA); divinity (M Div). *Application deadline:* For fall admission, 7/1; for spring admission, 11/15. Applications are processed on a rolling basis. *Application fee:* $20. *Application Contact:* Kheresa W. Harmon, Director of Admissions, 910-893-1830 Ext. 1865, Fax: 910-893-1835, E-mail: harmonk@mailcenter.campbell.edu. *Dean,* Dr. Michael Glenn Cogdill, 910-893-1830, Fax: 910-893-1835, E-mail: cogdill@mailcenter.campbell.edu.

Lundy-Fetterman School of Business Students: 5 full-time (3 women), 184 part-time (106 women); includes 21 minority (16 African Americans, 5 Hispanic Americans), 16 international. Average age 30. 145 applicants, 59% accepted. *Faculty:* 10 full-time (1 woman), 5 part-time/adjunct (0 women). Expenses: Contact institution. In 2001, 184 degrees awarded. *Degree program information:* Part-time and evening/weekend programs available. Offers business (MBA, MTIM). *Application deadline:* Applications are processed on a rolling basis. *Application fee:* $25. *Application Contact:* James S. Farthing, Director of Graduate Admissions, 910-893-1200 Ext. 1318, Fax: 910-893-1306, E-mail: farthing@mailcenter.campbell.edu. *Dean,* Dr. Christian Zinkhan, 910-893-1380, Fax: 910-814-4352, E-mail: zinkhan@mailcenter.campbell.edu.

Norman Adrian Wiggins School of Law Students: 311 full-time (147 women); includes 22 minority (8 African Americans, 5 Asian Americans or Pacific Islanders, 6 Hispanic Americans, 3 Native Americans), 2 international. Average age 26. 672 applicants, 33% accepted, 113 enrolled. *Faculty:* 20 full-time (3 women), 17 part-time/adjunct (4 women). Expenses: Contact institution. *Financial support:* In 2001–02, 264 students received support, including 13 research assistantships, 6 teaching assistantships (averaging $2,000 per year); career-related internships or fieldwork, Federal Work-Study, institutionally sponsored loans, and scholarships/grants also available. Financial award application deadline: 4/15; financial award applicants required to submit FAFSA. In 2001, 89 degrees awarded. Offers law (JD). *Application deadline:* For fall admission, 3/31 (priority date). Applications are processed on a rolling basis. *Application fee:* $50. *Application Contact:* Alan D. Woodlief, Associate Dean for Admissions, 910-893-1754, Fax: 910-893-1780, E-mail: woodlief@webster.campbell.edu. *Dean,* Willis Whichard, 910-893-1750, Fax: 910-893-1780, E-mail: whichard@webster.campbell.edu.

School of Education Students: 27 full-time (22 women), 163 part-time (137 women). Average age 32. *Faculty:* 9 full-time (5 women), 2 part-time/adjunct (0 women). Expenses: Contact institution. *Financial support:* In 2001–02, 66 students received support. Career-related internships or fieldwork and Federal Work-Study available. Financial award application deadline: 4/15; financial award applicants required to submit FAFSA. In 2001, 45 degrees awarded. *Degree program information:* Part-time and evening/weekend programs available. Offers administration (MSA); community counseling (MA); elementary education (M Ed); English education (M Ed); interdisciplinary studies (M Ed); mathematics education (M Ed); middle grades education (M Ed); physical education (M Ed); school counseling (M Ed); secondary education (M Ed); social science education (M Ed). *Application deadline:* For fall admission, 8/1 (priority date); for spring admission, 1/2 (priority date). Applications are processed on a rolling basis. *Application Contact:* James S. Farthing, Director of Graduate Admissions, 910-893-1200 Ext. 1318, Fax: 910-893-1306, E-mail: farthing@mailcenter.campbell.edu. *Dean,* Dr. Karen P. Nery, 910-893-1630, Fax: 910-893-1999, E-mail: nery@mailcenter.campbell.edu.

School of Pharmacy Students: 362 full-time (261 women), 95 part-time (68 women); includes 61 minority (30 African Americans, 28 Asian Americans or Pacific Islanders, 1 Hispanic American, 2 Native Americans), 10 international. Average age 24. 362 applicants, 39% accepted, 95 enrolled. *Faculty:* 38 full-time (12 women), 49 part-time/adjunct (24 women). Expenses: Contact institution. *Financial support:* In 2001–02, 214 students received support, including 4 research assistantships (averaging $3,000 per year), 2 teaching assistantships (averaging $3,000 per year); career-related internships or fieldwork, Federal Work-Study, and scholarships/grants also available. Financial award application deadline: 4/15; financial award applicants required to submit FAFSA. In 2001, 85 first professional degrees, 6 master's awarded. Offers clinical research (MS); pharmaceutical science (MS); pharmacy (Pharm D). *Application deadline:* For fall admission, 2/15 (priority date). Applications are processed on a rolling basis. *Application fee:* $50. Electronic applications accepted. *Application Contact:* Dr. Daniel W. Teat, Assistant Dean for Admissions, 910-893-1200 Ext. 1690, Fax: 910-893-1937, E-mail: pharmacy@camel.campbell.edu. *Dean,* Dr. Ronald W. Maddox, 910-893-1200 Ext. 1685, Fax: 910-893-1697, E-mail: pharmacy@camel.campbell.edu.

CANADIAN COLLEGE OF NATUROPATHIC MEDICINE, Toronto, ON M2K 1E2, Canada

General Information Independent, coed, primarily women, graduate-only institution. *Enrollment by degree level:* 539 doctoral. *Graduate faculty:* 2 full-time (1 woman), 2 part-time/adjunct (both women). *Graduate tuition:* Tuition charges are reported in Canadian dollars. *Tuition:* Full-time $15,175 Canadian dollars. *Graduate housing:* Room and/or apartments available on a first-come, first-served basis to single students; on-campus housing not available to married students. Housing application deadline: 1/1. *Student services:* Campus employment opportunities, campus safety program, career counseling, child daycare facilities, exercise/wellness program, free psychological counseling. *Library facilities:* Learning Resource Centre. *Online resources:* library catalog, web page. *Collection:* 5,000 titles, 80 serial subscriptions, 1,500 audiovisual materials.

Computer facilities: 15 computers available on campus for general student use. A campuswide network can be accessed. Internet access is available. *Web address:* http://www.ccnm.edu/.

General Application Contact: Mary Beth Michaels, Recruitment Coordinator, 416-498-1225 Ext. 241, Fax: 416-498-1643, E-mail: mbmichaels@ccnm.edu.

GRADUATE UNITS

Program in Naturopathic Medicine Students: 508 full-time, 31 part-time. Average age 25. 187 applicants, 58% accepted. *Faculty:* 2 full-time (1 woman), 2 part-time/adjunct (both women). Expenses: Contact institution. *Financial support:* In 2001–02, 448 students received support, including 3 research assistantships with full and partial tuition reimbursements available, 2 teaching assistantships; scholarships/grants also available. Financial award application deadline: 7/31. In 2001, 108 degrees awarded. Offers naturopathic medicine (ND). *Application deadline:* For fall admission, 1/31; for spring admission, 6/30. *Application fee:* $150. *Application Contact:* Mary Beth Michaels, Recruitment Coordinator, 416-498-1255 Ext. 241, Fax: 416-498-1643, E-mail: mbmichaels@ccnm.edu. *Registrar,* Jen Gouthro, 416-498-1255, Fax: 416-498-3197, E-mail: jgouthro@ccnm.edu.

CANADIAN MEMORIAL CHIROPRACTIC COLLEGE, Toronto, ON M4G 3E6, Canada

General Information Independent, coed, graduate-only institution. *Graduate housing:* On-campus housing not available. *Research affiliation:* University of Waterloo, University of Calgary, University of Toronto.

GRADUATE UNITS

Certificate Programs Offers chiropractic clinical sciences (Certificate); chiropractic radiology (Certificate); chiropractic sports sciences (Certificate).

Professional Program Offers chiropractic (DC).

CANADIAN THEOLOGICAL SEMINARY, Regina, SK S4T 0H8, Canada

General Information Independent-religious, coed, graduate-only institution. *Enrollment by degree level:* 28 first professional, 78 master's, 19 other advanced degrees. *Graduate faculty:* 18 full-time (3 women). *Graduate tuition:* Tuition and fees charges are reported in Canadian dollars. *Tuition:* Part-time $180 Canadian dollars per credit. *Required fees:* $30 Canadian dollars per semester. *Graduate housing:* Rooms and/or apartments available on a first-come, first-served basis to single and married students. Typical cost: $1,100 Canadian dollars per year ($3,040 Canadian dollars including board) for single students; $3,960 Canadian dollars per year for married students. Room and board charges vary according to board plan and housing facility selected. Housing application deadline: 8/15. *Student services:* Campus employment opportunities, campus safety program, career counseling, disabled student services, exercise/wellness program, free psychological counseling, international student services, teacher training, writing training. *Library facilities:* Archibald Foundation Library. *Online resources:* library catalog. *Collection:* 79,000 titles, 401 serial subscriptions, 2,482 audiovisual materials. *Research affiliation:* Christian and Missionary Alliance (theology and ministry training).

Computer facilities: 9 computers available on campus for general student use. A campuswide network can be accessed. Internet access is available. *Web address:* http://www.cbccts.ca/.

General Application Contact: Terry Symes, Assistant Director of Enrollment, 306-545-1515 Ext. 244, Fax: 306-545-0210, E-mail: tsymes@cbccts.ca.

GRADUATE UNITS

Graduate and Professional Programs Students: 59 full-time (14 women), 66 part-time (35 women); includes 24 minority (2 African Americans, 20 Asian Americans or Pacific Islanders, 1 Hispanic American, 1 Native American), 11 international. Average age 36. 53 applicants, 58% accepted. *Faculty:* 18 full-time (3 women). Expenses: Contact institution. *Financial support:* In 2001–02, 48 students received support. Career-related internships or fieldwork and scholarships/grants available. Support available to part-time students. Financial award application deadline: 3/30. In 2001, 15 first professional degrees, 20 master's, 3 other advanced degrees awarded. *Degree program information:* Part-time programs available. Postbaccalaureate distance learning degree programs offered (minimal on-campus study). Offers Christian studies (Diploma); church education (M Div); intercultural ministries (M Div, MA, Diploma); pastoral ministries (M Div); religion (MA); religious education (MRE). *Application deadline:* For fall admission, 7/31 (priority date); for winter admission, 11/30 (priority date). Applications are processed on a rolling basis. *Application fee:* $35. Electronic applications accepted. *Application Contact:* Terry Symes, Assistant Director of Enrollment, 306-545-1515 Ext. 244, Fax: 306-545-0210, E-mail: tsymes@cbccts.ca. *Interim Academic Dean,* Rod Remin, 306-545-1515 Ext. 263, Fax: 306-545-0210, E-mail: rremin@cbccts.ca.

CANISIUS COLLEGE, Buffalo, NY 14208-1098

General Information Independent-religious, coed, comprehensive institution. *Enrollment:* 680 full-time matriculated graduate/professional students (436 women), 812 part-time matriculated graduate/professional students (446 women). *Enrollment by degree level:* 1,492 master's. *Graduate faculty:* 74 full-time (18 women), 96 part-time/adjunct (28 women). *Tuition:* Full-time $11,640; part-time $485 per credit hour. *Required fees:* $234. Tuition and fees vary according to program. *Graduate housing:* Room and/or apartments available on a first-come, first-served basis to single students; on-campus housing not available to married students. Typical cost: $3,190 per year ($6,390 including board). Room and board charges vary according to board plan, campus/location and housing facility selected. Housing application deadline: 5/1. *Student services:* Campus employment opportunities, career counseling, disabled student services, exercise/wellness program, free psychological counseling, international student services, multicultural affairs office, teacher training. *Library facilities:* Andrew L. Bouwhuis Library plus 1 other. *Online resources:* library catalog, web page, access to other libraries' catalogs. *Collection:* 318,789 titles, 9,637 serial subscriptions, 7,357 audiovisual materials.

Computer facilities: 208 computers available on campus for general student use. A campuswide network can be accessed from student residence rooms and from off campus. Internet access and online class registration are available. *Web address:* http://www.canisius.edu/.

General Application Contact: Dr. Herbert J. Nelson, Vice President for Academic Affairs, 716-888-2120 Ext. 109, Fax: 716-888-2125, E-mail: nelson@canisius.edu.

GRADUATE UNITS

Graduate Division Students: 680 full-time (436 women), 812 part-time (446 women); includes 76 minority (49 African Americans, 13 Asian Americans or Pacific Islanders, 12 Hispanic Americans, 2 Native Americans), 236 international. Average age 30. 711 applicants, 73% accepted. *Faculty:* 74 full-time (18 women), 96 part-time/adjunct (28 women). Expenses: Contact institution. *Financial support:* In 2001–02, 26 research assistantships (averaging $5,650 per year) were awarded; career-related internships or fieldwork, Federal Work-Study, institutionally sponsored loans, tuition waivers (partial), and unspecified assistantships also available. Support available to part-time students. Financial award applicants required to submit FAFSA. In 2001, 448 degrees awarded. *Degree program information:* Part-time and evening/weekend programs available. *Application deadline:* Applications are processed on a rolling basis. *Application fee:* $25. Electronic applications accepted. *Vice President for Academic Affairs,* Dr. Herbert J. Nelson, 716-888-2120 Ext. 109, Fax: 716-888-2125, E-mail: nelson@canisius.edu.

College of Arts and Sciences Students: 3 full-time (all women), 31 part-time (24 women). *Faculty:* 6 full-time (2 women), 2 part-time/adjunct (1 woman). Expenses: Contact institution. *Financial support:* Applicants required to submit FAFSA. In 2001, 15 degrees awarded. *Degree program information:* Part-time and evening/weekend programs available. Offers arts and sciences (MS); organizational communication and development (MS). *Application deadline:* For fall admission, 7/15 (priority date); for winter admission, 11/15 (priority date); for spring admission, 4/15 (priority date). Applications are processed on a rolling basis. *Application fee:* $25. Electronic applications accepted. *Application Contact:* Stanton H. Hudson, Director, 716-888-2589, Fax: 716-888-3290, E-mail: hudsons@canisius.edu. *Dean,* Dr. James P. McDermott, 716-888-2130, E-mail: mcdermot@canisius.edu.

Richard J. Wehle School of Business Students: 73 full-time (26 women), 249 part-time (86 women). Average age 29. 187 applicants, 82% accepted, 117 enrolled. *Faculty:* 34 full-time (3 women), 12 part-time/adjunct (3 women). Expenses: Contact institution. *Financial support:* In 2001–02, 10 research assistantships with partial tuition reimbursements were awarded; career-related internships or fieldwork, institutionally sponsored loans, scholarships/grants, and unspecified assistantships also available. Support available to part-time students. Financial award application deadline: 6/15; financial award applicants required to submit FAFSA. In 2001, 85 degrees awarded. *Degree program information:* Part-time and evening/weekend programs available. Offers business (MBA, MBAPA, MTM); business administration (MBA, MBAPA); professional accounting (MBAPA); telecommunications management (MTM). *Application deadline:* For fall admission, 7/1 (priority date); for spring admission, 11/1 (priority date). Applications are processed on a rolling basis. *Application fee:* $25. Electronic applications accepted. *Application Contact:* Dr. James S. Valone, Associate Dean, 716-888-2140, Fax: 716-888-3211, E-mail: valone@canisius.edu. *Director, Graduate Business Programs,* Laura McEwen, 716-888-2140, Fax: 716-888-2145, E-mail: gradubus@canisius.edu.

School of Education and Human Services *Degree program information:* Part-time and evening/weekend programs available. Offers college student personnel administration (MS); counseling and human services (MS, CAS); education and human services (MS, MS Ed, CAS, SAS); educational administration (MS, SAS); physical education (MS); reading (MS Ed); secondary education (MS); special education—preparation of teachers of the deaf (MS); sport administration (MS); teacher education (MS Ed). Electronic applications accepted.

CAPELLA UNIVERSITY, Minneapolis, MN 55402

General Information Proprietary, coed, upper-level institution. *Enrollment:* 4,650 matriculated graduate/professional students. *Graduate faculty:* 35 full-time, 215 part-time/adjunct. *Tuition:* Part-time $1,210 per course. Tuition and fees vary according to degree level and program. *Library facilities:* University of Alabama in Huntsville. *Web address:* http://www.capellauniversity.edu/.

General Application Contact: Enrollment Services Office, 888-CAPELLA, Fax: 612-339-8022, E-mail: info@capella.edu.

GRADUATE UNITS

Graduate School Students: 4,650. Average age 41. 4,870 applicants, 78% accepted, 3288 enrolled. *Faculty:* 35 full-time, 215 part-time/adjunct. Expenses: Contact institution. *Financial support:* In 2001–02, 2,520 students received support. Institutionally sponsored loans and scholarships/grants available. Support available to part-time students. Financial award applicants required to submit FAFSA. In 2001, 136 master's, 61 doctorates awarded. *Degree program information:* Part-time and evening/weekend programs available. Postbaccalaureate distance learning degree programs offered (minimal on-campus study). Offers education (MS, PhD); human services (MS, PhD); information technology (MS); training and performance improvement (MS). *Application deadline:* Applications are processed on a rolling basis. *Application fee:* $50 ($150 for international students). Electronic applications accepted. *Application Contact:* Enrollment Services Office, 888-CAPELLA, Fax: 612-339-8022, E-mail: info@capella.edu. *President,* Dr. Michael Offerman, 888-CAPELLA, E-mail: mofferman@capella.edu.

School of Business Students: 1,347. Average age 39. 1,272 applicants, 81% accepted, 869 enrolled. *Faculty:* 5 full-time, 85 part-time/adjunct. Expenses: Contact institution. *Financial support:* Institutionally sponsored loans and scholarships/grants available. Support available to part-time students. Financial award applicants required to submit FAFSA. In 2001, 36 master's, 28 doctorates awarded. *Degree program information:* Part-time and evening/weekend programs available. Postbaccalaureate distance learning degree programs offered (minimal on-campus study). Offers business administration (MBA); organization and management (MS, PhD). *Application deadline:* Applications are processed on a rolling basis. *Application fee:* $50 ($150 for international students). Electronic applications accepted. *Application Contact:* Sara Peterson, Associate Director of Enrollment Services, 888-CAPELLA, Fax: 612-339-8022, E-mail: info@capella.edu. *Dean,* Paul Schroeder, 888-CAPELLA, Fax: 612-337-5396, E-mail: pschroeder@capella.edu.

School of Psychology Students: 978. Average age 41. 1,140 applicants, 63% accepted, 621 enrolled. *Faculty:* 20 full-time, 65 part-time/adjunct. Expenses: Contact institution. *Financial support:* Institutionally sponsored loans and scholarships/grants available. Support available to part-time students. Financial award applicants required to submit FAFSA. In 2001, 20 master's, 1 doctorate awarded. *Degree program information:* Part-time and evening/weekend programs available. Postbaccalaureate distance learning degree programs offered (minimal on-campus study). Offers psychology (MS, PhD). *Application deadline:* Applications are processed on a rolling basis. *Application fee:* $50 ($150 for international students). Electronic applications accepted. *Application Contact:* Kimberly Hanson, Associate Director of Enrollment Services, 612-278-0495 Ext. 372, Fax: 612-337-5396, E-mail: info@capella.edu. *Dean,* Dr. Karen Viechnicki, 888-CAPELLA, E-mail: kviechnicki@capella.edu.

CAPITAL BIBLE SEMINARY, Lanham, MD 20706-3599

General Information Independent-religious, coed, graduate-only institution. *Graduate housing:* Rooms and/or apartments available to single students and available on a first-come, first-served basis to married students. Housing application deadline: 7/15.

GRADUATE UNITS

Graduate and Professional Programs *Degree program information:* Part-time and evening/weekend programs available. Offers biblical studies (MA); Christian counseling (MA); ministry leadership (MA); theology (M Div, Th M).

CAPITAL UNIVERSITY, Columbus, OH 43209-2394

General Information Independent-religious, coed, comprehensive institution. *Enrollment:* 595 full-time matriculated graduate/professional students (278 women), 584 part-time matriculated graduate/professional students (268 women). *Enrollment by degree level:* 773 first professional, 406 master's. *Graduate faculty:* 55 full-time (19 women), 63 part-time/adjunct (11 women). *Tuition:* Part-time $641 per credit hour. Tuition and fees vary according to degree level and program. *Graduate housing:* On-campus housing not available. *Student services:* Campus employment opportunities, campus safety program, career counseling, free psychological counseling, international student services. *Library facilities:* Blackmore Library. *Online resources:* library catalog. *Collection:* 187,281 titles, 3,741 serial subscriptions, 6,048 audiovisual materials.

Computer facilities: 100 computers available on campus for general student use. A campuswide network can be accessed from student residence rooms and from off campus. Internet access is available. *Web address:* http://www.capital.edu/.

GRADUATE UNITS

Law School Students: 409 full-time (209 women), 353 part-time (159 women); includes 90 minority (60 African Americans, 13 Asian Americans or Pacific Islanders, 15 Hispanic Americans, 2 Native Americans), 2 international. Average age 29. 1,036 applicants, 58% accepted, 276 enrolled. *Faculty:* 29 full-time (6 women), 36 part-time/adjunct (7 women). Expenses: Contact institution. *Financial support:* In 2001–02, 624 students received support, including 17 research assistantships (averaging $2,800 per year), 20 teaching assistantships (averaging $4,000 per year); fellowships, career-related internships or fieldwork, Federal Work-Study, scholarships/grants, and tuition waivers (full and partial) also available. Support available to part-time students. Financial award application deadline: 4/1; financial award applicants required to submit FAFSA. In 2001, 199 first professional degrees, 23 master's awarded. *Degree program information:* Part-time and evening/weekend programs available. Offers business (LL M); business and taxation (LL M); law (JD, LL M, MT); taxation (LL M, MT). *Application deadline:* For fall admission, 5/1 (priority date). Applications are processed on a rolling basis. *Application fee:* $35. Electronic applications accepted. *Application Contact:* Linda J. Mihely, Assistant Dean of Admissions and Financial Aid, 614-236-6310, Fax: 614-236-6972, E-mail: admissions@law.capital.edu. *Dean,* Steven C. Bahls, 614-236-6500, Fax: 614-236-6972, E-mail: sbahls@law.capital.edu.

School of Management Students: 161 full-time (54 women), 99 part-time (33 women); includes 37 minority (23 African Americans, 10 Asian Americans or Pacific Islanders, 3 Hispanic Americans, 1 Native American), 4 international. Average age 29. 65 applicants, 77% accepted. *Faculty:* 17 full-time (7 women), 23 part-time/adjunct (1 woman). Expenses: Contact institution. *Financial support:* In 2001–02, 2 students received support, including 2 fellowships (averaging $1,000 per year); scholarships/grants and tuition waivers (full) also available. Support available to part-time students. Financial award application deadline: 8/1; financial award applicants required to submit FAFSA. In 2001, 57 degrees awarded. *Degree program information:* Part-time and evening/weekend programs available. Offers administration (MBA). *Application deadline:* For fall admission, 8/1 (priority date); for winter admission, 12/1 (priority date); for spring admission, 4/1. Applications are processed on a rolling basis. *Application fee:* $25. Electronic applications accepted. *Application Contact:* Trudy Riesser, Registrar, 614-236-6679, Fax: 614-236-6540, E-mail: mba@capital.edu. *Dean,* Dr. William A. Raabe, 614-236-6679, Fax: 614-296-6940, E-mail: wraabe@capital.edu.

School of Nursing Students: 11 full-time (all women), 40 part-time (all women). Average age 42. 8 applicants, 100% accepted. *Faculty:* 11 full-time (all women). Expenses: Contact institution. *Financial support:* Career-related internships or fieldwork available. Financial award applicants required to submit FAFSA. In 2001, 12 degrees awarded. *Degree program information:* Part-time and evening/weekend programs available. Offers administration (MSN); family and community (MSN); interdisciplinary family focused health care across cultures (MSN); legal studies (MSN); occupational health (MSN); parish nursing (MSN); school health nursing (MSN); theological studies (MSN). *Application deadline:* For fall admission, 8/1 (priority date); for spring admission, 12/1. Applications are processed on a rolling basis. *Application fee:* $25. *Acting Dean and Professor,* Dr. Elaine F. Haynes, 614-236-6703, Fax: 614-236-6157, E-mail: ehaynes@capital.edu.

CAPITOL COLLEGE, Laurel, MD 20708-9759

General Information Independent, coed, comprehensive institution. *Enrollment:* 6 full-time matriculated graduate/professional students (3 women), 625 part-time matriculated graduate/professional students (175 women). *Enrollment by degree level:* 631 master's. *Graduate faculty:* 3 full-time (0 women), 34 part-time/adjunct (4 women). *Tuition:* Part-time $354 per credit. *Graduate housing:* On-campus housing not available. *Student services:* Career counseling. *Library facilities:* Puente Library. *Online resources:* library catalog. *Collection:* 10,000 titles, 100 serial subscriptions, 117 audiovisual materials.

Computer facilities: 42 computers available on campus for general student use. A campuswide network can be accessed from off campus. Internet access is available. *Web address:* http://www.capitol-college.edu/.

Capitol College (continued)

General Application Contact: Ken Crockett, Director of Graduate Admissions, 301-369-2800 Ext. 3026, Fax: 301-953-3876, E-mail: gradschool@capitol-college.edu.

GRADUATE UNITS

Graduate Programs Students: 6 full-time (3 women), 625 part-time (175 women). Average age 35. 400 applicants, 75% accepted, 275 enrolled. *Faculty:* 3 full-time (0 women), 34 part-time/adjunct (4 women). Expenses: Contact institution. *Financial support:* In 2001–02, 2 students received support. Available to part-time students. Applicants required to submit FAFSA. In 2001, 52 degrees awarded. *Degree program information:* Part-time and evening/weekend programs available. Postbaccalaureate distance learning degree programs offered (no on-campus study). Offers computer science (MS); electrical engineering (MS); electronic commerce management (MS); information and telecommunications systems management (MS); information architecture (MS); network security (MS). *Application deadline:* For fall admission, 7/1 (priority date); for winter admission, 12/1 (priority date); for spring admission, 3/1 (priority date). Applications are processed on a rolling basis. *Application fee:* $100 for international students. Electronic applications accepted. *Application Contact:* Ken Crockett, Director of Graduate Admissions, 301-369-2800 Ext. 3026, Fax: 301-953-3876, E-mail: gradschool@capitol-college.edu. *Dean of Academics*, Pat Smit, 301-369-2800 Ext. 3044, Fax: 301-953-3876, E-mail: gradschool@capitol-college.edu.

CARDEAN UNIVERSITY, Deerfield, IL 60015-5609

General Information Proprietary, coed, graduate-only institution.

GRADUATE UNITS

MBA Program Offers finance and accounting (MBA); management and organizations (MBA); marketing and product development (MBA).

See in-depth description on page 781.

CARDINAL STRITCH UNIVERSITY, Milwaukee, WI 53217-3985

General Information Independent-religious, coed, comprehensive institution. *Enrollment:* 1,646 full-time matriculated graduate/professional students (1,031 women), 389 part-time matriculated graduate/professional students (305 women). *Enrollment by degree level:* 1,928 master's, 107 doctoral. *Graduate faculty:* 42 full-time (25 women), 154 part-time/adjunct (43 women). *Tuition:* Part-time $390 per credit. *Required fees:* $150; $75 per semester. One-time fee: $25. Tuition and fees vary according to program. *Graduate housing:* Room and/or apartments available on a first-come, first-served basis to single students; on-campus housing not available to married students. Typical cost: $4,840 (including board). Room and board charges vary according to board plan. *Student services:* Career counseling, disabled student services, international student services, multicultural affairs office, teacher training, writing training. *Library facilities:* Cardinal Stritch University Library. *Online resources:* library catalog, web page, access to other libraries' catalogs. *Collection:* 96,864 titles, 688 serial subscriptions, 6,138 audiovisual materials.

Computer facilities: 236 computers available on campus for general student use. A campuswide network can be accessed from student residence rooms and from off campus. Internet access is available. *Web address:* http://www.stritch.edu/.

General Application Contact: 800-347-8822 Ext. 4042, E-mail: gradadm@stritch.edu.

GRADUATE UNITS

College of Arts and Sciences Students: 34 full-time (29 women), 41 part-time (36 women); includes 10 minority (8 African Americans, 1 Asian American or Pacific Islander, 1 Hispanic American), 1 international. Average age 39. 57 applicants, 70% accepted, 38 enrolled. *Faculty:* 10 full-time (5 women), 3 part-time/adjunct (1 woman). Expenses: Contact institution. *Financial support:* In 2001–02, 2 students received support, including 2 research assistantships with partial tuition reimbursements available (averaging $1,500 per year); career-related internships or fieldwork, Federal Work-Study, and scholarships/grants also available. Financial award applicants required to submit FAFSA. In 2001, 18 degrees awarded. *Degree program information:* Part-time and evening/weekend programs available. Offers arts and sciences (MA, ME); clinical psychology (MA); religious studies (MA); visual studies (MA). *Application deadline:* For fall admission, 7/15 (priority date); for spring admission, 12/15 (priority date). Applications are processed on a rolling basis. *Application fee:* $25. *Application Contact:* 800-347-8822 Ext. 4042, E-mail: gradadm@stritch.edu. *Dean*, Dr. Dickson K. Smith, 414-410-4010.

College of Business and Management Students: 896 full-time (480 women); includes 191 minority (133 African Americans, 28 Asian Americans or Pacific Islanders, 26 Hispanic Americans, 4 Native Americans), 1 international. Average age 34. 133 applicants, 97% accepted, 83 enrolled. *Faculty:* 12 full-time (5 women), 127 part-time/adjunct (25 women). Expenses: Contact institution. *Financial support:* Career-related internships or fieldwork, Federal Work-Study, and scholarships/grants available. Financial award applicants required to submit FAFSA. In 2001, 215 degrees awarded. *Degree program information:* Part-time and evening/weekend programs available. Offers business administration (MBA); financial services (MS); health care executives (MBA); healthcare executives (MBA); management (MS). *Application deadline:* Applications are processed on a rolling basis. *Application fee:* $25. *Application Contact:* Shirley Hansen, Director of Marketing, 414-410-4315. *Interim Dean*, 414-410-4437.

College of Education Students: 714 full-time (520 women), 323 part-time (244 women); includes 146 minority (101 African Americans, 29 Asian Americans or Pacific Islanders, 12 Hispanic Americans, 4 Native Americans), 8 international. Average age 36. 394 applicants, 81% accepted, 289 enrolled. *Faculty:* 18 full-time (13 women), 21 part-time/adjunct (14 women). Expenses: Contact institution. *Financial support:* In 2001–02, 9 students received support, including 3 fellowships (averaging $5,000 per year), 6 research assistantships with partial tuition reimbursements available (averaging $1,500 per year); career-related internships or fieldwork, Federal Work-Study, and scholarships/grants also available. Financial award applicants required to submit FAFSA. In 2001, 205 master's, 26 doctorates awarded. *Degree program information:* Part-time and evening/weekend programs available. Offers computer science education (MS); education (MA, ME, MS, Ed D); educational computing (ME); educational leadership (MS); leadership (Ed D); professional development (ME); reading/language arts (MA); reading/learning disability (MA); special education (MA). *Application deadline:* For fall admission, 7/15 (priority date); for spring admission, 12/15 (priority date). Applications are processed on a rolling basis. *Application fee:* $25. *Application Contact:* 800-347-8822 Ext. 4042, E-mail: gradamd@stritch.edu. *Dean*, Dr. Tia Bojar, 414-410-4434.

College of Nursing Students: 2 full-time (both women), 25 part-time (all women); includes 1 minority (Hispanic American) Average age 39. 13 applicants, 77% accepted, 9 enrolled. *Faculty:* 2 full-time (both women), 3 part-time/adjunct (all women). Expenses: Contact institution. *Financial support:* Federal Work-Study and scholarships/grants available. Financial award applicants required to submit FAFSA. *Degree program information:* Part-time and evening/weekend programs available. Offers nursing (MSN). *Application deadline:* For fall admission, 6/15 (priority date); for spring admission, 11/15 (priority date). Applications are processed on a rolling basis. *Application fee:* $25. *Application Contact:* 800-347-8822 Ext. 4042, E-mail: gradadm@stritch.edu. *Dean*, Dr. Nancy Cervanansky, MSN, 414-410-4390.

CARIBBEAN UNIVERSITY, Bayamón, PR 00960-0493

General Information Independent, coed, comprehensive institution.

GRADUATE UNITS

Graduate Programs

CARLETON UNIVERSITY, Ottawa, ON K1S 5B6, Canada

General Information Province-supported, coed, university. *Graduate housing:* Room and/or apartments available to single students; on-campus housing not available to married students. Housing application deadline: 5/31. *Research affiliation:* Communications and Information Technology Ontario (VLSI, network access methods), Micronet Research and Development (high frequency circuits and systems, high-speed VLSI modules), TeleLearning Network of Centres of Excellence (telelearning), Materials and Manufacturing Ontario (polymers, design of castings, welds).

GRADUATE UNITS

Faculty of Graduate Studies *Degree program information:* Part-time and evening/weekend programs available. Electronic applications accepted.

College of Natural Sciences *Degree program information:* Part-time and evening/weekend programs available. Offers biology (M Sc, PhD); chemistry (M Sc, PhD); computer science (MCS, PhD); earth science (M Sc, PhD); information and systems science (M Sc); mathematics (M Sc, PhD); physics (M Sc, PhD); science (M Sc, MCS, PhD).

Faculty of Arts and Social Sciences *Degree program information:* Part-time and evening/weekend programs available. Offers anthropology (MA); applied language studies (MA); arts and social sciences (M Sc, MA, PhD); Canadian art history (MA); Canadian studies (MA, PhD); cognitive science (PhD); English (MA); film studies (MA); French (MA); geography (MA, PhD); history (MA, PhD); languages, literatures, and comparative literary studies (MA, PhD); philosophy (MA); psychology (M Sc, MA, PhD); sociology (MA, PhD).

Faculty of Engineering and Design Offers aerospace engineering (M Eng, PhD); civil and environmental engineering (M Eng, PhD); design studies (M Arch); electrical engineering (M Eng, PhD); engineering and design (M Arch, M Eng, M Sc, PhD); information and systems science (M Sc); materials engineering (M Eng); mechanical engineering (M Eng, PhD); telecommunications technology management (M Eng).

Faculty of Public Affairs and Management *Degree program information:* Part-time programs available. Offers business administration (MBA); central east/European and Russian area studies (MA); communication (MA, PhD); economics (MA, PhD); international affairs (MA); journalism (MJ); legal studies (MA); management (PhD); political economy (MA); political science (MA, PhD); public administration (MA, DPA); public affairs and management (MA, MBA, MJ, MSW, DPA, PhD); public policy (PhD); social work (MSW).

CARLOS ALBIZU UNIVERSITY, San Juan, PR 00902-3711

General Information Independent, coed, upper-level institution. *Graduate housing:* On-campus housing not available. *Research affiliation:* Consulorio Educativo Psicológico & Innovaciones (psychology), Lutheran Medical Center, Sunset Park (psychology).

GRADUATE UNITS

Graduate Programs in Psychology *Degree program information:* Part-time and evening/weekend programs available. Offers clinical psychology (PhD, Psy D); general psychology (PhD); industrial/organizational psychology (MS, PhD).

CARLOS ALBIZU UNIVERSITY, MIAMI CAMPUS, Miami, FL 33172-2209

General Information Independent, coed, primarily women, upper-level institution. *Enrollment:* 432 full-time matriculated graduate/professional students (322 women), 32 part-time matriculated graduate/professional students (22 women). *Enrollment by degree level:* 240 master's, 224 doctoral. *Graduate faculty:* 19 full-time (9 women), 37 part-time/adjunct (19 women). *Tuition:* Part-time $455 per credit. *Required fees:* $819; $273 per term. Tuition and fees vary according to course load and degree level. *Graduate housing:* On-campus housing not available. *Student services:* Campus employment opportunities, international student services, writing training. *Library facilities:* Albizu Library. *Online resources:* library catalog, web page, access to other libraries' catalogs. *Collection:* 16,634 titles, 220 serial subscriptions, 628 audiovisual materials.

Computer facilities: 26 computers available on campus for general student use. A campuswide network can be accessed from off campus. Internet access is available. *Web address:* http://www.albizu.edu/.

General Application Contact: Miriam Matos, Admissions Officer, 305-593-1223 Ext. 134, Fax: 305-593-1854, E-mail: mmatos@albizu.edu.

GRADUATE UNITS

Graduate Programs Students: 432 full-time (322 women), 32 part-time (22 women); includes 328 minority (58 African Americans, 7 Asian Americans or Pacific Islanders, 263 Hispanic Americans), 4 international. Average age 35. 189 applicants, 50% accepted, 69 enrolled. *Faculty:* 19 full-time (9 women), 37 part-time/adjunct (19 women). Expenses: Contact institution. *Financial support:* In 2001–02, 22 students received support. Federal Work-Study and scholarships/grants available. Financial award application deadline: 6/1; financial award applicants required to submit FAFSA. In 2001, 44 master's, 69 doctorates awarded. *Degree program information:* Part-time and evening/weekend programs available. Offers clinical psychology (Psy D); industrial/organizational psychology (MS); management (MBA); marriage and family therapy (MS); mental health counseling (MS); psychology (MS); school counseling (MS). *Application deadline:* For fall admission, 8/1 (priority date); for spring admission, 11/30 (priority date). Applications are processed on a rolling basis. *Application fee:* $50. *Application Contact:* Miriam Matos, Admissions Officer, 305-593-1223 Ext. 134, Fax: 305-593-1854, E-mail: mmatos@albizu.edu. *Chancellor*, Dr. Gerardo F. Rodriquez-Menedez, 305-593-1223 Ext. 120, Fax: 305-629-8052, E-mail: grodriguez@albizu.edu.

CARLOW COLLEGE, Pittsburgh, PA 15213-3165

General Information Independent-religious, coed, primarily women, comprehensive institution. *Enrollment:* 11 full-time matriculated graduate/professional students (all women), 298 part-time matriculated graduate/professional students (274 women). *Enrollment by degree level:* 309 master's. *Graduate faculty:* 14 full-time (12 women), 44 part-time/adjunct (33 women). *Tuition:* Part-time $444 per credit. *Required fees:* $27 per credit. *Graduate housing:* Room and/or apartments available on a first-come, first-served basis to single students; on-campus housing not available to married students. *Student services:* Campus safety program, career counseling, child daycare facilities, disabled student services, exercise/wellness program, free psychological counseling, international student services, multicultural affairs office. *Library facilities:* Grace Library. *Online resources:* library catalog, web page, access to other libraries' catalogs. *Collection:* 79,690 titles, 434 serial subscriptions, 4,542 audiovisual materials.

Computer facilities: 660 computers available on campus for general student use. A campuswide network can be accessed from student residence rooms and from off campus. Internet access and online class registration, applications software, e-mail are available. *Web address:* http://www.carlow.edu/.

General Application Contact: Maggie Golofski, Secretary, Graduate Studies, 412-578-8764, Fax: 412-578-8822, E-mail: mgolofski@carlow.edu.

GRADUATE UNITS

Division of Education Students: 2 full-time (both women), 60 part-time (58 women); includes 8 minority (6 African Americans, 1 Asian American or Pacific Islander, 1 Native American) Average age 37. 11 applicants, 91% accepted, 10 enrolled. *Faculty:* 5 full-time (all women), 14 part-time/adjunct (8 women). Expenses: Contact institution. *Financial support:* In 2001–02, 37 students received support. Career-related internships or fieldwork, Federal Work-Study, scholarships/grants, and tuition waivers (partial) available. Support available to part-time students. Financial award application deadline: 4/3; financial award applicants required to submit FAFSA. In 2001, 11 degrees awarded. *Degree program information:* Part-time and evening/weekend programs available. Offers art education (M Ed); early childhood education (M Ed); early childhood supervision (M Ed); education (M Ed); educational leadership (M Ed). *Application deadline:* For fall admission, 7/15 (priority date); for spring admission, 11/15 (priority date). Applications are processed on a rolling basis. *Application fee:* $35. *Application Contact:* Maggie Golofski, Secretary, Graduate Studies, 412-578-8764, Fax: 412-578-8822, E-mail: mgolofski@carlow.edu. *Chair*, Dr. Roberta Schomburg, 412-578-6312, Fax: 412-578-8816, E-mail: rschomburg@carlow.edu.

Division of Management Students: 2 full-time (both women), 66 part-time (57 women); includes 15 minority (all African Americans) Average age 38. 25 applicants, 92% accepted, 18 enrolled. *Faculty:* 4 full-time (3 women), 3 part-time/adjunct (1 woman). Expenses: Contact institution. *Financial support:* In 2001–02, 11 students received support. Federal Work-Study and scholarships/grants available. Support available to part-time students. Financial award application deadline: 4/3. In 2001, 6 degrees awarded. *Degree program information:* Part-time and evening/weekend programs available. Offers management and technology (MS). *Application deadline:* For fall admission, 6/15 (priority date); for spring admission, 11/15 (priority date). Applications are processed on a rolling basis. *Application fee:* $35. *Application Contact:* Maggie Golofski, Secretary, Graduate Studies, 412-578-8764, Fax: 412-578-8822, E-mail: mgolofski@carlow.edu. *Chair,* Dr. Mary Rothenberger, 412-578-6181, Fax: 412-587-6367, E-mail: mrothenberger@carlow.edu.

Division of Nursing Students: 2 full-time (both women), 53 part-time (51 women); includes 4 minority (all African Americans) Average age 40. 33 applicants, 70% accepted, 22 enrolled. *Faculty:* 2 full-time (both women), 11 part-time/adjunct (9 women). Expenses: Contact institution. *Financial support:* In 2001–02, 35 students received support. Career-related internships or fieldwork, Federal Work-Study, scholarships/grants, traineeships, and tuition waivers (partial) available. Support available to part-time students. Financial award application deadline: 4/3. In 2001, 27 degrees awarded. *Degree program information:* Part-time and evening/weekend programs available. Postbaccalaureate distance learning degree programs offered (minimal on-campus study). Offers case management/leadership (Certificate); home health advanced practice nursing (MSN, Certificate); nursing case management/leadership (MSN); nursing leadership (MSN). *Application deadline:* For fall admission, 6/15 (priority date); for spring admission, 11/15 (priority date). Applications are processed on a rolling basis. *Application fee:* $35. *Application Contact:* Maggie Golofski, Secretary, Graduate Studies, 412-578-8764, Fax: 412-578-8822, E-mail: mgolofski@carlow.edu. *Acting Chair,* Dr. Mary Lou Bost, 412-578-6116, Fax: 412-578-6114, E-mail: mbost@carlow.edu.

Division of Professional Leadership Students: 5 full-time (4 women), 119 part-time (109 women); includes 10 minority (all African Americans) Average age 39. 45 applicants, 73% accepted, 27 enrolled. *Faculty:* 3 full-time (2 women), 16 part-time/adjunct (15 women). Expenses: Contact institution. *Financial support:* In 2001–02, 47 students received support. Career-related internships or fieldwork, Federal Work-Study, and scholarships/grants available. Support available to part-time students. Financial award application deadline: 4/1. In 2001, 35 degrees awarded. *Degree program information:* Part-time and evening/weekend programs available. Offers health service education (MS); nonprofit management (MS); training and development (MS). *Application deadline:* For fall admission, 6/15 (priority date); for spring admission, 11/15 (priority date). Applications are processed on a rolling basis. *Application fee:* $35. *Application Contact:* Maggie Golofski, Secretary, Graduate Studies, 412-578-8764, Fax: 412-578-8822, E-mail: mgolofski@carlow.edu. *Director,* Dr. M. Sandie Turner, 412-578-6669, Fax: 412-578-8706, E-mail: mturner@carlow.edu.

CARNEGIE MELLON UNIVERSITY, Pittsburgh, PA 15213-3891

General Information Independent, coed, university. CGS member. *Graduate housing:* On-campus housing not available. *Research affiliation:* National Census Data Research Center (public policy), Robotics Engineering Consortium (computer science and engineering), Software Engineering Institute (computer science and engineering), Carnegie Bosch Institute for Applied Studies in International Management (business and management), Pittsburgh Supercomputer Center.

GRADUATE UNITS

Carnegie Institute of Technology *Degree program information:* Part-time and evening/weekend programs available. Offers bioengineering (MS, PhD); biomedical engineering (MS, PhD); chemical engineering (M Ch E, MS, PhD); civil engineering (MS, PhD); civil engineering and industrial management (MS); civil engineering and robotics (PhD); civil engineering/bioengineering (PhD); civil engineering/engineering and public policy (MS, PhD); colloids, polymers and surfaces (MS); electrical and computer engineering (MS, PhD); engineering and public policy (MS, PhD); materials science and engineering (ME, MS, PhD); mechanical engineering (ME, MS, PhD); technology (M Ch E, ME, MS, PhD).

Information Networking Institute Offers information networking (MS).

College of Fine Arts *Degree program information:* Part-time programs available. Offers art (MFA); fine arts (M Des, M Sc, MAM, MET, MFA, MM, MSA, PhD). Electronic applications accepted.

School of Architecture Offers architecture (MSA); building performance and diagnostics (M Sc, PhD); computational design (M Sc, PhD).

School of Design Offers communication planning and design (M Des); design theory (PhD); interaction design (M Des, PhD); new product development (PhD); typography and information design (PhD).

School of Drama Offers design (MFA); directing (MFA); dramatic writing (MFA); performance technology and management (MFA).

School of Music *Degree program information:* Part-time programs available. Offers composition (MM); conducting (MM); music education (MM); performance (MM).

College of Humanities and Social Sciences *Degree program information:* Part-time programs available. Offers behavioral decision theory (PhD); business (MAPW); cognitive neuropsychology (PhD); cognitive psychology (PhD); communication planning and design (M Des); computer-assisted language learning (MCALL); design (MAPW); developmental psychology (PhD); English (MA); history (MA, MS); history and policy (MA, PhD); humanities and social sciences (M Des, MA, MAPW, MCALL, MS, PhD); literary and cultural theory (MA, PhD); logic and computation (MS); marketing (MAPW); mathematical finance (PhD); organization science (PhD); philosophy (MA, MS); policy (MAPW); professional writing (MAPW); pure and applied logic (PhD); research (MAPW); rhetoric (MA, PhD); rhetorical theory (MAPW); science writing (MAPW); second language acquisition (PhD); social and cultural history (PhD); social and decision science (PhD); social/personality psychology (PhD); statistics (MS, PhD); technical (MAPW). Electronic applications accepted.

Center for Innovation in Learning Offers instructional science (PhD).

Graduate School of Industrial Administration *Degree program information:* Part-time programs available. Offers accounting (PhD); algorithms, combinatorics, and optimization (MS, PhD); business management and software engineering (MBMSE); civil engineering and industrial management (MS); computational finance (MSCF); economics (MS, PhD); electronic commerce (MS); environmental engineering and management (MEEM); finance (PhD); financial economics (PhD); industrial administration (MBA, PhD); information systems (PhD); management of manufacturing and automation (MOM, PhD); manufacturing (MOM); marketing (PhD); mathematical finance (PhD); operations research (PhD); organizational behavior and theory (PhD); political economy (PhD); production and operations management (PhD); public policy and management (MS, MSED); software engineering and business management (MS).

H. John Heinz III School of Public Policy and Management *Degree program information:* Part-time and evening/weekend programs available. Offers arts management (MAM); health care policy and management (MSHCPM); information systems management (MISM); medical management (MMM); public management (MPM); public policy analysis (PhD); public policy and management (MAM, MIS, MISM, MMM, MPM, MS, MSED, MSHCPM, PhD); sustainable economic development (MIS). Electronic applications accepted.

Mellon College of Science *Degree program information:* Part-time programs available. Offers algorithms, combinatorics, and optimization (PhD); applied physics (PhD); biochemistry (PhD); biophysics (PhD); cell biology (PhD); chemical instrumentation (MS); chemistry (MS, PhD); colloids, polymers and surfaces (MS); computational biology (MS, PhD); developmental biology (PhD); genetics (PhD); mathematical finance (PhD); mathematical sciences (MS, DA, PhD); molecular biology (PhD); neurobiology (PhD); physics (MS, PhD); polymer science (MS); pure and applied logic (PhD); science (MS, DA, PhD). Electronic applications accepted.

School of Computer Science Offers algorithms, combinatorics, and optimization (PhD); computer science (PhD); entertainment technology (MET); human-computer interaction (MHCI, PhD); knowledge discovery and data mining (MS); pure and applied logic (PhD); software engineering (MSE, PhD).

Language Technologies Institute Offers language technologies (MLT, PhD).

Robotics Institute Offers robotics (MS, PhD).

CARROLL COLLEGE, Waukesha, WI 53186-5593

General Information Independent-religious, coed, comprehensive institution. *Graduate housing:* On-campus housing not available.

GRADUATE UNITS

Graduate Program in Education *Degree program information:* Part-time and evening/weekend programs available. Offers education (M Ed).

Program in Physical Therapy Offers physical therapy (MPT).

Program in Software Engineering *Degree program information:* Part-time and evening/weekend programs available. Offers software engineering (MSE). Electronic applications accepted.

CARSON-NEWMAN COLLEGE, Jefferson City, TN 37760

General Information Independent-religious, coed, comprehensive institution. *Enrollment:* 124 full-time matriculated graduate/professional students (94 women), 80 part-time matriculated graduate/professional students (68 women). *Enrollment by degree level:* 204 master's. *Graduate faculty:* 7 full-time (4 women), 20 part-time/adjunct (12 women). *Tuition:* Part-time $200 per hour. *Graduate housing:* Rooms and/or apartments available to single and married students. Typical cost: $1,660 per year ($4,120 including board) for single students. Housing application deadline: 7/15. *Student services:* Campus employment opportunities, career counseling, free psychological counseling, international student services, low-cost health insurance. *Library facilities:* Stephens-Burnett Library plus 1 other. *Online resources:* library catalog, web page. *Collection:* 2,245 serial subscriptions, 14,008 audiovisual materials.

Computer facilities: 200 computers available on campus for general student use. A campuswide network can be accessed from student residence rooms and from off campus. Internet access is available. *Web address:* http://www.cn.edu/.

General Application Contact: Jane W. McGill, Graduate Admissions and Services Adviser, 865-471-3460, Fax: 865-471-3475.

GRADUATE UNITS

Department of Nursing Students: 7 full-time (6 women), 9 part-time (all women). Average age 32. *Faculty:* 2 full-time (both women), 10 part-time/adjunct (9 women). Expenses: Contact institution. In 2001, 7 degrees awarded. Offers family nurse practitioner (MSN). *Application deadline:* For fall admission, 7/15 (priority date). Applications are processed on a rolling basis. *Application fee:* $50. *Dean and Chair,* Dr. Ann Harley, 865-471-3426, E-mail: aharley@cn.edu.

Graduate Program in Education Students: 117 full-time (88 women), 71 part-time (59 women); includes 6 minority (4 African Americans, 1 Asian American or Pacific Islander, 1 Hispanic American), 29 international. Average age 32. 64 applicants, 95% accepted. *Faculty:* 5 full-time (2 women), 10 part-time/adjunct (3 women). Expenses: Contact institution. *Financial support:* In 2001–02, 129 students received support. Federal Work-Study and unspecified assistantships available. Financial award application deadline: 4/1; financial award applicants required to submit FAFSA. In 2001, 122 degrees awarded. *Degree program information:* Part-time and evening/weekend programs available. Offers curriculum and instruction (M Ed); elementary education (MAT); school counseling (M Ed); secondary education (MAT); teaching English as a second language (MATESL). *Application deadline:* For fall admission, 7/15 (priority date). Applications are processed on a rolling basis. *Application fee:* $25 ($50 for international students). *Application Contact:* Jane W. McGill, Graduate Admissions and Services Adviser, 865-471-3460, Fax: 865-471-3475. *Chair,* Dr. Margaret A. Hypes, 865-471-3461.

CARTHAGE COLLEGE, Kenosha, WI 53140-1994

General Information Independent-religious, coed, comprehensive institution. *Enrollment:* 124 part-time matriculated graduate/professional students (114 women). *Enrollment by degree level:* 124 master's. *Graduate faculty:* 3 full-time (2 women), 16 part-time/adjunct (11 women). *Tuition:* Part-time $255 per credit. *Graduate housing:* On-campus housing not available. *Student services:* Campus safety program, career counseling, free psychological counseling, international student services, low-cost health insurance. *Library facilities:* Hedberg Library. *Online resources:* library catalog, web page, access to other libraries' catalogs. *Collection:* 141,187 titles, 615 serial subscriptions, 3,194 audiovisual materials.

Computer facilities: 200 computers available on campus for general student use. A campuswide network can be accessed from student residence rooms and from off campus. Internet access is available. *Web address:* http://www.carthage.edu/.

General Application Contact: Dr. Judith B. Schaumberg, Director of Graduate Programs, 262-551-5876, Fax: 262-551-5704, E-mail: jschaumberg@carthage.edu.

GRADUATE UNITS

Division of Teacher Education Average age 35. 45 applicants, 100% accepted. *Faculty:* 3 full-time (2 women), 16 part-time/adjunct (11 women). Expenses: Contact institution. *Financial support:* In 2001–02, 6 students received support, including 6 teaching assistantships In 2001, 31 degrees awarded. *Degree program information:* Part-time and evening/weekend programs available. Offers classroom guidance and counseling (M Ed); creative arts (M Ed); gifted and talented children (M Ed); language arts (M Ed); modern language (M Ed); natural sciences (M Ed); reading (M Ed, Certificate); social sciences (M Ed); teacher leadership (M Ed, Certificate). *Application deadline:* Applications are processed on a rolling basis. *Application fee:* $25. *Director of Graduate Programs,* Dr. Judith B. Schaumberg, 262-551-5876, Fax: 262-551-5704, E-mail: jschaumberg@carthage.edu.

CASE WESTERN RESERVE UNIVERSITY, Cleveland, OH 44106

General Information Independent, coed, university. CGS member. *Graduate housing:* Room and/or apartments available to single students; on-campus housing not available to married students. Housing application deadline: 5/1. *Research affiliation:* University Hospitals of Cleveland (biomedical science), Cleveland Hearing and Speech Center (speech-language pathology and audiology), Dow Chemical Company (polymers), Corning Glass Works (sensors), E. I. du Pont de Nemours and Company (sensors), Cleveland Clinic Foundation (biomedical science).

GRADUATE UNITS

Frances Payne Bolton School of Nursing *Degree program information:* Part-time programs available. Offers acute care adult nurse practitioner (MSN); acute care pediatric nurse practitioner (MSN); adult practitioner (MSN); community health nursing (MSN); critical care nursing (MSN); family nurse practitioner (MSN); gerontological nurse practitioner (MSN); medical-surgical nursing (MSN); neonatal practitioner (MSN); nurse anesthesia (MSN); nurse midwifery (MSN); nurse practitioner (MSN); nursing (MSN, ND, PhD); oncology nursing (MSN); pediatric nurse practitioner (MSN); psychiatric-mental health nurse practitioner (MSN); women's health nurse practitioner (MSN).

Mandel School of Applied Social Sciences Expenses: Contact institution. *Financial support:* Career-related internships or fieldwork, Federal Work-Study, institutionally sponsored loans, and tuition waivers (partial) available. Support available to part-time students. Financial award application deadline: 4/27; financial award applicants required to submit FAFSA. In 2001, 189 degrees awarded. *Degree program information:* Evening/weekend programs available. Offers nonprofit organizations (MNO, CNM); social administration (MSSA); social welfare (PhD). *Application deadline:* Applications are processed on a rolling basis. *Application fee:* $30. *Application Contact:* Director of Recruitment and Admissions, 800-863-6772 Ext. 2280, Fax: 216-368-5065, E-mail: msassadmit@po.cwru.edu. *Dean,* Dr. Grover Cleveland Gilmore, 216-368-2256, E-mail: gcg@po.cwru.edu.

School of Dentistry Students: 321 full-time (94 women); includes 91 minority (6 African Americans, 78 Asian Americans or Pacific Islanders, 7 Hispanic Americans) Average age 27. 1,580 applicants, 18% accepted, 70 enrolled. *Faculty:* 33 full-time (5 women), 230 part-time/adjunct (50 women). Expenses: Contact institution. *Financial support:* In 2001–02, 248 students received support. Federal Work-Study, institutionally sponsored loans, and scholarships/grants available. Financial award application deadline: 4/30; financial award applicants required to submit FAFSA. In 2001, 72 DDSs, 14 master's awarded. Offers advanced general dentistry (Certificate); dentistry (DDS, MSD, Certificate); endodontics (MSD, Certificate); oral surgery (MSD, Certificate); orthodontics (MSD, Certificate); pedodontics (Certificate); periodontics (MSD, Certificate). *Application deadline:* For fall admission, 2/1. Applications are processed on a rolling basis. *Application fee:* $45. Electronic applica-

Case Western Reserve University (continued)

tions accepted. *Application Contact:* David A. Dalsky, Director of Admissions, 216-368-2460, Fax: 216-368-3204, E-mail: dad4@po.cwru.edu. *Dean,* Dr. Jerold S. Goldberg, 216-368-3266, Fax: 216-368-3204, E-mail: jsg@po.cwru.edu.

School of Graduate Studies *Degree program information:* Part-time and evening/weekend programs available. Offers acting (MFA); American studies (MA, PhD); analytical chemistry (MS, PhD); anthropology (MA, PhD); applied mathematics (MS, PhD); art education (MA); art history (MA, PhD); art history and museum studies (MA, PhD); astronomy (MS, PhD); bioethics (MA); biology (MS, PhD); clinical psychology (PhD); comparative literature (MA); contemporary dance (MFA); early music (D Mus A); English and American literature (MA, PhD); experimental psychology (PhD); French (MA, PhD); geological sciences (MS, PhD); gerontology (Certificate); history (MA, PhD); inorganic chemistry (MS, PhD); mathematics (MS, PhD); mental retardation (PhD); museum studies (MA); music (MA, PhD); music education (MA, PhD); organic chemistry (MS, PhD); physical chemistry (MS, PhD); physics (MS, PhD); political science (MA, PhD); sociology (PhD); speech-language pathology (MA, PhD); statistics (MS, PhD); theater (MFA).

The Case School of Engineering Students: 309 full-time (86 women), 296 part-time (58 women); includes 55 minority (7 African Americans, 42 Asian Americans or Pacific Islanders, 6 Hispanic Americans), 295 international. Average age 24. 1,912 applicants, 26% accepted, 116 enrolled. *Faculty:* 109 full-time (6 women), 80 part-time/adjunct (10 women). Expenses: Contact institution. *Financial support:* In 2001–02, 175 fellowships with full and partial tuition reimbursements (averaging $16,524 per year), 184 research assistantships with full and partial tuition reimbursements (averaging $16,413 per year), 5 teaching assistantships (averaging $18,600 per year) were awarded. Career-related internships or fieldwork, Federal Work-Study, and institutionally sponsored loans also available. Support available to part-time students. Financial award applicants required to submit FAFSA. In 2001, 131 master's, 51 doctorates awarded. *Degree program information:* Part-time and evening/weekend programs available. Postbaccalaureate distance learning degree programs offered. Offers aerospace engineering (MS, PhD); biomedical engineering (MS, PhD); ceramics and materials science (MS); chemical engineering (MS, PhD); civil engineering (MS, PhD); computer engineering (MS, PhD); computing and information science (MS, PhD); electrical engineering (MS, PhD); engineering (ME, MS, PhD); engineering mechanics (MS); fluid and thermal engineering sciences (MS); fluid and thermal engineering sciences (PhD); macromolecular science (MS, PhD); materials science and engineering (MS, PhD); mechanical engineering (MS, PhD); systems and control engineering (MS, PhD). *Application deadline:* Applications are processed on a rolling basis. *Application fee:* $25. *Interim Dean,* Dr. Robert F. Savinell, 216-368-4436, Fax: 216-368-6939, E-mail: rfs2@po.cwru.edu.

School of Law Students: 688 full-time (294 women), 55 part-time (27 women); includes 97 minority (33 African Americans, 52 Asian Americans or Pacific Islanders, 12 Hispanic Americans), 63 international. Average age 25. 1,547 applicants, 56% accepted. *Faculty:* 47 full-time (14 women), 104 part-time/adjunct (27 women). Expenses: Contact institution. *Financial support:* In 2001–02, 491 students received support. Career-related internships or fieldwork, Federal Work-Study, and scholarships/grants available. Support available to part-time students. Financial award application deadline: 3/15; financial award applicants required to submit FAFSA. In 2001, 186 first professional degrees, 53 master's awarded. *Degree program information:* Part-time programs available. Offers law (JD); taxation (LL M); U.S. legal studies (LL M). *Application deadline:* For fall admission, 4/1 (priority date). Applications are processed on a rolling basis. *Application fee:* $40. Electronic applications accepted. *Application Contact:* Christopher Lucak, Director of Admissions, 216-368-3600, Fax: 216-368-1042, E-mail: lawadmissions@po.cwru.edu. *Dean,* Gerald Korngold, 216-368-3283.

School of Medicine Students: 412. Expenses: Contact institution. *Financial support:* Fellowships, research assistantships, teaching assistantships, career-related internships or fieldwork, Federal Work-Study, institutionally sponsored loans, and tuition waivers (full and partial) available. Support available to part-time students. In 2001, 150 first professional degrees, 39 master's, 37 doctorates awarded. *Degree program information:* Part-time programs available. Offers biomedical sciences (PhD); medicine (MD, MA, MPH, MS, PhD). *Application deadline:* Applications are processed on a rolling basis. *Dean,* Dr. Nathan A. Berger, 216-368-2820.

Graduate Programs in Medicine Students: 338 full-time (173 women), 171 part-time (101 women); includes 45 minority (10 African Americans, 23 Asian Americans or Pacific Islanders, 8 Hispanic Americans, 4 Native Americans), 141 international. Average age 28. 928 applicants, 31% accepted. Expenses: Contact institution. *Financial support:* Fellowships, research assistantships, teaching assistantships, career-related internships or fieldwork, Federal Work-Study, institutionally sponsored loans, and tuition waivers (full and partial) available. Support available to part-time students. In 2001, 71 master's, 47 doctorates awarded. *Degree program information:* Part-time programs available. Offers anesthesiology (MS); applied anatomy (MS); biochemical research (MS); biochemistry (MS, PhD); biological anthropology (MS, PhD); biophysics and bioengineering (PhD); biostatistics (MS, PhD); cell biology (MS, PhD); cell physiology (PhD); cellular biology (MS, PhD); developmental biology (PhD); dietetics (MS); environmental toxicology (MS, PhD); epidemiology (MS, PhD); exerscise physiology (MS); genetic counseling (MS); human, molecular, and developmental genetics and genomics (PhD); immunology (MS, PhD); medicine (MA, MPH, MS, PhD); microbiology (PhD); molecular biology (PhD); molecular toxicology (MS, PhD); neurobiology (PhD); neuroscience (PhD); nutrition (MS, PhD); pathology (MS, PhD); pharmacology (MS, PhD); physiology and biophysics (PhD); physiology and biotechnology (MS); public health (MPH); public health nutrition (MS); systems physiology (PhD). *Application deadline:* Applications are processed on a rolling basis. *Application fee:* $25. *Dean, Graduate Studies,* Dr. Joyce E. Jentoft, 216-368-4400, Fax: 216-368-4250.

Weatherhead School of Management Students: 801 full-time (269 women), 695 part-time (275 women); includes 151 minority (78 African Americans, 51 Asian Americans or Pacific Islanders, 20 Hispanic Americans, 2 Native Americans), 404 international. Average age 28. 858 applicants, 51% accepted, 239 enrolled. *Faculty:* 93 full-time (17 women), 19 part-time/adjunct (4 women). Expenses: Contact institution. *Financial support:* In 2001–02, 524 students received support, including 4 fellowships with full and partial tuition reimbursements available (averaging $4,000 per year); career-related internships or fieldwork, Federal Work-Study, institutionally sponsored loans, scholarships/grants, tuition waivers (full and partial), unspecified assistantships, and awards also available. Financial award application deadline: 5/1; financial award applicants required to submit FAFSA. In 2001, 547 master's, 20 doctorates awarded. *Degree program information:* Part-time and evening/weekend programs available. Offers accountancy (M Acc, PhD); banking and finance (MBA, PhD); economics (MBA); information systems (MBA, MSM, PhD); labor and human resource policy (MBA, PhD); management (MS, EDM); management policy (MBA, PhD); marketing (MBA, PhD); operations research (PhD); organizational behavior and analysis (MBA, MS, PhD). *Application deadline:* For fall admission, 3/15 (priority date). Applications are processed on a rolling basis. *Application fee:* $50. Electronic applications accepted. *Application Contact:* Christine L. Gill, Director of Marketing and Admissions, 216-368-3845, Fax: 216-368-4776, E-mail: clg3@po.cwru.edu. *Dean,* Mohsen Anvari, 216-368-2046, Fax: 216-368-2845, E-mail: mxa104@po.cwru.edu.

Mandel Center for Nonprofit Organizations Students: 23 full-time (19 women), 40 part-time (35 women); includes 18 minority (10 African Americans, 6 Asian Americans or Pacific Islanders, 2 Hispanic Americans) Average age 32. 45 applicants, 47% accepted, 21 enrolled. *Faculty:* 4 full-time (2 women), 25 part-time/adjunct (5 women). Expenses: Contact institution. *Financial support:* In 2001–02, 3 fellowships with full and partial tuition reimbursements were awarded; career-related internships or fieldwork, Federal Work-Study, and scholarships/grants also available. Financial award application deadline: 5/1; financial award applicants required to submit FAFSA. In 2001, 24 degrees awarded. *Degree program information:* Part-time and evening/weekend programs available. Offers nonprofit organizations (MNO, CNM). *Application deadline:* For fall admission, 8/1 (priority date); for spring admission, 11/15 (priority date). Applications are processed on a rolling basis. *Application fee:* $25. *Application Contact:* Carol K. Willen, Director of Graduate Programs, 216-368-8566, Fax: 216-368-4793, E-mail: ckw3@po.cwru.edu. *Director,* Susan Lajoie Eagan, 216-368-2275, Fax: 216-368-8592, E-mail: sle7@po.cwru.edu.

See in-depth description on page 783.

CASTLETON STATE COLLEGE, Castleton, VT 05735

General Information State-supported, coed, comprehensive institution. *Enrollment:* 25 full-time matriculated graduate/professional students (23 women), 89 part-time matriculated graduate/professional students (60 women). *Enrollment by degree level:* 114 master's. *Graduate faculty:* 15 full-time (11 women), 7 part-time/adjunct (4 women). Tuition, state resident: full-time $4,404; part-time $184 per credit. Tuition, nonresident: full-time $10,320; part-time $430 per credit. *Required fees:* $838; $31 per credit. *Graduate housing:* Room and/or apartments available on a first-come, first-served basis to single students; on-campus housing not available to married students. Typical cost: $3,252 per year ($5,530 including board). Housing application deadline: 5/19. *Student services:* Campus employment opportunities, career counseling, free psychological counseling, low-cost health insurance. *Library facilities:* Calvin Coolidge Library. *Online resources:* library catalog, web page, access to other libraries' catalogs. *Collection:* 161,480 titles, 1,858 serial subscriptions, 2,626 audiovisual materials.

Computer facilities: 215 computers available on campus for general student use. A campuswide network can be accessed from student residence rooms. Internet access is available. *Web address:* http://www.castleton.edu/.

General Application Contact: Bill Allen, Dean of Enrollment, 802-468-1213, Fax: 802-468-1476, E-mail: info@castleton.edu.

GRADUATE UNITS

Division of Graduate Studies Students: 25 full-time (23 women), 89 part-time (60 women); includes 4 minority (1 Asian American or Pacific Islander, 1 Hispanic American, 2 Native Americans) Average age 30. *Faculty:* 15 full-time (11 women), 7 part-time/adjunct (4 women). Expenses: Contact institution. *Financial support:* Fellowships, teaching assistantships, career-related internships or fieldwork and Federal Work-Study available. Support available to part-time students. Financial award application deadline: 2/15; financial award applicants required to submit FAFSA. In 2001, 43 degrees awarded. *Degree program information:* Part-time and evening/weekend programs available. Offers curriculum and instruction (MA Ed); educational leadership (MA Ed, CAGS); forensic psychology (MA); language arts and reading (MA Ed, CAGS); special education (MA Ed, CAGS). *Application deadline:* For fall admission, 7/1. *Application fee:* $30. *Application Contact:* Bill Allen, Dean of Enrollment, 802-468-1213, Fax: 802-468-1476, E-mail: info@castleton.edu. *Associate Academic Dean,* John Tigue, 802-468-1243, Fax: 802-468-5237, E-mail: john.tigue@castleton.edu.

CATAWBA COLLEGE, Salisbury, NC 28144-2488

General Information Independent-religious, coed, comprehensive institution. *Enrollment:* 21 part-time matriculated graduate/professional students (19 women). *Enrollment by degree level:* 21 master's. *Graduate faculty:* 5 full-time (4 women), 3 part-time/adjunct (1 woman). *Tuition:* Part-time $115 per semester hour. *Graduate housing:* On-campus housing not available. *Student services:* Campus safety program, career counseling, teacher training. *Library facilities:* Corriher-Linn-Black Memorial Library plus 1 other. *Online resources:* library catalog, access to other libraries' catalogs. *Collection:* 144,788 titles, 3,661 serial subscriptions, 24,281 audiovisual materials.

Computer facilities: 80 computers available on campus for general student use. A campuswide network can be accessed from student residence rooms. Internet access is available. *Web address:* http://www.catawba.edu/.

General Application Contact: Dr. Lou W. Kasias, Director, Graduate Program, 704-637-4462, Fax: 704-637-4732, E-mail: lakasias@catawba.edu.

GRADUATE UNITS

Program in Education Average age 30. 3 applicants, 100% accepted. *Faculty:* 5 full-time (4 women), 3 part-time/adjunct (1 woman). Expenses: Contact institution. *Financial support:* Career-related internships or fieldwork and Federal Work-Study available. In 2001, 8 degrees awarded. *Degree program information:* Part-time and evening/weekend programs available. Offers elementary education (M Ed). *Application deadline:* For fall admission, 8/1 (priority date); for spring admission, 12/1 (priority date). Applications are processed on a rolling basis. *Application fee:* $15. Electronic applications accepted. *Application Contact:* Dr. Lou W. Kasias, Director, Graduate Program, 704-637-4462, Fax: 704-637-4732, E-mail: lakasias@catawba.edu. *Chair, Department of Teacher Education,* Dr. James K. Stringfield, 704-637-4461, Fax: 704-637-4732, E-mail: jstringf@catawba.edu.

THE CATHOLIC DISTANCE UNIVERSITY, Hamilton, VA 20158

General Information Independent-religious, coed, graduate-only institution. *Enrollment by degree level:* 127 master's. *Graduate faculty:* 8 part-time/adjunct (0 women). *Tuition:* Part-time $218 per semester hour. *Graduate housing:* On-campus housing not available. *Library facilities:* Catholic Distance University. *Collection:* 600 titles.

Computer facilities: A campuswide network can be accessed. *Web address:* http://www.cdu.edu/.

General Application Contact: Frank Degnan, Graduate Registrar, 540-338-2700, Fax: 540-338-4788, E-mail: cdu@cdu.edu.

GRADUATE UNITS

Graduate Programs Average age 48. *Faculty:* 8 part-time/adjunct (0 women). Expenses: Contact institution. In 2001, 6 degrees awarded. *Degree program information:* Part-time and evening/weekend programs available. Postbaccalaureate distance learning degree programs offered (no on-campus study). Offers religious studies (MA, MRS). *Application deadline:* Applications are processed on a rolling basis. *Application fee:* $100. *Application Contact:* Frank Degnan, Graduate Registrar, 540-338-2700, Fax: 540-338-4788, E-mail: cdu@cdu.edu. *Graduate Dean,* Rev. Leonard G. Obloy, 540-338-2700, Fax: 540-338-4788, E-mail: cdu@cdu.edu.

CATHOLIC THEOLOGICAL UNION AT CHICAGO, Chicago, IL 60615-5698

General Information Independent-religious, coed, graduate-only institution. *Enrollment by degree level:* 177 first professional, 176 master's, 33 doctoral, 10 other advanced degrees. *Graduate faculty:* 29 full-time (8 women), 15 part-time/adjunct (4 women). *Tuition:* Part-time $285 per credit hour. *Required fees:* $4 per credit hour. *Graduate housing:* Rooms and/or apartments available on a first-come, first-served basis to single and married students. Typical cost: $4,350 per year for single students; $4,350 per year for married students. Room charges vary according to housing facility selected. Housing application deadline: 7/1. *Student services:* Campus employment opportunities, campus safety program, career counseling, disabled student services, international student services, low-cost health insurance, writing training. *Library facilities:* Paul Bechtold Library. *Online resources:* library catalog, web page, access to other libraries' catalogs. *Collection:* 120,000 titles, 580 serial subscriptions.

Computer facilities: 14 computers available on campus for general student use. A campuswide network can be accessed. Internet access is available. *Web address:* http://www.ctu.edu/.

General Application Contact: Terry Stadler, Director of Admissions, 773-753-5316, Fax: 773-324-4360, E-mail: tstadler@ctu.edu.

GRADUATE UNITS

Graduate and Professional Programs Students: 248 full-time (52 women), 149 part-time (102 women); includes 80 minority (16 African Americans, 38 Asian Americans or Pacific Islanders, 22 Hispanic Americans, 4 Native Americans), 98 international. Average age 32. 200 applicants, 98% accepted, 188 enrolled. *Faculty:* 29 full-time (8 women), 15 part-time/adjunct (4 women). Expenses: Contact institution. *Financial support:* In 2001–02, 104 students received support. Career-related internships or fieldwork, scholarships/grants, and tuition waivers (full and partial) available. Support available to part-time students. Financial award application deadline: 7/15; financial award applicants required to submit CSS PROFILE. In 2001, 27 first professional degrees, 42 master's, 15 doctorates, 3 other advanced degrees awarded. *Degree program information:* Part-time and evening/weekend programs available. Offers biblical spirituality (Certificate); cross-cultural ministries (D Min); cross-cultural missions (Certificate); divinity (M Div); liturgical studies (Certificate); liturgy (D Min); pastoral studies (MAPS, Certificate); spiritual formation (Certificate); spirituality (D Min); theology (MA). *Application deadline:* For fall admission, 4/15 (priority date); for winter admission, 1/2; for spring admission, 3/15. Applications are processed on a rolling basis. *Application fee:* $35. *Application Contact:* Terry Stadler, Director of Admissions, 773-753-5316, Fax: 773-324-4360, E-mail: tstadler@ctu.edu. *Academic Dean and Vice President,* Rev. Gary Riebe-Estrella, SVD, 773-753-5307, Fax: 773-684-5817, E-mail: griebe@ctu.edu.

THE CATHOLIC UNIVERSITY OF AMERICA, Washington, DC 20064

General Information Independent-religious, coed, university. CGS member. *Enrollment:* 1,367 full-time matriculated graduate/professional students (695 women), 1,459 part-time matriculated graduate/professional students (731 women). *Graduate faculty:* 360 full-time (120 women), 285 part-time/adjunct (126 women). *Tuition:* Full-time $20,050; part-time $770 per credit. *Required fees:* $430 per term. Tuition and fees vary according to program. *Graduate housing:* Room and/or apartments available on a first-come, first-served basis to single students; on-campus housing not available to married students. Typical cost: $4,708 per year ($8,382 including board). Housing application deadline: 6/1. *Student services:* Campus employment opportunities, campus safety program, career counseling, child daycare facilities, disabled student services, exercise/wellness program, free psychological counseling, international student services, low-cost health insurance, multicultural affairs office, writing training. *Library facilities:* Mullen Library plus 7 others. *Online resources:* library catalog, web page, access to other libraries' catalogs. *Collection:* 1.4 million titles, 11,200 serial subscriptions, 38,200 audiovisual materials. *Research affiliation:* Folger Institute of Renaissance and Eighteenth-Century Studies, Folger Shakespeare Library, Dumbarton Oaks Center for Byzantine Studies, Oak Ridge Institute for Science and Education (science, business, education).

Computer facilities: 450 computers available on campus for general student use. A campuswide network can be accessed from student residence rooms and from off campus. Internet access and online class registration are available. *Web address:* http://www.cua.edu/.

General Application Contact: Dr. Kristy Lisle, Director of Graduate Admissions, 202-319-5057, Fax: 202-319-6171, E-mail: mccown@cua.edu.

GRADUATE UNITS

The Benjamin T. Rome School of Music Students: 40 full-time (32 women), 74 part-time (48 women); includes 19 minority (8 African Americans, 9 Asian Americans or Pacific Islanders, 2 Hispanic Americans), 33 international. Average age 34. 106 applicants, 58% accepted, 33 enrolled. *Faculty:* 15 full-time (4 women), 20 part-time/adjunct (7 women). Expenses: Contact institution. *Financial support:* In 2001–02, 65 students received support, including 2 research assistantships, 8 teaching assistantships; fellowships, career-related internships or fieldwork, Federal Work-Study, institutionally sponsored loans, scholarships/grants, and tuition waivers (full and partial) also available. Support available to part-time students. Financial award application deadline: 2/1; financial award applicants required to submit FAFSA. In 2001, 19 master's, 12 doctorates awarded. *Degree program information:* Part-time programs available. Offers accompanying and chamber music (MM); chamber music (DMA); composition (MM, DMA); instrumental conducting (MM, DMA); liturgical music (M Lit M, DMA); music (M Lit M, MA, MM, DMA, PhD); musicology (MA, PhD); orchestral instruments (MM, DMA); organ (MM, DMA); performance (MM, DMA); piano pedagogy (MM, DMA); vocal accompanying (DMA); vocal pedagogy (MM); vocal performance (MM); voice pedagogy and performance (DMA). *Application deadline:* For fall admission, 8/1 (priority date); for spring admission, 12/1. Applications are processed on a rolling basis. *Application fee:* $55. Electronic applications accepted. *Application Contact:* Dr. Paul G. Taylor, Assistant Dean, 202-319-5414, E-mail: taylorpg@cua.edu. *Dean,* Marilyn Neeley, 202-319-5417, E-mail: neeley@cua.edu.

Columbus School of Law Students: 654 full-time (356 women), 278 part-time (129 women); includes 202 minority (121 African Americans, 37 Asian Americans or Pacific Islanders, 43 Hispanic Americans, 1 Native American), 8 international. Average age 26. 2,165 applicants, 48% accepted. *Faculty:* 44 full-time (15 women), 49 part-time/adjunct (14 women). Expenses: Contact institution. *Financial support:* In 2001–02, 746 students received support; research assistantships, career-related internships or fieldwork, Federal Work-Study, institutionally sponsored loans, and scholarships/grants available. Support available to part-time students. Financial award application deadline: 3/1; financial award applicants required to submit FAFSA. In 2001, 279 degrees awarded. *Degree program information:* Part-time and evening/weekend programs available. Offers law (JD). *Application deadline:* For fall admission, 3/1. Applications are processed on a rolling basis. *Application fee:* $55. *Application Contact:* George P. Braxton, Director of Admissions, 202-319-5151, Fax: 202-319-4498, E-mail: braxton@law.edu. *Interim Dean,* Robert A. Destro, 202-319-5144, Fax: 202-319-5473.

National Catholic School of Social Service Students: 92 full-time (82 women), 115 part-time (96 women); includes 44 minority (31 African Americans, 4 Asian Americans or Pacific Islanders, 9 Hispanic Americans), 10 international. Average age 36. 145 applicants, 82% accepted, 80 enrolled. *Faculty:* 15 full-time (12 women), 19 part-time/adjunct (17 women). Expenses: Contact institution. *Financial support:* In 2001–02, 100 students received support; fellowships, career-related internships or fieldwork, Federal Work-Study, institutionally sponsored loans, and scholarships/grants available. Support available to part-time students. Financial award applicants required to submit FAFSA. In 2001, 64 master's, 3 doctorates awarded. *Degree program information:* Part-time programs available. Offers social service (MSW, PhD). *Application fee:* $55. Electronic applications accepted. *Application Contact:* Christine Sabatino, Director of Admission, 202-319-5496, Fax: 202-319-5093, E-mail: cua-ncss@cua.edu. *Dean,* Dr. Ann Patrick Conrad, 202-319-5454, Fax: 202-319-5093.

School of Architecture and Planning Students: 76 full-time (37 women), 7 part-time (3 women); includes 14 minority (6 African Americans, 5 Asian Americans or Pacific Islanders, 3 Hispanic Americans), 15 international. Average age 27. 80 applicants, 51% accepted, 23 enrolled. *Faculty:* 14 full-time (3 women), 16 part-time/adjunct (3 women). Expenses: Contact institution. *Financial support:* In 2001–02, 40 teaching assistantships were awarded; Federal Work-Study, scholarships/grants, and tuition waivers (partial) also available. Financial award application deadline: 1/22; financial award applicants required to submit FAFSA. In 2001, 45 degrees awarded. *Degree program information:* Part-time programs available. Offers architecture and planning (M Arch, M Arch Studies). *Application deadline:* For fall admission, 1/22 (priority date); for spring admission, 10/15. Applications are processed on a rolling basis. *Application fee:* $55. Electronic applications accepted. *Application Contact:* Dr. Terrance Williams, Associate Dean of Graduate Studies, 202-319-5188, Fax: 202-319-5728. *Dean,* Gregory K. Hunt, 202-319-5784, Fax: 202-238-2023, E-mail: huntg@cua.edu.

School of Arts and Sciences Students: 155 full-time (77 women), 393 part-time (179 women); includes 61 minority (29 African Americans, 11 Asian Americans or Pacific Islanders, 18 Hispanic Americans, 3 Native Americans), 62 international. Average age 33. 504 applicants, 59% accepted, 137 enrolled. *Faculty:* 154 full-time (49 women), 77 part-time/adjunct (51 women). Expenses: Contact institution. *Financial support:* Fellowships, research assistantships, teaching assistantships, career-related internships or fieldwork, Federal Work-Study, institutionally sponsored loans, scholarships/grants, and tuition waivers (full and partial) available. Support available to part-time students. Financial award application deadline: 2/1. In 2001, 115 master's, 28 doctorates awarded. *Degree program information:* Part-time and evening/weekend programs available. Offers accounting (MA); acting, directing, and playwriting (MFA); administration, curriculum, and policy studies (MA); American government (MA, PhD); anthropology (MA, PhD); applied experimental psychology (MA, PhD); arts and sciences (MA, MFA, MS, MTS, PhD, Certificate); Byzantine studies (MA, Certificate); Catholic school leadership (MA); cell and microbial biology (MS, PhD); cell biology (MS, PhD); chemistry (MS, PhD); classics (MA); clinical laboratory science (MS, PhD); clinical psychology (PhD); comparative literature (MA, PhD); congressional studies (MA); counselor education (MA); early Christian studies (MA, PhD, Certificate); economics (MA); educational administration (PhD); educational psychology (PhD); English as a second language (MA); English language and literature (MA, PhD); financial management (MA); French (MA, PhD); general psychology (MA); German (MA); Greek and Latin (PhD); history (MA, PhD); human development (PhD); human factors (MA); human resource management (MA); international affairs (MA); international political economics (MA); Irish studies (MA); Italian (MA); Latin (MA); learning and instruction (MA); medieval studies (MA, PhD, Certificate); microbiology (MS, PhD); physics (MS, PhD); policy studies (PhD); political theory (MA, PhD); rhetoric (MA, PhD); Romance languages and literatures (MA, PhD); Semitic and Egyptian languages and literature (MA, PhD); sociology (MA, PhD); Spanish (MA, PhD); teacher education (MA); theatre history and criticism (MA); world politics (MA, PhD). *Application deadline:* Applications are processed on a rolling basis. *Application fee:* $55. Electronic applications accepted. *Application Contact:* Dr. Hanna Marks, Associate Dean for Graduate Programs, 202-319-5254, Fax: 202-319-4463, E-mail: marks@cua.edu. *Dean,* Dr. Antanas Suziedelis, 202-319-5115, Fax: 202-319-4463.

School of Engineering Students: 21 full-time (2 women), 86 part-time (16 women); includes 16 minority (9 African Americans, 5 Asian Americans or Pacific Islanders, 2 Hispanic Americans), 42 international. Average age 33. 123 applicants, 60% accepted, 17 enrolled. *Faculty:* 26 full-time (2 women), 14 part-time/adjunct (2 women). Expenses: Contact institution. *Financial support:* Fellowships, research assistantships, teaching assistantships, career-related internships or fieldwork, Federal Work-Study, institutionally sponsored loans, tuition waivers (full and partial), and unspecified assistantships available. Support available to part-time students. Financial award application deadline: 2/1. In 2001, 47 master's, 7 doctorates awarded. *Degree program information:* Part-time and evening/weekend programs available. Offers biomedical engineering (MBE, MS Engr, PhD); civil engineering (MCE, D Engr); construction management (MCE, MS Engr); design (D Engr, PhD); design and robotics (MME, D Engr, PhD); electrical engineering and computer science (MEE, MS Engr, MSCS, D Engr, PhD); engineering (MBE, MCE, MEE, MME, MS Engr, MSCS, D Engr, PhD); engineering management (MS Engr); environmental engineering (MCE, MS Engr); fluid mechanics and thermal science (MME, D Engr, PhD); geotechnical engineering (MCE); mechanical design (MME); ocean and structural acoustics (MME, MS Engr, PhD); structures and structural mechanics (MCE). *Application deadline:* For fall admission, 7/31; for spring admission, 12/10. Applications are processed on a rolling basis. *Application fee:* $55. Electronic applications accepted. *Application Contact:* Peggy Wheeler, Administrative Assistant, 202-319-5160, Fax: 202-319-4499. *Dean,* Dr. Charles C. Nguyen, 202-319-5160, Fax: 202-319-4499.

School of Library and Information Science Students: 25 full-time (22 women), 175 part-time (134 women); includes 28 minority (23 African Americans, 3 Asian Americans or Pacific Islanders, 2 Hispanic Americans), 10 international. Average age 38. 111 applicants, 77% accepted, 52 enrolled. *Faculty:* 7 full-time (all women), 18 part-time/adjunct (11 women). Expenses: Contact institution. *Financial support:* Fellowships, research assistantships, career-related internships or fieldwork, Federal Work-Study, institutionally sponsored loans, tuition waivers (full and partial), and unspecified assistantships available. Support available to part-time students. Financial award application deadline: 2/1. In 2001, 63 degrees awarded. *Degree program information:* Part-time and evening/weekend programs available. Post-baccalaureate distance learning degree programs offered (minimal on-campus study). Offers library and information science (MSLS). *Application deadline:* For fall admission, 7/1 (priority date); for spring admission, 11/1. Applications are processed on a rolling basis. *Application fee:* $55. Electronic applications accepted. *Dean,* Dr. Peter Liebscher, 202-319-5085, E-mail: liebscher@cua.edu.

School of Nursing Students: 33 full-time (32 women), 56 part-time (55 women); includes 17 minority (12 African Americans, 3 Asian Americans or Pacific Islanders, 2 Hispanic Americans), 15 international. Average age 40. 42 applicants, 71% accepted, 22 enrolled. *Faculty:* 17 full-time (all women), 8 part-time/adjunct (all women). Expenses: Contact institution. *Financial support:* In 2001–02, 25 students received support, including 2 teaching assistantships; research assistantships, career-related internships or fieldwork, Federal Work-Study, institutionally sponsored loans, and tuition waivers (full and partial) also available. Support available to part-time students. Financial award application deadline: 4/1; financial award applicants required to submit FAFSA. In 2001, 19 master's, 9 doctorates awarded. *Degree program information:* Part-time programs available. Offers advanced practice nursing (MSN); clinical nursing (DN Sc). *Application deadline:* For fall admission, 8/1 (priority date); for spring admission, 12/1. Applications are processed on a rolling basis. *Application fee:* $55. Electronic applications accepted. *Dean,* Dr. Annmarie T Brooks, 202-319-5403, Fax: 202-319-6485.

School of Philosophy Students: 41 full-time (11 women), 63 part-time (11 women); includes 3 minority (1 Asian American or Pacific Islander, 2 Hispanic Americans), 15 international. Average age 32. 66 applicants, 76% accepted, 32 enrolled. *Faculty:* 15 full-time (2 women), 15 part-time/adjunct (3 women). Expenses: Contact institution. *Financial support:* Fellowships, career-related internships or fieldwork, Federal Work-Study, and tuition waivers (full and partial) available. Financial award application deadline: 2/1. In 2001, 12 master's, 6 doctorates awarded. *Degree program information:* Part-time programs available. Offers philosophy (MA, PhD, Ph L). *Application deadline:* For fall admission, 8/1 (priority date); for spring admission, 12/1. Applications are processed on a rolling basis. *Application fee:* $55. Electronic applications accepted. *Dean,* Rev. Kurt Pritzel, OP, 202-319-5259, Fax: 202-319-4731.

School of Religious Studies Students: 171 full-time (24 women), 179 part-time (50 women); includes 30 minority (6 African Americans, 12 Asian Americans or Pacific Islanders, 12 Hispanic Americans), 55 international. Average age 38. 174 applicants, 76% accepted, 79 enrolled. *Faculty:* 57 full-time (8 women), 15 part-time/adjunct (1 woman). Expenses: Contact institution. *Financial support:* Fellowships, research assistantships, teaching assistantships, career-related internships or fieldwork, Federal Work-Study, institutionally sponsored loans, and tuition waivers (full and partial) available. Support available to part-time students. Financial award application deadline: 2/1. In 2001, 5 first professional degrees, 45 master's, 25 doctorates awarded. *Degree program information:* Part-time programs available. Offers biblical studies (MA, PhD); canon law (JCD, JCL); church history (MA, PhD); liturgical studies (MA, PhD, STD, STL); religion (MA, MRE, PhD); religious education (MA, MRE, PhD); religious studies (M Div, STB, MA, MRE, D Min, JCD, PhD, STD, JCL, STL); theology (M Div, STB, MA, D Min, PhD, STD, STL). *Application deadline:* For fall admission, 8/1 (priority date). Applications are processed on a rolling basis. *Application fee:* $55. Electronic applications accepted. *Dean,* Rev. Stephen Happel, 202-319-5683, Fax: 202-319-4967, E-mail: happel@cua.edu.

See in-depth description on page 785.

CEDARVILLE UNIVERSITY, Cedarville, OH 45314-0601

General Information Independent-religious, coed, comprehensive institution. *Enrollment:* 5 part-time matriculated graduate/professional students (4 women). *Enrollment by degree level:* 5 master's. *Graduate faculty:* 7. *Tuition:* Part-time $260 per semester hour. *Library facilities:* Centennial Library. *Online resources:* library catalog, web page, access to other libraries' catalogs. *Collection:* 139,026 titles, 4,112 serial subscriptions, 14,717 audiovisual materials.

Computer facilities: 1,850 computers available on campus for general student use. A campuswide network can be accessed from student residence rooms and from off campus. Software packages available. *Web address:* http://www.cedarville.edu/.

General Application Contact: Rocoe Smith, Admissions Director, 937-766-7700, Fax: 937-766-7575, E-mail: smithr@cedarville.edu.

GRADUATE UNITS

Graduate Programs *Faculty:* 7. Expenses: Contact institution. *Application Contact:* Rocoe Smith, Admissions Director, 937-766-7700, Fax: 937-766-7575, E-mail: smithr@cedarville.edu. *Director,* Dr. Sharon Johnson, 888-CEDARVILLE.

CENTENARY COLLEGE, Hackettstown, NJ 07840-2100

General Information Independent-religious, coed, comprehensive institution. *Enrollment:* 16 full-time matriculated graduate/professional students, 165 part-time matriculated graduate/professional students. *Graduate faculty:* 35. *Tuition:* Full-time $10,320; part-time $430 per credit. *Graduate housing:* Room and/or apartments available on a first-come, first-served basis to single students; on-campus housing not available to married students. Housing application deadline: 6/1. *Student services:* Career counseling, disabled student services, international student services, low-cost health insurance, teacher training, writing training.

Centenary College (continued)

Library facilities: Taylor Memorial Learning Resource Center. *Online resources:* library catalog. *Collection:* 67,272 titles, 211 serial subscriptions, 4,965 audiovisual materials.

Computer facilities: 30 computers available on campus for general student use. A campuswide network can be accessed from student residence rooms and from off campus. Internet access, resident students have a computer and printer in their room. are available. *Web address:* http://www.centenarycollege.edu/.

General Application Contact: Prof. Terry L. Eason, Director of Graduate Studies, 908-852-1400 Ext. 2172, Fax: 908-813-1984, E-mail: easont@centenarycollege.edu.

GRADUATE UNITS

Program in Business Administration *Degree program information:* Part-time and evening/weekend programs available. Postbaccalaureate distance learning degree programs offered (minimal on-campus study). Offers business administration (MBA).

Program in Counseling Psychology *Degree program information:* Part-time and evening/weekend programs available. Postbaccalaureate distance learning degree programs offered (minimal on-campus study). Offers counseling (MA); counseling psychology (MA).

Program in Education *Degree program information:* Part-time and evening/weekend programs available. Postbaccalaureate distance learning degree programs offered (minimal on-campus study). Offers instructional leadership (MA); special education (MA).

Program in Professional Accounting *Degree program information:* Part-time and evening/weekend programs available. Postbaccalaureate distance learning degree programs offered (minimal on-campus study). Offers professional accounting (MS).

CENTENARY COLLEGE OF LOUISIANA, Shreveport, LA 71134-1188

General Information Independent-religious, coed, comprehensive institution. *Enrollment:* 5 full-time matriculated graduate/professional students (4 women), 134 part-time matriculated graduate/professional students (79 women). *Enrollment by degree level:* 139 master's. *Graduate faculty:* 7 full-time (5 women), 10 part-time/adjunct (7 women). *Tuition:* Full-time $15,400. *Required fees:* $400. *Graduate housing:* Room and/or apartments available on a first-come, first-served basis to single students; on-campus housing not available to married students. *Student services:* Career counseling. *Library facilities:* Magale Library plus 1 other. *Online resources:* library catalog, web page, access to other libraries' catalogs. *Collection:* 186,564 titles, 59,899 serial subscriptions, 5,945 audiovisual materials.

Computer facilities: A campuswide network can be accessed from student residence rooms and from off campus. Internet access is available. *Web address:* http://www.centenary.edu/.

General Application Contact: Dr. Darrel Colson, Head, 318-869-5104, Fax: 318-869-5026, E-mail: dcolson@centenary.edu.

GRADUATE UNITS

Graduate Programs *Degree program information:* Part-time and evening/weekend programs available. Offers administration (M Ed); elementary education (M Ed, MAT); secondary education (M Ed, MAT); supervision of instruction (M Ed).

Frost School of Business Average age 38. 68 applicants, 100% accepted. *Faculty:* 6 full-time (2 women). Expenses: Contact institution. In 2001, 32 degrees awarded. *Degree program information:* Part-time and evening/weekend programs available. Offers business (MBA). *Application deadline:* Applications are processed on a rolling basis. *Application fee:* $20. *Application Contact:* Kelly M. Schellinger, MBA Program Coordinator, 318-869-5149, Fax: 318-869-5139, E-mail: kschelli@centenary.edu. *Dean,* Dr. Chris L. Martin, 318-869-5141, Fax: 318-869-5139, E-mail: cmartin@centenary.edu.

CENTER FOR HUMANISTIC STUDIES, Detroit, MI 48202-3802

General Information Independent, coed, graduate-only institution. *Graduate faculty:* 4 full-time (2 women), 12 part-time/adjunct (5 women). *Tuition:* Full-time $14,060. *Graduate housing:* On-campus housing not available. *Library facilities:* Center for Humanistic Studies Library. *Collection:* 10,272 titles, 52 serial subscriptions, 185 audiovisual materials.

Computer facilities: 4 computers available on campus for general student use. Internet access is available. *Web address:* http://www.humanpsych.edu/.

General Application Contact: Ellen F. Blau, Admissions Adviser, 313-875-7440, Fax: 313-875-2610, E-mail: eblau@humanpsych.edu.

GRADUATE UNITS

Programs in Humanistic, Clinical, and Educational Psychology Students: 83 full-time (60 women); includes 15 minority (13 African Americans, 2 Asian Americans or Pacific Islanders) Average age 38. 90 applicants, 83% accepted. *Faculty:* 4 full-time (2 women), 12 part-time/adjunct (5 women). Expenses: Contact institution. *Financial support:* In 2001–02, 39 students received support. Application deadline: 6/30; In 2001, 30 degrees awarded. Offers humanistic and clinical psychology (MA, Psy D). *Application deadline:* For fall admission, 9/1 (priority date). Applications are processed on a rolling basis. *Application fee:* $75. *Application Contact:* Ellen F. Blau, Admissions Adviser, 313-875-7440, Fax: 313-875-2610, E-mail: eblau@humanpsych.edu.

CENTRAL BAPTIST THEOLOGICAL SEMINARY, Kansas City, KS 66102-3964

General Information Independent-religious, coed, graduate-only institution. *Graduate faculty:* 12 full-time (3 women), 12 part-time/adjunct (3 women). *Tuition:* Full-time $1,905; part-time $191 per credit hour. *Required fees:* $85 per semester. *Graduate housing:* Rooms and/or apartments available on a first-come, first-served basis to single and married students. Typical cost: $1,300 per year for single students; $1,300 per year for married students. *Student services:* Campus employment opportunities, career counseling, low-cost health insurance. *Library facilities:* Pratt-Journeycake Library. *Online resources:* library catalog. *Collection:* 85,500 titles, 520 serial subscriptions.

Computer facilities: 13 computers available on campus for general student use. Internet access is available. *Web address:* http://www.cbts.edu/.

General Application Contact: Dr. Bill Hill, Director of Student Life and Enrollment Services, 913-371-5313 Ext. 102, Fax: 913-371-8110, E-mail: bhill@cbts.edu.

GRADUATE UNITS

Graduate and Professional Programs Students: 64 full-time (31 women), 42 part-time (20 women); includes 28 minority (26 African Americans, 1 Asian American or Pacific Islander, 1 Native American), 13 international. Average age 41. 35 applicants, 71% accepted, 25 enrolled. *Faculty:* 12 full-time (3 women), 12 part-time/adjunct (3 women). Expenses: Contact institution. *Financial support:* In 2001–02, 42 students received support. Career-related internships or fieldwork and scholarships/grants available. Financial award application deadline: 8/2. In 2001, 17 first professional degrees, 5 master's awarded. *Degree program information:* Part-time programs available. Offers theology (M Div, MARS, Diploma). *Application deadline:* For fall admission, 8/2 (priority date); for winter admission, 12/2 (priority date); for spring admission, 1/2. Applications are processed on a rolling basis. *Application fee:* $30. *Application Contact:* Dr. Bill Hill, Director of Student Life and Enrollment Services, 913-371-5313 Ext. 102, Fax: 913-371-8110, E-mail: bhill@cbts.edu. *Academic Dean,* Dr. James F. Hines, 913-371-5313 Ext. 105, Fax: 913-371-8110, E-mail: jfhines@cbts.edu.

CENTRAL CONNECTICUT STATE UNIVERSITY, New Britain, CT 06050-4010

General Information State-supported, coed, comprehensive institution. CGS member. *Enrollment:* 497 full-time matriculated graduate/professional students (324 women), 1,578 part-time matriculated graduate/professional students (1,090 women). *Enrollment by degree level:* 1,498 master's, 577 other advanced degrees. *Graduate faculty:* 302 full-time (132 women), 244 part-time/adjunct (116 women). Tuition, state resident: full-time $2,772; part-time $245 per credit. Tuition, nonresident: full-time $7,726; part-time $245 per credit. *Required fees:* $2,102. Tuition and fees vary according to course level and degree level. *Graduate housing:* Room and/or apartments available on a first-come, first-served basis to single students; on-campus housing not available to married students. Typical cost: $2,530 per year ($6,030 including board). Housing application deadline: 5/1. *Student services:* Campus employment opportunities, campus safety program, career counseling, child daycare facilities, exercise/wellness program, free psychological counseling, international student services, low-cost health insurance, multicultural affairs office, teacher training. *Library facilities:* Burritt Library plus 1 other. *Online resources:* library catalog, access to other libraries' catalogs. *Collection:* 620,958 titles, 2,813 serial subscriptions, 5,224 audiovisual materials.

Computer facilities: 230 computers available on campus for general student use. A campuswide network can be accessed from student residence rooms and from off campus. Internet access is available. *Web address:* http://www.ccsu.edu/.

General Application Contact: Kevin Oliva, Graduate Admissions, 860-832-2350, Fax: 860-832-2362, E-mail: oliva@ccsu.edu.

GRADUATE UNITS

School of Graduate Studies Students: 497 full-time (324 women), 1,578 part-time (1,090 women); includes 222 minority (80 African Americans, 63 Asian Americans or Pacific Islanders, 73 Hispanic Americans, 6 Native Americans), 39 international. Average age 33. 890 applicants, 72% accepted. *Faculty:* 302 full-time (132 women), 244 part-time/adjunct (116 women). Expenses: Contact institution. *Financial support:* In 2001–02, 59 research assistantships (averaging $4,800 per year), 2 teaching assistantships (averaging $4,800 per year) were awarded. Fellowships, career-related internships or fieldwork, Federal Work-Study, and institutionally sponsored loans also available. Support available to part-time students. Financial award application deadline: 3/15; financial award applicants required to submit FAFSA. In 2001, 457 master's, 48 other advanced degrees awarded. *Degree program information:* Part-time and evening/weekend programs available. Offers international studies (MS); social science (MS). *Application deadline:* For fall admission, 8/10 (priority date); for spring admission, 12/10. Applications are processed on a rolling basis. *Application fee:* $40. *Application Contact:* Diane Abraham, Graduate Admissions, 860-832-2360, Fax: 860-832-2362, E-mail: abraham@ccsu.edu. *Graduate Admissions,* Kevin Oliva, 860-832-2350, Fax: 860-832-2362, E-mail: oliva@ccsu.edu.

School of Arts and Sciences Students: 279 full-time (187 women), 474 part-time (282 women); includes 105 minority (28 African Americans, 52 Asian Americans or Pacific Islanders, 21 Hispanic Americans, 4 Native Americans), 20 international. Average age 34. 319 applicants, 70% accepted. *Faculty:* 223 full-time (93 women), 181 part-time/adjunct (85 women). Expenses: Contact institution. *Financial support:* In 2001–02, 13 research assistantships (averaging $4,800 per year), 2 teaching assistantships (averaging $4,800 per year) were awarded. Career-related internships or fieldwork and Federal Work-Study also available. Financial award application deadline: 3/15; financial award applicants required to submit FAFSA. In 2001, 180 degrees awarded. *Degree program information:* Part-time and evening/weekend programs available. Offers art education (MS); arts and sciences (MA, MS, Certificate); biological sciences (MA, MS); cell and molecular biology (Certificate); community psychology (MA); computer science (MS); criminal justice (MS); earth science (MS); English (MA); French (MA); general science (MS); geography (MS); graphic information design (MA); history (MA); international studies (MA); mathematics (MA, MS); music education (MS); natural science chemistry (MS); natural sciences (MS); organizational communication (MS); physics (MS); pre health (Certificate); psychology (MA); public history (MS); science and science education (MS); Spanish (MA, MS); teaching English to speakers of other languages (MS). *Application deadline:* For fall admission, 8/10 (priority date); for spring admission, 12/10. Applications are processed on a rolling basis. *Application fee:* $40. *Application Contact:* Dr. Carol A. Jones, Associate to Dean, 860-832-2600. *Dean,* Dr. June B. Higgins, 860-832-2600.

School of Business Students: 42 full-time (19 women), 52 part-time (27 women); includes 9 minority (1 African American, 3 Asian Americans or Pacific Islanders, 5 Hispanic Americans), 14 international. Average age 32. 45 applicants, 78% accepted. *Faculty:* 12 full-time (2 women), 5 part-time/adjunct (2 women). Expenses: Contact institution. *Financial support:* In 2001–02, 25 research assistantships were awarded; Federal Work-Study also available. Financial award application deadline: 3/15; financial award applicants required to submit FAFSA. In 2001, 30 degrees awarded. *Degree program information:* Part-time and evening/weekend programs available. Offers business (MBA, MS); business education (MS); international business administration (MBA). *Application deadline:* For fall admission, 8/10 (priority date); for spring admission, 12/10. Applications are processed on a rolling basis. *Application fee:* $40. *Application Contact:* Dr. George Claffey, Associate Dean, 860-832-3210. *Dean,* Dr. Dan Miller, 860-832-3205.

School of Education and Professional Studies Students: 156 full-time (112 women), 936 part-time (745 women); includes 95 minority (43 African Americans, 7 Asian Americans or Pacific Islanders, 43 Hispanic Americans, 2 Native Americans), 5 international. Average age 33. 492 applicants, 74% accepted. *Faculty:* 63 full-time (37 women), 49 part-time/adjunct (26 women). Expenses: Contact institution. *Financial support:* In 2001–02, 15 research assistantships were awarded; fellowships, career-related internships or fieldwork and Federal Work-Study also available. Financial award application deadline: 3/15; financial award applicants required to submit FAFSA. In 2001, 285 master's, 48 other advanced degrees awarded. *Degree program information:* Part-time and evening/weekend programs available. Offers early childhood education (MS); education and professional studies (MS, Ed D, Sixth Year Certificate); education leadership (MS); educational foundations policy/secondary education (MS); educational leadership (Ed D, Sixth Year Certificate); educational technology (MS); educational technology and media (MS); elementary education (MS); marriage and family therapy (MS); physical education (MS); reading (MS, Sixth Year Certificate); rehabilitation/mental counseling (MS); school counseling (MS); special education (MS); student development in higher education (MS). *Application deadline:* For fall admission, 8/10 (priority date); for spring admission, 12/10. Applications are processed on a rolling basis. *Application fee:* $40. *Dean,* Dr. Ellen Whitford, 860-832-2102.

School of Technology Students: 16 full-time (3 women), 93 part-time (24 women); includes 11 minority (7 African Americans, 1 Asian American or Pacific Islander, 3 Hispanic Americans) Average age 37. 33 applicants, 70% accepted. *Faculty:* 4 full-time (0 women), 9 part-time/adjunct (3 women). Expenses: Contact institution. *Financial support:* In 2001–02, 6 research assistantships were awarded; Federal Work-Study also available. Financial award application deadline: 3/15; financial award applicants required to submit FAFSA. In 2001, 29 degrees awarded. *Degree program information:* Part-time and evening/weekend programs available. Offers construction management, technology management (MS); engineering technology (MS); technology (MS); technology education (MS). *Application deadline:* For fall admission, 8/10 (priority date); for spring admission, 12/10. Applications are processed on a rolling basis. *Application fee:* $40. *Application Contact:* Dr. Karen Tracey, Information Contact, 860-832-1800. *Dean,* Dr. Zdzislaw Kremens, 860-832-1800.

See in-depth description on page 787.

CENTRAL METHODIST COLLEGE, Fayette, MO 65248-1198

General Information Independent-religious, coed, comprehensive institution. *Graduate housing:* On-campus housing not available.

GRADUATE UNITS

Program in Education *Degree program information:* Part-time and evening/weekend programs available. Postbaccalaureate distance learning degree programs offered (no on-campus study). Offers education (M Ed). Electronic applications accepted.

CENTRAL MICHIGAN UNIVERSITY, Mount Pleasant, MI 48859

General Information State-supported, coed, university. CGS member. *Enrollment:* 1,010 full-time matriculated graduate/professional students (630 women), 1,150 part-time matriculated graduate/professional students (700 women). *Graduate faculty:* 707 full-time (243 women). Tuition, state resident: part-time $182 per unit. Tuition, nonresident: part-time $182 per unit. *Required fees:* $208 per semester. Part-time tuition and fees vary according to course load. *Graduate housing:* Rooms and/or apartments available on a first-come, first-served basis to single students and available to married students. *Student services:* Campus employment opportunities, campus safety program, career counseling, disabled student services, free psychological counseling, international student services, low-cost health insurance, multicultural affairs office. *Library facilities:* Park Library plus 1 other. *Online resources:* library catalog, web page. *Collection:* 941,543 titles, 4,358 serial subscriptions, 24,630 audiovisual materials.

Computer facilities: 1,500 computers available on campus for general student use. A campuswide network can be accessed from student residence rooms and from off campus. Internet access and online class registration are available. *Web address:* http://www.cmich.edu/.

General Application Contact: Dr. James Hageman, Dean, College of Graduate Studies, 989-774-6467, Fax: 989-774-3439, E-mail: grad@cmich.edu.

GRADUATE UNITS

College of Extended Learning Average age 38. 3,016 applicants, 99% accepted. *Faculty:* 1,800 part-time/adjunct (0 women). Expenses: Contact institution. *Financial support:* Available to part-time students. Applicants required to submit FAFSA. In 2001, 1,600 master's, 45 other advanced degrees awarded. *Degree program information:* Part-time and evening/weekend programs available. Postbaccalaureate distance learning degree programs offered (no on-campus study). Offers audiology (Au D); educational administration (MA); educational technology (MA); extended learning (MA, MSA, Au D, DHA, Certificate); general administration (MSA); health administration (DHA); health services administration (MSA, Certificate); hospitality and tourism (MSA, Certificate); human resources administration (MSA, Certificate); humanities (MA); information resource management (MSA, Certificate); international administration (MSA, Certificate); leadership (MSA, Certificate); public administration (MSA, Certificate); school principalship (MA); software engineering administration (MSA, Certificate). *Application deadline:* Applications are processed on a rolling basis. *Application fee:* $50. Electronic applications accepted. *Application Contact:* 800-950-1144 Ext. 1205, Fax: 989-774-2461, E-mail: celinfo@mail.cel.cmich.edu. *Dean,* Dr. Marcia Bankirer, 989-774-3865, Fax: 989-774-3542, E-mail: marcia.bankirer@cmich.edu.

College of Graduate Studies *Degree program information:* Part-time and evening/weekend programs available. Postbaccalaureate distance learning degree programs offered.

College of Business Administration *Degree program information:* Part-time programs available. Offers accounting (MBA); business administration (MA, MBA, MBE, MS); business education (MBE); economics (MA); finance and law (MBA); information systems (MS); management (MBA); marketing and hospitality services administration (MBA).

College of Communication and Fine Arts Offers art (MA, MFA); broadcast and cinematic arts (MA); communication and fine arts (MA, MFA, MM, MSA); interpersonal and public communication (MA); music education and supervision (MM); music performance (MM); oral interpretation (MA); theatre (MA).

College of Education and Human Services Offers classroom teaching (MA); community leadership (MA); counseling (MA); early childhood education (MA); education and human services (MA, MS, MSA, Ed D, Ed S); educational administration (MA, Ed S); educational leadership (Ed D); educational technology (MA); elementary education (MA); human development and family studies (MA); library media (MA); library, media, and technology (MA); media and technology (MA); middle level education (MA); nutrition and dietetics (MS); professional counseling (MA); reading improvement (MA); reading in the elementary school (MA); recreation and park administration (MA); school guidance personnel (MA); school principalship (MA); secondary education (MA); special education (MA); teaching senior high (MA); therapeutic recreation (MA).

College of Health Professions Offers athletic administration (MA); audiology (Au D); coaching (MA); exercise science (MA); health professions (MA, MS, MSA, Au D, Certificate); health promotion and program management (MA); physical therapy (MS); physician assistant (MS); speech and language pathology (MA); sport administration (MA); teaching (MA).

College of Humanities and Social and Behavioral Sciences *Degree program information:* Evening/weekend programs available. Offers applied experimental psychology (PhD); clinical psychology (Psy D); composition and communication (MA); creative writing (MA); English language and literature (MA); general, applied, and experimental psychology (MS, PhD); general/experimental psychology (MS); history (MA, PhD); humanities and social and behavioral sciences (MA, MPA, MS, PhD, Psy D, Certificate, S Psy S); industrial/organizational psychology (MA, PhD); political science (MA); public administration (MPA); public management (MPA); school psychology (PhD, S Psy S); social and criminal justice (MA); sociology (MA); Spanish (MA); state and local government (MPA); teaching English to speakers of other languages (MA).

College of Science and Technology *Degree program information:* Part-time programs available. Offers biology (MS); chemistry (MS); computer science (MS); conservation biology (MS); industrial education (MA); industrial management and technology (MA); mathematics (MA, MAT, PhD); physics (MS); science and technology (MA, MAT, MS, PhD); teaching chemistry (MA).

Interdisciplinary Programs Offers general administration (MSA); health service administration (MSA); hospitality and tourism administration (MSA); human resource administration (MSA); humanities (MA); information resource administration (MSA); interdisciplinary studies (MA, MSA); international administration (MSA); leadership (MSA); organizational communications (MSA); public administration (MSA); recreation and park administration (MSA); software engineering (MSA); sports administration (MSA).

See in-depth description on page 789.

CENTRAL MISSOURI STATE UNIVERSITY, Warrensburg, MO 64093

General Information State-supported, coed, comprehensive institution. CGS member. *Enrollment:* 1,239 matriculated graduate/professional students. *Graduate faculty:* 273 full-time (85 women), 40 part-time/adjunct (18 women). *Tuition, area resident:* Full-time $4,200; part-time $175 per credit hour. Tuition, nonresident: full-time $8,352; part-time $348 per credit hour. *Graduate housing:* Rooms and/or apartments available on a first-come, first-served basis to single and married students. *Student services:* Campus employment opportunities, campus safety program, career counseling, child daycare facilities, disabled student services, exercise/wellness program, free psychological counseling, international student services, low-cost health insurance, multicultural affairs office, teacher training, writing training. *Library facilities:* James C. Kirkpatrick Library. *Online resources:* library catalog, web page, access to other libraries' catalogs. *Collection:* 850,973 titles, 3,570 serial subscriptions, 23,412 audiovisual materials.

Computer facilities: 1,007 computers available on campus for general student use. A campuswide network can be accessed from student residence rooms and from off campus. Internet access and online class registration are available. *Web address:* http://www.cmsu.edu/.

General Application Contact: Dr. Novella Perrin, Dean of Graduate Studies/Assistant Vice-President for Academic Affairs, 660-543-4092, Fax: 660-543-8333, E-mail: perrin@cmsu1.cmsu.edu.

GRADUATE UNITS

School of Graduate Studies Students: 1,239. Average age 36. 392 applicants, 82% accepted. *Faculty:* 273 full-time (85 women), 40 part-time/adjunct (18 women). Expenses: Contact institution. *Financial support:* In 2001–02, 671 students received support, including 108 research assistantships with full and partial tuition reimbursements available (averaging $5,856 per year), 127 teaching assistantships with full and partial tuition reimbursements available (averaging $6,069 per year); career-related internships or fieldwork, Federal Work-Study, scholarships/grants, unspecified assistantships, and administrative assistantships, laboratory assistantships also available. Support available to part-time students. Financial award application deadline: 3/1; financial award applicants required to submit FAFSA. In 2001, 381 master's, 17 other advanced degrees awarded. *Degree program information:* Part-time programs available. Offers administration (Ed S); adult education (MSE); criminal justice (MS); curriculum and instruction (Ed S); education and human services (MA, MS, MSE, Ed S); education technology (MSE); education, administration and higher education (MSE); education, administration and higher education (MS, Ed S); elementary education (MSE); human services (Ed S); human services-public services (Ed S); human services/guidance and counseling (Ed S); human services/learning resources (Ed S); K–12 education (MSE); library information technology (MS); library science and information services (MS); physical education/exercise and sports science (MS); psychology (MS); reading (MSE); school administration (MSE); school counseling (MS); secondary education (MSE); social gerontology (MS); sociology (MA); special education (MSE, Ed S); special education/human services (Ed S); speech pathology and audiology (MS); student personnel administration (MS). *Application deadline:* Applications are processed on a rolling basis. *Application fee:* $25 ($50 for international students). Electronic applications accepted. *Dean of Graduate Studies/Assistant Vice President for Academic Affairs,* Dr. Novella Perrin, 660-543-4092, Fax: 660-543-8333, E-mail: perrin@cmsu1.cmsu.edu.

College of Applied Sciences and Technology Students: 45 full-time (16 women), 144 part-time (54 women); includes 16 minority (7 African Americans, 6 Hispanic Americans, 3 Native Americans), 23 international. Average age 35. 71 applicants, 76% accepted. *Faculty:* 43 full-time (12 women), 15 part-time/adjunct (5 women). Expenses: Contact institution. *Financial support:* In 2001–02, 1 fellowship with tuition reimbursement (averaging $12,000 per year), 7 research assistantships with full and partial tuition reimbursements (averaging $6,386 per year), 35 teaching assistantships with full and partial tuition reimbursements (averaging $6,552 per year) were awarded. Federal Work-Study, scholarships/grants, unspecified assistantships, and administrative and laboratory assistantships also available. Support available to part-time students. Financial award application deadline: 3/1; financial award applicants required to submit FAFSA. In 2001, 75 master's, 4 other advanced degrees awarded. *Degree program information:* Part-time programs available. Offers applied sciences and technology (MS, MSE, Ed S); aviation safety (MS); human services/industrial arts and technology (Ed S); human services/public services (Ed S); industrial hygiene (MS); industrial management (MS); industrial safety management (MS); industrial technology (MS); industrial, vocational, and technical education (MS); K-12 education/industrial arts and technology (MSE); occupational safety management (MS); public services administration (MS); rural and family nursing (MS); safety management (MS); secondary education/safety education (MSE); security (MS); transportation safety (MS). *Application deadline:* Applications are processed on a rolling basis. *Application fee:* $25 ($50 for international students). *Interim Dean,* Dr. Alice Greife, 660-543-4450, Fax: 660-543-8031, E-mail: greiffe@cmsu1.cmsu.edu.

College of Arts and Sciences Students: 20 full-time (13 women), 126 part-time (63 women); includes 9 minority (4 African Americans, 2 Asian Americans or Pacific Islanders, 3 Hispanic Americans), 33 international. Average age 33. 66 applicants, 83% accepted. *Faculty:* 103 full-time (32 women), 1 part-time/adjunct (0 women). Expenses: Contact institution. *Financial support:* In 2001–02, 18 research assistantships with full and partial tuition reimbursements (averaging $6,986 per year), 37 teaching assistantships with full and partial tuition reimbursements (averaging $6,675 per year) were awarded. Career-related internships or fieldwork, Federal Work-Study, scholarships/grants, unspecified assistantships, and administrative and laboratory assistantships also available. Support available to part-time students. Financial award application deadline: 3/1; financial award applicants required to submit FAFSA. In 2001, 44 degrees awarded. *Degree program information:* Part-time programs available. Offers applied mathematics (MS); arts and sciences (MA, MS, MSE); biology (MS); communication (MA); English (MA); English education (MSE); history (MA); mathematics (MS); mathematics education (MSE); music (MA); social studies (MSE); speech communication (MA, MSE); teaching English as a second language (MA, MSE); theatre (MA). *Application deadline:* Applications are processed on a rolling basis. *Application fee:* $25 ($50 for international students). *Dean,* Dr. Robert Schwartz, 660-543-4750, Fax: 660-543-8006, E-mail: schwartz@cmsu2.cmsu.edu.

Harmon College of Business Administration Students: 37 full-time (14 women), 70 part-time (27 women); includes 10 minority (4 African Americans, 4 Asian Americans or Pacific Islanders, 2 Hispanic Americans), 54 international. Average age 27. 46 applicants, 63% accepted. *Faculty:* 43 full-time (11 women), 1 (woman) part-time/adjunct. Expenses: Contact institution. *Financial support:* In 2001–02, 40 research assistantships with full and partial tuition reimbursements (averaging $5,461 per year), 14 teaching assistantships with full and partial tuition reimbursements (averaging $6,496 per year) were awarded. Career-related internships or fieldwork, Federal Work-Study, scholarships/grants, unspecified assistantships, and administrative and laboratory assistantships also available. Support available to part-time students. Financial award application deadline: 3/1; financial award applicants required to submit FAFSA. In 2001, 44 degrees awarded. *Degree program information:* Part-time programs available. Offers accounting (MA); business administration (MA, MBA, MS); computer and office information systems (MS); economics (MA); management and business communication (MBA). *Application deadline:* Applications are processed on a rolling basis. *Application fee:* $25 ($50 for international students). *Dean,* Dr. George Wilson, 660-543-4580, Fax: 660-543-8885, E-mail: gwilson@cmsu1.cmsu.edu.

See in-depth description on page 791.

CENTRAL STATE UNIVERSITY, Wilberforce, OH 45384

General Information State-supported, coed, comprehensive institution. *Enrollment:* 35 part-time matriculated graduate/professional students (25 women). *Enrollment by degree level:* 35 master's. *Graduate faculty:* 9 part-time/adjunct (5 women). Tuition, state resident: full-time $4,788; part-time $133 per credit hour. Tuition, nonresident: full-time $8,208; part-time $228 per credit hour. *Graduate housing:* Room and/or apartments available on a first-come, first-served basis to single students; on-campus housing not available to married students. Typical cost: $2,676 per year ($5,208 including board). Housing application deadline: 6/15. *Student services:* Campus employment opportunities, campus safety program, career counseling, exercise/wellness program, free psychological counseling, low-cost health insurance, teacher training, writing training. *Library facilities:* Hallie Q. Brown Memorial Library plus 1 other. *Online resources:* library catalog, access to other libraries' catalogs. *Collection:* 280,470 titles, 26,066 serial subscriptions, 497 audiovisual materials.

Computer facilities: 338 computers available on campus for general student use. A campuswide network can be accessed. Internet access is available. *Web address:* http://www.centralstate.edu/.

General Application Contact: Dr. Jerome Tillman, Dean, College of Education, 937-376-6225, E-mail: jhillman@csu.edu.

GRADUATE UNITS

Program in Education Average age 43. 8 applicants, 100% accepted. *Faculty:* 9 part-time/adjunct (5 women). Expenses: Contact institution. *Financial support:* In 2001–02, 1 student received support. Institutionally sponsored loans and scholarships/grants available. Financial award applicants required to submit FAFSA. In 2001, 1 degree awarded. *Degree program information:* Part-time and evening/weekend programs available. Offers educational technology (M Ed); leadership (M Ed); literacy (M Ed). *Application deadline:* For fall admission, 6/1 (priority date). Applications are processed on a rolling basis. *Application fee:* $15. *Dean, College of Education,* Dr. Jerome Tillman, 937-376-6225, E-mail: jhillman@csu.edu.

CENTRAL WASHINGTON UNIVERSITY, Ellensburg, WA 98926-7463

General Information State-supported, coed, comprehensive institution. CGS member. *Enrollment:* 216 full-time matriculated graduate/professional students (141 women), 208 part-time matriculated graduate/professional students (124 women). *Enrollment by degree level:* 424 master's. *Graduate faculty:* 266 full-time (84 women). Tuition, state resident: full-time $4,848; part-time $162 per credit. Tuition, nonresident: full-time $14,772; part-time $492 per credit. *Required fees:* $324. *Graduate housing:* Rooms and/or apartments available on a first-come, first-served basis to single and married students. Typical cost: $4,600 per year for single students; $5,900 per year for married students. Room charges vary according to board plan, campus/location and housing facility selected. *Student services:* Campus employment opportunities, campus safety program, career counseling, child daycare facilities, disabled student services, exercise/wellness program, free psychological counseling, grant writing training, international student services, low-cost health insurance, multicultural

Central Washington University (continued)

affairs office, teacher training, writing training. *Library facilities:* Central Washington University Library. *Online resources:* library catalog, web page, access to other libraries' catalogs. *Collection:* 537,718 titles, 1,469 serial subscriptions, 9,230 audiovisual materials. *Research affiliation:* East-West Center (Pacific area studies), Associated Western Universities (science and engineering).

Computer facilities: 659 computers available on campus for general student use. A campuswide network can be accessed from student residence rooms and from off campus. Internet access is available. *Web address:* http://www.cwu.edu/.

General Application Contact: Barbara Sisko, Office Assistant, Graduate Studies and Research, 509-963-3103, Fax: 509-963-1799, E-mail: masters@cwu.edu.

GRADUATE UNITS

Graduate Studies and Research Students: 216 full-time (141 women), 208 part-time (124 women); includes 52 minority (10 African Americans, 11 Asian Americans or Pacific Islanders, 19 Hispanic Americans, 12 Native Americans), 14 international. 312 applicants, 62% accepted, 152 enrolled. *Faculty:* 266 full-time (84 women). Expenses: Contact institution. *Financial support:* In 2001–02, 39 research assistantships with partial tuition reimbursements (averaging $7,120 per year), 63 teaching assistantships with partial tuition reimbursements (averaging $7,120 per year) were awarded. Career-related internships or fieldwork, Federal Work-Study, and unspecified assistantships also available. Financial award application deadline: 3/1; financial award applicants required to submit FAFSA. In 2001, 169 degrees awarded. *Degree program information:* Part-time and evening/weekend programs available. Offers business (MPA); individual studies (M Ed, MA, MS). *Application deadline:* For fall admission, 4/1 (priority date); for winter admission, 10/1 (priority date); for spring admission, 1/1 (priority date). Applications are processed on a rolling basis. *Application fee:* $35. *Application Contact:* Barbara Sisko, Office Assistant, Graduate Studies and Research, 509-963-3103, Fax: 509-963-1799, E-mail: masters@cwu.edu. *Interim Associate Vice President for Graduate Studies, Research and Faculty,* Dr. Richard S. Mack, 509-963-3103, Fax: 509-963-1799, E-mail: masters@cwu.edu.

College of Arts and Humanities Students: 46 full-time (27 women), 11 part-time (4 women); includes 8 minority (1 Asian American or Pacific Islander, 5 Hispanic Americans, 2 Native Americans), 3 international. 55 applicants, 56% accepted, 23 enrolled. *Faculty:* 81 full-time (24 women). Expenses: Contact institution. *Financial support:* In 2001–02, 5 research assistantships with partial tuition reimbursements (averaging $7,120 per year), 27 teaching assistantships with partial tuition reimbursements (averaging $7,120 per year) were awarded. Career-related internships or fieldwork, Federal Work-Study, and unspecified assistantships also available. Financial award application deadline: 3/1; financial award applicants required to submit FAFSA. In 2001, 32 degrees awarded. *Degree program information:* Part-time programs available. Offers art (MA, MFA); arts and humanities (MA, MFA, MM); English (MA); history (MA); music (MM); teaching English as a foreign language (MA); teaching English as a second language (MA); theatre production (MA). *Application deadline:* For fall admission, 4/1; for winter admission, 10/1 (priority date); for spring admission, 1/1 (priority date). Applications are processed on a rolling basis. *Application fee:* $35. *Application Contact:* Barbara Sisko, Office Assistant, Graduate Studies and Research, 509-963-3103, Fax: 509-963-1799, E-mail: masters@cwu.edu. *Dean,* Dr. Liahna Armstrong, 509-963-1858.

College of Education and Professional Studies Students: 50 full-time (35 women), 151 part-time (95 women); includes 25 minority (6 African Americans, 7 Asian Americans or Pacific Islanders, 7 Hispanic Americans, 5 Native Americans), 8 international. 91 applicants, 84% accepted, 65 enrolled. *Faculty:* 74 full-time (29 women). Expenses: Contact institution. *Financial support:* In 2001–02, 6 research assistantships with partial tuition reimbursements (averaging $7,120 per year), 17 teaching assistantships with partial tuition reimbursements (averaging $7,120 per year) were awarded. Federal Work-Study also available. Financial award application deadline: 3/1; financial award applicants required to submit FAFSA. In 2001, 78 degrees awarded. *Degree program information:* Part-time programs available. Offers apparel design (MS); business and distributive education (M Ed); curriculum and instruction (M Ed); education and professional studies (M Ed, MS); educational administration (M Ed); elementary education (M Ed); engineering technology (MS); family and consumer sciences education (MS); family studies (MS); health, physical education and recreation (MS); nutrition (MS); reading education (M Ed); special education (M Ed). *Application deadline:* For fall admission, 4/1 (priority date); for winter admission, 10/1; for spring admission, 1/1. Applications are processed on a rolling basis. *Application fee:* $35. *Application Contact:* Barbara Sisko, Office Assistant, Graduate Studies and Research, 509-963-3103, Fax: 509-963-1799, E-mail: masters@cwu.edu. *Dean,* Dr. Rebecca Bowers, 509-963-1411.

College of the Sciences Students: 112 full-time (72 women), 39 part-time (19 women); includes 15 minority (3 African Americans, 2 Asian Americans or Pacific Islanders, 5 Hispanic Americans, 5 Native Americans), 2 international. 144 applicants, 47% accepted, 51 enrolled. *Faculty:* 96 full-time (28 women). Expenses: Contact institution. *Financial support:* In 2001–02, 27 research assistantships with partial tuition reimbursements (averaging $7,120 per year), 19 teaching assistantships with partial tuition reimbursements (averaging $7,120 per year) were awarded. Career-related internships or fieldwork and Federal Work-Study also available. Financial award application deadline: 3/1; financial award applicants required to submit FAFSA. In 2001, 59 degrees awarded. *Degree program information:* Part-time and evening/weekend programs available. Offers biological sciences (MS); chemistry (MS); counseling psychology (MS); experimental psychology (MS); geological sciences (MS); guidance and counseling (M Ed); mathematics (MAT); organizational development (MS); resource management (MS); school psychology (M Ed); sciences (M Ed, MAT, MS). *Application deadline:* For fall admission, 4/1 (priority date). Applications are processed on a rolling basis. *Application fee:* $35. *Application Contact:* Barbara Sisko, Office Assistant, Graduate Studies and Research, 509-963-3103, Fax: 509-963-1799, E-mail: masters@cwu.edu. *Interim Dean,* Dr. Barney Erickson, 509-963-1866.

Announcement: CWU's mission is to enable graduate students to competently confront the complexities of modern global society and to prepare them for successful careers as well as for independent, lifelong learning. CWU provides quality graduate programs in selected fields, taught by faculty members dedicated to excellence in teaching and research. Classes are small, and the opportunity to work closely with professors is a hallmark of CWU, as is hands-on research activity. The University is located in an attractive and safe community on the eastern slopes of the Cascade Mountains, 2 hours from Seattle by car.

See in-depth description on page 793.

CENTRAL YESHIVA TOMCHEI TMIMIM-LUBAVITCH, Brooklyn, NY 11230

General Information Independent-religious, men only, comprehensive institution.

CENTRO DE ESTUDIOS AVANZADOS DE PUERTO RICO Y EL CARIBE, Old San Juan, PR 00902-3970

General Information Independent, coed, graduate-only institution. *Graduate housing:* On-campus housing not available. *Research affiliation:* Museo de las Americas, Museo Hombre Dominicano (Santo Domingo), Archivo General, Museo Universidad del Turabo.

GRADUATE UNITS

Graduate Program in Puerto Rican and Caribbean Studies *Degree program information:* Part-time and evening/weekend programs available. Offers Puerto Rican and Caribbean studies (MA, PhD).

CHADRON STATE COLLEGE, Chadron, NE 69337

General Information State-supported, coed, comprehensive institution. *Enrollment:* 44 full-time matriculated graduate/professional students (27 women), 366 part-time matriculated graduate/professional students (276 women). *Enrollment by degree level:* 410 master's. *Graduate faculty:* 72 full-time (17 women). Tuition, state resident: full-time $2,106; part-time $70 per credit hour. Tuition, nonresident: full-time $4,212; part-time $176 per credit hour. *Required fees:* $78; $11 per credit hour. $15 per term. *Graduate housing:* Rooms and/or apartments available on a first-come, first-served basis to single and married students. Typical cost: $1,644 per year ($3,430 including board) for single students; $3,600 per year for married students. Room and board charges vary according to board plan. Housing application deadline: 6/1. *Student services:* Campus employment opportunities, campus safety program, career counseling, child daycare facilities, exercise/wellness program, free psychological counseling, international student services, low-cost health insurance, teacher training. *Library facilities:* Reta King Library. *Online resources:* library catalog, access to other libraries' catalogs. *Collection:* 129,660 titles, 5,596 audiovisual materials.

Computer facilities: 200 computers available on campus for general student use. A campuswide network can be accessed from student residence rooms and from off campus. Internet access and online class registration are available. *Web address:* http://www.csc.edu/.

General Application Contact: Dr. Thomas P. Colgate, Dean, School of Education and Graduate Studies, 308-432-6330, Fax: 308-432-6454, E-mail: pcolgate@csc.edu.

GRADUATE UNITS

School of Education and Graduate Studies Students: 44 full-time (27 women), 366 part-time (276 women); includes 14 minority (1 African American, 2 Asian Americans or Pacific Islanders, 7 Hispanic Americans, 4 Native Americans), 3 international. Average age 40. 30 applicants, 100% accepted. *Faculty:* 72 full-time (17 women). Expenses: Contact institution. *Financial support:* In 2001–02, 23 teaching assistantships with tuition reimbursements (averaging $4,000 per year) were awarded; career-related internships or fieldwork, Federal Work-Study, scholarships/grants, and unspecified assistantships also available. Support available to part-time students. Financial award application deadline: 6/1; financial award applicants required to submit FAFSA. In 2001, 44 master's, 2 other advanced degrees awarded. *Degree program information:* Part-time and evening/weekend programs available. Postbaccalaureate distance learning degree programs offered (minimal on-campus study). Offers business (MA Ed); business and economics (MBA); counseling (MA Ed); educational administration (MS Ed, Sp Ed); elementary education (MS Ed); history (MA Ed); language and literature (MA Ed); secondary administration (MS Ed); secondary education (MS Ed). *Application deadline:* Applications are processed on a rolling basis. *Application fee:* $15. *Application Contact:* Mary Burke, Office Assistant, Graduate Office, 308-432-6214, Fax: 308-432-6454, E-mail: mburke@csc.edu. *Dean, School of Education and Graduate Studies,* Dr. Thomas P. Colgate, 308-432-6330, Fax: 308-432-6454, E-mail: pcolgate@csc.edu.

CHAMINADE UNIVERSITY OF HONOLULU, Honolulu, HI 96816-1578

General Information Independent-religious, coed, comprehensive institution. *Enrollment:* 367 full-time matriculated graduate/professional students (243 women), 257 part-time matriculated graduate/professional students (158 women). *Enrollment by degree level:* 624 master's. *Graduate faculty:* 25 full-time (13 women), 31 part-time/adjunct (16 women). *Graduate housing:* On-campus housing not available. *Student services:* Campus safety program, career counseling, free psychological counseling, international student services. *Library facilities:* Sullivan Library. *Online resources:* library catalog. *Collection:* 139,751 titles, 905 serial subscriptions.

Computer facilities: 50 computers available on campus for general student use. A campuswide network can be accessed from off campus. *Web address:* http://www.chaminade.edu/.

General Application Contact: Dr. Michael Fassiotto, Director, 808-739-4674, Fax: 808-739-4607, E-mail: mfassiot@chaminade.edu.

GRADUATE UNITS

Graduate Programs Students: 367 full-time (243 women), 257 part-time (158 women); includes 331 minority (28 African Americans, 290 Asian Americans or Pacific Islanders, 12 Hispanic Americans, 1 Native American), 35 international. Average age 31. 293 applicants, 58% accepted. *Faculty:* 25 full-time (13 women), 31 part-time/adjunct (16 women). Expenses: Contact institution. *Financial support:* In 2001–02, 175 students received support. Career-related internships or fieldwork, Federal Work-Study, institutionally sponsored loans, and tuition waivers (partial) available. Support available to part-time students. Financial award application deadline: 3/1. In 2001, 153 degrees awarded. *Degree program information:* Part-time and evening/weekend programs available. Offers business administration (MBA); counseling psychology (MSCP); criminal justice administration (MSCJA); management (MBA, MPA); pastoral leadership (MPL); public administration (MPA); social science via peace education (M Ed). *Application deadline:* For fall admission, 9/1 (priority date). Applications are processed on a rolling basis. *Application fee:* $50. Electronic applications accepted. *Director,* Dr. Michael Fassiotto, 808-739-4674, Fax: 808-739-4607, E-mail: mfassiot@chaminade.edu.

CHAMPLAIN COLLEGE, Burlington, VT 05402-0670

General Information Independent, coed, comprehensive institution.

GRADUATE UNITS

Program in Managing Innovation and Information Technology Offers management of technology (MS).

CHAPMAN UNIVERSITY, Orange, CA 92866

General Information Independent-religious, coed, comprehensive institution. *Enrollment:* 2,900 matriculated graduate/professional students. *Graduate faculty:* 313. *Tuition:* Part-time $450 per credit. *Required fees:* $450 per credit. Tuition and fees vary according to program. *Graduate housing:* On-campus housing not available. *Student services:* Campus employment opportunities, campus safety program, career counseling, child daycare facilities, disabled student services, free psychological counseling, international student services, low-cost health insurance. *Library facilities:* Thurmond Clarke Memorial Library plus 1 other. *Online resources:* library catalog, web page. *Collection:* 203,915 titles, 2,121 serial subscriptions, 3,350 audiovisual materials.

Computer facilities: 278 computers available on campus for general student use. A campuswide network can be accessed from off campus. Internet access is available. *Web address:* http://www.chapman.edu/.

GRADUATE UNITS

Graduate Studies Students: 2,900. Average age 28. *Faculty:* 313. Expenses: Contact institution. *Financial support:* Career-related internships or fieldwork, Federal Work-Study, scholarships/grants, and tuition waivers (partial) available. Support available to part-time students. Financial award application deadline: 3/1; financial award applicants required to submit FAFSA. *Degree program information:* Part-time and evening/weekend programs available. Offers food science and nutrition (MS); human resources (MSHRM). *Application deadline:* Applications are processed on a rolling basis. *Application fee:* $40. Electronic applications accepted. *Application Contact:* Saundra Hoover, Director of Graduate Admissions, 714-997-6786, Fax: 714-997-6713, E-mail: shoover@chapman.edu. *Vice Provost and Dean,* Dr. Barbara E. G. Mulch, 714-997-6733.

Department of Physical Therapy *Faculty:* 9 full-time (8 women). Expenses: Contact institution. *Financial support:* In 2001–02, 48 fellowships were awarded Financial award application deadline: 3/1. Offers physical therapy (DPT). *Application deadline:* For fall admission, 12/10 (priority date). *Application fee:* $80. *Application Contact:* Dorcas Tominaga, Admission Coordinator, 714-744-7624, E-mail: gabard@chapman.edu. *Chair,* Dr. Donald L. Gabard, 714-744-7620.

Division of Psychology *Faculty:* 11 full-time (5 women). Expenses: Contact institution. *Financial support:* Application deadline: 3/1. *Degree program information:* Part-time and evening/weekend programs available. Offers marriage and family therapy (MA); preclinical (MA). *Application deadline:* Applications are processed on a rolling basis. *Application fee:* $40. *Application Contact:* Susan Read-Weil, Coordinator, 714-744-7837, E-mail: sreadwei@chapman.edu. *Chair,* Dr. Gerhardt Eifert, 714-997-6776, E-mail: eifert@chapman.edu.

The George L. Argyros School of Business and Economics *Faculty:* 18 full-time (1 woman). Expenses: Contact institution. *Financial support:* Fellowships available. Financial award application deadline: 3/1. *Degree program information:* Part-time and evening/weekend programs available. Offers business and economics (Exec MBA, MBA). *Application deadline:* Applications are processed on a rolling basis. *Application fee:* $40. *Application Contact:* Dr. Debra Gonda, Associate Dean, 714-997-6894, E-mail: gonda@chapman.edu. *Dean,* Doug Tuggle, 714-997-6684.

Professional Studies *Faculty:* 3 full-time (2 women). Expenses: Contact institution. *Financial support:* Fellowships available. Financial award application deadline: 3/1. *Degree program information:* Part-time and evening/weekend programs available. Offers human resources (MS). *Application deadline:* Applications are processed on a rolling basis. *Application fee:* $40. *Application Contact:* Saundra Hoover, Director of Admission, 714-997-6786, E-mail: shoover@chapman.edu. *Vice Provost and Dean,* Dr. Barbara E. G. Mulch, 714-997-6733.

School of Communication Arts *Faculty:* 22 full-time (12 women). Expenses: Contact institution. *Financial support:* Fellowships available. Financial award application deadline: 3/1. *Degree program information:* Part-time programs available. Offers communication arts (MA, MFA); creative writing (MFA); literature (MA); teaching literature and composition (MA). *Application deadline:* Applications are processed on a rolling basis. *Application fee:* $40. *Application Contact:* Dr. Martin Nakell, Program Coordinator, 714-997-6609, E-mail: nakell@chapman.edu. *Dean,* Dr. Myron Yeager, 714-997-6653, E-mail: yeager@chapman.edu.

School of Education *Faculty:* 10 full-time (8 women). Expenses: Contact institution. *Financial support:* Fellowships available. Financial award application deadline: 3/1. *Degree program information:* Part-time and evening/weekend programs available. Offers curriculum and instruction (MA); education (MA, Ed S); educational administration (MA); educational psychology (MA, Ed S); learning handicapped (MA); reading education (MA); school counseling (MA); severely handicapped (MA); special education (MA). *Application deadline:* Applications are processed on a rolling basis. *Application fee:* $40. *Application Contact:* Rika Judd, Graduate Admission Counselor, 714-997-6786, Fax: 714-997-6713, E-mail: rjudd@chapman.edu. *Dean,* Dr. Jim Brown, 714-997-6781.

School of Film and Television *Faculty:* 10 full-time (2 women). Expenses: Contact institution. *Financial support:* Fellowships available. Financial award application deadline: 3/1. *Degree program information:* Part-time and evening/weekend programs available. Offers film and television (MA, MFA); film studies (MA); new media (MFA); producing (MFA); production (MFA); screenwriting (MFA). *Application deadline:* Applications are processed on a rolling basis. *Application fee:* $40. *Application Contact:* Dan Pavelin, Program Coordinator, 714-744-7866. *Dean,* Robert Bassett, 714-997-6765.

School of Law *Faculty:* 18 full-time (9 women), 4 part-time/adjunct. Expenses: Contact institution. *Financial support:* Application deadline: 3/1. Offers law (JD). *Application fee:* $50. *Application Contact:* Demetrius L. Greer, Office of Admissions, 888-242-1913, E-mail: greer@chapman.edu. *Dean,* Parham Williams, 714-628-2500.

See in-depth description on page 795.

CHARLES R. DREW UNIVERSITY OF MEDICINE AND SCIENCE, Los Angeles, CA 90059

General Information Independent, coed, comprehensive institution. *Graduate housing:* On-campus housing not available.

GRADUATE UNITS

College of Allied Health

Professional Program in Medicine Offers medicine (MD).

CHARLESTON SOUTHERN UNIVERSITY, Charleston, SC 29423-8087

General Information Independent-religious, coed, comprehensive institution. *Enrollment:* 15 full-time matriculated graduate/professional students (10 women), 223 part-time matriculated graduate/professional students (128 women). *Enrollment by degree level:* 238 master's. *Graduate faculty:* 40 full-time (15 women), 10 part-time/adjunct (5 women). *Tuition:* Full-time $6,184; part-time $200 per credit hour. Part-time tuition and fees vary according to program. *Graduate housing:* On-campus housing not available. *Student services:* Campus employment opportunities, campus safety program, career counseling, disabled student services, free psychological counseling, international student services. *Library facilities:* L. Mendel Rivers Library. *Online resources:* library catalog, web page, access to other libraries' catalogs. *Collection:* 195,563 titles, 1,267 serial subscriptions, 7,745 audiovisual materials. *Research affiliation:* Metro Charleston Chamber of Commerce (economic forecasting), Waccamaw Regional Planning and Development Council (economic forecasting), Santee Lynches Council of Governments (economic forecasting).

Computer facilities: 150 computers available on campus for general student use. A campuswide network can be accessed. Internet access is available. *Web address:* http://www.charlestonsouthern.edu/.

General Application Contact: Debbie Williamson, Executive Director of Enrollment Management, 804-863-7050, Fax: 804-863-7070, E-mail: enroll@csuniv.edu.

GRADUATE UNITS

Program in Business Students: 7 full-time (5 women), 92 part-time (50 women); includes 34 minority (27 African Americans, 2 Asian Americans or Pacific Islanders, 5 Hispanic Americans), 4 international. Average age 35. 61 applicants, 66% accepted, 38 enrolled. *Faculty:* 6 full-time (1 woman), 3 part-time/adjunct (1 woman). Expenses: Contact institution. *Financial support:* In 2001–02, 27 students received support, including 1 research assistantship with full tuition reimbursement available; Federal Work-Study also available. Financial award application deadline: 4/15; financial award applicants required to submit FAFSA. In 2001, 36 degrees awarded. *Degree program information:* Part-time and evening/weekend programs available. Offers accounting (MBA); finance (MBA); health care administration (MBA); information systems (MBA); organizational development (MBA). *Application deadline:* Applications are processed on a rolling basis. *Application fee:* $25. *Application Contact:* Heather Brooks, Graduate School Coordinator, 843-863-7534, Fax: 843-863-7070, E-mail: hbrooks@csuniv.edu. *MBA Director,* Dr. Al Parish, 843-863-7904, Fax: 843-863-7919, E-mail: aparish@awdd.com.

Program in Criminal Justice Students: 4 full-time (3 women), 24 part-time (15 women); includes 8 minority (all African Americans), 3 international. 23 applicants, 52% accepted, 12 enrolled. *Faculty:* 4 full-time (3 women), 2 part-time/adjunct (0 women). Expenses: Contact institution. *Financial support:* Research assistantships, institutionally sponsored loans available. Financial award application deadline: 4/15; financial award applicants required to submit FAFSA. In 2001, 2 degrees awarded. *Degree program information:* Part-time and evening/weekend programs available. Offers criminal justice (MSCJ). *Application fee:* $25. *Application Contact:* Heather Brooks, Graduate School Coordinator, 843-863-7534, Fax: 843-863-7070, E-mail: hbrooks@csuniv.edu. *Chair,* Dr. Beth McConnell, 843-863-7131, E-mail: bmcconne@csuniv.edu.

Programs in Education Students: 1 full-time (0 women), 84 part-time (52 women); includes 32 minority (26 African Americans, 6 Hispanic Americans) Average age 35. 55 applicants, 53% accepted, 28 enrolled. *Faculty:* 7 full-time (4 women), 7 part-time/adjunct (4 women). Expenses: Contact institution. *Financial support:* In 2001–02, 27 students received support, including 4 research assistantships with full tuition reimbursements available; career-related internships or fieldwork and Federal Work-Study also available. Financial award application deadline: 4/15; financial award applicants required to submit FAFSA. In 2001, 37 degrees awarded. *Degree program information:* Part-time and evening/weekend programs available. Offers administration and supervision (M Ed); elementary education (M Ed); English (MAT); science (MAT); secondary education (M Ed); social studies (MAT). *Application deadline:* Applications are processed on a rolling basis. *Application fee:* $25. *Application Contact:* Heather Brooks, Graduate School Coordinator, 843-863-7534, Fax: 843-863-7070, E-mail: hbrooks@csuniv.edu. *Graduate Director,* Dr. Gary Leonard, 843-863-7567.

CHATHAM COLLEGE, Pittsburgh, PA 15232-2826

General Information Independent, women only, comprehensive institution. *Enrollment:* 251 full-time matriculated graduate/professional students (209 women), 167 part-time matriculated graduate/professional students (148 women). *Enrollment by degree level:* 397 master's, 21 doctoral. *Graduate faculty:* 33 full-time (23 women), 56 part-time/adjunct (35 women). *Tuition:* Full-time $17,764; part-time $458 per credit. Tuition and fees vary according to program. *Graduate housing:* Rooms and/or apartments available on a first-come, first-served basis to single and married students. Typical cost: $3,344 per year ($6,494 including board) for single students. Room and board charges vary according to board plan and housing facility selected. *Student services:* Campus employment opportunities, campus safety program, career counseling, exercise/wellness program, free psychological counseling, international student services, low-cost health insurance, writing training. *Library facilities:* Jennie King Mellon Library. *Online resources:* library catalog, web page, access to other libraries' catalogs. *Collection:* 95,625 titles, 1,240 serial subscriptions, 321 audiovisual materials.

Computer facilities: 312 computers available on campus for general student use. A campuswide network can be accessed from student residence rooms and from off campus. Internet access, computer-aided instruction are available. *Web address:* http://www.chatham.edu/.

General Application Contact: Office of Graduate Admissions, 412-365-1290, Fax: 412-365-1609, E-mail: admissions@chatham.edu.

GRADUATE UNITS

Graduate and Professional Studies Students: 251 full-time (209 women), 167 part-time (148 women); includes 44 minority (27 African Americans, 12 Asian Americans or Pacific Islanders, 4 Hispanic Americans, 1 Native American), 6 international. Average age 30. 494 applicants, 60% accepted, 196 enrolled. *Faculty:* 34 full-time (23 women), 56 part-time/adjunct (35 women). Expenses: Contact institution. *Financial support:* In 2001–02, 315 students received support, including 48 research assistantships (averaging $5,900 per year); career-related internships or fieldwork also available. Support available to part-time students. Financial award applicants required to submit FAFSA. In 2001, 148 degrees awarded. *Degree program information:* Part-time and evening/weekend programs available. Postbaccalaureate distance learning degree programs offered (minimal on-campus study). Offers biology (MS Biol); business administration (MBA); computational science (MSCS); counseling psychology (MS); digital technology (MADT); elementary and special education (MAT); elementary education (MAT); environmental education (MAT); health science (MHS); landscape studies (MALS); liberal arts (MLA); occupational therapy (MOT); physical therapy (MPT, DPT); physician assistant studies (MPAS); secondary biology education (MAT); secondary chemistry education (MAT); secondary English education (MAT); secondary math education (MAT); secondary physics education (MAT); secondary social studies education (MAT); special education (MAT); writing (MA). *Application deadline:* Applications are processed on a rolling basis. *Application fee:* $35. Electronic applications accepted. *Application Contact:* Office of Graduate Admissions, 412-365-1290, Fax: 412-365-1609, E-mail: admissions@chatham.edu. *Director of Graduate and Professional Studies,* Dr. Anthony Goreczny, 412-365-1817, Fax: 412-365-1720, E-mail: goreczny@chatham.edu.

CHESTNUT HILL COLLEGE, Philadelphia, PA 19118-2693

General Information Independent-religious, coed, comprehensive institution. *Enrollment:* 80 full-time matriculated graduate/professional students (66 women), 522 part-time matriculated graduate/professional students (438 women). *Enrollment by degree level:* 529 master's, 73 doctoral. *Graduate faculty:* 18 full-time (13 women), 71 part-time/adjunct (50 women). *Tuition:* Full-time $8,880; part-time $370 per credit. Tuition and fees vary according to degree level and program. *Graduate housing:* On-campus housing not available. *Student services:* Campus employment opportunities, campus safety program, career counseling, exercise/wellness program, free psychological counseling, international student services, low-cost health insurance, writing training. *Library facilities:* Logue Library. *Online resources:* library catalog, web page, access to other libraries' catalogs. *Collection:* 141,430 titles, 596 serial subscriptions, 2,026 audiovisual materials.

Computer facilities: 185 computers available on campus for general student use. Internet access, e-mail are available. *Web address:* http://www.chc.edu/.

General Application Contact: JoAnn McVeigh, Administrative Assistant, 215-248-7161, Fax: 215-248-7161, E-mail: mcveigh@chc.edu.

GRADUATE UNITS

Graduate Division Students: 80 full-time (66 women), 522 part-time (438 women); includes 89 minority (71 African Americans, 6 Asian Americans or Pacific Islanders, 12 Hispanic Americans), 9 international. Average age 36. *Faculty:* 18 full-time (13 women), 71 part-time/adjunct (50 women). Expenses: Contact institution. *Financial support:* In 2001–02, 151 students received support. Career-related internships or fieldwork and unspecified assistantships available. Support available to part-time students. Financial award application deadline: 7/15; financial award applicants required to submit FAFSA. In 2001, 115 degrees awarded. *Degree program information:* Part-time and evening/weekend programs available. Postbaccalaureate distance learning degree programs offered (minimal on-campus study). Offers administration of human services (MS); applied technology (MS); clinical psychology (MA, MS, Psy D); counseling psychology and human services (MA, MS); early childhood education (M Ed); educational leadership (M Ed); elementary education (M Ed); holistic spirituality (MA); holistic spirituality and healthcare (MA); holistic spirituality and spiritual direction (MA). *Application deadline:* For fall admission, 7/17 (priority date); for spring admission, 2/15 (priority date). Applications are processed on a rolling basis. *Application fee:* $35. *Application Contact:* Sr. Regina Raphael Smith, SSJ, Director of Graduate Admissions, 215-248-7020, Fax: 215-248-7161, E-mail: graddiv@chc.edu. *Dean of the Graduate Division,* Sr. Roseann Quinn, SSJ, 215-248-7022, Fax: 215-248-7161, E-mail: quinn@che.edu.

See in-depth description on page 797.

CHEYNEY UNIVERSITY OF PENNSYLVANIA, Cheyney, PA 19319

General Information State-supported, coed, comprehensive institution. *Enrollment:* 34 full-time matriculated graduate/professional students (25 women), 204 part-time matriculated graduate/professional students (151 women). *Graduate faculty:* 9 full-time (3 women), 22 part-time/adjunct (14 women). Tuition, state resident: full-time $4,600; part-time $256 per credit hour. Tuition, nonresident: full-time $7,554; part-time $420 per credit hour. *Required fees:* $380; $191 per term. *Graduate housing:* On-campus housing not available. *Student services:* Career counseling, international student services, low-cost health insurance. *Library facilities:* Leslie Pickney Hill Library plus 1 other. *Online resources:* web page. *Collection:* 85,533 titles, 1,526 serial subscriptions, 1,379 audiovisual materials.

Computer facilities: 150 computers available on campus for general student use. A campuswide network can be accessed from student residence rooms and from off campus. Internet access and online class registration, various software packages are available. *Web address:* http://www.cheyney.edu/.

General Application Contact: Dr. Wesley Pugh, Dean of Graduate Studies, 610-399-2400, Fax: 610-399-2118, E-mail: wpugh@cheyney.edu.

GRADUATE UNITS

School of Education Students: 34 full-time (25 women), 204 part-time (151 women). Average age 39. *Faculty:* 9 full-time (3 women), 22 part-time/adjunct (14 women). Expenses: Contact institution. *Financial support:* Career-related internships or fieldwork, institutionally sponsored loans, tuition waivers (full), and unspecified assistantships available. Financial award application deadline: 5/1. In 2001, 202 degrees awarded. *Degree program information:* Part-time and evening/weekend programs available. Offers adult and continuing education (MS); early childhood education (Certificate); education (M Ed, MAT, MS, Certificate); educational administration and supervision (M Ed, Certificate); educational administration of adult and continuing education (M Ed, MS); elementary education (M Ed, MAT); special

Cheyney University of Pennsylvania (continued)

education (M Ed, MS). *Application deadline:* For fall admission, 8/1 (priority date); for spring admission, 12/15. Applications are processed on a rolling basis. *Application fee:* $25. Electronic applications accepted. *Dean of Graduate Studies*, Dr. Wesley Pugh, 610-399-2400, Fax: 610-399-2118, E-mail: wpugh@cheyney.edu.

CHICAGO SCHOOL OF PROFESSIONAL PSYCHOLOGY, Chicago, IL 60605-2024

General Information Independent, coed, graduate-only institution. *Graduate faculty:* 19 full-time (10 women), 43 part-time/adjunct (25 women). *Tuition:* Part-time $550 per credit hour. *Required fees:* $350 per year. Tuition and fees vary according to degree level and program. *Graduate housing:* On-campus housing not available. *Student services:* Campus employment opportunities, career counseling, disabled student services, international student services, low-cost health insurance, multicultural affairs office. *Library facilities:* Chicago School Library. *Online resources:* web page. *Collection:* 10,000 titles, 220 serial subscriptions, 395 audiovisual materials.

Computer facilities: 18 computers available on campus for general student use. A campuswide network can be accessed. Internet access is available. *Web address:* http://www.csopp.edu/.

General Application Contact: Magdelen Kellogg, Director of Admission, 312-786-9443 Ext. 3029, Fax: 312-322-3273, E-mail: mkellogg@csopp.edu.

GRADUATE UNITS

Graduate School Students: 216 full-time (162 women), 157 part-time (114 women); includes 75 minority (38 African Americans, 16 Asian Americans or Pacific Islanders, 21 Hispanic Americans), 25 international. Average age 25. 215 applicants, 74% accepted, 70 enrolled. *Faculty:* 19 full-time (10 women), 43 part-time/adjunct (25 women). Expenses: Contact institution. *Financial support:* In 2001–02, 16 research assistantships with partial tuition reimbursements, 32 teaching assistantships with partial tuition reimbursements were awarded. Career-related internships or fieldwork, Federal Work-Study, scholarships/grants, and tuition waivers (partial) also available. Support available to part-time students. Financial award application deadline: 5/1; financial award applicants required to submit FAFSA. In 2001, 48 degrees awarded. *Degree program information:* Part-time programs available. Offers clinical psychology (Psy D); forensic psychology (MA); industrial and organizational psychology (MA). *Application deadline:* For fall admission, 1/15 (priority date); for spring admission, 11/1 (priority date). Applications are processed on a rolling basis. *Application fee:* $50. *Application Contact:* Magdelen Kellogg, Director of Admission, 312-786-9443 Ext. 3029, Fax: 312-322-3273, E-mail: mkellogg@csopp.edu. *President*, Dr. Michael Horowitz, 312-786-9443 Ext. 3033, Fax: 312-322-3273, E-mail: mhorowitz@csopp.edu.

CHICAGO STATE UNIVERSITY, Chicago, IL 60628

General Information State-supported, coed, comprehensive institution. *Enrollment:* 312 full-time matriculated graduate/professional students (210 women), 1,542 part-time matriculated graduate/professional students (1,072 women). *Enrollment by degree level:* 1,854 master's. *Graduate faculty:* 133 full-time (67 women), 87 part-time/adjunct (49 women). *Graduate housing:* Room and/or apartments available on a first-come, first-served basis to single students; on-campus housing not available to married students. *Student services:* Campus employment opportunities, career counseling, child daycare facilities, disabled student services, free psychological counseling, international student services, low-cost health insurance, teacher training, writing training. *Library facilities:* Paul and Emily Douglas Library. *Collection:* 320,000 titles, 1,539 serial subscriptions.

Computer facilities: 40 computers available on campus for general student use. *Web address:* http://www.csu.edu/.

General Application Contact: Daphne G. Townsend, Admissions and Records Officer II, 773-995-2404, Fax: 773-995-3671, E-mail: g-studies1@csu.edu.

GRADUATE UNITS

Graduate Studies Students: 312 full-time (210 women), 1,542 part-time (1,072 women); includes 1,334 minority (1,166 African Americans, 17 Asian Americans or Pacific Islanders, 150 Hispanic Americans, 1 Native American), 3 international. Average age 39. 528 applicants, 53% accepted. *Faculty:* 133 full-time (67 women), 87 part-time/adjunct (49 women). Expenses: Contact institution. *Financial support:* In 2001–02, research assistantships with tuition reimbursements (averaging $5,400 per year), teaching assistantships with tuition reimbursements (averaging $5,400 per year) were awarded. Career-related internships or fieldwork and tuition waivers (full) also available. Support available to part-time students. Financial award applicants required to submit FAFSA. In 2001, 257 degrees awarded. *Degree program information:* Part-time and evening/weekend programs available. *Application deadline:* For fall admission, 3/15; for spring admission, 10/15. Applications are processed on a rolling basis. *Application fee:* $25. Electronic applications accepted. *Application Contact:* Daphne G. Townsend, Admissions and Records Officer II, 773-995-2404, Fax: 773-995-3671, E-mail: g-studies1@csu.edu. *Dean of Graduate Studies*, Dr. Ellen F. Rosen, 773-995-2404, Fax: 773-995-3671, E-mail: ef-rosen@csu.edu.

College of Arts and Sciences Students: 390 (239 women); includes 322 minority (301 African Americans, 6 Asian Americans or Pacific Islanders, 13 Hispanic Americans, 2 Native Americans) 13 international. Average age 39. *Faculty:* 38 full-time (10 women). Expenses: Contact institution. *Financial support:* Research assistantships available. *Degree program information:* Part-time and evening/weekend programs available. Offers arts and sciences (MA, MS, MSW); biological sciences (MS); counseling (MA); criminal justice (MS); English (MA); geography (MA); history, philosophy, and political science (MA); mathematics and computer science (MS); social work and sociology (MSW). *Application fee:* $25. *Application Contact:* Anika Miller, Graduate Studies Office, 773-995-2404, E-mail: g-studies1@csu.edu. *Dean*, Dr. Rachel Lindsey, 773-995-2105, Fax: 773-995-3767, E-mail: rw-lindsey@csu.edu.

College of Education Students: 618 (444 women); includes 416 minority (359 African Americans, 1 Asian American or Pacific Islander, 54 Hispanic Americans, 2 Native Americans) 2 international. *Faculty:* 48 full-time (25 women). Expenses: Contact institution. *Financial support:* In 2001–02, 6 research assistantships with partial tuition reimbursements (averaging $6,000 per year) were awarded *Degree program information:* Part-time programs available. Offers bilingual/bicultural education (MS Ed); early childhood education (MAT, MS Ed); education (MA, MAT, MS, MS Ed); educational leadership (MA); elementary education (MAT, MS Ed); general administration (MA); higher education administration (MA); library science and communications media (MS); physical education (MS Ed); reading (MS Ed); secondary education (MAT, MS Ed); special education (MS Ed); teaching in non-school settings (MS Ed); teaching of reading (MS Ed); technology and education (MS Ed). *Application deadline:* For fall admission, 7/1; for spring admission, 11/10. *Application fee:* $25. *Acting Dean*, Dr. Sandra Westbrooks, 773-995-2472, Fax: 773-995-2473.

CHICAGO THEOLOGICAL SEMINARY, Chicago, IL 60637-1507

General Information Independent-religious, coed, graduate-only institution. *Graduate faculty:* 9 full-time (1 woman), 11 part-time/adjunct (2 women). *Tuition:* Full-time $7,960; part-time $995 per course. *Required fees:* $120; $60 per semester. One-time fee: $125 full-time. Tuition and fees vary according to degree level and program. *Graduate housing:* Rooms and/or apartments available on a first-come, first-served basis to single students and available to married students. Typical cost: $4,950 per year for single students; $4,950 per year for married students. Housing application deadline: 8/1. *Student services:* Career counseling, international student services, low-cost health insurance. *Library facilities:* Hammond Library. *Collection:* 110,000 titles, 221 serial subscriptions.

Computer facilities: 2 computers available on campus for general student use. *Web address:* http://www.ctschicago.edu/.

General Application Contact: Rev. Alison Buttrick Patton, Director of Admissions, Recruitment and Financial Aid, 773-752-5757 Ext. 229, Fax: 773-752-1903, E-mail: apatton@ctschicago.edu.

GRADUATE UNITS

Graduate and Professional Programs Students: 99 full-time (43 women), 105 part-time (60 women); includes 47 minority (44 African Americans, 3 Asian Americans or Pacific Islanders), 33 international. Average age 41. *Faculty:* 9 full-time (1 woman), 11 part-time/adjunct (2 women). Expenses: Contact institution. *Financial support:* Fellowships, institutionally sponsored loans and scholarships/grants available. Support available to part-time students. Financial award application deadline: 4/1; financial award applicants required to submit FAFSA. *Degree program information:* Part-time programs available. Offers clinical pastoral education (D Min); Jewish-Christian studies (PhD); pastoral care (PhD); pastoral counseling (D Min); preaching (D Min); spiritual leadership (D Min); theology (M Div, MA); theology and the human sciences (PhD). *Application deadline:* For fall admission, 5/1; for winter admission, 11/1. Applications are processed on a rolling basis. *Application fee:* $50. *Application Contact:* Rev. Alison Buttrick Patton, Director of Admissions, Recruitment and Financial Aid, 773-752-5757 Ext. 229, Fax: 773-752-1903, E-mail: apatton@ctschicago.edu. *Dean*, Dr. Dow Edgerton, 773-752-5757, Fax: 773-752-5925, E-mail: dedgerton@ctschicago.edu.

CHRISTENDOM COLLEGE, Front Royal, VA 22630-5103

General Information Independent-religious, coed, comprehensive institution. *Graduate housing:* On-campus housing not available.

GRADUATE UNITS

Notre Dame Graduate School *Degree program information:* Part-time and evening/weekend programs available. Offers theological studies (MA). Electronic applications accepted.

CHRISTIAN BROTHERS UNIVERSITY, Memphis, TN 38104-5581

General Information Independent-religious, coed, comprehensive institution. *Enrollment:* 262 full-time matriculated graduate/professional students (166 women), 199 part-time matriculated graduate/professional students (116 women). *Enrollment by degree level:* 461 master's. *Graduate faculty:* 26 full-time (9 women), 17 part-time/adjunct (12 women). *Tuition:* Full-time $4,050; part-time $450 per hour. One-time fee: $50. *Graduate housing:* On-campus housing not available. *Student services:* Campus employment opportunities, career counseling, free psychological counseling, low-cost health insurance. *Library facilities:* Plough Memorial Library and Media Center. *Online resources:* library catalog, web page, access to other libraries' catalogs. *Collection:* 100,000 titles, 537 serial subscriptions. *Research affiliation:* Federal Express (information technology).

Computer facilities: 300 computers available on campus for general student use. A campuswide network can be accessed from student residence rooms and from off campus. Internet access and online class registration, on-line class listings, e-mail, course assignments are available. *Web address:* http://www.cbu.edu/.

General Application Contact: Information Contact, 901-321-3200.

GRADUATE UNITS

Graduate Programs Students: 262 full-time (166 women), 199 part-time (116 women); includes 240 minority (230 African Americans, 8 Asian Americans or Pacific Islanders, 1 Hispanic American, 1 Native American), 6 international. Average age 32. *Faculty:* 26 full-time (9 women), 17 part-time/adjunct (12 women). Expenses: Contact institution. *Financial support:* Institutionally sponsored loans available. Support available to part-time students. In 2001, 91 degrees awarded. *Degree program information:* Part-time and evening/weekend programs available. *Application deadline:* Applications are processed on a rolling basis. *Application fee:* $25. *Information Contact*, 901-321-3200.

School of Arts Students: 168 full-time (119 women), 91 part-time (70 women); includes 182 minority (180 African Americans, 2 Asian Americans or Pacific Islanders), 2 international. Average age 30. *Faculty:* 7 full-time (5 women), 12 part-time/adjunct (9 women). Expenses: Contact institution. In 2001, 29 degrees awarded. Offers liberal arts (M Ed). *Application deadline:* Applications are processed on a rolling basis. *Application fee:* $25. *Application Contact:* Dr. Ellen S. Faith, Director, 901-321-4350, Fax: 901-321-3408, E-mail: esfaith@cbu.edu. *Dean*, Dr. Kristin Pruitt, 901-321-3339, Fax: 901-321-3408, E-mail: kpruitt@cbu.edu.

School of Business Students: 78 full-time (41 women), 74 part-time (40 women); includes 45 minority (39 African Americans, 4 Asian Americans or Pacific Islanders, 1 Hispanic American, 1 Native American), 4 international. Average age 32. *Faculty:* 16 full-time (4 women), 1 part-time/adjunct (0 women). Expenses: Contact institution. *Financial support:* Institutionally sponsored loans available. Support available to part-time students. In 2001, 55 degrees awarded. *Degree program information:* Part-time and evening/weekend programs available. Offers business (MBA). *Application deadline:* Applications are processed on a rolling basis. *Application fee:* $25. *Application Contact:* Dr. John E. Megley, III, Director, MBA Program, 901-321-3319, Fax: 901-321-3494, E-mail: jmegley@cbu.edu. *Dean*, Dr. Thomas Dukes, 901-321-3316, Fax: 901-321-3494.

School of Engineering Students: 16 full-time (6 women), 34 part-time (6 women); includes 13 minority (11 African Americans, 2 Asian Americans or Pacific Islanders) Average age 32. *Faculty:* 3 full-time (0 women), 4 part-time/adjunct (3 women). Expenses: Contact institution. *Financial support:* Institutionally sponsored loans available. In 2001, 7 degrees awarded. *Degree program information:* Part-time and evening/weekend programs available. Offers engineering (MEM). *Application fee:* $25. *Application Contact:* Dr. Neal Jackson, Director, 901-321-3283, Fax: 901-321-3494, E-mail: njackson@cbu.edu. *Dean*, Dr. Sinipong Malasri, 901-321-3408, Fax: 901-321-3494.

CHRISTIAN THEOLOGICAL SEMINARY, Indianapolis, IN 46208-3301

General Information Independent-religious, coed, graduate-only institution. *Graduate faculty:* 20 full-time (7 women), 14 part-time/adjunct (5 women). *Tuition:* Full-time $6,480; part-time $1,620 per semester. *Required fees:* $80; $20 per semester. Tuition and fees vary according to course load. *Graduate housing:* Rooms and/or apartments available on a first-come, first-served basis to single and married students. Typical cost: $2,960 (including board) for single students; $5,720 (including board) for married students. Housing application deadline: 5/1. *Student services:* Campus employment opportunities, campus safety program, career counseling, international student services, writing training. *Library facilities:* CTS Library. *Online resources:* library catalog, access to other libraries' catalogs. *Collection:* 217,693 titles, 1,361 serial subscriptions, 5,144 audiovisual materials.

Computer facilities: 21 computers available on campus for general student use. A campuswide network can be accessed from student residence rooms and from off campus. Internet access is available. *Web address:* http://www.cts.edu/.

General Application Contact: Rev. Annette Barnes, Director of Admissions, 317-931-2300, Fax: 317-923-1961, E-mail: abarnes@cts.edu.

GRADUATE UNITS

Graduate and Professional Programs Students: 142 full-time (91 women), 138 part-time (80 women); includes 67 minority (60 African Americans, 4 Asian Americans or Pacific Islanders, 2 Hispanic Americans, 1 Native American), 4 international. 94 applicants, 95% accepted, 70 enrolled. *Faculty:* 20 full-time (7 women), 14 part-time/adjunct (5 women). Expenses: Contact institution. *Financial support:* In 2001–02, 156 students received support, including 15 fellowships (averaging $6,480 per year); career-related internships or fieldwork, Federal Work-Study, scholarships/grants, and tuition waivers (full and partial) also available. Financial award application deadline: 4/1; financial award applicants required to submit FAFSA. In 2001, 27 first professional degrees, 22 master's, 6 doctorates awarded. *Degree program information:* Part-time programs available. Offers Christian education (MA); church music (MA); marriage and family (MA); pastoral care and counseling (D Min); pastoral counseling (MA); practical theology (D Min); sacred theology (STM); theological studies (MTS); theology (M Div). *Application deadline:* For fall admission, 7/15; for spring admission, 11/15. Applications are processed on a rolling basis. *Application fee:* $30. Electronic applications accepted. *Application Contact:* Rev. Annette Barnes, Director of Admissions, 317-931-2300, Fax: 317-923-1961, E-mail: abarnes@cts.edu. *President*, Dr. Edward Wheeler, 317-931-2305, Fax: 317-923-1961, E-mail: wheeler@cts.edu.

CHRISTOPHER NEWPORT UNIVERSITY, Newport News, VA 23606-2998

General Information State-supported, coed, comprehensive institution. *Enrollment:* 39 full-time matriculated graduate/professional students (29 women), 118 part-time matriculated graduate/professional students (70 women). *Enrollment by degree level:* 157 master's. *Graduate faculty:* 69 full-time (21 women). Tuition, state resident: full-time $1,782; part-time $99 per credit. Tuition, nonresident: full-time $6,138; part-time $341 per credit. *Required fees:* $49 per credit hour. $20 per term. *Graduate housing:* Room and/or apartments available on a first-come, first-served basis to single students; on-campus housing not available to married students. Typical cost: $3,500 per year ($5,750 including board). Room and board charges vary according to housing facility selected. *Student services:* Campus employment opportunities, campus safety program, career counseling, disabled student services, exercise/wellness program, grant writing training, international student services, multicultural affairs office, teacher training, writing training. *Library facilities:* Captain John Smith Library. *Online resources:* library catalog, web page, access to other libraries' catalogs. *Collection:* 430,502 titles, 10,353 serial subscriptions, 9,292 audiovisual materials. *Research affiliation:* Science Application International (SAIC) (computer engineering), NASA–Institute for Computer Applications in Science and Engineering (flow visualization), Thomas Jefferson National Acceleration Facility (instrument and nuclear physics), Applied Research Center (biology, engineering, physics), JDH Technologies (computer software), National Science Foundation (science).

Computer facilities: 1,000 computers available on campus for general student use. A campuswide network can be accessed from student residence rooms and from off campus. Internet access is available. *Web address:* http://www.cnu.edu/.

General Application Contact: Susan R. Chittenden, Graduate Admissions, 757-594-7359, Fax: 757-594-7333, E-mail: gradstdy@cnu.edu.

GRADUATE UNITS

Graduate Studies Students: 39 full-time (29 women), 118 part-time (70 women); includes 24 minority (17 African Americans, 4 Asian Americans or Pacific Islanders, 3 Hispanic Americans) Average age 36. 103 applicants, 99% accepted. *Faculty:* 69 full-time (21 women). Expenses: Contact institution. *Financial support:* Research assistantships with full and partial tuition reimbursements, teaching assistantships, career-related internships or fieldwork, Federal Work-Study, institutionally sponsored loans, and scholarships/grants available. Support available to part-time students. Financial award application deadline: 3/1; financial award applicants required to submit FAFSA. In 2001, 33 degrees awarded. *Degree program information:* Part-time and evening/weekend programs available. Offers applied physics and computer science (MS); applied psychology (MS); environmental science (MS); history (MAT); leadership (MPSL); public safety (MPSL); teaching language arts (MAT); teaching mathematics (MAT); teaching science (MAT). *Application deadline:* For fall admission, 7/1; for spring admission, 11/15. Applications are processed on a rolling basis. *Application fee:* $40. Electronic applications accepted. *Application Contact:* Susan R. Chittenden, Graduate Admissions, 757-594-7359, Fax: 757-594-7333, E-mail: gradstdy@cnu.edu. *Director*, Dr. Dorothy C. Doolittle, 757-594-7544, Fax: 757-594-7649, E-mail: dolittle@cnu.edu.

See in-depth description on page 799.

CHRIST THE KING SEMINARY, East Aurora, NY 14052

General Information Independent-religious, coed, graduate-only institution. *Enrollment by degree level:* 30 first professional, 66 master's. *Graduate faculty:* 18 full-time (2 women), 8 part-time/adjunct (2 women). *Tuition:* Part-time $230 per credit hour. *Required fees:* $145; $110 per year. *Graduate housing:* Room and/or apartments available to single students; on-campus housing not available to married students. Typical cost: $7,250 (including board). *Student services:* Writing training. *Library facilities:* Main library plus 1 other. *Collection:* 150,000 titles, 430 serial subscriptions, 1,518 audiovisual materials.

Computer facilities: 1 computer available on campus for general student use. Online class registration is available.

General Application Contact: Rev. Lynn R. Morgan, Assistant to the Academic Dean, 716-652-8900, Fax: 716-652-8903, E-mail: lmorgan@cks.edu.

GRADUATE UNITS

Graduate and Professional Programs Students: 29 full-time (1 woman), 67 part-time (37 women); includes 9 minority (6 African Americans, 3 Hispanic Americans), 3 international. Average age 38. 21 applicants, 100% accepted, 20 enrolled. *Faculty:* 18 full-time (2 women), 8 part-time/adjunct (2 women). Expenses: Contact institution. *Financial support:* Career-related internships or fieldwork and scholarships/grants available. Support available to part-time students. Financial award application deadline: 8/1; financial award applicants required to submit FAFSA. In 2001, 3 first professional degrees, 17 master's awarded. *Degree program information:* Part-time and evening/weekend programs available. Offers divinity (M Div); pastoral ministry (MA); theology (MA). *Application deadline:* For fall admission, 8/15 (priority date); for spring admission, 1/5 (priority date). *Application fee:* $75. *Application Contact:* Rev. Lynn R. Morgan, Assistant to the Academic Dean, 716-652-8900, Fax: 716-652-8903, E-mail: lmorgan@cks.edu. *Academic Dean*, Dr. Dennis Castillo, 716-652-8900, Fax: 716-652-8903, E-mail: dcastillo@cks.edu.

CHURCH DIVINITY SCHOOL OF THE PACIFIC, Berkeley, CA 94709-1217

General Information Independent-religious, coed, graduate-only institution. *Enrollment by degree level:* 73 first professional, 21 master's, 11 doctoral, 26 other advanced degrees. *Graduate faculty:* 11 full-time (5 women), 6 part-time/adjunct (4 women). *Tuition:* Part-time $420 per unit. *Required fees:* $30 per semester. Tuition and fees vary according to course load, degree level and program. *Graduate housing:* Rooms and/or apartments available on a first-come, first-served basis to single and married students. Typical cost: $4,990 (including board) for single students. Housing application deadline: 5/1. *Student services:* Campus employment opportunities, low-cost health insurance. *Library facilities:* Flora Lamson Hewlett Library of the Graduate Theological Union. *Online resources:* web page. *Collection:* 500,000 titles.

Computer facilities: 4 computers available on campus for general student use. A campuswide network can be accessed from student residence rooms and from off campus. Internet access is available. *Web address:* http://www.cdsp.edu/.

General Application Contact: Rev. Stina Pope, Director of Admissions, 510-204-0715, Fax: 510-644-0712, E-mail: admissions@cdsp.edu.

GRADUATE UNITS

Graduate and Professional Programs Students: 73 full-time (40 women), 58 part-time (36 women). Average age 44. 80 applicants, 74% accepted, 42 enrolled. *Faculty:* 11 full-time (5 women), 6 part-time/adjunct (4 women). Expenses: Contact institution. *Financial support:* Career-related internships or fieldwork, Federal Work-Study, and scholarships/grants available. Support available to part-time students. Financial award application deadline: 3/1; financial award applicants required to submit FAFSA. In 2001, 24 first professional degrees, 7 master's, 6 other advanced degrees awarded. *Degree program information:* Part-time programs available. *Application deadline:* For fall admission, 5/1. Applications are processed on a rolling basis. *Application fee:* $30. Electronic applications accepted. *Application Contact:* Rev. Stina Pope, Director of Admissions, 510-204-0715, Fax: 510-644-0712, E-mail: admissions@cdsp.edu. *President and Dean*, Dr. Donn F. Morgan, 510-204-0733.

CHURCH OF GOD THEOLOGICAL SEMINARY, Cleveland, TN 37320-3330

General Information Independent-religious, coed, graduate-only institution. *Graduate housing:* Rooms and/or apartments available to single and married students.

GRADUATE UNITS

Graduate and Professional Programs *Degree program information:* Part-time programs available. Offers church ministries (MA); discipleship and Christian formations (MA); theology (M Div).

CINCINNATI BIBLE COLLEGE AND SEMINARY, Cincinnati, OH 45204-3200

General Information Independent-religious, coed, comprehensive institution. *Enrollment:* 136 full-time matriculated graduate/professional students (62 women), 177 part-time matriculated graduate/professional students (49 women). *Enrollment by degree level:* 55 first professional, 258 master's. *Graduate faculty:* 11 full-time (1 woman), 27 part-time/adjunct (8 women). *Tuition:* Full-time $4,320; part-time $240 per credit hour. *Graduate housing:* On-campus housing not available. *Student services:* Campus employment opportunities, career counseling, free psychological counseling, international student services, low-cost health insurance. *Library facilities:* Cincinnati Bible College Library. *Online resources:* library catalog, access to other libraries' catalogs. *Collection:* 93,000 titles, 656 serial subscriptions.

Computer facilities: 32 computers available on campus for general student use. A campuswide network can be accessed from student residence rooms and from off campus. Internet access is available. *Web address:* http://www.cincybible.edu/.

General Application Contact: Jeffrey Derico, Director of Admissions and Enrollment, 513-244-8612, Fax: 513-244-8434, E-mail: jeffrey.derico@cincybible.edu.

GRADUATE UNITS

Graduate School Students: 136 full-time (62 women), 177 part-time (49 women); includes 31 minority (29 African Americans, 1 Asian American or Pacific Islander, 1 Hispanic American), 22 international. Average age 26. 151 applicants, 75% accepted, 94 enrolled. *Faculty:* 11 full-time (1 woman), 27 part-time/adjunct (8 women). Expenses: Contact institution. *Financial support:* In 2001–02, 159 students received support. Career-related internships or fieldwork, Federal Work-Study, scholarships/grants, tuition waivers (full and partial), and unspecified assistantships available. Support available to part-time students. Financial award application deadline: 7/15; financial award applicants required to submit FAFSA. In 2001, 14 first professional degrees, 52 master's awarded. *Degree program information:* Part-time programs available. Offers biblical studies (MA); church history (MA); counseling (MAC); divinity (M Div); ministry (M Min); practical ministries (MA); theological studies (MA). *Application deadline:* For fall admission, 8/10 (priority date); for spring admission, 12/10 (priority date). Applications are processed on a rolling basis. *Application fee:* $35 ($75 for international students). Electronic applications accepted. *Application Contact:* Jeffrey Derico, Director of Admissions and Enrollment, 513-244-8612, Fax: 513-244-8434, E-mail: jeffrey.derico@cincybible.edu. *Dean*, Dr. William C. Weber, 513-244-8192, Fax: 513-244-8434, E-mail: bill.weber@cincybible.edu.

THE CITADEL, THE MILITARY COLLEGE OF SOUTH CAROLINA, Charleston, SC 29409

General Information State-supported, coed, primarily men, comprehensive institution. *Enrollment:* 150 full-time matriculated graduate/professional students (100 women), 628 part-time matriculated graduate/professional students (366 women). *Enrollment by degree level:* 703 master's, 75 other advanced degrees. *Graduate faculty:* 46 full-time (16 women), 14 part-time/adjunct (5 women). Tuition, state resident: full-time $1,314; part-time $141 per credit hour. Tuition, nonresident: full-time $2,619; part-time $285 per credit hour. *Graduate housing:* On-campus housing not available. *Student services:* Campus employment opportunities, career counseling, disabled student services, free psychological counseling, international student services, multicultural affairs office, teacher training, writing training. *Library facilities:* Daniel Library. *Online resources:* library catalog, web page, access to other libraries' catalogs. *Collection:* 173,765 titles, 1,318 serial subscriptions, 1,426 audiovisual materials.

Computer facilities: 350 computers available on campus for general student use. A campuswide network can be accessed from student residence rooms and from off campus. Internet access and online class registration are available. *Web address:* http://www.citadel.edu.

General Application Contact: Patricia Ezell, Assistant Dean, College of Graduate and Professional Studies, 843-953-5089, Fax: 843-953-7630, E-mail: ezellp@citadel.edu.

GRADUATE UNITS

College of Graduate and Professional Studies Students: 150 full-time (100 women), 628 part-time (366 women); includes 137 minority (115 African Americans, 12 Asian Americans or Pacific Islanders, 9 Hispanic Americans, 1 Native American), 7 international. Average age 31. *Faculty:* 46 full-time (16 women), 14 part-time/adjunct (5 women). Expenses: Contact institution. *Financial support:* Fellowships, research assistantships, teaching assistantships, career-related internships or fieldwork, unspecified assistantships, and incentive fellowships available. Support available to part-time students. Financial award applicants required to submit FAFSA. In 2001, 160 master's, 16 other advanced degrees awarded. *Degree program information:* Part-time and evening/weekend programs available. Offers biology education (MAE); business administration (MBA); computer and information science (MS); educational administration (M Ed, Ed S); English (MA); guidance and counseling (M Ed); health and physical education (M Ed); history (MA); mathematics education (MAE); psychology (MA); reading (M Ed); school psychology (Ed S); secondary education (MAT); social studies education (MAE). *Application deadline:* For fall admission, 8/1 (priority date). Applications are processed on a rolling basis. *Application fee:* $25. *Application Contact:* Patricia Ezell, Assistant Dean, College of Graduate and Professional Studies, 843-953-5089, Fax: 843-953-7630, E-mail: ezellp@citadel.edu. *Acting Dean*, Brig. Gen. Harrison Carter, 843-953-5089, Fax: 843-953-7118, E-mail: carterh@citadel.edu.

CITY COLLEGE OF THE CITY UNIVERSITY OF NEW YORK, New York, NY 10031-9198

General Information State and locally supported, coed, university. *Enrollment:* 230 full-time matriculated graduate/professional students (103 women), 1,463 part-time matriculated graduate/professional students (807 women). *Enrollment by degree level:* 1,693 master's. *Graduate faculty:* 482 full-time (142 women), 328 part-time/adjunct (126 women). Tuition, state resident: part-time $185 per credit. Tuition, nonresident: part-time $320 per credit. *Required fees:* $43 per term. *Graduate housing:* On-campus housing not available. *Student services:* Career counseling, child daycare facilities, free psychological counseling. *Library facilities:* Morris Raphael Cohen Library plus 3 others. *Online resources:* library catalog, web page, access to other libraries' catalogs. *Collection:* 1.4 million titles, 2,207 serial subscriptions, 19,586 audiovisual materials. *Research affiliation:* Brookhaven National Laboratory (physics), Museum of Natural History, Hospital for Joint Diseases (biomedical engineering), Lucent Laboratories (engineering).

Computer facilities: 3,000 computers available on campus for general student use. A campuswide network can be accessed from off campus. Internet access is available. *Web address:* http://www.ccny.cuny.edu/.

General Application Contact: 212-650-6977, Fax: 212-650-6417, E-mail: admissions@admin.ccny.cuny.edu.

GRADUATE UNITS

Graduate School Students: 230 full-time (103 women), 1,463 part-time (807 women). Expenses: Contact institution. *Financial support:* Fellowships, research assistantships, teaching assistantships, career-related internships or fieldwork, Federal Work-Study, institutionally sponsored loans, and tuition waivers (full and partial) available. Support available to part-time students. In 2001, 639 master's, 6 other advanced degrees awarded. *Degree program information:* Part-time and evening/weekend programs available. *Application fee:* $40. *Application Contact:* Graduate Admissions Office, 212-650-6977, E-mail: adocc@cunyvm.cuny.edu. *Assistant Provost for Graduate Studies and Research*, Joseph Barba, 212-650-8245.

College of Liberal Arts and Science Students: 805. 438 applicants, 66% accepted. Expenses: Contact institution. *Financial support:* Fellowships, research assistantships, teaching assistantships, career-related internships or fieldwork, Federal Work-Study, institutionally sponsored loans, and tuition waivers (full and partial) available. Support available to part-time students. In 2001, 99 degrees awarded. *Degree program information:* Part-time and evening/weekend programs available. Offers advertising design (MFA); applied urban anthropology (MA); art history (MA); art history and museum studies (MA); biochemistry

City College of the City University of New York (continued)

(MA, PhD); biology (MA, PhD); ceramic design (MFA); chemistry (MA, PhD); clinical psychology (PhD); creative writing (MA); earth and environmental science (PhD); earth systems science (MA); economics (MA); English and American literature (MA); experimental cognition (PhD); fine arts (MFA); general psychology (MA); history (MA); humanities and arts (MA, MFA); international relations (MA); language and literacy (MA); liberal arts and science (MA, MFA, MS, PhD); mathematics (MA); media arts production (MFA); museum studies (MA); music (MA); painting (MFA); physics (MA, PhD); printmaking (MFA); science (MA, PhD); sculpture (MFA); social science (MA, MS, PhD); sociology (MA); Spanish (MA); wood and metal design (MFA). *Application deadline:* For fall admission, 5/1; for spring admission, 12/1. *Application fee:* $40. *Application Contact:* 212-650-6977.

School of Architecture and Environmental Studies Students: 10. Expenses: Contact institution. *Financial support:* Fellowships, career-related internships or fieldwork and Federal Work-Study available. Support available to part-time students. In 2001, 8 degrees awarded. *Degree program information:* Part-time programs available. Offers architecture (PD); urban design (MUP). *Application fee:* $40. *Application Contact:* Director, 212-650-8734. *Chair*, Lance Brown, 212-650-7118.

School of Education Students: 687; includes 401 minority (172 African Americans, 40 Asian Americans or Pacific Islanders, 189 Hispanic Americans) Expenses: Contact institution. *Financial support:* Fellowships, research assistantships, teaching assistantships, career-related internships or fieldwork, Federal Work-Study, and tuition waivers (full and partial) available. Support available to part-time students. In 2001, 380 master's, 6 other advanced degrees awarded. *Degree program information:* Part-time and evening/weekend programs available. Offers bilingual education (MS); early childhood education (MS); education (MA, MS, MS Ed, AC); educational administration (MS, AC); elementary education (MS); environmental education (MA); reading (MS, AC); secondary science education (MA); special education (MS). *Application deadline:* For fall admission, 4/15; for winter admission, 11/15. *Application fee:* $40. *Application Contact:* Fareed Suarez, Graduate Admissions Adviser, 212-650-6236. *Interim Dean*, Alfred Posamentier, 212-650-5354.

School of Engineering Students: 424; includes 201 minority (45 African Americans, 131 Asian Americans or Pacific Islanders, 25 Hispanic Americans) 521 applicants, 45% accepted. Expenses: Contact institution. *Financial support:* Fellowships, research assistantships, teaching assistantships, Federal Work-Study, institutionally sponsored loans, and tuition waivers (full and partial) available. Support available to part-time students. In 2001, 152 degrees awarded. *Degree program information:* Part-time programs available. Offers chemical engineering (ME, MS, PhD); civil engineering (ME, MS, PhD); computer sciences (MS, PhD); electrical engineering (ME, MS, PhD); engineering (ME, MS, PhD); mechanical engineering (ME, MS, PhD). *Application deadline:* Applications are processed on a rolling basis. *Application fee:* $40. *Application Contact:* Graduate Admissions Office, 212-650-6977. *Associate Dean for Graduate Studies*, Dr. Muntaz G. Kassir, 212-650-8030.

See in-depth description on page 801.

CITY OF HOPE NATIONAL MEDICAL CENTER/BECKMAN RESEARCH INSTITUTE, Duarte, CA 91010

General Information Independent, coed, graduate-only institution. *Enrollment by degree level:* 35 doctoral. *Graduate faculty:* 54 full-time (15 women). *Graduate housing:* Rooms and/or apartments available on a first-come, first-served basis to single and married students. Typical cost: $400 per year for single students; $800 per year for married students. Housing application deadline: 7/14. *Student services:* Career counseling, free psychological counseling, grant writing training, international student services, writing training. *Library facilities:* Graff Medical Library. *Online resources:* library catalog, web page, access to other libraries' catalogs. *Collection:* 7,100 titles, 535 serial subscriptions.

Computer facilities: 45 computers available on campus for general student use. A campuswide network can be accessed from student residence rooms and from off campus. Internet access is available. *Web address:* http://gradschool.coh.org/.

General Application Contact: Dr. Steven J. Novak, Associate Dean for Administration, 626-256-8775, Fax: 626-301-8015, E-mail: snovak@coh.org.

GRADUATE UNITS

City of Hope Graduate School of Biological Sciences Students: 35 full-time (16 women); includes 21 minority (16 Asian Americans or Pacific Islanders, 5 Hispanic Americans) 88 applicants, 25% accepted, 9 enrolled. *Faculty:* 54 full-time (15 women). Expenses: Contact institution. *Financial support:* In 2001–02, 35 fellowships with full tuition reimbursements (averaging $23,000 per year) were awarded In 2001, 5 doctorates awarded. Offers biological sciences (PhD). *Application deadline:* For spring admission, 2/1 (priority date). *Application fee:* $0. *Application Contact:* Dr. Steven J. Novak, Associate Dean for Administration, 626-256-8775, Fax: 626-301-8105, E-mail: snovak@coh.org. *Dean*, Dr. John Rossi, 626-256-8775, Fax: 626-301-8105.

CITY UNIVERSITY, Bellevue, WA 98005

General Information Independent, coed, comprehensive institution. *Enrollment:* 967 full-time matriculated graduate/professional students (624 women), 4,050 part-time matriculated graduate/professional students (1,994 women). *Enrollment by degree level:* 5,017 master's, 173 other advanced degrees. *Graduate faculty:* 54 full-time (30 women), 1,117 part-time/adjunct (480 women). *Tuition:* Part-time $324 per credit. *Graduate housing:* On-campus housing not available. *Student services:* Campus employment opportunities, disabled student services, international student services. *Library facilities:* City University Library. *Online resources:* library catalog, web page, access to other libraries' catalogs. *Collection:* 32,329 titles, 1,518 serial subscriptions, 5,184 audiovisual materials.

Computer facilities: 145 computers available on campus for general student use. A campuswide network can be accessed from off campus. Internet access is available. *Web address:* http://www.cityu.edu/.

General Application Contact: 800-426-5596, Fax: 425-701-5361, E-mail: info@cityu.edu.

GRADUATE UNITS

Graduate Division Students: 967 full-time (624 women), 4,050 part-time (1,994 women); includes 964 minority (190 African Americans, 661 Asian Americans or Pacific Islanders, 79 Hispanic Americans, 34 Native Americans), 20 international. Average age 36. 1,491 applicants, 100% accepted, 439 enrolled. *Faculty:* 54 full-time (30 women), 1,117 part-time/adjunct (480 women). Expenses: Contact institution. *Financial support:* In 2001–02, 117 students received support. Federal Work-Study available. Support available to part-time students. Financial award applicants required to submit FAFSA. In 2001, 1503 degrees awarded. *Degree program information:* Part-time and evening/weekend programs available. Postbaccalaureate distance learning degree programs offered (no on-campus study). *Application deadline:* Applications are processed on a rolling basis. *Application fee:* $75 ($175 for international students). Electronic applications accepted. *Application Contact:* 800-426-5596, Fax: 425-709-5361, E-mail: info@cityu.edu. *Executive Vice President and Academic Dean*, Arthur C. Rogers, 425-637-1010 Ext. 5454, Fax: 425-709-5366, E-mail: arogers@cityu.edu.

Gordon Albright School of Education Students: 540 full-time, 981 part-time; includes 125 minority (47 African Americans, 37 Asian Americans or Pacific Islanders, 24 Hispanic Americans, 17 Native Americans) Average age 36. 645 applicants, 100% accepted, 217 enrolled. *Faculty:* 23 full-time (13 women), 345 part-time/adjunct (212 women). Expenses: Contact institution. *Financial support:* In 2001–02, 77 students received support. Federal Work-Study available. Support available to part-time students. Financial award applicants required to submit FAFSA. In 2001, 612 degrees awarded. *Degree program information:* Part-time and evening/weekend programs available. Postbaccalaureate distance learning degree programs offered (no on-campus study). Offers curriculum and instruction (M Ed); education technology (M Ed); educational leadership and principal certification (M Ed, Certificate); guidance and counseling (M Ed); professional certification-teachers (Certificate); reading and literacy (M Ed); teacher certification (MIT, Certificate). *Application deadline:* Applications are processed on a rolling basis. *Application fee:* $75 ($175 for international students). Electronic applications accepted. *Application Contact:* 800-426-5596, Fax: 425-709-5363, E-mail: info@cityu.edu. *Dean*, Dr. Margaret M. Davis, 425-637-1010 Ext. 5412, Fax: 425-709-5363, E-mail: mdavis@cityu.edu.

School of Business and Management Students: 289 full-time, 2,769 part-time; includes 819 minority (140 African Americans, 615 Asian Americans or Pacific Islanders, 49 Hispanic Americans, 15 Native Americans), 19 international. Average age 37. 786 applicants, 100% accepted, 215 enrolled. *Faculty:* 15 full-time (8 women), 513 part-time/adjunct (148 women). Expenses: Contact institution. *Financial support:* In 2001–02, 90 students received support. Federal Work-Study available. Support available to part-time students. Financial award applicants required to submit FAFSA. In 2001, 849 degrees awarded. *Degree program information:* Part-time and evening/weekend programs available. Postbaccalaureate distance learning degree programs offered (no on-campus study). Offers C++ programming (Certificate); computer systems—C++ programming (MS); computer systems—individual (MS); computer systems—web programming language (MS); computer systems-web development (MS); e-commerce (MBA, Certificate); financial management (MBA, Certificate); general management (MBA, MPA, Certificate); general management-Europe (MBA); human resource management (MBA, MPA); human resources management (Certificate); individualized study (MBA, MPA); information systems (MBA, MPA, Certificate); managerial leadership (MBA, MPA, Certificate); marketing (MBA, Certificate); organizational management-general management (MS); organizational management-human resource management (MS); organizational management-individualized study (MS); organizational management-project management (MS); personal financial planning (MBA, Certificate); project management (MBA, MPA, MS, Certificate); public administration (Certificate); web development (Certificate); web programming language (Certificate). *Application deadline:* Applications are processed on a rolling basis. *Application fee:* $75 ($175 for international students). Electronic applications accepted. *Application Contact:* 800-426-5596, Fax: 425-709-5363, E-mail: info@cityu.edu. *Dean*, Carl Adams, 425-637-1010 Ext. 5392, Fax: 425-709-5363, E-mail: ksmith@cityu.edu.

School of Human Services and Applied Behavioral Sciences Students: 105 full-time, 243 part-time; includes 40 minority (23 African Americans, 8 Asian Americans or Pacific Islanders, 7 Hispanic Americans, 2 Native Americans), 2 international. Average age 36. 60 applicants, 100% accepted, 7 enrolled. *Faculty:* 5 full-time (4 women), 58 part-time/adjunct (37 women). Expenses: Contact institution. *Financial support:* In 2001–02, 31 students received support. Federal Work-Study available. Support available to part-time students. Financial award applicants required to submit FAFSA. In 2001, 41 degrees awarded. *Degree program information:* Part-time and evening/weekend programs available. Postbaccalaureate distance learning degree programs offered (no on-campus study). Offers counseling psychology (MA). *Application deadline:* Applications are processed on a rolling basis. *Application fee:* $75 ($175 for international students). Electronic applications accepted. *Application Contact:* 800-426-5596, Fax: 425-709-5361, E-mail: info@cityu.edu. *Dean*, 425-637-1010 Ext. 5494, Fax: 425-709-5363.

See in-depth description on page 803.

CITY UNIVERSITY OF NEW YORK SCHOOL OF LAW AT QUEENS COLLEGE, Flushing, NY 11367-1358

General Information State and locally supported, coed, graduate-only institution. *Enrollment by degree level:* 446 first professional. *Graduate faculty:* 35 full-time (19 women), 20 part-time/adjunct (11 women). Tuition, state resident: full-time $5,700; part-time $240 per credit. Tuition, nonresident: full-time $8,930; part-time $375 per credit. *Required fees:* $1,052; $45 per credit. $26 per semester. *Graduate housing:* On-campus housing not available. *Student services:* Campus employment opportunities, career counseling, child daycare facilities, disabled student services, free psychological counseling, low-cost health insurance, writing training. *Library facilities:* City University of New York School of Law Library. *Online resources:* library catalog, web page, access to other libraries' catalogs. *Collection:* 93,980 titles, 2,955 serial subscriptions, 12 audiovisual materials.

Computer facilities: 60 computers available on campus for general student use. A campuswide network can be accessed from off campus. Internet access is available. *Web address:* http://www.law.cuny.edu/.

General Application Contact: Yvonne Cherena-Pacheco, Assistant Dean for Enrollment Management and Director of Admissions, 718-340-4210, Fax: 718-340-4435, E-mail: admissions@mail.law.cuny.edu.

GRADUATE UNITS

Professional Program Students: 442 full-time (264 women), 4 part-time (2 women); includes 189 minority (73 African Americans, 48 Asian Americans or Pacific Islanders, 64 Hispanic Americans, 4 Native Americans), 13 international. Average age 30. 1,267 applicants, 42% accepted, 165 enrolled. *Faculty:* 35 full-time (19 women), 20 part-time/adjunct (11 women). Expenses: Contact institution. *Financial support:* In 2001–02, 348 students received support, including 18 fellowships (averaging $2,700 per year); research assistantships, teaching assistantships, career-related internships or fieldwork, Federal Work-Study, scholarships/grants, and tuition waivers (partial) also available. Financial award application deadline: 5/1; financial award applicants required to submit FAFSA. In 2001, 97 degrees awarded. Offers law (JD). *Application deadline:* For fall admission, 3/15 (priority date). Applications are processed on a rolling basis. *Application fee:* $40. *Application Contact:* Yvonne Cherena-Pacheco, Assistant Dean for Enrollment Management and Director of Admissions, 718-340-4210, Fax: 718-340-4435, E-mail: admissions@mail.law.cuny.edu. *Dean*, Kristin Booth Glen, 718-340-4201, Fax: 718-340-4482, E-mail: glen@mail.law.cuny.edu.

CLAREMONT GRADUATE UNIVERSITY, Claremont, CA 91711-6160

General Information Independent, coed, graduate-only institution. CGS member. *Enrollment by degree level:* 803 master's, 1,097 doctoral, 58 other advanced degrees. *Graduate faculty:* 82 full-time (25 women), 67 part-time/adjunct (25 women). *Tuition:* Full-time $22,984; part-time $1,000 per unit. *Required fees:* $160; $80 per semester. *Graduate housing:* Rooms and/or apartments available on a first-come, first-served basis to single and married students. Typical cost: $4,500 per year for single students; $8,580 per year for married students. Room charges vary according to housing facility selected. *Student services:* Campus employment opportunities, campus safety program, career counseling, free psychological counseling, international student services, low-cost health insurance, multicultural affairs office, teacher training, writing training. *Library facilities:* Honnold Library plus 3 others. *Online resources:* library catalog, web page, access to other libraries' catalogs. *Collection:* 4.4 million titles, 7,437 serial subscriptions, 15,400 audiovisual materials. *Research affiliation:* Rancho Santa Ana Botanic Garden (botany/native plants), Tomas Rivera Policy Institute (Latino policy studies), California Institute of Public Affairs (political science), Claremont School of Theology (religion).

Computer facilities: 91 computers available on campus for general student use. A campuswide network can be accessed from off campus. Internet access is available. *Web address:* http://www.cgu.edu/.

General Application Contact: Rosa Delia Rosas, Admissions Coordinator, 909-621-8069, Fax: 909-607-7285, E-mail: admiss@cgu.edu.

GRADUATE UNITS

Graduate Programs Students: 1,195 full-time (600 women), 762 part-time (400 women); includes 536 minority (119 African Americans, 196 Asian Americans or Pacific Islanders, 211 Hispanic Americans, 10 Native Americans), 310 international. Average age 35. 1,335 applicants, 73% accepted. *Faculty:* 82 full-time (25 women), 67 part-time/adjunct (25 women). Expenses: Contact institution. *Financial support:* In 2001–02, 697 students received support; fellowships, research assistantships, teaching assistantships, career-related internships or fieldwork, Federal Work-Study, institutionally sponsored loans, scholarships/grants, and tuition waivers (full and partial) available. Support available to part-time students. Financial award application deadline: 2/15; financial award applicants required to submit FAFSA. In 2001, 451 master's, 105 doctorates awarded. *Degree program information:* Part-time programs available. Offers interdisciplinary studies (MA). *Application deadline:* For fall admission, 2/15 (priority date). Applications are processed on a rolling basis. *Application fee:* $50. Electronic applications accepted. *Application Contact:* Rosa Delia Rosas, Admissions Coordinator, 909-621-8069, Fax: 909-607-7285, E-mail: diane.guido@cgu.edu. *Vice President for Academic Affairs/Provost*, Dr. Ann Weaver Hart, 909-621-8068, Fax: 909-621-8390, E-mail: ann.hart@cgu.edu.

Center for the Arts Students: 89 full-time (49 women), 8 part-time (6 women); includes 12 minority (9 Asian Americans or Pacific Islanders, 2 Hispanic Americans, 1 Native American), 9 international. Average age 37. *Faculty:* 6 full-time (3 women), 13 part-time/adjunct (4 women). Expenses: Contact institution. *Financial support:* Fellowships, research assistantships, teaching assistantships, Federal Work-Study and institutionally sponsored loans available. Support available to part-time students. Financial award application deadline: 2/15; financial award applicants required to submit FAFSA. In 2001, 27 master's, 10 doctorates awarded. *Degree program information:* Part-time programs available. Offers arts (MA, MFA, DCM, DMA, PhD); church music (MA, DCM); composition (MA, DMA); drawing (MA, MFA); filmmaking (MA, MFA); history (MA); music education (MA); musicology (MA, PhD); painting (MA, MFA); performance (MA, DMA); performance/installation (MA, MFA); photography (MA, MFA); printmaking (MA, MFA); sculpture (MA, MFA). *Application deadline:* For fall admission, 2/15 (priority date). Applications are processed on a rolling basis. *Application fee:* $50. Electronic applications accepted. *Application Contact:* Rosa Delia Rosas, Admissions Coordinator, 909-621-8069, Fax: 909-607-7285, E-mail: diane.guido@cgu.edu.

Center for the Humanities Students: 180 full-time (110 women), 88 part-time (42 women); includes 69 minority (15 African Americans, 22 Asian Americans or Pacific Islanders, 29 Hispanic Americans, 3 Native Americans), 8 international. Average age 35. *Faculty:* 10 full-time (5 women), 13 part-time/adjunct (5 women). Expenses: Contact institution. *Financial support:* Fellowships, research assistantships, teaching assistantships, career-related internships or fieldwork, Federal Work-Study, and institutionally sponsored loans available. Support available to part-time students. Financial award application deadline: 2/15; financial award applicants required to submit FAFSA. In 2001, 34 master's, 11 doctorates awarded. *Degree program information:* Part-time programs available. Offers American studies (MA, PhD); ancient philosophy (MA, PhD); contemporary philosophy (MA, PhD); cultural studies (MA, PhD); English (M Phil, MA, PhD); European studies (MA, PhD); history (MA, PhD); humanities (M Phil, MA, PhD); literature and creative writing (MA); literature and film (MA); literature and theatre (MA); modern philosophy (MA, PhD). *Application deadline:* For fall admission, 2/15 (priority date). Applications are processed on a rolling basis. *Application fee:* $50. Electronic applications accepted. *Application Contact:* Pamela Hawkes, Program Administrator, 909-621-8612, Fax: 909-607-1221, E-mail: pamela.hawkes@cgu.edu. *Dean*, Constance Jordan, 909-621-8612, Fax: 909-607-1221, E-mail: humcen@gcu.edu.

Independent Programs Students: 49 full-time (20 women), 21 part-time (6 women); includes 14 minority (1 African American, 10 Asian Americans or Pacific Islanders, 3 Hispanic Americans), 15 international. Average age 34. *Faculty:* 7 full-time (1 woman), 1 part-time/adjunct (0 women). Expenses: Contact institution. *Financial support:* Fellowships, research assistantships, career-related internships or fieldwork, Federal Work-Study, institutionally sponsored loans, and tuition waivers (full and partial) available. Support available to part-time students. Financial award application deadline: 2/15; financial award applicants required to submit FAFSA. In 2001, 22 master's, 6 doctorates awarded. *Degree program information:* Part-time programs available. Offers applied women's studies (MA); computer science (PhD); engineering mathematics (PhD); financial engineering (MS); operations research and statistics (MA, MS); physical applied mathematics (MA, MS); pure mathematics (MA, MS, PhD); scientific computing (MA, MS); systematics and evolution of higher plants (MS, PhD); systems and control theory (MA, MS). *Application deadline:* For fall admission, 2/15 (priority date). Applications are processed on a rolling basis. *Application fee:* $50. Electronic applications accepted. *Application Contact:* Rosa Delia Rosas, Admissions Coordinator, 909-621-8069, Fax: 909-607-7285, E-mail: diane.guido@cgu.edu.

Peter F. Drucker Graduate School of Management Students: 139 full-time (48 women), 198 part-time (76 women); includes 75 minority (9 African Americans, 46 Asian Americans or Pacific Islanders, 19 Hispanic Americans, 1 Native American), 80 international. Average age 38. *Faculty:* 13 full-time (2 women), 9 part-time/adjunct (1 woman). Expenses: Contact institution. *Financial support:* Fellowships, research assistantships, teaching assistantships, career-related internships or fieldwork, Federal Work-Study, and institutionally sponsored loans available. Support available to part-time students. Financial award application deadline: 2/15; financial award applicants required to submit FAFSA. In 2001, 126 master's, 4 doctorates awarded. *Degree program information:* Part-time programs available. Offers advanced management (MSAM); business administration (MBA); executive management (EMBA, MA, MSAM, PhD, Certificate); finance (MBA); financial engineering (MS); international business (MBA); management (MBA); marketing (MBA); strategic management (MBA). *Application deadline:* For fall admission, 2/15 (priority date). Applications are processed on a rolling basis. *Application fee:* $50. Electronic applications accepted. *Application Contact:* Go Yoshida, Assistant Director/Market Research, 909-607-7810, Fax: 909-621-8543, E-mail: drucker@cgu.edu. *Dean*, Cornelis de Kluyver, 909-607-3778, Fax: 909-621-8543, E-mail: drucker@cgu.edu.

School of Behavioral and Organizational Sciences Students: 128 full-time (94 women), 41 part-time (30 women); includes 55 minority (8 African Americans, 24 Asian Americans or Pacific Islanders, 21 Hispanic Americans, 2 Native Americans), 10 international. Average age 32. *Faculty:* 6 full-time (2 women), 15 part-time/adjunct (8 women). Expenses: Contact institution. *Financial support:* Fellowships, research assistantships, teaching assistantships, career-related internships or fieldwork, Federal Work-Study, and tuition waivers (full and partial) available. Support available to part-time students. Financial award application deadline: 2/15; financial award applicants required to submit FAFSA. In 2001, 35 master's, 16 doctorates awarded. Offers behavioral and organizational sciences (MA, MS, PhD); cognitive psychology (MA, PhD); developmental psychology (MA, PhD); human resources design (MS); organizational behavior (MA, PhD); program design, management, and evaluation (MA); social environmental psychology (PhD); social psychology (MA). *Application deadline:* For fall admission, 2/15 (priority date). Applications are processed on a rolling basis. *Application fee:* $50. Electronic applications accepted. *Application Contact:* Jessica Johnson, Program Coordinator, 909-621-8084, Fax: 909-621-8905, E-mail: jessica.johnson@cgu.edu. *Dean*, Stewart Donaldson, 909-607-3707, E-mail: stewart.donaldson@cgu.edu.

School of Educational Studies Students: 156 full-time (113 women), 250 part-time (181 women); includes 191 minority (46 African Americans, 38 Asian Americans or Pacific Islanders, 104 Hispanic Americans, 3 Native Americans), 11 international. Average age 35. *Faculty:* 16 full-time (8 women), 4 part-time/adjunct (3 women). Expenses: Contact institution. *Financial support:* Fellowships, research assistantships, Federal Work-Study and institutionally sponsored loans available. Support available to part-time students. Financial award application deadline: 2/15; financial award applicants required to submit FAFSA. In 2001, 124 master's, 31 doctorates awarded. *Degree program information:* Part-time programs available. Offers comparative educational studies (MA, PhD); education policy issues (MA, PhD); higher education (MA, PhD); human development (MA, PhD); linguistics and anthropology (MA, PhD); organization and administration (PhD); public school administration (MA, PhD); reading and language development (MA, PhD); teacher education (MA, PhD); teaching and learning (MA, PhD); teaching/learning process (PhD); urban education administration (MA, PhD). *Application deadline:* For fall admission, 2/15 (priority date). Applications are processed on a rolling basis. *Application fee:* $50. Electronic applications accepted. *Application Contact:* Janet Alonzo, Secretary, 909-621-8075, Fax: 909-621-8734, E-mail: educ@cgu.edu. *Dean*, David Drew, 909-621-8075, Fax: 909-621-8734, E-mail: david.drew@cgu.edu.

School of Information Science Students: 65 full-time (16 women), 59 part-time (21 women); includes 38 minority (11 African Americans, 22 Asian Americans or Pacific Islanders, 5 Hispanic Americans), 42 international. Average age 35. 99 applicants, 60% accepted. *Faculty:* 6 full-time (0 women), 5 part-time/adjunct (1 woman). Expenses: Contact institution. *Financial support:* Fellowships, research assistantships, teaching assistantships, Federal Work-Study and institutionally sponsored loans available. Support available to part-time students. Financial award application deadline: 2/15; financial award applicants required to submit FAFSA. In 2001, 40 master's, 4 doctorates awarded. *Degree program information:* Part-time programs available. Offers electronic commerce (MSEC); information systems (MIS); management of information systems (MSMIS, PhD). *Application deadline:* For fall admission, 2/15 (priority date). Applications are processed on a rolling basis. *Application fee:* $50. Electronic applications accepted. *Application Contact:* Nancy Back, Program Coordinator, 909-621-8209, Fax: 909-621-8564, E-mail: infosci@cgu.edu. *Dean*, Lorne Olfman, 909-621-8209, Fax: 909-621-8564, E-mail: lorne.olfman@cgu.edu.

School of Politics and Economics Students: 222 full-time (80 women), 64 part-time (26 women); includes 48 minority (20 African Americans, 7 Asian Americans or Pacific Islanders, 21 Hispanic Americans), 102 international. Average age 33. *Faculty:* 14 full-time (2 women), 4 part-time/adjunct (1 woman). Expenses: Contact institution. *Financial support:* Fellowships, research assistantships, teaching assistantships, career-related internships or fieldwork, Federal Work-Study, and institutionally sponsored loans available. Support available to part-time students. Financial award application deadline: 2/15; financial award applicants required to submit FAFSA. In 2001, 36 master's, 17 doctorates awarded. *Degree program information:* Part-time programs available. Offers business and financial economics (MA, PhD); economics (PhD); international economic policy and management (MA, PhD); international political economy (MAIPE); international studies (MAIS); political economy and public policy (MA, PhD); political science (PhD); politics (MAP); politics and economics (MA, MAIPE, MAIS, MAP, MAPEB, MAPP, PhD); politics, economics, and business (MAPEB); public policy (MAPP). *Application deadline:* For fall admission, 2/15 (priority date). Applications are processed on a rolling basis. *Application fee:* $50. Electronic applications accepted. *Application Contact:* Sandra Seymor, Program Administrator, 908-621-8079, Fax: 909-621-8545, E-mail: sandra.seymor@cgu.edu. *Dean*, Arthur Denzau, 909-621-8074, Fax: 909-621-8545, E-mail: arthur.denzau@cgu.edu.

School of Religion Students: 117 full-time (20 women), 33 part-time (12 women); includes 34 minority (9 African Americans, 18 Asian Americans or Pacific Islanders, 7 Hispanic Americans), 33 international. Average age 38. *Faculty:* 4 full-time (2 women), 3 part-time/adjunct (2 women). Expenses: Contact institution. *Financial support:* Fellowships, research assistantships, teaching assistantships, Federal Work-Study and institutionally sponsored loans available. Support available to part-time students. Financial award application deadline: 2/15; financial award applicants required to submit FAFSA. In 2001, 7 master's, 6 doctorates awarded. *Degree program information:* Part-time programs available. Offers Hebrew Bible (MA, PhD); history of Christianity (MA, PhD); New Testament (MA, PhD); philosophy of religion and theology (MA, PhD); theology, ethics and culture (MA, PhD); women's studies in religion (MA, PhD). MA/PhD (philosophy of religion and theology) offered in cooperation with the Department of Philosophy. *Application deadline:* For fall admission, 2/15 (priority date). Applications are processed on a rolling basis. *Application fee:* $50. Electronic applications accepted. *Application Contact:* Jackie Huntzinger, Secretary, 909-621-8085, Fax: 909-607-9587, E-mail: religion@cgu.edu. *Dean*, Karen Jo Torjesen, 909-621-8085, Fax: 909-607-9587, E-mail: karen.torjesen@cgu.edu.

CLAREMONT SCHOOL OF THEOLOGY, Claremont, CA 91711-3199

General Information Independent-religious, coed, graduate-only institution. *Enrollment by degree level:* 166 first professional, 68 master's, 56 doctoral, 42 other advanced degrees. *Graduate faculty:* 20 full-time (8 women), 22 part-time/adjunct (7 women). *Tuition:* Part-time $335 per unit. *Required fees:* $35. *Graduate housing:* Rooms and/or apartments available on a first-come, first-served basis to single and married students. Typical cost: $4,620 per year for single students; $5,850 per year for married students. Housing application deadline: 6/1. *Student services:* Campus employment opportunities, career counseling, international student services, low-cost health insurance, writing training. *Online resources:* library catalog, web page, access to other libraries' catalogs. *Collection:* 181,698 titles, 635 serial subscriptions, 499 audiovisual materials. *Research affiliation:* Moore Multicultural Resource and Research Center, Institute for Antiquity and Christianity, Center for Process Studies, National United Methodist Native American Center, Center for Pacific and Asian-American Ministries, Ancient Biblical Manuscript Center.

Computer facilities: 20 computers available on campus for general student use. A campuswide network can be accessed. Internet access is available. *Web address:* http://www.cst.edu/.

General Application Contact: Mark Hobbs, Director of Admissions, 866-274-6500, Fax: 909-447-6291, E-mail: admissions@cst.edu.

GRADUATE UNITS

Graduate and Professional Programs Students: 110 full-time (53 women), 222 part-time (112 women); includes 94 minority (27 African Americans, 57 Asian Americans or Pacific Islanders, 8 Hispanic Americans, 2 Native Americans), 38 international. Average age 40. 163 applicants, 72% accepted, 86 enrolled. *Faculty:* 20 full-time (8 women), 22 part-time/adjunct (7 women). Expenses: Contact institution. *Financial support:* In 2001–02, 207 students received support, including 6 research assistantships (averaging $1,500 per year); career-related internships or fieldwork, Federal Work-Study, institutionally sponsored loans, and scholarships/grants also available. Support available to part-time students. Financial award application deadline: 4/1; financial award applicants required to submit FAFSA. In 2001, 31 first professional degrees, 12 master's, 15 doctorates awarded. *Degree program information:* Part-time programs available. Offers Bible and theology (PhD); divinity (M Div); ministry (D Min); religion (MA, PhD). *Application deadline:* For fall admission, 4/15 (priority date). *Application fee:* $30 ($50 for international students). *Application Contact:* Mark Hobbs, Director of Admissions, 866-274-6500, Fax: 909-447-6291, E-mail: admissions@cst.edu. *Vice President for Academic Affairs and Dean*, Dr. John R. Fitzmier, 909-447-2520, Fax: 909-447-6274, E-mail: fitzmier@cst.edu.

CLARION UNIVERSITY OF PENNSYLVANIA, Clarion, PA 16214

General Information State-supported, coed, comprehensive institution. CGS member. *Enrollment:* 459 matriculated graduate/professional students. *Graduate faculty:* 71. Tuition, state resident: full-time $4,600; part-time $256 per credit. Tuition, nonresident: full-time $7,554; part-time $420 per credit. *Required fees:* $908; $72 per credit. *Graduate housing:* Room and/or apartments available on a first-come, first-served basis to single students; on-campus housing not available to married students. Typical cost: $4,328 (including board). *Student services:* Campus employment opportunities, campus safety program, career counseling, child daycare facilities, disabled student services, free psychological counseling, international student services, low-cost health insurance. *Library facilities:* Carlson Library. *Online resources:* library catalog, web page, access to other libraries' catalogs. *Collection:* 2.2 million titles, 12,198 serial subscriptions, 223,570 audiovisual materials.

Computer facilities: 400 computers available on campus for general student use. A campuswide network can be accessed from student residence rooms and from off campus. Internet access and online class registration are available. *Web address:* http://www.clarion.edu/.

General Application Contact: Dr. Brenda Dédé, Assistant Vice President for Academic Affairs, 814-393-2337, Fax: 814-393-2030, E-mail: bdede@clarion.edu.

See in-depth description on page 805.

CLARK ATLANTA UNIVERSITY, Atlanta, GA 30314

General Information Independent-religious, coed, university. CGS member. *Graduate housing:* Room and/or apartments available to single students; on-campus housing not available to married students. Housing application deadline: 6/1.

GRADUATE UNITS

School of Arts and Sciences *Degree program information:* Part-time programs available. Offers African-American studies (MA); Africana women's studies (MA, DA); applied mathematics (MS); arts and sciences (MA, MPA, MS, DA, PhD); biology (MS, PhD); computer and information science (MS); computer science (MS); criminal justice (MA); economics (MA); English (MA); history (MA); humanities (DA); inorganic chemistry (MS, PhD); organic chemistry (MS, PhD); physical chemistry (MS, PhD); physics (MS); political science (MA, PhD); public administration (MPA); Romance languages (MA); science education (DA); sociology (MA).

Clark Atlanta University (continued)

School of Business Administration *Degree program information:* Part-time programs available. Offers business administration (MBA); decision science (MBA); finance (MBA); marketing (MBA).

School of Education *Degree program information:* Part-time and evening/weekend programs available. Offers counseling (MA, PhD); curriculum (MA, Ed S); education (MA, Ed D, PhD, Ed S); education psychology (MA); educational leadership (MA, Ed D, Ed S); exceptional student education (MA, Ed S).

School of International Affairs and Development Offers international affairs and development (PhD); international business and development (MA); international development administration (MA); international development education and planning (MA); international relations (MA); regional studies (MA).

School of Library and Information Studies *Degree program information:* Part-time and evening/weekend programs available. Offers library and information studies (MSLS, SLS).

School of Social Work *Degree program information:* Part-time programs available. Offers social work (MSW, PhD).

CLARKE COLLEGE, Dubuque, IA 52001-3198

General Information Independent-religious, coed, comprehensive institution. *Graduate housing:* On-campus housing not available.

GRADUATE UNITS

Department of Nursing and Health *Degree program information:* Part-time programs available. Offers administration of nursing systems (MSN); advanced practice nursing (MSN); education (MSN); family nurse practitioner (MSN, PMC).

Physical Therapy Program Offers physical therapy (MSPT). Freshman-entry master's degree program; entry to the MSPT is determined after junior year of the BS program.

Program in Education *Degree program information:* Part-time and evening/weekend programs available. Postbaccalaureate distance learning degree programs offered (minimal on-campus study). Offers early childhood/special education (MA); educational administration: elementary and secondary (MA); educational media: elementary and secondary (MA); multicategorical resource K–12 (MA); multidisciplinary studies (MA); reading: elementary (MA); technology in education (MA). Electronic applications accepted.

Program in Management *Degree program information:* Part-time and evening/weekend programs available. Offers management (MS). Electronic applications accepted.

CLARKSON COLLEGE, Omaha, NE 68131-2739

General Information Independent, coed, primarily women, comprehensive institution. *Enrollment:* 1 (woman) full-time matriculated graduate/professional student, 95 part-time matriculated graduate/professional students (89 women). *Enrollment by degree level:* 96 master's. *Graduate faculty:* 9 full-time (8 women). *Tuition:* Full-time $3,096; part-time $344 per semester hour. *Required fees:* $150; $75 per semester. Tuition and fees vary according to course load. *Graduate housing:* Room and/or apartments available on a first-come, first-served basis to single students; on-campus housing not available to married students. Typical cost: $2,800 per year. *Student services:* Campus employment opportunities, campus safety program, career counseling, child daycare facilities, free psychological counseling. *Library facilities:* Clarkson College Library. *Online resources:* library catalog, web page. *Collection:* 8,807 titles, 262 serial subscriptions, 530 audiovisual materials.

Computer facilities: 40 computers available on campus for general student use. A campuswide network can be accessed from off campus. Internet access is available. *Web address:* http://www.clarksoncollege.edu/.

General Application Contact: Tami Bartunek, Director of Admissions, 402-552-3100, Fax: 402-552-6057, E-mail: bartunek@clarksoncollege.edu.

GRADUATE UNITS

Graduate Programs Students: 1 (woman) full-time, 95 part-time (89 women); includes 7 minority (4 African Americans, 2 Asian Americans or Pacific Islanders, 1 Hispanic American), 1 international. Average age 28. 27 applicants, 74% accepted, 18 enrolled. *Faculty:* 9 full-time (8 women). Expenses: Contact institution. *Financial support:* In 2001–02, 14 students received support. Federal Work-Study, institutionally sponsored loans, and scholarships/grants available. Support available to part-time students. Financial award application deadline: 4/1; financial award applicants required to submit FAFSA. In 2001, 45 degrees awarded. *Degree program information:* Part-time and evening/weekend programs available. Postbaccalaureate distance learning degree programs offered (minimal on-campus study). Offers administration (MSN); education (MSN); family nurse practitioner (MSN). *Application deadline:* For fall admission, 7/13; for spring admission, 1/5. Applications are processed on a rolling basis. *Application fee:* $15. Electronic applications accepted. *Application Contact:* Tami Bartunek, Director of Admissions, 402-552-3100, Fax: 402-552-6057, E-mail: bartunek@clarksoncollege.edu. *Dean,* Linda Christensen, 402-552-3373, Fax: 402-552-6058, E-mail: christensen@clarksoncollege.edu.

CLARKSON UNIVERSITY, Potsdam, NY 13699

General Information Independent, coed, university. CGS member. *Enrollment:* 303 full-time matriculated graduate/professional students (106 women), 36 part-time matriculated graduate/professional students (8 women). *Enrollment by degree level:* 261 master's, 78 doctoral. *Graduate faculty:* 158 full-time (34 women), 20 part-time/adjunct (5 women). *Tuition:* Part-time $714 per credit. *Required fees:* $108 per semester. *Graduate housing:* On-campus housing not available. *Student services:* Campus employment opportunities, campus safety program, career counseling, disabled student services, free psychological counseling, international student services, low-cost health insurance. *Library facilities:* Andrew S. Schuler Educational Resources Center. *Online resources:* library catalog, web page. *Collection:* 235,876 titles, 845 serial subscriptions, 3,730 audiovisual materials.

Computer facilities: 250 computers available on campus for general student use. A campuswide network can be accessed from student residence rooms and from off campus. Internet access is available. *Web address:* http://www.clarkson.edu/.

General Application Contact: Donna Brockway, Assistant to Dean/Foreign Student Advisor, 315-268-6447, Fax: 315-268-7994, E-mail: brockway@clarkson.edu.

GRADUATE UNITS

Graduate School Students: 303 full-time (106 women), 36 part-time (8 women); includes 15 minority (5 African Americans, 5 Asian Americans or Pacific Islanders, 5 Hispanic Americans), 135 international. Average age 27. 1,069 applicants, 60% accepted. *Faculty:* 158 full-time (34 women), 20 part-time/adjunct (5 women). Expenses: Contact institution. *Financial support:* In 2001–02, 170 students received support, including 17 fellowships (averaging $20,000 per year), 71 research assistantships (averaging $17,000 per year), 82 teaching assistantships (averaging $17,000 per year); scholarships/grants and tuition waivers (full) also available. Financial award applicants required to submit FAFSA. In 2001, 144 master's, 21 doctorates awarded. *Degree program information:* Part-time and evening/weekend programs available. *Application deadline:* For fall admission, 5/15 (priority date); for spring admission, 10/15 (priority date). Applications are processed on a rolling basis. *Application fee:* $25 ($35 for international students). *Application Contact:* Donna Brockway, Assistant to Dean/Foreign Student Advisor, 315-268-6447, Fax: 315-268-7994, E-mail: brockway@clarkson.edu. *Provost,* Dr. Anthony G. Collins, 315-268-6445, Fax: 315-268-2308, E-mail: tony.collins@clarkson.edu.

Center for Health Science Students: 23 full-time (16 women); includes 1 minority (African American) Average age 29. *Faculty:* 5 full-time (3 women), 1 (woman) part-time/adjunct. Expenses: Contact institution. *Degree program information:* Part-time programs available. Offers basic science (MS); health science (MPT, MS); physical therapy (MPT). *Application deadline:* For fall admission, 5/15 (priority date); for spring admission, 10/15 (priority date). Applications are processed on a rolling basis. *Application fee:* $25 ($35 for international students). *Associate Dean of Health Sciences,* Dr. Samuel B. Feitelberg, 315-268-3786, Fax: 315-268-7118, E-mail: feitelsb@clarkson.edu.

Interdisciplinary Studies Students: 28 full-time (7 women), 25 part-time (4 women); includes 7 minority (2 African Americans, 2 Asian Americans or Pacific Islanders, 3 Hispanic Americans), 15 international. Average age 29. 104 applicants, 53% accepted. Expenses: Contact institution. *Financial support:* In 2001–02, 7 students received support, including 2 research assistantships, 5 teaching assistantships (averaging $17,000 per year) In 2001, 11 degrees awarded. Offers computer science (MS); engineering and management (MS); engineering and manufacturing management (MS); information technology (MS). *Application Contact:* Donna Brockway, Assistant to Dean/Foreign Student Advisor, 315-268-6447, Fax: 315-268-7994, E-mail: brockway@clarkson.edu.

School of Business Students: 76 full-time (28 women), 10 part-time (4 women); includes 3 minority (2 Asian Americans or Pacific Islanders, 1 Hispanic American), 13 international. Average age 26. 156 applicants, 56% accepted. *Faculty:* 22 full-time (3 women), 3 part-time/adjunct (0 women). Expenses: Contact institution. *Financial support:* In 2001–02, 73 students received support, including 73 teaching assistantships (averaging $17,000 per year); research assistantships, tuition waivers (full) also available. In 2001, 81 degrees awarded. *Degree program information:* Part-time and evening/weekend programs available. Offers business (MBA, MS); business administration (MBA); human resource management (MS); management information systems (MS); manufacturing management (MS). *Application deadline:* For fall admission, 5/15 (priority date); for spring admission, 10/15 (priority date). Applications are processed on a rolling basis. *Application fee:* $25 ($35 for international students). *Application Contact:* Dr. Brian F. O'Neil, Graduate Director, 315-268-6613, Fax: 315-268-3810, E-mail: oneilb@clarkson.edu. *Dean,* Dr. Timothy F. Sugrue, 315-268-2300, Fax: 315-268-3810, E-mail: sugrue@clarkson.edu.

School of Engineering Students: 136 full-time (39 women), 1 part-time; includes 2 minority (1 Asian American or Pacific Islander, 1 Hispanic American), 82 international. Average age 26. 679 applicants, 58% accepted. *Faculty:* 58 full-time (10 women), 5 part-time/adjunct (0 women). Expenses: Contact institution. *Financial support:* In 2001–02, 101 students received support, including 16 fellowships (averaging $20,000 per year), 56 research assistantships (averaging $17,000 per year), 29 teaching assistantships (averaging $17,000 per year); scholarships/grants and tuition waivers (partial) also available. In 2001, 45 master's, 16 doctorates awarded. *Degree program information:* Part-time programs available. Offers chemical engineering (ME, MS, PhD); civil and environmental engineering (PhD); civil engineering (ME, MS); computer engineering (ME, MS); electrical and computer engineering (PhD); electrical engineering (ME, MS); engineering (ME, MS, PhD); engineering science (MS, PhD); mechanical engineering (ME, MS, PhD). *Application deadline:* For fall admission, 5/15 (priority date); for spring admission, 10/15 (priority date). Applications are processed on a rolling basis. *Application fee:* $25 ($35 for international students). *Application Contact:* Donna Brockway, Assistant to Dean/Foreign Student Advisor, 315-268-6447, Fax: 315-268-7994, E-mail: brockway@clarkson.edu. *Dean,* Dr. Norbert L. Ackermann, 315-268-6446, Fax: 315-268-3841, E-mail: nla@clarkson.edu.

School of Science Students: 40 full-time (16 women); includes 2 minority (both African Americans), 18 international. Average age 28. 135 applicants, 79% accepted. *Faculty:* 41 full-time (6 women), 4 part-time/adjunct (1 woman). Expenses: Contact institution. *Financial support:* In 2001–02, 35 students received support, including 1 fellowship (averaging $20,000 per year), 12 research assistantships (averaging $17,000 per year), 22 teaching assistantships (averaging $17,000 per year); scholarships/grants and tuition waivers (partial) also available. In 2001, 7 master's, 5 doctorates awarded. *Degree program information:* Part-time programs available. Offers analytical chemistry (MS, PhD); computer science (MS); inorganic chemistry (MS, PhD); mathematics (MS, PhD); organic chemistry (MS, PhD); physical chemistry (MS, PhD); physics (MS, PhD); science (MS, PhD). *Application deadline:* For fall admission, 5/15 (priority date); for spring admission, 10/15 (priority date). Applications are processed on a rolling basis. *Application fee:* $25 ($35 for international students). *Application Contact:* Donna Brockway, Assistant to Dean/Foreign Student Advisor, 315-268-6447, Fax: 315-268-7994, E-mail: brockway@clarkson.edu. *Provost,* Dr. Anthony G. Collins, 315-268-6445, Fax: 315-268-2308, E-mail: tony.collins@clarkson.edu.

CLARK UNIVERSITY, Worcester, MA 01610-1477

General Information Independent, coed, university. CGS member. *Enrollment:* 496 full-time matriculated graduate/professional students (267 women), 277 part-time matriculated graduate/professional students (130 women). *Enrollment by degree level:* 585 master's, 185 doctoral. *Graduate faculty:* 172 full-time (61 women), 108 part-time/adjunct (48 women). *Tuition:* Full-time $24,400; part-time $763 per credit. *Required fees:* $10. *Graduate housing:* Rooms and/or apartments available to single and married students. Typical cost: $4,932 per year ($6,882 including board) for single students; $4,932 per year ($6,882 including board) for married students. *Student services:* Campus employment opportunities, career counseling, international student services, low-cost health insurance. *Library facilities:* Robert Hutchings Goddard Library plus 4 others. *Online resources:* library catalog, web page, access to other libraries' catalogs. *Collection:* 285,656 titles, 1,496 serial subscriptions, 970 audiovisual materials. *Research affiliation:* Worcester Foundation for Experimental Biology, Worcester Area Computation Center, Massachusetts Biotechnology Research Institute.

Computer facilities: 70 computers available on campus for general student use. A campuswide network can be accessed from student residence rooms and from off campus. Internet access, on-line course support are available. *Web address:* http://www.clarku.edu/.

General Application Contact: Audrey Rawson, Graduate School Coordinator, 508-793-7676, Fax: 508-793-8834, E-mail: arawson@clarku.edu.

GRADUATE UNITS

Graduate School Students: 496 full-time (267 women), 277 part-time (130 women); includes 28 minority (10 African Americans, 12 Asian Americans or Pacific Islanders, 5 Hispanic Americans, 1 Native American), 266 international. Average age 30. 1,107 applicants, 51% accepted, 233 enrolled. *Faculty:* 172 full-time (61 women), 108 part-time/adjunct (48 women). Expenses: Contact institution. *Financial support:* In 2001–02, 5 fellowships with full and partial tuition reimbursements (averaging $12,500 per year), 54 research assistantships with full and partial tuition reimbursements (averaging $12,500 per year), 102 teaching assistantships with full and partial tuition reimbursements (averaging $12,500 per year) were awarded. Career-related internships or fieldwork, Federal Work-Study, institutionally sponsored loans, scholarships/grants, and tuition waivers (full and partial) also available. Support available to part-time students. In 2001, 214 master's, 40 doctorates, 3 other advanced degrees awarded. *Degree program information:* Part-time and evening/weekend programs available. Offers biology (MA, PhD); chemistry (MA, PhD); clinical psychology (PhD); community development and planning (MA); developmental psychology (PhD); economics (PhD); education (MA Ed); English (MA); environmental science and policy (MA); geographic information science for development and environment (MA); geography (PhD); history (MA, CAGS); holocaust history (PhD); international development and social change (MA); physics (MA, PhD); social-personality psychology (PhD); women's studies (PhD). *Application deadline:* Applications are processed on a rolling basis. *Application fee:* $40. Electronic applications accepted. *Application Contact:* Audrey Rawson, Graduate School Coordinator, 508-793-7676, Fax: 508-793-8834, E-mail: arawson@clarku.edu. *Dean of Graduate Studies and Research,* David P. Angel, 508-793-7676.

College of Professional and Continuing Education Students: 18 full-time (16 women), 63 part-time (42 women); includes 4 minority (1 African American, 3 Asian Americans or Pacific Islanders), 6 international. Average age 35. 43 applicants, 100% accepted, 15 enrolled. *Faculty:* 19 part-time/adjunct (5 women). Expenses: Contact institution. *Financial support:* Career-related internships or fieldwork available. Support available to part-time students. In 2001, 57 master's, 3 other advanced degrees awarded. *Degree program information:* Part-time and evening/weekend programs available. Offers information technology (MIT); liberal studies (MALA); professional and continuing education (MALA, MIT, MPA, MSPC, CAGS, Certificate); professional communications (MSPC); public administration (MPA, Certificate). *Application deadline:* Applications are processed on a rolling basis. *Application fee:* $40. *Application Contact:* Julia Parent, Director of Marketing, Communications, and Admissions, 508-793-7217, Fax: 508-793-7232, E-mail: jparent@clarku.edu. *Director,* Dr. Thomas Massey, 508-793-7217.

Graduate School of Management Students: 111 full-time (43 women), 195 part-time (81 women); includes 13 minority (5 African Americans, 6 Asian Americans or Pacific Islanders,

2 Hispanic Americans), 111 international. Average age 29. 269 applicants, 87% accepted, 90 enrolled. *Faculty:* 17 full-time (5 women), 8 part-time/adjunct (3 women). Expenses: Contact institution. *Financial support:* In 2001–02, 12 research assistantships with partial tuition reimbursements (averaging $4,700 per year), 12 teaching assistantships with partial tuition reimbursements (averaging $4,700 per year) were awarded. Fellowships, career-related internships or fieldwork, Federal Work-Study, institutionally sponsored loans, and tuition waivers (partial) also available. Support available to part-time students. Financial award application deadline: 5/31. In 2001, 90 degrees awarded. *Degree program information:* Part-time and evening/weekend programs available. Offers accounting (MBA); finance (MBA, MSF); global business (MBA); health care management (MBA); management (MBA); management of information technology (MBA); marketing (MBA). *Application deadline:* For fall admission, 6/1 (priority date); for spring admission, 12/1 (priority date). Applications are processed on a rolling basis. *Application fee:* $50. Electronic applications accepted. *Application Contact:* Patricia Tollo, Admissions Director, 508-793-7406, Fax: 508-793-8822, E-mail: clarkmba@clarku.edu. *Dean,* Dr. Edward Ottensmeyer, 508-793-7406, Fax: 508-793-8822.

See in-depth description on page 807.

CLEARY UNIVERSITY, Ann Arbor, MI 48105-2659

General Information Independent, coed, comprehensive institution. *Enrollment:* 27 full-time matriculated graduate/professional students (14 women). *Enrollment by degree level:* 27 master's. *Graduate faculty:* 4 full-time (2 women), 6 part-time/adjunct (1 woman). *Tuition:* Full-time $12,750. *Graduate housing:* On-campus housing not available. *Library facilities:* Cleary College Library plus 1 other. *Online resources:* library catalog, web page. *Collection:* 6,000 titles, 35 serial subscriptions, 20 audiovisual materials.

Computer facilities: 60 computers available on campus for general student use. A campuswide network can be accessed from student residence rooms and from off campus. Internet access and online class registration are available. *Web address:* http://www.cleary.edu/.

General Application Contact: Carrie Bonofiglio, Director of Admissions, 800-589-1979 Ext. 2213, Fax: 517-552-7805, E-mail: cbono@cleary.edu.

GRADUATE UNITS

Program in Business Administration Students: 27 full-time (14 women); includes 7 minority (6 African Americans, 1 Hispanic American) Average age 42. 14 applicants, 79% accepted, 9 enrolled. *Faculty:* 4 full-time (2 women), 6 part-time/adjunct (1 woman). Expenses: Contact institution. *Financial support:* In 2001–02, 17 students received support. Federal Work-Study and scholarships/grants available. Support available to part-time students. Financial award application deadline: 8/31; financial award applicants required to submit FAFSA. In 2001, 31 degrees awarded. *Degree program information:* Evening/weekend programs available. Post-baccalaureate distance learning degree programs offered (minimal on-campus study). Offers accounting (MBA); management (MBA). *Application deadline:* For fall admission, 7/15 (priority date); for spring admission, 4/12 (priority date). Applications are processed on a rolling basis. *Application fee:* $50. Electronic applications accepted. *Application Contact:* Carrie Bonofiglio, Director of Admissions, 800-589-1979 Ext. 2213, Fax: 517-552-7805, E-mail: cbono@cleary.edu. *Graduate Program Chair,* Dr. Phil Bayster, 800-686-1883 Ext. 3336, Fax: 734-332-4646, E-mail: pbayster@cleary.edu.

CLEMSON UNIVERSITY, Clemson, SC 29634

General Information State-supported, coed, university. CGS member. *Enrollment:* 1,760 full-time matriculated graduate/professional students (652 women), 988 part-time matriculated graduate/professional students (526 women). *Enrollment by degree level:* 2,064 master's, 684 doctoral. *Graduate faculty:* 970 full-time (253 women), 23 part-time/adjunct (10 women). Tuition, state resident: full-time $5,310. Tuition, nonresident: full-time $11,284. *Graduate housing:* Rooms and/or apartments available to single and married students. Housing application deadline: 1/30. *Student services:* Campus safety program, career counseling, disabled student services, exercise/wellness program, free psychological counseling, international student services, low-cost health insurance. *Library facilities:* Robert Muldrow Cooper Library plus 1 other. *Online resources:* library catalog, web page, access to other libraries' catalogs. *Collection:* 1.6 million titles, 5,978 serial subscriptions, 94,641 audiovisual materials. *Research affiliation:* Oak Ridge National Laboratory, South Carolina Universities Research and Education Foundation (energy), Greenville Hospital System (biological sciences), National Textile Center (textile and fiber technology).

Computer facilities: 1,000 computers available on campus for general student use. A campuswide network can be accessed from student residence rooms and from off campus. *Web address:* http://www.clemson.edu/.

General Application Contact: Dr. Mark A. McKnew, Associate Dean of the Graduate School, 861-656-3195, Fax: 864-656-5344, E-mail: mamckn@clemson.edu.

GRADUATE UNITS

Graduate School Students: 1,760 full-time (652 women), 988 part-time (526 women); includes 179 minority (133 African Americans, 17 Asian Americans or Pacific Islanders, 26 Hispanic Americans, 3 Native Americans), 734 international. Average age 24. 4,173 applicants, 46% accepted. *Faculty:* 970 full-time (253 women), 23 part-time/adjunct (10 women). Expenses: Contact institution. *Financial support:* Fellowships, research assistantships, teaching assistantships, career-related internships or fieldwork, Federal Work-Study, institutionally sponsored loans, scholarships/grants, tuition waivers (full and partial), and unspecified assistantships available. Support available to part-time students. Financial award applicants required to submit FAFSA. In 2001, 887 master's, 100 doctorates, 14 other advanced degrees awarded. *Degree program information:* Part-time and evening/weekend programs available. Post-baccalaureate distance learning degree programs offered. Offers policy studies (PhD, Certificate). *Application deadline:* Applications are processed on a rolling basis. Electronic applications accepted. *Application Contact:* Kaye Rackley, Coordinator, 864-656-5340, Fax: 864-656-5344, E-mail: krackle@clemson.edu. *Dean,* Dr. Bonnie Holaday, 864-656-3196, Fax: 864-656-5344.

College of Agriculture, Forestry and Life Sciences Students: 330 full-time (140 women), 89 part-time (35 women); includes 18 minority (10 African Americans, 4 Asian Americans or Pacific Islanders, 2 Hispanic Americans, 2 Native Americans), 106 international. 426 applicants, 40% accepted. *Faculty:* 231 full-time (29 women), 1 (woman) part-time/adjunct. Expenses: Contact institution. *Financial support:* Fellowships, research assistantships, teaching assistantships, career-related internships or fieldwork, Federal Work-Study, institutionally sponsored loans, scholarships/grants, and unspecified assistantships available. Financial award applicants required to submit FAFSA. In 2001, 66 master's, 34 doctorates awarded. *Degree program information:* Part-time programs available. Offers agricultural and applied economics (MS); agriculture, forestry and life sciences (M Ag Ed, M Engr, MFR, MS, PhD); animal and food industries (MS); animal physiology (MS, PhD); applied economics (PhD); aquaculture, fisheries and wildlife (MS, PhD); biochemistry (MS, PhD); biology instruction and agricultural education (M Ag Ed); biosystems engineering (M Engr, MS, PhD); entomology (MS, PhD); environmental toxicology (MS, PhD); food technology (PhD); forest resources (MFR, MS, PhD); genetics (MS, PhD); microbiology (MS, PhD); plant and environmental studies (MS); zoology (MS, PhD). *Application deadline:* Applications are processed on a rolling basis. *Application fee:* $40. Electronic applications accepted. *Interim Dean,* Dr. Calvin Schoulties, 864-656-7592, Fax: 864-656-1286, E-mail: cshlts@clemson.edu.

College of Architecture, Arts, and Humanities Students: 196 full-time (77 women), 74 part-time (31 women); includes 15 minority (10 African Americans, 2 Asian Americans or Pacific Islanders, 2 Hispanic Americans, 1 Native American), 23 international. 278 applicants, 57% accepted, 88 enrolled. *Faculty:* 215 full-time (93 women), 5 part-time/adjunct (3 women). Expenses: Contact institution. *Financial support:* Fellowships, research assistantships, teaching assistantships, career-related internships or fieldwork, Federal Work-Study, scholarships/grants, and unspecified assistantships available. Financial award applicants required to submit FAFSA. In 2001, 68 degrees awarded. *Degree program information:* Part-time programs available. Offers architecture (M Arch, MS); architecture, arts, and humanities (M Arch, MA, MCRP, MFA, MFAC, MS); construction science and management); English (MA); environmental planning (MCRP); fine arts in computing (MFAC); history (MA); land development planning (MCRP); professional communication (MA); visual arts (MFA). *Application deadline:* Applications are processed on a rolling basis. *Application fee:* $40. Electronic applications accepted. *Dean,* Dr. Janice Schach, 864-656-3085, Fax: 864-656-0204.

College of Business and Behavioral Science Students: 223 full-time (93 women), 202 part-time (74 women); includes 22 minority (11 African Americans, 5 Asian Americans or Pacific Islanders, 6 Hispanic Americans), 71 international. 558 applicants, 45% accepted, 139 enrolled. *Faculty:* 145 full-time (31 women), 3 part-time/adjunct (0 women). Expenses: Contact institution. *Financial support:* Fellowships, research assistantships, teaching assistantships, career-related internships or fieldwork, Federal Work-Study, institutionally sponsored loans, and unspecified assistantships available. Support available to part-time students. Financial award applicants required to submit FAFSA. In 2001, 196 master's, 4 doctorates awarded. *Degree program information:* Part-time and evening/weekend programs available. Offers accountancy (MP Acc); applied economics (PhD); applied psychology (MS); applied sociology (MS); business administration (MBA); business and behavioral science (M E Com, MA, MBA, MP Acc, MPA, MS, PhD); economics (MA); electronic commerce (M E Com); graphic communications (MS); human factors (MS); industrial management (MS, PhD); industrial/organizational psychology (PhD); management science (PhD); public administration (MPA). *Application deadline:* Applications are processed on a rolling basis. *Application fee:* $40. *Dean,* Dr. Jerry Trapnell, 864-656-3177, Fax: 864-656-4468, E-mail: trapnel@clemson.edu.

College of Engineering and Science Students: 839 full-time (223 women), 114 part-time (23 women); includes 32 minority (22 African Americans, 4 Asian Americans or Pacific Islanders, 6 Hispanic Americans), 520 international. 2,606 applicants, 47% accepted, 296 enrolled. *Faculty:* 273 full-time (35 women), 13 part-time/adjunct (5 women). Expenses: Contact institution. *Financial support:* Fellowships, research assistantships, teaching assistantships, career-related internships or fieldwork, institutionally sponsored loans, and unspecified assistantships available. Support available to part-time students. Financial award applicants required to submit FAFSA. In 2001, 298 master's, 46 doctorates awarded. *Degree program information:* Part-time programs available. Offers applied and pure mathematics (MS, PhD); astronomy and astrophysics (MS, PhD); atmospheric physics (MS, PhD); bioengineering (MS, PhD); biophysics (MS, PhD); ceramic and materials engineering (MS, PhD); chemical engineering (MS, PhD); chemistry (MS, PhD); civil engineering (M Engr, MS, PhD); computational mathematics (MS, PhD); computer engineering (MS, PhD); computer science (MS, PhD); electrical engineering (M Engr, MS, PhD); engineering and science (M Engr, MS, PhD); environmental engineering and science (M Engr, MS, PhD); hydrogeology (MS); industrial engineering (MS, PhD); management science (PhD); materials science and engineering (MS, PhD); mechanical engineering (MS, PhD); operations research (MS, PhD); physics (MS, PhD); statistics (MS, PhD); textiles, fiber and polymer science (MS, PhD). *Application fee:* $40. Electronic applications accepted. *Application Contact:* Dr. Christian Przirembel, Associate Dean, 864-656-3200, Fax: 864-656-0859, E-mail: rutgers@clemson.edu. *Dean,* Dr. Thomas M. Keinath, 864-656-3202, Fax: 864-656-0859, E-mail: keinath@clemson.edu.

College of Health, Education, and Human Development Students: 172 full-time (119 women), 509 part-time (363 women); includes 92 minority (80 African Americans, 2 Asian Americans or Pacific Islanders, 10 Hispanic Americans), 14 international. 332 applicants, 61% accepted, 118 enrolled. *Faculty:* 106 full-time (65 women), 1 (woman) part-time/adjunct. Expenses: Contact institution. *Financial support:* Fellowships, research assistantships, teaching assistantships, career-related internships or fieldwork, Federal Work-Study, tuition waivers (full and partial), and unspecified assistantships available. Support available to part-time students. Financial award applicants required to submit FAFSA. In 2001, 255 master's, 17 doctorates, 14 other advanced degrees awarded. *Degree program information:* Part-time and evening/weekend programs available. Postbaccalaureate distance learning degree programs offered. Offers administration and supervision (M Ed, Ed S); career and technology education (MCTE); counseling and guidance services (M Ed); curriculum and instruction (PhD); educational leadership (PhD); elementary education (M Ed); English (M Ed); health, education, and human development (M Ed, MCTE, MHA, MHRD, MPRTM, MS, Ed D, PhD, Ed S); history and government (M Ed); human resource development (MHRD); mathematics (M Ed); natural sciences (M Ed); nursing (MS); parks, recreation, and tourism management (MPRTM, MS, PhD); public health (MHA); reading (M Ed); secondary education (M Ed); special education (M Ed); vocational/technical education (Ed D). *Application deadline:* Applications are processed on a rolling basis. *Application fee:* $40. Electronic applications accepted. *Dean,* Dr. Harold E. Cheatham, 864-656-7641, Fax: 864-656-5488.

CLEVELAND CHIROPRACTIC COLLEGE-KANSAS CITY CAMPUS, Kansas City, MO 64131-1181

General Information Independent, coed, upper-level institution. *Enrollment:* 405 full-time matriculated graduate/professional students (125 women), 10 part-time matriculated graduate/professional students (4 women). *Enrollment by degree level:* 415 first professional. *Graduate faculty:* 38 full-time (10 women), 13 part-time/adjunct (4 women). *Tuition:* Full-time $11,632; part-time $182 per hour. *Required fees:* $55 per trimester. *Graduate housing:* On-campus housing not available. *Student services:* Campus employment opportunities, campus safety program, career counseling, disabled student services, free psychological counseling, international student services. *Library facilities:* Ruth R. Cleveland Memorial Library. *Online resources:* library catalog, web page. *Collection:* 14,000 titles, 268 serial subscriptions, 12,320 audiovisual materials.

Computer facilities: 14 computers available on campus for general student use. A campuswide network can be accessed. Internet access, educational software are available. *Web address:* http://www.cleveland.edu/.

General Application Contact: Melissa Denton, Director of Admission, 816-501-0100, Fax: 816-501-0205.

GRADUATE UNITS

Professional Program Students: 405 full-time (125 women), 10 part-time (4 women); includes 51 minority (17 African Americans, 13 Asian Americans or Pacific Islanders, 14 Hispanic Americans, 7 Native Americans), 13 international. Average age 29. 127 applicants, 69% accepted, 48 enrolled. *Faculty:* 38 full-time (10 women), 13 part-time/adjunct (4 women). Expenses: Contact institution. *Financial support:* In 2001–02, 15 teaching assistantships (averaging $1,500 per year) were awarded; career-related internships or fieldwork, Federal Work-Study, and scholarships/grants also available. Support available to part-time students. Financial award applicants required to submit FAFSA. In 2001, 133 degrees awarded. Offers chiropractic (DC). *Application deadline:* For fall admission, 7/1 (priority date); for winter admission, 11/1 (priority date); for spring admission, 3/1 (priority date). Applications are processed on a rolling basis. *Application fee:* $50. Electronic applications accepted. *Application Contact:* Melissa Denton, Director of Admissions, 816-501-0100, Fax: 816-501-0205. *Academic Dean,* Dr. Ruth Sandefur, 816-501-0100, Fax: 816-501-0221.

CLEVELAND CHIROPRACTIC COLLEGE-LOS ANGELES CAMPUS, Los Angeles, CA 90004-2196

General Information Independent, coed, upper-level institution. *Enrollment by degree level:* 497 first professional. *Graduate faculty:* 30 full-time (9 women), 25 part-time/adjunct (4 women). *Tuition:* Full-time $19,350; part-time $1,955 per trimester. Tuition and fees vary according to course load. *Graduate housing:* On-campus housing not available. *Student services:* Campus employment opportunities, campus safety program, career counseling, free psychological counseling, international student services. *Web address:* http://www.clevelandchiropractic.edu/.

General Application Contact: K. Monty Jordan, Director of Admissions, 800-466-CCLA, Fax: 213-323, E-mail: jordanm@cleveland.edu.

GRADUATE UNITS

Professional Program in Chiropractic Medicine Students: 474 full-time (152 women), 23 part-time (7 women); includes 211 minority (24 African Americans, 132 Asian Americans or Pacific Islanders, 52 Hispanic Americans, 3 Native Americans), 48 international. Average age

Cleveland Chiropractic College-Los Angeles Campus (continued)
29. 110 applicants, 53% accepted, 29 enrolled. *Faculty:* 30 full-time (9 women), 25 part-time/adjunct (4 women). Expenses: Contact institution. *Financial support:* Research assistantships with partial tuition reimbursements, teaching assistantships with partial tuition reimbursements, Federal Work-Study, scholarships/grants, and tuition waivers (partial) available. Financial award application deadline: 6/15; financial award applicants required to submit FAFSA. In 2001, 162 degrees awarded. Offers chiropractic medicine (DC). *Application deadline:* Applications are processed on a rolling basis. *Application fee:* $50. Electronic applications accepted. *Application Contact:* K. Monty Jordan, Director of Admissions, 800-466-CCLA, Fax: 323-660-4195, E-mail: joardanm@cleveland.edu. *Executive Vice President,* Dr. Matthew Givrad, 323-660-6166, Fax: 323-660-5387.

THE CLEVELAND INSTITUTE OF ART, Cleveland, OH 44106-1700

General Information Independent, coed, comprehensive institution.

GRADUATE UNITS

Program in Medical Illustration

CLEVELAND INSTITUTE OF MUSIC, Cleveland, OH 44106-1776

General Information Independent, coed, comprehensive institution. *Enrollment:* 148 full-time matriculated graduate/professional students (81 women), 5 part-time matriculated graduate/professional students (2 women). *Enrollment by degree level:* 104 master's, 7 doctoral, 42 other advanced degrees. *Graduate faculty:* 31 full-time, 69 part-time/adjunct. *Tuition:* Full-time $19,550; part-time $875 per credit hour. *Required fees:* $1,522. *Graduate housing:* Room and/or apartments available on a first-come, first-served basis to single students; on-campus housing not available to married students. Typical cost: $3,475 per year ($6,675 including board). Room and board charges vary according to board plan. Housing application deadline: 5/30. *Student services:* Campus employment opportunities, campus safety program, career counseling, free psychological counseling, international student services, low-cost health insurance. *Online resources:* library catalog, web page, access to other libraries' catalogs. *Collection:* 47,500 titles, 110 serial subscriptions.

Computer facilities: 25 computers available on campus for general student use. A campuswide network can be accessed from student residence rooms and from off campus. Internet access is available. *Web address:* http://www.cim.edu/.

General Application Contact: E. William Fay, Director of Admissions, 216-795-3107, E-mail: cimadmission@po.cwru.edu.

GRADUATE UNITS

Graduate Programs Offers performance (MM, DMA, AD, CPS). Electronic applications accepted.

CLEVELAND STATE UNIVERSITY, Cleveland, OH 44115

General Information State-supported, coed, university. CGS member. *Enrollment:* 981 full-time matriculated graduate/professional students (510 women), 2,913 part-time matriculated graduate/professional students (1,680 women). *Enrollment by degree level:* 829 first professional, 2,744 master's, 321 doctoral. *Graduate faculty:* 440 full-time (125 women), 136 part-time/adjunct (34 women). Tuition, state resident: full-time $6,838; part-time $263 per credit hour. Tuition, nonresident: full-time $13,526; part-time $520 per credit hour. *Graduate housing:* Rooms and/or apartments available to single and married students. Typical cost: $3,336 per year ($5,550 including board) for single students; $3,336 per year ($5,550 including board) for married students. Room and board charges vary according to board plan. *Student services:* Campus employment opportunities, campus safety program, career counseling, child daycare facilities, free psychological counseling, international student services, low-cost health insurance. *Library facilities:* University Library plus 1 other. *Online resources:* library catalog, web page, access to other libraries' catalogs. *Collection:* 470,659 titles, 6,503 serial subscriptions, 159,934 audiovisual materials. *Research affiliation:* Cleveland Clinic Foundation, Metro Health System.

Computer facilities: 600 computers available on campus for general student use. *Web address:* http://www.csuohio.edu/.

General Application Contact: Dr. William C. Bailey, Director of Graduate Admissions and Associate Dean, College of Graduate Studies, 216-687-9370, Fax: 216-687-9214, E-mail: w.baily@csuohio.edu.

GRADUATE UNITS

Cleveland-Marshall College of Law Students: 529 full-time (239 women), 304 part-time (154 women); includes 87 minority (55 African Americans, 14 Asian Americans or Pacific Islanders, 17 Hispanic Americans, 1 Native American), 10 international. Average age 29. 1,205 applicants, 54% accepted, 292 enrolled. *Faculty:* 54 full-time (24 women), 27 part-time/adjunct (10 women). Expenses: Contact institution. *Financial support:* In 2001–02, 731 students received support, including 219 fellowships (averaging $3,917 per year), 40 research assistantships; career-related internships or fieldwork, Federal Work-Study, institutionally sponsored loans, scholarships/grants, tuition waivers (full and partial), and unspecified assistantships also available. Support available to part-time students. Financial award application deadline: 4/1; financial award applicants required to submit FAFSA. In 2001, 231 first professional degrees, 2 master's awarded. *Degree program information:* Part-time and evening/weekend programs available. Offers law (JD, LL M). *Application deadline:* For fall admission, 4/1. Applications are processed on a rolling basis. *Application fee:* $35. *Application Contact:* Margaret McNally, Assistant Dean for Admissions, 216-687-2304, Fax: 216-687-6881, E-mail: admissions@law.csuohio.edu. *Dean,* Steven H. Steinglass, 216-687-2300, Fax: 216-687-6881, E-mail: steven.steinglass@law.csuohio.edu.

College of Graduate Studies Students: 453 full-time (271 women), 2,612 part-time (1,527 women); includes 479 minority (375 African Americans, 55 Asian Americans or Pacific Islanders, 44 Hispanic Americans, 5 Native Americans), 530 international. Average age 32. 2,046 applicants, 68% accepted. *Faculty:* 440 full-time (125 women), 136 part-time/adjunct (34 women). Expenses: Contact institution. *Financial support:* In 2001–02, 3 fellowships (averaging $6,960 per year), 148 research assistantships with full tuition reimbursements (averaging $6,960 per year), 125 teaching assistantships with full tuition reimbursements (averaging $6,960 per year) were awarded. Career-related internships or fieldwork, Federal Work-Study, institutionally sponsored loans, tuition waivers (full and partial), and unspecified assistantships also available. Support available to part-time students. In 2001, 1,054 master's, 38 doctorates awarded. *Degree program information:* Part-time and evening/weekend programs available. Postbaccalaureate distance learning degree programs offered (minimal on-campus study). Offers molecular medicine (PhD). *Application deadline:* For fall admission, 7/24 (priority date); for spring admission, 12/13 (priority date). Applications are processed on a rolling basis. *Application fee:* $30 ($0 for international students). Electronic applications accepted. *Application Contact:* Dr. William C. Bailey, Director of Graduate Admissions and Associate Dean, College of Graduate Studies, 216-687-9370, Fax: 216-687-9214, E-mail: w.baily@csuohio.edu. *Vice Provost for Research and Dean, College of Graduate Studies,* Dr. Mark A. Tumeo, 216-687-3595, Fax: 216-687-9214, E-mail: m.tumeo@csuohio.edu.

College of Arts and Sciences Average age 32. Expenses: Contact institution. *Financial support:* Fellowships, research assistantships, teaching assistantships, career-related internships or fieldwork, Federal Work-Study, institutionally sponsored loans, tuition waivers (full and partial), and unspecified assistantships available. Support available to part-time students. *Degree program information:* Part-time and evening/weekend programs available. Offers analytical chemistry (MS, PhD); applied mathematics (MS); applied optics (MS); art history (MA); arts and sciences (MA, MACTM, MM, MS, MSN, MSW, PhD, Psy S); biological, geological, and environmental sciences (MS, PhD); clinical and counseling psychology (MA); clinical chemistry (MS, PhD); clinical/bioanalytical (PhD); communication (MACTM); composition (MM); condensed matter physics (MS); consumer/industrial research (MA); diversity management (MA); economics (MA); education and performance (MM); English (MA); history (MA); inorganic chemistry (MS); mathematics (MA); medical physics (MS); music history (MM); occupational therapy (MA); organic chemistry (MS); philosophy (MA); physical chemistry (MS); population health nursing (MSN); research psychology (MA); school psychology (Psy S); social work (MSW); sociology (MA); Spanish (MA); speech and hearing (MA); structural analysis (MS, PhD). *Application deadline:* Applications are processed on a rolling basis. *Application fee:* $25. Electronic applications accepted. *Application Contact:* Dr. William C. Bailey, Director of Graduate Admissions and Associate Dean, College of Graduate Studies, 216-687-5599, Fax: 216-687-9210, E-mail: w.bailey@csuohio.edu. *Interim Dean,* Dr. Earl Anderson, 216-687-3660.

College of Education Students: 67 full-time (55 women), 949 part-time (751 women); includes 205 minority (182 African Americans, 8 Asian Americans or Pacific Islanders, 14 Hispanic Americans, 1 Native American), 15 international. Average age 34. 199 applicants, 94% accepted. *Faculty:* 59 full-time (33 women). Expenses: Contact institution. *Financial support:* In 2001–02, 4 research assistantships, 9 teaching assistantships were awarded. Career-related internships or fieldwork, Federal Work-Study, and unspecified assistantships also available. Support available to part-time students. In 2001, 358 master's, 11 doctorates awarded. *Degree program information:* Part-time programs available. Offers administration (PhD); adult learning and development (M Ed); community health education (M Ed); counseling (PhD); curriculum and instruction (M Ed); education (M Ed, PhD, Ed S); educational administration and supervision (M Ed, Ed S); educational research (M Ed); exercise science (M Ed); gifted education (M Ed); health education (M Ed); human performance (M Ed); leadership and lifelong learning (PhD); learning and development (PhD); pedagogy (M Ed); policy studies (PhD); school and professional counseling (M Ed, Ed S); sport and exercise psychology (M Ed); sport management (M Ed); sport management/exercise science (M Ed); technology education (M Ed). *Application deadline:* For fall admission, 7/15 (priority date). *Application fee:* $25. *Application Contact:* Katie Glenn, Assistant Director, Education Student Services Center, 216-687-4625, E-mail: w.glenn@cusohio.edu. *Dean,* Dr. James McLoughlin, 216-523-7143, E-mail: j.mcloughlin@csuohio.edu.

Fenn College of Engineering Students: 22 full-time (3 women), 217 part-time (41 women); includes 11 minority (3 African Americans, 4 Asian Americans or Pacific Islanders, 4 Hispanic Americans), 157 international. Average age 28. 422 applicants, 69% accepted. *Faculty:* 46 full-time (3 women), 23 part-time/adjunct (3 women). Expenses: Contact institution. *Financial support:* In 2001–02, 34 students received support, including 1 fellowship with full tuition reimbursement available, 17 research assistantships with full tuition reimbursements available (averaging $14,000 per year), 16 teaching assistantships with full and partial tuition reimbursements available (averaging $12,000 per year); career-related internships or fieldwork, Federal Work-Study, institutionally sponsored loans, tuition waivers (full and partial), and unspecified assistantships also available. Support available to part-time students. Financial award application deadline: 3/30. In 2001, 29 master's, 9 doctorates awarded. *Degree program information:* Part-time and evening/weekend programs available. Offers applied biomedical engineering (D Eng); chemical engineering (MS, D Eng); civil engineering (MS, D Eng); electrical and computer engineering (MS, D Eng); engineering (D Eng); engineering mechanics (MS); environmental engineering (MS); industrial engineering (MS); mechanical engineering (MS, D Eng). *Application deadline:* For fall admission, 7/15 (priority date). Applications are processed on a rolling basis. *Application fee:* $25. Electronic applications accepted. *Application Contact:* Dr. Joanne Belovich, Associate Dean, 216-687-2555, E-mail: engineering@csvax.csuohio.edu. *Interim Dean,* Dr. John H, Hemann, 216-687-2555.

James J. Nance College of Business Administration Students: 135 full-time (55 women), 837 part-time (349 women); includes 108 minority (61 African Americans, 36 Asian Americans or Pacific Islanders, 9 Hispanic Americans, 2 Native Americans), 283 international. Average age 29. 868 applicants, 66% accepted. *Faculty:* 75 full-time (16 women). Expenses: Contact institution. *Financial support:* In 2001–02, 21 research assistantships, 8 teaching assistantships were awarded. Career-related internships or fieldwork, Federal Work-Study, tuition waivers (full), and unspecified assistantships also available. Financial award applicants required to submit FAFSA. In 2001, 421 master's, 6 doctorates awarded. *Degree program information:* Part-time and evening/weekend programs available. Offers accounting and financial information systems (MAC); business administration (MBA, DBA); health care administration (MBA); labor relations and human resources (MLRHR); management and organization analysis (MCIS); public health (MPH); systems programming (MCIS). *Application deadline:* For fall admission, 7/15 (priority date); for spring admission, 12/15 (priority date). Applications are processed on a rolling basis. *Application fee:* $30. *Application Contact:* Benoy W. Joseph, Associate Dean, 216-687-2019, Fax: 216-687-9354, E-mail: w.joseph@csuohio.edu. *Interim Dean,* Dr. Rosemary P. Ramsey, 216-687-2130, Fax: 216-687-9354, E-mail: rramsey@grail.cba.csuohio.edu.

Maxine Goodman Levin College of Urban Affairs Students: 57 full-time (33 women), 171 part-time (103 women); includes 68 minority (60 African Americans, 8 Hispanic Americans), 14 international. Average age 35. 83 applicants, 64% accepted. *Faculty:* 15 full-time (7 women). Expenses: Contact institution. *Financial support:* In 2001–02, 39 research assistantships were awarded; teaching assistantships, career-related internships or fieldwork, Federal Work-Study, institutionally sponsored loans, tuition waivers (full and partial), and unspecified assistantships also available. Support available to part-time students. Financial award application deadline: 3/1. In 2001, 78 degrees awarded. *Degree program information:* Part-time and evening/weekend programs available. Offers public administration (MPA, PhD); urban affairs (MA, MAES, MPA, MS, MUPDD, PhD); urban planning, design, and development (MUPDD); urban studies (MA, MS, PhD). *Application deadline:* For fall admission, 7/15 (priority date). Applications are processed on a rolling basis. *Application fee:* $25. *Application Contact:* Graduate Programs Coordinator, 216-523-7522, Fax: 216-687-5398, E-mail: gradprog@wolf.csuohio.edu. *Dean,* Dr. Mark Rosentraub, 216-687-2135.

See in-depth description on page 809.

COASTAL CAROLINA UNIVERSITY, Conway, SC 29528-6054

General Information State-supported, coed, comprehensive institution. *Enrollment:* 6 full-time matriculated graduate/professional students (5 women), 188 part-time matriculated graduate/professional students (163 women). *Enrollment by degree level:* 194 master's. *Graduate faculty:* 5 full-time (1 woman), 9 part-time/adjunct (8 women). Tuition, state resident: full-time $4,320; part-time $180 per credit hour. Tuition, nonresident: full-time $11,160; part-time $465 per credit hour. *Graduate housing:* On-campus housing not available. *Student services:* Campus safety program, career counseling, free psychological counseling, international student services, multicultural affairs office. *Library facilities:* Kimbel Library. *Online resources:* library catalog, web page, access to other libraries' catalogs. *Collection:* 189,468 titles, 1,736 serial subscriptions, 11,636 audiovisual materials.

Computer facilities: 220 computers available on campus for general student use. A campuswide network can be accessed from student residence rooms and from off campus. Internet access, on-line grades are available. *Web address:* http://www.coastal.edu/.

General Application Contact: Dr. Judy W. Vogt, Director of Financial Aid and Admissions, 843-349-2037, Fax: 843-349-2127, E-mail: jvogt@coastal.edu.

GRADUATE UNITS

College of Education and Graduate Studies Students: 6 full-time (5 women), 188 part-time (163 women); includes 13 minority (12 African Americans, 1 Native American) Average age 39. *Faculty:* 5 full-time (1 woman), 9 part-time/adjunct (8 women). Expenses: Contact institution. *Financial support:* Fellowships, research assistantships, unspecified assistantships available. Support available to part-time students. Financial award application deadline: 4/1; financial award applicants required to submit FAFSA. In 2001, 27 degrees awarded. *Degree program information:* Part-time and evening/weekend programs available. Offers early childhood education (M Ed); educational technology (M Ed); elementary education (M Ed); Secondary Education (MAT); secondary education (M Ed). *Application deadline:* For fall admission, 8/15 (priority date). Applications are processed on a rolling basis. *Application fee:* $35. Electronic applications accepted. *Application Contact:* Dr. Judy W Vogt, Associate Vice President, Enrollment Services, 843-349-2037, E-mail: jvogt@coastal.edu. *Dean,* Dr. Gilbert H. Hunt, 843-349-2607, Fax: 843-349-2940, E-mail: hunt@coastal.edu.

COE COLLEGE, Cedar Rapids, IA 52402-5092

General Information Independent-religious, coed, comprehensive institution. *Enrollment:* 57 part-time matriculated graduate/professional students. *Enrollment by degree level:*

57 master's. *Graduate faculty:* 8 full-time (5 women), 5 part-time/adjunct (3 women). *Tuition:* Part-time $333 per semester hour. *Graduate housing:* On-campus housing not available. *Student services:* Campus safety program, career counseling, international student services, teacher training, writing training. *Library facilities:* Stewart Memorial Library plus 1 other. *Online resources:* library catalog, web page. *Collection:* 206,290 titles, 818 serial subscriptions, 9,782 audiovisual materials.

Computer facilities: 189 computers available on campus for general student use. A campuswide network can be accessed from student residence rooms and from off campus. Internet access is available. *Web address:* http://www.coe.edu/.

General Application Contact: Dr. Terry F. McNabb, Associate Professor, 319-399-8870, Fax: 319-399-8721, E-mail: tmcnabb@coe.edu.

GRADUATE UNITS

Department of Education Average age 30. 10 applicants, 100% accepted, 10 enrolled. *Faculty:* 8 full-time (5 women), 5 part-time/adjunct (3 women). Expenses: Contact institution. *Financial support:* Institutionally sponsored loans and tuition waivers (partial) available. Support available to part-time students. Financial award applicants required to submit FAFSA. In 2001, 21 degrees awarded. *Degree program information:* Part-time programs available. Offers education (MAT). *Application deadline:* For fall admission, 8/1 (priority date); for spring admission, 4/1 (priority date). *Application fee:* $25. *Associate Professor,* Dr. Terry F. McNabb, 319-399-8870, Fax: 319-399-8721, E-mail: tmcnabb@coe.edu.

COLD SPRING HARBOR LABORATORY, WATSON SCHOOL OF BIOLOGICAL SCIENCES, Cold Spring Harbor, NY 11724

General Information Independent, coed, graduate-only institution. *Enrollment by degree level:* 20 doctoral. *Graduate faculty:* 53 full-time (7 women). *Graduate tuition:* All students receive a full tuition waiver, health coverage, and an annual stipend. *Graduate housing:* Room and/or apartments guaranteed to single students; on-campus housing not available to married students. *Student services:* Campus safety program, career counseling, child daycare facilities, exercise/wellness program, grant writing training, low-cost health insurance, writing training. *Library facilities:* Carnegie Library plus 8 others. *Online resources:* library catalog, web page. *Collection:* 20,000 titles, 846 serial subscriptions, 75 audiovisual materials.

Computer facilities: A campuswide network can be accessed from student residence rooms and from off campus. Internet access, compujtational biology applications/tools, online library sy are available. *Web address:* http://www.cshl.edu/gradschool/.

General Application Contact: Janet Duffy, Admissions and Academic Records Administrator, 516-367-6890, Fax: 516-367-6919, E-mail: duffy@cshl.edu.

GRADUATE UNITS

Graduate Program Students: 20 full-time (7 women). Average age 23. 252 applicants, 6% accepted, 6 enrolled. *Faculty:* 53 full-time (7 women). Expenses: Contact institution. *Financial support:* In 2001–02, 20 students received support, including 20 fellowships; health care benefits, tuition waivers (full), and housing and food subsidies and research support also available. Offers biological sciences (PhD). *Application deadline:* For fall admission, 1/1. *Application fee:* $50. *Application Contact:* Janet Duffy, Admissions and Academic Records Administrator, 516-367-6890, Fax: 516-367-6919, E-mail: duffy@cshl.edu. *Dean,* Dr. Winship Herr, 516-367-6909, Fax: 516-367-6919, E-mail: herr@cshl.edu.

COLEGIO PENTECOSTAL MIZPA, Río Piedras, PR 00928-0966

General Information Independent-religious, comprehensive institution.

GRADUATE UNITS

Program in Pastoral Theology Offers pastoral theology (MA).

COLEMAN COLLEGE, La Mesa, CA 91942-1532

General Information Independent, coed, comprehensive institution. *Enrollment:* 27 full-time matriculated graduate/professional students (5 women). *Enrollment by degree level:* 27 master's. *Graduate faculty:* 7 full-time (1 woman), 3 part-time/adjunct (1 woman). *Tuition:* Part-time $200 per credit. *Graduate housing:* On-campus housing not available. *Student services:* Campus employment opportunities, career counseling, international student services. *Library facilities:* Coleman College LaMesa Library. *Collection:* 66,800 titles, 69 serial subscriptions.

Computer facilities: 420 computers available on campus for general student use. A campuswide network can be accessed. Internet access is available. *Web address:* http://www.coleman.edu/.

General Application Contact: Debbie Coleman, Registrar, 619-465-3990 Ext. 102, Fax: 619-463-0162, E-mail: debcoleman@coleman.edu.

GRADUATE UNITS

Graduate Program in Information Technology Students: 27 full-time (5 women). Average age 35. 32 applicants, 91% accepted, 29 enrolled. *Faculty:* 7 full-time (1 woman), 3 part-time/adjunct (1 woman). Expenses: Contact institution. *Financial support:* Applicants required to submit FAFSA. *Degree program information:* Evening/weekend programs available. Offers information technology (MSIT). *Application deadline:* Applications are processed on a rolling basis. *Application fee:* $100. *Application Contact:* Debbie Coleman, Registrar, 619-465-3990 Ext. 102, Fax: 619-463-0162, E-mail: debcoleman@coleman.edu. *Director of Graduate Studies,* Dr. Marianne Liszkay, 619-465-3990 Ext. 168, Fax: 619-463-0162, E-mail: mliszkay@coleman.edu.

COLGATE ROCHESTER CROZER DIVINITY SCHOOL, Rochester, NY 14620-2530

General Information Independent-religious, coed, graduate-only institution. *Enrollment by degree level:* 83 first professional, 10 master's, 16 doctoral. *Graduate faculty:* 10 full-time (5 women), 6 part-time/adjunct (2 women). *Tuition:* Full-time $6,330; part-time $1,055 per course. *Required fees:* $165; $17 per unit. *Graduate housing:* Rooms and/or apartments available on a first-come, first-served basis to single and married students. Typical cost: $4,455 per year for single students; $5,049 per year for married students. Room charges vary according to housing facility selected. Housing application deadline: 4/1. *Student services:* Campus employment opportunities, career counseling. *Library facilities:* Ambrose Swasey Library plus 1 other. *Online resources:* library catalog, web page, access to other libraries' catalogs. *Collection:* 304,508 titles, 701 serial subscriptions, 3,677 audiovisual materials.

Computer facilities: 10 computers available on campus for general student use. A campuswide network can be accessed from student residence rooms and from off campus. Internet access is available. *Web address:* http://www.crcds.edu/.

General Application Contact: Robert Jones, Vice President for Enrollment, 585-271-1320, Fax: 585-271-8013, E-mail: rjones@crds.edu.

GRADUATE UNITS

Graduate and Professional Programs Students: 68 full-time, 56 part-time. Average age 44. *Faculty:* 10 full-time (5 women), 6 part-time/adjunct (2 women). Expenses: Contact institution. *Financial support:* In 2001–02, 44 students received support. Career-related internships or fieldwork, scholarships/grants, and tuition waivers (full and partial) available. Support available to part-time students. Financial award application deadline: 9/1; financial award applicants required to submit FAFSA. In 2001, 33 first professional degrees, 3 master's, 1 doctorate awarded. *Degree program information:* Part-time and evening/weekend programs available. Offers theology (M Div, MA, D Min, Certificate). *Application deadline:* For spring admission, 2/1. Applications are processed on a rolling basis. *Application fee:* $35. *Application Contact:* Robert Jones, Vice President for Enrollment, 585-271-1320, Fax: 585-271-8013, E-mail: rjones@crds.edu. *President,* Dr. G. Thomas Halbrooks, 585-271-1320, Fax: 585-271-8013, E-mail: thalbrooks@crds.edu.

COLGATE UNIVERSITY, Hamilton, NY 13346-1386

General Information Independent, coed, comprehensive institution. *Enrollment:* 2 full-time matriculated graduate/professional students (1 woman), 2 part-time matriculated graduate/professional students (1 woman). *Enrollment by degree level:* 3 master's. *Graduate faculty:* 10 full-time (5 women). *Tuition:* Part-time $2,982 per course. *Required fees:* $90 per term. *Graduate housing:* On-campus housing not available. *Student services:* Campus safety program, career counseling, disabled student services, exercise/wellness program, free psychological counseling, low-cost health insurance, teacher training, writing training. *Library facilities:* Everett Needham Case Library plus 1 other. *Online resources:* library catalog, web page, access to other libraries' catalogs. *Collection:* 634,874 titles, 2,314 serial subscriptions, 8,091 audiovisual materials.

Computer facilities: 577 computers available on campus for general student use. A campuswide network can be accessed from student residence rooms and from off campus. Internet access and online class registration, software applications are available. *Web address:* http://www.colgate.edu/.

General Application Contact: Jeffrey Baldani, Associate Dean of Faculty and Director of Graduate Studies, 315-228-7220, Fax: 315-228-7831, E-mail: jbaldani@mail.colgate.edu.

GRADUATE UNITS

Graduate Programs Students: 2 full-time (1 woman), 2 part-time (1 woman). 10 applicants, 70% accepted, 1 enrolled. *Faculty:* 10 full-time (5 women). Expenses: Contact institution. *Financial support:* In 2001–02, 3 students received support; research assistantships, career-related internships or fieldwork, Federal Work-Study, institutionally sponsored loans, tuition waivers (partial), and unspecified assistantships available. Support available to part-time students. Financial award applicants required to submit FAFSA. In 2001, 2 degrees awarded. *Degree program information:* Part-time programs available. Offers secondary education (MAT). *Application deadline:* For fall admission, 3/15 (priority date); for spring admission, 9/1. Applications are processed on a rolling basis. *Application fee:* $50. *Associate Dean of Faculty and Director of Graduate Studies,* Jeffrey Baldani, 315-228-7220, Fax: 315-228-7831, E-mail: jbaldani@mail.colgate.edu.

COLLÈGE DOMINICAIN DE PHILOSOPHIE ET DE THÉOLOGIE, Ottawa, ON K1R 7G3, Canada

General Information Independent-religious, coed, comprehensive institution. *Enrollment:* 54 full-time matriculated graduate/professional students (5 women), 5 part-time matriculated graduate/professional students. *Enrollment by degree level:* 33 master's, 26 doctoral. *Graduate faculty:* 7 full-time (1 woman), 6 part-time/adjunct (1 woman). *Graduate housing:* On-campus housing not available. *Student services:* Campus safety program. *Library facilities:* Bibliothèque du College Dominicain. *Online resources:* library catalog. *Collection:* 85,000 titles, 500 serial subscriptions.

Computer facilities: 1 computer available on campus for general student use.

General Application Contact: Fr. Jacques Lison, OP, Registrar, 613-233-5696, Fax: 613-233-6064, E-mail: registraire@collegedominicain.ca.

GRADUATE UNITS

Graduate Programs Students: 54 full-time (5 women), 5 part-time; includes 11 minority (3 African Americans, 3 Asian Americans or Pacific Islanders, 5 Hispanic Americans), 3 international. Average age 41. 9 applicants, 100% accepted. *Faculty:* 7 full-time (1 woman), 6 part-time/adjunct (1 woman). Expenses: Contact institution. In 2001, 2 master's awarded. *Degree program information:* Part-time and evening/weekend programs available. Offers pastoral theology (M Prof Past, M Th Past); philosophy (MA Ph, PhD); theology (M Th, MA Th, PhD, Th D, L Th). *Application deadline:* For fall admission, 8/1 (priority date). Applications are processed on a rolling basis. *Application fee:* $25. *Application Contact:* Fr. Jacques Lison, OP, Registrar, 613-233-5696, Fax: 613-233-6064, E-mail: registraire@collegedominicain.ca.

COLLEGE FOR FINANCIAL PLANNING, Greenwood Village, CO 80111-4707

General Information Proprietary, coed, primarily men, graduate-only institution. *Enrollment by degree level:* 625 master's. *Graduate faculty:* 8 full-time (3 women). *Tuition:* Part-time $200 per semester hour. *Graduate housing:* On-campus housing not available. *Library facilities:* Apollo Learning Resource Center. *Online resources:* web page. *Collection:* 500,000 titles, 17 million serial subscriptions.

Computer facilities: A campuswide network can be accessed from off campus. Internet access is available. *Web address:* http://www.fp.edu/.

General Application Contact: Gary BatongBacal, Enrollment Manager, 303-220-4955, Fax: 303-220-1810, E-mail: gcb@fp.edu.

GRADUATE UNITS

Program in Financial Planning Average age 41. 210 applicants, 95% accepted, 200 enrolled. *Faculty:* 8 full-time (3 women). Expenses: Contact institution. In 2001, 42 degrees awarded. *Degree program information:* Part-time programs available. Postbaccalaureate distance learning degree programs offered (no on-campus study). Offers personal financial planning (MS). *Application deadline:* Applications are processed on a rolling basis. *Application fee:* $225. Electronic applications accepted. *Application Contact:* Gary BatongBacal, Enrollment Manager, 303-220-4955, Fax: 303-220-1810, E-mail: gcb@fp.edu. *Vice President, Academic Affairs,* Jesse B. Arman, 303-220-4823, Fax: 303-220-4941, E-mail: jba@fp.edu.

COLLEGE MISERICORDIA, Dallas, PA 18612-1098

General Information Independent-religious, coed, comprehensive institution. *Enrollment:* 389 full-time matriculated graduate/professional students (327 women), 203 part-time matriculated graduate/professional students (156 women). *Enrollment by degree level:* 592 master's. *Graduate faculty:* 35 full-time (23 women), 30 part-time/adjunct (13 women). *Tuition:* Part-time $465 per credit. *Graduate housing:* On-campus housing not available. *Student services:* Campus safety program, career counseling, disabled student services, free psychological counseling, international student services, low-cost health insurance, multicultural affairs office. *Library facilities:* Mary Kintz Bevevina Library. *Online resources:* library catalog, web page, access to other libraries' catalogs. *Collection:* 72,836 titles, 782 serial subscriptions, 2,240 audiovisual materials.

Computer facilities: 50 computers available on campus for general student use. A campuswide network can be accessed from student residence rooms and from off campus. Internet access is available. *Web address:* http://www.miseri.edu/.

General Application Contact: Larree Brown, Coordinator of Part-Time Undergraduate and Graduate Programs, 570-674-6451, Fax: 570-674-6232, E-mail: lbrown@misericordia.edu.

GRADUATE UNITS

Division of Health Sciences Students: 499. 616 applicants, 37% accepted. *Faculty:* 22 full-time (13 women), 13 part-time/adjunct (9 women). Expenses: Contact institution. *Financial support:* Fellowships, research assistantships, teaching assistantships, career-related internships or fieldwork, Federal Work-Study, institutionally sponsored loans, traineeships, and tuition waivers (partial) available. Support available to part-time students. In 2001, 125 degrees awarded. *Degree program information:* Part-time and evening/weekend programs available. Offers health sciences (MSN, MSOT, MSPT); nursing (MSN); occupational therapy (MSOT); physical therapy (MSPT). *Application deadline:* Applications are processed on a rolling basis. *Application fee:* $25. *Application Contact:* Larree Brown, Coordinator of Part-Time Undergraduate and Graduate Programs, 570-674-6451, Fax: 570-674-6232, E-mail: lbrown@misericordia.edu. *Chair,* Dr. Catherine Perry Wilkinson, 570-674-6465.

Division of Professional Studies 21 applicants, 81% accepted. *Faculty:* 6 full-time (3 women), 12 part-time/adjunct (1 woman). Expenses: Contact institution. *Financial support:* Fellowships, research assistantships, teaching assistantships, career-related internships or fieldwork and institutionally sponsored loans available. Support available to part-time students. Financial award application deadline: 5/1. In 2001, 13 degrees awarded. *Degree program information:* Part-time and evening/weekend programs available. Offers education/curriculum

College Misericordia (continued)

(MS); organizational management (MS); professional studies (MS). *Application deadline:* For fall admission, 8/1 (priority date). Applications are processed on a rolling basis. *Application fee:* $25. *Application Contact:* Larree Brown, Coordinator of Part-Time Undergraduate and Graduate Programs, 570-674-6451, Fax: 570-674-6232, E-mail: lbrown@misericordia.edu. *Director of Adult Education,* Tom O'Neill.

COLLEGE OF CHARLESTON, Charleston, SC 29424-0001

General Information State-supported, coed, comprehensive institution. *Enrollment:* 251 full-time matriculated graduate/professional students (186 women), 259 part-time matriculated graduate/professional students (189 women). *Enrollment by degree level:* 510 master's. *Graduate faculty:* 224 full-time (67 women), 29 part-time/adjunct (13 women). Tuition, state resident: part-time $200 per hour. Tuition, nonresident: part-time $455 per hour. *Required fees:* $2 per hour. $15 per term. One-time fee: $45 part-time. *Graduate housing:* On-campus housing not available. *Student services:* Campus employment opportunities, campus safety program, career counseling, child daycare facilities, disabled student services, free psychological counseling, international student services, low-cost health insurance, multicultural affairs office, teacher training. *Library facilities:* Robert Scott Small Library plus 1 other. *Online resources:* library catalog, web page, access to other libraries' catalogs. *Collection:* 375,442 titles, 3,194 serial subscriptions, 4,901 audiovisual materials. *Research affiliation:* South Carolina Marine Resources Division (marine biology), NASA, Oak Ridge Associated Universities (science).

Computer facilities: 2,500 computers available on campus for general student use. A campuswide network can be accessed from off campus. Internet access and online class registration are available. *Web address:* http://www.cofc.edu/.

General Application Contact: Laura H. Hines, Graduate School Coordinator, 843-953-5614, Fax: 843-953-1434, E-mail: hinesl@cofc.edu.

GRADUATE UNITS

Graduate School Students: 251 full-time (186 women), 259 part-time (189 women); includes 56 minority (25 African Americans, 15 Asian Americans or Pacific Islanders, 16 Hispanic Americans), 12 international. Average age 29. 346 applicants, 51% accepted, 159 enrolled. *Faculty:* 224 full-time (67 women), 29 part-time/adjunct (13 women). Expenses: Contact institution. *Financial support:* Fellowships, research assistantships, teaching assistantships, career-related internships or fieldwork, Federal Work-Study, institutionally sponsored loans, tuition waivers (partial), and unspecified assistantships available. Support available to part-time students. Financial award applicants required to submit FAFSA. In 2001, 165 degrees awarded. *Degree program information:* Part-time and evening/weekend programs available. Offers computer and information sciences (MS). *Application fee:* $35. *Application Contact:* Laura H. Hines, Graduate School Coordinator, 843-953-5614, Fax: 843-953-1434, E-mail: hinesl@cofc.edu. *Dean of Graduate Studies,* Dr. Hugh Haynsworth, 843-953-5748, Fax: 843-953-1434, E-mail: pattersonw@cofc.edu.

School of Business and Economics Students: 12 full-time (4 women), 18 part-time (9 women), 1 international. Average age 29. 22 applicants, 82% accepted, 17 enrolled. *Faculty:* 9 full-time (3 women). Expenses: Contact institution. *Financial support:* In 2001–02, 2 research assistantships were awarded Support available to part-time students. Financial award applicants required to submit FAFSA. In 2001, 11 degrees awarded. Offers accountancy (MS); business and economics (MS). *Application deadline:* Applications are processed on a rolling basis. *Application fee:* $35. *Application Contact:* Laura H. Hines, Graduate School Coordinator, 843-953-5614, Fax: 843-953-1434, E-mail: hinesl@cofc.edu. *Dean,* Dr. Clarence Condon, 843-953-1356, Fax: 843-953-5697.

School of Education Students: 119 full-time (104 women), 120 part-time (112 women); includes 29 minority (21 African Americans, 3 Asian Americans or Pacific Islanders, 5 Hispanic Americans), 1 international. Average age 30. 113 applicants, 60% accepted, 59 enrolled. *Faculty:* 26 full-time (17 women), 6 part-time/adjunct (4 women). Expenses: Contact institution. *Financial support:* Research assistantships, teaching assistantships, career-related internships or fieldwork and Federal Work-Study available. Support available to part-time students. Financial award application deadline: 4/1; financial award applicants required to submit FAFSA. In 2001, 93 degrees awarded. *Degree program information:* Part-time and evening/weekend programs available. Offers early childhood education (M Ed, MAT); education (M Ed, MAT); elementary education (M Ed, MAT); science and mathematics for teachers (M Ed); special education (M Ed, MAT). *Application deadline:* Applications are processed on a rolling basis. *Application fee:* $35. *Application Contact:* Laura H. Hines, Graduate School Coordinator, 843-953-5614, Fax: 843-953-1434, E-mail: hinesl@cofc.edu. *Dean,* Dr. Nancy Sorenson, 843-953-5613, Fax: 843-953-5407.

School of Humanities and Social Sciences Students: 35 full-time (24 women), 50 part-time (36 women); includes 15 minority (3 African Americans, 2 Asian Americans or Pacific Islanders, 10 Hispanic Americans), 3 international. Average age 29. 66 applicants, 41% accepted, 23 enrolled. *Faculty:* 73 full-time (24 women), 6 part-time/adjunct (2 women). Expenses: Contact institution. *Financial support:* Fellowships, research assistantships, career-related internships or fieldwork and Federal Work-Study available. Support available to part-time students. Financial award applicants required to submit FAFSA. In 2001, 35 degrees awarded. *Degree program information:* Part-time and evening/weekend programs available. Offers bilingual legal interpreting (MA); English (MA); history (MA); humanities and social sciences (MA, MPA); public affairs and policy studies (MPA). *Application Contact:* Laura H. Hines, Graduate School Coordinator, 843-953-5614, Fax: 843-953-1434, E-mail: hinesl@cofc.edu. *Dean,* Dr. Samuel M. Hines, 843-953-5770, Fax: 843-953-5818.

School of Sciences and Mathematics Students: 85 full-time (54 women), 71 part-time (32 women); includes 12 minority (1 African American, 10 Asian Americans or Pacific Islanders, 1 Hispanic American), 7 international. Average age 27. 140 applicants, 45% accepted, 60 enrolled. *Faculty:* 116 full-time (23 women), 17 part-time/adjunct (7 women). Expenses: Contact institution. *Financial support:* Fellowships, research assistantships, teaching assistantships, career-related internships or fieldwork, Federal Work-Study, and institutionally sponsored loans available. Support available to part-time students. Financial award applicants required to submit FAFSA. In 2001, 41 degrees awarded. Offers environmental studies (MS); marine biology (MS); mathematics (MS); sciences and mathematics (MS). *Application deadline:* Applications are processed on a rolling basis. *Dean,* Dr. Gordon Jones, 843-953-5991.

See in-depth description on page 811.

COLLEGE OF EMMANUEL AND ST. CHAD, Saskatoon, SK S7N 0W6, Canada

General Information Independent-religious, coed, comprehensive institution. *Enrollment:* 16 full-time matriculated graduate/professional students (10 women), 3 part-time matriculated graduate/professional students. *Enrollment by degree level:* 16 first professional, 3 master's. *Graduate faculty:* 4 full-time (1 woman), 4 part-time/adjunct (1 woman). *Tuition:* Part-time $400 per credit. *Graduate housing:* Room and/or apartments available on a first-come, first-served basis to single students; on-campus housing not available to married students. Typical cost: $1,710 (including board). Housing application deadline: 6/15. *Student services:* Campus employment opportunities, campus safety program, career counseling, free psychological counseling, international student services, writing training. *Library facilities:* H. E. Sellers Library plus 11 others. *Collection:* 15,000 titles, 93 serial subscriptions.

Computer facilities: 1 computer available on campus for general student use. *Web address:* http://www.usask.ca/stu/emmanuel.

General Application Contact: Colleen Walker, Registrar's Assistant, 306-975-1558, Fax: 306-934-2683, E-mail: colleen.walker@usask.edu.

GRADUATE UNITS

Bachelor of Theology Program *Degree program information:* Part-time programs available. Postbaccalaureate distance learning degree programs offered (minimal on-campus study). Offers theology (B Th).

Graduate Programs *Degree program information:* Part-time programs available. Offers theology (M Div, MTS, STM).

COLLEGE OF MOUNT ST. JOSEPH, Cincinnati, OH 45233-1670

General Information Independent-religious, coed, comprehensive institution. *Enrollment:* 38 full-time matriculated graduate/professional students (27 women), 164 part-time matriculated graduate/professional students (121 women). *Enrollment by degree level:* 202 master's. *Graduate faculty:* 20 full-time (13 women). *Tuition:* Full-time $9,168; part-time $382 per credit hour. *Required fees:* $45 per semester. Tuition and fees vary according to program and reciprocity agreements. *Graduate housing:* Room and/or apartments available on a first-come, first-served basis to single students; on-campus housing not available to married students. Housing application deadline: 7/1. *Student services:* Campus employment opportunities, campus safety program, career counseling, child daycare facilities, disabled student services, exercise/wellness program, free psychological counseling, international student services, low-cost health insurance, multicultural affairs office, teacher training, writing training. *Library facilities:* Archbishop Alter Library. *Online resources:* library catalog, web page, access to other libraries' catalogs. *Collection:* 97,637 titles, 4,960 serial subscriptions, 1,305 audiovisual materials.

Computer facilities: 227 computers available on campus for general student use. A campuswide network can be accessed from student residence rooms and from off campus. Internet access and online class registration, computer-aided instruction are available. *Web address:* http://www.msj.edu/.

General Application Contact: Peggy Minnich, Director of Admission, 513-244-4814, Fax: 513-244-4601, E-mail: peggy_minnich@mail.msj.edu.

GRADUATE UNITS

Education Department *Faculty:* 11 full-time (7 women). Expenses: Contact institution. *Financial support:* In 2001–02, 52 students received support. Institutionally sponsored loans and scholarships/grants available. Support available to part-time students. Financial award application deadline: 6/1. In 2001, 16 degrees awarded. *Degree program information:* Part-time and evening/weekend programs available. Offers art (MA Ed); education (MA Ed); inclusive early childhood education (MA Ed); professional development (MA Ed); professional foundations (MA Ed); reading (MA Ed); special education (MA Ed). *Application deadline:* Applications are processed on a rolling basis. *Application fee:* $0. Electronic applications accepted. *Application Contact:* Marion Albertz, Graduate Secretary, 513-244-4801, Fax: 513-244-4867, E-mail: marion_albertz@mail.msj.edu. *Chair,* Dr. Clarissa Enio Rosas, 513-244-4858, Fax: 513-244-4867, E-mail: clarissa_rosas@mail.msj.edu.

Interdisciplinary Program in Organizational Leadership *Faculty:* 2 full-time (1 woman). Expenses: Contact institution. Offers organizational leadership (MS). *Application deadline:* Applications are processed on a rolling basis. Electronic applications accepted. *Director,* Dr. Lonnie Supnick, 513-244-4330, E-mail: lonnie_supnick@mail.msj.edu.

Physical Therapy Department Students: 38 full-time (27 women); includes 1 minority (Asian American or Pacific Islander) *Faculty:* 5 full-time (4 women). Expenses: Contact institution. In 2001, 25 degrees awarded. Offers physical therapy (MPT). *Application deadline:* Applications are processed on a rolling basis. Electronic applications accepted. *Application Contact:* Dr. Terri Glenn, Program Director, 513-244-4826, E-mail: terri_glenn@mail.msj.edu. *Chair, Health Science,* Dr. Gene Kritzky, 513-244-4891, Fax: 513-244-2547.

Religious Studies Department *Faculty:* 4 full-time (2 women). Expenses: Contact institution. In 2001, 4 degrees awarded. Offers religious studies (MA); spiritual and pastoral care (MA). *Application deadline:* For fall admission, 8/1. Applications are processed on a rolling basis. *Application fee:* $0. Electronic applications accepted. *Chair,* Dr. John Trokan, 513-244-4272, Fax: 513-244-4222, E-mail: john_trokan@mail.msj.edu.

See in-depth description on page 813.

COLLEGE OF MOUNT SAINT VINCENT, Riverdale, NY 10471-1093

General Information Independent, coed, comprehensive institution. *Enrollment:* 20 full-time matriculated graduate/professional students, 525 part-time matriculated graduate/professional students. *Enrollment by degree level:* 545 master's. *Graduate faculty:* 19 full-time (16 women), 6 part-time/adjunct (4 women). *Tuition:* Part-time $496 per credit. *Graduate housing:* Room and/or apartments available on a first-come, first-served basis to single students; on-campus housing not available to married students. Typical cost: $7,030 (including board). *Student services:* Campus employment opportunities, career counseling, exercise/wellness program, free psychological counseling, international student services, low-cost health insurance, teacher training, writing training. *Library facilities:* Elizabeth Seton Library. *Online resources:* library catalog, web page, access to other libraries' catalogs. *Collection:* 169,529 titles, 616 serial subscriptions, 6,642 audiovisual materials. *Research affiliation:* New York Zoological Society.

Computer facilities: 150 computers available on campus for general student use. A campuswide network can be accessed from student residence rooms and from off campus. E-mail available. *Web address:* http://www.cmsv.edu/.

General Application Contact: Alice E. Wylie, Associate Director of Transfer and Graduate Admissions, 718-405-3267, Fax: 718-549-7945, E-mail: admissions@cmsv.edu.

GRADUATE UNITS

Division of Nursing *Degree program information:* Part-time and evening/weekend programs available. Offers adult nurse practitioner (MSN, PMC); clinical nurse specialist (MSN); family nurse practitioner (MSN, PMC); nursing administration (MSN); nursing for the adult and aged (MSN).

Program in Allied Health Studies Students: 7 full-time (all women), 43 part-time (35 women); includes 33 minority (19 African Americans, 1 Asian American or Pacific Islander, 13 Hispanic Americans) Average age 36. *Faculty:* 7 full-time (4 women), 4 part-time/adjunct (1 woman). Expenses: Contact institution. *Financial support:* Career-related internships or fieldwork available. Support available to part-time students. Financial award applicants required to submit FAFSA. In 2001, 14 master's, 2 other advanced degrees awarded. *Degree program information:* Part-time and evening/weekend programs available. Offers allied health studies (MS); counseling (Certificate); health care management (Certificate); health care systems and policies (Certificate). *Application deadline:* For fall admission, 8/1 (priority date); for winter admission, 11/1 (priority date); for spring admission, 1/1 (priority date). Applications are processed on a rolling basis. *Application fee:* $50. *Application Contact:* Director of Transfer and Graduate Admissions, 718-405-3267, Fax: 718-549-7945, E-mail: admissns@cmsv.edu. *Director,* Dr. Rita Scher Dytell, 718-405-3788, Fax: 718-405-3734, E-mail: rdytell@cmsv.edu.

Program in Education *Degree program information:* Part-time and evening/weekend programs available. Offers instructional technology and global perspectives (MS Ed, Certificate); middle level education (MS Ed, Certificate); multicultural studies (MS Ed, Certificate); urban and multicultural education (MS Ed, Certificate).

See in-depth description on page 815.

THE COLLEGE OF NEW JERSEY, Ewing, NJ 08628

General Information State-supported, coed, comprehensive institution. CGS member. *Enrollment:* 103 full-time matriculated graduate/professional students (86 women), 771 part-time matriculated graduate/professional students (629 women). *Enrollment by degree level:* 874 master's. *Graduate faculty:* 41 full-time, 12 part-time/adjunct. Tuition, state resident: full-time $6,981; part-time $387 per credit. Tuition, nonresident: full-time $9,772; part-time $542 per credit. *Required fees:* $1,011. *Graduate housing:* On-campus housing not available. *Student services:* Campus employment opportunities, career counseling, child daycare facilities, disabled student services, exercise/wellness program, free psychological counseling, international student services, low-cost health insurance. *Library facilities:* Roscoe L. West Library. *Online resources:* library catalog, web page. *Collection:* 520,000 titles, 4,700 serial subscriptions, 2,500 audiovisual materials.

Computer facilities: 800 computers available on campus for general student use. A campuswide network can be accessed from student residence rooms and from off campus. Internet access and online class registration are available. *Web address:* http://www.tcnj.edu/.

General Application Contact: Frank Cooper, Director, Office of Graduate Studies, 609-771-2300, Fax: 609-637-5105, E-mail: graduate@tcnj.edu.

GRADUATE UNITS

Graduate Division Students: 103 full-time (86 women), 771 part-time (629 women); includes 118 minority (60 African Americans, 11 Asian Americans or Pacific Islanders, 43 Hispanic Americans, 4 Native Americans), 70 international. Average age 26. 581 applicants, 74% accepted, 331 enrolled. *Faculty:* 41 full-time, 12 part-time/adjunct. Expenses: Contact institution. *Financial support:* In 2001–02, 85 research assistantships with full tuition reimbursements (averaging $3,000 per year) were awarded; career-related internships or fieldwork, Federal Work-Study, and unspecified assistantships also available. Support available to part-time students. Financial award application deadline: 5/1; financial award applicants required to submit FAFSA. In 2001, 325 degrees awarded. *Degree program information:* Part-time and evening/weekend programs available. *Application deadline:* For fall admission, 10/15; for spring admission, 4/15. *Application fee:* $50. *Application Contact:* Frank Cooper, Director, Office of Graduate Studies, 609-771-2300, Fax: 609-637-5105, E-mail: graduate@tcnj.edu. *Dean of Graduate Studies,* Dr. Suzanne Pasch, 609-771-2515, Fax: 609-637-5117, E-mail: pasch@tcnj.edu.

School of Culture and Society *Faculty:* 6 full-time. Expenses: Contact institution. *Financial support:* Unspecified assistantships available. Financial award application deadline: 5/1; financial award applicants required to submit FAFSA. In 2001, 10 degrees awarded. *Degree program information:* Part-time and evening/weekend programs available. Offers culture and society (MA); English (MA). *Application deadline:* For fall admission, 4/15; for spring admission, 10/15. *Application fee:* $50. *Application Contact:* Frank Cooper, Director, Office of Graduate Studies, 609-771-2300, Fax: 609-637-5105, E-mail: graduate@tcnj.edu. *Dean,* Dr. Susan Albertine, 609-771-3434, Fax: 609-637-5183.

School of Education Students: 102 full-time (87 women), 540 part-time (436 women); includes 87 minority (42 African Americans, 9 Asian Americans or Pacific Islanders, 33 Hispanic Americans, 3 Native Americans), 51 international. *Faculty:* 32 full-time, 12 part-time/adjunct. Expenses: Contact institution. *Financial support:* Unspecified assistantships available. Financial award application deadline: 5/1; financial award applicants required to submit FAFSA. In 2001, 285 degrees awarded. *Degree program information:* Part-time and evening/weekend programs available. Offers audiology (MA); community counseling: human services (MA); community counseling: substance abuse and addiction (MA, Certificate); developmental reading (M Ed); education (M Ed, MA, MAT, MS, Certificate, Ed S); educational leadership (M Ed); educational technology (MS); elementary education (M Ed, MAT); elementary teaching (MAT); English as a second language (M Ed); health (MAT); health education (M Ed, MAT); instructional computing coordinator (Certificate); marriage and family therapy (Ed S); physical education (M Ed, MAT); school counseling (MA); school personnel licensure: preschool-grade 3 (M Ed); secondary education (MAT); special education (M Ed, MAT); special education with learning disabilities (M Ed); speech pathology (MA); teaching English as a second language (M Ed, Certificate). *Application deadline:* For fall admission, 4/15; for spring admission, 10/15. *Application fee:* $50. *Application Contact:* Frank Cooper, Director, Office of Graduate Studies, 609-771-2300, Fax: 609-637-5105, E-mail: graduate@tcnj.edu. *Dean,* Dr. Terence O'Connor, 609-771-2155, Fax: 609-637-5117.

School of Nursing *Faculty:* 3. Expenses: Contact institution. *Financial support:* Unspecified assistantships available. Financial award application deadline: 5/1; financial award applicants required to submit FAFSA. *Degree program information:* Part-time and evening/weekend programs available. Offers nursing (MSN); nursing: adult nurse practitioner (MSN); nursing: family nurse practitioner (MSN); school nurse certification (MSN). *Application deadline:* For fall admission, 3/15. *Application fee:* $50. *Application Contact:* Frank Cooper, Director, Office of Graduate Studies, 609-771-2300, Fax: 609-637-5105, E-mail: graduate@tcnj.edu. *Dean,* Dr. Susan Bakewell-Sachs, 609-771-2541, Fax: 609-637-5159, E-mail: sherwen@tcnj.edu.

See in-depth description on page 817.

THE COLLEGE OF NEW ROCHELLE, New Rochelle, NY 10805-2308

General Information Independent, women only, comprehensive institution. CGS member. *Graduate housing:* Room and/or apartments available on a first-come, first-served basis to single students; on-campus housing not available to married students. Housing application deadline: 8/1.

GRADUATE UNITS

Graduate School *Degree program information:* Part-time and evening/weekend programs available. Offers acute care nurse practitioner (MS, Certificate); art education (MA); art museum education (Certificate); art therapy (MS); clinical specialist in holistic nursing (MS, Certificate); communication studies (MS, Certificate); family nurse practitioner (MS, Certificate); fine art (MS); graphic art (MS); nursing and health care management (MS); nursing education (Certificate); studio art (MS).

Division of Education *Degree program information:* Part-time and evening/weekend programs available. Offers bilingual education (Certificate); elementary education/early childhood education (MS Ed); gifted education (MS Ed, Certificate); reading (MS Ed); reading/special education (MS Ed); school administration and supervision (MS Ed, Certificate, PD); special education (MS Ed); speech-language pathology (MS); teaching English as a second language (MS Ed, Certificate).

Division of Human Services *Degree program information:* Part-time and evening/weekend programs available. Offers career development (MS, Certificate); community-school psychology (MS); gerontology (MS, Certificate); guidance and counseling (MS); thanatology (Certificate).

See in-depth description on page 819.

COLLEGE OF NOTRE DAME OF MARYLAND, Baltimore, MD 21210-2476

General Information Independent-religious, women only, comprehensive institution. *Enrollment:* 140 full-time matriculated graduate/professional students (120 women), 1,200 part-time matriculated graduate/professional students (1,025 women). *Enrollment by degree level:* 1,340 master's. *Graduate faculty:* 40 full-time (25 women), 125 part-time/adjunct (100 women). *Tuition:* Part-time $320 per credit. *Required fees:* $30 per course. Full-time tuition and fees vary according to reciprocity agreements and student's religious affiliation. *Graduate housing:* On-campus housing not available. *Student services:* Campus safety program, career counseling, disabled student services, international student services, teacher training, writing training. *Library facilities:* Loyola/Notre Dame Library. *Online resources:* library catalog, web page, access to other libraries' catalogs.

Computer facilities: 80 computers available on campus for general student use. A campuswide network can be accessed from student residence rooms and from off campus. Internet access, online classroom assignments and information are available. *Web address:* http://www.ndm.edu/.

General Application Contact: Kathy Nikolaidis, Graduate Admissions Secretary, 410-532-5317, Fax: 410-532-5333, E-mail: gradadm@ndm.edu.

GRADUATE UNITS

Graduate Studies Average age 35. *Faculty:* 37 full-time (22 women), 83 part-time/adjunct (53 women). Expenses: Contact institution. *Financial support:* Career-related internships or fieldwork and institutionally sponsored loans available. Support available to part-time students. Financial award application deadline: 6/30; financial award applicants required to submit FAFSA. In 2001, 267 degrees awarded. *Degree program information:* Part-time and evening/weekend programs available. Offers communicating in contemporary culture (MA); leadership in teaching (MA); liberal studies (MA); management (MA); nonprofit management (MA); studies in aging (MA); teaching (MA); teaching English to speakers of other languages (MA). *Application deadline:* For fall admission, 8/15 (priority date); for winter admission, 12/15; for spring admission, 1/15. Applications are processed on a rolling basis. *Application fee:* $25. Electronic applications accepted. *Application Contact:* Kathy Nikolaidis, Graduate Admissions Secretary, 410-532-5317, Fax: 410-532-5333, E-mail: gradadm@ndm.edu. *Director,* Sr. Margaret E. Mahoney, 410-532-5316, Fax: 410-532-5333, E-mail: mmahoney@ndm.edu.

COLLEGE OF ST. CATHERINE, St. Paul, MN 55105-1789

General Information Independent-religious, women only, comprehensive institution. *Enrollment:* 589 full-time matriculated graduate/professional students (526 women), 433 part-time matriculated graduate/professional students (384 women). *Enrollment by degree level:* 1,022 master's. *Graduate faculty:* 93 full-time (74 women). *Tuition:* Part-time $375 per credit. *Required fees:* $60; $60 per year. Tuition and fees vary according to program. *Graduate housing:* Rooms and/or apartments available on a first-come, first-served basis to single and married students. Housing application deadline: 5/1. *Student services:* Campus employment opportunities, campus safety program, career counseling, free psychological counseling, international student services, low-cost health insurance, multicultural affairs office, writing training. *Library facilities:* St. Catherine Library plus 2 others. *Online resources:* library catalog, web page, access to other libraries' catalogs. *Collection:* 263,495 titles, 1,141 serial subscriptions, 13,627 audiovisual materials.

Computer facilities: 350 computers available on campus for general student use. A campuswide network can be accessed from student residence rooms and from off campus. Internet access, transcript are available. *Web address:* http://www.stkate.edu/.

General Application Contact: 651-690-6505.

GRADUATE UNITS

Graduate Program Students: 589 full-time (526 women), 433 part-time (384 women); includes 55 minority (19 African Americans, 14 Asian Americans or Pacific Islanders, 16 Hispanic Americans, 6 Native Americans), 6 international. Average age 35. 581 applicants, 78% accepted, 351 enrolled. *Faculty:* 93 full-time (74 women). Expenses: Contact institution. *Financial support:* In 2001–02, 485 students received support; research assistantships, career-related internships or fieldwork and institutionally sponsored loans available. Support available to part-time students. Financial award application deadline: 4/1; financial award applicants required to submit FAFSA. In 2001, 246 degrees awarded. *Degree program information:* Part-time and evening/weekend programs available. Offers education (MA); library and information science (MA); nursing (MA); occupational therapy (MA); organizational leadership (MA); physical therapy (MPT); social work (MSW); theology (MA). *Application fee:* $25. *Application Contact:* 651-690-6505. *Academic Dean,* Dr. Mary Margaret Smith, 651-690-6500, Fax: 651-690-6024.

See in-depth description on page 821.

COLLEGE OF SAINT ELIZABETH, Morristown, NJ 07960-6989

General Information Independent-religious, women only, comprehensive institution. *Enrollment:* 34 full-time matriculated graduate/professional students (30 women), 351 part-time matriculated graduate/professional students (313 women). *Enrollment by degree level:* 356 master's, 29 other advanced degrees. *Graduate faculty:* 18 full-time (14 women), 27 part-time/adjunct (16 women). *Tuition:* Full-time $8,100; part-time $450 per credit. *Required fees:* $195. Tuition and fees vary according to course load. *Graduate housing:* Room and/or apartments available on a first-come, first-served basis to single students; on-campus housing not available to married students. Typical cost: $7,200 (including board). Housing application deadline: 5/10. *Student services:* Campus employment opportunities, campus safety program, career counseling, disabled student services, international student services, low-cost health insurance. *Library facilities:* Mahoney Library. *Online resources:* library catalog. *Collection:* 169,765 titles, 852 serial subscriptions, 1,563 audiovisual materials. *Research affiliation:* National Institute of Mental Health (mental health service), KAP Foundation (religion), National Figure Skating Association (sports nutrition), Cornell University and University of Texas Houston (food biotechnology (attitude research)).

Computer facilities: 125 computers available on campus for general student use. A campuswide network can be accessed from student residence rooms and from off campus. Internet access is available. *Web address:* http://www.cse.edu/.

General Application Contact: Denise Yacullo, Director of Enrollment Management, 973-290-4112, Fax: 973-290-4167, E-mail: dyacullo@cse.edu.

GRADUATE UNITS

Department of Business Administration/Economics Students: 5 full-time (3 women), 100 part-time (91 women); includes 8 minority (1 African American, 1 Asian American or Pacific Islander, 5 Hispanic Americans, 1 Native American), 1 international. Average age 36. 25 applicants, 100% accepted, 20 enrolled. *Faculty:* 2 full-time (1 woman), 7 part-time/adjunct (4 women). Expenses: Contact institution. *Financial support:* Career-related internships or fieldwork, tuition waivers (partial), and unspecified assistantships available. Support available to part-time students. Financial award application deadline: 3/15; financial award applicants required to submit FAFSA. In 2001, 19 degrees awarded. *Degree program information:* Part-time and evening/weekend programs available. Offers management (MS). *Application deadline:* Applications are processed on a rolling basis. *Application fee:* $35. Electronic applications accepted. *Director of the Graduate Program in Management,* Dr. Peter Schneider, 973-290-4113, Fax: 973-290-4177, E-mail: pschneider@cse.edu.

Department of Education Students: 1 (woman) full-time, 102 part-time (93 women); includes 6 minority (4 African Americans, 1 Asian American or Pacific Islander, 1 Native American) Average age 39. 9 applicants, 89% accepted, 8 enrolled. *Faculty:* 4 full-time (3 women), 10 part-time/adjunct (6 women). Expenses: Contact institution. *Financial support:* In 2001–02, 22 students received support. Career-related internships or fieldwork, Federal Work-Study, tuition waivers (partial), and unspecified assistantships available. Support available to part-time students. Financial award application deadline: 3/15; financial award applicants required to submit FAFSA. In 2001, 20 master's, 6 other advanced degrees awarded. *Degree program information:* Part-time and evening/weekend programs available. Offers administration and supervision for teachers (Certificate); education: human services leadership (MA); educational technology (MA). *Application deadline:* For fall admission, 6/30 (priority date); for spring admission, 11/30. Applications are processed on a rolling basis. *Application fee:* $35. Electronic applications accepted. *Director of Graduate Education Programs,* Dr. Joan T. Walters, SC, 973-290-4374, Fax: 973-290-4389, E-mail: jwalters@cse.edu.

Department of Foods and Nutrition Students: 17 full-time (all women), 25 part-time (23 women); includes 10 minority (4 African Americans, 3 Asian Americans or Pacific Islanders, 3 Hispanic Americans), 1 international. 70 applicants, 43% accepted, 27 enrolled. *Faculty:* 2 full-time (both women), 5 part-time/adjunct (3 women). Expenses: Contact institution. *Financial support:* In 2001–02, 2 students received support. Federal Work-Study, tuition waivers (partial), and unspecified assistantships available. Support available to part-time students. Financial award application deadline: 3/15; financial award applicants required to submit FAFSA. In 2001, 9 master's, 18 other advanced degrees awarded. *Degree program information:* Part-time and evening/weekend programs available. Offers dietetic internship (Certificate); nutrition (MS). *Application deadline:* Applications are processed on a rolling basis. *Application fee:* $35. Electronic applications accepted. *Director of the Graduate Program in Nutrition,* Dr. Marie Struble, 973-290-4176, Fax: 973-290-4167, E-mail: nutrition@cse.edu.

Department of Health Professions and Related Sciences Students: 1 (woman) full-time, 45 part-time (43 women); includes 8 minority (4 African Americans, 3 Asian Americans or Pacific Islanders, 1 Hispanic American) Average age 43. 4 applicants, 100% accepted, 3 enrolled. *Faculty:* 3 full-time (2 women), 7 part-time/adjunct (4 women). Expenses: Contact institution. *Financial support:* In 2001–02, 1 student received support. Career-related internships or fieldwork, tuition waivers (partial), and unspecified assistantships available. Support available to part-time students. Financial award application deadline: 3/15; financial award applicants required to submit FAFSA. In 2001, 11 degrees awarded. *Degree program information:* Part-time and evening/weekend programs available. Offers health care management (MS). *Application deadline:* Applications are processed on a rolling basis. *Application*

College of Saint Elizabeth (continued)

fee: $35. Electronic applications accepted. *Director of the Graduate Program in Health Care Management*, Linda Hunter, 973-290-4040, Fax: 973-290-4167, E-mail: lhunter@cse.edu.

Department of Philosophy/Theology Average age 52. 10 applicants, 100% accepted, 10 enrolled. *Faculty:* 2 full-time (1 woman), 1 (woman) part-time/adjunct. Expenses: Contact institution. *Financial support:* In 2001–02, 10 students received support. Tuition waivers (partial) and unspecified assistantships available. Support available to part-time students. Financial award applicants required to submit FAFSA. In 2001, 7 degrees awarded. *Degree program information:* Part-time and evening/weekend programs available. Offers theology (MA). *Application deadline:* For fall admission, 3/1 (priority date); for spring admission, 9/1. Applications are processed on a rolling basis. *Application fee:* $35. Electronic applications accepted. *Director of the Graduate Program in Theology*, Sr. Ellen Joyce, 973-290-4371, Fax: 973-290-4312, E-mail: ejoyce@cse.edu.

Department of Psychology Students: 10 full-time (8 women), 41 part-time (38 women); includes 11 minority (6 African Americans, 1 Asian American or Pacific Islander, 4 Hispanic Americans), 1 international. Average age 38. 16 applicants, 100% accepted, 10 enrolled. *Faculty:* 5 full-time (4 women), 10 part-time/adjunct (5 women). Expenses: Contact institution. *Financial support:* In 2001–02, 1 student received support. Career-related internships or fieldwork, tuition waivers (partial), and unspecified assistantships available. Support available to part-time students. Financial award application deadline: 3/15; financial award applicants required to submit FAFSA. In 2001, 13 degrees awarded. *Degree program information:* Part-time and evening/weekend programs available. Offers counseling psychology (MA). *Application deadline:* For fall admission, 4/14 (priority date); for spring admission, 11/15. Applications are processed on a rolling basis. *Application fee:* $35. Electronic applications accepted. *Director of the Graduate Program in Counseling Psychology*, Dr. Valerie Scott, 973-290-4102, Fax: 973-290-4676, E-mail: vscott@cse.edu.

COLLEGE OF ST. JOSEPH, Rutland, VT 05701-3899

General Information Independent-religious, coed, comprehensive institution. *Enrollment:* 47 full-time matriculated graduate/professional students (36 women), 119 part-time matriculated graduate/professional students (82 women). *Enrollment by degree level:* 166 master's. *Graduate faculty:* 6 full-time (2 women), 10 part-time/adjunct (6 women). *Tuition:* Full-time $9,000; part-time $250 per credit. *Required fees:* $45 per semester. Part-time tuition and fees vary according to course load. *Graduate housing:* Room and/or apartments available on a first-come, first-served basis to single students; on-campus housing not available to married students. Typical cost: $6,300 (including board). Housing application deadline: 5/1. *Student services:* Career counseling, free psychological counseling, low-cost health insurance. *Library facilities:* St. Joseph Library plus 1 other. *Online resources:* library catalog, access to other libraries' catalogs. *Collection:* 45,000 titles, 256 serial subscriptions, 5,504 audiovisual materials.

Computer facilities: 30 computers available on campus for general student use. A campuswide network can be accessed from student residence rooms. Internet access is available. *Web address:* http://www.csj.edu/.

General Application Contact: Steve Soba, Dean of Admissions, 802-773-5900 Ext. 3206, Fax: 802-773-5900, E-mail: ssoba@csj.edu.

GRADUATE UNITS

Graduate Program Students: 47 full-time (36 women), 119 part-time (82 women); includes 3 minority (2 African Americans, 1 Asian American or Pacific Islander) Average age 34. *Faculty:* 6 full-time (2 women), 10 part-time/adjunct (6 women). Expenses: Contact institution. *Financial support:* In 2001–02, 7 students received support. Career-related internships or fieldwork, Federal Work-Study, and unspecified assistantships available. Support available to part-time students. Financial award application deadline: 3/1. In 2001, 45 degrees awarded. *Degree program information:* Part-time and evening/weekend programs available. Postbaccalaureate distance learning degree programs offered (minimal on-campus study). Offers business (MBA); business administration (MBA). *Application deadline:* Applications are processed on a rolling basis. *Application fee:* $35. *Application Contact:* Steve Soba, Dean of Admissions, 802-773-5900 Ext. 3206, Fax: 802-773-5900, E-mail: ssoba@csj.edu. *President*, Dr. Frank Miglorie, 802-773-5900.

Division of Education Students: 33 full-time, 38 part-time. Average age 34. *Faculty:* 3 full-time (2 women), 5 part-time/adjunct (all women). Expenses: Contact institution. *Financial support:* Career-related internships or fieldwork, Federal Work-Study, and unspecified assistantships available. Support available to part-time students. Financial award application deadline: 3/1. In 2001, 38 degrees awarded. *Degree program information:* Part-time and evening/weekend programs available. Offers elementary education (M Ed); general education (M Ed); reading (M Ed); special education (M Ed). *Application deadline:* Applications are processed on a rolling basis. *Application fee:* $35. *Application Contact:* Steve Soba, Dean of Admissions, 802-773-5900 Ext. 3206, Fax: 802-773-5900, E-mail: ssoba@csj.edu. *Chair*, Dr. Kapi Reith, 802-773-5900 Ext. 3243, Fax: 802-773-5900, E-mail: kreith@csj.edu.

Division of Psychology and Human Services Students: 14 full-time, 32 part-time; includes 3 minority (2 African Americans, 1 Asian American or Pacific Islander) Average age 34. *Faculty:* 3 full-time (0 women), 6 part-time/adjunct (3 women). Expenses: Contact institution. *Financial support:* Career-related internships or fieldwork, Federal Work-Study, and unspecified assistantships available. Support available to part-time students. Financial award application deadline: 3/1. In 2001, 7 degrees awarded. *Degree program information:* Part-time and evening/weekend programs available. Offers clinical psychology (MS); community counseling (MS); school guidance counseling (MS). *Application deadline:* Applications are processed on a rolling basis. *Application fee:* $35. *Application Contact:* Steve Soba, Dean of Admissions, 802-773-5900 Ext. 3206, Fax: 802-773-5900, E-mail: ssoba@csj.edu. *Chair*, Dr. Craig Knapp, 802-773-5900 Ext. 3219, Fax: 802-773-5900, E-mail: cknapp@csj.edu.

THE COLLEGE OF SAINT ROSE, Albany, NY 12203-1419

General Information Independent, coed, comprehensive institution. CGS member. *Enrollment:* 301 full-time matriculated graduate/professional students (238 women), 1,254 part-time matriculated graduate/professional students (913 women). *Enrollment by degree level:* 1,479 master's, 76 other advanced degrees. *Graduate faculty:* 159 full-time (90 women), 212 part-time/adjunct (123 women). *Tuition:* Full-time $8,712. *Required fees:* $190. *Graduate housing:* On-campus housing not available. *Student services:* Campus employment opportunities, campus safety program, career counseling, disabled student services, free psychological counseling, international student services, multicultural affairs office. *Library facilities:* Neil Hellman Library plus 1 other. *Online resources:* library catalog, web page. *Collection:* 200,987 titles, 975 serial subscriptions, 1,089 audiovisual materials.

Computer facilities: 322 computers available on campus for general student use. A campuswide network can be accessed from student residence rooms and from off campus. Internet access and online class registration are available. *Web address:* http://www.strose.edu/.

General Application Contact: Anne Tully, Dean of Graduate and Adult and Continuing Education Admissions, 518-454-5136, Fax: 518-458-5479, E-mail: ace@mail.strose.edu.

GRADUATE UNITS

Graduate Studies Students: 301 full-time (238 women), 1,254 part-time (913 women); includes 76 minority (35 African Americans, 17 Asian Americans or Pacific Islanders, 20 Hispanic Americans, 4 Native Americans), 54 international. Average age 30. 621 applicants, 90% accepted, 425 enrolled. *Faculty:* 159 full-time (90 women), 212 part-time/adjunct (123 women). Expenses: Contact institution. *Financial support:* Research assistantships, career-related internships or fieldwork and tuition waivers (partial) available. Support available to part-time students. Financial award application deadline: 3/1; financial award applicants required to submit FAFSA. In 2001, 505 master's, 18 other advanced degrees awarded. *Degree program information:* Part-time and evening/weekend programs available. *Application deadline:* Applications are processed on a rolling basis. *Application fee:* $30. *Application Contact:* Anne Tully, Dean of Graduate and Adult and Continuing Education Admissions, 518-454-5136, Fax: 518-458-5479, E-mail: ace@mail.strose.edu. *Vice President of Academic Affairs*, Dr. William Lowe, 518-454-5160, Fax: 518-337-2039.

School of Arts and Humanities Students: 12 full-time (5 women), 127 part-time (79 women); includes 5 minority (1 African American, 1 Asian American or Pacific Islander, 2 Hispanic Americans, 1 Native American), 4 international. Average age 32. 62 applicants, 89% accepted, 37 enrolled. *Faculty:* 58 full-time (32 women), 77 part-time/adjunct (42 women). Expenses: Contact institution. *Financial support:* Research assistantships, career-related internships or fieldwork and tuition waivers (partial) available. Support available to part-time students. Financial award application deadline: 3/1; financial award applicants required to submit FAFSA. In 2001, 37 degrees awarded. *Degree program information:* Part-time and evening/weekend programs available. Offers art education (MS Ed); arts and humanities (MA, MS Ed); English (MA); history/political science (MA); music (MA); music education (MS Ed); public communications (MA). *Application deadline:* For fall admission, 7/15 (priority date); for spring admission, 12/1 (priority date). Applications are processed on a rolling basis. *Application fee:* $30. *Application Contact:* 518-454-5136, Fax: 518-458-5479, E-mail: ace@mail.strose.edu.

School of Business Students: 28 full-time (15 women), 147 part-time (71 women); includes 13 minority (7 African Americans, 4 Asian Americans or Pacific Islanders, 2 Hispanic Americans), 10 international. Average age 33. 82 applicants, 100% accepted, 63 enrolled. *Faculty:* 15 full-time (8 women). Expenses: Contact institution. *Financial support:* Research assistantships, tuition waivers (partial) available. Support available to part-time students. Financial award application deadline: 3/1; financial award applicants required to submit FAFSA. In 2001, 32 degrees awarded. *Degree program information:* Part-time and evening/weekend programs available. Offers accounting (MS); business (MBA, MS, Certificate); business administration (MBA); not-for-profit management (Certificate). *Application deadline:* For fall admission, 7/15 (priority date); for spring admission, 12/1. Applications are processed on a rolling basis. *Application fee:* $30. *Application Contact:* 518-454-5136, Fax: 518-458-5479, E-mail: ace@mail.strose.edu. *Dean*, Dr. Severin C. Carlson, 518-454-2122.

School of Education Students: 260 full-time (217 women), 938 part-time (745 women); includes 47 minority (21 African Americans, 7 Asian Americans or Pacific Islanders, 16 Hispanic Americans, 3 Native Americans), 38 international. Average age 31. 465 applicants, 89% accepted, 314 enrolled. *Faculty:* 49 full-time (29 women), 78 part-time/adjunct (54 women). Expenses: Contact institution. *Financial support:* Research assistantships, career-related internships or fieldwork and tuition waivers (partial) available. Support available to part-time students. Financial award application deadline: 3/1; financial award applicants required to submit FAFSA. In 2001, 427 master's, 18 Certificates awarded. *Degree program information:* Part-time and evening/weekend programs available. Offers applied technology (Certificate); applied technology education (Certificate); college student personnel (MS Ed); communication disorders (MS Ed); community counseling (MS Ed); counseling (MS Ed); early childhood education (MS Ed); education (MS Ed, Certificate); educational administration and supervision (MS Ed, Certificate); educational computing (Certificate); educational psychology (MS Ed); elementary education (MS Ed); reading (MS Ed); school counseling (MS Ed); school psychology (MS Ed, Certificate); secondary education (MS Ed); special education (MS Ed); teacher education (MS Ed, Certificate). *Application deadline:* Applications are processed on a rolling basis. *Application fee:* $30. *Application Contact:* 518-454-5136, Fax: 518-458-5479, E-mail: ace@mail.strose.edu. *Dean*, Dr. Crystal J. Gips, 518-454-2147, Fax: 518-454-2083, E-mail: gipsc@mail.strose.edu.

School of Mathematics and Sciences Students: 1 (woman) full-time, 41 part-time (18 women); includes 10 minority (5 African Americans, 5 Asian Americans or Pacific Islanders), 2 international. Average age 34. 12 applicants, 92% accepted, 11 enrolled. *Faculty:* 31 full-time (18 women), 40 part-time/adjunct (19 women). Expenses: Contact institution. *Financial support:* Research assistantships, career-related internships or fieldwork and tuition waivers (partial) available. Support available to part-time students. Financial award application deadline: 3/1; financial award applicants required to submit FAFSA. In 2001, 9 degrees awarded. *Degree program information:* Part-time and evening/weekend programs available. Offers computer information systems (MS); mathematics and sciences (MS). *Application deadline:* For fall admission, 7/15 (priority date); for spring admission, 12/1 (priority date). Applications are processed on a rolling basis. *Application fee:* $30. Electronic applications accepted. *Application Contact:* 518-454-5136, Fax: 518-458-5479, E-mail: ace@mail.strose.edu. *Dean*, Dr. David Amey, 518-337-2332, E-mail: ameyd@mail.strose.edu.

See in-depth description on page 823.

THE COLLEGE OF ST. SCHOLASTICA, Duluth, MN 55811-4199

General Information Independent-religious, coed, comprehensive institution. *Enrollment:* 194 full-time matriculated graduate/professional students (141 women), 305 part-time matriculated graduate/professional students (218 women). *Graduate faculty:* 36 full-time (17 women), 31 part-time/adjunct (23 women). *Tuition:* Part-time $565 per credit. Tuition and fees vary according to course load and program. *Graduate housing:* Room and/or apartments available on a first-come, first-served basis to single students; on-campus housing not available to married students. Typical cost: $3,600 per year ($5,198 including board). *Student services:* Campus employment opportunities, campus safety program, career counseling, child daycare facilities, disabled student services, free psychological counseling, international student services. *Library facilities:* College of St. Scholastica Library plus 1 other. *Online resources:* library catalog, web page, access to other libraries' catalogs. *Collection:* 122,492 titles, 828 serial subscriptions.

Computer facilities: 160 computers available on campus for general student use. A campuswide network can be accessed from student residence rooms and from off campus. Internet access is available. *Web address:* http://www.css.edu/.

General Application Contact: Kathy D. Stinnett, Graduate Administrative Assistant, 218-723-6285, Fax: 218-723-6290, E-mail: kstinnet@css.edu.

GRADUATE UNITS

Graduate Studies Students: 194 full-time (141 women), 305 part-time (218 women); includes 8 minority (3 African Americans, 2 Asian Americans or Pacific Islanders, 1 Hispanic American, 2 Native Americans), 4 international. Average age 32. 658 applicants, 88% accepted, 499 enrolled. *Faculty:* 36 full-time (17 women), 31 part-time/adjunct (23 women). Expenses: Contact institution. *Financial support:* In 2001–02, 284 students received support. Scholarships/grants and traineeships available. Support available to part-time students. Financial award applicants required to submit FAFSA. In 2001, 250 degrees awarded. *Degree program information:* Part-time and evening/weekend programs available. Postbaccalaureate distance learning degree programs offered (minimal on-campus study). Offers education (M Ed); educational media and technology (M Ed); exercise physiology (MA); health information management (MA); management (MA); nursing (MA); occupational therapy (MA); physical therapy (MA). *Application deadline:* Applications are processed on a rolling basis. *Application fee:* $50. Electronic applications accepted. *Application Contact:* Kathy D. Stinnett, Graduate Administrative Assistant, 218-723-6285, Fax: 218-723-6290, E-mail: kstinnet@css.edu. *Interim Director*, Dr. Cecelia Taylor, 218-723-6024, Fax: 218-723-5991, E-mail: ctaylor@css.edu.

COLLEGE OF SANTA FE, Santa Fe, NM 87505-7634

General Information Independent, coed, comprehensive institution. *Graduate housing:* Room and/or apartments available on a first-come, first-served basis to single students; on-campus housing not available to married students.

GRADUATE UNITS

Department of Business Administration *Degree program information:* Part-time and evening/weekend programs available. Offers business administration (MBA). Program also available at Albuquerque campus.

Department of Education *Degree program information:* Part-time and evening/weekend programs available. Offers at-risk youth (MA); bilingual/multicultural education (MA); classroom teaching (MA); community counseling (MA); educational administration (MA); leadership (MA); multicultural special education (MA); school counseling (MA).

COLLEGE OF STATEN ISLAND OF THE CITY UNIVERSITY OF NEW YORK, Staten Island, NY 10314-6600

General Information State and locally supported, coed, comprehensive institution. *Enrollment:* 82 full-time matriculated graduate/professional students (41 women), 862 part-time matriculated graduate/professional students (689 women). *Enrollment by degree level:* 844 master's, 100 other advanced degrees. *Graduate faculty:* 116 full-time (43 women), 52 part-time/adjunct (21 women). Tuition, state resident: full-time $4,350; part-time $185 per credit. Tuition, nonresident: full-time $7,600; part-time $320 per credit. *Required fees:* $53 per semester. *Graduate housing:* On-campus housing not available. *Student services:* Campus employment opportunities, campus safety program, career counseling, child daycare facilities, disabled student services, exercise/wellness program, free psychological counseling, international student services, low-cost health insurance, multicultural affairs office, teacher training. *Library facilities:* College of Staten Island Library. *Online resources:* library catalog, web page, access to other libraries' catalogs. *Collection:* 203,368 titles, 11,074 serial subscriptions, 14,350 audiovisual materials. *Research affiliation:* Institute for Basic Research (developmental neurosciences).

Computer facilities: 120 computers available on campus for general student use. A campuswide network can be accessed from off campus. Internet access is available. *Web address:* http://www.csi.cuny.edu/.

General Application Contact: Mary Beth Reilly, Director of Admissions, 718-982-2010, Fax: 718-982-2500, E-mail: reilly@postbox.csi.cuny.edu.

GRADUATE UNITS

Graduate Programs Students: 82 full-time (41 women), 862 part-time (689 women); includes 103 minority (36 African Americans, 34 Asian Americans or Pacific Islanders, 28 Hispanic Americans, 5 Native Americans) Average age 33. *Faculty:* 116 full-time (43 women), 52 part-time/adjunct (21 women). Expenses: Contact institution. *Financial support:* Fellowships, research assistantships, teaching assistantships, career-related internships or fieldwork, Federal Work-Study, institutionally sponsored loans, traineeships, tuition waivers (full and partial), and unspecified assistantships available. Support available to part-time students. In 2001, 331 master's, 44 other advanced degrees awarded. *Degree program information:* Part-time and evening/weekend programs available. Offers adult health nursing (MS); biology (MS); cinema studies (MA); computer science (MS, PhD); educational supervision and administration (6th Year Certificate); elementary education (MS Ed); English (MA); environmental science (MS); history (MA); liberal studies (MA); physical therapy (MS); polymer chemistry (PhD); secondary education (MS Ed); special education (MS Ed). *Application deadline:* Applications are processed on a rolling basis. *Application fee:* $40. *Application Contact:* Mary Beth Reilly, Director of Admissions, 718-982-2010, Fax: 718-982-2500, E-mail: reilly@postbox.csi.cuny.edu. *Senior Vice President for Academic Affairs and Provost,* Dr. Mirella Affron, 718-982-2440, Fax: 718-982-2442, E-mail: affron@postbox.csi.cuny.edu.

Center for Developmental Neuroscience and Developmental Disabilities Expenses: Contact institution. *Financial support:* Fellowships, research assistantships, teaching assistantships, career-related internships or fieldwork and institutionally sponsored loans available. Offers biology (PhD); biopsychology (PhD); clinical psychology (PhD); developmental psychology (PhD); environmental psychology (PhD); experimental cognition (PhD); experimental psychology (PhD); learning processes (PhD); neuropsychology (PhD); neuroscience (PhD); psychology (PhD); social-personality psychology (PhD). *Application deadline:* Applications are processed on a rolling basis. *Application fee:* $40. *Deputy Director,* Dr. Ekkehart Trenkner, 718-982-3952, Fax: 718-982-3953, E-mail: trenkner@postbox.csi.cuny.edu.

See in-depth description on page 825.

COLLEGE OF THE ATLANTIC, Bar Harbor, ME 04609-1198

General Information Independent, coed, comprehensive institution. *Enrollment:* 5 full-time matriculated graduate/professional students (4 women). *Enrollment by degree level:* 5 master's. *Graduate faculty:* 22 full-time (6 women), 6 part-time/adjunct (3 women). *Tuition:* Full-time $14,844. *Required fees:* $270. *Graduate housing:* Room and/or apartments available to single students; on-campus housing not available to married students. Typical cost: $3,777 per year ($6,100 including board). Housing application deadline: 6/1. *Student services:* Campus employment opportunities, campus safety program, career counseling, grant writing training, international student services. *Library facilities:* Thorndike Library. *Online resources:* library catalog, web page, access to other libraries' catalogs. *Collection:* 35,000 titles, 475 serial subscriptions, 1,579 audiovisual materials. *Research affiliation:* Acadia National Park, National Park Service (research management, environmental education), Mount Desert Island Biological Laboratory, Jackson Laboratory (genetics), Society for Human Ecology (ecological decision making in society).

Computer facilities: 48 computers available on campus for general student use. A campuswide network can be accessed from student residence rooms and from off campus. *Web address:* http://www.coa.edu/.

General Application Contact: Dr. John G. Anderson, Dean for Advanced Studies, 207-288-5015 Ext. 269, Fax: 207-288-3780, E-mail: jga@ecology.coa.edu.

GRADUATE UNITS

Program in Human Ecology Offers human ecology (M Phil). Electronic applications accepted.

Program in Human Ecology Offers human ecology (M Phil).

COLLEGE OF THE SOUTHWEST, Hobbs, NM 88240-9129

General Information Independent, coed, comprehensive institution. *Enrollment:* 76 full-time matriculated graduate/professional students (62 women), 124 part-time matriculated graduate/professional students (99 women). *Enrollment by degree level:* 200 master's. *Graduate faculty:* 5 full-time (4 women), 10 part-time/adjunct (6 women). *Tuition:* Full-time $3,792; part-time $158 per term. *Required fees:* $95 per term. *Graduate housing:* On-campus housing not available. *Student services:* Campus employment opportunities. *Library facilities:* Scarborough Memorial Library plus 1 other. *Collection:* 68,941 titles, 301 serial subscriptions, 1,166 audiovisual materials.

Computer facilities: 20 computers available on campus for general student use. *Web address:* http://www.csw.edu/.

General Application Contact: Charlotte Smith, Director of Admissions, 505-392-6561 Ext. 1012, Fax: 505-592-6006, E-mail: csmith@csw.edu.

GRADUATE UNITS

School of Education and Professional Studies Students: 76 full-time (62 women), 124 part-time (99 women). Average age 38. *Faculty:* 5 full-time (4 women), 10 part-time/adjunct (6 women). Expenses: Contact institution. *Financial support:* In 2001–02, 74 students received support, including 1 research assistantship; Federal Work-Study, scholarships/grants, and tuition waivers (full) also available. Support available to part-time students. Financial award application deadline: 4/1; financial award applicants required to submit FAFSA. In 2001, 30 degrees awarded. *Degree program information:* Part-time and evening/weekend programs available. Postbaccalaureate distance learning degree programs offered. Offers curriculum and instruction (MS); educational administration (MS); educational counseling (MS); educational diagnostician (MS). *Application deadline:* For fall admission, 3/1 (priority date); for spring admission, 10/1. Applications are processed on a rolling basis. *Application fee:* $50. *Dean,* Dr. Elizabeth Posey, 505-392-6561, E-mail: eposey@csw.edu.

THE COLLEGE OF WILLIAM AND MARY, Williamsburg, VA 23187-8795

General Information State-supported, coed, university. CGS member. *Enrollment:* 1,390 full-time matriculated graduate/professional students (653 women), 495 part-time matriculated graduate/professional students (273 women). *Graduate faculty:* 577 full-time (178 women), 148 part-time/adjunct (73 women). Tuition, state resident: full-time $3,262; part-time $175 per credit hour. Tuition, nonresident: full-time $14,768; part-time $550 per credit hour. *Required fees:* $2,478. *Graduate housing:* Rooms and/or apartments available on a first-come, first-served basis to single and married students. Typical cost: $3,130 per year ($5,300 including board) for single students; $3,130 per year ($5,300 including board) for married students. *Student services:* Campus employment opportunities, campus safety program, career counseling, child daycare facilities, disabled student services, exercise/wellness program, free psychological counseling, grant writing training, international student services, low-cost health insurance, multicultural affairs office, teacher training. *Library facilities:* Swem Library plus 9 others. *Online resources:* library catalog, web page. *Collection:* 2 million titles, 11,541 serial subscriptions, 28,002 audiovisual materials. *Research affiliation:* Stanford Linear Accelerator Center (particles and fields physics), Fermi National Laboratory (nuclear physics), Applied Research Center (high-technology businesses).

Computer facilities: 300 computers available on campus for general student use. A campuswide network can be accessed from student residence rooms and from off campus. Internet access is available. *Web address:* http://www.wm.edu/.

General Application Contact: Dr. Eugene Tracy, Dean of Research and Graduate Studies, 757-221-2467, E-mail: tracy@physics.wm.edu.

GRADUATE UNITS

Faculty of Arts and Sciences Students: 309 full-time (137 women), 39 part-time (10 women); includes 31 minority (20 African Americans, 8 Asian Americans or Pacific Islanders, 3 Hispanic Americans), 77 international. Average age 28. 790 applicants, 34% accepted. *Faculty:* 402 full-time (130 women), 100 part-time/adjunct (49 women). Expenses: Contact institution. *Financial support:* Fellowships, research assistantships, teaching assistantships, career-related internships or fieldwork, Federal Work-Study, and institutionally sponsored loans available. Financial award applicants required to submit FAFSA. In 2001, 98 master's, 22 doctorates awarded. *Degree program information:* Part-time programs available. Offers American studies (MA, PhD); anthropology (MA, PhD); applied science (MS, PhD); arts and sciences (MA, MPP, MS, PhD, Psy D); biology (MA); chemistry (MA, MS); clinical psychology (Psy D); computational operations research (MS); computer science (MS, PhD); general experimental psychology (MA); history (MA, PhD); physics (MA, MS, PhD); public policy (MPP). *Application fee:* $30. *Application Contact:* Wanda Carter, Enrollment Services Assistant, 757-221-2467, Fax: 757-221-4874, E-mail: wanda@asci.wm.edu. *Dean of Research and Graduate Studies,* Dr. Eugene Tracy, 757-221-2467, E-mail: tracy@physics.wm.edu.

School of Business Students: 199 full-time (79 women), 138 part-time (32 women); includes 33 minority (8 African Americans, 17 Asian Americans or Pacific Islanders, 7 Hispanic Americans, 1 Native American), 54 international. Average age 37. 386 applicants, 65% accepted. *Faculty:* 51 full-time (13 women), 1 part-time/adjunct (0 women). Expenses: Contact institution. *Financial support:* In 2001–02, 47 research assistantships with full tuition reimbursements (averaging $2,277 per year) were awarded; career-related internships or fieldwork also available. Financial award application deadline: 3/1; financial award applicants required to submit FAFSA. In 2001, 180 degrees awarded. *Degree program information:* Part-time and evening/weekend programs available. Offers accounting (M Acc); business administration (MBA). *Application deadline:* For fall admission, 5/1 (priority date). Applications are processed on a rolling basis. *Application fee:* $50. Electronic applications accepted. *Application Contact:* Kathy Pattison, Director of Admissions, 757-221-2898, Fax: 757-221-2937, E-mail: kpattison@business.wm.edu. *Dean,* Dr. Lawrence Pulley, 757-221-2891, Fax: 757-221-2937.

School of Education Students: 159 full-time (116 women), 163 part-time (126 women); includes 46 minority (33 African Americans, 10 Asian Americans or Pacific Islanders, 3 Hispanic Americans), 8 international. Average age 30. 385 applicants, 56% accepted, 124 enrolled. *Faculty:* 38 full-time (16 women), 14 part-time/adjunct (13 women). Expenses: Contact institution. *Financial support:* In 2001–02, 2 fellowships with full tuition reimbursements (averaging $10,000 per year), 104 research assistantships with full and partial tuition reimbursements (averaging $10,000 per year) were awarded. Teaching assistantships, career-related internships or fieldwork, Federal Work-Study, institutionally sponsored loans, scholarships/grants, and unspecified assistantships also available. Support available to part-time students. Financial award application deadline: 2/1; financial award applicants required to submit FAFSA. In 2001, 115 master's, 17 doctorates, 11 other advanced degrees awarded. *Degree program information:* Part-time and evening/weekend programs available. Offers community and addictions counseling (M Ed); community counseling (M Ed); education (M Ed, MA Ed, Ed D, PhD, Ed S); educational counseling (M Ed, Ed D, PhD); educational leadership (M Ed); educational policy, planning, and leadership (Ed D, PhD); elementary education (MA Ed); family counseling (M Ed); gifted education (MA Ed); gifted education administration (M Ed); reading education (MA Ed); school counseling (M Ed); school psychology (M Ed, Ed S); secondary education (MA Ed); special education (MA Ed). *Application deadline:* For fall admission, 2/1; for spring admission, 10/1. *Application fee:* $30. *Application Contact:* Patricia Burleson, Director of Admissions, 757-221-2317, E-mail: paburl@wm.edu. *Dean,* Dr. Virginia McLaughlin, 757-221-2317, E-mail: vamcla@wm.edu.

William & Mary Law School Students: 539 full-time (222 women), 15 part-time (7 women); includes 82 minority (49 African Americans, 20 Asian Americans or Pacific Islanders, 10 Hispanic Americans, 3 Native Americans), 4 international. Average age 26. 2,479 applicants, 29% accepted. *Faculty:* 29 full-time (7 women), 32 part-time/adjunct (12 women). Expenses: Contact institution. *Financial support:* In 2001–02, 426 students received support, including 86 research assistantships with full tuition reimbursements available (averaging $4,326 per year), 26 teaching assistantships with full tuition reimbursements available (averaging $4,326 per year); fellowships, career-related internships or fieldwork, Federal Work-Study, institutionally sponsored loans, and scholarships/grants also available. Financial award application deadline: 2/15; financial award applicants required to submit FAFSA. In 2001, 161 first professional degrees, 5 master's awarded. Offers law (JD, LL M). *Application deadline:* For fall admission, 3/1 (priority date). *Application fee:* $40. *Application Contact:* Faye F. Shealy, Associate Dean for Admission, 757-221-3785, Fax: 757-221-3261, E-mail: ffshea@wm.edu. *Dean,* W. Taylor Reveley, 757-221-3800, Fax: 757-221-3261, E-mail: taylor@wm.edu.

See in-depth description on page 827.

COLLÈGE UNIVERSITAIRE DE SAINT-BONIFACE, Saint-Boniface, MB R2H 0H7, Canada

General Information Independent-religious, comprehensive institution.

GRADUATE UNITS

Department of Education Offers education (M Ed).

Program in Canadian Studies Offers Canadian studies (MA).

COLORADO CHRISTIAN UNIVERSITY, Lakewood, CO 80226-7499

General Information Independent-religious, coed, comprehensive institution. *Enrollment:* 78 full-time matriculated graduate/professional students (52 women), 8 part-time matriculated graduate/professional students (3 women). *Enrollment by degree level:* 86 master's. *Tuition:* Part-time $324 per hour. *Required fees:* $200; $200 per year. *Graduate housing:* On-campus housing not available. *Student services:* Campus employment opportunities, campus safety program, free psychological counseling. *Library facilities:* Clifton Fowler Library plus 1 other. *Online resources:* library catalog, web page. *Collection:* 71,565 titles, 1,192 serial subscriptions, 4,200 audiovisual materials.

Computer facilities: 13 computers available on campus for general student use. A campuswide network can be accessed from student residence rooms and from off campus. Internet access is available. *Web address:* http://www.ccu.edu/.

General Application Contact: Steve Mountjoy, Director, 303-963-3150, Fax: 303-274-7560, E-mail: smountjoy@ccu.edu.

THE COLORADO COLLEGE, Colorado Springs, CO 80903-3294

General Information Independent, coed, comprehensive institution. *Enrollment:* 18 full-time matriculated graduate/professional students (13 women). *Enrollment by degree level:* 18 master's. *Graduate faculty:* 4 full-time (2 women), 9 part-time/adjunct (6 women). *Tuition:* Full-time $17,584. *Required fees:* $1,145. *Graduate housing:* On-campus housing not available. *Student services:* Campus safety program, career counseling, child daycare facilities,

The Colorado College (continued)

exercise/wellness program, free psychological counseling, international student services, low-cost health insurance, teacher training, writing training. *Library facilities:* Tutt Library plus 2 others. *Online resources:* library catalog, web page, access to other libraries' catalogs. *Collection:* 481,050 titles, 4,010 serial subscriptions, 40,473 audiovisual materials.

Computer facilities: 237 computers available on campus for general student use. A campuswide network can be accessed from student residence rooms and from off campus. Internet access and online class registration are available. *Web address:* http://www.coloradocollege.edu/.

General Application Contact: Marsha E. Unruh, Education Services Manager, 719-389-6472, Fax: 719-389-6473, E-mail: munruh@coloradocollege.edu.

GRADUATE UNITS

Department of Education Students: 18 full-time (13 women); includes 2 minority (1 African American, 1 Asian American or Pacific Islander) Average age 26. 38 applicants, 66% accepted, 19 enrolled. *Faculty:* 4 full-time (2 women), 9 part-time/adjunct (6 women). Expenses: Contact institution. *Financial support:* In 2001–02, 19 teaching assistantships (averaging $12,000 per year) were awarded; career-related internships or fieldwork, institutionally sponsored loans, and tuition waivers (partial) also available. Financial award application deadline: 3/1; financial award applicants required to submit CSS PROFILE or FAFSA. In 2001, 23 degrees awarded. Offers art teaching (MAT); elementary education (MAT); elementary school teaching (MAT); English teaching (MAT); foreign language teaching (MAT); mathematics teaching (MAT); music teaching (MAT); science teaching (MAT); secondary education (MAT); social studies teaching (MAT). *Application deadline:* For fall admission, 2/1. *Application fee:* $50. *Application Contact:* Marsha E. Unruh, Education Services Manager, 719-389-6472, Fax: 719-389-6473, E-mail: munruh@coloradocollege.edu. *Chair,* Charlotte Mendoza, 719-389-6474, Fax: 719-389-6473, E-mail: cmendoza@coloradocollege.edu.

Programs for Experienced Teachers *Degree program information:* Part-time programs available. Offers humanities for secondary school teachers and administrators (MAT); liberal arts for elementary school teachers and administrators (MAT); Southwest studies (MAT). Offered during summer only.

COLORADO SCHOOL OF MINES, Golden, CO 80401-1887

General Information State-supported, coed, university. CGS member. *Enrollment:* 505 full-time matriculated graduate/professional students (161 women), 190 part-time matriculated graduate/professional students (43 women). *Enrollment by degree level:* 392 master's, 297 doctoral, 3 other advanced degrees. *Graduate faculty:* 274 full-time (83 women), 34 part-time/adjunct (15 women). Tuition, state resident: full-time $4,940; part-time $246 per credit. Tuition, nonresident: full-time $16,070; part-time $803 per credit. *Required fees:* $341 per semester. *Graduate housing:* Rooms and/or apartments available on a first-come, first-served basis to single and married students. Typical cost: $3,360 per year for single students; $6,672 per year for married students. Room charges vary according to campus/location and housing facility selected. *Student services:* Campus employment opportunities, campus safety program, career counseling, exercise/wellness program, free psychological counseling, international student services, low-cost health insurance, teacher training, writing training. *Library facilities:* Arthur Lakes Library. *Online resources:* library catalog, web page, access to other libraries' catalogs. *Collection:* 102,533 titles, 1,840 serial subscriptions, 48 audiovisual materials. *Research affiliation:* Abu Dhabi National Oil Company (petroleum), Bethlehem Steel (metallurgical and materials), Gas Research Institute (supply and distribution), Atlantic Richfield Company (gas/oil research), American Chemical Society, British Petroleum Amoco (petroleum).

Computer facilities: A campuswide network can be accessed from student residence rooms and from off campus. *Web address:* http://www.mines.edu/.

General Application Contact: Linda Powell, Graduate Admissions Officer, 303-273-3248, Fax: 303-273-3244, E-mail: lpowell@mines.edu.

GRADUATE UNITS

Graduate School Students: 505 full-time (161 women), 187 part-time (43 women); includes 39 minority (4 African Americans, 19 Asian Americans or Pacific Islanders, 13 Hispanic Americans, 3 Native Americans), 286 international. 777 applicants, 74% accepted, 180 enrolled. *Faculty:* 274 full-time (83 women), 34 part-time/adjunct (15 women). Expenses: Contact institution. *Financial support:* In 2001–02, 585 students received support, including 130 fellowships (averaging $4,651 per year), 359 research assistantships (averaging $4,987 per year), 311 teaching assistantships (averaging $5,262 per year); career-related internships or fieldwork, Federal Work-Study, institutionally sponsored loans, and unspecified assistantships also available. Support available to part-time students. Financial award applicants required to submit FAFSA. In 2001, 136 master's, 48 doctorates awarded. *Degree program information:* Part-time programs available. Offers applied chemistry (PhD); applied physics (PhD); chemical engineering and petroleum refining (MS, PhD); chemistry (MS, PhD); engineering geology (Diploma); exploration geosciences (Diploma); geochemistry (MS, PhD); geological engineering (ME, MS, PhD, Diploma); geology (MS, PhD); geophysical engineering (ME, MS, PhD); geophysics (MS, PhD, Diploma); hydrogeology (Diploma); materials science (MS, PhD); mathematical and computer sciences (MS, PhD); metallurgical and materials engineering (ME, MS, PhD); mining and earth systems engineering (ME, MS, PhD); petroleum engineering (ME, MS, PhD); physics (MS). *Application deadline:* For fall admission, 12/1 (priority date); for spring admission, 5/1 (priority date). Applications are processed on a rolling basis. *Application fee:* $40. Electronic applications accepted. *Application Contact:* Linda Powell, Graduate Admissions Officer, 303-273-3248, Fax: 303-273-3244, E-mail: lpowell@mines.edu. *Dean of Graduate Studies and Research,* Dr. Phillip R. Romig, 303-273-3247, Fax: 303-273-3244, E-mail: grad-school@mines.edu.

Division of Economics and Business Students: 58 full-time (11 women), 27 part-time (5 women); includes 6 minority (2 African Americans, 2 Asian Americans or Pacific Islanders, 2 Hispanic Americans), 37 international. 114 applicants, 94% accepted, 30 enrolled. *Faculty:* 13 full-time (2 women), 13 part-time/adjunct (5 women). Expenses: Contact institution. *Financial support:* In 2001–02, 32 students received support, including 5 fellowships (averaging $6,471 per year), 4 research assistantships (averaging $7,793 per year), 31 teaching assistantships (averaging $5,232 per year); unspecified assistantships also available. Support available to part-time students. Financial award applicants required to submit FAFSA. In 2001, 31 master's, 2 doctorates awarded. *Degree program information:* Part-time programs available. Offers engineering and technology management (MS); mineral economics (MS, PhD). *Application deadline:* For fall admission, 12/1 (priority date); for spring admission, 5/1 (priority date). Applications are processed on a rolling basis. *Application fee:* $40. Electronic applications accepted. *Application Contact:* Kathleen A. Feighny, Administrative Faculty, 303-273-3979, Fax: 303-273-3416, E-mail: kfeighny@mines.edu. *Head,* Dr. Roderick G. Eggert, 303-273-3981, Fax: 303-273-3416, E-mail: reggert@mines.edu.

Division of Engineering Students: 51 full-time (11 women), 11 part-time (1 woman); includes 3 minority (1 Asian American or Pacific Islander, 1 Hispanic American, 1 Native American), 16 international. 56 applicants, 82% accepted, 10 enrolled. *Faculty:* 33 full-time (3 women), 19 part-time/adjunct (4 women). Expenses: Contact institution. *Financial support:* In 2001–02, 4 fellowships (averaging $4,875 per year), 71 research assistantships (averaging $4,606 per year), 42 teaching assistantships (averaging $6,091 per year) were awarded. Federal Work-Study and unspecified assistantships also available. Financial award applicants required to submit FAFSA. In 2001, 11 master's, 4 doctorates awarded. *Degree program information:* Part-time programs available. Offers engineering systems (ME, MS, PhD). *Application deadline:* For fall admission, 12/1 (priority date); for spring admission, 5/1 (priority date). Applications are processed on a rolling basis. *Application fee:* $40. Electronic applications accepted. *Application Contact:* Leslie Urioste, Information Contact, 303-384-2394, Fax: 303-273-3278, E-mail: lurioste@mines.edu. *Head,* Dr. Joan Gosink, 303-273-3650, Fax: 303-273-3602, E-mail: jgosink@mines.edu.

Division of Environmental Science and Engineering Students: 42 full-time (22 women), 30 part-time (15 women); includes 3 minority (1 Asian American or Pacific Islander, 2 Hispanic Americans), 21 international. 63 applicants, 79% accepted, 27 enrolled. *Faculty:* 8 full-time (1 woman), 8 part-time/adjunct (1 woman). Expenses: Contact institution. *Financial support:* In 2001–02, 56 students received support, including 7 fellowships (averaging $2,818 per year), 23 research assistantships (averaging $3,880 per year), 24 teaching assistantships (averaging $4,738 per year); unspecified assistantships also available. Support available to part-time students. Financial award applicants required to submit FAFSA. In 2001, 18 master's, 3 doctorates awarded. *Degree program information:* Part-time programs available. Offers environmental science and engineering (MS, PhD). *Application deadline:* For fall admission, 12/1 (priority date); for spring admission, 5/1 (priority date). Applications are processed on a rolling basis. *Application fee:* $40. Electronic applications accepted. *Application Contact:* Juanita Chuven, Administrative Assistant, 303-273-3427, Fax: 303-273-3413, E-mail: jchuven@mines.edu. *Head,* Dr. Robert Seigrist, 303-384-2158, Fax: 303-273-3413, E-mail: rseigris@mines.edu.

See in-depth description on page 829.

COLORADO STATE UNIVERSITY, Fort Collins, CO 80523-0015

General Information State-supported, coed, university. CGS member. *Enrollment:* 2,295 full-time matriculated graduate/professional students (1,348 women), 3,145 part-time matriculated graduate/professional students (1,476 women). *Enrollment by degree level:* 528 first professional, 3,782 master's, 1,130 doctoral. *Graduate faculty:* 949 full-time (248 women), 46 part-time/adjunct (3 women). Tuition, state resident: full-time $2,880; part-time $160 per credit. Tuition, nonresident: full-time $11,412; part-time $634 per credit. *Required fees:* $750; $34 per credit. *Graduate housing:* Rooms and/or apartments available on a first-come, first-served basis to single students and available to married students. *Student services:* Campus employment opportunities, campus safety program, career counseling, child daycare facilities, disabled student services, exercise/wellness program, free psychological counseling, international student services, low-cost health insurance, multicultural affairs office. *Library facilities:* William E. Morgan Library plus 3 others. *Online resources:* library catalog, web page, access to other libraries' catalogs. *Collection:* 1.2 million titles, 21,208 serial subscriptions, 9,428 audiovisual materials. *Research affiliation:* Rocky Mountain Forest and Range Experiment Station, National Seed Storage Laboratory, Collaborative Radiological Health Laboratory, Bayer Corporation, Heska Corporation, Hoeschst Roussel Pharmaceutical Company.

Computer facilities: A campuswide network can be accessed from student residence rooms and from off campus. Internet access is available. *Web address:* http://www.colostate.edu/.

General Application Contact: Graduate School, 970-491-6817, Fax: 970-491-2194, E-mail: gschool@grad.colostate.edu.

GRADUATE UNITS

College of Veterinary Medicine and Biomedical Sciences Students: 744 full-time (475 women), 114 part-time (67 women); includes 103 minority (10 African Americans, 34 Asian Americans or Pacific Islanders, 42 Hispanic Americans, 17 Native Americans), 47 international. Average age 29. 1,455 applicants, 18% accepted, 229 enrolled. *Faculty:* 133 full-time (27 women). Expenses: Contact institution. *Financial support:* In 2001–02, 18 fellowships with full tuition reimbursements (averaging $20,000 per year), 79 research assistantships with full tuition reimbursements (averaging $18,000 per year), 20 teaching assistantships with partial tuition reimbursements (averaging $18,000 per year) were awarded. Career-related internships or fieldwork, Federal Work-Study, institutionally sponsored loans, traineeships, and tuition waivers (partial) also available. Support available to part-time students. Financial award applicants required to submit FAFSA. In 2001, 131 first professional degrees, 69 master's, 13 doctorates awarded. *Degree program information:* Part-time programs available. Offers anatomy and neurobiology (MS, PhD); cell and molecular biology (MS, PhD); cellular and molecular biology (MS, PhD); clinical sciences (MS, PhD); environmental health (MS, PhD); health physics (MS, PhD); immunology (MS, PhD); mammalian radiobiology (MS, PhD); microbiology (MS, PhD); nuclear-waste management (MS); pathology (MS, PhD); physiology (MS, PhD); radiobiology (MS); radioecology (MS, PhD); radiological health sciences (MS, PhD); radiology (MS, PhD); veterinary medicine (DVM); veterinary medicine and biomedical sciences (DVM, MS, PhD); veterinary radiology (MS). *Application deadline:* Applications are processed on a rolling basis. Electronic applications accepted. *Application Contact:* Dr. Sherry McConnell, Associate Dean of Admissions and Advising, 970-491-7052, Fax: 970-491-2250, E-mail: smcconnell@cvmbs.colostate.edu. *Dean,* Dr. Lance Perryman, 970-491-7051, Fax: 970-491-2250.

Graduate School Students: 1,767 full-time (964 women), 3,145 part-time (1,476 women); includes 394 minority (72 African Americans, 112 Asian Americans or Pacific Islanders, 153 Hispanic Americans, 57 Native Americans), 717 international. Average age 33. 5,410 applicants, 58% accepted, 1060 enrolled. *Faculty:* 949 full-time (248 women), 46 part-time/adjunct (3 women). Expenses: Contact institution. *Financial support:* In 2001–02, 161 fellowships, 613 research assistantships, 691 teaching assistantships were awarded. Career-related internships or fieldwork, Federal Work-Study, institutionally sponsored loans, traineeships, and tuition waivers (full and partial) also available. Support available to part-time students. In 2001, 805 master's, 100 doctorates awarded. *Degree program information:* Part-time programs available. Postbaccalaureate distance learning degree programs offered (no on-campus study). Offers cell and molecular biology (MS, PhD); ecology (MS, PhD). *Application deadline:* For fall admission, 2/15 (priority date); for spring admission, 11/15 (priority date). *Application fee:* $30. Electronic applications accepted. *Application Contact:* Graduate School, 970-491-6817, Fax: 970-491-2194, E-mail: gschool@grad.colostate.edu. *Dean,* James L. Fry, 970-491-6817, Fax: 970-491-2194.

College of Agricultural Sciences Students: 120 full-time (55 women), 130 part-time (58 women); includes 11 minority (3 African Americans, 1 Asian American or Pacific Islander, 2 Hispanic Americans, 5 Native Americans), 51 international. Average age 31. 165 applicants, 59% accepted, 53 enrolled. *Faculty:* 101 full-time (15 women). Expenses: Contact institution. *Financial support:* In 2001–02, 14 fellowships, 34 research assistantships, 21 teaching assistantships were awarded. Career-related internships or fieldwork, Federal Work-Study, institutionally sponsored loans, and traineeships also available. Support available to part-time students. In 2001, 43 master's, 10 doctorates awarded. *Degree program information:* Part-time programs available. Postbaccalaureate distance learning degree programs offered. Offers agricultural and resource economics (M Agr, MS, PhD); agricultural sciences (M Agr, MS, PhD); animal breeding and genetics (MS, PhD); animal nutrition (MS, PhD); animal reproduction (MS, PhD); animal sciences (M Agr); crop science (MS, PhD); entomology (MS, PhD); floriculture (M Agr, MS, PhD); horticultural food crops (M Agr, MS, PhD); livestock handling (MS, PhD); meats (MS, PhD); nursery and landscape management (M Agr, MS, PhD); plant genetics (MS, PhD); plant pathology (MS, PhD); plant physiology (MS, PhD); production management (MS, PhD); soil science (MS, PhD); turf management (M Agr, MS, PhD); weed science (MS, PhD). *Application deadline:* Applications are processed on a rolling basis. *Application fee:* $30. Electronic applications accepted. *Interim Vice Provost and Interim Dean,* Dr. James C. Heird, 970-491-6274, Fax: 970-491-4895, E-mail: jheird@agsci.colostate.edu.

College of Applied Human Sciences Students: 378 full-time (297 women), 478 part-time (316 women). Average age 35. 613 applicants, 69% accepted, 211 enrolled. *Faculty:* 109 full-time (50 women), 21 part-time/adjunct (2 women). Expenses: Contact institution. *Financial support:* In 2001–02, 14 fellowships, 27 research assistantships with partial tuition reimbursements, 40 teaching assistantships with full tuition reimbursements were awarded. Career-related internships or fieldwork, Federal Work-Study, institutionally sponsored loans, scholarships/grants, traineeships, and tuition waivers (full and partial) also available. Support available to part-time students. In 2001, 159 master's, 18 doctorates awarded. *Degree program information:* Part-time programs available. Postbaccalaureate distance learning degree programs offered. Offers apparel and merchandising (MS); applied human sciences (M Ed, MS, MSW, PhD); automotive pollution control (MS); construction management (MS); education and human resource studies (M Ed, PhD); food science (MS, PhD); health and exercise science (MS); historic preservation (MS); human development and family studies (MS); industrial technology management (MS); interior design (MS); nutrition (MS, PhD); occupational therapy (MS); social work (MSW); student affairs (MS); technology education and training (MS); technology of industry (PhD). *Application fee:* $30. Electronic applications accepted. *Application Contact:* Dr. Kevin Oltjenbruns, Head, 970-491-5811, Fax: 470-491-7859, E-mail: oltjenbrun@cahs.colostate.edu. *Dean,* Nancy Hartley, 970-491-5841, Fax: 970-491-7859.

College of Business Students: 45 full-time (23 women), 515 part-time (144 women); includes 45 minority (12 African Americans, 12 Asian Americans or Pacific Islanders, 14 Hispanic Americans, 7 Native Americans), 55 international. Average age 36. 397 applicants, 65% accepted, 179 enrolled. *Faculty:* 54 full-time (14 women), 3 part-time/adjunct (0 women). Expenses: Contact institution. *Financial support:* In 2001–02, 13 fellowships, 1 research assistantship with full and partial tuition reimbursement (averaging $4,410 per year), 37 teaching assistantships (averaging $4,410 per year) were awarded. Career-related internships or fieldwork and Federal Work-Study also available. Financial award application deadline: 2/1. In 2001, 229 degrees awarded. *Degree program information:* Part-time and evening/weekend programs available. Postbaccalaureate distance learning degree programs offered. Offers accounting (MS); business (MBA, MS); business administration (MBA); computer information systems (MS). *Application deadline:* For fall admission, 4/1. Applications are processed on a rolling basis. *Application fee:* $30. Electronic applications accepted. *Application Contact:* Dr. Ajay Menon, Associate Dean, 970-491-6471, Fax: 970-491-0596. *Dean*, Dr. Daniel Costello, 970-491-6471, Fax: 970-491-0596.

College of Engineering Students: 227 full-time (48 women), 318 part-time (58 women); includes 30 minority (2 African Americans, 16 Asian Americans or Pacific Islanders, 9 Hispanic Americans, 3 Native Americans), 230 international. Average age 30. 1,058 applicants, 58% accepted, 156 enrolled. *Faculty:* 98 full-time (7 women). Expenses: Contact institution. *Financial support:* In 2001–02, 21 fellowships with full tuition reimbursements (averaging $12,658 per year), 146 research assistantships with full tuition reimbursements (averaging $16,300 per year), 51 teaching assistantships with full tuition reimbursements (averaging $11,133 per year) were awarded. Career-related internships or fieldwork, Federal Work-Study, institutionally sponsored loans, and traineeships also available. In 2001, 62 master's, 16 doctorates awarded. *Degree program information:* Part-time programs available. Offers atmospheric science (M Eng, PhD); bioengineering (MS, PhD); bioresource and agricultural engineering (MS); bioresource and agriculture engineering (PhD); chemical engineering (MS, PhD); electrical and computer engineering (M Eng, MS, PhD); energy and environmental engineering (MS, PhD); energy conversion (MS, PhD); engineering (ME); engineering management (MS); environmental engineering (MS, PhD); heat and mass transfer (MS, PhD); hydraulics and wind engineering (MS, PhD); industrial and manufacturing systems engineering (MS, PhD); mechanical engineering (MS, PhD); mechanics and materials (MS, PhD); structural and geotechnical engineering (MS, PhD); water resources planning and management (MS, PhD); water resources, hydrologic and environmental sciences (MS, PhD). *Application deadline:* For fall admission, 2/1 (priority date). Applications are processed on a rolling basis. *Application fee:* $30. Electronic applications accepted. *Application Contact:* Dr. Steven Abt, Head, 970-491-6558, Fax: 970-491-3827, E-mail: sabt@engr.colostate.edu. *Dean*, Dr. Neal Gallagher, 970-491-3366, Fax: 970-491-5569, E-mail: nealg@engr.colostate.edu.

College of Liberal Arts Students: 276 full-time (175 women), 232 part-time (125 women); includes 36 minority (5 African Americans, 9 Asian Americans or Pacific Islanders, 16 Hispanic Americans, 6 Native Americans), 62 international. Average age 31. 536 applicants, 66% accepted, 150 enrolled. *Faculty:* 227 full-time (73 women), 54 part-time/adjunct (29 women). Expenses: Contact institution. *Financial support:* In 2001–02, 28 fellowships, 7 research assistantships, 166 teaching assistantships were awarded. Career-related internships or fieldwork, Federal Work-Study, institutionally sponsored loans, traineeships, and tuition waivers (full and partial) also available. Support available to part-time students. In 2001, 115 master's, 3 doctorates awarded. *Degree program information:* Part-time programs available. Offers American history (MA); anthropology (MA); applied music (MM); archival science (MA); Asian history (MA); communication development (MA); conducting (MM); creative writing (MFA); drawing (MFA); economics (MA, PhD); English (MA); English as a second language (MA); environmental politics and policy (PhD); European history (MA); fibers (MFA); French (MA); French/TESL (MA); German (MA); German/TESL (MA); graphic design (MFA); historic preservation (MA); Latin American history (MA); liberal arts (MA, MFA, MM, MS, PhD); literature (MA); metalsmithing (MFA); museum studies (MA); music education (MM); music therapy (MM); painting (MFA); philosophy (MA); political science (MA, PhD); printmaking (MFA); rhetoric and composition (MA); sculpture (MFA); sociology (MA, PhD); Spanish (MA); Spanish/TESL (MA); speech communication (MA); teaching (MA); technical communication (MS). *Application deadline:* Applications are processed on a rolling basis. *Application fee:* $30. Electronic applications accepted. *Dean*, Robert Hoffert, 970-491-5421, Fax: 970-491-0528, E-mail: robert.hoffert@colostate.edu.

College of Natural Resources Students: 121 full-time (58 women), 146 part-time (63 women); includes 20 minority (2 African Americans, 4 Asian Americans or Pacific Islanders, 9 Hispanic Americans, 5 Native Americans), 34 international. Average age 31. 178 applicants, 52% accepted, 45 enrolled. *Faculty:* 60 full-time (11 women), 10 part-time/adjunct (2 women). Expenses: Contact institution. *Financial support:* In 2001–02, 11 fellowships, 55 research assistantships (averaging $13,755 per year), 40 teaching assistantships with tuition reimbursements (averaging $9,724 per year) were awarded. Career-related internships or fieldwork, Federal Work-Study, institutionally sponsored loans, and traineeships also available. Support available to part-time students. In 2001, 42 master's, 5 doctorates awarded. *Degree program information:* Part-time programs available. Offers commercial recreation and tourism (MS); earth resources (PhD); fishery and wildlife biology (MS, PhD); fluvial geomorphology (MS); forestry (MF, MS, PhD); geology (MS, PhD); human dimensions in natural resources (PhD); hydrogeology (MS); natural resources (MF, MS, PhD); petrology/geochemistry and economic geology (MS); rangeland ecosystem science (MS, PhD); recreation resource management (MS, PhD); resource interpretation (MS); stratigraphy/sedimentology (MS); structure/tectonics (MS); watershed science (MS, PhD). *Application deadline:* Applications are processed on a rolling basis. *Application fee:* $30. Electronic applications accepted. *Application Contact:* Dr. Joyce Berry, Associate Dean, 970-491-5405, Fax: 970-491-0279, E-mail: joyceb@colostate.edu. *Dean*, A. A. Dyer, 970-491-6675, Fax: 970-491-0279, E-mail: al@cnr.colostate.edu.

College of Natural Sciences Students: 298 full-time (132 women), 284 part-time (113 women); includes 39 minority (2 African Americans, 18 Asian Americans or Pacific Islanders, 14 Hispanic Americans, 5 Native Americans), 164 international. Average age 29. 1,219 applicants, 28% accepted, 142 enrolled. *Faculty:* 184 full-time (32 women), 13 part-time/adjunct (0 women). Expenses: Contact institution. *Financial support:* In 2001–02, 42 fellowships, 142 research assistantships, 238 teaching assistantships were awarded. Career-related internships or fieldwork, Federal Work-Study, institutionally sponsored loans, traineeships, and tuition waivers (partial) also available. Support available to part-time students. Financial award applicants required to submit FAFSA. In 2001, 77 master's, 31 doctorates awarded. *Degree program information:* Part-time programs available. Offers applied social psychology (PhD); behavioral neuroscience (PhD); biochemistry and molecular biology (MS, PhD); botany (MS, PhD); chemistry (MS, PhD); cognitive psychology (PhD); computer science (MS, PhD); counseling psychology (PhD); industrial-organizational psychology (PhD); mathematics (MS, PhD); natural sciences (MS, PhD); physics (MS, PhD); statistics (MS, PhD); zoology (MS, PhD). *Application deadline:* Applications are processed on a rolling basis. *Application fee:* $30. Electronic applications accepted. *Dean*, John C. Raich, 970-491-6864, Fax: 970-491-6639, E-mail: jraich@lamar.colostate.edu.

COLORADO TECHNICAL UNIVERSITY, Colorado Springs, CO 80907-3896

General Information Proprietary, coed, comprehensive institution. *Enrollment:* 310 full-time matriculated graduate/professional students (94 women), 48 part-time matriculated graduate/professional students (11 women). *Enrollment by degree level:* 321 master's, 37 doctoral. *Graduate faculty:* 18 full-time (5 women), 25 part-time/adjunct (4 women). *Tuition:* Full-time $6,960; part-time $290 per credit. *Required fees:* $40 per quarter. One-time fee: $100. Tuition and fees vary according to course load and degree level. *Graduate housing:* On-campus housing not available. *Student services:* Campus employment opportunities, campus safety program, career counseling, exercise/wellness program, international student services, low-cost health insurance. *Library facilities:* Colorado Technical University Library. *Online resources:* library catalog, web page, access to other libraries' catalogs. *Collection:* 22,245 titles, 4,389 serial subscriptions, 620 audiovisual materials.

Computer facilities: 130 computers available on campus for general student use. A campuswide network can be accessed from off campus. Internet access is available. *Web address:* http://www.coloradotech.edu.

General Application Contact: Judy Galante, Graduate Admissions, 719-590-6720, Fax: 719-598-3740, E-mail: jgalante@coloradotech.edu.

GRADUATE UNITS

Graduate Studies Students: 310 full-time (94 women), 48 part-time (11 women); includes 57 minority (24 African Americans, 17 Asian Americans or Pacific Islanders, 16 Hispanic Americans), 9 international. Average age 38. 130 applicants, 94% accepted, 114 enrolled. *Faculty:* 18 full-time (5 women), 25 part-time/adjunct (4 women). Expenses: Contact institution. *Financial support:* Career-related internships or fieldwork and Federal Work-Study available. Financial award applicants required to submit FAFSA. In 2001, 154 master's, 3 doctorates awarded. *Degree program information:* Part-time and evening/weekend programs available. Offers business administration (MBA); business management (MSM); business technology (MSM); communication systems (MSEE); computer engineering (MSCE); computer science (DCS); computer systems security (MSCS); database management (MSM); electronic systems (MSEE); human resources management (MSM); information technology (MSM); logistics management (MSM); management (DM); organizational leadership (MSM); project management (MSM); software engineering (MSCS); software project management (MSCS). *Application deadline:* For fall admission, 10/2; for winter admission, 1/3; for spring admission, 4/3. Applications are processed on a rolling basis. *Application fee:* $100. *Application Contact:* Judy Galante, Graduate Admissions, 719-590-6720, Fax: 719-598-3740, E-mail: jgalante@coloradotech.edu. *President*, David D. O'Donnell, 719-590-6749, Fax: 719-598-6860, E-mail: dodonnell@coloradotech.edu.

COLORADO TECHNICAL UNIVERSITY DENVER CAMPUS, Greenwood Village, CO 80111

General Information Proprietary, coed, comprehensive institution. *Enrollment:* 70 full-time matriculated graduate/professional students (24 women), 8 part-time matriculated graduate/professional students (2 women). *Enrollment by degree level:* 74 master's. *Graduate faculty:* 5 full-time (2 women), 13 part-time/adjunct (4 women). *Tuition:* Full-time $6,960; part-time $290 per credit. *Required fees:* $40 per quarter. One-time fee: $100. Tuition and fees vary according to course load and degree level. *Graduate housing:* On-campus housing not available. *Student services:* Campus employment opportunities, campus safety program, career counseling, international student services, low-cost health insurance. *Library facilities:* Colorado Technical University Resource Center. *Collection:* 2,262 serial subscriptions, 15 audiovisual materials.

Computer facilities: 25 computers available on campus for general student use. A campuswide network can be accessed. Internet access is available. *Web address:* http://www.coloradotech.edu/.

General Application Contact: Suzanne Hyman, Director of Admissions, 303-694-6600, Fax: 303-694-6673, E-mail: shyman@coloradotech.edu.

GRADUATE UNITS

Program in Computer Science Students: 24 full-time (4 women), 2 part-time (1 woman); includes 9 minority (3 African Americans, 6 Asian Americans or Pacific Islanders) Average age 34. 6 applicants, 83% accepted, 5 enrolled. *Faculty:* 4 full-time (2 women), 4 part-time/adjunct (2 women). Expenses: Contact institution. *Financial support:* Federal Work-Study and scholarships/grants available. Support available to part-time students. Financial award applicants required to submit FAFSA. In 2001, 10 master's awarded. *Degree program information:* Part-time and evening/weekend programs available. Offers computer systems security (MSCS); software engineering (MSCS); software project management (MSCS). *Application deadline:* For fall admission, 10/2; for winter admission, 1/3; for spring admission, 4/3. Applications are processed on a rolling basis. *Application fee:* $100. *Application Contact:* Suzanne Hyman, Director of Admissions, 303-694-6600, Fax: 303-694-6673, E-mail: shyman@coloradotech.edu. *Dean of Computer Science*, Dr. Jack Klag, 719-590-6850, Fax: 719-598-3740, E-mail: jklag@coloradotech.edu.

Programs in Business Administration and Management Students: 46 full-time (20 women), 6 part-time (1 woman); includes 23 minority (5 African Americans, 16 Asian Americans or Pacific Islanders, 1 Hispanic American, 1 Native American), 7 international. Average age 34. 12 applicants, 83% accepted, 10 enrolled. *Faculty:* 1 full-time (0 women), 9 part-time/adjunct (2 women). Expenses: Contact institution. *Financial support:* Federal Work-Study and scholarships/grants available. Support available to part-time students. Financial award applicants required to submit FAFSA. In 2001, 35 master's awarded. *Degree program information:* Part-time and evening/weekend programs available. Offers business administration (MBA); business technology (MSM); database management (MSM); information technology (MSM); project management (MSM). *Application deadline:* For fall admission, 10/2; for winter admission, 1/3; for spring admission, 4/3. Applications are processed on a rolling basis. *Application fee:* $100. *Application Contact:* Suzanne Hyman, Director of Admissions, 303-694-6600, Fax: 303-694-6673, E-mail: shyman@coloradotech.edu. *Dean of Management*, Dr. Eric Goodman, 719-590-6772, Fax: 719-590-6790, E-mail: egoodman@cos.coloradotech.edu.

COLORADO TECHNICAL UNIVERSITY SIOUX FALLS CAMPUS, Sioux Falls, SD 57108

General Information Proprietary, coed, comprehensive institution. *Enrollment:* 73 full-time matriculated graduate/professional students (39 women). *Enrollment by degree level:* 73 master's. *Graduate faculty:* 6 full-time (1 woman), 13 part-time/adjunct (5 women). *Tuition:* Full-time $7,080. One-time fee: $100 full-time. *Graduate housing:* On-campus housing not available. *Student services:* Campus safety program, career counseling, disabled student services, international student services. *Library facilities:* Resource Center. *Online resources:* library catalog, web page.

Computer facilities: 55 computers available on campus for general student use. A campuswide network can be accessed from off campus. Internet access is available. *Web address:* http://www.colotechu.edu/.

General Application Contact: Catherine Taplett-Allen, Admissions Manager, 605-361-0200 Ext. 103, Fax: 605-361-5954, E-mail: callen@sp.coloradotech.edu.

GRADUATE UNITS

Programs in Business Administration and Management *Degree program information:* Evening/weekend programs available. Offers business administration (MBA); business management (MSM); health science management (MSM); human resources management (MSM); information technology (MSM); organizational leadership (MSM).

COLUMBIA COLLEGE, Columbia, MO 65216-0002

General Information Independent-religious, coed, comprehensive institution. *Enrollment:* 184 full-time matriculated graduate/professional students (121 women). *Graduate faculty:* 14 full-time (8 women), 11 part-time/adjunct (2 women). *Tuition:* Full-time $2,985; part-time $199 per credit hour. Full-time tuition and fees vary according to campus/location. *Graduate housing:* Room and/or apartments available to single students; on-campus housing not available to married students. Typical cost: $2,938 per year ($4,666 including board). *Student services:* Career counseling, exercise/wellness program, free psychological counseling, teacher training. *Library facilities:* Stafford Library. *Online resources:* library catalog, web page, access to other libraries' catalogs. *Collection:* 56,169 titles, 619 serial subscriptions, 3,366 audiovisual materials.

Computer facilities: 125 computers available on campus for general student use. A campuswide network can be accessed. Internet access is available. *Web address:* http://www.ccis.edu/.

General Application Contact: Regina Morin, Director of Admissions, 573-875-7354, Fax: 573-875-7506, E-mail: rmmorin@email.ccis.edu.

Columbia College (continued)
GRADUATE UNITS

Program in Business Administration Students: 97 full-time (59 women); includes 9 minority (6 African Americans, 1 Asian American or Pacific Islander, 1 Hispanic American, 1 Native American), 7 international. Average age 34. 24 applicants, 92% accepted. *Faculty:* 8 full-time (5 women), 7 part-time/adjunct (1 woman). Expenses: Contact institution. *Financial support:* Federal Work-Study and scholarships/grants available. Support available to part-time students. Financial award application deadline: 3/15; financial award applicants required to submit FAFSA. In 2001, 27 degrees awarded. *Degree program information:* Part-time and evening/weekend programs available. Offers business administration (MBA). *Application deadline:* For fall admission, 8/1 (priority date). Applications are processed on a rolling basis. *Application fee:* $25 ($50 for international students). *Application Contact:* Regina Morin, Director of Admissions, 573-875-7354, Fax: 573-875-7506, E-mail: rmmorin@email.ccis.edu. *Chair, Evening and Graduate Division,* Dr. Ken Middleton, 573-875-7535, Fax: 573-875-7209, E-mail: kamiddleton@email.ccis.edu.

Program in Criminal Justice Students: 35 full-time (19 women); includes 7 minority (5 African Americans, 2 Native Americans) Average age 34. 7 applicants, 100% accepted. *Faculty:* 1 full-time (0 women), 3 part-time/adjunct (1 woman). Expenses: Contact institution. *Financial support:* Career-related internships or fieldwork, institutionally sponsored loans, and scholarships/grants available. Support available to part-time students. Financial award applicants required to submit FAFSA. In 2001, 7 degrees awarded. *Degree program information:* Part-time and evening/weekend programs available. Offers criminal justice (MSCJ). *Application deadline:* For fall admission, 8/1 (priority date); for spring admission, 12/15 (priority date). Applications are processed on a rolling basis. *Application fee:* $25 ($50 for international students). *Application Contact:* Regina Morin, Director of Admissions, 573-875-7354, Fax: 573-875-7506, E-mail: rmmorin@email.ccis.edu. *Chairman,* Dr. Michael Lyman, 573-875-7472, Fax: 573-875-7209, E-mail: mlyman@email.ccis.edu.

Program in Teaching Students: 52 full-time (43 women); includes 2 minority (both African Americans) Average age 35. 19 applicants, 100% accepted. *Faculty:* 5 full-time (3 women), 1 part-time/adjunct (0 women). Expenses: Contact institution. *Financial support:* Career-related internships or fieldwork, Federal Work-Study, and institutionally sponsored loans available. Support available to part-time students. Financial award applicants required to submit FAFSA. In 2001, 7 degrees awarded. *Degree program information:* Part-time and evening/weekend programs available. Offers teaching (MAT). *Application deadline:* For fall admission, 8/1 (priority date). Applications are processed on a rolling basis. *Application fee:* $25 ($50 for international students). *Application Contact:* Regina Morin, Director of Admissions, 573-875-7354, Fax: 573-875-7506, E-mail: rmmorin@email.ccis.edu. *Chair, MAT Program,* Dr. Ron Taylor, 573-875-7615, Fax: 573-875-7209, E-mail: rdtaylor@email.ccis.edu.

COLUMBIA COLLEGE, Columbia, SC 29203-5998

General Information Independent-religious, women only, comprehensive institution. *Enrollment:* 163 full-time matriculated graduate/professional students (148 women), 28 part-time matriculated graduate/professional students (24 women). *Enrollment by degree level:* 191 master's. *Graduate faculty:* 7 full-time (6 women), 12 part-time/adjunct (3 women). *Tuition:* Full-time $230; part-time $230 per semester hour. Tuition and fees vary according to campus/location and program. *Graduate housing:* On-campus housing not available. *Student services:* Campus safety program, career counseling. *Library facilities:* Edens Library. *Online resources:* library catalog, web page, access to other libraries' catalogs. *Collection:* 645 serial subscriptions, 8,123 audiovisual materials.

Computer facilities: 182 computers available on campus for general student use. A campuswide network can be accessed from student residence rooms and from off campus. *Web address:* http://www.columbiacollegesc.edu/.

General Application Contact: Carol Williams, Graduate Director of Recruitment and Admissions, 803-786-3191, Fax: 803-786-3184, E-mail: cwms@colucoll.edu.

GRADUATE UNITS

Graduate Programs Students: 163 full-time (148 women), 28 part-time (24 women); includes 75 minority (72 African Americans, 2 Hispanic Americans, 1 Native American) Average age 35. 100 applicants, 84% accepted, 62 enrolled. *Faculty:* 7 full-time (6 women), 12 part-time/adjunct (3 women). Expenses: Contact institution. *Financial support:* Available to part-time students. Application deadline: 7/1; In 2001, 124 degrees awarded. *Degree program information:* Part-time and evening/weekend programs available. Postbaccalaureate distance learning degree programs offered (minimal on-campus study). Offers divergent learning (M Ed); human behavior and conflict management (MA); interpersonal relations/conflict management (Certificate); organizational behavior/conflict management (Certificate). *Application deadline:* For fall admission, 8/22 (priority date); for winter admission, 1/8 (priority date). Applications are processed on a rolling basis. *Application fee:* $50. Electronic applications accepted. *Application Contact:* Carol Williams, Graduate Director of Recruitment and Admissions, 803-786-3191, Fax: 803-786-3184, E-mail: cwms@colucoll.edu. *Interim Dean of the Graduate School,* Dr. Anne M. McCulloch, 803-786-3788, Fax: 803-786-3393, E-mail: amcculloch@colacoll.eldu.

COLUMBIA COLLEGE CHICAGO, Chicago, IL 60605-1996

General Information Independent, coed, comprehensive institution. CGS member. *Enrollment:* 214 full-time matriculated graduate/professional students (141 women), 291 part-time matriculated graduate/professional students (203 women). *Enrollment by degree level:* 499 master's, 6 other advanced degrees. *Graduate faculty:* 8 full-time, 24 part-time/adjunct. *Tuition:* Full-time $7,614; part-time $423 per credit hour. *Required fees:* $70 per semester. Tuition and fees vary according to course load. *Graduate housing:* Room and/or apartments available on a first-come, first-served basis to single students; on-campus housing not available to married students. Typical cost: $5,900 per year. Housing application deadline: 8/15. *Student services:* Campus employment opportunities, career counseling, international student services, low-cost health insurance. *Library facilities:* Columbia College Library. *Online resources:* library catalog, web page, access to other libraries' catalogs. *Collection:* 187,132 titles, 3,001 serial subscriptions, 127,494 audiovisual materials.

Computer facilities: 730 computers available on campus for general student use. A campuswide network can be accessed. Internet access is available. *Web address:* http://www.colum.edu/.

General Application Contact: Keith Cleveland, Associate Dean of the Graduate School, 312-663-1600 Ext. 5260, Fax: 312-344-8047, E-mail: kcleveland@colum.edu.

GRADUATE UNITS

Graduate School Students: 214 full-time (141 women), 291 part-time (203 women); includes 185 minority (85 African Americans, 30 Asian Americans or Pacific Islanders, 68 Hispanic Americans, 2 Native Americans), 23 international. Average age 33. Expenses: Contact institution. *Financial support:* Fellowships, career-related internships or fieldwork, Federal Work-Study, and scholarships/grants available. Support available to part-time students. Financial award application deadline: 8/15; financial award applicants required to submit FAFSA. In 2001, 134 degrees awarded. *Degree program information:* Part-time and evening/weekend programs available. Offers architectural studies (MFA); arts, entertainment, and media management (MA); creative writing (MFA); dance/movement therapy (MA); elementary (MAT); English (MAT); film and video (MFA); interdisciplinary arts (MA, MAT); interdisciplinary book and paper arts (MFA); interior design (MFA); multicultural education (MA); photography (MA, MFA); public affairs journalism (MA); teaching of writing (MA); urban teaching (MA). *Application fee:* $50. *Acting Dean of the Graduate School,* Keith Cleveland, 312-344-7261, Fax: 312-344-8047, E-mail: kcleveland@colum.edu.

Announcement: Using sophisticated equipment and contemporary facilities, graduate students pursue practical, professional curricula in the arts, media, communications, and education fields. A faculty of distinguished artists and successful professionals provides leadership, incentive, and direction, encouraging students to exert their individuality and creativity. Exceptionally well qualified applicants are eligible for fellowships and graduate opportunity awards.

See in-depth description on page 831.

COLUMBIA INTERNATIONAL UNIVERSITY, Columbia, SC 29230-3122

General Information Independent-religious, coed, comprehensive institution. *Enrollment:* 268 full-time matriculated graduate/professional students (125 women), 191 part-time matriculated graduate/professional students (73 women). *Enrollment by degree level:* 104 first professional, 230 master's, 49 doctoral, 76 other advanced degrees. *Graduate faculty:* 26 full-time (5 women), 29 part-time/adjunct (6 women). *Tuition:* Full-time $5,670; part-time $315 per hour. *Required fees:* $165. *Graduate housing:* Room and/or apartments available to single students; on-campus housing not available to married students. Typical cost: $4,750 (including board). Housing application deadline: 8/27. *Student services:* Campus employment opportunities, campus safety program, career counseling, child daycare facilities, international student services, low-cost health insurance. *Library facilities:* G. Allen Fleece Library. *Online resources:* library catalog. *Collection:* 99,052 titles, 425 serial subscriptions, 6,781 audiovisual materials.

Computer facilities: 42 computers available on campus for general student use. A campuswide network can be accessed from student residence rooms. *Web address:* http://www.ciu.edu/.

General Application Contact: Chad Jones, Director of Seminary Admissions, 803-754-4100 Ext. 3344, Fax: 803-786-4209, E-mail: yescbs@ciu.edu.

GRADUATE UNITS

Columbia Biblical Seminary and School of Missions Students: 212 full-time (83 women), 171 part-time (57 women); includes 53 minority (42 African Americans, 10 Asian Americans or Pacific Islanders, 1 Hispanic American), 43 international. Average age 32. 272 applicants, 72% accepted, 142 enrolled. *Faculty:* 19 full-time (2 women), 17 part-time/adjunct (1 woman). Expenses: Contact institution. *Financial support:* In 2001–02, 344 students received support. Career-related internships or fieldwork, Federal Work-Study, institutionally sponsored loans, and scholarships/grants available. Financial award application deadline: 3/20; financial award applicants required to submit FAFSA. In 2001, 36 first professional degrees, 100 master's, 5 doctorates, 7 other advanced degrees awarded. *Degree program information:* Part-time and evening/weekend programs available. Offers academic ministries (M Div); Bible (MA); biblical studies (Certificate); Christian education (M Div, MACE); evangelism (MAEV); general theological studies (MA); intercultural studies (MA); international theological education (MA); leadership for evangelism/discipleship (M Div, MALED); missiology (MA); missions (M Div, MAMIS, D Min); Muslim studies (M Div, MA); New Testament (MA); Old Testament (MA); pastoral counseling (M Div, MAPC); pastoral leadership (M Div); pastoral theology (D Min); teaching English as a foreign language/intercultural studies (MA). *Application deadline:* For fall admission, 8/15 (priority date); for winter admission, 12/15 (priority date); for spring admission, 1/15 (priority date). Applications are processed on a rolling basis. *Application fee:* $25. Electronic applications accepted. *Application Contact:* Chad Jones, Director of Seminary Admissions, 803-754-4100 Ext. 3344, Fax: 803-786-4209, E-mail: yescbs@ciu.edu. *Interim Dean,* Dr. Robert W. Ferris, 803-754-4100 Ext. 3330, Fax: 803-786-4209, E-mail: rferris@ciu.edu.

Columbia Graduate School Students: 56 full-time (42 women), 20 part-time (16 women); includes 8 minority (all African Americans), 6 international. 82 applicants, 59% accepted, 24 enrolled. *Faculty:* 7 full-time (3 women), 12 part-time/adjunct (5 women). Expenses: Contact institution. *Financial support:* In 2001–02, 31 students received support. Career-related internships or fieldwork, Federal Work-Study, institutionally sponsored loans, and scholarships/grants available. Financial award application deadline: 3/20; financial award applicants required to submit FAFSA. In 2001, 26 degrees awarded. *Degree program information:* Part-time and evening/weekend programs available. Offers counseling (MACN); curriculum and instruction (MA Ed); educational administration (MA Ed); teaching (MAT); teaching english as a foreign language (MATEFL). *Application deadline:* For fall admission, 8/15 (priority date); for winter admission, 12/15 (priority date); for spring admission, 1/15 (priority date). Applications are processed on a rolling basis. *Application fee:* $25. Electronic applications accepted. *Application Contact:* Chad Jones, Director of Seminary Admissions, 803-754-4100 Ext. 3344, Fax: 803-786-4209, E-mail: yescbs@ciu.edu. *Dean,* Dr. Milton Uecker, 803-754-4100 Ext. 3319, Fax: 803-786-4209, E-mail: muecker@ciu.edu.

COLUMBIA SOUTHERN UNIVERSITY, Orange Beach, AL 36561

General Information Proprietary, coed, comprehensive institution. *Enrollment:* 203 part-time matriculated graduate/professional students. *Enrollment by degree level:* 203 master's. *Graduate faculty:* 16 part-time/adjunct (5 women). *Tuition:* Part-time $175 per credit hour. *Student services:* International student services. *Web address:* http://www.columbiasouthern.edu/.

General Application Contact: Poché Waguespack, Dean of Students, 800-977-8449 Ext. 110, Fax: 251-981-3815, E-mail: poche@columbiasouthern.edu.

GRADUATE UNITS

MBA Program Students: 129. 203 applicants, 81% accepted, 129 enrolled. *Faculty:* 11 part-time/adjunct (3 women). Expenses: Contact institution. *Financial support:* Institutionally sponsored loans available. In 2001, 52 degrees awarded. *Degree program information:* Part-time and evening/weekend programs available. Postbaccalaureate distance learning degree programs offered (no on-campus study). Offers electronic business and technology (MBA); healthcare management (MBA); human resources management (MBA); international management (MBA); marketing (MBA); project management (MBA); public administration (MBA); sport management (MBA). *Application deadline:* Applications are processed on a rolling basis. *Application fee:* $25 ($50 for international students). Electronic applications accepted. *Application Contact:* Poché Waguespack, Dean of Students, 800-977-8449 Ext. 110, Fax: 251-981-3815, E-mail: poche@columbiasouthern.edu. *Director of Educational Services,* Dr. Tommy Boothe, 800-977-8449, Fax: 251-981-3771, E-mail: drtommymb@columbiasouthern.edu.

Program in Occupational Safety and Health 114 applicants, 80% accepted, 25 enrolled. *Faculty:* 5 part-time/adjunct (2 women). Expenses: Contact institution. In 2001, 38 degrees awarded. *Degree program information:* Part-time and evening/weekend programs available. Postbaccalaureate distance learning degree programs offered (no on-campus study). Offers environmental management (MS). *Application deadline:* Applications are processed on a rolling basis. *Application fee:* $50. Electronic applications accepted. *Application Contact:* Poché Waguespack, Dean of Students, 800-977-8449 Ext. 110, Fax: 251-981-3815, E-mail: poche@columbiasouthern.edu. *Academic Dean,* Dr. Joseph Manjone, 800-977-8449 Ext. 101, Fax: 251-981-3815, E-mail: drmanjone@colsouth.edu.

COLUMBIA THEOLOGICAL SEMINARY, Decatur, GA 30031-0520

General Information Independent-religious, coed, graduate-only institution. *Enrollment by degree level:* 166 first professional, 78 master's, 313 doctoral. *Graduate faculty:* 32 full-time (4 women), 15 part-time/adjunct (5 women). *Tuition:* Part-time $300 per credit hour. *Graduate housing:* Rooms and/or apartments available on a first-come, first-served basis to single students and available to married students. Housing application deadline: 4/30. *Student services:* Career counseling, exercise/wellness program, free psychological counseling, international student services, low-cost health insurance, writing training. *Library facilities:* John Bulow Campbell Library. *Online resources:* library catalog, web page, access to other libraries' catalogs. *Collection:* 139,500 titles, 664 serial subscriptions, 3,500 audiovisual materials.

Computer facilities: 27 computers available on campus for general student use. A campuswide network can be accessed from off campus. Internet access is available. *Web address:* http://www.ctsnet.edu/.

General Application Contact: Ann Clay Adams, Director of Admissions, 404-378-8821, Fax: 404-377-9696.

GRADUATE UNITS

Graduate and Professional Programs Students: 523 full-time (160 women), 87 part-time (44 women); includes 91 minority (43 African Americans, 44 Asian Americans or Pacific Islanders, 4 Hispanic Americans), 44 international. Average age 35. *Faculty:* 32 full-time (4 women), 15 part-time/adjunct (5 women). Expenses: Contact institution. *Financial support:* In 2001–02, 131 students received support. Career-related internships or fieldwork, Federal Work-Study, and scholarships/grants available. Financial award application deadline: 8/1; financial award applicants required to submit FAFSA. In 2001, 51 first professional degrees, 11 master's, 46 doctorates awarded. Offers theology (M Div, MATS, Th M, D Min, Th D). *Application deadline:* Applications are processed on a rolling basis. *Application fee:* $30. *Application Contact:* Ann Clay Adams, Director of Admissions, 404-378-8821, Fax: 404-377-9696. *Vice President for Academic Affairs*, Dr. Cameron Murchison, 404-378-8821, Fax: 404-377-9696.

COLUMBIA UNIVERSITY, New York, NY 10027

General Information Independent, coed, university. CGS member. *Enrollment by degree level:* 3,916 first professional, 5,978 master's, 2,599 doctoral, 149 other advanced degrees. *Graduate faculty:* 3,137 full-time (1,046 women), 995 part-time/adjunct (387 women). *Tuition:* Full-time $27,528. *Required fees:* $1,638. *Graduate housing:* Rooms and/or apartments available on a first-come, first-served basis to single and married students. Housing application deadline: 8/9. *Student services:* Campus employment opportunities, campus safety program, career counseling, disabled student services, exercise/wellness program, free psychological counseling, international student services, low-cost health insurance, multicultural affairs office, writing training. *Research affiliation:* Goddard Space Flight Center, Marine Biological Laboratory, American Museum of Natural History, New York Botanical Gardens, Brookhaven National Laboratory, Long Island Biological Laboratory. *Web address:* http://www.columbia.edu/.

General Application Contact: Information Contact, 212-854-1754.

GRADUATE UNITS

College of Physicians and Surgeons *Degree program information:* Part-time programs available. Offers medicine (MD, M Phil, MA, MS, DN Sc, PhD, Adv C); occupational therapy (professional) (MS); occupational therapy administration or education (post-professional) (MS); physical therapy (MS).

Graduate School of Arts and Sciences at the College of Physicians and Surgeons Offers anatomy (M Phil, MA, PhD); anatomy and cell biology (PhD); biochemistry and molecular biophysics (M Phil, PhD); biomedical sciences (M Phil, MA, PhD); biophysics (PhD); cellular, molecular and biophysical studies (M Phil, MA, PhD); genetics (M Phil, MA, PhD); medical informatics (M Phil, MA, PhD); medicine (M Phil, MA, PhD); neurobiology and behavior (M Phil, PhD); pathobiology (M Phil, MA, PhD); pharmacology (M Phil, MA, PhD); pharmacology-toxicology (M Phil, MA, PhD); physiology and cellular biophysics (M Phil, MA, PhD). Only candidates for the PhD are admitted.

Institute of Human Nutrition Students: 49 full-time (39 women), 9 part-time (7 women); includes 14 minority (5 African Americans, 7 Asian Americans or Pacific Islanders, 2 Hispanic Americans), 16 international. Average age 23. 86 applicants, 40% accepted, 24 enrolled. *Faculty:* 44 full-time (15 women). Expenses: Contact institution. *Financial support:* In 2001–02, 12 fellowships (averaging $24,575 per year), 20 research assistantships (averaging $24,575 per year) were awarded. Federal Work-Study, institutionally sponsored loans, and traineeships also available. Support available to part-time students. Financial award application deadline: 1/4; financial award applicants required to submit FAFSA. In 2001, 22 master's, 2 doctorates awarded. *Degree program information:* Part-time and evening/weekend programs available. Offers nutrition (M Phil, MA, MS, PhD). *Application fee:* $75. *Application Contact:* Dr. David Talmage, Student Adviser, 212-305-4808, Fax: 212-305-3079, E-mail: dat1@columbia.edu. *Director*, Dr. Richard Deckelbaum, 212-305-4808, Fax: 212-305-3079, E-mail: nutrition@columbia.edu.

Fu Foundation School of Engineering and Applied Science Students: 495 full-time (112 women), 327 part-time (70 women); includes 65 minority (6 African Americans, 54 Asian Americans or Pacific Islanders, 4 Hispanic Americans, 1 Native American), 543 international. Average age 24. 2,959 applicants, 31% accepted, 300 enrolled. *Faculty:* 129 full-time (7 women), 65 part-time/adjunct (4 women). Expenses: Contact institution. *Financial support:* In 2001–02, 42 fellowships (averaging $15,000 per year), 209 research assistantships (averaging $15,000 per year), 82 teaching assistantships (averaging $17,000 per year) were awarded. Career-related internships or fieldwork, Federal Work-Study, institutionally sponsored loans, scholarships/grants, unspecified assistantships, and outside fellowships also available. Support available to part-time students. Financial award application deadline: 1/5; financial award applicants required to submit FAFSA. In 2001, 276 master's, 64 doctorates awarded. *Degree program information:* Part-time programs available. Postbaccalaureate distance learning degree programs offered (no on-campus study). Offers applied physics (MS, PhD); applied physics and applied mathematics (Eng Sc D); biomedical engineering (MS, Eng Sc D); chemical engineering (MS, Eng Sc D, PhD, Engr); civil engineering (MS, Eng Sc D, PhD, Engr); computer science (MS, PhD, CSE); earth resources engineering (MS, PhD); electrical engineering (MS, Eng Sc D, PhD, EE); engineering and applied science (ME, MS, Eng Sc D, PhD, CSE, EE, EM, Engr, Met E); financial engineering (MS); industrial engineering (MS, Eng Sc D, PhD, Engr); materials science and engineering (MS, Eng Sc D, PhD); mechanical engineering (ME, MS, Eng Sc D, PhD); mechanics (MS, Eng Sc D, PhD, Engr); medical physics (MS); minerals engineering and materials science (Eng Sc D, PhD, Engr); operations research (MS, Eng Sc D, PhD); solid state science and engineering (MS, Eng Sc D, PhD); telecommunications (MS). *Application deadline:* For fall admission, 1/5 (priority date); for spring admission, 10/1 (priority date). Applications are processed on a rolling basis. *Application fee:* $55. Electronic applications accepted. *Application Contact:* Thomas P. Rock, Assistant Dean, 212-854-6438, Fax: 212-854-5900, E-mail: tpr4@columbia.edu. *Dean*, Zvi Galil, 212-854-2993, Fax: 212-854-5900, E-mail: seasgradmit@columbia.edu.

Graduate School of Architecture, Planning, and Preservation Students: 565 full-time (242 women). *Faculty:* 19 full-time (5 women), 115 part-time/adjunct (28 women). Expenses: Contact institution. *Financial support:* Fellowships, teaching assistantships with partial tuition reimbursements, career-related internships or fieldwork, Federal Work-Study, and institutionally sponsored loans available. In 2001, 266 degrees awarded. Offers advanced architectural design (MS); architecture (M Arch, PhD); architecture and urban design (MS); architecture, planning, and preservation (M Arch, MS, PhD); historic preservation (MS); real estate development (MS); urban planning (MS, PhD). PhD offered through the Graduate School of Arts and Sciences. *Application fee:* $60. *Application Contact:* Head, 212-854-3510. *Dean*, Bernard Tschumi, 212-854-3473.

Graduate School of Arts and Sciences Students: 2,827 full-time (1,352 women), 422 part-time (233 women); includes 378 minority (76 African Americans, 219 Asian Americans or Pacific Islanders, 78 Hispanic Americans, 5 Native Americans), 947 international. Average age 32. 6,307 applicants, 28% accepted. *Faculty:* 508 full-time, 158 part-time/adjunct. Expenses: Contact institution. *Financial support:* Fellowships, research assistantships, teaching assistantships, career-related internships or fieldwork, Federal Work-Study, and institutionally sponsored loans available. Support available to part-time students. Financial award application deadline: 1/5; financial award applicants required to submit FAFSA. In 2001, 392 master's, 360 doctorates awarded. *Degree program information:* Part-time and evening/weekend programs available. Offers African-American studies (MA); American studies (MA); arts and sciences (M Phil, MA, MS, DMA, PhD, Certificate); conservation biology (MA); East Asian regional studies (MA); East Asian studies (MA); French cultural studies (MA); human rights studies (MA); Islamic culture studies (MA); Jewish studies (MA); medieval studies (MA); modern European studies (MA); quantitative methods in the social sciences (MA); Russian, Eurasian and East European regional studies (MA); South Asian studies (MA); theatre (M Phil, MA, PhD); Yiddish studies (MA). *Application deadline:* For fall admission, 1/3. *Application fee:* $65. *Application Contact:* Robert Furno, Assistant Dean for Admissions, 212-854-4737, Fax: 212-854-2863, E-mail: jc12@columbia.edu. *Dean*, Dr. Henry C. Pinkham, 212-854-2861, Fax: 212-854-2863, E-mail: hcp3@columbia.edu.

Division of Humanities Students: 1,056 full-time (615 women), 127 part-time (78 women); includes 133 minority (25 African Americans, 72 Asian Americans or Pacific Islanders, 36 Hispanic Americans), 204 international. Average age 33. 1,988 applicants, 30% accepted. Expenses: Contact institution. *Financial support:* Fellowships, teaching assistantships, Federal Work-Study, and institutionally sponsored loans available. Support available to part-time students. Financial award application deadline: 1/5; financial award applicants required to submit FAFSA. In 2001, 136 master's, 89 doctorates awarded. *Degree program information:* Part-time programs available. Offers archaeology (M Phil, MA, PhD); art history and archaeology (M Phil, MA, PhD); classics (M Phil, MA, PhD); comparative literature (M Phil, MA, PhD); East Asian languages and cultures (M Phil, MA, PhD); English literature (M Phil, MA, PhD); French and Romance philology (M Phil, PhD); Germanic languages (M Phil, MA, PhD); Hebrew language and literature (M Phil, MA, PhD); humanities (M Phil, MA, DMA, PhD); Italian (M Phil, MA, PhD); Jewish studies (M Phil, MA, PhD); literature-writing (M Phil, MA, PhD); Middle Eastern languages and cultures (M Phil, MA, PhD); modern art (MA); music (M Phil, MA, DMA, PhD); Oriental studies (M Phil, MA, PhD); philosophy (M Phil, MA, PhD); religion (M Phil, MA, PhD); Romance languages (MA); Russian literature (M Phil, MA, PhD); Slavic languages (M Phil, MA, PhD); Spanish and Portuguese (M Phil, MA, PhD). *Application deadline:* For fall admission, 1/3; for spring admission, 11/30. *Application fee:* $65. *Application Contact:* Robert Furno, Assistant Dean for Admissions, 212-854-4737, Fax: 212-854-2863, E-mail: jc12@columbia.edu.

Division of Natural Sciences Students: 473 full-time (157 women), 69 part-time (21 women); includes 46 minority (7 African Americans, 31 Asian Americans or Pacific Islanders, 7 Hispanic Americans, 1 Native American), 269 international. Average age 31. 1,388 applicants, 22% accepted. Expenses: Contact institution. *Financial support:* Fellowships, research assistantships, teaching assistantships, career-related internships or fieldwork, Federal Work-Study, and institutionally sponsored loans available. Support available to part-time students. Financial award application deadline: 1/5; financial award applicants required to submit FAFSA. In 2001, 91 master's, 76 doctorates awarded. *Degree program information:* Part-time programs available. Offers astronomy (M Phil, MA, PhD); atmospheric and planetary science (M Phil, PhD); biological sciences (M Phil, MA, PhD); chemical physics (M Phil, PhD); conservation biology (Certificate); ecology and evolutionary biology (PhD); environmental policy (Certificate); epidemiology (M Phil, MA, PhD); experimental psychology (M Phil, MA, PhD); geochemistry (M Phil, MA, PhD); geodetic sciences (M Phil, MA, PhD); geophysics (M Phil, MA, PhD); inorganic chemistry (M Phil, MS, PhD); mathematics (M Phil, MA, PhD); natural sciences (M Phil, MA, MS, PhD, Certificate); oceanography (M Phil, MA, PhD); organic chemistry (M Phil, MS, PhD); philosophical foundations of physics (MA); physics (M Phil, PhD); psychobiology (M Phil, MA, PhD); social psychology (M Phil, MA, PhD); statistics (M Phil, MA, PhD). *Application deadline:* For fall admission, 1/3. *Application fee:* $65. *Application Contact:* Robert Furno, Assistant Dean for Admissions, 212-854-4737, Fax: 212-854-2863, E-mail: jc12@columbia.edu.

Division of Social Sciences Students: 894 full-time (386 women), 93 part-time (49 women); includes 105 minority (33 African Americans, 45 Asian Americans or Pacific Islanders, 23 Hispanic Americans, 4 Native Americans), 305 international. Average age 32. 1,668 applicants, 37% accepted. Expenses: Contact institution. *Financial support:* Fellowships, teaching assistantships, Federal Work-Study and institutionally sponsored loans available. Support available to part-time students. Financial award application deadline: 1/5; financial award applicants required to submit FAFSA. In 2001, 108 master's, 84 doctorates awarded. *Degree program information:* Part-time programs available. Offers American history (M Phil, MA, PhD); anthropology (M Phil, MA, PhD); economics (M Phil, MA, PhD); history (M Phil, MA, PhD); political science (M Phil, MA, PhD); social sciences (M Phil, MA, PhD); sociology (M Phil, MA, PhD). *Application deadline:* For fall admission, 1/3. *Application fee:* $65. *Application Contact:* Robert Furno, Assistant Dean for Admissions, 212-854-4737, Fax: 212-854-2863, E-mail: jc12@columbia.edu.

Graduate School of Business Students: 1,775 full-time (597 women). Average age 29. *Faculty:* 127 full-time (19 women), 80 part-time/adjunct (14 women). Expenses: Contact institution. *Financial support:* Fellowships, research assistantships, teaching assistantships, career-related internships or fieldwork, Federal Work-Study, institutionally sponsored loans, and scholarships/grants available. Financial award application deadline: 2/1; financial award applicants required to submit FAFSA. In 2001, 978 master's, 16 doctorates awarded. Offers accounting (MBA); business (PhD); business administration (EMBA, MBA); decision, risk, and operations (MBA); entrepreneurship (MBA); finance and economics (MBA); human resource management (MBA); international business (MBA); management (MBA); marketing (MBA); media, entertainment and communications (MBA); real estate (MBA); social enterprise (MBA). *Application deadline:* Applications are processed on a rolling basis. Electronic applications accepted. *Application Contact:* Linda B. Meehan, Assistant Dean and Executive Director of Admissions and Financial Aid, 212-854-1961, Fax: 212-662-6754, E-mail: apply@claven.gsb.columbia.edu. *Dean*, Prof. Meyer Feldberg, 212-854-6083, Fax: 212-932-0545, E-mail: mf7@columbia.edu.

Graduate School of Journalism Students: 208 full-time (124 women), 92 part-time (50 women); includes 44 minority (20 African Americans, 16 Asian Americans or Pacific Islanders, 8 Hispanic Americans), 42 international. Average age 28. 1,261 applicants, 19% accepted, 206 enrolled. *Faculty:* 19 full-time (7 women), 78 part-time/adjunct (26 women). Expenses: Contact institution. *Financial support:* Fellowships, research assistantships, career-related internships or fieldwork, institutionally sponsored loans, and scholarships/grants available. Financial award application deadline: 2/15; financial award applicants required to submit FAFSA. In 2001, 256 degrees awarded. *Degree program information:* Part-time programs available. Offers journalism (MS, PhD). *Application deadline:* For fall admission, 12/16. *Application fee:* $75. *Application Contact:* Robert MacDonald, Director of Admissions, 212-854-3828, Fax: 212-854-2352, E-mail: rm37@columbia.edu. *Dean*, Tom Goldstein, 212-854-4150.

School of Dental and Oral Surgery Offers clinical specialty (MA); dental and oral surgery (DDS, MA, MS).

School of International and Public Affairs Students: 776 full-time (465 women), 99 part-time (60 women). Average age 27. 2,150 applicants, 46% accepted, 453 enrolled. *Faculty:* 162 full-time (21 women), 63 part-time/adjunct (26 women). Expenses: Contact institution. *Financial support:* In 2001–02, 309 students received support, including 255 fellowships, 32 research assistantships, 22 teaching assistantships; career-related internships or fieldwork, Federal Work-Study, and institutionally sponsored loans also available. Financial award application deadline: 1/5; financial award applicants required to submit FAFSA. In 2001, 619 degrees awarded. *Degree program information:* Part-time programs available. Offers earth systems science, policy and management (MPA); international affairs (MIA); international and public affairs (MIA, MPA, Certificate); public policy and administration (MPA). *Application deadline:* For fall admission, 1/5 (priority date); for spring admission, 10/15. *Application fee:* $90 ($75 for international students). Electronic applications accepted. *Application Contact:* Robert Garris, Associate Director, 212-854-6216, Fax: 212-854-3010, E-mail: sipa_admission@columbia.edu. *Dean*, Dr. Lisa Anderson, 212-854-4604, Fax: 212-864-4847, E-mail: la8@columbia.edu.

East Asian Institute Expenses: Contact institution. *Financial support:* Application deadline: 1/15. Offers Asian studies (Certificate). Students must be enrolled in a separate graduate degree program at Columbia University. *Application deadline:* For fall admission, 1/5 (priority date); for spring admission, 10/15 (priority date). *Application fee:* $75. Electronic applications accepted. *Application Contact:* Robert Garris, Associate Director, 212-854-6216, Fax: 212-854-3010, E-mail: sipa_admission@columbia.edu. *Director*, Dr. Madeleine Zelin, 212-854-2591, Fax: 212-749-1497, E-mail: mhz1@columbia.edu.

Harriman Institute Expenses: Contact institution. *Financial support:* Fellowships, career-related internships or fieldwork and Federal Work-Study available. Financial award application deadline: 1/15. *Degree program information:* Part-time programs available. Students must be enrolled in a separate graduate degree program at Columbia University. *Application deadline:* For fall admission, 1/5 (priority date); for spring admission, 10/15 (priority date). *Application fee:* $75. Electronic applications accepted. *Application Contact:* Robert Garris, Associate Director, 212-854-4623, Fax: 212-854-3010, E-mail: sipa_admission@columbia.edu. *Director*, Dr. Mark L. von Hagen, 212-854-6216, Fax: 212-854-3010, E-mail: sipa_admission@columbia.edu.

Institute for the Study of Europe Expenses: Contact institution. *Financial support:* Application deadline: 1/15. Offers Europe (Certificate). Students must be enrolled in a separate graduate degree program at Columbia University. *Application deadline:* For fall admission,

Columbia University (continued)

1/5 (priority date); for spring admission, 10/15 (priority date). *Application fee:* $75. Electronic applications accepted. *Application Contact:* Robert Garris, Associate Director, 212-854-6216, Fax: 212-854-3010, E-mail: sipa_admission@columbia.edu. *Director*, Dr. John Micgiel, 212-854-4618, Fax: 212-854-8577, E-mail: jsm6@columbia.edu.

Institute of African Studies *Faculty:* 22 full-time, 14 part-time/adjunct. Expenses: Contact institution. *Financial support:* Application deadline: 1/15. Offers African studies (Certificate). Students must be enrolled in a separate graduate degree program at Columbia University. *Application deadline:* For fall admission, 1/5 (priority date); for spring admission, 10/15 (priority date). *Application fee:* $75. Electronic applications accepted. *Application Contact:* Robert Garris, Associate Director, 212-854-6216, Fax: 212-854-3010, E-mail: sipa_admission@columbia.edu. *Director*, Prof. Mahmood Mamdani, 212-854-4633, Fax: 212-854-4639, E-mail: mm1124@columbia.edu.

Institute of Latin American and Iberian Studies Students: 2. *Faculty:* 47 full-time, 17 part-time/adjunct. Expenses: Contact institution. *Financial support:* Application deadline: 1/15. Offers Latin American and Iberian studies (Certificate). Students must be enrolled in a separate graduate degree program at Columbia University. *Application deadline:* For fall admission, 1/5 (priority date); for spring admission, 10/15 (priority date). *Application fee:* $75. Electronic applications accepted. *Application Contact:* Robert Garris, Associate Director, 212-854-6216, Fax: 212-854-3010, E-mail: sipa_admission@columbia.edu. *Director*, Dr. Douglas Chalmers, 212-854-4643, Fax: 212-854-4607, E-mail: chalmers@columbia.edu.

Institute on East Central Europe *Faculty:* 10 full-time, 10 part-time/adjunct. Expenses: Contact institution. *Financial support:* In 2001–02, 1 research assistantship was awarded; fellowships, career-related internships or fieldwork and Federal Work-Study also available. Financial award application deadline: 1/15. Offers East Central Europe (Certificate). Students must be enrolled in a separate graduate degree program at Columbia University. *Application deadline:* For fall admission, 1/5 (priority date); for spring admission, 10/15 (priority date). *Application fee:* $75. Electronic applications accepted. *Application Contact:* Robert Garris, Associate Director, 212-854-6216, Fax: 212-854-3010, E-mail: sipa_admission@columbia.edu. *Director*, Dr. John Micgiel, 212-854-4618, Fax: 212-854-8577, E-mail: jsm6@columbia.edu.

Middle East Institute Expenses: Contact institution. *Financial support:* Application deadline: 1/5. Offers Middle East studies (Certificate). Students must be enrolled in a separate graduate degree program at Columbia University. *Application deadline:* For fall admission, 1/5 (priority date); for spring admission, 10/15 (priority date). *Application fee:* $75. Electronic applications accepted. *Application Contact:* Robert Garris, Associate Director, 212-854-6216, Fax: 212-854-3010, E-mail: sipa_admission@columbia.edu. *Director*, Dr. Gary Sick, 212-854-2584, Fax: 212-854-1413, E-mail: ggs2@columbia.edu.

Southern Asian Institute Students: 1. Expenses: Contact institution. *Financial support:* Application deadline: 1/15. Offers Southern Asian studies (Certificate). Students must be enrolled in a separate graduate degree program at Columbia University. *Application deadline:* For fall admission, 1/5 (priority date); for spring admission, 10/15 (priority date). *Application fee:* $75. Electronic applications accepted. *Application Contact:* Robert Garris, Associate Director, 212-854-6216, Fax: 212-854-3010, E-mail: sipa_admission@columbia.edu. *Director*, Dr. Giauri Viswanathan, 212-854-3616, Fax: 212-854-6987, E-mail: southasia@columbia.edu.

School of Law Students: 1,139 full-time (576 women); includes 363 minority (104 African Americans, 165 Asian Americans or Pacific Islanders, 88 Hispanic Americans, 6 Native Americans), 76 international. Average age 24. 6,614 applicants, 17% accepted, 356 enrolled. *Faculty:* 91 full-time (24 women), 138 part-time/adjunct (27 women). Expenses: Contact institution. *Financial support:* In 2001–02, 550 students received support, including 24 research assistantships; fellowships, teaching assistantships, career-related internships or fieldwork, Federal Work-Study, institutionally sponsored loans, scholarships/grants, and tuition waivers (full and partial) also available. Financial award application deadline: 3/1; financial award applicants required to submit FAFSA. In 2001, 381 first professional degrees, 171 master's, 5 doctorates awarded. Offers law (JD, LL M, JSD). *Application deadline:* For fall admission, 2/15. Applications are processed on a rolling basis. *Application fee:* $65. Electronic applications accepted. *Application Contact:* James Milligan, Dean of Admissions, 212-854-2674, Fax: 212-854-1109. *Dean of Faculty of Law*, David W. Leebron, 212-854-2675.

School of Nursing Students: 124 full-time (110 women), 263 part-time (234 women); includes 39 African Americans, 41 Asian Americans or Pacific Islanders, 16 Hispanic Americans Average age 34. 569 applicants, 76% accepted, 281 enrolled. *Faculty:* 42 full-time (39 women). Expenses: Contact institution. *Financial support:* In 2001–02, 120 students received support; research assistantships, teaching assistantships, Federal Work-Study and institutionally sponsored loans available. Support available to part-time students. Financial award applicants required to submit FAFSA. In 2001, 160 master's, 1 doctorate awarded. *Degree program information:* Part-time programs available. Offers acute care nurse practitioner (MS, Adv C); adult nurse practitioner (MS, Adv C); family nurse practitioner (MS, Adv C); geriatric nurse practitioner (MS, Adv C); HIV nursing (MS, Adv C); neonatal nurse practitioner (MS, Adv C); nurse anesthesia (MS, Adv C); nurse midwifery (MS); nursing (MS, DN Sc, Adv C); nursing science (DN Sc); oncology nursing (MS, Adv C); pediatric nurse practitioner (MS, Adv C); psychiatric-community mental health nursing (MS, Adv C); women's health nurse practitioner (MS, Adv C). *Application deadline:* Applications are processed on a rolling basis. *Application fee:* $75. Electronic applications accepted. *Dean*, Dr. Mary O. Mundinger, 212-305-3582.

School of Social Work Offers social work (MSSW, PhD). PhD offered through the Graduate School of Arts and Sciences.

School of the Arts Students: 738 full-time (386 women), 4 part-time (all women); includes 117 minority (44 African Americans, 48 Asian Americans or Pacific Islanders, 23 Hispanic Americans, 2 Native Americans), 99 international. Average age 27. 1,868 applicants, 17% accepted, 206 enrolled. *Faculty:* 44 full-time (16 women), 156 part-time/adjunct (68 women). Expenses: Contact institution. *Financial support:* In 2001–02, 386 students received support, including 275 fellowships (averaging $6,000 per year), 15 research assistantships (averaging $22,070 per year), 41 teaching assistantships with full and partial tuition reimbursements available; career-related internships or fieldwork, Federal Work-Study, institutionally sponsored loans, scholarships/grants, and tuition waivers (partial) also available. Financial award applicants required to submit FAFSA. In 2001, 162 master's, 1 doctorate awarded. Offers arts (MFA, DMA, PhD); digital media (MFA); directing (MFA); drawing (MFA); fiction (MFA); history/theory (MFA); installation (MFA); new genres (MFA); nonfiction (MFA); painting (MFA); photography (MFA); poetry (MFA); printmaking (MFA); producing (MFA); screen writing (MFA); sculpture (MFA). *Application deadline:* For fall admission, 1/1. *Application fee:* $90. Electronic applications accepted. *Application Contact:* Jamie Sosnow, Director of Admissions, 212-854-2134, E-mail: admissions-arts@columbia.edu. *Dean*, Bruce Ferguson, 212-854-2875.

Oscar Hammerstein Center for Theatre Studies Students: 137 (85 women). Average age 27. 263 applicants, 27% accepted, 41 enrolled. *Faculty:* 8 full-time (3 women), 17 part-time/adjunct (8 women). Expenses: Contact institution. *Financial support:* In 2001–02, 85 fellowships (averaging $5,097 per year), 8 research assistantships (averaging $22,070 per year) were awarded. Career-related internships or fieldwork, Federal Work-Study, institutionally sponsored loans, and tuition waivers (partial) also available. Financial award applicants required to submit FAFSA. In 2001, 43 master's, 1 doctorate awarded. Offers acting (MFA); directing (MFA); drama and theater arts (PhD); dramaturgy (MFA); playwriting (MFA); theater management (MFA). *Application deadline:* For fall admission, 1/1. *Application fee:* $90. Electronic applications accepted. *Application Contact:* Director of Admissions, 212-854-2134, E-mail: admissions-arts@columbia.edu. *Chair*, Kristin Linklater, 212-854-3408, E-mail: theatre@columbia.edu.

See in-depth description on page 833.

COLUMBUS STATE UNIVERSITY, Columbus, GA 31907-5645

General Information State-supported, coed, comprehensive institution. *Enrollment:* 218 full-time matriculated graduate/professional students (127 women), 679 part-time matriculated graduate/professional students (384 women). *Enrollment by degree level:* 781 master's, 116 other advanced degrees. *Graduate faculty:* 89 full-time (37 women), 7 part-time/adjunct (1 woman). Tuition, state resident: full-time $1,166. Tuition, nonresident: full-time $7,386. *Graduate housing:* Room and/or apartments available on a first-come, first-served basis to single students; on-campus housing not available to married students. Typical cost: $3,200 per year ($5,390 including board). Room and board charges vary according to board plan. Housing application deadline: 7/1. *Student services:* Campus employment opportunities, campus safety program, career counseling, disabled student services, exercise/wellness program, free psychological counseling, international student services, low-cost health insurance, multicultural affairs office, teacher training. *Library facilities:* Simon Schwob Memorial Library. *Online resources:* library catalog, web page, access to other libraries' catalogs. *Collection:* 250,000 titles, 1,400 serial subscriptions, 2,500 audiovisual materials. *Research affiliation:* University of Georgia Gerontology Center (memory), Southern Company (benthic response to sediment remediation), Georgia Department of Natural Resources (endangered mussels), Georgia Department of Human Resources (tobacco use), Bradley Turner Foundation (servant leadership), Muscogee County Schools (professional development materials).

Computer facilities: 300 computers available on campus for general student use. A campuswide network can be accessed from student residence rooms and from off campus. Internet access and online class registration are available. *Web address:* http://www.colstate.edu/.

General Application Contact: Katie Thornton, Graduate Admissions Specialist, 706-568-2279, Fax: 706-568-2462, E-mail: thornton_katie@colstate.edu.

GRADUATE UNITS

Graduate Studies Students: 218 full-time (127 women), 679 part-time (384 women); includes 228 minority (201 African Americans, 10 Asian Americans or Pacific Islanders, 16 Hispanic Americans, 1 Native American), 14 international. Average age 35. 272 applicants, 58% accepted. *Faculty:* 89 full-time (37 women), 7 part-time/adjunct (1 woman). Expenses: Contact institution. *Financial support:* In 2001–02, 389 students received support, including 4 fellowships with partial tuition reimbursements available (averaging $3,750 per year), 57 research assistantships with partial tuition reimbursements available (averaging $3,000 per year); career-related internships or fieldwork, Federal Work-Study, institutionally sponsored loans, scholarships/grants, tuition waivers (partial), and unspecified assistantships also available. Support available to part-time students. Financial award application deadline: 5/1; financial award applicants required to submit FAFSA. In 2001, 193 master's, 28 other advanced degrees awarded. *Degree program information:* Part-time and evening/weekend programs available. Postbaccalaureate distance learning degree programs offered (minimal on-campus study). *Application deadline:* For fall admission, 7/6 (priority date); for spring admission, 12/14. Applications are processed on a rolling basis. *Application fee:* $25. Electronic applications accepted. *Application Contact:* Katie Thornton, Graduate Admissions Specialist, 706-568-2279, Fax: 706-568-2462, E-mail: thornton_katie@colstate.edu. *Acting Vice President for Academic Affairs*, Dr. Paul J. Vander Gheynst, 706-568-2061, Fax: 706-569-3168, E-mail: vandergheynst_paul@colstate.edu.

College of Arts and Letters Students: 66 full-time (31 women), 171 part-time (46 women); includes 60 minority (56 African Americans, 4 Hispanic Americans), 1 international. Average age 37. 68 applicants, 51% accepted. *Faculty:* 36 full-time (15 women), 7 part-time/adjunct (1 woman). Expenses: Contact institution. *Financial support:* In 2001–02, 4 fellowships with partial tuition reimbursements (averaging $3,750 per year), 29 research assistantships with partial tuition reimbursements (averaging $3,000 per year) were awarded. Career-related internships or fieldwork, Federal Work-Study, institutionally sponsored loans, scholarships/grants, tuition waivers (partial), and unspecified assistantships also available. Support available to part-time students. Financial award application deadline: 5/1; financial award applicants required to submit FAFSA. *Degree program information:* Part-time and evening/weekend programs available. Postbaccalaureate distance learning degree programs offered (minimal on-campus study). Offers art education (M Ed); arts and letters (M Ed, MM, MPA); music education (MM); public administration (MPA). *Application deadline:* For fall admission, 7/6 (priority date); for spring admission, 12/14. Applications are processed on a rolling basis. *Application fee:* $25. Electronic applications accepted. *Application Contact:* Katie Thornton, Graduate Admissions Specialist, 706-568-2279, Fax: 706-568-2462, E-mail: thornton_katie@colstate.edu. *Acting Dean*, Dr. William L. Chappell, 706-568-2055, Fax: 706-569-3123, E-mail: chappell_william@colstate.edu.

College of Education Students: 109 full-time (81 women), 388 part-time (289 women); includes 136 minority (124 African Americans, 4 Asian Americans or Pacific Islanders, 7 Hispanic Americans, 1 Native American), 1 international. Average age 37. *Faculty:* 28 full-time (19 women). Expenses: Contact institution. *Financial support:* In 2001–02, 252 students received support, including 4 fellowships with partial tuition reimbursements available (averaging $3,750 per year), 43 research assistantships with partial tuition reimbursements available (averaging $3,000 per year); career-related internships or fieldwork, Federal Work-Study, institutionally sponsored loans, scholarships/grants, tuition waivers (partial), and unspecified assistantships also available. Support available to part-time students. Financial award application deadline: 5/1; financial award applicants required to submit FAFSA. In 2001, 94 master's, 28 other advanced degrees awarded. *Degree program information:* Part-time and evening/weekend programs available. Postbaccalaureate distance learning degree programs offered (minimal on-campus study). Offers community counseling (MS); early childhood education (M Ed, Ed S); education (M Ed, MS, Ed S); educational leadership (M Ed, Ed S); instructional technology (MS); middle grades education (M Ed, Ed S); physical education (M Ed); school counseling (M Ed, Ed S); secondary education (M Ed, Ed S); special education (Ed S). *Application deadline:* For fall admission, 7/6 (priority date); for spring admission, 12/14. Applications are processed on a rolling basis. *Application fee:* $25. *Application Contact:* Katie Thornton, Graduate Admissions Specialist, 706-568-2279, Fax: 706-568-2462, E-mail: thornton_katie@colstate.edu. *Dean*, Dr. Thomas E. Harrison, 706-568-2212, Fax: 706-569-3134, E-mail: harrison_thomas@colstate.edu.

College of Science Students: 32 full-time (10 women), 95 part-time (35 women); includes 28 minority (20 African Americans, 5 Asian Americans or Pacific Islanders, 3 Hispanic Americans), 9 international. Average age 37. 73 applicants, 47% accepted. *Faculty:* 14 full-time (0 women). Expenses: Contact institution. *Financial support:* In 2001–02, 49 students received support, including 23 research assistantships with partial tuition reimbursements available (averaging $3,000 per year); career-related internships or fieldwork, Federal Work-Study, institutionally sponsored loans, scholarships/grants, tuition waivers (partial), and unspecified assistantships also available. Support available to part-time students. Financial award application deadline: 5/1; financial award applicants required to submit FAFSA. In 2001, 21 degrees awarded. *Degree program information:* Part-time and evening/weekend programs available. Postbaccalaureate distance learning degree programs offered (no on-campus study). Offers applied computer science (MS); environmental science (MS); information technology management (MS); science (MS). *Application deadline:* For fall admission, 7/6 (priority date); for spring admission, 12/14. Applications are processed on a rolling basis. *Application fee:* $25. *Application Contact:* Katie Thornton, Graduate Admissions Specialist, 706-568-2279, Fax: 706-568-2462, E-mail: thornton_katie@colstate.edu. *Dean*, Dr. Arthur G. Cleveland, 706-568-2056, E-mail: cleveland_art@colstate.edu.

CONCORDIA LUTHERAN SEMINARY, Edmonton, AB T5B 4E3, Canada

General Information Independent-religious, coed, primarily men, graduate-only institution. *Enrollment by degree level:* 17 first professional, 2 master's. *Graduate faculty:* 5 full-time (0 women). *Tuition:* Full-time $6,125; part-time $175 per credit. *Required fees:* $15 per semester. One-time fee: $50 full-time. *Graduate housing:* On-campus housing not available. *Student services:* Campus employment opportunities. *Library facilities:* Concordia Lutheran Seminary Library. *Online resources:* library catalog. *Collection:* 24,900 titles, 4,069 serial subscriptions, 662 audiovisual materials.

Computer facilities: 1 computer available on campus for general student use. Internet access is available. *Web address:* http://www.concordiasem.ab.ca/.

General Application Contact: Dr. Vernon A. Raaflaub, Director of Admissions, 780-474-1468, Fax: 780-479-3067, E-mail: clsdean@connect.ab.ca.

GRADUATE UNITS

Graduate and Professional Programs Students: 19 full-time (2 women), 1 international. Average age 31. 3 applicants, 67% accepted, 2 enrolled. *Faculty:* 5 full-time (0 women). Expenses: Contact institution. *Financial support:* In 2001–02, 11 students received support. Scholarships/grants available. Financial award application deadline: 8/1. In 2001, 5 M Divs, 1 master's awarded. *Degree program information:* Part-time programs available. Offers theology (M Div, MTS). *Application deadline:* For fall admission, 4/1 (priority date); for winter admission, 10/30 (priority date). *Application fee:* $25. *Application Contact:* Dr. Vernon A. Raaflaub, Director of Admissions, 780-474-1468, Fax: 780-479-3067, E-mail: admissions@concordiasem.ab.ca. *Academic Dean*, Dr. Edward G. Kettner, 780-474-1468, Fax: 780-479-3067, E-mail: clsdean@connect.ab.ca.

CONCORDIA SEMINARY, St. Louis, MO 63105-3199

General Information Independent-religious, coed, primarily men, graduate-only institution. *Enrollment by degree level:* 420 first professional, 48 master's, 46 doctoral, 34 other advanced degrees. *Graduate faculty:* 40 full-time (0 women). *Tuition:* Full-time $11,070; part-time $410 per hour. *Graduate housing:* Rooms and/or apartments guaranteed to single students and available to married students. Typical cost: $1,655 per year ($4,965 including board) for single students; $6,660 per year for married students. Housing application deadline: 3/4. *Student services:* Campus employment opportunities, campus safety program, career counseling, disabled student services, exercise/wellness program, free psychological counseling, international student services, low-cost health insurance. *Library facilities:* Concordia Seminary Library. *Online resources:* library catalog, web page, access to other libraries' catalogs. *Collection:* 230,000 titles, 1,056 serial subscriptions, 20,500 audiovisual materials. *Research affiliation:* Center for Reformation Research, Concordia Historical Institute.

Computer facilities: 10 computers available on campus for general student use. A campuswide network can be accessed from student residence rooms and from off campus. Internet access is available. *Web address:* http://www.csl.edu/.

General Application Contact: Rev. Jeffery C. Moore, Director, Ministerial Recruitment, 314-505-7222, Fax: 314-505-7220, E-mail: csladmis@aol.com.

GRADUATE UNITS

Graduate Programs Students: 504 full-time (18 women), 44 part-time (5 women); includes 14 minority (2 African Americans, 7 Asian Americans or Pacific Islanders, 5 Hispanic Americans), 17 international. Average age 31. 170 applicants, 78% accepted, 121 enrolled. *Faculty:* 40 full-time (0 women). Expenses: Contact institution. *Financial support:* In 2001–02, 1 fellowship (averaging $12,000 per year), 5 research assistantships (averaging $3,000 per year), 5 teaching assistantships (averaging $1,680 per year) were awarded. Career-related internships or fieldwork, Federal Work-Study, and tuition waivers (full) also available. Support available to part-time students. Financial award application deadline: 8/1; financial award applicants required to submit FAFSA. In 2001, 86 first professional degrees, 13 master's, 3 doctorates, 15 other advanced degrees awarded. Offers theology (M Div, MA, STM, D Min, PhD, Certificate). *Application deadline:* For fall admission, 8/10; for winter admission, 10/10 (priority date); for spring admission, 2/10 (priority date). Applications are processed on a rolling basis. *Application fee:* $40. *Application Contact:* Rev. Jeffery C. Moore, Director, Ministerial Recruitment, 314-505-7222, Fax: 314-505-7220, E-mail: csladmis@aol.com. *President*, Dr. John F. Johnson, 314-505-7011, Fax: 314-505-7002.

CONCORDIA THEOLOGICAL SEMINARY, Fort Wayne, IN 46825-4996

General Information Independent-religious, coed, primarily men, graduate-only institution. *Graduate housing:* Room and/or apartments available to single students; on-campus housing not available to married students.

GRADUATE UNITS

Graduate and Professional Programs *Degree program information:* Part-time programs available. Offers theology (M Div, MA, STM, D Min, D Miss).

CONCORDIA UNIVERSITY, Irvine, CA 92612-3299

General Information Independent-religious, coed, comprehensive institution. *Enrollment:* 133 full-time matriculated graduate/professional students (82 women), 69 part-time matriculated graduate/professional students (44 women). *Enrollment by degree level:* 202 master's. *Graduate faculty:* 7 full-time (4 women), 18 part-time/adjunct (12 women). *Tuition:* Full-time $3,960; part-time $330 per unit. *Graduate housing:* Room and/or apartments available on a first-come, first-served basis to married students; on-campus housing not available to single students. *Student services:* Campus employment opportunities, campus safety program, career counseling, disabled student services, exercise/wellness program, free psychological counseling, international student services, low-cost health insurance, multicultural affairs office, teacher training, writing training. *Library facilities:* Concordia University Library. *Online resources:* library catalog, web page, access to other libraries' catalogs. *Collection:* 93,899 titles, 3,679 audiovisual materials.

Computer facilities: 42 computers available on campus for general student use. A campuswide network can be accessed from student residence rooms. *Web address:* http://www.cui.edu/.

General Application Contact: Dr. Heidi Aharonian, Assistant Director, Assessment and Distance Learning, 949-854-8002 Ext. 1274, Fax: 949-854-6879, E-mail: heidi.aharonian@cui.edu.

GRADUATE UNITS

School of Business Administration Students: 40 full-time (15 women), 7 part-time (2 women); includes 12 minority (1 African American, 9 Asian Americans or Pacific Islanders, 2 Hispanic Americans), 3 international. Average age 32. 40 applicants, 75% accepted. *Faculty:* 4 full-time (1 woman), 2 part-time/adjunct (0 women). Expenses: Contact institution. *Financial support:* Applicants required to submit FAFSA. *Degree program information:* Part-time and evening/weekend programs available. Postbaccalaureate distance learning degree programs offered (minimal on-campus study). Offers business administration (MBA). *Application deadline:* For fall admission, 8/10; for spring admission, 1/3. Applications are processed on a rolling basis. *Application fee:* $25. *Application Contact:* Donna Mork, Administrative Assistant, 949-854-8002 Ext. 1710. *Director*, Dr. Richard Harms, 949-854-8002 Ext. 1711, Fax: 949-854-6864, E-mail: richard.harms@cui.edu.

School of Education Students: 112 full-time (94 women), 62 part-time (50 women); includes 13 minority (6 Asian Americans or Pacific Islanders, 5 Hispanic Americans, 2 Native Americans) Average age 32. 60 applicants, 83% accepted. *Faculty:* 7 full-time (4 women), 18 part-time/adjunct (12 women). Expenses: Contact institution. *Financial support:* Application deadline: 7/1; In 2001, 28 degrees awarded. *Degree program information:* Part-time and evening/weekend programs available. *Application deadline:* For fall admission, 7/31 (priority date); for spring admission, 11/30 (priority date). Applications are processed on a rolling basis. *Application fee:* $0. *Application Contact:* Lindsay R. Gallacher, Coordinator of Postbaccalaureate Admissions, 949-854-8002 Ext. 1323, Fax: 949-854-6878, E-mail: lindsay.gallacher@cui.edu. *Dean*, Dr. Barbara Morton, 949-854-8002 Ext. 1326, Fax: 949-854-6878, E-mail: barbara.morton@cui.edu.

School of Theology Students: 34 full-time (3 women), 3 part-time (1 woman); includes 16 minority (12 Asian Americans or Pacific Islanders, 4 Hispanic Americans) Average age 39. 15 applicants, 80% accepted. *Faculty:* 5 full-time (0 women), 4 part-time/adjunct (1 woman). Expenses: Contact institution. *Financial support:* In 2001–02, 32 fellowships with full and partial tuition reimbursements (averaging $10,000 per year) were awarded; tuition waivers (partial) also available. In 2001, 8 degrees awarded. *Degree program information:* Part-time and evening/weekend programs available. Offers Christian leadership (MA); family life (MA); mission planting (MA); Reformation theology (MA); research and theology (MA); theology and culture (MA). *Application deadline:* For fall admission, 7/31 (priority date); for spring admission, 11/30 (priority date). *Application Contact:* Deborah Davis, Administrative Assistant, 949-854-8002 Ext. 1750, Fax: 949-854-6854, E-mail: deborah.davis@cui.edu. *Dean*, Rev. Dr. James V. Bachman, 949-854-8002 Ext. 1751, Fax: 949-854-6854, E-mail: james.bachman@cui.edu.

CONCORDIA UNIVERSITY, Montréal, QC H3G 1M8, Canada

General Information Province-supported, coed, university. CGS member. *Enrollment:* 2,970 full-time matriculated graduate/professional students (1,363 women), 756 part-time matriculated graduate/professional students (399 women). *Enrollment by degree level:* 2,559 master's, 510 doctoral, 657 other advanced degrees. *Graduate faculty:* 732. *Graduate housing:* Room and/or apartments available on a first-come, first-served basis to single students; on-campus housing not available to married students. *Student services:* Campus employment opportunities, campus safety program, career counseling, child daycare facilities, disabled student services, exercise/wellness program, free psychological counseling, grant writing training, international student services, multicultural affairs office, writing training. *Library facilities:* Webster Library plus 2 others. *Online resources:* library catalog, web page, access to other libraries' catalogs. *Collection:* 1.3 million titles, 5,894 serial subscriptions. *Research affiliation:* Centre de Recherche Informatique de Montreal, Picosecond Laser Spectroscopy Canadian Centre (chemistry).

Computer facilities: 350 computers available on campus for general student use. A campuswide network can be accessed from student residence rooms and from off campus. Internet access and online class registration, specialized software applications are available. *Web address:* http://www.concordia.ca/.

General Application Contact: Dr. Claude Bédard, Dean of Graduate Studies and Research, 514-848-3803, Fax: 514-848-2812, E-mail: sgscu@vax2.concordia.ca.

GRADUATE UNITS

School of Graduate Studies Students: 2,970 full-time (1,363 women), 756 part-time (399 women). Average age 33. Expenses: Contact institution. *Financial support:* Fellowships, research assistantships, teaching assistantships, career-related internships or fieldwork and institutionally sponsored loans available. In 2001, 654 master's, 54 doctorates, 280 other advanced degrees awarded. *Degree program information:* Part-time and evening/weekend programs available. Offers humanities (PhD); special individualized program (M Sc, MA, PhD). *Application fee:* $50. *Dean of Graduate Studies and Research*, Dr. Claude Bédard, 514-848-3803, Fax: 514-848-2812, E-mail: sgscu@vax2.concordia.ca.

Faculty of Arts and Science Students: 1,095 full-time (684 women), 256 part-time (188 women). Expenses: Contact institution. *Financial support:* Fellowships, research assistantships, teaching assistantships, career-related internships or fieldwork, institutionally sponsored loans, and scholarships/grants available. In 2001, 249 master's, 31 doctorates, 93 other advanced degrees awarded. Offers adult education (Diploma); anglais-français en langue et techniques de localization (Certificate); applied linguistics (MA); arts and science (M Sc, MA, MTM, PhD, Certificate, Diploma); biology (M Sc, PhD); chemistry (M Sc, PhD); child study (MA); communication (PhD); communication studies (Diploma); community economic development (Diploma); creative writing (MA); economic policy (Diploma); economics (MA, PhD); educational studies (MA); educational technology (MA, PhD); English (MA); environmental impact assessment (Diploma); history (MA, PhD); history and philosophy of religion (MA); human systems intervention (MA); instructional technology (Diploma); journalism (Diploma); Judaic studies (MA); mathematics (PhD); mathematics and statistics (M Sc, MA); media studies (MA); philosophy (MA); psychology (clinical) (MA, PhD); psychology (general) (MA, PhD); public policy and public administration (MA); religion (PhD); social and cultural anthropology (MA); sociology (MA); teaching of mathematics (MTM); theological studies (MA); traductologie (MA); translation (Diploma). *Application fee:* $50. *Dean*, Dr. M. Singer, 514-848-2081, Fax: 514-848-2877.

Faculty of Engineering and Computer Science Students: 1,066 full-time (247 women), 158 part-time (37 women). Expenses: Contact institution. In 2001, 183 master's, 16 doctorates, 102 other advanced degrees awarded. Offers aerospace engineering (M Eng); building (M Eng, MA Sc, PhD, Certificate); civil engineering (M Eng, MA Sc, PhD); composites (M Eng); computer science (M App Comp Sc, MCS, PhD, Diploma); electrical and computer engineering (M Eng, MA Sc, PhD, Certificate); engineering and computer science (M App Comp Sc, M Eng, MA Sc, MCS, PhD, Certificate, Diploma); environmental engineering (Certificate); mechanical engineering (M Eng, MA Sc, PhD, Certificate); software systems for mechanical and aerospace engineering (Certificate); user interface design for software systems (Certificate). *Application fee:* $50. *Dean*, Dr. N. Esmail, 514-848-3062, Fax: 514-848-4509.

Faculty of Fine Arts Students: 273 full-time (181 women), 31 part-time (25 women). Expenses: Contact institution. *Financial support:* Fellowships, research assistantships, teaching assistantships, career-related internships or fieldwork available. In 2001, 60 master's, 5 doctorates, 13 other advanced degrees awarded. *Degree program information:* Part-time programs available. Offers advanced music performance studies (Diploma); art education (MA, PhD); art history (MA, PhD); creative arts therapies (MA); digital technologies in design art practice (Certificate); film studies (MA); fine arts (MA, MFA, PhD, Certificate, Diploma); studio arts (MFA). *Application fee:* $50. *Dean*, Prof. C. Jackson, 514-848-4614, Fax: 514-848-4599.

John Molson School of Business Students: 463 full-time (210 women), 294 part-time (138 women). Expenses: Contact institution. *Financial support:* Fellowships, career-related internships or fieldwork available. In 2001, 162 master's, 2 doctorates, 72 other advanced degrees awarded. *Degree program information:* Part-time and evening/weekend programs available. Offers accountancy (Diploma); administration (M Sc, PhD, Diploma); business administration (Aviation MBA, MBA); community organizational development (Certificate); cultural affairs and event management (Certificate); e-business (Certificate); executive business administration (EMBA); investment management (MA, Diploma); management of healthcare organizations (Certificate); sport administration (Diploma). *Application fee:* $50. *Application Contact:* Dr. J. McGuire, Associate Dean, Graduate Programs, Research and Program Evaluation, 514-848-2958, Fax: 514-848-4208. *Interim Dean*, Dr. J. Tomberlin, 514-848-2700, Fax: 514-848-4502.

See in-depth description on page 835.

CONCORDIA UNIVERSITY, River Forest, IL 60305-1499

General Information Independent-religious, coed, comprehensive institution. CGS member. *Graduate housing:* Rooms and/or apartments available on a first-come, first-served basis to single and married students.

GRADUATE UNITS

Graduate Studies *Degree program information:* Part-time and evening/weekend programs available. Postbaccalaureate distance learning degree programs offered (no on-campus study). Offers church music (MCM, CAS); curriculum and instruction (MA, CAS); early childhood education (MA, Ed D, CAS); educational leadership (Ed D); gerontology (MA, CAS); human services (MA, CAS); professional counseling (MA, CAS); psychology (MA, CAS); reading education (MA, CAS); religion (MA, CAS); school administration (MA, CAS); school counseling (MA, CAS); supervision of instruction (MA, CAS); teaching (MAT, CAS); urban teaching (MA).

CONCORDIA UNIVERSITY, St. Paul, MN 55104-5494

General Information Independent-religious, coed, comprehensive institution. *Enrollment:* 324 full-time matriculated graduate/professional students (238 women). *Enrollment by degree level:* 324 master's. *Graduate faculty:* 14 full-time (4 women), 111 part-time/adjunct (55 women). *Tuition:* Part-time $300 per semester hour. Tuition and fees vary according to program. *Graduate housing:* Rooms and/or apartments available on a first-come, first-served basis to single students and available to married students. *Student services:* Campus employment opportunities, campus safety program, career counseling, free psychological counseling, low-cost health insurance, multicultural affairs office, writing training. *Library facilities:* Buenger Memorial Library plus 1 other. *Online resources:* library catalog, web page, access to other libraries' catalogs. *Collection:* 125,000 titles, 1,400 serial subscriptions, 6,000 audiovisual materials.

Concordia University (continued)

Computer facilities: 1,200 computers available on campus for general student use. A campuswide network can be accessed from student residence rooms and from off campus. Internet access is available. *Web address:* http://www.csp.edu/.

General Application Contact: Nathan Bostrom, Marketing Director, 651-641-8863, Fax: 651-641-8807, E-mail: bostrom@csp.edu.

GRADUATE UNITS

School of Accelerated Learning Students: 163 full-time (102 women). Average age 41. 140 applicants, 87% accepted. *Faculty:* 6 full-time (1 woman), 13 part-time/adjunct (4 women). Expenses: Contact institution. *Financial support:* In 2001–02, 1 student received support, including 1 research assistantship (averaging $9,000 per year); teaching assistantships, institutionally sponsored loans also available. Financial award applicants required to submit FAFSA. In 2001, 58 degrees awarded. *Degree program information:* Evening/weekend programs available. Offers human resource management (MAOM). *Application deadline:* Applications are processed on a rolling basis. *Application fee:* $50. Electronic applications accepted. *Application Contact:* Tim Utter, Admissions, 651-641-8863, Fax: 651-641-8807, E-mail: bostrom@csp.edu. *Associate Dean,* Thomas Hanson, 651-641-8863, Fax: 651-641-8807, E-mail: hanson@csp.edu.

School of Human Services Students: 161 full-time (136 women); includes 24 minority (20 African Americans, 2 Asian Americans or Pacific Islanders, 2 Hispanic Americans) Average age 34. 50 applicants, 90% accepted. *Faculty:* 8 full-time (3 women), 98 part-time/adjunct (51 women). Expenses: Contact institution. *Financial support:* Federal Work-Study available. Support available to part-time students. Financial award application deadline:4/6. In 2001, 18 degrees awarded. *Degree program information:* Evening/weekend programs available. Postbaccalaureate distance learning degree programs offered (minimal on-campus study). Offers community education (MA Ed); criminal justice (MAHS); early childhood education (MA Ed); family studies (MAHS); leadership (MAHS); parish education (MA Ed); school-age care (MA Ed); youth development (MA Ed). *Application deadline:* Applications are processed on a rolling basis. *Application fee:* $50. Electronic applications accepted. *Application Contact:* Gail Ann Wells, Marketing Coordinator, 651-603-6186, Fax: 651-603-6144, E-mail: wells@csp.edu. *Associate Dean,* James Ollhoff, 651-603-6148, E-mail: ollhoff@csp.edu.

CONCORDIA UNIVERSITY, Seward, NE 68434-1599

General Information Independent-religious, coed, comprehensive institution. *Enrollment:* 276 part-time matriculated graduate/professional students (145 women). *Enrollment by degree level:* 276 master's. *Graduate faculty:* 36 full-time (10 women). *Tuition:* Part-time $155 per credit hour. *Graduate housing:* Rooms and/or apartments available on a first-come, first-served basis to single and married students. *Student services:* Career counseling, free psychological counseling, international student services, multicultural affairs office. *Library facilities:* Link Library. *Online resources:* library catalog, web page, access to other libraries' catalogs. *Collection:* 171,688 titles, 575 serial subscriptions, 12,068 audiovisual materials.

Computer facilities: 75 computers available on campus for general student use. A campuswide network can be accessed from student residence rooms and from off campus. *Web address:* http://www.cune.edu/.

General Application Contact: Dr. Len Bassett, Dean of Graduate Studies, 402-643-7464, Fax: 402-643-3328, E-mail: lbassett@seward.cune.edu.

GRADUATE UNITS

Graduate Programs in Education Average age 40. 56 applicants, 100% accepted. *Faculty:* 36 full-time (10 women). Expenses: Contact institution. *Financial support:* Federal Work-Study and institutionally sponsored loans available. Support available to part-time students. Financial award applicants required to submit FAFSA. In 2001, 33 degrees awarded. *Degree program information:* Part-time and evening/weekend programs available. Offers early childhood education (M Ed); education (M Ed, MPE, MS); educational administration (M Ed); elementary education (M Ed); family life (MS); parish education (MPE); reading education (M Ed). *Application deadline:* For fall admission, 8/1 (priority date); for spring admission, 12/1. Applications are processed on a rolling basis. *Application fee:* $15. Electronic applications accepted. *Dean of Graduate Studies,* Dr. Len Bassett, 402-643-7464, Fax: 402-643-3328, E-mail: lbassett@seward.cune.edu.

CONCORDIA UNIVERSITY, Portland, OR 97211-6099

General Information Independent-religious, coed, comprehensive institution. *Enrollment:* 132 full-time matriculated graduate/professional students (81 women), 33 part-time matriculated graduate/professional students (20 women). *Enrollment by degree level:* 165 master's. *Graduate faculty:* 16 full-time (8 women), 16 part-time/adjunct (9 women). *Tuition:* Part-time $408 per credit. *Graduate housing:* Rooms and/or apartments available to single and married students. Typical cost: $3,600 per year for single students; $5,100 per year for married students. Housing application deadline: 8/1. *Library facilities:* Concordia Library plus 1 other. *Online resources:* library catalog, access to other libraries' catalogs. *Collection:* 56,040 titles, 418 serial subscriptions, 7,764 audiovisual materials.

Computer facilities: 60 computers available on campus for general student use. A campuswide network can be accessed from student residence rooms and from off campus. Internet access is available. *Web address:* http://www.cu-portland.edu/.

General Application Contact: Donna Hoyt, Director of Graduate Admissions, 503-280-8501, Fax: 503-280-8531, E-mail: dhoyt@cu-portland.edu.

GRADUATE UNITS

College of Education Offers curriculum and instruction (elementary) (M Ed); educational administration (M Ed); elementary education (MAT); secondary education (MAT).

CONCORDIA UNIVERSITY AT AUSTIN, Austin, TX 78705-2799

General Information Independent-religious, coed, comprehensive institution. *Enrollment:* 57 part-time matriculated graduate/professional students (43 women). *Enrollment by degree level:* 57 master's. *Graduate faculty:* 8 part-time/adjunct (4 women). *Tuition:* Part-time $325 per hour. *Student services:* Disabled student services, exercise/wellness program, teacher training. *Library facilities:* Founders Library. *Online resources:* library catalog, web page, access to other libraries' catalogs. *Collection:* 50,323 titles, 632 serial subscriptions, 1,683 audiovisual materials.

Computer facilities: 40 computers available on campus for general student use. Internet access is available. *Web address:* http://www.concordia.edu/.

General Application Contact: Richard Liedtke, Assistant Vice President of Enrollment Services, 512-486-1109, Fax: 512-459-8517, E-mail: liedtker@concordia.edu.

GRADUATE UNITS

School of Education *Degree program information:* Part-time and evening/weekend programs available. Offers education (M Ed).

CONCORDIA UNIVERSITY WISCONSIN, Mequon, WI 53097-2402

General Information Independent-religious, coed, comprehensive institution. *Graduate housing:* On-campus housing not available.

GRADUATE UNITS

School of Graduate Studies *Degree program information:* Part-time and evening/weekend programs available. Postbaccalaureate distance learning degree programs offered (minimal on-campus study). Offers church administration (MBA); church music (MCM); counseling (MS Ed); curriculum and instruction (MS Ed); early childhood (MS Ed); educational administration (MS); family nurse practitioner (MSN); family studies (MS Ed); finance (MBA); geriatric nurse practitioner (MSN); health care administration (MBA); human resource management (MBA); international business (MBA); management (MBA); management information services (MBA); managerial communications (MBA); marketing (MBA); nurse educator (MSN); occupational therapy (MOT); physical therapy (MPT, MSPT); public administration (MBA); reading (MS Ed); risk management (MBA); student personnel administration (MSSPA). Electronic applications accepted.

CONNECTICUT COLLEGE, New London, CT 06320-4196

General Information Independent, coed, comprehensive institution. *Graduate housing:* On-campus housing not available. *Research affiliation:* Hartford Hospital (neurophysiology).

GRADUATE UNITS

Graduate School *Degree program information:* Part-time programs available. Offers botany (MA, MAT); chemistry (MAT); dance (MFA); elementary education (MAT); English (MA, MAT); French and Italian (MA, MAT); German (MAT); Hispanic studies (MA); Latin (MAT); mathematics (MAT); music (MA, MAT); physics (MAT); psychology (MA); Russian studies (MAT); secondary education (MAT); zoology (MA, MAT).

CONVERSE COLLEGE, Spartanburg, SC 29302-0006

General Information Independent, women only, comprehensive institution. *Enrollment:* 131 full-time matriculated graduate/professional students (113 women), 584 part-time matriculated graduate/professional students (500 women). *Enrollment by degree level:* 715 master's. *Graduate faculty:* 74 full-time (38 women), 12 part-time/adjunct (8 women). *Tuition:* Part-time $225 per credit hour. One-time fee: $20 part-time. *Graduate housing:* On-campus housing not available. *Student services:* Campus employment opportunities, campus safety program, career counseling, international student services, teacher training. *Library facilities:* Mickel Library. *Online resources:* library catalog, web page, access to other libraries' catalogs. *Collection:* 129,411 titles, 1,467 serial subscriptions, 30,132 audiovisual materials.

Computer facilities: 65 computers available on campus for general student use. A campuswide network can be accessed from student residence rooms and from off campus. Internet access is available. *Web address:* http://www.converse.edu/.

General Application Contact: Dr. Martha Thomas Lovett, Dean, 864-596-9082, Fax: 864-596-9221, E-mail: martha.lovett@converse.edu.

GRADUATE UNITS

Carroll McDaniel Petrie School of Music Students: 2 full-time, 15 part-time. *Faculty:* 17 full-time (8 women), 8 part-time/adjunct (5 women). Expenses: Contact institution. *Financial support:* In 2001–02, 17 students received support, including 12 fellowships with full and partial tuition reimbursements available (averaging $3,600 per year); teaching assistantships, career-related internships or fieldwork, Federal Work-Study, institutionally sponsored loans, tuition waivers (full), and unspecified assistantships also available. Support available to part-time students. Financial award application deadline: 4/30; financial award applicants required to submit FAFSA. In 2001, 8 degrees awarded. *Degree program information:* Part-time programs available. Offers instrumental performance (M Mus); music education (M Mus); piano pedagogy (M Mus); vocal performance (M Mus). *Application deadline:* Applications are processed on a rolling basis. *Application fee:* $35. *Application Contact:* Director of Music Enrollment. *Interim Dean,* Lynn Stalnaker, 864-596-9021, Fax: 864-596-9167, E-mail: lynn.stalnaker@converse.edu.

Department of Education Students: 131 full-time (113 women), 584 part-time (500 women). Average age 35. *Faculty:* 57 full-time (30 women), 4 part-time/adjunct (3 women). Expenses: Contact institution. *Financial support:* In 2001–02, 500 students received support; research assistantships, career-related internships or fieldwork and scholarships/grants available. Support available to part-time students. Financial award applicants required to submit FAFSA. In 2001, 203 master's, 35 other advanced degrees awarded. *Degree program information:* Part-time and evening/weekend programs available. Postbaccalaureate distance learning degree programs offered. Offers administration and supervision (Ed S); curriculum and instruction (Ed S); economics (MLA); education (MAT, Ed S); elementary education (M Ed); English (MLA); gifted education (M Ed); history (MLA); leadership (M Ed); liberal arts (MLA); marriage and family therapy (Ed S); political science (MLA); secondary education (M Ed); sociology (MLA); special education (M Ed). *Application deadline:* Applications are processed on a rolling basis. *Application fee:* $35. *Dean,* Dr. Martha Thomas Lovett, 864-596-9082, Fax: 864-596-9221, E-mail: martha.lovett@converse.edu.

CONWAY SCHOOL OF LANDSCAPE DESIGN, Conway, MA 01341-0179

General Information Independent, coed, graduate-only institution. *Enrollment by degree level:* 18 master's. *Graduate faculty:* 2 full-time (1 woman), 5 part-time/adjunct (3 women). *Tuition:* Full-time $18,500. *Graduate housing:* On-campus housing not available. *Student services:* Career counseling. *Collection:* 3,068 titles, 35 serial subscriptions.

Computer facilities: 3 computers available on campus for general student use. Internet access is available. *Web address:* http://www.csld.edu/.

General Application Contact: Nancy E. Braxton, Administrative Director, 413-369-4044, Fax: 413-369-4032, E-mail: nebraxton@csld.edu.

GRADUATE UNITS

Graduate Program in Landscape Design Students: 18 full-time (12 women); includes 17 Hispanic Americans Average age 35. 25 applicants, 80% accepted. *Faculty:* 2 full-time (1 woman), 5 part-time/adjunct (3 women). Expenses: Contact institution. *Financial support:* In 2001–02, 10 students received support. Career-related internships or fieldwork and institutionally sponsored loans available. Financial award application deadline: 8/1; financial award applicants required to submit FAFSA. In 2001, 15 degrees awarded. Offers landscape design/environmental planning (MA). *Application deadline:* For fall admission, 3/15 (priority date). Applications are processed on a rolling basis. *Application fee:* $50. *Application Contact:* Ilze Meijers, Administrative Assistant, 413-369-4044, Fax: 413-369-4032, E-mail: ilze@csld.edu. *Academic Director,* Donald L. Walker, 413-369-4044, Fax: 413-369-4032, E-mail: don@csld.edu.

COPPIN STATE COLLEGE, Baltimore, MD 21216-3698

General Information State-supported, coed, comprehensive institution. CGS member. *Enrollment:* 31 full-time matriculated graduate/professional students (24 women), 598 part-time matriculated graduate/professional students (471 women). *Enrollment by degree level:* 629 master's. *Graduate faculty:* 26 full-time (15 women), 56 part-time/adjunct (36 women). Tuition, state resident: full-time $3,576; part-time $149 per credit. Tuition, nonresident: full-time $6,360; part-time $265 per credit. *Required fees:* $589; $589 per year. *Graduate housing:* On-campus housing not available. *Student services:* Campus employment opportunities, campus safety program, career counseling, disabled student services, free psychological counseling, international student services, low-cost health insurance, writing training. *Library facilities:* Parlett L. Moore Library. *Online resources:* library catalog. *Collection:* 134,983 titles, 665 serial subscriptions.

Computer facilities: 130 computers available on campus for general student use. A campuswide network can be accessed from off campus. Internet access is available. *Web address:* http://www.coppin.edu/.

General Application Contact: Vell Lyles, Associate Vice President for Enrollment Management, 410-951-3575, E-mail: vlyles@coppin.edu.

GRADUATE UNITS

Division of Graduate Studies Students: 31 full-time (24 women), 598 part-time (471 women); includes 416 minority (406 African Americans, 3 Asian Americans or Pacific Islanders, 6 Hispanic Americans, 1 Native American), 8 international. 305 applicants, 90% accepted. *Faculty:* 26 full-time (15 women), 56 part-time/adjunct (36 women). Expenses: Contact institution. *Financial support:* Career-related internships or fieldwork, Federal Work-Study, institutionally sponsored loans, and scholarships/grants available. Support available to part-time students. Financial award application deadline: 4/1; financial award applicants required to submit FAFSA. In 2001, 74 degrees awarded. *Degree program information:* Part-time and evening/weekend programs available. *Application deadline:* For fall admission, 7/15 (priority date); for spring admission, 12/15 (priority date). Applications are processed on a rolling basis. *Application fee:* $25. *Application Contact:* Vell Lyles, Associate Vice President for

Enrollment Management, 410-951-3575, E-mail: vlyles@coppin.edu. *Dean*, Dr. Mary Owens, 410-383-5535, Fax: 410-383-5454, E-mail: mowens@coppin.edu.

Division of Arts and Sciences Students: 15 full-time (12 women), 155 part-time (115 women); includes 162 minority (160 African Americans, 1 Hispanic American, 1 Native American), 4 international. 99 applicants, 81% accepted. *Faculty:* 9 full-time (3 women), 18 part-time/adjunct (9 women). Expenses: Contact institution. *Financial support:* Career-related internships or fieldwork, Federal Work-Study, institutionally sponsored loans, and scholarships/grants available. Support available to part-time students. Financial award application deadline: 4/1; financial award applicants required to submit FAFSA. In 2001, 31 degrees awarded. *Degree program information:* Part-time and evening/weekend programs available. Offers alcohol and substance abuse (MS); arts and sciences (M Ed, MS); criminal justice (MS); rehabilitation (M Ed); social sciences (MS). *Application deadline:* For fall admission, 7/15; for spring admission, 12/15. Applications are processed on a rolling basis. *Application fee:* $25. *Application Contact:* Vell Lyles, Associate Vice President for Enrollment Management, 410-951-3575, E-mail: vlyles@coppin.edu. *Dean*, Dr. Clyde Mathura, 410-951-3020, E-mail: cmathura@wye.coppin.edu.

Division of Education Students: 15 full-time (11 women), 430 part-time (345 women); includes 241 minority (233 African Americans, 3 Asian Americans or Pacific Islanders, 5 Hispanic Americans), 4 international. 206 applicants, 94% accepted. *Faculty:* 16 full-time (11 women), 31 part-time/adjunct (21 women). Expenses: Contact institution. *Financial support:* Career-related internships or fieldwork, Federal Work-Study, institutionally sponsored loans, and scholarships/grants available. Support available to part-time students. Financial award application deadline: 4/1; financial award applicants required to submit FAFSA. In 2001, 43 degrees awarded. *Degree program information:* Part-time and evening/weekend programs available. Offers adult and general education (M Ed, MS); curriculum and instruction (M Ed, MAT); special education (M Ed); teaching (MAT). *Application deadline:* For fall admission, 7/15 (priority date); for spring admission, 12/15 (priority date). Applications are processed on a rolling basis. *Application fee:* $25. *Application Contact:* Vell Lyles, Associate Vice President for Enrollment Management, 410-951-3575, E-mail: vlyles@coppin.edu. *Chair*, Dr. Julius Chapman, 410-951-3520, E-mail: jchapman@coppin.edu.

Helene Fuld School of Nursing Students: 1 (woman) full-time, 13 part-time (11 women); includes 13 minority (all African Americans) 11 applicants, 91% accepted. *Faculty:* 1 (woman) full-time, 7 part-time/adjunct (6 women). Expenses: Contact institution. *Financial support:* Federal Work-Study, institutionally sponsored loans, and scholarships/grants available. Support available to part-time students. Financial award application deadline: 4/1; financial award applicants required to submit FAFSA. *Degree program information:* Part-time and evening/weekend programs available. Offers nurse practitioner (MS). *Application deadline:* For fall admission, 7/15; for spring admission, 12/15. Applications are processed on a rolling basis. *Application fee:* $25. *Application Contact:* Vell Lyles, Associate Vice President for Enrollment Management, 410-951-3575, E-mail: vlyles@coppin.edu. *Dean*, Dr. Marcella Copes, 410-951-3991, Fax: 410-462-3032, E-mail: mcopes@wye.coppin.edu.

CORNELL UNIVERSITY, Ithaca, NY 14853-0001

General Information Independent, coed, university. CGS member. *Enrollment:* 5,619 full-time matriculated graduate/professional students (2,346 women). *Enrollment by degree level:* 864 first professional, 2,423 master's, 2,332 doctoral. *Graduate faculty:* 1,468 full-time (338 women), 82 part-time/adjunct (18 women). *Tuition:* Full-time $25,970. *Required fees:* $50. *Graduate housing:* Rooms and/or apartments available on a first-come, first-served basis to single and married students. Typical cost: $8,800 (including board) for single students. *Student services:* Campus employment opportunities, campus safety program, career counseling, disabled student services, exercise/wellness program, free psychological counseling, international student services, low-cost health insurance. *Library facilities:* Olin Library plus 17 others. *Online resources:* library catalog, web page. *Collection:* 6.3 million titles, 61,941 serial subscriptions, 140,443 audiovisual materials. *Research affiliation:* Boyce Thompson Institute for Plant Research, Fermi National Accelerator Laboratory, Brookhaven National Laboratory.

Computer facilities: 700 computers available on campus for general student use. A campuswide network can be accessed from student residence rooms and from off campus. Internet access is available. *Web address:* http://www.cornell.edu/.

General Application Contact: Graduate School Application Requests, Caldwell Hall, 607-255-4884, E-mail: gradadmissions@cornell.edu.

GRADUATE UNITS

Cornell Law School Students: 551 full-time (272 women); includes 136 minority (28 African Americans, 72 Asian Americans or Pacific Islanders, 29 Hispanic Americans, 7 Native Americans), 9 international. Average age 25. 3,717 applicants, 22% accepted. *Faculty:* 44 full-time (14 women), 16 part-time/adjunct (7 women). Expenses: Contact institution. *Financial support:* In 2001–02, 271 students received support. Career-related internships or fieldwork, Federal Work-Study, and scholarships/grants available. Financial award application deadline: 3/15; financial award applicants required to submit FAFSA. In 2001, 182 first professional degrees, 48 master's awarded. Offers law (JD, LL M). JD/MLLP offered jointly with Humboldt University, Berlin. *Application deadline:* For fall admission, 2/1. *Application fee:* $65. Electronic applications accepted. *Application Contact:* Richard D. Geiger, Dean of Admissions, 607-255-5141. *Dean*, Lee E. Teitelbaum, 607-255-3527.

Graduate School Students: 4,297 full-time (1,777 women); includes 557 minority (110 African Americans, 283 Asian Americans or Pacific Islanders, 143 Hispanic Americans, 21 Native Americans), 1,890 international. ###### applicants, 27% accepted, 0 enrolled. *Faculty:* 1,463 full-time (291 women), 69 part-time/adjunct (14 women). Expenses: Contact institution. *Financial support:* In 2001–02, 3,184 students received support, including 1,019 fellowships with full tuition reimbursements available, 1,044 research assistantships with full tuition reimbursements available, 1,121 teaching assistantships with full tuition reimbursements available; career-related internships or fieldwork, institutionally sponsored loans, scholarships/grants, traineeships, tuition waivers (full and partial), and unspecified assistantships also available. Financial award applicants required to submit FAFSA. In 2001, 1,102 master's, 397 doctorates awarded. *Application fee:* $65. Electronic applications accepted. *Application Contact:* Graduate School Application Requests, Caldwell Hall, 607-255-5816. *Dean*, Dr. Alison G. Power, 607-255-5816.

Field of Environmental Management Expenses: Contact institution. Offers environmental management (MPS). *Application Contact:* Tad McGalliard, Education Coordinator, 607-255-9996, Fax: 607-255-0238, E-mail: tnm2@cornell.edu.

Graduate Field in the Law School Students: 63 full-time (29 women); includes 2 minority (1 Asian American or Pacific Islander, 1 Hispanic American), 58 international. 1,105 applicants, 19% accepted. *Faculty:* 32 full-time. Expenses: Contact institution. *Financial support:* In 2001–02, 10 students received support, including 10 fellowships with full tuition reimbursements available; research assistantships with full tuition reimbursements available, teaching assistantships with full tuition reimbursements available, institutionally sponsored loans, scholarships/grants, tuition waivers (full and partial), and unspecified assistantships also available. Financial award applicants required to submit FAFSA. In 2001, 56 master's, 1 doctorate awarded. Offers law (LL M, JSD). *Application deadline:* For fall admission, 5/1 (priority date). *Application fee:* $65. Electronic applications accepted. *Application Contact:* Graduate Field Assistant, 607-255-5141, E-mail: gradlaw@law.mail.cornell.edu. *Director of Graduate Studies*, 607-255-5141.

Graduate Field of Management Students: 33 full-time (15 women); includes 4 minority (2 African Americans, 1 Asian American or Pacific Islander, 1 Native American), 21 international. 455 applicants, 5% accepted. *Faculty:* 46 full-time. Expenses: Contact institution. *Financial support:* In 2001–02, 29 students received support, including 4 fellowships with full tuition reimbursements available, 25 research assistantships with full tuition reimbursements available; teaching assistantships with full tuition reimbursements available, institutionally sponsored loans, scholarships/grants, tuition waivers (full and partial), and unspecified assistantships also available. Financial award applicants required to submit FAFSA. In 2001, 6 doctorates awarded. Offers accounting (PhD); behavioral decision theory (PhD); finance (PhD); managerial economics (PhD); marketing (PhD); organizational behavior (PhD); production and operations management (PhD). *Application deadline:* For fall admission, 1/3 (priority date). *Application fee:* $65. Electronic applications accepted. *Application Contact:* Graduate Field Assistant, 607-255-3669, E-mail: js_phd.cornell.edu. *Director of Graduate Studies*, 607-255-3669.

Graduate Fields of Architecture, Art and Planning Students: 193 full-time (89 women); includes 29 minority (5 African Americans, 11 Asian Americans or Pacific Islanders, 13 Hispanic Americans), 70 international. 585 applicants, 38% accepted. *Faculty:* 98 full-time. Expenses: Contact institution. *Financial support:* In 2001–02, 99 students received support, including 27 fellowships with full tuition reimbursements available, 5 research assistantships with full tuition reimbursements available, 67 teaching assistantships with full tuition reimbursements available; institutionally sponsored loans, scholarships/grants, tuition waivers (full and partial), and unspecified assistantships also available. Financial award applicants required to submit FAFSA. In 2001, 59 master's, 13 doctorates awarded. Offers architectural design (M Arch); architectural science (MS); architecture, art and planning (M Arch, MA, MFA, MLA, MPSRE, MRP, MS, PhD); city and regional planning (MRP, PhD); computer graphics (MS); creative visual arts (MFA); environmental studies (MA, MS, PhD); historic preservation planning (MA); history of architecture (MA, PhD); history of urban development (MA, PhD); international spatial problems (MA, MS, PhD); location theory (MA, MS, PhD); multiregional economic analysis (MA, MS, PhD); peace science (MA, MS, PhD); planning methods (MA, MS, PhD); planning theory and systems analysis (MRP, PhD); real estate (MPSRE); regional science (MRP, PhD); urban and regional economics (MA, MS, PhD); urban and regional theory (MRP, PhD); urban design (M Arch); urban planning history (MRP, PhD). *Application fee:* $65. Electronic applications accepted. *Application Contact:* Graduate School Application Requests, Caldwell Hall, 607-255-5816. *Interim Dean*, Dr. Porus Olpadwala.

Professional Field of the Johnson Graduate School of Management Students: 683 full-time (186 women); includes 150 minority (25 African Americans, 103 Asian Americans or Pacific Islanders, 21 Hispanic Americans, 1 Native American), 178 international. Average age 29. 2,130 applicants, 24% accepted, 254 enrolled. *Faculty:* 44 full-time (11 women), 4 part-time/adjunct (0 women). Expenses: Contact institution. *Financial support:* Fellowships, research assistantships, career-related internships or fieldwork, Federal Work-Study, institutionally sponsored loans, and tuition waivers (full and partial) available. Financial award application deadline: 2/15; financial award applicants required to submit FAFSA. In 2001, 340 master's awarded. Offers management (MBA). *Application deadline:* For fall admission, 4/1. *Application fee:* $80 ($120 for international students). *Application Contact:* 800-847-2082, Fax: 607-254-8886, E-mail: mba@johnson.cornell.edu. *Dean*, Robert J. Swieringa, 607-255-6418.

Professional School of Veterinary Medicine Students: 322 full-time (249 women); includes 68 minority (6 African Americans, 17 Asian Americans or Pacific Islanders, 39 Hispanic Americans, 6 Native Americans), 3 international. Average age 26. 921 applicants, 11% accepted, 84 enrolled. *Faculty:* 118 full-time (25 women), 6 part-time/adjunct (4 women). Expenses: Contact institution. *Financial support:* In 2001–02, 286 students received support, including fellowships (averaging $9,000 per year); Federal Work-Study, institutionally sponsored loans, and scholarships/grants also available. Financial award application deadline: 2/1; financial award applicants required to submit CSS PROFILE or FAFSA. In 2001, 78 degrees awarded. Offers veterinary medicine (DVM). *Application deadline:* For fall admission, 10/1. *Application fee:* $40. Electronic applications accepted. *Application Contact:* Joseph M. Piekunka, Director of DVM Admissions, 607-253-3700, Fax: 607-253-3709, E-mail: vet_admissions@cornell.edu. *Dean*, Dr. Donald F. Smith, 607-253-3771.

COVENANT COLLEGE, Lookout Mountain, GA 30750

General Information Independent-religious, coed, comprehensive institution. *Enrollment:* 60 full-time matriculated graduate/professional students (38 women), 6 part-time matriculated graduate/professional students (4 women). *Enrollment by degree level:* 66 master's. *Graduate faculty:* 8 full-time (1 woman), 4 part-time/adjunct (1 woman). *Tuition:* Full-time $2,835; part-time $345 per unit. *Required fees:* $96; $42 per course. Part-time tuition and fees vary according to course load. *Graduate housing:* Room and/or apartments guaranteed to single students; on-campus housing not available to married students. Typical cost: $376 per year. Housing application deadline: 5/1. *Student services:* Career counseling. *Library facilities:* Kresge Memorial Library. *Online resources:* library catalog, web page, access to other libraries' catalogs. *Collection:* 61,502 titles, 554 serial subscriptions, 11,500 audiovisual materials.

Computer facilities: 135 computers available on campus for general student use. A campuswide network can be accessed from off campus. Internet access is available. *Web address:* http://www.covenant.edu/.

General Application Contact: Rebecca Dodson, Assistant Director, Program in Education, 706-419-1406, Fax: 706-820-0672, E-mail: dodsonr@covenant.edu.

GRADUATE UNITS

Program in Education Students: 60 full-time (38 women), 6 part-time (4 women); includes 1 minority (African American) Average age 37. 24 applicants, 100% accepted, 22 enrolled. *Faculty:* 8 full-time (1 woman), 4 part-time/adjunct (1 woman). Expenses: Contact institution. *Financial support:* In 2001–02, 50 students received support. Institutionally sponsored loans, scholarships/grants, and tuition waivers (partial) available. Support available to part-time students. Financial award application deadline: 3/10; financial award applicants required to submit FAFSA. In 2001, 16 degrees awarded. *Degree program information:* Part-time programs available. Offers education (M Ed). *Application deadline:* For fall admission, 4/1 (priority date). Applications are processed on a rolling basis. *Application fee:* $35. *Application Contact:* Rebecca Dodson, Assistant Director, Program in Education, 706-419-1406, Fax: 706-820-0672, E-mail: dodsonr@covenant.edu. *Director*, Dr. Jack Fennema, 706-419-1402, Fax: 706-820-0672, E-mail: fennema@covenant.edu.

COVENANT THEOLOGICAL SEMINARY, St. Louis, MO 63141-8697

General Information Independent-religious, coed, graduate-only institution. *Enrollment by degree level:* 331 first professional, 287 master's, 150 doctoral, 64 other advanced degrees. *Graduate faculty:* 19 full-time (0 women), 25 part-time/adjunct (6 women). *Tuition:* Full-time $6,760; part-time $260 per hour. *Required fees:* $140; $30 per semester. Tuition and fees vary according to course load. *Graduate housing:* Rooms and/or apartments available on a first-come, first-served basis to single and married students. Typical cost: $1,632 per year for single students; $4,905 per year for married students. Room charges vary according to campus/location and housing facility selected. Housing application deadline: 4/1. *Student services:* Campus employment opportunities, career counseling, disabled student services, free psychological counseling, writing training. *Library facilities:* J. Oliver Buswell Jr. Library. *Online resources:* library catalog, web page, access to other libraries' catalogs. *Collection:* 66,992 titles, 362 serial subscriptions, 2,703 audiovisual materials.

Computer facilities: 18 computers available on campus for general student use. A campuswide network can be accessed from off campus. Internet access is available.

General Application Contact: John Gullett, Director of Admissions, 314-434-4044, Fax: 314-434-4819, E-mail: admissions@covenantseminary.edu.

GRADUATE UNITS

Graduate and Professional Programs Students: 339 full-time (69 women), 493 part-time (140 women); includes 84 minority (37 African Americans, 32 Asian Americans or Pacific Islanders, 13 Hispanic Americans, 2 Native Americans), 41 international. Average age 36. 292 applicants, 82% accepted, 199 enrolled. *Faculty:* 19 full-time (0 women), 25 part-time/adjunct (6 women). Expenses: Contact institution. *Financial support:* In 2001–02, 430 students received support. Career-related internships or fieldwork, institutionally sponsored loans, scholarships/grants, and tuition waivers (full and partial) available. Support available to part-time students. Financial award application deadline: 4/15; financial award applicants required to submit FAFSA. In 2001, 44 first professional degrees, 57 master's, 5 doctorates, 6 other advanced degrees awarded. *Degree program information:* Part-time and evening/weekend programs available. Postbaccalaureate distance learning degree programs offered (minimal on-campus study). Offers theology (M Div, MA, MAC, Th M, D Min, Certificate). *Application deadline:* Applications are processed on a rolling basis. *Application fee:* $25.

Covenant Theological Seminary (continued)

Electronic applications accepted. *Application Contact:* John Gullett, Director of Admissions, 314-434-4044, Fax: 314-434-4819, E-mail: admissions@covenantseminary.edu. *Vice President for Academics*, Dr. Donald Guthrie, 314-434-4044.

CRANBROOK ACADEMY OF ART, Bloomfield Hills, MI 48303-0801

General Information Independent, coed, graduate-only institution. *Enrollment by degree level:* 133 master's. *Graduate faculty:* 10 full-time (3 women). *Tuition:* Full-time $16,900. *Required fees:* $500. *Graduate housing:* Room and/or apartments available on a first-come, first-served basis to single students; on-campus housing not available to married students. Typical cost: $3,200 per year ($5,250 including board) ; $3,200 per year ($5,250 including board) for married students. Housing application deadline: 2/1. *Student services:* Campus employment opportunities, career counseling, free psychological counseling. *Online resources:* library catalog, web page, access to other libraries' catalogs. *Collection:* 30,000 titles, 95 serial subscriptions, 2,496 audiovisual materials.

Computer facilities: 10 computers available on campus for general student use. A campuswide network can be accessed from student residence rooms. Internet access is available. *Web address:* http://www.cranbrookart.edu/.

General Application Contact: Katharine E. Willman, Dean of Admissions and Financial Aid, 248-645-3360, Fax: 248-646-0046, E-mail: kwillman@cranbrook.edu.

GRADUATE UNITS

Graduate School Students: 133 full-time (65 women); includes 15 minority (1 African American, 10 Asian Americans or Pacific Islanders, 4 Hispanic Americans), 17 international. Average age 28. 364 applicants, 32% accepted. *Faculty:* 10 full-time (3 women). Expenses: Contact institution. *Financial support:* In 2001–02, 106 students received support. Federal Work-Study available. Financial award application deadline: 2/1; financial award applicants required to submit FAFSA. In 2001, 65 degrees awarded. Offers architecture (M Arch); ceramics (MFA); design (MFA); fiber arts (MFA); metalsmithing (MFA); painting (MFA); photography (MFA); printmaking (MFA); sculpture (MFA). *Application deadline:* For fall admission, 2/1 (priority date); for spring admission, 11/1. *Application fee:* $50. *Application Contact:* Katharine E. Willman, Dean of Admissions and Financial Aid, 248-645-3360, Fax: 248-646-0046, E-mail: kwillman@cranbrook.edu. *Director*, Gerhardt Knodel, 248-645-3301, Fax: 248-646-0046, E-mail: gknodel@cranbrook.edu.

CREIGHTON UNIVERSITY, Omaha, NE 68178-0001

General Information Independent-religious, coed, university. CGS member. *Enrollment:* 2,155 full-time matriculated graduate/professional students (1,089 women), 463 part-time matriculated graduate/professional students (257 women). *Enrollment by degree level:* 2,144 first professional, 269 master's, 41 doctoral, 144 other advanced degrees. *Graduate housing:* Rooms and/or apartments available to single and married students. *Student services:* Campus employment opportunities, campus safety program, career counseling, child daycare facilities, disabled student services, exercise/wellness program, free psychological counseling, international student services, low-cost health insurance, multicultural affairs office, teacher training. *Library facilities:* Reinert Alumni Memorial Library plus 2 others. *Online resources:* library catalog, web page, access to other libraries' catalogs. *Collection:* 481,848 titles, 1,666 serial subscriptions, 2,500 audiovisual materials. *Research affiliation:* St. Joseph Hospital, Children's Memorial Hospital, Boys Town Institute for Communication Disorders in Children, Omaha Veterans Administration Hospital, Global Weather Central.

Computer facilities: A campuswide network can be accessed from student residence rooms and from off campus. Internet access and online class registration, on-line grade information are available. *Web address:* http://www.creighton.edu/.

General Application Contact: Dr. Barbara J. Braden, Dean, Graduate School, 402-280-2870, Fax: 402-280-5762, E-mail: bbraden@creighton.edu.

GRADUATE UNITS

Graduate School Students: 178 full-time (79 women), 296 part-time (161 women); includes 27 minority (11 African Americans, 14 Asian Americans or Pacific Islanders, 1 Hispanic American, 1 Native American), 83 international. Average age 30. *Faculty:* 251. Expenses: Contact institution. *Financial support:* Research assistantships, teaching assistantships, career-related internships or fieldwork, institutionally sponsored loans, and tuition waivers (partial) available. Support available to part-time students. In 2001, 166 master's awarded. *Degree program information:* Part-time and evening/weekend programs available. *Application deadline:* For fall admission, 3/1 (priority date). Applications are processed on a rolling basis. *Application fee:* $40. *Application Contact:* Linda C. Hanson, Assistant to the Dean, 402-280-2870, Fax: 402-280-5762, E-mail: lhanson@creighton.edu. *Dean*, Dr. Barbara J. Braden, 402-280-2870, Fax: 402-280-5762, E-mail: bbraden@creighton.edu.

College of Arts and Sciences Students: 17 full-time (5 women), 94 part-time (59 women). Expenses: Contact institution. *Financial support:* Teaching assistantships available. In 2001, 68 degrees awarded. *Degree program information:* Part-time and evening/weekend programs available. Offers arts and sciences (MA, MCS, MLS, MS); atmospheric sciences (MS); Christian spirituality (MA); computer sciences (MCS); educational administration (MS); guidance and counseling (MS); international relations (MA); liberal studies (MLS); ministry (MA); physics (MS); theology (MA). *Application deadline:* For fall admission, 3/1. Applications are processed on a rolling basis. *Application fee:* $40. *Application Contact:* Dr. Barbara J. Braden, Dean, Graduate School, 402-280-2870, Fax: 402-280-5762, E-mail: bbraden@creighton.edu. *Dean*, Dr. Timothy R. Austin, 402-280-2431, E-mail: traustin@creighton.edu.

Eugene C. Eppley College of Business Administration Students: 54 full-time (16 women), 111 part-time (37 women); includes 10 minority (6 African Americans, 4 Asian Americans or Pacific Islanders), 36 international. *Faculty:* 40 full-time, 1 part-time/adjunct. Expenses: Contact institution. *Financial support:* Career-related internships or fieldwork and unspecified assistantships available. In 2001, 65 degrees awarded. *Degree program information:* Evening/weekend programs available. Offers business administration (MBA); electronic commerce (MS); information technology (MS); management (MS). *Application deadline:* For fall admission, 3/1. Applications are processed on a rolling basis. *Application fee:* $40. *Application Contact:* Gail Hafer, Coordinator, 402-280-2829. *Dean*, Dr. Robert Pitts, 402-280-2852.

School of Dentistry Offers dentistry (DDS).

School of Law Students: 444 full-time (185 women), 23 part-time (13 women); includes 54 minority (19 African Americans, 10 Asian Americans or Pacific Islanders, 20 Hispanic Americans, 5 Native Americans), 4 international. Average age 26. 681 applicants, 63% accepted, 170 enrolled. *Faculty:* 29 full-time (8 women), 44 part-time/adjunct (13 women). Expenses: Contact institution. *Financial support:* In 2001–02, 429 students received support. Career-related internships or fieldwork, institutionally sponsored loans, scholarships/grants, and unspecified assistantships available. Support available to part-time students. Financial award application deadline: 7/1; financial award applicants required to submit FAFSA. In 2001, 132 degrees awarded. *Degree program information:* Part-time programs available. Offers law (JD). *Application deadline:* For fall admission, 5/1 (priority date). Applications are processed on a rolling basis. *Application fee:* $45. Electronic applications accepted. *Application Contact:* Andrea D. Bashara, Assistant Dean, 402-280-2872, Fax: 402-280-3161, E-mail: bashara@culaw.creighton.edu. *Dean*, Patrick J. Borchers, 402-280-2874, Fax: 402-280-3161.

School of Medicine Students: 584 full-time (267 women), 3 part-time (2 women); includes 150 minority (16 African Americans, 113 Asian Americans or Pacific Islanders, 14 Hispanic Americans, 7 Native Americans), 76 international. Average age 24. 4,205 applicants, 6% accepted, 121 enrolled. *Faculty:* 289 full-time (55 women), 80 part-time/adjunct (19 women). Expenses: Contact institution. *Financial support:* In 2001–02, 458 students received support; fellowships with full tuition reimbursements available, research assistantships with tuition reimbursements available, teaching assistantships with tuition reimbursements available, career-related internships or fieldwork, Federal Work-Study, institutionally sponsored loans, and tuition waivers (full and partial) available. Support available to part-time students. Financial award application deadline: 4/1. In 2001, 114 first professional degrees, 13 master's, 13 doctorates awarded. Offers biomedical sciences (MS, PhD); medical microbiology and immunology (MS, PhD); medicine (MD, MS, PhD); pharmaceutical sciences (MS, PhD); pharmacology (MS, PhD). *Application deadline:* Applications are processed on a rolling basis. *Dean*, Dr. M. Roy Wilson, 402-280-2600, Fax: 402-280-2599.

School of Nursing Students: 20 full-time (17 women), 36 part-time (all women); includes 1 minority (Hispanic American) Average age 30. *Faculty:* 14 full-time (all women), 2 part-time/adjunct (both women). Expenses: Contact institution. *Financial support:* Career-related internships or fieldwork, Federal Work-Study, institutionally sponsored loans, and traineeships available. Financial award applicants required to submit FAFSA. In 2001, 18 degrees awarded. *Degree program information:* Part-time programs available. Postbaccalaureate distance learning degree programs offered (minimal on-campus study). Offers nursing (MS). *Application deadline:* For fall admission, 3/15 (priority date); for spring admission, 10/15 (priority date). Applications are processed on a rolling basis. *Application fee:* $30. Electronic applications accepted. *Application Contact:* Dr. Brenda Bergman-Evans, Director, Advanced Practice, 402-280-2041, Fax: 402-280-2045, E-mail: bbevans@creighton.edu. *Interim Dean*, Dr. Eleanor V. Howell, 402-280-2004, Fax: 402-280-2045, E-mail: howell@creighton.edu.

School of Pharmacy and Allied Health Professions Postbaccalaureate distance learning degree programs offered (no on-campus study). Offers occupational therapy (OTD); pharmaceutical sciences (MS); pharmacy (Pharm D); pharmacy and allied health (Pharm D, MS, DPT, OTD); physical therapy (DPT). Electronic applications accepted.

THE CRISWELL COLLEGE, Dallas, TX 75246-1537

General Information Independent-religious, coed, comprehensive institution. *Graduate housing:* On-campus housing not available.

GRADUATE UNITS

Graduate School of the Bible *Degree program information:* Part-time programs available. Offers biblical studies (M Div, MA); Christian leadership (MA); ministry (MA); New Testament (MA); Old Testament (MA); theological studies (MA); theology (MA). Electronic applications accepted.

CROWN COLLEGE, St. Bonifacius, MN 55375-9001

General Information Independent-religious, coed, comprehensive institution. *Enrollment:* 7 full-time matriculated graduate/professional students, 8 part-time matriculated graduate/professional students (1 woman). *Enrollment by degree level:* 15 master's. *Graduate faculty:* 8 part-time/adjunct (0 women). *Tuition:* Part-time $201 per credit. *Required fees:* $33 per semester. *Graduate housing:* Room and/or apartments available on a first-come, first-served basis to married students; on-campus housing not available to single students. Housing application deadline: 7/1. *Student services:* Campus employment opportunities, career counseling. *Library facilities:* Peter Watne Memorial Library. *Online resources:* library catalog, web page. *Collection:* 190,000 titles, 1,780 serial subscriptions, 2,400 audiovisual materials.

Computer facilities: 50 computers available on campus for general student use. A campuswide network can be accessed from student residence rooms and from off campus. Internet access is available. *Web address:* http://www.crown.edu/.

General Application Contact: Lorri Ague, Director of Adult Programs, 952-446-4330, Fax: 952-446-4349, E-mail: grad@crown.edu.

GRADUATE UNITS

Graduate Studies Students: 7 full-time (0 women), 8 part-time (1 woman). 40 applicants, 100% accepted. *Faculty:* 8 part-time/adjunct (0 women). Expenses: Contact institution. In 2001, 3 degrees awarded. *Degree program information:* Part-time and evening/weekend programs available. Offers church leadership (MA); intercultural studies (MA). *Application deadline:* For fall admission, 8/1 (priority date); for winter admission, 1/1 (priority date); for spring admission, 6/1 (priority date). Applications are processed on a rolling basis. *Application fee:* $25. *Director of Adult Programs*, Lorri Ague, 952-446-4330, Fax: 952-446-4349, E-mail: grad@crown.edu.

CUMBERLAND COLLEGE, Williamsburg, KY 40769-1372

General Information Independent-religious, coed, comprehensive institution. *Enrollment:* 8 full-time matriculated graduate/professional students (6 women), 133 part-time matriculated graduate/professional students (98 women). *Enrollment by degree level:* 138 master's. *Graduate faculty:* 4 full-time (2 women), 5 part-time/adjunct (2 women). *Tuition:* Part-time $180 per hour. *Graduate housing:* Room and/or apartments available to single students; on-campus housing not available to married students. *Student services:* Career counseling, low-cost health insurance. *Library facilities:* Norma Perkins Hagan Memorial Library. *Online resources:* library catalog, web page, access to other libraries' catalogs. *Collection:* 159,068 titles, 2,020 serial subscriptions, 6,906 audiovisual materials.

Computer facilities: 300 computers available on campus for general student use. A campuswide network can be accessed from student residence rooms and from off campus. Internet access and online class registration are available. *Web address:* http://cc.cumber.edu/.

General Application Contact: Dr. John Farris, Director, Graduate Programs in Education, 606-549-2200 Ext. 4432, Fax: 606-539-4014, E-mail: jfarris@cumberlandcollege.edu.

GRADUATE UNITS

Graduate Programs in Education *Degree program information:* Part-time and evening/weekend programs available. Offers early childhood education (MA Ed); early elementary K-4 (MA Ed); elementary education (MA Ed); elementary/secondary principalship (Certificate); elementary/secondary teaching (Certificate); middle school 5-8 (MA Ed); middle school education (MA Ed); reading specialist (MA Ed); secondary general education (MA Ed); special education (MA Ed).

CUMBERLAND UNIVERSITY, Lebanon, TN 37087-3554

General Information Independent, coed, comprehensive institution. *Enrollment:* 49 full-time matriculated graduate/professional students (25 women), 514 part-time matriculated graduate/professional students (412 women). *Enrollment by degree level:* 563 master's. *Graduate faculty:* 4 full-time (1 woman), 32 part-time/adjunct (17 women). *Tuition:* Part-time $467 per hour. Tuition and fees vary according to program. *Graduate housing:* Room and/or apartments available on a first-come, first-served basis to single students; on-campus housing not available to married students. Typical cost: $3,990 (including board). Room and board charges vary according to board plan and housing facility selected. *Student services:* Campus employment opportunities, career counseling, free psychological counseling, low-cost health insurance. *Library facilities:* Doris and Harry Vise Library. *Online resources:* web page. *Collection:* 50,000 titles, 130 serial subscriptions, 250 audiovisual materials.

Computer facilities: 50 computers available on campus for general student use. A campuswide network can be accessed from student residence rooms and from off campus. Internet access is available. *Web address:* http://www.cumberland.edu/.

General Application Contact: Edward Freytag, Director of Admissions, 615-444-2562 Ext. 1120, Fax: 615-444-2569, E-mail: efreytag@cumberland.edu.

GRADUATE UNITS

Division of Graduate Studies Students: 49 full-time (25 women), 514 part-time (412 women); includes 142 minority (132 African Americans, 4 Asian Americans or Pacific Islanders, 4 Hispanic Americans, 2 Native Americans), 5 international. Average age 28. *Faculty:* 4 full-time (1 woman), 32 part-time/adjunct (17 women). Expenses: Contact institution. *Financial support:* In 2001–02, 40 students received support. Career-related internships or fieldwork, institutionally sponsored loans, and scholarships/grants available. Support available to part-time students. Financial award application deadline: 8/1; financial award applicants required to submit FAFSA. In 2001, 233 degrees awarded. *Degree program information:* Part-time and evening/weekend programs available. Offers business administration (MBA); education (MAE); human relations management (MS); public service administration (MS). *Application fee:* $50. *Application Contact:* Edward Freytag, Director of Admissions, 615-444-2562 Ext. 1120, Fax: 615-444-

2569, E-mail: efreytag@cumberland.edu. *Director*, Dr. J. M. Galloway, 615-444-2562 Ext. 1170, Fax: 615-444-2569, E-mail: jgalloway@cumberland.edu.

CURRY COLLEGE, Milton, MA 02186-9984

General Information Independent, coed, comprehensive institution. *Graduate housing:* On-campus housing not available. *Research affiliation:* Public School Systems, Literacy Centers/GED Programs.

GRADUATE UNITS

Program in Education *Degree program information:* Part-time and evening/weekend programs available. Offers adult education (M Ed, Certificate); educational studies in and out of the classroom environment (M Ed); learning disabilities across the lifespan (Certificate); post-secondary learning disabilities (M Ed); reading (M Ed, Certificate). Electronic applications accepted.

THE CURTIS INSTITUTE OF MUSIC, Philadelphia, PA 19103-6107

General Information Independent, coed, comprehensive institution. *Graduate housing:* On-campus housing not available.

GRADUATE UNITS

Graduate Studies Offers opera (MM).

DAEMEN COLLEGE, Amherst, NY 14226-3592

General Information Independent, coed, comprehensive institution. *Enrollment:* 26 full-time matriculated graduate/professional students (20 women), 57 part-time matriculated graduate/professional students (47 women). *Enrollment by degree level:* 83 master's. *Graduate faculty:* 18 full-time (9 women), 14 part-time/adjunct (6 women). *Tuition:* Part-time $505 per credit hour. *Required fees:* $14 per credit hour. Part-time tuition and fees vary according to course load. *Graduate housing:* Room and/or apartments available on a first-come, first-served basis to single students; on-campus housing not available to married students. Typical cost: $6,700 (including board). Housing application deadline: 7/15. *Student services:* Campus employment opportunities, campus safety program, career counseling, disabled student services, low-cost health insurance, teacher training. *Library facilities:* Marian Library plus 1 other. *Online resources:* library catalog, web page, access to other libraries' catalogs. *Collection:* 123,835 titles, 983 serial subscriptions, 14,533 audiovisual materials.

Computer facilities: 154 computers available on campus for general student use. A campuswide network can be accessed from student residence rooms and from off campus. Internet access is available. *Web address:* http://www.daemen.edu/.

GRADUATE UNITS

Department of Nursing Students: 4 full-time (all women), 30 part-time (29 women); includes 1 minority (Native American), 1 international. Average age 41. 18 applicants, 44% accepted, 7 enrolled. *Faculty:* 5 full-time (all women), 5 part-time/adjunct (4 women). Expenses: Contact institution. *Financial support:* Scholarships/grants and tuition waivers (partial) available. Support available to part-time students. Financial award application deadline: 2/15; financial award applicants required to submit FAFSA. In 2001, 11 degrees awarded. *Degree program information:* Part-time programs available. Offers adult nurse practitioner (MS, Certificate); palliative care nursing (MS, Certificate). *Application deadline:* For fall admission, 3/1 (priority date); for spring admission, 10/1 (priority date). Applications are processed on a rolling basis. *Application fee:* $25. Electronic applications accepted. *Application Contact:* Susan Eiss, Graduate Admissions Coordinator, 716-839-8225, Fax: 716-839-8370, E-mail: seiss@daemen.edu. *Chair*, Mary Lou Rusin, 716-839-8387, Fax: 716-839-8314, E-mail: mrusin@daemen.edu.

DAKOTA STATE UNIVERSITY, Madison, SD 57042-1799

General Information State-supported, coed, comprehensive institution. *Enrollment:* 34 full-time matriculated graduate/professional students (12 women), 86 part-time matriculated graduate/professional students (51 women). *Enrollment by degree level:* 120 master's. *Graduate faculty:* 34 full-time (11 women). Tuition, state resident: part-time $95 per credit hour. Tuition, nonresident: part-time $182 per credit hour. Tuition and fees vary according to course load, campus/location and reciprocity agreements. *Graduate housing:* Room and/or apartments available on a first-come, first-served basis to single students; on-campus housing not available to married students. Typical cost: $2,300 per year ($5,500 including board). Room and board charges vary according to board plan and housing facility selected. Housing application deadline: 7/15. *Student services:* Campus employment opportunities, campus safety program, career counseling, disabled student services, exercise/wellness program, free psychological counseling, grant writing training, international student services, low-cost health insurance, multicultural affairs office, writing training. *Library facilities:* Karl E. Mundt Library plus 1 other. *Online resources:* library catalog, web page, access to other libraries' catalogs. *Collection:* 4.6 million titles, 7,456 serial subscriptions, 2,738 audiovisual materials.

Computer facilities: 391 computers available on campus for general student use. A campuswide network can be accessed from student residence rooms and from off campus. Internet access and online class registration are available. *Web address:* http://www.dsu.edu/.

General Application Contact: Laurie B. Dennis, Director, Graduate Programs, 605-256-5263, Fax: 605-256-5316, E-mail: laurie.dennis@dsu.edu.

GRADUATE UNITS

College of Business and Information Systems Students: 30 full-time (11 women), 49 part-time (20 women); includes 2 minority (1 African American, 1 Asian American or Pacific Islander), 16 international. Average age 34. 46 applicants, 83% accepted, 27 enrolled. *Faculty:* 12 full-time (0 women). Expenses: Contact institution. *Financial support:* In 2001–02, 30 students received support, including 13 research assistantships with partial tuition reimbursements available (averaging $4,035 per year), 5 teaching assistantships with partial tuition reimbursements available (averaging $5,800 per year); Federal Work-Study, scholarships/grants, and unspecified assistantships also available. Support available to part-time students. Financial award applicants required to submit FAFSA. In 2001, 22 degrees awarded. *Degree program information:* Part-time and evening/weekend programs available. Postbaccalaureate distance learning degree programs offered (minimal on-campus study). Offers business and information systems (MSIS). *Application deadline:* For fall admission, 8/1; for winter admission, 10/1. Applications are processed on a rolling basis. *Application fee:* $35 ($85 for international students). Electronic applications accepted. *Application Contact:* Laurie B. Dennis, Director, Graduate Programs, 605-256-5263, Fax: 605-256-5316, E-mail: laurie.dennis@dsu.edu. *Dean*, Dr. Richard Christoph, 605-256-5176, Fax: 605-256-5316.

College of Education Students: 4 full-time (1 woman), 37 part-time (31 women). Average age 39. 10 applicants, 90% accepted, 8 enrolled. *Faculty:* 9 full-time (2 women). Expenses: Contact institution. *Financial support:* In 2001–02, 6 students received support, including 3 research assistantships with partial tuition reimbursements available (averaging $4,035 per year); Federal Work-Study, scholarships/grants, and unspecified assistantships also available. Support available to part-time students. Financial award applicants required to submit FAFSA. In 2001, 8 degrees awarded. *Degree program information:* Part-time programs available. Postbaccalaureate distance learning degree programs offered (minimal on-campus study). Offers instructional/educational technology (MSCET). *Application deadline:* For fall admission, 8/1. Applications are processed on a rolling basis. *Application fee:* $35 ($85 for international students). Electronic applications accepted. *Application Contact:* Laurie B. Dennis, Director, Graduate Programs, 605-256-5263, Fax: 605-256-5316, E-mail: laurie.dennis@dsu.edu. *Dean*, Dr. W. Thomas Hawley, 605-256-5177, Fax: 605-256-7300, E-mail: tom.hawley@dsu.edu.

DALHOUSIE UNIVERSITY, Halifax, NS B3H 4R2, Canada

General Information Province-supported, coed, university. *Enrollment:* 1,823 full-time matriculated graduate/professional students (873 women), 876 part-time matriculated graduate/professional students (492 women). *Enrollment by degree level:* 74 first professional, 2,190 master's, 433 doctoral, 2 other advanced degrees. *Graduate faculty:* 1,320. *Graduate tuition:* Tuition charges are reported in Canadian dollars. *Tuition:* Part-time $4,752 Canadian dollars per degree program. Tuition and fees vary according to course load, degree level and program. *Graduate housing:* Rooms and/or apartments available on a first-come, first-served basis to single and married students. Housing application deadline: 7/15. *Student services:* Campus employment opportunities, campus safety program, career counseling, child daycare facilities, disabled student services, free psychological counseling, international student services. *Library facilities:* The Killam Memorial Library plus 4 others. *Online resources:* library catalog, web page, access to other libraries' catalogs. *Collection:* 1.7 million titles, 8,306 serial subscriptions, 6,001 audiovisual materials.

Computer facilities: 710 computers available on campus for general student use. A campuswide network can be accessed from student residence rooms and from off campus. Internet access is available. *Web address:* http://www.dal.ca/.

General Application Contact: Dr. Jan Kwak, Dean, Faculty of Graduate Studies, 902-494-2485, Fax: 902-494-8797, E-mail: graduate.studies@dal.ca.

GRADUATE UNITS

Faculty of Architecture Tuition charges are reported in Canadian dollars. Offers architecture (M Arch, MEDS, MURP); urban and rural planning (MURP).

Faculty of Dentistry Tuition charges are reported in Canadian dollars. Offers dentistry (DDS, Diploma).

Faculty of Graduate Studies Tuition charges are reported in Canadian dollars. *Degree program information:* Part-time programs available. Postbaccalaureate distance learning degree programs offered. Offers anatomy and neurobiology (M Sc, PhD); community health and epidemiology (M Sc); dentistry); interdisciplinary studies (PhD); marine affairs (MMM); medicine (M Sc, PhD); microbiology and immunology (M Sc, PhD); neuroscience (M Sc, PhD); pathology (M Sc); pharmacology (M Sc, PhD); physiology and biophysics (M Sc, PhD).

College of Arts and Science Tuition charges are reported in Canadian dollars. *Degree program information:* Part-time programs available. Offers arts and science (M Sc, MA, MDE, PhD); arts and social science (M Sc, MA, MDE, PhD); biology (M Sc, PhD); chemistry (M Sc, PhD); classics (MA, PhD); clinical psychology (PhD); earth sciences (M Sc, PhD); economics (MA, MDE, PhD); English (MA, PhD); French (MA, PhD); German (MA); history (MA, PhD); international development studies (MA); mathematics (M Sc, PhD); oceanography (M Sc, PhD); philosophy (MA, PhD); physics (M Sc, PhD); political science (MA, PhD); psychology (M Sc, PhD); psychology/neuroscience (M Sc, PhD); science (M Sc, MA, MDE, PhD); social anthropology (MA); sociology (MA, PhD); statistics (M Sc, PhD); women's studies (MA).

DalTech Tuition charges are reported in Canadian dollars. *Degree program information:* Part-time programs available. Offers biological engineering (M Eng, MA Sc, PhD); biomedical engineering (MA Sc); chemical engineering (M Eng, MA Sc, PhD); civil engineering (M Eng, MA Sc, PhD); computer science (MC Sc, PhD); electrical and computer engineering (M Eng, MA Sc, PhD); electronic commerce (MEC); engineering (M Eng, M Sc, MA Sc, PhD); engineering mathematics (M Sc, PhD); food science and technology (M Sc, PhD); industrial engineering (M Eng, MA Sc, PhD); internet working (M Eng); mechanical engineering (M Eng, MA Sc, PhD); metallurgical engineering (M Eng, MA Sc, PhD); mining (M Eng, MA Sc, PhD).

Faculty of Health Professions Tuition charges are reported in Canadian dollars. *Degree program information:* Part-time programs available. Postbaccalaureate distance learning degree programs offered. Offers health and human performance (M Sc, MA); health education (MA); health professions (M Sc, MA, MHSA, MN, MSW, PhD); health services administration (MHSA); human communication disorders (M Sc); kinesiology (M Sc); leisure studies (MA); nursing (MN); occupational therapy (M Sc); pharmacy (M Sc, PhD); social work (MSW).

Faculty of Law Tuition charges are reported in Canadian dollars. *Degree program information:* Part-time programs available. Offers law (LL M, JSD).

Faculty of Management Tuition charges are reported in Canadian dollars. *Degree program information:* Part-time programs available. Offers business administration (MBA); information technology (MBA); library and information studies (MLIS); management (MBA, MES, MLIS, MPA, Diploma); public administration (MPA); resource and environmental studies (MES).

Henson College of Public Affairs and Continuing Education Tuition charges are reported in Canadian dollars. Offers information technology education (MITE).

Nova Scotia Agricultural College *Degree program information:* Part-time programs available. Offers agriculture (M Sc).

Faculty of Medicine Students: 380. *Faculty:* 560. Expenses: Contact institution. *Financial support:* Fellowships, teaching assistantships, institutionally sponsored loans available. In 2001, 86 first professional degrees, 11 master's, 5 doctorates awarded. *Degree program information:* Part-time programs available. Offers biochemistry and molecular biology (M Sc, PhD); medicine (MD, M Sc, PhD). *Application deadline:* Applications are processed on a rolling basis. *Application fee:* $55. *Application Contact:* Sharon Graham, Director of Admissions, 902-494-1874. *Dean*, Dr. Noni MacDonald, 902-494-1846.

DALLAS BAPTIST UNIVERSITY, Dallas, TX 75211-9299

General Information Independent-religious, coed, comprehensive institution. *Enrollment:* 197 full-time matriculated graduate/professional students (133 women), 765 part-time matriculated graduate/professional students (507 women). *Enrollment by degree level:* 962 master's. *Graduate faculty:* 85 full-time (35 women), 49 part-time/adjunct (20 women). *Tuition:* Full-time $6,030; part-time $335 per credit. *Graduate housing:* Rooms and/or apartments available on a first-come, first-served basis to single and married students. Typical cost: $1,200 per year for single students; $1,200 per year for married students. *Student services:* Campus employment opportunities, campus safety program, career counseling, disabled student services, free psychological counseling, international student services, low-cost health insurance, writing training. *Library facilities:* Vance Memorial Library. *Online resources:* library catalog, web page. *Collection:* 213,072 titles, 664 serial subscriptions, 5,992 audiovisual materials.

Computer facilities: 109 computers available on campus for general student use. A campuswide network can be accessed from student residence rooms and from off campus. Internet access is available. *Web address:* http://www.dbu.edu/.

General Application Contact: Sarah R. Brancaccio, Director of Graduate Programs, 214-333-5242, Fax: 214-333-5579, E-mail: graduate@dbu.edu.

GRADUATE UNITS

College of Adult Education Students: 118 (84 women). 77 applicants, 47% accepted, 30 enrolled. *Faculty:* 30 full-time (7 women), 43 part-time/adjunct (15 women). Expenses: Contact institution. *Financial support:* Federal Work-Study, institutionally sponsored loans, scholarships/grants, and tuition waivers (full and partial) available. Support available to part-time students. In 2001, 43 degrees awarded. *Degree program information:* Part-time and evening/weekend programs available. Offers adult education (MA, MLA); liberal arts (MLA); professional development (MA). *Application deadline:* Applications are processed on a rolling basis. *Application fee:* $25. Electronic applications accepted. *Application Contact:* Sarah R. Brancaccio, Director of Graduate Programs, 214-333-5243, Fax: 214-333-5579, E-mail: graduate@dbu.edu. *Dean*, Kerry Webb, 214-333-5545, Fax: 214-333-5558, E-mail: caed@dbu.edu.

College of Business Students: 540 (292 women). 279 applicants, 67% accepted, 81 enrolled. *Faculty:* 14 full-time (5 women), 31 part-time/adjunct (10 women). Expenses: Contact institution. *Financial support:* Career-related internships or fieldwork, Federal Work-Study, institutionally sponsored loans, scholarships/grants, and tuition waivers (full and partial) available. Support available to part-time students. In 2001, 131 degrees awarded. *Degree program information:* Part-time and evening/weekend programs available. Postbaccalaureate distance learning degree programs offered (no on-campus study). Offers accounting (MBA); business (MA, MBA); conflict resolution management (MA); E. business (MBA); finance (MBA); general

Dallas Baptist University (continued)

management (MA); health care management (MA, MBA); human resource management (MA); international business (MBA); management (MBA); management information systems (MBA); marketing (MBA); technology and engineering management (MBA). *Application deadline:* Applications are processed on a rolling basis. *Application fee:* $25. Electronic applications accepted. *Application Contact:* Sarah R. Brancaccio, Director of Graduate Programs, 214-333-5243, Fax: 214-333-5579, E-mail: graduate@dbu.edu. *Acting Dean,* Dr. Denny Dowd, 214-333-5338, Fax: 214-333-5293, E-mail: graduate@dbu.edu.

College of Humanities and Social Sciences Students: 112 (86 women). 56 applicants, 61% accepted, 12 enrolled. *Faculty:* 3 full-time (1 woman), 7 part-time/adjunct (2 women). Expenses: Contact institution. *Financial support:* Career-related internships or fieldwork, Federal Work-Study, institutionally sponsored loans, scholarships/grants, and tuition waivers (full and partial) available. Support available to part-time students. Financial award applicants required to submit FAFSA. In 2001, 36 degrees awarded. *Degree program information:* Part-time and evening/weekend programs available. Offers counseling (MA); humanities and social sciences (MA). *Application deadline:* Applications are processed on a rolling basis. *Application fee:* $25. Electronic applications accepted. *Application Contact:* Sarah R. Brancaccio, Director of Graduate Programs, 214-333-5243, Fax: 214-333-5579, E-mail: graduate@dbu.edu. *Dean,* Dr. Michael E. Williams, 214-333-5238, Fax: 214-333-5323, E-mail: graduate@dbu.edu.

Dorothy M. Bush College of Education Students: 191 (161 women). 114 applicants, 63% accepted, 17 enrolled. *Faculty:* 9 full-time (6 women), 9 part-time/adjunct (6 women). Expenses: Contact institution. *Financial support:* Federal Work-Study, institutionally sponsored loans, scholarships/grants, and tuition waivers (full and partial) available. Support available to part-time students. In 2001, 38 degrees awarded. *Degree program information:* Part-time and evening/weekend programs available. Offers early childhood education (M Ed); education (M Ed, MAT); educational organization and administration (M Ed); elementary reading education (M Ed); general elementary education (M Ed); higher education (M Ed); reading specialist (M Ed); school counseling (M Ed); teaching (MAT). *Application deadline:* Applications are processed on a rolling basis. *Application fee:* $25. Electronic applications accepted. *Application Contact:* Sarah R. Brancaccio, Director of Graduate Programs, 214-333-5243, Fax: 214-333-5579, E-mail: graduate@dbu.edu. *Dean,* Dr. Mike Rosato, 214-333-5200, Fax: 214-333-5551, E-mail: graduate@dbu.edu.

DALLAS INSTITUTE OF ACUPUNCTURE AND ORIENTAL MEDICINE, Dallas, TX 75229

General Information Independent, coed, graduate-only institution.

DALLAS THEOLOGICAL SEMINARY, Dallas, TX 75204-6499

General Information Independent, coed, graduate-only institution. *Graduate housing:* Rooms and/or apartments available on a first-come, first-served basis to single and married students.

GRADUATE UNITS

Graduate Programs *Degree program information:* Part-time and evening/weekend programs available. Offers academic ministries (Th M); Bible translation (Th M); biblical and theological studies (CGS); biblical counseling (MA); biblical exegesis and linguistics (MA); biblical studies (MA, Th M, PhD, Th D); chaplaincy (Th M); Christian education (MA, D Min); corporate chaplaincy (MA); cross-cultural ministries (MA, Th M); educational leadership (Th M); evangelism and discipleship (Th M); interdisciplinary (Th M); media arts in ministry (Th M); ministry (D Min); pastoral ministries (Th M); sacred theology (STM); theological studies (Th M, PhD, Th D); women's ministry (Th M). MA (biblical exegesis and linguistics) offered jointly with the Summer Institute of Linguistics. Extension branches located in Chattanooga (TN), Houston (TX), Philadelphia (PA), San Antonio (TX), and the Tampa Bay area (FL). Electronic applications accepted.

DARKEI NOAM RABBINICAL COLLEGE, Brooklyn, NY 11210

General Information Independent-religious, men only, comprehensive institution.

DARTMOUTH COLLEGE, Hanover, NH 03755

General Information Independent, coed, university. CGS member. *Enrollment:* 1,289 full-time matriculated graduate/professional students (462 women), 64 part-time matriculated graduate/professional students (29 women). *Enrollment by degree level:* 279 first professional, 654 master's, 386 doctoral. *Graduate faculty:* 1,023 full-time, 1,211 part-time/adjunct. *Tuition:* Full-time $26,425. *Graduate housing:* Rooms and/or apartments available to single and married students. Typical cost: $14,400 (including board) for single students. *Student services:* Campus safety program, career counseling, disabled student services, free psychological counseling, international student services, low-cost health insurance, teacher training, writing training. *Library facilities:* Baker-Berry Library plus 10 others. *Online resources:* library catalog, web page, access to other libraries' catalogs. *Collection:* 2.4 million titles, 20,679 serial subscriptions, 78,471 audiovisual materials. *Research affiliation:* Cold Regions Research Engineering Laboratory.

Computer facilities: 12,000 computers available on campus for general student use. A campuswide network can be accessed from student residence rooms and from off campus. Internet access and online class registration are available. *Web address:* http://www.dartmouth.edu/.

General Application Contact: Lynn Foster-Johnson, Institutional Research, 603-646-1187, E-mail: v.lynn-foster@dartmouth.edu.

GRADUATE UNITS

Dartmouth Medical School Offers medicine (MD).

School of Arts and Sciences Students: 445 full-time (209 women), 57 part-time (29 women); includes 44 minority (8 African Americans, 25 Asian Americans or Pacific Islanders, 7 Hispanic Americans, 4 Native Americans), 135 international. 1,661 applicants, 21% accepted, 192 enrolled. *Faculty:* 162 full-time (46 women). Expenses: Contact institution. *Financial support:* In 2001–02, 502 students received support, including fellowships with full tuition reimbursements available (averaging $16,440 per year), research assistantships with full tuition reimbursements available (averaging $16,440 per year), teaching assistantships with full tuition reimbursements available (averaging $16,440 per year); career-related internships or fieldwork, Federal Work-Study, institutionally sponsored loans, scholarships/grants, traineeships, tuition waivers (full and partial), and unspecified assistantships also available. Support available to part-time students. Financial award applicants required to submit CSS PROFILE. In 2001, 115 master's, 44 doctorates awarded. *Degree program information:* Part-time programs available. Offers arts and sciences (AM, MALS, MS, PhD); biochemistry (PhD); biology (PhD); chemistry (PhD); cognitive neuroscience (PhD); comparative literature (AM); computer science (MS, PhD); earth sciences (MS, PhD); electro-acoustic music (AM); evaluative clinical sciences (MS, PhD); genetics (PhD); liberal studies (MALS); mathematics (PhD); pharmacology and toxicology (PhD); physics and astronomy (MS, PhD); physiology (PhD); psychology (PhD). Electronic applications accepted. *Application Contact:* Lynn Foster-Johnson, Institutional Research, 603-646-1187, E-mail: v.lynn-foster@dartmouth.edu. *Dean,* Dr. Roger D. Sloboda, 603-646-2106, E-mail: rds@dartmouth.edu.

Thayer School of Engineering Students: 136 full-time (27 women), 4 part-time; includes 20 minority (4 African Americans, 12 Asian Americans or Pacific Islanders, 4 Hispanic Americans), 57 international. Average age 24. 230 applicants, 43% accepted, 72 enrolled. *Faculty:* 33 full-time (4 women), 18 part-time/adjunct (1 woman). Expenses: Contact institution. *Financial support:* In 2001–02, 4 fellowships with full tuition reimbursements (averaging $16,920 per year), 64 research assistantships with full tuition reimbursements (averaging $18,120 per year), 27 teaching assistantships with partial tuition reimbursements (averaging $5,800 per year) were awarded. Career-related internships or fieldwork, institutionally sponsored loans, scholarships/grants, and tuition waivers (full and partial) also available. Financial award application deadline: 1/15; financial award applicants required to submit CSS PROFILE. In 2001, 46 master's, 6 doctorates awarded. Offers biomedical engineering (MS, PhD); biotechnology and biochemical engineering (MS, PhD); computer engineering (MS, PhD); electrical engineering (MS, PhD); engineering (MEM, MS, PhD); engineering management (MEM); environmental engineering (MS, PhD); materials sciences and engineering (MS, PhD); mechanical engineering (MS, PhD). *Application deadline:* For fall admission, 1/1 (priority date). *Application fee:* $40 ($50 for international students). Electronic applications accepted. *Application Contact:* Candace S. Potter, Graduate Admissions Administrator, 603-646-3844, Fax: 603-646-1620, E-mail: candace.potter@dartmouth.edu. *Dean,* Dr. Lewis M. Duncan, 603-646-2238, Fax: 603-646-2580, E-mail: lewis.m.duncan@dartmouth.edu.

Tuck School of Business at Dartmouth Students: 432 full-time (118 women); includes 70 minority (15 African Americans, 30 Asian Americans or Pacific Islanders, 24 Hispanic Americans, 1 Native American), 129 international. Average age 28. 2,329 applicants, 19% accepted. *Faculty:* 45 full-time (9 women), 22 part-time/adjunct (4 women). Expenses: Contact institution. *Financial support:* In 2001–02, 312 students received support, including 192 fellowships (averaging $7,500 per year); career-related internships or fieldwork, Federal Work-Study, institutionally sponsored loans, and scholarships/grants also available. Financial award application deadline: 3/1; financial award applicants required to submit FAFSA. In 2001, 187 degrees awarded. Offers business (MBA). *Application deadline:* For fall admission, 12/3; for winter admission, 1/18; for spring admission, 4/17. *Application fee:* $175. Electronic applications accepted. *Application Contact:* Kristine Laca, Director of Admissions, 603-646-3162, Fax: 603-646-1441, E-mail: tuck.admissions@dartmouth.edu. *Dean,* Paul Danos, 603-646-2460, Fax: 603-646-1308, E-mail: paul.danos@dartmouth.edu.

See in-depth description on page 837.

DAVENPORT UNIVERSITY, Dearborn, MI 48126-3799

General Information Independent, coed, comprehensive institution. *Graduate housing:* On-campus housing not available.

GRADUATE UNITS

Sneden Graduate School *Degree program information:* Part-time and evening/weekend programs available. Postbaccalaureate distance learning degree programs offered (no on-campus study). Offers accounting (MBA); e-business (MBA); finance (MBA); global business (MBA); health care management (MBA); human resources management (MBA); management (MBA); marketing (MBA).

DAVID N. MYERS UNIVERSITY, Cleveland, OH 44115-1096

General Information Independent, coed, comprehensive institution.

GRADUATE UNITS

McDonald School of Business

DEFIANCE COLLEGE, Defiance, OH 43512-1610

General Information Independent-religious, coed, comprehensive institution. *Enrollment:* 115 part-time matriculated graduate/professional students (57 women). *Enrollment by degree level:* 115 master's. *Graduate faculty:* 8 full-time (4 women), 4 part-time/adjunct (2 women). *Tuition:* Full-time $2,610; part-time $290 per credit. *Required fees:* $200; $25 per semester. Part-time tuition and fees vary according to course load. *Graduate housing:* On-campus housing not available. *Student services:* Career counseling, exercise/wellness program, multicultural affairs office, teacher training. *Library facilities:* Pilgrim Library. *Online resources:* library catalog, access to other libraries' catalogs. *Collection:* 88,000 titles, 424 serial subscriptions, 25,000 audiovisual materials.

Computer facilities: 100 computers available on campus for general student use. A campuswide network can be accessed from student residence rooms and from off campus. Internet access is available. *Web address:* http://www.defiance.edu/.

General Application Contact: Sally Bissell, Director of Continuing Education, 419-783-2350, Fax: 419-784-0426, E-mail: sbissell@defiance.edu.

GRADUATE UNITS

Program in Business and Organizational Leadership Average age 28. 11 applicants, 100% accepted. *Faculty:* 6 full-time (3 women), 4 part-time/adjunct (2 women). Expenses: Contact institution. In 2001, 14 degrees awarded. *Degree program information:* Part-time and evening/weekend programs available. Offers business and organizational leadership (MBOL). *Application deadline:* For fall admission, 8/1. Applications are processed on a rolling basis. *Application fee:* $25. *Application Contact:* Sally Bissell, Director of Continuing Education, 419-783-2350, Fax: 419-784-0426, E-mail: sbissell@defiance.edu. *Coordinator,* Dr. Susan Wajert, 419-783-2372, Fax: 419-784-0426, E-mail: swajert@definance.edu.

Program in Education Average age 28. 9 applicants, 100% accepted. *Faculty:* 5 full-time (3 women), 2 part-time/adjunct (1 woman). Expenses: Contact institution. In 2001, 21 degrees awarded. *Degree program information:* Part-time programs available. Offers education (MA). *Application deadline:* For fall admission, 8/1. Applications are processed on a rolling basis. *Application fee:* $25. *Application Contact:* Sally Bissell, Director of Continuing Education, 419-783-2350, Fax: 419-784-0426, E-mail: sbissell@defiance.edu. *Coordinator,* Dr. Suzanne McFarland, 419-783-2315, Fax: 419-784-0426, E-mail: smcfarland@defiance.edu.

DELAWARE STATE UNIVERSITY, Dover, DE 19901-2277

General Information State-supported, coed, comprehensive institution. *Enrollment:* 96 full-time matriculated graduate/professional students (73 women), 163 part-time matriculated graduate/professional students (107 women). *Enrollment by degree level:* 259 master's. *Graduate faculty:* 73 full-time (14 women), 3 part-time/adjunct (1 woman). *Tuition, area resident:* Full-time $3,420; part-time $190 per credit hour. *Required fees:* $180; $90 per semester. Full-time tuition and fees vary according to degree level and program. *Graduate housing:* On-campus housing not available. *Student services:* Campus employment opportunities, campus safety program, career counseling, free psychological counseling, international student services. *Library facilities:* William C. Jason Library. *Online resources:* library catalog. *Collection:* 204,127 titles, 3,094 serial subscriptions, 13,775 audiovisual materials.

Computer facilities: 641 computers available on campus for general student use. A campuswide network can be accessed from student residence rooms and from off campus. Internet access and online class registration, online grade access, e-mail are available. *Web address:* http://www.dsc.edu/.

General Application Contact: Dr. Hazell Reed, Dean of Graduate Studies and Research, 302-857-6800, Fax: 302-857-6802.

GRADUATE UNITS

Graduate Programs Students: 96 full-time (73 women), 163 part-time (107 women); includes 151 minority (148 African Americans, 1 Asian American or Pacific Islander, 2 Native Americans), 1 international. Average age 37. *Faculty:* 73 full-time (14 women), 3 part-time/adjunct (1 woman). Expenses: Contact institution. *Financial support:* In 2001–02, 33 research assistantships were awarded; fellowships, teaching assistantships, career-related internships or fieldwork, Federal Work-Study, institutionally sponsored loans, and tuition waivers (full and partial) also available. Support available to part-time students. In 2001, 77 degrees awarded. *Degree program information:* Part-time and evening/weekend programs available. Offers applied chemistry (MS); biology (MS); biology education (MS); business administration (MBA); chemistry (MS); curriculum and instruction (MA); education (MA); mathematics (MS); physics (MS); physics teaching (MS); science education (MA); social work (MSW); special education (MA). *Application deadline:* For fall admission, 6/30 (priority date); for winter admission, 9/4 (priority date); for spring admission, 1/17. Applications are processed on a rolling basis. *Application fee:* $15. *Dean of Graduate Studies and Research,* Dr. Hazell Reed, 302-857-6800, Fax: 302-857-6802.

access to other libraries' catalogs. *Collection:* 454,362 titles, 1,200 serial subscriptions, 250 audiovisual materials.

Computer facilities: 91 computers available on campus for general student use. A campuswide network can be accessed from student residence rooms and from off campus. Internet access and online class registration are available. *Web address:* http://www.dsl.edu/.

General Application Contact: Barbara W. Guillaume, Director, Law Admissions, 717-240-5207, Fax: 717-241-3503, E-mail: dsladmit@psu.edu.

GRADUATE UNITS

Graduate and Professional Programs Students: 534 full-time (246 women), 1 (woman) part-time. Average age 25. 1,718 applicants, 48% accepted. *Faculty:* 35 full-time (12 women), 57 part-time/adjunct (9 women). Expenses: Contact institution. *Financial support:* In 2001–02, 445 students received support. Federal Work-Study, institutionally sponsored loans, and scholarships/grants available. Support available to part-time students. Financial award application deadline: 2/15; financial award applicants required to submit FAFSA. In 2001, 168 first professional degrees, 8 master's awarded. Offers comparative law (LL M); law (JD). *Application deadline:* For fall admission, 3/1 (priority date). Applications are processed on a rolling basis. *Application fee:* $50. *Application Contact:* Barbara W. Guillaume, Director, Law Admissions, 717-240-5207, Fax: 717-241-3503, E-mail: dsladmit@psu.edu. *Dean,* Peter G. Glenn, 717-240-5000, Fax: 717-240-5213.

DOANE COLLEGE, Crete, NE 68333-2430

General Information Independent-religious, coed, comprehensive institution. *Enrollment:* 224 full-time matriculated graduate/professional students (162 women), 402 part-time matriculated graduate/professional students (305 women). *Enrollment by degree level:* 626 master's. *Graduate faculty:* 5 full-time (2 women), 31 part-time/adjunct (9 women). *Tuition:* Part-time $140 per credit hour. Tuition and fees vary according to program. *Graduate housing:* On-campus housing not available. *Student services:* Career counseling. *Library facilities:* Perkins Library. *Online resources:* library catalog, web page, access to other libraries' catalogs. *Collection:* 247,952 titles, 3,500 serial subscriptions, 1,313 audiovisual materials.

Computer facilities: 200 computers available on campus for general student use. A campuswide network can be accessed from student residence rooms and from off campus. Internet access and online class registration are available. *Web address:* http://www.doane.edu/.

General Application Contact: Lyn Forester, Dean of Graduate Studies in Education, 402-464-1223, Fax: 404-466-4228, E-mail: wdaddarino@doane.edu.

GRADUATE UNITS

Program in Counseling Students: 81 full-time, 17 part-time. Average age 36. *Faculty:* 2 full-time (0 women), 11 part-time/adjunct (6 women). Expenses: Contact institution. *Financial support:* Unspecified assistantships available. Financial award application deadline: 6/1; financial award applicants required to submit FAFSA. In 2001, 7 degrees awarded. *Degree program information:* Evening/weekend programs available. Postbaccalaureate distance learning degree programs offered. Offers counseling (MAC). *Application deadline:* Applications are processed on a rolling basis. *Application fee:* $25. *Dean,* Thomas Gilligan, 402-466-4774, Fax: 402-466-4228, E-mail: tgilligan@doane.edu.

Program in Education Students: 60 full-time, 382 part-time. Average age 37. Expenses: Contact institution. *Financial support:* Applicants required to submit FAFSA. *Degree program information:* Part-time and evening/weekend programs available. Offers curriculum and instruction (M Ed); educational leadership (M Ed). *Application deadline:* Applications are processed on a rolling basis. *Application fee:* $25. Electronic applications accepted. *Application Contact:* Wilma Daddario, Assistant Dean, 402-464-1223, Fax: 402-466-4228, E-mail: wdaddario@doane.edu. *Co-Dean,* Dr. Marilyn Kent Byrne, 402-826-8604, Fax: 402-826-8278, E-mail: mbyrne@doane.edu.

Program in Management Students: 83 full-time, 3 part-time. *Faculty:* 1 (woman) full-time, 8 part-time/adjunct (4 women). Expenses: Contact institution. *Financial support:* Application deadline: 6/1; *Degree program information:* Part-time and evening/weekend programs available. Offers management (MAM). *Application deadline:* Applications are processed on a rolling basis. *Application fee:* $25. *Application Contact:* Beverlee Linder, Student Coordinator, 402-826-8253, Fax: 402-466-4228, E-mail: blinder@doane.edu. *Acting Dean,* Frederic D. Brown.

DOMINICAN COLLEGE, Orangeburg, NY 10962-1210

General Information Independent, coed, comprehensive institution. *Enrollment:* 36 full-time matriculated graduate/professional students (22 women), 81 part-time matriculated graduate/professional students (71 women). *Graduate faculty:* 10 full-time (all women), 7 part-time/adjunct (all women). *Tuition:* Full-time $8,495; part-time $472 per credit. *Required fees:* $340; $15 per credit. Tuition and fees vary according to program. *Graduate housing:* On-campus housing not available. *Student services:* Campus employment opportunities, campus safety program, career counseling, free psychological counseling, international student services. *Library facilities:* Pius X Hall plus 1 other. *Online resources:* library catalog, access to other libraries' catalogs. *Collection:* 103,350 titles, 650 serial subscriptions.

Computer facilities: 38 computers available on campus for general student use. A campuswide network can be accessed from student residence rooms and from off campus. Internet access is available. *Web address:* http://www.dc.edu.

General Application Contact: Joyce Elbe, Director of Admissions, 845-359-7800 Ext. 208, Fax: 845-359-2313, E-mail: admissions@dc.edu.

GRADUATE UNITS

Department of Occupational Therapy Students: 39 full-time (35 women); includes 5 minority (3 African Americans, 2 Hispanic Americans) *Faculty:* 7 full-time (all women), 4 part-time/adjunct (all women). Expenses: Contact institution. In 2001, 18 degrees awarded. Offers occupational therapy (MS). *Application deadline:* Applications are processed on a rolling basis. *Application fee:* $50. *Application Contact:* Joyce Elbe, Director of Admissions, 845-359-7800 Ext. 208, Fax: 845-359-2313, E-mail: admissions@dc.edu. *Head,* Dr. Sandra Countee, 845-359-7800.

Division of Nursing *Faculty:* 2 full-time (both women), 1 (woman) part-time/adjunct. Expenses: Contact institution. In 2001, 7 degrees awarded. Offers nursing (MSN). *Application deadline:* Applications are processed on a rolling basis. *Application fee:* $50. *Application Contact:* Joyce Elbe, Director of Admissions, 845-359-7800 Ext. 208, Fax: 845-359-2313, E-mail: admissions@dc.edu. *Chair,* Dr. Maureen Creegan, 845-359-7800 Ext. 283, Fax: 845-359-2313.

Division of Physical Therapy Students: 9 full-time (5 women); includes 3 minority (all Asian Americans or Pacific Islanders) *Faculty:* 2 full-time (1 woman), 2 part-time/adjunct (1 woman). Expenses: Contact institution. In 2001, 7 degrees awarded. Offers physical therapy (MS). *Application deadline:* Applications are processed on a rolling basis. *Application fee:* $50. *Application Contact:* Joyce Elbe, Director of Admissions, 845-359-7800 Ext. 208, Fax: 845-359-2313, E-mail: admissions@dc.edu. *Head,* Dr. Valerie Olson, 845-359-7800 Ext. 405.

Division of Teacher Education *Faculty:* 2 full-time (both women), 3 part-time/adjunct (all women). Expenses: Contact institution. *Financial support:* Career-related internships or fieldwork, Federal Work-Study, and institutionally sponsored loans available. Support available to part-time students. In 2001, 14 degrees awarded. *Degree program information:* Part-time and evening/weekend programs available. Offers special education (MS Ed); teacher of visually impaired (MS Ed). *Application deadline:* Applications are processed on a rolling basis. *Application fee:* $50. *Application Contact:* Joyce Elbe, Director of Admissions, 845-359-7800 Ext. 208, Fax: 845-359-2313, E-mail: admissions@dc.edu. *Graduate Coordinator,* Dr. Rona Shaw, 845-359-7800, Fax: 845-359-2313.

See in-depth description on page 841.

DOMINICAN HOUSE OF STUDIES, Washington, DC 20017-1585

General Information Independent-religious, coed, primarily men, graduate-only institution. *Enrollment by degree level:* 43 first professional, 15 master's, 23 other advanced degrees. *Graduate faculty:* 12 full-time (1 woman), 11 part-time/adjunct (2 women). *Tuition:* Full-time $3,150; part-time $300 per semester. *Required fees:* $30. One-time fee: $25 full-time; $75 part-time. *Graduate housing:* On-campus housing not available. *Library facilities:* Dominican College Library. *Online resources:* web page. *Collection:* 75,570 titles, 450 serial subscriptions, 440 audiovisual materials.

Computer facilities: 5 computers available on campus for general student use. A campuswide network can be accessed. Internet access is available. *Web address:* http://www.dhs.edu/.

General Application Contact: Fr. Giles Dimock, OP, Academic Dean, 202-529-5300, Fax: 202-636-4460.

GRADUATE UNITS

Graduate and Professional Programs in Theology Students: 60 full-time (5 women), 21 part-time (6 women); includes 7 minority (4 African Americans, 1 Asian American or Pacific Islander, 2 Hispanic Americans), 13 international. *Faculty:* 12 full-time (1 woman), 11 part-time/adjunct (2 women). Expenses: Contact institution. *Financial support:* Teaching assistantships with partial tuition reimbursements, career-related internships or fieldwork available. In 2001, 6 first professional degrees, 3 master's, 3 other advanced degrees awarded. *Degree program information:* Part-time programs available. Offers theology (M Div, MA, STL). *Application deadline:* For fall admission, 9/1 (priority date); for spring admission, 1/20. Applications are processed on a rolling basis. *Application fee:* $25. *Application Contact:* Veronica D. Wynnyk, Registrar, 202-529-5300 Ext. 122, Fax: 202-636-4460, E-mail: vwynnyk@aol.com. *Academic Dean,* Fr. Giles Dimock, OP, 202-529-5300, Fax: 202-636-4460.

DOMINICAN SCHOOL OF PHILOSOPHY AND THEOLOGY, Berkeley, CA 94709-1295

General Information Independent-religious, coed, upper-level institution. *Enrollment:* 90 full-time matriculated graduate/professional students (19 women). *Enrollment by degree level:* 32 first professional, 58 master's. *Graduate faculty:* 12 full-time (1 woman), 10 part-time/adjunct (2 women). *Tuition:* Full-time $9,000. *Required fees:* $50. *Graduate housing:* Room and/or apartments available on a first-come, first-served basis to single students; on-campus housing not available to married students. Typical cost: $6,675 per year. Housing application deadline: 5/1. *Student services:* Campus employment opportunities, career counseling, low-cost health insurance. *Library facilities:* Flora Lamson Hewlett Library plus 1 other. *Online resources:* library catalog, web page. *Collection:* 401,086 titles, 1,526 serial subscriptions, 8,143 audiovisual materials.

Computer facilities: 4 computers available on campus for general student use. Internet access is available. *Web address:* http://www.dspt.edu/.

General Application Contact: Dr. Eugene Ludwig, Academic Dean, 510-883-2084, Fax: 510-849-1372, E-mail: eludwig@dspt.edu.

GRADUATE UNITS

Graduate Programs Students: 90 full-time (19 women); includes 31 minority (15 Asian Americans or Pacific Islanders, 16 Hispanic Americans) 35 applicants, 94% accepted, 25 enrolled. *Faculty:* 15 full-time (1 woman), 5 part-time/adjunct (2 women). Expenses: Contact institution. *Financial support:* In 2001–02, 12 students received support. Institutionally sponsored loans, scholarships/grants, and tuition waivers (partial) available. Financial award application deadline: 4/1; financial award applicants required to submit FAFSA. In 2001, 3 first professional degrees, 9 master's awarded. Offers philosophy (MA); theology (M Div, MA, Certificate). *Application deadline:* Applications are processed on a rolling basis. *Application fee:* $30. Electronic applications accepted. *Application Contact:* Susan M. McGinnis-Hardie, Director of Admissions and Recruitment, 510-883-2073, Fax: 510-849-1372, E-mail: smcginnishardie@dspt.edu. *Academic Dean,* Dr. Eugene Ludwig, 510-883-2084, Fax: 510-849-1372, E-mail: eludwig@dspt.edu.

DOMINICAN UNIVERSITY, River Forest, IL 60305-1099

General Information Independent-religious, coed, comprehensive institution. *Enrollment:* 186 full-time matriculated graduate/professional students (133 women), 1,158 part-time matriculated graduate/professional students (901 women). *Enrollment by degree level:* 1,344 master's. *Graduate faculty:* 27 full-time (14 women), 44 part-time/adjunct (23 women). *Tuition:* Part-time $395 per credit hour. *Graduate housing:* Room and/or apartments available on a first-come, first-served basis to single students; on-campus housing not available to married students. Typical cost: $5,000 (including board). Housing application deadline: 7/1. *Student services:* Campus employment opportunities, campus safety program, career counseling, child daycare facilities, free psychological counseling, international student services, low-cost health insurance, multicultural affairs office, teacher training, writing training. *Library facilities:* Rebecca Crown Library. *Online resources:* library catalog, web page, access to other libraries' catalogs. *Collection:* 280,475 titles, 4,422 serial subscriptions, 7,000 audiovisual materials.

Computer facilities: 199 computers available on campus for general student use. A campuswide network can be accessed from student residence rooms and from off campus. Internet access, email are available. *Web address:* http://www.dom.edu/.

GRADUATE UNITS

Graduate School of Business Students: 80 full-time (50 women), 187 part-time (96 women); includes 44 minority (20 African Americans, 14 Asian Americans or Pacific Islanders, 8 Hispanic Americans, 2 Native Americans), 91 international. Average age 32. *Faculty:* 14 full-time (3 women), 21 part-time/adjunct (5 women). Expenses: Contact institution. *Financial support:* Career-related internships or fieldwork, tuition waivers (partial), and unspecified assistantships available. Support available to part-time students. Financial award applicants required to submit FAFSA. In 2001, 76 degrees awarded. *Degree program information:* Part-time and evening/weekend programs available. Offers accounting (MSA); business administration (MBA); computer information systems (MSCIS); management information systems (MSMIS); organization management (MSOM). *Application deadline:* Applications are processed on a rolling basis. *Application fee:* $25. Electronic applications accepted. *Application Contact:* Roberta McMahon, Assistant Dean for Graduate Business Programs, 708-524-6507, Fax: 708-524-6939, E-mail: rmcmahon@email.dom.edu. *Dean,* Dr. Molly Burke, 708-524-6810, Fax: 708-524-6939, E-mail: burkemq@email.dom.edu.

Graduate School of Education Students: 16 full-time (14 women), 418 part-time (340 women); includes 80 minority (23 African Americans, 7 Asian Americans or Pacific Islanders, 50 Hispanic Americans), 2 international. Average age 36. *Faculty:* 10 full-time (8 women), 22 part-time/adjunct (18 women). Expenses: Contact institution. *Financial support:* In 2001–02, 157 students received support, including 34 teaching assistantships with full tuition reimbursements available; fellowships, career-related internships or fieldwork, institutionally sponsored loans, scholarships/grants, and tuition waivers (partial) also available. Support available to part-time students. Financial award application deadline: 8/15; financial award applicants required to submit FAFSA. In 2001, 89 degrees awarded. *Degree program information:* Part-time and evening/weekend programs available. Offers curriculum and instruction (MA Ed); early childhood education (MS); education (MAT); educational administration (MA); special education (MS). *Application deadline:* For fall admission, 8/15 (priority date); for spring admission, 1/16. Applications are processed on a rolling basis. *Application fee:* $25. Electronic applications accepted. *Application Contact:* Keven Hansen, Coordinator of Admissions and Recruitment, 708-524-6921, Fax: 708-524-6665, E-mail: educate@email.dom.edu. *Dean,* Sr. Colleen McNicholas, 708-524-6830, Fax: 708-524-6665, E-mail: educate@email.dom.edu.

Graduate School of Library and Information Science *Degree program information:* Part-time and evening/weekend programs available. Postbaccalaureate distance learning degree programs offered (minimal on-campus study). Offers library and information science (MLIS, MSMIS, CSS); management information systems (MSMIS).

Graduate School of Social Work Students: 14 full-time (11 women), 44 part-time (37 women); includes 30 minority (21 African Americans, 1 Asian American or Pacific Islander, 8

Dominican University (continued)

Hispanic Americans), 1 international. Average age 40. 72 applicants, 93% accepted, 55 enrolled. *Faculty:* 3 full-time (all women), 1 part-time/adjunct (0 women). Expenses: Contact institution. *Financial support:* Career-related internships or fieldwork, institutionally sponsored loans, and scholarships/grants available. Offers social work (MSW). *Application Contact:* Maria Talarico, Administrative Assistant, 708-366-3463, Fax: 708-366-3446, E-mail: msw@email.dom.edu. *Dean,* Vimala Pillari, 708-366-3316, E-mail: vpillari@email.dom.edu.

DOMINICAN UNIVERSITY OF CALIFORNIA, San Rafael, CA 94901-2298

General Information Independent-religious, coed, comprehensive institution. *Enrollment:* 249 full-time matriculated graduate/professional students (180 women), 194 part-time matriculated graduate/professional students (146 women). *Enrollment by degree level:* 224 master's, 199 other advanced degrees. *Graduate faculty:* 29 full-time (20 women), 84 part-time/adjunct (56 women). *Tuition:* Full-time $14,040; part-time $585 per unit. One-time fee: $335. Full-time tuition and fees vary according to program. *Graduate housing:* Room and/or apartments available on a first-come, first-served basis to single students; on-campus housing not available to married students. Typical cost: $8,440 (including board). Housing application deadline: 8/15. *Student services:* Campus employment opportunities, campus safety program, career counseling, free psychological counseling, international student services, low-cost health insurance. *Library facilities:* Archbishop Alemany Library plus 1 other. *Online resources:* library catalog, web page, access to other libraries' catalogs. *Collection:* 102,813 titles, 389 serial subscriptions, 1,107 audiovisual materials.

Computer facilities: 52 computers available on campus for general student use. A campuswide network can be accessed from student residence rooms and from off campus. Internet access is available. *Web address:* http://www.dominican.edu/.

General Application Contact: Lorrie Crivello, Director of Graduate and Pathways Admissions, 415-458-3754, Fax: 415-485-3293, E-mail: crivello@dominican.edu.

GRADUATE UNITS

Graduate Programs Students: 249 full-time (180 women), 194 part-time (146 women); includes 53 minority (7 African Americans, 18 Asian Americans or Pacific Islanders, 27 Hispanic Americans, 1 Native American), 26 international. Average age 38. 453 applicants, 85% accepted. *Faculty:* 29 full-time (20 women), 84 part-time/adjunct (56 women). Expenses: Contact institution. *Financial support:* In 2001–02, 77 students received support, including 77 fellowships (averaging $1,883 per year); career-related internships or fieldwork, Federal Work-Study, institutionally sponsored loans, scholarships/grants, tuition waivers (partial), and tuition discounts also available. Support available to part-time students. Financial award applicants required to submit FAFSA. In 2001, 110 master's, 120 other advanced degrees awarded. *Degree program information:* Part-time and evening/weekend programs available. *Application deadline:* For fall admission, 5/1; for spring admission, 11/1. Applications are processed on a rolling basis. *Application fee:* $40. *Application Contact:* Lorrie Crivello, Associate Director of Graduate Admissions, 415-485-3754, Fax: 415-485-3293, E-mail: crivello@dominican.edu. *Vice President for Academic Affairs,* Dr. Denise Lucy, 415-485-3291, Fax: 415-485-3205, E-mail: lucy@dominican.edu.

School of Arts and Sciences Students: 37 full-time (29 women), 72 part-time (61 women); includes 9 minority (3 African Americans, 2 Asian Americans or Pacific Islanders, 4 Hispanic Americans), 2 international. Average age 35. 62 applicants, 74% accepted, 31 enrolled. *Faculty:* 8 full-time (3 women), 23 part-time/adjunct (12 women). Expenses: Contact institution. *Financial support:* In 2001–02, 34 students received support, including 34 fellowships (averaging $2,299 per year); career-related internships or fieldwork, Federal Work-Study, institutionally sponsored loans, and tuition discounts also available. Support available to part-time students. Financial award applicants required to submit FAFSA. In 2001, 25 degrees awarded. *Degree program information:* Part-time programs available. Offers arts and sciences (MA, MS); counseling psychology (MS); health sciences (MS); humanities (MA); nursing (MS). *Application deadline:* For fall admission, 5/1; for spring admission, 11/1. Applications are processed on a rolling basis. *Application fee:* $40. *Application Contact:* Lorrie Crivello, Associate Director of Graduate Admissions, 415-485-3754, Fax: 415-485-3293, E-mail: crivello@dominican.edu. *Dean,* Dr. Martha Nelson, 415-257-1310, Fax: 415-257-0120, E-mail: nelson@dominican.edu.

School of Business, Education and Leadership Students: 152 full-time (115 women), 77 part-time (57 women); includes 24 minority (3 African Americans, 2 Asian Americans or Pacific Islanders, 18 Hispanic Americans, 1 Native American), 4 international. Average age 35. 208 applicants, 90% accepted. *Faculty:* 11 full-time (10 women), 20 part-time/adjunct (all women). Expenses: Contact institution. *Financial support:* In 2001–02, 11 students received support, including 11 fellowships (averaging $525 per year); Federal Work-Study, institutionally sponsored loans, tuition waivers (partial), and tuition discounts also available. Financial award applicants required to submit FAFSA. In 2001, 19 master's, 120 other advanced degrees awarded. *Degree program information:* Part-time programs available. Offers business (MBA); business, education and leadership (MBA, MS, Credential); curriculum and instruction (MS); education (MS, Credential); global strategic management (MBA); multiple subject credential (Credential); single subject credential (Credential); strategic leadership (MBA). Programs also offered in Ukiah, CA. *Application deadline:* For fall admission, 5/1; for spring admission, 11/1. Applications are processed on a rolling basis. *Application fee:* $40. *Application Contact:* Lorrie Crivello, Associate Director of Graduate Admissions, 415-485-3754, Fax: 415-485-3293, E-mail: crivello@dominican.edu. *Dean,* Dr. Ed Kujawa, 415-485-3245, Fax: 415-458-3790, E-mail: kujawa@dominican.edu.

DONGGUK ROYAL UNIVERSITY, Los Angeles, CA 90020

General Information Independent, coed, graduate-only institution. *Graduate housing:* On-campus housing not available.

GRADUATE UNITS

Program in Oriental Medicine *Degree program information:* Part-time and evening/weekend programs available. Offers Oriental medicine (MS).

DORDT COLLEGE, Sioux Center, IA 51250-1697

General Information Independent-religious, coed, comprehensive institution. *Graduate housing:* Rooms and/or apartments available to single and married students.

GRADUATE UNITS

Program in Education *Degree program information:* Part-time programs available. Offers education (M Ed).

DOWLING COLLEGE, Oakdale, NY 11769-1999

General Information Independent, coed, comprehensive institution. *Graduate housing:* Room and/or apartments available on a first-come, first-served basis to single students; on-campus housing not available to married students. Housing application deadline: 9/1.

GRADUATE UNITS

Graduate Programs in Education *Degree program information:* Part-time and evening/weekend programs available. Postbaccalaureate distance learning degree programs offered. Offers computers in education (PD); educational administration (Ed D, PD); elementary education (MS Ed); reading (MS Ed); reading/special education (MS Ed); school administration and supervision (PD); school district administration (PD); secondary education (MS Ed); special education (MS Ed). Electronic applications accepted.

School of Business *Degree program information:* Part-time and evening/weekend programs available. Offers aviation management (MBA, Certificate); banking and finance (MBA, Certificate); general management (MBA); public management (MBA, Certificate); total quality management (MBA, Certificate). Electronic applications accepted.

DRAKE UNIVERSITY, Des Moines, IA 50311-4516

General Information Independent, coed, university. *Enrollment:* 428 full-time matriculated graduate/professional students (219 women), 801 part-time matriculated graduate/professional students (459 women). *Enrollment by degree level:* 399 first professional, 830 master's. *Graduate faculty:* 255 full-time, 85 part-time/adjunct. *Tuition:* Full-time $17,830. *Required fees:* $220. Full-time tuition and fees vary according to class time and program. *Graduate housing:* Rooms and/or apartments available on a first-come, first-served basis to single and married students. Typical cost: $2,720 per year ($5,270 including board) for single students; $2,720 per year ($5,270 including board) for married students. Room and board charges vary according to housing facility selected. Housing application deadline: 8/1. *Student services:* Campus employment opportunities, campus safety program, career counseling, disabled student services, exercise/wellness program, free psychological counseling, international student services, low-cost health insurance. *Library facilities:* Cowles Library plus 1 other. *Online resources:* library catalog, web page, access to other libraries' catalogs. *Collection:* 559,764 titles, 2,120 serial subscriptions, 165 audiovisual materials.

Computer facilities: 1,081 computers available on campus for general student use. A campuswide network can be accessed from student residence rooms and from off campus. Internet access is available. *Web address:* http://www.drake.edu/.

General Application Contact: Ann J. Martin, Graduate Coordinator, 515-271-3871, Fax: 515-271-2831, E-mail: ajm@admin.drake.edu.

GRADUATE UNITS

College of Business and Public Administration Students: 101 full-time, 364 part-time. Average age 29. 119 applicants, 94% accepted, 99 enrolled. *Faculty:* 21 full-time (5 women), 3 part-time/adjunct (0 women). Expenses: Contact institution. *Financial support:* In 2001–02, 1 student received support. Career-related internships or fieldwork and institutionally sponsored loans available. Support available to part-time students. Financial award application deadline: 3/1; financial award applicants required to submit FAFSA. In 2001, 202 degrees awarded. *Degree program information:* Part-time and evening/weekend programs available. Offers business and public administration (M Acc, MBA, MPA). *Application deadline:* For fall admission, 7/15 (priority date); for winter admission, 12/20 (priority date); for spring admission, 12/1 (priority date). Applications are processed on a rolling basis. *Application fee:* $25. Electronic applications accepted. *Application Contact:* Danette Kenne, Director of Graduate Programs, 515-271-2188, Fax: 515-271-4518, E-mail: cbpa.gradprograms@drake.edu. *Dean, College of Business and Public Administration,* Dr. Antone F. Alber, 515-271-2871, Fax: 515-271-4518, E-mail: joe.alber@drake.edu.

College of Pharmacy and Health Sciences Students: 420 full-time (280 women); includes 62 minority (10 African Americans, 50 Asian Americans or Pacific Islanders, 2 Hispanic Americans) Average age 24. 206 applicants, 39% accepted. *Faculty:* 39 full-time (20 women), 6 part-time/adjunct (2 women). Expenses: Contact institution. *Financial support:* In 2001–02, 300 students received support, including 10 teaching assistantships (averaging $3,200 per year); career-related internships or fieldwork, Federal Work-Study, institutionally sponsored loans, and scholarships/grants also available. Support available to part-time students. Financial award application deadline: 3/1; financial award applicants required to submit FAFSA. In 2001, 71 degrees awarded. Offers pharmacy (Pharm D); pharmacy and health sciences (Pharm D). *Application deadline:* For fall admission, 3/1 (priority date). Applications are processed on a rolling basis. *Application fee:* $25. Electronic applications accepted. *Application Contact:* Dr. Renae J. Chesnut, Assistant Dean for Student Affairs, Fax: 515-271-4171, E-mail: renae.chesnut@drake.edu. *Dean,* Dr. Stephen G. Hoag, 515-271-2172, Fax: 515-271-4171, E-mail: stephen.hoag@drake.edu.

Law School Students: 374 full-time (189 women), 16 part-time (9 women); includes 41 minority (18 African Americans, 14 Asian Americans or Pacific Islanders, 8 Hispanic Americans, 1 Native American), 6 international. Average age 25. 748 applicants, 62% accepted, 144 enrolled. *Faculty:* 29 full-time (9 women), 24 part-time/adjunct (5 women). Expenses: Contact institution. *Financial support:* In 2001–02, 365 students received support, including 30 research assistantships (averaging $988 per year), 9 teaching assistantships (averaging $1,082 per year); career-related internships or fieldwork, Federal Work-Study, institutionally sponsored loans, scholarships/grants, tuition waivers (full and partial), and computer laboratory monitors, tutoring positions also available. Support available to part-time students. Financial award application deadline: 3/1; financial award applicants required to submit FAFSA. In 2001, 116 degrees awarded. Offers law (JD). *Application deadline:* For fall admission, 4/1 (priority date). Applications are processed on a rolling basis. *Application fee:* $40. Electronic applications accepted. *Application Contact:* J. Kara Blanchard, Director of Admission and Financial Aid, 800-44-DRAKE Ext. 2782, Fax: 515-271-2530, E-mail: lawadmit@drake.edu. *Dean,* C. Peter Goplerud, 515-271-3985, Fax: 515-271-4118, E-mail: peter.goplerud@drake.edu.

School of Education *Degree program information:* Part-time and evening/weekend programs available. Postbaccalaureate distance learning degree programs offered. Offers adult education (MS, MSE, Ed D, Ed S); adult education, training and development (MS); counseling (MSE); early childhood education (MSE); education (MAT, MS, MSE, MST, Ed D, Ed S); education leadership (MSE, Ed D, Ed S); elementary education (MSE, MST); guidance counseling (MSE); secondary education (MAT); special education (MSE); teacher education (MSE, Ed S); vocational rehabilitation (MS). Electronic applications accepted.

See in-depth description on page 843.

DREW UNIVERSITY, Madison, NJ 07940-1493

General Information Independent-religious, coed, university. CGS member. *Enrollment:* 449 full-time matriculated graduate/professional students (213 women), 398 part-time matriculated graduate/professional students (223 women). *Graduate faculty:* 160. *Tuition:* Full-time $23,238; part-time $1,291 per credit. *Required fees:* $690; $690 per year. One-time fee: $125. Tuition and fees vary according to program. *Graduate housing:* Rooms and/or apartments available to single and married students. Typical cost: $4,800 per year for single students; $8,098 per year for married students. Room charges vary according to housing facility selected. Housing application deadline: 7/1. *Student services:* Campus employment opportunities, campus safety program, career counseling, child daycare facilities, disabled student services, exercise/wellness program, free psychological counseling, international student services, low-cost health insurance, multicultural affairs office, writing training. *Library facilities:* Drew University Library. *Collection:* 487,562 titles, 3,066 serial subscriptions. *Research affiliation:* Center for Research Libraries (humanities), Dana Rise Institute (science), Raritan Bay Medical Center (medical humanities), Society for the History of Authorship, Readership and Publishing (book history), Methodist Archives (religion).

Computer facilities: 200 computers available on campus for general student use. A campuswide network can be accessed from student residence rooms and from off campus. Internet access and online class registration are available. *Web address:* http://www.drew.edu/.

General Application Contact: Carla J. Osit, Director of Graduate Admissions, 973-408-3110, Fax: 973-408-3242, E-mail: gradm@drew.edu.

GRADUATE UNITS

Caspersen School of Graduate Studies Students: 261 full-time (120 women), 280 part-time (179 women); includes 83 minority (28 African Americans, 34 Asian Americans or Pacific Islanders, 19 Hispanic Americans, 2 Native Americans), 94 international. Average age 41. 146 applicants, 55% accepted, 41 enrolled. *Faculty:* 117. Expenses: Contact institution. *Financial support:* Fellowships, research assistantships, teaching assistantships, career-related internships or fieldwork, Federal Work-Study, scholarships/grants, and tuition waivers (full and partial) available. Support available to part-time students. Financial award application deadline: 2/15; financial award applicants required to submit FAFSA. In 2001, 23 master's, 24 doctorates, 9 other advanced degrees awarded. *Degree program information:* Part-time and evening/weekend programs available. Offers anthropology of religion (MA, PhD); book history (MA); Christian social ethics (MA, PhD); English literature (MA, PhD); historical studies (MA, PhD); liberal studies (M Litt, D Litt); liturgical studies (MA, PhD); medical humanities (MMH, DMH, CMH); Methodist studies (PhD); modern history and literature (MA, PhD); philosophy of religion (MA, PhD); psychology and religion (MA, PhD); religion in ancient Israel (MA, PhD); sociology of religion (MA, PhD); systematic theology (MA, PhD); the New Testament and early Christianity (MA, PhD); theological ethics (MA, PhD); Wesleyan and Methodist studies (MA, PhD); women's studies (MA). *Application deadline:* For fall admission, 2/1. *Application fee:* $35. *Application Contact:* Carla J. Osit, Director of Graduate Admissions, 973-408-3110, Fax: 973-408-3242, E-mail: gradm@drew.edu. *Dean,* Dr. James Pain, 973-408-3285.

The Theological School Students: 188 full-time (93 women), 118 part-time (44 women); includes 107 minority (76 African Americans, 12 Asian Americans or Pacific Islanders, 19 Hispanic Americans), 28 international. Average age 36. 270 applicants, 54% accepted. *Faculty:* 26 full-time (9 women), 17 part-time/adjunct (6 women). Expenses: Contact institution. *Financial support:* Fellowships, career-related internships or fieldwork, Federal Work-Study, institutionally sponsored loans, and scholarships/grants available. Support available to part-time students. Financial award application deadline: 4/15. In 2001, 61 master's, 27 doctorates awarded. *Degree program information:* Part-time programs available. Postbaccalaureate distance learning degree programs offered (minimal on-campus study). Offers theology (M Div, MTS, STM, D Min, Certificate). *Application deadline:* For fall admission, 3/1 (priority date); for spring admission, 12/15 (priority date). Applications are processed on a rolling basis. *Application fee:* $35. Electronic applications accepted. *Application Contact:* Rev. Dr. Robert J. Duncan, Director of Admissions, 973-408-3111, Fax: 973-408-3242, E-mail: rduncan@drew.edu. *Dean,* Dr. Maxine Beach, 973-408-3258, Fax: 973-408-3534, E-mail: mbeach@drew.edu.

See in-depth description on page 845.

DREXEL UNIVERSITY, Philadelphia, PA 19104-2875

General Information Independent, coed, university. CGS member. *Enrollment:* 663 full-time matriculated graduate/professional students (320 women), 1,799 part-time matriculated graduate/professional students (735 women). *Enrollment by degree level:* 2,097 master's, 338 doctoral, 27 other advanced degrees. *Graduate faculty:* 499 full-time (140 women), 390 part-time/adjunct (135 women). *Tuition:* Full-time $20,088; part-time $558 per credit. *Required fees:* $78 per term. One-time fee: $200. Tuition and fees vary according to course load, degree level and program. *Graduate housing:* On-campus housing not available. *Student services:* Campus employment opportunities, campus safety program, career counseling, international student services, low-cost health insurance. *Library facilities:* W. W. Hagerty Library. *Online resources:* library catalog, web page, access to other libraries' catalogs. *Collection:* 258,243 titles, 7,048 serial subscriptions, 5,561 audiovisual materials.

Computer facilities: 6,500 computers available on campus for general student use. A campuswide network can be accessed from student residence rooms and from off campus. Internet access and online class registration, campuswide wireless network are available. *Web address:* http://www.drexel.edu/.

General Application Contact: Director of Graduate Admissions, 215-895-6700, Fax: 215-895-5939, E-mail: enroll@drexel.edu.

GRADUATE UNITS

College of Medicine Students: 1,213 full-time (635 women), 11 part-time (5 women); includes 465 minority (127 African Americans, 273 Asian Americans or Pacific Islanders, 60 Hispanic Americans, 5 Native Americans), 37 international. Average age 25. 7,816 applicants, 14% accepted, 369 enrolled. *Faculty:* 406 full-time (123 women), 359 part-time/adjunct (140 women). Expenses: Contact institution. *Financial support:* Fellowships, research assistantships, teaching assistantships, career-related internships or fieldwork, Federal Work-Study, institutionally sponsored loans, and tuition waivers (full and partial) available. Support available to part-time students. Financial award application deadline: 5/1; financial award applicants required to submit FAFSA. In 2001, 247 first professional degrees, 55 master's, 12 doctorates, 26 other advanced degrees awarded. *Degree program information:* Part-time programs available. Offers medicine (MD, MBS, MLAS, MMS, MS, PhD, Certificate). *Application deadline:* Applications are processed on a rolling basis. Electronic applications accepted. *Dean,* Dr. Warren E. Ross, 215-762-8900, E-mail: warren.ross@drexel.edu.

Biomedical Graduate Programs Students: 240 full-time (121 women), 11 part-time (5 women); includes 74 minority (21 African Americans, 44 Asian Americans or Pacific Islanders, 9 Hispanic Americans), 20 international. Average age 24. 425 applicants, 49% accepted, 132 enrolled. *Faculty:* 50 full-time (14 women), 6 part-time/adjunct (3 women). Expenses: Contact institution. *Financial support:* Fellowships, research assistantships, teaching assistantships, career-related internships or fieldwork, Federal Work-Study, institutionally sponsored loans, scholarships/grants, and tuition waivers (full and partial) available. Support available to part-time students. Financial award application deadline: 5/1; financial award applicants required to submit FAFSA. In 2001, 55 master's, 12 doctorates, 26 other advanced degrees awarded. *Degree program information:* Part-time programs available. Offers biochemistry (MS, PhD); biomedical sciences (MBS, MLAS, MMS, MS, PhD, Certificate); laboratory animal science (MLAS); medical science (MBS, MMS, Certificate); microbiology and immunology (MS, PhD); molecular and cell biology (MS, PhD); molecular and human genetics (MS, PhD); molecular pathobiology (PhD); neuroscience (PhD); pharmacology and physiology (MS, PhD); radiation (MS); radiation biology (MS); radiation physics (PhD); radiation science (PhD); radiopharmaceutical science (MS, PhD). *Application deadline:* For fall admission, 4/1. Applications are processed on a rolling basis. *Application fee:* $30. Electronic applications accepted. *Application Contact:* Dr. Barry D. Waterhouse, Associate Dean, 866-6BIOMED, Fax: 215-843-5810, E-mail: biomed.mcphu@drexel.edu. *Senior Associate Dean for Research and Biomedical Graduate Studies,* Dr. Abdul S. Rao, 215-762-8989, Fax: 215-843-5810, E-mail: abdul.s.rao@drexel.edu.

College of Nursing and Health Professions Students: 344 full-time (272 women), 202 part-time (170 women); includes 83 minority (47 African Americans, 23 Asian Americans or Pacific Islanders, 11 Hispanic Americans, 2 Native Americans), 20 international. Average age 31. 373 applicants, 47% accepted, 138 enrolled. *Faculty:* 54 full-time (34 women), 37 part-time/adjunct (27 women). Expenses: Contact institution. *Financial support:* Fellowships, research assistantships, teaching assistantships, career-related internships or fieldwork, Federal Work-Study, institutionally sponsored loans, and tuition waivers (partial) available. Support available to part-time students. Financial award application deadline: 5/1; financial award applicants required to submit FAFSA. In 2001, 162 master's, 30 doctorates, 55 other advanced degrees awarded. *Degree program information:* Part-time and evening/weekend programs available. Offers advanced physician assistant studies (MHS); art therapy (MA); couples and family therapy (PhD); dance/movement therapy (MA); emergency and public safety service (MS); family therapy (MFT); music therapy (MA); nurse anesthesia (MSN); nursing (MSN); nursing and health professions (MA, MFT, MHS, MS, MSN, DPT, PhD, Certificate). *Application deadline:* Applications are processed on a rolling basis. *Application fee:* $50. Electronic applications accepted. *Dean,* Dr. Gloria Donnelly, 215-762-1336.

Graduate School Students: 663 full-time (320 women), 1,799 part-time (735 women); includes 299 minority (122 African Americans, 144 Asian Americans or Pacific Islanders, 30 Hispanic Americans, 3 Native Americans), 599 international. Average age 31. 2,574 applicants, 66% accepted, 488 enrolled. *Faculty:* 499 full-time (140 women), 390 part-time/adjunct (135 women). Expenses: Contact institution. *Financial support:* Research assistantships, teaching assistantships, career-related internships or fieldwork, Federal Work-Study, institutionally sponsored loans, tuition waivers (full and partial), and unspecified assistantships available. Support available to part-time students. Financial award application deadline: 2/1. In 2001, 787 master's, 51 doctorates, 1 other advanced degree awarded. *Degree program information:* Part-time and evening/weekend programs available. *Application deadline:* Applications are processed on a rolling basis. *Application fee:* $50. Electronic applications accepted. *Application Contact:* Director of Graduate Admissions, 215-895-6700, Fax: 215-895-5939, E-mail: enroll@drexel.edu. *Associate Provost for Research and Graduate Studies,* Dr. Richard Haracz, 215-895-2498.

College of Arts and Sciences Students: 90 full-time (45 women), 323 part-time (157 women). Average age 29. 481 applicants, 54% accepted, 62 enrolled. *Faculty:* 179 full-time (58 women), 108 part-time/adjunct (61 women). Expenses: Contact institution. *Financial support:* Research assistantships, teaching assistantships, career-related internships or fieldwork, Federal Work-Study, institutionally sponsored loans, tuition waivers (full and partial), and unspecified assistantships available. Support available to part-time students. Financial award application deadline: 2/1. In 2001, 87 master's, 19 doctorates awarded. *Degree program information:* Part-time and evening/weekend programs available. Offers arts and sciences (MA, MS, MSSE, PhD); biological science (MS, PhD); chemistry (MS, PhD); clinical neuropsychology (PhD); clinical psychology (MA, MS); communication (MS); computer science (MS, PhD); educational leadership and learning technology (PhD); food science (MS); forensic psychology (PhD); health psychology (PhD); law-psychology (PhD); mathematics (MS, PhD); neuropsychology (PhD); nutrition and food sciences (MS, PhD); nutrition science (PhD); physics (MS, PhD); publication management (MS); science of instruction (MS); science, technology and society (MS); software engineering (MSSE). *Application deadline:* Applications are processed on a rolling basis. *Application fee:* $50. Electronic applications accepted. *Application Contact:* Director of Graduate Admissions, 215-895-6700, Fax: 215-895-5939, E-mail: enroll@drexel.edu. *Dean,* Dr. Richard Rosen, 215-895-2620.

College of Business and Administration Students: 299 full-time (130 women), 495 part-time (199 women); includes 82 minority (29 African Americans, 44 Asian Americans or Pacific Islanders, 8 Hispanic Americans, 1 Native American), 207 international. Average age 30. 607 applicants, 63% accepted, 146 enrolled. *Faculty:* 88 full-time (19 women), 11 part-time/adjunct (2 women). Expenses: Contact institution. *Financial support:* Research assistantships, teaching assistantships, career-related internships or fieldwork, tuition waivers (full), and unspecified assistantships available. Financial award application deadline:2/1. In 2001, 302 master's, 8 doctorates, 1 other advanced degree awarded. *Degree program information:* Part-time and evening/weekend programs available. Offers accounting (MS); business administration (MBA, PhD, APC); business and administration (MBA, MS, PhD, APC); decision sciences (MS); finance (MS); marketing (MS); taxation (MS). *Application deadline:* For fall admission, 8/21. Applications are processed on a rolling basis. *Application fee:* $50. Electronic applications accepted. *Application Contact:* Director of Graduate Admissions, 215-895-6700, Fax: 215-895-5939, E-mail: enroll@drexel.edu. *Associate Dean,* Dr. Tom Hindelang, 215-895-1030.

College of Engineering Students: 93 full-time (21 women), 374 part-time (66 women); includes 43 minority (12 African Americans, 23 Asian Americans or Pacific Islanders, 7 Hispanic Americans, 1 Native American), 188 international. Average age 31. 909 applicants, 66% accepted, 76 enrolled. *Faculty:* 100 full-time (9 women), 13 part-time/adjunct (1 woman). Expenses: Contact institution. *Financial support:* Research assistantships, teaching assistantships, career-related internships or fieldwork, Federal Work-Study, institutionally sponsored loans, tuition waivers (full and partial), and unspecified assistantships available. Support available to part-time students. Financial award application deadline:2/1. In 2001, 117 master's, 15 doctorates awarded. *Degree program information:* Part-time and evening/weekend programs available. Offers biochemical engineering (MS); chemical engineering (MS, PhD); civil engineering (MS, PhD); computer engineering (MS); electrical and computer engineering (PhD); electrical engineering (MSEE, PhD); engineering (MS, MSEE, PhD); engineering geology (MS); engineering management (MS, PhD); manufacturing engineering (MS, PhD); materials engineering (MS, PhD); mechanical engineering and mechanics (MS, PhD); telecommunications engineering (MSEE). *Application deadline:* For fall admission, 8/21. Applications are processed on a rolling basis. *Application fee:* $50. Electronic applications accepted. *Application Contact:* Director of Graduate Admissions, 215-895-6700, Fax: 215-895-5939, E-mail: enroll@drexel.edu. *Dean,* Dr. Selcuk Güçeri, 215-895-2210.

College of Information Science and Technology Students: 67 full-time (38 women), 460 part-time (235 women); includes 68 minority (31 African Americans, 34 Asian Americans or Pacific Islanders, 3 Hispanic Americans), 61 international. Average age 34. 298 applicants, 76% accepted, 118 enrolled. *Faculty:* 27 full-time (13 women), 11 part-time/adjunct (2 women). Expenses: Contact institution. *Financial support:* Research assistantships, teaching assistantships, career-related internships or fieldwork, Federal Work-Study, institutionally sponsored loans, traineeships, tuition waivers (partial), and unspecified assistantships available. Support available to part-time students. Financial award application deadline:2/1. In 2001, 178 master's awarded. *Degree program information:* Part-time and evening/weekend programs available. Postbaccalaureate distance learning degree programs offered (no on-campus study). Offers information science and technology (PhD); information studies (PhD, CAS); information systems (MSIS); library and information science (MS). *Application deadline:* For fall admission, 8/21. Applications are processed on a rolling basis. *Application fee:* $50. Electronic applications accepted. *Application Contact:* Director of Graduate Admissions, 215-895-6700, Fax: 215-895-5939, E-mail: info@cis.drexel.edu. *Associate Dean,* Dr. Tom Childers, 215-895-2474.

College of Media Arts and Design Students: 68 full-time (64 women), 33 part-time (28 women). Average age 30. 62 applicants, 77% accepted, 23 enrolled. *Faculty:* 67 full-time (32 women), 70 part-time/adjunct (31 women). Expenses: Contact institution. *Financial support:* Research assistantships, teaching assistantships, career-related internships or fieldwork and unspecified assistantships available. Support available to part-time students. Financial award application deadline: 2/1. In 2001, 34 degrees awarded. *Degree program information:* Part-time and evening/weekend programs available. Offers architecture (M Arch); arts administration (MS); design (MS); fashion design (MS); interior design (MS); media arts (MS); performing arts (MS). *Application deadline:* For fall admission, 8/21; for spring admission, 3/5. Applications are processed on a rolling basis. *Application fee:* $50. Electronic applications accepted. *Application Contact:* Director of Graduate Admissions, 215-895-6700, Fax: 215-895-5939, E-mail: enroll@drexel.edu. *Dean,* Jonathan Estrin, 215-895-2386.

School of Biomedical Engineering, Science and Health Systems Students: 36 full-time (15 women), 50 part-time (15 women); includes 16 minority (6 African Americans, 10 Asian Americans or Pacific Islanders), 28 international. Average age 28. 114 applicants, 75% accepted, 18 enrolled. *Faculty:* 11 full-time (2 women), 2 part-time/adjunct (0 women). Expenses: Contact institution. *Financial support:* Research assistantships, teaching assistantships, career-related internships or fieldwork, Federal Work-Study, institutionally sponsored loans, tuition waivers (full and partial), and unspecified assistantships available. Financial award application deadline: 2/1. In 2001, 7 master's, 2 doctorates awarded. Offers biomedical engineering (MS, PhD); biomedical science (MS, PhD); biostatistics (MS); clinical/rehabilitation engineering (MS). *Application deadline:* For fall admission, 8/21. Applications are processed on a rolling basis. *Application fee:* $50. Electronic applications accepted. *Application Contact:* Director of Graduate Admissions, 215-895-6700, Fax: 215-895-5939, E-mail: enroll@drexel.edu. *Director,* Dr. Banu Onaral, 215-895-2215.

School of Environmental Science, Engineering and Policy Students: 10 full-time (7 women), 64 part-time (35 women); includes 12 minority (6 African Americans, 3 Asian Americans or Pacific Islanders, 3 Hispanic Americans), 9 international. Average age 30. 65 applicants, 80% accepted, 19 enrolled. *Faculty:* 10 full-time (3 women), 5 part-time/adjunct (1 woman). Expenses: Contact institution. *Financial support:* Research assistantships, teaching assistantships, career-related internships or fieldwork and unspecified assistantships available. Financial award application deadline: 2/1. In 2001, 12 master's, 4 doctorates awarded. *Degree program information:* Part-time and evening/weekend programs available. Offers environmental engineering (MS, PhD); environmental policy (MS); environmental science (MS, PhD); environmental science, engineering and policy (MS, PhD). *Application deadline:* For fall admission, 8/21. Applications are processed on a rolling basis. *Application fee:* $50. Electronic applications accepted. *Application Contact:* Director of Graduate Admissions, 215-895-6700, Fax: 215-895-5939, E-mail: enroll@drexel.edu. *Director,* Dr. Susan Kilham, 215-895-2265.

School of Public Health Students: 59 full-time (49 women); includes 34 minority (16 African Americans, 14 Asian Americans or Pacific Islanders, 2 Hispanic Americans, 2 Native Americans), 4 international. Average age 28. 60 applicants, 38% accepted, 9 enrolled. *Faculty:* 11 full-time (9 women). Expenses: Contact institution. In 2001, 32 degrees awarded. Offers public health (MPH). *Application deadline:* Applications are processed on a rolling basis. *Application fee:* $30. Electronic applications accepted. *Application Contact:* Lenore Sherman, Associate Director of Student Affairs and Public Health, 215-762-8251, Fax: 215-762-4088. *Dean,* Dr. Robert Valdez, 215-762-6957, E-mail: robert.valdez@drexel.edu.

See in-depth description on page 847.

DRURY UNIVERSITY, Springfield, MO 65802-3791

General Information Independent, coed, comprehensive institution. *Enrollment:* 43 full-time matriculated graduate/professional students (28 women), 255 part-time matriculated graduate/

Drury University (continued)

professional students (176 women). *Enrollment by degree level:* 298 master's. *Graduate faculty:* 12 full-time (7 women), 13 part-time/adjunct (8 women). *Tuition:* Part-time $214 per credit hour. Tuition and fees vary according to program. *Graduate housing:* Rooms and/or apartments available on a first-come, first-served basis to single students and available to married students. *Student services:* Campus employment opportunities, campus safety program, career counseling, disabled student services, exercise/wellness program, international student services, teacher training, writing training. *Library facilities:* F. W. Olin Library plus 1 other. *Online resources:* library catalog, web page, access to other libraries' catalogs. *Collection:* 244,000 titles, 797 serial subscriptions, 56,583 audiovisual materials. *Research affiliation:* Yale University (child development).

Computer facilities: 205 computers available on campus for general student use. A campuswide network can be accessed from student residence rooms and from off campus. Internet access and online class registration, digital imaging lab are available. *Web address:* http://www.drury.edu/.

General Application Contact: Dr. Terry Hudson, Director of Teacher Education, 417-873-7271, Fax: 417-873-7269, E-mail: thudson@drury.edu.

GRADUATE UNITS

Breech School of Business Administration Average age 30. Expenses: Contact institution. *Financial support:* In 2001–02, 4 students received support; research assistantships with partial tuition reimbursements available, career-related internships or fieldwork available. Financial award application deadline: 5/15. *Degree program information:* Part-time and evening/weekend programs available. Offers business administration (MBA); business and international management (MBA). *Application deadline:* For fall admission, 7/30 (priority date); for spring admission, 12/15 (priority date). Applications are processed on a rolling basis. *Application fee:* $25. Electronic applications accepted. *Application Contact:* Dr. Alan F. Foltz, Assistant Director, 417-873-7508, Fax: 417-873-7537, E-mail: afoltz@drury.edu. *Director,* Dr. Thomas Zimmerer, 417-873-7241, Fax: 417-873-7537, E-mail: tzimmere@drury.edu.

Graduate Programs in Education Average age 29. Expenses: Contact institution. *Financial support:* Fellowships, teaching assistantships with full tuition reimbursements, career-related internships or fieldwork, institutionally sponsored loans, and minority fellowships available. Financial award applicants required to submit FAFSA. *Degree program information:* Part-time and evening/weekend programs available. Offers elementary education (M Ed); gifted education (M Ed); human services (M Ed); middle school teaching (M Ed); physical education (M Ed); secondary education (M Ed). *Application deadline:* For fall admission, 8/25 (priority date); for spring admission, 1/15 (priority date). Applications are processed on a rolling basis. *Application fee:* $20. *Application Contact:* Dr. Terry Hudson, Assistant Director, 417-873-7271, Fax: 417-873-7269, E-mail: thudson@drury.edu. *Director,* Dr. Daniel R. Beach, 417-873-7271, Fax: 417-873-7269, E-mail: dbeach@lib.drury.edu.

Program in Communication Average age 37. Expenses: Contact institution. *Financial support:* Application deadline: 10/15; *Degree program information:* Part-time and evening/weekend programs available. Offers communication (MA). *Application deadline:* For fall admission, 8/26 (priority date); for spring admission, 1/20 (priority date). Applications are processed on a rolling basis. *Application fee:* $20. *Graduate Director Communication,* Dr. Lynn Hinds, 417-873-7441, Fax: 417-873-7897, E-mail: lhinds@drury.edu.

Program in Criminology/Criminal Justice Average age 33. Expenses: Contact institution. *Financial support:* Application deadline: 10/15; *Degree program information:* Part-time and evening/weekend programs available. Offers criminal justice (MS); criminology (MA). *Application deadline:* For fall admission, 8/26 (priority date); for spring admission, 1/15 (priority date). Applications are processed on a rolling basis. *Application fee:* $25. Electronic applications accepted. *Application Contact:* Dr. Jane Bufkin, Director, 417-873-6948, Fax: 417-873-7529, E-mail: grad@drury.edu. *Graduate Director,* Dr. Victor Agruso, 417-873-7306, Fax: 417-873-7529, E-mail: vagruso@lib.drury.edu.

DUKE UNIVERSITY, Durham, NC 27708-0586

General Information Independent-religious, coed, university. CGS member. *Enrollment:* 5,767 full-time matriculated graduate/professional students (2,517 women), 334 part-time matriculated graduate/professional students (221 women). *Enrollment by degree level:* 1,706 first professional, 2,196 master's, 1,731 doctoral, 468 other advanced degrees. *Graduate faculty:* 2,145. *Tuition:* Full-time $24,600. *Graduate housing:* Rooms and/or apartments available to single and married students. Typical cost: $4,267 per year for single students; $8,515 per year for married students. *Student services:* Campus employment opportunities, campus safety program, career counseling, disabled student services, free psychological counseling, international student services, low-cost health insurance, multicultural affairs office, teacher training, writing training. *Library facilities:* Perkins Library plus 11 others. *Online resources:* library catalog, web page, access to other libraries' catalogs. *Collection:* 5 million titles, 31,941 serial subscriptions, 232,106 audiovisual materials. *Research affiliation:* Highlands Biological Station, U.S. Forest Sciences Laboratory, Organization for Tropical Studies.

Computer facilities: 600 computers available on campus for general student use. A campuswide network can be accessed from student residence rooms and from off campus. Internet access and online class registration are available. *Web address:* http://www.duke.edu/.

General Application Contact: Bertie S. Belvin, Associate Dean for Academic Services, 919-684-3913, E-mail: grad-admissions@duke.edu.

GRADUATE UNITS

Divinity School Students: 405 full-time (175 women), 54 part-time (32 women); includes 67 minority (53 African Americans, 6 Asian Americans or Pacific Islanders, 2 Hispanic Americans, 6 Native Americans), 12 international. Average age 27. *Faculty:* 50 full-time (17 women), 34 part-time/adjunct (17 women). Expenses: Contact institution. *Financial support:* Career-related internships or fieldwork, Federal Work-Study, institutionally sponsored loans, scholarships/grants, and field education stipends available. Financial award application deadline: 5/1; financial award applicants required to submit FAFSA. In 2001, 114 first professional degrees, 41 master's awarded. *Degree program information:* Part-time programs available. Offers theology (M Div, MCM, MTS, Th M). *Application deadline:* For fall admission, 4/1; for spring admission, 11/1. Applications are processed on a rolling basis. *Application fee:* $25. *Application Contact:* Donna Claycomb, Director of Admissions, 919-660-3436, Fax: 919-660-3535, E-mail: admissions@div.duke.edu. *Dean,* Dr. L. Gregory Jones, 919-660-3434, Fax: 919-660-3474.

Fuqua School of Business Students: 679 full-time (236 women). Average age 28. 3,207 applicants, 20% accepted. *Faculty:* 105 full-time (21 women), 10 part-time/adjunct (2 women). Expenses: Contact institution. *Financial support:* In 2001–02, 502 students received support, including 243 fellowships (averaging $11,450 per year); research assistantships, teaching assistantships, career-related internships or fieldwork, Federal Work-Study, institutionally sponsored loans, and scholarships/grants also available. Financial award application deadline: 3/1; financial award applicants required to submit FAFSA. In 2001, 332 degrees awarded. *Degree program information:* Evening/weekend programs available. Postbaccalaureate distance learning degree programs offered. Offers business (CCMBA, GEMBA, MBA, WEMBA, PhD); health sector management (MBA). *Application deadline:* For fall admission, 4/2. *Application fee:* $150. Electronic applications accepted. *Application Contact:* Liz M. Riley, Director of Admissions, 919-660-7705, Fax: 919-681-8026, E-mail: admissions-info@fuqua.duke.edu. *Dean,* Douglas T. Breeden, 919-660-7727, Fax: 919-684-8742, E-mail: breeden@mail.duke.edu.

Graduate School Students: 2,270 full-time, 17 part-time; includes 242 minority (103 African Americans, 76 Asian Americans or Pacific Islanders, 56 Hispanic Americans, 7 Native Americans), 723 international. Average age 29. 5,502 applicants, 25% accepted. *Faculty:* 1,177 full-time, 232 part-time/adjunct. Expenses: Contact institution. *Financial support:* In 2001–02, 1,980 students received support, including fellowships with full tuition reimbursements available (averaging $14,000 per year), research assistantships with full tuition reimbursements available (averaging $15,500 per year), teaching assistantships with full tuition reimbursements available (averaging $8,000 per year); career-related internships or fieldwork, Federal Work-Study, and institutionally sponsored loans also available. Support available to part-time students. Financial award application deadline: 4/15; financial award applicants required to submit FAFSA. In 2001, 205 master's, 247 doctorates awarded. *Degree program information:* Part-time and evening/weekend programs available. Offers art and art history (PhD); biological chemistry (Certificate); biological psychology (PhD); biology (PhD); business administration (PhD); cell biology (PhD); cellular and molecular biology (PhD); chemistry (PhD); classical studies (PhD); clinical psychology (PhD); cognitive psychology (PhD); computer science (MS, PhD); crystallography of macromolecules (PhD); developmental biology (Certificate); developmental psychology (PhD); East Asian studies (AM, Certificate); ecology (PhD, Certificate); economics (AM, PhD); English (PhD); enzyme mechanisms (PhD); experimental psychology (PhD); French (PhD); genetics (PhD); geology (MS, PhD); German studies (PhD); gross anatomy and physical anthropology (PhD); health psychology (PhD); history (PhD); human social development (PhD); humanities (AM); immunology (PhD); Latin American studies (PhD); liberal studies (AM); lipid biochemistry (PhD); literature (PhD); mathematics (PhD); medieval and Renaissance studies (Certificate); membrane structure and function (PhD); molecular biophysics (Certificate); molecular cancer biology (PhD); molecular genetics (PhD); molecular genetics and microbiology (PhD); music composition (AM, PhD); musicology (AM, PhD); natural resource economics/policy (AM, PhD); natural resource science/ecology (AM, PhD); natural resource systems science (AM, PhD); neuroanatomy (PhD); neurobiology (PhD); neurochemistry (PhD); nucleic acid structure and function (PhD); pathology (PhD); performance practice (AM, PhD); pharmacology and cancer biology (PhD); philosophy (PhD); physical anthropology (PhD); physics (PhD); political science (AM, PhD); protein structure and function (PhD); religion (MA, PhD); Slavic languages and literatures (AM); social/cultural anthropology (PhD); sociology (AM, PhD); Spanish (PhD); teaching (MAT); toxicology (Certificate); women's studies (Certificate). *Application fee:* $75. Electronic applications accepted. *Application Contact:* Bertie S. Belvin, Associate Dean for Academic Services, 919-684-3913, E-mail: grad-admissions@duke.edu. *Dean,* Lewis M. Siegel, 919-681-3267.

Center for Demographic Studies Expenses: Contact institution. *Financial support:* Application deadline: 12/31. Offers demographic studies (PhD). *Application deadline:* For fall admission, 12/31. *Application fee:* $75. *Director,* Dr. Ken Manton, 919-684-6126.

Center for International Development Students: 40; includes 1 minority (Asian American or Pacific Islander), 38 international. Average age 34. *Faculty:* 10 full-time (2 women), 14 part-time/adjunct (4 women). Expenses: Contact institution. *Financial support:* In 2001–02, 1 fellowship with partial tuition reimbursement (averaging $24,000 per year) was awarded; scholarships/grants and tuition waivers (full and partial) also available. Financial award application deadline: 12/31. In 2001, 14 degrees awarded. Offers international development (MA). *Application deadline:* For fall admission, 12/31 (priority date); for spring admission, 10/1. Applications are processed on a rolling basis. *Application fee:* $75. Electronic applications accepted. *Application Contact:* Stephanie Alt Lamm, Coordinator, 919-613-7356, Fax: 919-684-2861, E-mail: dcid@pps.duke.edu. *Director of Graduate Studies,* Dr. Francis Lethem, 919-613-7333, Fax: 919-684-2861.

Institute of Statistics and Decision Sciences Students: 26 full-time (12 women); includes 1 minority (Asian American or Pacific Islander), 16 international. 75 applicants, 35% accepted, 7 enrolled. *Faculty:* 12 full-time, 5 part-time/adjunct. Expenses: Contact institution. *Financial support:* Fellowships, research assistantships, teaching assistantships available. Financial award application deadline: 12/31. In 2001, 4 doctorates awarded. *Degree program information:* Part-time programs available. Offers statistics and decision sciences (PhD). *Application deadline:* For fall admission, 12/31. *Application fee:* $75. *Director of Graduate Studies,* Jim Berger, 919-684-8029, Fax: 919-684-8594, E-mail: dgs@stat.duke.edu.

School of Engineering Expenses: Contact institution. *Financial support:* Fellowships, research assistantships, teaching assistantships, Federal Work-Study available. Financial award application deadline: 12/31. In 2001, 45 master's, 35 doctorates awarded. *Degree program information:* Part-time programs available. Offers biomedical engineering (MS, PhD); civil and environmental engineering (MS, PhD); electrical and computer engineering (MS, PhD); engineering (MEM, MS, PhD); engineering management (MEM); environmental engineering (MS, PhD); materials science (MS, PhD); mechanical engineering (MS, PhD). *Dean,* Dr. Kristina M. Johnson, 919-660-5389, Fax: 919-684-4860.

Terry Sanford Institute of Public Policy Students: 75 full-time (40 women); includes 11 minority (5 African Americans, 4 Asian Americans or Pacific Islanders, 1 Hispanic American, 1 Native American), 8 international. 209 applicants, 65% accepted, 40 enrolled. *Faculty:* 35 full-time, 10 part-time/adjunct. Expenses: Contact institution. *Financial support:* Fellowships, research assistantships, teaching assistantships, career-related internships or fieldwork and Federal Work-Study available. Financial award application deadline: 12/31. In 2001, 22 degrees awarded. Offers public policy (MPP). *Application deadline:* For fall admission, 12/31 (priority date). *Application fee:* $75. *Director,* Bruce W. Jentleson, 919-613-7325, Fax: 919-681-8288, E-mail: mpp@pps.duke.edu.

Nicholas School of the Environment Students: 218 full-time (120 women), 2 part-time (1 woman). Average age 25. 342 applicants, 76% accepted. *Faculty:* 64 full-time (10 women), 23 part-time/adjunct (3 women). Expenses: Contact institution. *Financial support:* In 2001–02, 163 students received support, including 152 fellowships (averaging $10,000 per year), 40 research assistantships (averaging $2,700 per year), 15 teaching assistantships (averaging $6,000 per year); career-related internships or fieldwork, Federal Work-Study, institutionally sponsored loans, scholarships/grants, and unspecified assistantships also available. Financial award application deadline: 2/1; financial award applicants required to submit FAFSA. In 2001, 113 master's, 10 doctorates awarded. *Degree program information:* Part-time programs available. Offers coastal environmental management (MEM); environmental science and policy (PhD); environmental toxicology, chemistry, and risk assessment (MEM); forest resource management (MF); resource ecology (MEM); resource economics and policy (MEM); water and air resources (MEM). PhD offered through the Graduate School. *Application deadline:* For fall admission, 2/1; for spring admission, 10/15. Applications are processed on a rolling basis. *Application fee:* $75. Electronic applications accepted. *Application Contact:* Cynthia Peters, Associate Dean for Academic Services, 919-613-8070, Fax: 919-684-8741, E-mail: envadm@duke.edu. *Dean,* Dr. William Schlesinger, 919-613-8004, Fax: 919-684-8741.

School of Law Offers law (JD, LL M, MLS, SJD). LL M and SJD offered only to international students.

School of Medicine Students: 361 full-time (160 women); includes 123 minority (58 African Americans, 54 Asian Americans or Pacific Islanders, 10 Hispanic Americans, 1 Native American), 5 international. Average age 22. 5,249 applicants, 5% accepted, 99 enrolled. *Faculty:* 1,290 full-time (342 women). Expenses: Contact institution. *Financial support:* In 2001–02, 309 students received support. Institutionally sponsored loans and scholarships/grants available. Financial award application deadline: 5/1; financial award applicants required to submit CSS PROFILE or FAFSA. In 2001, 83 degrees awarded. Offers clinical research (MHS); medicine (MD, MHS, MS); pathologists' assistant (MHS); physical therapy (MS); physician assistant (MHS). *Application deadline:* For fall admission, 11/15. Applications are processed on a rolling basis. *Application fee:* $65. *Application Contact:* Dr. Brenda Armstrong, Director of Admissions, 919-684-2985, Fax: 919-684-8893, E-mail: medadm@mc.duke.edu. *Vice Dean of Medical Education,* Dr. Edward C. Halperin, 919-668-3381, Fax: 919-660-7040, E-mail: halperin@radonc.duke.edu.

School of Nursing Students: 99 full-time (92 women), 85 part-time (80 women); includes 28 minority (17 African Americans, 6 Asian Americans or Pacific Islanders, 4 Hispanic Americans, 1 Native American) Average age 37. 106 applicants, 74% accepted, 54 enrolled. *Faculty:* 29 full-time, 5 part-time/adjunct. Expenses: Contact institution. *Financial support:* Career-related internships or fieldwork, institutionally sponsored loans, scholarships/grants, and traineeships available. Support available to part-time students. Financial award application deadline: 6/30; financial award applicants required to submit FAFSA. In 2001, 89 master's, 17 other advanced degrees awarded. *Degree program information:* Part-time programs available. Postbaccalaureate distance learning degree programs offered (minimal on-campus study). Offers adult acute care (Certificate); adult cardiovascular (Certificate); adult oncology/HIV (Certificate); adult primary care (Certificate); clinical nurse specialist (MSN); clinical research management (MSN, Certificate); family (Certificate); gerontology (Certificate); health and nursing ministries (MSN, Certificate); health systems leadership and outcomes (MSN, Certificate); leadership in community based long term care (MSN, Certificate); neonatal (Certificate); nurse anesthetist

(MSN, Certificate); nurse practitioner (MSN); nursing informatics (Certificate); pediatric (Certificate); pediatric acute care (Certificate). *Application deadline:* For fall admission, 3/1 (priority date); for spring admission, 10/1 (priority date). Applications are processed on a rolling basis. *Application fee:* $50. *Application Contact:* Jennifer Avery, Admissions Officer, 919-684-4248, Fax: 919-681-8899, E-mail: avery014@mc.duke.edu. *Dean,* Dr. Mary T. Champagne, 919-684-3786, Fax: 919-681-8899, E-mail: champ001@mc.duke.edu.

See in-depth description on page 849.

DUQUESNE UNIVERSITY, Pittsburgh, PA 15282-0001

General Information Independent-religious, coed, university. CGS member. *Enrollment:* 2,173 full-time matriculated graduate/professional students (1,258 women), 1,874 part-time matriculated graduate/professional students (1,093 women). *Enrollment by degree level:* 1,174 first professional, 2,873 master's. *Tuition:* Part-time $566 per credit. *Required fees:* $56 per credit. Part-time tuition and fees vary according to degree level and program. *Graduate housing:* On-campus housing not available. *Student services:* Campus employment opportunities, campus safety program, career counseling, child daycare facilities, disabled student services, exercise/wellness program, free psychological counseling, international student services, low-cost health insurance, teacher training, writing training. *Library facilities:* Gumberg Library plus 1 other. *Online resources:* library catalog, web page, access to other libraries' catalogs. *Collection:* 325,377 titles, 4,135 serial subscriptions, 32,677 audiovisual materials.

Computer facilities: 650 computers available on campus for general student use. A campuswide network can be accessed from student residence rooms and from off campus. Internet access is available. *Web address:* http://www.duq.edu/.

General Application Contact: Dr. Ralph L. Pearson, Provost and Academic Vice President, 412-396-6054, Fax: 412-396-5644.

GRADUATE UNITS

Bayer School of Natural and Environmental Sciences Students: 73 full-time (42 women), 77 part-time (33 women); includes 5 minority (3 African Americans, 2 Asian Americans or Pacific Islanders), 26 international. Average age 27. 124 applicants, 65% accepted, 53 enrolled. *Faculty:* 31 full-time (3 women), 18 part-time/adjunct (5 women). Expenses: Contact institution. *Financial support:* In 2001–02, 3 fellowships with full tuition reimbursements (averaging $13,500 per year), 3 research assistantships with full tuition reimbursements (averaging $16,500 per year), 49 teaching assistantships with full tuition reimbursements (averaging $10,000 per year) were awarded. Career-related internships or fieldwork, scholarships/grants, tuition waivers (partial), and unspecified assistantships also available. Support available to part-time students. Financial award application deadline: 5/1; financial award applicants required to submit FAFSA. In 2001, 43 master's, 4 doctorates awarded. *Degree program information:* Part-time and evening/weekend programs available. Postbaccalaureate distance learning degree programs offered (no on-campus study). Offers biochemistry (MS, PhD); biology (MS, PhD); chemistry (MS, PhD); environmental management (Certificate); environmental science (Certificate); environmental science and management (MS); natural and environmental sciences (MS, PhD, Certificate). *Application deadline:* Applications are processed on a rolling basis. *Application fee:* $40. *Application Contact:* Mary Ann Quinn, Assistant to the Dean Graduate Affairs, 412-396-6339, Fax: 412-396-4881, E-mail: gradinfo@duq.edu. *Interim Dean,* Dr. David Seybert, 412-396-4877, Fax: 412-396-4881, E-mail: seybert@duq.edu.

Graduate School of Liberal Arts Students: 424 full-time (220 women), 323 part-time (157 women); includes 20 minority (15 African Americans, 1 Asian American or Pacific Islander, 4 Hispanic Americans), 115 international. 409 applicants, 72% accepted, 180 enrolled. *Faculty:* 117 full-time, 61 part-time/adjunct. Expenses: Contact institution. *Financial support:* In 2001–02, 30 research assistantships with full tuition reimbursements (averaging $9,000 per year), 55 teaching assistantships with full tuition reimbursements (averaging $9,000 per year) were awarded. Fellowships with full tuition reimbursements, career-related internships or fieldwork, Federal Work-Study, institutionally sponsored loans, scholarships/grants, and tuition waivers (full and partial) also available. Support available to part-time students. Financial award application deadline: 5/1. In 2001, 176 master's, 32 doctorates awarded. *Degree program information:* Part-time and evening/weekend programs available. Offers archival, museum, and editing studies (MA); clinical psychology (PhD); communication and rhetoric (MA, PhD); computational mathematics (MA); developmental psychology (PhD); English (MA, PhD); health care ethics (MA, DHCE, PhD); history (MA); liberal arts (M Phil, MA, MALS, MS, DHCE, PhD, Certificate); liberal studies (M Phil, MALS); multimedia technology (MS); pastoral ministry (MA); philosophy (MA, PhD); philosophy for theological studies (MA); religious education (MA); systematic theology (PhD); theology (MA). *Application deadline:* Applications are processed on a rolling basis. *Application fee:* $50. *Application Contact:* Linda L. Rendulic, Assistant to the Dean, 412-396-6400, Fax: 412-396-5265, E-mail: rendulic@duq.edu. *Dean,* Dr. Constance D. Ramirez, 412-396-6400.

Graduate Center for Social and Public Policy Students: 35 full-time (16 women), 17 part-time (6 women); includes 2 minority (1 African American, 1 Hispanic American), 26 international. Average age 31. 52 applicants, 58% accepted, 18 enrolled. *Faculty:* 15 full-time (3 women), 1 (woman) part-time/adjunct. Expenses: Contact institution. *Financial support:* In 2001–02, 20 students received support, including 12 research assistantships with full and partial tuition reimbursements available (averaging $9,000 per year), 4 teaching assistantships with full and partial tuition reimbursements available (averaging $9,000 per year); career-related internships or fieldwork, institutionally sponsored loans, scholarships/grants, and tuition waivers (full and partial) also available. Support available to part-time students. Financial award application deadline: 5/1. In 2001, 13 degrees awarded. *Degree program information:* Part-time and evening/weekend programs available. Offers conflict resolution and peace studies (Certificate); social and public policy (MA). Programs are a collaboration between the Departments of Political Science and Sociology. *Application deadline:* For fall admission, 4/30 (priority date); for spring admission, 10/31 (priority date). Applications are processed on a rolling basis. *Application fee:* $50. *Head,* Dr. Michael Irwin, 412-396-6488, Fax: 412-396-5197, E-mail: socialpolicy@duq.edu.

John F. Donahue Graduate School of Business Students: 109 full-time (40 women), 436 part-time (161 women); includes 31 minority (12 African Americans, 12 Asian Americans or Pacific Islanders, 7 Hispanic Americans), 23 international. Average age 30. 237 applicants, 75% accepted. *Faculty:* 46 full-time (3 women), 12 part-time/adjunct (2 women). Expenses: Contact institution. *Financial support:* In 2001–02, 27 students received support, including 27 research assistantships with partial tuition reimbursements available; career-related internships or fieldwork and unspecified assistantships also available. Support available to part-time students. Financial award application deadline: 7/1; financial award applicants required to submit FAFSA. In 2001, 223 degrees awarded. *Degree program information:* Part-time and evening/weekend programs available. Offers business administration (MBA); information systems management (MS); taxation (MS). *Application deadline:* For fall admission, 6/1 (priority date); for spring admission, 11/1. Applications are processed on a rolling basis. *Application fee:* $50. *Application Contact:* Dr. William Presutti, Associate Dean and Director, 412-396-6269, Fax: 412-396-1726, E-mail: presutti@duq2.cc.duq.edu. *Dean,* James C. Stalder, Fax: 412-396-5304, E-mail: stalder@duq.edu.

John G. Rangos, Sr. School of Health Sciences Students: 246 full-time (220 women), 74 part-time (37 women); includes 5 African Americans, 5 Asian Americans or Pacific Islanders, 4 Hispanic Americans Average age 24. 143 applicants, 38% accepted, 27 enrolled. *Faculty:* 32 full-time (20 women), 28 part-time/adjunct (9 women). Expenses: Contact institution. *Financial support:* Federal Work-Study available. In 2001, 149 degrees awarded. Offers health management systems (MHMS); occupational therapy (MOT); physical therapy (MPT, DPT); physician assistant (MPA); rehabilitation science (MS, PhD); speech-language pathology (MSLP). *Application deadline:* For fall admission, 12/1 (priority date); for winter admission, 1/15 (priority date). *Application fee:* $50. Electronic applications accepted. *Application Contact:* Deborah L. Durica, Director of Student and Alumni Services, 412-396-6652, Fax: 412-396-5554, E-mail: durica@duq.edu. *Dean,* Dr. Jerome L. Martin, 412-396-6012, Fax: 412-396-5554, E-mail: martin2@duq.edu.

Mary Pappert School of Music Students: 69 full-time (28 women), 20 part-time (12 women); includes 11 minority (2 African Americans, 1 Asian American or Pacific Islander, 8 Hispanic Americans), 22 international. Average age 23. 101 applicants, 73% accepted. *Faculty:* 25 full-time (7 women), 68 part-time/adjunct (25 women). Expenses: Contact institution. *Financial support:* In 2001–02, 50 fellowships with full and partial tuition reimbursements were awarded; career-related internships or fieldwork, Federal Work-Study, institutionally sponsored loans, and tuition waivers (full and partial) also available. Support available to part-time students. Financial award application deadline: 4/1. In 2001, 30 master's, 7 ADs awarded. *Degree program information:* Part-time programs available. Postbaccalaureate distance learning degree programs offered (minimal on-campus study). Offers music education (MM); music performance (MM, AD); music theory/composition (MM); sacred music (MM). *Application deadline:* For fall admission, 8/1 (priority date); for spring admission, 12/1. Applications are processed on a rolling basis. *Application fee:* $50. *Application Contact:* Joanna Karaczun, Administrative Assistant of Enrollment, 412-396-5064, Fax: 412-396-5479, E-mail: karaczun@duq.edu. *Director of Graduate Studies,* Dr. Robert Shankovich, 412-396-6676, Fax: 412-396-5479, E-mail: shankovi@duq2.cc.duq.edu.

School of Education *Degree program information:* Part-time and evening/weekend programs available. Offers community counseling (MS Ed); counselor education (MS Ed, Ed D); counselor education and supervision (Ed D); early childhood education (MS Ed); education (MS Ed, Ed D, CAGS); educational leaders (Ed D); educational studies (MS Ed); elementary education (MS Ed); instructional leadership excellence (Ed D); instructional technology (MS Ed); marriage and family therapy (MS Ed); reading and language arts (MS Ed); school administration (MS Ed); school administration and supervision (MS Ed); school counseling (MS Ed); school psychology (MS Ed, CAGS); school supervision (MS Ed); secondary education (MS Ed); special education (MS Ed).

School of Law *Degree program information:* Part-time and evening/weekend programs available. Offers law (JD).

School of Nursing Students: 3 full-time (all women), 128 part-time (all women). 51 applicants, 57% accepted, 27 enrolled. *Faculty:* 14 full-time (13 women), 4 part-time/adjunct (3 women). Expenses: Contact institution. *Financial support:* In 2001–02, 1 research assistantship with partial tuition reimbursement (averaging $3,600 per year), 2 teaching assistantships with partial tuition reimbursements (averaging $3,200 per year) were awarded. Institutionally sponsored loans, scholarships/grants, traineeships, tuition waivers (partial), and unspecified assistantships also available. Financial award applicants required to submit FAFSA. In 2001, 18 master's, 7 doctorates awarded. *Degree program information:* Part-time programs available. Postbaccalaureate distance learning degree programs offered (minimal on-campus study). Offers family nurse practitioner (MSN); nursing (MSN, PhD); nursing administration (MSN); nursing education (MSN). *Application deadline:* Applications are processed on a rolling basis. *Application fee:* $50. *Application Contact:* Cherith Simmer, Assistant Dean, 412-396-6556, Fax: 412-396-6346, E-mail: simmer@duq.edu. *Dean,* Mary deChesnay, 412-396-6553, Fax: 412-396-6346, E-mail: dechesna@duq.edu.

School of Pharmacy Students: 784 full-time (507 women), 92 part-time (49 women); includes 29 minority (11 African Americans, 18 Asian Americans or Pacific Islanders), 67 international. Expenses: Contact institution. *Financial support:* In 2001–02, 9 research assistantships with full tuition reimbursements, 30 teaching assistantships with full tuition reimbursements were awarded. Fellowships, career-related internships or fieldwork, Federal Work-Study, institutionally sponsored loans, and scholarships/grants also available. Support available to part-time students. Financial award applicants required to submit FAFSA. In 2001, 129 first professional degrees, 3 master's, 3 doctorates awarded. *Degree program information:* Part-time programs available. Postbaccalaureate distance learning degree programs offered (minimal on-campus study). Offers pharmacy (Pharm D, MS, PhD). *Dean,* Dr. R. Pete Vanderveen, 412-396-6380.

Graduate School of Pharmaceutical Sciences Students: 19 full-time (6 women), 45 part-time (18 women); includes 1 minority (African American), 42 international. 216 applicants, 13% accepted, 15 enrolled. *Faculty:* 15 full-time (2 women). Expenses: Contact institution. *Financial support:* In 2001–02, 39 students received support, including 9 research assistantships with full tuition reimbursements available, 30 teaching assistantships with full tuition reimbursements available; career-related internships or fieldwork also available. Financial award applicants required to submit FAFSA. In 2001, 3 master's, 3 doctorates awarded. *Degree program information:* Part-time programs available. Offers medicinal chemistry (MS, PhD); pharmaceutical administration (MS); pharmaceutical chemistry (MS, PhD); pharmaceutics (MS, PhD); pharmacology/toxicology (MS, PhD). *Application deadline:* For fall admission, 2/1 (priority date). Applications are processed on a rolling basis. *Application fee:* $50. *Application Contact:* Information Contact, 412-396-5662, E-mail: gsps-adm@duq.edu. *Director,* Dr. Aleem Gangjee, 412-396-5662.

See in-depth description on page 851.

D'YOUVILLE COLLEGE, Buffalo, NY 14201-1084

General Information Independent, coed, comprehensive institution. *Enrollment:* 1,103 full-time matriculated graduate/professional students (837 women), 422 part-time matriculated graduate/professional students (345 women). *Enrollment by degree level:* 863 master's, 662 other advanced degrees. *Graduate faculty:* 103 full-time (59 women), 83 part-time/adjunct (55 women). *Tuition:* Full-time $10,320; part-time $430 per credit hour. Tuition and fees vary according to course load. *Graduate housing:* Room and/or apartments available on a first-come, first-served basis to single students; on-campus housing not available to married students. Typical cost: $6,154 (including board). Housing application deadline: 8/1. *Student services:* Campus employment opportunities, campus safety program, career counseling, disabled student services, free psychological counseling, international student services, low-cost health insurance, multicultural affairs office, writing training. *Library facilities:* D'Youville College Library. *Online resources:* library catalog, web page, access to other libraries' catalogs. *Collection:* 93,413 titles, 1,235 serial subscriptions, 3,280 audiovisual materials.

Computer facilities: 70 computers available on campus for general student use. A campuswide network can be accessed from student residence rooms and from off campus. *Web address:* http://www.dyc.edu/.

General Application Contact: Linda Fisher, Graduate Admissions Director, 716-881-7676, Fax: 716-881-7790, E-mail: graduateadmissions@dyc.edu.

GRADUATE UNITS

Department of Business Students: 17 full-time (9 women), 9 part-time (6 women); includes 6 minority (3 African Americans, 1 Asian American or Pacific Islander, 2 Hispanic Americans), 8 international. Average age 33. 74 applicants, 76% accepted, 13 enrolled. *Faculty:* 7 full-time (3 women), 5 part-time/adjunct (2 women). Expenses: Contact institution. *Financial support:* In 2001–02, 1 research assistantship with partial tuition reimbursement (averaging $3,000 per year) was awarded; career-related internships or fieldwork, Federal Work-Study, and scholarships/grants also available. Support available to part-time students. Financial award application deadline: 3/1; financial award applicants required to submit FAFSA. In 2001, 3 degrees awarded. *Degree program information:* Part-time and evening/weekend programs available. Offers international business (MS). Combined BS/MS in international business also offered. *Application deadline:* Applications are processed on a rolling basis. *Application fee:* $25. Electronic applications accepted. *Application Contact:* Linda Fisher, Graduate Admissions Director, 716-881-7676, Fax: 716-881-7790, E-mail: graduateadmissions@dyc.edu. *Chair,* Dr. Kushnaod Haq, 716-881-3200, Fax: 716-881-7790.

Department of Education Students: 915 full-time (693 women), 186 part-time (135 women); includes 18 minority (12 African Americans, 2 Asian Americans or Pacific Islanders, 3 Hispanic Americans, 1 Native American), 791 international. Average age 28. 811 applicants, 73% accepted, 402 enrolled. *Faculty:* 23 full-time (10 women), 24 part-time/adjunct (18 women). Expenses: Contact institution. *Financial support:* In 2001–02, 1 research assistantship with partial tuition reimbursement (averaging $3,000 per year) was awarded; career-related internships or fieldwork and scholarships/grants also available. Support available to part-time students. Financial award application deadline: 3/1; financial award applicants required to submit FAFSA. In 2001, 123 degrees awarded. *Degree program information:* Part-time and evening/weekend programs available. Offers elementary education (MS Ed, Teaching Certificate); secondary education (MS Ed, Teaching Certificate); special education (MS Ed). *Application deadline:* Applications are processed on a rolling basis. *Application fee:* $25.

D'Youville College (continued)

Electronic applications accepted. *Application Contact:* Linda Fisher, Graduate Admissions Director, 716-881-7676, Fax: 716-881-7790, E-mail: graduateadmissions@dyc.edu. *Chair,* Dr. Sheila Dunn, 716-881-3200.

Department of Health Services Administration Students: 11 full-time (8 women), 69 part-time (58 women); includes 8 minority (2 African Americans, 1 Asian American or Pacific Islander, 4 Hispanic Americans, 1 Native American), 14 international. Average age 36. 46 applicants, 83% accepted, 23 enrolled. *Faculty:* 2 full-time (1 woman), 3 part-time/adjunct (1 woman). Expenses: Contact institution. *Financial support:* In 2001–02, 1 research assistantship with partial tuition reimbursement (averaging $3,000 per year) was awarded; career-related internships or fieldwork, Federal Work-Study, and scholarships/grants also available. Support available to part-time students. Financial award application deadline: 3/1; financial award applicants required to submit FAFSA. In 2001, 21 degrees awarded. *Degree program information:* Part-time and evening/weekend programs available. Offers clinical researach associate (Certificate); health services administration (MS, Certificate); long term care administration (Certificate). *Application deadline:* Applications are processed on a rolling basis. *Application fee:* $25. Electronic applications accepted. *Application Contact:* Linda Fisher, Graduate Admissions Director, 716-881-7676, Fax: 716-881-7790, E-mail: graduateadmissions@dyc.edu. *Chair,* Dr. Ardyce Lightner, 716-881-3200, Fax: 716-881-7790.

Department of Nursing Students: 32 full-time (28 women), 144 part-time (134 women); includes 12 minority (8 African Americans, 3 Hispanic Americans, 1 Native American), 114 international. Average age 34. 83 applicants, 76% accepted, 54 enrolled. *Faculty:* 15 full-time (14 women), 4 part-time/adjunct (all women). Expenses: Contact institution. *Financial support:* In 2001–02, 1 research assistantship with partial tuition reimbursement (averaging $3,000 per year) was awarded; Federal Work-Study and scholarships/grants also available. Support available to part-time students. Financial award application deadline: 3/1; financial award applicants required to submit FAFSA. In 2001, 22 master's, 2 other advanced degrees awarded. *Degree program information:* Part-time and evening/weekend programs available. Offers addictions in the community (Certificate); community health nursing (MSN); family nurse practitioner (Certificate); holistic nursing (Certificate); hospice and palliative care (Certificate); nurse practitioner (MS); nursing and health-related professions (Certificate). *Application deadline:* Applications are processed on a rolling basis. *Application fee:* $25. Electronic applications accepted. *Application Contact:* Linda Fisher, Graduate Admissions Director, 716-881-7676, Fax: 716-881-7790, E-mail: graduateadmissions@dyc.edu. *Chair,* Dr. Verna Kieffer, 716-881-3200, Fax: 716-881-7790.

Department of Physical Therapy Students: 65 full-time (45 women); includes 7 minority (5 African Americans, 1 Asian American or Pacific Islander, 1 Hispanic American), 14 international. Average age 23. 125 applicants, 75% accepted, 21 enrolled. *Faculty:* 10 full-time (6 women), 8 part-time/adjunct (6 women). Expenses: Contact institution. *Financial support:* Federal Work-Study and scholarships/grants available. Support available to part-time students. Financial award application deadline: 3/1; financial award applicants required to submit FAFSA. In 2001, 47 degrees awarded. *Degree program information:* Part-time programs available. Offers advanced orthopedic physical therapy (Certificate); manual physical therapy (Certificate); physical therapy (MPT, MS). Combined BS/MS in physical therapy also offered. *Application deadline:* Applications are processed on a rolling basis. *Application fee:* $25. Electronic applications accepted. *Application Contact:* Linda Fisher, Graduate Admissions Director, 716-881-7676, Fax: 716-881-7790, E-mail: graduateadmissions@dyc.edu. *Chair,* Lynn Rivers, 716-881-3200 Ext. 7708, Fax: 716-881-7790, E-mail: riversl@dyc.edu.

Occupational Therapy Department Students: 48 full-time (43 women), 5 part-time (4 women); includes 2 minority (both Asian Americans or Pacific Islanders), 3 international. Average age 26. 52 applicants, 71% accepted, 11 enrolled. *Faculty:* 10 full-time (9 women), 4 part-time/adjunct (all women). Expenses: Contact institution. In 2001, 46 degrees awarded. Offers occupational therapy (MS). Combined BS/MS in occupational therapy also offered. *Application fee:* $25. *Application Contact:* Linda Fisher, Graduate Admissions Director, 716-881-7676, Fax: 716-881-7790, E-mail: graduateadmissions@dyc.edu. *Chair,* Dr. Merlene Gingher, 716-881-3200, Fax: 716-881-7790.

See in-depth description on page 853.

EARLHAM SCHOOL OF RELIGION, Richmond, IN 47374-5360

General Information Independent-religious, coed, graduate-only institution. *Enrollment by degree level:* 68 master's. *Graduate faculty:* 9 full-time (3 women), 3 part-time/adjunct (1 woman). *Tuition:* Full-time $6,408; part-time $276 per credit. *Required fees:* $420; $210 per semester. *Graduate housing:* On-campus housing not available. *Student services:* Campus employment opportunities, career counseling, exercise/wellness program, international student services, low-cost health insurance. *Library facilities:* Lilly Library plus 2 others. *Online resources:* library catalog, web page, access to other libraries' catalogs. *Collection:* 381,739 titles, 1,339 serial subscriptions.

Computer facilities: 125 computers available on campus for general student use. A campuswide network can be accessed from off campus. Internet access and online class registration are available. *Web address:* http://www.esr.earlham.edu/.

General Application Contact: Susan G. Axtell, Director of Admissions, 800-432-1377, Fax: 765-983-1688, E-mail: axtelsu@earlham.edu.

GRADUATE UNITS

Graduate Programs Students: 92 full-time (50 women); includes 4 minority (3 African Americans, 1 Native American) Average age 47. 31 applicants, 90% accepted, 28 enrolled. *Faculty:* 9 full-time (3 women), 3 part-time/adjunct (1 woman). Expenses: Contact institution. *Financial support:* In 2001–02, 49 students received support. Scholarships/grants and tuition waivers (full and partial) available. Financial award applicants required to submit FAFSA. In 2001, 11 degrees awarded. *Degree program information:* Part-time programs available. Offers theology (M Div, M Min, MA). *Application deadline:* Applications are processed on a rolling basis. *Application fee:* $35. Electronic applications accepted. *Application Contact:* Susan G. Axtell, Director of Admissions, 765-983-1523, Fax: 765-983-1688, E-mail: axtelsu@earlham.edu. *Dean,* Jay W. Marshall, 765-983-1687, E-mail: marshja@earlham.edu.

EAST CAROLINA UNIVERSITY, Greenville, NC 27858-4353

General Information State-supported, coed, university. CGS member. *Enrollment:* 1,595 full-time matriculated graduate/professional students (964 women), 1,380 part-time matriculated graduate/professional students (877 women). *Enrollment by degree level:* 291 first professional, 2,501 master's, 156 doctoral, 27 other advanced degrees. *Graduate faculty:* 526 full-time (131 women), 4 part-time/adjunct (0 women). Tuition, state resident: full-time $2,636. Tuition, nonresident: full-time $11,365. *Graduate housing:* Room and/or apartments available on a first-come, first-served basis to single students; on-campus housing not available to married students. Housing application deadline: 5/1. *Student services:* Campus employment opportunities, campus safety program, career counseling, disabled student services, exercise/wellness program, free psychological counseling, grant writing training, international student services, low-cost health insurance, multicultural affairs office, teacher training, writing training. *Library facilities:* Joyner Library plus 1 other. *Online resources:* library catalog, web page, access to other libraries' catalogs. *Collection:* 1.2 million titles, 7,788 serial subscriptions.

Computer facilities: 1,465 computers available on campus for general student use. A campuswide network can be accessed from student residence rooms and from off campus. Internet access and online class registration are available. *Web address:* http://www.ecu.edu/.

General Application Contact: Dr. Paul D. Tschetter, Senior Associate Dean of the Graduate School, 252-328-6012, Fax: 252-328-6071, E-mail: gradschool@mail.ecu.edu.

GRADUATE UNITS

Brody School of Medicine Students: 314 full-time (154 women), 28 part-time (5 women); includes 106 minority (58 African Americans, 29 Asian Americans or Pacific Islanders, 9 Hispanic Americans, 10 Native Americans), 10 international. Average age 26. 1,264 applicants, 9% accepted. *Faculty:* 88 full-time (8 women), 2 part-time/adjunct (0 women). Expenses: Contact institution. *Financial support:* Fellowships with partial tuition reimbursements, institutionally sponsored loans available. Financial award application deadline: 6/1. In 2001, 68 first professional degrees, 4 doctorates awarded. Offers anatomy and cell biology (PhD); biochemistry (PhD); interdisciplinary biological sciences (PhD); medicine (MD, PhD); microbiology and immunology (PhD); pharmacology (PhD); physiology (PhD). *Application fee:* $45. *Application Contact:* Dr. Ed Lieberman, Associate Dean for Research and Graduate Studies, 252-816-2827, Fax: 252-816-3260, E-mail: liebermane@mail.ecu.edu. *Interim Dean,* Dr. Peter Kragel, 252-816-2201, Fax: 252-816-3616, E-mail: pkragel@brody.med.ecu.edu.

Graduate School Students: 1,595 full-time (964 women), 1,380 part-time (877 women); includes 478 minority (344 African Americans, 66 Asian Americans or Pacific Islanders, 40 Hispanic Americans, 28 Native Americans), 113 international. Average age 31. 2,022 applicants, 64% accepted. *Faculty:* 526 full-time (131 women), 4 part-time/adjunct (0 women). Expenses: Contact institution. *Financial support:* Fellowships with partial tuition reimbursements, research assistantships with partial tuition reimbursements, teaching assistantships with partial tuition reimbursements, career-related internships or fieldwork, Federal Work-Study, scholarships/grants, traineeships, and unspecified assistantships available. Support available to part-time students. Financial award application deadline: 6/1; financial award applicants required to submit FAFSA. In 2001, 853 master's, 9 doctorates, 7 other advanced degrees awarded. *Degree program information:* Part-time and evening/weekend programs available. Postbaccalaureate distance learning degree programs offered (no on-campus study). Offers coastal resource management (PhD). *Application deadline:* Applications are processed on a rolling basis. *Application fee:* $45. *Application Contact:* Dr. Paul D. Tschetter, Senior Associate Dean of the Graduate School, 252-328-6012, Fax: 252-328-6071, E-mail: gradschool@mail.ecu.edu. *Vice Chancellor for Research and Graduate Studies,* Dr. Thomas L. Feldbush, 252-328-6937, Fax: 252-328-6071, E-mail: feldbusht@mail.ecu.edu.

College of Arts and Sciences Students: 310 full-time (156 women), 253 part-time (126 women); includes 56 minority (31 African Americans, 11 Asian Americans or Pacific Islanders, 10 Hispanic Americans, 4 Native Americans), 34 international. Average age 29. 406 applicants, 62% accepted. *Faculty:* 198 full-time (38 women), 1 (woman) part-time/adjunct. Expenses: Contact institution. *Financial support:* Fellowships with partial tuition reimbursements, research assistantships with partial tuition reimbursements, teaching assistantships with partial tuition reimbursements, career-related internships or fieldwork, Federal Work-Study, scholarships/grants, traineeships, and unspecified assistantships available. Support available to part-time students. Financial award application deadline: 6/1. In 2001, 170 degrees awarded. *Degree program information:* Part-time and evening/weekend programs available. Offers American history (MA, MA Ed); anthropology (MA); applied and biomedical physics (MS); applied mathematics (MA); applied resource economics (MS); arts and sciences (MA, MA Ed, MPA, MS, PhD); biology (MS); chemistry (MS); clinical psychology (MA); English (MA, MA Ed); European history (MA, MA Ed); general psychology (MA); geography (MA); geology (MS); international studies (MA); maritime history (MA); mathematics (MA, MA Ed); medical physics (MS); molecular biology/biotechnology (MS); physics (PhD); public administration (MPA); school psychology); sociology (MA). *Application deadline:* Applications are processed on a rolling basis. *Application fee:* $45. *Application Contact:* Dr. Paul D. Tschetter, Senior Associate Dean of the Graduate School, 252-328-6012, Fax: 252-328-6071, E-mail: gradschool@mail.ecu.edu. *Dean,* Dr. Keats Sparrow, 252-328-6249, E-mail: asoffice@ecuvm.cis.ecu.edu.

School of Allied Health Sciences Students: 163 full-time (129 women), 55 part-time (40 women); includes 20 minority (12 African Americans, 1 Asian American or Pacific Islander, 5 Hispanic Americans, 2 Native Americans), 3 international. Average age 28. 301 applicants, 49% accepted. *Faculty:* 19 full-time (4 women). Expenses: Contact institution. *Financial support:* Research assistantships with partial tuition reimbursements, teaching assistantships with partial tuition reimbursements, career-related internships or fieldwork, Federal Work-Study, and scholarships/grants available. Support available to part-time students. Financial award application deadline: 6/1; financial award applicants required to submit FAFSA. In 2001, 114 master's, 3 doctorates awarded. *Degree program information:* Part-time and evening/weekend programs available. Postbaccalaureate distance learning degree programs offered (no on-campus study). Offers allied health sciences (MPT, MS, MSOT, PhD); communication sciences and disorders (PhD); occupational therapy (MSOT); physical therapy (MPT); rehabilitation studies (MS); speech, language and auditory pathology (MS); substance abuse (MS); vocational evaluation (MS). *Application fee:* $45. *Application Contact:* Dr. Paul D. Tschetter, Senior Associate Dean of the Graduate School, 252-328-6012, Fax: 252-328-6071, E-mail: gradschool@mail.ecu.edu. *Interim Dean,* Dr. Stephen Thomas, 252-328-6961, E-mail: thomass@mail.ecu.edu.

School of Art Students: 34 full-time (22 women), 13 part-time (10 women); includes 3 minority (1 African American, 1 Hispanic American, 1 Native American), 1 international. Average age 37. 43 applicants, 40% accepted. *Faculty:* 36 full-time (12 women). Expenses: Contact institution. *Financial support:* Research assistantships with partial tuition reimbursements, teaching assistantships with partial tuition reimbursements, Federal Work-Study available. Support available to part-time students. Financial award application deadline:6/1. In 2001, 8 degrees awarded. *Degree program information:* Part-time and evening/weekend programs available. Offers art (MA, MA Ed, MFA). *Application deadline:* For fall admission, 2/1; for spring admission, 10/1. Applications are processed on a rolling basis. *Application fee:* $45. *Application Contact:* Dr. Paul D. Tschetter, Senior Associate Dean of the Graduate School, 252-328-6012, Fax: 252-328-6071, E-mail: gradschool@mail.ecu.edu. *Director of Graduate Studies,* Jackie Leebrick, 252-328-6563, Fax: 252-328-6441, E-mail: leebrickj@mail.ecu.edu.

School of Business Students: 294 full-time (150 women), 135 part-time (66 women); includes 52 minority (38 African Americans, 11 Asian Americans or Pacific Islanders, 3 Hispanic Americans), 38 international. Average age 28. 283 applicants, 71% accepted. *Faculty:* 39 full-time (4 women). Expenses: Contact institution. *Financial support:* Research assistantships with partial tuition reimbursements, teaching assistantships with partial tuition reimbursements, Federal Work-Study available. Support available to part-time students. Financial award application deadline: 6/1. In 2001, 157 degrees awarded. *Degree program information:* Part-time and evening/weekend programs available. Offers business (MBA, MSA). *Application deadline:* For fall admission, 6/1 (priority date). Applications are processed on a rolling basis. *Application fee:* $45. *Application Contact:* Dr. Paul D. Tschetter, Senior Associate Dean of the Graduate School, 252-328-6012, Fax: 252-328-6071, E-mail: gradschool@mail.ecu.edu. *Director of Graduate Studies,* Dr. Rick Niswander, 252-328-6970, Fax: 252-328-6664, E-mail: niswanderr@mail.ecu.edu.

School of Computer Science and Communication Students: 8 full-time (2 women), 12 part-time (2 women); includes 1 minority (Asian American or Pacific Islander), 9 international. Average age 28. 23 applicants, 30% accepted. *Faculty:* 6 full-time (0 women). Expenses: Contact institution. In 2001, 3 degrees awarded. Offers computer science and communication (MS). *Application fee:* $45. *Application Contact:* Dr. Ronnie Smith, Director of Graduate Studies, 252-328-1905, Fax: 252-328-6414, E-mail: smithr@mail.ecu.edu. *Interim Dean,* Dr. Michael Poteat, 252-328-6461, Fax: 252-328-6071, E-mail: poteatg@mail.ecu.edu.

School of Education Students: 147 full-time (114 women), 565 part-time (442 women); includes 144 minority (128 African Americans, 5 Asian Americans or Pacific Islanders, 3 Hispanic Americans, 8 Native Americans), 12 international. Average age 37. 425 applicants, 78% accepted. *Faculty:* 42 full-time (17 women), 1 part-time/adjunct (0 women). Expenses: Contact institution. *Financial support:* Research assistantships with partial tuition reimbursements, teaching assistantships with partial tuition reimbursements, Federal Work-Study available. Support available to part-time students. Financial award application deadline:6/1. In 2001, 191 master's, 6 doctorates, 7 other advanced degrees awarded. *Degree program information:* Part-time and evening/weekend programs available. Offers adult education (MA Ed); behavior/emotional disabilities (MA Ed); counselor education (MS, Ed S); education (MA, MA Ed, MLS, MS, MSA, Ed D, CAS, Ed S); educational administration and supervision (Ed S); educational leadership (Ed D); elementary education (MA Ed); higher education administration (Ed D); information technologies (MS); instruction technology specialist (MA Ed); learning disabilities (MA Ed); library science (MLS, CAS); low incidence disabilities (MA Ed); mental retardation (MA Ed); middle grade education (MA Ed); reading education (MA Ed); school administration (MSA); science education (MA, MA Ed); supervision (MA Ed); vocation education (MA Ed). *Application deadline:* Applications are processed on a rolling basis. *Application fee:* $40. *Application Contact:* Dr. Mary Schmidt,

Associate Dean, 252-328-6191, Fax: 252-328-6071, E-mail: schmidtma@mail.ecu.edu. *Dean*, Dr. Marilyn Sheerer, 252-328-6172, E-mail: sheerer@mail.ecu.edu.

School of Health and Human Performance Students: 66 full-time (32 women), 40 part-time (26 women); includes 16 minority (13 African Americans, 1 Asian American or Pacific Islander, 2 Hispanic Americans), 1 international. Average age 27. 108 applicants, 63% accepted. *Faculty:* 23 full-time (8 women). Expenses: Contact institution. *Financial support:* Research assistantships, teaching assistantships, Federal Work-Study available. Support available to part-time students. Financial award application deadline: 6/1. In 2001, 37 degrees awarded. *Degree program information:* Part-time and evening/weekend programs available. Offers bioenergetics (PhD); exercise and sport science (MA, MA Ed); health and human performance (MA, MA Ed, MS, PhD); health education (MA, MA Ed); recreation and leisure services administration (MS); therapeutic recreation administration (MS). *Application deadline:* For fall admission, 6/1 (priority date). Applications are processed on a rolling basis. *Application fee:* $45. *Application Contact:* Dr. Sharon Knight, Director of Graduate Studies, 252-328-4648, Fax: 252-328-6562, E-mail: gradschool@mail.ecu.edu. *Dean*, Dr. Glen Gilbert, 252-328-4630, Fax: 252-328-4655.

School of Human Environmental Sciences Students: 53 full-time (45 women), 32 part-time (all women); includes 12 minority (9 African Americans, 3 Asian Americans or Pacific Islanders), 2 international. Average age 29. 78 applicants, 47% accepted. *Faculty:* 17 full-time (12 women). Expenses: Contact institution. *Financial support:* Fellowships, research assistantships, teaching assistantships, career-related internships or fieldwork and Federal Work-Study available. Support available to part-time students. Financial award application deadline: 6/1. In 2001, 29 degrees awarded. *Degree program information:* Part-time programs available. Offers child development and family relations (MS); human environmental sciences (MS); marriage and family therapy (MS); nutrition (MS). *Application deadline:* Applications are processed on a rolling basis. *Application fee:* $45. *Application Contact:* Dr. Paul D. Tschetter, Senior Associate Dean of the Graduate School, 252-328-6012, Fax: 252-328-6071, E-mail: gradschool@mail.ecu.edu. *Dean*, Dr. Karla Hughes, 252-328-6891, Fax: 252-328-4276.

School of Industry and Technology Students: 23 full-time (7 women), 116 part-time (21 women); includes 9 minority (7 African Americans, 2 Hispanic Americans), 1 international. Average age 34. 47 applicants, 68% accepted. *Faculty:* 9 full-time (1 woman), 1 part-time/adjunct (0 women). Expenses: Contact institution. *Financial support:* Fellowships, research assistantships, teaching assistantships, Federal Work-Study available. Support available to part-time students. Financial award application deadline: 6/1. In 2001, 27 degrees awarded. *Degree program information:* Part-time programs available. Offers environment health (MS); industrial technology (MS); industry and technology (MS); occupational safety (MS). *Application deadline:* For fall admission, 6/1 (priority date). Applications are processed on a rolling basis. *Application fee:* $45. *Application Contact:* Dr. Paul D. Tschetter, Senior Associate Dean of the Graduate School, 252-328-6012, Fax: 252-328-6071, E-mail: gradschool@mail.ecu.edu. *Dean*, Dr. Ruben M. Desmond, 252-328-6704, Fax: 252-328-4250, E-mail: desmondr@mail.ecu.edu.

School of Music Students: 34 full-time (19 women), 9 part-time (4 women); includes 6 minority (all African Americans), 1 international. Average age 28. 42 applicants, 71% accepted. *Faculty:* 23 full-time (4 women). Expenses: Contact institution. *Financial support:* Fellowships, research assistantships, teaching assistantships, Federal Work-Study available. Support available to part-time students. Financial award application deadline: 6/1. In 2001, 21 degrees awarded. *Degree program information:* Part-time programs available. Offers music education (MM); music therapy (MM); performance (MM); theory and composition (MM). *Application deadline:* For fall admission, 6/1 (priority date). Applications are processed on a rolling basis. *Application fee:* $45. *Application Contact:* Dr. Paul D. Tschetter, Senior Associate Dean of the Graduate School, 252-328-6012, Fax: 252-328-6071, E-mail: gradschool@mail.ecu.edu. *Director of Graduate Studies*, Dr. Rodney Schmidt, 252-328-6282, Fax: 252-328-6258, E-mail: schmidtr@mail.ecu.edu.

School of Nursing Students: 45 full-time (43 women), 47 part-time (45 women); includes 8 minority (4 African Americans, 1 Asian American or Pacific Islander, 1 Hispanic American, 2 Native Americans) Average age 37. 37 applicants, 73% accepted. *Faculty:* 21 full-time (19 women). Expenses: Contact institution. *Financial support:* Research assistantships with partial tuition reimbursements, teaching assistantships with partial tuition reimbursements, Federal Work-Study available. Support available to part-time students. Financial award application deadline: 6/1. In 2001, 31 degrees awarded. *Degree program information:* Part-time programs available. Offers nursing (MSN, PhD). *Application deadline:* For fall admission, 6/1 (priority date). Applications are processed on a rolling basis. *Application fee:* $45. *Application Contact:* Dr. Paul D. Tschetter, Senior Associate Dean of the Graduate School, 252-328-6012, Fax: 252-328-6071, E-mail: gradschool@mail.ecu.edu. *Director of Graduate Studies*, Dr. Judy Bernhardt, 252-328-4302, Fax: 252-328-4300, E-mail: bernhardtj@mail.ecu.edu.

School of Social Work and Criminal Justice Studies Students: 104 full-time (91 women), 75 part-time (58 women); includes 45 minority (37 African Americans, 3 Asian Americans or Pacific Islanders, 4 Hispanic Americans, 1 Native American), 1 international. Average age 32. 229 applicants, 59% accepted. *Faculty:* 11 full-time (6 women), 1 part-time/adjunct (0 women). Expenses: Contact institution. *Financial support:* Research assistantships with partial tuition reimbursements, teaching assistantships with partial tuition reimbursements, Federal Work-Study available. Support available to part-time students. Financial award application deadline: 6/1. In 2001, 63 degrees awarded. Offers criminal justice studies (MA); social work (MSW); social work and criminal justice studies (MA, MSW). *Application deadline:* For fall admission, 1/15 (priority date). *Application fee:* $45. *Application Contact:* Dr. Paul D. Tschetter, Senior Associate Dean of the Graduate School, 252-328-6012, Fax: 252-328-6071, E-mail: gradschool@mail.ecu.edu. *Dean*, Dr. David Harrison, 252-328-4199, Fax: 252-328-4196, E-mail: harrisonw@mail.ecu.edu.

See in-depth description on page 855.

EAST CENTRAL UNIVERSITY, Ada, OK 74820-6899

General Information State-supported, coed, comprehensive institution. CGS member. *Enrollment:* 147 full-time matriculated graduate/professional students (104 women), 324 part-time matriculated graduate/professional students (230 women). *Enrollment by degree level:* 471 master's. Tuition, state resident: part-time $96 per credit hour. Tuition, nonresident: part-time $225 per credit hour. Full-time tuition and fees vary according to course load. *Graduate housing:* Rooms and/or apartments available on a first-come, first-served basis to single students and available to married students. Typical cost: $910 per year ($2,360 including board) for single students; $910 per year ($2,360 including board) for married students. Room and board charges vary according to housing facility selected. *Student services:* Campus employment opportunities, career counseling, child daycare facilities, international student services. *Library facilities:* Linscheid Library. *Online resources:* library catalog, web page. *Collection:* 213,000 titles, 800 serial subscriptions.

Computer facilities: 40 computers available on campus for general student use. A campuswide network can be accessed. *Web address:* http://www.ecok.edu/.

General Application Contact: Dr. Jack W. Paschall, Dean of the Graduate School, 580-332-8000 Ext. 709, Fax: 580-332-8691, E-mail: jpaschil@mailclerk.ecok.edu.

GRADUATE UNITS

Graduate School Students: 147 full-time (104 women), 324 part-time (230 women); includes 73 minority (14 African Americans, 4 Hispanic Americans, 55 Native Americans), 2 international. Expenses: Contact institution. *Financial support:* Fellowships, teaching assistantships, career-related internships or fieldwork, Federal Work-Study, institutionally sponsored loans, and tuition waivers (partial) available. Support available to part-time students. In 2001, 173 degrees awarded. *Degree program information:* Part-time and evening/weekend programs available. Offers administration (MSHR); counseling (MSHR); criminal justice (MSHR); education (M Ed); psychology (MSPS); rehabilitation counseling (MSHR). *Application deadline:* Applications are processed on a rolling basis. *Application fee:* $0 ($50 for international students). *Dean*, Dr. Jack W. Paschall, 580-332-8000 Ext. 709, Fax: 580-332-3042, E-mail: jpaschll@mailclerk.ecok.edu.

EASTERN BAPTIST THEOLOGICAL SEMINARY, Wynnewood, PA 19096-3430

General Information Independent-religious, coed, graduate-only institution. *Graduate housing:* Rooms and/or apartments available to single and married students. Housing application deadline: 8/15.

GRADUATE UNITS

Graduate and Professional Programs *Degree program information:* Part-time and evening/weekend programs available. Offers marriage and family (D Min); renewal of the church for mission (D Min); theology (M Div, MTS, D Min).

EASTERN CONNECTICUT STATE UNIVERSITY, Willimantic, CT 06226-2295

General Information State-supported, coed, comprehensive institution. *Graduate housing:* On-campus housing not available. *Research affiliation:* Department of Education (early childhood education, mathematics and science education).

GRADUATE UNITS

School of Education and Professional Studies *Degree program information:* Part-time and evening/weekend programs available. Offers accounting (MS); early childhood education (MS); education and professional studies (MS); elementary education (MS); organizational management (MS); reading and language arts (MS); science education (MS).

Announcement: The School of Education/Professional Studies and the Graduate Division offer Master of Science degrees in the following areas: accounting, early childhood education, educational technology, elementary education, organizational management, reading/language arts, and science education. Eastern also offers graduate certification programs in early childhood education and elementary education.

EASTERN ILLINOIS UNIVERSITY, Charleston, IL 61920-3099

General Information State-supported, coed, comprehensive institution. CGS member. *Enrollment:* 505 full-time matriculated graduate/professional students (325 women), 801 part-time matriculated graduate/professional students (511 women). *Graduate faculty:* 448. *Tuition, area resident:* Full-time $2,521. Tuition, state resident: full-time $7,562; part-time $105 per semester hour. Tuition, nonresident: part-time $315 per semester hour. *Required fees:* $1,310; $49 per semester hour. *Graduate housing:* Rooms and/or apartments available to single and married students. Typical cost: $3,360 per year for single students; $3,360 per year for married students. Room charges vary according to board plan. *Student services:* Campus employment opportunities, campus safety program, career counseling, exercise/wellness program, free psychological counseling, international student services, low-cost health insurance, multicultural affairs office, teacher training, writing training. *Library facilities:* Booth Library. *Online resources:* library catalog, web page, access to other libraries' catalogs. *Collection:* 486,300 titles, 2,922 serial subscriptions, 20,321 audiovisual materials.

Computer facilities: 1,202 computers available on campus for general student use. A campuswide network can be accessed from student residence rooms and from off campus. Internet access and online class registration are available. *Web address:* http://www.eiu.edu/.

General Application Contact: Dr. Robert M. Augustine, Dean/Graduate School, 217-581-2220, Fax: 217-581-6020, E-mail: cfrma@eiu.edu.

GRADUATE UNITS

Graduate School *Degree program information:* Part-time and evening/weekend programs available. Electronic applications accepted.

College of Arts and Humanities *Degree program information:* Part-time programs available. Offers art (MA); arts and humanities (MA); English (MA); historical administration (MA); history (MA); music (MA); speech-communication (MA).

College of Education and Professional Studies *Degree program information:* Part-time and evening/weekend programs available. Offers education and professional studies (MS, MS Ed, Ed S); educational administration and supervision (MS Ed, Ed S); educational psychology and guidance (MS Ed); elementary education (MS Ed); junior high education (MS Ed); physical education (MS); special education (MS Ed).

College of Sciences *Degree program information:* Part-time programs available. Offers biological sciences (MS); botany (MS); chemistry (MS); clinical psychology (MA); communication disorders and sciences (MS); economics (MA); environmental biology (MS); mathematics (MA); mathematics education (MA); political science (MA); school psychology (SSP); sciences (MA, MS, SSP); zoology (MS).

Lumpkin College of Business and Applied Sciences *Degree program information:* Part-time and evening/weekend programs available. Offers business administration (MBA); business and applied sciences (MA, MBA, MS, MS Ed); dietetics (MS); gerontology (MA); home economics (MS); technology (MS).

See in-depth description on page 857.

EASTERN KENTUCKY UNIVERSITY, Richmond, KY 40475-3102

General Information State-supported, coed, comprehensive institution. CGS member. *Enrollment:* 400 full-time matriculated graduate/professional students (237 women), 1,493 part-time matriculated graduate/professional students (1,086 women). *Graduate faculty:* 680 full-time (318 women), 347 part-time/adjunct (189 women). Tuition, state resident: full-time $1,468; part-time $165 per credit hour. Tuition, nonresident: full-time $4,034; part-time $450 per credit hour. *Graduate housing:* Rooms and/or apartments guaranteed to single students and available to married students. *Student services:* Campus employment opportunities, campus safety program, career counseling, disabled student services, free psychological counseling, international student services, low-cost health insurance, multicultural affairs office. *Library facilities:* John Grant Crabbe Library plus 2 others. *Online resources:* library catalog, web page. *Collection:* 832,663 titles, 3,564 serial subscriptions.

Computer facilities: 500 computers available on campus for general student use. Internet access is available. *Web address:* http://www.eku.edu/.

General Application Contact: Dr. Bankole Thompson, Dean, 859-622-1744.

GRADUATE UNITS

The Graduate School Students: 400 full-time (237 women), 1,493 part-time (1,086 women); includes 89 minority (36 African Americans, 47 Asian Americans or Pacific Islanders, 2 Hispanic Americans, 4 Native Americans) *Faculty:* 680 full-time (318 women), 347 part-time/adjunct (189 women). Expenses: Contact institution. *Financial support:* Fellowships, research assistantships, teaching assistantships, career-related internships or fieldwork, Federal Work-Study, institutionally sponsored loans, and scholarships/grants available. Support available to part-time students. Financial award applicants required to submit FAFSA. In 2001, 367 master's, 9 other advanced degrees awarded. *Degree program information:* Part-time and evening/weekend programs available. Postbaccalaureate distance learning degree programs offered. *Application fee:* $0. *Dean*, Dr. Bankole Thompson, 859-622-1744.

College of Arts and Sciences Students: 167 full-time (99 women), 127 part-time (63 women). Average age 26. Expenses: Contact institution. *Financial support:* Research assistantships, teaching assistantships, career-related internships or fieldwork, Federal Work-Study, and institutionally sponsored loans available. Support available to part-time students. In 2001, 68 degrees awarded. *Degree program information:* Part-time and evening/weekend programs available. Offers arts and sciences (MA, MM, MPA, MS, PhD, Psy S); biological sciences (MS); chemistry (MS); choral conducting (MM); clinical psychology (MS); community development (MPA); community health administration (MPA); ecology (MS); English (MA); general public administration (MPA); geology (MS, PhD); history (MA); industrial/organizational psychology (MS); mathematical sciences (MS); performance (MM); political science (MA); school psychology (Psy S); theory/composition (MM). *Application fee:* $0. *Dean*, Dr. Dominick Hart, 859-622-1405.

College of Business and Technology Students: 24 full-time (9 women), 101 part-time (37 women). *Faculty:* 22 full-time (7 women). Expenses: Contact institution. *Financial support:*

Eastern Kentucky University (continued)

Research assistantships, teaching assistantships, Federal Work-Study available. Support available to part-time students. In 2001, 36 degrees awarded. *Degree program information:* Part-time programs available. Offers business administration (MBA); business and technology (MBA, MS); industrial education (MS); industrial technology (MS); occupational training and development (MS); technical administration (MS); technology education (MS). *Application fee:* $0. *Director*, Dr. Jack L. Dyer, 859-622-1775, Fax: 859-622-1413, E-mail: mba@eku.edu.

College of Education Students: 82 full-time (59 women), 727 part-time (459 women); includes 20 minority (15 African Americans, 1 Asian American or Pacific Islander, 4 Hispanic Americans) Average age 25. *Faculty:* 65 full-time (42 women), 29 part-time/adjunct (24 women). Expenses: Contact institution. *Financial support:* Fellowships, research assistantships, teaching assistantships, career-related internships or fieldwork, Federal Work-Study, and scholarships/grants available. Support available to part-time students. In 2001, 168 degrees awarded. *Degree program information:* Part-time programs available. Postbaccalaureate distance learning degree programs offered (minimal on-campus study). Offers agricultural education (MA Ed); allied health sciences education (MA Ed); art education (MA Ed); biological sciences education (MA Ed); business education (MA Ed); chemistry education (MA Ed); communication disorders (MA Ed); earth science education (MA Ed); education (MA, MA Ed); elementary education general (MA Ed); English education (MA Ed); general science education (MA Ed); geography education (MA Ed); history education (MA Ed); home economics education (MA Ed); human services (MA); industrial education (MA Ed); instructional leadership (MA Ed); mathematical sciences education (MA Ed); mental health counseling (MA); music education (MA Ed); physical education (MA Ed); physics education (MA Ed); political science education (MA Ed); psychology education (MA Ed); reading (MA Ed); school counseling (MA Ed); school health education (MA Ed); secondary and higher education (MA Ed); sociology education (MA Ed); special education (MA Ed). *Application fee:* $0. *Application Contact:* Office of Student Services, 859-622-1828, Fax: 859-622-1831, E-mail: coeadvising@eku.edu. *Dean*, Dr. M. Mark Wasicsko, 859-622-3515, Fax: 859-622-1831, E-mail: coedean@eku.edu.

College of Health Sciences Students: 78 full-time (51 women), 103 part-time (74 women). *Faculty:* 47 full-time (32 women), 8 part-time/adjunct (6 women). Expenses: Contact institution. *Financial support:* Career-related internships or fieldwork and institutionally sponsored loans available. Financial award applicants required to submit CSS PROFILE. In 2001, 66 degrees awarded. *Degree program information:* Part-time programs available. Offers chemical abuse and dependency (MPH); community health (MPH); community nutrition (MS); environmental health science (MPH); health sciences (MPH, MS, MSN); leisure studies (MS); occupational therapy (MS); physical education (MS); rural community health care (MSN); rural health family nurse practitioner (MSN); sports administration (MS). *Application fee:* $0. *Dean*, Dr. David D. Gale, 859-622-1523, Fax: 859-622-1140, E-mail: david.gale@eku.edu.

College of Justice and Safety Students: 37 full-time (9 women), 39 part-time (16 women). 93 applicants, 60% accepted. *Faculty:* 30 full-time (7 women), 1 (woman) part-time/adjunct. Expenses: Contact institution. *Financial support:* Research assistantships, teaching assistantships, career-related internships or fieldwork and Federal Work-Study available. Support available to part-time students. In 2001, 29 degrees awarded. *Degree program information:* Part-time programs available. Offers corrections and juvenile services (MS); criminal justice (MS); criminal justice education (MS); justice and safety (MS); loss prevention administration (MS); police studies (MS). *Application fee:* $0. *Dean*, Gary Cordner, 859-622-3565, Fax: 859-622-6561, E-mail: jus.dean@eku.edu.

EASTERN MENNONITE UNIVERSITY, Harrisonburg, VA 22802-2462

General Information Independent-religious, coed, comprehensive institution. *Enrollment:* 111 full-time matriculated graduate/professional students (53 women), 184 part-time matriculated graduate/professional students (120 women). *Enrollment by degree level:* 101 first professional, 194 master's. *Graduate faculty:* 31 full-time (12 women), 11 part-time/adjunct (1 woman). *Tuition:* Part-time $270 per credit hour. *Required fees:* $2 per credit hour. Tuition and fees vary according to degree level, program and student's religious affiliation. *Graduate housing:* Rooms and/or apartments available on a first-come, first-served basis to single and married students. Typical cost: $3,480 per year for single students; $4,500 per year for married students. Room charges vary according to housing facility selected. *Student services:* Campus employment opportunities, career counseling, disabled student services, exercise/wellness program, free psychological counseling, international student services, low-cost health insurance, multicultural affairs office. *Library facilities:* Sadie Hartzler Library. *Online resources:* library catalog, web page, access to other libraries' catalogs. *Collection:* 175,362 titles, 1,157 serial subscriptions, 10,723 audiovisual materials.

Computer facilities: 138 computers available on campus for general student use. A campuswide network can be accessed from student residence rooms. Internet access is available. *Web address:* http://www.emu.edu/.

General Application Contact: Don A. Yoder, Director of Admissions, 540-432-4257, Fax: 540-432-4444, E-mail: yoderda@emu.edu.

GRADUATE UNITS

Eastern Mennonite Seminary Students: 56 full-time (20 women), 45 part-time (25 women); includes 2 minority (both African Americans), 10 international. Average age 40. 51 applicants, 92% accepted, 42 enrolled. *Faculty:* 10 full-time (2 women), 6 part-time/adjunct (1 woman). Expenses: Contact institution. *Financial support:* In 2001–02, 87 students received support. Career-related internships or fieldwork, Federal Work-Study, and scholarships/grants available. Support available to part-time students. Financial award application deadline: 6/30; financial award applicants required to submit FAFSA. In 2001, 6 first professional degrees, 10 master's awarded. *Degree program information:* Part-time programs available. Offers church leadership (MA); divinity (M Div); religion (MA). *Application deadline:* For fall admission, 9/8 (priority date). Applications are processed on a rolling basis. *Application fee:* $25. *Application Contact:* Don A. Yoder, Director of Admissions, 540-432-4257, Fax: 540-432-4444, E-mail: yoderda@emu.edu. *Seminary Academic Dean*, Dr. Ervin R. Stutzman, 540-432-4261, Fax: 540-432-4444, E-mail: stutzerv@emu.edu.

Program in Business Administration Average age 37. 6 applicants, 100% accepted, 5 enrolled. *Faculty:* 6 full-time (2 women), 4 part-time/adjunct (0 women). Expenses: Contact institution. *Financial support:* In 2001–02, 2 students received support. Available to part-time students. Application deadline: 6/30; *Degree program information:* Part-time and evening/weekend programs available. Offers business (MBA). *Application deadline:* Applications are processed on a rolling basis. *Application fee:* $25. *Application Contact:* Don A. Yoder, Director of Admissions, 540-432-4257, Fax: 540-432-4444, E-mail: yoderda@emu.edu. *Director*, Dr. Lynden D. Krause, 540-432-4154, Fax: 540-432-4070, E-mail: krausel@emu.edu.

Program in Conflict Transformation Students: 35 full-time (19 women), 27 part-time (18 women); includes 3 minority (1 African American, 2 Hispanic Americans), 26 international. Average age 38. 52 applicants, 94% accepted, 28 enrolled. *Faculty:* 6 full-time (3 women), 1 part-time/adjunct (0 women). Expenses: Contact institution. *Financial support:* In 2001–02, 28 students received support. Federal Work-Study, scholarships/grants, and unspecified assistantships available. Support available to part-time students. Financial award application deadline: 6/30; financial award applicants required to submit FAFSA. In 2001, 13 degrees awarded. *Degree program information:* Part-time programs available. Offers conflict transformation (MA). *Application deadline:* For fall admission, 3/1 (priority date). Applications are processed on a rolling basis. *Application fee:* $25. *Application Contact:* Don A. Yoder, Director of Admissions, 540-432-4257, Fax: 540-432-4444, E-mail: yoderda@emu.edu. *Director*, Dr. Vernon E. Jantzi, 540-432-4490, Fax: 540-432-4449, E-mail: jantziv@emu.edu.

Program in Counseling Students: 18 full-time (13 women), 10 part-time (8 women); includes 1 minority (African American), 3 international. Average age 38. 21 applicants, 86% accepted, 14 enrolled. *Faculty:* 4 full-time (2 women). Expenses: Contact institution. *Financial support:* In 2001–02, 14 students received support. Federal Work-Study and scholarships/grants available. Support available to part-time students. Financial award application deadline: 6/30; financial award applicants required to submit FAFSA. In 2001, 11 degrees awarded. *Degree program information:* Part-time programs available. Offers counseling (MA). *Application deadline:* For fall admission, 2/15 (priority date). Applications are processed on a rolling basis. *Application fee:* $25. *Application Contact:* Don A. Yoder, Director of Admissions, 540-432-4257, Fax: 540-432-4444, E-mail: yoderda@emu.edu.

Program in Education Students: 2 full-time (1 woman), 85 part-time (62 women); includes 1 minority (Asian American or Pacific Islander) Average age 37. 37 applicants, 100% accepted, 34 enrolled. *Faculty:* 5 full-time (3 women). Expenses: Contact institution. *Financial support:* In 2001–02, 5 students received support. Federal Work-Study available. Support available to part-time students. Financial award application deadline: 6/30; financial award applicants required to submit FAFSA. In 2001, 17 degrees awarded. *Degree program information:* Part-time programs available. Offers education (MA). *Application deadline:* Applications are processed on a rolling basis. *Application fee:* $25. *Application Contact:* Evelyn Sauder, Education Secretary, 540-432-4350, Fax: 540-432-4444, E-mail: saudere@emu.edu. *Director*, Dr. Donovan D. Steiner, 540-432-4144, Fax: 540-432-4444, E-mail: steinerd@emu.edu.

EASTERN MICHIGAN UNIVERSITY, Ypsilanti, MI 48197

General Information State-supported, coed, comprehensive institution. CGS member. *Enrollment:* 5,401 matriculated graduate/professional students (3,507 women). *Enrollment by degree level:* 5,276 master's, 125 doctoral. *Graduate faculty:* 687 full-time (279 women). Tuition, state resident: part-time $285 per credit hour. Tuition, nonresident: part-time $510 per credit hour. *Graduate housing:* Rooms and/or apartments available on a first-come, first-served basis to single and married students. *Student services:* Campus employment opportunities, campus safety program, career counseling, child daycare facilities, disabled student services, exercise/wellness program, free psychological counseling, grant writing training, international student services, low-cost health insurance, multicultural affairs office, teacher training, writing training. *Library facilities:* Bruce T. Halle Library. *Online resources:* library catalog, web page, access to other libraries' catalogs. *Collection:* 951,062 titles, 6,244 serial subscriptions, 7,229 audiovisual materials. *Research affiliation:* Environmental Research Institute of Michigan (space and environmental education), KMS Optics (physics), Dow Chemical National Science Foundation Center (polymer technology), Pittsburgh Plate Glass National Science Foundation Center (coatings technology), DuPont Chrysler (odor emissions), Flint Ink National Science Foundation Center (odor emissions).

Computer facilities: 525 computers available on campus for general student use. A campuswide network can be accessed from student residence rooms and from off campus. Internet access is available. *Web address:* http://www.emich.edu/.

General Application Contact: Mary Ann Shichtman, Associate Director of Admissions, 734-487-3400, Fax: 734-487-1484.

GRADUATE UNITS

Graduate School Students: 5,401 (3,507 women). 3,428 applicants, 63% accepted. *Faculty:* 687 full-time (279 women). Expenses: Contact institution. *Financial support:* In 2001–02, 30 fellowships (averaging $4,000 per year), research assistantships with full tuition reimbursements (averaging $7,000 per year), teaching assistantships with full tuition reimbursements (averaging $7,000 per year) were awarded. Career-related internships or fieldwork, Federal Work-Study, institutionally sponsored loans, scholarships/grants, tuition waivers (partial), and unspecified assistantships also available. Support available to part-time students. Financial award application deadline: 3/15; financial award applicants required to submit FAFSA. In 2001, 1,072 master's, 5 doctorates, 13 other advanced degrees awarded. *Degree program information:* Part-time and evening/weekend programs available. Postbaccalaureate distance learning degree programs offered (minimal on-campus study). *Application deadline:* For fall admission, 5/15 (priority date); for winter admission, 11/1 (priority date); for spring admission, 3/15 (priority date). Applications are processed on a rolling basis. *Application fee:* $30. *Application Contact:* Graduate Admissions, 734-487-3400, Fax: 734-487-1484, E-mail: graduate.admissions@emich.edu. *Associate Vice President for Research and Graduate Studies*, Dr. Robert Holkeboer, 734-487-0042, Fax: 734-487-0050.

College of Arts and Sciences *Faculty:* 372 full-time (132 women). Expenses: Contact institution. *Financial support:* In 2001–02, fellowships (averaging $4,000 per year), research assistantships with full tuition reimbursements (averaging $6,200 per year), teaching assistantships with full tuition reimbursements (averaging $6,200 per year) were awarded. Career-related internships or fieldwork, Federal Work-Study, institutionally sponsored loans, and tuition waivers (partial) also available. Support available to part-time students. Financial award application deadline: 3/15; financial award applicants required to submit FAFSA. *Degree program information:* Part-time and evening/weekend programs available. Offers applied economics (MA); art (MA); art education (MA); arts administration (MA); arts and sciences (MA, MFA, MLS, MPA, MS, PhD); biology (MS); chemistry (MS); children's literature (MA); clinical psychology (PhD); clinical/behavioral services (MS); communication (MA); computer science (MS); criminology and criminal justice (MA); development, trade and planning (MA); drama/theatre for the young (MA, MFA); economics (MA); English (MA); English linguistics (MA); fine arts (MFA); foreign languages (MA); French (MA); general psychology (MS); general science (MS); geography (MA, MS); German (MA); historic preservation (MS); history (MA); interpretation/performance studies (MA); language and international trade (MA); literature (MA); mathematics (MA); music (MA); physics (MS); physics education (MS); psychology (MS); public administration (MPA); social science (MA, MLS); social science and American culture (MLS); sociology (MA); Spanish (MA); Spanish (bilingual-bicultural education) (MA); studio art (MA); teaching English to speakers of other languages (MA); theatre arts (MA); women's studies (MLS); written communication (MA). *Application deadline:* For fall admission, 5/15; for winter admission, 11/1; for spring admission, 3/15. Applications are processed on a rolling basis. *Application fee:* $30. *Interim Dean*, Dr. Nina Contis, 734-487-4344.

College of Business Students: 860 (395 women). *Faculty:* 71 full-time (17 women). Expenses: Contact institution. *Financial support:* In 2001–02, fellowships (averaging $4,000 per year), research assistantships with full tuition reimbursements (averaging $6,200 per year), teaching assistantships with full tuition reimbursements (averaging $6,200 per year) were awarded. Federal Work-Study also available. Support available to part-time students. Financial award application deadline: 3/15; financial award applicants required to submit FAFSA. In 2001, 217 degrees awarded. *Degree program information:* Part-time and evening/weekend programs available. Offers accounting (MSA); accounting and taxation (MBA); accounting, financial, and operational control (MBA); business (MBA, MSA, MSHROD, MSIS); business administration (MBA); computer information systems (MBA); computer-based information systems (MSIS); finance (MBA); human resources management and organizational development (MSHROD); international business (MBA); management of human resources (MBA); management organizational development (MBA); marketing (MBA); production and operations management (MBA); strategic quality management (MBA). *Application deadline:* For fall admission, 5/15; for spring admission, 3/15. Applications are processed on a rolling basis. *Application fee:* $30. *Application Contact:* Dr. Christy Montgomery, Coordinator, 734-487-4444. *Dean*, Dr. Earl Potter, 734-487-4140.

College of Education Students: 1,572 (1,185 women). 714 applicants, 50% accepted. *Faculty:* 111 full-time (67 women). Expenses: Contact institution. *Financial support:* In 2001–02, fellowships (averaging $4,000 per year), research assistantships with full tuition reimbursements (averaging $6,200 per year), teaching assistantships with full tuition reimbursements (averaging $6,200 per year) were awarded. Career-related internships or fieldwork and Federal Work-Study also available. Support available to part-time students. Financial award application deadline: 3/15; financial award applicants required to submit FAFSA. In 2001, 309 master's, 5 doctorates, 7 other advanced degrees awarded. *Degree program information:* Part-time and evening/weekend programs available. Offers advanced counseling (MA); community counseling (MA); curriculum and instruction (MA); early childhood education (MA); education (MA, MS, Ed D, Sp Ed); educational leadership (MA, Ed D, Sp Ed); educational psychology (MA); elementary education (MA); guidance and counseling (MA, Sp Ed); K–12 curriculum (MA); middle school education (MA); physical education (MS); reading (MA); school counseling (MA, Sp Ed); secondary curriculum (MA); secondary school teaching (MA); social foundations of education (MA); special education (MA, Sp Ed); speech and language pathology (MA). *Application deadline:* For fall admission, 5/15 (priority date); for winter admission, 11/1; for spring admission, 3/15.

Applications are processed on a rolling basis. *Application fee:* $30. *Dean,* Dr. Jerry Robbins, 734-487-1414.

College of Health and Human Services *Faculty:* 58 full-time (44 women). Expenses: Contact institution. *Financial support:* In 2001–02, fellowships (averaging $4,000 per year), research assistantships with full tuition reimbursements (averaging $6,200 per year), teaching assistantships with full tuition reimbursements (averaging $6,200 per year) were awarded. Federal Work-Study also available. Support available to part-time students. Financial award application deadline: 3/15; financial award applicants required to submit FAFSA. In 2001, 88 degrees awarded. *Degree program information:* Part-time and evening/weekend programs available. Offers health and human services (MOT, MS, MSN, MSW); human, environmental, and consumer resources (MS); nursing education (MSN); occupational therapy (MOT, MS); social work (MSW). *Application deadline:* For fall admission, 5/15; for winter admission, 11/1; for spring admission, 3/15. Applications are processed on a rolling basis. *Application fee:* $30. *Dean,* Dr. Elizabeth King, 734-487-0077.

College of Technology *Faculty:* 45 full-time (8 women). Expenses: Contact institution. *Financial support:* In 2001–02, fellowships (averaging $4,000 per year), research assistantships with full tuition reimbursements (averaging $6,200 per year), teaching assistantships with full tuition reimbursements (averaging $6,200 per year) were awarded. Federal Work-Study also available. Support available to part-time students. Financial award application deadline: 3/15; financial award applicants required to submit FAFSA. In 2001, 110 degrees awarded. *Degree program information:* Part-time and evening/weekend programs available. Offers business education (MBE); industrial technology (MS); liberal studies in technology (MLS); polymer technology (MS); technology (MA, MBE, MLS, MS); technology education (MA). *Application deadline:* For fall admission, 5/15; for winter admission, 11/1; for spring admission, 3/15. Applications are processed on a rolling basis. *Application fee:* $30. *Dean,* Dr. John Dugger, 734-487-4140.

EASTERN NAZARENE COLLEGE, Quincy, MA 02170-2999

General Information Independent-religious, coed, comprehensive institution. *Enrollment:* 50 full-time matriculated graduate/professional students (30 women), 120 part-time matriculated graduate/professional students (80 women). *Enrollment by degree level:* 170 master's. *Graduate faculty:* 8 full-time (3 women), 8 part-time/adjunct (5 women). *Tuition:* Part-time $360 per credit hour. *Required fees:* $50 per semester. *Graduate housing:* Room and/or apartments available to married students; on-campus housing not available to single students. *Student services:* Campus safety program, career counseling, exercise/wellness program, low-cost health insurance, multicultural affairs office, teacher training. *Library facilities:* Nease Library. *Online resources:* library catalog. *Collection:* 117,540 titles, 466 serial subscriptions, 1,290 audiovisual materials.

Computer facilities: 98 computers available on campus for general student use. A campuswide network can be accessed from student residence rooms and from off campus. Internet access is available. *Web address:* http://www.enc.edu/.

General Application Contact: Cleo P. Cakridas, Assistant Director of Graduate Studies, 617-774-6826, Fax: 617-774-6800, E-mail: cakridac@enc.edu.

GRADUATE UNITS

Graduate Studies Students: 50 full-time (30 women), 120 part-time (80 women). Average age 30. 26 applicants, 100% accepted. *Faculty:* 8 full-time (3 women), 8 part-time/adjunct (5 women). Expenses: Contact institution. *Financial support:* Career-related internships or fieldwork and scholarships/grants available. Support available to part-time students. Financial award applicants required to submit FAFSA. In 2001, 26 degrees awarded. *Degree program information:* Part-time and evening/weekend programs available. Offers family counseling (MS). *Application deadline:* Applications are processed on a rolling basis. *Application fee:* $35. *Application Contact:* Cleo P. Cakridas, Assistant Director/Coordinator of Graduate Studies, 617-774-6826, Fax: 617-774-6800, E-mail: cakridac@enc.edu. *Director of Graduate Studies,* 617-745-3558.

Division of Education Students: 135. Average age 35. 20 applicants, 100% accepted. *Faculty:* 9 full-time (5 women), 11 part-time/adjunct (5 women). Expenses: Contact institution. *Financial support:* Career-related internships or fieldwork available. Support available to part-time students. Financial award applicants required to submit FAFSA. In 2001, 2 degrees awarded. *Degree program information:* Part-time and evening/weekend programs available. Offers early childhood education (M Ed, Certificate); elementary education (M Ed, Certificate); English as a second language (M Ed, Certificate); instructional enrichment and development (M Ed, Certificate); middle school education (M Ed, Certificate); moderate special needs education (M Ed, Certificate); principal (Certificate); program development and supervision (M Ed, Certificate); secondary education (M Ed, Certificate); special education administrator (Certificate); supervisor (Certificate); teacher of reading (M Ed, Certificate). M Ed and Certificate also available through weekend program for administration, special needs, and reading only. *Application deadline:* Applications are processed on a rolling basis. *Application fee:* $35. *Chair,* Dr. Lorne Ranstrom, 617-745-3528.

EASTERN NEW MEXICO UNIVERSITY, Portales, NM 88130

General Information State-supported, coed, comprehensive institution. CGS member. *Enrollment:* 97 full-time matriculated graduate/professional students (55 women), 264 part-time matriculated graduate/professional students (194 women). *Enrollment by degree level:* 361 master's. *Graduate faculty:* 84 full-time (31 women), 9 part-time/adjunct (2 women). Tuition, state resident: full-time $1,740; part-time $73 per credit. Tuition, nonresident: full-time $7,296; part-time $304 per credit. *Required fees:* $588; $25 per credit. *Graduate housing:* Rooms and/or apartments available on a first-come, first-served basis to single students and available to married students. Typical cost: $1,850 per year ($4,160 including board) for single students. *Student services:* Campus employment opportunities, career counseling, child daycare facilities, disabled student services, free psychological counseling, international student services, low-cost health insurance, multicultural affairs office. *Library facilities:* Golden Library. *Online resources:* library catalog, web page, access to other libraries' catalogs. *Collection:* 506,751 titles, 8,795 serial subscriptions, 24,005 audiovisual materials.

Computer facilities: 266 computers available on campus for general student use. A campuswide network can be accessed from student residence rooms and from off campus. Internet access and online class registration are available. *Web address:* http://www.enmu.edu/.

General Application Contact: Dr. Phillip Shelley, Dean, Graduate School, 505-562-2150, Fax: 505-562-2168, E-mail: phillip.shelley@enmu.edu.

GRADUATE UNITS

Graduate School Students: 97 full-time (55 women), 264 part-time (194 women); includes 71 minority (11 African Americans, 4 Asian Americans or Pacific Islanders, 53 Hispanic Americans, 3 Native Americans), 14 international. 83 applicants, 94% accepted. *Faculty:* 84 full-time (31 women), 9 part-time/adjunct (2 women). Expenses: Contact institution. *Financial support:* In 2001–02, 5 fellowships (averaging $7,200 per year), 33 research assistantships (averaging $7,700 per year), 46 teaching assistantships (averaging $7,700 per year) were awarded. Career-related internships or fieldwork and Federal Work-Study also available. Support available to part-time students. Financial award application deadline: 3/1. In 2001, 84 degrees awarded. *Degree program information:* Part-time and evening/weekend programs available. Postbaccalaureate distance learning degree programs offered (minimal on-campus study). *Application deadline:* For fall admission, 8/20 (priority date). Applications are processed on a rolling basis. *Application fee:* $10. Electronic applications accepted. *Dean,* Dr. Phillip Shelley, 505-262-2150, Fax: 505-562-2168, E-mail: phillip.shelley@enmu.edu.

College of Business Students: 18 full-time (7 women), 17 part-time (12 women); includes 6 minority (2 Asian Americans or Pacific Islanders, 3 Hispanic Americans, 1 Native American), 7 international. Average age 36. 11 applicants, 100% accepted. *Faculty:* 13 full-time (2 women), 2 part-time/adjunct (0 women). Expenses: Contact institution. *Financial support:* In 2001–02, 1 fellowship (averaging $7,200 per year), 7 research assistantships (averaging $7,700 per year), 2 teaching assistantships (averaging $7,700 per year) were awarded. Federal Work-Study also available. Support available to part-time students. Financial award application deadline: 3/1. In 2001, 8 degrees awarded. *Degree program information:* Part-time and evening/weekend programs available. Postbaccalaureate distance learning degree programs offered (minimal on-campus study). Offers business (MBA). *Application deadline:* For fall admission, 8/20 (priority date). Applications are processed on a rolling basis. *Application fee:* $10. Electronic applications accepted. *Application Contact:* Dr. William Brunsen, Graduate Coordinator, 505-562-2744, E-mail: bill.brunsen@enmu.edu. *Dean,* Dr. Gerry Huybregts, 505-562-2343, E-mail: gerry.huybregts@enmu.edu.

College of Education and Technology Students: 35 full-time (22 women), 169 part-time (127 women); includes 43 minority (7 African Americans, 36 Hispanic Americans) Average age 35. 44 applicants, 100% accepted. *Faculty:* 23 full-time (13 women), 1 part-time/adjunct (0 women). Expenses: Contact institution. *Financial support:* In 2001–02, 3 fellowships (averaging $7,200 per year), 6 research assistantships (averaging $7,700 per year), 15 teaching assistantships (averaging $7,700 per year) were awarded. Career-related internships or fieldwork and Federal Work-Study also available. Support available to part-time students. Financial award application deadline: 3/1. In 2001, 51 degrees awarded. *Degree program information:* Part-time and evening/weekend programs available. Postbaccalaureate distance learning degree programs offered (minimal on-campus study). Offers counseling (MA); education (M Ed); education and technology (M Ed, M Sp Ed, MA, MS); physical education (MS); school guidance (M Ed); special education (M Sp Ed). *Application deadline:* For fall admission, 8/20 (priority date). Applications are processed on a rolling basis. *Application fee:* $10. Electronic applications accepted. *Dean,* Dr. Kenneth Moore, 505-562-2443, E-mail: kenneth.moore@enmu.edu.

College of Fine Arts *Faculty:* 7 full-time (4 women), 1 part-time/adjunct (0 women). Expenses: Contact institution. *Financial support:* Federal Work-Study available. Support available to part-time students. Financial award application deadline: 3/1. In 2001, 1 degree awarded. *Degree program information:* Part-time programs available. Offers fine arts (MM). *Application deadline:* For fall admission, 8/20 (priority date). Applications are processed on a rolling basis. *Application fee:* $10. Electronic applications accepted. *Application Contact:* Dr. John Olsen, Interim Director, 505-562-2377, E-mail: john.olsen@enmu.edu. *Dean,* Dr. David Gerig, 505-562-2373, E-mail: david.gerig@enmu.edu.

College of Liberal Arts and Sciences Students: 44 full-time (26 women), 78 part-time (55 women); includes 22 minority (4 African Americans, 2 Asian Americans or Pacific Islanders, 14 Hispanic Americans, 2 Native Americans), 7 international. Average age 33. 28 applicants, 82% accepted. *Faculty:* 41 full-time (12 women), 5 part-time/adjunct (2 women). Expenses: Contact institution. *Financial support:* In 2001–02, 1 fellowship (averaging $7,200 per year), 20 research assistantships (averaging $7,700 per year), 29 teaching assistantships (averaging $7,700 per year) were awarded. Career-related internships or fieldwork and Federal Work-Study also available. Support available to part-time students. Financial award application deadline: 3/1. In 2001, 24 degrees awarded. *Degree program information:* Part-time and evening/weekend programs available. Postbaccalaureate distance learning degree programs offered. Offers anthropology (MA); biology (MS); chemistry (MS); communication (MA); English (MA); liberal arts and sciences (MA, MS); mathematical sciences (MA); psychology and sociology (MA); speech pathology and audiology (MS). *Application deadline:* For fall admission, 8/20 (priority date). Applications are processed on a rolling basis. *Application fee:* $10. Electronic applications accepted. *Dean,* Dr. Thurman Elder, 505-562-2421, E-mail: thurman.elder@enmu.edu.

EASTERN OREGON UNIVERSITY, La Grande, OR 97850-2899

General Information State-supported, coed, comprehensive institution. *Enrollment:* 66 full-time matriculated graduate/professional students (46 women), 118 part-time matriculated graduate/professional students (73 women). *Enrollment by degree level:* 184 master's. *Graduate faculty:* 12 full-time (6 women), 7 part-time/adjunct (3 women). *Tuition:* Full-time $8,000. *Graduate housing:* Rooms and/or apartments available to single and married students. *Student services:* Career counseling, free psychological counseling, low-cost health insurance. *Library facilities:* Pierce Library plus 1 other. *Online resources:* library catalog, web page, access to other libraries' catalogs. *Collection:* 329,942 titles, 998 serial subscriptions, 35,556 audiovisual materials.

Computer facilities: 125 computers available on campus for general student use. A campuswide network can be accessed from student residence rooms and from off campus. Internet access and online class registration are available. *Web address:* http://www.eou.edu/.

General Application Contact: Dr. Kenneth M. Smith, Coordinator of Graduate Studies, 541-962-3772, Fax: 541-962-3701, E-mail: ksmith@eou.edu.

GRADUATE UNITS

School of Education and Business Students: 66 full-time (46 women), 118 part-time (73 women); includes 9 minority (8 Hispanic Americans, 1 Native American) Average age 28. 148 applicants, 60% accepted. *Faculty:* 12 full-time (6 women), 7 part-time/adjunct (3 women). Expenses: Contact institution. *Financial support:* Federal Work-Study, scholarships/grants, and tuition waivers (full and partial) available. Support available to part-time students. Financial award applicants required to submit FAFSA. In 2001, 35 degrees awarded. *Degree program information:* Part-time programs available. Postbaccalaureate distance learning degree programs offered (minimal on-campus study). Offers education and business (MTE); elementary education (MTE); secondary education (MTE). *Application deadline:* For fall admission, 1/1 (priority date). Applications are processed on a rolling basis. *Application fee:* $50. *Application Contact:* Dr. Kenneth M. Smith, Coordinator of Graduate Studies, 541-962-3772, Fax: 541-962-3701, E-mail: ksmith@eou.edu. *Dean,* Dr. Michael Jaeger, 541-962-3772, Fax: 541-962-3701, E-mail: mjaeger@eou.edu.

EASTERN UNIVERSITY, St. Davids, PA 19087-3696

General Information Independent-religious, coed, comprehensive institution. *Graduate housing:* On-campus housing not available.

GRADUATE UNITS

Graduate Business Programs *Degree program information:* Part-time and evening/weekend programs available. Offers business administration (MBA); economic development (MBA, MS); nonprofit management (MBA, MS).

Graduate Education Programs *Degree program information:* Part-time programs available. Offers English as a second or foreign language (Certificate); multicultural education (M Ed); school health services (M Ed).

Programs in Counseling Offers community/clinical counseling (MA); educational counseling (MA, MS); marriage and family (MA); school counseling (MA); school psychology (MS); student development (MA).

EASTERN VIRGINIA MEDICAL SCHOOL, Norfolk, VA 23501-1980

General Information Independent, coed, graduate-only institution. *Graduate faculty:* 292 full-time, 31 part-time/adjunct. *Graduate housing:* Rooms and/or apartments available to single and married students. *Student services:* Campus employment opportunities, campus safety program, career counseling, low-cost health insurance. *Library facilities:* Moorman Memorial Library. *Collection:* 77,202 titles, 966 serial subscriptions.

Computer facilities: A campuswide network can be accessed. Internet access is available. *Web address:* http://www.evms.edu/.

GRADUATE UNITS

Art Therapy Program Offers art therapy (MS).

Doctoral Program in Biomedical Sciences Students: 53. Expenses: Contact institution. *Financial support:* Research assistantships, career-related internships or fieldwork available. Offers biomedical sciences (PhD). *Application deadline:* For fall admission, 2/15. Applications are processed on a rolling basis. *Application fee:* $30. *Application Contact:* Toni Dorn, Administrator, 757-446-8480, Fax: 757-466-8449, E-mail: dornma@evms.edu. *Director,* Dr. William J. Wasilenko, 757-446-8480, Fax: 757-446-8449, E-mail: wasilewj@evms.edu.

Master of Public Health Program Students: 43. Expenses: Contact institution. *Financial support:* Career-related internships or fieldwork and institutionally sponsored loans available. *Degree program information:* Part-time and evening/weekend programs available. Offers public health (MPH). *Application deadline:* For spring admission, 5/30. *Application fee:* $50

Eastern Virginia Medical School (continued)

($100 for international students). *Application Contact:* Paula Swartz, Administrative Secretary, 757-446-6120, Fax: 757-446-6121, E-mail: swartzpm@evms.edu. *Director,* Dr. Robert R. Jacobs, 757-466-6120, Fax: 757-446-6121, E-mail: jacobsrr@evms.edu.

Master's Program in Biomedical Sciences Students: 13. Expenses: Contact institution. *Financial support:* Federal Work-Study and institutionally sponsored loans available. Offers biomedical sciences (MS). *Application deadline:* For fall admission, 4/1. *Application fee:* $60. *Application Contact:* Toni Dorn, Administrator, 757-446-8480, Fax: 757-466-8449, E-mail: dornma@evms.edu. *Director,* Dr. Donald Meyer, 757-446-8480, Fax: 757-446-8449, E-mail: meyerdc@evms.edu.

Professional Program in Medicine Students: 418. Expenses: Contact institution. *Financial support:* In 2001–02, 345 students received support. Federal Work-Study and institutionally sponsored loans available. Financial award application deadline: 3/15; financial award applicants required to submit CSS PROFILE or FAFSA. In 2001, 104 degrees awarded. Offers medicine (MD). *Application deadline:* For fall admission, 11/15 (priority date). Applications are processed on a rolling basis. *Application fee:* $85. *Application Contact:* Susan Castora, Director of Admissions, 757-446-5812, Fax: 757-446-5896, E-mail: castorsl@evms.edu. *Associate Dean for Admissions,* Dr. Donald Lewis, 757-446-5812, Fax: 757-446-5896, E-mail: lewisdw@evms.edu.

The Virginia Consortium Program in Clinical Psychology Students: 44. Expenses: Contact institution. Offers psychology (Psy D). *Application deadline:* For fall admission, 1/5. *Application fee:* $30. *Application Contact:* Eileen O'Neill, Administrative Coordinator, 757-518-2550, Fax: 757-518-2553, E-mail: exoneill@odu.edu. *Director,* Dr. John D. Ball, 757-518-2550, Fax: 757-518-2553, E-mail: balljd@evms.edu.

EASTERN WASHINGTON UNIVERSITY, Cheney, WA 99004-2431

General Information State-supported, coed, comprehensive institution. CGS member. *Enrollment:* 623 full-time matriculated graduate/professional students (427 women), 384 part-time matriculated graduate/professional students (256 women). *Enrollment by degree level:* 1,007 master's. *Graduate faculty:* 385 full-time (166 women). Tuition, state resident: full-time $1,586; part-time $159 per credit hour. Tuition, nonresident: full-time $4,677; part-time $468 per credit hour. *Required fees:* $222; $159 per credit. $74 per quarter. *Graduate housing:* Rooms and/or apartments available on a first-come, first-served basis to single and married students. Typical cost: $4,000 (including board) for single students; $1,773 per year for married students. Room and board charges vary according to board plan and housing facility selected. Housing application deadline: 5/1. *Student services:* Campus employment opportunities, campus safety program, career counseling, child daycare facilities, disabled student services, exercise/wellness program, free psychological counseling, international student services, low-cost health insurance, teacher training, writing training. *Library facilities:* John F. Kennedy Library plus 2 others. *Online resources:* library catalog, web page, access to other libraries' catalogs. *Collection:* 1.4 million titles, 6,429 serial subscriptions, 31,832 audiovisual materials.

Computer facilities: 125 computers available on campus for general student use. A campuswide network can be accessed from student residence rooms and from off campus. Internet access, e-mail are available. *Web address:* http://www.ewu.edu/.

General Application Contact: Dr. Larry Briggs, Associate Vice President for Graduate Studies, 509-359-6297, Fax: 509-359-6044, E-mail: gradprograms@mail.ewu.edu.

GRADUATE UNITS

Graduate School Studies Students: 623 full-time (427 women), 384 part-time (256 women); includes 91 minority (13 African Americans, 16 Asian Americans or Pacific Islanders, 43 Hispanic Americans, 19 Native Americans), 46 international. Average age 34. 883 applicants, 62% accepted, 343 enrolled. *Faculty:* 385 full-time (166 women). Expenses: Contact institution. *Financial support:* In 2001–02, teaching assistantships with partial tuition reimbursements (averaging $7,000 per year); career-related internships or fieldwork, Federal Work-Study, institutionally sponsored loans, scholarships/grants, health care benefits, tuition waivers (full and partial), and unspecified assistantships also available. Support available to part-time students. Financial award application deadline: 2/1; financial award applicants required to submit FAFSA. In 2001, 571 degrees awarded. *Degree program information:* Part-time and evening/weekend programs available. Offers arts and letters (M Ed, MA, MFA); college instruction (MA); composition (MA); creative writing (MFA); English (MA); French education (M Ed); instrumental/vocal performance (MA); interdisciplinary studies (MA, MS); music education (MA); music history and literature (MA). *Application deadline:* For fall admission, 3/1 (priority date). Applications are processed on a rolling basis. *Application fee:* $35. *Application Contact:* Dr. Larry Briggs, Associate Vice President for Graduate Studies, 509-359-6297, Fax: 509-359-6044, E-mail: gradprograms@mail.ewu.edu. *Dean,* Dr. Ronald Dalla, 509-359-6566, Fax: 509-359-6044.

College of Business Administration and Public Administration Students: 47 full-time (20 women), 61 part-time (30 women); includes 14 minority (2 African Americans, 1 Asian American or Pacific Islander, 6 Hispanic Americans, 5 Native Americans), 5 international. 103 applicants, 37% accepted, 21 enrolled. *Faculty:* 31 full-time (11 women). Expenses: Contact institution. *Financial support:* In 2001–02, 4 teaching assistantships with partial tuition reimbursements (averaging $7,000 per year) were awarded; career-related internships or fieldwork, Federal Work-Study, institutionally sponsored loans, scholarships/grants, health care benefits, tuition waivers (partial), and unspecified assistantships also available. Support available to part-time students. Financial award application deadline:2/1. In 2001, 53 degrees awarded. *Degree program information:* Part-time and evening/weekend programs available. Offers business administration (MBA, MPA, MURP); public administration (MPA); urban and regional planning (MURP). *Application deadline:* For fall admission, 4/1 (priority date); for spring admission, 1/15. Applications are processed on a rolling basis. *Application fee:* $35. *Application Contact:* Prof. M. David Gorton, MBA Director, 509-358-2270, Fax: 509-358-2267, E-mail: mgorton@mailserver.ewu.edu. *Dean,* Dr. Dolores Martin, 509-358-2237, Fax: 509-359-4656.

College of Education and Human Development Students: 148 full-time (110 women), 137 part-time (95 women); includes 11 minority (3 African Americans, 5 Hispanic Americans, 3 Native Americans), 16 international. 199 applicants, 40% accepted, 61 enrolled. *Faculty:* 64 full-time (31 women). Expenses: Contact institution. *Financial support:* In 2001–02, 16 teaching assistantships with partial tuition reimbursements (averaging $7,000 per year) were awarded; career-related internships or fieldwork, Federal Work-Study, institutionally sponsored loans, scholarships/grants, health care benefits, tuition waivers (partial), and unspecified assistantships also available. Support available to part-time students. Financial award application deadline: 2/1; financial award applicants required to submit FAFSA. In 2001, 153 degrees awarded. *Degree program information:* Part-time programs available. Offers adult education (M Ed); college instruction (MA, MS); college instruction in physical education (MS); counseling psychology (MS); curriculum and instruction (M Ed); developing psychology (MS); early childhood education (M Ed); education and human development (M Ed, MA, MS); educational leadership (M Ed); elementary teaching (M Ed); foundations of education (M Ed); literacy specialist (M Ed); physical education (MS); school counseling (MS); school library media administration (M Ed); school psychology (MS); science education (M Ed); social science education (M Ed); special education (M Ed); supervising (clinic) teaching (M Ed). *Application deadline:* Applications are processed on a rolling basis. *Application fee:* $35. *Dean,* Dr. Foritz Erikson, 509-359-6492, Fax: 509-359-4822.

College of Science, Mathematics and Technology Students: 114 full-time (76 women), 29 part-time (14 women); includes 6 minority (2 Asian Americans or Pacific Islanders, 2 Hispanic Americans, 2 Native Americans), 3 international. 114 applicants, 54% accepted, 40 enrolled. *Faculty:* 116 full-time (51 women). Expenses: Contact institution. *Financial support:* In 2001–02, 29 teaching assistantships with partial tuition reimbursements (averaging $7,000 per year) were awarded; career-related internships or fieldwork, Federal Work-Study, institutionally sponsored loans, scholarships/grants, health care benefits, tuition waivers (partial), and unspecified assistantships also available. Support available to part-time students. Financial award application deadline: 2/1; financial award applicants required to submit FAFSA. In 2001, 69 degrees awarded. *Degree program information:* Part-time programs available. Offers biology (MS); communication disorders (MS); computer science (M Ed, MS); geology (MS); mathematics (MS); physical therapy (MPT); science, mathematics and technology (M Ed, MA, MPT, MS). *Application deadline:* Applications are processed on a rolling basis. *Application fee:* $35. *Dean,* Dr. Ray Soltero, 509-359-6244, Fax: 509-359-6950.

College of Social and Behavioral Sciences Students: 49 full-time (29 women), 39 part-time (27 women); includes 6 minority (2 Asian Americans or Pacific Islanders, 2 Hispanic Americans, 2 Native Americans), 3 international. 70 applicants, 46% accepted, 24 enrolled. *Faculty:* 49 full-time (14 women). Expenses: Contact institution. *Financial support:* In 2001–02, 21 teaching assistantships with partial tuition reimbursements (averaging $7,000 per year) were awarded; research assistantships, career-related internships or fieldwork, Federal Work-Study, institutionally sponsored loans, scholarships/grants, health care benefits, tuition waivers (partial), and unspecified assistantships also available. Support available to part-time students. Financial award application deadline: 2/1; financial award applicants required to submit FAFSA. In 2001, 45 degrees awarded. *Degree program information:* Part-time and evening/weekend programs available. Offers communications (MS); history (MA); letters and social sciences (MA, MS); psychology (MS); school psychology (MS). *Application deadline:* Applications are processed on a rolling basis. *Application fee:* $35. *Dean,* Dr. Jeffers Chertok, 509-359-2287, Fax: 509-359-6732.

Intercollegiate College for Nursing (ICN) *Faculty:* 19 full-time (17 women). Expenses: Contact institution. *Financial support:* Application deadline: 2/1. Offers nursing education (MN). *Application deadline:* For fall admission, 4/1 (priority date). Applications are processed on a rolling basis. *Application fee:* $35. *Application Contact:* Dr. Anne Hirsch, Associate Dean, 509-324-7334. *Dean,* Dr. Dorothy Detlor, 509-324-7334, Fax: 509-324-7341.

School of Social Work and Human Services Students: 165 full-time (127 women), 78 part-time (64 women); includes 38 minority (6 African Americans, 6 Asian Americans or Pacific Islanders, 20 Hispanic Americans, 6 Native Americans), 2 international. 233 applicants, 73% accepted, 93 enrolled. *Faculty:* 49 full-time (29 women). Expenses: Contact institution. *Financial support:* In 2001–02, 4 teaching assistantships with partial tuition reimbursements (averaging $7,000 per year) were awarded; career-related internships or fieldwork, Federal Work-Study, institutionally sponsored loans, scholarships/grants, health care benefits, tuition waivers (partial), and unspecified assistantships also available. Support available to part-time students. Financial award application deadline: 2/1; financial award applicants required to submit FAFSA. In 2001, 213 degrees awarded. *Degree program information:* Part-time programs available. Offers social work and human services (MSW). *Application deadline:* Applications are processed on a rolling basis. *Application fee:* $35. *Application Contact:* Diane Somerday, Program Coordinator, 509-359-6482. *Dean,* Dr. Michael Frumkin, 509-359-6885, Fax: 509-359-6475.

See in-depth description on page 859.

EAST STROUDSBURG UNIVERSITY OF PENNSYLVANIA, East Stroudsburg, PA 18301-2999

General Information State-supported, coed, comprehensive institution. *Enrollment:* 271 full-time matriculated graduate/professional students (167 women), 542 part-time matriculated graduate/professional students (397 women). *Enrollment by degree level:* 813 master's. *Graduate faculty:* 80 full-time (28 women), 5 part-time/adjunct (4 women). Tuition, state resident: full-time $4,600; part-time $256 per credit. Tuition, nonresident: full-time $7,554; part-time $420 per credit. *Required fees:* $806; $45 per credit. *Graduate housing:* Room and/or apartments available to single students; on-campus housing not available to married students. *Student services:* Campus employment opportunities, campus safety program, career counseling, child daycare facilities, disabled student services, exercise/wellness program, free psychological counseling, international student services, low-cost health insurance. *Library facilities:* Kemp Library. *Online resources:* library catalog, web page, access to other libraries' catalogs. *Collection:* 1,758 serial subscriptions, 12,506 audiovisual materials.

Computer facilities: 164 computers available on campus for general student use. A campuswide network can be accessed from off campus. Internet access is available. *Web address:* http://www.esu.edu/.

General Application Contact: Dr. James A. Fagin, Dean of Graduate Studies and Continuing Education, 570-423-3536, Fax: 570-423-1906, E-mail: jfagin@po-box.esu.edu.

GRADUATE UNITS

Graduate School Students: 271 full-time (167 women), 542 part-time (397 women); includes 40 minority (11 African Americans, 12 Asian Americans or Pacific Islanders, 16 Hispanic Americans, 1 Native American), 21 international. Average age 32. *Faculty:* 80 full-time (28 women), 5 part-time/adjunct (4 women). Expenses: Contact institution. *Financial support:* In 2001–02, 144 research assistantships with full tuition reimbursements (averaging $3,750 per year) were awarded; career-related internships or fieldwork, Federal Work-Study, and institutionally sponsored loans also available. Financial award application deadline: 3/1; financial award applicants required to submit FAFSA. In 2001, 265 degrees awarded. *Degree program information:* Part-time and evening/weekend programs available. *Application deadline:* For fall admission, 7/31 (priority date); for spring admission, 11/30. Applications are processed on a rolling basis. *Application fee:* $25. *Dean,* Dr. James A. Fagin, 570-422-3536, Fax: 570-422-3506, E-mail: jfagin@po-box.esu.edu.

School of Arts and Sciences Students: 57 full-time (27 women), 62 part-time (30 women); includes 4 minority (3 African Americans, 1 Asian American or Pacific Islander), 7 international. Average age 30. *Faculty:* 29 full-time (9 women), 7 part-time/adjunct (2 women). Expenses: Contact institution. *Financial support:* In 2001–02, 43 research assistantships with full tuition reimbursements (averaging $2,500 per year) were awarded; career-related internships or fieldwork, Federal Work-Study, and institutionally sponsored loans also available. Financial award application deadline: 3/1; financial award applicants required to submit FAFSA. In 2001, 34 degrees awarded. *Degree program information:* Part-time and evening/weekend programs available. Offers arts and sciences (M Ed, MA, MS); biology (M Ed, MS); computer science (MS); general science (M Ed, MS); history (M Ed, MA); political science (M Ed, MA). *Application deadline:* For fall admission, 7/31; for spring admission, 11/30. Applications are processed on a rolling basis. *Application fee:* $15 ($25 for international students). *Interim Dean,* Dr. Michael Liberman, 570-422-3494, Fax: 570-422-3506.

School of Health Sciences and Human Performance Students: 99 full-time (66 women), 82 part-time (55 women); includes 13 minority (5 African Americans, 4 Asian Americans or Pacific Islanders, 4 Hispanic Americans), 2 international. Average age 30. *Faculty:* 25 full-time (11 women), 4 part-time/adjunct (3 women). Expenses: Contact institution. *Financial support:* In 2001–02, 65 research assistantships with full tuition reimbursements (averaging $5,000 per year) were awarded; career-related internships or fieldwork, Federal Work-Study, and institutionally sponsored loans also available. Financial award application deadline: 3/1; financial award applicants required to submit FAFSA. In 2001, 87 degrees awarded. *Degree program information:* Part-time and evening/weekend programs available. Offers cardiac rehabilitation and exercise science (MS); community health education (MPH); health and physical education (M Ed); health education (MS); health sciences and human performance (M Ed, MPH, MS); physical education (MS); speech pathology and audiology (MS). *Application deadline:* For fall admission, 7/31 (priority date); for spring admission, 11/30. Applications are processed on a rolling basis. *Application fee:* $25. *Dean,* Dr. Mark Kilker, 530-422-1425, Fax: 530-422-3347, E-mail: mkilker@po-box.esu.edu.

School of Professional Studies Students: 117 full-time (82 women), 401 part-time (317 women); includes 21 minority (4 African Americans, 5 Asian Americans or Pacific Islanders, 11 Hispanic Americans, 1 Native American), 2 international. Average age 33. *Faculty:* 22 full-time (12 women), 1 (woman) part-time/adjunct. Expenses: Contact institution. *Financial support:* In 2001–02, 36 research assistantships with full tuition reimbursements (averaging $2,500 per year) were awarded; career-related internships or fieldwork, Federal Work-Study, and institutionally sponsored loans also available. Financial award application deadline: 3/1; financial award applicants required to submit FAFSA. In 2001, 144 degrees awarded. *Degree program information:* Part-time and evening/weekend programs available. Offers elementary education (M Ed); instructional technology (M Ed); professional and secondary education (M Ed); professional studies (M Ed); reading (M Ed); special education (M Ed).

Application deadline: For fall admission, 7/31 (priority date); for spring admission, 11/30. Applications are processed on a rolling basis. *Application fee:* $25. *Dean,* Dr. Sam Hausfather, 530-422-3377, Fax: 530-422-3506, E-mail: shausfather@po-box.esu.edu.

See in-depth description on page 861.

EAST TENNESSEE STATE UNIVERSITY, Johnson City, TN 37614

General Information State-supported, coed, university. CGS member. *Enrollment:* 1,036 full-time matriculated graduate/professional students (620 women), 906 part-time matriculated graduate/professional students (578 women). *Enrollment by degree level:* 238 first professional, 1,498 master's, 177 doctoral, 29 other advanced degrees. *Graduate faculty:* 433 full-time (152 women), 50 part-time/adjunct (8 women). Tuition, state resident: part-time $181 per hour. Tuition, nonresident: part-time $270 per hour. *Required fees:* $220 per term. *Graduate housing:* Rooms and/or apartments available on a first-come, first-served basis to single and married students. Typical cost: $1,840 per year ($4,008 including board) for single students; $3,600 per year ($5,768 including board) for married students. Housing application deadline: 7/1. *Student services:* Campus employment opportunities, campus safety program, career counseling, child daycare facilities, disabled student services, exercise/wellness program, free psychological counseling, grant writing training, international student services, low-cost health insurance, multicultural affairs office, teacher training. *Library facilities:* Sherrod Library plus 2 others. *Online resources:* library catalog, web page. *Collection:* 594,080 titles, 3,403 serial subscriptions. *Research affiliation:* Oak Ridge National Laboratory (biomedical physical science), Eastman Chemical Corporation (biomedical science), Tennessee Mouse Genome Consortium (biomedical science), Tennessee Biotechnology Association (biotechnology), Siemens (scientific and biomedical manufacturing), Marshall Space Flight Center.

Computer facilities: 550 computers available on campus for general student use. A campuswide network can be accessed. Internet access and online class registration are available. *Web address:* http://www.etsu.edu/.

General Application Contact: Dr. Roberta Herrin, Associate Dean, 423-439-4221, Fax: 423-439-5624, E-mail: gradsch@etsu.edu.

GRADUATE UNITS

James H. Quillen College of Medicine Students: 265 full-time (136 women), 8 part-time (5 women); includes 55 minority (27 African Americans, 19 Asian Americans or Pacific Islanders, 8 Hispanic Americans, 1 Native American), 7 international. Average age 27. *Faculty:* 142 full-time (36 women), 48 part-time/adjunct (7 women). Expenses: Contact institution. *Financial support:* Research assistantships with full tuition reimbursements, teaching assistantships with full tuition reimbursements, career-related internships or fieldwork, Federal Work-Study, institutionally sponsored loans, scholarships/grants, and tuition waivers (full) available. Financial award applicants required to submit FAFSA. In 2001, 53 first professional degrees, 3 master's, 4 doctorates awarded. *Degree program information:* Part-time programs available. Offers anatomy (MS, PhD); biochemistry (MS, PhD); biophysics (MS, PhD); medicine (MD, MS, PhD); microbiology (MS, PhD); pharmacology (MS, PhD); physiology (MS, PhD). *Application deadline:* Applications are processed on a rolling basis. *Application fee:* $25. *Application Contact:* Edwin D. Taylor, Assistant Dean for Admissions and Records, 423-439-4753, Fax: 423-439-8206, E-mail: dougt@etsu.edu. *Vice President for Health Affairs, Dean,* Dr. Ronald Franks, 423-439-6315, Fax: 423-439-8090, E-mail: franksr@etsu.edu.

School of Graduate Studies Students: 771 full-time (484 women), 898 part-time (573 women); includes 105 minority (75 African Americans, 18 Asian Americans or Pacific Islanders, 7 Hispanic Americans, 5 Native Americans), 80 international. Average age 34. *Faculty:* 291 full-time (116 women), 2 part-time/adjunct (1 woman). Expenses: Contact institution. *Financial support:* Research assistantships with full tuition reimbursements, teaching assistantships with full tuition reimbursements, career-related internships or fieldwork, Federal Work-Study, institutionally sponsored loans, scholarships/grants, tuition waivers (full), and unspecified assistantships available. Support available to part-time students. Financial award applicants required to submit FAFSA. In 2001, 490 master's, 10 doctorates, 22 other advanced degrees awarded. *Degree program information:* Part-time and evening/weekend programs available. *Application fee:* $25 ($35 for international students). *Application Contact:* Admissions and Records Clerk, 423-439-4221, Fax: 423-439-5624, E-mail: gradsch@etsu.edu. *Dean,* Dr. Wesley Brown, 423-439-6146, Fax: 423-439-5624, E-mail: gradsch@etsu.edu.

College of Applied Science and Technology Students: 74 full-time (25 women), 41 part-time (10 women); includes 6 minority (2 African Americans, 4 Asian Americans or Pacific Islanders), 21 international. Average age 32. *Faculty:* 28 full-time (6 women). Expenses: Contact institution. *Financial support:* Research assistantships with full tuition reimbursements, teaching assistantships with full tuition reimbursements, career-related internships or fieldwork, Federal Work-Study, scholarships/grants, and unspecified assistantships available. Support available to part-time students. Financial award application deadline: 7/1; financial award applicants required to submit FAFSA. In 2001, 48 degrees awarded. *Degree program information:* Part-time and evening/weekend programs available. Postbaccalaureate distance learning degree programs offered (no on-campus study). Offers applied science and technology (MS); clinical nutrition (MS); computer science (MS); engineering technology (MS); industrial arts/technology education (MS); information systems science (MS); software engineering (MS). *Application deadline:* Applications are processed on a rolling basis. *Application fee:* $25 ($35 for international students). *Interim Dean,* Dr. Carroll Hyder, 423-439-7500, Fax: 423-439-7868, E-mail: hyder@etsu.edu.

College of Arts and Sciences Students: 152 full-time (83 women), 102 part-time (57 women); includes 19 minority (13 African Americans, 4 Asian Americans or Pacific Islanders, 1 Hispanic American, 1 Native American), 13 international. Average age 30. *Faculty:* 127 full-time (42 women). Expenses: Contact institution. *Financial support:* Research assistantships with full tuition reimbursements, teaching assistantships with full tuition reimbursements, career-related internships or fieldwork, Federal Work-Study, institutionally sponsored loans, scholarships/grants, tuition waivers (full), and unspecified assistantships available. In 2001, 74 degrees awarded. *Degree program information:* Part-time and evening/weekend programs available. Offers applied sociology (MA); art education (MA); art history (MA); arts and sciences (M Mu Ed, MA, MFA, MS, MSW); biology (MS); chemistry (MS); clinical psychology (MA); communication (MA); criminal justice and criminology (MA); English (MA); general psychology (MA); general sociology (MA); history (MA); mathematics (MS); microbiology (MS); music (M Mu Ed); social work (MSW); studio art (MA, MFA). *Application fee:* $25 ($35 for international students). *Interim Dean,* Dr. Rebecca A. Pyles, 423-439-5671, Fax: 423-439-4645, E-mail: pylesr@etsu.edu.

College of Business Students: 90 full-time (37 women), 82 part-time (35 women); includes 13 minority (8 African Americans, 4 Asian Americans or Pacific Islanders, 1 Hispanic American), 21 international. Average age 31. *Faculty:* 30 full-time (4 women). Expenses: Contact institution. *Financial support:* Research assistantships with full tuition reimbursements, Federal Work-Study and scholarships/grants available. Financial award application deadline: 8/15. In 2001, 83 master's, 7 other advanced degrees awarded. *Degree program information:* Part-time and evening/weekend programs available. Offers accountancy (M Acc); business (M Acc, MBA, MCM, MPM, Certificate); business administration (MBA, Certificate); city management (MCM); community development (MPM); general administration (MPM); health care management (Certificate); municipal service management (MPM); urban and regional economic development (MPM); urban and regional planning (MPM). *Application deadline:* For fall admission, 7/1 (priority date); for spring admission, 12/1. Applications are processed on a rolling basis. *Application fee:* $25 ($35 for international students). *Dean,* Dr. Linda Garceau, 423-439-5276, Fax: 423-439-5274, E-mail: garceaul@etsu.edu.

College of Education Students: 251 full-time (187 women), 381 part-time (275 women); includes 39 minority (30 African Americans, 3 Asian Americans or Pacific Islanders, 3 Hispanic Americans, 3 Native Americans), 12 international. Average age 35. *Faculty:* 48 full-time (24 women), 2 part-time/adjunct (1 woman). Expenses: Contact institution. *Financial support:* Research assistantships with full tuition reimbursements, teaching assistantships with full tuition reimbursements, career-related internships or fieldwork, Federal Work-Study, institutionally sponsored loans, scholarships/grants, and unspecified assistantships available. In 2001, 171 master's, 10 doctorates, 1 other advanced degree awarded. *Degree program information:* Part-time and evening/weekend programs available. Offers 7-12 (MAT); administrative endorsement (M Ed, Ed D, Ed S); advanced practitioner (M Ed); classroom leadership (Ed D); classroom technology (M Ed); community agency counseling (M Ed, MA); comprehensive concentration (M Ed); counseling (M Ed, MA); early childhood education (M Ed, MA); early childhood general (M Ed); early childhood special education (M Ed); early childhood teaching (M Ed); education (M Ed, MA, MAT, Ed D, Ed S); educational communication (M Ed); educational leadership (M Ed, Ed D, Ed S); educational media/educational technology (M Ed); elementary and secondary (school counseling) (M Ed, MA); elementary education (M Ed, MAT); exercise physiology (MA); fitness leadership (MA); K-12 (MAT); marriage and family therapy (M Ed, MA); modified concentration (M Ed); physical education (M Ed, MA); post secondary and private sector leadership (Ed D); reading and storytelling (M Ed, MA); reading education (M Ed, MA); school leadership (Ed D); school library media (M Ed); school system leadership (Ed S); secondary education (M Ed, MAT); sports management (MA); sports sciences (MA); teacher leadership (Ed S). *Application deadline:* For fall admission, 7/15 (priority date). Applications are processed on a rolling basis. *Application fee:* $25 ($35 for international students). *Application Contact:* Dr. Hal Knight, Associate Dean, 423-439-4159, Fax: 423-439-7560, E-mail: knighth@etsu.edu. *Dean,* Dr. Martha Collins, 423-439-7627, Fax: 423-439-7560, E-mail: collinsm@etsu.edu.

College of Nursing Students: 50 full-time (39 women), 57 part-time (47 women); includes 2 minority (both African Americans) Average age 36. *Faculty:* 27 full-time (26 women). Expenses: Contact institution. *Financial support:* Research assistantships with full tuition reimbursements, teaching assistantships with full tuition reimbursements, career-related internships or fieldwork, traineeships, and unspecified assistantships available. Support available to part-time students. Financial award application deadline: 7/1. In 2001, 36 master's, 14 other advanced degrees awarded. *Degree program information:* Part-time programs available. Offers advanced nursing practice (Post Master's Certificate); health care management (Certificate); nursing (MSN, DSN). *Application deadline:* For fall admission, 1/15 (priority date). Applications are processed on a rolling basis. *Application fee:* $25 ($35 for international students). *Dean,* Dr. Joellen Edwards, 423-439-7051, Fax: 423-439-4522, E-mail: edwardsj@etsu.edu.

College of Public and Allied Health Students: 108 full-time (78 women), 32 part-time (20 women); includes 8 minority (4 African Americans, 2 Asian Americans or Pacific Islanders, 1 Hispanic American, 1 Native American), 10 international. Average age 29. *Faculty:* 27 full-time (13 women). Expenses: Contact institution. *Financial support:* Research assistantships with full tuition reimbursements, teaching assistantships with full tuition reimbursements, career-related internships or fieldwork, Federal Work-Study, institutionally sponsored loans, scholarships/grants, tuition waivers (full), and unspecified assistantships available. Support available to part-time students. In 2001, 69 degrees awarded. *Degree program information:* Part-time and evening/weekend programs available. Offers audiology (MS); communicative disorders (MS); community health (MPH); environmental health (MSEH); gerontology (Certificate); health care management (Certificate); physical therapy (MPT); public and allied health (MPH, MPT, MS, MSEH, Certificate); public health (MPH); public health administration (MPH); special education audiology pre-K-12 (MS); special education speech pathology pre-K-12 (MS); speech pathology (MS). *Application fee:* $25 ($35 for international students). *Dean,* Dr. Wilsie Bishop, 423-439-4243, Fax: 423-439-5238, E-mail: bishopws@etsu.edu.

Division of Cross-Disciplinary Studies Students: 14 full-time (9 women), 34 part-time (18 women); includes 9 minority (all African Americans), 2 international. Average age 41. *Faculty:* 4 full-time (1 woman). Expenses: Contact institution. *Financial support:* Research assistantships with full tuition reimbursements, teaching assistantships with full tuition reimbursements available. In 2001, 9 degrees awarded. Offers liberal studies (MALS). *Application fee:* $25. *Associate Dean,* Dr. Rick E. Osborn, 423-439-4223, Fax: 423-439-7091, E-mail: osbornr@etsu.edu.

See in-depth description on page 863.

ÉCOLE DES HAUTES ÉTUDES COMMERCIALES DE MONTRÉAL, Montréal, QC H3T 2A7, Canada

General Information Province-supported, coed, comprehensive institution. *Enrollment:* 1,150 full-time matriculated graduate/professional students (545 women), 1,540 part-time matriculated graduate/professional students (703 women). *Enrollment by degree level:* 1,419 master's, 115 doctoral, 1,156 other advanced degrees. *Graduate faculty:* 191 full-time (50 women). *Graduate tuition:* Tuition and fees charges are reported in Canadian dollars. *International tuition:* $9,168 Canadian dollars full-time. Tuition, province resident: full-time $1,668 Canadian dollars; part-time $56 Canadian dollars per credit. Tuition, Canadian resident: full-time $3,850 Canadian dollars; part-time $129 Canadian dollars per credit. *Required fees:* $155 Canadian dollars. Tuition and fees vary according to course load and program. *Graduate housing:* Rooms and/or apartments available on a first-come, first-served basis to single and married students. Typical cost: $2,736 Canadian dollars per year for single students; $4,860 Canadian dollars per year for married students. Room charges vary according to campus/location. Housing application deadline: 3/31. *Student services:* Campus employment opportunities, campus safety program, career counseling, child daycare facilities, disabled student services, exercise/wellness program, international student services, multicultural affairs office. *Library facilities:* Myriam et J.-Robert Ouimet Library plus 1 other. *Online resources:* library catalog, web page, access to other libraries' catalogs. *Collection:* 343,456 titles, 6,018 serial subscriptions, 2,211 audiovisual materials. *Research affiliation:* Centre Francophone de Recherche en Informatisation des Organisations (information systems), Ad Opt (operational research), Hydro Quebec, Center for InterUniversity Research and Analysis on Organizations (organizational analysis).

Computer facilities: 250 computers available on campus for general student use. A campuswide network can be accessed from off campus. Internet access and online class registration are available. *Web address:* http://www.hec.ca/.

General Application Contact: Daniel Zizian, Acting Registrar, 514-340-6110, Fax: 514-340-5640, E-mail: registraire.info@hec.ca.

GRADUATE UNITS

School of Business Administration Students: 1,150 full-time (545 women), 1,531 part-time (698 women). Average age 29. 2,548 applicants, 61% accepted, 1040 enrolled. *Faculty:* 191 full-time (50 women). Expenses: Contact institution. *Financial support:* Fellowships, research assistantships, teaching assistantships, scholarships/grants available. In 2001, 251 master's, 9 doctorates, 308 other advanced degrees awarded. *Degree program information:* Part-time and evening/weekend programs available. Offers administration (LL M, M Sc, PhD, Diploma); applied economics (M Sc); applied financial economics (M Sc); business administration (LL M, M Sc, MBA, PhD, Diploma); business administration and management (MBA); business intelligence (M Sc); controllership (M Sc); electronic commerce (Diploma); finance (M Sc); financial engineering (M Sc); human resources management (M Sc); information systems (M Sc); international management (M Sc); logistics (M Sc); management (M Sc, Diploma); management of cultural organizations (Diploma); marketing (M Sc); marketing communication (Diploma); modeling and decision making (M Sc); production and operations management (M Sc); public accountancy (Diploma); supply chain management (Diploma); taxation (LL M, Diploma). Most courses are given in French. *Application fee:* $40. *Application Contact:* Daniel Zizian, Acting Registrar, 514-340-6110, Fax: 514-340-5640, E-mail: registraire.info@hec.ca. *Director,* Dr. Jean-Marie Toulouse, 514-340-6110, Fax: 514-340-5640.

ÉCOLE POLYTECHNIQUE DE MONTRÉAL, Montréal, QC H3C 3A7, Canada

General Information Province-supported, coed, graduate-only institution. *Graduate housing:* Room and/or apartments available to single students; on-campus housing not available to married students. Housing application deadline: 2/1. *Research affiliation:* Energy Research Institute (Quebec), CRIM (computer sciences and engineering), Center for Research on Computation and its Applications (computer science), Center for InterUniversity Research and Analysis on Organization (organizations analysis), Centre Québécois de Valorisation des Biotechnologies (biotechnological process engineering), Metropolitan Gas (natural gas).

École Polytechnique de Montréal (continued)

GRADUATE UNITS

Graduate Programs *Degree program information:* Part-time and evening/weekend programs available. Offers advanced materials (M Eng, M Sc A, PhD); aerothermics (M Eng, M Sc A, PhD); applied mechanics (M Eng, M Sc A, PhD); automation (M Eng, M Sc A, PhD); chemical engineering (M Eng, M Sc A, PhD, DESS); chemical metallurgy (M Eng, M Sc A, PhD); computer science (M Eng, M Sc A, PhD); electrotechnology (M Eng, M Sc A, PhD); environmental engineering (M Eng, M Sc A, PhD); ergonomy (M Eng, M Sc A, DESS); geotechnical engineering (M Eng, M Sc A, PhD); hydraulics engineering (M Eng, M Sc A, PhD); mathematical method in CA engineering (M Eng, M Sc A, PhD); microelectronics (M Eng, M Sc A, PhD); microwave technology (M Eng, M Sc A, PhD); mining engineering and geological engineering (M Eng, M Sc A, PhD); operational research (M Eng, M Sc A, PhD); optical engineering (M Eng, M Sc A, PhD); physical metallurgy (M Eng, M Sc A, PhD); production (M Eng, M Sc A); solid-state physics and engineering (M Eng, M Sc A, PhD); structural engineering (M Eng, M Sc A, PhD); technology management (M Eng, M Sc A); tool design (M Eng, M Sc A, PhD); transportation engineering (M Eng, M Sc A, PhD).

Institute of Biomedical Engineering *Degree program information:* Part-time programs available. Offers biomedical engineering (M Eng, M Sc A, PhD, DESS).

Institute of Nuclear Engineering Offers nuclear engineering (M Eng, PhD); nuclear engineering, socio-economics of energy (M Sc A).

ECUMENICAL THEOLOGICAL SEMINARY, Detroit, MI 48201

General Information Independent-religious, coed, graduate-only institution. *Enrollment by degree level:* 90 first professional, 54 doctoral. *Graduate faculty:* 13. *Tuition:* Part-time $975 per course. *Required fees:* $10 per course. $45 per term. Part-time tuition and fees vary according to course load, degree level and program. *Graduate housing:* On-campus housing not available. *Library facilities:* Biesdorf Library plus 1 other. *Web address:* http://www.etseminary.org/.

General Application Contact: Beverly Schneider, Registrar, Admissions and Financial Aid, 313-831-5200 Ext. 203, Fax: 313-831-1353, E-mail: bschneider@etseminary.org.

GRADUATE UNITS

Professional Program Students: 109 full-time. *Faculty:* 10. Expenses: Contact institution. Offers theology (M Div). *Application deadline:* Applications are processed on a rolling basis. *Application fee:* $25. *Application Contact:* Beverly Schneider, Registrar, Admissions and Financial Aid, 313-831-5200 Ext. 203, Fax: 313-831-1353, E-mail: bschneider@etseminary.org. *Director*, Dr. Charles Mabee, 313-831-5200 Ext. 217, E-mail: cmabee@etseminary.org.

Program in Ministry Students: 54 full-time. *Faculty:* 10. Expenses: Contact institution. Offers ministry (D Min). *Application deadline:* Applications are processed on a rolling basis. *Application fee:* $25. *Application Contact:* Beverly Schneider, Registrar, Admissions and Financial Aid, 313-831-5200 Ext. 203, Fax: 313-831-1353, E-mail: bschneider@etseminary.org. *Director*, Dr. James Perkinson, 313-831-5200 Ext. 215, E-mail: jperkinson@etseminary.org.

EDEN THEOLOGICAL SEMINARY, St. Louis, MO 63119-3192

General Information Independent-religious, coed, graduate-only institution. *Enrollment by degree level:* 112 first professional, 18 master's, 40 doctoral. *Graduate faculty:* 12 full-time (5 women), 2 part-time/adjunct (0 women). *Tuition:* Full-time $7,260; part-time $220 per credit hour. *Required fees:* $225. *Graduate housing:* Rooms and/or apartments available on a first-come, first-served basis to single and married students. Typical cost: $3,255 per year for single students; $3,510 per year for married students. Housing application deadline: 7/30. *Student services:* Campus employment opportunities, child daycare facilities. *Library facilities:* Eden-Webster Library. *Online resources:* library catalog, web page, access to other libraries' catalogs. *Collection:* 260,000 titles, 1,360 serial subscriptions, 8,845 audiovisual materials.

Computer facilities: 2 computers available on campus for general student use. A campuswide network can be accessed from student residence rooms and from off campus. Internet access is available. *Web address:* http://www.eden.edu/.

General Application Contact: Rev. Diane Windler, Admissions Office, 314-918-2501, Fax: 314-918-2640, E-mail: dwindler@eden.edu.

GRADUATE UNITS

Graduate and Professional Programs Students: 163 full-time (87 women), 7 part-time (6 women); includes 25 minority (23 African Americans, 2 Hispanic Americans), 7 international. Average age 35. 71 applicants, 90% accepted. *Faculty:* 12 full-time (5 women), 2 part-time/adjunct (0 women). Expenses: Contact institution. *Financial support:* In 2001–02, 36 students received support. Career-related internships or fieldwork and scholarships/grants available. Financial award application deadline: 7/30; financial award applicants required to submit FAFSA. In 2001, 21 first professional degrees, 7 master's, 3 doctorates awarded. Offers theology (M Div, MAPS, MTS, D Min). *Application deadline:* For fall admission, 7/15; for spring admission, 12/1. Applications are processed on a rolling basis. *Application fee:* $25. *Application Contact:* Rev. Diane Windler, Admissions Office, 314-918-2501, Fax: 314-918-2640, E-mail: dwindler@eden.edu. *President*, Dr. David M. Greenhaw, 314-961-3627.

EDGEWOOD COLLEGE, Madison, WI 53711-1997

General Information Independent-religious, coed, comprehensive institution. *Enrollment:* 73 full-time matriculated graduate/professional students (55 women), 405 part-time matriculated graduate/professional students (246 women). *Enrollment by degree level:* 478 master's. *Graduate faculty:* 20 full-time (5 women), 24 part-time/adjunct (10 women). *Tuition:* Full-time $10,200; part-time $425 per credit. *Graduate housing:* On-campus housing not available. *Student services:* Career counseling, free psychological counseling, international student services, low-cost health insurance. *Library facilities:* Oscar Rennebohm Library. *Online resources:* library catalog, web page, access to other libraries' catalogs. *Collection:* 90,253 titles, 447 serial subscriptions, 4,359 audiovisual materials.

Computer facilities: 85 computers available on campus for general student use. A campuswide network can be accessed from student residence rooms and from off campus. Internet access is available. *Web address:* http://www.edgewood.edu/.

General Application Contact: Dr. Raymond Schultz, Associate Dean of Graduate Programs, 608-663-2377, Fax: 608-663-3291, E-mail: schultz@edgewood.edu.

GRADUATE UNITS

Program in Business Students: 32 full-time (23 women), 212 part-time (102 women); includes 17 minority (5 African Americans, 6 Asian Americans or Pacific Islanders, 6 Hispanic Americans), 13 international. Average age 33. *Faculty:* 11 full-time (2 women), 12 part-time/adjunct (4 women). Expenses: Contact institution. *Financial support:* Career-related internships or fieldwork available. In 2001, 58 degrees awarded. *Degree program information:* Part-time and evening/weekend programs available. Offers business (MBA). *Application deadline:* For fall admission, 8/1 (priority date); for spring admission, 1/10 (priority date). Applications are processed on a rolling basis. *Application fee:* $25. *Application Contact:* Paula O'Malley, Graduate Student Admissions Counselor, 608-663-2282, Fax: 608-663-3291, E-mail: gradprograms@edgewood.edu. *Chair*, Dr. Gary Schroeder, 608-663-3374, Fax: 608-663-3291, E-mail: gschroeder@edgewood.edu.

Program in Education Students: 25 full-time (19 women), 116 part-time (83 women); includes 5 minority (2 African Americans, 2 Hispanic Americans, 1 Native American), 1 international. Average age 36. *Faculty:* 6 full-time (1 woman), 5 part-time/adjunct (1 woman). Expenses: Contact institution. In 2001, 23 degrees awarded. *Degree program information:* Part-time and evening/weekend programs available. Offers director of instruction (Certificate); director of special education and pupil services (Certificate); education (MA Ed); educational administration (MA); emotional disturbances (MA, Certificate); learning disabilities (MA, Certificate); learning disabilities and emotional disturbances (MA, Certificate); school business administration (Certificate); school principalship K-12 (Certificate). *Application deadline:* For fall admission, 8/1 (priority date); for spring admission, 1/10 (priority date). Applications are processed on a rolling basis. *Application fee:* $25. *Application Contact:* Paula O'Malley, Graduate Student Admissions Counselor, 608-663-2282, Fax: 608-663-3291, E-mail: gradprograms@edgewood.edu. *Chair*, Dr. Joseph Schmiedicke, 608-663-2293, Fax: 608-663-3291, E-mail: schmied@edgewood.edu.

Program in Marriage and Family Therapy Students: 14 full-time (12 women), 15 part-time (13 women); includes 3 minority (1 African American, 2 Asian Americans or Pacific Islanders) Average age 32. *Faculty:* 2 full-time (1 woman), 6 part-time/adjunct (4 women). Expenses: Contact institution. In 2001, 9 degrees awarded. *Degree program information:* Part-time and evening/weekend programs available. Offers marriage and family therapy (MS). *Application deadline:* For fall admission, 3/1. *Application fee:* $25. *Application Contact:* Paula O'Malley, Graduate Student Admissions Counselor, 608-663-2282, Fax: 608-663-3291, E-mail: gradprograms@edgewood.edu. *Director*, Dr. Peter Fabian, 608-663-2233, Fax: 608-663-3291, E-mail: fabian@edgewood.edu.

Program in Nursing Average age 41. *Faculty:* 1 (woman) full-time, 1 (woman) part-time/adjunct. Expenses: Contact institution. In 2001, 2 degrees awarded. Offers nursing (MS). *Application deadline:* For fall admission, 8/1 (priority date); for spring admission, 1/10 (priority date). Applications are processed on a rolling basis. *Application fee:* $25. *Application Contact:* Paula O'Malley, Graduate Student Admissions Counselor, 608-663-2282, Fax: 608-663-3291, E-mail: gradprograms@edgewood.edu. *Chair*, Dr. Mary Kelly-Powell, 608-663-2292, Fax: 608-663-3291, E-mail: mkellypowell@edgewood.edu.

Program in Religious Studies Average age 48. *Faculty:* 3 full-time (2 women). Expenses: Contact institution. *Financial support:* Career-related internships or fieldwork, institutionally sponsored loans, scholarships/grants, and tuition waivers (partial) available. Support available to part-time students. In 2001, 3 degrees awarded. *Degree program information:* Part-time and evening/weekend programs available. Offers religious studies (MA). *Application deadline:* For fall admission, 8/1 (priority date); for spring admission, 1/10 (priority date). Applications are processed on a rolling basis. *Application fee:* $25. *Application Contact:* Paula O'Malley, Graduate Student Admissions Counselor, 608-663-2282, Fax: 608-663-3291, E-mail: gradprograms@edgewood.edu. *Chairperson*, Dr. Barbara B. Miller, 608-663-2824, Fax: 608-663-3291, E-mail: bmiller@edgewood.edu.

EDINBORO UNIVERSITY OF PENNSYLVANIA, Edinboro, PA 16444

General Information State-supported, coed, comprehensive institution. *Enrollment:* 355 full-time matriculated graduate/professional students (262 women), 420 part-time matriculated graduate/professional students (280 women). *Enrollment by degree level:* 616 master's, 159 other advanced degrees. *Graduate faculty:* 70 full-time (39 women), 6 part-time/adjunct (3 women). Tuition, state resident: full-time $4,600; part-time $256 per credit. Tuition, nonresident: full-time $7,554; part-time $420 per credit. *Required fees:* $68 per credit. *Graduate housing:* Room and/or apartments available on a first-come, first-served basis to single students; on-campus housing not available to married students. Typical cost: $2,520 per year ($4,384 including board). Room and board charges vary according to board plan. Housing application deadline: 7/1. *Student services:* Campus employment opportunities, campus safety program, career counseling, child daycare facilities, disabled student services, exercise/wellness program, free psychological counseling, international student services, low-cost health insurance, multicultural affairs office, teacher training. *Library facilities:* Baron-Forness Library plus 1 other. *Online resources:* library catalog, web page, access to other libraries' catalogs. *Collection:* 468,977 titles, 1,829 serial subscriptions, 12,796 audiovisual materials.

Computer facilities: 700 computers available on campus for general student use. A campuswide network can be accessed from student residence rooms and from off campus. Internet access and online class registration, e-mail are available. *Web address:* http://www.edinboro.edu/.

General Application Contact: Dr. Mary Margaret Bevevino, Dean of Graduate Studies, 814-732-2856, Fax: 814-732-2611, E-mail: mbevevino@edinboro.edu.

GRADUATE UNITS

Graduate Studies Students: 355 full-time (262 women), 420 part-time (280 women); includes 29 minority (22 African Americans, 3 Asian Americans or Pacific Islanders, 3 Hispanic Americans, 1 Native American), 13 international. Average age 31. 324 applicants, 81% accepted, 174 enrolled. *Faculty:* 70 full-time (39 women), 6 part-time/adjunct (3 women). Expenses: Contact institution. *Financial support:* In 2001–02, 136 students received support, including 136 research assistantships with full and partial tuition reimbursements available (averaging $3,150 per year); career-related internships or fieldwork, Federal Work-Study, institutionally sponsored loans, scholarships/grants, and unspecified assistantships also available. Support available to part-time students. Financial award application deadline: 5/1; financial award applicants required to submit FAFSA. In 2001, 146 degrees awarded. *Degree program information:* Part-time and evening/weekend programs available. Certificate issued by State Agency: Elementary Guidance, Secondary School Guidance, Elementary School Administration, Secondary School Administration, Reading Specialist, School Psychology, School Supervision (Art Communication, Elementary Education, Mathematics, Science, Social Studies, Special Education. *Application deadline:* Applications are processed on a rolling basis. *Application fee:* $25. Electronic applications accepted. *Dean of Graduate Studies*, Dr. Mary Margaret Bevevino, 814-732-2856, Fax: 814-732-2611, E-mail: mbevevino@edinboro.edu.

School of Education Students: 185 full-time (133 women), 332 part-time (228 women); includes 23 minority (18 African Americans, 2 Asian Americans or Pacific Islanders, 3 Hispanic Americans), 4 international. Average age 31. *Faculty:* 31 full-time (20 women), 3 part-time/adjunct (1 woman). Expenses: Contact institution. *Financial support:* In 2001–02, 68 students received support, including research assistantships with full and partial tuition reimbursements available (averaging $3,150 per year); career-related internships or fieldwork, Federal Work-Study, institutionally sponsored loans, scholarships/grants, and unspecified assistantships also available. Support available to part-time students. Financial award application deadline: 5/1; financial award applicants required to submit FAFSA. In 2001, 109 degrees awarded. *Degree program information:* Part-time and evening/weekend programs available. Offers behavior management (Certificate); counseling (MA, Certificate); early childhood (M Ed); education (M Ed, MA, Certificate); educational psychology (M Ed); elementary education (M Ed); elementary education clinical (M Ed); elementary school administration (M Ed, Certificate); health and physical education (Certificate); language arts (M Ed); mathematics (M Ed); middle and secondary instruction (M Ed); reading (M Ed, Certificate); reading specialist (Certificate); school administration (M Ed, Certificate); school psychology (Certificate); science (M Ed); secondary school administration (M Ed, Certificate); social studies (M Ed); special education (M Ed). *Application deadline:* Applications are processed on a rolling basis. *Application fee:* $25. Electronic applications accepted. *Application Contact:* Dr. Mary Margaret Bevevino, Dean of Graduate Studies, 814-732-2856, Fax: 814-732-2611, E-mail: mbevevino@edinboro.edu. *Dean of Education*, Dr. R. Scott Baldwin, 814-732-2752, Fax: 814-732-2268, E-mail: sbaldwin@edinboro.edu.

School of Liberal Arts Students: 115 full-time (96 women), 46 part-time (28 women); includes 3 minority (2 African Americans, 1 Asian American or Pacific Islander), 8 international. Average age 29. *Faculty:* 29 full-time (14 women), 3 part-time/adjunct (2 women). Expenses: Contact institution. *Financial support:* In 2001–02, 62 students received support. Career-related internships or fieldwork, Federal Work-Study, institutionally sponsored loans, scholarships/grants, and unspecified assistantships available. Support available to part-time students. Financial award application deadline: 5/1; financial award applicants required to submit FAFSA. In 2001, 22 degrees awarded. *Degree program information:* Part-time and evening/weekend programs available. Offers art (MA); ceramics (MFA); clinical psychology (MA); communication studies (MA); jewelry (MFA); liberal arts (MA, MFA, MSW); painting (MFA); printmaking (MFA); sculpture (MFA); social sciences (MA); social work (MSW); speech-language pathology (MA). *Application deadline:* Applications are processed on a rolling basis. *Application fee:* $25. Electronic applications accepted. *Application Contact:* Dr. Mary Margaret Bevevino, Dean of Graduate Studies, 814-732-2856, Fax: 814-732-2611, E-mail: mbevevino@edinboro.edu. *Dean of Liberal Arts*, Dr. Terry L. Smith, 814-732-2477, Fax: 814-732-2629, E-mail: tlsmith@edinboro.edu.

School of Science, Management and Technology Students: 13 full-time (6 women), 24 part-time (12 women); includes 1 minority (Native American), 2 international. Average age 33. *Faculty:* 10 full-time (5 women). Expenses: Contact institution. *Financial support:* In

2001–02, 5 students received support. Career-related internships or fieldwork, Federal Work-Study, institutionally sponsored loans, scholarships/grants, and unspecified assistantships available. Support available to part-time students. Financial award application deadline: 5/1; financial award applicants required to submit FAFSA. In 2001, 15 degrees awarded. *Degree program information:* Part-time and evening/weekend programs available. Offers biology (MS); family nurse practitioner (MSN); information technology (Certificate); mathematics and computer science (Certificate); public accounting (Certificate); science, management and technology (MS, MSN, Certificate). *Application deadline:* Applications are processed on a rolling basis. *Application fee:* $25. Electronic applications accepted. *Application Contact:* Dr. Mary Margaret Bevevino, Dean of Graduate Studies, 814-732-2856, Fax: 814-732-2611, E-mail: mbevevino@edinboro.edu. *Dean,* Dr. Eric Randall, 814-732-2400, Fax: 814-732-2422, E-mail: erandall@edinboro.edu.

ELIZABETH CITY STATE UNIVERSITY, Elizabeth City, NC 27909-7806

General Information State-supported, coed, comprehensive institution.

GRADUATE UNITS

Program in Elementary Education

ELMHURST COLLEGE, Elmhurst, IL 60126-3296

General Information Independent-religious, coed, comprehensive institution. *Enrollment:* 130 part-time matriculated graduate/professional students (59 women). *Enrollment by degree level:* 130 master's. *Graduate faculty:* 9 full-time (6 women), 5 part-time/adjunct (4 women). *Tuition:* Part-time $555 per hour. *Graduate housing:* Room and/or apartments available to single students. *Student services:* Campus employment opportunities, campus safety program, career counseling, child daycare facilities, disabled student services, exercise/wellness program, free psychological counseling, international student services, low-cost health insurance, multicultural affairs office, writing training. *Library facilities:* Buehler Library. *Online resources:* library catalog, web page, access to other libraries' catalogs. *Collection:* 211,151 titles, 2,000 serial subscriptions, 6,531 audiovisual materials.

Computer facilities: 345 computers available on campus for general student use. A campuswide network can be accessed from student residence rooms and from off campus. *Web address:* http://www.elmhurst.edu/.

General Application Contact: Elizabeth D. Kuebler, Director of Graduate Admission, 630-617-3069, Fax: 630-617-5501, E-mail: gradadm@elmhurst.edu.

GRADUATE UNITS

Graduate Programs Average age 32. 169 applicants, 71% accepted, 83 enrolled. *Faculty:* 9 full-time (6 women), 5 part-time/adjunct (4 women). Expenses: Contact institution. *Financial support:* In 2001–02, 21 students received support. Federal Work-Study and scholarships/grants available. Support available to part-time students. Financial award application deadline: 6/1; financial award applicants required to submit FAFSA. In 2001, 54 degrees awarded. *Degree program information:* Part-time and evening/weekend programs available. Offers computer network systems (MS); early childhood special education (M Ed); industrial/organizational psychology (MA); professional accountancy (MPA); professional writing (MA); supply chain management (MS). *Application deadline:* For fall admission, 4/1 (priority date). Applications are processed on a rolling basis. *Application fee:* $25. *Director of Graduate Admission,* Elizabeth D. Kuebler, 630-617-3069, Fax: 630-617-5501, E-mail: gradadm@elmhurst.edu.

ELMS COLLEGE, Chicopee, MA 01013-2839

General Information Independent-religious, coed, primarily women, comprehensive institution. *Enrollment:* 23 full-time matriculated graduate/professional students (19 women), 65 part-time matriculated graduate/professional students (58 women). *Enrollment by degree level:* 78 master's, 10 other advanced degrees. *Graduate faculty:* 21 full-time (13 women), 11 part-time/adjunct (6 women). *Tuition:* Full-time $6,660; part-time $370 per credit. *Required fees:* $40; $20 per term. *Graduate housing:* Room and/or apartments guaranteed to single students; on-campus housing not available to married students. Typical cost: $5,900 (including board). Housing application deadline: 8/15. *Student services:* Career counseling, low-cost health insurance. *Library facilities:* Alumnae Library. *Online resources:* library catalog. *Collection:* 116,889 titles, 503 serial subscriptions, 10,286 audiovisual materials.

Computer facilities: 76 computers available on campus for general student use. A campuswide network can be accessed from student residence rooms and from off campus. Internet access is available. *Web address:* http://www.elms.edu/.

General Application Contact: Joseph Wagner, Director of Admission Office, 413-594-2761 Ext. 238, Fax: 413-594-2781, E-mail: crowleym@elms.edu.

GRADUATE UNITS

Division of Education Students: 20 full-time (18 women), 57 part-time (52 women); includes 2 minority (1 African American, 1 Hispanic American) Average age 36. 43 applicants, 98% accepted, 31 enrolled. *Faculty:* 9 full-time (6 women), 4 part-time/adjunct (2 women). Expenses: Contact institution. *Financial support:* In 2001–02, 10 teaching assistantships with partial tuition reimbursements were awarded; tuition waivers (partial) also available. Support available to part-time students. Financial award applicants required to submit FAFSA. In 2001, 42 master's, 2 other advanced degrees awarded. *Degree program information:* Part-time and evening/weekend programs available. Offers early childhood education (MAT); education (M Ed, CAGS); elementary education (MAT); English as a second language (MAT); reading (MAT); secondary education (MAT); special education (MAT). *Application deadline:* Applications are processed on a rolling basis. *Application fee:* $30. *Director,* Dr. Mary Janeczek, 413-594-2761 Ext. 291, Fax: 413-592-4871, E-mail: janeczekm@elms.edu.

Program in Liberal Arts Students: 2 full-time (0 women), 6 part-time (4 women). Average age 35. 8 applicants, 100% accepted. *Faculty:* 7 full-time (3 women), 3 part-time/adjunct (1 woman). Expenses: Contact institution. *Financial support:* Teaching assistantships with partial tuition reimbursements, unspecified assistantships available. Support available to part-time students. Financial award applicants required to submit FAFSA. In 2001, 2 degrees awarded. *Degree program information:* Part-time and evening/weekend programs available. Offers liberal arts (MALA). *Application deadline:* Applications are processed on a rolling basis. *Application fee:* $30. *Director of MALA/MAAT Programs,* Dr. Martin Pion, 413-594-2761 Ext. 389, Fax: 413-594-3951, E-mail: pionm@elms.edu.

Religious Studies Department Students: 1 (woman) full-time, 7 part-time (6 women). Average age 49. 2 applicants, 100% accepted. *Faculty:* 2 full-time (1 woman), 2 part-time/adjunct (0 women). Expenses: Contact institution. *Financial support:* Tuition waivers (partial) available. Financial award applicants required to submit FAFSA. In 2001, 6 degrees awarded. *Degree program information:* Part-time and evening/weekend programs available. Offers religious studies (MAAT). *Application deadline:* Applications are processed on a rolling basis. *Application fee:* $30. *Director of MALA/MAAT Programs,* Dr. Martin Pion, 413-594-2761 Ext. 389, Fax: 413-594-3951, E-mail: pionm@elms.edu.

ELON UNIVERSITY, Elon, NC 27244-2010

General Information Independent-religious, coed, comprehensive institution. *Enrollment:* 85 full-time matriculated graduate/professional students (53 women), 96 part-time matriculated graduate/professional students (53 women). *Enrollment by degree level:* 181 master's. *Graduate faculty:* 40 full-time (19 women), 9 part-time/adjunct (6 women). *Tuition:* Part-time $253 per credit. Tuition and fees vary according to program. *Graduate housing:* On-campus housing not available. *Student services:* Campus employment opportunities, campus safety program, career counseling, disabled student services, exercise/wellness program, free psychological counseling, international student services, low-cost health insurance, multicultural affairs office, teacher training, writing training. *Library facilities:* Carol Grotnes Belk. *Online resources:* library catalog, web page, access to other libraries' catalogs. *Collection:* 145,056 titles, 4,858 serial subscriptions, 8,164 audiovisual materials.

Computer facilities: 500 computers available on campus for general student use. A campuswide network can be accessed from student residence rooms and from off campus. Internet access, e-mail are available. *Web address:* http://www.elon.edu/.

General Application Contact: Art Fadde, Director of Graduate Admissions, 800-334-8448, Fax: 336-278-7699, E-mail: afadde@elon.edu.

GRADUATE UNITS

Program in Business Administration Students: 13 full-time (5 women), 68 part-time (25 women); includes 7 minority (5 African Americans, 1 Hispanic American, 1 Native American), 3 international. Average age 34. 37 applicants, 76% accepted, 26 enrolled. *Faculty:* 22 full-time (6 women), 3 part-time/adjunct (2 women). Expenses: Contact institution. *Financial support:* In 2001–02, 8 students received support. Federal Work-Study available. Support available to part-time students. Financial award application deadline: 8/1; financial award applicants required to submit FAFSA. In 2001, 49 degrees awarded. *Degree program information:* Part-time and evening/weekend programs available. Offers business administration (MBA). *Application deadline:* For fall admission, 8/1 (priority date); for spring admission, 1/5 (priority date). Applications are processed on a rolling basis. *Application fee:* $35. Electronic applications accepted. *Application Contact:* Art Fadde, Director of Graduate Admissions, 800-334-8448, Fax: 336-278-7699, E-mail: afadde@elon.edu. *Chair,* Dr. Kevin J. O'Mara, 336-278-6000, Fax: 336-278-5952, E-mail: omarak@elon.edu.

Program in Education Students: 2 full-time (1 woman), 28 part-time (all women); includes 4 minority (3 African Americans, 1 Hispanic American) Average age 32. 18 applicants, 83% accepted, 9 enrolled. *Faculty:* 10 full-time (9 women), 2 part-time/adjunct (1 woman). Expenses: Contact institution. *Financial support:* In 2001–02, 7 students received support. Available to part-time students. Application deadline: 8/1; In 2001, 24 degrees awarded. *Degree program information:* Part-time and evening/weekend programs available. Offers elementary education (M Ed); special education (M Ed). *Application deadline:* For fall admission, 8/15 (priority date); for spring admission, 1/15 (priority date). Applications are processed on a rolling basis. *Application fee:* $35. Electronic applications accepted. *Application Contact:* Art Fadde, Director of Graduate Admissions, 800-334-8448, Fax: 336-278-7699, E-mail: afadde@elon.edu. *Director,* Dr. Judith B. Howard, 336-278-5889, Fax: 336-278-5919, E-mail: howardj@elon.edu.

Program in Physical Therapy Students: 70 full-time (47 women); includes 11 minority (7 African Americans, 1 Asian American or Pacific Islander, 3 Hispanic Americans), 1 international. Average age 26. 57 applicants, 60% accepted, 25 enrolled. *Faculty:* 8 full-time (4 women), 4 part-time/adjunct (all women). Expenses: Contact institution. *Financial support:* Application deadline: 10/1; Offers physical therapy (DPT). *Application deadline:* Applications are processed on a rolling basis. *Application fee:* $50. Electronic applications accepted. *Application Contact:* Art Fadde, Director of Graduate Admissions, 800-334-8448, Fax: 336-278-7699, E-mail: afadde@elon.edu. *Director,* Dr. Elizabeth A. Rogers, 336-278-6400, Fax: 336-278-6414, E-mail: rogers@elon.edu.

EMBRY-RIDDLE AERONAUTICAL UNIVERSITY, Prescott, AZ 86301-3720

General Information Independent, coed, primarily men, comprehensive institution.

GRADUATE UNITS

Program in Safety Science

EMBRY-RIDDLE AERONAUTICAL UNIVERSITY, Daytona Beach, FL 32114-3900

General Information Independent, coed, primarily men, comprehensive institution. *Enrollment:* 120 full-time matriculated graduate/professional students (27 women), 171 part-time matriculated graduate/professional students (54 women). *Enrollment by degree level:* 291 master's. *Graduate faculty:* 42 full-time (6 women), 4 part-time/adjunct (1 woman). *Tuition:* Full-time $13,140; part-time $730 per credit. *Required fees:* $250; $250 per year. $125 per semester. Tuition and fees vary according to program. *Graduate housing:* Rooms and/or apartments available on a first-come, first-served basis to single and married students. Typical cost: $3,050 per year ($5,480 including board) for single students; $3,050 per year ($5,480 including board) for married students. Room and board charges vary according to board plan and housing facility selected. Housing application deadline: 6/30. *Student services:* Campus employment opportunities, campus safety program, career counseling, disabled student services, free psychological counseling, international student services, low-cost health insurance. *Library facilities:* Jack R. Hunt Memorial Library. *Online resources:* library catalog, web page. *Collection:* 66,557 titles, 1,504 serial subscriptions, 6,484 audiovisual materials. *Research affiliation:* Boeing (future mission concepts), Universal Systems and Technology (airport capacities), Command and Control Technology (air traffic management), National Aviation and Research Institute (air traffic management), Society of Manufacturing Engineering (aircraft manufacturing training), Honeywell International (aviation weather information network project).

Computer facilities: A campuswide network can be accessed from student residence rooms and from off campus. *Web address:* http://www.embryriddle.edu/.

General Application Contact: Christine Castetter, Graduate Admissions, 800-388-3728, Fax: 386-226-7111, E-mail: gradmit@erau.edu.

GRADUATE UNITS

Daytona Beach Campus Graduate Program Students: 120 full-time (27 women), 171 part-time (54 women); includes 33 minority (21 African Americans, 6 Asian Americans or Pacific Islanders, 5 Hispanic Americans, 1 Native American), 132 international. Average age 28. 214 applicants, 50% accepted, 64 enrolled. *Faculty:* 42 full-time (6 women), 4 part-time/adjunct (1 woman). Expenses: Contact institution. *Financial support:* In 2001–02, 127 students received support, including 3 fellowships with partial tuition reimbursements available (averaging $15,744 per year), 38 research assistantships with partial tuition reimbursements available (averaging $8,100 per year), 24 teaching assistantships with partial tuition reimbursements available (averaging $8,100 per year); career-related internships or fieldwork, Federal Work-Study, and unspecified assistantships also available. Support available to part-time students. Financial award application deadline: 4/15; financial award applicants required to submit FAFSA. In 2001, 97 degrees awarded. *Degree program information:* Part-time and evening/weekend programs available. Offers aeronautical science (MAS); aeronautics (MAS, MBAA, MSAE, MSE, MSHFS, MSSS); aerospace engineering (MSAE); business administration in aviation (MBAA); human factors engineering (MSHFS); software engineering (MSE); systems engineering (MSHFS). *Application deadline:* For fall admission, 8/1 (priority date); for spring admission, 12/1 (priority date). Applications are processed on a rolling basis. *Application fee:* $30 ($50 for international students). Electronic applications accepted. *Application Contact:* Christine Castetter, Graduate Admissions, 800-388-3728, Fax: 386-226-7111, E-mail: gradmit@erau.edu. *Dean of Student Academics,* Dr. John Watret, 386-226-4943, Fax: 386-226-7111, E-mail: watretj@erau.edu.

Department of Physical Sciences Offers space science (MS).

EMBRY-RIDDLE AERONAUTICAL UNIVERSITY, EXTENDED CAMPUS, Daytona Beach, FL 32114-3900

General Information Independent, coed, primarily men, comprehensive institution. *Enrollment:* 73 full-time matriculated graduate/professional students (17 women), 2,230 part-time matriculated graduate/professional students (358 women). *Enrollment by degree level:* 2,303 master's. *Graduate faculty:* 73 full-time (5 women), 339 part-time/adjunct (29 women). *Tuition:* Full-time $5,880; part-time $245 per credit. *Graduate housing:* On-campus housing not available. *Student services:* Career counseling, international student services. *Library facilities:* Jack R. Hunt Memorial Library. *Online resources:* library catalog, web page. *Collection:* 66,557 titles, 1,504 serial subscriptions, 6,484 audiovisual materials. *Web address:* http://www.embryriddle.edu/.

General Application Contact: Pam Thomas, Director of Admissions and Records, 386-226-6910, Fax: 386-226-6984, E-mail: ecinfo@erau.edu.

Embry-Riddle Aeronautical University, Extended Campus (continued)

GRADUATE UNITS

Graduate Resident Centers Students: 73 full-time (17 women), 2,230 part-time (358 women); includes 342 minority (148 African Americans, 61 Asian Americans or Pacific Islanders, 108 Hispanic Americans, 25 Native Americans), 47 international. Average age 36. 611 applicants, 92% accepted, 288 enrolled. *Faculty:* 73 full-time (5 women), 339 part-time/adjunct (29 women). Expenses: Contact institution. *Financial support:* In 2001–02, 57 students received support. Available to part-time students. Applicants required to submit FAFSA. In 2001, 1044 degrees awarded. *Degree program information:* Part-time and evening/weekend programs available. Postbaccalaureate distance learning degree programs offered (minimal on-campus study). Offers aeronautical science (MAS); aviation administration and management (MBAA); technical management (MSTM). *Application deadline:* Applications are processed on a rolling basis. *Application fee:* $30 ($50 for international students). Electronic applications accepted. *Application Contact:* Pam Thomas, Director of Admissions and Records, 386-226-6910, Fax: 386-226-6984, E-mail: ecinfo@erau.edu. *Chancellor,* Dr. Leon E. Flancher, 386-226-6961, Fax: 386-226-6949, E-mail: flancher@erau.edu.

EMERSON COLLEGE, Boston, MA 02116-4624

General Information Independent, coed, comprehensive institution. CGS member. *Enrollment:* 713 full-time matriculated graduate/professional students (559 women), 214 part-time matriculated graduate/professional students (147 women). *Enrollment by degree level:* 927 master's. *Graduate faculty:* 124 full-time, 232 part-time/adjunct. *Tuition:* Part-time $632 per credit. *Graduate housing:* On-campus housing not available. *Student services:* Campus employment opportunities, campus safety program, career counseling, disabled student services, exercise/wellness program, free psychological counseling, international student services, low-cost health insurance, multicultural affairs office, teacher training, writing training. *Library facilities:* Emerson Library plus 1 other. *Online resources:* library catalog, web page, access to other libraries' catalogs. *Collection:* 193,000 titles, 7,430 serial subscriptions, 8,579 audiovisual materials. *Research affiliation:* Children's Hospital Medical Center, Eunice Kennedy Shriver Center.

Computer facilities: 265 computers available on campus for general student use. A campuswide network can be accessed from student residence rooms and from off campus. Internet access and online class registration are available. *Web address:* http://www.emerson.edu/.

General Application Contact: Lynn Terrell, Director of Graduate Admission, 617-824-8610, Fax: 617-824-8614, E-mail: gradapp@emerson.edu.

GRADUATE UNITS

Graduate Studies Students: 713 full-time (559 women), 214 part-time (147 women); includes 76 minority (31 African Americans, 24 Asian Americans or Pacific Islanders, 19 Hispanic Americans, 2 Native Americans), 156 international. Average age 27. 1,340 applicants, 68% accepted. *Faculty:* 124 full-time, 232 part-time/adjunct. Expenses: Contact institution. *Financial support:* Fellowships with partial tuition reimbursements, research assistantships with partial tuition reimbursements, teaching assistantships with partial tuition reimbursements, career-related internships or fieldwork, Federal Work-Study, institutionally sponsored loans, scholarships/grants, and unspecified assistantships available. Support available to part-time students. Financial award application deadline: 2/1; financial award applicants required to submit FAFSA. *Degree program information:* Part-time and evening/weekend programs available. *Application deadline:* For fall admission, 2/1; for spring admission, 11/1. *Application fee:* $55 ($75 for international students). Electronic applications accepted. *Application Contact:* Lynn Terrell, Director of Graduate Admissions, 617-824-8608, Fax: 617-824-8614, E-mail: lynn_terrell@emerson.edu. *Dean,* Donna Schroth, 617-824-8612.

School of Communication Average age 26. 727 applicants, 78% accepted. Expenses: Contact institution. *Financial support:* Fellowships with partial tuition reimbursements, research assistantships with partial tuition reimbursements, teaching assistantships with partial tuition reimbursements, career-related internships or fieldwork, Federal Work-Study, institutionally sponsored loans, scholarships/grants, and unspecified assistantships available. Support available to part-time students. Financial award application deadline: 2/1; financial award applicants required to submit FAFSA. Offers broadcast journalism (MA); communication (MA, MS); communication sciences and disorders (MS); global marketing communication and advertising (MA); health communication (MA); integrated journalism (MA); integrated marketing communication (MA); management and organizational communication (MA); political communication (MA); print/multimedia journalism (MA); print/multimedia journalism, broadcast journalism, integrated journalism (MA); speech-language pathology (MS). *Application deadline:* For fall admission, 2/1 (priority date); for spring admission, 11/1 (priority date). *Application fee:* $55 ($75 for international students). Electronic applications accepted. *Application Contact:* Lynn Terrell, Director of Graduate Admissions, 617-824-8608, Fax: 617-824-8614, E-mail: lynn_terrell@emerson.edu. *Dean,* Dr. Stuart J. Sigman, 617-824-8354.

School of the Arts 613 applicants, 56% accepted. Expenses: Contact institution. *Financial support:* Fellowships with partial tuition reimbursements, research assistantships with partial tuition reimbursements, teaching assistantships with partial tuition reimbursements, career-related internships or fieldwork, Federal Work-Study, institutionally sponsored loans, scholarships/grants, and unspecified assistantships available. Support available to part-time students. Financial award application deadline: 2/1; financial award applicants required to submit FAFSA. *Degree program information:* Part-time programs available. Offers arts (MA, MFA); audio production (MA); audio, television/video, and new media production (MA); creative writing (MFA); new media production (MA); publishing and writing (MA); television/video production (MA); theatre education (MA). *Application deadline:* For fall admission, 2/1; for spring admission, 11/1 (priority date). *Application fee:* $55 ($75 for international students). Electronic applications accepted. *Application Contact:* Lynn Terrell, Director of Graduate Admissions, 617-824-8608, Fax: 617-824-8614, E-mail: lynn_terrell@emerson.edu. *Dean,* Grafton J. Nunes, 617-824-8983.

See in-depth description on page 865.

EMMANUEL COLLEGE, Boston, MA 02115

General Information Independent-religious, coed, comprehensive institution. *Enrollment:* 650 part-time matriculated graduate/professional students. *Graduate faculty:* 4 full-time, 150 part-time/adjunct. *Tuition:* Part-time $1,395 per course. *Graduate housing:* On-campus housing not available. *Student services:* Campus safety program, career counseling, free psychological counseling, international student services, low-cost health insurance, teacher training. *Library facilities:* Cardinal Cushing Library. *Online resources:* library catalog, web page, access to other libraries' catalogs. *Collection:* 98,513 titles, 876 serial subscriptions, 515 audiovisual materials.

Computer facilities: 115 computers available on campus for general student use. A campuswide network can be accessed from student residence rooms. Internet access, software applications are available. *Web address:* http://www.emmanuel.edu/.

General Application Contact: Suzanne Sergi, Graduate and Professional Programs, 617-735-9802, Fax: 617-735-9708, E-mail: sergis@emmanuel.edu.

GRADUATE UNITS

Graduate Programs *Degree program information:* Part-time and evening/weekend programs available. Offers elementary education (MAT); human resource management (MA); management (MSM); multi-cultural education (MAT); school administration (M Ed); secondary education (MAT). Electronic applications accepted.

EMMANUEL SCHOOL OF RELIGION, Johnson City, TN 37601-9438

General Information Independent-religious, coed, primarily men, graduate-only institution. *Graduate faculty:* 12 full-time (1 woman), 1 part-time/adjunct (0 women). *Tuition:* Part-time $240 per hour. *Required fees:* $75 per term. *Graduate housing:* Rooms and/or apartments available on a first-come, first-served basis to single and married students. Housing application deadline: 8/1. *Student services:* Campus employment opportunities, career counseling, low-cost health insurance. *Library facilities:* Main library plus 1 other. *Online resources:* library catalog. *Collection:* 127,000 titles, 733 serial subscriptions. *Research affiliation:* Disciples of Christ Historical Society, American Schools of Oriental Research (ancient Near East).

Computer facilities: 20 computers available on campus for general student use. A campuswide network can be accessed from off campus. Internet access is available.

General Application Contact: David Fulks, Director of Admissions, 423-461-1536, Fax: 423-926-6198, E-mail: fulks@emmanuel.johnson-city.tn.us.

GRADUATE UNITS

Graduate and Professional Programs Students: 97 full-time (30 women), 59 part-time (9 women). Average age 32. 50 applicants, 94% accepted. *Faculty:* 12 full-time (1 woman), 1 part-time/adjunct (0 women). Expenses: Contact institution. *Financial support:* In 2001–02, 100 students received support, including 1 teaching assistantship (averaging $3,600 per year); career-related internships or fieldwork, Federal Work-Study, institutionally sponsored loans, scholarships/grants, and tuition waivers (partial) also available. Support available to part-time students. Financial award application deadline: 4/1. In 2001, 14 first professional degrees, 6 master's, 2 doctorates awarded. *Degree program information:* Part-time programs available. Offers religion (M Div, MAR, D Min). *Application deadline:* For fall admission, 8/1 (priority date). Applications are processed on a rolling basis. *Application fee:* $25. *Application Contact:* David Fulks, Director of Admissions, 423-461-1536, Fax: 423-926-6198, E-mail: fulks@emmanuel.johnson-city.tn.us. *Dean and Registrar,* Dr. Eleanor A. Daniel, 423-461-1521, Fax: 423-926-6198, E-mail: daniele@esr.edu.

EMORY & HENRY COLLEGE, Emory, VA 24327-0947

General Information Independent-religious, coed, comprehensive institution. *Enrollment:* 18 part-time matriculated graduate/professional students (all women). *Enrollment by degree level:* 18 master's. *Graduate faculty:* 4 part-time/adjunct (1 woman). *Tuition:* Part-time $215 per hour. *Required fees:* $10 per hour. *Student services:* Campus employment opportunities, teacher training. *Library facilities:* Kelly Library. *Online resources:* library catalog, web page, access to other libraries' catalogs. *Collection:* 176,450 titles, 5,129 serial subscriptions, 6,169 audiovisual materials.

Computer facilities: 121 computers available on campus for general student use. A campuswide network can be accessed from student residence rooms and from off campus. Internet access is available. *Web address:* http://www.ehc.edu/.

General Application Contact: Dr. Jack Roper, Director of Graduate Studies, 276-944-6188, Fax: 276-944-5223.

GRADUATE UNITS

Graduate Programs Average age 26. 18 applicants. *Faculty:* 4 part-time/adjunct (1 woman). Expenses: Contact institution. In 2001, 7 degrees awarded. *Degree program information:* Part-time programs available. *Application fee:* $25. *Director of Graduate Studies,* Dr. Jack Roper, 276-944-6188, Fax: 276-944-5223.

EMORY UNIVERSITY, Atlanta, GA 30322-1100

General Information Independent-religious, coed, university. CGS member. *Enrollment:* 4,334 full-time matriculated graduate/professional students (2,402 women), 735 part-time matriculated graduate/professional students (470 women). *Enrollment by degree level:* 1,601 first professional, 3,468 doctoral. *Graduate faculty:* 2,252 full-time, 531 part-time/adjunct. *Tuition:* Full-time $24,770. *Required fees:* $100. Tuition and fees vary according to program and student level. *Graduate housing:* Rooms and/or apartments available on a first-come, first-served basis to single and married students. Typical cost: $6,984 per year for single students; $10,560 per year for married students. Room charges vary according to housing facility selected. *Student services:* Career counseling, free psychological counseling, low-cost health insurance. *Library facilities:* Robert W. Woodruff Library plus 7 others. *Online resources:* library catalog, web page, access to other libraries' catalogs. *Collection:* 2.3 million titles, 24,687 serial subscriptions. *Research affiliation:* Highlands Biological Station, Centers for Disease Control, Georgia Mental Health Institute, Oak Ridge Associated Universities (energy, health and environment), Emory and Georgia Technical Biomedical Research Center, Georgia Research Consortium.

Computer facilities: 600 computers available on campus for general student use. A campuswide network can be accessed from student residence rooms and from off campus. Internet access and online class registration are available. *Web address:* http://www.emory.edu/.

General Application Contact: Kharen Fulton, Director of Admissions, 404-727-0184, Fax: 404-727-4990, E-mail: gradkef@emory.edu.

GRADUATE UNITS

Candler School of Theology Students: 440 full-time (213 women), 90 part-time (49 women); includes 127 minority (115 African Americans, 5 Asian Americans or Pacific Islanders, 5 Hispanic Americans, 2 Native Americans), 41 international. Average age 34. 577 applicants, 72% accepted, 204 enrolled. *Faculty:* 49 full-time (13 women), 24 part-time/adjunct (9 women). Expenses: Contact institution. *Financial support:* In 2001–02, 488 students received support, including 456 fellowships (averaging $9,563 per year); career-related internships or fieldwork, Federal Work-Study, institutionally sponsored loans, and scholarships/grants also available. Support available to part-time students. Financial award application deadline: 8/1; financial award applicants required to submit CSS PROFILE or FAFSA. In 2001, 117 first professional degrees, 39 master's, 2 doctorates awarded. *Degree program information:* Part-time programs available. Offers theology (M Div, MTS, Th M, Th D). *Application deadline:* For fall admission, 7/1; for spring admission, 12/1. Applications are processed on a rolling basis. *Application fee:* $25. *Application Contact:* Mary Lou Greenwood Boice, Dean of Admissions, 404-727-6326, Fax: 404-727-2915. *Registrar,* Matthew L. King, 404-727-6480, Fax: 404-727-2915, E-mail: mking4@emory.edu.

Graduate School of Arts and Sciences Students: 1,393 full-time (813 women), 15 part-time (10 women); includes 191 minority (116 African Americans, 41 Asian Americans or Pacific Islanders, 33 Hispanic Americans, 1 Native American), 252 international. 2,944 applicants, 19% accepted, 260 enrolled. *Faculty:* 655. Expenses: Contact institution. *Financial support:* Fellowships, research assistantships, teaching assistantships, career-related internships or fieldwork, Federal Work-Study, institutionally sponsored loans, scholarships/grants, and tuition waivers (full and partial) available. Support available to part-time students. Financial award application deadline: 1/20; financial award applicants required to submit FAFSA. In 2001, 94 master's, 163 doctorates awarded. Offers anthropology (PhD); art history (PhD); arts and sciences (M Ed, MA, MAT, MM, MS, MSM, PhD, Certificate, DAST); biostatistics (PhD); chemistry (PhD); clinical psychology (PhD); cognition and development (PhD); comparative literature (Certificate); economics (PhD); English (PhD); film studies (MA); French (PhD); history (PhD); Jewish studies (MA); mathematics (PhD); mathematics/computer science (MS); music (MM, MSM); nursing (PhD); philosophy (PhD); physics (PhD); political science (PhD); psychobiology (PhD); sociology (PhD); Spanish (PhD); women's studies (Certificate). *Application deadline:* For fall admission, 1/20 (priority date). *Application fee:* $50. Electronic applications accepted. *Application Contact:* Kharen Fulton, Director of Admissions, 404-727-0184, Fax: 404-727-4990, E-mail: gradkef@emory.edu. *Acting Dean,* Dr. Gary S Wihl, 404-727-2669, Fax: 404-727-4990, E-mail: gwihl@emory.edu.

Department of Epidemiology Students: 27 full-time (19 women); includes 1 minority (Asian American or Pacific Islander), 4 international. 63 applicants, 22% accepted, 6 enrolled. *Faculty:* 17 full-time (6 women). Expenses: Contact institution. *Financial support:* In 2001–02, 25 fellowships were awarded; career-related internships or fieldwork, institutionally sponsored loans, scholarships/grants, and tuition waivers (partial) also available. Financial award application deadline: 1/20. In 2001, 4 degrees awarded. Offers quantitative epidemiology (PhD). *Application deadline:* For fall admission, 1/20 (priority date). *Application fee:* $50. Electronic applications accepted. *Application Contact:* Melanie Chastain, Assistant Director of Academic Programs, 404-727-8729, E-mail: mchasta@sph.emory.edu. *Director,* Dr. John Boring, 404-727-8710.

Division of Biological and Biomedical Sciences Students: 288 full-time (168 women); includes 30 minority (12 African Americans, 14 Asian Americans or Pacific Islanders, 3

Hispanic Americans, 1 Native American), 38 international. Average age 27. 811 applicants, 19% accepted, 66 enrolled. *Faculty:* 262 full-time (51 women). Expenses: Contact institution. *Financial support:* In 2001–02, 173 students received support, including 173 fellowships with full tuition reimbursements available (averaging $19,000 per year); institutionally sponsored loans, health care benefits, and tuition waivers (full) also available. In 2001, 45 doctorates awarded. Offers biochemistry, cell and developmental biology (PhD); biological and biomedical sciences (PhD); genetics and molecular biology (PhD); immunology and molecular pathogenesis (PhD); microbiology and molecular genetics (PhD); molecular and systems pharmacology (PhD); neuroscience (PhD); nutrition and health sciences (PhD); population biology, ecology, and evolution (PhD). *Application deadline:* For fall admission, 1/20. *Application fee:* $50. Electronic applications accepted. *Application Contact:* 404-727-2545, Fax: 404-727-3322, E-mail: gdbbs@emory.edu. *Director of Recruitment and Admissions,* Kathy Smith, 404-727-2547, Fax: 404-727-3322, E-mail: kathy_smith@emory.edu.

Division of Educational Studies Students: 50 full-time (38 women); includes 23 minority (22 African Americans, 1 Asian American or Pacific Islander), 4 international. 31 applicants, 13% accepted, 3 enrolled. *Faculty:* 11 full-time (3 women). Expenses: Contact institution. *Financial support:* In 2001–02, 10 fellowships were awarded; research assistantships, teaching assistantships, career-related internships or fieldwork, scholarships/grants, and tuition waivers (full and partial) also available. Financial award application deadline: 1/20. In 2001, 16 master's, 4 doctorates awarded. Offers educational studies (MA, PhD, DAST); middle grades teaching (M Ed, MAT); secondary teaching (M Ed, MAT). *Application deadline:* For fall admission, 1/20; for spring admission, 3/15. *Application fee:* $45. Electronic applications accepted. *Application Contact:* Dr. Glen Avant, Program Development Coordinator, 404-727-0612, E-mail: gavant@emory.edu. *Director,* Dr. Eleanor C. Main, 404-727-2674, E-mail: ecmain@emory.edu.

Division of Religion Students: 133 full-time (73 women); includes 14 minority (8 African Americans, 2 Asian Americans or Pacific Islanders, 4 Hispanic Americans), 13 international. 196 applicants, 13% accepted, 12 enrolled. *Faculty:* 54 full-time (12 women). Expenses: Contact institution. *Financial support:* In 2001–02, 65 fellowships were awarded; teaching assistantships, scholarships/grants also available. Financial award application deadline: 1/20. In 2001, 16 degrees awarded. Offers religion (PhD). *Application deadline:* For fall admission, 1/20 (priority date). *Application fee:* $50. Electronic applications accepted. *Application Contact:* Pescha Penso, Assistant Director, 404-727-6333, E-mail: ppenso@emory.edu. *Director,* Dr. Steven M. Tipton, 404-727-6333, Fax: 404-727-7594.

Graduate Institute of Liberal Arts Students: 62 full-time (33 women); includes 15 minority (11 African Americans, 2 Asian Americans or Pacific Islanders, 2 Hispanic Americans), 8 international. 84 applicants, 8% accepted, 6 enrolled. *Faculty:* 16 full-time (7 women). Expenses: Contact institution. *Financial support:* In 2001–02, 36 fellowships were awarded; research assistantships, teaching assistantships, career-related internships or fieldwork, Federal Work-Study, scholarships/grants, and tuition waivers (full and partial) also available. Financial award application deadline: 1/20. In 2001, 4 doctorates awarded. Offers liberal arts (PhD). *Application deadline:* For fall admission, 1/20 (priority date). *Application fee:* $50. Electronic applications accepted. *Application Contact:* Dr. Cate Nickerson, Director of Graduate Studies, 404-727-7396, E-mail: cniker@emory.edu. *Acting Chair,* Dr. Dana White, 404-727-7601, Fax: 404-727-2370.

Nell Hodgson Woodruff School of Nursing Students: 90 full-time, 76 part-time; includes 44 minority (38 African Americans, 4 Asian Americans or Pacific Islanders, 2 Hispanic Americans) Average age 31. 259 applicants, 53% accepted, 105 enrolled. *Faculty:* 28 full-time (26 women), 19 part-time/adjunct (18 women). Expenses: Contact institution. *Financial support:* In 2001–02, 160 students received support; fellowships, career-related internships or fieldwork, Federal Work-Study, institutionally sponsored loans, scholarships/grants, and traineeships available. Support available to part-time students. Financial award application deadline: 3/15; financial award applicants required to submit CSS PROFILE or FAFSA. In 2001, 86 degrees awarded. *Degree program information:* Part-time programs available. Postbaccalaureate distance learning degree programs offered (minimal on-campus study). Offers adult health (MSN); family nurse midwifery (MSN); family nurse practitioner (MSN); gerontology (MSN); international health (MSN); leadership in healthcare (MSN); public health nursing (MSN); women's health nurse practitioner (MSN). *Application deadline:* For fall admission, 2/15 (priority date); for spring admission, 11/1 (priority date). Applications are processed on a rolling basis. *Application fee:* $50. Electronic applications accepted. *Application Contact:* Dr. Nancy H. Halloran, Director, Student Affairs and Admissions, 404-727-7980, Fax: 404-727-8509, E-mail: nhallor@emory.edu. *Dean,* Dr. Marla E. Salmon, 404-727-7976, Fax: 404-727-0536, E-mail: msalmon@emory.edu.

Roberto C. Goizueta Business School Students: 455 full-time (117 women), 129 part-time (28 women); includes 77 minority (36 African Americans, 23 Asian Americans or Pacific Islanders, 18 Hispanic Americans), 144 international. Average age 27. 1,161 applicants, 32% accepted, 171 enrolled. *Faculty:* 77 full-time (22 women), 6 part-time/adjunct (1 woman). Expenses: Contact institution. *Financial support:* In 2001–02, 231 students received support, including 33 research assistantships (averaging $8,320 per year), 37 teaching assistantships (averaging $8,320 per year); career-related internships or fieldwork, Federal Work-Study, institutionally sponsored loans, and scholarships/grants also available. Support available to part-time students. Financial award application deadline: 4/15; financial award applicants required to submit FAFSA. In 2001, 298 degrees awarded. *Degree program information:* Part-time and evening/weekend programs available. Offers business (EMBA, MBA, PhD). *Application deadline:* For fall admission, 3/31 (priority date); for winter admission, 10/1 (priority date); for spring admission, 3/1 (priority date). Applications are processed on a rolling basis. *Application fee:* $100. Electronic applications accepted. *Application Contact:* Julie Barefoot, Assistant Dean, 404-727-6311, Fax: 404-727-4612, E-mail: admissions@bus.emory.edu. *Dean,* Thomas S. Robertson, 404-727-6377, Fax: 404-727-0868, E-mail: tom_robertson@bus.emory.edu.

The Rollins School of Public Health Students: 476 full-time (375 women), 203 part-time (148 women); includes 255 minority (141 African Americans, 93 Asian Americans or Pacific Islanders, 21 Hispanic Americans), 49 international. Average age 29. 968 applicants, 77% accepted. *Faculty:* 108 full-time (51 women), 223 part-time/adjunct (73 women). Expenses: Contact institution. *Financial support:* In 2001–02, 300 students received support; fellowships, research assistantships, teaching assistantships, career-related internships or fieldwork, Federal Work-Study, institutionally sponsored loans, scholarships/grants, and traineeships available. Support available to part-time students. Financial award application deadline: 2/1; financial award applicants required to submit FAFSA. In 2001, 293 master's, 6 doctorates awarded. *Degree program information:* Part-time programs available. Postbaccalaureate distance learning degree programs offered (minimal on-campus study). Offers behavioral sciences and health education (MPH); biostatistics (MPH, MSPH, PhD); environmental/occupational health (MPH, MSPH); epidemiology (MPH, MS, MSPH, PhD); health policy and management (MPH); international health (MPH); public health (MPH, MS, MSPH, PhD); public health informatics (MSPH). *Application deadline:* For fall admission, 2/1 (priority date). Applications are processed on a rolling basis. *Application fee:* $50. *Application Contact:* Shannon Shelton, Associate Director of Student Services/Acting Director of Admissions, 404-727-3410, Fax: 404-727-3996, E-mail: admit@sph.emory.edu. *Director, Student Services,* John Youngblood, 404-454-7005, Fax: 404-727-3996, E-mail: jyoung@sph.emory.edu.

School of Law Students: 649 full-time (348 women). Average age 24. 2,983 applicants, 35% accepted, 227 enrolled. *Faculty:* 44 full-time (12 women), 65 part-time/adjunct (16 women). Expenses: Contact institution. *Financial support:* In 2001–02, 605 students received support, including 15 fellowships with full tuition reimbursements available (averaging $3,000 per year), 78 research assistantships (averaging $530 per year), 12 teaching assistantships; career-related internships or fieldwork, Federal Work-Study, institutionally sponsored loans, scholarships/grants, and tuition waivers (full and partial) also available. Financial award application deadline: 3/1; financial award applicants required to submit FAFSA. In 2001, 218 first professional degrees, 10 master's awarded. Offers law (JD, LL M, Certificate). *Application deadline:* For fall admission, 3/1. Applications are processed on a rolling basis. *Application fee:* $65. Electronic applications accepted. *Application Contact:* Lynell A. Cadray, Assistant Dean for Admissions, 404-727-6802, Fax: 404-727-2477. *Interim,* Peter H. Hay, 404-727-6896, Fax: 404-727-0866.

School of Medicine Students: 746 (417 women); includes 177 minority (59 African Americans, 88 Asian Americans or Pacific Islanders, 23 Hispanic Americans, 7 Native Americans) 12 international. Average age 24. *Faculty:* 1,462 full-time (439 women), 1,381 part-time/adjunct (319 women). Expenses: Contact institution. *Financial support:* In 2001–02, 660 students received support; fellowships, research assistantships, teaching assistantships, career-related internships or fieldwork, institutionally sponsored loans, and scholarships/grants available. Support available to part-time students. Financial award applicants required to submit CSS PROFILE or FAFSA. In 2001, 110 first professional degrees, 103 master's awarded. Offers anesthesiology/patient monitoring systems (MM Sc); medicine (MD, MM Sc, DPT); ophthalmic technology (MM Sc); physical therapy (DPT); physician assistant (MM Sc); radiation oncology physics (MM Sc). *Application Contact:* Dr. John William Eley, Associate Dean of Student Affairs and Director of Admissions, 404-727-5660, Fax: 404-727-5456, E-mail: medschadmiss@medadm.emory.edu. *Executive Associte Dean, Medical Education and Student Affairs,* Dr. Jonas A. Shulman, 404-727-5655, Fax: 404-727-0045, E-mail: jshulman@medadm.emory.edu.

See in-depth description on page 867.

EMPEROR'S COLLEGE OF TRADITIONAL ORIENTAL MEDICINE, Santa Monica, CA 90403

General Information Private, coed, graduate-only institution. *Graduate housing:* On-campus housing not available. *Research affiliation:* Lotus Herbs (herbs), LA Free Clinic (herbs), USC (stroke), Daniel Freeman Hospital (stroke).

GRADUATE UNITS

Program in Chinese Medicine and Acupuncture *Degree program information:* Part-time and evening/weekend programs available. Offers Chinese medicine and acupuncture (MTOM).

EMPORIA STATE UNIVERSITY, Emporia, KS 66801-5087

General Information State-supported, coed, comprehensive institution. CGS member. *Enrollment:* 335 full-time matriculated graduate/professional students (214 women), 686 part-time matriculated graduate/professional students (525 women). *Enrollment by degree level:* 988 master's, 23 doctoral, 10 other advanced degrees. *Graduate faculty:* 232 full-time (74 women), 89 part-time/adjunct (58 women). Tuition, state resident: full-time $2,632; part-time $119 per credit hour. Tuition, nonresident: full-time $6,734; part-time $290 per credit hour. *Graduate housing:* Rooms and/or apartments available to single and married students. Typical cost: $1,914 per year ($3,874 including board) for single students; $1,710 per year ($3,670 including board) for married students. Housing application deadline: 8/25. *Student services:* Campus employment opportunities, career counseling, child daycare facilities, disabled student services, free psychological counseling, grant writing training, international student services, low-cost health insurance, multicultural affairs office, teacher training, writing training. *Library facilities:* William Allen White Library. *Online resources:* library catalog, web page. *Collection:* 620,077 titles, 1,405 serial subscriptions, 8,340 audiovisual materials.

Computer facilities: 283 computers available on campus for general student use. A campuswide network can be accessed from student residence rooms and from off campus. Internet access and online class registration, various software packages are available. *Web address:* http://www.emporia.edu/.

General Application Contact: Mary McKenna, Admissions Coordinator, 800-950-GRAD, Fax: 620-341-5909, E-mail: mckennam@emporia.edu.

GRADUATE UNITS

School of Graduate Studies Students: 335 full-time (214 women), 686 part-time (525 women); includes 36 minority (13 African Americans, 3 Asian Americans or Pacific Islanders, 16 Hispanic Americans, 4 Native Americans), 59 international. 332 applicants, 72% accepted. *Faculty:* 232 full-time (74 women), 89 part-time/adjunct (58 women). Expenses: Contact institution. *Financial support:* In 2001–02, 10 fellowships (averaging $1,459 per year), 15 research assistantships (averaging $5,632 per year), 102 teaching assistantships with full tuition reimbursements (averaging $5,273 per year) were awarded. Career-related internships or fieldwork, Federal Work-Study, institutionally sponsored loans, scholarships/grants, health care benefits, and unspecified assistantships also available. Financial award application deadline: 3/15; financial award applicants required to submit FAFSA. In 2001, 303 master's, 3 doctorates, 8 other advanced degrees awarded. *Degree program information:* Part-time programs available. Postbaccalaureate distance learning degree programs offered. *Application deadline:* Applications are processed on a rolling basis. *Application fee:* $30 ($75 for international students). Electronic applications accepted. *Application Contact:* Mary McKenna, Admissions Coordinator, 800-950-GRAD, Fax: 620-341-5909, E-mail: mckennam@emporia.edu. *Dean, School of Graduate Studies,* Dr. Timothy M. Downs, 620-341-5403, Fax: 620-341-5909, E-mail: downstim@emporia.edu.

College of Liberal Arts and Sciences Students: 58 full-time (28 women), 33 part-time (18 women); includes 3 minority (2 African Americans, 1 Hispanic American), 13 international. 31 applicants, 68% accepted. *Faculty:* 93 full-time (19 women), 18 part-time/adjunct (10 women). Expenses: Contact institution. *Financial support:* In 2001–02, 5 fellowships (averaging $1,459 per year), 8 research assistantships (averaging $5,632 per year), 37 teaching assistantships with full tuition reimbursements (averaging $5,273 per year) were awarded. Career-related internships or fieldwork, Federal Work-Study, institutionally sponsored loans, health care benefits, and unspecified assistantships also available. Financial award application deadline: 3/15; financial award applicants required to submit FAFSA. In 2001, 30 degrees awarded. *Degree program information:* Part-time programs available. Offers American history (MAT); anthropology (MAT); botany (MS); chemistry (MS); earth science (MS); economics (MAT); English (MA); environmental biology (MS); general biology (MS); geography (MAT); history (MA); liberal arts and sciences (MA, MAT, MM, MS); mathematics (MS); microbial and cellular biology (MS); music education (MM); performance (MM); physical science (MS); physics (MS); political science (MAT); social sciences (MAT); social studies education (MAT); sociology (MAT); world history (MAT); zoology (MS). *Application deadline:* For fall admission, 8/15 (priority date). Applications are processed on a rolling basis. *Application fee:* $30 ($75 for international students). Electronic applications accepted. *Dean,* Dr. Lendley C. Black, 620-341-5278, Fax: 620-341-5681, E-mail: blacklen@emporia.edu.

School of Business Students: 45 full-time (19 women), 41 part-time (30 women); includes 2 minority (both Hispanic Americans), 26 international. 35 applicants, 71% accepted. *Faculty:* 29 full-time (4 women). Expenses: Contact institution. *Financial support:* In 2001–02, 2 fellowships (averaging $1,459 per year), 1 research assistantship (averaging $5,632 per year), 9 teaching assistantships with full tuition reimbursements (averaging $5,273 per year) were awarded. Career-related internships or fieldwork, Federal Work-Study, institutionally sponsored loans, health care benefits, and unspecified assistantships also available. Financial award application deadline: 3/15; financial award applicants required to submit FAFSA. In 2001, 27 degrees awarded. *Degree program information:* Part-time programs available. Offers business (MBA, MS); business administration (MBA); business education (MS). *Application deadline:* For fall admission, 8/15 (priority date). Applications are processed on a rolling basis. *Application fee:* $30 ($75 for international students). Electronic applications accepted. *Dean,* Dr. Sajjad Hashmi, 620-341-5274, Fax: 620-341-5892, E-mail: hashmisa@emporia.edu.

School of Library and Information Management Students: 48 full-time (37 women), 219 part-time (187 women); includes 8 minority (2 African Americans, 2 Asian Americans or Pacific Islanders, 4 Hispanic Americans), 2 international. 123 applicants, 85% accepted. *Faculty:* 19 full-time (11 women), 41 part-time/adjunct (30 women). Expenses: Contact institution. *Financial support:* In 2001–02, 1 research assistantship (averaging $5,632 per year), 17 teaching assistantships with full tuition reimbursements (averaging $5,273 per year) were awarded. Career-related internships or fieldwork, Federal Work-Study, institutionally sponsored loans, health care benefits, and unspecified assistantships also available. Financial award application deadline: 3/15; financial award applicants required to submit FAFSA. In 2001, 78 master's, 3 doctorates awarded. *Degree program information:* Part-time programs available. Offers library and information science (PhD); library science (MLS). *Application deadline:* For fall admission, 8/15 (priority date). Applications are processed on a rolling basis. *Application fee:* $30 ($75 for international students). Electronic

Emporia State University (continued)

applications accepted. *Application Contact:* Daniel Rowland, Director of Communications, 800-552-4770, Fax: 620-341-5233, E-mail: sliminfo@emporia.edu. *Dean,* Dr. Robert J. Grover, 800-552-4770, Fax: 620-341-5233, E-mail: groverro@emporia.edu.

The Teachers College Students: 184 full-time (130 women), 393 part-time (290 women); includes 23 minority (9 African Americans, 1 Asian American or Pacific Islander, 9 Hispanic Americans, 4 Native Americans), 18 international. 143 applicants, 62% accepted. *Faculty:* 91 full-time (40 women), 30 part-time/adjunct (18 women). Expenses: Contact institution. *Financial support:* In 2001–02, 3 fellowships (averaging $1,459 per year), 5 research assistantships (averaging $5,632 per year), 39 teaching assistantships with full tuition reimbursements (averaging $5,273 per year) were awarded. Career-related internships or fieldwork, Federal Work-Study, institutionally sponsored loans, health care benefits, and unspecified assistantships also available. Financial award application deadline: 3/15; financial award applicants required to submit FAFSA. In 2001, 168 master's, 8 other advanced degrees awarded. *Degree program information:* Part-time programs available. Postbaccalaureate distance learning degree programs offered. Offers art therapy (MS); behavior disorders (MS); clinical psychology (MS); counselor education (MS); curriculum and instruction (MS); early childhood education (MS); education (MS, Ed S); educational administration (MS); elementary education (MS); general psychology (MS); gifted, talented, and creative (MS); health, physical education and recreation (MS); industrial/organizational psychology (MS); instructional design and technology (MS); interrelated special education (MS); learning disabilities (MS); mental health counseling (MS); mental retardation (MS); psychology (MS); rehabilitation counseling (MS); school counseling (MS); school psychology (MS, Ed S); secondary education (MS); special education (MS); student personnel (MS). *Application deadline:* Applications are processed on a rolling basis. *Application fee:* $30 ($75 for international students). Electronic applications accepted. *Dean,* Dr. Teresa Mehring, 620-341-5367, Fax: 620-341-5785, E-mail: mehringt@emporia.edu.

See in-depth description on page 869.

ENDICOTT COLLEGE, Beverly, MA 01915-2096

General Information Independent, coed, comprehensive institution. *Enrollment:* 100 full-time matriculated graduate/professional students (78 women), 191 part-time matriculated graduate/professional students (140 women). *Enrollment by degree level:* 291 master's. *Graduate faculty:* 2 full-time (1 woman), 45 part-time/adjunct (25 women). *Tuition:* Part-time $240 per credit. *Graduate housing:* On-campus housing not available. *Student services:* Campus employment opportunities, campus safety program, career counseling, child daycare facilities, disabled student services, exercise/wellness program, grant writing training, international student services, low-cost health insurance, multicultural affairs office, teacher training, writing training. *Library facilities:* Endicott College Library. *Online resources:* library catalog, web page, access to other libraries' catalogs. *Collection:* 115,000 titles, 2,100 serial subscriptions, 500 audiovisual materials. *Research affiliation:* Peabody Essex Museum (history), North Shore Consortium (special needs).

Computer facilities: 100 computers available on campus for general student use. A campuswide network can be accessed from student residence rooms and from off campus. Internet access, e-mail, on-line instructional courses are available. *Web address:* http://www.endicott.edu/.

General Application Contact: Dr. Paul Squarcia, Acting Dean of Graduate and Professional Studies, 978-232-2269, Fax: 978-232-3000, E-mail: psquarcia@endicott.edu.

GRADUATE UNITS

School of Graduate and Professional Studies Students: 100 full-time (78 women), 191 part-time (140 women). Average age 35. *Faculty:* 2 full-time (1 woman), 45 part-time/adjunct (25 women). Expenses: Contact institution. *Financial support:* Career-related internships or fieldwork, Federal Work-Study, institutionally sponsored loans, and tuition waivers (partial) available. *Degree program information:* Part-time and evening/weekend programs available. Postbaccalaureate distance learning degree programs offered (minimal on-campus study). Offers arts and learning (M Ed); business administration (MBA); elementary education (M Ed); hospitality organizational training and management (M Ed); integrated studies (M Ed); international education (M Ed); organizational management (M Ed); reading and literacy (M Ed); special education (M Ed). *Application deadline:* Applications are processed on a rolling basis. *Application fee:* $50. Electronic applications accepted. *Acting Dean of Graduate and Professional Studies,* Dr. Paul Squarcia, 978-232-2269, Fax: 978-232-3000, E-mail: psquarcia@endicott.edu.

EPISCOPAL DIVINITY SCHOOL, Cambridge, MA 02138-3494

General Information Independent-religious, coed, graduate-only institution. *Enrollment by degree level:* 65 first professional, 11 master's, 10 doctoral, 11 other advanced degrees. *Graduate faculty:* 16 full-time (8 women), 11 part-time/adjunct (7 women). *Tuition:* Full-time $13,500; part-time $6,730 per semester. *Required fees:* $1,470; $1,470 per year. *Graduate housing:* Rooms and/or apartments available on a first-come, first-served basis to single and married students. Typical cost: $2,487 per year ($3,787 including board) for single students; $4,073 per year ($5,373 including board) for married students. Room and board charges vary according to board plan and housing facility selected. Housing application deadline: 7/31. *Student services:* Campus employment opportunities, career counseling, exercise/wellness program, free psychological counseling, international student services, low-cost health insurance, writing training. *Library facilities:* Episcopal Divinity School/Weston Jesuit School of Theology Library. *Online resources:* library catalog, web page, access to other libraries' catalogs. *Collection:* 224,987 titles, 1,177 serial subscriptions, 518 audiovisual materials. *Research affiliation:* Boston Theological Institute.

Computer facilities: 4 computers available on campus for general student use. A campuswide network can be accessed from off campus. Internet access is available. *Web address:* http://www.episdivschool.edu/.

General Application Contact: Christopher J. Medeiros, Director of Admissions, Recruitment, and Financial Aid, 617-868-3450 Ext. 307, Fax: 617-864-5385, E-mail: admissions@episdivschool.edu.

GRADUATE UNITS

Graduate and Professional Programs *Degree program information:* Part-time programs available.

EPISCOPAL THEOLOGICAL SEMINARY OF THE SOUTHWEST, Austin, TX 78768-2247

General Information Independent-religious, coed, graduate-only institution. *Enrollment by degree level:* 58 first professional, 42 master's, 7 other advanced degrees. *Graduate faculty:* 8 full-time (3 women), 21 part-time/adjunct (6 women). *Tuition:* Full-time $10,420; part-time $303 per credit hour. *Required fees:* $50. *Graduate housing:* Rooms and/or apartments available on a first-come, first-served basis to single students and available to married students. Typical cost: $4,800 (including board) for single students; $9,000 (including board) for married students. Housing application deadline: 8/1. *Student services:* Campus employment opportunities, international student services, low-cost health insurance, writing training. *Library facilities:* Episcopal Theological Seminary of the Southwest Bosher Library plus 1 other. *Online resources:* library catalog, web page, access to other libraries' catalogs. *Collection:* 102,116 titles, 308 serial subscriptions, 1,631 audiovisual materials.

Computer facilities: 8 computers available on campus for general student use. A campuswide network can be accessed. Internet access is available. *Web address:* http://www.etss.edu/.

General Application Contact: Joseph Liro, Director of Admissions, 512-472-4133 Ext. 307, Fax: 512-472-3098, E-mail: jwallace@etss.edu.

GRADUATE UNITS

Graduate and Professional Programs Students: 60 full-time (23 women), 47 part-time (36 women); includes 11 minority (6 African Americans, 5 Hispanic Americans), 1 international. Average age 47. 43 applicants, 88% accepted, 27 enrolled. *Faculty:* 8 full-time (3 women), 21 part-time/adjunct (6 women). Expenses: Contact institution. *Financial support:* Career-related internships or fieldwork and scholarships/grants available. Support available to part-time students. Financial award application deadline: 8/1. In 2001, 16 first professional degrees, 7 master's awarded. *Degree program information:* Part-time and evening/weekend programs available. Offers theology (M Div, MAPM, MAR, CITS, CSS). *Application deadline:* For fall admission, 7/5; for spring admission, 12/20 (priority date). Applications are processed on a rolling basis. *Application fee:* $30. *Application Contact:* Joseph Liro, Director of Admissions, 512-472-4133 Ext. 307, Fax: 512-472-3098, E-mail: jwallace@etss.edu. *Dean,* Very Rev. Durstan R. McDonald, 512-472-4133 Ext. 307, Fax: 512-472-3098, E-mail: dmcdonald@etss.edu.

ERIKSON INSTITUTE, Chicago, IL 60611-5627

General Information Independent, coed, primarily women, graduate-only institution. *Enrollment by degree level:* 125 master's, 21 other advanced degrees. *Graduate faculty:* 10 full-time (8 women), 11 part-time/adjunct (all women). *Tuition:* Full-time $18,852; part-time $460 per credit. *Required fees:* $150. One-time fee: $115 part-time. Tuition and fees vary according to course load and program. *Student services:* Career counseling, international student services, teacher training, writing training. *Library facilities:* Edward Neisser Library and Learning Center. *Online resources:* library catalog, access to other libraries' catalogs. *Collection:* 8,300 titles, 75 serial subscriptions, 600 audiovisual materials.

Computer facilities: 16 computers available on campus for general student use. A campuswide network can be accessed from off campus. Internet access, online "course area" with course syllabi, course reading are available. *Web address:* http://www.erikson.edu/.

General Application Contact: Melanie K. Miller, Associate Director of Recruitment and Financial Aid, 312-755-2250 Ext. 2276, Fax: 312-755-0928, E-mail: mmiller@erikson.edu.

GRADUATE UNITS

Academic Programs Students: 40 full-time (39 women), 106 part-time (100 women); includes 48 minority (31 African Americans, 7 Asian Americans or Pacific Islanders, 10 Hispanic Americans), 1 international. Average age 30. 102 applicants, 84% accepted, 60 enrolled. *Faculty:* 10 full-time (8 women), 11 part-time/adjunct (all women). Expenses: Contact institution. *Financial support:* In 2001–02, 80 students received support, including 80 fellowships (averaging $3,534 per year); career-related internships or fieldwork, institutionally sponsored loans, and scholarships/grants also available. Support available to part-time students. Financial award application deadline: 4/1; financial award applicants required to submit FAFSA. In 2001, 16 master's, 14 other advanced degrees awarded. *Degree program information:* Part-time and evening/weekend programs available. Offers child development (MS); director's leadership (Certificate); early childhood education (MS); infant studies (Certificate). *Application deadline:* For fall admission, 4/1 (priority date). Applications are processed on a rolling basis. *Application fee:* $30. *Application Contact:* Melanie K. Miller, Associate Director of Recruitment and Financial Aid, 312-755-2250 Ext. 2276, Fax: 312-755-0928, E-mail: mmiller@erikson.edu. *Vice President/Dean of Academic Programs,* Dr. Fran Stott, 312-755-2250 Ext. 2280, Fax: 312-755-0928, E-mail: fstott@erikson.edu.

ERSKINE THEOLOGICAL SEMINARY, Due West, SC 29639-0668

General Information Independent-religious, coed, graduate-only institution. *Graduate faculty:* 13 full-time (1 woman), 12 part-time/adjunct (0 women). *Graduate housing:* Room and/or apartments available to single students; on-campus housing not available to married students. *Student services:* Career counseling, low-cost health insurance. *Library facilities:* McCain Library plus 1 other. *Collection:* 550,000 titles, 50 serial subscriptions.

Computer facilities: 56 computers available on campus for general student use. A campuswide network can be accessed. Internet access is available. *Web address:* http://www.erskine.edu/seminary/index.html.

General Application Contact: Bruce Wayne Cooley, Associate Director of Admissions, 864-379-6653, Fax: 864-379-2171, E-mail: cooley@erskine.edu.

GRADUATE UNITS

Graduate and Professional Programs Students: 121 full-time (20 women), 254 part-time (70 women); includes 118 minority (103 African Americans, 12 Asian Americans or Pacific Islanders, 2 Hispanic Americans, 1 Native American) *Faculty:* 13 full-time (1 woman), 12 part-time/adjunct (0 women). Expenses: Contact institution. *Financial support:* Career-related internships or fieldwork, institutionally sponsored loans, and scholarships/grants available. Financial award application deadline: 8/1; financial award applicants required to submit FAFSA. *Degree program information:* Part-time and evening/weekend programs available. Offers theology (M Div, MACE, MAPM, MATS, MCM, D Min). *Application deadline:* For fall admission, 8/15 (priority date); for spring admission, 1/15. Applications are processed on a rolling basis. *Application fee:* $15. *Application Contact:* Sherry B. Martin, Director of Academic Services and Registrar, 864-379-8779, Fax: 864-379-2171, E-mail: smartin@erskine.edu. *Associate Director of Admissions,* Bruce Wayne Cooley, 864-379-6653, Fax: 864-379-2171, E-mail: cooley@erskine.edu.

EVANGELICAL SCHOOL OF THEOLOGY, Myerstown, PA 17067-1212

General Information Independent-religious, coed, graduate-only institution. *Enrollment by degree level:* 105 first professional, 46 master's. *Graduate faculty:* 6 full-time (0 women), 5 part-time/adjunct (1 woman). *Tuition:* Full-time $7,600; part-time $320 per credit. *Required fees:* $50. One-time fee: $150 full-time. Tuition and fees vary according to program. *Graduate housing:* Rooms and/or apartments available on a first-come, first-served basis to single and married students. Typical cost: $1,800 per year for single students; $4,050 per year for married students. Housing application deadline: 6/1. *Student services:* Campus employment opportunities, career counseling, international student services, low-cost health insurance. *Library facilities:* Rostad Library. *Online resources:* library catalog, web page. *Collection:* 70,000 titles, 550 serial subscriptions, 506 audiovisual materials.

Computer facilities: 17 computers available on campus for general student use. A campuswide network can be accessed from student residence rooms and from off campus. Internet access, library searching, course selection are available. *Web address:* http://www.evangelical.edu/.

General Application Contact: Tom M. Maiello, Dean of Admissions, 800-532-5775 Ext. 109, Fax: 717-866-4667, E-mail: admissions@evangelical.edu.

GRADUATE UNITS

Graduate and Professional Programs Students: 16 full-time (5 women), 135 part-time (35 women). Average age 40. 42 applicants, 90% accepted, 38 enrolled. *Faculty:* 6 full-time (0 women), 5 part-time/adjunct (1 woman). Expenses: Contact institution. *Financial support:* Career-related internships or fieldwork, scholarships/grants, and tuition waivers (full) available. Support available to part-time students. Financial award application deadline: 6/1; financial award applicants required to submit FAFSA. In 2001, 5 first professional degrees, 10 master's, 3 other advanced degrees awarded. *Degree program information:* Part-time programs available. Offers divinity (M Div); educational ministries (MA); marriage and family therapy (MA); ministry (Certificate); religion (MAR); theology (Diploma). *Application deadline:* For fall admission, 6/1 (priority date); for spring admission, 11/1 (priority date). Applications are processed on a rolling basis. *Application fee:* $30. Electronic applications accepted. *Application Contact:* Tom M. Maiello, Dean of Admissions, 800-532-5775 Ext. 109, Fax: 717-866-4667, E-mail: admissions@evangelical.edu. *Vice President, Academic Affairs,* Rev. Dr. Rodney H. Shearer, 717-866-5775 Ext. 105, Fax: 717-866-4667, E-mail: rshearer@evangelical.edu.

EVANGELICAL SEMINARY OF PUERTO RICO, San Juan, PR 00925-2207

General Information Independent-religious, coed, graduate-only institution. *Graduate housing:* Rooms and/or apartments available on a first-come, first-served basis to single and married students.

GRADUATE UNITS

Graduate and Professional Programs *Degree program information:* Part-time programs available. Offers theology (M Div, MAR).

EVANGEL UNIVERSITY, Springfield, MO 65802-2191

General Information Independent-religious, coed, comprehensive institution. *Enrollment:* 34 full-time matriculated graduate/professional students (30 women), 11 part-time matriculated graduate/professional students (7 women). *Enrollment by degree level:* 45 master's. *Graduate faculty:* 8 full-time (3 women), 8 part-time/adjunct (4 women). *Tuition:* Full-time $3,040; part-time $190 per credit. *Required fees:* $240. Tuition and fees vary according to program. *Graduate housing:* Rooms and/or apartments available on a first-come, first-served basis to single and married students. Typical cost: $3,410 per year ($5,500 including board) for single students; $4,200 per year for married students. Housing application deadline: 5/1. *Student services:* Campus employment opportunities, campus safety program, career counseling, exercise/wellness program, international student services, multicultural affairs office, teacher training, writing training. *Library facilities:* Claude Kendrick Library. *Online resources:* library catalog, access to other libraries' catalogs. *Collection:* 96,487 titles, 748 serial subscriptions.

Computer facilities: 77 computers available on campus for general student use. *Web address:* http://www.evangel.edu/.

General Application Contact: Jackie Eutsler, Administrative Assistant of Graduate Studies, 417-865-2815, Fax: 417-520-0545, E-mail: eutslerj@evangel.edu.

GRADUATE UNITS

Department of Education Students: 22 full-time (21 women). Average age 35. 3 applicants, 100% accepted. *Faculty:* 4 full-time (2 women), 4 part-time/adjunct (3 women). Expenses: Contact institution. *Financial support:* In 2001–02, 6 students received support; fellowships with partial tuition reimbursements available, research assistantships with partial tuition reimbursements available, teaching assistantships with partial tuition reimbursements available, career-related internships or fieldwork, institutionally sponsored loans, and scholarships/grants available. Support available to part-time students. Financial award application deadline: 3/1; financial award applicants required to submit FAFSA. *Degree program information:* Part-time and evening/weekend programs available. Offers elementary education (M Ed); reading education (M Ed). *Application deadline:* For fall admission, 7/15 (priority date); for spring admission, 11/19 (priority date). Applications are processed on a rolling basis. *Application fee:* $25. *Application Contact:* Jackie Eutsler, Administrative Assistant of Graduate Studies, 417-865-2815, Fax: 417-520-0545, E-mail: eutslerj@evangel.edu. *Chair,* Dr. Rebecca Huechteman, 417-865-2815 Ext. 8244, E-mail: huechtemanb@evangel.edu.

Department of Psychology Students: 12 full-time (9 women), 11 part-time (7 women); includes 1 minority (Asian American or Pacific Islander) Average age 29. 10 applicants, 100% accepted. *Faculty:* 4 full-time (1 woman), 4 part-time/adjunct (1 woman). Expenses: Contact institution. *Financial support:* In 2001–02, 6 students received support; research assistantships, teaching assistantships, career-related internships or fieldwork, institutionally sponsored loans, and scholarships/grants available. Financial award application deadline: 5/1; financial award applicants required to submit FAFSA. In 2001, 4 degrees awarded. *Degree program information:* Part-time and evening/weekend programs available. Offers clinical psychology (MS); general psychology (MS); guidance and counseling (MS). *Application deadline:* For fall admission, 7/15 (priority date); for spring admission, 11/19 (priority date). Applications are processed on a rolling basis. *Application fee:* $25. *Application Contact:* Jackie Eutsler, Administrative Assistant of Graduate Studies, 417-865-2815, Fax: 417-520-0545, E-mail: eutslerj@evangel.edu. *Supervisor of Graduate Psychology,* Dr. Jeffrey Fulks, 417-865-2815 Ext. 7915.

THE EVERGREEN STATE COLLEGE, Olympia, WA 98505

General Information State-supported, coed, comprehensive institution. *Enrollment:* 112 full-time matriculated graduate/professional students (74 women), 114 part-time matriculated graduate/professional students (62 women). *Enrollment by degree level:* 226 master's. *Graduate faculty:* 18 full-time (9 women), 5 part-time/adjunct (2 women). Tuition, state resident: full-time $4,848; part-time $161 per credit. Tuition, nonresident: full-time $14,769; part-time $492 per credit. Tuition and fees vary according to course load. *Graduate housing:* Rooms and/or apartments available on a first-come, first-served basis to single and married students. Typical cost: $5,610 (including board) for single students; $5,610 (including board) for married students. Housing application deadline: 5/15. *Student services:* Campus employment opportunities, campus safety program, career counseling, child daycare facilities, disabled student services, exercise/wellness program, free psychological counseling, grant writing training, international student services, multicultural affairs office, teacher training, writing training. *Library facilities:* Daniel J. Evans Library. *Online resources:* library catalog, web page, access to other libraries' catalogs. *Collection:* 320,100 titles, 5,100 serial subscriptions, 85,344 audiovisual materials. *Research affiliation:* Washington State Institute for Public Policy.

Computer facilities: 150 computers available on campus for general student use. A campuswide network can be accessed from student residence rooms and from off campus. Internet access is available. *Web address:* http://www.evergreen.edu/.

General Application Contact: J. T. Austin, Graduate Studies Office, 360-867-6707, Fax: 360-867-5430, E-mail: graduatestudies@evergreen.edu.

GRADUATE UNITS

Graduate Programs *Degree program information:* Part-time and evening/weekend programs available. Offers environmental studies (MES); public administration (MPA); teaching (MIT).

EXCELSIOR COLLEGE, Albany, NY 12203-5159

General Information Independent, coed, comprehensive institution. *Enrollment:* 10 full-time matriculated graduate/professional students (all women), 206 part-time matriculated graduate/professional students (153 women). *Enrollment by degree level:* 216 master's. *Graduate faculty:* 2 full-time (1 woman), 55 part-time/adjunct (38 women). *Tuition:* Part-time $275 per credit hour. *Required fees:* $190 per year. Tuition and fees vary according to program. *Library facilities:* Excelsior College Virtual Library. *Online resources:* web page.

Computer facilities: A campuswide network can be accessed from off campus. *Web address:* http://www.excelsior.edu/.

General Application Contact: Dr. Daniel Eisenberg, Associate Dean, 518-464-8699, Fax: 518-464-8777, E-mail: dan@excelsior.edu.

GRADUATE UNITS

Program in Liberal Studies Average age 47. 75 applicants, 83% accepted, 50 enrolled. *Faculty:* 2 full-time (1 woman), 15 part-time/adjunct (3 women). Expenses: Contact institution. In 2001, 1 degree awarded. *Degree program information:* Part-time and evening/weekend programs available. Postbaccalaureate distance learning degree programs offered (no on-campus study). Offers liberal studies (MA). *Application deadline:* Applications are processed on a rolling basis. *Application fee:* $100. *Application Contact:* Susan Carlson, Administrative Assistant, 518-464-8500 Ext. 1323, Fax: 518-464-8777, E-mail: mls@excelsior.edu. *Associate Dean,* Dr. Daniel Eisenberg, 518-464-8699, Fax: 518-464-8777, E-mail: dan@excelsior.edu.

School of Nursing Students: 10 full-time (all women), 129 part-time (117 women); includes 22 minority (14 African Americans, 7 Asian Americans or Pacific Islanders, 1 Hispanic American) Average age 45. *Faculty:* 40 part-time/adjunct (35 women). Expenses: Contact institution. *Financial support:* Available to part-time students. *Degree program information:* Part-time and evening/weekend programs available. Postbaccalaureate distance learning degree programs offered (no on-campus study). Offers nursing (MSN). *Application deadline:* Applications are processed on a rolling basis. *Application fee:* $100. *Application Contact:* Lynne Dooley, Graduate Advisor, 518-464-8500, Fax: 518-464-8777, E-mail: msn@excelsior.edu. *Director, Graduate Program in Nursing and Healthcare,* Deborah Sopczyk, 518-464-8500, Fax: 518-464-8777, E-mail: msn@excelsior.edu.

FAIRFIELD UNIVERSITY, Fairfield, CT 06824

General Information Independent-religious, coed, comprehensive institution. *Enrollment:* 153 full-time matriculated graduate/professional students (105 women), 837 part-time matriculated graduate/professional students (470 women). *Enrollment by degree level:* 990 master's. *Graduate faculty:* 98 full-time (40 women), 46 part-time/adjunct (16 women). *Tuition:* Full-time $9,550; part-time $390 per credit hour. *Required fees:* $25 per term. Tuition and fees vary according to program. *Graduate housing:* On-campus housing not available. *Student services:* Campus employment opportunities, campus safety program, career counseling, disabled student services, free psychological counseling, international student services, multicultural affairs office, teacher training. *Library facilities:* Dimenna-Nyselius Library. *Online resources:* library catalog, web page. *Collection:* 293,191 titles, 1,790 serial subscriptions, 9,924 audiovisual materials.

Computer facilities: 150 computers available on campus for general student use. A campuswide network can be accessed from student residence rooms and from off campus. Internet access and online class registration are available. *Web address:* http://www.fairfield.edu/.

General Application Contact: 866-333-8648.

GRADUATE UNITS

Charles F. Dolan School of Business Students: 24 full-time (12 women), 175 part-time (64 women); includes 9 minority (3 African Americans, 5 Asian Americans or Pacific Islanders, 1 Hispanic American), 7 international. Average age 27. 94 applicants, 79% accepted. *Faculty:* 40 full-time (15 women), 3 part-time/adjunct (1 woman). Expenses: Contact institution. In 2001, 60 degrees awarded. *Degree program information:* Part-time and evening/weekend programs available. Offers accounting (MBA, CAS); finance (MBA, CAS); financial management (MSFM); healthcare management (MBA); human resource management (CAS); information technology (MBA, CAS); international business (MBA, CAS); marketing (MBA, CAS); taxation (MBA, CAS). *Application deadline:* For fall admission, 7/15; for spring admission, 11/15. Applications are processed on a rolling basis. *Application fee:* $55. Electronic applications accepted. *Application Contact:* Pamela Ann Curry, Assistant Director of Graduate Programs, 203-254-4070, Fax: 203-254-4029, E-mail: mba@fair1.fairfield.edu. *Dean,* Dr. Norman A. Solomon, 203-254-4070, Fax: 203-254-4105, E-mail: nsolomon@mail.fairfield.edu.

College of Arts and Sciences Students: 2 full-time (0 women), 31 part-time (22 women); includes 2 minority (1 African American, 1 Hispanic American) Average age 41. 20 applicants, 100% accepted, 17 enrolled. *Faculty:* 34 full-time (10 women). Expenses: Contact institution. *Financial support:* Tuition waivers (partial) available. Financial award applicants required to submit FAFSA. In 2001, 3 degrees awarded. *Degree program information:* Part-time and evening/weekend programs available. Offers American studies (MA); arts and sciences (MA, MS); mathematics and quantitative methods (MS). *Application deadline:* For fall admission, 7/1; for spring admission, 12/1. Applications are processed on a rolling basis. *Application fee:* $55. *Application Contact:* Sue Peterson, Assistant to the Dean, 203-254-4000 Ext. 2246, Fax: 203-254-4119, E-mail: speterson@mail.fairfield.edu. *Dean,* Dr. Timothy L. Snyder, 203-254-4000 Ext. 2221, Fax: 203-254-4119, E-mail: tsnyder@mail.fairfield.edu.

Graduate School of Education and Allied Professions Students: 117 full-time (90 women), 384 part-time (309 women); includes 60 minority (17 African Americans, 5 Asian Americans or Pacific Islanders, 38 Hispanic Americans), 11 international. Average age 30. 293 applicants, 70% accepted, 137 enrolled. *Faculty:* 17 full-time (10 women), 25 part-time/adjunct (11 women). Expenses: Contact institution. *Financial support:* In 2001–02, 10 research assistantships with full and partial tuition reimbursements were awarded; career-related internships or fieldwork and tuition waivers (partial) also available. Support available to part-time students. Financial award applicants required to submit FAFSA. In 2001, 141 master's, 15 other advanced degrees awarded. *Degree program information:* Part-time and evening/weekend programs available. Offers applied psychology (MA); community counseling (MA); computers in education (MA, CAS); counselor education (CAS); early childhood education (MA, CAS); education and allied professions (MA, CAS); educational media (MA, CAS); elementary education (MA); marriage and family therapy (MA); school counseling (MA); school psychology (MA, CAS); special education (MA, CAS); teaching and foundation (MA, CAS); TESOL, foreign language and bilingual/multicultural education (MA, CAS). *Application deadline:* Applications are processed on a rolling basis. *Application fee:* $55. Electronic applications accepted. *Application Contact:* Karen L Creecy, Assistant Dean, 203-254-4000 Ext. 2414, Fax: 203-254-4241, E-mail: klcreecy@mail.fairfield.edu. *Dean,* Dr. Margaret C. Deignan, 203-254-4000 Ext. 4250, Fax: 203-254-4241, E-mail: mcdeignan@mail.fairfield.edu.

School of Engineering Students: 9 full-time (2 women), 215 part-time (43 women); includes 35 minority (8 African Americans, 21 Asian Americans or Pacific Islanders, 6 Hispanic Americans), 39 international. 53 applicants, 100% accepted, 42 enrolled. *Faculty:* 2 full-time (0 women), 16 part-time/adjunct (2 women). Expenses: Contact institution. *Financial support:* Tuition waivers (partial) available. Financial award applicants required to submit FAFSA. In 2001, 47 degrees awarded. *Degree program information:* Part-time and evening/weekend programs available. Offers management of technology (MS); software engineering (MS). *Application deadline:* For fall admission, 6/30 (priority date). Applications are processed on a rolling basis. *Application fee:* $55. *Application Contact:* Dr. Richard G. Weber, Associate Dean, 203-254-4000 Ext. 4147, Fax: 203-254-4013, E-mail: rweber@fair1.fairfield.edu. *Dean,* Dr. Evangelos Hadjimichael, 203-254-4000 Ext. 4147, Fax: 203-254-4013, E-mail: hadjm@fair1.fairfield.edu.

School of Nursing Students: 1 (woman) full-time, 32 part-time (all women); includes 5 minority (2 African Americans, 2 Asian Americans or Pacific Islanders, 1 Hispanic American) Average age 42. 11 applicants, 45% accepted, 4 enrolled. *Faculty:* 5 full-time (all women), 2 part-time/adjunct (both women). Expenses: Contact institution. *Financial support:* Traineeships and tuition waivers (partial) available. Financial award applicants required to submit FAFSA. In 2001, 15 degrees awarded. *Degree program information:* Part-time and evening/weekend programs available. Offers adult nurse practitioner (MSN, CAS); family nurse practitioner (MSN, CAS); psychiatric nurse practitioner (MSN, CAS). *Application deadline:* For fall admission, 5/1 (priority date); for spring admission, 12/1 (priority date). Applications are processed on a rolling basis. *Application fee:* $55. *Application Contact:* Kathy Borrelli, Graduate Program Assistant, 203-254-4000 Ext. 2702, Fax: 203-254-4126, E-mail: kborrelli@mail.fairfield.edu. *Dean,* Dr. Jeanne M. Novotny, 203-254-4000 Ext. 2701, Fax: 203-254-4126, E-mail: jnovotny@mail.fairfield.edu.

FAIRLEIGH DICKINSON UNIVERSITY, COLLEGE AT FLORHAM, Madison, NJ 07940-1099

General Information Independent, coed, comprehensive institution. *Enrollment:* 208 full-time matriculated graduate/professional students (137 women), 548 part-time matriculated graduate/professional students (319 women). *Enrollment by degree level:* 756 master's. *Tuition:* Full-time $11,484; part-time $638 per credit. *Required fees:* $420. One-time fee: $97 part-time. *Library facilities:* Friendship Library plus 1 other. *Online resources:* library catalog. *Collection:* 176,222 titles, 1,259 serial subscriptions, 591 audiovisual materials.

Computer facilities: 300 computers available on campus for general student use. A campuswide network can be accessed from student residence rooms and from off campus. *Web address:* http://www.fdu.edu/.

General Application Contact: Jeanine Whalen, Associate Director of Adult and Graduate Admissions, 973-443-8905, Fax: 973-443-8088, E-mail: globaleducation@fdu.edu.

GRADUATE UNITS

Maxwell Becton College of Arts and Sciences Students: 103 full-time (73 women), 185 part-time (143 women); includes 35 minority (15 African Americans, 10 Asian Americans or Pacific Islanders, 10 Hispanic Americans), 27 international. Average age 33. 207 applicants, 81% accepted, 92 enrolled. Expenses: Contact institution. In 2001, 78 degrees awarded. Offers applied social and community psychology (MA); arts and sciences (MA, MFA, MS); biology (MS); chemistry (MS); clinical/counseling psychology (MA); corporate and organizational communication (MA); creative writing (MFA); general experimental psychology (MA); industrial/organizational psychology (MA); mathematics (MA); organizational behavior (MA).

Fairleigh Dickinson University, College at Florham (continued)

Application deadline: Applications are processed on a rolling basis. *Application fee:* $40. *Dean*, Dr. Barbara Salmore, 973-443-8750, E-mail: salmore@fdu.edu.

New College of General and Continuing Studies Students: 4 full-time (2 women), 9 part-time (all women); includes 3 minority (1 African American, 2 Hispanic Americans), 5 international. Average age 35. 11 applicants, 73% accepted, 5 enrolled. Expenses: Contact institution. *Application deadline:* Applications are processed on a rolling basis. *Application fee:* $40. *Dean*, Kenneth T. Vehrkens, 201-692-2671, Fax: 201-692-2503, E-mail: vehrkens@fdu.edu.

School of Hotel, Restaurant and Tourism Management Students: 4 full-time (2 women), 9 part-time (all women); includes 3 minority (1 African American, 2 Hispanic Americans), 5 international. Average age 35. 11 applicants, 73% accepted, 5 enrolled. Expenses: Contact institution. Offers hospitality management studies (MS). *Application deadline:* Applications are processed on a rolling basis. *Application fee:* $40. *Director*, Richard Wisch, 201-692-7271, Fax: 201-692-7279, E-mail: wisch@fdu.edu.

Samuel J. Silberman College of Business Administration Students: 101 full-time (62 women), 354 part-time (167 women); includes 60 minority (16 African Americans, 31 Asian Americans or Pacific Islanders, 13 Hispanic Americans), 19 international. Average age 32. 149 applicants, 74% accepted, 79 enrolled. Expenses: Contact institution. In 2001, 132 degrees awarded. *Degree program information:* Part-time and evening/weekend programs available. Offers accounting (MS); business administration (MBA, MS); finance (MBA); human resource management (MBA); information systems management (MBA); international business (MBA); management (MBA); marketing (MBA); pharmaceutical-chemical studies (MBA); taxation (MS). *Application deadline:* Applications are processed on a rolling basis. *Application fee:* $40. *Dean*, Leo Rogers, 201-692-7200, Fax: 201-692-7199, E-mail: rogers@fdu.edu.

George Rothman Institute of Entrepreneurial Studies Students: 1 (woman) full-time, 7 part-time. Average age 34. 3 applicants, 67% accepted, 0 enrolled. Expenses: Contact institution. In 2001, 3 degrees awarded. Offers entrepreneurial studies (MBA). *Application deadline:* Applications are processed on a rolling basis. *Application fee:* $40. *Dean*, Leo Rogers, 973-443-8842, Fax: 973-443-8847, E-mail: rogers@fdu.edu.

See in-depth description on page 871.

FAIRLEIGH DICKINSON UNIVERSITY, METROPOLITAN CAMPUS, Teaneck, NJ 07666-1914

General Information Independent, coed, comprehensive institution. *Enrollment:* 846 full-time matriculated graduate/professional students (414 women), 1,300 part-time matriculated graduate/professional students (814 women). *Enrollment by degree level:* 2,026 master's, 120 doctoral. *Graduate faculty:* 675. *Tuition:* Full-time $11,484; part-time $638 per credit. *Required fees:* $420; $97. *Library facilities:* Weiner Library plus 2 others. *Online resources:* library catalog. *Collection:* 435,718 titles, 15,508 serial subscriptions, 3,779 audiovisual materials.

Computer facilities: 210 computers available on campus for general student use. A campuswide network can be accessed from student residence rooms and from off campus. *Web address:* http://www.fdu.edu/.

General Application Contact: Andrew G. Nelson, Director of Adult and Graduate Admissions, 800-338-8803, Fax: 201-692-7309, E-mail: globaleducation@fdu.edu.

GRADUATE UNITS

New College of General and Continuing Studies Students: 48 full-time (34 women), 356 part-time (172 women); includes 42 minority (26 African Americans, 6 Asian Americans or Pacific Islanders, 9 Hispanic Americans, 1 Native American), 24 international. Average age 39. 228 applicants, 97% accepted, 111 enrolled. Expenses: Contact institution. In 2001, 109 degrees awarded. *Application deadline:* Applications are processed on a rolling basis. *Application fee:* $40. *Dean*, Kenneth T. Vehrkens, 201-692-2671, Fax: 201-692-2503, E-mail: vehrkens@fdu.edu.

Public Administration Institute Students: 34 full-time (23 women), 330 part-time (159 women); includes 38 minority (23 African Americans, 6 Asian Americans or Pacific Islanders, 8 Hispanic Americans, 1 Native American), 16 international. Average age 39. 204 applicants, 98% accepted, 98 enrolled. Expenses: Contact institution. In 2001, 109 degrees awarded. Offers administrative science (MAS); public administration (MPA). *Application deadline:* Applications are processed on a rolling basis. *Application fee:* $40. *Director*, Dr. William Roberts, 201-692-7171, Fax: 201-692-7179, E-mail: wroberts@fdu.edu.

School of Hotel, Restaurant and Tourism Management Students: 14 full-time (11 women), 26 part-time (13 women); includes 4 minority (3 African Americans, 1 Hispanic American), 8 international. Average age 38. 24 applicants, 88% accepted, 13 enrolled. Expenses: Contact institution. Offers hospitality management (MS). *Application deadline:* Applications are processed on a rolling basis. *Application fee:* $40. *Director*, Richard Wisch, 201-692-7271, Fax: 201-692-7279, E-mail: wisch@fdu.edu.

Silberman College of Business Administration Students: 143 full-time (74 women), 241 part-time (117 women); includes 62 minority (20 African Americans, 30 Asian Americans or Pacific Islanders, 12 Hispanic Americans), 77 international. Average age 33. 316 applicants, 77% accepted, 87 enrolled. Expenses: Contact institution. In 2001, 136 degrees awarded. Offers accounting (MS); business administration (MBA, MS); finance (MBA); global management (MBA); human resource management (MBA); information systems management (MBA); international business (MBA); management (MBA); management for executives (MBA); management for health systems executives (MBA); management for informations systems professionals (MBA); marketing (MBA); pharmaceutical-chemical studies (MBA); taxation (MS). *Application deadline:* Applications are processed on a rolling basis. *Application fee:* $40. *Dean*, Leo Rogers, 973-692-8842, Fax: 973-443-8847, E-mail: rogers@fdu.edu.

George Rothman Institute of Entrepreneurial Studies Students: 1 (woman) full-time; minority (Hispanic American) Average age 25. 4 applicants, 75% accepted, 1 enrolled. Expenses: Contact institution. In 2001, 1 degree awarded. Offers entrepreneurial studies (MBA). *Application deadline:* Applications are processed on a rolling basis. *Application fee:* $40. *Dean*, Leo Rogers, 973-692-8842, Fax: 973-443-8847, E-mail: rogers@fdu.edu.

University College: Arts, Sciences, and Professional Studies Students: 655 full-time (306 women), 703 part-time (525 women); includes 157 minority (58 African Americans, 55 Asian Americans or Pacific Islanders, 41 Hispanic Americans, 3 Native Americans), 427 international. Average age 31. 1,395 applicants, 80% accepted, 430 enrolled. Expenses: Contact institution. In 2001, 318 master's, 13 doctorates awarded. Offers arts, sciences, and professional studies (MA, MAS, MAT, MPA, MS, MSEE, MSN, PhD, Psy D); systems science (MS). *Application deadline:* Applications are processed on a rolling basis. *Application fee:* $40. *Dean*, Dr. John Snyder, 201-692-2132, Fax: 201-692-2729, E-mail: rednys@fdu.edu.

Henry P. Becton School of Nursing and Allied Health Students: 3 full-time (2 women), 33 part-time (29 women); includes 18 minority (6 African Americans, 10 Asian Americans or Pacific Islanders, 1 Hispanic American, 1 Native American), 1 international. Average age 41. 15 applicants, 87% accepted, 7 enrolled. Expenses: Contact institution. In 2001, 4 degrees awarded. Offers medical technology (MS); nursing (MSN). *Application deadline:* Applications are processed on a rolling basis. *Application fee:* $40. *Director*, Dr. Minerva Guttman, 201-692-2888, Fax: 201-692-2388, E-mail: guttman@fdu.edu.

Peter Sammartino School of Education Students: 113 full-time (94 women), 411 part-time (355 women); includes 53 minority (25 African Americans, 6 Asian Americans or Pacific Islanders, 21 Hispanic Americans, 1 Native American), 13 international. Average age 35. 294 applicants, 91% accepted, 204 enrolled. Expenses: Contact institution. In 2001, 138 degrees awarded. *Degree program information:* Part-time programs available. Offers education for certified teachers (MA); educational leadership (MA); learning disabilities (MA); multilingual education (MA); teaching (MAT). *Application deadline:* Applications are processed on a rolling basis. *Application fee:* $40. *Director*, Dr. Eloise Forster, 201-692-2834, Fax: 201-692-2603, E-mail: forster@fdu.edu.

School of Communication Arts Students: 2 full-time (1 woman), 6 part-time (4 women); includes 1 minority (African American), 1 international. Average age 32. 3 applicants, 67% accepted, 1 enrolled. Expenses: Contact institution. In 2001, 1 degree awarded. Offers English and comparative literature (MA). *Application deadline:* Applications are processed on a rolling basis. *Application fee:* $40. *Director*, Dr. Duane Edwards, 201-692-2263, Fax: 201-692-2265, E-mail: edwards@fdu.edu.

School of Computer Science and Information Systems Students: 277 full-time (74 women), 115 part-time (39 women); includes 31 minority (10 African Americans, 19 Asian Americans or Pacific Islanders, 1 Hispanic American, 1 Native American), 306 international. Average age 28. 593 applicants, 70% accepted, 89 enrolled. Expenses: Contact institution. In 2001, 90 degrees awarded. Offers computer science (MS); e-commerce (MS); management information systems (MS). *Application deadline:* Applications are processed on a rolling basis. *Application fee:* $40. *Interim Director*, Dr. Gilbert Steiner, 201-692-2261, Fax: 201-692-2773, E-mail: steiner@fdu.edu.

School of Engineering and Engineering Technology Students: 85 full-time (8 women), 16 part-time (3 women); includes 5 minority (1 African American, 3 Asian Americans or Pacific Islanders, 1 Hispanic American), 86 international. Average age 26. 300 applicants, 87% accepted, 50 enrolled. Expenses: Contact institution. In 2001, 10 degrees awarded. Offers computer engineering (MS); electrical engineering (MSEE). *Application deadline:* Applications are processed on a rolling basis. *Application fee:* $40. *Director*, Dr. Alfredo Tan, 201-692-2347, Fax: 201-692-2130, E-mail: tan@fdu.edu.

School of History, Political, and International Studies Students: 6 full-time (3 women), 12 part-time (4 women); includes 2 minority (both African Americans), 4 international. Average age 34. 13 applicants, 92% accepted, 4 enrolled. Expenses: Contact institution. In 2001, 5 degrees awarded. Offers history (MA); international studies (MA); political science (MA). *Application deadline:* Applications are processed on a rolling basis. *Application fee:* $40. *Director*, Dr. Faramarz Fatemi, 201-692-2272, Fax: 201-692-9096, E-mail: fatemi@fdu.edu.

School of Natural Sciences Students: 15 full-time (10 women), 70 part-time (56 women); includes 25 minority (9 African Americans, 12 Asian Americans or Pacific Islanders, 4 Hispanic Americans), 6 international. Average age 31. 73 applicants, 90% accepted, 32 enrolled. Expenses: Contact institution. In 2001, 28 degrees awarded. Offers biology (MS); science (MA). *Application deadline:* Applications are processed on a rolling basis. *Application fee:* $40. *Director*, Dr. Anne Anastasia, 201-692-2389, Fax: 201-692-7349, E-mail: anastasi@fdu.edu.

School of Psychology Students: 152 full-time (114 women), 38 part-time (35 women); includes 22 minority (4 African Americans, 5 Asian Americans or Pacific Islanders, 13 Hispanic Americans), 8 international. Average age 30. 93 applicants, 77% accepted, 36 enrolled. Expenses: Contact institution. In 2001, 35 master's, 13 doctorates awarded. Offers clinical psychology (PhD); general-theoretical psychology (MA); school psychology (MA, Psy D). *Application deadline:* Applications are processed on a rolling basis. *Application fee:* $40. *Director*, Dr. Christopher Capuano, 201-692-2811, Fax: 201-692-2304, E-mail: capuano@fdu.edu.

See in-depth description on page 871.

FAIRMONT STATE COLLEGE, Fairmont, WV 26554

General Information State-supported, coed, comprehensive institution.

GRADUATE UNITS

Program in Criminal Justice

FAITH BAPTIST BIBLE COLLEGE AND THEOLOGICAL SEMINARY, Ankeny, IA 50021-2152

General Information Independent-religious, coed, comprehensive institution. *Enrollment:* 30 full-time matriculated graduate/professional students (5 women), 85 part-time matriculated graduate/professional students (31 women). *Enrollment by degree level:* 24 first professional, 12 master's. *Graduate faculty:* 4 full-time (0 women), 6 part-time/adjunct (0 women). *Tuition:* Full-time $8,232; part-time $300 per credit hour. One-time fee: $50. *Graduate housing:* Rooms and/or apartments available on a first-come, first-served basis to single and married students. Typical cost: $1,616 per year ($3,466 including board) for single students. Room and board charges vary according to housing facility selected. Housing application deadline: 8/1. *Student services:* Campus employment opportunities, career counseling, free psychological counseling, international student services, low-cost health insurance. *Library facilities:* Patten Hall plus 1 other. *Online resources:* library catalog. *Collection:* 60,700 titles, 423 serial subscriptions, 3,768 audiovisual materials.

Computer facilities: 41 computers available on campus for general student use. A campuswide network can be accessed from student residence rooms. Internet access is available. *Web address:* http://www.faith.edu/.

General Application Contact: Tim Nilius, Vice President of Enrollment, 888-FAITH4U, Fax: 515-964-1638, E-mail: niliust@faith.edu.

GRADUATE UNITS

Graduate Program Students: 30 full-time (5 women), 85 part-time (31 women); includes 2 minority (both Hispanic Americans), 6 international. Average age 29. 30 applicants, 97% accepted, 27 enrolled. *Faculty:* 4 full-time (0 women), 6 part-time/adjunct (0 women). Expenses: Contact institution. *Financial support:* In 2001–02, 45 students received support. Career-related internships or fieldwork and scholarships/grants available. Support available to part-time students. Financial award applicants required to submit FAFSA. In 2001, 6 first professional degrees, 10 master's awarded. *Degree program information:* Part-time programs available. Offers biblical studies (MA); pastoral studies (M Div); pastoral training (MA); religion (MA); theological studies (MA); theology (Th D). *Application deadline:* For fall admission, 8/1 (priority date); for spring admission, 12/15. Applications are processed on a rolling basis. *Application fee:* $25. *Application Contact:* Tim Nilius, Vice President of Enrollment, 888-FAITH4U, Fax: 515-964-1638, E-mail: niliust@faith.edu. *Dean of Seminary*, Dr. John Hartog, 515-964-0601, Fax: 515-964-1638, E-mail: hartogj3@faith.edu.

FAITH EVANGELICAL LUTHERAN SEMINARY, Tacoma, WA 98407

General Information Independent-religious, coed, graduate-only institution. *Graduate faculty:* 7 full-time (0 women), 17 part-time/adjunct (0 women). *Library facilities:* Main library plus 1 other. *Collection:* 20,000 titles. *Web address:* http://www.faithseminary.edu/.

GRADUATE UNITS

Graduate and Professional Programs Students: 70 full-time (25 women), 40 part-time (15 women); includes 59 minority (12 African Americans, 45 Asian Americans or Pacific Islanders, 2 Hispanic Americans) Expenses: Contact institution. Offers theology (M Div, MCM). *Application fee:* $40.

FASHION INSTITUTE OF TECHNOLOGY, New York, NY 10001-5992

General Information State and locally supported, coed, comprehensive institution. *Enrollment:* 41 full-time matriculated graduate/professional students (all women), 65 part-time matriculated graduate/professional students (56 women). *Enrollment by degree level:* 106 master's. *Graduate faculty:* 3 full-time (2 women), 15 part-time/adjunct (12 women). *Tuition, area resident:* Full-time $4,654; part-time $228 per credit. Tuition, nonresident: full-time $10,396; part-time $486 per credit. *Required fees:* $270. *Graduate housing:* Room and/or apartments available to single students; on-campus housing not available to married students. *Student services:* Career counseling, exercise/wellness program, free psychological counseling, international student services. *Library facilities:* Gladys Marcus Library. *Collection:* 154,015 titles, 1,770 audiovisual materials.

Computer facilities: 450 computers available on campus for general student use. A campuswide network can be accessed from student residence rooms and from off campus. Internet access and online class registration are available. *Web address:* http://www.fitnyc.suny.edu/.

General Application Contact: Dr. Maria Ann Conelli, Dean, 212-217-5714.

GRADUATE UNITS

Division of Graduate Studies Students: 41 full-time (all women), 65 part-time (56 women); includes 7 minority (1 African American, 4 Asian Americans or Pacific Islanders, 2 Hispanic Americans), 20 international. Average age 30. 121 applicants, 63% accepted. *Faculty:* 3 full-time (2 women), 15 part-time/adjunct (12 women). Expenses: Contact institution. In 2001, 20 degrees awarded. Offers cosmetics and fragrance marketing and management (MPS); gallery and retail art administration (MA); museum studies: applied arts (MA); museum studies: costume and textiles (MA). *Application deadline:* For fall admission, 2/15 (priority date). *Application fee:* $25. *Dean,* Dr. Maria Ann Conelli, 212-217-5714.

FAULKNER UNIVERSITY, Montgomery, AL 36109-3398

General Information Independent-religious, coed, comprehensive institution. *Enrollment:* 83 full-time matriculated graduate/professional students (36 women), 139 part-time matriculated graduate/professional students (60 women). *Enrollment by degree level:* 222 first professional. *Graduate faculty:* 14 full-time (3 women), 6 part-time/adjunct (1 woman). *Tuition:* Full-time $12,000; part-time $3,600 per semester. Tuition and fees vary according to course load. *Graduate housing:* On-campus housing not available. *Student services:* Career counseling, disabled student services. *Library facilities:* Gus Nichols Library plus 2 others. *Online resources:* library catalog, web page, access to other libraries' catalogs. *Collection:* 118,039 titles, 1,183 serial subscriptions, 730 audiovisual materials.

Computer facilities: 85 computers available on campus for general student use. A campuswide network can be accessed. Internet access is available. *Web address:* http://www.faulkner.edu/.

General Application Contact: Paul M. Smith, Assistant Dean, 334-386-7212, Fax: 334-386-7223, E-mail: psmith@faulkner.edu.

GRADUATE UNITS

Thomas Goode Jones School of Law Students: 83 full-time (36 women), 139 part-time (60 women); includes 22 minority (20 African Americans, 1 Asian American or Pacific Islander, 1 Hispanic American) Average age 31. 128 applicants, 73% accepted, 73 enrolled. *Faculty:* 14 full-time (3 women), 6 part-time/adjunct (1 woman). Expenses: Contact institution. *Financial support:* In 2001–02, 161 students received support. Career-related internships or fieldwork and Federal Work-Study available. Support available to part-time students. Financial award application deadline: 5/1; financial award applicants required to submit FAFSA. In 2001, 55 degrees awarded. *Degree program information:* Part-time and evening/weekend programs available. Offers law (JD). *Application deadline:* For fall admission, 7/15. Applications are processed on a rolling basis. *Application fee:* $25. *Application Contact:* Paul M. Smith, Assistant Dean, 334-386-7212, Fax: 334-386-7223, E-mail: psmith@faulkner.edu. *Dean,* Wendell W. Mitchell, 334-386-7210, Fax: 334-386-7223, E-mail: wmitchell@faulkner.edu.

FAYETTEVILLE STATE UNIVERSITY, Fayetteville, NC 28301-4298

General Information State-supported, coed, comprehensive institution. CGS member. *Enrollment:* 81 full-time matriculated graduate/professional students (58 women), 171 part-time matriculated graduate/professional students (128 women). *Enrollment by degree level:* 197 master's, 55 doctoral. *Graduate faculty:* 97. Tuition, state resident: full-time $810; part-time $426 per year. Tuition, nonresident: full-time $4,445; part-time $2,223 per year. Tuition and fees vary according to course load. *Graduate housing:* On-campus housing not available. *Student services:* Career counseling, child daycare facilities, free psychological counseling, low-cost health insurance. *Library facilities:* Charles W. Chestnut Library. *Online resources:* library catalog, web page. *Collection:* 197,814 titles, 2,769 serial subscriptions. *Research affiliation:* Research Triangle Park.

Computer facilities: 300 computers available on campus for general student use. A campuswide network can be accessed from student residence rooms and from off campus. Internet access is available. *Web address:* http://www.uncfsu.edu/.

General Application Contact: Dr. LaDelle Olion, Director of the Graduate Center, 910-672-1498, Fax: 910-672-1782, E-mail: lolion@uncfsu.edu.

GRADUATE UNITS

Graduate School Students: 81 full-time (58 women), 171 part-time (128 women); includes 130 minority (119 African Americans, 3 Asian Americans or Pacific Islanders, 2 Hispanic Americans, 6 Native Americans) 80 applicants, 100% accepted. Expenses: Contact institution. *Financial support:* Institutionally sponsored loans available. Support available to part-time students. In 2001, 107 master's, 4 doctorates awarded. *Degree program information:* Part-time and evening/weekend programs available. Offers biology (MA Ed, MS); business administration (MBA); educational leadership (Ed D); elementary education (MA Ed); English (MA); history (MA, MA Ed); mathematics (MA Ed, MS); middle grades (MA Ed); political science (MA, MA Ed); psychology (MA); school administration (MSA); sociology (MA, MA Ed); special education (MA Ed). *Application deadline:* For fall admission, 8/1; for spring admission, 12/15. Applications are processed on a rolling basis. *Application fee:* $25. *Director of the Graduate Center,* Dr. LaDelle Olion, 910-672-1498, Fax: 910-672-1782, E-mail: lolion@uncfsu.edu.

FELICIAN COLLEGE, Lodi, NJ 07644-2117

General Information Independent-religious, coed, comprehensive institution. *Enrollment:* 3 full-time matriculated graduate/professional students (all women), 93 part-time matriculated graduate/professional students (77 women). *Enrollment by degree level:* 96 master's. *Graduate faculty:* 9 full-time (8 women), 21 part-time/adjunct (15 women). *Tuition:* Part-time $415 per credit. *Graduate housing:* Rooms and/or apartments available on a first-come, first-served basis to single and married students. *Student services:* Campus employment opportunities, career counseling, child daycare facilities, disabled student services, free psychological counseling, writing training. *Library facilities:* Felician College Library. *Online resources:* library catalog, web page. *Collection:* 133,322 titles, 726 serial subscriptions, 14,845 audiovisual materials. *Research affiliation:* Hackensack University Medical Center, Department of Nursing (nursing), University of Medicine and Dentistry of New Jersey, School of Nursing (nursing).

Computer facilities: 100 computers available on campus for general student use. A campuswide network can be accessed from student residence rooms and from off campus. Internet access is available. *Web address:* http://www.felician.edu/.

General Application Contact: Cynthia Sievewright, Director of Admissions, 201-559-6131 Ext. 6131, Fax: 201-559-6188, E-mail: admissions@inet.felician.edu.

GRADUATE UNITS

Program in Advanced Practice Nursing Students: 1 (woman) full-time, 33 part-time (28 women). Average age 35. 24 applicants, 83% accepted. *Faculty:* 7 full-time (all women), 10 part-time/adjunct (9 women). Expenses: Contact institution. *Financial support:* Scholarships/grants, traineeships, and tuition waivers (partial) available. *Degree program information:* Part-time programs available. Offers adult nurse practitioner (MSN); family nurse practitioner (MSN). *Application deadline:* Applications are processed on a rolling basis. *Application fee:* $40. *Application Contact:* Rosalie Santaniello, Director of Adult and Graduate Admission, 201-559-6055, Fax: 201-559-6188, E-mail: santaniellor@inet.felician.edu. *Dean, Division of Health Sciences,* Dr. Muriel Shore, 201-559-6030, E-mail: shorem@inet.felician.edu.

Program in Education Students: 2 full-time (both women), 42 part-time (37 women). 12 applicants, 83% accepted. *Faculty:* 2 full-time (1 woman). Expenses: Contact institution. *Financial support:* Scholarships/grants available. Support available to part-time students. *Degree program information:* Part-time and evening/weekend programs available. Offers education (MA). *Application deadline:* Applications are processed on a rolling basis. *Application fee:* $40. *Application Contact:* Rosalie Santaniello, Director of Adult and Graduate Admission, 201-559-6055, Fax: 201-559-6131, E-mail: santaniellor@inet.felician.edu. *Chairperson,* Dr. JoAnn Looney, 201-559-3545.

Program in Religious Education Average age 38. 20 applicants, 85% accepted. *Faculty:* 11 part-time/adjunct (6 women). Expenses: Contact institution. *Financial support:* Scholarships/grants and tuition waivers (partial) available. Support available to part-time students. *Degree program information:* Part-time and evening/weekend programs available. Offers religious education (MA). *Application deadline:* Applications are processed on a rolling basis. *Application fee:* $40. *Application Contact:* Rosalie Santaniello, Director of Adult and Graduate Admission, 201-559-6055, Fax: 201-559-6131, E-mail: santaniellor@inet.felician.edu. *Director,* Dr. Dolores M. Henchy, 201-559-6053, Fax: 973-472-8936, E-mail: henchyd@inet.felician.edu.

FERRIS STATE UNIVERSITY, Big Rapids, MI 49307

General Information State-supported, coed, comprehensive institution. *Enrollment:* 737 matriculated graduate/professional students. *Enrollment by degree level:* 409 first professional, 328 master's. *Graduate faculty:* 69 full-time (22 women), 68 part-time/adjunct (25 women). Tuition, state resident: full-time $2,335; part-time $196 per credit hour. Tuition, nonresident: full-time $4,945; part-time $414 per credit hour. *Required fees:* $200 per semester. *Graduate housing:* Rooms and/or apartments available on a first-come, first-served basis to single and married students. *Student services:* Campus employment opportunities, campus safety program, career counseling, child daycare facilities, disabled student services, free psychological counseling, international student services, low-cost health insurance. *Library facilities:* Ferris Library for Information, Technology and Education. *Online resources:* library catalog, web page, access to other libraries' catalogs. *Collection:* 339,164 titles, 10,000 serial subscriptions, 10,136 audiovisual materials. *Research affiliation:* Research Technology Institute (materials science, manufacturing sciences), Vistakon–Johnson & Johnson (optometry), Allergan-Hydron (optometry), Bausch & Lomb (optometry), Ciba Vision Care (optometry).

Computer facilities: 276 computers available on campus for general student use. A campuswide network can be accessed from student residence rooms and from off campus. Internet access and online class registration are available. *Web address:* http://www.ferris.edu/.

General Application Contact: Craig Westman, Associate Dean Enrollment Services/Director Admissions and Records, 231-581-2100, Fax: 231-591-2978, E-mail: admissions@ferris.edu.

GRADUATE UNITS

College of Business Students: 81 full-time (26 women), 73 part-time (25 women); includes 26 minority (11 African Americans, 13 Asian Americans or Pacific Islanders, 2 Hispanic Americans), 56 international. 223 applicants, 76% accepted, 59 enrolled. *Faculty:* 6 full-time (1 woman), 2 part-time/adjunct (0 women). Expenses: Contact institution. *Financial support:* In 2001–02, 40 research assistantships, 10 teaching assistantships were awarded. Career-related internships or fieldwork also available. Support available to part-time students. In 2001, 81 degrees awarded. *Degree program information:* Part-time and evening/weekend programs available. Offers business (MSISM); information systems management (MSISM). *Application deadline:* For fall admission, 7/1; for winter admission, 11/1; for spring admission, 3/1. *Application fee:* $30. Electronic applications accepted. *Dean,* David Nicol, 231-591-2422, Fax: 231-591-2973.

College of Education and Human Services Students: 169 (77 women); includes 22 minority (13 African Americans, 3 Asian Americans or Pacific Islanders, 3 Hispanic Americans, 3 Native Americans) 4 international. Average age 31. *Faculty:* 15 full-time (8 women), 13 part-time/adjunct (7 women). Expenses: Contact institution. *Financial support:* In 2001–02, 8 students received support, including research assistantships with full tuition reimbursements available (averaging $3,960 per year), 1 teaching assistantship with partial tuition reimbursement available (averaging $3,800 per year); career-related internships or fieldwork and tuition waivers (full and partial) also available. Support available to part-time students. In 2001, 38 degrees awarded. *Degree program information:* Part-time and evening/weekend programs available. Postbaccalaureate distance learning degree programs offered. Offers education and human services (M Ed, MS, MSCTE). *Application deadline:* For fall admission, 8/31; for winter admission, 12/10. Applications are processed on a rolling basis. *Application fee:* $20. *Dean,* Michelle Johnston, 616-591-3646, Fax: 616-592-3792, E-mail: michelle_johnston@ferris.edu.

School of Criminal Justice Students: 27 full-time (15 women), 43 part-time (10 women); includes 16 minority (12 African Americans, 1 Asian American or Pacific Islander, 1 Hispanic American, 2 Native Americans), 3 international. Average age 26. *Faculty:* 5 full-time (2 women). Expenses: Contact institution. *Financial support:* In 2001–02, 4 students received support, including research assistantships (averaging $3,960 per year); career-related internships or fieldwork also available. In 2001, 15 degrees awarded. *Degree program information:* Part-time programs available. Offers criminal justice (MS). *Application deadline:* For fall admission, 8/23 (priority date); for winter admission, 12/10 (priority date). Applications are processed on a rolling basis. *Application fee:* $30. Electronic applications accepted. *Application Contact:* Dr. Nancy L. Hogan, Assistant Professor, 231-591-2664, Fax: 231-591-3792, E-mail: nancy_hogan@ferris.edu. *Acting Director,* Dr. Frank Crowe, 231-591-2840, Fax: 231-591-3792, E-mail: crowef@ferris.edu.

School of Education Students: 104 (53 women); includes 8 minority (3 African Americans, 2 Asian Americans or Pacific Islanders, 2 Hispanic Americans, 1 Native American) 2 international. Average age 35. 40 applicants, 75% accepted. *Faculty:* 11 full-time (7 women), 13 part-time/adjunct (7 women). Expenses: Contact institution. *Financial support:* Career-related internships or fieldwork and tuition waivers (full and partial) available. Support available to part-time students. Financial award applicants required to submit FAFSA. In 2001, 28 degrees awarded. *Degree program information:* Part-time and evening/weekend programs available. Postbaccalaureate distance learning degree programs offered. Offers administration (MSCTE); curriculum and instruction (M Ed); education technology (MSCTE); instructor (MSCTE); post-secondary administration (MSCTE); training and development (MSCTE). *Application deadline:* For fall admission, 7/1 (priority date); for winter admission, 12/10 (priority date). Applications are processed on a rolling basis. *Application fee:* $30. *Application Contact:* Kathy Cairns, Secretary, 231-591-3511, Fax: 231-591-2041, E-mail: cairnsk@ferris.edu. *Director,* Dr. Susanne Chandler, 231-591-5362, Fax: 231-591-2041, E-mail: chandles@ferris.edu.

College of Pharmacy Students: 279 full-time (184 women); includes 24 minority (6 African Americans, 15 Asian Americans or Pacific Islanders, 1 Hispanic American, 2 Native Americans) Average age 23. 365 applicants, 33% accepted. *Faculty:* 28 full-time (10 women), 3 part-time/adjunct (2 women). Expenses: Contact institution. *Financial support:* Institutionally sponsored loans and scholarships/grants available. Financial award applicants required to submit FAFSA. In 2001, 14 degrees awarded. Offers pharmacy (Pharm D). *Application deadline:* For fall admission, 1/31. *Application fee:* $30. *Application Contact:* Dr. Rodney A. Larson, Assistant Dean, 231-591-3780, Fax: 231-591-3829, E-mail: larsonr@ferris.edu. *Dean,* Dr. Ian Mathison, 231-591-2254, Fax: 231-591-3829, E-mail: mathisol@ferris.edu.

Michigan College of Optometry Students: 130 full-time; includes 11 minority (10 Asian Americans or Pacific Islanders, 1 Hispanic American), 3 international. Average age 23. 205 applicants, 17% accepted. *Faculty:* 19 full-time (2 women), 50 part-time/adjunct (16 women). Expenses: Contact institution. *Financial support:* In 2001–02, 104 students received support. Career-related internships or fieldwork, Federal Work-Study, and scholarships/grants available. Financial award application deadline: 4/1. In 2001, 30 degrees awarded. Offers optometry (OD). *Application deadline:* For fall admission, 2/1. Applications are processed on a rolling basis. *Application fee:* $30. Electronic applications accepted. *Application Contact:* Dr. Thomas R. Colladay, Associate Dean, 231-591-3703, Fax: 231-591-2394, E-mail: colladat@ferris.edu. *Dean,* Dr. Kevin L. Alexander, 231-591-3706, Fax: 231-591-2394, E-mail: alexandk@ferris.edu.

FIELDING GRADUATE INSTITUTE, Santa Barbara, CA 93105-3538

General Information Independent, coed, graduate-only institution. CGS member. *Enrollment by degree level:* 146 master's, 1,161 doctoral. *Graduate faculty:* 81 full-time (39 women), 62 part-time/adjunct (27 women). *Tuition:* Full-time $14,100. *Graduate housing:* On-campus housing not available. *Library facilities:* The Fielding Graduate Institute Library Services. *Online resources:* web page. *Collection:* 1,900 titles.

Fielding Graduate Institute (continued)

Computer facilities: 6 computers available on campus for general student use. A campuswide network can be accessed from off campus. Internet access and online class registration are available. *Web address:* http://www.fielding.edu/.

General Application Contact: Marine Dumas, Admissions Manager, 805-898-4039, Fax: 805-687-4590, E-mail: mdumas@fielding.edu.

GRADUATE UNITS

Graduate Programs Students: 1,307 full-time (889 women); includes 352 minority (207 African Americans, 43 Asian Americans or Pacific Islanders, 60 Hispanic Americans, 42 Native Americans), 25 international. Average age 44. 324 applicants, 59% accepted, 161 enrolled. *Faculty:* 81 full-time (39 women), 62 part-time/adjunct (27 women). Expenses: Contact institution. *Financial support:* In 2001–02, 709 students received support. Career-related internships or fieldwork, institutionally sponsored loans, scholarships/grants, and tuition waivers (partial) available. Financial award application deadline: 3/1; financial award applicants required to submit FAFSA. In 2001, 115 master's, 115 doctorates awarded. *Degree program information:* Evening/weekend programs available. Postbaccalaureate distance learning degree programs offered. Offers clinical psychology (PhD); educational leadership (Ed D); human and organizational systems (PhD); human development (MA, PhD); human organization development (Ed D); human services (MA); organization development (MA); organizational design and effectiveness/organizational management (MA); psychology (MA). *Application deadline:* For fall admission, 3/5; for spring admission, 9/5. *Application fee:* $75. Electronic applications accepted. *Application Contact:* Marine Dumas, Admissions Manager, 805-898-4039, Fax: 805-687-4590, E-mail: mdumas@fielding.edu. *President,* Dr. Judith Kuipers, 805-898-2903, Fax: 805-687-4590, E-mail: jkuipers@fielding.edu.

FINCH UNIVERSITY OF HEALTH SCIENCES/THE CHICAGO MEDICAL SCHOOL, North Chicago, IL 60064-3095

General Information Independent, coed, upper-level institution. CGS member. *Enrollment:* 1,461 matriculated graduate/professional students. *Graduate faculty:* 57 full-time, 28 part-time/adjunct. *Tuition:* Part-time $416 per credit hour. *Required fees:* $25. Part-time tuition and fees vary according to program. *Graduate housing:* On-campus housing not available. *Student services:* Free psychological counseling, low-cost health insurance. *Library facilities:* Boxer University Library. *Online resources:* library catalog, web page. *Collection:* 94,045 titles, 1,063 serial subscriptions, 282 audiovisual materials. *Research affiliation:* Veterans Administration Hospital, Lutheran General Hospital, Northern Illinois Medical Center, St. Francis Hospital, Fermi National Accelerator Laboratory, Argonne National Laboratory.

Computer facilities: 39 computers available on campus for general student use. A campuswide network can be accessed from off campus. *Web address:* http://www.finchcms.edu/.

General Application Contact: Dana Frederick, Admissions Officer, 847-578-3209.

GRADUATE UNITS

School of Graduate and Postdoctoral Studies Students: 230 full-time (121 women), 1 (woman) part-time; includes 78 minority (3 African Americans, 68 Asian Americans or Pacific Islanders, 7 Hispanic Americans), 18 international. Average age 23. *Faculty:* 57 full-time, 28 part-time/adjunct. Expenses: Contact institution. *Financial support:* In 2001–02, fellowships (averaging $16,500 per year); research assistantships, teaching assistantships, career-related internships or fieldwork, scholarships/grants, and tuition waivers (full and partial) also available. Financial award application deadline: 7/10; financial award applicants required to submit FAFSA. In 2001, 74 master's, 24 doctorates awarded. *Degree program information:* Part-time programs available. Offers anatomy (MS, PhD); applied physiology (MS); biochemistry (MS, PhD); cell biology (MS, PhD); cellular and molecular pharmacology (MS, PhD); clinical psychology (MS, PhD); medical microbiology (MS, PhD); medical radiation physics (MS, PhD); microbiology and immunology (MS, PhD); neuroscience (PhD); pathology (MS, PhD); physiology (MS, PhD). *Application deadline:* Applications are processed on a rolling basis. *Application fee:* $25. *Application Contact:* Dana Frederick, Admissions Officer, 847-578-3209. *Dean/Vice President for Research,* Dr. Velayudhan Nair, 847-578-3250, Fax: 847-578-3332, E-mail: nairv@finchcms.edu.

School of Medicine Students: 738 full-time (266 women); includes 367 minority (46 African Americans, 309 Asian Americans or Pacific Islanders, 10 Hispanic Americans, 2 Native Americans), 7 international. Average age 26. 7,688 applicants, 7% accepted, 193 enrolled. *Faculty:* 294 full-time (100 women), 380 part-time/adjunct (79 women). Expenses: Contact institution. *Financial support:* Application deadline: 6/8; In 2001, 172 degrees awarded. Offers medicine (MD). *Application deadline:* For fall admission, 11/15. Applications are processed on a rolling basis. *Application fee:* $90. Electronic applications accepted. *Application Contact:* Kristine A. Jones, Director of Admissions/Registrar, 847-578-3204, Fax: 847-578-3284, E-mail: jonesk@finchcms.edu. *Interim Dean,* Dr. Charles P. Barsano, 847-578-3000, Fax: 847-578-3320, E-mail: barsanoc@finchcms.edu.

School of Related Health Sciences Students: 120 full-time (89 women), 124 part-time (105 women). *Faculty:* 26 full-time (19 women), 9 part-time/adjunct (5 women). Expenses: Contact institution. *Financial support:* Teaching assistantships, career-related internships or fieldwork, institutionally sponsored loans, scholarships/grants, and tuition waivers (partial) available. Support available to part-time students. Financial award applicants required to submit FAFSA. In 2001, 77 degrees awarded. *Degree program information:* Part-time and evening/weekend programs available. Postbaccalaureate distance learning degree programs offered (minimal on-campus study). Offers clinical education (MS); clinical laboratory science (MS); clinical nutrition (MS); healthcare management (MS); healthcare risk management (MS); pathologist assistant (MS); physical therapy (MS, TDPT); physician assistant (MS); physician assistant studies (MS); related health sciences (MS, TDPT). *Application deadline:* Applications are processed on a rolling basis. *Application fee:* $25. *Dean,* Dr. Cynthia Adams, 847-578-3304, Fax: 847-578-3015, E-mail: adamsc@finchcms.edu.

FISK UNIVERSITY, Nashville, TN 37208-3051

General Information Independent-religious, coed, comprehensive institution. *Enrollment:* 59 full-time matriculated graduate/professional students (41 women). *Graduate faculty:* 28 full-time (6 women), 1 (woman) part-time/adjunct. *Tuition:* Full-time $9,790. *Graduate housing:* Rooms and/or apartments available on a first-come, first-served basis to single and married students. Typical cost: $3,008 per year ($5,182 including board) for single students; $4,800 per year for married students. Housing application deadline: 4/6. *Student services:* Campus employment opportunities, campus safety program, career counseling, free psychological counseling, international student services, low-cost health insurance. *Library facilities:* Fisk University Main Library. *Online resources:* library catalog, web page, access to other libraries' catalogs. *Collection:* 210,000 titles, 425 serial subscriptions. *Research affiliation:* Oak Ridge Associated Universities (chemical physics).

Computer facilities: 40 computers available on campus for general student use. A campuswide network can be accessed from student residence rooms and from off campus. *Web address:* http://www.fisk.edu/.

General Application Contact: William Carter, Director of Admissions, 615-329-8819, Fax: 615-329-8774, E-mail: bcarter@fisk.edu.

FITCHBURG STATE COLLEGE, Fitchburg, MA 01420-2697

General Information State-supported, coed, comprehensive institution. CGS member. *Enrollment:* 168 full-time matriculated graduate/professional students (127 women), 539 part-time matriculated graduate/professional students (416 women). *Enrollment by degree level:* 707 master's. *Graduate faculty:* 150 part-time/adjunct. Tuition, state resident: part-time $150 per credit. *Required fees:* $7 per credit. $65 per term. Tuition and fees vary according to course load. *Graduate housing:* Room and/or apartments available on a first-come, first-served basis to single students; on-campus housing not available to married students. Typical cost: $4,858 (including board). Room and board charges vary according to board plan and housing facility selected. *Student services:* Campus employment opportunities, campus safety program, career counseling, disabled student services, international student services, low-cost health insurance, teacher training. *Library facilities:* Hammond Library. *Online resources:* library catalog, web page, access to other libraries' catalogs. *Collection:* 229,505 titles, 11,799 serial subscriptions, 2,159 audiovisual materials.

Computer facilities: 500 computers available on campus for general student use. A campuswide network can be accessed from student residence rooms and from off campus. Internet access is available. *Web address:* http://www.fsc.edu/.

General Application Contact: Director of Admissions, 978-665-3144, Fax: 978-665-4540, E-mail: admissions@fsc.edu.

GRADUATE UNITS

Division of Graduate and Continuing Education Students: 168 full-time (127 women), 539 part-time (416 women); includes 23 minority (7 African Americans, 5 Asian Americans or Pacific Islanders, 9 Hispanic Americans, 2 Native Americans), 51 international. Average age 35. *Faculty:* 150 part-time/adjunct. Expenses: Contact institution. *Financial support:* In 2001–02, research assistantships with partial tuition reimbursements (averaging $5,500 per year), teaching assistantships with partial tuition reimbursements (averaging $5,500 per year) were awarded. Federal Work-Study and unspecified assistantships also available. Support available to part-time students. Financial award application deadline: 3/1; financial award applicants required to submit FAFSA. In 2001, 277 master's, 27 other advanced degrees awarded. *Degree program information:* Part-time and evening/weekend programs available. Offers adolescent and family therapy (Certificate); arts in education (M Ed); business administration (MBA); child protective services (Certificate); communications/media (MS); computer science (MS); criminal justice (MS); early childhood education (M Ed); educational leadership and management (M Ed, CAGS); elementary education (M Ed); elementary school guidance counseling (MS); forensic case work (Certificate); forensic nursing (MS); general studies education (M Ed); guided study (M Ed); interdisciplinary studies (CAGS); mental health counseling (MS); middle school education (M Ed); occupational education (M Ed); school guidance counselor (Certificate); science education (M Ed); secondary education (M Ed); secondary school guidance counseling (MS); teacher leadership (CAGS); teaching biology (MA, MAT); teaching earth science (MAT); teaching English (MA, MAT); teaching history (MA, MAT); teaching mathematics (MAT); teaching students with intensive special needs (M Ed); teaching students with special needs (M Ed); technology education (M Ed). *Application deadline:* Applications are processed on a rolling basis. *Application fee:* $10. *Application Contact:* Director of Admissions, 978-665-3144, Fax: 978-665-4540, E-mail: admissions@fsc.edu. *Dean of Graduate Studies,* Dr. Dorothy Boisvert, 978-665-3240, Fax: 978-665-3658, E-mail: gce@fsc.edu.

See in-depth description on page 873.

FIVE BRANCHES INSTITUTE: COLLEGE OF TRADITIONAL CHINESE MEDICINE, Santa Cruz, CA 95062

General Information Independent, coed, graduate-only institution. *Enrollment by degree level:* 200 master's. *Graduate faculty:* 37 part-time/adjunct (20 women). *Tuition:* Full-time $9,000; part-time $191 per unit. *Required fees:* $250. *Graduate housing:* On-campus housing not available. *Student services:* Campus employment opportunities. *Library facilities:* Five Branches Institute Library. *Online resources:* web page. *Collection:* 1,600 titles, 784 serial subscriptions.

Computer facilities: 4 computers available on campus for general student use. Internet access is available. *Web address:* http://www.fivebranches.edu/.

General Application Contact: Eleonor Mendelson, Admissions Director, 408-476-9424, Fax: 408-476-8928, E-mail: tcm@fivebranches.com.

FIVE TOWNS COLLEGE, Dix Hills, NY 11746-6055

General Information Independent, coed, comprehensive institution. *Enrollment:* 2 full-time matriculated graduate/professional students, 52 part-time matriculated graduate/professional students (17 women). *Enrollment by degree level:* 54 master's. *Graduate faculty:* 4 full-time (1 woman), 12 part-time/adjunct (3 women). *Tuition:* Full-time $10,500; part-time $440 per credit. *Required fees:* $450; $30 per credit. Part-time tuition and fees vary according to course load and program. *Graduate housing:* On-campus housing not available. *Student services:* Campus employment opportunities, campus safety program, career counseling, international student services, low-cost health insurance, teacher training, writing training. *Library facilities:* Five Towns College Library. *Online resources:* library catalog, access to other libraries' catalogs. *Collection:* 32,000 titles, 550 serial subscriptions, 6,000 audiovisual materials.

Computer facilities: 84 computers available on campus for general student use. A campuswide network can be accessed. Internet access is available. *Web address:* http://www.fivetowns.edu/.

General Application Contact: Jerry Cohen, Admissions Coordinator, 631-424-7000, Fax: 631-424-7008, E-mail: admissions@ftc.edu.

GRADUATE UNITS

Department of Music Students: 2 full-time (0 women), 52 part-time (17 women); includes 5 minority (4 African Americans, 1 Hispanic American) Average age 25. 54 applicants, 100% accepted. *Faculty:* 3 full-time (0 women), 9 part-time/adjunct (2 women). Expenses: Contact institution. *Financial support:* Tuition waivers (partial) available. Financial award applicants required to submit FAFSA. In 2001, 10 degrees awarded. *Degree program information:* Part-time programs available. Offers jazz/commercial music (MM); music education (MM). *Application deadline:* Applications are processed on a rolling basis. *Application fee:* $50. *Application Contact:* Jerry Cohen, Admissions Coordinator, 631-424-7000 Ext. 121, Fax: 631-424-7008, E-mail: admissions@ftc.edu. *Chair,* Jeffrey Lipton, 631-424-7000 Ext. 122, Fax: 631-424-7008.

FLORIDA AGRICULTURAL AND MECHANICAL UNIVERSITY, Tallahassee, FL 32307-3200

General Information State-supported, coed, university. CGS member. *Graduate housing:* Rooms and/or apartments available on a first-come, first-served basis to single and married students. Housing application deadline: 6/1. *Research affiliation:* The Boeing Company (aerospace science), Minority Health Professions Foundation (health science), Pfizer, Inc..

GRADUATE UNITS

Division of Graduate Studies, Research, and Continuing Education *Degree program information:* Part-time and evening/weekend programs available.

College of Arts and Sciences *Degree program information:* Part-time programs available. Offers applied social science (MASS); arts and sciences (MASS, MS); biology (MS); chemistry (MS); community psychology (MS); physics (MS); school psychology (MS); social and behavioral sciences (MASS).

College of Education *Degree program information:* Part-time and evening/weekend programs available. Offers administration and supervision (M Ed, MS Ed, PhD); adult education (M Ed, MS Ed); business education (MBE); early childhood and elementary education (M Ed, MS Ed); education (M Ed, MBE, MS Ed, PhD); guidance and counseling (M Ed, MS Ed); health, physical education, and recreation (M Ed, MS Ed); industrial education (M Ed, MS Ed); secondary education (M Ed, MS Ed).

College of Engineering Science, Technology, and Agriculture Offers agricultural and extension education (M Ed, MS Ed); engineering science, technology, and agriculture (M Ed, MS Ed).

College of Pharmacy and Pharmaceutical Sciences Offers environmental toxicology (PhD); medicinal chemistry (MS, PhD); pharmaceutics (MS, PhD); pharmacology/toxicology (MS, PhD); pharmacy administration (MS); pharmacy and pharmaceutical sciences (Pharm D, MPH, MS, PhD); public health (MPH).

FAMU-FSU College of Engineering Offers chemical engineering (MS, PhD); civil engineering (MS, PhD); electrical engineering (MS, PhD); engineering (MS, PhD); environmental engineering (MS, PhD); industrial engineering (MS, PhD); mechanical engineering (MS, PhD). College administered jointly by Florida State University.

School of Allied Health Sciences

School of Architecture *Degree program information:* Part-time programs available. Offers architecture (M Arch, MS Arch).

School of Business and Industry Offers accounting (MBA); finance (MBA); management information systems (MBA); marketing (MBA).

School of Journalism Media and Graphic Arts Offers journalism (MS).

FLORIDA ATLANTIC UNIVERSITY, Boca Raton, FL 33431-0991

General Information State-supported, coed, university. CGS member. *Enrollment:* 1,117 full-time matriculated graduate/professional students (624 women), 1,636 part-time matriculated graduate/professional students (1,070 women). *Enrollment by degree level:* 2,305 master's, 411 doctoral, 37 other advanced degrees. *Graduate faculty:* 879 full-time (364 women), 16 part-time/adjunct (5 women). Tuition, state resident: full-time $3,098; part-time $172 per credit. Tuition, nonresident: full-time $10,427; part-time $579 per credit. *Graduate housing:* Rooms and/or apartments available on a first-come, first-served basis to single and married students. Typical cost: $6,134 (including board) for single students; $6,134 (including board) for married students. Housing application deadline: 5/1. *Student services:* Campus employment opportunities, campus safety program, career counseling, child daycare facilities, disabled student services, exercise/wellness program, free psychological counseling, international student services, low-cost health insurance, multicultural affairs office, teacher training. *Library facilities:* S. E. Wimberly Library. *Online resources:* library catalog, web page, access to other libraries' catalogs. *Collection:* 808,239 titles, 4,184 serial subscriptions, 9,511 audiovisual materials. *Research affiliation:* Company of Biologists, LTD, Shell Oil Co. (engineering), Children's Services Council (urban redevelopment), Motorola Corporation (engineering), Harbor Branch Oceanographic Institution (marine resources characterization), Smithsonian Marine Station (marine resources characterization).

Computer facilities: 400 computers available on campus for general student use. A campuswide network can be accessed from student residence rooms and from off campus. Internet access and online class registration are available. *Web address:* http://www.fau.edu/.

General Application Contact: Steve Todish, Graduate Studies—Admissions, 561-297-3624, Fax: 561-297-2117, E-mail: stodish@fau.edu.

GRADUATE UNITS

Charles E. Schmidt College of Science Students: 210 full-time (110 women), 87 part-time (46 women); includes 44 minority (11 African Americans, 13 Asian Americans or Pacific Islanders, 19 Hispanic Americans, 1 Native American), 63 international. Average age 32. 268 applicants, 51% accepted, 102 enrolled. *Faculty:* 110 full-time (15 women), 3 part-time/adjunct (0 women). Expenses: Contact institution. *Financial support:* In 2001–02, 20 research assistantships with partial tuition reimbursements (averaging $15,000 per year), 149 teaching assistantships with partial tuition reimbursements (averaging $15,000 per year) were awarded. Fellowships with partial tuition reimbursements, career-related internships or fieldwork, Federal Work-Study, institutionally sponsored loans, tuition waivers (partial), and unspecified assistantships also available. In 2001, 74 master's, 6 doctorates awarded. *Degree program information:* Part-time programs available. Offers biological sciences (MBS, MS, MST); chemistry and biochemistry (MS, MST, PhD); environmental sciences (MS); geography (MA, MAT); geology (MS); mathematical science (MS, MST, PhD); physics (MS, MST, PhD); psychology (MA, PhD); science (MA, MAT, MBS, MS, MST, PhD). *Application deadline:* Applications are processed on a rolling basis. *Application fee:* $20. Electronic applications accepted. *Application Contact:* Dr. Ingrid Johanson, Associate Dean of Student Services, 561-297-3700, Fax: 561-297-3792, E-mail: johanson@fau.edu. *Dean,* Dr. John Wiesenfeld, 561-297-3035, Fax: 561-297-3792.

Center for Complex Systems and Brain Sciences Students: 17 full-time (4 women), 2 part-time (1 woman); includes 3 minority (2 Asian Americans or Pacific Islanders, 1 Hispanic American), 6 international. Average age 32. 15 applicants, 20% accepted, 3 enrolled. *Faculty:* 12 full-time (1 woman). Expenses: Contact institution. *Financial support:* In 2001–02, 5 fellowships with full tuition reimbursements (averaging $16,060 per year), 5 research assistantships with partial tuition reimbursements (averaging $16,060 per year), 9 teaching assistantships with partial tuition reimbursements (averaging $16,060 per year) were awarded. Federal Work-Study also available. In 2001, 3 degrees awarded. Offers complex systems and brain sciences (PhD). *Application deadline:* For fall admission, 2/15 (priority date). *Application fee:* $20. *Application Contact:* Dr. Betty Tuller, Associate Director, 561-297-2227, Fax: 561-297-3634, E-mail: tuller@walt.ccs.fau.edu. *Director,* Dr. J. A. Scott Kelso, 561-297-2230, Fax: 561-297-3634, E-mail: kelso@walt.ccs.fau.edu.

College of Architecture, Urban and Public Affairs Students: 81 full-time (49 women), 151 part-time (83 women); includes 64 minority (39 African Americans, 5 Asian Americans or Pacific Islanders, 19 Hispanic Americans, 1 Native American), 9 international. Average age 36. 175 applicants, 67% accepted, 96 enrolled. *Faculty:* 35 full-time (15 women), 14 part-time/adjunct (4 women). Expenses: Contact institution. *Financial support:* In 2001–02, 27 students received support, including 3 fellowships with partial tuition reimbursements available (averaging $10,500 per year), 5 research assistantships with partial tuition reimbursements available (averaging $7,500 per year), 15 teaching assistantships with partial tuition reimbursements available (averaging $13,000 per year); career-related internships or fieldwork, Federal Work-Study, and institutionally sponsored loans also available. Support available to part-time students. Financial award application deadline: 4/1. In 2001, 56 master's, 6 doctorates awarded. *Degree program information:* Part-time and evening/weekend programs available. Offers architecture, urban and public affairs (MJPM, MNM, MPA, MSW, MURP, PhD); criminology and criminal justice (MJPM); social work (MSW); urban and regional planning (MURP). *Application deadline:* Applications are processed on a rolling basis. *Application fee:* $20. *Application Contact:* Anna G. Plotkin, Academic Adviser, 954-762-5662, E-mail: aplotkin@fau.edu. *Dean,* Dr. Rosalyn Carter, 954-762-5660, Fax: 954-762-5673, E-mail: rcarter@fau.edu.

School of Public Administration Students: 28 full-time (6 women), 93 part-time (44 women); includes 33 minority (21 African Americans, 3 Asian Americans or Pacific Islanders, 8 Hispanic Americans, 1 Native American), 6 international. Average age 37. 62 applicants, 61% accepted, 35 enrolled. *Faculty:* 13 full-time (4 women), 14 part-time/adjunct (4 women). Expenses: Contact institution. *Financial support:* In 2001–02, 17 students received support, including 4 fellowships with full tuition reimbursements available (averaging $16,000 per year), 3 research assistantships with partial tuition reimbursements available (averaging $7,500 per year), 10 teaching assistantships with partial tuition reimbursements available (averaging $12,000 per year); career-related internships or fieldwork, Federal Work-Study, institutionally sponsored loans, and tuition waivers (partial) also available. Support available to part-time students. Financial award application deadline: 4/1. In 2001, 38 master's, 6 doctorates awarded. *Degree program information:* Part-time and evening/weekend programs available. Offers public administration (MNM, MPA, PhD). *Application deadline:* For fall admission, 4/1 (priority date); for spring admission, 11/1. Applications are processed on a rolling basis. *Application fee:* $20. *Application Contact:* Anna G. Plotkin, Academic Adviser, 954-762-5662, E-mail: aplotkin@fau.edu. *Director,* Dr. Hugh T. Miller, 954-762-5650, Fax: 954-762-5693, E-mail: hmiller@fau.edu.

College of Business Students: 198 full-time (83 women), 382 part-time (193 women); includes 118 minority (35 African Americans, 25 Asian Americans or Pacific Islanders, 57 Hispanic Americans, 1 Native American), 60 international. Average age 31. 463 applicants, 54% accepted, 155 enrolled. *Faculty:* 123 full-time (33 women), 31 part-time/adjunct (7 women). Expenses: Contact institution. *Financial support:* In 2001–02, 46 students received support, including 19 research assistantships with partial tuition reimbursements available, 15 teaching assistantships with full tuition reimbursements available (averaging $12,000 per year); fellowships with partial tuition reimbursements available, career-related internships or fieldwork, Federal Work-Study, institutionally sponsored loans, tuition waivers (full and partial), and unspecified assistantships also available. Support available to part-time students. Financial award application deadline: 3/1. In 2001, 200 master's, 5 doctorates awarded. *Degree program information:* Part-time and evening/weekend programs available. Postbaccalaureate distance learning degree programs offered (minimal on-campus study). Offers business (Exec MBA, M Ac, M Tax, MBA, MS, MSIB, MST, MT, PhD); business administration (Exec MBA, MBA, PhD); economics (MS, MST); international business (MSIB); sport management (MBA). *Application deadline:* For fall admission, 6/15 (priority date); for spring admission, 10/15 (priority date). Applications are processed on a rolling basis. *Application fee:* $20. *Application Contact:* Ella Smith, Graduate Adviser, 561-297-3196, E-mail: smith@fau.edu. *Dean,* Dr. Bruce Mallen, 561-297-3630, Fax: 561-297-3686.

School of Accounting Students: 10 full-time (6 women), 52 part-time (33 women); includes 11 minority (5 African Americans, 2 Asian Americans or Pacific Islanders, 4 Hispanic Americans) Average age 33. 63 applicants, 52% accepted, 26 enrolled. *Faculty:* 13 full-time (3 women), 2 part-time/adjunct (0 women). Expenses: Contact institution. *Financial support:* In 2001–02, 1 student received support, including 1 research assistantship with partial tuition reimbursement available (averaging $6,000 per year); fellowships, teaching assistantships, career-related internships or fieldwork, Federal Work-Study, institutionally sponsored loans, scholarships/grants, and tuition waivers (partial) also available. Support available to part-time students. Financial award application deadline: 3/1. In 2001, 18 degrees awarded. *Degree program information:* Part-time and evening/weekend programs available. Postbaccalaureate distance learning degree programs offered (minimal on-campus study). Offers accounting (M Ac, M Tax, MT); taxation (M Tax, MT). *Application deadline:* For fall admission, 6/15 (priority date); for spring admission, 10/15 (priority date). Applications are processed on a rolling basis. *Application fee:* $20. *Application Contact:* Ella Smith, Graduate Adviser, 561-297-3196, E-mail: smith@fau.edu. *Director, School of Accounting,* Dr. Carl Borgia, 561-297-3636, Fax: 561-297-7023, E-mail: borgiac@fau.edu.

College of Education Students: 245 full-time (195 women), 574 part-time (471 women); includes 176 minority (87 African Americans, 15 Asian Americans or Pacific Islanders, 73 Hispanic Americans, 1 Native American), 12 international. Average age 36. 535 applicants, 56% accepted, 248 enrolled. *Faculty:* 78 full-time (41 women), 36 part-time/adjunct (18 women). Expenses: Contact institution. *Financial support:* In 2001–02, 29 students received support, including 17 research assistantships with partial tuition reimbursements available (averaging $7,500 per year), 12 teaching assistantships with partial tuition reimbursements available (averaging $7,500 per year); fellowships with partial tuition reimbursements available, career-related internships or fieldwork, Federal Work-Study, and unspecified assistantships also available. In 2001, 226 master's, 5 doctorates, 32 other advanced degrees awarded. *Degree program information:* Part-time and evening/weekend programs available. Offers adult/community education (M Ed, Ed D, Ed S); art teacher education (M Ed); counselor education (M Ed, Ed S); curriculum and instruction (M Ed, Ed D, Ed S); education (M Ed, MA, MAT, MS, Ed D, Ed S); educational leadership (M Ed, Ed D, Ed S); elementary education (M Ed); exceptional student education (M Ed); exercise science and health promotion (M Ed, MS); foundations of education (M Ed); foundations-educational research (M Ed); foundations-educational technology (M Ed); higher education management (Ed D); reading teacher education (M Ed); special education (Ed D); speech-language pathology (MS). *Application deadline:* Applications are processed on a rolling basis. *Application fee:* $20. Electronic applications accepted. *Application Contact:* Dr. Wayne Hill, Director, Office for Academic and Student Services, 561-297-3574, Fax: 561-297-2991, E-mail: whill@fau.edu. *Dean,* Dr. Gregory Aloia, 561-297-3564.

College of Engineering Students: 189 full-time (58 women), 123 part-time (23 women); includes 63 minority (10 African Americans, 30 Asian Americans or Pacific Islanders, 23 Hispanic Americans), 180 international. Average age 30. 490 applicants, 69% accepted, 95 enrolled. *Faculty:* 70 full-time (4 women), 5 part-time/adjunct (0 women). Expenses: Contact institution. *Financial support:* In 2001–02, research assistantships with partial tuition reimbursements (averaging $15,000 per year), teaching assistantships with partial tuition reimbursements (averaging $15,000 per year) were awarded. Fellowships, career-related internships or fieldwork, Federal Work-Study, and unspecified assistantships also available. Support available to part-time students. Financial award applicants required to submit FAFSA. In 2001, 106 master's, 12 doctorates awarded. *Degree program information:* Part-time and evening/weekend programs available. Postbaccalaureate distance learning degree programs offered (minimal on-campus study). Offers civil engineering (MS); computer engineering (MS, PhD); computer science (MS, PhD); electrical engineering (MS, PhD); engineering (MS, PhD); manufacturing systems engineering (MS); mechanical engineering (MS, PhD); ocean engineering (MS, PhD). *Application deadline:* Applications are processed on a rolling basis. *Application fee:* $20. *Interim Dean,* Dr. Karl Stevens, 561-297-3400, Fax: 561-297-2659, E-mail: stevens@fau.edu.

College of Nursing Students: 29 full-time (26 women), 113 part-time (107 women); includes 26 minority (16 African Americans, 1 Asian American or Pacific Islander, 9 Hispanic Americans), 2 international. Average age 40. 76 applicants, 76% accepted, 57 enrolled. *Faculty:* 20 full-time (19 women), 13 part-time/adjunct (10 women). Expenses: Contact institution. *Financial support:* In 2001–02, 62 students received support, including 11 research assistantships with partial tuition reimbursements available, 6 teaching assistantships with partial tuition reimbursements available; career-related internships or fieldwork, Federal Work-Study, institutionally sponsored loans, scholarships/grants, and traineeships also available. Support available to part-time students. In 2001, 38 master's awarded. *Degree program information:* Part-time programs available. Offers family nurse practitioner (MS, Post Master's Certificate); family/school nurse practitioner (MS); nursing (DNS); nursing administration (MS). *Application deadline:* For fall admission, 6/2; for spring admission, 10/20. Applications are processed on a rolling basis. *Application fee:* $20. *Application Contact:* Dr. Lynne M. Dunphy, Graduate Coordinator, 561-297-3261, Fax: 561-297-0088, E-mail: ldunphy@fau.edu. *Dean,* Dr. Anne Boykin, 561-297-3206, Fax: 561-297-3687, E-mail: boykina@acc.fau.edu.

Dorothy F. Schmidt College of Arts and Letters Students: 157 full-time (96 women), 192 part-time (136 women); includes 63 minority (24 African Americans, 10 Asian Americans or Pacific Islanders, 28 Hispanic Americans, 1 Native American), 27 international. Average age 35. 219 applicants, 72% accepted, 123 enrolled. *Faculty:* 110 full-time (35 women). Expenses: Contact institution. *Financial support:* In 2001–02, 5 fellowships with partial tuition reimbursements (averaging $12,000 per year), 100 teaching assistantships (averaging $7,500 per year) were awarded. Research assistantships, career-related internships or fieldwork, Federal Work-Study, institutionally sponsored loans, and tuition waivers (partial) also available. Support available to part-time students. In 2001, 73 degrees awarded. *Degree program information:* Part-time programs available. Offers American literature (MA); anthropology (MA, MAT); art education (MAT); arts and letters (MA, MAT, MFA, PhD, Certificate); ceramics (MFA); communication (MA); comparative literature (MA); comparative studies (PhD); English literature (MA); fantasy and science fiction (MA); French (MA); German (MA); history (MA); multicultural literature (MA); music (MA); painting (MFA); political science (MA, MAT); sociology (MA, MAT); Spanish (MA); teaching French (MAT); teaching German (MAT); teaching Spanish (MAT); theatre (MFA). *Application deadline:* For fall admission, 6/1 (priority date). Applications are processed on a rolling basis. *Application fee:* $20. Electronic applications accepted. *Application Contact:* Dr. Ken Keaton, Associate Dean, 561-297-3802, Fax: 561-297-2744, E-mail: keaton@fau.edu. *Interim Dean,* Dr. William Covino, 561-297-3803.

Women's Studies Center Students: 5 full-time (all women), 5 part-time (all women); includes 4 minority (1 African American, 2 Asian Americans or Pacific Islanders, 1 Hispanic American) Average age 35. 9 applicants, 56% accepted, 5 enrolled. *Faculty:* 4 full-time (all women), 1 (woman) part-time/adjunct. Expenses: Contact institution. *Financial support:* In 2001–02, 8 students received support, including 4 fellowships with full and partial tuition reimbursements available (averaging $750 per year), 4 teaching assistantships with full and partial tuition reimbursements available (averaging $6,012 per year); career-related internships or fieldwork, Federal Work-Study, institutionally sponsored loans, scholarships/grants, and unspecified assistantships also available. Support available to part-time students. In 2001, 3 degrees awarded. Offers women's studies (MA, Certificate). *Application deadline:* Applications are processed on a rolling basis. *Application fee:* $20. *Application Contact:* Dr. Jane Caputi, Associate Professor, 954-297-3865, Fax: 561-297-2127, E-mail: jcaputi@fau.edu. *Chair,* Dr. Mary M. Cameron, 561-297-3865, Fax: 561-297-2127, E-mail: mcameron@fau.edu.

FLORIDA COASTAL SCHOOL OF LAW, Jacksonville, FL 32216

General Information Proprietary, coed, graduate-only institution. *Enrollment by degree level:* 452 first professional. *Graduate faculty:* 27 full-time (9 women), 29 part-time/adjunct (5 women). *Tuition:* Full-time $19,340; part-time $7,735 per semester. *Required fees:* $455 per semester. Tuition and fees vary according to course load. *Student services:* Campus employment opportunities, campus safety program, career counseling, disabled student

Florida Coastal School of Law (continued)

services, grant writing training, international student services, low-cost health insurance, multicultural affairs office, teacher training, writing training. *Library facilities:* Law Library. *Online resources:* library catalog, web page, access to other libraries' catalogs. *Collection:* 16,306 titles, 2,617 serial subscriptions, 175 audiovisual materials.

Computer facilities: 51 computers available on campus for general student use. A campuswide network can be accessed from off campus. Internet access, online grades are available. *Web address:* http://www.fcsl.edu/.

General Application Contact: 904-680-7710, Fax: 904-680-7776, E-mail: admissions@fcsl.edu.

GRADUATE UNITS

Professional Program Students: 248 full-time (115 women), 204 part-time (95 women); includes 94 minority (55 African Americans, 17 Asian Americans or Pacific Islanders, 17 Hispanic Americans, 5 Native Americans), 4 international. Average age 27. 1,846 applicants, 28% accepted, 122 enrolled. *Faculty:* 27 full-time (9 women), 29 part-time/adjunct (5 women). Expenses: Contact institution. *Financial support:* In 2001–02, 341 students received support, including 14 research assistantships (averaging $2,000 per year), 12 teaching assistantships (averaging $2,000 per year); scholarships/grants and tuition waivers (full and partial) also available. Support available to part-time students. Financial award applicants required to submit FAFSA. In 2001, 99 degrees awarded. *Degree program information:* Part-time and evening/weekend programs available. Offers law (JD). *Application deadline:* Applications are processed on a rolling basis. *Application fee:* $50. Electronic applications accepted. *Application Contact:* 904-680-7710, Fax: 904-680-7776, E-mail: admissions@fcsl.edu. *Dean,* J. Richard Hurt, E-mail: jrhurt@fcsl.edu.

FLORIDA GULF COAST UNIVERSITY, Fort Myers, FL 33965-6565

General Information State-supported, coed, comprehensive institution. *Enrollment:* 194 full-time matriculated graduate/professional students (110 women), 384 part-time matriculated graduate/professional students (272 women). *Enrollment by degree level:* 811 master's. *Graduate faculty:* 175 full-time (94 women), 130 part-time/adjunct (65 women). Tuition, state resident: part-time $164 per credit hour. Tuition, nonresident: part-time $571 per credit hour. *Required fees:* $36 per semester. *Graduate housing:* Room and/or apartments available on a first-come, first-served basis to single students; on-campus housing not available to married students. Typical cost: $4,000 per year ($7,000 including board). Housing application deadline: 5/15. *Student services:* Campus employment opportunities, campus safety program, career counseling, child daycare facilities, disabled student services, exercise/wellness program, free psychological counseling, international student services, low-cost health insurance, multicultural affairs office, teacher training. *Library facilities:* Library Services. *Online resources:* library catalog, web page, access to other libraries' catalogs. *Collection:* 139,999 titles, 2,414 serial subscriptions, 1,655 audiovisual materials.

Computer facilities: 323 computers available on campus for general student use. A campuswide network can be accessed from student residence rooms and from off campus. Internet access and online class registration, online admissions and advising are available. *Web address:* http://www.fgcu.edu/.

General Application Contact: Paula Dumas, Coordinator, High School, Community College Relations, 941-590-5878, Fax: 941-590-7894, E-mail: oar@fgcu.edu.

GRADUATE UNITS

College of Business Students: 68 full-time (29 women), 110 part-time (57 women); includes 24 minority (6 African Americans, 3 Asian Americans or Pacific Islanders, 12 Hispanic Americans, 3 Native Americans), 9 international. Average age 33. 90 applicants, 77% accepted, 60 enrolled. *Faculty:* 31 full-time (9 women), 14 part-time/adjunct (3 women). Expenses: Contact institution. *Financial support:* Career-related internships or fieldwork, Federal Work-Study, and unspecified assistantships available. Support available to part-time students. Financial award application deadline: 5/1; financial award applicants required to submit FAFSA. In 2001, 65 degrees awarded. *Degree program information:* Part-time and evening/weekend programs available. Offers accounting and taxation (MS); business (MBA, MS); business administration (MBA); computer and information systems (MS). *Application deadline:* For fall admission, 7/1 (priority date); for spring admission, 11/15. Applications are processed on a rolling basis. *Application fee:* $20. Electronic applications accepted. *Application Contact:* Carol Burnette, Assistant Dean, 239-590-7350, Fax: 239-590-7330, E-mail: burnette@fgcu.edu. *Dean,* Richard Pegnetter, 239-590-7310, Fax: 239-590-7330, E-mail: epegnett@fgcu.edu.

College of Education Students: 37 full-time (26 women), 159 part-time (139 women); includes 11 minority (3 African Americans, 1 Asian American or Pacific Islander, 7 Hispanic Americans) Average age 36. 107 applicants, 91% accepted, 69 enrolled. *Faculty:* 31 full-time (20 women), 33 part-time/adjunct (26 women). Expenses: Contact institution. In 2001, 80 degrees awarded. *Degree program information:* Part-time and evening/weekend programs available. Postbaccalaureate distance learning degree programs offered (minimal on-campus study). Offers behavior disorders (MA); biology (MAT); counselor education (M Ed, MA); education (M Ed, MA, MAT); educational leadership (M Ed); educational technology (M Ed, MA); elementary education (M Ed, MA); English (MAT); mathematics (MAT); mental retardation (MA); reading education (M Ed); social sciences (MAT); specific learning disabilities (MA); varying exceptionalities (MA). *Application deadline:* Applications are processed on a rolling basis. *Application fee:* $20. Electronic applications accepted. *Application Contact:* Edward Beckett, Adviser/Counselor, 239-590-7759, Fax: 239-590-7801, E-mail: ebeckett@fgcu.edu. *Dean,* Lawrence Byrnes, 239-590-7822, Fax: 239-590-7801, E-mail: lbyrnes@fgcu.edu.

College of Health Professions Students: 69 full-time (40 women), 52 part-time (41 women); includes 14 minority (3 African Americans, 4 Asian Americans or Pacific Islanders, 7 Hispanic Americans) Average age 43. 119 applicants, 66% accepted, 65 enrolled. *Faculty:* 35 full-time (28 women), 14 part-time/adjunct (7 women). Expenses: Contact institution. *Financial support:* Career-related internships or fieldwork, Federal Work-Study, and institutionally sponsored loans available. In 2001, 20 degrees awarded. *Degree program information:* Part-time and evening/weekend programs available. Postbaccalaureate distance learning degree programs offered. Offers health professions (MS, MSN); health science (MS); nursing (MSN); physical therapy (MS). *Application deadline:* Applications are processed on a rolling basis. *Application fee:* $20. Electronic applications accepted. *Application Contact:* Lynn O'Hare, Administrative Assistant, 239-590-7451, Fax: 239-590-7474, E-mail: lohare@fgcu.edu. *Dean,* Cecilia Rokusek, 239-590-7452, Fax: 239-590-7474, E-mail: crokusek@fgcu.edu.

College of Public and Social Services Students: 21 full-time (15 women), 63 part-time (35 women); includes 10 minority (4 African Americans, 1 Asian American or Pacific Islander, 4 Hispanic Americans, 1 Native American), 2 international. Average age 37. 48 applicants, 92% accepted, 30 enrolled. *Faculty:* 16 full-time (9 women), 7 part-time/adjunct (1 woman). Expenses: Contact institution. *Financial support:* Research assistantships, career-related internships or fieldwork and tuition waivers (full and partial) available. Support available to part-time students. In 2001, 34 degrees awarded. *Degree program information:* Part-time and evening/weekend programs available. Offers criminal justice (MPA); environmental policy (MPA); general public administration (MPA); management (MPA); public and social services (MPA, MSW); social work (MSW). *Application deadline:* Applications are processed on a rolling basis. *Application fee:* $20. Electronic applications accepted. *Dean,* Dr. John McGaha, 239-590-7823, Fax: 239-590-7846, E-mail: jmcgaha@fgcu.edu.

FLORIDA INSTITUTE OF TECHNOLOGY, Melbourne, FL 32901-6975

General Information Independent, coed, university. CGS member. *Enrollment:* 394 full-time matriculated graduate/professional students (183 women), 1,692 part-time matriculated graduate/professional students (610 women). *Enrollment by degree level:* 1,820 master's, 266 doctoral. *Graduate faculty:* 163 full-time (24 women), 185 part-time/adjunct (23 women). *Tuition:* Part-time $650 per credit. *Graduate housing:* Room and/or apartments available on a first-come, first-served basis to single students; on-campus housing not available to married students. Typical cost: $2,850 per year ($5,550 including board). *Student services:* Campus employment opportunities, career counseling, disabled student services, free psychological counseling, international student services, low-cost health insurance, teacher training, writing training. *Library facilities:* Evans Library. *Online resources:* library catalog, web page, access to other libraries' catalogs. *Collection:* 138,503 titles, 5,325 serial subscriptions, 4,734 audiovisual materials. *Research affiliation:* Lockheed Martin Corporation (biological sciences), Microsoft Corporation (simulation software development), General Electric-Harris (software testing), Boeing Corporation (digital signal processing aeronautics), Arthur D. Little, Inc/U.S. Navy (oceanography/trace metal studies), IBM (software technology).

Computer facilities: 600 computers available on campus for general student use. A campuswide network can be accessed from student residence rooms and from off campus. Internet access and online class registration are available. *Web address:* http://www.fit.edu/.

General Application Contact: Carolyn P. Farrior, Director of Graduate Admissions, 321-674-7118, Fax: 321-723-9468, E-mail: cfarrior@fit.edu.

GRADUATE UNITS

Graduate Programs Students: 394 full-time (183 women), 1,692 part-time (610 women); includes 364 minority (210 African Americans, 65 Asian Americans or Pacific Islanders, 83 Hispanic Americans, 6 Native Americans), 328 international. Average age 34. 2,028 applicants, 49% accepted. *Faculty:* 163 full-time (24 women), 185 part-time/adjunct (23 women). Expenses: Contact institution. *Financial support:* In 2001–02, 232 students received support, including 5 fellowships with full and partial tuition reimbursements available (averaging $13,000 per year), 96 research assistantships with full and partial tuition reimbursements available (averaging $10,830 per year), 131 teaching assistantships with full and partial tuition reimbursements available (averaging $7,683 per year); career-related internships or fieldwork, institutionally sponsored loans, tuition waivers (partial), and tuition remissions also available. Support available to part-time students. Financial award application deadline: 3/1; financial award applicants required to submit FAFSA. In 2001, 614 master's, 35 doctorates awarded. *Degree program information:* Part-time and evening/weekend programs available. Postbaccalaureate distance learning degree programs offered (no on-campus study). *Application deadline:* Applications are processed on a rolling basis. *Application fee:* $50. Electronic applications accepted. *Application Contact:* Carolyn P. Farrior, Director of Graduate Admissions, 321-674-7118, Fax: 321-723-9468, E-mail: cfarrior@fit.edu. *Vice President for Research and Graduate Programs,* Dr. Robert L. Sullivan, 321-674-8960, Fax: 407-674-8969, E-mail: sullivan@fit.edu.

College of Engineering Students: 145 full-time (32 women), 326 part-time (73 women); includes 49 minority (10 African Americans, 17 Asian Americans or Pacific Islanders, 22 Hispanic Americans), 231 international. Average age 30. 1,146 applicants, 54% accepted. *Faculty:* 65 full-time (3 women), 23 part-time/adjunct (3 women). Expenses: Contact institution. *Financial support:* In 2001–02, 125 students received support, including 2 fellowships with full and partial tuition reimbursements available (averaging $13,000 per year), 60 research assistantships with full and partial tuition reimbursements available (averaging $8,398 per year), 64 teaching assistantships with full and partial tuition reimbursements available (averaging $9,120 per year); career-related internships or fieldwork, institutionally sponsored loans, and tuition remissions also available. Financial award application deadline: 3/1; financial award applicants required to submit FAFSA. In 2001, 105 master's, 6 doctorates awarded. *Degree program information:* Part-time and evening/weekend programs available. Offers aerospace engineering (MS, PhD); biological oceanography (MS); chemical engineering (MS, PhD); chemical oceanography (MS); civil engineering (MS, PhD); coastal zone management (MS); computer engineering (MS, PhD); computer information systems (MS); computer science (MS, PhD); electrical engineering (MS, PhD); engineering (MS, PhD); engineering management (MS); environmental resource management (MS); environmental science (MS, PhD); geological oceanography (MS); mechanical engineering (MS, PhD); meteorology (MS); ocean engineering (MS, PhD); oceanography (MS, PhD); physical oceanography (MS); software engineering (MS). *Application deadline:* Applications are processed on a rolling basis. *Application fee:* $50. Electronic applications accepted. *Application Contact:* Carolyn P. Farrior, Director of Graduate Admissions, 321-674-7118, Fax: 321-723-9468, E-mail: cfarrior@fit.edu. *Dean,* Dr. J. Ronald Bailey, 321-674-7318, Fax: 321-674-7270, E-mail: jrbailey@fit.edu.

College of Science and Liberal Arts Students: 58 full-time (27 women), 121 part-time (56 women); includes 5 Asian Americans or Pacific Islanders, 55 international. Average age 32. 334 applicants, 42% accepted. *Faculty:* 58 full-time (10 women), 8 part-time/adjunct (2 women). Expenses: Contact institution. *Financial support:* In 2001–02, 70 students received support, including 2 fellowships with full and partial tuition reimbursements available (averaging $13,000 per year), 9 research assistantships with full and partial tuition reimbursements available (averaging $11,461 per year), 59 teaching assistantships with full and partial tuition reimbursements available (averaging $7,752 per year); career-related internships or fieldwork and tuition remissions also available. Financial award application deadline: 3/1; financial award applicants required to submit FAFSA. In 2001, 35 master's, 11 doctorates awarded. *Degree program information:* Part-time and evening/weekend programs available. Offers applied mathematics (MS, PhD); biological sciences (PhD); biotechnology (MS); cell and molecular biology (PhD); chemistry (MS, PhD); computer science education (MS); ecology (MS); environmental education (MS); marine biology (MS); mathematics education (MS, Ed D, PhD, Ed S); operations research (MS, PhD); physics (MS, PhD); science and liberal arts (MS, Ed D, PhD, Ed S); science education (MS, Ed D, PhD, Ed S); space science (MS, PhD); technical and professional communication (MS). *Application deadline:* Applications are processed on a rolling basis. *Application fee:* $50. Electronic applications accepted. *Application Contact:* Carolyn P. Farrior, Director of Graduate Admissions, 321-674-7118, Fax: 321-723-9468, E-mail: cfarrior@fit.edu. *Dean,* Dr. Gordon L. Nelson, 321-674-7260, Fax: 321-674-8864, E-mail: nelson@fit.edu.

School of Aeronautics Students: 9 full-time (5 women), 8 part-time (4 women); includes 3 minority (1 African American, 2 Hispanic Americans), 8 international. Average age 26. 26 applicants, 65% accepted. *Faculty:* 6 full-time (1 woman). Expenses: Contact institution. *Financial support:* In 2001–02, 1 student received support, including 1 teaching assistantship with full and partial tuition reimbursement available (averaging $6,840 per year); research assistantships with full and partial tuition reimbursements available, career-related internships or fieldwork, institutionally sponsored loans, unspecified assistantships, and tuition remissions also available. Financial award application deadline: 3/1. In 2001, 4 degrees awarded. *Degree program information:* Part-time and evening/weekend programs available. Offers airport development and management (MSA); applied aviation safety (MSA); aviation human factors (MS). *Application deadline:* For fall admission, 8/1; for spring admission, 12/1. Applications are processed on a rolling basis. *Application fee:* $50. Electronic applications accepted. *Application Contact:* Carolyn P. Farrior, Director of Graduate Admissions, 321-674-7118, Fax: 321-723-9468, E-mail: cfarrior@fit.edu. *Chairman of Graduate Studies,* Dr. Nathaniel Villaire, 321-674-8120, Fax: 321-674-8059, E-mail: villaire@fit.edu.

School of Extended Graduate Studies Students: 57 full-time (29 women), 1,198 part-time (455 women); includes 277 minority (183 African Americans, 38 Asian Americans or Pacific Islanders, 51 Hispanic Americans, 5 Native Americans), 16 international. Average age 37. 299 applicants, 42% accepted. *Faculty:* 10 full-time (2 women), 131 part-time/adjunct (15 women). Expenses: Contact institution. *Financial support:* Institutionally sponsored loans available. Financial award application deadline: 3/1; financial award applicants required to submit FAFSA. In 2001, 434 degrees awarded. *Degree program information:* Part-time and evening/weekend programs available. Postbaccalaureate distance learning degree programs offered (no on-campus study). Offers acquisition and contract management (MS, MSM, PMBA); aerospace engineering (MS); business administration (PMBA); computer information systems (MS); computer science (MS); ebusiness (MSM); electrical engineering (MS); engineering management (MS); health management (MS); human resource management (MSM, PMBA); human resources management (MS); information systems (MSM, PMBA); logistics management (MS, MSM); management (MS); material acquisition management (MS); mechanical engineering (MS); operations research (MS); project management (MS); public administration (MPA); software engineering (MS); space systems (MS); space systems management (MS); systems management (MS); transportation management (MSM). *Application deadline:* Applications are processed on a rolling basis. *Application fee:* $50. Electronic

Florida International University (continued)

Islander, 33 Hispanic Americans), 15 international. Average age 32. 166 applicants, 33% accepted, 35 enrolled. *Faculty:* 17 full-time (8 women). Expenses: Contact institution. *Financial support:* Application deadline: 4/1. In 2001, 16 degrees awarded. *Degree program information:* Part-time and evening/weekend programs available. Offers mass communication (MS). *Application deadline:* For fall admission, 4/1 (priority date); for spring admission, 10/1. Applications are processed on a rolling basis. *Application fee:* $20. *Dean,* Dr. J. Arthur Heise, 305-919-5625, Fax: 305-919-5203, E-mail: heisea@fiu.edu.

See in-depth description on page 877.

FLORIDA METROPOLITAN UNIVERSITY–BRANDON CAMPUS, Tampa, FL 33619

General Information Proprietary, coed, comprehensive institution.

GRADUATE UNITS

Program in Business Administration Offers business administration (MBA).

Program in Criminal Justice Offers criminal justice (MS).

FLORIDA METROPOLITAN UNIVERSITY–FORT LAUDERDALE CAMPUS, Fort Lauderdale, FL 33304-2522

General Information Proprietary, coed, comprehensive institution. *Graduate housing:* On-campus housing not available.

GRADUATE UNITS

MBA Program *Degree program information:* Part-time and evening/weekend programs available. Offers business administration (MBA).

FLORIDA METROPOLITAN UNIVERSITY–MELBOURNE CAMPUS, Melbourne, FL 32935-6657

General Information Proprietary, coed, comprehensive institution.

GRADUATE UNITS

Program in Business Administration Offers business administration (MBA).

FLORIDA METROPOLITAN UNIVERSITY–NORTH ORLANDO CAMPUS, Orlando, FL 32810-5674

General Information Proprietary, coed, comprehensive institution. *Enrollment:* 3 full-time matriculated graduate/professional students (2 women), 40 part-time matriculated graduate/professional students (23 women). *Enrollment by degree level:* 43 master's. *Graduate faculty:* 1 full-time (0 women), 6 part-time/adjunct (0 women). *Tuition:* Full-time $7,560; part-time $315 per credit. *Required fees:* $600. *Graduate housing:* On-campus housing not available. *Student services:* Career counseling. *Library facilities:* Orlando College Library. *Collection:* 10,000 titles, 105 serial subscriptions.

Computer facilities: 25 computers available on campus for general student use. A campuswide network can be accessed. Internet access is available. *Web address:* http://www.fmu.edu/.

General Application Contact: Charlene Donnelly, Director of Admissions, 407-628-5870 Ext. 108, Fax: 407-628-1344, E-mail: cdonnelly@cci.edu.

GRADUATE UNITS

Division of Business Administration *Degree program information:* Part-time and evening/weekend programs available. Offers business administration (MBA).

FLORIDA METROPOLITAN UNIVERSITY–PINELLAS CAMPUS, Clearwater, FL 33759

General Information Proprietary, coed, comprehensive institution.

GRADUATE UNITS

Program in Business Administration Offers business administration (MBA).

Program in Criminal Justice Offers criminal justice (MS).

FLORIDA METROPOLITAN UNIVERSITY–TAMPA CAMPUS, Tampa, FL 33614-5899

General Information Proprietary, coed, comprehensive institution. *Graduate housing:* On-campus housing not available.

GRADUATE UNITS

Department of Business Administration *Degree program information:* Part-time and evening/weekend programs available. Offers human resources (MBA); international business (MBA).

FLORIDA SOUTHERN COLLEGE, Lakeland, FL 33801-5698

General Information Independent-religious, coed, comprehensive institution. *Enrollment:* 48 part-time matriculated graduate/professional students (25 women). *Enrollment by degree level:* 48 master's. *Graduate faculty:* 8 full-time (1 woman), 2 part-time/adjunct (both women). *Tuition:* Part-time $324 per hour. *Graduate housing:* On-campus housing not available. *Student services:* Campus employment opportunities, campus safety program, career counseling, free psychological counseling, international student services, multicultural affairs office. *Library facilities:* E. T. Roux Library plus 1 other. *Online resources:* library catalog, web page, access to other libraries' catalogs. *Collection:* 167,633 titles, 667 serial subscriptions, 9,205 audiovisual materials.

Computer facilities: 191 computers available on campus for general student use. A campuswide network can be accessed from student residence rooms and from off campus. Internet access and online class registration are available. *Web address:* http://www.flsouthern.edu/.

General Application Contact: Bill Walker, Coordinator of External Programs, 863-680-4205, Fax: 863-680-3088, E-mail: hwalker@flsouthern.edu.

GRADUATE UNITS

Program in Business Administration Average age 34. 21 applicants, 67% accepted. *Faculty:* 8 full-time (1 woman), 2 part-time/adjunct (both women). Expenses: Contact institution. *Financial support:* In 2001–02, 9 students received support. Scholarships/grants available. Support available to part-time students. Financial award applicants required to submit FAFSA. In 2001, 12 degrees awarded. *Degree program information:* Part-time programs available. Offers accounting (MBA); business administration (MBA). *Application deadline:* For fall admission, 8/1; for spring admission, 12/1. Applications are processed on a rolling basis. *Application fee:* $30. *Application Contact:* Bill Walker, Coordinator of External Programs, 863-680-4205, Fax: 863-680-3088, E-mail: hwalker@flsouthern.edu.

FLORIDA STATE UNIVERSITY, Tallahassee, FL 32306

General Information State-supported, coed, university. CGS member. *Enrollment:* 4,268 full-time matriculated graduate/professional students (2,221 women), 2,049 part-time matriculated graduate/professional students (1,272 women). *Graduate faculty:* 1,795 full-time (557 women), 130 part-time/adjunct (37 women). Tuition, state resident: part-time $163 per credit hour. Tuition, nonresident: part-time $570 per credit hour. Tuition and fees vary according to program. *Graduate housing:* Rooms and/or apartments available to single and married students. *Student services:* Campus employment opportunities, campus safety program, career counseling, child daycare facilities, disabled student services, exercise/wellness program, free psychological counseling, international student services, low-cost health insurance, multicultural affairs office. *Library facilities:* Robert Manning Strozier Library plus 6 others. *Online resources:* library catalog, web page, access to other libraries' catalogs. *Collection:* 2.3 million titles, 15,446 serial subscriptions, 43,275 audiovisual materials. *Research affiliation:* National Center for Atmospheric Research, Fermi National Accelerator Laboratory, Southeastern Archaeological Studies, Center for the Study of Southern Culture and Religion.

Computer facilities: 1,249 computers available on campus for general student use. A campuswide network can be accessed from student residence rooms and from off campus. Internet access and online class registration, Web pages are available. *Web address:* http://www.fsu.edu/.

General Application Contact: Melanie Booker, Assistant Director for Graduate Admissions, 850-644-3420.

GRADUATE UNITS

College of Law Students: 714 full-time (331 women); includes 155 minority (64 African Americans, 21 Asian Americans or Pacific Islanders, 65 Hispanic Americans, 5 Native Americans), 3 international. Average age 26. 2,209 applicants, 35% accepted. *Faculty:* 41 full-time (13 women), 31 part-time/adjunct (9 women). Expenses: Contact institution. *Financial support:* In 2001–02, 73 fellowships (averaging $1,342 per year), 58 research assistantships (averaging $3,300 per year), 6 teaching assistantships (averaging $2,069 per year) were awarded. Scholarships/grants also available. Financial award application deadline: 4/1. In 2001, 226 degrees awarded. Offers law (JD). *Application deadline:* For fall admission, 2/15 (priority date). Applications are processed on a rolling basis. *Application fee:* $20. Electronic applications accepted. *Application Contact:* Sharon J. Booker, Director of Admissions and Records, 850-644-3787, Fax: 850-644-7284, E-mail: admissions@law.fsu.edu. *Dean,* Donald J. Weidner, 850-644-3400, Fax: 850-644-5487, E-mail: dweidner@law.fsu.edu.

Graduate Studies Students: 3,545 full-time (1,892 women), 2,046 part-time (1,271 women); includes 886 minority (519 African Americans, 132 Asian Americans or Pacific Islanders, 217 Hispanic Americans, 18 Native Americans) Average age 31. *Faculty:* 1,751 full-time (541 women), 127 part-time/adjunct (36 women). Expenses: Contact institution. *Financial support:* Fellowships, research assistantships, teaching assistantships, career-related internships or fieldwork, Federal Work-Study, institutionally sponsored loans, scholarships/grants, traineeships, and unspecified assistantships available. Support available to part-time students. Financial award applicants required to submit FAFSA. In 2001, 1,388 master's, 233 doctorates awarded. *Degree program information:* Part-time and evening/weekend programs available. *Application fee:* $20. Electronic applications accepted. *Application Contact:* Melanie Booker, Assistant Director for Graduate Admissions, 850-644-3420. *Interim Dean of Graduate Studies,* Dr. Dianne F. Harrison, 850-644-3500, E-mail: dfharris@mailer.fsu.edu.

College of Arts and Sciences Students: 1,027 full-time (446 women), 438 part-time (190 women). Average age 31. *Faculty:* 446 full-time (138 women), 40 part-time/adjunct (14 women). Expenses: Contact institution. *Financial support:* Fellowships, research assistantships, teaching assistantships, career-related internships or fieldwork, Federal Work-Study, institutionally sponsored loans, scholarships/grants, traineeships, tuition waivers (full), and unspecified assistantships available. Support available to part-time students. In 2001, 178 master's, 94 doctorates awarded. *Degree program information:* Part-time programs available. Offers American and Florida studies (MA); analytical chemistry (MS, PhD); anthropology (MA, MS, PhD); applied behavior analysis (MS); applied mathematics (MA, MS, PhD); applied statistics (MS); arts and sciences (MA, MS, PhD); biochemistry (MS, PhD); cell biology (MS, PhD); chemical physics (MS, PhD); classical archaeology (MA); classical civilization (MA, PhD); classics (MA); clinical psychology (PhD); cognitive and behavioral science (PhD); computer and network system administration (MA, MS); computer science (MA, MS, PhD); developmental biology (MS, PhD); ecology (MS, PhD); English (MA, PhD); evolutionary biology (MS, PhD); financial mathematics (PhD); French (MA, PhD); genetics (MS, PhD); geological sciences (MS, PhD); geophysical fluid dynamics (PhD); German (MA); Greek (MA); Greek and Latin (MA); historical administration (MA); history (MA, PhD); humanities (MA, PhD); immunology (MS, PhD); inorganic chemistry (MS, PhD); Italian (MA); Italian studies (MA); Latin (MA); literature (MA, PhD); marine biology (MS, PhD); mathematical sciences (MA, MS); mathematical statistics (MS, PhD); meteorology (MS, PhD); microbiology (MS, PhD); molecular and cell biology (PhD); molecular biology (MS, PhD); molecular biophysics (PhD); neuroscience (PhD); oceanography (MS, PhD); organic chemistry (MS, PhD); philosophy (MA, PhD); physical chemistry (MS, PhD); physics (MS, PhD); physiology (MS, PhD); plant sciences (MS, PhD); pure mathematics (MA, MS, PhD); radiation biology (MS, PhD); religion (MA, PhD); Slavic languages and literatures (MA); Slavic languages/Russian (MA); software engineering (MA, MS); Spanish (MA, PhD); writing (MA, PhD). *Application fee:* $20. *Application Contact:* Jon Bridges, Academic Coordinator, 850-644-0714, Fax: 850-644-9656, E-mail: jbridges@mailer.fsu.edu. *Dean,* Dr. Donald J. Foss, 850-644-1081.

College of Business Students: 152 full-time (62 women), 196 part-time (81 women); includes 65 minority (37 African Americans, 16 Asian Americans or Pacific Islanders, 12 Hispanic Americans), 18 international. Average age 31. 362 applicants, 54% accepted, 139 enrolled. *Faculty:* 85 full-time. Expenses: Contact institution. *Financial support:* In 2001–02, 96 students received support, including 18 fellowships with partial tuition reimbursements available (averaging $4,000 per year), 48 research assistantships with partial tuition reimbursements available (averaging $6,000 per year), 18 teaching assistantships with partial tuition reimbursements available (averaging $10,000 per year); unspecified assistantships also available. Support available to part-time students. Financial award application deadline: 1/1. In 2001, 125 master's, 14 doctorates awarded. *Degree program information:* Part-time and evening/weekend programs available. Postbaccalaureate distance learning degree programs offered (no on-campus study). Offers accounting (M Acc); business administration (MBA, PhD); hospitality and tourism (MS); information science (MS); insurance (MS); management (MS). *Application deadline:* For fall admission, 5/1; for spring admission, 10/1. Applications are processed on a rolling basis. *Application fee:* $20. Electronic applications accepted. *Application Contact:* Scheri L. Martin, Graduate Coordinator, 850-644-6458, Fax: 850-644-0915, E-mail: smartin@cob.fsu.edu. *Associate Dean for Graduate Studies,* Dr. Pamela L. Perrewé, 850-644-3090, Fax: 850-644-0915, E-mail: pperrew@cob.fsu.edu.

College of Communication Students: 132 full-time (99 women), 73 part-time (44 women); includes 34 minority (14 African Americans, 11 Asian Americans or Pacific Islanders, 9 Hispanic Americans), 2 international. Average age 26. 293 applicants, 40% accepted. *Faculty:* 32 full-time (13 women), 8 part-time/adjunct (5 women). Expenses: Contact institution. *Financial support:* In 2001–02, 50 students received support, including 16 research assistantships, 34 teaching assistantships; fellowships, career-related internships or fieldwork, Federal Work-Study, and institutionally sponsored loans also available. Support available to part-time students. Financial award applicants required to submit FAFSA. In 2001, 41 master's, 4 doctorates awarded. *Degree program information:* Part-time programs available. Offers communication (Adv M, MA, MS, PhD); communication sciences and disorders (Adv M, MS, PhD); interactive and new communication technology (MA, MS); management communication (MA, MS); mass communication (MA, MS, PhD); policy and political communications (MA, MS); rhetorical and communication theory (MA, MS); speech communication (PhD). *Application deadline:* For fall admission, 2/1 (priority date). Applications are processed on a rolling basis. *Application fee:* $20. Electronic applications accepted. *Dean,* Dr. John K. Mayo, 850-644-9698, Fax: 850-644-0611.

College of Education Students: 843 full-time (530 women), 387 part-time (266 women); includes 250 minority (155 African Americans, 22 Asian Americans or Pacific Islanders, 67 Hispanic Americans, 6 Native Americans), 62 international. 1,024 applicants, 55% accepted. *Faculty:* 90 full-time (44 women), 22 part-time/adjunct (4 women). Expenses: Contact institution. *Financial support:* In 2001–02, 10 fellowships, 3 teaching assistantships were awarded. Research assistantships, career-related internships or fieldwork and traineeships also available. Financial award applicants required to submit FAFSA. In 2001, 363 master's, 58 doctorates, 35 other advanced degrees awarded. *Degree program information:* Part-time and evening/weekend programs available. Postbaccalaureate distance learning degree programs offered. Offers adapted physical education (MS); adult education (MS, Ed D, PhD, Ed S); comprehensive vocational education (PhD, Ed S); counseling and human systems (MS, Ed S); counseling psychology (PhD); early childhood education (MS, Ed D, PhD, Ed S); education (MS, Ed D, PhD, Ed S); educational administration/leadership (MS, Ed D, PhD, Ed S); educational leadership and policy studies (MS); educational psychology (MS, PhD, Ed S); elementary education (MS, Ed D, PhD, Ed S); emotional disturbance/learning disabilities (MS); English education (MS, PhD, Ed S); foundations of education

applications accepted. *Application Contact:* Carolyn P. Farrior, Director of Graduate Admissions, 321-674-7118, Fax: 321-723-9468, E-mail: cfarrior@fit.edu. *Dean, School of Extended Graduate Studies,* Dr. Ronald L. Marshall, 321-674-8880.

School of Management Students: 8 full-time (3 women), 29 part-time (16 women); includes 3 minority (1 African American, 1 Asian American or Pacific Islander, 1 Hispanic American), 8 international. Average age 32. 40 applicants, 55% accepted. *Faculty:* 12 full-time (4 women), 7 part-time/adjunct (2 women). Expenses: Contact institution. *Financial support:* In 2001–02, 2 students received support, including 1 research assistantship with full and partial tuition reimbursement available (averaging $6,080 per year), 1 teaching assistantship with full and partial tuition reimbursement available (averaging $6,080 per year); institutionally sponsored loans, unspecified assistantships, and tuition remissions also available. Financial award application deadline: 3/1; financial award applicants required to submit FAFSA. In 2001, 10 degrees awarded. *Degree program information:* Part-time and evening/weekend programs available. Offers management (MBA). *Application deadline:* Applications are processed on a rolling basis. *Application fee:* $50. Electronic applications accepted. *Application Contact:* Carolyn P. Farrior, Director of Graduate Admissions, 321-674-7118, Fax: 321-723-9468, E-mail: cfarrior@fit.edu. *Dean,* Dr. A. Thomas Hollingsworth, 321-674-7327, Fax: 321-674-8896, E-mail: aholling@fit.edu.

School of Psychology Students: 117 full-time (87 women), 10 part-time (6 women); includes 14 minority (6 African Americans, 4 Asian Americans or Pacific Islanders, 4 Hispanic Americans), 10 international. Average age 29. 183 applicants, 34% accepted. *Faculty:* 12 full-time (4 women), 16 part-time/adjunct (1 woman). Expenses: Contact institution. *Financial support:* In 2001–02, 32 students received support, including 26 research assistantships with full and partial tuition reimbursements available (averaging $3,600 per year), 6 teaching assistantships with partial tuition reimbursements available (averaging $3,600 per year); career-related internships or fieldwork, institutionally sponsored loans, tuition waivers (partial), unspecified assistantships, and tuition remissions also available. Financial award application deadline: 3/1; financial award applicants required to submit FAFSA. In 2001, 26 degrees awarded. *Degree program information:* Part-time programs available. Offers applied behavior analysis (MS); clinical psychology (Psy D); industrial/organizational psychology (MS, PhD). *Application deadline:* For fall admission, 3/15. Applications are processed on a rolling basis. *Application fee:* $50. Electronic applications accepted. *Application Contact:* Carolyn P. Farrior, Director of Graduate Admissions, 321-674-7118, Fax: 321-723-9468, E-mail: cfarrior@fit.edu. *Dean,* Dr. Mary Beth Kenkel, 321-674-8142, Fax: 321-674-7105.

See in-depth description on page 875.

FLORIDA INTERNATIONAL UNIVERSITY, Miami, FL 33199

General Information State-supported, coed, university. CGS member. *Enrollment:* 2,107 full-time matriculated graduate/professional students (1,135 women), 2,146 part-time matriculated graduate/professional students (1,330 women). *Enrollment by degree level:* 3,381 master's, 736 doctoral, 65 other advanced degrees. *Graduate faculty:* 825 full-time (290 women). Tuition, state resident: full-time $2,916; part-time $162 per credit hour. Tuition, nonresident: full-time $10,245; part-time $569 per credit hour. *Required fees:* $168 per term. *Graduate housing:* Rooms and/or apartments available on a first-come, first-served basis to single and married students. Typical cost: $3,704 per year for single students; $3,704 per year for married students. *Student services:* Campus employment opportunities, campus safety program, career counseling, child daycare facilities, disabled student services, free psychological counseling, international student services, low-cost health insurance, multicultural affairs office. *Library facilities:* University Park Library plus 2 others. *Online resources:* library catalog, web page, access to other libraries' catalogs. *Collection:* 2.2 million titles, 14,978 serial subscriptions, 121,173 audiovisual materials. *Research affiliation:* Jefferson Laboratories (physics), Everglades National Park (environmental studies), Fairchild Tropical Gardens (botany), Cordis Corporation (bioengineering), Miami Children's Hospital (biomedical science), Sea World Shark Institute (shark tissue).

Computer facilities: 600 computers available on campus for general student use. A campuswide network can be accessed from student residence rooms and from off campus. Internet access and online class registration are available. *Web address:* http://www.fiu.edu/.

General Application Contact: Carmen Brown, Director of Admissions, 305-348-2363, Fax: 305-348-3648, E-mail: admiss@fiu.edu.

GRADUATE UNITS

College of Arts and Sciences Students: 533 full-time (288 women), 351 part-time (201 women); includes 334 minority (64 African Americans, 19 Asian Americans or Pacific Islanders, 250 Hispanic Americans, 1 Native American), 203 international. Average age 33. 1,169 applicants, 41% accepted, 234 enrolled. *Faculty:* 392 full-time (123 women). Expenses: Contact institution. *Financial support:* Fellowships, research assistantships, teaching assistantships, career-related internships or fieldwork, Federal Work-Study, institutionally sponsored loans, and tuition waivers (full and partial) available. Support available to part-time students. Financial award application deadline: 4/1. In 2001, 155 master's, 39 doctorates awarded. *Degree program information:* Part-time and evening/weekend programs available. Offers African-new world studies (MA); arts and sciences (MA, MFA, MM, MS, PhD); biological management (MS); biological sciences (MS, PhD); biology (MS, PhD); chemistry (MS, PhD); comparative sociology (MA); creative writing (MFA); developmental psychology (PhD); earth sciences (MS, PhD); economics (MA, PhD); energy (MS); English (MA); forensic science (MS); general psychology (MS); history (MA, PhD); international relations (PhD); international studies (MA); Latin American and Caribbean studies (MA); linguistics (MA); mathematical sciences (MS); physics (MS, PhD); political science (MS, PhD); pollution (MS); psychology (MS); religious studies (MA); sociology (PhD); Spanish (MA, PhD); statistics (MS); visual arts (MFA). *Application deadline:* Applications are processed on a rolling basis. *Application fee:* $20. *Dean,* Dr. Arthur W. Herriott, 305-348-2864, Fax: 305-348-4172, E-mail: herriott@fiu.edu.

School of Computer Science Students: 32 full-time (12 women), 8 part-time (3 women); includes 6 minority (all Hispanic Americans), 29 international. Average age 30. 278 applicants, 46% accepted, 30 enrolled. *Faculty:* 25 full-time (3 women). Expenses: Contact institution. *Financial support:* Application deadline: 4/1. In 2001, 27 master's, 4 doctorates awarded. *Degree program information:* Part-time and evening/weekend programs available. Offers computer science (MS, PhD). *Application deadline:* For fall admission, 4/1 (priority date); for spring admission, 10/1. Applications are processed on a rolling basis. *Application fee:* $20. *Director,* Dr. Jainendra Navlakha, 305-348-2744, Fax: 305-348-3549, E-mail: navlakha@cs.fiu.edu.

School of Music Students: 50 full-time (24 women), 12 part-time (6 women); includes 24 minority (7 African Americans, 17 Hispanic Americans), 21 international. Average age 31. 62 applicants, 55% accepted, 29 enrolled. *Faculty:* 20 full-time (2 women). Expenses: Contact institution. In 2001, 12 degrees awarded. *Degree program information:* Part-time and evening/weekend programs available. Offers music (MM); music education (MS). *Application fee:* $20. *Director,* Fredrick Kaufman, 305-348-2896, Fax: 305-348-4073, E-mail: kaufmanf@scvrms.fiu.edu.

College of Business Administration Students: 481 full-time (202 women), 416 part-time (173 women); includes 499 minority (53 African Americans, 36 Asian Americans or Pacific Islanders, 410 Hispanic Americans), 209 international. 836 applicants, 47% accepted, 280 enrolled. *Faculty:* 89 full-time (22 women). Expenses: Contact institution. *Financial support:* Fellowships, research assistantships, teaching assistantships, Federal Work-Study available. In 2001, 452 master's, 2 doctorates awarded. *Degree program information:* Part-time and evening/weekend programs available. Offers business administration (M Acc, MBA, MIB, MS, MSF, MST, PhD); decision sciences and information systems (PhD); finance (MSF); international business (MIB). *Application deadline:* For fall admission, 4/1 (priority date); for spring admission, 10/1. Applications are processed on a rolling basis. *Application fee:* $20. *Dean,* Dr. Joyce J. Elam, 305-348-2751, Fax: 305-348-3278, E-mail: elamj@fiu.edu.

School of Accounting Students: 50 full-time (24 women), 140 part-time (75 women); includes 137 minority (10 African Americans, 10 Asian Americans or Pacific Islanders, 117 Hispanic Americans), 15 international. Average age 30. 118 applicants, 56% accepted, 51 enrolled. *Faculty:* 19 full-time (5 women). Expenses: Contact institution. In 2001, 153 degrees awarded. *Degree program information:* Part-time and evening/weekend programs available. Offers accounting (M Acc); taxation (MST). *Application deadline:* For fall admission, 4/1 (priority date); for spring admission, 10/1. Applications are processed on a rolling basis. *Application fee:* $20. *Director,* Dr. Dana Forgione, 305-348-2581, Fax: 305-348-2914, E-mail: forgione@fiu.edu.

College of Education Students: 179 full-time (135 women), 715 part-time (566 women); includes 560 minority (150 African Americans, 23 Asian Americans or Pacific Islanders, 386 Hispanic Americans, 1 Native American), 36 international. Average age 35. 543 applicants, 40% accepted, 147 enrolled. *Faculty:* 74 full-time (33 women). Expenses: Contact institution. *Financial support:* In 2001–02, 4 research assistantships, 25 teaching assistantships were awarded. Fellowships, career-related internships or fieldwork, Federal Work-Study, institutionally sponsored loans, and tuition waivers (full and partial) also available. Support available to part-time students. In 2001, 292 master's, 12 doctorates, 18 other advanced degrees awarded. *Degree program information:* Part-time and evening/weekend programs available. Offers administration and supervision of vocational education (MS); adult education (MS, Ed D); art education (MS, Ed D); counselor education (MS); curriculum and instruction (MS, Ed D, Ed S); early childhood education (MS); education (MA, MS, Ed D, Ed S); educational administration and supervision (Ed D); educational leadership (MS, Ed S); elementary education (MS); emotional disturbances (MS); English education (MS, Ed D); English for non-English speakers (MS); exceptional student education (Ed D); health education (MS); higher education administration (Ed D); home economics education (MS); human resource development (MS); international development education (MS); mathematics education (MS); modern language education (MS, Ed D); non-school based home economics education (MS); parks and recreation administration (MS); parks/recreation/sports management (MS); physical education (MS); reading education (MS); school psychology (Ed S); science education (MS, Ed D); social studies education (MS); specific learning disabilities (MS); urban education (MS); vocational home economics education (MS); vocational industrial education (MS). *Application deadline:* For fall admission, 4/1 (priority date); for spring admission, 10/1. Applications are processed on a rolling basis. *Application fee:* $20. *Dean,* Dr. Linda P. Blanton, 305-348-3202, Fax: 305-348-3205, E-mail: blantonl@fiu.edu.

College of Engineering Students: 226 full-time (38 women), 179 part-time (46 women); includes 142 minority (15 African Americans, 7 Asian Americans or Pacific Islanders, 120 Hispanic Americans), 222 international. Average age 32. 758 applicants, 46% accepted, 125 enrolled. *Faculty:* 53 full-time (6 women). Expenses: Contact institution. *Financial support:* Fellowships, research assistantships, teaching assistantships, career-related internships or fieldwork, Federal Work-Study, and institutionally sponsored loans available. In 2001, 76 master's, 5 doctorates awarded. *Degree program information:* Part-time and evening/weekend programs available. Offers biomedical engineering (MS); civil engineering (MS, PhD); computer engineering (MS); construction management (MS); electrical engineering (MS, PhD); engineering (MS, PhD); environmental and urban systems (MS); environmental engineering (MS); industrial engineering (MS); mechanical engineering (MS, PhD). *Application deadline:* For fall admission, 4/1 (priority date); for spring admission, 10/1. Applications are processed on a rolling basis. *Application fee:* $20. *Acting Dean,* Dr. Vish Prasad, 305-348-6050, Fax: 305-348-1401, E-mail: prasad@fiu.edu.

College of Health and Urban Affairs Students: 510 full-time (367 women), 403 part-time (294 women); includes 582 minority (221 African Americans, 32 Asian Americans or Pacific Islanders, 328 Hispanic Americans, 1 Native American), 59 international. Average age 36. 717 applicants, 55% accepted, 205 enrolled. *Faculty:* 94 full-time (54 women). Expenses: Contact institution. *Financial support:* Fellowships, research assistantships, career-related internships or fieldwork, Federal Work-Study, and institutionally sponsored loans available. In 2001, 397 master's, 3 doctorates awarded. *Degree program information:* Part-time and evening/weekend programs available. Offers health and urban affairs (MHSA, MPA, MPH, MS, MSN, MSW, PhD). *Application deadline:* For fall admission, 4/1 (priority date); for spring admission, 10/1. Applications are processed on a rolling basis. *Application fee:* $20. *Dean,* Dr. Ronald M. Berkman, 305-348-5840, Fax: 305-348-5980, E-mail: berkmanr@fiu.edu.

School of Health Students: 252 full-time (179 women), 111 part-time (85 women); includes 214 minority (70 African Americans, 17 Asian Americans or Pacific Islanders, 126 Hispanic Americans, 1 Native American), 49 international. Average age 34. 357 applicants, 62% accepted, 102 enrolled. *Faculty:* 34 full-time (27 women). Expenses: Contact institution. *Financial support:* In 2001–02, 1 fellowship, 1 research assistantship, 1 teaching assistantship were awarded. Career-related internships or fieldwork, Federal Work-Study, and institutionally sponsored loans also available. In 2001, 104 master's, 1 doctorate awarded. *Degree program information:* Part-time programs available. Offers communication sciences and disorders (MS); dietetics and nutrition (MS, PhD); health (MPH, MS, MSN, PhD); occupational therapy (MS); physical therapy (MS); public health (MPH). *Application deadline:* For fall admission, 4/1 (priority date); for spring admission, 10/1. Applications are processed on a rolling basis. *Application fee:* $20. *Director,* Dr. Norma B. Anderson, 305-348-3446, Fax: 305-348-5980.

School of Nursing Students: 62 full-time (45 women), 37 part-time (32 women); includes 64 minority (29 African Americans, 6 Asian Americans or Pacific Islanders, 29 Hispanic Americans), 1 international. Average age 38. 76 applicants, 22% accepted, 14 enrolled. *Faculty:* 21 full-time (17 women). Expenses: Contact institution. In 2001, 67 degrees awarded. *Degree program information:* Part-time programs available. Offers nursing (MSN). *Application deadline:* For fall admission, 4/1 (priority date); for spring admission, 10/1. Applications are processed on a rolling basis. *Application fee:* $20.

School of Policy and Management Students: 85 full-time (52 women), 165 part-time (100 women); includes 186 minority (82 African Americans, 6 Asian Americans or Pacific Islanders, 98 Hispanic Americans), 4 international. Average age 33. 180 applicants, 46% accepted, 49 enrolled. *Faculty:* 28 full-time (7 women). Expenses: Contact institution. *Financial support:* In 2001–02, 2 fellowships were awarded; career-related internships or fieldwork, Federal Work-Study, and institutionally sponsored loans also available. In 2001, 107 master's, 1 doctorate awarded. *Degree program information:* Part-time and evening/weekend programs available. Offers criminal justice (MS); health services administration (MHSA); policy and management (MHSA, MPA, MS, PhD); public administration (MPA, PhD). *Application deadline:* For fall admission, 4/1 (priority date); for spring admission, 10/1. Applications are processed on a rolling basis. *Application fee:* $20. *Director,* Dr. Terry Buss, 305-348-2653, Fax: 305-348-5848, E-mail: busst@fiu.edu.

School of Social Work Students: 111 full-time (91 women), 90 part-time (77 women); includes 118 minority (40 African Americans, 3 Asian Americans or Pacific Islanders, 75 Hispanic Americans), 5 international. Average age 38. 104 applicants, 70% accepted, 40 enrolled. *Faculty:* 11 full-time (3 women). Expenses: Contact institution. In 2001, 119 master's, 1 doctorate awarded. *Degree program information:* Part-time and evening/weekend programs available. Offers social work (MSW, PhD). *Application deadline:* For fall admission, 4/1 (priority date); for spring admission, 10/1. Applications are processed on a rolling basis. *Application fee:* $20. *Director,* Dr. Ray Thomlison, 305-919-5880, Fax: 305-919-5313, E-mail: thomlisr@fiu.edu.

School of Architecture Students: 50 full-time (21 women), 27 part-time (11 women); includes 48 minority (1 African American, 2 Asian Americans or Pacific Islanders, 45 Hispanic Americans), 10 international. Average age 31. 80 applicants, 48% accepted, 21 enrolled. *Faculty:* 17 full-time (7 women). Expenses: Contact institution. In 2001, 10 degrees awarded. *Degree program information:* Part-time and evening/weekend programs available. Offers architecture (MS); landscape architecture (MS). *Application deadline:* For fall admission, 4/1 (priority date); for spring admission, 10/1. Applications are processed on a rolling basis. *Application fee:* $20. *Dean,* Juan A. Bueno, 305-348-3176, Fax: 305-348-6716, E-mail: buenoj@fiu.edu.

School of Hospitality Management Students: 91 full-time (53 women), 31 part-time (18 women); includes 20 minority (6 African Americans, 1 Asian American or Pacific Islander, 13 Hispanic Americans), 80 international. Average age 29. 92 applicants, 77% accepted, 37 enrolled. *Faculty:* 22 full-time (6 women). Expenses: Contact institution. In 2001, 60 degrees awarded. Offers hotel and food service management (MS). *Application fee:* $20. *Dean,* Dr. Joseph West, 305-919-4500, Fax: 305-919-4555, E-mail: jwest@fiu.edu.

School of Journalism and Mass Communication Students: 37 full-time (31 women), 24 part-time (21 women); includes 37 minority (3 African Americans, 1 Asian American or Pacific

are processed on a rolling basis. *Application fee:* $25 ($35 for international students). Electronic applications accepted. *Dean*, Dr. Tony Fernandez, 785-628-4200.

FORT VALLEY STATE UNIVERSITY, Fort Valley, GA 31030-4313

General Information State-supported, coed, comprehensive institution. *Graduate housing:* Room and/or apartments available on a first-come, first-served basis to single students; on-campus housing not available to married students. Housing application deadline: 7/21.

GRADUATE UNITS

Graduate Division *Degree program information:* Part-time programs available. Offers early childhood education (MS); guidance and counseling (MS, Ed S); mental health counseling (MS); middle grades education (MS); vocational rehabilitation counseling (MS).

FRAMINGHAM STATE COLLEGE, Framingham, MA 01701-9101

General Information State-supported, coed, comprehensive institution. *Graduate housing:* On-campus housing not available.

GRADUATE UNITS

Graduate Programs Students: 33 full-time, 767 part-time. *Faculty:* 24 full-time, 39 part-time/adjunct. Expenses: Contact institution. In 2001, 182 degrees awarded. *Degree program information:* Part-time and evening/weekend programs available. Offers business administration (MA); counseling (MA); curriculum and instructional technology (M Ed); educational leadership (MA); English (M Ed); food science and nutrition science (MS); health care administration (MA); history (M Ed); human resources administration (MA); human services administration (MA); literacy and language (M Ed); mathematics (M Ed); nutrition education (M Ed); public administration (MA); special education (M Ed); teaching English as a second language (M Ed). *Application deadline:* Applications are processed on a rolling basis. *Application Contact:* 508-626-4550. *Associate Dean*, Dr. Arnold Good, 508-626-4562.

FRANCISCAN SCHOOL OF THEOLOGY, Berkeley, CA 94709-1294

General Information Independent-religious, coed, graduate-only institution. *Enrollment by degree level:* 40 first professional, 37 master's, 20 other advanced degrees. *Graduate faculty:* 11 full-time (4 women), 9 part-time/adjunct (0 women). *Tuition:* Full-time $8,320; part-time $465 per credit. *Required fees:* $25 per term. *Graduate housing:* Rooms and/or apartments available on a first-come, first-served basis to single and married students. Typical cost: $7,320 per year for single students; $8,750 per year for married students. Room charges vary according to housing facility selected. Housing application deadline: 5/15. *Student services:* Campus employment opportunities, career counseling, international student services, low-cost health insurance, multicultural affairs office, writing training. *Library facilities:* Graduate Theological Union Library. *Online resources:* library catalog, web page. *Collection:* 418,767 titles, 1,453 serial subscriptions, 8,880 audiovisual materials.

Computer facilities: 7 computers available on campus for general student use. A campuswide network can be accessed from off campus. Internet access is available. *Web address:* http://www.fst.edu/.

General Application Contact: Ernesto Zamora, Recruitment Director, 510-848-5232 Ext. 28, Fax: 510-549-9466, E-mail: info@fst.edu.

GRADUATE UNITS

Graduate and Professional Programs Students: 67 full-time (36 women), 30 part-time (19 women); includes 31 minority (2 African Americans, 16 Asian Americans or Pacific Islanders, 13 Hispanic Americans), 9 international. Average age 40. 58 applicants, 81% accepted, 37 enrolled. *Faculty:* 11 full-time (4 women), 9 part-time/adjunct (0 women). Expenses: Contact institution. *Financial support:* In 2001–02, 51 students received support. Career-related internships or fieldwork, institutionally sponsored loans, scholarships/grants, and tuition waivers (partial) available. Financial award application deadline: 5/1. In 2001, 7 first professional degrees, 9 master's awarded. *Degree program information:* Part-time programs available. Offers ministry (Certificate); ministry for a multicultural church (MA); theological studies (MTS); theology (M Div, MA). *Application deadline:* For fall admission, 6/1 (priority date); for spring admission, 11/1 (priority date). Applications are processed on a rolling basis. *Application fee:* $30. Electronic applications accepted. *Application Contact:* Ernesto Zamora, Recruitment Director, 510-848-5232 Ext. 28, Fax: 510-549-9466, E-mail: info@fst.edu. *President*, Dr. William M. Cieslak, OFM, 510-848-5232, Fax: 510-549-9466, E-mail: wcieslak@fst.edu.

FRANCISCAN UNIVERSITY OF STEUBENVILLE, Steubenville, OH 43952-1763

General Information Independent-religious, coed, comprehensive institution. *Enrollment:* 154 full-time matriculated graduate/professional students (83 women), 321 part-time matriculated graduate/professional students (180 women). *Enrollment by degree level:* 475 master's. *Graduate faculty:* 9 full-time (3 women), 36 part-time/adjunct (5 women). *Tuition:* Part-time $470 per credit hour. *Required fees:* $10 per credit. Part-time tuition and fees vary according to course level and program. *Graduate housing:* On-campus housing not available. *Student services:* Campus employment opportunities, career counseling, disabled student services, exercise/wellness program, free psychological counseling, international student services, low-cost health insurance. *Library facilities:* John Paul II Library. *Online resources:* library catalog, web page, access to other libraries' catalogs. *Collection:* 222,425 titles, 737 serial subscriptions, 896 audiovisual materials.

Computer facilities: 126 computers available on campus for general student use. A campuswide network can be accessed. Internet access is available. *Web address:* http://www.franuniv.edu/.

General Application Contact: Mark McGuire, Director of Graduate Enrollment, 800-783-6220, Fax: 740-284-5456, E-mail: mmcguire@franuniv.edu.

GRADUATE UNITS

Graduate Programs Students: 154 full-time (83 women), 321 part-time (180 women); includes 6 minority (1 African American, 1 Asian American or Pacific Islander, 3 Hispanic Americans, 1 Native American), 33 international. Average age 34. 208 applicants, 90% accepted. *Faculty:* 9 full-time (3 women), 36 part-time/adjunct (5 women). Expenses: Contact institution. *Financial support:* Career-related internships or fieldwork and Federal Work-Study available. Support available to part-time students. Financial award application deadline: 7/1; financial award applicants required to submit FAFSA. In 2001, 109 degrees awarded. *Degree program information:* Part-time and evening/weekend programs available. Postbaccalaureate distance learning degree programs offered (minimal on-campus study). Offers administration (MS Ed); business (MBA); counseling (MA); nursing (MSN); philosophy (MA); teaching (MS Ed); theology and Christian ministry (MA). *Application deadline:* For fall admission, 7/1. Applications are processed on a rolling basis. *Application fee:* $20. *Application Contact:* Mark McGuire, Director of Graduate Enrollment, 800-783-6220, Fax: 740-284-5456, E-mail: mmcguire@franuniv.edu. *Dean of Faculty*, Dr. Stephen Miletic, 740-283-6228 Ext. 2305, Fax: 740-283-6401, E-mail: smiletic@franuniv.edu.

FRANCIS MARION UNIVERSITY, Florence, SC 29501-0547

General Information State-supported, coed, comprehensive institution. *Enrollment:* 45 full-time matriculated graduate/professional students (39 women), 646 part-time matriculated graduate/professional students (534 women). *Enrollment by degree level:* 691 master's. *Graduate faculty:* 101 full-time (18 women), 2 part-time/adjunct (1 woman). Tuition, state resident: full-time $3,820; part-time $191 per semester hour. Tuition, nonresident: full-time $7,640; part-time $382 per semester hour. *Required fees:* $170; $4 per semester hour. $30 per semester. *Graduate housing:* Room and/or apartments available on a first-come, first-served basis to single students; on-campus housing not available to married students. Typical cost: $4,002 (including board). Room and board charges vary according to board plan. Housing application deadline: 8/1. *Student services:* Campus employment opportunities, campus safety program, career counseling, disabled student services, free psychological counseling, international student services, low-cost health insurance, multicultural affairs office, teacher training. *Library facilities:* James A. Rogers Library plus 1 other. *Online resources:* library catalog, web page. *Collection:* 305,352 titles, 1,691 serial subscriptions.

Computer facilities: 170 computers available on campus for general student use. A campuswide network can be accessed. *Web address:* http://www.fmarion.edu/.

General Application Contact: 843-661-1284, Fax: 843-661-4688, E-mail: graduate@fmarion.edu.

GRADUATE UNITS

Graduate Programs Students: 45 full-time (39 women), 646 part-time (534 women); includes 191 minority (187 African Americans, 1 Asian American or Pacific Islander, 1 Hispanic American, 2 Native Americans), 11 international. Average age 36. *Faculty:* 101 full-time (18 women), 2 part-time/adjunct (1 woman). Expenses: Contact institution. *Financial support:* In 2001–02, fellowships (averaging $6,000 per year); career-related internships or fieldwork and unspecified assistantships also available. Support available to part-time students. Financial award application deadline: 3/1; financial award applicants required to submit FAFSA. In 2001, 86 degrees awarded. *Degree program information:* Part-time and evening/weekend programs available. Offers applied clinical psychology (MS); applied community psychology (MS); early childhood education (M Ed); elementary education (M Ed); learning disabilities (M Ed, MAT); remediation education (M Ed); school psychology (MS); secondary education (M Ed). *Application deadline:* For fall admission, 4/15 (priority date); for spring admission, 10/15 (priority date). Applications are processed on a rolling basis. *Application fee:* $30. *Provost Office*, 843-661-1284, Fax: 843-661-4688.

School of Business Students: 63. Average age 36. *Faculty:* 16 full-time (3 women). Expenses: Contact institution. *Financial support:* Fellowships, unspecified assistantships available. Support available to part-time students. Financial award application deadline: 3/1; financial award applicants required to submit FAFSA. In 2001, 19 degrees awarded. *Degree program information:* Part-time and evening/weekend programs available. Offers business (MBA); health management (MBA). *Application deadline:* For fall admission, 4/15 (priority date); for spring admission, 10/15 (priority date). Applications are processed on a rolling basis. *Application fee:* $30. *Dean*, Dr. M. Barry O'Brien, 843-661-1419, Fax: 843-661-1432, E-mail: mbobrien@fmarion.edu.

FRANKLIN PIERCE COLLEGE, Rindge, NH 03461-0060

General Information Independent, coed, comprehensive institution. *Graduate housing:* On-campus housing not available.

GRADUATE UNITS

Graduate Studies *Degree program information:* Part-time and evening/weekend programs available. Offers leadership (MBA). Electronic applications accepted.

FRANKLIN PIERCE LAW CENTER, Concord, NH 03301-4197

General Information Independent, coed, graduate-only institution. *Enrollment by degree level:* 63 master's, 57 doctoral. *Graduate faculty:* 24 full-time, 40 part-time/adjunct. *Tuition:* Full-time $19,987. Full-time tuition and fees vary according to degree level and program. *Graduate housing:* On-campus housing not available. *Student services:* Career counseling, low-cost health insurance. *Library facilities:* Franklin Pierce Law Center Library. *Online resources:* library catalog, web page, access to other libraries' catalogs. *Collection:* 54,646 titles, 3,331 serial subscriptions, 328 audiovisual materials. *Research affiliation:* Patent, Trademark, and Copyright Research Foundation, Institute for Health Law and Ethics, Academy of Applied Science.

Computer facilities: 46 computers available on campus for general student use. A campuswide network can be accessed from off campus. Internet access and online class registration are available. *Web address:* http://www.piercelaw.edu/.

General Application Contact: Katie McDonald, Director of Admissions, 603-228-9217, Fax: 603-228-1074, E-mail: kmcdonald@piercelaw.edu.

GRADUATE UNITS

Professional Program Students: 473 full-time (205 women), 36 part-time (19 women); includes 45 minority (13 African Americans, 17 Asian Americans or Pacific Islanders, 13 Hispanic Americans, 2 Native Americans), 121 international. Average age 29. 768 applicants, 60% accepted. *Faculty:* 24 full-time, 40 part-time/adjunct. Expenses: Contact institution. *Financial support:* In 2001–02, 249 students received support, including 1 fellowship (averaging $7,500 per year), 4 research assistantships (averaging $2,000 per year), 70 teaching assistantships (averaging $2,200 per year); Federal Work-Study, institutionally sponsored loans, and scholarships/grants also available. Financial award application deadline: 4/15; financial award applicants required to submit FAFSA. In 2001, 122 first professional degrees, 71 master's awarded. Offers education law (MEL, CAES, CAGS); intellectual property (JD, LL M, MIP, Diploma); law (JD). Diploma awarded as part of Intellectual Property Summer Institute. *Application deadline:* For fall admission, 5/1 (priority date). Applications are processed on a rolling basis. *Application fee:* $45. Electronic applications accepted. *Application Contact:* Katie McDonald, Director of Admissions, 603-228-9217, Fax: 603-228-1074, E-mail: kmcdonald@piercelaw.edu. *Dean*, John D. Hutson, 603-228-1541, Fax: 603-228-1074, E-mail: dhutson@piercelaw.edu.

FRANKLIN UNIVERSITY, Columbus, OH 43215-5399

General Information Independent, coed, comprehensive institution. *Enrollment:* 560 full-time matriculated graduate/professional students (257 women), 327 part-time matriculated graduate/professional students (174 women). *Enrollment by degree level:* 887 master's. *Graduate faculty:* 11 full-time (1 woman), 50 part-time/adjunct (11 women). *Tuition:* Part-time $315 per credit hour. Tuition and fees vary according to program. *Graduate housing:* On-campus housing not available. *Student services:* Campus employment opportunities, disabled student services, international student services, writing training. *Library facilities:* Franklin University Library. *Online resources:* library catalog, access to other libraries' catalogs. *Collection:* 95,291 titles, 3,878 serial subscriptions, 289 audiovisual materials.

Computer facilities: 194 computers available on campus for general student use. A campuswide network can be accessed. Internet access and online class registration are available. *Web address:* http://www.franklin.edu/.

General Application Contact: Graduate Services Office, 614-797-4700, Fax: 614-221-7723, E-mail: gradschl@franklin.edu.

GRADUATE UNITS

Graduate School of Business Students: 500 full-time (216 women), 100 part-time (50 women); includes 91 minority (57 African Americans, 23 Asian Americans or Pacific Islanders, 7 Hispanic Americans, 4 Native Americans), 38 international. Average age 34. 285 applicants, 65% accepted, 125 enrolled. *Faculty:* 6 full-time (0 women), 37 part-time/adjunct (7 women). Expenses: Contact institution. *Financial support:* In 2001–02, 85 students received support. Institutionally sponsored loans available. Financial award application deadline: 6/30; financial award applicants required to submit FAFSA. In 2001, 296 degrees awarded. *Degree program information:* Part-time and evening/weekend programs available. Postbaccalaureate distance learning degree programs offered (no on-campus study). Offers business (MBA). *Application deadline:* For fall admission, 7/15 (priority date); for winter admission, 11/6 (priority date); for spring admission, 2/26 (priority date). Applications are processed on a rolling basis. *Application fee:* $30. Electronic applications accepted. *Application Contact:* Graduate Services Office, 614-797-4700, Fax: 614-221-7723, E-mail: gradschl@franklin.edu. *Dean*, Dr. Betty Young, 614-341-6367, Fax: 614-224-4025, E-mail: youngb@franklin.edu.

Human Services Management Program Students: 52 full-time (36 women), 9 part-time (7 women); includes 23 minority (22 African Americans, 1 Asian American or Pacific Islander), 1 international. Average age 36. 41 applicants, 71% accepted, 22 enrolled. *Faculty:* 1 full-time (0 women), 4 part-time/adjunct (2 women). Expenses: Contact institution. *Financial support:* In 2001–02, 16 students received support. Scholarships/grants available. Financial award application deadline: 6/30. In 2001, 34 degrees awarded. *Degree program information:* Part-time and evening/weekend programs available. Offers human services management (MS). *Application deadline:* For fall admission, 7/15 (priority date); for winter admission, 11/6 (priority date); for spring admission, 2/26 (priority date). Applications are processed on a

Franklin University (continued)

rolling basis. *Application fee:* $30. Electronic applications accepted. *Application Contact:* Graduate Services Office, 614-797-4700, E-mail: gradschl@franklin.edu. *Program Chair*, Dr. Terry Boyd, 614-797-4700, Fax: 614-224-4025, E-mail: boydf@franklin.edu.

Marketing and Communications Program Students: 3 full-time (all women), 123 part-time (86 women); includes 20 minority (19 African Americans, 1 Hispanic American), 6 international. Average age 33. 30 applicants, 87% accepted, 17 enrolled. *Faculty:* 3 full-time (0 women), 6 part-time/adjunct (1 woman). Expenses: Contact institution. *Financial support:* In 2001–02, 11 students received support. Application deadline: 6/30. In 2001, 41 degrees awarded. *Degree program information:* Part-time and evening/weekend programs available. Offers marketing and communications (MS). *Application deadline:* For fall admission, 7/15 (priority date); for winter admission, 11/6 (priority date); for spring admission, 2/26 (priority date). Applications are processed on a rolling basis. *Application fee:* $30. Electronic applications accepted. *Application Contact:* Graduate Services Office, 614-797-4700, Fax: 614-224-7723, E-mail: gradschl@franklin.edu.

FRANK LLOYD WRIGHT SCHOOL OF ARCHITECTURE, Scottsdale, AZ 85261-4430

General Information Independent, coed, graduate-only institution. *Graduate housing:* Rooms and/or apartments guaranteed to single students and available on a first-come, first-served basis to married students.

GRADUATE UNITS

Graduate Program Offers architecture (M Arch). Summer session held in Spring Green, WI.

FREED-HARDEMAN UNIVERSITY, Henderson, TN 38340-2399

General Information Independent-religious, coed, comprehensive institution. *Enrollment:* 76 full-time matriculated graduate/professional students (51 women), 373 part-time matriculated graduate/professional students (239 women). *Enrollment by degree level:* 449 master's. *Graduate faculty:* 30 full-time (5 women), 15 part-time/adjunct (8 women). *Tuition:* Part-time $215 per hour. *Graduate housing:* Room and/or apartments available on a first-come, first-served basis to single students; on-campus housing not available to married students. Typical cost: $2,560 per year ($4,710 including board). Room and board charges vary according to board plan. Housing application deadline: 8/22. *Student services:* Campus employment opportunities, campus safety program, career counseling, child daycare facilities, disabled student services, exercise/wellness program, free psychological counseling, grant writing training, international student services, teacher training. *Library facilities:* Loden-Daniel Library. *Online resources:* library catalog, web page. *Collection:* 155,394 titles, 1,634 serial subscriptions, 41,478 audiovisual materials.

Computer facilities: 238 computers available on campus for general student use. A campuswide network can be accessed from student residence rooms and from off campus. Internet access is available. *Web address:* http://www.fhu.edu/.

General Application Contact: Dr. W. Stephen Johnson, Director of Graduate Studies and Vice President for Academic Affairs, 731-989-6004, Fax: 731-989-6945, E-mail: sjohnson@fhu.edu.

GRADUATE UNITS

Program in Counseling Students: 13 full-time (7 women), 44 part-time (32 women); includes 16 minority (15 African Americans, 1 Native American) *Faculty:* 9 full-time (2 women), 4 part-time/adjunct (3 women). Expenses: Contact institution. *Financial support:* Career-related internships or fieldwork, Federal Work-Study, tuition waivers (partial), and unspecified assistantships available. Support available to part-time students. Financial award application deadline: 8/1; financial award applicants required to submit FAFSA. In 2001, 10 degrees awarded. *Degree program information:* Part-time and evening/weekend programs available. Offers counseling (MS). *Application deadline:* For fall admission, 8/1 (priority date); for spring admission, 12/1. Applications are processed on a rolling basis. *Application fee:* $30. *Graduate Director*, Dr. Mike Cravens, 731-989-6666, Fax: 731-989-6065, E-mail: mcravens@fhu.edu.

Program in Education Students: 56 full-time (44 women), 261 part-time (206 women); includes 124 minority (121 African Americans, 2 Asian Americans or Pacific Islanders, 1 Native American), 1 international. 82 applicants, 82% accepted. *Faculty:* 9 full-time (3 women), 6 part-time/adjunct (4 women). Expenses: Contact institution. *Financial support:* Career-related internships or fieldwork, Federal Work-Study, tuition waivers (partial), and unspecified assistantships available. Support available to part-time students. Financial award application deadline: 8/1; financial award applicants required to submit FAFSA. In 2001, 115 degrees awarded. *Degree program information:* Part-time and evening/weekend programs available. Offers curriculum and instruction (M Ed); school counseling (M Ed). *Application deadline:* For fall admission, 8/1; for spring admission, 12/1. Applications are processed on a rolling basis. *Application fee:* $30. *Graduate Director*, Dr. James Murphy, 731-989-6082, Fax: 731-989-6065, E-mail: jmurphy@fhu.edu.

School of Biblical Studies Students: 7 full-time (0 women), 68 part-time (1 woman); includes 6 minority (1 African American, 5 Asian Americans or Pacific Islanders) 22 applicants, 91% accepted, 18 enrolled. *Faculty:* 5 full-time (0 women), 1 part-time/adjunct (0 women). Expenses: Contact institution. *Financial support:* Career-related internships or fieldwork, Federal Work-Study, tuition waivers (partial), and unspecified assistantships available. Support available to part-time students. Financial award application deadline: 8/1; financial award applicants required to submit FAFSA. In 2001, 18 degrees awarded. *Degree program information:* Part-time programs available. Offers biblical studies (M Min, MA); ministry (M Min); New Testament (MA). *Application deadline:* For fall admission, 8/1 (priority date); for spring admission, 12/1. Applications are processed on a rolling basis. *Application fee:* $25. *Director of Graduate Studies*, Dr. Earl Edwards, 731-989-6626, Fax: 731-989-6059, E-mail: eedwards@fhu.edu.

FRESNO PACIFIC UNIVERSITY, Fresno, CA 93702-4709

General Information Independent-religious, coed, comprehensive institution. *Enrollment:* 63 full-time matriculated graduate/professional students (48 women), 463 part-time matriculated graduate/professional students (320 women). *Enrollment by degree level:* 526 master's. *Graduate faculty:* 29 full-time (13 women), 47 part-time/adjunct (20 women). *Tuition:* Full-time $5,760; part-time $320 per unit. Tuition and fees vary according to course level and program. *Graduate housing:* On-campus housing not available. *Student services:* Campus employment opportunities, career counseling, grant writing training, international student services, teacher training. *Library facilities:* Hiebert Library. *Online resources:* library catalog, web page, access to other libraries' catalogs. *Collection:* 148,000 titles, 2,000 serial subscriptions, 6,000 audiovisual materials.

Computer facilities: 68 computers available on campus for general student use. A campuswide network can be accessed from student residence rooms and from off campus. *Web address:* http://www.fresno.edu/.

General Application Contact: Edith D. Thiessen, Director of Graduate Admissions, 559-453-2256, Fax: 559-453-2001, E-mail: edthiess@fresno.edu.

GRADUATE UNITS

Graduate School Students: 63 full-time (48 women), 463 part-time (320 women); includes 106 minority (10 African Americans, 17 Asian Americans or Pacific Islanders, 74 Hispanic Americans, 5 Native Americans), 10 international. Average age 40. 134 applicants, 73% accepted, 90 enrolled. *Faculty:* 29 full-time (13 women), 47 part-time/adjunct (20 women). Expenses: Contact institution. *Financial support:* In 2001–02, 165 students received support. Career-related internships or fieldwork, scholarships/grants, and tuition waivers (full and partial) available. Support available to part-time students. Financial award applicants required to submit FAFSA. In 2001, 168 degrees awarded. *Degree program information:* Part-time and evening/weekend programs available. Offers administration (MA Ed); administrative services (MA Ed); bilingual/cross-cultural education (MA Ed); conflict management and peacemaking (MA); curriculum and teaching (MA Ed); educational technology (MA Ed); foundations, curriculum and teaching (MA Ed); individualized study (MA); integrated mathematics/science education (MA Ed); language development (MA Ed); language, literacy, and culture (MA Ed); leadership and organizational studies (MA); learning handicapped (MA Ed); mathematics education (MA Ed); mathematics/science/computer education (MA Ed); middle school mathematics (MA Ed); multilingual contexts (MA Ed); physical and health impairments (MA Ed); pupil personnel (MA Ed); reading (MA Ed); reading/English as a second language (MA Ed); reading/language arts (MA Ed); school counseling (MA Ed); school library and information technology (MA Ed); school psychology (MA Ed); secondary school mathematics (MA Ed); severely handicapped (MA Ed); special education (MA Ed); teaching English to speakers of other languages (MA). *Application deadline:* Applications are processed on a rolling basis. *Application fee:* $90. Electronic applications accepted. *Application Contact:* Edith D. Thiessen, Director of Graduate Admissions, 559-453-2256, Fax: 559-453-2001, E-mail: edthiess@fresno.edu. *Interim Dean*, Dr. Rod Janzen, 559-453-2248, Fax: 559-453-2001, E-mail: rajanzen@fresno.edu.

FRIENDS UNIVERSITY, Wichita, KS 67213

General Information Independent, coed, comprehensive institution. *Enrollment:* 563 matriculated graduate/professional students. *Enrollment by degree level:* 563 master's. *Graduate faculty:* 61. *Tuition:* Part-time $399 per credit hour. Full-time tuition and fees vary according to campus/location and program. *Graduate housing:* Rooms and/or apartments available on a first-come, first-served basis to single and married students. Housing application deadline: 8/1. *Student services:* Campus employment opportunities, campus safety program, career counseling, disabled student services, free psychological counseling, international student services, writing training. *Library facilities:* Edmund Stanley Library plus 3 others. *Online resources:* library catalog. *Collection:* 105,989 titles, 857 serial subscriptions.

Computer facilities: 190 computers available on campus for general student use. A campuswide network can be accessed from student residence rooms and from off campus. *Web address:* http://www.friends.edu/.

General Application Contact: Tony Myers, Director of Graduate Admissions, 800-794-6945 Ext. 5583.

GRADUATE UNITS

Graduate Programs Students: 563 full-time. *Faculty:* 61. Expenses: Contact institution. In 2001, 261 degrees awarded. *Degree program information:* Evening/weekend programs available. *Application deadline:* Applications are processed on a rolling basis. *Application fee:* $45 ($80 for international students). *Application Contact:* Director of Graduate Admissions, 800-794-6945 Ext. 5583. *Vice President of Academic Affairs*, Dr. G. Robert Dove, 800-794-6945 Ext. 5881.

College of Arts and Sciences Students: 196. *Faculty:* 29. Expenses: Contact institution. *Degree program information:* Evening/weekend programs available. Offers arts and sciences (MACM, MAT, MSES, MSFT, MSL); Christian ministries (MACM); elementary education (MAT); environmental studies (MSES); family therapy (MSFT); school leadership (MSL); secondary education (MAT). *Application deadline:* Applications are processed on a rolling basis. *Application fee:* $45 ($80 for international students). *Application Contact:* Director of Graduate Admissions, 800-794-6945 Ext. 5583.

College of Business Students: 298 full-time. *Faculty:* 22. Expenses: Contact institution. *Degree program information:* Evening/weekend programs available. Offers business (EMBA, MMIS, MSM); executive business administration (EMBA); management (MSM); management information systems (MMIS). *Application deadline:* For fall admission, 8/15 (priority date). Applications are processed on a rolling basis. *Application fee:* $125. *Application Contact:* Director of Graduate Admissions, 800-794-6945 Ext. 5800. *Dean*, Dr. Al Saber, 800-794-6945 Ext. 5685.

College of Continuing Education Students: 67 full-time. *Faculty:* 11. Expenses: Contact institution. *Degree program information:* Evening/weekend programs available. Offers human resource development/occupational development (MHRDOD). *Application deadline:* Applications are processed on a rolling basis. *Application fee:* $45 ($65 for international students). *Application Contact:* Director of Graduate Admissions, 800-794-6945 Ext. 5300. *Dean*, 800-794-6945 Ext. 5682.

FROSTBURG STATE UNIVERSITY, Frostburg, MD 21532-1099

General Information State-supported, coed, comprehensive institution. *Enrollment:* 202 full-time matriculated graduate/professional students (116 women), 665 part-time matriculated graduate/professional students (377 women). *Enrollment by degree level:* 867 master's. *Graduate faculty:* 89 full-time (37 women), 14 part-time/adjunct (7 women). *Tuition, area resident:* Part-time $187 per credit hour. Tuition, state resident: full-time $3,366; part-time $187 per credit hour. Tuition, nonresident: full-time $3,906; part-time $217 per credit hour. *Required fees:* $812; $34 per credit hour. One-time fee: $9 full-time. *Graduate housing:* Room and/or apartments available to single students; on-campus housing not available to married students. Typical cost: $2,730 per year ($5,424 including board). Housing application deadline: 6/1. *Student services:* Career counseling, child daycare facilities, free psychological counseling, international student services. *Library facilities:* Lewis J. Ort Library. *Online resources:* library catalog, web page, access to other libraries' catalogs. *Collection:* 256,977 titles, 3,353 serial subscriptions, 72,490 audiovisual materials.

Computer facilities: 577 computers available on campus for general student use. A campuswide network can be accessed from student residence rooms and from off campus. Internet access and online class registration are available. *Web address:* http://www.frostburg.edu/.

General Application Contact: Patricia C. Spiker, Director of Graduate Services, 301-687-7053, Fax: 301-687-4597, E-mail: pspiker@frostburg.edu.

GRADUATE UNITS

Graduate School Students: 202 full-time (116 women), 665 part-time (377 women); includes 49 minority (28 African Americans, 6 Asian Americans or Pacific Islanders, 14 Hispanic Americans, 1 Native American), 26 international. Average age 33. 629 applicants, 81% accepted. *Faculty:* 89 full-time (37 women), 14 part-time/adjunct (7 women). Expenses: Contact institution. *Financial support:* In 2001–02, 245 students received support, including 81 research assistantships with full tuition reimbursements available (averaging $5,000 per year); career-related internships or fieldwork, Federal Work-Study, scholarships/grants, and international fellowships also available. Financial award application deadline: 4/1; financial award applicants required to submit FAFSA. In 2001, 233 degrees awarded. *Degree program information:* Part-time and evening/weekend programs available. *Application deadline:* Applications are processed on a rolling basis. *Application fee:* $30. Electronic applications accepted. *Director of Graduate Services*, Patricia C. Spiker, 301-687-7053, Fax: 301-687-4597, E-mail: pspiker@frostburg.edu.

College of Business Students: 59 full-time (28 women), 314 part-time (134 women); includes 36 minority (23 African Americans, 5 Asian Americans or Pacific Islanders, 7 Hispanic Americans, 1 Native American), 10 international. Average age 35. 152 applicants, 90% accepted. *Faculty:* 16 full-time (8 women), 6 part-time/adjunct (2 women). Expenses: Contact institution. *Financial support:* In 2001–02, 7 research assistantships with full tuition reimbursements (averaging $5,000 per year) were awarded; career-related internships or fieldwork and Federal Work-Study also available. Financial award application deadline: 4/1; financial award applicants required to submit FAFSA. In 2001, 103 degrees awarded. *Degree program information:* Part-time and evening/weekend programs available. Offers business (MBA); business administration (MBA). *Application deadline:* For fall admission, 7/15 (priority date). Applications are processed on a rolling basis. *Application fee:* $30. Electronic applications accepted. *Application Contact:* Patricia C. Spiker, Director of Graduate Services, 301-687-7053, Fax: 301-687-4597, E-mail: pspiker@frostburg.edu. *Interim Dean*, Connie Groer, 301-687-4019.

College of Education Students: 85 full-time (54 women), 313 part-time (229 women); includes 9 minority (4 African Americans, 5 Hispanic Americans), 3 international. Average age 32. 280 applicants, 85% accepted. *Faculty:* 29 full-time (15 women), 9 part-time/adjunct (4 women). Expenses: Contact institution. *Financial support:* In 2001–02, 29 research assistantships with full tuition reimbursements (averaging $5,000 per year) were awarded; career-related internships or fieldwork and Federal Work-Study also available. Financial award application deadline: 4/1; financial award applicants required to submit FAFSA. In 2001, 82 degrees awarded. *Degree program information:* Part-time and evening/weekend programs available. Offers curriculum and instruction (M Ed); education (M Ed, MA, MS); educational administration (M Ed); educational technology (M Ed); elementary (M Ed); elementary education (M Ed); elementary teaching (MA); human performance (MS); interdisciplinary education (M Ed); parks and recreational management (MS); reading (M Ed); school counseling (M Ed); secondary (M Ed); secondary education (M Ed); special education (M Ed). *Application deadline:* For fall admission, 7/15 (priority date). Applications are processed on a rolling basis. *Application fee:* $30. Electronic applications accepted. *Application Contact:* Patricia C. Spiker, Director of Graduate Services, 301-687-7053, Fax: 301-687-4597, E-mail: pspiker@frostburg.edu. *Dean,* Dr. Susan Arisman, 301-687-4759.

College of Liberal Arts and Sciences Students: 58 full-time (34 women), 38 part-time (14 women); includes 4 minority (1 African American, 1 Asian American or Pacific Islander, 2 Hispanic Americans), 13 international. Average age 29. *Faculty:* 50 full-time (16 women), 14 part-time/adjunct (2 women). Expenses: Contact institution. *Financial support:* In 2001–02, 22 research assistantships with full tuition reimbursements (averaging $5,000 per year) were awarded; career-related internships or fieldwork and Federal Work-Study also available. Financial award application deadline: 4/1; financial award applicants required to submit FAFSA. In 2001, 21 degrees awarded. *Degree program information:* Part-time and evening/weekend programs available. Offers applied computer science (MS); applied ecology and conservation biology (MS); counseling psychology (MS); fisheries and wildlife management (MS); liberal arts and sciences (MA, MS); modern humanities (MA). *Application deadline:* Applications are processed on a rolling basis. *Application fee:* $30. Electronic applications accepted. *Application Contact:* Patricia C. Spiker, Director of Graduate Services, 301-687-7053, Fax: 301-687-4597, E-mail: pspiker@frostburg.edu. *Dean,* Dr. Fred Yaffe, 301-687-4120.

FULLER THEOLOGICAL SEMINARY, Pasadena, CA 91182

General Information Independent-religious, coed, graduate-only institution. *Graduate housing:* Rooms and/or apartments available on a first-come, first-served basis to single students and available to married students.

GRADUATE UNITS

Graduate School of Psychology Offers clinical psychology (PhD, Psy D); marital/family therapy (MS); psychology (MA, MS).

Graduate School of Theology *Degree program information:* Part-time and evening/weekend programs available. Offers theology (M Div, MACL, MAT, Th M, D Min, PhD). M Div offered jointly with Denver Conservative Baptist Seminary.

Graduate School of World Mission *Degree program information:* Part-time and evening/weekend programs available. Offers global ministries (D Min); intercultural studies (MA, Th M, PhD); missiology (D Miss, PhD); world mission (MA, Th M, D Min, D Miss, PhD).

FURMAN UNIVERSITY, Greenville, SC 29613

General Information Independent, coed, comprehensive institution. *Enrollment:* 332 full-time matriculated graduate/professional students (276 women), 188 part-time matriculated graduate/professional students (154 women). *Enrollment by degree level:* 82 master's. *Graduate faculty:* 12 full-time (6 women). *Tuition:* Part-time $230 per credit hour. *Graduate housing:* On-campus housing not available. *Student services:* Campus safety program, career counseling. *Library facilities:* James Buchanan Duke Library plus 2 others. *Online resources:* library catalog, web page, access to other libraries' catalogs. *Collection:* 445,900 titles, 3,347 serial subscriptions, 4,200 audiovisual materials.

Computer facilities: 340 computers available on campus for general student use. A campuswide network can be accessed from student residence rooms and from off campus. Internet access and online class registration are available. *Web address:* http://www.furman.edu/.

General Application Contact: Dr. Hazel W. Harris, Director of Graduate Studies, 864-294-2213.

GRADUATE UNITS

Graduate Division Students: 332 full-time (276 women), 188 part-time (154 women). Expenses: Contact institution. *Financial support:* Fellowships available. Offers chemistry (MS); early childhood education (MA); elementary education (MA); reading (MA); school administration (MA); special education (MA). *Application deadline:* Applications are processed on a rolling basis. *Application fee:* $30. *Director,* Dr. Hazel W. Harris, 864-294-2213.

GALLAUDET UNIVERSITY, Washington, DC 20002-3625

General Information Independent, coed, university. CGS member. *Graduate housing:* Rooms and/or apartments available on a first-come, first-served basis to single students and available to married students. Housing application deadline: 4/1. *Research affiliation:* George Washington University (minority involvement in science), Georgia State University (vocabulary development in deaf children), Medical College of Virginia (genetics and deafness), University of Maryland College Park (audiology and speech science), University of Wisconsin (telecommunications access for deaf and hard of hearing people), Delmarva Foundation for Medical Care (cultural competence for health service providers).

GRADUATE UNITS

The Graduate School *Degree program information:* Part-time programs available.

College of Arts and Sciences Offers arts and sciences (MA, MSW, PhD, Psy S); clinical psychology (PhD); developmental psychology (MA); school psychology (MA, Psy S); social work (MSW).

School of Communication *Degree program information:* Part-time programs available. Offers audiology (Au D); communication (MA, MS, Au D); interpretation (MA); linguistics (MA); speech and language pathology (MS).

School of Education and Human Services Offers administration (MS); administration and supervision (PhD, Ed S); community counseling (MA); early childhood education (MA, Ed S); education and human services (MA, MS, PhD, Certificate, Ed S); education of deaf and hard of hearing students and multihandicapped deaf and hard of hearing students (MA, Ed S); elementary education (MA, Ed S); individualized program of study (PhD); instructional supervision (Ed S); integrating technology in the classroom (Certificate); leadership training (MS); leisure services administration (MS); mental health counseling (MA); parent/infant specialty (MA, Ed S); school counseling (MA); secondary education (MA, Ed S); special education administration (PhD).

GANNON UNIVERSITY, Erie, PA 16541-0001

General Information Independent-religious, coed, comprehensive institution. *Graduate housing:* On-campus housing not available. *Research affiliation:* General Electric (computer-controlled locomotives), Allegheny Ludlum (metal coating research), Snap-Tite (hose and coupling materials), Zurn Industries (energy systems), American Sterilizer (computerized sterilizers), Ericz Magnetics (metal detectors).

GRADUATE UNITS

School of Graduate Studies *Degree program information:* Part-time and evening/weekend programs available.

College of Humanities, Business, and Education *Degree program information:* Part-time and evening/weekend programs available. Offers accounting (Certificate); business (MBA, Certificate); business administration (MBA, Certificate); counseling psychology (MS, PhD); curriculum and instruction (M Ed); early intervention (MS, Certificate); education (M Ed, MS, PhD, Certificate); educational computing technology (M Ed); English (M Ed, MA); finance (Certificate); gerontology (Certificate); human resources management (Certificate); humanities (M Ed, MA, MPA, MS, PhD, Certificate); humanities, business, and education (M Ed, MA, MBA, MPA, MS, PhD, Certificate); pastoral studies (MA, Certificate); public administration (MPA, Certificate); reading (M Ed, Certificate); secondary education (M Ed).

College of Sciences, Engineering, and Health Sciences *Degree program information:* Part-time and evening/weekend programs available. Offers administration (MSN); anesthesia (MSN); electrical engineering (MS); embedded software engineering (MS); engineering and computer science (MS); family nurse practitioner (MSN, Certificate); gerontology (MSN); health sciences (MOT, MPT, MS, Certificate); mechanical engineering (MS); medical-surgical nursing (MSN); natural sciences/environmental education (M Ed, Certificate); occupational therapy (MOT); physical therapy (MPT); physician assistant (MS); sciences (M Ed, Certificate); sciences, engineering, and health sciences (M Ed, MOT, MPT, MS, MSN, Certificate).

GARDNER-WEBB UNIVERSITY, Boiling Springs, NC 28017

General Information Independent-religious, coed, comprehensive institution. *Enrollment:* 117 full-time matriculated graduate/professional students (67 women), 818 part-time matriculated graduate/professional students (455 women). *Enrollment by degree level:* 157 first professional, 778 master's. *Graduate faculty:* 40 full-time (12 women), 7 part-time/adjunct (1 woman). *Tuition:* Part-time $210 per hour. Part-time tuition and fees vary according to program. *Graduate housing:* Room and/or apartments available to single students; on-campus housing not available to married students. Typical cost: $1,220 per year ($2,440 including board). *Student services:* Campus employment opportunities, campus safety program, career counseling, disabled student services, exercise/wellness program, free psychological counseling, international student services, low-cost health insurance, teacher training, writing training. *Library facilities:* Dover Memorial Library. *Online resources:* library catalog. *Collection:* 210,000 titles, 5,600 serial subscriptions, 9,065 audiovisual materials.

Computer facilities: 150 computers available on campus for general student use. A campuswide network can be accessed from student residence rooms and from off campus. Internet access and online class registration are available. *Web address:* http://www.gardner-webb.edu/.

General Application Contact: Dr. Darlene J. Gravett, Dean, Graduate School, 704-406-4723, Fax: 704-406-4329, E-mail: gradschool@gardner-webb.edu.

GRADUATE UNITS

Graduate School Students: 4 full-time (all women), 430 part-time (301 women); includes 38 minority (37 African Americans, 1 Hispanic American) Average age 32. 248 applicants, 85% accepted, 200 enrolled. *Faculty:* 9 full-time (4 women), 9 part-time/adjunct (6 women). Expenses: Contact institution. *Financial support:* Fellowships, Federal Work-Study, institutionally sponsored loans, and unspecified assistantships available. Support available to part-time students. In 2001, 89 degrees awarded. *Degree program information:* Part-time and evening/weekend programs available. Offers elementary education (MA); English (MA); English education (MA); mental health counseling (MA); middle grades education (MA); physical education (MA); school administration (MA); school counseling (MA). *Application deadline:* Applications are processed on a rolling basis. *Application fee:* $25. Electronic applications accepted. *Dean,* Dr. Darlene J. Gravett, 704-406-4723, Fax: 704-406-4329, E-mail: gradschool@gardner-webb.edu.

Graduate School of Business Students: 7 full-time (3 women), 337 part-time (171 women); includes 49 minority (43 African Americans, 3 Asian Americans or Pacific Islanders, 3 Hispanic Americans), 2 international. Average age 33. 147 applicants, 80% accepted, 117 enrolled. *Faculty:* 15 full-time (2 women), 1 part-time/adjunct (0 women). Expenses: Contact institution. *Financial support:* In 2001–02, 23 students received support. Unspecified assistantships available. Support available to part-time students. Financial award applicants required to submit FAFSA. In 2001, 61 degrees awarded. *Degree program information:* Part-time and evening/weekend programs available. Postbaccalaureate distance learning degree programs offered (no on-campus study). Offers business (M Acc, MBA). *Application deadline:* For fall admission, 8/29; for spring admission, 1/13. Applications are processed on a rolling basis. *Application fee:* $25. Electronic applications accepted. *Application Contact:* Kristen J. Setzer, Director of Admissions, 800-457-4622, Fax: 704-434-3895, E-mail: ksetzer@gardner-webb.edu. *Director,* Dr. Anthony Negbenebor, 704-406-4622, Fax: 704-406-3895, E-mail: anegbenebor@gardner-webb.edu.

M. Christopher White School of Divinity Students: 92 full-time (28 women), 59 part-time (16 women); includes 18 minority (15 African Americans, 3 Asian Americans or Pacific Islanders) Average age 34. 81 applicants, 98% accepted. *Faculty:* 11 full-time (2 women), 4 part-time/adjunct (2 women). Expenses: Contact institution. *Financial support:* In 2001–02, 120 students received support; fellowships, institutionally sponsored loans and unspecified assistantships available. Support available to part-time students. Financial award application deadline: 5/15. In 2001, 17 degrees awarded. *Degree program information:* Part-time programs available. Offers Christian education (M Div); church music (M Div); ministry (D Min); missiology (M Div); pastoral care and counseling (M Div); pastoral ministry (M Div). *Application deadline:* For fall admission, 8/1 (priority date); for spring admission, 12/15 (priority date). Applications are processed on a rolling basis. *Application fee:* $25. *Application Contact:* Dr. Jack Buchanan, Information Contact, 704-406-4396, Fax: 704-406-3935, E-mail: divinity@gardner-webb.edu. *Dean,* Dr. R. Wayne Stacy, 704-406-4400, Fax: 704-406-3935, E-mail: wstacy@gardner-webb.edu.

GARRETT-EVANGELICAL THEOLOGICAL SEMINARY, Evanston, IL 60201-2926

General Information Independent-religious, coed, graduate-only institution. *Enrollment by degree level:* 142 first professional, 64 master's, 50 doctoral. *Graduate faculty:* 25 full-time (8 women), 30 part-time/adjunct (7 women). *Tuition:* Full-time $11,232; part-time $416 per credit. Full-time tuition and fees vary according to degree level. *Graduate housing:* Rooms and/or apartments guaranteed to single students and available to married students. Typical cost: $5,175 (including board) for single students; $5,805 per year for married students. Housing application deadline: 7/1. *Student services:* Campus employment opportunities, disabled student services, international student services, low-cost health insurance, writing training. *Library facilities:* United Library. *Online resources:* library catalog, web page, access to other libraries' catalogs. *Collection:* 316,709 titles, 1,910 serial subscriptions, 432 audiovisual materials.

Computer facilities: 19 computers available on campus for general student use. A campuswide network can be accessed from off campus. Internet access is available. *Web address:* http://www.garrett.nwu.edu/.

General Application Contact: Sean Recroft, Director of Admissions, 847-866-3926, Fax: 847-866-3957.

GRADUATE UNITS

Graduate and Professional Programs Students: 256 (155 women). Average age 37. *Faculty:* 25 full-time (8 women), 30 part-time/adjunct (7 women). Expenses: Contact institution. *Financial support:* In 2001–02, 183 students received support, including 25 fellowships (averaging $4,818 per year); career-related internships or fieldwork, Federal Work-Study, and scholarships/grants also available. Support available to part-time students. Financial award application deadline: 5/31; financial award applicants required to submit CSS PROFILE or FAFSA. In 2001, 39 first professional degrees, 27 master's, 12 doctorates awarded. *Degree program information:* Part-time programs available. Offers Bible and culture (PhD); Christian education (MA); Christian education and congregational studies (PhD); contemporary theology and culture (PhD); divinity (M Div); ethics, church, and society (MA); liturgical studies (PhD); ministry (D Min); music ministry (MA); pastoral care and counseling (MA); pastoral theology, personality, and culture (PhD); spiritual formation and evangelism (MA); theological studies (MTS). *Application deadline:* For fall admission, 7/20 (priority date). Applications are processed on a rolling basis. *Application fee:* $0. *Application Contact:* Sean Recroft, Director of Admissions, 847-866-3926, Fax: 847-866-3957. *Academic Dean,* Dr. Jack L. Seymour, 847-866-3904, Fax: 847-866-3957, E-mail: jack.seymour@nwu.edu.

GENERAL THEOLOGICAL SEMINARY, New York, NY 10011-4977

General Information Independent-religious, coed, graduate-only institution. *Graduate faculty:* 13 full-time (4 women), 4 part-time/adjunct (3 women). *Tuition:* Full-time $9,200. *Graduate housing:* Rooms and/or apartments available to single and married students. Housing application deadline: 6/1. *Student services:* Campus employment opportunities, career counseling, child daycare facilities, low-cost health insurance. *Library facilities:* St. Mark's Library. *Online*

General Theological Seminary (continued)

resources: library catalog, web page. *Collection:* 230,000 titles, 650 serial subscriptions, 100 audiovisual materials.

Computer facilities: 17 computers available on campus for general student use. A campuswide network can be accessed from off campus. Internet access is available.

General Application Contact: Antoinette J. Daniels, Director of Admissions, 212-243-5150 Ext. 280, Fax: 212-727-3907, E-mail: daniels@gts.edu.

GRADUATE UNITS

Graduate and Professional Programs Students: 112 full-time (54 women), 45 part-time (30 women). Average age 43. 86 applicants, 100% accepted. *Faculty:* 13 full-time (4 women), 4 part-time/adjunct (3 women). Expenses: Contact institution. *Financial support:* In 2001–02, 63 students received support. Career-related internships or fieldwork, institutionally sponsored loans, and tuition waivers (full and partial) available. Financial award application deadline: 5/1; financial award applicants required to submit FAFSA. In 2001, 23 first professional degrees, 15 master's, 1 doctorate awarded. *Degree program information:* Part-time and evening/weekend programs available. Offers Anglican studies (STM, Th D); divinity (M Div); spiritual direction (MASD, STM); theology (MA). *Application deadline:* For fall admission, 6/1 (priority date). Applications are processed on a rolling basis. *Application fee:* $35. *Application Contact:* Antoinette J. Daniels, Director of Admissions, 212-243-5150 Ext. 280, Fax: 212-727-3907, E-mail: daniels@gts.edu. *Sub-Dean, Academic Affairs,* Dr. Bruce Mullin, 212-243-5150 Ext. 231, Fax: 212-242-4451, E-mail: mullin@gts.edu.

GENEVA COLLEGE, Beaver Falls, PA 15010-3599

General Information Independent-religious, coed, comprehensive institution. *Enrollment:* 206 full-time matriculated graduate/professional students (104 women), 93 part-time matriculated graduate/professional students (52 women). *Enrollment by degree level:* 299 master's. *Graduate faculty:* 19 full-time (6 women), 32 part-time/adjunct (11 women). *Tuition:* Part-time $445 per credit hour. *Graduate housing:* On-campus housing not available. *Student services:* Campus employment opportunities, career counseling, international student services, multicultural affairs office. *Library facilities:* McCartney Library plus 5 others. *Online resources:* library catalog, web page, access to other libraries' catalogs. *Collection:* 160,000 titles, 916 serial subscriptions, 23,403 audiovisual materials.

Computer facilities: 150 computers available on campus for general student use. A campuswide network can be accessed from off campus. *Web address:* http://www.geneva.edu/.

General Application Contact: Dr. Robin Ware, Director of Graduate Student Services, 724-847-6697, Fax: 724-847-6101, E-mail: mba@geneva.edu.

GRADUATE UNITS

Program in Business Administration Average age 30. 6 applicants, 100% accepted, 6 enrolled. *Faculty:* 8 full-time (1 woman), 1 part-time/adjunct (0 women). Expenses: Contact institution. *Financial support:* Applicants required to submit FAFSA. In 2001, 1 degree awarded. *Degree program information:* Part-time and evening/weekend programs available. Offers business administration (MBA). *Application deadline:* For fall admission, 3/1 (priority date); for spring admission, 11/1 (priority date). Applications are processed on a rolling basis. *Application fee:* $50. Electronic applications accepted. *Application Contact:* Dr. Robin Ware, Director of Graduate Student Services, 724-847-6697, Fax: 724-847-6101, E-mail: mba@geneva.edu. *Chairperson,* Dr. J. Randall Nutter, 724-847-6613, E-mail: jrn@geneva.edu.

Program in Counseling Students: 16 full-time (14 women), 31 part-time (23 women). Average age 26. *Faculty:* 5 full-time (2 women), 2 part-time/adjunct (0 women). Expenses: Contact institution. *Financial support:* In 2001–02, 6 teaching assistantships (averaging $2,500 per year) were awarded; career-related internships or fieldwork and unspecified assistantships also available. In 2001, 4 degrees awarded. *Degree program information:* Part-time and evening/weekend programs available. Offers marriage and family (MA); mental health (MA); school counseling (MA). *Application deadline:* For fall admission, 7/1 (priority date); for spring admission, 11/1 (priority date). Applications are processed on a rolling basis. *Application fee:* $50. Electronic applications accepted. *Application Contact:* Dr. Robin Ware, Director of Graduate Student Services, 724-847-6697, Fax: 724-847-6101, E-mail: counseling@geneva.edu. *Director,* Dr. Carol Luce, 724-847-6622, Fax: 724-847-6101, E-mail: cbluce@geneva.edu.

Program in Higher Education Students: 29 full-time (16 women), 41 part-time (21 women); includes 9 minority (all African Americans) Average age 24. 40 applicants, 98% accepted, 38 enrolled. *Faculty:* 1 full-time (0 women), 10 part-time/adjunct (4 women). Expenses: Contact institution. *Financial support:* In 2001–02, 16 students received support, including 1 research assistantship with partial tuition reimbursement available (averaging $4,500 per year), 1 teaching assistantship with partial tuition reimbursement available (averaging $4,500 per year); career-related internships or fieldwork and unspecified assistantships also available. Support available to part-time students. Financial award application deadline: 9/1; financial award applicants required to submit FAFSA. In 2001, 17 degrees awarded. *Degree program information:* Part-time and evening/weekend programs available. Postbaccalaureate distance learning degree programs offered (minimal on-campus study). Offers college teaching (MA); educational leadership (MA); student affairs administration (MA). *Application deadline:* For fall admission, 9/1 (priority date); for winter admission, 1/2 (priority date); for spring admission, 5/15 (priority date). Applications are processed on a rolling basis. Electronic applications accepted. *Application Contact:* Krista Purcell, Coordinator, 724-847-5564, Fax: 724-847-6696, E-mail: hed@geneva.edu. *Director,* Dr. David S. Guthrie, 724-847-5564, Fax: 724-847-6696, E-mail: hed@geneva.edu.

Program in Organizational Leadership *Degree program information:* Part-time and evening/weekend programs available. Offers organizational leadership (MS). Electronic applications accepted.

Program in Special Education 5 applicants, 40% accepted, 2 enrolled. *Faculty:* 2 full-time (1 woman), 2 part-time/adjunct (both women). Expenses: Contact institution. *Degree program information:* Part-time programs available. Offers special education (M Ed). *Application deadline:* For fall admission, 3/1 (priority date); for spring admission, 11/1 (priority date). Applications are processed on a rolling basis. *Application fee:* $0. *Application Contact:* Dr. Robin Ware, Director of Graduate Student Services, 724-847-6697, Fax: 724-847-6101, E-mail: counseling@geneva.edu. *Director,* Dr. Richard Belcastro, 724-847-6534, E-mail: speced@geneva.edu.

GEORGE FOX UNIVERSITY, Newberg, OR 97132-2697

General Information Independent-religious, coed, university. *Enrollment:* 300 full-time matriculated graduate/professional students (189 women), 673 part-time matriculated graduate/professional students (398 women). *Graduate faculty:* 44 full-time (17 women), 48 part-time/adjunct (25 women). *Tuition:* Full-time $13,312; part-time $416 per semester. *Required fees:* $140; $35 per semester. Part-time tuition and fees vary according to campus/location and program. *Graduate housing:* On-campus housing not available. *Student services:* Free psychological counseling, international student services, low-cost health insurance, teacher training. *Library facilities:* Murdock Learning Resource Center plus 1 other. *Online resources:* library catalog, web page, access to other libraries' catalogs. *Collection:* 123,734 titles, 1,323 serial subscriptions, 2,687 audiovisual materials.

Computer facilities: 1,300 computers available on campus for general student use. A campuswide network can be accessed from student residence rooms and from off campus. Internet access and online class registration are available. *Web address:* http://www.georgefox.edu/.

General Application Contact: Dr. Andrea Cook, Vice President for Enrollment Services, 800-631-0921, Fax: 503-554-3856, E-mail: acook@georgefox.edu.

GRADUATE UNITS

Graduate and Professional Studies Students: 300 full-time (189 women), 673 part-time (398 women); includes 71 minority (20 African Americans, 21 Asian Americans or Pacific Islanders, 19 Hispanic Americans, 11 Native Americans), 23 international. *Faculty:* 43 full-time (17 women), 49 part-time/adjunct (25 women). Expenses: Contact institution. *Degree program information:* Part-time and evening/weekend programs available. Postbaccalaureate distance learning degree programs offered. Offers business administration (MBA); counseling (MA); marriage and family therapy (MA); organizational leadership (MAOL); teacher education (M Ed, MAT, Ed D). *Dean,* Dr. James Foster, 503-554-6149.

George Fox Evangelical Seminary Students: 59 full-time (24 women), 101 part-time (61 women); includes 11 minority (8 African Americans, 3 Asian Americans or Pacific Islanders), 6 international. 70 applicants, 80% accepted, 42 enrolled. *Faculty:* 8 full-time (2 women), 6 part-time/adjunct (1 woman). Expenses: Contact institution. *Financial support:* In 2001–02, 8 research assistantships, 8 teaching assistantships were awarded. Career-related internships or fieldwork and scholarships/grants also available. Support available to part-time students. Financial award application deadline: 5/1; financial award applicants required to submit FAFSA. In 2001, 6 first professional degrees, 7 master's awarded. *Degree program information:* Part-time programs available. Offers Christian education (MA); divinity (M Div); ministry (D Min); theological studies (MA). *Application deadline:* For fall admission, 7/1; for spring admission, 10/15. Applications are processed on a rolling basis. *Application fee:* $40. Electronic applications accepted. *Application Contact:* Sheila Bartlett, Admissions Counselor, 800-493-4937, Fax: 503-554-3856, E-mail: sbartlett@georgefox.edu. *Dean of George Fox Evangelical Seminary,* Dr. Jules Glanzer, 503-554-6152, E-mail: jglanzer@georgefox.edu.

Graduate School of Clinical Psychology Students: 72 full-time (32 women), 12 part-time (6 women); includes 11 minority (2 African Americans, 2 Asian Americans or Pacific Islanders, 3 Hispanic Americans, 4 Native Americans), 3 international. 36 applicants, 75% accepted, 21 enrolled. *Faculty:* 5 full-time (2 women), 3 part-time/adjunct (2 women). Expenses: Contact institution. *Financial support:* Teaching assistantships, career-related internships or fieldwork available. Financial award applicants required to submit FAFSA. In 2001, 16 master's, 16 doctorates awarded. Offers clinical psychology (Psy D); psychology (MA). *Application deadline:* For fall admission, 1/1. *Application fee:* $40. Electronic applications accepted. *Application Contact:* Dr. Andrea Cook, Vice President for Enrollment Services, 800-631-0921, Fax: 503-554-3856, E-mail: acook@georgefox.edu. *Director,* Dr. Wayne Adams, 800-765-4369 Ext. 2760, E-mail: wadams@georgefox.edu.

See in-depth description on page 883.

GEORGE MASON UNIVERSITY, Fairfax, VA 22030-4444

General Information State-supported, coed, university. CGS member. *Enrollment:* 2,038 full-time matriculated graduate/professional students (1,080 women), 5,143 part-time matriculated graduate/professional students (2,720 women). *Enrollment by degree level:* 763 first professional, 5,115 master's, 1,303 doctoral. *Graduate faculty:* 965 full-time (355 women), 696 part-time/adjunct (346 women). Tuition, state resident: full-time $3,168; part-time $132 per credit hour. Tuition, nonresident: full-time $11,280; part-time $470 per credit hour. *Required fees:* $1,416; $59 per credit hour. *Graduate housing:* Rooms and/or apartments available to single and married students. Typical cost: $3,280 per year ($5,400 including board) for single students. Housing application deadline: 6/1. *Student services:* Campus employment opportunities, campus safety program, career counseling, child daycare facilities, disabled student services, exercise/wellness program, free psychological counseling, international student services, low-cost health insurance, multicultural affairs office, writing training. *Library facilities:* Fenwick Library plus 1 other. *Online resources:* library catalog, web page, access to other libraries' catalogs. *Collection:* 947,288 titles, 18,820 serial subscriptions, 233,891 audiovisual materials. *Research affiliation:* Medical Sciences Research Institute, Science Applications Internation Corporation (science, technology), Bellcore (software), Chi Associates (biotechnology).

Computer facilities: 1,500 computers available on campus for general student use. A campuswide network can be accessed from student residence rooms and from off campus. Internet access, telephone registration are available. *Web address:* http://www.gmu.edu/.

General Application Contact: Beverly Davis, Director of Graduate Admissions, 703-993-2407, Fax: 703-993-2392, E-mail: http://admissions.gmu.edu/Email/.

GRADUATE UNITS

College of Arts and Sciences Students: 320 full-time (192 women), 1,162 part-time (661 women); includes 212 minority (96 African Americans, 55 Asian Americans or Pacific Islanders, 57 Hispanic Americans, 4 Native Americans), 95 international. Average age 34. 1,471 applicants, 52% accepted, 405 enrolled. *Faculty:* 416 full-time (154 women), 338 part-time/adjunct (181 women). Expenses: Contact institution. *Financial support:* Fellowships, research assistantships, teaching assistantships, career-related internships or fieldwork and Federal Work-Study available. Support available to part-time students. Financial award application deadline: 3/1; financial award applicants required to submit FAFSA. In 2001, 36 master's, 51 doctorates awarded. *Degree program information:* Part-time and evening/weekend programs available. Offers applied and engineering physics (MS); arts and sciences (MA, MAIS, MFA, MPA, MS, PhD); bioinformatics (MS); biology (MS); chemistry (MS); clinical psychology (PhD); creative writing (MFA); cultural studies (PhD); developmental psychology (PhD); ecology, systematics and evolution (MS); economics (MA, PhD); English (MA); English literature (MA); environmental science and public policy (MS, PhD); experimental neuropsychology (MA); foreign languages (MA); geography and cartographic sciences (MS); history (MA); human factors engineering psychology (MA, PhD); industrial/organizational psychology (MA, PhD); interdisciplinary studies (MAIS); interpretive biology (MS); liberal studies (MAIS); life-span development psychology (MA); linguistics (MA); mathematics (MS); molecular, microbial, and cellular biology (MS); organismal biology (MS); professional writing and editing (MA); public administration (MPA); school psychology (MA); sociology (MA); teaching writing and literature (MA); telecommunications (MA). *Application fee:* $30. Electronic applications accepted. *Application Contact:* Susan Swett, Director of Graduate Admissions, 703-993-2423, Fax: 703-993-8714, E-mail: artsandsciences@gmu.edu. *Dean,* Danielle Struppa, 703-993-8715, Fax: 703-993-8714, E-mail: dstruppa@gmu.edu.

College of Nursing and Health Science Students: 61 full-time (51 women), 234 part-time (220 women); includes 56 minority (30 African Americans, 20 Asian Americans or Pacific Islanders, 6 Hispanic Americans), 21 international. Average age 40. 140 applicants, 90% accepted, 100 enrolled. *Faculty:* 45 full-time (39 women), 29 part-time/adjunct (25 women). Expenses: Contact institution. *Financial support:* Fellowships, research assistantships, teaching assistantships, tuition waivers (partial) available. Support available to part-time students. Financial award application deadline: 3/1; financial award applicants required to submit FAFSA. In 2001, 77 master's, 6 doctorates awarded. Offers advanced clinical nursing (MSN); nurse practitioner (MSN); nursing (MSN, PhD); nursing administration (MSN). *Application deadline:* For fall admission, 5/1; for spring admission, 11/1. *Application fee:* $30. Electronic applications accepted. *Application Contact:* Dr. James D. Vail, Associate Dean, Graduate Programs and Research, 703-993-1947, Fax: 703-993-1942, E-mail: nursinfo@gmu.edu. *Dean,* Dr. Rita M. Carty, 703-993-1918.

College of Visual and Performing Arts Students: 25 full-time (16 women), 48 part-time (36 women); includes 8 minority (3 African Americans, 2 Asian Americans or Pacific Islanders, 3 Hispanic Americans), 4 international. Average age 32. 80 applicants, 54% accepted, 24 enrolled. *Faculty:* 36 full-time (15 women), 40 part-time/adjunct (27 women). Expenses: Contact institution. *Financial support:* Fellowships, teaching assistantships, career-related internships or fieldwork, Federal Work-Study, and institutionally sponsored loans available. Support available to part-time students. Financial award application deadline: 3/1; financial award applicants required to submit FAFSA. In 2001, 34 degrees awarded. Offers dance (MFA); music (MA); music education (MA); visual and performing arts (MA, MFA); visual information technologies (MA). *Application deadline:* For fall admission, 5/1; for spring admission, 11/1. *Application fee:* $30. Electronic applications accepted. *Application Contact:* Dr. Scott M. Martin, Director, 703-993-4574, Fax: 703-993-8798, E-mail: avt@gmu.edu. *Dean,* William Reeder, 703-993-8877, Fax: 703-993-8883.

Graduate School of Education Students: 316 full-time (270 women), 1,318 part-time (1,053 women); includes 277 minority (162 African Americans, 49 Asian Americans or Pacific Islanders, 61 Hispanic Americans, 5 Native Americans), 38 international. Average age 37. 899 applicants, 84% accepted, 520 enrolled. *Faculty:* 81 full-time (47 women), 85 part-time/adjunct (64 women). Expenses: Contact institution. *Financial support:* Fellowships, research assistantships, teaching assistantships, career-related internships or fieldwork and Federal Work-Study available. Support available to part-time students. Financial award application deadline: 3/1; financial award applicants required to submit FAFSA. In 2001, 683 master's, 24 doctorates awarded. *Degree program information:* Part-time and evening/weekend programs available. Offers bilingual/multicultural/English as a second language education (M Ed); counseling and development (M Ed); early childhood education (M Ed); education (M Ed, MA, MS, DA Ed, PhD); education leadership (M Ed); educational transformation (MA); exercise, fitness and health promotion (MS); instructional technology (M Ed); middle education (M Ed); reading (M Ed); secondary education (M Ed); special education (M Ed). *Application deadline:* For fall admission, 5/1; for spring admission, 11/1. *Application fee:* $30. Electronic applications accepted. *Application Contact:* Dr. Mark Goor, Information Contact, 703-993-4648, E-mail: gseinfo@gmu.edu. Jeffrey Gorrell, Fax: 703-993-2004, E-mail: gseinfo@gmu.edu.

The National Center for Community College Education Students: 1 (woman) full-time, 85 part-time (27 women); includes 18 minority (11 African Americans, 3 Asian Americans or Pacific Islanders, 4 Hispanic Americans), 2 international. Average age 49. 1 applicant, 100% accepted, 0 enrolled. *Faculty:* 2 part-time/adjunct (1 woman). Expenses: Contact institution. *Financial support:* Fellowships available. Support available to part-time students. Financial award application deadline: 3/1; financial award applicants required to submit FAFSA. In 2001, 10 degrees awarded. Offers community college education (DA Ed). *Application deadline:* For fall admission, 5/1; for spring admission, 11/1. *Application fee:* $30. Electronic applications accepted. *Head,* 703-993-2310, Fax: 703-993-2307.

Institute for Conflict Analysis and Resolution Students: 55 full-time (40 women), 75 part-time (44 women); includes 18 minority (12 African Americans, 3 Asian Americans or Pacific Islanders, 3 Hispanic Americans), 33 international. Average age 36. 190 applicants, 37% accepted, 40 enrolled. *Faculty:* 11 full-time (3 women), 8 part-time/adjunct (5 women). Expenses: Contact institution. *Financial support:* Fellowships, research assistantships, teaching assistantships, career-related internships or fieldwork available. Support available to part-time students. Financial award application deadline: 3/1; financial award applicants required to submit FAFSA. In 2001, 16 master's, 4 doctorates awarded. *Degree program information:* Part-time programs available. Offers conflict analysis and resolution (MS, PhD). *Application deadline:* For fall admission, 3/1; for spring admission, 11/1. *Application fee:* $35. Electronic applications accepted. *Director,* Dr. Sara Cobb, 703-993-1300, Fax: 703-993-1302, E-mail: icarinfo@gmu.edu.

School of Computational Sciences Students: 117 full-time (36 women), 215 part-time (43 women). Average age 30. 116 applicants, 65% accepted. *Faculty:* 28 full-time (4 women), 10 part-time/adjunct (1 woman). Expenses: Contact institution. *Financial support:* In 2001–02, 22 fellowships with tuition reimbursements (averaging $2,800 per year), 56 research assistantships with full tuition reimbursements (averaging $12,600 per year) were awarded. Teaching assistantships, career-related internships or fieldwork, Federal Work-Study, institutionally sponsored loans, and tuition waivers (partial) also available. Financial award application deadline: 2/1; financial award applicants required to submit FAFSA. In 2001, 5 doctorates, 3 other advanced degrees awarded. *Degree program information:* Part-time and evening/weekend programs available. Offers computational sciences (MS); computational sciences and informatics (PhD); computational techniques and applications (Certificate). *Application deadline:* For fall admission, 3/1 (priority date); for spring admission, 11/1 (priority date). Applications are processed on a rolling basis. *Application fee:* $50. *Application Contact:* Dr. Peter A. Becker, Graduate Coordinator, 703-993-3619, Fax: 703-993-1980, E-mail: pbecker@science.gmu.edu. *Dean,* Dr. W. Murray Black, 703-993-1990, Fax: 703-993-1993, E-mail: mblack@gmu.edu.

School of Information Technology and Engineering Students: 345 full-time (130 women), 1,582 part-time (438 women); includes 464 minority (106 African Americans, 309 Asian Americans or Pacific Islanders, 45 Hispanic Americans, 4 Native Americans), 608 international. Average age 32. 1,531 applicants, 71% accepted, 658 enrolled. *Faculty:* 100 full-time (15 women), 68 part-time/adjunct (12 women). Expenses: Contact institution. *Financial support:* Fellowships, research assistantships, teaching assistantships, career-related internships or fieldwork, Federal Work-Study, institutionally sponsored loans, and unspecified assistantships available. Support available to part-time students. Financial award application deadline: 3/1; financial award applicants required to submit FAFSA. In 2001, 322 master's, 29 doctorates awarded. *Degree program information:* Part-time and evening/weekend programs available. Offers computer science (MS, PhD); electrical and computer engineering (PhD); electrical engineering (MS); information systems (MS); information technology and engineering (MS, PhD); operations research and management science (MS); software systems engineering (MS); statistical science (MS); systems engineering (MS). *Application deadline:* For fall admission, 5/1; for spring admission, 11/1. *Application fee:* $30. Electronic applications accepted. *Application Contact:* Dr. Stephen G. Nash, Information Contact, 703-993-1505, Fax: 703-993-1734, E-mail: itegrad@gmu.edu. *Dean,* Lloyd Griffiths, 703-993-1500, Fax: 703-993-1734, E-mail: lgriffiths@gmu.edu.

School of Law Students: 714 full-time (301 women), 49 part-time (23 women); includes 74 minority (9 African Americans, 46 Asian Americans or Pacific Islanders, 16 Hispanic Americans, 3 Native Americans), 4 international. Average age 29. 1,965 applicants, 36% accepted. *Faculty:* 38 full-time (8 women), 49 part-time/adjunct (13 women). Expenses: Contact institution. *Financial support:* Fellowships available. In 2001, 206 degrees awarded. *Degree program information:* Part-time and evening/weekend programs available. Offers law (JD). *Application deadline:* For fall admission, 5/1; for spring admission, 11/1. *Application fee:* $30. Electronic applications accepted. *Application Contact:* 703-993-8010. *Dean,* Dr. Mark F. Grady, 703-993-8006, Fax: 703-993-8088.

School of Management Students: 61 full-time (17 women), 200 part-time (60 women); includes 43 minority (7 African Americans, 28 Asian Americans or Pacific Islanders, 8 Hispanic Americans), 7 international. Average age 33. 237 applicants, 55% accepted, 79 enrolled. *Faculty:* 56 full-time (21 women), 36 part-time/adjunct (7 women). Expenses: Contact institution. *Financial support:* Fellowships, research assistantships, teaching assistantships, career-related internships or fieldwork and Federal Work-Study available. Support available to part-time students. Financial award application deadline: 3/1; financial award applicants required to submit FAFSA. In 2001, 136 degrees awarded. *Degree program information:* Part-time and evening/weekend programs available. Offers business administration (EMBA, MBA); management (EMBA, MBA, MS); technology management (MS). *Application deadline:* For fall admission, 5/1; for spring admission, 11/1. Applications are processed on a rolling basis. *Application fee:* $30. Electronic applications accepted. *Application Contact:* Dr. Andres Fortino, Director, 703-993-1872, Fax: 703-993-1867, E-mail: masonmba@som.gmu.edu. *Dean,* Richard Klimoski, 703-993-1807, E-mail: rklimosk@gmu.edu.

School of Public Policy Offers enterprise engineering and policy (MS); international commerce and policy (MA); organizational learning (MSNPS); peace operations (MAIS); professional studies: organizational learning (MS); public policy (MA, MAIS, MS, MSNPS, PhD); regional economic development and technology (MAIS); transportation policy, operations and logistics (MSNPS). Electronic applications accepted.

See in-depth description on page 885.

GEORGETOWN COLLEGE, Georgetown, KY 40324-1696

General Information Independent-religious, coed, comprehensive institution. *Enrollment:* 1 (woman) full-time matriculated graduate/professional student, 341 part-time matriculated graduate/professional students (304 women). *Enrollment by degree level:* 342 master's. *Graduate faculty:* 6 full-time (3 women), 9 part-time/adjunct (1 woman). *Tuition:* Part-time $200 per hour. One-time fee: $50 part-time. *Graduate housing:* On-campus housing not available. *Student services:* Career counseling. *Library facilities:* Anna Ashcraft Ensor Learning Resource Center plus 1 other. *Online resources:* library catalog, web page, access to other libraries' catalogs. *Collection:* 145,794 titles, 833 serial subscriptions, 3,009 audiovisual materials.

Computer facilities: 150 computers available on campus for general student use. A campuswide network can be accessed from student residence rooms and from off campus. Internet access is available. *Web address:* http://www.georgetowncollege.edu/.

General Application Contact: Dr. Taylor Thompson, Director of Graduate Studies, 502-863-8176, Fax: 502-868-7741, E-mail: taylor_thompson@georgetowncollege.edu.

GRADUATE UNITS

Graduate Studies Students: 1 (woman) full-time, 341 part-time (304 women); includes 13 minority (9 African Americans, 4 Hispanic Americans) Average age 32. 85 applicants, 100% accepted. *Faculty:* 6 full-time (3 women), 9 part-time/adjunct (1 woman). Expenses: Contact institution. *Financial support:* Federal Work-Study available. Support available to part-time students. In 2001, 108 degrees awarded. *Degree program information:* Part-time programs available. Offers education (MA Ed). *Application deadline:* For fall admission, 9/1 (priority date); for spring admission, 1/10 (priority date). Applications are processed on a rolling basis. *Application fee:* $0. *Dean of Education,* Dr. Ben R. Oldham, 502-863-8176, Fax: 502-868-7741, E-mail: boldham@georgetowncollege.edu.

GEORGETOWN UNIVERSITY, Washington, DC 20057

General Information Independent-religious, coed, university. CGS member. *Graduate housing:* On-campus housing not available.

GRADUATE UNITS

Graduate School of Arts and Sciences Offers American government (MA, PhD); analytical chemistry (MS, PhD); Arab studies (MA, Certificate); Arabic language, literature, and linguistics (MS, PhD); arts and sciences (MA, MALS, MAT, MBA, MPP, MS, PhD, Certificate); bilingual education (Certificate); biochemistry (MS, PhD); biochemistry and molecular biology (PhD); biology (MS, PhD); biomedical sciences (MS, PhD); biostatistics and epidemiology (MS); British and American literature (MA); cell biology (PhD); chemical physics (MS, PhD); communication, culture, and technology (MA); comparative government (PhD); demography (MA); economics (PhD); German (MS, PhD); health physics (MS); history (MA, PhD); inorganic chemistry (MS, PhD); international relations (PhD); linguistics (MS, PhD); microbiology and immunology (PhD); national security studies (MA); neuroscience (PhD); organic chemistry (MS, PhD); pathology (MS, PhD); pharmacology (PhD); philosophy (MA, PhD); physical chemistry (MS, PhD); physiology and biophysics (MS, PhD); political theory (PhD); psychology (PhD); radiobiology (MS); Russian and East European studies (MA); Spanish (MS, PhD); teaching English as a second language (MAT, Certificate); teaching English as a second language and bilingual education (MAT); theoretical chemistry (MS, PhD).

BMW Center for German and European Studies Offers German and European studies (MA).

Center for Latin American Studies Offers Latin American studies (MA).

Edmund A. Walsh School of Foreign Service Offers foreign service (MS).

The Georgetown Public Policy Institute Offers public policy (MPP).

McDonough School of Business Offers business administration (MBA).

School for Summer and Continuing Education Offers summer and continuing education (MALS).

School of Nursing and Health Studies Offers nursing (MS).

Law Center *Degree program information:* Part-time and evening/weekend programs available. Offers advocacy (LL M); common law studies (LL M); general (LL M); international and comparative law (LL M); labor and employment law (LL M); law (JD, SJD); securities regulation (LL M); taxation (LL M).

School of Medicine Offers medicine (MD).

THE GEORGE WASHINGTON UNIVERSITY, Washington, DC 20052

General Information Independent, coed, university. CGS member. *Enrollment:* 5,249 full-time matriculated graduate/professional students (2,724 women), 5,773 part-time matriculated graduate/professional students (3,007 women). *Enrollment by degree level:* 2,120 first professional, 6,189 master's, 1,626 doctoral, 476 other advanced degrees. *Graduate faculty:* 1,236 full-time (439 women), 2,339 part-time/adjunct (709 women). *Tuition:* Part-time $810 per credit. *Required fees:* $1 per credit. *Graduate housing:* On-campus housing not available. *Student services:* Campus employment opportunities, campus safety program, career counseling, disabled student services, exercise/wellness program, free psychological counseling, international student services, low-cost health insurance, multicultural affairs office, teacher training, writing training. *Library facilities:* Gelman Library plus 2 others. *Online resources:* library catalog, web page, access to other libraries' catalogs. *Collection:* 1.8 million titles, 14,729 serial subscriptions, 17,246 audiovisual materials. *Research affiliation:* NASA–Langley Research Center (aeroacoustics, aeronautics, astronautics), National Institutes of Health (biostatistics), Smithsonian Institution, Library of Congress, Goddard Space Flight Center (radar modeling analysis, space systems technologies), Children's Hospital National Medical Center.

Computer facilities: 550 computers available on campus for general student use. A campuswide network can be accessed from student residence rooms and from off campus. *Web address:* http://www.gwu.edu/.

General Application Contact: Kristin Williams, Director, Graduate Enrollment Support Services, 202-994-0467, Fax: 202-994-0709.

GRADUATE UNITS

Columbian College of Arts and Sciences Students: 959 full-time (644 women), 1,135 part-time (656 women); includes 271 minority (103 African Americans, 103 Asian Americans or Pacific Islanders, 60 Hispanic Americans, 5 Native Americans), 257 international. Average age 30. 2,928 applicants, 60% accepted. *Faculty:* 250 full-time (84 women), 78 part-time/adjunct (23 women). Expenses: Contact institution. *Financial support:* In 2001–02, 233 fellowships with tuition reimbursements (averaging $6,700 per year), 186 teaching assistantships with tuition reimbursements (averaging $4,000 per year) were awarded. Research assistantships, career-related internships or fieldwork, Federal Work-Study, scholarships/grants, and unspecified assistantships also available. Support available to part-time students. Financial award application deadline: 2/1. In 2001, 487 master's, 81 doctorates, 14 other advanced degrees awarded. *Degree program information:* Part-time and evening/weekend programs available. Offers American (MA); American literature (MA, PhD); American studies (MA, PhD); analytical chemistry (MS, PhD); anthropology (MA); applied mathematics (MA, MS); applied social psychology (PhD); applied statistics (MS); art history (MA); art history-museum training (MA); art therapy (MA); arts and sciences (MA, MFA, MFS, MPP, MS, MSFS, PhD, Psy D, Certificate); baroque (MA); biochemistry and molecular biology (MS, PhD); biology (MS, PhD); biostatistics (MS, PhD); ceramics (MFA); chemical toxicology (MS); classical acting (MFA); classical art and archaeology (MA); clinical psychology (PhD, Psy D); cognitive neuropsychology (PhD); computational mathematics (MS); computational physics (MS); computational science (MS); computational statistics and stochastic modeling (MS); contemporary (MA); crime and commerce (MA); criminal justice (MA); design (MFA); economics (MA, PhD); eighteenth-century art (MA); English literature (MA, PhD); environmental and resource policy (MA); epidemiology and biostatistics (MS, PhD); folklife (MA); forensic molecular biology (MFS); forensic sciences (MFS, MSFS); geochemistry (MS); geography and regional science (MA); geology (MS, PhD); Hinduism and Islam (MA); historic preservation (MA); history (MA, PhD); history and public policy (MA); history of religion (MA); hominid paleobiology (MS, PhD); human resource management (MA); human sciences (PhD); industrial and engineering statistics (MS); industrial-organizational psychology (PhD); inorganic chemistry (MS, PhD); interior design (MFA); legislative affairs (MA); material culture (MA); materials science (MS, PhD); mathematical statistics (MS); mathematics (MA, PhD); medieval (MA); museum studies (MA, Certificate); nineteenth-century art (MA); organic chemistry (MS, PhD); organizational management (MA); painting (MFA); philosophy and social policy (MA); photography (MFA); physical chemistry (MS, PhD); physics (PhD); political science (MA, PhD); printmaking (MFA); public policy (MA, MPP, PhD); public policy-women's studies (MA); Renaissance (MA); sculpture (MFA); security management (MA); sociology (MA); speech pathology (MA); statistical computing (MS); statistics (MS, PhD); telecommunication studies (MA); theatre/design (MFA); visual communication (MFA); women's studies (MA). *Application fee:* $55. *Application Contact:* 202-994-6210, Fax: 202-994-6213, E-mail: csasgrad@gwu.edu. *Interim Dean,* Jean Folkerts, 202-994-6226.

Graduate School of Political Management Students: 79 full-time (42 women), 86 part-time (44 women); includes 15 minority (7 African Americans, 2 Asian Americans or Pacific Islanders, 6 Hispanic Americans), 13 international. Average age 26. 125 applicants, 89% accepted. Expenses: Contact institution. *Financial support:* Research assistantships, career-related internships or fieldwork and scholarships/grants available. Financial award application deadline: 2/1. In 2001, 54 degrees awarded. Offers political management (MA).

The George Washington University (continued)

Application fee: $55. *Application Contact:* Admissions Office, 202-994-6000. *Dean*, Dr. Christopher Arterton, 202-994-5843, Fax: 202-994-5806.

Institute for Biomedical Sciences Students: 16 full-time (11 women), 8 part-time (4 women); includes 1 minority (Hispanic American), 7 international. Average age 28. 188 applicants, 24% accepted. Expenses: Contact institution. *Financial support:* Fellowships, Federal Work-Study and institutionally sponsored loans available. *Degree program information:* Part-time and evening/weekend programs available. Offers biochemistry and molecular biology (PhD); genetics (MS, PhD); microbiology and immunology (PhD); molecular and cellular oncology (PhD); neuroscience (PhD); pharmacology (PhD). *Application fee:* $55. *Application Contact:* 202-994-2179, Fax: 202-994-0967.

School of Media and Public Affairs Students: 13 full-time (11 women), 10 part-time (6 women); includes 4 minority (2 African Americans, 1 Asian American or Pacific Islander, 1 Native American), 3 international. Average age 27. 85 applicants, 33% accepted. Expenses: Contact institution. *Financial support:* In 2001–02, 9 fellowships with tuition reimbursements (averaging $6,000 per year), 8 teaching assistantships with tuition reimbursements (averaging $4,800 per year) were awarded. In 2001, 11 degrees awarded. Offers media and public affairs (MA). *Application fee:* $55. *Director*, Jerry Maniteim, 202-994-6227, Fax: 202-994-5806.

Elliott School of International Affairs Students: 373 full-time (227 women), 143 part-time (85 women); includes 85 minority (18 African Americans, 30 Asian Americans or Pacific Islanders, 36 Hispanic Americans, 1 Native American), 80 international. Average age 27. 1,092 applicants, 76% accepted. *Faculty:* 11 full-time (0 women), 19 part-time/adjunct (5 women). Expenses: Contact institution. *Financial support:* In 2001–02, 27 fellowships with tuition reimbursements (averaging $6,500 per year), 8 teaching assistantships with tuition reimbursements (averaging $2,700 per year) were awarded. Research assistantships with tuition reimbursements, career-related internships or fieldwork, Federal Work-Study, institutionally sponsored loans, and tuition waivers (full and partial) also available. Financial award application deadline: 1/15; financial award applicants required to submit FAFSA. In 2001, 196 degrees awarded. *Degree program information:* Part-time and evening/weekend programs available. Offers Asian studies (MA); European and Eurasian studies (MA); international affairs (MA, MIS); international development studies (MA); international policy and practice (MIS); international trade and investment policy (MA); Latin American studies (MA); Russian and East European studies (MA); science, technology, and public policy (MA); security policy studies (MA). *Application deadline:* For fall admission, 2/1. *Application fee:* $55. Electronic applications accepted. *Application Contact:* Jeff V. Miles, Director of Graduate Admissions, 202-994-7050, Fax: 202-994-9537, E-mail: esiagrad@gwu.edu. *Dean*, Dr. Harry Harding, 202-994-6241.

Graduate School of Education and Human Development Students: 405 full-time (294 women), 985 part-time (697 women); includes 442 minority (342 African Americans, 42 Asian Americans or Pacific Islanders, 51 Hispanic Americans, 7 Native Americans), 51 international. Average age 37. 892 applicants, 95% accepted. *Faculty:* 72 full-time (38 women), 64 part-time/adjunct (43 women). Expenses: Contact institution. *Financial support:* In 2001–02, 20 fellowships with tuition reimbursements (averaging $3,700 per year), 17 teaching assistantships with tuition reimbursements (averaging $3,400 per year) were awarded. Research assistantships with tuition reimbursements, career-related internships or fieldwork, Federal Work-Study, and tuition waivers (full and partial) also available. Support available to part-time students. In 2001, 369 master's, 49 doctorates, 42 other advanced degrees awarded. *Degree program information:* Part-time and evening/weekend programs available. Postbaccalaureate distance learning degree programs offered (no on-campus study). Offers counseling (PhD, Ed S); counseling: school, community and rehabilitation (MA Ed, PhD); curriculum and instruction (MA Ed, Ed D, Ed S); education administration and policy studies (Ed D); education and human development (M Ed, MA Ed, MAT, Ed D, PhD, Certificate, Ed S); education policy studies (MA Ed); educational human development (MA Ed); educational leadership and administration (MA Ed); educational technology leadership (MA Ed); elementary education (M Ed); executive leadership (Ed D); higher education administration (MA Ed, Ed D, Ed S); human resource development (MA Ed, Ed D, Ed S); infant special education (MA Ed); international education (MA Ed); museum education (MAT); secondary education (M Ed); special education (Ed D, Ed S); special education of seriously emotionally disturbed students (MA Ed); special education/early childhood (MA Ed); transitional special education (MA Ed, Certificate). *Application deadline:* For fall admission, 1/15 (priority date); for spring admission, 10/1. Applications are processed on a rolling basis. *Application fee:* $55. Electronic applications accepted. *Application Contact:* Debra Bright Harris, Director of Graduate Admissions, 202-994-6160, Fax: 202-994-7207, E-mail: dbharris@gwu.edu. *Dean*, Dr. Mary Hatwood Futrell, 202-994-1445, Fax: 202-994-7207, E-mail: mfutrell@gwu.edu.

Law School Students: 1,364 full-time (647 women), 392 part-time (157 women); includes 534 minority (220 African Americans, 155 Asian Americans or Pacific Islanders, 149 Hispanic Americans, 10 Native Americans), 80 international. Average age 28. 178 applicants, 100% accepted. *Faculty:* 71 full-time (21 women), 90 part-time/adjunct (23 women). Expenses: Contact institution. *Financial support:* In 2001–02, 550 students received support; research assistantships, career-related internships or fieldwork, Federal Work-Study, institutionally sponsored loans, scholarships/grants, and tuition waivers (full and partial) available. Support available to part-time students. Financial award application deadline: 3/1; financial award applicants required to submit CSS PROFILE or FAFSA. In 2001, 461 first professional degrees, 124 master's, 2 doctorates awarded. *Degree program information:* Part-time and evening/weekend programs available. Offers law (JD, LL M, SJD). *Application deadline:* For fall admission, 3/1. Applications are processed on a rolling basis. *Application fee:* $65. *Application Contact:* Robert V. Stanek, Assistant Dean of Admissions and Financial Aid, 202-739-0648, Fax: 202-739-0624, E-mail: jd@admit.nlc.gwu.edu. *Dean*, Michael K. Young, 202-994-6288.

School of Business and Public Management, Full Time MBA Program Students: 865 full-time (390 women), 1,333 part-time (565 women); includes 453 minority (197 African Americans, 189 Asian Americans or Pacific Islanders, 63 Hispanic Americans, 4 Native Americans), 428 international. Average age 32. 1,970 applicants, 68% accepted. *Faculty:* 111 full-time (20 women), 48 part-time/adjunct (8 women). Expenses: Contact institution. *Financial support:* In 2001–02, 92 fellowships with tuition reimbursements (averaging $3,600 per year), 81 teaching assistantships with tuition reimbursements (averaging $3,500 per year) were awarded. Career-related internships or fieldwork, Federal Work-Study, institutionally sponsored loans, and tuition waivers (partial) also available. Financial award application deadline: 4/1. In 2001, 853 master's, 13 doctorates awarded. *Degree program information:* Part-time and evening/weekend programs available. Offers accountancy (M Accy, PhD); budget and public finance (MPA); business and public management (M Accy, MBA, MPA, MS, MSF, MSIST, MTA, PhD); business economics and public policy (MBA); destination management (MTA); event management (MTA); executive, legislative, and regulatory management (MPA); finance (MSF, PhD); finance and investments (MBA); human resources management (MBA); information systems management (MBA); international business (MBA, PhD); logistics, operations, and materials management (MBA); management and organizations (PhD); management decision making (MBA, PhD); management information systems (MSIST); management information systems technology (MSIST); management of science, technology, and innovation (MBA); managing public organizations (MPA); managing state and local governments (MPA); marketing (MBA, PhD); organizational behavior and development (MBA); policy analysis and evaluation (MPA); project management (MS); public administration (MBA, MPA, PhD); real estate development (MBA); sport management (MTA); strategic management and public policy (PhD); tourism administration (MTA); tourism and hospitality management (MBA); travel marketing (MTA). *Application deadline:* For fall admission, 4/1 (priority date); for spring admission, 10/1. Applications are processed on a rolling basis. *Application fee:* $55. Electronic applications accepted. *Application Contact:* David Toomer, Director Enrollment Management, 202-994-6584, Fax: 202-994-6382. *Dean*, Dr. Susan Philips, 202-994-6380, Fax: 202-994-6382.

School of Engineering and Applied Science Students: 435 full-time (98 women), 1,138 part-time (316 women); includes 309 minority (131 African Americans, 122 Asian Americans or Pacific Islanders, 51 Hispanic Americans, 5 Native Americans), 515 international. Average age 34. 963 applicants, 90% accepted. *Faculty:* 76 full-time (10 women), 83 part-time/adjunct (5 women). Expenses: Contact institution. *Financial support:* In 2001–02, 77 fellowships with full and partial tuition reimbursements (averaging $6,200 per year), 133 research assistantships with full and partial tuition reimbursements, 71 teaching assistantships with full and partial tuition reimbursements (averaging $3,800 per year) were awarded. Career-related internships or fieldwork, Federal Work-Study, institutionally sponsored loans, and tuition waivers (full and partial) also available. Financial award application deadline: 3/1; financial award applicants required to submit FAFSA. In 2001, 381 master's, 13 doctorates, 2 other advanced degrees awarded. *Degree program information:* Part-time and evening/weekend programs available. Offers civil and environmental engineering (MS, D Sc, App Sc, Engr); computer science (MS, D Sc, App Sc, Engr); electrical and computer engineering (MS, D Sc, App Sc, Engr); engineering and applied science (MEM, MS, D Sc, App Sc, Engr); engineering management and systems engineering (MEM, MS, D Sc, App Sc, Engr); mechanical and aerospace engineering (MS, D Sc, App Sc, Engr). *Application deadline:* For fall admission, 3/1; for spring admission, 10/1. Applications are processed on a rolling basis. *Application fee:* $55. *Application Contact:* Howard M. Davis, Manager, Office of Admissions and Student Records, 202-994-6158, Fax: 202-994-0909, E-mail: data:adms@seas.gwu.edu. *Dean*, Dr. Timothy Tong, 202-994-6080, Fax: 202-994-4522, E-mail: tong@seas.gwu.edu.

School of Medicine and Health Sciences Students: 816 full-time (454 women), 103 part-time (74 women); includes 179 minority (50 African Americans, 103 Asian Americans or Pacific Islanders, 25 Hispanic Americans, 1 Native American), 26 international. Average age 28. 337 applicants, 44% accepted. *Faculty:* 696 full-time (252 women), 1,902 part-time/adjunct (445 women). Expenses: Contact institution. *Financial support:* Career-related internships or fieldwork, Federal Work-Study, and institutionally sponsored loans available. In 2001, 141 first professional degrees, 94 master's, 63 other advanced degrees awarded. Offers medicine (MD); medicine and health sciences (MD, MSHS, Certificate); oral biology (MSHS); physical therapy (MSHS); physician assistant (MSHS). *Application deadline:* Applications are processed on a rolling basis. *Application Contact:* Admissions, 202-994-3748, Fax: 202-994-1753, E-mail: medadmit@gwu.edu. *Vice President for Academic Affairs*, Dr. John F. Williams, 202-994-3727.

School of Public Health and Health Services Students: 215 full-time (153 women), 361 part-time (274 women); includes 244 minority (127 African Americans, 88 Asian Americans or Pacific Islanders, 28 Hispanic Americans, 1 Native American), 51 international. Average age 30. 803 applicants, 92% accepted. *Faculty:* 50 full-time (20 women), 25 part-time/adjunct (10 women). Expenses: Contact institution. *Financial support:* In 2001–02, 8 research assistantships, 25 teaching assistantships were awarded. Career-related internships or fieldwork, Federal Work-Study, institutionally sponsored loans, scholarships/grants, and tuition waivers (partial) also available. Support available to part-time students. In 2001, 230 master's, 8 other advanced degrees awarded. *Degree program information:* Part-time and evening/weekend programs available. Postbaccalaureate distance learning degree programs offered (minimal on-campus study). Offers administrative medicine (MPH); community-oriented primary care (MPH); environmental-occupational health (MPH); epidemiology-biostatistics (MPH); exercise science (MS); health promotion (MPH); health promotion-disease prevention (MPH); health services management and policy (MHSA, Specialist); international health (MPH); management (MPH); maternal and child health (MPH); policy (MPH); policy and programs (MPH); public health (Dr PH); public health and health services (MHSA, MPH, MS, MSHS, Dr PH, Specialist). *Application deadline:* For fall admission, 5/15 (priority date); for spring admission, 11/15. Applications are processed on a rolling basis. *Application fee:* $55. *Application Contact:* Michelle Sparacino, Director of Recruitment, 202-994-2160, Fax: 202-994-3773, E-mail: sphhs-info@gwumc.edu. *Dean*, Dr. Richard Riegelman, 202-994-4772, Fax: 202-994-3773, E-mail: sphrkr@gwumc.edu.

See in-depth description on page 887.

GEORGIA COLLEGE & STATE UNIVERSITY, Milledgeville, GA 31061

General Information State-supported, coed, comprehensive institution. *Enrollment:* 248 full-time matriculated graduate/professional students (159 women), 761 part-time matriculated graduate/professional students (525 women). *Enrollment by degree level:* 1,009 master's. *Graduate faculty:* 249. Tuition, state resident: full-time $2,286. Tuition, nonresident: full-time $9,108. *Required fees:* $500. *Graduate housing:* Room and/or apartments available on a first-come, first-served basis to single students; on-campus housing not available to married students. Typical cost: $2,600 per year ($4,494 including board). Room and board charges vary according to board plan and housing facility selected. Housing application deadline: 6/15. *Student services:* Campus employment opportunities, campus safety program, career counseling, disabled student services, exercise/wellness program, free psychological counseling, grant writing training, international student services, multicultural affairs office. *Library facilities:* Ina Dillard Russell Library. *Online resources:* library catalog, web page, access to other libraries' catalogs. *Collection:* 140,593 titles, 1,037 serial subscriptions, 4,169 audiovisual materials.

Computer facilities: 375 computers available on campus for general student use. A campuswide network can be accessed from student residence rooms and from off campus. Internet access and online class registration are available. *Web address:* http://www.gcsu.edu/.

General Application Contact: Dr. Ken Jones, Dean of the Graduate School, 478-445-1228, Fax: 478-445-1229, E-mail: kjones@gcsu.edu.

GRADUATE UNITS

Graduate School Students: 248 full-time (159 women), 761 part-time (525 women); includes 272 minority (216 African Americans, 45 Asian Americans or Pacific Islanders, 9 Hispanic Americans, 2 Native Americans) Average age 35. Expenses: Contact institution. *Financial support:* In 2001–02, 99 research assistantships with tuition reimbursements (averaging $5,900 per year) were awarded; career-related internships or fieldwork, Federal Work-Study, and unspecified assistantships also available. Support available to part-time students. Financial award application deadline: 3/1; financial award applicants required to submit FAFSA. In 2001, 362 master's, 52 other advanced degrees awarded. *Degree program information:* Part-time and evening/weekend programs available. *Application deadline:* For fall admission, 7/15 (priority date). Applications are processed on a rolling basis. *Application fee:* $25. Electronic applications accepted. *Dean of the Graduate School*, Dr. Ken Jones, 478-445-1228, Fax: 478-445-1229, E-mail: kjones@gcsu.edu.

College of Arts and Sciences Students: 65 full-time (40 women), 156 part-time (89 women); includes 74 minority (62 African Americans, 8 Asian Americans or Pacific Islanders, 3 Hispanic Americans, 1 Native American) Average age 34. Expenses: Contact institution. *Financial support:* In 2001–02, 34 research assistantships with tuition reimbursements were awarded; career-related internships or fieldwork, Federal Work-Study, and unspecified assistantships also available. Support available to part-time students. Financial award application deadline: 3/1; financial award applicants required to submit FAFSA. In 2001, 88 degrees awarded. *Degree program information:* Part-time programs available. Offers arts and sciences (MA, MPA, MS, MSA, MSLS); biology (MS); English, speech, and journalism (MA); history (MA); logistics (MSA, MSLS); logistics management (MSA); logistics systems (MSLS); psychology (MS); public administration (MPA); public administration and public affairs (MPA, MS); public affairs (MS). *Application deadline:* For fall admission, 7/15 (priority date). Applications are processed on a rolling basis. *Application fee:* $25. Electronic applications accepted. *Dean*, Dr. Bernie L. Patterson, 478-445-4441, E-mail: bpatters@mail.gcsu.edu.

The J. Whitney Bunting School of Business Students: 108 full-time (32 women), 126 part-time (86 women); includes 60 minority (25 African Americans, 30 Asian Americans or Pacific Islanders, 4 Hispanic Americans, 1 Native American) Average age 32. Expenses: Contact institution. *Financial support:* In 2001–02, 38 research assistantships with tuition reimbursements were awarded; career-related internships or fieldwork, Federal Work-Study, and unspecified assistantships also available. Support available to part-time students. Financial award application deadline: 3/1; financial award applicants required to submit FAFSA. In 2001, 56 degrees awarded. *Degree program information:* Part-time and evening/weekend programs available. Offers business (MBA, MIS). *Application deadline:* For fall admission, 7/15 (priority date); for spring admission, 12/1 (priority date). Applications are processed on a rolling basis. *Application fee:* $25. Electronic applications accepted. *Application Contact:* Lynn Hanson, Graduate Director of Programs, 478-445-5115, E-mail: lhanson@mail.gcsu.edu. *Dean,* Dr. Jo Ann Jones, 478-445-5497, E-mail: jjones@mail.gcsu.edu.

School of Education Students: 104 full-time (88 women), 356 part-time (283 women); includes 121 minority (116 African Americans, 2 Asian Americans or Pacific Islanders, 2 Hispanic Americans, 1 Native American), 2 international. Average age 35. Expenses: Contact institution. *Financial support:* In 2001–02, 8 research assistantships were awarded; career-related internships or fieldwork, Federal Work-Study, and unspecified assistantships also available. Support available to part-time students. Financial award application deadline: 3/1; financial award applicants required to submit FAFSA. In 2001, 195 master's, 42 other advanced degrees awarded. *Degree program information:* Part-time programs available. Offers administration and supervision (M Ed, Ed S); behavior disorders (M Ed); early childhood education (M Ed, Ed S); education (M Ed, MAT, Ed S); English education (M Ed); instructional technology (M Ed); interrelated teaching (M Ed); learning disabilities (M Ed); mathematics education (M Ed); mental retardation (M Ed); middle grades education (M Ed, Ed S); natural science education (M Ed, Ed S); secondary education (MAT); social science education (M Ed, Ed S); special education (M Ed). *Application deadline:* For fall admission, 7/15 (priority date). Applications are processed on a rolling basis. *Application fee:* $25. Electronic applications accepted. *Application Contact:* Dr. W. Bee Crews, Graduate Coordinator, E-mail: bcrews@mail.gcsu.edu. *Dean,* Dr. Janet Fields, E-mail: jfields@gcsu.edu.

School of Health Sciences Students: 14 full-time (7 women), 59 part-time (47 women); includes 17 minority (all African Americans) Average age 35. *Faculty:* 11 full-time, 14 part-time/adjunct. Expenses: Contact institution. *Financial support:* In 2001–02, 19 research assistantships with tuition reimbursements were awarded; career-related internships or fieldwork, Federal Work-Study, and unspecified assistantships also available. Support available to part-time students. Financial award application deadline: 3/1; financial award applicants required to submit FAFSA. In 2001, 23 master's, 4 other advanced degrees awarded. Offers health and physical education (M Ed, Ed S); health sciences (M Ed, MSN, Ed S); nursing (MSN). *Application deadline:* For fall admission, 7/15 (priority date). Applications are processed on a rolling basis. *Application fee:* $25. Electronic applications accepted. *Dean,* Dr. Pamela Levi, 478-445-4004, E-mail: plevi@mail.gcsu.edu.

GEORGIA INSTITUTE OF TECHNOLOGY, Atlanta, GA 30332-0001

General Information State-supported, coed, university. CGS member. *Graduate housing:* Rooms and/or apartments available to single and married students. Housing application deadline: 5/1. *Research affiliation:* Oak Ridge National Laboratory (energy, health, environment), Yerkes Regional Primate Research Center (biomedicine, physiology and behavior), Skidaway Institute of Oceanography (marine geology), Southeastern Universities Research Association (high-energy physics), Emory University Medical School (biomedical engineering), Zoo Atlanta (environmental design, environmental psychology).

GRADUATE UNITS

Graduate Studies and Research *Degree program information:* Part-time and evening/weekend programs available. Postbaccalaureate distance learning degree programs offered. Offers algorithms, combinatorics, and optimization (PhD); statistics (MS Stat). Electronic applications accepted.

College of Architecture Offers architecture (M Arch, MCP, MS, PhD); city planning (MCP); facility and property management (MS, PhD); project delivery systems (MS, PhD). Electronic applications accepted.

College of Computing *Degree program information:* Part-time programs available. Offers algorithms, combinatorics, and optimization (PhD); computer science (MS, MSCS, PhD); human computer interaction (MSHCI).

College of Engineering *Degree program information:* Part-time programs available. Postbaccalaureate distance learning degree programs offered. Offers aerospace engineering (MS, MSAE, PhD); algorithms, combinatorics, and optimization (PhD); biomedical engineering (MS Bio E); ceramic engineering (MSMSE, PhD); chemical engineering (MS Ch E, PhD); civil engineering (MS, MS Bio E, MSCE, PhD); construction management (MS, MSCE, PhD); electrical and computer engineering (MS, MSEE, PhD); engineering (MS, MS Bio E, MS Ch E, MS Env E, MS Poly, MS Stat, MS Text, MSAE, MSCE, MSEE, MSESM, MSHP, MSHS, MSIE, MSME, MSMSE, MSNE, MSOR, MST Ch, MSTE, PhD, Certificate); engineering science and mechanics (MS, MSESM, PhD); environmental engineering (MS, MS Env E, PhD); health physics (MSHP); health systems (MSHS); industrial and systems engineering (MS, MS Stat, MSIE, PhD); industrial engineering (MS, MSIE); materials engineering (MS); mechanical engineering (MS, MS Bio E, MSME, PhD); metallurgy (MSMSE, PhD); nuclear engineering (MSNE, PhD); nuclear engineering and health physics (MSHP, MSNE, PhD); operations research (MSOR); polymers (MS Poly); pulp and paper engineering (Certificate); statistics (MS Stat); textile chemistry (MS, MST Ch); textile engineering (MS, MSTE, PhD); textiles (MS, MS Text). Electronic applications accepted.

College of Sciences *Degree program information:* Part-time programs available. Offers algorithms, combinatorics, and optimization (PhD); applied mathematics (MS); applied physics (MSA Phy); atmospheric chemistry (MS, PhD); atmospheric dynamics and physics (MS, PhD); biology (MS, MS Biol, PhD); chemistry and biochemistry (MS, MS Chem, PhD); earth and atmospheric sciences (MSEAS); geochemistry (MS, PhD); human computer interaction (MSHCI); mathematics (MS Math, PhD); physics (MS, MS Phys, PhD); psychology (MS, MS Psy, PhD); sciences (MS, MS Biol, MS Chem, MS Math, MS Phys, MS Psy, MS Stat, MSA Phy, MSEAS, MSHCI, PhD); solid-earth geophysics (MS, PhD); statistics (MS Stat). Electronic applications accepted.

Dupree College of Management *Degree program information:* Part-time and evening/weekend programs available. Offers management (MS, MS Mgt, MSMOT, PhD); management of technology (MSMOT). Electronic applications accepted.

Ivan Allen College of Policy and International Affairs *Degree program information:* Part-time and evening/weekend programs available. Offers economics (MS); history of technology (MSHT, PhD); human computer interaction (MSHCI); information design and technology (MSIDT); international affairs (MS Int A); policy and international affairs (MS, MS Int A, MS Pub P, MSHCI, MSHT, MSIDT, PhD); public policy (MS Pub P, PhD). Electronic applications accepted.

GEORGIAN COURT COLLEGE, Lakewood, NJ 08701-2697

General Information Independent-religious, women only, comprehensive institution. *Enrollment:* 87 full-time matriculated graduate/professional students (58 women), 585 part-time matriculated graduate/professional students (482 women). *Enrollment by degree level:* 672 master's. *Graduate faculty:* 9 full-time (5 women), 31 part-time/adjunct (16 women). *Tuition:* Full-time $7,308; part-time $406 per credit. *Required fees:* $70; $35 per term. Tuition and fees vary according to course load. *Graduate housing:* Room and/or apartments available on a first-come, first-served basis to single students; on-campus housing not available to married students. Typical cost: $3,120 per year ($5,200 including board). Room and board charges vary according to board plan. Housing application deadline: 5/1. *Student services:* Career counseling, free psychological counseling. *Library facilities:* Georgian Court College Library. *Online resources:* library catalog, web page. *Collection:* 121,724 titles, 1,076 serial subscriptions.

Computer facilities: 131 computers available on campus for general student use. A campuswide network can be accessed from student residence rooms. Internet access, intranet are available. *Web address:* http://www.georgian.edu/.

General Application Contact: Michael Backes, Vice President for Enrollment, 732-364-2200 Ext. 760, Fax: 732-364-4442, E-mail: admissions@georgian.edu.

GRADUATE UNITS

Graduate School Students: 87 full-time (58 women), 585 part-time (482 women); includes 37 minority (15 African Americans, 7 Asian Americans or Pacific Islanders, 15 Hispanic Americans), 20 international. Average age 36. 291 applicants, 84% accepted, 201 enrolled. *Faculty:* 9 full-time (5 women), 31 part-time/adjunct (16 women). Expenses: Contact institution. *Financial support:* In 2001–02, 218 students received support; teaching assistantships, tuition waivers (partial), unspecified assistantships, and vouchers, stipends available. Support available to part-time students. Financial award application deadline: 4/15; financial award applicants required to submit FAFSA. In 2001, 142 degrees awarded. *Degree program information:* Part-time and evening/weekend programs available. Offers administration, supervision and curriculum planning (management specialization) (MA); administration, supervision, and curriculum planning (MA); biology (MS); business administration (MBA); counseling psychology (MA); early intervention studies (Certificate); education (MA); instructional technology (MA); mathematics (MA); reading specialization (MA); special education (MA); substance awareness (Certificate); theology (MA). *Application deadline:* For fall admission, 8/25; for spring admission, 1/15. Applications are processed on a rolling basis. *Application fee:* $40. *Application Contact:* Michael Backes, Vice President for Enrollment, 732-364-2200 Ext. 760, Fax: 732-364-4442, E-mail: admissions@georgian.edu. *Vice President for Academic and Student Affairs,* Dr. Eduardo Paderón, 732-364-2200 Ext. 314, Fax: 732-905-8571.

GEORGIA SOUTHERN UNIVERSITY, Statesboro, GA 30460

General Information State-supported, coed, comprehensive institution. CGS member. *Enrollment:* 390 full-time matriculated graduate/professional students (261 women), 900 part-time matriculated graduate/professional students (634 women). *Enrollment by degree level:* 954 master's, 190 doctoral, 146 other advanced degrees. *Graduate faculty:* 427 full-time (169 women), 69 part-time/adjunct (27 women). Tuition, state resident: full-time $1,746; part-time $97 per credit hour. Tuition, nonresident: full-time $6,966; part-time $387 per credit hour. *Required fees:* $294 per semester. *Graduate housing:* Room and/or apartments available on a first-come, first-served basis to single students; on-campus housing not available to married students. Housing application deadline: 5/1. *Student services:* Campus employment opportunities, campus safety program, career counseling, disabled student services, exercise/wellness program, free psychological counseling, grant writing training, international student services, low-cost health insurance. *Library facilities:* Henderson Library. *Online resources:* library catalog, web page, access to other libraries' catalogs. *Collection:* 3,511 serial subscriptions, 29,296 audiovisual materials. *Research affiliation:* Skidaway Institute of Oceanography (marine sciences), St. Catherine's Island Research Foundation (marine sciences, life sciences), Space Telescope Science Institute (astronomy physics), Mount Desert Island Biological Laboratory (marine biology), Oak Ridge National Laboratory (physical sciences).

Computer facilities: 1,100 computers available on campus for general student use. A campuswide network can be accessed from student residence rooms and from off campus. Internet access is available. *Web address:* http://www.gasou.edu/.

General Application Contact: Dr. John R. Diebolt, Associate Graduate Dean, 912-681-5384, Fax: 912-681-0740, E-mail: diebolt@gasou.edu.

GRADUATE UNITS

Jack N. Averitt College of Graduate Studies Students: 390 full-time (261 women), 900 part-time (634 women); includes 182 minority (151 African Americans, 16 Asian Americans or Pacific Islanders, 12 Hispanic Americans, 3 Native Americans), 55 international. Average age 34. 470 applicants, 88% accepted, 304 enrolled. Expenses: Contact institution. *Financial support:* In 2001–02, 524 students received support, including 169 research assistantships with partial tuition reimbursements available (averaging $5,200 per year), 54 teaching assistantships with partial tuition reimbursements available (averaging $5,600 per year); career-related internships or fieldwork, Federal Work-Study, scholarships/grants, traineeships, unspecified assistantships, and doctoral stipends also available. Support available to part-time students. Financial award application deadline: 4/15; financial award applicants required to submit FAFSA. In 2001, 365 master's, 9 doctorates, 42 other advanced degrees awarded. *Degree program information:* Part-time and evening/weekend programs available. *Application deadline:* For fall admission, 7/1 (priority date); for spring admission, 11/15 (priority date). Applications are processed on a rolling basis. *Application fee:* $0. Electronic applications accepted. *Application Contact:* Dr. John R. Diebolt, Associate Graduate Dean, 912-681-5384, Fax: 912-681-0740, E-mail: diebolt@gasou.edu. *Interim Dean of Graduate Studies and Research,* Dr. Charles J. Hardy, 912-681-0578, Fax: 912-681-0605, E-mail: chardy@gasou.edu.

Allen E. Paulson College of Science and Technology Students: 46 full-time (28 women), 30 part-time (15 women); includes 11 minority (8 African Americans, 3 Asian Americans or Pacific Islanders), 10 international. Average age 29. 40 applicants, 95% accepted, 26 enrolled. *Faculty:* 77 full-time (17 women), 7 part-time/adjunct (3 women). Expenses: Contact institution. *Financial support:* In 2001–02, 35 students received support, including 3 research assistantships with partial tuition reimbursements available (averaging $5,700 per year), 29 teaching assistantships with partial tuition reimbursements available (averaging $6,100 per year); career-related internships or fieldwork, Federal Work-Study, and unspecified assistantships also available. Support available to part-time students. Financial award application deadline: 4/15; financial award applicants required to submit FAFSA. In 2001, 20 degrees awarded. *Degree program information:* Part-time and evening/weekend programs available. Offers biology (MS); mathematics (MS); science and technology (M Tech, MS); technology (M Tech). *Application deadline:* For fall admission, 7/1 (priority date); for spring admission, 11/15 (priority date). Applications are processed on a rolling basis. *Application fee:* $0. Electronic applications accepted. *Application Contact:* Dr. John R. Diebolt, Associate Graduate Dean, 912-681-5384, Fax: 912-681-0740, E-mail: gradschool@gasou.edu. *Dean,* Dr. Jimmy Solomon, 912-681-5111, Fax: 912-681-0836, E-mail: jsolomon@gasou.edu.

College of Business Administration Students: 84 full-time (47 women), 143 part-time (67 women); includes 33 minority (21 African Americans, 7 Asian Americans or Pacific Islanders, 4 Hispanic Americans, 1 Native American), 31 international. Average age 29. 90 applicants, 91% accepted, 69 enrolled. *Faculty:* 60 full-time (17 women), 13 part-time/adjunct (1 woman). Expenses: Contact institution. *Financial support:* In 2001–02, 84 students received support, including 22 research assistantships with partial tuition reimbursements available (averaging $5,000 per year); career-related internships or fieldwork, Federal Work-Study, and unspecified assistantships also available. Support available to part-time students. Financial award application deadline: 4/15; financial award applicants required to submit FAFSA. In 2001, 90 degrees awarded. *Degree program information:* Part-time and evening/weekend programs available. Offers accounting (M Acc); business administration (M Acc, MBA, WMBA). *Application deadline:* For fall admission, 7/1 (priority date); for spring admission, 11/15 (priority date). Applications are processed on a rolling basis. *Application fee:* $0. Electronic applications accepted. *Application Contact:* Dr. John R. Diebolt, Associate Graduate Dean, 912-681-5384, Fax: 912-681-0740, E-mail: gradschool@gasou.edu. *Dean,* Dr. Ron Shiffler, 912-681-5106, Fax: 912-681-0292, E-mail: jsimons@gasou.edu.

College of Education Students: 87 full-time (76 women), 594 part-time (465 women); includes 79 minority (73 African Americans, 1 Asian American or Pacific Islander, 5 Hispanic Americans), 2 international. Average age 37. 174 applicants, 86% accepted, 100 enrolled. *Faculty:* 108 full-time (57 women), 26 part-time/adjunct (11 women). Expenses: Contact institution. *Financial support:* In 2001–02, 219 students received support, including 17 research assistantships with partial tuition reimbursements available (averaging $5,000 per year), 3 teaching assistantships with partial tuition reimbursements available (averaging $9,000 per year); career-related internships or fieldwork, Federal Work-Study, unspecified assistantships, and doctoral stipends also available. Support available to part-time students. Financial award application deadline: 4/15; financial award applicants required to submit FAFSA. In 2001, 153 master's, 9 doctorates, 42 other advanced degrees awarded. *Degree program information:* Part-time and evening/weekend programs available. Offers art education (M Ed, Ed S); business education (M Ed); counselor education (M Ed, Ed S); curriculum studies (Ed D); early childhood education (M Ed, Ed S); education (M Ed, Ed D, Ed S); educational administration (Ed D); educational leadership (M Ed, Ed D, Ed S); English education (M Ed, Ed S); French education (M Ed); health and physical education (M Ed, Ed S); higher education (M Ed); instructional technology (M Ed, Ed S); mathematics (M Ed, Ed S); middle grades education (M Ed, Ed S); music education (Ed S); reading

Georgia Southern University (continued)

education (M Ed, Ed S); school psychology (M Ed, Ed S); science education (M Ed, Ed S); social science education (M Ed, Ed S); Spanish education (M Ed); special education (M Ed, Ed S); technology education (M Ed, Ed S). *Application deadline:* For fall admission, 7/1 (priority date); for spring admission, 11/15 (priority date). Applications are processed on a rolling basis. *Application fee:* $0. Electronic applications accepted. *Application Contact:* Dr. John R. Diebolt, Associate Graduate Dean, 912-681-5384, Fax: 912-681-0740, E-mail: gradschool@gasou.edu. *Dean*, Dr. Lucindia Chance, 912-681-5648, Fax: 912-681-5093, E-mail: lchance@gasou.edu.

College of Health and Professional Studies Students: 91 full-time (58 women), 61 part-time (42 women); includes 21 minority (17 African Americans, 2 Asian Americans or Pacific Islanders, 2 Hispanic Americans), 7 international. Average age 29. 102 applicants, 85% accepted, 56 enrolled. *Faculty:* 46 full-time (24 women), 5 part-time/adjunct (3 women). Expenses: Contact institution. *Financial support:* In 2001–02, 92 students received support, including 8 research assistantships with partial tuition reimbursements available (averaging $5,000 per year), 24 teaching assistantships with tuition reimbursements available (averaging $5,000 per year); career-related internships or fieldwork, Federal Work-Study, traineeships, and unspecified assistantships also available. Support available to part-time students. Financial award application deadline: 4/15; financial award applicants required to submit FAFSA. In 2001, 47 degrees awarded. *Degree program information:* Part-time and evening/weekend programs available. Offers health and professional studies (MHSA, MPH, MS, MSN, Certificate); health services administration (MHSA); kinesiology (MS); public health (MPH); recreation administration (MS); rural community health nurse specialist (MSN, Certificate); rural family nurse practitioner (MSN, Certificate); sport management (MS); women's health nurse practitioner (Certificate). *Application deadline:* For fall admission, 7/1 (priority date); for spring admission, 11/15 (priority date). Applications are processed on a rolling basis. *Application fee:* $0. Electronic applications accepted. *Application Contact:* Dr. John R. Diebolt, Associate Graduate Dean, 912-681-5384, Fax: 912-681-0740, E-mail: gradschool@gasou.edu. *Dean*, Dr. Frederick Whitt, 912-681-5322, Fax: 912-681-5349, E-mail: fwhitt@gasou.edu.

College of Liberal Arts and Social Sciences Students: 82 full-time (52 women), 72 part-time (45 women); includes 38 minority (32 African Americans, 3 Asian Americans or Pacific Islanders, 1 Hispanic American, 2 Native Americans), 5 international. Average age 32. 64 applicants, 86% accepted, 46 enrolled. *Faculty:* 136 full-time (54 women), 18 part-time/adjunct (9 women). Expenses: Contact institution. *Financial support:* In 2001–02, 94 students received support, including 47 research assistantships with partial tuition reimbursements available (averaging $5,000 per year); career-related internships or fieldwork, Federal Work-Study, and unspecified assistantships also available. Support available to part-time students. Financial award application deadline: 4/15; financial award applicants required to submit FAFSA. In 2001, 55 degrees awarded. *Degree program information:* Part-time programs available. Offers English (MA); fine arts (MFA); history (MA); liberal arts and social sciences (MA, MFA, MM, MPA, MS); music (MM); political science (MA); psychology (MS); public administration (MPA); sociology (MA). *Application deadline:* For fall admission, 7/1 (priority date); for spring admission, 11/15 (priority date). Applications are processed on a rolling basis. *Application fee:* $0. Electronic applications accepted. *Application Contact:* Dr. John R. Diebolt, Associate Graduate Dean, 912-681-5384, Fax: 912-681-0740, E-mail: gradschool@gasou.edu. *Dean*, Dr. Katherine Conway-Turner, 912-681-5434, Fax: 912-681-5346, E-mail: kgtect@gasou.edu.

GEORGIA SOUTHWESTERN STATE UNIVERSITY, Americus, GA 31709-4693

General Information State-supported, coed, comprehensive institution. *Enrollment:* 102 full-time matriculated graduate/professional students (70 women), 476 part-time matriculated graduate/professional students (409 women). *Enrollment by degree level:* 517 master's, 61 other advanced degrees. *Graduate faculty:* 71 full-time (26 women). *Tuition, area resident:* Part-time $97 per semester hour. Tuition, state resident: full-time $1,160. Tuition, nonresident: full-time $4,640; part-time $387 per semester hour. *Required fees:* $277; $217 per year. *Graduate housing:* Room and/or apartments available on a first-come, first-served basis to single students; on-campus housing not available to married students. Housing application deadline: 8/1. *Student services:* Campus employment opportunities, campus safety program, career counseling, disabled student services, exercise/wellness program, international student services, multicultural affairs office. *Library facilities:* James Earl Carter Library. *Online resources:* library catalog, web page, access to other libraries' catalogs. *Collection:* 190,000 titles, 59 serial subscriptions, 1,849 audiovisual materials.

Computer facilities: 336 computers available on campus for general student use. A campuswide network can be accessed from off campus. Internet access and online class registration are available. *Web address:* http://www.gsw.edu/.

General Application Contact: Dr. Cathy L. Rozmus, Vice President for Academic Affairs, 913-931-2275, E-mail: clr@canes.gsw.edu.

GRADUATE UNITS

Graduate Studies Students: 102 full-time (70 women), 476 part-time (409 women); includes 114 minority (111 African Americans, 2 Asian Americans or Pacific Islanders, 1 Hispanic American), 24 international. Average age 34. *Faculty:* 71 full-time (26 women). Expenses: Contact institution. *Financial support:* In 2001–02, 121 students received support, including 10 research assistantships, 10 teaching assistantships with full tuition reimbursements available; fellowships, Federal Work-Study, institutionally sponsored loans, and scholarships/grants also available. Support available to part-time students. Financial award application deadline: 9/1. In 2001, 168 master's, 30 other advanced degrees awarded. *Degree program information:* Part-time programs available. *Application deadline:* For fall admission, 8/1; for spring admission, 12/15. Applications are processed on a rolling basis. *Application fee:* $20. *Application Contact:* Lois Oliver, Graduate Admissions Specialist, 912-931-2002, Fax: 912-931-2021, E-mail: loliver@canes.gsw.edu. *Vice President for Academic Affairs*, Dr. Cathy L. Rozmus, 913-931-2275, E-mail: clr@canes.gsw.edu.

School of Business Students: 31 full-time (21 women), 55 part-time (31 women); includes 28 minority (all African Americans), 5 international. Average age 30. Expenses: Contact institution. *Financial support:* Application deadline: 9/1. In 2001, 36 degrees awarded. Offers business administration (MSA); computer information systems (MSA); social administration (MSA). *Application deadline:* For fall admission, 8/1; for spring admission, 12/15. Applications are processed on a rolling basis. *Application fee:* $20. *Application Contact:* Lois Oliver, Graduate Admissions Specialist, 912-931-2002, Fax: 912-931-2021, E-mail: loliver@canes.gsw.edu. *Dean*, Dr. John G. Kooti, 912-931-2090.

School of Computer and Information Science Students: 18 full-time (3 women), 16 part-time (10 women); includes 8 minority (6 African Americans, 2 Asian Americans or Pacific Islanders), 17 international. Average age 29. 20 applicants, 25% accepted. *Faculty:* 5 full-time (0 women). Expenses: Contact institution. *Financial support:* In 2001–02, 10 students received support, including 10 teaching assistantships with full tuition reimbursements available; fellowships, scholarships/grants also available. Financial award application deadline: 9/1. In 2001, 9 degrees awarded. *Degree program information:* Part-time programs available. Offers computer information systems (MS); computer science (MS). *Application deadline:* For fall admission, 8/1; for spring admission, 12/15. Applications are processed on a rolling basis. *Application fee:* $20. *Application Contact:* Lois Oliver, Graduate Admissions Specialist, 912-931-2002, Fax: 912-931-2021, E-mail: loliver@canes.gsw.edu. *Interim Dean*, Dr. Boris V. Peltsverger, 912-931-2818 Ext. 2113, Fax: 912-931-2270, E-mail: plz@canes.gsw.edu.

School of Education Students: 53 full-time (46 women), 405 part-time (368 women); includes 78 minority (77 African Americans, 1 Hispanic American), 2 international. Average age 36. *Faculty:* 21 full-time (11 women), 13 part-time/adjunct (5 women). Expenses: Contact institution. *Financial support:* Application deadline: 9/1. In 2001, 123 master's, 30 other advanced degrees awarded. Offers business education (M Ed); early childhood education (M Ed, Ed S); health and physical education (M Ed); middle grades education (M Ed, Ed S); reading (M Ed); secondary education (M Ed). *Application deadline:* For fall admission, 8/1; for spring admission, 12/15. Applications are processed on a rolling basis. *Application fee:* $20. *Application Contact:* Lois Oliver, Graduate Admissions Specialist, 912-931-2002, Fax: 912-931-2021, E-mail: loliver@canes.gsw.edu. *Dean*, Dr. Julia Dorminey, 912-931-2145.

GEORGIA STATE UNIVERSITY, Atlanta, GA 30303-3083

General Information State-supported, coed, university. CGS member. *Enrollment:* 3,530 full-time matriculated graduate/professional students (2,073 women), 3,430 part-time matriculated graduate/professional students (1,899 women). *Enrollment by degree level:* 629 first professional, 5,104 master's, 933 doctoral, 294 other advanced degrees. *Graduate faculty:* 981 full-time (424 women), 59 part-time/adjunct (41 women). Tuition, state resident: full-time $8,156; part-time $132 per hour. Tuition, nonresident: full-time $12,624; part-time $526 per hour. *Required fees:* $660; $330 per semester. *Graduate housing:* Room and/or apartments available on a first-come, first-served basis to single students; on-campus housing not available to married students. Typical cost: $4,680 per year. Housing application deadline: 3/15. *Student services:* Campus employment opportunities, campus safety program, career counseling, child daycare facilities, exercise/wellness program, free psychological counseling, international student services. *Library facilities:* Pullen Library plus 1 other. *Online resources:* library catalog, web page, access to other libraries' catalogs. *Collection:* 12,053 serial subscriptions, 14,615 audiovisual materials.

Computer facilities: 500 computers available on campus for general student use. A campuswide network can be accessed from student residence rooms and from off campus. *Web address:* http://www.gsu.edu/.

General Application Contact: Gretchen Young, Interim Director of Admissions, 404-651-2469, Fax: 404-651-4811, E-mail: admissions@gsu.edu.

GRADUATE UNITS

Andrew Young School of Policy Studies *Degree program information:* Part-time and evening/weekend programs available. Offers economics (MA, PhD); human resource development (MS, PhD); policy studies (MA, MPA, MS, PhD); public administration (MPA); public policy (PhD); urban policy studies (MS).

College of Arts and Sciences *Degree program information:* Part-time and evening/weekend programs available. Offers anthropology (MA); applied and environmental microbiology (MS, PhD); applied linguistics (MA); arts and sciences (M Mu, MA, MA Ed, MAT, MFA, MHP, MS, PhD, Certificate); astronomy (PhD); cell biology and physiology (MS, PhD); chemistry (MS, PhD); communication (MA, PhD); composition (MA, PhD); computer science (MS, PhD); creative writing (MA, MFA, PhD); English (MA, PhD); fiction (MFA); French (MA, Certificate); geography (MA); geology (MS); German (MA, Certificate); heritage preservation (MHP); history (MA, PhD); literature (MA, PhD); mathematics (MA, MAT, MS); molecular genetics and biochemistry (MS, PhD); neurobiology (MS, PhD); philosophy (MA); physics (MS, PhD); poetry (MFA); political science (MA, PhD); psychology (PhD); rhetoric (MA, PhD); sociology (MA, PhD); Spanish (MA, Certificate); technical and professional writing (MA, PhD); translation and interpretation (Certificate). Electronic applications accepted.

School of Art and Design *Degree program information:* Part-time programs available. Offers art education (MA Ed); art history (MA); studio art (MFA). Electronic applications accepted.

School of Music *Degree program information:* Part-time and evening/weekend programs available. Offers music (M Mu). Electronic applications accepted.

Women's Studies Institute *Degree program information:* Part-time and evening/weekend programs available. Offers women's studies (MA). Electronic applications accepted.

College of Education Students: 665 full-time (548 women), 904 part-time (707 women); includes 346 minority (286 African Americans, 25 Asian Americans or Pacific Islanders, 21 Hispanic Americans, 14 Native Americans), 47 international. Average age 33. 809 applicants, 67% accepted. *Faculty:* 121 full-time (74 women), 74 part-time/adjunct (54 women). Expenses: Contact institution. *Financial support:* In 2001–02, 194 research assistantships, 28 teaching assistantships were awarded. Fellowships, career-related internships or fieldwork, Federal Work-Study, institutionally sponsored loans, and tuition waivers (partial) also available. Support available to part-time students. In 2001, 421 master's, 49 doctorates, 100 other advanced degrees awarded. *Degree program information:* Part-time and evening/weekend programs available. Offers art education (Ed S); communication disorders (M Ed); counseling (PhD); counseling psychology (PhD); early childhood education (M Ed, PhD, Ed S); education (M Ed, MLM, MS, PhD, Ed S); education of behavior/learning disabled (M Ed); education of the hearing impaired (M Ed); educational leadership (M Ed, PhD, Ed S); educational psychology (MS, PhD); educational research (MS, PhD); English education (M Ed, Ed S); exceptionalities (PhD); exercise science (MS); foreign language education (Ed S); health and physical education (M Ed); higher education (PhD); instructional technology (MS, PhD, Ed S); language and literacy education (M Ed, PhD); library media technology (MLM, PhD, Ed S); library science/media (MLM, MS, PhD, Ed S); mathematics education (M Ed, PhD, Ed S); middle childhood education (M Ed, PhD, Ed S); multiple/severe disabilities (M Ed); music education (Ed S); professional counseling (MS, PhD, Ed S); reading instruction (M Ed, Ed S); rehabilitation counseling (MS, Ed S); research, measurements and statistics (PhD); school counseling (M Ed, Ed S); school psychology (M Ed, PhD, Ed S); science education (M Ed, PhD, Ed S); secondary education (M Ed, PhD, Ed S); social foundations of education (MS, PhD); social science education (Ed S); social studies education (M Ed, PhD); special education (Ed S); sport science (PhD); sports administration (MS); sports medicine (MS); teaching English as a second language (M Ed); urban teacher leadership (MS); vocational education (M Ed). *Application fee:* $25. *Interim Dean*, Dr. Ron P. Colarusso, 404-651-2310.

College of Health and Human Sciences *Degree program information:* Part-time and evening/weekend programs available. Offers advanced nutrition (MS); advanced physical therapy (MS); advanced respiratory care (MS); community partnerships (MSW); criminal justice (MS); health and human sciences (MPT, MS, MSW, PhD); physical therapy (MPT).

School of Nursing *Degree program information:* Part-time and evening/weekend programs available. Offers adult health (MS); child health (MS); family nurse practitioner (MS); health promotion, protection and restoration (PhD); perinatal/women's health (MS); psychiatric/mental health (MS).

College of Law *Degree program information:* Part-time and evening/weekend programs available. Offers law (JD). Electronic applications accepted.

J. Mack Robinson College of Business *Degree program information:* Part-time and evening/weekend programs available. Offers actuarial science (MAS, MBA); business (MAS, MBA, MHA, MIB, MPA, MS, MSHA, MSRE, MTX, PhD); computer information systems (MBA, MS, PhD); decision sciences (MBA, MS); entrepreneurship (MBA); finance (MBA, MS, PhD); general business administration (MBA); management (MBA, MS, PhD); marketing (MBA, MS, PhD); operations management (PhD); personal financial planning (MBA, MS); real estate (MBA, MSRE, PhD); risk management and insurance (MBA, MS, PhD). Electronic applications accepted.

Institute of Health Administration Offers health administration (MBA, MHA, MSHA, PhD). Electronic applications accepted.

Institute of International Business *Degree program information:* Part-time and evening/weekend programs available. Offers international business (MBA, MIB, PhD). Electronic applications accepted.

School of Accountancy *Degree program information:* Part-time and evening/weekend programs available. Offers accountancy (MBA, MPA, MTX, PhD); taxation (MTX). Electronic applications accepted.

W. T. Beebe Institute of Personnel and Employee Relations *Degree program information:* Part-time and evening/weekend programs available. Offers personnel and employee relations (MBA, MS, PhD).

GLOBAL UNIVERSITY OF THE ASSEMBLIES OF GOD, Springfield, MO 65804

General Information Independent-religious, coed, comprehensive institution. *Enrollment:* 80 full-time matriculated graduate/professional students (19 women), 108 part-time matriculated graduate/professional students (32 women). *Enrollment by degree level:* 154 master's. *Graduate faculty:* 14 full-time (0 women), 47 part-time/adjunct (2 women). *Tuition:* Part-time $139 per credit hour. *Graduate housing:* On-campus housing not available. *Library facilities:* Global University Library. *Online resources:* web page. *Collection:* 180 serial subscriptions, 3,000 audiovisual materials. *Web address:* http://www.globaluniversity.edu/.

General Application Contact: Carmen Burgess, Graduate Student Representative, 417-862-9533 Ext. 2347, Fax: 417-865-7167, E-mail: gradenroll@globaluniversity.edu.

GRADUATE UNITS

Graduate Studies Students: 80 full-time (19 women), 108 part-time (32 women). Average age 41. 54 applicants, 80% accepted. *Faculty:* 14 full-time (0 women), 47 part-time/adjunct (2 women). Expenses: Contact institution. In 2001, 22 degrees awarded. *Degree program information:* Part-time and evening/weekend programs available. Postbaccalaureate distance learning degree programs offered (no on-campus study). Offers biblical studies (MA); ministerial studies (MA). *Application deadline:* Applications are processed on a rolling basis. *Application fee:* $45. Electronic applications accepted. *Application Contact:* Carmen Burgess, Graduate Student Representative, 417-862-9533 Ext. 2347, Fax: 417-865-7167, E-mail: gradenroll@globaluniversity.edu. *Dean,* Dr. Carl Gibbs, 417-862-9533 Ext. 2223, Fax: 417-862-0863, E-mail: cgibbs@globaluniversity.edu.

GODDARD COLLEGE, Plainfield, VT 05667-9432

General Information Independent, coed, comprehensive institution. *Graduate housing:* On-campus housing not available.

GRADUATE UNITS

Graduate Programs Postbaccalaureate distance learning degree programs offered (minimal on-campus study). Offers health arts and sciences (MA); individually designed liberal arts (MA); interdisciplinary arts (MFA); organizational development (MA); psychology and counseling (MA); social ecology (MA); teacher education (MA); writing (MFA). Electronic applications accepted.

GOLDEN GATE BAPTIST THEOLOGICAL SEMINARY, Mill Valley, CA 94941-3197

General Information Independent-religious, coed, graduate-only institution. *Enrollment by degree level:* 346 first professional, 98 master's, 93 doctoral. *Graduate faculty:* 25 full-time (2 women), 18 part-time/adjunct (8 women). *Tuition:* Part-time $120 per unit. Tuition and fees vary according to student's religious affiliation. *Graduate housing:* Rooms and/or apartments available on a first-come, first-served basis to single and married students. Housing application deadline: 6/15. *Student services:* Campus employment opportunities, career counseling, child daycare facilities, international student services, low-cost health insurance. *Collection:* 146,003 titles, 860 serial subscriptions.

Computer facilities: 15 computers available on campus for general student use. A campuswide network can be accessed from off campus. Internet access and online class registration are available. *Web address:* http://www.ggbts.edu/.

General Application Contact: Karen White, Director of Admissions and International Student Advancement, 415-380-1600, Fax: 415-380-1602, E-mail: admissions@ggbts.edu.

GRADUATE UNITS

Graduate and Professional Programs Students: 329 full-time (50 women), 208 part-time (57 women); includes 185 minority (42 African Americans, 119 Asian Americans or Pacific Islanders, 23 Hispanic Americans, 1 Native American), 49 international. Average age 34. 173 applicants, 87% accepted. *Faculty:* 25 full-time (2 women), 18 part-time/adjunct (8 women). Expenses: Contact institution. *Financial support:* In 2001–02, 6 fellowships were awarded Financial award application deadline: 6/1. In 2001, 52 first professional degrees, 25 master's, 18 doctorates awarded. *Degree program information:* Part-time programs available. Offers Christian education (MACE, Dip CS); church music (MACM, MMCM); divinity (M Div); early childhood education (Certificate); intercultural ministries (MAIM); ministry (D Min); theological studies (MATS); theology (Th M, Dip CS); worship leadership (MA). *Application deadline:* For fall admission, 7/15; for spring admission, 12/27. Applications are processed on a rolling basis. *Application fee:* $25. *Application Contact:* Karen White, Director of Admissions and International Student Advancement, 415-380-1600, Fax: 415-380-1602, E-mail: admissions@ggbts.edu. *Dean of Academic Affairs,* Dr. Rodrick Durst, 415-380-1508, Fax: 415-383-0723, E-mail: rickdurst@ggbts.edu.

GOLDEN GATE UNIVERSITY, San Francisco, CA 94105-2968

General Information Independent, coed, university. *Graduate housing:* On-campus housing not available.

GRADUATE UNITS

School of Business *Degree program information:* Part-time and evening/weekend programs available. Offers accounting (M Ac, MBA); business administration (EMBA, DBA); economics (MS); finance (MBA, MS); financial planning (Certificate); human resource management (MS); human resources management (Certificate); information systems (MBA); international business (MBA); management (MBA); marketing (MBA, MS); operations management (MBA); public relations (MS, Certificate); telecommunications (MBA).

School of Law Students: 418 full-time (251 women), 334 part-time (176 women); includes 208 minority (51 African Americans, 105 Asian Americans or Pacific Islanders, 45 Hispanic Americans, 7 Native Americans), 28 international. Average age 28. 1,546 applicants, 64% accepted, 233 enrolled. *Faculty:* 39 full-time (14 women), 121 part-time/adjunct (52 women). Expenses: Contact institution. *Financial support:* In 2001–02, 531 students received support; fellowships, research assistantships, teaching assistantships, career-related internships or fieldwork, Federal Work-Study, institutionally sponsored loans, and tuition waivers (full and partial) available. Support available to part-time students. Financial award application deadline: 11/15; financial award applicants required to submit FAFSA. In 2001, 158 first professional degrees, 90 master's awarded. *Degree program information:* Part-time and evening/weekend programs available. Offers environmental law (LL M); intellectual property law (LL M); international legal studies (LL M, SJD); law (JD); taxation (LL M); U.S. legal studies (LL M). *Application deadline:* For fall admission, 4/15 (priority date); for spring admission, 11/15. Applications are processed on a rolling basis. *Application fee:* $40. Electronic applications accepted. *Application Contact:* Tracy Simmons, Assistant Dean for Admissions and Financial Aid, 415-442-6630, Fax: 415-442-6631, E-mail: lawadmit@ggu.edu. *Dean,* Peter G. Keane, 415-442-6660, Fax: 415-442-6609.

School of Professional Programs and Undergraduate Studies *Degree program information:* Part-time and evening/weekend programs available. Offers applied psychology (Certificate); counseling (MA); industrial/organizational psychology (MA); liberal studies and public affairs (MA, MPA, Certificate); marriage, family and child counseling (MA); public administration (MPA).

School of Taxation *Degree program information:* Part-time and evening/weekend programs available. Offers taxation (MS, Certificate).

School of Technology and Industry *Degree program information:* Part-time and evening/weekend programs available. Offers hospitality administration and tourism (MS); information systems (MS, Certificate); telecommunications management (MS, Certificate).

GOLDEY-BEACOM COLLEGE, Wilmington, DE 19808-1999

General Information Independent, coed, comprehensive institution. *Enrollment:* 10 full-time matriculated graduate/professional students (2 women), 239 part-time matriculated graduate/professional students (119 women). *Enrollment by degree level:* 249 master's. *Graduate faculty:* 6 full-time (3 women), 4 part-time/adjunct (1 woman). *Tuition:* Full-time $14,436; part-time $401 per credit. *Required fees:* $5 per credit. *Student services:* Campus employment opportunities, campus safety program, career counseling, free psychological counseling, international student services. *Library facilities:* J. Wilbur Hirons Library. *Online resources:* web page. *Collection:* 29,700 titles, 817 serial subscriptions.

Computer facilities: 136 computers available on campus for general student use. A campuswide network can be accessed from student residence rooms and from off campus. Internet access is available. *Web address:* http://www.gbc.edu/.

General Application Contact: Alison Boord White, Director of Graduate Programs/Assistant Academic Dean, 302-225-6257, Fax: 302-996-5408, E-mail: graduate@gbc.edu.

GRADUATE UNITS

MBA Program Students: 10 full-time (2 women), 239 part-time (119 women); includes 20 minority (8 African Americans, 9 Asian Americans or Pacific Islanders, 3 Hispanic Americans), 26 international. Average age 33. 86 applicants, 78% accepted, 64 enrolled. *Faculty:* 6 full-time (3 women), 4 part-time/adjunct (1 woman). Expenses: Contact institution. *Financial support:* Application deadline: 4/1; *Degree program information:* Part-time and evening/weekend programs available. Offers business administration (MBA); financial management (MBA); human resource management (MBA); information technology (MBA); marketing management (MBA). *Application deadline:* Applications are processed on a rolling basis. *Application fee:* $30. Electronic applications accepted. *Director of Graduate Programs/Assistant Academic Dean,* Alison Boord White, 302-225-6257, Fax: 302-996-5408, E-mail: whitea@gbc.edu.

GONZAGA UNIVERSITY, Spokane, WA 99258

General Information Independent-religious, coed, comprehensive institution. *Enrollment:* 1,146 full-time matriculated graduate/professional students (751 women). *Graduate faculty:* 154 full-time (34 women), 45 part-time/adjunct (15 women). *Graduate housing:* Rooms and/or apartments available to single students and available on a first-come, first-served basis to married students. *Student services:* Campus employment opportunities, career counseling, disabled student services, free psychological counseling, grant writing training, low-cost health insurance, multicultural affairs office, writing training. *Library facilities:* Ralph E. and Helen Higgins Foley Center plus 1 other. *Online resources:* library catalog, web page, access to other libraries' catalogs. *Collection:* 351,616 titles, 1,470 serial subscriptions, 2,597 audiovisual materials.

Computer facilities: 340 computers available on campus for general student use. A campuswide network can be accessed from student residence rooms and from off campus. Internet access and online class registration are available. *Web address:* http://www.gonzaga.edu/.

General Application Contact: Dr. Leonard Doohan, Dean of the Graduate School, 509-328-4220 Ext. 3546, Fax: 509-324-5399.

GRADUATE UNITS

Graduate School Students: 1,146 full-time (751 women); includes 104 minority (10 African Americans, 63 Asian Americans or Pacific Islanders, 21 Hispanic Americans, 10 Native Americans), 228 international. 531 applicants, 64% accepted. *Faculty:* 92 full-time (27 women), 52 part-time/adjunct (23 women). Expenses: Contact institution. *Financial support:* Fellowships, teaching assistantships, Federal Work-Study and tuition waivers (full and partial) available. Support available to part-time students. Financial award application deadline: 3/1; financial award applicants required to submit FAFSA. In 2001, 334 master's, 13 doctorates awarded. *Degree program information:* Part-time and evening/weekend programs available. Offers teaching English as a second language (MATESL). *Application fee:* $40. *Dean,* Dr. Leonard Doohan, 509-328-4220 Ext. 3546, Fax: 509-324-5399.

College of Arts and Sciences Students: 62 full-time (31 women); includes 7 minority (2 African Americans, 2 Asian Americans or Pacific Islanders, 2 Hispanic Americans, 1 Native American), 6 international. 27 applicants, 67% accepted. *Faculty:* 44 full-time (5 women). Expenses: Contact institution. *Financial support:* Fellowships, teaching assistantships, Federal Work-Study available. Support available to part-time students. Financial award application deadline: 3/1. In 2001, 8 master's awarded. *Degree program information:* Part-time programs available. Offers arts and sciences (M Div, MA); pastoral ministry (MA); philosophy (MA); religious studies (M Div, MA); spirituality (MA). *Application deadline:* For fall admission, 7/20 (priority date); for spring admission, 11/1. Applications are processed on a rolling basis. *Application fee:* $40. *Application Contact:* Dr. Leonard Doohan, Dean of the Graduate School, 509-328-4220 Ext. 3546, Fax: 509-324-5399. *Dean,* 509-328-4220.

School of Business Administration Students: 164 full-time (57 women). Average age 31. 133 applicants, 56% accepted. *Faculty:* 24 full-time (1 woman). Expenses: Contact institution. *Financial support:* Teaching assistantships, Federal Work-Study available. Support available to part-time students. Financial award application deadline: 3/1. In 2001, 60 degrees awarded. *Degree program information:* Part-time and evening/weekend programs available. Offers accounting (M Acc); business administration (M Acc, MBA). *Application deadline:* For fall admission, 7/20 (priority date); for spring admission, 11/1. Applications are processed on a rolling basis. *Application fee:* $40. *Application Contact:* Dr. Larry Lewis, Assistant Dean, 509-328-4220 Ext. 3430. *Dean,* Dr. Clarence H. Barnes, 509-328-4220 Ext. 5502.

School of Education Students: 653 full-time (450 women); includes 75 minority (6 African Americans, 54 Asian Americans or Pacific Islanders, 12 Hispanic Americans, 3 Native Americans), 174 international. Average age 39. 295 applicants, 63% accepted. *Faculty:* 50 full-time (20 women), 44 part-time/adjunct (15 women). Expenses: Contact institution. *Financial support:* Teaching assistantships, Federal Work-Study and tuition waivers (full and partial) available. Support available to part-time students. Financial award application deadline: 3/1. In 2001, 198 master's, 13 doctorates awarded. *Degree program information:* Part-time and evening/weekend programs available. Offers administration and curriculum (MAA); anesthesiology education (M Anesth Ed); counseling psychology (MAC, MAP); educational administration (MA Ed Ad); educational leadership (PhD); initial teaching (MIT); special education (MES); sports and athletic administration (MASPAA); teaching (MTA). *Application fee:* $40. *Dean,* Dr. Corrine McGuigan, 509-328-4220 Ext. 3503, Fax: 509-324-5812.

School of Professional Studies Students: 235 full-time (193 women); includes 10 minority (1 African American, 2 Asian Americans or Pacific Islanders, 3 Hispanic Americans, 4 Native Americans), 1 international. Average age 38. 64 applicants, 80% accepted. *Faculty:* 20 full-time (6 women). Expenses: Contact institution. *Financial support:* Application deadline: 3/1. In 2001, 59 degrees awarded. Offers nursing (MSN); organizational leadership (MOL); professional studies (MOL, MSN). *Application deadline:* For fall admission, 7/20 (priority date); for spring admission, 11/1. Applications are processed on a rolling basis. *Application fee:* $40. *Application Contact:* Dr. Joseph Albert, Contact, 509-328-4220 Ext. 3564. *Dean,* Dr. Richard Wolfe, 509-328-4220 Ext. 3542.

School of Law Students: 446 full-time (213 women), 26 part-time (12 women); includes 72 minority (14 African Americans, 28 Asian Americans or Pacific Islanders, 17 Hispanic Americans, 13 Native Americans) Average age 28. 1,002 applicants, 60% accepted. *Faculty:* 30 full-time (12 women), 35 part-time/adjunct (7 women). Expenses: Contact institution. *Financial support:* In 2001–02, 425 students received support. Career-related internships or fieldwork, Federal Work-Study, institutionally sponsored loans, and scholarships/grants available. Support available to part-time students. Financial award application deadline: 3/15; financial award applicants required to submit FAFSA. In 2001, 141 degrees awarded. *Degree program information:* Part-time programs available. Offers law (JD). *Application deadline:* For fall admission, 4/1 (priority date). Applications are processed on a rolling basis. *Application fee:* $40. *Application Contact:* Tamara D. Martinez-Anderson, Assistant Dean for Admissions, 509-323-5532, Fax: 509-323-3857, E-mail: admissions@lawschool.gonzaga.edu. *Dean,* John E. Clute, 509-328-4220 Ext. 6090.

GOODING INSTITUTE OF NURSE ANESTHESIA, Panama City, FL 32401

General Information Independent, coed, graduate-only institution. *Enrollment by degree level:* 20 master's. *Graduate faculty:* 21 full-time (7 women), 1 (woman) part-time/adjunct. *Tuition:* Full-time $7,100. One-time fee: $700 full-time. *Graduate housing:* On-campus housing not available. *Student services:* Campus safety program, career counseling, exercise/wellness program. *Library facilities:* Gooding Institute Library plus 2 others. *Collection:* 312 titles, 22 serial subscriptions, 30 audiovisual materials.

Computer facilities: 3 computers available on campus for general student use. Internet access is available. *Web address:* http://www.baymedical.org/Gooding/gooding_main.htm.

General Application Contact: Dr. David Ely, Director, 850-747-6223, Fax: 850-747-6115, E-mail: dely@baymedical.org.

Gooding Institute of Nurse Anesthesia (continued)

GRADUATE UNITS

Program in Nurse Anesthesia Students: 20 full-time (13 women); includes 2 minority (1 African American, 1 Native American) Average age 29. 77 applicants, 13% accepted, 10 enrolled. *Faculty:* 21 full-time (7 women), 1 (woman) part-time/adjunct. Expenses: Contact institution. *Financial support:* In 2001–02, 17 students received support. Scholarships/grants and traineeships available. Financial award application deadline: 8/1; financial award applicants required to submit FAFSA. In 2001, 10 degrees awarded. Offers nurse anesthesia (MS). *Application deadline:* For fall admission, 10/1. Applications are processed on a rolling basis. *Application fee:* $40. *Director*, Dr. David Ely, 850-747-6223, Fax: 850-747-6115, E-mail: dely@baymedical.org.

GORDON COLLEGE, Wenham, MA 01984-1899

General Information Independent-religious, coed, comprehensive institution. *Enrollment:* 4 full-time matriculated graduate/professional students (all women), 76 part-time matriculated graduate/professional students (62 women). *Enrollment by degree level:* 80 master's. *Graduate faculty:* 7 full-time (6 women), 9 part-time/adjunct (5 women). *Tuition:* Full-time $2,100; part-time $700 per course. *Required fees:* $35; $35 per year. *Graduate housing:* On-campus housing not available. *Student services:* Career counseling, free psychological counseling, teacher training, writing training. *Library facilities:* Jenks Learning Resource Center. *Online resources:* library catalog, access to other libraries' catalogs. *Collection:* 136,625 titles, 563 serial subscriptions, 9,078 audiovisual materials.

Computer facilities: 75 computers available on campus for general student use. A campuswide network can be accessed from student residence rooms and from off campus. Internet access and online class registration are available. *Web address:* http://www.gordon.edu/.

General Application Contact: Dr. Malcolm L. Patterson, Dean of Graduate Studies, 978-927-2306 Ext. 4322, Fax: 978-524-3734, E-mail: mpatterson@gordon.edu.

GRADUATE UNITS

Division of Education Students: 4 full-time (all women), 76 part-time (62 women); includes 7 minority (2 African Americans, 4 Asian Americans or Pacific Islanders, 1 Hispanic American) Average age 31. 8 applicants, 100% accepted, 8 enrolled. *Faculty:* 7 full-time (6 women), 9 part-time/adjunct (5 women). Expenses: Contact institution. In 2001, 13 degrees awarded. *Degree program information:* Part-time and evening/weekend programs available. Offers education (M Ed). *Application deadline:* Applications are processed on a rolling basis. *Application fee:* $40. *Application Contact:* Lois S. Wells, Administrative Coordinator, 978-927-2306 Ext. 4322, Fax: 978-524-3734, E-mail: lwells@gordon.edu. *Dean of Graduate Studies*, Dr. Malcolm L. Patterson, 978-927-2306 Ext. 4322, Fax: 978-524-3734, E-mail: mpatterson@gordon.edu.

GORDON-CONWELL THEOLOGICAL SEMINARY, South Hamilton, MA 01982-2395

General Information Independent-religious, coed, graduate-only institution. *Graduate housing:* Rooms and/or apartments available to single and married students. Housing application deadline: 4/1.

GRADUATE UNITS

Graduate and Professional Programs *Degree program information:* Part-time and evening/weekend programs available. Offers Christian education (MACE); church history (MACH); counseling (MACO); ministry (D Min); missions/evangelism (MAME); New Testament (MANT); Old Testament (MAOT); religion (MAR); theology (M Div, MATH, Th M).

GOUCHER COLLEGE, Baltimore, MD 21204-2794

General Information Independent, coed, comprehensive institution. *Enrollment:* 100 full-time matriculated graduate/professional students (84 women), 675 part-time matriculated graduate/professional students (548 women). *Graduate faculty:* 12 full-time (5 women), 83 part-time/adjunct (56 women). *Tuition:* Full-time $4,635; part-time $280 per credit. Tuition and fees vary according to course load and program. *Graduate housing:* On-campus housing not available. *Student services:* Career counseling, low-cost health insurance. *Library facilities:* Julia Rogers Library. *Online resources:* library catalog, web page. *Collection:* 295,593 titles, 1,138 serial subscriptions, 8,532 audiovisual materials. *Research affiliation:* Sheppard-Pratt Hospital (education).

Computer facilities: 150 computers available on campus for general student use. A campuswide network can be accessed from student residence rooms and from off campus. Internet access is available. *Web address:* http://www.goucher.edu/.

General Application Contact: Frederick Mauk, Associate Dean for Graduate and Professional Studies, 410-337-6242, Fax: 410-337-6085, E-mail: fmaul@goucher.edu.

GRADUATE UNITS

Historic Preservation Program Average age 43. *Faculty:* 10 part-time/adjunct (3 women). Expenses: Contact institution. *Financial support:* In 2001–02, 15 students received support. Career-related internships or fieldwork available. Support available to part-time students. Financial award application deadline: 1/31; financial award applicants required to submit FAFSA. In 2001, 6 degrees awarded. *Degree program information:* Part-time and evening/weekend programs available. Postbaccalaureate distance learning degree programs offered (minimal on-campus study). Offers historic preservation (MA). *Application deadline:* For fall admission, 2/15. *Application fee:* $50. *Application Contact:* Richard Wagner, Director, 410-337-6200, Fax: 410-337-6085, E-mail: rwagner@goucher.edu. *Executive Director*, Deborah R. Culbertson, 410-337-6200, Fax: 410-337-6085, E-mail: dculbert@goucher.edu.

Premedical Studies Concentration Students: 17 full-time (13 women), 2 part-time (both women). Average age 25. *Faculty:* 11 full-time (6 women), 1 part-time/adjunct (0 women). Expenses: Contact institution. *Financial support:* In 2001–02, 15 students received support. Institutionally sponsored loans and scholarships/grants available. Financial award application deadline: 3/1; financial award applicants required to submit FAFSA. Offers premedical studies (Certificate). *Application deadline:* Applications are processed on a rolling basis. *Application fee:* $50. *Director*, Liza Thompson, 800-414-3437, Fax: 410-337-6085, E-mail: lthompso@goucher.edu.

Program in Arts Administration Students: 25 full-time (23 women), 19 part-time (11 women); includes 6 minority (3 African Americans, 3 Hispanic Americans) Average age 35. *Faculty:* 11 part-time/adjunct (8 women). Expenses: Contact institution. *Financial support:* In 2001–02, 19 students received support. Institutionally sponsored loans available. Financial award application deadline: 3/15. In 2001, 5 degrees awarded. *Degree program information:* Part-time programs available. Postbaccalaureate distance learning degree programs offered (minimal on-campus study). Offers arts administration (MA). *Application deadline:* For fall admission, 3/15. *Application fee:* $50. *Director*, Dr. Jean Wilhelm, 410-337-6200, Fax: 410-337-6085, E-mail: jwilhelm@goucher.edu.

Program in Creative Nonfiction Students: 29 full-time (23 women); includes 2 minority (both African Americans) Average age 46. *Faculty:* 6 part-time/adjunct (4 women). Expenses: Contact institution. *Financial support:* Career-related internships or fieldwork and institutionally sponsored loans available. Financial award application deadline: 2/15; financial award applicants required to submit FAFSA. In 2001, 11 degrees awarded. *Degree program information:* Part-time and evening/weekend programs available. Postbaccalaureate distance learning degree programs offered (minimal on-campus study). Offers creative nonfiction (MFA). *Application deadline:* For fall admission, 4/1. *Application fee:* $50. *Director*, Patsy Sims, 410-337-6200, Fax: 410-337-6085, E-mail: psims@goucher.edu.

Programs in Education Students: 24 full-time (21 women), 539 part-time (459 women); includes 74 minority (65 African Americans, 2 Asian Americans or Pacific Islanders, 6 Hispanic Americans, 1 Native American), 1 international. Average age 36. *Faculty:* 6 full-time (5 women), 33 part-time/adjunct (22 women). Expenses: Contact institution. *Financial support:* In 2001–02, 3 research assistantships with tuition reimbursements (averaging $4,500 per year) were awarded; career-related internships or fieldwork and need-based awards also available. Support available to part-time students. Financial award application deadline: 8/15; financial award applicants required to submit FAFSA. In 2001, 58 degrees awarded. *Degree program information:* Part-time and evening/weekend programs available. Offers education (M Ed, MAT). *Application deadline:* For fall admission, 9/1 (priority date); for spring admission, 1/15. Applications are processed on a rolling basis. *Application fee:* $25. *Application Contact:* Shirley Gray, Coordinator of Admission and Registration, 410-337-6392, Fax: 410-337-6394, E-mail: sgray@goucher.edu. *Director*, Phyllis Sunshine, 410-337-6047, Fax: 410-337-6394, E-mail: psunshin@goucher.edu.

GOVERNORS STATE UNIVERSITY, University Park, IL 60466-0975

General Information State-supported, coed, upper-level institution. *Enrollment:* 171 full-time matriculated graduate/professional students (102 women), 2,709 part-time matriculated graduate/professional students (1,998 women). *Enrollment by degree level:* 2,880 master's. *Graduate faculty:* 147 full-time (53 women), 147 part-time/adjunct (68 women). Tuition, state resident: part-time $111 per hour. Tuition, nonresident: part-time $333 per hour. *Graduate housing:* On-campus housing not available. *Student services:* Campus employment opportunities, campus safety program, career counseling, child daycare facilities, disabled student services, exercise/wellness program, free psychological counseling, international student services, low-cost health insurance, teacher training. *Library facilities:* University Library. *Online resources:* library catalog, web page. *Collection:* 246,000 titles, 2,200 serial subscriptions, 2,700 audiovisual materials.

Computer facilities: 142 computers available on campus for general student use. A campuswide network can be accessed from off campus. *Web address:* http://www.govst.edu/.

General Application Contact: William T. Craig, Admissions Officer, 708-534-4492, Fax: 708-534-1640, E-mail: b-craig@govst.edu.

GRADUATE UNITS

College of Arts and Sciences Students: 50 full-time, 394 part-time. Average age 33. 309 applicants, 80% accepted. *Faculty:* 48 full-time (16 women), 51 part-time/adjunct (23 women). Expenses: Contact institution. *Financial support:* In 2001–02, 11 research assistantships were awarded; career-related internships or fieldwork, Federal Work-Study, institutionally sponsored loans, and scholarships/grants also available. Support available to part-time students. Financial award application deadline: 5/1. In 2001, 97 degrees awarded. *Degree program information:* Part-time and evening/weekend programs available. Offers arts and sciences (MA, MS). *Application deadline:* For fall admission, 7/15; for spring admission, 11/10. Applications are processed on a rolling basis. *Application fee:* $0. *Dean*, Dr. Roger Oden, 708-534-4101.

Division of Liberal Arts Students: 297 (206 women). Average age 34. *Faculty:* 13 full-time (6 women), 18 part-time/adjunct (8 women). Expenses: Contact institution. *Financial support:* Research assistantships, Federal Work-Study, institutionally sponsored loans, and scholarships/grants available. Support available to part-time students. Financial award application deadline: 5/1. In 2001, 62 degrees awarded. *Degree program information:* Part-time and evening/weekend programs available. Offers art (MA); communication studies (MA); English (MA); instructional and training technology (MA); liberal arts (MA); media communication (MA); political and justice studies (MA). *Application deadline:* For fall admission, 7/15 (priority date); for spring admission, 11/10. Applications are processed on a rolling basis. *Application fee:* $0. *Chairperson*, Dr. Joyce Kennedy, 708-534-4010.

Division of Science Students: 147 (65 women). Average age 32. *Faculty:* 19 full-time (5 women), 11 part-time/adjunct (2 women). Expenses: Contact institution. *Financial support:* Research assistantships, career-related internships or fieldwork, Federal Work-Study, institutionally sponsored loans, and scholarships/grants available. Support available to part-time students. Financial award application deadline: 5/1. In 2001, 35 degrees awarded. *Degree program information:* Part-time and evening/weekend programs available. Offers analytical chemistry (MS); computer science (MS); environmental biology (MS); science (MS). *Application deadline:* For fall admission, 7/15 (priority date); for spring admission, 11/10. Applications are processed on a rolling basis. *Application fee:* $0. *Chairperson*, Dr. Edwin Cehelnik, 708-534-4520.

College of Business and Public Administration Students: 15 full-time, 220 part-time. Average age 35. 201 applicants, 81% accepted. *Faculty:* 34 full-time (6 women), 29 part-time/adjunct (10 women). Expenses: Contact institution. *Financial support:* Fellowships, research assistantships, career-related internships or fieldwork, Federal Work-Study, institutionally sponsored loans, scholarships/grants, and tuition waivers (full and partial) available. Support available to part-time students. Financial award application deadline: 5/1. In 2001, 61 degrees awarded. *Degree program information:* Part-time and evening/weekend programs available. Offers accounting (MS); business administration (MBA); business and public administration (MBA, MPA, MS); management information systems (MS); public administration (MPA). *Application deadline:* For fall admission, 7/15 (priority date); for spring admission, 11/10. Applications are processed on a rolling basis. *Application fee:* $0. *Application Contact:* Dorothy Calvin, Adviser, 708-534-4930. *Dean*, Dr. William Nowlin, 708-534-4930.

College of Education Students: 40 full-time, 1,215 part-time. Average age 35. 208 applicants, 74% accepted. *Faculty:* 35 full-time (14 women), 53 part-time/adjunct (25 women). Expenses: Contact institution. *Financial support:* Career-related internships or fieldwork, Federal Work-Study, institutionally sponsored loans, tuition waivers (full and partial), and unspecified assistantships available. Support available to part-time students. Financial award application deadline: 5/1. In 2001, 306 degrees awarded. *Degree program information:* Part-time and evening/weekend programs available. Offers education (MA). *Application deadline:* For fall admission, 7/15 (priority date); for spring admission, 11/10. Applications are processed on a rolling basis. *Application fee:* $0. *Application Contact:* Kathy Borem, Adviser, 708-534-4394. *Dean*, Dr. Diane Alexander, 708-534-4050.

Division of Education Students: 16 full-time, 963 part-time. Average age 35. *Faculty:* 20 full-time (8 women), 29 part-time/adjunct (13 women). Expenses: Contact institution. *Financial support:* Career-related internships or fieldwork, Federal Work-Study, institutionally sponsored loans, tuition waivers (full and partial), and unspecified assistantships available. Support available to part-time students. Financial award application deadline: 5/1. In 2001, 228 degrees awarded. *Degree program information:* Part-time and evening/weekend programs available. Offers early childhood education (MA); education (MA); educational administration and supervision (MA); multi-categorical special education (MA); reading (MA). *Application deadline:* For fall admission, 7/15 (priority date); for spring admission, 11/10. Applications are processed on a rolling basis. *Application fee:* $0. *Application Contact:* Nick Battaglia, Adviser, 708-534-4393. *Chairperson*, Dr. Larry Freeman, 708-534-4360.

Division of Psychology and Counseling Students: 24 full-time, 252 part-time. Average age 33. *Faculty:* 15 full-time (6 women), 24 part-time/adjunct (12 women). Expenses: Contact institution. *Financial support:* Career-related internships or fieldwork, Federal Work-Study, institutionally sponsored loans, tuition waivers (full and partial), and unspecified assistantships available. Support available to part-time students. Financial award application deadline: 5/1. In 2001, 78 degrees awarded. *Degree program information:* Part-time and evening/weekend programs available. Offers counseling (MA); psychology (MA); psychology and counseling (MA). *Application deadline:* For fall admission, 7/15 (priority date); for spring admission, 11/10. Applications are processed on a rolling basis. *Application fee:* $0. *Chairperson*, Dr. Addison Woodward, 708-534-4840.

College of Health Professions Students: 371 (308 women). Average age 34. 226 applicants, 33% accepted. *Faculty:* 29 full-time (10 women), 28 part-time/adjunct (17 women). Expenses: Contact institution. *Financial support:* Research assistantships, career-related internships or fieldwork, Federal Work-Study, institutionally sponsored loans, scholarships/grants, and tuition waivers (full and partial) available. Support available to part-time students. Financial award application deadline: 5/1. In 2001, 124 degrees awarded. *Degree program information:* Part-time and evening/weekend programs available. Offers health professions (MHA, MHS, MOT, MPT, MSN, MSW); social work (MSW). *Application deadline:* Applications are processed on a rolling basis. *Application fee:* $0. *Interim Dean*, Dr. Amerfil Wang, 708-534-4388.

Division of Health Administration and Human Services Students: 9 full-time, 99 part-time. Average age 36. *Faculty:* 6 full-time (1 woman), 8 part-time/adjunct (2 women). Expenses:

Contact institution. *Financial support:* Research assistantships, career-related internships or fieldwork, Federal Work-Study, institutionally sponsored loans, scholarships/grants, and tuition waivers (full and partial) available. Support available to part-time students. Financial award application deadline: 5/1. In 2001, 60 degrees awarded. *Degree program information:* Part-time and evening/weekend programs available. Offers addictions studies (MHS); health administration (MHA); health administration and human services (MHA, MHS). *Application deadline:* For fall admission, 7/15 (priority date); for spring admission, 11/10. Applications are processed on a rolling basis. *Application fee:* $0. *Chairperson*, Dr. Cheryl Mejta, 708-534-4030.

Division of Nursing, Communication Disorders, Occupational Therapy, and Physical Therapy Students: 41 full-time, 222 part-time. Average age 33. Expenses: Contact institution. *Financial support:* Research assistantships, career-related internships or fieldwork, Federal Work-Study, institutionally sponsored loans, scholarships/grants, and tuition waivers (full and partial) available. Support available to part-time students. Financial award application deadline: 5/1. In 2001, 86 degrees awarded. *Degree program information:* Part-time and evening/weekend programs available. Offers communication disorders (MHS); nursing (MSN); nursing and health science (MHS, MOT, MPT, MSN); occupational therapy (MOT); physical therapy (MPT). *Application deadline:* Applications are processed on a rolling basis. *Application fee:* $0. *Chairperson*, Dr. Sandra Mayfield, 708-534-4590.

GRACE COLLEGE, Winona Lake, IN 46590-1294

General Information Independent-religious, coed, comprehensive institution. *Enrollment:* 6 full-time matriculated graduate/professional students (3 women), 38 part-time matriculated graduate/professional students (22 women). *Enrollment by degree level:* 44 master's. *Graduate faculty:* 3 full-time (1 woman), 2 part-time/adjunct (0 women). *Tuition:* Part-time $335 per credit hour. *Required fees:* $30 per semester. *Graduate housing:* On-campus housing not available. *Student services:* Campus employment opportunities, campus safety program, career counseling, free psychological counseling. *Library facilities:* Morgan Library. *Online resources:* library catalog, web page, access to other libraries' catalogs. *Collection:* 140,202 titles, 7,178 serial subscriptions, 850 audiovisual materials.

Computer facilities: 45 computers available on campus for general student use. A campuswide network can be accessed from student residence rooms and from off campus. Internet access is available. *Web address:* http://www.grace.edu/.

General Application Contact: Shilo A. Maack, Admissions Counselor, 800-54 GRACE Ext. 6001, Fax: 574-372-5120, E-mail: macslg@grace.edu.

GRADUATE UNITS

Program in Counseling Students: 6 full-time (3 women), 38 part-time (22 women). 15 applicants, 100% accepted. *Faculty:* 3 full-time (1 woman), 2 part-time/adjunct (0 women). Expenses: Contact institution. *Financial support:* In 2001–02, 2 teaching assistantships (averaging $2,000 per year) were awarded In 2001, 4 degrees awarded. *Degree program information:* Part-time and evening/weekend programs available. Offers clinical counseling (MA); ministry (MA). *Application deadline:* For fall admission, 7/1 (priority date). Applications are processed on a rolling basis. *Application fee:* $25. *Application Contact:* Shilo A. Maack, Admissions Counselor, 800-54 GRACE Ext. 6001, Fax: 574-372-5120, E-mail: macslg@grace.edu. *Head*, Dr. Thomas J. Edgington, 800-54-GRACE Ext. 6052, Fax: 574-372-5143, E-mail: edgingtj@grace.edu.

GRACELAND UNIVERSITY, Lamoni, IA 50140

General Information Independent-religious, coed, comprehensive institution. *Enrollment:* 11 full-time matriculated graduate/professional students (10 women), 229 part-time matriculated graduate/professional students (192 women). *Enrollment by degree level:* 240 master's. *Tuition:* Part-time $170 per credit hour. *Graduate housing:* On-campus housing not available. *Student services:* Campus safety program, career counseling, free psychological counseling. *Library facilities:* Frederick Madison Smith Library. *Online resources:* library catalog, web page, access to other libraries' catalogs. *Collection:* 110,862 titles, 567 serial subscriptions, 2,827 audiovisual materials.

Computer facilities: 138 computers available on campus for general student use. A campuswide network can be accessed from student residence rooms and from off campus. Internet access is available. *Web address:* http://www2.graceland.edu/.

General Application Contact: Judy Luffman, Office Manager, 816-833-0524, Fax: 816-833-2990, E-mail: luffman@graceland.edu.

GRADUATE UNITS

Community of Christ Seminary Average age 35. 20 applicants, 75% accepted, 2 enrolled. *Faculty:* 12 part-time/adjunct (1 woman). Expenses: Contact institution. *Financial support:* Application deadline: 12/15. In 2001, 6 degrees awarded. *Degree program information:* Part-time and evening/weekend programs available. Offers religion (MAR). *Application deadline:* For fall admission, 8/15 (priority date); for winter admission, 12/15 (priority date); for spring admission, 4/15 (priority date). Applications are processed on a rolling basis. *Application fee:* $30. *Provost*, Dr. Donald Compier, 800-833-0524, Fax: 816-833-2990, E-mail: dcompier@graceland.edu.

School of Education 64 applicants, 94% accepted, 60 enrolled. *Faculty:* 2 full-time (1 woman). Expenses: Contact institution. *Financial support:* In 2001–02, 21 students received support. Scholarships/grants available. Support available to part-time students. Financial award application deadline: 12/15. In 2001, 21 degrees awarded. *Degree program information:* Part-time and evening/weekend programs available. Postbaccalaureate distance learning degree programs offered (minimal on-campus study). Offers education (M Ed). *Application deadline:* For spring admission, 1/15. *Application fee:* $30. Electronic applications accepted. *Application Contact:* Jim Robinson, Education Coordinator, 800-833-0524 Ext. 4520, Fax: 816-833-2990, E-mail: jrobinson@graceland.edu. *Dean*, Dr. William Armstrong, 515-784-5000, E-mail: billa@graceland.edu.

School of Nursing Students: 16 full-time (12 women), 126 part-time (108 women); includes 13 minority (5 African Americans, 3 Asian Americans or Pacific Islanders, 2 Hispanic Americans, 3 Native Americans) Average age 42. 78 applicants, 67% accepted. *Faculty:* 6 full-time (all women), 2 part-time/adjunct (both women). Expenses: Contact institution. *Financial support:* Institutionally sponsored loans and traineeships available. Support available to part-time students. Financial award applicants required to submit FAFSA. In 2001, 15 master's, 2 other advanced degrees awarded. *Degree program information:* Part-time programs available. Postbaccalaureate distance learning degree programs offered (minimal on-campus study). Offers clinical nurse specialist/family nursing (educator) (MSN); family nurse practitioner (MSN, PMC); health care administration (MSN). *Application deadline:* Applications are processed on a rolling basis. *Application fee:* $100. Electronic applications accepted. *Application Contact:* Paul Binnicker, Student Support Services, 800-833-0524 Ext. 4800, Fax: 816-833-2990, E-mail: binnicke@graceland.edu. *Associate Dean*, Dr. Karen Fernengel, 816-833-0524, Fax: 816-833-2990, E-mail: karenf@graceland.edu.

GRACE THEOLOGICAL SEMINARY, Winona Lake, IN 46590-9907

General Information Independent-religious, coed, primarily men, graduate-only institution. *Graduate faculty:* 4 full-time (0 women), 5 part-time/adjunct (0 women). *Tuition:* Full-time $5,000; part-time $250 per credit hour. *Required fees:* $60; $30 per semester. *Graduate housing:* On-campus housing not available. *Student services:* Campus employment opportunities, career counseling, low-cost health insurance. *Library facilities:* Betty Zimmer Morgan Library. *Online resources:* library catalog, web page, access to other libraries' catalogs. *Collection:* 146,000 titles, 588 serial subscriptions.

Computer facilities: 36 computers available on campus for general student use. A campuswide network can be accessed from student residence rooms. Internet access is available. *Web address:* http://www.grace.edu/.

General Application Contact: Roger E. Peugh, Director of Admissions, 574-372-5100 Ext. 6431, Fax: 574-372-5117, E-mail: peughdr@grace.edu.

GRADUATE UNITS

Graduate and Professional Programs Students: 29 full-time (1 woman), 37 part-time (6 women); includes 10 minority (7 African Americans, 2 Hispanic Americans, 1 Native American), 3 international. Average age 26. 39 applicants, 85% accepted, 30 enrolled. *Faculty:* 4 full-time (0 women), 5 part-time/adjunct (0 women). Expenses: Contact institution. *Financial support:* In 2001–02, 24 students received support. Career-related internships or fieldwork, Federal Work-Study, scholarships/grants, and tuition waivers (partial) available. Support available to part-time students. Financial award application deadline: 4/1; financial award applicants required to submit FAFSA. In 2001, 6 first professional degrees, 14 master's, 6 doctorates awarded. *Degree program information:* Part-time programs available. Postbaccalaureate distance learning degree programs offered (no on-campus study). Offers biblical studies (Certificate, Diploma); counseling (M Div); ministry (MA); missions (M Div, MA); theology (M Div, MA, D Min). *Application deadline:* For fall admission, 4/1 (priority date). Applications are processed on a rolling basis. *Application fee:* $25. Electronic applications accepted. *Application Contact:* Roger E. Peugh, Director of Admissions, 574-372-5100 Ext. 6431, Fax: 574-372-5117, E-mail: peughdr@grace.edu. *Vice President for Academic Affairs*, Dr. David R. Plaster, 574-372-5100 Ext. 6132, Fax: 574-372-5117, E-mail: drplaster@grace.edu.

GRACE UNIVERSITY, Omaha, NE 68108

General Information Independent-religious, coed, comprehensive institution. *Enrollment:* 33 full-time matriculated graduate/professional students (18 women), 39 part-time matriculated graduate/professional students (12 women). *Enrollment by degree level:* 72 master's. *Graduate faculty:* 8 full-time (1 woman), 2 part-time/adjunct (0 women). *Tuition:* Part-time $330 per credit hour. *Required fees:* $200; $200 per year. *Graduate housing:* Room and/or apartments available to single students; on-campus housing not available to married students. *Student services:* Campus employment opportunities, campus safety program, career counseling, disabled student services, free psychological counseling, international student services, low-cost health insurance. *Library facilities:* Grace University Library. *Online resources:* library catalog, web page, access to other libraries' catalogs. *Collection:* 43,900 titles, 2,777 serial subscriptions, 3,882 audiovisual materials.

Computer facilities: 45 computers available on campus for general student use. A campuswide network can be accessed. *Web address:* http://www.graceuniversity.edu/.

General Application Contact: Jen Mulder, Graduate Admissions Counselor, 402-449-2917, Fax: 402-341-9587, E-mail: admissions@graceu.edu.

GRADUATE UNITS

College of Graduate Studies Students: 33 full-time (18 women), 39 part-time (12 women); includes 5 minority (4 African Americans, 1 Native American), 1 international. *Faculty:* 8 full-time (1 woman), 2 part-time/adjunct (0 women). Expenses: Contact institution. *Financial support:* In 2001–02, 2 teaching assistantships were awarded; career-related internships or fieldwork and institutionally sponsored loans also available. Support available to part-time students. Financial award applicants required to submit FAFSA. In 2001, 12 degrees awarded. *Degree program information:* Part-time and evening/weekend programs available. Offers biblical studies (MA); counseling (MA). *Application deadline:* For fall admission, 8/15 (priority date); for spring admission, 1/1. Applications are processed on a rolling basis. *Application fee:* $50. Electronic applications accepted. *Application Contact:* Cynthia Fitzgerald, Graduate Admissions Counselor, 402-449-2917, Fax: 402-341-9587, E-mail: admissions@graceu.edu. *Dean*, Dr. Dick Dahlquist, 402-449-2846, Fax: 402-341-9587, E-mail: ddahlquist@mail.graceu.edu.

GRADUATE SCHOOL AND UNIVERSITY CENTER OF THE CITY UNIVERSITY OF NEW YORK, New York, NY 10016-4039

General Information State and locally supported, coed, graduate-only institution. CGS member. *Enrollment by degree level:* 135 master's, 3,360 doctoral. *Graduate faculty:* 1,471 full-time (318 women). Tuition, state resident: part-time $245 per credit. Tuition, nonresident: part-time $425 per credit. *Required fees:* $72 per semester. *Graduate housing:* Rooms and/or apartments available to single and married students. Housing application deadline: 5/1. *Student services:* Career counseling, free psychological counseling, low-cost health insurance. *Library facilities:* Mina Rees Library. *Collection:* 204,000 titles, 1,680 serial subscriptions. *Research affiliation:* American Museum of Natural History (anthropology), Roche Institute of Molecular Biology (biological sciences), New York Botanical Gardens (biological sciences). *Web address:* http://www.gc.cuny.edu/.

General Application Contact: Les Gribben, Director of Admissions, 212-817-7470, Fax: 212-817-1624, E-mail: lgribben@gc.cuny.edu.

GRADUATE UNITS

Graduate Studies Students: 3,173 full-time (1,782 women), 322 part-time (170 women); includes 543 minority (196 African Americans, 124 Asian Americans or Pacific Islanders, 219 Hispanic Americans, 4 Native Americans), 817 international. Average age 36. 2,881 applicants, 49% accepted, 603 enrolled. *Faculty:* 1,471 full-time (318 women). Expenses: Contact institution. *Financial support:* In 2001–02, 1,656 students received support, including 941 fellowships, 48 research assistantships, 30 teaching assistantships; career-related internships or fieldwork, Federal Work-Study, institutionally sponsored loans, and tuition waivers (full and partial) also available. Financial award application deadline: 2/1; financial award applicants required to submit FAFSA. In 2001, 38 master's, 330 doctorates awarded. Offers accounting (PhD); anthropological linguistics (PhD); archaeology (PhD); architecture (PhD); basic applied neurocognition (PhD); behavioral science (PhD); biochemistry (PhD); biology (PhD); biomedical science (PhD); biopsychology (PhD); chemical engineering (PhD); chemistry (PhD); civil engineering (PhD); classical studies (MA, PhD); clinical psychology (PhD); comparative literature (MA, PhD); computer science (PhD); criminal justice (PhD); cultural anthropology (PhD); developmental psychology (PhD); earth and environmental sciences (PhD); economics (PhD); educational psychology (PhD); electrical engineering (PhD); English (PhD); environmental psychology (PhD); experimental psychology (PhD); finance (PhD); French (PhD); Germanic languages and literatures (MA, PhD); graphic arts (PhD); Hispanic and Luso-Brazilian literatures (PhD); history (PhD); industrial psychology (PhD); learning processes (PhD); liberal studies (MA); linguistics (MA, PhD); management planning systems (PhD); mathematics (PhD); mechanical engineering (PhD); music (DMA, PhD); neuropsychology (PhD); painting (PhD); philosophy (MA, PhD); photography (PhD); physical anthropology (PhD); physics (PhD); political science (MA, PhD); psychology (PhD); sculpture (PhD); social personality (PhD); social welfare (DSW); sociology (PhD); speech and hearing sciences (PhD); theatre (PhD); urban education (PhD). *Application fee:* $40. *Application Contact:* Les Gribben, Director of Admissions, 212-817-7470, Fax: 212-817-1624, E-mail: lgribben@gc.cuny.edu. *Provost and Senior Vice President for Academic Affairs*, Dr. William Kelly, 212-817-7200, Fax: 212-817-1612, E-mail: provost@gc.cuny.edu.

Interdisciplinary Studies Expenses: Contact institution. *Financial support:* Application deadline: 2/1. Offers language in social context (PhD); medieval studies (PhD); public policy (MA, PhD); urban studies (MA, PhD); women's studies (MA, PhD). *Application deadline:* For fall admission, 2/1. *Application fee:* $40. *Chairman*, 212-642-2430.

See in-depth description on page 889.

GRADUATE SCHOOL OF FIGURATIVE ART OF THE NEW YORK ACADEMY OF ART, New York, NY 10013-2911

General Information Independent, coed, graduate-only institution. *Enrollment by degree level:* 119 master's. *Graduate faculty:* 5 full-time (1 woman), 28 part-time/adjunct (4 women). *Tuition:* Full-time $15,000; part-time $500 per credit. *Required fees:* $500; $150 per semester. *Graduate housing:* On-campus housing not available. *Student services:* Campus employment opportunities, teacher training. *Library facilities:* New York Academy of Art Library. *Online resources:* web page. *Collection:* 4,500 titles, 12 serial subscriptions, 88 audiovisual materials.

Computer facilities: 5 computers available on campus for general student use. A campuswide network can be accessed. Internet access is available. *Web address:* http://www.nyaa.edu/.

General Application Contact: Michael Gormley, Vice President, Academic Affairs, 212-966-0300, Fax: 212-966-3217, E-mail: info@nyaa.edu.

Graduate School of Figurative Art of the New York Academy of Art (continued)

GRADUATE UNITS

Program in Figurative Art Students: 103 full-time (50 women), 16 part-time (6 women); includes 14 minority (3 African Americans, 8 Asian Americans or Pacific Islanders, 3 Hispanic Americans), 6 international. Average age 27. 187 applicants, 42% accepted. *Faculty:* 5 full-time (1 woman), 28 part-time/adjunct (4 women). Expenses: Contact institution. *Financial support:* In 2001–02, 5 fellowships with partial tuition reimbursements (averaging $37,500 per year), 1 research assistantship (averaging $7,500 per year) were awarded. Career-related internships or fieldwork, scholarships/grants, and tuition waivers (partial) also available. Financial award application deadline: 4/15; financial award applicants required to submit FAFSA. In 2001, 59 degrees awarded. *Degree program information:* Part-time programs available. Offers drawing (MFA); painting (MFA); sculpting (MFA). *Application deadline:* For fall admission, 4/15 (priority date). Applications are processed on a rolling basis. *Application fee:* $50. Electronic applications accepted. *Application Contact:* Michael Gormley, Dean, 212-966-0300, Fax: 212-966-3217, E-mail: info@nyaa.edu. *Executive Director*, Stephen Farthing, 212-966-0300, Fax: 212-966-3217, E-mail: info@nyaa.edu.

See in-depth description on page 891.

GRADUATE THEOLOGICAL UNION, Berkeley, CA 94709-1212

General Information Independent-religious, coed, graduate-only institution. *Enrollment by degree level:* 107 master's, 233 doctoral, 7 other advanced degrees. *Graduate faculty:* 80 full-time (29 women), 14 part-time/adjunct (3 women). *Tuition:* Full-time $16,000. Tuition and fees vary according to degree level. *Graduate housing:* Rooms and/or apartments available on a first-come, first-served basis to single and married students. *Student services:* Campus employment opportunities, international student services, low-cost health insurance. *Library facilities:* Flora Lamson Hewlett Library. *Online resources:* library catalog, web page, access to other libraries' catalogs. *Collection:* 418,779 titles, 1,453 serial subscriptions, 5,233 audiovisual materials.

Computer facilities: 40 computers available on campus for general student use. Internet access is available. *Web address:* http://www.gtu.edu/.

General Application Contact: Dr. Kathleen Kook, Assistant Dean for Admissions, 800-826-4488, Fax: 510-649-1730, E-mail: gtuadm@gtu.edu.

GRADUATE UNITS

Graduate Programs Students: 308 full-time (154 women), 39 part-time (13 women); includes 48 minority (9 African Americans, 28 Asian Americans or Pacific Islanders, 9 Hispanic Americans, 2 Native Americans), 60 international. Average age 42. 193 applicants, 65% accepted, 76 enrolled. *Faculty:* 80 full-time (29 women), 14 part-time/adjunct (3 women). Expenses: Contact institution. *Financial support:* In 2001–02, 160 students received support, including 15 fellowships (averaging $19,000 per year), 22 research assistantships (averaging $4,000 per year); teaching assistantships, Federal Work-Study, scholarships/grants, and tuition waivers (full and partial) also available. Support available to part-time students. Financial award application deadline: 2/1; financial award applicants required to submit FAFSA. In 2001, 28 master's, 20 doctorates awarded. Offers arts and religion (MA, Th D); biblical languages (MA); biblical studies (Old and New Testament) (MA, PhD, Th D); Buddhist studies (MA); Christian spirituality (MA); cultural and historical studies (MA, PhD); ethics and social theory (PhD); historical studies (MA, PhD, Th D); history of art and religion (PhD); homiletics (MA, PhD, Th D); interdisciplinary studies (PhD, Th D); Jewish studies (MA, PhD, Certificate); liturgical studies (MA, PhD, Th D); Near Eastern religions (PhD); religion and psychology (MA, PhD); religion and society (MA); systematic and philosophical theology (MA, PhD, Th D); theology (MA, PhD, Th D, Certificate). MA/M Div offered jointly with individual denominations. *Application deadline:* For fall admission, 12/15; for winter admission, 2/15; for spring admission, 9/30. *Application fee:* $40. Electronic applications accepted. *Application Contact:* Dr. Kathleen Kook, Assistant Dean for Admissions, 800-826-4488, Fax: 510-649-1730, E-mail: gtuadm@gtu.edu. *Interim Dean*, Dr. Eldon G. Ernst, 510-649-2440, Fax: 510-649-1417, E-mail: eernst@gtu.edu.

GRAMBLING STATE UNIVERSITY, Grambling, LA 71245

General Information State-supported, coed, comprehensive institution. CGS member. *Graduate housing:* Rooms and/or apartments available to single and married students. Housing application deadline: 7/15. *Research affiliation:* U.S. Army Research Office (advanced distributed simulation), NASA (high-performance plastics).

GRADUATE UNITS

Division of Graduate Studies *Degree program information:* Part-time and evening/weekend programs available. Postbaccalaureate distance learning degree programs offered.

College of Education *Degree program information:* Part-time and evening/weekend programs available. Postbaccalaureate distance learning degree programs offered. Offers curriculum and instruction (Ed D); developmental education (MS, Ed D); early childhood education (MS); educational leadership (Ed D); elementary education (MS); sports administration (MS).

College of Liberal Arts *Degree program information:* Part-time and evening/weekend programs available. Offers criminal justice (MS); humanities (MA); mass communication (MA); public administration (MPA); social sciences (MAT).

College of Science and Technology *Degree program information:* Part-time and evening/weekend programs available. Offers natural sciences (MAT).

School of Nursing *Degree program information:* Evening/weekend programs available. Offers family nurse practitioner (MSN).

School of Social Work *Degree program information:* Part-time and evening/weekend programs available. Offers social work (MSW).

GRAND CANYON UNIVERSITY, Phoenix, AZ 85061-1097

General Information Independent-religious, coed, comprehensive institution. *Enrollment:* 53 full-time matriculated graduate/professional students (36 women), 2,451 part-time matriculated graduate/professional students (1,899 women). *Enrollment by degree level:* 2,504 master's. *Graduate faculty:* 19 full-time (12 women), 104 part-time/adjunct (72 women). *Tuition:* Full-time $9,500; part-time $438 per hour. Tuition and fees vary according to course load. *Graduate housing:* Rooms and/or apartments available on a first-come, first-served basis to single and married students. Typical cost: $4,800 (including board) for single students; $6,300 per year for married students. Room and board charges vary according to housing facility selected. Housing application deadline: 3/15. *Student services:* Campus employment opportunities, campus safety program, career counseling, free psychological counseling, international student services, low-cost health insurance, multicultural affairs office, teacher training. *Library facilities:* Fleming Library. *Online resources:* library catalog. *Collection:* 75,905 titles, 1,174 serial subscriptions, 404 audiovisual materials.

Computer facilities: 119 computers available on campus for general student use. Internet access is available. *Web address:* http://www.grand-canyon.edu/.

General Application Contact: April Chapman, Director of Admissions, 602-589-2855 Ext. 2811, Fax: 602-589-2580.

GRADUATE UNITS

College of Business Students: 13 full-time (7 women), 20 part-time (13 women); includes 6 minority (3 African Americans, 3 Hispanic Americans), 15 international. *Faculty:* 10 full-time (5 women). Expenses: Contact institution. *Financial support:* In 2001–02, 4 fellowships (averaging $375 per year) were awarded; institutionally sponsored loans also available. Support available to part-time students. Financial award application deadline: 3/15; financial award applicants required to submit FAFSA. In 2001, 15 degrees awarded. *Degree program information:* Part-time and evening/weekend programs available. Offers business (MBA). *Application deadline:* Applications are processed on a rolling basis. *Application fee:* $25. *Director, MBA Program*, Dr. Rob Jones, 602-589-2867, Fax: 602-589-2532, E-mail: rjones@grand-canyon.edu.

College of Education Students: 40 full-time (29 women), 2,431 part-time (1,886 women). *Faculty:* 9 full-time (7 women), 104 part-time/adjunct (72 women). Expenses: Contact institution. *Financial support:* In 2001–02, 23 fellowships (averaging $1,250 per year) were awarded; career-related internships or fieldwork, Federal Work-Study, and institutionally sponsored loans also available. Support available to part-time students. Financial award application deadline: 3/15. In 2001, 991 degrees awarded. *Degree program information:* Part-time and evening/weekend programs available. Postbaccalaureate distance learning degree programs offered (no on-campus study). Offers elementary education (M Ed, MA); reading education (MA); secondary education (M Ed); teaching (MAT); teaching English as a second language (MA). *Application deadline:* Applications are processed on a rolling basis. *Application fee:* $25. *Associate Dean*, Dr. Marilyn Wells, 602-589-2472.

GRAND RAPIDS BAPTIST SEMINARY OF CORNERSTONE UNIVERSITY, Grand Rapids, MI 49525-5897

General Information Independent-religious, coed, graduate-only institution. *Graduate faculty:* 8 full-time (0 women), 5 part-time/adjunct (0 women). *Tuition:* Part-time $295 per credit hour. *Graduate housing:* Rooms and/or apartments available on a first-come, first-served basis to single students and available to married students. Housing application deadline: 6/1. *Student services:* Campus employment opportunities, career counseling, international student services, low-cost health insurance. *Library facilities:* Miller Library. *Online resources:* web page. *Collection:* 119,943 titles, 1,107 serial subscriptions, 3,761 audiovisual materials.

Computer facilities: A campuswide network can be accessed from student residence rooms and from off campus. Internet access and online class registration are available. *Web address:* http://www.grbs.edu/.

General Application Contact: Peter G. Osborn, Director of Admissions, 616-222-1422 Ext. 1251, Fax: 616-222-1400, E-mail: peter_g_osborn@cornerstone.edu.

GRADUATE UNITS

Graduate Programs Students: 148 full-time (30 women), 77 part-time (16 women); includes 18 minority (12 African Americans, 5 Asian Americans or Pacific Islanders, 1 Hispanic American), 15 international. Average age 30. 108 applicants, 91% accepted, 75 enrolled. *Faculty:* 8 full-time (0 women), 5 part-time/adjunct (0 women). Expenses: Contact institution. *Financial support:* In 2001–02, 98 students received support. Career-related internships or fieldwork and scholarships/grants available. Support available to part-time students. Financial award application deadline: 8/15; financial award applicants required to submit FAFSA. In 2001, 10 first professional degrees, 32 master's, 6 doctorates awarded. *Degree program information:* Part-time programs available. Postbaccalaureate distance learning degree programs offered (minimal on-campus study). Offers biblical counseling (MA); chaplaincy (M Div); Christian education (M Div, MA, MRE); education/management (D Min); intercultural studies (MA); missions (M Div, MRE); New Testament (MA, MTS, Th M); Old Testament (MA, MTS, Th M); pastoral studies (M Div, MRE); religious education (MRE); systematic theology (MA); theology (MTS, Th M). *Application deadline:* For fall admission, 8/15; for spring admission, 1/15. Applications are processed on a rolling basis. *Application fee:* $25. *Application Contact:* Peter G. Osborn, Director of Admissions, 616-222-1422 Ext. 1251, Fax: 616-222-1400, E-mail: peter_g_osborn@cornerstone.edu. *Executive Vice President*, Dr. Robert W. Nienhuis, 616-222-1415, Fax: 616-222-1540, E-mail: rnienhuis@cornerstone.edu.

GRAND VALLEY STATE UNIVERSITY, Allendale, MI 49401-9403

General Information State-supported, coed, comprehensive institution. *Enrollment:* 627 full-time matriculated graduate/professional students (455 women), 1,405 part-time matriculated graduate/professional students (970 women). *Enrollment by degree level:* 2,032 master's. *Graduate faculty:* 140 full-time (67 women), 126 part-time/adjunct (50 women). Tuition, state resident: part-time $202 per credit hour. Tuition, nonresident: part-time $437 per credit hour. *Graduate housing:* Rooms and/or apartments available on a first-come, first-served basis to single and married students. Housing application deadline: 2/1. *Student services:* Campus employment opportunities, campus safety program, career counseling, child daycare facilities, disabled student services, exercise/wellness program, free psychological counseling, grant writing training, international student services, low-cost health insurance, multicultural affairs office, teacher training, writing training. *Library facilities:* James H. Zumberge Library plus 2 others. *Online resources:* library catalog, web page. *Collection:* 620,000 titles, 3,207 serial subscriptions.

Computer facilities: 2,600 computers available on campus for general student use. A campuswide network can be accessed from student residence rooms and from off campus. Internet access and online class registration, transcript, degree audit are available. *Web address:* http://www.gvsu.edu/.

General Application Contact: Tory Parsons, Associate Director for Graduate Recruitment, 616-895-2025, Fax: 616-486-6476, E-mail: parsonst@gvsu.edu.

GRADUATE UNITS

Division of Arts and Humanities Students: 4 full-time (3 women), 11 part-time (7 women), 2 international. Average age 32. 2 applicants, 100% accepted, 2 enrolled. *Faculty:* 2 full-time (0 women), 1 part-time/adjunct (0 women). Expenses: Contact institution. *Financial support:* In 2001–02, 3 students received support, including 3 research assistantships with tuition reimbursements available (averaging $4,400 per year); career-related internships or fieldwork, Federal Work-Study, and institutionally sponsored loans also available. Support available to part-time students. Financial award application deadline: 3/1. In 2001, 2 degrees awarded. *Degree program information:* Part-time and evening/weekend programs available. Offers arts and humanities (MS). *Application deadline:* For fall admission, 8/15 (priority date); for winter admission, 12/15 (priority date); for spring admission, 4/15 (priority date). Applications are processed on a rolling basis. *Application fee:* $20. *Application Contact:* Dr. Alex Nesterenko, Director, 616-895-3668, Fax: 616-895-2700, E-mail: nesterea@gvsu.edu. *Dean*, Jon Jellema, 616-895-2111, Fax: 616-895-2520, E-mail: jellemaj@gvsu.edu.

School of Communications Students: 4 full-time (3 women), 11 part-time (7 women), 2 international. Average age 32. 2 applicants, 100% accepted, 2 enrolled. *Faculty:* 2 full-time (0 women), 1 part-time/adjunct (0 women). Expenses: Contact institution. *Financial support:* In 2001–02, 3 students received support, including 3 research assistantships with tuition reimbursements available (averaging $4,400 per year); career-related internships or fieldwork, Federal Work-Study, and institutionally sponsored loans also available. Support available to part-time students. Financial award application deadline: 3/1. In 2001, 2 degrees awarded. *Degree program information:* Part-time and evening/weekend programs available. Offers communications (MS). *Application deadline:* For fall admission, 8/15 (priority date); for winter admission, 12/15 (priority date); for spring admission, 4/15 (priority date). Applications are processed on a rolling basis. *Application fee:* $20. *Director*, Dr. Alex Nesterenko, 616-895-3668, Fax: 616-895-2700, E-mail: nesterea@gvsu.edu.

Russell B. Kirkhof School of Nursing Students: 122; includes 4 minority (2 African Americans, 1 Hispanic American, 1 Native American) Average age 40. 50 applicants, 78% accepted. *Faculty:* 15 full-time (all women). Expenses: Contact institution. *Financial support:* In 2001–02, 19 research assistantships were awarded; career-related internships or fieldwork, Federal Work-Study, institutionally sponsored loans, and traineeships also available. Financial award application deadline: 2/15. In 2001, 37 degrees awarded. *Degree program information:* Part-time programs available. Offers nursing (MSN). *Application deadline:* For fall admission, 3/15 (priority date). Applications are processed on a rolling basis. *Application fee:* $20. Electronic applications accepted. *Application Contact:* Dr. Jean Martin, Director of Graduate Programs, 616-336-7167, E-mail: martinj@gvsu.edu. *Dean*, Dr. Phyllis Gendler, 616-336-7161, Fax: 616-336-7362, E-mail: gendlerp@gvsu.edu.

School of Education Students: 102 full-time (74 women), 754 part-time (593 women); includes 38 minority (20 African Americans, 5 Asian Americans or Pacific Islanders, 10 Hispanic Americans, 3 Native Americans) Average age 33. 734 applicants, 96% accepted. *Faculty:* 25 full-time (15 women), 41 part-time/adjunct (23 women). Expenses: Contact institution. *Financial support:* In 2001–02, 5 research assistantships with full and partial tuition reimbursements (averaging $3,000 per year) were awarded; career-related internships or fieldwork, Federal Work-Study, scholarships/grants, and unspecified assistantships also available. In 2001, 300 degrees awarded. *Degree program information:* Part-time and evening/

weekend programs available. Postbaccalaureate distance learning degree programs offered (minimal on-campus study). Offers adult and higher education (M Ed); early childhood education (M Ed); education (M Ed); education of the gifted and talented (M Ed); educational leadership (M Ed); educational technology (M Ed); elementary education (M Ed); learning disabilities (M Ed); middle and high school education (M Ed); pre-primary impaired (M Ed); reading/language arts (M Ed); special education administration (M Ed); teaching English to speakers of other languages (M Ed). *Application deadline:* Applications are processed on a rolling basis. *Application fee:* $20. Electronic applications accepted. *Application Contact:* 616-895-2025, Fax: 616-895-2000. *Interim Dean,* Dr. Anne Mulder, 616-895-2091, Fax: 616-895-2330.

School of Social Work Students: 126 full-time (108 women), 197 part-time (170 women); includes 31 minority (19 African Americans, 1 Asian American or Pacific Islander, 5 Hispanic Americans, 6 Native Americans), 18 international. Average age 36. 136 applicants, 75% accepted. *Faculty:* 24 full-time (15 women), 9 part-time/adjunct (6 women). Expenses: Contact institution. *Financial support:* In 2001–02, 20 research assistantships with partial tuition reimbursements (averaging $3,000 per year) were awarded; career-related internships or fieldwork, Federal Work-Study, and institutionally sponsored loans also available. In 2001, 90 degrees awarded. *Degree program information:* Part-time programs available. Offers social work (MSW). *Application deadline:* For fall admission, 5/1 (priority date); for winter admission, 10/1 (priority date); for spring admission, 3/15 (priority date). Applications are processed on a rolling basis. *Application fee:* $20. Electronic applications accepted. *Application Contact:* Dr. Lois Smith Owens, Chair, Admissions, 616-771-6550, Fax: 616-771-6570. *Dean,* Dr. Rodney Mulder, 616-771-6550, Fax: 616-771-6570.

Science and Mathematics Division Students: 353 full-time (255 women), 42 part-time (7 women); includes 23 minority (5 African Americans, 14 Asian Americans or Pacific Islanders, 3 Hispanic Americans, 1 Native American), 3 international. Average age 28. 322 applicants, 44% accepted, 98 enrolled. *Faculty:* 34 full-time (13 women), 53 part-time/adjunct (18 women). Expenses: Contact institution. *Financial support:* In 2001–02, 2 research assistantships with full and partial tuition reimbursements (averaging $11,000 per year), 3 teaching assistantships with full and partial tuition reimbursements (averaging $8,000 per year) were awarded. Fellowships, career-related internships or fieldwork, Federal Work-Study, institutionally sponsored loans, scholarships/grants, and unspecified assistantships also available. In 2001, 133 degrees awarded. *Degree program information:* Part-time programs available. Offers biomedical and health sciences (MHS); information systems (MS); science and mathematics (MHS, MPAS, MS, MSE); software engineering (MS). *Application fee:* $20. Electronic applications accepted. *Dean,* Dr. P. Douglas Kindschi, 616-895-2261.

School of Health Professions Students: 260 full-time (194 women); includes 14 minority (3 African Americans, 8 Asian Americans or Pacific Islanders, 2 Hispanic Americans, 1 Native American), 1 international. Average age 25. 185 applicants, 48% accepted, 83 enrolled. *Faculty:* 19 full-time (10 women), 18 part-time/adjunct (11 women). Expenses: Contact institution. *Financial support:* Research assistantships, career-related internships or fieldwork, Federal Work-Study, institutionally sponsored loans, and scholarships/grants available. In 2001, 102 degrees awarded. *Degree program information:* Part-time programs available. Offers health professions (MPAS, MS); occupational therapy (MS); physical therapy (MS); physician assistant studies (MPAS). *Application fee:* $20. Electronic applications accepted. *Application Contact:* Chris Lewis, Outreach Coordinator, 616-895-3958, Fax: 616-895-3350, E-mail: lewisch@gvsu.edu. *Director,* Dr. Jane Toot, 616-895-3356, E-mail: tootj@gvsu.edu.

Seymour and Esther Padnos School of Engineering Students: 5 full-time (1 woman), 42 part-time (7 women); includes 4 minority (1 African American, 2 Asian Americans or Pacific Islanders, 1 Hispanic American), 2 international. Average age 31. 37 applicants, 57% accepted, 15 enrolled. *Faculty:* 10 full-time (1 woman), 3 part-time/adjunct (1 woman). Expenses: Contact institution. *Financial support:* In 2001–02, 2 research assistantships with full tuition reimbursements (averaging $11,000 per year), 3 teaching assistantships with full tuition reimbursements (averaging $8,000 per year) were awarded. Career-related internships or fieldwork, Federal Work-Study, institutionally sponsored loans, scholarships/grants, and unspecified assistantships also available. In 2001, 2 degrees awarded. *Degree program information:* Part-time programs available. Offers manufacturing engineering (MSE); manufacturing operations (MSE); mechanical engineering (MSE). *Application deadline:* Applications are processed on a rolling basis. *Application fee:* $20. *Application Contact:* Dr. Hugh Jack, Graduate Coordinator, 616-771-6750, Fax: 616-336-7215, E-mail: jackh@gvsu.edu. *Director,* Dr. Paul Plotkowski, 616-771-6750, Fax: 616-336-7215, E-mail: plotkowp@gvsu.edu.

Seidman School of Business Students: 40 full-time (13 women), 300 part-time (96 women); includes 9 minority (4 African Americans, 2 Asian Americans or Pacific Islanders, 2 Hispanic Americans, 1 Native American), 20 international. Average age 32. 194 applicants, 78% accepted. *Faculty:* 19 full-time (3 women), 15 part-time/adjunct (0 women). Expenses: Contact institution. *Financial support:* In 2001–02, 80 students received support, including 11 research assistantships with full tuition reimbursements available (averaging $6,200 per year); fellowships, Federal Work-Study and institutionally sponsored loans also available. Support available to part-time students. Financial award application deadline: 4/1; financial award applicants required to submit FAFSA. In 2001, 78 degrees awarded. *Degree program information:* Part-time and evening/weekend programs available. Offers business (MBA, MST); business administration (MBA); taxation (MST). *Application deadline:* For fall admission, 6/1 (priority date); for winter admission, 12/1 (priority date); for spring admission, 4/1 (priority date). Applications are processed on a rolling basis. *Application fee:* $20. Electronic applications accepted. *Application Contact:* Claudia J. Bajema, Director, 616-336-7387, Fax: 616-336-7389, E-mail: seidman_mba@gvsu.edu. *Dean,* Dr. David E. Mielke, 616-336-7379, Fax: 616-336-7389.

Social Science Division Students: 154 (97 women); includes 24 minority (14 African Americans, 4 Asian Americans or Pacific Islanders, 5 Hispanic Americans, 1 Native American) Average age 35. 76 applicants, 89% accepted. *Faculty:* 21 full-time (6 women), 7 part-time/adjunct (3 women). Expenses: Contact institution. *Financial support:* In 2001–02, 20 students received support, including research assistantships with full and partial tuition reimbursements available (averaging $6,000 per year); fellowships, teaching assistantships, career-related internships or fieldwork, Federal Work-Study, institutionally sponsored loans, scholarships/grants, and unspecified assistantships also available. Financial award application deadline: 5/1. In 2001, 32 degrees awarded. *Degree program information:* Part-time and evening/weekend programs available. Postbaccalaureate distance learning degree programs offered (no on-campus study). Offers social science (MPA, MS). *Application deadline:* For fall admission, 5/1; for winter admission, 11/1; for spring admission, 4/10. Applications are processed on a rolling basis. *Application fee:* $20. Electronic applications accepted. *Dean,* Dr. Ericka G. King, 616-895-2291, Fax: 616-895-3288.

School of Criminal Justice Students: 6 full-time (all women), 22 part-time (11 women); includes 4 minority (2 African Americans, 1 Hispanic American, 1 Native American) Average age 36. 26 applicants, 88% accepted, 18 enrolled. *Faculty:* 10 full-time (2 women). Expenses: Contact institution. *Financial support:* In 2001–02, research assistantships with full tuition reimbursements (averaging $4,000 per year); career-related internships or fieldwork, Federal Work-Study, and scholarships/grants also available. Financial award application deadline: 5/1. In 2001, 2 degrees awarded. *Degree program information:* Part-time and evening/weekend programs available. Postbaccalaureate distance learning degree programs offered (no on-campus study). Offers criminal justice (MS). *Application deadline:* For fall admission, 7/30 (priority date); for winter admission, 12/10 (priority date); for spring admission, 4/10 (priority date). *Application fee:* $20. *Application Contact:* Dr. John Hewitt, Professor, 616-336-7145, Fax: 616-336-7155, E-mail: hewittj@gvsu.edu. *Director,* Dr. James Houston, 616-336-7131, Fax: 616-336-7155, E-mail: houstonj@gvsu.edu.

School of Public and Nonprofit Administration Students: 126 (80 women); includes 20 minority (12 African Americans, 4 Asian Americans or Pacific Islanders, 4 Hispanic Americans) Average age 35. 50 applicants, 90% accepted. *Faculty:* 11 full-time (4 women), 7 part-time/adjunct (3 women). Expenses: Contact institution. *Financial support:* In 2001–02, 20 students received support, including research assistantships with partial tuition reimbursements available (averaging $2,000 per year); career-related internships or fieldwork, Federal Work-Study, scholarships/grants, and unspecified assistantships also available. Financial award application deadline: 5/1. In 2001, 30 degrees awarded. *Degree program information:* Part-time and evening/weekend programs available. Offers public and nonprofit administration (MPA). *Application deadline:* For fall admission, 5/1 (priority date); for winter admission, 11/1 (priority date). Applications are processed on a rolling basis. *Application fee:* $20. Electronic applications accepted. *Director,* Dr. Danny L. Balfour, 616-771-6594, Fax: 616-336-7120, E-mail: balfourd@gvsu.edu.

See in-depth description on page 893.

GRATZ COLLEGE, Melrose Park, PA 19027

General Information Independent-religious, coed, comprehensive institution. *Enrollment:* 13 full-time matriculated graduate/professional students (8 women), 580 part-time matriculated graduate/professional students (498 women). *Enrollment by degree level:* 593 master's. *Graduate faculty:* 7 full-time (3 women), 57 part-time/adjunct (42 women). *Tuition:* Full-time $9,950; part-time $466 per credit. *Graduate housing:* On-campus housing not available. *Student services:* Campus employment opportunities, career counseling, low-cost health insurance. *Library facilities:* Tuttleman Library. *Online resources:* library catalog. *Collection:* 100,000 titles, 175 serial subscriptions, 380 audiovisual materials.

Computer facilities: 2 computers available on campus for general student use. A campuswide network can be accessed from off campus. *Web address:* http://www.gratzcollege.edu/.

General Application Contact: Adena E. Johnston, Director of Admissions, 215-635-7300 Ext. 140, Fax: 215-635-7320, E-mail: admissions@gratz.edu.

GRADUATE UNITS

Graduate Programs Students: 13 full-time (8 women), 580 part-time (498 women); includes 24 minority (17 African Americans, 2 Asian Americans or Pacific Islanders, 5 Hispanic Americans) Average age 35. 125 applicants, 87% accepted, 102 enrolled. *Faculty:* 7 full-time (3 women), 57 part-time/adjunct (42 women). Expenses: Contact institution. *Financial support:* Fellowships, career-related internships or fieldwork, Federal Work-Study, scholarships/grants, and tuition waivers (partial) available. Support available to part-time students. In 2001, 98 degrees awarded. *Degree program information:* Part-time and evening/weekend programs available. Offers classical studies (MA); education (MA); Israel studies (Certificate); Jewish communal studies (MA, Certificate); Jewish education (MA, Certificate); Jewish music (MA, Certificate); Jewish studies (MA); Judaica librarianship (Certificate); modern studies (MA). *Application deadline:* Applications are processed on a rolling basis. *Application fee:* $50. *Application Contact:* Adena E. Johnston, Director of Admissions, 215-635-7300 Ext. 140, Fax: 215-635-7320, E-mail: admissions@gratz.edu. *Dean for Academic Affairs,* Dr. Jerome Kutnick, 215-635-7300 Ext. 137, Fax: 215-635-7320, E-mail: jkutnick@gratz.edu.

See in-depth description on page 895.

GREENVILLE COLLEGE, Greenville, IL 62246-0159

General Information Independent-religious, coed, comprehensive institution. *Graduate housing:* On-campus housing not available.

GRADUATE UNITS

Leadership and Ministry Program Offers leadership and ministry (MA).

GWYNEDD-MERCY COLLEGE, Gwynedd Valley, PA 19437-0901

General Information Independent-religious, coed, comprehensive institution. *Graduate housing:* Room and/or apartments available on a first-come, first-served basis to single students; on-campus housing not available to married students.

GRADUATE UNITS

School of Education *Degree program information:* Part-time and evening/weekend programs available. Offers educational administration (MS); mental health counseling (MS); reading (MS); school counseling (MS); teaching (MS).

School of Nursing *Degree program information:* Part-time programs available. Offers gerontology (MSN); nurse practitioner (MSN).

HAMLINE UNIVERSITY, St. Paul, MN 55104-1284

General Information Independent-religious, coed, comprehensive institution. *Enrollment:* 1,309 full-time matriculated graduate/professional students, 1,457 part-time matriculated graduate/professional students. *Graduate faculty:* 159. *Tuition:* Full-time $6,900; part-time $1,155 per course. One-time fee: $150. Tuition and fees vary according to course load, degree level and program. *Graduate housing:* Rooms and/or apartments available on a first-come, first-served basis to single and married students. Typical cost: $5,100 per year ($6,100 including board) for single students. Room and board charges vary according to board plan and housing facility selected. *Student services:* Campus employment opportunities, campus safety program, career counseling, free psychological counseling, international student services, low-cost health insurance, multicultural affairs office. *Library facilities:* Bush Library plus 1 other. *Online resources:* library catalog, web page, access to other libraries' catalogs. *Collection:* 445,902 titles, 3,803 serial subscriptions, 2,040 audiovisual materials. *Research affiliation:* Minnesota Women Elected Officials.

Computer facilities: 326 computers available on campus for general student use. A campuswide network can be accessed from student residence rooms and from off campus. Internet access and online class registration are available. *Web address:* http://www.hamline.edu/.

General Application Contact: Gwenn M. Sherburne, Assistant Director, Graduate Admission, 651-523-2900, Fax: 651-523-2458, E-mail: gradprog@gw.hamline.edu.

GRADUATE UNITS

Graduate Liberal Studies Program Students: 746 full-time (440 women), 901 part-time (662 women); includes 132 minority (57 African Americans, 44 Asian Americans or Pacific Islanders, 22 Hispanic Americans, 9 Native Americans), 79 international. Average age 25. 47 applicants, 91% accepted, 32 enrolled. *Faculty:* 62 full-time (35 women), 45 part-time/adjunct (25 women). Expenses: Contact institution. *Financial support:* Federal Work-Study available. Financial award applicants required to submit FAFSA. In 2001, 258 master's, 161 other advanced degrees awarded. *Degree program information:* Part-time and evening/weekend programs available. Offers liberal studies (MALS, MFA, CALS). *Application deadline:* For fall admission, 7/15 (priority date); for spring admission, 12/1 (priority date). Applications are processed on a rolling basis. *Application fee:* $30. Electronic applications accepted. *Application Contact:* Gwenn M. Sherburne, Assistant Director, Graduate Admission, 651-523-2900, Fax: 651-523-2458, E-mail: gradprog@gw.hamline.edu. *Director,* Mary Francóis Rockcastle, 651-523-2047, Fax: 651-523-2490.

Graduate School of Education Students: 10 full-time, 320 part-time. 291 applicants, 85% accepted, 205 enrolled. *Faculty:* 7 full-time, 10 part-time/adjunct. Expenses: Contact institution. *Financial support:* Federal Work-Study available. Financial award applicants required to submit FAFSA. *Degree program information:* Part-time and evening/weekend programs available. Offers education (MA Ed, MAESL, MAT, Ed D). *Application deadline:* For fall admission, 7/15 (priority date); for spring admission, 12/15 (priority date). Applications are processed on a rolling basis. *Application fee:* $30. *Application Contact:* Gwenn M. Sherburne, Assistant Director, Graduate Admission, 651-523-2900, Fax: 651-523-2458, E-mail: gradprog@gw.hamline.edu. *Interim Dean,* Deirde Kramer, 651-523-2900, Fax: 651-523-2458.

Graduate School of Public Administration and Management Students: 80 full-time, 156 part-time. 121 applicants, 76% accepted, 66 enrolled. *Faculty:* 4 full-time, 25 part-time/adjunct. Expenses: Contact institution. *Financial support:* Federal Work-Study available. Financial award applicants required to submit FAFSA. *Degree program information:* Part-time and evening/weekend programs available. Offers management (MAM); nonprofit management (MANM); public administration (MAPA). *Application deadline:* For fall admission, 7/15 (priority date); for spring admission, 12/1 (priority date). Applications are processed on a rolling basis. *Application fee:* $30. Electronic applications accepted. *Application Contact:* Gwenn M. Sherburne, Assistant Director, Graduate Admission, 651-523-2900, Fax: 651-523-2458, E-mail: gradprog@gw.hamline.edu. *Dean,* Dr. Jane McPeak, 651-523-2900, Fax: 651-523-3098.

Hamline University (continued)

School of Law Students: 473 full-time (263 women), 80 part-time (44 women); includes 64 minority (20 African Americans, 26 Asian Americans or Pacific Islanders, 13 Hispanic Americans, 5 Native Americans), 10 international. Average age 25. 981 applicants, 65% accepted, 219 enrolled. *Faculty:* 32 full-time (14 women), 35 part-time/adjunct (12 women). Expenses: Contact institution. *Financial support:* In 2001–02, 10 fellowships (averaging $3,000 per year) were awarded; career-related internships or fieldwork, Federal Work-Study, and scholarships/grants also available. Support available to part-time students. Financial award applicants required to submit FAFSA. In 2001, 161 first professional degrees, 6 master's awarded. *Degree program information:* Part-time and evening/weekend programs available. Offers law (JD, LL M). *Application deadline:* For fall admission, 5/1 (priority date). Applications are processed on a rolling basis. *Application fee:* $40. Electronic applications accepted. *Application Contact:* Michael J. States, Director of Admissions, 800-388-3688, Fax: 651-523-3064, E-mail: mstates@gw.hamline.edu. *Dean,* Edwin J. Butterfoss, 651-523-2968, Fax: 651-523-2435, E-mail: ebutterfoss@gw.hamline.edu.

HAMPTON UNIVERSITY, Hampton, VA 23668

General Information Independent, coed, university. CGS member. *Graduate housing:* Rooms and/or apartments available to single and married students. Housing application deadline: 6/1. *Research affiliation:* NASA–Langley Research Center (physical sciences), Southeastern Universities Research Association (science), Continuous Electron Beam Accelerator Facility (science).

GRADUATE UNITS

Graduate College *Degree program information:* Part-time and evening/weekend programs available. Offers applied mathematics (MS); biological sciences (MA, MS); business (MBA); chemistry (MS); college student development (MA); communicative sciences and disorders (MA); community agency counseling (MA); computer science (MS); counseling (MA); elementary education (MA); museum studies (MA); nursing (MS); physical therapy (DPT); physics (MS, PhD); special education (MA); teaching (MT).

See in-depth description on page 897.

HARDING UNIVERSITY, Searcy, AR 72149-0001

General Information Independent-religious, coed, comprehensive institution. *Enrollment:* 160 full-time matriculated graduate/professional students (95 women), 178 part-time matriculated graduate/professional students (118 women). *Graduate faculty:* 33. *Tuition:* Full-time $5,238; part-time $291 per credit hour. *Required fees:* $300; $291 per credit hour. $150 per semester. Tuition and fees vary according to course load, degree level, reciprocity agreements, student level and student's religious affiliation. *Graduate housing:* Rooms and/or apartments available on a first-come, first-served basis to single and married students. Typical cost: $2,100 per year ($4,498 including board) for single students. Housing application deadline: 3/30. *Student services:* Campus employment opportunities, campus safety program, career counseling, child daycare facilities, disabled student services, exercise/wellness program, free psychological counseling, international student services, low-cost health insurance, writing training. *Library facilities:* Brackett Library plus 1 other. *Online resources:* library catalog, web page, access to other libraries' catalogs. *Collection:* 321,928 titles, 1,368 serial subscriptions, 7,481 audiovisual materials.

Computer facilities: 150 computers available on campus for general student use. A campuswide network can be accessed from student residence rooms and from off campus. Internet access and online class registration are available. *Web address:* http://www.harding.edu/.

General Application Contact: Dr. Jim Nichols, Director of Graduate Studies, 501-279-4315, Fax: 501-279-4685, E-mail: jnichols@harding.edu.

GRADUATE UNITS

College of Bible and Religion Students: 31 full-time (16 women); includes 2 minority (1 African American, 1 Asian American or Pacific Islander) Average age 28. 20 applicants, 80% accepted, 14 enrolled. *Faculty:* 3 full-time (0 women), 4 part-time/adjunct (1 woman). Expenses: Contact institution. *Financial support:* Career-related internships or fieldwork, Federal Work-Study, and institutionally sponsored loans available. Financial award application deadline: 3/31. In 2001, 10 degrees awarded. *Degree program information:* Part-time programs available. Offers Bible and religion (MA, MS); marriage and family therapy (MS); ministry (MA). *Application deadline:* For fall admission, 4/15 (priority date). *Application fee:* $25. *Dean,* Dr. Tom Alexander, 501-279-4291, Fax: 501-279-4042, E-mail: talexander@harding.edu.

College of Nursing Average age 27. 4 applicants, 100% accepted, 3 enrolled. *Faculty:* 6 full-time (5 women), 1 (woman) part-time/adjunct. Expenses: Contact institution. *Financial support:* In 2001–02, 4 students received support, including 2 teaching assistantships with tuition reimbursements available; institutionally sponsored loans, scholarships/grants, and tuition waivers (partial) also available. Support available to part-time students. Financial award application deadline: 7/2. *Degree program information:* Part-time and evening/weekend programs available. Offers nursing (MSN). *Application deadline:* For fall admission, 7/1 (priority date); for spring admission, 11/1 (priority date). *Application fee:* $25. *Application Contact:* Debbie Kemper, Assistant to Dean, 501-279-4682, Fax: 501-305-8902, E-mail: dkemper@harding.edu. *Dean,* Dr. Cathleen M. Schultz, 501-279-4475, Fax: 501-305-8902, E-mail: shultz@harding.edu.

School of Business Students: 43 full-time (17 women), 33 part-time (11 women); includes 9 minority (4 African Americans, 2 Asian Americans or Pacific Islanders, 1 Hispanic American, 2 Native Americans), 5 international. Average age 28. 26 applicants, 73% accepted, 17 enrolled. *Faculty:* 7 part-time/adjunct (1 woman). Expenses: Contact institution. In 2001, 22 degrees awarded. *Degree program information:* Part-time and evening/weekend programs available. Postbaccalaureate distance learning degree programs offered. Offers business (MBA). *Application deadline:* For fall admission, 8/1 (priority date); for spring admission, 12/1 (priority date). *Application fee:* $25. *Application Contact:* Dr. Steve L. Williams, Graduate Director, 501-279-4095, Fax: 501-279-4665, E-mail: slwilliams@harding.edu. *Dean,* Dr. Randy McLeod, 501-279-4240, Fax: 501-279-4665, E-mail: rmmcleod@harding.edu.

School of Education Students: 86 full-time (62 women), 136 part-time (99 women); includes 8 minority (7 African Americans, 1 Hispanic American) Average age 32. 106 applicants, 94% accepted, 100 enrolled. *Faculty:* 12 part-time/adjunct (8 women). Expenses: Contact institution. *Financial support:* Scholarships/grants and unspecified assistantships available. Support available to part-time students. In 2001, 53 degrees awarded. *Degree program information:* Part-time programs available. Offers education (M Ed, MSE); elementary education (M Ed); elementary school administration (M Ed); secondary education (M Ed, MSE). *Application deadline:* For fall admission, 8/1; for spring admission, 1/15. Applications are processed on a rolling basis. *Application fee:* $25. *Director of Graduate Studies,* Dr. Jim Nichols, 501-279-4315, Fax: 501-279-4685, E-mail: jnichols@harding.edu.

HARDING UNIVERSITY GRADUATE SCHOOL OF RELIGION, Memphis, TN 38117-5499

General Information Independent-religious, coed, primarily men, graduate-only institution. *Enrollment by degree level:* 85 first professional, 71 master's, 27 doctoral. *Graduate faculty:* 9 full-time (0 women), 12 part-time/adjunct (2 women). *Tuition:* Full-time $6,174; part-time $343 per semester hour. *Required fees:* $270; $15 per semester hour. $11 per semester. *Graduate housing:* Rooms and/or apartments available to single and married students. Typical cost: $2,340 (including board) for single students; $5,559 (including board) for married students. *Student services:* Career counseling, low-cost health insurance. *Library facilities:* L. M. Graves Memorial Library. *Online resources:* library catalog, web page, access to other libraries' catalogs. *Collection:* 113,325 titles, 660 serial subscriptions, 2,638 audiovisual materials.

Computer facilities: 6 computers available on campus for general student use. Internet access and online class registration are available. *Web address:* http://www.hugsr.edu/.

General Application Contact: Mark K. Parker, Director of Admissions, 901-761-1356, Fax: 901-761-1358, E-mail: mparker@hugsr.edu.

GRADUATE UNITS

Graduate Programs Students: 55 full-time (10 women), 128 part-time (16 women). Average age 35. 58 applicants, 78% accepted, 41 enrolled. *Faculty:* 9 full-time (0 women), 12 part-time/adjunct (2 women). Expenses: Contact institution. *Financial support:* In 2001–02, 43 students received support, including 4 research assistantships with full and partial tuition reimbursements available (averaging $2,000 per year); career-related internships or fieldwork, institutionally sponsored loans, scholarships/grants, tuition waivers (partial), and unspecified assistantships also available. Support available to part-time students. Financial award applicants required to submit FAFSA. In 2001, 7 first professional degrees, 14 master's, 5 doctorates awarded. *Degree program information:* Part-time programs available. *Application deadline:* For fall admission, 12/7 (priority date); for spring admission, 5/3 (priority date). Applications are processed on a rolling basis. *Application fee:* $40. Electronic applications accepted. *Application Contact:* Mark K. Parker, Director of Admissions, 901-761-1356, Fax: 901-761-1358, E-mail: mparker@hugsr.edu. *Dean and Executive Director,* Dr. Evertt W. Huffard, 901-761-1352, Fax: 901-761-1358, E-mail: dean@hugsr.edu.

HARDIN-SIMMONS UNIVERSITY, Abilene, TX 79698-0001

General Information Independent-religious, coed, comprehensive institution. *Enrollment:* 159 full-time matriculated graduate/professional students (83 women), 175 part-time matriculated graduate/professional students (93 women). *Enrollment by degree level:* 59 first professional, 275 master's. *Graduate faculty:* 75 full-time (20 women), 13 part-time/adjunct (3 women). *Tuition:* Full-time $6,120; part-time $340 per credit. *Required fees:* $750. *Graduate housing:* Rooms and/or apartments available on a first-come, first-served basis to single students and available to married students. Typical cost: $1,730 per year ($3,663 including board) for single students. Room and board charges vary according to board plan. *Student services:* Campus employment opportunities, career counseling, free psychological counseling. *Library facilities:* Richardson Library plus 1 other. *Online resources:* library catalog, web page, access to other libraries' catalogs. *Collection:* 194,433 titles, 4,015 serial subscriptions, 16,007 audiovisual materials.

Computer facilities: 224 computers available on campus for general student use. A campuswide network can be accessed from student residence rooms and from off campus. Internet access is available. *Web address:* http://www.hsutx.edu/.

General Application Contact: Dr. Gary Stanlake, Dean of Graduate Studies, 915-670-1298, Fax: 915-670-1564, E-mail: gradoff@hsutx.edu.

GRADUATE UNITS

Graduate School Students: 159 full-time (83 women), 175 part-time (93 women); includes 29 minority (14 African Americans, 1 Asian American or Pacific Islander, 14 Hispanic Americans) Average age 30. 83 applicants, 99% accepted, 55 enrolled. *Faculty:* 75 full-time (20 women), 13 part-time/adjunct (3 women). Expenses: Contact institution. *Financial support:* In 2001–02, 208 students received support, including 42 fellowships with full and partial tuition reimbursements available (averaging $943 per year); research assistantships, teaching assistantships, career-related internships or fieldwork, Federal Work-Study, scholarships/grants, tuition waivers (full and partial), unspecified assistantships, and recreation assistantships, coaching assistantships also available. Support available to part-time students. Financial award application deadline: 3/15; financial award applicants required to submit FAFSA. In 2001, 13 first professional degrees, 81 master's awarded. *Degree program information:* Part-time programs available. Offers English (MA); environmental management (MS); family psychology (MA); history (MA); physical therapy (MPT). *Application deadline:* Applications are processed on a rolling basis. *Application fee:* $25 ($100 for international students). *Dean of Graduate Studies,* Dr. Gary Stanlake, 915-670-1298, Fax: 915-670-1564, E-mail: gradoff@hsutx.edu.

Irvin School of Education Students: 39 full-time (25 women), 82 part-time (54 women); includes 19 minority (12 African Americans, 7 Hispanic Americans) Average age 31. 33 applicants, 97% accepted, 26 enrolled. *Faculty:* 9 full-time (3 women), 3 part-time/adjunct (all women). Expenses: Contact institution. *Financial support:* In 2001–02, 72 students received support, including 6 fellowships with full and partial tuition reimbursements available (averaging $1,100 per year); research assistantships, teaching assistantships, career-related internships or fieldwork, Federal Work-Study, scholarships/grants, tuition waivers (full and partial), unspecified assistantships, and coaching assistantships also available. Support available to part-time students. Financial award application deadline: 3/15; financial award applicants required to submit FAFSA. In 2001, 25 degrees awarded. *Degree program information:* Part-time programs available. Offers counseling and human development (M Ed); education (M Ed); gifted education (M Ed); reading specialist (M Ed); secondary physical education (M Ed); sports and recreation management (M Ed). *Application deadline:* For fall admission, 8/15 (priority date); for spring admission, 1/5 (priority date). Applications are processed on a rolling basis. *Application fee:* $25 ($100 for international students). *Application Contact:* Dr. Gary Stanlake, Dean of Graduate Studies, 915-670-1298, Fax: 915-670-1564, E-mail: gradoff@hsutx.edu. *Dean,* Dr. Pam Williford, 915-670-1347, Fax: 915-670-5859, E-mail: pwilliford@hsutx.edu.

Logsdon School of Theology Students: 33 full-time (4 women), 36 part-time (9 women); includes 3 minority (1 African American, 1 Asian American or Pacific Islander, 1 Hispanic American) Average age 32. 14 applicants, 100% accepted, 14 enrolled. *Faculty:* 13 full-time (1 woman), 8 part-time/adjunct (1 woman). Expenses: Contact institution. *Financial support:* In 2001–02, 29 students received support, including 14 fellowships with full and partial tuition reimbursements available (averaging $988 per year); career-related internships or fieldwork, Federal Work-Study, scholarships/grants, and tuition waivers (full and partial) also available. Support available to part-time students. Financial award application deadline: 3/15; financial award applicants required to submit FAFSA. In 2001, 13 first professional degrees, 5 master's awarded. *Degree program information:* Part-time and evening/weekend programs available. Offers family ministry (MA); religion (MA); theology (M Div). *Application deadline:* For fall admission, 8/15 (priority date); for spring admission, 1/5 (priority date). Applications are processed on a rolling basis. *Application fee:* $25 ($100 for international students). *Application Contact:* Dr. Gary Stanlake, Dean of Graduate Studies, 915-670-1298, Fax: 915-670-1564, E-mail: gradoff@hsutx.edu. *Dean,* Dr. M. Vernon Davis, 915-670-5866, Fax: 915-670-1406, E-mail: theo@hsutx.edu.

School of Business Students: 11 full-time (6 women), 22 part-time (9 women); includes 2 minority (1 African American, 1 Hispanic American) Average age 33. 11 applicants, 100% accepted, 6 enrolled. *Faculty:* 9 full-time (1 woman), 2 part-time/adjunct (0 women). Expenses: Contact institution. *Financial support:* In 2001–02, 13 students received support; fellowships with full and partial tuition reimbursements available, career-related internships or fieldwork, Federal Work-Study, scholarships/grants, and tuition waivers (full and partial) available. Support available to part-time students. Financial award application deadline: 3/15; financial award applicants required to submit FAFSA. In 2001, 1 degree awarded. *Degree program information:* Part-time and evening/weekend programs available. Offers business (MBA). *Application deadline:* For fall admission, 8/15 (priority date); for spring admission, 1/5 (priority date). Applications are processed on a rolling basis. *Application fee:* $25 ($100 for international students). *Application Contact:* Dr. Gary Stanlake, Dean of Graduate Studies, 915-670-1298, Fax: 915-670-1564, E-mail: gradoff@hsutx.edu. *Dean,* Dr. Jimmie Monhollan, 915-670-1508, Fax: 915-670-1523, E-mail: jmonholl@hsutx.edu.

School of Music Students: 1 (woman) full-time, 4 part-time (2 women). Average age 28. 2 applicants, 100% accepted, 1 enrolled. *Faculty:* 11 full-time (4 women). Expenses: Contact institution. *Financial support:* In 2001–02, 5 students received support, including 3 fellowships with partial tuition reimbursements available (averaging $1,027 per year); career-related internships or fieldwork, Federal Work-Study, scholarships/grants, and tuition waivers (full and partial) also available. Support available to part-time students. Financial award application deadline: 3/15; financial award applicants required to submit FAFSA. *Degree program information:* Part-time programs available. Offers church music (MM); music education (MM); music performance (MM); theory-composition (MM). *Application deadline:* For fall admission, 8/15 (priority date); for spring admission, 1/5 (priority date). Applications are processed on a rolling basis. *Application fee:* $25 ($100 for international students). *Application Contact:* Dr. Gary Stanlake, Dean of Graduate Studies, 915-670-1298, Fax:

915-670-1564, E-mail: gradoff@hsutx.edu. *Director*, Dr. Leigh Anne Hunsaker, 915-670-1391, Fax: 915-670-5873, E-mail: hunsaker@hsutx.edu.

School of Nursing Students: 1 (woman) full-time, 7 part-time (all women); includes 1 minority (Hispanic American) Average age 36. 2 applicants, 100% accepted, 1 enrolled. *Faculty:* 3 full-time (all women), 1 part-time/adjunct (0 women). Expenses: Contact institution. *Financial support:* In 2001–02, 2 students received support. Career-related internships or fieldwork, Federal Work-Study, scholarships/grants, and tuition waivers (full and partial) available. Support available to part-time students. Financial award application deadline: 3/15; financial award applicants required to submit FAFSA. In 2001, 2 degrees awarded. *Degree program information:* Part-time programs available. Offers advanced healthcare delivery (MSN); family nurse practitioner (MSN). *Application deadline:* For fall admission, 8/15 (priority date); for spring admission, 1/5 (priority date). Applications are processed on a rolling basis. *Application fee:* $25 ($100 for international students). *Application Contact:* Dr. Gary Stanlake, Dean of Graduate Studies, 915-670-1298, Fax: 915-670-1564, E-mail: gradoff@hsutx.edu. *Dean*, Dr. Cecilia Tiller, 915-672-2441, Fax: 915-670-1564, E-mail: aisn@abilene.com.

HARTFORD SEMINARY, Hartford, CT 06105-2279

General Information Independent-religious, coed, graduate-only institution. *Graduate faculty:* 31. *Tuition:* Part-time $975 per course. *Required fees:* $1,020 per course. *Graduate housing:* On-campus housing not available. *Student services:* Career counseling, international student services. *Collection:* 72,000 titles, 300 serial subscriptions.

Computer facilities: 4 computers available on campus for general student use. A campuswide network can be accessed. Internet access is available. *Web address:* http://www.hartsem.edu/.

General Application Contact: Marilyn Garcia, Administrative Assistant, Admissions, 860-509-9512, Fax: 860-509-9509, E-mail: garcia@hartsem.edu.

GRADUATE UNITS

Graduate Programs Students: 132. *Faculty:* 12 full-time (5 women), 19 part-time/adjunct (7 women). Expenses: Contact institution. *Financial support:* In 2001–02, 33 students received support. Tuition waivers (partial) available. Support available to part-time students. Financial award application deadline: 7/15. *Degree program information:* Part-time and evening/weekend programs available. Offers black ministry (Certificate); Islamic studies (MA); ministerios Hispanos (Certificate); ministry (D Min); religious studies (MA); women's leadership institute (Certificate). *Application deadline:* Applications are processed on a rolling basis. *Application fee:* $35. *Application Contact:* Dr. Kelton Cobb, Academic Adviser, 860-509-9513, Fax: 860-509-9509, E-mail: kcobb@hartsem.edu. *Dean*, Dr. Ian Markham, 860-509-9554.

HARVARD UNIVERSITY, Cambridge, MA 02138

General Information Independent, coed, university. CGS member. *Enrollment:* 11,555 full-time matriculated graduate/professional students (5,391 women), 977 part-time matriculated graduate/professional students (575 women). *Enrollment by degree level:* 2,715 first professional, 5,167 master's, 4,230 doctoral, 420 other advanced degrees. *Graduate faculty:* 2,378. *Tuition:* Full-time $23,370. *Required fees:* $816. Full-time tuition and fees vary according to program and student level. *Graduate housing:* Rooms and/or apartments available to single and married students. Housing application deadline: 5/1. *Student services:* Campus employment opportunities, campus safety program, career counseling, child daycare facilities, disabled student services, exercise/wellness program, free psychological counseling, grant writing training, international student services, low-cost health insurance, multicultural affairs office, teacher training, writing training. *Library facilities:* Widener Library plus 90 others. *Collection:* 13.4 million titles, 97,568 serial subscriptions. *Research affiliation:* Woods Hole Oceanographic Institution (biology), Villa i Tatti (Italian and Renaissance studies), Dumbarton Oaks (pre-Columbian civilization, landscape architecture, international relations, Byzantine art), Center for Hellenic Studies (Greek studies).

Computer facilities: A campuswide network can be accessed from student residence rooms and from off campus. Internet access is available. *Web address:* http://www.harvard.edu/.

GRADUATE UNITS

Business School Students: 1,912 full-time (664 women). Expenses: Contact institution. *Financial support:* Fellowships, research assistantships, teaching assistantships, career-related internships or fieldwork, institutionally sponsored loans, and tuition waivers (full) available. Offers business (MBA, DBA, PhD); business administration (DBA); business economics (PhD); health policy management (PhD); information and technology management (PhD); organizational behavior (PhD). *Dean*, Prof. Kim B. Clark, 617-495-6000.

Divinity School Students: 478 (271 women); includes 86 minority (41 African Americans, 23 Asian Americans or Pacific Islanders, 18 Hispanic Americans, 4 Native Americans) 52 international. Average age 31. 629 applicants, 42% accepted. *Faculty:* 37 full-time (12 women), 39 part-time/adjunct (16 women). Expenses: Contact institution. *Financial support:* In 2001–02, 356 students received support, including 324 fellowships with tuition reimbursements available (averaging $11,388 per year); teaching assistantships, career-related internships or fieldwork, Federal Work-Study, and scholarships/grants also available. Support available to part-time students. Financial award application deadline: 2/1; financial award applicants required to submit CSS PROFILE or FAFSA. In 2001, 63 first professional degrees, 102 master's, 6 doctorates awarded. Offers divinity (M Div, MTS, Th M, PhD, Th D). *Application deadline:* For fall admission, 2/1 (priority date); for spring admission, 12/1. *Application fee:* $50. *Application Contact:* Anne S. Gardner, Assistant Dean for Admissions and Financial Aid, 617-495-5796, Fax: 617-495-0345, E-mail: anne_gardner@harvard.edu. *Acting Dean*, William A. Graham, 917-495-4513, Fax: 617-496-8026.

Extension School Average age 33. *Faculty:* 450 part-time/adjunct. Expenses: Contact institution. *Financial support:* In 2001–02, 213 students received support. Scholarships/grants available. Support available to part-time students. Financial award application deadline: 8/11; financial award applicants required to submit FAFSA. In 2001, 79 master's, 303 Diplomas awarded. *Degree program information:* Part-time and evening/weekend programs available. Offers applied sciences (CAS); English for graduate and professional studies (DGP); environmental management (CEM); information technology (ALM); liberal arts (ALM); museum studies (CMS); premedical studies (Diploma); public health (CPH); publication and communication (CPC); special studies in administration and management (CSS); technologies of education (CTE). *Application deadline:* Applications are processed on a rolling basis. *Application fee:* $75. *Application Contact:* Program Director, 617-495-4024, Fax: 617-495-9176. *Dean*, Michael Shinagel.

Graduate School of Arts and Sciences Offers African history (PhD); Akkadian and Sumerian (AM, PhD); American history (PhD); ancient art (PhD); ancient Near Eastern art (PhD); ancient, medieval, early modern, and modern Europe (PhD); anthropology and Middle Eastern studies (PhD); Arabic (AM, PhD); archaeology (PhD); architecture (PhD); Armenian (AM, PhD); arts and sciences (MD, AM, ME, MFS, SM, PhD, Sc D); astronomy (AM, PhD); astrophysics (AM, PhD); baroque art (PhD); biblical history (AM, PhD); biochemical chemistry (AM, PhD); biological anthropology (PhD); biological chemistry and molecular pharmacology (PhD); biological sciences in public health (PhD); biology (PhD); biophysics (PhD); business economics (AM, PhD); Byzantine art (PhD); Byzantine Greek (PhD); cell biology (PhD); chemical physics (PhD); chemistry (AM); Chinese (AM, PhD); Chinese studies (AM); classical archaeology (AM, PhD); classical art (PhD); classical philology (AM, PhD); classical philosophy (PhD); comparative literature (PhD); composition (AM, PhD); critical theory (AM, PhD); descriptive linguistics (AM, PhD); diplomatic history (PhD); earth and planetary sciences (AM, PhD); East Asian history (PhD); economic and social history (PhD); economics (AM, PhD); economics and Middle Eastern studies (PhD); eighteenth-century literature (AM, PhD); experimental pathology (PhD); experimental physics (AM, PhD); fine arts and Middle Eastern studies (PhD); forest science (MFS); French (AM, PhD); genetics (PhD); German (AM, PhD); health policy (PhD); Hebrew (AM, PhD); historical linguistics (AM, PhD); history and East Asian languages (PhD); history and Middle Eastern studies (PhD); history of American civilization (PhD); history of science (AM, PhD); immunology (PhD); Indian art (PhD); Indian philosophy (AM, PhD); Indo-Muslim culture (AM, PhD); Inner Asian and Altaic studies (PhD); inorganic chemistry (AM, PhD); intellectual history (PhD); Iranian (AM, PhD); Irish (AM, PhD); Islamic art (PhD); Italian (AM, PhD); Japanese (AM, PhD); Japanese and Chinese art (PhD); Japanese studies (AM); Jewish history and literature (AM, PhD); Korean (AM, PhD); Korean studies (AM); landscape architecture (PhD); Latin American history (PhD); legal anthropology (AM); literature: nineteenth-century to the present (AM, PhD); mathematics (AM, PhD); medical anthropology (AM); medical engineering/medical physics (PhD, Sc D); medieval art (PhD); medieval Latin (PhD); medieval literature and language (AM, PhD); microbiology and molecular genetics (PhD); modern art (PhD); modern British and American literature (AM, PhD); molecular and cellular biology (PhD); Mongolian (AM, PhD); Mongolian studies (AM); musicology (AM); musicology and ethnomusicology (PhD); Near Eastern history (PhD); neurobiology (PhD); oceanic history (PhD); oral literature (PhD); organic chemistry (AM, PhD); organizational behavior (PhD); Pali (AM, PhD); pathology (PhD); Persian (AM, PhD); philosophy (PhD); physical chemistry (AM, PhD); physics (AM); Polish (AM, PhD); political economy and government (PhD); political science (AM, PhD); Portuguese (AM, PhD); psychology (AM, PhD); public policy (PhD); regional studies–Middle East (AM); regional studies–Russia, Eastern Europe, and Central Asia (AM); Renaissance and modern architecture (PhD); Renaissance art (PhD); Renaissance literature (AM, PhD); Russian (AM, PhD); Sanskrit (AM, PhD); Scandinavian (AM, PhD); Semitic philology (AM, PhD); Serbo-Croatian (AM, PhD); Slavic philology (AM, PhD); social anthropology (AM, PhD); social change and development (AM); social psychology (AM, PhD); sociology (AM, PhD); Spanish (AM, PhD); statistics (AM, PhD); study of religion (AM, PhD); Syro-Palestinian archaeology (AM, PhD); theoretical linguistics (AM, PhD); theoretical physics (AM, PhD); theory (AM, PhD); Tibetan (AM, PhD); Turkish (AM, PhD); Ukrainian (AM, PhD); urban planning (PhD); Urdu (AM, PhD); Vietnamese (AM, PhD); Vietnamese studies (AM); virology (PhD); Welsh (AM, PhD). Electronic applications accepted.

Division of Engineering and Applied Sciences Offers applied mathematics (ME, SM, PhD); applied physics (ME, SM, PhD); computer science (ME, SM, PhD); computing technology (PhD); engineering science (ME); engineering sciences (SM, PhD); medical engineering/medical physics (PhD, Sc D).

Graduate School of Design Students: 540 full-time (251 women); includes 120 minority (15 African Americans, 81 Asian Americans or Pacific Islanders, 22 Hispanic Americans, 2 Native Americans), 203 international. Average age 30. 1,135 applicants, 29% accepted. *Faculty:* 38 full-time (13 women), 104 part-time/adjunct (21 women). Expenses: Contact institution. *Financial support:* Fellowships, research assistantships, teaching assistantships, Federal Work-Study available. Support available to part-time students. Financial award application deadline: 1/1; financial award applicants required to submit CSS PROFILE or FAFSA. In 2001, 220 master's, 9 doctorates awarded. Offers architecture (M Arch); design (M Arch, M Des S, MAUD, MLA, MLAUD, MUP, Dr DES); design studies (M Des S); landscape architecture (MLA); urban planning (MUP); urban planning and design (MAUD, MLAUD). *Application fee:* $60. Electronic applications accepted. *Application Contact:* Gail Gustafson, Director of Admissions, 617-496-1238, Fax: 617-495-8949, E-mail: ggustafson@gsd.harvard.edu. *Dean*, Dr. Peter G. Rowe, 617-495-4237.

Graduate School of Education Students: 888 full-time (648 women), 208 part-time (157 women); includes 269 minority (85 African Americans, 88 Asian Americans or Pacific Islanders, 87 Hispanic Americans, 9 Native Americans), 122 international. Average age 32. 1,747 applicants, 48% accepted, 631 enrolled. *Faculty:* 50 full-time (29 women), 67 part-time/adjunct (35 women). Expenses: Contact institution. *Financial support:* In 2001–02, 757 students received support, including 85 fellowships (averaging $20,915 per year), 33 research assistantships, 236 teaching assistantships; career-related internships or fieldwork, Federal Work-Study, and scholarships/grants also available. Support available to part-time students. Financial award application deadline: 2/3; financial award applicants required to submit FAFSA. In 2001, 599 master's, 54 doctorates, 5 other advanced degrees awarded. *Degree program information:* Part-time programs available. Offers administration, planning and social policy (Ed M, CAS); arts in education (Ed M); community and schools (Ed D); education (Ed M, Ed D, CAS); education in the community (Ed D); elementary and secondary education (Ed D); gender studies (Ed M); higher education (Ed M, Ed D); human development and psychology (Ed M, Ed D, CAS); individualized program (Ed M); international education (Ed D); international education policy (Ed M); language and literacy (Ed M, Ed D, CAS); learning and teaching (Ed M, Ed D); mid-career mathematics and science (teaching certification) (Ed M, CAS); mind brain and education (Ed M); philosophy of education and curriculum theory (Ed D); research (Ed D); risk and prevention (Ed M, CAS); schools and schooling (Ed D); teaching and curriculum (teaching certification) (Ed M); technology in education (Ed M); urban superintendency (Ed D). *Application deadline:* For fall admission, 1/2. *Application fee:* $65. *Application Contact:* Roland A. Hence, Director of Admissions, 617-495-3414, Fax: 617-496-3577, E-mail: gseadmissions@harvard.edu. *Dean*, Ellen C. Lagemann, 617-495-3401.

John F. Kennedy School of Government Students: 558 full-time (236 women); includes 105 minority (34 African Americans, 36 Asian Americans or Pacific Islanders, 30 Hispanic Americans, 5 Native Americans), 229 international. Average age 31. 1,886 applicants, 44% accepted, 558 enrolled. *Faculty:* 70. Expenses: Contact institution. *Financial support:* Fellowships, research assistantships, teaching assistantships, career-related internships or fieldwork, Federal Work-Study, institutionally sponsored loans, and scholarships/grants available. Support available to part-time students. Financial award applicants required to submit CSS PROFILE or FAFSA. Offers government (MPA, MPAID, MPP, MPPUP, PhD); political economy and government (PhD); public administration (MPA); public administration and international development (MPAID); public policy (MPP, PhD); public policy and urban planning (MPPUP). *Application fee:* $80. Electronic applications accepted. *Application Contact:* Office of Admissions, 617-495-1155, E-mail: ksg_admissions@harvard.edu. *Dean*, Dr. Joseph Nye.

Law School Offers law (JD, LL M, SJD).

Medical School Students: 728 full-time (338 women); includes 342 minority (86 African Americans, 182 Asian Americans or Pacific Islanders, 65 Hispanic Americans, 9 Native Americans), 24 international. 4,589 applicants, 5% accepted, 167 enrolled. *Faculty:* 5,787 full-time, 2,881 part-time/adjunct. Expenses: Contact institution. *Financial support:* In 2001–02, 500 students received support; fellowships, research assistantships, teaching assistantships, career-related internships or fieldwork, Federal Work-Study, institutionally sponsored loans, scholarships/grants, and tuition waivers (full and partial) available. Financial award application deadline: 3/31; financial award applicants required to submit CSS PROFILE or FAFSA. In 2001, 165 degrees awarded. Offers medicine (MD, SM, PhD, Sc D). *Application deadline:* For fall admission, 10/15. *Application fee:* $75. Electronic applications accepted. *Application Contact:* 617-432-1550, Fax: 617-432-3307, E-mail: admissions_office@hms.harvard.edu. *Dean*, Dr. Joseph B. Martin, 617-432-1501.

Division of Health Sciences and Technology Offers applied physics (PhD); engineering sciences (PhD); medical engineering/medical physics (PhD, Sc D); medical informatics (SM); medical sciences (MD); physics (PhD); speech and hearing sciences (PhD, Sc D).

Division of Medical Sciences Offers medical sciences (PhD).

School of Dental Medicine Students: 258 full-time. Expenses: Contact institution. *Financial support:* Federal Work-Study, institutionally sponsored loans, and scholarships/grants available. Financial award applicants required to submit CSS PROFILE or FAFSA. In 2001, 28 first professional degrees, 16 master's, 7 doctorates awarded. Offers advanced general dentistry (Certificate); dental medicine (DMD, M Med Sc, D Med Sc, Certificate); dental public health (Certificate); endodontics (Certificate); general practice residency (Certificate); oral biology (M Med Sc, D Med Sc); oral pathology (Certificate); oral surgery (Certificate); orthodontics (Certificate); pediatric dentistry (Certificate); periodontics (Certificate); prosthodontics (Certificate). *Application Contact:* Director of Admissions and Student Affairs, 617-432-1443, Fax: 617-432-3881, E-mail: hsdm_admissions@hsdm.harvard.edu. *Dean*, Dr. R. Bruce Donoff, 617-432-1401, Fax: 617-432-4266, E-mail: bruce_donoff@hsdm.harvard.edu.

School of Public Health Students: 619 full-time (413 women), 161 part-time (73 women); includes 145 minority (37 African Americans, 83 Asian Americans or Pacific Islanders, 22 Hispanic Americans, 3 Native Americans), 205 international. Average age 33. 1,243 applicants, 58% accepted, 442 enrolled. *Faculty:* 136 full-time (40 women), 210 part-time/adjunct (59 women). Expenses: Contact institution. *Financial support:* Fellowships, research assistantships, teaching assistantships, career-related internships or fieldwork, Federal Work-Study, scholarships/grants, traineeships, tuition waivers (partial), and unspecified assistantships

Harvard University (continued)

available. Support available to part-time students. Financial award application deadline: 2/12; financial award applicants required to submit FAFSA. In 2001, 344 master's, 49 doctorates awarded. *Degree program information:* Part-time programs available. Offers biostatistics (SM, SD); cancer cell biology (PhD); clinical effectiveness (MPH); environmental epidemiology (SM, DPH, SD); environmental health (SM); environmental science and engineering (SM, SD); epidemiology (SM, DPH, SD); epidemiology/international nutrition (DPH, SD); family and community health (MPH); health and social behavior (SM, DPH, SD); health care management (MPH); health policy and management (SM, DPH, SD); immunology and infectious diseases (DPH, SD); international health (MPH); law and public health (MPH); maternal and child health (SM, DPH, SD); occupational and environmental health (MPH); occupational health (MOH, SM, DPH, SD); physiology (SD); population and international health (SM, DPH, SD); public health (MOH, MPH, SM, DPH, PhD, SD); quantitative methods (MPH). *Application deadline:* For fall admission, 12/15. *Application fee:* $60. Electronic applications accepted. *Application Contact:* Vincent W. James, Director of Admissions, 617-432-1031, Fax: 617-432-2009, E-mail: admisofc@hsph.harvard.edu. *Dean,* Dr. Barry R. Bloom, 617-432-1025, Fax: 617-277-5320.

Division of Biological Sciences Students: 37 full-time (21 women); includes 18 minority (4 African Americans, 10 Asian Americans or Pacific Islanders, 4 Hispanic Americans), 4 international. Average age 31. 69 applicants, 22% accepted. *Faculty:* 51 full-time (10 women), 3 part-time/adjunct (1 woman). Expenses: Contact institution. *Financial support:* Fellowships with full tuition reimbursements, teaching assistantships, scholarships/grants, traineeships, tuition waivers (partial), and unspecified assistantships available. In 2001, 2 degrees awarded. Offers biological sciences (PhD). *Application deadline:* For fall admission, 12/15. *Application fee:* $60. Electronic applications accepted. *Application Contact:* Ruth Kenworthy, Program Administrator, 617-432-4470, Fax: 617-432-0433, E-mail: kenworthy@cvlab.harvard.edu. *Director,* Dr. Dyann F. Wirth, 617-432-4470, Fax: 617-432-0433, E-mail: rkenwort@hsph.harvard.edu.

See in-depth description on page 899.

HASTINGS COLLEGE, Hastings, NE 68901-7696

General Information Independent-religious, coed, comprehensive institution. *Graduate housing:* On-campus housing not available.

GRADUATE UNITS

Program in Teacher Education *Degree program information:* Part-time programs available. Offers teacher education (MAT).

HAWAI'I PACIFIC UNIVERSITY, Honolulu, HI 96813-2785

General Information Independent, coed, comprehensive institution. *Enrollment:* 691 full-time matriculated graduate/professional students (317 women), 583 part-time matriculated graduate/professional students (255 women). *Enrollment by degree level:* 1,274 master's. *Graduate faculty:* 47 full-time (19 women), 38 part-time/adjunct (18 women). *Tuition:* Full-time $7,380; part-time $410 per credit. *Graduate housing:* Room and/or apartments available to single students; on-campus housing not available to married students. Typical cost: $8,530 (including board). Housing application deadline: 8/1. *Student services:* Campus employment opportunities, campus safety program, career counseling, international student services, low-cost health insurance. *Library facilities:* Meader Library plus 2 others. *Online resources:* library catalog, web page, access to other libraries' catalogs. *Collection:* 160,000 titles, 11,000 serial subscriptions, 8,695 audiovisual materials. *Research affiliation:* Oceanic Institute (marine science), Hawaii Institute of Marine Biology (marine science).

Computer facilities: 418 computers available on campus for general student use. A campuswide network can be accessed from student residence rooms and from off campus. Internet access is available. *Web address:* http://www.hpu.edu/.

General Application Contact: Jose Rosal, Admissions Coordinator, 808-544-1135, Fax: 800-544-0280, E-mail: gradservctr@hpu.edu.

GRADUATE UNITS

Division of Arts and Sciences Students: 66. Average age 30. 34 applicants, 91% accepted, 18 enrolled. *Faculty:* 2 full-time (0 women), 3 part-time/adjunct (1 woman). Expenses: Contact institution. *Financial support:* Career-related internships or fieldwork, Federal Work-Study, and unspecified assistantships available. Support available to part-time students. Financial award application deadline: 3/1; financial award applicants required to submit FAFSA. In 2001, 1 degree awarded. Offers diplomacy and military studies (MA); political science (MA). *Application deadline:* Applications are processed on a rolling basis. *Application fee:* $50. Electronic applications accepted. *Application Contact:* Jose Rosal, Admissions Coordinator, 808-544-1135, Fax: 800-544-0280, E-mail: gradservctr@hpu.edu. *Associate Vice President and Dean,* Dr. Leslie Correa, 808-549-9340, Fax: 808-544-9306, E-mail: lcorrea@hpu.edu.

Division of Business Administration Students: 568. Average age 30. 321 applicants, 78% accepted, 133 enrolled. *Faculty:* 15 full-time (3 women), 20 part-time/adjunct (6 women). Expenses: Contact institution. *Financial support:* Research assistantships, career-related internships or fieldwork, Federal Work-Study, and unspecified assistantships available. Support available to part-time students. Financial award application deadline: 3/1; financial award applicants required to submit FAFSA. In 2001, 243 degrees awarded. *Degree program information:* Part-time and evening/weekend programs available. Offers accounting (MBA); finance (MBA); human resource management (MBA); information systems (MBA); international business (MBA); management (MBA); marketing (MBA); not-for-profit management (MBA); quality management (MBA); travel industry management (MBA). *Application deadline:* Applications are processed on a rolling basis. *Application fee:* $50. Electronic applications accepted. *Application Contact:* Jose Rosal, Admissions Coordinator, 808-544-1135, Fax: 800-544-0280, E-mail: gradservctr@hpu.edu. *Dean,* Dr. Rodney Romig, 808-544-0283, E-mail: rromig@hpu.edu.

Division of Communication Students: 71. 70 applicants, 99% accepted, 39 enrolled. *Faculty:* 3 full-time (2 women), 5 part-time/adjunct (4 women). Expenses: Contact institution. *Financial support:* Career-related internships or fieldwork, Federal Work-Study, and unspecified assistantships available. Support available to part-time students. Financial award application deadline: 3/1; financial award applicants required to submit FAFSA. *Degree program information:* Part-time and evening/weekend programs available. Offers communication (MA). *Application deadline:* Applications are processed on a rolling basis. *Application fee:* $50. Electronic applications accepted. *Application Contact:* Jose Rosal, Admissions Coordinator, 808-544-1135, Fax: 800-544-0280, E-mail: gradservctr@hpu.edu. *Dean,* Dr. Helen Varner, 808-544-0824, Fax: 808-544-0835, E-mail: hvarner@hpu.edu.

Division of International Studies Students: 33. 20 applicants, 70% accepted, 12 enrolled. *Faculty:* 6 full-time (4 women), 2 part-time/adjunct (both women). Expenses: Contact institution. *Financial support:* Career-related internships or fieldwork, Federal Work-Study, and unspecified assistantships available. Support available to part-time students. Financial award application deadline: 3/1; financial award applicants required to submit FAFSA. *Degree program information:* Part-time and evening/weekend programs available. Offers teaching English as a second language (MA). *Application deadline:* Applications are processed on a rolling basis. *Application fee:* $50. Electronic applications accepted. *Application Contact:* Jose Rosal, Admissions Coordinator, 808-544-1135, Fax: 800-544-0280, E-mail: gradservctr@hpu.edu. *Dean,* Dr. Jeanne Rellahan, 808-544-9392, Fax: 808-544-0834, E-mail: jrellaha@hpu.edu.

Division of Nursing Students: 46. Average age 32. 34 applicants, 94% accepted, 28 enrolled. *Faculty:* 8 full-time (7 women), 4 part-time/adjunct (3 women). Expenses: Contact institution. *Financial support:* Career-related internships or fieldwork, Federal Work-Study, and unspecified assistantships available. Support available to part-time students. Financial award application deadline: 3/1; financial award applicants required to submit FAFSA. In 2001, 4 degrees awarded. *Degree program information:* Part-time and evening/weekend programs available. Offers community clinical nurse specialist (MSN); family nurse practitioner (MSN). *Application deadline:* Applications are processed on a rolling basis. *Application fee:* $50. Electronic applications accepted. *Application Contact:* Jose Rosal, Admissions Coordinator, 808-544-1135, Fax: 800-544-0280, E-mail: gradservctr@hpu.edu. *Dean,* Dr. Carol Winters-Moorhead, 808-236-3552, Fax: 808-236-5818, E-mail: cwinters@hpu.edu.

Division of Professional Studies Students: 490. 363 applicants, 85% accepted, 132 enrolled. *Faculty:* 13 full-time (3 women), 4 part-time/adjunct (2 women). Expenses: Contact institution. *Financial support:* Career-related internships or fieldwork, Federal Work-Study, and unspecified assistantships available. Support available to part-time students. Financial award application deadline: 3/1; financial award applicants required to submit FAFSA. In 2001, 150 degrees awarded. *Degree program information:* Part-time and evening/weekend programs available. Offers human resource management (MA); information systems management (MSIS); information systems technology (MSIS); management (MA); organizational change (MA). *Application deadline:* Applications are processed on a rolling basis. *Application fee:* $50. Electronic applications accepted. *Application Contact:* Jose Rosal, Admissions Coordinator, 808-544-1135, Fax: 800-544-0280, E-mail: gradservctr@hpu.edu. *Dean,* Dr. Larry Zimmerman, 808-544-9373, Fax: 808-544-0247, E-mail: lzimmerm@hpu.edu.

See in-depth description on page 901.

HEBREW COLLEGE, Newton Centre, MA 02459

General Information Independent-religious, coed, comprehensive institution. *Graduate faculty:* 6 full-time (1 woman), 19 part-time/adjunct (7 women). *Tuition:* Part-time $550 per credit. *Graduate housing:* On-campus housing not available. *Student services:* Career counseling, international student services, low-cost health insurance, teacher training. *Library facilities:* Jacob and Rose Grossman Library. *Online resources:* web page. *Collection:* 110,000 titles, 275 serial subscriptions, 1,454 audiovisual materials.

Computer facilities: 4 computers available on campus for general student use. Internet access is available. *Web address:* http://www.hebrewcollege.edu/.

General Application Contact: Melissa Roiter, Assistant to the Dean of Students, 617-559-8610, Fax: 617-559-8601, E-mail: admissions@hebrewcollege.edu.

GRADUATE UNITS

Program in Jewish Studies Average age 30. 20 applicants, 100% accepted, 19 enrolled. *Faculty:* 6 full-time (1 woman), 19 part-time/adjunct (7 women). Expenses: Contact institution. *Financial support:* Fellowships, teaching assistantships, tuition waivers (partial) available. Support available to part-time students. Financial award application deadline: 4/15. *Degree program information:* Part-time and evening/weekend programs available. Postbaccalaureate distance learning degree programs offered. Offers Jewish cantorial arts (Certificate); Jewish communal and clinical social work (Certificate); Jewish music (Certificate); Jewish studies (MA); management of Jewish philanthropic and community organizations (Certificate). *Application deadline:* For fall admission, 5/31 (priority date). Applications are processed on a rolling basis. *Application fee:* $40. *Application Contact:* Melissa Roiter, Assistant to Dean of Students, 617-559-8610, Fax: 617-559-8601, E-mail: admissions@hebrewcollege.edu. *Provost,* Dr. Barry Mesch, 617-559-8600, Fax: 617-559-8601, E-mail: bmesch@hebrewcollege.edu.

Shoolman Graduate School of Education Average age 37. 10 applicants, 100% accepted, 10 enrolled. *Faculty:* 6 full-time (1 woman), 19 part-time/adjunct (7 women). Expenses: Contact institution. *Financial support:* Fellowships, teaching assistantships, career-related internships or fieldwork and tuition waivers (partial) available. Support available to part-time students. Financial award application deadline: 4/15. In 2001, 5 degrees awarded. *Degree program information:* Part-time and evening/weekend programs available. Postbaccalaureate distance learning degree programs offered. Offers early childhood Jewish education (Certificate); Jewish day school education (Certificate); Jewish education (MJ Ed); Jewish family education (Certificate); Jewish special education (Certificate); Jewish youth education, informal education and camping (Certificate). *Application deadline:* For fall admission, 5/1 (priority date). Applications are processed on a rolling basis. *Application fee:* $40. *Application Contact:* Melissa Roiter, Assistant to Dean of Students, 617-559-8610, Fax: 617-559-8601, E-mail: admissions@hebrewcollege.edu. *Dean,* Dr. Harvey Shapiro, 617-559-8600, Fax: 617-559-8601, E-mail: hshapiro@hebrewcollege.edu.

See in-depth description on page 903.

HEBREW THEOLOGICAL COLLEGE, Skokie, IL 60077-3263

General Information Independent-religious, men only, comprehensive institution. *Library facilities:* Saul Silber Memorial Library plus 2 others. *Collection:* 63,000 titles, 60 serial subscriptions.

Computer facilities: 30 computers available on campus for general student use. A campuswide network can be accessed. Internet access is available. *Web address:* http://www.htcnet.edu/.

GRADUATE UNITS

Department of Talmud and Rabbinics Expenses: Contact institution. Offers Talmud and rabbinics (Rabbi).

HEBREW UNION COLLEGE–JEWISH INSTITUTE OF RELIGION, Los Angeles, CA 90007-3796

General Information Independent-religious, coed, graduate-only institution. *Graduate faculty:* 20 full-time (9 women), 20 part-time/adjunct (8 women). *Tuition:* Full-time $8,500; part-time $355 per unit. *Required fees:* $373; $348 per unit. *Graduate housing:* On-campus housing not available. *Student services:* Campus employment opportunities, career counseling, grant writing training, international student services, low-cost health insurance. *Library facilities:* Frances-Henry Library plus 1 other. *Online resources:* library catalog, web page, access to other libraries' catalogs. *Collection:* 115,000 titles, 850 serial subscriptions, 2,000 audiovisual materials.

Computer facilities: 12 computers available on campus for general student use. A campuswide network can be accessed from off campus. Internet access is available. *Web address:* http://www.huc.edu/.

General Application Contact: Lisa Kaplan, Director of Admissions and Recruitment, 213-749-3424, Fax: 213-747-6128, E-mail: lkaplan@huc.edu.

GRADUATE UNITS

Edgar F. Magnin School of Graduate Studies Students: 4 full-time (all women), 2 part-time (both women). Average age 45. 3 applicants, 100% accepted, 2 enrolled. Expenses: Contact institution. *Financial support:* In 2001–02, 2 students received support, including teaching assistantships (averaging $12,000 per year); fellowships, career-related internships or fieldwork, scholarships/grants, and unspecified assistantships also available. Financial award application deadline: 3/15; financial award applicants required to submit FAFSA. *Degree program information:* Part-time programs available. *Application deadline:* For fall admission, 3/1. Applications are processed on a rolling basis. *Application fee:* $55. *Application Contact:* Lisa Kaplan, Director of Admissions and Recruitment, 213-749-3424, Fax: 213-747-6128, E-mail: lkaplan@huc.edu. *Director,* Dr. Reuven Firestone, 213-749-3424, Fax: 213-747-6128, E-mail: rfirestone@huc.edu.

Irwin Daniels School of Jewish Communal Services Students: 22 full-time (17 women), 1 (woman) part-time. Average age 26. 24 applicants, 71% accepted, 11 enrolled. *Faculty:* 3 full-time (1 woman), 9 part-time/adjunct (2 women). Expenses: Contact institution. *Financial support:* Career-related internships or fieldwork and scholarships/grants available. Financial award application deadline: 3/1; financial award applicants required to submit FAFSA. In 2001, 10 degrees awarded. Offers Jewish communal services (MAJCS, Certificate, MAJCS/MAJS). *Application deadline:* For fall admission, 2/15. *Application fee:* $55. *Application Contact:* Lisa Kaplan, Director of Admissions and Recruitment, 213-749-3424, Fax: 213-747-6128, E-mail: lkaplan@huc.edu. *Director,* Dr. Steven Windmueller, 213-749-3424, Fax: 213-747-6128, E-mail: swindmueller@huc.edu.

Rhea Hirsch School of Education Students: 9 full-time (7 women). Average age 25. 7 applicants, 71% accepted, 5 enrolled. *Faculty:* 3 full-time (2 women), 5 part-time/adjunct (3 women). Expenses: Contact institution. *Financial support:* Career-related internships or fieldwork and scholarships/grants available. Support available to part-time students. Financial award application deadline: 3/15; financial award applicants required to submit FAFSA. In 2001, 14 degrees awarded. Offers education (MAJE, PhD). *Application deadline:* For fall admission, 2/15. *Application fee:* $55. *Application Contact:* Lisa Kaplan, Director of Admissions and Recruitment, 213-749-3424, Fax: 213-747-6128, E-mail: lkaplan@huc.edu. *Director*, Sara Lee, 213-749-3424, Fax: 213-747-6128, E-mail: slee@huc.edu.

School of Rabbinic Studies Students: 33 full-time (19 women), 1 part-time, 2 international. 95 applicants, 67% accepted, 60 enrolled. *Faculty:* 14 full-time (5 women), 9 part-time/adjunct (3 women). Expenses: Contact institution. *Financial support:* Career-related internships or fieldwork and scholarships/grants available. Financial award application deadline: 3/15; financial award applicants required to submit FAFSA. In 2001, 10 degrees awarded. Offers rabbinic studies (MAHL). *Application deadline:* For fall admission, 10/31. *Application fee:* $75. *Application Contact:* Lisa Kaplan, Director of Admissions and Recruitment, 213-749-3424, Fax: 213-747-6128, E-mail: lkaplan@huc.edu. *Director*, Rabbi Richard Levy, 213-749-3424, Fax: 213-747-6128, E-mail: rlevy@huc.edu.

HEBREW UNION COLLEGE–JEWISH INSTITUTE OF RELIGION, New York, NY 10012-1186

General Information Independent-religious, coed, graduate-only institution. *Enrollment by degree level:* 61 first professional, 46 master's, 32 doctoral. *Graduate faculty:* 14 full-time (6 women), 43 part-time/adjunct (17 women). *Tuition:* Full-time $8,500; part-time $355 per credit hour. *Required fees:* $3,000; $355 per credit hour. One-time fee: $225 full-time. Part-time tuition and fees vary according to course load, degree level and program. *Graduate housing:* On-campus housing not available. *Student services:* Campus employment opportunities, career counseling, low-cost health insurance. *Library facilities:* Klau Library plus 1 other. *Online resources:* library catalog, access to other libraries' catalogs. *Collection:* 140,000 titles, 245 serial subscriptions.

Computer facilities: 4 computers available on campus for general student use. Internet access is available. *Web address:* http://www.huc.edu/.

General Application Contact: Cantor Ellen Dreskin, Associate Dean, 212-674-5300 Ext. 217, Fax: 212-388-1720, E-mail: edreskin@huc.edu.

GRADUATE UNITS

Rabbinical School Students: 60 full-time (36 women), 1 (woman) part-time. Average age 26. *Faculty:* 12 full-time (5 women), 23 part-time/adjunct (10 women). Expenses: Contact institution. *Financial support:* In 2001–02, 55 fellowships (averaging $10,000 per year) were awarded; career-related internships or fieldwork and scholarships/grants also available. Financial award application deadline: 6/1; financial award applicants required to submit FAFSA. Offers rabbinic studies (MAHL). *Application deadline:* For winter admission, 1/1 (priority date). *Application fee:* $35. *Application Contact:* Cantor Ellen Dreskin, Associate Dean, 212-674-5300 Ext. 217, Fax: 212-388-1720, E-mail: edreskin@huc.edu. *Dean*, Rabbi Aaron Panken, 212-674-5300 Ext. 219, Fax: 212-388-1720, E-mail: apanken@huc.edu.

School of Education Students: 6 full-time (4 women), 6 part-time (all women). Average age 32. *Faculty:* 10 full-time (4 women), 4 part-time/adjunct (2 women). Expenses: Contact institution. *Financial support:* Career-related internships or fieldwork and scholarships/grants available. Financial award application deadline: 6/1; financial award applicants required to submit FAFSA. In 2001, 4 degrees awarded. *Degree program information:* Part-time programs available. Offers education (MARE). *Application deadline:* Applications are processed on a rolling basis. *Application fee:* $35. *Application Contact:* Stacey Siepmann, Academic Assistant, 212-824-2252, Fax: 212-388-1720, E-mail: ssiepmann@huc.edu. *Director*, Jo Kay, 212-824-2213 Ext. 223, Fax: 212-388-1720, E-mail: jkay@huc.edu.

School of Graduate Studies Students: 22 full-time (9 women), 26 part-time (11 women). Average age 38. *Faculty:* 4 full-time (2 women), 28 part-time/adjunct (8 women). Expenses: Contact institution. *Financial support:* Applicants required to submit FAFSA. In 2001, 4 master's, 6 doctorates awarded. *Degree program information:* Part-time programs available. Offers Hebrew letters (DHL); Judaic studies (MAJS); pastoral counseling (D Min). *Application fee:* $35. *Coordinator*, Dr. Carol Ochs, 212-674-5300 Ext. 267, Fax: 212-388-1720.

School of Sacred Music Students: 30 full-time (21 women). Average age 26. 21 applicants, 57% accepted. *Faculty:* 4 full-time (2 women), 16 part-time/adjunct (7 women). Expenses: Contact institution. *Financial support:* Scholarships/grants available. Financial award application deadline: 6/1; financial award applicants required to submit FAFSA. In 2001, 11 degrees awarded. Offers sacred music (MSM). *Application deadline:* For winter admission, 1/5 (priority date). Applications are processed on a rolling basis. *Application fee:* $75. *Application Contact:* Cantor Ellen Dreskin, Associate Dean, 212-674-5300 Ext. 217, Fax: 212-388-1720, E-mail: edreskin@huc.edu. *Director*, Cantor Israel Goldstein, 212-674-5300 Ext. 225, Fax: 212-388-1720, E-mail: igoldstein@huc.edu.

HEBREW UNION COLLEGE–JEWISH INSTITUTE OF RELIGION, Cincinnati, OH 45220-2488

General Information Independent-religious, coed, graduate-only institution. CGS member. *Enrollment by degree level:* 61 master's, 62 doctoral. *Graduate faculty:* 18 full-time (2 women), 7 part-time/adjunct (3 women). *Tuition:* Full-time $8,500; part-time $355 per credit hour. *Required fees:* $355 per credit hour. *Graduate housing:* Room and/or apartments available on a first-come, first-served basis to single students; on-campus housing not available to married students. Typical cost: $2,000 per year. Housing application deadline: 7/31. *Student services:* Campus employment opportunities, campus safety program, career counseling, child daycare facilities, low-cost health insurance. *Library facilities:* Klau Library. *Online resources:* library catalog, web page. *Collection:* 430,000 titles, 2,250 serial subscriptions. *Research affiliation:* Union of American Hebrew Congregations (Jewish education, survey and analysis of reform education), Oriental Institute (neo-Babylonian texts).

Computer facilities: 4 computers available on campus for general student use. A campuswide network can be accessed from off campus. Internet access, CD-ROM databases are available. *Web address:* http://www.huc.edu/.

General Application Contact: Rabbi Kenneth E. Ehrlich, Dean of Rabbinic School, 513-221-1875, Fax: 513-221-0321, E-mail: kehrlich@huc.edu.

GRADUATE UNITS

Rabbinic School Students: 58 full-time (24 women); includes 1 minority (Hispanic American) Average age 30. 73 applicants, 71% accepted. *Faculty:* 18 full-time (2 women), 7 part-time/adjunct (3 women). Expenses: Contact institution. *Financial support:* In 2001–02, 42 students received support, including 1 teaching assistantship (averaging $2,000 per year); career-related internships or fieldwork, institutionally sponsored loans, and scholarships/grants also available. Financial award application deadline: 6/1; financial award applicants required to submit FAFSA. Offers rabbinic studies (MAHL). *Application deadline:* For fall admission, 11/1 (priority date); for spring admission, 12/18. *Application fee:* $75. *Application Contact:* Rabbi Roxanne J. Schneider, Dean of Admissions, 513-221-1875, Fax: 513-221-5372, E-mail: rschneider@huc.edu. *Dean*, Rabbi Kenneth E. Ehrlich, 513-221-1875 Ext. 227, Fax: 513-221-0321, E-mail: kehrlich@huc.edu.

School of Graduate Studies Students: 65 full-time (16 women), 1 part-time; includes 2 minority (1 African American, 1 Asian American or Pacific Islander), 8 international. Average age 35. 22 applicants, 64% accepted, 6 enrolled. *Faculty:* 17 full-time (2 women), 1 part-time/adjunct (0 women). Expenses: Contact institution. *Financial support:* In 2001–02, 30 students received support, including 20 fellowships with full and partial tuition reimbursements available (averaging $6,000 per year), 4 teaching assistantships with full and partial tuition reimbursements available (averaging $2,000 per year); institutionally sponsored loans, scholarships/grants, and tuition waivers (full and partial) also available. Financial award application deadline: 2/15; financial award applicants required to submit FAFSA. In 2001, 5 master's, 3 doctorates awarded. Offers Bible and the ancient Near East (M Phil, MA, PhD); Hebrew letters (DHL); history of biblical interpretation (M Phil, MA, PhD); Jewish and Christian studies in the Greco-Roman period (M Phil, PhD); Jewish and cognate studies (M Phil); Judaic and cognate studies (MA, PhD); modern Jewish history (M Phil, MA, PhD); philosophy and Jewish religious thought (M Phil, MA, PhD); rabbinics (M Phil, MA, PhD). *Application deadline:* For fall admission, 2/15. *Application fee:* $35. *Director of School of Graduate Studies*, Dr. Adam Kamesar, 513-221-1875, Fax: 513-221-0321, E-mail: akamesar@huc.edu.

HEIDELBERG COLLEGE, Tiffin, OH 44883-2462

General Information Independent-religious, coed, comprehensive institution. *Enrollment:* 14 full-time matriculated graduate/professional students (11 women), 158 part-time matriculated graduate/professional students (118 women). *Enrollment by degree level:* 172 master's. *Graduate faculty:* 3 full-time (1 woman), 13 part-time/adjunct (5 women). *Tuition:* Part-time $385 per credit hour. Tuition and fees vary according to program. *Graduate housing:* On-campus housing not available. *Student services:* Campus employment opportunities, career counseling, exercise/wellness program, free psychological counseling, international student services, multicultural affairs office, teacher training. *Library facilities:* Beeghly Library plus 1 other. *Online resources:* library catalog, web page. *Collection:* 260,055 titles, 829 serial subscriptions.

Computer facilities: 125 computers available on campus for general student use. A campuswide network can be accessed from student residence rooms and from off campus. Internet access and online class registration are available. *Web address:* http://www.heidelberg.edu/.

General Application Contact: 419-448-2288, Fax: 419-448-2124, E-mail: sallen@heidelberg.

GRADUATE UNITS

Department of Business Administration *Faculty:* 2 full-time (0 women), 4 part-time/adjunct (1 woman). Expenses: Contact institution. *Financial support:* Available to part-time students. Application deadline: 4/15; In 2001, 32 degrees awarded. *Degree program information:* Part-time and evening/weekend programs available. Offers business administration (MBA). *Application deadline:* For fall admission, 8/10. Applications are processed on a rolling basis. *Application fee:* $25. Electronic applications accepted. *Director of Graduate Studies in Business*, Dr. Henry G. Rennie, 419-448-2221, Fax: 419-448-2124, E-mail: hrennie@nike.heidelberg.edu.

Program in Counseling Students: 5 full-time (all women), 27 part-time (24 women). *Faculty:* 2 full-time (1 woman), 6 part-time/adjunct (4 women). Expenses: Contact institution. *Financial support:* In 2001–02, 1 teaching assistantship was awarded Support available to part-time students. Financial award application deadline: 4/15; financial award applicants required to submit FAFSA. In 2001, 6 degrees awarded. *Degree program information:* Part-time and evening/weekend programs available. Offers counseling (MA). *Application deadline:* Applications are processed on a rolling basis. *Application fee:* $25. Electronic applications accepted. *Interim Director*, Dr. Jo-Ann Lipford Sanders, 419-448-2312, Fax: 419-448-2124, E-mail: jsanders@heidelberg.edu.

Program in Education Students: 8 full-time (6 women), 75 part-time (65 women). *Faculty:* 5 part-time/adjunct (2 women). Expenses: Contact institution. *Financial support:* Available to part-time students. Application deadline: 4/15; In 2001, 26 degrees awarded. *Degree program information:* Part-time and evening/weekend programs available. Offers education (MA). *Application deadline:* Applications are processed on a rolling basis. *Application fee:* $25. Electronic applications accepted. *Interim Director of Graduate Studies in Education*, Dr. Jim Getz, 419-448-2068, Fax: 419-448-2124, E-mail: jgetz@heidelberg.edu.

HENDERSON STATE UNIVERSITY, Arkadelphia, AR 71999-0001

General Information State-supported, coed, comprehensive institution. *Enrollment:* 40 full-time matriculated graduate/professional students (31 women), 228 part-time matriculated graduate/professional students (151 women). *Enrollment by degree level:* 268 master's. *Graduate faculty:* 51 full-time (17 women), 9 part-time/adjunct (2 women). Tuition, state resident: part-time $150 per credit hour. Tuition, nonresident: part-time $300 per credit hour. *Required fees:* $120 per semester. *Graduate housing:* Room and/or apartments available to single students; on-campus housing not available to married students. *Student services:* Campus employment opportunities, career counseling, disabled student services, free psychological counseling, international student services. *Library facilities:* Huie Library. *Online resources:* library catalog, web page, access to other libraries' catalogs. *Collection:* 274,639 titles, 11,500 serial subscriptions, 18,254 audiovisual materials.

Computer facilities: 125 computers available on campus for general student use. A campuswide network can be accessed from student residence rooms and from off campus. *Web address:* http://www.hsu.edu/.

General Application Contact: Dr. Marck L. Beggs, MLA Director/Graduate Dean, 870-230-5126, Fax: 870-230-5479, E-mail: beggsm@hsu.edu.

GRADUATE UNITS

Graduate Studies Students: 40 full-time (31 women), 228 part-time (151 women); includes 43 minority (26 African Americans, 14 Asian Americans or Pacific Islanders, 1 Hispanic American, 2 Native Americans), 5 international. Average age 33. 156 applicants, 96% accepted. *Faculty:* 51 full-time (17 women), 9 part-time/adjunct (2 women). Expenses: Contact institution. *Financial support:* In 2001–02, 168 students received support, including teaching assistantships with full tuition reimbursements available (averaging $4,000 per year); research assistantships, Federal Work-Study and institutionally sponsored loans also available. Support available to part-time students. Financial award application deadline: 7/31; financial award applicants required to submit FAFSA. In 2001, 22 degrees awarded. *Degree program information:* Part-time programs available. Offers arts and sciences (MLA); English (MLA); social studies (MLA). *Application deadline:* For fall admission, 5/1 (priority date); for spring admission, 12/1 (priority date). Applications are processed on a rolling basis. *Application fee:* $0 ($30 for international students). *Application Contact:* Missie Bell, Administrative Assistant I, 870-230-5126, Fax: 870-230-5479, E-mail: bellm@hsu.edu. *Graduate*, Dr. Marck L. Beggs, 870-230-5126, Fax: 870-230-5479, E-mail: beggsm@hsu.edu.

School of Business Administration Students: 9 full-time (6 women), 16 part-time (11 women); includes 1 minority (Hispanic American), 4 international. Average age 33. *Faculty:* 7 full-time (2 women), 2 part-time/adjunct (0 women). Expenses: Contact institution. *Financial support:* In 2001–02, 11 teaching assistantships with tuition reimbursements (averaging $4,000 per year) were awarded; research assistantships, Federal Work-Study and institutionally sponsored loans also available. Support available to part-time students. Financial award application deadline: 7/31. In 2001, 4 degrees awarded. *Degree program information:* Part-time programs available. Offers business administration (MBA). *Application deadline:* For fall admission, 5/1 (priority date); for spring admission, 12/1 (priority date). Applications are processed on a rolling basis. *Application fee:* $0 ($30 for international students). *Application Contact:* Dr. Marck L. Beggs, MLA Director/Graduate Dean, 870-230-5126, Fax: 870-230-5479, E-mail: beggsm@hsu.edu. *Dean*, Dr. Gary Linn, 870-230-5310, Fax: 870-230-5286, E-mail: linng@hsu.edu.

School of Education Students: 23 full-time (19 women), 189 part-time (126 women); includes 40 minority (24 African Americans, 14 Asian Americans or Pacific Islanders, 2 Native Americans), 1 international. 28 applicants, 82% accepted. *Faculty:* 31 full-time (11 women), 4 part-time/adjunct (2 women). Expenses: Contact institution. *Financial support:* Research assistantships, teaching assistantships, Federal Work-Study and institutionally sponsored loans available. Support available to part-time students. Financial award application deadline: 7/31. In 2001, 18 degrees awarded. *Degree program information:* Part-time programs available. Offers art education (MSE); biology education (MSE); community counseling (MS); early childhood/special education (MSE); education (MS, MSE); education of the mildly handicapped (MSE); educational leadership (MSE); elementary school administration (MSE); elementary school counseling (MSE); English education (MSE); general elementary education (MSE); mathematics education (MSE); physical education (MSE); reading (MSE); secondary school administration (MSE); secondary school counseling (MSE); social sciences education (MSE). *Application deadline:* For fall admission, 5/1 (priority date); for spring admission, 12/1 (priority date). Applications are processed on a rolling basis. *Application fee:* $0 ($30 for international students). *Dean*, Dr. Charles Green, 870-230-5394, Fax: 870-230-5455, E-mail: green@hsu.edu.

HENDRIX COLLEGE, Conway, AR 72032-3080

General Information Independent-religious, coed, comprehensive institution.

GRADUATE UNITS

Program in Accounting

HERITAGE BAPTIST COLLEGE AND HERITAGE THEOLOGICAL SEMINARY, Cambridge, ON N3C 3T2, Canada

General Information Independent-religious, coed, comprehensive institution.

GRADUATE UNITS

Program in Theological Studies Offers divinity (MA); theological studies (MA, Certificate).

HERITAGE COLLEGE, Toppenish, WA 98948-9599

General Information Independent, coed, comprehensive institution. *Graduate housing:* On-campus housing not available.

GRADUATE UNITS

Graduate Programs in Education *Degree program information:* Part-time and evening/weekend programs available. Offers bilingual education/ESL (M Ed); community and human resource development (M Ed); counseling (M Ed); early childhood education (M Ed); educational administration (M Ed); professional development (M Ed); special education (M Ed).

HIGH POINT UNIVERSITY, High Point, NC 27262-3598

General Information Independent-religious, coed, comprehensive institution. CGS member. *Enrollment:* 18 full-time matriculated graduate/professional students (11 women), 150 part-time matriculated graduate/professional students (92 women). *Enrollment by degree level:* 168 master's. *Graduate faculty:* 20 full-time (5 women). *Tuition:* Full-time $6,403; part-time $337 per credit. *Required fees:* $100; $50 per semester. *Graduate housing:* Room and/or apartments available on a first-come, first-served basis to single students; on-campus housing not available to married students. Typical cost: $2,580 per year ($6,030 including board). Room and board charges vary according to board plan and housing facility selected. *Student services:* Campus safety program, career counseling, disabled student services, exercise/wellness program, free psychological counseling, low-cost health insurance. *Library facilities:* Herman and Louise Smith Library. *Online resources:* library catalog, web page, access to other libraries' catalogs. *Collection:* 105,040 titles, 7,081 serial subscriptions, 11,000 audiovisual materials.

Computer facilities: 176 computers available on campus for general student use. A campuswide network can be accessed from student residence rooms and from off campus. Internet access is available. *Web address:* http://www.highpoint.edu/.

General Application Contact: Dr. Alberta Haynes Herron, Dean of Graduate Studies, 336-841-9198, Fax: 336-841-4599, E-mail: aherron@highpoint.edu.

GRADUATE UNITS

Graduate Studies Students: 18 full-time (11 women), 150 part-time (92 women); includes 41 African Americans, 12 international. Average age 33. 75 applicants, 81% accepted, 47 enrolled. *Faculty:* 20 full-time (5 women). Expenses: Contact institution. *Financial support:* In 2001–02, 80 students received support. Institutionally sponsored loans available. Support available to part-time students. Financial award application deadline: 3/1; financial award applicants required to submit FAFSA. In 2001, 53 degrees awarded. *Degree program information:* Part-time and evening/weekend programs available. Offers business administration (MBA); international management (MS); management (MS); nonprofit organizations (MPA). *Application deadline:* For fall admission, 4/15 (priority date); for spring admission, 10/15 (priority date). Applications are processed on a rolling basis. *Application fee:* $35 ($50 for international students). *Dean of Graduate Studies,* Dr. Alberta Haynes Herron, 336-841-9198, Fax: 336-841-4599, E-mail: aherron@highpoint.edu.

HOFSTRA UNIVERSITY, Hempstead, NY 11549

General Information Independent, coed, university. CGS member. *Enrollment:* 1,329 full-time matriculated graduate/professional students (721 women), 2,454 part-time matriculated graduate/professional students (1,716 women). *Enrollment by degree level:* 818 first professional, 2,289 master's, 301 doctoral, 375 other advanced degrees. *Graduate faculty:* 182 full-time (70 women), 145 part-time/adjunct (67 women). *Tuition:* Full-time $12,408. Tuition and fees vary according to course load and program. *Graduate housing:* Room and/or apartments available on a first-come, first-served basis to single students; on-campus housing not available to married students. *Student services:* Campus employment opportunities, campus safety program, career counseling, child daycare facilities, disabled student services, exercise/wellness program, free psychological counseling, international student services, low-cost health insurance, teacher training, writing training. *Library facilities:* Axinn Library plus 1 other. *Online resources:* library catalog, web page, access to other libraries' catalogs. *Collection:* 1.6 million titles, 7,017 serial subscriptions, 7,000 audiovisual materials.

Computer facilities: 600 computers available on campus for general student use. A campuswide network can be accessed from student residence rooms. Internet access is available. *Web address:* http://www.hofstra.edu/.

General Application Contact: Mary Beth Carey, Vice President of Enrollment Services, Fax: 516-560-7660, E-mail: hofstra@hofstra.edu.

GRADUATE UNITS

College of Liberal Arts and Sciences Students: 148 full-time (108 women), 367 part-time (265 women); includes 8 minority (2 African Americans, 6 Asian Americans or Pacific Islanders) Average age 30. *Faculty:* 54 full-time (17 women), 22 part-time/adjunct (10 women). Expenses: Contact institution. *Financial support:* Fellowships, research assistantships, teaching assistantships, career-related internships or fieldwork, Federal Work-Study, institutionally sponsored loans, scholarships/grants, tuition waivers (partial), and tutoring assistantships available. Support available to part-time students. Financial award applicants required to submit FAFSA. In 2001, 122 master's, 32 doctorates awarded. *Degree program information:* Part-time and evening/weekend programs available. Offers liberal arts and sciences (MA, MS, PhD, Psy D, Certificate, Post-Doctoral Certificate). *Application deadline:* Applications are processed on a rolling basis. *Application fee:* $40 ($75 for international students). *Application Contact:* Mary Beth Carey, Vice President of Enrollment Services, Fax: 516-560-7660, E-mail: hofstra@hofstra.edu. *Dean,* Dr. Bernard J. Firestone, 516-463-5411, Fax: 516-463-4861, E-mail: lasbjf@hofstra.edu.

Division of Humanities Students: 2 full-time (0 women), 58 part-time (48 women); includes 1 minority (African American) Average age 32. *Faculty:* 15 full-time (3 women), 3 part-time/adjunct (1 woman). Expenses: Contact institution. *Financial support:* Fellowships, research assistantships, career-related internships or fieldwork, Federal Work-Study, institutionally sponsored loans, and scholarships/grants available. Support available to part-time students. In 2001, 10 degrees awarded. *Degree program information:* Part-time and evening/weekend programs available. Offers applied linguistics (MA); audiology (MA); audiology and speech-language pathology (MA); bilingualism (MA); biological extension of speech-language pathology (MA); English (MA); English and creative writing (MA); humanities (MA); speech-language pathology (MA); teachers of speech and hearing handicapped (MA). *Application deadline:* Applications are processed on a rolling basis. *Application fee:* $40 ($75 for international students). *Application Contact:* Mary Beth Carey, Vice President of Enrollment Services, Fax: 516-560-7660, E-mail: hofstra@hofstra.edu.

Division of Natural Sciences, Mathematics, Engineering, and Computer Science Students: 7 full-time (3 women), 82 part-time (35 women); includes 2 minority (both Asian Americans or Pacific Islanders) Average age 32. *Faculty:* 13 full-time (5 women), 2 part-time/adjunct (0 women). Expenses: Contact institution. *Financial support:* Fellowships, research assistantships, teaching assistantships, career-related internships or fieldwork, Federal Work-Study, institutionally sponsored loans, tuition waivers (partial), and tutoring assistantships available. Support available to part-time students. Financial award applicants required to submit FAFSA. In 2001, 25 degrees awarded. *Degree program information:* Part-time and evening/weekend programs available. Offers applied mathematics (MA, MS); biology (MA, MS); computer science (MA, MS); human cytogenetics (MS); natural sciences, mathematics, engineering, and computer science (MA, MS, Certificate); physicians assistant (Certificate). MS (engineering) offered jointly with Columbia University. *Application deadline:* Applications are processed on a rolling basis. *Application fee:* $40 ($75 for international students). *Application Contact:* Mary Beth Carey, Vice President of Enrollment Services, Fax: 516-560-7660, E-mail: hofstra@hofstra.edu.

Division of Social Sciences Students: 139 full-time (105 women), 227 part-time (182 women); includes 5 minority (1 African American, 4 Asian Americans or Pacific Islanders) Average age 29. *Faculty:* 26 full-time (9 women), 17 part-time/adjunct (9 women). Expenses: Contact institution. *Financial support:* Fellowships, research assistantships, teaching assistantships, career-related internships or fieldwork, Federal Work-Study, and institutionally sponsored loans available. Support available to part-time students. Financial award applicants required to submit FAFSA. In 2001, 87 master's, 32 doctorates awarded. *Degree program information:* Part-time and evening/weekend programs available. Offers clinical and school psychology (MA, PhD, Post-Doctoral Certificate); industrial/organizational psychology (MA); school-community psychology (MS, Psy D); social sciences (MA, MS, PhD, Psy D, Post-Doctoral Certificate). *Application deadline:* Applications are processed on a rolling basis. *Application fee:* $40 ($75 for international students). *Application Contact:* Mary Beth Carey, Vice President of Enrollment Services, Fax: 516-560-7660, E-mail: hofstra@hofstra.edu.

Frank G. Zarb School of Business Students: 113 full-time (41 women), 392 part-time (155 women); includes 2 minority (both African Americans) Average age 30. *Faculty:* 37 full-time (7 women), 4 part-time/adjunct (0 women). Expenses: Contact institution. *Financial support:* Fellowships, research assistantships, career-related internships or fieldwork, Federal Work-Study, and tuition waivers (partial) available. Financial award application deadline: 4/1; financial award applicants required to submit FAFSA. In 2001, 164 degrees awarded. *Degree program information:* Part-time and evening/weekend programs available. Offers accounting (MBA, MS); accounting information systems (MS); business (EMBA, Exec MBA, MBA, MS); business computer information systems/quantitative methods (MBA); computer information systems (MS); finance (MBA, MS); human resource management (MS); international business (MBA); management (EMBA); marketing (MBA, MS); taxation (MBA, MS). *Application deadline:* Applications are processed on a rolling basis. *Application fee:* $40 ($75 for international students). *Application Contact:* Dr. Stuart L. Bass, Director of Graduate Programs, 516-463-5145, E-mail: actslb@hofstra.edu. *Dean of Academics,* Dr. Ralph Polimeni, 516-463-5685, Fax: 516-463-5268, E-mail: bizrsp@hofstra.edu.

New College Average age 32. *Faculty:* 2 full-time (1 woman). Expenses: Contact institution. *Financial support:* Fellowships, research assistantships, career-related internships or fieldwork and Federal Work-Study available. Support available to part-time students. Financial award applicants required to submit FAFSA. In 2001, 1 degree awarded. *Degree program information:* Part-time and evening/weekend programs available. Offers interdisciplinary studies (MA). *Application deadline:* Applications are processed on a rolling basis. *Application fee:* $40 ($75 for international students). *Application Contact:* Heather E. Johnson, Senior Assistant Dean, 516-463-5824, Fax: 516-463-4832, E-mail: nuchef@hofstra.edu. *Dean,* David C. Christman, 516-463-5820, Fax: 516-463-4832.

School of Education and Allied Human Services Students: 234 full-time (174 women), 1,351 part-time (1,057 women); includes 12 minority (7 African Americans, 2 Asian Americans or Pacific Islanders, 3 Hispanic Americans), 1 international. Average age 32. *Faculty:* 51 full-time (36 women), 89 part-time/adjunct (49 women). Expenses: Contact institution. *Financial support:* Fellowships, research assistantships, teaching assistantships, career-related internships or fieldwork, Federal Work-Study, institutionally sponsored loans, scholarships/grants, tuition waivers (full and partial), and unspecified assistantships available. Support available to part-time students. Financial award applicants required to submit FAFSA. In 2001, 625 master's, 10 doctorates, 50 other advanced degrees awarded. *Degree program information:* Part-time and evening/weekend programs available. Offers art (MS Ed); art education (MA, MS Ed); art therapy and special education (MA); biology (MS Ed); biology education (MA); business (MS Ed); business and distributive education (MA); chemistry (MA, MS Ed); consultation in special education (CAS); counseling (MS Ed, CAS, Professional Diploma); creative arts therapy (MA); deaf education (CAS); early childhood education (MA); early childhood special education (MS Ed, CAS); education and allied human services (MA, MPS, MS, MS Ed, Mus Doc, Ed D, PhD, CAS, Certificate, PD, Postgraduate Diploma, Professional Diploma); education of gifted/talented children (Professional Diploma); educational administration (MS Ed, Mus Doc, Ed D, CAS); elementary and early childhood education (MA, MS Ed); elementary education (MA, MS Ed); English (MA, MS Ed); family therapy (Certificate); foundations of education (MS Ed, CAS); foundations of education and elementary education (CAS); French (MA, MS Ed); geology (MA, MS Ed); German (MA, MS Ed); gerontology (MS, CAS); health administration (MA); health education (MS Ed); literary studies (MS Ed); literary studies and special education (MS Ed); managed care (Professional Diploma); marriage and family therapy (MA, Professional Diploma); mathematics (MA, MS Ed); mathematics, science, and technology in elementary education (MA); middle school 7-9 extension (CAS); music (MS Ed); music education (MA, MS Ed); physical education (MS); physics (MA, MS Ed); postsecondary transition specialist (CAS); program evaluation (MS Ed); reading, language and cognition (MA, Ed D, PhD, CAS); rehabilitation administration (Professional Diploma); rehabilitation counseling (MS Ed, Professional Diploma); Russian (MA, MS Ed); school counselor-bilingual extension (CAS); secondary education (MA, MS Ed); sex counseling (CAS); social studies (MA); Spanish (MA, MS Ed); special education (MA, MPS, MS Ed, CAS, Professional Diploma); special education assessment and diagnosis (CAS); teaching English as a second language (MS Ed); teaching of writing (MA, CAS). *Application deadline:* Applications are processed on a rolling basis. *Application fee:* $40 ($75 for international students). *Application Contact:* Mary Beth Carey, Vice President of Enrollment Services, Fax: 516-560-7660, E-mail: hofstra@hofstra.edu. *Dean,* James Johnson, 516-463-5740, Fax: 516-463-6503, E-mail: soejrj@hofstra.edu.

School of Law Students: 812 full-time (386 women), 14 part-time (4 women). Average age 27. *Faculty:* 31 full-time (6 women), 28 part-time/adjunct (8 women). Expenses: Contact institution. *Financial support:* Fellowships, research assistantships, career-related internships or fieldwork, Federal Work-Study, institutionally sponsored loans, and tuition waivers (full and partial) available. Financial award application deadline: 5/15; financial award applicants required to submit FAFSA. In 2001, 269 first professional degrees, 3 master's awarded. Offers American legal studies (LL M); international law (LL M); law (JD). *Application deadline:* For fall admission, 4/15 (priority date). Applications are processed on a rolling basis. *Application fee:* $60. *Application Contact:* Deborah M. Martin, Director of Law School Admissions, 516-463-5916, Fax: 516-463-6091, E-mail: lawadmissions@hofstra.edu. *Dean,* Dr. David N. Yellen, 516-463-5854, E-mail: lawdny@hofstra.edu.

HOLLINS UNIVERSITY, Roanoke, VA 24020-1603

General Information Independent, women only, comprehensive institution. *Enrollment:* 147 full-time matriculated graduate/professional students (118 women), 159 part-time matriculated graduate/professional students (130 women). *Enrollment by degree level:* 289 master's, 17 other advanced degrees. *Graduate faculty:* 50 full-time (25 women), 28 part-time/adjunct (18 women). *Tuition:* Part-time $765 per course. *Graduate housing:* On-campus housing not available. *Student services:* Campus safety program, career counseling, international student services, low-cost health insurance, teacher training, writing training. *Library facilities:* Wyndham Robertson Library plus 1 other. *Online resources:* library catalog, web page, access to other libraries' catalogs. *Collection:* 186,835 titles, 6,382 serial subscriptions, 3,402 audiovisual materials.

Computer facilities: 100 computers available on campus for general student use. A campuswide network can be accessed from student residence rooms and from off campus. Internet access, applications software are available. *Web address:* http://www.hollins.edu/.

General Application Contact: Cathy S. Koon, Coordinator of Graduate Studies, 540-362-6575, Fax: 540-362-6288, E-mail: hugrad@hollins.edu.

GRADUATE UNITS

Graduate Programs Students: 147 full-time (118 women), 159 part-time (130 women); includes 30 minority (15 African Americans, 4 Asian Americans or Pacific Islanders, 8 Hispanic Americans, 3 Native Americans) Average age 33. 235 applicants, 63% accepted, 121 enrolled. *Faculty:* 50 full-time (25 women), 28 part-time/adjunct (18 women). Expenses: Contact institution. *Financial support:* In 2001–02, 143 students received support, including fellowships (averaging $19,270 per year); Federal Work-Study and scholarships/grants also available. Support available to part-time students. Financial award application deadline: 7/15; financial award applicants required to submit FAFSA. In 2001, 82 master's, 2 other advanced degrees awarded. *Degree program information:* Part-time and evening/weekend programs available. Offers children's literature (MA); computer studies (MALS); creative writing (MA); English (MA); humanities (MALS); interdisciplinary studies (MALS); liberal studies (CAS); screenwriting and film studies (MA); social science (MALS); teaching (MAT). *Application deadline:* For fall admission, 2/2 (priority date). Applications are processed on a rolling basis. *Application fee:* $35. Electronic applications accepted. *Application Contact:* Cathy S. Koon, Coordinator of Graduate Studies, 540-362-6575, Fax: 540-362-6288, E-mail: hugrad@hollins.edu. *Dean of Graduate Studies*, Dr. Leslie V. Willett, 540-362-7431, Fax: 540-362-6288, E-mail: lwillett@hollins.edu.

HOLY APOSTLES COLLEGE AND SEMINARY, Cromwell, CT 06416-2005

General Information Independent-religious, coed, comprehensive institution. *Enrollment:* 67 full-time matriculated graduate/professional students (2 women), 145 part-time matriculated graduate/professional students (55 women). *Enrollment by degree level:* 212 master's. *Graduate faculty:* 14 full-time (2 women), 15 part-time/adjunct (6 women). *Tuition:* Full-time $7,920; part-time $195 per credit. One-time fee: $175 full-time; $20 part-time. Full-time tuition and fees vary according to course load. *Graduate housing:* Room and/or apartments available to single students; on-campus housing not available to married students. Typical cost: $6,400 (including board) ; $6,400 (including board) for married students. *Student services:* Free psychological counseling, writing training. *Library facilities:* Holy Apostles College and Seminary Library. *Collection:* 84,584 titles, 250 serial subscriptions.

Computer facilities: 10 computers available on campus for general student use. Internet access is available. *Web address:* http://www.holyapostles.edu/.

General Application Contact: Peggy Sitarz, Registrar, 860-632-3033, Fax: 860-632-3075, E-mail: registrar@holyapostles.edu.

GRADUATE UNITS

Department of Theology Students: 67 full-time (2 women), 145 part-time (55 women); includes 5 minority (4 Hispanic Americans, 1 Native American), 5 international. Average age 43. *Faculty:* 14 full-time (2 women), 15 part-time/adjunct (6 women). Expenses: Contact institution. *Financial support:* In 2001–02, 18 students received support. Career-related internships or fieldwork available. Support available to part-time students. Financial award applicants required to submit FAFSA. In 2001, 12 first professional degrees, 10 master's awarded. *Degree program information:* Part-time and evening/weekend programs available. Offers bioethics (MA, Certificate, Post Master's Certificate); church history (MA, Certificate, Post Master's Certificate); dogmatic theology (MA, Certificate, Post Master's Certificate); liturgical music (MA, Certificate, Post Master's Certificate); liturgy (MA, Certificate, Post Master's Certificate); moral theology (MA, Certificate, Post Master's Certificate); philosophical theology (MA, Certificate, Post Master's Certificate); religious education (MA, Certificate, Post Master's Certificate); sacred scripture (MA, Post Master's Certificate); sacred scriptures (Certificate); theology (M Div). *Application deadline:* For fall admission, 8/15 (priority date). Applications are processed on a rolling basis. *Application fee:* $50. *Application Contact:* Rev. Douglas L. Mosey, President and Rector, 860-632-3012, Fax: 860-632-0176, E-mail: rector@holyapostles.edu. *Academic Dean*, Maurice Sheehan, OFM, 860-632-3001, Fax: 860-632-3075.

HOLY CROSS GREEK ORTHODOX SCHOOL OF THEOLOGY, Brookline, MA 02445-7496

General Information Independent-religious, coed, graduate-only institution. *Graduate faculty:* 11 full-time (1 woman), 14 part-time/adjunct (0 women). *Tuition:* Full-time $9,450; part-time $394 per credit hour. *Required fees:* $215. *Graduate housing:* Rooms and/or apartments available on a first-come, first-served basis to single and married students. Typical cost: $7,350 (including board) for single students. *Student services:* Campus employment opportunities, career counseling, free psychological counseling, international student services, low-cost health insurance. *Library facilities:* Archbishop Iakoros Library. *Online resources:* library catalog, web page. *Collection:* 11,900 titles, 765 serial subscriptions, 1,415 audiovisual materials.

Computer facilities: 1 computer available on campus for general student use. *Web address:* http://www.hchc.edu/.

General Application Contact: Rev. James Katinas, Co-Director of Admissions and Records, 617-731-3500 Ext. 1260, Fax: 617-850-1460, E-mail: admissions@hchc.edu.

GRADUATE UNITS

Theological Programs Students: 106 full-time (7 women), 12 part-time (6 women), 9 international. Average age 29. 66 applicants, 77% accepted. *Faculty:* 11 full-time (1 woman), 14 part-time/adjunct (0 women). Expenses: Contact institution. *Financial support:* Federal Work-Study, scholarships/grants, and tuition waivers (partial) available. Financial award application deadline: 5/1; financial award applicants required to submit FAFSA. In 2001, 15 first professional degrees, 12 master's awarded. *Degree program information:* Part-time programs available. Offers theology (M Div, MA, MTS, Th M). *Application deadline:* For fall admission, 8/15; for spring admission, 1/3. *Application fee:* $35. *Application Contact:* Rev. James Katinas, Co-Director of Admissions and Records, 617-731-3500 Ext. 1260, Fax: 617-850-1460, E-mail: katinas@hchc.edu. *Acting Dean*, Dr. James Skedros, 617-731-3500 Ext. 1213, Fax: 617-850-1460.

HOLY FAMILY COLLEGE, Philadelphia, PA 19114-2094

General Information Independent-religious, coed, comprehensive institution. *Enrollment:* 55 full-time matriculated graduate/professional students (47 women), 643 part-time matriculated graduate/professional students (506 women). *Graduate faculty:* 15 full-time (8 women), 40 part-time/adjunct (15 women). *Tuition:* Full-time $7,650; part-time $425 per credit. *Required fees:* $340; $170 per term. *Graduate housing:* On-campus housing not available. *Student services:* Campus employment opportunities, campus safety program, career counseling, disabled student services, free psychological counseling. *Library facilities:* Holy Family College Library plus 1 other. *Online resources:* library catalog. *Collection:* 115,000 titles, 840 serial subscriptions, 1,556 audiovisual materials.

Computer facilities: 148 computers available on campus for general student use. A campuswide network can be accessed. Internet access is available. *Web address:* http://www.hfc.edu/.

General Application Contact: Dr. Antoinette M. Schiavo, Dean, Graduate Studies, 215-637-7700 Ext. 3230, Fax: 215-637-1478, E-mail: schiavo@hfc.edu.

GRADUATE UNITS

Graduate Studies Students: 55 full-time (47 women), 643 part-time (506 women); includes 56 minority (20 African Americans, 19 Asian Americans or Pacific Islanders, 16 Hispanic Americans, 1 Native American) Average age 32. 296 applicants, 99% accepted. *Faculty:* 15 full-time (8 women), 40 part-time/adjunct (15 women). Expenses: Contact institution. *Financial support:* Research assistantships with partial tuition reimbursements, Federal Work-Study available. Support available to part-time students. Financial award application deadline: 2/15; financial award applicants required to submit FAFSA. In 2001, 209 degrees awarded. *Degree program information:* Part-time and evening/weekend programs available. *Application deadline:* Applications are processed on a rolling basis. *Application fee:* $25. *Application Contact:* Joseph Canaday, Director of Graduate Admissions, 215-637-7203, Fax: 215-637-1478, E-mail: jcanaday@hfc.edu. *Dean*, Dr. Antoinette M. Schiavo, 215-637-7700 Ext. 3230, Fax: 215-637-1478, E-mail: schiavo@hfc.edu.

School of Business 21 applicants, 100% accepted. *Faculty:* 3 full-time (0 women), 3 part-time/adjunct (0 women). Expenses: Contact institution. *Financial support:* Federal Work-Study available. Support available to part-time students. Financial award application deadline: 2/15; financial award applicants required to submit FAFSA. *Degree program information:* Part-time and evening/weekend programs available. Offers computer communications management (MS); human resources management (MS). *Application deadline:* For fall admission, 7/1 (priority date); for winter admission, 11/1 (priority date); for spring admission, 4/1 (priority date). Applications are processed on a rolling basis. *Application fee:* $25. *Application Contact:* Joseph Canaday, Director of Graduate Admissions, 215-637-7203, Fax: 215-637-1478, E-mail: jcanaday@hfc.edu. *Dean*, Dr. Anthony DiPrimio, 215-637-7700 Ext. 3415, Fax: 215-637-5937, E-mail: odiprimio@hfc.edu.

School of Education Students: 52 full-time (44 women), 540 part-time (429 women); includes 30 minority (11 African Americans, 10 Asian Americans or Pacific Islanders, 9 Hispanic Americans) Average age 27. 247 applicants, 99% accepted. *Faculty:* 11 full-time (7 women), 33 part-time/adjunct (13 women). Expenses: Contact institution. *Financial support:* Research assistantships, Federal Work-Study available. Support available to part-time students. Financial award application deadline: 2/15; financial award applicants required to submit FAFSA. In 2001, 196 degrees awarded. *Degree program information:* Part-time and evening/weekend programs available. Offers education (M Ed); elementary education (M Ed); reading specialist (M Ed); secondary education (M Ed). *Application deadline:* For fall admission, 7/1 (priority date); for winter admission, 11/1 (priority date). Applications are processed on a rolling basis. *Application fee:* $25. *Application Contact:* Joseph Canaday, Director of Graduate Admissions, 215-637-7203, Fax: 215-637-1478, E-mail: jcanaday@hfc.edu. *Chair*, Dr. Leonard Soroka, 215-637-7700 Ext. 3565, Fax: 215-824-2438, E-mail: lsoroka@hfc.edu.

School of Nursing Average age 37. 9 applicants, 100% accepted. *Faculty:* 1 (woman) full-time. Expenses: Contact institution. *Financial support:* Federal Work-Study available. Support available to part-time students. Financial award application deadline: 2/15; financial award applicants required to submit FAFSA. *Degree program information:* Part-time and evening/weekend programs available. Offers nursing (MSN). *Application deadline:* For fall admission, 7/1 (priority date); for winter admission, 11/1 (priority date); for spring admission, 4/1 (priority date). Applications are processed on a rolling basis. *Application fee:* $25. *Application Contact:* Joseph Canaday, Director of Graduate Admissions, 215-637-7203, Fax: 215-637-1478, E-mail: jcanaday@hfc.edu. *Graduate Coordinator*, Sara Wuthnow, 215-637-7700 Ext. 3277, Fax: 215-637-6598, E-mail: swuthnow@hfc.edu.

School of Social and Behavioral Sciences Students: 3 full-time (all women), 33 part-time (26 women); includes 1 minority (Asian American or Pacific Islander) Average age 29. 17 applicants, 100% accepted. *Faculty:* 1 (woman) full-time, 4 part-time/adjunct (2 women). Expenses: Contact institution. *Financial support:* Research assistantships with full and partial tuition reimbursements, Federal Work-Study available. Support available to part-time students. Financial award application deadline: 2/15; financial award applicants required to submit FAFSA. In 2001, 9 degrees awarded. *Degree program information:* Part-time and evening/weekend programs available. Offers counseling psychology (MS). *Application deadline:* For fall admission, 4/15 (priority date). Applications are processed on a rolling basis. *Application fee:* $25. *Application Contact:* Joseph Canaday, Director of Graduate Admissions, 215-637-7203, Fax: 215-637-1478, E-mail: jcanaday@hfc.edu. *Graduate Coordinator*, Dr. Jane McGarrahan, 215-504-2000, Fax: 215-504-2050, E-mail: jmc.garrahan@hfc.edu.

HOLY NAMES COLLEGE, Oakland, CA 94619-1699

General Information Independent-religious, coed, primarily women, comprehensive institution. *Enrollment:* 107 full-time matriculated graduate/professional students (86 women), 219 part-time matriculated graduate/professional students (182 women). *Graduate faculty:* 18 full-time (13 women), 48 part-time/adjunct (33 women). *Tuition:* Part-time $460 per unit. *Required fees:* $120. *Graduate housing:* Room and/or apartments available on a first-come, first-served basis to single students; on-campus housing not available to married students. Typical cost: $6,800 (including board). Housing application deadline: 8/15. *Student services:* Campus employment opportunities, campus safety program, career counseling, free psychological counseling, international student services, low-cost health insurance. *Library facilities:* Cushing Library. *Online resources:* web page. *Collection:* 111,062 titles, 376 serial subscriptions, 4,350 audiovisual materials.

Computer facilities: 69 computers available on campus for general student use. A campuswide network can be accessed from student residence rooms and from off campus. Internet access is available. *Web address:* http://www.hnc.edu/.

General Application Contact: 510-436-1317, Fax: 510-436-1325, E-mail: hall@hnc.edu.

GRADUATE UNITS

Graduate Division Students: 107 full-time (86 women), 219 part-time (182 women); includes 108 minority (56 African Americans, 19 Asian Americans or Pacific Islanders, 31 Hispanic Americans, 2 Native Americans), 15 international. Average age 41. 172 applicants, 66% accepted. *Faculty:* 18 full-time (13 women), 48 part-time/adjunct (33 women). Expenses: Contact institution. *Financial support:* In 2001–02, 143 students received support. Scholarships/grants available. Support available to part-time students. Financial award application deadline: 3/2; financial award applicants required to submit FAFSA. In 2001, 59 master's, 58 other advanced degrees awarded. *Degree program information:* Part-time and evening/weekend programs available. Offers advanced curriculum studies (M Ed); community health nursing/case manager (MS); counseling psychology with emphasis in pastoral counseling (MA); educational therapy (M Ed); English (MA); family nurse practitioner (MS); Kodály music education (Certificate); management (MBA); mild/moderate disabilities (Ed S); multiple subject credential program (M Ed); music education with a Kodály emphasis (MM); pastoral counseling (MA, Certificate); pastoral ministry (MA); performance (MM); piano pedagogy (MM); piano pedagogy with Suzuki emphasis (Certificate); single subject credential program (M Ed); special education (M Ed); teaching English as a second language (M Ed, Certificate); urban education (M Ed). *Application deadline:* For fall admission, 8/1 (priority date); for spring admission, 12/1 (priority date). Applications are processed on a rolling basis. *Application fee:* $50. *Application Contact:* 800-430-1321, Fax: 510-436-1317, E-mail: hall@hnc.edu. *Vice President for Academic Affairs*, Dr. David Fike, 510-436-1040, Fax: 510-436-1199, E-mail: fike@academ.hnc.edu.

Sophia Center: Spirituality for the New Millennium Students: 10 full-time (6 women), 24 part-time (21 women); includes 1 minority (Native American), 3 international. Average age 52. 26 applicants, 77% accepted. *Faculty:* 1 full-time (0 women), 13 part-time/adjunct (9 women). Expenses: Contact institution. *Financial support:* In 2001–02, 16 students received support. Available to part-time students. Application deadline: 3/2; In 2001, 20 master's, 5 other advanced degrees awarded. Offers creation spirituality (Certificate); culture and creation spirituality (MA). *Application deadline:* For fall admission, 8/1 (priority date); for spring admission, 12/1 (priority date). Applications are processed on a rolling basis. *Application fee:* $35. *Application Contact:* 800-430-1321, Fax: 510-436-1317, E-mail: hall@hnc.edu. *Program Director*, Dr. James Conlon, 510-436-1046.

HOOD COLLEGE, Frederick, MD 21701-8575

General Information Independent, women only, comprehensive institution. CGS member. *Enrollment:* 36 full-time matriculated graduate/professional students (22 women), 666 part-time matriculated graduate/professional students (422 women). *Enrollment by degree level:* 702 master's, 32 other advanced degrees. *Graduate faculty:* 30 full-time (13 women), 27 part-time/adjunct (12 women). *Tuition:* Full-time $5,670; part-time $315 per credit. *Required fees:* $20 per term. *Graduate housing:* On-campus housing not available. *Student services:* Campus safety program, career counseling, disabled student services, international student services, multicultural affairs office. *Library facilities:* Beneficial-Hodson Library and Information Technology Center. *Online resources:* library catalog, web page, access to other libraries' catalogs. *Collection:* 200,000 titles, 6,300 serial subscriptions, 3,293 audiovisual materials.

Computer facilities: 222 computers available on campus for general student use. A campuswide network can be accessed from student residence rooms and from off campus. Internet access is available. *Web address:* http://www.hood.edu/.

General Application Contact: Dr. Ann Boyd, Dean of the Graduate School, 301-696-3600, Fax: 301-696-3597, E-mail: boyd@hood.edu.

GRADUATE UNITS

Graduate School Students: 36 full-time (22 women), 666 part-time (422 women); includes 72 minority (34 African Americans, 20 Asian Americans or Pacific Islanders, 12 Hispanic Americans, 6 Native Americans), 13 international. Average age 32. 278 applicants, 82% accepted, 142 enrolled. *Faculty:* 30 full-time (13 women), 27 part-time/adjunct (12 women). Expenses: Contact institution. *Financial support:* Institutionally sponsored loans available. Financial award applicants required to submit FAFSA. In 2001, 149 master's, 15 other

Hood College (continued)

advanced degrees awarded. *Degree program information:* Part-time and evening/weekend programs available. Offers administration and management (MBA); biomedical science (MS); computer science (MS); curriculum and instruction (MS); educational leadership (MS); environmental biology (MS); information technology (MS); management information technology (MS); psychology (MA); regulatory compliance (Certificate); thanatology (MA). *Application deadline:* Applications are processed on a rolling basis. *Application fee:* $30. *Application Contact:* Margot Rhoades, Graduate School Office, 301-696-3600, Fax: 301-696-3597, E-mail: hoodgrad@hood.edu. *Dean*, Dr. Ann Boyd, 301-696-3600, Fax: 301-696-3597, E-mail: boyd@hood.edu.

HOOD THEOLOGICAL SEMINARY, Salisbury, NC 28144

General Information Independent-religious, coed, primarily men, graduate-only institution. *Enrollment by degree level:* 123 master's. *Graduate faculty:* 9 full-time (2 women), 7 part-time/adjunct (3 women). *Tuition:* Full-time $5,700; part-time $190 per credit hour. *Required fees:* $430. *Graduate housing:* Rooms and/or apartments guaranteed to single students and available on a first-come, first-served basis to married students. Typical cost: $1,560 per year for single students; $2,262 per year for married students. Housing application deadline: 8/15. *Student services:* Campus employment opportunities, writing training. *Library facilities:* Hood Seminary Library. *Online resources:* library catalog. *Collection:* 25,522 titles, 133 serial subscriptions, 175 audiovisual materials.

Computer facilities: 5 computers available on campus for general student use. A campuswide network can be accessed from student residence rooms.

General Application Contact: Rev. Melissa C. Neal, Dean of Admissions, 704-216-6112, Fax: 704-216-6844, E-mail: mneal@livingstone.edu.

GRADUATE UNITS

Graduate and Professional Programs Students: 98 full-time (39 women), 25 part-time (11 women); includes 78 minority (all African Americans), 1 international. 58 applicants, 72% accepted, 30 enrolled. *Faculty:* 9 full-time (2 women), 7 part-time/adjunct (3 women). Expenses: Contact institution. *Financial support:* In 2001–02, 30 students received support. Scholarships/grants and resident assistantships available. Financial award application deadline: 6/1; financial award applicants required to submit FAFSA. In 2001, 12 degrees awarded. *Degree program information:* Evening/weekend programs available. Offers theology (M Div, MTS, D Min). *Application deadline:* For fall admission, 8/15 (priority date); for spring admission, 12/15. *Application fee:* $25. *Application Contact:* Rev. Melissa C. Neal, Dean of Admissions, 704-216-6112, Fax: 704-216-6844, E-mail: mneal@livingstone.edu. *President*, Dr. Albert J. D. Aymer, 704-216-6113, Fax: 704-216-6844, E-mail: aaymer@livingstone.edu.

HOPE INTERNATIONAL UNIVERSITY, Fullerton, CA 92831-3138

General Information Independent-religious, coed, comprehensive institution. *Graduate housing:* Room and/or apartments available on a first-come, first-served basis to single students; on-campus housing not available to married students. Housing application deadline: 7/15.

GRADUATE UNITS

School of Graduate Studies *Degree program information:* Part-time and evening/weekend programs available. Postbaccalaureate distance learning degree programs offered (minimal on-campus study). Offers church music (MA, MCM); congregational leadership (MA); counseling (MA); education (ME); intercultural studies/urban ministries (MA); international development (MBA, MSM); marriage and family therapy (MFT); marriage, family, and child counseling (MA); nonprofit management (MBA); psychology (MA). Electronic applications accepted.

HOUSTON BAPTIST UNIVERSITY, Houston, TX 77074-3298

General Information Independent-religious, coed, comprehensive institution. *Enrollment:* 624 full-time matriculated graduate/professional students (457 women), 252 part-time matriculated graduate/professional students (182 women). *Enrollment by degree level:* 876 master's. *Graduate faculty:* 116 full-time, 85 part-time/adjunct. *Tuition:* Part-time $990 per course. *Required fees:* $250 per quarter. *Graduate housing:* Rooms and/or apartments available on a first-come, first-served basis to single and married students. *Student services:* Campus employment opportunities, career counseling, exercise/wellness program, free psychological counseling, international student services, low-cost health insurance, teacher training, writing training. *Library facilities:* Moody Library. *Collection:* 140,292 titles, 1,415 serial subscriptions, 9,700 audiovisual materials.

Computer facilities: 115 computers available on campus for general student use. A campuswide network can be accessed from off campus. *Web address:* http://www.hbu.edu/.

General Application Contact: Ida Thompson, Director of Graduate Admissions, E-mail: ithompson@hbu.edu.

GRADUATE UNITS

College of Arts and Humanities Students: 12 full-time (4 women), 37 part-time (21 women); includes 14 minority (10 African Americans, 1 Asian American or Pacific Islander, 3 Hispanic Americans) 7 applicants, 57% accepted. Expenses: Contact institution. *Financial support:* Federal Work-Study and scholarships/grants available. Support available to part-time students. Financial award application deadline: 4/15; financial award applicants required to submit FAFSA. In 2001, 23 degrees awarded. *Degree program information:* Part-time and evening/weekend programs available. Offers arts and humanities (MATS, MLA); liberal arts (MLA); theological studies (MATS). *Application deadline:* For fall admission, 7/1 (priority date); for winter admission, 10/1 (priority date); for spring admission, 1/1 (priority date). Applications are processed on a rolling basis. *Application fee:* $25 ($100 for international students). *Application Contact:* Dr. Joe Blair, Program Director, 281-649-3288. *Dean*, Dr. James Taylor, 281-649-3337.

College of Business and Economics Students: 111 full-time (63 women), 54 part-time (30 women); includes 77 minority (35 African Americans, 32 Asian Americans or Pacific Islanders, 10 Hispanic Americans), 16 international. 122 applicants, 54% accepted. *Faculty:* 24 full-time (4 women), 35 part-time/adjunct (5 women). Expenses: Contact institution. *Financial support:* Federal Work-Study and scholarships/grants available. Support available to part-time students. Financial award application deadline: 4/15; financial award applicants required to submit FAFSA. In 2001, 66 degrees awarded. *Degree program information:* Part-time and evening/weekend programs available. Offers accountancy and information technology (MS Acct); accounting (MBA); business administration (MSM); business and economics (MBA, MS Acct, MSHRM, MSM, MSMCS); finance (MBA); human resource management (MBA); human resources management (MSHRM); information technology (MBA); international management (MBA); management, computing and systems (MSMCS). *Application deadline:* For fall admission, 7/1 (priority date); for winter admission, 10/1 (priority date); for spring admission, 1/1 (priority date). Applications are processed on a rolling basis. *Application fee:* $25 ($100 for international students). *Application Contact:* Dr. Carter L. Franklin, Associate Dean, 281-649-3429. *Dean*, Dr. Lynn Gillette, 281-649-3325.

College of Education and Behavioral Sciences Students: 428 full-time (340 women), 116 part-time (95 women). 104 applicants, 75% accepted. Expenses: Contact institution. *Financial support:* Career-related internships or fieldwork, Federal Work-Study, and scholarships/grants available. Support available to part-time students. Financial award application deadline: 4/15; financial award applicants required to submit FAFSA. In 2001, 92 degrees awarded. *Degree program information:* Part-time and evening/weekend programs available. Offers bilingual education (M Ed); Christian counseling (MAPCP); counselor education (M Ed); curriculum instruction (M Ed); education (M Ed); education and behavioral sciences (M Ed, MAP, MAPCP); educational administration (M Ed); educational diagnostician (M Ed); elementary education (M Ed); generic special education (M Ed); psychology (MAP); reading education (M Ed); secondary education (M Ed). *Application deadline:* For fall admission, 7/1 (priority date); for spring admission, 1/1 (priority date). Applications are processed on a rolling basis. *Application fee:* $25 ($100 for international students). *Application Contact:* Judy Ferguson, Program Secretary, 281-649-3000 Ext. 3241. *Dean*, John Alexander, 281-649-3000 Ext. 2237.

College of Nursing Students: 73 full-time (50 women), 45 part-time (36 women); includes 75 minority (47 African Americans, 24 Asian Americans or Pacific Islanders, 4 Hispanic Americans), 8 international. 45 applicants, 64% accepted. *Faculty:* 2 full-time (both women), 5 part-time/adjunct (all women). Expenses: Contact institution. *Financial support:* Federal Work-Study available. Financial award application deadline: 4/15; financial award applicants required to submit FAFSA. In 2001, 14 degrees awarded. *Degree program information:* Part-time and evening/weekend programs available. Offers congregational care nurse (MSN); family nurse practitioner (MSN); family nurse practitioner-congregational nurse (MSN); health administration (MSHA); nursing (MSHA, MSN). *Application deadline:* For fall admission, 7/1 (priority date); for winter admission, 10/1 (priority date); for spring admission, 1/1 (priority date). Applications are processed on a rolling basis. *Application fee:* $25 ($100 for international students). *Dean*, Dr. Nancy Yuill, 281-649-3300, E-mail: nyuill@hbu.edu.

HOUSTON GRADUATE SCHOOL OF THEOLOGY, Houston, TX 77004

General Information Independent-religious, coed, graduate-only institution. *Enrollment by degree level:* 55 first professional, 129 master's, 32 doctoral. *Graduate faculty:* 11 full-time (3 women), 15 part-time/adjunct (3 women). *Tuition:* Part-time $200 per credit hour. *Required fees:* $100 per semester. *Graduate housing:* On-campus housing not available. *Student services:* Campus employment opportunities, career counseling, international student services. *Online resources:* library catalog, access to other libraries' catalogs. *Collection:* 24,608 titles, 48 serial subscriptions, 636 audiovisual materials.

Computer facilities: 10 computers available on campus for general student use. A campuswide network can be accessed from student residence rooms and from off campus. Internet access is available.

General Application Contact: Dr. Ronald D. Worden, Vice President for Academic Affairs, 713-942-9505, Fax: 713-942-9506, E-mail: rdworden@hgst.edu.

GRADUATE UNITS

Graduate School Students: 57 full-time (19 women), 159 part-time (66 women). Average age 45. 48 applicants, 85% accepted. *Faculty:* 11 full-time (3 women), 15 part-time/adjunct (3 women). Expenses: Contact institution. In 2001, 12 first professional degrees, 26 master's, 4 doctorates awarded. *Degree program information:* Part-time and evening/weekend programs available. Offers pastoral ministry (M Div, D Min); theological studies (MTS); theology (MA). *Application deadline:* For fall admission, 8/1 (priority date). *Application fee:* $35. *Application Contact:* Dr. Ronald D. Worden, Vice President for Academic Affairs, 713-942-9505, Fax: 713-942-9506, E-mail: rdworden@hgst.edu. *President*, Dr. David J. Robinson, 713-942-9505, Fax: 713-942-9506, E-mail: hgst@flash.net.

HOWARD UNIVERSITY, Washington, DC 20059-0002

General Information Independent, coed, university. CGS member. *Graduate housing:* Rooms and/or apartments available on a first-come, first-served basis to single and married students. Housing application deadline: 4/1. *Research affiliation:* AT&T (physics).

GRADUATE UNITS

College of Dentistry Students: 346 full-time (177 women); includes 227 minority (165 African Americans, 50 Asian Americans or Pacific Islanders, 12 Hispanic Americans), 81 international. Average age 25. 1,323 applicants, 13% accepted, 73 enrolled. *Faculty:* 79 full-time (31 women), 16 part-time/adjunct (3 women). Expenses: Contact institution. *Financial support:* In 2001–02, 262 students received support. Federal Work-Study, institutionally sponsored loans, and scholarships/grants available. Financial award application deadline: 4/1; financial award applicants required to submit FAFSA. In 2001, 74 DDSs, 21 other advanced degrees awarded. Offers advanced education program general dentistry (Certificate); dentistry (DDS); general dentistry (Certificate); oral and matillo surgery (Certificate); orthodontics (Certificate); pediatric dentistry (Certificate). *Application deadline:* For fall admission, 3/1. Applications are processed on a rolling basis. *Application fee:* $45. *Application Contact:* Doris Williams, Director of Admissions, 202-806-0400. *Dean*, Dr. Charles F. Sanders, 202-806-0440, Fax: 202-806-0354.

College of Engineering, Architecture, and Computer Sciences Students: 50 full-time (19 women), 36 part-time (11 women); includes 42 minority (38 African Americans, 1 Asian American or Pacific Islander, 2 Hispanic Americans, 1 Native American), 44 international. 125 applicants, 50% accepted, 18 enrolled. *Faculty:* 44 full-time, 12 part-time/adjunct. Expenses: Contact institution. *Financial support:* Fellowships, research assistantships, teaching assistantships, career-related internships or fieldwork, Federal Work-Study, institutionally sponsored loans, scholarships/grants, and unspecified assistantships available. Financial award application deadline: 4/1; financial award applicants required to submit FAFSA. In 2001, 16 master's, 4 doctorates awarded. *Degree program information:* Part-time programs available. Offers engineering, architecture, and computer sciences (M Eng, MCS, MS, PhD). *Application deadline:* For fall admission, 4/1; for spring admission, 11/1. *Application fee:* $45. Electronic applications accepted. *Application Contact:* Dr. Clayton W. Bates, Associate Dean for Graduate Education and Research, 202-806-6147, Fax: 202-806-5258, E-mail: bates@msrce.howard.edu. *Dean*, Dr. James H. Johnson, 202-806-6565, Fax: 202-462-1810, E-mail: jj@scs.howard.edu.

School of Engineering and Computer Science Students: 50 full-time (19 women), 36 part-time (11 women); includes 42 minority (38 African Americans, 1 Asian American or Pacific Islander, 2 Hispanic Americans, 1 Native American), 44 international. 125 applicants, 50% accepted, 18 enrolled. *Faculty:* 44 full-time (4 women), 12 part-time/adjunct (1 woman). Expenses: Contact institution. *Financial support:* In 2001–02, 20 research assistantships with full tuition reimbursements, 14 teaching assistantships with full and partial tuition reimbursements were awarded. Fellowships with full tuition reimbursements, career-related internships or fieldwork, institutionally sponsored loans, scholarships/grants, and unspecified assistantships also available. Financial award application deadline: 4/1; financial award applicants required to submit FAFSA. In 2001, 16 master's, 4 doctorates awarded. *Degree program information:* Part-time programs available. Offers chemical engineering (MS); civil engineering (M Eng); electrical engineering (M Eng, PhD); engineering and computer science (M Eng, MCS, MS, PhD); mechanical engineering (M Eng, PhD); systems and computer science (MCS). *Application deadline:* For fall admission, 4/1; for spring admission, 11/1. Applications are processed on a rolling basis. *Application fee:* $45. Electronic applications accepted.

College of Fine Arts *Degree program information:* Part-time programs available. Offers applied music (MM); art history (MA); ceramics (MFA); design (MFA); experimental studio (MFA); fine arts (MFA); jazz studies (MM); music (MM Ed); music education (MM Ed); painting (MFA); performance (MM); photography (MFA); printmaking (MFA); sculpture (MFA).

College of Medicine Offers biochemistry and molecular biology (PhD); biotechnology (MS); medicine (MD, MS, PhD).

College of Pharmacy, Nursing and Allied Health Sciences *Degree program information:* Part-time programs available. Offers pharmacy, nursing and allied health sciences (Pharm D, MSN, Certificate). Electronic applications accepted.

Division of Nursing *Degree program information:* Part-time programs available. Offers nurse practitioner (Certificate); primary family health nursing (MSN).

Division of Pharmacy Offers pharmacy (Pharm D). Electronic applications accepted.

Graduate School of Arts and Sciences *Degree program information:* Part-time and evening/weekend programs available. Offers African studies (MA, PhD); analytical chemistry (MS, PhD); anatomy (MS, PhD); applied mathematics (MS, PhD); arts and sciences (M Eng, MA, MAPA, MCS, MS, PhD); atmospheric (MS, PhD); atmospheric sciences (MS, PhD); biochemistry (MS, PhD); biology (MS, PhD); biophysics (PhD); clinical psychology (PhD); developmental psychology (PhD); economics (MA, PhD); English (MA, PhD); environmental (MS, PhD); exercise physiology (MS); experimental psychology (PhD); French (MA); genetics and human genetics (MS, PhD); history (MA, PhD); inorganic chemistry (MS, PhD); mathematics (MS, PhD); microbiology (PhD); neuropsychology (PhD); nutrition (MS, PhD); organic chemistry (MS, PhD); personality psychology (PhD); pharmacology (MS, PhD); philosophy (MA); physical chemistry (MS, PhD); physics (MS, PhD); physiology (PhD); political science

(MA, PhD); polymer chemistry (MS, PhD); psychology (MS); public administration (MAPA); public affairs (MA); recreation and leisure studies (MS); school and community health education (MS); social psychology (PhD); sociology (MA, PhD); Spanish (MA). Electronic applications accepted.

School of Business Students: 77 full-time (33 women), 16 part-time (11 women); includes 56 minority (all African Americans), 37 international. Average age 26. 207 applicants, 29% accepted, 36 enrolled. *Faculty:* 32 full-time (6 women), 5 part-time/adjunct (1 woman). Expenses: Contact institution. *Financial support:* In 2001–02, 12 research assistantships with full tuition reimbursements (averaging $10,000 per year) were awarded; career-related internships or fieldwork, institutionally sponsored loans, and scholarships/grants also available. Support available to part-time students. Financial award application deadline: 2/15; financial award applicants required to submit FAFSA. In 2001, 54 degrees awarded. *Degree program information:* Part-time and evening/weekend programs available. Postbaccalaureate distance learning degree programs offered (no on-campus study). Offers accounting (MBA); business (MBA); entrepreneurship (MBA); finance (MBA); information systems (MBA); international business (MBA); marketing (MBA); supply chain management (MBA). *Application deadline:* For fall admission, 4/30. *Application fee:* $45. *Application Contact:* Donna K. Mason, Administrative Assistant, 202-806-1725, Fax: 202-986-4435, E-mail: dmason@howard.edu. *Dean,* Dr. Barron H. Harvey, 202-806-1508, Fax: 202-797-6393, E-mail: bharvey@howard.edu.

School of Communications *Degree program information:* Part-time and evening/weekend programs available. Offers audiology (MS); communication sciences and disorders (PhD); communications (MA, MFA, MS, PhD); film (MFA); intercultural communication (MA, PhD); mass communication (MA, PhD); organizational communication (MA, PhD); speech pathology (MS).

School of Divinity Students: 229 full-time (84 women), 88 part-time (56 women); includes 308 minority (290 African Americans, 18 Asian Americans or Pacific Islanders), 1 international. Average age 44. 202 applicants, 72% accepted. *Faculty:* 12 full-time (4 women), 18 part-time/adjunct (3 women). Expenses: Contact institution. *Financial support:* In 2001–02, 40 fellowships with partial tuition reimbursements (averaging $5,613 per year), 9 research assistantships (averaging $4,000 per year) were awarded. Career-related internships or fieldwork, Federal Work-Study, institutionally sponsored loans, scholarships/grants, and traineeships also available. Support available to part-time students. Financial award application deadline: 4/1. In 2001, 46 master's, 25 doctorates awarded. *Degree program information:* Part-time and evening/weekend programs available. Offers theology (M Div, MARS, D Min). *Application deadline:* For fall admission, 4/1 (priority date); for spring admission, 11/1. Applications are processed on a rolling basis. *Application fee:* $45. Electronic applications accepted. *Application Contact:* Cassandra Newsome, Director of Student Services, 202-806-0500, Fax: 202-806-0711. *Dean,* Dr. Clarence G. Newsome, 202-806-0500, Fax: 202-806-0711.

School of Education *Degree program information:* Part-time and evening/weekend programs available. Offers counseling psychology (M Ed, MA, Ed D, PhD, CAGS); early childhood education (M Ed, MA, MAT, CAGS); education (M Ed, MA, MAT, MS, Ed D, PhD, CAGS); educational administration (M Ed, MA, CAGS); educational psychology (M Ed, MA, Ed D, PhD, CAGS); educational supervision (M Ed, MA, CAGS); elementary education (M Ed); guidance and counseling (M Ed, MA, Ed D, PhD, CAGS); human development (MS); reading (M Ed, MA, MAT, CAGS); school psychology (M Ed, MA, Ed D, PhD, CAGS); secondary curriculum and instruction (M Ed, MA, MAT, CAGS); special education (M Ed, MA, CAGS).

School of Law Students: 425 full-time (259 women), 2 part-time (1 woman); includes 368 minority (348 African Americans, 9 Asian Americans or Pacific Islanders, 11 Hispanic Americans), 38 international. Average age 25. 1,457 applicants, 35% accepted, 212 enrolled. *Faculty:* 35 full-time (16 women), 21 part-time/adjunct (5 women). Expenses: Contact institution. *Financial support:* In 2001–02, 133 students received support, including 1 fellowship (averaging $5,000 per year), 20 research assistantships (averaging $5,200 per year), 5 teaching assistantships (averaging $5,200 per year); Federal Work-Study and scholarships/grants also available. Support available to part-time students. Financial award application deadline: 2/15; financial award applicants required to submit FAFSA. In 2001, 119 first professional degrees, 12 master's awarded. Offers law (JD, LL M). *Application deadline:* For fall admission, 3/31. Applications are processed on a rolling basis. *Application fee:* $60. Electronic applications accepted. *Application Contact:* Nyurka Willis, Assistant Dean of Admissions and Financial Aid, 202-806-8008, Fax: 202-806-8162, E-mail: rjsherrod@law.howard.edu. *Assistant Dean of Admissions and Financial Aid,* Ruby Sherrod, 202-806-8008, Fax: 202-806-8424.

School of Social Work *Degree program information:* Part-time programs available. Offers social work (MSW, PhD).

HSI LAI UNIVERSITY, Rosemead, CA 91770

General Information Independent, coed, comprehensive institution. *Enrollment by degree level:* 27 master's, 23 doctoral. *Graduate faculty:* 7 full-time (1 woman), 5 part-time/adjunct (1 woman). *Tuition:* Full-time $3,000; part-time $100 per credit. *Required fees:* $135; $45 per semester. Part-time tuition and fees vary according to course load. *Graduate housing:* Room and/or apartments guaranteed to single students; on-campus housing not available to married students. Typical cost: $5,000 (including board). *Student services:* Campus employment opportunities, campus safety program, career counseling, disabled student services, exercise/wellness program, free psychological counseling, international student services, low-cost health insurance. *Web address:* http://www.hlu.edu/.

General Application Contact: Grace Su-Wen Hsiao, Registrar (Admissions), 626-571-8811, Fax: 626-571-1413, E-mail: info@hlu.edu.

GRADUATE UNITS

Department of Business Administration Students: 25 full-time (16 women), 4 part-time (1 woman); includes 28 minority (all Asian Americans or Pacific Islanders) 10 applicants, 100% accepted, 5 enrolled. Expenses: Contact institution. *Financial support:* In 2001–02, 15 students received support. Career-related internships or fieldwork, scholarships/grants, and tuition waivers (partial) available. In 2001, 2 degrees awarded. *Degree program information:* Part-time and evening/weekend programs available. Offers business administration (EMBA); finance (MBA); information technology and management (MBA); international business (MBA); nonprofit organization management (MBA). *Application deadline:* Applications are processed on a rolling basis. *Application fee:* $45 ($100 for international students). *Application Contact:* Grace Su-Wen Hsiao, Registrar (Admissions), 626-571-8811, Fax: 626-571-1413, E-mail: info@hlu.edu. *Chair,* Dr. Bill Yue-Yun Chen, 626-656-2125, Fax: 626-571-1413, E-mail: billchen@hlu.edu.

Department of Religious Studies Students: 19 full-time (12 women), 31 part-time (13 women); includes 45 minority (all Asian Americans or Pacific Islanders) Average age 25. 8 applicants, 100% accepted, 8 enrolled. *Faculty:* 6 full-time (0 women), 5 part-time/adjunct (1 woman). Expenses: Contact institution. *Financial support:* In 2001–02, 25 students received support, including 2 fellowships (averaging $6,500 per year); scholarships/grants and tuition waivers (partial) also available. In 2001, 8 master's awarded. *Degree program information:* Part-time and evening/weekend programs available. Offers Buddhist studies (MA); Budhhist studies (DBS); comparative religions (MA); religious studies (PhD). *Application deadline:* Applications are processed on a rolling basis. *Application fee:* $45 ($100 for international students). *Application Contact:* Melissa Rhodes, Registrar, 626-656-2121, E-mail: info@hlu.edu. *Chair,* Dr. An-Hue Thich, 626-571-8811, Fax: 626-571-1413, E-mail: info@hlu.edu.

HUMBOLDT STATE UNIVERSITY, Arcata, CA 95521-8299

General Information State-supported, coed, comprehensive institution. CGS member. *Enrollment:* 307 full-time matriculated graduate/professional students (180 women), 149 part-time matriculated graduate/professional students (77 women). *Enrollment by degree level:* 456 master's. *Graduate faculty:* 308 full-time (98 women), 252 part-time/adjunct (130 women). Tuition, state resident: full-time $1,969. Tuition, nonresident: part-time $246 per unit. *Graduate housing:* Room and/or apartments available to single students; on-campus housing not available to married students. Typical cost: $3,825 per year ($6,690 including board). *Student services:* Campus employment opportunities, campus safety program, career counseling, child daycare facilities, disabled student services, free psychological counseling, low-cost health insurance, multicultural affairs office. *Online resources:* library catalog, web page, access to other libraries' catalogs. *Collection:* 528,680 titles, 3,169 serial subscriptions, 46,391 audiovisual materials. *Research affiliation:* California Cooperative Fisheries Research Unit, Redwood Sciences Laboratory of the Pacific Southwest Forest and Range Experiment Station, U.S. Fish and Wildlife Service–Wildlife Field Station, National Sea Grant, McIntire-Stennis (forestry).

Computer facilities: 600 computers available on campus for general student use. A campuswide network can be accessed from student residence rooms and from off campus. Internet access and online class registration are available. *Web address:* http://www.humboldt.edu/.

General Application Contact: Carla Douglas, Research and Graduate Studies, 707-826-3949, E-mail: cpd1@humboldt.edu.

GRADUATE UNITS

Graduate Studies Students: 307 full-time (180 women), 149 part-time (77 women). Average age 32. 412 applicants, 58% accepted, 168 enrolled. *Faculty:* 308 full-time (98 women), 252 part-time/adjunct (130 women). Expenses: Contact institution. *Financial support:* Fellowships, research assistantships, teaching assistantships, career-related internships or fieldwork, Federal Work-Study, and institutionally sponsored loans available. Support available to part-time students. Financial award application deadline: 3/1; financial award applicants required to submit FAFSA. In 2001, 118 degrees awarded. *Degree program information:* Part-time and evening/weekend programs available. *Application deadline:* Applications are processed on a rolling basis. *Application fee:* $55. Electronic applications accepted. *Dean,* Dr. Donna Schafer, 707-826-3949, E-mail: schafer@humboldt.edu.

College of Arts, Humanities, and Social Sciences Students: 106 full-time (65 women), 36 part-time (20 women); includes 16 minority (2 African Americans, 5 Asian Americans or Pacific Islanders, 7 Hispanic Americans, 2 Native Americans), 2 international. Average age 33. 129 applicants, 71% accepted, 61 enrolled. Expenses: Contact institution. *Financial support:* Fellowships, teaching assistantships, career-related internships or fieldwork, Federal Work-Study, and institutionally sponsored loans available. Support available to part-time students. Financial award application deadline: 3/1; financial award applicants required to submit FAFSA. In 2001, 29 degrees awarded. Offers arts, humanities, and social sciences (MA, MFA); English (MA); social science (MA); sociology (MA); theatre arts (MA, MFA). *Application deadline:* Applications are processed on a rolling basis. *Application fee:* $55. Electronic applications accepted. *Dean,* Dr. Karen Carlton, 707-826-3116, E-mail: kac7@humboldt.edu.

College of Natural Resources and Sciences Students: 157 full-time (96 women), 63 part-time (26 women); includes 22 minority (1 African American, 8 Asian Americans or Pacific Islanders, 11 Hispanic Americans, 2 Native Americans), 8 international. Average age 30. 214 applicants, 45% accepted, 69 enrolled. Expenses: Contact institution. *Financial support:* Fellowships, career-related internships or fieldwork and Federal Work-Study available. Support available to part-time students. Financial award application deadline: 3/1; financial award applicants required to submit FAFSA. In 2001, 68 degrees awarded. *Degree program information:* Part-time programs available. Offers biological sciences (MA); environmental systems (MS); natural resources (MS); natural resources and sciences (MA, MS); psychology (MA). *Application deadline:* Applications are processed on a rolling basis. *Application fee:* $55. *Dean,* Dr. Jim Howard, 707-826-3256, E-mail: howard@humboldt.edu.

College of Professional Studies Students: 44 full-time (19 women), 50 part-time (31 women); includes 11 minority (2 African Americans, 2 Asian Americans or Pacific Islanders, 4 Hispanic Americans, 3 Native Americans), 3 international. Average age 34. 69 applicants, 75% accepted, 38 enrolled. Expenses: Contact institution. *Financial support:* Fellowships, teaching assistantships, career-related internships or fieldwork, Federal Work-Study, and institutionally sponsored loans available. Support available to part-time students. Financial award application deadline: 3/1; financial award applicants required to submit FAFSA. In 2001, 21 degrees awarded. *Degree program information:* Part-time and evening/weekend programs available. Offers business and economics (MBA); physical education (MA); professional studies (MA, MBA). *Application deadline:* Applications are processed on a rolling basis. *Application fee:* $55. *Dean,* Dr. John Costello, 707-826-3961, Fax: 826-3963, E-mail: costello@humboldt.edu.

HUMPHREYS COLLEGE, Stockton, CA 95207-3896

General Information Independent, coed, comprehensive institution. *Enrollment:* 60 full-time matriculated graduate/professional students (26 women). *Enrollment by degree level:* 60 first professional. *Graduate faculty:* 1 full-time (0 women), 17 part-time/adjunct (7 women). *Graduate housing:* Rooms and/or apartments available on a first-come, first-served basis to single and married students. *Student services:* Campus employment opportunities, career counseling, child daycare facilities. *Library facilities:* Humphreys College Library plus 1 other. *Collection:* 20,500 titles, 115 serial subscriptions.

Computer facilities: 40 computers available on campus for general student use. Internet access is available. *Web address:* http://www.humphreys.edu/.

General Application Contact: Santa Lopez, Admission Counselor, 209-478-0800 Ext. 102, Fax: 209-478-8721, E-mail: slopez@humphreys.edu.

GRADUATE UNITS

School of Law Students: 60 full-time (26 women); includes 20 minority (3 African Americans, 7 Asian Americans or Pacific Islanders, 9 Hispanic Americans, 1 Native American) Average age 36. 59 applicants, 56% accepted. *Faculty:* 1 full-time (0 women), 17 part-time/adjunct (7 women). Expenses: Contact institution. *Financial support:* In 2001–02, 50 students received support. Federal Work-Study available. Support available to part-time students. Financial award application deadline: 7/1; financial award applicants required to submit FAFSA. In 2001, 11 degrees awarded. Offers law (JD). *Application deadline:* For fall admission, 7/1 (priority date). Applications are processed on a rolling basis. *Application fee:* $35. *Application Contact:* Santa Lopez, Admission Counselor, 209-478-0800 Ext. 102, Fax: 209-478-8721, E-mail: slopez@humphreys.edu. *Dean,* Nels B. Fransen, 209-478-0800 Ext. 116, Fax: 209-478-8721.

HUNTER COLLEGE OF THE CITY UNIVERSITY OF NEW YORK, New York, NY 10021-5085

General Information State and locally supported, coed, comprehensive institution. *Enrollment:* 811 full-time matriculated graduate/professional students (639 women), 3,884 part-time matriculated graduate/professional students (3,053 women). *Enrollment by degree level:* 3,626 master's. *Graduate faculty:* 584 full-time (300 women), 665 part-time/adjunct (378 women). Tuition, state resident: full-time $2,175; part-time $185 per credit. Tuition, nonresident: full-time $3,800; part-time $320 per credit. *Graduate housing:* Room and/or apartments available on a first-come, first-served basis to single students; on-campus housing not available to married students. *Student services:* Campus employment opportunities, campus safety program, career counseling, child daycare facilities, disabled student services, exercise/wellness program, free psychological counseling, international student services, teacher training, writing training. *Library facilities:* Hunter College Library. *Online resources:* library catalog, web page, access to other libraries' catalogs. *Collection:* 521,955 titles, 2,419 serial subscriptions, 12,515 audiovisual materials. *Research affiliation:* Bellevue Hospital Center, The Mount Sinai Medical Center, New York Hospital, Cornell University Medical Center.

Computer facilities: 600 computers available on campus for general student use. A campuswide network can be accessed. Internet access is available. *Web address:* http://www.hunter.cuny.edu/.

General Application Contact: William Zlata, Director for Graduate Admissions, 212-772-4288, Fax: 212-650-3336, E-mail: admissions@hunter.cuny.edu.

Hunter College of the City University of New York (continued)

GRADUATE UNITS

Graduate School Students: 811 full-time (639 women), 3,884 part-time (3,053 women); includes 975 minority (409 African Americans, 164 Asian Americans or Pacific Islanders, 393 Hispanic Americans, 9 Native Americans), 84 international. Average age 33. 3,791 applicants, 46% accepted. *Faculty:* 584 full-time (300 women), 665 part-time/adjunct (378 women). Expenses: Contact institution. *Financial support:* Fellowships with full and partial tuition reimbursements, research assistantships with partial tuition reimbursements, teaching assistantships, career-related internships or fieldwork, Federal Work-Study, institutionally sponsored loans, scholarships/grants, traineeships, tuition waivers (full and partial), unspecified assistantships, and lesson stipends available. Support available to part-time students. Financial award applicants required to submit FAFSA. In 2001, 997 master's, 26 other advanced degrees awarded. *Degree program information:* Part-time and evening/weekend programs available. *Application fee:* $40. *Application Contact:* Michael Goldstein, Assistant Director for Graduate Admissions, 212-772-4288, Fax: 212-650-3336, E-mail: admissions@hunter.cuny.edu. *Director of Admissions*, William Zlata, 212-772-4288, Fax: 212-650-3336, E-mail: michael.goldstein@t.zayid.hunter.cuny.edu.

School of Arts and Sciences Students: 91 full-time (55 women), 633 part-time (406 women); includes 119 minority (25 African Americans, 28 Asian Americans or Pacific Islanders, 66 Hispanic Americans), 59 international. Average age 32. 839 applicants, 41% accepted. *Faculty:* 387 full-time (218 women), 509 part-time/adjunct (235 women). Expenses: Contact institution. *Financial support:* Fellowships, research assistantships, teaching assistantships, career-related internships or fieldwork, Federal Work-Study, institutionally sponsored loans, scholarships/grants, tuition waivers (full and partial), unspecified assistantships, and lesson stipends available. Support available to part-time students. In 2001, 218 degrees awarded. *Degree program information:* Part-time and evening/weekend programs available. Offers analytical geography (MA); anthropology (MA); applied and evaluative psychology (MA); applied mathematics (MA); applied social research (MS); art history (MA); arts and sciences (MA, MFA, MS, MSSR, MSW, MUP, DSW, PhD, AC, Certificate); biochemistry (MA); biological sciences (MA, PhD); biopsychology and comparative psychology (MA); creative writing (MFA); earth system science (MA); economics (MA); English and American literature (MA); English education (MA); environmental and social issues (MA); fine arts (MFA); French (MA); French education (MA); geographic information science (Certificate); geographic information systems (MA); history (MA); integrated media arts (MA); Italian (MA); Italian education (MA); mathematics for secondary education (MA); music (MA); music education (MA); physics (MA, PhD); pure mathematics (MA); social work (MSW, DSW); social, cognitive, and developmental psychology (MA); sociology (MSSR); Spanish (MA); Spanish education (MA); studio art (MFA); teaching earth science (MA); teaching Latin (MA); theater (MA); urban affairs (MS); urban planning (MUP). *Application fee:* $40. *Application Contact:* William Zlata, Director for Graduate Admissions, 212-772-4288, Fax: 212-650-3336, E-mail: admissions@hunter.cuny.edu. *Acting Dean*, Dr. Judith Friedlander, 212-772-5121, Fax: 212-772-5138, E-mail: judith.friedlander@hunter.cuny.edu.

School of Education Students: 136 full-time (108 women), 1,425 part-time (1,233 women); includes 354 minority (108 African Americans, 80 Asian Americans or Pacific Islanders, 166 Hispanic Americans), 14 international. Average age 33. 1,148 applicants, 57% accepted. *Faculty:* 62 full-time (42 women), 72 part-time/adjunct (50 women). Expenses: Contact institution. *Financial support:* Fellowships, career-related internships or fieldwork, Federal Work-Study, institutionally sponsored loans, and tuition waivers (full and partial) available. Support available to part-time students. In 2001, 443 master's, 22 other advanced degrees awarded. Offers bilingual education (MS); biology education (MA); blind or visually impaired (MS Ed); chemistry education (MA); corrective reading (K–12) (MS Ed); deaf or hard of hearing (MS Ed); early childhood education (MS); earth science (MA); education (MA, MS, MS Ed, AC); educational supervision and administration (AC); elementary education (MS); English education (MA); French education (MA); Italian education (MA); literacy (MS); mathematics education (MA); music education (MA); physics education (MA); rehabilitation counseling (MS Ed); school counselor (MS Ed); severe/multiple disabilities (MS Ed); social studies education (MA); Spanish education (MA); special education (MS Ed); teaching English as a second language (MA). *Application deadline:* For fall admission, 4/1; for spring admission, 11/1. Applications are processed on a rolling basis. *Application fee:* $40. *Application Contact:* William Zlata, Director for Graduate Admissions, 212-772-4288, Fax: 212-650-3336, E-mail: admissions@hunter.cuny.edu. *Acting Dean*, Dr. David J. Hodges, 212-772-4623.

Hunter-Bellevue School of Nursing Students: 10 full-time (6 women), 216 part-time (197 women); includes 86 minority (56 African Americans, 22 Asian Americans or Pacific Islanders, 8 Hispanic Americans), 1 international. Average age 38. 111 applicants, 85% accepted. *Faculty:* 21 full-time (19 women), 6 part-time/adjunct (5 women). Expenses: Contact institution. *Financial support:* In 2001–02, 9 students received support. Federal Work-Study, scholarships/grants, traineeships, and tuition waivers (partial) available. Support available to part-time students. Financial award application deadline: 5/1; financial award applicants required to submit FAFSA. In 2001, 65 master's, 7 other advanced degrees awarded. *Degree program information:* Part-time programs available. Offers adult nurse practitioner (MS); community health nursing (MS); gerontological nurse practitioner (MS); maternal child-health nursing (MS); medical/surgical nursing (MS); nursing (MS, AC); pediatric nurse practitioner (MS, AC); psychiatric nursing (MS). *Application deadline:* For fall admission, 4/15; for spring admission, 11/21. Applications are processed on a rolling basis. *Application fee:* $40. *Application Contact:* William Zlata, Director for Graduate Admissions, 212-772-4288, Fax: 212-650-3336, E-mail: admissions@hunter.cuny.edu. *Director*, Dr. Diane Rendon, 212-481-4312, Fax: 212-481-5078.

See in-depth description on page 905.

HUNTINGTON COLLEGE, Huntington, IN 46750-1299

General Information Independent-religious, coed, comprehensive institution. *Enrollment:* 3 full-time matriculated graduate/professional students (1 woman), 52 part-time matriculated graduate/professional students (11 women). *Enrollment by degree level:* 55 master's. *Graduate faculty:* 2 full-time (0 women), 10 part-time/adjunct (1 woman). *Tuition:* Full-time $5,000; part-time $256 per credit hour. *Required fees:* $60 per semester. One-time fee: $20. *Graduate housing:* On-campus housing not available. *Student services:* Career counseling, low-cost health insurance. *Library facilities:* RichLyn Library. *Collection:* 76,954 titles, 553 serial subscriptions.

Computer facilities: 75 computers available on campus for general student use. A campuswide network can be accessed from student residence rooms. Internet access is available. *Web address:* http://www.huntington.edu/.

General Application Contact: Dr. Gary House, Assistant Professor of Education, 260-359-4036, Fax: 260-359-4126, E-mail: ghouse@huntington.edu.

GRADUATE UNITS

Graduate School of Christian Ministries Students: 3 full-time (1 woman), 52 part-time (11 women); includes 2 minority (both African Americans), 1 international. Average age 38. *Faculty:* 3 full-time (0 women), 9 part-time/adjunct (1 woman). Expenses: Contact institution. *Financial support:* In 2001–02, 30 students received support, including 1 research assistantship with full tuition reimbursement available; career-related internships or fieldwork, institutionally sponsored loans, and scholarships/grants also available. Support available to part-time students. In 2001, 8 degrees awarded. *Degree program information:* Part-time programs available. Offers educational ministry (MA); pastoral ministry (MA); youth ministry (MA). *Application deadline:* For fall admission, 8/1 (priority date); for spring admission, 12/1 (priority date). Applications are processed on a rolling basis. *Application fee:* $20. Electronic applications accepted. *Application Contact:* Gary House, Graduate Admissions Department/Recruitment, 260-359-4036, Fax: 260-359-4126, E-mail: ghouse@huntington.edu. *Associate Dean for the Graduate School of Christian Ministries*, Dr. Ray A. Seilhamer, 260-359-4128, Fax: 260-359-4126, E-mail: rseilhamer@huntington.edu.

HURON UNIVERSITY USA IN LONDON, London, SW7 2PG, United Kingdom

General Information Independent, coed, comprehensive institution. *Enrollment:* 100 full-time matriculated graduate/professional students (50 women). *Enrollment by degree level:* 100 master's. *Graduate faculty:* 8 full-time (1 woman), 10 part-time/adjunct (4 women). *Tuition:* Full-time $10,000. Tuition and fees vary according to course level and program. *Graduate housing:* Rooms and/or apartments available on a first-come, first-served basis to single and married students. Typical cost: $6,000 per year for single students; $6,000 per year for married students. Room charges vary according to housing facility selected. *Student services:* Campus employment opportunities, campus safety program, career counseling, international student services, low-cost health insurance, writing training. *Web address:* http://www.huron.ac.uk/.

General Application Contact: Carolyne Miller, Assistant Director of Admissions, 20-7589-9696, Fax: 20-7589-9406, E-mail: carolyne@huron.ac.uk.

GRADUATE UNITS

Program in Business Administration Students: 65 full-time (35 women). Average age 25. 120 applicants, 33% accepted, 25 enrolled. *Faculty:* 4 full-time (0 women), 2 part-time/adjunct (both women). Expenses: Contact institution. *Financial support:* In 2001–02, 20 students received support. Scholarships/grants and tuition waivers (partial) available. In 2001, 50 degrees awarded. *Degree program information:* Part-time programs available. Offers entrepreneurship (MBA); global financial institutions and markets (MBA); international business (MBA); management information systems (MBA); marketing (MBA). *Application deadline:* For fall admission, 5/1 (priority date); for winter admission, 11/1 (priority date); for spring admission, 3/15 (priority date). Applications are processed on a rolling basis. *Application fee:* $35. Electronic applications accepted. *Application Contact:* Arvind Vepa, Assistant Director of Admissions, E-mail: arvind@huron.ac.uk. *Director*, Dr. Karl Roberts.

Program in International Relations Students: 12 full-time (8 women), 3 part-time (2 women). 65 applicants, 28% accepted, 15 enrolled. *Faculty:* 2 full-time (0 women), 2 part-time/adjunct (1 woman). Expenses: Contact institution. *Financial support:* In 2001–02, 4 students received support. Scholarships/grants and tuition waivers (partial) available. In 2001, 5 degrees awarded. *Degree program information:* Part-time programs available. Offers conflict resolution (MA); diplomacy (MA); international public law (MA); international relations (MA); politics (MA). *Application deadline:* For fall admission, 5/1 (priority date); for winter admission, 11/1 (priority date); for spring admission, 4/15 (priority date). Applications are processed on a rolling basis. *Application fee:* $35. Electronic applications accepted. *Application Contact:* Arvind Vepa, Assistant Director of Admissions, E-mail: arvind@huron.ac.uk. *Director*, Dr. Bruce Stanley.

HUSSON COLLEGE, Bangor, ME 04401-2999

General Information Independent, coed, comprehensive institution. *Graduate housing:* Room and/or apartments available to single students; on-campus housing not available to married students. Housing application deadline: 6/1.

GRADUATE UNITS

Graduate Studies Division *Degree program information:* Part-time and evening/weekend programs available. Offers business (MSB); family nurse practitioner (MSN); nursing (MSN); physical therapy (MSPT); psychiatric nursing (MSN).

ICR GRADUATE SCHOOL, Santee, CA 92071

General Information Independent-religious, coed, graduate-only institution. *Enrollment by degree level:* 37 master's. *Graduate faculty:* 5 full-time (0 women), 8 part-time/adjunct (0 women). *Tuition:* Part-time $150 per semester hour. *Graduate housing:* On-campus housing not available. *Student services:* Campus employment opportunities, campus safety program, career counseling. *Collection:* 23,242 titles, 560 serial subscriptions.

Computer facilities: 8 computers available on campus for general student use. Internet access is available. *Web address:* http://www.icr.org/.

General Application Contact: Dr. Jack Kriege, Registrar, 619-448-0900 Ext. 6016, Fax: 619-448-3469, E-mail: jkriege@icr.org.

GRADUATE UNITS

Graduate Programs Students: 15 full-time (7 women), 22 part-time (10 women); includes 3 minority (all Asian Americans or Pacific Islanders) Average age 42. *Faculty:* 5 full-time (0 women), 8 part-time/adjunct (0 women). Expenses: Contact institution. *Degree program information:* Part-time programs available. Offers astro/geophysics (MS); biology (MS); geology (MS); science education (MS). *Application deadline:* Applications are processed on a rolling basis. *Application fee:* $30. *Application Contact:* Dr. Jack Kriege, Registrar, 619-448-0900 Ext. 6016, Fax: 619-448-3469, E-mail: jkriege@icr.org. *Dean*, Kenneth B. Cumming, 619-448-0900, Fax: 619-448-3469.

IDAHO STATE UNIVERSITY, Pocatello, ID 83209

General Information State-supported, coed, university. CGS member. *Enrollment:* 841 full-time matriculated graduate/professional students (427 women), 598 part-time matriculated graduate/professional students (315 women). *Enrollment by degree level:* 224 first professional, 967 master's, 248 doctoral. *Graduate faculty:* 278 full-time (78 women), 11 part-time/adjunct (3 women). *International tuition:* $9,672 full-time. *Tuition, area resident:* Full-time $3,432. Tuition, state resident: part-time $172 per credit. Tuition, nonresident: full-time $10,196; part-time $262 per credit. Part-time tuition and fees vary according to course load, program and reciprocity agreements. *Graduate housing:* Rooms and/or apartments available on a first-come, first-served basis to single and married students. Typical cost: $2,660 per year ($4,950 including board) for single students; $4,450 per year for married students. Room and board charges vary according to board plan, campus/location and housing facility selected. Housing application deadline: 5/1. *Student services:* Campus employment opportunities, campus safety program, career counseling, child daycare facilities, disabled student services, exercise/wellness program, free psychological counseling, grant writing training, international student services, low-cost health insurance, multicultural affairs office, teacher training, writing training. *Library facilities:* Eli M. Oboler Library. *Online resources:* library catalog, web page. *Collection:* 345,066 titles, 3,336 serial subscriptions, 4,500 audiovisual materials. *Research affiliation:* Environmental Science and Research Foundation (waste management, ecology), Bechtel BWXT ID, LLC (environmental management, nuclear sciences), J. R. Simplot Company, Idaho (plant sciences, environmental studies), Inland Northwest Research Alliance (science), AMI Semiconductor (computer sciences, environmental management), S. M. Stoller Corporation (ecology, waste management).

Computer facilities: 300 computers available on campus for general student use. A campuswide network can be accessed from student residence rooms and from off campus. *Web address:* http://www.isu.edu/.

General Application Contact: Dr. Paul Tate, Dean, 208-282-2150, Fax: 208-282-4847, E-mail: graddean@isu.edu.

GRADUATE UNITS

Office of Graduate Studies Students: 841 full-time (427 women), 598 part-time (315 women); includes 88 minority (10 African Americans, 33 Asian Americans or Pacific Islanders, 32 Hispanic Americans, 13 Native Americans), 135 international. Average age 34. 2,665 applicants. *Faculty:* 278 full-time (78 women), 11 part-time/adjunct (3 women). Expenses: Contact institution. *Financial support:* In 2001–02, 24 fellowships with full and partial tuition reimbursements (averaging $10,874 per year), 53 research assistantships with full and partial tuition reimbursements (averaging $8,819 per year), 192 teaching assistantships with full and partial tuition reimbursements (averaging $8,385 per year) were awarded. Career-related internships or fieldwork, Federal Work-Study, institutionally sponsored loans, scholarships/grants, traineeships, and tuition waivers (full and partial) also available. Support available to part-time students. In 2001, 66 first professional degrees, 281 master's, 23 doctorates, 11 other advanced degrees awarded. *Degree program information:* Part-time and evening/weekend programs available. Postbaccalaureate distance learning degree programs offered. Offers biology (MNS); chemistry (MNS); general interdisciplinary (M Ed, MA); geology (MNS);

industrial training management (M Ed); mathematics (MNS); physics (MNS); technology (M Ed, MTD); training and development (MTD); vocational program management (M Ed); waste management and environmental science (MS). *Application deadline:* Applications are processed on a rolling basis. *Application fee:* $35. *Dean*, Dr. Paul Tate, 208-282-2150, Fax: 208-282-4847, E-mail: graddean@isu.edu.

College of Arts and Sciences Students: 197 full-time (92 women), 71 part-time (32 women); includes 14 minority (2 Asian Americans or Pacific Islanders, 7 Hispanic Americans, 5 Native Americans), 17 international. Average age 34. *Faculty:* 150 full-time (34 women), 5 part-time/adjunct (2 women). Expenses: Contact institution. *Financial support:* In 2001–02, 23 fellowships with full and partial tuition reimbursements (averaging $10,826 per year), 34 research assistantships with full and partial tuition reimbursements (averaging $7,839 per year), 91 teaching assistantships with full and partial tuition reimbursements (averaging $7,920 per year) were awarded. Career-related internships or fieldwork, Federal Work-Study, institutionally sponsored loans, and tuition waivers (full and partial) also available. Support available to part-time students. In 2001, 58 master's, 14 doctorates awarded. *Degree program information:* Part-time programs available. Offers anthropology (MA, MS); art (MFA); arts and sciences (MA, MFA, MNS, MPA, MS, DA, PhD, Certificate); biology (MS, DA, PhD); chemistry (MNS, MS); clinical psychology (PhD); English (MA, DA); geology (MS); geophysics/hydrology (MS); geotechnology (Certificate); mathematics (MS, DA); microbiology (MS); natural science (MNS); physics (MS); political science (MA, DA); psychology (MS); public administration (MPA); sociology (MA); speech communication (MA); theatre (MA). *Application deadline:* Applications are processed on a rolling basis. *Application fee:* $35. *Application Contact:* Bonnie Hall, Graduate School Admissions Clerk, 208-282-2150. *Interim Dean*, Dr. Bob Swanson, 208-282-3204.

College of Business Students: 41 full-time (13 women), 83 part-time (21 women). Average age 33. *Faculty:* 24 full-time (3 women), 1 part-time/adjunct (0 women). Expenses: Contact institution. *Financial support:* In 2001–02, 15 teaching assistantships with full and partial tuition reimbursements (averaging $7,846 per year) were awarded; Federal Work-Study and tuition waivers (full and partial) also available. Support available to part-time students. In 2001, 22 degrees awarded. *Degree program information:* Part-time and evening/weekend programs available. Offers business administration (MBA); computer information systems (MS). *Application deadline:* For fall admission, 7/1 (priority date); for spring admission, 12/1. Applications are processed on a rolling basis. *Application fee:* $35. *Dean*, William Stratton, 208-282-2135.

College of Education Students: 77 full-time (46 women), 259 part-time (144 women); includes 17 minority (4 African Americans, 3 Asian Americans or Pacific Islanders, 8 Hispanic Americans, 2 Native Americans), 59 international. Average age 38. *Faculty:* 30 full-time (15 women). Expenses: Contact institution. *Financial support:* In 2001–02, 1 fellowship with full and partial tuition reimbursement (averaging $12,000 per year), 31 teaching assistantships with full and partial tuition reimbursements (averaging $9,723 per year) were awarded. Research assistantships with full and partial tuition reimbursements, career-related internships or fieldwork, Federal Work-Study, institutionally sponsored loans, and tuition waivers (full) also available. Support available to part-time students. In 2001, 68 master's, 5 doctorates, 6 other advanced degrees awarded. *Degree program information:* Part-time and evening/weekend programs available. Postbaccalaureate distance learning degree programs offered (no on-campus study). Offers athletic administration (MPE); child and family studies (M Ed); curriculum and instruction (M Ed); education (M Ed, MPE, Ed D, Ed S); educational administration (M Ed, Ed S); educational leadership (Ed D); human exceptionality (M Ed); instructional technology (M Ed); literacy (M Ed); school psychology (Ed S); special education (Ed S). *Application deadline:* For fall admission, 7/1 (priority date); for spring admission, 12/1. Applications are processed on a rolling basis. *Application fee:* $35. *Application Contact:* Dr. Stephanie Salzman, Director, Office of Standards and Assessment, 208-282-3114, Fax: 208-282-4697, E-mail: salzstep@isu.edu. *Dean*, Dr. Larry Harris, 208-282-3259, Fax: 208-282-4697, E-mail: harris@isu.edu.

College of Engineering Students: 34 full-time (8 women), 18 part-time (1 woman); includes 7 minority (1 African American, 5 Asian Americans or Pacific Islanders, 1 Hispanic American), 15 international. Average age 34. *Faculty:* 13 full-time (0 women), 1 part-time/adjunct (0 women). Expenses: Contact institution. *Financial support:* In 2001–02, 7 research assistantships with full and partial tuition reimbursements (averaging $10,740 per year), 16 teaching assistantships with full and partial tuition reimbursements (averaging $6,775 per year) were awarded. Federal Work-Study and institutionally sponsored loans also available. Support available to part-time students. Financial award application deadline: 2/15. In 2001, 12 master's, 1 doctorate awarded. *Degree program information:* Part-time programs available. Offers engineering and applied science (PhD); engineering structures and mechanics (MS); environmental engineering (MS); measurement and control engineering (MS); nuclear science and engineering (MS); waste management and environmental science (MS). *Application deadline:* For fall admission, 7/1 (priority date); for spring admission, 12/1. Applications are processed on a rolling basis. *Application fee:* $35. *Dean*, Dr. Jay Kunze, 208-282-2902, Fax: 208-282-4538.

College of Health Professions Students: 236 full-time (151 women), 72 part-time (62 women); includes 13 minority (1 African American, 5 Asian Americans or Pacific Islanders, 5 Hispanic Americans, 2 Native Americans), 15 international. Average age 33. *Faculty:* 36 full-time (19 women), 3 part-time/adjunct (0 women). Expenses: Contact institution. *Financial support:* In 2001–02, 5 research assistantships with full and partial tuition reimbursements (averaging $8,098 per year), 30 teaching assistantships with full and partial tuition reimbursements (averaging $9,241 per year) were awarded. Fellowships, career-related internships or fieldwork, Federal Work-Study, institutionally sponsored loans, scholarships/grants, traineeships, and tuition waivers (full and partial) also available. Support available to part-time students. In 2001, 94 master's, 4 doctorates, 2 other advanced degrees awarded. *Degree program information:* Part-time programs available. Offers advanced general dentistry (Post-Doctoral Certificate); audiology (MS); counseling (M Coun, Ed S); counselor education and counseling (PhD); deaf education (MS); family medicine (Certificate); health education (MHE); health professions (M Coun, MHE, MOT, MPAS, MPH, MPT, MS, PhD, Certificate, Ed S, Post-Doctoral Certificate); marriage and family counseling (M Coun); mental health counseling (M Coun); nursing (MS, Certificate); occupational therapy (MOT); physical therapy (MPT); physician assistant studies (MPAS); public health (MPH); school counseling (M Coun); speech language pathology (MS); student affairs and college counseling (M Coun). *Application fee:* $35. *Dean*, Dr. Linda Hatzenbuehler, 208-282-3287, Fax: 208-282-4000.

College of Pharmacy Students: 217 full-time (97 women), 25 part-time (16 women); includes 26 minority (2 African Americans, 18 Asian Americans or Pacific Islanders, 3 Hispanic Americans, 3 Native Americans), 15 international. Average age 28. *Faculty:* 19 full-time (6 women), 1 (woman) part-time/adjunct. Expenses: Contact institution. *Financial support:* In 2001–02, 6 research assistantships with full and partial tuition reimbursements (averaging $12,366 per year), 5 teaching assistantships with full and partial tuition reimbursements (averaging $10,397 per year) were awarded. Federal Work-Study also available. Support available to part-time students. In 2001, 66 first professional degrees, 2 doctorates awarded. *Degree program information:* Part-time programs available. Offers biopharmaceutical analysis (PhD); biopharmaceutics (PhD); pharmaceutical chemistry (MS); pharmaceutical science (PhD); pharmaceutics (MS); pharmacognosy (MS); pharmacokinetics (PhD); pharmacology (MS, PhD); pharmacy (Pharm D); pharmacy administration (MS, PhD). *Application deadline:* For fall admission, 8/1 (priority date). *Application fee:* $35. *Dean*, Dr. Joseph Steiner, 208-282-2175.

ILIFF SCHOOL OF THEOLOGY, Denver, CO 80210-4798

General Information Independent-religious, coed, graduate-only institution. *Enrollment by degree level:* 157 first professional, 156 master's. *Graduate faculty:* 21 full-time (4 women), 33 part-time/adjunct (21 women). *Tuition:* Full-time $10,320; part-time $430. *Required fees:* $30. Part-time tuition and fees vary according to course load, degree level and program. *Graduate housing:* Rooms and/or apartments available on a first-come, first-served basis to single and married students. Typical cost: $3,278 (including board) for single students; $3,678 (including board) for married students. Room and board charges vary according to housing facility selected. *Student services:* Campus employment opportunities, career counseling, disabled student services, free psychological counseling, international student services, writing training. *Library facilities:* Ira J. Taylor Library. *Online resources:* library catalog, web page. *Collection:* 203,000 titles, 900 serial subscriptions, 2,580 audiovisual materials.

Computer facilities: 16 computers available on campus for general student use. A campuswide network can be accessed from off campus. Internet access is available. *Web address:* http://www.iliff.edu/.

General Application Contact: Matthew R. Wehrly, Vice President for Student Services, 303-765-3118, Fax: 303-777-0164, E-mail: mwehrly@iliff.edu.

GRADUATE UNITS

Graduate and Professional Programs Students: 147 full-time (96 women), 166 part-time (91 women); includes 41 minority (22 African Americans, 11 Asian Americans or Pacific Islanders, 4 Hispanic Americans, 4 Native Americans), 19 international. Average age 38. 116 applicants, 70% accepted. *Faculty:* 24 full-time (6 women), 20 part-time/adjunct (8 women). Expenses: Contact institution. *Financial support:* In 2001–02, 232 students received support, including 1 fellowship (averaging $10,105 per year), 13 research assistantships (averaging $2,889 per year), 8 teaching assistantships (averaging $3,271 per year); career-related internships or fieldwork, Federal Work-Study, institutionally sponsored loans, scholarships/grants, tuition waivers (partial), and unspecified assistantships also available. Financial award application deadline: 5/15; financial award applicants required to submit FAFSA. In 2001, 28 master's, 4 doctorates awarded. *Degree program information:* Part-time programs available. Offers biblical studies (MA); church history (MA); religion (MA); specialized ministry (MASM); theology (M Div, MTS, D Min, PhD); theology/ethics (MA). *Application deadline:* For fall admission, 7/1 (priority date); for winter admission, 11/1 (priority date); for spring admission, 1/1 (priority date). Applications are processed on a rolling basis. *Application fee:* $25. *Application Contact:* Matthew R. Wehrly, Director of Admissions, 303-765-3118, Fax: 303-777-0164, E-mail: mwehrly@iliff.edu. *President*, Dr. David Maldonado, 303-765-3102, Fax: 303-777-3387.

ILLINOIS COLLEGE OF OPTOMETRY, Chicago, IL 60616-3878

General Information Independent, coed, graduate-only institution. *Enrollment by degree level:* 635 first professional. *Graduate faculty:* 46 full-time (27 women), 27 part-time/adjunct (11 women). *Tuition:* Full-time $22,668; part-time $475 per hour. *Required fees:* $188. *Graduate housing:* Rooms and/or apartments guaranteed to single students and available on a first-come, first-served basis to married students. Typical cost: $7,761 (including board) for single students; $10,497 per year for married students. Room and board charges vary according to housing facility selected. Housing application deadline: 6/1. *Student services:* Campus employment opportunities, campus safety program, career counseling, disabled student services, exercise/wellness program, free psychological counseling, international student services, low-cost health insurance. *Library facilities:* Carl F. Shepard Library. *Online resources:* library catalog, web page, access to other libraries' catalogs. *Collection:* 31,978 titles, 210 serial subscriptions, 1,170 audiovisual materials. *Research affiliation:* University of Chicago (vision science), Rush University (cataract development), Alcon Labs (glaucoma).

Computer facilities: 33 computers available on campus for general student use. A campuswide network can be accessed from student residence rooms and from off campus. Internet access is available. *Web address:* http://www.ico.edu/.

General Application Contact: Dr. Mark Colip, Dean for Student Affairs, 312-949-7400, Fax: 312-949-7680, E-mail: mcolip@eyecare.ico.edu.

GRADUATE UNITS

Professional Program Students: 634 full-time (362 women), 1 (woman) part-time; includes 182 minority (4 African Americans, 158 Asian Americans or Pacific Islanders, 20 Hispanic Americans), 79 international. Average age 24. 737 applicants, 45% accepted, 148 enrolled. *Faculty:* 46 full-time (27 women), 27 part-time/adjunct (11 women). Expenses: Contact institution. *Financial support:* In 2001–02, 580 students received support. Career-related internships or fieldwork, Federal Work-Study, and scholarships/grants available. Support available to part-time students. Financial award application deadline: 3/15; financial award applicants required to submit FAFSA. In 2001, 159 degrees awarded. Offers optometry (OD). *Application deadline:* For fall admission, 3/15. Applications are processed on a rolling basis. *Application fee:* $75. Electronic applications accepted. *Application Contact:* Dr. Mark Colip, Dean for Student Affairs, 312-949-7400, Fax: 312-949-7680, E-mail: mcolip@eyecare.ico.edu. *President*, Dr. Charles F. Mullen, 312-949-7701, Fax: 312-949-7670, E-mail: cmullen@eyecare.ico.edu.

ILLINOIS INSTITUTE OF TECHNOLOGY, Chicago, IL 60616-3793

General Information Independent, coed, university. CGS member. *Enrollment:* 1,239 full-time matriculated graduate/professional students (360 women), 1,510 part-time matriculated graduate/professional students (410 women). *Graduate faculty:* 280 full-time (52 women), 220 part-time/adjunct (40 women). *Tuition:* Part-time $590 per credit hour. *Graduate housing:* Rooms and/or apartments available on a first-come, first-served basis to single and married students. Housing application deadline: 7/15. *Student services:* Campus employment opportunities, campus safety program, career counseling, free psychological counseling, international student services, low-cost health insurance, multicultural affairs office. *Library facilities:* Paul V. Galvin Library plus 5 others. *Online resources:* library catalog, web page, access to other libraries' catalogs. *Collection:* 829,386 titles, 7,512 serial subscriptions, 52,251 audiovisual materials. *Research affiliation:* Fermi National Accelerator Laboratory, Los Alamos National Laboratory, Argonne National Laboratory, Brookhaven National Laboratory.

Computer facilities: 450 computers available on campus for general student use. A campuswide network can be accessed from student residence rooms and from off campus. Internet access and online class registration are available. *Web address:* http://www.iit.edu/.

General Application Contact: Dr. Ali Cinar, Dean of Graduate College, 312-567-3637, Fax: 312-567-7517, E-mail: gradstu@iit.edu.

GRADUATE UNITS

Center for Law and Financial Markets Students: 22 full-time (7 women), 50 part-time (9 women); includes 8 minority (2 African Americans, 5 Asian Americans or Pacific Islanders, 1 Hispanic American), 18 international. Average age 32. 120 applicants, 79% accepted. *Faculty:* 4 full-time (0 women), 35 part-time/adjunct (10 women). Expenses: Contact institution. *Financial support:* In 2001–02, 35 students received support. Career-related internships or fieldwork, institutionally sponsored loans, and scholarships/grants available. Support available to part-time students. Financial award applicants required to submit FAFSA. In 2001, 31 degrees awarded. *Degree program information:* Part-time and evening/weekend programs available. Offers financial markets (MS); financial markets and trading (MS); financial services law (LL M). *Application deadline:* For fall admission, 8/1; for winter admission, 10/15; for spring admission, 2/15. Applications are processed on a rolling basis. *Application fee:* $50. *Application Contact:* Melanie Winter, Director, 312-906-6508, Fax: 312-906-6511, E-mail: mwinter@elfm.iit.edu. *Executive Director*, Dr. Pamela Reardon, 312-906-6507, Fax: 312-906-6511, E-mail: pamela.reardon@iit.edu.

Chicago-Kent College of Law Students: 773 full-time (386 women), 319 part-time (138 women). Average age 26. 2,484 applicants, 46% accepted, 316 enrolled. *Faculty:* 63 full-time (19 women), 119 part-time/adjunct (24 women). Expenses: Contact institution. *Financial support:* In 2001–02, 925 students received support, including 27 research assistantships, 41 teaching assistantships; career-related internships or fieldwork, institutionally sponsored loans, scholarships/grants, and tuition waivers (full) also available. Support available to part-time students. Financial award application deadline: 3/15; financial award applicants required to submit FAFSA. In 2001, 289 first professional degrees, 19 master's awarded. *Degree program information:* Part-time and evening/weekend programs available. Offers environmental management (JD, LL M); financial markets and trading (JD, LL M); financial services (LL M); international law (LL M); law (JD); taxation (LL M). *Application deadline:* For fall admission, 3/1 (priority date). Applications are processed on a rolling basis. *Application fee:* $45. Electronic applications accepted. *Application Contact:* Michael S. Burns, Assistant Dean, 312-906-5020, Fax: 312-906-5274, E-mail: admit@kentlaw.edu. *Dean*, Henry H. Perritt, 312-906-5010, Fax: 312-906-5335, E-mail: hperritt@kentlaw.edu.

Illinois Institute of Technology (continued)

Graduate College Students: 1,056 full-time (296 women), 1,144 part-time (293 women); includes 245 minority (59 African Americans, 136 Asian Americans or Pacific Islanders, 48 Hispanic Americans, 2 Native Americans), 1,379 international. Average age 31. 5,102 applicants, 53% accepted. *Faculty:* 199 full-time (29 women), 127 part-time/adjunct (22 women). Expenses: Contact institution. *Financial support:* In 2001–02, 45 fellowships, 90 research assistantships, 177 teaching assistantships were awarded. Career-related internships or fieldwork, Federal Work-Study, institutionally sponsored loans, scholarships/grants, and unspecified assistantships also available. Financial award applicants required to submit FAFSA. In 2001, 570 master's, 55 doctorates awarded. *Degree program information:* Part-time and evening/weekend programs available. Postbaccalaureate distance learning degree programs offered (no on-campus study). *Application deadline:* For fall admission, 7/1; for spring admission, 11/1. Applications are processed on a rolling basis. *Application fee:* $30. Electronic applications accepted. *Dean of Graduate College*, Dr. Ali Cinar, 312-567-3637, Fax: 312-567-7517, E-mail: gradstu@iit.edu.

Armour College of Engineering and Sciences Students: 794 full-time (164 women), 1,010 part-time (227 women); includes 189 minority (37 African Americans, 117 Asian Americans or Pacific Islanders, 34 Hispanic Americans, 1 Native American), 1,227 international. Average age 28. 4,568 applicants, 53% accepted. *Faculty:* 153 full-time (18 women), 85 part-time/adjunct (10 women). Expenses: Contact institution. *Financial support:* In 2001–02, 12 fellowships, 90 research assistantships, 129 teaching assistantships were awarded. Career-related internships or fieldwork, Federal Work-Study, institutionally sponsored loans, scholarships/grants, and unspecified assistantships also available. Support available to part-time students. Financial award application deadline: 3/1; financial award applicants required to submit FAFSA. In 2001, 488 master's, 38 doctorates awarded. *Degree program information:* Part-time and evening/weekend programs available. Postbaccalaureate distance learning degree programs offered (no on-campus study). Offers analytical chemistry (MAC, MS, PhD); applied mathematics (MS, PhD); biochemistry (MS); biology (MS, PhD); biomedical engineering (PhD); biotechnology (MS); cell biology (MS); chemical engineering (M Ch E, MS, PhD); chemistry (M Chem, MAC, MS, PhD); civil and architectural engineering (M Geoenv E, M Trans E, MCEM, MGE, MPW, MS, MSE, PhD); computer science (MS, PhD); computer systems engineering (MS); electrical and computer engineering (MECE); electrical engineering (MS, PhD); engineering and sciences (M Ch E, M Chem, M Eng, M Env E, M Geoenv E, M Trans E, MAC, MCEM, MECE, MGE, MHP, MMAE, MME, MMME, MPA, MPW, MS, MSE, MST, MTSE, PhD); environmental engineering (M Env E, MS, PhD); food safety and technology (M Eng, MS); health physics (MHP); inorganic chemistry (MS, PhD); manufacturing engineering (MME, MS); mechanical and aerospace engineering (MMAE, MS, PhD); metallurgical and materials engineering (MMME, MS, PhD); microbiology (MS); organic chemistry (MS, PhD); physical chemistry (MS, PhD); physics (MHP, MS, PhD); polymer chemistry (MS, PhD); social sciences (MPA, MPW); teaching (MST); technical communication and information design (MS); telecommunications and software engineering (MTSE); theoretical chemistry (MS, PhD). *Application deadline:* For fall admission, 7/1; for spring admission, 11/1. Applications are processed on a rolling basis. *Application fee:* $30. Electronic applications accepted. *Application Contact:* Dr. Ali Cinar, Dean of Graduate College, 312-567-3637, Fax: 312-567-7517, E-mail: gradstu@iit.edu. *Dean*, Dr. Allan Myerson, 312-567-3163, Fax: 312-567-7018, E-mail: myerson@iit.edu.

College of Architecture Students: 101 full-time (37 women), 52 part-time (12 women); includes 15 minority (5 African Americans, 4 Asian Americans or Pacific Islanders, 6 Hispanic Americans), 94 international. Average age 31. 300 applicants, 65% accepted. *Faculty:* 26 full-time (5 women), 31 part-time/adjunct (6 women). Expenses: Contact institution. *Financial support:* In 2001–02, research assistantships (averaging $5,000 per year), 33 teaching assistantships (averaging $2,000 per year) were awarded. Fellowships, Federal Work-Study, institutionally sponsored loans, and scholarships/grants also available. Financial award application deadline: 3/1; financial award applicants required to submit FAFSA. In 2001, 24 master's, 1 doctorate awarded. *Degree program information:* Part-time programs available. Offers architecture (M Arch, PhD). *Application deadline:* For fall admission, 2/1. Applications are processed on a rolling basis. *Application fee:* $30. Electronic applications accepted. *Application Contact:* Dr. Stephen Sennott, Assistant Dean of Academic Affairs, 312-567-3230, Fax: 312-567-5820, E-mail: sennott@iit.edu. *Dean*, Donna Robertson, 312-567-3230, Fax: 312-567-5820, E-mail: robertson@iit.edu.

Institute of Design Students: 77 full-time (39 women), 7 part-time (3 women); includes 9 minority (2 African Americans, 5 Asian Americans or Pacific Islanders, 2 Hispanic Americans), 43 international. Average age 30. 74 applicants, 57% accepted. *Faculty:* 10 full-time (1 woman), 4 part-time/adjunct (0 women). Expenses: Contact institution. *Financial support:* In 2001–02, 1 fellowship was awarded; institutionally sponsored loans and scholarships/grants also available. Financial award application deadline: 2/15; financial award applicants required to submit FAFSA. In 2001, 37 master's, 1 doctorate awarded. Offers communication design (M Des, MS, PhD); photography (M Des); product design (M Des, MS, PhD). *Application deadline:* For fall admission, 2/15 (priority date); for spring admission, 10/15. Applications are processed on a rolling basis. *Application fee:* $30. Electronic applications accepted. *Application Contact:* Julia Chase, Graduate Admissions, 312-808-5300, Fax: 312-808-5322, E-mail: design@id.iit.edu. *Director*, Patrick Whitney, 312-808-5300, Fax: 312-808-5322, E-mail: whitney@id.iit.edu.

Institute of Psychology Students: 84 full-time (56 women), 75 part-time (51 women); includes 32 minority (15 African Americans, 10 Asian Americans or Pacific Islanders, 6 Hispanic Americans, 1 Native American), 15 international. Average age 30. 157 applicants, 49% accepted. *Faculty:* 17 full-time (7 women), 4 part-time/adjunct (2 women). Expenses: Contact institution. *Financial support:* In 2001–02, 32 fellowships, 18 teaching assistantships were awarded. Research assistantships, career-related internships or fieldwork, Federal Work-Study, institutionally sponsored loans, scholarships/grants, and unspecified assistantships also available. Financial award application deadline: 3/1; financial award applicants required to submit FAFSA. In 2001, 21 master's, 15 doctorates awarded. Offers clinical psychology (PhD); industrial/organizational psychology (PhD); personnel/human resource development (MS); psychology (MS); rehabilitation counseling (MS); rehabilitation psychology (PhD). *Application deadline:* For fall admission, 1/15 (priority date); for spring admission, 11/1. Applications are processed on a rolling basis. *Application fee:* $30. Electronic applications accepted. *Application Contact:* Dr. Ali Cinar, Dean of Graduate College, 312-567-3637, Fax: 312-567-7517, E-mail: gradstu@iit.edu. *Chairman*, Dr. M. Ellen Mitchell, 312-567-3362, Fax: 312-567-3493, E-mail: mitchell@itt.edu.

Stuart Graduate School of Business Students: 161 full-time (57 women), 316 part-time (108 women); includes 75 minority (25 African Americans, 39 Asian Americans or Pacific Islanders, 10 Hispanic Americans, 1 Native American), 200 international. Average age 30. 374 applicants, 64% accepted. *Faculty:* 18 full-time (0 women), 13 part-time/adjunct (2 women). Expenses: Contact institution. *Financial support:* Fellowships, teaching assistantships, Federal Work-Study, institutionally sponsored loans, scholarships/grants, and unspecified assistantships available. Financial award application deadline: 3/1; financial award applicants required to submit FAFSA. In 2001, 179 master's, 2 doctorates awarded. *Degree program information:* Part-time and evening/weekend programs available. Offers business (MBA, MS, PhD); environmental management (MS); finance (MBA); information management (MBA); international business (MBA); management science (MBA, PhD); marketing (MBA); marketing communication (MS); operations and technology management (MS); operations management (MBA); organization and management (MBA); strategic management (MBA); telecommunications management (MBA). *Application deadline:* For fall admission, 8/1; for spring admission, 4/15. Applications are processed on a rolling basis. *Application fee:* $50. Electronic applications accepted. *Application Contact:* Lynn Miller, Director, Admission, 312-906-6544, Fax: 312-906-6549, E-mail: degrees@stuart.iit.edu. *Dean*, Dr. M. Zia Hassan, 312-906-6500, Fax: 312-906-6549, E-mail: hassan@stuart.iit.edu.

See in-depth description on page 907.

ILLINOIS STATE UNIVERSITY, Normal, IL 61790-2200

General Information State-supported, coed, university. CGS member. *Enrollment:* 1,001 full-time matriculated graduate/professional students (612 women), 1,353 part-time matriculated graduate/professional students (863 women). *Enrollment by degree level:* 1,913 master's, 420 doctoral, 21 other advanced degrees. *Graduate faculty:* 564 full-time (194 women), 13 part-time/adjunct (3 women). Tuition, state resident: full-time $2,691; part-time $112 per credit hour. Tuition, nonresident: full-time $5,880; part-time $245 per credit hour. *Required fees:* $1,146; $48 per credit hour. *Graduate housing:* Rooms and/or apartments available to single and married students. Typical cost: $4,758 (including board) for single students. *Student services:* Campus employment opportunities, campus safety program, career counseling, child daycare facilities, disabled student services, exercise/wellness program, free psychological counseling, international student services, low-cost health insurance, multicultural affairs office, teacher training. *Library facilities:* Milner Library. *Online resources:* library catalog, web page, access to other libraries' catalogs. *Collection:* 1.5 million titles, 8,915 serial subscriptions, 59,272 audiovisual materials.

Computer facilities: 2,100 computers available on campus for general student use. A campuswide network can be accessed from student residence rooms and from off campus. Internet access is available. *Web address:* http://www.ilstu.edu/.

General Application Contact: Dr. Gary McGinnis, Associate Vice President of Research, Graduate Studies, and International Education, 309-438-2583, Fax: 309-438-7912.

GRADUATE UNITS

Graduate School Students: 1,001 full-time (612 women), 1,353 part-time (863 women); includes 247 minority (135 African Americans, 38 Asian Americans or Pacific Islanders, 66 Hispanic Americans, 8 Native Americans), 291 international. 1,164 applicants, 66% accepted. *Faculty:* 564 full-time (194 women), 13 part-time/adjunct (3 women). Expenses: Contact institution. *Financial support:* In 2001–02, 563 students received support, including 436 research assistantships, 379 teaching assistantships; fellowships, career-related internships or fieldwork, Federal Work-Study, institutionally sponsored loans, tuition waivers (full and partial), and unspecified assistantships also available. Support available to part-time students. Financial award application deadline: 4/1. In 2001, 670 master's, 32 doctorates, 5 other advanced degrees awarded. *Degree program information:* Part-time programs available. *Application deadline:* Applications are processed on a rolling basis. *Application fee:* $30. *Associate Vice President of Research, Graduate Studies and International Education*, Dr. Gary McGinnis, 309-438-2583, Fax: 309-438-9712.

College of Applied Science and Technology Students: 177 full-time (93 women), 189 part-time (88 women); includes 16 minority (1 African American, 8 Asian Americans or Pacific Islanders, 5 Hispanic Americans, 2 Native Americans), 90 international. 264 applicants, 54% accepted. *Faculty:* 73 full-time (27 women), 1 (woman) part-time/adjunct. Expenses: Contact institution. *Financial support:* In 2001–02, 102 students received support, including 92 research assistantships, 67 teaching assistantships; fellowships, career-related internships or fieldwork, Federal Work-Study, institutionally sponsored loans, tuition waivers (full and partial), and unspecified assistantships also available. Support available to part-time students. Financial award application deadline: 4/1. In 2001, 98 degrees awarded. *Degree program information:* Part-time programs available. Offers agribusiness (MS); applied computer science (MS); applied science and technology (MA, MS); criminal justice sciences (MA, MS); environmental health and safety (MS); family and consumer sciences (MA, MS); health education (MS); physical education (MS); technology (MS). *Application deadline:* Applications are processed on a rolling basis. *Application fee:* $30. *Dean*, Dr. J. Robert Rossman, 309-438-7602.

College of Arts and Sciences Students: 547 full-time (359 women), 286 part-time (179 women); includes 84 minority (51 African Americans, 10 Asian Americans or Pacific Islanders, 19 Hispanic Americans, 4 Native Americans), 101 international. 593 applicants, 66% accepted. *Faculty:* 274 full-time (87 women), 4 part-time/adjunct (0 women). Expenses: Contact institution. *Financial support:* In 2001–02, 169 research assistantships, 262 teaching assistantships were awarded. Career-related internships or fieldwork, Federal Work-Study, institutionally sponsored loans, tuition waivers (full and partial), and unspecified assistantships also available. Support available to part-time students. Financial award application deadline: 4/1. In 2001, 229 master's, 16 doctorates, 4 other advanced degrees awarded. *Degree program information:* Part-time programs available. Offers arts and sciences (MA, MS, MSW, PhD, SSP); biological sciences (MS); biology (PhD); biotechnology (MS); botany (PhD); chemistry (MS); communication (MA, MS); ecology (PhD); economics (MA, MS); English (MA, MS, PhD); English studies (PhD); French (MA); French and German (MA); French and Spanish (MA); genetics (PhD); geohydrology (MS); German (MA); German and Spanish (MA); history (MA, MS); mathematics (MA, MS); mathematics education (PhD); microbiology (PhD); physiology (PhD); politics and government (MA, MS); psychology (MA, MS); school psychology (PhD, SSP); social work (MSW); sociology (MA, MS); Spanish (MA); speech pathology and audiology (MA, MS); writing (MA, MS); zoology (PhD). *Application deadline:* Applications are processed on a rolling basis. *Application fee:* $30. *Interim Dean*, Dr. John Freed, 309-438-5669.

College of Business Students: 70 full-time (31 women), 158 part-time (61 women); includes 23 minority (9 African Americans, 12 Asian Americans or Pacific Islanders, 2 Hispanic Americans), 34 international. 87 applicants, 83% accepted. *Faculty:* 37 full-time (11 women), 2 part-time/adjunct (0 women). Expenses: Contact institution. *Financial support:* In 2001–02, 56 research assistantships, 3 teaching assistantships were awarded. Career-related internships or fieldwork, Federal Work-Study, institutionally sponsored loans, and tuition waivers (full and partial) also available. Support available to part-time students. Financial award application deadline: 4/1. In 2001, 85 degrees awarded. *Degree program information:* Part-time programs available. Offers accounting (MPA, MS); business (MBA, MPA, MS); business administration (MBA). *Application deadline:* Applications are processed on a rolling basis. *Application fee:* $30. *Dean*, Dr. Dixie Mills, 309-438-2251.

College of Education Students: 91 full-time (63 women), 665 part-time (492 women); includes 79 minority (60 African Americans, 5 Asian Americans or Pacific Islanders, 12 Hispanic Americans, 2 Native Americans), 46 international. 120 applicants, 88% accepted. *Faculty:* 51 full-time (26 women), 4 part-time/adjunct (1 woman). Expenses: Contact institution. *Financial support:* In 2001–02, 63 research assistantships, 2 teaching assistantships were awarded. Career-related internships or fieldwork, Federal Work-Study, institutionally sponsored loans, tuition waivers (full and partial), and unspecified assistantships also available. Support available to part-time students. Financial award application deadline:4/1. In 2001, 198 master's, 16 doctorates awarded. *Degree program information:* Part-time programs available. Offers curriculum and instruction (MS, MS Ed, Ed D); education (MS, MS Ed, Ed D, PhD); educational administration and foundations (MS, MS Ed, Ed D, PhD); educational policies (Ed D); guidance and counseling (MS, MS Ed); postsecondary education (Ed D); reading education (MS Ed); special education (MS, MS Ed, Ed D); supervision (Ed D). *Application deadline:* Applications are processed on a rolling basis. *Application fee:* $30. *Dean*, Dr. Dianne Ashby, 309-438-5415.

College of Fine Arts Students: 107 full-time (57 women), 36 part-time (24 women); includes 7 minority (4 African Americans, 2 Asian Americans or Pacific Islanders, 1 Hispanic American), 20 international. 93 applicants, 57% accepted. *Faculty:* 76 full-time (29 women), 2 part-time/adjunct (1 woman). Expenses: Contact institution. *Financial support:* In 2001–02, 90 students received support, including 53 research assistantships, 45 teaching assistantships; career-related internships or fieldwork, Federal Work-Study, institutionally sponsored loans, tuition waivers (full and partial), and unspecified assistantships also available. Support available to part-time students. Financial award application deadline: 4/1. In 2001, 47 degrees awarded. *Degree program information:* Part-time programs available. Offers art history (MA, MS); arts technology (MS); ceramics (MFA, MS); drawing (MFA, MS); fibers (MFA, MS); fine arts (MA, MFA, MM, MM Ed, MS); glass (MFA, MS); graphic design (MFA, MS); metals (MFA, MS); music (MM, MM Ed); painting (MFA, MS); photography (MFA, MS); printmaking (MFA, MS); sculpture (MFA, MS); theater (MA, MFA, MS). *Application deadline:* Applications are processed on a rolling basis. *Application fee:* $30. *Dean*, Dr. Roosevelt Newson, 309-438-8321.

Mennonite College of Nursing Students: 9 full-time (all women), 19 part-time (all women); all minorities (1 Asian American or Pacific Islander, 27 Hispanic Americans) 7 applicants, 86% accepted. *Faculty:* 8 full-time (all women). Expenses: Contact institution. *Financial support:* In 2001–02, 3 research assistantships (averaging $4,800 per year) were awarded; teaching assistantships In 2001, 13 master's, 1 other advanced degree awarded. Offers family nurse practitioner (PMC); nursing (MSN). *Application fee:* $30. *Dean*, Nancy Ridenour, 309-438-7400, Fax: 309-438-2620.

See in-depth description on page 909.

IMCA–INTERNATIONAL MANAGEMENT CENTRES ASSOCIATION, Buckingham, MK18 1BP, United Kingdom

General Information Independent, graduate-only institution.

GRADUATE UNITS

Programs in Business Administration Postbaccalaureate distance learning degree programs offered (no on-campus study). Offers business administration (M Phil, MBA, D Phil, DBA).

IMMACULATA UNIVERSITY, Immaculata, PA 19345

General Information Independent-religious, women only, comprehensive institution. *Enrollment:* 72 full-time matriculated graduate/professional students (60 women), 574 part-time matriculated graduate/professional students (454 women). *Graduate faculty:* 48. *Tuition:* Part-time $390 per credit. *Graduate housing:* Room and/or apartments available on a first-come, first-served basis to single students; on-campus housing not available to married students. Typical cost: $2,800 per year. *Student services:* Campus employment opportunities, career counseling. *Library facilities:* Gabriele Library. *Online resources:* library catalog, web page. *Collection:* 1.1 million titles, 982 serial subscriptions, 1,749 audiovisual materials.

Computer facilities: 150 computers available on campus for general student use. A campuswide network can be accessed from student residence rooms and from off campus. Internet access is available. *Web address:* http://www.immaculata.edu/.

General Application Contact: Sr. Ann M. Heath, Dean, 610-647-4400 Ext. 3211, Fax: 610-993-8550.

GRADUATE UNITS

College of Graduate Studies Students: 72 full-time (60 women), 574 part-time (454 women); includes 42 minority (31 African Americans, 6 Asian Americans or Pacific Islanders, 4 Hispanic Americans, 1 Native American), 8 international. Average age 33. 184 applicants, 80% accepted, 117 enrolled. *Faculty:* 48. Expenses: Contact institution. *Financial support:* Career-related internships or fieldwork and Federal Work-Study available. Support available to part-time students. Financial award application deadline: 5/1; financial award applicants required to submit FAFSA. In 2001, 72 master's, 22 doctorates awarded. *Degree program information:* Part-time and evening/weekend programs available. Offers clinical psychology (Psy D); counseling psychology (MA, Certificate); cultural and linguistic diversity (MA); educational leadership and administration (MA, Ed D); elementary education (Certificate); intermediate unit director (Certificate); music therapy (MA); nutrition education (MA); nutrition education/approved pre-professional practice program (MA); organization leadership (MA); school principal (Certificate); school psychology (Psy D); school superintendent (Certificate); seondary education (Certificate); special education (Certificate). *Application deadline:* Applications are processed on a rolling basis. *Application fee:* $25. *Application Contact:* Office of Graduate Admission, 610-647-4400 Ext. 3211. *Dean*, Sr. Ann M. Heath, 610-647-4400 Ext. 3211, Fax: 610-993-8550.

See in-depth description on page 911.

INDIANA INSTITUTE OF TECHNOLOGY, Fort Wayne, IN 46803-1297

General Information Independent, coed, comprehensive institution. *Enrollment:* 202 full-time matriculated graduate/professional students (79 women), 179 part-time matriculated graduate/professional students (79 women). *Enrollment by degree level:* 381 master's. *Graduate faculty:* 12 full-time (5 women), 26 part-time/adjunct (4 women). *Tuition:* Full-time $6,696; part-time $279 per credit. *Graduate housing:* On-campus housing not available. *Student services:* Career counseling. *Library facilities:* McMillen Library. *Online resources:* library catalog, web page, access to other libraries' catalogs. *Collection:* 60,000 titles, 175 serial subscriptions.

Computer facilities: 79 computers available on campus for general student use. A campuswide network can be accessed from off campus. *Web address:* http://www.indtech.edu/.

General Application Contact: Kathleen Stahl, Campus Director, 260-422-TECH Ext. 2278, Fax: 260-422-1518, E-mail: stahl@indtech.edu.

GRADUATE UNITS

Program in Business Administration Students: 202 full-time (79 women), 179 part-time (79 women); includes 76 minority (66 African Americans, 9 Asian Americans or Pacific Islanders, 1 Hispanic American), 63 international. Average age 38. *Faculty:* 12 full-time (5 women), 26 part-time/adjunct (4 women). Expenses: Contact institution. *Financial support:* In 2001–02, 41 students received support. Application deadline: 3/1; In 2001, 65 degrees awarded. *Degree program information:* Part-time and evening/weekend programs available. Offers entrepreneurship (MBA); human resources (MBA); management (MBA); marketing (MBA). *Application deadline:* Applications are processed on a rolling basis. *Application fee:* $25 ($35 for international students). Electronic applications accepted. *Application Contact:* Kathleen Stahl, Campus Director, 260-422-TECH Ext. 2278, Fax: 260-422-1518, E-mail: stahl@indtech.edu. *Vice President, Extended Studies*, Jim Bishop, 260-422-5561 Ext. 2209, Fax: 260-422-6309, E-mail: bishop@indtech.edu.

INDIANA STATE UNIVERSITY, Terre Haute, IN 47809-1401

General Information State-supported, coed, university. CGS member. *Graduate housing:* Rooms and/or apartments available on a first-come, first-served basis to single and married students. *Research affiliation:* NASA–Stennis Space Center (remote sensing), Indiana University School of Medicine (microbiology), Walther Cancer Institute (psychosocial impacts of cancer).

GRADUATE UNITS

School of Graduate Studies *Degree program information:* Part-time and evening/weekend programs available. Postbaccalaureate distance learning degree programs offered (minimal on-campus study). Electronic applications accepted.

College of Arts and Sciences *Degree program information:* Part-time and evening/weekend programs available. Offers art history (MA); arts and sciences (MA, MFA, MM, MME, MPA, MS, PhD, Psy D, CAS); ceramics (MA, MFA, MS); chemistry (MS); child and family relations (MS); clinical laboratory sciences (MS); clinical psychology (Psy D); clothing and textiles (MS); communication studies (MA, MS); composition (MA); criminology (MA, MS); dietetics (MS); drawing (MA, MFA, MS); earth sciences (MS); ecology (MA, MS, PhD); economic geography (PhD); economics (MA, MS); English (MA, MS); French (MA, MS); general psychology (MA, MS); geography (MA); graphic design (MA, MFA, MS); history (MA, MS); home management (MS); interdisciplinary humanities (MA); language (CAS); linguistics/teaching English as a second language (MA, MS); literature (CAS); mathematics (MA, MS); metalry (MA, MFA, MS); microbiology (MA, MS, PhD); music (MM); music education (MA, MME, MS); music history and literature (MA); music performance (MS); music theory (MA); nutrition and foods (MS); painting (MA, MFA, MS); photography (MA, MFA, MS); physical geography (PhD); physics (MA, MS); physiology (MA, MS, PhD); political science (MA, MS); printmaking (MA, MFA, MS); public administration (MPA); radio, television and film (MA, MS); religion (MA); rhetoric (CAS); science education (MA, MS); sculpture (MA, MFA, MS); sociology (MA, MS); Spanish (MA, MS); theatre (MA, MS). Electronic applications accepted.

School of Business *Degree program information:* Part-time and evening/weekend programs available. Offers business (MA, MBA, MS, PhD, Ed S). Electronic applications accepted.

School of Education *Degree program information:* Part-time and evening/weekend programs available. Offers counseling psychology (PhD); counselor education (PhD); curriculum and instruction (M Ed, PhD); director of special education (M Ed); early childhood education (M Ed, PhD, Ed S); education (M Ed, MA, MS, PhD, Ed S); educational administration (PhD, Ed S); educational media (MA, MS, Ed S); educational psychology (MA, MS); elementary education (M Ed, PhD, Ed S); elementary school administration (M Ed); gifted/talented education (MA, MS, Ed S); guidance (PhD, Ed S); higher education (MA, MS); industrial arts education (PhD); marriage and family counseling (MA, MS); reading education (M Ed, PhD, Ed S); school counseling (M Ed); school psychology (M Ed, PhD, Ed S); secondary education (M Ed, MS, PhD, Ed S); secondary school administration (M Ed); special education (MA, MS, PhD); speech pathology and audiology (MA, MS). Electronic applications accepted.

School of Health and Human Performance Offers athletic training (MA, MS); health and human performance (MA, MS); health program and facility administration (MA, MS); occupational safety management (MA, MS); physical education (MA, MS); recreation and sport management (MA, MS); school health and safety (MA, MS). Electronic applications accepted.

School of Nursing *Degree program information:* Part-time programs available. Offers nursing (MS). Electronic applications accepted.

School of Technology Offers curriculum and instruction (PhD); electronics and computer technology (MA, MS); human resource development (MS); industrial technology (MA, MS); technology (MA, MS, PhD); technology education (MA, MS); vocational technical education (MA, MS). Electronic applications accepted.

See in-depth description on page 913.

INDIANA UNIVERSITY BLOOMINGTON, Bloomington, IN 47405

General Information State-supported, coed, university. CGS member. *Enrollment:* 4,780 full-time matriculated graduate/professional students (2,271 women), 2,564 part-time matriculated graduate/professional students (1,372 women). *Graduate faculty:* 1,071 full-time (267 women), 5 part-time/adjunct (4 women). Tuition, state resident: full-time $4,720; part-time $197 per credit. Tuition, nonresident: full-time $13,748; part-time $573 per credit. *Required fees:* $642. *Graduate housing:* Rooms and/or apartments available to single and married students. Typical cost: $6,690 (including board) for single students. *Student services:* Campus employment opportunities, campus safety program, career counseling, child daycare facilities, disabled student services, exercise/wellness program, free psychological counseling, international student services, low-cost health insurance, multicultural affairs office, writing training. *Library facilities:* Indiana University Library plus 32 others. *Online resources:* library catalog, web page, access to other libraries' catalogs. *Collection:* 6.3 million titles, 45,596 serial subscriptions, 635,574 audiovisual materials. *Research affiliation:* AT&T (communications technology, education), Eli Lilly & Company (biology), Martin Marietta Corporation (environmental science), Ciba Vision Corporation (optometry), Motorola Government Electronics (computer science), The Procter & Gamble Company (chemistry).

Computer facilities: 1,500 computers available on campus for general student use. A campuswide network can be accessed from student residence rooms and from off campus. Internet access, various software packages are available.

General Application Contact: 812-855-2666.

GRADUATE UNITS

Graduate School Average age 30. Expenses: Contact institution. *Financial support:* In 2001–02, 127 fellowships with full and partial tuition reimbursements (averaging $7,811 per year) were awarded; research assistantships, teaching assistantships, career-related internships or fieldwork, Federal Work-Study, institutionally sponsored loans, and tuition waivers (full and partial) also available. Support available to part-time students. In 2001, 1,582 master's, 404 doctorates, 38 other advanced degrees awarded. *Degree program information:* Part-time programs available. PhD offered through the University Graduate School; MD/MS and MD/PhD offered jointly with the Indiana University School of Medicine. *Application deadline:* For fall admission, 1/15 (priority date); for spring admission, 9/1. *Application fee:* $45 ($55 for international students). Electronic applications accepted. *Application Contact:* Nancy Remillard, Graduate School, 812-855-8853, Fax: 812-856-5226, E-mail: grdschl@indiana.edu. *Vice President for Research and Dean*, George E. Walker, 812-855-8852, Fax: 812-855-4266.

College of Arts and Sciences Students: 1,477 full-time (729 women), 1,214 part-time (593 women); includes 226 minority (75 African Americans, 58 Asian Americans or Pacific Islanders, 82 Hispanic Americans, 11 Native Americans), 685 international. Average age 30. *Faculty:* 697 full-time (167 women), 2 part-time/adjunct (both women). Expenses: Contact institution. *Financial support:* In 2001–02, fellowships (averaging $9,825 per year); research assistantships, teaching assistantships, career-related internships or fieldwork, Federal Work-Study, institutionally sponsored loans, scholarships/grants, traineeships, tuition waivers (full and partial), and unspecified assistantships also available. Support available to part-time students. In 2001, 365 master's, 235 doctorates awarded. *Degree program information:* Part-time programs available. Offers acting (MFA); Afro-American studies (MA); analytical chemistry (PhD); anthropology (MA, PhD); apparel studies (MS); applied linguistics (teaching English as a second language) (MA, Certificate); applied mathematics–numerical analysis (MA, PhD); art education (MAT); arts administration (MA); arts and sciences (MA, MAT, MFA, MS, PhD, Certificate); astronomy (MA, PhD); astrophysics (PhD); biochemistry and molecular biology (MS, PhD); biogeochemistry (MS, PhD); biological chemistry (PhD); biology and behavior (PhD); biology teaching (MAT); Central Eurasian studies (MA, PhD); ceramics (MFA); chemistry (MAT, MS); Chinese language and literature (MA, PhD); classical studies (MA, MAT, PhD); clinical science (PhD); cognitive psychology (PhD); communication and culture (MA, MAT, PhD); comparative literature (MA, MAT, PhD); computer science (MS, PhD); computer science/cognitive science (PhD); computer science/logic (PhD); costume design (MFA); creative writing (MFA); cross-cultural studies of crime and justice (MA, PhD); developmental psychology (PhD); directing (MFA); East Asian studies (MA); East European studies (Certificate); ecology (MA, PhD); economics (MA, MAT, PhD); English (MA, PhD); English education (MAT); environmental geosciences (MS, PhD); evolution, ecology, and behavior (MA, PhD); evolutionary biology (MA, PhD); fine arts (MA, MAT, MFA, PhD); folklore (MA, PhD); French (MA, MAT, PhD); French linguistics (MA, PhD); French literature (MA, PhD); genetics (PhD); geobiology, stratigraphy, and sedimentology (MS, PhD); geochemistry (MS, PhD); geochemistry, mineralogy, and petrology (MS, PhD); geography (MA, MAT, PhD); geophysics (MS, PhD); geophysics, tectonics, and structural geology (MS, PhD); German literature and studies (PhD); German studies (MA, PhD); graphic design (MFA); Hispanic linguistics (MA, PhD); Hispanic literature (MA, PhD); history (MA, MAT, PhD); history and philosophy of science (MA, PhD); history of art (MA, PhD); inorganic chemistry (PhD); interior design (MS); Italian (MA, PhD); Japanese language and literature (MA, PhD); jewelry/metalsmithing (MFA); justice systems and processes (MA, PhD); Latin American and Caribbean studies (MA); law and society (MA, PhD); lighting design (MFA); linguistics (MA, PhD); literature (MA, PhD); Luso-Brazilian literature (MA, PhD); mass communication (PhD); mathematics education (MAT); medieval German studies (PhD); microbiology (MA, PhD); molecular, cellular, and developmental biology (PhD); nature of crime (MA, PhD); Near Eastern languages and cultures (MA, PhD); neural sciences (PhD); painting (MFA); philosophy (MA, PhD); photography (MFA); physical chemistry (PhD); physics (MAT, MS, PhD); plant sciences, molecular and organismal biology (MA, PhD); playwriting (MFA); political science (MA, PhD); printmaking (MFA); probability-statistics (MA, PhD); religious studies (MA, PhD); Russian and East European studies (MA); Russian area studies (Certificate); scenic design (MFA); sculpture (MFA); Slavic languages and literatures (MA, MAT, PhD); social psychology (PhD); sociology (MA, PhD); speech and hearing sciences (MA, MAT, PhD); teaching French (MAT); teaching German (MAT); teaching Spanish (MAT); technology (MFA); telecommunications (MA, MS); textiles (MFA); theatre and drama (MAT); theatre history (MA, PhD); theory (MA, PhD); West European studies (MA, PhD, Certificate); zoology (MA, PhD). PhD offered through the University Graduate School. *Application deadline:* Applications are processed on a rolling basis. *Application fee:* $45 ($55 for international students). Electronic applications accepted. *Application Contact:* Mitchell Byler, Assistant Dean, 812-855-8931, Fax: 812-855-2060, E-mail: byler@indiana.edu. *Dean*, 812-855-2392, Fax: 812-855-2060.

School of Journalism Students: 15 full-time (10 women), 10 part-time (6 women), 7 international. Average age 29. *Faculty:* 18 full-time (6 women). Expenses: Contact institution. *Financial support:* In 2001–02, 14 fellowships (averaging $5,337 per year), 2 research assistantships with full tuition reimbursements, 16 teaching assistantships with partial

Indiana University Bloomington (continued)

tuition reimbursements (averaging $6,260 per year) were awarded. Career-related internships or fieldwork, Federal Work-Study, institutionally sponsored loans, and tuition waivers (full) also available. Financial award application deadline: 1/15. In 2001, 27 degrees awarded. Offers journalism (MA); mass communication (PhD). PhD offered through the University Graduate School. *Application deadline:* For fall admission, 1/15 (priority date); for spring admission, 9/1 (priority date). Applications are processed on a rolling basis. *Application fee:* $45 ($55 for international students). *Application Contact:* Dan Drew, Associate Dean of Graduate Studies, 812-855-1701, Fax: 812-855-0901, E-mail: drew@indiana.edu. *Dean,* Trevor Brown, 812-855-9247, Fax: 812-855-0901.

Kelley School of Business Students: 780 full-time (177 women), 25 part-time (9 women); includes 108 minority (38 African Americans, 43 Asian Americans or Pacific Islanders, 27 Hispanic Americans), 271 international. Average age 28. *Faculty:* 100 full-time (15 women), 1 part-time/adjunct (0 women). Expenses: Contact institution. *Financial support:* In 2001–02, fellowships (averaging $5,403 per year); research assistantships, teaching assistantships, career-related internships or fieldwork, institutionally sponsored loans, and tuition waivers (full and partial) also available. Financial award application deadline: 3/1; financial award applicants required to submit FAFSA. In 2001, 391 master's, 16 doctorates awarded. Offers accounting (DBA, PhD); business (EMBA, MBA, MPA, MS, MSIS, DBA, PhD); business economics and public policy (DBA, PhD); decision systems (DBA, PhD); entrepreneurship (MBA); finance (MBA, DBA, PhD); human resources management (MBA); international business (MBA); management (MBA, DBA, PhD); management information systems (MBA, DBA, PhD); marketing (MBA, DBA, PhD); operations management (MBA, DBA, PhD); organizational behavior (DBA, PhD); production/operations leaders program (MBA); professional accountancy (MPA); systems and accounting (MS, MSIS). PhD offered through the University Graduate School. *Application fee:* $75 ($55 for international students). Electronic applications accepted. *Dean,* Dr. Dan R. Dalton, 812-855-8100, Fax: 812-855-8983, E-mail: dalton@indiana.edu.

Medical Sciences Program Students: 14 full-time (4 women), 9 part-time (5 women); includes 4 minority (1 African American, 3 Asian Americans or Pacific Islanders), 2 international. Average age 28. *Faculty:* 12 full-time (3 women). Expenses: Contact institution. *Financial support:* In 2001–02, fellowships (averaging $4,635 per year) In 2001, 1 master's, 2 doctorates awarded. Offers anatomy and cell biology (MA, PhD); pharmacology (MS, PhD); physiology (MA, PhD). *Application deadline:* For fall admission, 1/15. *Application fee:* $45 ($55 for international students). *Application Contact:* Kimberly Bunch, Director of Graduate Admissions, 812-855-1119, E-mail: kbunch@indiana.edu.

School of Education Students: 497 full-time (329 women), 629 part-time (408 women); includes 119 minority (63 African Americans, 28 Asian Americans or Pacific Islanders, 24 Hispanic Americans, 4 Native Americans), 257 international. Average age 33. *Faculty:* 89 full-time (34 women). Expenses: Contact institution. *Financial support:* In 2001–02, 61 fellowships with tuition reimbursements (averaging $8,061 per year), 24 research assistantships with tuition reimbursements (averaging $11,500 per year), 167 teaching assistantships with tuition reimbursements (averaging $10,400 per year) were awarded. Career-related internships or fieldwork, Federal Work-Study, institutionally sponsored loans, tuition waivers (full and partial), and unspecified assistantships also available. Support available to part-time students. In 2001, 319 master's, 86 doctorates awarded. *Degree program information:* Part-time and evening/weekend programs available. Postbaccalaureate distance learning degree programs offered. Offers art education (MS Ed); counseling/counselor education (MS Ed, Ed D, PhD); curriculum and instruction (Ed D, PhD); education (MM Ed, MS Ed, D Mus Ed, Ed D, PhD, Ed S); educational leadership and policy (PhD); educational psychology (MS Ed, Ed D, PhD); elementary education (MS Ed, Ed S); higher education (Ed D, PhD); higher education and student affairs administration (MS Ed); history and philosophy of education (MS Ed); history, philosophy, and policy studies in education (PhD); instructional systems technology (MS Ed, PhD, Ed S); international and comparative education (MS Ed); language education (MS Ed, Ed D, PhD, Ed S); music education (MM Ed, D Mus Ed); school administration (MS Ed, Ed D, Ed S); school psychology (Ed S); science and environmental education (Ed D); secondary education (MS Ed, Ed S); social studies education (MS Ed); special education (MS Ed, Ed D, PhD, Ed S). PhD offered through the University Graduate School. *Application deadline:* For fall admission, 6/1. Applications are processed on a rolling basis. *Application fee:* $45 ($55 for international students). Electronic applications accepted. *Application Contact:* Barbara Hayes, Graduate Admissions, 812-856-8504. *Dean,* Gerardo Gonzalez, 812-856-8001, Fax: 812-856-8440.

School of Health, Physical Education and Recreation Students: 160 full-time (92 women), 103 part-time (49 women); includes 26 minority (16 African Americans, 4 Asian Americans or Pacific Islanders, 5 Hispanic Americans, 1 Native American), 52 international. Average age 29. *Faculty:* 42 full-time (14 women). Expenses: Contact institution. *Financial support:* In 2001–02, 115 students received support, including 13 fellowships with tuition reimbursements available (averaging $6,527 per year), 3 research assistantships with tuition reimbursements available (averaging $10,000 per year), 93 teaching assistantships with tuition reimbursements available (averaging $9,500 per year); career-related internships or fieldwork, Federal Work-Study, institutionally sponsored loans, tuition waivers (partial), unspecified assistantships, and fee scholarships, fee remissions also available. Financial award application deadline: 3/1. In 2001, 100 master's, 15 doctorates awarded. *Degree program information:* Part-time programs available. Postbaccalaureate distance learning degree programs offered (no on-campus study). Offers adapted physical education (MS); administration (MS); applied health science (MS); applied sport science (MS); athletic administration/sport management (MS); athletic training (MS); biomechanics (MS); clinical exercise physiology (MS); exercise physiology (MS); health and safety (HSD, HS Dir); health behavior (PhD); health, physical education and recreation (MPH, MS, HSD, PED, PhD, Re D, HS Dir, PE Dir, Re Dir); human performance (PhD); leisure behavior (PhD); motor control (MS); motor development (MS); motor learning (MS); outdoor recreation and resource management (MS); park and recreation management (MS); physical education (PED, PE Dir); public health (MPH); recreation (Re D, Re Dir); social science of sport (MS); sport management (MS); sports management (MS); therapeutic recreation (MS). PhD offered through the University Graduate School. *Application deadline:* Applications are processed on a rolling basis. *Application fee:* $45 ($55 for international students). *Application Contact:* David Gallahue, Associate Dean/Academic Program Administration, 812-855-1561, Fax: 812-855-4983, E-mail: hper@indiana.edu. *Dean,* Tony Mobley, 812-855-1561, Fax: 812-855-4983.

School of Informatics Students: 13 full-time (4 women), 2 part-time (1 woman); includes 2 minority (both Asian Americans or Pacific Islanders), 5 international. Average age 30. Expenses: Contact institution. *Financial support:* In 2001–02, fellowships (averaging $5,000 per year) Offers bioinformatics (MS); chemical informatics (MS); human computer interaction (MS); media arts and science (MS); new media (MS). *Application fee:* $45 ($55 for international students). *Dean,* J. Michael Dunn.

School of Library and Information Science Students: 168 full-time (105 women), 104 part-time (75 women); includes 30 minority (12 African Americans, 10 Asian Americans or Pacific Islanders, 7 Hispanic Americans, 1 Native American), 20 international. Average age 31. *Faculty:* 13 full-time (5 women), 1 part-time/adjunct (0 women). Expenses: Contact institution. *Financial support:* In 2001–02, fellowships with partial tuition reimbursements (averaging $9,811 per year); career-related internships or fieldwork and tuition waivers (partial) also available. In 2001, 115 master's, 7 doctorates awarded. *Degree program information:* Part-time programs available. Offers library and information science (MIS, MLS, PhD, Spec). PhD offered through the University Graduate School. *Application deadline:* For fall admission, 5/15 (priority date); for spring admission, 11/1 (priority date). Applications are processed on a rolling basis. *Application fee:* $45 ($55 for international students). *Application Contact:* Rhonda Spencer, Information Contact, 812-855-2018, Fax: 812-855-6166. *Dean,* Dr. Blaise Cronin, 812-855-2018, Fax: 812-855-6166.

School of Music Students: 491 full-time (251 women), 254 part-time (122 women); includes 67 minority (15 African Americans, 32 Asian Americans or Pacific Islanders, 20 Hispanic Americans), 236 international. Average age 28. *Faculty:* 25 full-time (7 women). Expenses: Contact institution. *Financial support:* In 2001–02, 375 students received support, including 34 fellowships with full tuition reimbursements available (averaging $5,319 per year), 220 teaching assistantships with full tuition reimbursements available (averaging $12,000 per year); research assistantships, Federal Work-Study, scholarships/grants, tuition waivers (full and partial), and unspecified assistantships also available. Financial award application deadline: 3/1; financial award applicants required to submit FAFSA. In 2001, 129 master's, 33 doctorates awarded. Offers ballet (MS); instrumentation science (MS); music (MA, MAT, MM, MS, DM, PhD); musicology (MA, PhD). *Application fee:* $45 ($55 for international students). *Application Contact:* Gwyn Richards, Associate Dean for Admissions, 812-855-7998, E-mail: musicadm@indiana.edu. *Dean,* 812-855-1582.

School of Optometry Students: 237 full-time (133 women), 61 part-time (38 women); includes 40 minority (5 African Americans, 30 Asian Americans or Pacific Islanders, 5 Hispanic Americans), 22 international. Average age 25. *Faculty:* 15 full-time (3 women), 1 (woman) part-time/adjunct. Expenses: Contact institution. *Financial support:* In 2001–02, 7 fellowships with tuition reimbursements (averaging $2,852 per year), 3 research assistantships with tuition reimbursements (averaging $3,000 per year), 47 teaching assistantships with full tuition reimbursements (averaging $3,220 per year) were awarded. Federal Work-Study, institutionally sponsored loans, and scholarships/grants also available. Support available to part-time students. Financial award application deadline: 3/1; financial award applicants required to submit FAFSA. In 2001, 67 first professional degrees, 5 master's, 1 doctorate awarded. Offers optometry (OD, MS, PhD); visual sciences and physiological optics (MS, PhD). PhD offered through the University Graduate School. *Application deadline:* Applications are processed on a rolling basis. *Application fee:* $45 ($55 for international students). *Application Contact:* Jacqueline S. Olson, Director of Student Affairs, 812-855-1917, Fax: 812-855-4389, E-mail: iubopt@indiana.edu. *Dean,* Gerald E. Lowther, 812-855-4447, Fax: 812-855-8664, E-mail: glowther@indiana.edu.

School of Public and Environmental Affairs Students: 281 full-time (160 women), 66 part-time (31 women); includes 30 minority (14 African Americans, 10 Asian Americans or Pacific Islanders, 4 Hispanic Americans, 2 Native Americans), 88 international. Average age 28. *Faculty:* 39 full-time (10 women). Expenses: Contact institution. *Financial support:* In 2001–02, 135 students received support, including fellowships (averaging $10,499 per year); research assistantships, teaching assistantships, career-related internships or fieldwork, Federal Work-Study, institutionally sponsored loans, and minority fellowships, Peace Corps assistantships also available. Financial award application deadline: 2/1; financial award applicants required to submit FAFSA. In 2001, 164 master's, 16 doctorates awarded. *Degree program information:* Part-time programs available. Offers environmental science (MSES, PhD); public affairs (EMPA, MPA, PhD); public and environmental affairs (EMPA, MPA, MSES, PhD); public policy (PhD). *Application deadline:* For fall admission, 2/1 (priority date). Applications are processed on a rolling basis. *Application fee:* $45 ($55 for international students). *Application Contact:* David Jones, Graduate Program Director, 812-765-7755, Fax: 812-855-7802, E-mail: speainfo@indiana.edu. *Dean,* A. James Barnes, 812-855-1432.

INDIANA UNIVERSITY KOKOMO, Kokomo, IN 46904-9003

General Information State-supported, coed, comprehensive institution. *Graduate housing:* On-campus housing not available.

GRADUATE UNITS

Division of Business and Economics *Degree program information:* Part-time and evening/weekend programs available. Offers business and economics (MBA).

Division of Education *Degree program information:* Part-time and evening/weekend programs available. Offers elementary education (MS); secondary education (MS).

INDIANA UNIVERSITY NORTHWEST, Gary, IN 46408-1197

General Information State-supported, coed, comprehensive institution. *Enrollment:* 59 full-time matriculated graduate/professional students (42 women), 332 part-time matriculated graduate/professional students (226 women). *Enrollment by degree level:* 327 master's, 64 other advanced degrees. *Graduate faculty:* 38 full-time (11 women). Tuition, state resident: full-time $3,827. Tuition, nonresident: full-time $8,567. *Required fees:* $416. *Graduate housing:* On-campus housing not available. *Student services:* Campus employment opportunities, campus safety program, career counseling, child daycare facilities, free psychological counseling, international student services, low-cost health insurance. *Library facilities:* IUN Library. *Online resources:* library catalog, web page, access to other libraries' catalogs. *Collection:* 242,667 titles, 1,786 serial subscriptions, 1,224 audiovisual materials.

Computer facilities: 250 computers available on campus for general student use. A campuswide network can be accessed from off campus. Internet access and online class registration are available. *Web address:* http://www.indiana.edu/.

General Application Contact: Marilyn Vasquez, Interim Executive Vice Chancellor for Academic Affairs, 219-980-6967, Fax: 219-980-7103.

GRADUATE UNITS

Program in Social Work Students: 25 full-time (21 women), 84 part-time (74 women); includes 41 minority (31 African Americans, 10 Hispanic Americans) Average age 37. Expenses: Contact institution. *Financial support:* In 2001–02, 43 students received support. Career-related internships or fieldwork, Federal Work-Study, tuition waivers (partial), and tuition remissions available. Support available to part-time students. Financial award application deadline: 6/1; financial award applicants required to submit FAFSA. *Degree program information:* Part-time and evening/weekend programs available. Offers social work (MSW). *Application deadline:* For fall admission, 2/1. *Application fee:* $25. *Director,* Dr. Grafton Hull, 219-980-7111, Fax: 219-981-4264, E-mail: ghull@iunhaw1.iun.indiana.edu.

School of Business and Economics Students: 15 full-time (7 women), 66 part-time (21 women); includes 15 minority (9 African Americans, 1 Asian American or Pacific Islander, 5 Hispanic Americans), 1 international. Average age 33. *Faculty:* 2 full-time (0 women). Expenses: Contact institution. *Financial support:* In 2001–02, 9 students received support. Federal Work-Study, institutionally sponsored loans, and unspecified assistantships available. Support available to part-time students. Financial award application deadline: 7/15. In 2001, 36 degrees awarded. *Degree program information:* Part-time and evening/weekend programs available. Offers accountancy (M Acc); accounting (Certificate); business administration (MBA). *Application deadline:* For fall admission, 7/15 (priority date); for spring admission, 11/15. Applications are processed on a rolling basis. *Application fee:* $25. *Application Contact:* Kathryn M. Lantz, Director of Graduate Programs, 219-980-6635, Fax: 219-980-6916. *Dean,* Dr. Donald A. Coffin, 219-980-6633, Fax: 219-980-6916.

School of Education Students: 8 full-time (5 women), 92 part-time (72 women); includes 47 minority (43 African Americans, 4 Hispanic Americans) Average age 36. *Faculty:* 6 full-time (2 women). Expenses: Contact institution. In 2001, 10 degrees awarded. *Degree program information:* Part-time and evening/weekend programs available. Offers elementary education (MS Ed); secondary education (MS Ed). *Application deadline:* For fall admission, 7/15 (priority date); for spring admission, 11/15. *Application fee:* $25. *Application Contact:* Dr. Kenneth Schoon, Assistant Dean, 219-980-7766, Fax: 219-981-4208, E-mail: kschoon@iunhaw1.iun.indiana.edu. *Dean,* Dr. Stanley E. Wigle, 219-981-4278, Fax: 219-981-4208, E-mail: jwigle@iunhaw1.iun.indiana.edu.

School of Public and Environmental Affairs Students: 11 full-time (9 women), 88 part-time (58 women); includes 55 minority (45 African Americans, 10 Hispanic Americans) Average age 38. *Faculty:* 2 full-time (1 woman). Expenses: Contact institution. *Financial support:* Career-related internships or fieldwork, Federal Work-Study, and tuition waivers (partial) available. Support available to part-time students. Financial award application deadline: 3/1. In 2001, 25 master's, 13 other advanced degrees awarded. *Degree program information:* Part-time programs available. Offers criminal justice (MPA); health services administration (MPA); human services administration (MPA); management of public affairs (MPA); non-profit management (NPMC); public management (PMC). *Application deadline:* For fall admission, 8/15 (priority date). Applications are processed on a rolling basis. *Application fee:* $25. *Application Contact:* Suzanne Green, Recorder, 219-980-6695, Fax: 219-980-6737, E-mail: sgreen@iunhaw1.iun.indiana.edu. *Director,* Joseph M. Pellicciotti, 219-980-6695, Fax: 219-980-6737, E-mail: jpelli@iunhaw1.iun.indiana.edu.

INDIANA UNIVERSITY OF PENNSYLVANIA, Indiana, PA 15705-1087

General Information State-supported, coed, university. CGS member. *Enrollment:* 793 full-time matriculated graduate/professional students (531 women), 901 part-time matriculated graduate/professional students (541 women). *Enrollment by degree level:* 1,219 master's, 475 doctoral. *Graduate faculty:* 348 full-time (133 women). Tuition, state resident: full-time $4,600; part-time $256 per credit hour. Tuition, nonresident: full-time $7,554; part-time $420 per credit hour. *Required fees:* $800. Part-time tuition and fees vary according to course load. *Graduate housing:* Room and/or apartments available on a first-come, first-served basis to single students; on-campus housing not available to married students. Typical cost: $2,492 per year. Housing application deadline: 4/15. *Student services:* Campus employment opportunities, campus safety program, career counseling, disabled student services, free psychological counseling, international student services, low-cost health insurance, multicultural affairs office. *Library facilities:* Stapleton Library. *Online resources:* library catalog, web page, access to other libraries' catalogs. *Collection:* 542,832 titles, 3,611 serial subscriptions, 224,613 audiovisual materials.

Computer facilities: 3,200 computers available on campus for general student use. A campuswide network can be accessed from student residence rooms and from off campus. *Web address:* http://www.iup.edu/.

General Application Contact: Donna Griffith, Assistant Dean, 724-357-2222, Fax: 724-357-4862, E-mail: graduate_admissions@iup.edu.

GRADUATE UNITS

Graduate School and Research Students: 793 full-time (531 women), 901 part-time (541 women); includes 119 minority (80 African Americans, 17 Asian Americans or Pacific Islanders, 18 Hispanic Americans, 4 Native Americans), 243 international. Average age 33. 1,990 applicants, 75% accepted. *Faculty:* 348 full-time (133 women). Expenses: Contact institution. *Financial support:* In 2001–02, 15 fellowships with full tuition reimbursements (averaging $5,000 per year), 296 research assistantships with full and partial tuition reimbursements (averaging $5,500 per year), 25 teaching assistantships with partial tuition reimbursements (averaging $17,001 per year) were awarded. Career-related internships or fieldwork, Federal Work-Study, scholarships/grants, and tuition waivers (full) also available. Support available to part-time students. Financial award application deadline: 3/15; financial award applicants required to submit FAFSA. In 2001, 533 master's, 75 doctorates, 9 other advanced degrees awarded. *Degree program information:* Part-time and evening/weekend programs available. *Application deadline:* Applications are processed on a rolling basis. *Application fee:* $30. *Application Contact:* Donna Griffith, Assistant Dean, 724-357-2222, Fax: 724-357-4862, E-mail: graduate_admissions@iup.edu. *Dean,* Dr. James C. Petersen, 724-357-2244, E-mail: jpetersn@iup.edu.

College of Education and Educational Technology Students: 251 full-time (186 women), 437 part-time (340 women); includes 45 minority (36 African Americans, 5 Asian Americans or Pacific Islanders, 3 Hispanic Americans, 1 Native American), 12 international. Average age 33. 620 applicants, 69% accepted. *Faculty:* 63 full-time (31 women). Expenses: Contact institution. *Financial support:* In 2001–02, 4 fellowships with full tuition reimbursements (averaging $5,000 per year), 87 research assistantships, 9 teaching assistantships with partial tuition reimbursements (averaging $17,001 per year) were awarded. Career-related internships or fieldwork and Federal Work-Study also available. Support available to part-time students. Financial award application deadline: 3/15; financial award applicants required to submit FAFSA. In 2001, 198 master's, 25 doctorates, 9 other advanced degrees awarded. *Degree program information:* Part-time and evening/weekend programs available. Offers administration and leadership studies (D Ed); adult education and communication technology (MA); communications technology (MA); community counseling (MA); counselor education (M Ed); curriculum and instruction (M Ed, D Ed); early childhood education (M Ed); education (M Ed, Certificate); education and educational technology (M Ed, MA, MS, D Ed, Certificate); education of exceptional persons (M Ed); educational psychology (M Ed, Certificate); literacy (M Ed); principal (Certificate); reading (M Ed); school psychology (D Ed); speech-language pathology (MS); student affairs in higher education (MA). *Application deadline:* Applications are processed on a rolling basis. *Application fee:* $30. *Application Contact:* Dr. Edward Nardi, Interim Associate Dean, 724-357-2480, E-mail: ewnardi@iup.edu. *Dean,* Dr. John Butzow, 724-357-2480, E-mail: jwbutzow@iup.edu.

College of Fine Arts Students: 17 full-time (11 women), 6 part-time (5 women). Average age 33. 28 applicants, 57% accepted. *Faculty:* 24 full-time (9 women). Expenses: Contact institution. *Financial support:* In 2001–02, 10 research assistantships (averaging $4,740 per year) were awarded; career-related internships or fieldwork and Federal Work-Study also available. Support available to part-time students. Financial award application deadline: 3/15; financial award applicants required to submit FAFSA. In 2001, 10 degrees awarded. *Degree program information:* Part-time programs available. Offers art (MA, MFA); fine arts (MA, MFA); music (MA); music education (MA); music history and literature (MA); music theory and composition (MA); performance (MA). *Application deadline:* For fall admission, 7/1 (priority date); for spring admission, 11/1. Applications are processed on a rolling basis. *Application fee:* $30. *Application Contact:* Dr. Douglas Bish, Associate Dean, 724-357-2397, E-mail: dbish@iup.edu. *Dean,* Michael Hood, 724-357-2397, E-mail: mhood@iup.edu.

College of Health and Human Services Students: 63 full-time (36 women), 88 part-time (49 women); includes 7 minority (4 African Americans, 1 Asian American or Pacific Islander, 1 Hispanic American, 1 Native American), 11 international. Average age 31. 125 applicants, 78% accepted. *Faculty:* 45 full-time (27 women). Expenses: Contact institution. *Financial support:* In 2001–02, 32 research assistantships (averaging $5,100 per year) were awarded; career-related internships or fieldwork and Federal Work-Study also available. Support available to part-time students. Financial award application deadline: 3/15; financial award applicants required to submit FAFSA. In 2001, 67 degrees awarded. *Degree program information:* Part-time and evening/weekend programs available. Offers aquatics administration and facilities management (MS); exercise science (MS); food and nutrition (MS); health and human services (MA, MS); industrial and labor relations (MA); nursing (MS); nursing and allied health (MS); safety sciences (MS); sport management (MS); sport science (MS). *Application deadline:* For fall admission, 7/1 (priority date); for spring admission, 11/1. Applications are processed on a rolling basis. *Application fee:* $30. *Application Contact:* Dr. Kathleen Rourke, Associate Dean, 724-357-2560, E-mail: kmrourke@iup.edu. *Dean,* Dr. Carleen Zoni, 724-357-2555, E-mail: cczoni@iup.edu.

College of Humanities and Social Sciences Students: 351 full-time (197 women), 148 part-time (77 women); includes 57 minority (35 African Americans, 8 Asian Americans or Pacific Islanders, 13 Hispanic Americans, 1 Native American), 112 international. Average age 34. 375 applicants, 73% accepted. *Faculty:* 98 full-time (35 women). Expenses: Contact institution. *Financial support:* In 2001–02, 8 fellowships (averaging $5,000 per year), 92 research assistantships (averaging $5,500 per year), 16 teaching assistantships (averaging $17,001 per year) were awarded. Career-related internships or fieldwork, Federal Work-Study, and tuition waivers (full) also available. Support available to part-time students. Financial award application deadline: 3/15; financial award applicants required to submit FAFSA. In 2001, 86 master's, 40 doctorates awarded. *Degree program information:* Part-time and evening/weekend programs available. Offers administration and leadership studies (PhD); composition and teaching English to speakers of other languages (MA, MAT, PhD); criminology (MA, PhD); generalist (MA); geography (MA, MS); history (MA); humanities and social sciences (MA, MAT, MS, PhD); literature (MA); literature and criticism (MA, PhD); public affairs (MA); rhetoric and linguistics (PhD); sociology (MA); teaching English (MAT); teaching English to speakers of other languages (MA). *Application deadline:* For fall admission, 7/1 (priority date); for spring admission, 11/1. Applications are processed on a rolling basis. *Application fee:* $30. *Dean,* Dr. Brenda Carter, 724-357-5764, E-mail: blcarter@iup.edu.

College of Natural Sciences and Mathematics Students: 93 full-time (60 women), 31 part-time (17 women); includes 7 minority (2 African Americans, 3 Asian Americans or Pacific Islanders, 1 Hispanic American, 1 Native American), 16 international. Average age 30. 180 applicants, 33% accepted. *Faculty:* 81 full-time (23 women). Expenses: Contact institution. *Financial support:* In 2001–02, 3 fellowships (averaging $5,000 per year), 54 research assistantships (averaging $5,800 per year), 1 teaching assistantship (averaging $17,001 per year) were awarded. Career-related internships or fieldwork, Federal Work-Study, and outside grants and professional employment also available. Support available to part-time students. Financial award application deadline: 3/15; financial award applicants required to submit FAFSA. In 2001, 41 master's, 10 doctorates awarded. *Degree program information:* Part-time programs available. Offers applied mathematics (MS); biology (MS); chemistry (MA, MS); elementary and middle school mathematics education (M Ed); mathematics education (M Ed); natural sciences and mathematics (M Ed, MA, MS, Psy D); physics (MA, MS); psychology (MA, Psy D). *Application deadline:* Applications are processed on a rolling basis. *Application fee:* $30. *Application Contact:* Dr. Raymond Pavloski, Dean's Associate, 724-357-2609. *Dean,* Dr. John S. Eck, 724-357-2609, E-mail: jseck@iup.edu.

Eberly College of Business and Information Technology Students: 123 full-time (48 women), 32 part-time (16 women); includes 2 minority (both African Americans), 84 international. Average age 28. 143 applicants, 66% accepted. *Faculty:* 37 full-time (8 women). Expenses: Contact institution. *Financial support:* In 2001–02, 22 research assistantships with full and partial tuition reimbursements (averaging $5,240 per year) were awarded; career-related internships or fieldwork and Federal Work-Study also available. Support available to part-time students. Financial award application deadline: 3/15; financial award applicants required to submit FAFSA. In 2001, 131 degrees awarded. *Degree program information:* Part-time and evening/weekend programs available. Offers business (M Ed, MBA); business administration (MBA); business/workforce development (M Ed). *Application deadline:* For fall admission, 7/1 (priority date); for spring admission, 11/1. Applications are processed on a rolling basis. *Application fee:* $30. *Dean,* Dr. Robert Camp, 724-357-4783, E-mail: bobcamp@iup.edu.

See in-depth description on page 915.

INDIANA UNIVERSITY–PURDUE UNIVERSITY FORT WAYNE, Fort Wayne, IN 46805-1499

General Information State-supported, coed, comprehensive institution. *Enrollment:* 56 full-time matriculated graduate/professional students (29 women), 606 part-time matriculated graduate/professional students (358 women). *Enrollment by degree level:* 662 master's. *Graduate faculty:* 88 full-time (34 women), 17 part-time/adjunct (5 women). Tuition, state resident: full-time $2,845; part-time $158 per credit hour. Tuition, nonresident: full-time $6,323; part-time $351 per credit hour. *Required fees:* $9 per credit hour. Tuition and fees vary according to course load. *Graduate housing:* On-campus housing not available. *Student services:* Campus employment opportunities, campus safety program, career counseling, child daycare facilities, disabled student services, exercise/wellness program, free psychological counseling, international student services, low-cost health insurance, multicultural affairs office, teacher training, writing training. *Library facilities:* Helmke Library. *Online resources:* library catalog, web page, access to other libraries' catalogs. *Collection:* 451,969 titles, 3,079 serial subscriptions, 962 audiovisual materials. *Research affiliation:* The Nature Company (environmental issues), Johnson and Johnson Consumes Products (dental health), Earthwatch (biology), Nugent Sand and Gravel Company (archaeology), Harza Engineering (archaeology), Church and Dwight Company, Inc. (dental health).

Computer facilities: 285 computers available on campus for general student use. A campuswide network can be accessed from off campus. Internet access and online class registration, students academic records are available. *Web address:* http://www.ipfw.edu/.

General Application Contact: Sandy Franke, Secretary for Graduate Studies, 260-481-6144, Fax: 260-481-6880, E-mail: ipfwadms@ipfw.edu.

GRADUATE UNITS

Division of Public and Environmental Affairs Students: 5 full-time (3 women), 34 part-time (23 women); includes 2 minority (1 African American, 1 Hispanic American) Average age 36. 21 applicants, 76% accepted, 13 enrolled. *Faculty:* 9 full-time (3 women). Expenses: Contact institution. *Financial support:* Career-related internships or fieldwork, Federal Work-Study, and scholarships/grants available. Support available to part-time students. Financial award application deadline: 3/1; financial award applicants required to submit FAFSA. In 2001, 7 degrees awarded. *Degree program information:* Part-time programs available. Offers public affairs (MPA); public management (Certificate). *Application deadline:* For fall admission, 8/1 (priority date); for spring admission, 12/1. Applications are processed on a rolling basis. *Application fee:* $30. *Application Contact:* Dr. Jane A. Grant, Director of Graduate Studies, 260-481-6349, Fax: 260-481-6346, E-mail: grant@iptw.edu. *Assistant Dean and Director,* Dr. William G. Ludwin, 260-481-6351, Fax: 260-481-6346, E-mail: ludwin@ipfw.edu.

School of Arts and Sciences Students: 20 full-time (10 women), 91 part-time (63 women); includes 15 minority (8 African Americans, 3 Asian Americans or Pacific Islanders, 2 Hispanic Americans, 2 Native Americans) Average age 36. 76 applicants, 79% accepted, 44 enrolled. *Faculty:* 45 full-time (18 women), 1 (woman) part-time/adjunct. Expenses: Contact institution. *Financial support:* In 2001–02, research assistantships with partial tuition reimbursements (averaging $7,350 per year), teaching assistantships with partial tuition reimbursements (averaging $7,350 per year) were awarded. Career-related internships or fieldwork, Federal Work-Study, institutionally sponsored loans, and scholarships/grants also available. Support available to part-time students. Financial award application deadline: 3/1; financial award applicants required to submit FAFSA. In 2001, 30 degrees awarded. *Degree program information:* Part-time and evening/weekend programs available. Offers applied mathematics (MS); arts and sciences (MA, MAT, MLS, MS); biology (MS); English (MA, MAT); liberal studies (MLS); mathematics (MS); operations research (MS); professional communication (MA, MS); sociological practice (MA). *Application deadline:* Applications are processed on a rolling basis. *Application fee:* $30. *Dean,* Dr. Van Coufoudakis, 260-481-6897, Fax: 260-481-6985, E-mail: coufouda@ipfw.edu.

School of Business and Management Sciences Students: 15 full-time (7 women), 104 part-time (28 women); includes 5 minority (1 African American, 2 Asian Americans or Pacific Islanders, 1 Hispanic American, 1 Native American), 3 international. Average age 30. 43 applicants, 95% accepted, 37 enrolled. *Faculty:* 11 full-time (2 women), 3 part-time/adjunct (0 women). Expenses: Contact institution. *Financial support:* In 2001–02, teaching assistantships with partial tuition reimbursements (averaging $7,350 per year); Federal Work-Study, scholarships/grants, and unspecified assistantships also available. Support available to part-time students. Financial award application deadline: 3/1; financial award applicants required to submit FAFSA. In 2001, 33 degrees awarded. *Degree program information:* Part-time programs available. Offers business administration (MBA). *Application deadline:* For fall admission, 7/1; for spring admission, 11/1. Applications are processed on a rolling basis. *Application fee:* $30. *Application Contact:* Janet Iden Kamdar, Executive Director of Graduate Studies, 260-481-6945, Fax: 260-481-6879, E-mail: kamdarj@ipfw.edu. *Dean,* Dr. John L. Wellington, 260-481-6461, Fax: 260-481-6879, E-mail: wellingj@ipfw.edu.

School of Education Students: 14 full-time (8 women), 344 part-time (230 women); includes 23 minority (17 African Americans, 1 Asian American or Pacific Islander, 3 Hispanic Americans, 2 Native Americans) Average age 37. 119 applicants, 67% accepted, 79 enrolled. *Faculty:* 15 full-time (8 women), 9 part-time/adjunct (3 women). Expenses: Contact institution. *Financial support:* Federal Work-Study and scholarships/grants available. Support available to part-time students. Financial award application deadline: 3/1; financial award applicants required to submit FAFSA. In 2001, 96 degrees awarded. *Degree program information:* Part-time programs available. Offers counselor education (MS Ed); education (MS Ed); elementary education (MS Ed); school administration (MS Ed); secondary education (MS Ed). *Application deadline:* For fall admission, 7/1 (priority date); for spring admission, 12/1. Applications are processed on a rolling basis. *Application fee:* $30. *Application Contact:* Vicky L. Schmidt, Graduate Recorder, 260-481-6450, Fax: 260-481-5408, E-mail: schmidt@ipfw.edu. *Dean,* Dr. Roberta B. Wiener, 260-481-4146, Fax: 260-481-5408, E-mail: wienerr@ipfw.edu.

School of Engineering, Technology, and Computer Science Students: 2 full-time (1 woman), 27 part-time (8 women); includes 4 minority (3 Asian Americans or Pacific Islanders, 1 Hispanic American), 3 international. Average age 36. 22 applicants, 68% accepted, 12 enrolled. *Faculty:* 4 full-time (0 women). Expenses: Contact institution. *Financial support:*

Indiana University–Purdue University Fort Wayne (continued)

In 2001–02, teaching assistantships (averaging $7,350 per year); career-related internships or fieldwork, Federal Work-Study, scholarships/grants, and unspecified assistantships also available. Support available to part-time students. Financial award application deadline: 3/1; financial award applicants required to submit FAFSA. In 2001, 6 degrees awarded. *Degree program information:* Part-time programs available. Offers applied computer science (MS); engineering, technology, and computer science (MS). *Application deadline:* For fall admission, 8/1 (priority date); for spring admission, 11/1. Applications are processed on a rolling basis. *Application fee:* $30. *Application Contact:* Dr. David Erbach, Chair of Computer Science, 260-481-6867, Fax: 260-481-5734, E-mail: erbach@ipfw.edu. *Dean, Interim,* Dr. C. Wayne Unsell, 260-481-6839, Fax: 260-481-5734, E-mail: unsell@ipfw.edu.

School of Health Sciences Average age 43. 8 applicants, 88% accepted, 5 enrolled. *Faculty:* 3 full-time (all women). Expenses: Contact institution. *Financial support:* Federal Work-Study and scholarships/grants available. Support available to part-time students. Financial award application deadline: 3/1; financial award applicants required to submit FAFSA. In 2001, 1 degree awarded. *Degree program information:* Part-time programs available. Offers health sciences (MS); nursing administration (MS). *Application deadline:* For fall admission, 8/1 (priority date); for spring admission, 12/1. Applications are processed on a rolling basis. *Application fee:* $30. *Application Contact:* Dr. Judith A. LeMire, Graduate Director, 260-481-6282, Fax: 260-481-5707, E-mail: lemirej@ipfw.edu. *Dean,* Dr. James E. Jones, 260-481-6967, Fax: 260-481-5701, E-mail: jonesj@ipfw.edu.

INDIANA UNIVERSITY–PURDUE UNIVERSITY INDIANAPOLIS, Indianapolis, IN 46202-2896

General Information State-supported, coed, university. *Enrollment:* 2,939 full-time matriculated graduate/professional students (1,453 women), 2,488 part-time matriculated graduate/professional students (1,282 women). *Enrollment by degree level:* 2,356 first professional, 2,622 master's, 256 doctoral. *Graduate faculty:* 516 full-time (149 women), 3 part-time/adjunct (0 women). Tuition, state resident: full-time $4,480; part-time $187 per credit. Tuition, nonresident: full-time $12,926; part-time $539 per credit. *Required fees:* $177. *Graduate housing:* Rooms and/or apartments available on a first-come, first-served basis to single and married students. *Student services:* Campus employment opportunities, campus safety program, career counseling, child daycare facilities, disabled student services, exercise/wellness program, free psychological counseling, international student services, low-cost health insurance, multicultural affairs office, writing training. *Library facilities:* University Library plus 5 others. *Online resources:* library catalog, web page, access to other libraries' catalogs. *Collection:* 1.4 million titles, 14,931 serial subscriptions, 434,863 audiovisual materials. *Research affiliation:* Indianapolis Center for Advanced Research, Regenstrief Institute for Health Care, Walther Oncology Research Institute.

Computer facilities: 500 computers available on campus for general student use. A campuswide network can be accessed from off campus. Internet access is available. *Web address:* http://www.indiana.edu/.

General Application Contact: Dr. Sheila Cooper, Director, Graduate Studies and Associate Dean, 317-274-4023, Fax: 317-278-2380, E-mail: smcoope@iupi.edu.

GRADUATE UNITS

Center on Philanthropy Students: 18 full-time (16 women), 17 part-time (15 women); includes 7 minority (2 African Americans, 1 Asian American or Pacific Islander, 4 Hispanic Americans), 2 international. Average age 32. Expenses: Contact institution. *Financial support:* In 2001–02, 17 students received support, including 2 fellowships with full and partial tuition reimbursements available (averaging $13,000 per year), 16 research assistantships with full and partial tuition reimbursements available (averaging $7,500 per year); career-related internships or fieldwork, Federal Work-Study, institutionally sponsored loans, and scholarships/grants also available. Financial award applicants required to submit FAFSA. In 2001, 13 degrees awarded. *Degree program information:* Part-time and evening/weekend programs available. Postbaccalaureate distance learning degree programs offered (minimal on-campus study). Offers nonprofit management (MPA); philanthropic studies (MA). *Application fee:* $45 ($55 for international students). *Application Contact:* Melissa Grider, Assistant Director for Student Services, 317-274-4200, Fax: 317-684-8900. *Executive Director,* Dr. Eugene Tempel, 317-274-4200.

Herron School of Art Average age 38. Expenses: Contact institution. *Financial support:* Career-related internships or fieldwork, Federal Work-Study, and tuition waivers (partial) available. In 2001, 6 degrees awarded. *Degree program information:* Part-time and evening/weekend programs available. Offers art education (MAE). *Application deadline:* For fall admission, 3/1 (priority date); for spring admission, 11/1. Applications are processed on a rolling basis. *Application fee:* $45 ($55 for international students). *Application Contact:* Cindy Borgmann, Program Coordinator, 317-920-2451, Fax: 317-920-2401, E-mail: cborgman@iupui.edu. *Dean,* Valerie Eickmeier, 317-920-2403, Fax: 317-920-2401, E-mail: veickmei@iupui.edu.

Kelley School of Business Students: 61 full-time (30 women), 495 part-time (102 women); includes 36 minority (10 African Americans, 21 Asian Americans or Pacific Islanders, 5 Hispanic Americans), 69 international. Average age 31. *Faculty:* 13 full-time (2 women). Expenses: Contact institution. *Financial support:* In 2001–02, fellowships (averaging $7,500 per year); Federal Work-Study also available. Support available to part-time students. Financial award application deadline: 3/1; financial award applicants required to submit FAFSA. In 2001, 52 degrees awarded. *Degree program information:* Part-time and evening/weekend programs available. Postbaccalaureate distance learning degree programs offered (minimal on-campus study). Offers business (MBA, MPA). *Application deadline:* For fall admission, 5/1; for spring admission, 11/1. *Application fee:* $45 ($55 for international students). *Application Contact:* Julie L. Moore, Recorder/Admission Coordinator, 317-274-4895, Fax: 317-274-2483, E-mail: mbaindy@iupui.edu. *Associate Dean, Indianapolis Programs,* Roger W. Schmenner, 317-274-4895.

School of Dentistry Students: 458 full-time (157 women), 73 part-time (24 women); includes 75 minority (4 African Americans, 55 Asian Americans or Pacific Islanders, 13 Hispanic Americans, 3 Native Americans), 66 international. Average age 28. *Faculty:* 20 full-time (5 women). Expenses: Contact institution. *Financial support:* In 2001–02, 43 students received support, including fellowships (averaging $5,306 per year); research assistantships, teaching assistantships, Federal Work-Study and institutionally sponsored loans also available. Financial award application deadline: 3/1; financial award applicants required to submit FAFSA. In 2001, 89 first professional degrees, 17 master's, 2 doctorates awarded. Offers dental materials (MS, MSD); dental sciences (PhD); dentistry (DDS, MS, MSD, PhD); diagnostic sciences (MS, MSD); endodontics (MSD); operative dentistry (MSD); oral and maxillofacial surgery (MSD); oral biology (PhD); orthodontics (MS, MSD); pediatric dentistry (MSD); periodontics (MSD); preventive dentistry (MS, MSD); prosthodontics (MSD). *Application fee:* $45 ($55 for international students). *Application Contact:* Barb Lerner, Coordinator of Student Services, 317-274-8173, Fax: 317-274-2419, E-mail: blerner@iupui.edu. *Dean,* Lawrence I. Goldblatt, 317-274-7461.

School of Education Students: 47 full-time (41 women), 266 part-time (188 women); includes 32 minority (25 African Americans, 4 Asian Americans or Pacific Islanders, 2 Hispanic Americans, 1 Native American), 10 international. Average age 34. *Faculty:* 16 full-time (9 women). Expenses: Contact institution. *Financial support:* Fellowships, research assistantships with partial tuition reimbursements, teaching assistantships, career-related internships or fieldwork, Federal Work-Study, and tuition waivers (partial) available. In 2001, 69 degrees awarded. *Degree program information:* Part-time and evening/weekend programs available. Offers counseling and counselor education (MS); education (MS); educational leadership and school administration (MS); elementary education (MS); higher education and student affairs (MS); instructional systems technology (MS); language education (MS); secondary education (MS); special education (MS). *Application deadline:* For fall admission, 3/1 (priority date); for spring admission, 11/1. *Application fee:* $45 ($55 for international students). *Application Contact:* Dr. Linda L. Houser, Assistant Dean for Education Student Services, 317-274-6841, Fax: 317-274-6864, E-mail: lhouser@iupui.edu. *Executive Associate Dean,* Dr. Barbara Wilcox, 317-274-6862, Fax: 317-274-6864, E-mail: wilcoxb@indiana.edu.

School of Engineering and Technology Students: 45 full-time (12 women), 59 part-time (17 women); includes 8 minority (2 African Americans, 3 Asian Americans or Pacific Islanders, 1 Hispanic American, 2 Native Americans), 73 international. Average age 29. *Faculty:* 1 full-time (0 women). Expenses: Contact institution. *Financial support:* In 2001–02, 16 students received support; fellowships with tuition reimbursements available, research assistantships with full and partial tuition reimbursements available, teaching assistantships, Federal Work-Study, institutionally sponsored loans, and tuition waivers (full and partial) available. Support available to part-time students. Financial award application deadline: 3/1. In 2001, 31 degrees awarded. *Degree program information:* Part-time and evening/weekend programs available. Offers biomedical engineering (MS Bm E, PhD); electrical engineering (MSEE); engineering (MS, MSE); engineering and technology (MS, MS Bm E, MSE, MSEE, MSME, PhD); mechanical engineering (MSME). *Application deadline:* For fall admission, 5/1. *Application fee:* $45 ($55 for international students). *Application Contact:* Valerie Lim, Graduate Program, 317-278-4960, Fax: 317-278-1671, E-mail: grad@engr.iupui.edu. *Dean,* Dr. H. Oner Yurtseven, 317-274-0802, Fax: 317-274-4567.

School of Informatics Students: 22 full-time (11 women), 64 part-time (21 women); includes 10 minority (7 African Americans, 2 Asian Americans or Pacific Islanders, 1 Hispanic American), 14 international. Average age 34. Expenses: Contact institution. *Financial support:* In 2001–02, teaching assistantships (averaging $3,500 per year); Federal Work-Study and scholarships/grants also available. Support available to part-time students. In 2001, 16 degrees awarded. *Degree program information:* Part-time and evening/weekend programs available. Offers media arts and science (MS). *Application deadline:* For fall admission, 3/15; for spring admission, 11/15. *Application fee:* $45 ($55 for international students). *Associate Dean,* Dr. Darrell L. Bailey, 317-278-7666, Fax: 317-278-7769, E-mail: dbailey@iupui.edu.

School of Liberal Arts Students: 26 full-time (19 women), 39 part-time (21 women); includes 1 minority (Asian American or Pacific Islander), 17 international. Average age 30. *Faculty:* 114 full-time (35 women). Expenses: Contact institution. *Financial support:* Fellowships with partial tuition reimbursements, research assistantships with partial tuition reimbursements, teaching assistantships with tuition reimbursements, career-related internships or fieldwork available. In 2001, 18 degrees awarded. Offers economics (MA); English (MA); history (MA); liberal arts (MA); public history (MA); teaching English (MA). *Application fee:* $45 ($55 for international students). *Application Contact:* William Schneider, Director of Research and Graduate Programs, 317-274-8305. *Dean,* Dr. Herman J. Saatkamp, 317-274-8305.

School of Library and Information Science Students: 24 full-time (19 women), 155 part-time (120 women); includes 4 minority (all African Americans), 1 international. Average age 37. *Faculty:* 1 (woman) full-time. Expenses: Contact institution. *Financial support:* Career-related internships or fieldwork available. In 2001, 67 degrees awarded. *Degree program information:* Part-time and evening/weekend programs available. Offers library and information science (MIS, MLS). *Application deadline:* For fall admission, 5/15 (priority date). Applications are processed on a rolling basis. *Application fee:* $45 ($55 for international students). *Application Contact:* Dr. Debora Shaw, Associate Dean, 317-278-2375, Fax: 317-278-1807, E-mail: shawd@indiana.edu. *Dean,* Dr. Blaise Cronin, 317-278-2375.

School of Medicine Students: 1,229 full-time (531 women), 114 part-time (68 women); includes 191 minority (82 African Americans, 84 Asian Americans or Pacific Islanders, 23 Hispanic Americans, 2 Native Americans), 53 international. Average age 26. *Faculty:* 225 full-time (40 women), 3 part-time/adjunct (0 women). Expenses: Contact institution. *Financial support:* In 2001–02, fellowships with full and partial tuition reimbursements (averaging $4,091 per year); research assistantships with full and partial tuition reimbursements, teaching assistantships with full tuition reimbursements, career-related internships or fieldwork, Federal Work-Study, institutionally sponsored loans, scholarships/grants, traineeships, tuition waivers (full and partial), unspecified assistantships, and stipends also available. Support available to part-time students. In 2001, 261 first professional degrees, 60 master's, 24 doctorates awarded. Offers anatomy and cell biology (MS, PhD); biochemistry and molecular biology (MS, PhD); health sciences education (MS); medical and molecular genetics (MS, PhD); medical biophysics (MS, PhD); medical neurobiology (MS, PhD); medical physiology (MS, PhD); medicine (MD, MS, PhD); microbiology and immunology (MS, PhD); nutrition and dietetics (MS); pathology and laboratory medicine (MS, PhD); pharmacology (MS, PhD); physical therapy (MS); therapeutic outcomes research (MS); toxicology (MS, PhD). *Application deadline:* Applications are processed on a rolling basis. *Application fee:* $45 ($55 for international students). *Application Contact:* 317-274-3772, Fax: 317-278-0211, E-mail: medschl@iupui.edu. *Dean,* Dr. Robert W. Holden, 317-274-8157.

School of Music Students: 3 full-time (1 woman), 14 part-time (7 women); includes 5 minority (3 African Americans, 1 Asian American or Pacific Islander, 1 Hispanic American), 1 international. Average age 36. Expenses: Contact institution. *Financial support:* In 2001–02, 3 teaching assistantships with full tuition reimbursements (averaging $5,000 per year) were awarded Financial award application deadline: 11/15. In 2001, 50 degrees awarded. *Degree program information:* Part-time and evening/weekend programs available. Postbaccalaureate distance learning degree programs offered. Offers music technology (MS). *Application deadline:* For fall admission, 4/15 (priority date); for spring admission, 11/15 (priority date). Applications are processed on a rolling basis. *Application fee:* $45 ($55 for international students). *Application Contact:* Dr. G. David Peters, Professor, 317-278-2591. *Associate Dean,* Dr. Darrell L. Bailey, 317-278-2594, E-mail: dbailey@iupui.edu.

School of Nursing Students: 24 full-time (23 women), 191 part-time (183 women); includes 10 minority (6 African Americans, 2 Asian Americans or Pacific Islanders, 2 Hispanic Americans), 5 international. Average age 39. *Faculty:* 42 full-time (40 women). Expenses: Contact institution. *Financial support:* In 2001–02, 93 students received support, including fellowships with full tuition reimbursements available (averaging $10,000 per year), 50 research assistantships with full tuition reimbursements available (averaging $3,000 per year), 10 teaching assistantships with full tuition reimbursements available (averaging $3,500 per year); Federal Work-Study, scholarships/grants, traineeships, and tuition waivers (full) also available. Support available to part-time students. Financial award application deadline: 5/1. In 2001, 50 master's, 7 doctorates awarded. *Degree program information:* Part-time programs available. Offers acute care nurse practitioner (MSN); adult clinical nurse specialist (MSN); adult nurse practitioner (MSN); community health nursing (MSN); family nurse practitioner (MSN); nursing (MSN, PhD); nursing administration (MSN); nursing science (PhD); pediatric (MSN); pediatric nursing practitioner (MSN); psychiatric and mental health nursing (MSN); women's health nurse practitioner (MSN). *Application fee:* $45 ($55 for international students). *Application Contact:* Bernice Mercier, Graduate Recorder, 317-274-2806, Fax: 317-274-2996, E-mail: bmercier@iupui.edu. *Associate Dean for Graduate Programs,* Dr. Linda Finke, 317-274-2806, Fax: 317-274-2996.

School of Public and Environmental Affairs Students: 85 full-time (60 women), 336 part-time (132 women); includes 53 minority (37 African Americans, 11 Asian Americans or Pacific Islanders, 5 Hispanic Americans), 12 international. Average age 36. *Faculty:* 9 full-time (2 women). Expenses: Contact institution. *Financial support:* In 2001–02, research assistantships with full and partial tuition reimbursements (averaging $7,600 per year); fellowships with full and partial tuition reimbursements, career-related internships or fieldwork and Federal Work-Study also available. Support available to part-time students. Financial award application deadline: 3/1. In 2001, 92 master's, 87 other advanced degrees awarded. *Degree program information:* Part-time and evening/weekend programs available. Offers environmental planning (M Pl); health administration (MHA); health planning (M Pl); planning and public policy (M Pl); public affairs (MPA, Certificate); public and environmental affairs (M Pl, MHA, MPA, Certificate); urban development planning (M Pl). *Application deadline:* For fall admission, 7/15 (priority date); for spring admission, 11/15. Applications are processed on a rolling basis. *Application fee:* $45 ($55 for international students). *Application Contact:* 317-274-4656, Fax: 317-274-5153, E-mail: speainfo@speanet.iupui.edu. *Associate Dean,* Dr. Mark Rosentraub, 317-274-8483, Fax: 317-274-5153.

School of Science Students: 90 full-time (50 women), 152 part-time (60 women); includes 22 minority (5 African Americans, 11 Asian Americans or Pacific Islanders, 5 Hispanic Americans, 1 Native American), 57 international. Average age 28. *Faculty:* 56 full-time (7 women). Expenses: Contact institution. *Financial support:* In 2001–02, 17 fellowships with full and partial tuition reimbursements, 41 research assistantships with full and partial tuition reimbursements, 57 teaching assistantships with full and partial tuition reimbursements were awarded. Career-related internships or fieldwork, Federal Work-Study, institutionally sponsored loans, scholarships/grants, tuition waivers (full and partial), and co-op positions also available. Support available to part-time students. Financial award applicants required to submit FAFSA. In 2001, 83 master's, 5 doctorates awarded. *Degree program information:* Part-time and evening/weekend programs available. Offers applied mathematics (MS, PhD); applied statistics (MS); biology (MS, PhD); chemistry (MS, PhD); clinical rehabilitation psychology (MS, PhD); computer science (MS); geology (MS); industrial/organizational psychology (MS); mathematics (MS, PhD); physics (MS, PhD); psychobiology of addictions (PhD); science (MS, PhD). *Application fee:* $45 ($55 for international students). Electronic applications accepted. *Dean,* David L. Stocum, 317-274-0625, Fax: 317-274-0628, E-mail: science@iupui.edu.

School of Social Work Students: 242 full-time (214 women), 170 part-time (153 women); includes 69 minority (56 African Americans, 2 Asian Americans or Pacific Islanders, 11 Hispanic Americans) Average age 32. *Faculty:* 12 full-time (6 women). Expenses: Contact institution. *Financial support:* In 2001–02, 27 students received support; fellowships with full tuition reimbursements available, research assistantships with partial tuition reimbursements available, teaching assistantships, career-related internships or fieldwork, Federal Work-Study, institutionally sponsored loans, and tuition waivers (partial) available. Support available to part-time students. Financial award applicants required to submit FAFSA. In 2001, 231 degrees awarded. *Degree program information:* Part-time and evening/weekend programs available. Offers social work (MSW, PhD). *Application fee:* $45 ($55 for international students). *Application Contact:* Rhonda Brock, Student Services Secretary, 317-274-8364, Fax: 317-274-8630, E-mail: rbrock@iupui.edu. *Dean,* Dr. Sheldon Siegel, 317-274-8362, Fax: 317-274-8630.

INDIANA UNIVERSITY SCHOOL OF LAW-BLOOMINGTON, Bloomington, IN 47405

General Information State-supported, coed, graduate-only institution. *Graduate faculty:* 47 full-time (15 women), 12 part-time/adjunct (4 women). Tuition, state resident: full-time $9,045; part-time $276 per credit hour. Tuition, nonresident: full-time $21,347; part-time $707 per credit hour. *Graduate housing:* Rooms and/or apartments available on a first-come, first-served basis to single and married students. Typical cost: $6,292 (including board) for single students. Housing application deadline: 5/1. *Student services:* Campus employment opportunities, campus safety program, career counseling, child daycare facilities, disabled student services, exercise/wellness program, free psychological counseling, international student services, low-cost health insurance, multicultural affairs office, teacher training, writing training. *Library facilities:* Indiana University Libraries plus 36 others. *Online resources:* library catalog, web page, access to other libraries' catalogs. *Collection:* 156,541 titles, 7,471 serial subscriptions, 1,595 audiovisual materials.

Computer facilities: 1,254 computers available on campus for general student use. A campuswide network can be accessed from student residence rooms and from off campus. Internet access is available. *Web address:* http://www.law.indiana.edu/.

General Application Contact: Kevin Robling, Assistant Dean for Admissions, 812-855-4765, Fax: 812-855-0555, E-mail: lawadmis@indiana.edu.

GRADUATE UNITS

School of Law Students: 614 full-time (255 women), 94 part-time (41 women); includes 99 minority (48 African Americans, 23 Asian Americans or Pacific Islanders, 28 Hispanic Americans), 100 international. Average age 24. 2,003 applicants, 39% accepted, 214 enrolled. *Faculty:* 47 full-time (15 women), 12 part-time/adjunct (4 women). Expenses: Contact institution. *Financial support:* In 2001–02, 389 students received support, including 9 fellowships with full and partial tuition reimbursements available (averaging $8,000 per year), 39 research assistantships, 4 teaching assistantships (averaging $2,000 per year); career-related internships or fieldwork, Federal Work-Study, institutionally sponsored loans, and scholarships/grants also available. Financial award application deadline: 3/1; financial award applicants required to submit FAFSA. In 2001, 215 first professional degrees, 62 master's awarded. Offers law (JD, LL M, MCL, SJD, Certificate). *Application deadline:* For fall admission, 3/1 (priority date). Applications are processed on a rolling basis. *Application fee:* $35 ($45 for international students). *Application Contact:* Kevin Robling, Assistant Dean for Admissions, 812-855-4765, Fax: 812-855-0555, E-mail: lawadmis@indiana.edu. *Acting Dean,* Lauren K. Robel, 812-855-8885, Fax: 812-855-7057, E-mail: lrobel@indiana.edu.

INDIANA UNIVERSITY SCHOOL OF LAW-INDIANAPOLIS, Indianapolis, IN 46202-3225

General Information State-supported, coed, graduate-only institution. *Enrollment by degree level:* 841 first professional. *Graduate faculty:* 42 full-time (14 women), 41 part-time/adjunct (12 women). Tuition, state resident: full-time $8,569; part-time $5,520 per year. Tuition, nonresident: full-time $19,696; part-time $12,707 per year. *Required fees:* $531; $531 per year. Tuition and fees vary according to course load. *Graduate housing:* On-campus housing not available. *Student services:* Campus employment opportunities, campus safety program, career counseling, child daycare facilities, disabled student services, exercise/wellness program, free psychological counseling, international student services, low-cost health insurance, multicultural affairs office, teacher training, writing training. *Library facilities:* Indiana University School of Law Library–Indianapolis plus 3 others. *Online resources:* library catalog, web page, access to other libraries' catalogs. *Collection:* 337,531 titles, 7,229 serial subscriptions, 772 audiovisual materials.

Computer facilities: 1,139 computers available on campus for general student use. A campuswide network can be accessed from student residence rooms and from off campus. Internet access and online class registration are available. *Web address:* http://www.iulaw.indy.indiana.edu/.

General Application Contact: Angela M. Espada, Assistant Dean for Admissions, 317-274-2459, Fax: 317-274-3955, E-mail: amespada@iupui.edu.

GRADUATE UNITS

School of Law Students: 550 full-time (262 women), 291 part-time (137 women); includes 126 minority (81 African Americans, 26 Asian Americans or Pacific Islanders, 16 Hispanic Americans, 3 Native Americans), 16 international. Average age 30. 1,085 applicants, 50% accepted. *Faculty:* 42 full-time (14 women), 41 part-time/adjunct (12 women). Expenses: Contact institution. *Financial support:* In 2001–02, 625 students received support. Career-related internships or fieldwork, Federal Work-Study, and scholarships/grants available. Support available to part-time students. Financial award applicants required to submit FAFSA. In 2001, 262 degrees awarded. *Degree program information:* Part-time and evening/weekend programs available. Offers law (JD). *Application deadline:* For fall admission, 3/1 (priority date). Applications are processed on a rolling basis. *Application fee:* $35. *Application Contact:* Angela M. Espada, Assistant Dean for Admissions, 317-274-2459, Fax: 317-274-3955, E-mail: amespada@iupui.edu. *Dean,* Norman Lefstein, 317-274-2581, Fax: 317-274-3955, E-mail: nlefstei@iupui.edu.

INDIANA UNIVERSITY SOUTH BEND, South Bend, IN 46634-7111

General Information State-supported, coed, comprehensive institution. *Enrollment:* 187 full-time matriculated graduate/professional students (110 women), 768 part-time matriculated graduate/professional students (497 women). *Enrollment by degree level:* 827 master's. *Graduate faculty:* 83 full-time (30 women), 35 part-time/adjunct (24 women). Tuition, state resident: full-time $3,664; part-time $153. Tuition, nonresident: full-time $8,929; part-time $372. *Required fees:* $390. Tuition and fees vary according to program. *Graduate housing:* On-campus housing not available. *Student services:* Campus employment opportunities, campus safety program, career counseling, child daycare facilities, disabled student services, exercise/wellness program, free psychological counseling, international student services, low-cost health insurance. *Library facilities:* Franklin D. Schurz Library plus 1 other. *Collection:* 592,095 titles, 2,116 serial subscriptions, 29,613 audiovisual materials.

Computer facilities: 200 computers available on campus for general student use. Internet access is available. *Web address:* http://www.iusb.edu/.

General Application Contact: Dr. Linda M. Fritshner, Acting Associate Vice Chancellor for Academic Affairs, 574-2374338, Fax: 574-2376549, E-mail: grad_admit@iusb.edu.

GRADUATE UNITS

College of Liberal Arts and Sciences Students: 2 full-time (0 women), 30 part-time (23 women); includes 3 minority (2 African Americans, 1 Hispanic American) Average age 38. *Faculty:* 6 full-time (1 woman). Expenses: Contact institution. *Financial support:* Career-related internships or fieldwork, Federal Work-Study, and institutionally sponsored loans available. Support available to part-time students. Financial award application deadline: 3/1; financial award applicants required to submit FAFSA. In 2001, 10 degrees awarded. *Degree program information:* Part-time and evening/weekend programs available. Offers applied mathematics and computer science (MS); applied psychology (MA); liberal arts and sciences (MA, MLS, MS); liberal studies (MLS). *Application deadline:* For fall admission, 7/15; for spring admission, 11/1. Applications are processed on a rolling basis. *Application fee:* $40 ($50 for international students). *Dean,* Dr. Miriam Shillingsburg, 574-237-4270, Fax: 574-237-4538, E-mail: shilling@iusb.edu.

Program in Social Work Students: 34 full-time (31 women), 59 part-time (50 women); includes 12 minority (8 African Americans, 2 Asian Americans or Pacific Islanders, 2 Hispanic Americans), 1 international. Average age 35. *Faculty:* 5 full-time (2 women). Expenses: Contact institution. *Financial support:* Career-related internships or fieldwork and Federal Work-Study available. Support available to part-time students. Financial award application deadline: 3/1; financial award applicants required to submit FAFSA. In 2001, 25 degrees awarded. *Degree program information:* Part-time and evening/weekend programs available. Offers social work (MSW). *Application deadline:* For fall admission, 2/1. *Application fee:* $40 ($50 for international students). *Director,* Dr. Paul R. Newcomb, 574-237-4464, Fax: 574-237-4876, E-mail: socw@iusb.edu.

School of Business and Economics Students: 55 full-time (16 women), 155 part-time (52 women); includes 17 minority (2 African Americans, 10 Asian Americans or Pacific Islanders, 5 Hispanic Americans), 53 international. Average age 32. *Faculty:* 32 full-time (5 women), 5 part-time/adjunct (2 women). Expenses: Contact institution. *Financial support:* Federal Work-Study and institutionally sponsored loans available. Support available to part-time students. Financial award application deadline: 3/1; financial award applicants required to submit FAFSA. In 2001, 45 degrees awarded. *Degree program information:* Part-time and evening/weekend programs available. Offers accounting (MSA); business administration (MBA); business and economics (MBA, MIT, MSA); management information technologies (MIT). *Application deadline:* For fall admission, 7/1 (priority date); for spring admission, 11/1. Applications are processed on a rolling basis. *Application fee:* $40 ($50 for international students). *Application Contact:* Dr. Katherine Jackson, Director of Graduate Business Programs, 574-237-4138, Fax: 574-237-4866, E-mail: gradbus@iusb.edu. *Dean,* Dr. Bill N. Schwartz, 574-2374346, Fax: 574-2374866, E-mail: bschwartz@iusb.edu.

School of Education Students: 81 full-time (52 women), 485 part-time (346 women); includes 48 minority (37 African Americans, 3 Asian Americans or Pacific Islanders, 7 Hispanic Americans, 1 Native American), 6 international. Average age 36. *Faculty:* 26 full-time (17 women), 28 part-time/adjunct (20 women). Expenses: Contact institution. *Financial support:* Federal Work-Study available. Support available to part-time students. Financial award application deadline: 3/1; financial award applicants required to submit FAFSA. In 2001, 122 degrees awarded. *Degree program information:* Part-time and evening/weekend programs available. Offers counseling and human services (MS Ed); education (MS Ed); elementary education (MS Ed); secondary education (MS Ed); special education (MS Ed). *Application deadline:* For fall admission, 7/1; for spring admission, 11/1. Applications are processed on a rolling basis. *Application fee:* $40 ($50 for international students). *Application Contact:* Dr. Jannette G. Shaw, Assistant Dean for Graduate Programs, 574-237-4127, Fax: 574-237-4550, E-mail: jshaw@iusb.edu. *Interim Dean,* Dr. Gwynn Mettetal, 219-237-4507, Fax: 219-237-1550, E-mail: jmetteta@iusb.edu.

School of Public and Environmental Affairs Students: 6 full-time (4 women), 26 part-time (16 women); includes 6 minority (5 African Americans, 1 Hispanic American), 1 international. Average age 35. *Faculty:* 10 full-time (4 women), 1 (woman) part-time/adjunct. Expenses: Contact institution. *Financial support:* Fellowships, research assistantships, career-related internships or fieldwork, Federal Work-Study, and institutionally sponsored loans available. Support available to part-time students. Financial award application deadline: 3/1; financial award applicants required to submit FAFSA. In 2001, 20 degrees awarded. *Degree program information:* Part-time and evening/weekend programs available. Offers public affairs (MPA); public and environmental affairs (MPA). *Application deadline:* For fall admission, 7/1 (priority date); for spring admission, 11/1. Applications are processed on a rolling basis. *Application fee:* $40 ($50 for international students). *Application Contact:* Dr. J. Paul Herr, Director, 574-237-4592, Fax: 574-237-6514, E-mail: jherr@iusb.edu. *Assistant Dean,* Dr. Leda M Hall, 574-237-4131, Fax: 574-237-6514.

School of the Arts Students: 9 full-time (7 women), 4 part-time (3 women), 7 international. Average age 29. *Faculty:* 4 full-time (1 woman), 1 (woman) part-time/adjunct. Expenses: Contact institution. *Financial support:* Fellowships, teaching assistantships, Federal Work-Study available. Support available to part-time students. Financial award application deadline: 3/1; financial award applicants required to submit FAFSA. In 2001, 3 degrees awarded. *Degree program information:* Part-time programs available. Offers music (MM). *Application deadline:* For fall admission, 7/1 (priority date); for spring admission, 11/1. Applications are processed on a rolling basis. *Application fee:* $40 ($50 for international students). *Application Contact:* Mike Esselstrom, Graduate Program Director, 574-237-4562, Fax: 574-237-4317, E-mail: messelt@iusb.edu. *Dean,* Dr. Thomas Miller, 574-237-4170, Fax: 574-237-4317, E-mail: messelst@iusb.edu.

INDIANA UNIVERSITY SOUTHEAST, New Albany, IN 47150-6405

General Information State-supported, coed, comprehensive institution. *Enrollment:* 29 full-time matriculated graduate/professional students (19 women), 691 part-time matriculated graduate/professional students (426 women). *Enrollment by degree level:* 720 master's. *Graduate faculty:* 21 full-time (14 women), 14 part-time/adjunct (7 women). Tuition, state resident: full-time $3,644; part-time $152 per credit. Tuition, nonresident: full-time $8,311; part-time $346 per credit. *Required fees:* $386; $386 per year. *Graduate housing:* On-campus housing not available. *Student services:* Campus employment opportunities, campus safety program, career counseling, child daycare facilities, disabled student services, free psychological counseling, low-cost health insurance, multicultural affairs office. *Library facilities:* Main library plus 1 other. *Collection:* 202,111 titles, 1,037 serial subscriptions, 15,676 audiovisual materials.

Computer facilities: 200 computers available on campus for general student use. A campuswide network can be accessed from off campus. Internet access is available. *Web address:* http://www.indiana.edu/.

General Application Contact: Dr. Carolyn A. Babione, Graduate Coordinator, 812-941-2594, Fax: 812-941-2667, E-mail: cbabione@ius.edu.

GRADUATE UNITS

School of Education Students: 15 full-time (11 women), 444 part-time (345 women); includes 34 minority (27 African Americans, 1 Asian American or Pacific Islander, 6 Hispanic Americans), 2 international. Average age 33. *Faculty:* 21 full-time (14 women), 14 part-time/adjunct (7 women). Expenses: Contact institution. *Financial support:* In 2001–02, 29 students received support. Career-related internships or fieldwork, Federal Work-Study, and institutionally sponsored loans available. Support available to part-time students. Financial award applicants required to submit FAFSA. In 2001, 121 degrees awarded. *Degree program information:* Part-time and evening/weekend programs available. Offers counselor education (MS Ed); elementary education (MS Ed); secondary education (MS Ed). *Application deadline:* Applications are processed on a rolling basis. *Application fee:* $30. *Application Contact:* Dr. Carolyn A. Babione, Graduate Coordinator, 812-941-2594, Fax: 812-941-2667, E-mail: cbabione@ius.edu. *Dean,* Dr. Gloria Murray, 812-941-2385, Fax: 812-941-2667, E-mail: glomurra@ius.edu.

INDIANA WESLEYAN UNIVERSITY, Marion, IN 46953-4974

General Information Independent-religious, coed, comprehensive institution. *Graduate housing:* Rooms and/or apartments available to single and married students. Housing application deadline: 4/10.

GRADUATE UNITS

College of Adult and Professional Studies Students: 2,220 full-time (1,220 women); includes 404 minority (337 African Americans, 30 Asian Americans or Pacific Islanders, 27 Hispanic Americans, 10 Native Americans) Average age 35. 1,490 applicants, 99% accepted. *Faculty:* 21 full-time (6 women), 294 part-time/adjunct (85 women). Expenses: Contact institution. *Financial support:* Available to part-time students. Applicants required to submit FAFSA. In 2001, 826 degrees awarded. *Degree program information:* Evening/weekend programs available. Postbaccalaureate distance learning degree programs offered (minimal on-campus study). Offers business administration (MBA); community counseling (MA); community/addiction counseling (MA); counseling (MA); curriculum and instruction (M Ed); management (MS); marriage and family counseling (MA); teacher education (M Ed). *Application deadline:* Applications are processed on a rolling basis. *Application fee:* $25. Electronic applications accepted. *Application Contact:* R. David Rose, Marketing Manager, 800-234-5327, Fax: 765-674-8028, E-mail: drose@indwes.edu. *Vice President,* Dr. Mark Smith, 765-677-2390, Fax: 765-677-2380, E-mail: msmith@indwes.edu.

Graduate Programs *Degree program information:* Part-time and evening/weekend programs available. Offers counseling (MA); ministry (MA); nursing education (MS, Post Master's Certificate). Electronic applications accepted.

Division of Nursing Education *Degree program information:* Part-time and evening/weekend programs available. Offers community health development (MS); community health nursing (MS); nursing (Post Master's Certificate); nursing education (MS); primary care nursing (MS). Electronic applications accepted.

INSTITUTE FOR CHRISTIAN STUDIES, Toronto, ON M5T 1R4, Canada

General Information Independent-religious, coed, graduate-only institution. *Enrollment by degree level:* 51 master's, 17 doctoral. *Graduate faculty:* 7 full-time (2 women), 3 part-time/adjunct (2 women). *Graduate tuition:* Tuition and fees charges are reported in Canadian dollars. *Tuition:* Full-time $3,150 Canadian dollars; part-time $395 Canadian dollars per course. *Required fees:* $150 Canadian dollars; $100 Canadian dollars per year. $25 Canadian dollars per term. Full-time tuition and fees vary according to degree level and program. *Graduate housing:* On-campus housing not available. *Student services:* Campus employment opportunities, career counseling, international student services, low-cost health insurance, writing training. *Online resources:* library catalog, web page. *Collection:* 25,000 titles, 80 serial subscriptions.

Computer facilities: 3 computers available on campus for general student use. A campuswide network can be accessed from off campus. Internet access is available. *Web address:* http://www.icscanada.edu/.

General Application Contact: Pam Trondson, Director of Student Services, 888-326-5347 Ext. 239, Fax: 416-979-2332, E-mail: studentservices@icscanada.edu.

GRADUATE UNITS

Graduate Programs Students: 35 full-time (3 women), 33 part-time (11 women). Average age 30. 15 applicants, 87% accepted. *Faculty:* 7 full-time (2 women), 3 part-time/adjunct (2 women). Expenses: Contact institution. *Financial support:* In 2001–02, 12 students received support, including 9 research assistantships (averaging $1,000 per year), 1 teaching assistantship (averaging $3,000 per year); Federal Work-Study, scholarships/grants, and tuition waivers (full and partial) also available. Financial award application deadline: 3/31. In 2001, 6 degrees awarded. *Degree program information:* Part-time programs available. Postbaccalaureate distance learning degree programs offered (minimal on-campus study). Offers aesthetics (M Phil F, PhD); biblical hermeneutical studies (M Phil F, PhD); education (M Phil F, PhD); hermeneutics (M Phil F); history of philosophy (M Phil F, PhD); philosophical theology (M Phil F, PhD); philosophy of science and technology (M Phil F); political theory (M Phil F, PhD); systematic philosophy (M Phil F, PhD); systematic theology (M Phil F, PhD); worldview studies (MWS). PhD offered jointly with Free University in Amsterdam, the Netherlands. *Application deadline:* For fall admission, 3/31 (priority date). Applications are processed on a rolling basis. *Application fee:* $40. *Application Contact:* Pam Trondson, Director of Student Services, 888-326-5347 Ext. 239, Fax: 416-979-2332, E-mail: studentservices@icscanada.edu. *President,* Dr. Harry Fernhout, 416-979-2331 Ext. 222, Fax: 416-979-2332, E-mail: hfernhout@icscanada.edu.

INSTITUTE FOR CLINICAL SOCIAL WORK, Chicago, IL 60601

General Information Independent, coed, primarily women, graduate-only institution. *Enrollment by degree level:* 84 doctoral. *Graduate faculty:* 67 part-time/adjunct (40 women). *Tuition:* Full-time $11,000; part-time $880 per course. *Graduate housing:* On-campus housing not available. *Student services:* Writing training. *Online resources:* web page. *Collection:* 3,000 titles, 23 serial subscriptions.

Computer facilities: 2 computers available on campus for general student use. Internet access is available. *Web address:* http://www.icsw.com/.

General Application Contact: Dr. Barbara Berger, Dean of Admissions, 312-726-8480 Ext. 31, Fax: 312-726-7216.

GRADUATE UNITS

Graduate Programs Students: 65 full-time (47 women), 19 part-time (15 women); includes 16 minority (9 African Americans, 2 Asian Americans or Pacific Islanders, 4 Hispanic Americans, 1 Native American) Average age 38. 20 applicants, 95% accepted. *Faculty:* 67 part-time/adjunct (40 women). Expenses: Contact institution. *Financial support:* In 2001–02, 23 students received support. Institutionally sponsored loans available. Financial award application deadline: 9/1; financial award applicants required to submit FAFSA. In 2001, 7 degrees awarded. *Degree program information:* Part-time programs available. Offers clinical social work (PhD). *Application deadline:* For fall admission, 5/1 (priority date). Applications are processed on a rolling basis. *Application fee:* $50. *Application Contact:* Dr. Barbara Berger, Dean of Admissions, 312-726-8480 Ext. 31, Fax: 312-726-7216. *President,* Thomas K. Kenemore, 312-726-8480 Ext. 22, Fax: 312-726-7216, E-mail: tkenemore@aol.com.

INSTITUTE OF PAPER SCIENCE AND TECHNOLOGY, Atlanta, GA 30318-5794

General Information Independent, coed, graduate-only institution. *Graduate housing:* Rooms and/or apartments available on a first-come, first-served basis to single and married students. Housing application deadline: 5/1. *Research affiliation:* Fort James Corporation (pulp and paper technology), Union Camp Corporation (pulp and paper technology), Weyerhaeuser Company (pulp and paper technology), Georgia-Pacific Corporation (pulp and paper technology), Champion International Corporation (pulp and paper technology), The Procter & Gamble Company (pulp and paper technology).

GRADUATE UNITS

Graduate Programs *Degree program information:* Part-time programs available. Offers biology (MS, PhD); chemical engineering (MS, PhD); chemistry (MS, PhD); mechanical engineering (MS, PhD); physics/mathematics (MS, PhD). Electronic applications accepted.

INSTITUTE OF PUBLIC ADMINISTRATION, Dublin, 4, Ireland

General Information Proprietary, coed, comprehensive institution.

GRADUATE UNITS

Programs in Public Administration Offers healthcare management (MA); local government management (MA); public management (MA, Diploma).

INSTITUTE OF TEXTILE TECHNOLOGY, Charlottesville, VA 22903-4614

General Information Independent, coed, graduate-only institution. *Enrollment by degree level:* 16 master's. *Graduate faculty:* 17 full-time (2 women), 5 part-time/adjunct (2 women). *Graduate tuition:* All students automatically receive a full fellowship which covers tuition and fees. *Graduate housing:* On-campus housing not available. *Student services:* Campus employment opportunities, campus safety program, career counseling, exercise/wellness program, writing training. *Library facilities:* Roger Milliken Library. *Online resources:* library catalog, web page. *Collection:* 35,000 titles, 500 serial subscriptions. *Research affiliation:* British Petroleum Fabrics and Fibers (textiles).

Computer facilities: 30 computers available on campus for general student use. A campuswide network can be accessed from student residence rooms and from off campus. Internet access is available. *Web address:* http://www.itt.edu/.

General Application Contact: Peggy S. Ehrenberg, Administrative Assistant to Academic Affairs, 434-296-5511 Ext. 275, Fax: 434-296-2957, E-mail: peggye@itt.edu.

GRADUATE UNITS

Program in Textile Technology Students: 16 full-time (6 women); includes 2 minority (1 African American, 1 Hispanic American) Average age 25. 35 applicants, 31% accepted. *Faculty:* 17 full-time (2 women), 5 part-time/adjunct (2 women). Expenses: Contact institution. *Financial support:* In 2001–02, 16 fellowships with full tuition reimbursements (averaging $20,000 per year) were awarded; career-related internships or fieldwork and tuition waivers (full) also available. Financial award application deadline: 2/15; financial award applicants required to submit FAFSA. In 2001, 12 degrees awarded. Offers textile technology (MS). *Application deadline:* For fall admission, 3/15. Applications are processed on a rolling basis. *Application fee:* $0. Electronic applications accepted. *Application Contact:* Peggy S. Ehrenberg, Administrative Assistant to Academic Affairs, 434-296-5511 Ext. 275, Fax: 434-296-2957, E-mail: peggye@itt.edu. *Executive Vice President and Dean of Academic Affairs,* Dan J. McCreight, 434-296-5511 Ext. 266, Fax: 434-297-3873, E-mail: danm@itt.edu.

INSTITUTE OF TRANSPERSONAL PSYCHOLOGY, Palo Alto, CA 94303

General Information Independent, coed, graduate-only institution. *Enrollment by degree level:* 137 master's, 160 doctoral, 54 other advanced degrees. *Graduate faculty:* 15 full-time (7 women), 44 part-time/adjunct (28 women). *Tuition:* Full-time $17,784. *Required fees:* $30. Tuition and fees vary according to degree level, campus/location and program. *Graduate housing:* On-campus housing not available. *Student services:* Campus employment opportunities, international student services. *Library facilities:* Institute of Transpersonal Psychology Library. *Online resources:* library catalog, web page, access to other libraries' catalogs. *Collection:* 13,000 titles, 140 serial subscriptions.

Computer facilities: 10 computers available on campus for general student use. A campuswide network can be accessed. Internet access is available. *Web address:* http://www.itp.edu/.

General Application Contact: 650-493-4430 Ext. 16, Fax: 650-493-6835, E-mail: itpinfo@itp.edu.

GRADUATE UNITS

Global Division Students: 83 full-time (67 women), 20 part-time (15 women); includes 9 minority (2 African Americans, 1 Asian American or Pacific Islander, 3 Hispanic Americans, 3 Native Americans), 12 international. Average age 43. 80 applicants, 78% accepted. *Faculty:* 3 full-time (1 woman), 31 part-time/adjunct (25 women). Expenses: Contact institution. *Financial support:* In 2001–02, 55 students received support. Federal Work-Study available. Support available to part-time students. Financial award application deadline: 6/30; financial award applicants required to submit FAFSA. In 2001, 16 degrees awarded. Postbaccalaureate distance learning degree programs offered (minimal on-campus study). Offers creative expression (Certificate); spiritual psychology (Certificate); transpersonal psychology (MTP, PhD); transpersonal studies (MA, Certificate); wellness counseling and body-mind consciousness (Certificate); women's spiritual development (Certificate). *Application deadline:* Applications are processed on a rolling basis. *Application fee:* $55. *Application Contact:* Edith Parker, Admissions Assistant, 650-493-4430 Ext. 40, Fax: 650-493-6835, E-mail: itpinfo@itp.edu. *Dean,* Prof. Kurtick Patel, 650-493-4430, Fax: 650-493-6835, E-mail: kpatel@itp.edu.

Residential Division Students: 236 full-time (173 women), 12 part-time (10 women); includes 30 minority (7 African Americans, 9 Asian Americans or Pacific Islanders, 11 Hispanic Americans, 3 Native Americans), 13 international. Average age 41. 122 applicants, 78% accepted, 58 enrolled. *Faculty:* 18 full-time (10 women), 22 part-time/adjunct (7 women). Expenses: Contact institution. *Financial support:* In 2001–02, 141 students received support; teaching assistantships, career-related internships or fieldwork and Federal Work-Study available. Support available to part-time students. Financial award application deadline: 7/1; financial award applicants required to submit FAFSA. In 2001, 48 master's, 12 doctorates awarded. *Degree program information:* Part-time and evening/weekend programs available. Offers counseling psychology (MA); transpersonal psychology (MA, PhD). *Application deadline:* For fall admission, 4/15 (priority date). Applications are processed on a rolling basis. *Application fee:* $55. *Application Contact:* John Hofmann, Admissions Office, 650-493-4430 Ext. 30, Fax: 650-493-6835, E-mail: itpinfo@itp.edu. *Academic Dean,* Dr. Paul Roy, 650-493-4430, Fax: 650-493-6835, E-mail: proy@itp.edu.

INSTITUT FRANCO-EUROPEAN DE CHIROPRATIQUE, 94200 Ivry-sur-Seine, France

General Information Independent, coed, graduate-only institution.

GRADUATE UNITS

Professional Program Offers chiropractic (DC).

INSTITUTO CENTROAMERICANO DE ADMINISTRACIÓN DE EMPRESAS, La Garita, Alajuela, Costa Rica

General Information Independent, coed, graduate-only institution. *Graduate housing:* Rooms and/or apartments guaranteed to single students and available on a first-come, first-served basis to married students. Housing application deadline: 7/30. *Research affiliation:* Tropical Agricultural Research and Higher Education Center (agribusiness), Harvard Institute for International Development (macroeconomics and environment), Earth University (agribusiness), Inter-American Institute for Cooperation on Agriculture (agribusiness), David Rockefeller Center for Latin American Studies (competitiveness), Zamarono (agribusiness).

GRADUATE UNITS

MBA Program Offers business administration (EMBA); entrepreneurial economics (MBA); industry and technology (MBA); sustainable development (MBA).

INSTITUTO TECNOLÓGICO Y DE ESTUDIOS SUPERIORES DE MONTERREY, CAMPUS CENTRAL DE VERACRUZ, 94500 Córdoba, Veracruz, Mexico

General Information Independent, coed, comprehensive institution.

GRADUATE UNITS

Graduate Programs *Degree program information:* Part-time and evening/weekend programs available. Postbaccalaureate distance learning degree programs offered (minimal on-campus study). Electronic applications accepted.

INSTITUTO TECNOLÓGICO Y DE ESTUDIOS SUPERIORES DE MONTERREY, CAMPUS CHIAPAS, 29000 Tuxtla Gutiérrez, Chiapas, Mexico

General Information Independent, coed, comprehensive institution.

INSTITUTO TECNOLÓGICO Y DE ESTUDIOS SUPERIORES DE MONTERREY, CAMPUS CHIHUAHUA, 31300 Chihuahua, Chihuahua, Mexico

General Information Independent, coed, comprehensive institution.

GRADUATE UNITS

Graduate Programs Offers computer systems engineering (Ingeniero); electrical engineering (Ingeniero); electromechanical engineering (Ingeniero); electronic engineering (Ingeniero); engineering administration (MEA); industrial engineering (MIE, Ingeniero); international trade (MIT); mechanical engineering (Ingeniero).

INSTITUTO TECNOLÓGICO Y DE ESTUDIOS SUPERIORES DE MONTERREY, CAMPUS CIUDAD DE MÉXICO, 14380 Ciudad de Mexico, DF, Mexico

General Information Independent, coed, comprehensive institution. *Graduate housing:* On-campus housing not available. *Research affiliation:* McGill University (management), Concordia University (business and management), Eli Lilly S.A. de C.U. (technological development), Ford Motor Company (industrial organization), German Research Center on Artificial Intelligence (informatics), Brent University (telecommunications).

GRADUATE UNITS

Division of Business *Degree program information:* Part-time and evening/weekend programs available. Postbaccalaureate distance learning degree programs offered (minimal on-campus study). Offers business administration (EMBA, MBA, PhD); economy (MBA); finance (MBA).

Division of Engineering and Architecture *Degree program information:* Part-time and evening/weekend programs available. Postbaccalaureate distance learning degree programs offered (minimal on-campus study). Offers management (MA); telecommunications (MA).

Division of Humanities and Social Sciences *Degree program information:* Part-time and evening/weekend programs available. Offers humanities and social sciences (LL B).

Virtual University Division *Degree program information:* Part-time and evening/weekend programs available. Postbaccalaureate distance learning degree programs offered (minimal on-campus study).

INSTITUTO TECNOLÓGICO Y DE ESTUDIOS SUPERIORES DE MONTERREY, CAMPUS CIUDAD JUÁREZ, 32320 Ciudad Juárez, Chihuahua, Mexico

General Information Independent, coed, comprehensive institution.

GRADUATE UNITS

Program in Administration of Information Technology Offers administration of information technology (MAIT).

Program in Business Administration Offers business administration (MBA).

Program in Education Offers education (M Ed).

Program in Financial Administration Offers financial administration (MFA).

Program in Industrial Engineering Offers industrial engineering (MIE).

Program in Quality Management Offers quality management (MQM).

Program in Telecommunications Offers telecommunications (MTEL).

INSTITUTO TECNOLÓGICO Y DE ESTUDIOS SUPERIORES DE MONTERREY, CAMPUS CIUDAD OBREGÓN, 85000 Ciudad Obregón, Sonora, Mexico

General Information Independent, coed, comprehensive institution.

GRADUATE UNITS

Program in Administration Offers administration (MA).

Program in Administration of Information Technology Offers administration of information technology (MATI).

Program in Administration of Telecommunications Offers administration of telecommunications (MAT).

Program in Engineering Offers engineering (ME).

Program in Finance Offers finance (MF).

Program in International Relations Offers international relations (MIR).

Program in Marketing Technology Offers marketing technology (MMT).

Programs in Education Offers cognitive development (ME); communications (ME); mathematics (ME).

INSTITUTO TECNOLÓGICO Y DE ESTUDIOS SUPERIORES DE MONTERREY, CAMPUS COLIMA, 28010 Colima, Colima, Mexico

General Information Independent, coed, comprehensive institution.

INSTITUTO TECNOLÓGICO Y DE ESTUDIOS SUPERIORES DE MONTERREY, CAMPUS CUERNAVACA, 62000 Temixco, Morelos, Mexico

General Information Independent, coed, comprehensive institution.

GRADUATE UNITS

Programs in Business Administration Offers finance (MA); human resources management (MA); international business (MA); marketing (MA).

Programs in Information Science Offers administration of information technology (MATI); computer science (MCC, DCC); information technology (MTI).

INSTITUTO TECNOLÓGICO Y DE ESTUDIOS SUPERIORES DE MONTERREY, CAMPUS ESTADO DE MÉXICO, Estado de Mexico, 52926, Mexico

General Information Independent, coed, comprehensive institution. *Enrollment:* 69 full-time matriculated graduate/professional students (18 women), 804 part-time matriculated graduate/professional students (257 women). *Enrollment by degree level:* 858 master's, 15 doctoral. *Graduate faculty:* 35 full-time (6 women), 25 part-time/adjunct (0 women). *Graduate housing:* On-campus housing not available. *Student services:* Campus employment opportunities, campus safety program, career counseling, exercise/wellness program, free psychological counseling, international student services. *Online resources:* library catalog, web page. *Collection:* 132,321 titles, 1,213 serial subscriptions. *Research affiliation:* Academy Assembly of Collegiate Schools of Business (business), American Marketing Association (marketing), Asociación de Lingüística y Filogogía de las América Lafino (literature), Asociación Filosófica de México (philosophy).

Computer facilities: 934 computers available on campus for general student use. A campuswide network can be accessed from off campus. Internet access and online class registration are available. *Web address:* http://www.cem.itesm.mx/.

General Application Contact: Andrea Dueñas Alfaro, Registrar, 5-864-5780, Fax: 5-864-5781, E-mail: aduenas@campus.cem.itesm.mx.

GRADUATE UNITS

Professional and Graduate Division Students: 69 full-time (18 women), 804 part-time (257 women). Average age 30. 271 applicants, 74% accepted. *Faculty:* 35 full-time (6 women), 25 part-time/adjunct (0 women). Expenses: Contact institution. *Financial support:* In 2001–02, 199 teaching assistantships with tuition reimbursements were awarded; fellowships with partial tuition reimbursements In 2001, 18 degrees awarded. *Degree program information:* Part-time programs available. Postbaccalaureate distance learning degree programs offered (minimal on-campus study). *Application deadline:* For fall admission, 1/13 (priority date); for spring admission, 4/4. Applications are processed on a rolling basis. *Application fee:* 750 Mexican pesos for international students. *Application Contact:* Lic. Lourdes Turrubiates, Admissions Officer, 5-864-5784, Fax: 5-864-5781, E-mail: lturrubi@campus.cem.itesm.mx. *Headmaster*, Ing. Emilio Alvarado Badillo, 5-864-5500, Fax: 5-864-5507, E-mail: ealvarad@campus.cem.itesm.mx.

INSTITUTO TECNOLÓGICO Y DE ESTUDIOS SUPERIORES DE MONTERREY, CAMPUS GUADALAJARA, 45140 Zapopan, Jalisco, Mexico

General Information Independent, coed, comprehensive institution. *Graduate housing:* Rooms and/or apartments available to single and married students. Housing application deadline: 8/30.

GRADUATE UNITS

Program in Business Administration *Degree program information:* Part-time and evening/weekend programs available. Postbaccalaureate distance learning degree programs offered. Offers business administration (MBA).

Program in Finance Offers finance (MF).

INSTITUTO TECNOLÓGICO Y DE ESTUDIOS SUPERIORES DE MONTERREY, CAMPUS HIDALGO, 42090 Pachuca, Hidalgo, Mexico

General Information Independent, coed, comprehensive institution.

INSTITUTO TECNOLÓGICO Y DE ESTUDIOS SUPERIORES DE MONTERREY, CAMPUS IRAPUATO, 36660 Irapuato, Guanajuato, Mexico

General Information Independent, coed, comprehensive institution.

GRADUATE UNITS

Graduate Programs Offers administration (MBA); administration of information technology (MAIT); administration of telecommunications (MAT); architecture (M Arch); computer science (MCS); education (M Ed); educational administration (MEA); educational innovation and technology (DEIT); educational technology (MET); electronic commerce (MBA); environmental administration and planning (MEAP); environmental systems (MES); finances (MBA); humanistic studies (MHS); international management for Latin American executives (MIMLAE); library and information science (MLIS); manufacturing quality management (MMQM); marketing research (MBA).

INSTITUTO TECNOLÓGICO Y DE ESTUDIOS SUPERIORES DE MONTERREY, CAMPUS LAGUNA, 27250 Torreón, Coahuila, Mexico

General Information Independent, coed, comprehensive institution. *Graduate housing:* On-campus housing not available.

GRADUATE UNITS

Graduate School *Degree program information:* Part-time programs available. Offers business administration (MBA); industrial engineering (MIE); management information systems (MS).

INSTITUTO TECNOLÓGICO Y DE ESTUDIOS SUPERIORES DE MONTERREY, CAMPUS LEÓN, 37120 León, Guanajuato, Mexico

General Information Independent, coed, comprehensive institution.

GRADUATE UNITS

Program in Business Administration *Degree program information:* Part-time programs available. Offers business administration (MBA).

INSTITUTO TECNOLÓGICO Y DE ESTUDIOS SUPERIORES DE MONTERREY, CAMPUS MAZATLÁN, 82000 Mazatlán, Sinaloa, Mexico

General Information Independent, coed, comprehensive institution.

INSTITUTO TECNOLÓGICO Y DE ESTUDIOS SUPERIORES DE MONTERREY, CAMPUS MONTERREY, 64849 Monterrey, Nuevo León, Mexico

General Information Independent, coed, university. *Graduate housing:* Room and/or apartments available to single students; on-campus housing not available to married students. *Research affiliation:* IBM de México (computer science), Southwest Research Institute (environment), Hylsa (steel), Vitro (glass products), Cydsa (petrochemicals), Cemex (cement).

GRADUATE UNITS

Graduate and Research Division *Degree program information:* Part-time and evening/weekend programs available. Offers agricultural parasitology (PhD); agricultural sciences (MS); applied statistics (M Eng); artificial intelligence (PhD); automation engineering (M Eng); biotechnology (MS); chemical engineering (M Eng); chemistry (MS, PhD); civil engineering (M Eng); communications (MS); computer science (MS); education (MA); electrical engineering (M Eng); electronic engineering (M Eng); environmental engineering (M Eng); farming productivity (MS); food processing engineering (MS); industrial engineering (M Eng, PhD); informatics (PhD); information systems (MS); information technology (MS); manufacturing engineering (M Eng); mechanical engineering (M Eng); phytopathology (MS); systems and quality engineering (M Eng).

Graduate School of Business Administration and Leadership *Degree program information:* Part-time programs available. Offers business administration (MA, MBA); finance (M Sc); international business (M Sc); management (PhD); management and leadership (M Sc, MA, MBA, PhD); marketing (M Sc).

INSTITUTO TECNOLÓGICO Y DE ESTUDIOS SUPERIORES DE MONTERREY, CAMPUS QUERÉTARO, 76130 Querétaro, Querétaro, Mexico

General Information Independent, coed, comprehensive institution. *Graduate housing:* On-campus housing not available. *Research affiliation:* Transmisiones y Equipos Mecanicos (manufacturing designing).

GRADUATE UNITS

School of Business Offers business (MBA).

INSTITUTO TECNOLÓGICO Y DE ESTUDIOS SUPERIORES DE MONTERREY, CAMPUS SALTILLO, 25270 Saltillo, Coahuila, Mexico

General Information Independent, coed, comprehensive institution.

INSTITUTO TECNOLÓGICO Y DE ESTUDIOS SUPERIORES DE MONTERREY, CAMPUS SAN LUIS POTOSÍ, 78140 San Luis Potosí, SLP, Mexico

General Information Independent, coed, comprehensive institution.

INSTITUTO TECNOLÓGICO Y DE ESTUDIOS SUPERIORES DE MONTERREY, CAMPUS SINALOA, 80800 Culiacán, Sinaloa, Mexico

General Information Independent, coed, comprehensive institution.

INSTITUTO TECNOLÓGICO Y DE ESTUDIOS SUPERIORES DE MONTERREY, CAMPUS SONORA NORTE, 83000 Hermosillo, Sonora, Mexico

General Information Independent, coed, comprehensive institution. *Graduate housing:* On-campus housing not available. *Research affiliation:* National Council for Science and Technology (engineering).

GRADUATE UNITS

Program in Business Offers business (MA).

Program in Education Offers education (MA).

Program in Technological Information Management Offers technological information management (MA).

INSTITUTO TECNOLÓGICO Y DE ESTUDIOS SUPERIORES DE MONTERREY, CAMPUS TAMPICO, 89120 Altimira, Tamaulipas, Mexico

General Information Independent, coed, comprehensive institution.

INSTITUTO TECNOLÓGICO Y DE ESTUDIOS SUPERIORES DE MONTERREY, CAMPUS TOLUCA, 50252 Toluca, Estado de Mexico, Mexico

General Information Independent, coed, comprehensive institution.

GRADUATE UNITS

Graduate Programs *Degree program information:* Part-time and evening/weekend programs available.

INSTITUTO TECNOLÓGICO Y DE ESTUDIOS SUPERIORES DE MONTERREY, CAMPUS ZACATECAS, 98000 Zacatecas, Zacatecas, Mexico

General Information Independent, coed, comprehensive institution.

INTER AMERICAN UNIVERSITY OF PUERTO RICO, ARECIBO CAMPUS, Arecibo, PR 00614-4050

General Information Independent, coed, comprehensive institution.

GRADUATE UNITS

Program in Anesthesia Offers anesthesia (MS).

Programs in Education Offers administration and educational supervision (MA Ed); orientation and counseling (MA Ed).

INTER AMERICAN UNIVERSITY OF PUERTO RICO, METROPOLITAN CAMPUS, San Juan, PR 00919-1293

General Information Independent, coed, comprehensive institution. CGS member. *Graduate housing:* On-campus housing not available. *Research affiliation:* Innovation Technology (electronics).

GRADUATE UNITS

Division of Science and Technology *Degree program information:* Part-time and evening/weekend programs available. Offers educational computing (MA); medical technology (MS); open information systems (MS). Electronic applications accepted.

Graduate Programs *Degree program information:* Part-time and evening/weekend programs available. Electronic applications accepted.

Division of Behavioral Science and Allied Professions *Degree program information:* Part-time and evening/weekend programs available. Offers criminal justice (MA); psychology (MA); social work (MA). Electronic applications accepted.

Division of Education *Degree program information:* Part-time and evening/weekend programs available. Offers administration and supervision (MA); education (Ed D); elementary education (MA); guidance and counseling (MA); health and physical education (MA); higher education (MA Ed); occupational education (MA); special education (MA Ed); teaching of science (MA Ed); vocational evaluation (MA). Electronic applications accepted.

Faculty of Economics and Administrative Sciences *Degree program information:* Part-time and evening/weekend programs available. Offers accounting (MBA); business and management development (PhD); business education (MA); finance (MBA); human resources (MBA); industrial management (MBA); labor relations (MA); marketing (MBA). Electronic applications accepted.

School of Humanistic Studies *Degree program information:* Part-time and evening/weekend programs available. Offers humanistic studies (MA); Spanish (MA); teaching English as a second language (MA). Electronic applications accepted.

School of Law *Degree program information:* Part-time and evening/weekend programs available. Offers law (JD).

INTER AMERICAN UNIVERSITY OF PUERTO RICO, SAN GERMÁN CAMPUS, San Germán, PR 00683-5008

General Information Independent, coed, university. *Enrollment:* 749 matriculated graduate/professional students. *Graduate faculty:* 36 full-time (21 women), 41 part-time/adjunct (15 women). *Tuition:* Part-time $165 per credit. *Required fees:* $390; $195 per semester. Tuition and fees vary according to degree level and program. *Graduate housing:* Room and/or apartments available on a first-come, first-served basis to single students; on-campus housing not available to married students. Typical cost: $900 per year ($2,400 including board). Room and board charges vary according to board plan. Housing application deadline: 6/15. *Student services:* Campus employment opportunities, campus safety program, career counseling, child daycare facilities, international student services, low-cost health insurance. *Library facilities:* Juan Cancio Ortiz Library. *Online resources:* library catalog, web page, access to other libraries' catalogs. *Collection:* 162,544 titles, 1,748 serial subscriptions, 2,836 audiovisual materials.

Computer facilities: 520 computers available on campus for general student use. A campuswide network can be accessed. Internet access and online class registration are available. *Web address:* http://www.sg.inter.edu/.

General Application Contact: Dr. Waldemar Velez, Director of Graduate Program Center, 787-892-4300 Ext. 7358, Fax: 787-892-6350, E-mail: wvelez@sg.inter.edu.

GRADUATE UNITS

Graduate Programs Students: 749. Average age 31. 344 applicants, 86% accepted, 239 enrolled. *Faculty:* 36 full-time (21 women), 41 part-time/adjunct (15 women). Expenses: Contact institution. *Financial support:* Fellowships, research assistantships, teaching assistantships, Federal Work-Study available. In 2001, 176 master's, 30 other advanced degrees awarded. *Degree program information:* Part-time and evening/weekend programs available. Offers accounting (MBA); administration of higher education institutions (MA); art (MA); business administration (MBA); business education (MA); counseling psychology (PhD); curriculum and instruction (MA Ed); educational administration (MA Ed); environmental sciences (MS); finance (MBA); guidance and counseling (MA Ed); health sciences (Certificate); human resources (MBA); industrial relations (MBA); library science (MA); management sciences (PhD); marketing (MBA); physical education and scientific analysis of human body movement (MA Ed); psychology (MA, MS); quality organizational design (MBA); school psychology (PhD); science education (MA); special education (MS Ed); teaching English as a second language (MA). *Application deadline:* For fall admission, 4/30 (priority date); for spring admission, 11/15. Applications are processed on a rolling basis. *Application fee:* $31. *Director of Graduate Program Center,* Dr. Waldemar Velez, 787-892-4300 Ext. 7358, Fax: 787-892-6350, E-mail: wvelez@sg.inter.edu.

INTER AMERICAN UNIVERSITY OF PUERTO RICO SCHOOL OF OPTOMETRY, San Juan, PR 00919

General Information Independent, coed, graduate-only institution.

GRADUATE UNITS

Professional Program in Optometry Students: 169 full-time (98 women), 3 part-time (1 woman); includes 119 minority (5 African Americans, 18 Asian Americans or Pacific Islanders, 96 Hispanic Americans), 9 international. Average age 23. 88 applicants, 69% accepted, 40 enrolled. *Faculty:* 16 full-time (6 women), 22 part-time/adjunct (8 women). Expenses: Contact institution. *Financial support:* In 2001–02, 2 fellowships with partial tuition reimbursements (averaging $7,500 per year) were awarded; Federal Work-Study, institutionally sponsored loans, and scholarships/grants also available. Financial award application deadline: 4/30; financial award applicants required to submit FAFSA. In 2001, 49 degrees awarded. Offers optometry (OD). *Application deadline:* For fall admission, 4/1 (priority date). *Application fee:* $31. Electronic applications accepted. *Application Contact:* José Colón, Director of Admissions, 787-765-1915 Ext. 2511, Fax: 787-767-3920, E-mail: jcolon@inter.edu. *Dean,* Dr. Hector C. Santiago, 787-765-1915 Ext. 2500, Fax: 787-767-3920, E-mail: hsantiag@inter.edu.

INTERDENOMINATIONAL THEOLOGICAL CENTER, Atlanta, GA 30314-4112

General Information Independent-religious, coed, graduate-only institution. *Graduate housing:* Rooms and/or apartments available to single and married students. *Research affiliation:* Emory University Library, Candler School of Theology Library, Columbia Theological Seminary Library, Atlanta University Center, Inc..

GRADUATE UNITS

Graduate and Professional Programs *Degree program information:* Part-time programs available. Offers theology (M Div, MACE, MACM, D Min, Th D).

INTERNATIONAL BAPTIST COLLEGE, Tempe, AZ 85282

General Information Independent-religious, coed, comprehensive institution. *Enrollment:* 5 full-time matriculated graduate/professional students, 18 part-time matriculated graduate/professional students (2 women). *Graduate faculty:* 4 full-time (0 women), 4 part-time/adjunct (0 women). *Graduate housing:* Room and/or apartments available on a first-come, first-served basis to single students; on-campus housing not available to married students. *Student services:* Campus employment opportunities, career counseling, child daycare facilities, international student services, writing training.

Computer facilities: 6 computers available on campus for general student use.

General Application Contact: Dr. Stan Bushey, Administrative Service Director, 480-838-7070, Fax: 480-838-5430.

GRADUATE UNITS

Program in Biblical Studies Students: 5 full-time (0 women), 3 part-time. *Faculty:* 3 full-time (0 women). Expenses: Contact institution. *Financial support:* Scholarships/grants available. Offers biblical studies (MA). *Application deadline:* Applications are processed on a rolling basis. *Application fee:* $25. *Administrative Service Director,* Dr. Stan Bushey, 480-838-7070, Fax: 480-838-5430.

Program in Ministry *Faculty:* 1 full-time (0 women), 4 part-time/adjunct (0 women). Expenses: Contact institution. *Financial support:* Scholarships/grants available. Offers ministry (M Min, D Min). *Application deadline:* Applications are processed on a rolling basis. *Application fee:* $25. *Application Contact:* Dr. Jerry Tetreau, College President, 480-838-7070. *Director,* Dr. James Singleton.

INTERNATIONAL COLLEGE AND GRADUATE SCHOOL, Honolulu, HI 96817

General Information Independent-religious, coed, upper-level institution. *Enrollment:* 9 full-time matriculated graduate/professional students (3 women), 14 part-time matriculated graduate/professional students (6 women). *Graduate faculty:* 3 full-time (0 women), 29 part-time/adjunct (0 women). *Tuition:* Full-time $3,690; part-time $615 per course. *Required fees:* $180; $90 per term. *Graduate housing:* On-campus housing not available. *Student services:* Career counseling, international student services. *Library facilities:* J. W. Cook Memorial Library. *Collection:* 16,669 titles, 65 serial subscriptions, 703 audiovisual materials.

Computer facilities: 6 computers available on campus for general student use. A campuswide network can be accessed from off campus. *Web address:* http://www.icgshawaii.org/.

General Application Contact: Harvey C.W. Ching, Director of Graduate Programs, 808-595-4247, Fax: 808-595-4799, E-mail: internatc001@hawaii.rr.com.

GRADUATE UNITS

Graduate Studies *Degree program information:* Part-time and evening/weekend programs available. Offers ministry (D Min); religion (MAR); theology (M Div).

INTERNATIONAL COLLEGE OF THE CAYMAN ISLANDS, Newlands, Grand Cayman, Cayman Islands

General Information Independent, coed, comprehensive institution. *Enrollment:* 15 full-time matriculated graduate/professional students (11 women), 20 part-time matriculated graduate/professional students (16 women). *Enrollment by degree level:* 35 master's. *Graduate faculty:* 5 full-time (2 women), 6 part-time/adjunct (2 women). *Tuition:* Full-time $3,300. *Required fees:* $110 per credit. $67 per quarter. One-time fee: $53. *Graduate housing:* Room and/or apartments available on a first-come, first-served basis to single students; on-campus housing not available to married students. Typical cost: $2,400 per year. *Student services:* Campus employment opportunities, career counseling. *Library facilities:* ICCI Library. *Collection:* 16,677 titles, 140 serial subscriptions.

Computer facilities: 16 computers available on campus for general student use. Internet access is available. *Web address:* http://cayman.com.ky/pub/icci/.

General Application Contact: Dr. Eileen Dounce, Director of Graduate Studies, 345-947-1100 Ext. 202, Fax: 345-947-1210.

INTERNATIONAL FINE ARTS COLLEGE, Miami, FL 33132-1121

General Information Proprietary, coed, comprehensive institution. *Enrollment:* 40 full-time matriculated graduate/professional students. *Enrollment by degree level:* 40 master's. *Graduate faculty:* 10. *Tuition:* Part-time $416 per credit hour. *Student services:* Career counseling, free psychological counseling, international student services. *Library facilities:* Daniel Stack Memorial Library plus 2 others. *Collection:* 14,022 titles, 87 serial subscriptions.

Computer facilities: 144 computers available on campus for general student use. Internet access is available. *Web address:* http://www.ifac.edu/.

General Application Contact: Elsia Suarez, Director of Admission, 305-995-5000, Fax: 305-374-5933, E-mail: admissions@ifac.edu.

GRADUATE UNITS

Computer Animation Program Students: 40 full-time. *Faculty:* 10. Expenses: Contact institution. Offers computer animation (MFA). *Application fee:* $50. *Head of Graduate Programs,* Dr. Liz Shearn-Maggio, 305-995-5048.

INTERNATIONAL INSTITUTE OF CHINESE MEDICINE, Santa Fe, NM 87592-9988

General Information Independent, coed, primarily women, graduate-only institution. *Enrollment by degree level:* 316 master's, 22 other advanced degrees. *Graduate faculty:* 21 full-time (12 women), 29 part-time/adjunct (12 women). *Tuition:* Part-time $170 per credit hour. *Required fees:* $140 per semester. *Graduate housing:* On-campus housing not available. *Student services:* Campus employment opportunities, exercise/wellness program, international student services. *Library facilities:* IICM Library plus 1 other. *Online resources:* web page. *Collection:* 1,500 titles, 14 serial subscriptions, 2 audiovisual materials.

Computer facilities: 2 computers available on campus for general student use. A campuswide network can be accessed. Internet access is available. *Web address:* http://www.iicm.org/.

General Application Contact: Emily Dai, Administrator, 505-473-5233 Ext. 108, Fax: 505-473-9279, E-mail: sfinfo@iicm.org.

GRADUATE UNITS

Program in Oriental Bodywork Students: 16 full-time (14 women), 6 part-time (3 women); includes 5 minority (2 African Americans, 2 Asian Americans or Pacific Islanders, 1 Native American) 1 applicant, 100% accepted. *Faculty:* 2 full-time (both women), 5 part-time/adjunct (4 women). Expenses: Contact institution. *Financial support:* Federal Work-Study and scholarships/grants available. Support available to part-time students. Financial award applicants required to submit FAFSA. In 2001, 8 degrees awarded. *Degree program information:* Part-time programs available. Offers Oriental bodywork (Certificate). *Application deadline:* For fall admission, 7/26 (priority date); for winter admission, 12/4 (priority date); for spring admission, 4/4 (priority date). Applications are processed on a rolling basis. *Application fee:* $50. *Application Contact:* John Werenko, Admissions Officer, 505-883-5569, Fax: 505-880-1775, E-mail: jwerenko@iicm.com. *Campus Director,* Robert Zeng, 505-883-5569, Fax: 505-880-1775, E-mail: rzeng@iicm.com.

Program in Oriental Medicine Students: 243 full-time (174 women), 73 part-time (49 women). Average age 40. 53 applicants, 81% accepted, 29 enrolled. *Faculty:* 21 full-time (12 women), 29 part-time/adjunct (12 women). Expenses: Contact institution. *Financial support:* In 2001–02, 60 students received support. Career-related internships or fieldwork, Federal Work-Study, scholarships/grants, and tuition waivers (partial) available. Support available to part-time students. Financial award applicants required to submit FAFSA. In 2001, 90 degrees awarded. *Degree program information:* Part-time programs available. Offers Oriental medicine (MOM). *Application deadline:* For fall admission, 7/26 (priority date); for winter admission, 12/4 (priority date); for spring admission, 4/4 (priority date). Applications are processed on a rolling basis. *Application fee:* $50. *Application Contact:* Emily Dai, Administrator, 505-473-5233 Ext. 108, Fax: 505-473-9279, E-mail: sfinfo@iicm.org. *President,* Dr. Michael Zeng, 505-473-5233 Ext. 105, Fax: 505-473-9279, E-mail: mzeng@iicm.org.

INTERNATIONAL SCHOOL OF THEOLOGY, Fontana, CA 92336

General Information Independent-religious, coed, graduate-only institution. *Graduate housing:* On-campus housing not available.

GRADUATE UNITS

Graduate School *Degree program information:* Part-time and evening/weekend programs available. Offers theology (M Div, MAPS, MATS).

INTERNATIONAL TECHNOLOGICAL UNIVERSITY, Santa Clara, CA 95050

General Information Independent, coed, upper-level institution. *Enrollment by degree level:* 113 master's, 6 doctoral. *Graduate faculty:* 4 full-time (0 women), 42 part-time/adjunct (8 women). *Tuition:* Full-time $6,800; part-time $425 per unit. *Student services:* Campus employment opportunities, career counseling, international student services, low-cost health insurance, teacher training, writing training. *Research affiliation:* Linux Works, Inc. (software), @Channel (software), New Trends Technology, Inc. (hardware), Pico Turbo, Inc. (hardware). *Web address:* http://www.itu.edu/.

General Application Contact: Dr. Chun-Mou Peng, Director of Research and Development Center, 408-556-9010, Fax: 408-556-9212, E-mail: chunmou@itu.edu.

GRADUATE UNITS

MBA Program Students: 12 full-time (8 women), 6 part-time (5 women). *Faculty:* 1 full-time (0 women), 5 part-time/adjunct (1 woman). Expenses: Contact institution. In 2001, 6 degrees awarded. *Degree program information:* Part-time and evening/weekend programs available. Offers business administration (MBA). *Application deadline:* For fall admission, 8/31 (priority date); for winter admission, 12/31 (priority date); for spring admission, 3/30 (priority date). *Application fee:* $30 ($80 for international students). *Application Contact:* Dr. Chun-Mou Peng, Director of Research and Development Center, 408-556-9010, Fax: 408-556-9212, E-mail: chunmou@itu.edu. *Director MBA Program,* Dr. Bjorn Fragner, 408-556-9013, Fax: 408-556-9212, E-mail: bfragner@itu.edu.

Program in Computer Engineering Students: 7 full-time (1 woman), 2 part-time (1 woman). *Faculty:* 1 full-time (0 women), 15 part-time/adjunct (3 women). Expenses: Contact institution. In 2001, 3 degrees awarded. Offers computer engineering (MSCE). *Application deadline:* For fall admission, 8/31 (priority date); for winter admission, 12/31 (priority date); for spring admission, 3/30 (priority date). *Application fee:* $30 ($80 for international students). *Application Contact:* Dr. Chun-Mou Peng, Director of Research and Development Center, 408-556-9010, Fax: 408-556-9212, E-mail: chunmou@itu.edu. *Chairman of Computer Engineering,* Dr. Russell Quong, 408-556-9010, Fax: 408-556-9012.

Program in Electrical Engineering Students: 9 full-time (1 woman), 8 part-time (1 woman). *Faculty:* 3 full-time (0 women), 9 part-time/adjunct (1 woman). Expenses: Contact institution. In 2001, 1 degree awarded. *Degree program information:* Part-time and evening/weekend programs available. Offers electrical engineering (MSEE). *Application deadline:* For fall admission, 8/31 (priority date); for winter admission, 12/31 (priority date); for spring admission, 3/30 (priority date). *Application fee:* $30 ($80 for international students). *Application Contact:* Dr. Chun-Mou Peng, Director of Research and Development Center, 408-556-9010, Fax: 408-556-9212, E-mail: chunmou@itu.edu. *Vice President,* Wai-kai Chen, 408-556-9010, Fax: 408-556-2012.

Program in Software Engineering Students: 45 full-time (20 women), 19 part-time (2 women). *Faculty:* 1 full-time (0 women), 15 part-time/adjunct (3 women). Expenses: Contact institution. In 2001, 19 degrees awarded. Offers software engineering (MSSE). *Application deadline:* For fall admission, 8/31 (priority date); for winter admission, 12/31 (priority date); for spring admission, 3/30 (priority date). *Application fee:* $30 ($80 for international students). *Application Contact:* Dr. Chun-Mou Peng, Director of Research and Development Center, 408-556-9010, Fax: 408-556-9212, E-mail: chunmou@itu.edu. *Chairman of Computer Engineering,* Dr. Russell Quong, 408-556-9010, Fax: 408-556-9012.

IONA COLLEGE, New Rochelle, NY 10801-1890

General Information Independent-religious, coed, comprehensive institution. *Enrollment:* 53 full-time matriculated graduate/professional students (35 women), 918 part-time matriculated graduate/professional students (550 women). *Enrollment by degree level:* 957 master's, 14 other advanced degrees. *Graduate faculty:* 66 full-time (19 women), 52 part-time/adjunct (15 women). *Tuition:* Part-time $525 per credit. *Graduate housing:* On-campus housing not available. *Student services:* Campus employment opportunities, career counseling, free psychological counseling, international student services. *Library facilities:* Ryan Library plus 1 other. *Online resources:* library catalog, web page, access to other libraries' catalogs. *Collection:* 264,917 titles, 803 serial subscriptions, 2,852 audiovisual materials. *Research affiliation:* IBM (teacher preparation).

Computer facilities: 425 computers available on campus for general student use. A campuswide network can be accessed from student residence rooms and from off campus. Internet access is available. *Web address:* http://www.iona.edu/.

General Application Contact: Thomas Delahunt, Vice Provost, 914-633-2461, E-mail: tdelahunt@iona.edu.

GRADUATE UNITS

Hagan School of Business Students: 28 full-time (13 women), 297 part-time (130 women); includes 12 minority (2 African Americans, 8 Asian Americans or Pacific Islanders, 2 Hispanic Americans), 4 international. Average age 31. 146 applicants, 106 enrolled. *Faculty:* 23 full-time (7 women), 3 part-time/adjunct (2 women). Expenses: Contact institution. *Financial support:* Federal Work-Study, tuition waivers (partial), and unspecified assistantships available. Support available to part-time students. In 2001, 100 master's, 16 other advanced degrees awarded. *Degree program information:* Part-time and evening/weekend programs available. Offers business (MBA, PMC); financial management (MBA, PMC); human resource management (MBA, PMC); information and decision technology management (MBA, PMC); international business (PMC); management (MBA, PMC); marketing (MBA, PMC). *Application deadline:* Applications are processed on a rolling basis. *Application fee:* $50. *Application Contact:* Tara Feller, Director of MBA Admissions, 914-633-2288, Fax: 914-633-2012, E-mail: tfeller@iona.edu. *Dean,* Dr. Nicholas J. Beutell, 914-633-2256.

School of Arts and Science Students: 25 full-time (22 women), 621 part-time (420 women); includes 103 minority (55 African Americans, 17 Asian Americans or Pacific Islanders, 29 Hispanic Americans, 2 Native Americans), 3 international. Average age 30. *Faculty:* 43 full-time (12 women), 49 part-time/adjunct (13 women). Expenses: Contact institution. *Financial support:* Career-related internships or fieldwork, tuition waivers (partial), and unspecified assistantships available. Support available to part-time students. In 2001, 242 degrees awarded. *Degree program information:* Part-time and evening/weekend programs available. Offers arts and science (MA, MS, MS Ed, MST, Certificate, PMC); biology education (MS Ed, MST); business education (MST); communication (PMC); computer science (MS); criminal justice (MS); educational administration (MS Ed); educational technology (MS, Certificate); English (MA); English education (MS Ed, MST); family counseling (MS, Certificate); health service administration (MS, Certificate); history (MA); journalism (MS); mathematics education (MS Ed, MST); multicultural education (MS Ed); pastoral counseling (MS); psychology (MA); school counseling (MA); school psychologist (MA); science (MS Ed); social studies education (MS Ed, MST); Spanish (MA); Spanish education (MS Ed, MST); teaching elementary education (MST); telecommunications (MS, Certificate). *Application deadline:* Applications are processed on a rolling basis. *Application fee:* $25. *Application Contact:* Alyce Ware, Associate Director of Graduate Recruitment, 914-633-2420, Fax: 914-633-2023, E-mail: aware@iona.edu. *Dean,* Dr. Alex Eodice, 914-633-2328, Fax: 914-633-2023, E-mail: arts@science@iona.edu.

See in-depth description on page 917.

IOWA STATE UNIVERSITY OF SCIENCE AND TECHNOLOGY, Ames, IA 50011

General Information State-supported, coed, university. CGS member. *Enrollment:* 2,335 full-time matriculated graduate/professional students (899 women), 2,028 part-time matriculated graduate/professional students (892 women). *Graduate faculty:* 1,401 full-time, 99 part-time/adjunct. Tuition, state resident: full-time $1,851. Tuition, nonresident: full-time $5,449. Tuition and fees vary according to program. *Graduate housing:* Rooms and/or apartments available on a first-come, first-served basis to single and married students. Typical cost: $2,500 per year ($4,905 including board) for single students; $4,300 per year for married students. Room and board charges vary according to board plan, campus/location and housing facility selected. Housing application deadline: 6/15. *Student services:* Campus employment opportunities, campus safety program, career counseling, child daycare facilities, disabled student services, exercise/wellness program, free psychological counseling, international student services, low-cost health insurance, multicultural affairs office, teacher training. *Library facilities:* University Library plus 1 other. *Online resources:* library catalog, web page, access to other libraries' catalogs. *Collection:* 2.3 million titles, 21,239 serial subscriptions, 925,593 audiovisual materials. *Research affiliation:* U.S. Department of Energy–Ames Laboratory, North Central Regional Center for Rural Development, National Soil Tilth Laboratory, National Animal Disease Center, National Veterinary Services Laboratories.

Computer facilities: 2,600 computers available on campus for general student use. A campuswide network can be accessed from student residence rooms and from off campus. E-mail, network services available. *Web address:* http://www.iastate.edu/.

General Application Contact: 515-294-5836, Fax: 515-294-2592, E-mail: grad_admissions@iastate.edu.

GRADUATE UNITS

College of Veterinary Medicine Students: 445 full-time (279 women), 37 part-time (12 women); includes 13 minority (1 African American, 7 Asian Americans or Pacific Islanders, 3 Hispanic Americans, 2 Native Americans), 31 international. Expenses: Contact institution. *Financial support:* In 2001–02, 37 research assistantships with partial tuition reimbursements (averaging $16,483 per year), 5 teaching assistantships with partial tuition reimbursements (averaging $13,356 per year) were awarded. Fellowships, career-related internships or fieldwork, Federal Work-Study, institutionally sponsored loans, scholarships/grants, health care benefits, and unspecified assistantships also available. In 2001, 97 first professional degrees, 11 master's, 9 doctorates awarded. *Degree program information:* Part-time programs available. Offers biomedical sciences (MS, PhD); veterinary anatomy (MS, PhD); veterinary clinical sciences (MS); veterinary diagnostic and production animal medicine (MS); veterinary medicine (DVM, MS, PhD); veterinary microbiology (MS, PhD); veterinary microbiology and preventive medicine (MS, PhD); veterinary pathology (MS, PhD); veterinary physiology (MS, PhD). Electronic applications accepted. *Dean,* Dr. Norman Cheville, 515-294-1250.

Graduate College Students: 2,249 full-time (867 women), 1,592 part-time (692 women); includes 207 minority (90 African Americans, 58 Asian Americans or Pacific Islanders, 51 Hispanic Americans, 8 Native Americans), 1,393 international. 6,703 applicants, 31% accepted, 1172 enrolled. *Faculty:* 1,401 full-time, 99 part-time/adjunct. Expenses: Contact institution. *Financial support:* In 2001–02, 1,499 research assistantships with partial tuition reimbursements (averaging $14,709 per year), 657 teaching assistantships with partial tuition reimbursements (averaging $12,156 per year) were awarded. Fellowships, career-related internships or fieldwork, Federal Work-Study, institutionally sponsored loans, scholarships/grants, traineeships, health care benefits, and unspecified assistantships also available. Support available to part-time students. In 2001, 772 master's, 232 doctorates awarded. *Degree program information:* Part-time and evening/weekend programs available. Postbaccalaureate distance learning degree programs offered (minimal on-campus study). Offers bioinformatics and computational biology (PhD); ecology and evolutionary biology (MS, PhD); family and consumer sciences (MFCS); genetics (MS, PhD); immunobiology (MS, PhD); industrial relations (MS); information assurance (MS); interdisciplinary graduate studies (MA, MS); interdisciplinary studies (M Eng, MA, MFCS, MS, PhD); molecular, cellular, and developmental biology (MS, PhD); neuroscience (MS, PhD); plant physiology (MS, PhD); systems engineering (M Eng); toxicology (MS, PhD); transportation (MS); water resources (MS, PhD). *Application deadline:* Applications are processed on a rolling basis. *Application fee:* $20 ($50 for international students). Electronic applications accepted. *Dean of the Graduate College,* Dr. James R. Bloedel, 515-294-6344, Fax: 515-294-6100, E-mail: grad_admissions@iastate.edu.

College of Agriculture Students: 402 full-time (155 women), 179 part-time (51 women); includes 22 minority (7 African Americans, 6 Asian Americans or Pacific Islanders, 9 Hispanic Americans), 166 international. 413 applicants, 40% accepted, 109 enrolled. *Faculty:* 279 full-time, 18 part-time/adjunct. Expenses: Contact institution. *Financial support:* In 2001–02, 359 research assistantships with partial tuition reimbursements (averaging $15,379 per year), 28 teaching assistantships with partial tuition reimbursements (averaging $14,335 per year) were awarded. Fellowships, Federal Work-Study, scholarships/grants, health care benefits, and unspecified assistantships also available. Support available to part-time students. In 2001, 89 master's, 39 doctorates awarded. *Degree program information:*

Iowa State University of Science and Technology (continued)

Part-time programs available. Postbaccalaureate distance learning degree programs offered (no on-campus study). Offers agricultural education and studies (MS, PhD); agricultural meteorology (MS, PhD); agriculture (M Ag, MS, PhD); agronomy (MS); animal breeding and genetics (MS, PhD); animal ecology (MS, PhD); animal nutrition (MS, PhD); animal physiology (MS); animal psychology (PhD); animal science (MS, PhD); biochemistry (MS, PhD); biophysics (MS, PhD); crop production and physiology (MS, PhD); entomology (MS, PhD); fisheries biology (MS, PhD); forestry (MS, PhD); genetics (MS, PhD); horticulture (MS, PhD); meat science (MS, PhD); microbiology (MS, PhD); molecular, cellular, and developmental biology (MS, PhD); plant breeding (MS, PhD); plant pathology (MS, PhD); soil science (MS, PhD); toxicology (MS, PhD); wildlife biology (MS, PhD). *Application deadline:* Applications are processed on a rolling basis. *Application fee:* $20 ($50 for international students). Electronic applications accepted. *Dean*, Dr. Catherine E. Woteki, 515-294-2518, Fax: 515-294-6800.

College of Business Students: 90 full-time (32 women), 187 part-time (70 women); includes 13 minority (4 African Americans, 2 Asian Americans or Pacific Islanders, 6 Hispanic Americans, 1 Native American), 46 international. 318 applicants, 44% accepted, 107 enrolled. *Faculty:* 64 full-time. Expenses: Contact institution. *Financial support:* In 2001–02, 46 research assistantships with partial tuition reimbursements (averaging $11,070 per year), 4 teaching assistantships with partial tuition reimbursements (averaging $13,050 per year) were awarded. Fellowships, scholarships/grants, health care benefits, and unspecified assistantships also available. In 2001, 87 degrees awarded. Offers accounting (M Acc); business (M Acc, MBA, MS); business administration (MBA, MS); informations system (MS). *Application fee:* $20 ($50 for international students). Electronic applications accepted. *Interim Dean*, Dr. Labh S. Hira, 515-294-8118, E-mail: busgrad@iastate.edu.

College of Design Students: 126 full-time (59 women); includes 12 minority (4 African Americans, 5 Asian Americans or Pacific Islanders, 3 Hispanic Americans), 41 international. Average age 32. 177 applicants, 36% accepted, 35 enrolled. *Faculty:* 92. Expenses: Contact institution. *Financial support:* In 2001–02, 70 students received support, including 13 research assistantships with partial tuition reimbursements available (averaging $7,363 per year), 52 teaching assistantships with partial tuition reimbursements available (averaging $7,205 per year); career-related internships or fieldwork, Federal Work-Study, institutionally sponsored loans, tuition waivers (partial), and unspecified assistantships also available. Support available to part-time students. Financial award applicants required to submit FAFSA. In 2001, 32 degrees awarded. *Degree program information:* Part-time programs available. Offers architectural studies (MSAS); architecture (M Arch); art and design (MA); art education (MA); community and regional planning (MCRP); design (M Arch, MA, MCRP, MFA, MLA, MS, MSAS); graphic design (MFA); integrated visual arts (MFA); interior design (MFA); landscape architecture (MLA); transportation (MS). *Application deadline:* For fall admission, 2/1 (priority date). Applications are processed on a rolling basis. *Application fee:* $20 ($50 for international students). Electronic applications accepted. *Application Contact:* Kate Schwennsen, Associate Dean, 515-294-7427, Fax: 515-294-9755, E-mail: kschwenn@iastate.edu. *Dean*, Mark Engelbrecht, 515-294-7427, Fax: 515-294-9755, E-mail: mengelbr@iastate.edu.

College of Education Students: 129 full-time (81 women), 335 part-time (207 women); includes 44 minority (27 African Americans, 7 Asian Americans or Pacific Islanders, 9 Hispanic Americans, 1 Native American), 41 international. 312 applicants, 45% accepted, 93 enrolled. *Faculty:* 76 full-time, 9 part-time/adjunct. Expenses: Contact institution. *Financial support:* In 2001–02, 44 research assistantships with partial tuition reimbursements (averaging $12,217 per year), 27 teaching assistantships with partial tuition reimbursements (averaging $10,600 per year) were awarded. Fellowships, career-related internships or fieldwork, Federal Work-Study, scholarships/grants, health care benefits, and unspecified assistantships also available. Support available to part-time students. In 2001, 147 master's, 22 doctorates awarded. *Degree program information:* Part-time programs available. Offers counselor education (M Ed, MS); curriculum and instructional technology (M Ed, MS, PhD); education (M Ed); educational administration (M Ed, MS); educational leadership (PhD); elementary education (M Ed, MS); exercise and sport science (MS); health and human performance (PhD); higher education (M Ed, MS); historial, philosophical, and comparative studies in education (MS); historical, philosophical, and comparative studies in education (M Ed); industrial education and technology (MS, PhD); organizational learning and human resource development (M Ed, MS); research and evaluation (MS); special education (M Ed, MS). *Application fee:* $20 ($50 for international students). Electronic applications accepted. *Dean*, Dr. Walter H. Gmelch, 515-294-7000, E-mail: wgmelch@iastate.edu.

College of Engineering Students: 506 full-time (94 women), 234 part-time (35 women); includes 23 minority (11 African Americans, 7 Asian Americans or Pacific Islanders, 5 Hispanic Americans), 446 international. 1,870 applicants, 19% accepted, 163 enrolled. *Faculty:* 218 full-time, 18 part-time/adjunct. Expenses: Contact institution. *Financial support:* In 2001–02, 398 research assistantships with partial tuition reimbursements (averaging $14,220 per year), 126 teaching assistantships with partial tuition reimbursements (averaging $11,758 per year) were awarded. Fellowships, Federal Work-Study, scholarships/grants, health care benefits, and unspecified assistantships also available. Support available to part-time students. In 2001, 145 master's, 42 doctorates awarded. *Degree program information:* Part-time programs available. Offers aerospace engineering (M Eng, MS, PhD); agricultural and biosystems engineering (M Eng, MS, PhD); chemical engineering (M Eng, MS, PhD); civil engineering (MS, PhD); computer engineering (MS, PhD); electrical engineering (MS, PhD); engineering (M Eng, MS, PhD); engineering mechanics (M Eng, MS, PhD); industrial engineering (MS, PhD); materials science and engineering (MS, PhD); mechanical engineering (MS, PhD); operations research (MS). *Application fee:* $20 ($50 for international students). Electronic applications accepted. *Application Contact:* Nancy Knight, Information Contact, 515-294-3241. *Dean*, Dr. James L. Melsa, 515-294-5933, E-mail: melsa@iastate.edu.

College of Family and Consumer Sciences Students: 83 full-time (63 women), 98 part-time (79 women); includes 15 minority (3 African Americans, 5 Asian Americans or Pacific Islanders, 6 Hispanic Americans, 1 Native American), 52 international. 203 applicants, 28% accepted, 34 enrolled. *Faculty:* 87 full-time, 4 part-time/adjunct. Expenses: Contact institution. *Financial support:* In 2001–02, 60 research assistantships with partial tuition reimbursements (averaging $13,714 per year), 21 teaching assistantships with partial tuition reimbursements (averaging $11,483 per year) were awarded. Fellowships, Federal Work-Study, scholarships/grants, health care benefits, and unspecified assistantships also available. Support available to part-time students. In 2001, 32 master's, 24 doctorates awarded. *Degree program information:* Part-time programs available. Offers family and consumer science education and studies (M Ed); family and consumer sciences (M Ed, MFCS, MS, PhD); family and consumer sciences education and studies (MS, PhD); food science and technology (MS, PhD); foodservice and lodging management (MFCS, MS, PhD); human development and family studies (MFCS, MS, PhD); marriage and family therapy (PhD); nutrition (MS, PhD); textiles and clothing (MFCS, MS, PhD). *Application fee:* $20 ($50 for international students). Electronic applications accepted. *Dean*, Dr. Carol B. Meeks, 515-294-5980, Fax: 515-294-6775, E-mail: cbmeeks@iastate.edu.

College of Liberal Arts and Sciences Students: 765 full-time (305 women), 334 part-time (153 women); includes 48 minority (16 African Americans, 18 Asian Americans or Pacific Islanders, 11 Hispanic Americans, 3 Native Americans), 483 international. 2,015 applicants, 29% accepted, 240 enrolled. *Faculty:* 461 full-time, 19 part-time/adjunct. Expenses: Contact institution. *Financial support:* In 2001–02, 375 research assistantships with partial tuition reimbursements (averaging $14,480 per year), 386 teaching assistantships with partial tuition reimbursements (averaging $12,269 per year) were awarded. Fellowships, Federal Work-Study, institutionally sponsored loans, scholarships/grants, health care benefits, and unspecified assistantships also available. Support available to part-time students. In 2001, 174 master's, 83 doctorates awarded. *Degree program information:* Part-time programs available. Offers agricultural economics (MS, PhD); agricultural history and rural studies (PhD); anthropology (MA); applied mathematics (MS, PhD); applied physics (MS, PhD); astrophysics (MS, PhD); botany (MS, PhD); chemistry (MS, PhD); cognitive psychology (PhD); computer science (MS, PhD); condensed matter physics (MS, PhD); counseling psychology (PhD); earth science (MS, PhD); economics (MS, PhD); English (MA); general psychology (MS); geology (MS, PhD); high energy physics (MS, PhD); history (MA); history of technology and science (MA, PhD); journalism and mass communication (MS); liberal arts and sciences (MA, MPA, MS, MSM, PhD); mathematics (MS, PhD); meteorology (MS, PhD); nuclear physics (MS, PhD); physics (MS, PhD); political science (MA); public administration (MPA); rhetoric and professional communication (PhD); rural sociology (MS, PhD); school mathematics (MSM); social psychology (PhD); sociology (MS, PhD); statistics (MS, PhD); water resources (MS, PhD); zoology and genetics (MS, PhD). *Application fee:* $20 ($50 for international students). Electronic applications accepted. *Dean*, Dr. Peter Rabideau, 515-294-3220, Fax: 515-294-1303.

See in-depth description on page 919.

ISIM UNIVERSITY, Denver, CO 80246

General Information Independent, coed, graduate-only institution. *Graduate faculty:* 1 full-time (0 women), 16 part-time/adjunct (7 women). *Tuition:* Part-time $1,245 per course. *Graduate housing:* On-campus housing not available. *Web address:* http://www.isim.edu/.

General Application Contact: Robin Thompson, Admissions Mentor, 303-333-4224 Ext. 177, Fax: 303-336-1144, E-mail: rthompson@isim.edu.

GRADUATE UNITS

Programs in Information Management Average age 37. *Faculty:* 17 part-time/adjunct (8 women). Expenses: Contact institution. In 2001, 20 degrees awarded. *Degree program information:* Part-time and evening/weekend programs available. Postbaccalaureate distance learning degree programs offered (no on-campus study). Offers business administration (MBA); information management (MBA, MS); information technology (MS); project management (MBA). *Application deadline:* Applications are processed on a rolling basis. *Application fee:* $75. Electronic applications accepted. *Application Contact:* Robin Thompson, Admissions Mentor, 303-333-4224 Ext. 177, Fax: 303-336-1144, E-mail: rthompson@isim.edu. *Dean*, Tina Parscal, 800-441-4746 Ext. 185, Fax: 303-336-1144, E-mail: tinaparscal@isim.edu.

ITHACA COLLEGE, Ithaca, NY 14850-7020

General Information Independent, coed, comprehensive institution. CGS member. *Enrollment:* 235 full-time matriculated graduate/professional students (184 women), 27 part-time matriculated graduate/professional students (17 women). *Enrollment by degree level:* 262 master's. *Graduate faculty:* 103 full-time (42 women), 6 part-time/adjunct (3 women). *Tuition:* Full-time $15,096; part-time $629 per credit hour. *Graduate housing:* On-campus housing not available. *Student services:* Campus employment opportunities, campus safety program, career counseling, disabled student services, exercise/wellness program, free psychological counseling, international student services, low-cost health insurance, multicultural affairs office, writing training. *Library facilities:* Ithaca College Library. *Online resources:* library catalog, web page, access to other libraries' catalogs. *Collection:* 238,613 titles, 2,400 serial subscriptions, 31,556 audiovisual materials. *Research affiliation:* Ithaca Talent Agency/Suzuki Institute (strings, piano), Biotechnology Institute of Göd0110 (Hungary) (biotechnology), Ornithology Laboratory of Cornell University (biology), University of Limerick, Ireland: The Irish World Music Center (strings, voice, dance, musicology).

Computer facilities: 584 computers available on campus for general student use. A campuswide network can be accessed from student residence rooms and from off campus. Internet access and online class registration are available. *Web address:* http://www.ithaca.edu/.

General Application Contact: Dr. Garry Brodhead, Associate Provost and Dean of Graduate Studies, 607-274-3527, Fax: 607-274-1263, E-mail: gradstudies@ithaca.edu.

GRADUATE UNITS

Graduate Studies Students: 235 full-time (184 women), 27 part-time (17 women); includes 16 minority (4 African Americans, 7 Asian Americans or Pacific Islanders, 1 Hispanic American, 4 Native Americans), 28 international. Average age 24. 271 applicants, 63% accepted, 174 enrolled. *Faculty:* 103 full-time (42 women), 6 part-time/adjunct (3 women). Expenses: Contact institution. *Financial support:* In 2001–02, 208 students received support, including 85 teaching assistantships (averaging $17,772 per year); career-related internships or fieldwork, institutionally sponsored loans, scholarships/grants, and unspecified assistantships also available. Financial award application deadline: 3/1; financial award applicants required to submit FAFSA. In 2001, 196 degrees awarded. *Degree program information:* Part-time programs available. *Application deadline:* Applications are processed on a rolling basis. *Application fee:* $40. *Associate Provost and Dean*, Dr. Garry Brodhead, 607-274-3527, Fax: 607-274-1263, E-mail: gradstudies@ithaca.edu.

Roy H. Park School of Communications Students: 19 full-time (14 women), 7 part-time (5 women); includes 3 minority (2 African Americans, 1 Native American), 11 international. Average age 30. 21 applicants, 76% accepted, 8 enrolled. *Faculty:* 9 full-time (5 women). Expenses: Contact institution. *Financial support:* In 2001–02, 19 students received support, including 17 teaching assistantships (averaging $17,792 per year); career-related internships or fieldwork, scholarships/grants, and unspecified assistantships also available. Financial award application deadline: 3/1; financial award applicants required to submit FAFSA. In 2001, 19 degrees awarded. *Degree program information:* Part-time programs available. Offers communications (MS). *Application deadline:* For fall admission, 3/1 (priority date); for spring admission, 12/1. Applications are processed on a rolling basis. *Application fee:* $40. *Dean*, Dr. Thomas W. Bohn, 607-274-3895, Fax: 607-274-1664.

School of Business Students: 10 full-time (3 women), 4 part-time (1 woman), 2 international. Average age 26. 26 applicants, 54% accepted, 11 enrolled. *Faculty:* 14 full-time (4 women). Expenses: Contact institution. *Financial support:* In 2001–02, 7 students received support. Application deadline: 3/1; *Degree program information:* Part-time programs available. Offers business (MBA); management (MBA). *Application deadline:* For fall admission, 3/1 (priority date); for spring admission, 12/1. Applications are processed on a rolling basis. *Application fee:* $40. *Dean*, Dr. Robert A. Ullrich, 607-274-3117, Fax: 607-274-1152.

School of Health Sciences and Human Performance Students: 174 full-time (144 women), 10 part-time (8 women); includes 10 minority (1 African American, 6 Asian Americans or Pacific Islanders, 1 Hispanic American, 2 Native Americans), 10 international. Average age 23. *Faculty:* 35 full-time (18 women), 4 part-time/adjunct (3 women). Expenses: Contact institution. *Financial support:* In 2001–02, 147 students received support, including 38 teaching assistantships (averaging $18,794 per year); career-related internships or fieldwork, institutionally sponsored loans, scholarships/grants, and unspecified assistantships also available. Financial award application deadline: 3/1; financial award applicants required to submit FAFSA. In 2001, 154 degrees awarded. *Degree program information:* Part-time programs available. Offers exercise and sport sciences (MS); health sciences and human performance (MS); occupational therapy (MS); physical therapy (MS); speech pathology (MS); teacher of the speech and hearing handicapped (MS). *Application fee:* $40. *Acting Dean*, Dr. John Bonaguro, 607-274-3237, Fax: 607-274-1137.

School of Music Students: 32 full-time (23 women), 6 part-time (3 women); includes 3 minority (1 African American, 1 Asian American or Pacific Islander, 1 Native American), 5 international. Average age 26. 76 applicants, 54% accepted, 15 enrolled. *Faculty:* 45 full-time (15 women), 2 part-time/adjunct (0 women). Expenses: Contact institution. *Financial support:* In 2001–02, 35 students received support, including 29 teaching assistantships (averaging $16,848 per year); career-related internships or fieldwork, scholarships/grants, and unspecified assistantships also available. Financial award application deadline: 3/1; financial award applicants required to submit FAFSA. In 2001, 23 degrees awarded. *Degree program information:* Part-time programs available. Offers composition (MM); conducting (MM); music (MM, MS); music education (MM, MS); music theory (MM); performance (MM); strings, woodwinds, or brasses (MM); Suzuki pedagogy (MM). *Application deadline:* For fall admission, 3/1 (priority date); for spring admission, 12/1. Applications are processed on a rolling basis. *Application fee:* $40. *Dean*, Dr. Arthur Ostrander, 607-274-3343.

See in-depth description on page 921.

ITI-INFORMATION TECHNOLOGY INSTITUTE, Halifax, NS B3J 3T1, Canada

General Information Proprietary, graduate-only institution.

GRADUATE UNITS

Programs in Information Technology Offers information technology (MBA); information technology education (MITE).

JACKSON STATE UNIVERSITY, Jackson, MS 39217

General Information State-supported, coed, university. CGS member. *Graduate housing:* Room and/or apartments available on a first-come, first-served basis to single students; on-campus housing not available to married students. Housing application deadline: 7/15. *Research affiliation:* Lawrence A. Berkeley Laboratories (biology, chemistry), U.S. Department of Energy (biology), National Science Foundation (biology, chemistry), U.S. Environmental Protection Agency, Oak Ridge Associated Universities (science), Raytheon Systems Company (computer science).

GRADUATE UNITS

Graduate School *Degree program information:* Part-time and evening/weekend programs available. Postbaccalaureate distance learning degree programs offered (minimal on-campus study).

School of Allied Health Offers allied health (MS).

School of Business *Degree program information:* Part-time and evening/weekend programs available. Offers accounting (MPA); business (M Bus Ed, MBA, MPA, MSSM, PhD); business administration (MBA); business education (M Bus Ed); systems management (MSSM).

School of Education *Degree program information:* Part-time and evening/weekend programs available. Offers community and agency counseling (MS); early childhood education (MS Ed, Ed D); education (MS, MS Ed, Ed D, PhD, Ed S); education administration (Ed S); educational administration (MS Ed, PhD); elementary education (MS Ed, Ed S); guidance and counseling (MS, MS Ed, Ed S); health, physical education and recreation (MS Ed); rehabilitative counseling service (MS Ed); secondary education (MS Ed, Ed S); special education (MS Ed, Ed S).

School of Liberal Arts *Degree program information:* Part-time and evening/weekend programs available. Offers clinical psychology (PhD); criminology and justice service (MA); English (MA); history (MA); liberal arts (MA, MAT, MM Ed, MPPA, MS, PhD); mass communications (MS); music education (MM Ed); political science (MA); public policy and administration (MPPA, PhD); sociology (MA); teaching English (MAT); urban and regional planning (MS).

School of Science and Technology *Degree program information:* Part-time and evening/weekend programs available. Offers biology education (MST); chemistry (MS, PhD); computer science (MS); environmental science (MS, PhD); hazardous materials management (MS); industrial arts education (MS Ed); mathematics (MS); mathematics education (MST); science and technology (MS, MS Ed, MST, PhD); science education (MST).

School of Social Work *Degree program information:* Evening/weekend programs available. Offers social work (MSW, PhD).

JACKSONVILLE STATE UNIVERSITY, Jacksonville, AL 36265-1602

General Information State-supported, coed, comprehensive institution. *Enrollment:* 267 full-time matriculated graduate/professional students (174 women), 1,101 part-time matriculated graduate/professional students (737 women). *Enrollment by degree level:* 1,042 master's, 326 other advanced degrees. *Graduate faculty:* 157 full-time (48 women). Tuition, state resident: part-time $147 per hour. Tuition, nonresident: part-time $294 per hour. One-time fee: $20 part-time. Tuition and fees vary according to course load. *Graduate housing:* Rooms and/or apartments available to single and married students. *Student services:* Campus employment opportunities, campus safety program, career counseling, free psychological counseling, international student services. *Library facilities:* Houston Cole Library. *Online resources:* library catalog, web page, access to other libraries' catalogs. *Collection:* 420,583 titles, 4,791 serial subscriptions, 32,875 audiovisual materials.

Computer facilities: 330 computers available on campus for general student use. A campuswide network can be accessed from off campus. Internet access is available. *Web address:* http://www.jsu.edu/.

General Application Contact: Dr. William D. Carr, Dean of the College of Graduate Studies and Continuing Education, 256-782-5329, Fax: 256-782-5321, E-mail: graduate@jsucc.jsu.edu.

GRADUATE UNITS

College of Graduate Studies and Continuing Education *Degree program information:* Part-time and evening/weekend programs available. Offers general studies (MA); public administration (MPA).

College of Arts and Sciences *Degree program information:* Part-time and evening/weekend programs available. Offers arts and sciences (MA, MS); biology (MS); computer systems and software design (MS); criminal justice (MS); English (MA); history (MA); mathematics (MS); music (MA); political science (MA); psychology (MS).

College of Commerce and Business Administration *Degree program information:* Part-time and evening/weekend programs available. Offers commerce and business administration (MBA).

College of Education *Degree program information:* Part-time and evening/weekend programs available. Offers early childhood education (MS Ed, Ed S); education (MA, MS, MS Ed, Ed S); elementary education (MS Ed, Ed S); guidance and counseling (MS, Ed S); health and physical education (MS Ed, Ed S); instructional media (MS Ed); music education (MA); school administration (MS Ed, Ed S); secondary education (MS Ed, Ed S); special education (MS Ed, Ed S).

College of Nursing Offers nursing (MSN). Electronic applications accepted.

Announcement: Jacksonville State University (JSU), committed to excellence in education since it was founded in 1883, is the ideal place for graduate education. Located in northeast Alabama, just 75 miles from Birmingham and 100 miles from Atlanta, JSU offers a range of cultural and social activities, mild climate, low cost of living, and rich historical heritage. Programs at Jacksonville State University are designed to meet the personal and professional needs of the students. JSU is one of the best educational values in the Southeast.

JACKSONVILLE UNIVERSITY, Jacksonville, FL 32211-3394

General Information Independent, coed, comprehensive institution. *Enrollment:* 85 full-time matriculated graduate/professional students (40 women), 221 part-time matriculated graduate/professional students (127 women). *Enrollment by degree level:* 306 master's. *Graduate faculty:* 108 full-time, 113 part-time/adjunct. *Tuition:* Full-time $16,540; part-time $550 per credit. *Required fees:* $240. Tuition and fees vary according to course load. *Graduate housing:* Room and/or apartments guaranteed to single students; on-campus housing not available to married students. Typical cost: $2,700 per year ($5,900 including board). Housing application deadline: 8/1. *Student services:* Campus employment opportunities, campus safety program, career counseling, disabled student services, exercise/wellness program, free psychological counseling, international student services, low-cost health insurance, teacher training. *Library facilities:* Carl S. Swisher Library. *Online resources:* web page. *Collection:* 306,090 titles, 780 serial subscriptions.

Computer facilities: 300 computers available on campus for general student use. A campuswide network can be accessed from student residence rooms and from off campus. *Web address:* http://www.ju.edu/.

General Application Contact: John P. Grundig, Director of Enrollment Operations, 904-745-7000, E-mail: jgrundi@ju.edu.

GRADUATE UNITS

College of Arts and Sciences Students: 67. Average age 39. Expenses: Contact institution. *Financial support:* Career-related internships or fieldwork, Federal Work-Study, and institutionally sponsored loans available. Support available to part-time students. Financial award application deadline: 3/15; financial award applicants required to submit FAFSA. *Degree program information:* Part-time and evening/weekend programs available. Offers arts and sciences (MAT, Certificate). *Application deadline:* For fall admission, 8/1 (priority date); for spring admission, 11/1. Applications are processed on a rolling basis. *Application fee:* $25. *Application Contact:* Dr. Harry M. Teitelbaum, Director, 904-745-7132, E-mail: hteitel@ju.ed. *Dean,* Dr. A. Quinton White, 904-745-7100.

School of Education Students: 67. Average age 39. Expenses: Contact institution. *Financial support:* Career-related internships or fieldwork, Federal Work-Study, and institutionally sponsored loans available. Support available to part-time students. Financial award application deadline: 3/15; financial award applicants required to submit FAFSA. *Degree program information:* Part-time and evening/weekend programs available. Offers art (MAT); computer education (MAT); early childhood education (Certificate); educational leadership (MAT); elementary education (MAT); English (MAT); exceptional child education (Certificate); foreign language (MAT); French (MAT); gifted education (Certificate); integrated learning with educational technology (MAT); mathematics (MAT); music (MAT); reading (MAT); secondary education (Certificate); Spanish (MAT). *Application deadline:* For fall admission, 8/1 (priority date); for spring admission, 11/1. Applications are processed on a rolling basis. *Application fee:* $25. *Director,* Dr. Harry M. Teitelbaum, 904-745-7132, E-mail: hteitel@ju.ed.

Davis College of Business Students: 72 full-time (20 women), 69 part-time (32 women); includes 26 minority (22 African Americans, 3 Asian Americans or Pacific Islanders, 1 Hispanic American), 8 international. Average age 37. Expenses: Contact institution. *Financial support:* Federal Work-Study, institutionally sponsored loans, scholarships/grants, and graduate resident assistantships available. Support available to part-time students. Financial award application deadline: 3/15. *Degree program information:* Part-time and evening/weekend programs available. Offers business (Exec MBA, MBA); business administration (Exec MBA, MBA). *Application deadline:* Applications are processed on a rolling basis. *Interim Dean,* Dr. William M. Crosby, 904-745-7431, Fax: 904-745-7467, E-mail: wcrosby@ju.edu.

JAMES MADISON UNIVERSITY, Harrisonburg, VA 22807

General Information State-supported, coed, comprehensive institution. CGS member. *Enrollment:* 416 full-time matriculated graduate/professional students (286 women), 354 part-time matriculated graduate/professional students (174 women). *Enrollment by degree level:* 708 master's, 31 doctoral, 31 other advanced degrees. *Graduate faculty:* 166 full-time (72 women), 20 part-time/adjunct (8 women). Tuition, state resident: part-time $143 per credit hour. Tuition, nonresident: part-time $465 per credit hour. *Graduate housing:* Room and/or apartments available to single students; on-campus housing not available to married students. *Student services:* Campus employment opportunities, campus safety program, career counseling, disabled student services, free psychological counseling, international student services, multicultural affairs office, teacher training. *Library facilities:* Carrier Library plus 2 others. *Online resources:* library catalog, web page. *Collection:* 1.3 million titles, 3,367 serial subscriptions, 28,465 audiovisual materials.

Computer facilities: 500 computers available on campus for general student use. A campuswide network can be accessed from student residence rooms and from off campus. Internet access and online class registration are available. *Web address:* http://www.jmu.edu/.

General Application Contact: Dr. N. William Walker, Interim Dean, College of Graduate and Professional Programs, 540-568-6131, Fax: 540-568-6266, E-mail: grad-school@jmu.edu.

GRADUATE UNITS

College of Graduate and Professional Programs Students: 416 full-time (286 women), 354 part-time (174 women); includes 61 minority (33 African Americans, 16 Asian Americans or Pacific Islanders, 11 Hispanic Americans, 1 Native American), 34 international. Average age 29. 585 applicants, 65% accepted, 208 enrolled. *Faculty:* 166 full-time (72 women), 20 part-time/adjunct (8 women). Expenses: Contact institution. *Financial support:* In 2001–02, 2 research assistantships with full tuition reimbursements (averaging $6,110 per year), 69 teaching assistantships with full tuition reimbursements (averaging $7,170 per year) were awarded. Career-related internships or fieldwork, Federal Work-Study, and unspecified assistantships also available. Financial award application deadline: 3/1; financial award applicants required to submit FAFSA. In 2001, 298 master's, 9 doctorates, 18 other advanced degrees awarded. *Degree program information:* Part-time and evening/weekend programs available. Postbaccalaureate distance learning degree programs offered (no on-campus study). *Application deadline:* For fall admission, 7/1 (priority date). Applications are processed on a rolling basis. *Application fee:* $55. *Interim Dean, College of Graduate and Professional Programs,* Dr. N. William Walker, 540-568-6131, Fax: 540-568-6266, E-mail: grad-school@jmu.edu.

College of Arts and Letters Students: 86 full-time (54 women), 34 part-time (19 women); includes 9 minority (7 African Americans, 1 Asian American or Pacific Islander, 1 Hispanic American), 4 international. Average age 29. *Faculty:* 46 full-time (20 women), 3 part-time/adjunct (0 women). Expenses: Contact institution. *Financial support:* In 2001–02, 26 teaching assistantships with full tuition reimbursements (averaging $7,170 per year) were awarded; Federal Work-Study and unspecified assistantships also available. Financial award application deadline: 3/1; financial award applicants required to submit FAFSA. In 2001, 46 degrees awarded. *Degree program information:* Part-time programs available. Offers art education (MA); art history (MA); arts and letters (MA, MFA, MM, MPA, MS); ceramics (MFA); conducting (MM); drawing/painting (MFA); English (MA); history (MA); metal/jewelry (MFA); music education (MM); performance (MM); photography (MFA); printmaking (MFA); public administration (MPA); sculpture (MFA); studio art (MA); technical and scientific communication (MA, MS); theory-composition (MM); weaving/fibers (MFA). *Application deadline:* For fall admission, 7/1 (priority date). Applications are processed on a rolling basis. *Application fee:* $55. *Dean,* Dr. Richard F. Whitman, 540-568-6472.

College of Business Students: 17 full-time (6 women), 60 part-time (27 women); includes 7 minority (3 African Americans, 3 Asian Americans or Pacific Islanders, 1 Hispanic American), 11 international. Average age 29. *Faculty:* 22 full-time (8 women). Expenses: Contact institution. *Financial support:* In 2001–02, 3 teaching assistantships with full tuition reimbursements (averaging $7,170 per year) were awarded; Federal Work-Study and unspecified assistantships also available. Financial award application deadline: 3/1; financial award applicants required to submit FAFSA. In 2001, 47 degrees awarded. *Degree program information:* Part-time and evening/weekend programs available. Postbaccalaureate distance learning degree programs offered (no on-campus study). Offers accounting (MS); business (MBA, MS); business administration (MBA). *Application deadline:* For fall admission, 7/1 (priority date). Applications are processed on a rolling basis. *Application fee:* $55. *Dean,* Dr. Robert D. Reid, 540-568-3254.

College of Education Students: 40 full-time (30 women), 73 part-time (49 women); includes 4 minority (2 African Americans, 1 Asian American or Pacific Islander, 1 Hispanic American) Average age 29. *Faculty:* 28 full-time (16 women), 5 part-time/adjunct (2 women). Expenses: Contact institution. *Financial support:* Research assistantships with full tuition reimbursements, teaching assistantships, career-related internships or fieldwork, Federal Work-Study, and unspecified assistantships available. Financial award application deadline: 3/1; financial award applicants required to submit FAFSA. In 2001, 62 degrees awarded. *Degree program information:* Part-time and evening/weekend programs available. Offers early childhood education (M Ed); education (M Ed, MAT, MS Ed); educational leadership (M Ed); middle education (M Ed); reading education (M Ed); secondary education (M Ed); special education (M Ed); vocational education (MS Ed). *Application deadline:* For fall admission, 7/1 (priority date). Applications are processed on a rolling basis. *Application fee:* $55. *Interim Dean,* Dr. Sharon E. Lovell, 540-568-6572.

College of Integrated Science and Technology Students: 263 full-time (192 women), 181 part-time (75 women); includes 39 minority (20 African Americans, 10 Asian Americans or

James Madison University (continued)

Pacific Islanders, 8 Hispanic Americans, 1 Native American), 19 international. Average age 29. *Faculty:* 64 full-time (26 women), 12 part-time/adjunct (6 women). Expenses: Contact institution. *Financial support:* In 2001–02, 40 teaching assistantships with full tuition reimbursements (averaging $7,170 per year) were awarded; Federal Work-Study and unspecified assistantships also available. Financial award application deadline: 3/1; financial award applicants required to submit FAFSA. In 2001, 140 master's, 9 doctorates, 18 other advanced degrees awarded. *Degree program information:* Part-time programs available. Postbaccalaureate distance learning degree programs offered (no on-campus study). Offers computer science (MS); counseling psychology (M Ed, MA, Ed S); general psychology (MA, Psy D); health sciences (MS, MS Ed); hearing disorders (M Ed); integrated science and technology (M Ed, MA, MS, MS Ed, Psy D, Ed S); kinesiology and recreation studies (MS); school psychology (MA, Ed S); speech pathology (MS). *Application deadline:* For fall admission, 7/1 (priority date). Applications are processed on a rolling basis. *Application fee:* $55. *Dean,* Dr. A. Jerry Benson, 540-568-3283.

College of Science and Mathematics Students: 10 full-time (4 women), 6 part-time (4 women); includes 2 minority (1 African American, 1 Asian American or Pacific Islander) Average age 29. *Faculty:* 6 full-time (2 women). Expenses: Contact institution. *Financial support:* In 2001–02, 2 research assistantships with full tuition reimbursements (averaging $6,110 per year) were awarded; teaching assistantships, Federal Work-Study and unspecified assistantships also available. Financial award application deadline: 3/1; financial award applicants required to submit FAFSA. In 2001, 3 degrees awarded. *Degree program information:* Part-time programs available. Offers biology (MS); science and mathematics (MS). *Application deadline:* For fall admission, 7/1 (priority date). Applications are processed on a rolling basis. *Application fee:* $55. *Dean,* Dr. David F. Brakke, 540-568-3508.

JESUIT SCHOOL OF THEOLOGY AT BERKELEY, Berkeley, CA 94709-1193

General Information Independent-religious, coed, graduate-only institution. *Enrollment by degree level:* 50 first professional, 67 master's, 12 doctoral. *Graduate faculty:* 16 full-time (3 women), 9 part-time/adjunct (4 women). *Tuition:* Full-time $9,990; part-time $437 per unit. Tuition and fees vary according to degree level and program. *Graduate housing:* Room and/or apartments available to single students; on-campus housing not available to married students. *Student services:* Campus employment opportunities, career counseling, low-cost health insurance, writing training. *Library facilities:* Graduate Theological Union Library.

Computer facilities: 3 computers available on campus for general student use. Internet access is available. *Web address:* http://www.jstb.edu/.

General Application Contact: Linda A. Menes, Director of Admissions, 800-824-0122, Fax: 510-841-8536, E-mail: admissions@jstb.edu.

GRADUATE UNITS

Graduate and Professional Programs Students: 107 full-time (19 women), 22 part-time (8 women); includes 19 minority (2 African Americans, 14 Asian Americans or Pacific Islanders, 3 Hispanic Americans), 49 international. 69 applicants, 86% accepted. *Faculty:* 16 full-time (3 women), 9 part-time/adjunct (4 women). Expenses: Contact institution. *Financial support:* In 2001–02, 56 students received support. Scholarships/grants and tuition waivers (partial) available. Financial award application deadline: 3/15. In 2001, 18 first professional degrees, 30 master's, 2 doctorates awarded. *Degree program information:* Part-time programs available. Offers theology (M Div, MA, MTS, Th M, STD, STL). *Application deadline:* Applications are processed on a rolling basis. *Application fee:* $35. *Application Contact:* Linda A. Menes, Director of Admissions, 800-824-0122, Fax: 510-841-8536, E-mail: admissions@jstb.edu. *Acting Academic Dean,* Sr. Mary Ann Donovan, SC, 510-841-8804, Fax: 510-841-8536, E-mail: mdonovan@jstb.edu.

JEWISH HOSPITAL COLLEGE OF NURSING AND ALLIED HEALTH, St. Louis, MO 63110-1091

General Information Independent, coed, primarily women, comprehensive institution. *Enrollment:* 31 full-time matriculated graduate/professional students (27 women), 45 part-time matriculated graduate/professional students (42 women). *Enrollment by degree level:* 76 master's. *Graduate faculty:* 13 full-time (12 women), 4 part-time/adjunct (2 women). *Tuition:* Part-time $360 per credit hour. *Graduate housing:* Rooms and/or apartments available on a first-come, first-served basis to single students and available to married students. Typical cost: $2,220 per year for single students. *Student services:* Campus employment opportunities, campus safety program, disabled student services, international student services. *Library facilities:* George and Juanita Way Library plus 4 others. *Online resources:* library catalog, access to other libraries' catalogs. *Collection:* 2,801 titles, 187 serial subscriptions.

Computer facilities: 21 computers available on campus for general student use. A campuswide network can be accessed from off campus. Software, research databases available. *Web address:* http://jhconah.edu.

General Application Contact: Christie N. Schneider, Chief Admissions Officer, 314-454-7538, Fax: 314-454-5239, E-mail: cns5347@bjc.org.

GRADUATE UNITS

Division of Allied Health Average age 38. 16 applicants, 100% accepted. *Faculty:* 1 part-time/adjunct (0 women). Expenses: Contact institution. *Financial support:* Institutionally sponsored loans and scholarships/grants available. *Degree program information:* Part-time and evening/weekend programs available. Offers education (MSAH); management (MSAH). *Application deadline:* For fall admission, 6/30 (priority date); for spring admission, 11/30 (priority date). Applications are processed on a rolling basis. *Application fee:* $25. *Application Contact:* Christie N. Schneider, Chief Admissions Officer, 314-454-7538, Fax: 314-454-5239, E-mail: cns5347@bjc.org. *Academic Dean, Nursing Division,* Dr. Michael D. Ward, 314-454-8987, E-mail: mdw7263@bjc.org.

Division of Nursing Students: 31 full-time (27 women), 38 part-time (37 women); includes 7 minority (4 African Americans, 1 Asian American or Pacific Islander, 2 Hispanic Americans) Average age 38. 6 applicants, 83% accepted. *Faculty:* 13 full-time (12 women), 4 part-time/adjunct (2 women). Expenses: Contact institution. *Financial support:* In 2001–02, 10 students received support, including 2 teaching assistantships with partial tuition reimbursements available (averaging $1,000 per year); fellowships with tuition reimbursements available, institutionally sponsored loans and scholarships/grants also available. Support available to part-time students. Financial award application deadline: 4/15; financial award applicants required to submit FAFSA. In 2001, 26 degrees awarded. *Degree program information:* Part-time and evening/weekend programs available. Offers adult nurse practitioner (MSN); education (MSN); gerontology nurse practitioner (MSN); holistics (MSN); neonatal nurse practitioner (MSN). *Application deadline:* For fall admission, 6/30 (priority date); for spring admission, 11/30 (priority date). Applications are processed on a rolling basis. *Application fee:* $25. *Application Contact:* Christie N. Schneider, Chief Admissions Officer, 314-454-7538, Fax: 314-454-5239, E-mail: cns5347@bjc.org. *Academic Dean,* Dr. Elizabeth A. Buck, 314-454-8416, Fax: 314-454-5239.

JEWISH THEOLOGICAL SEMINARY OF AMERICA, New York, NY 10027-4649

General Information Independent-religious, coed, university. *Enrollment:* 205 full-time matriculated graduate/professional students (104 women), 151 part-time matriculated graduate/professional students (91 women). *Enrollment by degree level:* 157 first professional, 95 master's, 104 doctoral. *Graduate faculty:* 61 full-time (15 women), 56 part-time/adjunct (23 women). *Tuition:* Full-time $17,680; part-time $620 per credit. *Required fees:* $4,180. One-time fee: $2,310 part-time. *Graduate housing:* Rooms and/or apartments available on a first-come, first-served basis to single and married students. Housing application deadline: 5/15. *Student services:* Campus employment opportunities, career counseling, free psychological counseling, low-cost health insurance. *Library facilities:* Library of the Jewish Theological Seminary. *Online resources:* library catalog, web page, access to other libraries' catalogs. *Collection:* 271,000 titles, 720 serial subscriptions.

Computer facilities: 20 computers available on campus for general student use. A campuswide network can be accessed from student residence rooms and from off campus. Internet access is available. *Web address:* http://www.jtsa.edu/.

General Application Contact: Dr. Stephen Garfinkel, Dean of the Graduate School, 212-678-8022, Fax: 212-678-8947, E-mail: gradschool@jtsa.edu.

GRADUATE UNITS

Graduate School Students: 24 full-time (16 women), 154 part-time (84 women). Average age 28. 113 applicants, 78% accepted. *Faculty:* 61 full-time (15 women), 56 part-time/adjunct (23 women). Expenses: Contact institution. *Financial support:* In 2001–02, 58 fellowships were awarded; career-related internships or fieldwork and tuition waivers (full and partial) also available. Support available to part-time students. Financial award application deadline: 3/1; financial award applicants required to submit FAFSA. In 2001, 22 master's, 8 doctorates awarded. *Degree program information:* Part-time programs available. Offers ancient Judaism (MA, DHL, PhD); Bible (MA, DHL, PhD); Jewish education (PhD); Jewish history (MA, DHL, PhD); Jewish literature (MA, DHL, PhD); Jewish philosophy (MA, DHL, PhD); liturgy (DHL, PhD); medieval Jewish studies (MA, DHL, PhD); Midrash (MA, DHL, PhD); modern Jewish studies (MA, DHL, PhD); Talmud and rabbinics (MA, DHL, PhD). *Application deadline:* For fall admission, 1/30 (priority date). Applications are processed on a rolling basis. *Application fee:* $50. *Dean,* Dr. Stephen Garfinkel, 212-678-8024, Fax: 212-678-8947, E-mail: gradschool@jtsa.edu.

H. L. Miller Cantorial School and College of Jewish Music Students: 33 full-time (21 women), 4 part-time (1 woman). Average age 30. 12 applicants, 92% accepted. *Faculty:* 3 full-time (0 women), 14 part-time/adjunct (3 women). Expenses: Contact institution. *Financial support:* Career-related internships or fieldwork available. Support available to part-time students. Financial award application deadline: 3/1; financial award applicants required to submit FAFSA. In 2001, 8 master's awarded. Offers Jewish music (MSM, DSM). *Application fee:* $50. *Dean,* Hazzan Henry Rosenblum, 212-678-8036, Fax: 212-678-8947.

Rabbinical School Students: 125 full-time (51 women), 13 part-time (8 women). Average age 26. 32 applicants, 88% accepted. *Faculty:* 46 full-time, 50 part-time/adjunct. Expenses: Contact institution. *Financial support:* Career-related internships or fieldwork available. Support available to part-time students. Financial award application deadline: 3/1; financial award applicants required to submit FAFSA. In 2001, 12 master's, 35 other advanced degrees awarded. Offers theology (MA, Rabbi). *Application deadline:* For fall admission, 12/31. Applications are processed on a rolling basis. *Application fee:* $50. *Dean,* Rabbi William Lebeau, 212-678-8067.

William Davidson Graduate School of Jewish Education Students: 34 full-time (26 women), 27 part-time (17 women). Average age 31. 26 applicants, 88% accepted. *Faculty:* 10 full-time (2 women), 3 part-time/adjunct (2 women). Expenses: Contact institution. *Financial support:* Fellowships, career-related internships or fieldwork available. Financial award application deadline: 3/1. In 2001, 6 master's, 1 doctorate awarded. *Degree program information:* Part-time programs available. Offers Jewish education (MA, Ed D, PhD). Offered in conjunction with Rabbinical School; H. L. Miller Cantorial School and College of Jewish Music; Teacher's College, Columbia University; and Union Theological Seminary. *Application deadline:* For fall admission, 2/15 (priority date). Applications are processed on a rolling basis. *Application fee:* $50. *Dean,* Dr. Aryeh Davidson, 212-678-8030, Fax: 212-749-9085.

JEWISH UNIVERSITY OF AMERICA, Skokie, IL 60077-3248

General Information Independent-religious, men only, graduate-only institution. *Graduate housing:* On-campus housing not available.

GRADUATE UNITS

Graduate School *Degree program information:* Part-time and evening/weekend programs available. Offers Jewish education (MJ Ed, DJ Ed).

Abrams Institute of Pastoral Counseling Offers counseling (MA); pastoral counseling (MPC, DPC).

Graduate Research Division *Degree program information:* Part-time programs available. Offers Bible (MHL, DHL); Hebrew (MHL, DHL); history (MHL, DHL); Jewish studies (MHL, DHL); philosophy (MHL, DHL); rabbinics (MHL, DHL).

JOAN AND SANFORD I. WEILL MEDICAL COLLEGE AND GRADUATE SCHOOL OF MEDICAL SCIENCES OF CORNELL UNIVERSITY, New York, NY 10021-4896

General Information Independent, coed, graduate-only institution. *Graduate faculty:* 683 full-time (150 women), 2 part-time/adjunct (0 women). *Tuition:* Full-time $28,500. *Required fees:* $1,090. *Graduate housing:* Rooms and/or apartments guaranteed to single students and available to married students. Typical cost: $4,463 per year ($8,543 including board) for single students. Housing application deadline: 3/28. *Student services:* Campus safety program, career counseling, low-cost health insurance, multicultural affairs office. *Library facilities:* Samuel J. Wood Library.

Computer facilities: 110 computers available on campus for general student use. A campuswide network can be accessed from student residence rooms and from off campus. Internet access is available. *Web address:* http://www.med.cornell.edu/.

General Application Contact: Liliana Montano, Assistant Dean of Admissions, 212-746-1067, Fax: 212-746-8052, E-mail: cumc-admissions@med.cornell.edu.

GRADUATE UNITS

Graduate School of Medical Sciences Students: 258 full-time (146 women); includes 54 minority (10 African Americans, 35 Asian Americans or Pacific Islanders, 9 Hispanic Americans), 91 international. Average age 22. 437 applicants, 23% accepted. *Faculty:* 205 full-time (47 women). Expenses: Contact institution. *Financial support:* In 2001–02, 4 fellowships (averaging $16,500 per year) were awarded; scholarships/grants, health care benefits, tuition waivers (full), and stipends also available. In 2001, 5 master's, 33 doctorates awarded. Offers biochemistry and structural biology (PhD); cell biology and genetics (PhD); clinical epidemiology and health services research (MS); immunology (MS, PhD); medical sciences (MS, PhD); molecular biology (MS, PhD); neuroscience (PhD); pharmacology (PhD); physiology, biophysics, and molecular medicine (PhD). *Application deadline:* For fall admission, 12/15. *Application fee:* $50. Electronic applications accepted. *Dean,* Dr. David P. Hajjar, 212-746-6900, E-mail: dphajjar@med.cornell.edu.

Medical College Students: 418 full-time (207 women); includes 193 minority (48 African Americans, 109 Asian Americans or Pacific Islanders, 36 Hispanic Americans), 6 international. Average age 27. 5,766 applicants, 4% accepted, 101 enrolled. *Faculty:* 277 full-time (57 women). Expenses: Contact institution. *Financial support:* Federal Work-Study, institutionally sponsored loans, and scholarships/grants available. Financial award application deadline: 5/15. In 2001, 88 degrees awarded. Offers medicine (MD). *Application deadline:* For fall admission, 10/15. *Application fee:* $75. Electronic applications accepted. *Application Contact:* Liliana Montano, Assistant Dean of Admissions, 212-746-1067, Fax: 212-746-8052, E-mail: cumc-admissions@med.cornell.edu. *Dean,* Dr. Antonio Gotto, 212-746-6005, Fax: 212-746-8424.

JOHN BROWN UNIVERSITY, Siloam Springs, AR 72761-2121

General Information Independent-religious, coed, comprehensive institution. *Enrollment:* 103 full-time matriculated graduate/professional students (57 women), 39 part-time matriculated graduate/professional students (20 women). *Enrollment by degree level:* 142 master's. *Graduate faculty:* 11 full-time (3 women), 5 part-time/adjunct (1 woman). *Tuition:* Full-time $5,940; part-time $330 per hour. *Graduate housing:* Rooms and/or apartments available on a first-come, first-served basis to single and married students. Typical cost: $2,650 per year for single students; $2,650 per year for married students. *Student services:* Career counseling, disabled student services, exercise/wellness program, free psychological counseling, international student services. *Library facilities:* Arutunoff Learning Resource Center plus 4 others.

Online resources: library catalog, web page, access to other libraries' catalogs. *Collection:* 93,190 titles, 1,580 serial subscriptions, 8,310 audiovisual materials.

Computer facilities: 75 computers available on campus for general student use. A campuswide network can be accessed from student residence rooms and from off campus. Internet access is available. *Web address:* http://www.jbu.edu/.

General Application Contact: Dr. Ida M. Adolphson, Graduate Business Coordinator, 479-524-7291, Fax: 479-524-9548, E-mail: idolphs@jbu.edu.

GRADUATE UNITS

Department of Counseling Students: 59 full-time (36 women), 39 part-time (20 women); includes 3 minority (1 African American, 2 Native Americans) Average age 32. 32 applicants, 81% accepted, 19 enrolled. *Faculty:* 7 full-time (2 women), 2 part-time/adjunct (0 women). Expenses: Contact institution. *Financial support:* In 2001–02, 12 students received support, including 3 research assistantships (averaging $8,100 per year); scholarships/grants, tuition waivers (full), and unspecified assistantships also available. Financial award applicants required to submit FAFSA. In 2001, 27 degrees awarded. *Degree program information:* Part-time and evening/weekend programs available. Offers licensed professional counseling (MS); marriage and family therapy (MS); school counseling (MS). *Application deadline:* For fall admission, 8/15 (priority date); for spring admission, 1/8. Applications are processed on a rolling basis. *Application fee:* $25. Electronic applications accepted. *Application Contact:* Dr. Ida M. Adolphson, Graduate Business Coordinator, 479-524-7291, Fax: 479-524-9548, E-mail: idolphs@jbu.edu. *Chair,* Dr. John V. Carmack, 479-524-7460, Fax: 479-524-9548, E-mail: jcarmack@jbu.edu.

Department of Leadership and Management Students: 44 full-time (21 women); includes 2 minority (1 African American, 1 Native American), 2 international. Average age 30. 34 applicants, 79% accepted, 21 enrolled. *Faculty:* 4 full-time (1 woman), 3 part-time/adjunct (1 woman). Expenses: Contact institution. *Financial support:* In 2001–02, 10 students received support, including 1 research assistantship with tuition reimbursement available (averaging $8,100 per year); scholarships/grants, tuition waivers (full), and unspecified assistantships also available. Financial award applicants required to submit FAFSA. In 2001, 19 degrees awarded. *Degree program information:* Part-time and evening/weekend programs available. Offers business administration (MBA); leadership and ethics (MS). *Application deadline:* For fall admission, 8/15 (priority date); for spring admission, 1/8 (priority date). Applications are processed on a rolling basis. *Application fee:* $25. Electronic applications accepted. *Application Contact:* Dr. Delia J. Haak, Graduate Business Coordinator, 479-524-7170, Fax: 479-524-9548, E-mail: dhaak@jbu.edu. *Chair,* Dr. Joe F. Walenciak, 479-524-7281, Fax: 479-524-9548, E-mail: jwalenci@jbu.edu.

JOHN CARROLL UNIVERSITY, University Heights, OH 44118-4581

General Information Independent-religious, coed, comprehensive institution. CGS member. *Enrollment:* 203 full-time matriculated graduate/professional students (147 women), 599 part-time matriculated graduate/professional students (357 women). *Enrollment by degree level:* 793 master's. *Graduate faculty:* 133 full-time (37 women), 55 part-time/adjunct (32 women). *Tuition:* Full-time $9,900; part-time $550 per credit hour. *Required fees:* $10 per credit hour. Tuition and fees vary according to program. *Graduate housing:* On-campus housing not available. *Student services:* Career counseling, exercise/wellness program, free psychological counseling, international student services, multicultural affairs office, writing training. *Library facilities:* Grasselli Library. *Online resources:* library catalog, web page, access to other libraries' catalogs. *Collection:* 620,000 titles, 2,198 serial subscriptions, 5,820 audiovisual materials.

Computer facilities: 210 computers available on campus for general student use. A campuswide network can be accessed from student residence rooms and from off campus. Internet access and online class registration are available. *Web address:* http://www.jcu.edu/.

General Application Contact: Revona Spicuzza, Admissions Secretary, 216-397-1925, Fax: 216-397-3009, E-mail: rspicuzza@jcu.edu.

GRADUATE UNITS

Graduate School Students: 203 full-time (147 women), 599 part-time (357 women); includes 72 minority (53 African Americans, 12 Asian Americans or Pacific Islanders, 6 Hispanic Americans, 1 Native American), 10 international. 316 applicants, 75% accepted. *Faculty:* 133 full-time (37 women), 55 part-time/adjunct (32 women). Expenses: Contact institution. *Financial support:* In 2001–02, 71 students received support, including 22 research assistantships with tuition reimbursements available (averaging $8,700 per year), 33 teaching assistantships (averaging $8,700 per year); career-related internships or fieldwork, institutionally sponsored loans, tuition waivers (partial), and unspecified assistantships also available. Support available to part-time students. Financial award application deadline: 4/1; financial award applicants required to submit FAFSA. In 2001, 284 degrees awarded. *Degree program information:* Part-time and evening/weekend programs available. Offers administration (M Ed, MA); biology (MA, MS); chemistry (MS); clinical counseling (Certificate); communications management (MA); community counseling (MA); educational and school psychology (M Ed, MA); English (MA); history (MA); humanities (MA); mathematics (MA, MS); physics (MS); professional teacher education (M Ed, MA); religious studies (MA); school based elementary education (M Ed); school based secondary education (M Ed); school counseling (M Ed, MA). *Application deadline:* Applications are processed on a rolling basis. *Application fee:* $25 ($35 for international students). *Admissions Secretary,* Revona Spicuzza, 216-397-1925, Fax: 216-397-3009, E-mail: rspicuzza@jcu.edu.

John M. and Mary Jo Boler School of Business Students: 19 full-time (5 women), 237 part-time (102 women); includes 19 minority (12 African Americans, 5 Asian Americans or Pacific Islanders, 2 Hispanic Americans) Average age 29. 84 applicants, 74% accepted, 51 enrolled. *Faculty:* 33 full-time (5 women), 4 part-time/adjunct (2 women). Expenses: Contact institution. *Financial support:* In 2001–02, 6 research assistantships with full tuition reimbursements (averaging $8,000 per year) were awarded; scholarships/grants and unspecified assistantships also available. Financial award application deadline: 3/1; financial award applicants required to submit FAFSA. In 2001, 88 degrees awarded. *Degree program information:* Part-time and evening/weekend programs available. Offers business (MBA). *Application deadline:* For fall admission, 8/15 (priority date); for spring admission, 1/3. Applications are processed on a rolling basis. *Application fee:* $25 ($35 for international students). *Associate Dean,* Dr. James M. Daley, 216-397-4391, Fax: 216-397-1728, E-mail: jdaley@jcu.edu.

JOHN F. KENNEDY UNIVERSITY, Orinda, CA 94563-2603

General Information Independent, coed, comprehensive institution. *Enrollment:* 599 full-time matriculated graduate/professional students (410 women), 695 part-time matriculated graduate/professional students (546 women). *Enrollment by degree level:* 289 first professional, 891 master's, 114 doctoral. *Graduate faculty:* 29 full-time (13 women), 805 part-time/adjunct (483 women). *Tuition:* Full-time $9,396; part-time $348 per unit. *Required fees:* $9 per quarter. Tuition and fees vary according to degree level and program. *Graduate housing:* On-campus housing not available. *Student services:* Campus safety program, career counseling, international student services, low-cost health insurance. *Library facilities:* Robert M. Fisher Library. *Online resources:* library catalog, web page. *Collection:* 91,170 titles, 811 serial subscriptions, 1,854 audiovisual materials.

Computer facilities: 50 computers available on campus for general student use. *Web address:* http://www.jfku.edu/.

General Application Contact: Ellena Bloedorn, Director of Admissions, 925-258-2213, Fax: 925-254-6964, E-mail: proginfo@jfku.edu.

GRADUATE UNITS

Graduate School for Holistic Studies Students: 137 full-time (116 women), 292 part-time (227 women); includes 63 minority (15 African Americans, 20 Asian Americans or Pacific Islanders, 25 Hispanic Americans, 3 Native Americans) Average age 38. 150 applicants, 93% accepted. *Faculty:* 6 full-time (3 women), 186 part-time/adjunct (120 women). Expenses: Contact institution. *Financial support:* Fellowships, career-related internships or fieldwork and institutionally sponsored loans available. Support available to part-time students. Financial award application deadline: 3/2. In 2001, 101 degrees awarded. *Degree program information:* Part-time and evening/weekend programs available. Offers arts and consciousness (MA); consciousness studies (MA, Certificate); holistic health education (MA); holistic studies (MA, MFA, Certificate); studio arts (MFA); transformative arts (MA); transpersonal counseling psychology (MA). *Application deadline:* For fall admission, 8/1 (priority date); for spring admission, 3/1. *Application fee:* $50. *Application Contact:* Ellena Bloedorn, Director of Admissions, 925-258-2213, Fax: 925-254-6964, E-mail: proginfo@jfku.edu. *Dean,* K. Sue Duncan, 925-254-0105.

Graduate School of Professional Psychology Students: 149 full-time (115 women), 271 part-time (217 women); includes 112 minority (46 African Americans, 32 Asian Americans or Pacific Islanders, 30 Hispanic Americans, 4 Native Americans) Average age 38. 164 applicants, 88% accepted. *Faculty:* 16 full-time (6 women), 316 part-time/adjunct (206 women). Expenses: Contact institution. *Financial support:* Fellowships, career-related internships or fieldwork and institutionally sponsored loans available. Support available to part-time students. Financial award application deadline: 3/2. In 2001, 114 master's, 23 doctorates, 6 other advanced degrees awarded. *Degree program information:* Part-time and evening/weekend programs available. Offers conflict resolution (Certificate); counseling psychology (MA); organizational psychology (MA, Certificate); professional psychology (MA, Psy D, Certificate); psychology (Psy D); sport psychology (MA). *Application deadline:* Applications are processed on a rolling basis. *Application fee:* $50. *Application Contact:* Ellena Bloedorn, Director of Admissions, 925-258-2213, Fax: 925-254-6964, E-mail: proginfo@jfku.edu. *Dean,* Dr. H. Keith McConnell, 925-254-0110.

School of Law Students: 274 full-time (150 women), 15 part-time (8 women); includes 111 minority (62 African Americans, 26 Asian Americans or Pacific Islanders, 19 Hispanic Americans, 4 Native Americans) Average age 37. 106 applicants, 77% accepted. *Faculty:* 1 full-time (0 women), 120 part-time/adjunct (51 women). Expenses: Contact institution. *Financial support:* Fellowships, institutionally sponsored loans available. Support available to part-time students. Financial award application deadline: 3/2. In 2001, 55 degrees awarded. *Degree program information:* Part-time and evening/weekend programs available. Offers law (JD). *Application deadline:* For fall admission, 5/30; for spring admission, 11/30. Applications are processed on a rolling basis. *Application fee:* $50. *Application Contact:* Ellena Bloedorn, Director of Admissions, 925-258-2213, Fax: 925-254-6964, E-mail: proginfo@jfku.edu. *Dean,* Michael Guarino, 925-295-1800.

School of Liberal Arts Students: 28 full-time (23 women), 41 part-time (35 women); includes 13 minority (9 African Americans, 3 Hispanic Americans, 1 Native American) Average age 33. 37 applicants, 78% accepted. *Faculty:* 3 full-time (2 women), 53 part-time/adjunct (38 women). Expenses: Contact institution. *Financial support:* Fellowships, institutionally sponsored loans available. Support available to part-time students. Financial award applicants required to submit FAFSA. In 2001, 16 master's, 4 other advanced degrees awarded. *Degree program information:* Part-time and evening/weekend programs available. Offers liberal arts (MA, MAT, Certificate); museum studies (MA, Certificate); teaching (MAT). *Application deadline:* Applications are processed on a rolling basis. *Application fee:* $50. *Application Contact:* Ellena Bloedorn, Director of Admissions, 925-258-2213, Fax: 925-254-6964, E-mail: proginfo@jfku.edu. *Dean,* Jeremiah Hallisey, 925-258-2232.

School of Management Students: 11 full-time (6 women), 77 part-time (60 women); includes 24 minority (12 African Americans, 8 Asian Americans or Pacific Islanders, 4 Hispanic Americans) Average age 40. 39 applicants, 95% accepted. *Faculty:* 3 full-time (2 women), 130 part-time/adjunct (68 women). Expenses: Contact institution. *Financial support:* Fellowships, institutionally sponsored loans available. Support available to part-time students. Financial award application deadline: 3/2. In 2001, 44 degrees awarded. *Degree program information:* Part-time and evening/weekend programs available. Offers business administration (MBA); career development (MA, Certificate); management (MA, MBA, Certificate); organizational leadership (Certificate). *Application deadline:* Applications are processed on a rolling basis. *Application fee:* $50. *Application Contact:* Ellena Bloedorn, Director of Admissions, 925-258-2213, Fax: 925-254-6964, E-mail: proginfo@jfku.edu. *Dean,* Josephina Baltodano, 925-295-0600, Fax: 925-295-0604.

See in-depth description on page 923.

JOHN JAY COLLEGE OF CRIMINAL JUSTICE OF THE CITY UNIVERSITY OF NEW YORK, New York, NY 10019-1093

General Information State and locally supported, coed, comprehensive institution. *Enrollment:* 233 full-time matriculated graduate/professional students (174 women), 793 part-time matriculated graduate/professional students (466 women). *Enrollment by degree level:* 1,049 master's, 1,026 doctoral. *Graduate faculty:* 45 full-time, 14 part-time/adjunct. Tuition, state resident: full-time $4,350; part-time $185 per credit. Tuition, nonresident: full-time $7,600; part-time $285 per credit. *Required fees:* $80; $40 per semester. Tuition and fees vary according to degree level. *Graduate housing:* On-campus housing not available. *Student services:* Campus employment opportunities, campus safety program, career counseling, child daycare facilities, disabled student services, exercise/wellness program, free psychological counseling, international student services, low-cost health insurance, multicultural affairs office. *Library facilities:* Lloyd George Sealy Library. *Online resources:* library catalog. *Collection:* 310,000 titles, 1,325 serial subscriptions. *Research affiliation:* Criminal Justice Center, Criminal Justice Research and Evaluation Center, Center on Violence and Human Survival, Center for Dispute Resolution, The Fire Science Institute, The Institute For Criminal Justice Ethics.

Computer facilities: 250 computers available on campus for general student use. A campuswide network can be accessed from off campus. Internet access is available. *Web address:* http://www.jjay.cuny.edu/.

General Application Contact: Shirley Rodriguez-Melendez, Admissions Assistant, 212-237-8863, Fax: 212-237-8777, E-mail: srodrigu@jjay.cuny.edu.

GRADUATE UNITS

Graduate Studies Students: 233 full-time (174 women), 793 part-time (466 women); includes 359 minority (189 African Americans, 47 Asian Americans or Pacific Islanders, 122 Hispanic Americans, 1 Native American), 36 international. Average age 29. 750 applicants, 60% accepted, 322 enrolled. *Faculty:* 45 full-time, 14 part-time/adjunct. Expenses: Contact institution. *Financial support:* Career-related internships or fieldwork, Federal Work-Study, institutionally sponsored loans, and scholarships/grants available. Support available to part-time students. Financial award applicants required to submit FAFSA. In 2001, 311 degrees awarded. *Degree program information:* Part-time and evening/weekend programs available. Offers criminal justice (MA, PhD); criminology and deviance (PhD); forensic psychology (MA, PhD); forensic science (MS, PhD); law and philosophy (PhD); organizational behavior (PhD); protection management (MS); public administration (MPA); public policy (PhD). *Application deadline:* For fall admission, 6/30 (priority date); for spring admission, 12/1. Applications are processed on a rolling basis. *Application fee:* $40. *Application Contact:* Shirley Rodriguez-Melendez, Admissions Assistant, 212-237-8863, Fax: 212-237-8777, E-mail: srodrigu@jjay.cuny.edu. *Dean,* Dr. James P. Levine, 212-237-8422, Fax: 212-237-8309.

JOHN MARSHALL LAW SCHOOL, Chicago, IL 60604-3968

General Information Independent, coed, graduate-only institution. *Enrollment by degree level:* 1,219 first professional, 223 master's. *Graduate faculty:* 58 full-time (18 women), 123 part-time/adjunct (27 women). *Tuition:* Full-time $25,500; part-time $850 per semester hour. *Required fees:* $50 per term. Tuition and fees vary according to degree level. *Graduate housing:* On-campus housing not available. *Student services:* Campus employment opportunities, campus safety program, career counseling, international student services, multicultural affairs office, writing training. *Library facilities:* The John Marshall Law School Library. *Online resources:* library catalog, web page, access to other libraries' catalogs. *Collection:* 227,891 titles, 5,034 serial subscriptions, 1,632 audiovisual materials.

Computer facilities: 122 computers available on campus for general student use. A campuswide network can be accessed from off campus. Internet access is available. *Web address:* http://www.jmls.edu/.

John Marshall Law School (continued)

General Application Contact: William B. Powers, Associate Dean of Admission and Student Affairs, 800-537-4280, Fax: 312-427-5136, E-mail: admission@jmls.edu.

GRADUATE UNITS

Graduate and Professional Programs Students: 900 full-time (401 women), 542 part-time (250 women); includes 256 minority (116 African Americans, 56 Asian Americans or Pacific Islanders, 77 Hispanic Americans, 7 Native Americans), 54 international. Average age 27. 1,897 applicants, 48% accepted, 275 enrolled. *Faculty:* 58 full-time (18 women), 123 part-time/adjunct (27 women). Expenses: Contact institution. *Financial support:* In 2001–02, 1,143 students received support. Scholarships/grants and tuition waivers (full and partial) available. Support available to part-time students. Financial award applicants required to submit FAFSA. In 2001, 307 first professional degrees, 104 master's awarded. *Degree program information:* Part-time and evening/weekend programs available. Offers comparative legal studies (LL M); employee benefits (LL M); information technology (LL M, MS); intellectual property (LL M); international business and trade (LL M); law (JD); real estate (LL M); taxation (LL M). *Application deadline:* For fall admission, 3/1 (priority date); for spring admission, 10/1 (priority date). Applications are processed on a rolling basis. *Application fee:* $50 ($60 for international students). Electronic applications accepted. *Application Contact:* William B. Powers, Associate Dean of Admission and Student Affairs, 800-537-4280, Fax: 312-427-5136, E-mail: admission@jmls.edu. *Dean,* Robert Gilbert Johnson, 312-427-2737.

JOHNS HOPKINS UNIVERSITY, Baltimore, MD 21218-2699

General Information Independent, coed, university. CGS member. *Enrollment:* 4,514 full-time matriculated graduate/professional students (2,299 women), 6,409 part-time matriculated graduate/professional students (3,247 women). *Graduate faculty:* 2,425 full-time (833 women), 3,438 part-time/adjunct (1,013 women). *Tuition:* Full-time $27,390. *Graduate housing:* Rooms and/or apartments available to single and married students. Housing application deadline:6/1. *Student services:* Campus employment opportunities, campus safety program, career counseling, disabled student services, exercise/wellness program, free psychological counseling, international student services, low-cost health insurance, multicultural affairs office, teacher training, writing training. *Library facilities:* Milton S. Eisenhower Library plus 6 others. *Online resources:* library catalog, web page, access to other libraries' catalogs. *Collection:* 3.4 million titles, 23,043 serial subscriptions, 295,952 audiovisual materials. *Research affiliation:* Space Telescope Science Institute (astronomy), Howard Hughes Medical Institute (biomedical sciences), Bristol-Myers Squibb (human nutrition), SmithKline Beecham (asthma and allergy), Carnegie Institution of Washington (biological sciences), General Electric (medical technology).

Computer facilities: 185 computers available on campus for general student use. A campuswide network can be accessed from student residence rooms and from off campus. Internet access is available. *Web address:* http://www.jhu.edu/.

General Application Contact: Nicole Kendzejewki, Graduate Admissions Coordinator, 410-516-8174, Fax: 410-516-8480, E-mail: grad_adm@jhu.edu.

GRADUATE UNITS

G. W. C. Whiting School of Engineering Students: 449 full-time (124 women), 23 part-time (3 women); includes 33 minority (5 African Americans, 19 Asian Americans or Pacific Islanders, 9 Hispanic Americans), 257 international. Average age 27. 1,743 applicants, 19% accepted, 168 enrolled. *Faculty:* 123 full-time (11 women), 43 part-time/adjunct (2 women). Expenses: Contact institution. *Financial support:* In 2001–02, 463 students received support, including 103 fellowships with full and partial tuition reimbursements available (averaging $17,041 per year), 200 research assistantships with full tuition reimbursements available (averaging $16,825 per year), 68 teaching assistantships with full and partial tuition reimbursements available (averaging $15,787 per year); Federal Work-Study, institutionally sponsored loans, scholarships/grants, tuition waivers (full), unspecified assistantships, and training grants also available. Support available to part-time students. Financial award applicants required to submit FAFSA. In 2001, 137 master's, 46 doctorates awarded. *Degree program information:* Part-time and evening/weekend programs available. Offers biomedical engineering (MSE); chemical engineering (MSE, PhD); civil engineering (MCE, MSE, PhD); computer science (MSE, PhD); discrete mathematics (MA, MSE, PhD); electrical and computer engineering (MSE, PhD); engineering (M Mat SE, MA, MCE, MS, MSE, PhD); geography and environmental engineering (MA, MS, MSE, PhD); materials science and engineering (M Mat SE, MSE, PhD); mechanical engineering (MS, MSE, PhD); operations research/optimization/decision science (MA, MSE, PhD); statistics/probability/stochastic processes (MA, MSE, PhD). *Application fee:* $0. Electronic applications accepted. *Dean,* Dr. Ilene J. Busch-Vishniac, 410-516-8350 Ext. 3, Fax: 410-516-8627, E-mail: jeannie@jhu.edu.

Paul H. Nitze School of Advanced International Studies Students: 567 full-time (275 women), 17 part-time (8 women); includes 71 minority (14 African Americans, 46 Asian Americans or Pacific Islanders, 10 Hispanic Americans, 1 Native American) Average age 27. 1,288 applicants, 35% accepted. *Faculty:* 44 full-time (13 women), 113 part-time/adjunct (29 women). Expenses: Contact institution. *Financial support:* In 2001–02, 431 fellowships (averaging $5,500 per year) were awarded; career-related internships or fieldwork and Federal Work-Study also available. Financial award application deadline: 2/1; financial award applicants required to submit FAFSA. In 2001, 294 master's, 13 doctorates, 34 other advanced degrees awarded. Offers emerging markets (Certificate); interdisciplinary studies (MA, PhD); international public policy (MIPP). MBA/MA offered jointly with the University of Pennsylvania–Wharton School and INSEAD in France. *Application deadline:* For fall admission, 1/15. *Application fee:* $75. Electronic applications accepted. *Application Contact:* Bonnie Wilson, Associate Dean of Student Affairs, 202-663-5700, Fax: 202-663-7788, E-mail: admissions.sais@jhu.edu. *Dean,* Dr. Jessica Einhorn, 202-663-5624, Fax: 202-663-5621.

Peabody Conservatory of Music Students: 269 full-time (165 women), 53 part-time (29 women); includes 39 minority (8 African Americans, 26 Asian Americans or Pacific Islanders, 5 Hispanic Americans), 121 international. Average age 27. 522 applicants, 56% accepted. *Faculty:* 66 full-time (18 women), 60 part-time/adjunct (20 women). Expenses: Contact institution. *Financial support:* Federal Work-Study, scholarships/grants, and unspecified assistantships available. Financial award application deadline: 2/1; financial award applicants required to submit FAFSA. In 2001, 100 master's, 8 doctorates, 34 GPDs awarded. Offers music (MM, DMA, AD, GPD). *Application deadline:* For fall admission, 12/15. *Application fee:* $55. *Application Contact:* David Lane, Director of Admissions, 800-368-2521, Fax: 410-659-8102, E-mail: admissions@peabody.jhu.edu. *Director,* Dr. Robert Sirota, 410-659-8100 Ext. 3060, Fax: 410-659-8129.

Program in Molecular Biophysics Offers molecular biophysics (PhD).

School of Medicine Students: 983 full-time (439 women); includes 260 minority (58 African Americans, 177 Asian Americans or Pacific Islanders, 23 Hispanic Americans, 2 Native Americans), 191 international. 5,427 applicants, 4% accepted. *Faculty:* 1,994 full-time (628 women), 1,270 part-time/adjunct (332 women). Expenses: Contact institution. *Financial support:* In 2001–02, fellowships with full tuition reimbursements (averaging $20,000 per year) research assistantships, teaching assistantships, career-related internships or fieldwork, Federal Work-Study, institutionally sponsored loans, and tuition waivers (full) also available. In 2001, 116 first professional degrees, 8 master's, 79 doctorates awarded. Offers art as applied to medicine (MA); medicine (MD, MA, MS, MSE, PhD). *Application deadline:* Applications are processed on a rolling basis. Electronic applications accepted. *Application Contact:* Dr. James Weiss, Associate Dean of Admissions, 410-955-3182. *Dean of Medical Faculty and Chief Executive Officer,* Dr. Edward D. Miller, 410-955-3180.

Graduate Programs in Medicine Students: 509 full-time (229 women); includes 88 minority (10 African Americans, 66 Asian Americans or Pacific Islanders, 11 Hispanic Americans, 1 Native American), 183 international. 774 applicants, 16% accepted. *Faculty:* 206 full-time (52 women), 32 part-time/adjunct (8 women). Expenses: Contact institution. *Financial support:* In 2001–02, fellowships with full tuition reimbursements (averaging $20,000 per year); research assistantships, teaching assistantships with tuition reimbursements, career-related internships or fieldwork, Federal Work-Study, institutionally sponsored loans, and tuition waivers (full) also available. Financial award applicants required to submit FAFSA. In 2001, 8 master's, 79 doctorates awarded. Offers biochemistry, cellular and molecular biology (PhD); biological chemistry (PhD); biophysics and biophysical chemistry (MS, PhD); cellular and molecular medicine (PhD); cellular and molecular physiology (PhD); functional anatomy and evolution (PhD); human genetics and molecular biology (PhD); immunology (PhD); medicine (MA, MS, PhD); molecular biology and genetics (PhD); neuroscience (PhD); pathobiology (PhD); pharmacology and molecular sciences (PhD); physiology (PhD). *Application deadline:* Applications are processed on a rolling basis. *Application fee:* $60. Electronic applications accepted. *Associate Dean for Graduate Student Affairs,* Dr. Peter Maloney, 410-955-8325.

School of Nursing Students: 57 full-time (54 women), 160 part-time (148 women); includes 41 minority (14 African Americans, 17 Asian Americans or Pacific Islanders, 4 Hispanic Americans, 6 Native Americans), 4 international. Average age 30. 271 applicants, 77% accepted. *Faculty:* 58. Expenses: Contact institution. *Financial support:* In 2001–02, 84 students received support, including 3 research assistantships with full tuition reimbursements available (averaging $15,000 per year), 6 teaching assistantships with full tuition reimbursements available (averaging $7,500 per year); fellowships, career-related internships or fieldwork, Federal Work-Study, institutionally sponsored loans, scholarships/grants, and traineeships also available. Support available to part-time students. Financial award application deadline: 5/1; financial award applicants required to submit FAFSA. In 2001, 58 master's, 4 doctorates awarded. *Degree program information:* Part-time programs available. Offers advanced practice nursing-nurse practitioner (MSN); clinical specialist (MSN); clinical specialist and health systems management (MSN); community health nursing (MSN); health systems management (MSN); nurse practitioner (Certificate); nursing (MSN, DN Sc, PhD, Certificate); nursing science (DN Sc). *Application deadline:* Applications are processed on a rolling basis. *Application fee:* $50. *Application Contact:* Mary O'Rourke, Director of Admissions/Student Services, 410-955-7548, Fax: 410-614-7086, E-mail: orourke@son.jhmi.edu. *Interim Dean,* Dr. Martha N. Hill, 410-955-7544, Fax: 410-955-4890, E-mail: mnhill@son.jhmi.edu.

School of Professional Studies in Business and Education Students: 657 full-time (398 women), 3,290 part-time (1,882 women); includes 830 minority (565 African Americans, 163 Asian Americans or Pacific Islanders, 91 Hispanic Americans, 11 Native Americans), 180 international. Average age 34. 2,124 applicants, 84% accepted, 1588 enrolled. *Faculty:* 57 full-time (35 women), 496 part-time/adjunct (178 women). Expenses: Contact institution. *Financial support:* In 2001–02, 1,145 students received support. Scholarships/grants available. Support available to part-time students. Financial award application deadline: 6/1; financial award applicants required to submit FAFSA. In 2001, 1,334 master's, 1 doctorate, 359 other advanced degrees awarded. *Degree program information:* Part-time and evening/weekend programs available. Offers continuing studies (MAT, MBA, MS, Ed D, CAGS, Certificate, Post Master's Certificate). *Application deadline:* Applications are processed on a rolling basis. *Application fee:* $55. Electronic applications accepted. *Application Contact:* Kumari Adams, Admissions Coordinator, 410-872-1234, Fax: 410-872-1251, E-mail: emsspsbe@jhu.edu. *Dean,* Dr. Ralph Fessler, 410-516-7820.

Division of Business and Management Students: 332 full-time (141 women), 2,228 part-time (1,011 women); includes 552 minority (359 African Americans, 124 Asian Americans or Pacific Islanders, 61 Hispanic Americans, 8 Native Americans), 165 international. Average age 34. 1,112 applicants, 85% accepted, 804 enrolled. *Faculty:* 14 full-time (3 women), 382 part-time/adjunct (104 women). Expenses: Contact institution. *Financial support:* In 2001–02, 460 students received support. Scholarships/grants available. Support available to part-time students. Financial award application deadline: 6/1; financial award applicants required to submit FAFSA. In 2001, 893 master's, 211 other advanced degrees awarded. *Degree program information:* Part-time and evening/weekend programs available. Offers advanced technology (Post Master's Certificate); business administration (MBA); change management (Certificate); electronic commerce (Post Master's Certificate); electronics business (Post Master's Certificate); finance (MS); information and telecommunication systems (Certificate); information and telecommunication systems for business (MS); information systems (Post Master's Certificate); investments (Certificate); leadership development (Certificate); marketing (MS); organization development and human resources (MS); police executive leadership (MS); real estate (MS); senior and housing care (Certificate); skilled facilitator (Certificate); telecommunication systems (Post Master's Certificate); the business of medicine (Certificate); the business of nursing (Certificate). *Application deadline:* Applications are processed on a rolling basis. *Application fee:* $55. Electronic applications accepted. *Application Contact:* Kumari Adams, Admissions Coordinator, 410-872-1234, Fax: 410-872-1251, E-mail: emsspsbe@jhu.edu. *Associate Dean,* Dr. Lynda de la Viña, 410-516-0755.

Division of Education Students: 325 full-time (257 women), 1,062 part-time (871 women); includes 278 minority (206 African Americans, 39 Asian Americans or Pacific Islanders, 30 Hispanic Americans, 3 Native Americans), 15 international. Average age 34. 1,012 applicants, 83% accepted, 784 enrolled. *Faculty:* 43 full-time (32 women), 114 part-time/adjunct (74 women). Expenses: Contact institution. *Financial support:* In 2001–02, 685 students received support. Scholarships/grants available. Support available to part-time students. Financial award application deadline: 6/1; financial award applicants required to submit FAFSA. In 2001, 441 master's, 1 doctorate, 148 other advanced degrees awarded. *Degree program information:* Part-time and evening/weekend programs available. Offers addictions counseling (Post Master's Certificate); administration and supervision (MS); assistive technology (Certificate); autism (Certificate); career counseling (Post Master's Certificate); clinical community counseling (Post Master's Certificate); counseling (MS, Ed D, CAGS); counseling at-risk students (Post Master's Certificate); discipline and positive behavior management (Certificate); early childhood education (MAT); earth and space science education/mathematics education (MS); earth/space science (Certificate); education (MAT, MS, Ed D, CAGS, Certificate, Post Master's Certificate); elementary education (MAT); general education (MS, Ed D); gifted education (MS, Certificate); inclusion (Certificate); instructional technology for web-based professional development and training (Certificate); leadership in technology integration (Certificate); learning disabilities (CAGS); organizational counseling (Post Master's Certificate); reading (MS, Certificate); school administration and supervision (Certificate); secondary education (MAT); severe disabilities (Certificate); severely and profoundly handicapped (CAGS); special education (MS, Ed D); teacher leadership (MS); teaching in higher education (Certificate); technology for educators (MS); technology for internet-based and mulitmedia instruction (Certificate); technology-based curriculum design and development (Certificate); transition planning (Certificate). *Application deadline:* Applications are processed on a rolling basis. *Application fee:* $55. Electronic applications accepted. *Application Contact:* Kumari Adams, Admissions Coordinator, 410-872-1234, Fax: 410-872-1251, E-mail: emsspsbe@jhu.edu. *Associate Dean,* Dr. Rochelle Ingram, 410-516-4957.

School of Public Health Students: 692 full-time (477 women), 577 part-time (367 women); includes 278 minority (84 African Americans, 154 Asian Americans or Pacific Islanders, 37 Hispanic Americans, 3 Native Americans), 314 international. Average age 30. 2,219 applicants, 54% accepted, 677 enrolled. *Faculty:* 442 full-time (195 women), 576 part-time/adjunct (215 women). Expenses: Contact institution. *Financial support:* In 2001–02, 1,119 students received support, including 40 fellowships (averaging $16,792 per year); research assistantships, teaching assistantships, Federal Work-Study, institutionally sponsored loans, scholarships/grants, and stipends also available. Support available to part-time students. Financial award application deadline: 4/15; financial award applicants required to submit FAFSA. In 2001, 437 master's, 109 doctorates awarded. *Degree program information:* Part-time and evening/weekend programs available. Postbaccalaureate distance learning degree programs offered (minimal on-campus study). Offers biochemistry (MPH, PhD); biostatistics (MPH); cancer epidemiology (MHS, Sc M, Dr PH, PhD, Sc D); clinical epidemiology (MHS, Sc M, Dr PH, PhD, Sc D); clinical investigation (MHS, Sc M, PhD, Certificate); clinical trials (MHS, Sc M, Dr PH, PhD, Sc D); disease prevention and control (MHS, PhD, Sc D); environmental health engineering (MHS, Sc M, Dr PH, PhD, Sc D); environmental health sciences (MPH); epidemiology (MHS, MPH, Sc M, Dr PH, PhD, Sc D); finance and administration (MHS); genetic counseling (Sc M); genetics (MHS, Sc M, Dr PH, Sc D); health and public policy (MHS, PhD, Sc D); health economics (PhD, Sc D); health education (MHS); health policy (MHS); health policy and management (MPH); health policy/prevention policy (PhD, Sc D); health services research (MHS, PhD, Sc D); health systems (MHS, PhD, Sc D); human nutrition (MHS, PhD, Sc D); infectious disease epidemiology (MHS, Sc M, Dr PH, PhD, Sc D); international health (MPH, Dr PH); long-term care (PhD, Sc D); mental hygiene (MHS, MPH,

Sc M, Dr PH, PhD, Sc D); molecular biology (PhD); molecular microbiology and immunology (MHS, MPH, Sc M, PhD); occupational and environmental health (Dr PH, PhD); occupational/environmental epidemiology (MHS, Sc M, Dr PH, PhD, Sc D); physiology (Sc M, PhD); population and family health sciences (MHS, MPH, Dr PH, PhD); public health (MHS, MPH, Sc M, Dr PH, PhD, Sc D, Certificate); radiation health sciences (MHS, Sc M, Dr PH, PhD, Sc D); reproductive biology (MHS, Sc M, PhD); social and behavioral interventions (MHS, PhD, Sc D); social and behavioral sciences (MHS, Sc M, PhD, Sc D); toxicological sciences (PhD). *Application deadline:* Applications are processed on a rolling basis. *Application fee:* $60. Electronic applications accepted. *Application Contact:* Michelle Sparacino, Director of Admissions, 410-955-3543, Fax: 410-955-0464, E-mail: msparaci@jhsph.edu. *Dean,* Dr. Alfred Sommer, 410-955-3540, Fax: 410-955-0121, E-mail: asommer@jhsph.edu.

Zanvyl Krieger School of Arts and Sciences Students: 987 full-time (460 women), 4 part-time (1 woman); includes 125 minority (26 African Americans, 75 Asian Americans or Pacific Islanders, 22 Hispanic Americans, 2 Native Americans), 279 international. Average age 26. 2,584 applicants, 21% accepted, 271 enrolled. *Faculty:* 267 full-time (61 women), 10 part-time/adjunct (7 women). Expenses: Contact institution. *Financial support:* In 2001–02, 90 fellowships, 250 research assistantships, 354 teaching assistantships were awarded. Career-related internships or fieldwork, Federal Work-Study, institutionally sponsored loans, scholarships/grants, and tuition waivers (full and partial) also available. Support available to part-time students. Financial award applicants required to submit FAFSA. In 2001, 149 master's, 134 doctorates awarded. Offers anthropology (PhD); arts and sciences (MA, MLA, PhD, CAGS); astronomy (PhD); biochemistry (PhD); biophysics (MA, PhD); cell biology (PhD); chemistry (MA, PhD); classics (MA, PhD); cognitive science (PhD); developmental biology (PhD); economics (PhD); English and American literature (PhD); experimental psychology (PhD); French (PhD); genetic biology (PhD); geochemistry (MA, PhD); geology (MA, PhD); geophysics (MA, PhD); German (PhD); groundwater (MA, PhD); history (PhD); history of art (MA, PhD); history of science (PhD); Italian (MA, PhD); liberal arts (MLA, CAGS); mathematics (PhD); molecular biology (PhD); Near Eastern studies (MA, PhD); oceanography (MA, PhD); philosophy (MA, PhD); physics (PhD); planetary atmosphere (MA, PhD); political science (PhD); psychology (PhD); sociology (PhD); Spanish (MA, PhD); writing (MA). *Application deadline:* Applications are processed on a rolling basis. *Application fee:* $55. Electronic applications accepted. *Application Contact:* Jeanine Majewski, Graduate Admissions Coordinator, 410-516-8174, Fax: 410-516-8480, E-mail: grad_adm@jhu.edu. *Dean,* Dr. Daniel Weiss, 410-516-8212, Fax: 410-516-6017.

Humanities Center Students: 20 full-time (9 women), 1 part-time; includes 4 minority (all Asian Americans or Pacific Islanders), 1 international. Average age 25. 43 applicants, 5% accepted, 2 enrolled. *Faculty:* 5 full-time (2 women), 1 (woman) part-time/adjunct. Expenses: Contact institution. *Financial support:* In 2001–02, 1 research assistantship, 5 teaching assistantships were awarded. Fellowships, Federal Work-Study, institutionally sponsored loans, and tuition waivers (partial) also available. Financial award application deadline: 3/14; financial award applicants required to submit FAFSA. Offers comparative literature and intellectual history (PhD). *Application deadline:* For fall admission, 1/15. *Application fee:* $55. Electronic applications accepted. *Application Contact:* Marva Philip, Administrator, 410-516-7619, Fax: 410-516-4897, E-mail: mphilip@jhunix.hcf.jhu.edu. *Chair,* Michael Fried, 410-516-7618, Fax: 410-516-4897, E-mail: mmf8@jhu.edu.

Institute for Policy Studies Students: 39 full-time (23 women), 1 part-time; includes 4 minority (2 African Americans, 2 Hispanic Americans), 7 international. Average age 27. 95 applicants, 57% accepted, 19 enrolled. *Faculty:* 4 part-time/adjunct (2 women). Expenses: Contact institution. *Financial support:* In 2001–02, 12 fellowships, 30 research assistantships, 5 teaching assistantships were awarded. Career-related internships or fieldwork, Federal Work-Study, and unspecified assistantships also available. Financial award application deadline: 4/15; financial award applicants required to submit FAFSA. In 2001, 22 degrees awarded. Offers policy studies (MA). *Application deadline:* For fall admission, 2/1. *Application fee:* $55. Electronic applications accepted. *Application Contact:* Angel Burgos, Program Coordinator, 410-516-7174, Fax: 410-516-8233, E-mail: aburgos@jhu.edu. *Director,* Dr. Sandra J. Newman, 410-516-7174, Fax: 410-516-8233, E-mail: jhuips@jhunix.hcf.jhu.edu.

See in-depth description on page 925.

JOHNSON & WALES UNIVERSITY, Providence, RI 02903-3703

General Information Independent, coed, comprehensive institution. CGS member. *Enrollment:* 456 full-time matriculated graduate/professional students (210 women), 170 part-time matriculated graduate/professional students (84 women). *Graduate faculty:* 13 full-time (4 women), 16 part-time/adjunct (4 women). *Tuition:* Part-time $216 per credit hour. Tuition and fees vary according to degree level. *Graduate housing:* Room and/or apartments available to single students; on-campus housing not available to married students. Typical cost: $6,150 (including board). *Student services:* Campus employment opportunities, campus safety program, career counseling, free psychological counseling, international student services, low-cost health insurance. *Library facilities:* Johnson & Wales University Library plus 2 others. *Online resources:* library catalog, web page, access to other libraries' catalogs. *Collection:* 85,523 titles, 1,921 serial subscriptions, 531 audiovisual materials. *Research affiliation:* Consortium of Rhode Island Academic and Research Libraries, Association of Institutional Research.

Computer facilities: 340 computers available on campus for general student use. A campuswide network can be accessed from student residence rooms and from off campus. Internet access is available. *Web address:* http://www.jwu.edu/.

General Application Contact: Dr. Allan G. Freedman, Director of Graduate Admissions, 401-598-1015, Fax: 401-598-4773, E-mail: clifb@jwu.edu.

GRADUATE UNITS

The Alan Shawn Feinstein Graduate School Students: 456 full-time (210 women), 170 part-time (84 women); includes 45 minority (21 African Americans, 12 Asian Americans or Pacific Islanders, 12 Hispanic Americans), 299 international. *Faculty:* 13 full-time (4 women), 16 part-time/adjunct (4 women). Expenses: Contact institution. *Financial support:* Career-related internships or fieldwork, institutionally sponsored loans, tuition waivers (partial), and unspecified assistantships available. Support available to part-time students. Financial award application deadline: 5/1. In 2001, 264 master's, 18 doctorates awarded. *Degree program information:* Part-time and evening/weekend programs available. Offers accounting (MBA); business administration (MAT); educational leadership (Ed D); food service (MAT); hospitality administration (MBA); international business (MBA); management (MBA). *Application deadline:* For fall admission, 8/21 (priority date). Applications are processed on a rolling basis. *Application fee:* $0. *Application Contact:* Dr. Allan G. Freedman, Director of Graduate Admissions, 401-598-1015, Fax: 401-598-4773, E-mail: clifb@jwu.edu. *Dean,* Dr. Joe Goldblatt, 401-598-4760, Fax: 401-598-1125.

See in-depth description on page 927.

JOHNSON BIBLE COLLEGE, Knoxville, TN 37998-1001

General Information Independent-religious, coed, comprehensive institution. *Enrollment:* 30 full-time matriculated graduate/professional students (21 women), 58 part-time matriculated graduate/professional students (16 women). *Enrollment by degree level:* 88 master's. *Graduate faculty:* 11 full-time (5 women), 15 part-time/adjunct (1 woman). *Tuition:* Full-time $2,250. Tuition and fees vary according to program. *Graduate housing:* Rooms and/or apartments available to single and married students. Typical cost: $3,800 (including board) for single students. Housing application deadline: 8/1. *Student services:* Campus employment opportunities, career counseling, child daycare facilities, free psychological counseling, low-cost health insurance. *Library facilities:* Glass Memorial Library plus 1 other. *Online resources:* library catalog, web page. *Collection:* 94,178 titles, 421 serial subscriptions, 11,542 audiovisual materials.

Computer facilities: 18 computers available on campus for general student use. A campuswide network can be accessed from student residence rooms and from off campus. *Web address:* http://www.jbc.edu/.

General Application Contact: Richard Beam, Vice President of Academics, 865-251-2358, Fax: 865-251-2337, E-mail: rbeam@jbc.edu.

GRADUATE UNITS

Department of Marriage and Family Therapy Students: 13 full-time (6 women), 5 part-time (2 women); includes 1 minority (Asian American or Pacific Islander) Average age 32. *Faculty:* 2 full-time (0 women), 3 part-time/adjunct (0 women). Expenses: Contact institution. *Financial support:* In 2001–02, 11 students received support. Scholarships/grants available. Financial award application deadline: 8/1; financial award applicants required to submit FAFSA. In 2001, 7 degrees awarded. Offers marriage and family therapy (MA). *Application deadline:* For fall admission, 4/15. *Application fee:* $50. *Chair,* Dr. Rick Townsend, 865-573-4517, Fax: 865-251-2337, E-mail: rtownsen@jbc.edu.

Program in Educational Technology Students: 6 full-time (all women), 11 part-time (8 women); includes 1 minority (African American), 1 international. Average age 41. 6 applicants, 100% accepted. *Faculty:* 2 full-time (1 woman), 5 part-time/adjunct (0 women). Expenses: Contact institution. *Financial support:* Career-related internships or fieldwork available. Support available to part-time students. Financial award application deadline: 5/1; financial award applicants required to submit FAFSA. In 2001, 2 degrees awarded. *Degree program information:* Part-time programs available. Postbaccalaureate distance learning degree programs offered (minimal on-campus study). Offers Bible and educational technology (MA). *Application deadline:* For winter admission, 9/1 (priority date). Applications are processed on a rolling basis. *Application fee:* $50. *Chairperson,* Dr. Chris Templar, 865-251-2348, Fax: 865-251-2337, E-mail: ctemplar@jbc.edu.

Program in Holistic Education Students: 9 full-time (all women), 2 part-time (both women). Average age 22. 13 applicants, 92% accepted, 12 enrolled. *Faculty:* 6 full-time (4 women), 3 part-time/adjunct (1 woman). Expenses: Contact institution. *Financial support:* Fellowships available. In 2001, 9 degrees awarded. Offers holistic education (MA). *Application deadline:* For fall admission, 5/1. *Application fee:* $0. *Chairperson,* Dr. Chris Templar, 865-251-2348, Fax: 865-251-2337, E-mail: ctemplar@jbc.edu.

Program in New Testament Students: 2 full-time, 40 part-time (4 women); includes 2 minority (both African Americans) Average age 38. *Faculty:* 1 full-time (0 women), 4 part-time/adjunct (0 women). Expenses: Contact institution. *Financial support:* Career-related internships or fieldwork, Federal Work-Study, and institutionally sponsored loans available. Financial award application deadline: 8/1. In 2001, 8 degrees awarded. *Degree program information:* Part-time and evening/weekend programs available. Postbaccalaureate distance learning degree programs offered (no on-campus study). Offers New Testament (MA). *Application deadline:* For fall admission, 6/1 (priority date); for spring admission, 11/15. *Application fee:* $50. *Director of Distance Learning,* Dr. John Ketchen, 800-669-7889, Fax: 865-251-2337, E-mail: jketchen@jbc.edu.

JOHNSON STATE COLLEGE, Johnson, VT 05656-9405

General Information State-supported, coed, comprehensive institution. *Enrollment:* 40 full-time matriculated graduate/professional students (28 women), 176 part-time matriculated graduate/professional students (135 women). *Enrollment by degree level:* 216 master's. *Graduate faculty:* 14 full-time (9 women), 8 part-time/adjunct (5 women). Tuition, state resident: part-time $184 per credit. Tuition, nonresident: part-time $430 per credit. *Required fees:* $18 per credit. $5 per term. *Graduate housing:* Rooms and/or apartments available on a first-come, first-served basis to single and married students. Housing application deadline: 8/1. *Student services:* Child daycare facilities, low-cost health insurance. *Library facilities:* Library and Learning Center. *Online resources:* library catalog, access to other libraries' catalogs. *Collection:* 100,053 titles, 522 serial subscriptions, 7,200 audiovisual materials.

Computer facilities: 131 computers available on campus for general student use. A campuswide network can be accessed from student residence rooms and from off campus. Internet access is available. *Web address:* http://www.jsc.vsc.edu/.

General Application Contact: Catherine H. Higley, Administrative Assistant for Graduate Programs, 800-635-2356 Ext. 5, Fax: 802-635-1248, E-mail: higleyc@badger.jsc.vsc.edu.

GRADUATE UNITS

Graduate Program in Education Students: 19 full-time (10 women), 102 part-time (74 women). *Faculty:* 6 full-time (4 women), 4 part-time/adjunct (2 women). Expenses: Contact institution. *Financial support:* Career-related internships or fieldwork, Federal Work-Study, institutionally sponsored loans, and unspecified assistantships available. Support available to part-time students. Financial award application deadline: 3/1; financial award applicants required to submit FAFSA. *Degree program information:* Part-time programs available. Offers children's mental health (MA Ed); curriculum and instruction (MA Ed); developmental disabilities (MA Ed); education (MA Ed); education of the gifted (MA Ed); reading education (MA Ed); special education (MA Ed). *Application deadline:* For fall admission, 7/15 (priority date); for spring admission, 11/1 (priority date). Applications are processed on a rolling basis. *Application fee:* $30. *Application Contact:* Catherine H. Higley, Administrative Assistant for Graduate Programs, 800-635-2356 Ext. 5, Fax: 802-635-1248, E-mail: higleyc@badger.jsc.vsc.edu.

Program in Counseling Students: 24 full-time (18 women), 38 part-time (34 women). *Faculty:* 5 full-time (3 women), 4 part-time/adjunct (3 women). Expenses: Contact institution. *Financial support:* Career-related internships or fieldwork, Federal Work-Study, and institutionally sponsored loans available. Financial award application deadline: 3/1; financial award applicants required to submit FAFSA. *Degree program information:* Part-time programs available. Offers counseling (MA). *Application deadline:* For fall admission, 4/1 (priority date); for spring admission, 11/1 (priority date). *Application fee:* $30. *Application Contact:* Catherine H. Higley, Administrative Assistant for Graduate Programs, 800-635-2356 Ext. 5, Fax: 802-635-1248, E-mail: higleyc@badger.jsc.vsc.edu.

Program in Fine Arts Students: 8 full-time (5 women), 17 part-time (12 women). *Faculty:* 3 full-time (2 women). Expenses: Contact institution. Offers drawing (MFA); painting (MFA); sculpture (MFA). *Application deadline:* For fall admission, 2/15. *Application fee:* $30. *Application Contact:* Catherine H. Higley, Administrative Assistant for Graduate Programs, 800-635-2356 Ext. 5, Fax: 802-635-1248, E-mail: higleyc@badger.jsc.vsc.edu.

JOINT MILITARY INTELLIGENCE COLLEGE, Washington, DC 20340-5100

General Information Federally supported, coed, graduate-only institution. *Graduate housing:* On-campus housing not available.

GRADUATE UNITS

School of Intelligence Studies *Degree program information:* Part-time and evening/weekend programs available. Offers intelligence studies (MSSI, Certificate). Open only to federal government employees.

JONES INTERNATIONAL UNIVERSITY, Englewood, CO 80112

General Information Independent, coed. *Graduate faculty:* 400. *Tuition:* Part-time $925 per course. *Graduate housing:* On-campus housing not available.

Computer facilities: Online class registration is available. *Web address:* http://www.jonesinternational.edu/.

General Application Contact: Lori Patik, Enrollment Counselor, 800-811-JONES (5663), Fax: 303-799-0966, E-mail: lpatik@international.edu.

GRADUATE UNITS

Education in e-Learning Offers e-learning (M Ed).

Graduate School of Business and e-Learning Postbaccalaureate distance learning degree programs offered (no on-campus study). Offers business communication (MA, MBA); electric commerce (MBA); entrepreneurship (MBA); global enterprise management (MBA); health care management (MBA); information technology management (MBA); negotiation and conflict management (MBA); project management (MBA). Program offered through the Internet only.

See in-depth description on page 929.

THE JUDGE ADVOCATE GENERAL'S SCHOOL, U.S. ARMY, Charlottesville, VA 22903-1781

General Information Federally supported, coed, primarily men, graduate-only institution. *Enrollment by degree level:* 86 master's. *Graduate faculty:* 36 full-time (7 women), 34 part-time/adjunct (5 women). *Graduate housing:* On-campus housing not available. *Student services:* Career counseling, exercise/wellness program, free psychological counseling, international student services, low-cost health insurance, multicultural affairs office, teacher training, writing training. *Library facilities:* TJAGSA Library plus 3 others. *Collection:* 7 million titles, 40,326 serial subscriptions, 89,000 audiovisual materials.

Computer facilities: 50 computers available on campus for general student use. A campuswide network can be accessed. Internet access is available.

General Application Contact: Col. Calvin Lewis, Deputy Comandant, 434-972-6303, Fax: 434-972-6338, E-mail: calvin.lewis@hqda.army.mil.

GRADUATE UNITS

Graduate Programs Offers military law (LL M). Only active duty military lawyers attend this school.

THE JUILLIARD SCHOOL, New York, NY 10023-6588

General Information Independent, coed, comprehensive institution. *Graduate housing:* Rooms and/or apartments available on a first-come, first-served basis to single students and available to married students. Housing application deadline: 5/1.

GRADUATE UNITS

Program in Music Offers music (MM, DMA, Adv C).

KANSAS STATE UNIVERSITY, Manhattan, KS 66506

General Information State-supported, coed, university. CGS member. *Enrollment:* 3,156 matriculated graduate/professional students. *Enrollment by degree level:* 333 first professional, 1,504 master's, 841 doctoral. *Graduate faculty:* 852. Tuition, state resident: part-time $113 per credit hour. Tuition, nonresident: part-time $358 per credit hour. *Graduate housing:* Rooms and/or apartments available to single students and available on a first-come, first-served basis to married students. Typical cost: $3,400 per year ($5,900 including board) for single students; $4,000 per year ($6,500 including board) for married students. Housing application deadline: 2/1. *Student services:* Campus employment opportunities, campus safety program, career counseling, child daycare facilities, disabled student services, exercise/wellness program, free psychological counseling, grant writing training, international student services, low-cost health insurance, multicultural affairs office, teacher training. *Library facilities:* Hale Library plus 3 others. *Online resources:* library catalog, web page, access to other libraries' catalogs. *Collection:* 1.5 million titles, 9,443 serial subscriptions, 3,899 audiovisual materials. *Research affiliation:* Chevron Corporation, U.S. Grain Marketing Research Laboratory, NASA-Research Center.

Computer facilities: 556 computers available on campus for general student use. A campuswide network can be accessed from student residence rooms and from off campus. Internet access and online class registration are available. *Web address:* http://www.ksu.edu/.

General Application Contact: Dr. James Guikema, Associate Dean, 785-532-7927, Fax: 785-532-2983, E-mail: guikema@gradresearch.grad.ksu.edu.

GRADUATE UNITS

College of Veterinary Medicine Students: 464. 23 applicants, 57% accepted, 13 enrolled. *Faculty:* 72. Expenses: Contact institution. *Financial support:* Research assistantships, teaching assistantships, Federal Work-Study, institutionally sponsored loans, and scholarships/grants available. Financial award application deadline: 3/1; financial award applicants required to submit FAFSA. In 2001, 6 master's, 5 doctorates awarded. Offers anatomy (MS); anatomy and physiology (MS, PhD); clinical sciences (MS); diagnostic medicine/pathobiology (MS, PhD); physiology (MS, PhD); veterinary medicine (DVM, MS, PhD); veterinary medicine and surgery (MS). *Application deadline:* For fall admission, 2/1 (priority date). Applications are processed on a rolling basis. *Application fee:* $0 ($25 for international students). Electronic applications accepted. *Application Contact:* Barbara Perry, Administrative Officer, 785-532-4005, Fax: 785-532-5884, E-mail: perry@vet.ksu.edu. *Dean,* Ralph Richardson, 785-532-4005, Fax: 785-532-5884, E-mail: dean@vet.ksu.edu.

Graduate School Students: 2,692. Average age 26. Expenses: Contact institution. *Financial support:* Fellowships, research assistantships, teaching assistantships, career-related internships or fieldwork, Federal Work-Study, institutionally sponsored loans, scholarships/grants, and tuition waivers (full and partial) available. Support available to part-time students. Financial award application deadline: 3/1; financial award applicants required to submit FAFSA. In 2001, 235 master's, 242 doctorates awarded. *Degree program information:* Part-time and evening/weekend programs available. Postbaccalaureate distance learning degree programs offered (minimal on-campus study). Offers food science (MS, PhD); genetics (MS, PhD). *Application deadline:* Applications are processed on a rolling basis. *Application fee:* $0 ($25 for international students). Electronic applications accepted. *Application Contact:* Dr. James Guikema, Associate Dean, 785-532-7927, Fax: 785-532-2983, E-mail: guikema@gradresearch.grad.ksu.edu. *Dean,* Ron Trewyn, 785-532-5110.

College of Agriculture Students: 342 full-time (108 women), 23 part-time (9 women); includes 11 minority (3 African Americans, 2 Asian Americans or Pacific Islanders, 4 Hispanic Americans, 2 Native Americans), 131 international. 202 applicants, 42% accepted, 61 enrolled. *Faculty:* 229 full-time (25 women). Expenses: Contact institution. *Financial support:* In 2001–02, 250 research assistantships, 18 teaching assistantships were awarded. Fellowships, career-related internships or fieldwork, Federal Work-Study, institutionally sponsored loans, scholarships/grants, and tuition waivers (partial) also available. Support available to part-time students. Financial award application deadline: 3/1; financial award applicants required to submit FAFSA. In 2001, 60 master's, 29 doctorates awarded. *Degree program information:* Part-time programs available. Postbaccalaureate distance learning degree programs offered (minimal on-campus study). Offers agricultural economics (MAB, MS, PhD); agriculture (MAB, MS, PhD); animal nutrition (MS, PhD); animal reproduction (MS, PhD); animal sciences and industry (MS, PhD); crop science (MS, PhD); entomology (MS, PhD); genetics (MS, PhD); grain science and industry (MS, PhD); horticulture (MS, PhD); meat science (MS, PhD); plant pathology (MS, PhD); range management (MS, PhD); soil science (MS, PhD); weed science (MS, PhD). *Application deadline:* For fall admission, 2/1; for spring admission, 10/1. *Application fee:* $0 ($25 for international students). Electronic applications accepted. *Dean,* Marc Johnson, 785-532-7137, Fax: 785-532-6563, E-mail: mjohnson@ksu.edu.

College of Architecture, Planning and Design Students: 51 full-time (21 women), 12 part-time (5 women); includes 2 minority (1 African American, 1 Hispanic American), 27 international. 104 applicants, 46% accepted, 23 enrolled. *Faculty:* 44 full-time (9 women). Expenses: Contact institution. *Financial support:* In 2001–02, 1 research assistantship (averaging $9,000 per year), 31 teaching assistantships with full tuition reimbursements (averaging $6,900 per year) were awarded. Fellowships, career-related internships or fieldwork, Federal Work-Study, institutionally sponsored loans, and scholarships/grants also available. Support available to part-time students. Financial award application deadline: 3/1; financial award applicants required to submit FAFSA. In 2001, 14 degrees awarded. *Degree program information:* Part-time and evening/weekend programs available. Postbaccalaureate distance learning degree programs offered (minimal on-campus study). Offers architecture (M Arch); architecture, planning and design (M Arch, MA, MLA, MRCP); environmental planning and management (MA); landscape architecture (MLA); regional and community planning (MRCP). *Application deadline:* For fall admission, 2/1; for spring admission, 10/1. Applications are processed on a rolling basis. *Application fee:* $30. Electronic applications accepted. *Dean,* Dennis Law, 785-532-5950, Fax: 785-532-6722, E-mail: dela@ksu.edu.

College of Arts and Sciences Students: 569 full-time (229 women), 90 part-time (38 women); includes 59 minority (16 African Americans, 22 Asian Americans or Pacific Islanders, 18 Hispanic Americans, 3 Native Americans), 182 international. 745 applicants, 48% accepted, 175 enrolled. *Faculty:* 376. Expenses: Contact institution. *Financial support:* In 2001–02, 1 fellowship, 147 research assistantships (averaging $10,722 per year), 263 teaching assistantships (averaging $9,022 per year) were awarded. Career-related internships or fieldwork, Federal Work-Study, institutionally sponsored loans, scholarships/grants, and tuition waivers also available. Support available to part-time students. Financial award application deadline: 3/1; financial award applicants required to submit FAFSA. In 2001, 124 master's, 46 doctorates awarded. *Degree program information:* Part-time programs available. Postbaccalaureate distance learning degree programs offered (minimal on-campus study). Offers analytical chemistry (MS); art (MFA); arts and sciences (MA, MFA, MM, MPA, MS, PhD); biochemistry (MS, PhD); cell biology (MS, PhD); chemistry (PhD); developmental biology and physiology (MS, PhD); economics (MA, PhD); English (MA); French (MA); geography (MA, PhD); geology (MS); German (MA); history (MA, PhD); inorganic chemistry (MS); international relations (MA); kinesiology (MS); mass communications (MS); mathematics (MS, PhD); microbiology and immunology (MS, PhD); molecular biology and genetics (MS, PhD); music education (MM); music history and literature (MM); organic chemistry (MS); performance (MM); performance with pedagogy emphasis (MM); physical chemistry (MS); physics (MS, PhD); political science (MA); psychology (MS, PhD); public administration (MPA); sociology (MA, PhD); Spanish (MA); speech (MA); statistics (MS, PhD); systematics and ecology (MS, PhD); theory and composition (MM); virology and oncology (MS, PhD). *Application deadline:* Applications are processed on a rolling basis. *Application fee:* $0 ($25 for international students). Electronic applications accepted. *Dean,* Peter Nicholls, 785-532-6900, Fax: 785-532-7004, E-mail: nicholls@ksu.edu.

College of Business Administration Students: 98 full-time (40 women), 19 part-time (8 women); includes 12 minority (7 African Americans, 4 Asian Americans or Pacific Islanders, 1 Hispanic American), 18 international. 114 applicants, 70% accepted, 56 enrolled. *Faculty:* 32 full-time (0 women). Expenses: Contact institution. *Financial support:* In 2001–02, 7 research assistantships with partial tuition reimbursements, 8 teaching assistantships with partial tuition reimbursements were awarded. Fellowships, Federal Work-Study, institutionally sponsored loans, and scholarships/grants also available. Support available to part-time students. Financial award application deadline: 3/1; financial award applicants required to submit FAFSA. In 2001, 73 degrees awarded. *Degree program information:* Part-time programs available. Offers accounting (M Acc); business administration (M Acc, MBA). *Application deadline:* For fall admission, 3/1; for spring admission, 9/1. Applications are processed on a rolling basis. *Application fee:* $45. *Application Contact:* Cynthia S. McCahon, Information Contact, 785-532-7227, Fax: 785-532-7024, E-mail: cmccahan@ksu.edu. *Interim Dean,* Yar M. Ebadi, 785-532-7227, Fax: 785-532-7024, E-mail: ebadi@ksu.edu.

College of Education Students: 631 (442 women); includes 64 minority (29 African Americans, 4 Asian Americans or Pacific Islanders, 29 Hispanic Americans, 2 Native Americans) 24 international. Average age 25. 158 applicants, 80% accepted, 78 enrolled. *Faculty:* 73. Expenses: Contact institution. *Financial support:* In 2001–02, 3 research assistantships, 16 teaching assistantships were awarded. Fellowships, career-related internships or fieldwork, Federal Work-Study, institutionally sponsored loans, and scholarships/grants also available. Support available to part-time students. Financial award application deadline: 3/1; financial award applicants required to submit FAFSA. In 2001, 190 master's, 30 doctorates awarded. *Degree program information:* Part-time and evening/weekend programs available. Postbaccalaureate distance learning degree programs offered. Offers counselor education (Ed D, PhD); curriculum and instruction (Ed D, PhD); education (MS, Ed D, PhD); educational administration and leadership (MS, Ed D); educational psychology (Ed D); elementary education (MS); foundations and adult education (MS, Ed D, PhD); school counseling (MS); secondary education (MS); student affairs in higher education (PhD); student personnel services (MS). *Application deadline:* Applications are processed on a rolling basis. *Application fee:* $0 ($25 for international students). Electronic applications accepted. *Application Contact:* Dr. Paul R. Burden, Assistant Dean, 785-532-5595, Fax: 785-532-7304, E-mail: burden@ksu.edu. *Dean,* Michael Holen, 785-532-5525, Fax: 785-532-7304, E-mail: mholen@ksu.edu.

College of Engineering Students: 332 full-time (82 women), 134 part-time (20 women); includes 9 minority (7 Asian Americans or Pacific Islanders, 2 Hispanic Americans), 310 international. 1,349 applicants, 31% accepted, 159 enrolled. *Faculty:* 134. Expenses: Contact institution. *Financial support:* In 2001–02, 160 research assistantships (averaging $12,476 per year), 52 teaching assistantships (averaging $12,555 per year) were awarded. Fellowships, career-related internships or fieldwork, Federal Work-Study, institutionally sponsored loans, and scholarships/grants also available. Support available to part-time students. Financial award application deadline: 3/1; financial award applicants required to submit FAFSA. In 2001, 93 master's, 18 doctorates awarded. *Degree program information:* Part-time programs available. Postbaccalaureate distance learning degree programs offered (minimal on-campus study). Offers architectural engineering (MS); bioengineering (MS, PhD); biological and agricultural engineering (MS, PhD); chemical engineering (MS, PhD); civil engineering (MS, PhD); communications (MS, PhD); computer engineering (MS, PhD); computer science (MS, PhD); control systems (MS, PhD); electric energy systems (MS, PhD); engineering (PhD); engineering management (MEM); industrial and manufacturing systems engineering (PhD); industrial engineering (MS); instrumentation (MS, PhD); mechanical engineering (MS); nuclear engineering (MS); operations research (MS); signal processing (MS, PhD); software engineering (MSE). *Application deadline:* Applications are processed on a rolling basis. *Application fee:* $0 ($25 for international students). Electronic applications accepted. *Application Contact:* Jan Rundquist, Secretary, 785-532-5846, Fax: 785-532-7810, E-mail: janr@ksu.edu. *Dean,* Terry S. King, 785-532-5590, Fax: 785-532-7810, E-mail: tsking@ksu.edu.

College of Human Ecology Students: 193 full-time (142 women), 119 part-time (85 women); includes 32 minority (19 African Americans, 4 Asian Americans or Pacific Islanders, 7 Hispanic Americans, 2 Native Americans), 79 international. 197 applicants, 66% accepted, 79 enrolled. *Faculty:* 55 full-time (37 women). Expenses: Contact institution. *Financial support:* In 2001–02, 1 fellowship with partial tuition reimbursement, 99 research assistantships with partial tuition reimbursements (averaging $9,000 per year), 30 teaching assistantships with partial tuition reimbursements (averaging $9,000 per year) were awarded. Career-related internships or fieldwork, Federal Work-Study, institutionally sponsored loans, scholarships/grants, and tuition waivers (full) also available. Support available to part-time students. Financial award application deadline: 3/1; financial award applicants required to submit FAFSA. In 2001, 46 master's, 13 doctorates awarded. *Degree program information:* Part-time programs available. Postbaccalaureate distance learning degree programs offered. Offers apparel and textiles (MS); dietetics (MS); family studies and human services (MS); food science (MS, PhD); food service and hospitality management (MS, PhD); human ecology (PhD); nutrition (MS, PhD). *Application deadline:* For fall admission, 2/1 (priority date); for spring admission, 10/1. *Application fee:* $0 ($25 for international students). Electronic applications accepted. *Application Contact:* Carol W. Shanklin, Graduate Program Director, 785-532-2206, Fax: 785-532-5522, E-mail: shanklin@humec.ksu.edu. *Dean,* Dr. Carol Kellett, 785-532-5500, Fax: 785-532-5504, E-mail: heinfo@ksu.edu.

Announcement: Kansas State University is a comprehensive, research, land-grant university offering innovative, interdisciplinary graduate programs and certificates that prepare graduates to be responsive to the needs of a rapidly changing world. Distance education opportunities are available for some of the programs. Check out the exciting opportunities for graduate study at www.ksu.edu/grad.

See in-depth description on page 931.

KANSAS WESLEYAN UNIVERSITY, Salina, KS 67401-6196

General Information Independent-religious, coed, comprehensive institution. *Enrollment:* 31 full-time matriculated graduate/professional students (13 women), 31 part-time matriculated graduate/professional students (18 women). *Enrollment by degree level:* 62 master's. *Graduate faculty:* 5 full-time (2 women), 1 part-time/adjunct (0 women). *Tuition:* Full-time $4,320; part-time $360 per credit hour. Tuition and fees vary according to course load. *Graduate housing:* Rooms and/or apartments available to single and married students. Typical cost: $4,400 (including board) for single students. *Student services:* Career counseling, exercise/wellness program, free psychological counseling, international student services, teacher training, writing training. *Library facilities:* Memorial Library. *Online resources:* library catalog, web page, access to other libraries' catalogs. *Collection:* 370 serial subscriptions, 1,055 audiovisual materials.

Computer facilities: 72 computers available on campus for general student use. A campuswide network can be accessed from student residence rooms and from off campus. Internet access is available. *Web address:* http://www.kwu.edu/.

General Application Contact: Tina Thayer, Director of Admissions, 785-827-5541 Ext. 1283, Fax: 785-827-0927.

GRADUATE UNITS

Program in Business Administration Students: 31 full-time (13 women), 31 part-time (18 women); includes 7 minority (4 African Americans, 2 Asian Americans or Pacific Islanders, 1 Hispanic American), 21 international. Average age 36. *Faculty:* 5 full-time (2 women), 1 part-time/adjunct (0 women). Expenses: Contact institution. *Financial support:* In 2001–02, 22 students received support. Applicants required to submit FAFSA. In 2001, 23 degrees awarded. *Degree program information:* Part-time and evening/weekend programs available. Offers business administration (MBA). *Application deadline:* For fall admission, 8/1 (priority date). Applications are processed on a rolling basis. *Application fee:* $30. *Application Contact:* Tina Thayer, Director of Admissions, 785-827-5541 Ext. 1283, Fax: 785-827-0927. *Director,* Dr. Carol Ahlvers, 785-827-5541, Fax: 785-827-0927, E-mail: mba@diamond.kwu.edu.

KEAN UNIVERSITY, Union, NJ 07083

General Information State-supported, coed, comprehensive institution. CGS member. *Enrollment:* 411 full-time matriculated graduate/professional students (295 women), 1,282 part-time matriculated graduate/professional students (958 women). *Enrollment by degree level:* 1,693 master's. *Graduate faculty:* 376 full-time (178 women), 555 part-time/adjunct. Tuition, state resident: full-time $7,372. Tuition, nonresident: full-time $9,004. *Required fees:* $1,006. *Graduate housing:* Room and/or apartments available on a first-come, first-served basis to single students; on-campus housing not available to married students. Typical cost: $4,838 per year ($6,038 including board). Housing application deadline: 6/15. *Student services:* Campus employment opportunities, campus safety program, career counseling, child daycare facilities, disabled student services, free psychological counseling, international student services, low-cost health insurance, multicultural affairs office, teacher training. *Library facilities:* Nancy Thompson Library plus 1 other. *Online resources:* library catalog, web page, access to other libraries' catalogs. *Collection:* 272,000 titles, 14,500 serial subscriptions. *Research affiliation:* University of Medicine and Dentistry of New Jersey, Montefiore Hospital, Beth Israel Hospital, J. F. Kennedy Hospital, Greenbrook Regional Center, Saint Barnabas Medical Center.

Computer facilities: 600 computers available on campus for general student use. A campuswide network can be accessed from student residence rooms and from off campus. Internet access and online class registration are available. *Web address:* http://www.kean.edu/.

General Application Contact: Joanne Morris, Director of Graduate Admissions, 908-527-2665, Fax: 908-527-2286, E-mail: grad_adm@kean.edu.

GRADUATE UNITS

College of Arts, Humanities and Social Sciences Students: 126 full-time (100 women), 193 part-time (129 women); includes 93 minority (41 African Americans, 9 Asian Americans or Pacific Islanders, 43 Hispanic Americans), 11 international. Average age 34. 370 applicants, 59% accepted. *Faculty:* 106 full-time (48 women), 162 part-time/adjunct. Expenses: Contact institution. *Financial support:* In 2001–02, 63 research assistantships with full tuition reimbursements (averaging $3,072 per year) were awarded; career-related internships or fieldwork, institutionally sponsored loans, scholarships/grants, and unspecified assistantships also available. In 2001, 106 master's, 12 other advanced degrees awarded. *Degree program information:* Part-time and evening/weekend programs available. Offers arts, humanities and social sciences (MA, MSW, Diploma, PMC); behavioral sciences (MA); business and industry counseling (PMC); educational psychology (MA); graphic communications (MA); liberal studies (MA); marriage and family therapy (Diploma); school psychology (Diploma); social work (MSW). *Application deadline:* For fall admission, 6/15; for spring admission, 11/15. *Application fee:* $35. *Application Contact:* Joanne Morris, Director of Graduate Admissions, 908-527-2665, Fax: 908-527-2286, E-mail: grad_adm@kean.edu. *Dean,* Dr. José Adames, 908-527-2034, Fax: 908-527-6254.

School of Visual and Performing Arts Students: 9 full-time (8 women), 30 part-time (all women); includes 5 minority (1 African American, 1 Asian American or Pacific Islander, 3 Hispanic Americans), 1 international. Average age 36. 9 applicants, 89% accepted. *Faculty:* 41 full-time (13 women), 32 part-time/adjunct. Expenses: Contact institution. *Financial support:* In 2001–02, 5 research assistantships with full tuition reimbursements (averaging $2,880 per year) were awarded; unspecified assistantships also available. In 2001, 13 degrees awarded. *Degree program information:* Part-time programs available. Offers fine arts education (MA). *Application deadline:* For fall admission, 6/15; for spring admission, 11/15. *Application fee:* $35. *Application Contact:* Joanne Morris, Director of Graduate Admissions, 908-527-2665, Fax: 908-527-2286, E-mail: grad_adm@kean.edu. *Coordinator,* Richard Buncamper, 908-527-2831, Fax: 908-527-2804.

College of Business and Public Administration Students: 117 full-time (64 women), 171 part-time (87 women); includes 121 minority (63 African Americans, 31 Asian Americans or Pacific Islanders, 27 Hispanic Americans), 67 international. Average age 32. 81 applicants, 68% accepted. *Faculty:* 70 full-time (26 women), 43 part-time/adjunct. Expenses: Contact institution. *Financial support:* In 2001–02, 57 research assistantships with full tuition reimbursements (averaging $2,880 per year) were awarded; career-related internships or fieldwork, institutionally sponsored loans, and unspecified assistantships also available. In 2001, 66 degrees awarded. *Degree program information:* Part-time and evening/weekend programs available. Offers health services administration (MPA); management systems analysis (MSMSA); public administration (MPA). *Application deadline:* For fall admission, 6/15; for spring admission, 11/15. *Application fee:* $35. Electronic applications accepted. *Application Contact:* Joanne Morris, Director of Graduate Admissions, 908-527-2665, Fax: 908-527-2286, E-mail: grad_adm@kean.edu. *Dean,* Dr. Charles Anderson, 908-527-2413, Fax: 908-354-2883.

College of Education Students: 139 full-time (112 women), 854 part-time (693 women); includes 172 minority (93 African Americans, 9 Asian Americans or Pacific Islanders, 69 Hispanic Americans, 1 Native American), 2 international. Average age 35. 303 applicants, 79% accepted. *Faculty:* 105 full-time (72 women), 164 part-time/adjunct. Expenses: Contact institution. *Financial support:* In 2001–02, 34 research assistantships with full tuition reimbursements (averaging $3,413 per year) were awarded; career-related internships or fieldwork and unspecified assistantships also available. In 2001, 277 degrees awarded. *Degree program information:* Part-time programs available. Offers administration in early childhood and family studies (MA); advanced curriculum and teaching (MA); alcohol and drug abuse counseling (MA); bilingual education (Certificate); bilingual/bicultural education (MA); business and industry counseling (MA, PMC); classroom instruction (MA); community/agency counseling (MA); counselor education (MA, PMC); developmental disabilities (MA); earth science (MA); education (MA, Certificate, PMC); education for family living (MA); educational administration (MA, Certificate); educational media specialist (MA); emotionally disturbed and socially maladjusted (MA); English as a second language (Certificate); exercise science (MA); instruction and curriculum (MA, Certificate); learning disabilities (MA); mathematics/science/computer education (MA); pre-school handicapped (MA); reading specialization (MA); school counseling (MA); special education (MA); speech pathology (MA); teaching (MA); teaching English as a second language (MA); teaching of reading (Certificate). *Application deadline:* For fall admission, 6/15; for spring admission, 11/15. *Application fee:* $35. Electronic applications accepted. *Application Contact:* Joanne Morris, Director of Graduate Admissions, 908-527-2665, Fax: 908-527-2286, E-mail: grad_adm@kean.edu. *Dean,* Dr. Ana Maria Schuhmann, 908-527-2136, Fax: 908-527-1808.

School of Natural, Applied and Health Sciences Students: 29 full-time (19 women), 64 part-time (49 women); includes 36 minority (14 African Americans, 16 Asian Americans or Pacific Islanders, 6 Hispanic Americans), 5 international. Average age 37. *Faculty:* 58 full-time (30 women), 81 part-time/adjunct. Expenses: Contact institution. *Financial support:* In 2001–02, 3 research assistantships with full tuition reimbursements (averaging $2,880 per year) were awarded; unspecified assistantships also available. In 2001, 25 degrees awarded. *Degree program information:* Part-time and evening/weekend programs available. Offers biotechnology (MS); computing, statistics and mathematics (MS); mathematics education (MA); natural, applied and health sciences (MA, MS, MSN); nursing (MSN); nursing and public administration); occupational therapy (MS). *Application deadline:* For fall admission, 6/15; for spring admission, 11/15. *Application fee:* $35. *Application Contact:* Joanne Morris, Director of Graduate Admissions, 908-527-2665, Fax: 908-527-2286, E-mail: grad_adm@kean.edu. *Dean,* Dr. Betty Barber, 908-527-2138.

See in-depth description on page 933.

KECK GRADUATE INSTITUTE OF APPLIED LIFE SCIENCES, Claremont, CA 91711

General Information Independent, coed, graduate-only institution. *Enrollment by degree level:* 58 master's. *Graduate faculty:* 12 full-time (3 women), 1 part-time/adjunct (0 women). *Tuition:* Full-time $28,800. *Graduate housing:* On-campus housing not available. *Student services:* Campus employment opportunities, campus safety program, career counseling, free psychological counseling, international student services, low-cost health insurance, multicultural affairs office. *Library facilities:* Honnold/Mudd Library plus 4 others. *Online resources:* library catalog, web page, access to other libraries' catalogs. *Collection:* 2.2 million titles, 5,592 serial subscriptions, 15,400 audiovisual materials. *Research affiliation:* Claremont Colleges Consortium.

Computer facilities: 60 computers available on campus for general student use. A campuswide network can be accessed from off campus. Internet access is available. *Web address:* http://www.kgi.edu/.

General Application Contact: John Friesman, Director of Admissions and Student Services, 909-607-8590, Fax: 909-607-8086, E-mail: admissions@kgi.edu.

GRADUATE UNITS

Program in Biosciences Students: 58 full-time (28 women). Average age 25. 130 applicants, 35% accepted. *Faculty:* 12 full-time (3 women), 1 part-time/adjunct (0 women). Expenses: Contact institution. *Financial support:* In 2001–02, 58 students received support, including 49 fellowships with full and partial tuition reimbursements available (averaging $7,000 per year); career-related internships or fieldwork, institutionally sponsored loans, scholarships/grants, and tuition waivers (full and partial) also available. Offers bioscience (MBS). *Application deadline:* For fall admission, 2/15 (priority date). Applications are processed on a rolling basis. *Application fee:* $60. Electronic applications accepted. *Application Contact:* John Friesman, Director of Admissions and Student Services, 909-607-8590, Fax: 909-607-8086, E-mail: admissions@kgi.edu. *President,* Henry E. Riggs, 909-607-7855, Fax: 909-607-8086.

KEENE STATE COLLEGE, Keene, NH 03435

General Information State-supported, coed, comprehensive institution. *Enrollment:* 36 full-time matriculated graduate/professional students (23 women), 86 part-time matriculated graduate/professional students (65 women). *Enrollment by degree level:* 122 master's. *Graduate faculty:* 13 full-time (6 women), 13 part-time/adjunct (11 women). Tuition, state resident: full-time $4,220; part-time $195 per credit. Tuition, nonresident: full-time $9,720; part-time $230 per credit. *Required fees:* $1,334; $54 per credit. *Graduate housing:* Rooms and/or apartments available on a first-come, first-served basis to single and married students. Typical cost: $5,726 (including board) for single students. Housing application deadline: 3/1. *Student services:* Campus employment opportunities, campus safety program, career counseling, child daycare facilities, disabled student services, free psychological counseling, international student services, low-cost health insurance. *Library facilities:* Mason Library. *Online resources:* library catalog, web page, access to other libraries' catalogs. *Collection:* 958 serial subscriptions.

Computer facilities: 285 computers available on campus for general student use. A campuswide network can be accessed from student residence rooms and from off campus. Internet access, e-mail, personal web pages are available. *Web address:* http://www.keene.edu/.

General Application Contact: Peggy Richmond, Director of Admissions, 603-358-2276, Fax: 603-358-2767, E-mail: admissions@keene.edu.

GRADUATE UNITS

Division of Graduate and Professional Studies Students: 36 full-time (23 women), 86 part-time (65 women); includes 2 minority (both Asian Americans or Pacific Islanders), 2 international. Average age 34. 75 applicants, 76% accepted, 46 enrolled. *Faculty:* 13 full-time (6 women), 13 part-time/adjunct (11 women). Expenses: Contact institution. *Financial support:* Research assistantships, career-related internships or fieldwork, Federal Work-Study, institutionally sponsored loans, and unspecified assistantships available. Support available to part-time students. Financial award application deadline: 3/1; financial award applicants required to submit FAFSA. In 2001, 32 degrees awarded. *Degree program information:* Part-time and evening/weekend programs available. Offers curriculum and instruction (M Ed); educational administration (M Ed); educational leadership (PMC); school counselor (M Ed, PMC); special education (M Ed, PMC). *Application deadline:* For fall admission, 6/15; for spring admission, 10/15. Applications are processed on a rolling basis. *Application fee:* $25 ($35 for international students). *Application Contact:* Peggy Richmond, Director of Admissions, 603-358-2276, Fax: 603-358-2767, E-mail: admissions@keene.edu. *Acting Dean,* Dr. David Hill, 603-358-2331, E-mail: dhill@keene.edu.

KEHILATH YAKOV RABBINICAL SEMINARY, Brooklyn, NY 11211-7207

General Information Independent-religious, men only, comprehensive institution.

KENNESAW STATE UNIVERSITY, Kennesaw, GA 30144-5591

General Information State-supported, coed, comprehensive institution. CGS member. *Enrollment:* 448 full-time matriculated graduate/professional students (252 women), 794 part-time matriculated graduate/professional students (408 women). *Enrollment by degree level:* 1,242 master's. *Graduate faculty:* 116 full-time (59 women), 17 part-time/adjunct (9 women). Tuition, state resident: part-time $97 per credit hour. Tuition, nonresident: part-time $387 per credit hour. *Required fees:* $178 per semester. *Graduate housing:* On-campus housing not available. *Student services:* Campus employment opportunities, campus safety program, career counseling, disabled student services, exercise/wellness program, free psychological counseling, international student services, low-cost health insurance, multicultural affairs office, teacher training, writing training. *Library facilities:* Horace W. Sturgis Library. *Online resources:* library catalog, web page, access to other libraries' catalogs. *Collection:* 565,000 titles, 3,500 serial subscriptions.

Computer facilities: 542 computers available on campus for general student use. A campuswide network can be accessed from off campus. Internet access and online class registration are available. *Web address:* http://www.kennesaw.edu/.

General Application Contact: Sinem Hamitoglu, Assistant Director of Graduate Admissions, 770-420-4377, Fax: 770-420-4435, E-mail: ksugrad@kennesaw.edu.

GRADUATE UNITS

College of Health and Human Services Students: 69 full-time (65 women), 7 part-time (6 women); includes 17 minority (15 African Americans, 1 Asian American or Pacific Islander, 1 Native American) Average age 34. 60 applicants, 88% accepted, 40 enrolled. *Faculty:* 11 full-time (8 women), 10 part-time/adjunct (7 women). Expenses: Contact institution. *Financial support:* In 2001–02, 2 research assistantships with full tuition reimbursements (averaging $15,000 per year) were awarded; Federal Work-Study also available. Support available to part-time students. Financial award application deadline: 6/15; financial award applicants required to submit FAFSA. In 2001, 36 degrees awarded. *Degree program information:* Part-time and evening/weekend programs available. Offers health and social service (MSN); primary care nurse practitioner (MSN). *Application deadline:* For fall admission, 7/7 (priority date); for spring admission, 10/20 (priority date). Applications are processed on a roll-

Kennesaw State University (continued)

ing basis. *Application fee:* $20. Electronic applications accepted. *Application Contact:* Sinem Hamitoglu, Assistant Director of Graduate Admissions, 770-420-4377, Fax: 770-420-4435, E-mail: ksugrad@kennesaw.edu. *Dean*, Dr. Richard Sowell, 770-423-6565, Fax: 770-423-6627, E-mail: rsowell@kennesaw.edu.

College of Humanities and Social Sciences Students: 64 full-time (43 women), 128 part-time (84 women); includes 45 minority (38 African Americans, 1 Asian American or Pacific Islander, 5 Hispanic Americans, 1 Native American), 3 international. Average age 34. 115 applicants, 62% accepted, 38 enrolled. *Faculty:* 16 full-time (7 women). Expenses: Contact institution. *Financial support:* In 2001–02, 2 research assistantships with full tuition reimbursements (averaging $15,000 per year) were awarded; Federal Work-Study also available. Support available to part-time students. Financial award application deadline: 6/15; financial award applicants required to submit FAFSA. In 2001, 28 degrees awarded. *Degree program information:* Part-time and evening/weekend programs available. Offers conflict management (MSCM); humanities and social sciences (MAPW, MPA, MSCM); professional writing (MAPW); public administration (MPA). *Application deadline:* For fall admission, 7/7 (priority date); for spring admission, 10/20 (priority date). Applications are processed on a rolling basis. *Application fee:* $20. Electronic applications accepted. *Application Contact:* Sinem Hamitoglu, Assistant Director of Graduate Admissions, 770-420-4377, Fax: 770-420-4435, E-mail: ksugrad@kennesaw.edu. *Dean*, Dr. Linda M. Noble, 770-423-6124, E-mail: lnoble@kennesaw.edu.

College of Science and Mathematics Students: 52 full-time (15 women), 75 part-time (21 women); includes 23 minority (12 African Americans, 9 Asian Americans or Pacific Islanders, 2 Hispanic Americans), 39 international. Average age 34. 90 applicants, 79% accepted, 36 enrolled. *Faculty:* 5 full-time (1 woman), 3 part-time/adjunct (1 woman). Expenses: Contact institution. *Financial support:* In 2001–02, 2 research assistantships with full tuition reimbursements (averaging $15,000 per year) were awarded In 2001, 13 degrees awarded. Offers information systems (MSIS); science and mathematics (MSIS). *Application deadline:* For fall admission, 7/7; for spring admission, 10/20. Applications are processed on a rolling basis. *Application fee:* $20. Electronic applications accepted. *Application Contact:* Sinem Hamitoglu, Assistant Director of Graduate Admissions, 770-420-4377, Fax: 770-420-4435, E-mail: ksugrad@kennesaw.edu. *Dean*, Dr. Laurence I. Peterson, 770-423-6160, Fax: 770-423-6530, E-mail: lpeterso@kennesaw.edu.

Leland and Clarice C. Bagwell College of Education Students: 24 full-time (23 women), 104 part-time (91 women). Average age 34. 131 applicants, 82% accepted, 30 enrolled. *Faculty:* 38 full-time (24 women), 2 part-time/adjunct (both women). Expenses: Contact institution. *Financial support:* Federal Work-Study available. Support available to part-time students. Financial award application deadline: 6/15; financial award applicants required to submit FAFSA. In 2001, 60 degrees awarded. *Degree program information:* Part-time programs available. Offers early childhood (M Ed); education (M Ed); middle grades (M Ed); special education (M Ed). *Application deadline:* For fall admission, 7/7 (priority date); for spring admission, 10/20 (priority date). *Application fee:* $20. Electronic applications accepted. *Application Contact:* Dawn Mann, Assistant Director of Graduate Admissions, 770-420-4377, Fax: 770-420-4435, E-mail: ksug@kennesaw.edu. *Dean*, Dr. Yiping Wan, 770-423-6117, Fax: 770-423-6567, E-mail: ywan@kennesaw.edu.

Michael J. Coles College of Business Students: 238 full-time (105 women), 486 part-time (205 women); includes 126 minority (89 African Americans, 19 Asian Americans or Pacific Islanders, 13 Hispanic Americans, 5 Native Americans), 63 international. Average age 34. 231 applicants, 82% accepted, 115 enrolled. *Faculty:* 51 full-time (14 women), 5 part-time/adjunct (0 women). Expenses: Contact institution. *Financial support:* Federal Work-Study available. Support available to part-time students. Financial award application deadline: 6/15; financial award applicants required to submit FAFSA. In 2001, 319 degrees awarded. *Degree program information:* Part-time and evening/weekend programs available. Offers accounting (M Acc, MBA); business (M Acc, MBA, MBA-EP, MBA-PE); business administration (MBA, MBA-EP, MBA-PE); business information systems management (MBA); entrepreneurship (MBA); finance (MBA); human resources management and development (MBA); marketing (MBA). *Application deadline:* For fall admission, 7/7 (priority date); for spring admission, 10/20 (priority date). Applications are processed on a rolling basis. *Application fee:* $20. Electronic applications accepted. *Application Contact:* Dawn Mann, Assistant Director of Graduate Admissions, 770-420-4377, Fax: 770-420-4435, E-mail: ksug@kennesaw.edu. *Dean*, Dr. Timothy Mescon, 770-423-6425, Fax: 770-423-6141, E-mail: tmescon@coles2.kennesaw.edu.

KENRICK-GLENNON SEMINARY, St. Louis, MO 63119-4330

General Information Independent-religious, men only, graduate-only institution. *Enrollment by degree level:* 77 first professional. *Graduate faculty:* 16 full-time (3 women), 9 part-time/adjunct (2 women). *Tuition:* Full-time $11,674. *Required fees:* $200. *Graduate housing:* Room and/or apartments available to single students; on-campus housing not available to married students. Typical cost: $5,454 (including board). *Student services:* Free psychological counseling, writing training. *Library facilities:* Charles L. Souvay Memorial Library. *Online resources:* library catalog, access to other libraries' catalogs. *Collection:* 70,518 titles, 290 serial subscriptions.

Computer facilities: 7 computers available on campus for general student use. A campuswide network can be accessed from student residence rooms and from off campus. Internet access is available. *Web address:* http://www.kenrick.edu/.

General Application Contact: Rev. Lawrence C. Brennan, Academic Dean, 314-792-6109, Fax: 314-792-6500, E-mail: revbrennan@kenrick.edu.

GRADUATE UNITS

Graduate and Professional Programs Students: 77 full-time (0 women); includes 8 minority (6 African Americans, 2 Asian Americans or Pacific Islanders), 2 international. Average age 28. 26 applicants, 100% accepted. *Faculty:* 16 full-time (3 women), 9 part-time/adjunct (2 women). Expenses: Contact institution. *Financial support:* In 2001–02, 8 students received support. Applicants required to submit FAFSA. In 2001, 9 first professional degrees, 4 master's awarded. Offers theology (M Div, MA, Certificate). *Application deadline:* For fall admission, 8/1 (priority date). *Application Contact:* Kathleen M. Raterman, Registrar, 314-792-6111, Fax: 314-792-6500, E-mail: raterman@kenrick.edu. *Academic Dean*, Rev. Lawrence C. Brennan, 314-792-6109, Fax: 314-792-6500, E-mail: revbrennan@kenrick.edu.

KENT STATE UNIVERSITY, Kent, OH 44242-0001

General Information State-supported, coed, university. CGS member. *Graduate housing:* Rooms and/or apartments available on a first-come, first-served basis to single students and available to married students.

GRADUATE UNITS

College of Arts and Sciences *Degree program information:* Part-time programs available. Offers American politics (MA, PhD); analytical chemistry (MS, PhD); anthropology (MA); applied mathematics (MA, MS, PhD); arts and sciences (MA, MLS, MPA, MS, PhD); biochemistry (PhD); botany (MA, MS, PhD); chemical physics (MS, PhD); chemistry (MA, MS, PhD); clinical psychology (MA, PhD); comparative politics (MA); computer science (MA, MS, PhD); ecology (MS, PhD); English (MA, PhD); experimental psychology (MA, PhD); French (MA); geography (MA, PhD); geology (MS, PhD); German (MA); history (MA, PhD); inorganic chemistry (MS, PhD); international politics (PhD); international relations (MA); justice studies (MA); Latin (MA); liberal studies (MLS); organic chemistry (MS, PhD); philosophy (MA); physical chemistry (MS, PhD); physics (MA, MS, PhD); physiology (MS, PhD); political theory (MA, PhD); public administration (MPA); pure mathematics (MA, MS, PhD); sociology (MA, PhD); Spanish (MA); zoology (MA, PhD). Electronic applications accepted.

College of Fine and Professional Arts Offers fine and professional arts (M Arch, MA, MFA, MLS, MM, MPH, MS, PhD). Electronic applications accepted.

Hugh A. Glauser School of Music Offers composition (MA); conducting (MM); ethnomusicology (MA, PhD); music education (MM, PhD); musicology (MA, PhD); performance (MM); piano pedagogy (MM); theory (MA); theory and composition (PhD). Electronic applications accepted.

School of Architecture and Environmental Design Offers architecture (M Arch). Electronic applications accepted.

School of Art Offers art (MA, MFA); art education (MA); fiber arts (MA, MFA); visual communication design (MA, MFA). Electronic applications accepted.

School of Communication Studies Offers communication studies (MA, PhD). Electronic applications accepted.

School of Exercise, Leisure and Sport Offers exercise physiology (PhD); physical education (MA). Electronic applications accepted.

School of Family and Consumer Studies Offers child and family relations (MA); nutrition (MS). Electronic applications accepted.

School of Journalism and Mass Communication Offers journalism and mass communication (MA). Electronic applications accepted.

School of Library and Information Science Offers library and information science (MLS, MS).

School of Public Health *Degree program information:* Part-time programs available. Offers public health (MPH).

School of Speech Pathology and Audiology Offers speech pathology and audiology (MA, PhD). Electronic applications accepted.

School of Theatre and Dance Offers theatre (MA, MFA). Electronic applications accepted.

College of Nursing Offers clinical nursing (MSN); nursing administration (MSN); nursing education (MSN); parent-child nursing (MSN).

Graduate School of Education Students: 556 full-time (439 women), 617 part-time (482 women); includes 122 minority (100 African Americans, 10 Asian Americans or Pacific Islanders, 11 Hispanic Americans, 1 Native American), 56 international. 253 applicants, 74% accepted, 165 enrolled. *Faculty:* 94 full-time (49 women), 112 part-time/adjunct (72 women). Expenses: Contact institution. *Financial support:* In 2001–02, 59 fellowships with full tuition reimbursements (averaging $9,500 per year), 17 research assistantships with full tuition reimbursements, 39 teaching assistantships with full tuition reimbursements were awarded. Career-related internships or fieldwork, Federal Work-Study, institutionally sponsored loans, scholarships/grants, health care benefits, and unspecified assistantships also available. Support available to part-time students. Financial award application deadline: 4/1. In 2001, 361 master's, 34 doctorates, 25 other advanced degrees awarded. *Degree program information:* Part-time and evening/weekend programs available. Offers community counseling (M Ed, MA); counseling and human development services (PhD); cultural foundations (M Ed, MA, PhD); curriculum and instruction (M Ed, MA, PhD, Ed S); early childhood education (M Ed, MA, MAT); early childhood intervention (M Ed, MA); education (M Ed, MA, MAT, PhD, Ed S); educational administration (M Ed, MA, PhD, Ed S); educational foundations (M Ed, MA, PhD); educational psychology (M Ed, MA, PhD); evaluation and measurement (M Ed, MA, PhD); gifted education (M Ed, MA); health and safety education (PhD); health education and promotion (M Ed, MA); hearing impaired education (M Ed, MA); higher education administration and student personnel (M Ed, MA, PhD, Ed S); instructional technology (M Ed, MA, PhD); K–12 leadership (M Ed, MA, PhD, Ed S); learning and development (M Ed, MA); middle childhood education (M Ed, MA); mild/moderate (M Ed, MA); moderate/intensive (M Ed, MA); reading (M Ed, MA); rehabilitation counseling (M Ed, MA, Ed S); school counseling (M Ed, MA); school psychology (M Ed, PhD, Ed S); secondary education (M Ed, MA, MAT); special education (M Ed, MA, PhD, Ed S); vocational and technical education (M Ed, MA, Ed S); vocational education (M Ed, MA, Ed S). *Application deadline:* Applications are processed on a rolling basis. *Application fee:* $30. Electronic applications accepted. *Application Contact:* Deborah Barber, Director, Office of Academic Services, 330-672-2862, Fax: 330-672-3549, E-mail: oas@educ.kent.edu. *Dean*, Dr. Joanne R. Schwartz, 330-672-2808, Fax: 330-672-3407, E-mail: jrschwar@kent.edu.

Graduate School of Management Students: 185 full-time (77 women), 276 part-time (102 women); includes 23 minority (15 African Americans, 6 Asian Americans or Pacific Islanders, 2 Hispanic Americans), 71 international. Average age 27. 305 applicants, 72% accepted, 155 enrolled. *Faculty:* 54 full-time (14 women), 4 part-time/adjunct (2 women). Expenses: Contact institution. *Financial support:* In 2001–02, 94 students received support, including 74 research assistantships with full tuition reimbursements available (averaging $4,875 per year), 32 teaching assistantships with full tuition reimbursements available (averaging $12,000 per year); fellowships with full tuition reimbursements available, career-related internships or fieldwork, Federal Work-Study, scholarships/grants, and tuition waivers (full) also available. Financial award applicants required to submit FAFSA. In 2001, 144 master's, 7 doctorates awarded. *Degree program information:* Part-time and evening/weekend programs available. Offers accounting (MS, PhD); business administration (MBA); economics (MA); finance (PhD); financial engineering (MSFE); management (MA, MBA, MS, MSFE, PhD); management systems (PhD); marketing (PhD). *Application deadline:* Applications are processed on a rolling basis. *Application fee:* $30. Electronic applications accepted. *Application Contact:* Louise M. Ditchey, Director, 330-672-2282, Fax: 330-672-7303, E-mail: gradbus@bsa3.kent.edu. *Associate Dean*, Dr. Frederick W. Schroath, 330-672-2282, Fax: 330-672-7303, E-mail: fschroat@bsa3.kent.edu.

School of Biomedical Sciences Students: 74 full-time (40 women), 16 part-time (8 women). 124 applicants, 40% accepted. *Faculty:* 66 full-time (13 women). Expenses: Contact institution. *Financial support:* In 2001–02, 76 students received support, including 63 teaching assistantships; fellowships, research assistantships, Federal Work-Study, institutionally sponsored loans, scholarships/grants, and tuition waivers (full) also available. Financial award application deadline: 2/1. In 2001, 6 master's, 11 doctorates awarded. Offers biological anthropology (PhD); biomedical sciences (MS, PhD); cellular and molecular biology (MS, PhD); neuroscience (MS, PhD); pharmacology (MS, PhD); physiology (MS, PhD). Offered in cooperation with Northeastern Ohio Universities College of Medicine. *Application deadline:* For fall admission, 6/1. Applications are processed on a rolling basis. *Application fee:* $30. *Director*, Dr. James L. Blank, 330-672-2263, Fax: 330-672-9391, E-mail: jimb@biology.kent.edu.

School of Technology Offers technology (MA).

KENTUCKY CHRISTIAN COLLEGE, Grayson, KY 41143-2205

General Information Independent-religious, coed, comprehensive institution.

KENTUCKY STATE UNIVERSITY, Frankfort, KY 40601

General Information State-related, coed, comprehensive institution. *Graduate housing:* Room and/or apartments available on a first-come, first-served basis to single students; on-campus housing not available to married students. Housing application deadline: 7/15.

GRADUATE UNITS

College of Arts and Sciences *Degree program information:* Part-time programs available. Offers aquaculture (MS).

School of Public Administration *Degree program information:* Part-time and evening/weekend programs available. Offers public administration (MPA).

KETTERING UNIVERSITY, Flint, MI 48504-4898

General Information Independent, coed, comprehensive institution. *Enrollment:* 9 full-time matriculated graduate/professional students (2 women), 684 part-time matriculated graduate/professional students (187 women). *Enrollment by degree level:* 693 master's. *Graduate faculty:* 35 full-time (5 women). *Tuition:* Full-time $8,370; part-time $465 per credit. *Graduate housing:* Room and/or apartments available on a first-come, first-served basis to single students; on-campus housing not available to married students. Typical cost: $2,500 per year ($4,200 including board). Housing application deadline: 7/15. *Student services:* Campus employment opportunities, disabled student services, exercise/wellness program, free psychological counseling, international student services, low-cost health insurance, multicultural affairs office. *Library facilities:* Kettering University Library plus 1 other. *Online resources:* library catalog, web page, access to other libraries' catalogs. *Collection:* 100,339 titles, 1,011 serial subscriptions, 778 audiovisual materials.

Computer facilities: 300 computers available on campus for general student use. A campuswide network can be accessed from student residence rooms and from off campus. Internet access and online class registration are available. *Web address:* http://www.kettering.edu/.

General Application Contact: Mary Sue Morris, Secretary, Graduate Students and Extension Services, 810-762-7953, Fax: 810-762-9935, E-mail: mmorris@kettering.edu.

GRADUATE UNITS

Graduate School Students: 9 full-time (2 women), 684 part-time (187 women); includes 88 minority (63 African Americans, 13 Asian Americans or Pacific Islanders, 11 Hispanic Americans, 1 Native American), 55 international. 437 applicants, 72% accepted. *Faculty:* 35 full-time (5 women). Expenses: Contact institution. *Financial support:* Fellowships with full tuition reimbursements, research assistantships with full tuition reimbursements, teaching assistantships with full tuition reimbursements, Federal Work-Study, scholarships/grants, and tuition waivers (partial) available. Support available to part-time students. Financial award application deadline: 7/15; financial award applicants required to submit CSS PROFILE or FAFSA. In 2001, 194 degrees awarded. *Degree program information:* Part-time and evening/weekend programs available. Postbaccalaureate distance learning degree programs offered (no on-campus study). Offers automotive systems (MS Eng); manufacturing (MS Eng); manufacturing management (MSMM, MSMO); manufacturing systems engineering (MS Eng); mechanical cognate (MS Eng); mechanical design (MS Eng); operations management (MSOM). *Application deadline:* For fall admission, 7/15. Applications are processed on a rolling basis. *Application fee:* $0. Electronic applications accepted. *Application Contact:* Betty L. Bedore, Coordinator of Publicity, 810-762-7494, Fax: 810-762-9935, E-mail: bbedore@kettering.edu. *Dean, Graduate Studies,* Dr. Tony Hain, 810-762-9616, Fax: 810-762-9935, E-mail: thain@kettering.edu.

KEUKA COLLEGE, Keuka Park, NY 14478-0098

General Information Independent-religious, coed, comprehensive institution.

GRADUATE UNITS

Office of Graduate Education

KING COLLEGE, Bristol, TN 37620-2699

General Information Independent-religious, coed, comprehensive institution.

GRADUATE UNITS

School of Business and Economics

KING'S COLLEGE, Wilkes-Barre, PA 18711-0801

General Information Independent-religious, coed, comprehensive institution. *Enrollment:* 56 full-time matriculated graduate/professional students (44 women), 102 part-time matriculated graduate/professional students (71 women). *Enrollment by degree level:* 158 master's. *Graduate faculty:* 20 full-time (10 women), 2 part-time/adjunct (1 woman). *Tuition:* Full-time $20,850; part-time $512 per credit. *Required fees:* $730. *Graduate housing:* On-campus housing not available. *Student services:* Career counseling, free psychological counseling, multicultural affairs office. *Library facilities:* D. Leonard Corgan Library. *Online resources:* library catalog, web page. *Collection:* 163,239 titles, 839 serial subscriptions, 4,740 audiovisual materials.

Computer facilities: 273 computers available on campus for general student use. A campuswide network can be accessed from student residence rooms and from off campus. Internet access is available. *Web address:* http://www.kings.edu/.

General Application Contact: Dr. Elizabeth S. Lott, Director of Graduate Programs, 570-208-5991, Fax: 570-825-9049, E-mail: eslott@kings.edu.

GRADUATE UNITS

College of Arts and Sciences Students: 56 full-time (44 women), 41 part-time (38 women); includes 7 minority (3 African Americans, 3 Asian Americans or Pacific Islanders, 1 Hispanic American) Average age 29. *Faculty:* 12 full-time (8 women), 1 (woman) part-time/adjunct. Expenses: Contact institution. In 2001, 15 degrees awarded. *Degree program information:* Part-time and evening/weekend programs available. Offers physician assistant studies (MSPAS); reading (M Ed). *Application deadline:* For fall admission, 12/15 (priority date). Applications are processed on a rolling basis. *Application fee:* $35. *Application Contact:* Dr. Elizabeth S. Lott, Director of Graduate Programs, 570-208-5991, Fax: 570-825-9049, E-mail: eslott@kings.edu. *Head,* 570-208-5901, Fax: 570-825-9049.

William G. McGowan School of Business Average age 35. *Faculty:* 8 full-time (2 women), 1 part-time/adjunct (0 women). Expenses: Contact institution. In 2001, 21 degrees awarded. *Degree program information:* Part-time and evening/weekend programs available. Offers finance (MS); health care administration (MS). *Application deadline:* For fall admission, 7/31 (priority date); for spring admission, 12/1 (priority date). Applications are processed on a rolling basis. *Application fee:* $35. *Application Contact:* Dr. Elizabeth S. Lott, Director of Graduate Programs, 570-208-5991, Fax: 570-825-9049, E-mail: eslott@kings.edu. *Director,* Dr. David Martin, 570-208-5932, Fax: 570-826-5989, E-mail: dgmartin@kings.edu.

KIRKSVILLE COLLEGE OF OSTEOPATHIC MEDICINE, Kirksville, MO 63501

General Information Independent, coed, graduate-only institution. *Enrollment by degree level:* 625 first professional, 313 master's, 202 doctoral. *Graduate faculty:* 118 full-time (36 women), 126 part-time/adjunct (61 women). *Tuition:* Full-time $24,950. *Required fees:* $690. *Graduate housing:* Rooms and/or apartments available on a first-come, first-served basis to single and married students. Typical cost: $4,140 per year for single students; $4,620 per year for married students. Housing application deadline: 4/1. *Student services:* Campus employment opportunities, career counseling, disabled student services, exercise/wellness program, free psychological counseling. *Library facilities:* A. T. Still Memorial Library. *Online resources:* library catalog, web page, access to other libraries' catalogs. *Collection:* 88,027 titles, 752 serial subscriptions, 4,606 audiovisual materials. *Research affiliation:* Robert Wood Johnson Pharmaceutical Research Foundation, Texas A&M Research Foundation.

Computer facilities: 35 computers available on campus for general student use. A campuswide network can be accessed from student residence rooms and from off campus. Internet access is available. *Web address:* http://www.kcom.edu/.

General Application Contact: Lori A. Haxton, Assistant Dean for Student Affairs/Director of Admissions, 660-626-2237, Fax: 660-626-2969, E-mail: admissions@kcom.edu.

GRADUATE UNITS

Arizona School of Health Sciences Students: 313 full-time (213 women), 189 part-time (141 women); includes 60 minority (12 African Americans, 27 Asian Americans or Pacific Islanders, 15 Hispanic Americans, 6 Native Americans), 2 international. Average age 32. 735 applicants, 43% accepted. *Faculty:* 34 full-time (19 women), 50 part-time/adjunct (25 women). Expenses: Contact institution. *Financial support:* In 2001–02, 314 students received support. Federal Work-Study available. Financial award application deadline: 6/1; financial award applicants required to submit FAFSA. In 2001, 91 master's, 191 doctorates awarded. Postbaccalaureate distance learning degree programs offered (no on-campus study). Offers audiology (Au D); medical informatics (MS); occupational therapy (MS); physical therapy (MS, DPT); physician assistant (MS); sports health care (MS). *Application deadline:* For fall admission, 2/1 (priority date). Applications are processed on a rolling basis. *Application fee:* $50. *Application Contact:* Lori A. Haxton, Assistant Dean for Student Affairs/Director of Admissions, 660-626-2237, Fax: 660-626-2969, E-mail: admissions@kcom.edu. *Provost,* Dr. Craig Phelps, 480-219-6000, Fax: 480-219-6110, E-mail: cphelps@ashs.edu.

Professional Program in Osteopathic Medicine Students: 625 full-time (180 women); includes 93 minority (4 African Americans, 84 Asian Americans or Pacific Islanders, 3 Hispanic Americans, 2 Native Americans), 3 international. Average age 26. 2,558 applicants, 6% accepted. *Faculty:* 72 full-time (14 women), 60 part-time/adjunct (32 women). Expenses: Contact institution. *Financial support:* In 2001–02, 535 students received support, including 5 fellowships (averaging $4,500 per year); career-related internships or fieldwork, Federal Work-Study, institutionally sponsored loans, scholarships/grants, and tuition waivers (full) also available. Financial award application deadline: 5/1; financial award applicants required to submit FAFSA. In 2001, 139 degrees awarded. Offers osteopathic medicine (DO). *Application deadline:* For fall admission, 2/1. Applications are processed on a rolling basis. *Application fee:* $50. *Application Contact:* Lori A. Haxton, Assistant Dean for Student Affairs/Director of Admissions, 660-626-2237, Fax: 660-626-2969, E-mail: admissions@kcom.edu. *President,* Dr. James J. McGovern, 660-626-2391, Fax: 660-626-2672, E-mail: jmcgovern@kcom.edu.

Program in Biomedical Sciences Students: 2 full-time (1 woman), 1 part-time. Average age 33. 3 applicants, 100% accepted. *Faculty:* 9 full-time (3 women). Expenses: Contact institution. *Financial support:* Fellowships, research assistantships, teaching assistantships, Federal Work-Study available. Financial award application deadline: 6/1; financial award applicants required to submit FAFSA. Offers biomedical sciences (MS). *Application deadline:* For fall admission, 6/1 (priority date); for winter admission, 10/1 (priority date); for spring admission, 1/1 (priority date). Applications are processed on a rolling basis. *Application fee:* $50. *Application Contact:* Lori A. Haxton, Assistant Dean for Student Affairs/Director of Admissions, 660-626-2237, Fax: 660-626-2969, E-mail: admissions@kcom.edu. *President,* Dr. James J. McGovern, 660-626-2391, Fax: 660-626-2672, E-mail: jmcgovern@kcom.edu.

School of Health Management Average age 30. 12 applicants, 83% accepted. *Faculty:* 3 full-time (0 women), 16 part-time/adjunct (4 women). Expenses: Contact institution. *Financial support:* Application deadline: 6/1; *Degree program information:* Part-time and evening/weekend programs available. Postbaccalaureate distance learning degree programs offered (no on-campus study). Offers geriatric health management (MGH); health administration (MHA); medical office management (Certificate); public health (MPH). *Application deadline:* For fall admission, 7/31 (priority date); for winter admission, 10/30 (priority date); for spring admission, 2/5 (priority date). *Application fee:* $50. *Application Contact:* Lori A. Haxton, Assistant Dean for Student Affairs/Director of Admissions, 660-626-2237, Fax: 660-626-2969, E-mail: admissions@kcom.edu. *Dean,* Dr. D. Kent Mulford, 660-626-2820, Fax: 660-626-2826, E-mail: shm@shm-kcom.edu.

KNOWLEDGE SYSTEMS INSTITUTE, Skokie, IL 60076

General Information Independent, coed, graduate-only institution. *Enrollment by degree level:* 96 master's. *Graduate faculty:* 5 full-time (0 women), 14 part-time/adjunct (4 women). *Tuition:* Full-time $5,670; part-time $315 per credit. *Required fees:* $30; $5 per course. $50 per term. One-time fee: $5. *Graduate housing:* Rooms and/or apartments available on a first-come, first-served basis to single and married students. *Student services:* Campus employment opportunities, career counseling, international student services, low-cost health insurance, writing training. *Library facilities:* Knowledge Systems Institute Library. *Online resources:* library catalog, web page. *Collection:* 2,900 titles, 2,100 serial subscriptions.

Computer facilities: 90 computers available on campus for general student use. A campuswide network can be accessed from student residence rooms and from off campus. Internet access is available. *Web address:* http://www.ksi.edu/.

General Application Contact: Judy Pan, Executive Director, 847-679-3135, Fax: 847-679-3166, E-mail: office@ksi.edu.

GRADUATE UNITS

Program in Computer and Information Sciences Students: 69 full-time (21 women), 27 part-time (7 women); includes 15 minority (4 African Americans, 10 Asian Americans or Pacific Islanders, 1 Hispanic American), 62 international. Average age 28. 59 applicants, 93% accepted. *Faculty:* 5 full-time (0 women), 14 part-time/adjunct (4 women). Expenses: Contact institution. *Financial support:* In 2001–02, 15 students received support. Federal Work-Study available. Financial award applicants required to submit FAFSA. In 2001, 14 degrees awarded. *Degree program information:* Part-time and evening/weekend programs available. Postbaccalaureate distance learning degree programs offered (minimal on-campus study). Offers computer and information sciences (MS). *Application deadline:* Applications are processed on a rolling basis. *Application fee:* $40. Electronic applications accepted. *Application Contact:* Margaret M. Price, Office Manager, 847-679-3135, Fax: 847-679-3166, E-mail: mprice@ksi.edu. *Executive Director,* Judy Pan, 847-679-3135, Fax: 847-679-3166, E-mail: office@ksi.edu.

KNOX COLLEGE, Toronto, ON M5S 2E6, Canada

General Information Independent-religious, coed, graduate-only institution. *Graduate housing:* Room and/or apartments available on a first-come, first-served basis to single students; on-campus housing not available to married students. Housing application deadline: 5/31.

GRADUATE UNITS

College of Theology *Degree program information:* Part-time programs available. Offers theology (M Div, Th M, D Min, Th D). Applicants for D Min, Th M, and Th D must apply to Toronto School of Theology.

KOL YAAKOV TORAH CENTER, Monsey, NY 10952-2954

General Information Independent-religious, men only, comprehensive institution. *Graduate housing:* Room and/or apartments available to single students; on-campus housing not available to married students.

GRADUATE UNITS

Graduate Program *Degree program information:* Part-time and evening/weekend programs available.

KUTZTOWN UNIVERSITY OF PENNSYLVANIA, Kutztown, PA 19530-0730

General Information State-supported, coed, comprehensive institution. CGS member. *Enrollment:* 185 full-time matriculated graduate/professional students (124 women), 790 part-time matriculated graduate/professional students (587 women). *Enrollment by degree level:* 753 master's, 222 other advanced degrees. *Graduate faculty:* 7 full-time (6 women), 99 part-time/adjunct (37 women). Tuition, state resident: full-time $4,600; part-time $256 per credit. Tuition, nonresident: full-time $7,554; part-time $420 per credit. *Required fees:* $835. *Graduate housing:* On-campus housing not available. *Student services:* Campus employment opportunities, career counseling, child daycare facilities, disabled student services, exercise/wellness program, free psychological counseling, international student services, low-cost health insurance, multicultural affairs office. *Library facilities:* Rohrbach Library. *Online resources:* library catalog, web page. *Collection:* 492,117 titles, 1,308 serial subscriptions, 15,981 audiovisual materials.

Computer facilities: 650 computers available on campus for general student use. A campuswide network can be accessed from student residence rooms and from off campus. Internet access is available. *Web address:* http://www.kutztown.edu/.

General Application Contact: Dr. Charles Cullum, Dean of Graduate Studies and Extended Learning, 610-683-4201, Fax: 610-683-1393, E-mail: ccullum@kutztown.edu.

GRADUATE UNITS

College of Graduate Studies and Extended Learning Students: 185 full-time (124 women), 790 part-time (587 women); includes 89 minority (62 African Americans, 6 Asian Americans or Pacific Islanders, 19 Hispanic Americans, 2 Native Americans), 35 international. Average age 32. *Faculty:* 7 full-time (6 women), 99 part-time/adjunct (37 women). Expenses: Contact institution. *Financial support:* In 2001–02, 25 research assistantships with full tuition reimbursements (averaging $5,000 per year) were awarded; career-related internships or fieldwork, Federal Work-Study, and unspecified assistantships also available. Financial award application deadline: 3/15; financial award applicants required to submit FAFSA. In 2001, 251 master's awarded. *Degree program information:* Part-time and evening/weekend programs available. Offers agency counseling (MA); counselor education (M Ed); marital and family therapy (MA); student affairs in higher education (M Ed). *Application deadline:* Applications are processed on a rolling basis. *Application fee:* $35. Electronic applications accepted. *Dean of Graduate Studies and Extended Learning,* Dr. Charles Cullum, 610-683-4201, Fax: 610-683-1393, E-mail: ccullum@kutztown.edu.

College of Business Students: 23 full-time (11 women), 101 part-time (37 women); includes 7 minority (5 African Americans, 2 Asian Americans or Pacific Islanders), 21 international.

Kutztown University of Pennsylvania (continued)

Average age 33. *Faculty:* 18 part-time/adjunct (1 woman). Expenses: Contact institution. *Financial support:* Career-related internships or fieldwork, Federal Work-Study, and unspecified assistantships available. Financial award application deadline: 3/15; financial award applicants required to submit FAFSA. In 2001, 35 degrees awarded. *Degree program information:* Part-time and evening/weekend programs available. Offers business (MBA); business administration (MBA). *Application deadline:* Applications are processed on a rolling basis. *Application fee:* $35. *Dean,* Theodore Hartz, 610-683-4575, Fax: 610-683-4573, E-mail: hartz@kutztown.edu.

College of Education Students: 85 full-time (55 women), 376 part-time (313 women); includes 57 minority (51 African Americans, 1 Asian American or Pacific Islander, 4 Hispanic Americans, 1 Native American), 1 international. Average age 32. *Faculty:* 28 part-time/adjunct (20 women). Expenses: Contact institution. *Financial support:* Career-related internships or fieldwork, Federal Work-Study, and unspecified assistantships available. Financial award application deadline: 3/15; financial award applicants required to submit FAFSA. In 2001, 127 degrees awarded. *Degree program information:* Part-time and evening/weekend programs available. Offers biology (M Ed); curriculum and instruction (M Ed); early childhood education (Certificate); education (M Ed, MLS, Certificate); elementary education (M Ed, Certificate); English (M Ed); library science (MLS, Certificate); mathematics (M Ed); reading (M Ed); secondary education (Certificate); social studies (M Ed); special education (Certificate). *Application deadline:* Applications are processed on a rolling basis. *Application fee:* $35. *Dean,* Dr. Eileen Shultz, 610-683-4253, Fax: 610-683-4255, E-mail: shultz@kutztown.edu.

College of Liberal Arts and Sciences Students: 22 full-time (14 women), 63 part-time (41 women); includes 2 minority (both Hispanic Americans), 13 international. Average age 33. *Faculty:* 47 part-time/adjunct (12 women). Expenses: Contact institution. *Financial support:* Career-related internships or fieldwork, Federal Work-Study, and unspecified assistantships available. Financial award application deadline: 3/15; financial award applicants required to submit FAFSA. In 2001, 33 master's awarded. *Degree program information:* Part-time and evening/weekend programs available. Offers computer and information science (MS); English (MA); liberal arts and sciences (MA, MPA, MS, Certificate); public administration (MPA); school nursing (Certificate); telecommunications (MS). *Application deadline:* Applications are processed on a rolling basis. *Application fee:* $35. *Dean,* Dr. Carl E. Brunner, 610-683-4305, Fax: 610-683-4633, E-mail: brunner@kutztown.edu.

College of Visual and Performing Arts Students: 12 full-time (8 women), 26 part-time (21 women). *Faculty:* 6 part-time/adjunct (4 women). Expenses: Contact institution. *Financial support:* Career-related internships or fieldwork, Federal Work-Study, and unspecified assistantships available. Financial award application deadline: 3/15; financial award applicants required to submit FAFSA. In 2001, 15 degrees awarded. *Degree program information:* Part-time programs available. Offers art education (M Ed, Certificate); visual and performing arts (M Ed, Certificate). *Application deadline:* Applications are processed on a rolling basis. *Application fee:* $35. *Dean,* Dr. William Mowder, 610-683-4500, Fax: 610-683-4547, E-mail: mowder@kutztown.edu.

See in-depth description on page 935.

KYUNG SAN UNIVERSITY USA, Garden Grove, CA 92844-1103

General Information Private, coed, graduate-only institution.

GRADUATE UNITS

School of Oriental Medicine *Degree program information:* Part-time programs available. Offers Oriental medicine (MSOM).

LAGRANGE COLLEGE, LaGrange, GA 30240-2999

General Information Independent-religious, coed, comprehensive institution. *Enrollment:* 26 full-time matriculated graduate/professional students (14 women), 14 part-time matriculated graduate/professional students (7 women). *Enrollment by degree level:* 40 master's. *Graduate faculty:* 24 part-time/adjunct (8 women). *Tuition:* Full-time $6,036; part-time $260 per quarter hour. Tuition and fees vary according to program. *Graduate housing:* Room and/or apartments available to single students; on-campus housing not available to married students. Typical cost: $5,136 (including board). Housing application deadline: 7/15. *Student services:* Campus employment opportunities, campus safety program, career counseling, free psychological counseling, international student services, low-cost health insurance. *Library facilities:* William and Evelyn Banks Library. *Online resources:* library catalog, web page. *Collection:* 135,522 titles, 7,294 serial subscriptions, 337 audiovisual materials.

Computer facilities: 169 computers available on campus for general student use. A campuswide network can be accessed from student residence rooms and from off campus. *Web address:* http://www.lgc.edu/.

General Application Contact: Andy Geeter, Director of Admission, 706-880-8253, Fax: 706-880-8010, E-mail: ageeter@lgc.edu.

GRADUATE UNITS

Graduate Programs Students: 26 full-time (14 women), 14 part-time (7 women); includes 1 minority (Hispanic American), 2 international. Average age 34. 21 applicants, 76% accepted. *Faculty:* 24 part-time/adjunct (8 women). Expenses: Contact institution. *Financial support:* Fellowships, teaching assistantships, career-related internships or fieldwork and tuition waivers (full and partial) available. Support available to part-time students. Financial award applicants required to submit FAFSA. In 2001, 27 degrees awarded. *Degree program information:* Part-time and evening/weekend programs available. Offers early childhood education (M Ed); education (M Ed, MAT); middle childhood education (M Ed). *Application deadline:* For fall admission, 8/1 (priority date). Applications are processed on a rolling basis. *Application fee:* $20 ($25 for international students). Electronic applications accepted. *Application Contact:* Andy Geeter, Director of Admission, 706-880-8253, Fax: 706-880-8010, E-mail: ageeter@lgc.edu. *Vice President for Academic Affairs and Dean,* Dr. Jay K. Simmons, 706-812-7235, Fax: 706-812-7358, E-mail: jsimmons@lgc.edu.

LAKE ERIE COLLEGE, Painesville, OH 44077-3389

General Information Independent, coed, comprehensive institution. *Enrollment:* 126 part-time matriculated graduate/professional students (97 women). *Enrollment by degree level:* 126 master's. *Graduate faculty:* 8 full-time (4 women), 5 part-time/adjunct (1 woman). *Tuition:* Part-time $420 per credit. *Required fees:* $30 per credit. *Graduate housing:* Room and/or apartments available on a first-come, first-served basis to single students; on-campus housing not available to married students. *Student services:* Campus safety program, career counseling, disabled student services, teacher training. *Library facilities:* Lincoln Library plus 2 others. *Online resources:* library catalog, web page. *Collection:* 85,978 titles, 767 serial subscriptions.

Computer facilities: A campuswide network can be accessed from student residence rooms and from off campus. Internet access is available. *Web address:* http://www.lec.edu/.

General Application Contact: 440-639-7879, Fax: 440-352-3533, E-mail: admissions@lec.edu.

GRADUATE UNITS

Division of Education Average age 37. 12 applicants, 100% accepted. *Faculty:* 3 full-time (2 women), 3 part-time/adjunct (1 woman). Expenses: Contact institution. *Financial support:* Scholarships/grants available. Financial award applicants required to submit FAFSA. In 2001, 9 degrees awarded. *Degree program information:* Part-time and evening/weekend programs available. Offers education (MS Ed); effective teaching (MS Ed); reading (MS Ed). *Application deadline:* For fall admission, 8/1 (priority date); for spring admission, 12/15. Applications are processed on a rolling basis. *Application fee:* $20 ($50 for international students). *Application Contact:* 440-639-7879, Fax: 440-352-3533, E-mail: lecadmit@lakeerie.edu. *Associate Dean of Teacher Education and Certification,* Dr. Carol Ramsay, 440-639-4749, Fax: 440-352-3533, E-mail: ramsay@lec.edu.

Division of Management Studies Average age 37. 28 applicants, 96% accepted. *Faculty:* 5 full-time (2 women), 2 part-time/adjunct (0 women). Expenses: Contact institution. *Financial support:* Career-related internships or fieldwork available. Financial award applicants required to submit FAFSA. In 2001, 18 degrees awarded. *Degree program information:* Part-time and evening/weekend programs available. Offers general management (MBA); management healthcare administration (MBA). *Application deadline:* For fall admission, 8/1 (priority date); for spring admission, 12/15. Applications are processed on a rolling basis. *Application fee:* $20 ($50 for international students). *Application Contact:* Admissions Office, 440-639-7879, Fax: 440-352-3533, E-mail: lecadmit@lakeerie.edu. *Associate Dean,* Dr. David Dumpe, 440-639-7845, Fax: 440-352-3533, E-mail: ddumpe@lec.edu.

LAKE ERIE COLLEGE OF OSTEOPATHIC MEDICINE, Erie, PA 16509-1025

General Information Independent, coed, graduate-only institution. *Enrollment by degree level:* 640 first professional. *Graduate faculty:* 46 full-time (8 women), 123 part-time/adjunct (17 women). *Tuition:* Full-time $21,760. *Required fees:* $1,000. *Graduate housing:* On-campus housing not available. *Student services:* Campus safety program, career counseling, exercise/wellness program, free psychological counseling, international student services, low-cost health insurance. *Library facilities:* Lecom Learning Resource Center. *Online resources:* library catalog, web page, access to other libraries' catalogs. *Collection:* 9,000 titles, 152 serial subscriptions, 700 audiovisual materials.

Computer facilities: 18 computers available on campus for general student use. A campuswide network can be accessed from off campus. Internet access is available. *Web address:* http://www.lecom.edu.

General Application Contact: Elaine Morse, Admissions Coordinator, 814-866-6641, Fax: 814-866-8123, E-mail: emorse@lecom.edu.

GRADUATE UNITS

Professional Program Students: 640 full-time (270 women); includes 77 minority (13 African Americans, 63 Asian Americans or Pacific Islanders, 1 Hispanic American), 2 international. Average age 25. 2,360 applicants, 12% accepted. *Faculty:* 46 full-time (8 women), 123 part-time/adjunct (17 women). Expenses: Contact institution. *Financial support:* In 2001–02, 394 students received support. Institutionally sponsored loans and scholarships/grants available. Financial award application deadline: 6/30; financial award applicants required to submit FAFSA. In 2001, 131 degrees awarded. Offers osteopathic medicine (DO, Pharm D, Certificate). *Application deadline:* For fall admission, 2/1. Applications are processed on a rolling basis. *Application fee:* $50. *Application Contact:* Elaine Morse, Admissions Coordinator, 814-866-6641, Fax: 814-866-8123, E-mail: emorse@lecom.edu. *Dean and Vice President of Academic Affairs,* Dr. Silvia M. Ferretti, 814-866-6641, Fax: 814-866-8123.

LAKE FOREST COLLEGE, Lake Forest, IL 60045-2399

General Information Independent, coed, comprehensive institution. *Enrollment:* 1 (woman) full-time matriculated graduate/professional student, 37 part-time matriculated graduate/professional students (21 women). *Enrollment by degree level:* 38 master's. *Graduate faculty:* 16 full-time (6 women), 1 part-time/adjunct (0 women). *Tuition:* Full-time $10,500; part-time $2,100 per course. *Graduate housing:* On-campus housing not available. *Student services:* Campus safety program, career counseling, multicultural affairs office, writing training. *Library facilities:* Donnelley Library plus 1 other. *Online resources:* library catalog, web page, access to other libraries' catalogs. *Collection:* 268,760 titles, 1,133 serial subscriptions, 11,911 audiovisual materials.

Computer facilities: 120 computers available on campus for general student use. A campuswide network can be accessed from student residence rooms and from off campus. Internet access is available. *Web address:* http://www.lakeforest.edu/.

General Application Contact: Carol Gayle, Associate Director, 847-735-5083, Fax: 847-735-6291, E-mail: gayle@lfc.edu.

GRADUATE UNITS

Graduate Program in Liberal Studies Students: 1 (woman) full-time, 37 part-time (21 women); includes 3 minority (1 Asian American or Pacific Islander, 2 Hispanic Americans) Average age 40. 21 applicants, 57% accepted, 7 enrolled. *Faculty:* 16 full-time (6 women), 1 part-time/adjunct (0 women). Expenses: Contact institution. *Financial support:* In 2001–02, 6 students received support, including 6 fellowships (averaging $1,000 per year); scholarships/grants and tuition waivers (partial) also available. Support available to part-time students. Financial award application deadline: 8/15; financial award applicants required to submit FAFSA. In 2001, 7 degrees awarded. *Degree program information:* Part-time and evening/weekend programs available. Offers liberal studies (MLS). *Application deadline:* For fall admission, 8/20; for spring admission, 1/1. Applications are processed on a rolling basis. *Application fee:* $20. Electronic applications accepted. *Application Contact:* Carol Gayle, Associate Director, 847-735-5083, Fax: 847-735-6291, E-mail: gayle@lfc.edu. *Director,* Rosemary Cowler, 847-735-5274, Fax: 847-735-6291, E-mail: cowler@lfc.edu.

LAKE FOREST GRADUATE SCHOOL OF MANAGEMENT, Lake Forest, IL 60045-2497

General Information Independent, coed, graduate-only institution. *Enrollment by degree level:* 771 master's. *Graduate faculty:* 159 part-time/adjunct (26 women). *Tuition:* Part-time $2,010 per course. *Graduate housing:* On-campus housing not available.

Computer facilities: 28 computers available on campus for general student use. A campuswide network can be accessed. Internet access is available. *Web address:* http://www.lfgsm.edu/.

General Application Contact: Dawn Peterson, Director of Admissions, Lake Forest Campus, 800-737-4MBA, Fax: 847-259-3656, E-mail: admiss@lfgsm.edu.

GRADUATE UNITS

Graduate Programs Average age 37. 174 applicants, 89% accepted, 155 enrolled. *Faculty:* 159 part-time/adjunct (26 women). Expenses: Contact institution. *Financial support:* In 2001–02, 113 students received support. Scholarships/grants available. Support available to part-time students. Financial award applicants required to submit FAFSA. In 2001, 202 degrees awarded. *Degree program information:* Part-time and evening/weekend programs available. Offers management (MBA). *Application deadline:* For fall admission, 7/13 (priority date); for spring admission, 12/21 (priority date). Applications are processed on a rolling basis. *Application fee:* $0. Electronic applications accepted. *Application Contact:* Dawn Peterson, Director of Admissions, Lake Forest Campus, 800-737-4MBA, Fax: 847-259-3656, E-mail: admiss@lfgsm.edu. *President and Chief Executive Officer,* John N. Popoli, 847-234-5005, Fax: 847-295-3656, E-mail: jpopoli@lfgsm.edu.

LAKEHEAD UNIVERSITY, Thunder Bay, ON P7B 5E1, Canada

General Information Province-supported, coed, comprehensive institution. *Graduate housing:* Rooms and/or apartments available to single students and available on a first-come, first-served basis to married students. Housing application deadline: 3/10. *Research affiliation:* Bowater Inc. (chemistry), Thunder Bay Regional Cancer Centre (psychosocial oncology), Centre for Northern Forest Ecosystem Research (biology, forestry, tourism), Bowater Inc. (engineering), Placer Dome (biology), Falcon bridge (biology).

GRADUATE UNITS

Graduate Studies *Degree program information:* Part-time and evening/weekend programs available. Offers clinical psychology (MA, PhD); experimental psychology (MA); geology (M Sc); history (MA); native Canadian philosophy (MA); physics (M Sc); social work (MSW); specialization gerontology (M Ed, M Sc, MA, MSW); women's studies (M Ed, MA, MSW).

Faculty of Arts and Science *Degree program information:* Part-time and evening/weekend programs available. Offers arts and science (M Sc, MA, MSW, PhD); biology (M Sc); chemistry (M Sc); economics (MA); English (MA); sociology (MA).

Faculty of Education *Degree program information:* Part-time and evening/weekend programs available. Offers curriculum development (M Ed); education administration (M Ed); educational studies (PhD).

Faculty of Engineering *Degree program information:* Part-time programs available. Offers control engineering (M Sc Engr).

Faculty of Forestry *Degree program information:* Part-time programs available. Offers forestry (M Sc F, MF).

School of Kinesiology *Degree program information:* Part-time programs available. Offers applied sport science and coaching (M Sc, MA).

School of Mathematical Sciences *Degree program information:* Part-time and evening/weekend programs available. Offers computer science (M Sc, MA); mathematics and statistics (M Sc, MA).

LAKELAND COLLEGE, Sheboygan, WI 53082-0359

General Information Independent-religious, coed, comprehensive institution. *Graduate housing:* On-campus housing not available.

GRADUATE UNITS

Graduate Studies Division *Degree program information:* Part-time and evening/weekend programs available. Offers business administration (MBA); education (M Ed); theology (MAT).

LAMAR UNIVERSITY, Beaumont, TX 77710

General Information State-supported, coed, university. CGS member. *Enrollment:* 485 full-time matriculated graduate/professional students (167 women), 458 part-time matriculated graduate/professional students (277 women). *Enrollment by degree level:* 915 master's, 28 doctoral. *Graduate faculty:* 182 full-time (45 women), 20 part-time/adjunct (7 women). Tuition, state resident: full-time $1,114. Tuition, nonresident: full-time $3,670. *Graduate housing:* Room and/or apartments available to single students; on-campus housing not available to married students. Typical cost: $1,922 per year ($3,732 including board). Housing application deadline: 9/1. *Student services:* Campus employment opportunities, career counseling, child daycare facilities, disabled student services, exercise/wellness program, free psychological counseling, grant writing training, international student services, low-cost health insurance, teacher training, writing training. *Library facilities:* Mary and John Gray Library. *Online resources:* library catalog, web page. *Collection:* 600,000 titles, 2,900 serial subscriptions. *Research affiliation:* Texas Technology Transfer Association (engineering, science), Texaco, Inc. (engineering), E. I. du Pont de Nemours and Company (engineering), Mobil Corporation (science).

Computer facilities: 120 computers available on campus for general student use. A campuswide network can be accessed from student residence rooms and from off campus. *Web address:* http://www.lamar.edu/.

General Application Contact: Sandy Drane, Coordinator of Graduate Admissions, 409-880-8356, Fax: 409-880-8414, E-mail: gradmissions@hal.lamar.edu.

GRADUATE UNITS

College of Graduate Studies Students: 485 full-time (167 women), 458 part-time (277 women); includes 126 minority (69 African Americans, 20 Asian Americans or Pacific Islanders, 34 Hispanic Americans, 3 Native Americans), 332 international. Average age 32. 1,179 applicants, 44% accepted, 261 enrolled. *Faculty:* 182 full-time (45 women), 20 part-time/adjunct (7 women). Expenses: Contact institution. *Financial support:* Fellowships with partial tuition reimbursements, research assistantships, teaching assistantships, career-related internships or fieldwork, Federal Work-Study, institutionally sponsored loans, scholarships/grants, and tuition waivers (partial) available. Support available to part-time students. Financial award application deadline: 4/1; financial award applicants required to submit FAFSA. In 2001, 290 master's, 7 doctorates awarded. *Degree program information:* Part-time and evening/weekend programs available. *Application deadline:* For fall admission, 5/15; for spring admission, 10/1. Applications are processed on a rolling basis. *Application fee:* $25 ($50 for international students). *Application Contact:* Sandy Drane, Coordinator of Graduate Admissions, 409-880-8356, Fax: 409-880-8414, E-mail: gradmissions@hal.lamar.edu. *Associate Vice President for Research and Dean,* Dr. James W. Westgate, 800-458-7558, Fax: 409-880-1723, E-mail: westgate@hal.lamar.edu.

College of Arts and Sciences Students: 41 full-time (20 women), 65 part-time (45 women); includes 22 minority (13 African Americans, 3 Asian Americans or Pacific Islanders, 6 Hispanic Americans), 7 international. Average age 36. 95 applicants, 29% accepted, 25 enrolled. *Faculty:* 56 full-time (12 women), 4 part-time/adjunct (1 woman). Expenses: Contact institution. *Financial support:* Fellowships, research assistantships, teaching assistantships with tuition reimbursements, career-related internships or fieldwork, Federal Work-Study, institutionally sponsored loans, scholarships/grants, and tuition waivers (partial) available. Support available to part-time students. Financial award application deadline:4/1. In 2001, 34 degrees awarded. *Degree program information:* Part-time and evening/weekend programs available. Offers applied criminology (MS); arts and sciences (MA, MPA, MS, MSN); biology (MS); chemistry (MS); community/clinical psychology (MS); English (MA); history (MA); industrial/organizational psychology (MS); nursing administration (MSN); public administration (MPA). *Application deadline:* For fall admission, 8/1 (priority date); for spring admission, 12/1 (priority date). Applications are processed on a rolling basis. *Application fee:* $25 ($50 for international students). *Application Contact:* Dr. James W. Westgate, Associate Vice President for Research and Dean, 800-458-7558, Fax: 409-880-1723, E-mail: westgate@hal.lamar.edu. *Dean,* Dr. Brenda S. Nichols, 409-880-8285.

College of Business Students: 31 full-time (16 women), 33 part-time (13 women); includes 11 minority (4 African Americans, 5 Asian Americans or Pacific Islanders, 2 Hispanic Americans), 10 international. Average age 29. 49 applicants, 45% accepted, 19 enrolled. *Faculty:* 21 full-time (3 women). Expenses: Contact institution. *Financial support:* In 2001–02, 12 students received support, including 3 research assistantships with partial tuition reimbursements available; fellowships with tuition reimbursements available, career-related internships or fieldwork, Federal Work-Study, institutionally sponsored loans, scholarships/grants, and tuition waivers (partial) also available. Support available to part-time students. Financial award application deadline: 4/1; financial award applicants required to submit FAFSA. In 2001, 23 degrees awarded. *Degree program information:* Part-time and evening/weekend programs available. Offers accounting (MBA); information systems (MBA); management (MBA). *Application deadline:* For fall admission, 3/15 (priority date); for spring admission, 10/1 (priority date). Applications are processed on a rolling basis. *Application fee:* $25 ($50 for international students). *Associate Dean,* Dr. Robert A. Swerdlow, 409-880-8604, Fax: 409-880-8088, E-mail: swerdlowra@hal.lamar.edu.

College of Education and Human Development Students: 51 full-time (40 women), 267 part-time (180 women); includes 58 minority (38 African Americans, 4 Asian Americans or Pacific Islanders, 14 Hispanic Americans, 2 Native Americans) Average age 39. 129 applicants, 40% accepted, 43 enrolled. *Faculty:* 34 full-time (17 women), 10 part-time/adjunct (4 women). Expenses: Contact institution. *Financial support:* Fellowships, research assistantships, teaching assistantships, career-related internships or fieldwork, Federal Work-Study, institutionally sponsored loans, and scholarships/grants available. Support available to part-time students. Financial award application deadline: 4/1. In 2001, 77 degrees awarded. *Degree program information:* Part-time and evening/weekend programs available. Postbaccalaureate distance learning degree programs offered. Offers counseling and development (M Ed, Certificate); counselor (Certificate); education administration (M Ed, Certificate); education and human development (M Ed, MS, Certificate); educational diagnostician (Certificate); elementary education (M Ed, Certificate); family and consumer sciences (MS); kinesiology (MS); mental retardation (Certificate); principal (Certificate); reading (Certificate); secondary education (M Ed, Certificate); special education (M Ed, Certificate); superintendent (Certificate); supervision (M Ed, Certificate). *Application deadline:* For fall admission, 8/1; for spring admission, 12/1. Applications are processed on a rolling basis. *Application fee:* $25 ($50 for international students). *Dean,* Dr. R. Carl Westerfield, 409-880-8661, E-mail: westerfirc@hal.lamar.edu.

College of Engineering Students: 281 full-time (29 women), 60 part-time (16 women); includes 9 minority (2 African Americans, 5 Asian Americans or Pacific Islanders, 2 Hispanic Americans), 313 international. Average age 26. 821 applicants, 45% accepted, 151 enrolled. *Faculty:* 40 full-time (3 women), 2 part-time/adjunct (0 women). Expenses: Contact institution. *Financial support:* In 2001–02, fellowships with partial tuition reimbursements (averaging $6,000 per year), research assistantships with partial tuition reimbursements (averaging $7,500 per year), teaching assistantships with partial tuition reimbursements (averaging $7,500 per year) were awarded. Career-related internships or fieldwork, Federal Work-Study, institutionally sponsored loans, scholarships/grants, tuition waivers (full and partial), and laboratory assistantships, graders also available. Support available to part-time students. Financial award application deadline: 4/1. In 2001, 123 master's, 5 doctorates awarded. *Degree program information:* Part-time and evening/weekend programs available. Offers chemical engineering (ME, MES, DE); civil engineering (ME, MES, DE); computer science (MS); electrical engineering (ME, MES, DE); engineering (ME, MEM, MES, MS, DE); engineering management (MEM); environmental engineering (MS); environmental studies (MS); industrial engineering (ME, MES, DE); mathematics (MS); mechanical engineering (ME, MES, DE). *Application deadline:* For fall admission, 5/15 (priority date); for spring admission, 10/1 (priority date). Applications are processed on a rolling basis. *Application fee:* $25 ($50 for international students). *Application Contact:* Sandy Drane, Coordinator of Graduate Admissions, 409-880-8356, Fax: 409-880-8414, E-mail: gradmissions@hal.lamar.edu. *Chair,* Dr. Jack Hopper, 409-880-8784, Fax: 409-880-2197, E-mail: che_dept@hal.lamar.edu.

College of Fine Arts and Communication Students: 81 full-time (62 women), 33 part-time (23 women); includes 26 minority (12 African Americans, 3 Asian Americans or Pacific Islanders, 10 Hispanic Americans, 1 Native American), 2 international. Average age 32. 85 applicants, 54% accepted, 29 enrolled. *Faculty:* 31 full-time (10 women), 4 part-time/adjunct (2 women). Expenses: Contact institution. *Financial support:* Fellowships, research assistantships, teaching assistantships, career-related internships or fieldwork, Federal Work-Study, institutionally sponsored loans, and tuition waivers (partial) available. Support available to part-time students. Financial award application deadline: 4/1. In 2001, 33 master's, 2 doctorates awarded. *Degree program information:* Part-time and evening/weekend programs available. Offers art history (MA); audiology (MS); deaf education (MS, Ed D); fine arts and communication (MA, MM, MM Ed, MS, Ed D); music education (MM Ed); music performance (MM); photography (MA); speech language pathology (MS); studio art (MA); theatre (MS); visual design (MA). *Application deadline:* For fall admission, 8/1; for spring admission, 12/1. Applications are processed on a rolling basis. *Application fee:* $25 ($50 for international students). *Application Contact:* Sandy Drane, Coordinator of Graduate Admissions, 409-880-8356, Fax: 409-880-8414, E-mail: gradmissions@hal.lamar.edu. *Dean,* Dr. Russ A. Schultz, 409-880-8137, Fax: 409-880-2286, E-mail: schulra@lub002.lamar.edu.

See in-depth description on page 937.

LANCASTER BIBLE COLLEGE, Lancaster, PA 17608-3403

General Information Independent-religious, coed, comprehensive institution. *Enrollment:* 3 full-time matriculated graduate/professional students (2 women), 101 part-time matriculated graduate/professional students (51 women). *Enrollment by degree level:* 104 master's. *Graduate faculty:* 7 full-time (1 woman), 14 part-time/adjunct (4 women). *Tuition:* Part-time $275 per credit. *Required fees:* $35 per term. *Graduate housing:* On-campus housing not available. *Student services:* Campus employment opportunities, career counseling, international student services. *Library facilities:* Lancaster Bible College Library. *Online resources:* library catalog, access to other libraries' catalogs. *Collection:* 118,519 titles, 1,273 serial subscriptions, 3,943 audiovisual materials.

Computer facilities: 20 computers available on campus for general student use. A campuswide network can be accessed from student residence rooms. Internet access is available. *Web address:* http://www.lbc.edu/.

General Application Contact: Dr. Miles A. Lewis, Dean of Graduate Education, 717-560-8297, Fax: 717-560-8236, E-mail: gradschool@lbc.edu.

GRADUATE UNITS

Graduate School Students: 3 full-time (2 women), 101 part-time (51 women); includes 12 minority (6 African Americans, 5 Asian Americans or Pacific Islanders, 1 Hispanic American), 4 international. Average age 40. 90 applicants, 58% accepted. *Faculty:* 7 full-time (1 woman), 14 part-time/adjunct (4 women). Expenses: Contact institution. *Financial support:* In 2001–02, 32 students received support. Available to part-time students. Application deadline: 6/1; In 2001, 7 degrees awarded. *Degree program information:* Part-time and evening/weekend programs available. Offers Bible (MA); counseling (M Ed); ministry (MA); school counseling (M Ed). *Application deadline:* For fall admission, 8/1 (priority date); for spring admission, 1/5. Applications are processed on a rolling basis. *Application fee:* $25. *Dean of Graduate Education,* Dr. Miles A. Lewis, 717-560-8297, Fax: 717-560-8236, E-mail: gradschool@lbc.edu.

LANCASTER THEOLOGICAL SEMINARY, Lancaster, PA 17603-2812

General Information Independent-religious, coed, graduate-only institution. *Graduate faculty:* 13 full-time (3 women), 9 part-time/adjunct (4 women). *Tuition:* Full-time $8,900; part-time $290 per credit. *Required fees:* $13 per term. *Graduate housing:* Rooms and/or apartments available on a first-come, first-served basis to single students and available to married students. Housing application deadline: 8/1. *Student services:* Campus employment opportunities, international student services, low-cost health insurance. *Library facilities:* Philip Schaff Library. *Online resources:* library catalog. *Collection:* 122,000 titles, 385 serial subscriptions.

Computer facilities: 12 computers available on campus for general student use. A campuswide network can be accessed. Internet access is available. *Web address:* http://www.lts.org/.

General Application Contact: Rev. Susan Minasian, Director of Admissions, Recruitment, and Financial Aid, 717-290-8737, Fax: 717-393-0423, E-mail: sminasian@lts.org.

GRADUATE UNITS

Graduate and Professional Programs Offers biblical studies (M Div, MAR); church life and work (M Div, MAR); historical studies (M Div, MAR); integrated ministry studies (M Div, MAR); theological studies (M Div, MAR); theology (D Min).

LANDER UNIVERSITY, Greenwood, SC 29649-2099

General Information State-supported, coed, comprehensive institution. *Enrollment:* 10 full-time matriculated graduate/professional students (9 women), 60 part-time matriculated graduate/professional students (54 women). *Enrollment by degree level:* 70 master's. *Graduate faculty:* 8 full-time (4 women), 4 part-time/adjunct (3 women). Tuition, state resident: full-time $2,280; part-time $190 per semester hour. Tuition, nonresident: full-time $4,692; part-time $391 per semester hour. *Graduate housing:* Room and/or apartments available on a first-come, first-served basis to single students; on-campus housing not available to married students. Typical cost: $2,876 per year ($4,376 including board) ; $2,876 per year ($6,376 including board) for married students. Room and board charges vary according to board plan and housing facility selected. *Student services:* Campus employment opportunities, career counseling, disabled student services, free psychological counseling, low-cost health insurance, multicultural affairs office, teacher training. *Library facilities:* Jackson Library. *Online resources:* library catalog, web page. *Collection:* 169,919 titles, 692 serial subscriptions, 2,089 audiovisual materials.

Computer facilities: 150 computers available on campus for general student use. A campuswide network can be accessed from student residence rooms and from off campus. Internet access and online class registration are available. *Web address:* http://www.lander.edu/.

General Application Contact: Dr. Robert Taylor, Director of Graduate Studies, School of Education, 864-388-8225, E-mail: btaylor@lander.edu.

GRADUATE UNITS

School of Education Students: 10 full-time (9 women), 60 part-time (54 women); includes 9 minority (8 African Americans, 1 Asian American or Pacific Islander), 1 international. Average age 34. 60 applicants, 92% accepted, 49 enrolled. *Faculty:* 8 full-time (4 women), 4 part-time/adjunct (3 women). Expenses: Contact institution. *Financial support:* Federal Work-Study available. Support available to part-time students. Financial award application deadline: 4/15;

Lander University (continued)

financial award applicants required to submit FAFSA. In 2001, 32 degrees awarded. *Degree program information:* Part-time and evening/weekend programs available. Offers elementary education (M Ed); teaching (MAT). *Application deadline:* Applications are processed on a rolling basis. *Application fee:* $25. *Application Contact:* Dr. Robert Taylor, Director of Graduate Studies, School of Education, 864-388-8318, E-mail: btaylor@lander.edu. *Dean,* Dr. Danny McKanzie, 864-388-8225, E-mail: dmckenzie@lander.edu.

LANGSTON UNIVERSITY, Langston, OK 73050-0907

General Information State-supported, coed, comprehensive institution. CGS member. *Enrollment:* 81 full-time matriculated graduate/professional students (52 women). *Enrollment by degree level:* 81 master's. *Graduate faculty:* 21 full-time (11 women), 13 part-time/adjunct (8 women). Tuition, state resident: part-time $71 per credit hour. Tuition, nonresident: part-time $119 per credit hour. *Graduate housing:* Rooms and/or apartments available to single and married students. *Student services:* Campus employment opportunities, campus safety program, career counseling, child daycare facilities, disabled student services, exercise/wellness program, free psychological counseling, international student services, teacher training. *Library facilities:* Main library plus 1 other. *Collection:* 236,000 titles, 1,732 serial subscriptions.

Computer facilities: 200 computers available on campus for general student use. A campuswide network can be accessed from student residence rooms and from off campus. Internet access is available. *Web address:* http://www.lunet.edu/.

General Application Contact: Dr. Alex O. Lewis, Dean, 405-466-3379, Fax: 405-466-3270, E-mail: aolewis@lunet.edu.

GRADUATE UNITS

School of Education and Behavioral Sciences Students: 81 full-time (52 women). 52 applicants, 79% accepted. *Faculty:* 21 full-time (11 women), 13 part-time/adjunct (8 women). Expenses: Contact institution. *Financial support:* In 2001–02, 4 teaching assistantships (averaging $5,000 per year) were awarded; research assistantships, institutionally sponsored loans and tuition waivers (partial) also available. Financial award application deadline: 5/15. In 2001, 6 degrees awarded. *Degree program information:* Part-time programs available. Offers education and behavioral sciences (M Ed). *Application deadline:* For fall admission, 7/15 (priority date); for spring admission, 12/15 (priority date). *Application fee:* $0. *Dean,* Dr. Alex O. Lewis, 405-466-3379, Fax: 405-466-3270, E-mail: aolewis@lunet.edu.

LA ROCHE COLLEGE, Pittsburgh, PA 15237-5898

General Information Independent-religious, coed, comprehensive institution. *Enrollment:* 95 full-time matriculated graduate/professional students (51 women), 152 part-time matriculated graduate/professional students (109 women). *Enrollment by degree level:* 247 master's. *Graduate faculty:* 8 full-time (5 women), 13 part-time/adjunct (7 women). *Tuition:* Full-time $8,280; part-time $460 per credit. *Required fees:* $7 per credit. *Graduate housing:* On-campus housing not available. *Student services:* Campus employment opportunities, career counseling, free psychological counseling, international student services, low-cost health insurance. *Library facilities:* John J. Wright Library. *Online resources:* library catalog. *Collection:* 62,361 titles, 2,220 serial subscriptions, 935 audiovisual materials.

Computer facilities: 95 computers available on campus for general student use. A campuswide network can be accessed from student residence rooms and from off campus. Internet access and online class registration are available. *Web address:* http://www.laroche.edu/.

General Application Contact: Renee Bowers, Director of Admissions for Graduate and Continuing Education, 412-536-1265, Fax: 412-536-1283, E-mail: bowersr1@laroche.edu.

GRADUATE UNITS

Graduate Studies Students: 95 full-time (51 women), 152 part-time (109 women); includes 14 minority (10 African Americans, 2 Asian Americans or Pacific Islanders, 1 Hispanic American, 1 Native American), 3 international. Average age 35. 96 applicants, 88% accepted, 65 enrolled. *Faculty:* 8 full-time (5 women), 13 part-time/adjunct (7 women). Expenses: Contact institution. *Financial support:* Career-related internships or fieldwork and unspecified assistantships available. Support available to part-time students. Financial award application deadline: 3/31; financial award applicants required to submit FAFSA. In 2001, 64 degrees awarded. *Degree program information:* Part-time and evening/weekend programs available. Offers community health nursing (MSN); critical care nursing (MSN); family nurse practitioner (MSN); gerontological nursing (MSN); human resources management (MS); nurse anesthesia (MS); nursing management (MSN). *Application deadline:* Applications are processed on a rolling basis. *Application fee:* $35. Electronic applications accepted. *Application Contact:* Renee Bowers, Director of Admissions for Graduate and Continuing Education, 412-536-1265, Fax: 412-536-1283, E-mail: bowersr1@laroche.edu. *Vice President for Academic Affairs and Graduate Dean,* Dr. Ronald Gilardi, 412-536-1281, Fax: 412-536-1290, E-mail: gilardi1@laroche.edu.

LA SALLE UNIVERSITY, Philadelphia, PA 19141-1199

General Information Independent-religious, coed, comprehensive institution. *Enrollment:* 182 full-time matriculated graduate/professional students (94 women), 1,343 part-time matriculated graduate/professional students (812 women). *Enrollment by degree level:* 1,440 master's, 85 doctoral. *Graduate faculty:* 90 full-time (41 women), 60 part-time/adjunct (22 women). *Tuition:* Part-time $405 per credit. *Required fees:* $75 per semester. *Graduate housing:* Room and/or apartments available on a first-come, first-served basis to single students; on-campus housing not available to married students. Typical cost: $4,010 per year ($7,470 including board). Housing application deadline: 7/1. *Student services:* Campus employment opportunities, campus safety program, career counseling, child daycare facilities, exercise/wellness program, free psychological counseling, international student services, multicultural affairs office, teacher training. *Library facilities:* Connelly Library. *Online resources:* library catalog, web page, access to other libraries' catalogs. *Collection:* 365,000 titles, 1,700 serial subscriptions, 5,200 audiovisual materials.

Computer facilities: 350 computers available on campus for general student use. A campuswide network can be accessed from student residence rooms and from off campus. Internet access and online class registration are available. *Web address:* http://www.lasalle.edu/.

General Application Contact: Paul J. Reilly, Director of Marketing/Graduate Enrollment, 215-951-1946, Fax: 215-951-1886, E-mail: reilly@lasalle.edu.

GRADUATE UNITS

Business Administration Program Students: 69 full-time (19 women), 504 part-time (208 women); includes 63 minority (38 African Americans, 14 Asian Americans or Pacific Islanders, 9 Hispanic Americans, 2 Native Americans), 2 international. Average age 33. 285 applicants, 59% accepted, 110 enrolled. *Faculty:* 27 full-time (7 women), 15 part-time/adjunct (1 woman). Expenses: Contact institution. *Financial support:* In 2001–02, 10 students received support. Career-related internships or fieldwork and scholarships/grants available. Financial award application deadline: 8/15. In 2001, 211 degrees awarded. *Degree program information:* Part-time and evening/weekend programs available. Offers business administration (MBA, Certificate); global management of technology (MS). *Application deadline:* For fall admission, 8/30 (priority date); for spring admission, 1/10. Applications are processed on a rolling basis. *Application fee:* $30. Electronic applications accepted. *Application Contact:* Paul J. Reilly, Director of Marketing/Graduate Enrollment, 215-951-1946, Fax: 215-951-1886, E-mail: reilly@lasalle.edu. *Associate Dean,* Joseph Y. Ugras, 215-951-1057, Fax: 215-951-1886, E-mail: ugras@lasalle.edu.

Program in Nursing Students: 11 full-time (6 women), 179 part-time (165 women); includes 12 minority (8 African Americans, 2 Asian Americans or Pacific Islanders, 2 Hispanic Americans) Average age 37. 93 applicants, 85% accepted, 75 enrolled. *Faculty:* 13 full-time (12 women), 8 part-time/adjunct (5 women). Expenses: Contact institution. *Financial support:* In 2001–02, 49 students received support; teaching assistantships, institutionally sponsored loans, scholarships/grants, and traineeships available. Support available to part-time students. Financial award application deadline: 7/1. In 2001, 30 degrees awarded. *Degree program information:* Part-time programs available. Postbaccalaureate distance learning degree programs offered (minimal on-campus study). Offers adult health and illness, clinical nurse specialist (MSN); clinical research (Certificate); nursing administration (MSN); nursing education (Certificate); nursing informatics (Certificate); primary care of adults-nurse practitioner (MSN); public health nursing (MSN); school nurse (Certificate); wound, ostomy, and continence nursing (MSN, Certificate). *Application deadline:* Applications are processed on a rolling basis. *Application fee:* $30. *Application Contact:* Dr. Janice Beitz, Graduate Director, 215-951-1430, Fax: 215-951-1896, E-mail: beitz@lasalle.edu. *Dean,* Dr. Zane R. Wolf, 215-951-1430, Fax: 215-951-1896, E-mail: wolf@lasalle.edu.

LASELL COLLEGE, Newton, MA 02466-2709

General Information Independent, coed, comprehensive institution. *Tuition:* Part-time $530 per credit. *Graduate housing:* On-campus housing not available. *Student services:* Campus employment opportunities, campus safety program, career counseling, disabled student services, exercise/wellness program, free psychological counseling, international student services, writing training. *Library facilities:* Brennan Library. *Online resources:* library catalog, access to other libraries' catalogs. *Collection:* 51,219 titles, 521 serial subscriptions, 2,145 audiovisual materials. *Research affiliation:* Lasell Village (elder care), Lasell College Center for Research on Aging and Intergenerational Studies (elder care).

Computer facilities: 150 computers available on campus for general student use. A campuswide network can be accessed from student residence rooms and from off campus. *Web address:* http://www.lasell.edu/.

General Application Contact: Wendy T. Ferrucci, Director of Graduate Admission, 617-243-2400, E-mail: wferrucci@lasell.edu.

GRADUATE UNITS

Program in Elder Care Management and Marketing Offers management (MS).

LA SIERRA UNIVERSITY, Riverside, CA 92515-8247

General Information Independent-religious, coed, comprehensive institution. *Graduate housing:* Rooms and/or apartments available on a first-come, first-served basis to single students and available to married students.

GRADUATE UNITS

College of Arts and Sciences *Degree program information:* Part-time programs available. Offers arts and sciences (MA); English (MA).

School of Business and Management Offers business administration and management (MBA); executive business administration (EMBA); leadership, values, and ethics for business and management (Certificate).

School of Education *Degree program information:* Part-time and evening/weekend programs available. Offers administration and leadership (MA, Ed D, Ed S); counseling (MA); curriculum and instruction (MA, Ed D, Ed S); education (MA, Ed D, Ed S); educational psychology (Ed S); school psychology (Ed S); special education (MA).

School of Religion *Degree program information:* Part-time programs available. Offers religion (MA); religious education (MA); religious studies (MA).

LAURA AND ALVIN SIEGAL COLLEGE OF JUDAIC STUDIES, Beachwood, OH 44122-7116

General Information Independent, coed, comprehensive institution. *Enrollment:* 8 full-time matriculated graduate/professional students (6 women), 105 part-time matriculated graduate/professional students (81 women). *Enrollment by degree level:* 113 master's. *Graduate faculty:* 13 full-time (4 women), 22 part-time/adjunct (17 women). *Tuition:* Full-time $4,050; part-time $225 per credit. *Required fees:* $25; $25 per year. Tuition and fees vary according to course load and program. *Graduate housing:* On-campus housing not available. *Student services:* Career counseling, international student services, teacher training. *Library facilities:* Aaron Garber Library. *Online resources:* library catalog, access to other libraries' catalogs. *Collection:* 28,000 titles, 100 serial subscriptions.

Computer facilities: 5 computers available on campus for general student use. *Web address:* http://www.siegalcollege.edu/.

General Application Contact: Linda L. Rosen, Director of Student Services, 216-464-4050 Ext. 101, Fax: 216-464-5827, E-mail: lrosen@siegalcollege.edu.

GRADUATE UNITS

Graduate Programs Students: 8 full-time (6 women), 105 part-time (81 women). Average age 37. 35 applicants, 66% accepted. *Faculty:* 13 full-time (4 women), 22 part-time/adjunct (17 women). Expenses: Contact institution. *Financial support:* In 2001–02, 6 students received support; fellowships, career-related internships or fieldwork and scholarships/grants available. Support available to part-time students. In 2001, 2 degrees awarded. *Degree program information:* Part-time and evening/weekend programs available. Postbaccalaureate distance learning degree programs offered (no on-campus study). Offers religious education (MAJS). *Application deadline:* For fall admission, 9/1 (priority date); for spring admission, 1/5 (priority date). Applications are processed on a rolling basis. *Application fee:* $50. *Application Contact:* Linda L. Rosen, Director of Student Services, 216-464-4050 Ext. 101, Fax: 216-464-5827, E-mail: lrosen@siegalcollege.edu. *President,* Dr. David S. Ariel, 216-464-4050 Ext. 108, Fax: 216-464-5827, E-mail: dsariel@siegalcollege.edu.

LAURENTIAN UNIVERSITY, Sudbury, ON P3E 2C6, Canada

General Information Independent-religious, coed, comprehensive institution. *Enrollment:* 170 full-time matriculated graduate/professional students (85 women), 126 part-time matriculated graduate/professional students (73 women). *Enrollment by degree level:* 296 master's. *Graduate faculty:* 179 full-time (40 women), 91 part-time/adjunct (10 women). *International tuition:* $2,620 full-time. *Tuition, area resident:* Full-time $1,333. *Required fees:* $199. *Graduate housing:* Rooms and/or apartments available on a first-come, first-served basis to single and married students. Typical cost: $3,015 per year for single students. *Student services:* Campus employment opportunities, campus safety program, career counseling, child daycare facilities, disabled student services, exercise/wellness program, free psychological counseling, international student services, low-cost health insurance, multicultural affairs office, writing training. *Library facilities:* J. N. Desmarais Library plus 3 others. *Online resources:* web page. *Collection:* 696,838 titles.

Computer facilities: 125 computers available on campus for general student use. Internet access is available. *Web address:* http://www.laurentian.ca/.

General Application Contact: 705-675-1151 Ext. 3909, Fax: 705-675-4843, E-mail: admissions@nickel.laurentian.ca.

GRADUATE UNITS

School of Graduate Studies and Research Students: 170 full-time (85 women), 126 part-time (73 women). 185 applicants, 100% accepted, 120 enrolled. *Faculty:* 179 full-time (40 women), 91 part-time/adjunct (10 women). Expenses: Contact institution. *Financial support:* In 2001–02, 44 fellowships (averaging $2,000 per year), 101 teaching assistantships (averaging $6,750 per year) were awarded. Research assistantships, career-related internships or fieldwork, institutionally sponsored loans, and scholarships/grants also available. In 2001, 86 degrees awarded. *Degree program information:* Part-time and evening/weekend programs available. Offers applied physics (M Sc); biology (M Sc); chemistry and biochemistry (M Sc); geology (M Sc); history (MA); human development (M Sc, MA); humanities: interpretation and values (MA); sociology (MA). *Application fee:* $50. *Application Contact:* 705-675-4843, Fax: 705-675-4891, E-mail: admissions@nickel.laurentian.ca. *Director,* Dr. Paul Colilli, 705-675-1151 Ext. 3423, Fax: 705-671-3840, E-mail: pcolilli@nickel.laurentian.ca.

École de Service Social Students: 3 full-time (2 women), 15 part-time (11 women). 12 applicants, 100% accepted, 4 enrolled. *Faculty:* 11 full-time (4 women), 1 (woman) part-time/adjunct. Expenses: Contact institution. In 2001, 1 degree awarded. *Degree program information:* Part-time programs available. Offers social service (MSS). Open only to French-speaking students. *Application deadline:* For fall admission, 5/28. *Application fee:* $50. *Application Contact:* 705-675-4843, Fax: 705-675-4891, E-mail: admissions@nickel.

laurentian.ca. *Director*, Dr. Marie-Luce Garceau, 705-673-6560 Ext. 5050, Fax: 705-671-3832, E-mail: mgarceau@nickel.laurentian.ca.

School of Commerce and Administration Students: 6 full-time (0 women), 18 part-time (5 women). 41 applicants, 100% accepted, 36 enrolled. *Faculty:* 9 full-time (2 women), 1 part-time/adjunct (0 women). Expenses: Contact institution. *Financial support:* In 2001–02, 1 fellowship, 6 teaching assistantships (averaging $6,750 per year) were awarded. Institutionally sponsored loans and scholarships/grants also available. In 2001, 18 degrees awarded. *Degree program information:* Part-time and evening/weekend programs available. Offers commerce and administration (MBA). *Application deadline:* For fall admission, 5/28 (priority date); for spring admission, 1/29. *Application fee:* $50. *Application Contact:* 705-675-4843, Fax: 705-675-4891, E-mail: admissions@nickel.laurentian.ca. *Director*, Dr. Bernadette Schell, 705-675-1151 Ext. 2123, Fax: 705-673-6518.

School of Engineering Students: 11 full-time (0 women), 12 part-time (2 women). 11 applicants, 100% accepted, 7 enrolled. *Faculty:* 18 full-time (0 women), 18 part-time/adjunct (0 women). Expenses: Contact institution. *Financial support:* In 2001–02, 2 fellowships (averaging $2,000 per year), 6 teaching assistantships (averaging $6,750 per year) were awarded. Scholarships/grants also available. In 2001, 2 degrees awarded. *Degree program information:* Part-time programs available. Offers metallurgy (MA Sc); mineral resource engineering (MA Sc); mineral resources engineering (M Eng). *Application deadline:* For fall admission, 9/1. *Application fee:* $50. *Application Contact:* 705-675-4843, Fax: 705-675-4891, E-mail: admissions@nickel.laurentian.ca. *Director*, Dr. Paul Lindon, 705-675-1151 Ext. 2244, Fax: 705-675-4862, E-mail: plindon@nickel.laurentian.ca.

School of Social Work 14 applicants, 100% accepted, 10 enrolled. *Faculty:* 15 full-time (7 women), 3 part-time/adjunct (1 woman). Expenses: Contact institution. *Financial support:* Teaching assistantships available. In 2001, 9 degrees awarded. *Degree program information:* Part-time programs available. Offers social work (MSW). *Application deadline:* For fall admission, 5/28. *Application fee:* $50. *Application Contact:* 705-675-4843, Fax: 705-675-4891, E-mail: admissions@nickel.laurentian.ca. *Director*, Dr. Marie-Luce Garceau, 705-673-6560 Ext. 5050, Fax: 705-671-3832, E-mail: mgarceau@nickel.laurentian.ca.

LAWRENCE TECHNOLOGICAL UNIVERSITY, Southfield, MI 48075-1058

General Information Independent, coed, comprehensive institution. *Enrollment:* 98 full-time matriculated graduate/professional students (21 women), 1,104 part-time matriculated graduate/professional students (392 women). *Enrollment by degree level:* 1,202 master's. *Graduate faculty:* 72 full-time (17 women), 88 part-time/adjunct (18 women). *Tuition:* Part-time $460 per credit hour. *Graduate housing:* Rooms and/or apartments available on a first-come, first-served basis to single and married students. Typical cost: $3,101 per year for single students; $3,101 per year for married students. Housing application deadline: 5/1. *Student services:* Campus employment opportunities, career counseling, exercise/wellness program, international student services, low-cost health insurance, writing training. *Library facilities:* Lawrence Technological University Library plus 1 other. *Online resources:* library catalog, web page. *Collection:* 107,000 titles, 665 serial subscriptions.

Computer facilities: 400 computers available on campus for general student use. A campuswide network can be accessed from student residence rooms and from off campus. *Web address:* http://www.ltu.edu/.

General Application Contact: Jane Rohrback, Interim Director of Admissions, 248-204-3160, Fax: 248-204-3188, E-mail: admission@ltu.edu.

GRADUATE UNITS

College of Architecture and Design Students: 5 full-time (0 women), 72 part-time (15 women); includes 3 minority (1 African American, 2 Asian Americans or Pacific Islanders), 8 international. Average age 28. 63 applicants, 25 enrolled. *Faculty:* 11 full-time (4 women), 17 part-time/adjunct (2 women). Expenses: Contact institution. *Financial support:* Application deadline: 3/1; In 2001, 25 degrees awarded. *Degree program information:* Part-time and evening/weekend programs available. Offers architecture and design (M Arch). *Application deadline:* For fall admission, 8/1 (priority date); for winter admission, 12/1 (priority date); for spring admission, 2/1. Applications are processed on a rolling basis. *Application fee:* $50. Electronic applications accepted. *Application Contact:* Jane Rohrback, Interim Director of Admissions, 248-204-3160, Fax: 248-204-3188, E-mail: admission@ltu.edu. *Dean*, Dr. Neville Clouten, 248-204-2800, Fax: 248-204-2900, E-mail: clouten@ltu.edu.

College of Arts and Sciences Students: 15 full-time (2 women), 133 part-time (55 women); includes 38 minority (4 African Americans, 28 Asian Americans or Pacific Islanders, 1 Hispanic American, 5 Native Americans), 33 international. Average age 34. 100 applicants, 97 enrolled. *Faculty:* 26 full-time (7 women), 14 part-time/adjunct (4 women). Expenses: Contact institution. *Financial support:* Application deadline: 3/1; In 2001, 41 degrees awarded. *Degree program information:* Part-time and evening/weekend programs available. Offers computer science (MS); science education (MSE); technical communication (MS). *Application deadline:* For fall admission, 8/1 (priority date); for winter admission, 12/1 (priority date); for spring admission, 5/1. Applications are processed on a rolling basis. *Application fee:* $50. Electronic applications accepted. *Application Contact:* Jane Rohrback, Interim Director of Admissions, 248-204-3160, Fax: 248-204-3188, E-mail: admission@ltu.edu. *Dean*, Dr. James Rodgers, 248-204-3500, Fax: 248-204-3518, E-mail: scidean@ltu.edu.

College of Engineering Average age 32. 133 applicants, 38 enrolled. *Faculty:* 27 full-time (2 women), 11 part-time/adjunct (1 woman). Expenses: Contact institution. *Financial support:* Institutionally sponsored loans available. Support available to part-time students. Financial award application deadline: 3/1; financial award applicants required to submit FAFSA. In 2001, 43 degrees awarded. *Degree program information:* Part-time and evening/weekend programs available. Offers automotive engineering (MAE); civil engineering (MCE); electrical and computer engineering (MS); manufacturing systems (MEMS, DE). *Application deadline:* For fall admission, 8/1 (priority date); for winter admission, 12/1 (priority date); for spring admission, 5/1. Applications are processed on a rolling basis. *Application fee:* $50. Electronic applications accepted. *Application Contact:* Jane Rohrback, Interim Director of Admissions, 248-204-3160, Fax: 248-204-3188, E-mail: admission@ltu.edu. *Dean*, Dr. Laird Johnston, 248-204-2500, Fax: 248-204-2509, E-mail: lejohnston@ltu.edu.

College of Management Students: 78 full-time (19 women), 758 part-time (302 women); includes 171 minority (65 African Americans, 81 Asian Americans or Pacific Islanders, 4 Hispanic Americans, 21 Native Americans), 91 international. Average age 35. 463 applicants, 287 enrolled. *Faculty:* 8 full-time (4 women), 46 part-time/adjunct (11 women). Expenses: Contact institution. *Financial support:* Institutionally sponsored loans available. Support available to part-time students. Financial award application deadline: 3/1; financial award applicants required to submit FAFSA. In 2001, 276 degrees awarded. *Degree program information:* Part-time and evening/weekend programs available. Offers business administration (MBA); industrial operations (MS); information systems (MS). *Application deadline:* For fall admission, 8/1 (priority date); for winter admission, 12/1 (priority date); for spring admission, 5/1. Applications are processed on a rolling basis. *Application fee:* $50. Electronic applications accepted. *Application Contact:* Jane Rohrback, Interim Director of Admissions, 248-204-3160, Fax: 248-204-3188, E-mail: admission@ltu.edu. *Dean*, Dr. Lou DeGennaro, 248-204-3050, E-mail: degennaro@ltu.edu.

THE LEADERSHIP INSTITUTE OF SEATTLE, Kenmore, WA 98028-4966

General Information Independent, coed, upper-level institution. *Enrollment by degree level:* 152 master's. *Graduate faculty:* 11 full-time (6 women), 9 part-time/adjunct (6 women). *Tuition:* Full-time $12,818. *Required fees:* $2,600. Full-time tuition and fees vary according to course load and program. *Graduate housing:* On-campus housing not available. *Student services:* Campus employment opportunities, career counseling, disabled student services, international student services.

Computer facilities: 2 computers available on campus for general student use. Internet access is available. *Web address:* http://www.lios.org/.

General Application Contact: Carolyn R. Pedersen, Admissions Director, 425-939-8124, Fax: 425-939-8110, E-mail: cpedersen@lios.org.

GRADUATE UNITS

School of Applied Behavioral Science Students: 152 full-time (120 women); includes 21 minority (6 African Americans, 5 Asian Americans or Pacific Islanders, 7 Hispanic Americans, 3 Native Americans), 8 international. Average age 40. 92 applicants, 96% accepted, 79 enrolled. *Faculty:* 11 full-time (6 women), 9 part-time/adjunct (6 women). Expenses: Contact institution. *Financial support:* In 2001–02, 97 students received support. Career-related internships or fieldwork, Federal Work-Study, and scholarships/grants available. Financial award applicants required to submit FAFSA. In 2001, 71 degrees awarded. Offers consulting and coaching in organizations (MAABS); systems counseling (MAABS). *Application deadline:* Applications are processed on a rolling basis. *Application fee:* $65. *Application Contact:* Carolyn R. Pedersen, Admissions Director, 425-939-8124, Fax: 425-939-8110, E-mail: cpedersen@lios.org. *Executive Dean*, Daniel D. Leahy, 425-939-8173, Fax: 425-939-8110, E-mail: dleahy@lios.org.

LEBANESE AMERICAN UNIVERSITY, Beirut, , Lebanon

General Information Private, comprehensive institution.

GRADUATE UNITS

School of Arts and Sciences Offers computer science (MS); international affairs (MA).

School of Business Offers business (MBA).

School of Pharmacy Offers pharmacy (Pharm D).

LEBANON VALLEY COLLEGE, Annville, PA 17003-1400

General Information Independent-religious, coed, comprehensive institution. *Enrollment:* 211 part-time matriculated graduate/professional students. *Enrollment by degree level:* 211 master's. *Graduate faculty:* 3 full-time (2 women), 27 part-time/adjunct (8 women). *Tuition:* Part-time $305 per credit. Part-time tuition and fees vary according to program. *Graduate housing:* On-campus housing not available. *Student services:* Career counseling. *Library facilities:* Bishop Library. *Online resources:* library catalog, web page, access to other libraries' catalogs. *Collection:* 165,642 titles, 6,160 serial subscriptions, 3,346 audiovisual materials.

Computer facilities: 194 computers available on campus for general student use. A campuswide network can be accessed from student residence rooms and from off campus. Internet access is available. *Web address:* http://www.lvc.edu/.

General Application Contact: Cheryl L. Batdorf, Assistant Director, 717-867-6335, Fax: 717-867-6018, E-mail: batdorf@lvc.edu.

GRADUATE UNITS

Graduate Studies and Continuing Education 113 applicants, 96% accepted, 108 enrolled. *Faculty:* 3 full-time (2 women), 27 part-time/adjunct (8 women). Expenses: Contact institution. *Financial support:* Application deadline: 5/1; In 2001, 90 degrees awarded. *Degree program information:* Part-time and evening/weekend programs available. Offers business administration (MBA); music education (MME); science education (MSE). *Application deadline:* Applications are processed on a rolling basis. *Application fee:* $25. Electronic applications accepted. *Associate Dean for Graduate and Continuing Education*, Dr. Barbara J. Denison, 717-867-6214, Fax: 717-867-6018, E-mail: denison@lvc.edu.

LEE UNIVERSITY, Cleveland, TN 37320-3450

General Information Independent-religious, coed, comprehensive institution.

GRADUATE UNITS

Department of Behavioral Sciences Offers counseling psychology (MS).

Program in Church Music *Degree program information:* Part-time programs available. Offers church music (MCM).

Program in Education Offers education (M Ed).

Program in Liberal Arts Offers liberal arts (MLA).

LEHIGH UNIVERSITY, Bethlehem, PA 18015-3094

General Information Independent, coed, university. CGS member. *Enrollment:* 797 full-time matriculated graduate/professional students (326 women), 1,032 part-time matriculated graduate/professional students (483 women). *Enrollment by degree level:* 1,035 master's, 511 doctoral, 283 other advanced degrees. *Graduate faculty:* 393 full-time (80 women), 100 part-time/adjunct (43 women). *Tuition:* Part-time $468 per credit hour. *Required fees:* $200; $100 per semester. Tuition and fees vary according to program. *Graduate housing:* Rooms and/or apartments available to single and married students. Typical cost: $4,740 per year for single students; $6,300 per year for married students. *Student services:* Campus employment opportunities, campus safety program, career counseling, child daycare facilities, exercise/wellness program, free psychological counseling, international student services, low-cost health insurance, multicultural affairs office. *Library facilities:* E. W. Fairchild-Martindale Library plus 1 other. *Online resources:* library catalog, web page, access to other libraries' catalogs. *Collection:* 1.2 million titles, 6,271 serial subscriptions, 8,415 audiovisual materials.

Computer facilities: 516 computers available on campus for general student use. A campuswide network can be accessed from student residence rooms and from off campus. Internet access and online class registration are available. *Web address:* http://www.lehigh.edu/.

GRADUATE UNITS

College of Arts and Sciences Students: 228 full-time (117 women), 217 part-time (106 women). 364 applicants, 41% accepted. *Faculty:* 206. Expenses: Contact institution. *Financial support:* In 2001–02, 10 fellowships with full tuition reimbursements (averaging $15,000 per year), 21 research assistantships with full tuition reimbursements, 119 teaching assistantships with full tuition reimbursements (averaging $12,500 per year) were awarded. Career-related internships or fieldwork, Federal Work-Study, institutionally sponsored loans, scholarships/grants, tuition waivers (full and partial), and unspecified assistantships also available. Support available to part-time students. Financial award application deadline: 1/15. In 2001, 57 master's, 27 doctorates awarded. *Degree program information:* Part-time programs available. Postbaccalaureate distance learning degree programs offered (no on-campus study). Offers American studies (MA); applied mathematics (MS, PhD); arts and sciences (MA, MS, DA, PhD); behavioral and evolutionary bioscience (PhD); behavioral neuroscience (PhD); biochemistry (PhD); biology (PhD); chemistry (MS, DA, PhD); earth and environmental sciences (MS, PhD); English (MA, PhD); experimental psychology (PhD); history (MA, PhD); mathematics (MS, PhD); molecular biology (PhD); photonics (MS); physics (MS, PhD); political science (MA); sociology and anthropology (MA); statistics (MS). *Application deadline:* For fall admission, 7/15; for spring admission, 12/30. Applications are processed on a rolling basis. *Application fee:* $50. Electronic applications accepted. *Application Contact:* Mary Anne Haller, Coordinator, 610-758-4280, Fax: 610-758-6232, E-mail: mh0h@lehigh.edu. *Dean*, Dr. Bobb Carson, 610-758-3300.

College of Business and Economics Students: 70 full-time (22 women), 283 part-time (95 women); includes 43 minority (6 African Americans, 33 Asian Americans or Pacific Islanders, 3 Hispanic Americans, 1 Native American), 36 international. Average age 30. 262 applicants, 76% accepted, 136 enrolled. *Faculty:* 53 full-time (7 women), 7 part-time/adjunct (1 woman). Expenses: Contact institution. *Financial support:* In 2001–02, 57 students received support, including 2 fellowships with full tuition reimbursements available (averaging $12,000 per year), 1 research assistantship with full and partial tuition reimbursement available (averaging $1,000 per year), 24 teaching assistantships with full tuition reimbursements available (averaging $11,350 per year); career-related internships or fieldwork, scholarships/grants, and tuition waivers (full and partial) also available. Support available to part-time students. Financial award application deadline: 1/15. In 2001, 108 master's, 2 doctorates awarded. *Degree program information:* Part-time and evening/weekend programs available. Postbaccalaureate distance learning degree programs offered (minimal on-campus study). Offers accounting and information analysis (MS); business (MBA, PhD); business administration (MBA); business administration and engineering); economics (MS, PhD); new ventures (Certificate); project management (Certificate); supply chain management (Certificate). *Application deadline:* For fall admission, 7/15; for spring admission, 12/1. Applications are processed on a roll-

Lehigh University (continued)

ing basis. *Application fee:* $50. Electronic applications accepted. *Application Contact:* Mary-Theresa Taglang, Director of Recruitment and Admissions, 610-758-5285, Fax: 610-758-5283, E-mail: mtt4@lehigh.edu. *Associate Dean and Director*, Kathleen A. Trexler, 610-758-4450, Fax: 610-758-5283, E-mail: kat3@lehigh.edu.

College of Education Students: 157 full-time (123 women), 311 part-time (226 women). 438 applicants, 48% accepted. *Faculty:* 23 full-time (10 women), 11 part-time/adjunct (5 women). Expenses: Contact institution. *Financial support:* Fellowships with full and partial tuition reimbursements, research assistantships with full and partial tuition reimbursements, teaching assistantships with full and partial tuition reimbursements, career-related internships or fieldwork, Federal Work-Study, institutionally sponsored loans, scholarships/grants, tuition waivers (full and partial), and unspecified assistantships available. Financial award application deadline: 1/31. In 2001, 144 master's, 24 doctorates, 6 other advanced degrees awarded. *Degree program information:* Part-time and evening/weekend programs available. Postbaccalaureate distance learning degree programs offered (minimal on-campus study). Offers counseling and human services (M Ed); counseling psychology (M Ed, PhD, Certificate); curriculum and instruction (Ed D); education (M Ed, MA, MS, Ed D, PhD, Certificate, Ed S); educational leadership (M Ed, Ed D, Certificate); educational technology (MS, Ed D); elementary education (M Ed, Ed D, Certificate); school counseling (M Ed, Certificate); school psychology (PhD, Certificate, Ed S); secondary education (M Ed, MA, Certificate); special education (M Ed, PhD, Certificate); technology–based teacher education (M Ed, Ed D, Certificate); technology-based teacher education (MA). *Application fee:* $50. Electronic applications accepted. *Application Contact:* Doris Woynicki, Executive Secretary, 610-758-3221, Fax: 610-758-6223, E-mail: daw2@lehigh.edu. *Dean*, Dr. Sally A. White, 610-758-3221, Fax: 610-758-6223, E-mail: saw8@lehigh.edu.

P.C. Rossin College of Engineering and Applied Science Students: 386 full-time (66 women), 123 part-time (21 women); includes 62 minority (13 African Americans, 36 Asian Americans or Pacific Islanders, 13 Hispanic Americans), 216 international. Average age 24. 1,986 applicants, 25% accepted, 134 enrolled. *Faculty:* 121 full-time (4 women), 8 part-time/adjunct (0 women). Expenses: Contact institution. *Financial support:* In 2001–02, 36 fellowships with full and partial tuition reimbursements (averaging $12,600 per year), 148 research assistantships with full and partial tuition reimbursements (averaging $16,500 per year), 39 teaching assistantships with full and partial tuition reimbursements (averaging $12,330 per year) were awarded. Career-related internships or fieldwork, Federal Work-Study, institutionally sponsored loans, scholarships/grants, and tuition waivers (full and partial) also available. Support available to part-time students. Financial award application deadline: 1/15. In 2001, 109 master's, 43 doctorates awarded. *Degree program information:* Part-time and evening/weekend programs available. Postbaccalaureate distance learning degree programs offered (no on-campus study). Offers applied mathematics (MS, PhD); chemical engineering (M Eng, MS, PhD); civil and environmental engineering (M Eng, MS, PhD); computer engineering (MS); computer science (MS, PhD); electrical engineering (M Eng, MS, PhD); engineering and applied science (M Eng, MS, PhD); industrial engineering (M Eng, MS, PhD); management science (MS); manufacturing systems engineering (MS); materials science and engineering (M Eng, MS, PhD); mechanical engineering (M Eng, MS, PhD); mechanics (M Eng, MS, PhD); quality engineering (MS). *Application deadline:* For fall admission, 7/15; for spring admission, 12/1. Applications are processed on a rolling basis. *Application fee:* $50. Electronic applications accepted. *Application Contact:* Lynn M. Walters, Administrative Coordinator, 610-758-6310, Fax: 610-758-5623, E-mail: lmw7@lehigh.edu. *Associate Dean*, Dr. John P. Coulter, 610-758-6310, Fax: 610-758-5623, E-mail: john.coulter@lehigh.edu.

Center for Polymer Science and Engineering Students: 20 full-time (7 women), 25 part-time (11 women); includes 20 minority (19 Asian Americans or Pacific Islanders, 1 Hispanic American) Average age 30. *Faculty:* 24 full-time (2 women). Expenses: Contact institution. *Financial support:* Fellowships, research assistantships, teaching assistantships available. Financial award application deadline: 1/15. In 2001, 5 master's, 3 doctorates awarded. *Degree program information:* Part-time and evening/weekend programs available. Postbaccalaureate distance learning degree programs offered (no on-campus study). Offers polymer science and engineering (MS, PhD). Programs are interdisciplinary. *Application deadline:* For fall admission, 7/15; for spring admission, 12/1. Applications are processed on a rolling basis. *Application fee:* $40. *Application Contact:* James E. Roberts, Chair, Polymer Education Committee, 610-758-4841, Fax: 610-758-6536, E-mail: jer1@lehigh.edu. *Director*, Dr. Raymond A. Pearson, 610-758-3857, Fax: 610-758-3526, E-mail: rp02@lehigh.edu.

LEHMAN COLLEGE OF THE CITY UNIVERSITY OF NEW YORK, Bronx, NY 10468-1589

General Information State and locally supported, coed, comprehensive institution. *Enrollment:* 114 full-time matriculated graduate/professional students (78 women), 1,853 part-time matriculated graduate/professional students (1,342 women). *Enrollment by degree level:* 1,967 master's. *Graduate faculty:* 110 full-time, 36 part-time/adjunct. Tuition, state resident: part-time $185 per credit. Tuition, nonresident: part-time $320 per credit. *Required fees:* $40 per term. *Graduate housing:* On-campus housing not available. *Student services:* Campus employment opportunities, campus safety program, career counseling, child daycare facilities, disabled student services, exercise/wellness program, international student services, low-cost health insurance, teacher training. *Library facilities:* Lehman College Library plus 1 other. *Online resources:* library catalog, web page, access to other libraries' catalogs. *Collection:* 541,944 titles, 1,350 serial subscriptions. *Research affiliation:* New York Botanical Gardens, Montefiore Hospital and Medical Center.

Computer facilities: 600 computers available on campus for general student use. Internet access is available. *Web address:* http://www.lehman.cuny.edu/.

General Application Contact: Roland Valaz, Deputy Director of Admissions and Recruitment, 718-960-8856, Fax: 718-960-8172.

GRADUATE UNITS

Division of Arts and Humanities Students: 45 full-time (38 women), 176 part-time (114 women); includes 51 minority (14 African Americans, 2 Asian Americans or Pacific Islanders, 35 Hispanic Americans) Average age 37. *Faculty:* 54 full-time (19 women), 4 part-time/adjunct (all women). Expenses: Contact institution. *Financial support:* Fellowships, teaching assistantships, career-related internships or fieldwork, Federal Work-Study, scholarships/grants, tuition waivers (full and partial), and unspecified assistantships available. Support available to part-time students. Financial award application deadline: 5/15; financial award applicants required to submit FAFSA. In 2001, 66 degrees awarded. *Degree program information:* Part-time and evening/weekend programs available. Offers art (MA, MFA); arts and humanities (MA, MAT, MFA); English (MA); history (MA); music (MAT); Spanish (MA); speech-language pathology and audiology (MA). *Application deadline:* For fall admission, 4/1; for spring admission, 11/1. Applications are processed on a rolling basis. *Application fee:* $40. *Acting Dean*, Marlene Gottlieb, 718-960-8675.

Division of Education Students: 8 full-time (7 women), 802 part-time (619 women); includes 194 minority (76 African Americans, 2 Asian Americans or Pacific Islanders, 116 Hispanic Americans), 1 international. Average age 35. *Faculty:* 40 full-time, 27 part-time/adjunct. Expenses: Contact institution. *Financial support:* Fellowships, career-related internships or fieldwork, Federal Work-Study, institutionally sponsored loans, and tuition waivers (full and partial) available. Support available to part-time students. Financial award application deadline: 5/15; financial award applicants required to submit FAFSA. In 2001, 305 degrees awarded. *Degree program information:* Part-time and evening/weekend programs available. Offers bilingual special education (MS Ed); business education (MS Ed); early childhood education (MS Ed); early special education (MS Ed); education (MA, MS Ed); elementary education (MS Ed); emotional handicaps (MS Ed); English education (MS Ed); guidance and counseling (MS Ed); learning disabilities (MS Ed); mathematics 7–12 (MS Ed); mental retardation (MS Ed); reading teacher (MS Ed); science education (MS Ed); social studies 7–12 (MA); special education (MS Ed); teaching English to speakers of other languages (MS Ed). *Application deadline:* For fall admission, 4/1; for spring admission, 11/1. Applications are processed on a rolling basis. *Application fee:* $40. *Dean*, James V. Bruni, 718-960-8401.

Division of Natural and Social Sciences Students: 56 full-time (30 women), 251 part-time (168 women); includes 82 minority (52 African Americans, 7 Asian Americans or Pacific Islanders, 23 Hispanic Americans), 1 international. *Faculty:* 16 full-time (3 women), 5 part-time/adjunct (0 women). Expenses: Contact institution. *Financial support:* Fellowships, research assistantships, teaching assistantships, career-related internships or fieldwork, Federal Work-Study, and tuition waivers (full and partial) available. Support available to part-time students. Financial award application deadline: 5/15; financial award applicants required to submit FAFSA. In 2001, 106 degrees awarded. *Degree program information:* Part-time and evening/weekend programs available. Offers accounting (MS); adult health nursing (MS); approved preprofessional practice (MS); biology (MA); clinical nutrition (MS); community nutrition (MS); computer science (MS); health education and promotion (MA); health N–12 teacher (MS Ed); mathematics (MA); natural and social sciences (MA, MS, MS Ed, PhD); nursing of old adults (MS); nutrition (MS); parent-child nursing (MS); pediatric nurse practitioner (MS); plant sciences (PhD); recreation (MA, MS Ed); recreation education (MA, MS Ed). *Application deadline:* For fall admission, 4/1; for spring admission, 11/1. Applications are processed on a rolling basis. *Application fee:* $40. *Dean*, Joseph Rachlin, 718-960-8764.

LE MOYNE COLLEGE, Syracuse, NY 13214-1399

General Information Independent-religious, coed, comprehensive institution. *Enrollment:* 52 full-time matriculated graduate/professional students (37 women), 408 part-time matriculated graduate/professional students (233 women). *Enrollment by degree level:* 460 master's. *Graduate faculty:* 32 full-time (13 women), 31 part-time/adjunct (19 women). *Tuition:* Full-time $7,920; part-time $440 per credit hour. Tuition and fees vary according to program. *Graduate housing:* On-campus housing not available. *Student services:* Campus employment opportunities, career counseling, free psychological counseling, teacher training. *Library facilities:* Noreen Reale Falcone Library. *Online resources:* library catalog, web page, access to other libraries' catalogs. *Collection:* 159,323 titles, 1,308 serial subscriptions, 10,129 audiovisual materials.

Computer facilities: 225 computers available on campus for general student use. A campuswide network can be accessed from student residence rooms and from off campus. Internet access is available. *Web address:* http://www.lemoyne.edu/.

GRADUATE UNITS

Department of Business Students: 9 full-time (3 women), 185 part-time (76 women); includes 13 minority (6 African Americans, 4 Asian Americans or Pacific Islanders, 3 Hispanic Americans), 2 international. Average age 37. 48 applicants, 100% accepted, 48 enrolled. *Faculty:* 21 full-time (6 women), 3 part-time/adjunct (1 woman). Expenses: Contact institution. *Financial support:* In 2001–02, 27 students received support. Career-related internships or fieldwork available. Support available to part-time students. Financial award applicants required to submit FAFSA. In 2001, 84 degrees awarded. *Degree program information:* Part-time and evening/weekend programs available. Offers business (MBA). *Application deadline:* Applications are processed on a rolling basis. *Application fee:* $0. *Director of MBA Program*, Dr. Wally Elmer, 315-445-4786, Fax: 315-445-4787, E-mail: elmer@lemoyne.edu.

Department of Education Students: 43 full-time (34 women), 223 part-time (157 women); includes 11 minority (8 African Americans, 2 Asian Americans or Pacific Islanders, 1 Hispanic American) Average age 31. 85 applicants, 100% accepted, 85 enrolled. *Faculty:* 11 full-time (7 women), 28 part-time/adjunct (18 women). Expenses: Contact institution. *Financial support:* In 2001–02, 133 students received support. Career-related internships or fieldwork available. Support available to part-time students. Financial award applicants required to submit FAFSA. In 2001, 87 degrees awarded. *Degree program information:* Part-time and evening/weekend programs available. Offers education (MS Ed, MST). *Application deadline:* Applications are processed on a rolling basis. *Application fee:* $25. *Chair, Education Department and Director of Graduate Education*, Dr. Robert P. Anderson, 315-445-4376, Fax: 315-445-4755, E-mail: andersrp@lemoyne.edu.

LENOIR-RHYNE COLLEGE, Hickory, NC 28603

General Information Independent-religious, coed, comprehensive institution. *Enrollment:* 3 full-time matriculated graduate/professional students, 85 part-time matriculated graduate/professional students. *Graduate faculty:* 2 full-time (both women), 11 part-time/adjunct (5 women). *Tuition:* Full-time $8,100; part-time $225 per credit hour. *Required fees:* $50; $25 per semester. Tuition and fees vary according to program. *Graduate housing:* On-campus housing not available. *Student services:* Campus employment opportunities, campus safety program, career counseling, disabled student services, exercise/wellness program, free psychological counseling, international student services, low-cost health insurance, multicultural affairs office, teacher training, writing training. *Library facilities:* Carl Rudisill Library plus 3 others. *Online resources:* library catalog, web page, access to other libraries' catalogs. *Collection:* 139,726 titles, 2,335 serial subscriptions, 36,728 audiovisual materials.

Computer facilities: 94 computers available on campus for general student use. A campuswide network can be accessed from student residence rooms and from off campus. Internet access is available. *Web address:* http://www.lrc.edu/.

General Application Contact: Gabriela Abad, Administrative Assistant, 828-328-7275, Fax: 828-328-7368, E-mail: abadg@lre.edu.

GRADUATE UNITS

The Graduate School Students: 3 full-time, 85 part-time. 28 applicants, 89% accepted, 25 enrolled. *Faculty:* 2 full-time (both women), 11 part-time/adjunct (5 women). Expenses: Contact institution. *Financial support:* Career-related internships or fieldwork, Federal Work-Study, institutionally sponsored loans, and tuition waivers (partial) available. Support available to part-time students. Financial award application deadline: 3/1; financial award applicants required to submit FAFSA. In 2001, 49 degrees awarded. *Degree program information:* Part-time and evening/weekend programs available. Offers community/agency counseling (MA); school counseling (MA). *Application deadline:* For fall admission, 8/1 (priority date); for spring admission, 12/1 (priority date). Applications are processed on a rolling basis. *Application fee:* $25. Electronic applications accepted. *Application Contact:* Gabriela Abad, Administrative Assistant, 828-328-7275, Fax: 828-328-7368, E-mail: abadg@lre.edu. *Associate Dean for Academic Affairs*, Dr. Regis Gilman, 828-328-7275, Fax: 828-328-7368, E-mail: gilmanr@lre.edu.

Charles M. Snipes School of Business Students: 2 full-time, 43 part-time. 10 applicants, 90% accepted, 9 enrolled. *Faculty:* 6 part-time/adjunct (3 women). Expenses: Contact institution. *Financial support:* In 2001–02, 45 students received support. In 2001, 24 degrees awarded. *Degree program information:* Part-time and evening/weekend programs available. Offers business (MBA). *Application deadline:* For fall admission, 8/1 (priority date); for spring admission, 12/1 (priority date). Applications are processed on a rolling basis. *Application fee:* $25. Electronic applications accepted. *Application Contact:* Gabriela Abad, Administrative Assistant, 828-328-7275, Fax: 828-328-7368, E-mail: abadg@lre.edu. *Chair*, Dr. Jerald Gober, 828-328-7197, Fax: 828-328-7368, E-mail: goberj@lrc.edu.

School of Education *Faculty:* 3 part-time/adjunct (2 women). Expenses: Contact institution. *Financial support:* Career-related internships or fieldwork, Federal Work-Study, and institutionally sponsored loans available. Support available to part-time students. In 2001, 1 degree awarded. *Degree program information:* Part-time and evening/weekend programs available. Offers birth through kindergarten education (MA); elementary education (MA). *Application deadline:* For fall admission, 8/1 (priority date); for spring admission, 12/1 (priority date). Applications are processed on a rolling basis. *Application fee:* $25. Electronic applications accepted. *Application Contact:* Gabriela Abad, Administrative Assistant, 828-328-7275, Fax: 828-328-7368, E-mail: abadg@lre.edu. *Chair*, Dr. Kathleena Whitesell, 828-328-7035, Fax: 828-328-7368, E-mail: whitesellk@lrc.edu.

LESLEY UNIVERSITY, Cambridge, MA 02138-2790

General Information Independent, coed, primarily women, comprehensive institution. CGS member. *Enrollment:* 261 full-time matriculated graduate/professional students (200 women), 3,441 part-time matriculated graduate/professional students (2,979 women). *Enrollment by degree level:* 3,618 master's, 44 doctoral, 40 other advanced degrees. *Graduate faculty:* 114 full-time (91 women), 366 part-time/adjunct (235 women). *Tuition:* Part-time $330 per credit. *Required fees:* $15 per term. Part-time tuition and fees vary according to campus/location and program. *Graduate housing:* On-campus housing not available. *Student services:* Campus employment opportunities, campus safety program, career counseling, disabled student services, free psychological counseling, international student services, teacher training. *Library facilities:* Eleanor DeWolfe Ludcke Library. *Online resources:* library catalog, web page, access to other libraries' catalogs. *Collection:* 100,992 titles, 91,873 serial subscriptions, 1,308 audiovisual materials.

Computer facilities: 150 computers available on campus for general student use. A campuswide network can be accessed from student residence rooms and from off campus. Internet access is available. *Web address:* http://www.lesley.edu/.

General Application Contact: Hugh Norwood, Dean of Admissions and Enrollment Planning, 800-999-1959, Fax: 617-349-8366, E-mail: hnorwood@mail.lesley.edu.

GRADUATE UNITS

Graduate School of Arts and Social Sciences Students: 108 full-time (97 women), 1,190 part-time (1,084 women); includes 134 minority (81 African Americans, 23 Asian Americans or Pacific Islanders, 26 Hispanic Americans, 4 Native Americans), 16 international. Average age 36. 639 applicants, 91% accepted, 313 enrolled. *Faculty:* 73 full-time (58 women), 137 part-time/adjunct (95 women). Expenses: Contact institution. *Financial support:* In 2001–02, 47 students received support; research assistantships, teaching assistantships, career-related internships or fieldwork, Federal Work-Study, and unspecified assistantships available. Support available to part-time students. Financial award application deadline: 4/1; financial award applicants required to submit FAFSA. In 2001, 1106 degrees awarded. *Degree program information:* Part-time and evening/weekend programs available. Postbaccalaureate distance learning degree programs offered (minimal on-campus study). Offers clinical mental health counseling (MA); counseling psychology (MA, CAGS); creative arts in learning (M Ed, CAGS); development project administration (MA); ecological literacy (MS); environmental education (MS); expressive therapies (MA, PhD, CAGS); independent studies (M Ed); independent study (MA); individually designed (MA); intercultural conflict resolution (MA); intercultural health and human services (MA); intercultural relations (MA, CAGS); intercultural training and consulting (MA); interdisciplinary studies (MA); international education exchange (MA); international student advising (MA); managing culturally diverse human resources (MA); multicultural education (MA); visual arts and creative writing (MFA). MS (environmental education) offered jointly with the Audubon Society Expedition Institute. *Application deadline:* Applications are processed on a rolling basis. *Application fee:* $50. *Application Contact:* Hugh Norwood, Dean of Admissions and Enrollment Planning, 800-999-1959, Fax: 617-349-8366, E-mail: hnorwood@mail.lesley.edu. *Dean,* Dr. Martha B. McKenna, 617-349-8467, Fax: 617-349-8366.

School of Education Students: 74 full-time (66 women), 2,108 part-time (1,781 women); includes 157 minority (76 African Americans, 28 Asian Americans or Pacific Islanders, 42 Hispanic Americans, 11 Native Americans), 8 international. Average age 36. 878 applicants, 86% accepted, 513 enrolled. *Faculty:* 51 full-time (40 women), 197 part-time/adjunct (130 women). Expenses: Contact institution. *Financial support:* In 2001–02, 33 students received support; research assistantships, teaching assistantships, career-related internships or fieldwork, Federal Work-Study, scholarships/grants, and unspecified assistantships available. Support available to part-time students. Financial award application deadline: 4/1; financial award applicants required to submit FAFSA. In 2001, 1,366 master's, 2 doctorates, 2 other advanced degrees awarded. *Degree program information:* Part-time and evening/weekend programs available. Postbaccalaureate distance learning degree programs offered (no on-campus study). Offers art education (M Ed); computers in education (M Ed, CAGS); curriculum and instruction (M Ed, CAGS); early childhood education (M Ed); educational administration (M Ed, CAGS); educational studies (PhD); elementary education (M Ed); individually designed (M Ed); intensive special needs (M Ed); middle school education (M Ed); reading (M Ed, CAGS); special needs (M Ed, CAGS). *Application deadline:* Applications are processed on a rolling basis. *Application fee:* $50. *Application Contact:* Hugh Norwood, Dean of Admissions and Enrollment Planning, 800-999-1959, Fax: 617-349-8366, E-mail: hnorwood@mail.lesley.edu. *Dean,* Dr. William L. Dandridge, 617-349-8375.

School of Management Students: 80 full-time (38 women), 143 part-time (114 women); includes 25 minority (9 African Americans, 10 Asian Americans or Pacific Islanders, 6 Hispanic Americans), 5 international. Average age 35. 92 applicants, 80% accepted, 39 enrolled. *Faculty:* 10 full-time (5 women), 32 part-time/adjunct (10 women). Expenses: Contact institution. *Financial support:* In 2001–02, 1 student received support. Career-related internships or fieldwork, Federal Work-Study, scholarships/grants, and unspecified assistantships available. Support available to part-time students. Financial award application deadline: 4/1; financial award applicants required to submit FAFSA. In 2001, 97 degrees awarded. *Degree program information:* Part-time and evening/weekend programs available. Postbaccalaureate distance learning degree programs offered (no on-campus study). Offers fundraising management (MSM); health services management (MSM); human resources management (MSM); management (MSM); management of information technology (MSM); training and development (MS). *Application deadline:* Applications are processed on a rolling basis. *Application fee:* $50. *Application Contact:* Hugh Norwood, Dean of Admissions and Enrollment Planning, 800-999-1959, Fax: 617-349-8366, E-mail: hnorwood@mail.lesley.edu. *Dean,* George Kaye, 617-349-8658.

See in-depth description on page 939.

LETOURNEAU UNIVERSITY, Longview, TX 75607-7001

General Information Independent-religious, coed, comprehensive institution. *Enrollment:* 32 full-time matriculated graduate/professional students (12 women), 259 part-time matriculated graduate/professional students (134 women). *Enrollment by degree level:* 291 master's. *Graduate faculty:* 8 full-time, 57 part-time/adjunct. *Tuition:* Part-time $365 per credit hour. *Graduate housing:* Room and/or apartments available on a first-come, first-served basis to married students; on-campus housing not available to single students. *Student services:* Teacher training. *Library facilities:* Margaret Estes Resource Center. *Online resources:* library catalog, web page. *Collection:* 72,957 titles, 459 serial subscriptions, 3,136 audiovisual materials.

Computer facilities: 120 computers available on campus for general student use. A campuswide network can be accessed from student residence rooms and from off campus. *Web address:* http://www.letu.edu/.

General Application Contact: Director of Marketing and Enrollment Management, 903-233-3250, Fax: 903-233-3105.

GRADUATE UNITS

Graduate and Professional Studies Students: 32 full-time (12 women), 259 part-time (134 women); includes 42 minority (31 African Americans, 4 Asian Americans or Pacific Islanders, 6 Hispanic Americans, 1 Native American), 3 international. 238 applicants, 88% accepted. *Faculty:* 8 full-time, 57 part-time/adjunct. Expenses: Contact institution. *Financial support:* Applicants required to submit FAFSA. In 2001, 99 degrees awarded. *Degree program information:* Evening/weekend programs available. Offers business administration (MBA); health care (MBA). *Application deadline:* Applications are processed on a rolling basis. *Application fee:* $50. *Application Contact:* Director of Marketing and Enrollment Management, 903-233-3250, Fax: 903-233-3227. *Vice President of Graduate and Professional Studies,* Dr. Robert W. Hudson, 903-233-3250.

LEWIS & CLARK COLLEGE, Portland, OR 97219-7899

General Information Independent, coed, comprehensive institution. *Graduate housing:* On-campus housing not available. *Research affiliation:* Oregon Museum of Science and Industry.

GRADUATE UNITS

Graduate School of Professional Studies *Degree program information:* Part-time and evening/weekend programs available. Offers counseling psychology (MA, MS); counseling psychology/school counseling (MA); educational administration (Certificate); elementary education (MAT); music education (MAT); school psychology (MS); secondary education (MAT); special education—hearing impaired (M Ed).

Northwestern School of Law Students: 486 full-time (248 women), 189 part-time (85 women); includes 109 minority (17 African Americans, 44 Asian Americans or Pacific Islanders, 34 Hispanic Americans, 14 Native Americans), 18 international. Average age 27. 1,758 applicants, 50% accepted, 232 enrolled. *Faculty:* 41 full-time (14 women), 27 part-time/adjunct (11 women). Expenses: Contact institution. *Financial support:* In 2001–02, 624 students received support, including 26 research assistantships (averaging $1,643 per year); career-related internships or fieldwork, Federal Work-Study, scholarships/grants, and tuition waivers (partial) also available. Support available to part-time students. Financial award application deadline: 3/1; financial award applicants required to submit FAFSA. In 2001, 218 first professional degrees, 13 master's awarded. *Degree program information:* Part-time and evening/weekend programs available. Offers environmental and natural resources law (LL M); law (JD). *Application deadline:* For fall admission, 3/15 (priority date). Applications are processed on a rolling basis. *Application fee:* $50. Electronic applications accepted. *Application Contact:* Emily Allen, Director of Admissions, 503-768-6613, Fax: 503-768-6793, E-mail: lawadmss@lclark.edu. *Dean,* James L. Huffman, 503-768-6602, Fax: 503-768-6671.

LEWIS UNIVERSITY, Romeoville, IL 60446

General Information Independent-religious, coed, comprehensive institution. *Enrollment:* 142 full-time matriculated graduate/professional students (76 women), 780 part-time matriculated graduate/professional students (454 women). *Enrollment by degree level:* 922 master's. *Graduate faculty:* 43 full-time (17 women), 79 part-time/adjunct (21 women). *Tuition:* Part-time $425. Tuition and fees vary according to program. *Graduate housing:* Room and/or apartments available on a first-come, first-served basis to single students; on-campus housing not available to married students. Housing application deadline: 8/1. *Student services:* Campus employment opportunities, campus safety program, career counseling, exercise/wellness program, international student services, low-cost health insurance, multicultural affairs office, teacher training, writing training. *Library facilities:* Lewis University Library. *Online resources:* library catalog, web page, access to other libraries' catalogs. *Collection:* 95,887 titles, 799 serial subscriptions, 2,818 audiovisual materials.

Computer facilities: 287 computers available on campus for general student use. A campuswide network can be accessed from student residence rooms and from off campus. Internet access and online class registration are available. *Web address:* http://www.lewisu.edu/.

General Application Contact: Director, Graduate Admissions, 800-897-9000, Fax: 815-836-5002, E-mail: admissions@lewisu.edu.

GRADUATE UNITS

College of Arts and Sciences Students: 97 full-time (62 women), 470 part-time (282 women); includes 107 minority (77 African Americans, 3 Asian Americans or Pacific Islanders, 26 Hispanic Americans, 1 Native American), 8 international. Average age 35. *Faculty:* 24 full-time (14 women), 36 part-time/adjunct (10 women). Expenses: Contact institution. *Financial support:* Research assistantships, career-related internships or fieldwork, scholarships/grants, tuition waivers (partial), and unspecified assistantships available. Support available to part-time students. Financial award application deadline: 4/1; financial award applicants required to submit FAFSA. In 2001, 172 degrees awarded. *Degree program information:* Part-time and evening/weekend programs available. Offers administration/education (MA); arts and sciences (M Ed, MA, MAE, MPSA, MS, CAS); counseling psychology (MA); crinimal/social justice (MS); curriculum and instruction (MA); education (M Ed, MAE); education administration (CAS); leadership studies (MA); philosophy (MA); public safety (MPSA); school counseling and guidance (MA); special education (MA). *Application fee:* $35. *Dean,* Dr. Katherine Delaney, 815-838-0500 Ext. 5240, Fax: 815-836-5995.

College of Business Students: 13 full-time (4 women), 389 part-time (189 women). Average age 33. 138 applicants, 93% accepted, 108 enrolled. *Faculty:* 19 full-time (4 women), 29 part-time/adjunct (6 women). Expenses: Contact institution. *Financial support:* Career-related internships or fieldwork available. Support available to part-time students. In 2001, 71 degrees awarded. *Degree program information:* Part-time and evening/weekend programs available. Offers business (MBA). *Application deadline:* For fall admission, 8/15 (priority date). Applications are processed on a rolling basis. *Application fee:* $35 ($30 for international students). Electronic applications accepted. *Executive Director of Graduate School of Management,* Robert E. Tucker, 800-897-9000, Fax: 815-838-3330, E-mail: tuckerro@lewisu.edu.

LEXINGTON THEOLOGICAL SEMINARY, Lexington, KY 40508-3218

General Information Independent-religious, coed, graduate-only institution. *Graduate faculty:* 11 full-time (3 women), 6 part-time/adjunct (1 woman). *Tuition:* Part-time $235 per credit hour. *Required fees:* $8 per credit hour. $20 per semester. *Graduate housing:* Rooms and/or apartments available on a first-come, first-served basis to single and married students. Housing application deadline: 6/15. *Student services:* Campus employment opportunities, career counseling, writing training. *Library facilities:* Bosworth Memorial Library. *Online resources:* library catalog, web page, access to other libraries' catalogs. *Collection:* 150,000 titles, 1,200 serial subscriptions.

Computer facilities: 6 computers available on campus for general student use. A campuswide network can be accessed from off campus. Internet access is available. *Web address:* http://www.lextheo.edu/.

General Application Contact: Jeannette Matthews, Admissions Counselor, 859-252-0361, Fax: 859-281-6042, E-mail: jmatthews@lextheo.edu.

GRADUATE UNITS

Graduate and Professional Programs Students: 146 (77 women); includes 9 African Americans, 2 Hispanic Americans Average age 36. 50 applicants, 88% accepted. *Faculty:* 11 full-time (3 women), 6 part-time/adjunct (1 woman). Expenses: Contact institution. *Financial support:* Fellowships with full and partial tuition reimbursements, research assistantships, career-related internships or fieldwork, scholarships/grants, and tuition waivers (full and partial) available. Support available to part-time students. Financial award application deadline: 7/1. *Degree program information:* Part-time and evening/weekend programs available. Offers theology (M Div, MA, MAPS, D Min). *Application deadline:* For fall admission, 7/17; for spring admission, 12/15. Applications are processed on a rolling basis. *Application fee:* $20. *Application Contact:* Jeannette Matthews, Admissions Counselor, 859-252-0361, Fax: 859-281-6042, E-mail: jmatthews@lextheo.edu. *Dean,* Dr. Philip N. Dare, 859-252-0361 Ext. 235, Fax: 859-281-6042, E-mail: pdare@lextheo.edu.

LIBERTY UNIVERSITY, Lynchburg, VA 24502

General Information Independent-religious, coed, comprehensive institution. *Enrollment:* 275 full-time matriculated graduate/professional students (78 women), 499 part-time matriculated graduate/professional students (217 women). *Enrollment by degree level:* 87 first professional, 637 master's, 50 doctoral. *Graduate faculty:* 29 full-time (5 women), 16 part-time/adjunct (3 women). *Tuition:* Full-time $5,130; part-time $285 per credit. *Required fees:* $500. Tuition and fees vary according to degree level and program. *Graduate housing:* Room and/or apartments guaranteed to single students; on-campus housing not available to married students. Typical cost: $5,100 (including board). Housing application deadline: 8/1. *Student services:* Campus employment opportunities, career counseling. *Library facilities:* A. Pierre Guillermin Library plus 1 other. *Online resources:* library catalog, web page. *Collection:* 296,601 titles, 7,739 serial subscriptions, 5,555 audiovisual materials.

Computer facilities: 245 computers available on campus for general student use. A campuswide network can be accessed from student residence rooms and from off campus. Internet access and online class registration are available. *Web address:* http://www.liberty.edu/.

General Application Contact: Dr. William E. Wegert, Coordinator of Graduate Admissions, 434-582-2175, Fax: 434-582-2421, E-mail: wewegert@liberty.edu.

GRADUATE UNITS

College of Arts and Science Students: 68 full-time (42 women), 203 part-time (134 women). *Faculty:* 9 full-time (4 women), 2 part-time/adjunct (0 women). Expenses: Contact institution.

Liberty University (continued)
Financial support: Federal Work-Study available. Financial award application deadline: 4/15; financial award applicants required to submit FAFSA. *Degree program information:* Part-time programs available. Postbaccalaureate distance learning degree programs offered (minimal on-campus study). Offers counseling (MA); nursing (MSN). *Application deadline:* For fall admission, 6/1 (priority date); for spring admission, 11/1. Applications are processed on a rolling basis. *Application fee:* $35. *Application Contact:* Dr. William E. Wegert, Coordinator of Graduate Admissions, 434-582-2175, Fax: 434-582-2421, E-mail: wewegert@liberty.edu. *Dean*, Dr. Ronald E. Hawkins, 434-582-2490, Fax: 434-582-2468, E-mail: rehawkin@liberty.edu.

Liberty Baptist Theological Seminary Students: 190 full-time (27 women), 192 part-time (23 women). *Faculty:* 6 full-time (0 women), 4 part-time/adjunct (0 women). Expenses: Contact institution. *Financial support:* Career-related internships or fieldwork and Federal Work-Study available. Financial award application deadline: 4/15; financial award applicants required to submit FAFSA. *Degree program information:* Part-time programs available. Postbaccalaureate distance learning degree programs offered (minimal on-campus study). Offers theology (M Div, MAR, MRE, Th M, D Min). *Application deadline:* For fall admission, 6/1 (priority date); for spring admission, 11/1. Applications are processed on a rolling basis. *Application fee:* $35. *Application Contact:* Dr. William E. Wegert, Coordinator of Graduate Admissions, 434-582-2175, Fax: 434-582-2421, E-mail: wewegert@liberty.edu. *Dean*, Dr. Danny Lovett, 434-582-2326, Fax: 434-582-2766, E-mail: jdlovett@liberty.edu.

School of Business and Government Students: 6 full-time (2 women), 25 part-time (13 women). *Faculty:* 5 full-time (0 women). Expenses: Contact institution. *Financial support:* Application deadline: 4/15; *Degree program information:* Part-time programs available. Postbaccalaureate distance learning degree programs offered (minimal on-campus study). Offers business and government (MBA). *Application deadline:* For fall admission, 6/1; for spring admission, 11/1. Applications are processed on a rolling basis. *Application fee:* $35. *Application Contact:* Dr. William E. Wegert, Coordinator of Graduate Admissions, 434-582-2175, Fax: 434-582-2421, E-mail: wewegert@liberty.edu. *Dean*, Dr. Bruce K. Bell, 434-582-2480, Fax: 434-582-2366, E-mail: bkbell@liberty.edu.

School of Education Students: 10 full-time (7 women), 76 part-time (44 women). *Faculty:* 3 full-time (1 woman), 6 part-time/adjunct (3 women). Expenses: Contact institution. *Financial support:* Federal Work-Study available. Financial award application deadline: 4/15; financial award applicants required to submit FAFSA. *Degree program information:* Part-time programs available. Postbaccalaureate distance learning degree programs offered (minimal on-campus study). Offers administration and supervision (M Ed); early childhood education (M Ed); educational leadership (Ed D); elementary education (M Ed); gifted education (M Ed); reading specialist (M Ed); school counseling (M Ed); secondary education (M Ed); special education (M Ed). *Application deadline:* For fall admission, 6/1 (priority date); for spring admission, 11/1. Applications are processed on a rolling basis. *Application fee:* $35. *Application Contact:* Dr. William E. Wegert, Coordinator of Graduate Admissions, 434-582-2175, Fax: 434-582-2421, E-mail: wewegert@liberty.edu. *Dean*, Dr. Karen L. Parker, 434-582-2445, Fax: 434-582-2468, E-mail: kparker@liberty.edu.

School of Religion Students: 1 full-time (0 women), 2 part-time. *Faculty:* 2 full-time (0 women), 4 part-time/adjunct (0 women). Expenses: Contact institution. *Financial support:* Federal Work-Study available. Financial award application deadline: 4/15; financial award applicants required to submit FAFSA. *Degree program information:* Part-time programs available. Postbaccalaureate distance learning degree programs offered (minimal on-campus study). Offers religious studies (MA). *Application deadline:* For fall admission, 6/1 (priority date); for spring admission, 11/1. Applications are processed on a rolling basis. *Application fee:* $35. *Application Contact:* Dr. William E. Wegert, Coordinator of Graduate Admissions, 434-582-2175, Fax: 434-582-2421, E-mail: wewegert@liberty.edu. *Dean*, Dr. Elmer Towns, 434-582-2169, Fax: 434-582-2575.

See in-depth description on page 941.

LIFE CHIROPRACTIC COLLEGE WEST, Hayward, CA 94545

General Information Independent, coed, graduate-only institution. *Enrollment by degree level:* 599 first professional. *Graduate faculty:* 39 full-time (14 women), 25 part-time/adjunct (10 women). *Tuition:* Full-time $13,950. *Graduate housing:* On-campus housing not available. *Student services:* Campus employment opportunities, campus safety program, free psychological counseling, international student services. *Library facilities:* Life West Library plus 1 other. *Online resources:* library catalog. *Collection:* 22,000 titles, 1,100 serial subscriptions. *Research affiliation:* Orthopedic System, Inc., Foundation for Chiropractic Education and Research, Foundation for the Advancement of Chiropractic Tenets, San Francisco Spine Center.

Computer facilities: 26 computers available on campus for general student use. A campuswide network can be accessed from student residence rooms and from off campus. Internet access is available. *Web address:* http://www.lifewest.edu/.

General Application Contact: Ann C. McDonald, Director of Admissions, 800-788-4476, Fax: 510-276-4893, E-mail: amcdonal@lifewest.edu.

GRADUATE UNITS

Professional Program Students: 599 full-time (210 women); includes 122 minority (3 African Americans, 82 Asian Americans or Pacific Islanders, 35 Hispanic Americans, 2 Native Americans), 84 international. Average age 28. 120 applicants, 54% accepted. *Faculty:* 39 full-time (14 women), 25 part-time/adjunct (10 women). Expenses: Contact institution. *Financial support:* In 2001–02, 3 research assistantships, 1 teaching assistantship were awarded. Career-related internships or fieldwork, Federal Work-Study, and scholarships/grants also available. Financial award applicants required to submit FAFSA. In 2001, 200 degrees awarded. Offers chiropractic (DC). *Application deadline:* For fall admission, 8/1 (priority date). Applications are processed on a rolling basis. *Application fee:* $45. *Application Contact:* Ann C. McDonald, Director of Admissions, 800-788-4476, Fax: 510-276-4893, E-mail: amcdonal@lifewest.edu. *President*, Dr. Gerard W. Clum, 800-788-4476.

LIFE UNIVERSITY, Marietta, GA 30060-2903

General Information Independent, coed, comprehensive institution. *Enrollment:* 1,616 full-time matriculated graduate/professional students (525 women), 667 part-time matriculated graduate/professional students (224 women). *Graduate faculty:* 209 full-time (72 women), 45 part-time/adjunct (13 women). *Tuition:* Part-time $196 per credit hour. *Required fees:* $49 per quarter. Tuition and fees vary according to program. *Graduate housing:* Rooms and/or apartments available on a first-come, first-served basis to single and married students. Typical cost: $2,600 per year for single students; $5,800 per year for married students. Room charges vary according to housing facility selected. *Student services:* Campus employment opportunities, campus safety program, career counseling, disabled student services, exercise/wellness program, free psychological counseling, international student services. *Research affiliation:* Zebris Corporation (biomechanical assessment). *Web address:* http://www.life.edu/.

General Application Contact: Denise Gordon, Director of Admissions, 800-543-3202, Fax: 770-426-2895, E-mail: dgordon@life.edu.

LINCOLN CHRISTIAN SEMINARY, Lincoln, IL 62656-2167

General Information Independent-religious, coed, graduate-only institution. *Enrollment by degree level:* 82 first professional, 158 master's. *Graduate faculty:* 9 full-time (0 women), 12 part-time/adjunct (3 women). *Tuition:* Full-time $4,302; part-time $239 per semester hour. *Required fees:* $630; $35 per semester hour. *Graduate housing:* Rooms and/or apartments available on a first-come, first-served basis to single students and available to married students. Typical cost: $4,100 (including board) for single students. *Student services:* Campus employment opportunities, career counseling, disabled student services, free psychological counseling, low-cost health insurance. *Library facilities:* Jessie C. Eury Library. *Online resources:* library catalog, web page, access to other libraries' catalogs. *Collection:* 128,000 titles, 500 serial subscriptions, 30,000 audiovisual materials.

Computer facilities: 45 computers available on campus for general student use. A campuswide network can be accessed from student residence rooms and from off campus. Internet access is available. *Web address:* http://www.lccs.edu/.

General Application Contact: Lyle Swanson, Director of Admissions, 217-732-3168 Ext. 2275, Fax: 217-732-5914, E-mail: lswanson@lccs.edu.

GRADUATE UNITS

Graduate and Professional Programs Students: 97 full-time (30 women), 143 part-time (31 women); includes 13 minority (7 African Americans, 3 Asian Americans or Pacific Islanders, 3 Hispanic Americans), 21 international. Average age 25. 97 applicants, 96% accepted, 74 enrolled. *Faculty:* 9 full-time (0 women), 12 part-time/adjunct (3 women). Expenses: Contact institution. *Financial support:* In 2001–02, 150 students received support, including 5 teaching assistantships (averaging $2,000 per year); career-related internships or fieldwork, Federal Work-Study, and scholarships/grants also available. Support available to part-time students. Financial award applicants required to submit FAFSA. In 2001, 15 first professional degrees, 29 master's awarded. *Degree program information:* Part-time programs available. Offers Bible and theology (MA); Bible translation (MA); counseling ministry (MA); divinity (M Div); leadership ministry (MA). MA (Bible translation) offered jointly with Pioneer Bible Translators (Dallas, TX). *Application deadline:* Applications are processed on a rolling basis. *Application fee:* $20. *Application Contact:* Lyle Swanson, Director of Admissions, 217-732-3168 Ext. 2275, Fax: 217-732-5914, E-mail: lswanson@lccs.edu. *Vice President of Academics*, Dr. Thomas Tanner, 217-732-3168 Ext. 2240, Fax: 217-732-5718, E-mail: ttanner@lccs.edu.

LINCOLN MEMORIAL UNIVERSITY, Harrogate, TN 37752-1901

General Information Independent, coed, comprehensive institution. *Graduate housing:* Rooms and/or apartments available on a first-come, first-served basis to single and married students. Housing application deadline: 8/1.

GRADUATE UNITS

Program in Business Administration *Degree program information:* Part-time and evening/weekend programs available. Offers business administration (MBA).

Program in Education *Degree program information:* Part-time and evening/weekend programs available. Offers administration and supervision (M Ed, Ed S); counseling and guidance (M Ed); curriculum and instruction (M Ed, Ed S).

LINCOLN UNIVERSITY, Oakland, CA 94612

General Information Independent, coed, comprehensive institution. *Graduate housing:* On-campus housing not available.

GRADUATE UNITS

Business Administration Program Offers business administration (MBA). Electronic applications accepted.

LINCOLN UNIVERSITY, Jefferson City, MO 65102

General Information State-supported, coed, comprehensive institution. *Enrollment:* 25 full-time matriculated graduate/professional students (12 women), 140 part-time matriculated graduate/professional students (110 women). *Enrollment by degree level:* 165 master's. *Graduate faculty:* 3 full-time (1 woman), 26 part-time/adjunct (7 women). Tuition, state resident: part-time $136 per credit hour. Tuition, nonresident: part-time $272 per credit hour. *Required fees:* $50 per term. *Graduate housing:* Room and/or apartments available to single students; on-campus housing not available to married students. Typical cost: $1,940 per year ($3,790 including board). Housing application deadline: 6/30. *Student services:* Campus employment opportunities, campus safety program, career counseling, disabled student services, free psychological counseling, international student services. *Library facilities:* Inman Page Library. *Collection:* 151,595 titles, 761 serial subscriptions.

Computer facilities: 175 computers available on campus for general student use. A campuswide network can be accessed from off campus. Internet access is available. *Web address:* http://www.lincolnu.edu/.

General Application Contact: Nathan H. Cook, Vice President for Academic Affairs and Dean of Graduate Studies, 573-681-5074, Fax: 573-681-5078, E-mail: cook@lincolnu.edu.

GRADUATE UNITS

Graduate School Students: 25 full-time (12 women), 140 part-time (110 women); includes 23 minority (all African Americans), 15 international. 35 applicants, 100% accepted, 35 enrolled. *Faculty:* 3 full-time (1 woman), 26 part-time/adjunct (7 women). Expenses: Contact institution. *Financial support:* Fellowships available. In 2001, 65 degrees awarded. *Degree program information:* Part-time and evening/weekend programs available. *Application deadline:* For fall admission, 7/1 (priority date); for spring admission, 12/1. Applications are processed on a rolling basis. *Application fee:* $17. *Application Contact:* Deb J. Hanlin, Administrative Assistant, 573-681-5076, Fax: 573-681-5078, E-mail: gradschool@lincolnu.edu. *Vice President for Academic Affairs and Dean of Graduate Studies*, Nathan H. Cook, 573-681-5074, Fax: 573-681-5078, E-mail: cook@lincolnu.edu.

College of Business and Professional Studies Students: 16 full-time (8 women), 15 part-time (7 women); includes 7 minority (all African Americans), 12 international. Average age 33. 13 applicants, 100% accepted, 13 enrolled. *Faculty:* 6 part-time/adjunct (1 woman). Expenses: Contact institution. *Financial support:* Fellowships available. In 2001, 6 degrees awarded. *Degree program information:* Part-time and evening/weekend programs available. Offers accounting (MBA); business (MBA); management (MBA). *Application deadline:* For fall admission, 7/1 (priority date); for spring admission, 12/1. Applications are processed on a rolling basis. *Application fee:* $17. *Dean*, Dr. Kojo Quartey, 573-681-5489, E-mail: quarteyk@lincolnu.edu.

College of Education Students: 7 full-time (3 women), 104 part-time (88 women); includes 9 minority (all African Americans), 1 international. 19 applicants, 100% accepted, 19 enrolled. *Faculty:* 3 full-time (1 woman), 10 part-time/adjunct (5 women). Expenses: Contact institution. In 2001, 47 degrees awarded. *Degree program information:* Part-time and evening/weekend programs available. Offers education (M Ed); elementary and secondary teaching (M Ed); guidance and counseling (M Ed); school administration and supervision (M Ed). *Application deadline:* For fall admission, 7/1; for spring admission, 12/1. Applications are processed on a rolling basis. *Application fee:* $17. *Dean*, Patrick Henry, 573-681-5250, E-mail: henryp@lincoln.edu.

College of Liberal Arts, Science, and Agriculture Students: 2 full-time (1 woman), 21 part-time (15 women); includes 7 minority (all African Americans), 2 international. 3 applicants, 100% accepted, 3 enrolled. *Faculty:* 10 part-time/adjunct (1 woman). Expenses: Contact institution. *Financial support:* Fellowships available. In 2001, 12 degrees awarded. *Degree program information:* Part-time and evening/weekend programs available. Offers history (MA); liberal arts, science, and agriculture (MA); sociology (MA); sociology/criminal justice (MA). *Application deadline:* For fall admission, 7/1; for spring admission, 12/1. *Application fee:* $17. *Dean*, Dr. Douglas Nancarrow, 573-681-5280.

LINCOLN UNIVERSITY, Lincoln University, PA 19352

General Information State-related, coed, comprehensive institution. *Graduate housing:* On-campus housing not available.

GRADUATE UNITS

Graduate Program in Human Services *Degree program information:* Evening/weekend programs available. Offers human services (M Hum Svcs).

LINDENWOOD UNIVERSITY, St. Charles, MO 63301-1695

General Information Independent-religious, coed, comprehensive institution. *Enrollment:* 752 full-time matriculated graduate/professional students (493 women), 795 part-time matriculated graduate/professional students (450 women). *Graduate faculty:* 50 full-time (13 women), 48 part-time/adjunct (22 women). *Tuition:* Full-time $10,800; part-time $300 per hour. Tuition and fees vary according to course load and program. *Graduate housing:* Rooms and/or apartments available to single and married students. Typical cost: $8,960 (including board) for single students; $8,960 (including board) for married students. Housing application deadline: 6/30. *Student services:* Campus employment opportunities, career counseling, international student services, writing training. *Library facilities:* Butler Library. *Collection:* 222,071 titles, 519 serial subscriptions.

Computer facilities: 160 computers available on campus for general student use. A campuswide network can be accessed. *Web address:* http://www.lindenwood.edu/.

General Application Contact: John Guffey, Dean of Admissions, 636-949-4934, Fax: 636-949-4910, E-mail: jguffey@lindenwood.edu.

GRADUATE UNITS

Graduate Programs Students: 752 full-time (493 women), 1,495 part-time (1,150 women); includes 279 minority (246 African Americans, 8 Asian Americans or Pacific Islanders, 16 Hispanic Americans, 9 Native Americans), 60 international. Average age 34. *Faculty:* 50 full-time (13 women), 48 part-time/adjunct (22 women). Expenses: Contact institution. *Financial support:* Career-related internships or fieldwork, Federal Work-Study, institutionally sponsored loans, tuition waivers (partial), and unspecified assistantships available. Financial award application deadline: 6/30. In 2001, 807 degrees awarded. *Degree program information:* Part-time and evening/weekend programs available. Offers administration (MSA); business administration (MBA); corporate communication (MS); counseling psychology (MA); gerontology (MA); health management (MS); human resource management (MS); human service agency management (MS); management (MSA); marketing (MSA); mass communication (MS). *Application deadline:* For fall admission, 6/30. Applications are processed on a rolling basis. *Application fee:* $25. Electronic applications accepted. *Application Contact:* John Guffey, Dean of Admissions, 636-949-4934, Fax: 636-949-4910, E-mail: jguffey@lindenwood.edu. *Provost*, Dr. James D. Evans, 636-949-4708, Fax: 636-949-4992, E-mail: jevans@lindenwood.edu.

Division of Arts and Communication Arts Students: 19 full-time (10 women), 24 part-time (14 women); includes 3 minority (all African Americans), 8 international. Average age 33. *Faculty:* 11 full-time (4 women), 1 (woman) part-time/adjunct. Expenses: Contact institution. *Financial support:* Career-related internships or fieldwork, institutionally sponsored loans, tuition waivers (partial), and unspecified assistantships available. Financial award application deadline: 6/30. In 2001, 29 degrees awarded. *Degree program information:* Part-time programs available. Offers communication arts (MA); theatre arts (MA, MFA). *Application deadline:* For fall admission, 6/30 (priority date); for spring admission, 11/30. Applications are processed on a rolling basis. *Application fee:* $25. *Application Contact:* John Guffey, Dean of Admissions, 636-949-4934, Fax: 636-949-4910, E-mail: jguffey@lindenwood.edu. *Dean of Fine Arts*, Marsha Parker, 636-949-4906, Fax: 636-949-4910, E-mail: mparker@lindenwood.edu.

Division of Business Administration Students: 55 full-time (24 women), 195 part-time (98 women); includes 24 minority (13 African Americans, 3 Asian Americans or Pacific Islanders, 6 Hispanic Americans, 2 Native Americans), 32 international. Average age 36. *Faculty:* 16 full-time (1 woman), 20 part-time/adjunct (6 women). Expenses: Contact institution. *Financial support:* Career-related internships or fieldwork, Federal Work-Study, institutionally sponsored loans, and tuition waivers (partial) available. Financial award application deadline: 6/30. In 2001, 135 degrees awarded. *Degree program information:* Part-time programs available. Offers business administration (MBA, MS). *Application deadline:* For fall admission, 6/30; for spring admission, 11/30. Applications are processed on a rolling basis. *Application fee:* $25. Electronic applications accepted. *Application Contact:* John Guffey, Dean of Admissions, 636-949-4934, Fax: 636-949-4910, E-mail: jguffey@lindenwood.edu. *Dean*, James Hardman, 636-949-4951, Fax: 636-949-4910, E-mail: jhardman@lindenwood.edu.

Division of Education Students: 163 full-time (119 women), 1,010 part-time (806 women); includes 135 minority (123 African Americans, 4 Asian Americans or Pacific Islanders, 5 Hispanic Americans, 3 Native Americans), 9 international. Average age 35. *Faculty:* 15 full-time (6 women), 16 part-time/adjunct (11 women). Expenses: Contact institution. *Financial support:* Career-related internships or fieldwork, institutionally sponsored loans, and tuition waivers (partial) available. Financial award application deadline: 6/30. In 2001, 345 degrees awarded. *Degree program information:* Part-time programs available. Offers education (MA, Ed S). *Application deadline:* For fall admission, 6/30. Applications are processed on a rolling basis. *Application fee:* $25. Electronic applications accepted. *Application Contact:* John Guffey, Dean of Admissions, 636-949-4934, Fax: 636-949-4910, E-mail: jguffey@lindenwood.edu. *Dean*, Dr. Richard Boyle, 636-949-4844.

LINDSEY WILSON COLLEGE, Columbia, KY 42728-1298

General Information Independent-religious, coed, comprehensive institution. *Enrollment:* 41 full-time matriculated graduate/professional students (32 women). *Enrollment by degree level:* 41 master's. *Graduate faculty:* 6 full-time (4 women). *Tuition:* Part-time $396 per credit hour. *Graduate housing:* Rooms and/or apartments available on a first-come, first-served basis to single students and available to married students. *Student services:* Campus employment opportunities, campus safety program, career counseling, disabled student services, free psychological counseling, international student services. *Library facilities:* Katie Murrell Library. *Collection:* 80,000 titles, 1,500 serial subscriptions.

Computer facilities: 80 computers available on campus for general student use. A campuswide network can be accessed from student residence rooms and from off campus. Internet access is available. *Web address:* http://www.lindsey.edu/.

General Application Contact: Dr. John Rigney, Graduate Director, 800-264-0138, Fax: 502-384-8152, E-mail: rigneyj@lindsey.edu.

GRADUATE UNITS

Department of Human Services and Counseling Offers counseling and human development (M Ed).

LIPSCOMB UNIVERSITY, Nashville, TN 37204-3951

General Information Independent-religious, coed, comprehensive institution. *Enrollment:* 55 full-time matriculated graduate/professional students (23 women), 173 part-time matriculated graduate/professional students (53 women). *Enrollment by degree level:* 27 first professional, 201 master's. *Graduate faculty:* 23 full-time (2 women), 12 part-time/adjunct (2 women). *Tuition:* Part-time $408 per semester hour. *Required fees:* $169 per semester. *Graduate housing:* Room and/or apartments available on a first-come, first-served basis to single students; on-campus housing not available to married students. Housing application deadline: 7/15. *Student services:* Campus employment opportunities, career counseling, exercise/wellness program, free psychological counseling, multicultural affairs office, teacher training. *Library facilities:* Beaman Library plus 1 other. *Online resources:* library catalog, access to other libraries' catalogs. *Collection:* 199,400 titles, 886 serial subscriptions, 724 audiovisual materials.

Computer facilities: 232 computers available on campus for general student use. A campuswide network can be accessed from student residence rooms and from off campus. Internet access and online class registration are available. *Web address:* http://www.lipscomb.edu/.

General Application Contact: Dr. Gary Holloway, Director of Graduate Bible Studies, 615-269-1000 Ext. 5761, Fax: 615-269-1808, E-mail: gary.holloway@lipscomb.edu.

GRADUATE UNITS

Graduate Program in Bible Studies Students: 17 full-time (4 women), 94 part-time (10 women); includes 4 minority (all African Americans), 3 international. Average age 34. 19 applicants, 100% accepted. *Faculty:* 14 full-time (0 women). Expenses: Contact institution. *Financial support:* Scholarships/grants available. Support available to part-time students. In 2001, 3 first professional degrees, 23 master's awarded. *Degree program information:* Part-time and evening/weekend programs available. Offers biblical studies (MA, MAR); divinity (M Div). *Application deadline:* For fall admission, 8/14 (priority date); for spring admission, 12/31. *Application fee:* $0. *Director*, Dr. Gary Holloway, 615-269-1000 Ext. 5761, Fax: 615-269-1808, E-mail: gary.holloway@lipscomb.edu.

Graduate Program in Education Students: 3 full-time (1 woman), 33 part-time (22 women); includes 2 minority (both African Americans) Average age 34. 9 applicants, 100% accepted. *Faculty:* 8 full-time (2 women), 1 part-time/adjunct (0 women). Expenses: Contact institution. *Financial support:* Federal Work-Study, tuition waivers (full), and unspecified assistantships available. Support available to part-time students. Financial award applicants required to submit FAFSA. In 2001, 16 degrees awarded. *Degree program information:* Part-time and evening/weekend programs available. Offers education (M Ed). *Application deadline:* For fall admission, 8/29 (priority date); for spring admission, 1/16. Applications are processed on a rolling basis. *Application fee:* $0. *Application Contact:* Jackie Sanders, Administrative Assistant, 615-269-1000 Ext. 6081, Fax: 615-386-7628, E-mail: jackie.sanders@lipscomb.edu. *Director*, Dr. Carolyn Tucker, 615-269-1000 Ext. 5772, Fax: 615-386-7628, E-mail: carolyn.tucker@lipscomb.edu.

MBA Program Students: 34 full-time (18 women), 52 part-time (24 women); includes 7 minority (4 African Americans, 2 Asian Americans or Pacific Islanders, 1 Hispanic American), 1 international. *Faculty:* 12 full-time (2 women), 4 part-time/adjunct (0 women). Expenses: Contact institution. *Financial support:* Federal Work-Study and unspecified assistantships available. Support available to part-time students. In 2001, 38 degrees awarded. *Degree program information:* Part-time and evening/weekend programs available. Offers business administration (MBA). *Director*, Dr. Perry G. Moore, 615-269-1000 Ext. 5795, Fax: 615-269-1818, E-mail: perry.moore@lipscomb.edu.

LOCK HAVEN UNIVERSITY OF PENNSYLVANIA, Lock Haven, PA 17745-2390

General Information State-supported, coed, comprehensive institution. *Enrollment:* 73 full-time matriculated graduate/professional students (46 women), 49 part-time matriculated graduate/professional students (37 women). *Enrollment by degree level:* 122 master's. *Graduate faculty:* 5 full-time (2 women), 22 part-time/adjunct (7 women). Tuition, state resident: full-time $4,600; part-time $335 per credit hour. Tuition, nonresident: full-time $7,554; part-time $420 per credit hour. *Required fees:* $1,031; $100 per credit hour. *Graduate housing:* Room and/or apartments available on a first-come, first-served basis to single students; on-campus housing not available to married students. Typical cost: $2,624 per year ($4,776 including board). Room and board charges vary according to board plan. Housing application deadline: 6/1. *Student services:* Campus employment opportunities, campus safety program, career counseling, free psychological counseling, international student services, low-cost health insurance. *Library facilities:* Stevenson Library. *Online resources:* library catalog, web page, access to other libraries' catalogs. *Collection:* 366,342 titles, 1,510 serial subscriptions, 8,158 audiovisual materials.

Computer facilities: 270 computers available on campus for general student use. A campuswide network can be accessed from student residence rooms and from off campus. *Web address:* http://www.lhup.edu/.

General Application Contact: C. Ginger Frankenberger, Secretary,Enrollment Services Office, 570-893-2124, Fax: 570-893-2734, E-mail: dbierly@lhup.edu.

GRADUATE UNITS

Office of Graduate Studies Students: 73 full-time (46 women), 49 part-time (37 women); includes 3 minority (all Asian Americans or Pacific Islanders), 2 international. Average age 31. 177 applicants, 44% accepted, 61 enrolled. *Faculty:* 5 full-time (2 women), 22 part-time/adjunct (7 women). Expenses: Contact institution. *Financial support:* In 2001–02, 10 students received support, including 10 fellowships (averaging $4,500 per year); tuition waivers (full and partial) and unspecified assistantships also available. Financial award application deadline: 8/1; financial award applicants required to submit FAFSA. In 2001, 47 degrees awarded. *Degree program information:* Part-time and evening/weekend programs available. Postbaccalaureate distance learning degree programs offered. Offers curriculum and instruction (M Ed); liberal arts (MLA); physician assistant in rural primary care (MHS). *Application deadline:* For fall admission, 8/1 (priority date); for spring admission, 12/1 (priority date). Applications are processed on a rolling basis. *Application fee:* $25. Electronic applications accepted. *Application Contact:* C. Ginger Frankenberger, Secretary, Enrollment Services, 570-893-2124, Fax: 570-893-2734, E-mail: cfranken@lhup.edu. *Director of Enrollment Services*, Dr. James K. Smalley, 570-893-2008, Fax: 257-893-2734, E-mail: jsmalley@eagle.lhup.edu.

LOGAN UNIVERSITY-COLLEGE OF CHIROPRACTIC, Chesterfield, MO 63006-1065

General Information Independent, coed, upper-level institution. *Enrollment:* 707 full-time matriculated graduate/professional students (228 women), 29 part-time matriculated graduate/professional students (11 women). *Enrollment by degree level:* 736 first professional. *Graduate faculty:* 54 full-time (12 women), 41 part-time/adjunct (18 women). *Tuition:* Full-time $10,000; part-time $95 per credit hour. *Required fees:* $270; $270 per year. *Graduate housing:* On-campus housing not available. *Student services:* Campus employment opportunities, career counseling, disabled student services, exercise/wellness program, free psychological counseling, international student services, low-cost health insurance, multicultural affairs office. *Library facilities:* Learning Resources Center. *Online resources:* library catalog, web page. *Collection:* 13,500 titles, 300 serial subscriptions, 2,100 audiovisual materials.

Computer facilities: 250 computers available on campus for general student use. A campuswide network can be accessed. Internet access is available. *Web address:* http://www.logan.edu/.

General Application Contact: Dr. Patrick M. Brown, Vice President of Admissions and Enrollment, 636-227-2100, Fax: 636-227-9338, E-mail: loganadm@logan.edu.

GRADUATE UNITS

Division of Basic Science, Chiropractic Science, Clinical Sciences, and Clinics Students: 707 full-time (228 women), 29 part-time (11 women); includes 55 minority (20 African Americans, 20 Asian Americans or Pacific Islanders, 14 Hispanic Americans, 1 Native American), 64 international. Average age 27. 166 applicants, 60% accepted. *Faculty:* 54 full-time (12 women), 41 part-time/adjunct (18 women). Expenses: Contact institution. *Financial support:* In 2001–02, 661 students received support. Federal Work-Study and scholarships/grants available. Support available to part-time students. Financial award applicants required to submit FAFSA. In 2001, 213 degrees awarded. Offers basic science, chiropractic science, clinical sciences, and clinics (DC). *Application deadline:* For fall admission, 7/15 (priority date); for winter admission, 11/15 (priority date); for spring admission, 3/15 (priority date). Applications are processed on a rolling basis. *Application fee:* $50. Electronic applications accepted. *Application Contact:* Dr. Patrick M. Brown, Vice President of Admissions and Enrollment, 636-227-2100, Fax: 636-227-9338, E-mail: loganadm@logan.edu. *Vice President of Academic Affairs and Executive Vice President*, Dr. William L. Ramsey, 636-227-2100, Fax: 636-227-9338, E-mail: wramsey@logan.edu.

LOMA LINDA UNIVERSITY, Loma Linda, CA 92350

General Information Independent-religious, coed, university. CGS member. *Enrollment:* 1,952 full-time matriculated graduate/professional students (982 women), 311 part-time matriculated graduate/professional students (209 women). *Graduate faculty:* 1,005 full-time (310 women), 1,074 part-time/adjunct (219 women). *Tuition:* Part-time $420 per unit. *Graduate housing:* Room and/or apartments available on a first-come, first-served basis to single students; on-campus housing not available to married students. *Student services:* Campus employment opportunities, campus safety program, career counseling, child daycare facilities, exercise/wellness program, free psychological counseling, international student services, low-cost health insurance, multicultural affairs office, writing training. *Library facilities:* Del E. Webb Memorial Library. *Online resources:* library catalog, web page. *Collection:* 322,657 titles, 1,394 serial subscriptions. *Research affiliation:* City of Hope Hospital (cancer research).

Computer facilities: A campuswide network can be accessed from student residence rooms and from off campus. Internet access and online class registration, on-line courses are available. *Web address:* http://www.llu.edu/.

General Application Contact: Dr. W. Barton Rippon, Dean of the Graduate School, 909-824-4528, Fax: 909-824-4859, E-mail: brippon@univ.llu.edu.

Loma Linda University (continued)

GRADUATE UNITS

Graduate School Students: 400 full-time (274 women), 150 part-time (112 women); includes 194 minority (60 African Americans, 54 Asian Americans or Pacific Islanders, 76 Hispanic Americans, 4 Native Americans), 75 international. 610 applicants, 48% accepted. *Faculty:* 39 full-time (16 women), 63 part-time/adjunct (22 women). Expenses: Contact institution. *Financial support:* In 2001–02, 50 students received support, including 45 fellowships; teaching assistantships, career-related internships or fieldwork, Federal Work-Study, institutionally sponsored loans, scholarships/grants, tuition waivers (full and partial), and unspecified assistantships also available. Support available to part-time students. In 2001, 130 master's, 14 doctorates awarded. *Degree program information:* Part-time and evening/weekend programs available. Offers adult and aging family nursing (MS); biology (MS, PhD); biomedical and clinical ethics (MA); clinical nutrition (MS); clinical psychology (PhD, Psy D); counseling and family science (MA, MS, DMFT, PhD, Certificate); endodontics (MS, Certificate); family studies (MA, Certificate); geology (MS); growing family nursing (MS); implant dentistry (MS, Certificate); marriage and family therapy (MS, DMFT, PhD); natural sciences (MS, PhD); nursing administration (MS, Certificate); nutrition care management (MS); nutritional science (MS); oral and maxillofacial surgery (MS, Certificate); orthodontics (MS, Certificate); periodontics (MS); social policy and research (PhD); social work (MSW). *Application Contact:* Dr. Edmond A. Haddad, Associate Dean for Academic Affairs, 909-824-4734, Fax: 909-824-4859, E-mail: eahaddad@univ.llu.edu. *Dean,* Dr. W. Barton Rippon, 909-824-4528, Fax: 909-824-4859, E-mail: brippon@univ.llu.edu.

Graduate Programs in Biological Science Students: 650 full-time (267 women). *Faculty:* 719 full-time (192 women), 547 part-time/adjunct (109 women). Expenses: Contact institution. *Financial support:* Tuition waivers (full and partial) available. Support available to part-time students. *Degree program information:* Part-time programs available. Offers anatomy (MS, PhD); biochemistry (MS, PhD); biomedical science (MS, PhD); microbiology (MS, PhD); pharmacology (MS, PhD); physiology (MS, PhD). *Application deadline:* Applications are processed on a rolling basis. *Application fee:* $40. *Associate Dean,* Dr. Daniel Giang, 909-824-4466.

School of Allied Health Professions Students: 258 full-time (149 women), 123 part-time (105 women); includes 138 minority (11 African Americans, 72 Asian Americans or Pacific Islanders, 54 Hispanic Americans, 1 Native American), 7 international. 485 applicants, 46% accepted. *Faculty:* 88 full-time (55 women), 162 part-time/adjunct (101 women). Expenses: Contact institution. In 2001, 68 degrees awarded. Offers allied health professions (MHIS, MPT, MRED, MS, DPT); health information systems (MHIS); physical therapy (MPT, DPT); physician assistant (MRED); speech-language pathology and audiology (MS). *Application deadline:* Applications are processed on a rolling basis. *Application fee:* $50. *Application Contact:* Helen Greenwood, Director, Admissions and Records, 909-824-4599, Fax: 909-824-4809, E-mail: hgreenwood@sahp.llu.edu. *Dean,* Dr. Joyce Hopp, 909-824-4545, Fax: 909-824-4809, E-mail: jhopp@sahp.llu.edu.

School of Dentistry Students: 450 full-time (157 women), 3 part-time; includes 241 minority (10 African Americans, 201 Asian Americans or Pacific Islanders, 28 Hispanic Americans, 2 Native Americans), 15 international. Average age 27. 1,305 applicants, 9% accepted. *Faculty:* 84 full-time (20 women), 189 part-time/adjunct (50 women). Expenses: Contact institution. *Financial support:* Fellowships, career-related internships or fieldwork, Federal Work-Study, and institutionally sponsored loans available. In 2001, 79 degrees awarded. Offers dentistry (DDS, Certificate). *Application deadline:* Applications are processed on a rolling basis. *Dean,* Dr. Charles Goodacre, 909-824-4683, Fax: 909-824-4211.

School of Medicine Students: 663 full-time (274 women); includes 235 minority (39 African Americans, 168 Asian Americans or Pacific Islanders, 25 Hispanic Americans, 3 Native Americans), 23 international. Average age 27. 4,284 applicants, 5% accepted. *Faculty:* 675 full-time (156 women), 34 part-time/adjunct (13 women). Expenses: Contact institution. *Financial support:* Fellowships, research assistantships, teaching assistantships, career-related internships or fieldwork, Federal Work-Study, institutionally sponsored loans, and tuition waivers (full and partial) available. Support available to part-time students. In 2001, 141 degrees awarded. Offers medicine (MD). *Application deadline:* For fall admission, 11/15. *Application fee:* $100. *Dean,* Dr. Brian Bull, 909-824-4462, Fax: 909-824-4146.

School of Public Health Students: 257 full-time (159 women), 96 part-time (67 women); includes 224 minority (104 African Americans, 91 Asian Americans or Pacific Islanders, 29 Hispanic Americans), 40 international. Average age 27. 284 applicants, 79% accepted. *Faculty:* 67 full-time (27 women), 102 part-time/adjunct (51 women). Expenses: Contact institution. *Financial support:* In 2001–02, 80 students received support; fellowships, research assistantships, teaching assistantships, career-related internships or fieldwork, Federal Work-Study, institutionally sponsored loans, tuition waivers (partial), and unspecified assistantships available. Support available to part-time students. Financial award application deadline: 5/15. In 2001, 114 master's, 4 doctorates awarded. *Degree program information:* Part-time programs available. Offers biostatistics (MPH, MSPH); environmental and occupational health (MPH, MSPH); epidemiology (MPH, Dr PH); health administration (MHA, MPH); health promotion and education (MPH, Dr PH); international health (MPH); public health (MHA, MPH, MSPH, Dr PH); public health nutrition (MPH, Dr PH). *Application deadline:* Applications are processed on a rolling basis. *Application fee:* $100. *Application Contact:* Terri Tamayose, Director of Admissions and Academic Records, 909-824-4694, Fax: 909-824-8087, E-mail: ttamayose@sph.llu.edu. *Dean,* Dr. Patricia K. Johnston, 909-824-4694.

LONG ISLAND UNIVERSITY, BRENTWOOD CAMPUS, Brentwood, NY 11717

General Information Independent, coed, upper-level institution. *Enrollment:* 151 full-time matriculated graduate/professional students (106 women), 662 part-time matriculated graduate/professional students (523 women). *Enrollment by degree level:* 813 master's. *Graduate faculty:* 20 full-time (5 women), 100 part-time/adjunct (35 women). *Tuition:* Part-time $572 per credit. Part-time tuition and fees vary according to program. *Graduate housing:* On-campus housing not available. *Student services:* Campus employment opportunities, career counseling, disabled student services, teacher training. *Web address:* http://www.liunet.edu/cwis/brent/brent.htm.

General Application Contact: John P. Metcalfe, Director of Admissions, 631-273-5112 Ext. 26, Fax: 631-952-0809, E-mail: john.metcalfe@liu.edu.

GRADUATE UNITS

School of Business Students: 46 full-time (23 women). Average age 40. 25 applicants, 68% accepted, 13 enrolled. Expenses: Contact institution. *Financial support:* Scholarships/grants, tuition waivers (partial), and unspecified assistantships available. Support available to part-time students. In 2001, 50 degrees awarded. *Degree program information:* Evening/weekend programs available. Offers business (MBA). *Application deadline:* Applications are processed on a rolling basis. *Application fee:* $0. *Head,* Dr. Herbert Sherman, 631-287-8284.

School of Education Students: 131 full-time (99 women), 602 part-time (482 women); includes 74 minority (47 African Americans, 1 Asian American or Pacific Islander, 26 Hispanic Americans) Average age 33. 290 applicants, 98% accepted, 262 enrolled. Expenses: Contact institution. *Financial support:* Federal Work-Study, scholarships/grants, and unspecified assistantships available. *Degree program information:* Part-time and evening/weekend programs available. Offers elementary education (MS); reading (MS); school counseling (MS); school district administration and supervision (MS); special education (MS). *Application deadline:* Applications are processed on a rolling basis. *Application fee:* $0. *Dean,* Dr. Robert Manheimer, 516-299-2210.

School of Public Service Average age 39. Expenses: Contact institution. *Financial support:* Scholarships/grants and unspecified assistantships available. Support available to part-time students. *Degree program information:* Part-time and evening/weekend programs available. Offers criminal justice (MS); health administration (MPA); public administration (MPA). *Application deadline:* Applications are processed on a rolling basis. *Application fee:* $0. *Head,* Dr. Robert Sanatore, 516-299-3017.

LONG ISLAND UNIVERSITY, BROOKLYN CAMPUS, Brooklyn, NY 11201-8423

General Information Independent, coed, university. *Graduate housing:* Rooms and/or apartments available to single and married students. Housing application deadline: 9/1.

GRADUATE UNITS

Arnold and Marie Schwartz College of Pharmacy and Health Sciences Students: 147 full-time (42 women), 94 part-time (44 women); includes 42 minority (11 African Americans, 29 Asian Americans or Pacific Islanders, 2 Hispanic Americans), 161 international. Average age 25. *Faculty:* 53 full-time (18 women), 8 part-time/adjunct (2 women). Expenses: Contact institution. *Financial support:* In 2001–02, 5 fellowships with full tuition reimbursements (averaging $13,500 per year), 30 teaching assistantships with full and partial tuition reimbursements (averaging $6,000 per year) were awarded. Federal Work-Study and institutionally sponsored loans also available. Support available to part-time students. Financial award applicants required to submit FAFSA. In 2001, 85 master's, 2 doctorates awarded. *Degree program information:* Part-time and evening/weekend programs available. Offers cosmetic science (MS); drug regulatory affairs (MS); industrial pharmacy (MS); pharmaceutical and health care marketing administration (MS); pharmaceutics (PhD); pharmaceutics and industrial pharmacy (MS, PhD); pharmacology/toxicology (MS); pharmacology/toxicology/medicinal chemistry (MS); pharmacy and health sciences (Pharm D, MS, PhD); pharmacy practice (MS); social and administrative sciences (MS). *Application deadline:* Applications are processed on a rolling basis. *Application fee:* $30. *Application Contact:* Bernard W. Sullivan, Associate Director of Admissions, 718-488-1011, Fax: 718-797-2399, E-mail: attend@liu.edu. *Dean,* Dr. Stephen M. Gross, 718-488-1004, Fax: 718-488-0628, E-mail: sgross@liu.edu.

Richard L. Conolly College of Liberal Arts and Sciences *Degree program information:* Part-time and evening/weekend programs available. Offers arts and sciences (MA, MS, PhD, Certificate); biology (MS); chemistry (MS); clinical psychology (PhD); economics (MA); English literature (MA); history (MS); political science (MA); professional and creative writing (MA); psychology (MA); speech-language pathology (MS); teaching of writing (MA); United Nations studies (Certificate); urban studies (MA). Electronic applications accepted.

School of Business, Public Administration and Information Sciences *Degree program information:* Part-time and evening/weekend programs available. Offers accounting (MS); business administration (MBA); business and public administration (MBA, MPA, MS); computer science (MS); human resources management (MS); public administration (MPA); taxation (MS). Electronic applications accepted.

School of Education *Degree program information:* Part-time and evening/weekend programs available. Offers bilingual education (MS Ed); computers in education (MS); counseling and development (MS, MS Ed, Certificate); education (MS, MS Ed, Certificate); elementary education (MS Ed); leadership and policy (MS); mathematics education (MS Ed); reading (MS Ed); school psychology (MS Ed); secondary education (MS Ed); special education (MS Ed); teaching English to speakers of other languages (MS Ed). Electronic applications accepted.

School of Health Professions *Degree program information:* Part-time and evening/weekend programs available. Offers adapted physical education (MS); athletic training and sports sciences (MS); community mental health (MS); exercise physiology (MS); family health (MS); health management (MS); health professions (MS); health sciences (MS); physical therapy (MS). Electronic applications accepted.

School of Nursing Offers adult nurse practitioner (MS, Certificate); nurse executive (MS); nursing (MS, Certificate). Electronic applications accepted.

LONG ISLAND UNIVERSITY, C.W. POST CAMPUS, Brookville, NY 11548-1300

General Information Independent, coed, comprehensive institution. *Enrollment:* 853 full-time matriculated graduate/professional students (595 women), 2,701 part-time matriculated graduate/professional students (1,981 women). *Enrollment by degree level:* 3,404 master's, 72 doctoral, 78 other advanced degrees. *Graduate faculty:* 313 full-time (123 women), 639 part-time/adjunct (264 women). *Tuition:* Full-time $10,296; part-time $572 per credit. *Required fees:* $380; $190 per semester. *Graduate housing:* Room and/or apartments available on a first-come, first-served basis to single students; on-campus housing not available to married students. Typical cost: $1,990 per year ($4,400 including board). Housing application deadline: 6/1. *Student services:* Campus employment opportunities, career counseling, child daycare facilities, disabled student services, exercise/wellness program, free psychological counseling, international student services, low-cost health insurance. *Library facilities:* B. Davis Schwartz Memorial Library. *Online resources:* library catalog, web page. *Collection:* 859,212 titles, 11,446 serial subscriptions, 34,530 audiovisual materials.

Computer facilities: 357 computers available on campus for general student use. A campuswide network can be accessed from student residence rooms and from off campus. Internet access is available. *Web address:* http://www.liu.edu/.

General Application Contact: Beth Carson, Associate Director of Graduate Admissions, 516-299-2900, Fax: 516-299-2137, E-mail: enroll@cwpost.liu.edu.

GRADUATE UNITS

Palmer School of Library and Information Science Students: 72 full-time (37 women), 333 part-time (233 women). 133 applicants, 88% accepted. *Faculty:* 14 full-time (3 women), 30 part-time/adjunct (10 women). Expenses: Contact institution. *Financial support:* Fellowships, research assistantships, career-related internships or fieldwork, Federal Work-Study, institutionally sponsored loans, and tuition waivers (partial) available. Support available to part-time students. Financial award application deadline: 5/15; financial award applicants required to submit CSS PROFILE or FAFSA. In 2001, 113 master's, 1 doctorate, 1 other advanced degree awarded. *Degree program information:* Part-time and evening/weekend programs available. Postbaccalaureate distance learning degree programs offered (minimal on-campus study). Offers archives (Certificate); information studies (PhD); library and information science (MS); records management (Certificate); schooll library media specialist (MS). *Application deadline:* For fall admission, 2/15; for spring admission, 10/15. *Application fee:* $30. Electronic applications accepted. *Application Contact:* Rosemary Chu, Graduate Admissions, 516-299-2866, Fax: 516-299-4168, E-mail: palmer@cwpost.liu.edu. *Dean,* Dr. Michael E. D. Koening, 516-299-2866, Fax: 516-299-4168, E-mail: palmer@cwpost.liu.edu.

College of Liberal Arts and Sciences Students: 81 full-time (67 women), 111 part-time (65 women). Average age 27. 272 applicants, 46% accepted, 51 enrolled. *Faculty:* 96 full-time (33 women), 31 part-time/adjunct (6 women). Expenses: Contact institution. *Financial support:* In 2001–02, 10 fellowships, 12 research assistantships, 7 teaching assistantships were awarded. Career-related internships or fieldwork, Federal Work-Study, institutionally sponsored loans, tuition waivers (full and partial), and unspecified assistantships also available. Support available to part-time students. Financial award application deadline: 5/15; financial award applicants required to submit CSS PROFILE or FAFSA. In 2001, 89 master's, 10 doctorates awarded. *Degree program information:* Part-time and evening/weekend programs available. Offers applied mathematics (MS); biology (MS); biology secondary education (MS); clinical psychology (Psy D); English (MA); English secondary education (MS); environmental management (MS); environmental science (MS); general experimental psychology (MA); history (MA); interdisciplinary studies (MA, MS); liberal arts and sciences (MA, MS, PhD, Psy D); mathematics education (MS); mathematics for secondary school teachers (MS); political science/international studies (MA); social studies (MS); social studies secondary education (MS); Spanish (MA); Spanish education (MS). *Application deadline:* Applications are processed on a rolling basis. *Application fee:* $30. Electronic applications accepted. *Application Contact:* Beth Carson, Associate Director of Graduate Admissions, 516-299-2900, Fax: 516-299-2137, E-mail: enroll@cwpost.liu.edu. *Acting Dean,* Dr. Katherine Hill-Miller, 516-299-2233, Fax: 516-299-4140.

College of Management Students: 143 full-time (65 women), 422 part-time (215 women). Average age 31. 273 applicants, 74% accepted, 122 enrolled. *Faculty:* 63 full-time (19 women), 79 part-time/adjunct (22 women). Expenses: Contact institution. *Financial support:* Fellowships, research assistantships, teaching assistantships, career-related internships or fieldwork, Federal Work-Study, institutionally sponsored loans, scholarships/grants, tuition waivers (partial), and unspecified assistantships available. Support available to part-time students. Financial award application deadline: 5/15; financial award applicants required to submit CSS PROFILE or FAFSA. In 2001, 259 master's, 5 other advanced degrees awarded. *Degree program information:* Part-time and evening/weekend programs available. Offers management (MBA, MPA, MS, Certificate). *Application deadline:* Applications are processed on a rolling basis. *Application fee:* $30. Electronic applications accepted. *Application Contact:* Beth Carson, Associate Director of Graduate Admissions, 516-299-2900, Fax: 516-299-2137, E-mail: enroll@cwpost.liu.edu. *Dean*, Dr. Robert J. Sanator, 516-299-3017, Fax: 516-299-2786, E-mail: rsanator@titan.liunet.edu.

School of Business(MBA Programs) Students: 95 full-time (35 women), 202 part-time (74 women). Average age 28. 163 applicants, 72% accepted, 57 enrolled. *Faculty:* 25 full-time (1 woman), 7 part-time/adjunct (2 women). Expenses: Contact institution. *Financial support:* Fellowships, research assistantships, tuition waivers (partial) and unspecified assistantships available. Support available to part-time students. Financial award application deadline: 5/15; financial award applicants required to submit CSS PROFILE or FAFSA. In 2001, 136 degrees awarded. *Degree program information:* Part-time and evening/weekend programs available. Offers business administration (Certificate); chain management (MBA); finance (MBA, Certificate); general business administration (MBA); human resource management (Certificate); international business (MBA, Certificate); logistical supply chain (Certificate); logistics and supply (MBA); management (MBA, Certificate); management information systems (MBA, Certificate); marketing (MBA, Certificate). *Application deadline:* For fall admission, 8/20; for spring admission, 1/10. Applications are processed on a rolling basis. *Application fee:* $30. Electronic applications accepted. *Application Contact:* Colleen Pisano, Graduate Advisor, 516-299-2719, Fax: 516-299-2137, E-mail: colleen.pisano@liu.edu. *MBA Program Director*, Salvatore Cordo, 516-299-2722, Fax: 516-299-2786, E-mail: sal.cordo@liu.edu.

School of Professional Accountancy Students: 8 full-time (5 women), 46 part-time (22 women). Average age 34. 30 applicants, 57% accepted, 13 enrolled. *Faculty:* 9 full-time (2 women), 4 part-time/adjunct (1 woman). Expenses: Contact institution. *Financial support:* Career-related internships or fieldwork, Federal Work-Study, institutionally sponsored loans, and unspecified assistantships available. Support available to part-time students. Financial award application deadline: 5/15; financial award applicants required to submit CSS PROFILE or FAFSA. In 2001, 46 degrees awarded. *Degree program information:* Part-time and evening/weekend programs available. Offers accountancy/information system (MS); accounting (MS); taxation (MS). *Application deadline:* For fall admission, 8/15; for spring admission, 12/15. Applications are processed on a rolling basis. *Application fee:* $30. Electronic applications accepted. *Application Contact:* Fred Tobias, Adviser, 516-299-2098, Fax: 516-299-2297, E-mail: fred.tobias@liu.edu. *Director*, Dr. Lawrence P. Kalbers, 516-299-2364, Fax: 516-299-3221, E-mail: lkalbers@liu.edu.

School of Public Service Students: 40 full-time (25 women), 174 part-time (119 women). 73 applicants, 88% accepted, 48 enrolled. *Faculty:* 15 full-time (6 women), 25 part-time/adjunct (5 women). Expenses: Contact institution. *Financial support:* Research assistantships with partial tuition reimbursements, career-related internships or fieldwork, Federal Work-Study, institutionally sponsored loans, scholarships/grants, and unspecified assistantships available. Support available to part-time students. Financial award application deadline: 5/15; financial award applicants required to submit CSS PROFILE or FAFSA. In 2001, 77 degrees awarded. *Degree program information:* Part-time and evening/weekend programs available. Offers fraud examination (MS); gerontology (Certificate); health care administration (MPA); health care administration/gerontology (MPA); public administration (MPA); public service (MPA, MS, Certificate); security administration (MS). *Application deadline:* For fall admission, 8/15; for spring admission, 12/15. Applications are processed on a rolling basis. *Application fee:* $30. Electronic applications accepted. *Application Contact:* Beth Carson, Associate Director of Graduate Admissions, 516-299-2900, Fax: 516-299-2137, E-mail: enroll@cwpost.liu.edu.

School of Education Students: 409 full-time (317 women), 1,518 part-time (1,239 women). Average age 28. 946 applicants, 78% accepted, 519 enrolled. *Faculty:* 44 full-time (19 women), 103 part-time/adjunct (39 women). Expenses: Contact institution. *Financial support:* In 2001–02, 29 research assistantships were awarded; teaching assistantships, career-related internships or fieldwork and Federal Work-Study also available. Support available to part-time students. Financial award application deadline: 5/15; financial award applicants required to submit CSS PROFILE or FAFSA. In 2001, 559 master's, 48 other advanced degrees awarded. *Degree program information:* Part-time and evening/weekend programs available. Offers adolescence (MS); art education (MS); bilingual education (MS); biology education (MS); childhood (MS); computers in education (MS); early childhood (MS); early childhood/literacy (MS); early childhood/special ed (MS); earth science education (MS); education (MA, MS, MS Ed, PD); English education (MS); French education (MS); Italian education (MS); literacy (MS); marriage and family therapy (PD); mathematics education (MS); mental health counseling (MS); music education (MS); reading (MS Ed); school administration and supervision (MS Ed); school business administration (PD); school counseling (MS); school district administration (PD); social studies (MS); Spanish education (MS); special education (MS Ed, PD); speech-language pathology (MA). *Application deadline:* Applications are processed on a rolling basis. *Application fee:* $30. Electronic applications accepted. *Application Contact:* Beth Carson, Associate Director of Graduate Admissions, 516-299-2900, Fax: 516-299-2137, E-mail: enroll@cwpost.liu.edu. *Acting Dean*, Dr. Robert Manheimer, 516-299-2210, Fax: 516-299-4167, E-mail: rmanheimer@liu.edu.

School of Health Professions and Nursing Students: 36 full-time (23 women), 107 part-time (90 women). Average age 30. 136 applicants, 63% accepted, 57 enrolled. *Faculty:* 14 full-time (9 women), 38 part-time/adjunct (25 women). Expenses: Contact institution. *Financial support:* In 2001–02, 45 students received support, including 4 fellowships with partial tuition reimbursements available, 6 teaching assistantships with partial tuition reimbursements available; career-related internships or fieldwork, Federal Work-Study, institutionally sponsored loans, tuition waivers (partial), and unspecified assistantships also available. Support available to part-time students. Financial award application deadline: 5/15; financial award applicants required to submit CSS PROFILE or FAFSA. In 2001, 18 master's, 1 other advanced degree awarded. *Degree program information:* Part-time and evening/weekend programs available. Postbaccalaureate distance learning degree programs offered. Offers advanced practice nursing (MS); cardiovascular perfusion (MS, Certificate); clinical laboratory management (MS); dietetic internship (Certificate); family nurse practitioner (MS, Certificate); health professions and nursing (MS, Certificate); hematology (MS); immunology (MS); medical biology (MS); medical chemistry (MS); microbiology (MS); nutrition (MS). *Application deadline:* Applications are processed on a rolling basis. *Application fee:* $30. Electronic applications accepted. *Application Contact:* Beth Carson, Associate Director of Graduate Admissions, 516-299-2900, Fax: 516-299-2137, E-mail: enroll@cwpost.liu.edu. *Dean*, Dr. Theodora T. Grauer, 516-299-2485, Fax: 516-299-2527, E-mail: healprof@liu.edu.

School of Visual and Performing Arts Students: 112 full-time (86 women), 136 part-time (95 women). Average age 25. 148 applicants, 82% accepted, 79 enrolled. *Faculty:* 27 full-time (11 women), 34 part-time/adjunct (18 women). Expenses: Contact institution. *Financial support:* Fellowships, teaching assistantships, career-related internships or fieldwork, Federal Work-Study, institutionally sponsored loans, scholarships/grants, and unspecified assistantships available. Support available to part-time students. Financial award application deadline: 5/15; financial award applicants required to submit CSS PROFILE or FAFSA. In 2001, 93 degrees awarded. *Degree program information:* Part-time and evening/weekend programs available. Offers art (MA); art education (MS); clinical art therapy (MA); fine art and design (MFA); interactive multimedia arts (MA); music (MA); music education (MS); theatre (MA); visual and performing arts (MA, MFA, MS). *Application deadline:* Applications are processed on a rolling basis. *Application fee:* $30. Electronic applications accepted. *Application Contact:* Beth Carson, Associate Director of Graduate Admissions, 516-299-2900, Fax: 516-299-2137, E-mail: enroll@cwpost.liu.edu. *Dean*, Lynn Croton, 516-299-2395, Fax: 516-299-4180, E-mail: vparts@liu.edu.

See in-depth description on page 943.

LONG ISLAND UNIVERSITY, ROCKLAND GRADUATE CAMPUS, Orangeburg, NY 10962

General Information Independent, coed, graduate-only institution. *Enrollment by degree level:* 434 master's. *Graduate faculty:* 12 full-time (3 women), 37 part-time/adjunct (9 women). *Tuition:* Part-time $572 per credit. *Required fees:* $70 per semester. *Graduate housing:* On-campus housing not available. *Student services:* Campus employment opportunities, career counseling, teacher training. *Library facilities:* Long Island University, Rockland Campus Library. *Online resources:* library catalog. *Collection:* 10,700 titles, 560 serial subscriptions, 45 audiovisual materials.

Computer facilities: 33 computers available on campus for general student use. A campuswide network can be accessed from off campus. Internet access is available. *Web address:* http://www.liu.edu/.

General Application Contact: Stacey Gargiulo, Director of Admissions/Marketing, 845-359-7200, Fax: 845-359-7248, E-mail: stacey.schepis@liu.edu.

GRADUATE UNITS

Graduate School Students: 37 full-time (31 women), 397 part-time (332 women). 176 applicants, 64% accepted. *Faculty:* 12 full-time (3 women), 37 part-time/adjunct (9 women). Expenses: Contact institution. *Financial support:* In 2001–02, 200 students received support. Scholarships/grants available. Support available to part-time students. Financial award applicants required to submit FAFSA. In 2001, 118 degrees awarded. Offers business administration (MBA); elementary education (MS Ed); health administration (MPA); reading teacher (MS Ed); school administration and supervision (MS Ed); school counseling (MS); special education (MS Ed). *Application deadline:* Applications are processed on a rolling basis. *Application fee:* $30. *Application Contact:* Stacey Gargiulo, Director of Admissions/Marketing, 845-359-7200, Fax: 845-359-7248, E-mail: stacey.schepis@liu.edu. *Associate Provost*, Nancy Low-Hogan, 845-359-7200, Fax: 845-359-7248, E-mail: nlow@liu.edu.

LONG ISLAND UNIVERSITY, SOUTHAMPTON COLLEGE, Southampton, NY 11968-4198

General Information Independent, coed, comprehensive institution. *Graduate housing:* Room and/or apartments available to single students; on-campus housing not available to married students.

GRADUATE UNITS

Education Division *Degree program information:* Part-time and evening/weekend programs available. Offers education (MS Ed); elementary education (MS Ed); reading (MS Ed). Electronic applications accepted.

Gerontology Division *Degree program information:* Part-time programs available. Postbaccalaureate distance learning degree programs offered (minimal on-campus study). Offers gerontology (MPS, AC).

Humanities Division *Degree program information:* Part-time programs available. Postbaccalaureate distance learning degree programs offered (minimal on-campus study). Offers English and writing (MFA).

LONG ISLAND UNIVERSITY, WESTCHESTER GRADUATE CAMPUS, Purchase, NY 10577

General Information Independent, coed, graduate-only institution. *Enrollment by degree level:* 104 master's. *Graduate faculty:* 5 full-time, 20 part-time/adjunct. *Tuition:* Part-time $572 per credit. *Graduate housing:* On-campus housing not available. *Student services:* Campus employment opportunities, career counseling, international student services, low-cost health insurance. *Library facilities:* Long Island University Library System. *Collection:* 2.3 million titles. *Web address:* http://www.liu.edu/westchester/.

General Application Contact: Carol A. Messar, Director of Admissions, 914-251-6510, Fax: 914-251-5959, E-mail: cmessar@liu.edu.

GRADUATE UNITS

Program in Business Administration Students: 5 full-time (3 women). Expenses: Contact institution. Offers business administration (MBA). *Application fee:* $30. *Application Contact:* Carol A. Messar, Director of Admissions, 914-251-6510, Fax: 914-251-5959, E-mail: cmessar@liu.edu. *Head*, Dr. Lynn Johnson, 914-251-6510.

Program in Education-Teaching Students: 1 (woman) full-time, 41 part-time (30 women). Expenses: Contact institution. Offers bi-lingual education (MS Ed); elementary education (MS Ed); reading teacher (MS Ed); special education (MS Ed); teaching English to speakers of other languages (MS Ed). *Application fee:* $30. *Application Contact:* Carol A. Messar, Director of Admissions, 914-251-6510, Fax: 914-251-5959, E-mail: cmessar@liu.edu. *Program Coordinator*, Dr. Sylvia Blake, 914-251-6510.

Program in Health Sciences/Exercise Physiology Expenses: Contact institution. In 2001, 10 degrees awarded. Offers health science (MS). *Application deadline:* Applications are processed on a rolling basis. *Application fee:* $30. *Application Contact:* Carol A. Messar, Director of Admissions, 914-251-6510, Fax: 914-251-5959, E-mail: cmessar@liu.edu. *Program Coordinator*, Skip Latella, 914-251-6510.

Program in Pharmaceutics/Industrial Pharmacy Expenses: Contact institution. In 2001, 3 degrees awarded. Offers pharmaceuticals (MS). *Application Contact:* Carol A. Messar, Director of Admissions, 914-251-6510, Fax: 914-251-5959, E-mail: cmessar@liu.edu. *Program Coordinator*, Dr. Almas Babar, 914-251-6510.

LONGWOOD COLLEGE, Farmville, VA 23909-1800

General Information State-supported, coed, comprehensive institution. *Graduate housing:* Room and/or apartments available to single students; on-campus housing not available to married students.

GRADUATE UNITS

Graduate Programs *Degree program information:* Part-time and evening/weekend programs available. Offers administration/supervision (MS); community and college counseling (MS); criminal justice (MS); curriculum and instruction specialist-elementary (MS); curriculum and instruction specialist-secondary (MS); English education and writing (MA); environmental studies (MS); guidance and counseling (MS); library science media specialist (MS); literature (MA); reading specialist (MS).

LONGY SCHOOL OF MUSIC, Cambridge, MA 02138

General Information Independent, coed, graduate-only institution. *Enrollment by degree level:* 77 master's, 50 other advanced degrees. *Graduate faculty:* 85 part-time/adjunct (40 women). *Tuition:* Full-time $16,500; part-time $925 per credit. *Required fees:* $295. Full-time tuition and fees vary according to course load, degree level and program. *Graduate housing:* Room and/or apartments available on a first-come, first-served basis to single students; on-campus housing not available to married students. Housing application deadline: 5/15. *Student services:* Campus employment opportunities, career counseling, international student services, low-cost health insurance. *Library facilities:* Bakalar Library. *Collection:* 17,000 titles, 26 serial subscriptions, 12,400 audiovisual materials.

Computer facilities: 6 computers available on campus for general student use. A campuswide network can be accessed. Internet access is available. *Web address:* http://www.longy.edu/.

General Application Contact: Alexandra Tucker, Director of Admissions, 617-876-0956 Ext. 521, Fax: 617-876-9326, E-mail: music@longy.edu.

GRADUATE UNITS

Professional Studies Division Students: 94 full-time (56 women), 33 part-time (24 women); includes 8 minority (5 African Americans, 3 Asian Americans or Pacific Islanders), 66 international. Average age 29. 130 applicants, 80% accepted. *Faculty:* 85 part-time/adjunct (40 women). Expenses: Contact institution. *Financial support:* In 2001–02, 97 students received support; fellowships with partial tuition reimbursements available, teaching assistantships with partial tuition reimbursements available, scholarships/grants, tuition waivers, and unspeci-

Longy School of Music (continued)

fied assistantships available. Financial award application deadline: 3/1; financial award applicants required to submit FAFSA. In 2001, 22 master's, 21 GPDs awarded. *Degree program information:* Part-time programs available. Offers chamber ensemble (Artist Diploma); collaboratiave piano (Artist Diploma); collaborative piano (MM, GPD); composition (MM); Dalcroze eurhythmics (MM); early music (MM, Artist Diploma, GPD); instrumental performance (MM, Artist Diploma, GPD); opera performance (MM, GPD); organ performance (MM); piano performance (MM, Artist Diploma, GPD); vocal performance (MM, Artist Diploma, GPD). *Application deadline:* For fall admission, 2/1 (priority date); for spring admission, 12/1. Applications are processed on a rolling basis. *Application fee:* $75. *Application Contact:* Alexandra Tucker, Director of Admissions, 617-876-0956, Fax: 617-876-9326, E-mail: music@longy.edu. *President*, Dr. Kwang-Wu Kim, 617-876-0956, Fax: 617-876-9326.

LORAS COLLEGE, Dubuque, IA 52004-0178

General Information Independent-religious, coed, comprehensive institution. *Enrollment:* 6 full-time matriculated graduate/professional students (5 women), 69 part-time matriculated graduate/professional students (47 women). *Enrollment by degree level:* 75 master's. *Graduate faculty:* 32 full-time (14 women), 5 part-time/adjunct (1 woman). *Tuition:* Part-time $375 per credit hour. *Graduate housing:* On-campus housing not available. *Student services:* Career counseling, disabled student services. *Library facilities:* Wahlert Memorial Library plus 1 other. *Online resources:* library catalog, web page, access to other libraries' catalogs. *Collection:* 283,000 titles, 963 serial subscriptions.

Computer facilities: 100 computers available on campus for general student use. A campuswide network can be accessed from student residence rooms and from off campus. Internet access is available. *Web address:* http://www.loras.edu/.

General Application Contact: Barb Harrington, Graduate Admissions Coordinator, 563-588-4915, Fax: 563-588-7119, E-mail: bharring@loras.edu.

GRADUATE UNITS

Graduate Division Students: 6 full-time (5 women), 69 part-time (47 women), 2 international. Average age 33. 27 applicants, 70% accepted. *Faculty:* 32 full-time (14 women), 5 part-time/adjunct (1 woman). Expenses: Contact institution. *Financial support:* In 2001–02, 20 students received support. Tuition waivers (full) and unspecified assistantships available. Financial award applicants required to submit FAFSA. In 2001, 38 degrees awarded. *Degree program information:* Part-time and evening/weekend programs available. Offers applied psychology (MA); educational administration: elementary and secondary (MA); educational counseling: elementary and secondary (MA); effective teaching (MA); English (MA); pastoral studies (MM); physical education (MA); religious education (MM); special education (MA); theology (MA). *Application deadline:* Applications are processed on a rolling basis. *Application fee:* $25. Electronic applications accepted. *Application Contact:* Barb Harrington, Graduate Admissions Coordinator, 563-588-4915, Fax: 563-588-7119, E-mail: bharring@loras.edu.

LOUISIANA STATE UNIVERSITY AND AGRICULTURAL AND MECHANICAL COLLEGE, Baton Rouge, LA 70803

General Information State-supported, coed, university. CGS member. *Enrollment:* 2,925 full-time matriculated graduate/professional students (1,490 women), 1,424 part-time matriculated graduate/professional students (796 women). *Enrollment by degree level:* 319 first professional, 2,403 master's, 1,627 doctoral. *Graduate faculty:* 1,094 full-time (219 women), 23 part-time/adjunct (3 women). Tuition, state resident: full-time $2,551. Tuition, nonresident: full-time $5,551. *Required fees:* $854. Part-time tuition and fees vary according to course load. *Graduate housing:* Rooms and/or apartments available on a first-come, first-served basis to single and married students. Typical cost: $2,650 per year ($4,546 including board) for single students. Housing application deadline: 3/15. *Student services:* Campus employment opportunities, campus safety program, career counseling, disabled student services, free psychological counseling, international student services, low-cost health insurance. *Library facilities:* Troy H. Middleton Library plus 7 others. *Online resources:* library catalog, web page, access to other libraries' catalogs. *Collection:* 1.1 million titles, 17,975 serial subscriptions, 2,043 audiovisual materials. *Research affiliation:* Delta Regional Primate Center, Center for Research Libraries.

Computer facilities: 7,000 computers available on campus for general student use. A campuswide network can be accessed from student residence rooms and from off campus. Internet access and online class registration, e-mail are available. *Web address:* http://www.lsu.edu/.

General Application Contact: Jennifer Whalen, Office of Graduate Admissions, 225-578-1128, Fax: 225-578-2112, E-mail: jwhalen@lsu.edu.

GRADUATE UNITS

Graduate School Students: 2,925 full-time (1,490 women), 1,424 part-time (796 women); includes 478 minority (334 African Americans, 53 Asian Americans or Pacific Islanders, 74 Hispanic Americans, 17 Native Americans), 973 international. Average age 30. 3,491 applicants, 43% accepted. *Faculty:* 1,094 full-time (219 women), 23 part-time/adjunct (3 women). Expenses: Contact institution. *Financial support:* In 2001–02, 1,720 students received support, including 163 fellowships with full tuition reimbursements available (averaging $15,410 per year), 681 research assistantships with partial tuition reimbursements available (averaging $13,434 per year), 625 teaching assistantships with partial tuition reimbursements available (averaging $12,925 per year); career-related internships or fieldwork, Federal Work-Study, institutionally sponsored loans, scholarships/grants, traineeships, tuition waivers (full and partial), unspecified assistantships, and contracts also available. Support available to part-time students. Financial award application deadline: 12/15; financial award applicants required to submit FAFSA. In 2001, 944 master's, 226 doctorates, 20 other advanced degrees awarded. *Degree program information:* Part-time and evening/weekend programs available. Postbaccalaureate distance learning degree programs offered. Offers linguistics (MA, PhD). *Application deadline:* For fall admission, 1/24 (priority date); for spring admission, 10/14. Applications are processed on a rolling basis. *Application fee:* $25. Electronic applications accepted. *Application Contact:* Marie Hamilton, Assistant Dean, 225-578-1640, Fax: 225-578-2112, E-mail: mhamil3@lsu.edu. *Interim Dean*, Kevin Smith, 225-578-3885, Fax: 225-578-2112, E-mail: kmsmith@lsu.edu.

College of Agriculture Students: 295 full-time (140 women), 176 part-time (90 women); includes 29 minority (18 African Americans, 3 Asian Americans or Pacific Islanders, 5 Hispanic Americans, 3 Native Americans), 146 international. Average age 32. 258 applicants, 45% accepted, 85 enrolled. *Faculty:* 190 full-time (28 women), 1 part-time/adjunct (0 women). Expenses: Contact institution. *Financial support:* In 2001–02, 77 students received support, including 10 fellowships with full tuition reimbursements available (averaging $14,267 per year), 181 research assistantships with partial tuition reimbursements available (averaging $13,600 per year), 32 teaching assistantships with partial tuition reimbursements available (averaging $11,137 per year); career-related internships or fieldwork, Federal Work-Study, institutionally sponsored loans, tuition waivers (full), and unspecified assistantships also available. Support available to part-time students. In 2001, 64 master's, 34 doctorates awarded. *Degree program information:* Part-time programs available. Offers agricultural economics and agribusiness (MS, PhD); agriculture (M App St, MS, MSBAE, PhD); agronomy (MS, PhD); animal science (MS, PhD); applied statistics (M App St); biological and agricultural engineering (MSBAE); comprehensive vocational education (MS, PhD); dairy science (MS, PhD); engineering science (MS, PhD); entomology (MS, PhD); extension and international education (MS, PhD); fisheries (MS); food science (MS, PhD); forestry (MS, PhD); horticulture (MS, PhD); human ecology (MS, PhD); industrial education (MS); plant health (MS, PhD); vocational agriculture education (MS, PhD); vocational business education (MS); vocational home economics education (MS); wildlife (MS); wildlife and fisheries science (PhD). *Application deadline:* Applications are processed on a rolling basis. *Application fee:* $25. *Application Contact:* Paula Beecher, Recruiting Coordinator, 225-578-2468, E-mail: pbeeche@lsu.edu. *Dean*, Dr. Kenneth Koonce, 225-578-2362, Fax: 225-578-2526, E-mail: kkoonce@lsu.edu.

College of Art and Design Students: 103 full-time (60 women), 27 part-time (17 women); includes 7 minority (2 African Americans, 1 Asian American or Pacific Islander, 1 Hispanic American, 3 Native Americans), 19 international. Average age 31. 90 applicants, 48% accepted, 32 enrolled. *Faculty:* 52 full-time (13 women), 2 part-time/adjunct (1 woman). Expenses: Contact institution. *Financial support:* In 2001–02, 20 research assistantships with partial tuition reimbursements (averaging $6,456 per year), 6 teaching assistantships with partial tuition reimbursements (averaging $6,325 per year) were awarded. Fellowships, career-related internships or fieldwork, Federal Work-Study, institutionally sponsored loans, scholarships/grants, and unspecified assistantships also available. Support available to part-time students. Financial award applicants required to submit FAFSA. In 2001, 30 degrees awarded. *Degree program information:* Part-time programs available. Offers architecture (M Arch, MS); art and design (M Arch, MA, MFA, MLA, MS); art history (MA); ceramics (MFA); graphic design (MFA); landscape architecture (MLA); painting and drawing (MFA); photography (MFA); printmaking (MFA); sculpture (MFA); studio art (MFA). *Application deadline:* For fall admission, 1/25 (priority date). Applications are processed on a rolling basis. *Application fee:* $25. *Application Contact:* Theresa Mooney, Academic Counselor, 225-578-5400, Fax: 225-578-1445, E-mail: deacon1@lsu.edu. *Interim Dean*, Dr. Ken Carpenter, 225-578-5400, Fax: 225-578-5040, E-mail: kenc@lsu.edu.

College of Arts and Sciences Students: 490 full-time (269 women), 235 part-time (112 women); includes 74 minority (49 African Americans, 5 Asian Americans or Pacific Islanders, 19 Hispanic Americans, 1 Native American), 79 international. Average age 31. 653 applicants, 38% accepted, 137 enrolled. *Faculty:* 270 full-time (67 women), 3 part-time/adjunct (1 woman). Expenses: Contact institution. *Financial support:* In 2001–02, 33 fellowships with full tuition reimbursements (averaging $15,257 per year), 56 research assistantships with partial tuition reimbursements (averaging $12,552 per year), 237 teaching assistantships with partial tuition reimbursements (averaging $11,963 per year) were awarded. Career-related internships or fieldwork, Federal Work-Study, institutionally sponsored loans, scholarships/grants, traineeships, tuition waivers (full), unspecified assistantships, and contracts also available. Support available to part-time students. Financial award applicants required to submit FAFSA. In 2001, 118 master's, 70 doctorates awarded. *Degree program information:* Part-time and evening/weekend programs available. Offers anthropology (MA); arts and sciences (MA, MALA, MFA, MS, PhD); biological psychology (MA, PhD); clinical psychology (MA, PhD); cognitive psychology (MA, PhD); communication sciences and disorders (MA, PhD); comparative literature (MA, PhD); creative writing (MFA); developmental psychology (MA, PhD); English (MA, PhD); French literature and linguistics (MA, PhD); geography (MA, MS, PhD); history (MA, PhD); industrial/organizational psychology (MA, PhD); liberal arts (MALA); mathematics (MS, PhD); philosophy (MA); political science (MA, PhD); school psychology (MA, PhD); sociology (MA, PhD); Spanish (MA); speech communication (MA, PhD). *Application fee:* $25. *Application Contact:* Dr. William W. Demastes, Associate Dean, 225-578-8273, Fax: 225-587-6447, E-mail: wdemast@lsu.edu. *Dean*, Dr. Mary Jane Collins, 225-578-8273, Fax: 225-578-6447, E-mail: collins@lsu.edu.

College of Basic Sciences Students: 380 full-time (143 women), 66 part-time (24 women); includes 57 minority (43 African Americans, 8 Asian Americans or Pacific Islanders, 6 Hispanic Americans), 196 international. Average age 28. 490 applicants, 34% accepted, 87 enrolled. *Faculty:* 157 full-time (18 women), 8 part-time/adjunct (0 women). Expenses: Contact institution. *Financial support:* In 2001–02, 53 fellowships (averaging $17,800 per year), 98 research assistantships with partial tuition reimbursements (averaging $16,088 per year), 151 teaching assistantships with partial tuition reimbursements (averaging $16,844 per year) were awarded. Career-related internships or fieldwork, Federal Work-Study, institutionally sponsored loans, and unspecified assistantships also available. Support available to part-time students. Financial award applicants required to submit FAFSA. In 2001, 73 master's, 46 doctorates awarded. *Degree program information:* Part-time programs available. Offers astronomy (PhD); astrophysics (PhD); basic sciences (MNS, MS, MSSS, PhD); biochemistry (MS, PhD); chemistry (MS, PhD); computer science (MSSS, PhD); geology and geophysics (MS, PhD); microbiology (MS, PhD); natural sciences (MNS); physics (MS, PhD); plant biology (MS, PhD); systems science (MSSS); zoology (MS, PhD). *Application deadline:* Applications are processed on a rolling basis. *Application fee:* $25. *Application Contact:* Dr. Frank Cartledge, Associate Dean, 225-578-4200, Fax: 225-578-8826, E-mail: fcartledge@lsu.edu. *Chairman*, Dr. Harold Silverman, 225-578-8859, Fax: 225-578-8826, E-mail: cxsiv@lsu.edu.

College of Education Students: 222 full-time (159 women), 282 part-time (222 women); includes 110 minority (90 African Americans, 9 Asian Americans or Pacific Islanders, 10 Hispanic Americans, 1 Native American), 14 international. Average age 33. 177 applicants, 57% accepted, 78 enrolled. *Faculty:* 55 full-time (28 women), 2 part-time/adjunct (0 women). Expenses: Contact institution. *Financial support:* In 2001–02, 93 students received support, including 39 fellowships (averaging $11,932 per year), 31 research assistantships with partial tuition reimbursements available (averaging $10,048 per year), 34 teaching assistantships with partial tuition reimbursements available (averaging $8,599 per year); career-related internships or fieldwork, Federal Work-Study, institutionally sponsored loans, tuition waivers (partial), and unspecified assistantships also available. Support available to part-time students. Financial award applicants required to submit FAFSA. In 2001, 126 master's, 26 doctorates, 17 other advanced degrees awarded. *Degree program information:* Part-time and evening/weekend programs available. Offers counseling (M Ed, MA, Ed S); curriculum and instruction (MA, PhD, Ed S); education (M Ed, MA, MS, PhD, Ed S); educational administration (M Ed, MA, PhD, Ed S); educational technology (MA); elementary education (M Ed); higher education (PhD); kinesiology (MS, PhD); research methodology (PhD); secondary education (M Ed). *Application deadline:* For fall admission, 1/25 (priority date). Applications are processed on a rolling basis. *Application fee:* $25. *Application Contact:* Dr. Rita Culross, Associate Dean, 225-578-2208, Fax: 225-578-2267, E-mail: acrita@lsu.edu. *Dean*, Dr. Barbara Fuhrmann, 225-578-1258, Fax: 225-578-2267, E-mail: fuhrma@lsu.edu.

College of Engineering Students: 337 full-time (67 women), 88 part-time (20 women); includes 15 minority (8 African Americans, 3 Asian Americans or Pacific Islanders, 3 Hispanic Americans, 1 Native American), 326 international. Average age 28. 810 applicants, 37% accepted, 100 enrolled. *Faculty:* 98 full-time (2 women), 2 part-time/adjunct (0 women). Expenses: Contact institution. *Financial support:* In 2001–02, 10 fellowships (averaging $17,637 per year), 172 research assistantships with partial tuition reimbursements (averaging $13,928 per year), 67 teaching assistantships with partial tuition reimbursements (averaging $12,107 per year) were awarded. Career-related internships or fieldwork, Federal Work-Study, institutionally sponsored loans, scholarships/grants, tuition waivers (full and partial), and unspecified assistantships also available. Financial award applicants required to submit FAFSA. In 2001, 109 master's, 17 doctorates awarded. *Degree program information:* Part-time and evening/weekend programs available. Offers chemical engineering (MS Ch E, PhD); electrical and computer engineering (MSEE, PhD); engineering (MS Ch E, MS Pet E, MSCE, MSEE, MSES, MSIE, MSME, PhD); engineering science (MSES, PhD); environmental engineering (MSCE, PhD); geotechnical engineering (MSCE, PhD); industrial engineering (MSIE); mechanical engineering (MSME, PhD); petroleum engineering (MS Pet E, PhD); structural engineering and mechanics (MSCE, PhD); transportation engineering (MSCE, PhD); water resources (MSCE, PhD). *Application deadline:* For fall admission, 1/25 (priority date). Applications are processed on a rolling basis. *Application fee:* $25. *Application Contact:* Dr. Mehmet T. Tumay, Associate Dean, 225-578-9165, Fax: 225-578-9162, E-mail: mtumay@lsu.edu. *Dean*, Dr. Pius J. Egbelu, 225-578-6003, Fax: 225-578-9162, E-mail: pegbelu@eng.lsu.edu.

College of Music and Dramatic Arts Students: 137 full-time (59 women), 57 part-time (28 women); includes 18 minority (12 African Americans, 2 Asian Americans or Pacific Islanders, 4 Hispanic Americans), 43 international. Average age 31. 107 applicants, 58% accepted, 32 enrolled. *Faculty:* 52 full-time (18 women), 3 part-time/adjunct (0 women). Expenses: Contact institution. *Financial support:* In 2001–02, 35 students received support, including 11 fellowships (averaging $14,202 per year), 1 research assistantship with partial tuition reimbursement available (averaging $21,500 per year), 3 teaching assistantships with partial tuition reimbursements available (averaging $20,667 per year); Federal Work-Study, tuition waivers (full and partial), and unspecified assistantships also available. Financial award applicants required to submit FAFSA. In 2001, 26 master's, 9 doctorates awarded. *Degree program information:* Part-time programs available. Offers acting (MFA); directing (MFA); music (MM, DMA, PhD); music and dramatic arts (MFA, MM, DMA, PhD); music education (PhD); theatre (PhD); theatre design/technology (MFA). *Application deadline:* For fall admission, 3/15 (priority date). Applications are processed on a rolling basis. *Application fee:* $25. *Application Contact:* Dr. Bill Grimes, Graduate Adviser and Professor, 225-578-2572, Fax: 225-578-2562, E-mail: bgrimes@lsu.edu. *Dean,* Dr. Ronald Ross, 225-578-3261, Fax: 225-578-2562, E-mail: rross@lsu.edu.

E.J. Ourso College of Business Administration Students: 319 full-time (146 women), 242 part-time (100 women); includes 73 minority (49 African Americans, 14 Asian Americans or Pacific Islanders, 9 Hispanic Americans, 1 Native American), 89 international. Average age 29. 592 applicants, 49% accepted, 203 enrolled. *Faculty:* 73 full-time (13 women), 1 part-time/adjunct (0 women). Expenses: Contact institution. *Financial support:* In 2001–02, 2 fellowships (averaging $15,167 per year), 52 research assistantships with partial tuition reimbursements (averaging $10,820 per year), 21 teaching assistantships with partial tuition reimbursements (averaging $13,919 per year) were awarded. Career-related internships or fieldwork, Federal Work-Study, institutionally sponsored loans, and unspecified assistantships also available. Financial award applicants required to submit FAFSA. In 2001, 199 master's, 7 doctorates awarded. *Degree program information:* Part-time and evening/weekend programs available. Offers accounting (MS, PhD); business administration (PhD); economics (MS, PhD); finance (MS); information systems and decision sciences (MS); marketing (MS); public administration (MPA). *Application deadline:* For fall admission, 1/25 (priority date). Applications are processed on a rolling basis. *Application fee:* $25. *Dean,* Dr. Thomas D. Clark, 225-578-5297, Fax: 225-578-3211, E-mail: tclark@lsu.edu.

Manship School of Mass Communication Students: 27 full-time (15 women), 24 part-time (13 women); includes 8 minority (4 African Americans, 4 Hispanic Americans), 11 international. Average age 31. 58 applicants, 34% accepted, 12 enrolled. *Faculty:* 19 full-time (4 women). Expenses: Contact institution. *Financial support:* In 2001–02, 4 students received support, including 1 research assistantship with partial tuition reimbursement available (averaging $21,500 per year), 3 teaching assistantships with partial tuition reimbursements available (averaging $20,667 per year); fellowships, career-related internships or fieldwork, Federal Work-Study, institutionally sponsored loans, and unspecified assistantships also available. Financial award application deadline: 3/1; financial award applicants required to submit FAFSA. In 2001, 17 degrees awarded. *Degree program information:* Part-time programs available. Postbaccalaureate distance learning degree programs offered (minimal on-campus study). Offers mass communication (MMC). *Application deadline:* For fall admission, 1/25 (priority date). Applications are processed on a rolling basis. *Application fee:* $25. *Application Contact:* Louis Day, Associate Dean of Graduate Studies, 225-578-6811, Fax: 225-578-2125, E-mail: lday@lsu.edu. *Dean,* Dr. John Maxwell Hamilton, 225-578-2002, Fax: 225-578-2125, E-mail: jhamilt@lsu.edu.

School of Library and Information Science Students: 55 full-time (40 women), 109 part-time (99 women); includes 27 minority (23 African Americans, 2 Hispanic Americans, 2 Native Americans), 10 international. Average age 36. 64 applicants, 64% accepted, 25 enrolled. *Faculty:* 9 full-time (5 women). Expenses: Contact institution. *Financial support:* In 2001–02, 16 students received support, including 11 research assistantships with partial tuition reimbursements available (averaging $8,588 per year), 2 teaching assistantships with partial tuition reimbursements available (averaging $10,338 per year); fellowships, career-related internships or fieldwork and unspecified assistantships also available. Support available to part-time students. Financial award applicants required to submit FAFSA. In 2001, 61 master's, 3 other advanced degrees awarded. *Degree program information:* Evening/weekend programs available. Offers library and information science (MLIS, CAS). *Application deadline:* For fall admission, 1/25 (priority date). Applications are processed on a rolling basis. *Application fee:* $25. *Application Contact:* Admissions Secretary, 225-578-3158. *Dean,* Dr. Beth M. Paskoff, 225-578-3158, Fax: 225-578-4581, E-mail: lspask@lsu.edu.

School of Social Work Students: 156 full-time (141 women), 61 part-time (49 women); includes 37 minority (31 African Americans, 2 Asian Americans or Pacific Islanders, 1 Hispanic American, 3 Native Americans), 4 international. Average age 30. 117 applicants, 67% accepted, 62 enrolled. *Faculty:* 14 full-time (8 women). Expenses: Contact institution. *Financial support:* In 2001–02, 7 students received support, including 1 teaching assistantship with partial tuition reimbursement available (averaging $9,500 per year); fellowships, research assistantships with partial tuition reimbursements available, career-related internships or fieldwork and unspecified assistantships also available. Support available to part-time students. Financial award applicants required to submit FAFSA. In 2001, 80 master's, 4 doctorates awarded. *Degree program information:* Part-time programs available. Offers social work (MSW, PhD). *Application deadline:* For fall admission, 3/1. *Application fee:* $25. *Application Contact:* Denise Chiasson Breaux, Director of Student Services, 225-578-1234, E-mail: dchiass@lsu.edu. *Interim Director,* Dr. Steven Rose, 225-578-1351, Fax: 225-578-1357, E-mail: swrose@lsu.edu.

School of the Coast and Environment Students: 60 full-time (26 women), 35 part-time (10 women); includes 3 minority (1 African American, 1 Asian American or Pacific Islander, 1 Native American), 21 international. Average age 30. 52 applicants, 56% accepted, 21 enrolled. *Faculty:* 40 full-time (3 women). Expenses: Contact institution. *Financial support:* In 2001–02, 3 fellowships (averaging $16,666 per year), 39 research assistantships with partial tuition reimbursements (averaging $13,668 per year), 1 teaching assistantship with partial tuition reimbursement (averaging $9,500 per year) were awarded. Career-related internships or fieldwork, Federal Work-Study, institutionally sponsored loans, and unspecified assistantships also available. Financial award applicants required to submit FAFSA. In 2001, 17 master's, 7 doctorates awarded. *Degree program information:* Part-time programs available. Offers environmental planning and management (MS); environmental toxicology (MS); oceanography and coastal sciences (MS, PhD); the coast and environment (MS, PhD). *Application deadline:* For fall admission, 1/25 (priority date). Applications are processed on a rolling basis. *Application fee:* $25. *Dean,* Dr. Russell L. Chapman, 225-578-6316, Fax: 225-578-5328, E-mail: chapman@lsu.edu.

Paul M. Hebert Law Center Students: 649 full-time (302 women); includes 84 minority (64 African Americans, 6 Asian Americans or Pacific Islanders, 11 Hispanic Americans, 3 Native Americans), 8 international. Average age 26. 998 applicants, 55% accepted, 259 enrolled. *Faculty:* 27 full-time (4 women), 18 part-time/adjunct (2 women). Expenses: Contact institution. *Financial support:* In 2001–02, 4 fellowships with tuition reimbursements were awarded; scholarships/grants and tuition waivers (full and partial) also available. In 2001, 224 first professional degrees, 4 master's awarded. Offers law (JD, LL M, MCL). *Application deadline:* For fall admission, 2/1 (priority date). Applications are processed on a rolling basis. *Application fee:* $25. Electronic applications accepted. *Application Contact:* Michele Forbes, Director of Admissions and Student Affairs, 225-578-8646, Fax: 225-578-8647, E-mail: mforbe1@lsu.edu. *Chancellor,* John J. Costonis, 225-578-8491, Fax: 225-578-8202, E-mail: jcoston@lsu.edu.

School of Veterinary Medicine Students: 346 full-time (229 women), 24 part-time (14 women); includes 21 minority (5 African Americans, 5 Asian Americans or Pacific Islanders, 10 Hispanic Americans, 1 Native American), 14 international. Average age 27. 115 applicants, 89% accepted, 95 enrolled. *Faculty:* 64 full-time (12 women). Expenses: Contact institution. *Financial support:* In 2001–02, 20 students received support, including 1 fellowship (averaging $18,000 per year), 20 research assistantships with partial tuition reimbursements available (averaging $17,960 per year), 10 teaching assistantships with partial tuition reimbursements available (averaging $24,986 per year); career-related internships or fieldwork, Federal Work-Study, institutionally sponsored loans, and unspecified assistantships also available. Financial award applicants required to submit FAFSA. In 2001, 75 first professional degrees, 5 master's, 7 doctorates awarded. Offers comparative biomedical sciences (MS, PhD); epidemiology and community health (MS, PhD); pathobiological sciences (MS, PhD); veterinary clinical sciences (MS); veterinary medicine (DVM, MS, PhD); veterinary science (MS, PhD). *Application deadline:* For fall admission, 3/1 (priority date). Applications are processed on a rolling basis. *Application fee:* $25. *Application Contact:* Dr. Peter Haynes, Executive Associate Dean, 225-578-9903, Fax: 225-578-9916, E-mail: pfhaynes@vetmed.lsu.edu. *Dean,* Dr. Michael G. Groves, 225-578-9903, Fax: 225-578-9916, E-mail: mgroves@lsu.edu.

LOUISIANA STATE UNIVERSITY HEALTH SCIENCES CENTER, New Orleans, LA 70112-2223

General Information State-supported, coed, university. CGS member. *Enrollment:* 1,775 full-time matriculated graduate/professional students (856 women), 196 part-time matriculated graduate/professional students (169 women). *Enrollment by degree level:* 1,315 first professional, 321 master's, 213 doctoral, 39 other advanced degrees. *Graduate faculty:* 1,680. Tuition, state resident: full-time $3,146. Tuition, nonresident: full-time $6,270. *Graduate housing:* Rooms and/or apartments available to single and married students. Housing application deadline: 6/1. *Student services:* Campus safety program, free psychological counseling, low-cost health insurance. *Library facilities:* John P. Ische Library plus 2 others. *Online resources:* library catalog, web page. *Collection:* 389,486 titles, 3,500 serial subscriptions, 9,454 audiovisual materials.

Computer facilities: 100 computers available on campus for general student use. A campuswide network can be accessed from student residence rooms and from off campus. *Web address:* http://www.lsumc.edu/.

General Application Contact: Nancy W. Rhodes, Director, Student Affairs, 504-568-2211, Fax: 504-568-5588, E-mail: nrhode@lsuhsc.edu.

GRADUATE UNITS

School of Allied Health Professions Students: 214 full-time (189 women), 36 part-time (29 women); includes 20 minority (9 African Americans, 4 Asian Americans or Pacific Islanders, 7 Hispanic Americans) Average age 24. 220 applicants, 60% accepted, 119 enrolled. *Faculty:* 48 full-time (32 women), 10 part-time/adjunct (8 women). Expenses: Contact institution. *Financial support:* Fellowships, work assistantships available. Financial award applicants required to submit FAFSA. In 2001, 109 degrees awarded. *Degree program information:* Part-time and evening/weekend programs available. Offers allied health professions (MCD, MHS, MOT, MPT); audiology (MCD); clinical concepts (MHS); education (MHS); management administration (MHS); physical therapy (MPT); rehabilitation counseling (MHS); speech pathology (MCD). *Application fee:* $50. *Application Contact:* Joan Dockworth, Office of Student Affairs, 504-568-4254, Fax: 504-568-4949, E-mail: alhpjbs@lsuhsc.edu. *Dean,* Dr. John Snyder, 504-568-4246, Fax: 504-568-4249, E-mail: jsnyde@lsuhsc.edu.

School of Dentistry Offers dentistry (DDS).

School of Graduate Studies in New Orleans Students: 80 full-time (36 women), 29 part-time (20 women); includes 19 minority (10 African Americans, 1 Asian American or Pacific Islander, 8 Hispanic Americans), 26 international. Average age 26. 197 applicants, 24% accepted. *Faculty:* 138 full-time (27 women), 29 part-time/adjunct (8 women). Expenses: Contact institution. *Financial support:* In 2001–02, 30 students received support, including 2 fellowships with full tuition reimbursements available (averaging $15,000 per year), 28 research assistantships with full tuition reimbursements available (averaging $15,000 per year), 27 teaching assistantships with full tuition reimbursements available (averaging $15,000 per year); Federal Work-Study, scholarships/grants, and tuition waivers (full) also available. In 2001, 3 master's, 16 doctorates awarded. *Degree program information:* Part-time and evening/weekend programs available. Offers biochemistry (MS, PhD); biometry (MPH, MS); cell biology and anatomy (MS, PhD); human genetics (MS, PhD); medicine (MPH, MS, PhD); microbiology and immunology (MS, PhD); neuroscience (PhD); pathology (MS, PhD); pharmacology and experimental therapeutics (MS, PhD); physiology (MS, PhD); public health and preventive medicine (MPH). *Application deadline:* Applications are processed on a rolling basis. *Application fee:* $30. *Application Contact:* Nancy W. Rhodes, Director, Student Affairs, 504-568-2211, Fax: 504-568-5588, E-mail: nrhode@lsuhsc.edu. *Head,* Dr. Joseph M. Moerschbaecher, 504-568-4740, Fax: 504-568-2361.

School of Graduate Studies in Shreveport Offers biochemistry and molecular biology (MS, PhD); cellular biology and anatomy (MS, PhD); medicine (MS, PhD); microbiology/immunology (MS, PhD); pharmacology (MS, PhD); physiology (MS, PhD).

School of Medicine in New Orleans Offers medicine (MD, MPH). Open only to residents of Louisiana. Electronic applications accepted.

School of Medicine in Shreveport Offers medicine (MD).

School of Nursing *Degree program information:* Part-time programs available. Offers adult health and illness (MN); adult health and nursing (DNS); neonatal nurse practitioner (MN); nursing (MN); nursing service administration (MN, DNS); parent-child health nursing (MN); primary care nurse practitioner (MN); psychiatric/community mental health nursing (MN, DNS); public health/community health nursing (MN, DNS).

LOUISIANA STATE UNIVERSITY IN SHREVEPORT, Shreveport, LA 71115-2399

General Information State-supported, coed, comprehensive institution. *Enrollment:* 126 full-time matriculated graduate/professional students (85 women), 568 part-time matriculated graduate/professional students (375 women). *Enrollment by degree level:* 678 master's, 16 other advanced degrees. *Graduate faculty:* 78 full-time (28 women), 25 part-time/adjunct (11 women). *Tuition, area resident:* Full-time $1,890; part-time $105 per credit. Tuition, nonresident: full-time $6,000; part-time $175 per credit. *Required fees:* $220; $55 per credit. *Graduate housing:* Rooms and/or apartments available on a first-come, first-served basis to single students and available to married students. *Student services:* Campus employment opportunities, career counseling, disabled student services, exercise/wellness program, free psychological counseling, teacher training. *Library facilities:* Noel Memorial Library. *Online resources:* library catalog, web page, access to other libraries' catalogs. *Collection:* 279,821 titles, 1,190 serial subscriptions, 1,914 audiovisual materials. *Research affiliation:* Cotton, Inc. (plant physiology), Biomedical Research Institute, Louisiana Manufacturing Science Center (robotics), Department of Agriculture (crop science), Micromanufacturing Institute (manufacturing technology).

Computer facilities: A campuswide network can be accessed from off campus. Internet access is available. *Web address:* http://www.lsus.edu/.

General Application Contact: Julie A. Wilkins, Registrar and Director of Admissions, 318-797-5061, Fax: 318-797-5286, E-mail: admissions@pilot.lsus.edu.

GRADUATE UNITS

College of Business Administration *Degree program information:* Part-time and evening/weekend programs available. Offers business administration (MBA).

College of Education Students: 38 full-time (31 women), 314 part-time (235 women); includes 90 minority (86 African Americans, 2 Asian Americans or Pacific Islanders, 2 Hispanic Americans), 2 international. Average age 34. Expenses: Contact institution. *Financial support:* In 2001–02, 2 research assistantships with partial tuition reimbursements were awarded; teaching assistantships, career-related internships or fieldwork and Federal Work-Study also available. Support available to part-time students. Financial award applicants required to submit FAFSA. In 2001, 38 degrees awarded. *Degree program information:* Part-time and evening/weekend programs available. Offers education (M Ed, SSP); school psychology (SSP). *Application deadline:* For fall admission, 8/5 (priority date); for spring admission, 12/15 (priority date). Applications are processed on a rolling basis. *Application fee:* $10. *Application Contact:* Dr. David B. Gustavson, Chair, 318-797-5032, Fax: 318-798-4144, E-mail: dgustav@pilot.lsus.edu. *Dean,* Dr. Charles Manges, 318-795-4279.

College of Liberal Arts *Degree program information:* Part-time and evening/weekend programs available. Postbaccalaureate distance learning degree programs offered. Offers human services administration (MS); liberal arts (MA, MS).

College of Sciences *Degree program information:* Part-time and evening/weekend programs available. Offers systems technology (MST).

See in-depth description on page 945.

LOUISIANA TECH UNIVERSITY, Ruston, LA 71272

General Information State-supported, coed, university. *Graduate housing:* Rooms and/or apartments available to single and married students. Housing application deadline: 7/15.

Louisiana Tech University (continued)

GRADUATE UNITS

Graduate School *Degree program information:* Part-time programs available.

College of Administration and Business *Degree program information:* Part-time programs available. Offers administration and business (MBA, MPA, DBA); business administration (MBA); business economics (MBA, DBA); finance (MBA, DBA); management (MBA, DBA); marketing (MBA, DBA); professional accountancy (MBA, MPA, DBA); quantitative analysis (MBA, DBA).

College of Applied and Natural Sciences *Degree program information:* Part-time programs available. Offers applied and natural sciences (MS); biological sciences (MS); dietetics (MS); human ecology (MS).

College of Education *Degree program information:* Part-time programs available. Offers counseling (MA, Ed S); counseling psychology (PhD); curriculum and instruction (MS, Ed D); education (M Ed, MA, MS, Ed D, PhD, Ed S); educational leadership (Ed D); health and physical education (MS); industrial/organizational psychology (MA); reading (Ed S); secondary education (M Ed); special education (MA).

College of Engineering and Science *Degree program information:* Part-time programs available. Offers applied computational analysis and modeling (PhD); biomedical engineering (MS, PhD); chemical engineering (MS, D Eng); chemistry (MS); civil engineering (MS, D Eng); computer science (MS); electrical engineering (MS, D Eng); engineering (D Eng); engineering and science (MS, D Eng, PhD); industrial engineering (MS, D Eng); manufacturing systems engineering (MS); mathematics and statistics (MS); mechanical engineering (MS, D Eng); operations research (MS); physics (MS).

College of Liberal Arts *Degree program information:* Part-time programs available. Offers art and graphic design (MFA); English (MA); history (MA); interior design (MFA); liberal arts (MA, MFA); photography (MFA); speech (MA); speech pathology and audiology (MA); studio art (MFA).

LOUISVILLE PRESBYTERIAN THEOLOGICAL SEMINARY, Louisville, KY 40205-1798

General Information Independent-religious, coed, graduate-only institution. *Enrollment by degree level:* 114 first professional, 33 master's, 72 doctoral. *Graduate faculty:* 21 full-time (9 women), 30 part-time/adjunct (11 women). *Tuition:* Full-time $7,200; part-time $240 per credit. *Required fees:* $455; $250 per term. One-time fee: $65. *Graduate housing:* Rooms and/or apartments available to single students and available on a first-come, first-served basis to married students. Typical cost: $2,250 per year ($3,405 including board) for single students; $3,240 per year ($4,395 including board) for married students. Room and board charges vary according to board plan and housing facility selected. Housing application deadline: 4/15. *Student services:* Campus employment opportunities, career counseling, disabled student services, free psychological counseling, international student services, low-cost health insurance, writing training. *Library facilities:* Ernest White Library. *Online resources:* library catalog, web page, access to other libraries' catalogs. *Collection:* 143,385 titles, 561 serial subscriptions, 5,878 audiovisual materials. *Research affiliation:* Louisville Institute (American religion).

Computer facilities: 13 computers available on campus for general student use. A campuswide network can be accessed. Internet access is available. *Web address:* http://www.lpts.edu/.

General Application Contact: Rev. Marilyn S. Gamm, Director of Admissions, 502-895-3411, Fax: 502-895-1096, E-mail: mgamm@lpts.edu.

GRADUATE UNITS

Graduate and Professional Programs Students: 120 full-time (61 women), 115 part-time (46 women); includes 30 minority (21 African Americans, 6 Asian Americans or Pacific Islanders, 2 Hispanic Americans, 1 Native American), 10 international. Average age 38. 140 applicants, 63% accepted, 61 enrolled. *Faculty:* 21 full-time (9 women), 30 part-time/adjunct (11 women). Expenses: Contact institution. *Financial support:* Career-related internships or fieldwork, Federal Work-Study, institutionally sponsored loans, and scholarships/grants available. Financial award application deadline: 4/15; financial award applicants required to submit CSS PROFILE or FAFSA. In 2001, 27 first professional degrees, 12 master's, 7 doctorates awarded. *Degree program information:* Part-time programs available. Offers Bible (MAR); divinity (M Div); ministry (D Min); religious thought (MAR); theology (Th M). *Application deadline:* For fall admission, 6/1 (priority date); for spring admission, 11/15 (priority date). Applications are processed on a rolling basis. *Application fee:* $30. Electronic applications accepted. *Application Contact:* Rev. Marilyn S. Gamm, Director of Admissions, 502-895-3411, Fax: 502-895-1096, E-mail: mgamm@lpts.edu. *Dean,* Dr. Dianne Reistroffer, 502-895-3411 Ext. 294, Fax: 502-895-1096, E-mail: dreistroffer@lpts.edu.

LOYOLA COLLEGE IN MARYLAND, Baltimore, MD 21210-2699

General Information Independent-religious, coed, comprehensive institution. *Enrollment:* 610 full-time matriculated graduate/professional students (349 women), 2,057 part-time matriculated graduate/professional students (1,270 women). *Graduate faculty:* 99 full-time (41 women), 110 part-time/adjunct (40 women). *Tuition:* Part-time $244 per unit. Tuition and fees vary according to degree level, program and student level. *Graduate housing:* On-campus housing not available. *Student services:* Campus employment opportunities, campus safety program, career counseling, disabled student services, exercise/wellness program, international student services, low-cost health insurance, multicultural affairs office. *Library facilities:* Loyola/Notre Dame Library. *Online resources:* library catalog, web page, access to other libraries' catalogs. *Collection:* 380,000 titles, 2,100 serial subscriptions, 30,000 audiovisual materials.

Computer facilities: 292 computers available on campus for general student use. A campuswide network can be accessed from student residence rooms and from off campus. Internet access is available. *Web address:* http://www.loyola.edu/.

General Application Contact: Scott Greatorex, Director, Graduate Admissions, 410-617-5020 Ext. 2407, Fax: 410-617-2002, E-mail: sgreatorex@loyola.edu.

GRADUATE UNITS

Graduate Programs Students: 610 full-time (349 women), 2,057 part-time (1,270 women); includes 305 minority (210 African Americans, 58 Asian Americans or Pacific Islanders, 36 Hispanic Americans, 1 Native American), 79 international. *Faculty:* 99 full-time (41 women), 110 part-time/adjunct (40 women). Expenses: Contact institution. *Financial support:* Research assistantships, career-related internships or fieldwork, scholarships/grants, and college/university gift aid from institutional funds available. Financial award applicants required to submit FAFSA. In 2001, 875 master's, 18 doctorates, 18 other advanced degrees awarded. *Degree program information:* Part-time and evening/weekend programs available. *Application deadline:* For fall admission, 8/20 (priority date). Applications are processed on a rolling basis. *Application Contact:* Scott Greatorex, Director, Graduate Admissions, 410-617-5020 Ext. 2407, Fax: 410-617-2002, E-mail: sgreatorex@loyola.edu. *President,* Rev. Harold Ridley, SJ, 410-617-2201.

College of Arts and Sciences Expenses: Contact institution. *Financial support:* Research assistantships, career-related internships or fieldwork available. Financial award applicants required to submit FAFSA. In 2001, 518 master's, 18 doctorates, 18 other advanced degrees awarded. *Degree program information:* Part-time and evening/weekend programs available. Offers arts and sciences (M Ed, MA, MES, MS, PhD, Psy D, CAS); clinical psychology (MA, MS, Psy D, CAS); counseling psychology (MA, MS, CAS); curriculum and instruction (M Ed, MA, CAS); education technology (M Ed); educational management and supervision (M Ed, MA, CAS); employee assistance and substance abuse (CAS); engineering science (MES, MS); foundations of education (M Ed, MA, CAS); general psychology (MA, CAS); guidance and counseling (M Ed, MA, CAS); modern studies (MA); Montessori education (M Ed, CAS); pastoral counseling (MS, PhD, CAS); reading (M Ed, MA, CAS); special education (M Ed, MA, CAS); speech pathology and audiology (MS, CAS); spiritual and pastoral care (MA). *Application deadline:* Applications are processed on a rolling basis. *Application Contact:* Scott Greatorex, Director, Graduate Admissions, 410-617-5020 Ext. 2407, Fax: 410-617-2002, E-mail: sgreatorex@loyola.edu. *Dean,* Dr. James Buckley, 410-617-2563, E-mail: jbuckley@loyola.edu.

The Joseph A. Sellinger S.J. School of Business and Management Expenses: Contact institution. *Financial support:* Research assistantships, career-related internships or fieldwork available. Financial award applicants required to submit FAFSA. In 2001, 357 degrees awarded. *Degree program information:* Part-time and evening/weekend programs available. Offers business and management (MBA, MIB, MSF, XMBA); decision sciences (MBA); economics (MBA); executive business administration (MBA, XMBA); finance (MBA, MSF); international business (MIB); marketing/management (MBA). *Application deadline:* For fall admission, 8/20 (priority date); for spring admission, 11/20 (priority date). Applications are processed on a rolling basis. *Application fee:* $50. *Application Contact:* Scott Greatorex, Director, Graduate Admissions, 410-617-5020 Ext. 2407, Fax: 410-617-2002, E-mail: sgreatorex@loyola.edu. *Associate Dean,* John Moran, 410-617-2457, E-mail: jmoran@loyola.edu.

LOYOLA MARYMOUNT UNIVERSITY, Los Angeles, CA 90045-2659

General Information Independent-religious, coed, comprehensive institution. CGS member. *Enrollment:* 1,015 full-time matriculated graduate/professional students (556 women), 409 part-time matriculated graduate/professional students (250 women). *Graduate faculty:* 311 full-time (104 women), 355 part-time/adjunct (162 women). *Tuition:* Part-time $612 per credit hour. *Required fees:* $86 per term. Tuition and fees vary according to program. *Graduate housing:* On-campus housing not available. *Student services:* Campus employment opportunities, campus safety program, career counseling, disabled student services, free psychological counseling, international student services, low-cost health insurance, multicultural affairs office, teacher training, writing training. *Library facilities:* Charles von der Ahe Library plus 1 other. *Collection:* 487,232 titles, 9,505 serial subscriptions.

Computer facilities: 200 computers available on campus for general student use. A campuswide network can be accessed from student residence rooms and from off campus. Internet access is available. *Web address:* http://www.lmu.edu/.

General Application Contact: Chake Kouyoumjian, Director, Graduate Admissions, 310-338-2721, Fax: 310-338-6086, E-mail: ckouyoum@lmu.edu.

GRADUATE UNITS

Graduate Division Students: 1,015 full-time (556 women), 409 part-time (250 women); includes 472 minority (96 African Americans, 156 Asian Americans or Pacific Islanders, 213 Hispanic Americans, 7 Native Americans), 106 international. 1,056 applicants, 76% accepted, 530 enrolled. *Faculty:* 311 full-time (104 women), 355 part-time/adjunct (162 women). Expenses: Contact institution. *Financial support:* In 2001–02, 26 research assistantships (averaging $11,788 per year) were awarded; fellowships, career-related internships or fieldwork, Federal Work-Study, scholarships/grants, and staff assistantships, teaching associateships also available. Support available to part-time students. Financial award application deadline: 7/1; financial award applicants required to submit FAFSA. In 2001, 396 degrees awarded. *Degree program information:* Part-time and evening/weekend programs available. *Application deadline:* Applications are processed on a rolling basis. *Application fee:* $45. Electronic applications accepted. *Application Contact:* Chake Kouyoumjian, Director, Graduate Admissions, 310-338-2721, Fax: 310-338-6086, E-mail: ckouyoum@lmu.edu. *Academic Vice President and Chair of Graduate Council,* Dr. Joseph G. Jabbra, 310-338-2733, E-mail: jjabbra@lmu.edu.

College of Business Administration Students: 389 full-time (158 women), 67 part-time (25 women); includes 133 minority (21 African Americans, 70 Asian Americans or Pacific Islanders, 41 Hispanic Americans, 1 Native American), 64 international. Average age 27. 381 applicants, 71% accepted. *Faculty:* 44 full-time (8 women), 40 part-time/adjunct (6 women). Expenses: Contact institution. *Financial support:* In 2001–02, 41 research assistantships (averaging $4,105 per year) were awarded; Federal Work-Study, scholarships/grants, and rain grants also available. Support available to part-time students. Financial award application deadline: 7/1; financial award applicants required to submit FAFSA. In 2001, 176 degrees awarded. *Degree program information:* Part-time and evening/weekend programs available. Offers business administration (MBA). *Application deadline:* Applications are processed on a rolling basis. *Application fee:* $45. Electronic applications accepted. *Application Contact:* Dr. Rachelle Katz, Associate Dean and Director of MBA Program, 310-338-2848, E-mail: rkatz@lmu.edu. *Dean,* Dr. John T. Wholihan, 310-338-7504, Fax: 310-338-2899.

College of Communication and Fine Arts Students: 100 full-time (35 women), 16 part-time (5 women); includes 33 minority (11 African Americans, 8 Asian Americans or Pacific Islanders, 11 Hispanic Americans, 3 Native Americans), 13 international. 91 applicants, 80% accepted, 33 enrolled. *Faculty:* 55 full-time (22 women), 122 part-time/adjunct (61 women). Expenses: Contact institution. *Financial support:* In 2001–02, 22 research assistantships (averaging $5,496 per year), 6 teaching assistantships were awarded. Career-related internships or fieldwork and scholarships/grants also available. Support available to part-time students. Financial award application deadline: 7/1; financial award applicants required to submit FAFSA. In 2001, 17 degrees awarded. Offers communication and fine arts (MA); film production (MA); screen writing (MA); television production (MA). *Application deadline:* For fall admission, 3/15. *Application fee:* $45. Electronic applications accepted. *Application Contact:* Dr. Richard Hadley, Graduate Director, 310-338-2779, Fax: 310-338-3030, E-mail: rhadley@lmu.edu. *Dean,* Thomas P. Kelly, 310-338-7430, Fax: 310-338-3030, E-mail: tkelly@lmu.edu.

College of Liberal Arts Students: 110 full-time (75 women), 60 part-time (29 women); includes 44 minority (11 African Americans, 10 Asian Americans or Pacific Islanders, 21 Hispanic Americans, 2 Native Americans), 5 international. 110 applicants, 83% accepted, 64 enrolled. *Faculty:* 130 full-time (50 women), 108 part-time/adjunct (55 women). Expenses: Contact institution. *Financial support:* In 2001–02, 24 fellowships (averaging $12,944 per year), 19 research assistantships (averaging $2,518 per year) were awarded. Federal Work-Study and scholarships/grants also available. Support available to part-time students. Financial award application deadline: 7/1; financial award applicants required to submit FAFSA. In 2001, 46 degrees awarded. *Degree program information:* Part-time and evening/weekend programs available. Offers counseling psychology (MA); creative writing (MA); liberal arts (MA); literature (MA); marital and family therapy (MA); pastoral studies (MA); theology (MA). *Application fee:* $45. Electronic applications accepted. *Dean,* Dr. Kenyon Chan, 310-338-2716, Fax: 310-338-2704, E-mail: kchan@lmu.edu.

College of Science and Engineering Students: 46 full-time (9 women), 46 part-time (9 women); includes 37 minority (8 African Americans, 20 Asian Americans or Pacific Islanders, 9 Hispanic Americans), 15 international. 97 applicants, 59% accepted, 31 enrolled. *Faculty:* 61 full-time (13 women), 44 part-time/adjunct (11 women). Expenses: Contact institution. *Financial support:* In 2001–02, 23 students received support, including 4 research assistantships (averaging $2,717 per year); Federal Work-Study, scholarships/grants, and instructorships also available. Support available to part-time students. Financial award application deadline: 7/1; financial award applicants required to submit FAFSA. In 2001, 39 degrees awarded. *Degree program information:* Part-time and evening/weekend programs available. Offers civil engineering (MS, MSE); computer science (MS); electrical engineering (MSE); engineering and production management (MS); environmental science (MS); mechanical engineering (MSE); science and engineering (MS, MSE). *Application fee:* $45. Electronic applications accepted. *Application Contact:* Dr. Bo A. Oppenheim, Director, 310-338-2825, E-mail: boppenhe@lmu.edu. *Dean,* Dr. Gerald S. Jakubowski, 310-338-2834, Fax: 310-338-7399, E-mail: gjakubow@lmu.edu.

School of Education Students: 239 full-time (192 women), 128 part-time (102 women); includes 146 minority (31 African Americans, 35 Asian Americans or Pacific Islanders, 79 Hispanic Americans, 1 Native American), 3 international. 347 applicants, 82% accepted, 239 enrolled. *Faculty:* 19 full-time (9 women), 41 part-time/adjunct (29 women). Expenses: Contact institution. *Financial support:* In 2001–02, 211 students received support, including 21 research assistantships (averaging $3,724 per year); Federal Work-Study and scholarships/grants also available. Support available to part-time students. Financial award application deadline: 7/1; financial award applicants required to submit FAFSA. In 2001,

142 degrees awarded. *Degree program information:* Part-time and evening/weekend programs available. Offers administration (M Ed); bilingual and bicultural education (MA); biology education (MAT); Catholic school administration (MA); child/adolescent literacy (MA); communications (MAT); counseling (MA); education (M Ed, MA, MAT); elementary education (MA); English education (MAT); general education (M Ed); history education (MAT); learning and teaching (MAT); literacy and language (M Ed); mathematics education (MAT); multicultural education (MA); reading/language arts (M Ed); school psychology (MA); secondary education (MA); social studies education (MAT); special education (MA). *Application deadline:* For fall admission, 7/15; for spring admission, 11/15. *Application fee:* $45. Electronic applications accepted. *Dean*, Dr. Albert P. Koppes, 310-338-7301, Fax: 310-338-1976, E-mail: akoppes@lmu.edu.

Loyola Law School Students: 1,012 full-time (554 women), 341 part-time (156 women); includes 496 minority (62 African Americans, 275 Asian Americans or Pacific Islanders, 149 Hispanic Americans, 10 Native Americans), 5 international. 3,284 applicants, 39% accepted, 425 enrolled. *Faculty:* 66 full-time (29 women), 69 part-time/adjunct (18 women). Expenses: Contact institution. *Financial support:* In 2001–02, 1,145 students received support, including 50 research assistantships (averaging $3,500 per year); career-related internships or fieldwork, Federal Work-Study, and scholarships/grants also available. Support available to part-time students. Financial award application deadline: 3/1; financial award applicants required to submit FAFSA. In 2001, 408 degrees awarded. *Degree program information:* Part-time and evening/weekend programs available. Offers law (JD); taxation (LL M). *Application deadline:* For fall admission, 2/1 (priority date). Applications are processed on a rolling basis. *Application fee:* $50. Electronic applications accepted. *Application Contact:* Matthew Riojas, Acting Director of Admissions, 213-736-8129, Fax: 213-736-6523, E-mail: admissions@lls.edu. *Dean*, David W. Burcham, 213-736-1028, Fax: 213-487-6736, E-mail: david.burcham@lls.edu.

See in-depth description on page 947.

LOYOLA UNIVERSITY CHICAGO, Chicago, IL 60611-2196

General Information Independent-religious, coed, university. CGS member. *Enrollment:* 2,959 full-time matriculated graduate/professional students (1,766 women), 2,505 part-time matriculated graduate/professional students (1,685 women). *Enrollment by degree level:* 1,224 first professional, 2,715 master's, 1,189 doctoral, 336 other advanced degrees. *Graduate faculty:* 1,382. *Tuition:* Part-time $529 per credit hour. *Graduate housing:* Room and/or apartments available on a first-come, first-served basis to single students; on-campus housing not available to married students. *Student services:* Campus employment opportunities, campus safety program, career counseling, child daycare facilities, free psychological counseling, international student services, low-cost health insurance. *Library facilities:* Cudahy Library plus 3 others. *Online resources:* library catalog, web page. *Collection:* 983,023 titles, 110,502 serial subscriptions, 32,777 audiovisual materials. *Research affiliation:* Erikson Institute for Early Education, St. Joseph Seminary, Argonne National Laboratory.

Computer facilities: 318 computers available on campus for general student use. A campuswide network can be accessed from student residence rooms and from off campus. Internet access is available. *Web address:* http://www.luc.edu/.

General Application Contact: Marianne Gramza, Assistant Dean and Director of Graduate Admissions, 773-508-3396, Fax: 773-508-2460, E-mail: grad-phd-ma-ms@luc.edu.

GRADUATE UNITS

Graduate School Students: 1,091 full-time (643 women), 675 part-time (457 women); includes 276 minority (123 African Americans, 80 Asian Americans or Pacific Islanders, 70 Hispanic Americans, 3 Native Americans), 233 international. 2,604 applicants, 47% accepted. *Faculty:* 543. Expenses: Contact institution. *Financial support:* In 2001–02, 45 fellowships with tuition reimbursements (averaging $10,000 per year), 457 research assistantships with tuition reimbursements (averaging $10,000 per year) were awarded. Teaching assistantships, career-related internships or fieldwork, Federal Work-Study, institutionally sponsored loans, and scholarships/grants also available. Support available to part-time students. Financial award applicants required to submit FAFSA. In 2001, 12 first professional degrees, 393 master's, 110 doctorates awarded. *Degree program information:* Part-time and evening/weekend programs available. Postbaccalaureate distance learning degree programs offered. Offers American politics and policy (MA, PhD); applied social psychology (MA, PhD); applied sociology (MA); biochemistry (MS, PhD); biology (MS); cell and molecular physiology (MS, PhD); cell biology, neurobiology and anatomy (MS, PhD); chemistry (MS, PhD); classical studies (PhD); clinical psychology (PhD); computer science (MS); criminal justice (MA); developmental psychology (PhD); English (MA, PhD); Greek (MA); history (MA, PhD); immunology (MS, PhD); international studies (MA, PhD); Latin (MA); mathematical sciences (MS); microbiology (MS, PhD); molecular biology (PhD); neurochemistry (PhD); neuroscience (MS, PhD); organizational development (MSOD); perception (PhD); pharmacology and experimental therapeutics (MS, PhD); philosophy (MA, PhD); political theory and philosophy (MA, PhD); sociology (MA, PhD); Spanish (MA); theology (MA, PhD); training and development (MSTD); virology (MS, PhD). *Application deadline:* Applications are processed on a rolling basis. *Application fee:* $40. Electronic applications accepted. *Application Contact:* Marianne Gramza, Assistant Dean and Director of Graduate Admissions, 773-508-3396, Fax: 773-508-2460, E-mail: grad-phd-ma-ms@luc.edu. *Acting Dean*, Dr. William Yost, 773-508-3396.

Institute of Human Resources and Industrial Relations Students: 31 full-time (23 women), 119 part-time (87 women); includes 34 minority (19 African Americans, 10 Asian Americans or Pacific Islanders, 5 Hispanic Americans), 7 international. Average age 29. 58 applicants, 88% accepted. *Faculty:* 8 full-time, 10 part-time/adjunct. Expenses: Contact institution. *Financial support:* In 2001–02, 3 research assistantships were awarded; career-related internships or fieldwork and Federal Work-Study also available. Support available to part-time students. Financial award applicants required to submit FAFSA. In 2001, 54 degrees awarded. *Degree program information:* Part-time programs available. Offers human resources and industrial relations (MSHR, MSIR). *Application deadline:* Applications are processed on a rolling basis. *Application fee:* $40. *Application Contact:* Dr. Fran Daly, Associate Director, 312-915-6595, Fax: 312-915-6231, E-mail: fdaly@luc.edu. *Director*, Dr. Homer H. Johnson, 312-915-6595, Fax: 312-915-6231, E-mail: hjohnso@wpo.it.luc.edu.

Institute of Pastoral Studies Students: 81 full-time (54 women), 147 part-time (107 women); includes 15 minority (7 African Americans, 2 Asian Americans or Pacific Islanders, 6 Hispanic Americans), 34 international. Average age 41. 112 applicants, 86% accepted. *Faculty:* 10 full-time (4 women), 58 part-time/adjunct (28 women). Expenses: Contact institution. *Financial support:* In 2001–02, 64 students received support, including 13 research assistantships with tuition reimbursements available (averaging $9,800 per year); fellowships, career-related internships or fieldwork, Federal Work-Study, institutionally sponsored loans, and scholarships/grants also available. Support available to part-time students. Financial award application deadline: 3/1; financial award applicants required to submit FAFSA. In 2001, 12 first professional degrees, 89 master's awarded. *Degree program information:* Part-time and evening/weekend programs available. Offers divinity (M Div); pastoral counseling (MA); pastoral studies (MPS); religious education (M Rel Ed). *Application deadline:* For fall admission, 2/15. Applications are processed on a rolling basis. *Application fee:* $40. *Application Contact:* Carita M. Kempner, Admissions Secretary, 773-508-2320 Ext. 2326, Fax: 773-508-2319, E-mail: akempne@luc.edu. *Director*, Dr. Camilla Burns, 773-508-2320, Fax: 773-508-2319.

Marcella Niehoff School of Nursing Students: 45 full-time (42 women), 126 part-time (119 women); includes 21 minority (11 African Americans, 6 Asian Americans or Pacific Islanders, 4 Hispanic Americans), 1 international. Average age 34. 107 applicants, 92% accepted. *Faculty:* 30 full-time (all women), 1 part-time/adjunct (0 women). Expenses: Contact institution. *Financial support:* In 2001–02, 1 fellowship with tuition reimbursement, 7 research assistantships with tuition reimbursements, 1 teaching assistantship with tuition reimbursement were awarded. Career-related internships or fieldwork, Federal Work-Study, institutionally sponsored loans, traineeships, and unspecified assistantships also available. Support available to part-time students. Financial award applicants required to submit FAFSA. In 2001, 36 master's, 5 doctorates awarded. *Degree program information:* Part-time programs available. Postbaccalaureate distance learning degree programs offered (no on-campus study). Offers acute care clinical nurse specialist (MSN); acute care nurse practitioner (MSN); adult nurse practitioner (MSN); cardiovascular health and disease clinical nurse specialist (MSN); emergency nurse practitioner (MSN); family nurse practitioner (MSN); health systems management (MSN); nurse midwifery (MSN); nursing (PhD); oncology clinical nurse specialist (MSN); pediatric clinical nurse specialist (MSN); pediatric nurse practitioner (MSN); women's health (MSN); women's health nurse practitioner (MSN). *Application deadline:* Applications are processed on a rolling basis. *Application fee:* $40. Electronic applications accepted. *Application Contact:* Dr. Marcia C. Maurer, Associate Dean Academic Programs, 773-508-3261, Fax: 773-508-3241, E-mail: mmaurer@luc.edu.

Graduate School of Business Students: 174 full-time (32 women), 483 part-time (199 women); includes 84 minority (25 African Americans, 38 Asian Americans or Pacific Islanders, 20 Hispanic Americans, 1 Native American), 115 international. Average age 27. 379 applicants, 85% accepted. *Faculty:* 49 full-time (11 women), 11 part-time/adjunct (3 women). Expenses: Contact institution. *Financial support:* In 2001–02, 37 students received support, including fellowships with partial tuition reimbursements available (averaging $1,100 per year), 14 research assistantships with partial tuition reimbursements available (averaging $5,000 per year); career-related internships or fieldwork, Federal Work-Study, and institutionally sponsored loans also available. Support available to part-time students. Financial award application deadline: 4/15; financial award applicants required to submit FAFSA. In 2001, 291 degrees awarded. *Degree program information:* Part-time and evening/weekend programs available. Offers accountancy (MS); business administration (MBA); information systems and operations management (MS); information systems management (MS); integrated marketing communications (MS); marketing (MS). *Application deadline:* For fall admission, 7/1; for winter admission, 10/1; for spring admission, 1/1. Applications are processed on a rolling basis. *Application fee:* $50. Electronic applications accepted. *Application Contact:* Alan Young, Director of Admissions, 312-915-6120, Fax: 312-915-6127, E-mail: ayoung3@luc.edu. *Associate Dean*, Dr. Faruk Guder, 312-915-6120.

School of Education Students: 482 full-time (358 women), 716 part-time (540 women); includes 368 minority (248 African Americans, 32 Asian Americans or Pacific Islanders, 87 Hispanic Americans, 1 Native American), 26 international. Average age 36. 679 applicants, 77% accepted, 320 enrolled. *Faculty:* 37 full-time (16 women), 32 part-time/adjunct (21 women). Expenses: Contact institution. *Financial support:* Fellowships, research assistantships, teaching assistantships, career-related internships or fieldwork, Federal Work-Study, institutionally sponsored loans, tuition waivers (partial), and unspecified assistantships available. Support available to part-time students. Financial award applicants required to submit FAFSA. In 2001, 145 master's, 50 doctorates awarded. *Degree program information:* Part-time and evening/weekend programs available. Offers administration/supervision (M Ed, MA, Ed D, PhD); community counseling (M Ed, MA); comparative-international education (M Ed, MA, Ed D, PhD); counseling psychology (PhD); cultural and educational policy studies (M Ed, MA, Ed D, PhD); curriculum and instruction (M Ed, MA, Ed D); education (M Ed, MA, Ed D, PhD, Ed S); educational psychology (M Ed, MA, PhD); higher education (M Ed, Ed D, PhD); history of education (M Ed, MA, Ed D, PhD); instructional leadership (M Ed); philosophy of education (M Ed, MA, Ed D, PhD); research methods (M Ed, MA, PhD); school counseling (M Ed); school psychology (M Ed, PhD, Ed S); sociology of education (M Ed, MA, Ed D, PhD); special education (M Ed). *Application deadline:* For fall admission, 7/1; for spring admission, 11/1. Applications are processed on a rolling basis. *Application fee:* $35. Electronic applications accepted. *Application Contact:* Marie Rosin-Dittmar, Information Contact, 312-915-6722, E-mail: schleduc@luc.edu. *Dean*, Dr. Margaret L. Fong, 312-915-6992, E-mail: mfong@luc.edu.

School of Law Students: 511 full-time (309 women), 220 part-time (129 women); includes 110 minority (30 African Americans, 44 Asian Americans or Pacific Islanders, 36 Hispanic Americans), 36 international. Average age 26. 2,461 applicants, 38% accepted, 263 enrolled. *Faculty:* 32 full-time (12 women), 108 part-time/adjunct (48 women). Expenses: Contact institution. *Financial support:* In 2001–02, 630 students received support; fellowships, research assistantships, teaching assistantships, Federal Work-Study, institutionally sponsored loans, scholarships/grants, and tuition waivers (partial) available. Support available to part-time students. Financial award application deadline: 3/1; financial award applicants required to submit FAFSA. In 2001, 335 first professional degrees, 60 master's awarded. *Degree program information:* Part-time and evening/weekend programs available. Offers business law (LL M, MJ); child and family law (LL M, MJ); health law (LL M, MJ, D Law, SJD); law (JD). *Application deadline:* For fall admission, 4/1. Applications are processed on a rolling basis. *Application fee:* $50. Electronic applications accepted. *Application Contact:* Pamela A. Bloomquist, Assistant Dean, Law Admission and Financial Assistance, 312-915-7170, Fax: 312-915-7906, E-mail: law-admissions@luc.edu. *Dean*, Nina S. Appel, 312-915-7120.

School of Social Work Students: 212 full-time (185 women), 250 part-time (208 women); includes 108 minority (64 African Americans, 12 Asian Americans or Pacific Islanders, 29 Hispanic Americans, 3 Native Americans) Average age 28. 450 applicants, 73% accepted. *Faculty:* 20 full-time (13 women), 23 part-time/adjunct (18 women). Expenses: Contact institution. *Financial support:* In 2001–02, 130 students received support, including 2 fellowships (averaging $10,000 per year), 31 research assistantships with tuition reimbursements available (averaging $4,050 per year); career-related internships or fieldwork, scholarships/grants, and tuition waivers (full and partial) also available. Support available to part-time students. Financial award application deadline: 2/28; financial award applicants required to submit FAFSA. In 2001, 147 master's, 4 doctorates awarded. *Degree program information:* Part-time programs available. Offers social work (MSW, PhD). *Application deadline:* Applications are processed on a rolling basis. *Application fee:* $50. *Application Contact:* Jude Gonzales, Director of Admissions, 312-915-7005, Fax: 312-915-7645, E-mail: socialwork@luc.edu. *Dean*, Dr. Joseph A. Walsh, 312-915-7005, Fax: 312-915-7645, E-mail: jwalsh3@luc.edu.

Stritch School of Medicine Students: 517 full-time (237 women); includes 77 minority (15 African Americans, 52 Asian Americans or Pacific Islanders, 10 Hispanic Americans) 3,619 applicants, 9% accepted. *Faculty:* 618 full-time (198 women), 809 part-time/adjunct (201 women). Expenses: Contact institution. *Financial support:* In 2001–02, 461 students received support. Federal Work-Study, institutionally sponsored loans, and scholarships/grants available. Financial award application deadline: 3/1; financial award applicants required to submit FAFSA. In 2001, 125 degrees awarded. Offers medicine (MD). *Application deadline:* For fall admission, 11/15. Applications are processed on a rolling basis. *Application fee:* $60. *Application Contact:* LaDonna E. Norstrom, Assistant Dean for Admissions, 708-216-3229. *Dean*, Dr. Stephen Slogoff, 708-216-9949, Fax: 708-216-4305.

See in-depth description on page 949.

LOYOLA UNIVERSITY NEW ORLEANS, New Orleans, LA 70118-6195

General Information Independent-religious, coed, comprehensive institution. *Enrollment:* 609 full-time matriculated graduate/professional students (353 women), 1,057 part-time matriculated graduate/professional students (666 women). *Enrollment by degree level:* 780 first professional, 886 master's. *Graduate faculty:* 263 full-time (102 women), 140 part-time/adjunct (57 women). *Tuition:* Part-time $764 per hour. *Required fees:* $122 per semester. Tuition and fees vary according to degree level and program. *Graduate housing:* Room and/or apartments available on a first-come, first-served basis to single students; on-campus housing not available to married students. Housing application deadline: 8/1. *Student services:* Campus safety program, career counseling, child daycare facilities, disabled student services, free psychological counseling, international student services, low-cost health insurance. *Library facilities:* University Library plus 1 other. *Online resources:* library catalog, web page, access to other libraries' catalogs. *Collection:* 384,774 titles, 5,111 serial subscriptions, 13,829 audiovisual materials. *Research affiliation:* New Orleans Museum of Art (communications, history, visual arts).

Computer facilities: 300 computers available on campus for general student use. A campuswide network can be accessed from student residence rooms and from off campus. Internet access and online class registration are available. *Web address:* http://www.loyno.edu/.

General Application Contact: Deborah C. Stieffel, Dean of Admissions and Enrollment Management, 504-865-3240, Fax: 504-865-3383, E-mail: admit@loyno.edu.

Loyola University New Orleans (continued)

GRADUATE UNITS

College of Arts and Sciences Students: 68 full-time (46 women), 80 part-time (61 women). Average age 32. 90 applicants, 94% accepted, 82 enrolled. *Faculty:* 163 full-time (64 women), 75 part-time/adjunct (38 women). Expenses: Contact institution. *Financial support:* Research assistantships, teaching assistantships, career-related internships or fieldwork, Federal Work-Study, scholarships/grants, and tuition waivers (partial) available. Support available to part-time students. Financial award application deadline: 5/1; financial award applicants required to submit FAFSA. In 2001, 28 degrees awarded. *Degree program information:* Part-time and evening/weekend programs available. Offers arts and sciences (MA, MCJ, MS); counseling (MS); criminal justice (MCJ); elementary education (MS); mass communication (MA); reading education (MS); religious studies (MA); secondary education (MS). *Application fee:* $20. Electronic applications accepted. *Application Contact:* Office of Graduate Admissions, 800-4LOYOLA, Fax: 504-865-3383, E-mail: admit@loyno.edu. *Dean,* Dr. Frank E. Scully, 504-865-3244, Fax: 504-865-2059, E-mail: fescully@loyno.edu.

College of Music Students: 11 full-time (9 women), 5 part-time (3 women). Average age 31. 15 applicants, 80% accepted, 12 enrolled. *Faculty:* 24 full-time (8 women), 36 part-time/adjunct (11 women). Expenses: Contact institution. *Financial support:* In 2001–02, 6 research assistantships (averaging $1,800 per year) were awarded; career-related internships or fieldwork and tuition waivers (full and partial) also available. Support available to part-time students. Financial award application deadline: 5/1; financial award applicants required to submit FAFSA. In 2001, 11 degrees awarded. *Degree program information:* Part-time programs available. Offers music (MM, MME, MMT). *Application deadline:* For fall admission, 5/1 (priority date). Applications are processed on a rolling basis. *Application fee:* $20. Electronic applications accepted. *Application Contact:* Dr. Anthony A. Decuir, Associate Dean, 504-865-3037, Fax: 504-865-2852, E-mail: decuir@loyno.edu. *Dean,* Dr. Edward J. Kvet, 504-865-3037, Fax: 504-865-2852, E-mail: ekvet@loyno.edu.

Institute for Ministry Students: 3 full-time (2 women), 576 part-time (414 women). Average age 46. 179 applicants, 100% accepted, 179 enrolled. *Faculty:* 6 full-time (3 women), 17 part-time/adjunct (5 women). Expenses: Contact institution. *Financial support:* Scholarships/grants available. Support available to part-time students. Financial award application deadline: 5/1; financial award applicants required to submit FAFSA. In 2001, 119 degrees awarded. *Degree program information:* Part-time and evening/weekend programs available. Postbaccalaureate distance learning degree programs offered (no on-campus study). Offers ministry (MPS, MRE). *Application deadline:* For fall admission, 8/6 (priority date); for spring admission, 10/15 (priority date). Applications are processed on a rolling basis. *Application fee:* $20. *Application Contact:* Dr. Billie S. Baladouni, Assistant Director, 504-865-3728, Fax: 504-865-2066, E-mail: lim@loyno.edu. *Director,* Dr. Barbara J. Fleischer, 504-865-3728, Fax: 504-865-2066, E-mail: lim@loyno.edu.

Joseph A. Butt, S.J., College of Business Administration Students: 28 full-time (8 women), 56 part-time (22 women); includes 20 minority (3 African Americans, 2 Asian Americans or Pacific Islanders, 9 Hispanic Americans, 6 Native Americans) Average age 29. 13 applicants, 100% accepted, 10 enrolled. *Faculty:* 34 full-time (10 women), 8 part-time/adjunct (1 woman). Expenses: Contact institution. *Financial support:* Research assistantships, career-related internships or fieldwork and Federal Work-Study available. Support available to part-time students. Financial award application deadline: 5/1; financial award applicants required to submit FAFSA. In 2001, 37 degrees awarded. *Degree program information:* Part-time and evening/weekend programs available. Postbaccalaureate distance learning degree programs offered. Offers business administration (MBA, MQM). *Application fee:* $50. Electronic applications accepted. *Application Contact:* Jan A. Moppert, Graduate Program Coordinator, 504-864-7965, Fax: 504-864-7970, E-mail: jamopper@loyno.edu. *Dean,* Dr. J. Patrick O'Brien, 504-864-7990, Fax: 504-864-7970, E-mail: pobrien@loyno.edu.

Program in Nursing Students: 8 full-time (7 women), 51 part-time (46 women). Average age 35. 46 applicants, 100% accepted, 46 enrolled. *Faculty:* 7 full-time (all women), 1 (woman) part-time/adjunct. Expenses: Contact institution. *Financial support:* Scholarships/grants available. Support available to part-time students. Financial award application deadline: 5/1; financial award applicants required to submit FAFSA. In 2001, 15 degrees awarded. Offers family nurse practitioner (MSN). *Application deadline:* For fall admission, 3/1 (priority date). *Application fee:* $20. *Application Contact:* Connie Gay, Assistant to the Director, 504-865-3142, Fax: 504-865-3254, E-mail: nurs@loyno.edu. *Director,* Dr. Billie Ann Wilson, 504-865-3142, Fax: 504-865-3254, E-mail: bwilson@loyno.edu.

School of Law Students: 491 full-time (281 women), 289 part-time (120 women). Average age 27. 1,406 applicants, 60% accepted, 313 enrolled. *Faculty:* 29 full-time (10 women), 4 part-time/adjunct (2 women). Expenses: Contact institution. *Financial support:* In 2001–02, 18 research assistantships (averaging $1,000 per year), 36 teaching assistantships (averaging $2,000 per year) were awarded. Career-related internships or fieldwork, Federal Work-Study, scholarships/grants, and unspecified assistantships also available. Support available to part-time students. Financial award application deadline: 5/1; financial award applicants required to submit FAFSA. In 2001, 199 degrees awarded. *Degree program information:* Part-time and evening/weekend programs available. Offers law (JD). *Application deadline:* For fall admission, 5/1 (priority date). Applications are processed on a rolling basis. *Application fee:* $40. Electronic applications accepted. *Application Contact:* Michele K. Allison-Davis, Assistant Dean, Admissions, 504-861-5575, Fax: 504-861-5772, E-mail: maldavis@loyno.edu. *Interim Dean,* James M. Klebba, 504-861-5550, Fax: 504-861-5739, E-mail: klebba@loyno.edu.

LUBBOCK CHRISTIAN UNIVERSITY, Lubbock, TX 79407-2099

General Information Independent-religious, coed, comprehensive institution. *Enrollment:* 1 full-time matriculated graduate/professional student, 23 part-time matriculated graduate/professional students. *Graduate faculty:* 8 full-time (0 women), 2 part-time/adjunct (0 women). *Tuition:* Part-time $105 per hour. *Required fees:* $100 per semester. *Graduate housing:* Rooms and/or apartments available to single and married students. Housing application deadline: 8/15. *Student services:* Career counseling, exercise/wellness program, free psychological counseling. *Library facilities:* University Library. *Collection:* 108,000 titles, 556 serial subscriptions.

Computer facilities: 130 computers available on campus for general student use. A campuswide network can be accessed from student residence rooms and from off campus. Internet access and online class registration, e-mail are available.

General Application Contact: Donna G. Taylor, Administrative Assistant, 806-720-7662 Ext. 369, Fax: 806-796-8917.

GRADUATE UNITS

Graduate Biblical Studies Students: 1 full-time, 23 part-time. Average age 30. 14 applicants, 100% accepted. *Faculty:* 8 full-time (0 women), 2 part-time/adjunct (0 women). Expenses: Contact institution. *Financial support:* Career-related internships or fieldwork, Federal Work-Study, institutionally sponsored loans, and tuition waivers (partial) available. Support available to part-time students. Financial award application deadline: 5/15. In 2001, 9 degrees awarded. *Degree program information:* Part-time programs available. Offers Bible and ministry (MS); biblical interpretation (MA). *Application deadline:* For fall admission, 5/15 (priority date); for spring admission, 1/15. Applications are processed on a rolling basis. *Application fee:* $10.

LUTHERAN SCHOOL OF THEOLOGY AT CHICAGO, Chicago, IL 60615-5199

General Information Independent-religious, coed, graduate-only institution. *Graduate faculty:* 22 full-time, 15 part-time/adjunct. *Tuition:* Full-time $7,035; part-time $782 per course. *Required fees:* $24; $8 per quarter. Full-time tuition and fees vary according to degree level and student's religious affiliation. *Graduate housing:* Rooms and/or apartments available to single and married students. *Student services:* Career counseling, low-cost health insurance. *Library facilities:* Jesuit-Krauss-McCormick Library. *Collection:* 334,388 titles. *Research affiliation:* Zygon Center for Religion and Science, Chicago Center for Public Ministry. *Web address:* http://www.lstc.edu/.

General Application Contact: Rev. Brian K. Halverson, Director of Admissions and Financial Aid, 773-256-0726, Fax: 773-256-0782, E-mail: admissions@lstc.edu.

GRADUATE UNITS

Graduate and Professional Programs Students: 198 full-time, 167 part-time. *Faculty:* 22 full-time, 15 part-time/adjunct. Expenses: Contact institution. *Financial support:* Career-related internships or fieldwork available. Support available to part-time students. *Degree program information:* Part-time programs available. Offers ministry (D Min); ministry, pastoral care, and counseling (D Min PCC); theological studies (MA, PhD); theology (M Div, Th M). *Application deadline:* Applications are processed on a rolling basis. *Application fee:* $25. *Application Contact:* Rev. Brian K. Halverson, Director of Admissions and Financial Aid, 773-256-0726, Fax: 773-256-0782, E-mail: admissions@lstc.edu. *Dean,* Dr. Kathleen Billman, 773-256-0721, Fax: 773-256-0782, E-mail: admissions@lstc.edu.

LUTHERAN THEOLOGICAL SEMINARY, Saskatoon, SK S7N 0X3, Canada

General Information Independent-religious, coed, graduate-only institution. *Graduate faculty:* 6 full-time (2 women), 3 part-time/adjunct (1 woman). *Graduate tuition:* Tuition and fees charges are reported in Canadian dollars. *Tuition:* Full-time $4,000 Canadian dollars. *Required fees:* $70 Canadian dollars. *Graduate housing:* Room and/or apartments available to single students; on-campus housing not available to married students. Typical cost: $4,980 Canadian dollars (including board). Room and board charges vary according to campus/location. Housing application deadline: 4/30. *Student services:* Career counseling, free psychological counseling. *Library facilities:* Otto Olson Memorial Library. *Collection:* 45,000 titles, 210 serial subscriptions. *Web address:* http://www.usask.ca./stu/luther/.

General Application Contact: Susan Avant, Registrar, 306-966-7856, Fax: 306-966-7852, E-mail: avant@duke.usask.ca.

GRADUATE UNITS

Graduate and Professional Programs *Degree program information:* Part-time programs available. Offers history (MTS, STM); New Testament (MTS, STM); Old Testament (MTS, STM); pastoral counseling (MTS, STM); systematics (MTS, STM).

LUTHERAN THEOLOGICAL SEMINARY AT GETTYSBURG, Gettysburg, PA 17325-1795

General Information Independent-religious, coed, graduate-only institution. *Graduate faculty:* 16 full-time (6 women), 8 part-time/adjunct (1 woman). *Tuition:* Full-time $7,000; part-time $310 per credit hour. *Required fees:* $720; $235 per semester. Full-time tuition and fees vary according to program. *Graduate housing:* Rooms and/or apartments available on a first-come, first-served basis to single and married students. Housing application deadline: 4/1. *Student services:* Campus employment opportunities, child daycare facilities, free psychological counseling, international student services, low-cost health insurance, multicultural affairs office. *Library facilities:* A. R. Wentz Library. *Online resources:* library catalog. *Collection:* 170,000 titles, 600 serial subscriptions, 2,782 audiovisual materials.

Computer facilities: 10 computers available on campus for general student use. A campuswide network can be accessed from student residence rooms and from off campus. Internet access is available. *Web address:* http://www.ltsg.edu/.

General Application Contact: Nancy E. Gable, Associate Dean for Admissions and Diaconal Ministry, 717-334-6286, Fax: 717-334-3469, E-mail: ngables@ltsg.edu.

GRADUATE UNITS

Graduate and Professional Programs Average age 35. 100 applicants, 85% accepted. *Faculty:* 16 full-time (6 women), 8 part-time/adjunct (1 woman). Expenses: Contact institution. *Financial support:* In 2001–02, 102 students received support, including 7 fellowships (averaging $8,171 per year), 1 teaching assistantship (averaging $1,000 per year); career-related internships or fieldwork, institutionally sponsored loans, and scholarships/grants also available. Support available to part-time students. Financial award application deadline: 4/15; financial award applicants required to submit FAFSA. *Degree program information:* Part-time programs available. Postbaccalaureate distance learning degree programs offered (no on-campus study). Offers theology (M Div, MAMS, MAR, STM). *Application deadline:* For fall admission, 6/1 (priority date); for winter admission, 12/1 (priority date); for spring admission, 1/15 (priority date). Applications are processed on a rolling basis. *Application fee:* $35. *Application Contact:* Nancy E. Gable, Associate Dean for Church Vocations and Diaconal Ministry, 717-334-6286, Fax: 717-334-3469, E-mail: ngable@ltsg.edu. *Dean,* Dr. Norma S. Wood, 717-334-6286 Ext. 3007, Fax: 717-334-3469, E-mail: nwood@gettysburg.edu.

THE LUTHERAN THEOLOGICAL SEMINARY AT PHILADELPHIA, Philadelphia, PA 19119-1794

General Information Independent-religious, coed, graduate-only institution. *Enrollment by degree level:* 203 first professional, 52 master's, 98 doctoral, 16 other advanced degrees. *Graduate faculty:* 18 full-time (6 women), 28 part-time/adjunct (8 women). *Tuition:* Full-time $6,992; part-time $874 per unit. *Required fees:* $1,612; $25 per term. Tuition and fees vary according to degree level, program and student's religious affiliation. *Graduate housing:* Rooms and/or apartments available on a first-come, first-served basis to single and married students. Typical cost: $5,760 (including board) for single students; $5,000 (including board) for married students. Room and board charges vary according to housing facility selected. Housing application deadline: 4/15. *Student services:* Campus employment opportunities, campus safety program, exercise/wellness program, free psychological counseling, low-cost health insurance. *Library facilities:* Krauth Memorial Library. *Online resources:* library catalog, access to other libraries' catalogs. *Collection:* 187,950 titles, 472 serial subscriptions, 5,250 audiovisual materials.

Computer facilities: 3 computers available on campus for general student use. A campuswide network can be accessed from student residence rooms and from off campus. Internet access is available. *Web address:* http://www.ltsp.edu/.

General Application Contact: Rev. Richard H. Summy, Director of Admissions, 800-286-4616 Ext. 6304, Fax: 215-248-4577, E-mail: rsummy@ltsp.edu.

GRADUATE UNITS

Graduate School Students: 119 full-time (61 women), 250 part-time (97 women); includes 105 minority (87 African Americans, 7 Asian Americans or Pacific Islanders, 10 Hispanic Americans, 1 Native American), 10 international. Average age 35. 124 applicants, 88% accepted, 95 enrolled. *Faculty:* 18 full-time (6 women), 28 part-time/adjunct (8 women). Expenses: Contact institution. *Financial support:* In 2001–02, 85 students received support, including 1 fellowship with tuition reimbursement available (averaging $4,500 per year); career-related internships or fieldwork also available. Financial award application deadline: 7/1; financial award applicants required to submit FAFSA. In 2001, 23 first professional degrees, 10 master's, 12 doctorates awarded. *Degree program information:* Part-time and evening/weekend programs available. Offers divinity (M Div); ministry (D Min); religion (MAR); social ministry (Certificate); theology (STM). *Application deadline:* For fall admission, 6/1 (priority date). Applications are processed on a rolling basis. *Application fee:* $35. *Application Contact:* Rev. Richard H. Summy, Director of Admissions, 800-286-4616 Ext. 6304, Fax: 215-248-4577, E-mail: rsummy@ltsp.edu. *Dean,* Dr. J. Paul Rajashekar, 215-248-6379, Fax: 215-248-4577, E-mail: rajashekar@ltsp.edu.

LUTHERAN THEOLOGICAL SOUTHERN SEMINARY, Columbia, SC 29203-5863

General Information Independent-religious, coed, graduate-only institution. *Enrollment by degree level:* 118 first professional, 33 master's, 1 doctoral. *Graduate faculty:* 15 full-time (4 women), 5 part-time/adjunct (0 women). *Tuition:* Full-time $7,267; part-time $260 per credit hour. *Required fees:* $125; $600 per course. One-time fee: $35 full-time. Full-time tuition and fees vary according to student's religious affiliation. *Graduate housing:* Rooms and/or apartments available on a first-come, first-served basis to single students and available to married students. Typical cost: $1,940 per year for single students. Room charges vary according to housing facility selected. Housing application deadline: 5/1. *Student services:* Campus employment opportunities, campus safety program, exercise/wellness program, low-cost health insurance. *Library facilities:* Lineberger Library. *Online resources:* library catalog, web page. *Collection:* 119,000 titles, 488 serial subscriptions, 1,039 audiovisual materials.

Computer facilities: 12 computers available on campus for general student use. A campuswide network can be accessed from student residence rooms and from off campus. Internet access and online class registration are available. *Web address:* http://www.ltss.edu/.

General Application Contact: Rev. Thomas M. Henderson, Director of Admissions, 803-786-5150, Fax: 803-786-6499, E-mail: thenderson@ltss.edu.

GRADUATE UNITS

Graduate and Professional Programs Students: 128 full-time (52 women), 23 part-time (13 women); includes 20 minority (17 African Americans, 2 Asian Americans or Pacific Islanders, 1 Hispanic American), 1 international. Average age 31. 63 applicants, 98% accepted, 50 enrolled. *Faculty:* 15 full-time (4 women), 5 part-time/adjunct (0 women). Expenses: Contact institution. *Financial support:* In 2001–02, 80 students received support, including 18 teaching assistantships; career-related internships or fieldwork, institutionally sponsored loans, scholarships/grants, tuition waivers (partial), and on-campus employment also available. Support available to part-time students. Financial award application deadline: 3/15; financial award applicants required to submit FAFSA. In 2001, 18 first professional degrees, 12 master's awarded. *Degree program information:* Part-time programs available. Postbaccalaureate distance learning degree programs offered. Offers theology (M Div, MAR, STM, D Min). *Application deadline:* For fall admission, 5/15 (priority date); for spring admission, 12/1 (priority date). Applications are processed on a rolling basis. *Application fee:* $35. *Application Contact:* Rev. Thomas M. Henderson, Director of Admissions, 803-786-5150, Fax: 803-786-6499, E-mail: thenderson@ltss.edu. *President,* Dr. H. Frederick Reisz, 803-786-5150, Fax: 803-786-6499.

LUTHER RICE BIBLE COLLEGE AND SEMINARY, Lithonia, GA 30038-2454

General Information Independent-religious, coed, comprehensive institution. *Enrollment:* 137 full-time matriculated graduate/professional students (27 women), 837 part-time matriculated graduate/professional students (74 women). *Graduate faculty:* 7 full-time (0 women), 9 part-time/adjunct (2 women). *Tuition:* Full-time $2,088; part-time $116 per semester hour. Full-time tuition and fees vary according to degree level. *Graduate housing:* On-campus housing not available. *Student services:* Campus employment opportunities, career counseling, low-cost health insurance. *Library facilities:* Bertha Smith Library. *Collection:* 45,200 titles, 70 serial subscriptions.

Computer facilities: 8 computers available on campus for general student use. *Web address:* http://www.lrs.edu/.

General Application Contact: Dr. Bruce Kreutzer, Director of Admissions and Records, 770-484-1204, Fax: 770-484-1155, E-mail: bkreutzer@lrs.edu.

GRADUATE UNITS

Graduate Programs Students: 137 full-time (27 women), 837 part-time (74 women); includes 380 minority (166 African Americans, 175 Asian Americans or Pacific Islanders, 39 Hispanic Americans), 91 international. 480 applicants, 96% accepted. *Faculty:* 7 full-time (0 women), 9 part-time/adjunct (2 women). Expenses: Contact institution. In 2001, 62 master's, 17 doctorates awarded. *Degree program information:* Part-time programs available. Postbaccalaureate distance learning degree programs offered (no on-campus study). Offers Bible/theology (M Div); biblical studies/theology (MA); Christian counseling (MA); Christian education (M Div, MRE); church ministry (D Min); counseling (M Div); ministry (M Div, MA); missions/evangelism (M Div). *Application deadline:* Applications are processed on a rolling basis. *Application fee:* $50. *Application Contact:* Dr. Bruce Kreutzer, Director of Admissions and Records, 770-484-1204, Fax: 770-484-1155, E-mail: bkreutzer@lrs.edu. *Dean,* Dr. James Kinnebrew, 770-484-1204.

LUTHER SEMINARY, St. Paul, MN 55108-1445

General Information Independent-religious, coed, graduate-only institution. *Graduate housing:* Rooms and/or apartments available on a first-come, first-served basis to single and married students.

GRADUATE UNITS

Graduate and Professional Programs *Degree program information:* Part-time programs available. Offers theology (M Div, M Th, MA, MSM, D Min, PhD).

LYNCHBURG COLLEGE, Lynchburg, VA 24501-3199

General Information Independent-religious, coed, comprehensive institution. *Enrollment:* 74 full-time matriculated graduate/professional students (49 women), 130 part-time matriculated graduate/professional students (91 women). *Enrollment by degree level:* 204 master's. *Graduate faculty:* 34 full-time (11 women), 7 part-time/adjunct (2 women). *Tuition:* Full-time $5,220; part-time $240 per credit. *Graduate housing:* Room and/or apartments available on a first-come, first-served basis to single students; on-campus housing not available to married students. Typical cost: $4,600 (including board). Room and board charges vary according to board plan. Housing application deadline: 8/1. *Student services:* Campus employment opportunities, career counseling, disabled student services, exercise/wellness program, free psychological counseling, grant writing training, international student services, multicultural affairs office, teacher training, writing training. *Library facilities:* Knight-Capron Library. *Online resources:* library catalog, web page, access to other libraries' catalogs. *Collection:* 287,601 titles, 636 serial subscriptions, 9,360 audiovisual materials.

Computer facilities: 217 computers available on campus for general student use. A campuswide network can be accessed from student residence rooms. Internet access is available. *Web address:* http://www.lynchburg.edu/.

General Application Contact: Dr. Edward Polloway, Vice President for Graduate and Community Advancement, 434-544-8655, E-mail: polloway@lynchburg.edu.

GRADUATE UNITS

Graduate Studies *Degree program information:* Part-time and evening/weekend programs available.

School of Business and Economics *Degree program information:* Evening/weekend programs available. Offers administration (M Ad); business (MBA).

School of Education and Human Development Offers agency counseling (M Ed); counseling (M Ed); curriculum and instruction (M Ed); curriculum and instruction: early childhood education (M Ed); curriculum and instruction: middle education (M Ed); early childhood education (M Ed); early childhood special education (M Ed); English education (M Ed); mental retardation (M Ed); middle school education (M Ed); reading (M Ed); school administration (M Ed); school counseling (M Ed); secondary education (M Ed); severely/profoundly handicapped education (M Ed); special education (M Ed); supervision (M Ed); teaching children with learning disabilities (M Ed); teaching the emotionally disturbed (M Ed).

LYNDON STATE COLLEGE, Lyndonville, VT 05851-0919

General Information State-supported, coed, comprehensive institution. *Enrollment:* 1 (woman) full-time matriculated graduate/professional student, 22 part-time matriculated graduate/professional students (18 women). *Enrollment by degree level:* 23 master's. *Graduate faculty:* 4 full-time (2 women), 1 (woman) part-time/adjunct. Tuition, state resident: full-time $4,404; part-time $184 per credit. Tuition, nonresident: full-time $10,320; part-time $430 per credit. *Required fees:* $700; $30 per credit. *Graduate housing:* On-campus housing not available. *Student services:* Campus employment opportunities, campus safety program, career counseling, child daycare facilities, disabled student services, free psychological counseling, international student services, low-cost health insurance, teacher training, writing training. *Library facilities:* Samuel Read Hall Library. *Online resources:* library catalog, web page, access to other libraries' catalogs. *Collection:* 101,872 titles, 16,468 serial subscriptions, 4,883 audiovisual materials.

Computer facilities: 125 computers available on campus for general student use. A campuswide network can be accessed from student residence rooms and from off campus. Internet access is available. *Web address:* http://www.lsc.vsc.edu/.

General Application Contact: 802-626-6413, E-mail: admissions@lsc.vsc.edu.

GRADUATE UNITS

Graduate Programs in Education Students: 1 (woman) full-time, 22 part-time (18 women). Average age 35. 3 applicants, 100% accepted. *Faculty:* 4 full-time (2 women), 1 (woman) part-time/adjunct. Expenses: Contact institution. *Financial support:* Career-related internships or fieldwork available. Financial award applicants required to submit FAFSA. In 2001, 2 degrees awarded. *Degree program information:* Part-time and evening/weekend programs available. Offers curriculum and instruction (M Ed); education (M Ed); natural sciences (MST); reading specialist (M Ed); science education (MST); special education (M Ed); teaching and counseling (M Ed). *Application deadline:* For fall admission, 2/28 (priority date); for spring admission, 10/31. *Application fee:* $30. *Application Contact:* 802-626-6413, E-mail: admissions@lsc.vsc.edu. *Academic Dean,* Dr. Michael Fishbein, 802-626-6406, Fax: 802-626-4804, E-mail: fishbeinm@mail.lsc.vsc.edu.

LYNN UNIVERSITY, Boca Raton, FL 33431-5598

General Information Independent, coed, comprehensive institution. *Enrollment:* 23 full-time matriculated graduate/professional students (18 women), 162 part-time matriculated graduate/professional students (86 women). *Graduate faculty:* 44 full-time (14 women), 19 part-time/adjunct (7 women). *Tuition:* Full-time $10,560; part-time $440 per credit. *Required fees:* $120; $30 per term. One-time fee: $50. *Graduate housing:* Room and/or apartments available on a first-come, first-served basis to single students; on-campus housing not available to married students. Typical cost: $4,590 per year ($7,650 including board). *Student services:* Campus employment opportunities, campus safety program, career counseling, exercise/wellness program, free psychological counseling, international student services, low-cost health insurance, multicultural affairs office. *Library facilities:* Eugene M. and Christine E. Lynn Library. *Online resources:* library catalog, access to other libraries' catalogs. *Collection:* 80,341 titles, 840 serial subscriptions.

Computer facilities: 150 computers available on campus for general student use. A campuswide network can be accessed from student residence rooms and from off campus. *Web address:* http://www.lynn.edu/.

General Application Contact: Sally Sites, Director of Graduate Admission, 561-237-7223, Fax: 561-237-7100, E-mail: ssites@lynn.edu.

GRADUATE UNITS

School of Graduate Studies *Degree program information:* Part-time programs available. Offers aging studies (Certificate); biomechanical trauma (MS); criminal justice administration (MS); health care administration (MS, Certificate); music performance (Diploma). Electronic applications accepted.

College of Education *Degree program information:* Part-time and evening/weekend programs available. Offers educational leadership with a global perspective (PhD); ESOL and varying exceptionalities (M Ed); varying exceptionalities (M Ed). Electronic applications accepted.

School of Business *Degree program information:* Part-time and evening/weekend programs available. Offers hospitality administration (MBA); international business (MBA); sports and athletics administration (MBA). Electronic applications accepted.

See in-depth description on page 951.

MACHZIKEI HADATH RABBINICAL COLLEGE, Brooklyn, NY 11204-1805

General Information Independent-religious, men only, comprehensive institution. *Graduate housing:* Room and/or apartments available to single students; on-campus housing not available to married students.

MADONNA UNIVERSITY, Livonia, MI 48150-1173

General Information Independent-religious, coed, comprehensive institution. *Enrollment:* 840 matriculated graduate/professional students. *Graduate faculty:* 56 full-time, 27 part-time/adjunct. *Tuition:* Part-time $325 per credit hour. *Graduate housing:* Room and/or apartments available on a first-come, first-served basis to single students; on-campus housing not available to married students. *Student services:* Campus safety program, career counseling, child daycare facilities, disabled student services, international student services, low-cost health insurance, multicultural affairs office, writing training. *Library facilities:* Madonna University Library. *Online resources:* library catalog, web page, access to other libraries' catalogs. *Collection:* 199,144 titles, 1,679 serial subscriptions.

Computer facilities: 175 computers available on campus for general student use. A campuswide network can be accessed from student residence rooms and from off campus. Internet access is available. *Web address:* http://www.munet.edu/.

General Application Contact: Sandra Kellums, Coordinator of Graduate Admissions, 734-432-5667, Fax: 734-432-5862, E-mail: kellums@smtp.munet.edu.

GRADUATE UNITS

Department of English 6 applicants, 83% accepted. *Faculty:* 1 full-time (0 women), 2 part-time/adjunct (0 women). Expenses: Contact institution. *Financial support:* Institutionally sponsored loans available. Support available to part-time students. Financial award application deadline: 3/1; financial award applicants required to submit FAFSA. *Degree program information:* Part-time and evening/weekend programs available. Offers teaching English to speakers of other languages (MTESOL). *Application deadline:* For fall admission, 8/1 (priority date); for winter admission, 12/1 (priority date); for spring admission, 4/1 (priority date). Applications are processed on a rolling basis. *Application fee:* $0 ($25 for international students). Electronic applications accepted. *Application Contact:* Sandra Kellums, Coordinator of Graduate Admissions, 734-432-5667, Fax: 734-432-5862, E-mail: kellums@smtp.munet.edu. *Director,* Dr. Andrew Domzalski, 734-432-5420, E-mail: domzalsk@smtp.munet.edu.

Department of Psychology 28 applicants, 89% accepted. *Faculty:* 3 full-time (1 woman), 3 part-time/adjunct (1 woman). Expenses: Contact institution. *Financial support:* Institutionally sponsored loans available. Support available to part-time students. *Degree program information:* Part-time and evening/weekend programs available. Offers clinical psychology (MS). *Application deadline:* For fall admission, 3/1. *Application fee:* $0 ($25 for international students). Electronic applications accepted. *Application Contact:* Sandra Kellums, Coordinator of Graduate Admissions, 734-432-5667, Fax: 734-432-5862, E-mail: kellums@smtp.munet.edu. *Chairperson,* Dr. Robert Cohen, 734-432-5736.

Program in Health Services Students: 4 full-time (3 women), 37 part-time (29 women). 6 applicants, 100% accepted. *Faculty:* 4 full-time (2 women), 2 part-time/adjunct (both women). Expenses: Contact institution. *Financial support:* Institutionally sponsored loans and scholarships/grants available. Support available to part-time students. In 2001, 5 degrees awarded. *Degree program information:* Part-time programs available. Offers health services (MS). *Application deadline:* For fall admission, 8/1 (priority date); for winter admission, 12/1 (priority date); for spring admission, 4/1 (priority date). Applications are processed on a rolling basis. *Application fee:* $0 ($25 for international students). Electronic applications accepted. *Application Contact:* Sandra Kellums, Coordinator of Graduate Admissions, 734-432-5667, Fax: 734-432-5862, E-mail: kellums@smtp.munet.edu. *Dean,* Dr. Ted Biermann, 734-432-5515.

Program in Hospice Students: 2 full-time (both women), 26 part-time (20 women). 9 applicants, 78% accepted. *Faculty:* 2 full-time (1 woman), 2 part-time/adjunct (1 woman). Expenses: Contact institution. *Financial support:* Institutionally sponsored loans and scholarships/grants available. Support available to part-time students. In 2001, 2 degrees awarded. *Degree program information:* Part-time and evening/weekend programs available. Offers hospice (MSH). *Application deadline:* For fall admission, 8/1 (priority date); for winter admission, 12/1 (priority date); for spring admission, 4/1 (priority date). Applications are processed on a rolling basis.

Madonna University (continued)

Application fee: $0 ($25 for international students). Electronic applications accepted. *Application Contact:* Sandra Kellums, Coordinator of Graduate Admissions, 734-432-5667, Fax: 734-432-5862, E-mail: kellums@smtp.munet.edu. *Director*, Dr. Kelly Rhoades, 734-432-5471, Fax: 734-432-5463, E-mail: rhoades@smtp.munet.edu.

Program in Nursing Students: 2 full-time (1 woman), 98 part-time (93 women). Average age 36. 13 applicants, 77% accepted. *Faculty:* 13 full-time (all women), 3 part-time/adjunct (1 woman). Expenses: Contact institution. *Financial support:* Career-related internships or fieldwork, Federal Work-Study, institutionally sponsored loans, and scholarships/grants available. Support available to part-time students. In 2001, 23 degrees awarded. *Degree program information:* Part-time programs available. Offers adult health: chronic health conditions (MSN); adult nurse practitioner (MSN); nursing administration (MSN). *Application deadline:* For fall admission, 8/1 (priority date); for winter admission, 12/1 (priority date); for spring admission, 4/1 (priority date). Applications are processed on a rolling basis. *Application fee:* $0 ($25 for international students). Electronic applications accepted. *Application Contact:* Sandra Kellums, Coordinator of Graduate Admissions, 734-432-5667, Fax: 734-432-5862, E-mail: kellums@smtp.munet.edu. *Chairperson*, Dr. Nancy O'Connor, 734-432-5461, Fax: 734-432-5463, E-mail: brauste@smtp.munet.edu.

Programs in Education Students: 2 full-time (both women), 136 part-time (122 women). 52 applicants, 96% accepted. *Faculty:* 7 full-time (4 women), 3 part-time/adjunct (2 women). Expenses: Contact institution. *Financial support:* Career-related internships or fieldwork, Federal Work-Study, institutionally sponsored loans, and scholarships/grants available. Support available to part-time students. In 2001, 12 degrees awarded. *Degree program information:* Part-time and evening/weekend programs available. Offers Catholic school leadership (MSA); educational leadership (MSA); learning disabilities (MAT); literacy education (MAT); teaching and learning (MAT). *Application deadline:* For fall admission, 8/1 (priority date); for winter admission, 12/1 (priority date); for spring admission, 4/1 (priority date). Applications are processed on a rolling basis. *Application fee:* $0 ($25 for international students). Electronic applications accepted. *Application Contact:* Sandra Kellums, Coordinator of Graduate Admissions, 734-432-5667, Fax: 734-432-5862, E-mail: kellums@smtp.munet.edu. *Dean*, Dr. Robert Kimball, 734-432-5652, E-mail: kimball@smtp.munet.edu.

School of Business Students: 115 full-time (15 women), 369 part-time (293 women). 92 applicants, 98% accepted. *Faculty:* 8 full-time (2 women), 13 part-time/adjunct (2 women). Expenses: Contact institution. *Financial support:* Career-related internships or fieldwork, institutionally sponsored loans, and scholarships/grants available. Support available to part-time students. In 2001, 113 degrees awarded. *Degree program information:* Part-time and evening/weekend programs available. Postbaccalaureate distance learning degree programs offered (minimal on-campus study). Offers business administration (MBA); international business (MSBA); leadership studies (MSBA); leadership studies in criminal justice (MSBA); quality and operations management (MSBA). *Application deadline:* For fall admission, 8/1 (priority date); for winter admission, 12/1 (priority date); for spring admission, 4/1 (priority date). Applications are processed on a rolling basis. *Application fee:* $0 ($25 for international students). Electronic applications accepted. *Application Contact:* Sandra Kellums, Coordinator of Graduate Admissions, 734-432-5667, Fax: 734-432-5862, E-mail: kellums@smtp.munet.edu. *Dean of Business School*, Dr. Stuart Arends, 734-432-5366, Fax: 734-432-5364, E-mail: arends@smtp.munet.edu.

MAHARISHI UNIVERSITY OF MANAGEMENT, Fairfield, IA 52557

General Information Independent, coed, university. *Graduate housing:* Rooms and/or apartments available to single and married students. Housing application deadline: 8/1. *Research affiliation:* Center for Nuclear Research, Switzerland (unified field theories), Los Alamos National Laboratory (unified field theories), American Cyanamid Company.

GRADUATE UNITS

Graduate Studies *Degree program information:* Evening/weekend programs available. Offers art (MA); business administration (MBA, PhD); ceramics/sculpture (MFA); computer science (MS); drawing/painting (MFA); elementary education (MA); English (MA); foundations of education (MA); mathematics (MS); neuroscience of human consciousness (MS, PhD); physiology, molecular, and cell biology (MS, PhD); professional writing (MA); psychology (MS, PhD); science of creative intelligence (MA, PhD); secondary education (MA).

MAINE COLLEGE OF ART, Portland, ME 04101-3987

General Information Independent, coed, comprehensive institution. *Enrollment:* 27 full-time matriculated graduate/professional students (17 women). *Enrollment by degree level:* 27 master's. *Graduate faculty:* 2 full-time (1 woman), 21 part-time/adjunct (14 women). *Tuition:* Full-time $18,270. *Graduate housing:* Room and/or apartments available to single students; on-campus housing not available to married students. *Student services:* Career counseling, teacher training, writing training. *Library facilities:* Joanne Waxman Library at the Main College of Art. *Online resources:* library catalog, web page, access to other libraries' catalogs. *Collection:* 20,797 titles, 98 serial subscriptions, 182 audiovisual materials.

Computer facilities: 40 computers available on campus for general student use. A campuswide network can be accessed. Internet access is available. *Web address:* http://www.meca.edu/.

General Application Contact: Rachel A. Katz, Assistant to Graduate Studies, 207-775-5154 Ext. 30, Fax: 207-772-5069, E-mail: rkatz@meca.edu.

GRADUATE UNITS

Program in Studio Arts Students: 27 full-time (17 women); includes 1 minority (Asian American or Pacific Islander) Average age 34. 58 applicants, 43% accepted. *Faculty:* 2 full-time (1 woman), 21 part-time/adjunct (14 women). Expenses: Contact institution. *Financial support:* Available to part-time students. Application deadline: 3/1; In 2001, 10 degrees awarded. Offers studio arts (MFA). *Application deadline:* Applications are processed on a rolling basis. *Application fee:* $40. *Application Contact:* Rachel A. Katz, Assistant to Graduate Studies, 207-775-5154 Ext. 30, Fax: 207-772-5069, E-mail: rkatz@meca.edu.

MAINE MARITIME ACADEMY, Castine, ME 04420

General Information State-supported, coed, primarily men, comprehensive institution. *Enrollment:* 21 full-time matriculated graduate/professional students (2 women), 25 part-time matriculated graduate/professional students (2 women). *Enrollment by degree level:* 44 master's. *Graduate faculty:* 6 full-time (2 women), 3 part-time/adjunct (0 women). *Tuition, area resident:* Full-time $17,415; part-time $386 per credit hour. *Required fees:* $384; $45 per semester. *Graduate housing:* Rooms and/or apartments available on a first-come, first-served basis to single students and available to married students. Typical cost: $5,490 per year for single students; $5,490 per year for married students. *Student services:* Campus employment opportunities, campus safety program, career counseling, disabled student services, exercise/wellness program, free psychological counseling, international student services, low-cost health insurance. *Library facilities:* Nutting Memorial Library. *Online resources:* library catalog, web page. *Collection:* 68,200 titles, 453 serial subscriptions.

Computer facilities: 40 computers available on campus for general student use. A campuswide network can be accessed from student residence rooms. Internet access and online class registration are available. *Web address:* http://www.mainemaritime.edu/.

General Application Contact: Carolyn J. Ulrich, Administrative Assistant, 207-326-2485, Fax: 207-326-2411, E-mail: gradschl@mma.edu.

GRADUATE UNITS

Department of Graduate Studies Students: 21 full-time (2 women), 25 part-time (2 women), 19 international. Average age 28. 19 applicants, 47% accepted, 7 enrolled. *Faculty:* 6 full-time (2 women), 3 part-time/adjunct (0 women). Expenses: Contact institution. *Financial support:* In 2001–02, 3 students received support; teaching assistantships, career-related internships or fieldwork, Federal Work-Study, and institutionally sponsored loans available. Support available to part-time students. Financial award applicants required to submit FAFSA. In 2001, 8 degrees awarded. *Degree program information:* Part-time programs available. Offers logistics management (MS, Certificate, Diploma); maritime management (MS, Certificate, Diploma). *Application deadline:* Applications are processed on a rolling basis. *Application fee:* $40. *Application Contact:* Carolyn J. Ulrich, Administrative Assistant, 207-326-2485, Fax: 207-326-2411, E-mail: gradschl@mma.edu. *Director*, Dr. Donna G. Fricke, 207-326-2485, Fax: 207-326-2411, E-mail: dfricke@mma.edu.

MALONE COLLEGE, Canton, OH 44709-3897

General Information Independent-religious, coed, comprehensive institution. *Enrollment:* 13 full-time matriculated graduate/professional students (7 women), 202 part-time matriculated graduate/professional students (116 women). *Enrollment by degree level:* 215 master's. *Graduate faculty:* 23 full-time (6 women), 22 part-time/adjunct (10 women). *Tuition:* Part-time $330 per semester hour. *Graduate housing:* On-campus housing not available. *Student services:* Career counseling. *Library facilities:* Everett L. Cattell Library. *Online resources:* library catalog, access to other libraries' catalogs. *Collection:* 154,226 titles, 1,850 serial subscriptions, 13,511 audiovisual materials.

Computer facilities: 145 computers available on campus for general student use. A campuswide network can be accessed from student residence rooms and from off campus. Internet access is available. *Web address:* http://www.malone.edu/.

General Application Contact: Dan DePasquale, Director of Graduate Student Services, 330-471-8381, Fax: 330-471-8343, E-mail: depasquale@malone.edu.

GRADUATE UNITS

Graduate School Students: 13 full-time (7 women), 202 part-time (116 women); includes 16 minority (14 African Americans, 1 Asian American or Pacific Islander, 1 Native American), 1 international. Average age 35. *Faculty:* 23 full-time (6 women), 22 part-time/adjunct (10 women). Expenses: Contact institution. *Financial support:* In 2001–02, 101 students received support. Tuition waivers (partial) available. Support available to part-time students. Financial award application deadline: 6/30; financial award applicants required to submit FAFSA. In 2001, 93 degrees awarded. *Degree program information:* Part-time and evening/weekend programs available. Offers business (MBA); Christian ministries (MA); community counseling (MA); curriculum and instruction (MA); curriculum, instruction, and professional development (MA); family and youth ministries (MA); instructional technology (MA); intervention specialist (MA); leadership in Christian church (MA); pastoral counseling (MA); reading (MA); school counseling (MA). *Application deadline:* Applications are processed on a rolling basis. *Application fee:* $20. Electronic applications accepted. *Application Contact:* Dan DePasquale, Director of Graduate Student Services, 330-471-8381, Fax: 330-471-8343, E-mail: depasquale@malone.edu. *Dean*, Dr. Marietta Daulton, 330-471-8225, Fax: 330-471-8343, E-mail: mdaulton@malone.edu.

See in-depth description on page 953.

MANCHESTER COLLEGE, North Manchester, IN 46962-1225

General Information Independent-religious, coed, comprehensive institution. *Enrollment:* 13 full-time matriculated graduate/professional students (5 women). *Enrollment by degree level:* 13 master's. *Graduate faculty:* 9 full-time (2 women). *Tuition:* Part-time $530 per semester hour. *Graduate housing:* Room and/or apartments available to single students; on-campus housing not available to married students. Housing application deadline: 6/1. *Student services:* Campus employment opportunities, campus safety program, career counseling, exercise/wellness program, free psychological counseling, international student services, low-cost health insurance, multicultural affairs office. *Library facilities:* Funderburg Library. *Online resources:* library catalog, web page, access to other libraries' catalogs. *Collection:* 172,822 titles, 740 serial subscriptions, 5,278 audiovisual materials.

Computer facilities: 165 computers available on campus for general student use. A campuswide network can be accessed from student residence rooms and from off campus. Internet access is available. *Web address:* http://www.manchester.edu/.

General Application Contact: Dr. Jo Young Switzer, Vice President for Academic Affairs, 260-982-5051, Fax: 260-982-5043, E-mail: jyswitzer@manchester.edu.

GRADUATE UNITS

Division of Graduate Studies Students: 13 full-time (5 women). Average age 22. 16 applicants, 81% accepted. *Faculty:* 9 full-time (2 women). Expenses: Contact institution. *Financial support:* In 2001–02, 11 students received support; teaching assistantships, career-related internships or fieldwork and unspecified assistantships available. Financial award application deadline: 5/1; financial award applicants required to submit FAFSA. In 2001, 11 degrees awarded. *Degree program information:* Part-time programs available. Offers accounting (M Acc); contemporary leadership (MA). *Application deadline:* Applications are processed on a rolling basis. *Application fee:* $25. *Vice President for Academic Affairs*, Dr. Jo Young Switzer, 260-982-5051, Fax: 260-982-5043, E-mail: jyswitzer@manchester.edu.

MANHATTAN COLLEGE, Riverdale, NY 10471

General Information Independent-religious, coed, comprehensive institution. *Enrollment:* 69 full-time matriculated graduate/professional students (31 women), 269 part-time matriculated graduate/professional students (133 women). *Enrollment by degree level:* 338 master's. *Graduate faculty:* 61. *Tuition, area resident:* Part-time $415 per credit. Full-time tuition and fees vary according to program. *Graduate housing:* Room and/or apartments available to single students; on-campus housing not available to married students. Typical cost: $8,025 (including board). Housing application deadline: 5/1. *Student services:* Career counseling, disabled student services, free psychological counseling, low-cost health insurance. *Library facilities:* Cardinal Hayes Library plus 1 other. *Online resources:* library catalog, access to other libraries' catalogs. *Collection:* 193,100 titles, 1,527 serial subscriptions, 3,680 audiovisual materials.

Computer facilities: 375 computers available on campus for general student use. A campuswide network can be accessed from student residence rooms and from off campus. Internet access is available. *Web address:* http://www.manhattan.edu/.

General Application Contact: Dr. Weldon Jackson, Provost, 718-862-7303, Fax: 718-862-8014, E-mail: weldon.jackson@manhattan.edu.

GRADUATE UNITS

Graduate Division *Degree program information:* Part-time and evening/weekend programs available.

School of Education *Degree program information:* Part-time and evening/weekend programs available. Offers administration and supervision (MS Ed, Diploma); counseling (MA, Diploma); special education (MS Ed, Diploma).

School of Engineering *Degree program information:* Part-time and evening/weekend programs available. Offers chemical engineering (MS); civil engineering (MS); computer engineering (MS); electrical engineering (MS); environmental engineering (ME, MS); mechanical engineering (MS).

School of Science Offers biotechnology (MS).

See in-depth description on page 955.

MANHATTAN SCHOOL OF MUSIC, New York, NY 10027-4698

General Information Independent, coed, comprehensive institution. *Enrollment:* 380 full-time matriculated graduate/professional students (229 women), 14 part-time matriculated graduate/professional students (10 women). *Graduate faculty:* 60 full-time (20 women), 190 part-time/adjunct (70 women). *Tuition:* Full-time $21,100; part-time $850 per credit. *Required fees:* $400; $400 per year. Part-time tuition and fees vary according to course load. *Graduate housing:* Room and/or apartments available on a first-come, first-served basis to single students; on-campus housing not available to married students. Typical cost: $7,200 per year ($11,400 including board). Housing application deadline: 5/1. *Student services:* Campus employment opportunities, campus safety program, career counseling, international student services, low-cost health insurance. *Library facilities:* Francis Hall Ballard Library. *Online resources:* library catalog. *Collection:* 71,400 titles, 93 serial subscriptions, 19,600 audiovisual materials.

Computer facilities: 10 computers available on campus for general student use. Internet access is available. *Web address:* http://www.msmnyc.edu/.

General Application Contact: Amy A. Anderson, Dean of Enrollment and Alumni, 917-493-4501, E-mail: aanderson@msmnyc.edu.

GRADUATE UNITS

Graduate Programs in Music Students: 380 full-time (229 women), 14 part-time (10 women). Average age 26. 1,239 applicants, 32% accepted. *Faculty:* 60 full-time (20 women), 190 part-time/adjunct (70 women). Expenses: Contact institution. *Financial support:* In 2001–02, 223 students received support, including 14 teaching assistantships with partial tuition reimbursements available (averaging $3,600 per year); Federal Work-Study, scholarships/grants, and tuition waivers (full and partial) also available. Support available to part-time students. Financial award application deadline: 3/15; financial award applicants required to submit CSS PROFILE or FAFSA. In 2001, 194 master's, 17 doctorates awarded. Offers composition (MM, DMA); conducting (MM); jazz (MM); music performance (MM, DMA). *Application deadline:* For fall admission, 12/3 (priority date). *Application fee:* $100. *Application Contact:* Amy A. Anderson, Director of Admission and Financial Aid, 212-749-2802 Ext. 2, Fax: 212-749-3025, E-mail: aanderson@msmnyc.edu. *Dean of Academics*, Dr. David Noon, 212-749-2802 Ext. 4506, Fax: 212-749-5471, E-mail: dnoon@msmnyc.edu.

MANHATTANVILLE COLLEGE, Purchase, NY 10577-2132

General Information Independent, coed, comprehensive institution. *Enrollment:* 149 full-time matriculated graduate/professional students (131 women), 741 part-time matriculated graduate/professional students (622 women). *Enrollment by degree level:* 890 master's. *Graduate faculty:* 51 full-time (23 women), 102 part-time/adjunct (70 women). *Tuition:* Part-time $435 per credit. Tuition and fees vary according to program. *Graduate housing:* Rooms and/or apartments available on a first-come, first-served basis to single students and available to married students. Typical cost: $4,850 per year ($8,320 including board) for single students. Housing application deadline: 7/1. *Student services:* Campus employment opportunities, career counseling, free psychological counseling, international student services. *Library facilities:* Manhattanville College Library plus 1 other. *Online resources:* library catalog, web page, access to other libraries' catalogs. *Collection:* 182,789 titles, 912 serial subscriptions, 3,096 audiovisual materials.

Computer facilities: 83 computers available on campus for general student use. A campuswide network can be accessed from student residence rooms and from off campus. Internet access is available. *Web address:* http://www.mville.edu/.

General Application Contact: Barry Ward, Vice President of Enrollment and Student Development, 914-323-5153, Fax: 914-694-2386.

GRADUATE UNITS

Graduate Programs Students: 149 full-time (131 women), 741 part-time (622 women); includes 56 minority (27 African Americans, 8 Asian Americans or Pacific Islanders, 21 Hispanic Americans), 5 international. Average age 33. 251 applicants, 87% accepted. *Faculty:* 51 full-time (23 women), 102 part-time/adjunct (70 women). Expenses: Contact institution. *Financial support:* Career-related internships or fieldwork, institutionally sponsored loans, tuition waivers (partial), and unspecified assistantships available. Support available to part-time students. Financial award applicants required to submit FAFSA. In 2001, 283 degrees awarded. *Degree program information:* Part-time and evening/weekend programs available. Offers leadership and strategic management (MS); liberal studies (MA); management communications (MS); organization development and human resources management (MS); writing (MA). *Application deadline:* Applications are processed on a rolling basis. *Application fee:* $45. *Application Contact:* Barry Ward, Vice President of Enrollment and Student Development, 914-323-5153, Fax: 914-694-2386. *Provost and Dean of Faculty*, Dr. Cate Myers, 914-323-5208, Fax: 914-694-2386.

School of Education Students: 148 full-time (130 women), 511 part-time (443 women); includes 26 minority (12 African Americans, 3 Asian Americans or Pacific Islanders, 11 Hispanic Americans), 2 international. Average age 33. 395 applicants, 86% accepted. *Faculty:* 10 full-time (5 women), 61 part-time/adjunct (44 women). Expenses: Contact institution. *Financial support:* Career-related internships or fieldwork and institutionally sponsored loans available. Support available to part-time students. In 2001, 216 degrees awarded. *Degree program information:* Part-time and evening/weekend programs available. Offers art education (MAT); education (MAT, MPS); elementary education (MAT); elementary education and special education (MPS); English (MAT); languages (MAT); mathematics (MAT); music education (MAT); reading and writing (MPS); science (MAT); secondary and special education (MPS); social studies (MAT); special education (MPS); special education and reading (MPS); teaching English as a second language (MPS). *Application deadline:* For fall admission, 9/1 (priority date); for spring admission, 3/1. Applications are processed on a rolling basis. *Application fee:* $45. *Application Contact:* Rebecca Strauser, Coordinator of Admissions, 914-323-5214, Fax: 914-323-5493, E-mail: strausera@mville.edu. *Dean*, Dr. Kathryn Podavano, 914-323-5137, Fax: 914-323-5493, E-mail: podavanok@mville.edu.

See in-depth description on page 957.

MANNES COLLEGE OF MUSIC, NEW SCHOOL UNIVERSITY, New York, NY 10024-4402

General Information Independent, coed, comprehensive institution. *Enrollment:* 167 full-time matriculated graduate/professional students (100 women). *Enrollment by degree level:* 103 master's, 64 other advanced degrees. *Graduate faculty:* 3 full-time, 163 part-time/adjunct. *Tuition:* Full-time $19,800; part-time $650 per credit. *Required fees:* $230; $115 per term. Part-time tuition and fees vary according to degree level. *Graduate housing:* Rooms and/or apartments available on a first-come, first-served basis to single and married students. Typical cost: $7,570 per year for single students. Housing application deadline: 8/1. *Student services:* Campus employment opportunities, career counseling, disabled student services, international student services, low-cost health insurance, writing training. *Library facilities:* Fogelman Library plus 2 others. *Collection:* 368,390 titles, 1,155 serial subscriptions, 433,123 audiovisual materials.

Computer facilities: 475 computers available on campus for general student use. *Web address:* http://www.mannes.edu/.

General Application Contact: Georgia Schmitt, Admission Counselor, 212-580-0210 Ext. 247, Fax: 212-580-1738, E-mail: mannesadmissions@newschool.edu.

GRADUATE UNITS

Graduate Program Students: 167 full-time (100 women). Average age 25. 712 applicants, 25% accepted. *Faculty:* 3 full-time, 163 part-time/adjunct. Expenses: Contact institution. *Financial support:* In 2001–02, 151 students received support. Career-related internships or fieldwork, Federal Work-Study, and scholarships/grants available. Financial award application deadline: 3/1; financial award applicants required to submit FAFSA. In 2001, 52 master's, 24 Certificates awarded. Offers music (MM, Certificate). *Application deadline:* For fall admission, 12/1 (priority date); for spring admission, 12/1. Applications are processed on a rolling basis. *Application fee:* $100. Electronic applications accepted. *Application Contact:* Georgia Schmitt, Admission Counselor, 212-580-0210 Ext. 247, Fax: 212-580-1738, E-mail: mannesadmissions@newschool.edu. *Dean*, Joel Lester, 212-580-0210, Fax: 212-580-1738.

MANSFIELD UNIVERSITY OF PENNSYLVANIA, Mansfield, PA 16933

General Information State-supported, coed, comprehensive institution. *Enrollment:* 51 full-time matriculated graduate/professional students (37 women), 180 part-time matriculated graduate/professional students (155 women). *Graduate faculty:* 35 part-time/adjunct (16 women). Tuition, state resident: full-time $2,300; part-time $256 per credit. Tuition, nonresident: full-time $3,777; part-time $470 per credit. *Required fees:* $230. *Graduate housing:* Room and/or apartments available to single students; on-campus housing not available to married students. Housing application deadline: 4/3. *Student services:* Campus safety program, career counseling, child daycare facilities, free psychological counseling, grant writing training, international student services, low-cost health insurance, multicultural affairs office. *Library facilities:* North Hill Library. *Online resources:* library catalog, web page, access to other libraries' catalogs. *Collection:* 237,911 titles, 3,110 serial subscriptions, 2,693 audiovisual materials.

Computer facilities: 371 computers available on campus for general student use. A campuswide network can be accessed from student residence rooms and from off campus. Internet access is available. *Web address:* http://www.mansfield.edu/.

General Application Contact: Dr. Nancy J. Cooledge, Associate Provost, 570-662-4807, Fax: 570-662-4115, E-mail: ncooledg@mnsfld.edu.

GRADUATE UNITS

Graduate Studies Students: 55 full-time (39 women), 230 part-time (192 women); includes 5 minority (4 Hispanic Americans, 1 Native American), 2 international. Average age 34. 156 applicants, 100% accepted. *Faculty:* 35 part-time/adjunct (16 women). Expenses: Contact institution. *Financial support:* In 2001–02, 85 students received support. Career-related internships or fieldwork and unspecified assistantships available. Support available to part-time students. Financial award application deadline: 5/1; financial award applicants required to submit FAFSA. In 2001, 44 degrees awarded. *Degree program information:* Part-time and evening/weekend programs available. Postbaccalaureate distance learning degree programs offered (no on-campus study). Offers art/communications (M Ed); elementary education (M Ed); music (MM); school library and information technologies (MS); secondary education (MS). *Application deadline:* Applications are processed on a rolling basis. *Application fee:* $25. Electronic applications accepted. *Director of Teacher Education*, Dr. Anne Pautz, 570-662-4565, E-mail: apautz@mnsfld.edu.

Announcement: MS program available in education. M Ed programs offered in art, elementary education, school library and information technologies, and special education. MM program offered in music education. Excellent opportunities for study and research in a rural environment. Assistantships available. Members of equity groups encouraged to apply.

MAPLE SPRINGS BAPTIST BIBLE COLLEGE AND SEMINARY, Capitol Heights, MD 20743

General Information Independent-religious, comprehensive institution. *Graduate housing:* On-campus housing not available.

GRADUATE UNITS

Graduate and Professional Programs Offers biblical studies (MA, Certificate); Christian counseling (MA); church administration (MA); divinity (M Div); ministry (D Min); religious education (MA).

MARANATHA BAPTIST BIBLE COLLEGE, Watertown, WI 53094

General Information Independent-religious, coed, comprehensive institution. *Enrollment:* 11 full-time matriculated graduate/professional students (1 woman), 14 part-time matriculated graduate/professional students (2 women). *Enrollment by degree level:* 25 master's. *Graduate faculty:* 6 full-time (0 women), 3 part-time/adjunct (0 women). *Tuition:* Part-time $135 per credit hour. *Required fees:* $15 per semester. Full-time tuition and fees vary according to course load. *Graduate housing:* Room and/or apartments available on a first-come, first-served basis to single students; on-campus housing not available to married students. Typical cost: $2,025 (including board). *Student services:* Campus employment opportunities. *Library facilities:* Cedarholm Library and Resource Center plus 1 other. *Online resources:* library catalog, access to other libraries' catalogs. *Collection:* 99,390 titles, 515 serial subscriptions, 3,441 audiovisual materials.

Computer facilities: 61 computers available on campus for general student use. A campuswide network can be accessed from student residence rooms and from off campus. Internet access is available. *Web address:* http://www.mbbc.edu/.

General Application Contact: Dr. Larry Oats, Chair, Department of Bible and Graduate Studies, 920-206-2324, Fax: 920-621-9109, E-mail: loats@mbbc.edu.

GRADUATE UNITS

Program in Biblical Studies Students: 11 full-time (1 woman), 14 part-time (2 women). Average age 31. 18 applicants, 100% accepted. *Faculty:* 6 full-time (0 women), 3 part-time/adjunct (0 women). Expenses: Contact institution. *Financial support:* In 2001–02, 7 students received support. Scholarships/grants and tuition waivers (full and partial) available. Support available to part-time students. Financial award application deadline: 8/15. In 2001, 8 degrees awarded. *Degree program information:* Part-time programs available. Postbaccalaureate distance learning degree programs offered (minimal on-campus study). Offers biblical studies (MA). *Application deadline:* Applications are processed on a rolling basis. *Application fee:* $40. *Application Contact:* Jim Harrison, Director of Admissions, 920-206-2327, Fax: 920-261-9109, E-mail: admissions@mbbc.edu. *President*, Dr. David B. Jaspers, 920-206-9300, Fax: 920-261-9109, E-mail: president@mbbc.edu.

MARIAN COLLEGE, Indianapolis, IN 46222-1997

General Information Independent-religious, coed, comprehensive institution.

GRADUATE UNITS

Department of Education

MARIAN COLLEGE OF FOND DU LAC, Fond du Lac, WI 54935-4699

General Information Independent-religious, coed, comprehensive institution. *Enrollment:* 49 full-time matriculated graduate/professional students (28 women), 881 part-time matriculated graduate/professional students (573 women). *Enrollment by degree level:* 930 master's. *Graduate faculty:* 13 full-time (5 women), 49 part-time/adjunct (19 women). *Tuition:* Part-time $249 per credit. Full-time tuition and fees vary according to program. *Graduate housing:* Room and/or apartments available on a first-come, first-served basis to single students; on-campus housing not available to married students. *Student services:* Campus employment opportunities, campus safety program, career counseling, disabled student services, exercise/wellness program, free psychological counseling, multicultural affairs office, teacher training, writing training. *Library facilities:* Cardinal Meyer Library. *Online resources:* library catalog, web page, access to other libraries' catalogs. *Collection:* 91,000 titles, 750 serial subscriptions, 397 audiovisual materials.

Computer facilities: 125 computers available on campus for general student use. A campuswide network can be accessed from student residence rooms. Internet access and online class registration are available. *Web address:* http://www.mariancollege.edu/.

GRADUATE UNITS

Business Division Students: 37 full-time (22 women), 59 part-time (30 women); includes 7 minority (2 African Americans, 3 Asian Americans or Pacific Islanders, 1 Hispanic American, 1 Native American) Average age 40. 49 applicants, 86% accepted. *Faculty:* 2 full-time (0 women), 8 part-time/adjunct (0 women). Expenses: Contact institution. *Financial support:* In 2001–02, 15 students received support. Institutionally sponsored loans available. Support available to part-time students. Financial award applicants required to submit FAFSA. In 2001, 38 degrees awarded. *Degree program information:* Part-time and evening/weekend programs available. Postbaccalaureate distance learning degree programs offered (no on-campus study). Offers organizational leadership and quality (MS). *Application deadline:* Applications are processed on a rolling basis. *Application fee:* $25. Electronic applications accepted. *Application Contact:* Elizabeth Nagler, Director of Marketing and Admission-MAAP, 920-923-8783, Fax: 920-923-7167, E-mail: lnagler@mariancollege.edu. *Dean of Lifelong Learning*, David McPhail, 920-923-8760, Fax: 920-923-7167, E-mail: dmcphail@mariancollege.edu.

Education Division Students: 12 full-time (6 women), 822 part-time (543 women); includes 23 minority (16 African Americans, 1 Asian American or Pacific Islander, 2 Hispanic Americans, 4 Native Americans) Average age 37. 128 applicants, 77% accepted. *Faculty:* 11 full-time (5 women), 41 part-time/adjunct (19 women). Expenses: Contact institution. *Financial support:* In 2001–02, 26 students received support. Federal Work-Study available. Support available to part-time students. Financial award application deadline: 3/1; financial award applicants

Marian College of Fond du Lac (continued)

required to submit FAFSA. In 2001, 292 degrees awarded. *Degree program information:* Part-time programs available. Offers educational leadership (MA); teacher development (MA). *Application deadline:* Applications are processed on a rolling basis. *Application fee:* $25. *Application Contact:* Robert Bohnsack, Graduate Education Admissions, 920-923-8100, Fax: 920-923-7154. *Chair, Educational Studies,* Dr. Donna Innes, 920-923-7140, Fax: 920-923-7154, E-mail: dinnes@mariancollege.edu.

MARIETTA COLLEGE, Marietta, OH 45750-4000

General Information Independent, coed, comprehensive institution. *Enrollment:* 6 full-time matriculated graduate/professional students (2 women), 67 part-time matriculated graduate/professional students (50 women). *Enrollment by degree level:* 73 master's. *Graduate faculty:* 11 full-time (6 women), 5 part-time/adjunct (all women). *Tuition:* Part-time $306 per credit hour. *Graduate housing:* Room and/or apartments available to single students; on-campus housing not available to married students. *Student services:* Campus safety program, career counseling, disabled student services, free psychological counseling, international student services, teacher training, writing training. *Library facilities:* Dawes Memorial Library. *Online resources:* library catalog, web page, access to other libraries' catalogs. *Collection:* 250,000 titles, 1,300 serial subscriptions, 7,300 audiovisual materials.

Computer facilities: 200 computers available on campus for general student use. A campuswide network can be accessed from student residence rooms and from off campus. Internet access is available. *Web address:* http://www.marietta.edu/.

General Application Contact: Cathy J. Brown, Registrar, 740-376-4740, Fax: 740-376-4729, E-mail: brownc@marietta.edu.

GRADUATE UNITS

Program in Education Students: 4 full-time (2 women), 48 part-time (39 women). Average age 37. *Faculty:* 5 full-time (3 women), 5 part-time/adjunct (all women). Expenses: Contact institution. *Financial support:* Available to part-time students. *Degree program information:* Part-time and evening/weekend programs available. Offers education (MA). *Application deadline:* For fall admission, 8/23 (priority date). *Application fee:* $25. *Chair,* Dr. Dorothy Erb, 740-376-4761.

Program in Liberal Learning Students: 2 full-time (1 woman), 19 part-time (11 women). Average age 37. *Faculty:* 6 full-time (3 women). Expenses: Contact institution. *Financial support:* Available to part-time students. *Degree program information:* Part-time and evening/weekend programs available. Offers liberal learning (MALL). *Application deadline:* For fall admission, 8/25. *Application fee:* $25. *Director,* Dr. James H. O'Donnell, 740-376-4625.

MARIST COLLEGE, Poughkeepsie, NY 12601-1387

General Information Independent, coed, comprehensive institution. *Enrollment:* 137 full-time matriculated graduate/professional students (76 women), 648 part-time matriculated graduate/professional students (324 women). *Enrollment by degree level:* 685 master's, 100 other advanced degrees. *Graduate faculty:* 33 full-time (11 women), 30 part-time/adjunct (14 women). *Tuition:* Full-time $4,320; part-time $480 per credit. *Required fees:* $30 per semester. *Graduate housing:* On-campus housing not available. *Student services:* Campus employment opportunities, career counseling, free psychological counseling, low-cost health insurance. *Library facilities:* Marist College Library. *Online resources:* library catalog, web page. *Collection:* 283,941 titles, 115,661 serial subscriptions, 5,646 audiovisual materials. *Research affiliation:* Hudson River Psychiatric Center, Harlem Valley Psychiatric Center, St. Francis Hospital, Dutchess County Community Mental Health Center.

Computer facilities: 450 computers available on campus for general student use. A campuswide network can be accessed from student residence rooms and from off campus. Internet access is available. *Web address:* http://www.marist.edu/.

General Application Contact: Dr. John DeJoy, Acting Dean of Graduate and Continuing Education, 845-575-3530, Fax: 845-575-3640, E-mail: john.dejoy@marist.edu.

GRADUATE UNITS

Graduate Programs Students: 137 full-time (76 women), 648 part-time (324 women); includes 110 minority (23 African Americans, 72 Asian Americans or Pacific Islanders, 14 Hispanic Americans, 1 Native American), 2 international. Average age 31. *Faculty:* 33 full-time (11 women), 30 part-time/adjunct (14 women). Expenses: Contact institution. *Financial support:* In 2001–02, 97 students received support. Career-related internships or fieldwork, Federal Work-Study, and tuition waivers (partial) available. Support available to part-time students. Financial award application deadline: 8/15; financial award applicants required to submit FAFSA. In 2001, 268 degrees awarded. *Degree program information:* Part-time and evening/weekend programs available. *Application deadline:* For fall admission, 8/1 (priority date); for spring admission, 12/15. Applications are processed on a rolling basis. *Application fee:* $30. *Application Contact:* Dr. John DeJoy, Acting Dean of Graduate and Continuing Education, 845-575-3530, Fax: 845-575-3640, E-mail: john.dejoy@marist.edu. *Academic Vice President,* Dr. Artin Arslanian, 845-575-3000 Ext. 2629, E-mail: artin.arslanian@marist.edu.

School of Computer Science and Mathematics Students: 50 full-time (15 women), 93 part-time (28 women); includes 63 minority (4 African Americans, 57 Asian Americans or Pacific Islanders, 2 Hispanic Americans), 2 international. Average age 33. *Faculty:* 11 full-time (3 women), 5 part-time/adjunct (1 woman). Expenses: Contact institution. *Financial support:* Federal Work-Study and tuition waivers (partial) available. Support available to part-time students. Financial award application deadline: 8/15; financial award applicants required to submit FAFSA. In 2001, 34 degrees awarded. *Degree program information:* Part-time and evening/weekend programs available. Offers computer science (MS). *Application deadline:* For fall admission, 8/1 (priority date); for spring admission, 12/15. Applications are processed on a rolling basis. *Application fee:* $30. *Application Contact:* Dr. John DeJoy, Acting Dean of Graduate and Continuing Education, 845-575-3530, Fax: 845-575-3640, E-mail: john.dejoy@marist.edu. *Dean,* Dr. Roger Norton, 845-575-3000, E-mail: roger.norton@marist.edu.

School of Management Students: 21 full-time (12 women), 406 part-time (183 women); includes 36 minority (14 African Americans, 14 Asian Americans or Pacific Islanders, 8 Hispanic Americans) Average age 29. 121 applicants, 74% accepted. *Faculty:* 14 full-time (5 women), 5 part-time/adjunct (2 women). Expenses: Contact institution. *Financial support:* Federal Work-Study and tuition waivers (partial) available. Support available to part-time students. Financial award application deadline: 8/15; financial award applicants required to submit FAFSA. In 2001, 133 degrees awarded. *Degree program information:* Part-time and evening/weekend programs available. Offers business administration (MBA, PGC); management (MBA, MPA, Certificate, PGC); public administration (MPA, Certificate). *Application deadline:* For fall admission, 8/1 (priority date); for spring admission, 12/15. Applications are processed on a rolling basis. *Application fee:* $30. *Application Contact:* Dr. John DeJoy, Acting Dean of Graduate and Continuing Education, 845-575-3530, Fax: 845-575-3640, E-mail: john.dejoy@marist.edu. *Dean,* Dr. Gordon Badovick, 845-575-3225, E-mail: gordon.badovick@marist.edu.

School of Social/Behavioral Sciences Students: 66 full-time (49 women), 149 part-time (113 women); includes 11 minority (5 African Americans, 1 Asian American or Pacific Islander, 4 Hispanic Americans, 1 Native American) Average age 30. 104 applicants, 79% accepted. *Faculty:* 8 full-time (3 women), 20 part-time/adjunct (11 women). Expenses: Contact institution. *Financial support:* Career-related internships or fieldwork, Federal Work-Study, and tuition waivers (partial) available. Support available to part-time students. Financial award application deadline: 8/15; financial award applicants required to submit FAFSA. In 2001, 62 degrees awarded. *Degree program information:* Part-time and evening/weekend programs available. Offers counseling/community psychology (MA); education psychology (MA); school psychology (MA, Adv C). *Application deadline:* For fall admission, 8/1 (priority date); for spring admission, 12/15. Applications are processed on a rolling basis. *Application fee:* $30. *Application Contact:* Dr. John DeJoy, Acting Dean of Graduate and Continuing Education, 845-575-3530, Fax: 845-575-3640, E-mail: john.dejoy@marist.edu. *Dean,* Margaret Calista, 845-575-3000 Ext. 2960, E-mail: margaret.calista@marist.edu.

MARLBORO COLLEGE, Marlboro, VT 05344

General Information Independent, coed, comprehensive institution. *Enrollment:* 51 full-time matriculated graduate/professional students (25 women), 19 part-time matriculated graduate/professional students (16 women). *Enrollment by degree level:* 51 master's, 19 other advanced degrees. *Graduate faculty:* 3 full-time (1 woman), 22 part-time/adjunct (12 women). *Tuition:* Part-time $3,000 per term. Tuition and fees vary according to program. *Graduate housing:* On-campus housing not available. *Student services:* Career counseling, child daycare facilities, free psychological counseling, low-cost health insurance. *Library facilities:* Rice Memorial Library. *Online resources:* library catalog, web page, access to other libraries' catalogs. *Collection:* 54,289 titles, 250 serial subscriptions, 746 audiovisual materials.

Computer facilities: 42 computers available on campus for general student use. A campuswide network can be accessed from student residence rooms and from off campus. Internet access is available. *Web address:* http://www.marlboro.edu/.

General Application Contact: Margaret J. Donahue, Admissions Officer, 802-258-9209, Fax: 802-258-9201, E-mail: mdonahue@gradcenter.marlboro.edu.

GRADUATE UNITS

The Graduate Center of Marlboro College Students: 51 full-time (25 women), 19 part-time (16 women). 240 applicants, 60% accepted. *Faculty:* 3 full-time (1 woman), 22 part-time/adjunct (12 women). Expenses: Contact institution. *Financial support:* Application deadline: 5/1; In 2001, 65 degrees awarded. *Degree program information:* Evening/weekend programs available. Postbaccalaureate distance learning degree programs offered (minimal on-campus study). Offers Internet engineering (MS); Internet strategy management (MS); internet teaching (Certificate); system integration management (MS); teaching with Internet technologies (MAT). *Application deadline:* For fall admission, 3/1 (priority date). Applications are processed on a rolling basis. *Application fee:* $0. Electronic applications accepted. *Application Contact:* Margaret J. Donahue, Admissions Officer, 802-268-9209, Fax: 802-258-9201, E-mail: mdonahue@gradcenter.marlboro.edu. *Director of Academic Programs,* Claudine Keenan, 802-258-9200, Fax: 802-258-9201, E-mail: ckeenan@marlboro.edu.

MARQUETTE UNIVERSITY, Milwaukee, WI 53201-1881

General Information Independent-religious, coed, university. CGS member. *Enrollment:* 890 full-time matriculated graduate/professional students (448 women), 1,324 part-time matriculated graduate/professional students (730 women). *Graduate faculty:* 519 full-time, 290 part-time/adjunct. *Tuition:* Full-time $10,170; part-time $445 per credit hour. Tuition and fees vary according to course load. *Graduate housing:* Rooms and/or apartments available on a first-come, first-served basis to single and married students. Typical cost: $4,400 per year ($6,662 including board) for single students; $4,400 per year for married students. Room and board charges vary according to board plan, campus/location and housing facility selected. *Student services:* Campus employment opportunities, campus safety program, career counseling, child daycare facilities, disabled student services, exercise/wellness program, free psychological counseling, grant writing training, international student services, low-cost health insurance, multicultural affairs office, teacher training, writing training. *Library facilities:* Memorial Library plus 2 others. *Online resources:* library catalog, web page, access to other libraries' catalogs. *Collection:* 719,906 titles, 9,225 serial subscriptions, 7,276 audiovisual materials. *Research affiliation:* American Educational Research Association, Argonne National Laboratory, Milwaukee Museum, NASA.

Computer facilities: 600 computers available on campus for general student use. A campuswide network can be accessed from student residence rooms and from off campus. Internet access is available. *Web address:* http://www.marquette.edu/.

General Application Contact: Erin Fox, Assistant Director for Recruitment, 414-288-5319, Fax: 414-288-1902.

GRADUATE UNITS

Graduate School Students: 890 full-time (442 women), 1,324 part-time (594 women); includes 220 minority (103 African Americans, 72 Asian Americans or Pacific Islanders, 39 Hispanic Americans, 6 Native Americans), 336 international. Average age 33. 1,900 applicants, 63% accepted. *Faculty:* 482 full-time (103 women), 118 part-time/adjunct (30 women). Expenses: Contact institution. *Financial support:* Fellowships, research assistantships with full tuition reimbursements, teaching assistantships with full tuition reimbursements, career-related internships or fieldwork, Federal Work-Study, institutionally sponsored loans, scholarships/grants, and tuition waivers (full and partial) available. Support available to part-time students. Financial award application deadline: 2/15. In 2001, 457 master's, 56 doctorates awarded. *Degree program information:* Part-time and evening/weekend programs available. Offers bioinformatics (MS); computing (MS); interdisciplinary studies (PhD). *Application deadline:* Applications are processed on a rolling basis. *Application fee:* $40. Electronic applications accepted. *Application Contact:* Rev. David A. Zampino, Manager, Graduate Inquiry Systems, 414-288-6302, Fax: 414-288-1902, E-mail: mugs@grad.mu.edu. *Interim Dean,* Dr. Lynn Miner, 414-288-1531, Fax: 414-288-1578.

College of Arts and Sciences Students: 353 full-time (153 women), 139 part-time (51 women); includes 34 minority (10 African Americans, 11 Asian Americans or Pacific Islanders, 10 Hispanic Americans, 3 Native Americans), 80 international. Average age 33. 452 applicants, 54% accepted. *Faculty:* 257 full-time (85 women), 7 part-time/adjunct (4 women). Expenses: Contact institution. *Financial support:* In 2001–02, 9 fellowships, 48 research assistantships, 196 teaching assistantships were awarded. Career-related internships or fieldwork, Federal Work-Study, institutionally sponsored loans, scholarships/grants, and tuition waivers (full and partial) also available. Support available to part-time students. Financial award application deadline: 2/15. In 2001, 57 master's, 35 doctorates awarded. *Degree program information:* Part-time programs available. Offers algebra (PhD); American literature (PhD); analytical chemistry (MS, PhD); ancient philosophy (MA, PhD); arts and sciences (MA, MAT, MS, PhD); bio-mathematical modeling (PhD); bioanalytical chemistry (MS, PhD); biophysical chemistry (MS, PhD); British and American literature (MA); British empiricism and analytic philosophy (MA, PhD); British literature (PhD); cell biology (MS, PhD); chemical physics (MS, PhD); Christian philosophy (MA, PhD); clinical psychology (MS); computers (MS); developmental biology (MS, PhD); early modern European philosophy (MA, PhD); ecology (MS, PhD); endocrinology (MS, PhD); ethics (MA, PhD); European history (MA, PhD); evolutionary biology (MS, PhD); genetics (MS, PhD); German philosophy (MA, PhD); historical theology (MA, PhD); inorganic chemistry (MS, PhD); international affairs (MA); mathematics (MS); mathematics education (MS); medieval history (MA); medieval philosophy (MA, PhD); microbiology (MS, PhD); molecular biology (MS, PhD); muscle and exercise physiology (MS, PhD); neurobiology (MS, PhD); organic chemistry (MS, PhD); phenomenology and existentialism (MA, PhD); philosophy of religion (MA, PhD); physical chemistry (MS, PhD); political science (MA); psychology (PhD); religious studies (PhD); Renaissance and Reformation (MA); reproductive physiology (MS, PhD); social and applied philosophy (MA); Spanish (MA, MAT); statistics (MS); systematic theology (MA, PhD); theology (MA); theology and society (PhD); United States (MA, PhD). *Application fee:* $40. *Application Contact:* Rev. David A. Zampino, Manager, Graduate Inquiry Systems, 414-288-6302, Fax: 414-288-1902, E-mail: mugs@grad.mu.edu. *Dean,* Dr. Michael A. McKinney, 414-288-7472.

College of Business Administration Students: 137 full-time (52 women), 550 part-time (176 women); includes 45 minority (14 African Americans, 21 Asian Americans or Pacific Islanders, 8 Hispanic Americans, 2 Native Americans), 67 international. Average age 31. 405 applicants, 79% accepted. *Faculty:* 42 full-time (7 women), 3 part-time/adjunct (0 women). Expenses: Contact institution. *Financial support:* In 2001–02, 4 research assistantships, 13 teaching assistantships were awarded. Federal Work-Study, institutionally sponsored loans, scholarships/grants, and tuition waivers (full and partial) also available. Support available to part-time students. Financial award application deadline: 2/15. In 2001, 192 degrees awarded. *Degree program information:* Part-time and evening/weekend programs available. Offers accounting (MSA); business administration (MBA, MSA, MSAE, MSHR); business economics (MSAE); financial economics (MSAE); human resources (MSHR); international economics (MSAE); public policy economics (MSAE). *Application fee:* $40. *Dean,* Dr. David Shrock, 414-288-7141, Fax: 414-288-1578.

College of Communication Students: 31 full-time (21 women), 19 part-time (14 women); includes 5 minority (3 African Americans, 2 Asian Americans or Pacific Islanders), 10 international. Average age 31. 52 applicants, 67% accepted. *Faculty:* 31. Expenses: Contact institution. *Financial support:* In 2001–02, 6 research assistantships, 12 teaching assistantships were awarded. Career-related internships or fieldwork, Federal Work-Study, institutionally sponsored loans, scholarships/grants, and tuition waivers (full and partial) also available. Support available to part-time students. Financial award application deadline: 2/15. In 2001, 19 degrees awarded. *Degree program information:* Part-time and evening/weekend programs available. Offers advertising and public relations (MA); broadcasting and electronic communications (MA); communications studies (MA); journalism (MA); mass communications (MA); religious communications (MA); science, health and environmental communications (MA). *Application fee:* $40. *Application Contact:* Dr. Ana Garner, Director of Graduate Studies, 414-288-7383. *Dean,* Dr. William R. Elliot, 414-288-7132, Fax: 414-288-1578.

College of Engineering Students: 124 full-time (33 women), 166 part-time (23 women); includes 21 minority (6 African Americans, 11 Asian Americans or Pacific Islanders, 3 Hispanic Americans, 1 Native American), 80 international. 276 applicants, 60% accepted. *Faculty:* 45 full-time (4 women), 51 part-time/adjunct (6 women). Expenses: Contact institution. *Financial support:* In 2001–02, 55 students received support, including 21 fellowships with tuition reimbursements available, 24 research assistantships with tuition reimbursements available, 31 teaching assistantships with tuition reimbursements available; Federal Work-Study, institutionally sponsored loans, scholarships/grants, and tuition waivers (full and partial) also available. Support available to part-time students. Financial award application deadline: 2/15. In 2001, 28 master's, 6 doctorates awarded. *Degree program information:* Part-time and evening/weekend programs available. Offers bioinstrumentation/computers (MS, PhD); biomechanics/biomaterials (MS, PhD); computing (MS); construction and public works management (MS, PhD); electrical engineering (MS, PhD); engineering (MS, PhD); engineering management (MS); environmental/water resources engineering (MS, PhD); functional imaging (PhD); healthcare technologies management (MS); mechanical engineering (MS, PhD); structural/geotechnical engineering (MS, PhD); systems physiology (MS, PhD); transportational planning and engineering (MS, PhD). *Application deadline:* Applications are processed on a rolling basis. *Application fee:* $40. Electronic applications accepted. *Application Contact:* Craig Pierce, Director of Admissions, 414-288-7137, Fax: 414-288-1902, E-mail: mugs@vms.csd.mu.edu. *Dean,* Dr. Douglas M. Green, 414-288-6591, Fax: 414-288-6025, E-mail: douglas.green@marquette.edu.

College of Health Sciences Students: 33 full-time (all women), 1 (woman) part-time. Average age 24. 80 applicants, 58% accepted. Expenses: Contact institution. In 2001, 25 degrees awarded. Offers health sciences (MPT, MS); physical therapy (MPT); physician assistant studies (MS); speech-language pathology (MS). *Dean,* Dr. Jack C. Brooks, 414-288-7948, E-mail: jack.brooks@mu.edu.

College of Nursing Students: 58 full-time (55 women), 82 part-time (78 women); includes 1 minority (African American), 4 international. Average age 35. 59 applicants, 90% accepted. *Faculty:* 24 full-time (23 women), 5 part-time/adjunct (4 women). Expenses: Contact institution. *Financial support:* In 2001–02, 6 research assistantships, 1 teaching assistantship were awarded. Career-related internships or fieldwork, Federal Work-Study, institutionally sponsored loans, scholarships/grants, and tuition waivers (full and partial) also available. Support available to part-time students. Financial award application deadline: 2/15. In 2001, 35 degrees awarded. *Degree program information:* Part-time and evening/weekend programs available. Offers adult nurse practitioner (Certificate); advanced practice nursing (MSN); gerontological nurse practitioner (Certificate); neonatal nurse practitioner (Certificate); nurse-midwifery (Certificate); pediatric nurse practitioner (Certificate). *Application fee:* $40. *Application Contact:* Dr. Judy Miller, Director of Graduate Studies, 414-288-3810, Fax: 414-288-1578. *Dean,* Dr. Madeline Wake, 414-288-3812, Fax: 414-288-1578.

School of Education Students: 24 full-time (13 women), 206 part-time (155 women); includes 68 minority (56 African Americans, 4 Asian Americans or Pacific Islanders, 8 Hispanic Americans), 10 international. Average age 39. 203 applicants, 77% accepted. *Faculty:* 17 full-time (7 women), 7 part-time/adjunct (0 women). Expenses: Contact institution. *Financial support:* In 2001–02, 5 research assistantships, 5 teaching assistantships were awarded. Federal Work-Study, institutionally sponsored loans, scholarships/grants, and tuition waivers (full and partial) also available. Support available to part-time students. Financial award application deadline: 2/15. In 2001, 34 master's, 11 doctorates awarded. *Degree program information:* Part-time programs available. Offers education (MA, Ed D, PhD, Spec). *Application fee:* $40. *Application Contact:* Dr. William Pink, Assistant Dean, 414-288-1421, Fax: 414-288-5333. *Dean,* Dr. Mary P. Hoy, 414-288-7376, Fax: 414-288-1578.

Law School Students: 480 full-time (192 women), 150 part-time (80 women); includes 47 minority (17 African Americans, 17 Asian Americans or Pacific Islanders, 12 Hispanic Americans, 1 Native American), 3 international. Average age 25. 984 applicants, 50% accepted, 202 enrolled. *Faculty:* 31 full-time (13 women), 67 part-time/adjunct (20 women). Expenses: Contact institution. *Financial support:* In 2001–02, 490 students received support. Career-related internships or fieldwork, Federal Work-Study, and scholarships/grants available. Support available to part-time students. Financial award application deadline: 3/1; financial award applicants required to submit FAFSA. In 2001, 188 degrees awarded. *Degree program information:* Part-time and evening/weekend programs available. Offers law (JD). *Application deadline:* For fall admission, 4/1. Applications are processed on a rolling basis. *Application fee:* $40. *Application Contact:* Edward A. Kawczynski, Assistant Dean for Admissions, 414-288-6767, Fax: 414-288-0676, E-mail: edward.kawczynski@marquette.edu. *Dean,* Howard B. Eisenberg, 414-288-7090, Fax: 414-288-6403, E-mail: howard.eisenberg@marquette.edu.

School of Dentistry Students: 320 full-time (115 women), 3 part-time (1 woman); includes 37 minority (5 African Americans, 6 Asian Americans or Pacific Islanders, 25 Hispanic Americans, 1 Native American), 3 international. Average age 26. 1,800 applicants, 6% accepted. *Faculty:* 46 full-time (6 women), 235 part-time/adjunct (20 women). Expenses: Contact institution. *Financial support:* In 2001–02, 2 research assistantships with partial tuition reimbursements (averaging $5,000 per year), 14 teaching assistantships with partial tuition reimbursements (averaging $5,000 per year) were awarded. Career-related internships or fieldwork, Federal Work-Study, institutionally sponsored loans, and tuition waivers (full and partial) also available. Support available to part-time students. In 2001, 10 degrees awarded. *Degree program information:* Part-time programs available. Offers advanced training in general dentistry (MS); dental biomaterials (MS); dentistry (DDS, MS); endodontics (MS); orthodontics (MS); prosthodontics (MS). *Application deadline:* Applications are processed on a rolling basis. *Application fee:* $40. *Application Contact:* Dr. Anthony M. Iacopino, Associate Dean for Research and Graduate Studies, 414-288-5670, Fax: 414-288-3586, E-mail: anthony.iacopino@marquette.edu. *Dean,* Dr. William L. Lobb, 414-288-7780, Fax: 414-288-3586.

See in-depth description on page 959.

MARSHALL UNIVERSITY, Huntington, WV 25755

General Information State-supported, coed, university. CGS member. *Enrollment:* 1,210 full-time matriculated graduate/professional students (742 women), 2,283 part-time matriculated graduate/professional students (1,594 women). *Enrollment by degree level:* 197 first professional, 3,150 master's, 31 doctoral, 115 other advanced degrees. *Graduate faculty:* 348 full-time, 110 part-time/adjunct. Tuition, state resident: part-time $147 per credit. Tuition, nonresident: part-time $468 per credit. Tuition and fees vary according to campus/location and reciprocity agreements. *Graduate housing:* Rooms and/or apartments available on a first-come, first-served basis to single students and available to married students. Typical cost: $2,688 per year ($5,108 including board) for single students. Room and board charges vary according to board plan and housing facility selected. *Student services:* Campus employment opportunities, campus safety program, career counseling, child daycare facilities, disabled student services, exercise/wellness program, free psychological counseling, grant writing training, international student services, low-cost health insurance, multicultural affairs office, teacher training, writing training. *Library facilities:* John Deaver Drinko Library plus 2 others. *Online resources:* library catalog, web page. *Collection:* 1.4 million titles, 13,405 serial subscriptions, 18,524 audiovisual materials. *Research affiliation:* U.S. Army Corps of Engineers (business practices and field research), West Virginia Department of Transportation.

Computer facilities: 1,330 computers available on campus for general student use. A campuswide network can be accessed from student residence rooms and from off campus. Internet access and online class registration are available. *Web address:* http://www.marshall.edu/.

General Application Contact: Ken O'Neal, Assistant Vice President, Adult Student Services, 304-746-2500 Ext. 1907, Fax: 304-746-1902, E-mail: oneal@marshall.edu.

GRADUATE UNITS

Graduate College Students: 971 full-time (599 women), 2,131 part-time (1,500 women); includes 115 minority (78 African Americans, 22 Asian Americans or Pacific Islanders, 6 Hispanic Americans, 9 Native Americans), 70 international. *Faculty:* 288 full-time (103 women), 102 part-time/adjunct (46 women). Expenses: Contact institution. *Financial support:* Fellowships, research assistantships, teaching assistantships, career-related internships or fieldwork, Federal Work-Study, tuition waivers (full and partial), and unspecified assistantships available. Support available to part-time students. In 2001, 774 master's, 29 other advanced degrees awarded. *Degree program information:* Part-time and evening/weekend programs available. Electronic applications accepted. *Application Contact:* Ken O'Neal, Assistant Vice President, Adult Student Services, 304-746-2500 Ext. 1907, Fax: 304-746-1902, E-mail: oneal@marshall.edu. *Dean,* Dr. Leonard J. Deutsch, 304-696-6606, Fax: 304-696-3316, E-mail: deutschl@marshall.edu.

College of Education and Human Services Students: 460 full-time (304 women), 1,540 part-time (1,183 women); includes 84 minority (62 African Americans, 13 Asian Americans or Pacific Islanders, 3 Hispanic Americans, 6 Native Americans), 28 international. *Faculty:* 70 full-time (28 women), 45 part-time/adjunct (21 women). Expenses: Contact institution. *Financial support:* Career-related internships or fieldwork, Federal Work-Study, tuition waivers (full and partial), and unspecified assistantships available. Support available to part-time students. In 2001, 420 master's, 29 other advanced degrees awarded. *Degree program information:* Evening/weekend programs available. Offers adult and technical education (MS); counseling (MA, Ed S); early childhood education (MA); education (MAT); education and human services (MA, MAT, MS, Ed D, Ed S); education and professional development (MA, Ed D, Ed S); elementary education (MA); exercise science (MS); exercise science, sports and recreation (MS); family and consumer sciences (MA); health and physical education (MS); human development and allied technology (MA, MS); leadership studies (MA, Ed S); reading education (MA, Ed S); school psychology (Ed S); secondary education (MA); special education (MA). *Application Contact:* Ken O'Neal, Assistant Vice President, Adult Student Services, 304-746-2500 Ext. 1907, Fax: 304-746-1902, E-mail: oneal@marshall.edu. *Interim Dean,* Dr. Tony Williams, 304-696-2858, E-mail: williamt@marshall.edu.

College of Fine Arts Students: 14 full-time (4 women), 18 part-time (14 women), 2 international. *Faculty:* 24 full-time (8 women), 4 part-time/adjunct (3 women). Expenses: Contact institution. In 2001, 14 degrees awarded. *Degree program information:* Evening/weekend programs available. Offers art (MA); fine arts (MA); music (MA). *Application Contact:* Ken O'Neal, Assistant Vice President, Adult Student Services, 304-746-2500 Ext. 1907, Fax: 304-746-1902, E-mail: oneal@marshall.edu. *Dean,* Dr. Donald Van Horn, 304-696-6433, E-mail: vanhorn@marshall.edu.

College of Information, Technology and Engineering Students: 60 full-time (19 women), 163 part-time (37 women); includes 10 minority (4 African Americans, 3 Asian Americans or Pacific Islanders, 1 Hispanic American, 2 Native Americans), 15 international. Average age 36. *Faculty:* 15 full-time (1 woman), 13 part-time/adjunct (3 women). Expenses: Contact institution. *Financial support:* Fellowships, tuition waivers (full) available. Support available to part-time students. Financial award application deadline: 8/1; financial award applicants required to submit FAFSA. In 2001, 51 degrees awarded. *Degree program information:* Part-time and evening/weekend programs available. Offers engineering (MSE); environmental science (MS); environmental science and safety technology (MS); information systems (MS); information systems and technology management (MS); information, technology and engineering (MS, MSE); safety (MS); technology management (MS). *Application Contact:* Ken O'Neal, Assistant Vice President, Adult Student Services, 304-746-2500 Ext. 1907, Fax: 304-746-1902, E-mail: oneal@marshall.edu. *Dean,* Dr. James Hooper, 304-696-6204, E-mail: hooper@marshall.edu.

College of Liberal Arts Students: 196 full-time (128 women), 176 part-time (112 women); includes 12 minority (8 African Americans, 2 Asian Americans or Pacific Islanders, 1 Hispanic American, 1 Native American), 6 international. *Faculty:* 78 full-time (34 women), 31 part-time/adjunct (17 women). Expenses: Contact institution. *Financial support:* Fellowships, teaching assistantships with tuition reimbursements available. In 2001, 121 degrees awarded. *Degree program information:* Evening/weekend programs available. Offers clinical psychology (MA); communication studies (MA); criminal justice (MS); English (MA); general psychology (MA); geography (MA, MS); history (MA); humanities (MA); industrial and organizational psychology (MA); liberal arts (MA, MS, Psy D); political science (MA); psychology (Psy D); sociology and anthropology (MA). *Application Contact:* Ken O'Neal, Assistant Vice President, Adult Student Services, 304-746-2500 Ext. 1907, Fax: 304-746-1902, E-mail: oneal@marshall.edu. *Dean,* Dr. Christina Murphy, 304-696-2731, E-mail: murphyc@marshall.edu.

College of Nursing and Health Professions Students: 41 full-time (40 women), 72 part-time (66 women); includes 1 minority (Native American) *Faculty:* 16 full-time (15 women), 2 part-time/adjunct (1 woman). Expenses: Contact institution. In 2001, 52 degrees awarded. Offers communication disorders (MA); nursing (MSN); nursing and health professions (MA, MSN). *Application Contact:* Ken O'Neal, Assistant Vice President, Adult Student Services, 304-746-2500 Ext. 1907, Fax: 304-746-1902, E-mail: oneal@marshall.edu. *Dean,* Dr. Lynne Welch, 304-696-6750, E-mail: welch@marshall.edu.

College of Science Students: 61 full-time (28 women), 27 part-time (14 women); includes 3 minority (1 African American, 2 Asian Americans or Pacific Islanders), 7 international. *Faculty:* 46 full-time (9 women), 2 part-time/adjunct (0 women). Expenses: Contact institution. *Financial support:* Career-related internships or fieldwork available. In 2001, 23 degrees awarded. Offers biological science (MA, MS); chemistry (MS); mathematics (MA, MS); physical science (MS); science (MA, MS). *Application Contact:* Ken O'Neal, Assistant Vice President, Adult Student Services, 304-746-2500 Ext. 1907, Fax: 304-746-1902, E-mail: oneal@marshall.edu. *Dean,* Dr. Ralph Taylor, 304-696-3167, E-mail: taylorr@marshall.edu.

Lewis College of Business Students: 123 full-time (66 women), 115 part-time (63 women); includes 3 African Americans, 2 Asian Americans or Pacific Islanders, 10 international. *Faculty:* 38 full-time (7 women), 4 part-time/adjunct (1 woman). Expenses: Contact institution. *Financial support:* Career-related internships or fieldwork and tuition waivers (full) available. Support available to part-time students. Financial award applicants required to submit FAFSA. In 2001, 86 degrees awarded. *Degree program information:* Part-time and evening/weekend programs available. Offers business (MBA, MS); business administration (MBA); health care administration (MS); industrial and employee relations (MS); management (MBA, MS). *Application deadline:* Applications are processed on a rolling basis. *Application fee:* $0. *Application Contact:* Ken O'Neal, Assistant Vice President, Adult Student Services, 304-746-2500 Ext. 1907, Fax: 304-746-1902, E-mail: oneal@marshall.edu. *Dean,* Dr. Calvin Kent, 304-696-2615, Fax: 304-696-4344, E-mail: kentc@marshall.edu.

School of Journalism and Mass Communications Students: 16 full-time (10 women), 20 part-time (11 women); includes 1 minority (Hispanic American), 2 international. *Faculty:* 5 full-time (1 woman), 1 part-time/adjunct (0 women). Expenses: Contact institution. In 2001, 7 degrees awarded. Offers journalism and mass communications (MAJ). *Application Contact:* Ken O'Neal, Assistant Vice President, Adult Student Services, 304-746-2500 Ext. 1907, Fax: 304-746-1902, E-mail: oneal@marshall.edu. *Director,* Dr. Harold C. Shaver, 304-696-2360, E-mail: shaver@marshall.edu.

Joan C. Edwards School of Medicine Students: 268 full-time (127 women), 1 (woman) part-time; includes 29 minority (5 African Americans, 21 Asian Americans or Pacific Islanders, 2 Hispanic Americans, 1 Native American), 6 international. Average age 25. 1,045 applicants, 8% accepted. *Faculty:* 172 full-time (50 women), 21 part-time/adjunct (9 women). Expenses: Contact institution. *Financial support:* In 2001–02, 186 students received support; research assistantships, career-related internships or fieldwork, Federal Work-Study, institutionally sponsored loans, and scholarships/grants available. Support available to part-time students.

Marshall University (continued)

Financial award application deadline: 5/1; financial award applicants required to submit FAFSA. In 2001, 50 first professional degrees, 18 master's, 2 doctorates awarded. *Degree program information:* Part-time programs available. Offers biomedical sciences (MS, PhD); forensic science (MS); medicine (MD, MS, PhD). *Application deadline:* Applications are processed on a rolling basis. *Application Contact:* Cynthia A. Warren, Assistant Dean for Admissions, 304-691-1738, Fax: 304-691-1744, E-mail: warren@marshall.edu. *Dean and Vice President,* Dr. Charles H. McKown, 304-691-1700, Fax: 304-691-1726.

See in-depth description on page 961.

MARTIN UNIVERSITY, Indianapolis, IN 46218-3867

General Information Independent, coed, comprehensive institution. *Enrollment:* 47 full-time matriculated graduate/professional students (32 women), 37 part-time matriculated graduate/professional students (26 women). *Enrollment by degree level:* 84 master's. *Graduate faculty:* 6 full-time (1 woman), 4 part-time/adjunct (1 woman). *Tuition:* Part-time $275 per credit hour. *Graduate housing:* On-campus housing not available. *Student services:* Campus employment opportunities, career counseling, exercise/wellness program, free psychological counseling, grant writing training, international student services.

Computer facilities: 20 computers available on campus for general student use.

General Application Contact: Sr. Jane Schilling, Vice President, Academic Affairs, 317-543-4890.

GRADUATE UNITS

Division of Psychology Students: 35 full-time (23 women), 17 part-time (13 women); includes 42 minority (all African Americans), 1 international. Average age 41. *Faculty:* 4 full-time (1 woman), 2 part-time/adjunct (1 woman). Expenses: Contact institution. *Financial support:* In 2001–02, 9 students received support. Applicants required to submit FAFSA. In 2001, 11 degrees awarded. *Degree program information:* Part-time and evening/weekend programs available. Offers community psychology (MS). *Application deadline:* Applications are processed on a rolling basis. *Application fee:* $55. *Application Contact:* Brenda Shaheed, Director of Enrollment Management, 317-543-3237, Fax: 317-543-4790, E-mail: rlelder@iupui.edu. *Chairperson,* Dr. Richard L. Elder, 317-917-3321, Fax: 317-543-4790, E-mail: relder@martin.edu.

Graduate School of Urban Ministry Students: 36 full-time (26 women), 1 (woman) part-time; includes 31 minority (all African Americans), 1 international. Average age 38. *Faculty:* 4 full-time (1 woman), 1 part-time/adjunct (0 women). Expenses: Contact institution. *Financial support:* Scholarships/grants and tuition waivers (partial) available. Support available to part-time students. Financial award applicants required to submit FAFSA. In 2001, 7 degrees awarded. *Degree program information:* Part-time and evening/weekend programs available. Offers urban ministry studies (MA). *Application deadline:* Applications are processed on a rolling basis. *Application fee:* $55. *Chair,* Dr. L. Wayne Smith, 317-543-4797, Fax: 317-917-3300.

MARY BALDWIN COLLEGE, Staunton, VA 24401-3610

General Information Independent-religious, coed, primarily women, comprehensive institution. *Enrollment:* 26 full-time matriculated graduate/professional students (20 women), 56 part-time matriculated graduate/professional students (49 women). *Enrollment by degree level:* 82 master's. *Graduate faculty:* 1 (woman) full-time, 29 part-time/adjunct (16 women). *Tuition, area resident:* Part-time $335 per credit hour. *Graduate housing:* On-campus housing not available. *Student services:* Campus employment opportunities, campus safety program, career counseling, international student services, low-cost health insurance, multicultural affairs office, teacher training, writing training. *Library facilities:* Grafton Library. *Online resources:* library catalog, web page, access to other libraries' catalogs. *Collection:* 166,797 titles, 7,000 serial subscriptions, 9,000 audiovisual materials.

Computer facilities: 175 computers available on campus for general student use. A campuswide network can be accessed from student residence rooms and from off campus. Internet access and online class registration are available. *Web address:* http://www.mbc.edu/.

General Application Contact: Dr. Carole Grove, Director, MAT Program, 540-887-7333, Fax: 540-887-7303, E-mail: cgrove@mbc.edu.

GRADUATE UNITS

Graduate Studies Students: 26 full-time (20 women), 56 part-time (49 women); includes 8 minority (7 African Americans, 1 Asian American or Pacific Islander), 1 international. Average age 30. 41 applicants, 85% accepted. *Faculty:* 1 (woman) full-time, 29 part-time/adjunct (16 women). Expenses: Contact institution. *Financial support:* In 2001–02, 43 students received support. Career-related internships or fieldwork and scholarships/grants available. Support available to part-time students. Financial award application deadline: 5/15; financial award applicants required to submit FAFSA. In 2001, 34 degrees awarded. *Degree program information:* Part-time and evening/weekend programs available. Postbaccalaureate distance learning degree programs offered (minimal on-campus study). Offers elementary education (MAT); middle grades education (MAT). *Application deadline:* For fall admission, 7/15; for spring admission, 11/15. Applications are processed on a rolling basis. *Application fee:* $35. *Application Contact:* Lori Allen, Administrative Assistant, E-mail: lallen@mbc.edu. *Director, MAT Program,* Dr. Carole Grove, 540-887-7333, Fax: 540-887-7303, E-mail: cgrove@mbc.edu.

MARYGROVE COLLEGE, Detroit, MI 48221-2599

General Information Independent-religious, coed, primarily women, comprehensive institution. *Enrollment:* 1,269 full-time matriculated graduate/professional students (1,026 women), 154 part-time matriculated graduate/professional students (92 women). *Enrollment by degree level:* 1,423 master's. *Graduate faculty:* 8 full-time (6 women), 32 part-time/adjunct (25 women). *Graduate housing:* On-campus housing not available. *Student services:* Campus employment opportunities, campus safety program, career counseling. *Online resources:* library catalog, access to other libraries' catalogs. *Collection:* 160,230 titles, 550 serial subscriptions.

Computer facilities: 115 computers available on campus for general student use. *Web address:* http://www.marygrove.edu/.

General Application Contact: Dr. Richard-Laurent Barnett, Director of Graduate Studies, 313-864-8000 Ext. 445, Fax: 313-864-6670, E-mail: rlbarnett@marygrove.edu.

GRADUATE UNITS

Graduate Division Students: 1,269 full-time (1,026 women), 154 part-time (92 women); includes 308 minority (305 African Americans, 3 Asian Americans or Pacific Islanders), 1 international. Average age 39. 782 applicants, 92% accepted. *Faculty:* 8 full-time (6 women), 32 part-time/adjunct (25 women). Expenses: Contact institution. *Financial support:* In 2001–02, 258 students received support. Career-related internships or fieldwork available. Support available to part-time students. Financial award applicants required to submit FAFSA. In 2001, 64 degrees awarded. *Degree program information:* Part-time and evening/weekend programs available. Postbaccalaureate distance learning degree programs offered (no on-campus study). Offers educational administration (MA); human resources management (MA); pastoral ministry (MA). *Application fee:* $25. *Application Contact:* Graduate Admissions Adviser, 313-862-8000 Ext. 446, Fax: 313-862-3093. *Dean of Graduate Studies,* Dr. Richard-Laurent Barnett, 313-927-1497, E-mail: rlbarnett@marygrove.edu.

Division of Education Students: 1,104 full-time (887 women), 80 part-time (65 women). Average age 43. 366 applicants, 91% accepted. *Faculty:* 7 full-time (6 women), 27 part-time/adjunct (22 women). Expenses: Contact institution. *Financial support:* Career-related internships or fieldwork available. Support available to part-time students. In 2001, 8 degrees awarded. *Degree program information:* Part-time and evening/weekend programs available. Postbaccalaureate distance learning degree programs offered (no on-campus study). Offers art of teaching (MAT); early childhood education (M Ed); education of the emotionally impaired (M Ed); modern language translation (M Ed); reading education (M Ed); special education (M Ed). *Application fee:* $25. *Application Contact:* Graduate Admissions Adviser, 313-862-8000 Ext. 446, Fax: 313-862-3093. *Chairperson,* Dr. Virginia Jones, 313-862-8000 Ext. 305, Fax: 313-864-6670.

MARYLAND INSTITUTE COLLEGE OF ART, Baltimore, MD 21217-4191

General Information Independent, coed, comprehensive institution. *Enrollment:* 137 full-time matriculated graduate/professional students (86 women), 1 (woman) part-time matriculated graduate/professional student. *Enrollment by degree level:* 129 master's, 9 other advanced degrees. *Graduate faculty:* 13 full-time (8 women), 12 part-time/adjunct (9 women). *Tuition:* Full-time $20,640; part-time $860 per credit. *Required fees:* $440; $220 per term. *Graduate housing:* Rooms and/or apartments available on a first-come, first-served basis to single and married students. Typical cost: $6,880 (including board) for single students; $5,300 per year for married students. Room and board charges vary according to board plan and housing facility selected. Housing application deadline: 5/1. *Student services:* Campus employment opportunities, campus safety program, career counseling, disabled student services, exercise/wellness program, free psychological counseling, grant writing training, international student services, low-cost health insurance, multicultural affairs office, teacher training, writing training. *Library facilities:* Decker Library plus 1 other. *Online resources:* library catalog, web page, access to other libraries' catalogs. *Collection:* 50,000 titles, 305 serial subscriptions, 4,600 audiovisual materials.

Computer facilities: 240 computers available on campus for general student use. A campuswide network can be accessed from student residence rooms and from off campus. Internet access, email are available. *Web address:* http://www.mica.edu/.

General Application Contact: Scott Kelly, Director of Graduate Admission, 410-225-2255, Fax: 410-225-2408, E-mail: micagrad@mica.edu.

GRADUATE UNITS

Graduate Studies Students: 137 full-time (86 women), 1 (woman) part-time; includes 20 minority (13 African Americans, 2 Asian Americans or Pacific Islanders, 5 Hispanic Americans), 21 international. Average age 30. 608 applicants, 21% accepted, 77 enrolled. *Faculty:* 13 full-time (8 women), 12 part-time/adjunct (9 women). Expenses: Contact institution. *Financial support:* In 2001–02, 50 teaching assistantships (averaging $1,200 per year) were awarded; fellowships, career-related internships or fieldwork and scholarships/grants also available. Financial award application deadline: 3/1; financial award applicants required to submit FAFSA. In 2001, 68 master's, 21 other advanced degrees awarded. *Degree program information:* Part-time programs available. Offers art (Certificate); art education (MAT, MFA); digital arts (MA); photography (MFA). *Application deadline:* For fall admission, 3/1; for spring admission, 10/1. *Application fee:* $50. *Dean,* Dr. Leslie King-Hammond, 410-225-2255, Fax: 410-225-2408, E-mail: graduate@mica.edu.

Hoffberger School of Painting Students: 14 full-time (6 women); includes 3 minority (2 African Americans, 1 Hispanic American), 4 international. Average age 30. *Faculty:* 1 (woman) full-time, 1 (woman) part-time/adjunct. Expenses: Contact institution. *Financial support:* In 2001–02, teaching assistantships (averaging $1,200 per year); fellowships, career-related internships or fieldwork and scholarships/grants also available. Financial award application deadline: 3/1; financial award applicants required to submit FAFSA. In 2001, 8 degrees awarded. Offers painting (MFA). *Application deadline:* For fall admission, 3/1. *Application fee:* $50. *Director,* Grace Hartigan, 410-225-2255.

Mount Royal Graduate School of Art Students: 27 full-time (15 women); includes 3 minority (1 African American, 1 Asian American or Pacific Islander, 1 Hispanic American), 3 international. Average age 30. *Faculty:* 1 full-time (0 women), 1 (woman) part-time/adjunct. Expenses: Contact institution. *Financial support:* In 2001–02, teaching assistantships (averaging $1,200 per year); fellowships, career-related internships or fieldwork and scholarships/grants also available. Financial award application deadline: 3/1; financial award applicants required to submit FAFSA. In 2001, 14 degrees awarded. Offers painting (MFA). *Application deadline:* For fall admission, 3/1. *Application fee:* $50. *Coordinator,* Dennis Farber, 410-225-2255.

Rinehart Graduate School of Sculpture Students: 10 full-time (5 women). Average age 30. *Faculty:* 1 (woman) full-time, 1 (woman) part-time/adjunct. Expenses: Contact institution. *Financial support:* In 2001–02, teaching assistantships (averaging $1,200 per year); fellowships, career-related internships or fieldwork and scholarships/grants also available. Financial award application deadline: 3/1; financial award applicants required to submit FAFSA. In 2001, 4 degrees awarded. Offers sculpture (MFA). *Application deadline:* For fall admission, 3/1. *Application fee:* $50. *Director,* Maren Hassinger, 410-225-2271.

MARYLHURST UNIVERSITY, Marylhurst, OR 97036-0261

General Information Independent-religious, coed, comprehensive institution. *Enrollment:* 75 full-time matriculated graduate/professional students (54 women), 195 part-time matriculated graduate/professional students (122 women). *Enrollment by degree level:* 270 master's. *Graduate faculty:* 5 full-time (3 women), 27 part-time/adjunct (14 women). *Tuition:* Full-time $8,235; part-time $305 per credit. *Required fees:* $195; $40 per quarter. Tuition and fees vary according to course load. *Graduate housing:* Room and/or apartments available on a first-come, first-served basis to single students; on-campus housing not available to married students. *Student services:* Campus employment opportunities, campus safety program, career counseling, disabled student services, grant writing training, international student services, low-cost health insurance, writing training. *Library facilities:* Shoen Library. *Online resources:* library catalog, web page, access to other libraries' catalogs. *Collection:* 1,449 audiovisual materials.

Computer facilities: 40 computers available on campus for general student use. A campuswide network can be accessed. Internet access and online class registration are available. *Web address:* http://www.marylhurst.edu/.

General Application Contact: Marylee King, Dean of Admissions, 800-634-9982 Ext. 4430, Fax: 503-635-6585, E-mail: admissions@marylhurst.edu.

GRADUATE UNITS

Graduate Program in Applied Theology Students: 34 full-time (30 women). Average age 40. *Faculty:* 1 full-time (0 women), 4 part-time/adjunct (3 women). Expenses: Contact institution. *Financial support:* In 2001–02, 12 students received support. Federal Work-Study and scholarships/grants available. Support available to part-time students. Financial award application deadline: 5/1; financial award applicants required to submit FAFSA. *Degree program information:* Evening/weekend programs available. Offers theology (MAAT). *Application deadline:* For fall admission, 6/30 (priority date); for winter admission, 11/30 (priority date); for spring admission, 3/30 (priority date). Applications are processed on a rolling basis. *Application fee:* $40 ($50 for international students). *Chair-Religious Studies Department,* Dr. Jerry Roussell, 503-699-6305, Fax: 503-697-5597, E-mail: jroussell@marylhurst.edu.

Graduate Program in Art Therapy Students: 6 full-time (all women), 24 part-time (23 women). Average age 30. *Faculty:* 1 (woman) full-time, 18 part-time/adjunct (17 women). Expenses: Contact institution. *Financial support:* In 2001–02, 30 students received support. Career-related internships or fieldwork, Federal Work-Study, institutionally sponsored loans, and scholarships/grants available. Support available to part-time students. Financial award application deadline: 5/1. *Degree program information:* Part-time programs available. Offers art therapy (MA). *Application deadline:* For fall admission, 2/15 (priority date). Applications are processed on a rolling basis. *Application fee:* $40 ($50 for international students). *Application Contact:* Laurie Perkin, Staff Assistant, 503-699-6244, Fax: 503-636-1957, E-mail: lperkin@marylhurst.edu. *Chairperson,* Christine Turner, 503-699-2244, Fax: 503-636-1957, E-mail: cturner@marylhurst.edu.

Graduate Program in Management Students: 40 full-time (21 women), 118 part-time (57 women). Average age 35. 50 applicants, 96% accepted, 46 enrolled. *Faculty:* 1 full-time (0 women), 21 part-time/adjunct (7 women). Expenses: Contact institution. *Financial support:* In 2001–02, 37 students received support. Federal Work-Study and scholarships/grants available. Support available to part-time students. Financial award applicants required to submit FAFSA. In 2001, 50 degrees awarded. *Degree program information:* Part-time and evening/weekend programs available. Postbaccalaureate distance learning degree programs offered (minimal on-campus study). Offers management (MBA). *Application deadline:* Applications are processed on a rolling basis. *Application fee:* $40 ($50 for international students). *Application Contact:* Ria Gerritsen, Graduate Admissions Advisor, 503-699-6268, E-mail: rgerritsen@marylhurst.edu. *Chair,* Bert Desmond, 503-675-3961, Fax: 503-697-5597, E-mail: mba@marylhurst.edu.

Master of Arts in Interdisciplinary Studies Students: 5 full-time (4 women), 44 part-time (36 women). Average age 42. *Faculty:* 1 (woman) full-time, 5 part-time/adjunct (3 women). Expenses: Contact institution. *Financial support:* In 2001–02, 25 students received support. Federal Work-Study and scholarships/grants available. Support available to part-time students. Financial award applicants required to submit FAFSA. In 2001, 11 degrees awarded. *Degree program information:* Part-time and evening/weekend programs available. Offers gerontology (MA); liberal arts (MA); organizational communications (MA); spiritual traditions (MA). *Application deadline:* Applications are processed on a rolling basis. *Application fee:* $40 ($55 for international students). *Chair,* Dr. Debrah B. Bokowski, 503-636-8141 Ext. 3338, Fax: 503-697-5597, E-mail: dbokowski@marylhurst.edu.

MARYMOUNT UNIVERSITY, Arlington, VA 22207-4299

General Information Independent-religious, coed, comprehensive institution. *Enrollment:* 373 full-time matriculated graduate/professional students (275 women), 902 part-time matriculated graduate/professional students (612 women). *Enrollment by degree level:* 935 master's, 140 other advanced degrees. *Graduate faculty:* 67 full-time (39 women), 58 part-time/adjunct (32 women). *Tuition:* Part-time $512 per credit. *Required fees:* $5 per credit. *Graduate housing:* On-campus housing not available. *Student services:* Campus employment opportunities, campus safety program, career counseling, international student services, low-cost health insurance, teacher training. *Library facilities:* Emerson C. Reinsch Library plus 1 other. *Online resources:* library catalog, access to other libraries' catalogs. *Collection:* 176,986 titles, 1,067 serial subscriptions, 920 audiovisual materials.

Computer facilities: 260 computers available on campus for general student use. A campuswide network can be accessed from off campus. On-line registration for graduate students available. *Web address:* http://www.marymount.edu/.

General Application Contact: Eileen Collins, Director, Graduate Admissions, 703-284-5901, Fax: 703-527-3815, E-mail: admissions@marymount.edu.

GRADUATE UNITS

School of Arts and Sciences Students: 25 full-time (21 women), 67 part-time (38 women); includes 18 minority (6 African Americans, 8 Asian Americans or Pacific Islanders, 4 Hispanic Americans), 19 international. Average age 33. 58 applicants, 97% accepted, 35 enrolled. *Faculty:* 10 full-time (9 women), 6 part-time/adjunct (4 women). Expenses: Contact institution. *Financial support:* Research assistantships with full and partial tuition reimbursements, career-related internships or fieldwork and scholarships/grants available. Support available to part-time students. Financial award applicants required to submit FAFSA. In 2001, 11 degrees awarded. *Degree program information:* Part-time and evening/weekend programs available. Offers arts and sciences (MA, MS, Certificate); computer science (MS, Certificate); humanities (MA); interior design (MA); literature and language (MA). *Application deadline:* Applications are processed on a rolling basis. *Application fee:* $35. Electronic applications accepted. *Dean,* Dr. Rosemary Hubbard, 703-284-1560, Fax: 703-284-3859, E-mail: rosemary.hubbard@marymount.edu.

School of Business Administration Students: 127 full-time (71 women), 588 part-time (364 women); includes 196 minority (113 African Americans, 46 Asian Americans or Pacific Islanders, 36 Hispanic Americans, 1 Native American), 50 international. Average age 35. 264 applicants, 95% accepted, 202 enrolled. *Faculty:* 27 full-time (8 women), 20 part-time/adjunct (4 women). Expenses: Contact institution. *Financial support:* Research assistantships with full tuition reimbursements, career-related internships or fieldwork and scholarships/grants available. Support available to part-time students. Financial award applicants required to submit FAFSA. In 2001, 204 master's, 3 other advanced degrees awarded. *Degree program information:* Part-time and evening/weekend programs available. Offers business administration (MBA); business technologies (MS, Certificate); health care management (MS); human performance systems (MA); human resource management (MA); information management (MS); information resources management (Certificate); instructional design (Certificate); international business (Certificate); leading and managing change (Certificate); legal administration (MA); management studies (Certificate); organization development (MA, Certificate); organizational leadership and innovation (MS); paralegal studies (Certificate). *Application deadline:* Applications are processed on a rolling basis. *Application fee:* $35. Electronic applications accepted. *Dean,* Dr. Robert Sigethy, 703-284-5910, Fax: 703-527-3830, E-mail: robert.sigethy@marymount.edu.

School of Education and Human Services Students: 137 full-time (117 women), 197 part-time (165 women); includes 35 minority (21 African Americans, 1 Asian American or Pacific Islander, 10 Hispanic Americans, 3 Native Americans), 8 international. Average age 33. 120 applicants, 97% accepted, 87 enrolled. *Faculty:* 21 full-time (17 women), 21 part-time/adjunct (16 women). Expenses: Contact institution. *Financial support:* Research assistantships with full tuition reimbursements, career-related internships or fieldwork and scholarships/grants available. Support available to part-time students. Financial award applicants required to submit FAFSA. In 2001, 180 degrees awarded. *Degree program information:* Part-time and evening/weekend programs available. Postbaccalaureate distance learning degree programs offered (minimal on-campus study). Offers alternative licensure certification (Certificate); Catholic school leadership (M Ed); counseling psychology (MA, Certificate); education and human services (M Ed, MA, Certificate); English as a second language (M Ed); forensic psychology (MA); learning disabilities (M Ed); pre-K-6 (M Ed); school counseling (MA); secondary (M Ed). *Application deadline:* Applications are processed on a rolling basis. *Application fee:* $35. Electronic applications accepted. *Dean,* Dr. Wayne Lesko, 703-284-1620, Fax: 703-284-1631, E-mail: wayne.lesko@marymount.edu.

School of Health Professions Students: 84 full-time (66 women), 50 part-time (45 women); includes 46 minority (21 African Americans, 16 Asian Americans or Pacific Islanders, 9 Hispanic Americans), 4 international. Average age 32. 97 applicants, 99% accepted, 37 enrolled. *Faculty:* 8 full-time (7 women), 12 part-time/adjunct (11 women). Expenses: Contact institution. *Financial support:* Research assistantships with full tuition reimbursements, career-related internships or fieldwork and scholarships/grants available. Support available to part-time students. Financial award applicants required to submit FAFSA. In 2001, 48 degrees awarded. *Degree program information:* Part-time and evening/weekend programs available. Offers critical care nursing (MSN, Certificate); family nurse practitioner (MSN, Certificate); health and nursing administration (MSN, Certificate); health professions (MS, MSN, MSPT, Certificate); health promotion management (MS); physical therapy (MSPT). *Application deadline:* Applications are processed on a rolling basis. *Application fee:* $35. Electronic applications accepted. *Acting Dean,* Dr. Tess Cappello, 703-284-1580, Fax: 703-284-3819, E-mail: tess.cappello@marymount.edu.

See in-depth description on page 963.

MARYVILLE UNIVERSITY OF SAINT LOUIS, St. Louis, MO 63141-7299

General Information Independent, coed, comprehensive institution. *Enrollment:* 134 full-time matriculated graduate/professional students (100 women), 396 part-time matriculated graduate/professional students (282 women). *Enrollment by degree level:* 530 master's. *Graduate faculty:* 41 full-time (27 women), 40 part-time/adjunct (21 women). *Tuition:* Full-time $14,400; part-time $408 per credit hour. *Required fees:* $120; $30 per semester. *Graduate housing:* Room and/or apartments available on a first-come, first-served basis to single students; on-campus housing not available to married students. Typical cost: $6,000 (including board). Room and board charges vary according to housing facility selected. *Student services:* Campus employment opportunities, campus safety program, career counseling, disabled student services, exercise/wellness program, free psychological counseling, international student services, low-cost health insurance, multicultural affairs office. *Library facilities:* Maryville University Library. *Online resources:* library catalog, web page, access to other libraries' catalogs. *Collection:* 125,742 titles, 7,721 serial subscriptions, 10,039 audiovisual materials. *Research affiliation:* Monsanto Fund (early childhood, science, mathematics curriculum development and teacher enrichment), Southwestern Bell Foundation (secondary education curriculum and teacher education).

Computer facilities: 260 computers available on campus for general student use. A campuswide network can be accessed from student residence rooms and from off campus. Internet access, e-mail, specialized software are available. *Web address:* http://www.maryville.edu/.

General Application Contact: Dr. Beth Triplett, Vice President for Enrollment, 314-529-9350, Fax: 314-529-9927, E-mail: gradinfo@maryville.du.

GRADUATE UNITS

The John E. Simon School of Business Students: 41 full-time (22 women), 179 part-time (93 women); includes 14 minority (7 African Americans, 4 Asian Americans or Pacific Islanders, 2 Hispanic Americans, 1 Native American), 16 international. Average age 34. 69 applicants, 100% accepted, 63 enrolled. *Faculty:* 13 full-time (6 women), 11 part-time/adjunct (1 woman). Expenses: Contact institution. *Financial support:* Career-related internships or fieldwork, Federal Work-Study, tuition waivers (partial), and campus employment available. Financial award application deadline: 7/31; financial award applicants required to submit FAFSA. In 2001, 60 degrees awarded. *Degree program information:* Part-time and evening/weekend programs available. Offers accounting (MBA, PGC); business studies (PGC); e-business (MBA, PGC); information systems (MBA, PGC); international business (MBA, PGC); management (MBA, PGC); marketing (MBA, PGC). *Application deadline:* Applications are processed on a rolling basis. *Application fee:* $35. Electronic applications accepted. *Application Contact:* Kathy Dougherty, Director of MBA Admissions and Enrollment, 314-529-9382, Fax: 314-529-9975, E-mail: business@marville.edu. *Dean,* Dr. Pamela Horwitz, 314-529-9418, Fax: 314-529-9975, E-mail: horwitz@maryville.edu.

School of Education Students: 45 full-time (35 women), 176 part-time (152 women); includes 16 minority (13 African Americans, 3 Asian Americans or Pacific Islanders), 1 international. Average age 34. 86 applicants, 84% accepted, 53 enrolled. *Faculty:* 10 full-time (6 women), 22 part-time/adjunct (18 women). Expenses: Contact institution. *Financial support:* Career-related internships or fieldwork, Federal Work-Study, tuition waivers (partial), and professional educator discounts available. Financial award application deadline: 7/31; financial award applicants required to submit FAFSA. In 2001, 75 degrees awarded. *Degree program information:* Part-time and evening/weekend programs available. Offers art education (MA Ed); early childhood education (MA Ed); elementary education (MA Ed); environmental education (MA Ed); gifted education (MA Ed); middle grades education (MA Ed); secondary education (MA Ed). *Application deadline:* Applications are processed on a rolling basis. *Application fee:* $20. Electronic applications accepted. *Application Contact:* Jan Horner, Graduate Admissions Coordinator, 314-529-9542, Fax: 314-529-9921, E-mail: teachered@maryville.edu. *Dean,* Dr. Kathe Rasch, 314-529-9466, Fax: 314-529-9921, E-mail: krasch@maryville.edu.

School of Health Professions Students: 48 full-time (43 women), 41 part-time (37 women); includes 2 minority (both African Americans), 1 international. Average age 33. *Faculty:* 18 full-time (15 women), 7 part-time/adjunct (2 women). Expenses: Contact institution. *Financial support:* Career-related internships or fieldwork, Federal Work-Study, and campus employment available. Financial award application deadline: 7/31. In 2001, 89 degrees awarded. *Degree program information:* Part-time and evening/weekend programs available. Offers health administration (MHA); health professions (MARC, MHA, MOT, MPT, MSN); nursing (MSN); occupational therapy (MOT); physical therapy (MPT); rehabilitation counseling (MARC). *Application deadline:* Applications are processed on a rolling basis. Electronic applications accepted. *Application Contact:* School of Health Professions—Graduate Programs, 314-529-9625, Fax: 314-529-9139, E-mail: hlthprofessions@maryville.edu. *Director,* Dr. Lance Carlucci, 314-529-9625, E-mail: lcarlucc@maryville.edu.

MARY WASHINGTON COLLEGE, Fredericksburg, VA 22401-5358

General Information State-supported, coed, comprehensive institution. *Enrollment:* 304 part-time matriculated graduate/professional students (182 women). *Enrollment by degree level:* 304 master's. *Graduate faculty:* 8 full-time (4 women), 23 part-time/adjunct (8 women). Tuition, state resident: part-time $117 per credit. Tuition, nonresident: part-time $395 per credit. Part-time tuition and fees vary according to course load, degree level and program. *Graduate housing:* On-campus housing not available. *Student services:* Campus employment opportunities, career counseling, disabled student services, free psychological counseling, international student services, multicultural affairs office, teacher training. *Library facilities:* Simpson Library. *Online resources:* library catalog, web page, access to other libraries' catalogs. *Collection:* 354,326 titles, 1,713 serial subscriptions, 342 audiovisual materials.

Computer facilities: 238 computers available on campus for general student use. A campuswide network can be accessed from student residence rooms and from off campus. *Web address:* http://www.mwc.edu/.

General Application Contact: Elizabeth P. Harper, Associate Dean of Admissions for Adult Programs, 540-654-1616, Fax: 540-654-2107, E-mail: eharper@mwc.edu.

GRADUATE UNITS

James Monroe Center for Graduate and Professional Studies Average age 35. 119 applicants, 100% accepted, 115 enrolled. *Faculty:* 8 full-time (4 women), 23 part-time/adjunct (8 women). Expenses: Contact institution. *Financial support:* In 2001–02, 46 students received support. Scholarships/grants available. Support available to part-time students. Financial award application deadline: 3/15; financial award applicants required to submit FAFSA. In 2001, 4 degrees awarded. *Degree program information:* Part-time and evening/weekend programs available. Offers liberal studies (MALS). *Application deadline:* For fall admission, 6/1 (priority date); for spring admission, 10/1. *Application fee:* $35. *Application Contact:* Elizabeth P. Harper, Associate Dean of Admissions for Adult Programs, 540-654-1616, Fax: 540-654-2107, E-mail: eharper@mwc.edu. *Vice President for Graduate and Professional Studies and Dean of the Faculty,* Dr. Meta R. Braymer, 540-286-8000, Fax: 540-286-8005, E-mail: mbraymer@mwc.edu.

MARYWOOD UNIVERSITY, Scranton, PA 18509-1598

General Information Independent-religious, coed, comprehensive institution. *Enrollment:* 432 full-time matriculated graduate/professional students (352 women), 838 part-time matriculated graduate/professional students (653 women). *Enrollment by degree level:* 935 master's, 81 doctoral. *Graduate faculty:* 96 full-time (54 women), 92 part-time/adjunct (48 women). *Graduate housing:* Room and/or apartments available to single students; on-campus housing not available to married students. *Student services:* Campus employment opportunities, career counseling, child daycare facilities, disabled student services, exercise/wellness program, free psychological counseling, international student services, teacher training, writing training. *Library facilities:* Learning Resources Center. *Online resources:* library catalog, web page, access to other libraries' catalogs. *Collection:* 219,852 titles, 984 serial subscriptions, 43,717 audiovisual materials.

Computer facilities: 350 computers available on campus for general student use. A campuswide network can be accessed from student residence rooms and from off campus. Internet access and online class registration are available. *Web address:* http://www.marywood.edu/.

General Application Contact: Deborah M. Flynn, Coordinator of Admissions, 570-340-6002, Fax: 570-961-4745, E-mail: gsas_adm@ac.marywood.edu.

GRADUATE UNITS

Graduate School of Arts and Sciences Students: 181 full-time (142 women), 466 part-time (358 women); includes 20 minority (9 African Americans, 6 Asian Americans or Pacific Islanders, 2 Hispanic Americans, 3 Native Americans), 3 international. 271 applicants, 80% accepted. *Faculty:* 80 full-time (42 women), 63 part-time/adjunct (27 women). Expenses: Contact institution. *Financial support:* In 2001–02, 17 research assistantships were awarded; career-related internships or fieldwork, scholarships/grants, and tuition waivers (partial) also available. Support available to part-time students. Financial award application deadline: 2/15; financial award applicants required to submit FAFSA. In 2001, 175 master's, 4 doctorates awarded. *Degree program information:* Part-time and evening/weekend programs available. Offers art education (MA); art therapy (MA); arts and sciences (M Ed, MA, MAT, MBA,

Marywood University (continued)

MFA, MHSA, MPA, MS, PhD, Psy D); church music (MA); communication arts (MA); counseling (MA); counselor education-elementary (MS); counselor education-secondary (MS); criminal justice (MS); early childhood intervention (MS); education (M Ed); elementary education (MAT, MS); finance and investments (MBA); general management (MBA); health services administration (MHSA); human development (PhD); instructional technology (MS); management information systems (MBA, MS); music education (MA); musicology (MA); nutrition and dietetics (MS); psychology (MA); psychology and counseling (Psy D); public administration (MPA); reading education (MS); school leadership (MS); special education (MS); special education administration and supervision (MS); speech language pathology (MS); studio art (MA); visual arts (MFA). *Application deadline:* Applications are processed on a rolling basis. *Application fee:* $20. Electronic applications accepted. *Application Contact:* Deborah M. Flynn, Coordinator of Admissions, 570-340-6002, Fax: 570-961-4745, E-mail: gsas_adm@ac.marywood.edu. *Chairperson*, Dr. Lois King Draina, 570-348-6230, Fax: 570-961-4745.

School of Nursing Expenses: Contact institution. Offers nursing (MS). *Application deadline:* For fall admission, 4/15; for spring admission, 11/15 (priority date). Applications are processed on a rolling basis. *Application fee:* $20. Electronic applications accepted. *Application Contact:* Meghan Cruciani, Coordinator of Admissions, 570-340-6002, Fax: 570-961-4745, E-mail: gsas_adm@ac.maryland.edu. *Chairperson*, Dr. MaryAlice Golden, 570-348-6211 Ext. 2675.

Graduate School of Social Work Students: 194 full-time (164 women), 175 part-time (143 women); includes 19 minority (7 African Americans, 2 Asian Americans or Pacific Islanders, 7 Hispanic Americans, 3 Native Americans), 1 international. 196 applicants, 62% accepted. *Faculty:* 14 full-time (10 women), 29 part-time/adjunct (21 women). Expenses: Contact institution. *Financial support:* In 2001–02, 5 research assistantships were awarded; career-related internships or fieldwork, scholarships/grants, and tuition waivers (partial) also available. Support available to part-time students. Financial award application deadline: 5/1; financial award applicants required to submit FAFSA. In 2001, 149 degrees awarded. *Degree program information:* Part-time and evening/weekend programs available. Offers social work (MSW). *Application deadline:* For fall admission, 5/15; for spring admission, 10/15. *Application fee:* $20. *Application Contact:* Virginia Haskett, Director of Admissions, 717-348-6282, Fax: 717-961-4742. *Dean*, Dr. William Whitaker, 570-348-6282, Fax: 570-348-1817.

See in-depth description on page 965.

MASSACHUSETTS COLLEGE OF ART, Boston, MA 02115-5882

General Information State-supported, coed, comprehensive institution. *Enrollment:* 58 full-time matriculated graduate/professional students (38 women), 46 part-time matriculated graduate/professional students (36 women). *Enrollment by degree level:* 104 master's. *Graduate faculty:* 16 full-time (7 women), 18 part-time/adjunct (13 women). Tuition, state resident: full-time $8,820; part-time $275 per credit. *Required fees:* $950; $10 per credit. $60 per term. *Graduate housing:* On-campus housing not available. *Student services:* Campus employment opportunities, campus safety program, career counseling, free psychological counseling, international student services, low-cost health insurance. *Library facilities:* Morton R. Godine Library. *Collection:* 231,586 titles, 757 serial subscriptions, 125,000 audiovisual materials.

Computer facilities: 250 computers available on campus for general student use. A campuswide network can be accessed from off campus. *Web address:* http://www.massart.edu/.

General Application Contact: Kay Ransdell, Dean for Admissions and Retention, 617-879-7225, Fax: 617-879-7250.

GRADUATE UNITS

Graduate Programs Students: 58 full-time (38 women), 46 part-time (36 women); includes 7 minority (1 African American, 5 Asian Americans or Pacific Islanders, 1 Hispanic American), 16 international. Average age 30. 385 applicants, 19% accepted, 51 enrolled. *Faculty:* 16 full-time (7 women), 18 part-time/adjunct (13 women). Expenses: Contact institution. *Financial support:* In 2001–02, 60 research assistantships (averaging $800 per year), 67 teaching assistantships were awarded. Career-related internships or fieldwork, Federal Work-Study, unspecified assistantships, and clerical/technical assistantships also available. Support available to part-time students. Financial award application deadline: 5/1; financial award applicants required to submit FAFSA. In 2001, 39 degrees awarded. *Degree program information:* Part-time programs available. Offers art education (MSAE); ceramics (MFA); design (MFA); fibers (MFA); film (MFA); glass (MFA); media and performing arts (MFA); metals (MFA); painting (MFA); photography (MFA); printmaking (MFA); sculpture (MFA). *Application deadline:* For fall admission, 2/1. Applications are processed on a rolling basis. *Application fee:* $75. *Application Contact:* Kay Ransdell, Dean for Admissions and Retention, 617-879-7225, Fax: 617-879-7250. *Director*, George Creamer, 617-879-7163, Fax: 617-879-7171, E-mail: creamer@massart.edu.

MASSACHUSETTS COLLEGE OF LIBERAL ARTS, North Adams, MA 01247-4100

General Information State-supported, coed, comprehensive institution. *Graduate housing:* On-campus housing not available.

GRADUATE UNITS

Program in Education *Degree program information:* Part-time and evening/weekend programs available. Offers curriculum and instruction (M Ed); educational administration (M Ed); reading (M Ed); special education (M Ed).

MASSACHUSETTS COLLEGE OF PHARMACY AND HEALTH SCIENCES, Boston, MA 02115-5896

General Information Independent, coed, university. *Enrollment:* 34 full-time matriculated graduate/professional students (15 women), 80 part-time matriculated graduate/professional students (53 women). *Enrollment by degree level:* 98 master's, 16 doctoral. *Graduate faculty:* 20 full-time (2 women), 9 part-time/adjunct (2 women). *Tuition:* Part-time $660 per credit hour. *Graduate housing:* On-campus housing not available. *Student services:* Campus employment opportunities, campus safety program, career counseling, disabled student services, exercise/wellness program, free psychological counseling, grant writing training, international student services, low-cost health insurance, multicultural affairs office, teacher training, writing training. *Library facilities:* Shepard Library. *Online resources:* library catalog, web page, access to other libraries' catalogs. *Collection:* 60,000 titles, 790 serial subscriptions, 750 audiovisual materials. *Research affiliation:* Center for Analytical Science (analytical medicinal chemistry), Center for Brain Sciences (neuropharmacology), Longwood Pharmaceutical Research (analytical chemistry, pharmaceutical manufacturing), Longwood Pharmacology Research (analytical chemistry, pharmacology, toxicology).

Computer facilities: 60 computers available on campus for general student use. A campuswide network can be accessed from student residence rooms and from off campus. Internet access is available. *Web address:* http://www.mcp.edu/.

General Application Contact: Lovie Condrick, Coordinator of Graduate Admissions, 617-732-2986, Fax: 617-732-2801, E-mail: admissions@mcp.edu.

GRADUATE UNITS

Graduate Studies Students: 34 full-time (15 women), 80 part-time (53 women). Average age 30. 77 applicants, 75% accepted, 37 enrolled. *Faculty:* 20 full-time (2 women), 9 part-time/adjunct (2 women). Expenses: Contact institution. *Financial support:* In 2001–02, 2 fellowships with partial tuition reimbursements (averaging $11,000 per year), 2 research assistantships with partial tuition reimbursements (averaging $11,000 per year), 20 teaching assistantships with partial tuition reimbursements (averaging $11,000 per year) were awarded. Scholarships/grants, tuition waivers (partial), unspecified assistantships, and animal caretaker also available. Financial award application deadline: 3/1. In 2001, 4 master's, 2 doctorates awarded. Offers chemistry (MS, PhD); drug regulatory affairs and health policy (MS); pharmaceutical sciences (MS, PhD); pharmacology (MS, PhD); pharmacy and allied health sciences (MS, PhD). *Application deadline:* For fall admission, 3/1 (priority date). *Application fee:* $100. *Application Contact:* Lovie Condrick, Coordinator of Graduate Admissions, 617-732-2986, Fax: 617-732-2801, E-mail: admissions@mcp.edu. *Dean for Research and Graduate Studies*, Dr. Timothy J. Maher, 617-732-2940, Fax: 617-732-2963, E-mail: tmaher@mcp.edu.

MASSACHUSETTS INSTITUTE OF TECHNOLOGY, Cambridge, MA 02139-4307

General Information Independent, coed, university. CGS member. *Enrollment:* 5,596 full-time matriculated graduate/professional students (1,607 women), 178 part-time matriculated graduate/professional students (44 women). *Enrollment by degree level:* 2,611 master's, 3,163 doctoral. *Graduate faculty:* 945 full-time (152 women), 11 part-time/adjunct (2 women). *Tuition:* Full-time $26,960. Full-time tuition and fees vary according to program. *Graduate housing:* Rooms and/or apartments available to single students and available on a first-come, first-served basis to married students. Typical cost: $12,750 (including board) for single students. Housing application deadline: 4/30. *Student services:* Campus employment opportunities, campus safety program, career counseling, child daycare facilities, disabled student services, exercise/wellness program, free psychological counseling, grant writing training, international student services, low-cost health insurance, teacher training, writing training. *Library facilities:* Main library plus 10 others. *Online resources:* library catalog, web page. *Collection:* 2.6 million titles, 20,207 serial subscriptions, 590,664 audiovisual materials. *Research affiliation:* Charles Stark Draper Laboratory (guidance navigation and control, computer science, data and signal processing), Whitehead Institute (developmental biology), Howard Hughes Medical Institute (biomedical research), Dibner Institute for the History of Science and Technology, Northeast Radio Observatory Corporation (radio astronomy).

Computer facilities: 950 computers available on campus for general student use. A campuswide network can be accessed from student residence rooms and from off campus. *Web address:* http://web.mit.edu/.

General Application Contact: Marilee Jones, Dean of Admissions, 617-253-2917, Fax: 617-258-8304, E-mail: mitgrad@mit.edu.

GRADUATE UNITS

Joint Program with Woods Hole Oceanographic Institution in Oceanography/Applied Ocean Science and Engineering Students: 119 full-time (59 women); includes 4 minority (2 African Americans, 2 Asian Americans or Pacific Islanders), 27 international. Average age 27. 125 applicants, 30% accepted, 24 enrolled. *Faculty:* 185 full-time (60 women). Expenses: Contact institution. *Financial support:* In 2001–02, 13 fellowships (averaging $35,948 per year), 69 research assistantships (averaging $35,948 per year) were awarded. Teaching assistantships, institutionally sponsored loans, health care benefits, and unspecified assistantships also available. Financial award application deadline: 1/15. In 2001, 10 master's, 11 doctorates awarded. Offers applied ocean sciences (PhD); biological oceanography (PhD, Sc D); chemical oceanography (PhD, Sc D); civil and environmental and oceanographic engineering (PhD); electrical and oceanographic engineering (PhD); geochemistry (PhD); geophysics (PhD); marine biology (PhD); marine geochemistry (PhD, Sc D); marine geology (PhD, Sc D); marine geophysics (PhD); mechanical and oceanographic engineering (PhD); ocean engineering (PhD); oceanographic engineering (M Eng, MS, PhD, Sc D, Eng); paleoceanography (PhD); physical oceanography (PhD, Sc D). MS, PhD, and Sc D offered jointly with Woods Hole Oceanographic Institution. *Application deadline:* For fall admission, 1/15 (priority date). *Application fee:* $60. Electronic applications accepted. *Application Contact:* Ronni Schwartz, Administrator, 617-253-7544, Fax: 617-253-9784, E-mail: mspiggy@mit.edu. *Director*, Prof. Paola Rizzoli, 617-253-2451, E-mail: rizzoli@mit.edu.

Operations Research Center Students: 47 full-time (14 women); includes 1 minority (African American), 25 international. Average age 22. 117 applicants, 20% accepted. *Faculty:* 44 full-time (2 women). Expenses: Contact institution. *Financial support:* In 2001–02, 45 students received support, including 10 fellowships (averaging $14,670 per year), 29 research assistantships (averaging $14,670 per year), 6 teaching assistantships (averaging $14,670 per year); Federal Work-Study, institutionally sponsored loans, scholarships/grants, and tuition waivers also available. Financial award application deadline: 12/31. In 2001, 10 master's, 4 doctorates awarded. Offers operations research (SM, PhD). *Application deadline:* For fall admission, 12/31. *Application fee:* $60. Electronic applications accepted. *Application Contact:* Laura A. Rose, Admissions Coordinator, 617-253-9303, Fax: 617-258-9214, E-mail: lrose@mit.edu. *Co-Director*, Dr. James B. Orlin, 617-253-6606, Fax: 617-258-9214, E-mail: jorlin@mit.edu.

School of Architecture and Planning Students: 539 full-time (245 women), 25 part-time (13 women); includes 67 minority (21 African Americans, 34 Asian Americans or Pacific Islanders, 12 Hispanic Americans), 222 international. *Faculty:* 88 full-time (21 women), 44 part-time/adjunct (12 women). Expenses: Contact institution. *Financial support:* Fellowships, research assistantships, teaching assistantships, career-related internships or fieldwork, Federal Work-Study, institutionally sponsored loans, scholarships/grants, and tuition waivers (partial) available. In 2001, 147 master's, 34 doctorates awarded. Offers architecture (M Arch, SM Arch S, SM Vis S, SMBT, PhD); architecture and planning (M Arch, MCP, MS, MSRED, SM Arch S, SM Vis S, SMBT, PhD); city planning (MCP); media arts and sciences (MS, PhD); urban and regional planning (PhD); urban and regional studies (PhD); urban studies and planning (MS). *Application fee:* $60. *Dean*, William J. Mitchell, 617-253-4402, Fax: 617-253-9417.

Center for Real Estate Students: 28 full-time (12 women); includes 2 minority (both African Americans), 10 international. Average age 30. *Faculty:* 8 full-time (3 women), 1 part-time/adjunct (0 women). Expenses: Contact institution. *Financial support:* In 2001–02, 8 fellowships were awarded In 2001, 30 degrees awarded. Offers real estate (MSRED). *Application deadline:* For fall admission, 2/15. *Application fee:* $60. *Application Contact:* Maria Vieira, Associate Director of Education, 617-253-4373. *Director*, William C. Wheaton, 617-253-4373, Fax: 617-258-6991.

School of Engineering Students: 2,584 full-time (593 women), 14 part-time (3 women); includes 402 minority (54 African Americans, 291 Asian Americans or Pacific Islanders, 53 Hispanic Americans, 4 Native Americans), 1,023 international. Average age 23. 5,523 applicants, 30% accepted, 830 enrolled. *Faculty:* 343 full-time (35 women), 5 part-time/adjunct (0 women). Expenses: Contact institution. *Financial support:* In 2001–02, 2,378 students received support, including 588 fellowships, 1,624 research assistantships, 272 teaching assistantships; career-related internships or fieldwork, Federal Work-Study, institutionally sponsored loans, scholarships/grants, traineeships, health care benefits, and unspecified assistantships also available. Financial award applicants required to submit FAFSA. In 2001, 872 master's, 243 doctorates awarded. Offers aeronautics and astronautics (M Eng, SM, PhD, Sc D, EAA); bioengineering (PhD); biomedical engineering (M Eng); chemical engineering (SM, PhD, Sc D); civil and environmental engineering (M Eng, SM, PhD, Sc D, CE, EE); computer science (EE); electrical engineering (EE); electrical engineering and computer science (M Eng, SM, PhD, Sc D); engineering (M Eng, MST, SM, PhD, Sc D, CE, EAA, EE, EE, Mat E, Mech E, Met E, NE, Naval E, Ocean E); materials engineering (Mat E); materials science and engineering (SM, PhD, Sc D); mechanical engineering (SM, PhD, Sc D, Mech E); metallurgical engineering (Met E); naval architecture and marine engineering (SM); naval engineering (Naval E); nuclear engineering (SM, PhD, Sc D, NE); nuclear systems engineering (M Eng); ocean engineering (M Eng, SM, PhD, Sc D, Ocean E); ocean systems management (SM); radiological health and industrial radiation engineering (M Eng); radiological sciences (PhD, Sc D); toxicology (SM, PhD, Sc D). *Application fee:* $60. Electronic applications accepted. *Dean*, Thomas L. Magnanti, 617-253-6604, Fax: 617-253-8549, E-mail: magnanti@mit.edu.

Engineering Systems Division Students: 133 full-time (37 women); includes 10 minority (9 Asian Americans or Pacific Islanders, 1 Hispanic American), 71 international. Average age 28. 219 applicants, 52% accepted, 64 enrolled. Expenses: Contact institution. *Financial support:* In 2001–02, 116 students received support, including 6 fellowships, 69 research assistantships, 15 teaching assistantships; career-related internships or fieldwork, Federal Work-Study, institutionally sponsored loans, scholarships/grants, health care benefits, and unspecified assistantships also available. Financial award applicants required to submit FAFSA. In 2001, 75 master's, 9 doctorates awarded. Offers engineering and management (SM); engineering systems (M Eng, MST, SM, PhD); logistics (M Eng); manufacturing); technology and policy (SM, PhD); transportation (MST, PhD). *Associate Dean for Engineering Systems*, Prof. Daniel Roos, 617-253-1661, Fax: 617-258-7733.

School of Humanities, Arts and Social Sciences Students: 323 full-time (135 women); includes 30 minority (4 African Americans, 22 Asian Americans or Pacific Islanders, 3 Hispanic Americans, 1 Native American), 129 international. *Faculty:* 93 full-time (20 women), 18 part-time/adjunct (7 women). Expenses: Contact institution. *Financial support:* Fellowships, research assistantships, teaching assistantships, Federal Work-Study and institutionally sponsored loans available. Support available to part-time students. In 2001, 15 master's, 54 doctorates awarded. Offers comparative media studies (SM); economics (MA, PhD); history and social study of science and technology (PhD); humanities, arts and social science (MA, SM, PhD); linguistics (PhD); philosophy (PhD); political science (SM, PhD). *Application deadline:* For fall admission, 1/15. *Application Contact:* Graduate Admissions Office, 617-253-4897. *Dean,* Philip S. Khoury, 617-253-3450.

School of Science Students: 1,025 full-time (326 women), 7 part-time (1 woman); includes 92 minority (16 African Americans, 59 Asian Americans or Pacific Islanders, 14 Hispanic Americans, 3 Native Americans), 347 international. Average age 25. 2,373 applicants, 20% accepted, 201 enrolled. *Faculty:* 259 full-time (32 women), 1 part-time/adjunct (0 women). Expenses: Contact institution. *Financial support:* In 2001–02, 1,030 students received support, including 236 fellowships, 468 research assistantships (averaging $21,600 per year), 190 teaching assistantships (averaging $16,650 per year); Federal Work-Study, institutionally sponsored loans, scholarships/grants, health care benefits, and unspecified assistantships also available. Financial award applicants required to submit FAFSA. In 2001, 30 master's, 144 doctorates awarded. Offers atmospheric chemistry (PhD, Sc D); atmospheric science (SM, PhD, Sc D); biochemistry (PhD); biological chemistry (PhD, Sc D); biological oceanography (PhD); biophysical chemistry and molecular structure (PhD); cellular/molecular neuroscience (PhD); climate physics and chemistry (PhD, Sc D); cognitive neuroscience (PhD); cognitive science (PhD); computational cognitive science (PhD); computational neuroscience (PhD); developmental biology (PhD); earth and planetary sciences (SM); genetics (PhD); genetics/microbiology (PhD); geochemistry (PhD, Sc D); geology (PhD, Sc D); geophysics (PhD, Sc D); geosystems (SM); immunology (PhD); inorganic chemistry (PhD, Sc D); mathematics (PhD); neurobiology (PhD); oceanography (SM, PhD, Sc D); organic chemistry (PhD, Sc D); physical chemistry (PhD, Sc D); physics (SM, PhD); planetary sciences (PhD, Sc D); science (SM, PhD, Sc D); systems neuroscience (PhD). *Application fee:* $60. Electronic applications accepted. *Application Contact:* Graduate Admissions Office, 617-253-2917, Fax: 617-253-9894. *Dean,* Robert J. Silbey, 617-253-8900.

Sloan School of Management Students: 733 full-time (194 women); includes 135 minority (23 African Americans, 93 Asian Americans or Pacific Islanders, 19 Hispanic Americans), 260 international. Average age 28. 2,940 applicants, 18% accepted, 372 enrolled. *Faculty:* 91 full-time (15 women), 5 part-time/adjunct (0 women). Expenses: Contact institution. *Financial support:* Fellowships with tuition reimbursements, research assistantships with tuition reimbursements, teaching assistantships with tuition reimbursements, institutionally sponsored loans available. Postbaccalaureate distance learning degree programs offered. Offers management (MBA, MS, SM, PhD). *Application fee:* $175 ($200 for international students). Electronic applications accepted. *Application Contact:* Rod Garcia, Director of Admissions, MBA Program, 617-253-0272, Fax: 617-253-6405, E-mail: mbaadmissions@sloan.mit.edu. *Dean,* Richard L. Schmalensee, 617-253-2957, Fax: 617-258-6617, E-mail: rschmal@mit.edu.

Whitaker College of Health Sciences and Technology Offers health sciences and technology (MD, SM, PhD, Sc D); medical engineering (PhD); medical engineering and medical physics (Sc D); medical informatics (SM); medical physics (PhD); medical sciences (MD); speech and hearing bioscience and technology (PhD, Sc D).

MASSACHUSETTS SCHOOL OF LAW AT ANDOVER, Andover, MA 01810

General Information Independent, coed, graduate-only institution. *Enrollment by degree level:* 500 first professional. *Graduate faculty:* 20 full-time (10 women), 65 part-time/adjunct (25 women). *Tuition:* Full-time $12,300; part-time $410 per credit. *Graduate housing:* On-campus housing not available. *Student services:* Campus employment opportunities, campus safety program, career counseling, disabled student services, free psychological counseling, low-cost health insurance, multicultural affairs office, writing training. *Library facilities:* Law Library plus 1 other. *Online resources:* library catalog, web page, access to other libraries' catalogs.

Computer facilities: 30 computers available on campus for general student use. A campuswide network can be accessed from student residence rooms and from off campus. Internet access, westlaw/LexisNexis are available. *Web address:* http://www.mslaw.edu/.

General Application Contact: Paula M. Colby-Clements, Director of Admissions, 978-681-0800, Fax: 978-681-6330, E-mail: pcolby@mslaw.edu.

GRADUATE UNITS

Professional Program Students: 250 full-time (125 women), 250 part-time (125 women). *Faculty:* 20 full-time (10 women), 65 part-time/adjunct (25 women). Expenses: Contact institution. Offers law (JD). *Application Contact:* Paula M. Colby-Clements, Director of Admissions, 978-681-0800, Fax: 978-681-6330, E-mail: pcolby@mslaw.edu.

MASSACHUSETTS SCHOOL OF PROFESSIONAL PSYCHOLOGY, Boston, MA 02132

General Information Independent, coed, graduate-only institution. *Enrollment by degree level:* 150 doctoral. *Graduate faculty:* 36 part-time/adjunct (13 women). *Tuition:* Full-time $20,260; part-time $633 per credit. *Graduate housing:* On-campus housing not available. *Student services:* Campus employment opportunities, career counseling, international student services, writing training. *Library facilities:* Mintz Library plus 1 other. *Online resources:* library catalog. *Collection:* 5,500 titles, 59 serial subscriptions, 132 audiovisual materials.

Computer facilities: 10 computers available on campus for general student use. A campuswide network can be accessed. Internet access is available. *Web address:* http://www.mspp.edu/.

General Application Contact: Katie Phalan, Admissions Coordinator, 617-327-6777, Fax: 617-627-4447, E-mail: admissions@mspp.edu.

GRADUATE UNITS

Graduate Program Students: 114 full-time (95 women), 36 part-time (30 women); includes 13 minority (1 African American, 8 Asian Americans or Pacific Islanders, 3 Hispanic Americans, 1 Native American), 17 international. Average age 28. 182 applicants, 43% accepted, 44 enrolled. *Faculty:* 36 part-time/adjunct (13 women). Expenses: Contact institution. *Financial support:* In 2001–02, 93 students received support, including 12 teaching assistantships (averaging $2,500 per year); career-related internships or fieldwork, institutionally sponsored loans, and scholarships/grants also available. Financial award application deadline: 2/8; financial award applicants required to submit FAFSA. In 2001, 36 degrees awarded. *Degree program information:* Part-time programs available. Offers clinical psychology (Psy D, Certificate); clinical psychopharmacology (Post-Doctoral MS). *Application deadline:* For fall admission, 1/11. *Application fee:* $50. *Application Contact:* 617-327-6777, Fax: 617-327-4447, E-mail: admissions@mspp.edu. *President,* Dr. Bruce J. Weiss, 617-327-6777, Fax: 617-327-4447.

THE MASTER'S COLLEGE AND SEMINARY, Santa Clarita, CA 91321-1200

General Information Independent-religious, coed, comprehensive institution. *Enrollment:* 191 full-time matriculated graduate/professional students, 134 part-time matriculated graduate/professional students. *Enrollment by degree level:* 261 first professional, 35 master's, 16 other advanced degrees. *Graduate faculty:* 17 full-time (0 women), 11 part-time/adjunct (0 women). *Tuition:* Part-time $250 per unit. *Graduate housing:* On-campus housing not available. *Student services:* Campus employment opportunities, campus safety program, career counseling, international student services, low-cost health insurance, writing training. *Library facilities:* Powell Library plus 1 other. *Online resources:* library catalog, web page, access to other libraries' catalogs. *Collection:* 106,701 titles, 1,450 serial subscriptions, 10,326 audiovisual materials.

Computer facilities: 57 computers available on campus for general student use. A campuswide network can be accessed from student residence rooms. Internet access is available. *Web address:* http://www.masters.edu/.

General Application Contact: Richard Oliver, Director of Admissions and Placement, 818-792-6488, Fax: 818-909-5725, E-mail: cwahler@tms.edu.

GRADUATE UNITS

The Master's Seminary Students: 191 full-time (0 women), 134 part-time; includes 47 minority (8 African Americans, 28 Asian Americans or Pacific Islanders, 10 Hispanic Americans, 1 Native American), 20 international. Average age 29. 131 applicants, 77% accepted, 92 enrolled. *Faculty:* 17 full-time (0 women), 11 part-time/adjunct (0 women). Expenses: Contact institution. *Financial support:* In 2001–02, 97 students received support. Career-related internships or fieldwork and scholarships/grants available. Support available to part-time students. Financial award application deadline: 6/1. In 2001, 71 first professional degrees, 8 master's awarded. Offers biblical counseling (MABC); new testament (Th D); old testament (Th D); theology (M Div, M Th, Th D). *Application deadline:* For fall admission, 6/1 (priority date); for winter admission, 10/1 (priority date); for spring admission, 1/1. Applications are processed on a rolling basis. *Application fee:* $30. *Application Contact:* Richard Oliver, Director of Admissions and Placement, 818-792-6488, Fax: 818-909-5725, E-mail: cwahler@tms.edu. *Senior Vice President and Dean,* Dr. Richard L. Mayhue, 818-782-6488 Ext. 5632, E-mail: ttenpas@tms.edu.

MAYO GRADUATE SCHOOL, Rochester, MN 55905

General Information Independent, coed, graduate-only institution. *Enrollment by degree level:* 119 doctoral. *Graduate faculty:* 236 full-time (34 women). *Tuition:* Full-time $17,900. *Graduate housing:* On-campus housing not available. *Student services:* Campus safety program, career counseling, free psychological counseling, grant writing training, international student services, low-cost health insurance, writing training. *Library facilities:* Plummer Library plus 7 others. *Online resources:* library catalog, web page, access to other libraries' catalogs. *Collection:* 348,845 titles, 4,284 serial subscriptions, 16,293 audiovisual materials.

Computer facilities: A campuswide network can be accessed from off campus. Internet access is available. *Web address:* http://www.mayo.edu/mgs/gs.html.

General Application Contact: Melissa L. Berg, Admissions Coordinator, 507-538-1160, Fax: 507-284-0999, E-mail: phd.training@mayo.edu.

GRADUATE UNITS

Graduate Programs in Biomedical Sciences Students: 119 full-time (66 women); includes 22 minority (1 African American, 3 Asian Americans or Pacific Islanders, 18 Hispanic Americans), 40 international. Average age 26. *Faculty:* 236 full-time (34 women). Expenses: Contact institution. *Financial support:* In 2001–02, 97 students received support, including 97 fellowships with full tuition reimbursements available; tuition waivers (full) also available. In 2001, 25 doctorates awarded. Offers biochemistry (PhD); biomedical engineering (PhD); biomedical sciences (PhD); immunology (PhD); molecular biology (PhD); molecular neuroscience (PhD); pharmacology (PhD); tumor biology (PhD). *Application deadline:* For fall admission, 12/31 (priority date). Applications are processed on a rolling basis. *Application fee:* $0. Electronic applications accepted. *Application Contact:* Melissa L. Berg, Admissions Coordinator, 507-538-1160, Fax: 507-284-0999, E-mail: phd.training@mayo.edu. *Dean,* Dr. Paul J. Leibson, 507-538-1160, Fax: 507-284-0999.

MAYO MEDICAL SCHOOL, Rochester, MN 55905

General Information Independent, coed, graduate-only institution. *Enrollment by degree level:* 165 first professional. *Graduate faculty:* 2,100. *Tuition:* Full-time $20,500. *Graduate housing:* On-campus housing not available. *Student services:* Campus employment opportunities, campus safety program, career counseling, disabled student services, exercise/wellness program, free psychological counseling, low-cost health insurance, multicultural affairs office, writing training. *Library facilities:* Plummer Medical Library plus 4 others. *Online resources:* library catalog. *Collection:* 337,000 titles, 4,250 serial subscriptions.

Computer facilities: A campuswide network can be accessed from off campus. Internet access is available. *Web address:* http://www.mayo.edu/education/mms/MMS_Home_Page.html.

General Application Contact: Barbara L. Porter, Assistant Dean for Student Affairs, 507-284-0916, Fax: 507-284-2634, E-mail: porter.barbara@mayo.edu.

GRADUATE UNITS

Professional Program Students: 165 full-time (93 women); includes 157 minority (15 African Americans, 17 Asian Americans or Pacific Islanders, 123 Hispanic Americans, 2 Native Americans) Average age 24. 2,828 applicants, 1% accepted. *Faculty:* 2,100. Expenses: Contact institution. *Financial support:* In 2001–02, 160 students received support. Institutionally sponsored loans, scholarships/grants, and health care benefits available. Financial award application deadline: 5/1; financial award applicants required to submit FAFSA. In 2001, 40 degrees awarded. Offers medicine (MD). MD offered through the Mayo Foundation's Division of Education. *Application deadline:* For fall admission, 11/1. Applications are processed on a rolling basis. *Application fee:* $60. *Application Contact:* Barbara L. Porter, Assistant Dean for Student Affairs, 507-284-0916, Fax: 507-284-2634, E-mail: porter.barbara@mayo.edu. *Dean,* Dr. Anthony J. Windebank.

MAYO SCHOOL OF HEALTH SCIENCES, Rochester, MN 55905

General Information Independent, coed, upper-level institution. *Enrollment:* 199 full-time matriculated graduate/professional students (117 women). *Enrollment by degree level:* 199 master's. *Graduate faculty:* 4 full-time (1 woman), 7 part-time/adjunct (4 women). *Tuition:* Full-time $2,875. Tuition and fees vary according to program and student level. *Student services:* Campus employment opportunities, campus safety program, career counseling, exercise/wellness program, free psychological counseling, low-cost health insurance, multicultural affairs office. *Library facilities:* Mayo Medical Library plus 3 others.

Computer facilities: A campuswide network can be accessed from off campus. Internet access is available. *Web address:* http://www.mayo.edu/hrs/hrs.htm.

General Application Contact: Valerie Eggers, Administrative Secretary, 507-284-3293.

GRADUATE UNITS

Program in Nurse Anesthesia Students: 90 full-time (46 women); includes 10 minority (2 African Americans, 4 Asian Americans or Pacific Islanders, 3 Hispanic Americans, 1 Native American) Average age 30. 112 applicants, 30 enrolled. *Faculty:* 2 part-time/adjunct (1 woman). Expenses: Contact institution. *Financial support:* Scholarships/grants and stipends available. In 2001, 30 degrees awarded. Offers nurse anesthesia (MNA). *Application deadline:* For fall admission, 10/15. Applications are processed on a rolling basis. *Application fee:* $50. *Application Contact:* Val Martin, Information Contact, 507-284-3678, Fax: 507-284-0656. *Director,* Mary E. Marienau, 507-284-3293, Fax: 507-284-0656, E-mail: marienau.mary@mayo.edu.

Program in Physical Therapy Students: 103 full-time; includes 1 Asian American or Pacific Islander *Faculty:* 4 full-time (0 women), 2 part-time/adjunct (both women). Expenses: Contact institution. In 2001, 35 degrees awarded. Offers physical therapy (MPT). *Application deadline:* For winter admission, 1/15. *Application fee:* $50. *Application Contact:* Rosalie Fountain, Secretary, 507-284-2054, E-mail: fountain.rosalie@mayo.edu. *Director,* Dr. John P. Cummings, 507-284-8487.

MCCORMICK THEOLOGICAL SEMINARY, Chicago, IL 60637-1693

General Information Independent-religious, coed, graduate-only institution. *Enrollment by degree level:* 165 first professional, 27 master's, 292 doctoral, 1 other advanced degree. *Graduate faculty:* 22 full-time (7 women), 29 part-time/adjunct (12 women). *Tuition:* Part-time $775 per credit hour. Tuition and fees vary according to degree level. *Graduate housing:* Rooms and/or apartments available on a first-come, first-served basis to single and married students. Typical cost: $2,700 per year for single students; $5,400 per year for married

McCormick Theological Seminary (continued)

students. Housing application deadline: 7/1. *Student services:* Campus employment opportunities, campus safety program, career counseling, free psychological counseling, grant writing training, international student services, low-cost health insurance, multicultural affairs office, writing training. *Library facilities:* Jesuit-Krauss-McCormick Library. *Online resources:* library catalog, web page, access to other libraries' catalogs. *Collection:* 349,087 titles, 983 serial subscriptions, 1,378 audiovisual materials.

Computer facilities: Internet access is available. *Web address:* http://www.mccormick.edu/.

General Application Contact: Rev. Craig Howard, Director of Recruitment and Admissions, 773-947-6314, Fax: 773-947-6273, E-mail: choward@mccormick.edu.

GRADUATE UNITS

Graduate and Professional Programs Students: 392 full-time (116 women), 93 part-time (48 women); includes 145 minority (81 African Americans, 32 Asian Americans or Pacific Islanders, 32 Hispanic Americans), 153 international. Average age 36. 193 applicants, 82% accepted. *Faculty:* 22 full-time (7 women), 29 part-time/adjunct (12 women). Expenses: Contact institution. *Financial support:* In 2001–02, 4 fellowships were awarded; teaching assistantships, career-related internships or fieldwork, Federal Work-Study, and scholarships/grants also available. Support available to part-time students. Financial award application deadline: 5/30; financial award applicants required to submit FAFSA. In 2001, 33 first professional degrees, 21 master's, 88 doctorates, 3 other advanced degrees awarded. Offers ministry (D Min); theological studies (MATS, Certificate); theology (M Div). *Application deadline:* For fall admission, 8/6. Applications are processed on a rolling basis. *Application fee:* $30. *Application Contact:* Rev. Craig Howard, Director of Recruitment and Admissions, 773-947-6314, Fax: 773-947-6273, E-mail: choward@mccormick.edu. *Vice President for Academic Affairs,* Dr. David Esterline, 773-947-6306, E-mail: desterline@mccormick.edu.

MCDANIEL COLLEGE, Westminster, MD 21157-4390

General Information Independent, coed, comprehensive institution. *Enrollment:* 145 full-time matriculated graduate/professional students (106 women), 1,338 part-time matriculated graduate/professional students (1,039 women). *Enrollment by degree level:* 1,483 master's. *Graduate faculty:* 26 full-time (13 women), 96 part-time/adjunct (61 women). *Tuition:* Part-time $240 per course. *Required fees:* $315 per year. Tuition and fees vary according to campus/location. *Graduate housing:* On-campus housing not available. *Student services:* Campus safety program, career counseling, disabled student services, free psychological counseling, international student services, multicultural affairs office. *Library facilities:* Hoover Library. *Online resources:* library catalog, web page. *Collection:* 214,259 titles, 1,090 serial subscriptions, 9,968 audiovisual materials.

Computer facilities: 162 computers available on campus for general student use. A campuswide network can be accessed from student residence rooms and from off campus. Internet access is available. *Web address:* http://www.wmdc.edu/.

General Application Contact: Dr. Kenneth W. Pool, Dean of Graduate Affairs, 410-857-2500, Fax: 410-857-2515, E-mail: kpool@wmdc.edu.

GRADUATE UNITS

Graduate Studies Students: 145 full-time (106 women), 1,338 part-time (1,039 women); includes 106 minority (77 African Americans, 9 Asian Americans or Pacific Islanders, 18 Hispanic Americans, 2 Native Americans), 10 international. Average age 34. 172 applicants, 100% accepted, 112 enrolled. *Faculty:* 26 full-time (13 women), 96 part-time/adjunct (61 women). Expenses: Contact institution. *Financial support:* In 2001–02, 36 students received support. Career-related internships or fieldwork, institutionally sponsored loans, and scholarships/grants available. Support available to part-time students. Financial award application deadline: 3/1; financial award applicants required to submit FAFSA. In 2001, 399 degrees awarded. *Degree program information:* Part-time and evening/weekend programs available. Offers education of the deaf (MS); educational administration (MS); elementary and secondary education (MS); guidance and counseling (MS); human resources development (MS); liberal studies (MLA); media/library science (MS); physical education (MS); reading education (MS); sensory impairment (MS); special education (MS). *Application deadline:* Applications are processed on a rolling basis. *Application fee:* $40. *Application Contact:* Crystal L. Perry, Administrator of Graduate Records, 410-857-2513, Fax: 410-857-2515, E-mail: cperry@wmdc.edu. *Dean of Graduate Affairs,* Dr. Kenneth W. Pool, 410-857-2500, Fax: 410-857-2515, E-mail: kpool@wmdc.edu.

MCGILL UNIVERSITY, Montréal, QC H3A 2T5, Canada

General Information Independent, coed, university. *Enrollment:* 4,596 full-time matriculated graduate/professional students, 1,017 part-time matriculated graduate/professional students. *Graduate faculty:* 5,213. *Graduate tuition:* Tuition charges are reported in Canadian dollars. *Tuition:* Full-time $9,073 Canadian dollars. *Graduate housing:* Rooms and/or apartments available to single and married students. *Student services:* Campus employment opportunities, career counseling, child daycare facilities, disabled student services, free psychological counseling, international student services, low-cost health insurance. *Library facilities:* Humanities and Social Sciences Library plus 16 others. *Online resources:* library catalog, web page, access to other libraries' catalogs. *Collection:* 3 million titles, 15,919 serial subscriptions, 553,469 audiovisual materials.

Computer facilities: 1,500 computers available on campus for general student use. A campuswide network can be accessed from student residence rooms and from off campus. Internet access and online class registration are available. *Web address:* http://www.mcgill.ca/.

General Application Contact: Dr. Pierre Belanger, Dean, Faculty of Graduate Studies and Research, 514-398-3991, Fax: 514-398-8257.

GRADUATE UNITS

Faculty of Graduate Studies and Research Students: 4,596 full-time, 1,017 part-time. 3,947 applicants, 57% accepted. Expenses: Contact institution. *Financial support:* Fellowships, research assistantships, teaching assistantships, career-related internships or fieldwork, Federal Work-Study, institutionally sponsored loans, and tuition waivers (full and partial) available. Support available to part-time students. In 2001, 1,325 master's, 351 doctorates awarded. *Degree program information:* Part-time and evening/weekend programs available. *Application deadline:* Applications are processed on a rolling basis. *Application Contact:* Charlotte E. Légaré, Information Contact. *Dean,* Dr. Pierre Belanger, 514-398-3991, Fax: 514-398-8257.

Faculty of Agricultural and Environmental Sciences Students: 335 full-time (168 women), 4 part-time (3 women), 101 international. Average age 28. 228 applicants, 61% accepted. *Faculty:* 93 full-time (22 women), 46 part-time/adjunct (9 women). Expenses: Contact institution. *Financial support:* In 2001–02, fellowships (averaging $9,000 per year), 55 research assistantships (averaging $10,800 per year), 84 teaching assistantships (averaging $1,300 per year) were awarded. Career-related internships or fieldwork, institutionally sponsored loans, scholarships/grants, and tuition waivers also available. In 2001, 65 master's, 33 doctorates, 28 other advanced degrees awarded. *Degree program information:* Part-time programs available. Offers agricultural and environmental sciences (M Sc, M Sc A, PhD, Certificate); agricultural economics (M Sc, PhD); agrometeorology (M Sc, PhD); animal science (M Sc, M Sc A, PhD); biotechnology (Certificate); computer applications (M Sc, M Sc A, PhD); dietetics and human nutrition (M Sc, M Sc A, PhD); entomology (M Sc, PhD); food engineering (M Sc, M Sc A, PhD); food science and agricultural chemistry (M Sc, PhD); forest science (M Sc, PhD); grain drying (M Sc, M Sc A, PhD); irrigation and drainage (M Sc, M Sc A, PhD); machinery (M Sc, M Sc A, PhD); microbiology (M Sc, PhD); neotropical environment (M Sc, PhD); parasitology (M Sc, PhD); plant science (M Sc, M Sc A, PhD); pollution control (M Sc, M Sc A, PhD); postharvest (M Sc, M Sc A, PhD); soil dynamics (M Sc, M Sc A, PhD); soil science (M Sc, PhD); structure and environment (M Sc, M Sc A, PhD); vegetable and fruit storage (M Sc, M Sc A, PhD); wildlife biology (M Sc, PhD). *Application deadline:* For fall admission, 1/1 (priority date); for winter admission, 5/1 (priority date); for spring admission, 9/1 (priority date). Applications are processed on a rolling basis. *Application fee:* $60 Canadian dollars. *Application Contact:* Student Affairs Office, 514-398-7925, Fax: 514-398-7968, E-mail: grad@macdonald.mcgill.ca. *Dean,* Dr. Deborah J. Buszard, 514-398-7707, Fax: 514-398-7766, E-mail: buszard@macdonald.mcgill.ca.

Faculty of Arts Students: 836 full-time (471 women), 5 part-time (3 women). 1,585 applicants, 36% accepted. *Faculty:* 208 full-time (69 women), 83 part-time/adjunct (14 women). Expenses: Contact institution. *Financial support:* Fellowships, research assistantships, teaching assistantships, career-related internships or fieldwork, institutionally sponsored loans, and tuition waivers (full and partial) available. Support available to part-time students. In 2001, 197 master's, 60 doctorates awarded. *Degree program information:* Part-time and evening/weekend programs available. Offers anthropology (MA, PhD); art history and communication studies (MA, PhD); arts (MA, MSW, PhD); East Asian studies (MA, PhD); economics (MA, PhD); English (MA, PhD); French language and literature (MA, PhD); German studies (MA, PhD); Hispanic studies (MA, PhD); history (MA, PhD); history of medicine (MA); Islamic studies (MA, PhD); Italian (MA, PhD); Jewish studies (MA, PhD); linguistics (MA, PhD); medical anthropology (MA); medical sociology (MA); philosophy (MA, PhD); political science (MA, PhD); Russian language (MA, PhD); Russian literature (MA, PhD); social work (MSW, PhD); sociology (MA, PhD). *Application fee:* $60 Canadian dollars. *Application Contact:* Charlotte E. Légaré, Information Contact.

Faculty of Dentistry Students: 11 full-time (3 women), 1 (woman) part-time. Average age 27. 10 applicants, 30% accepted. *Faculty:* 11 full-time (3 women), 7 part-time/adjunct (2 women). Expenses: Contact institution. *Financial support:* In 2001–02, 1 student received support. Tuition waivers (partial) and paid residencies available. In 2001, 1 degree awarded. Offers dentistry (M Sc, PhD); oral and maxillofacial surgery (M Sc, PhD). *Application deadline:* For fall admission, 3/1; for winter admission, 11/1. Applications are processed on a rolling basis. *Application fee:* $60 Canadian dollars. *Application Contact:* Mary Farmus, Graduate Secretary, 514-398-7203 Ext. 7226, Fax: 514-398-8900, E-mail: mfarmus@med.mcgill.ca. *Dean,* Dr. James P. Lund, 514-398-7219, Fax: 514-398-8900, E-mail: lund@med.mcgill.ca.

Faculty of Education Students: 502 full-time (403 women), 222 part-time (196 women). 597 applicants, 71% accepted. *Faculty:* 99 full-time (47 women), 86 part-time/adjunct (49 women). Expenses: Contact institution. *Financial support:* Fellowships, research assistantships, teaching assistantships, career-related internships or fieldwork, institutionally sponsored loans, and tuition waivers (full and partial) available. In 2001, 247 master's, 35 doctorates awarded. *Degree program information:* Part-time and evening/weekend programs available. Offers counseling psychology (MA, PhD); culture and values in education (MA, PhD); curriculum (MA); education (M Ed, MA, MLIS, PhD, Certificate, Diploma); educational leadership (Certificate); educational psychology (M Ed, MA, PhD); educational studies (PhD); kinesiology and physical education (MA); leadership (MA); library and information studies (MLIS, PhD, Certificate, Diploma); school psychology (MA, PhD); school/applied child psychology and applied developmental psychology (MA, PhD); second language education (MA, PhD). *Application deadline:* Applications are processed on a rolling basis. *Application fee:* $60 Canadian dollars. *Dean,* A. E. Wall, 514-398-7037, Fax: 514-398-1527, E-mail: walla@education.mcgill.ca.

Faculty of Engineering Students: 467 full-time (133 women), 95 part-time (24 women). 876 applicants, 47% accepted. *Faculty:* 109 full-time (6 women), 53 part-time/adjunct (7 women). Expenses: Contact institution. *Financial support:* Fellowships, research assistantships, teaching assistantships, institutionally sponsored loans, tuition waivers (full and partial), and teaching and research assistantships available. In 2001, 129 master's, 31 doctorates, 1 other advanced degree awarded. *Degree program information:* Part-time and evening/weekend programs available. Offers architecture (PhD); chemical engineering (M Eng, M Sc, PhD); electrical and computer engineering (M Eng, PhD); engineering (M Arch, M Eng, M Sc, MMM, MUP, PhD, Diploma); environmental engineering (M Eng, M Sc, PhD); environmental planning (MUP); fluid mechanics (M Sc); fluid mechanics and hydraulic engineering (M Eng, PhD); history and theory of architecture (M Arch); housing (M Arch, MUP, Diploma); manufacturing management (MMM); materials engineering (M Eng, PhD); mechanical engineering (M Eng, PhD); metals and materials (M Eng, PhD); mining engineering (M Eng, M Sc, PhD, Diploma); professional architecture (M Arch); rehabilitation (M Eng, PhD); soil behavior (M Eng, PhD); soil mechanics and foundations (M Eng, PhD); structures and structural mechanics (M Eng, PhD); transportation (MUP); urban planning and design (MUP); water resources (M Sc); water resources engineering (M Eng, PhD). *Application deadline:* Applications are processed on a rolling basis. *Application fee:* $60. *Application Contact:* Judy Pharo, Student Advisor, 514-398-7256, Fax: 514-398-7379, E-mail: judy@eng1.lan.mcgill.ca. *Dean,* Prof. John E. Gruzleski, 514-398-7251, Fax: 514-398-7379, E-mail: johng@eng1.lan.mcgill.ca.

Faculty of Law Students: 144 full-time (62 women). Average age 25. 236 applicants, 54% accepted, 63 enrolled. *Faculty:* 37 full-time (10 women), 5 part-time/adjunct (0 women). Expenses: Contact institution. *Financial support:* In 2001–02, 15 students received support, including 5 fellowships (averaging $10,000 per year), 6 research assistantships (averaging $13,000 per year); teaching assistantships, institutionally sponsored loans and tuition waivers (partial) also available. Financial award application deadline: 2/1. In 2001, 47 master's, 4 doctorates, 3 other advanced degrees awarded. Offers air and space law (LL M, DCL, Certificate); comparative law (LL M, DCL, Certificate). *Application deadline:* For fall admission, 2/1. *Application fee:* $100 Canadian dollars. Electronic applications accepted. *Application Contact:* Graduate Programs in Law, 514-398-3544, Fax: 514-398-8197, E-mail: gradadmissions.law@mcgill.ca. *Associate Dean, Graduate Studies and Research,* Lionel Smith, 514-398-3544, Fax: 514-398-8197, E-mail: lionel.smith@mcgill.ca.

Faculty of Management Students: 441 full-time (174 women), 232 part-time (48 women). Average age 28. 1,033 applicants, 38% accepted, 244 enrolled. *Faculty:* 51 full-time (15 women), 23 part-time/adjunct (4 women). Expenses: Contact institution. *Financial support:* In 2001–02, 74 students received support; fellowships, research assistantships, scholarships/grants and unspecified assistantships available. Financial award application deadline: 2/1. In 2001, 267 master's, 10 doctorates awarded. *Degree program information:* Part-time programs available. Offers management (MBA, MMM, PhD). *Application deadline:* For fall admission, 2/15. Applications are processed on a rolling basis. *Application fee:* $100 Canadian dollars. Electronic applications accepted. *Application Contact:* Susanne Major, Director of Recruiting, 514-398-3196, Fax: 514-398-2499, E-mail: mba@management.mcgill.ca. *Dean,* Dr. Gerald Ross, 514-398-4001.

Faculty of Medicine Students: 1,019 full-time. 907 applicants, 51% accepted, 343 enrolled. *Faculty:* 396 full-time, 1,383 part-time/adjunct. Expenses: Contact institution. *Financial support:* Fellowships, research assistantships, teaching assistantships, career-related internships or fieldwork, Federal Work-Study, institutionally sponsored loans, scholarships/grants, tuition waivers (full and partial), and demonstratorships, fee waivers, stipends available. In 2001, 179 master's, 92 doctorates awarded. *Degree program information:* Part-time programs available. Offers anatomy (M Sc, PhD); biochemistry (M Sc, PhD); bioethics (M Sc); biomedical engineering (M Eng, PhD); communication sciences and disorders (M Sc, M Sc A, PhD); community health (M Sc); environmental health (M Sc); epidemiology (M Sc); epidemiology and biostatistics (PhD, Diploma); experimental medicine (M Sc, PhD); genetic counseling (M Sc); health care evaluation (M Sc); human genetics (M Sc, PhD); medical radiation physics (M Sc, PhD); medical statistics (M Sc); medicine (M Eng, M Sc, M Sc A, PhD, Diploma); microbiology and immunology (M Sc, PhD); neurology and neurosurgery (M Sc, PhD); nursing (M Sc, M Sc A, PhD); occupational health (M Sc); otolaryngology (M Sc); pathology (M Sc, PhD); pharmacology and therapeutics (M Sc, PhD); physiology (M Sc, PhD); psychiatry (M Sc); rehabilitation science (M Sc, M Sc A, PhD); surgery (M Sc, PhD). *Application deadline:* Applications are processed on a rolling basis. *Application fee:* $60 Canadian dollars. *Application Contact:* Marlene Kristian, Admissions Officer, 514-398-3517, Fax: 514-398-4631, E-mail: marlene@med.mcgill.ca. *Dean,* Dr. A. Fuks, 514-398-3524, Fax: 514-398-8368, E-mail: dean@med.mcgill.ca.

Faculty of Music Students: 157 full-time (80 women). 234 applicants, 51% accepted, 70 enrolled. *Faculty:* 45 full-time (9 women), 31 part-time/adjunct (7 women). Expenses: Contact institution. *Financial support:* Fellowships, research assistantships, teaching assistantships, career-related internships or fieldwork and tuition waivers (partial) available. In 2001, 39 master's, 5 doctorates awarded. Offers composition (M Mus, D Mus); music education (MA, PhD); music technology (MA); musicology (MA, PhD); performance

(M Mus); performance studies (D Mus); sound recording (M Mus); theory (MA, PhD). *Application deadline:* For fall admission, 1/15 (priority date). Applications are processed on a rolling basis. *Application fee:* $60 Canadian dollars. *Application Contact:* Veronica Slobodian, Admissions Officer, 514-398-4546, Fax: 514-398-8061, E-mail: veronica.slobodian@mcgill.ca. *Dean,* Don McLean, 514-398-4538, Fax: 514-398-8061, E-mail: mclean@music.mcgill.ca.

Faculty of Religious Studies Students: 74 full-time (27 women), 3 part-time. 49 applicants, 69% accepted. *Faculty:* 13 full-time (2 women), 3 part-time/adjunct (0 women). Expenses: Contact institution. *Financial support:* In 2001–02, 8 fellowships (averaging $4,000 per year), 38 teaching assistantships (averaging $2,218 per year) were awarded. Research assistantships, career-related internships or fieldwork and tuition waivers (partial) also available. Financial award application deadline: 2/15. In 2001, 11 master's, 7 doctorates awarded. Offers religious studies and theology (MA, STM, PhD). *Application deadline:* For fall admission, 2/15 (priority date); for winter admission, 10/1. Applications are processed on a rolling basis. *Application fee:* $60 Canadian dollars. Electronic applications accepted. *Application Contact:* Luvana DiFrancesco, Administrative Assistant, 514-398-4125, Fax: 514-398-4125, E-mail: ldifra@po-box.mcgill.ca. *Chair, Graduate Committee,* Prof. Richard Hayes, 514-398-3291, Fax: 514-398-6665, E-mail: rhayes@po-box.mcgill.ca.

Faculty of Science Students: 496 full-time (217 women). 744 applicants, 28% accepted. *Faculty:* 176 full-time (34 women), 26 part-time/adjunct (6 women). Expenses: Contact institution. *Financial support:* Fellowships, research assistantships, teaching assistantships, career-related internships or fieldwork, institutionally sponsored loans, tuition waivers (partial), and bursaries, stipends available. In 2001, 52 master's, 46 doctorates awarded. Offers atmospheric science (M Sc, PhD); biology (M Sc, PhD); chemistry (M Sc, PhD); clinical psychology (PhD); earth and planetary sciences (M Sc, PhD, Diploma); experimental psychology (M Sc, MA, PhD); geography (M Sc, MA, PhD); mathematics and statistics (M Sc, MA, PhD); physical oceanography (M Sc, PhD); physics (M Sc, PhD); science (M Sc, MA, PhD, Diploma). *Application deadline:* Applications are processed on a rolling basis. *Application fee:* $60 Canadian dollars. *Application Contact:* Charlotte E. Légaré, Information Contact.

School of Computer Science Students: 115 full-time (32 women), 7 part-time (1 woman), 32 international. 171 applicants, 44% accepted. *Faculty:* 19 full-time (2 women), 4 part-time/adjunct (0 women). Expenses: Contact institution. *Financial support:* In 2001–02, 26 research assistantships (averaging $15,000 per year), teaching assistantships (averaging $2,386 per year) were awarded. Financial award application deadline: 2/1. In 2001, 22 master's, 6 doctorates awarded. Offers computer science (M Sc, PhD). *Application deadline:* For fall admission, 2/1 (priority date). Applications are processed on a rolling basis. *Application fee:* $60 Canadian dollars. *Application Contact:* Graduate Program Secretary, 514-398-7071 Ext. 3744, Fax: 514-398-3883, E-mail: grad-sec@cs.mcgill.ca. *Director,* D. Thérien, 514-398-7071 Ext. 3744, Fax: 514-398-3883, E-mail: grad@cs.mcgill.ca.

Professional Program in Dentistry Tuition charges are reported in Canadian dollars. Offers dentistry (DMD). Electronic applications accepted.

Professional Program in Medicine Tuition charges are reported in Canadian dollars. Offers medicine (MD). Electronic applications accepted.

MCMASTER UNIVERSITY, Hamilton, ON L8S 4M2, Canada

General Information Province-supported, coed, university. *Enrollment:* 1,843 full-time matriculated graduate/professional students, 596 part-time matriculated graduate/professional students. *Enrollment by degree level:* 1,682 master's, 757 doctoral. *Graduate faculty:* 879 full-time, 83 part-time/adjunct. *Graduate tuition:* Tuition and fees charges are reported in Canadian dollars. *Tuition:* Full-time $4,422 Canadian dollars; part-time $737 Canadian dollars per term. *Required fees:* $336 Canadian dollars; $128 Canadian dollars per term. *Graduate housing:* Room and/or apartments available to single students; on-campus housing not available to married students. Typical cost: $3,900 Canadian dollars per year. Housing application deadline: 6/30. *Student services:* Campus employment opportunities, campus safety program, career counseling, child daycare facilities, disabled student services, exercise/wellness program, free psychological counseling, international student services, low-cost health insurance, multicultural affairs office, writing training. *Library facilities:* Mills Memorial Library plus 4 others. *Online resources:* library catalog, web page, access to other libraries' catalogs. *Collection:* 1.7 million titles, 11,976 serial subscriptions. *Research affiliation:* Commonwealth Development (telecommunications), Canadian Centre for Inland Waters (chemical and civil engineering).

Computer facilities: 400 computers available on campus for general student use. A campuswide network can be accessed from student residence rooms and from off campus. Internet access is available. *Web address:* http://www.mcmaster.ca/.

General Application Contact: John A. Scime, Graduate Registar and Secretary, 905-525-9140 Ext. 23684, Fax: 905-521-0689, E-mail: askgrad@mcmaster.ca.

GRADUATE UNITS

Faculty of Health Sciences Students: 254. *Faculty:* 150. Expenses: Contact institution. *Financial support:* Teaching assistantships available. *Degree program information:* Part-time programs available. Offers cell biology and metabolism (M Sc, PhD); clinical health sciences/health research methodology (M Sc, PhD); clinical health sciences/nursing (M Sc, PhD); clinical health sciences/rehabilitation science (M Sc); health sciences (M Sc, MCHS, PhD); hemostasis, thromboembolism, and atherosclerosis (M Sc, PhD); molecular biology, genetics, and cancer (M Sc, PhD); molecular immunology, virology, and inflammation (M Sc, PhD); neurosciences and behavioral sciences (M Sc, PhD); occupational therapy (MCHS); physiology/pharmacology (M Sc, PhD); physiotherapy (MCHS). *Application Contact:* Dr. Carl Richards, Associate Dean, 905-525-9140 Ext. 27718, Fax: 905-546-1129. *Dean/Vice President,* Dr. John G. Kelton, Fax: 905-546-0800.

McMaster Divinity College Tuition and fees charges are reported in Canadian dollars. *Degree program information:* Part-time programs available. Offers theology (M Div, M Th, MRE, MTS, D Min). Affiliated with the Toronto School of Theology.

School of Graduate Studies Students: 1,843 full-time, 596 part-time. *Faculty:* 879 full-time (244 women), 83 part-time/adjunct. Expenses: Contact institution. *Financial support:* In 2001–02, 1,400 fellowships (averaging $5,000 per year), 100 research assistantships (averaging $2,000 per year), 700 teaching assistantships (averaging $8,073 per year) were awarded. Career-related internships or fieldwork, Federal Work-Study, institutionally sponsored loans, scholarships/grants, and tuition waivers (partial) also available. In 2001, 601 master's, 94 doctorates awarded. *Degree program information:* Part-time programs available. Offers applied statistics (M Sc); graduate studies (M Eng, M Sc, MA, MA Sc, MBA, MSW, PhD); medical statistics (M Sc); statistical theory (M Sc); urban studies (MA, PhD). *Application fee:* $75. *Application Contact:* John A. Scime, Graduate Registrar and Secretary, 905-525-9140 Ext. 23684, Fax: 905-521-0689, E-mail: askgrad@mcmaster.ca. *Dean,* Dr. Fred L. Hall, 905-525-9140 Ext. 23683, Fax: 905-521-0689, E-mail: deangrad@mcmaster.ca.

Faculty of Business Students: 338 full-time, 197 part-time. *Faculty:* 51 full-time (4 women). Expenses: Contact institution. *Financial support:* In 2001–02, teaching assistantships (averaging $8,073 per year); fellowships, research assistantships, career-related internships or fieldwork, Federal Work-Study, and scholarships/grants also available. In 2001, 295 master's, 2 doctorates awarded. *Degree program information:* Part-time programs available. Offers business (MBA, PhD); human resources and management (MBA, PhD); management science/systems (PhD). *Application deadline:* For fall admission, 6/1. *Application fee:* $75. *Application Contact:* Denise Anderson, Manager, Recruiting and Admissions, 905-525-9140 Ext. 23940, Fax: 905-521-8995, E-mail: anderd@mcmaster.ca. *Dean,* Dr. Vishwanath Baba, 905-525-9140, Fax: 905-526-0852, E-mail: deanbus@mcmaster.ca.

Faculty of Engineering Students: 343 full-time, 121 part-time. *Faculty:* 118 full-time (4 women), 32 part-time/adjunct (0 women). Expenses: Contact institution. *Financial support:* In 2001–02, teaching assistantships (averaging $8,073 per year); fellowships, research assistantships, career-related internships or fieldwork, Federal Work-Study, and scholarships/grants also available. In 2001, 79 master's, 23 doctorates awarded. *Degree program information:* Part-time programs available. Offers bioengineering (M Eng, MA Sc, PhD); chemical engineering (M Eng, MA Sc, PhD); civil engineering (M Eng, MA Sc, PhD); electrical engineering (M Eng, MA Sc, PhD); engineering (M Eng, M Sc, MA Sc, PhD); engineering physics (M Eng, MA Sc, PhD); materials engineering (M Eng, MA Sc, PhD); materials science (M Eng, M Sc, PhD); mechanical engineering (M Eng, MA Sc, PhD); nuclear engineering (PhD). *Application deadline:* For fall admission, 3/1 (priority date). Applications are processed on a rolling basis. *Application fee:* $75. *Dean of the Faculty of Engineering,* Dr. M. Elbestawi, 905-525-9140 Ext. 24288, Fax: 905-540-1149, E-mail: deaneng@mcmaster.ca.

Faculty of Humanities Students: 142 full-time, 31 part-time. *Faculty:* 127 full-time (32 women), 1 part-time/adjunct (0 women). Expenses: Contact institution. *Financial support:* In 2001–02, teaching assistantships (averaging $8,234 per year); fellowships, research assistantships, career-related internships or fieldwork, Federal Work-Study, institutionally sponsored loans, and scholarships/grants also available. In 2001, 45 master's, 11 doctorates awarded. *Degree program information:* Part-time and evening/weekend programs available. Offers classics (MA, PhD); English (MA, PhD); French (MA); history (MA, PhD); humanities (MA, PhD); music criticism (MA); philosophy (MA, PhD). *Application deadline:* Applications are processed on a rolling basis. *Application fee:* $75. *Dean,* Dr. Daniel Woolf, 905-525-9140 Ext. 24603, Fax: 905-528-6733, E-mail: deanhum@mcmaster.ca.

Faculty of Science Tuition and fees charges are reported in Canadian dollars. *Degree program information:* Part-time and evening/weekend programs available. Offers analytical chemistry (M Sc, PhD); astrophysics (PhD); biochemistry (M Sc, PhD); biology (M Sc, PhD); chemical physics (M Sc, PhD); chemistry (M Sc, PhD); computer science (M Sc); geochemistry (PhD); geology (M Sc, PhD); health and radiation physics (M Sc); human geography (MA, PhD); inorganic chemistry (M Sc, PhD); mathematics (PhD); mathematics and statistics (M Sc); organic chemistry (M Sc, PhD); physical chemistry (M Sc, PhD); physical geography (M Sc, PhD); physics (PhD); polymer chemistry (M Sc, PhD); psychology (M Sc, PhD); science (M Sc, MA, PhD).

Faculty of Social Sciences Students: 221 full-time, 80 part-time. 687 applicants, 20% accepted. *Faculty:* 184 full-time (45 women), 14 part-time/adjunct (4 women). Expenses: Contact institution. *Financial support:* Fellowships, research assistantships, teaching assistantships, tuition waivers (partial) available. In 2001, 90 master's, 11 doctorates awarded. *Degree program information:* Part-time and evening/weekend programs available. Offers analysis of social welfare policy (MSW); analysis of social work practice (MSW); anthropology (MA, PhD); economics (MA, PhD); human biodynamics (PhD); kinesiology (M Sc); political science (MA); public and the global economy (MA); public policy and administration (MA); religious studies (MA, PhD); social sciences (M Sc, MA, MSW, PhD); sociology (MA, PhD). *Application fee:* $75. *Dean,* Dr. A. J. Harrison, 905-525-9140 Ext. 24727.

MCNEESE STATE UNIVERSITY, Lake Charles, LA 70609

General Information State-supported, coed, comprehensive institution. *Enrollment:* 234 full-time matriculated graduate/professional students (126 women), 426 part-time matriculated graduate/professional students (319 women). *Enrollment by degree level:* 630 master's, 30 other advanced degrees. *Graduate faculty:* 111 full-time (33 women), 13 part-time/adjunct (11 women). Tuition, state resident: part-time $1,208 per semester. Tuition, nonresident: part-time $4,378 per semester. *Graduate housing:* Rooms and/or apartments available on a first-come, first-served basis to single students and available to married students. Housing application deadline: 8/15. *Student services:* Campus employment opportunities, campus safety program, career counseling, disabled student services, exercise/wellness program, free psychological counseling, international student services, low-cost health insurance. *Library facilities:* Frazer Memorial Library plus 2 others. *Online resources:* library catalog, web page, access to other libraries' catalogs. *Collection:* 365,259 titles, 1,679 serial subscriptions, 1,395 audiovisual materials.

Computer facilities: 354 computers available on campus for general student use. A campuswide network can be accessed from off campus. Internet access and online class registration are available. *Web address:* http://www.mcneese.edu/.

General Application Contact: Tammie Pettis, Director of Admissions, 337-475-5148, E-mail: tpettis@mail.mcneese.edu.

GRADUATE UNITS

Graduate School Students: 234 full-time (126 women), 426 part-time (319 women); includes 123 minority (107 African Americans, 4 Asian Americans or Pacific Islanders, 9 Hispanic Americans, 3 Native Americans), 76 international. *Faculty:* 111 full-time (33 women), 13 part-time/adjunct (11 women). Expenses: Contact institution. *Financial support:* Fellowships, research assistantships, teaching assistantships, career-related internships or fieldwork, Federal Work-Study, institutionally sponsored loans, and unspecified assistantships available. Support available to part-time students. In 2001, 178 degrees awarded. *Degree program information:* Part-time and evening/weekend programs available. *Application deadline:* For fall admission, 7/15 (priority date). Applications are processed on a rolling basis. *Application fee:* $20 ($30 for international students). *Dean,* Dr. Hugh Frugé, 318-475-5394, Fax: 337-475-5467, E-mail: hfruge@mail.mcneese.edu.

College of Business Students: 40 full-time (12 women), 55 part-time (34 women); includes 18 minority (16 African Americans, 1 Asian American or Pacific Islander, 1 Hispanic American), 18 international. *Faculty:* 8 full-time (1 woman). Expenses: Contact institution. *Financial support:* Research assistantships, teaching assistantships, Federal Work-Study available. Support available to part-time students. Financial award application deadline:5/1. In 2001, 20 degrees awarded. *Degree program information:* Part-time and evening/weekend programs available. Offers business (MBA); business administration (MBA). *Application deadline:* For fall admission, 7/15 (priority date). Applications are processed on a rolling basis. *Application fee:* $20 ($30 for international students). *Application Contact:* Dr. Bruce Swindle, MBA Director, 337-475-5576, Fax: 337-475-5986, E-mail: mbaprog@acc.mcneese.edu. *Acting Dean,* Dr. Doug McNiel, 337-475-5514.

College of Education Students: 80 full-time (62 women), 281 part-time (224 women); includes 78 minority (71 African Americans, 2 Asian Americans or Pacific Islanders, 2 Hispanic Americans, 3 Native Americans), 6 international. *Faculty:* 39 full-time (14 women), 11 part-time/adjunct (9 women). Expenses: Contact institution. *Financial support:* Fellowships, research assistantships, teaching assistantships, Federal Work-Study available. Support available to part-time students. Financial award application deadline: 5/1. In 2001, 124 degrees awarded. *Degree program information:* Part-time and evening/weekend programs available. Offers administration and supervision (M Ed, Ed S); counseling and guidance (M Ed); early childhood education (M Ed); education (M Ed, MA, Ed S); educational technology (M Ed); elementary education (M Ed); health and physical education (M Ed); psychology (MA); reading education (M Ed); secondary education (M Ed); special education (M Ed). *Application deadline:* For fall admission, 7/15 (priority date). Applications are processed on a rolling basis. *Application fee:* $20 ($30 for international students). *Dean,* Joe E. Savoie, 337-475-5432, Fax: 337-475-5467, E-mail: jsavoie@mail.mcneese.edu.

College of Engineering and Technology Students: 24 full-time (5 women), 5 part-time; includes 1 minority (Asian American or Pacific Islander), 23 international. *Faculty:* 14 full-time (1 woman). Expenses: Contact institution. *Financial support:* Federal Work-Study available. Support available to part-time students. Financial award application deadline:5/1. In 2001, 5 degrees awarded. *Degree program information:* Part-time and evening/weekend programs available. Offers chemical engineering (M Eng); civil engineering (M Eng); electrical engineering (M Eng); mechanical engineering (M Eng). *Application deadline:* For fall admission, 7/15 (priority date). Applications are processed on a rolling basis. *Application fee:* $20 ($30 for international students). *Application Contact:* Dr. Jay O. Uppot, Director of Graduate Studies, 337-475-5874, Fax: 37-475-5286, E-mail: juppot@mail.mcneese.edu. *Dean,* Dr. O. C. Karkalits, 337-475-5875, Fax: 337-475-5237, E-mail: ckarkal@mail.mcneese.edu.

College of Liberal Arts Students: 36 full-time (22 women), 12 part-time (10 women); includes 6 minority (4 African Americans, 2 Hispanic Americans), 4 international. *Faculty:* 21 full-time (8 women), 1 (woman) part-time/adjunct. Expenses: Contact institution. *Financial support:* Teaching assistantships, Federal Work-Study available. Support available to part-time students. In 2001, 9 degrees awarded. *Degree program information:* Part-time and evening/weekend programs available. Offers creative writing (MFA); English (MA); liberal arts (MA, MFA, MM Ed); music education (MM Ed). *Application deadline:* For fall admission, 7/15 (priority date). Applications are processed on a rolling basis. *Application fee:* $20

McNeese State University (continued)

($30 for international students). *Dean,* Dr. Ray Miles, 337-475-5192, Fax: 337-475-5594, E-mail: rmiles@mail.mcneese.edu.

College of Nursing Students: 11 full-time (8 women), 43 part-time (36 women); includes 9 minority (8 African Americans, 1 Hispanic American), 1 international. Average age 35. *Faculty:* 5 full-time (all women), 1 (woman) part-time/adjunct. Expenses: Contact institution. In 2001, 6 degrees awarded. Offers nursing (MSN). *Application deadline:* For fall admission, 7/15 (priority date). Applications are processed on a rolling basis. *Application fee:* $20 ($30 for international students). *Dean,* Dr. Peggy L. Wolfe, 337-475-5820, Fax: 337-475-5924, E-mail: pwolfe@mail.mcneese.edu.

College of Science Students: 43 full-time (17 women), 30 part-time (15 women); includes 11 minority (8 African Americans, 3 Hispanic Americans), 24 international. *Faculty:* 24 full-time (4 women). Expenses: Contact institution. *Financial support:* Teaching assistantships, Federal Work-Study available. Support available to part-time students. Financial award application deadline: 5/1. In 2001, 14 degrees awarded. *Degree program information:* Part-time and evening/weekend programs available. Offers biology (MS); chemistry (MS); computer science (MS); environmental sciences (MS); mathematics (MS); science (MS); statistics (MS). *Application deadline:* For fall admission, 7/15 (priority date). Applications are processed on a rolling basis. *Application fee:* $20 ($30 for international students). *Dean,* Dr. George F. Mead, 337-475-5785, Fax: 337-475-5249, E-mail: mead@mail.mcneese.edu.

MEADVILLE LOMBARD THEOLOGICAL SCHOOL, Chicago, IL 60637-1602

General Information Independent-religious, coed, graduate-only institution. *Graduate faculty:* 5 full-time (3 women), 11 part-time/adjunct (5 women). *Tuition:* Full-time $9,900. *Graduate housing:* Rooms and/or apartments available on a first-come, first-served basis to single and married students. Typical cost: $3,900 per year for single students; $8,400 per year for married students. Housing application deadline: 5/15. *Student services:* Campus employment opportunities, campus safety program, career counseling, international student services, low-cost health insurance, multicultural affairs office. *Library facilities:* Wiggin Library. *Collection:* 103,000 titles, 90 serial subscriptions, 100 audiovisual materials.

Computer facilities: 5 computers available on campus for general student use. Internet access and online class registration are available. *Web address:* http://www.meadville.edu/.

General Application Contact: Susan A. Grubb, Director of Admissions and Recruitment, 773-256-3000 Ext. 237, Fax: 773-256-3006, E-mail: sgrubb@meadville.edu.

GRADUATE UNITS

Graduate and Professional Programs Students: 36 full-time (20 women), 53 part-time (41 women); includes 8 minority (5 African Americans, 1 Asian American or Pacific Islander, 2 Hispanic Americans) Average age 32. *Faculty:* 5 full-time (3 women), 11 part-time/adjunct (5 women). Expenses: Contact institution. *Financial support:* Career-related internships or fieldwork and scholarships/grants available. Support available to part-time students. Financial award application deadline: 3/1. In 2001, 2 doctorates awarded. *Degree program information:* Part-time programs available. Offers divinity (M Div); ministry (D Min). *Application deadline:* For fall admission, 3/1. Applications are processed on a rolling basis. *Application fee:* $25. *Application Contact:* Susan A. Grubb, Director of Admissions and Recruitment, 773-256-3000 Ext. 237, Fax: 773-256-3006, E-mail: sgrubb@meadville.edu. *President and Academic Dean,* William R. Murry, 773-256-3000, Fax: 773-753-1323.

MEDAILLE COLLEGE, Buffalo, NY 14214-2695

General Information Independent, coed, comprehensive institution. *Enrollment:* 124 full-time matriculated graduate/professional students (65 women), 152 part-time matriculated graduate/professional students (100 women). *Enrollment by degree level:* 276 master's. *Graduate faculty:* 16 full-time (7 women), 8 part-time/adjunct (1 woman). *Tuition:* Full-time $11,352; part-time $473 per credit. *Required fees:* $19 per credit. Full-time tuition and fees vary according to campus/location and program. *Graduate housing:* Rooms and/or apartments available on a first-come, first-served basis to single and married students. Typical cost: $5,800 (including board) for single students; $5,800 (including board) for married students. Housing application deadline: 8/15. *Student services:* Campus employment opportunities, campus safety program, career counseling, disabled student services, exercise/wellness program, free psychological counseling, low-cost health insurance, multicultural affairs office, teacher training, writing training. *Library facilities:* Medaille College Library. *Online resources:* library catalog, web page, access to other libraries' catalogs. *Collection:* 53,848 titles, 240 serial subscriptions, 2,063 audiovisual materials.

Computer facilities: 105 computers available on campus for general student use. A campuswide network can be accessed from student residence rooms and from off campus. Internet access is available. *Web address:* http://www.medaille.edu/.

General Application Contact: Jacqueline Matheny, Director of Enrollment Management, 716-884-3281 Ext. 302, Fax: 716-884-0291, E-mail: jmatheny@medaille.edu.

GRADUATE UNITS

Program in Business Administration Students: 24 full-time (13 women), 80 part-time (40 women); includes 22 minority (20 African Americans, 1 Asian American or Pacific Islander, 1 Hispanic American), 3 international. Average age 36. 48 applicants, 79% accepted. *Faculty:* 11 full-time (3 women), 5 part-time/adjunct (0 women). Expenses: Contact institution. *Financial support:* In 2001–02, 45 students received support. Federal Work-Study available. Financial award applicants required to submit FAFSA. In 2001, 10 degrees awarded. *Degree program information:* Part-time and evening/weekend programs available. Offers business administration (MBA). *Application deadline:* For fall admission, 8/15 (priority date); for spring admission, 1/15 (priority date). Applications are processed on a rolling basis. *Application fee:* $35. Electronic applications accepted. *Application Contact:* Jacqueline Matheny, Director of Enrollment Management, 716-884-3281 Ext. 302, Fax: 716-884-0291, E-mail: jmatheny@medaille.edu. *Chairperson,* Dr. Faith Burke, 716-884-3281 Ext. 161, Fax: 716-884-0291, E-mail: fburke@medaille.edu.

Program in Business Administration—Amherst Students: 114 full-time (59 women); includes 35 minority (30 African Americans, 1 Asian American or Pacific Islander, 3 Hispanic Americans, 1 Native American) Average age 36. 55 applicants, 93% accepted, 51 enrolled. *Faculty:* 11 full-time (3 women), 3 part-time/adjunct (1 woman). Expenses: Contact institution. *Financial support:* In 2001–02, 72 students received support. Federal Work-Study available. Financial award applicants required to submit FAFSA. *Degree program information:* Evening/weekend programs available. Offers business administration (MBA). *Application deadline:* Applications are processed on a rolling basis. *Application fee:* $100. *Application Contact:* Rose Hollander, Marketing Support, 716-631-1061 Ext. 101, Fax: 716-631-1380, E-mail: rahollan@apollogrp.edu. *Associate Dean for Special Programs,* Jennifer Bavifard, 716-631-1061, Fax: 716-631-1380, E-mail: jbavifar@medaille.edu.

Program in Education Students: 6 full-time (4 women), 77 part-time (62 women); includes 15 minority (11 African Americans, 4 Hispanic Americans), 1 international. Average age 29. 34 applicants, 74% accepted. *Faculty:* 3 full-time (1 woman), 6 part-time/adjunct (2 women). Expenses: Contact institution. *Financial support:* In 2001–02, 48 students received support. Federal Work-Study available. Financial award applicants required to submit FAFSA. In 2001, 10 degrees awarded. *Degree program information:* Part-time and evening/weekend programs available. Offers education (MS Ed). *Application deadline:* For fall admission, 8/15 (priority date); for spring admission, 1/15 (priority date). Applications are processed on a rolling basis. *Application fee:* $35. Electronic applications accepted. *Application Contact:* Jacqueline Matheny, Director of Enrollment Management, 716-884-3281 Ext. 302, Fax: 716-884-0291, E-mail: jmatheny@medaille.edu. *Chairperson,* Dr. Jerry Mosey, 716-884-3281 Ext. 313, Fax: 716-884-0291, E-mail: jmosey@medaille.edu.

Announcement: Medaille College offers a Master of Business Administration and 3 Master of Science in Education programs. The MBA provides strategic decision making for business professionals. The MS Ed programs (certification: grades 1–6; literacy; and curriculum and instruction) prepare graduates to enter the classroom or administration.

MEDICAL COLLEGE OF GEORGIA, Augusta, GA 30912

General Information State-supported, coed, upper-level institution. CGS member. *Enrollment:* 1,175 full-time matriculated graduate/professional students (460 women), 95 part-time matriculated graduate/professional students (68 women). *Graduate faculty:* 617 full-time (193 women), 105 part-time/adjunct (50 women). *International tuition:* $6,312 full-time. Tuition, nonresident: full-time $1,578. *Required fees:* $618. *Graduate housing:* Rooms and/or apartments available on a first-come, first-served basis to single and married students. Typical cost: $2,600 per year for single students; $2,900 per year for married students. Room charges vary according to housing facility selected. *Student services:* Campus employment opportunities, campus safety program, career counseling, child daycare facilities, free psychological counseling, international student services, low-cost health insurance, multicultural affairs office. *Library facilities:* Robert B. Greenblatt MD Library. *Online resources:* library catalog, web page, access to other libraries' catalogs. *Collection:* 176,646 titles, 1,672 serial subscriptions, 12,928 audiovisual materials. *Research affiliation:* Medical College of Georgia Research Institute, Inc. (biomedical research), Advanced Technology Development Center (biotechnology transfer), Educational Research and Development Association of Georgia Universities (university health and safety), Georgia Research Alliance (science and technology development), Georgia Medical Center Authority (biotechnology and economic development), Georgia Tech Research Center (technology development).

Computer facilities: 58 computers available on campus for general student use. A campuswide network can be accessed. *Web address:* http://www.mcg.edu/.

General Application Contact: Elizabeth Griffin, Director of Academic Admissions, 706-721-2725, Fax: 706-721-7279, E-mail: gradadm@mail.mcg.edu.

GRADUATE UNITS

School of Dentistry Offers dentistry (DMD).

School of Graduate Studies Students: 126 full-time (49 women), 87 part-time (61 women); includes 21 minority (12 African Americans, 6 Asian Americans or Pacific Islanders, 3 Hispanic Americans), 29 international. Average age 29. 269 applicants, 53% accepted, 67 enrolled. *Faculty:* 155 full-time (47 women). Expenses: Contact institution. *Financial support:* In 2001–02, 161 students received support, including 71 research assistantships with partial tuition reimbursements available (averaging $18,500 per year); fellowships, teaching assistantships, career-related internships or fieldwork, Federal Work-Study, institutionally sponsored loans, scholarships/grants, traineeships, and unspecified assistantships also available. Support available to part-time students. Financial award application deadline: 3/31; financial award applicants required to submit FAFSA. In 2001, 55 master's, 14 doctorates awarded. *Degree program information:* Part-time programs available. Postbaccalaureate distance learning degree programs offered (no on-campus study). Offers adult nursing (MSN); biochemistry and molecular biology (MS, PhD); cellular biology and anatomy (MS, PhD); community nursing (MSN); medical illustration (MSMI); mental health nursing (MSN); molecular medicine (PhD); nurse practitioner (MN); nursing (PhD); nursing anesthesia (MN); oral biology (MS, PhD); parent-child nursing (MSN); pharmacology and toxicology (MS, PhD); physiology (MS, PhD); vascular biology (PhD). *Application deadline:* For fall admission, 6/30. Applications are processed on a rolling basis. *Application fee:* $25. *Application Contact:* Carol Nobles, Director of Student Recruitment and Admissions, 706-721-2725, Fax: 706-721-7279, E-mail: cnobles@mail.mcg.edu. *Dean,* Dr. Matthew J. Kluger, 706-721-3278, Fax: 706-721-6829, E-mail: mkluger@mail.mcg.edu.

Programs in Allied Health Sciences Students: 20 full-time (10 women), 12 part-time (9 women). 72 applicants, 69% accepted, 18 enrolled. *Faculty:* 20 full-time (12 women). Expenses: Contact institution. *Financial support:* Federal Work-Study, institutionally sponsored loans, and unspecified assistantships available. Support available to part-time students. Financial award application deadline: 3/31; financial award applicants required to submit FAFSA. In 2001, 15 degrees awarded. *Degree program information:* Part-time programs available. Postbaccalaureate distance learning degree programs offered (no on-campus study). Offers allied health sciences (MHE, MS); dental hygiene (MHE, MS); health information management (MHE, MS); medical technology (MHE, MS); occupational therapy (MHE, MS); physical therapy (MHE, MS); physician assistant (MHE, MS); radiologic sciences (MHE, MS); respiratory therapy (MHE, MS). *Application deadline:* For fall admission, 6/30 (priority date). Applications are processed on a rolling basis. *Application fee:* $25. *Application Contact:* Dr. Carol Campbell, Interim Associate Dean, 706-721-2621, E-mail: cacampbe@mail.mcg.edu. *Dean,* Dr. Leona Mishoe, 706-721-2621, E-mail: smishoe@mail.mcg.edu.

School of Medicine Offers medicine (MD).

MEDICAL COLLEGE OF OHIO, Toledo, OH 43614-5805

General Information State-supported, coed, graduate-only institution. CGS member. *Graduate housing:* On-campus housing not available. *Research affiliation:* Cordis Corporation (clinical trials), Genetech (clinical trials), Glaxo Wellcome (clinical trials), RxKinetix, Inc. (vaccine development), Wyeth-Ayerst (clinical trials), Biocheck Laboratories (immunology).

GRADUATE UNITS

Graduate School *Degree program information:* Part-time and evening/weekend programs available. Offers anatomy (MS); cellular and molecular neurobiology (MS, PhD); medical sciences (MS); medicine (MS); microbiology (MS); molecular and cellular biology (PhD); molecular basis of disease (PhD); oral biology (MS); orthopedic science (MS); pathology (MS); pharmacology (MS); physiology (MS); public health (MPH); radiation therapy (MS); radiological science (MS); surgery (MS); urological science (MS).

School of Allied Health *Degree program information:* Part-time programs available. Offers allied health (MOT, MS, MSBS, Certificate); occupational health (MS, Certificate); occupational therapy (MOT); physician assistant studies (MSBS).

School of Nursing *Degree program information:* Part-time programs available. Offers advanced practice nursing (MSN).

School of Medicine Offers medicine (MD).

MEDICAL COLLEGE OF WISCONSIN, Milwaukee, WI 53226-0509

General Information Independent, coed, graduate-only institution. CGS member. *Enrollment by degree level:* 190 master's, 132 doctoral. *Tuition:* Full-time $9,693; part-time $540 per credit. *Graduate housing:* On-campus housing not available. *Student services:* Campus employment opportunities, campus safety program, career counseling, child daycare facilities, free psychological counseling, international student services, low-cost health insurance. *Library facilities:* Todd Wehr Library plus 2 others. *Online resources:* library catalog. *Collection:* 236,700 titles, 1,550 serial subscriptions, 1,692 audiovisual materials. *Research affiliation:* General Electric Medical Systems (biophysics, radiology).

Computer facilities: 150 computers available on campus for general student use. A campuswide network can be accessed from student residence rooms and from off campus. Internet access, multimedia resources, i.e., CDROM books are available. *Web address:* http://www.mcw.edu/.

General Application Contact: Susan K. Barnes, Manager of Admissions and Registrar, 414-456-8603, Fax: 414-456-6555, E-mail: sbarnes@mcw.edu.

GRADUATE UNITS

Graduate School of Biomedical Sciences Students: 161 full-time (84 women), 276 part-time (114 women); includes 44 minority (7 African Americans, 29 Asian Americans or Pacific Islanders, 8 Hispanic Americans), 83 international. Average age 25. 418 applicants, 18% accepted. Expenses: Contact institution. *Financial support:* In 2001–02, 113 students received support, including 28 fellowships with full tuition reimbursements available (averaging $19,845 per year), 28 research assistantships with full tuition reimbursements available (averaging $19,845 per year); career-related internships or fieldwork, Federal Work-Study, institutionally sponsored loans, scholarships/grants, and annual stipends also available. Support available to part-time students. Financial award application deadline: 2/15; financial award applicants required to submit FAFSA. In 2001, 66 master's, 16 doctorates awarded. *Degree program information:* Part-time and evening/weekend programs available. Postbaccalaureate distance learning degree programs offered (minimal on-campus study). Offers biochemistry (MS,

PhD); bioethics (MA); biomedical sciences (MA, MPH, MS, PhD); biophysics (PhD); biostatistics (PhD); cell and developmental biology (MS, PhD); epidemiology (MS); functional imaging (PhD); health care technologies (PhD); medical informatics (MS); microbiology and molecular genetics (MS, PhD); pathology (MS, PhD); pharmacology and toxicology (MS, PhD); physiology (MS, PhD). *Application deadline:* For fall admission, 2/15 (priority date). Applications are processed on a rolling basis. *Application fee:* $40. Electronic applications accepted. *Application Contact:* Susan K. Barnes, Manager of Admissions and Registrar, 414-456-8603, Fax: 414-456-6555, E-mail: sbarnes@mcw.edu. *Dean,* Dr. William R. Hendee, 414-456-8218, E-mail: gradschool@mcw.edu.

Medical School *Degree program information:* Part-time programs available. Postbaccalaureate distance learning degree programs offered (no on-campus study). Offers general preventive medicine and public health (MPH); medicine (MD, MPH); occupational medicine (MPH).

MEDICAL UNIVERSITY OF SOUTH CAROLINA, Charleston, SC 29425-0002

General Information State-supported, coed, upper-level institution. CGS member. *Enrollment:* 1,762 full-time matriculated graduate/professional students, 170 part-time matriculated graduate/professional students. *Graduate faculty:* 1,115 full-time (413 women), 119 part-time/adjunct (55 women). Tuition, state resident: part-time $210 per term. Tuition, nonresident: part-time $279 per term. *Required fees:* $70 per term. Tuition and fees vary according to degree level and program. *Graduate housing:* On-campus housing not available. *Student services:* Campus employment opportunities, campus safety program, exercise/wellness program, free psychological counseling, grant writing training, international student services, low-cost health insurance, multicultural affairs office, writing training. *Library facilities:* Medical University of South Carolina Library plus 1 other. *Online resources:* library catalog, web page, access to other libraries' catalogs. *Collection:* 217,841 titles, 2,180 serial subscriptions, 6,596 audiovisual materials. *Research affiliation:* Ross Products of Abbott Laboratories (type 2 diabetes), ICON Research Inc./Kyowa Pharmaceutical Inc. (recurrent or advanced ovarian cancer), Covance Inc./Yamanouchi Inc. (male and female overactive bladder), Sanofi-Synthelabo Inc. (maintenance of sinus rhythm), Merck and Company (major depressive disorders), Statprobe Inc./Pfizer Inc. (minority postmenopausal women).

Computer facilities: 189 computers available on campus for general student use. A campuswide network can be accessed from off campus. Internet access is available. *Web address:* http://www.musc.edu/.

General Application Contact: Wendy L. Stephens, Enrollment Services, 843-792-8710, Fax: 843-792-3764, E-mail: stephewl@musc.edu.

GRADUATE UNITS

College of Dental Medicine Students: 211 full-time (77 women); includes 27 minority (11 African Americans, 13 Asian Americans or Pacific Islanders, 3 Hispanic Americans) Average age 27. 539 applicants, 13% accepted, 55 enrolled. *Faculty:* 54 full-time (6 women), 21 part-time/adjunct (5 women). Expenses: Contact institution. *Financial support:* In 2001–02, 181 students received support. Federal Work-Study, scholarships/grants, and tuition waivers (partial) available. Financial award application deadline: 4/1; financial award applicants required to submit FAFSA. In 2001, 52 degrees awarded. Offers dental medicine (DMD). *Application deadline:* For fall admission, 12/1. *Application fee:* $55. *Application Contact:* Wendy L. Stephens, Enrollment Services, 843-792-8710, Fax: 843-792-3764, E-mail: stephewl@musc.edu. *Dean,* Dr. Richard W. DeChamplain, 843-792-3811, Fax: 843-792-1376, E-mail: dechampr@musc.edu.

College of Graduate Studies Students: 219 full-time (121 women); includes 25 minority (10 African Americans, 14 Asian Americans or Pacific Islanders, 1 Native American), 29 international. Average age 30. 203 applicants, 54% accepted, 67 enrolled. *Faculty:* 318 part-time/adjunct (83 women). Expenses: Contact institution. *Financial support:* In 2001–02, 51 students received support; fellowships, research assistantships, teaching assistantships, Federal Work-Study, scholarships/grants, and tuition waivers (partial) available. Support available to part-time students. Financial award application deadline: 4/1; financial award applicants required to submit FAFSA. In 2001, 36 master's, 19 doctorates awarded. Offers biochemistry and molecular biology (MS, PhD); biometrics (MS, PhD); biostatistics (MS, PhD); cell and molecular pharmacology and experimental therapeutics (MS, PhD); cell biology and anatomy (PhD); clinical research (MS); epidemiology (MS, PhD); manufacturing pharmacy (PhD); marine biomedicine (PhD); microbiology and immunology (MS, PhD); natural products/pharmaceutical chemistry (PhD); nursing science (PhD); pathology and laboratory medicine (MS, PhD); pharmaceutics/biopharmaceuticals (PhD); pharmacokinetics (PhD); physiology and neuroscience (MS, PhD). *Application deadline:* For fall admission, 1/15. Applications are processed on a rolling basis. *Application fee:* $55. Electronic applications accepted. *Application Contact:* Hester Young, Director of Student Programs, 800-589-2003, Fax: 843-792-6590, E-mail: youngh@musc.edu. *Dean,* Dr. Perry V. Halushka, 843-792-3102, Fax: 843-792-6590, E-mail: halushpv@musc.edu.

College of Health Professions Students: 449 full-time (341 women), 78 part-time (41 women); includes 70 minority (59 African Americans, 9 Asian Americans or Pacific Islanders, 2 Native Americans), 4 international. Average age 28. 338 applicants, 66% accepted, 167 enrolled. *Faculty:* 85 full-time (41 women), 11 part-time/adjunct (9 women). Expenses: Contact institution. *Financial support:* In 2001–02, 402 students received support. Career-related internships or fieldwork, Federal Work-Study, institutionally sponsored loans, scholarships/grants, traineeships, tuition waivers (partial), and unspecified assistantships available. Support available to part-time students. Financial award application deadline: 3/15; financial award applicants required to submit FAFSA. In 2001, 149 master's, 8 doctorates, 1 other advanced degree awarded. *Degree program information:* Part-time and evening/weekend programs available. Postbaccalaureate distance learning degree programs offered (minimal on-campus study). Offers anesthesia for nurses (MHS); clinical laboratory sciences (MS); communication sciences and disorders (MSR); cytotechnology (MS); health administration (MHA, DHA); health information administration (MHS); health management (Certificate); health professions (MHA, MHS, MS, MSR, DHA, Certificate); occupational therapy (MHS, MSR); periodontics (MHS); physical therapy (MHS, MSR); physician assistant (MHS). *Application deadline:* Applications are processed on a rolling basis. *Application fee:* $55. *Application Contact:* Dr. Jerry L. Blackwell, Associate Dean, 843-792-3326, Fax: 843-792-0253, E-mail: blackwjl@musc.edu. *Dean,* Dr. Danielle N. Ripich, 843-792-3328, Fax: 843-792-3322, E-mail: ripichd@musc.edu.

College of Medicine Students: 576 full-time (249 women); includes 112 minority (67 African Americans, 44 Asian Americans or Pacific Islanders, 1 Hispanic American), 9 international. Average age 28. 1,738 applicants, 12% accepted, 140 enrolled. *Faculty:* 825 full-time (258 women), 69 part-time/adjunct (29 women). Expenses: Contact institution. *Financial support:* In 2001–02, 484 students received support. Federal Work-Study, scholarships/grants, and tuition waivers (partial) available. Financial award application deadline: 3/15; financial award applicants required to submit FAFSA. In 2001, 135 degrees awarded. Offers medicine (MD). *Application deadline:* For fall admission, 12/1. *Application fee:* $55. *Application Contact:* Wanda Taylor, Director of Admissions, 843-792-2055, Fax: 843-792-4262, E-mail: taylorwl@musc.edu. *Dean,* Dr. Jerry G. Reves, 843-792-2842, Fax: 843-792-2967, E-mail: revesj@musc.edu.

College of Nursing Students: 56 full-time, 74 part-time; includes 27 minority (25 African Americans, 2 Asian Americans or Pacific Islanders), 1 international. Average age 33. 75 applicants, 96% accepted, 45 enrolled. *Faculty:* 23 full-time (22 women), 24 part-time/adjunct (all women). Expenses: Contact institution. *Financial support:* Federal Work-Study, institutionally sponsored loans, and traineeships available. Financial award application deadline: 5/1; financial award applicants required to submit FAFSA. In 2001, 55 degrees awarded. *Degree program information:* Part-time programs available. Offers adult health (MSN, Post Master's Certificate); gerontological nursing (MSN, Post Master's Certificate); family nurse practitioner (MSN, Post Master's Certificate); neonatal nurse practitioner (MSN, Post Master's Certificate); nurse-midwifery (MSN); nursing (MSN, Post Master's Certificate); nursing systems management (MSN, Post Master's Certificate); parent-child nursing (MSN, Post Master's Certificate); psychiatric mental health nursing (MSN, Post Master's Certificate). *Application deadline:* For fall admission, 2/1 (priority date); for spring admission, 10/15 (priority date). Applications are processed on a rolling basis. *Application fee:* $75. Electronic applications accepted. *Application Contact:* Carolyn F. Page, Coordinator, 843-792-3844, Fax: 843-792-3726, E-mail: pagecf@musc.edu.

College of Pharmacy Students: 226 full-time (172 women); includes 60 minority (33 African Americans, 22 Asian Americans or Pacific Islanders, 3 Hispanic Americans, 2 Native Americans), 1 international. Average age 26. 120 applicants, 65% accepted, 60 enrolled. *Faculty:* 43 full-time (17 women), 1 part-time/adjunct (0 women). Expenses: Contact institution. *Financial support:* In 2001–02, 201 students received support. Career-related internships or fieldwork, Federal Work-Study, institutionally sponsored loans, and scholarships/grants available. Financial award application deadline: 3/15; financial award applicants required to submit FAFSA. In 2001, 36 degrees awarded. Offers pharmacy (Pharm D). *Application deadline:* For fall admission, 1/15. *Application fee:* $55. Electronic applications accepted. *Application Contact:* Susan Coates, Pharmacy Admission Specialist, 843-792-8722, Fax: 843-792-3764, E-mail: coatess@musc.edu. *Acting Dean,* Dr. John F. Cormier, 843-792-8450, Fax: 843-792-9081, E-mail: cormierj@musc.edu.

MEHARRY MEDICAL COLLEGE, Nashville, TN 37208-9989

General Information Independent-religious, coed, graduate-only institution. CGS member. *Graduate faculty:* 273 full-time (69 women), 46 part-time/adjunct (11 women). *Tuition:* Full-time $23,208. *Required fees:* $3,916. Full-time tuition and fees vary according to degree level, program and student level. *Graduate housing:* Rooms and/or apartments available on a first-come, first-served basis to single and married students. *Student services:* Campus employment opportunities, campus safety program, career counseling, child daycare facilities, exercise/wellness program, free psychological counseling, international student services, low-cost health insurance. *Library facilities:* Meharry Medical College Library. *Online resources:* library catalog, web page. *Collection:* 98,000 titles, 1,011 serial subscriptions, 382 audiovisual materials.

Computer facilities: 100 computers available on campus for general student use. A campuswide network can be accessed from student residence rooms and from off campus. Internet access is available. *Web address:* http://www.mmc.edu/.

General Application Contact: Allen D. Mosley, Director of Admissions and Records, 615-327-6223, Fax: 615-327-6228, E-mail: amosley@mmc.edu.

GRADUATE UNITS

School of Dentistry Students: 220 full-time (123 women); includes 201 minority (172 African Americans, 27 Asian Americans or Pacific Islanders, 1 Hispanic American, 1 Native American), 6 international. Average age 26. 1,089 applicants, 8% accepted, 53 enrolled. *Faculty:* 39 full-time (10 women), 16 part-time/adjunct (5 women). Expenses: Contact institution. *Financial support:* Career-related internships or fieldwork, Federal Work-Study, and institutionally sponsored loans available. Financial award application deadline: 4/15; financial award applicants required to submit FAFSA. In 2001, 60 degrees awarded. Offers dentistry (DDS). *Application deadline:* For fall admission, 3/1. Applications are processed on a rolling basis. *Application fee:* $60. *Application Contact:* Allen D. Mosley, Director of Admissions and Records, 615-327-6223, Fax: 615-327-6228, E-mail: amosley@mmc.edu. *Dean,* Dr. William B. Butler, 615-327-6207, Fax: 615-327-6213.

School of Graduate Studies Students: 139 full-time (86 women); includes 124 minority (117 African Americans, 6 Asian Americans or Pacific Islanders, 1 Hispanic American), 10 international. Average age 30. 105 applicants, 61% accepted, 41 enrolled. Expenses: Contact institution. *Financial support:* Fellowships, research assistantships, teaching assistantships, career-related internships or fieldwork, Federal Work-Study, institutionally sponsored loans, scholarships/grants, and tuition waivers (full) available. Support available to part-time students. Financial award applicants required to submit FAFSA. In 2001, 15 master's, 14 doctorates awarded. *Degree program information:* Part-time and evening/weekend programs available. Offers biochemistry (PhD); biomedical sciences (PhD); general preventive medicine (MSPH); health services administration (MSPH); microbiology (PhD); occupational medicine (MSPH); pharmacology (MS, PhD); physiology (PhD); public health administration (MSPH). *Application deadline:* For fall admission, 6/1. Applications are processed on a rolling basis. *Application fee:* $45. *Interim Director,* Dr. Maria F Lima, 615-327-6533, Fax: 615-327-2933, E-mail: mflima@mmc.edu.

School of Medicine Students: 362 full-time (190 women); includes 326 minority (266 African Americans, 30 Asian Americans or Pacific Islanders, 24 Hispanic Americans, 6 Native Americans), 10 international. Average age 26. 3,542 applicants, 4% accepted, 80 enrolled. *Faculty:* 234 full-time (59 women), 30 part-time/adjunct (6 women). Expenses: Contact institution. *Financial support:* Federal Work-Study, institutionally sponsored loans, and tuition waivers (partial) available. Financial award application deadline: 4/15; financial award applicants required to submit FAFSA. In 2001, 77 degrees awarded. Offers medicine (MD). *Application deadline:* For fall admission, 12/15. Applications are processed on a rolling basis. *Application fee:* $60. *Application Contact:* Allen D. Mosley, Director of Admissions and Records, 615-327-6223, Fax: 615-327-6228, E-mail: amosley@mmc.edu. *Dean,* Dr. A. Cherrie Epps, 615-327-6204, Fax: 615-327-6568, E-mail: meharrysom@ccvax.edu.

MEIJI COLLEGE OF ORIENTAL MEDICINE, Berkeley, CA 94704

General Information Independent, coed, graduate-only institution. *Enrollment by degree level:* 59 master's. *Graduate faculty:* 5 full-time (2 women), 15 part-time/adjunct (3 women). *Tuition:* Full-time $9,000; part-time $11 per hour. *Graduate housing:* On-campus housing not available. *Online resources:* library catalog. *Collection:* 1,850 titles, 38 serial subscriptions, 100 audiovisual materials.

Computer facilities: 1 computer available on campus for general student use. Medline available.

General Application Contact: Linda Flanagan, Admissions Officer, 510-666-8248, Fax: 510-666-0111, E-mail: admissions@msn.com.

GRADUATE UNITS

Program in Oriental Medicine Students: 51 full-time (36 women), 8 part-time (7 women); includes 18 minority (17 Asian Americans or Pacific Islanders, 1 Hispanic American), 4 international. Average age 34. 33 applicants, 79% accepted, 21 enrolled. *Faculty:* 5 full-time (2 women), 15 part-time/adjunct (3 women). Expenses: Contact institution. *Financial support:* In 2001–02, 34 students received support. Available to part-time students. Application deadline: 7/31. In 2001, 12 degrees awarded. *Degree program information:* Part-time programs available. Offers Oriental medicine (MS). *Application deadline:* For fall admission, 7/31. Applications are processed on a rolling basis. *Application fee:* $50. *Application Contact:* Linda Flanagan, Admissions Officer, 510-666-8248, Fax: 510-666-0111, E-mail: meijiadmissions@msu.com. *President,* Hirohisa Oda, 510-666-8248, Fax: 510-666-0111.

MEMORIAL UNIVERSITY OF NEWFOUNDLAND, St. John's, NF A1C 5S7, Canada

General Information Province-supported, coed, university. *Enrollment:* 1,019 full-time matriculated graduate/professional students (533 women), 602 part-time matriculated graduate/professional students (310 women). *Enrollment by degree level:* 1,623 master's, 244 doctoral, 14 other advanced degrees. *Graduate faculty:* 800. *Graduate tuition:* Tuition and fees charges are reported in Canadian dollars. Tuition, province resident: part-time $858 Canadian dollars per semester. Tuition, Canadian resident: part-time $953 Canadian dollars per semester. *Required fees:* $180 Canadian dollars. Full-time tuition and fees vary according to degree level and program. *Graduate housing:* Rooms and/or apartments available on a first-come, first-served basis to single and married students. Typical cost: $2,800 Canadian dollars per year ($5,400 Canadian dollars including board) for single students; $6,600 Canadian dollars per year ($9,400 Canadian dollars including board) for married students. *Student services:* Campus employment opportunities, campus safety program, career counseling, child daycare facilities, disabled student services, free psychological counseling, international student services, low-cost health insurance, teacher training, writing training. *Library facilities:* Queen Elizabeth II Library plus 2 others. *Online resources:* library catalog, web page, access to other libraries' catalogs. *Collection:* 1.2 million titles, 17,000 serial subscriptions.

Memorial University of Newfoundland (continued)

Computer facilities: 800 computers available on campus for general student use. A campuswide network can be accessed from student residence rooms and from off campus. Internet access is available. *Web address:* http://www.mun.ca/.

General Application Contact: Kim Hearn, Admissions, 709-737-2445, Fax: 709-737-4702, E-mail: sgs@mun.ca.

GRADUATE UNITS

Faculty of Medicine Students: 306 full-time (154 women), 52 part-time (36 women), 64 international. 796 applicants, 11% accepted. *Faculty:* 114 full-time (34 women), 49 part-time/adjunct (16 women). Expenses: Contact institution. *Financial support:* In 2001–02, 70 students received support, including 5 fellowships (averaging $14,000 per year); research assistantships, external awards also available. Financial award application deadline: 5/31. In 2001, 57 first professional degrees, 12 master's, 4 doctorates, 1 other advanced degree awarded. *Degree program information:* Part-time programs available. Postbaccalaureate distance learning degree programs offered (no on-campus study). Offers medicine (MD, M Sc, PhD, Diploma). *Application deadline:* Applications are processed on a rolling basis. Electronic applications accepted. *Application Contact:* Assistant Dean of Research and Graduate Studies, 709-737-6762, Fax: 709-737-5033. *Dean of Medicine,* Dr. M. Ian Bowmer, 709-737-6602, Fax: 709-737-6746, E-mail: bowmer@morgan.ucs.mun.ca.

Graduate Programs in Medicine Students: 75 full-time (47 women), 69 part-time (45 women), 12 international. 54 applicants, 46% accepted. *Faculty:* 179 full-time (58 women), 25 part-time/adjunct (12 women). Expenses: Contact institution. *Financial support:* Research assistantships, external awards available. Financial award application deadline: 3/31. In 2001, 13 master's, 1 doctorate, 1 other advanced degree awarded. *Degree program information:* Part-time programs available. Offers basic medical sciences (M Sc, PhD); clinical epidemiology (M Sc, PhD, Diploma); community health (M Sc, PhD, Diploma); human genetics (M Sc, PhD); medicine (M Sc, PhD, Diploma). *Application deadline:* For fall admission, 3/31 (priority date); for winter admission, 10/15 (priority date); for spring admission, 2/15 (priority date). Applications are processed on a rolling basis. *Application fee:* $40. Electronic applications accepted. *Application Contact:* Information Contact, E-mail: rgs@mun.ca. *Assistant Dean of Research and Graduate Studies,* Dr. Penny Moody-Corbett, 709-777-6762, Fax: 709-777-7501, E-mail: pmoody@mun.ca.

School of Graduate Studies Students: 1,019 full-time (533 women), 602 part-time (310 women), 229 international. 1,469 applicants, 32% accepted. Expenses: Contact institution. *Financial support:* In 2001–02, 600 fellowships (averaging $8,000 per year) were awarded; research assistantships, teaching assistantships, career-related internships or fieldwork, Federal Work-Study, institutionally sponsored loans, and scholarships/grants also available. In 2001, 371 master's, 23 doctorates, 4 other advanced degrees awarded. *Degree program information:* Part-time and evening/weekend programs available. Postbaccalaureate distance learning degree programs offered (minimal on-campus study). Offers anthropology (MA, PhD); applied social psychology (MASP); aquaculture (M Sc); atomic and molecular physics (PhD); biochemistry (M Sc, PhD); biology (M Sc, PhD); biopsychology (M Sc, PhD); chemistry (M Sc, PhD); classics (MA); computational science (M Sc); computational science (cooperative) (M Sc); computer science (M Sc, PhD); condensed matter physics (PhD); economics (MA); English language and literature (MA, PhD); environmental engineering and applied science (MA Sc); environmental science (M Env Sc, M Sc); experimental psychology (M Sc, PhD); fisheries resource management (MMS); folklore (MA, PhD); food science (M Sc, PhD); French studies (MA); geography (M Sc, MA, PhD); geology (M Sc, PhD); geophysics (M Sc, PhD); German language and literature (M Phil, MA); history (MA, PhD); humanities (M Phil); instrumental analysis (M Sc); linguistics (MA, PhD); marine biology (M Sc, PhD); mathematics (M Sc, PhD); mathematics and statistics (MAS); philosophy (MA); physical oceanography (M Sc, PhD); physics (M Sc); political science (MA); religious studies (MA); sociology (MA, PhD); statistics (M Sc, PhD); women's studies (MWS). *Application deadline:* Applications are processed on a rolling basis. *Application fee:* $40 Canadian dollars. Electronic applications accepted. *Application Contact:* Kim Hearn, Admissions, 709-737-2445, Fax: 709-737-4702, E-mail: sgs@mun.ca. *Interim Dean,* Dr. Chet R. Jablonski, 709-737-2478, Fax: 709-737-4702, E-mail: cjablons@mun.ca.

Faculty of Business Administration Students: 58 full-time (26 women), 99 part-time (40 women), 20 international. 110 applicants, 65% accepted, 71 enrolled. Expenses: Contact institution. *Financial support:* Fellowships available. In 2001, 83 degrees awarded. *Degree program information:* Part-time programs available. Offers business administration (EMBA, MBA). *Application deadline:* For fall admission, 5/15 (priority date); for winter admission, 10/15; for spring admission, 2/15. Applications are processed on a rolling basis. *Application fee:* $40. Electronic applications accepted. *Application Contact:* Dr. John Usher, Associate Dean, 709-737-8522, Fax: 709-737-2467, E-mail: business@mun.ca. *Dean,* Dr. R. W. Blake, 709-737-8851, E-mail: bblake@mun.ca.

Faculty of Education Students: 67 full-time (47 women), 213 part-time (110 women), 6 international. 104 applicants, 38% accepted, 39 enrolled. Expenses: Contact institution. *Financial support:* Fellowships, research assistantships, teaching assistantships, career-related internships or fieldwork available. In 2001, 129 degrees awarded. *Degree program information:* Part-time programs available. Offers counseling psychology (M Ed); educational leadership studies (M Ed); information technology (M Ed); post-secondary studies (M Ed); teaching and learning studies (M Ed). *Application deadline:* For fall admission, 2/1; for winter admission, 9/15. Applications are processed on a rolling basis. *Application fee:* $40. Electronic applications accepted. *Application Contact:* Dr. Roberta Hammett, Associate Dean, 709-737-8587, Fax: 709-737-4379, E-mail: hammett@mun.ca. *Acting Dean,* Dr. Alice Collins, 709-737-8588, Fax: 709-737-4379, E-mail: alicec@mun.ca.

Faculty of Engineering and Applied Science Students: 98 full-time (18 women), 44 part-time (8 women), 39 international. 233 applicants, 23% accepted, 54 enrolled. Expenses: Contact institution. *Financial support:* Fellowships, research assistantships, teaching assistantships available. In 2001, 29 master's, 6 doctorates awarded. *Degree program information:* Part-time programs available. Offers civil engineering (M Eng, PhD); electrical engineering (M Eng, PhD); mechanical engineering (M Eng, PhD); naval architecture and ocean engineering (M Eng, PhD). *Application deadline:* Applications are processed on a rolling basis. *Application fee:* $40 Canadian dollars. Electronic applications accepted. *Application Contact:* Dr. M. Haddara, Associate Dean, 709-737-8900, Fax: 709-737-3480, E-mail: mhaddara@engr.mun.ca. *Dean,* Dr. Rangaswany Seshadri, 709-737-8810, Fax: 709-737-8975, E-mail: sesh@engr.mun.ca.

School of Human Kinetics and Recreation Students: 18 full-time (7 women), 7 part-time (3 women), 1 international. 19 applicants, 79% accepted, 12 enrolled. Expenses: Contact institution. *Financial support:* In 2001–02, 6 students received support; fellowships, research assistantships, teaching assistantships available. Financial award application deadline:5/1. In 2001, 2 degrees awarded. *Degree program information:* Part-time programs available. Offers human kinetics and recreation (MPE). *Application deadline:* Applications are processed on a rolling basis. *Application fee:* $40 Canadian dollars. Electronic applications accepted. *Application Contact:* Dr. Matthew White, Graduate Officer, 709-737-8676, Fax: 709-737-3979, E-mail: mdwhite@mun.ca. *Director,* Dr. Colin Higgs, 709-737-8129, Fax: 709-737-3979, E-mail: chiggs@mun.ca.

School of Nursing Students: 14 full-time (13 women), 39 part-time (38 women), 4 international. 36 applicants, 47% accepted, 17 enrolled. Expenses: Contact institution. *Financial support:* Fellowships, research assistantships, teaching assistantships available. Financial award application deadline: 12/31. In 2001, 11 degrees awarded. *Degree program information:* Part-time programs available. Offers nursing (MN). *Application deadline:* For fall admission, 12/31 (priority date). Applications are processed on a rolling basis. *Application fee:* $40. Electronic applications accepted. *Application Contact:* Dr. Sandra LeFort, Graduate Officer, 709-777-6679, E-mail: nursing@mun.ca. *Director,* Dr. Carole Orchard, 709-777-6972, Fax: 709-777-7037, E-mail: corchard@mun.ca.

School of Pharmacy Students: 9 full-time (4 women), 1 (woman) part-time, 7 international. 47 applicants, 6% accepted, 3 enrolled. Expenses: Contact institution. *Financial support:* Fellowships, research assistantships available. *Degree program information:* Part-time programs available. Offers pharmacy (MSCPharm, PhD). *Application deadline:* Applications are processed on a rolling basis. *Application fee:* $40 Canadian dollars. Electronic applications accepted. *Application Contact:* Dr. Hu Liu, Graduate Officer, 709-777-6382, Fax: 709-777-7044, E-mail: hliu@mun.ca. *Acting Director,* Dr. Linda Hensman, 709-777-5153, Fax: 709-777-7044, E-mail: lindah@mun.ca.

School of Social Work Students: 34 full-time (25 women), 32 part-time (27 women), 4 international. 43 applicants, 47% accepted, 18 enrolled. Expenses: Contact institution. *Financial support:* Fellowships, career-related internships or fieldwork available. In 2001, 13 master's, 1 doctorate awarded. *Degree program information:* Part-time and evening/weekend programs available. Offers social work (MSW, PhD). *Application deadline:* Applications are processed on a rolling basis. *Application fee:* $40. Electronic applications accepted. *Application Contact:* Dr. S. Birnie-Lefcovitch, Graduate Officer, 709-737-8146, Fax: 709-737-4512, E-mail: slefcovi@mun.ca. *Acting Director,* Dr. Janet Fitzpatrick, 709-737-8044, Fax: 709-737-2405, E-mail: jfitzpat@mun.ca.

See in-depth description on page 967.

MEMPHIS COLLEGE OF ART, Memphis, TN 38104-2764

General Information Independent, coed, comprehensive institution. *Enrollment:* 31 full-time matriculated graduate/professional students (12 women), 3 part-time matriculated graduate/professional students (all women). *Enrollment by degree level:* 34 master's. *Graduate faculty:* 12 full-time (4 women), 3 part-time/adjunct (2 women). *Tuition:* Full-time $12,940. *Required fees:* $250. *Graduate housing:* Room and/or apartments available on a first-come, first-served basis to single students; on-campus housing not available to married students. Typical cost: $3,000 per year ($4,500 including board). Room and board charges vary according to housing facility selected. Housing application deadline: 8/15. *Student services:* Career counseling, free psychological counseling, international student services, teacher training. *Library facilities:* G. Pillow Lewis Library. *Collection:* 14,500 titles, 102 serial subscriptions.

Computer facilities: 40 computers available on campus for general student use. Internet access is available. *Web address:* http://www.mca.edu/.

General Application Contact: Annette James Moore, Director of Admissions, 800-727-1088, Fax: 901-272-5158, E-mail: info@mca.edu.

GRADUATE UNITS

Graduate Programs Students: 31 full-time (12 women), 3 part-time (all women); includes 5 minority (all African Americans), 13 international. Average age 28. 74 applicants, 68% accepted, 17 enrolled. *Faculty:* 12 full-time (4 women), 3 part-time/adjunct (2 women). Expenses: Contact institution. *Financial support:* In 2001–02, 30 students received support, including 5 teaching assistantships with partial tuition reimbursements available; career-related internships or fieldwork, Federal Work-Study, institutionally sponsored loans, scholarships/grants, unspecified assistantships, and merit awards also available. Support available to part-time students. Financial award application deadline: 8/1; financial award applicants required to submit FAFSA. In 2001, 12 degrees awarded. *Degree program information:* Part-time programs available. Offers computer arts (MFA); fiber/surface design (MFA); painting (MFA); papermaking (MFA); photography (MFA); printmaking (MFA); sculpture (MFA); studio art (MFA). *Application deadline:* For fall admission, 6/1 (priority date); for spring admission, 12/15 (priority date). Applications are processed on a rolling basis. *Application fee:* $25. Electronic applications accepted. *Application Contact:* Annette James Moore, Director of Admissions, 800-727-1088, Fax: 901-272-5158, E-mail: info@mca.edu. *Dean,* Ken Strickland, 901-272-5100, Fax: 901-272-5104, E-mail: info@mca.edu.

MEMPHIS THEOLOGICAL SEMINARY, Memphis, TN 38104-4395

General Information Independent-religious, coed, graduate-only institution. *Enrollment by degree level:* 197 first professional, 26 master's, 26 doctoral. *Graduate faculty:* 11 full-time (4 women), 7 part-time/adjunct (0 women). *Tuition:* Part-time $290 per credit hour. *Graduate housing:* Rooms and/or apartments available on a first-come, first-served basis to single and married students. Housing application deadline: 7/15. *Student services:* Campus employment opportunities, career counseling, international student services. *Library facilities:* Memphis Theological Seminary Library. *Online resources:* library catalog, access to other libraries' catalogs. *Collection:* 93,367 titles, 428 serial subscriptions, 425 audiovisual materials. *Research affiliation:* Lilly Foundation (technology/religion), Wabash Center for Teaching and Learning (theology, religion).

Computer facilities: 12 computers available on campus for general student use. A campuswide network can be accessed. Internet access is available. *Web address:* http://www.mtscampus.edu/.

General Application Contact: Barry L. Anderson, Director of Admissions, 901-458-8232 Ext. 109, Fax: 901-452-4501, E-mail: banderson@mtscampus.edu.

GRADUATE UNITS

Graduate and Professional Programs *Degree program information:* Part-time programs available. Offers theology (M Div, MAR, D Min).

MENNONITE BRETHREN BIBLICAL SEMINARY, Fresno, CA 93727-5097

General Information Independent-religious, coed, graduate-only institution. *Enrollment by degree level:* 61 first professional, 63 master's, 29 other advanced degrees. *Graduate faculty:* 8 full-time (2 women), 6 part-time/adjunct (4 women). *Tuition:* Part-time $260 per unit. *Graduate housing:* Rooms and/or apartments available on a first-come, first-served basis to single and married students. *Student services:* Campus employment opportunities, campus safety program, career counseling, free psychological counseling, international student services. *Library facilities:* Hiebert Library. *Online resources:* library catalog, access to other libraries' catalogs. *Collection:* 150,000 titles, 2,350 serial subscriptions, 6,000 audiovisual materials.

Computer facilities: 3 computers available on campus for general student use. Internet access is available. *Web address:* http://www.mbseminary.com/.

General Application Contact: Jim Holm, Director of Constituency Relations, 559-452-1702, Fax: 559-251-7212, E-mail: jimmbbs@aol.com.

GRADUATE UNITS

School of Theology Students: 54 full-time (14 women), 99 part-time (42 women); includes 13 minority (6 African Americans, 1 Asian American or Pacific Islander, 6 Hispanic Americans), 21 international. Average age 36. 52 applicants, 75% accepted. Expenses: Contact institution. *Financial support:* In 2001–02, 105 students received support, including 12 teaching assistantships; career-related internships or fieldwork, institutionally sponsored loans, scholarships/grants, and tuition waivers (partial) also available. Support available to part-time students. Financial award application deadline: 5/1; financial award applicants required to submit FAFSA. In 2001, 17 first professional degrees, 11 master's awarded. *Degree program information:* Part-time programs available. Postbaccalaureate distance learning degree programs offered (minimal on-campus study). Offers church ministry (MA); divinity (M Div); marriage, family, and child counseling (MAMFCC, Diploma); New Testament (MA); Old Testament (MA); theology (MA). *Application deadline:* For fall admission, 8/1 (priority date); for spring admission, 12/1 (priority date). Applications are processed on a rolling basis. *Application fee:* $35. *Application Contact:* Cam Rowland, Admissions Counselor, 559-452-1798, Fax: 559-251-7212, E-mail: mbbsrec@aol.com. *Academic Dean,* Dr. James N. Pankratz, 559-452-1791, Fax: 559-452-1763, E-mail: jpankratz@fresno.edu.

MERCER UNIVERSITY, Macon, GA 31207-0003

General Information Independent-religious, coed, comprehensive institution. *Enrollment:* 1,635 full-time matriculated graduate/professional students (970 women), 683 part-time matriculated graduate/professional students (407 women). *Enrollment by degree level:* 1,324 first professional, 956 master's, 21 doctoral, 17 other advanced degrees. *Tuition:* Part-time $228 per credit hour. Tuition and fees vary according to degree level, campus/location and program. *Graduate housing:* Rooms and/or apartments available on a first-come, first-served basis to single and married students. *Student services:* Campus employment opportunities, campus safety program, career counseling, disabled student services, free psychological counseling, international student services, low-cost health insurance. *Library facilities:*

Jack Tarver Library plus 3 others. *Online resources:* library catalog, web page. *Collection:* 439,121 titles, 9,567 serial subscriptions, 60,024 audiovisual materials. *Research affiliation:* Central State Hospital of Milledgeville, Georgia (schizophrenia, treatment of psychosis, tumor necrosis), MedCen Foundation (basic clinical investigations).

Computer facilities: 140 computers available on campus for general student use. A campuswide network can be accessed from student residence rooms and from off campus. Internet access is available. *Web address:* http://www.mercer.edu/.

General Application Contact: 478-301-2700.

GRADUATE UNITS

Graduate Studies, Cecil B. Day Campus Students: 888 full-time (574 women), 461 part-time (299 women). Average age 30. *Faculty:* 69 full-time (28 women), 22 part-time/adjunct (9 women). Expenses: Contact institution. *Financial support:* Teaching assistantships, career-related internships or fieldwork, Federal Work-Study, and scholarships/grants available. Support available to part-time students. In 2001, 140 first professional degrees, 418 master's, 19 other advanced degrees awarded. *Degree program information:* Part-time and evening/weekend programs available. Postbaccalaureate distance learning degree programs offered (no on-campus study).

James and Carolyn McAfee School of Theology Students: 87 full-time (35 women), 58 part-time (30 women); includes 20 minority (18 African Americans, 2 Asian Americans or Pacific Islanders), 7 international. Average age 32. 93 applicants, 86% accepted, 42 enrolled. *Faculty:* 7 full-time (2 women), 3 part-time/adjunct (1 woman). Expenses: Contact institution. *Financial support:* Career-related internships or fieldwork, Federal Work-Study, institutionally sponsored loans, and scholarships/grants available. Support available to part-time students. In 2001, 14 degrees awarded. *Degree program information:* Part-time programs available. Offers theology (M Div). *Application deadline:* Applications are processed on a rolling basis. *Application fee:* $35. *Application Contact:* Dock Hollingsworth, Director of Admissions, 678-547-6474, Fax: 678-547-6478, E-mail: hollingsw_jn@mercer.edu. *Dean,* Dr. R. Alan Culpepper, 678-547-6470, Fax: 678-547-6478, E-mail: culpepper_ra@mercer.edu.

Southern School of Pharmacy Students: 538 full-time (395 women), 16 part-time (10 women); includes 144 minority (66 African Americans, 69 Asian Americans or Pacific Islanders, 9 Hispanic Americans), 20 international. Average age 26. 818 applicants, 27% accepted, 141 enrolled. *Faculty:* 31 full-time (15 women), 2 part-time/adjunct (1 woman). Expenses: Contact institution. *Financial support:* In 2001–02, 350 students received support; teaching assistantships, career-related internships or fieldwork, Federal Work-Study, institutionally sponsored loans, and scholarships/grants available. Support available to part-time students. Financial award application deadline: 5/1. In 2001, 115 first professional degrees, 1 doctorate awarded. Offers pharmacy (Pharm D, PhD). *Application deadline:* For fall admission, 2/1. Applications are processed on a rolling basis. *Application fee:* $25. Electronic applications accepted. *Application Contact:* Dr. James W. Bartling, Associate Dean for Student Affairs and Admissions, 678-547-6232, Fax: 678-547-6063, E-mail: bartling_jw@mercer.edu. *Dean,* Dr. Hewitt W. Matthews, 678-547-6304, Fax: 678-547-6315, E-mail: matthews_h@mercer.edu.

Stetson School of Business and Economics Students: 229 full-time (111 women), 224 part-time (110 women); includes 167 minority (135 African Americans, 23 Asian Americans or Pacific Islanders, 9 Hispanic Americans), 69 international. Average age 31. 193 applicants, 87% accepted, 121 enrolled. *Faculty:* 24 full-time (8 women), 7 part-time/adjunct (1 woman). Expenses: Contact institution. *Financial support:* Federal Work-Study available. In 2001, 175 degrees awarded. *Degree program information:* Part-time and evening/weekend programs available. Offers business administration (MBA, XMBA); health care management (MS); technology management (MS). *Application deadline:* For fall admission, 7/1 (priority date); for spring admission, 11/1 (priority date). Applications are processed on a rolling basis. *Application fee:* $35 ($50 for international students). *Application Contact:* Dr. Argy S. Russell, Director, 678-547-6417, Fax: 678-547-6367, E-mail: russell_a@mercer.edu. *Dean,* Dr. W. Carl Joiner, 478-301-2832, Fax: 478-301-2635, E-mail: joiner_wc@mercer.edu.

Tift College of Education Students: 34 full-time (33 women), 163 part-time (149 women); includes 75 minority (70 African Americans, 5 Asian Americans or Pacific Islanders) Average age 34. 49 applicants, 96% accepted, 36 enrolled. *Faculty:* 7 full-time (3 women), 10 part-time/adjunct (6 women). Expenses: Contact institution. *Financial support:* Career-related internships or fieldwork and Federal Work-Study available. Support available to part-time students. Financial award application deadline: 5/1. In 2001, 81 master's, 9 other advanced degrees awarded. *Degree program information:* Part-time and evening/weekend programs available. Offers community counseling (M Ed); early childhood education (M Ed, Ed S); middle grades education (M Ed, Ed S); reading education (M Ed); secondary education (M Ed). *Application deadline:* For fall admission, 8/1; for spring admission, 12/1. Applications are processed on a rolling basis. *Application fee:* $25. *Application Contact:* Dr. Allison Gilmore, Associate Dean and Director of Graduate Education, 678-547-6330, Fax: 678-547-6055, E-mail: gilmore_a@mercer.edu. *Dean,* Dr. Richard T. Sietsema, 478-301-5397, Fax: 478-301-2280, E-mail: sietsema_rt@mercer.edu.

Graduate Studies, Macon Campus Students: 28 full-time (17 women), 193 part-time (86 women). Average age 33. *Faculty:* 29 full-time (9 women), 8 part-time/adjunct (3 women). Expenses: Contact institution. *Financial support:* Career-related internships or fieldwork, Federal Work-Study, and institutionally sponsored loans available. Support available to part-time students. In 2001, 74 master's, 2 other advanced degrees awarded. *Degree program information:* Part-time and evening/weekend programs available. *Application Contact:* Director, 912-301-2700.

School of Education Students: 1 (woman) full-time, 23 part-time (19 women); includes 1 minority (African American), 1 international. Average age 35. 7 applicants, 100% accepted, 5 enrolled. *Faculty:* 8 full-time (5 women), 2 part-time/adjunct (both women). Expenses: Contact institution. *Financial support:* Career-related internships or fieldwork, Federal Work-Study, and institutionally sponsored loans available. Support available to part-time students. Financial award application deadline: 5/1. In 2001, 6 master's, 1 other advanced degree awarded. *Degree program information:* Part-time and evening/weekend programs available. Offers early childhood education (M Ed, Ed S); English education (M Ed); mathematics education (M Ed); middle grades education (M Ed, Ed S); reading specialist (M Ed); science education (M Ed); social sciences education (M Ed). *Application deadline:* For fall admission, 8/1 (priority date); for spring admission, 12/1. Applications are processed on a rolling basis. *Application fee:* $25. *Application Contact:* Dr. Carolyn R. Garvin, Director, 478-301-2585, Fax: 478-301-2576, E-mail: garvin_cr@mercer.edu. *Dean,* Dr. Richard T. Sietsema, 478-301-5397, Fax: 478-301-2280, E-mail: sietsema_rt@mercer.edu.

School of Engineering Students: 3 full-time (2 women), 104 part-time (31 women); includes 19 minority (13 African Americans, 6 Asian Americans or Pacific Islanders), 5 international. Average age 36. 31 applicants, 97% accepted, 27 enrolled. *Faculty:* 10 full-time (1 woman), 5 part-time/adjunct (1 woman). Expenses: Contact institution. *Financial support:* Federal Work-Study available. In 2001, 32 degrees awarded. *Degree program information:* Part-time and evening/weekend programs available. Offers biomedical engineering (MSE); electrical engineering (MSE); engineering management (MSE); mechanical engineering (MSE); software engineering (MSE); software systems (MS); technical communications management (MS); technical management (MS). *Application deadline:* For fall admission, 7/1; for spring admission, 11/15. Applications are processed on a rolling basis. *Application fee:* $35 ($50 for international students). *Application Contact:* Kathy Olivier, Graduate Administrative Coordinator, 478-301-2196, E-mail: olivier_kk@mercer.edu. *Dean,* Dr. M. Dayne Aldridge, 478-301-2459, Fax: 478-301-5593, E-mail: aldridge_md@mercer.edu.

Stetson School of Business and Economics Students: 24 full-time (14 women), 66 part-time (36 women); includes 8 minority (6 African Americans, 1 Asian American or Pacific Islander, 1 Native American), 6 international. Average age 30. 19 applicants, 100% accepted, 19 enrolled. *Faculty:* 11 full-time (3 women), 1 part-time/adjunct (0 women). Expenses: Contact institution. *Financial support:* Federal Work-Study and institutionally sponsored loans available. Support available to part-time students. In 2001, 28 degrees awarded. *Degree program information:* Part-time and evening/weekend programs available. Offers business and economics (MBA). *Application deadline:* For fall admission, 8/1. Applications are processed on a rolling basis. *Application fee:* $35 ($50 for international students). *Application Contact:* Dr. Robert Holland, Director, Academic Administrator, 478-301-2835, Fax: 478-301-2635, E-mail: holland_r@mercer.edu. *Dean,* Dr. W. Carl Joiner, 478-301-2832, Fax: 478-301-2635, E-mail: joiner_wc@mercer.edu.

School of Medicine Students: 307 full-time. Expenses: Contact institution. *Financial support:* Institutionally sponsored loans available. Financial award applicants required to submit FAFSA. Offers medicine (MD, MFS, MPH). *Application deadline:* For fall admission, 11/1. Applications are processed on a rolling basis. *Application fee:* $40. *Application Contact:* Dr. A. Peter Eveland, Associate Dean for Admissions and Student Affairs/Registrar, 478-301-2542, Fax: 478-301-2547, E-mail: eveland_ap@mercer.edu. *Dean,* Dr. Ann C. Jobe, 478-301-5570, Fax: 478-301-2547.

Walter F. George School of Law Students: 432 full-time (215 women), 3 part-time (2 women); includes 60 minority (40 African Americans, 11 Asian Americans or Pacific Islanders, 6 Hispanic Americans, 3 Native Americans) Average age 25. 954 applicants, 38% accepted, 136 enrolled. *Faculty:* 29 full-time (6 women), 25 part-time/adjunct (8 women). Expenses: Contact institution. *Financial support:* In 2001–02, 353 students received support, including 1 fellowship (averaging $4,000 per year), 48 research assistantships (averaging $600 per year); career-related internships or fieldwork, Federal Work-Study, institutionally sponsored loans, scholarships/grants, tuition waivers (partial), and institutional work study also available. Support available to part-time students. Financial award application deadline: 4/1; financial award applicants required to submit FAFSA. In 2001, 116 degrees awarded. *Degree program information:* Part-time programs available. Offers law (JD). *Application deadline:* For fall admission, 3/15 (priority date). Applications are processed on a rolling basis. *Application fee:* $45. Electronic applications accepted. *Application Contact:* Susan Martin, Admissions Assistant, 478-301-2605, Fax: 478-301-2989, E-mail: martin_sv@mercer.edu. *Dean,* R. Lawrence Dessem, 478-301-2602, Fax: 478-301-2101, E-mail: dessem_rl@mercer.edu.

MERCY COLLEGE, Dobbs Ferry, NY 10522-1189

General Information Independent, coed, comprehensive institution. *Enrollment:* 715 full-time matriculated graduate/professional students (525 women), 1,823 part-time matriculated graduate/professional students (1,319 women). *Enrollment by degree level:* 2,538 master's. *Graduate faculty:* 156. *Tuition:* Part-time $450 per credit. Part-time tuition and fees vary according to program. *Graduate housing:* Room and/or apartments available to single students; on-campus housing not available to married students. Typical cost: $4,960 per year ($7,700 including board). Housing application deadline: 6/1. *Student services:* Campus employment opportunities, career counseling, disabled student services, free psychological counseling, international student services. *Library facilities:* Mercy College Library. *Online resources:* library catalog, web page. *Collection:* 322,610 titles, 1,765 serial subscriptions.

Computer facilities: 138 computers available on campus for general student use. A campuswide network can be accessed from off campus. Internet access is available. *Web address:* http://www.mercy.edu/.

General Application Contact: Joy Colelli, Vice President of Enrollment Management, 914-674-7600, Fax: 914-693-7832, E-mail: jcolelli@mercy.edu.

GRADUATE UNITS

Division of Business and Accounting Students: 84 full-time (51 women), 306 part-time (159 women); includes 197 minority (120 African Americans, 28 Asian Americans or Pacific Islanders, 49 Hispanic Americans), 19 international. Average age 32. *Faculty:* 25 full-time (5 women), 40 part-time/adjunct (24 women). Expenses: Contact institution. Offers banking (MS); business administration (MBA); direct marketing (MS); finance (MBA); human resource management (MS); international business (MBA); internet business systems (MS); management (MBA); marketing (MBA); organizational leadership (MS); securities (MS). *Application deadline:* For fall admission, 2/1. *Application fee:* $35. *Application Contact:* Wayne L. Cioffari, Associate Chairperson, 914-674-7481, Fax: 914-674-7488, E-mail: wcioffari@mercy.edu. *Chairperson,* Dr. Tom Milton, 914-374-7479, Fax: 914-674-7488, E-mail: tmilton@mercy.edu.

Division of Education Students: 311 full-time (240 women), 997 part-time (756 women); includes 730 minority (338 African Americans, 38 Asian Americans or Pacific Islanders, 353 Hispanic Americans, 1 Native American), 26 international. Average age 32. 300 applicants, 87% accepted. *Faculty:* 23 full-time (9 women), 77 part-time/adjunct (41 women). Expenses: Contact institution. *Financial support:* Institutionally sponsored loans, scholarships/grants, and unspecified assistantships available. Support available to part-time students. In 2001, 235 master's, 10 other advanced degrees awarded. Offers administration and supervision (PD); education (MS); learning technology (MS); reading education (MS); school administration and supervision (MS); teaching English to speakers of other languages (MS); urban education (MS). *Application deadline:* For fall admission, 2/1. Applications are processed on a rolling basis. *Application fee:* $35. *Chairperson,* Dr. William Prattella, 914-674-7350, Fax: 914-674-7352, E-mail: wpratella@mercy.edu.

Division of Health Sciences Expenses: Contact institution. Offers acupuncture and Oriental medicine (MPS); adult nurse practitioner (MS); family clinical nurse specialist (MS); nursing (MS); occupational therapy (MS); physical therapy (MS); physician assistant (MPS).

Division of Literature, Language, and Communication Students: 42 full-time (31 women); includes 17 minority (12 African Americans, 1 Asian American or Pacific Islander, 4 Hispanic Americans) Average age 35. 5 applicants, 100% accepted, 5 enrolled. *Faculty:* 4 full-time (1 woman), 4 part-time/adjunct (3 women). Expenses: Contact institution. *Financial support:* In 2001–02, 1 student received support, including 1 research assistantship with full tuition reimbursement available (averaging $1,200 per year) In 2001, 5 degrees awarded. *Degree program information:* Part-time and evening/weekend programs available. Postbaccalaureate distance learning degree programs offered (minimal on-campus study). Offers English literature (MA). *Application deadline:* Applications are processed on a rolling basis. *Application fee:* $35. *Application Contact:* Admissions Office, 800-MERCY-NY, Fax: 914-674-7382, E-mail: admission@merlin.mercy.edu. *Program Director,* Dr. Joel Feimer, 914-245-6100 Ext. 2235, Fax: 914-674-7433, E-mail: jfeimer@mercy.edu.

Division of Social and Behavioral Sciences Students: 51 full-time (41 women), 105 part-time (81 women); includes 104 minority (47 African Americans, 7 Asian Americans or Pacific Islanders, 50 Hispanic Americans), 10 international. Expenses: Contact institution. Offers alcohol and substance abuse counseling (AC); family counseling (AC); health services management (MPA, MS); psychology (MS); retirement counseling (AC); school counseling (MS); school psychology (MS). *Application fee:* $35. *Application Contact:* Information Contact, 800-MERCY-NY. *Chairperson,* Dr. Frances T.M. Mahoney, 914-674-7438, Fax: 914-674-7542, E-mail: fmahoney@mercy.edu.

MERCYHURST COLLEGE, Erie, PA 16546

General Information Independent-religious, coed, comprehensive institution. *Enrollment:* 77 full-time matriculated graduate/professional students (48 women), 88 part-time matriculated graduate/professional students (51 women). *Enrollment by degree level:* 165 master's. *Graduate faculty:* 4 full-time (1 woman), 19 part-time/adjunct (7 women). *Graduate housing:* Room and/or apartments available on a first-come, first-served basis to single students; on-campus housing not available to married students. *Student services:* Campus employment opportunities, campus safety program, career counseling, child daycare facilities, disabled student services, exercise/wellness program, free psychological counseling, grant writing training, international student services, low-cost health insurance, multicultural affairs office, teacher training, writing training. *Library facilities:* Hammermill Library plus 1 other. *Online resources:* library catalog, web page, access to other libraries' catalogs. *Collection:* 123,467 titles, 849 serial subscriptions, 8,051 audiovisual materials.

Computer facilities: 350 computers available on campus for general student use. A campuswide network can be accessed from student residence rooms and from off campus. Internet access is available. *Web address:* http://www.mercyhurst.edu/.

General Application Contact: Lynda Schaaf, Director, Office of Adult and Graduate Programs, 814-824-2294, Fax: 814-824-2055, E-mail: lschaaf@mercyhurst.edu.

Mercyhurst College (continued)

GRADUATE UNITS

Graduate Program Average age 29. 86 applicants, 90% accepted. *Faculty:* 4 full-time (1 woman), 19 part-time/adjunct (7 women). Expenses: Contact institution. *Financial support:* In 2001–02, 4 fellowships with tuition reimbursements, 46 research assistantships with tuition reimbursements were awarded. Career-related internships or fieldwork, institutionally sponsored loans, scholarships/grants, and unspecified assistantships also available. Support available to part-time students. Financial award applicants required to submit FAFSA. In 2001, 31 degrees awarded. *Degree program information:* Part-time and evening/weekend programs available. Offers administration of justice (MS); applied intelligence (MS); bilingual/bicultural special education (MS); educational leadership (Certificate); organizational leadership (MS, Certificate); special education (MS). *Application deadline:* For fall admission, 8/1 (priority date). Applications are processed on a rolling basis. *Application fee:* $35. Electronic applications accepted. *Application Contact:* Lynda Schaaf, Director, Office of Adult and Graduate Programs, 814-824-2294, Fax: 814-824-2055, E-mail: lschaaf@mercyhurst.edu. *Dean,* Dr. Joseph F. Gower, 814-824-2311, Fax: 814-824-2055, E-mail: jgower@mercyhurst.edu.

MEREDITH COLLEGE, Raleigh, NC 27607-5298

General Information Independent, women only, comprehensive institution. CGS member. *Enrollment:* 1 (woman) full-time matriculated graduate/professional student, 108 part-time matriculated graduate/professional students (95 women). *Enrollment by degree level:* 109 master's. *Graduate faculty:* 16 full-time (10 women), 4 part-time/adjunct (3 women). *Tuition:* Part-time $310 per credit hour. *Required fees:* $25 per credit hour. Tuition and fees vary according to program. *Graduate housing:* On-campus housing not available. *Student services:* Campus safety program, career counseling, disabled student services, free psychological counseling, international student services. *Library facilities:* Carlyle Campbell Library plus 1 other. *Online resources:* library catalog, web page, access to other libraries' catalogs. *Collection:* 113,179 titles, 4,952 serial subscriptions, 11,751 audiovisual materials.

Computer facilities: 150 computers available on campus for general student use. A campuswide network can be accessed from student residence rooms. Internet access is available. *Web address:* http://www.meredith.edu/.

General Application Contact: Deborah Horvitz, Dean, John E. Weems Graduate School, 919-760-8423, Fax: 919-760-2898, E-mail: horvitz@meredith.edu.

GRADUATE UNITS

John E. Weems Graduate School Students: 1 (woman) full-time, 108 part-time (95 women); includes 12 minority (7 African Americans, 2 Asian Americans or Pacific Islanders, 2 Hispanic Americans, 1 Native American), 3 international. Average age 33. 65 applicants, 78% accepted, 33 enrolled. *Faculty:* 16 full-time (10 women), 4 part-time/adjunct (3 women). Expenses: Contact institution. *Financial support:* In 2001–02, 45 students received support. Career-related internships or fieldwork, institutionally sponsored loans, scholarships/grants, and tuition waivers (partial) available. Support available to part-time students. Financial award application deadline: 2/15; financial award applicants required to submit FAFSA. In 2001, 46 degrees awarded. *Degree program information:* Part-time and evening/weekend programs available. Offers education (M Ed); music (MM). *Application deadline:* For fall admission, 8/1 (priority date); for spring admission, 12/1. Applications are processed on a rolling basis. *Application fee:* $50. Electronic applications accepted. *Director,* Deborah Horvitz, 919-760-8423, Fax: 919-760-8389, E-mail: horvitz@meredith.edu.

School of Business Students: 1 (woman) full-time, 67 part-time (54 women); includes 8 minority (5 African Americans, 1 Asian American or Pacific Islander, 1 Hispanic American, 1 Native American) Average age 31. 43 applicants, 72% accepted, 19 enrolled. *Faculty:* 3 full-time (1 woman), 1 (woman) part-time/adjunct. Expenses: Contact institution. *Financial support:* Career-related internships or fieldwork, institutionally sponsored loans, scholarships/grants, and tuition waivers (partial) available. Support available to part-time students. Financial award application deadline: 2/15; financial award applicants required to submit FAFSA. In 2001, 40 degrees awarded. *Degree program information:* Part-time and evening/weekend programs available. Offers business administration (MBA). *Application deadline:* For fall admission, 8/1 (priority date); for spring admission, 12/1. Applications are processed on a rolling basis. *Application fee:* $50. Electronic applications accepted. *Application Contact:* Wendy Dedzins, Coordinator, 919-760-2281, Fax: 919-760-2898, E-mail: dedzinsw@meredith.edu. *Dean,* Dr. Sidney Adkins, 919-760-8471, Fax: 919-760-8470.

MERRIMACK COLLEGE, North Andover, MA 01845-5800

General Information Independent-religious, coed, comprehensive institution. *Enrollment:* 25 part-time matriculated graduate/professional students (23 women). *Enrollment by degree level:* 25 master's. *Graduate faculty:* 5 part-time/adjunct (3 women). *Tuition:* Part-time $329 per credit. *Required fees:* $329 per credit. *Graduate housing:* On-campus housing not available. *Student services:* Campus safety program, disabled student services, international student services, teacher training. *Library facilities:* McQuade Library. *Online resources:* library catalog, web page, access to other libraries' catalogs. *Collection:* 120,369 titles, 967 serial subscriptions, 1,300 audiovisual materials.

Computer facilities: 175 computers available on campus for general student use. A campuswide network can be accessed from student residence rooms and from off campus. Internet access is available. *Web address:* http://www.merrimack.edu/.

General Application Contact: Diane Aprile, Associate Director, Continuing and Professional Education, 978-837-5101, Fax: 978-837-5226, E-mail: diane.aprile@merrimack.edu.

GRADUATE UNITS

Department of Education 12 applicants, 100% accepted. *Faculty:* 5 full-time (3 women). Expenses: Contact institution. *Financial support:* Career-related internships or fieldwork available. In 2001, 1 degree awarded. *Degree program information:* Part-time and evening/weekend programs available. Offers education (M Ed). *Application deadline:* For fall admission, 8/15 (priority date); for spring admission, 1/15. Applications are processed on a rolling basis. *Application fee:* $50. *Application Contact:* Diane Aprile, Associate Director, Continuing and Professional Education, 978-837-5101, Fax: 978-837-5226, E-mail: diane.aprile@merrimack.edu. *Director,* Dr. Brenda B. Brown, 978-837-5000 Ext. 4367, Fax: 978-837-5069, E-mail: brenda.brown@merrimack.edu.

MESA STATE COLLEGE, Grand Junction, CO 81501

General Information State-supported, coed, comprehensive institution. *Enrollment:* 29 part-time matriculated graduate/professional students (16 women). *Graduate faculty:* 7 part-time/adjunct (0 women). Tuition, state resident: part-time $234 per course. Tuition, nonresident: part-time $1,139 per course. *Required fees:* $89 per course. *Graduate housing:* Room and/or apartments available on a first-come, first-served basis to single students; on-campus housing not available to married students. Housing application deadline: 6/1. *Student services:* Campus safety program, disabled student services, exercise/wellness program, free psychological counseling, international student services, low-cost health insurance, multicultural affairs office. *Library facilities:* John U. Tomlinson Library. *Online resources:* library catalog, web page. *Collection:* 329,681 titles, 1,010 serial subscriptions, 25,578 audiovisual materials.

Computer facilities: 350 computers available on campus for general student use. A campuswide network can be accessed from off campus. Internet access and online class registration are available. *Web address:* http://www2.mesastate.edu/.

General Application Contact: Mary Vail, Graduate Admissions Counselor, 970-248-1778, Fax: 970-248-1730, E-mail: mvail@mesastate.edu.

GRADUATE UNITS

School of Business and Professional Studies Average age 36. 29 applicants. *Faculty:* 7 part-time/adjunct (0 women). Expenses: Contact institution. In 2001, 10 degrees awarded. *Degree program information:* Part-time and evening/weekend programs available. Offers business administration (MBA). *Application deadline:* For fall admission, 8/19 (priority date); for spring admission, 1/13 (priority date). Applications are processed on a rolling basis. *Application fee:* $50. Electronic applications accepted. *Application Contact:* Mary Vail, Graduate Admissions Counselor, 970-248-1778, Fax: 970-248-1730, E-mail: mvail@mesastate.edu. *Dean,* Dr. John C. Rogers, 970-248-1656, Fax: 970-248-1730, E-mail: jcrogers@mesastate.edu.

MESIVTA OF EASTERN PARKWAY RABBINICAL SEMINARY, Brooklyn, NY 11218-5559

General Information Independent-religious, men only, comprehensive institution.

GRADUATE UNITS

Graduate Programs

MESIVTA TIFERETH JERUSALEM OF AMERICA, New York, NY 10002-6301

General Information Independent-religious, men only, comprehensive institution.

GRADUATE UNITS

Graduate Programs

MESIVTA TORAH VODAATH RABBINICAL SEMINARY, Brooklyn, NY 11218-5299

General Information Independent-religious, men only, comprehensive institution.

GRADUATE UNITS

Graduate Programs

METHODIST THEOLOGICAL SCHOOL IN OHIO, Delaware, OH 43015-8004

General Information Independent-religious, coed, graduate-only institution. *Graduate housing:* Rooms and/or apartments available on a first-come, first-served basis to single students and available to married students. Housing application deadline: 8/15.

GRADUATE UNITS

Graduate and Professional Programs *Degree program information:* Part-time programs available. Offers theology (M Div, MACE, MACM, MASM, MTS).

METROPOLITAN STATE UNIVERSITY, St. Paul, MN 55106-5000

General Information State-supported, coed, comprehensive institution. *Graduate housing:* On-campus housing not available.

GRADUATE UNITS

College of Arts and Sciences Offers technical communication (MS).

College of Management *Degree program information:* Part-time and evening/weekend programs available. Offers finance (MBA); human resource management (MBA); information management (MMIS); international business (MBA); law enforcement (MPNA); management information systems (MBA); marketing (MBA); nonprofit management (MPNA); organizational studies (MBA); public administration (MPNA); purchasing management (MBA); systems management (MMIS).

School of Nursing *Degree program information:* Part-time programs available. Offers nursing (MSN).

MGH INSTITUTE OF HEALTH PROFESSIONS, Boston, MA 02129

General Information Independent, coed, primarily women, graduate-only institution. *Enrollment by degree level:* 336 master's, 128 doctoral, 19 other advanced degrees. *Graduate faculty:* 42 full-time (34 women), 29 part-time/adjunct (22 women). *Tuition:* Part-time $605 per credit. *Graduate housing:* On-campus housing not available. *Student services:* Campus employment opportunities, campus safety program, career counseling, disabled student services, international student services, low-cost health insurance. *Library facilities:* Treadwell Library. *Online resources:* library catalog, web page, access to other libraries' catalogs. *Collection:* 50,000 titles, 700 serial subscriptions, 75 audiovisual materials. *Research affiliation:* Massachusetts General Hospital, Spaulding Rehabilitation Hospital, McLean Psychiatric Hospital, Partners Health Care System, Inc., Brigham and Women's Hospital.

Computer facilities: 25 computers available on campus for general student use. A campuswide network can be accessed from off campus. Internet access is available. *Web address:* http://www.mghihp.edu/.

General Application Contact: Alice Taggart, Admissions Coordinator, 617-726-3140, Fax: 617-726-8010, E-mail: ataggart@partners.org.

GRADUATE UNITS

Graduate Programs Students: 324 full-time (292 women), 160 part-time (130 women); includes 34 minority (8 African Americans, 20 Asian Americans or Pacific Islanders, 4 Hispanic Americans, 2 Native Americans), 6 international. 451 applicants, 82% accepted, 255 enrolled. *Faculty:* 42 full-time (34 women), 29 part-time/adjunct (22 women). Expenses: Contact institution. *Financial support:* In 2001–02, 275 students received support, including 7 research assistantships (averaging $1,200 per year), 7 teaching assistantships (averaging $1,200 per year); career-related internships or fieldwork, scholarships/grants, traineeships, tuition waivers (partial), and unspecified assistantships also available. Support available to part-time students. Financial award application deadline: 3/1; financial award applicants required to submit FAFSA. In 2001, 160 master's, 7 other advanced degrees awarded. *Degree program information:* Part-time and evening/weekend programs available. Postbaccalaureate distance learning degree programs offered. Offers clinical investigation (MS, Certificate); nursing (MSN, Certificate); physical therapy (MS, DPT, Certificate); speech-language pathology (MS). *Application fee:* $50. Electronic applications accepted. *Application Contact:* Alice Taggart, Admissions Coordinator, 617-726-3140, Fax: 617-726-8010, E-mail: ataggart@partners.org. *President,* Ann W. Caldwell, 617-726-8002, Fax: 617-726-3716, E-mail: caldwell.ann@mgh.harvard.edu.

MIAMI UNIVERSITY, Oxford, OH 45056

General Information State-related, coed, university. CGS member. *Enrollment:* 1,087 full-time matriculated graduate/professional students (609 women), 261 part-time matriculated graduate/professional students (211 women). *Graduate faculty:* 270 full-time (56 women), 189 part-time/adjunct (63 women). Tuition, state resident: full-time $7,155; part-time $295 per semester hour. Tuition, nonresident: full-time $14,829; part-time $615 per semester hour. Tuition and fees vary according to degree level and campus/location. *Graduate housing:* Rooms and/or apartments available on a first-come, first-served basis to single and married students. Housing application deadline: 3/1. *Student services:* Campus employment opportunities, campus safety program, career counseling, child daycare facilities, disabled student services, exercise/wellness program, free psychological counseling, international student services, low-cost health insurance, multicultural affairs office, writing training. *Library facilities:* King Library plus 3 others. *Online resources:* library catalog, web page, access to other libraries' catalogs. *Collection:* 2.7 million titles, 12,234 serial subscriptions, 134,404 audiovisual materials.

Computer facilities: 1,000 computers available on campus for general student use. A campuswide network can be accessed from student residence rooms and from off campus. Internet access and online class registration are available. *Web address:* http://www.muohio.edu/.

General Application Contact: Dr. Robert C. Johnson, Associate Provost and Dean of the Graduate School, 513-529-4125, Fax: 513-529-4127, E-mail: johnsorc@muohio.edu.

GRADUATE UNITS

Graduate School Students: 1,189 full-time (667 women), 222 part-time (169 women); includes 142 minority (84 African Americans, 37 Asian Americans or Pacific Islanders, 15 Hispanic Americans, 6 Native Americans), 162 international. 1,456 applicants, 77% accepted,

474 enrolled. *Faculty:* 270 full-time (56 women), 189 part-time/adjunct (63 women). Expenses: Contact institution. *Financial support:* In 2001–02, 815 students received support, including 550 fellowships (averaging $8,535 per year), 19 research assistantships (averaging $12,513 per year), 115 teaching assistantships (averaging $12,245 per year); career-related internships or fieldwork, Federal Work-Study, and tuition waivers (full) also available. Financial award application deadline: 3/1; financial award applicants required to submit FAFSA. In 2001, 494 master's, 33 doctorates awarded. *Degree program information:* Part-time programs available. *Application fee:* $35. Electronic applications accepted. *Application Contact:* Cyndi E. Stevens, Assistant to the Dean, 513-529-4126, Fax: 513-529-4127, E-mail: stevence@muohio.edu. *Associate Provost and Dean of The Graduate School,* Dr. Robert C. Johnson, 513-529-4125, Fax: 513-529-4127, E-mail: johnsorc@muohio.edu.

College of Arts and Sciences Students: 682 full-time (384 women), 30 part-time (22 women); includes 63 minority (33 African Americans, 15 Asian Americans or Pacific Islanders, 12 Hispanic Americans, 3 Native Americans), 111 international. 821 applicants, 74% accepted, 231 enrolled. *Faculty:* 156 full-time (32 women), 104 part-time/adjunct (33 women). Expenses: Contact institution. *Financial support:* In 2001–02, 329 fellowships (averaging $9,671 per year), 19 research assistantships (averaging $12,513 per year), 106 teaching assistantships (averaging $12,329 per year) were awarded. Career-related internships or fieldwork, Federal Work-Study, and tuition waivers (full) also available. Financial award application deadline: 3/1. In 2001, 197 master's, 35 doctorates awarded. *Degree program information:* Part-time programs available. Offers analytical chemistry (MS, PhD); arts and sciences (MA, MAT, MGS, MS, MS Stat, MTSC, PhD); biochemistry (MS, PhD); biological sciences (MAT); botany (MA, MS, PhD); chemical education (MS, PhD); chemistry (MS, PhD); clinical psychology (PhD); comparative religion (MA); composition and rhetoric (MA, PhD); creative writing (MA); criticism (PhD); English and American literature and language (PhD); English education (MAT); experimental psychology (PhD); French (MA); geography (MA); geology (MA, MS, PhD); gerontology (MGS); history (MA); inorganic chemistry (MS, PhD); library theory (PhD); literature (MA, MAT, PhD); mass communication (MA); mathematics (MA, MAT, MS); mathematics/operations research (MS); microbiology (MS, PhD); organic chemistry (MS, PhD); philosophy (MA); physical chemistry (MS, PhD); physics (MS); political science (MA, MAT, PhD); social psychology (PhD); Spanish (MA); speech communication (MA); speech pathology and audiology (MA, MS); statistics (MS Stat); technical and scientific communication (MTSC); zoology (MA, MS, PhD). *Application fee:* $35. *Dean,* Dr. John Skillings, 513-529-1234, Fax: 513-529-5026.

Institute of Environmental Sciences Students: 65 full-time (36 women), 2 part-time (both women); includes 4 minority (2 African Americans, 1 Asian American or Pacific Islander, 1 Native American), 11 international. 68 applicants, 75% accepted, 19 enrolled. Expenses: Contact institution. *Financial support:* In 2001–02, 13 fellowships (averaging $6,501 per year) were awarded; research assistantships, teaching assistantships, career-related internships or fieldwork, Federal Work-Study, and tuition waivers (full) also available. In 2001, 12 degrees awarded. *Degree program information:* Part-time programs available. Offers environmental sciences (M En S). *Application deadline:* For fall admission, 2/1. *Application fee:* $35. *Director,* Dr. Gene Willeke, 513-529-5811, Fax: 513-529-5814, E-mail: environ@muohio.edu.

Richard T. Farmer School of Business Administration Students: 131 full-time (58 women), 24 part-time (10 women); includes 12 minority (7 African Americans, 3 Asian Americans or Pacific Islanders, 1 Hispanic American, 1 Native American), 30 international. 189 applicants, 83% accepted, 76 enrolled. *Faculty:* 48 full-time (5 women), 28 part-time/adjunct (3 women). Expenses: Contact institution. *Financial support:* In 2001–02, 55 fellowships (averaging $3,762 per year) were awarded; research assistantships, Federal Work-Study and tuition waivers (full) also available. Financial award application deadline: 3/1. In 2001, 96 degrees awarded. *Degree program information:* Part-time programs available. Offers accountancy (M Acc); business administration (MBA); economics (MA); finance (MBA); general management (MBA); management information systems (MBA); marketing (MBA); quality and process improvement (MBA). *Application deadline:* For fall admission, 3/1 (priority date). Applications are processed on a rolling basis. *Application fee:* $35. *Dean,* Dr. Daniel Short, 513-529-3631, E-mail: miamimba@muohio.edu.

School of Education and Allied Professions Students: 260 full-time (174 women), 147 part-time (123 women); includes 48 minority (38 African Americans, 8 Asian Americans or Pacific Islanders, 2 Hispanic Americans), 2 international. 244 applicants, 80% accepted, 108 enrolled. *Faculty:* 29 full-time (11 women), 36 part-time/adjunct (19 women). Expenses: Contact institution. *Financial support:* In 2001–02, 81 fellowships (averaging $7,862 per year), 9 teaching assistantships (averaging $11,313 per year) were awarded. Research assistantships, career-related internships or fieldwork, Federal Work-Study, and tuition waivers (full) also available. Financial award application deadline: 3/1. In 2001, 135 master's, 18 doctorates awarded. *Degree program information:* Part-time programs available. Offers adolescent education (MAT); child and family studies (MS); college student personnel services (MS); curriculum and teacher leadership (M Ed); education and allied professions (M Ed, MA, MAT, MS, Ed D, PhD, Ed S); educational administration (Ed D, PhD); educational leadership (M Ed, MS); educational psychology (M Ed); elementary education (M Ed, MAT); elementary mathematics education (M Ed); physical education, health, and sports studies (MS); reading education (M Ed); school psychology (MS, Ed S); secondary education (M Ed, MAT); special education (M Ed, MA). *Application deadline:* For fall admission, 3/1 (priority date). Applications are processed on a rolling basis. *Application fee:* $35. *Acting Dean,* Dr. Curtis Ellison, 513-529-6317, Fax: 513-529-7270.

School of Engineering and Applied Science Students: 30 full-time (9 women); includes 8 minority (all Asian Americans or Pacific Islanders), 14 international. 74 applicants, 66% accepted, 13 enrolled. *Faculty:* 12 full-time (0 women), 4 part-time/adjunct (1 woman). Expenses: Contact institution. *Financial support:* In 2001–02, 22 fellowships (averaging $10,057 per year) were awarded; research assistantships, teaching assistantships, Federal Work-Study and tuition waivers (full) also available. Financial award application deadline: 3/1. In 2001, 23 degrees awarded. Offers engineering and applied science (MS); paper science and engineering (MS); systems analysis (MS). *Application deadline:* For fall admission, 3/1 (priority date). Applications are processed on a rolling basis. *Application fee:* $35. *Chair,* Dr. Marek Dollár, 513-529-4036.

School of Fine Arts Students: 86 full-time (42 women), 21 part-time (14 women); includes 11 minority (6 African Americans, 3 Asian Americans or Pacific Islanders, 2 Native Americans), 5 international. 128 applicants, 87% accepted, 46 enrolled. *Faculty:* 25 full-time (8 women), 17 part-time/adjunct (7 women). Expenses: Contact institution. *Financial support:* In 2001–02, 61 fellowships (averaging $7,085 per year) were awarded; research assistantships, teaching assistantships, career-related internships or fieldwork, Federal Work-Study, and tuition waivers (full) also available. Financial award application deadline: 3/1. In 2001, 43 degrees awarded. *Degree program information:* Part-time programs available. Offers architecture (M Arch); art education (MA); fine arts (M Arch, MA, MFA, MM); music education (MM); music performance (MM); studio art (MFA); theatre (MA). *Application fee:* $35. *Dean,* Dr. Pamela Fox, 513-529-6010.

See in-depth description on page 969.

MICHIGAN STATE UNIVERSITY, East Lansing, MI 48824

General Information State-supported, coed, university. CGS member. *Enrollment:* 5,827 full-time matriculated graduate/professional students (3,091 women), 3,526 part-time matriculated graduate/professional students (2,156 women). *Enrollment by degree level:* 1,378 first professional, 5,141 master's, 2,834 doctoral. *Graduate faculty:* 1,977 full-time (534 women). Tuition, state resident: part-time $244 per credit hour. Tuition, nonresident: part-time $494 per credit hour. *Required fees:* $268 per semester. Tuition and fees vary according to course load, degree level and program. *Graduate housing:* Rooms and/or apartments available on a first-come, first-served basis to single and married students. *Student services:* Campus employment opportunities, campus safety program, career counseling, child daycare facilities, disabled student services, exercise/wellness program, free psychological counseling, grant writing training, international student services, low-cost health insurance, multicultural affairs office. *Library facilities:* Main Library plus 14 others. *Online resources:* library catalog, web page, access to other libraries' catalogs. *Collection:* 4.4 million titles, 27,324 serial subscriptions, 278,968 audiovisual materials. *Research affiliation:* Argonne National Laboratory (high-energy physics), Association of Sea Grant Programs (fresh water ecosystems), Michigan Biotechnology Institute, Michigan Technology Council (broad spectrum of high technology), Center for Nuclear Research (particle physics), Neogen Corporation (biotechnology).

Computer facilities: 2,000 computers available on campus for general student use. A campuswide network can be accessed from student residence rooms and from off campus. Internet access and online class registration are available. *Web address:* http://www.msu.edu/.

General Application Contact: Dr. Karen Klomparens,, Dean of the Graduate School, 517-355-3220, Fax: 517-353-3355.

GRADUATE UNITS

College of Human Medicine Students: 510 (290 women); includes 160 minority (54 African Americans, 62 Asian Americans or Pacific Islanders, 39 Hispanic Americans, 5 Native Americans) 10 international. Average age 27. 200 applicants, 96% accepted. *Faculty:* 104. Expenses: Contact institution. *Financial support:* In 2001–02, 102 fellowships with tuition reimbursements (averaging $3,698 per year), 48 research assistantships with tuition reimbursements (averaging $12,058 per year), 1 teaching assistantship with tuition reimbursement (averaging $10,944 per year) were awarded. Career-related internships or fieldwork, Federal Work-Study, and institutionally sponsored loans also available. Support available to part-time students. Financial award applicants required to submit FAFSA. In 2001, 99 first professional degrees, 14 master's, 2 doctorates awarded. *Degree program information:* Part-time programs available. Offers anatomy (MS); anthropology (MA); biochemistry (MS, PhD); epidemiology (MS); human medicine (MD, MA, MS, PhD); human pathology (MS, PhD); medicine); microbiology (MS, PhD); pharmacology/toxicology (MS, PhD); physiology (MS, PhD); psychology (MA); sociology (MA); surgery (MS); zoology (MS). *Application deadline:* Applications are processed on a rolling basis. *Application fee:* $30 ($40 for international students). Electronic applications accepted. *Application Contact:* Dr. Christine L. Shafer, Assistant Dean, 517-353-9620, Fax: 517-432-0021, E-mail: mdadmissions@msu.edu. *Dean,* Dr. Glenn C. Davis, 517-353-1730, Fax: 517-355-0340.

College of Osteopathic Medicine Students: 528 full-time (249 women); includes 105 minority (14 African Americans, 68 Asian Americans or Pacific Islanders, 20 Hispanic Americans, 3 Native Americans), 1 international. Average age 24. 1,692 applicants, 11% accepted, 125 enrolled. *Faculty:* 88 full-time (11 women), 2 part-time/adjunct (0 women). Expenses: Contact institution. *Financial support:* In 2001–02, 514 students received support; fellowships, research assistantships, teaching assistantships, career-related internships or fieldwork, Federal Work-Study, institutionally sponsored loans, and tuition waivers (partial) available. Support available to part-time students. Financial award applicants required to submit FAFSA. In 2001, 126 first professional degrees, 1 doctorate awarded. *Degree program information:* Part-time programs available. Offers anatomy (MS, PhD); biochemistry (MS, PhD); microbiology (PhD); osteopathic medicine (DO, MS, PhD); pathology (MS, PhD); pharmacology/toxicology (MS, PhD); physiology (MS, PhD). *Application deadline:* For winter admission, 12/1. *Application fee:* $75. *Application Contact:* Kathie Schafer, Director of Admissions, 517-353-7740, Fax: 517-355-3296, E-mail: comadm@msu.edu. *Dean,* Dr. William D. Strampel, 517-355-9616, Fax: 517-432-2125, E-mail: strampe3@msu.edu.

College of Veterinary Medicine Students: 514 full-time (381 women); includes 49 minority (8 African Americans, 20 Asian Americans or Pacific Islanders, 15 Hispanic Americans, 6 Native Americans), 20 international. 1,153 applicants, 11% accepted, 114 enrolled. *Faculty:* 107. Expenses: Contact institution. *Financial support:* Fellowships, research assistantships, Federal Work-Study available. Support available to part-time students. In 2001, 91 first professional degrees, 6 master's, 6 doctorates awarded. Offers comparative medicine and integrative biology (MS, PhD); large animal clinical sciences (MS, PhD); microbiology and molecular genetics (MS, PhD); pathobiology and diagnostic investigation (MS, PhD); pharmacology/toxicology (MS, PhD); small animal clinical sciences (MS); veterinary medicine (DVM, MS, PhD). *Dean,* Dr. Lonnie J. King, 517-335-6509, Fax: 517-432-1037, E-mail: kinglonn@cvm.msu.edu.

Institute for Environmental Toxicology Students: 47 full-time (5 women). Expenses: Contact institution. *Financial support:* Research assistantships with tuition reimbursements, teaching assistantships, career-related internships or fieldwork and Federal Work-Study available. Financial award applicants required to submit FAFSA. Offers environmental toxicology (PhD). *Application fee:* $30 ($40 for international students). *Director,* Dr. Lawrence J. Fischer, 517-355-4603, Fax: 517-355-4603, E-mail: lfischer@pilot.msu.edu.

Graduate School Students: 4,473 full-time (2,251 women), 3,502 part-time (2,141 women); includes 956 minority (471 African Americans, 250 Asian Americans or Pacific Islanders, 198 Hispanic Americans, 37 Native Americans), 2,092 international. Average age 30. ###### applicants, 29% accepted. *Faculty:* 1,977. Expenses: Contact institution. *Financial support:* In 2001–02, 1,995 fellowships (averaging $3,274 per year), 1,860 research assistantships (averaging $12,283 per year), 1,339 teaching assistantships (averaging $11,570 per year) were awarded. Career-related internships or fieldwork, Federal Work-Study, institutionally sponsored loans, scholarships/grants, tuition waivers (partial), and unspecified assistantships also available. Support available to part-time students. Financial award application deadline: 2/1; financial award applicants required to submit CSS PROFILE or FAFSA. In 2001, 1,776 master's, 434 doctorates awarded. *Degree program information:* Part-time and evening/weekend programs available. Postbaccalaureate distance learning degree programs offered. *Application deadline:* Applications are processed on a rolling basis. *Application fee:* $30 ($40 for international students). Electronic applications accepted. *Application Contact:* 517-355-8332, E-mail: admis@msu.edu. *Dean of the Graduate School,* Dr. Karen Klomparens,, 517-355-3220, Fax: 517-353-3355.

College of Agriculture and Natural Resources Students: 382 full-time (161 women), 291 part-time (152 women); includes 69 minority (27 African Americans, 18 Asian Americans or Pacific Islanders, 21 Hispanic Americans, 3 Native Americans), 245 international. Average age 30. 644 applicants, 27% accepted. *Faculty:* 290. Expenses: Contact institution. *Financial support:* In 2001–02, 203 fellowships (averaging $3,217 per year), 439 research assistantships (averaging $11,715 per year), 46 teaching assistantships with tuition reimbursements (averaging $11,297 per year) were awarded. Career-related internships or fieldwork, Federal Work-Study, institutionally sponsored loans, and tuition waivers (partial) also available. Support available to part-time students. Financial award applicants required to submit FAFSA. In 2001, 103 master's, 46 doctorates awarded. *Degree program information:* Part-time and evening/weekend programs available. Postbaccalaureate distance learning degree programs offered. Offers agricultural and extension education (MS, PhD); agricultural economics (MS, PhD); agricultural engineering (MS, PhD); agricultural technology and systems management (MS, PhD); agriculture and natural resources (MS, PhD); animal science (MS, PhD); animal science-environmental toxicology (PhD); biosystems engineering (MS, PhD); building construction management (MS); crop and soil science (MS, PhD); crop and soil science-environmental toxicology (PhD); entomology (MS, PhD); entomology-environmental toxicology (PhD); entomology-urban studies (MS, PhD); fisheries and wildlife (MS, PhD); forestry (MS, PhD); forestry-environmental toxicology (PhD); forestry-urban studies (MS, PhD); horticulture (MS, PhD); packaging (MS, PhD); park, recreation and tourism resources (MS, PhD); park, recreation and tourism resources-urban studies (MS, PhD); plant breeding and genetics-crop and soil sciences (MS, PhD); plant breeding and genetics-forestry (MS, PhD); plant breeding and genetics-horticulture (MS, PhD); plant pathology (MS, PhD); recreation (PhD); resource development (MS, PhD); resource development—environmental toxicology (PhD); resource development-urban studies (MS, PhD). *Application deadline:* Applications are processed on a rolling basis. *Application fee:* $30 ($40 for international students). Electronic applications accepted. *Dean,* Dr. Jeffrey Armstrong, 517-355-0232, Fax: 517-353-9856.

College of Arts and Letters Students: 395 full-time (217 women), 286 part-time (182 women); includes 76 minority (44 African Americans, 15 Asian Americans or Pacific Islanders, 13 Hispanic Americans, 4 Native Americans), 218 international. Average age 32. 717 applicants, 43% accepted. *Faculty:* 293. Expenses: Contact institution. *Financial support:* In 2001–02, 182 fellowships with tuition reimbursements (averaging $3,134 per year), 19 research assistantships with tuition reimbursements (averaging $10,850 per year), 295 teaching assistantships with tuition reimbursements (averaging $10,363 per year) were

Michigan State University (continued)

awarded. Career-related internships or fieldwork, Federal Work-Study, institutionally sponsored loans, and scholarships/grants also available. Support available to part-time students. Financial award applicants required to submit FAFSA. In 2001, 92 master's, 53 doctorates awarded. *Degree program information:* Part-time and evening/weekend programs available. Offers adult language learning (MA); American studies (PhD); applied music (M Mus, DMA, PhD); arts and letters (M Mus, MA, MFA, DMA, PhD); ceramics (MFA); comparative literature (MA); conducting (M Mus, DMA); creative writing (MA); critical studies (MA); English (MA, PhD); English and American literature (MA); French (MA); French language and literature (PhD); German (MA, PhD); German language and literature (PhD); German studies (MA, PhD); graphic design (MFA); health and humanities (MA); history (MA, PhD); history of art (MA); history-urban studies (MA, PhD); linguistics (MA, PhD); literature in English (MA); music composition (M Mus, DMA, PhD); music education (M Mus, PhD); music theory (M Mus, PhD); music therapy (M Mus); music, performance, and conducting (DMA); musicology (MA, PhD); painting (MFA); performance (M Mus); philosophy (MA, PhD); piano (M Mus); piano pedagogy (M Mus); printmaking (MFA); Russian (MA); sculpture (MFA); secondary school/community college teaching (MA); Spanish (MA); Spanish language and literature (PhD); studio art (MA, MFA); teaching English in secondary school (MA); teaching of English to speakers of other languages (MA); theatre (MA, MFA, PhD). *Application deadline:* Applications are processed on a rolling basis. *Application fee:* $30 ($40 for international students). Electronic applications accepted. *Application Contact:* Patrick McConeghy, Acting Director, 517-355-0366, Fax: 517-432-0129. *Dean,* Dr. Wendy Wilkins, 517-355-4597, Fax: 517-432-0129.

College of Communication Arts and Sciences Students: 189 full-time (130 women), 183 part-time (109 women); includes 49 minority (28 African Americans, 15 Asian Americans or Pacific Islanders, 6 Hispanic Americans), 138 international. Average age 28. 672 applicants, 38% accepted. *Faculty:* 64. Expenses: Contact institution. *Financial support:* In 2001–02, 245 fellowships (averaging $4,080 per year), 23 research assistantships (averaging $11,498 per year), 60 teaching assistantships with tuition reimbursements (averaging $11,360 per year) were awarded. Career-related internships or fieldwork, Federal Work-Study, and institutionally sponsored loans also available. Support available to part-time students. Financial award applicants required to submit FAFSA. In 2001, 125 master's, 23 doctorates awarded. *Degree program information:* Part-time and evening/weekend programs available. Postbaccalaureate distance learning degree programs offered (no on-campus study). Offers advertising (MA); audiology and speech sciences (MA, PhD); audiology and speech sciences-urban studies (PhD); communication (MA, PhD); communication arts and sciences (MA, PhD); communication-urban studies (MA); digital media arts and technology (MA); health communication (MA); information and telecommunication management (MA); information policy and society (MA); journalism (MA); mass media (PhD); public relations (MA); telecommunication (MA). *Application deadline:* Applications are processed on a rolling basis. *Application fee:* $30 ($40 for international students). Electronic applications accepted. *Application Contact:* Graduate Student Affairs Office, 517-355-3410. *Dean,* Dr. James Spaniolo, 517-355-3410, Fax: 517-432-1244.

College of Education Students: 449 full-time (302 women), 777 part-time (561 women); includes 159 minority (106 African Americans, 23 Asian Americans or Pacific Islanders, 24 Hispanic Americans, 6 Native Americans), 122 international. Average age 32. 919 applicants, 50% accepted. *Faculty:* 127. Expenses: Contact institution. *Financial support:* In 2001–02, 174 fellowships (averaging $3,471 per year), 143 research assistantships with tuition reimbursements (averaging $12,106 per year), 121 teaching assistantships with tuition reimbursements (averaging $11,860 per year) were awarded. Career-related internships or fieldwork, Federal Work-Study, and institutionally sponsored loans also available. Support available to part-time students. Financial award applicants required to submit FAFSA. In 2001, 499 master's, 63 doctorates, 20 other advanced degrees awarded. *Degree program information:* Part-time and evening/weekend programs available. Postbaccalaureate distance learning degree programs offered (no on-campus study). Offers adult and continuing education (MA, Ed D, PhD, Ed S); college and university administration (MA, PhD); counseling (MA, Ed D, Ed S); counseling psychology (MA, PhD); counselor education (PhD); curriculum and teaching (MA); curriculum, teaching and education policy (PhD, Ed S); curriculum, teaching, and education policy (Ed D); education (MA, MS, Ed D, PhD, Ed S); educational psychology (MA, Ed D, PhD, Ed S); educational system design (Ed S); educational system development (MA, Ed D); educational technology and instructional design (MA); educational technology and system design (MA); health and physical education (Ed D, PhD); health education and human performance (MA, PhD); higher education (Ed D, Ed S); higher, adult and lifelong education (PhD); K–12 educational administration (MA, PhD, Ed S); K-12 education administration (Ed D); kinesiology (MS, PhD); kinesiology-urban studies (MS); literacy instruction (MA); measurement and quantitative methods (MA, PhD); measurement, evaluation and research design (Ed D, PhD); physical education and exercise science (Ed D, PhD); physical education and exercise science-urban studies (MS); physical education and exercises science (MA); physical education-urban studies (MS); reading instruction (MA); rehabilitation counseling (MA); rehabilitation counseling and school counseling (PhD); school psychology (PhD, Ed S); special education (MA, Ed D, PhD, Ed S); student affairs administration (MA). *Application deadline:* Applications are processed on a rolling basis. *Application fee:* $30 ($40 for international students). Electronic applications accepted. *Dean,* Dr. Carole Ames, 517-355-1734, Fax: 517-353-6393.

College of Engineering Students: 376 full-time (67 women), 214 part-time (39 women); includes 82 minority (27 African Americans, 32 Asian Americans or Pacific Islanders, 23 Hispanic Americans), 365 international. Average age 27. 2,244 applicants, 14% accepted. *Faculty:* 128. Expenses: Contact institution. *Financial support:* In 2001–02, 174 fellowships with tuition reimbursements (averaging $3,471 per year), 235 research assistantships with tuition reimbursements (averaging $13,915 per year), 156 teaching assistantships with tuition reimbursements (averaging $13,076 per year) were awarded. Federal Work-Study also available. Support available to part-time students. Financial award applicants required to submit FAFSA. In 2001, 173 master's, 50 doctorates awarded. *Degree program information:* Part-time programs available. Postbaccalaureate distance learning degree programs offered (minimal on-campus study). Offers chemical engineering (MS, PhD); civil engineering (MS, PhD); civil engineering-environmental toxicology (PhD); civil engineering-urban studies (MS); computer science (MS, PhD); electrical and computer engineering (MS, PhD); engineering (MS, PhD); engineering mechanics (MS, PhD); environmental engineering (MS, PhD); environmental engineering-environmental toxicology (PhD); materials science and engineering (MS, PhD); mechanical engineering (MS, PhD); mechanics (PhD); metallurgy (MS, PhD). *Application deadline:* Applications are processed on a rolling basis. *Application fee:* $30 ($40 for international students). Electronic applications accepted. *Application Contact:* Dr. Anthony Wojcik, Associate Dean for Graduate Studies and Research, 517-432-2464, Fax: 517-353-7782, E-mail: egrgrad@egr.msu.edu. *Dean,* Dr. Janie Fouke, 517-355-5113, Fax: 517-355-2288.

College of Human Ecology Students: 115 full-time (89 women), 134 part-time (109 women); includes 40 minority (25 African Americans, 9 Asian Americans or Pacific Islanders, 6 Hispanic Americans), 75 international. Average age 34. 173 applicants, 36% accepted. *Faculty:* 54. Expenses: Contact institution. *Financial support:* In 2001–02, 109 fellowships (averaging $3,600 per year), 32 research assistantships (averaging $11,393 per year), 21 teaching assistantships with tuition reimbursements (averaging $10,730 per year) were awarded. Career-related internships or fieldwork and Federal Work-Study also available. Support available to part-time students. Financial award applicants required to submit FAFSA. In 2001, 50 master's, 10 doctorates awarded. *Degree program information:* Part-time and evening/weekend programs available. Postbaccalaureate distance learning degree programs offered. Offers apparel and textiles (MA); child development (MA); clothing and textiles (MA); community service-urban studies (MS); community services (MS); family and child ecology (PhD); family consumer sciences education (MA); family ecology (PhD); family economics and management (MA); family studies (MA); food science (MS, PhD); home economics education (MA); human design and management (PhD); human ecology (MA, MS, PhD); human nutrition (MS, PhD); human nutrition-environmental toxicology (PhD); interior design and facilities management (MA); interior design and human environment (MA); marriage and family therapy (MA); merchandising management (MS). *Application deadline:* Applications are processed on a rolling basis. *Application fee:* $30 ($40 for international students). Electronic applications accepted. *Dean,* Dr. Julia R. Miller, 517-355-7714, Fax: 517-353-9426, E-mail: jrmiller@msu.edu.

College of Natural Science Students: 668 full-time (269 women), 247 part-time (108 women); includes 52 minority (12 African Americans, 17 Asian Americans or Pacific Islanders, 22 Hispanic Americans, 1 Native American), 407 international. Average age 27. 1,371 applicants, 34% accepted. *Faculty:* 301. Expenses: Contact institution. *Financial support:* In 2001–02, 274 fellowships with tuition reimbursements (averaging $3,422 per year), 319 research assistantships with tuition reimbursements (averaging $13,365 per year), 421 teaching assistantships with tuition reimbursements (averaging $12,283 per year) were awarded. Career-related internships or fieldwork, Federal Work-Study, institutionally sponsored loans, scholarships/grants, and unspecified assistantships also available. Support available to part-time students. Financial award applicants required to submit CSS PROFILE or FAFSA. In 2001, 97 master's, 81 doctorates awarded. *Degree program information:* Part-time programs available. Offers analytical chemistry (PhD); applied mathematics (MS, PhD); applied statistics (MS); astrophysics and astronomy (MS, PhD); beam physics (PhD); biochemistry (PhD); biochemistry and molecular biology (MS, PhD); biochemistry-environmental toxicology (PhD); botany and plant pathology (PhD); cell and molecular biology (PhD); cellular and molecular biology (PhD); chemical physics (MS, PhD); chemistry (MS, PhD); chemistry-environmental toxicology (PhD); clinical laboratory science (MS); computational chemistry (MS); computational mathematics (MS); computational statistics (MS); environmental geosciences (MS, PhD); environmental geosciences-environmental toxicology (PhD); environmental toxicology (PhD); genetics (PhD); genetics-environmental toxicology (PhD); geological sciences (MS, PhD); horticulture (PhD); industrial mathematics (MS); inorganic chemistry (MS, PhD); mathematics (MA, MAT, MS, PhD); mathematics education (PhD); microbiology (PhD); natural science (MA, MAT, MS, PhD); neuroscience (PhD); operations research-statistics (MS); organic chemistry (MS, PhD); physics (MAT, MS, PhD); plant biology (MS, PhD); statistics (MA, MS, PhD); zoology (MS, PhD); zoology-environmental toxicology (PhD). *Application deadline:* Applications are processed on a rolling basis. *Application fee:* $30 ($40 for international students). Electronic applications accepted. *Application Contact:* Dr. Estelle McGroarty, Associate Dean, 517-355-4470, Fax: 517-432-1054. *Dean,* Dr. George E. Leroi, 517-355-4470, Fax: 517-432-1054.

College of Nursing Students: 15 full-time (12 women), 92 part-time (86 women); includes 14 minority (12 African Americans, 2 Asian Americans or Pacific Islanders) Average age 37. 60 applicants, 72% accepted. *Faculty:* 20 full-time (17 women). Expenses: Contact institution. *Financial support:* In 2001–02, 39 fellowships with tuition reimbursements (averaging $2,626 per year), 10 research assistantships with tuition reimbursements (averaging $11,655 per year) were awarded. Teaching assistantships with tuition reimbursements, Federal Work-Study also available. Support available to part-time students. Financial award applicants required to submit FAFSA. In 2001, 44 degrees awarded. *Degree program information:* Part-time programs available. Offers nursing (MSN, PhD). *Application deadline:* For fall admission, 1/15. Applications are processed on a rolling basis. *Application fee:* $30 ($40 for international students). *Application Contact:* Audrey Gift, Associate Dean for Research and Doctoral Programs, 517-432-6220, Fax: 517-353-9553, E-mail: nurse@msu.edu. *Dean,* Dr. Marilyn Rothert, 517-355-6523, Fax: 517-353-9553, E-mail: nurse@msu.edu.

College of Social Science Students: 546 full-time (345 women), 361 part-time (239 women); includes 169 minority (98 African Americans, 30 Asian Americans or Pacific Islanders, 32 Hispanic Americans, 9 Native Americans), 125 international. Average age 30. 1,254 applicants, 37% accepted. *Faculty:* 250 full-time (75 women). Expenses: Contact institution. *Financial support:* In 2001–02, 236 fellowships with tuition reimbursements (averaging $3,178 per year), 180 research assistantships with tuition reimbursements (averaging $11,530 per year), 186 teaching assistantships with tuition reimbursements (averaging $11,018 per year) were awarded. Career-related internships or fieldwork, Federal Work-Study, and institutionally sponsored loans also available. Support available to part-time students. Financial award applicants required to submit FAFSA. In 2001, 224 master's, 54 doctorates awarded. *Degree program information:* Part-time and evening/weekend programs available. Postbaccalaureate distance learning degree programs offered (minimal on-campus study). Offers administration and program evaluation (MSW); administration and program evaluation-urban studies (MSW); anthropology (MA, PhD); applied developmental science (MA, PhD); clinical social work (MSW); clinical social work-urban studies (MSW); cricimal justice-urban studies (MS); criminal justice (MS, PhD); economics (MA, PhD); geography (MA, MS, PhD); geography-urban studies (MA); industrial relations and human resources (PhD); infant studies (MA, PhD); interdisciplinary social science/social work (PhD); labor relations and human resources (MLRHR); labor relations and human resources-urban studies (MLRHR); neuroscience-psychology (MA, PhD); organizational and community practice (MSW); political science (MA, PhD); political science-urban studies (PhD); program evaluation-urban studies (MSW); psychology (MA, PhD); psychology-urban studies (MA, PhD); public administration (MPA); public administration-urban studies (MPA); social science (MA, MLRHR, MPA, MS, MSW, MUP, MURP, PhD); sociology (MA, PhD); sociology-urban studies (MA, PhD); urban and regional planning (MURP); urban planning (MUP). *Application deadline:* Applications are processed on a rolling basis. *Application fee:* $30 ($40 for international students). Electronic applications accepted. *Dean,* Dr. Marietta Baba, 517-355-6676.

Eli Broad Graduate School of Business and Management Students: 627 full-time (160 women), 28 part-time (14 women); includes 95 minority (25 African Americans, 61 Asian Americans or Pacific Islanders, 7 Hispanic Americans, 2 Native Americans), 164 international. Average age 29. 1,613 applicants, 25% accepted. *Faculty:* 104. Expenses: Contact institution. *Financial support:* In 2001–02, 182 fellowships (averaging $3,134 per year), 66 research assistantships (averaging $10,836 per year), 122 teaching assistantships with tuition reimbursements (averaging $11,231 per year) were awarded. Career-related internships or fieldwork, Federal Work-Study, institutionally sponsored loans, and unspecified assistantships also available. Support available to part-time students. Financial award applicants required to submit FAFSA. In 2001, 365 master's, 8 doctorates awarded. *Degree program information:* Part-time and evening/weekend programs available. Offers accounting (PhD); business administration (MBA); business and management (MBA, MS, PhD); business information systems (MBA); business management (MS); business management of manufacturing (MS); entrepreneurship (MBA); finance (MBA, PhD); food service management (MS); hospitality business (MBA); hotel, restaurant, and institution management (MBA); human resources management (MBA); leadership and change management (MBA); logistics (PhD); management policy and strategy (PhD); marketing (MBA, PhD); operations and sourcing management (PhD); organizational behavior-personnel (PhD); production and operations management (PhD); professional accounting (MBA, MS); supply chain management (MBA). *Application deadline:* Applications are processed on a rolling basis. *Application fee:* $30 ($40 for international students). Electronic applications accepted. *Dean,* Dr. Robert B. Duncan, 517-355-7604, Fax: 517-355-1649, E-mail: mba@msu.edu.

Urban Affairs Programs Offers administration and program evaluation-urban studies (MSW); audiology and speech sciences-urban studies (PhD); civil engineering-urban studies (MS); clinical social work-urban studies (MSW); communication-urban studies (MA); entomology-urban studies (MS, PhD); environmental engineering-urban studies (MS); forestry-urban studies (MS, PhD); geography-urban studies (MA); history-urban studies (MA, PhD); labor relations and human resources-urban studies (MLRHR); park, recreation and tourism resources-urban studies (MS, PhD); physical education and exercise science-urban studies (MS); political science-urban studies (PhD); psychology-urban studies (PhD); public administration-urban studies (MPA); resource development-urban studies (MS, PhD); sociology-urban studies (PhD); telecommunication-urban studies (MA); urban studies (MA, MLRHR, MPA, MS, MSW, PhD). Electronic applications accepted.

See in-depth description on page 971.

MICHIGAN STATE UNIVERSITY-DETROIT COLLEGE OF LAW, East Lansing, MI 48824-1300

General Information Independent, coed, graduate-only institution. *Enrollment by degree level:* 780 first professional. *Graduate faculty:* 34 full-time (11 women), 37 part-time/adjunct (12 women). Tuition, state resident: part-time $669 per credit hour. *Graduate housing:*

Rooms and/or apartments available on a first-come, first-served basis to single students and available to married students. Housing application deadline: 4/1. *Student services:* Campus employment opportunities, campus safety program, career counseling, exercise/wellness program, international student services, low-cost health insurance, multicultural affairs office, writing training. *Library facilities:* Michigan State University-Detroit College of Law plus 5 others. *Online resources:* library catalog, web page, access to other libraries' catalogs. *Collection:* 118,631 titles, 3,657 serial subscriptions, 860 audiovisual materials.

Computer facilities: 60 computers available on campus for general student use. A campuswide network can be accessed from student residence rooms and from off campus. Internet access and online class registration are available. *Web address:* http://www.law.msu.edu/.

General Application Contact: Andrea Heatley, Assistant Dean of Admissions, 517-432-0222, Fax: 517-432-0098, E-mail: heatleya@law.msu.edu.

GRADUATE UNITS

Professional Program Students: 596 full-time (256 women), 184 part-time (88 women); includes 135 minority (65 African Americans, 49 Asian Americans or Pacific Islanders, 14 Hispanic Americans, 7 Native Americans) Average age 28. 1,200 applicants, 60% accepted. *Faculty:* 34 full-time (11 women), 37 part-time/adjunct (12 women). Expenses: Contact institution. *Financial support:* In 2001–02, 202 students received support, including 202 fellowships with full and partial tuition reimbursements available (averaging $17,024 per year), 7 research assistantships with tuition reimbursements available (averaging $4,000 per year), 5 teaching assistantships (averaging $4,000 per year); career-related internships or fieldwork, Federal Work-Study, institutionally sponsored loans, and scholarships/grants also available. Support available to part-time students. Financial award application deadline: 4/15; financial award applicants required to submit FAFSA. In 2001, 181 degrees awarded. *Degree program information:* Part-time and evening/weekend programs available. Offers law (JD). *Application deadline:* For fall admission, 4/15 (priority date). Applications are processed on a rolling basis. *Application fee:* $50. Electronic applications accepted. *Application Contact:* Andrea Heatley, Assistant Dean of Admissions, 517-432-0222, Fax: 517-432-0098, E-mail: heatleya@law.msu.edu. *Dean,* Terence L. Blackburn, 517-432-6804, Fax: 517-432-6801, E-mail: blackb14@law.msu.edu.

MICHIGAN TECHNOLOGICAL UNIVERSITY, Houghton, MI 49931-1295

General Information State-supported, coed, university. CGS member. *Enrollment:* 542 full-time matriculated graduate/professional students (168 women), 128 part-time matriculated graduate/professional students (40 women). *Enrollment by degree level:* 392 master's, 278 doctoral. *Graduate faculty:* 303 full-time (60 women), 16 part-time/adjunct (5 women). Tuition, state resident: full-time $5,354; part-time $447 per credit. Tuition, nonresident: full-time $10,998; part-time $917 per credit. *Required fees:* $524. *Graduate housing:* Rooms and/or apartments available on a first-come, first-served basis to single and married students. Typical cost: $2,409 per year ($5,201 including board) for single students; $3,294 per year for married students. Housing application deadline: 7/15. *Student services:* Campus employment opportunities, campus safety program, career counseling, child daycare facilities, disabled student services, exercise/wellness program, free psychological counseling, grant writing training, international student services, low-cost health insurance, teacher training, writing training. *Library facilities:* J. R. Van Pelt Library. *Online resources:* library catalog, web page, access to other libraries' catalogs. *Collection:* 992,197 titles, 10,585 serial subscriptions, 3,790 audiovisual materials. *Research affiliation:* Michigan Biotechnology Institute, Michigan Aquatic Sciences Consortium (biology).

Computer facilities: 1,235 computers available on campus for general student use. A campuswide network can be accessed from student residence rooms and from off campus. Internet access and online class registration are available. *Web address:* http://www.mtu.edu/.

General Application Contact: Dr. Marilyn J. Urion, Assistant Dean of the Graduate School, 906-487-2327, Fax: 906-487-2245, E-mail: mjurion@mtu.edu.

GRADUATE UNITS

Graduate School *Degree program information:* Part-time programs available. Electronic applications accepted.

College of Engineering *Degree program information:* Part-time programs available. Offers chemical engineering (MS, PhD); civil engineering (ME, MS, PhD); computational science and engineering (PhD); electrical engineering (ME, MS, PhD); engineering (ME, MS, PhD); engineering mechanics (MS); engineering physics (PhD); environmental engineering (ME, MS, PhD); environmental engineering science (MS); geological engineering (MS, PhD); geology (MS, PhD); geophysics (MS); geotechnical engineering (PhD); materials science and engineering (MS, PhD); mechanical engineering (MS, PhD); mechanical engineering-engineering mechanics (PhD); mining engineering (MS, PhD); sensing and signal processing (PhD); structural engineering (PhD). Electronic applications accepted.

College of Sciences and Arts *Degree program information:* Part-time programs available. Offers applied science education (MS-ASE); biological sciences (MS, PhD); chemistry (MS, PhD); computational science and engineering (PhD); computer science (MS, PhD); environmental policy (MS); industrial archaeology (MS); mathematical sciences (PhD); mathematics (MS); physics (MS, PhD); rhetoric and technical writing (MS, PhD); sciences and arts (MS, MS-ASE, PhD). Electronic applications accepted.

School of Business and Economics *Degree program information:* Part-time programs available. Offers business administration (MS); business and economics (MS); mineral economics (MS); operations management (MS). Electronic applications accepted.

School of Forestry and Wood Products *Degree program information:* Part-time programs available. Offers forest molecular genetics and biotechnology (MS, PhD); forest science (PhD); forestry (MS, PhD). Electronic applications accepted.

Announcement: Since its charter in 1885, Michigan Technological University has built a tradition of excellence in science and engineering education. Students may study for advanced degrees in all the major science and engineering disciplines, as well as in humanities, social sciences, and forestry. Most programs offer both the MS and PhD, and some offer accelerated professional master's programs. Graduate students also have access to a number of co-op, internship, and international exchange opportunities.

See in-depth description on page 973.

MICHIGAN THEOLOGICAL SEMINARY, Plymouth, MI 48170

General Information Independent-religious, coed, graduate-only institution. *Graduate housing:* On-campus housing not available.

GRADUATE UNITS

Graduate Programs *Degree program information:* Part-time and evening/weekend programs available. Offers Christian education (MA); counseling psychology (MA); divinity (M Div); expository communication (D Min); theological studies (MA).

MID-AMERICA BAPTIST THEOLOGICAL SEMINARY, Germantown, TN 38183-1528

General Information Independent-religious, coed, primarily men. *Enrollment:* 233 full-time matriculated graduate/professional students (22 women), 63 part-time matriculated graduate/professional students (7 women). *Enrollment by degree level:* 141 first professional, 56 master's. *Graduate faculty:* 19 full-time (0 women), 8 part-time/adjunct (1 woman). *Tuition:* Full-time $1,600. *Graduate housing:* Rooms and/or apartments available on a first-come, first-served basis to single and married students. *Student services:* Career counseling, low-cost health insurance. *Library facilities:* Ora Byram Allison Memorial Library. *Online resources:* library catalog, web page. *Collection:* 119,000 titles, 931 serial subscriptions.

Computer facilities: 10 computers available on campus for general student use. A campuswide network can be accessed. *Web address:* http://www.mabts.edu/.

General Application Contact: Louise Burnett, Registrar, 901-751-8453, Fax: 901-751-8454, E-mail: lburnett@mabts.edu.

GRADUATE UNITS

Graduate and Professional Programs Students: 235 full-time (22 women), 61 part-time (7 women); includes 19 minority (all African Americans), 11 international. Average age 29. *Faculty:* 19 full-time (0 women), 8 part-time/adjunct (1 woman). Expenses: Contact institution. In 2001, 30 first professional degrees, 8 master's, 11 doctorates awarded. Offers theology (M Div, MACCS, MARE, D Min, PhD). *Application deadline:* For fall admission, 7/20 (priority date). Applications are processed on a rolling basis. *Application fee:* $25. Electronic applications accepted. *Application Contact:* Louise Burnett, Registrar, 901-751-8453, Fax: 901-751-8454, E-mail: lburnett@mabts.edu. *President,* Dr. Michael R. Spradlin, 901-751-8453.

MID-AMERICA BAPTIST THEOLOGICAL SEMINARY NORTHEAST BRANCH, Schenectady, NY 12303-3463

General Information Independent-religious, coed, primarily men, graduate-only institution. *Graduate housing:* On-campus housing not available.

GRADUATE UNITS

Program in Theology *Degree program information:* Part-time and evening/weekend programs available. Offers theology (M Div).

MIDAMERICA NAZARENE UNIVERSITY, Olathe, KS 66062-1899

General Information Independent-religious, coed, comprehensive institution. *Enrollment:* 213 full-time matriculated graduate/professional students (133 women), 8 part-time matriculated graduate/professional students (6 women). *Enrollment by degree level:* 221 master's. *Graduate faculty:* 18 full-time (5 women), 19 part-time/adjunct (7 women). *Tuition:* Full-time $13,400. Full-time tuition and fees vary according to program. *Graduate housing:* On-campus housing not available. *Student services:* Campus safety program, career counseling, free psychological counseling, international student services. *Library facilities:* Mabee Library. *Online resources:* library catalog, web page, access to other libraries' catalogs. *Collection:* 80,560 titles, 1,025 serial subscriptions.

Computer facilities: 85 computers available on campus for general student use. A campuswide network can be accessed from student residence rooms and from off campus. Internet access is available. *Web address:* http://www.mnu.edu/.

General Application Contact: Gina Harvey, Secretary, Graduate Studies in Management, 913-782-3276, Fax: 913-791-3409, E-mail: mba@mnu.edu.

GRADUATE UNITS

Graduate Studies in Counseling Students: 31 full-time (22 women), 8 part-time (6 women); includes 1 minority (African American) 30 applicants, 67% accepted. *Faculty:* 3 full-time (0 women), 8 part-time/adjunct (2 women). Expenses: Contact institution. Offers counseling (MAC). *Application deadline:* For fall admission, 6/15. *Application fee:* $75. *Application Contact:* Aileen Douglas, Secretary, 913-791-3449, Fax: 913-791-3402, E-mail: adouglas@mnu.edu. *Director,* Roy Rotz, 913-791-3449, Fax: 913-791-3402, E-mail: rrotz@mnu.edu.

Graduate Studies in Education Students: 99 full-time (78 women); includes 5 minority (1 African American, 4 Native Americans) 111 applicants, 88% accepted, 98 enrolled. *Faculty:* 8 full-time (2 women), 8 part-time/adjunct (4 women). Expenses: Contact institution. *Financial support:* Application deadline: 5/1; In 2001, 53 degrees awarded. *Degree program information:* Evening/weekend programs available. Offers curriculum and instruction (M Ed); educational technology (MET). *Application deadline:* Applications are processed on a rolling basis. *Application fee:* $75. *Application Contact:* Melissa Jones, Administrative Assistant, 913-791-3292, Fax: 913-791-3407, E-mail: mjones@mnu.edu. *Chair, Division of Education,* Dr. Verla R. Powers, 913-791-3292, Fax: 913-791-3407, E-mail: vpowers@mnu.edu.

Graduate Studies in Management Students: 83 full-time (33 women); includes 6 minority (4 African Americans, 1 Asian American or Pacific Islander, 1 Hispanic American) Average age 37. 48 applicants, 100% accepted. *Faculty:* 7 full-time (3 women), 3 part-time/adjunct (1 woman). Expenses: Contact institution. *Financial support:* Application deadline: 5/1; In 2001, 57 degrees awarded. *Degree program information:* Evening/weekend programs available. Offers management (MBA). *Application deadline:* For fall admission, 9/1 (priority date); for spring admission, 2/1. Applications are processed on a rolling basis. *Application fee:* $75. Electronic applications accepted. *Application Contact:* Gina Harvey, Secretary, 913-791-3276, Fax: 913-791-3409, E-mail: mba@mnu.edu. *Director,* Dr. Willadee Wehmeyer, 913-791-3276, Fax: 913-791-3409, E-mail: wwehmeye@mnu.edu.

Announcement: MidAmerica Nazarene University (MNU) offers 4 accelerated master's degrees. Courses are held one night per week, in cohort groups. The Master of Business Administration, Master of Education, Master of Educational Technology, and Master of Arts in Counseling admit students 25 and over with regionally accredited bachelor's degrees and work experience.

MIDDLEBURY COLLEGE, Middlebury, VT 05753-6002

General Information Independent, coed, comprehensive institution. *Enrollment:* 824 full-time matriculated graduate/professional students (596 women). *Graduate faculty:* 107 full-time (42 women). *Graduate housing:* Room and/or apartments available on a first-come, first-served basis to single students; on-campus housing not available to married students. *Student services:* Campus employment opportunities, campus safety program, career counseling, disabled student services, free psychological counseling, international student services, teacher training. *Library facilities:* Egbert Starr Library plus 3 others. *Online resources:* library catalog, web page, access to other libraries' catalogs. *Collection:* 1.5 million titles, 2,496 serial subscriptions, 27,697 audiovisual materials.

Computer facilities: 225 computers available on campus for general student use. A campuswide network can be accessed from student residence rooms and from off campus. Internet access and online class registration, computer helpline are available. *Web address:* http://www.middlebury.edu/.

General Application Contact: Kara Gennarelli, Language School Office, 802-443-5510, Fax: 802-443-2075, E-mail: kgennare@middlebury.edu.

GRADUATE UNITS

Bread Loaf School of English Students: 475 full-time (335 women); includes 43 minority (25 African Americans, 3 Asian Americans or Pacific Islanders, 8 Hispanic Americans, 7 Native Americans), 16 international. Average age 34. 225 applicants, 73% accepted. *Faculty:* 51 full-time (20 women). Expenses: Contact institution. *Financial support:* In 2001–02, 174 students received support. Scholarships/grants available. Support available to part-time students. In 2001, 60 master's awarded. Offers English (M Litt, MA). Offered during summer only. *Application deadline:* Applications are processed on a rolling basis. *Application fee:* $50. *Director,* Dr. James Maddox, 802-443-5418, Fax: 802-443-2060, E-mail: blse@breadnet.middlebury.edu.

Language Schools Students: 349 full-time (261 women); includes 48 minority (14 African Americans, 4 Asian Americans or Pacific Islanders, 30 Hispanic Americans) *Faculty:* 56 full-time (22 women). Expenses: Contact institution. *Financial support:* Fellowships, scholarships/grants available. In 2001, 50 master's, 3 doctorates awarded. Offers French (MA, DML); German (MA, DML); Italian (MA, DML); language (MA, DML); Russian (MA, DML); Spanish (MA, DML). *Application deadline:* Applications are processed on a rolling basis. *Application fee:* $50. *Application Contact:* Kara Gennarelli, Language School Office, 802-443-5510, Fax: 802-443-2075, E-mail: kgennare@middlebury.edu. *Dean, Languages and International Studies,* Dr. Michael R. Katz, 802-443-5508.

MIDDLE TENNESSEE SCHOOL OF ANESTHESIA, Madison, TN 37116

General Information Independent, coed, graduate-only institution. *Enrollment by degree level:* 83 master's. *Graduate faculty:* 8 full-time (3 women), 13 part-time/adjunct (3 women). *Tuition:* Full-time $8,000. *Required fees:* $1,200. Full-time tuition and fees vary according to

Middle Tennessee School of Anesthesia (continued)

student level. *Graduate housing:* On-campus housing not available. *Student services:* Free psychological counseling, low-cost health insurance. *Library facilities:* Nelda Ackerman Learning Resource Center. *Collection:* 834 titles, 17 serial subscriptions.

Computer facilities: 5 computers available on campus for general student use. A campuswide network can be accessed from off campus. Internet access is available. *Web address:* http://www.mtsa.edu/.

General Application Contact: Mary E. DeVasher, Vice President and Dean, 615-868-6503, Fax: 615-868-9885, E-mail: ikey@mtsa.edu.

GRADUATE UNITS

Program in Nurse Anesthesia Students: 83 full-time (40 women); includes 5 minority (1 African American, 2 Asian Americans or Pacific Islanders, 2 Hispanic Americans) Average age 30. 200 applicants, 22% accepted. *Faculty:* 8 full-time (3 women), 13 part-time/adjunct (3 women). Expenses: Contact institution. *Financial support:* Traineeships available. In 2001, 35 degrees awarded. Offers nurse anesthesia (MS). *Application deadline:* For fall admission, 10/31. Applications are processed on a rolling basis. *Application fee:* $25. *Vice President and Dean,* Mary E. DeVasher, 615-868-6503, Fax: 615-868-9885, E-mail: ikey@mtsa.edu.

MIDDLE TENNESSEE STATE UNIVERSITY, Murfreesboro, TN 37132

General Information State-supported, coed, university. CGS member. *Enrollment:* 156 full-time matriculated graduate/professional students (86 women), 1,581 part-time matriculated graduate/professional students (942 women). *Graduate faculty:* 290 full-time (110 women). Tuition, state resident: full-time $1,716; part-time $191 per hour. Tuition, nonresident: full-time $4,952; part-time $461 per hour. *Required fees:* $14 per hour. $58 per semester. *Graduate housing:* Rooms and/or apartments available on a first-come, first-served basis to single and married students. Typical cost: $1,070 per year for single students. *Student services:* Campus employment opportunities, campus safety program, career counseling, disabled student services, exercise/wellness program, free psychological counseling, international student services, low-cost health insurance, multicultural affairs office. *Library facilities:* University Library. *Online resources:* library catalog, web page, access to other libraries' catalogs. *Collection:* 651,744 titles, 3,608 serial subscriptions.

Computer facilities: 2,200 computers available on campus for general student use. A campuswide network can be accessed from off campus. Internet access and online class registration are available. *Web address:* http://www.mtsu.edu/.

General Application Contact: Dr. Donald L. Curry, Dean and Vice Provost for Research, 615-898-2840, Fax: 615-904-8020, E-mail: dcurry@mtsu.edu.

GRADUATE UNITS

College of Graduate Studies Students: 156 full-time (86 women), 1,481 part-time (842 women); includes 290 minority (170 African Americans, 89 Asian Americans or Pacific Islanders, 23 Hispanic Americans, 8 Native Americans) Average age 32. 947 applicants, 95% accepted. *Faculty:* 290 full-time (110 women). Expenses: Contact institution. *Financial support:* In 2001–02, 7 fellowships with full tuition reimbursements (averaging $10,000 per year) were awarded; research assistantships, teaching assistantships, career-related internships or fieldwork, institutionally sponsored loans, and tuition waivers (partial) also available. Support available to part-time students. Financial award application deadline: 5/1; financial award applicants required to submit FAFSA. In 2001, 518 master's, 16 doctorates, 33 other advanced degrees awarded. *Degree program information:* Part-time and evening/weekend programs available. *Application deadline:* For fall admission, 8/1 (priority date). Applications are processed on a rolling basis. *Application fee:* $25. Electronic applications accepted. *Vice Provost for Research and Dean,* Dr. Donald L. Curry, 615-898-2840, Fax: 615-904-8020, E-mail: dcurry@mtsu.edu.

College of Basic and Applied Sciences Students: 51 full-time (20 women), 223 part-time (98 women); includes 71 minority (20 African Americans, 46 Asian Americans or Pacific Islanders, 4 Hispanic Americans, 1 Native American) Average age 32. 55 applicants, 96% accepted. *Faculty:* 98 full-time (30 women), 6 part-time/adjunct (0 women). Expenses: Contact institution. *Financial support:* Teaching assistantships, institutionally sponsored loans available. Support available to part-time students. Financial award application deadline: 5/1; financial award applicants required to submit FAFSA. In 2001, 53 master's, 2 doctorates awarded. *Degree program information:* Part-time and evening/weekend programs available. Offers aerospace education (M Ed); airport/airline management (MS); asset management (MS); aviation administration (MS); basic and applied sciences (M Ed, MS, MST, MVTE, DA); biology (MS, MST); chemistry (MS, DA); computer science (MS); engineering technology and industrial studies (MS, MVTE); mathematics (MS); mathematics education (MST); natural science (MS). *Application deadline:* For fall admission, 8/1 (priority date). Applications are processed on a rolling basis. *Application fee:* $25. Electronic applications accepted. *Interim Dean,* Dr. Thomas Cheatham, 615-898-2613, Fax: 615-898-2615.

College of Business Students: 118 full-time (61 women), 397 part-time (167 women); includes 114 minority (61 African Americans, 42 Asian Americans or Pacific Islanders, 7 Hispanic Americans, 4 Native Americans) Average age 31. 148 applicants, 100% accepted. *Faculty:* 64 full-time (15 women), 4 part-time/adjunct (1 woman). Expenses: Contact institution. *Financial support:* Teaching assistantships, institutionally sponsored loans available. Support available to part-time students. Financial award application deadline: 5/1; financial award applicants required to submit FAFSA. In 2001, 124 master's awarded. Offers accounting (MS); business (MA, MBA, MBE, MS, DA); business education (MBE); computer information systems (MS); economics (MA, DA); industrial relations (MA); information systems (MS); management and marketing (MBA). *Application deadline:* For fall admission, 8/1 (priority date). Applications are processed on a rolling basis. *Application fee:* $25. Electronic applications accepted. *Dean,* Dr. James E. Burton, 615-898-2764, Fax: 615-898-4736, E-mail: relam@mtsu.edu.

College of Education and Behavioral Science Students: 111 full-time (83 women), 1,242 part-time (920 women); includes 163 minority (122 African Americans, 21 Asian Americans or Pacific Islanders, 15 Hispanic Americans, 5 Native Americans) Average age 31. *Faculty:* 107 full-time (51 women), 19 part-time/adjunct (6 women). Expenses: Contact institution. *Financial support:* Research assistantships, teaching assistantships, career-related internships or fieldwork and institutionally sponsored loans available. Support available to part-time students. Financial award application deadline: 5/1; financial award applicants required to submit FAFSA. In 2001, 221 master's, 3 doctorates, 26 other advanced degrees awarded. *Degree program information:* Part-time and evening/weekend programs available. Offers administration and supervision (M Ed, Ed S); child development and family studies (MS); criminal justice administration (MCJ); curriculum and instruction (M Ed, Ed S); curriculum specialist (M Ed, Ed S); early childhood education (M Ed); education and behavioral science (M Ed, MA, MAT, MCJ, MS, DA, Ed S); elementary education (M Ed, Ed S); exercise science and health promotion (MS); health, physical education, recreation and safety (MS); industrial/organizational psychology (MA); middle school education (M Ed); nutrition and food science (MS); physical education (DA); psychology (MA); reading (M Ed); school counseling (M Ed, Ed S); school psychology (Ed S); secondary education (M Ed, Ed S); special education (M Ed). *Application deadline:* For fall admission, 8/1 (priority date). Applications are processed on a rolling basis. *Application fee:* $25. Electronic applications accepted. *Dean,* Dr. Gloria Bonner, 615-898-2874, Fax: 615-898-2530, E-mail: gbonner@mtsu.edu.

College of Liberal Arts Students: 13 full-time (8 women), 203 part-time (129 women); includes 17 minority (10 African Americans, 4 Asian Americans or Pacific Islanders, 2 Hispanic Americans, 1 Native American) Average age 32. 72 applicants, 94% accepted. *Faculty:* 104 full-time (41 women), 9 part-time/adjunct (2 women). Expenses: Contact institution. *Financial support:* Teaching assistantships, career-related internships or fieldwork and institutionally sponsored loans available. Support available to part-time students. Financial award application deadline: 5/1; financial award applicants required to submit FAFSA. In 2001, 41 master's, 3 doctorates awarded. *Degree program information:* Part-time and evening/weekend programs available. Offers English (MA, DA); foreign languages and literatures (MAT); historic preservation (DA); history (MA, DA); liberal arts (MA, MAT, DA); music (MA); sociology (MA). *Application deadline:* For fall admission, 8/1 (priority date). Applications are processed on a rolling basis. *Application fee:* $25. Electronic applications accepted. *Dean,* Dr. John McDaniel, 615-898-2534, Fax: 615-898-5907, E-mail: mcdaniel@mtsu.edu.

College of Mass Communications Students: 3 full-time (1 woman), 36 part-time (22 women); includes 13 minority (11 African Americans, 2 Asian Americans or Pacific Islanders) Average age 30. 15 applicants, 87% accepted. *Faculty:* 17 full-time (5 women). Expenses: Contact institution. *Financial support:* Institutionally sponsored loans and unspecified assistantships available. Support available to part-time students. Financial award application deadline: 5/1; financial award applicants required to submit FAFSA. In 2001, 10 degrees awarded. *Degree program information:* Part-time and evening/weekend programs available. Offers mass communications (MS). *Application deadline:* For fall admission, 8/1 (priority date). Applications are processed on a rolling basis. *Application fee:* $25. Electronic applications accepted. *Interim Dean,* Dr. Larry Burriss, 615-898-2813, Fax: 615-898-5682.

MIDWEST COLLEGE OF ORIENTAL MEDICINE, Racine, WI 53403-9747

General Information Proprietary, coed, graduate-only institution. *Enrollment by degree level:* 177 master's, 40 other advanced degrees. *Graduate faculty:* 7 full-time (2 women), 25 part-time/adjunct (11 women). *Tuition:* Full-time $8,895; part-time $2,965 per quarter. Tuition and fees vary according to program. *Graduate housing:* On-campus housing not available. *Student services:* Career counseling, writing training. *Library facilities:* Racine. *Collection:* 6,202 titles, 62 serial subscriptions, 55 audiovisual materials. *Research affiliation:* Guangzhou University of Traditional Chinese Medicine (pharmacology).

Computer facilities: 6 computers available on campus for general student use. Internet access is available. *Web address:* http://www.acupuncture.edu/midwest/.

General Application Contact: Pam Taylor, Administrative Coordinator, 800-593-2320, Fax: 262-554-7475, E-mail: pamelalt@aol.com.

GRADUATE UNITS

Graduate Programs Students: 123 full-time (70 women), 94 part-time (52 women); includes 64 minority (4 African Americans, 55 Asian Americans or Pacific Islanders, 4 Hispanic Americans, 1 Native American) Average age 41. 51 applicants, 100% accepted, 44 enrolled. *Faculty:* 7 full-time (2 women), 25 part-time/adjunct (11 women). Expenses: Contact institution. *Financial support:* Available to part-time students. Applicants required to submit FAFSA. In 2001, 30 master's, 22 Certificates awarded. *Degree program information:* Part-time and evening/weekend programs available. Offers acupuncture (Certificate); oriental medicine (MSOM). *Application deadline:* For fall admission, 9/1 (priority date); for winter admission, 11/1 (priority date); for spring admission, 3/1 (priority date). Applications are processed on a rolling basis. *Application fee:* $65. *Application Contact:* Pam Taylor, Administrative Coordinator, 800-593-2320, Fax: 262-554-7475, E-mail: pamelalt@aol.com. *Administrative Director,* Robert Chelnick, 773-975-1295, Fax: 773-975-6511, E-mail: 75703.3001@compuserve.com.

MIDWESTERN BAPTIST THEOLOGICAL SEMINARY, Kansas City, MO 64118-4697

General Information Independent-religious, coed, graduate-only institution. *Graduate housing:* Rooms and/or apartments guaranteed to single and married students.

GRADUATE UNITS

Graduate and Professional Programs *Degree program information:* Part-time programs available. Postbaccalaureate distance learning degree programs offered (minimal on-campus study). Offers Biblical studies (MA); Christian education (MACE); divinity/ministry (M Div); ministry (D Min); sacred music (MCM). Electronic applications accepted.

MIDWESTERN STATE UNIVERSITY, Wichita Falls, TX 76308

General Information State-supported, coed, comprehensive institution. *Enrollment:* 131 full-time matriculated graduate/professional students (80 women), 547 part-time matriculated graduate/professional students (354 women). *Enrollment by degree level:* 678 master's. *Graduate faculty:* 67 full-time (22 women), 9 part-time/adjunct (6 women). Tuition, state resident: full-time $936. Tuition, nonresident: full-time $4,734. *Required fees:* $1,280. One-time fee: $190. Tuition and fees vary according to course load. *Graduate housing:* Rooms and/or apartments available to single and married students. Typical cost: $2,150 per year ($4,188 including board) for single students; $3,100 per year ($5,138 including board) for married students. Housing application deadline: 6/23. *Student services:* Campus employment opportunities, career counseling, disabled student services, free psychological counseling, international student services, low-cost health insurance, teacher training. *Library facilities:* Moffett Library. *Online resources:* library catalog, web page, access to other libraries' catalogs. *Collection:* 366,350 titles, 1,100 serial subscriptions.

Computer facilities: 220 computers available on campus for general student use. A campuswide network can be accessed from student residence rooms and from off campus. *Web address:* http://www.mwsu.edu/.

General Application Contact: Barbara Ramos Merkle, Assistant Registrar, 940-397-4334, Fax: 940-397-4672, E-mail: admissions@mwsu.edu.

GRADUATE UNITS

Graduate Studies Students: 131 full-time (80 women), 547 part-time (354 women); includes 86 minority (40 African Americans, 13 Asian Americans or Pacific Islanders, 29 Hispanic Americans, 4 Native Americans), 58 international. Average age 34. 318 applicants, 100% accepted. *Faculty:* 67 full-time (22 women), 9 part-time/adjunct (6 women). Expenses: Contact institution. *Financial support:* In 2001–02, 5 research assistantships, 28 teaching assistantships with partial tuition reimbursements (averaging $5,952 per year) were awarded. Career-related internships or fieldwork, Federal Work-Study, institutionally sponsored loans, scholarships/grants, tuition waivers (partial), and unspecified assistantships also available. Support available to part-time students. In 2001, 164 degrees awarded. *Degree program information:* Part-time and evening/weekend programs available. *Application deadline:* For fall admission, 8/7; for spring admission, 12/15. *Application fee:* $0 ($50 for international students). *Application Contact:* Barbara Ramos Merkle, Director of Admissions, 940-397-4334, Fax: 940-397-4672, E-mail: admissions@mwsu.edu. *Vice President for Academic Affairs,* Dr. Robert Clark, 940-397-4226, Fax: 940-397-4042.

College of Business Administration Students: 23 full-time (15 women), 53 part-time (21 women); includes 15 minority (6 African Americans, 3 Asian Americans or Pacific Islanders, 6 Hispanic Americans), 18 international. Average age 30. 32 applicants, 100% accepted. *Faculty:* 11 full-time (1 woman). Expenses: Contact institution. *Financial support:* Teaching assistantships, career-related internships or fieldwork, Federal Work-Study, institutionally sponsored loans, tuition waivers (partial), and unspecified assistantships available. Support available to part-time students. In 2001, 43 degrees awarded. *Degree program information:* Part-time and evening/weekend programs available. Offers business administration (MBA). *Application deadline:* For fall admission, 8/7; for spring admission, 12/15. *Application fee:* $0 ($50 for international students). *Application Contact:* Dr. Henry Van Geem, Graduate Advisor, 940-397-4367. *Dean,* Dr. Yoshi Fukasawa, 940-397-4248, Fax: 940-397-4280.

College of Education Students: 46 full-time (34 women), 248 part-time (184 women); includes 46 minority (25 African Americans, 4 Asian Americans or Pacific Islanders, 15 Hispanic Americans, 2 Native Americans), 3 international. Average age 35. 79 applicants, 100% accepted. *Faculty:* 11 full-time (5 women), 8 part-time/adjunct (6 women). Expenses: Contact institution. *Financial support:* Teaching assistantships, career-related internships or fieldwork, Federal Work-Study, institutionally sponsored loans, tuition waivers (partial), and unspecified assistantships available. Support available to part-time students. In 2001, 74 degrees awarded. *Degree program information:* Part-time and evening/weekend programs available. Offers curriculum and instruction (M Ed); education (M Ed, MA); educational leadership (M Ed); elementary education (M Ed); general counseling (MA); human resource development (MA); reading education (M Ed); school counseling (M Ed); special education (M Ed); training and development (M Ed). *Application deadline:* For fall admission, 8/7; for spring admission, 12/15. *Application fee:* $0 ($50 for international students). *Application Contact:* Dr. Ann Estrada, Graduate Coordinator, 940-397-4136, Fax: 940-397-4694. *Dean,* Dr. Grant Simpson, 940-397-4564, Fax: 940-397-4694.

College of Health and Human Services Students: 21 full-time (9 women), 99 part-time (69 women); includes 11 minority (5 African Americans, 2 Asian Americans or Pacific Islanders, 4 Hispanic Americans), 2 international. Average age 36. 43 applicants, 100% accepted. *Faculty:* 13 full-time (9 women). Expenses: Contact institution. In 2001, 15 degrees awarded. Offers family nurse practitioner (MSN); health and human services (MA, MPA, MSK, MSN, MSR); health services administration (MA); kinesiology (MSK); nurse educator (MSN); public administration (MA, MPA); radiologic administration (MSR); radiologic education (MSR); radiologic services (MSR). *Application deadline:* For fall admission, 8/7; for spring admission, 12/15. *Application fee:* $0 ($50 for international students). *Dean,* Dr. Susan Sportsman, 940-397-4597, Fax: 940-397-4513.

College of Liberal Arts Students: 22 full-time (16 women), 63 part-time (35 women); includes 6 minority (3 African Americans, 2 Hispanic Americans, 1 Native American), 5 international. Average age 33. 29 applicants, 100% accepted. *Faculty:* 21 full-time (5 women), 1 part-time/adjunct (0 women). Expenses: Contact institution. *Financial support:* In 2001–02, 21 teaching assistantships with partial tuition reimbursements were awarded; research assistantships, career-related internships or fieldwork, Federal Work-Study, institutionally sponsored loans, tuition waivers (partial), and unspecified assistantships also available. Support available to part-time students. In 2001, 14 degrees awarded. *Degree program information:* Part-time and evening/weekend programs available. Offers English (MA); history (MA); liberal arts (MA); political science (MA); psychology (MA). *Application deadline:* For fall admission, 8/7; for spring admission, 12/15. *Application fee:* $0 ($50 for international students). *Dean,* Dr. Michael Collins, 940-397-4030, Fax: 940-397-4929.

College of Science and Mathematics Students: 14 full-time (2 women), 49 part-time (23 women); includes 7 minority (1 African American, 4 Asian Americans or Pacific Islanders, 2 Hispanic Americans), 30 international. Average age 30. 20 applicants, 95% accepted. *Faculty:* 11 full-time (2 women). Expenses: Contact institution. *Financial support:* In 2001–02, 2 research assistantships, 5 teaching assistantships with partial tuition reimbursements were awarded. Federal Work-Study, institutionally sponsored loans, tuition waivers (partial), and unspecified assistantships also available. Support available to part-time students. In 2001, 18 degrees awarded. *Degree program information:* Part-time and evening/weekend programs available. Offers biology (MS); computer science (MS); science (MS). *Application deadline:* For fall admission, 8/7; for spring admission, 12/15. *Application fee:* $0 ($50 for international students). *Application Contact:* Dr. Stewart Carpenter, Graduate Coordinator, Computer Science, 940-397-4279. *Dean,* Dr. Norman Horner, 940-397-4164, Fax: 940-397-4442.

MIDWESTERN UNIVERSITY, DOWNERS GROVE CAMPUS, Downers Grove, IL 60515-1235

General Information Independent, coed, graduate-only institution. *Enrollment by degree level:* 902 first professional, 229 master's. *Graduate faculty:* 201 full-time (72 women), 370 part-time/adjunct (74 women). Tuition, state resident: full-time $24,185. Tuition, nonresident: full-time $29,374. *Required fees:* $285. Tuition and fees vary according to program. *Graduate housing:* Rooms and/or apartments available on a first-come, first-served basis to single students and available to married students. *Student services:* Campus employment opportunities, campus safety program, career counseling, exercise/wellness program, free psychological counseling, low-cost health insurance. *Library facilities:* Library Technology Center. *Online resources:* web page. *Collection:* 84,097 titles, 1,450 serial subscriptions.

Computer facilities: 23 computers available on campus for general student use. A campuswide network can be accessed from student residence rooms and from off campus. Internet access is available. *Web address:* http://www.midwestern.edu/.

General Application Contact: Raelene Brower, Director of Admissions, 630-515-6171, Fax: 630-971-6086, E-mail: mwuinfo@mwu.edu.

GRADUATE UNITS

Chicago College of Osteopathic Medicine Students: 646 full-time (275 women); includes 176 minority (17 African Americans, 139 Asian Americans or Pacific Islanders, 18 Hispanic Americans, 2 Native Americans) Average age 26. 2,697 applicants, 15% accepted. *Faculty:* 141 full-time (29 women), 244 part-time/adjunct (35 women). Expenses: Contact institution. *Financial support:* In 2001–02, 568 students received support; fellowships with partial tuition reimbursements available, career-related internships or fieldwork, Federal Work-Study, institutionally sponsored loans, and tuition waivers (full and partial) available. Financial award application deadline: 6/1; financial award applicants required to submit FAFSA. In 2001, 142 degrees awarded. Offers osteopathic medicine (DO). *Application deadline:* For fall admission, 2/1. Applications are processed on a rolling basis. *Application fee:* $50. *Application Contact:* Raelene Brower, Director of Admissions, 630-515-6171, Fax: 630-971-6086, E-mail: mwuinfo@mwu.edu. *Dean,* Dr. John J. Fernandes, 630-515-6059.

Chicago College of Pharmacy Students: 217 full-time (156 women), 39 part-time (26 women); includes 98 minority (15 African Americans, 75 Asian Americans or Pacific Islanders, 8 Hispanic Americans) Average age 31. 489 applicants, 54% accepted. *Faculty:* 36 full-time (27 women), 12 part-time/adjunct (5 women). Expenses: Contact institution. *Financial support:* Federal Work-Study and institutionally sponsored loans available. Support available to part-time students. Financial award applicants required to submit FAFSA. In 2001, 108 degrees awarded. Offers pharmacy (Pharm D). *Application deadline:* For fall admission, 2/28. *Application fee:* $30. *Application Contact:* Raelene Brower, Director of Admissions, 630-515-6171, Fax: 630-971-6086, E-mail: mwuinfo@mwu.edu. *Dean,* Dr. Mary W. L. Lee, 630-971-6417.

College of Health Sciences, Illinois Campus Students: 224 full-time (174 women), 5 part-time (4 women); includes 26 minority (4 African Americans, 17 Asian Americans or Pacific Islanders, 5 Hispanic Americans) Average age 26. 603 applicants, 42% accepted. *Faculty:* 22 full-time (11 women), 61 part-time/adjunct (17 women). Expenses: Contact institution. *Financial support:* In 2001–02, 229 students received support. Federal Work-Study, institutionally sponsored loans, and scholarships/grants available. Financial award applicants required to submit FAFSA. In 2001, 99 degrees awarded. Offers biomedical sciences (MBS); health sciences (MBS, MMS, MOT, MPT); occupational therapy (MOT); physical therapy (MPT); physician assistant studies (MMS). *Application deadline:* Applications are processed on a rolling basis. *Application fee:* $30. *Application Contact:* Raelene Brower, Director of Admissions, 630-515-6171, Fax: 630-971-6086, E-mail: mwuinfo@mwu.edu. *Dean,* Dr. Dennis J. Paulson, 630-515-6388, E-mail: dpauls@midwestern.edu.

MIDWESTERN UNIVERSITY, GLENDALE CAMPUS, Glendale, AZ 85308

General Information Independent, coed, graduate-only institution. *Enrollment by degree level:* 844 first professional, 122 master's. *Graduate faculty:* 178 full-time (129 women), 474 part-time/adjunct (82 women). *Tuition, area resident:* Full-time $28,302. *Required fees:* $150. *Web address:* http://www.midwestern.edu/.

General Application Contact: James Walter, Director of Admissions, 800-458-6253, Fax: 630-971-6086, E-mail: mwuinfo@mwu.edu.

GRADUATE UNITS

Arizona College of Osteopathic Medicine Students: 514 full-time (184 women), 2 part-time; includes 107 minority (3 African Americans, 93 Asian Americans or Pacific Islanders, 10 Hispanic Americans, 1 Native American) Average age 28. 2,438 applicants, 13% accepted. *Faculty:* 145 full-time (114 women), 426 part-time/adjunct (62 women). Expenses: Contact institution. *Financial support:* Fellowships with partial tuition reimbursements, career-related internships or fieldwork, Federal Work-Study, institutionally sponsored loans, and tuition waivers (full and partial) available. Financial award application deadline: 6/12; financial award applicants required to submit FAFSA. In 2001, 95 degrees awarded. Offers osteopathic medicine (DO). *Application deadline:* For fall admission, 11/1 (priority date); for winter admission, 2/1. Applications are processed on a rolling basis. *Application fee:* $50. Electronic applications accepted. *Application Contact:* James Walter, Director of Admissions, 623-572-3215, E-mail: mwuinfo@mwu.edu. *Dean,* Dr. James W. Cole, 623-572-3202.

College of Health Sciences, Arizona Campus Students: 111 full-time (83 women), 11 part-time (9 women); includes 27 minority (2 African Americans, 13 Asian Americans or Pacific Islanders, 11 Hispanic Americans, 1 Native American) Average age 28. 389 applicants, 35% accepted. *Faculty:* 11 full-time (5 women), 46 part-time/adjunct (20 women). Expenses: Contact institution. *Financial support:* Applicants required to submit FAFSA. In 2001, 45 degrees awarded. *Degree program information:* Part-time programs available. Offers bioethics (Certificate); biomedical sciences (MBS); cardiovascular science (MCVS); health professions education (MHPE); health sciences (MBS, MCVS, MHPE, MMS, MOT, Certificate); occupational therapy (MOT); physician assistant studies (MMS). *Application deadline:* Applications are processed on a rolling basis. *Application Contact:* James Walter, Director of Admissions, 623-572-3215, E-mail: mwuinfo@mwu.edu. *Dean,* Dr. Dennis J. Paulson, 630-515-6388, E-mail: dpauls@midwestern.edu.

College of Pharmacy-Glendale Students: 300 full-time (180 women), 28 part-time (20 women); includes 122 minority (13 African Americans, 84 Asian Americans or Pacific Islanders, 22 Hispanic Americans, 3 Native Americans) Average age 28. 250 applicants, 59% accepted. *Faculty:* 22 full-time (10 women), 2 part-time/adjunct (0 women). Expenses: Contact institution. *Financial support:* Applicants required to submit FAFSA. Offers pharmacy (Pharm D). *Application Contact:* James Walter, Director of Admissions, 623-572-3215, E-mail: mwuinfo@mwu.edu. *Dean,* Dr. David J. Slatkin, 623-572-3500.

MILLERSVILLE UNIVERSITY OF PENNSYLVANIA, Millersville, PA 17551-0302

General Information State-supported, coed, comprehensive institution. CGS member. *Enrollment:* 89 full-time matriculated graduate/professional students (65 women), 417 part-time matriculated graduate/professional students (314 women). *Enrollment by degree level:* 506 master's. *Graduate faculty:* 202 full-time (90 women), 79 part-time/adjunct (35 women). Tuition, state resident: part-time $256 per credit. Tuition, nonresident: full-time $7,554; part-time $420 per credit. *Required fees:* $1,037; $44 per credit. *Graduate housing:* On-campus housing not available. *Student services:* Campus employment opportunities, campus safety program, career counseling, child daycare facilities, disabled student services, exercise/wellness program, free psychological counseling, international student services, low-cost health insurance, teacher training. *Library facilities:* Helen A. Ganser Library. *Online resources:* library catalog, web page. *Collection:* 496,162 titles, 2,557 serial subscriptions, 30,163 audiovisual materials. *Research affiliation:* Marine Science Consortium.

Computer facilities: 425 computers available on campus for general student use. A campuswide network can be accessed from student residence rooms and from off campus. *Web address:* http://www.millersville.edu/.

General Application Contact: Dr. Duncan M. Perry, Dean of Graduate Studies, Professional Training and Education, 717-872-3030, E-mail: duncan.perry@millersville.edu.

GRADUATE UNITS

Graduate School Students: 89 full-time (65 women), 417 part-time (314 women); includes 26 minority (9 African Americans, 5 Asian Americans or Pacific Islanders, 12 Hispanic Americans), 2 international. Average age 31. 124 applicants, 73% accepted, 75 enrolled. *Faculty:* 202 full-time (90 women), 79 part-time/adjunct (35 women). Expenses: Contact institution. *Financial support:* In 2001–02, 94 research assistantships with full and partial tuition reimbursements (averaging $4,000 per year) were awarded; career-related internships or fieldwork, Federal Work-Study, institutionally sponsored loans, and unspecified assistantships also available. Support available to part-time students. Financial award application deadline: 3/15. In 2001, 183 degrees awarded. *Degree program information:* Part-time and evening/weekend programs available. *Application deadline:* For fall admission, 5/1 (priority date). Applications are processed on a rolling basis. *Application fee:* $30. *Dean of Graduate Studies, Professional Training and Education,* Dr. Duncan M. Perry, 717-872-3030, E-mail: duncan.perry@millersville.edu.

School of Education Students: 77 full-time (59 women), 348 part-time (261 women); includes 22 minority (7 African Americans, 5 Asian Americans or Pacific Islanders, 10 Hispanic Americans), 1 international. Average age 31. 106 applicants, 72% accepted, 67 enrolled. *Faculty:* 90 full-time (45 women), 45 part-time/adjunct (15 women). Expenses: Contact institution. *Financial support:* In 2001–02, 88 research assistantships with full and partial tuition reimbursements (averaging $4,000 per year) were awarded; career-related internships or fieldwork, Federal Work-Study, institutionally sponsored loans, and unspecified assistantships also available. Support available to part-time students. Financial award application deadline: 3/15; financial award applicants required to submit FAFSA. In 2001, 146 degrees awarded. *Degree program information:* Part-time and evening/weekend programs available. Offers athletic coaching (M Ed); athletic management (M Ed); clinical psychology (MS); early childhood education (M Ed); education (M Ed, MS); elementary education (M Ed); gifted education (M Ed); industrial arts/technology education (M Ed); leadership for teaching and learning (M Ed); psychology (MS); reading education (M Ed); reading/language arts education (M Ed); school counseling (M Ed); school psychology (MS); special education (M Ed); sport management (M Ed). *Application deadline:* For fall admission, 5/1 (priority date). Applications are processed on a rolling basis. *Application fee:* $30. *Application Contact:* Dr. Duncan M. Perry, Dean of Graduate Studies, Professional Training and Education, 717-872-3030, E-mail: duncan.perry@millersville.edu. *Dean,* Dr. Jane S. Bray, 717-872-3379, E-mail: jane.bray@millersville.edu.

School of Humanities and Social Sciences Students: 8 full-time (3 women), 35 part-time (22 women); includes 3 minority (1 African American, 2 Hispanic Americans) Average age 32. 9 applicants, 67% accepted, 1 enrolled. *Faculty:* 58 full-time (30 women), 20 part-time/adjunct (10 women). Expenses: Contact institution. *Financial support:* In 2001–02, 4 research assistantships with full tuition reimbursements (averaging $4,000 per year) were awarded; career-related internships or fieldwork, Federal Work-Study, institutionally sponsored loans, and unspecified assistantships also available. Support available to part-time students. Financial award application deadline: 3/15; financial award applicants required to submit FAFSA. In 2001, 23 degrees awarded. *Degree program information:* Part-time and evening/weekend programs available. Offers art education (M Ed); English (MA); English education (M Ed); French (M Ed, MA); German (M Ed, MA); history (MA); humanities and social sciences (M Ed, MA); Spanish (M Ed, MA). *Application deadline:* For fall admission, 5/1 (priority date). Applications are processed on a rolling basis. *Application fee:* $30. *Application Contact:* Dr. Duncan M. Perry, Dean of Graduate Studies, Professional Training and Education, 717-872-3030, E-mail: duncan.perry@millersville.edu. *Dean,* Dr. Rita D. Marinho, 717-872-3553, E-mail: rita.marinho@millersville.edu.

School of Science and Mathematics Students: 4 full-time (3 women), 34 part-time (31 women); includes 1 minority (African American), 1 international. Average age 34. 9 applicants, 89% accepted, 7 enrolled. *Faculty:* 54 full-time (15 women), 14 part-time/adjunct (10 women). Expenses: Contact institution. *Financial support:* In 2001–02, 2 research assistantships with full tuition reimbursements (averaging $4,000 per year) were awarded; career-related internships or fieldwork, Federal Work-Study, institutionally sponsored loans, and unspecified assistantships also available. Support available to part-time students. Financial award application deadline: 3/15; financial award applicants required to submit FAFSA. In 2001, 14 degrees awarded. *Degree program information:* Part-time and evening/weekend programs available. Offers biology (MS); mathematics (M Ed); nursing (MSN); science and mathematics (M Ed, MS, MSN). *Application deadline:* For fall admission, 5/1 (priority date). Applications are processed on a rolling basis. *Application fee:* $30. *Application Contact:* Dr. Duncan M. Perry, Dean of Graduate Studies, Professional Training and Education, 717-872-3030, E-mail: duncan.perry@millersville.edu. *Dean,* Dr. Edward C. Shane, 717-872-3407, Fax: 817-872-3985, E-mail: edward.shane@millersville.edu.

See in-depth description on page 975.

MILLIGAN COLLEGE, Milligan College, TN 37682

General Information Independent-religious, coed, comprehensive institution. *Graduate housing:* Rooms and/or apartments available on a first-come, first-served basis to single and married students. Housing application deadline: 4/1.

Milligan College (continued)

GRADUATE UNITS

Area of Teacher Education Students: 71 (51 women); includes 3 minority (2 African Americans, 1 Hispanic American) Average age 30. 18 applicants, 83% accepted, 12 enrolled. *Faculty:* 7 full-time (6 women), 4 part-time/adjunct (2 women). Expenses: Contact institution. *Financial support:* In 2001–02, 54 students received support. Career-related internships or fieldwork, institutionally sponsored loans, and scholarships/grants available. Financial award application deadline: 4/15; financial award applicants required to submit FAFSA. In 2001, 47 degrees awarded. *Degree program information:* Part-time programs available. Offers teacher education (M Ed). *Application deadline:* For fall admission, 8/1 (priority date); for winter admission, 11/15 (priority date); for spring admission, 4/1 (priority date). Applications are processed on a rolling basis. *Application fee:* $30 ($91 for international students). Electronic applications accepted. *Application Contact:* Carrie Davidson, Director of Graduate Admissions, 423-461-8306, Fax: 423-461-8789, E-mail: cdavidson@milligan.edu. *Director*, Dr. Billye Joyce Fine, 423-461-3576, Fax: 423-461-3103, E-mail: bjfine@milligan.edu.

Program in Occupational Therapy Students: 21 full-time (19 women), 4 part-time (all women); includes 2 minority (both African Americans) Average age 30. 60 applicants, 25% accepted, 14 enrolled. *Faculty:* 5 full-time (3 women), 3 part-time/adjunct (all women). Expenses: Contact institution. *Financial support:* In 2001–02, 22 students received support. Institutionally sponsored loans available. Financial award application deadline: 4/15; financial award applicants required to submit FAFSA. In 2001, 24 degrees awarded. Offers occupational therapy (MSOT). *Application deadline:* Applications are processed on a rolling basis. *Application fee:* $30. Electronic applications accepted. *Application Contact:* Carrie Davidson, Director of Graduate Admissions, 423-461-8306, Fax: 423-461-8789, E-mail: cdavidson@milligan.edu. *Director*, Dr. Daniel Poff, 800-262-8337, Fax: 423-975-8019, E-mail: dwpoff@milligan.edu.

MILLSAPS COLLEGE, Jackson, MS 39210-0001

General Information Independent-religious, coed, comprehensive institution. *Graduate housing:* Room and/or apartments available to single students; on-campus housing not available to married students. Housing application deadline: 6/1. *Research affiliation:* Mississippi Research and Development Center, Jackson Enterprise Center (new business start-up).

GRADUATE UNITS

School of Management *Degree program information:* Part-time and evening/weekend programs available. Offers accounting (M Acc); business administration (MBA).

MILLS COLLEGE, Oakland, CA 94613-1000

General Information Independent, women only, comprehensive institution. *Enrollment:* 373 full-time matriculated graduate/professional students (299 women), 61 part-time matriculated graduate/professional students (47 women). *Enrollment by degree level:* 380 master's, 40 doctoral, 14 other advanced degrees. *Graduate faculty:* 60 full-time (34 women), 43 part-time/adjunct (32 women). *Tuition:* Full-time $12,700; part-time $3,250 per credit. *Required fees:* $480. One-time fee: $480 part-time. *Graduate housing:* Rooms and/or apartments available on a first-come, first-served basis to single and married students. Typical cost: $4,500 per year ($8,500 including board) for single students; $4,900 per year ($8,920 including board) for married students. Room and board charges vary according to board plan and housing facility selected. Housing application deadline: 9/1. *Student services:* Campus employment opportunities, campus safety program, career counseling, child daycare facilities, disabled student services, exercise/wellness program, free psychological counseling, international student services, low-cost health insurance, teacher training, writing training. *Library facilities:* F. W. Olin Library plus 1 other. *Online resources:* library catalog, web page, access to other libraries' catalogs. *Collection:* 189,814 titles, 2,029 serial subscriptions, 6,046 audiovisual materials.

Computer facilities: 66 computers available on campus for general student use. A campuswide network can be accessed from student residence rooms and from off campus. *Web address:* http://www.mills.edu/.

General Application Contact: Ron B. Clement, Associate Director of Graduate Studies, 510-430-2355, Fax: 510-430-2159, E-mail: rclement@mills.edu.

GRADUATE UNITS

Graduate Studies Students: 373 full-time (299 women), 61 part-time (47 women); includes 102 minority (41 African Americans, 34 Asian Americans or Pacific Islanders, 22 Hispanic Americans, 5 Native Americans), 23 international. Average age 32. 578 applicants, 60% accepted, 242 enrolled. *Faculty:* 60 full-time (34 women), 43 part-time/adjunct (32 women). Expenses: Contact institution. *Financial support:* In 2001–02, 272 students received support, including 181 fellowships with partial tuition reimbursements available (averaging $1,785 per year), 115 teaching assistantships with partial tuition reimbursements available (averaging $4,337 per year); career-related internships or fieldwork, institutionally sponsored loans, scholarships/grants, and residence awards also available. Support available to part-time students. Financial award application deadline: 2/1; financial award applicants required to submit CSS PROFILE or FAFSA. In 2001, 89 master's, 49 other advanced degrees awarded. *Degree program information:* Part-time and evening/weekend programs available. Offers administration (Ed D); ceramics (MFA); childlife in health care settings (MA); computer science (Certificate); creative writing (MFA); dance (MA, MFA); early childhood education (MA); education (MA); English (MA, MFA); management (MBA); multimedia/art (MFA); multimedia/music (MFA); music (MA, MFA); painting (MFA); photography (MFA); pre-med (Certificate); sculpture (MFA). *Application deadline:* For fall admission, 2/1; for spring admission, 11/1. Applications are processed on a rolling basis. *Application fee:* $50. *Application Contact:* Ron B. Clement, Associate Director of Graduate Studies, 510-430-2355, Fax: 510-430-2159, E-mail: rclement@mills.edu. *Director*, Marianne B. Sheldon, 510-430-2345, Fax: 510-430-2159, E-mail: mshel@mills.edu.

See in-depth description on page 977.

MILWAUKEE SCHOOL OF ENGINEERING, Milwaukee, WI 53202-3109

General Information Independent, coed, primarily men, comprehensive institution. *Enrollment:* 20 full-time matriculated graduate/professional students (8 women), 297 part-time matriculated graduate/professional students (55 women). *Enrollment by degree level:* 317 master's. *Graduate faculty:* 12 full-time (2 women), 47 part-time/adjunct (2 women). *Tuition:* Part-time $440 per credit. Tuition and fees vary according to course load. *Graduate housing:* Room and/or apartments available on a first-come, first-served basis to single students; on-campus housing not available to married students. Typical cost: $4,865 (including board). Room and board charges vary according to board plan. *Student services:* Campus employment opportunities, campus safety program, career counseling, disabled student services, exercise/wellness program, free psychological counseling, international student services, low-cost health insurance, multicultural affairs office, writing training. *Library facilities:* Walter Schroeder Library. *Online resources:* library catalog, web page, access to other libraries' catalogs. *Collection:* 45,638 titles, 430 serial subscriptions, 467 audiovisual materials. *Research affiliation:* Milwaukee Public Schools (education), Caterpillar, Inc. (electrohydraulics), The Procter & Gamble Company (rapid tooling), State of Wisconsin (energy conservation), Rochester Institute of Technology (software engineering).

Computer facilities: 105 computers available on campus for general student use. A campuswide network can be accessed from student residence rooms and from off campus. Internet access, e-mail are available. *Web address:* http://www.msoe.edu/.

General Application Contact: Paul Borens, Admissions Director, 800-332-6763, Fax: 414-277-7475, E-mail: borens@msoe.edu.

GRADUATE UNITS

Department of Architectural Engineering and Building Construction Students: 2 full-time (0 women), 25 part-time (6 women). Average age 25. 18 applicants, 61% accepted, 2 enrolled. *Faculty:* 2 full-time (1 woman), 11 part-time/adjunct (0 women). Expenses: Contact institution. *Financial support:* In 2001–02, 3 students received support, including 2 research assistantships; career-related internships or fieldwork also available. Support available to part-time students. Financial award applicants required to submit FAFSA. In 2001, 8 degrees awarded. *Degree program information:* Part-time and evening/weekend programs available. Offers environmental engineering (MS); structural engineering (MS). *Application deadline:* Applications are processed on a rolling basis. *Application fee:* $35. Electronic applications accepted. *Application Contact:* Paul Borens, Admissions Director, 800-332-6763, Fax: 414-277-7475, E-mail: borens@msoe.edu. *Chairman*, Matt Fuchs, 414-277-7302, Fax: 414-277-7479, E-mail: fuchs@msoe.edu.

Department of Electrical Engineering and Computer Science Students: 9 full-time (4 women), 42 part-time (1 woman); includes 1 minority (African American), 2 international. Average age 25. 39 applicants, 36% accepted, 12 enrolled. *Faculty:* 8 full-time (0 women), 13 part-time/adjunct (1 woman). Expenses: Contact institution. *Financial support:* In 2001–02, 8 students received support; research assistantships, career-related internships or fieldwork available. Support available to part-time students. Financial award applicants required to submit FAFSA. In 2001, 21 degrees awarded. *Degree program information:* Part-time and evening/weekend programs available. Offers engineering (MS); perfusion (MS). *Application deadline:* Applications are processed on a rolling basis. *Application fee:* $30. Electronic applications accepted. *Application Contact:* Paul Borens, Admissions Director, 800-332-6763, Fax: 414-277-7475, E-mail: borens@msoe.edu. *Chairman*, Ray Palmer, 414-277-7325, Fax: 414-277-7465, E-mail: palmer@msoe.edu.

School of Business Students: 9 full-time (4 women), 230 part-time (48 women); includes 9 minority (5 African Americans, 4 Asian Americans or Pacific Islanders), 4 international. Average age 25. 80 applicants, 60% accepted, 31 enrolled. *Faculty:* 4 full-time (1 woman), 27 part-time/adjunct (2 women). Expenses: Contact institution. *Financial support:* In 2001–02, 10 students received support. Career-related internships or fieldwork available. Support available to part-time students. Financial award applicants required to submit FAFSA. *Degree program information:* Part-time and evening/weekend programs available. Offers engineering management (MS); medical informatics (MS). *Application deadline:* Applications are processed on a rolling basis. *Application fee:* $35. Electronic applications accepted. *Application Contact:* Paul Borens, Admissions Director, 800-332-6763, Fax: 414-277-7475, E-mail: borens@msoe.edu. *Chairman*, Joseph Papp, 414-277-7352, Fax: 414-277-7479, E-mail: papp@msoe.edu.

MINNEAPOLIS COLLEGE OF ART AND DESIGN, Minneapolis, MN 55404-4347

General Information Independent, coed, comprehensive institution. *Enrollment:* 22 full-time matriculated graduate/professional students (11 women), 3 part-time matriculated graduate/professional students (2 women). *Enrollment by degree level:* 25 master's. *Graduate faculty:* 32 full-time (12 women). *Tuition:* Full-time $21,300; part-time $710 per credit. *Required fees:* $470; $235 per term. Tuition and fees vary according to course load. *Graduate housing:* Rooms and/or apartments available on a first-come, first-served basis to single and married students. Typical cost: $3,420 per year for single students; $3,420 per year for married students. Room charges vary according to housing facility selected. Housing application deadline: 6/1. *Student services:* Campus employment opportunities, campus safety program, career counseling, disabled student services, free psychological counseling, grant writing training, international student services, low-cost health insurance, writing training. *Library facilities:* Minneapolis College of Art and Design Library. *Online resources:* web page. *Collection:* 47,166 titles, 196 serial subscriptions, 139,245 audiovisual materials.

Computer facilities: 110 computers available on campus for general student use. A campuswide network can be accessed from off campus. Internet access is available. *Web address:* http://www.mcad.edu/.

General Application Contact: Brad Nuorala, Acting Director of Admissions and Recruitment, 612-874-3762, Fax: 612-874-3701, E-mail: brad_nuorala@mcad.edu.

GRADUATE UNITS

Program in Visual Studies Students: 44 full-time (29 women), 6 part-time (5 women); includes 2 minority (1 African American, 1 Asian American or Pacific Islander), 3 international. Average age 27. 77 applicants, 32% accepted. *Faculty:* 23 full-time (7 women), 9 part-time/adjunct (4 women). Expenses: Contact institution. *Financial support:* In 2001–02, 23 students received support. Career-related internships or fieldwork, Federal Work-Study, scholarships/grants, and unspecified assistantships available. Support available to part-time students. Financial award application deadline: 4/1; financial award applicants required to submit FAFSA. In 2001, 15 master's, 12 other advanced degrees awarded. *Degree program information:* Part-time programs available. Offers advertising design (MFA); animation (MFA); comic art (MFA); drawing (MFA); film making (MFA); fine arts (MFA); furniture design (MFA); graphic design (MFA); illustration (MFA); interactive media (MFA); painting (MFA); photography (MFA); printmaking (MFA); sculpture (MFA); studio studies (Certificate); visualization (Certificate). *Application deadline:* For fall admission, 2/15; for spring admission, 10/1. Applications are processed on a rolling basis. *Application fee:* $50. Electronic applications accepted. *Application Contact:* Patricia Gibbs, Dean of Enrollment Services, 612-874-3762, Fax: 612-874-3701, E-mail: patty_gibbs@mcad.edu. *Graduate Director*, Carole Fisher, 612-874-3629, Fax: 612-874-3704, E-mail: carole_fisher@mn.mcad.edu.

MINNESOTA STATE UNIVERSITY, MANKATO, Mankato, MN 56001

General Information State-supported, coed, comprehensive institution. CGS member. *Enrollment:* 1,611 matriculated graduate/professional students (1,026 women). *Graduate faculty:* 405 full-time (150 women), 120 part-time/adjunct (58 women). Tuition, state resident: full-time $3,253; part-time $157 per credit. Tuition, nonresident: full-time $4,893; part-time $248 per credit. *Required fees:* $24 per credit. Tuition and fees vary according to reciprocity agreements. *Graduate housing:* Room and/or apartments available to single students; on-campus housing not available to married students. *Student services:* Campus employment opportunities, campus safety program, career counseling, child daycare facilities, disabled student services, exercise/wellness program, free psychological counseling, international student services, low-cost health insurance, multicultural affairs office, teacher training. *Library facilities:* Memorial Library. *Online resources:* library catalog, web page. *Collection:* 1.1 million titles, 4,396 serial subscriptions, 129,006 audiovisual materials.

Computer facilities: 525 computers available on campus for general student use. A campuswide network can be accessed from student residence rooms and from off campus. Internet access and online class registration are available. *Web address:* http://www.mnsu.edu.

General Application Contact: Joni Roberts, Admissions Coordinator, 507-389-5244, Fax: 507-389-5974, E-mail: grad@mankato.msus.edu.

GRADUATE UNITS

College of Graduate Studies Students: 467 full-time (298 women), 1,144 part-time (728 women). Average age 33. *Faculty:* 405 full-time (150 women), 120 part-time/adjunct (58 women). Expenses: Contact institution. *Financial support:* In 2001–02, 550 students received support; fellowships with full tuition reimbursements available, research assistantships with full tuition reimbursements available, teaching assistantships with full tuition reimbursements available, career-related internships or fieldwork, Federal Work-Study, and institutionally sponsored loans available. Support available to part-time students. Financial award application deadline: 3/15; financial award applicants required to submit FAFSA. In 2001, 458 master's, 53 other advanced degrees awarded. *Degree program information:* Part-time and evening/weekend programs available. Offers multidisciplinary studies (MS). *Application deadline:* For fall admission, 7/9 (priority date); for spring admission, 11/27. Applications are processed on a rolling basis. *Application fee:* $20. *Application Contact:* Joni Roberts, Admissions Coordinator, 507-389-5244, Fax: 507-389-5974, E-mail: grad@mankato.msus.edu. *Chairperson*, Dr. Anthony J. Filipovitch, 507-389-2321.

College of Allied Health and Nursing Students: 11 full-time (all women), 41 part-time (35 women). Average age 33. *Faculty:* 46 full-time (31 women), 1 (woman) part-time/adjunct. Expenses: Contact institution. *Financial support:* Fellowships, research assistantships with full tuition reimbursements, teaching assistantships with full tuition reimbursements, career-related internships or fieldwork, Federal Work-Study, and institutionally sponsored loans available. Support available to part-time students. Financial award application deadline: 3/15; financial award applicants required to submit FAFSA. In 2001, 70 master's awarded. *Degree program information:* Part-time programs available. Offers allied health and nursing (MA, MS, MSN, MT, SP); communication disorders (MS); community health (MS); family consumer science and interior design (MS, MT); family nursing (MSN); health science (MS, MT); human performance (MA, MS, MT, SP); managed care (MSN); rehabilitation counseling (MS). *Application deadline:* For fall admission, 7/9 (priority date); for spring admission, 11/27. Applications are processed on a rolling basis. *Application fee:* $20. *Application Contact:* Joni Roberts, Admissions Coordinator, 507-389-5244, Fax: 507-389-5974, E-mail: grad@mankato.msus.edu. *Interim Dean,* Dr. Sharon Aodalen, 507-389-6315.

College of Arts and Humanities Students: 152 (91 women). Average age 32. *Faculty:* 61 full-time (23 women). Expenses: Contact institution. *Financial support:* Research assistantships with full tuition reimbursements, teaching assistantships with full tuition reimbursements, career-related internships or fieldwork, Federal Work-Study, and institutionally sponsored loans available. Support available to part-time students. Financial award application deadline: 3/15; financial award applicants required to submit FAFSA. In 2001, 51 degrees awarded. *Degree program information:* Part-time and evening/weekend programs available. Offers art education (MS); arts and humanities (MA, MAT, MFA, MM, MS, MT); creative writing (MFA); English (MA, MS); French (MAT, MS); German (MAT); music (MM, MT); Spanish (MAT, MS); speech communication (MA, MS, MT); studio art (MA); teaching art (MAT, MT); teaching English (MS, MT); theatre arts (MA, MFA). *Application deadline:* For fall admission, 7/9 (priority date); for spring admission, 11/27. Applications are processed on a rolling basis. *Application fee:* $20. *Application Contact:* Joni Roberts, Admissions Coordinator, 507-389-5244, Fax: 507-389-5974, E-mail: grad@mankato.msus.edu. *Dean,* Dr. Jane F. Earley, 507-389-1712.

College of Education Students: 673 (451 women). Average age 35. *Faculty:* 50 full-time (19 women). Expenses: Contact institution. *Financial support:* Fellowships with partial tuition reimbursements, research assistantships with full tuition reimbursements, teaching assistantships with full tuition reimbursements, career-related internships or fieldwork, Federal Work-Study, and institutionally sponsored loans available. Support available to part-time students. Financial award application deadline: 3/15; financial award applicants required to submit FAFSA. In 2001, 458 master's, 53 other advanced degrees awarded. *Degree program information:* Part-time and evening/weekend programs available. Offers bilingual/bicultural education (MS); computer services administration (MS); counseling and student personnel (MS); curriculum and instruction (MAT, MT); early childhood education (MS); early education for exceptional children (MS); education (MA, MAT, MS, MT, Certificate, SP); education of the gifted and talented (MS); education technology (MS); educational administration (Certificate); educational leadership (MS, Certificate, SP); elementary education (MS, SP); elementary school administration (MS, SP); emotional disturbance (MS); experiential education (MS); general educational administration (MS); higher education administration (MS); learning disabilities (MS); library media education (MS, SP); mental retardation (MS); reading consultant (MS); secondary administration (MS, SP); secondary teaching (MA, MS, SP); severely handicapped (MS); vocational-technical administration (MS). *Application deadline:* For fall admission, 7/9 (priority date); for spring admission, 11/27. Applications are processed on a rolling basis. *Application fee:* $20. *Application Contact:* Joni Roberts, Admissions Coordinator, 507-389-5244, Fax: 507-389-5974, E-mail: grad@mankato.msus.edu. *Interim Dean,* Dr. Joanne Brandt, 507-389-1215.

College of Science, Engineering and Technology Students: 82 (31 women). Average age 28. *Faculty:* 78 full-time (13 women). Expenses: Contact institution. *Financial support:* Fellowships with full tuition reimbursements, research assistantships with full tuition reimbursements, teaching assistantships with full tuition reimbursements, career-related internships or fieldwork, Federal Work-Study, and institutionally sponsored loans available. Support available to part-time students. Financial award application deadline: 3/15; financial award applicants required to submit FAFSA. In 2001, 56 degrees awarded. *Degree program information:* Part-time programs available. Offers biology (MS); chemistry (MA, MS); computer science (MS); computers (MS); ecology (MS); economic and political systems (MS); electrical engineering and electronic engineering technology (MSE); environmental science (MS); human ecosystems (MS); manufacturing (MS); mathematics (MA, MS); mathematics: computer science (MS); mechanical engineering (MS); physical science (MS); physics and astronomy (MS, MT); science, engineering and technology (MA, MS, MSE, MT); statistics (MS); teaching mathematics (MT); technology (MS). *Application deadline:* For fall admission, 7/9 (priority date); for spring admission, 11/27. Applications are processed on a rolling basis. *Application fee:* $20. *Application Contact:* Joni Roberts, Admissions Coordinator, 507-389-5244, Fax: 507-389-5974, E-mail: grad@mankato.msus.edu. *Dean,* Dr. John Frey, 507-389-5998.

College of Social and Behavioral Sciences Students: 207 (139 women). Average age 27. *Faculty:* 68 full-time (20 women). Expenses: Contact institution. *Financial support:* Fellowships with partial tuition reimbursements, research assistantships with full tuition reimbursements, teaching assistantships with full tuition reimbursements, career-related internships or fieldwork, Federal Work-Study, and institutionally sponsored loans available. Support available to part-time students. Financial award application deadline: 3/15; financial award applicants required to submit FAFSA. In 2001, 66 degrees awarded. *Degree program information:* Part-time programs available. Offers anthropology (MS); clinical psychology (MA); geography (MA, MS, MT); gerontology (MS); history (MA, MS); industrial psychology (MA); political science (MA, MS, MT); psychology (MT); public administration (MAPA); public administration and law); social and behavioral sciences (MA, MAPA, MS, MT); social studies (MS); sociology (MA, MT); sociology: corrections (MS); teaching history (MS, MT); urban and regional studies (MA); women's studies (MS). *Application deadline:* For fall admission, 7/9 (priority date); for spring admission, 11/27. Applications are processed on a rolling basis. *Application fee:* $20. *Application Contact:* Joni Roberts, Admissions Coordinator, 507-389-5244, Fax: 507-389-5974, E-mail: grad@mankato.msus.edu. *Acting Dean,* Dr. Susan Coultrap-McQuin, 507-389-5717.

MINNESOTA STATE UNIVERSITY, MOORHEAD, Moorhead, MN 56563-0002

General Information State-supported, coed, comprehensive institution. *Enrollment:* 93 full-time matriculated graduate/professional students (71 women), 290 part-time matriculated graduate/professional students (215 women). *Graduate faculty:* 124. *Tuition, area resident:* Part-time $148 per credit. Tuition, nonresident: part-time $234 per credit. *Graduate housing:* Room and/or apartments available to single students; on-campus housing not available to married students. Typical cost: $3,706 (including board). Room and board charges vary according to board plan. Housing application deadline: 3/1. *Student services:* Campus employment opportunities, campus safety program, career counseling, child daycare facilities, disabled student services, free psychological counseling, international student services, low-cost health insurance, multicultural affairs office, writing training. *Library facilities:* Livingston Lord Library. *Online resources:* library catalog, web page, access to other libraries' catalogs. *Collection:* 367,334 titles, 1,539 serial subscriptions. *Research affiliation:* West Central Minnesota Business Innovation Center.

Computer facilities: 450 computers available on campus for general student use. A campuswide network can be accessed from student residence rooms and from off campus. Internet access and online class registration are available. *Web address:* http://www.mnstate.edu/.

General Application Contact: Karla Wenger, Graduate Studies Office, 218-236-2344, Fax: 218-236-2482, E-mail: wengerk@mnstate.edu.

GRADUATE UNITS

Graduate Studies Students: 93 full-time (71 women), 290 part-time (215 women); includes 11 minority (1 African American, 5 Asian Americans or Pacific Islanders, 2 Hispanic Americans, 3 Native Americans), 4 international. Average age 33. 141 applicants, 82% accepted. *Faculty:* 124. Expenses: Contact institution. *Financial support:* Career-related internships or fieldwork, Federal Work-Study, and unspecified assistantships available. Support available to part-time students. Financial award application deadline: 7/15; financial award applicants required to submit FAFSA. In 2001, 78 degrees awarded. *Degree program information:* Part-time and evening/weekend programs available. Offers counseling and student affairs (MS); creative writing (MFA); curriculum and instruction (MS); educational administration (MS, Ed S); liberal studies (MLA); music (MA, MS); music education (MS); nursing (MS); public, human services, and health administration (MS); reading (MS); school psychology (MS, Psy S); special education (MS); speech pathology and audiology (MS). *Application fee:* $20 ($35 for international students). Electronic applications accepted. *Application Contact:* Karla Wenger, Graduate Studies Office, 218-236-2344, Fax: 218-236-2482, E-mail: wengerk@mnstate.edu. *Director of Graduate Studies,* Dr. Dorothy Suomala, 218-236-2026.

MINOT STATE UNIVERSITY, Minot, ND 58707-0002

General Information State-supported, coed, comprehensive institution. *Graduate housing:* Rooms and/or apartments available to single and married students. Housing application deadline: 6/30.

GRADUATE UNITS

Graduate School Offers audiology (MS); criminal justice (MS); education of the deaf (MS); elementary education (MS); English (MAT); learning disabilities (MS); management (MS); mathematics (MAT); music education (MME); psychology (Ed Sp); science (MAT); special education (MS); speech-language pathology (MS).

MIRRER YESHIVA, Brooklyn, NY 11223-2010

General Information Independent-religious, men only, comprehensive institution.

MISSISSIPPI COLLEGE, Clinton, MS 39058

General Information Independent-religious, coed, comprehensive institution. *Graduate housing:* Rooms and/or apartments available on a first-come, first-served basis to single students and available to married students. *Research affiliation:* Gulf Coast Research Laboratory.

GRADUATE UNITS

Graduate School *Degree program information:* Part-time and evening/weekend programs available.

College of Arts and Sciences *Degree program information:* Part-time and evening/weekend programs available. Offers administration of justice (MSS); applied music performance (MM); art (MA, MFA); arts and sciences (M Ed, MA, MCS, MFA, MLS, MM, MS, MSC, MSS, MSS); biology (MCS); chemistry (MCS); communication (MSC); computer science (MS); conducting (MM); counseling psychology (MS); English (M Ed, MA); history (M Ed, MA, MSS); liberal studies (MLS); mathematics (MCS, MS); music education (MM); political science (MSS); psychology (MS); psychometry (M Ed); social sciences (M Ed, MSS); sociology (MSS); theory and composition (MM); vocal pedagogy (MM).

School of Business Administration *Degree program information:* Part-time and evening/weekend programs available. Offers accounting (MBA); business administration (MBA); health services administration (MHSA).

School of Education *Degree program information:* Part-time and evening/weekend programs available. Offers art education (M Ed); biology education (M Ed); business education (M Ed); computer science education (M Ed); counseling psychology (MCP); education (M Ed, MCP, Ed S); educational leadership (M Ed); elementary education (M Ed); guidance and counseling (M Ed, Ed S); mathematics education (M Ed); sciences education (M Ed); secondary education (M Ed).

School of Law Students: 383 full-time (159 women). 574 applicants, 60% accepted, 143 enrolled. *Faculty:* 12 full-time (4 women), 16 part-time/adjunct (3 women). Expenses: Contact institution. *Financial support:* In 2001–02, 341 students received support. Career-related internships or fieldwork, Federal Work-Study, and scholarships/grants available. Financial award application deadline: 5/1. In 2001, 119 degrees awarded. Offers law (JD). *Application deadline:* For fall admission, 5/1 (priority date). Applications are processed on a rolling basis. *Application fee:* $40. Electronic applications accepted. *Application Contact:* Patricia H. Evans, Director of Admissions, 601-925-7150, Fax: 601-925-7185, E-mail: pevans@mc.edu. *Dean,* J. Larry Lee, 601-925-7104, Fax: 601-925-7115, E-mail: llee@mc.edu.

MISSISSIPPI STATE UNIVERSITY, Mississippi State, MS 39762

General Information State-supported, coed, university. CGS member. *Enrollment:* 1,695 full-time matriculated graduate/professional students (777 women), 1,579 part-time matriculated graduate/professional students (883 women). *Enrollment by degree level:* 193 first professional, 2,297 master's, 699 doctoral, 85 other advanced degrees. *Graduate faculty:* 883 full-time (267 women), 182 part-time/adjunct (106 women). Tuition, state resident: full-time $3,586; part-time $150 per credit hour. Tuition, nonresident: full-time $8,128; part-time $339 per credit hour. Tuition and fees vary according to course load and campus/location. *Graduate housing:* Rooms and/or apartments available on a first-come, first-served basis to single students and available to married students. Typical cost: $2,669 per year ($5,704 including board) for single students. Room and board charges vary according to board plan and housing facility selected. Housing application deadline: 8/1. *Student services:* Campus employment opportunities, campus safety program, career counseling, disabled student services, exercise/wellness program, free psychological counseling, international student services, low-cost health insurance, multicultural affairs office. *Library facilities:* Mitchell Memorial Library plus 2 others. *Online resources:* library catalog, web page, access to other libraries' catalogs. *Collection:* 1.6 million titles, 15,574 serial subscriptions, 14,665 audiovisual materials. *Research affiliation:* Mississippi Research Consortium (interdisciplinary research), John C. Stennis Space Center (interdisciplinary research), Mississippi Mineral Resources Institute (geology–sciences and engineering), Mississippi Research and Technology Park (engineering—interdisciplinary), Oak Ridge Associated Universities (energy related research–interdisciplinary), Southeastern Universities Research Association (interdisciplinary research).

Computer facilities: 2,000 computers available on campus for general student use. A campuswide network can be accessed from student residence rooms and from off campus. Internet access and online class registration are available. *Web address:* http://www.msstate.edu/.

General Application Contact: Jerry B. Inmon, Director of Admissions, 662-325-2224, Fax: 662-325-7360, E-mail: admit@admissions.msstate.edu.

GRADUATE UNITS

College of Agriculture and Life Sciences Students: 150 full-time (66 women), 98 part-time (37 women); includes 17 minority (14 African Americans, 1 Asian American or Pacific Islander, 2 Hispanic Americans), 69 international. Average age 30. 112 applicants, 49% accepted. *Faculty:* 125. Expenses: Contact institution. *Financial support:* Research assistantships, teaching assistantships, career-related internships or fieldwork, Federal Work-Study, institutionally sponsored loans, scholarships/grants, tuition waivers (partial), and unspecified assistantships available. Financial award applicants required to submit FAFSA. In 2001, 68 master's, 23 doctorates awarded. *Degree program information:* Part-time programs available. Offers agribusiness management (MABM); agricultural pest management (MS); agriculture and extension education (MS); agriculture and life sciences (MABM, MLA, MS, Ed D, PhD, Ed S); agronomy (MS, PhD); applied economics (PhD); biochemistry (MS); entomology (MS, PhD); food science and technology (MS, PhD); horticulture (MS, PhD); landscape architecture (MLA); molecular biology (PhD); plant pathology (MS, PhD); poultry science (MS); weed science (MS, PhD). *Application deadline:* For fall admission, 7/1; for spring admission, 11/1. Applications are processed on a rolling basis. *Application fee:* $25 for international students. *Application Contact:* Jerry B. Inmon, Director of Admissions, 662-325-2224, Fax: 662-325-7360, E-mail: admit@admissions.msstate.edu. *Dean and Vice President,* Dr. Vance Watson, 662-325-2110, E-mail: vwatson@dafvm.msstate.edu.

College of Arts and Sciences Students: 316 full-time (143 women), 322 part-time (182 women); includes 68 minority (47 African Americans, 8 Asian Americans or Pacific Islanders, 8 Hispanic Americans, 5 Native Americans), 87 international. Average age 33. 444 applicants, 49% accepted. *Faculty:* 211 full-time (45 women), 21 part-time/adjunct (7 women). Expenses: Contact institution. *Financial support:* In 2001–02, 226 students received support, including

Mississippi State University (continued)
research assistantships with full tuition reimbursements available (averaging $11,000 per year), teaching assistantships with full tuition reimbursements available (averaging $7,500 per year); fellowships with full tuition reimbursements available, Federal Work-Study, institutionally sponsored loans, scholarships/grants, tuition waivers (partial), and unspecified assistantships also available. Financial award applicants required to submit FAFSA. In 2001, 108 master's, 17 doctorates awarded. *Degree program information:* Part-time and evening/weekend programs available. Offers arts and sciences (MA, MFA, MPPA, MS, PhD); biological sciences (MS, PhD); chemistry (MS, PhD); clinical psychology (MS); cognitive science (PhD); electronic visualization (MFA); engineering physics (PhD); English (MA); experimental psychology (MS); French (MA); French/German (MA); geosciences (MS); German (MA); history (MA, PhD); mathematical sciences (PhD); mathematics (MS); physics (MS); political science (MA); public policy and administration (MPPA, PhD); sociology (MS, PhD); Spanish (MA); Spanish/French (MA); Spanish/German (MA); statistics (MS). *Application deadline:* For fall admission, 7/1; for spring admission, 11/1. Applications are processed on a rolling basis. *Application fee:* $0 ($25 for international students). *Application Contact:* Jerry B. Inmon, Director of Admissions, 662-325-2224, Fax: 662-325-7360, E-mail: admit@admissions.msstate.edu. *Interim Head*, Dr. Philip B. Oldham, 662-325-2646, Fax: 662-325-9075.

College of Business and Industry Students: 152 full-time (65 women), 90 part-time (30 women); includes 29 minority (23 African Americans, 4 Asian Americans or Pacific Islanders, 2 Hispanic Americans), 45 international. Average age 29. 211 applicants, 64% accepted, 93 enrolled. *Faculty:* 58. Expenses: Contact institution. *Financial support:* In 2001–02, 43 research assistantships with full tuition reimbursements (averaging $5,940 per year), 25 teaching assistantships with full tuition reimbursements (averaging $10,200 per year) were awarded. Fellowships with full tuition reimbursements, career-related internships or fieldwork, Federal Work-Study, institutionally sponsored loans, and unspecified assistantships also available. Financial award applicants required to submit FAFSA. In 2001, 115 master's, 5 doctorates awarded. *Degree program information:* Part-time and evening/weekend programs available. Postbaccalaureate distance learning degree programs offered (no on-campus study). Offers applied economics (PhD); business administration (MBA, PhD); business and industry (MA, MBA, MPA, MSBA, MSIS, MTX, PhD); economics (MA); finance (MSBA); information systems (MSIS); project management (MBA). *Application deadline:* For fall admission, 7/1; for spring admission, 11/1. Applications are processed on a rolling basis. *Application fee:* $25. *Application Contact:* Jerry B. Inmon, Director of Admissions, 662-325-2224, Fax: 662-325-7360, E-mail: admit@admissions.msstate.edu. *Director of Graduate Studies in Business*, Dr. Barbara Spencer, 662-325-1891, Fax: 662-325-7360, E-mail: gsb@cobilan.msstate.edu.

School of Accountancy Students: 36 full-time (19 women), 4 part-time (2 women); includes 5 minority (3 African Americans, 1 Asian American or Pacific Islander, 1 Hispanic American), 1 international. Average age 25. 43 applicants, 63% accepted, 22 enrolled. *Faculty:* 10 full-time (1 woman), 1 (woman) part-time/adjunct. Expenses: Contact institution. *Financial support:* In 2001–02, 20 students received support, including fellowships (averaging $6,000 per year), 5 research assistantships with tuition reimbursements available (averaging $5,940 per year), 5 teaching assistantships with partial tuition reimbursements available (averaging $10,200 per year); career-related internships or fieldwork, Federal Work-Study, institutionally sponsored loans, and unspecified assistantships also available. Support available to part-time students. Financial award applicants required to submit FAFSA. In 2001, 33 degrees awarded. Offers accountancy (MPA, MTX, PhD). *Application deadline:* For fall admission, 7/1; for spring admission, 11/1. Applications are processed on a rolling basis. *Application fee:* $25. *Application Contact:* Jerry B. Inmon, Director of Admissions, 662-325-2224, Fax: 662-325-7360, E-mail: admit@admissions.msstate.edu. *Director*, Dr. Dan P. Hollingsworth, 662-325-3710, Fax: 662-325-1646, E-mail: dhollingsworth@cobilan.msstate.edu.

College of Education Students: 290 full-time (213 women), 547 part-time (410 women); includes 276 minority (262 African Americans, 3 Asian Americans or Pacific Islanders, 7 Hispanic Americans, 4 Native Americans), 14 international. Average age 34. 233 applicants, 74% accepted. *Faculty:* 103 full-time (48 women), 27 part-time/adjunct (18 women). Expenses: Contact institution. *Financial support:* In 2001–02, 12 fellowships with full tuition reimbursements (averaging $6,500 per year), 22 research assistantships (averaging $6,500 per year), 18 teaching assistantships (averaging $6,500 per year) were awarded. Career-related internships or fieldwork, Federal Work-Study, institutionally sponsored loans, scholarships/grants, and unspecified assistantships also available. Financial award applicants required to submit FAFSA. In 2001, 300 master's, 33 doctorates, 39 other advanced degrees awarded. *Degree program information:* Part-time and evening/weekend programs available. Postbaccalaureate distance learning degree programs offered (minimal on-campus study). Offers community college leadership (PhD); counselor education (MS, PhD, Ed S); curriculum and instruction (PhD); education (MS, MSIT, Ed D, PhD, Ed S); educational leadership (PhD); educational psychology (MS, PhD, Ed S); elementary education (MS, Ed D, PhD, Ed S); exercise science (MS); health education/health promotion (MS); instructional technology (MSIT); school administration (MS, Ed S); secondary education (MS, Ed D, PhD, Ed S); special education (MS, Ed S); sports administration (MS); teaching/coaching (MS); technology (MS, Ed D, PhD, Ed S); workforce education leadership (MS). *Application deadline:* For fall admission, 7/1; for spring admission, 11/1. Applications are processed on a rolling basis. *Application fee:* $25 for international students. *Application Contact:* Jerry B. Inmon, Director of Admissions, 662-325-2224, Fax: 662-325-7360, E-mail: admit@admissions.msstate.edu. *Interim Dean*, Dr. Roy Ruby, 662-325-3717, Fax: 662-325-8784.

College of Engineering Students: 392 full-time (83 women), 165 part-time (32 women); includes 43 minority (23 African Americans, 15 Asian Americans or Pacific Islanders, 3 Hispanic Americans, 2 Native Americans), 358 international. Average age 27. 1,327 applicants, 35% accepted, 125 enrolled. *Faculty:* 115 full-time (11 women), 12 part-time/adjunct (4 women). Expenses: Contact institution. *Financial support:* In 2001–02, 27 fellowships with full tuition reimbursements (averaging $9,240 per year), 247 research assistantships with full tuition reimbursements (averaging $12,850 per year), 61 teaching assistantships with full tuition reimbursements (averaging $12,000 per year) were awarded. Federal Work-Study, institutionally sponsored loans, and unspecified assistantships also available. Financial award applicants required to submit FAFSA. In 2001, 97 master's, 15 doctorates awarded. *Degree program information:* Part-time programs available. Postbaccalaureate distance learning degree programs offered (no on-campus study). Offers aerospace engineering (MS); biological engineering (MS); biomedical engineering (MS, PhD); civil engineering (MS, PhD); computational engineering (MS, PhD); computer engineering (MS, PhD); computer science (MS, PhD); electrical engineering (MS, PhD); engineering (PhD); engineering mechanics (MS); industrial engineering (MS, PhD); mechanical engineering (MS, PhD). *Application deadline:* For fall admission, 7/1; for spring admission, 11/1. Applications are processed on a rolling basis. *Application fee:* $25 for international students. *Application Contact:* Jerry B. Inmon, Director of Admissions, 662-325-2224, Fax: 662-325-7360, E-mail: admit@admissions.msstate.edu. *Dean*, Dr. A. Wayne Bennett, 662-325-2270, Fax: 662-325-8573, E-mail: bennet@engr.msstate.edu.

David C. Swalm School of Chemical Engineering Students: 19 full-time (6 women), 4 part-time; includes 2 minority (1 African American, 1 Hispanic American), 15 international. Average age 26. 79 applicants, 32% accepted, 2 enrolled. *Faculty:* 11 full-time (2 women). Expenses: Contact institution. *Financial support:* In 2001–02, 3 fellowships with full tuition reimbursements (averaging $16,000 per year), 19 research assistantships with full tuition reimbursements (averaging $13,200 per year) were awarded. Teaching assistantships with tuition reimbursements, Federal Work-Study, institutionally sponsored loans, and unspecified assistantships also available. Financial award applicants required to submit FAFSA. In 2001, 4 degrees awarded. Offers chemical engineering (MS); engineering (PhD). *Application deadline:* For fall admission, 4/1 (priority date); for spring admission, 8/1 (priority date). Applications are processed on a rolling basis. *Application fee:* $25 for international students. *Application Contact:* Jerry B. Inmon, Director of Admissions, 662-325-2224, Fax: 662-325-7360, E-mail: admit@admissions.msstate.edu. *Director*, Dr. Kirk H. Schulz, 662-325-2480, Fax: 662-325-2482.

College of Forest Resources Students: 94 full-time (21 women), 43 part-time (4 women); includes 3 minority (1 Asian American or Pacific Islander, 2 Hispanic Americans), 16 international. Average age 29. 12 applicants, 67% accepted, 6 enrolled. *Faculty:* 47 full-time (5 women), 45 part-time/adjunct (5 women). Expenses: Contact institution. *Financial support:* In 2001–02, 22 research assistantships with full tuition reimbursements (averaging $11,200 per year), 5 teaching assistantships with full tuition reimbursements (averaging $10,560 per year) were awarded. Career-related internships or fieldwork, Federal Work-Study, institutionally sponsored loans, and unspecified assistantships also available. Financial award applicants required to submit FAFSA. In 2001, 16 master's, 5 doctorates awarded. *Degree program information:* Part-time programs available. Offers forest products (MS); forest resources (MS, PhD); forestry (MS); wildlife and fisheries science (MS). *Application deadline:* For fall admission, 7/1; for spring admission, 11/1. Applications are processed on a rolling basis. *Application fee:* $25 for international students. Electronic applications accepted. *Application Contact:* Jerry B. Inmon, Director of Admissions, 662-325-2224, Fax: 662-325-7360, E-mail: admit@admissions.msstate.edu. *Head*, Dr. G. Sam Foster, 662-325-2953, Fax: 662-325-8726, E-mail: sfoster@cfr.msstate.edu.

College of Veterinary Medicine Students: 211 full-time (133 women), 5 part-time (3 women); includes 11 minority (5 African Americans, 3 Asian Americans or Pacific Islanders, 3 Hispanic Americans), 6 international. Average age 25. 432 applicants, 14% accepted, 58 enrolled. Expenses: Contact institution. *Financial support:* In 2001–02, 17 students received support, including 17 research assistantships with full tuition reimbursements available (averaging $15,000 per year); career-related internships or fieldwork, Federal Work-Study, and subsidized and unsubsidized loans also available. Financial award application deadline: 6/30; financial award applicants required to submit FAFSA. In 2001, 46 first professional degrees, 7 master's, 1 doctorate awarded. Offers environmental toxicology (PhD); veterinary medical science (MS, PhD); veterinary medicine (DVM, MS, PhD). *Application deadline:* For fall admission, 10/1. *Application fee:* $30. Electronic applications accepted. *Application Contact:* Barbara R. Coats, Student Affairs Coordinator, 662-325-1278, Fax: 662-325-8714, E-mail: coats@cvm.msstate.edu. *Dean*, Dr. John U. Thomson, 662-325-3432, Fax: 662-325-1498, E-mail: thomson@cvm.msstate.edu.

School of Architecture Students: 7 full-time (2 women), 3 part-time (1 woman), 8 international. Average age 31. 20 applicants, 30% accepted, 5 enrolled. *Faculty:* 2 full-time (0 women), 1 part-time/adjunct (0 women). Expenses: Contact institution. *Financial support:* In 2001–02, 7 students received support, including 5 fellowships with full tuition reimbursements available (averaging $6,000 per year), 1 research assistantship with full tuition reimbursement available (averaging $6,000 per year), 1 teaching assistantship with full tuition reimbursement available (averaging $8,000 per year); career-related internships or fieldwork, Federal Work-Study, institutionally sponsored loans, and unspecified assistantships also available. Financial award application deadline: 3/1; financial award applicants required to submit FAFSA. Offers architecture (MS). *Application deadline:* For fall admission, 3/1 (priority date). Applications are processed on a rolling basis. *Application fee:* $25 for international students. Electronic applications accepted. *Application Contact:* Jerry B. Inmon, Director of Admissions, 662-325-2224, Fax: 662-325-7360, E-mail: admit@admissions.msstate.edu. *Dean*, James L. West, 662-325-2202, Fax: 662-325-8872, E-mail: jwest@sarc.msstate.edu.

MISSISSIPPI UNIVERSITY FOR WOMEN, Columbus, MS 39701-9998

General Information State-supported, coed, primarily women, comprehensive institution. *Graduate housing:* Rooms and/or apartments available on a first-come, first-served basis to single and married students.

GRADUATE UNITS

Graduate School *Degree program information:* Part-time programs available.

Division of Education and Human Sciences *Degree program information:* Part-time programs available. Offers gifted studies (M Ed); instructional management (M Ed); speech/language pathology (MS).

Division of Health and Kinesiology Offers health education (MS).

Division of Nursing *Degree program information:* Part-time programs available. Offers nursing (MSN, Certificate).

MISSISSIPPI VALLEY STATE UNIVERSITY, Itta Bena, MS 38941-1400

General Information State-supported, coed, comprehensive institution. *Graduate housing:* Room and/or apartments available to single students; on-campus housing not available to married students. Housing application deadline: 8/1.

GRADUATE UNITS

Department of Criminal Justice and Social Work *Degree program information:* Part-time and evening/weekend programs available. Offers criminal justice (MS). Electronic applications accepted.

Department of Education Offers education (MAT); elementary education (MA).

Department of Natural Science and Environmental Health *Degree program information:* Evening/weekend programs available. Offers environmental health (MS).

MOLLOY COLLEGE, Rockville Centre, NY 11571-5002

General Information Independent, coed, comprehensive institution. *Enrollment:* 11 full-time matriculated graduate/professional students (all women), 195 part-time matriculated graduate/professional students (191 women). *Graduate faculty:* 16 full-time (15 women), 5 part-time/adjunct (4 women). *Tuition:* Full-time $9,360; part-time $520 per credit. *Required fees:* $570; $155 per semester. Tuition and fees vary according to degree level. *Graduate housing:* On-campus housing not available. *Student services:* Campus employment opportunities, career counseling, writing training. *Library facilities:* James Edward Tobin Library. *Online resources:* library catalog. *Collection:* 135,000 titles, 9,675 audiovisual materials.

Computer facilities: 246 computers available on campus for general student use. A campuswide network can be accessed. Internet access is available.

General Application Contact: Dr. Carol A. Clifford, Director, Graduate Program, 516-256-2218, Fax: 516-678-9718, E-mail: cclifford@molloy.edu.

GRADUATE UNITS

Department of Nursing Students: 11 full-time (all women), 195 part-time (191 women); includes 81 minority (42 African Americans, 30 Asian Americans or Pacific Islanders, 8 Hispanic Americans, 1 Native American) Average age 36. 60 applicants, 63% accepted. *Faculty:* 16 full-time (15 women), 5 part-time/adjunct (4 women). Expenses: Contact institution. *Financial support:* In 2001–02, 2 students received support, including 1 research assistantship with partial tuition reimbursement available; teaching assistantships with partial tuition reimbursements available, institutionally sponsored loans and tuition waivers (partial) also available. Support available to part-time students. Financial award application deadline: 5/1; financial award applicants required to submit FAFSA. In 2001, 24 master's, 6 other advanced degrees awarded. *Degree program information:* Part-time and evening/weekend programs available. Offers adult nurse practitioner (MSN, Advanced Certificate); clinical nurse specialist: adult health (MSN, Advanced Certificate); family nurse practitioner (MSN, Advanced Certificate); nurse practitioner psychiatry (MSN, Advanced Certificate); nursing (MSN); nursing administration (Advanced Certificate); nursing administration with informatics (MSN); nursing education (MSN, Advanced Certificate); pediatric nurse practitioner (MSN, Advanced Certificate). *Application deadline:* For fall admission, 9/2 (priority date); for spring admission, 1/20 (priority date). Applications are processed on a rolling basis. *Application fee:* $60. *Application Contact:* Linda Finley Albanese, Vice President for Enrollment Management, 516-678-5000 Ext. 240, Fax: 516-256-2247, E-mail: lalbanese@molloy.edu. *Director, Graduate Program*, Dr. Carol A. Clifford, 516-256-2218, Fax: 516-678-9718, E-mail: cclifford@molloy.edu.

MONMOUTH UNIVERSITY, West Long Branch, NJ 07764-1898

General Information Independent, coed, comprehensive institution. *Enrollment:* 409 full-time matriculated graduate/professional students (299 women), 1,165 part-time matriculated graduate/professional students (750 women). *Enrollment by degree level:* 1,574 master's.

Graduate faculty: 97 full-time (32 women), 57 part-time/adjunct (29 women). *Tuition:* Full-time $9,900; part-time $549 per credit. *Required fees:* $568. *Graduate housing:* On-campus housing not available. *Student services:* Campus employment opportunities, campus safety program, career counseling, disabled student services, exercise/wellness program, free psychological counseling, international student services, low-cost health insurance, multicultural affairs office, writing training. *Library facilities:* Murry and Leonie Guggenheim Memorial Library. *Online resources:* library catalog, web page. *Collection:* 230,000 titles, 1,300 serial subscriptions.

Computer facilities: 400 computers available on campus for general student use. A campuswide network can be accessed from student residence rooms and from off campus. *Web address:* http://www.monmouth.edu/.

General Application Contact: Kevin Roane, Director, Office of Graduate Admissions, 732-571-3452, Fax: 732-263-5123, E-mail: gradadm@monmouth.edu.

GRADUATE UNITS

Graduate School Students: 409 full-time (299 women), 1,165 part-time (750 women); includes 152 minority (65 African Americans, 58 Asian Americans or Pacific Islanders, 26 Hispanic Americans, 3 Native Americans), 128 international. 1,473 applicants, 54% accepted, 495 enrolled. *Faculty:* 97 full-time (32 women), 57 part-time/adjunct (29 women). Expenses: Contact institution. *Financial support:* In 2001–02, 558 students received support, including 509 fellowships (averaging $1,701 per year), 92 research assistantships (averaging $4,810 per year); career-related internships or fieldwork, scholarships/grants, tuition waivers (full and partial), and unspecified assistantships also available. Support available to part-time students. Financial award application deadline: 3/1; financial award applicants required to submit FAFSA. In 2001, 416 degrees awarded. *Degree program information:* Part-time and evening/weekend programs available. Offers community and international development (MSW); computer science (MS); corporate and public communication (MA); criminal justice administration (MA, Certificate); history (MA); human resources communication (Certificate); liberal arts (MA); media studies (Certificate); practice with families and children (MSW); professional counseling (PMC); psychological counseling (MA); public relations (Certificate); software development (Certificate); software engineering (MS, Certificate). *Application deadline:* For fall admission, 8/15 (priority date); for spring admission, 12/15 (priority date). Applications are processed on a rolling basis. *Application fee:* $35. Electronic applications accepted. *Application Contact:* Kevin Roane, Director, Office of Graduate Admissions, 732-571-3452, Fax: 732-263-5123, E-mail: gradadm@monmouth.edu. *Dean,* Dr. Datta V. Naik, 732-571-7550, Fax: 732-263-5142.

The Marjorie K. Unterberg School of Nursing and Health Studies Students: 11 full-time (all women), 54 part-time (51 women); includes 9 minority (3 African Americans, 6 Asian Americans or Pacific Islanders) Average age 39. 34 applicants, 79% accepted, 21 enrolled. *Faculty:* 5 full-time (all women), 2 part-time/adjunct (1 woman). Expenses: Contact institution. *Financial support:* In 2001–02, 53 students received support, including 52 fellowships (averaging $1,756 per year), 3 research assistantships (averaging $3,606 per year); career-related internships or fieldwork, scholarships/grants, tuition waivers (partial), and unspecified assistantships also available. Support available to part-time students. Financial award application deadline: 3/1; financial award applicants required to submit FAFSA. In 2001, 22 degrees awarded. *Degree program information:* Part-time and evening/weekend programs available. Offers advanced practice nursing (MSN, Certificate); nursing (MSN); school nursing (Certificate); substance awareness coordinator (Certificate). *Application deadline:* For fall admission, 8/15 (priority date); for spring admission, 12/15 (priority date). Applications are processed on a rolling basis. *Application fee:* $35. Electronic applications accepted. *Application Contact:* Kevin Roane, Director, Office of Graduate Admissions, 732-571-3452, Fax: 732-263-5123, E-mail: gradadm@monmouth.edu. *Director,* Dr. Janet Mahoney, 732-571-3443, Fax: 732-263-5131, E-mail: jmahoney@monmouth.edu.

School of Business Administration Students: 28 full-time (13 women), 241 part-time (94 women); includes 28 minority (8 African Americans, 15 Asian Americans or Pacific Islanders, 4 Hispanic Americans, 1 Native American), 10 international. Average age 31. 249 applicants, 60% accepted, 71 enrolled. *Faculty:* 23 full-time (4 women), 8 part-time/adjunct (3 women). Expenses: Contact institution. *Financial support:* In 2001–02, 69 students received support, including 67 fellowships (averaging $1,392 per year), 10 research assistantships (averaging $3,955 per year); career-related internships or fieldwork, scholarships/grants, tuition waivers (partial), and unspecified assistantships also available. Support available to part-time students. Financial award application deadline: 3/1; financial award applicants required to submit FAFSA. In 2001, 87 degrees awarded. *Degree program information:* Part-time and evening/weekend programs available. Offers accounting (MBA); business administration (MBA); health care management (MBA); healthcare management (Certificate). *Application deadline:* For fall admission, 8/15 (priority date); for spring admission, 12/15 (priority date). Applications are processed on a rolling basis. *Application fee:* $35. Electronic applications accepted. *Application Contact:* Kevin Roane, Director, Office of Graduate Admissions, 732-571-3452, Fax: 732-263-5123, E-mail: gradadm@monmouth.edu. *Director of MBA Program,* Catherine Bianchi, 732-571-3434, Fax: 732-263-5517, E-mail: cbianchi@monmouth.edu.

School of Education Students: 118 full-time (97 women), 305 part-time (245 women); includes 23 minority (17 African Americans, 2 Asian Americans or Pacific Islanders, 3 Hispanic Americans, 1 Native American), 1 international. Average age 32. 388 applicants, 71% accepted, 168 enrolled. *Faculty:* 12 full-time (7 women), 17 part-time/adjunct (10 women). Expenses: Contact institution. *Financial support:* In 2001–02, 105 students received support, including 96 fellowships (averaging $1,517 per year), 10 research assistantships (averaging $4,130 per year); career-related internships or fieldwork, scholarships/grants, tuition waivers (partial), and unspecified assistantships also available. Support available to part-time students. Financial award application deadline: 3/1; financial award applicants required to submit FAFSA. In 2001, 143 degrees awarded. *Degree program information:* Part-time and evening/weekend programs available. Offers educational counseling (MS Ed); elementary education (MAT); learning disabilities-teacher consultant (Certificate); principal studies (MS Ed); reading specialist (MS Ed, Certificate); special education (MS Ed); supervisor (Certificate); teacher of the handicapped (Certificate). *Application deadline:* For fall admission, 8/15 (priority date); for spring admission, 12/15 (priority date). Applications are processed on a rolling basis. *Application fee:* $35. Electronic applications accepted. *Application Contact:* Kevin Roane, Director, Office of Graduate Admissions, 732-571-3452, Fax: 732-263-5123, E-mail: gradadm@monmouth.edu. *Dean,* Dr. Bernice Willis, 732-571-7518, Fax: 732-263-5277, E-mail: bwillis@monmouth.edu.

See in-depth description on page 979.

MONTANA STATE UNIVERSITY–BILLINGS, Billings, MT 59101-0298

General Information State-supported, coed, comprehensive institution. *Enrollment:* 136 full-time matriculated graduate/professional students (103 women), 147 part-time matriculated graduate/professional students (111 women). *Enrollment by degree level:* 283 master's. *Graduate faculty:* 74 full-time (26 women), 2 part-time/adjunct (0 women). Tuition, state resident: full-time $3,560; part-time $1,164 per semester. Tuition, nonresident: full-time $8,498; part-time $2,810 per semester. *Graduate housing:* Rooms and/or apartments available on a first-come, first-served basis to single and married students. *Student services:* Campus employment opportunities, campus safety program, career counseling, disabled student services, exercise/wellness program, free psychological counseling, grant writing training, international student services, low-cost health insurance, multicultural affairs office, teacher training, writing training. *Library facilities:* Montana State University-Billings Library. *Online resources:* library catalog, access to other libraries' catalogs. *Collection:* 418,000 titles, 865 serial subscriptions, 1,907 audiovisual materials. *Research affiliation:* Northwest College and University Association for Science (natural sciences).

Computer facilities: 450 computers available on campus for general student use. A campuswide network can be accessed from student residence rooms and from off campus. Internet access and online class registration, on-line degree programs are available. *Web address:* http://www.msubillings.edu/.

General Application Contact: Dr. George White, Director of Graduate Studies and Research, 406-657-2238, Fax: 406-657-2299, E-mail: skraft@msubillings.edu.

GRADUATE UNITS

College of Arts and Sciences Offers arts and sciences (MS); psychology (MS); public relations (MS).

College of Business Offers business (MSIPC); information processing and communications (MSIPC).

College of Education and Human Services *Degree program information:* Part-time programs available. Postbaccalaureate distance learning degree programs offered (minimal on-campus study). Offers community counseling (MS, MS Sp Ed); early childhood education (M Ed); education and human services (M Ed, MS, MS Sp Ed, MSRC); educational technology (M Ed); emotionally disturbed (MS Sp Ed); general curriculum (M Ed); interdisciplinary studies (M Ed); mental retardation (MS Sp Ed); reading (M Ed); rehabilitation counseling (MSRC); school counseling (M Ed); secondary education (M Ed); special education (MS Sp Ed); special education generalist (MS Sp Ed); sport management (MS).

College of Professional Studies and Lifelong Learning Offers health administration (MHA); professional studies and lifelong learning (MHA).

MONTANA STATE UNIVERSITY–BOZEMAN, Bozeman, MT 59717

General Information State-supported, coed, university. CGS member. *Enrollment:* 449 full-time matriculated graduate/professional students (181 women), 505 part-time matriculated graduate/professional students (247 women). *Enrollment by degree level:* 713 master's, 241 doctoral. *International tuition:* $10,811 full-time. Tuition, state resident: full-time $3,894; part-time $198 per credit. Tuition, nonresident: full-time $10,661; part-time $480 per credit. Tuition and fees vary according to course load and program. *Graduate housing:* Rooms and/or apartments available on a first-come, first-served basis to single and married students. Typical cost: $4,068 per year for single students; $4,455 per year for married students. Room charges vary according to housing facility selected. *Student services:* Campus employment opportunities, campus safety program, career counseling, child daycare facilities, disabled student services, exercise/wellness program, free psychological counseling, international student services, low-cost health insurance, multicultural affairs office, teacher training, writing training. *Library facilities:* Renne Library plus 1 other. *Online resources:* library catalog, web page, access to other libraries' catalogs. *Collection:* 574,634 titles, 3,790 serial subscriptions, 2,925 audiovisual materials. *Research affiliation:* ILX Lightwave (laser diodes, electro-optical test equipment), Scientific Materials (laser crystals), Cytoclonal Pharmaceutics, Inc., Exegenics Inc., Eli Lilly & Company (antifungal technology), IBM (optical data storage), Sheridan Research, Inc. (anti-cancer technology).

Computer facilities: 850 computers available on campus for general student use. A campuswide network can be accessed from student residence rooms and from off campus. Internet access and online class registration, e-mail are available. *Web address:* http://www.montana.edu/.

General Application Contact: Dr. Bruce McLeod, Dean, 406-994-4145, Fax: 406-994-4733, E-mail: gradstudy@montana.edu.

GRADUATE UNITS

College of Graduate Studies Students: 449 full-time (181 women), 505 part-time (247 women); includes 33 minority (2 African Americans, 8 Asian Americans or Pacific Islanders, 6 Hispanic Americans, 17 Native Americans), 99 international. Average age 31. 836 applicants, 87% accepted, 463 enrolled. Expenses: Contact institution. *Financial support:* Fellowships with full and partial tuition reimbursements, research assistantships with full and partial tuition reimbursements, teaching assistantships with full and partial tuition reimbursements, career-related internships or fieldwork, Federal Work-Study, institutionally sponsored loans, scholarships/grants, traineeships, tuition waivers (full and partial), and unspecified assistantships available. Support available to part-time students. Financial award application deadline: 3/1; financial award applicants required to submit FAFSA. In 2001, 327 master's, 30 doctorates awarded. *Degree program information:* Part-time programs available. Postbaccalaureate distance learning degree programs offered (minimal on-campus study). *Application deadline:* For fall admission, 7/15 (priority date); for spring admission, 12/1 (priority date). Applications are processed on a rolling basis. *Application fee:* $50. Electronic applications accepted. *Dean, Graduate Studies,* Dr. Bruce McLeod, 406-994-4145, Fax: 406-994-7433, E-mail: gradstudy@montana.edu.

College of Agriculture Students: 40 full-time (18 women), 91 part-time (51 women); includes 3 minority (1 Hispanic American, 2 Native Americans), 17 international. Average age 29. 71 applicants, 77% accepted, 35 enrolled. Expenses: Contact institution. *Financial support:* Fellowships, research assistantships, teaching assistantships, career-related internships or fieldwork, Federal Work-Study, scholarships/grants, and tuition waivers (full and partial) available. Financial award application deadline: 3/1; financial award applicants required to submit FAFSA. In 2001, 22 master's, 2 doctorates awarded. *Degree program information:* Part-time programs available. Offers agriculture (MS, PhD); animal and range science (MS); applied economics (MS); entomology (MS); land rehabilitation (MS); land resources and environmental sciences (MS, PhD); plant pathology (MS); plant science (MS, PhD); veterinary molecular biology (MS, PhD). *Application deadline:* Applications are processed on a rolling basis. *Application fee:* $50. Electronic applications accepted. *Dean,* Dr. Sharron Quisenberry, 406-994-3681, Fax: 406-994-6579, E-mail: agdean@montana.edu.

College of Arts and Architecture Students: 71 full-time (21 women), 14 part-time (3 women); includes 1 minority (Hispanic American), 6 international. Average age 27. 107 applicants, 80% accepted, 72 enrolled. Expenses: Contact institution. *Financial support:* Research assistantships, teaching assistantships with full tuition reimbursements, career-related internships or fieldwork, Federal Work-Study, scholarships/grants, and tuition waivers (partial) available. Financial award application deadline: 3/1; financial award applicants required to submit FAFSA. In 2001, 53 degrees awarded. *Degree program information:* Part-time programs available. Offers architecture (M Arch); art (MFA); arts and architecture (M Arch, MFA); science and natural history filmmaking (MFA). *Application deadline:* Applications are processed on a rolling basis. *Application fee:* $50. Electronic applications accepted. *Dean,* Jerry Bancroft, 406-994-4405, Fax: 406-994-3680, E-mail: jb@montana.edu.

College of Business Students: 28 full-time (20 women), 9 part-time (8 women); includes 1 minority (Asian American or Pacific Islander), 1 international. Average age 28. 24 applicants, 100% accepted, 19 enrolled. Expenses: Contact institution. *Financial support:* In 2001–02, 8 students received support, including 5 teaching assistantships with full and partial tuition reimbursements available (averaging $2,600 per year) Financial award application deadline: 3/1; financial award applicants required to submit FAFSA. In 2001, 33 degrees awarded. *Degree program information:* Part-time programs available. Offers professional accountancy (MP Ac). *Application deadline:* For fall admission, 6/30; for spring admission, 11/15. Applications are processed on a rolling basis. *Application fee:* $50. Electronic applications accepted. *Dean,* Dr. Richard J. Semenik, 406-994-4421, Fax: 406-994-6206, E-mail: busgrad@montana.edu.

College of Education, Health, and Human Development Students: 54 full-time (43 women), 114 part-time (66 women); includes 12 minority (2 African Americans, 2 Asian Americans or Pacific Islanders, 2 Hispanic Americans, 6 Native Americans), 3 international. Average age 39. 81 applicants, 94% accepted, 45 enrolled. Expenses: Contact institution. *Financial support:* In 2001–02, 2 research assistantships with partial tuition reimbursements (averaging $6,000 per year), 14 teaching assistantships with full and partial tuition reimbursements (averaging $6,938 per year) were awarded. Career-related internships or fieldwork, Federal Work-Study, and scholarships/grants also available. Financial award application deadline: 3/1; financial award applicants required to submit FAFSA. In 2001, 77 master's, 9 doctorates awarded. *Degree program information:* Part-time programs available. Postbaccalaureate distance learning degree programs offered (minimal on-campus study). Offers education (M Ed, PhD); education, health, and human development (M Ed, MS, PhD); health and human development (MS); science education (MS). *Application deadline:* For fall admission, 6/1; for spring admission, 11/1. Applications are processed on a rolling basis. Electronic

Montana State University–Bozeman (continued)

applications accepted. *Dean,* Dr. Greg Weisenstein, 406-994-4133, Fax: 406-994-1854, E-mail: gweisens@montana.edu.

College of Engineering Students: 97 full-time (21 women), 58 part-time (21 women); includes 3 minority (all Asian Americans or Pacific Islanders), 39 international. Average age 28. 165 applicants, 80% accepted, 59 enrolled. Expenses: Contact institution. *Financial support:* Fellowships with partial tuition reimbursements, research assistantships with partial tuition reimbursements, teaching assistantships with partial tuition reimbursements, career-related internships or fieldwork, Federal Work-Study, scholarships/grants, and tuition waivers (full and partial) available. Financial award application deadline: 3/1; financial award applicants required to submit FAFSA. In 2001, 70 degrees awarded. *Degree program information:* Part-time programs available. Offers computer science (MS); computer sciences (PhD); electrical engineering (MS); engineering (PhD); industrial and management engineering (MS); mechanical engineering (MS). *Application deadline:* For fall admission, 6/1; for spring admission, 11/1. Applications are processed on a rolling basis. *Application fee:* $50. Electronic applications accepted. *Interim Dean,* Dr. Robert Marley, 406-994-2272, Fax: 406-994-6665, E-mail: rmarley@montana.edu.

College of Letters and Science Students: 143 full-time (46 women), 211 part-time (93 women); includes 12 minority (2 Asian Americans or Pacific Islanders, 2 Hispanic Americans, 8 Native Americans), 33 international. Average age 31. 205 applicants, 82% accepted, 84 enrolled. Expenses: Contact institution. *Financial support:* Application deadline: 3/1; In 2001, 64 master's, 17 doctorates awarded. *Degree program information:* Part-time programs available. Offers applied psychology (MS); biochemistry (MS, PhD); biological science (MS); biological sciences (MS, PhD); cell biology (PhD); chemistry (MS, PhD); complex biological systems (PhD); earth sciences (MS); English (MA); fish and wildlife biology (PhD); fish and wildlife management (MS); history (MA); land rehabilitation (MS); letters and science (MA, MPA, MS, PhD); mathematics (MS, PhD); microbiology (MS, PhD); Native American studies (MA); neuroscience (PhD); physics (MS, PhD); public administration (MPA); statistics (MS, PhD). *Application deadline:* Applications are processed on a rolling basis. *Application fee:* $50. Electronic applications accepted. *Dean,* Dr. James McMillan, 406-494-4288, Fax: 406-994-6879, E-mail: jamc@montana.edu.

College of Nursing Students: 15 full-time (12 women), 4 part-time (2 women); includes 1 minority (Native American) Average age 39. 6 applicants, 100% accepted, 5 enrolled. Expenses: Contact institution. *Financial support:* In 2001–02, 14 students received support, including 4 teaching assistantships with partial tuition reimbursements available (averaging $5,120 per year); institutionally sponsored loans, scholarships/grants, and traineeships also available. Financial award application deadline: 3/1; financial award applicants required to submit FAFSA. In 2001, 10 degrees awarded. *Degree program information:* Part-time programs available. Postbaccalaureate distance learning degree programs offered (minimal on-campus study). Offers nursing (MN). *Application deadline:* For fall admission, 2/15; for spring admission, 6/15. Applications are processed on a rolling basis. *Application fee:* $50. Electronic applications accepted. *Dean,* Dr. Lea Acord, 406-994-3783, Fax: 406-994-6020, E-mail: lynnt@montana.edu.

MONTANA STATE UNIVERSITY–NORTHERN, Havre, MT 59501-7751

General Information State-supported, coed, comprehensive institution. *Enrollment:* 90 full-time matriculated graduate/professional students (74 women), 30 part-time matriculated graduate/professional students (20 women). *Enrollment by degree level:* 120 master's. *Graduate faculty:* 5 full-time (2 women), 9 part-time/adjunct (3 women). *Graduate housing:* Rooms and/or apartments available on a first-come, first-served basis to single students and available to married students. Housing application deadline: 8/22. *Student services:* Campus employment opportunities, career counseling, child daycare facilities, exercise/wellness program, low-cost health insurance, multicultural affairs office, teacher training. *Library facilities:* VandeBogart Libraries. *Online resources:* library catalog, web page, access to other libraries' catalogs. *Collection:* 128,000 titles, 1,729 serial subscriptions.

Computer facilities: 140 computers available on campus for general student use. A campuswide network can be accessed from student residence rooms and from off campus. Internet access and online class registration are available. *Web address:* http://www.msun.edu/.

General Application Contact: Dr. Darlene Sellers, Dean, College of Education and Graduate Programs, 406-265-3745, Fax: 406-265-3777, E-mail: sellersd@msun.edu.

GRADUATE UNITS

College of Education and Graduate Programs Students: 90 full-time (74 women), 30 part-time (20 women); includes 16 minority (all Native Americans) Average age 35. *Faculty:* 5 full-time (2 women), 9 part-time/adjunct (3 women). Expenses: Contact institution. *Financial support:* In 2001–02, 3 research assistantships with partial tuition reimbursements (averaging $4,000 per year), 1 teaching assistantship with partial tuition reimbursement (averaging $4,000 per year) were awarded. Career-related internships or fieldwork, Federal Work-Study, institutionally sponsored loans, and unspecified assistantships also available. Support available to part-time students. Financial award application deadline: 4/1; financial award applicants required to submit FAFSA. In 2001, 55 degrees awarded. *Degree program information:* Part-time and evening/weekend programs available. Postbaccalaureate distance learning degree programs offered (minimal on-campus study). Offers counselor education (M Ed); elementary education (M Ed); general science (M Ed); learning development (M Ed); vocational education (M Ed). *Application deadline:* For fall admission, 9/20 (priority date). Applications are processed on a rolling basis. *Application fee:* $30. Electronic applications accepted. *Application Contact:* Dr. Darlene Sellers, Dean, College of Education and Graduate Programs, 406-265-3745, Fax: 406-265-3777, E-mail: sellersd@msun.edu. *Dean, College of Education and Graduate Programs,* Dr. Darlene Sellers, 406-265-3745, Fax: 406-265-3777, E-mail: sellersd@msun.edu.

MONTANA TECH OF THE UNIVERSITY OF MONTANA, Butte, MT 59701-8997

General Information State-supported, coed, comprehensive institution. *Enrollment:* 64 full-time matriculated graduate/professional students (22 women), 16 part-time matriculated graduate/professional students (9 women). *Enrollment by degree level:* 80 master's. *Graduate faculty:* 46 full-time (6 women). Tuition, state resident: full-time $3,717; part-time $196 per credit. Tuition, nonresident: full-time $11,770; part-time $324 per credit. *Graduate housing:* Rooms and/or apartments guaranteed to single students and available on a first-come, first-served basis to married students. Typical cost: $2,504 (including board) for single students. Room and board charges vary according to board plan. Housing application deadline: 8/25. *Student services:* Campus employment opportunities, campus safety program, career counseling, child daycare facilities, exercise/wellness program, free psychological counseling, grant writing training, international student services, low-cost health insurance. *Library facilities:* Montana Tech Library plus 1 other. *Online resources:* library catalog, web page, access to other libraries' catalogs. *Collection:* 161,187 titles, 495 serial subscriptions, 38 audiovisual materials. *Research affiliation:* MSE-TA (environmental restoration), Montana Technology Companies, Inc. (environmental restoration), Montana Technology Enterprise Center (sonic technology), Stillwater Mining (minerals production).

Computer facilities: 500 computers available on campus for general student use. A campuswide network can be accessed from student residence rooms and from off campus. Internet access and online class registration are available. *Web address:* http://www.mtech.edu/.

General Application Contact: Cindy Dunstan, Administrator, Graduate School, 406-496-4304, Fax: 406-496-4334, E-mail: cdunstan@mtech.edu.

GRADUATE UNITS

Graduate School Students: 64 full-time (22 women), 16 part-time (9 women); includes 3 minority (1 Asian American or Pacific Islander, 2 Hispanic Americans) 76 applicants, 78% accepted, 29 enrolled. *Faculty:* 46 full-time (6 women). Expenses: Contact institution. *Financial support:* In 2001–02, 61 students received support, including 13 research assistantships with full tuition reimbursements available (averaging $8,000 per year), 40 teaching assistantships with partial tuition reimbursements available (averaging $5,440 per year); career-related internships or fieldwork, institutionally sponsored loans, and tuition waivers (full and partial) also available. Financial award application deadline: 4/1; financial award applicants required to submit FAFSA. In 2001, 46 degrees awarded. *Degree program information:* Part-time and evening/weekend programs available. Postbaccalaureate distance learning degree programs offered (no on-campus study). Offers engineering (MS); environmental engineering (MS); geochemistry (MS); geological engineering (MS); geology (MS); geophysical engineering (MS); hydrogeological engineering (MS); hydrogeology (MS); industrial hygiene (MS); metallurgical/mineral processing engineering (MS); mineral economics (MS); mining engineering (MS); petroleum engineering (MS); project engineering and management (MPEM); technical communications (MS). *Application deadline:* For fall admission, 4/1 (priority date); for spring admission, 10/1 (priority date). Applications are processed on a rolling basis. *Application fee:* $30. *Application Contact:* Cindy Dunstan, Administrator, Graduate School, 406-496-4304, Fax: 406-496-4334, E-mail: cdunstan@mtech.edu. *Vice Chancellor, Research and Graduate Studies,* Dr. Joseph Figueira, 406-496-4102.

MONTCLAIR STATE UNIVERSITY, Upper Montclair, NJ 07043-1624

General Information State-supported, coed, comprehensive institution. CGS member. *Graduate housing:* Room and/or apartments available on a first-come, first-served basis to single students; on-campus housing not available to married students. Housing application deadline: 3/23.

GRADUATE UNITS

The School of Graduate, Professional and Continuing Education *Degree program information:* Part-time and evening/weekend programs available. Electronic applications accepted.

College of Education and Human Services *Degree program information:* Part-time and evening/weekend programs available. Offers administration and supervision (MA); art (MAT); biological science (MAT); business education (MAT); coaching and sports administration (MA); counseling and guidance (MA); critical thinking (M Ed); early childhood education (MAT); early childhood special education (MA); earth science (MAT); education (M Ed, Ed D); education and human services (M Ed, MA, MAT, Ed D); educator/trainer (MA); English (MAT); exercise science (MA); family life education (MA); family relations/child development (MA); French (MAT); health and physical education (MAT); health education (MA, MAT); home economics (MAT); home economics education (MA); home management/consumer economics (MA); human services (MA); industrial arts (MAT); learning disabilities (MA); mathematics (MAT); mathematics education (Ed D); music (MAT); nutrition education (MA); philosophy for children (M Ed, Ed D); physical education (MA, MAT); physical science (MAT); reading (MA); social studies (MAT); Spanish (MAT); teacher of ESL (MAT); teacher of handicapped (MAT); teaching (MAT); teaching and administration of physical education (MA); teaching middle school philosophy (MAT); technology education (MA). Electronic applications accepted.

College of Humanities and Social Sciences *Degree program information:* Part-time and evening/weekend programs available. Offers anthropology (MA); applied linguistics (MA); applied sociology (MA); child advocacy (Certificate); child/adolescent clinical psychology (MA); clinical psychology for Spanish/English bilinguals (MA); dispute resolution (MA); economics (MA); educational psychology (MA); English (MA); French (MA); history (MA); humanities and social sciences (MA, Certificate); industrial and organizational psychology (MA); law office management and technology (MA); legal studies (MA); paralegal (Certificate); practical anthropology (MA); psychology (MA); Spanish (MA); speech/language pathology (MA). Electronic applications accepted.

College of Science and Mathematics *Degree program information:* Part-time and evening/weekend programs available. Offers applied mathematics (MS); applied statistics (MS); biology science education (MS); chemistry (MS); computer science (MS); environmental studies (MS); geoscience (MS, Certificate); informatics (MS); mathematics (MS); mathematics education (MS); molecular biology (Certificate); object oriented computing (Certificate); pure and applied mathematics (MS); science and mathematics (MS, Certificate); statistics (MS); water resource management (Certificate).

School of Business *Degree program information:* Part-time and evening/weekend programs available. Offers accounting (MBA); business (MA, MBA); business economics (MBA); business education (MA); economics (MA); finance (MBA); international business (MBA); management (MBA); management information systems (MBA); marketing (MBA); social science (MA).

School of the Arts *Degree program information:* Part-time and evening/weekend programs available. Offers art history (MA); arts (MA, MFA); communication arts (MA); music education (MA); music therapy (MA); performance (MA); studio arts (MA, MFA); theatre (MA); theory/composition (MA). Electronic applications accepted.

See in-depth description on page 981.

MONTEREY INSTITUTE OF INTERNATIONAL STUDIES, Monterey, CA 93940-2691

General Information Independent, coed, graduate-only institution. *Enrollment:* 555 full-time matriculated graduate/professional students (385 women), 65 part-time matriculated graduate/professional students (38 women). *Enrollment by degree level:* 620 master's. *Graduate faculty:* 64 full-time (29 women), 21 part-time/adjunct (10 women). *Tuition:* Full-time $19,988; part-time $840 per unit. *Required fees:* $50. Part-time tuition and fees vary according to course load and reciprocity agreements. *Graduate housing:* On-campus housing not available. *Student services:* Campus employment opportunities, career counseling, disabled student services, exercise/wellness program, international student services, low-cost health insurance, writing training. *Library facilities:* William Tell Coleman Library. *Online resources:* library catalog, web page, access to other libraries' catalogs. *Collection:* 87,000 titles, 550 serial subscriptions.

Computer facilities: 122 computers available on campus for general student use. A campuswide network can be accessed from off campus. Internet access is available. *Web address:* http://www.miis.edu/.

General Application Contact: Admissions Office, 831-647-4123, Fax: 831-647-6405, E-mail: admit@miis.edu.

GRADUATE UNITS

Fisher Graduate School of International Business Students: 66 full-time (32 women), 6 part-time (2 women); includes 6 minority (2 African Americans, 4 Asian Americans or Pacific Islanders), 36 international. Average age 28. 83 applicants, 92% accepted, 34 enrolled. *Faculty:* 9 full-time (2 women), 1 part-time/adjunct (0 women). Expenses: Contact institution. *Financial support:* In 2001–02, 2 research assistantships with partial tuition reimbursements (averaging $4,000 per year) were awarded; career-related internships or fieldwork, Federal Work-Study, institutionally sponsored loans, scholarships/grants, tuition waivers (partial), and unspecified assistantships also available. Support available to part-time students. Financial award applicants required to submit FAFSA. In 2001, 58 degrees awarded. Offers international business (MBA). *Application deadline:* For fall admission, 3/15 (priority date); for spring admission, 10/1 (priority date). Applications are processed on a rolling basis. *Application fee:* $50. Electronic applications accepted. *Application Contact:* 831-647-4123, Fax: 831-647-6405, E-mail: admit@miis.edu. *Acting Dean,* Dr. Ernest J. Scalberg, 831-647-4140, Fax: 831-647-6506, E-mail: ernest.scalberg@miis.edu.

Graduate School of International Policy Studies Students: 247 full-time (147 women), 14 part-time (7 women); includes 24 minority (6 African Americans, 8 Asian Americans or Pacific Islanders, 10 Hispanic Americans), 95 international. Average age 28. 263 applicants, 96% accepted, 116 enrolled. *Faculty:* 15 full-time (6 women), 5 part-time/adjunct (1 woman). Expenses: Contact institution. *Financial support:* In 2001–02, 253 students received support, including 60 research assistantships with partial tuition reimbursements available (averaging $4,000 per year); career-related internships or fieldwork, Federal Work-Study, institutionally sponsored loans, scholarships/grants, and tuition waivers (partial) also available. Support available to part-time students. Financial award applicants required to submit FAFSA. In 2001, 135 degrees awarded. Offers commercial diplomacy (MA); international environmental policy (MPA); international management (MPA); international policy studies (MA, MPA). *Application deadline:* For fall admission, 3/15 (priority date); for spring admission, 10/1 (priority date). Applications are processed on a rolling basis. *Application fee:* $50. Electronic applications accepted. *Application Contact:* 831-647-4123, Fax: 831-647-6405, E-mail: admit@miis.edu. *Dean*, Dr. Philip Morgan, 831-647-4155, Fax: 831-647-4199, E-mail: philip.morgan@miis.edu.

Graduate School of Language and Educational Linguistics Students: 47 full-time (40 women), 40 part-time (25 women); includes 8 minority (1 African American, 7 Asian Americans or Pacific Islanders), 17 international. Average age 28. 64 applicants, 86% accepted, 30 enrolled. *Faculty:* 19 full-time (9 women), 3 part-time/adjunct (2 women). Expenses: Contact institution. *Financial support:* In 2001–02, 8 research assistantships with partial tuition reimbursements (averaging $4,000 per year) were awarded; career-related internships or fieldwork, Federal Work-Study, institutionally sponsored loans, scholarships/grants, tuition waivers (partial), and unspecified assistantships also available. Support available to part-time students. Financial award applicants required to submit FAFSA. In 2001, 54 degrees awarded. Offers language and educational linguistics (MATESOL, MATFL); peace corps master's internationalist in TESOL (MATESOL); teaching English to speakers of other languages (MATESOL); teaching foreign language (MATFL). *Application deadline:* For fall admission, 3/15 (priority date); for spring admission, 10/1 (priority date). Applications are processed on a rolling basis. *Application fee:* $50. Electronic applications accepted. *Application Contact:* 831-647-4123, Fax: 831-647-6405, E-mail: admit@miis.edu. *Dean*, Dr. Ruth Larimer, 831-647-4185, Fax: 831-647-6650.

Graduate School of Translation and Interpretation Students: 167 full-time (166 women), 33 part-time (4 women); includes 23 minority (11 Asian Americans or Pacific Islanders, 12 Hispanic Americans), 124 international. Average age 26. 190 applicants, 83% accepted, 110 enrolled. *Faculty:* 21 full-time (12 women), 12 part-time/adjunct (7 women). Expenses: Contact institution. *Financial support:* In 2001–02, 138 students received support, including 16 research assistantships with partial tuition reimbursements available (averaging $4,000 per year); career-related internships or fieldwork, Federal Work-Study, institutionally sponsored loans, scholarships/grants, tuition waivers (partial), and unspecified assistantships also available. Support available to part-time students. Financial award applicants required to submit FAFSA. In 2001, 87 degrees awarded. Offers conference interpretation (MA); translation (MA); translation and interpretation (MA). *Application deadline:* For fall admission, 3/15 (priority date); for spring admission, 10/1 (priority date). Applications are processed on a rolling basis. *Application fee:* $50. Electronic applications accepted. *Application Contact:* 831-647-4123, Fax: 831-647-6405, E-mail: admit@miis.edu. *Dean*, Dr. Diane De Terra, 831-647-4170, Fax: 831-647-3560, E-mail: ddeterra@miis.edu.

MONTREAT COLLEGE, Montreat, NC 28757-1267

General Information Independent-religious, coed, comprehensive institution. *Enrollment:* 92 full-time matriculated graduate/professional students (36 women). *Enrollment by degree level:* 92 master's. *Graduate faculty:* 5 full-time (1 woman), 4 part-time/adjunct (1 woman). *Tuition:* Part-time $240 per credit hour. *Graduate housing:* On-campus housing not available. *Library facilities:* L. Nelson Bell Library. *Online resources:* library catalog, access to other libraries' catalogs. *Collection:* 67,378 titles, 426 serial subscriptions.

Computer facilities: 60 computers available on campus for general student use. A campuswide network can be accessed from student residence rooms and from off campus. Internet access is available. *Web address:* http://www.montreat.edu/.

General Application Contact: Dr. Gary Harris, Director of Recruitment, 828-667-5044 Ext. 315, Fax: 828-667-9079, E-mail: gary.harris@apollogrp.edu.

GRADUATE UNITS

Business Division Students: 92 full-time (36 women). Average age 34. 50 applicants, 92% accepted. *Faculty:* 5 full-time (1 woman), 4 part-time/adjunct (1 woman). Expenses: Contact institution. *Financial support:* Available to part-time students. Applicants required to submit FAFSA. In 2001, 11 degrees awarded. *Degree program information:* Evening/weekend programs available. Offers business (MBA). *Application deadline:* Applications are processed on a rolling basis. *Application fee:* $25. *Application Contact:* Dr. Gary Harris, Director of Recruitment, 828-667-5044 Ext. 315, Fax: 828-667-9079, E-mail: gary.harris@apollogrp.edu. *Chair*, Dr. David Walters, 828-669-8012 Ext. 3653, Fax: 828-669-9554, E-mail: dwalters@montreat.edu.

MOODY BIBLE INSTITUTE, Chicago, IL 60610-3284

General Information Independent-religious, coed, comprehensive institution. *Enrollment:* 113 full-time matriculated graduate/professional students (54 women), 159 part-time matriculated graduate/professional students (51 women). *Enrollment by degree level:* 88 first professional, 173 master's. *Graduate faculty:* 10 full-time (1 woman), 17 part-time/adjunct (5 women). *Tuition:* Full-time $3,720; part-time $155 per hour. *Required fees:* $227; $13 per semester. One-time fee: $125 full-time; $185 part-time. *Graduate housing:* Rooms and/or apartments guaranteed to single students and available on a first-come, first-served basis to married students. Typical cost: $3,900 per year ($6,400 including board) for single students; $6,800 per year ($9,300 including board) for married students. Housing application deadline: 6/1. *Student services:* Campus employment opportunities, campus safety program, career counseling, exercise/wellness program, international student services, low-cost health insurance. *Library facilities:* Henry Crowell Learning Center plus 1 other. *Collection:* 135,000 titles, 987 serial subscriptions.

Computer facilities: 26 computers available on campus for general student use. A campuswide network can be accessed from student residence rooms and from off campus. Internet access is available. *Web address:* http://www.moody.edu/.

General Application Contact: Annette Moy, Associate Dean of Enrollment Management/Admissions, 312-329-4267, Fax: 312-329-8987, E-mail: amoy@moody.edu.

GRADUATE UNITS

Graduate School Students: 113 full-time (54 women), 159 part-time (51 women); includes 28 African Americans, 27 Asian Americans or Pacific Islanders, 8 Hispanic Americans, 34 international. Average age 28. 136 applicants, 66% accepted. *Faculty:* 10 full-time (1 woman), 17 part-time/adjunct (5 women). Expenses: Contact institution. *Financial support:* Scholarships/grants available. In 2001, 38 degrees awarded. *Degree program information:* Part-time programs available. Offers biblical studies (MABS, Certificate); intercultural studies (MAIS); ministry (M Div, MA Min, MAUM); spiritual formation (MASF); teaching English to speakers of other languages (Certificate); urban ministry (MAUM). *Application deadline:* For fall admission, 3/1 (priority date); for spring admission, 12/1 (priority date). Applications are processed on a rolling basis. *Application fee:* $35. *Application Contact:* Annette Moy, Associate Dean of Enrollment Management/Admissions, 312-329-4267, Fax: 312-329-8987, E-mail: amoy@moody.edu. *Vice President and Dean*, Dr. Joseph Henriques, 312-329-4341, Fax: 312-329-4344.

MORAVIAN COLLEGE, Bethlehem, PA 18018-6650

General Information Independent-religious, coed, comprehensive institution. *Enrollment:* 111 part-time matriculated graduate/professional students (61 women). *Enrollment by degree level:* 111 master's. *Graduate faculty:* 11 full-time (0 women), 8 part-time/adjunct (2 women). *Tuition:* Part-time $493 per credit. *Graduate housing:* On-campus housing not available. *Student services:* Career counseling, disabled student services, multicultural affairs office, teacher training. *Library facilities:* Reeves Library. *Online resources:* library catalog, web page, access to other libraries' catalogs. *Collection:* 247,841 titles, 1,268 serial subscriptions, 1,462 audiovisual materials. *Research affiliation:* Northeast Tier–Ben Franklin Technology Center.

Computer facilities: 150 computers available on campus for general student use. A campuswide network can be accessed from student residence rooms and from off campus. Internet access is available. *Web address:* http://www.moravian.edu/.

General Application Contact: Dr. Linda H. Heindel, Dean, Continuing and Graduate Studies, 610-861-1386, Fax: 610-861-1466, E-mail: melhh01@moravian.edu.

GRADUATE UNITS

Division of Continuing and Graduate Studies *Degree program information:* Part-time and evening/weekend programs available. Offers business administration (MBA); continuing and graduate studies (M Ed, MBA); curriculum and instruction (M Ed).

MORAVIAN THEOLOGICAL SEMINARY, Bethlehem, PA 18018-6614

General Information Independent-religious, coed, graduate-only institution. *Enrollment by degree level:* 34 first professional, 42 master's. *Graduate faculty:* 5 full-time (1 woman), 15 part-time/adjunct (5 women). *Tuition:* Part-time $362 per credit hour. *Required fees:* $30 per term. *Graduate housing:* Rooms and/or apartments available to single and married students. Housing application deadline: 2/15. *Student services:* Campus safety program, career counseling, free psychological counseling, international student services, low-cost health insurance. *Library facilities:* Reeves Library. *Online resources:* library catalog, web page, access to other libraries' catalogs. *Collection:* 252,061 titles, 1,344 serial subscriptions, 1,567 audiovisual materials.

Computer facilities: 80 computers available on campus for general student use. A campuswide network can be accessed from student residence rooms and from off campus. Internet access is available. *Web address:* http://www.moravianseminary.edu/.

General Application Contact: Thom Stapleton, Associate Dean and Director of Admissions, 610-861-1525, Fax: 610-861-1569, E-mail: thom@moravian.edu.

GRADUATE UNITS

Graduate and Professional Programs Students: 30 full-time (15 women), 46 part-time (33 women); includes 3 minority (all African Americans), 5 international. Average age 43. 22 applicants, 86% accepted, 15 enrolled. *Faculty:* 5 full-time (1 woman), 15 part-time/adjunct (5 women). Expenses: Contact institution. *Financial support:* In 2001–02, 44 students received support. Career-related internships or fieldwork and institutionally sponsored loans available. Support available to part-time students. Financial award application deadline: 4/1; financial award applicants required to submit FAFSA. In 2001, 6 first professional degrees, 4 master's awarded. *Degree program information:* Part-time programs available. Offers theology (M Div, MAPC, MATS). *Application deadline:* For fall admission, 7/31 (priority date); for spring admission, 12/31. Applications are processed on a rolling basis. *Application fee:* $25. *Application Contact:* Thom Stapleton, Associate Dean and Director of Admissions, 610-861-1525, Fax: 610-861-1569, E-mail: thom@moravian.edu. *Dean and Vice President*, Dr. Frank L. Crouch.

MOREHEAD STATE UNIVERSITY, Morehead, KY 40351

General Information State-supported, coed, comprehensive institution. CGS member. *Enrollment:* 243 full-time matriculated graduate/professional students (145 women), 771 part-time matriculated graduate/professional students (528 women). *Enrollment by degree level:* 1,008 master's, 6 other advanced degrees. *Graduate faculty:* 142 full-time (48 women). *International tuition:* $4,247 full-time. Tuition, state resident: part-time $176 per hour. Tuition, nonresident: full-time $1,584; part-time $472 per hour. *Graduate housing:* Rooms and/or apartments available on a first-come, first-served basis to single and married students. Housing application deadline: 8/1. *Student services:* Campus employment opportunities, campus safety program, career counseling, child daycare facilities, disabled student services, exercise/wellness program, free psychological counseling, grant writing training, international student services, low-cost health insurance, multicultural affairs office, teacher training, writing training. *Library facilities:* Camden Carroll Library. *Online resources:* library catalog, web page, access to other libraries' catalogs. *Collection:* 299,290 titles, 13,570 serial subscriptions, 21,033 audiovisual materials.

Computer facilities: 1,000 computers available on campus for general student use. A campuswide network can be accessed from student residence rooms and from off campus. Internet access and online class registration are available. *Web address:* http://www.moreheadstate.edu/.

General Application Contact: Betty R. Cowsert, Graduate Admissions/Records Manager, 606-783-2039, Fax: 606-783-5061, E-mail: b.cowsert@moreheadstate.edu.

GRADUATE UNITS

Graduate Programs Students: 243 full-time (145 women), 771 part-time (528 women); includes 14 minority (7 African Americans, 3 Asian Americans or Pacific Islanders, 4 Hispanic Americans), 106 international. Average age 25. 335 applicants, 96% accepted. *Faculty:* 142 full-time (48 women). Expenses: Contact institution. *Financial support:* In 2001–02, 29 research assistantships (averaging $5,000 per year), 48 teaching assistantships (averaging $5,000 per year) were awarded. Career-related internships or fieldwork and Federal Work-Study also available. Financial award application deadline: 4/1; financial award applicants required to submit FAFSA. In 2001, 318 degrees awarded. *Degree program information:* Part-time and evening/weekend programs available. Postbaccalaureate distance learning degree programs offered (minimal on-campus study). *Application deadline:* For fall admission, 7/1 (priority date); for spring admission, 12/1 (priority date). Applications are processed on a rolling basis. *Application fee:* $0. *Application Contact:* Betty R. Cowsert, Graduate Admissions/Records Manager, 606-783-2039, Fax: 606-783-5061, E-mail: b.cowsert@moreheadstate.edu. *Associate Vice President for Graduate and Undergraduate Programs*, Dr. Deborah Abell, 606-782-2004, Fax: 606-783-5061, E-mail: d.abell@moreheadstate.edu.

Caudill College of Humanities Students: 74 full-time (54 women), 43 part-time (36 women); includes 3 minority (1 African American, 2 Hispanic Americans), 48 international. Average age 25. 43 applicants, 91% accepted. *Faculty:* 49 full-time (15 women). Expenses: Contact institution. *Financial support:* In 2001–02, 29 teaching assistantships (averaging $5,000 per year) were awarded; career-related internships or fieldwork and Federal Work-Study also available. Financial award application deadline: 4/1; financial award applicants required to submit FAFSA. In 2001, 25 degrees awarded. *Degree program information:* Part-time and evening/weekend programs available. Postbaccalaureate distance learning degree programs offered. Offers advertising/publications (MA); art education (MA); criminology (MA); electronic media (MA); English (MA); general sociology (MA); gerontology (MA); humanities (MA, MM); journalism (MA); music education (MM); music performance (MM); speech (MA); studio art (MA); theatre (MA). *Application deadline:* For fall admission, 8/1 (priority date); for spring admission, 12/1 (priority date). Applications are processed on a rolling basis. *Application fee:* $0. *Application Contact:* Betty R. Cowsert, Graduate Admissions/Records Manager, 606-783-2039, Fax: 606-783-5061, E-mail: b.cowsert@moreheadstate.edu. *Dean*, Dr. Michael Seelig, 606-783-2045, Fax: 606-783-5046, E-mail: m.seelig@moreheadstate.edu.

College of Business Students: 71 full-time (30 women), 202 part-time (99 women); includes 4 minority (2 African Americans, 2 Asian Americans or Pacific Islanders), 33 international. Average age 25. 92 applicants, 92% accepted. *Faculty:* 17 full-time (5 women). Expenses: Contact institution. *Financial support:* In 2001–02, 5 teaching assistantships (averaging $5,000 per year) were awarded; career-related internships or fieldwork and Federal Work-Study also available. Financial award application deadline: 4/1; financial award applicants required to submit FAFSA. In 2001, 44 degrees awarded. *Degree program information:* Part-time and evening/weekend programs available. Postbaccalaureate distance learning degree programs offered (minimal on-campus study). Offers business (MBA). *Application deadline:* For fall admission, 8/1 (priority date); for spring admission, 12/1 (priority date). Applications are processed on a rolling basis. *Application fee:* $0. *Application Contact:* Betty R. Cowsert, Graduate Admissions/Records Manager, 606-783-2039, Fax: 606-783-5061, E-mail: b.cowsert@moreheadstate.edu. *Dean*, Dr. Robert L. Albert, 606-783-2797, Fax: 606-783-5025, E-mail: r.albert@moreheadstate.edu.

College of Education Students: 51 full-time (34 women), 505 part-time (387 women); includes 5 minority (2 African Americans, 1 Asian American or Pacific Islander, 2 Hispanic Americans), 21 international. Average age 25. 183 applicants, 98% accepted. *Faculty:* 49 full-time (23 women). Expenses: Contact institution. *Financial support:* In 2001–02, research assistantships (averaging $5,000 per year), 8 teaching assistantships (averaging $5,000

Morehead State University (continued)

per year) were awarded. Career-related internships or fieldwork and Federal Work-Study also available. Financial award application deadline: 4/1; financial award applicants required to submit FAFSA. In 2001, 216 degrees awarded. *Degree program information:* Part-time and evening/weekend programs available. Offers adult and higher education (MA, Ed S); curriculum and instruction (Ed S); education (MA, MA Ed, MS, Ed S); elementary education (MA Ed); exercise physiology (MA); guidance and counseling (MA Ed, Ed S); health, physical education and recreation (MA); instructional leadership (Ed S); middle school education (MA Ed); reading (MA Ed); recreation and sports administration (MA); school administration (MA); secondary education (MA Ed); special education (MA Ed). *Application deadline:* For fall admission, 7/1 (priority date); for spring admission, 12/1 (priority date). Applications are processed on a rolling basis. *Application fee:* $0. *Application Contact:* Betty R. Cowsert, Graduate Admissions/Records Manager, 606-783-2039, Fax: 606-783-5061, E-mail: b.cowsert@moreheadstate.edu. *Interim Dean,* Dr. Dan Branham, 606-783-2040, Fax: 606-783-5029, E-mail: m.seelig@moreheadstate.edu.

College of Science and Technology Students: 47 full-time (27 women), 21 part-time (6 women); includes 2 minority (both African Americans), 4 international. Average age 25. 17 applicants, 94% accepted. *Faculty:* 27 full-time (5 women). Expenses: Contact institution. *Financial support:* In 2001–02, 29 research assistantships (averaging $5,000 per year), 6 teaching assistantships (averaging $5,000 per year) were awarded. Career-related internships or fieldwork and Federal Work-Study also available. Financial award application deadline: 4/1; financial award applicants required to submit FAFSA. In 2001, 33 degrees awarded. *Degree program information:* Part-time and evening/weekend programs available. Offers biology (MS); clinical psychology (MA); counseling psychology (MA); experimental/general psychology (MA); science and technology (MA, MS); vocational education/technology (MS). *Application deadline:* For fall admission, 8/1 (priority date); for spring admission, 12/1 (priority date). Applications are processed on a rolling basis. *Application fee:* $0. *Application Contact:* Betty R. Cowsert, Graduate Admissions/Records Manager, 606-783-2039, Fax: 606-783-5061, E-mail: b.cowsert@moreheadstate.edu. *Dean,* Dr. Gerald DeMoss, 606-783-2158, Fax: 606-783-5039, E-mail: g.demoss@moreheadstate.edu.

MOREHOUSE SCHOOL OF MEDICINE, Atlanta, GA 30310-1495

General Information Independent, coed, graduate-only institution. *Graduate housing:* On-campus housing not available. *Research affiliation:* Parke-Davis (HIV, AIDS), Pharma Pacific (oral infections), Amgen, Inc. (filagrastin study), Merck and Company (hypertension), Dialysis Clinics, Inc. (renal disease kidney disorders), Pfizer (women's health).

GRADUATE UNITS

Master of Public Health Program *Degree program information:* Part-time programs available. Offers public health (MPH).

Professional Program Offers medicine (MD).

Program in Biomedical Sciences Offers biomedical sciences (PhD).

MORGAN STATE UNIVERSITY, Baltimore, MD 21251

General Information State-supported, coed, university. CGS member. *Enrollment:* 281 full-time matriculated graduate/professional students, 243 part-time matriculated graduate/professional students. *Enrollment by degree level:* 324 master's, 200 doctoral. *Graduate faculty:* 172 full-time, 10 part-time/adjunct. Tuition, state resident: part-time $193 per credit. Tuition, nonresident: part-time $364 per credit. *Required fees:* $40 per credit. *Graduate housing:* On-campus housing not available. *Student services:* Campus employment opportunities, campus safety program, career counseling, child daycare facilities, disabled student services, grant writing training, international student services, low-cost health insurance, teacher training, writing training. *Library facilities:* Morris Soper Library. *Online resources:* library catalog. *Collection:* 333,101 titles, 2,526 serial subscriptions.

Computer facilities: 65 computers available on campus for general student use. A campuswide network can be accessed from student residence rooms and from off campus. Internet access and online class registration, engineering lab supercomputer are available. *Web address:* http://www.morgan.edu/.

General Application Contact: Dr. James E. Waller, Admissions and Programs Officer, 443-885-3185, Fax: 443-319-3837, E-mail: jwaller@moac.morgan.edu.

GRADUATE UNITS

School of Graduate Studies Students: 281 full-time, 243 part-time. *Faculty:* 172 full-time, 10 part-time/adjunct. Expenses: Contact institution. *Financial support:* In 2001–02, 250 students received support, including fellowships with full tuition reimbursements available (averaging $16,000 per year), research assistantships with full tuition reimbursements available (averaging $10,500 per year), teaching assistantships with full tuition reimbursements available (averaging $10,500 per year); career-related internships or fieldwork, Federal Work-Study, scholarships/grants, and tuition waivers (partial) also available. Support available to part-time students. In 2001, 105 master's, 11 doctorates awarded. *Degree program information:* Part-time and evening/weekend programs available. Offers public health (Dr PH). *Application deadline:* Applications are processed on a rolling basis. *Application fee:* $0. *Application Contact:* Dr. James E. Waller, Admissions and Programs Officer, 443-885-3185, Fax: 443-319-3837, E-mail: jwaller@moac.morgan.edu. *Dean, Graduate Studies,* Dr. Maurice C. Taylor, 443-885-3185, E-mail: mctaylor@moac.morgan.edu.

College of Liberal Arts Students: 88 (49 women); includes 82 minority (all African Americans) 6 international. Expenses: Contact institution. *Financial support:* Fellowships, research assistantships, teaching assistantships available. Financial award application deadline:4/1. *Degree program information:* Part-time and evening/weekend programs available. Offers African-American studies (MA); economics (MA); English (MA, PhD); history (MA, PhD); international studies (MA); liberal arts (MA, MS, PhD); music (MA); sociology (MA, MS); telecommunications management (MS). *Application deadline:* For fall admission, 2/1; for spring admission, 10/1. Applications are processed on a rolling basis. *Application fee:* $0. *Application Contact:* Dr. James E. Waller, Admissions Officer, 410-319-3185, Fax: 410-319-3837, E-mail: jwaller@moac.morgan.edu. *Dean,* Dr. Burney J. Hollis, 443-885-3090.

Earl G. Graves School of Business and Management Students: 72 (36 women); includes 52 minority (51 African Americans, 1 Asian American or Pacific Islander) 19 international. Average age 29. 105 applicants, 57% accepted. *Faculty:* 42 full-time, 3 part-time/adjunct. Expenses: Contact institution. *Financial support:* Application deadline: 4/1. In 2001, 17 degrees awarded. *Degree program information:* Part-time and evening/weekend programs available. Offers business administration (PhD); business and management (MBA, PhD). *Application deadline:* For fall admission, 2/1; for spring admission, 10/1. Applications are processed on a rolling basis. *Application fee:* $0. *Application Contact:* Dr. Mildred Glover, Assistant Dean/Graduate Director, 443-885-3396, Fax: 443-319-3651, E-mail: mba@moac.morgan.edu. *Dean,* Dr. Otis A. Thomas, 443-885-3160, Fax: 443-319-3358, E-mail: athomas@moac.morgan.edu.

Institute of Architecture and Planning Students: 68; includes 34 minority (33 African Americans, 1 Hispanic American), 12 international. Average age 29. *Faculty:* 11 full-time (2 women), 13 part-time/adjunct (4 women). Expenses: Contact institution. *Financial support:* Fellowships, research assistantships, teaching assistantships, Federal Work-Study and scholarships/grants available. Financial award application deadline: 4/1. Offers architecture (M Arch, MS Arch); city and regional planning (MCRP); landscape architecture (MASLA, MLA). *Application deadline:* For fall admission, 2/1; for spring admission, 10/1. Applications are processed on a rolling basis. *Application fee:* $0. *Application Contact:* Dr. James E. Waller, Admissions and Programs Officer, 443-885-3185, Fax: 443-319-3837, E-mail: jwaller@moac.morgan.edu. *Director,* Melvin L. Mitchell, 443-885-3225, E-mail: mmitchell@moac.morgan.edu.

School of Computer, Mathematical, and Natural Sciences Students: 17 (12 women); includes 16 minority (all African Americans) 1 international. Expenses: Contact institution. In 2001, 2 degrees awarded. Offers bio-environmental science (PhD); biology (MS); chemistry (MS); computer, mathematical, and natural sciences (MA, MS, PhD); mathematics (MA); physics (MS); science (MS, PhD). *Application deadline:* For fall admission, 2/1; for spring admission, 10/1. Applications are processed on a rolling basis. *Application fee:* $0. *Dean,* Dr. T. Joan Robinson, 443-885-4515, E-mail: jrobinson@moac.morgan.edu.

School of Education and Urban Studies Students: 150 (104 women); includes 125 minority (122 African Americans, 3 Asian Americans or Pacific Islanders) 6 international. *Faculty:* 10. Expenses: Contact institution. *Financial support:* Fellowships, research assistantships, career-related internships or fieldwork and Federal Work-Study available. Financial award application deadline: 4/1. In 2001, 59 master's, 5 doctorates awarded. *Degree program information:* Part-time and evening/weekend programs available. Offers education and urban studies (MAT, MS, Ed D, PhD); educational administration and supervision (MS); elementary and middle school education (MS); higher education administration (PhD); mathematics education (Ed D); teaching (MAT); urban educational leadership (Ed D). *Application deadline:* For fall admission, 2/1; for spring admission, 10/1. Applications are processed on a rolling basis. *Application fee:* $0. *Application Contact:* Dr. James E. Waller, Admissions and Programs Officer, 443-885-3185, Fax: 443-319-3837, E-mail: jwaller@moac.morgan.edu. *Dean,* Dr. Patricia L. Welch, 443-885-3385, Fax: 410-319-3871, E-mail: pmorris@moac.morgan.edu.

School of Engineering Students: 82 (26 women); includes 43 minority (36 African Americans, 2 Asian Americans or Pacific Islanders, 5 Hispanic Americans) 17 international. Expenses: Contact institution. *Financial support:* Fellowships, research assistantships, career-related internships or fieldwork and Federal Work-Study available. Financial award application deadline: 4/1. In 2001, 7 degrees awarded. *Degree program information:* Part-time and evening/weekend programs available. Offers engineering (MS, D Eng); transportation (MS). *Application deadline:* For fall admission, 2/1; for spring admission, 10/1. Applications are processed on a rolling basis. *Application fee:* $0. *Application Contact:* Dr. James E. Waller, Admissions and Programs Officer, 443-885-3185, Fax: 443-319-3837, E-mail: jwaller@moac.morgan.edu. *Dean,* Dr. Eugene DeLoatch, 443-885-3231.

MORNINGSIDE COLLEGE, Sioux City, IA 51106-1751

General Information Independent-religious, coed, comprehensive institution. *Graduate housing:* Rooms and/or apartments available to single and married students. Housing application deadline: 7/1. *Research affiliation:* Iowa Public Service Company (biology, chemistry, physics).

GRADUATE UNITS

Graduate Division *Degree program information:* Part-time and evening/weekend programs available. Offers elementary education (MAT); reading specialist (MAT); special education (MAT); technology based learning (MAT).

MORRISON UNIVERSITY, Reno, NV 89503-5600

General Information Proprietary, coed, comprehensive institution. *Graduate housing:* On-campus housing not available.

GRADUATE UNITS

Graduate School *Degree program information:* Part-time and evening/weekend programs available. Electronic applications accepted.

MOUNTAIN STATE UNIVERSITY, Beckley, WV 25802-9003

General Information Independent, coed, comprehensive institution. *Enrollment:* 87 full-time matriculated graduate/professional students (55 women), 16 part-time matriculated graduate/professional students (13 women). *Enrollment by degree level:* 103 master's. *Graduate faculty:* 21 full-time (13 women). *Tuition:* Part-time $210 per credit hour. Part-time tuition and fees vary according to program. *Graduate housing:* Room and/or apartments available on a first-come, first-served basis to single students; on-campus housing not available to married students. Typical cost: $2,382 per year ($3,812 including board). Room and board charges vary according to board plan and housing facility selected. *Student services:* Campus employment opportunities, campus safety program, career counseling, disabled student services, exercise/wellness program, grant writing training, international student services. *Library facilities:* Robert C. Byrd Learning Resource Center plus 1 other. *Online resources:* library catalog, access to other libraries' catalogs. *Collection:* 90,929 titles, 2,300 serial subscriptions, 2,405 audiovisual materials.

Computer facilities: 90 computers available on campus for general student use. A campuswide network can be accessed from off campus. Internet access and online class registration are available. *Web address:* http://www.mountainstate.edu/.

General Application Contact: Christy Bishop, Graduate Studies Coordinator, 304-929-1588, Fax: 304-929-1601, E-mail: cbishop@mountainstate.edu.

GRADUATE UNITS

Graduate Studies *Degree program information:* Part-time programs available. Offers criminal justice administration (MS); interdisciplinary studies (MA, MS); physician assistant (MSPA). Electronic applications accepted.

School of Health Sciences Offers administration (MHS); administration/education (MSN); classroom teaching (MHS); clinical teaching (MHS); community/rural medicine (MHS); diagnostic ultrasound (MHS); emergency medicine (MHS); family medicine (MHS); family nurse practitioner (MSN); geriatric medicine (MHS); special topics (MHS). Electronic applications accepted.

See in-depth description on page 983.

MOUNT ALLISON UNIVERSITY, Sackville, NB E4L 1E4, Canada

General Information Province-supported, coed, comprehensive institution. *Enrollment:* 2 full-time matriculated graduate/professional students (both women). *Enrollment by degree level:* 2 master's. *Graduate faculty:* 18 full-time (4 women). *Graduate tuition:* Tuition charges are reported in Canadian dollars. Tuition, province resident: full-time $500 Canadian dollars. Tuition, Canadian resident: full-time $500 Canadian dollars. *Graduate housing:* Room and/or apartments available to single students; on-campus housing not available to married students. *Student services:* Campus employment opportunities, campus safety program, child daycare facilities, disabled student services, exercise/wellness program, free psychological counseling, international student services, low-cost health insurance. *Library facilities:* Ralph Pickard Bell Library plus 3 others. *Online resources:* library catalog, web page, access to other libraries' catalogs. *Collection:* 400,000 titles, 1,700 serial subscriptions. *Research affiliation:* Huntsman Marine Science Centre (marine biology).

Computer facilities: 100 computers available on campus for general student use. A campuswide network can be accessed from student residence rooms and from off campus. Internet access is available. *Web address:* http://www.mta.ca/.

General Application Contact: Dr. Irena Kaczmarska, Professor, 506-364-2500, Fax: 506-364-2505, E-mail: iehrman@mta.ca.

GRADUATE UNITS

Faculty of Science Students: 2 full-time (both women). Average age 24. 10 applicants, 0% accepted. *Faculty:* 18 full-time (4 women). Expenses: Contact institution. *Financial support:* In 2001–02, 2 fellowships (averaging $12,000 per year) were awarded; research assistantships Offers biology (M Sc); chemistry (M Sc); science (M Sc). *Application deadline:* Applications are processed on a rolling basis. *Application Contact:* Dr. Irena Kaczmarska, Professor, 506-364-2500, Fax: 506-364-2505, E-mail: iehrman@mta.ca. *Dean,* Jean–Guy Godin, 506-364-2507.

MOUNT ANGEL SEMINARY, Saint Benedict, OR 97373

General Information Independent-religious, men only, comprehensive institution. *Graduate housing:* Room and/or apartments guaranteed to single students; on-campus housing not available to married students.

GRADUATE UNITS

Program in Theology *Degree program information:* Part-time programs available. Offers theology (M Div, MA).

MOUNT MARTY COLLEGE, Yankton, SD 57078-3724

General Information Independent-religious, coed, comprehensive institution. *Enrollment:* 73 full-time matriculated graduate/professional students (38 women). *Enrollment by degree level:* 73 master's. *Graduate faculty:* 1 full-time (0 women), 2 part-time/adjunct (0 women). *Tuition:* Full-time $16,000. Full-time tuition and fees vary according to course load and student level. *Graduate housing:* On-campus housing not available. *Student services:* Career counseling, free psychological counseling, low-cost health insurance. *Library facilities:* Mount Marty College Library. *Online resources:* library catalog, access to other libraries' catalogs. *Collection:* 78,684 titles, 446 serial subscriptions, 8,336 audiovisual materials. *Research affiliation:* Sacred Heart Hospital (anesthesia), University of Nebraska Medical Center (anesthesia), Marion Health Center (anesthesia), Sioux Valley Hospital (anesthesia), McKennan Hospital (anesthesia), Immanuel Medical Center (anesthesia).

Computer facilities: 53 computers available on campus for general student use. A campuswide network can be accessed from student residence rooms. Internet access is available. *Web address:* http://www.mtmc.edu/.

General Application Contact: Larry Lee Dahlen, Director of Nurse Anesthesia Program, 605-322-8090, Fax: 605-322-8095, E-mail: msna@mtmc.edu.

GRADUATE UNITS

Graduate Studies Division Students: 73 full-time (38 women); includes 5 minority (3 African Americans, 2 Asian Americans or Pacific Islanders) 86 applicants, 45% accepted. *Faculty:* 1 full-time (0 women), 2 part-time/adjunct (0 women). Expenses: Contact institution. *Financial support:* In 2001–02, 27 students received support. Career-related internships or fieldwork, institutionally sponsored loans, and scholarships/grants available. Financial award application deadline: 8/1; financial award applicants required to submit FAFSA. In 2001, 27 degrees awarded. Offers nursing anesthesia (MS). *Application deadline:* For fall admission, 12/15 (priority date). Applications are processed on a rolling basis. *Application fee:* $35. *Director of Nurse Anesthesia Program,* Larry Lee Dahlen, 605-322-8090, Fax: 605-322-8095, E-mail: idahlen@mtmc.edu.

MOUNT MARY COLLEGE, Milwaukee, WI 53222-4597

General Information Independent-religious, women only, comprehensive institution. *Enrollment:* 21 full-time matriculated graduate/professional students (all women), 115 part-time matriculated graduate/professional students (107 women). *Enrollment by degree level:* 136 master's. *Graduate faculty:* 7 full-time (6 women), 11 part-time/adjunct (all women). *Tuition:* Full-time $7,254; part-time $403 per credit. *Required fees:* $160; $35 per semester. *Graduate housing:* Room and/or apartments available on a first-come, first-served basis to single students; on-campus housing not available to married students. Typical cost: $4,630 (including board). Housing application deadline: 8/1. *Student services:* Campus employment opportunities, campus safety program, career counseling, child daycare facilities, free psychological counseling, international student services, low-cost health insurance, teacher training. *Library facilities:* Haggerty Library. *Online resources:* library catalog, web page, access to other libraries' catalogs. *Collection:* 104,000 titles, 675 serial subscriptions, 8,910 audiovisual materials.

Computer facilities: 74 computers available on campus for general student use. A campuswide network can be accessed from student residence rooms and from off campus. Internet access is available. *Web address:* http://www.mtmary.edu/.

General Application Contact: Director of Center for Educational and Professional Advancement, 414-256-1252, Fax: 414-256-1224, E-mail: ockerm@mtmary.edu.

GRADUATE UNITS

Graduate Programs Students: 21 full-time (all women), 115 part-time (107 women); includes 9 minority (5 African Americans, 3 Asian Americans or Pacific Islanders, 1 Hispanic American), 2 international. Average age 35. 68 applicants, 94% accepted, 42 enrolled. *Faculty:* 7 full-time (6 women), 11 part-time/adjunct (all women). Expenses: Contact institution. *Financial support:* In 2001–02, 39 students received support. Career-related internships or fieldwork, Federal Work-Study, and unspecified assistantships available. Support available to part-time students. Financial award application deadline: 5/1; financial award applicants required to submit FAFSA. In 2001, 36 degrees awarded. *Degree program information:* Part-time and evening/weekend programs available. Offers administrative dietetics (MS); art therapy (MS); clinical dietetics (MS); education (MA); gerontology (MA); nutrition education (MS); occupational therapy (MS); professional development (MA). *Application deadline:* Applications are processed on a rolling basis. *Application fee:* $35. Electronic applications accepted. *Application Contact:* Marci Ocker, Director of Center for Educational and Professional Advancement, 414-256-1252, Fax: 414-256-1224, E-mail: ockerm@mtmary.edu. *Vice President for Academics and Student Affairs,* Sr. Jane Forni, SSND, 414-256-0183, Fax: 414-256-0182, E-mail: fornij@mtmary.edu.

MOUNT SAINT MARY COLLEGE, Newburgh, NY 12550-3494

General Information Independent, coed, comprehensive institution. *Enrollment:* 25 full-time matriculated graduate/professional students (15 women), 420 part-time matriculated graduate/professional students (340 women). *Enrollment by degree level:* 445 master's. *Graduate faculty:* 14 full-time (9 women), 21 part-time/adjunct (14 women). *Tuition:* Full-time $3,879; part-time $431 per credit. *Required fees:* $15 per credit. *Graduate housing:* On-campus housing not available. *Student services:* Campus employment opportunities, campus safety program, career counseling, free psychological counseling, international student services, low-cost health insurance. *Library facilities:* Curtin Memorial Library plus 1 other. *Collection:* 119,146 titles, 1,117 serial subscriptions.

Computer facilities: 150 computers available on campus for general student use. A campuswide network can be accessed from student residence rooms and from off campus. Internet access, intranet are available. *Web address:* http://www.msmc.edu/.

General Application Contact: Graduate Coordinator, 845-561-0800, Fax: 845-562-6762.

GRADUATE UNITS

Division of Business Students: 8 full-time (1 woman), 45 part-time (21 women); includes 13 minority (8 African Americans, 2 Asian Americans or Pacific Islanders, 3 Hispanic Americans), 1 international. Average age 31. 20 applicants, 85% accepted. *Faculty:* 5 full-time (2 women), 4 part-time/adjunct (0 women). Expenses: Contact institution. In 2001, 16 degrees awarded. *Degree program information:* Part-time and evening/weekend programs available. Offers business (MBA). *Application fee:* $30. *Application Contact:* Janice Banker, Secretary, 845-569-3582, Fax: 845-569-3885, E-mail: banker@msmc.edu. *Coordinator,* Dr. James Griesemer, 845-569-3120, Fax: 845-562-6762, E-mail: grieseme@msmc.edu.

Division of Education Students: 16 full-time (13 women), 349 part-time (295 women); includes 23 minority (13 African Americans, 3 Asian Americans or Pacific Islanders, 7 Hispanic Americans) Average age 33. 188 applicants, 89% accepted. *Faculty:* 6 full-time (5 women), 14 part-time/adjunct (11 women). Expenses: Contact institution. *Financial support:* Career-related internships or fieldwork and Federal Work-Study available. Support available to part-time students. Financial award application deadline: 9/30. In 2001, 123 degrees awarded. *Degree program information:* Part-time and evening/weekend programs available. Offers elementary education (MS Ed); elementary/special education (MS Ed); literacy (MS Ed); literacy/childhood (MS Ed); secondary education (MS Ed); special education (MS Ed). *Application deadline:* Applications are processed on a rolling basis. *Application fee:* $30. *Coordinator,* Dr. Lucy DiPaola, 845-569-3528, Fax: 845-562-6762, E-mail: dipaola@msmc.edu.

Division of Nursing Students: 1 (woman) full-time, 26 part-time (24 women); includes 5 minority (3 African Americans, 2 Hispanic Americans) Average age 41. 12 applicants, 100% accepted, 7 enrolled. *Faculty:* 3 full-time (2 women), 3 part-time/adjunct (all women). Expenses: Contact institution. *Financial support:* In 2001–02, 5 students received support. Scholarships/grants, traineeships, and nursing lab assistant available. Financial award applicants required to submit FAFSA. In 2001, 7 degrees awarded. *Degree program information:* Part-time and evening/weekend programs available. Offers adult nurse practitioner (MS); clinical nurse specialist-adult health (MS). *Application deadline:* For fall admission, 6/3 (priority date); for spring admission, 10/31 (priority date). Applications are processed on a rolling basis. *Application fee:* $30. *Coordinator,* Sr. Leona DeBoer, 845-569-3138, Fax: 845-562-6762, E-mail: deboer@msmc.edu.

MOUNT ST. MARY'S COLLEGE, Los Angeles, CA 90049-1599

General Information Independent-religious, coed, primarily women, comprehensive institution. *Graduate housing:* On-campus housing not available.

GRADUATE UNITS

Graduate Division *Degree program information:* Part-time and evening/weekend programs available. Offers administrative studies (MS); counseling psychology (MS); elementary education (MS); physical therapy (DPT); religious studies (MA); secondary education (MS); special education (MS).

MOUNT SAINT MARY'S COLLEGE AND SEMINARY, Emmitsburg, MD 21727-7799

General Information Independent-religious, coed, comprehensive institution. *Enrollment:* 211 full-time matriculated graduate/professional students (43 women), 216 part-time matriculated graduate/professional students (110 women). *Enrollment by degree level:* 117 first professional, 310 master's. *Graduate faculty:* 27 full-time (7 women), 25 part-time/adjunct (10 women). *Tuition:* Part-time $243 per credit hour. *Required fees:* $200; $5 per credit. Tuition and fees vary according to degree level and program. *Graduate housing:* Room and/or apartments available on a first-come, first-served basis to single students; on-campus housing not available to married students. Typical cost: $3,600 per year ($7,300 including board). *Student services:* Campus employment opportunities, campus safety program, career counseling, disabled student services, exercise/wellness program, free psychological counseling, international student services, low-cost health insurance, multicultural affairs office, teacher training, writing training. *Library facilities:* Phillips Library. *Online resources:* library catalog, web page, access to other libraries' catalogs. *Collection:* 207,557 titles, 920 serial subscriptions, 4,440 audiovisual materials.

Computer facilities: 118 computers available on campus for general student use. A campuswide network can be accessed from student residence rooms and from off campus. Internet access and online class registration are available. *Web address:* http://www.msmary.edu/.

General Application Contact: Dr. Stan Werne, Dean of Academic Services, 301-447-5355, Fax: 301-447-5755, E-mail: werne@msmary.edu.

GRADUATE UNITS

Graduate Seminary Students: 147 full-time (0 women), 1 part-time; includes 16 minority (1 African American, 10 Asian Americans or Pacific Islanders, 5 Hispanic Americans), 26 international. Average age 31. *Faculty:* 11 full-time (4 women), 10 part-time/adjunct (2 women). Expenses: Contact institution. *Financial support:* Career-related internships or fieldwork and scholarships/grants available. Financial award applicants required to submit CSS PROFILE. In 2001, 35 first professional degrees, 6 master's awarded. Offers theology (M Div, MA). *Application deadline:* Applications are processed on a rolling basis. *Application fee:* $25. *Vice President/Rector,* Rev. Kevin Rhoades, 301-447-5295, Fax: 301-447-5636.

Program in Business Students: 42 full-time (22 women), 152 part-time (61 women); includes 6 minority (3 African Americans, 2 Asian Americans or Pacific Islanders, 1 Hispanic American), 3 international. Average age 32. 67 applicants, 93% accepted. *Faculty:* 11 full-time (0 women), 4 part-time/adjunct (0 women). Expenses: Contact institution. *Financial support:* In 2001–02, research assistantships with full tuition reimbursements (averaging $6,000 per year); career-related internships or fieldwork also available. Financial award applicants required to submit CSS PROFILE. In 2001, 52 degrees awarded. *Degree program information:* Part-time and evening/weekend programs available. Offers business (MBA). *Application deadline:* For fall admission, 8/15 (priority date). Applications are processed on a rolling basis. *Application fee:* $35. *Application Contact:* Sandy Kauffman, Administrative Assistant, 301-447-5326, Fax: 301-447-5335, E-mail: kauffman@msmary.edu. *Director,* Lori White Drega, 301-447-5326, Fax: 301-447-5335, E-mail: drega@msmary.edu.

Program in Education Students: 22 full-time (21 women), 63 part-time (49 women); includes 6 minority (2 African Americans, 2 Asian Americans or Pacific Islanders, 1 Hispanic American, 1 Native American) Average age 35. *Faculty:* 5 full-time (3 women), 10 part-time/adjunct (7 women). Expenses: Contact institution. *Financial support:* In 2001–02, 3 students received support, including research assistantships with full tuition reimbursements available (averaging $6,000 per year); career-related internships or fieldwork also available. Financial award applicants required to submit CSS PROFILE. In 2001, 17 degrees awarded. *Degree program information:* Part-time and evening/weekend programs available. Offers education (M Ed). *Application deadline:* For fall admission, 8/15 (priority date). Applications are processed on a rolling basis. *Application fee:* $20. *Director,* Liz Monahan, 301-447-5371, Fax: 301-447-5250, E-mail: monahan@msmary.edu.

MOUNT SAINT VINCENT UNIVERSITY, Halifax, NS B3M 2J6, Canada

General Information Province-supported, coed, primarily women, comprehensive institution. *Enrollment:* 672 matriculated graduate/professional students (568 women). *Enrollment by degree level:* 672 master's. *Graduate faculty:* 105. *Graduate tuition:* Tuition and fees charges are reported in Canadian dollars. *Tuition:* Part-time $1,185 Canadian dollars per credit. *Required fees:* $26 Canadian dollars per credit. $233 Canadian dollars per year. Full-time tuition and fees vary according to course load. *Graduate housing:* Room and/or apartments available on a first-come, first-served basis to single students; on-campus housing not available to married students. Typical cost: $5,260 Canadian dollars (including board). Room and board charges vary according to board plan and housing facility selected. Housing application deadline: 5/15. *Student services:* Campus employment opportunities, career counseling, child daycare facilities, disabled student services, exercise/wellness program, free psychological counseling, international student services, low-cost health insurance, teacher training, writing training. *Library facilities:* E. Margaret Fulton Communications Centre Library plus 3 others. *Online resources:* library catalog, web page, access to other libraries' catalogs. *Collection:* 194,531 titles, 2,682 serial subscriptions, 967 audiovisual materials.

Computer facilities: 125 computers available on campus for general student use. A campuswide network can be accessed from student residence rooms. Internet access and online class registration are available. *Web address:* http://www.msvu.ca/.

General Application Contact: Tara Wigglesworth-Hines, Assistant Registrar, 902-457-6363, Fax: 902-443-4727, E-mail: tara.wigglesworth-hines@msvu.ca.

GRADUATE UNITS

Graduate Programs Students: 672 (568 women). Average age 36. 842 applicants, 74% accepted. *Faculty:* 105. Expenses: Contact institution. *Financial support:* In 2001–02, 30 research assistantships were awarded; fellowships, scholarships/grants also available. Support available to part-time students. Financial award application deadline: 5/1. In 2001, 323 degrees awarded. *Degree program information:* Part-time and evening/weekend programs available. Postbaccalaureate distance learning degree programs offered (minimal on-campus study). Offers adult education (M Ed, MA Ed, MA(R)); applied human nutrition (M Sc AHN, MAHN); child and youth study (MA); curriculum studies (M Ed, MA Ed, MA(R)); education of the blind or visually impaired (M Ed, MA Ed); education of the deaf or hard of hearing (M Ed, MA Ed); education of young adolescents (M Ed, MA Ed, MA(R)); educational foundations (M Ed, MA Ed, MA(R)); educational psychology (M Ed, MA Ed, MA(R)); elementary education (M Ed, MA Ed, MA(R)); family studies and gerontology (MA); general studies (M Ed, MA Ed, MA(R)); human relations (M Ed, MA Ed); literacy education (M Ed, MA Ed, MA(R)); school psychology (MASP); TESC (M Ed, MA Ed, MA(R)); women's studies (MA). *Application deadline:* For fall admission, 3/1 (priority date). Applications are processed on a rolling basis. *Application fee:* $50. Electronic applications accepted. *Application Contact:* Tara Wigglesworth-Hines, Assistant Registrar, 902-457-6363, Fax: 902-443-4727, E-mail: tara.wigglesworth-hines@msvu.ca. *Dean of Professional Studies,* Dr. Mary E. Lyon, 902-457-6124, Fax: 902-443-8211, E-mail: mary.lyon@msvu.ca.

MOUNT SINAI SCHOOL OF MEDICINE OF NEW YORK UNIVERSITY, New York, NY 10029-6504

General Information Independent, coed, graduate-only institution. *Enrollment by degree level:* 426 first professional, 210 doctoral. *Graduate faculty:* 1,196 full-time, 252 part-time/adjunct. *Graduate housing:* Rooms and/or apartments guaranteed to single and married students. *Student services:* Career counseling, international student services. *Library facilities:* Levy Library. *Online resources:* library catalog, web page, access to other libraries' catalogs. *Collection:* 156,000 titles, 2,600 serial subscriptions.

Computer facilities: 75 computers available on campus for general student use. A campuswide network can be accessed from off campus. Internet access is available. *Web address:* http://www.mssm.edu/.

General Application Contact: C. Gita Bosch, Administrative Manager and Associate Dean, 212-241-6546, Fax: 212-241-0651, E-mail: grads@mssm.edu.

GRADUATE UNITS

Graduate School of Biological Sciences Students: 215 full-time (97 women); includes 58 minority (7 African Americans, 41 Asian Americans or Pacific Islanders, 10 Hispanic Americans), 65 international. Average age 30. 528 applicants, 23% accepted, 38 enrolled. *Faculty:* 212 full-time. Expenses: Contact institution. *Financial support:* In 2001–02, 215 fellowships with full tuition reimbursements (averaging $22,000 per year) were awarded; scholarships/grants also available. In 2001, 22 degrees awarded. Offers biological sciences (PhD); biomathematical sciences (PhD); biophysics, structural biology and biomathematics (PhD); genetics and genomic sciences (PhD); mechanisms of disease and therapy (PhD); microbiology (PhD); molecular, cellular, and environmental pathology (PhD); molecular, cellular, biochemical and developmental sciences (PhD); neurosciences (PhD); pharmacology (PhD); physiology and biophysics (PhD). *Application deadline:* For fall admission, 4/15. *Application fee:* $60. *Application Contact:* C. Gita Bosch, Administrative Manager and Associate Dean, 212-241-6546, Fax: 212-241-0651, E-mail: grads@mssm.edu. *Dean,* Dr. Terry Ann Krulwich, 212-241-6546, Fax: 212-241-0651, E-mail: terry.krulwich@mssm.edu.

School of Medicine Students: 426 full-time (217 women); includes 152 minority (35 African Americans, 95 Asian Americans or Pacific Islanders, 15 Hispanic Americans, 7 Native Americans), 8 international. Average age 25. 4,182 applicants, 3% accepted, 106 enrolled. *Faculty:* 2,110 full-time, 250 part-time/adjunct. Expenses: Contact institution. *Financial support:* In 2001–02, 331 students received support, including 19 fellowships with full tuition reimbursements available (averaging $23,750 per year); Federal Work-Study, institutionally sponsored loans, scholarships/grants, and unspecified assistantships also available. Financial award application deadline: 5/1; financial award applicants required to submit CSS PROFILE or FAFSA. In 2001, 109 degrees awarded. Offers medicine (MD). *Application deadline:* For fall admission, 11/1. Applications are processed on a rolling basis. *Application fee:* $100. Electronic applications accepted. *Application Contact:* Dr. Richard D. Kayne, Associate Dean for Admissions, 212-241-6696, Fax: 212-828-4135, E-mail: admissions@mssm.edu. *Interim Dean and Interim CEO,* Dr. Nathan Kase, 212-659-9000, Fax: 212-828-4135.

MOUNT VERNON NAZARENE UNIVERSITY, Mount Vernon, OH 43050-9500

General Information Independent-religious, coed, comprehensive institution. *Enrollment:* 145 part-time matriculated graduate/professional students (88 women). *Enrollment by degree level:* 145 master's. *Graduate faculty:* 9 full-time (4 women), 13 part-time/adjunct (6 women). *Tuition:* Part-time $284 per credit hour. Part-time tuition and fees vary according to program. *Graduate housing:* On-campus housing not available. *Student services:* Campus employment opportunities, campus safety program, career counseling, disabled student services, free psychological counseling, multicultural affairs office, teacher training. *Library facilities:* Thorne Library/Learning Resource Center. *Online resources:* library catalog, web page, access to other libraries' catalogs. *Collection:* 93,743 titles, 560 serial subscriptions, 3,382 audiovisual materials.

Computer facilities: 212 computers available on campus for general student use. A campuswide network can be accessed from student residence rooms and from off campus. Internet access is available. *Web address:* http://www.mvnc.edu/.

General Application Contact: Dr. Henry L. Smith, Vice President for Academic Affairs, 740-392-6868 Ext. 4200, Fax: 740-397-9129, E-mail: henry.smith@mvnu.edu.

GRADUATE UNITS

Department of Education *Faculty:* 5 full-time (3 women), 11 part-time/adjunct (6 women). Expenses: Contact institution. *Financial support:* In 2001–02, 1 student received support. Tuition waivers (partial) available. Support available to part-time students. Financial award application deadline: 8/1. In 2001, 14 degrees awarded. *Degree program information:* Part-time programs available. Offers education (MA Ed). *Application deadline:* For fall admission, 8/1; for spring admission, 12/1. Applications are processed on a rolling basis. *Application fee:* $20. *Director,* Dr. John Hollingsworth, 740-392-6868 Ext. 3421, Fax: 740-397-2769, E-mail: john.hollingsworth@mvnu.edu.

Master of Ministry Program *Faculty:* 4 full-time (1 woman), 2 part-time/adjunct (0 women). Expenses: Contact institution. *Financial support:* Tuition waivers (partial) available. Support available to part-time students. Financial award application deadline: 8/1. In 2001, 7 degrees awarded. *Degree program information:* Part-time and evening/weekend programs available. Offers ministry (M Min). *Application deadline:* For fall admission, 8/1; for spring admission, 12/1. Applications are processed on a rolling basis. *Application fee:* $20. *Director,* Dr. Bruce L. Petersen, 740-392-6868 Ext. 3608, Fax: 740-397-2769, E-mail: bruce.petersen@mvnu.edu.

MULTNOMAH BIBLE COLLEGE AND BIBLICAL SEMINARY, Portland, OR 97220-5898

General Information Independent-religious, coed, comprehensive institution. *Graduate housing:* Rooms and/or apartments available on a first-come, first-served basis to single and married students. Housing application deadline: 7/1.

GRADUATE UNITS

Multnomah Biblical Seminary *Degree program information:* Part-time and evening/weekend programs available. Offers biblical studies (MA, Certificate); divinity (M Div); pastoral studies (MA); theology (M Div, MA, Certificate).

MURRAY STATE UNIVERSITY, Murray, KY 42071-0009

General Information State-supported, coed, comprehensive institution. CGS member. *Enrollment:* 553 full-time matriculated graduate/professional students (300 women), 1,329 part-time matriculated graduate/professional students (946 women). *Enrollment by degree level:* 1,882 master's. *Graduate faculty:* 319 full-time (77 women). Tuition, state resident: full-time $1,440; part-time $169 per hour. Tuition, nonresident: full-time $4,004; part-time $450 per hour. *Graduate housing:* Rooms and/or apartments available on a first-come, first-served basis to single and married students. *Student services:* Campus employment opportunities, campus safety program, career counseling, disabled student services, free psychological counseling, international student services, low-cost health insurance, multicultural affairs office. *Library facilities:* Harry Lee Waterfield Library plus 1 other. *Online resources:* library catalog, web page, access to other libraries' catalogs. *Collection:* 470,000 titles, 3,000 serial subscriptions.

Computer facilities: 1,500 computers available on campus for general student use. A campuswide network can be accessed from student residence rooms and from off campus. Internet access is available. *Web address:* http://www.murraystate.edu/.

General Application Contact: Dr. Sandra Flynn, University Coordinator of Graduate Studies, 270-762-3895, Fax: 270-762-3799, E-mail: sandra.flynn@coe.murraystate.edu.

GRADUATE UNITS

College of Business and Public Affairs Students: 208 full-time (96 women), 190 part-time (92 women); includes 40 minority (20 African Americans, 5 Asian Americans or Pacific Islanders, 15 Hispanic Americans), 125 international. 150 applicants, 96% accepted. *Faculty:* 61 full-time (10 women). Expenses: Contact institution. *Financial support:* Research assistantships, teaching assistantships, career-related internships or fieldwork and Federal Work-Study available. Financial award application deadline: 4/1. In 2001, 71 degrees awarded. *Degree program information:* Part-time and evening/weekend programs available. Offers business administration (MBA); business and public affairs (MA, MBA, MPA, MPAC, MS); economics (MS); mass communications (MA, MS); organizational communication (MA, MS); professional accounting (MPAC); public affairs (MPA); telecommunications systems management (MS). *Application deadline:* Applications are processed on a rolling basis. *Application fee:* $25. *Dean,* Dr. Dannie Harrison, 270-762-4183, Fax: 270-762-3482, E-mail: dannie.harrison@murraystate.edu.

College of Education Students: 67 full-time (50 women), 899 part-time (720 women); includes 63 minority (55 African Americans, 2 Asian Americans or Pacific Islanders, 4 Hispanic Americans, 2 Native Americans), 20 international. 196 applicants, 100% accepted. *Faculty:* 41 full-time (15 women). Expenses: Contact institution. *Financial support:* Research assistantships, teaching assistantships, Federal Work-Study available. Financial award application deadline: 4/1. *Degree program information:* Part-time programs available. Offers community and agency counseling (Ed S); early childhood education (MS); education (MA, MA Ed, MS, Ed D, PhD, Ed S); elementary education (MA Ed, Ed S); guidance and counseling (MA Ed, Ed S); health, physical education, and recreation (MA); human development and leadership (MS); industrial and technical education (MS); learning disabilities (MA Ed); middle school education (MA Ed, Ed S); physical education (MA); reading and writing (MA Ed); school administration (MA Ed, Ed S); secondary education (MA Ed, Ed S); special education (MA Ed). *Application deadline:* Applications are processed on a rolling basis. *Application fee:* $20. *Dean,* Dr. Jack Rose, 270-762-3818, Fax: 270-762-3889, E-mail: jack.rose@coe.murraystate.edu.

College of Health Sciences and Human Services Students: 96 full-time (65 women), 99 part-time (75 women); includes 3 minority (all African Americans), 4 international. 60 applicants, 97% accepted. *Faculty:* 30 full-time (15 women). Expenses: Contact institution. *Financial support:* Research assistantships, teaching assistantships, Federal Work-Study available. Financial award application deadline: 4/1. *Degree program information:* Part-time programs available. Offers health sciences and human services (MA, MS, MSN); nursing (MSN); occupational safety and health (MS); recreation and leisure services (MA); speech language pathology (MS). *Application deadline:* Applications are processed on a rolling basis. *Application fee:* $25. *Dean,* Dr. Elizabeth Blodgett, 270-762-3970, Fax: 270-762-5403, E-mail: betty.blodgett@murraystate.edu.

College of Humanities and Fine Arts Students: 58 full-time (38 women), 58 part-time (33 women). 38 applicants, 82% accepted. *Faculty:* 88 full-time (28 women). Expenses: Contact institution. *Financial support:* Research assistantships, teaching assistantships, Federal Work-Study available. Financial award application deadline: 4/1. In 2001, 45 degrees awarded. *Degree program information:* Part-time programs available. Offers clinical psychology (MA, MS); English (MA); history (MA); humanities and fine arts (MA, MME, MS); music education (MME); psychology (MA, MS); teaching English to speakers of other languages (MA). *Application deadline:* Applications are processed on a rolling basis. *Application fee:* $25. *Dean,* Dr. Sandra Jordan, 270-762-6936, Fax: 270-762-3424, E-mail: sandra.jordan@murraystate.edu.

College of Science, Engineering and Technology Students: 87 full-time (34 women), 61 part-time (18 women). 57 applicants, 100% accepted. *Faculty:* 89 full-time (9 women). Expenses: Contact institution. *Financial support:* Research assistantships, teaching assistantships, Federal Work-Study available. Financial award application deadline: 4/1. In 2001, 40 degrees awarded. *Degree program information:* Part-time programs available. Offers biological sciences (MAT, MS, PhD); chemistry (MAT, MS); geosciences (MA, MS); management of technology (MS); mathematics (MA, MAT, MS); science, engineering and technology (MA, MAT, MS, PhD); water science (MS). *Application deadline:* Applications are processed on a rolling basis. *Application fee:* $25. *Interim Dean,* Dr. Neil V. Weber, 270-762-3391, Fax: 270-762-6277, E-mail: neil.weber@murraystate.edu.

School of Agriculture Students: 37 full-time (17 women), 22 part-time (8 women); includes 1 minority (African American), 1 international. 18 applicants, 94% accepted. *Faculty:* 10 full-time (0 women). Expenses: Contact institution. *Financial support:* Research assistantships, teaching assistantships, Federal Work-Study available. Financial award application deadline: 4/1. In 2001, 15 degrees awarded. *Degree program information:* Part-time programs available. Offers agriculture (MS). *Application deadline:* Applications are processed on a rolling basis. *Application fee:* $25. *Application Contact:* Dr. Tony Brannon, Graduate Coordinator, 270-762-6923, Fax: 270-762-5454, E-mail: tony.brannon@murraystate.edu. *Head,* Dr. James Rudolph, 270-762-6925, Fax: 270-762-5454, E-mail: jim.rudolph@murraystate.edu.

See in-depth description on page 985.

MUSKINGUM COLLEGE, New Concord, OH 43762

General Information Independent-religious, coed, comprehensive institution. *Graduate housing:* On-campus housing not available.

GRADUATE UNITS

Graduate Program in Education *Degree program information:* Part-time programs available. Offers education (MAE).

NAROPA UNIVERSITY, Boulder, CO 80302-6697

General Information Independent, coed, comprehensive institution. *Enrollment:* 404 full-time matriculated graduate/professional students (277 women), 228 part-time matriculated graduate/professional students (172 women). *Graduate faculty:* 34 full-time (14 women), 175 part-time/adjunct (128 women). *Tuition:* Full-time $10,766; part-time $489 per credit. *Required fees:* $560; $280 per semester. Tuition and fees vary according to course load and campus/location. *Graduate housing:* On-campus housing not available. *Student services:* Campus employment opportunities, campus safety program, career counseling, disabled student services, international student services, multicultural affairs office, writing training. *Library facilities:* Allen Ginsberg Library. *Online resources:* library catalog, web page. *Collection:* 30,000 titles, 111 serial subscriptions, 11,916 audiovisual materials.

Computer facilities: 18 computers available on campus for general student use. A campuswide network can be accessed. Internet access is available. *Web address:* http://www.naropa.edu/.

General Application Contact: Susan Elizabeth Boyle, Director of Admissions, 303-546-3572, Fax: 303-546-3583, E-mail: sboyle@naropa.edu.

GRADUATE UNITS

Graduate Programs Students: 404 full-time (277 women), 233 part-time (177 women); includes 51 minority (12 African Americans, 18 Asian Americans or Pacific Islanders, 17 Hispanic Americans, 4 Native Americans), 31 international. Average age 37. 485 applicants, 82% accepted, 242 enrolled. *Faculty:* 34 full-time (14 women), 175 part-time/adjunct (128 women). Expenses: Contact institution. *Financial support:* In 2001–02, 82 students received support. Career-related internships or fieldwork, Federal Work-Study, scholarships/grants, health care benefits, and tuition waivers (partial) available. Support available to part-time students. Financial award application deadline: 3/1; financial award applicants required to submit FAFSA. In 2001, 160 degrees awarded. Offers art therapy (MA); body psychotherapy (MA); Buddhist studies (MA); contemplative education (MA); creation spirituality (MLA); dance/movement therapy (MA); divinity (M Div); engaged Buddhism (MA); environmental leadership (MA); gerontology (MA); Indo-Tibetan Buddhism (MA); Indo-Tibetan Buddhism with language (MA); music therapy (MA); psychology: contemplative psychotherapy (MA); religious studies (MA); transpersonal counseling psychology (MA); transpersonal psychology (MA); wilderness therapy (MA); writing and poetics (MFA). *Application deadline:* For fall admission, 2/1 (priority date); for spring admission, 11/1 (priority date). Applications are processed on a rolling basis. *Application fee:* $50 ($0 for international students). Electronic applications accepted. *Application Contact:* Susan Elizabeth Boyle, Director of Admissions, 303-546-3572, Fax: 303-546-3583, E-mail: sboyle@naropa.edu. *President,* John Cobb, 303-444-0202.

NASHOTAH HOUSE, Nashotah, WI 53058-9793

General Information Independent-religious, coed, primarily men, graduate-only institution. *Enrollment by degree level:* 30 first professional, 3 master's, 25 other advanced degrees. *Graduate faculty:* 7 full-time (0 women), 5 part-time/adjunct (1 woman). *Tuition:* Full-time $12,000; part-time $330 per credit hour. Part-time tuition and fees vary according to course load. *Graduate housing:* Rooms and/or apartments available on a first-come, first-served basis to single students and available to married students. Typical cost: $2,300 per year ($5,500 including board) for single students; $6,300 per year ($9,500 including board) for married students. Room and board charges vary according to housing facility selected. Housing application deadline: 8/15. *Student services:* Campus employment opportunities, career counseling. *Library facilities:* Frances Donaldson Library. *Online resources:* web page. *Collection:* 123,000 titles, 296 serial subscriptions, 410 audiovisual materials.

Computer facilities: 3 computers available on campus for general student use. Internet access is available. *Web address:* http://www.nashotah.edu/.

General Application Contact: Judith Mills Gray, Registrar/Financial Aid Officer/Acting Director of Admissions, 262-646-6547, Fax: 262-646-6504, E-mail: jmgray@nashotah.edu.

GRADUATE UNITS

School of Theology Students: 33 full-time (3 women), 25 part-time (3 women), 3 international. Average age 35. 15 applicants, 80% accepted, 12 enrolled. *Faculty:* 7 full-time (0 women), 5 part-time/adjunct (1 woman). Expenses: Contact institution. *Financial support:* In 2001–02, 35 students received support; teaching assistantships, career-related internships or fieldwork, scholarships/grants, and tuition waivers (partial) available. Financial award application deadline: 9/15; financial award applicants required to submit FAFSA. In 2001, 6 M Divs, 3 other advanced degrees awarded. *Degree program information:* Part-time programs available. Offers theology (M Div, MTS, STM, Certificate). *Application deadline:* For fall admission, 7/1 (priority date). Applications are processed on a rolling basis. *Application fee:* $0. *Application Contact:* Judith Mills Gray, Registrar/Financial Aid Officer/Acting Director of Admissions, 262-646-6547, Fax: 262-646-6504, E-mail: jmgray@nashotah.edu. *Dean,* Very Rev. Robert S. Munday, 262-646-6500, Fax: 262-646-6504, E-mail: nashotah@nashotah.edu.

NATIONAL AMERICAN UNIVERSITY, Rapid City, SD 57701

General Information Proprietary, coed, comprehensive institution. *Enrollment:* 9 full-time matriculated graduate/professional students (4 women), 51 part-time matriculated graduate/professional students (24 women). *Enrollment by degree level:* 60 master's. *Graduate faculty:* 1 full-time (0 women), 4 part-time/adjunct (0 women). *Tuition:* Full-time $4,860; part-time $270 per semester hour. *Graduate housing:* Room and/or apartments available on a first-come, first-served basis to single students. Housing application deadline: 6/1. *Student services:* Campus employment opportunities, career counseling, disabled student services, international student services, multicultural affairs office. *Library facilities:* Jefferson Library. *Online resources:* web page. *Collection:* 31,018 titles, 268 serial subscriptions.

Computer facilities: 50 computers available on campus for general student use. A campuswide network can be accessed. Internet access is available. *Web address:* http://www.national.edu/.

General Application Contact: Carrie Fischer, Admissions, 605-394-4800, Fax: 605-394-4871, E-mail: cfischer@rc.national.edu.

GRADUATE UNITS

MBA Program Students: 9 full-time (4 women), 51 part-time (24 women); includes 12 minority (3 African Americans, 2 Asian Americans or Pacific Islanders, 4 Hispanic Americans, 3 Native Americans) Average age 28. *Faculty:* 1 full-time (0 women), 4 part-time/adjunct (0 women). Expenses: Contact institution. *Financial support:* In 2001–02, 13 students received support. Applicants required to submit FAFSA. *Degree program information:* Part-time and evening/weekend programs available. Offers business administration (MBA). *Application deadline:* For fall admission, 7/30 (priority date); for winter admission, 10/29 (priority date); for spring admission, 2/11 (priority date). Applications are processed on a rolling basis. *Application fee:* $45. Electronic applications accepted. *Application Contact:* Erica Vollmer, Information Contract, 605-394-4800, Fax: 605-394-4871, E-mail: evollmer@rc.national.edu. *Dean of Graduate Studies,* Dr. Mike Madden, 605-394-4959, Fax: 605-394-4871, E-mail: mmadden@national.edu.

NATIONAL COLLEGE OF NATUROPATHIC MEDICINE, Portland, OR 97201

General Information Independent, coed, graduate-only institution. *Enrollment by degree level:* 36 master's, 460 doctoral. *Graduate faculty:* 22 full-time, 68 part-time/adjunct. *Tuition:* Full-time $15,756. *Required fees:* $2,840. One-time fee: $1,340 full-time. *Graduate housing:* On-campus housing not available. *Student services:* Campus employment opportunities, campus safety program, career counseling, disabled student services, free psychological counseling, low-cost health insurance. *Library facilities:* National College of Naturopathic Medicine Library. *Collection:* 10,000 titles, 125 serial subscriptions.

Computer facilities: 10 computers available on campus for general student use. A campuswide network can be accessed. Internet access is available. *Web address:* http://www.ncnm.edu/.

General Application Contact: Phil Reid, Director of Admissions, 503-552-1660, Fax: 503-499-0027, E-mail: admissions@ncnm.edu.

GRADUATE UNITS

Program in Chinese Medicine Students: 36 full-time (28 women). Average age 29. 47 applicants, 70% accepted, 27 enrolled. *Faculty:* 3 full-time (0 women), 8 part-time/adjunct (3 women). Expenses: Contact institution. *Financial support:* Federal Work-Study available. Financial award applicants required to submit FAFSA. In 2001, 17 degrees awarded. Offers Oriental medicine (MS). *Application deadline:* For fall admission, 4/15. *Application fee:* $60. *Application Contact:* Phil Reid, Director of Admissions, 503-552-1660, Fax: 503-499-0027, E-mail: admissions@ncnm.edu. *Program Administrator,* Andrea C. Smith, 503-552-1692, Fax: 503-499-0027, E-mail: ccm@ncnm.edu.

Program in Naturopathic Medicine Students: 457 full-time (345 women), 3 part-time (all women). Average age 29. 228 applicants, 77% accepted, 83 enrolled. *Faculty:* 22 full-time, 68 part-time/adjunct. Expenses: Contact institution. *Financial support:* In 2001–02, 381 students received support. Federal Work-Study available. Support available to part-time students. Financial award application deadline: 4/15; financial award applicants required to submit FAFSA. In 2001, 124 degrees awarded. Offers naturopathic medicine (ND). *Application deadline:* For fall admission, 2/1 (priority date); for winter admission, 10/15. Applications are processed on a rolling basis. *Application fee:* $60. *Application Contact:* Phil Reid, Director of Admissions, 503-552-1660, Fax: 503-499-0027, E-mail: admissions@ncnm.edu. *Dean,* Dr. Chris Meletis, 503-552-1620 Ext. 108, Fax: 503-499-0022.

NATIONAL COLLEGE OF ORIENTAL MEDICINE, Orlando, FL 32809

General Information Proprietary, coed, graduate-only institution. *Enrollment by degree level:* 110 master's. *Graduate faculty:* 5 full-time (4 women), 5 part-time/adjunct (2 women). *Tuition:* Full-time $9,600. *Graduate housing:* On-campus housing not available. *Student services:* Career counseling, exercise/wellness program, international student services. *Library facilities:* National College of Oriental Medicine Library. *Online resources:* web page. *Collection:* 2,000 titles, 48 serial subscriptions, 200 audiovisual materials.

Computer facilities: 2 computers available on campus for general student use. A campuswide network can be accessed. Internet access is available. *Web address:* http://www.acupuncureschool.com/.

General Application Contact: Lloyd J. Buss, Admissions Officer, 407-888-8689, Fax: 407-888-8211, E-mail: lloyd@acupunctureschool.com.

GRADUATE UNITS

Graduate Program Students: 110 full-time (77 women); includes 30 minority (4 African Americans, 17 Asian Americans or Pacific Islanders, 9 Hispanic Americans), 2 international. Average age 35. 35 applicants, 77% accepted. *Faculty:* 5 full-time (4 women), 5 part-time/adjunct (2 women). Expenses: Contact institution. *Financial support:* Application deadline: 6/15; In 2001, 16 degrees awarded. Offers Oriental medicine (MSOM). *Application deadline:* For fall admission, 6/15 (priority date); for winter admission, 11/15 (priority date). Applications are processed on a rolling basis. *Application fee:* $25. *Application Contact:* Lloyd J. Buss, Admissions Officer, 407-888-8689, Fax: 407-888-8211, E-mail: lloyd@acupunctureschool.com. *Academic Dean,* Dr. Michael Miller, 407-888-8689, Fax: 407-888-8211.

NATIONAL DEFENSE UNIVERSITY, Washington, DC 20319-5066

General Information Federally supported, graduate-only institution. *Graduate faculty:* 353 full-time, 48 part-time/adjunct. *Student services:* Exercise/wellness program, international student services, writing training. *Library facilities:* NDU Library plus 1 other. *Online resources:* web page. *Collection:* 500,000 titles.

Computer facilities: A campuswide network can be accessed from off campus. Internet access is available. *Web address:* http://www.ndu.edu/.

GRADUATE UNITS

Industrial College of the Armed Forces Students: 299 full-time. *Faculty:* 85 full-time. Expenses: Contact institution. In 2001, 299 degrees awarded. Offers national resource strategy (MS). Open only to Department of Defense employees and specific federal agencies. *Commandant,* Maj. Gen. Harold Mashburn.

National War College Students: 195 full-time. *Faculty:* 60 full-time. Expenses: Contact institution. In 2001, 189 degrees awarded. Offers national security strategy (MS). Open only to Department of Defense employees and specific federal agencies. *Application Contact:* Col. David H. McIntyre, Dean of Faculty and Academic Programs. *Commandant,* Maj. Reginal Clemmons.

THE NATIONAL GRADUATE SCHOOL OF QUALITY MANAGEMENT, Falmouth, MA 02541

General Information Independent, coed, graduate-only institution.

GRADUATE UNITS

Program in Quality Systems Management Offers e-commerce (MS); management (MS); six sigma (MS).

NATIONAL-LOUIS UNIVERSITY, Chicago, IL 60603

General Information Independent, coed, university. *Enrollment:* 1,490 full-time matriculated graduate/professional students (1,151 women), 3,086 part-time matriculated graduate/professional students (2,497 women). *Enrollment by degree level:* 4,525 master's, 51 doctoral. *Tuition:* Full-time $13,830; part-time $461 per credit hour. *Graduate housing:* Room and/or apartments available on a first-come, first-served basis to single students; on-campus housing not available to married students. Typical cost: $2,687 per year ($6,013 including board). Room and board charges vary according to board plan. *Student services:* Campus employment opportunities, career counseling, disabled student services, international student services, low-cost health insurance, teacher training, writing training. *Library facilities:* NLU Library plus 5 others. *Online resources:* library catalog. *Collection:* 5,043 audiovisual materials.

Computer facilities: A campuswide network can be accessed from off campus. Internet access is available. *Web address:* http://www.nl.edu/.

General Application Contact: David McCulloch, Vice President for University Services, 800-443-5522 Ext. 5127, Fax: 847-465-0593, E-mail: dmcc@wheeling1.nl.edu.

GRADUATE UNITS

College of Arts and Sciences *Degree program information:* Part-time and evening/weekend programs available. Postbaccalaureate distance learning degree programs offered (minimal on-campus study). Offers arts and sciences (M Ad Ed, MA, MS, Ed D, Certificate).

Division of Health and Human Services *Degree program information:* Part-time programs available. Offers addictions counseling (MS, Certificate); addictions treatment (Certificate); career counseling and development studies (Certificate); community wellness and prevention (MS, Certificate); counseling (MS, Certificate); eating disorders counseling (Certificate); employee assistance programs (MS, Certificate); gerontology administration (Certificate); gerontology counseling (MS, Certificate); human services administration (MS, Certificate); long-term care administration (Certificate).

Division of Language and Academic Development *Degree program information:* Part-time programs available. Postbaccalaureate distance learning degree programs offered (minimal on-campus study). Offers adult education (M Ad Ed, Ed D, Certificate); adult education and developmental studies (M Ad Ed, Certificate); developmental studies (M Ad Ed).

Division of Liberal Arts and Sciences Offers cultural psychology (MA); health psychology (MA); human development (MA); liberal arts and sciences (MA, MS, Certificate); organizational psychology (MA); psychology (Certificate); written communication (MS).

College of Management and Business *Degree program information:* Part-time and evening/weekend programs available. Offers business administration (MBA); human resource management and development (MS); management and business (MBA, MS); managerial leadership (MS).

National College of Education, McGaw Graduate School *Degree program information:* Part-time and evening/weekend programs available. Offers administration and supervision (M Ed, CAS, Ed S); curriculum and instruction (M Ed, MS Ed, CAS, Ed S); curriculum and social inquiry (Ed D); early childhood administration (M Ed, CAS); early childhood curriculum and instruction specialist (M Ed, MS Ed, CAS); early childhood education (M Ed, MAT, CAS); early childhood leadership and advocacy (M Ed); education (M Ed, MAT, MS Ed, Ed D, CAS, Ed S); educational leadership (Ed D); educational leadership/superintendent endorsement (Ed D); educational psychology (CAS); educational psychology/human learning and development (M Ed, MS Ed); educational psychology/school psychology (M Ed, Ed D, Ed S); elementary education (MAT); general special education (M Ed, MS Ed, CAS); human learning and development (Ed D); language and literacy (M Ed, MS Ed, CAS); learning disabilities (M Ed, MS Ed, CAS); learning disabilities/behavior disorders (M Ed, MAT, MS Ed, CAS); mathematics education (M Ed, MS Ed, CAS); reading and language (Ed D); reading recovery (CAS); reading specialist (M Ed, MS Ed, CAS); science education (M Ed, MS Ed, CAS); secondary education (MAT); technology in education (M Ed, MS Ed, CAS).

NATIONAL TECHNOLOGICAL UNIVERSITY, Fort Collins, CO 80526-1842

General Information Independent, coed, primarily men, graduate-only institution. *Enrollment by degree level:* 674 master's. *Graduate faculty:* 230. *Tuition:* Part-time $660 per credit hour. Part-time tuition and fees vary according to course load, campus/location and program. *Graduate housing:* On-campus housing not available. *Student services:* Career counseling. *Web address:* http://www.ntu.edu/.

General Application Contact: Rhonda Bonham, Admissions Officer, 970-495-6400, Fax: 970-498-0601, E-mail: rhonda@ntu.edu.

GRADUATE UNITS

Program in International Business Administration Expenses: Contact institution. *Degree program information:* Part-time programs available. Postbaccalaureate distance learning degree programs offered (no on-campus study). Offers international business administration (IMBA, MBA). *Application deadline:* Applications are processed on a rolling basis. *Application fee:* $50. Electronic applications accepted. *Application Contact:* Rhonda Bonham, Admissions Officer, 970-495-6409, Fax: 970-498-0601, E-mail: rhonda@ntu.edu. *Chair,* Greg Mosier, 405-744-5118, Fax: 405-744-5180, E-mail: gmosier@okway.okstate.edu.

Programs in Engineering Expenses: Contact institution. In 2001, 114 degrees awarded. *Degree program information:* Part-time programs available. Postbaccalaureate distance learning degree programs offered (no on-campus study). Offers chemical engineering (MS); computer engineering (MS); computer science (MS); electrical engineering (MS); engineering management (MS); environmental systems management (MS); management of technology

National Technological University (continued)

(MS); manufacturing systems engineering (MS); materials science and engineering (MS); mechanical engineering (MS); microelectronics and semiconductor engineering (MS); software engineering (MS); special majors (MS); systems engineering (MS). *Application deadline:* Applications are processed on a rolling basis. *Application fee:* $50. Electronic applications accepted. *Application Contact:* Rhonda Bonham, Admissions Officer, 970-495-6400, Fax: 970-498-0601, E-mail: rhonda@ntu.edu. *President*, Dr. Andre Vacroux, 970-495-6400, Fax: 970-484-0668, E-mail: andre@ntu.edu.

NATIONAL THEATRE CONSERVATORY, Denver, CO 80204-2157

General Information Independent, coed, graduate-only institution. *Enrollment by degree level:* 22 master's. *Graduate faculty:* 4 full-time (1 woman), 12 part-time/adjunct (2 women). *Graduate housing:* On-campus housing not available. *Student services:* Campus employment opportunities, career counseling, free psychological counseling, low-cost health insurance. *Library facilities:* National Theatre Conservatory Library. *Online resources:* library catalog, web page, access to other libraries' catalogs. *Collection:* 16,000 titles, 15 serial subscriptions, 2,105 audiovisual materials.

Computer facilities: 2 computers available on campus for general student use. A campuswide network can be accessed from student residence rooms and from off campus. Internet access and online class registration are available.

General Application Contact: Marti J. Steger, Registrar/Administrator, 303-446-4855, Fax: 303-825-2117, E-mail: ntc@dcpa.org.

GRADUATE UNITS

Department of Acting Students: 22 full-time (9 women); includes 4 minority (all African Americans) Average age 28. 400 applicants, 2% accepted. *Faculty:* 4 full-time (1 woman), 12 part-time/adjunct (2 women). Expenses: Contact institution. *Financial support:* Career-related internships or fieldwork and scholarships/grants available. In 2001, 8 degrees awarded. Offers acting (MFA, Certificate). *Application deadline:* For fall admission, 1/31. *Application fee:* $50. *Application Contact:* Marti J. Steger, Registrar/Administrator, 303-446-4855, Fax: 303-825-2117, E-mail: ntc@dcpa.org. *Director of Education*, Daniel Renner, 303-446-4855, Fax: 303-825-2117, E-mail: renner@dcpa.org.

NATIONAL UNIVERSITY, La Jolla, CA 92037-1011

General Information Independent, coed, comprehensive institution. CGS member. *Enrollment:* 8,455 full-time matriculated graduate/professional students (5,316 women), 4,452 part-time matriculated graduate/professional students (2,612 women). *Graduate faculty:* 108 full-time (47 women), 2,171 part-time/adjunct (1,016 women). *Tuition:* Part-time $221 per quarter hour. *Graduate housing:* On-campus housing not available. *Student services:* Campus employment opportunities, career counseling, disabled student services, international student services, multicultural affairs office, writing training. *Library facilities:* Central Library. *Online resources:* library catalog, web page. *Collection:* 195,783 titles, 19,851 serial subscriptions, 5,198 audiovisual materials.

Computer facilities: 2,152 computers available on campus for general student use. A campuswide network can be accessed from off campus. Internet access and online class registration are available. *Web address:* http://www.nu.edu/.

General Application Contact: Nancy Rohland, Director of Enrollment Management, 858-642-8180, Fax: 858-642-8710, E-mail: advisor@nu.edu.

GRADUATE UNITS

Academic Affairs Average age 34. 4,615 applicants, 100% accepted. *Faculty:* 108 full-time (47 women), 2,171 part-time/adjunct (1,016 women). Expenses: Contact institution. *Financial support:* Institutionally sponsored loans, scholarships/grants, and tuition waivers (full and partial) available. Support available to part-time students. Financial award applicants required to submit FAFSA. In 2001, 2773 degrees awarded. *Degree program information:* Part-time and evening/weekend programs available. Postbaccalaureate distance learning degree programs offered (minimal on-campus study). *Application deadline:* Applications are processed on a rolling basis. *Application fee:* $60 ($100 for international students). *Application Contact:* Nancy Rohland, Director of Enrollment Management, 858-642-8180, Fax: 858-642-8710, E-mail: advisor@nu.edu. *Vice President*, Dr. Susan Harris, 858-642-8106, Fax: 858-642-8719, E-mail: sharris@nu.edu.

School of Arts and Sciences Students: 359 full-time (269 women), 125 part-time (95 women); includes 176 minority (73 African Americans, 30 Asian Americans or Pacific Islanders, 69 Hispanic Americans, 4 Native Americans), 2 international. Average age 34. 147 applicants, 100% accepted. *Faculty:* 19 full-time (11 women), 359 part-time/adjunct (196 women). Expenses: Contact institution. *Financial support:* Institutionally sponsored loans, scholarships/grants, and tuition waivers (full and partial) available. Support available to part-time students. Financial award applicants required to submit FAFSA. In 2001, 249 degrees awarded. *Degree program information:* Part-time and evening/weekend programs available. Postbaccalaureate distance learning degree programs offered (minimal on-campus study). Offers art therapy (Certificate); arts and sciences (MA, MFA, MS, Certificate); counseling psychology (MA); film studies (MFA); human behavior (MA); instructional technology (MS); nursing (MS). *Application deadline:* Applications are processed on a rolling basis. *Application fee:* $60 ($100 for international students). *Application Contact:* Nancy Rohland, Director of Enrollment Management, 858-642-8180, Fax: 858-642-8710, E-mail: advisor@nu.edu. *Dean*, Dr. Mary Elizabeth Shutler, 858-642-8460.

School of Business and Technology Students: 1,180 full-time (535 women), 505 part-time (198 women); includes 560 minority (195 African Americans, 194 Asian Americans or Pacific Islanders, 161 Hispanic Americans, 10 Native Americans), 289 international. 493 applicants, 100% accepted. *Faculty:* 40 full-time (7 women), 555 part-time/adjunct (116 women). Expenses: Contact institution. *Financial support:* Scholarships/grants and tuition waivers (full and partial) available. Support available to part-time students. Financial award application deadline: 5/1; financial award applicants required to submit FAFSA. In 2001, 756 degrees awarded. *Degree program information:* Part-time and evening/weekend programs available. Postbaccalaureate distance learning degree programs offered (minimal on-campus study). Offers accounting (MBA); biotechnology (MBA); business and technology (GMBA, MA, MBA, MCJ, MFS, MHCA, MPA, MS); criminal justice (MCJ, MPA); electronic commerce (MBA, MS); environmental management (MBA); financial management (MBA); forensic science (MFS); general business administration (MBA); global business administration (GMBA); health care administration (MBA, MHCA); human resource management (MA); human resources administration (MBA); international business (MBA); management (MA); marketing (MBA); public administration (MBA, MPA); software engineering (MS); space commerce (MBA); technology management (MBA, MS); telecommunications systems management (MS). *Application deadline:* Applications are processed on a rolling basis. *Application fee:* $60 ($100 for international students). *Application Contact:* Nancy Rohland, Director of Enrollment Management, 858-642-8180, Fax: 858-642-8710, E-mail: advisor@nu.edu. *Dean*, Dr. Shahram Azordegan, 858-642-8418, Fax: 858-642-8716, E-mail: sazordeg@nu.edu.

School of Education Students: 6,915 full-time (4,512 women), 3,822 part-time (2,319 women); includes 3,276 minority (864 African Americans, 594 Asian Americans or Pacific Islanders, 1,728 Hispanic Americans, 90 Native Americans), 17 international. 2,726 applicants, 100% accepted. *Faculty:* 48 full-time (29 women), 1,255 part-time/adjunct (703 women). Expenses: Contact institution. *Financial support:* Institutionally sponsored loans, scholarships/grants, and tuition waivers (full and partial) available. Support available to part-time students. Financial award application deadline: 5/1. In 2001, 1792 degrees awarded. *Degree program information:* Part-time and evening/weekend programs available. Postbaccalaureate distance learning degree programs offered (minimal on-campus study). Offers cross-cultural teaching (M Ed); education (MS); educational administration (MS); educational counseling (MS); educational technology (MS); school psychology (MS); special education (MS); teaching (MA). *Application deadline:* Applications are processed on a rolling basis. *Application fee:* $60 ($100 for international students). *Application Contact:* Nancy Rohland, Director of Enrollment Management, 858-642-8180, Fax: 858-642-8710, E-mail: advisor@nu.edu. *Dean*, Dr. Marie Schrup, 858-642-8330, Fax: 858-642-8724, E-mail: mschrup@nu.edu.

See in-depth description on page 987.

NATIONAL UNIVERSITY OF HEALTH SCIENCES, Lombard, IL 60148-4583

General Information Independent, coed, graduate-only institution. *Enrollment:* 524 full-time matriculated graduate/professional students (179 women). *Enrollment by degree level:* 524 first professional. *Graduate faculty:* 55 full-time, 7 part-time/adjunct. *Tuition:* Part-time $6,500 per trimester. *Graduate housing:* Rooms and/or apartments available on a first-come, first-served basis to single and married students. *Student services:* Campus employment opportunities, campus safety program, career counseling. *Web address:* http://www.nuhs.edu/.

General Application Contact: Michael Brickman, Director of Admissions, 800-826-6285, Fax: 630-889-6554, E-mail: mbrickman@nuhs.edu.

GRADUATE UNITS

College of Professional Studies Students: 524 full-time (179 women). Average age 26. *Faculty:* 55 full-time, 7 part-time/adjunct. Expenses: Contact institution. *Financial support:* Fellowships, research assistantships, teaching assistantships, Federal Work-Study and scholarships/grants available. Support available to part-time students. Financial award applicants required to submit FAFSA. In 2001, 218 degrees awarded. Offers chiropractic (DC). *Application deadline:* Applications are processed on a rolling basis. *Application fee:* $55. Electronic applications accepted. *Application Contact:* Michael Brickman, Director of Admissions, 800-826-6285, Fax: 630-889-6554, E-mail: mbrickman@nuhs.edu. *President*, Dr. James F. Winterstein, 800-826-6285.

NAVAL POSTGRADUATE SCHOOL, Monterey, CA 93943

General Information Federally supported, coed, graduate-only institution. CGS member. *Graduate faculty:* 348 full-time, 34 part-time/adjunct. *Graduate housing:* Rooms and/or apartments available to single and married students. *Student services:* Career counseling, child daycare facilities. *Library facilities:* Dudley Knox Library. *Online resources:* library catalog, web page, access to other libraries' catalogs. *Collection:* 500,000 titles, 1,200 serial subscriptions.

Computer facilities: 260 computers available on campus for general student use. A campuswide network can be accessed from student residence rooms and from off campus. Internet access is available. *Web address:* http://www.nps.navy.mil/.

General Application Contact: Tracy Hammond, Acting Director of Admissions, 831-656-3059, Fax: 831-656-2891, E-mail: thammond@bps.navy.mil.

GRADUATE UNITS

Graduate Programs Students: 1,439 full-time, 253 international. *Faculty:* 348 full-time, 34 part-time/adjunct. Expenses: Contact institution. In 2001, 740 master's, 10 doctorates, 10 other advanced degrees awarded. *Degree program information:* Part-time programs available. Postbaccalaureate distance learning degree programs offered (minimal on-campus study). Offers aeronautics and astronautics (MS, D Eng, PhD, Eng); command, control, communications, computers and intelligence (MS); computer science (MS, PhD); electrical and computer engineering (MS, PhD, Eng); engineering acoustics (MS, D Eng, PhD); information systems (MS); information systems and operations (MS); information warfare and electronic warfare systems technology (MS); mathematics (MS, PhD); mechanical engineering (MS, D Eng, PhD, Eng); meteorology (MS, PhD); modeling virtual environments and simulations (MS, PhD); national security affairs (MA); oceanography (MS, PhD); operations research (MS, PhD); physics (MS, PhD); product development for the twenty-first century (MS); space systems (MS); special operations (MS); systems engineering and integration (MS); undersea warfare (MS). Programs only open to commissioned officers of the United States and friendly nations and selected United States federal civilian employees. *Application Contact:* Information Contact, 831-656-3059, Fax: 831-656-2891, E-mail: thammond@bps.navy.mil. *Acting Director of Admissions*, Tracy Hammond, 831-656-3059, Fax: 831-656-2891, E-mail: thammond@nps.navy.mil.

School of Business and Public Policy Students: 334 full-time, 49 international. Expenses: Contact institution. In 2001, 162 degrees awarded. *Degree program information:* Part-time programs available. Postbaccalaureate distance learning degree programs offered (minimal on-campus study). Offers systems management (MS). Program only open to commissioned officers of the United States and friendly nations and selected United States federal civilian employees. *Application Contact:* Tracy Hammond, Acting Director of Admissions, 831-656-3059, Fax: 831-656-2891, E-mail: thammond@bps.navy.mil. *Chairman*, Dr. Reuben T. Harris, 831-656-2161.

NAVAL WAR COLLEGE, Newport, RI 02841-1207

General Information Federally supported, coed, primarily men, graduate-only institution.

GRADUATE UNITS

Program in National Security and Strategic Studies Offers national security and strategic studies (MA). Program open only to full-time military personnel.

NAZARENE THEOLOGICAL SEMINARY, Kansas City, MO 64131-1263

General Information Independent-religious, coed, primarily men, graduate-only institution. *Graduate faculty:* 17 full-time (1 woman), 14 part-time/adjunct (2 women). *Tuition:* Part-time $265 per credit hour. *Required fees:* $100 per semester. Tuition and fees vary according to student's religious affiliation. *Graduate housing:* On-campus housing not available. *Student services:* Campus employment opportunities, career counseling, international student services, low-cost health insurance. *Library facilities:* William Broadhurst Library. *Online resources:* library catalog, web page, access to other libraries' catalogs. *Collection:* 98,338 titles, 520 serial subscriptions, 2,829 audiovisual materials.

Computer facilities: 9 computers available on campus for general student use. A campuswide network can be accessed from off campus. Internet access is available. *Web address:* http://www.nts.edu/.

General Application Contact: Director of Admissions, 816-333-6251 Ext. 211, Fax: 816-333-6271.

GRADUATE UNITS

Graduate and Professional Programs Students: 236 full-time (56 women), 114 part-time (37 women); includes 13 minority (3 African Americans, 4 Asian Americans or Pacific Islanders, 5 Hispanic Americans, 1 Native American), 15 international. Average age 25. 142 applicants, 94% accepted. *Faculty:* 17 full-time (1 woman), 14 part-time/adjunct (2 women). Expenses: Contact institution. *Financial support:* In 2001–02, 229 students received support, including 15 teaching assistantships (averaging $1,400 per year); institutionally sponsored loans and scholarships/grants also available. Support available to part-time students. Financial award application deadline: 3/1; financial award applicants required to submit FAFSA. In 2001, 47 first professional degrees, 6 master's, 5 doctorates awarded. *Degree program information:* Part-time programs available. Offers Christian education (MACE); theological studies (MA(R)); theology (M Div, D Min). *Application deadline:* For fall admission, 8/1 (priority date); for spring admission, 12/1. Applications are processed on a rolling basis. *Application fee:* $20. Electronic applications accepted. *Application Contact:* Director of Admissions, 816-333-6251 Ext. 211, Fax: 816-333-6271. *Dean*, Dr. Roger Hahn, 816-333-6254 Ext. 220, Fax: 816-333-6271, E-mail: rlhahn@nts.edu.

The Terrell C. Sanders School of World Mission and Evangelism Students: 34 full-time (8 women), 16 part-time (9 women); includes 1 minority (Asian American or Pacific Islander), 9 international. Average age 25. 24 applicants, 96% accepted. *Faculty:* 17 full-time (1 woman), 14 part-time/adjunct (2 women). Expenses: Contact institution. *Financial support:* In 2001–02, 47 students received support, including 3 teaching assistantships (averaging $1,400 per year); institutionally sponsored loans and scholarships/grants also available. Support available to part-time students. Financial award application deadline: 3/1; financial award applicants required to submit FAFSA. In 2001, 5 first professional degrees, 4 master's awarded. *Degree program information:* Part-time programs available. Offers evangelism (M Div); missiology (MA). *Application deadline:* For fall admission, 8/1 (priority date); for spring admission, 12/1. Applications are processed on a rolling basis. *Application fee:* $20. Electronic applications accepted.

Application Contact: Director of Admissions, 816-333-6251 Ext. 211, Fax: 816-333-6271. *Director*, Dr. Bill Selvidge, 816-333-6251, Fax: 816-333-6271, E-mail: bselvidge@nts.edu.

NAZARETH COLLEGE OF ROCHESTER, Rochester, NY 14618-3790

General Information Independent, coed, comprehensive institution. *Enrollment:* 248 full-time matriculated graduate/professional students (214 women), 961 part-time matriculated graduate/professional students (796 women). *Enrollment by degree level:* 1,209 master's. *Graduate faculty:* 36 full-time (23 women), 72 part-time/adjunct (49 women). *Tuition:* Part-time $466 per credit hour. *Required fees:* $20 per semester. *Graduate housing:* On-campus housing not available. *Student services:* Campus employment opportunities, campus safety program, career counseling, child daycare facilities, free psychological counseling, multicultural affairs office. *Library facilities:* Lorette Wilmot Library. *Online resources:* library catalog, web page, access to other libraries' catalogs. *Collection:* 283,810 titles, 1,959 serial subscriptions, 18,503 audiovisual materials.

Computer facilities: 190 computers available on campus for general student use. A campuswide network can be accessed from student residence rooms and from off campus. Internet access is available. *Web address:* http://www.naz.edu/.

General Application Contact: Dr. Kay F. Marshman, Dean, 585-389-2815, Fax: 585-389-2817, E-mail: gradstudies@naz.edu.

GRADUATE UNITS

Graduate Studies Students: 248 full-time (214 women), 961 part-time (796 women); includes 81 minority (49 African Americans, 17 Asian Americans or Pacific Islanders, 15 Hispanic Americans) Average age 27. 386 applicants, 89% accepted, 267 enrolled. *Faculty:* 36 full-time (23 women), 72 part-time/adjunct (49 women). Expenses: Contact institution. *Financial support:* In 2001–02, 15 students received support, including 10 research assistantships with partial tuition reimbursements available (averaging $2,500 per year); career-related internships or fieldwork and scholarships/grants also available. Support available to part-time students. Financial award applicants required to submit FAFSA. In 2001, 453 degrees awarded. *Degree program information:* Part-time and evening/weekend programs available. Postbaccalaureate distance learning degree programs offered. Offers art education (MS Ed); art therapy (MS); business education (MS Ed); computer education (MS Ed); early childhood education (MS Ed); educational technology specialist (MS Ed); elementary education (MS Ed); general secondary education (MS Ed); gerontological nurse practitioner (MS); inclusive education (MS Ed); liberal studies (MA); literacy education (MS Ed); management (MS); music education (MS Ed); social work (MSW); special education (MS Ed); speech pathology (MS); teaching English to speakers of other languages (MS Ed). *Application deadline:* For spring admission, 10/1. Applications are processed on a rolling basis. *Application fee:* $40. *Application Contact:* Dr. Kay F. Marshman, Dean, 585-389-2815, Fax: 585-389-2817, E-mail: gradstudies@naz.edu. *Dean*, Dr. Kay F. Marshman, 716-389-2815, Fax: 716-389-2871, E-mail: gradstudies@naz.edu.

NEBRASKA METHODIST COLLEGE, Omaha, NE 68114-3426

General Information Independent-religious, coed, comprehensive institution. *Enrollment:* 43 full-time matriculated graduate/professional students (37 women). *Enrollment by degree level:* 43 master's. *Graduate faculty:* 9 full-time (all women), 19 part-time/adjunct (9 women). *Tuition:* Full-time $6,750. *Required fees:* $450. *Graduate housing:* Room and/or apartments available on a first-come, first-served basis to single students; on-campus housing not available to married students. Typical cost: $2,660 per year. Housing application deadline:4/1. *Student services:* Campus employment opportunities, campus safety program, career counseling, disabled student services, exercise/wellness program, free psychological counseling, grant writing training, international student services, low-cost health insurance, teacher training, writing training. *Library facilities:* John Moritz Library plus 1 other. *Collection:* 8,656 titles, 468 serial subscriptions, 964 audiovisual materials.

Computer facilities: 45 computers available on campus for general student use. A campuswide network can be accessed. Internet access is available. *Web address:* http://www.methodistcollege.edu/.

General Application Contact: Deann Sterner, Director of Admissions, 402-354-4879, Fax: 402-354-8875, E-mail: admissions@methodistcollege.edu.

GRADUATE UNITS

Program in Health Promotion Students: 17 full-time (14 women); includes 3 minority (2 African Americans, 1 Hispanic American) Average age 35. 9 applicants, 100% accepted. *Faculty:* 2 full-time (both women), 16 part-time/adjunct (7 women). Expenses: Contact institution. *Financial support:* In 2001–02, 12 students received support, including 6 research assistantships with full and partial tuition reimbursements available (averaging $2,768 per year); scholarships/grants also available. Support available to part-time students. Financial award applicants required to submit FAFSA. In 2001, 10 degrees awarded. *Degree program information:* Evening/weekend programs available. Postbaccalaureate distance learning degree programs offered (minimal on-campus study). Offers health promotion (MS). *Application deadline:* For fall admission, 8/1. Applications are processed on a rolling basis. *Application fee:* $25. *Application Contact:* Deann Sterner, Director of Admissions, 402-354-4879, Fax: 402-354-8875, E-mail: admissions@methodistcollege.edu. *Chairperson*, Dr. Kay Ryan, 402-354-4953, Fax: 402-354-8875, E-mail: kyan@methodistcollege.edu.

Program in Nursing Students: 26 full-time (23 women); includes 1 minority (African American) Average age 34. 11 applicants, 100% accepted. *Faculty:* 7 full-time (all women), 3 part-time/adjunct (2 women). Expenses: Contact institution. *Financial support:* In 2001–02, 13 students received support, including 4 research assistantships with full and partial tuition reimbursements available (averaging $1,309 per year); scholarships/grants also available. Support available to part-time students. Financial award applicants required to submit FAFSA. *Degree program information:* Evening/weekend programs available. Postbaccalaureate distance learning degree programs offered (minimal on-campus study). Offers nursing (MSN). *Application deadline:* For spring admission, 12/1. Applications are processed on a rolling basis. *Application fee:* $25. *Application Contact:* Deann Sterner, Director of Admissions, 402-354-4879, Fax: 402-354-8875, E-mail: admissions@methodistcollege.edu. *Chairperson*, Nancy Mockelstrom, 402-354-4981, Fax: 402-354-8875.

NEBRASKA WESLEYAN UNIVERSITY, Lincoln, NE 68504-2796

General Information Independent-religious, coed, comprehensive institution.

GRADUATE UNITS

Office of Graduate and Extended Programs

NER ISRAEL RABBINICAL COLLEGE, Baltimore, MD 21208

General Information Independent-religious, men only, comprehensive institution. *Enrollment:* 162 full-time matriculated graduate/professional students, 17 part-time matriculated graduate/professional students. *Enrollment by degree level:* 26 first professional, 114 master's, 23 doctoral. *Graduate faculty:* 7 full-time (0 women), 6 part-time/adjunct (0 women). *Tuition:* Full-time $6,500. *Graduate housing:* Rooms and/or apartments guaranteed to single students and available on a first-come, first-served basis to married students. Typical cost: $3,000 per year ($6,000 including board) for single students.

General Application Contact: H. A. Levine, 410-484-7200, Fax: 410-484-3060.

GRADUATE UNITS

Graduate Programs Students: 162 full-time (0 women), 17 part-time. *Faculty:* 7 full-time (0 women), 6 part-time/adjunct (0 women). Expenses: Contact institution. *Application Contact:* Rabbi Ezra Neuberger, Dean, 410-484-7200.

NER ISRAEL YESHIVA COLLEGE OF TORONTO, Thornhill, ON L4J 8A7, Canada

General Information Independent-religious, men only, comprehensive institution.

NEUMANN COLLEGE, Aston, PA 19014-1298

General Information Independent-religious, coed, comprehensive institution. *Enrollment:* 72 full-time matriculated graduate/professional students (44 women), 201 part-time matriculated graduate/professional students (157 women). *Enrollment by degree level:* 273 master's. *Graduate faculty:* 24 full-time (13 women), 21 part-time/adjunct (16 women). *Tuition:* Full-time $7,920; part-time $440 per credit. *Graduate housing:* On-campus housing not available. *Student services:* Campus employment opportunities, campus safety program, career counseling, child daycare facilities, disabled student services, exercise/wellness program, free psychological counseling, writing training. *Library facilities:* Neumann College Library. *Online resources:* library catalog, access to other libraries' catalogs. *Collection:* 95,216 titles, 1,702 serial subscriptions, 52,305 audiovisual materials.

Computer facilities: 121 computers available on campus for general student use. A campuswide network can be accessed from student residence rooms and from off campus. Internet access, e-mail are available. *Web address:* http://www.neumann.edu/.

General Application Contact: Scott Bogard, Director of Admissions, 610-558-5616, Fax: 610-558-5652, E-mail: sbogard@neumann.edu.

GRADUATE UNITS

Program in Education Students: 12 full-time (9 women), 130 part-time (104 women); includes 23 minority (22 African Americans, 1 Asian American or Pacific Islander) Average age 37. 30 applicants, 100% accepted, 20 enrolled. *Faculty:* 5 full-time (1 woman), 2 part-time/adjunct (1 woman). Expenses: Contact institution. *Financial support:* Available to part-time students. Application deadline: 3/15; In 2001, 10 degrees awarded. *Degree program information:* Part-time programs available. Offers education (MS). *Application deadline:* Applications are processed on a rolling basis. *Application fee:* $50. *Application Contact:* Louise Bank, Assistant Director of Admissions, Graduate and Evening Programs, 610-558-5604, Fax: 610-459-1370, E-mail: bankl@neumann.edu. *Dean, Division of Education and Human Services*, Dr. Joseph Gillespie, 610-558-5640, Fax: 610-459-1370, E-mail: gillespj@neumann.edu.

Program in Nursing and Health Sciences Students: 1 full-time (0 women), 7 part-time (6 women). Average age 39. 1 applicant, 100% accepted. *Faculty:* 5 full-time (4 women), 1 part-time/adjunct (0 women). Expenses: Contact institution. *Financial support:* Available to part-time students. Application deadline: 3/15; In 2001, 1 degree awarded. *Degree program information:* Part-time programs available. Offers nursing (MS). *Application deadline:* Applications are processed on a rolling basis. *Application fee:* $50. *Application Contact:* Louise Bank, Assistant Director of Admissions, Graduate and Evening Programs, 610-558-5604, Fax: 610-459-1370, E-mail: bankl@neumann.edu. *Chair, Division of Nursing and Health Services*, Dr. Gregg Newschwander, 610-558-5561, Fax: 610-459-1370, E-mail: newschwg@neumann.edu.

Program in Pastoral Counseling Students: 5 full-time (4 women), 51 part-time (40 women); includes 9 minority (7 African Americans, 2 Asian Americans or Pacific Islanders) Average age 48. 12 applicants, 100% accepted. *Faculty:* 4 full-time (3 women), 7 part-time/adjunct (6 women). Expenses: Contact institution. *Financial support:* In 2001–02, 8 students received support. Available to part-time students. Application deadline: 3/15; In 2001, 17 degrees awarded. *Degree program information:* Part-time and evening/weekend programs available. Offers pastoral counseling (MS, CAS); spiritual direction (CSD). *Application deadline:* Applications are processed on a rolling basis. *Application fee:* $50. *Application Contact:* Louise Bank, Assistant Director of Admissions, Graduate and Evening Programs, 610-558-5604, Fax: 610-459-1370, E-mail: bankl@neumann.edu. *Executive Director*, Leonard DiPaul, 610-558-5572, Fax: 610-459-1370.

Program in Physical Therapy Students: 54 full-time (32 women), 5 part-time (3 women); includes 5 minority (3 African Americans, 2 Asian Americans or Pacific Islanders) Average age 31. 30 applicants, 60% accepted, 15 enrolled. *Faculty:* 5 full-time (3 women), 10 part-time/adjunct (8 women). Expenses: Contact institution. *Financial support:* Available to part-time students. Application deadline: 3/15; In 2001, 21 degrees awarded. *Degree program information:* Evening/weekend programs available. Offers physical therapy (MS). *Application deadline:* For fall admission, 12/1. *Application fee:* $50. *Application Contact:* Louise Bank, Assistant Director of Admissions, Graduate and Evening Programs, 610-558-5604, Fax: 610-459-1370, E-mail: bankl@neumann.edu. *Director*, Dr. Robert Post, 610-558-5233, Fax: 610-459-1370, E-mail: postr@neumann.edu.

Program in Sports Management 1 applicant, 100% accepted. *Faculty:* 5 full-time (2 women). Expenses: Contact institution. *Financial support:* Available to part-time students. Applicants required to submit FAFSA. *Degree program information:* Part-time programs available. Offers sports management (MS). *Application deadline:* Applications are processed on a rolling basis. *Application fee:* $50. *Application Contact:* Louise Bank, Assistant Director of Admissions, Graduate and Evening Programs, 610-558-5604, Fax: 610-459-1370, E-mail: bankl@neumann.edu. *Coordinator*, Dr. Sandra L. Slabik, 610-361-5291, Fax: 610-558-5574, E-mail: slabiks@neumann.edu.

NEW BRUNSWICK THEOLOGICAL SEMINARY, New Brunswick, NJ 08901-1196

General Information Independent-religious, coed, graduate-only institution. *Enrollment by degree level:* 163 first professional, 58 master's, 19 doctoral. *Graduate faculty:* 12 full-time (2 women), 35 part-time/adjunct (11 women). *Tuition:* Part-time $265 per credit hour. *Required fees:* $106. Full-time tuition and fees vary according to course load, degree level and student's religious affiliation. *Graduate housing:* Rooms and/or apartments available to single and married students. Typical cost: $2,767 per year ($5,779 including board) for single students; $2,767 per year ($5,179 including board) for married students. Room and board charges vary according to housing facility selected. *Student services:* Campus employment opportunities, career counseling, international student services, low-cost health insurance. *Library facilities:* Gardner Sage Library. *Collection:* 152,800 titles, 310 serial subscriptions.

Computer facilities: 8 computers available on campus for general student use. A campuswide network can be accessed. Internet access is available. *Web address:* http://www.nbts.edu/.

General Application Contact: Laura Tarbous, Student Services, 732-246-5595, Fax: 732-245-5412, E-mail: lkt@nbts.edu.

GRADUATE UNITS

Graduate and Professional Programs Students: 41 full-time (20 women), 200 part-time (103 women); includes 150 minority (119 African Americans, 25 Asian Americans or Pacific Islanders, 6 Hispanic Americans), 8 international. Average age 45. 75 applicants, 68% accepted. *Faculty:* 12 full-time (2 women), 35 part-time/adjunct (11 women). Expenses: Contact institution. *Financial support:* In 2001–02, 65 students received support. Career-related internships or fieldwork, scholarships/grants, and tuition waivers (full and partial) available. Support available to part-time students. Financial award application deadline: 7/28; financial award applicants required to submit FAFSA. In 2001, 23 first professional degrees, 7 master's, 7 doctorates awarded. *Degree program information:* Part-time and evening/weekend programs available. Offers metro-urban ministry (D Min); theological studies (M Div, MA, D Min). *Application deadline:* For fall admission, 7/15; for spring admission, 12/7. Applications are processed on a rolling basis. *Application fee:* $25. Electronic applications accepted. *Application Contact:* Laura Tarbous, Student Services, 732-246-5595, Fax: 732-245-5412, E-mail: lkt@nbts.edu. *Dean*, Dr. Paul Fries, 732-246-5591, Fax: 732-249-5412.

NEW COLLEGE OF CALIFORNIA, San Francisco, CA 94102-5206

General Information Independent, coed, comprehensive institution. *Graduate housing:* On-campus housing not available.

New College of California (continued)

GRADUATE UNITS

Division of Humanities *Degree program information:* Part-time and evening/weekend programs available. Offers culture, ecology, and sustainable community (MA); humanities and leadership (MA); media studies (MA); poetics (MA, MFA); poetics and writing (MFA); psychology (MA); women's spirituality (MA); writing and consciousness (MA).

School of Law Students: 100. Average age 30. 100 applicants, 50% accepted. *Faculty:* 6 full-time (4 women), 18 part-time/adjunct (6 women). Expenses: Contact institution. *Financial support:* Career-related internships or fieldwork, Federal Work-Study, and scholarships/grants available. Support available to part-time students. Financial award application deadline: 3/1; financial award applicants required to submit FAFSA. In 2001, 22 degrees awarded. *Degree program information:* Part-time programs available. Offers law (JD). *Application deadline:* For fall admission, 3/1 (priority date). Applications are processed on a rolling basis. *Application fee:* $45. *Application Contact:* Sabrina Baptiste, Associate Dean for Admissions, 415-241-1374, Fax: 415-241-1353. *Dean,* Debrenia Madison, 415-241-1325, Fax: 415-241-1353, E-mail: madison@ncgate.newcollege.edu.

School of Psychology Students: 43 full-time (32 women). Average age 28. 60 applicants, 77% accepted, 40 enrolled. *Faculty:* 6 full-time (3 women), 10 part-time/adjunct (7 women). Expenses: Contact institution. *Financial support:* In 2001–02, 4 students received support, including 2 teaching assistantships (averaging $900 per year); career-related internships or fieldwork and Federal Work-Study also available. Financial award application deadline: 7/15; financial award applicants required to submit FAFSA. *Degree program information:* Evening/weekend programs available. Offers feminist clinical psychology (MA); social-clinical psychology (MA). *Application deadline:* For fall admission, 4/1 (priority date). Applications are processed on a rolling basis. *Application fee:* $50 ($75 for international students). *Application Contact:* Carmen Gonzalez, Admissions Director, 415-437-3421. *Dean,* Dr. Ali Chavoshian, 415-437-3435.

See in-depth description on page 989.

NEW ENGLAND COLLEGE, Henniker, NH 03242-3293

General Information Independent, coed, comprehensive institution. *Graduate housing:* On-campus housing not available.

GRADUATE UNITS

Program in Creative Writing Expenses: Contact institution. *Application Contact:* Richard S. Keating, Director of Graduate Studies, 603-428-2479, Fax: 603-428-8123, E-mail: rkeating@nec.edu.

Program in Education Offers literacy and language arts (M Ed); meeting the needs of all learners/special education (M Ed); teacher leadership/school reform (M Ed).

Program in Organizational Management *Degree program information:* Part-time and evening/weekend programs available. Offers business (MS); community mental health counseling (MS); health care (MS); health care management (Certificate); human resource management (Certificate); human services (MS). Electronic applications accepted.

THE NEW ENGLAND COLLEGE OF OPTOMETRY, Boston, MA 02115-1100

General Information Independent, coed, graduate-only institution. *Enrollment by degree level:* 422 first professional. *Graduate faculty:* 37 full-time (12 women), 52 part-time/adjunct (20 women). *Tuition:* Full-time $23,964. *Required fees:* $480. *Graduate housing:* On-campus housing not available. *Student services:* Campus employment opportunities, career counseling, free psychological counseling, international student services, low-cost health insurance. *Library facilities:* Library. *Online resources:* library catalog, web page. *Collection:* 13,206 titles, 235 serial subscriptions, 11,778 audiovisual materials. *Research affiliation:* Brookfield Optical Systems.

Computer facilities: 28 computers available on campus for general student use. A campuswide network can be accessed from off campus. Internet access is available. *Web address:* http://www.ne-optometry.edu/.

General Application Contact: Lawrence Shattuck, Director of Admissions, 617-236-6210, Fax: 617-369-0162, E-mail: shattuck@ne-optometry.edu.

GRADUATE UNITS

Professional Program Students: 421 full-time (271 women), 1 (woman) part-time; includes 160 minority (20 African Americans, 126 Asian Americans or Pacific Islanders, 13 Hispanic Americans, 1 Native American), 62 international. Average age 25. 711 applicants, 29% accepted. Expenses: Contact institution. *Financial support:* In 2001–02, 355 students received support, including 2 fellowships; career-related internships or fieldwork, Federal Work-Study, institutionally sponsored loans, and scholarships/grants also available. Financial award application deadline: 4/1; financial award applicants required to submit FAFSA. In 2001, 107 degrees awarded. Offers optometry (OD). *Application deadline:* For fall admission, 3/31. Applications are processed on a rolling basis. *Application fee:* $75. *Application Contact:* Lawrence Shattuck, Director of Admissions, 617-236-6210, Fax: 617-369-0162, E-mail: shattuck@ne-optometry.edu.

NEW ENGLAND CONSERVATORY OF MUSIC, Boston, MA 02115-5000

General Information Independent, coed, comprehensive institution. *Enrollment:* 364 full-time matriculated graduate/professional students (219 women), 27 part-time matriculated graduate/professional students (20 women). *Enrollment by degree level:* 304 master's, 29 doctoral, 58 other advanced degrees. *Graduate faculty:* 76 full-time (23 women), 130 part-time/adjunct (40 women). *Tuition:* Full-time $23,000; part-time $1,400 per credit. *Required fees:* $250; $250 per year. *Graduate housing:* Room and/or apartments available to single students; on-campus housing not available to married students. Typical cost: $9,400 (including board) ; $9,400 (including board) for married students. Housing application deadline: 6/15. *Student services:* Campus employment opportunities, career counseling, disabled student services, free psychological counseling, international student services, low-cost health insurance. *Library facilities:* Spaulding Library plus 1 other. *Online resources:* library catalog, web page, access to other libraries' catalogs. *Collection:* 75,674 titles, 255 serial subscriptions, 1,238 audiovisual materials.

Computer facilities: 48 computers available on campus for general student use. A campuswide network can be accessed. Internet access is available. *Web address:* http://www.newenglandconservatory.edu/.

General Application Contact: Tom Novak, Director of Admissions, 617-585-1106, Fax: 617-585-1115, E-mail: tnovak@newenglandconservatory.edu.

GRADUATE UNITS

Graduate Program in Music Students: 364 full-time (219 women), 27 part-time (20 women); includes 45 minority (5 African Americans, 33 Asian Americans or Pacific Islanders, 7 Hispanic Americans), 122 international. Average age 26. 789 applicants, 47% accepted, 187 enrolled. *Faculty:* 76 full-time (23 women), 130 part-time/adjunct (40 women). Expenses: Contact institution. *Financial support:* In 2001–02, 222 students received support, including 222 fellowships with tuition reimbursements available (averaging $11,218 per year); Federal Work-Study, scholarships/grants, and tuition waivers (partial) also available. Support available to part-time students. Financial award application deadline: 12/1; financial award applicants required to submit FAFSA. In 2001, 121 master's, 9 doctorates, 16 Diplomas awarded. Offers music (MM, DMA, Diploma). *Application deadline:* For fall admission, 12/2 (priority date); for spring admission, 11/1. Applications are processed on a rolling basis. *Application fee:* $100. *Application Contact:* Tom Novak, Director of Admissions, 617-585-1106, Fax: 617-585-1115, E-mail: tnovak@newenglandconservatory.edu. *Provost,* Peter Row, 617-585-1304, Fax: 617-585-1303, E-mail: prow@newenglandconservatory.edu.

NEW ENGLAND SCHOOL OF ACUPUNCTURE, Watertown, MA 02472

General Information Independent, coed, graduate-only institution. *Enrollment by degree level:* 274 master's. *Graduate faculty:* 1 (woman) full-time, 82 part-time/adjunct (46 women). *Tuition:* Full-time $9,546; part-time $258 per credit. *Required fees:* $300; $100 per term. Full-time tuition and fees vary according to program and student level. *Graduate housing:* On-campus housing not available. *Student services:* Campus employment opportunities, international student services, low-cost health insurance. *Library facilities:* Kelly Library Information Center. *Online resources:* library catalog. *Collection:* 2,060 titles, 61 serial subscriptions, 158 audiovisual materials.

Computer facilities: 1 computer available on campus for general student use. *Web address:* http://www.nesa.edu/.

General Application Contact: Lucille Petringa, Director of Admissions, 617-926-1788 Ext. 110, Fax: 617-924-4167, E-mail: lpetringa@nesa.edu.

GRADUATE UNITS

Program in Acupuncture and Oriental Medicine Students: 220 full-time (164 women), 54 part-time (43 women); includes 38 minority (4 African Americans, 28 Asian Americans or Pacific Islanders, 5 Hispanic Americans, 1 Native American), 14 international. Average age 35. 189 applicants, 72% accepted, 101 enrolled. *Faculty:* 1 (woman) full-time, 82 part-time/adjunct (46 women). Expenses: Contact institution. *Financial support:* In 2001–02, 165 students received support. Available to part-time students. Application deadline: 7/1; In 2001, 80 degrees awarded. *Degree program information:* Part-time programs available. Offers acupuncture (M Ac); acupuncture and Oriental medicine (MAOM). *Application deadline:* For fall admission, 5/1 (priority date). Applications are processed on a rolling basis. *Application fee:* $50. *Application Contact:* Lucille Petringa, Director of Admissions, 617-926-1788 Ext. 110, Fax: 617-924-4167, E-mail: lpetringa@nesa.edu. *Academic Dean,* Amy Hull, 617-926-1788 Ext. 118, Fax: 617-924-4167, E-mail: efowler@nesa.edu.

NEW ENGLAND SCHOOL OF LAW, Boston, MA 02116-5687

General Information Independent, coed, graduate-only institution. *Enrollment by degree level:* 956 first professional. *Graduate faculty:* 33 full-time (11 women), 69 part-time/adjunct (12 women). *Tuition:* Full-time $18,560. *Required fees:* $165; $165 per year. One-time fee: $100. *Graduate housing:* On-campus housing not available. *Student services:* Campus employment opportunities, career counseling, disabled student services, free psychological counseling, low-cost health insurance, writing training. *Library facilities:* New England School of Law Library. *Online resources:* library catalog, web page, access to other libraries' catalogs. *Collection:* 190,027 titles, 3,181 serial subscriptions, 2,359 audiovisual materials.

Computer facilities: 87 computers available on campus for general student use. A campuswide network can be accessed from off campus. Internet access is available. *Web address:* http://www.nesl.edu/.

General Application Contact: Pamela Jorgensen, Director of Admissions, 617-422-7210, Fax: 617-422-7200, E-mail: admit@admin.nesl.edu.

GRADUATE UNITS

Professional Program Students: 611 full-time (354 women), 345 part-time (181 women); includes 143 minority (42 African Americans, 48 Asian Americans or Pacific Islanders, 51 Hispanic Americans, 2 Native Americans), 15 international. Average age 26. 2,080 applicants, 68% accepted, 342 enrolled. *Faculty:* 33 full-time (11 women), 69 part-time/adjunct (12 women). Expenses: Contact institution. *Financial support:* In 2001–02, 430 students received support. Federal Work-Study, scholarships/grants, and tuition waivers (full and partial) available. Support available to part-time students. Financial award application deadline: 4/17; financial award applicants required to submit FAFSA. In 2001, 282 degrees awarded. *Degree program information:* Part-time and evening/weekend programs available. Offers law (JD). *Application deadline:* For fall admission, 6/1. Applications are processed on a rolling basis. *Application fee:* $50. Electronic applications accepted. *Application Contact:* Pamela Jorgensen, Director of Admissions, 617-422-7210, Fax: 617-422-7200, E-mail: admit@admin.nesl.edu. *Dean,* John F. O'Brien, 617-422-7221, Fax: 617-422-7333, E-mail: jobrien@admin.nesl.edu.

NEW JERSEY CITY UNIVERSITY, Jersey City, NJ 07305-1597

General Information State-supported, coed, comprehensive institution. *Enrollment:* 1,142 matriculated graduate/professional students. *Graduate faculty:* 51 full-time (19 women), 10 part-time/adjunct (4 women). Tuition, state resident: full-time $5,062. Tuition, nonresident: full-time $8,663. *Graduate housing:* On-campus housing not available. *Student services:* Campus employment opportunities, campus safety program, career counseling, child daycare facilities, free psychological counseling, international student services. *Library facilities:* Congressman Frank J. Guarini Library. *Online resources:* library catalog. *Collection:* 710,875 titles, 11,260 serial subscriptions, 2,286 audiovisual materials.

Computer facilities: 1,400 computers available on campus for general student use. *Web address:* http://www.njcu.edu/core.htm.

General Application Contact: Dr. Peter J. Donnelly, Director of Graduate Studies and Special Programs, 201-200-3409, Fax: 201-200-3411, E-mail: pdonnelly@njcu.edu.

GRADUATE UNITS

Graduate Studies Students: 1,142. Average age 32. *Faculty:* 51 full-time (19 women), 10 part-time/adjunct (4 women). Expenses: Contact institution. *Financial support:* Fellowships, research assistantships, teaching assistantships, career-related internships or fieldwork available. In 2001, 4 degrees awarded. *Degree program information:* Part-time and evening/weekend programs available. *Application deadline:* For fall admission, 8/1 (priority date); for spring admission, 12/1. Applications are processed on a rolling basis. *Application fee:* $0. *Director,* Dr. Peter J. Donnelly, 201-200-3409, Fax: 201-200-3411, E-mail: pdonnelly@njcu.edu.

College of Arts and Sciences Students: 232 (170 women); includes 86 minority (31 African Americans, 8 Asian Americans or Pacific Islanders, 47 Hispanic Americans) Average age 32. 130 applicants, 80% accepted. *Faculty:* 17 full-time, 3 part-time/adjunct. Expenses: Contact institution. *Financial support:* In 2001–02, 4 teaching assistantships were awarded; career-related internships or fieldwork also available. In 2001, 69 master's, 4 other advanced degrees awarded. *Degree program information:* Part-time and evening/weekend programs available. Offers art (MA); art education (MA); arts and sciences (MA, PD); counseling (MA); educational psychology (MA, PD); mathematics education (MA); music education (MA); school psychology (PD). *Application deadline:* For fall admission, 8/1 (priority date); for spring admission, 12/1. Applications are processed on a rolling basis. *Application fee:* $0. *Acting Dean,* Dr. Lisa Fiol-Mata, 201-200-3001.

College of Education Students: 748 (543 women); includes 204 minority (78 African Americans, 18 Asian Americans or Pacific Islanders, 108 Hispanic Americans) Expenses: Contact institution. *Financial support:* Fellowships, teaching assistantships, career-related internships or fieldwork available. In 2001, 226 degrees awarded. Offers administration, curriculum and instruction (MA); basics and urban studies (MA); bilingual/bicultural education and English as a second language (MA); early childhood education (MA); education (MA); educational technology (MA); literary education (MA); special education (MA); urban education (MA). *Application deadline:* For fall admission, 8/1; for spring admission, 12/1. *Application fee:* $0. *Acting Dean,* Dr. Muriel Rand, 201-200-2102.

College of Professional Studies Students: 162 (114 women); includes 66 minority (33 African Americans, 9 Asian Americans or Pacific Islanders, 24 Hispanic Americans) Average age 32. 312 applicants, 83% accepted. *Faculty:* 34 full-time, 7 part-time/adjunct. Expenses: Contact institution. *Financial support:* In 2001–02, 11 teaching assistantships were awarded; fellowships, research assistantships, career-related internships or fieldwork also available. In 2001, 58 degrees awarded. *Degree program information:* Evening/weekend programs available. Offers accounting (MS); community health education (MS); criminal justice (MS); health administration (MS); holistic medicine (MS); professional studies (MA, MS, Certificate); urban medicine (MS). *Application deadline:* For fall admission, 8/1 (priority date); for spring admission, 12/1. Applications are processed on a rolling basis. *Application fee:* $0. *Dean,* Dr. Sandra Bloomberg, 201-200-3321.

NEW JERSEY INSTITUTE OF TECHNOLOGY, Newark, NJ 07102

General Information State-supported, coed, university. CGS member. *Enrollment:* 1,253 full-time matriculated graduate/professional students (382 women), 1,391 part-time matriculated graduate/professional students (345 women). *Enrollment by degree level:* 2,138 master's, 379 doctoral. *Graduate faculty:* 418 full-time (71 women), 272 part-time/adjunct (47 women). Tuition, state resident: full-time $7,812; part-time $434 per credit. Tuition, nonresident: full-time $10,746; part-time $597 per credit. *Required fees:* $47 per credit. $76 per semester. *Graduate housing:* Room and/or apartments available to single students; on-campus housing not available to married students. Housing application deadline: 3/31. *Student services:* Campus employment opportunities, campus safety program, career counseling, child daycare facilities, free psychological counseling, international student services, low-cost health insurance. *Library facilities:* Van Houten Library plus 1 other. *Online resources:* library catalog, web page, access to other libraries' catalogs. *Collection:* 160,000 titles, 1,100 serial subscriptions. *Research affiliation:* Lucent Technologies (communications), Virginia Semiconductor, Inc. (semiconductors).

Computer facilities: 4,500 computers available on campus for general student use. A campuswide network can be accessed from student residence rooms and from off campus. *Web address:* http://www.njit.edu/.

General Application Contact: Kathryn Kelly, Director of Admissions, 973-596-3300, Fax: 973-596-3461, E-mail: admissions@njit.edu.

GRADUATE UNITS

Office of Graduate Studies Students: 1,253 full-time (382 women), 1,391 part-time (345 women); includes 584 minority (135 African Americans, 339 Asian Americans or Pacific Islanders, 108 Hispanic Americans, 2 Native Americans), 1,194 international. Average age 30. 5,061 applicants, 49% accepted, 847 enrolled. *Faculty:* 418 full-time (71 women), 272 part-time/adjunct (47 women). Expenses: Contact institution. *Financial support:* Fellowships with full and partial tuition reimbursements, research assistantships with full and partial tuition reimbursements, teaching assistantships with full and partial tuition reimbursements, career-related internships or fieldwork, Federal Work-Study, institutionally sponsored loans, and unspecified assistantships available. Financial award application deadline: 3/15. In 2001, 905 master's, 65 doctorates, 64 other advanced degrees awarded. *Degree program information:* Part-time and evening/weekend programs available. Offers applied mathematics (MS); applied physics (MS, PhD); applied statistics (MS); biology (MS, PhD); biomedical engineering (MS); chemical engineering (MS, PhD); chemistry (MS, PhD); civil engineering (MS, PhD); computational biology (MS); computer engineering (MS, PhD); electrical engineering (MS, PhD); engineering management (MS); engineering science (MS); environmental engineering (MS, PhD); environmental policy studies (MS, PhD); environmental science (MS, PhD); history (MA, MAT); history of technology, environment and medicine (MA); industrial/manufacturing engineering (MS, PhD); Internet engineering (MS); materials science and engineering (MS, PhD); mathematics science (PhD); mechanical engineering (MS, PhD, Engineer); occupational safety and health engineering (MS); occupational safety and industrial hygiene (MS); pharmaceutical engineering (MS); professional and technical communication (MS); public health (MS); transportation (MS, PhD). *Application deadline:* For fall admission, 6/5 (priority date); for spring admission, 10/15. Applications are processed on a rolling basis. Electronic applications accepted. *Application Contact:* Kathryn Kelly, Director of Admissions, 973-596-3300, Fax: 973-596-3461, E-mail: admissions@njit.edu. *Dean of Graduate Studies,* Dr. Ron Kane, 973-596-3462, Fax: 973-596-6479, E-mail: ronald.kane@njit.edu.

College of Computing Science Students: 466 full-time (166 women), 529 part-time (132 women); includes 238 minority (25 African Americans, 186 Asian Americans or Pacific Islanders, 26 Hispanic Americans, 1 Native American), 513 international. Average age 29. 1,942 applicants, 40% accepted, 278 enrolled. *Faculty:* 62 full-time (10 women). Expenses: Contact institution. *Financial support:* Fellowships with full and partial tuition reimbursements, research assistantships with full and partial tuition reimbursements, teaching assistantships with full and partial tuition reimbursements, career-related internships or fieldwork, Federal Work-Study, institutionally sponsored loans, and unspecified assistantships available. Financial award application deadline: 3/15. In 2001, 392 master's, 5 doctorates awarded. *Degree program information:* Part-time and evening/weekend programs available. Offers computer science (MS, PhD); information systems (MS, PhD); telecommunication (MS). *Application deadline:* For fall admission, 6/5 (priority date); for spring admission, 10/15. Applications are processed on a rolling basis. *Application fee:* $50. Electronic applications accepted. *Application Contact:* Kathryn Kelly, Director of Admissions, 973-596-3300, Fax: 973-596-3461, E-mail: admissions@njit.edu. *Dean,* Dr. Stephen B. Seidman, 973-596-5488, E-mail: stephen.siedman@njit.edu.

School of Architecture Students: 78 full-time (33 women), 28 part-time (12 women); includes 22 minority (5 African Americans, 10 Asian Americans or Pacific Islanders, 7 Hispanic Americans), 33 international. Average age 32. 173 applicants, 57% accepted, 50 enrolled. *Faculty:* 27 full-time (6 women). Expenses: Contact institution. *Financial support:* Fellowships with full and partial tuition reimbursements, research assistantships with full and partial tuition reimbursements, teaching assistantships with full and partial tuition reimbursements, career-related internships or fieldwork, Federal Work-Study, institutionally sponsored loans, and unspecified assistantships available. Financial award application deadline: 3/15. In 2001, 27 degrees awarded. *Degree program information:* Part-time and evening/weekend programs available. Offers architectural studies (MS); architecture (M Arch); infrastructure planning (MIP); urban system (PhD). *Application deadline:* For fall admission, 6/5 (priority date); for spring admission, 10/15. Applications are processed on a rolling basis. *Application fee:* $50. Electronic applications accepted. *Application Contact:* Kathryn Kelly, Director of Admissions, 973-596-3300, Fax: 973-596-3461, E-mail: admissions@njit.edu. *Dean,* Urs P. Gauchat, 973-596-3079, E-mail: urs.p.gauchat@njit.edu.

School of Management Students: 121 full-time (45 women), 201 part-time (71 women); includes 56 minority (18 African Americans, 25 Asian Americans or Pacific Islanders, 13 Hispanic Americans), 111 international. Average age 32. 346 applicants, 52% accepted, 111 enrolled. *Faculty:* 29 full-time (7 women). Expenses: Contact institution. *Financial support:* Fellowships with full and partial tuition reimbursements, research assistantships with full and partial tuition reimbursements, teaching assistantships with full and partial tuition reimbursements, career-related internships or fieldwork, Federal Work-Study, institutionally sponsored loans, and unspecified assistantships available. Financial award application deadline: 3/15. In 2001, 197 master's, 3 doctorates awarded. *Degree program information:* Part-time and evening/weekend programs available. Offers management of business administration (MBA); management of technology (MS, PhD). *Application deadline:* For fall admission, 6/5 (priority date); for spring admission, 10/15. Applications are processed on a rolling basis. *Application fee:* $50. Electronic applications accepted. *Application Contact:* Kathryn Kelly, Director of Admissions, 973-596-3300, Fax: 973-596-3461, E-mail: admissions@njit.edu. *Dean,* Mark Somers, 973-596-3279, E-mail: mark.somers@njit.edu.

NEWMAN THEOLOGICAL COLLEGE, Edmonton, AB T6V 1H3, Canada

General Information Independent-religious, coed, graduate-only institution. *Enrollment by degree level:* 59 first professional, 33 master's, 79 other advanced degrees. *Graduate faculty:* 9 full-time (3 women), 17 part-time/adjunct (6 women). *Graduate tuition:* Tuition and fees charges are reported in Canadian dollars. *Tuition:* Full-time $4,050 Canadian dollars; part-time $400 Canadian dollars per unit. One-time fee: $50 Canadian dollars full-time; $25 Canadian dollars part-time. *Graduate housing:* On-campus housing not available. *Student services:* Career counseling, exercise/wellness program. *Library facilities:* Library. *Online resources:* library catalog, access to other libraries' catalogs. *Collection:* 26,500 titles, 240 serial subscriptions, 210 audiovisual materials.

Computer facilities: 10 computers available on campus for general student use. A campuswide network can be accessed. Internet access, e-mail are available. *Web address:* http://www.newman.edu/.

General Application Contact: Sharon P. Gauthier, Registrar, 780-447-2993 Ext. 227, Fax: 78—447-2685, E-mail: registrar@newman.edu.

GRADUATE UNITS

Religious Education Program Tuition and fees charges are reported in Canadian dollars. *Degree program information:* Part-time programs available. Postbaccalaureate distance learning degree programs offered (no on-campus study). Offers Catholic school administration (CCSA); religious education (MRE, GDRE).

Theology Program Tuition and fees charges are reported in Canadian dollars. *Degree program information:* Part-time programs available. Offers theology (M Div, M Th, MTS).

NEWMAN UNIVERSITY, Wichita, KS 67213-2097

General Information Independent-religious, coed, comprehensive institution. *Graduate housing:* Rooms and/or apartments available on a first-come, first-served basis to single and married students. Housing application deadline: 8/1.

GRADUATE UNITS

Division of Nursing *Degree program information:* Part-time and evening/weekend programs available. Offers nurse anesthesia (MS); nursing (MS).

Graduate School of Social Work Offers social work (MSW).

Masters in Business Administration *Degree program information:* Part-time and evening/weekend programs available. Offers organizational leadership (MS).

Program in Education *Degree program information:* Part-time and evening/weekend programs available. Offers adult education (MS Ed); building leadership (MS Ed); elementary/middle-level education (MS Ed); English as a second language (MS Ed).

NEW MEXICO HIGHLANDS UNIVERSITY, Las Vegas, NM 87701

General Information State-supported, coed, comprehensive institution. CGS member. *Enrollment:* 310 full-time matriculated graduate/professional students (221 women), 319 part-time matriculated graduate/professional students (224 women). *Enrollment by degree level:* 629 master's. *Graduate faculty:* 109 full-time (44 women), 14 part-time/adjunct (11 women). Tuition, state resident: full-time $2,238. Tuition, nonresident: full-time $9,366. *Graduate housing:* Rooms and/or apartments available to single and married students. Typical cost: $2,952 per year ($4,112 including board) for single students; $3,580 per year for married students. Housing application deadline: 8/1. *Student services:* Career counseling, child daycare facilities, free psychological counseling, low-cost health insurance. *Library facilities:* Donnelly Library. *Online resources:* library catalog, web page, access to other libraries' catalogs. *Collection:* 429,978 titles, 47,100 serial subscriptions, 807 audiovisual materials.

Computer facilities: 500 computers available on campus for general student use. A campuswide network can be accessed from student residence rooms and from off campus. Internet access and online class registration are available. *Web address:* http://www.nmhu.edu/.

General Application Contact: Dr. Linda LaGrange, Associate Dean of Graduate Studies, 505-454-3266, Fax: 505-454-3558, E-mail: lagrange_l@nmhu.edu.

GRADUATE UNITS

Graduate Studies Students: 310 full-time (221 women), 319 part-time (224 women); includes 322 minority (20 African Americans, 4 Asian Americans or Pacific Islanders, 251 Hispanic Americans, 47 Native Americans), 26 international. Average age 36. *Faculty:* 109 full-time (44 women), 14 part-time/adjunct (11 women). Expenses: Contact institution. *Financial support:* Fellowships, research assistantships with full and partial tuition reimbursements, teaching assistantships with full and partial tuition reimbursements, career-related internships or fieldwork, Federal Work-Study, institutionally sponsored loans, and tuition waivers (full) available. Support available to part-time students. Financial award application deadline: 3/1. In 2001, 86 degrees awarded. *Degree program information:* Part-time programs available. *Application deadline:* For fall admission, 8/1 (priority date). Applications are processed on a rolling basis. *Application fee:* $15. *Application Contact:* Prescilla S. Ortega-Mathis, Administrative Assistant, 505-454-3266, Fax: 505-454-3558, E-mail: pmathis@nmhu.edu. *Associate Dean of Graduate Studies,* Dr. Linda LaGrange, 505-454-3266, Fax: 505-454-3558, E-mail: lagrange_l@nmhu.edu.

College of Arts and Sciences Students: 73 full-time (39 women), 53 part-time (35 women); includes 50 minority (6 African Americans, 2 Asian Americans or Pacific Islanders, 41 Hispanic Americans, 1 Native American), 19 international. Average age 34. *Faculty:* 62 full-time (23 women). Expenses: Contact institution. *Financial support:* Research assistantships with full and partial tuition reimbursements, teaching assistantships with full and partial tuition reimbursements, Federal Work-Study available. Financial award application deadline: 3/1. In 2001, 13 degrees awarded. *Degree program information:* Part-time programs available. Offers administration (MA); anthropology (MA); applied chemistry (MS); applied sociology (MA); arts and sciences (MA, MS); biology (MS); cognitive science (MA, MS); computer graphics (MA, MS); design studies (MA); digital audio and video production (MA); English (MA); environmental science and management (MS); Hispanic language and literature (MA); historical and cross-cultural perspective (MA); history and political science (MA); multimedia systems (MS); networking technology (MA, MS); political and governmental processes (MA); psychology (MS). *Application deadline:* For fall admission, 8/1 (priority date). Applications are processed on a rolling basis. *Application fee:* $15. Electronic applications accepted. *Application Contact:* Dr. Linda LaGrange, Associate Dean of Graduate Studies, 505-454-3266, Fax: 505-454-3558, E-mail: lagrange_l@nmhu.edu. *Dean,* Dr. Tomas Salazar, 505-454-3080, Fax: 505-454-3389, E-mail: salazar_t@nmhu.edu.

School of Business Students: 26 full-time (15 women), 57 part-time (35 women); includes 47 minority (41 Hispanic Americans, 6 Native Americans), 5 international. Average age 34. *Faculty:* 10 full-time (3 women). Expenses: Contact institution. *Financial support:* Research assistantships with full and partial tuition reimbursements, Federal Work-Study available. Financial award application deadline: 3/1. In 2001, 15 degrees awarded. Offers business (MBA). *Application deadline:* For fall admission, 8/1 (priority date). Applications are processed on a rolling basis. *Application fee:* $15. *Application Contact:* Dr. Linda LaGrange, Associate Dean of Graduate Studies, 505-454-3266, Fax: 505-454-3558, E-mail: lagrange_l@nmhu.edu. *Dean,* Dr. Margaret Young, 505-454-3344, Fax: 505-454-3354, E-mail: young_m@nmhu.edu.

School of Education Students: 45 full-time (30 women), 115 part-time (70 women); includes 100 minority (5 African Americans, 90 Hispanic Americans, 5 Native Americans) Average age 37. *Faculty:* 25 full-time (13 women), 1 part-time/adjunct (0 women). Expenses: Contact institution. *Financial support:* Research assistantships with full and partial tuition reimbursements, teaching assistantships with full and partial tuition reimbursements, Federal Work-Study available. Financial award application deadline: 3/1. In 2001, 14 degrees awarded. *Degree program information:* Part-time programs available. Offers curriculum and instruction (MA); education administration (MA); guidance and counseling (MA); human performance, leisure and sport (MA); special education (MA). *Application deadline:* For fall admission, 8/1 (priority date). Applications are processed on a rolling basis. *Application fee:* $15. *Application Contact:* Dr. Linda LaGrange, Associate Dean of Graduate Studies, 505-454-3266, Fax: 505-454-3558, E-mail: lagrange_l@nmhu.edu. *Dean,* Dr. James Abreu, 505-454-3357, Fax: 505-454-3384, E-mail: abreu_james@nmhu.edu.

School of Social Work Students: 166 full-time (137 women), 94 part-time (84 women); includes 125 minority (9 African Americans, 2 Asian Americans or Pacific Islanders, 79 Hispanic Americans, 35 Native Americans), 2 international. Average age 37. *Faculty:* 12 full-time (5 women), 13 part-time/adjunct (11 women). Expenses: Contact institution. *Financial support:* Research assistantships with full and partial tuition reimbursements, Federal Work-Study available. Financial award application deadline: 3/1. In 2001, 44 degrees awarded. *Degree program information:* Part-time programs available. Offers social work (MSW). *Application deadline:* For fall admission, 8/1 (priority date). Applications are processed on a rolling basis. *Application fee:* $15. *Application Contact:* Dr. Linda LaGrange, Associate Dean of Graduate Studies, 505-454-3266, Fax: 505-454-3558, E-mail: lagrange_l@nmhu.edu. *Dean,* Dr. Alfredo Garcia, 505-454-3307, Fax: 505-454-3290, E-mail: a_garcia@nmhu.edu.

NEW MEXICO INSTITUTE OF MINING AND TECHNOLOGY, Socorro, NM 87801

General Information State-supported, coed, university. *Enrollment:* 232 full-time matriculated graduate/professional students (71 women), 58 part-time matriculated graduate/professional students (30 women). *Enrollment by degree level:* 220 master's, 70 doctoral. *Graduate faculty:* 85 full-time, 9 part-time/adjunct. Tuition, state resident: part-time $1,084 per semester. Tuition, nonresident: part-time $4,367 per semester. *Required fees:* $429 per semester. *Graduate housing:* Rooms and/or apartments available on a first-come, first-served basis to single and married students. *Student services:* Campus employment opportunities, career counseling, child daycare facilities, disabled student services, free psychological counseling, grant writing training, international student services, low-cost health insurance, multicultural affairs office. *Library facilities:* New Mexico Tech Library plus 1 other. *Online resources:* web page. *Collection:* 89,725 titles, 766 serial subscriptions, 2,065 audiovisual materials. *Research affiliation:* National Center for Atmospheric Research, National Radio Astronomy Observatory, Joint Center for Materials Research.

Computer facilities: 225 computers available on campus for general student use. A campuswide network can be accessed from student residence rooms and from off campus. Internet access is available. *Web address:* http://www.nmt.edu/.

General Application Contact: Dr. David B. Johnson, Dean of Graduate Studies, 505-835-5513, Fax: 505-835-5476, E-mail: graduate@nmt.edu.

GRADUATE UNITS

Graduate Studies Students: 232 full-time (71 women), 58 part-time (30 women); includes 19 minority (2 Asian Americans or Pacific Islanders, 16 Hispanic Americans, 1 Native American), 103 international. Average age 30. 482 applicants, 72% accepted. Expenses: Contact institution. *Financial support:* In 2001–02, 122 research assistantships (averaging $9,670 per year), 61 teaching assistantships with full and partial tuition reimbursements (averaging $9,670 per year) were awarded. Fellowships, career-related internships or fieldwork, Federal Work-Study, and institutionally sponsored loans also available. Support available to part-time students. Financial award application deadline: 3/1; financial award applicants required to submit CSS PROFILE or FAFSA. In 2001, 58 master's, 11 doctorates awarded. Offers astrophysics (MS, PhD); atmospheric physics (MS, PhD); biochemistry (MS); biology (MS); chemistry (MS); computer science (MS, PhD); engineering science in mechanics (MS); environmental chemistry (PhD); environmental engineering (MS); explosives technology and atmospheric chemistry (PhD); geochemistry (MS, PhD); geology (MS, PhD); geology and geochemistry (MS, PhD); geophysics (MS, PhD); hydrology (MS, PhD); instrumentation (MS); material engineering (MS, PhD); mathematical physics (PhD); mathematics (MS); operations research (MS); petroleum engineering (MS, PhD); science teaching (MST). *Application deadline:* For fall admission, 3/1 (priority date); for spring admission, 6/1. Applications are processed on a rolling basis. *Application fee:* $16. Electronic applications accepted. *Application Contact:* Mary C. Watson-Finley, Administrative Secretary, 505-835-5513, Fax: 505-835-5476, E-mail: mwatson@admin.nmt.edu. *Dean,* Dr. David B. Johnson, 505-835-5513, Fax: 505-835-5476, E-mail: graduate@nmt.edu.

See in-depth description on page 991.

NEW MEXICO STATE UNIVERSITY, Las Cruces, NM 88003-8001

General Information State-supported, coed, university. CGS member. *Enrollment:* 1,276 full-time matriculated graduate/professional students (638 women), 932 part-time matriculated graduate/professional students (528 women). *Enrollment by degree level:* 1,602 master's, 554 doctoral, 52 other advanced degrees. *Graduate faculty:* 482 full-time (133 women), 105 part-time/adjunct (26 women). Tuition, state resident: full-time $3,234; part-time $135 per credit. Tuition, nonresident: full-time $9,420; part-time $428 per credit. *Required fees:* $858. *Graduate housing:* Rooms and/or apartments available on a first-come, first-served basis to single students and available to married students. Typical cost: $2,216 per year ($4,296 including board) for single students. *Student services:* Campus employment opportunities, campus safety program, career counseling, disabled student services, free psychological counseling, international student services, low-cost health insurance. *Library facilities:* New Library plus 1 other. *Online resources:* library catalog, web page. *Collection:* 11,784 serial subscriptions, 320 audiovisual materials. *Research affiliation:* Astrophysical Research Consortium, Corporation for Public Broadcasting, Sandia National Laboratories, Los Alamos National Laboratory, Jet Propulsion Laboratory, Westinghouse Corporation.

Computer facilities: 500 computers available on campus for general student use. A campuswide network can be accessed from student residence rooms and from off campus. Internet access and online class registration are available. *Web address:* http://www.nmsu.edu/.

General Application Contact: Christine Marlow, Associate Dean of the Graduate School, 505-646-5746, Fax: 505-646-7721, E-mail: cmarlow@nmsu.edu.

GRADUATE UNITS

Graduate School Students: 1,276 full-time (638 women), 932 part-time (528 women); includes 621 minority (37 African Americans, 35 Asian Americans or Pacific Islanders, 523 Hispanic Americans, 26 Native Americans), 440 international. Average age 34. 1,217 applicants, 69% accepted, 387 enrolled. *Faculty:* 486 full-time (133 women), 105 part-time/adjunct (26 women). Expenses: Contact institution. *Financial support:* In 2001–02, 225 research assistantships, 609 teaching assistantships were awarded. Fellowships, career-related internships or fieldwork, Federal Work-Study, scholarships/grants, and traineeships also available. Support available to part-time students. In 2001, 551 master's, 79 doctorates, 3 other advanced degrees awarded. *Degree program information:* Part-time and evening/weekend programs available. Postbaccalaureate distance learning degree programs offered (no on-campus study). Offers interdisciplinary studies (MA, MS, PhD); molecular biology (MS, PhD). *Application fee:* $15 ($35 for international students). Electronic applications accepted. *Application Contact:* Christine Marlow, Associate Dean of the Graduate School, 505-646-5746, Fax: 505-646-7721, E-mail: cmarlow@nmsu.edu. *Dean,* Dr. Linda Lacey, 505-646-5746, Fax: 505-646-7721, E-mail: lacey@nmsu.edu.

College of Agriculture and Home Economics Students: 145 full-time (64 women), 89 part-time (46 women); includes 45 minority (4 Asian Americans or Pacific Islanders, 37 Hispanic Americans, 4 Native Americans), 51 international. Average age 33. 91 applicants, 55% accepted, 37 enrolled. *Faculty:* 94 full-time (28 women), 21 part-time/adjunct (1 woman). Expenses: Contact institution. *Financial support:* In 2001–02, 63 research assistantships, 46 teaching assistantships were awarded. Career-related internships or fieldwork and Federal Work-Study also available. Support available to part-time students. Financial award application deadline: 3/1. In 2001, 54 master's, 11 doctorates awarded. *Degree program information:* Part-time and evening/weekend programs available. Offers agricultural economics (MS); agriculture and extension education (MA); agriculture and home economics (M Ag, MA, MS, PhD); animal science (M Ag, MS, PhD); economics (MA); entomology, plant pathology and weed science (MS); family and consumer sciences (MS); general agronomy (MS, PhD); horticulture (MS, PhD); range science (M Ag, MS, PhD); wildlife science (MS). *Application deadline:* For spring admission, 11/1. Applications are processed on a rolling basis. *Application fee:* $15 ($35 for international students). Electronic applications accepted. *Dean,* Dr. Jerry Schickedanz, 505-646-1806, Fax: 505-646-5975, E-mail: agdean@nmsu.edu.

College of Arts and Sciences Students: 527 full-time (255 women), 179 part-time (90 women); includes 127 minority (12 African Americans, 14 Asian Americans or Pacific Islanders, 96 Hispanic Americans, 5 Native Americans), 176 international. Average age 30. 525 applicants, 73% accepted, 160 enrolled. *Faculty:* 205 full-time (56 women), 47 part-time/adjunct (11 women). Expenses: Contact institution. *Financial support:* In 2001–02, 85 research assistantships, 346 teaching assistantships were awarded. Fellowships, career-related internships or fieldwork, Federal Work-Study, and scholarships/grants also available. Support available to part-time students. In 2001, 131 master's, 22 doctorates awarded. *Degree program information:* Part-time programs available. Postbaccalaureate distance learning degree programs offered. Offers anthropology (MA); art (MA, MFA); arts and sciences (MA, MAG, MCJ, MFA, MM, MPA, MS, PhD); astronomy (MS, PhD); biology (MS, PhD); chemistry and biochemistry (MS, PhD); communication studies (MA); computer science (MS, PhD); creative writing (MFA); criminal justice (MCJ); English (MA, PhD); geography (MAG); geological sciences (MS); government (MA, MPA); history (MA); mathematical sciences (MS, PhD); music (MM); physics (MS, PhD); psychology (MA, PhD); sociology (MA); Spanish (MA). *Application fee:* $15 ($35 for international students). Electronic applications accepted. *Interim Dean,* Dr. Jeffrey Brown, 505-646-2001, Fax: 505-646-6096, E-mail: jbrown@nmsu.edu.

College of Business Administration and Economics Students: 87 full-time (36 women), 63 part-time (27 women); includes 34 minority (5 African Americans, 2 Asian Americans or Pacific Islanders, 25 Hispanic Americans, 2 Native Americans), 36 international. Average age 32. 86 applicants, 55% accepted, 41 enrolled. *Faculty:* 63 full-time (13 women), 7 part-time/adjunct (3 women). Expenses: Contact institution. *Financial support:* In 2001–02, 5 research assistantships, 53 teaching assistantships were awarded. Fellowships, career-related internships or fieldwork, Federal Work-Study, institutionally sponsored loans, scholarships/grants, and unspecified assistantships also available. Support available to part-time students. Financial award application deadline: 3/1. In 2001, 71 master's, 7 doctorates awarded. *Degree program information:* Part-time programs available. Offers accounting and business computer systems (M Acct); business administration (MBA); business administration and economics (M Acct, MA, MBA, MS, PhD); economics (MA, MBA, MS); experimental statistics (MS); management (PhD); marketing (PhD). *Application deadline:* For fall admission, 7/1 (priority date); for spring admission, 11/1. Applications are processed on a rolling basis. *Application fee:* $15 ($35 for international students). Electronic applications accepted. *Dean,* Dr. Danny Arnold, 505-646-2821, Fax: 505-646-6155, E-mail: darnold@nmsu.edu.

College of Education Students: 219 full-time (156 women), 445 part-time (310 women); includes 293 minority (13 African Americans, 6 Asian Americans or Pacific Islanders, 266 Hispanic Americans, 8 Native Americans), 23 international. Average age 38. 111 applicants, 64% accepted, 50 enrolled. *Faculty:* 41 full-time (21 women), 14 part-time/adjunct (6 women). Expenses: Contact institution. *Financial support:* In 2001–02, 10 research assistantships, 56 teaching assistantships were awarded. Fellowships, career-related internships or fieldwork and Federal Work-Study also available. Support available to part-time students. Financial award application deadline: 3/1. In 2001, 141 master's, 24 doctorates, 3 other advanced degrees awarded. *Degree program information:* Part-time and evening/weekend programs available. Postbaccalaureate distance learning degree programs offered (minimal on-campus study). Offers counseling and guidance (MA, Ed S); counseling psychology (PhD); curriculum and instruction (MAT, Ed D, PhD, Ed S); education (MA, MAT, Ed D, PhD, Ed S); educational administration (MA, PhD, Ed S); educational management and development (Ed D); general education (MA); reading (Ed S); special education/communication disorders (MA). *Application deadline:* Applications are processed on a rolling basis. *Application fee:* $15 ($35 for international students). Electronic applications accepted. *Dean,* Dr. Robert Moulton, 505-646-3404, Fax: 505-646-6032, E-mail: moulton@nmsu.edu.

College of Engineering Students: 180 full-time (36 women), 109 part-time (19 women); includes 58 minority (2 African Americans, 6 Asian Americans or Pacific Islanders, 46 Hispanic Americans, 4 Native Americans), 137 international. Average age 30. 327 applicants, 75% accepted, 71 enrolled. *Faculty:* 59 full-time (3 women), 11 part-time/adjunct (2 women). Expenses: Contact institution. *Financial support:* In 2001–02, 54 research assistantships, 79 teaching assistantships were awarded. Fellowships, career-related internships or fieldwork and Federal Work-Study also available. Support available to part-time students. Financial award application deadline: 3/1. In 2001, 97 master's, 12 doctorates awarded. *Degree program information:* Part-time programs available. Offers chemical engineering (MS Ch E, PhD); civil engineering (MSCE, PhD); electrical and computer engineering (MSEE, PhD); engineering (MS Ch E, MS Env E, MSCE, MSEE, MSIE, MSME, PhD); environmental engineering (MS Env E); industrial engineering (MSIE, PhD); mechanical engineering (MSME, PhD). *Application deadline:* For fall admission, 7/1 (priority date); for spring admission, 11/1. Applications are processed on a rolling basis. *Application fee:* $15 ($35 for international students). Electronic applications accepted. *Interim Dean,* Dr. Kenneth White, 505-646-2914, Fax: 505-646-3549, E-mail: krwhite@nmsu.edu.

College of Health and Social Services Students: 91 full-time (74 women), 40 part-time (33 women); includes 56 minority (4 African Americans, 2 Asian Americans or Pacific Islanders, 49 Hispanic Americans, 1 Native American), 6 international. Average age 34. 47 applicants, 64% accepted, 19 enrolled. *Faculty:* 20 full-time (12 women), 5 part-time/adjunct (3 women). Expenses: Contact institution. *Financial support:* In 2001–02, 6 research assistantships, 16 teaching assistantships were awarded. Fellowships, career-related internships or fieldwork, Federal Work-Study, scholarships/grants, and traineeships also available. Financial award application deadline: 3/1. In 2001, 52 degrees awarded. *Degree program information:* Part-time and evening/weekend programs available. Postbaccalaureate distance learning degree programs offered. Offers health and social services (MPH, MSN, MSW); health science (MPH); nursing (MSN); social work (MSW). *Application deadline:* For fall admission, 7/1 (priority date). Applications are processed on a rolling basis. *Application fee:* $15 ($35 for international students). Electronic applications accepted. *Application Contact:* Dr. Larry K. Olsen, Associate Dean, 505-646-3526, E-mail: lolsen@nmsu.edu. *Dean,* Dr. Jeffrey Brandon, 505-646-3526, Fax: 505-646-6166, E-mail: jbrandon@nmsu.edu.

NEW ORLEANS BAPTIST THEOLOGICAL SEMINARY, New Orleans, LA 70126-4858

General Information Independent-religious, coed, primarily men, comprehensive institution. *Graduate housing:* Rooms and/or apartments available to single and married students.

GRADUATE UNITS

Graduate and Professional Programs *Degree program information:* Evening/weekend programs available. Offers biblical studies (M Div, D Min, PhD); Christian education (M Div, MACE, D Min, DEM, PhD); church music ministries (MMCM, DMA); pastoral ministries (M Div, MAMFC, D Min, PhD); theological and historical studies (M Div, D Min, PhD); theology (M Div, MACE, MAMFC, MMCM, D Min, DEM, DMA, PhD).

NEWSCHOOL OF ARCHITECTURE & DESIGN, San Diego, CA 92101-6634

General Information Proprietary, coed, primarily men, comprehensive institution. *Graduate housing:* On-campus housing not available. *Research affiliation:* Center City Development Corporation.

GRADUATE UNITS

Program in Architecture *Degree program information:* Part-time and evening/weekend programs available. Offers architecture (M Arch, MS).

NEW SCHOOL UNIVERSITY, New York, NY 10011-8603

General Information Independent, coed, university. *Enrollment by degree level:* 2,649 master's, 471 doctoral. *Graduate faculty:* 103 full-time, 423 part-time/adjunct. *Tuition:* Full-time $18,720; part-time $1,040 per credit. *Required fees:* $450; $115 per term. Tuition and fees vary according to program. *Graduate housing:* Rooms and/or apartments available on a first-come, first-served basis to single students and available to married students. Typical cost: $6,984 per year ($9,612 including board) for married students. Housing application deadline: 5/1. *Student services:* Campus employment opportunities, campus safety program, career counseling, disabled student services, free psychological counseling, grant writing training, international student services, low-cost health insurance, multicultural affairs office, teacher training, writing training. *Web address:* http://www.newschool.edu/.

General Application Contact: Emily Johnson, Information Contact, 877-5AVE-321, E-mail: customer@newschool.edu.

GRADUATE UNITS

Actors Studio Drama School Students: 204 full-time (111 women), 5 part-time (1 woman); includes 29 minority (4 African Americans, 10 Asian Americans or Pacific Islanders, 15 Hispanic Americans), 27 international. Average age 28. 250 applicants, 45% accepted, 71 enrolled. Expenses: Contact institution. *Financial support:* In 2001–02, 187 students received support; fellowships with full tuition reimbursements available, research assistantships, teaching assistantships, Federal Work-Study, institutionally sponsored loans, scholarships/grants, and tuition waivers (partial) available. Financial award application deadline: 3/1; financial award applicants required to submit FAFSA. In 2001, 73 degrees awarded. Offers acting (MFA); directing (MFA); playwriting (MFA). *Application deadline:* For fall admission, 1/10 (priority date). *Application fee:* $40. *Application Contact:* Lisa Formosa, Director of Admissions, 212-229-5859, E-mail: formosal@newschool.edu. *Dean,* James Lipton, 212-229-5612.

Graduate Faculty of Political and Social Science Students: 857 full-time (433 women), 184 part-time (105 women); includes 161 minority (56 African Americans, 39 Asian Americans or Pacific Islanders, 63 Hispanic Americans, 3 Native Americans), 304 international. Average age 34. 761 applicants, 87% accepted, 216 enrolled. *Faculty:* 64 full-time, 19 part-time/adjunct. Expenses: Contact institution. *Financial support:* In 2001–02, 77 fellowships with full and partial tuition reimbursements (averaging $5,800 per year), 59 research assistantships with full and partial tuition reimbursements (averaging $4,700 per year), 67 teaching assistantships with full and partial tuition reimbursements (averaging $2,400 per year) were awarded. Career-related internships or fieldwork, Federal Work-Study, scholarships/grants, and tuition waivers (full and partial) also available. Financial award application deadline: 1/15; financial award applicants required to submit FAFSA. In 2001, 101 master's, 51 doctorates awarded. *Degree program information:* Part-time and evening/weekend programs available. Offers anthropology (MA, DS Sc, PhD); clinical psychology (PhD); economics (MA, DS Sc, PhD); general psychology (MA, PhD); historical studies (MA, PhD); liberal studies (MA); philosophy (MA, DS Sc, PhD); political and social science (MA, MS Sc, DS Sc, PhD); political science (MA, DS Sc, PhD); psychoanalytic studies (MS Sc); sociology (MA, DS Sc, PhD). *Application deadline:* For fall admission, 1/15 (priority date). Applications are processed on a rolling basis. *Application fee:* $40. *Application Contact:* Emanuel Lomax, Director of Admissions, 800-523-5411, Fax: 212-989-7102, E-mail: gfadmit@newschool.edu. *Dean,* Dr. Kenneth Prewitt, 212-229-5777.

New School Students: 377 full-time (262 women), 246 part-time (163 women); includes 129 minority (47 African Americans, 33 Asian Americans or Pacific Islanders, 47 Hispanic Americans, 2 Native Americans), 122 international. Average age 31. 675 applicants, 60% accepted, 257 enrolled. *Faculty:* 1 full-time, 105 part-time/adjunct. Expenses: Contact institution. *Financial support:* In 2001–02, 480 students received support, including 16 research assistantships (averaging $4,600 per year); fellowships, teaching assistantships, career-related internships or fieldwork, Federal Work-Study, institutionally sponsored loans, scholarships/grants, and tuition waivers (full and partial) also available. Support available to part-time students. Financial award applicants required to submit FAFSA. In 2001, 172 degrees awarded. *Degree program information:* Part-time and evening/weekend programs available. Postbaccalaureate distance learning degree programs offered (no on-campus study). Offers communication theory (MA); creative writing (MFA); global management, trade, and finance (MA, MS); international development (MA, MS); international media and communication (MA, MS); international politics and diplomacy (MA, MS); media studies (MA); service, civic, and non-profit management (MA, MS); teacher education (MST). *Application deadline:* Applications are processed on a rolling basis. *Application fee:* $40. *Dean,* Ann Louise Shapiro, 212-229-5613.

Parsons School of Design Students: 347 full-time (209 women), 75 part-time (71 women); includes 61 minority (14 African Americans, 28 Asian Americans or Pacific Islanders, 18 Hispanic Americans, 1 Native American), 172 international. Average age 31. 780 applicants, 59% accepted, 221 enrolled. Expenses: Contact institution. *Financial support:* In 2001–02, 248 students received support; fellowships, career-related internships or fieldwork, Federal Work-Study, institutionally sponsored loans, scholarships/grants, tuition waivers (partial), and unspecified assistantships available. Support available to part-time students. Financial award application deadline: 4/1; financial award applicants required to submit FAFSA. In 2001, 123 degrees awarded. Offers architecture (M Arch); design (M Arch, MA, MFA, MS Ed); design and technology (MFA); history of decorative arts (MA); lighting design (MFA); painting (MFA); sculpture (MFA). *Application deadline:* For fall admission, 3/1 (priority date). Applications are processed on a rolling basis. *Application fee:* $40. *Application Contact:* Nadine M. Bourgeois, Assistant Dean and Director of Admissions, 212-229-8910, Fax: 212-229-8975, E-mail: bourgeon@newschool.edu. *Dean,* H. Randolph Swearer, 212-229-8950.

Robert J. Milano Graduate School of Management and Urban Policy Students: 202 full-time (149 women), 462 part-time (359 women); includes 284 minority (173 African Americans, 33 Asian Americans or Pacific Islanders, 77 Hispanic Americans, 1 Native American), 26 international. Average age 34. 379 applicants, 86% accepted. *Faculty:* 24 full-time, 48 part-time/adjunct. Expenses: Contact institution. *Financial support:* In 2001–02, 387 students received support, including 19 fellowships (averaging $10,422 per year), 5 research assistantships (averaging $10,000 per year); teaching assistantships, career-related internships or fieldwork, Federal Work-Study, scholarships/grants, and tuition waivers (full and partial) also available. Support available to part-time students. Financial award application deadline: 3/1; financial award applicants required to submit FAFSA. In 2001, 13 degrees awarded. *Degree program information:* Part-time and evening/weekend programs available. Postbaccalaureate distance learning degree programs offered (minimal on-campus study). Offers career planning and development (Adv C); health services management and policy (MS); human resources management (MS); management and urban policy (MS, PhD, Adv C); medical group practice management (Adv C); nonprofit management (MS); organization development (Adv C); organizational change management (MS); public and urban policy (PhD); training and development (Adv C); urban policy analysis and management (MS). *Application deadline:* For fall admission, 9/1 (priority date). Applications are processed on a rolling basis. *Application fee:* $30. *Application Contact:* Mario Johnson, Director of Admissions, 212-229-5462, Fax: 212-229-8935, E-mail: mgsinfo@newschool.edu. *Dean,* Dr. Edward J. Blakely, 212-229-5311 Ext. 1222, Fax: 212-229-8935.

See in-depth description on page 993.

NEW YORK CHIROPRACTIC COLLEGE, Seneca Falls, NY 13148-0800

General Information Independent, coed, graduate-only institution. *Enrollment by degree level:* 729 first professional. *Graduate faculty:* 45 full-time (21 women), 36 part-time/adjunct (12 women). *Tuition:* Full-time $11,700. *Graduate housing:* Rooms and/or apartments available on a first-come, first-served basis to single and married students. Typical cost: $3,400 per year ($5,000 including board) for single students; $4,250 per year for married students. Room and board charges vary according to board plan. *Student services:* Campus employment opportunities, campus safety program, career counseling, disabled student services, exercise/wellness program, free psychological counseling, low-cost health insurance. *Library facilities:* New York Chiropractic College Library. *Online resources:* library catalog, web page. *Collection:* 30,532 titles, 265 serial subscriptions, 35,855 audiovisual materials. *Research affiliation:* Foot Levelers, Inc. (gait research), Foundation for Chiropractic Education and Research (bio-med/chiropractic research), Consortium Center of Chiropractic Research/National Institutes of Health (neuroscience).

Computer facilities: 75 computers available on campus for general student use. A campuswide network can be accessed from student residence rooms and from off campus. Internet access is available. *Web address:* http://www.nycc.edu/.

General Application Contact: Diane Dixon, Executive Director of Enrollment Management, 315-568-3065, Fax: 315-568-3015, E-mail: enrolnow@nycc.edu.

GRADUATE UNITS

Professional Program Students: 726 full-time (239 women), 3 part-time; includes 65 minority (17 African Americans, 23 Asian Americans or Pacific Islanders, 24 Hispanic Americans, 1 Native American), 144 international. Average age 26. 286 applicants, 80% accepted, 113 enrolled. *Faculty:* 45 full-time (21 women), 36 part-time/adjunct (12 women). Expenses: Contact institution. *Financial support:* In 2001–02, 670 students received support. Federal Work-Study, institutionally sponsored loans, and scholarships/grants available. Financial award application deadline: 4/15; financial award applicants required to submit FAFSA. In 2001, 232 degrees awarded. Offers chiropractic (DC). *Application deadline:* Applications are processed on a rolling basis. *Application fee:* $60. Electronic applications accepted. *Application Contact:* Diane Dixon, Executive Director of Enrollment Management, 315-568-3065, Fax: 315-568-3015, E-mail: enrolnow@nycc.edu. *Chief Financial Officer and Controller,* Sean Anglim, 315-568-3092, Fax: 315-568-3012, E-mail: sanglim@nycc.edu.

THE NEW YORK COLLEGE OF HEALTH PROFESSIONS, Syosset, NY 11791-4413

General Information Independent, coed. *Enrollment:* 151 full-time matriculated graduate/professional students (85 women), 97 part-time matriculated graduate/professional students (58 women). *Enrollment by degree level:* 248 master's. *Graduate faculty:* 11 full-time (4 women), 23 part-time/adjunct (6 women). *Tuition:* Full-time $9,900; part-time $275 per credit. Tuition and fees vary according to program. *Graduate housing:* On-campus housing not available. *Student services:* Campus employment opportunities, campus safety program, career counseling, international student services. *Library facilities:* James and Lenore Jacobson Library at the New Center. *Online resources:* library catalog. *Collection:* 4,600 titles, 100 serial subscriptions. *Research affiliation:* North Shore Hospital (acupuncture).

Computer facilities: 3 computers available on campus for general student use. *Web address:* http://www.nycollege.edu/.

General Application Contact: Joe Bubenas, Director of Admissions, 516-364-0808 Ext. 232, Fax: 516-364-0989, E-mail: jbubenas@nycollege.edu.

GRADUATE UNITS

School for Oriental Medicine Students: 151 full-time (85 women), 97 part-time (58 women); includes 39 minority (10 African Americans, 17 Asian Americans or Pacific Islanders, 11 Hispanic Americans, 1 Native American) Average age 37. 97 applicants, 75% accepted. *Faculty:* 11 full-time (4 women), 23 part-time/adjunct (6 women). Expenses: Contact institution. *Financial support:* In 2001–02, 2 students received support. Federal Work-Study and scholarships/grants available. Support available to part-time students. Financial award applicants required to submit FAFSA. *Degree program information:* Part-time programs available. Offers acupuncture (MS); Oriental medicine (MS). *Application deadline:* For fall admission, 8/1 (priority date); for winter admission, 12/1 (priority date); for spring admission, 4/1 (priority date). Applications are processed on a rolling basis. *Application fee:* $85. *Application Contact:* Joe Bubenas, Director of Admissions, 516-364-0808 Ext. 232, Fax: 516-364-0989, E-mail: jbubenas@nycollege.edu. *Dean,* 516-364-0808, Fax: 516-364-0989.

NEW YORK COLLEGE OF PODIATRIC MEDICINE, New York, NY 10035-1815

General Information Independent, coed, graduate-only institution. *Graduate housing:* Rooms and/or apartments available to single and married students.

GRADUATE UNITS

Professional Program Offers podiatric medicine (DPM).

NEW YORK INSTITUTE OF TECHNOLOGY, Old Westbury, NY 11568-8000

General Information Independent, coed, comprehensive institution. CGS member. *Enrollment:* 1,897 full-time matriculated graduate/professional students (868 women), 1,488 part-time matriculated graduate/professional students (759 women). *Enrollment by degree level:* 1,075 first professional, 2,310 master's. *Graduate faculty:* 260 full-time (79 women), 519 part-time/adjunct (188 women). *Tuition:* Part-time $545 per credit. Tuition and fees vary according to course load, degree level, program and student level. *Graduate housing:* Room and/or apartments available on a first-come, first-served basis to single students; on-campus housing not available to married students. Typical cost: $3,880 per year ($6,880 including board). Room and board charges vary according to board plan, campus/location and housing facility selected. *Student services:* Campus employment opportunities, career counseling, disabled student services, exercise/wellness program, free psychological counseling, international student services, low-cost health insurance, multicultural affairs office, teacher training, writing training. *Library facilities:* George and Gertrude Wisser Memorial Library plus 4 others. *Online resources:* library catalog, web page. *Collection:* 213,646 titles, 2,971 serial subscriptions, 44,448 audiovisual materials.

Computer facilities: 634 computers available on campus for general student use. A campuswide network can be accessed from student residence rooms and from off campus. Internet access, e-mail are available. *Web address:* http://www.nyit.edu/.

General Application Contact: Jacquelyn Nealon, Dean of Admissions and Financial Aid, 516-686-7925, Fax: 516-686-7613, E-mail: jnealon@nyit.edu.

GRADUATE UNITS

Graduate Division Students: 822 full-time (340 women), 1,488 part-time (759 women); includes 302 minority (114 African Americans, 132 Asian Americans or Pacific Islanders, 54 Hispanic Americans, 2 Native Americans), 570 international. Average age 32. 1,250 applicants, 70% accepted, 328 enrolled. *Faculty:* 233 full-time (79 women), 519 part-time/adjunct (188 women). Expenses: Contact institution. *Financial support:* Fellowships with partial tuition reimbursements, research assistantships with partial tuition reimbursements, career-related internships or fieldwork, Federal Work-Study, institutionally sponsored loans, tuition waivers (full and partial), and unspecified assistantships available. Support available to part-time students. Financial award applicants required to submit FAFSA. In 2001, 743 master's, 1 other advanced degree awarded. *Degree program information:* Part-time and evening/weekend programs available. Postbaccalaureate distance learning degree programs offered (minimal on-campus study). *Application deadline:* For fall admission, 7/1 (priority date); for spring admission, 12/1 (priority date). Applications are processed on a rolling basis. *Application fee:* $50. Electronic applications accepted. *Application Contact:* Jacquelyn Nealon, Dean of Admissions and Financial Aid, 516-686-7925, Fax: 516-686-7613, E-mail: jnealon@nyit.edu. *Vice President for Academic Affairs,* Dr. Alexandra W. Logue, 516-686-7631, Fax: 516-686-7631, E-mail: alogue@nyit.edu.

School of Allied Health and Life Sciences Students: 160 full-time (105 women), 42 part-time (26 women); includes 46 minority (18 African Americans, 20 Asian Americans or Pacific Islanders, 8 Hispanic Americans), 14 international. Average age 28. 85 applicants, 71% accepted, 31 enrolled. Expenses: Contact institution. *Financial support:* In 2001–02, 4 research assistantships with partial tuition reimbursements were awarded; fellowships, career-related internships or fieldwork, institutionally sponsored loans, tuition waivers (full and partial), and unspecified assistantships also available. Support available to part-time students. Financial award applicants required to submit FAFSA. In 2001, 74 degrees awarded. *Degree program information:* Part-time and evening/weekend programs available. Postbaccalaureate distance learning degree programs offered. Offers allied health and life sciences (MPS, MS); clinical nutrition (MS); human relations (MPS); occupational therapy (MS); physical therapy (MS). *Application deadline:* For fall admission, 7/1 (priority date); for spring admission, 12/1 (priority date). Applications are processed on a rolling basis. *Application fee:* $50. Electronic applications accepted. *Application Contact:* Jacquelyn Nealon, Dean of Admissions and Financial Aid, 516-686-7925, Fax: 516-686-7613, E-mail: jnealon@nyit.edu. *Dean,* Dr. Barbara Ross-Lee, 516-686-3889, Fax: 516-686-3854, E-mail: brosslee@nyit.edu.

School of Architecture Students: 5 full-time (0 women), 1 (woman) part-time, 4 international. Average age 32. 26 applicants, 42% accepted, 3 enrolled. Expenses: Contact institution. *Financial support:* Research assistantships with partial tuition reimbursements, institutionally sponsored loans and tuition waivers (full and partial) available. Support available to part-time students. Financial award applicants required to submit FAFSA. In 2001, 2 degrees awarded. *Degree program information:* Part-time programs available. Offers urban and regional design (M Arch). *Application deadline:* For fall admission, 7/1 (priority date); for spring admission, 12/1 (priority date). Applications are processed on a rolling basis. *Application fee:* $50. Electronic applications accepted. *Application Contact:* Jacquelyn Nealon, Dean of Admissions and Financial Aid, 516-686-7925, Fax: 516-686-7613, E-mail: jnealon@nyit.edu. *Dean,* Judith DiMaio, 516-686-7594, Fax: 516-686-7921, E-mail: jdimaio@nyit.edu.

School of Arts, Sciences, and Communication Students: 88 full-time (41 women), 111 part-time (70 women); includes 25 minority (8 African Americans, 8 Asian Americans or

New York Institute of Technology (continued)

Pacific Islanders, 9 Hispanic Americans), 97 international. Average age 29. 115 applicants, 83% accepted, 60 enrolled. Expenses: Contact institution. *Financial support:* In 2001–02, 2 research assistantships with partial tuition reimbursements were awarded; career-related internships or fieldwork, Federal Work-Study, institutionally sponsored loans, tuition waivers (partial), and unspecified assistantships also available. Support available to part-time students. Financial award applicants required to submit FAFSA. In 2001, 109 degrees awarded. *Degree program information:* Part-time and evening/weekend programs available. Offers arts, sciences, and communication (MA); communication arts (MA). *Application deadline:* For fall admission, 7/1 (priority date); for spring admission, 12/1 (priority date). Applications are processed on a rolling basis. *Application fee:* $50. Electronic applications accepted. *Application Contact:* Jacquelyn Nealon, Dean of Admissions and Financial Aid, 516-686-7925, Fax: 516-686-7613, E-mail: jnealon@nyit.edu. *Dean*, Dr. Robert C. Vogt, 516-686-7700, Fax: 516-626-3655.

School of Education and Professional Services Students: 22 full-time (16 women), 488 part-time (336 women); includes 45 minority (25 African Americans, 3 Asian Americans or Pacific Islanders, 17 Hispanic Americans), 6 international. Average age 34. 225 applicants, 74% accepted, 99 enrolled. Expenses: Contact institution. *Financial support:* In 2001–02, 8 research assistantships with partial tuition reimbursements were awarded; career-related internships or fieldwork, institutionally sponsored loans, and tuition waivers (full and partial) also available. Support available to part-time students. Financial award applicants required to submit FAFSA. In 2001, 217 master's, 1 other advanced degree awarded. *Degree program information:* Part-time and evening/weekend programs available. Postbaccalaureate distance learning degree programs offered. Offers distance learning (Advanced Certificate); district leadership and technology (Professional Diploma); education and professional services (MS, Advanced Certificate, Professional Diploma); elementary education (MS); instructional technology (MS); mental health counseling (MS); multimedia (Advanced Certificate); school counseling (MS); school leadership and technology (Professional Diploma). *Application deadline:* For fall admission, 7/1 (priority date); for spring admission, 12/1 (priority date). Applications are processed on a rolling basis. *Application fee:* $50. Electronic applications accepted. *Application Contact:* Jacquelyn Nealon, Dean of Admissions and Financial Aid, 516-686-7925, Fax: 516-686-7613, E-mail: jnealon@nyit.edu. *Dean*, Dr. Helen Greene, 516-686-7706, Fax: 516-686-7655.

School of Engineering and Technology Students: 268 full-time (66 women), 279 part-time (53 women); includes 96 minority (23 African Americans, 66 Asian Americans or Pacific Islanders, 7 Hispanic Americans), 268 international. Average age 33. 456 applicants, 65% accepted, 113 enrolled. Expenses: Contact institution. *Financial support:* In 2001–02, 42 research assistantships with partial tuition reimbursements were awarded; fellowships, career-related internships or fieldwork, institutionally sponsored loans, tuition waivers (full and partial), and unspecified assistantships also available. Support available to part-time students. Financial award applicants required to submit FAFSA. In 2001, 150 degrees awarded. *Degree program information:* Part-time and evening/weekend programs available. Postbaccalaureate distance learning degree programs offered. Offers computer science (MS); electrical engineering and computer engineering (MS); energy management (MS); energy technology (Advanced Certificate); engineering and technology (MS, Advanced Certificate); environmental management (Advanced Certificate); environmental technology (MS); facilities management (Advanced Certificate). *Application deadline:* For fall admission, 7/1 (priority date); for spring admission, 12/1 (priority date). Applications are processed on a rolling basis. *Application fee:* $50. Electronic applications accepted. *Application Contact:* Jacquelyn Nealon, Dean of Admissions and Financial Aid, 516-686-7925, Fax: 516-686-7613, E-mail: jnealon@nyit.edu. *Dean*, Dr. Heskia Heskiaoff, 516-686-7931, Fax: 516-625-5801.

School of Management Students: 213 full-time (91 women), 320 part-time (138 women); includes 67 minority (30 African Americans, 27 Asian Americans or Pacific Islanders, 9 Hispanic Americans, 1 Native American), 174 international. Average age 30. 319 applicants, 76% accepted, 127 enrolled. Expenses: Contact institution. *Financial support:* In 2001–02, 11 research assistantships with partial tuition reimbursements were awarded; fellowships, career-related internships or fieldwork, institutionally sponsored loans, tuition waivers (full and partial), and unspecified assistantships also available. Support available to part-time students. Financial award applicants required to submit FAFSA. In 2001, 190 degrees awarded. *Degree program information:* Part-time and evening/weekend programs available. Postbaccalaureate distance learning degree programs offered. Offers accounting (Advanced Certificate); business administration (MBA); finance (Advanced Certificate); human resources administration (Advanced Certificate); human resources management and labor relations (MS); international business (Advanced Certificate); labor relations (Advanced Certificate); management (MBA, MS, Advanced Certificate); management of information systems (Advanced Certificate); marketing (Advanced Certificate). *Application deadline:* For fall admission, 7/1 (priority date); for spring admission, 12/1 (priority date). Applications are processed on a rolling basis. *Application fee:* $50. Electronic applications accepted. *Application Contact:* Jacquelyn Nealon, Dean of Admissions and Financial Aid, 516-686-7925, Fax: 516-686-7613, E-mail: jnealon@nyit.edu. *Dean*, Dr. David R. Decker, 516-686-7423, Fax: 516-686-7655.

New York College of Osteopathic Medicine Students: 1,075 full-time (528 women); includes 454 minority (75 African Americans, 319 Asian Americans or Pacific Islanders, 58 Hispanic Americans, 2 Native Americans), 2 international. Average age 25. 2,743 applicants, 18% accepted, 264 enrolled. *Faculty:* 46 full-time (15 women), 40 part-time/adjunct. Expenses: Contact institution. *Financial support:* In 2001–02, 914 students received support, including 38 fellowships with partial tuition reimbursements available (averaging $17,200 per year); tuition waivers (full and partial) also available. Financial award application deadline: 4/1; financial award applicants required to submit FAFSA. In 2001, 252 degrees awarded. Offers osteopathic medicine (DO). *Application deadline:* For fall admission, 2/1. *Application fee:* $60. *Application Contact:* Michael J. Schaefer, Director of Admissions, 516-626-6947, Fax: 516-686-3831, E-mail: mschaefer@nyit.edu. *Dean*, Dr. Stanley Schiowitz, 516-686-3722, Fax: 516-686-3830, E-mail: sschiowi@nyit.edu.

See in-depth description on page 995.

NEW YORK LAW SCHOOL, New York, NY 10013

General Information Independent, coed, graduate-only institution. *Enrollment by degree level:* 1,397 first professional. *Graduate faculty:* 50 full-time (13 women), 65 part-time/adjunct (25 women). *Tuition:* Full-time $26,654; part-time $9,996 per semester. Part-time tuition and fees vary according to course load. *Graduate housing:* Room and/or apartments available on a first-come, first-served basis to single students; on-campus housing not available to married students. Typical cost: $8,000 per year. *Student services:* Campus employment opportunities, campus safety program, career counseling, disabled student services, free psychological counseling, international student services, low-cost health insurance, writing training. *Library facilities:* Mendik Library. *Online resources:* library catalog, web page, access to other libraries' catalogs. *Collection:* 475,188 titles, 5,329 serial subscriptions.

Computer facilities: 110 computers available on campus for general student use. A campuswide network can be accessed from off campus. Internet access is available. *Web address:* http://www.nyls.edu/.

General Application Contact: Thomas Matos, Director of Admissions, 212-431-2888, Fax: 212-966-1522, E-mail: admissions@nyls.edu.

GRADUATE UNITS

Professional Program Students: 920 full-time (465 women), 476 part-time (210 women); includes 351 minority (135 African Americans, 88 Asian Americans or Pacific Islanders, 127 Hispanic Americans, 1 Native American) Average age 28. 3,508 applicants, 55% accepted, 492 enrolled. *Faculty:* 50 full-time (13 women), 65 part-time/adjunct (25 women). Expenses: Contact institution. *Financial support:* In 2001–02, 1,270 students received support. Career-related internships or fieldwork, Federal Work-Study, institutionally sponsored loans, and scholarships/grants available. Support available to part-time students. Financial award application deadline: 4/16; financial award applicants required to submit FAFSA. In 2001, 401 degrees awarded. *Degree program information:* Part-time and evening/weekend programs available. Offers law (JD). *Application deadline:* For fall admission, 4/1 (priority date). Applications are processed on a rolling basis. *Application fee:* $50. Electronic applications accepted. *Application Contact:* Thomas Matos, Director of Admissions, 212-431-2888, Fax: 212-966-1522, E-mail: admissions@nyls.edu. *President and Dean*, Richard A. Matasar, 212-431-2840.

NEW YORK MEDICAL COLLEGE, Valhalla, NY 10595-1691

General Information Independent, coed, graduate-only institution. CGS member. *Graduate housing:* Rooms and/or apartments available on a first-come, first-served basis to single and married students. *Research affiliation:* American Health Foundation.

GRADUATE UNITS

Graduate School of Basic Medical Sciences Students: 105 full-time (60 women), 32 part-time (18 women); includes 32 minority (4 African Americans, 23 Asian Americans or Pacific Islanders, 5 Hispanic Americans), 35 international. Average age 30. 142 applicants, 49% accepted. *Faculty:* 83 full-time (19 women). Expenses: Contact institution. *Financial support:* In 2001–02, 46 research assistantships with full tuition reimbursements were awarded; career-related internships or fieldwork, Federal Work-Study, institutionally sponsored loans, scholarships/grants, and tuition waivers (full) also available. Support available to part-time students. Financial award applicants required to submit FAFSA. In 2001, 21 master's, 12 doctorates awarded. *Degree program information:* Part-time and evening/weekend programs available. Offers basic medical sciences (MS, PhD); biochemistry and molecular biology (MS, PhD); cell biology and neuroscience (MS, PhD); experimental pathology (MS, PhD); microbiology and immunology (MS, PhD); pharmacology (MS, PhD); physiology (MS, PhD). *Application deadline:* For fall admission, 7/1 (priority date); for spring admission, 12/1 (priority date). Applications are processed on a rolling basis. *Application fee:* $35 ($60 for international students). *Application Contact:* Nina Pelella-Doyle, Admission Coordinator, 914-594-4110, Fax: 914-594-4944. *Dean*, Dr. Francis L. Belloni, 914-594-4110, Fax: 914-594-4944, E-mail: francis_belloni@nymc.edu.

Professional Program Students: 768 full-time (381 women); includes 341 minority (30 African Americans, 277 Asian Americans or Pacific Islanders, 31 Hispanic Americans, 3 Native Americans), 3 international. Average age 26. 8,256 applicants, 8% accepted, 188 enrolled. *Faculty:* 1,248 full-time (405 women), 1,568 part-time/adjunct (369 women). Expenses: Contact institution. *Financial support:* In 2001–02, 50 research assistantships with full tuition reimbursements (averaging $17,000 per year) were awarded; Federal Work-Study, institutionally sponsored loans, scholarships/grants, and tuition waivers (full) also available. Support available to part-time students. Financial award application deadline: 4/20; financial award applicants required to submit FAFSA. In 2001, 204 degrees awarded. Offers medicine (MD). *Application deadline:* For fall admission, 12/15. Applications are processed on a rolling basis. *Application fee:* $100. *Application Contact:* Dr. Fern Juster, Admissions Office, 914-594-4507, Fax: 914-594-4613, E-mail: mdadmit@nymc.edu. *Provost and Dean, School of Medicine*, Dr. Ralph A. O'Connell, 914-594-4900, Fax: 914-594-4145.

School of Public Health Students: 134 full-time, 418 part-time; includes 111 minority (50 African Americans, 44 Asian Americans or Pacific Islanders, 17 Hispanic Americans), 17 international. Average age 33. 156 applicants, 65% accepted, 76 enrolled. *Faculty:* 15 full-time (9 women), 177 part-time/adjunct (90 women). Expenses: Contact institution. *Financial support:* In 2001–02, 110 students received support. Career-related internships or fieldwork, Federal Work-Study, institutionally sponsored loans, tuition waivers (partial), and tuition reimbursements available. Support available to part-time students. Financial award applicants required to submit FAFSA. In 2001, 118 degrees awarded. *Degree program information:* Part-time and evening/weekend programs available. Offers assistive technology (CGS); behavioral sciences and health promotion (MPH); biostatistics (MPH, MS); clinical research administration (MS); early intervention (CGS); emergency medical services (MPH, MS, CGS); environmental health science (MPH, MS); epidemiology (MPH, MS); gerontology (MPH, CGS); health informatics (MPH); health policy and management (MPH, MS); international health (MPH, MS, CGS); maternal and child health (MPH, CGS); physical therapy (MS, DPT); public health (MPH, MS, DPT, CGS); speech-language pathology (MS). *Application deadline:* For fall admission, 7/20 (priority date); for spring admission, 12/1 (priority date). Applications are processed on a rolling basis. *Application fee:* $35 ($60 for international students). *Application Contact:* Marian McGowan, Assistant Dean, 914-594-4510, Fax: 914-594-4292, E-mail: gshs_admissions@nymc.edu. *Dean*, Sheila M. Smythe, 914-594-4531, Fax: 914-594-4292, E-mail: sheila_smythe@nymc.edu.

NEW YORK SCHOOL OF INTERIOR DESIGN, New York, NY 10021-5110

General Information Independent, coed, comprehensive institution. *Enrollment:* 9 full-time matriculated graduate/professional students (6 women). *Enrollment by degree level:* 9 master's. *Graduate faculty:* 2 full-time (0 women), 9 part-time/adjunct (3 women). *Tuition:* Full-time $18,000. *Graduate housing:* On-campus housing not available. *Student services:* Campus employment opportunities, career counseling, international student services, low-cost health insurance. *Library facilities:* NYSID Library. *Online resources:* library catalog, web page, access to other libraries' catalogs. *Collection:* 10,000 titles, 88 serial subscriptions, 100 audiovisual materials. *Research affiliation:* Metropolitan New York Library Council–Research Consortium.

Computer facilities: 50 computers available on campus for general student use. A campuswide network can be accessed from off campus. Internet access is available. *Web address:* http://www.nysid.edu/.

General Application Contact: Scott Ageloff, Dean, 212-472-1500 Ext. 301, Fax: 212-288-6577.

GRADUATE UNITS

Program in Interior Design Students: 9 full-time (6 women), 7 international. Average age 30. 53 applicants, 36% accepted, 4 enrolled. *Faculty:* 2 full-time (0 women), 9 part-time/adjunct (3 women). Expenses: Contact institution. *Financial support:* In 2001–02, 6 fellowships (averaging $5,000 per year) were awarded; career-related internships or fieldwork, Federal Work-Study, institutionally sponsored loans, and scholarships/grants also available. Financial award application deadline: 5/1; financial award applicants required to submit FAFSA. In 2001, 6 degrees awarded. Offers interior design (MFA). *Application deadline:* For fall admission, 3/15 (priority date). Applications are processed on a rolling basis. *Application fee:* $50 ($75 for international students). *Application Contact:* David T. Sprouls, Director of Admissions, 212-472-1500 Ext. 202, Fax: 212-472-1867, E-mail: david@nysid.edu. *Dean*, Scott Ageloff, 212-472-1500 Ext. 301, Fax: 212-288-6577.

NEW YORK THEOLOGICAL SEMINARY, New York, NY 10115

General Information Independent-religious, coed, graduate-only institution. *Enrollment by degree level:* 238 first professional, 65 doctoral. *Graduate faculty:* 13 full-time (5 women), 37 part-time/adjunct (7 women). *Tuition:* Part-time $275 per credit. *Required fees:* $324 per year. *Graduate housing:* On-campus housing not available. *Student services:* Campus employment opportunities, career counseling, international student services, writing training. *Library facilities:* Saint Mark's Library plus 1 other. *Online resources:* library catalog, web page, access to other libraries' catalogs. *Collection:* 221,000 titles, 600 serial subscriptions, 6 audiovisual materials. *Research affiliation:* Bellevue Hospital Center, Goldwater Memorial Hospital, Institutes of Religion and Health, Lutheran Medical Center, Postgraduate Center for Mental Health.

Computer facilities: 6 computers available on campus for general student use. A campuswide network can be accessed from off campus. Internet access is available. *Web address:* http://www.nyts.edu/.

General Application Contact: Yon Su Kang, Registrar, 212-532-4012, Fax: 212-684-0757, E-mail: skang@nyts.edu.

GRADUATE UNITS

Graduate and Professional Programs Students: 179 full-time (89 women), 124 part-time (46 women); includes 239 minority (151 African Americans, 69 Asian Americans or Pacific Islanders, 19 Hispanic Americans), 22 international. Average age 42. 178 applicants, 61%

accepted, 89 enrolled. *Faculty:* 13 full-time (5 women), 37 part-time/adjunct (7 women). Expenses: Contact institution. *Financial support:* In 2001–02, 102 students received support, including 91 fellowships (averaging $1,375 per year); career-related internships or fieldwork and scholarships/grants also available. Support available to part-time students. Financial award application deadline: 4/1. In 2001, 59 first professional degrees, 12 doctorates awarded. *Degree program information:* Part-time and evening/weekend programs available. Offers theology (M Div, MPS, MSW, D Min). *Application deadline:* For fall admission, 4/1 (priority date); for spring admission, 11/30. Applications are processed on a rolling basis. *Application fee:* $50. *Application Contact:* Yon Su Kang, Registrar, 212-532-4012, Fax: 212-684-0757, E-mail: skang@nyts.edu. *Acting President,* Dr. Ileana Rodriquez, 212-532-4012, Fax: 212-684-0757.

NEW YORK UNIVERSITY, New York, NY 10012-1019

General Information Independent, coed, university. CGS member. *Enrollment:* 10,031 full-time matriculated graduate/professional students (5,667 women), 7,521 part-time matriculated graduate/professional students (4,361 women). *Enrollment by degree level:* 3,324 first professional, 11,651 master's, 2,078 doctoral, 499 other advanced degrees. *Graduate faculty:* 2,778 full-time, 2,121 part-time/adjunct. *Tuition:* Full-time $19,536; part-time $814 per credit. *Required fees:* $1,330; $38 per credit. Tuition and fees vary according to course load and program. *Graduate housing:* Rooms and/or apartments available on a first-come, first-served basis to single and married students. Typical cost: $10,236 per year ($13,226 including board) for single students; $18,606 per year for married students. *Student services:* Campus employment opportunities, campus safety program, career counseling, disabled student services, exercise/wellness program, free psychological counseling, grant writing training, international student services, low-cost health insurance, multicultural affairs office, teacher training, writing training. *Library facilities:* Elmer H. Bobst Library plus 11 others. *Online resources:* library catalog, web page, access to other libraries' catalogs. *Collection:* 4.5 million titles, 32,766 serial subscriptions, 58,500 audiovisual materials. *Research affiliation:* New York Botanical Gardens, American Research Center (Egypt), American Museum of Natural History, British Museum of Natural History (London, England), Metropolitan Museum of Art, Smithsonian Institute.

Computer facilities: 1,400 computers available on campus for general student use. A campuswide network can be accessed from student residence rooms and from off campus. Internet access and online class registration are available. *Web address:* http://www.nyu.edu/.

General Application Contact: New York University Information, 212-998-1212.

GRADUATE UNITS

College of Dentistry Students: 1,438 full-time, 7 part-time; includes 744 minority (34 African Americans, 618 Asian Americans or Pacific Islanders, 92 Hispanic Americans), 12 international. Average age 28. 2,772 applicants, 25% accepted. *Faculty:* 136 full-time, 503 part-time/adjunct. Expenses: Contact institution. *Financial support:* In 2001–02, 916 students received support, including 6 fellowships (averaging $20,000 per year), 12 teaching assistantships (averaging $5,500 per year); Federal Work-Study, institutionally sponsored loans, scholarships/grants, and unspecified assistantships also available. Support available to part-time students. Financial award application deadline: 3/1; financial award applicants required to submit FAFSA. In 2001, 300 first professional degrees, 41 other advanced degrees awarded. Offers clinical research (MS); dentistry (DDS, MS, Advanced Certificate); endodontics (Advanced Certificate); general dentistry (Advanced Certificate); oral and maxillofacial surgery (Advanced Certificate); orthodontics (Advanced Certificate); pediatric dentistry (Advanced Certificate); periodontics (Advanced Certificate); prosthodontics (Advanced Certificate); prosthodontics (implantology) (Advanced Certificate). *Application deadline:* For fall admission, 4/1 (priority date). Applications are processed on a rolling basis. *Application fee:* $35. *Application Contact:* Novella L. Jones, Assistant Dean for Student Affairs and Admissions, 212-998-9818, Fax: 212-995-4240, E-mail: novella.jones@nyu.edu. *Dean,* Dr. Michael C. Alfano, 212-998-9898, Fax: 212-995-4240, E-mail: michael.alfano@nyu.edu.

Gallatin School of Individualized Study Students: 43 full-time (34 women), 139 part-time (101 women); includes 48 minority (23 African Americans, 10 Asian Americans or Pacific Islanders, 15 Hispanic Americans), 8 international. Average age 30. 235 applicants, 41% accepted, 51 enrolled. *Faculty:* 24 full-time (12 women), 29 part-time/adjunct (17 women). Expenses: Contact institution. *Financial support:* In 2001–02, 110 students received support, including 2 fellowships with partial tuition reimbursements available, 4 research assistantships with full tuition reimbursements available (averaging $6,375 per year); career-related internships or fieldwork, Federal Work-Study, institutionally sponsored loans, and scholarships/grants also available. Support available to part-time students. Financial award application deadline: 3/1; financial award applicants required to submit FAFSA. In 2001, 47 degrees awarded. *Degree program information:* Part-time and evening/weekend programs available. Offers individualized study (MA). *Application deadline:* For fall admission, 2/1 (priority date); for spring admission, 11/1 (priority date). Applications are processed on a rolling basis. *Application fee:* $45. *Application Contact:* Frances R. Levin, Director of Graduate Admissions, 212-998-7364, Fax: 212-995-4150, E-mail: gallatin.gradadmissions@nyu.edu. *Dean,* Dr. E. Frances White, 212-998-7370.

Graduate School of Arts and Science Students: 2,442 full-time (1,334 women), 1,543 part-time (862 women); includes 549 minority (126 African Americans, 277 Asian Americans or Pacific Islanders, 142 Hispanic Americans, 4 Native Americans), 1,243 international. Average age 27. 8,749 applicants, 30% accepted. *Faculty:* 597 full-time (159 women), 393 part-time/adjunct. Expenses: Contact institution. *Financial support:* In 2001–02, 707 fellowships with tuition reimbursements, 131 research assistantships with tuition reimbursements, 587 teaching assistantships with tuition reimbursements were awarded. Career-related internships or fieldwork, Federal Work-Study, institutionally sponsored loans, tuition waivers (partial), unspecified assistantships, and instructorships also available. Financial award applicants required to submit FAFSA. In 2001, 780 master's, 225 doctorates, 22 other advanced degrees awarded. *Degree program information:* Part-time and evening/weekend programs available. Offers Africana studies (MA); American studies (MA, PhD); anthropology (MA, PhD); anthropology and French studies (PhD); applied economic analysis (Advanced Certificate); archival management and historical editing (Advanced Certificate); arts and science (MA, MFA, MS, PhD, Advanced Certificate, PhD/Advanced Certificate); biochemistry (MS, PhD); biology (PhD); biomaterials (MS); biomedical journalism (MS); cell biology (MS, PhD); chemistry (MS, PhD); classics (MA, PhD); clinical psychology (PhD); cognition and perception (PhD); community psychology (PhD); comparative literature (MA, PhD); creative writing (MFA); culture and media (PhD/Advanced Certificate); early music performance (Advanced Certificate); economics (MA, PhD); English and American literature (MA, PhD); French studies and politics (PhD); French studies and sociology (PhD); French studies/history (PhD); French studies/journalism (MA); general biology (MS); general psychology (MA); Germanic languages and literatures (MA, PhD); Hebrew and Judaic studies (MA, PhD); Hebrew and Judaic studies/history (PhD); Hebrew and Judaic studies/museum studies (MA); history (MA, PhD); humanities and social thought (MA); industrial/organizational psychology (MA, PhD); international politics and international business (MA); Italian (MA, PhD); Italian studies (MA); journalism (MA); journalism (cultural reporting and criticism) (MA); Latin American and Caribbean studies/journalism (MA); linguistics (MA, PhD); microbiology (MS, PhD); Middle Eastern studies/history (PhD); museum studies (Advanced Certificate); museum studies and Africana studies (MA); museum studies and Hebrew and Judaic studies (MA); museum studies and Latin American and Caribbean studies (MA); music (ethnomusicology) (MA, PhD); music (theory, composition and musicology) (MA, PhD); Near Eastern studies/journalism (MA); neural sciences and physiology (PhD); parasitology (PhD); pathology (MS, PhD); pharmacology (PhD); philosophy (MA, PhD); physics (MS, PhD); physiology (MS, PhD); poetics and theory (Advanced Certificate); politics (MA, PhD); politics (Near Eastern studies) (PhD); Portuguese (MA, PhD); psychoanalysis (Advanced Certificate); public history (MA, Advanced Certificate); religion (Advanced Certificate); religious studies (MA); Romance languages and literatures (MA); Russian literature (MA); science and environmental reporting (Advanced Certificate); science and environmental reporting/journalism (MA); Slavic literature (MA); social theory (Advanced Certificate); social/personality psychology (PhD); sociology (MA, PhD); Spanish (MA, PhD); world history (MA). *Application Contact:* Roberta Popik, Assistant Dean of Enrollment, 212-998-8050, Fax: 212-995-4557, E-mail: gsas.admissions@nyu.edu. *Dean,* Catharine R. Stimpson, 212-998-8040.

Center for European Studies Students: 9 full-time (6 women), 1 part-time; includes 3 minority (1 Asian American or Pacific Islander, 1 Hispanic American, 1 Native American), 3 international. Average age 24. 27 applicants, 78% accepted, 4 enrolled. *Faculty:* 4 full-time (0 women). Expenses: Contact institution. *Financial support:* Fellowships with tuition reimbursements, teaching assistantships with tuition reimbursements, career-related internships or fieldwork, Federal Work-Study, and institutionally sponsored loans available. Financial award application deadline: 1/4; financial award applicants required to submit FAFSA. In 2001, 4 degrees awarded. Offers European studies (MA). *Application deadline:* For fall admission, 1/4 (priority date). *Application fee:* $60. *Application Contact:* Jan Gross, Associate Chair, 212-998-3838, Fax: 212-995-4188. *Director,* Martin Schain, 212-998-3838, Fax: 212-995-4188, E-mail: gsas.admissions@nyu.edu.

Center for French Civilization and Culture Students: 94 full-time (66 women), 27 part-time (20 women); includes 9 minority (3 African Americans, 4 Asian Americans or Pacific Islanders, 2 Hispanic Americans), 31 international. Average age 26. 110 applicants, 64% accepted, 40 enrolled. Expenses: Contact institution. *Financial support:* Fellowships with tuition reimbursements, research assistantships with tuition reimbursements, teaching assistantships with tuition reimbursements, Federal Work-Study, institutionally sponsored loans, and instructorships available. Financial award application deadline: 1/4; financial award applicants required to submit FAFSA. In 2001, 23 master's, 14 doctorates awarded. *Degree program information:* Part-time and evening/weekend programs available. Offers French (PhD); French civilization and culture (MA, PhD, Advanced Certificate); French language and civilization (MA); French literature (MA); French Studies (PhD); French studies (MA, PhD, Advanced Certificate); French studies and anthropology (PhD); French studies and history (PhD); French studies and journalism (MA); French studies and politics (PhD); French studies and sociology (PhD); Romance languages and literatures (MA). *Application deadline:* For fall admission, 1/4. *Application fee:* $60. *Application Contact:* Charles Affron, Director of Graduate Studies, 212-998-8700, Fax: 212-995-3539. *Director,* Thomas Bishop, 212-998-8700, Fax: 212-995-3539, E-mail: french.web@nyu.edu.

Center for Latin American and Caribbean Studies Students: 19 full-time (15 women), 15 part-time (11 women); includes 10 minority (1 African American, 2 Asian Americans or Pacific Islanders, 7 Hispanic Americans), 5 international. Average age 34. 63 applicants, 83% accepted, 14 enrolled. *Faculty:* 2 full-time (0 women), 5 part-time/adjunct. Expenses: Contact institution. *Financial support:* Fellowships with tuition reimbursements, teaching assistantships with tuition reimbursements, Federal Work-Study, institutionally sponsored loans, and unspecified assistantships available. Financial award application deadline: 1/4; financial award applicants required to submit FAFSA. In 2001, 19 degrees awarded. *Degree program information:* Part-time programs available. Offers Latin American and Caribbean studies (MA); Latin American and Caribbean studies/journalism (MA); Latin American and Caribbean studies/museum studies (MA). *Application deadline:* For fall admission, 1/4 (priority date); for spring admission, 11/1. *Application fee:* $60. *Director,* George Yudice, 212-998-8686, Fax: 212-995-4163, E-mail: clacs.info@nyu.edu.

Center for Neural Science Students: 27 full-time (15 women), 14 part-time (5 women); includes 7 minority (1 African American, 2 Asian Americans or Pacific Islanders, 3 Hispanic Americans, 1 Native American), 12 international. Average age 25. 92 applicants, 14% accepted, 5 enrolled. *Faculty:* 15 full-time (3 women), 4 part-time/adjunct. Expenses: Contact institution. *Financial support:* Fellowships with tuition reimbursements, research assistantships with tuition reimbursements, career-related internships or fieldwork and Federal Work-Study available. Financial award application deadline: 1/4; financial award applicants required to submit FAFSA. In 2001, 2 degrees awarded. Offers neural science (PhD). *Application deadline:* For fall admission, 1/4. *Application fee:* $60. *Application Contact:* Samuel Feldman, Director of Graduate Studies, 212-998-7780, Fax: 212-995-4011, E-mail: cns@nyu.edu. *Chairman,* Daniel Sanes, 212-998-7780.

Courant Institute of Mathematical Sciences Students: 281 full-time (63 women), 388 part-time (114 women); includes 77 minority (4 African Americans, 62 Asian Americans or Pacific Islanders, 11 Hispanic Americans), 345 international. Average age 26. 1,373 applicants, 46% accepted, 199 enrolled. *Faculty:* 76 full-time (1 woman). Expenses: Contact institution. *Financial support:* Fellowships with tuition reimbursements, research assistantships with tuition reimbursements, teaching assistantships with tuition reimbursements, Federal Work-Study, institutionally sponsored loans, and tuition waivers (full and partial) available. Financial award application deadline: 1/4; financial award applicants required to submit FAFSA. In 2001, 161 master's, 22 doctorates awarded. *Degree program information:* Part-time and evening/weekend programs available. Offers atmosphere-ocean science and mathematics (PhD); computer science (MS, PhD); information systems (MS); mathematics (MS, PhD); mathematics and statistics/operations research (MS); mathematics in finance (MS); scientific computing (MS). *Application deadline:* For fall admission, 1/4. *Application fee:* $60. *Associate Director,* Charles Newman, 212-998-3223, Fax: 212-995-4121.

Hagop Kevorkian Center for Near Eastern Studies Students: 53 full-time (35 women), 12 part-time (4 women); includes 6 minority (1 African American, 3 Asian Americans or Pacific Islanders, 2 Hispanic Americans), 14 international. Average age 27. 75 applicants, 43% accepted, 17 enrolled. *Faculty:* 32 full-time (11 women). Expenses: Contact institution. *Financial support:* Fellowships with tuition reimbursements, teaching assistantships with tuition reimbursements, Federal Work-Study and institutionally sponsored loans available. Financial award application deadline: 1/4; financial award applicants required to submit FAFSA. In 2001, 10 master's, 6 doctorates awarded. *Degree program information:* Part-time and evening/weekend programs available. Offers Middle Eastern studies (MA, PhD); Middle Eastern studies/history (PhD); Near Eastern studies (MA); Near Eastern studies/journalism (MA); Near Eastern studies/museum studies (MA). *Application deadline:* For fall admission, 1/4. *Application fee:* $60. *Chair,* Timothy Mitchell, 212-998-8877, Fax: 212-995-4144, E-mail: kevorkian.center@nyu.edu.

Institute for Law and Society Students: 12 full-time (8 women); includes 4 minority (1 African American, 2 Asian Americans or Pacific Islanders, 1 Hispanic American), 3 international. Average age 25. 40 applicants, 18% accepted, 3 enrolled. *Faculty:* 3 full-time (1 woman). Expenses: Contact institution. *Financial support:* Fellowships with tuition reimbursements, teaching assistantships with tuition reimbursements, career-related internships or fieldwork, Federal Work-Study, and institutionally sponsored loans available. Financial award application deadline: 1/4; financial award applicants required to submit FAFSA. In 2001, 2 degrees awarded. Offers law and society (PhD). *Application deadline:* For fall admission, 1/4. *Application fee:* $60. *Application Contact:* Wolf Heydebrand, Information Contact, 212-998-8536, Fax: 212-995-4034, E-mail: law.society@nyu.edu. *Director,* Christine Harrington, 212-998-8536, Fax: 212-995-4034.

Institute of Fine Arts Students: 167 full-time (139 women), 101 part-time (85 women); includes 20 minority (11 Asian Americans or Pacific Islanders, 9 Hispanic Americans), 42 international. Average age 29. 284 applicants, 31% accepted, 36 enrolled. *Faculty:* 19 full-time (5 women). Expenses: Contact institution. *Financial support:* Fellowships with tuition reimbursements, research assistantships with tuition reimbursements, teaching assistantships with tuition reimbursements, career-related internships or fieldwork, Federal Work-Study, institutionally sponsored loans, and tuition waivers (partial) available. Financial award application deadline: 1/4; financial award applicants required to submit FAFSA. In 2001, 17 degrees awarded. *Degree program information:* Part-time programs available. Offers classical art and archaeology (PhD); history of art and archaeology (MA, PhD); Near Eastern art and archaeology (PhD). *Application deadline:* For fall admission, 1/4. *Application fee:* $60. *Application Contact:* Donald Hansen, Director of Graduate Studies, 212-992-5800, Fax: 212-992-5807, E-mail: ifa.program@nyu.edu. *Chair,* James McCredie, 212-992-5800.

Nelson Institute of Environmental Medicine Students: 30 full-time (15 women), 17 part-time (8 women); includes 5 minority (1 African American, 3 Asian Americans or Pacific Islanders, 1 Hispanic American), 17 international. Average age 26. 69 applicants, 55% accepted, 23 enrolled. *Faculty:* 26 full-time (7 women). Expenses: Contact institution. *Financial support:* Fellowships with tuition reimbursements, teaching assistantships with tuition reimbursements, career-related internships or fieldwork, Federal Work-Study, and institutionally sponsored loans available. Financial award application deadline: 2/1; financial

New York University (continued)

award applicants required to submit FAFSA. In 2001, 5 master's, 4 doctorates awarded. *Degree program information:* Part-time programs available. Offers environmental health sciences (MS, PhD). *Application deadline:* For fall admission, 2/1. *Application fee:* $60. *Application Contact:* Jerry Solomon, Director of Graduate Studies, 845-731-3661, Fax: 914-351-3317, E-mail: ehs@env.med.nyu.edu. *Director,* Dr. Max Costa, 845-731-3661, Fax: 914-351-3317.

Leonard N. Stern School of Business *Degree program information:* Part-time and evening/weekend programs available. Offers accounting (MBA, PhD, APC); business (MBA, MS, PhD, APC); economics (MBA, PhD, APC); executive finance (MBA); executive general management (MBA); finance (MBA, PhD); information systems (MBA, MS, PhD, APC); international business (MBA, PhD, APC); management (MBA, PhD, APC); marketing (MBA, PhD, APC); operations management (MBA); statistics and operations research (MBA, MS, PhD, APC). MBA/Certificate offered jointly with the Community of European Management Schools. Electronic applications accepted.

Robert F. Wagner Graduate School of Public Service Students: 394 full-time (278 women), 432 part-time (305 women); includes 250 minority (99 African Americans, 93 Asian Americans or Pacific Islanders, 58 Hispanic Americans), 98 international. Average age 27. 981 applicants, 76% accepted, 299 enrolled. *Faculty:* 30 full-time (11 women), 75 part-time/adjunct (40 women). Expenses: Contact institution. *Financial support:* In 2001–02, 331 students received support, including 305 fellowships (averaging $5,071 per year), 26 research assistantships with partial tuition reimbursements available (averaging $7,761 per year); career-related internships or fieldwork, Federal Work-Study, institutionally sponsored loans, scholarships/grants, and tuition waivers (full and partial) also available. Support available to part-time students. Financial award application deadline: 2/15; financial award applicants required to submit FAFSA. In 2001, 336 master's, 6 doctorates awarded. *Degree program information:* Part-time and evening/weekend programs available. Offers advanced management program for clinicians (MS); financial management (MPA); health policy analysis (MPA); health services management (MPA); housing (Advanced Certificate); infrastructure management (MS); international public service management (MS); management (MS); public administration (PhD); public and nonprofit management and policy (MPA, Advanced Certificate); public economics (Advanced Certificate); public service (MPA, MS, MUP, PhD, Advanced Certificate); quantitative analysis and computer applications for policy and planning (Advanced Certificate); urban planning (MUP). *Application deadline:* For fall admission, 7/15; for spring admission, 1/1. Applications are processed on a rolling basis. *Application fee:* $50. *Application Contact:* James Short, Director, Admissions and Financial Aid, 212-998-7414, Fax: 212-995-4164, E-mail: wagner.admissions@nyu.edu. *Dean,* Dr. Jo Ivey Boufford, 212-998-7400, Fax: 212-995-4161.

School of Continuing and Professional Studies Students: 279 full-time (145 women), 569 part-time (248 women); includes 81 minority (20 African Americans, 39 Asian Americans or Pacific Islanders, 22 Hispanic Americans), 147 international. Average age 33. 551 applicants, 77% accepted, 316 enrolled. *Faculty:* 16 full-time (8 women), 149 part-time/adjunct (47 women). Expenses: Contact institution. *Financial support:* In 2001–02, 66 fellowships (averaging $2,000 per year), 9 research assistantships were awarded. Career-related internships or fieldwork, Federal Work-Study, institutionally sponsored loans, scholarships/grants, and tuition waivers (partial) also available. Support available to part-time students. Financial award application deadline: 3/1; financial award applicants required to submit FAFSA. In 2001, 216 master's, 25 other advanced degrees awarded. *Degree program information:* Part-time and evening/weekend programs available. Postbaccalaureate distance learning degree programs offered (no on-campus study). Offers continuing and professional studies (MS, Advanced Certificate); digital imaging and design (MS); information technology (Advanced Certificate); management and systems (MS); translation (MS). *Application deadline:* For fall admission, 6/1 (priority date); for spring admission, 10/15 (priority date). Applications are processed on a rolling basis. *Application fee:* $50. Electronic applications accepted. *Dean,* Dr. David F. Finney, 212-998-7000, Fax: 212-995-4130.

Center for Direct and Interactive Marketing Students: 21 full-time (19 women), 81 part-time (52 women); includes 15 minority (5 African Americans, 6 Asian Americans or Pacific Islanders, 4 Hispanic Americans), 23 international. Average age 30. 70 applicants, 69% accepted, 39 enrolled. *Faculty:* 1 (woman) full-time, 16 part-time/adjunct (5 women). Expenses: Contact institution. *Financial support:* In 2001–02, 28 fellowships (averaging $1,690 per year) were awarded; career-related internships or fieldwork and scholarships/grants also available. Support available to part-time students. Financial award application deadline: 3/1; financial award applicants required to submit FAFSA. In 2001, 28 degrees awarded. *Degree program information:* Part-time programs available. Offers direct and interactive marketing (MS). *Application deadline:* For fall admission, 6/1 (priority date); for spring admission, 10/15 (priority date). Applications are processed on a rolling basis. *Application fee:* $50. *Application Contact:* Fadia Saint-Juste, Program Coordinator, 212-790-3220, Fax: 212-790-1650, E-mail: fs20@nyu.edu. *Director,* Renee Harris, 212-790-3220, Fax: 212-790-1650, E-mail: rlh1@nyu.edu.

Center for Hospitality, Tourism and Travel Administration Students: 61 full-time (50 women), 53 part-time (35 women); includes 6 minority (1 African American, 3 Asian Americans or Pacific Islanders, 2 Hispanic Americans), 63 international. Average age 26. 81 applicants, 64% accepted, 40 enrolled. *Faculty:* 5 full-time (4 women), 25 part-time/adjunct (10 women). Expenses: Contact institution. *Financial support:* In 2001–02, 107 students received support, including 9 research assistantships; career-related internships or fieldwork, Federal Work-Study, institutionally sponsored loans, and scholarships/grants also available. Support available to part-time students. Financial award application deadline: 3/1; financial award applicants required to submit FAFSA. In 2001, 66 degrees awarded. *Degree program information:* Part-time and evening/weekend programs available. Postbaccalaureate distance learning degree programs offered. Offers customer relationship management (Advanced Certificate); hospitality industry studies (MS, Advanced Certificate); tourism and travel management (MS). *Application deadline:* For fall admission, 6/1 (priority date); for spring admission, 10/15 (priority date). Applications are processed on a rolling basis. *Application fee:* $50. *Associate Dean,* Dr. Lalia Rach, 212-998-9100, Fax: 212-995-4676, E-mail: erl@nyu.edu.

Center for Publishing Students: 15 full-time (all women), 89 part-time (64 women); includes 9 minority (5 African Americans, 1 Asian American or Pacific Islander, 3 Hispanic Americans), 20 international. Average age 29. 50 applicants, 70% accepted, 30 enrolled. *Faculty:* 1 full-time (0 women), 22 part-time/adjunct (6 women). Expenses: Contact institution. *Financial support:* In 2001–02, 14 fellowships (averaging $2,800 per year) were awarded; career-related internships or fieldwork, Federal Work-Study, institutionally sponsored loans, and scholarships/grants also available. Support available to part-time students. Financial award application deadline: 3/1; financial award applicants required to submit FAFSA. In 2001, 23 degrees awarded. *Degree program information:* Part-time and evening/weekend programs available. Offers book publishing (MS); electronic publishing (MS); magazine publishing (MS). *Application deadline:* For fall admission, 6/1 (priority date); for spring admission, 10/15 (priority date). Applications are processed on a rolling basis. *Application fee:* $50. *Application Contact:* Heidi Johnson, Associate Director, 212-790-3236, Fax: 212-790-3233, E-mail: pub.center@nyu.edu. *Director,* Robert E. Baensch, 212-790-3232, Fax: 212-790-3233, E-mail: pub.center@nyu.edu.

Real Estate Institute Students: 45 full-time (13 women), 284 part-time (67 women); includes 18 minority (5 African Americans, 8 Asian Americans or Pacific Islanders, 5 Hispanic Americans), 26 international. Average age 30. 210 applicants, 83% accepted, 130 enrolled. *Faculty:* 5 full-time (1 woman), 47 part-time/adjunct (5 women). Expenses: Contact institution. *Financial support:* Career-related internships or fieldwork and scholarships/grants available. Support available to part-time students. Financial award application deadline: 3/1; financial award applicants required to submit FAFSA. In 2001, 84 degrees awarded. *Degree program information:* Part-time and evening/weekend programs available. Offers construction management (MS, Advanced Certificate); real estate (MS, Advanced Certificate). *Application deadline:* For fall admission, 6/1 (priority date); for spring admission, 10/15 (priority date). Applications are processed on a rolling basis. *Application fee:* $50. *Application Contact:* Marcie Burros, Associate Director, 212-790-1335, Fax: 212-790-1686, E-mail: gradadmissions.scps@nyu.edu. *Associate Dean,* D. Kenneth Patton, 212-790-1335, Fax: 212-790-1686.

School of Law Students: 1,296 full-time (652 women); includes 311 minority (84 African Americans, 144 Asian Americans or Pacific Islanders, 81 Hispanic Americans, 2 Native Americans), 38 international. 6,887 applicants, 21% accepted, 385 enrolled. *Faculty:* 92 full-time (24 women), 56 part-time/adjunct (14 women). Expenses: Contact institution. *Financial support:* In 2001–02, 432 students received support; fellowships, research assistantships, teaching assistantships, career-related internships or fieldwork, Federal Work-Study, institutionally sponsored loans, scholarships/grants, tuition waivers (partial), and loan repayment assistance available. Financial award application deadline: 4/15; financial award applicants required to submit FAFSA. In 2001, 473 degrees awarded. Offers law (JD, LL M, JSD). PhD offered through the Graduate School of Arts and Science. *Application deadline:* For fall admission, 2/1. Applications are processed on a rolling basis. *Application fee:* $70. Electronic applications accepted. *Application Contact:* Kenneth Kleinrock, Assistant Dean for Admissions, 212-998-6060. *Dean,* Richard Revesz, 212-998-6000, Fax: 212-995-3150.

School of Medicine Students: 906 full-time (406 women); includes 359 minority (56 African Americans, 259 Asian Americans or Pacific Islanders, 44 Hispanic Americans), 66 international. Average age 24. *Faculty:* 967 full-time, 293 part-time/adjunct. Expenses: Contact institution. *Financial support:* Fellowships, research assistantships, teaching assistantships, Federal Work-Study, institutionally sponsored loans, scholarships/grants, and tuition waivers (full) available. Financial award application deadline: 6/15. In 2001, 177 first professional degrees, 28 doctorates awarded. Offers medicine (MD, PhD). *Application deadline:* Applications are processed on a rolling basis. Electronic applications accepted. *Application Contact:* Raymond Brienza, Associate Dean, Admissions, 212-263-5290, Fax: 212-725-2140. *Dean,* Dr. Robert M. Glickman, 212-263-5370, Fax: 212-263-8622.

Sackler Institute of Graduate Biomedical Sciences Students: 214 full-time (95 women); includes 76 minority (18 African Americans, 41 Asian Americans or Pacific Islanders, 17 Hispanic Americans), 56 international. Average age 25. 562 applicants, 18% accepted. *Faculty:* 150 full-time (35 women). Expenses: Contact institution. *Financial support:* In 2001–02, 122 research assistantships with tuition reimbursements (averaging $24,000 per year), 56 teaching assistantships with tuition reimbursements (averaging $24,000 per year) were awarded. Fellowships, tuition waivers (full) also available. Financial award application deadline: 2/1; financial award applicants required to submit FAFSA. In 2001, 21 degrees awarded. Offers biochemistry (PhD); biomedical sciences (PhD); cell biology (PhD); immunology (PhD); medical and molecular parasitology (PhD); microbiology (PhD); molecular oncology (PhD); neuroscience (PhD); pathology (PhD); pharmacology (PhD); physiology (PhD). *Application deadline:* For fall admission, 2/1 (priority date). Applications are processed on a rolling basis. *Application fee:* $60. *Application Contact:* Debra E. Stalk, Administrative Manager, 212-263-5648, Fax: 212-263-7600, E-mail: stalkd01@popmail.med.nyu.edu. *Associate Dean for Graduate Studies,* Dr. Joel D. Oppenheim, 212-263-8001, Fax: 212-263-7600.

Shirley M. Ehrenkranz School of Social Work Students: 570 full-time (503 women), 402 part-time (343 women); includes 332 minority (163 African Americans, 43 Asian Americans or Pacific Islanders, 124 Hispanic Americans, 2 Native Americans), 18 international. Average age 27. 1,532 applicants, 74% accepted, 523 enrolled. *Faculty:* 46 full-time (36 women), 128 part-time/adjunct (88 women). Expenses: Contact institution. *Financial support:* In 2001–02, 480 students received support, including 5 research assistantships with full tuition reimbursements available (averaging $5,000 per year); career-related internships or fieldwork, Federal Work-Study, scholarships/grants, and tuition waivers (partial) also available. Support available to part-time students. Financial award application deadline: 3/1; financial award applicants required to submit FAFSA. In 2001, 557 master's, 23 doctorates awarded. Offers social work (MSW, PhD). *Application deadline:* For fall admission, 7/1; for spring admission, 11/15. Applications are processed on a rolling basis. *Application fee:* $50. *Application Contact:* Stuart Gitlin, Director of Admissions, 212-998-5910, Fax: 212-995-4171, E-mail: essw.admissions@nyu.edu. *Dean,* Suzanne England, 212-998-5959, Fax: 212-995-4172.

The Steinhardt School of Education Students: 1,722 full-time (1,401 women), 2,231 part-time (1,767 women); includes 946 minority (419 African Americans, 283 Asian Americans or Pacific Islanders, 235 Hispanic Americans, 9 Native Americans) Average age 25. 3,727 applicants, 45% accepted, 1181 enrolled. *Faculty:* 233 full-time (135 women), 521 part-time/adjunct (346 women). Expenses: Contact institution. *Financial support:* In 2001–02, fellowships with full and partial tuition reimbursements (averaging $15,000 per year); research assistantships with partial tuition reimbursements, teaching assistantships with partial tuition reimbursements, career-related internships or fieldwork, Federal Work-Study, institutionally sponsored loans, scholarships/grants, traineeships, tuition waivers (partial), and unspecified assistantships also available. Support available to part-time students. Financial award application deadline: 3/1; financial award applicants required to submit FAFSA. In 2001, 1,315 master's, 126 doctorates, 21 other advanced degrees awarded. *Degree program information:* Part-time and evening/weekend programs available. Offers administration and management of technology and industry oriented programs (MA, Ed D, PhD, Advanced Certificate); adolescence special education (MA); advanced occupational therapy (MA); alternative certification program (MA); applied psychology (MA, PhD, Psy D, Advanced Certificate); art education (MA, Ed D, PhD); art therapy (MA); arts and humanities education (MA, PhD); bilingual education (MA, PhD, Advanced Certificate); business education (MA, Ed D, PhD, Advanced Certificate); childhood and bilingual special education (MA); childhood special education (MA); community health education (MPH, Ed D, PhD); costume studies (MA); counseling and guidance (MA, PhD, Advanced Certificate); counseling psychology (PhD); counselor education (MA, PhD, Advanced Certificate); dance education (MA, Ed D, PhD); deafness rehabilitation (MA); drama therapy (MA); early childhood and elementary education (MA, PhD, Advanced Certificate); early childhood special education (MA); education (MA, MFA, MM, MPH, MS, DA, DPT, Ed D, PhD, Psy D, Advanced Certificate); educational administration (MA, Ed D, PhD, Advanced Certificate); educational communication and technology (MA, Ed D, PhD, Advanced Certificate); educational psychology (MA); educational theatre (MA, Ed D, PhD, Advanced Certificate); educational theatre with English 7-12 (MA); English education (MA, PhD, Advanced Certificate); environmental conservation education (MA); folk art studies (MA); food and food management (MA, PhD); food management (MA); food studies (MA); for-profit sector (MA); foreign language education (MA, Advanced Certificate); graphic communications management and technology (MA, Ed D, PhD, Advanced Certificate); health education (MA, MPH, Ed D, PhD, Advanced Certificate); higher education (MA, Ed D, PhD); history of education (MA, PhD); human sexuality education (MA, Ed D, PhD); international education (MA, PhD); literacy 5-12 (MA); literacy 8-6 (MA); mathematics education (MA, PhD); media ecology (MA, PhD); middle childhood education (MA); multilingual/multicultural studies (MA, PhD, Advanced Certificate); music business (MA); music education (MA, Ed D, PhD, Advanced Certificate); music performance and composition (MA, PhD); music technology (MM); music therapy (MA, DA); nutrition and dietetics (MS, PhD); occupational therapy (MA); pathokinesiology (MA); performing arts administration (MA); philosophy of education (MA, PhD); physical therapy (DPT); practicing physical therapist (DPT); professional child/school psychology (Psy D); professional program in health education (Advanced Certificate); psychological development (PhD); public health nutrition (MPH); recreation services and resources management (MA, PhD, Advanced Certificate); rehabilitation counseling (MA, PhD); research in occupational therapy (PhD); research in physical therapy (PhD); school and college health education (MA, Ed D, PhD); school business administrator (Advanced Certificate); school psychologist (Advanced Certificate); school psychology (PhD); science education (MA); services and management (MA); services and resources management (PhD, Advanced Certificate); severe disabilities (Advanced Certificate); social studies (MA); social studies education (MA); sociology of education (MA, PhD); special education (MA, Advanced Certificate); special education hearing consultant (Advanced Certificate); speech communication (MA, Advanced Certificate); speech-language pathology and audiology (MA, PhD); student personnel administration in higher education (MA); studio art (MA, MFA); teachers of business subjects in higher education (MA, Ed D, PhD, Advanced Certificate); teaching and learning (Ed D, PhD); teaching English to speakers of other languages (MA, PhD, Advanced Certificate); visual arts administration (MA); visual culture (MA); workplace learning (Advanced Certificate). *Application deadline:* For fall admission, 2/1 (priority date); for spring admission, 12/1. Applications are processed on a rolling basis. *Application fee:* $40 ($60 for international students). *Application Contact:* 212-998-5030, Fax: 212-995-4328, E-mail: edgradadmissions@nyu.edu. *Dean,* Dr. Ann Marcus, 212-998-5000.

Division of Nursing Students: 49 full-time (45 women), 421 part-time (402 women); includes 112 minority (47 African Americans, 43 Asian Americans or Pacific Islanders, 22 Hispanic Americans) 167 applicants, 83% accepted, 104 enrolled. *Faculty:* 29 full-time (26 women), 84 part-time/adjunct (77 women). Expenses: Contact institution. *Financial support:* In 2001–02, 2 research assistantships with partial tuition reimbursements were awarded; fellowships with full and partial tuition reimbursements, career-related internships or fieldwork, Federal Work-Study, institutionally sponsored loans, scholarships/grants, and tuition waivers (partial) also available. Support available to part-time students. Financial award application deadline: 3/1; financial award applicants required to submit FAFSA. In 2001, 90 master's, 7 doctorates, 14 other advanced degrees awarded. *Degree program information:* Part-time and evening/weekend programs available. Offers advance practice nursing: adult primary care nurse practitioner (MA); advanced practice nursing: adult acute care nurse practitioner (MA, Advanced Certificate); advanced practice nursing: adult primary care nurse practitioner (Advanced Certificate); advanced practice nursing: adult primary care/geriatrics (Advanced Certificate); advanced practice nursing: children with special needs (Advanced Certificate); advanced practice nursing: geriatrics (MA, Advanced Certificate); advanced practice nursing: holistic nursing (MA, Advanced Certificate); advanced practice nursing: home health nursing (Advanced Certificate); advanced practice nursing: mental health (MA, Advanced Certificate); advanced practice nursing: pediatrics (Advanced Certificate); advanced practice nursing: pediatrics/children with special needs (MA); midwifery (MA, Advanced Certificate); nursing (MA, PhD, Advanced Certificate); nursing administration (MA, Advanced Certificate); nursing informatics (MA, Advanced Certificate); palliative care (MA, Advanced Certificate); research and theory development in nursing science (PhD); teaching of nursing (MA). *Application deadline:* For fall admission, 2/1 (priority date); for spring admission, 12/1. Applications are processed on a rolling basis. *Application fee:* $40 ($60 for international students). *Application Contact:* 212-998-5030, Fax: 212-995-4328, E-mail: grad.admissions@nyu.edu. *Acting Chairperson,* Dr. Terry Fulmer, 212-998-5300.

Tisch School of the Arts Students: 777 full-time (395 women), 38 part-time (23 women); includes 207 minority (52 African Americans, 99 Asian Americans or Pacific Islanders, 54 Hispanic Americans, 2 Native Americans), 157 international. Average age 26. 2,527 applicants, 22% accepted. *Faculty:* 81 full-time (35 women), 177 part-time/adjunct (78 women). Expenses: Contact institution. *Financial support:* Fellowships, research assistantships, teaching assistantships, career-related internships or fieldwork, Federal Work-Study, institutionally sponsored loans, scholarships/grants, tuition waivers (full and partial), and unspecified assistantships available. Support available to part-time students. Financial award application deadline: 2/1; financial award applicants required to submit CSS PROFILE or FAFSA. In 2001, 322 master's, 20 doctorates awarded. *Degree program information:* Part-time programs available. Offers acting (MFA); arts (MA, MFA, MPS, PhD); cinema studies (MA, PhD); dance (MFA); design (MFA); dramatic writing (MFA); film and television (MFA); moving image archiving and preservation (MA); musical theatre writing (MFA); performance studies (MA, PhD); telecommunications (MPS). *Application fee:* $50. *Application Contact:* Dan Sandford, Director of Graduate Admissions, 212-998-1918, Fax: 212-995-4060, E-mail: tisch.gradadmissions@nyu.edu. *Dean,* Mary Schmidt Campbell, 212-998-1800.

See in-depth descriptions on pages 997 and 999.

NIAGARA UNIVERSITY, Niagara Falls, Niagara University, NY 14109

General Information Independent-religious, coed, comprehensive institution. *Enrollment:* 458 full-time matriculated graduate/professional students (321 women), 360 part-time matriculated graduate/professional students (242 women). *Enrollment by degree level:* 814 master's, 4 other advanced degrees. *Graduate faculty:* 27 full-time (10 women), 24 part-time/adjunct (11 women). *Tuition:* Part-time $350 per credit. Full-time tuition and fees vary according to program. *Graduate housing:* Room and/or apartments available to single students; on-campus housing not available to married students. Typical cost: $6,950 (including board). Housing application deadline: 8/1. *Student services:* Campus employment opportunities, campus safety program, career counseling, disabled student services, free psychological counseling, international student services, low-cost health insurance, multicultural affairs office. *Library facilities:* Our Lady of Angels Library. *Online resources:* library catalog. *Collection:* 313,895 titles, 4,500 serial subscriptions. *Research affiliation:* Roswell Park Memorial Institute.

Computer facilities: 150 computers available on campus for general student use. A campuswide network can be accessed from student residence rooms. *Web address:* http://www.niagara.edu/.

General Application Contact: Mark Wojnowski, Assistant Dean for Graduate Recruitment, 716-286-8718, Fax: 716-286-8170, E-mail: mew@niagara.edu.

GRADUATE UNITS

Graduate Division of Arts and Sciences Students: 7 full-time (5 women), 18 part-time (7 women); includes 1 minority (African American), 6 international. *Faculty:* 4 full-time (1 woman). Expenses: Contact institution. *Financial support:* Fellowships, career-related internships or fieldwork and Federal Work-Study available. Support available to part-time students. In 2001, 8 degrees awarded. *Degree program information:* Part-time and evening/weekend programs available. Offers arts and sciences (MS); criminal justice administration (MS). *Application deadline:* For fall admission, 8/1. Applications are processed on a rolling basis. *Application fee:* $30.

Graduate Division of Business Administration Students: 52 full-time (16 women), 40 part-time (12 women); includes 4 minority (1 African American, 2 Hispanic Americans, 1 Native American), 38 international. Average age 30. 89 applicants, 73% accepted. *Faculty:* 6 full-time (2 women), 1 part-time/adjunct (0 women). Expenses: Contact institution. *Financial support:* In 2001–02, 3 fellowships, 2 research assistantships were awarded. Career-related internships or fieldwork and Federal Work-Study also available. Support available to part-time students. Financial award application deadline: 8/1; financial award applicants required to submit FAFSA. In 2001, 14 degrees awarded. *Degree program information:* Part-time and evening/weekend programs available. Offers business (MBA); commerce (MBA). *Application deadline:* For fall admission, 8/1; for spring admission, 11/1. Applications are processed on a rolling basis. *Application fee:* $30. *Director,* Dr. Philip Scherer, 716-286-8165.

Graduate Division of Education Students: 393 full-time (296 women), 299 part-time (220 women); includes 15 minority (10 African Americans, 5 Native Americans), 270 international. Average age 37. 382 applicants, 75% accepted. *Faculty:* 10 full-time (2 women), 18 part-time/adjunct (8 women). Expenses: Contact institution. *Financial support:* In 2001–02, 2 fellowships, 3 research assistantships were awarded. Career-related internships or fieldwork, Federal Work-Study, scholarships/grants, and unspecified assistantships also available. Support available to part-time students. Financial award application deadline: 3/15. In 2001, 238 master's, 2 other advanced degrees awarded. *Degree program information:* Part-time and evening/weekend programs available. Offers administration and supervision (MS Ed, PD); biology (MAT); elementary education (MS Ed); foundations and teaching (MA, MS Ed); inclusive education (MS Ed); literacy instruction (MS Ed); mental health counseling (MS Ed); school counseling (MS Ed, PD); secondary education (MS Ed); teacher education (MS Ed). *Application deadline:* For fall admission, 8/1. Applications are processed on a rolling basis. *Application fee:* $30. *Dean,* Dr. Debra A. Colley, 716-286-8560, Fax: 716-286-8561, E-mail: dcolley@niagara.edu.

Graduate Division of Nursing Students: 6 full-time (4 women), 3 part-time (all women), 2 international. Expenses: Contact institution. *Financial support:* Career-related internships or fieldwork and Federal Work-Study available. Support available to part-time students. In 2001, 3 degrees awarded. Offers family nurse practitioner (MS). *Application deadline:* For fall admission, 8/1. Applications are processed on a rolling basis. *Application fee:* $30.

See in-depth description on page 1001.

NICHOLLS STATE UNIVERSITY, Thibodaux, LA 70310

General Information State-supported, coed, comprehensive institution. *Graduate housing:* Rooms and/or apartments available on a first-come, first-served basis to single and married students. Housing application deadline: 4/13.

GRADUATE UNITS

Graduate Studies Students: 78 full-time (50 women), 306 part-time (213 women); includes 38 minority (32 African Americans, 3 Asian Americans or Pacific Islanders, 1 Hispanic American, 2 Native Americans), 1 international. Average age 34. *Faculty:* 57 full-time (17 women), 5 part-time/adjunct (1 woman). Expenses: Contact institution. *Financial support:* In 2001–02, 70 research assistantships with full tuition reimbursements (averaging $4,000 per year), 23 teaching assistantships with full tuition reimbursements (averaging $6,000 per year) were awarded. Unspecified assistantships also available. Support available to part-time students. In 2001, 88 master's, 3 other advanced degrees awarded. *Degree program information:* Part-time and evening/weekend programs available. *Application deadline:* Applications are processed on a rolling basis. *Application fee:* $20 ($30 for international students). *Director,* Dr. J. B. Stroud, 985-449-7014, Fax: 985-448-4922, E-mail: ba-mba@nicholls.edu.

College of Arts and Sciences Students: 9 full-time (6 women), 9 part-time (6 women); includes 1 minority (African American) Average age 23. 9 applicants, 100% accepted. *Faculty:* 35 full-time (8 women), 1 part-time/adjunct (0 women). Expenses: Contact institution. *Financial support:* In 2001–02, 4 students received support, including teaching assistantships with full tuition reimbursements available (averaging $6,000 per year); unspecified assistantships also available. Financial award application deadline: 6/17. In 2001, 5 degrees awarded. *Degree program information:* Part-time and evening/weekend programs available. Offers applied mathematics (MS); arts and sciences (MS). *Application deadline:* For fall admission, 6/17 (priority date); for spring admission, 11/15. Applications are processed on a rolling basis. *Application fee:* $20 ($30 for international students). *Dean,* Dr. Thomas Mortillaro, 985-448-4385, Fax: 985-448-4927, E-mail: math-dmb@nicholls.edu.

College of Business Administration Students: 29 full-time (12 women), 76 part-time (36 women); includes 7 minority (3 African Americans, 1 Asian American or Pacific Islander, 3 Hispanic Americans) 55 applicants, 100% accepted, 32 enrolled. *Faculty:* 28 full-time (7 women). Expenses: Contact institution. *Financial support:* In 2001–02, 15 research assistantships with full tuition reimbursements (averaging $4,000 per year) were awarded; unspecified assistantships also available. Financial award application deadline: 6/1. In 2001, 26 degrees awarded. *Degree program information:* Part-time and evening/weekend programs available. Offers business administration (MBA). *Application deadline:* For fall admission, 8/1 (priority date); for spring admission, 12/1 (priority date). Applications are processed on a rolling basis. *Application fee:* $20 ($30 for international students). Electronic applications accepted. *Dean,* Dr. Ridley Gros, 985-448-4170, Fax: 985-448-4922, E-mail: ba-rjg@nicholls.edu.

College of Education Students: 40 full-time (32 women), 221 part-time (171 women); includes 33 minority (28 African Americans, 2 Asian Americans or Pacific Islanders, 1 Hispanic American, 2 Native Americans), 1 international. *Faculty:* 24 full-time (10 women), 5 part-time/adjunct (1 woman). Expenses: Contact institution. *Financial support:* In 2001–02, research assistantships with tuition reimbursements (averaging $4,000 per year), teaching assistantships with tuition reimbursements (averaging $6,000 per year) were awarded. Financial award application deadline: 6/17. In 2001, 61 master's, 3 other advanced degrees awarded. *Degree program information:* Part-time and evening/weekend programs available. Offers administration and supervision (M Ed); counselor education (M Ed); curriculum and instruction (M Ed); education (M Ed, MA, SSP); psychological counseling (MA); school psychology (SSP). *Application deadline:* For fall admission, 6/17 (priority date); for spring admission, 11/15 (priority date). Applications are processed on a rolling basis. *Application fee:* $20 ($30 for international students). Electronic applications accepted. *Dean,* Dr. O. Cleveland Hill, 985-448-4325.

NICHOLS COLLEGE, Dudley, MA 01571-5000

General Information Independent, coed, comprehensive institution. *Graduate housing:* On-campus housing not available.

GRADUATE UNITS

Graduate Program in Business Administration *Degree program information:* Part-time and evening/weekend programs available. Offers accounting (MBA); finance (MBA); international business (MBA); management (MBA); marketing (MBA).

THE NIGERIAN BAPTIST THEOLOGICAL SEMINARY, Ogbomoso, Oyo, Nigeria

General Information Independent-religious, coed, primarily men, comprehensive institution. *Graduate housing:* Rooms and/or apartments available to single and married students.

GRADUATE UNITS

Graduate Studies *Degree program information:* Part-time programs available. Offers church music (Diploma); divinity (M Div); theological studies (MATS); theology (M Th).

NIPISSING UNIVERSITY, North Bay, ON P1B 8L7, Canada

General Information Province-supported, coed, comprehensive institution. *Enrollment:* 669 full-time matriculated graduate/professional students (463 women), 2,120 part-time matriculated graduate/professional students (1,528 women). *Enrollment by degree level:* 312 master's, 2,477 doctoral. *Graduate faculty:* 52 full-time (31 women), 21 part-time/adjunct (8 women). *Graduate tuition:* Tuition charges are reported in Canadian dollars. Tuition, province resident: part-time $550 Canadian dollars per course. *Graduate housing:* On-campus housing not available. *Student services:* Campus safety program, career counseling, disabled student services, exercise/wellness program, free psychological counseling, low-cost health insurance, teacher training. *Library facilities:* Education Centre Library. *Online resources:* library catalog, web page, access to other libraries' catalogs. *Collection:* 166,675 titles, 4,083 serial subscriptions, 229 audiovisual materials. *Research affiliation:* Community Partners Group (sociology and economics).

Computer facilities: 163 computers available on campus for general student use. A campuswide network can be accessed from student residence rooms and from off campus. Internet access and online class registration are available. *Web address:* http://www.nipissingu.ca/.

General Application Contact: Maureen Knight, Assistant Registrar-Admissions, 705-474-3461 Ext. 4292, Fax: 705-495-1772, E-mail: maureenk@nipissingu.ca.

GRADUATE UNITS

Faculty of Education Students: 669 full-time (463 women), 2,120 part-time (1,528 women). 3,807 applicants, 20% accepted. *Faculty:* 52 full-time (31 women), 21 part-time/adjunct (8 women). Expenses: Contact institution. In 2001, 33 degrees awarded. *Degree program information:* Part-time and evening/weekend programs available. Offers education (M Ed, Certificate). *Application deadline:* For fall admission, 6/7; for winter admission, 10/18; for spring admission, 3/29. *Application fee:* $50. *Application Contact:* Maureen Knight, Assistant Registrar-Admissions, 705-474-3461 Ext. 4292, Fax: 705-495-1772, E-mail: maureenk@nipissingu.ca. *Dean of Education,* Dr. Ronald Common, 705-474-3461 Ext. 4268, Fax: 705-474-3264, E-mail: ronaldc@nipissingu.ca.

NORFOLK STATE UNIVERSITY, Norfolk, VA 23504

General Information State-supported, coed, comprehensive institution. CGS member. *Enrollment:* 241 full-time matriculated graduate/professional students (199 women), 166 part-time matriculated graduate/professional students (119 women). *Graduate faculty:* 68 full-time (22 women), 41 part-time/adjunct (20 women). *Tuition, area resident:* Part-time $197 per credit. Tuition, nonresident: part-time $503 per credit. *Graduate housing:* On-campus housing not available. *Student services:* Campus safety program, career counseling. *Library facilities:* Lymon Beecher Brooks Library. *Online resources:* library catalog, access to other libraries' catalogs. *Collection:* 597,878 titles.

Computer facilities: 512 computers available on campus for general student use. A campuswide network can be accessed from student residence rooms and from off campus. Internet access and online class registration are available. *Web address:* http://www.nsu.edu/.

Norfolk State University (continued)

General Application Contact: Dr. Jennifer M. Keane-Dawes, Director, Office of Graduate Studies, 757-823-8015, Fax: 757-823-2849, E-mail: jkeane-dawes@nsu.edu.

GRADUATE UNITS

School of Graduate Studies Students: 241 full-time (199 women), 166 part-time (119 women); includes 328 minority (313 African Americans, 9 Asian Americans or Pacific Islanders, 4 Hispanic Americans, 2 Native Americans), 2 international. Average age 28. *Faculty:* 68 full-time (22 women), 41 part-time/adjunct (20 women). Expenses: Contact institution. *Financial support:* In 2001–02, 2 teaching assistantships (averaging $1,989 per year) were awarded; fellowships, career-related internships or fieldwork and institutionally sponsored loans also available. Financial award application deadline: 4/1; financial award applicants required to submit FAFSA. In 2001, 185 master's, 2 doctorates awarded. *Degree program information:* Part-time programs available. *Application deadline:* For fall admission, 3/1; for spring admission, 10/1. *Application fee:* $30. Electronic applications accepted. *Application Contact:* Phyllis A. Williams, Program Practitioner, 757-823-8015, Fax: 757-823-2849, E-mail: pawilliams@nsu.edu. *Director,* Dr. Jennifer M. Keane-Dawes, 757-683-8015, Fax: 757-683-2849, E-mail: jkeane-dawes@nsu.edu.

School of Education Expenses: Contact institution. *Financial support:* Fellowships, career-related internships or fieldwork, Federal Work-Study, and unspecified assistantships available. Financial award applicants required to submit FAFSA. *Degree program information:* Part-time programs available. Offers early childhood education (MAT); education (MA, MAT); education of the gifted (MA); pre-elementary education (MA); principal preparation (MA); secondary education (MAT); severe disabilities (MA); urban education/administration (MA). *Application deadline:* For fall admission, 3/1; for spring admission, 10/1. *Application fee:* $30. *Application Contact:* Phyllis A. Williams, Program Practitioner, 757-823-8015, Fax: 757-823-2849, E-mail: pawilliams@nsu.edu. *Dean,* Dr. Jean Braxton, 757-823-8701, E-mail: jbraxton@nsu.edu.

School of Liberal Arts Expenses: Contact institution. *Financial support:* Fellowships with partial tuition reimbursements, teaching assistantships with partial tuition reimbursements, unspecified assistantships available. *Degree program information:* Part-time programs available. Offers applied sociology (MS); communication (MA); community/clinical psychology (MA); liberal arts (MA, MFA, MM, MS, Psy D); media and communication (MA); music (MM); music education (MM); performance (MM); psychology (Psy D); theory and composition (MM); urban affairs (MA); visual studies (MA, MFA). *Application deadline:* For fall admission, 3/1; for spring admission, 10/1. *Application fee:* $30. *Dean,* Dr. Elsie Barnes, 757-683-8118, Fax: 757-823-2512, E-mail: embarnes@nsu.edu.

School of Science and Technology Offers health related professions and natural sciences (MS); materials science (MS).

School of Social Work 137 applicants, 74% accepted, 102 enrolled. *Faculty:* 21 full-time, 9 part-time/adjunct. Expenses: Contact institution. *Financial support:* Fellowships, research assistantships, teaching assistantships, career-related internships or fieldwork, Federal Work-Study, scholarships/grants, traineeships, and unspecified assistantships available. Financial award applicants required to submit FAFSA. *Degree program information:* Part-time programs available. Offers social work (MSW, DSW). *Application deadline:* For fall admission, 3/1; for spring admission, 10/1. *Application fee:* $30. *Application Contact:* Margaret Kerekes, Coordinator, 757-823-8696, E-mail: mdkerekes@nsu.edu. *Dean,* Dr. Marvin Feit, 757-823-8668.

See in-depth description on page 1003.

NORTH AMERICAN BAPTIST SEMINARY, Sioux Falls, SD 57105-1599

General Information Independent-religious, coed, graduate-only institution. *Graduate faculty:* 8 full-time (1 woman), 12 part-time/adjunct (3 women). *Tuition:* Full-time $9,900; part-time $412 per hour. *Required fees:* $40; $20 per semester. *Graduate housing:* Rooms and/or apartments available to single and married students. Housing application deadline: 7/1. *Student services:* Campus employment opportunities, career counseling, exercise/wellness program, free psychological counseling, international student services, low-cost health insurance. *Library facilities:* Kaiser-Ramaker Library. *Online resources:* library catalog, access to other libraries' catalogs. *Collection:* 68,898 titles, 304 serial subscriptions, 8,997 audiovisual materials.

Computer facilities: Internet access is available. *Web address:* http://www.nabs.edu/.

General Application Contact: Melissa M. Hiatt, Director of Admissions, 605-336-6588, Fax: 605-335-9090, E-mail: melissah@nabs.edu.

GRADUATE UNITS

Graduate and Professional Programs Students: 93 full-time (34 women), 23 part-time (10 women). *Faculty:* 8 full-time (1 woman), 12 part-time/adjunct (3 women). Expenses: Contact institution. *Financial support:* Career-related internships or fieldwork and scholarships/grants available. Support available to part-time students. *Degree program information:* Part-time programs available. Offers Bible and theology (MA); church music (MA); counseling (MA); marriage and family therapy (MA); ministry (D Min); pastoral ministry (M Div); religious studies (MA); theological studies (Certificate). *Application deadline:* Applications are processed on a rolling basis. *Application fee:* $35. *Application Contact:* Melissa M. Hiatt, Director of Admissions, 605-336-6588, Fax: 605-335-9090, E-mail: melissah@nabs.edu. *Academic Vice President,* Dr. Benjamin C. Leslie, 605-336-6588, Fax: 605-335-9090, E-mail: bleslie@nabs.edu.

NORTH CAROLINA AGRICULTURAL AND TECHNICAL STATE UNIVERSITY, Greensboro, NC 27411

General Information State-supported, coed, university. CGS member. *Graduate housing:* Room and/or apartments available on a first-come, first-served basis to single students; on-campus housing not available to married students. Housing application deadline: 5/8. *Research affiliation:* North Carolina Biotechnology Research Center (biotechnology research), The Boeing Company (aerospace engineering), Northrop Grumman Corporation (high performance computing), Research Triangle Institute (environmental protection, advanced technology), Rockwell Inc. (avionics technology, communications technology), Honeywell (industrial automation control).

GRADUATE UNITS

Graduate School *Degree program information:* Part-time and evening/weekend programs available.

College of Arts and Sciences *Degree program information:* Part-time and evening/weekend programs available. Offers art education (MS); arts and sciences (MA, MS, MSW); biology (MS); chemistry (MS); English (MA); English and Afro-American literature (MA); history education (MS); mathematics education (MS); social science education (MS); sociology and social work (MSW).

College of Engineering Students: 270 full-time (113 women), 7 part-time (2 women); includes 187 minority (167 African Americans, 20 Asian Americans or Pacific Islanders), 61 international. Average age 25. 790 applicants, 82% accepted, 339 enrolled. *Faculty:* 74 full-time (4 women), 15 part-time/adjunct (1 woman). Expenses: Contact institution. *Financial support:* Fellowships, research assistantships, teaching assistantships, career-related internships or fieldwork and unspecified assistantships available. Support available to part-time students. In 2001, 83 master's, 5 doctorates awarded. *Degree program information:* Part-time programs available. Offers architectural, agricultural, civil and environmental engineering (MSAE, MSCE, MSE); chemical engineering (MSE); computer science (MSCS); electrical engineering (MSEE, PhD); engineering (MSAE, MSCE, MSCS, MSE, MSEE, MSISE, MSME, PhD); industrial and systems engineering (MSISE, PhD); mechanical engineering (MSME, PhD). *Application deadline:* For fall admission, 7/1 (priority date); for spring admission, 1/9. Applications are processed on a rolling basis. *Application fee:* $35. *Application Contact:* Dr. Kenneth Murray, Interim Dean of the Graduate School, 336-334-7920, Fax: 336-334-7282, E-mail: kmurray@ncat.edu. *Dean,* Dr. Joseph Monroe, 336-334-7589, Fax: 336-334-7540, E-mail: monroe@ncat.edu.

School of Agriculture and Environmental and Allied Sciences *Degree program information:* Part-time and evening/weekend programs available. Offers agricultural economics (MS); agricultural education (MS); agriculture and environmental and allied sciences (MS); food and nutrition (MS); plant science (MS).

School of Education *Degree program information:* Part-time and evening/weekend programs available. Offers adult education (MS); biology education (MS); chemistry education (MS); early childhood education (MS); education (MS); educational administration (MS); educational media (MS); elementary education (MS); English education (MS); guidance and counseling (MS); health and physical education (MS); history education (MS); human resources (MS); intermediate education (MS); reading (MS); social science education (MS).

School of Technology *Degree program information:* Part-time and evening/weekend programs available. Offers industrial arts education (MS); industrial technology (MS, MSIT); safety and driver education (MS); technology (MS, MSIT); technology education (MS); vocational-industrial education (MS).

NORTH CAROLINA CENTRAL UNIVERSITY, Durham, NC 27707-3129

General Information State-supported, coed, comprehensive institution. CGS member. *Enrollment:* 644 full-time matriculated graduate/professional students (427 women), 616 part-time matriculated graduate/professional students (457 women). *Enrollment by degree level:* 345 first professional, 915 master's. *Graduate faculty:* 208 full-time (94 women), 61 part-time/adjunct (27 women). Tuition, state resident: full-time $1,424. Tuition, nonresident: full-time $9,492. *Required fees:* $1,054. *Graduate housing:* Room and/or apartments available to single students; on-campus housing not available to married students. Typical cost: $1,742 per year ($3,284 including board). Housing application deadline: 7/1. *Student services:* Career counseling, child daycare facilities, disabled student services, free psychological counseling, low-cost health insurance. *Library facilities:* Shepherd Library plus 1 other. *Online resources:* library catalog, access to other libraries' catalogs.

Computer facilities: 400 computers available on campus for general student use. *Web address:* http://www.nccu.edu/.

General Application Contact: Dr. Walter Harris, Vice Chancellor for Academic Affairs and Provost, 919-560-6230, Fax: 919-560-5012, E-mail: harris@wpo.nccu.edu.

GRADUATE UNITS

Division of Academic Affairs Students: 644 full-time (427 women), 616 part-time (457 women); includes 849 minority (787 African Americans, 28 Asian Americans or Pacific Islanders, 13 Hispanic Americans, 21 Native Americans) Average age 32. 1,272 applicants, 45% accepted. *Faculty:* 208 full-time (94 women), 61 part-time/adjunct (27 women). Expenses: Contact institution. *Financial support:* Fellowships, research assistantships, teaching assistantships, career-related internships or fieldwork, Federal Work-Study, institutionally sponsored loans, and scholarships/grants available. Support available to part-time students. Financial award application deadline: 5/1. In 2001, 100 first professional degrees, 293 master's awarded. *Degree program information:* Part-time and evening/weekend programs available. *Application fee:* $30. *Vice Chancellor for Academic Affairs and Provost,* Dr. Walter Harris, 919-560-6320, Fax: 919-560-5012, E-mail: harris@wpo.nccu.edu.

College of Arts and Sciences Students: 114 full-time (86 women), 275 part-time (182 women); includes 346 minority (339 African Americans, 1 Asian American or Pacific Islander, 3 Hispanic Americans, 3 Native Americans) Average age 31. 158 applicants, 94% accepted. *Faculty:* 118 full-time (49 women), 36 part-time/adjunct (20 women). Expenses: Contact institution. *Financial support:* Fellowships, research assistantships, teaching assistantships, career-related internships or fieldwork, Federal Work-Study, institutionally sponsored loans, and scholarships/grants available. Support available to part-time students. Financial award application deadline: 5/1. In 2001, 82 degrees awarded. *Degree program information:* Part-time and evening/weekend programs available. Offers arts and sciences (MA, MPA, MS); biology (MS); chemistry (MS); criminal justice (MS); earth sciences (MS); English (MA); general physical education (MS); history (MA); human sciences (MS); mathematics (MS); psychology (MA); public administration (MPA); recreation administration (MS); sociology (MA); special physical education (MS); therapeutic recreation (MS). *Application deadline:* For fall admission, 8/1. *Application fee:* $30. *Dean,* Dr. Bernice D. Johnson, 919-560-6368, Fax: 919-530-5361, E-mail: bjohnson@wpo.nccu.edu.

School of Business Students: 25 full-time (10 women), 29 part-time (14 women); includes 40 minority (38 African Americans, 2 Asian Americans or Pacific Islanders) Average age 29. 39 applicants, 97% accepted. *Faculty:* 28 full-time (9 women), 8 part-time/adjunct (3 women). Expenses: Contact institution. *Financial support:* Teaching assistantships, Federal Work-Study and institutionally sponsored loans available. Support available to part-time students. Financial award application deadline: 5/1. In 2001, 13 degrees awarded. *Degree program information:* Part-time and evening/weekend programs available. Offers business (MBA). *Application deadline:* For fall admission, 8/1. *Application fee:* $30. *Application Contact:* Dr. Mary Phillips, Associate Dean, 919-530-7378, Fax: 919-530-6163, E-mail: mphillips@wpo.nccu.edu. *Dean,* Dr. H. James Williams, 919-560-6458, Fax: 919-530-7961, E-mail: hwilliam@wpo.nccu.edu.

School of Education Students: 83 full-time (76 women), 189 part-time (159 women); includes 175 minority (166 African Americans, 3 Asian Americans or Pacific Islanders, 2 Hispanic Americans, 4 Native Americans) Average age 32. 101 applicants, 91% accepted. *Faculty:* 32 full-time (21 women), 6 part-time/adjunct (2 women). Expenses: Contact institution. *Financial support:* Fellowships, research assistantships, teaching assistantships, career-related internships or fieldwork, Federal Work-Study, institutionally sponsored loans, and scholarships/grants available. Support available to part-time students. Financial award application deadline: 5/1. In 2001, 102 degrees awarded. *Degree program information:* Part-time and evening/weekend programs available. Offers agency counseling (MA); career counseling (MA); development leadership and professional studies (MA); education (M Ed, MA); education of the emotionally handicapped (M Ed); education of the mentally handicapped (M Ed); elementary education (M Ed, MA); instructional media (MA); school counseling (MA); speech pathology and audiology (M Ed). *Application deadline:* For fall admission, 8/1. *Application fee:* $30. *Application Contact:* Dr. Janice A. Harper, Interim Associate Dean of Graduate Studies and Administration, 919-530-7297, Fax: 919-530-7681, E-mail: jharper@wpo.nccu.edu. *Interim Dean,* Dr. Cecelia Steppe-Jones, 919-560-6466, Fax: 919-530-7971, E-mail: csteppej@wpo.nccu.edu.

School of Law Students: 339 full-time (202 women), 6 part-time (4 women); includes 181 minority (161 African Americans, 4 Asian Americans or Pacific Islanders, 8 Hispanic Americans, 8 Native Americans) Average age 30. 895 applicants, 24% accepted. *Faculty:* 23 full-time (12 women), 4 part-time/adjunct (0 women). Expenses: Contact institution. *Financial support:* Career-related internships or fieldwork, Federal Work-Study, and institutionally sponsored loans available. Support available to part-time students. Financial award application deadline: 5/1. In 2001, 100 degrees awarded. *Degree program information:* Part-time and evening/weekend programs available. Offers law (JD, LL B). *Application deadline:* For fall admission, 4/15. *Application fee:* $30. *Application Contact:* Adrienne Meddock, Assistant Dean, 919-560-5249. *Dean,* Janice Mills, 919-530-7161, Fax: 919-560-6339, E-mail: jmills@wpo.nccu.edu.

School of Library and Information Sciences Students: 72 full-time (44 women), 128 part-time (107 women); includes 107 minority (83 African Americans, 18 Asian Americans or Pacific Islanders, 6 Native Americans) Average age 36. 79 applicants, 99% accepted. *Faculty:* 7 full-time (3 women), 7 part-time/adjunct (2 women). Expenses: Contact institution. *Financial support:* Fellowships, research assistantships, career-related internships or fieldwork, institutionally sponsored loans, and scholarships/grants available. Support available to part-time students. Financial award application deadline: 5/1. In 2001, 96 degrees awarded. *Degree program information:* Part-time and evening/weekend programs available. Offers library and information sciences (MIS, MLS). *Application deadline:* For fall admission, 8/1. *Application fee:* $30. *Dean,* Dr. Benjamin F. Speller, 919-560-6485, Fax: 919-560-6402, E-mail: bspeller@wpo.nccu.edu.

NORTH CAROLINA SCHOOL OF THE ARTS, Winston-Salem, NC 27127-2188

General Information State-supported, coed, comprehensive institution. *Enrollment:* 77 full-time matriculated graduate/professional students (48 women), 4 part-time matriculated graduate/professional students (2 women). *Enrollment by degree level:* 81 master's. *Graduate faculty:* 47 full-time (9 women), 6 part-time/adjunct (3 women). Tuition, state resident: full-time $1,761. Tuition, nonresident: full-time $11,340. *Required fees:* $1,215. *Graduate housing:* Room and/or apartments available on a first-come, first-served basis to single students; on-campus housing not available to married students. *Student services:* Campus employment opportunities, campus safety program, career counseling, disabled student services, exercise/wellness program, free psychological counseling, grant writing training, international student services, low-cost health insurance, writing training. *Library facilities:* Semans Library plus 1 other. *Collection:* 85,672 titles, 48,546 serial subscriptions, 12,597 audiovisual materials.

Computer facilities: 20 computers available on campus for general student use. *Web address:* http://www.ncarts.edu/.

General Application Contact: Sheeler Lawson, Director of Admissions, 336-770-3290, Fax: 336-770-3370, E-mail: admissions@ncarts.edu.

GRADUATE UNITS

School of Design and Production Students: 31 full-time (19 women), 1 (woman) part-time; includes 3 minority (all African Americans), 2 international. Average age 25. 27 applicants, 78% accepted, 16 enrolled. *Faculty:* 19 full-time (4 women). Expenses: Contact institution. *Financial support:* In 2001–02, 24 teaching assistantships with partial tuition reimbursements (averaging $3,000 per year) were awarded; career-related internships or fieldwork, Federal Work-Study, and unspecified assistantships also available. Support available to part-time students. Financial award application deadline: 3/15; financial award applicants required to submit FAFSA. In 2001, 10 degrees awarded. Offers costume design (MFA); costume technology (MFA); film production design (MFA); scene design (MFA); scene painting/properties (MFA); sound design (MFA); technical direction (MFA); wig and make-up design (MFA). *Application deadline:* For fall admission, 4/1 (priority date). Applications are processed on a rolling basis. *Application fee:* $45 ($90 for international students). *Application Contact:* Sheeler Lawson, Director of Admissions, 336-770-3290, Fax: 336-770-3370, E-mail: admissions@ncarts.edu. *Dean,* John A. Sneden, 336-770-3214 Ext. 103, Fax: 336-770-3213, E-mail: snedej@ncarts.edu.

School of Music Students: 46 full-time (29 women), 3 part-time (1 woman); includes 5 minority (3 African Americans, 1 Asian American or Pacific Islander, 1 Hispanic American), 11 international. Average age 25. 39 applicants, 87% accepted, 23 enrolled. *Faculty:* 28 full-time (5 women), 6 part-time/adjunct (3 women). Expenses: Contact institution. *Financial support:* In 2001–02, 10 fellowships with partial tuition reimbursements (averaging $5,000 per year), 9 teaching assistantships with partial tuition reimbursements (averaging $2,000 per year) were awarded. Career-related internships or fieldwork and Federal Work-Study also available. Support available to part-time students. Financial award application deadline: 3/15; financial award applicants required to submit FAFSA. In 2001, 22 degrees awarded. Offers film music composition (MM); music performance (MM); orchestral conducting (MM). *Application deadline:* For fall admission, 4/1 (priority date). Applications are processed on a rolling basis. *Application fee:* $45 ($90 for international students). *Application Contact:* Sheeler Lawson, Director of Admissions, 336-770-3290, Fax: 336-770-3370, E-mail: admissions@ncarts.edu. *Dean,* Dr. Robert Yekovich, 336-770-3251, Fax: 336-770-3248, E-mail: yekovb@ncarts.edu.

NORTH CAROLINA STATE UNIVERSITY, Raleigh, NC 27695

General Information State-supported, coed, university. CGS member. *Enrollment:* 3,670 full-time matriculated graduate/professional students (1,479 women), 1,932 part-time matriculated graduate/professional students (877 women). *Enrollment by degree level:* 3,443 master's, 2,159 doctoral. *Graduate faculty:* 1,602 full-time (291 women), 818 part-time/adjunct (86 women). Tuition, state resident: full-time $1,748. Tuition, nonresident: full-time $6,904. *Graduate housing:* Rooms and/or apartments available on a first-come, first-served basis to single and married students. Typical cost: $3,335 per year for single students; $4,066 per year for married students. Room charges vary according to board plan, campus/location and housing facility selected. *Student services:* Campus employment opportunities, campus safety program, career counseling, child daycare facilities, free psychological counseling, international student services, low-cost health insurance. *Library facilities:* D. H. Hill Library plus 4 others. *Online resources:* library catalog, web page, access to other libraries' catalogs. *Collection:* 951,788 titles, 35,882 serial subscriptions, 142,831 audiovisual materials. *Research affiliation:* Triangle Universities Nuclear Laboratory, Research Triangle Institute, Highlands Biological Station, National Humanities Center, North Carolina Microelectronics Center, North Carolina-Japan Center.

Computer facilities: 4,600 computers available on campus for general student use. A campuswide network can be accessed from student residence rooms and from off campus. Internet access is available. *Web address:* http://www.ncsu.edu/.

General Application Contact: Graduate Admissions, 919-515-2871, Fax: 919-515-2873, E-mail: graduate_admissions@ncsu.edu.

GRADUATE UNITS

College of Veterinary Medicine Students: 94 full-time (50 women), 15 part-time (5 women); includes 15 minority (9 African Americans, 3 Asian Americans or Pacific Islanders, 3 Hispanic Americans), 27 international. Average age 32. 53 applicants, 51% accepted. *Faculty:* 127 full-time (34 women), 53 part-time/adjunct (6 women). Expenses: Contact institution. *Financial support:* In 2001–02, 10 fellowships (averaging $8,068 per year), 64 research assistantships (averaging $7,363 per year), 1 teaching assistantship (averaging $5,545 per year) were awarded. Federal Work-Study also available. In 2001, 65 first professional degrees, 14 master's, 8 doctorates awarded. *Degree program information:* Part-time programs available. Offers cell biology and morphology (MS, PhD); epidemiology and population medicine (MS, PhD); immunology (MS, PhD); microbiology and immunology (MS, PhD); pathology (MS, PhD); pharmacology (MS, PhD); specialized veterinary medicine (MS); veterinary medicine (DVM, MLS, MS, PhD). *Application deadline:* Applications are processed on a rolling basis. *Application Contact:* Sandra Poole, Administrative Assistant, 919-513-6210, Fax: 919-513-6452, E-mail: sandra_poole@ncsu.edu. *Dean,* Dr. Oscar J. Fletcher, 919-513-6210, Fax: 919-513-6452, E-mail: oscar_fletcher@ncsu.edu.

Graduate School Students: 3,670 full-time (1,479 women), 1,932 part-time (877 women); includes 751 minority (420 African Americans, 225 Asian Americans or Pacific Islanders, 85 Hispanic Americans, 21 Native Americans), 1,467 international. Average age 31. 6,477 applicants, 41% accepted. *Faculty:* 1,602 full-time (291 women), 818 part-time/adjunct (86 women). Expenses: Contact institution. *Financial support:* In 2001–02, 216 fellowships (averaging $6,314 per year), 1,485 research assistantships (averaging $5,878 per year), 726 teaching assistantships (averaging $5,363 per year) were awarded. Career-related internships or fieldwork, Federal Work-Study, institutionally sponsored loans, scholarships/grants, traineeships, tuition waivers (full and partial), and minority grants also available. Support available to part-time students. In 2001, 1,137 master's, 290 doctorates awarded. *Degree program information:* Part-time and evening/weekend programs available. Postbaccalaureate distance learning degree programs offered. Offers bioinformatics (MB, PhD); functional genomics (MFG, MS, PhD). *Application deadline:* Applications are processed on a rolling basis. *Application fee:* $45. *Application Contact:* 919-515-2871, Fax: 919-515-2873, E-mail: graduate_admissions@ncsu.edu. *Dean,* Dr. Robert S. Sowell, 919-515-2394, Fax: 919-515-2873, E-mail: robert_sowell@ncsu.edu.

College of Agriculture and Life Sciences Students: 622 full-time (310 women), 160 part-time (84 women); includes 72 minority (36 African Americans, 16 Asian Americans or Pacific Islanders, 19 Hispanic Americans, 1 Native American), 123 international. Average age 30. 686 applicants, 36% accepted. *Faculty:* 465 full-time (68 women), 249 part-time/adjunct (19 women). Expenses: Contact institution. *Financial support:* In 2001–02, 67 fellowships (averaging $6,968 per year), 404 research assistantships (averaging $5,433 per year), 69 teaching assistantships (averaging $5,811 per year) were awarded. Career-related internships or fieldwork, Federal Work-Study, institutionally sponsored loans, traineeships, and tuition waivers (partial) also available. Support available to part-time students. In 2001, 99 master's, 63 doctorates awarded. *Degree program information:* Part-time programs available. Offers agricultural economics (M Econ, MS, PhD); agricultural education (MAEE, MS); agriculture and life sciences (M Ag, M Econ, M Ed, M Tox, MAEE, MAWB, MBAE, MLS, MS, Ed D, PhD); animal science (M Ag, MS, PhD); biochemistry (MS, PhD); biological and agricultural engineering (MBAE, MS, PhD); botany (MLS, MS, PhD); crop science (M Ag, MS, PhD); entomology (M Ag, MS, PhD); extension education (MAEE, MS); food science (M Ag, MS, PhD); genetics (MS, PhD); horticultural science (M Ag, MS, PhD); microbiology (MLS, MS, PhD); nutrition (MS, PhD); physiology (MLS, MS, PhD); plant pathology (M Ag, MLS, MS, PhD); poultry science (MS); soil science (M Ag, MS, PhD); toxicology (M Tox, MS, PhD); zoology (MAWB, MLS, MS, PhD). *Application fee:* $45. *Application Contact:* Bee Smith, Administrative Assistant, 919-515-2668, Fax: 919-515-6980, E-mail: bee_smith@ncsu.edu. *Interim Dean,* Dr. James L. Oblinger, 919-515-2668, Fax: 919-515-6980, E-mail: james_oblinger@ncsu.edu.

College of Design Students: 176 full-time (88 women), 10 part-time (7 women); includes 18 minority (6 African Americans, 5 Asian Americans or Pacific Islanders, 5 Hispanic Americans, 2 Native Americans), 24 international. Average age 31. 276 applicants, 49% accepted. *Faculty:* 47 full-time (11 women), 6 part-time/adjunct (1 woman). Expenses: Contact institution. *Financial support:* In 2001–02, 11 fellowships (averaging $2,182 per year), 12 research assistantships (averaging $3,764 per year), 25 teaching assistantships (averaging $2,244 per year) were awarded. Career-related internships or fieldwork and Federal Work-Study also available. In 2001, 48 degrees awarded. *Degree program information:* Part-time programs available. Offers architecture (M Arch); design (M Arch, MGD, MID, MLA, PhD); graphic design (MGD); industrial design (MID); landscape architecture (MLA). *Application fee:* $45. *Application Contact:* Dottie Haynes, Administrative Assistant, 919-515-8302, Fax: 919-515-7330, E-mail: dottie_haynes@ncsu.edu. *Dean,* Prof. Marvin Malecha, 919-515-8310, Fax: 919-515-7330, E-mail: marvin_malecha@ncsu.edu.

College of Education Students: 291 full-time (198 women), 625 part-time (401 women); includes 215 minority (187 African Americans, 7 Asian Americans or Pacific Islanders, 12 Hispanic Americans, 9 Native Americans), 9 international. Average age 38. 482 applicants, 61% accepted. *Faculty:* 105 full-time (40 women), 77 part-time/adjunct (26 women). Expenses: Contact institution. *Financial support:* In 2001–02, 13 fellowships (averaging $2,659 per year), 32 research assistantships (averaging $5,362 per year), 17 teaching assistantships (averaging $5,174 per year) were awarded. Career-related internships or fieldwork, Federal Work-Study, institutionally sponsored loans, tuition waivers (full), and minority grants also available. Support available to part-time students. In 2001, 181 master's, 42 doctorates awarded. *Degree program information:* Part-time programs available. Offers agency counseling (M Ed, MS); agricultural education (M Ed, MS, CAGS); counselor education (PhD, CAGS); curriculum and instruction (M Ed, MS, Ed D); education (M Ed, MS, MSA, Ed D, PhD, CAGS, Certificate); educational administration and supervision (Ed D); educational research and policy analysis (Ed D); health occupations and teacher education (M Ed, MS); health occupations education (M Ed, MS); higher education administration (M Ed, MS, Ed D); mathematics education (M Ed, MS, PhD); middle years education (M Ed, MS); occupational education (M Ed, MS, Ed D, CAGS); psychology (MS, PhD); school administration (MSA); science education (M Ed, MS, PhD); special education (M Ed, MS); technology education (M Ed, MS, Ed D); training and development (M Ed, MS). *Application deadline:* Applications are processed on a rolling basis. *Application fee:* $45. *Application Contact:* Sue Bullard, Administrative Assistant, 919-515-2231, Fax: 919-515-5836, E-mail: bullard@poe.coe.ncsu.edu. *Dean,* Kathryn M. Moore, 919-515-5900, Fax: 919-515-5901, E-mail: kay_moore@ncsu.edu.

College of Engineering Students: 1,250 full-time (267 women), 504 part-time (86 women); includes 219 minority (59 African Americans, 131 Asian Americans or Pacific Islanders, 26 Hispanic Americans, 3 Native Americans), 904 international. Average age 28. 3,094 applicants, 35% accepted. *Faculty:* 244 full-time (17 women), 171 part-time/adjunct (4 women). Expenses: Contact institution. *Financial support:* In 2001–02, 52 fellowships (averaging $7,336 per year), 519 research assistantships (averaging $6,078 per year), 246 teaching assistantships (averaging $5,773 per year) were awarded. Career-related internships or fieldwork, Federal Work-Study, institutionally sponsored loans, scholarships/grants, and traineeships also available. In 2001, 401 master's, 85 doctorates awarded. *Degree program information:* Part-time programs available. Offers aerospace engineering (MS, PhD); chemical engineering (M Ch E, MS, PhD); civil engineering (MCE, MS, PhD); computer engineering (MS, PhD); computer networking (MS); computer science (MC Sc, MS, PhD); electrical engineering (MS, PhD); engineering (M Ch E, M Eng, MBAE, MC Sc, MCE, MIE, MIMS, MME, MMSE, MNE, MOR, MS, MSIE, PhD, PD); industrial engineering (MIE, MSIE, PhD); integrated manufacturing systems engineering (MIMS); materials science and engineering (MMSE, MS, PhD); mechanical engineering (MME, MS, PhD); nuclear engineering (MNE, MS, PhD); operations research (MOR, MS, PhD). *Application deadline:* Applications are processed on a rolling basis. *Application fee:* $45. *Application Contact:* Fran Coats, Administrative Assistant, 919-515-2311, Fax: 919-515-7951, E-mail: fran_coats@ncsu.edu. *Dean,* Dr. Nino A. Masnari, 919-515-2311, Fax: 919-515-7951, E-mail: nino_masnari@ncsu.edu.

College of Humanities and Social Sciences Students: 266 full-time (188 women), 305 part-time (184 women); includes 74 minority (55 African Americans, 12 Asian Americans or Pacific Islanders, 5 Hispanic Americans, 2 Native Americans), 16 international. Average age 33. 468 applicants, 49% accepted. *Faculty:* 172 full-time (60 women), 55 part-time/adjunct (15 women). Expenses: Contact institution. *Financial support:* In 2001–02, 16 fellowships (averaging $3,563 per year), 24 research assistantships (averaging $5,596 per year), 123 teaching assistantships (averaging $4,430 per year) were awarded. Career-related internships or fieldwork, Federal Work-Study, institutionally sponsored loans, traineeships, and minority grants also available. Support available to part-time students. In 2001, 118 master's, 11 doctorates awarded. *Degree program information:* Part-time and evening/weekend programs available. Offers English (MA); history (MA); humanities and social sciences (M Soc, MA, MAIS, MPA, MS, PhD); international studies (MAIS); liberal studies (MA); organizational communication (MS); public administration (MPA, PhD); public history (MA); rural sociology (MS); sociology (M Soc, PhD); technical communication (MS). *Application deadline:* Applications are processed on a rolling basis. *Application fee:* $45. *Application Contact:* Amy Roberson, Administrative Assistant, 919-515-2467, Fax: 919-515-9419, E-mail: amy_roberson@ncsu.edu. *Dean,* Linda P. Brady, 919-515-0402, Fax: 919-515-9419, E-mail: linda_brady@ncsu.edu.

College of Management Students: 198 full-time (88 women), 164 part-time (53 women); includes 46 minority (19 African Americans, 21 Asian Americans or Pacific Islanders, 6 Hispanic Americans), 72 international. Average age 31. 498 applicants, 45% accepted. *Faculty:* 96 full-time (15 women), 3 part-time/adjunct (0 women). Expenses: Contact institution. *Financial support:* In 2001–02, 3 fellowships (averaging $3,918 per year), 13 research assistantships (averaging $5,323 per year), 63 teaching assistantships (averaging $3,626 per year) were awarded. In 2001, 130 master's, 5 doctorates awarded. *Degree program information:* Part-time programs available. Offers accounting (MAC); biotechnology (MS); computer science (MS); economics (M Econ, MA, PhD); engineering (MS); forest resources management (MS); general business (MS); management (MS); management information systems (MS); operations research (MS); statistics (MS); telecommunications systems engineering (MS); textile management (MS); total quality management (MS). *Application deadline:* Applications are processed on a rolling basis. *Application fee:* $45. *Application Contact:* Christine Miller, Administrative Assistant, 919-515-5560, Fax: 919-515-5564, E-mail: christine_miller@ncsu.edu. *Interim Dean,* Dr. Jon W. Bartley, 919-515-5560, Fax: 919-515-1078, E-mail: jon_bartley@ncsu.edu.

College of Natural Resources Students: 131 full-time (49 women), 66 part-time (28 women); includes 13 minority (5 African Americans, 3 Asian Americans or Pacific Islanders, 4 Hispanic Americans, 1 Native American), 39 international. Average age 31. 112 applicants, 54% accepted. *Faculty:* 85 full-time (13 women), 56 part-time/adjunct (3 women). Expenses: Contact institution. *Financial support:* In 2001–02, 3 fellowships (averaging $4,407 per year), 77 research assistantships (averaging $4,554 per year), 11 teaching assistantships (averaging $4,192 per year) were awarded. Career-related internships or fieldwork and institutionally sponsored loans also available. Support available to part-time students. In 2001, 45 master's, 8 doctorates awarded. *Degree program information:* Part-time

North Carolina State University (continued)

programs available. Offers fisheries and wildlife sciences (MS); forestry (MF, MS, PhD); geographic information systems (MS); maintenance management (MRRA, MS); natural resources (MF, MNR, MRRA, MS, MWPS, PhD); recreation planning (MRRA, MS); recreation resources administration/public administration (MRRA); recreation/park management (MRRA, MS); sports management (MRRA, MS); travel and tourism management (MS); wood and paper science (MS, MWPS, PhD). *Application deadline:* Applications are processed on a rolling basis. *Application fee:* $45. *Application Contact:* Dawn Silsbee, Administrative Assistant, 919-515-2883, Fax: 919-515-7231, E-mail: dawn_silsbee@ncsu.edu. *Dean,* Larry A. Nielsen, 919-515-2883, Fax: 919-515-7231, E-mail: larry_neilsen@ncsu.edu.

College of Physical and Mathematical Sciences Students: 536 full-time (197 women), 64 part-time (21 women); includes 73 minority (41 African Americans, 26 Asian Americans or Pacific Islanders, 4 Hispanic Americans, 2 Native Americans), 182 international. Average age 29. 701 applicants, 43% accepted. *Faculty:* 216 full-time (25 women), 104 part-time/adjunct (7 women). Expenses: Contact institution. *Financial support:* In 2001–02, 41 fellowships (averaging $7,169 per year), 271 research assistantships (averaging $6,385 per year), 163 teaching assistantships (averaging $6,549 per year) were awarded. Career-related internships or fieldwork, Federal Work-Study, and institutionally sponsored loans also available. Financial award application deadline: 3/1. In 2001, 79 master's, 53 doctorates awarded. *Degree program information:* Part-time programs available. Offers applied mathematics (MS, PhD); biomathematics (M Biomath, MS, PhD); chemistry (MCH, MS, PhD); ecology (PhD); geology (MS, PhD); geophysics (MS, PhD); marine, earth, and atmospheric sciences (MS, PhD); mathematics (MS, PhD); meteorology (MS, PhD); oceanography (MS, PhD); physical and mathematical sciences (M Biomath, M Stat, MCH, MS, PhD); physics (MS, PhD); statistics (M Stat, MS, PhD). *Application deadline:* Applications are processed on a rolling basis. *Application fee:* $45. *Application Contact:* Winnie D. Ellis, Administrative Assistant, 919-515-7277, Fax: 919-515-7855, E-mail: winnie_ellis@ncsu.edu. *Dean,* Dr. Daniel L. Solomon, 919-515-7277, Fax: 919-515-7855, E-mail: d_solomon@ncsu.edu.

College of Textiles Students: 106 full-time (44 women), 19 part-time (8 women); includes 6 minority (3 African Americans, 1 Asian American or Pacific Islander, 1 Hispanic American, 1 Native American), 71 international. Average age 29. 93 applicants, 44% accepted. *Faculty:* 44 full-time (7 women), 46 part-time/adjunct (5 women). Expenses: Contact institution. *Financial support:* In 2001–02, 1 fellowship (averaging $6,774 per year), 71 research assistantships (averaging $5,344 per year) were awarded. Teaching assistantships, career-related internships or fieldwork, Federal Work-Study, and institutionally sponsored loans also available. Support available to part-time students. Financial award application deadline: 6/1. In 2001, 25 master's, 11 doctorates awarded. *Degree program information:* Part-time and evening/weekend programs available. Postbaccalaureate distance learning degree programs offered. Offers fiber and polymer sciences (PhD); textile chemistry (MS, MT); textile engineering (MS); textile management and technology (MS, MT); textile materials science (MS); textile technology management (PhD); textiles (MTE); textiles materials science (MT). *Application deadline:* For fall admission, 6/25. *Application fee:* $45. *Application Contact:* Cindy Maciejewski, Administrative Assistant, 919-515-6640, Fax: 919-515-3057, E-mail: cindy_maciejewski@ncsu.edu. *Acting Dean,* A. Blanton Godfrey, 919-515-6500, Fax: 919-515-3057, E-mail: blanton_godfrey@ncsu.edu.

NORTH CENTRAL COLLEGE, Naperville, IL 60566-7063

General Information Independent-religious, coed, comprehensive institution. *Enrollment:* 73 full-time matriculated graduate/professional students (31 women), 375 part-time matriculated graduate/professional students (192 women). *Enrollment by degree level:* 448 master's. *Graduate faculty:* 40 full-time, 22 part-time/adjunct. *Tuition:* Full-time $8,145; part-time $552 per credit hour. *Graduate housing:* On-campus housing not available. *Student services:* Campus employment opportunities, campus safety program, career counseling, free psychological counseling, international student services, multicultural affairs office, writing training. *Library facilities:* Oesterle Library. *Online resources:* library catalog, web page, access to other libraries' catalogs. *Collection:* 132,322 titles, 736 serial subscriptions, 3,546 audiovisual materials.

Computer facilities: 200 computers available on campus for general student use. A campuswide network can be accessed from student residence rooms and from off campus. Internet access, software packages are available. *Web address:* http://www.noctrl.edu/.

General Application Contact: Frank Johnson, Director of Graduate Programs, 630-637-5840, Fax: 630-637-5844, E-mail: frjohnson@noctrl.edu.

GRADUATE UNITS

Graduate Programs Students: 73 full-time (31 women), 375 part-time (192 women); includes 58 minority (15 African Americans, 33 Asian Americans or Pacific Islanders, 10 Hispanic Americans) Average age 32. 203 applicants, 81% accepted. *Faculty:* 40 full-time, 22 part-time/adjunct. Expenses: Contact institution. *Financial support:* Scholarships/grants available. Support available to part-time students. In 2001, 121 degrees awarded. *Degree program information:* Part-time and evening/weekend programs available. Offers business administration (MBA); computer science (MS); education (MA Ed); leadership studies (MLD); liberal studies (MALS); management information systems (MS). *Application deadline:* For fall admission, 8/15; for winter admission, 12/1; for spring admission, 2/1. Applications are processed on a rolling basis. *Application fee:* $25. *Application Contact:* Frank Johnson, Director of Graduate Programs, 630-637-5840, Fax: 630-637-5844, E-mail: frjohnson@noctrl.edu. *Associate Dean,* Barbara E. Illg, 630-637-5362, Fax: 630-637-5360, E-mail: bei@noctrl.edu.

NORTH DAKOTA STATE UNIVERSITY, Fargo, ND 58105

General Information State-supported, coed, university. CGS member. *Enrollment:* 1,083 matriculated graduate/professional students (447 women). *Enrollment by degree level:* 862 master's, 221 doctoral. *Graduate faculty:* 432 full-time (65 women), 21 part-time/adjunct (6 women). Tuition, state resident: part-time $124 per credit. Tuition, nonresident: part-time $325 per credit. *Required fees:* $22 per credit. Tuition and fees vary according to reciprocity agreements. *Graduate housing:* Rooms and/or apartments available on a first-come, first-served basis to single and married students. *Student services:* Career counseling, child daycare facilities, disabled student services, free psychological counseling, international student services, low-cost health insurance, multicultural affairs office. *Library facilities:* North Dakota State University Library plus 3 others. *Online resources:* library catalog, web page, access to other libraries' catalogs. *Collection:* 400,000 titles, 4,500 serial subscriptions, 3,200 audiovisual materials. *Research affiliation:* U.S. Department of Agriculture–Metabolism and Radiation Laboratory.

Computer facilities: 500 computers available on campus for general student use. A campuswide network can be accessed from student residence rooms and from off campus. Internet access is available. *Web address:* http://www.ndsu.edu/.

General Application Contact: Velmer S. Burton, Dean, 701-231-7033, Fax: 701-231-6524.

GRADUATE UNITS

The Graduate School Students: 1,083 full-time (447 women); includes 183 minority (20 African Americans, 152 Asian Americans or Pacific Islanders, 3 Hispanic Americans, 8 Native Americans), 72 international. Average age 25. 685 applicants, 80% accepted. *Faculty:* 432 full-time (65 women), 21 part-time/adjunct (6 women). Expenses: Contact institution. *Financial support:* Fellowships with full tuition reimbursements, research assistantships with full tuition reimbursements, teaching assistantships with full tuition reimbursements, career-related internships or fieldwork, Federal Work-Study, institutionally sponsored loans, scholarships/grants, traineeships, tuition waivers (full and partial), and unspecified assistantships available. Support available to part-time students. Financial award applicants required to submit FAFSA. In 2001, 202 master's, 25 doctorates, 3 other advanced degrees awarded. *Degree program information:* Part-time and evening/weekend programs available. Postbaccalaureate distance learning degree programs offered (minimal on-campus study). Offers natural resources management (MS, PhD); nursing (MS). *Application fee:* $35. Electronic applications accepted. *Dean,* Velmer S. Burton, 701-231-7033, Fax: 701-231-6524.

College of Agriculture Students: 177 (62 women); includes 9 minority (2 African Americans, 1 Asian American or Pacific Islander, 3 Hispanic Americans, 3 Native Americans) 42 international. Average age 26. *Faculty:* 134. Expenses: Contact institution. *Financial support:* Fellowships with full tuition reimbursements, research assistantships with full tuition reimbursements, teaching assistantships with full tuition reimbursements, career-related internships or fieldwork, Federal Work-Study, and institutionally sponsored loans available. Support available to part-time students. In 2001, 32 master's, 8 doctorates awarded. *Degree program information:* Part-time programs available. Offers agricultural economics (MS); agriculture (MS, PhD); animal science (MS, PhD); cellular and molecular biology (PhD); cereal science (MS, PhD); crop and weed sciences (MS); entomology (MS, PhD); horticulture (MS); microbiology (MS); natural resources management (MS, PhD); plant pathology (MS, PhD); plant sciences (PhD); range science (MS, PhD); soil sciences (MS, PhD); veterinary sciences (MS). *Application deadline:* Applications are processed on a rolling basis. *Application fee:* $35. Electronic applications accepted. *Dean for Agricultural Affairs,* Patricia A. Jensen, 701-231-7656, Fax: 701-231-7566, E-mail: pjensen@ndsuext.nodak.edu.

College of Arts, Humanities and Social Sciences Students: 8 full-time (6 women), 134 part-time (85 women). *Faculty:* 65 full-time (18 women), 2 part-time/adjunct (0 women). Expenses: Contact institution. *Financial support:* In 2001–02, 2 fellowships with full tuition reimbursements (averaging $10,608 per year), 45 teaching assistantships with full tuition reimbursements (averaging $7,037 per year) were awarded. Research assistantships with full tuition reimbursements, career-related internships or fieldwork, Federal Work-Study, institutionally sponsored loans, scholarships/grants, and tuition waivers (full) also available. Support available to part-time students. In 2001, 18 degrees awarded. *Degree program information:* Part-time and evening/weekend programs available. Offers communication (PhD); criminal justice (PhD); English (MA, MS); history (MA, MS); humanities and social sciences (MA, MS, PhD); mass communication (MA, MS); political science (MA, MS); social science (MA, MS); speech communication (MA, MS). *Application deadline:* Applications are processed on a rolling basis. *Application fee:* $35. *Dean,* Dr. Thomas J. Riley, 701-231-9588, Fax: 701-231-1047, E-mail: thomas.riley@ndsu.nodak.edu.

College of Business Administration Students: 22 full-time (8 women), 57 part-time (26 women); includes 8 minority (2 African Americans, 4 Asian Americans or Pacific Islanders, 2 Hispanic Americans), 6 international. Average age 27. 50 applicants, 84% accepted. *Faculty:* 22 full-time (4 women). Expenses: Contact institution. *Financial support:* In 2001–02, 13 students received support, including 13 research assistantships; teaching assistantships, career-related internships or fieldwork, Federal Work-Study, and institutionally sponsored loans also available. Support available to part-time students. Financial award application deadline: 6/15; financial award applicants required to submit FAFSA. In 2001, 29 degrees awarded. *Degree program information:* Part-time and evening/weekend programs available. Offers business administration (MBA). *Application deadline:* For fall admission, 7/15 (priority date); for spring admission, 11/15. Applications are processed on a rolling basis. *Application fee:* $35. *Application Contact:* Paul R. Brown, Director, 701-231-7681, Fax: 701-231-7508, E-mail: paul.brown@ndsu.nodak.edu. *Dean,* Dr. Jay Leitch, 701-231-7577.

College of Engineering and Architecture Students: 33 full-time (6 women), 40 part-time (5 women); includes 38 minority (1 African American, 34 Asian Americans or Pacific Islanders, 3 Native Americans), 10 international. Average age 25. *Faculty:* 68 full-time (2 women). Expenses: Contact institution. *Financial support:* In 2001–02, 40 students received support, including 20 research assistantships with full tuition reimbursements available (averaging $6,000 per year), 20 teaching assistantships with full tuition reimbursements available (averaging $5,000 per year); fellowships with full tuition reimbursements available, career-related internships or fieldwork, Federal Work-Study, institutionally sponsored loans, scholarships/grants, and tuition waivers (full) also available. Support available to part-time students. Financial award application deadline: 4/15. In 2001, 12 master's, 1 doctorate awarded. *Degree program information:* Part-time and evening/weekend programs available. Postbaccalaureate distance learning degree programs offered (minimal on-campus study). Offers agricultural and biosystems engineering (MS); civil engineering (MS); electrical and computer engineering (MS); engineering (PhD); engineering and architecture (MS, PhD); environmental engineering (MS); industrial engineering and management (MS); mechanical engineering and applied mechanics (MS); natural resource management (MS). *Application deadline:* Applications are processed on a rolling basis. *Application fee:* $35. *Application Contact:* Velmer S. Burton, Dean, 701-231-7033, Fax: 701-231-8098. *Dean,* Dr. Otto J. Helweg, 701-231-7525, Fax: 701-231-8957, E-mail: otto.nelweg@ndsu.nodak.edu.

College of Human Development and Education Students: 191. Average age 32. Expenses: Contact institution. *Financial support:* Fellowships, research assistantships, teaching assistantships, career-related internships or fieldwork, Federal Work-Study, institutionally sponsored loans, and tuition waivers (full) available. Support available to part-time students. In 2001, 65 master's, 2 other advanced degrees awarded. *Degree program information:* Part-time and evening/weekend programs available. Postbaccalaureate distance learning degree programs offered (minimal on-campus study). Offers agricultural education (M Ed, MS); agricultural extension education (MS); child development and family science (MS); counselor education (M Ed, MA, MS); education (M Ed, MA, MS, Ed S); educational administration (MS, Ed S); family and consumer sciences education (M Ed, MS); gerontology (PhD); human development and education (M Ed, MA, MS, PhD, Ed S); pedagogy (M Ed, MS); physical education and athletic administration (M Ed, MS). *Application deadline:* Applications are processed on a rolling basis. *Application fee:* $35. *Dean,* Dr. Virginia L. Clark, 701-231-8211, Fax: 701-231-7174, E-mail: vclark@badlands.nodak.edu.

College of Pharmacy Students: 16 full-time (8 women), 2 part-time, 9 international. Average age 30. 46 applicants, 4% accepted. *Faculty:* 8 full-time (1 woman). Expenses: Contact institution. *Financial support:* In 2001–02, 16 research assistantships with full tuition reimbursements (averaging $12,000 per year) were awarded; career-related internships or fieldwork, Federal Work-Study, institutionally sponsored loans, and scholarships/grants also available. Financial award application deadline: 4/1. In 2001, 1 degree awarded. *Degree program information:* Part-time programs available. Offers pharmaceutical sciences (MS, PhD); pharmacy (MS, PhD). *Application deadline:* For fall admission, 4/1. Applications are processed on a rolling basis. *Application fee:* $35. *Application Contact:* Dr. John J. Wagner, Interim Chair, 701-231-7605, Fax: 701-231-8333, E-mail: janelle.fortier@ndsu.nodak.edu. *Dean,* Dr. Charles D. Peterson, 701-231-6469, Fax: 701-231-7606.

College of Science and Mathematics Students: 265. *Faculty:* 102. Expenses: Contact institution. *Financial support:* Fellowships with full tuition reimbursements, research assistantships with full tuition reimbursements, teaching assistantships with full tuition reimbursements, career-related internships or fieldwork, Federal Work-Study, institutionally sponsored loans, scholarships/grants, traineeships, tuition waivers (full and partial), and unspecified assistantships available. Support available to part-time students. Financial award applicants required to submit FAFSA. *Degree program information:* Part-time programs available. Offers applied mathematics (MS, PhD); applied statistics (MS); biochemistry and molecular biology (MS, PhD); botany (MS, PhD); cellular and molecular biology (PhD); chemistry (MS, PhD); clinical psychology (MS, PhD); computer science (MS, PhD); computer science and statistics (MS); general psychology (MS); mathematics (MS, PhD); natural resources management (MS); operations research (MS); physics (MS, PhD); polymers and coatings (MS, PhD); psychology (MS); science and mathematics (MS, PhD); statistics (PhD); zoology (MS, PhD). *Application deadline:* Applications are processed on a rolling basis. *Application fee:* $35. Electronic applications accepted. *Application Contact:* Velmer S. Burton, Dean, 701-231-7033, Fax: 701-231-6524. *Dean,* Dr. Alan R. White, 701-231-7411, Fax: 701-231-7149, E-mail: alan.white@ndsu.nodak.edu.

See in-depth description on page 1005.

NORTHEASTERN ILLINOIS UNIVERSITY, Chicago, IL 60625-4699

General Information State-supported, coed, comprehensive institution. CGS member. *Enrollment:* 242 full-time matriculated graduate/professional students (149 women), 1,453 part-time matriculated graduate/professional students (1,055 women). *Enrollment by degree level:* 1,695 master's. *Graduate faculty:* 259 full-time (110 women), 170 part-time/adjunct (85 women). *International tuition:* $8,646 full-time. *Tuition, area resident:* Full-time $2,882; part-time $107 per semester hour. Tuition, nonresident: part-time $320 per semester hour. *Required* *fees:* $20 per semester hour. *Graduate housing:* On-campus housing not available. *Student services:* Campus employment opportunities, campus safety program, career counseling, child daycare facilities, disabled student services, exercise/wellness program, free psychological counseling, grant writing training, international student services, low-cost health insurance, teacher training. *Library facilities:* Ronald Williams Library. *Online resources:* library catalog, web page, access to other libraries' catalogs. *Collection:* 498,940 titles, 3,451 serial subscriptions, 5,389 audiovisual materials. *Research affiliation:* Advocate Health Care Network (health care cost containment), Lutheran General Hospital (clinical cardiology), Advocate Medical Group (health care outcomes research).

Computer facilities: 300 computers available on campus for general student use. A campuswide network can be accessed from off campus. Internet access and online class registration, productivity software are available. *Web address:* http://www.neiu.edu/.

General Application Contact: Dr. Mohan K. Sood, Dean of the Graduate College, 773-442-6010, Fax: 773-442-6020, E-mail: m-sood@neiu.edu.

GRADUATE UNITS

Graduate College Students: 242 full-time (149 women), 1,443 part-time (1,045 women). Average age 34. 702 applicants, 79% accepted. *Faculty:* 259 full-time (110 women), 173 part-time/adjunct (85 women). Expenses: Contact institution. *Financial support:* In 2001–02, 509 students received support, including 86 research assistantships with full tuition reimbursements available (averaging $6,600 per year); career-related internships or fieldwork, Federal Work-Study, institutionally sponsored loans, and tuition waivers (full and partial) also available. Support available to part-time students. Financial award applicants required to submit FAFSA. In 2001, 515 degrees awarded. *Degree program information:* Part-time and evening/weekend programs available. *Application deadline:* For fall admission, 4/1 (priority date); for spring admission, 8/15. Applications are processed on a rolling basis. *Application fee:* $25. *Application Contact:* Diane O'Cherony, Administrative Aide, 773-642-6003, Fax: 773-442-6020, E-mail: dsochero@neiu.edu. *Dean of the Graduate College,* Dr. Mohan K. Sood, 773-442-6010, Fax: 773-442-6020, E-mail: m-sood@neiu.edu.

College of Arts and Sciences Students: 74 full-time (27 women), 390 part-time (217 women). Average age 32. 207 applicants, 66% accepted. *Faculty:* 139 full-time (47 women), 65 part-time/adjunct (23 women). Expenses: Contact institution. *Financial support:* In 2001–02, 270 students received support, including 57 research assistantships with full tuition reimbursements available (averaging $6,600 per year); career-related internships or fieldwork, Federal Work-Study, institutionally sponsored loans, and tuition waivers (full and partial) also available. Support available to part-time students. Financial award applicants required to submit FAFSA. In 2001, 114 degrees awarded. *Degree program information:* Part-time and evening/weekend programs available. Offers arts and sciences (MA, MS); biology (MS); chemistry (MS); composition/writing (MA); computer science (MS); earth science (MS); English (MA); geography and environmental studies (MA); gerontology (MA); history (MA); linguistics (MA); literature (MA); mathematics (MA, MS); mathematics for elementary school teachers (MA); music (MA); political science (MA); speech (MA). *Application deadline:* For fall admission, 4/1 (priority date); for spring admission, 8/15. Applications are processed on a rolling basis. *Application fee:* $25. *Application Contact:* Dr. Mohan K. Sood, Dean of the Graduate College, 773-442-6010, Fax: 773-442-6020, E-mail: m-sood@neiu.edu. *Acting Dean,* Dr. Charles Pastors, 773-443-5702, Fax: 773-442-4920, E-mail: c-pastors@neiu.edu.

College of Business and Management Students: 25 full-time (15 women), 26 part-time (12 women); includes 14 minority (6 African Americans, 4 Asian Americans or Pacific Islanders, 3 Hispanic Americans, 1 Native American), 6 international. Average age 31. 40 applicants, 18% accepted. *Faculty:* 24 full-time (3 women), 13 part-time/adjunct (4 women). Expenses: Contact institution. *Financial support:* In 2001–02, 20 students received support, including 8 research assistantships with full tuition reimbursements available (averaging $6,600 per year); career-related internships or fieldwork, Federal Work-Study, institutionally sponsored loans, and tuition waivers (full and partial) also available. Support available to part-time students. In 2001, 9 degrees awarded. *Degree program information:* Part-time and evening/weekend programs available. Offers accounting (MBA, MSA); accounting, business law, and finance (MSA); finance (MBA); management (MBA); marketing (MBA). *Application deadline:* For fall admission, 4/1 (priority date); for spring admission, 8/15. Applications are processed on a rolling basis. *Application fee:* $25. *Application Contact:* Mohan K. Sood, Dean of the Graduate College, 773-442-6010, Fax: 773-442-6020, E-mail: m-sood@neiu.edu. *Acting Dean,* Dr. Allen N. Shub, 773-442-6100, Fax: 773-442-6110, E-mail: a-shub@neiu.edu.

College of Education Students: 143 full-time (107 women), 1,037 part-time (826 women); includes 316 minority (131 African Americans, 31 Asian Americans or Pacific Islanders, 154 Hispanic Americans), 3 international. Average age 35. 455 applicants, 90% accepted. *Faculty:* 83 full-time (47 women), 64 part-time/adjunct (40 women). Expenses: Contact institution. *Financial support:* In 2001–02, 219 students received support, including 21 research assistantships with full tuition reimbursements available (averaging $6,600 per year); career-related internships or fieldwork, Federal Work-Study, institutionally sponsored loans, and tuition waivers (full and partial) also available. Support available to part-time students. Financial award applicants required to submit FAFSA. In 2001, 431 degrees awarded. *Degree program information:* Part-time and evening/weekend programs available. Offers bilingual/bicultural education (MAT, MSI); early childhood special education (MA); educating children with behavior disorders (MA); educating individuals with mental retardation (MA); education (M Ed, MA, MAT, MSI); educational administration and supervision (MA); educational leadership (MA); gifted education (MA); guidance and counseling (MA); human resource development (MA); inner city studies (MA); instruction (MSI); language arts (MAT, MSI); reading (MA); special education (MA); teaching (MAT); teaching children with learning disabilities (MA). *Application deadline:* For fall admission, 4/1 (priority date); for spring admission, 8/15. Applications are processed on a rolling basis. *Application fee:* $25. *Application Contact:* Dr. Mohan K. Sood, Dean of the Graduate College, 773-442-6010, Fax: 773-442-6020, E-mail: m-sood@neiu.edu. *Dean,* Dr. Nan Giblin, 773-442-5500, Fax: 773-442-5510, E-mail: n-giblin@neiu.edu.

NORTHEASTERN OHIO UNIVERSITIES COLLEGE OF MEDICINE, Rootstown, OH 44272-0095

General Information State-supported, coed, graduate-only institution. *Enrollment by degree level:* 427 first professional. *Graduate faculty:* 247 full-time (51 women), 1,577 part-time/adjunct (271 women). Tuition, state resident: full-time $15,738. Tuition, nonresident: full-time $31,476. *Required fees:* $966. *Graduate housing:* On-campus housing not available. *Student services:* Campus employment opportunities, career counseling, disabled student services, free psychological counseling, low-cost health insurance, multicultural affairs office. *Library facilities:* Oliver Ocasek Regional Medical Information Center. *Online resources:* library catalog, web page, access to other libraries' catalogs. *Collection:* 106,559 titles, 1,036 serial subscriptions, 3,182 audiovisual materials. *Research affiliation:* National Institutes of Health (anatomy, biochemistry, immunology, neurobiology), Aventis (biochemistry, rheumatology), Amgen, Inc. (biochemistry), Eli Lilly and Company (endocrinology, anatomy), Pfizer Pharmaceutical Group (family medicine), Wyeth-Ayerst Pharmaceuticals (rheumatology).

Computer facilities: 50 computers available on campus for general student use. A campuswide network can be accessed from off campus. Internet access is available. *Web address:* http://www.neoucom.edu/.

General Application Contact: Dr. Steve Manuel, Director of Admissions and Institutional Research, 330-325-6270, E-mail: admission@neoucom.edu.

GRADUATE UNITS

Professional Program Students: 427 full-time (217 women); includes 200 minority (20 African Americans, 163 Asian Americans or Pacific Islanders, 15 Hispanic Americans, 2 Native Americans) Average age 23. 859 applicants, 12% accepted. *Faculty:* 247 full-time (51 women), 1,577 part-time/adjunct (271 women). Expenses: Contact institution. *Financial support:* In 2001–02, 330 students received support; fellowships, Federal Work-Study, institutionally sponsored loans, and scholarships/grants available. Support available to part-time students. Financial award application deadline: 4/15; financial award applicants required to submit FAFSA. In 2001, 95 degrees awarded. Offers medicine (MD). *Application deadline:* For fall admission, 11/1. Applications are processed on a rolling basis. *Application fee:* $30. Electronic applications accepted. *Application Contact:* Dr. Steve Manuel, Director of Admissions and Institutional Research, 330-325-6270, E-mail: admission@neoucom.edu. *President and Dean,* Dr. Robert S. Blacklow, 330-325-6255.

NORTHEASTERN SEMINARY AT ROBERTS WESLEYAN COLLEGE, Rochester, NY 14624

General Information Independent-religious, coed, graduate-only institution. *Enrollment by degree level:* 98 master's. *Graduate faculty:* 4 full-time (0 women), 10 part-time/adjunct (2 women). *Tuition:* Part-time $280 per credit hour. *Graduate housing:* On-campus housing not available. *Student services:* Campus employment opportunities, campus safety program, disabled student services, exercise/wellness program. *Library facilities:* Roberts Wesleyan College Library. *Online resources:* library catalog, web page.

Computer facilities: A campuswide network can be accessed from student residence rooms and from off campus. Internet access is available. *Web address:* http://www.nes.edu/.

General Application Contact: Tracy Patrice Johnson, Director of Admissions, 716-594-6802, Fax: 716-594-6801, E-mail: johnson_tracy@roberts.edu.

GRADUATE UNITS

Graduate and Professional Programs Students: 98 full-time (36 women); includes 22 minority (16 African Americans, 2 Asian Americans or Pacific Islanders, 4 Hispanic Americans) *Faculty:* 4 full-time (0 women), 10 part-time/adjunct (2 women). Expenses: Contact institution. *Financial support:* In 2001–02, 48 students received support, including 48 fellowships with tuition reimbursements available (averaging $1,000 per year); career-related internships or fieldwork, institutionally sponsored loans, scholarships/grants, and tuition waivers (partial) also available. Financial award applicants required to submit FAFSA. In 2001, 5 master's awarded. *Degree program information:* Evening/weekend programs available. Offers theological studies (MA); theology (M Div). *Application deadline:* For fall admission, 8/1 (priority date); for spring admission, 3/1 (priority date). Applications are processed on a rolling basis. *Application fee:* $35. *Application Contact:* Tracy Patrice Johnson, Director of Admissions, 716-594-6802, Fax: 716-594-6801, E-mail: johnson_tracy@roberts.edu. *Dean,* Dr. Wayne G. McCown.

NORTHEASTERN STATE UNIVERSITY, Tahlequah, OK 74464-2399

General Information State-supported, coed, comprehensive institution. *Enrollment:* 390 full-time matriculated graduate/professional students (253 women), 419 part-time matriculated graduate/professional students (279 women). *Enrollment by degree level:* 99 first professional. *Graduate faculty:* 153 full-time (23 women), 10 part-time/adjunct (5 women). *Tuition, area resident:* Part-time $87 per credit hour. Tuition, state resident: part-time $206 per credit hour. *Graduate housing:* Rooms and/or apartments available to single and married students. Housing application deadline: 6/1. *Student services:* Campus employment opportunities, career counseling, disabled student services, free psychological counseling, international student services, low-cost health insurance, multicultural affairs office, teacher training. *Library facilities:* John Vaughn Library. *Online resources:* library catalog, web page. *Collection:* 379,173 titles, 3,442 serial subscriptions.

Computer facilities: 300 computers available on campus for general student use. A campuswide network can be accessed from student residence rooms and from off campus. Internet access is available. *Web address:* http://www.nsuok.edu/.

General Application Contact: Dr. Kenneth L. Collins, Dean of the Graduate College, 918-456-5511 Ext. 2093, Fax: 918-458-2061, E-mail: collins@cherokee.nsuok.edu.

GRADUATE UNITS

College of Optometry Students: 99 full-time (49 women); includes 19 minority (1 African American, 6 Asian Americans or Pacific Islanders, 3 Hispanic Americans, 9 Native Americans) Average age 25. 127 applicants, 23% accepted, 26 enrolled. *Faculty:* 24 full-time (10 women), 10 part-time/adjunct (5 women). Expenses: Contact institution. *Financial support:* In 2001–02, 92 students received support. Federal Work-Study, institutionally sponsored loans, scholarships/grants, tuition waivers (full and partial), unspecified assistantships, and residencies available. Financial award application deadline: 5/1; financial award applicants required to submit FAFSA. In 2001, 24 degrees awarded. Offers optometry (OD). Applicants must be residents of Oklahoma, Arkansas, Kansas, Colorado, New Mexico, Missouri, Texas, or Nebraska. *Application deadline:* For fall admission, 2/1. Applications are processed on a rolling basis. *Application fee:* $25. *Application Contact:* Tricia Grindstaff, Coordinator of Student Affairs, 918-456-5511 Ext. 4036, Fax: 918-458-2104, E-mail: mallett@nsuok.edu. *Dean,* Dr. George E. Foster, 918-456-5511 Ext. 4000, Fax: 918-458-2104, E-mail: fosterg@cherokee.nsuok.edu.

Graduate College Students: 291 full-time (204 women), 419 part-time (279 women); includes 189 minority (38 African Americans, 7 Asian Americans or Pacific Islanders, 3 Hispanic Americans, 141 Native Americans), 4 international. Average age 35. *Faculty:* 82 full-time (25 women). Expenses: Contact institution. *Financial support:* Research assistantships, teaching assistantships, career-related internships or fieldwork, Federal Work-Study, scholarships/grants, and tuition waivers (partial) available. Financial award application deadline: 3/1. In 2001, 218 degrees awarded. *Degree program information:* Part-time and evening/weekend programs available. *Application deadline:* Applications are processed on a rolling basis. *Application fee:* $0. *Application Contact:* Margie Railey, Administrative Assistant, 918-456-5511 Ext. 2093, Fax: 918-458-2061, E-mail: railey@nsuok.edu. *Dean,* Dr. Kenneth L. Collins, 918-456-5511 Ext. 2093, Fax: 918-458-2061, E-mail: collins@cherokee.nsuok.edu.

College of Arts and Letters Students: 9 full-time (6 women), 5 part-time (4 women); includes 3 minority (all Native Americans) *Faculty:* 26 full-time (6 women). Expenses: Contact institution. *Financial support:* Teaching assistantships, Federal Work-Study available. Financial award application deadline: 3/1. In 2001, 5 degrees awarded. *Degree program information:* Part-time and evening/weekend programs available. Offers arts and letters (MA); communication (MA); English (MA). *Application deadline:* For fall admission, 6/1 (priority date). Applications are processed on a rolling basis. *Application fee:* $0. *Dean,* Dr. Kathryn Robinson, 918-456-5511 Ext. 3619, Fax: 918-458-2348, E-mail: robinska@cherokee.nsuok.edu.

College of Behavioral and Social Sciences Students: 87 full-time (63 women), 102 part-time (76 women); includes 51 minority (11 African Americans, 1 Hispanic American, 39 Native Americans), 1 international. *Faculty:* 30 full-time (8 women). Expenses: Contact institution. *Financial support:* Teaching assistantships, career-related internships or fieldwork and Federal Work-Study available. Financial award application deadline: 3/1. In 2001, 54 degrees awarded. *Degree program information:* Part-time and evening/weekend programs available. Offers American studies (MA); behavioral and social sciences (M Ed, MA, MS); counseling psychology (MS); criminal justice (MS); school counseling (M Ed). *Application deadline:* Applications are processed on a rolling basis. *Application fee:* $0. *Dean,* Dr. Lyle Haskins, 918-456-5511 Ext. 3500, Fax: 918-458-2390, E-mail: haskins@cherokee.nsuok.edu.

College of Business and Industry Students: 25 full-time (14 women), 83 part-time (28 women); includes 23 minority (5 African Americans, 2 Asian Americans or Pacific Islanders, 16 Native Americans), 3 international. *Faculty:* 12 full-time (2 women). Expenses: Contact institution. *Financial support:* Teaching assistantships, Federal Work-Study available. Financial award application deadline: 3/1. In 2001, 40 degrees awarded. *Degree program information:* Part-time and evening/weekend programs available. Offers business administration (MBA); business and industry (MBA, MS); industrial management (MS). *Application deadline:* For fall admission, 6/1 (priority date). Applications are processed on a rolling basis. *Application fee:* $0. *Dean,* Dr. Penny Dotson, 918-456-5511 Ext. 2900, Fax: 918-458-2337, E-mail: dotson@cherokee.nsuok.edu.

College of Education Students: 170 full-time (121 women), 229 part-time (171 women); includes 112 minority (22 African Americans, 5 Asian Americans or Pacific Islanders, 2 Hispanic Americans, 83 Native Americans), 1 international. *Faculty:* 26 full-time (11 women). Expenses: Contact institution. *Financial support:* Teaching assistantships, career-related internships or fieldwork and Federal Work-Study available. Financial award application deadline: 3/1. In 2001, 124 degrees awarded. *Degree program information:* Part-time and

Northeastern State University (continued)

evening/weekend programs available. Offers college teaching (MS); early childhood education (M Ed); education (M Ed, MS); health and human performance (MS); reading (M Ed); school administration (M Ed); special education (M Ed); special education/speech language pathology (M Ed); teaching (M Ed). *Application deadline:* For fall admission, 6/1 (priority date). Applications are processed on a rolling basis. *Application fee:* $0. *Head,* Dr. Kay Grant, 918-456-5511 Ext. 3700, Fax: 918-458-2351.

NORTHEASTERN UNIVERSITY, Boston, MA 02115-5096

General Information Independent, coed, university. CGS member. *Enrollment:* 2,646 full-time matriculated graduate/professional students (1,455 women), 1,571 part-time matriculated graduate/professional students (701 women). *Enrollment by degree level:* 565 first professional, 2,586 master's, 599 doctoral, 101 other advanced degrees. *Graduate faculty:* 774 full-time (271 women). *Tuition:* Part-time $535 per credit hour. *Required fees:* $56. Tuition and fees vary according to program. *Graduate housing:* Room and/or apartments available on a first-come, first-served basis to single students; on-campus housing not available to married students. Typical cost: $3,600 per year ($5,955 including board). *Student services:* Campus employment opportunities, campus safety program, career counseling, child daycare facilities, disabled student services, exercise/wellness program, free psychological counseling, international student services, low-cost health insurance, multicultural affairs office, teacher training. *Library facilities:* Snell Library plus 6 others. *Online resources:* library catalog, web page, access to other libraries' catalogs. *Collection:* 681,972 titles, 8,590 serial subscriptions, 15,928 audiovisual materials. *Research affiliation:* Stanford Linear Accelerator Center (physics), Fermi National Accelerator Laboratory (physics), European Laboratory for Particle Physics (CERN) (physics), Massachusetts Microelectronics Center (engineering), Argonne National Laboratory (physics), University Research Associations (physics).

Computer facilities: A campuswide network can be accessed from student residence rooms and from off campus. Internet access is available. *Web address:* http://www.northeastern.edu/.

GRADUATE UNITS

Bouvé College of Health Sciences Graduate School Students: 637 full-time (508 women), 266 part-time (228 women). 1,264 applicants, 54% accepted. *Faculty:* 54 full-time (20 women). Expenses: Contact institution. *Financial support:* In 2001–02, 25 teaching assistantships with full tuition reimbursements (averaging $11,025 per year) were awarded; fellowships, research assistantships with full tuition reimbursements, career-related internships or fieldwork, Federal Work-Study, tuition waivers (partial), and administrative assistantships also available. Support available to part-time students. Financial award application deadline: 3/1; financial award applicants required to submit FAFSA. In 2001, 38 first professional degrees, 318 master's, 8 doctorates, 11 other advanced degrees awarded. *Degree program information:* Part-time and evening/weekend programs available. Offers applied behavior analysis (MS); applied educational psychology (MS); audiology (MS); biomedical sciences (MS); cardiopulmonary science (perfusion technology) (MS); clinical exercise physiology (MS); college student development and counseling (MS); counseling psychology (MS, PhD, CAGS); medical laboratory science (MS, PhD); medicinal chemistry (MS, PhD); pharmaceutics (PhD); pharmacology (MS, PhD); pharmacy (Pharm D); pharmacy and health sciences (Pharm D, MS, MS Ed, PhD, CAGS, CAS); physician assistant (MS); rehabilitation counseling (MS); school counseling (MS); school psychology (MS, PhD, CAGS); special needs and intensive special needs (MS Ed); speech-language pathology (MS); toxicology (MS, PhD). *Application deadline:* Applications are processed on a rolling basis. *Application fee:* $50. *Application Contact:* Bill Purnell, Director of Graduate Admissions, 617-373-2708, Fax: 617-373-4701, E-mail: w.purnell@neu.edu. *Director,* Dr. Ena Vazquez-Nuttall, 617-373-2708, Fax: 617-373-4701.

School of Nursing Students: 45 full-time (41 women), 100 part-time (94 women). Average age 38. 53 applicants, 89% accepted. *Faculty:* 25 full-time (all women), 13 part-time/adjunct (11 women). Expenses: Contact institution. *Financial support:* In 2001–02, 34 students received support, including 7 research assistantships with full tuition reimbursements available (averaging $10,700 per year); fellowships, teaching assistantships with full tuition reimbursements available, career-related internships or fieldwork, institutionally sponsored loans, tuition waivers (full and partial), and unspecified assistantships also available. Support available to part-time students. Financial award application deadline: 7/1; financial award applicants required to submit FAFSA. In 2001, 57 degrees awarded. *Degree program information:* Part-time programs available. Offers community health nursing (MS, CAS); critical care-acute care nurse practitioner (MS, CAS); critical care-neonatal nurse practitioner (MS, CAS); nurse anesthesia (MS); nursing (MS, CAS); nursing administration (MS); primary care nursing (MS, CAS); psychiatric-mental health nursing (MS, CAS). *Application deadline:* Applications are processed on a rolling basis. *Application fee:* $50. *Application Contact:* Bill Purnell, Director of Graduate Admissions, 617-373-2708, Fax: 617-373-4701, E-mail: w.purnell@neu.edu. *Interim Dean,* Dr. Margery Chisholm, 617-373-3649, Fax: 617-373-8675, E-mail: m.chisholm@neu.edu.

College of Arts and Sciences Students: 499 full-time (257 women), 181 part-time (114 women); includes 56 minority (22 African Americans, 14 Asian Americans or Pacific Islanders, 19 Hispanic Americans, 1 Native American), 183 international. Average age 26. 1,064 applicants, 46% accepted, 232 enrolled. *Faculty:* 234 full-time, 25 part-time/adjunct. Expenses: Contact institution. *Financial support:* Fellowships with tuition reimbursements, research assistantships with tuition reimbursements, teaching assistantships with tuition reimbursements, career-related internships or fieldwork, Federal Work-Study, institutionally sponsored loans, tuition waivers (full and partial), and unspecified assistantships available. Support available to part-time students. Financial award applicants required to submit FAFSA. In 2001, 168 master's, 49 doctorates awarded. *Degree program information:* Part-time and evening/weekend programs available. Offers American government and politics (MA); analytical chemistry (PhD); arts and sciences (M Ed, MA, MAT, MAW, MPA, MS, MTPW, PhD, Certificate); biology (MS, PhD); chemistry (MS, PhD); comparative government and politics (MA); development administration (MPA); economics (MA); English (MA, PhD); experimental psychology (MA, PhD); health administration and policy (MPA); history (MA, PhD); inorganic chemistry (PhD); international relations (MA); law, policy, and society (MS, PhD); management information systems (MPA); mathematics (MS, PhD); organic chemistry (PhD); physical chemistry (PhD); physics (MS, PhD); political theory (MA); public administration (MPA); public and international affairs (PhD); public history (MA); sociology and anthropology (MA, PhD); state and local government (MPA); technical and professional writing (MTPW, Certificate); technical writing training (Certificate); writing (MA, MAW). *Application deadline:* Applications are processed on a rolling basis. *Application fee:* $50. Electronic applications accepted. *Application Contact:* Graduate School of Arts and Sciences, 617-373-3982, Fax: 617-373-2942, E-mail: gsas@neu.edu. *Interim Associate Dean and Director of the Graduate School,* Dr. Edward L. Jarroll, 617-373-5173, Fax: 617-373-2942.

School of Education Students: 20 full-time (14 women), 40 part-time (33 women); includes 8 minority (6 African Americans, 2 Asian Americans or Pacific Islanders), 1 international. Average age 29. 59 applicants, 71% accepted. *Faculty:* 8 full-time (2 women), 3 part-time/adjunct (2 women). Expenses: Contact institution. *Financial support:* Career-related internships or fieldwork, Federal Work-Study, tuition waivers (full and partial), and unspecified assistantships available. Support available to part-time students. Financial award application deadline: 3/1; financial award applicants required to submit FAFSA. In 2001, 17 degrees awarded. *Degree program information:* Part-time and evening/weekend programs available. Offers biology (MAT); chemistry (MAT); curriculum and instruction (M Ed); economics (MAT); English (MAT); history (MAT); mathematics (MAT); physics (MAT); political science (MAT); sociology (MAT). *Application deadline:* For fall admission, 7/15; for spring admission, 2/1. Applications are processed on a rolling basis. *Application fee:* $50. *Application Contact:* Dr. Joan Fitzgerald, Graduate Coordinator, 617-373-4216, Fax: 617-373-8924, E-mail: graded@neu.edu. *Dean/Director,* Dr. James W. Fraser, 617-373-3302, Fax: 617-373-5261.

School of Journalism Students: 15 full-time (10 women), 5 part-time (3 women), 6 international. Average age 28. 82 applicants, 34% accepted. *Faculty:* 7 full-time (2 women), 6 part-time/adjunct (2 women). Expenses: Contact institution. *Financial support:* Research assistantships, career-related internships or fieldwork, Federal Work-Study, institutionally sponsored loans, tuition waivers (partial), and unspecified assistantships available. Financial award application deadline: 4/1; financial award applicants required to submit FAFSA. In 2001, 13 degrees awarded. *Degree program information:* Part-time and evening/weekend programs available. Offers journalism (MA). *Application deadline:* For fall admission, 6/1 (priority date); for spring admission, 3/1. Applications are processed on a rolling basis. *Application fee:* $50. *Application Contact:* Carol Medige, Graduate Assistant, 617-373-3236, Fax: 617-373-8773, E-mail: gradjourn@neu.edu. *Graduate Coordinator,* Prof. Alan Schroeder, 617-373-3236, Fax: 617-373-8773.

College of Computer Science Students: 110 full-time (44 women), 44 part-time (10 women); includes 4 minority (1 African American, 2 Asian Americans or Pacific Islanders, 1 Native American), 107 international. Average age 29. 313 applicants, 59% accepted. *Faculty:* 18 full-time (5 women), 3 part-time/adjunct (0 women). Expenses: Contact institution. *Financial support:* In 2001–02, 23 research assistantships with full tuition reimbursements (averaging $13,125 per year), 10 teaching assistantships with full tuition reimbursements (averaging $13,125 per year) were awarded. Fellowships, career-related internships or fieldwork, Federal Work-Study, and institutionally sponsored loans also available. Financial award application deadline: 2/15. In 2001, 50 master's, 2 doctorates awarded. *Degree program information:* Part-time and evening/weekend programs available. Offers computer science (MS, PhD). *Application deadline:* For fall admission, 8/15; for winter admission, 11/1; for spring admission, 2/1. Applications are processed on a rolling basis. *Application fee:* $50. *Application Contact:* Dr. Agnes Chan, Associate Dean and Director of Graduate Program, 617-373-2462, Fax: 617-373-5121. *Dean,* Dr. Larry A. Finkelstein, 617-373-2462, Fax: 617-373-5121.

College of Criminal Justice Students: 35 full-time (23 women), 10 part-time (4 women); includes 3 minority (2 African Americans, 1 Asian American or Pacific Islander), 2 international. Average age 26. 110 applicants, 64% accepted. *Faculty:* 14 full-time (5 women), 5 part-time/adjunct (1 woman). Expenses: Contact institution. *Financial support:* In 2001–02, 1 fellowship with tuition reimbursement (averaging $10,500 per year), 12 teaching assistantships with tuition reimbursements (averaging $10,800 per year) were awarded. Research assistantships with partial tuition reimbursements, career-related internships or fieldwork, Federal Work-Study, institutionally sponsored loans, and minority fellowships also available. Support available to part-time students. Financial award application deadline: 3/31; financial award applicants required to submit FAFSA. In 2001, 35 degrees awarded. *Degree program information:* Part-time and evening/weekend programs available. Offers criminal justice (MS). *Application deadline:* For fall admission, 6/1; for winter admission, 11/1; for spring admission, 2/1. Applications are processed on a rolling basis. *Application fee:* $50. *Application Contact:* Laurie A. Mastone, Assistant to the Director, 617-373-2813, Fax: 617-373-8723, E-mail: l.mastone@neu.edu. *Director,* Jack McDevitt, 617-373-2813, Fax: 617-373-8723.

College of Engineering Students: 498 full-time (199 women), 403 part-time (77 women); includes 86 minority (17 African Americans, 42 Asian Americans or Pacific Islanders, 26 Hispanic Americans, 1 Native American), 435 international. Average age 25. 1,265 applicants, 49% accepted, 216 enrolled. *Faculty:* 80 full-time (6 women), 29 part-time/adjunct (2 women). Expenses: Contact institution. *Financial support:* In 2001–02, 258 students received support, including 5 fellowships with tuition reimbursements available, 120 research assistantships with full tuition reimbursements available (averaging $13,560 per year), 88 teaching assistantships with full tuition reimbursements available (averaging $13,560 per year); career-related internships or fieldwork, Federal Work-Study, scholarships/grants, tuition waivers (full), and unspecified assistantships also available. Support available to part-time students. Financial award application deadline: 2/15; financial award applicants required to submit FAFSA. In 2001, 296 master's, 18 doctorates awarded. *Degree program information:* Part-time programs available. Offers chemical engineering (MS, PhD); civil and environmental engineering (MS, PhD); computer systems engineering (MS); electrical and computer engineering (MS, PhD); engineering (MS, PhD); engineering management (MS); industrial engineering (MS, PhD); information systems (MS); mechanical engineering (MS, PhD); operations research (MS). *Application deadline:* For fall admission, 2/15 (priority date). Applications are processed on a rolling basis. *Application fee:* $50. Electronic applications accepted. *Application Contact:* Stephen L. Gibson, Associate Director, 617-373-2711, Fax: 617-373-2501, E-mail: grad-eng@coe.neu.edu. *Associate Dean of Engineering for Research and Graduate Studies,* Dr. Yaman Yener, 617-373-2711, Fax: 617-373-2501.

Graduate School of Business Administration Students: 305 full-time (105 women), 634 part-time (254 women). Average age 29. 517 applicants, 70% accepted. *Faculty:* 94 full-time, 46 part-time/adjunct. Expenses: Contact institution. *Financial support:* In 2001–02, 22 fellowships (averaging $9,700 per year), 61 research assistantships (averaging $10,000 per year), 18 teaching assistantships (averaging $9,700 per year) were awarded. Career-related internships or fieldwork, Federal Work-Study, institutionally sponsored loans, and unspecified assistantships also available. Support available to part-time students. Financial award application deadline: 3/1; financial award applicants required to submit FAFSA. In 2001, 389 master's, 13 other advanced degrees awarded. *Degree program information:* Part-time and evening/weekend programs available. Offers business administration (EMBA, MBA, MSF, MST, CAGS); finance (MSF). *Application deadline:* Applications are processed on a rolling basis. *Application fee:* $50. Electronic applications accepted. *Application Contact:* Program Director, 617-373-5960, Fax: 617-373-8564, E-mail: gsba@neu.edu. *Associate Dean and Director,* Therese M. Hofmann, 617-373-5417, Fax: 617-373-8564, E-mail: gsba@cba.neu.edu.

Graduate School of Professional Accounting Students: 34 full-time (15 women), 102 part-time (58 women). Average age 32. 58 applicants, 90% accepted. *Faculty:* 15 full-time (4 women), 1 part-time/adjunct (0 women). Expenses: Contact institution. *Financial support:* In 2001–02, 15 research assistantships (averaging $5,250 per year), 7 teaching assistantships (averaging $10,500 per year) were awarded. Career-related internships or fieldwork, Federal Work-Study, institutionally sponsored loans, and scholarships/grants also available. Support available to part-time students. Financial award application deadline: 3/1; financial award applicants required to submit FAFSA. In 2001, 80 degrees awarded. Offers professional accounting (MST, CAGS); taxation (MST, CAGS). *Application deadline:* For fall admission, 5/1 (priority date). Applications are processed on a rolling basis. *Application fee:* $50. Electronic applications accepted. *Director,* Cynthia Spies, 617-373-5072.

School of Law Students: 567 full-time (324 women); includes 123 minority (33 African Americans, 41 Asian Americans or Pacific Islanders, 45 Hispanic Americans, 4 Native Americans), 7 international. Average age 28. 2,000 applicants, 40% accepted. *Faculty:* 33 full-time (16 women), 18 part-time/adjunct (11 women). Expenses: Contact institution. *Financial support:* In 2001–02, research assistantships (averaging $3,155 per year), 38 teaching assistantships (averaging $3,500 per year) were awarded. Fellowships, career-related internships or fieldwork, Federal Work-Study, institutionally sponsored loans, scholarships/grants, and tuition waivers (full and partial) also available. Financial award application deadline: 3/1; financial award applicants required to submit CSS PROFILE or FAFSA. In 2001, 213 degrees awarded. Offers law (JD). *Application deadline:* For fall admission, 3/1. Applications are processed on a rolling basis. *Application fee:* $65. Electronic applications accepted. *Application Contact:* Carol Figueroa, Information Contact, 617-373-2395, Fax: 617-373-8865. *Dean,* Roger I. Abrams, 617-373-3307, Fax: 617-373-8793, E-mail: r.abrams@nunet.neu.edu.

See in-depth descriptions on pages 1007 and 1009.

NORTHERN ARIZONA UNIVERSITY, Flagstaff, AZ 86011

General Information State-supported, coed, university. CGS member. *Enrollment:* 1,547 full-time matriculated graduate/professional students (1,070 women), 3,004 part-time matriculated graduate/professional students (2,234 women). *Graduate faculty:* 553 full-time (207 women), 327 part-time/adjunct (151 women). Tuition, state resident: full-time $2,488. Tuition, nonresident: full-time $10,354. *Graduate housing:* Rooms and/or apartments available to single and married students. Typical cost: $2,440 per year ($4,910 including board) for single students. *Student services:* Campus employment opportunities, campus safety program, career counseling, child daycare facilities, disabled student services, exercise/wellness program, free psychological counseling, grant writing training, international student services, low-cost health insurance, multicultural affairs office, teacher training, writing training. *Library facilities:* Cline Library. *Online resources:* library catalog, web page, access to other libraries' catalogs. *Collection:* 523,860 titles, 6,253 serial subscriptions, 28,535 audiovisual materials. *Research affiliation:* Museum of Northern Arizona, Lowell Observatory, Rocky Mountain Forest and

Range Experiment Station, U.S. Naval Observatory, U.S. Geological Survey, W. L. Gore and Associates, Inc.

Computer facilities: 620 computers available on campus for general student use. A campuswide network can be accessed from student residence rooms and from off campus. Internet access and online class registration are available. *Web address:* http://www.nau.edu/.

General Application Contact: Dr. Patricia Baron, Director of Graduate Admissions, 928-523-4348, Fax: 928-523-8950, E-mail: graduate.college@nau.edu.

GRADUATE UNITS

Graduate College Students: 1,547 full-time (1,070 women), 3,004 part-time (2,234 women); includes 1,052 minority (112 African Americans, 51 Asian Americans or Pacific Islanders, 624 Hispanic Americans, 265 Native Americans), 69 international. Average age 36. 2,329 applicants, 66% accepted, 1209 enrolled. *Faculty:* 553 full-time (207 women), 327 part-time/adjunct (151 women). Expenses: Contact institution. *Financial support:* In 2001–02, 205 research assistantships, 198 teaching assistantships were awarded. Fellowships, career-related internships or fieldwork, Federal Work-Study, institutionally sponsored loans, scholarships/grants, traineeships, tuition waivers (full and partial), and unspecified assistantships also available. Support available to part-time students. In 2001, 1,905 master's, 42 doctorates awarded. *Degree program information:* Part-time and evening/weekend programs available. *Application fee:* $45. Electronic applications accepted. *Application Contact:* Dr. Patricia Baron, Director of Graduate Admissions, 928-523-4348, Fax: 928-523-8950, E-mail: graduate.college@nau.edu. *Vice Provost for Research and Graduate Studies*, Dr. Carl Fox, 520-523-4340, E-mail: carl.fox@nau.edu.

Center for Excellence in Education Students: 770 full-time (599 women), 2,654 part-time (2,037 women); includes 895 minority (99 African Americans, 36 Asian Americans or Pacific Islanders, 542 Hispanic Americans, 218 Native Americans), 20 international. Average age 36. 1,354 applicants, 76% accepted, 873 enrolled. *Faculty:* 85 full-time (47 women), 230 part-time/adjunct (125 women). Expenses: Contact institution. *Financial support:* In 2001–02, 16 research assistantships, 25 teaching assistantships were awarded. Fellowships, career-related internships or fieldwork, Federal Work-Study, tuition waivers (full and partial), and unspecified assistantships also available. In 2001, 1,574 master's, 23 doctorates awarded. *Degree program information:* Part-time and evening/weekend programs available. Offers bilingual multicultural education (M Ed); community college (M Ed); counseling (M Ed, MA); counseling psychology (Ed D); curriculum and instruction (Ed D); early childhood education (M Ed); educational leadership (Ed D); educational technology (M Ed); elementary education (M Ed); English as a Second Language/Teaching English as a second language (Certificate); excellence in education (M Ed, MA, MVE, Ed D, Certificate); learning and instruction (Ed D); reading and learning disabilities (M Ed); school leadership (M Ed); school psychology (MA, Ed D); secondary education (M Ed); special education (M Ed); vocational education (MVE). *Application fee:* $45. *Executive Director*, Dr. Melvin E. Hall, 928-523-7113.

College of Arts and Sciences Students: 303 full-time (186 women), 137 part-time (76 women); includes 45 minority (3 African Americans, 6 Asian Americans or Pacific Islanders, 27 Hispanic Americans, 9 Native Americans), 22 international. Average age 32. 380 applicants, 54% accepted, 135 enrolled. *Faculty:* 194 full-time (57 women), 50 part-time/adjunct (12 women). Expenses: Contact institution. *Financial support:* In 2001–02, 76 research assistantships, 136 teaching assistantships were awarded. Fellowships, career-related internships or fieldwork, Federal Work-Study, institutionally sponsored loans, tuition waivers (full and partial), and unspecified assistantships also available. Support available to part-time students. In 2001, 115 master's, 10 doctorates awarded. *Degree program information:* Part-time programs available. Offers applied linguistics (PhD); applied physics (MS); arts and sciences (MA, MAT, MLS, MS, PhD, Certificate); biology (MS, PhD); biology education (MAT); chemistry (MS); conservation ecology (Certificate); creative writing (MA); earth science (MAT, MS); English (MA); environmental sciences and policy (MS); general English (MA); geology (MS); history (MA, PhD); liberal studies (MLS); literature (MA); mathematics (MAT, MS); physical science (MAT); quaternary studies (MS); rhetoric (MA); statistics (MS); teaching English as a second language (MA); teaching English as a second language/applied linguistics (MA, PhD); Teaching English as a Second Language/English as a Second Language (Certificate); teaching English as a second language/English as a second language (Certificate). *Application fee:* $45. *Interim Dean*, David Best, 928-323-2701.

College of Business Administration Students: 44 full-time (11 women), 47 part-time (21 women); includes 12 minority (1 African American, 1 Asian American or Pacific Islander, 6 Hispanic Americans, 4 Native Americans), 9 international. Average age 32. 87 applicants, 31% accepted, 19 enrolled. *Faculty:* 43 full-time (9 women), 1 part-time/adjunct (0 women). Expenses: Contact institution. *Financial support:* In 2001–02, 10 research assistantships, 3 teaching assistantships were awarded. Federal Work-Study, institutionally sponsored loans, and tuition waivers (full and partial) also available. Financial award application deadline: 3/1. In 2001, 51 degrees awarded. *Degree program information:* Part-time programs available. Offers general management (MBA); management (MSM); management information systems (MBA). *Application deadline:* For fall admission, 3/1 (priority date). Applications are processed on a rolling basis. *Application fee:* $45. *Interim Dean*, Dr. Mason Gerety, 928-523-7345, Fax: 928-523-7331, E-mail: mba@nau.edu.

College of Ecosystem Science and Management Students: 57 full-time (27 women), 39 part-time (15 women); includes 8 minority (1 Asian American or Pacific Islander, 3 Hispanic Americans, 4 Native Americans), 3 international. Average age 33. 68 applicants, 40% accepted, 24 enrolled. *Faculty:* 33 full-time (10 women), 19 part-time/adjunct (4 women). Expenses: Contact institution. *Financial support:* In 2001–02, 53 research assistantships were awarded; fellowships, teaching assistantships, tuition waivers (full and partial) also available. In 2001, 22 master's, 6 doctorates awarded. *Degree program information:* Part-time programs available. Offers ecosystem science and management (MA, MSF, PhD, Certificate); forestry (MSF, PhD); geographic information systems (Certificate); rural geography (MA). *Application deadline:* Applications are processed on a rolling basis. *Application fee:* $45. *Interim Dean*, Dr. Donald G. Arganbright, 928-523-8247.

College of Engineering Students: 9 full-time (3 women), 7 part-time (4 women); includes 2 minority (both Hispanic Americans), 1 international. 25 applicants, 64% accepted, 10 enrolled. *Faculty:* 34 full-time (6 women). Expenses: Contact institution. In 2001, 1 degree awarded. Offers engineering (M Eng). *Application fee:* $45. *Application Contact:* Ernesto Penado, Graduate Coordinator, 928-523-9453, E-mail: m.eng@nau.edu. *Dean*, Dr. Mason Somerville, 928-523-5252.

College of Health Professions Students: 206 full-time (153 women), 38 part-time (32 women); includes 37 minority (1 African American, 3 Asian Americans or Pacific Islanders, 21 Hispanic Americans, 12 Native Americans), 2 international. Average age 31. 170 applicants, 64% accepted, 79 enrolled. *Faculty:* 50 full-time (36 women). Expenses: Contact institution. *Financial support:* In 2001–02, 4 research assistantships, 5 teaching assistantships were awarded. Fellowships, career-related internships or fieldwork, traineeships, tuition waivers (full and partial), and unspecified assistantships also available. In 2001, 85 master's, 1 doctorate awarded. *Degree program information:* Part-time programs available. Offers case management (Certificate); communications sciences and disorders (MS); exercise science (MS); health education and health promotion (MPH); health professions (MPH, MPT, MS, MSN, DPT, Certificate); nursing (MSN); physical education (MS); physical therapy (MPT, DPT). *Application fee:* $45. *Dean*, Dr. James Blagg, 928-523-4331.

College of Social and Behavioral Sciences Students: 137 full-time (81 women), 83 part-time (51 women); includes 51 minority (8 African Americans, 4 Asian Americans or Pacific Islanders, 21 Hispanic Americans, 18 Native Americans), 12 international. Average age 32. 224 applicants, 41% accepted, 55 enrolled. *Faculty:* 83 full-time (36 women), 16 part-time/adjunct (5 women). Expenses: Contact institution. *Financial support:* In 2001–02, 39 research assistantships, 21 teaching assistantships were awarded. Fellowships, career-related internships or fieldwork, Federal Work-Study, and tuition waivers (full and partial) also available. In 2001, 47 master's, 2 doctorates awarded. *Degree program information:* Part-time programs available. Offers anthropology (MA); applied health psychology (MA); applied sociology (MA); archaeology (MA); criminal justice (MS); criminal justice policy and planning (Certificate); general (MA); political science (MA, PhD); public administration (MPA); public management (Certificate); public policy (PhD); social and behavioral sciences (MA, MPA, MS, PhD, Certificate). *Application deadline:* Applications are processed on a rolling basis. *Application fee:* $45. *Dean*, Kathryn Cruz-Uribe, 928-523-2672.

School of Performing Arts Students: 21 full-time (10 women), 4 part-time (3 women); includes 2 Hispanic Americans Average age 30. 21 applicants, 81% accepted, 14 enrolled. *Faculty:* 31 full-time (6 women), 11 part-time/adjunct (5 women). Expenses: Contact institution. *Financial support:* In 2001–02, 13 teaching assistantships were awarded; tuition waivers (full and partial) also available. In 2001, 10 degrees awarded. Offers choral conducting (MM); instrumental conducting (MM); instrumental performance (MM); music education (MM); music history (MM); theory and composition (MM); vocal performance (MM). *Application deadline:* For fall admission, 3/15 (priority date). Applications are processed on a rolling basis. *Application fee:* $45. *Application Contact:* Dr. Victor Liva, Coordinator, 928-523-1863, E-mail: master.music@nau.edu. *Interim Dean*, Dr. John Burton, 928-523-3731.

NORTHERN BAPTIST THEOLOGICAL SEMINARY, Lombard, IL 60148-5698

General Information Independent-religious, coed, graduate-only institution. *Enrollment by degree level:* 119 first professional, 48 master's, 88 doctoral. *Graduate faculty:* 13 full-time (3 women), 26 part-time/adjunct (6 women). *Tuition:* Part-time $295 per hour. *Required fees:* $70 per quarter. Tuition and fees vary according to degree level. *Graduate housing:* Rooms and/or apartments available on a first-come, first-served basis to single and married students. Typical cost: $5,100 per year for single students; $9,000 per year for married students. Housing application deadline: 6/30. *Student services:* Free psychological counseling, low-cost health insurance. *Library facilities:* Brimsom-Grow Library. *Online resources:* library catalog, web page, access to other libraries' catalogs. *Collection:* 46,963 titles, 295 serial subscriptions, 1,486 audiovisual materials.

Computer facilities: 18 computers available on campus for general student use. A campuswide network can be accessed from student residence rooms. Internet access is available. *Web address:* http://www.seminary.edu/.

General Application Contact: Rev. Karen Walker-Freeburg, Director of Admissions, 630-620-2128, Fax: 630-620-2190, E-mail: walkerfreeburg@northern.seminary.edu.

GRADUATE UNITS

Graduate and Professional Programs Students: 150 full-time (32 women), 107 part-time (47 women); includes 100 minority (58 African Americans, 23 Asian Americans or Pacific Islanders, 19 Hispanic Americans), 16 international. Average age 40. 71 applicants, 90% accepted. *Faculty:* 13 full-time (3 women), 26 part-time/adjunct (6 women). Expenses: Contact institution. *Financial support:* Career-related internships or fieldwork and scholarships/grants available. Support available to part-time students. Financial award application deadline: 9/1. In 2001, 20 first professional degrees, 7 master's, 15 doctorates awarded. *Degree program information:* Part-time programs available. Offers Bible (MA); Christian ministries (MACM); divinity (M Div); ethics (MA); history (MA); ministry (D Min); theology (MA); worship/spirituality (MAWS); youth ministry (MAYM). *Application deadline:* For fall admission, 9/1 (priority date); for winter admission, 12/1 (priority date); for spring admission, 3/1 (priority date). Applications are processed on a rolling basis. *Application fee:* $35. Electronic applications accepted. *Application Contact:* Rev. Karen Walker-Freeburg, Director of Admissions, 630-620-2128, Fax: 630-620-2190, E-mail: walkerfreeburg@northern.seminary.edu. *Dean*, Dr. Timothy Weber, 630-620-2103.

NORTHERN ILLINOIS UNIVERSITY, De Kalb, IL 60115-2854

General Information State-supported, coed, university. CGS member. *Enrollment:* 1,904 full-time matriculated graduate/professional students (1,012 women), 2,969 part-time matriculated graduate/professional students (1,838 women). *Enrollment by degree level:* 303 first professional, 3,595 master's, 849 doctoral, 126 other advanced degrees. *Graduate faculty:* 703 full-time (252 women), 60 part-time/adjunct (15 women). Tuition, state resident: full-time $5,124; part-time $148 per credit hour. Tuition, nonresident: full-time $8,666; part-time $295 per credit hour. *Required fees:* $51 per term. *Graduate housing:* Rooms and/or apartments available on a first-come, first-served basis to single and married students. Typical cost: $5,330 (including board) for single students. *Student services:* Campus employment opportunities, campus safety program, career counseling, child daycare facilities, disabled student services, exercise/wellness program, free psychological counseling, international student services, low-cost health insurance, teacher training, writing training. *Library facilities:* Founders Memorial Library plus 8 others. *Online resources:* library catalog, web page, access to other libraries' catalogs. *Collection:* 1.6 million titles, 17,000 serial subscriptions, 49,270 audiovisual materials. *Research affiliation:* Argonne National Laboratory, Fermi National Accelerator Laboratory, Roper Center, Field Museum of Natural History.

Computer facilities: 1,200 computers available on campus for general student use. A campuswide network can be accessed from student residence rooms and from off campus. *Web address:* http://www.niu.edu/.

General Application Contact: Graduate School Office, 815-753-0395, E-mail: gradsch@niu.edu.

GRADUATE UNITS

College of Law Students: 297 full-time (137 women), 6 part-time (5 women); includes 52 minority (19 African Americans, 12 Asian Americans or Pacific Islanders, 19 Hispanic Americans, 2 Native Americans) Average age 28. *Faculty:* 22 full-time (11 women). Expenses: Contact institution. *Financial support:* In 2001–02, 22 teaching assistantships were awarded; research assistantships, career-related internships or fieldwork, Federal Work-Study, tuition waivers (full and partial), and unspecified assistantships also available. Support available to part-time students. In 2001, 90 degrees awarded. Offers law (JD). *Application deadline:* For fall admission, 6/1. *Application fee:* $35. *Application Contact:* Judith L. Malen, Director of Admissions and Financial Aid, 815-753-1420. *Dean*, LeRoy Pernell, 815-753-1067, Fax: 815-753-1310.

Graduate School Students: 1,607 full-time (875 women), 2,963 part-time (1,833 women); includes 698 minority (307 African Americans, 201 Asian Americans or Pacific Islanders, 175 Hispanic Americans, 15 Native Americans), 512 international. Average age 33. 3,970 applicants, 51% accepted, 1137 enrolled. *Faculty:* 681 full-time (241 women), 60 part-time/adjunct (15 women). Expenses: Contact institution. *Financial support:* In 2001–02, 244 research assistantships with full tuition reimbursements, 689 teaching assistantships with full tuition reimbursements were awarded. Fellowships with full tuition reimbursements, career-related internships or fieldwork, Federal Work-Study, scholarships/grants, tuition waivers (full), and unspecified assistantships also available. Support available to part-time students. Financial award applicants required to submit FAFSA. In 2001, 1,261 master's, 94 doctorates, 19 other advanced degrees awarded. *Degree program information:* Part-time and evening/weekend programs available. Postbaccalaureate distance learning degree programs offered (minimal on-campus study). *Application deadline:* Applications are processed on a rolling basis. *Application fee:* $30. *Application Contact:* Graduate School Office, 815-753-0395, E-mail: gradsch@niu.edu. *Dean and Vice Provost for Graduate Studies and Research*, Dr. Jerrold Zar, 815-753-1883, Fax: 815-753-6366.

College of Business Students: 222 full-time (90 women), 571 part-time (228 women); includes 68 minority (10 African Americans, 46 Asian Americans or Pacific Islanders, 12 Hispanic Americans), 61 international. Average age 32. *Faculty:* 53 full-time (15 women), 4 part-time/adjunct (0 women). Expenses: Contact institution. *Financial support:* In 2001–02, 20 research assistantships with full tuition reimbursements were awarded; fellowships with full tuition reimbursements, teaching assistantships with full tuition reimbursements, career-related internships or fieldwork, Federal Work-Study, tuition waivers (full), and unspecified assistantships also available. Support available to part-time students. In 2001, 278 degrees awarded. *Degree program information:* Part-time and evening/weekend programs available. Offers accountancy (MAS, MST); business (MAS, MBA, MS, MST); business administration (MBA); management information systems (MS). *Application deadline:* Applications are processed on a rolling basis. *Application fee:* $30. *Application Contact:* Harry Wright, Director of Graduate Studies, 815-753-6301. *Dean*, Dr. David K. Graf, 815-753-6176, Fax: 815-753-5305.

Northern Illinois University (continued)

College of Education Students: 225 full-time (157 women), 1,690 part-time (1,224 women); includes 245 minority (163 African Americans, 21 Asian Americans or Pacific Islanders, 57 Hispanic Americans, 4 Native Americans), 35 international. Average age 37. 584 applicants, 65% accepted. *Faculty:* 105 full-time (61 women), 4 part-time/adjunct (3 women). Expenses: Contact institution. *Financial support:* Fellowships with full tuition reimbursements, research assistantships with full tuition reimbursements, teaching assistantships with full tuition reimbursements, career-related internships or fieldwork, Federal Work-Study, tuition waivers (full), and unspecified assistantships available. Support available to part-time students. In 2001, 510 master's, 62 doctorates, 9 other advanced degrees awarded. *Degree program information:* Part-time and evening/weekend programs available. Postbaccalaureate distance learning degree programs offered (minimal on-campus study). Offers adult continuing education (MS Ed, Ed D); counseling (MS Ed, Ed D); curriculum and instruction (MS Ed, Ed D); curriculum and leadership (MS Ed); early childhood education (MS Ed); education (MS Ed, Ed D, Ed S); educational administration (MS Ed, Ed D, Ed S); educational psychology (MS Ed, Ed D); elementary education (MS Ed, Ed D); foundations of education (MS Ed); instructional technology (MS Ed, Ed D); outdoor teacher education (MS Ed); physical education (MS Ed); reading (MS Ed, Ed D); school business management (MS Ed); secondary education (MS Ed, Ed D); special education (MS Ed). *Application deadline:* For spring admission, 11/1. Applications are processed on a rolling basis. *Application fee:* $30. *Acting Dean,* Dr. Christine Sorensen, 815-753-9056, Fax: 815-753-2100.

College of Engineering and Engineering Technology Students: 108 full-time (21 women), 78 part-time (9 women); includes 14 minority (1 African American, 13 Asian Americans or Pacific Islanders), 111 international. Average age 26. *Faculty:* 34 full-time (1 woman), 3 part-time/adjunct (0 women). Expenses: Contact institution. *Financial support:* Fellowships with full tuition reimbursements, research assistantships with full tuition reimbursements, teaching assistantships with full tuition reimbursements, career-related internships or fieldwork, Federal Work-Study, tuition waivers (full), and unspecified assistantships available. Support available to part-time students. In 2001, 43 degrees awarded. *Degree program information:* Part-time and evening/weekend programs available. Offers electrical engineering (MS); engineering and engineering technology (MS); industrial engineering (MS); industrial management (MS); mechanical engineering (MS). *Application deadline:* For fall admission, 6/1; for spring admission, 11/1. Applications are processed on a rolling basis. *Application fee:* $30. *Dean,* Dr. Romualdas Kasuba, 815-753-1281, Fax: 815-753-1310.

College of Health and Human Sciences Students: 211 full-time (187 women), 177 part-time (167 women); includes 42 minority (17 African Americans, 13 Asian Americans or Pacific Islanders, 11 Hispanic Americans, 1 Native American), 20 international. Average age 30. 457 applicants, 40% accepted. *Faculty:* 49 full-time (38 women), 3 part-time/adjunct (all women). Expenses: Contact institution. *Financial support:* Fellowships with full tuition reimbursements, research assistantships with full tuition reimbursements, teaching assistantships with full tuition reimbursements, career-related internships or fieldwork, Federal Work-Study, tuition waivers (full), and unspecified assistantships available. Support available to part-time students. In 2001, 99 degrees awarded. *Degree program information:* Part-time and evening/weekend programs available. Offers applied family and child studies (MS); communicative disorders (MA); health and human sciences (MA, MPH, MPT, MS); nursing (MS); nutrition and dietetics (MS); physical therapy (MPT); public health (MPH). *Application deadline:* Applications are processed on a rolling basis. *Application fee:* $30. *Dean,* Dr. Shirley Richmond, 815-753-6155.

College of Liberal Arts and Sciences Students: 723 full-time (346 women), 447 part-time (193 women); includes 114 minority (35 African Americans, 47 Asian Americans or Pacific Islanders, 28 Hispanic Americans, 4 Native Americans), 254 international. Average age 30. *Faculty:* 341 full-time (96 women), 34 part-time/adjunct (6 women). Expenses: Contact institution. *Financial support:* Fellowships with full tuition reimbursements, research assistantships with full tuition reimbursements, teaching assistantships with full tuition reimbursements, career-related internships or fieldwork, Federal Work-Study, tuition waivers (full), and unspecified assistantships available. Support available to part-time students. In 2001, 265 master's, 32 doctorates awarded. *Degree program information:* Part-time and evening/weekend programs available. Offers anthropology (MA); biological sciences (MS, PhD); chemistry (MS, PhD); communication studies (MA); computer science (MS); economics (MA, PhD); English (MA, PhD); French (MA); geography (MS); geology (MS, PhD); history (MA, PhD); liberal arts and sciences (MA, MPA, MS, PhD); mathematical sciences (PhD); mathematics (MS); philosophy (MA); physics (MS, PhD); political science (MA, PhD); psychology (MA, PhD); public administration (MPA); sociology (MA); Spanish (MA); statistics (MS). *Application deadline:* For spring admission, 11/1. Applications are processed on a rolling basis. *Application fee:* $30. *Dean,* Dr. Frederick Kitterle, 815-753-1061, Fax: 815-753-7950.

College of Visual and Performing Arts Students: 149 full-time (85 women), 102 part-time (71 women); includes 18 minority (8 African Americans, 6 Asian Americans or Pacific Islanders, 4 Hispanic Americans), 35 international. Average age 32. *Faculty:* 99 full-time (30 women), 12 part-time/adjunct (3 women). Expenses: Contact institution. *Financial support:* Fellowships with full tuition reimbursements, research assistantships with full tuition reimbursements, teaching assistantships with full tuition reimbursements, career-related internships or fieldwork, Federal Work-Study, tuition waivers (full), and unspecified assistantships available. Support available to part-time students. In 2001, 66 master's, 10 other advanced degrees awarded. *Degree program information:* Part-time and evening/weekend programs available. Offers art (MA, MFA, MS); music (MM, Performer's Certificate); theatre and dance (MFA); visual and performing arts (MA, MFA, MM, MS, Performer's Certificate). *Application deadline:* Applications are processed on a rolling basis. *Application fee:* $30. *Dean,* Dr. Harold Kafer, 815-753-1138, Fax: 815-753-8372.

See in-depth description on page 1011.

NORTHERN KENTUCKY UNIVERSITY, Highland Heights, KY 41099

General Information State-supported, coed, comprehensive institution. *Enrollment:* 300 full-time matriculated graduate/professional students (148 women), 788 part-time matriculated graduate/professional students (454 women). *Enrollment by degree level:* 374 first professional, 714 master's. *Graduate faculty:* 116 full-time (54 women). Tuition, state resident: full-time $2,958; part-time $149 per credit hour. Tuition, nonresident: full-time $7,872; part-time $422 per credit hour. *Graduate housing:* Room and/or apartments available to single students; on-campus housing not available to married students. Typical cost: $4,460 (including board). *Student services:* Campus employment opportunities, campus safety program, career counseling, child daycare facilities, disabled student services, exercise/wellness program, free psychological counseling, international student services, low-cost health insurance, multicultural affairs office. *Library facilities:* Steely Library plus 2 others. *Online resources:* library catalog, web page. *Collection:* 524,802 titles, 3,554 serial subscriptions, 1,490 audiovisual materials.

Computer facilities: 600 computers available on campus for general student use. A campuswide network can be accessed from student residence rooms and from off campus. Internet access and online class registration are available. *Web address:* http://www.nku.edu/.

General Application Contact: Peg Griffin, Graduate Coordinator, 859-572-6364, E-mail: griffinp@nku.edu.

GRADUATE UNITS

Salmon P. Chase College of Law Students: 212 full-time (100 women), 162 part-time (73 women); includes 21 minority (14 African Americans, 5 Asian Americans or Pacific Islanders, 2 Hispanic Americans) Average age 30. *Faculty:* 26 full-time (8 women). Expenses: Contact institution. *Financial support:* Research assistantships, career-related internships or fieldwork, scholarships/grants, and tuition waivers (partial) available. Support available to part-time students. Financial award application deadline: 4/1; financial award applicants required to submit FAFSA. In 2001, 81 degrees awarded. *Degree program information:* Part-time and evening/weekend programs available. Offers law (JD). *Application deadline:* For fall admission, 3/1. Applications are processed on a rolling basis. *Application fee:* $30. *Application Contact:* Gina Bray, Admissions Specialist, 859-572-5384. *Dean,* Prof. Gerald A. St. Amand, 859-572-6406.

School of Graduate Programs Students: 88 full-time (48 women), 626 part-time (381 women); includes 36 minority (16 African Americans, 15 Asian Americans or Pacific Islanders, 4 Hispanic Americans, 1 Native American), 17 international. Average age 33. *Faculty:* 116 full-time (54 women). Expenses: Contact institution. *Financial support:* Fellowships, research assistantships with tuition reimbursements, career-related internships or fieldwork, Federal Work-Study, institutionally sponsored loans, tuition waivers (full), and unspecified assistantships available. Support available to part-time students. In 2001, 196 degrees awarded. *Degree program information:* Part-time and evening/weekend programs available. Offers accountancy (M Acct); business administration (MBA); computer science (MSCS); information systems (MSIS); nursing (MSN); public administration (MPA); technology (MST). *Application deadline:* Applications are processed on a rolling basis. *Application fee:* $25. *Application Contact:* Peg Griffin, Graduate Coordinator, 859-572-6364, E-mail: griffinp@nku.edu. *Associate Provost,* Dr. Paul Reichardt, 859-572-5379.

College of Education Students: 7 full-time (3 women), 309 part-time (251 women); includes 9 minority (6 African Americans, 1 Asian American or Pacific Islander, 1 Hispanic American, 1 Native American) Average age 33. *Faculty:* 19 full-time (11 women). Expenses: Contact institution. *Financial support:* In 2001–02, 3 research assistantships were awarded; Federal Work-Study also available. In 2001, 122 degrees awarded. *Degree program information:* Part-time and evening/weekend programs available. Offers elementary education (MA Ed); middle school education (MA Ed); secondary education (MA Ed). *Application deadline:* For fall admission, 8/1; for spring admission, 12/1. Applications are processed on a rolling basis. *Application fee:* $25. *Application Contact:* Peg Griffin, Graduate Coordinator, 859-572-6364, E-mail: griffinp@nku.edu. *Interim Chairperson,* Dr. Linda Olasov, 859-572-5365.

NORTHERN MICHIGAN UNIVERSITY, Marquette, MI 49855-5301

General Information State-supported, coed, comprehensive institution. CGS member. *Enrollment:* 547 matriculated graduate/professional students. *Graduate faculty:* 114 full-time (51 women), 27 part-time/adjunct (8 women). Tuition, state resident: full-time $158. Tuition, nonresident: full-time $260. Tuition and fees vary according to course load. *Graduate housing:* Rooms and/or apartments available to single and married students. Typical cost: $1,700 (including board) for single students; $1,133 (including board) for married students. *Student services:* Campus employment opportunities, campus safety program, career counseling, disabled student services, free psychological counseling, international student services, low-cost health insurance. *Library facilities:* Lydia Olson Library plus 1 other. *Online resources:* library catalog, web page, access to other libraries' catalogs. *Collection:* 1,492 titles, 1,748 serial subscriptions, 39,924 audiovisual materials.

Computer facilities: 450 computers available on campus for general student use. A campuswide network can be accessed from student residence rooms and from off campus. Internet access and online class registration are available. *Web address:* http://www.nmu.edu/.

General Application Contact: Dr. Sara L. Doubledee, Dean of Graduate Studies, 906-227-2300, Fax: 906-227-2315, E-mail: sdoubled@nmu.edu.

GRADUATE UNITS

College of Graduate Studies Students: 547. Average age 36. 163 applicants, 89% accepted. *Faculty:* 114 full-time (51 women), 27 part-time/adjunct (8 women). Expenses: Contact institution. *Financial support:* Research assistantships, teaching assistantships, career-related internships or fieldwork, Federal Work-Study, institutionally sponsored loans, tuition waivers (full), and unspecified assistantships available. Support available to part-time students. In 2001, 152 degrees awarded. *Degree program information:* Part-time and evening/weekend programs available. Postbaccalaureate distance learning degree programs offered. *Application deadline:* Applications are processed on a rolling basis. *Application fee:* $25. Electronic applications accepted. *Interim Dean,* Dr. Sara L. Doubledee, 906-227-2300, Fax: 906-227-2315, E-mail: sdoubled@nmu.edu.

College of Arts and Sciences Students: 117 full-time (61 women), 118 part-time (66 women); includes 25 minority (11 African Americans, 6 Asian Americans or Pacific Islanders, 8 Native Americans) *Faculty:* 62 full-time (17 women), 16 part-time/adjunct (3 women). Expenses: Contact institution. *Financial support:* Career-related internships or fieldwork, Federal Work-Study, institutionally sponsored loans, tuition waivers (full), and unspecified assistantships available. Support available to part-time students. Financial award application deadline: 3/1. In 2001, 53 degrees awarded. *Degree program information:* Part-time programs available. Postbaccalaureate distance learning degree programs offered (minimal on-campus study). Offers administrative services (MA); arts and sciences (MA, MFA, MPA, MS); biochemistry (MS); biology (MS); chemistry (MS); creative writing (MFA); literature (MA); mathematics education (MS); pedagogy (MA); public administration (MPA); science education (MS); writing (MA). *Application deadline:* For fall admission, 7/1 (priority date); for spring admission, 11/1. Applications are processed on a rolling basis. *Application fee:* $25. *Dean,* Dr. Terrence Scethogg, 906-227-2700.

College of Professional Studies Students: 312. *Faculty:* 26 full-time (12 women), 2 part-time/adjunct (1 woman). Expenses: Contact institution. *Financial support:* Teaching assistantships, career-related internships or fieldwork, Federal Work-Study, institutionally sponsored loans, tuition waivers (full), and unspecified assistantships available. Support available to part-time students. Financial award application deadline: 3/1. In 2001, 76 degrees awarded. *Degree program information:* Part-time programs available. Offers administration and supervision (MA Ed, Ed S); behavioral sciences and human services (MA, MA Ed, MS, MSN, Ed S); communication disorders (MA); criminal justice (MS); elementary education (MA Ed); exercise science (MS); nursing (MSN); psychology (MS); secondary education (MA Ed); special education (MA Ed). *Application deadline:* For fall admission, 7/1 (priority date); for spring admission, 11/1. Applications are processed on a rolling basis. *Application fee:* $25. *Dean,* Dr. M. Cameron Howes, 906-227-2400.

NORTHERN STATE UNIVERSITY, Aberdeen, SD 57401-7198

General Information State-supported, coed, comprehensive institution. *Enrollment:* 30 full-time matriculated graduate/professional students (16 women), 63 part-time matriculated graduate/professional students (43 women). *Enrollment by degree level:* 90 master's. *Graduate faculty:* 83 full-time (18 women). Tuition, state resident: full-time $2,376; part-time $99 per credit hour. Tuition, nonresident: full-time $7,005; part-time $291 per credit hour. *Required fees:* $1,380. One-time fee: $35 part-time. Full-time tuition and fees vary according to course load, degree level and reciprocity agreements. *Graduate housing:* Room and/or apartments available on a first-come, first-served basis to single students; on-campus housing not available to married students. Typical cost: $1,447 per year ($2,837 including board). *Student services:* Campus employment opportunities, campus safety program, career counseling, child daycare facilities, exercise/wellness program, free psychological counseling, international student services, low-cost health insurance. *Library facilities:* Beulah Williams Library. *Online resources:* library catalog, web page, access to other libraries' catalogs. *Collection:* 187,961 titles, 1,084 serial subscriptions.

Computer facilities: 800 computers available on campus for general student use. A campuswide network can be accessed from student residence rooms and from off campus. Internet access and online class registration are available. *Web address:* http://www.northern.edu/.

General Application Contact: Tammy K. Griffith, Senior Secretary, 605-626-2558, Fax: 605-626-3022, E-mail: griffith@northern.edu.

GRADUATE UNITS

Division of Graduate Studies in Education Students: 30 full-time (16 women), 63 part-time (43 women). Average age 32. *Faculty:* 80 full-time (20 women). Expenses: Contact institution. *Financial support:* In 2001–02, 51 students received support; teaching assistantships, career-related internships or fieldwork, Federal Work-Study, institutionally sponsored loans, and scholarships/grants available. Support available to part-time students. Financial award application deadline: 3/1; financial award applicants required to submit FAFSA. In 2001, 48 degrees awarded. *Degree program information:* Part-time and evening/weekend programs available. Offers education (MS Ed); educational studies (MS Ed); elementary classroom teaching (MS Ed); elementary school administration (MS Ed); guidance and counseling (MS Ed); health, physical education, and coaching (MS Ed); language and literacy (MS Ed); secondary classroom teaching (MS Ed); secondary school administration (MS Ed); special education (MS Ed). *Application deadline:* For fall admission, 8/15 (priority date); for spring admission, 12/15. Applications are processed on a rolling basis. *Application fee:* $35. *Application Contact:* Tammy K. Griffith, Senior Secretary, 605-626-2558, Fax: 605-626-3022, E-mail: griffith@northern.edu. *Head,* Dr. Ruth A. Johnson, 605-626-2558, Fax: 605-626-3022, E-mail: johnsonr@northern.edu.

NORTH GEORGIA COLLEGE & STATE UNIVERSITY, Dahlonega, GA 30597-1001

General Information State-supported, coed, comprehensive institution. *Enrollment:* 96 full-time matriculated graduate/professional students (67 women), 336 part-time matriculated graduate/professional students (259 women). *Enrollment by degree level:* 432 master's. *Graduate faculty:* 95 full-time (45 women), 10 part-time/adjunct (6 women). Tuition, state resident: full-time $1,160. Tuition, nonresident: full-time $4,640. *Graduate housing:* On-campus housing not available. *Student services:* Campus employment opportunities, campus safety program, career counseling, disabled student services, exercise/wellness program, free psychological counseling, international student services, low-cost health insurance, multicultural affairs office, writing training. *Library facilities:* Stewart Library. *Online resources:* library catalog, web page, access to other libraries' catalogs. *Collection:* 116,676 titles, 2,464 serial subscriptions, 4,496 audiovisual materials. *Research affiliation:* Northeast Georgia Medical Center, Morehouse School of Medicine, St. Joseph's Hospital, Mettler Electronic Corporation.

Computer facilities: 500 computers available on campus for general student use. A campuswide network can be accessed from student residence rooms and from off campus. *Web address:* http://www.ngcsu.edu/.

General Application Contact: Dr. Steve Ross, Coordinator of Graduate Admissions, 706-864-1916, Fax: 706-864-1874, E-mail: sross@ngcsu.edu.

GRADUATE UNITS

Graduate School Students: 96 full-time (67 women), 336 part-time (259 women). Average age 34. *Faculty:* 95 full-time (45 women), 10 part-time/adjunct (6 women). Expenses: Contact institution. *Financial support:* Teaching assistantships with partial tuition reimbursements, career-related internships or fieldwork, scholarships/grants, and unspecified assistantships available. Support available to part-time students. Financial award application deadline: 5/1; financial award applicants required to submit FAFSA. In 2001, 134 degrees awarded. *Degree program information:* Part-time and evening/weekend programs available. Postbaccalaureate distance learning degree programs offered. Offers community counseling (MS); early childhood education (M Ed); educational administration (Ed S); family practitioner (MSN); middle grades education (M Ed); physical therapy (MS); public administration (MPA); secondary education (M Ed); special education (M Ed). *Application deadline:* For fall admission, 7/1 (priority date); for spring admission, 12/1 (priority date). Applications are processed on a rolling basis. *Application fee:* $25. *Application Contact:* Dr. Steve Ross, Coordinator of Graduate Admissions, 706-864-1916, Fax: 706-864-1874, E-mail: sross@ngcsu.edu.

NORTH PARK THEOLOGICAL SEMINARY, Chicago, IL 60625-4895

General Information Independent-religious, coed, graduate-only institution. *Graduate faculty:* 17 full-time (4 women), 13 part-time/adjunct (3 women). *Graduate housing:* Rooms and/or apartments available to single and married students. Housing application deadline: 9/1. *Student services:* Campus employment opportunities, campus safety program, career counseling, free psychological counseling, international student services, low-cost health insurance, multicultural affairs office, writing training. *Library facilities:* North Park Consolidated Library. *Online resources:* library catalog. *Collection:* 251,732 titles, 1,197 serial subscriptions, 6,492 audiovisual materials. *Research affiliation:* Northside Chicago Theological Institute, Covenant Archives and Historical Society, American Theological Library Association.

Computer facilities: A campuswide network can be accessed from off campus. Internet access is available. *Web address:* http://www.northpark.edu/sem/.

General Application Contact: Mark Washington, Associate Director, 800-964-0101, Fax: 773-244-6244, E-mail: semadmissions@northpark.edu.

GRADUATE UNITS

Graduate and Professional Programs Students: 145. Average age 35. 90 applicants, 79% accepted. *Faculty:* 17 full-time (4 women), 13 part-time/adjunct (3 women). Expenses: Contact institution. *Financial support:* In 2001–02, 54 students received support, including 17 teaching assistantships; career-related internships or fieldwork and tuition waivers (full and partial) also available. Financial award application deadline: 9/7; financial award applicants required to submit FAFSA. In 2001, 12 first professional degrees, 4 master's, 3 doctorates awarded. *Degree program information:* Part-time programs available. Offers Christian studies (Certificate); preaching (D Min); religious education (MACE); theological studies (MATS); theology (M Div). *Application deadline:* Applications are processed on a rolling basis. *Application fee:* $25. *Application Contact:* Mark Washington, Associate Director, 800-964-0101, Fax: 773-244-6244, E-mail: semadmissions@northpark.edu. *President and Dean,* Dr. John E. Phelan, 773-244-6214, Fax: 773-244-6244.

NORTH PARK UNIVERSITY, Chicago, IL 60625-4895

General Information Independent-religious, coed, comprehensive institution. *Graduate housing:* Rooms and/or apartments available to single and married students.

GRADUATE UNITS

Center for Management Education *Degree program information:* Part-time and evening/weekend programs available. Offers management education (MBA, MM).

School of Community Development Offers community development (MA).

School of Education Offers education (MA).

School of Nursing *Degree program information:* Part-time and evening/weekend programs available. Offers nursing (MS).

NORTHWEST BAPTIST SEMINARY, Tacoma, WA 98407

General Information Independent-religious, coed, primarily men, graduate-only institution. *Enrollment by degree level:* 69 first professional, 9 master's. *Graduate faculty:* 6 full-time (0 women), 1 part-time/adjunct (0 women). *Tuition:* Part-time $169 per credit hour. Tuition and fees vary according to course load and reciprocity agreements. *Graduate housing:* On-campus housing not available. *Student services:* Career counseling. *Library facilities:* Robert Powell Memorial Library. *Online resources:* library catalog, access to other libraries' catalogs. *Collection:* 17,000 titles, 29,765 serial subscriptions, 1,097 audiovisual materials.

Computer facilities: 4 computers available on campus for general student use. A campuswide network can be accessed. Internet access is available. *Web address:* http://www.nbs.edu/.

General Application Contact: Gene Haithcox, Dean of Students, 253-759-6104 Ext. 108, Fax: 253-759-3299, E-mail: ghaithcox@nbs.edu.

GRADUATE UNITS

Programs in Theology Students: 30 full-time (2 women), 48 part-time (8 women); includes 13 minority (1 African American, 4 Asian Americans or Pacific Islanders, 8 Hispanic Americans), 4 international. Average age 33. 29 applicants, 97% accepted, 25 enrolled. *Faculty:* 6 full-time (0 women), 1 part-time/adjunct (0 women). Expenses: Contact institution. *Financial support:* Scholarships/grants available. In 2001, 10 first professional degrees, 1 master's awarded. *Degree program information:* Part-time programs available. Offers theology (M Div, M Min, MTS, STM, Th M). *Application deadline:* For fall admission, 8/15 (priority date); for winter admission, 12/5 (priority date); for spring admission, 2/25 (priority date). Applications are processed on a rolling basis. *Application fee:* $35. *Application Contact:* Gene Haithcox, Dean of Students, 253-759-6104 Ext. 108, Fax: 253-759-3299, E-mail: ghaithcox@nbs.edu. *President,* Dr. Mark Wagner, 253-759-6107, Fax: 253-759-3299, E-mail: nbs@nbs.edu.

NORTHWEST CHRISTIAN COLLEGE, Eugene, OR 97401-3745

General Information Independent-religious, coed, comprehensive institution. *Graduate housing:* Rooms and/or apartments available on a first-come, first-served basis to single students and available to married students.

GRADUATE UNITS

Department of Business and Management *Degree program information:* Part-time and evening/weekend programs available. Offers business and management (MBA).

Department of Education and Counseling *Degree program information:* Part-time and evening/weekend programs available. Postbaccalaureate distance learning degree programs offered (minimal on-campus study). Offers school counseling/consulting (MA). Electronic applications accepted.

NORTHWESTERN HEALTH SCIENCES UNIVERSITY, Bloomington, MN 55431-1599

General Information Independent, coed, graduate-only institution. *Enrollment by degree level:* 697 first professional, 108 master's, 32 other advanced degrees. *Graduate faculty:* 55 full-time (21 women), 29 part-time/adjunct (14 women). *Tuition:* Part-time $5,810 per term. *Graduate housing:* On-campus housing not available. *Student services:* Campus employment opportunities, campus safety program, career counseling, disabled student services, free psychological counseling, international student services, low-cost health insurance. *Library facilities:* Greenwalt Library. *Online resources:* library catalog, web page. *Collection:* 13,200 titles, 320 serial subscriptions, 685 audiovisual materials. *Research affiliation:* Berman Center for Outcomes and Clinical Research (outcomes and clinical research), Pain Assessment and Rehabilitation Center (pain management), University of Minnesota, School of Medicine (orthopedic surgery).

Computer facilities: 40 computers available on campus for general student use. A campuswide network can be accessed from off campus. Internet access and online class registration are available. *Web address:* http://www.nwhealth.edu/.

General Application Contact: Lynn Heieie, Associate Director of Admissions, 952-888-4777, Fax: 952-888-6713, E-mail: admit@nwhealth.edu.

GRADUATE UNITS

Minnesota College of Acupuncture and Oriental Medicine Students: 73 full-time (56 women), 24 part-time (18 women); includes 10 minority (9 Asian Americans or Pacific Islanders, 1 Native American), 2 international. Average age 38. 29 applicants, 97% accepted. *Faculty:* 7 full-time (2 women), 10 part-time/adjunct (8 women). Expenses: Contact institution. *Financial support:* Career-related internships or fieldwork, Federal Work-Study, and scholarships/grants available. Support available to part-time students. Offers acupuncture (M Ac); oriental medicine (MOM). *Application deadline:* For fall admission, 5/1 (priority date); for winter admission, 9/1 (priority date). Applications are processed on a rolling basis. *Application fee:* $50. Electronic applications accepted. *Application Contact:* Susan Weldy, Admissions Counselor, 952-888-4777 Ext. 248, Fax: 952-888-6713, E-mail: admit@nwhealth.edu. *Acting Dean,* Rosemary Haywood, 952-888-4777 Ext. 359, Fax: 952-889-1398, E-mail: rhaywood@nwhealth.edu.

Northwestern College of Chiropractic Students: 653 full-time (239 women), 44 part-time (22 women); includes 39 minority (10 African Americans, 17 Asian Americans or Pacific Islanders, 4 Hispanic Americans, 8 Native Americans), 61 international. Average age 26. 187 applicants, 105% accepted. *Faculty:* 48 full-time (19 women), 19 part-time/adjunct (6 women). Expenses: Contact institution. *Financial support:* Career-related internships or fieldwork, Federal Work-Study, and scholarships/grants available. Support available to part-time students. In 2001, 213 degrees awarded. Offers chiropractic (DC). *Application deadline:* For fall admission, 5/1 (priority date); for winter admission, 9/1 (priority date); for spring admission, 1/1 (priority date). Applications are processed on a rolling basis. *Application fee:* $50. Electronic applications accepted. *Application Contact:* Lynn Heieie, Associate Director of Admissions, 952-888-4777, Fax: 952-888-6713, E-mail: admit@nwhealth.edu. *Senior Vice President,* Dr. Charles E. Sawyer, 952-888-4777 Ext. 470, Fax: 952-888-6713.

NORTHWESTERN OKLAHOMA STATE UNIVERSITY, Alva, OK 73717-2799

General Information State-supported, coed, comprehensive institution. *Graduate housing:* Room and/or apartments available to single students; on-campus housing not available to married students.

GRADUATE UNITS

School of Education, Psychology, and Health and Physical Education *Degree program information:* Part-time programs available. Offers behavioral sciences (MBS); education: non-certificate option (M Ed); elementary education (M Ed); guidance and counseling K–12 (M Ed); psychometry (M Ed); reading specialist (M Ed); secondary education (M Ed).

NORTHWESTERN POLYTECHNIC UNIVERSITY, Fremont, CA 94539-7482

General Information Independent, coed, comprehensive institution. *Enrollment:* 284 full-time matriculated graduate/professional students (146 women), 239 part-time matriculated graduate/professional students (124 women). *Enrollment by degree level:* 523 master's. *Graduate faculty:* 8 full-time (0 women), 64 part-time/adjunct (5 women). *Tuition:* Full-time $8,100; part-time $450 per unit. *Required fees:* $45; $15 per term. *Graduate housing:* Room and/or apartments available on a first-come, first-served basis to single students; on-campus housing not available to married students. Typical cost: $4,800 per year. *Student services:* Campus employment opportunities, career counseling, disabled student services, exercise/wellness program, international student services, low-cost health insurance, multicultural affairs office, writing training. *Library facilities:* NPU Library plus 1 other. *Collection:* 12,000 titles, 200 serial subscriptions, 200 audiovisual materials.

Computer facilities: 150 computers available on campus for general student use. A campuswide network can be accessed from student residence rooms and from off campus. Internet access is available. *Web address:* http://www.npu.edu/.

General Application Contact: Jack Xie, Director of Admissions, 510-657-5913, Fax: 510-657-8975, E-mail: jack@npu.edu.

GRADUATE UNITS

School of Business and Information Technology Students: 45 full-time (27 women), 29 part-time (16 women). Average age 30. 49 applicants, 76% accepted. *Faculty:* 1 full-time (0 women), 11 part-time/adjunct (1 woman). Expenses: Contact institution. *Financial support:* In 2001–02, 8 teaching assistantships with partial tuition reimbursements (averaging $2,400 per year) were awarded; career-related internships or fieldwork and unspecified assistantships also available. In 2001, 32 degrees awarded. *Degree program information:* Part-time and evening/weekend programs available. Offers business and information technology (MBA). *Application deadline:* For fall admission, 8/12 (priority date); for spring admission, 12/11 (priority date). Applications are processed on a rolling basis. *Application fee:* $50 ($75 for international students). *Application Contact:* Jack Xie, Director of Admissions, 510-657-5913, Fax: 510-657-8975, E-mail: jack@npu.edu. *Dean,* Paul Jensen, 510-657-5911, Fax: 510-657-8975, E-mail: npuadm@npu.edu.

School of Engineering Students: 239 full-time (119 women), 210 part-time (108 women). Average age 30. 132 applicants, 55% accepted. *Faculty:* 7 full-time (0 women), 53 part-time/adjunct (4 women). Expenses: Contact institution. *Financial support:* In 2001–02, 160 teaching assistantships with full and partial tuition reimbursements (averaging $1,000 per year) were awarded; career-related internships or fieldwork and unspecified assistantships also available. In 2001, 148 degrees awarded. *Degree program information:* Part-time and evening/weekend programs available. Offers computer science (MS); computer systems engineering (MS); electrical engineering (MS). *Application deadline:* For fall admission, 8/12 (priority

Northwestern Polytechnic University (continued)

date); for spring admission, 2/11 (priority date). Applications are processed on a rolling basis. *Application fee:* $50 ($75 for international students). *Application Contact:* Jack Xie, Director of Admissions, 510-657-5913, Fax: 510-657-8975, E-mail: jack@npu.edu. *Dean*, Dr. Pochang Hsu, 510-657-5911, Fax: 510-657-8975, E-mail: npuadm@npu.edu.

NORTHWESTERN STATE UNIVERSITY OF LOUISIANA, Natchitoches, LA 71497

General Information State-supported, coed, comprehensive institution. CGS member. *Enrollment:* 249 full-time matriculated graduate/professional students (181 women), 793 part-time matriculated graduate/professional students (618 women). *Enrollment by degree level:* 687 master's, 354 other advanced degrees. *Graduate faculty:* 55 full-time (32 women), 12 part-time/adjunct (8 women). Tuition, state resident: full-time $2,280. Tuition, nonresident: full-time $8,154. *Required fees:* $134 per semester. *Graduate housing:* Rooms and/or apartments available on a first-come, first-served basis to single and married students. Housing application deadline: 7/30. *Student services:* Campus employment opportunities, campus safety program, career counseling, disabled student services, exercise/wellness program, free psychological counseling, low-cost health insurance. *Library facilities:* Eugene P. Watson Memorial Library. *Online resources:* library catalog, access to other libraries' catalogs. *Collection:* 330,145 titles, 1,749 serial subscriptions, 5,282 audiovisual materials. *Research affiliation:* Federal Records and Archives Services, Central State Hospital, NASA (strategic defense initiative).

Computer facilities: 687 computers available on campus for general student use. A campuswide network can be accessed from student residence rooms and from off campus. Internet access and online class registration are available. *Web address:* http://www.nsula.edu/.

General Application Contact: Dr. Anthony J. Scheffler, Dean, Graduate Studies, Research, and Information Systems, 318-357-5851, Fax: 318-357-5019, E-mail: grad_school@alpha.nsula.edu.

GRADUATE UNITS

Graduate Studies and Research and Associate Provost Students: 249 full-time (181 women), 793 part-time (618 women); includes 239 minority (209 African Americans, 5 Asian Americans or Pacific Islanders, 12 Hispanic Americans, 13 Native Americans), 12 international. Average age 36. *Faculty:* 55 full-time (32 women), 12 part-time/adjunct (8 women). Expenses: Contact institution. *Financial support:* Fellowships, research assistantships, teaching assistantships, career-related internships or fieldwork and Federal Work-Study available. Support available to part-time students. Financial award application deadline: 7/15. In 2001, 206 master's, 8 other advanced degrees awarded. *Degree program information:* Part-time and evening/weekend programs available. Offers art (MA); clinical psychology (MS); English (MA); English education (M Ed); health promotion (M Ed); history (MA); music (MM); social sciences education (M Ed); sport administration (M Ed). *Application deadline:* For fall admission, 8/1 (priority date); for spring admission, 1/10. Applications are processed on a rolling basis. *Application fee:* $20 ($30 for international students). Electronic applications accepted. *Dean, Graduate Studies, Research, and Information Systems*, Dr. Anthony J. Scheffler, 318-357-5851, Fax: 318-357-5019, E-mail: grad_school@alpha.nsula.edu.

College of Education Students: 117 full-time (92 women), 371 part-time (293 women); includes 129 minority (119 African Americans, 1 Asian American or Pacific Islander, 3 Hispanic Americans, 6 Native Americans), 4 international. Average age 35. *Faculty:* 10 full-time (7 women), 4 part-time/adjunct (2 women). Expenses: Contact institution. *Financial support:* Career-related internships or fieldwork and Federal Work-Study available. Financial award application deadline: 7/15. In 2001, 124 master's, 8 other advanced degrees awarded. Offers adult and continuing education (M Ed); business and distributive education (M Ed); counseling and guidance (M Ed, Ed S); early childhood education (M Ed); educational administration/supervision (M Ed, Ed S); educational technology (M Ed, Ed S); elementary teaching (M Ed, Ed S); health and physical education (M Ed); home economics education (M Ed); human services (M Ed, MA, Ed S); mathematics education (M Ed); professional secondary studies: alternate certification 5th-year program (M Ed); reading (M Ed, Ed S); science education (M Ed); secondary teaching (M Ed, Ed S); special education (M Ed, Ed S); student personnel services (MA). *Application deadline:* For fall admission, 8/1 (priority date); for spring admission, 1/10. Applications are processed on a rolling basis. *Application fee:* $20 ($30 for international students). *Application Contact:* Dr. Anthony J. Scheffler, Dean, Graduate Studies, Research, and Information Systems, 318-357-5851, Fax: 318-357-5019, E-mail: grad_school@alpha.nsula.edu. *Chair*, Dr. John Tollett, 318-357-5195, Fax: 318-357-6275, E-mail: education@nsula.edu.

College of Nursing Students: 8 full-time (7 women), 86 part-time (72 women); includes 15 minority (11 African Americans, 1 Asian American or Pacific Islander, 1 Hispanic American, 2 Native Americans) Average age 36. *Faculty:* 5 full-time (all women). Expenses: Contact institution. *Financial support:* Career-related internships or fieldwork and Federal Work-Study available. Support available to part-time students. Financial award application deadline: 7/15. In 2001, 11 degrees awarded. *Degree program information:* Part-time programs available. Offers nursing (MSN). *Application deadline:* For fall admission, 8/1 (priority date); for spring admission, 1/10. Applications are processed on a rolling basis. *Application fee:* $20 ($30 for international students). *Application Contact:* Dr. Anthony J. Scheffler, Dean, Graduate Studies, Research, and Information Systems, 318-357-5851, Fax: 318-357-5019, E-mail: grad_school@alpha.nsula.edu. *Director*, Dr. Norann Planchock, 318-677-3100, Fax: 318-676-7887, E-mail: planchockn@alpha.nsula.edu.

NORTHWESTERN UNIVERSITY, Evanston, IL 60208

General Information Independent, coed, university. CGS member. *Enrollment:* 6,057 full-time matriculated graduate/professional students (2,691 women), 1,776 part-time matriculated graduate/professional students (622 women). *Graduate faculty:* 2,001 full-time (541 women), 136 part-time/adjunct (38 women). *Tuition:* Full-time $26,526. *Graduate housing:* Rooms and/or apartments available to single and married students. Housing application deadline: 9/1. *Student services:* Campus employment opportunities, campus safety program, career counseling, disabled student services, exercise/wellness program, free psychological counseling, grant writing training, international student services, low-cost health insurance, multicultural affairs office, teacher training, writing training. *Library facilities:* University Library plus 6 others. *Online resources:* library catalog, web page, access to other libraries' catalogs. *Collection:* 4.1 million titles, 37,467 serial subscriptions, 65,024 audiovisual materials. *Research affiliation:* Amoco Oil Company (materials science and engineering), Dow Chemical Company (materials science and engineering), E. I. du Pont de Nemours and Company (physics), Exxon Chemical Company (chemical engineering), Ford Motor Company (mechanical engineering), Medtronics, Inc. (cardiology).

Computer facilities: 661 computers available on campus for general student use. A campuswide network can be accessed from student residence rooms and from off campus. Internet access and online class registration are available. *Web address:* http://www.northwestern.edu/.

General Application Contact: Dorothea Reid, Coordinator of Graduate Admissions, 847-491-8532, Fax: 847-491-5070, E-mail: gradapp@northwestern.edu.

GRADUATE UNITS

The Graduate School Students: 6,057 full-time (2,691 women), 1,776 part-time (622 women); includes 1,336 minority (328 African Americans, 772 Asian Americans or Pacific Islanders, 212 Hispanic Americans, 24 Native Americans), 1,584 international. 7,592 applicants, 22% accepted. *Faculty:* 2,001 full-time (541 women), 136 part-time/adjunct (38 women). Expenses: Contact institution. *Financial support:* In 2001–02, 410 fellowships with full tuition reimbursements (averaging $16,800 per year), 515 research assistantships with partial tuition reimbursements (averaging $23,000 per year), 475 teaching assistantships with full tuition reimbursements (averaging $13,419 per year) were awarded. Career-related internships or fieldwork, Federal Work-Study, institutionally sponsored loans, scholarships/grants, traineeships, tuition waivers (full and partial), and unspecified assistantships also available. Support available to part-time students. Financial award application deadline: 12/30; financial award applicants required to submit FAFSA. In 2001, 434 first professional degrees, 2,282 master's, 350 doctorates, 50 other advanced degrees awarded. *Degree program information:* Part-time and evening/weekend programs available. Offers biochemistry (PhD); biochemistry, molecular biology, and cell biology (PhD); biotechnology (PhD); cell and molecular biology (PhD); clinical investigations (MSCI, Certificate); clinical psychology (PhD); developmental biology and genetics (PhD); education and social policy-counseling psychology (MA); genetic counseling (MS); hormone action and signal transduction (PhD); law and social science (Certificate); liberal studies (MA); literature (MA); management and organizations and sociology (PhD); marital and family therapy (MS); mathematical methods in social science (MS); molecular biophysics (PhD); neuroscience (PhD); public health (MPH); structural biology (PhD); structural biology, biochemistry, and biophysics (PhD); telecommunications science, management, and policy (Certificate). MBA, MMM offered through Kellogg School of Management; DPT offered through the Medical School; MSC offered through the School of Speech. *Application deadline:* For fall admission, 12/31 (priority date). Applications are processed on a rolling basis. *Application fee:* $60 ($75 for international students). Electronic applications accepted. *Application Contact:* Dorothea Reid, Coordinator of Graduate Admissions, 847-491-8532, Fax: 847-491-5070, E-mail: gradapp@northwestern.edu. *Dean*, Richard I. Morimoto, 847-491-8502, Fax: 847-467-7600.

Center for International and Comparative Studies Expenses: Contact institution. Offers international and comparative studies (Certificate). *Application fee:* $50 ($55 for international students). *Director*, Kenneth W. Abbott, 847-467-2770, Fax: 847-467-1996, E-mail: k-abbott@northwestern.edu.

Institute for Neuroscience Students: 80 full-time (49 women); includes 9 minority (2 African Americans, 5 Asian Americans or Pacific Islanders, 2 Hispanic Americans), 19 international. 135 applicants, 27% accepted. *Faculty:* 124 full-time (31 women). Expenses: Contact institution. *Financial support:* In 2001–02, 16 fellowships with full tuition reimbursements (averaging $20,000 per year), 35 research assistantships with partial tuition reimbursements (averaging $20,000 per year), 10 teaching assistantships with full tuition reimbursements (averaging $12,843 per year) were awarded. Scholarships/grants and traineeships also available. Financial award application deadline: 12/31; financial award applicants required to submit FAFSA. In 2001, 10 degrees awarded. Offers neuroscience (PhD). Admissions and degree offered through The Graduate School. *Application deadline:* For fall admission, 1/15 (priority date). *Application fee:* $50 ($55 for international students). *Application Contact:* Robert Harper-Mangels, Assistant Director, NUIN, 312-503-4300, Fax: 312-503-7345, E-mail: r_mangels@northwestern.edu. *Director*, Enrico Mugnaini, 312-503-4300, Fax: 312-503-7345, E-mail: e-mugnaini@northwestern.edu.

Judd A. and Marjorie Weinberg College of Arts and Sciences Students: 4,235 full-time (1,759 women), 576 part-time (250 women). *Faculty:* 402 full-time. Expenses: Contact institution. *Financial support:* Fellowships with full tuition reimbursements, research assistantships with partial tuition reimbursements, teaching assistantships with full tuition reimbursements, career-related internships or fieldwork, Federal Work-Study, institutionally sponsored loans, traineeships, and tuition waivers (full and partial) available. Financial award application deadline: 1/15; financial award applicants required to submit FAFSA. In 2001, 135 master's, 128 doctorates awarded. *Degree program information:* Part-time and evening/weekend programs available. Offers anthropology (PhD); art history (PhD); arts and sciences (MA, MFA, MS, PhD, Certificate); astrophysics (PhD); brain, behavior and cognition (PhD); chemistry (PhD); clinical psychology (PhD); cognitive psychology (PhD); comparative literary studies (PhD); economics (MA, PhD); eighteenth-century studies (Certificate); English (MA, PhD); French (PhD); French and comparative literature (PhD); geological sciences (MS, PhD); German literature and critical thought (PhD); history (PhD); Italian studies (Certificate); linguistics (MA, PhD); mathematics (PhD); neurobiology and physiology (MS); personality (PhD); philosophy (PhD); physics (MS, PhD); political science (MA, PhD); Slavic languages and literature (PhD); social psychology (PhD); sociology (PhD); statistics (MS, PhD); visual arts (MFA). *Application deadline:* Applications are processed on a rolling basis. *Application fee:* $50 ($55 for international students). *Application Contact:* Graduate School, 847-491-7264, E-mail: gradapp@northwestern.edu. *Dean*, Eric J. Sundquist, 847-491-3276.

Kellogg School of Management Students: 718 full-time (196 women), 1,173 part-time (352 women); includes 367 minority (67 African Americans, 251 Asian Americans or Pacific Islanders, 47 Hispanic Americans, 2 Native Americans), 217 international. Average age 28. 8,850 applicants, 17% accepted. *Faculty:* 134 full-time (29 women), 90 part-time/adjunct. Expenses: Contact institution. *Financial support:* In 2001–02, 1,544 students received support. Career-related internships or fieldwork, institutionally sponsored loans, and scholarships/grants available. Support available to part-time students. Financial award application deadline: 4/30; financial award applicants required to submit FAFSA. In 2001, 611 degrees awarded. *Degree program information:* Part-time and evening/weekend programs available. Offers accounting (PhD); business administration (MBA); finance (PhD); management (MBA, MMM, MS, PhD); management and organizations (PhD); managerial economics and strategy (PhD); manufacturing management (MMM); marketing (PhD). PhD admissions and degree offered through The Graduate School. *Application fee:* $160. *Application Contact:* Michele Rogers, Assistant Dean, Director of Admissions and Financial Aid, 847-491-3308, Fax: 847-491-4960, E-mail: kellogg_admissions@northwestern.edu. *Dean*, Dipak Jain, 847-491-3300.

Program in African Studies Expenses: Contact institution. *Financial support:* In 2001–02, 3 fellowships with full tuition reimbursements were awarded Offers African studies (Certificate). *Application fee:* $50 ($55 for international students). *Application Contact:* Dr. Akbar Virmani, Associate Director, 847-491-7323, Fax: 847-491-3739, E-mail: a-virmani@northwestern.edu. *Interim Director*, Dr. David Lee Schoenbrun, 847-491-7323, Fax: 847-491-3739, E-mail: dls@northwestern.edu.

School of Communication Students: 269 full-time, 112 part-time. *Faculty:* 95 full-time. Expenses: Contact institution. *Financial support:* In 2001–02, 23 fellowships with full tuition reimbursements (averaging $16,680 per year), 72 teaching assistantships with full tuition reimbursements (averaging $13,329 per year) were awarded. Research assistantships, career-related internships or fieldwork, Federal Work-Study, and institutionally sponsored loans also available. Financial award application deadline: 1/15; financial award applicants required to submit FAFSA. *Degree program information:* Part-time programs available. Offers audiology and hearing sciences (MA, PhD); communication (MA, MFA, MSC, PhD); communication studies (MA, PhD); communication systems (MSC); directing (MFA); learning disabilities (MA, PhD); managerial communication (MSC); performance studies (MA, PhD); radio/television/film (MA, MFA, PhD); speech and language pathology (MA, PhD); speech and language pathology and learning disabilities (MA); stage design (MFA); theatre (MA); theatre and drama (PhD). MA, MFA, and PhD admissions and degrees offered through The Graduate School; MSC admissions and degrees offered through the School of Speech. *Application deadline:* For fall admission, 8/30. *Application fee:* $50 ($55 for international students). *Dean*, Barbara O'Keefe, 847-491-7023, Fax: 847-467-1464.

School of Education and Social Policy Students: 127 full-time (96 women); includes 30 minority (14 African Americans, 13 Asian Americans or Pacific Islanders, 2 Hispanic Americans, 1 Native American), 14 international. Average age 30. *Faculty:* 23 full-time (9 women), 6 part-time/adjunct (3 women). Expenses: Contact institution. *Financial support:* In 2001–02, 23 fellowships with full tuition reimbursements (averaging $17,400 per year), 44 research assistantships with full tuition reimbursements (averaging $15,408 per year), 24 teaching assistantships with full tuition reimbursements (averaging $13,420 per year) were awarded. Career-related internships or fieldwork, Federal Work-Study, institutionally sponsored loans, scholarships/grants, and tuition waivers (partial) also available. Financial award application deadline: 1/15; financial award applicants required to submit FAFSA. In 2001, 103 master's, 13 doctorates awarded. *Degree program information:* Part-time and evening/weekend programs available. Offers advanced teaching (MS); education (MS); education and social policy (MS); education and social policy-learning sciences (MA, PhD); higher education administration (MS); human development and social policy (PhD); learning and organizational change (MS); secondary teaching (MS). MA and PhD admissions and degrees offered through The Graduate School. *Application fee:* $50 ($55 for international students). Electronic applications accepted. *Application Contact:* Aaron Akins, Office of Student Affairs, 847-491-3790, Fax: 847-467-2495, E-mail: sesp@northwestern.

edu. *Assistant Dean*, Mark P. Hoffman, 847-491-3790, Fax: 847-467-2495, E-mail: markhoffman@northwestern.edu.

Law School Offers law (JD, LL M). Electronic applications accepted.

McCormick School of Engineering and Applied Science Students: 777 full-time (183 women), 181 part-time (31 women); includes 154 minority (18 African Americans, 106 Asian Americans or Pacific Islanders, 29 Hispanic Americans, 1 Native American), 347 international. Average age 26. 2,762 applicants, 23% accepted. *Faculty:* 155 full-time. Expenses: Contact institution. *Financial support:* In 2001–02, 128 fellowships with full tuition reimbursements (averaging $19,800 per year), 358 research assistantships with partial tuition reimbursements (averaging $19,200 per year), 88 teaching assistantships with full tuition reimbursements (averaging $12,845 per year) were awarded. Career-related internships or fieldwork, Federal Work-Study, and institutionally sponsored loans also available. Financial award application deadline: 1/15; financial award applicants required to submit FAFSA. In 2001, 251 master's, 106 doctorates awarded. *Degree program information:* Part-time and evening/weekend programs available. Offers applied mathematics (MS, PhD); biomedical engineering (MS, PhD); chemical engineering (MS, PhD); computer science (MS, PhD); electrical and computer engineering (MS, PhD); electronic materials (MS, PhD, Certificate); engineering and applied science (MEM, MIT, MME, MMM, MPM, MS, PhD, Certificate); engineering management (MEM); environmental engineering and science (MS, PhD); fluid mechanics (MS, PhD); geotechnical engineering (MS, PhD); industrial engineering and management science (MS, PhD); information technology (MIT); manufacturing engineering (MME); materials science and engineering (MS, PhD); mechanical engineering (MS, PhD); mechanics of materials and solids (MS, PhD); operations research (MS, PhD); project management (MPM); solid mechanics (MS, PhD); structural engineering and materials (MS, PhD); theoretical and applied mechanics (MS, PhD); transportation systems analysis and planning (MS, PhD). MS and PhD admissions and degrees offered through The Graduate School. *Application deadline:* Applications are processed on a rolling basis. *Application fee:* $50 ($55 for international students). Electronic applications accepted. *Application Contact:* Melissa W. Grady, Information Contact, 847-491-3553, Fax: 847-491-5341, E-mail: m-grady@northwestern.edu. *Dean*, John Birge, 847-491-5520.

Medical School Offers cancer biology (PhD); cell biology (PhD); clinical investigation (MSCI); developmental biology (PhD); evolutionary biology (PhD); immunology and microbial pathogenesis (PhD); medicine (MD, MS, MSCI, DPT, PhD); molecular biology and genetics (PhD); neurobiology (PhD); pharmacology and toxicology (PhD); physical therapy (DPT, PhD); structural biology and biochemistry (PhD).

Medill School of Journalism Students: 240 full-time (160 women). Average age 25. *Faculty:* 43 full-time (7 women), 5 part-time/adjunct (2 women). Expenses: Contact institution. *Financial support:* In 2001–02, 152 students received support. Career-related internships or fieldwork, Federal Work-Study, institutionally sponsored loans, and scholarships/grants available. Financial award applicants required to submit FAFSA. In 2001, 240 degrees awarded. Offers advertising/sales promotion (MSIMC); broadcast journalism (MSJ); direct, database and e-commerce marketing (MSIMC); general studies (MSIMC); integrated marketing communications (MSIMC); magazine publishing (MSJ); new media (MSJ); public relations (MSIMC); reporting and writing (MSJ). *Application deadline:* For fall admission, 1/15 (priority date); for winter admission, 9/1 (priority date); for spring admission, 12/1 (priority date). *Application fee:* $50. *Application Contact:* Office of Graduate Admissions and Financial Aid, 847-491-5228, Fax: 847-467-7342, E-mail: medill-admis@northwestern.edu. *Dean*, Loren Ghiglione, 847-491-2050.

School of Music Students: 244 full-time (130 women), 4 part-time (1 woman); includes 43 minority (5 African Americans, 28 Asian Americans or Pacific Islanders, 10 Hispanic Americans), 20 international. 733 applicants, 31% accepted, 158 enrolled. *Faculty:* 64 full-time (19 women), 54 part-time/adjunct (17 women). Expenses: Contact institution. *Financial support:* In 2001–02, 178 students received support; fellowships, research assistantships, teaching assistantships, career-related internships or fieldwork, Federal Work-Study, institutionally sponsored loans, scholarships/grants, and unspecified assistantships available. Financial award application deadline: 2/15; financial award applicants required to submit FAFSA. In 2001, 75 master's, 10 doctorates, 6 other advanced degrees awarded. Offers collaborative arts (DM); conducting (MM, DM); jazz pedagogy (MM); keyboard (MM, DM, CP); music (MM, DM, PhD, CP); music cognition (PhD); music composition (MM, DM); music education (MM, PhD); music technology (MM, PhD); music theory (MM, PhD); musicology (MM, PhD); opera production (MM); performance (MM); piano performance and pedagogy (MM); string performance and pedagogy (MM); strings (MM, DM); strings, winds and percussion (CP); voice (MM, DM, CP); winds and percussion (MM, DM). PhD admissions and degree offered through The Graduate School. *Application deadline:* For fall admission, 1/15; for winter admission, 10/1 (priority date). *Application fee:* $50. *Application Contact:* Heather A. Landes, Assistant Dean, Music Admission and Financial Aid, 847-491-3141, Fax: 847-467-7440, E-mail: hlandes@northwestern.edu. *Dean*, Bernard J. Dobroski, 847-491-7552, Fax: 847-491-5260, E-mail: b-dobroski@northwestern.edu.

NORTHWEST GRADUATE SCHOOL OF THE MINISTRY, Seattle, WA 98104

General Information Independent-religious, coed, primarily men, graduate-only institution. *Enrollment by degree level:* 66 master's, 102 doctoral. *Graduate faculty:* 4 full-time (1 woman), 14 part-time/adjunct (0 women). *Tuition:* Part-time $170 per credit hour. *Graduate housing:* On-campus housing not available. *Student services:* Career counseling, writing training. *Library facilities:* Northwest Graduate School Library. *Online resources:* web page. *Collection:* 5,000 titles, 69 serial subscriptions, 125 audiovisual materials.

Computer facilities: 2 computers available on campus for general student use. A campuswide network can be accessed. Internet access is available. *Web address:* http://www.nwgs.edu/.

General Application Contact: Jeorily K. Martin, Admissions Coordinator, 206-246-9100, Fax: 206-624-0613, E-mail: nwgs@nwgs.edu.

GRADUATE UNITS

Program in Pastoral Ministry Average age 36. 7 applicants, 71% accepted. *Faculty:* 4 full-time (1 woman), 14 part-time/adjunct (0 women). Expenses: Contact institution. *Financial support:* In 2001–02, 20 students received support, including 20 fellowships (averaging $300 per year); tuition waivers (partial) also available. Support available to part-time students. Financial award application deadline: 4/1. In 2001, 3 master's, 12 doctorates awarded. *Degree program information:* Part-time programs available. Postbaccalaureate distance learning degree programs offered (minimal on-campus study). Offers pastoral ministry (MTS, D Min). *Application deadline:* For fall admission, 7/1 (priority date); for winter admission, 12/1; for spring admission, 3/15. Applications are processed on a rolling basis. *Application fee:* $25. Electronic applications accepted. *Application Contact:* Jeorily K. Martin, Admissions Coordinator, 206-246-9100, Fax: 206-624-0613, E-mail: nwgs@nwgs.edu. *Director of Academic Services*, Dr. Bill A. Payne, 206-264-9100, Fax: 206-624-0613, E-mail: payne@nwgs.edu.

NORTHWEST INSTITUTE OF ACUPUNCTURE AND ORIENTAL MEDICINE, Seattle, WA 98103

General Information Independent, coed, graduate-only institution. *Enrollment by degree level:* 206 master's. *Graduate faculty:* 2 full-time (1 woman), 34 part-time/adjunct (22 women). *Tuition:* Full-time $3,000; part-time $162 per credit. *Required fees:* $45; $5 per quarter. Tuition and fees vary according to program. *Graduate housing:* On-campus housing not available. *Student services:* Campus employment opportunities, exercise/wellness program, international student services. *Library facilities:* Northwest Institute of Acupuncture and Oriental Medicine Library. *Online resources:* library catalog. *Collection:* 2,300 titles, 35 serial subscriptions, 350 audiovisual materials.

Computer facilities: 4 computers available on campus for general student use. A campuswide network can be accessed from off campus. Internet access is available. *Web address:* http://www.niaom.edu/.

General Application Contact: Maritza Julia, Admissions Manager, 206-633-2419 Ext. 128, Fax: 206-633-5578, E-mail: admissions@niaom.edu.

GRADUATE UNITS

Program in Acupuncture Students: 147 full-time (112 women), 59 part-time (39 women); includes 30 minority (2 African Americans, 18 Asian Americans or Pacific Islanders, 7 Hispanic Americans, 3 Native Americans), 7 international. Average age 32. 203 applicants, 67% accepted. *Faculty:* 2 full-time (1 woman), 34 part-time/adjunct (22 women). Expenses: Contact institution. *Financial support:* Available to part-time students. Applicants required to submit FAFSA. In 2001, 51 degrees awarded. Offers acupuncture (M Ac); traditional Chinese medicine (MTCM). *Application deadline:* For fall admission, 5/1 (priority date); for spring admission, 12/1 (priority date). Applications are processed on a rolling basis. *Application fee:* $50. *Application Contact:* Maritza Julia, Admissions Manager, 206-633-2419 Ext. 128, Fax: 206-633-5578, E-mail: admissions@niaom.edu. *President*, Robert Shook, 206-633-2419 Ext. 120, Fax: 206-633-5578, E-mail: rshook@niaom.edu.

NORTHWEST MISSOURI STATE UNIVERSITY, Maryville, MO 64468-6001

General Information State-supported, coed, comprehensive institution. *Enrollment:* 160 full-time matriculated graduate/professional students (76 women), 353 part-time matriculated graduate/professional students (227 women). *Enrollment by degree level:* 1,023 master's, 43 other advanced degrees. *Graduate faculty:* 180 full-time (65 women). Tuition, state resident: full-time $2,777; part-time $154 per hour. Tuition, nonresident: full-time $4,626; part-time $257 per hour. Tuition and fees vary according to course level and course load. *Graduate housing:* Room and/or apartments available on a first-come, first-served basis to single students; on-campus housing not available to married students. Typical cost: $2,342 per year ($4,322 including board). Room and board charges vary according to board plan. Housing application deadline: 7/1. *Student services:* Campus employment opportunities, campus safety program, career counseling, disabled student services, free psychological counseling, international student services, low-cost health insurance, multicultural affairs office, writing training. *Library facilities:* B. D. Owens Library plus 1 other. *Online resources:* library catalog, web page, access to other libraries' catalogs. *Collection:* 305,982 titles, 1,469 serial subscriptions.

Computer facilities: 2,450 computers available on campus for general student use. A campuswide network can be accessed from student residence rooms and from off campus. Internet access is available. *Web address:* http://www.nwmissouri.edu/.

General Application Contact: Dr. Frances Shipley, Dean of Graduate School, 660-562-1145, Fax: 660-562-0000, E-mail: gradsch@mail.nwmissouri.edu.

GRADUATE UNITS

Graduate School Students: 160 full-time (76 women), 353 part-time (227 women). 221 applicants, 100% accepted, 141 enrolled. *Faculty:* 180 full-time (65 women). Expenses: Contact institution. *Financial support:* In 2001–02, 111 research assistantships with full tuition reimbursements (averaging $5,250 per year), 26 teaching assistantships with full tuition reimbursements (averaging $5,250 per year) were awarded. Career-related internships or fieldwork, Federal Work-Study, institutionally sponsored loans, and administrative assistantships, tutorial assistantships also available. Financial award application deadline: 3/1; financial award applicants required to submit FAFSA. In 2001, 197 master's, 23 other advanced degrees awarded. *Degree program information:* Part-time programs available. *Application deadline:* For fall admission, 7/1; for spring admission, 11/15. Applications are processed on a rolling basis. *Application fee:* $0 ($50 for international students). Electronic applications accepted. *Dean of Graduate School*, Dr. Frances Shipley, 660-562-1145, Fax: 660-562-0000, E-mail: gradsch@mail.nwmissouri.edu.

College of Arts and Sciences Students: 25 full-time (10 women), 31 part-time (17 women); includes 1 minority (Asian American or Pacific Islander), 2 international. 23 applicants, 100% accepted, 12 enrolled. *Faculty:* 64 full-time (21 women). Expenses: Contact institution. *Financial support:* In 2001–02, 21 research assistantships (averaging $5,250 per year), 8 teaching assistantships (averaging $5,250 per year) were awarded. Administrative assistantships, tutorial assistantships also available. Financial award application deadline: 3/1. In 2001, 21 degrees awarded. *Degree program information:* Part-time programs available. Offers agriculture (MS); arts and sciences (MA, MS, MS Ed); biology (MS); English (MA); English with speech emphasis (MA); history (MA); teaching agriculture (MS Ed); teaching English with speech emphasis (MS Ed); teaching history (MS Ed); teaching mathematics (MS Ed); teaching music (MS Ed). *Application deadline:* For fall admission, 7/1; for spring admission, 11/15. Applications are processed on a rolling basis. *Application fee:* $0 ($50 for international students). Electronic applications accepted. *Application Contact:* Dr. Frances Shipley, Dean of Graduate School, 660-562-1145, Fax: 660-562-0000, E-mail: gradsch@mail.nwmissouri.edu. *Dean*, Dr. Theophil W. Ross, 660-562-1197.

College of Education and Human Services Students: 62 full-time (38 women), 260 part-time (170 women). 82 applicants, 100% accepted, 56 enrolled. *Faculty:* 56 full-time (34 women). Expenses: Contact institution. *Financial support:* In 2001–02, 8 research assistantships (averaging $5,250 per year), 46 teaching assistantships (averaging $5,250 per year) were awarded. Unspecified assistantships also available. Financial award application deadline: 3/1. In 2001, 128 master's, 23 other advanced degrees awarded. *Degree program information:* Part-time programs available. Offers counseling psychology (MS); early childhood education (MS Ed); education and human services (MS, MS Ed, Ed S); educational leadership (MS Ed, Ed S); educational leadership: elementary (MS Ed); educational leadership: secondary (MS Ed); elementary education (MS Ed); elementary principalship (Ed S); guidance and counseling (MS Ed); health and physical education (MS Ed); learning disabilities: elementary (MS Ed); learning disabilities: elementary/secondary (MS Ed); learning disabilities: secondary (MS Ed); learning disabled and mentally handicapped (MS Ed); mentally handicapped: elementary (MS Ed); mentally handicapped: elementary/secondary (MS Ed); mentally handicapped: secondary (MS Ed); middle school education (MS Ed); reading education (MS Ed); science education (MS Ed); secondary education (MS Ed); secondary individualized prescribed programs (MS Ed); secondary principalship (Ed S); superintendency (Ed S); teaching secondary (MS Ed). *Application deadline:* For fall admission, 7/1; for spring admission, 11/15. *Application fee:* $0 ($50 for international students). Electronic applications accepted. *Application Contact:* Dr. Frances Shipley, Dean of Graduate School, 660-562-1145, Fax: 660-562-0000, E-mail: gradsch@mail.nwmissouri.edu. *Dean*, Dr. Max Ruhl, 660-562-1231.

Melvin and Valorie Booth College of Business and Professional Studies Students: 73 full-time (28 women), 62 part-time (40 women). 88 applicants, 100% accepted, 42 enrolled. *Faculty:* 21 full-time (5 women). Expenses: Contact institution. *Financial support:* In 2001–02, 18 research assistantships (averaging $5,250 per year), 14 teaching assistantships (averaging $5,250 per year) were awarded. Career-related internships or fieldwork and administrative assistantships, tutorial assistantships also available. Financial award application deadline: 3/1. In 2001, 48 degrees awarded. *Degree program information:* Part-time programs available. Offers accounting (MBA); agricultural economics (MBA); business administration (MBA); business and professional studies (MBA, MS, MS Ed); management information systems (MBA); school computer studies (MS); teaching instructional technology (MS Ed). *Application deadline:* Applications are processed on a rolling basis. *Application fee:* $0 ($50 for international students). Electronic applications accepted. *Application Contact:* Dr. Frances Shipley, Dean of Graduate School, 660-562-1145, Fax: 660-562-0000, E-mail: gradsch@mail.nwmissouri.edu. *Dean*, Dr. Ron DeYoung, 660-562-1277.

NORTHWEST NAZARENE UNIVERSITY, Nampa, ID 83686-5897

General Information Independent-religious, coed, comprehensive institution. *Enrollment:* 185 full-time matriculated graduate/professional students (121 women), 91 part-time matriculated graduate/professional students (60 women). *Enrollment by degree level:* 276 master's. *Graduate faculty:* 69. *Tuition:* Full-time $1,770; part-time $295 per credit. One-time fee: $25. Tuition and fees vary according to program. *Graduate housing:* Rooms and/or apartments available to single and married students. Housing application deadline: 4/1. *Student services:* Career counseling, free psychological counseling, multicultural affairs office, teacher training. *Library facilities:* John E. Riley Library. *Online resources:* library catalog, web page, access to other libraries' catalogs. *Collection:* 100,966 titles, 821 serial subscriptions.

Northwest Nazarene University (continued)

Computer facilities: 400 computers available on campus for general student use. A campuswide network can be accessed from student residence rooms and from off campus. Internet access, various software packages are available. *Web address:* http://www.nnu.edu/.

General Application Contact: Dr. Dennis D. Cartwright, Director, Graduate and Continuing Studies, 208-467-8345, Fax: 208-467-8426.

GRADUATE UNITS

Graduate Studies Students: 185 full-time (121 women), 91 part-time (60 women); includes 13 minority (1 African American, 12 Hispanic Americans) Average age 38. *Faculty:* 69. Expenses: Contact institution. *Financial support:* In 2001–02, 193 students received support. Career-related internships or fieldwork available. In 2001, 79 degrees awarded. *Degree program information:* Part-time and evening/weekend programs available. Offers business administration (MBA); curriculum and instruction (M Ed); educational leadership (M Ed); exceptional child (M Ed); religion (M Min); school counseling (M Ed); social work (MSW). *Application deadline:* Applications are processed on a rolling basis. *Application fee:* $25. Electronic applications accepted. *Director,* Dr. Dennis D. Cartwright, 208-467-8366, Fax: 208-467-8562.

NORTHWOOD UNIVERSITY, Midland, MI 48640-2398

General Information Independent, coed, comprehensive institution. *Enrollment:* 54 full-time matriculated graduate/professional students (17 women), 186 part-time matriculated graduate/professional students (55 women). *Enrollment by degree level:* 240 master's. *Graduate faculty:* 5 full-time (1 woman). *Tuition:* Full-time $18,000. Tuition and fees vary according to program. *Graduate housing:* Room and/or apartments available to single students; on-campus housing not available to married students. Typical cost: $3,939 per year ($6,611 including board). Housing application deadline: 7/30. *Student services:* Campus employment opportunities, campus safety program, career counseling, free psychological counseling, international student services, low-cost health insurance, multicultural affairs office. *Library facilities:* Strosacker Library. *Online resources:* library catalog, web page, access to other libraries' catalogs. *Collection:* 45,913 titles, 410 serial subscriptions.

Computer facilities: 95 computers available on campus for general student use. A campuswide network can be accessed from student residence rooms and from off campus. Internet access is available. *Web address:* http://www.northwood.edu/.

General Application Contact: Matt Bennett, Director of Enrollment, 989-837-4178, Fax: 989-837-4800, E-mail: mba@northwood.edu.

GRADUATE UNITS

Richard DeVos Graduate School of Management Students: 54 full-time (17 women), 186 part-time (55 women); includes 35 minority (19 African Americans, 7 Asian Americans or Pacific Islanders, 8 Hispanic Americans, 1 Native American), 20 international. Average age 32. 75 applicants, 100% accepted, 67 enrolled. *Faculty:* 5 full-time (1 woman). Expenses: Contact institution. *Financial support:* In 2001–02, 23 students received support, including fellowships (averaging $5,000 per year); career-related internships or fieldwork, Federal Work-Study, scholarships/grants, and tuition waivers (full and partial) also available. Support available to part-time students. Financial award application deadline: 2/15; financial award applicants required to submit FAFSA. In 2001, 67 degrees awarded. *Degree program information:* Part-time programs available. Offers management (EMBA, MBA, MMBA). *Application deadline:* For fall admission, 7/1 (priority date). Applications are processed on a rolling basis. *Application fee:* $50. Electronic applications accepted. *Application Contact:* Matt Bennett, Director of Enrollment, 517-837-4820, Fax: 517-837-4800, E-mail: mba@northwood.edu. *Dean,* Dr. Timothy G. Nash, 989-837-4488, Fax: 989-837-4800.

NORWICH UNIVERSITY, Northfield, VT 05663

General Information Independent, coed, comprehensive institution.

GRADUATE UNITS

Military Graduate Program *Degree program information:* Part-time and evening/weekend programs available. Postbaccalaureate distance learning degree programs offered (minimal on-campus study). Offers diplomacy and military science (MA). Electronic applications accepted.

Program in Business Administration Postbaccalaureate distance learning degree programs offered (no on-campus study). Offers business administration (MBA). Program offered online. Electronic applications accepted.

NOTRE DAME COLLEGE, South Euclid, OH 44121-4293

General Information Independent-religious, coed, comprehensive institution. *Graduate housing:* Room and/or apartments available to single students; on-campus housing not available to married students. Housing application deadline: 6/30.

GRADUATE UNITS

Graduate Studies *Degree program information:* Part-time and evening/weekend programs available. Offers accounting (Certificate); creative critical thinking (M Ed); financial services management (Certificate); information systems (Certificate); learning disabilities (M Ed); management (Certificate); paralegal (Certificate); pastoral ministry (Certificate); reading (M Ed); teacher education (Certificate).

NOTRE DAME DE NAMUR UNIVERSITY, Belmont, CA 94002-1997

General Information Independent-religious, coed, comprehensive institution. CGS member. *Enrollment:* 227 full-time matriculated graduate/professional students (172 women), 518 part-time matriculated graduate/professional students (397 women). *Enrollment by degree level:* 511 master's, 234 other advanced degrees. *Graduate faculty:* 19 full-time (15 women), 102 part-time/adjunct (70 women). *Tuition:* Full-time $9,450; part-time $525 per unit. *Required fees:* $35 per term. *Graduate housing:* Rooms and/or apartments available on a first-come, first-served basis to single and married students. Typical cost: $8,476 (including board) for single students; $8,476 (including board) for married students. Housing application deadline: 7/1. *Student services:* Campus employment opportunities, career counseling, free psychological counseling, international student services, low-cost health insurance, teacher training, writing training. *Library facilities:* College of Notre Dame Library. *Online resources:* library catalog, access to other libraries' catalogs. *Collection:* 726 serial subscriptions, 8,314 audiovisual materials.

Computer facilities: 50 computers available on campus for general student use. A campuswide network can be accessed from off campus. Internet access is available. *Web address:* http://www.ndnu.edu/.

General Application Contact: Barbara Sterner, Assistant Director of Graduate Admissions, 650-508-3527, Fax: 650-508-3662, E-mail: grad.admit@ndnu.edu.

GRADUATE UNITS

Graduate School Students: 227 full-time (172 women), 518 part-time (397 women). Average age 35. 377 applicants, 76% accepted. *Faculty:* 19 full-time (15 women), 102 part-time/adjunct (70 women). Expenses: Contact institution. *Financial support:* Career-related internships or fieldwork and scholarships/grants available. Support available to part-time students. Financial award applicants required to submit FAFSA. In 2001, 198 degrees awarded. *Degree program information:* Part-time and evening/weekend programs available. Offers art therapy psychology (MAAT, MAMFT); arts and humanities (MA, MM); business administration (MBA); business and management (MBA, MPA, MSEBM, MSM); chemical dependency (MACP); counseling psychology (MACP); curriculum and instruction (M Ed); education and leadership (M Ed, MA, MAT, MSETA, Certificate); educational technology administration (MSETA, Certificate); electronic business management (MSEBM); English (MA); gerontology (MA, Certificate); management (MSM); marital and family therapy (MACP, MAMFT); music (MM); pedagogy (MM); performance (MM); premedical studies (Certificate); public administration (MPA); sciences (MA, MAAT, MACP, MAMFT, Certificate); special education (MA, Certificate); teaching (MAT). *Application deadline:* For fall admission, 8/1 (priority date); for spring admission, 12/1 (priority date). Applications are processed on a rolling basis. *Application fee:* $50 ($500 for international students). Electronic applications accepted. *Application Contact:* Barbara Sterner, Assistant Director of Graduate Admissions, 650-508-3527, Fax: 650-508-3662, E-mail: grad.admit@ndnu.edu. *Dean,* Dr. Elaine L. Cohen, 650-508-3528.

NOTRE DAME SEMINARY, New Orleans, LA 70118-4391

General Information Independent-religious, coed, primarily men, graduate-only institution. *Enrollment by degree level:* 117 first professional, 56 master's. *Graduate faculty:* 13 full-time (2 women), 17 part-time/adjunct (2 women). *Tuition:* Full-time $8,776; part-time $280 per hour. *Required fees:* $500; $280 per hour. *Graduate housing:* Room and/or apartments available to single students; on-campus housing not available to married students. Typical cost: $6,450 (including board). *Library facilities:* Robert J. Stahl Memorial Library. *Online resources:* library catalog. *Collection:* 100,000 titles.

Computer facilities: 6 computers available on campus for general student use. Internet access is available.

General Application Contact: Rev. José I. Lavastida, Dean of the Graduate School of Theology, 504-866-7426 Ext. 3107, Fax: 504-861-1301.

GRADUATE UNITS

Graduate School of Theology Students: 148 full-time (0 women), 40 part-time (27 women); includes 38 minority (7 African Americans, 28 Asian Americans or Pacific Islanders, 3 Hispanic Americans), 26 international. Average age 32. 47 applicants, 100% accepted. *Faculty:* 13 full-time (2 women), 17 part-time/adjunct (2 women). Expenses: Contact institution. *Financial support:* In 2001–02, 30 students received support. Federal Work-Study available. Financial award applicants required to submit FAFSA. In 2001, 25 first professional degrees, 9 master's awarded. *Degree program information:* Part-time programs available. Offers theology (M Div, MA). *Application deadline:* For fall admission, 8/1 (priority date); for spring admission, 1/3. Applications are processed on a rolling basis. *Application fee:* $40. *Dean,* Rev. José I. Lavastida, 504-866-7426 Ext. 3107, Fax: 504-861-1301.

NOVA SCOTIA AGRICULTURAL COLLEGE, Truro, NS B2N 5E3, Canada

General Information Province-supported, coed, comprehensive institution. *Enrollment:* 33 full-time matriculated graduate/professional students (21 women), 18 part-time matriculated graduate/professional students (13 women). *Enrollment by degree level:* 51 master's. *Graduate faculty:* 34 full-time (4 women), 14 part-time/adjunct (1 woman). *Graduate tuition:* Tuition and fees charges are reported in Canadian dollars. *International tuition:* $8,100 Canadian dollars full-time. Tuition, Canadian resident: full-time $5,400 Canadian dollars; part-time $600 Canadian dollars per semester. *Required fees:* $254 Canadian dollars; $10 Canadian dollars per course. *Graduate housing:* Room and/or apartments available on a first-come, first-served basis to single students; on-campus housing not available to married students. Housing application deadline: 6/30. *Student services:* Campus employment opportunities, campus safety program, career counseling, child daycare facilities, exercise/wellness program, free psychological counseling, international student services, low-cost health insurance, teacher training. *Library facilities:* MacRae Library. *Collection:* 23,000 titles, 800 serial subscriptions. *Research affiliation:* Crop Development Institute, Atlantic Poultry Research Institute, Organic Agriculture Centre of Canada, Performance Genomics, Inc. (animal genomics).

Computer facilities: 110 computers available on campus for general student use. A campuswide network can be accessed. Internet access is available. *Web address:* http://www.nsac.ns.ca/.

General Application Contact: Jill L. Rogers, Manager, Research and Graduate Studies Office, 902-893-6502, Fax: 902-897-9399, E-mail: jrogers@nsac.ns.ca.

GRADUATE UNITS

Research and Graduate Studies Students: 33 full-time (21 women), 18 part-time (13 women); includes 1 minority (Asian American or Pacific Islander) 56 applicants, 66% accepted, 14 enrolled. *Faculty:* 34 full-time (4 women), 14 part-time/adjunct (1 woman). Expenses: Contact institution. *Financial support:* In 2001–02, 29 students received support, including research assistantships (averaging $13,500 per year), teaching assistantships (averaging $900 per year); career-related internships or fieldwork, scholarships/grants, and unspecified assistantships also available. In 2001, 16 degrees awarded. *Degree program information:* Part-time programs available. Offers agriculture (M Sc). *Application deadline:* For fall admission, 6/1; for winter admission, 11/15; for spring admission, 2/28. Applications are processed on a rolling basis. *Application fee:* $65. *Application Contact:* Marie Law, Assistant, 902-893-6502, Fax: 902-893-3430, E-mail: mlaw@nsac.ns.ca. *Manager,* Jill L. Rogers, 902-893-6360, Fax: 902-893-3430, E-mail: jrogers@nsac.ns.ca.

NOVA SCOTIA COLLEGE OF ART AND DESIGN, Halifax, NS B3J 3J6, Canada

General Information Province-supported, coed, comprehensive institution. *Enrollment:* 15 full-time matriculated graduate/professional students (12 women), 10 part-time matriculated graduate/professional students (9 women). *Enrollment by degree level:* 25 master's. *Graduate faculty:* 41 full-time (16 women). *Graduate tuition:* Tuition charges are reported in Canadian dollars. *International tuition:* $7,884 Canadian dollars full-time. *Tuition, area resident:* Full-time $4,436 Canadian dollars; part-time $174 Canadian dollars per credit. Tuition, Canadian resident: part-time $325 Canadian dollars per credit. *Graduate housing:* On-campus housing not available. *Student services:* Campus employment opportunities, disabled student services, free psychological counseling, international student services, low-cost health insurance, teacher training, writing training. *Library facilities:* Nova Scotia College of Art and Design Library. *Online resources:* library catalog, access to other libraries' catalogs. *Collection:* 32,000 titles, 235 serial subscriptions, 120,000 audiovisual materials.

Computer facilities: 60 computers available on campus for general student use. Internet access, CD Rom data bases are available. *Web address:* http://www.nscad.ns.ca/.

General Application Contact: Terrence Bailey, Coordinator of Admissions, 902-494-8188, Fax: 902-425-2987, E-mail: tbailey@nscad.ns.ca.

GRADUATE UNITS

Program in Art Education Average age 43. *Faculty:* 4 full-time (1 woman). Expenses: Contact institution. *Financial support:* Teaching assistantships, institutionally sponsored loans available. Support available to part-time students. In 2001, 2 degrees awarded. *Degree program information:* Part-time and evening/weekend programs available. Offers art education (MA). *Application deadline:* For fall admission, 6/3; for spring admission, 10/2. *Application fee:* $35. *Chair,* Dr. Nick Webb, 902-494-8152, Fax: 902-425-4172, E-mail: nwebb@nscad.ns.ca.

Program in Fine Arts Students: 15 full-time (12 women). Average age 32. 196 applicants, 4% accepted. *Faculty:* 41 full-time (16 women). Expenses: Contact institution. *Financial support:* In 2001–02, 14 students received support, including 14 fellowships (averaging $1,500 per year), 14 teaching assistantships (averaging $5,000 per year); institutionally sponsored loans also available. In 2001, 5 degrees awarded. Offers craft (MFA); design (MFA); fine and media arts (MFA). *Application deadline:* For fall admission, 1/31. *Application fee:* $35. *Application Contact:* Terrence Bailey, Coordinator of Admissions, 902-494-8188, Fax: 902-425-2987, E-mail: tbailey@nscad.ns.ca. *Chair,* Bruce Barber, 902-494-8155, Fax: 902-425-2420, E-mail: bbarber@nscad.ns.ca.

NOVA SOUTHEASTERN UNIVERSITY, Fort Lauderdale, FL 33314-7721

General Information Independent, coed, university. CGS member. *Enrollment:* 6,392 full-time matriculated graduate/professional students, 8,656 part-time matriculated graduate/professional students. *Enrollment by degree level:* 3,179 first professional. *Graduate faculty:* 486 full-time, 772 part-time/adjunct. *Tuition:* Full-time $7,380; part-time $432 per credit. *Required fees:* $200. Tuition and fees vary according to campus/location and program. *Graduate housing:* Rooms and/or apartments available on a first-come, first-served basis to single and married students. Typical cost: $3,664 per year ($6,484 including board) for single students. *Student services:* Campus employment opportunities, campus safety program, career counseling, disabled student services, exercise/wellness program, international student services, low-cost health insurance, teacher training. *Library facilities:* Einstein Library plus 4 others. *Online resources:* library catalog, web page, access to other libraries' catalogs. *Collection:* 362,611 titles, 8,821 serial subscriptions, 2,591 audiovisual materials.

Computer facilities: 800 computers available on campus for general student use. A campuswide network can be accessed from student residence rooms and from off campus. Internet access and online class registration are available. *Web address:* http://www.nova.edu/.

General Application Contact: 800-541-6682.

GRADUATE UNITS

Center for Psychological Studies Students: 941 full-time (744 women). Average age 34. *Faculty:* 33 full-time (10 women), 37 part-time/adjunct (17 women). Expenses: Contact institution. *Financial support:* In 2001–02, 4 research assistantships, 17 teaching assistantships (averaging $1,000 per year) were awarded. Career-related internships or fieldwork, Federal Work-Study, and institutionally sponsored loans also available. Support available to part-time students. Financial award application deadline: 4/1. In 2001, 155 master's, 223 doctorates awarded. *Degree program information:* Part-time and evening/weekend programs available. Offers clinical psychology (PhD, Psy D, SPS); mental health counseling (MS); psychological studies (MS, PhD, Psy D, SPS); psychopharmacology (MS); school guidance and counseling (MS). *Application deadline:* Applications are processed on a rolling basis. *Application fee:* $50. *Application Contact:* Nancy L. Smith, Supervisor, 954-262-5760, Fax: 954-262-3893, E-mail: cpsinfo@cps.nova.edu. *Dean,* Dr. Ronald F. Levant, 954-262-5701, Fax: 954-262-3859.

Fischler Graduate School of Education and Human Services Students: 6,887 (5,187 women); includes 2,827 minority (1,997 African Americans, 54 Asian Americans or Pacific Islanders, 748 Hispanic Americans, 28 Native Americans) 109 international. Average age 41. Expenses: Contact institution. *Financial support:* Fellowships, career-related internships or fieldwork and Federal Work-Study available. Support available to part-time students. In 2001, 1,477 master's, 313 doctorates, 188 other advanced degrees awarded. *Degree program information:* Part-time and evening/weekend programs available. Postbaccalaureate distance learning degree programs offered. Offers adult education (Ed D); audiology (Au D); child and youth care administration (MS); child and youth studies (Ed D); computer science education (MS, Ed S); computing and information technology (Ed D); early childhood education administration (MS); education and human services (MA, MS, Au D, Ed D, SLPD, Ed S); education technology (MS, Ed S); educational leaders (Ed D); educational leadership (administration K–12) (MS, Ed S); educational media (MS, Ed S); educational technology (MS); elementary education (MS, Ed S); English (MS, Ed S); family support studies (MS); gifted education (MS); health care education (Ed D); higher education (Ed D); instructional technology and distance education (MS, Ed D); mathematics (MS, Ed S); pre-kindergarten/primary (Ed S); prekindergarten/primary (MS); reading (MS, Ed S); science (MS, Ed S); social studies (MS, Ed S); Spanish language (MS); speech-language pathology (MS, SLPD); substance abuse counseling and education (MS); teaching and learning (MA); teaching English to speakers of other languages (MS, Ed S); varying exceptionalities (MS, Ed S); vocational, occupational and technical education (Ed D). *Application deadline:* Applications are processed on a rolling basis. *Application fee:* $50. *Application Contact:* Dr. Jean Lewis, Dean of Student Services and Admissions, 800-986-3223 Ext. 8650, Fax: 954-262-3908, E-mail: lewisj@fgse.nova.edu. *Provost/Dean,* Dr. H. Wells Singleton, 954-262-8730, Fax: 954-262-3912, E-mail: singlew@fgse.nova.edu.

Graduate School of Humanities and Social Sciences Students: 339 (260 women); includes 101 minority (64 African Americans, 4 Asian Americans or Pacific Islanders, 32 Hispanic Americans, 1 Native American) 28 international. Average age 37. *Faculty:* 17 full-time (10 women), 10 part-time/adjunct (8 women). Expenses: Contact institution. *Financial support:* Research assistantships with partial tuition reimbursements, teaching assistantships, career-related internships or fieldwork, Federal Work-Study, institutionally sponsored loans, scholarships/grants, and clinical assistantships, graduate assistantships available. Support available to part-time students. Financial award application deadline: 4/1; financial award applicants required to submit CSS PROFILE. In 2001, 30 master's, 5 doctorates awarded. *Degree program information:* Part-time and evening/weekend programs available. Postbaccalaureate distance learning degree programs offered (minimal on-campus study). Offers conflict analysis and resolution (MS, PhD, Certificate); family therapy (MS, PhD, Certificate); humanities and social sciences (MS, PhD, Certificate). *Application deadline:* Applications are processed on a rolling basis. *Application fee:* $50. *Application Contact:* 800-262-7978, Fax: 954-262-3968, E-mail: shss@nova.edu. *Dean,* Dr. Honggang Yang, 954-262-3000, Fax: 954-262-3968, E-mail: ssss@nova.edu.

Health Professions Division Students: 2,588 (1,393 women); includes 979 minority (144 African Americans, 378 Asian Americans or Pacific Islanders, 447 Hispanic Americans, 10 Native Americans) 110 international. Average age 30. *Faculty:* 212 full-time, 7 part-time/adjunct. Expenses: Contact institution. *Financial support:* Fellowships, teaching assistantships, career-related internships or fieldwork, Federal Work-Study, institutionally sponsored loans, scholarships/grants, and unspecified assistantships available. Support available to part-time students. In 2001, 449 first professional degrees, 172 master's awarded. Postbaccalaureate distance learning degree programs offered (minimal on-campus study). Offers health professions (DMD, DO, OD, Pharm D, MBS, MOT, MPH, MPT, DPT, Dr OT, PhD). *Application deadline:* Applications are processed on a rolling basis. *Application fee:* $50. *Chancellor,* Dr. Morton Terry, 954-262-1100 Ext. 1507.

College of Allied Health Students: 283 (197 women). Expenses: Contact institution. *Financial support:* Teaching assistantships, institutionally sponsored loans and unspecified assistantships available. In 2001, 159 master's, 2 doctorates awarded. Postbaccalaureate distance learning degree programs offered (minimal on-campus study). Offers allied health (MOT, MPT, DPT, Dr OT, PhD); occupational therapy (MOT, Dr OT, PhD); physical therapy (MPT, DPT, PhD). *Application deadline:* Applications are processed on a rolling basis. *Application fee:* $50. *Application Contact:* Carla Straus, Admissions Counselor, 954-262-1100. *Director,* Dr. Raul Cuadrado, 954-262-1203.

College of Dental Medicine Students: 395 full-time (152 women); includes 102 minority (7 African Americans, 54 Asian Americans or Pacific Islanders, 41 Hispanic Americans), 61 international. Average age 25. 1,639 applicants, 9% accepted, 96 enrolled. *Faculty:* 74 full-time, 133 part-time/adjunct. Expenses: Contact institution. *Financial support:* Applicants required to submit FAFSA. In 2001, 106 degrees awarded. Offers dental medicine (DMD). *Application deadline:* For fall admission, 3/1. Applications are processed on a rolling basis. *Application fee:* $50. *Application Contact:* Su-Ann Zarrett, Dental Admissions Counselor, 954-262-1108, Fax: 954-262-2282, E-mail: zarrett@nova.edu. *Dean,* Dr. Seymour Oliet, 954-262-7312, Fax: 954-262-1782, E-mail: soliet@nova.edu.

College of Medical Sciences Students: 23 full-time (12 women); includes 8 minority (3 African Americans, 1 Asian American or Pacific Islander, 4 Hispanic Americans) Average age 28. 76 applicants, 30% accepted. *Faculty:* 30 full-time (10 women), 1 (woman) part-time/adjunct. Expenses: Contact institution. *Financial support:* Applicants required to submit FAFSA. Offers biomedical sciences (MBS). *Application deadline:* For spring admission, 5/1. Applications are processed on a rolling basis. *Application fee:* $50. *Application Contact:* Jodie Berman, Admissions Counselor, 954-262-1111, Fax: 954-262-2282, E-mail: jodie@nova.edu. *Dean,* Dr. Harold E. Laubach, 954-262-1303, Fax: 954-262-1802, E-mail: harold@nova.edu.

College of Optometry Students: 383 full-time (207 women); includes 140 minority (15 African Americans, 87 Asian Americans or Pacific Islanders, 36 Hispanic Americans, 2 Native Americans), 7 international. Average age 26. *Faculty:* 41 full-time (18 women), 9 part-time/adjunct (5 women). Expenses: Contact institution. *Financial support:* Federal Work-Study, institutionally sponsored loans, and scholarships/grants available. Support available to part-time students. Financial award application deadline: 4/1. In 2001, 91 degrees awarded. Offers optometry (OD). *Application deadline:* For fall admission, 4/1. Applications are processed on a rolling basis. *Application fee:* $50. Electronic applications accepted. *Application Contact:* Tracy Templin, Admissions Counselor, 954-262-1112, Fax: 954-262-2282, E-mail: dpetracy@nova.edu. *Dean,* Dr. David S. Loshin, 954-262-1402, Fax: 954-262-1818.

College of Osteopathic Medicine Students: 734 full-time (298 women); includes 231 minority (34 African Americans, 131 Asian Americans or Pacific Islanders, 62 Hispanic Americans, 4 Native Americans), 12 international. 2,236 applicants, 14% accepted, 225 enrolled. *Faculty:* 56 full-time (19 women), 654 part-time/adjunct (98 women). Expenses: Contact institution. *Financial support:* In 2001–02, 607 students received support, including 12 fellowships with partial tuition reimbursements available; teaching assistantships, career-related internships or fieldwork, Federal Work-Study, institutionally sponsored loans, scholarships/grants, and unspecified assistantships also available. Financial award application deadline: 4/15; financial award applicants required to submit FAFSA. In 2001, 151 first professional degrees, 12 master's awarded. Offers osteopathic medicine (DO, MPH); public health (MPH). *Application deadline:* For fall admission, 3/1. Applications are processed on a rolling basis. *Application fee:* $50. *Application Contact:* Lynne Cawley, Associate Director of Admissions and Student Affairs, 954-262-1113. *Dean,* Dr. Anthony J. Silavgni, 954-262-1407, E-mail: silvagni@hpd.nova.edu.

College of Pharmacy Students: 651 full-time (450 women). Average age 27. 476 applicants, 51% accepted. *Faculty:* 49 full-time (28 women), 3 part-time/adjunct (1 woman). Expenses: Contact institution. *Financial support:* Career-related internships or fieldwork, Federal Work-Study, institutionally sponsored loans, and scholarships/grants available. Financial award application deadline: 4/1. In 2001, 99 degrees awarded. Postbaccalaureate distance learning degree programs offered (minimal on-campus study). Offers pharmacy (Pharm D). *Application deadline:* For fall admission, 4/1. Applications are processed on a rolling basis. *Application fee:* $50. *Application Contact:* Margaret Brown, Admissions Counselor, 954-262-1114, Fax: 954-262-2282, E-mail: mbrown@nova.edu. *Dean,* Dr. William Hardigan, 954-262-1300, Fax: 954-262-2278, E-mail: hardigan@hpd.nova.edu.

Oceanographic Center Students: 130 (79 women). Average age 30. 67 applicants, 75% accepted. *Faculty:* 14 full-time (1 woman), 5 part-time/adjunct (0 women). Expenses: Contact institution. *Financial support:* In 2001–02, 6 research assistantships (averaging $4,000 per year), 3 teaching assistantships (averaging $3,500 per year) were awarded. Career-related internships or fieldwork, Federal Work-Study, scholarships/grants, tuition waivers (partial), and unspecified assistantships also available. Support available to part-time students. Financial award applicants required to submit FAFSA. In 2001, 15 degrees awarded. *Degree program information:* Part-time and evening/weekend programs available. Offers coastal-zone management (MS); marine biology (MS, PhD); marine environmental science (MS); oceanography (PhD). *Application deadline:* Applications are processed on a rolling basis. *Application fee:* $50. *Application Contact:* Dr. Andrew Rogerson, Director, Graduate Programs, 954-262-3600, Fax: 954-262-4020, E-mail: arogerso@nova.edu. *Dean,* Dr. Richard Dodge, 954-262-3600, Fax: 954-262-4020, E-mail: dodge@ocean.nova.edu.

School of Computer and Information Sciences Students: 832 full-time (297 women); includes 195 minority (97 African Americans, 39 Asian Americans or Pacific Islanders, 56 Hispanic Americans, 3 Native Americans), 63 international. Average age 41. 286 applicants, 80% accepted, 169 enrolled. *Faculty:* 18 full-time (4 women), 12 part-time/adjunct (3 women). Expenses: Contact institution. *Financial support:* In 2001–02, 2 teaching assistantships with full tuition reimbursements (averaging $25,000 per year) were awarded; Federal Work-Study, scholarships/grants, and unspecified assistantships also available. Support available to part-time students. Financial award application deadline: 5/1. In 2001, 114 master's, 27 doctorates awarded. *Degree program information:* Part-time and evening/weekend programs available. Postbaccalaureate distance learning degree programs offered (no on-campus study). Offers computer information systems (MS, PhD); computer science (MS, PhD); computing technology in education (MS, Ed D, PhD); information science (PhD); information systems (PhD); management information systems (MS). *Application deadline:* Applications are processed on a rolling basis. *Application fee:* $50. *Application Contact:* Sherese Young, Marketing Coordinator, 954-262-2005, Fax: 954-262-3915, E-mail: scisinfo@nova.edu. *Dean,* Dr. Edward Lieblein.

Shepard Broad Law Center Students: 778 full-time (404 women), 228 part-time (109 women); includes 333 minority (103 African Americans, 30 Asian Americans or Pacific Islanders, 198 Hispanic Americans, 2 Native Americans) Average age 28. 1,512 applicants, 49% accepted, 365 enrolled. *Faculty:* 48 full-time (21 women), 61 part-time/adjunct (13 women). Expenses: Contact institution. *Financial support:* In 2001–02, 120 students received support, including 117 fellowships (averaging $14,413 per year), 84 research assistantships, 13 teaching assistantships; career-related internships or fieldwork, Federal Work-Study, scholarships/grants, tuition waivers (full and partial), and mediation programs also available. Support available to part-time students. Financial award application deadline: 3/1; financial award applicants required to submit FAFSA. In 2001, 287 degrees awarded. *Degree program information:* Part-time and evening/weekend programs available. Offers law (JD, MHL). *Application deadline:* For fall admission, 3/1 (priority date). Applications are processed on a rolling basis. *Application fee:* $50. Electronic applications accepted. *Application Contact:* Nancy Kelly Sanguigni, Director of Admissions, 954-262-6120, Fax: 954-262-3844, E-mail: sanguignin@nsu.law.nova.edu. *Dean,* Joseph D. Harbaugh, 954-262-6105, Fax: 954-262-3834, E-mail: harbaughj@nsu.law.nova.edu.

Wayne Huizenga Graduate School of Business and Entrepreneurship Students: 2,331 (1,283 women); includes 1,066 minority (599 African Americans, 75 Asian Americans or Pacific Islanders, 384 Hispanic Americans, 8 Native Americans) 346 international. Average age 38. 567 applicants, 74% accepted. Expenses: Contact institution. *Financial support:* Career-related internships or fieldwork, Federal Work-Study, institutionally sponsored loans, and scholarships/grants available. Support available to part-time students. In 2001, 763 master's, 82 doctorates awarded. *Degree program information:* Part-time and evening/weekend programs available. Offers accounting (M Acc); business administration (MBA, DBA); business and entrepreneurship (M Acc, MBA, MIBA, MPA, MS, MSHRM, MT, DBA, DIBA, DPA); health services administration (MBA, MS); human resources management (MSHRM); international business administration (MIBA, DIBA); public administration (MPA, DPA). *Application deadline:* For fall admission, 8/15; for spring admission, 2/10. Applications are processed on a rolling basis. *Application fee:* $50. *Application Contact:* Dr. Karen Goldberg, Assistant Director, 954-262-5039, Fax: 954-262-3822, E-mail: karen@nova.edu. *Dean,* Dr. Randolph A. Pohlman, 954-262-5005, E-mail: pohlman@huizenga.nova.edu.

OAKLAND CITY UNIVERSITY, Oakland City, IN 47660-1099

General Information Independent-religious, coed, comprehensive institution. *Enrollment:* 113 full-time matriculated graduate/professional students (54 women), 200 part-time matriculated graduate/professional students (104 women). *Enrollment by degree level:* 21 first professional, 284 master's, 8 doctoral. *Graduate faculty:* 4 full-time (1 woman), 32 part-time/adjunct (9 women). *Tuition:* Full-time $10,950. *Graduate housing:* Room and/or apartments available to single students; on-campus housing not available to married students. Housing application deadline: 7/1. *Student services:* Campus employment opportunities, career counseling, free psychological counseling. *Library facilities:* Founders Memorial Library. *Online resources:* library catalog, access to other libraries' catalogs. *Collection:* 75,000 titles, 350 serial subscriptions.

Computer facilities: 70 computers available on campus for general student use. Internet access is available. *Web address:* http://www.oak.edu/.

General Application Contact: Counselor for Graduate Admissions, 812-749-1241, Fax: 812-749-1233.

GRADUATE UNITS

Chapman School of Religious Studies Students: 20 full-time (2 women), 9 part-time (4 women); includes 1 minority (African American) Average age 33. 4 applicants, 100% accepted. *Faculty:* 2 full-time (0 women), 4 part-time/adjunct (1 woman). Expenses: Contact institution. *Financial support:* In 2001–02, 10 students received support. Career-related internships or fieldwork and Federal Work-Study available. Support available to part-time students. Financial award applicants required to submit FAFSA. In 2001, 4 degrees awarded. *Degree program information:* Part-time programs available. Offers religious studies (M Div, D Min). *Application deadline:* Applications are processed on a rolling basis. *Application fee:* $25. *Application Contact:* Counselor for Graduate Admissions, 812-749-1241, Fax: 812-749-1233. *Dean,* Dr. Ray Barber, 812-749-1289, Fax: 812-749-1233, E-mail: rbarber@oak.edu.

Oakland City University (continued)

School of Adult Degrees Students: 137 full-time (59 women), 18 part-time (7 women); includes 31 minority (21 African Americans, 5 Asian Americans or Pacific Islanders, 5 Hispanic Americans) Average age 35. 65 applicants, 100% accepted. *Faculty:* 1 full-time (0 women), 18 part-time/adjunct (3 women). Expenses: Contact institution. *Financial support:* Institutionally sponsored loans available. Financial award application deadline: 3/10; financial award applicants required to submit FAFSA. In 2001, 121 degrees awarded. *Degree program information:* Part-time and evening/weekend programs available. Offers management (MS Mgt). *Application deadline:* Applications are processed on a rolling basis. *Application fee:* $35. *Application Contact:* Wanda M. Johnson, Administrator Adult Degrees, 812-749-1241, Fax: 812-749-1233, E-mail: wjohnson@oak.edu. *Executive Vice President*, Dr. Ora Johnson, 812-749-1409, Fax: 812-749-1294, E-mail: ojohnson@oak.edu.

School of Education Students: 120 full-time (75 women); includes 17 minority (14 African Americans, 1 Asian American or Pacific Islander, 2 Hispanic Americans) Average age 29. 153 applicants, 88% accepted, 120 enrolled. *Faculty:* 1 (woman) full-time, 10 part-time/adjunct (5 women). Expenses: Contact institution. *Financial support:* Applicants required to submit FAFSA. In 2001, 92 degrees awarded. Offers teaching (MA). *Application deadline:* For spring admission, 5/1. Applications are processed on a rolling basis. *Application fee:* $35. *Application Contact:* Dr. Earlene Holland, Associate Professor/Director, 812-749-1509, Fax: 812-749-1415, E-mail: eholland@oak.edu. *Dean*, Dr. Patricia A. Swails, 812-749-1232, Fax: 812-749-1233, E-mail: pswails@oak.edu.

OAKLAND UNIVERSITY, Rochester, MI 48309-4401

General Information State-supported, coed, university. CGS member. *Enrollment:* 946 full-time matriculated graduate/professional students (625 women), 2,400 part-time matriculated graduate/professional students (1,540 women). *Enrollment by degree level:* 2,437 master's, 185 doctoral, 120 other advanced degrees. *Graduate faculty:* 441 full-time (177 women), 80 part-time/adjunct (42 women). Tuition, state resident: full-time $5,904; part-time $246 per credit hour. Tuition, nonresident: full-time $12,192; part-time $508 per credit hour. *Required fees:* $472; $236 per term. *Graduate housing:* Rooms and/or apartments available on a first-come, first-served basis to single and married students. Typical cost: $5,832 (including board) for single students. *Student services:* Campus employment opportunities, campus safety program, career counseling, child daycare facilities, disabled student services, exercise/wellness program, free psychological counseling, international student services, low-cost health insurance, multicultural affairs office. *Library facilities:* Kresge Library plus 1 other. *Online resources:* library catalog, web page, access to other libraries' catalogs. *Collection:* 688,000 titles, 2,600 serial subscriptions, 4,361 audiovisual materials. *Research affiliation:* Henry Ford Health Systems (medical physics), Beaumont Hospital Corporation (eye research, nursing).

Computer facilities: 640 computers available on campus for general student use. A campuswide network can be accessed from student residence rooms and from off campus. *Web address:* http://www.oakland.edu/.

General Application Contact: Christina J. Grabowski, Associate Director of Graduate Study and Lifelong Learning, 248-370-3167, Fax: 248-370-4114, E-mail: grabowsk@oakland.edu.

GRADUATE UNITS

Graduate Study and Lifelong Learning Students: 946 full-time (625 women), 2,400 part-time (1,540 women); includes 308 minority (142 African Americans, 117 Asian Americans or Pacific Islanders, 34 Hispanic Americans, 15 Native Americans), 251 international. Average age 34. 1,543 applicants, 82% accepted. *Faculty:* 441 full-time (177 women), 80 part-time/adjunct (42 women). Expenses: Contact institution. *Financial support:* Fellowships, research assistantships, teaching assistantships, career-related internships or fieldwork, Federal Work-Study, institutionally sponsored loans, and tuition waivers (full) available. Financial award application deadline: 3/1; financial award applicants required to submit FAFSA. In 2001, 785 master's, 17 doctorates, 13 other advanced degrees awarded. *Degree program information:* Part-time and evening/weekend programs available. *Application deadline:* Applications are processed on a rolling basis. *Application fee:* $30. Electronic applications accepted. *Associate Director of Graduate Study and Lifelong Learning*, Christina J. Grabowski, 248-370-3167, Fax: 248-370-4114, E-mail: grabowsk@oakland.edu.

College of Arts and Sciences Students: 81 full-time (55 women), 157 part-time (96 women); includes 25 minority (8 African Americans, 15 Asian Americans or Pacific Islanders, 1 Hispanic American, 1 Native American), 23 international. Average age 33. 126 applicants, 73% accepted. *Faculty:* 220 full-time (83 women), 6 part-time/adjunct (3 women). Expenses: Contact institution. *Financial support:* Fellowships, research assistantships, teaching assistantships, career-related internships or fieldwork, Federal Work-Study, institutionally sponsored loans, and tuition waivers (full) available. Financial award application deadline: 3/1; financial award applicants required to submit FAFSA. In 2001, 33 master's, 2 doctorates awarded. *Degree program information:* Part-time and evening/weekend programs available. Offers applied mathematical science (PhD); applied statistics (MS, PhD); arts and sciences (MA, MM, MPA, MS, PhD, Certificate); biological sciences (MA, MS); cellular biology of aging (MS); chemistry (MS, PhD); English (MA); health and environmental chemistry (PhD); history (MA); industrial applied mathematics (MS); liberal studies (MA); linguistics (MA); mathematics (MA); medical physics (PhD); music (MM); physics (MS); public administration (MPA); statistical methods (Certificate). *Application deadline:* For fall admission, 7/15 (priority date); for winter admission, 12/1 (priority date); for spring admission, 3/15 (priority date). Applications are processed on a rolling basis. *Application fee:* $30. Electronic applications accepted. *Dean*, Dr. David Downing, 248-370-2140.

School of Business Administration Students: 52 full-time (23 women), 484 part-time (164 women); includes 38 minority (11 African Americans, 18 Asian Americans or Pacific Islanders, 7 Hispanic Americans, 2 Native Americans), 39 international. Average age 31. 250 applicants, 76% accepted. *Faculty:* 55 full-time (10 women), 13 part-time/adjunct (2 women). Expenses: Contact institution. *Financial support:* Career-related internships or fieldwork, Federal Work-Study, institutionally sponsored loans, and tuition waivers (full) available. Financial award application deadline: 3/1; financial award applicants required to submit FAFSA. In 2001, 152 master's, 7 other advanced degrees awarded. *Degree program information:* Part-time and evening/weekend programs available. Offers accounting (M Acc); business administration (MBA, Certificate); information technology management (MS). *Application deadline:* For fall admission, 8/15 (priority date); for winter admission, 12/1 (priority date); for spring admission, 4/15 (priority date). Applications are processed on a rolling basis. *Application fee:* $30. Electronic applications accepted. *Application Contact:* Darla Null, Coordinator, 248-370-3281. *Dean*, Dr. John Gardner, 248-370-3286.

School of Education and Human Services Students: 459 full-time (406 women), 1,246 part-time (1,099 women); includes 137 minority (96 African Americans, 14 Asian Americans or Pacific Islanders, 18 Hispanic Americans, 9 Native Americans), 13 international. Average age 36. 670 applicants, 89% accepted. *Faculty:* 70 full-time (41 women), 43 part-time/adjunct (34 women). Expenses: Contact institution. *Financial support:* Career-related internships or fieldwork, Federal Work-Study, institutionally sponsored loans, and tuition waivers (full) available. Financial award application deadline: 3/1; financial award applicants required to submit FAFSA. In 2001, 352 master's, 7 doctorates, 20 other advanced degrees awarded. *Degree program information:* Part-time and evening/weekend programs available. Offers counseling (MA, PhD); curriculum, instruction and leadership (M Ed, PhD, Certificate); early childhood education (M Ed, PhD, Certificate); education and human services (M Ed, MA, MAT, MTD, PhD, Certificate, Ed S); educational specialist (Ed S); microcomputer applications in education (Certificate); reading (MAT, PhD, Certificate); special education (M Ed); training and development (MTD). *Application deadline:* Applications are processed on a rolling basis. *Application fee:* $30. Electronic applications accepted. *Dean*, Dr. Mary L. Otto, 248-370-3050.

School of Engineering and Computer Science Students: 270 full-time (75 women), 378 part-time (76 women); includes 89 minority (17 African Americans, 65 Asian Americans or Pacific Islanders, 5 Hispanic Americans, 2 Native Americans), 167 international. Average age 30. 404 applicants, 81% accepted. *Faculty:* 39 full-time (6 women), 10 part-time/adjunct (0 women). Expenses: Contact institution. *Financial support:* Federal Work-Study, institutionally sponsored loans, and tuition waivers (full) available. Financial award application deadline: 3/1; financial award applicants required to submit FAFSA. In 2001, 173 master's, 8 doctorates awarded. *Degree program information:* Part-time and evening/weekend programs available. Offers computer science (MS); electrical and computer engineering (MS); embedded systems (MS); engineering and computer science (MS, PhD); engineering management (MS); mechanical engineering (MS); software engineering (MS); systems engineering (MS, PhD). *Application deadline:* For fall admission, 8/1 (priority date); for winter admission, 12/1 (priority date); for spring admission, 4/1 (priority date). Applications are processed on a rolling basis. *Application fee:* $30. Electronic applications accepted. *Application Contact:* Information Contact, 248-370-2233. *Dean*, Dr. Pieter Frick, 248-370-2233.

School of Health Sciences Students: 85 full-time (69 women), 29 part-time (18 women); includes 6 minority (3 African Americans, 3 Asian Americans or Pacific Islanders), 7 international. Average age 29. 32 applicants, 63% accepted. *Faculty:* 19 full-time (10 women), 1 (woman) part-time/adjunct. Expenses: Contact institution. *Financial support:* Fellowships, Federal Work-Study, institutionally sponsored loans, and tuition waivers (full) available. Financial award application deadline: 3/1; financial award applicants required to submit FAFSA. In 2001, 44 master's, 3 other advanced degrees awarded. Offers complementary wellness (Certificate); exercise science (MS); health sciences (MS, DPT, Dr Sc PT, Certificate); orthopedic manual physical therapy (Certificate); pediatric rehabilitation (Certificate); physical therapy (MS, DPT, Dr Sc PT). *Application deadline:* For fall admission, 7/15. Applications are processed on a rolling basis. *Application fee:* $30. Electronic applications accepted. *Dean*, Dr. Ronald E. Olson, 248-370-3562.

School of Nursing Students: 21 full-time (17 women), 106 part-time (87 women); includes 13 minority (7 African Americans, 2 Asian Americans or Pacific Islanders, 3 Hispanic Americans, 1 Native American), 2 international. Average age 33. 61 applicants, 64% accepted. *Faculty:* 21 full-time (20 women), 6 part-time/adjunct (4 women). Expenses: Contact institution. *Financial support:* Federal Work-Study, institutionally sponsored loans, and tuition waivers (full) available. Financial award application deadline: 3/1; financial award applicants required to submit FAFSA. In 2001, 21 master's, 1 other advanced degree awarded. *Degree program information:* Part-time and evening/weekend programs available. Offers adult health (MSN); family nurse practitioner (MSN, Certificate); nurse anesthetist (MSN, Certificate); nursing (MSN, Certificate). *Application fee:* $30. Electronic applications accepted. *Acting Dean*, Dr. Kathleen Emrich, 248-370-4081.

See in-depth description on page 1013.

OBERLIN COLLEGE, Oberlin, OH 44074

General Information Independent, coed, comprehensive institution. *Enrollment:* 5 full-time matriculated graduate/professional students (3 women). *Enrollment by degree level:* 5 master's. *Graduate faculty:* 68 full-time, 12 part-time/adjunct. *Tuition:* Full-time $27,880. *Graduate housing:* Room and/or apartments available on a first-come, first-served basis to single students; on-campus housing not available to married students. Typical cost: $3,570 per year ($7,830 including board). Housing application deadline: 6/15. *Student services:* Campus employment opportunities, campus safety program, career counseling, disabled student services, exercise/wellness program, free psychological counseling, international student services, multicultural affairs office, writing training. *Library facilities:* Mudd Center Library plus 3 others. *Online resources:* library catalog, web page, access to other libraries' catalogs. *Collection:* 1.5 million titles, 4,560 serial subscriptions, 59,186 audiovisual materials.

Computer facilities: 275 computers available on campus for general student use. A campuswide network can be accessed from student residence rooms and from off campus. *Web address:* http://www.oberlin.edu/.

General Application Contact: Michael C. Mandersen, Director of Admissions, 440-775-8413, Fax: 440-775-6972, E-mail: conservatory.admissions@oberlin.edu.

GRADUATE UNITS

Conservatory of Music Offers music (MM, MM Ed, MMT).

OBLATE SCHOOL OF THEOLOGY, San Antonio, TX 78216-6693

General Information Independent-religious, coed, graduate-only institution. *Enrollment by degree level:* 54 first professional, 33 master's, 64 doctoral. *Graduate faculty:* 17 full-time (4 women), 2 part-time/adjunct (0 women). *Tuition:* Part-time $331 per semester hour. Tuition and fees vary according to course level, course load, degree level and program. *Graduate housing:* On-campus housing not available. *Collection:* 90,000 titles, 360 serial subscriptions.

Computer facilities: 2 computers available on campus for general student use. A campuswide network can be accessed. Internet access is available. *Web address:* http://www.texas.net/~square1/oblate/.

General Application Contact: Christiane B. Scheel, Director of Admissions/Registrar, 210-341-1366, Fax: 210-341-4519, E-mail: registrar@ost.edu.

GRADUATE UNITS

Graduate and Professional Programs *Degree program information:* Part-time programs available. Offers divinity (M Div); Hispanic ministry (D Min); pastoral ministry (MAP Min); supervision (D Min); theology (MA Th).

OCCIDENTAL COLLEGE, Los Angeles, CA 90041-3314

General Information Independent, coed, comprehensive institution. *Enrollment:* 10 full-time matriculated graduate/professional students (all women), 6 part-time matriculated graduate/professional students (4 women). *Enrollment by degree level:* 16 master's. *Graduate faculty:* 133 full-time (60 women), 54 part-time/adjunct (27 women). *Tuition:* Full-time $25,030; part-time $1,029 per unit. *Required fees:* $528; $264 per semester. *Graduate housing:* On-campus housing not available. *Student services:* Campus employment opportunities, campus safety program, career counseling, child daycare facilities, free psychological counseling, low-cost health insurance, multicultural affairs office, teacher training. *Library facilities:* Mary Norton Clapp Library plus 2 others. *Online resources:* library catalog, web page, access to other libraries' catalogs. *Collection:* 481,822 titles, 1,135 serial subscriptions.

Computer facilities: 131 computers available on campus for general student use. A campuswide network can be accessed from student residence rooms and from off campus. Internet access and online class registration are available. *Web address:* http://www.oxy.edu/.

General Application Contact: Susan Molik, Administrative Assistant, Graduate Office, 323-259-2921, E-mail: molik@oxy.edu.

GRADUATE UNITS

Graduate Studies Students: 10 full-time (all women), 6 part-time (4 women); includes 4 minority (all Hispanic Americans) Average age 25. 15 applicants, 80% accepted. *Faculty:* 133 full-time (60 women), 54 part-time/adjunct (27 women). Expenses: Contact institution. *Financial support:* Fellowships, Federal Work-Study, institutionally sponsored loans, and scholarships/grants available. Support available to part-time students. Financial award application deadline: 3/1; financial award applicants required to submit FAFSA. In 2001, 18 degrees awarded. *Degree program information:* Part-time programs available. Offers biology (MA); elementary education (MAT); English and comparative literary studies (MAT); history (MAT); liberal studies (MAT); life science (MAT); mathematics (MAT); physical science (MAT); secondary education (MAT); social science (MAT); Spanish (MAT). *Application deadline:* For fall admission, 3/1; for spring admission, 10/1. Applications are processed on a rolling basis. *Application fee:* $50. *Application Contact:* Susan Molik, Administrative Assistant, Graduate Office, 323-259-2921, E-mail: molik@oxy.edu. *Director*, 323-259-2921.

OGI SCHOOL OF SCIENCE & ENGINEERING AT OREGON HEALTH & SCIENCE UNIVERSITY, Beaverton, OR 97006-8921

General Information Independent, coed, graduate-only institution. *Enrollment by degree level:* 240 master's, 104 doctoral. *Graduate faculty:* 75 full-time (7 women), 102 part-time/adjunct (9 women). *Tuition:* Full-time $4,905; part-time $545 per credit hour. *Required fees:* $466. *Graduate housing:* On-campus housing not available. *Student services:* Campus employment opportunities, campus safety program, international student services. *Library facilities:*

Samuel L. Diack Memorial Library. *Online resources:* library catalog, web page, access to other libraries' catalogs. *Collection:* 45,000 titles, 400 serial subscriptions. *Research affiliation:* Pacific Northwest Laboratory (computer science, biotechnology, membrane chemistry).

Computer facilities: A campuswide network can be accessed. Internet access and online class registration are available. *Web address:* http://www.ogi.edu/.

General Application Contact: Enrollment Manager, 800-685-2423, Fax: 503-748-1285, E-mail: admissions@admin.ogi.edu.

GRADUATE UNITS

Graduate Studies Students: 170 full-time, 393 part-time. Average age 31. *Faculty:* 75 full-time (7 women), 102 part-time/adjunct (9 women). Expenses: Contact institution. *Financial support:* Fellowships with full and partial tuition reimbursements, research assistantships with full and partial tuition reimbursements, teaching assistantships with full and partial tuition reimbursements, career-related internships or fieldwork, Federal Work-Study, and scholarships/grants available. In 2001, 132 master's, 11 doctorates, 14 other advanced degrees awarded. *Degree program information:* Part-time and evening/weekend programs available. Offers biochemistry and molecular biology (MS, PhD); computational finance (MS, Certificate); computer engineering (MS, PhD); computer science and engineering (MS, PhD); ecosystem management and restoration (MS); electrical engineering (MS, PhD); environmental information technology (PhD); environmental science (MS, PhD); environmental science and engineering (MS, PhD); environmental systems management (MS); management in science and technology (MS). *Application deadline:* Applications are processed on a rolling basis. *Application fee:* $50. Electronic applications accepted. *Application Contact:* Enrollment Manager, 800-685-2423, Fax: 503-748-1285, E-mail: admissions@admin.ogi.edu. *Dean,* Dr. Edward W. Thompson, 503-690-1128, Fax: 503-690-1029, E-mail: thompsed@ohsu.edu.

OGLALA LAKOTA COLLEGE, Kyle, SD 57752-0490

General Information State and locally supported, coed, comprehensive institution. *Graduate housing:* On-campus housing not available.

GRADUATE UNITS

Graduate Studies *Degree program information:* Part-time and evening/weekend programs available. Offers educational administration (MA); Lakota leadership and management (MA).

OGLETHORPE UNIVERSITY, Atlanta, GA 30319-2797

General Information Independent, coed, comprehensive institution. *Enrollment:* 23 full-time matriculated graduate/professional students (15 women), 60 part-time matriculated graduate/professional students (38 women). *Enrollment by degree level:* 83 master's. *Graduate faculty:* 10 full-time (5 women), 3 part-time/adjunct (2 women). *Tuition:* Part-time $395 per hour. Part-time tuition and fees vary according to program. *Graduate housing:* On-campus housing not available. *Student services:* Campus employment opportunities, campus safety program, career counseling, exercise/wellness program, free psychological counseling, international student services, low-cost health insurance. *Library facilities:* Philip Weltner Library. *Online resources:* library catalog, web page, access to other libraries' catalogs. *Collection:* 135,000 titles, 950 serial subscriptions, 520 audiovisual materials.

Computer facilities: 60 computers available on campus for general student use. A campuswide network can be accessed from student residence rooms and from off campus. *Web address:* http://www.oglethorpe.edu/.

General Application Contact: Josh Waller, Graduate Admissions Counselor, 404-364-8314, Fax: 404-364-8500, E-mail: jwaller@facstaff.oglethorpe.edu.

GRADUATE UNITS

Division of Business Administration Students: 18 full-time (10 women), 32 part-time (14 women). Average age 31. 23 applicants, 78% accepted. *Faculty:* 6 full-time (1 woman). Expenses: Contact institution. Offers business administration (MBA). *Application deadline:* For fall admission, 8/15. *Application fee:* $30. *Application Contact:* Josh Waller, Graduate Admissions Counselor, 404-364-8314, Fax: 404-364-8500, E-mail: jwaller@facstaff.oglethorpe.edu. *Director,* William Straley, 404-364-8353, Fax: 404-364-8500.

Division of Education Students: 5 full-time (all women), 28 part-time (24 women). Average age 30. 28 applicants, 82% accepted. *Faculty:* 4 full-time (all women), 3 part-time/adjunct (2 women). Expenses: Contact institution. In 2001, 23 degrees awarded. *Degree program information:* Part-time programs available. Offers early childhood education (MAT). *Application deadline:* Applications are processed on a rolling basis. *Application fee:* $30. *Application Contact:* Josh Waller, Graduate Admissions Counselor, 404-364-8314, Fax: 404-364-8500, E-mail: jwaller@facstaff.oglethorpe.edu. *Chair,* Dr. Beth Roberts, 404-364-8387, Fax: 404-364-8500.

OHIO COLLEGE OF PODIATRIC MEDICINE, Cleveland, OH 44106-3082

General Information Independent, coed, graduate-only institution. *Enrollment by degree level:* 291 first professional. *Graduate faculty:* 16 full-time (7 women), 8 part-time/adjunct (5 women). *Tuition:* Full-time $18,000. *Required fees:* $1,135. *Graduate housing:* On-campus housing not available. *Student services:* Campus employment opportunities, campus safety program, career counseling, disabled student services, free psychological counseling, low-cost health insurance. *Library facilities:* Medical Library. *Online resources:* library catalog, web page. *Collection:* 17,651 titles, 154 serial subscriptions, 689 audiovisual materials. *Research affiliation:* Biolitec, Inc. (medical diode lasers), Sulzer Biologics, Inc. (orthopedic and cardiovascular).

Computer facilities: 33 computers available on campus for general student use. A campuswide network can be accessed from off campus. Internet access is available. *Web address:* http://www.ocpm.edu/.

General Application Contact: Kelly W. Lie, Director of Admissions, 216-231-3300 Ext. 8130, Fax: 216-231-1005, E-mail: klie@ocpm.edu.

GRADUATE UNITS

Professional Program Students: 291 full-time (106 women); includes 68 minority (40 African Americans, 22 Asian Americans or Pacific Islanders, 4 Hispanic Americans, 2 Native Americans) Average age 26. 260 applicants, 43% accepted, 59 enrolled. *Faculty:* 16 full-time (7 women), 8 part-time/adjunct (5 women). Expenses: Contact institution. *Financial support:* Career-related internships or fieldwork, Federal Work-Study, institutionally sponsored loans, and scholarships/grants available. Financial award application deadline: 5/30; financial award applicants required to submit FAFSA. In 2001, 110 degrees awarded. Offers podiatric medicine (DPM). *Application deadline:* For fall admission, 6/1 (priority date). Applications are processed on a rolling basis. *Application fee:* $95. Electronic applications accepted. *Application Contact:* Brian Sherman, Director of Student Recruitment, 216-231-3300, Fax: 216-231-1005, E-mail: bsherman@ocpm.edu. *President,* Dr. Thomas Melillo, 216-231-3300.

OHIO NORTHERN UNIVERSITY, Ada, OH 45810-1599

General Information Independent-religious, coed, comprehensive institution. *Enrollment:* 1,084 full-time matriculated graduate/professional students (629 women), 38 part-time matriculated graduate/professional students (20 women). *Graduate faculty:* 41 full-time (15 women), 24 part-time/adjunct (8 women). *Tuition:* Full-time $19,740. *Graduate housing:* Room and/or apartments available on a first-come, first-served basis to single students; on-campus housing not available to married students. *Student services:* Campus employment opportunities, campus safety program, career counseling, child daycare facilities, disabled student services, exercise/wellness program, free psychological counseling, international student services, multicultural affairs office. *Library facilities:* Heterick Memorial Library plus 1 other. *Online resources:* library catalog, web page, access to other libraries' catalogs. *Collection:* 246,103 titles, 1,038 serial subscriptions, 8,655 audiovisual materials.

Computer facilities: 461 computers available on campus for general student use. A campuswide network can be accessed from student residence rooms and from off campus. Internet access and online class registration are available. *Web address:* http://www.onu.edu/.

GRADUATE UNITS

Claude W. Pettit College of Law Students: 273 full-time (109 women). Average age 25. 775 applicants, 59% accepted, 120 enrolled. *Faculty:* 23 full-time (8 women), 12 part-time/adjunct (4 women). Expenses: Contact institution. *Financial support:* In 2001–02, 245 students received support, including 25 research assistantships; career-related internships or fieldwork, Federal Work-Study, institutionally sponsored loans, and scholarships/grants also available. Financial award application deadline: 5/1; financial award applicants required to submit FAFSA. In 2001, 100 degrees awarded. Offers law (JD). *Application deadline:* Applications are processed on a rolling basis. *Application fee:* $40. Electronic applications accepted. *Application Contact:* Linda English, Assistant Dean and Director of Law Admissions, 419-772-2210, Fax: 419-772-3042, E-mail: l-english@onu.edu. *Dean,* Dr. David C. Crago, 419-772-2205, Fax: 419-772-1875, E-mail: c-crago@onu.edu.

Raabe College of Pharmacy Students: 811 full-time (520 women), 38 part-time (20 women); includes 69 minority (19 African Americans, 40 Asian Americans or Pacific Islanders, 9 Hispanic Americans, 1 Native American), 6 international. Average age 21. 462 applicants, 80% accepted. *Faculty:* 22 full-time (7 women), 22 part-time/adjunct (9 women). Expenses: Contact institution. *Financial support:* Federal Work-Study, institutionally sponsored loans, and scholarships/grants available. Financial award applicants required to submit FAFSA. In 2001, 150 degrees awarded. Postbaccalaureate distance learning degree programs offered (no on-campus study). Offers pharmacy (Pharm D). Students enter the program as undergraduates. *Application deadline:* For fall admission, 3/1 (priority date). Applications are processed on a rolling basis. *Application fee:* $30. Electronic applications accepted. *Application Contact:* Dr. Robert McCurdy, Assistant Dean and Director of Pharmacy Student Services, 419-772-2278, Fax: 419-772-2720, E-mail: r-mccurdy@onu.edu. *Dean,* Dr. Bobby G. Bryant, 419-772-2275, Fax: 419-772-2720, E-mail: b.bryant@onu.edu.

THE OHIO STATE UNIVERSITY, Columbus, OH 43210

General Information State-supported, coed, university. CGS member. *Graduate housing:* Rooms and/or apartments available to single students and available on a first-come, first-served basis to married students. *Research affiliation:* Cleveland Clinic (biomedical engineering), Children's Hospital (pediatrics), Transportation Research Center, Midwest Universities Consortium for International Activities, Science and Technology Campus.

GRADUATE UNITS

College of Dentistry Students: 490 full-time (164 women); includes 68 minority (5 African Americans, 51 Asian Americans or Pacific Islanders, 12 Hispanic Americans), 15 international. Average age 28. 1,398 applicants, 10% accepted. *Faculty:* 93 full-time (23 women), 71 part-time/adjunct (13 women). Expenses: Contact institution. *Financial support:* In 2001–02, 1 fellowship with tuition reimbursement, 8 research assistantships with tuition reimbursements (averaging $10,000 per year), 90 teaching assistantships with tuition reimbursements (averaging $10,000 per year) were awarded. Federal Work-Study and institutionally sponsored loans also available. Financial award application deadline: 3/1. In 2001, 84 first professional degrees, 19 master's, 3 doctorates awarded. Offers dentistry (DDS, MS, PhD); oral biology (PhD). *Application deadline:* Applications are processed on a rolling basis. *Application fee:* $30 ($40 for international students). *Application Contact:* Dr. Michael Rowland, Director of Admissions, 614-292-3361, Fax: 614-292-0813, E-mail: dentadmit@osu.edu. *Dean,* Jan E. Kronmiller, 614-292-9755, Fax: 614-292-7619.

College of Medicine and Public Health Students: 825 full-time (349 women); includes 229 minority (40 African Americans, 157 Asian Americans or Pacific Islanders, 30 Hispanic Americans, 2 Native Americans) Average age 23. 2,998 applicants, 14% accepted, 210 enrolled. *Faculty:* 802 full-time (190 women), 305 part-time/adjunct (89 women). Expenses: Contact institution. *Financial support:* In 2001–02, 725 students received support. Federal Work-Study, institutionally sponsored loans, and scholarships/grants available. Support available to part-time students. Financial award application deadline: 3/1; financial award applicants required to submit FAFSA. In 2001, 196 degrees awarded. Offers medicine (MD); medicine and public health (MD, PhD); neuroscience (PhD). *Application deadline:* For fall admission, 11/1. Applications are processed on a rolling basis. *Application fee:* $30 ($40 for international students). Electronic applications accepted. *Application Contact:* Dr. Mark Notestine, Assistant Dean of Admissions and Records, 614-292-7137, Fax: 614-292-7959, E-mail: admiss-med@osu.edu. *Dean and Vice President for Health Sciences,* Dr. Fred Sanfilippo, 614-292-1200, Fax: 614-292-1301.

College of Optometry Expenses: Contact institution. *Financial support:* Research assistantships with full tuition reimbursements, teaching assistantships with full tuition reimbursements, Federal Work-Study, institutionally sponsored loans, and scholarships/grants available. Financial award application deadline: 2/1; financial award applicants required to submit FAFSA. In 2001, 63 first professional degrees, 5 master's awarded. Offers optometry (OD, MS, PhD); vision science (MS, PhD). *Application fee:* $30 ($40 for international students). Electronic applications accepted. *Dean,* Dr. John Schoessler, 614-292-3246, Fax: 614-292-7493.

College of Pharmacy Students: 367 full-time (222 women), 9 part-time (5 women); includes 69 minority (18 African Americans, 46 Asian Americans or Pacific Islanders, 5 Hispanic Americans), 51 international. Average age 24. 493 applicants, 39% accepted, 150 enrolled. *Faculty:* 34 full-time (4 women), 4 part-time/adjunct (0 women). Expenses: Contact institution. *Financial support:* In 2001–02, 183 students received support, including 11 fellowships with full tuition reimbursements available (averaging $17,500 per year), 48 research assistantships with full tuition reimbursements available (averaging $19,000 per year), 32 teaching assistantships with full tuition reimbursements available (averaging $16,000 per year); career-related internships or fieldwork, Federal Work-Study, institutionally sponsored loans, scholarships/grants, and traineeships also available. In 2001, 16 master's, 10 doctorates awarded. *Degree program information:* Part-time programs available. Offers hospital pharmacy (MS); medicinal chemistry and pharmacognosy (MS, PhD); pharmaceutical administration (MS, PhD); pharmaceutics (MS, PhD); pharmacology (MS, PhD); pharmacy (MS, PhD); pharmacy practice and administration (MS, PhD). *Application deadline:* For fall admission, 2/1 (priority date). *Application fee:* $30 ($40 for international students). Electronic applications accepted. *Application Contact:* Kathy I. Brooks, Graduate Program Coordinator, 614-292-6822, Fax: 614-292-2588, E-mail: gadmbrks@dendrite.pharmacy.ohio-state.edu. *Dean,* Dr. John M. Cassady, 614-292-2266, Fax: 614-292-2588, E-mail: cassady.1@osu.edu.

College of Veterinary Medicine *Degree program information:* Part-time programs available. Offers anatomy and cellular biology (MS, PhD); pathobiology (MS, PhD); pharmacology (MS, PhD); toxicology (MS, PhD); veterinary biosciences (MS, PhD); veterinary clinical sciences (MS, PhD); veterinary medicine (DVM, MS, PhD); veterinary physiology (MS, PhD); veterinary preventive medicine (MS, PhD).

Graduate Programs in the Basic Medical Sciences Students: 332 full-time (234 women), 58 part-time (40 women); includes 63 minority (30 African Americans, 27 Asian Americans or Pacific Islanders, 5 Hispanic Americans, 1 Native American), 62 international. Average age 24. 549 applicants, 50% accepted, 152 enrolled. *Faculty:* 269 full-time (76 women), 23 part-time/adjunct (4 women). Expenses: Contact institution. *Financial support:* In 2001–02, 95 students received support, including 20 fellowships with full tuition reimbursements available (averaging $15,360 per year), 83 research assistantships with full tuition reimbursements available (averaging $13,342 per year), 14 teaching assistantships with full tuition reimbursements available (averaging $14,053 per year); Federal Work-Study, institutionally sponsored loans, scholarships/grants, traineeships, and unspecified assistantships also available. Support available to part-time students. Financial award application deadline: 1/15; financial award applicants required to submit FAFSA. In 2001, 88 master's, 20 doctorates awarded. *Degree program information:* Part-time and evening/weekend programs available. Offers anatomy (MS, PhD); basic medical sciences (MHA, MPH, MPT, MS, PhD); experimental pathobiology (MS); integrated biomedical science (PhD); molecular virology, immunology and medical genetics (MS, PhD); pathology assistant (MS); pharmacology (MS); physiology (MS). *Application deadline:* Applications are processed on a rolling basis. *Application fee:* $30 ($40 for international students). Electronic applications accepted. *Associate Dean for Graduate Education,* Dr. James S. King, 614-292-8725, Fax: 614-292-6226, E-mail: king.11@osu.edu.

Division of Health Services Management and Policy Students: 49 full-time (30 women), 3 part-time (all women); includes 20 minority (10 African Americans, 9 Asian Americans or

The Ohio State University (continued)

Pacific Islanders, 1 Native American), 3 international. Average age 25. 110 applicants, 25% accepted. *Faculty:* 8 full-time (3 women), 4 part-time/adjunct (2 women). Expenses: Contact institution. *Financial support:* In 2001–02, 25 students received support, including 9 fellowships with tuition reimbursements available (averaging $14,400 per year), 3 research assistantships with tuition reimbursements available (averaging $8,100 per year); Federal Work-Study, institutionally sponsored loans, scholarships/grants, traineeships, and administrative assistantships, associateships also available. Support available to part-time students. Financial award application deadline: 1/15; financial award applicants required to submit FAFSA. In 2001, 27 degrees awarded. *Degree program information:* Part-time programs available. Offers health administration (MHA). *Application deadline:* For fall admission, 3/1 (priority date). *Application fee:* $30 ($40 for international students). Electronic applications accepted. *Application Contact:* Sandra L. Daly, Director of Admissions, 614-292-8193, Fax: 614-292-3572, E-mail: daly.6@osu.edu. *Chairman*, Dr. Stephen F. Loebs, 614-292-9708, Fax: 614-292-3572, E-mail: loebs.1@osu.edu.

School of Allied Medical Professions Students: 85 full-time (71 women), 6 part-time (all women); includes 5 minority (3 African Americans, 2 Hispanic Americans), 2 international. Average age 28. 62 applicants, 81% accepted. *Faculty:* 25 full-time (14 women), 2 part-time/adjunct (1 woman). Expenses: Contact institution. *Financial support:* In 2001–02, 11 students received support, including 8 research assistantships with full tuition reimbursements available (averaging $8,200 per year), 3 teaching assistantships with full tuition reimbursements available (averaging $8,200 per year); fellowships, traineeships and administrative assistantships also available. Financial award application deadline: 3/1. In 2001, 17 degrees awarded. *Degree program information:* Part-time programs available. Offers allied medicine (MS); physical therapy (MPT). *Application deadline:* For fall admission, 8/15; for winter admission, 12/1; for spring admission, 3/1. Applications are processed on a rolling basis. *Application fee:* $30 ($40 for international students). Electronic applications accepted. *Application Contact:* Jill Clutter, Director of Graduate Student Services, 614-292-9579, Fax: 614-292-0210, E-mail: clutter.1@osu.edu. *Director*, Dr. Stephen L. Wilson, 614-292-5645, Fax: 614-292-0210.

School of Public Health Students: 89 full-time (70 women), 46 part-time (30 women); includes 23 minority (15 African Americans, 7 Asian Americans or Pacific Islanders, 1 Hispanic American), 27 international. Average age 25. 184 applicants, 70% accepted, 59 enrolled. *Faculty:* 28 full-time (12 women), 1 part-time/adjunct (0 women). Expenses: Contact institution. *Financial support:* In 2001–02, 5 fellowships with full tuition reimbursements (averaging $14,400 per year), 19 research assistantships with full tuition reimbursements (averaging $12,000 per year) were awarded. Federal Work-Study, institutionally sponsored loans, traineeships, and unspecified assistantships also available. Support available to part-time students. Financial award application deadline: 7/1. In 2001, 35 master's, 5 doctorates awarded. *Degree program information:* Part-time and evening/weekend programs available. Offers public health (MPH, MS, PhD). *Application deadline:* For fall admission, 3/1 (priority date). *Application fee:* $30 ($40 for international students). Electronic applications accepted. *Application Contact:* Judy Dawson, Graduate Studies Office, 614-293-3907, Fax: 614-293-3937, E-mail: dawson.6@osu.edu. *Interim Dean*, Dr. Ronald L. St. Pierre, 614-293-3907, Fax: 614-293-3937.

Graduate School *Degree program information:* Part-time and evening/weekend programs available. Offers Slavic and East European studies (MA).

College of Biological Sciences *Degree program information:* Part-time programs available. Offers biochemistry (MS, PhD); biological sciences (MS, PhD); biophysics (MS, PhD); cell and developmental biology (MS, PhD); entomology (MS, PhD); evolution, ecology, and organismal biology (MS, PhD); genetics (MS, PhD); microbiology (MS, PhD); molecular biology (MS, PhD); molecular, cellular and developmental biology (MS, PhD); plant biology (MS, PhD).

College of Education Students: 1,647 (1,197 women); includes 215 minority (161 African Americans, 27 Asian Americans or Pacific Islanders, 20 Hispanic Americans, 7 Native Americans) 184 international. 1,100 applicants, 71% accepted, 644 enrolled. *Faculty:* 131 full-time, 3 part-time/adjunct. Expenses: Contact institution. *Financial support:* In 2001–02, 42 fellowships with tuition reimbursements (averaging $9,900 per year), 90 research assistantships with tuition reimbursements (averaging $9,900 per year), 144 teaching assistantships with tuition reimbursements (averaging $9,900 per year) were awarded. Career-related internships or fieldwork, Federal Work-Study, institutionally sponsored loans, scholarships/grants, traineeships, health care benefits, and unspecified assistantships also available. Support available to part-time students. In 2001, 722 master's, 73 doctorates awarded. Offers education (M Ed, MA, PhD, Certificate); educational administration (Certificate); educational policy and leadership (M Ed, MA, PhD); physical activity and educational services (M Ed, MA, PhD); teaching and learning (M Ed, MA, PhD). *Application fee:* $40 ($50 for international students). *Application Contact:* Jogy Das, Information Contact, 614-292-5732, E-mail: das.1@osu.edu. *Dean*, Dr. Donna Evans, 614-292-2581, Fax: 614-292-8052.

College of Engineering *Degree program information:* Part-time and evening/weekend programs available. Offers aeronautical and astronautical engineering (MS, PhD); architecture (M Arch, M Land Arch, MCRP, PhD); biomedical engineering (MS, PhD); chemical engineering (MS, PhD); city and regional planning (MCRP, PhD); civil engineering (MS, PhD); computer and information science (MS, PhD); electrical engineering (MS, PhD); engineering (M Arch, M Land Arch, MCRP, MS, PhD); engineering mechanics (MS, PhD); environmental science (MS, PhD); geodetic science and surveying (MS, PhD); industrial and systems engineering (MS, PhD); landscape architecture (M Land Arch); materials science and engineering (MS, PhD); mechanical engineering (MS, PhD); nuclear engineering (MS, PhD); welding engineering (MS, PhD).

College of Food, Agricultural, and Environmental Sciences *Degree program information:* Part-time programs available. Offers agricultural economics and rural sociology (MS, PhD); agricultural education (MS, PhD); animal sciences (MS, PhD); food science and nutrition (MS, PhD); food, agricultural, and biological engineering (MS, PhD); food, agricultural, and environmental sciences (MS, PhD); horticulture and crop science (MS, PhD); natural resources (MS, PhD); plant pathology (MS, PhD); soil science (MS, PhD); vocational education (PhD).

College of Human Ecology *Degree program information:* Part-time programs available. Offers family and consumer sciences education (M Ed, MS, PhD); family relations and human development (MS, PhD); family resource management (MS, PhD); food service management (MS, PhD); foods (MS, PhD); human ecology (M Ed, MS, PhD); nutrition (MS, PhD); textiles and clothing (MS, PhD).

College of Humanities *Degree program information:* Part-time programs available. Offers African-American and African studies (MA); comparative studies (MA); East Asian languages and literatures (MA, PhD); English (MA, MFA, PhD); French and Italian (MA, PhD); Germanic languages and literatures (MA, PhD); Greek and Latin (MA, PhD); history (MA, PhD); humanities (MA, MFA, PhD, Certificate); Latin American studies (Certificate); linguistics (MA, PhD); Near Eastern languages and cultures (MA); philosophy (MA, PhD); Russian area studies (Certificate); Slavic and East European languages and literatures (MA, PhD); Spanish and Portuguese (MA, PhD); women's studies (MA).

College of Mathematical and Physical Sciences *Degree program information:* Part-time programs available. Offers astronomy (MS, PhD); biostatistics (PhD); chemical physics (MS, PhD); chemistry (MS, PhD); geological sciences (MS, PhD); mathematical and physical sciences (M Appl Stat, MA, MS, PhD); mathematics (MA, MS, PhD); physics (MS, PhD); statistics (M Appl Stat, MS, PhD).

College of Nursing *Degree program information:* Part-time programs available. Offers nursing (MS, PhD).

College of Social and Behavioral Sciences *Degree program information:* Part-time programs available. Offers anthropology (MA, PhD); atmospheric sciences (MS, PhD); clinical psychology (PhD); cognitive/experimental psychology (PhD); communication (PhD); counseling psychology (PhD); developmental psychology (PhD); economics (MA, PhD); geography (MA, PhD); journalism and communication (MA); Latin American studies (Certificate); mental retardation and developmental disabilities (PhD); political science (MA, PhD); psychobiology (PhD); public policy and management (MA, MPA, PhD); quantitative psychology (PhD); Russian area studies (Certificate); social and behavioral sciences (MA, MPA, MS, PhD, Certificate); social psychology (PhD); sociology (MA, PhD); speech and hearing science (MA, PhD).

College of Social Work *Degree program information:* Part-time programs available. Offers social work (MSW, PhD).

College of the Arts *Degree program information:* Part-time programs available. Offers art (MA, MFA); art education (MA, PhD); arts (M Mus, MA, MFA, DMA, PhD); arts policy and administration (MA); dance (MA, MFA); history of art (MA, PhD); industrial, interior, and visual communication design (MA, MFA); music (M Mus, MA, DMA, PhD); theatre (MA, MFA, PhD).

Max M. Fisher College of Business *Degree program information:* Part-time programs available. Offers accounting and management information systems (M Acc, MA, PhD); business (M Acc, MA, MBA, MLHR, PhD); business administration (MA, MBA, PhD); labor and human resources (MLHR, PhD).

Moritz College of Law Students: 661 full-time (304 women); includes 122 minority (69 African Americans, 31 Asian Americans or Pacific Islanders, 19 Hispanic Americans, 3 Native Americans), 14 international. Average age 24. 1,902 applicants, 32% accepted, 225 enrolled. *Faculty:* 42 full-time (13 women), 47 part-time/adjunct (23 women). Expenses: Contact institution. *Financial support:* In 2001–02, 470 students received support. Career-related internships or fieldwork, Federal Work-Study, institutionally sponsored loans, and scholarships/grants available. Financial award application deadline: 3/1; financial award applicants required to submit FAFSA. In 2001, 195 degrees awarded. Offers law (JD). *Application deadline:* For fall admission, 3/15 (priority date). Applications are processed on a rolling basis. *Application fee:* $30 ($40 for international students). Electronic applications accepted. *Application Contact:* Kathy S. Northern, Associate Dean, 614-292-8810, Fax: 614-292-1492, E-mail: lawadmit@osu.edu. *Dean*, Nancy H. Rogers, 614-292-2631, Fax: 614-292-1383, E-mail: rogers.23@osu.edu.

OHIO UNIVERSITY, Athens, OH 45701-2979

General Information State-supported, coed, university. CGS member. *Enrollment:* 1,993 full-time matriculated graduate/professional students (982 women), 550 part-time matriculated graduate/professional students (287 women). *Graduate faculty:* 1,042 full-time (355 women), 661 part-time/adjunct (260 women). Tuition, state resident: full-time $6,585. Tuition, nonresident: full-time $12,254. *Graduate housing:* Rooms and/or apartments available to single students and available on a first-come, first-served basis to married students. Housing application deadline: 5/1. *Student services:* Campus employment opportunities, campus safety program, career counseling, child daycare facilities, disabled student services, exercise/wellness program, free psychological counseling, international student services, low-cost health insurance, multicultural affairs office. *Library facilities:* Alden Library. *Online resources:* library catalog, web page, access to other libraries' catalogs. *Collection:* 2.3 million titles, 20,808 serial subscriptions, 368,484 audiovisual materials.

Computer facilities: 1,500 computers available on campus for general student use. A campuswide network can be accessed from student residence rooms and from off campus. *Web address:* http://www.ohio.edu/.

General Application Contact: Dr. Katherine Tadlock, Director, Graduate Student Services, 740-593-2800, Fax: 740-593-4625, E-mail: tadlockk@ohio.edu.

GRADUATE UNITS

College of Osteopathic Medicine Students: 423 full-time (180 women); includes 111 minority (40 African Americans, 46 Asian Americans or Pacific Islanders, 23 Hispanic Americans, 2 Native Americans) Average age 25. 2,031 applicants, 8% accepted. *Faculty:* 95 full-time (24 women), 20 part-time/adjunct (9 women). Expenses: Contact institution. *Financial support:* In 2001–02, 389 students received support, including 7 fellowships with full tuition reimbursements available (averaging $6,600 per year); career-related internships or fieldwork, Federal Work-Study, institutionally sponsored loans, scholarships/grants, tuition waivers (partial), and research fellowships also available. Financial award application deadline: 4/1; financial award applicants required to submit FAFSA. In 2001, 99 degrees awarded. Offers osteopathic medicine (DO). *Application deadline:* For fall admission, 1/2. Applications are processed on a rolling basis. *Application fee:* $30. *Application Contact:* John D. Schriner, Director of Admissions, 740-593-4313, Fax: 740-593-2256, E-mail: admissions@exchange.oucom.ohiou.edu. *Dean*, Dr. John A. Brose, 740-593-2178, Fax: 740-593-0761.

Graduate Studies 3,728 applicants, 51% accepted. *Faculty:* 1,042 full-time (355 women), 661 part-time/adjunct (260 women). Expenses: Contact institution. *Financial support:* In 2001–02, 48 fellowships with full tuition reimbursements, 293 research assistantships with full and partial tuition reimbursements, 450 teaching assistantships with full and partial tuition reimbursements were awarded. Career-related internships or fieldwork, Federal Work-Study, institutionally sponsored loans, scholarships/grants, traineeships, tuition waivers (full and partial), unspecified assistantships, and associateships, graduate assistantships, graduate scholarships/stipends also available. Financial award applicants required to submit FAFSA. In 2001, 1,006 master's, 106 doctorates awarded. *Degree program information:* Part-time and evening/weekend programs available. Offers interdisciplinary studies (MA, MS, PhD). *Application fee:* $30. Electronic applications accepted. *Application Contact:* Graduate Student Services, 740-593-2800, Fax: 740-593-4625, E-mail: gradstu@www.ohiou.edu. *Interim Associate Provost for Graduate Studies*, Dr. Raymie E. McKerrow, 740-593-4122, E-mail: mckerrow@ohio.edu.

Center for International Studies Students: 122 full-time (66 women), 7 part-time (5 women); includes 12 minority (6 African Americans, 1 Asian American or Pacific Islander, 5 Hispanic Americans), 78 international. 255 applicants, 76% accepted, 81 enrolled. *Faculty:* 1 full-time (0 women). Expenses: Contact institution. *Financial support:* In 2001–02, 16 fellowships with full tuition reimbursements, 38 research assistantships with full and partial tuition reimbursements, 5 teaching assistantships with full and partial tuition reimbursements were awarded. Career-related internships or fieldwork, Federal Work-Study, institutionally sponsored loans, scholarships/grants, and tuition waivers (full) also available. Financial award application deadline: 1/15. In 2001, 65 degrees awarded. Offers African studies (MA); communications and development studies (MA); development studies (MA); international studies (MA); Latin American studies (MA); Southeast Asian studies (MA). *Application deadline:* For fall admission, 3/1 (priority date). *Application fee:* $30. *Application Contact:* Joan Kraynanski, Administrative Assistant, 740-593-1840, Fax: 740-593-1837, E-mail: kraynans@ohio.edu. *Director*, Dr. Josep Rota, 740-593-1839, Fax: 740-593-1837, E-mail: rota@ohio.edu.

College of Arts and Sciences Students: 692 full-time (315 women), 138 part-time (64 women); includes 22 minority (9 African Americans, 8 Asian Americans or Pacific Islanders, 3 Hispanic Americans, 2 Native Americans), 387 international. 977 applicants, 46% accepted. *Faculty:* 387 full-time (110 women), 45 part-time/adjunct (20 women). Expenses: Contact institution. *Financial support:* In 2001–02, 13 fellowships with full tuition reimbursements, 71 research assistantships with full tuition reimbursements, 291 teaching assistantships with full tuition reimbursements were awarded. Career-related internships or fieldwork, Federal Work-Study, institutionally sponsored loans, scholarships/grants, traineeships, tuition waivers (full and partial), and unspecified assistantships also available. In 2001, 228 master's, 40 doctorates awarded. *Degree program information:* Part-time programs available. Offers applied linguistics/TESOL (MA); arts and sciences (MA, MPA, MS, MSS, MSW, PhD); biological sciences (MS, PhD); chemistry and biochemistry (MS, PhD); clinical psychology (PhD); economics (MA); English language and literature (MA, PhD); environmental and plant biology (MS, PhD); environmental studies (MS); experimental psychology (PhD); French (MA); geography (MA); geological sciences (MS); history (MA, PhD); industrial and organizational psychology (PhD); mathematics (MS, PhD); microbiology (MS, PhD); molecular and cellular biology (MS, PhD); neuroscience (MS); philosophy (MA); physics (MS, PhD); political science (MA); public administration (MPA); social sciences (MSS); social work (MSW); sociology (MA); Spanish (MA); zoology (MS, PhD). *Application fee:* $30. Electronic applications accepted. *Dean*, Dr. Leslie Flemming, 740-593-2850, Fax: 740-593-0053.

College of Business Students: 147 full-time (45 women), 7 part-time (5 women); includes 14 minority (4 African Americans, 8 Asian Americans or Pacific Islanders, 1 Hispanic American, 1 Native American), 35 international. 165 applicants, 62% accepted. *Faculty:* 53 full-time (19 women), 17 part-time/adjunct (7 women). Expenses: Contact institution. *Financial support:* In 2001–02, 30 research assistantships with full and partial tuition reimbursements were awarded; career-related internships or fieldwork, Federal Work-Study, institutionally sponsored loans, tuition waivers (full and partial), and associateships also available. In 2001, 92 degrees awarded. *Degree program information:* Part-time and evening/weekend programs available. Offers business (EMBA, MBA, MSA); business administration (EMBA, MBA, MSA). *Application fee:* $30. *Application Contact:* Jan Ross, Assistant Director, 740-593-2007, Fax: 740-597-2995, E-mail: rossj@ohio.edu. *Assistant Dean,* Dr. Hugh Sherman, 740-593-2007, Fax: 740-597-2995.

College of Communication Students: 104 full-time (56 women), 30 part-time (11 women); includes 14 minority (8 African Americans, 4 Asian Americans or Pacific Islanders, 1 Hispanic American, 1 Native American), 63 international. 211 applicants, 56% accepted, 58 enrolled. *Faculty:* 48 full-time (17 women), 6 part-time/adjunct (4 women). Expenses: Contact institution. *Financial support:* In 2001–02, 7 fellowships, 18 research assistantships with full tuition reimbursements, 26 teaching assistantships with full tuition reimbursements were awarded. Career-related internships or fieldwork, Federal Work-Study, institutionally sponsored loans, and tuition waivers (full and partial) also available. Financial award applicants required to submit FAFSA. In 2001, 30 master's, 18 doctorates awarded. *Degree program information:* Part-time and evening/weekend programs available. Offers communication (MA, MS, PhD); interpersonal communication (MA, PhD); journalism (MS, PhD); telecommunications (MA, PhD); visual communication (MA). *Application deadline:* Applications are processed on a rolling basis. *Application fee:* $30. *Dean,* Dr. Kathy Krendl, 740-593-4883.

College of Education Students: 246 full-time (143 women), 284 part-time (166 women); includes 33 minority (24 African Americans, 2 Asian Americans or Pacific Islanders, 4 Hispanic Americans, 3 Native Americans), 204 international. 348 applicants, 65% accepted. *Faculty:* 47 full-time (26 women), 19 part-time/adjunct (7 women). Expenses: Contact institution. *Financial support:* In 2001–02, 126 students received support, including 97 research assistantships with full tuition reimbursements available (averaging $6,500 per year), 13 teaching assistantships with full tuition reimbursements available (averaging $7,200 per year); Federal Work-Study, institutionally sponsored loans, tuition waivers (full), and unspecified assistantships also available. Financial award application deadline: 3/15. In 2001, 168 master's, 44 doctorates awarded. *Degree program information:* Part-time and evening/weekend programs available. Offers adolescent to young adult education (M Ed); college student personnel (M Ed); community/agency counseling (M Ed); computer education and technology (M Ed); counselor education (PhD); cultural studies (M Ed); curriculum and instruction (M Ed, PhD); education (M Ed, Ed D, PhD); educational administration (M Ed, Ed D); educational research and evaluation (M Ed, PhD); elementary education (M Ed); gifted and talented (M Ed); higher education (M Ed, PhD); instructional technology (PhD); mathematics education (PhD); middle child education (M Ed); middle level education (PhD); reading and language arts (PhD); reading education (M Ed); rehabilitation counseling (M Ed); school counseling (M Ed); secondary mathematics education (M Ed); social studies education (PhD); special education (M Ed, PhD); supervision (PhD). *Application deadline:* For fall admission, 4/1 (priority date). *Application fee:* $30. *Application Contact:* Lynn Graham, Assistant Director, Graduate Services, 740-593-4420, Fax: 740-593-9310, E-mail: graham-m@ohio.edu. *Dean,* Dr. James L. Heap, 740-593-9449, E-mail: heap@ohiou.edu.

College of Fine Arts Students: 240 full-time (121 women), 32 part-time (22 women); includes 17 minority (9 African Americans, 3 Asian Americans or Pacific Islanders, 4 Hispanic Americans, 1 Native American), 73 international. 460 applicants, 35% accepted. *Faculty:* 85 full-time (26 women), 8 part-time/adjunct (5 women). Expenses: Contact institution. *Financial support:* In 2001–02, 48 research assistantships with full and partial tuition reimbursements, 70 teaching assistantships with full and partial tuition reimbursements were awarded. Career-related internships or fieldwork, Federal Work-Study, institutionally sponsored loans, scholarships/grants, tuition waivers (full and partial), and associateships also available. In 2001, 70 master's, 3 doctorates awarded. Postbaccalaureate distance learning degree programs offered (minimal on-campus study). Offers art education (MA); art history (MFA); art history/studio (MFA); ceramics (MFA); comparative arts (PhD); conducting (MM); film (MA, MFA); fine arts (MA, MFA, MM, PhD); history (MM); literature (MM); music education (MM); painting (MFA); performance (MM); photography (MFA); printmaking (MFA); sculpture (MFA); theater (MA, MFA); theory (MM). *Application fee:* $30. Electronic applications accepted. *Dean,* Dr. Raymond Tymas-Jones, 740-593-1808, Fax: 740-593-0570.

College of Health and Human Services Students: 251 full-time (159 women), 29 part-time (23 women); includes 11 minority (8 African Americans, 1 Asian American or Pacific Islander, 2 Native Americans), 50 international. 416 applicants, 41% accepted. *Faculty:* 41 full-time (19 women), 17 part-time/adjunct (11 women). Expenses: Contact institution. *Financial support:* In 2001–02, 3 fellowships, 55 research assistantships with tuition reimbursements, 32 teaching assistantships with tuition reimbursements were awarded. Career-related internships or fieldwork, Federal Work-Study, institutionally sponsored loans, scholarships/grants, tuition waivers (full), and graduate scholarships/stipends also available. Financial award application deadline: 3/15. In 2001, 195 master's, 1 doctorate awarded. *Degree program information:* Part-time programs available. Offers athletics/training education (MS); child development and family life (MSHCS); coaching education (MS); food and nutrition (MSHCS); health and human services (MA, MBA, MHA, MPT, MS, MSA, MSHCS, MSP Ex, PhD); health sciences (MHA); physical education (MS); physical education pedagogy (MS); physical therapy (MPT); physiology of exercise (MSP Ex); recreation studies (MS); speech pathology and audiology (MA, PhD); sport physiology and adult fitness (MS); sports administration (MBA, MSA). *Application fee:* $30. *Dean,* Dr. Gary Neiman, 740-593-9336, Fax: 740-593-0285.

Russ College of Engineering and Technology Students: 237 full-time (40 women), 78 part-time (17 women); includes 10 minority (4 African Americans, 6 Asian Americans or Pacific Islanders), 250 international. 933 applicants, 66% accepted. *Faculty:* 106 full-time (5 women), 15 part-time/adjunct (4 women). Expenses: Contact institution. *Financial support:* In 2001–02, 16 fellowships with full tuition reimbursements (averaging $14,000 per year), 46 research assistantships with full tuition reimbursements (averaging $10,000 per year), 37 teaching assistantships with full tuition reimbursements (averaging $9,500 per year) were awarded. Career-related internships or fieldwork, Federal Work-Study, institutionally sponsored loans, tuition waivers (full and partial), and unspecified assistantships also available. In 2001, 83 master's, 14 doctorates awarded. *Degree program information:* Part-time programs available. Offers chemical engineering (MS, PhD); computer science (MS); electrical engineering (MS, PhD); engineering and technology (MS, PhD); geotechnical and environmental engineering (MS, PhD); industrial and manufacturing systems engineering (MS); intelligent systems (PhD); manufacturing engineering (MS); materials processing (PhD); mechanical engineering (MS, PhD); water resources and structures (MS). *Application fee:* $30. Electronic applications accepted. *Application Contact:* Roger Radcliff, Associate Dean, Fax: 740-593-0007, E-mail: radcliff@ohio.edu. *Interim Dean,* Dr. Dennis Irwin, 740-593-1482, Fax: 740-593-0659, E-mail: mitchell@ohio.edu.

OHR HAMEIR THEOLOGICAL SEMINARY, Peekskill, NY 10566

General Information Independent-religious, men only, comprehensive institution.

OKLAHOMA BAPTIST UNIVERSITY, Shawnee, OK 74804

General Information Independent-religious, coed, comprehensive institution. *Enrollment:* 10 full-time matriculated graduate/professional students (9 women), 10 part-time matriculated graduate/professional students (7 women). *Enrollment by degree level:* 20 master's. *Graduate faculty:* 4 full-time (0 women), 3 part-time/adjunct (1 woman). *Tuition:* Full-time $7,680; part-time $320 per credit. *Required fees:* $200; $100 per semester. *Graduate housing:* Rooms and/or apartments available to single and married students. Housing application deadline: 4/15. *Student services:* Campus employment opportunities, campus safety program, career counseling, free psychological counseling, international student services, low-cost health insurance. *Library facilities:* Mabee Learning Center. *Online resources:* library catalog, web page, access to other libraries' catalogs. *Collection:* 230,000 titles, 1,800 serial subscriptions, 1,600 audiovisual materials.

Computer facilities: 170 computers available on campus for general student use. A campuswide network can be accessed from student residence rooms. Internet access is available. *Web address:* http://www.okbu.edu/.

General Application Contact: Dr. D. Christopher Estes, Director of Graduate Studies in Marriage and Family Therapy, 405-878-2225, Fax: 405-878-2069, E-mail: chris_estes@mail.okbu.edu.

GRADUATE UNITS

Graduate Studies in Marriage and Family Therapy Students: 10 full-time (9 women), 10 part-time (7 women). Average age 36. 14 applicants, 86% accepted. *Faculty:* 4 full-time (0 women), 3 part-time/adjunct (1 woman). Expenses: Contact institution. *Financial support:* In 2001–02, 16 students received support. Career-related internships or fieldwork, Federal Work-Study, and institutionally sponsored loans available. Support available to part-time students. Financial award application deadline: 3/31; financial award applicants required to submit FAFSA. In 2001, 9 degrees awarded. *Degree program information:* Part-time and evening/weekend programs available. Postbaccalaureate distance learning degree programs offered (minimal on-campus study). Offers marriage and family therapy (MS). *Application deadline:* For fall admission, 3/31 (priority date). *Application fee:* $50. *Director of Graduate Studies in Marriage and Family Therapy,* 405-878-2225, Fax: 405-878-2069, E-mail: chris_estes@mail.okbu.edu.

OKLAHOMA CHRISTIAN UNIVERSITY, Oklahoma City, OK 73136-1100

General Information Independent-religious, coed, comprehensive institution. *Enrollment:* 10 full-time matriculated graduate/professional students, 24 part-time matriculated graduate/professional students. *Enrollment by degree level:* 34 master's. *Graduate faculty:* 12 full-time (0 women). *Graduate housing:* On-campus housing not available. *Student services:* Campus employment opportunities, campus safety program, exercise/wellness program, free psychological counseling, international student services. *Library facilities:* Mabee Learning Center. *Online resources:* library catalog. *Collection:* 95,789 titles, 415 serial subscriptions.

Computer facilities: 135 computers available on campus for general student use. A campuswide network can be accessed from student residence rooms and from off campus. Internet access is available. *Web address:* http://www.oc.edu/.

General Application Contact: Dr. Glenn D. Pemberton, Chair, Graduate Bible, 405-425-5378, Fax: 405-425-5076, E-mail: glenn.pemberton@oc.edu.

GRADUATE UNITS

Graduate School Students: 10 full-time (0 women), 24 part-time; includes 1 minority (African American), 2 international. Average age 30. 8 applicants, 100% accepted. *Faculty:* 12 full-time (0 women). Expenses: Contact institution. *Financial support:* Career-related internships or fieldwork, Federal Work-Study, scholarships/grants, and tuition waivers (partial) available. Support available to part-time students. Financial award application deadline: 3/1. In 2001, 8 degrees awarded. *Degree program information:* Part-time programs available. Postbaccalaureate distance learning degree programs offered (minimal on-campus study). Offers family life ministry (MA); ministry (MA); youth ministry (MA). *Application deadline:* Applications are processed on a rolling basis. *Professor,* Dr. Glenn Pemberton, 405-425-5378, Fax: 405-425-5076, E-mail: glenn.pemberton@oc.edu.

OKLAHOMA CITY UNIVERSITY, Oklahoma City, OK 73106-1402

General Information Independent-religious, coed, comprehensive institution. *Enrollment:* 1,101 full-time matriculated graduate/professional students (417 women), 712 part-time matriculated graduate/professional students (298 women). *Enrollment by degree level:* 534 first professional, 1,279 master's. *Graduate faculty:* 127 full-time (41 women), 129 part-time/adjunct (45 women). *Tuition:* Full-time $9,960; part-time $415 per credit hour. *Required fees:* $400. *Graduate housing:* Rooms and/or apartments available on a first-come, first-served basis to single and married students. Typical cost: $2,800 (including board) for single students. Housing application deadline: 8/15. *Student services:* Campus employment opportunities, campus safety program, career counseling, disabled student services, exercise/wellness program, free psychological counseling, international student services, low-cost health insurance, teacher training, writing training. *Library facilities:* Dulaney Browne Library plus 1 other. *Online resources:* library catalog, web page, access to other libraries' catalogs. *Collection:* 280,457 titles, 5,699 serial subscriptions, 10,605 audiovisual materials.

Computer facilities: 264 computers available on campus for general student use. A campuswide network can be accessed from student residence rooms and from off campus. Internet access is available. *Web address:* http://www.okcu.edu/.

General Application Contact: Sherry Boyles, Director of Admissions, 800-633-7242 Ext. 4, Fax: 405-521-5356, E-mail: gadmissions@okcu.edu.

GRADUATE UNITS

Meinders School of Business *Degree program information:* Part-time and evening/weekend programs available. Offers accounting (MSA); arts management (MBA); finance (MBA); health administration (MBA); information systems management (MBA); integrated marketing communications (MBA); international business (MBA); management (MBA); management and business sciences (MBA, MSA); marketing (MBA); public administration (MBA).

Petree College of Arts and Sciences *Degree program information:* Part-time and evening/weekend programs available. Offers art (MLA); arts and sciences (M Ed, MA, MCJA, MLA, MS); international studies (MLA); leadership management (MLA); literature (MLA); philosophy (MLA); writing (MLA).

Division of Education Students: 54 full-time (36 women), 46 part-time (40 women); includes 23 minority (9 African Americans, 1 Asian American or Pacific Islander, 4 Hispanic Americans, 9 Native Americans), 49 international. Average age 34. 69 applicants, 91% accepted. *Faculty:* 5 full-time (3 women), 14 part-time/adjunct (9 women). Expenses: Contact institution. *Financial support:* Fellowships with partial tuition reimbursements, career-related internships or fieldwork, Federal Work-Study, institutionally sponsored loans, and tuition waivers (full and partial) available. Support available to part-time students. Financial award application deadline: 8/1; financial award applicants required to submit FAFSA. In 2001, 41 degrees awarded. *Degree program information:* Part-time and evening/weekend programs available. Offers curriculum and instruction (M Ed); early childhood education (M Ed); education (M Ed, MA); elementary education (M Ed); teaching English as a second language (MA). *Application deadline:* For fall admission, 8/25 (priority date); for spring admission, 1/15. Applications are processed on a rolling basis. *Application fee:* $35 ($70 for international students). *Application Contact:* Stacy Messinger, Assistant Director of Admissions, 800-633-7242 Ext. 4, Fax: 405-521-5356, E-mail: gadmissions@okcu.edu. *Director,* Dr. Donna C. Richardson, 405-521-5371.

Division of Mathematics and Science *Degree program information:* Part-time and evening/weekend programs available. Offers computer science (MS).

Division of Social Sciences *Degree program information:* Part-time and evening/weekend programs available. Offers criminal justice administration (MCJA).

Division of Theatre *Degree program information:* Part-time programs available. Offers costume design (MA); technical theatre (MA); theatre (MA); theatre for young audiences (MA).

School of Law *Degree program information:* Part-time and evening/weekend programs available. Offers law (JD).

School of Music *Degree program information:* Part-time programs available. Offers music composition (MM); musical theatre (MM); opera performance (MM); performance (MM).

School of Religion and Church Vocations Students: 1 full-time (0 women), 8 part-time (5 women). Average age 34. 7 applicants, 100% accepted. *Faculty:* 4 full-time (2 women), 5

Oklahoma City University (continued)

part-time/adjunct (2 women). Expenses: Contact institution. *Financial support:* Fellowships with partial tuition reimbursements, career-related internships or fieldwork, Federal Work-Study, institutionally sponsored loans, and tuition waivers (partial) available. Support available to part-time students. Financial award applicants required to submit FAFSA. In 2001, 2 degrees awarded. *Degree program information:* Part-time and evening/weekend programs available. Offers church business management (MAR); religious education (M Rel); religious studies (MAR). *Application deadline:* For fall admission, 8/20 (priority date); for spring admission, 1/9. Applications are processed on a rolling basis. *Application fee:* $35 ($70 for international students). *Application Contact:* Stacy Messinger, Assistant Director of Admissions, 800-633-7242 Ext. 4, Fax: 405-521-5356, E-mail: gadmissions@okcu.edu. *Dean,* Dr. Donald Emler, 405-521-5284, E-mail: dgemler@okcu.edu.

OKLAHOMA STATE UNIVERSITY, Stillwater, OK 74078

General Information State-supported, coed, university. CGS member. *Enrollment:* 1,892 full-time matriculated graduate/professional students (815 women), 2,250 part-time matriculated graduate/professional students (997 women). *Enrollment by degree level:* 289 first professional, 2,649 master's, 1,204 doctoral. *Graduate faculty:* 977 full-time (277 women), 179 part-time/adjunct (76 women). Tuition, state resident: part-time $92 per credit hour. Tuition, nonresident: part-time $297 per credit hour. *Required fees:* $21 per credit hour. $14 per semester. One-time fee: $20. Tuition and fees vary according to course load. *Graduate housing:* Rooms and/or apartments available on a first-come, first-served basis to single and married students. Typical cost: $2,286 per year ($4,856 including board) for single students; $5,244 per year for married students. *Student services:* Campus employment opportunities, campus safety program, career counseling, disabled student services, exercise/wellness program, free psychological counseling, grant writing training, international student services, low-cost health insurance, multicultural affairs office, teacher training. *Library facilities:* Edmon Low Library plus 4 others. *Online resources:* library catalog, web page, access to other libraries' catalogs. *Collection:* 2.1 million titles, 35,698 serial subscriptions, 6,529 audiovisual materials. *Research affiliation:* Howard Hughes Foundation, Kellogg Foundation, Seagate Technology, Noble Research Foundation, American Heart Association, Phillips Petroleum Company.

Computer facilities: 2,000 computers available on campus for general student use. A campuswide network can be accessed from student residence rooms and from off campus. Internet access and online class registration are available. *Web address:* http://www.okstate.edu/.

General Application Contact: Dr. Timothy J Pettibone, Interim Dean, 405-744-6368, Fax: 405-744-0355, E-mail: grad_i@okstate.edu.

GRADUATE UNITS

College of Veterinary Medicine Students: 323 full-time (191 women), 3 part-time (1 woman). Average age 27. *Faculty:* 158 full-time (42 women), 5 part-time/adjunct (2 women). Expenses: Contact institution. *Financial support:* Fellowships, research assistantships, teaching assistantships, career-related internships or fieldwork, Federal Work-Study, and tuition waivers (partial) available. Support available to part-time students. Financial award application deadline: 3/1; financial award applicants required to submit FAFSA. In 2001, 76 first professional degrees, 1 master's, 7 doctorates awarded. Postbaccalaureate distance learning degree programs offered. Offers veterinary biomedical sciences (MS, PhD); veterinary medicine (DVM, MS, PhD). *Application deadline:* Applications are processed on a rolling basis. *Application Contact:* Pat Stormont, Coordinator, 405-744-6653, Fax: 405-744-6633. *Dean,* Dr. Joseph W. Alexander, 405-744-6648.

Graduate College Students: 1,892 full-time (815 women), 2,250 part-time (997 women); includes 462 minority (120 African Americans, 81 Asian Americans or Pacific Islanders, 69 Hispanic Americans, 192 Native Americans), 1,122 international. Average age 32. *Faculty:* 977 full-time (277 women), 179 part-time/adjunct (76 women). Expenses: Contact institution. *Financial support:* Fellowships, research assistantships, teaching assistantships, career-related internships or fieldwork, Federal Work-Study, and tuition waivers (full and partial) available. Support available to part-time students. Financial award application deadline: 3/1. *Degree program information:* Part-time programs available. Offers environmental sciences (MS, PhD); international studies (MS); natural and applied science (MS). *Application fee:* $25. *Application Contact:* Dr. Craig Satterfield, Director of Student Services. *Interim Dean,* Dr. Timothy J Pettibone, 405-744-6368, Fax: 405-744-0355, E-mail: grad_i@okstate.edu.

College of Agricultural Sciences and Natural Resources Students: 144 full-time (50 women), 177 part-time (71 women); includes 22 minority (4 African Americans, 6 Hispanic Americans, 12 Native Americans), 118 international. Average age 30. 217 applicants, 58% accepted. *Faculty:* 239 full-time (36 women), 9 part-time/adjunct (0 women). Expenses: Contact institution. *Financial support:* In 2001–02, 245 students received support, including 234 research assistantships (averaging $13,268 per year), 18 teaching assistantships (averaging $11,300 per year); fellowships, career-related internships or fieldwork, Federal Work-Study, and tuition waivers (partial) also available. Support available to part-time students. Financial award application deadline: 3/1. In 2001, 67 master's, 29 doctorates awarded. *Degree program information:* Part-time programs available. Offers agricultural economics (M Ag, MS, PhD); agricultural education, communication and 4H (M Ag, MS, Ed D, PhD); agricultural sciences and natural resources (M Ag, M Bio E, MS, Ed D, PhD); agronomy (M Ag, MS, PhD); animal breeding (PhD); animal nutrition (PhD); animal sciences (M Ag, MS); biochemistry and molecular biology (MS, PhD); biosystems and agricultural engineering (M Bio E, MS, PhD); crop science (PhD); entomology (MS, PhD); food science (MS, PhD); forestry (M Ag, MS); horticulture and landscape architecture (M Ag, MS); plant pathology (M Ag, MS, PhD); plant science (PhD); soil science (PhD). *Application fee:* $25. *Dean,* Dr. Samuel E. Curl, 405-744-5398, Fax: 405-744-5339, E-mail: securl@okstate.edu.

College of Arts and Sciences Students: 331 full-time (138 women), 511 part-time (223 women); includes 103 minority (19 African Americans, 26 Asian Americans or Pacific Islanders, 14 Hispanic Americans, 44 Native Americans), 264 international. Average age 31. 740 applicants, 61% accepted. *Faculty:* 417 full-time (117 women), 63 part-time/adjunct (31 women). Expenses: Contact institution. *Financial support:* In 2001–02, 489 students received support, including 179 research assistantships (averaging $14,083 per year), 320 teaching assistantships (averaging $11,408 per year); fellowships, career-related internships or fieldwork, Federal Work-Study, and tuition waivers (full and partial) also available. Support available to part-time students. Financial award application deadline: 3/1. In 2001, 145 master's, 37 doctorates awarded. Offers applied mathematics (MS); arts and sciences (MA, MM, MS, Ed D, PhD); botany (MS, PhD); chemistry (MS, PhD); clinical psychology (PhD); communications sciences and disorders (MA); computer education (Ed D); computer science (MS, PhD); corrections (MS); English (MA, PhD); experimental psychology (PhD); fire protection and safety (MS); general psychology (MS); geography (MS); geology (MS); history (MA, PhD); mass communication (MS, Ed D); mathematics (MS, Ed D, PhD); microbiology and molecular genetics (MS, PhD); music pedagogy (MM); philosophy (MA, PhD); physics (MS, PhD); political science (MA); sociology (MS, PhD); statistics (MS, PhD); theatre (MA); wildlife and fisheries ecology (MS, PhD); zoology (MS, PhD). *Application fee:* $25. *Dean,* Dr. John M. Dobson, 405-744-5663, Fax: 405-744-7074, E-mail: jdobson@okstate.edu.

College of Business Administration Students: 241 full-time (100 women), 242 part-time (80 women); includes 39 minority (8 African Americans, 15 Asian Americans or Pacific Islanders, 3 Hispanic Americans, 13 Native Americans), 111 international. Average age 30. 369 applicants, 72% accepted. *Faculty:* 101 full-time (18 women), 12 part-time/adjunct (2 women). Expenses: Contact institution. *Financial support:* In 2001–02, 50 research assistantships (averaging $11,800 per year), 109 teaching assistantships (averaging $5,305 per year) were awarded. Career-related internships or fieldwork, Federal Work-Study, and tuition waivers (partial) also available. Support available to part-time students. Financial award application deadline: 3/1. In 2001, 141 master's, 20 doctorates awarded. Offers accounting (MS, PhD); business administration (MBA, MS, PhD); economics and legal studies in business (MS, PhD); finance (MBA, PhD); management (MBA, MS, PhD); management science and information systems (MBA); marketing (MBA, PhD); telecommunications management (MS). *Application deadline:* For fall admission, 7/1 (priority date). *Application fee:* $25. *Dean,* Dr. James Lumpkin, 405-744-5064.

College of Education Students: 260 full-time (173 women), 592 part-time (377 women); includes 117 minority (59 African Americans, 10 Asian Americans or Pacific Islanders, 17 Hispanic Americans, 31 Native Americans), 45 international. Average age 37. 291 applicants, 84% accepted. *Faculty:* 101 full-time (58 women), 47 part-time/adjunct (22 women). Expenses: Contact institution. *Financial support:* In 2001–02, 107 research assistantships (averaging $8,073 per year), 13 teaching assistantships (averaging $7,490 per year) were awarded. Career-related internships or fieldwork, Federal Work-Study, and tuition waivers (partial) also available. Support available to part-time students. Financial award application deadline: 3/1. In 2001, 155 master's, 82 doctorates awarded. Offers applied behavioral studies (MS, Ed D, PhD); counseling and student personnel (MS, PhD); curriculum and educational leadership (MS, PhD); education (MS, Ed D, PhD, Ed S); educational administration (MS, Ed S); educational psychology (PhD); health (MS, Ed D); higher education (MS, Ed D); leisure sciences (MS, Ed D); physical education (MS, Ed D); physical education and leisure sciences (Ed D); technical education (MS, Ed D, Ed S); trade and industrial education (MS, Ed D, Ed S). *Application deadline:* For fall admission, 7/1 (priority date). *Application fee:* $25. *Dean,* Dr. Ann C. Candler-Lotven, 405-744-6350.

College of Engineering, Architecture and Technology Students: 368 full-time (52 women), 341 part-time (43 women); includes 42 minority (9 African Americans, 12 Asian Americans or Pacific Islanders, 10 Hispanic Americans, 11 Native Americans), 415 international. Average age 29. 1,158 applicants, 66% accepted. *Faculty:* 123 full-time (5 women), 14 part-time/adjunct (0 women). Expenses: Contact institution. *Financial support:* In 2001–02, 260 students received support, including 148 research assistantships (averaging $10,566 per year), 110 teaching assistantships (averaging $6,869 per year); fellowships, career-related internships or fieldwork, Federal Work-Study, and tuition waivers (partial) also available. Support available to part-time students. Financial award application deadline:3/1. In 2001, 137 master's, 19 doctorates awarded. Offers architectural engineering (M Arch E); architecture (M Arch, M Arch E); biophotonics (MS, PhD); chemical engineering (M En, MS, PhD); civil engineering (M En, MS, PhD); electrical and computer engineering (M En, MS, PhD); engineering, architecture and technology (M Arch, M Arch E, M Bio E, M En, M Gen E, MIE Mgmt, MS, PhD); environmental engineering (M En, MS, PhD); industrial engineering and management (M En, MIE Mgmt, MS, PhD); manufacturing systems engineering (M En); mechanical engineering (M En, MS, PhD). *Application deadline:* For fall admission, 7/1 (priority date). *Application fee:* $25. *Dean,* Dr. Karl N. Reid, 405-744-5140.

College of Human Environmental Sciences Students: 95 full-time (71 women), 109 part-time (90 women); includes 22 minority (9 African Americans, 3 Asian Americans or Pacific Islanders, 10 Native Americans), 48 international. Average age 32. 96 applicants, 92% accepted. *Faculty:* 47 full-time (34 women), 3 part-time/adjunct (2 women). Expenses: Contact institution. *Financial support:* In 2001–02, 83 students received support, including 58 research assistantships (averaging $8,770 per year), 15 teaching assistantships (averaging $7,332 per year); career-related internships or fieldwork, Federal Work-Study, and tuition waivers (partial) also available. Support available to part-time students. Financial award application deadline: 3/1. In 2001, 27 master's, 8 doctorates awarded. Offers design, housing and merchandising (MS, PhD); design, housing, and merchandising (PhD); family relations and child development (MS, PhD); hotel and restaurant administration (MS, PhD); human environmental sciences (MS, PhD); nutritional sciences (MS, PhD). *Application deadline:* For fall admission, 7/1 (priority date). *Application fee:* $25. *Dean,* Dr. Patricia Knaub, 405-744-5053.

See in-depth description on page 1015.

OKLAHOMA STATE UNIVERSITY CENTER FOR HEALTH SCIENCES, Tulsa, OK 74107-1898

General Information State-supported, coed, graduate-only institution. *Enrollment by degree level:* 345 first professional, 10 master's, 14 doctoral. *Graduate faculty:* 64 full-time (13 women), 273 part-time/adjunct (59 women). Tuition, state resident: full-time $10,507; part-time $92 per credit hour. Tuition, nonresident: full-time $26,669; part-time $297 per credit hour. *Graduate housing:* On-campus housing not available. *Student services:* Campus safety program, career counseling, disabled student services, free psychological counseling, low-cost health insurance. *Library facilities:* Oklahoma State University Medical Library plus 1 other. *Online resources:* library catalog, web page, access to other libraries' catalogs. *Collection:* 54,770 titles, 515 serial subscriptions, 126,254 audiovisual materials. *Research affiliation:* Sun River, Inc. (cognitive rehabilitation), Merck and Company (pharmaceutical sciences), Viropharma (pharmaceutical sciences), Ingenex (pharmaceutical sciences), Serono Laboratories (pharmaceutical sciences), Cook Urological, Inc. (pharmaceutical sciences).

Computer facilities: 66 computers available on campus for general student use. A campuswide network can be accessed from off campus. Internet access is available. *Web address:* http://osu.com.okstate.edu/.

General Application Contact: Michele Bartlett, Assistant Registrar, 918-582-1972, Fax: 918-561-8243, E-mail: bartlem@chs.okstate.edu.

GRADUATE UNITS

College of Osteopathic Medicine Offers osteopathic medicine (DO).

Program in Biomedical Sciences Offers biomedical sciences (PhD). Electronic applications accepted.

OLD DOMINION UNIVERSITY, Norfolk, VA 23529

General Information State-supported, coed, university. CGS member. *Enrollment:* 1,280 full-time matriculated graduate/professional students (683 women), 2,324 part-time matriculated graduate/professional students (1,243 women). *Enrollment by degree level:* 3,002 master's, 571 doctoral, 31 other advanced degrees. *Graduate faculty:* 603 full-time (206 women), 331 part-time/adjunct (176 women). Tuition, state resident: part-time $202 per credit. Tuition, nonresident: part-time $534 per credit. *Required fees:* $76 per semester. *Graduate housing:* Room and/or apartments available to single students; on-campus housing not available to married students. Typical cost: $3,102 per year ($5,364 including board). Housing application deadline: 5/1. *Student services:* Campus employment opportunities, campus safety program, career counseling, disabled student services, free psychological counseling, grant writing training, international student services, low-cost health insurance, multicultural affairs office, teacher training. *Library facilities:* Douglas and Patricia Perry Library plus 2 others. *Online resources:* library catalog, web page, access to other libraries' catalogs. *Collection:* 585,396 titles, 7,985 serial subscriptions, 39,050 audiovisual materials. *Research affiliation:* Virginia Center for Innovative Technology (technology development), Life Net (biological materials for transplantation), Thomas Jefferson National Accelerator Facility (high energy physics and laser processing), Virginia Space Grant Consortium (aerospace education and research), NASA–Langley Research Center (aerodynamic testing and evaluation), Virginia Modeling Analysis and Simulation Center (applied research in modeling and simulation).

Computer facilities: 790 computers available on campus for general student use. A campuswide network can be accessed from student residence rooms and from off campus. Internet access and online class registration, on-line courses are available. *Web address:* http://www.odu.edu/.

General Application Contact: Alice McAdory, Director of Admissions, 757-683-3685, Fax: 757-683-3255, E-mail: admit@odu.edu.

GRADUATE UNITS

College of Arts and Letters Students: 90 full-time (52 women), 148 part-time (78 women); includes 34 minority (24 African Americans, 4 Asian Americans or Pacific Islanders, 6 Hispanic Americans), 25 international. Average age 34. 225 applicants, 89% accepted. *Faculty:* 149 full-time (63 women), 87 part-time/adjunct (50 women). Expenses: Contact institution. *Financial support:* In 2001–02, 211 students received support, including 3 fellowships (averaging $3,500 per year), 45 research assistantships with tuition reimbursements available (averaging $8,500 per year), 28 teaching assistantships with partial tuition reimbursements available (averaging $8,500 per year); career-related internships or fieldwork, institutionally sponsored loans, scholarships/grants, and tuition waivers (partial) also available. Support available to part-time students. Financial award application deadline: 2/15; financial award applicants required to submit CSS PROFILE or FAFSA. In 2001, 87 master's, 5 doctorates awarded. *Degree program information:* Part-time and evening/weekend programs available. Offers applied linguistics (MA); applied sociology (MA); arts and letters (MA, MFA, PhD); creative writing (MFA); English (MA); history (MA); humanities (MA); international studies (MA, PhD); visual studies (MA, MFA). *Application fee:* $30. Electronic applications accepted. *Interim Dean,* Dr. Janet Katz, 757-683-3925, Fax: 757-683-5746, E-mail: jkatz@odu.edu.

College of Business and Public Administration Students: 206 full-time (98 women), 490 part-time (228 women); includes 107 minority (76 African Americans, 12 Asian Americans or Pacific Islanders, 15 Hispanic Americans, 4 Native Americans), 169 international. Average age 33. 570 applicants, 88% accepted. *Faculty:* 86 full-time (26 women), 24 part-time/adjunct (8 women). Expenses: Contact institution. *Financial support:* In 2001–02, 230 students received support, including 5 fellowships (averaging $4,896 per year), 53 research assistantships with tuition reimbursements available (averaging $7,130 per year), 7 teaching assistantships with tuition reimbursements available (averaging $8,322 per year); career-related internships or fieldwork, scholarships/grants, and tuition waivers (partial) also available. Support available to part-time students. Financial award application deadline: 2/15; financial award applicants required to submit FAFSA. In 2001, 208 master's, 8 doctorates awarded. *Degree program information:* Part-time and evening/weekend programs available. Postbaccalaureate distance learning degree programs offered (no on-campus study). Offers accounting (MS); business administration (MBA, PhD); business and public administration (MA, MBA, MPA, MS, MTX, MUS, PhD); e-commerce systems (MS); economics (MA); policy analysis/program evaluation (MUS); public administration (MPA); public planning analysis (MUS); taxation (MTX); urban administration (MUS); urban services/urban management (PhD). *Application fee:* $30. Electronic applications accepted. *Application Contact:* Dr. Ali Ardalan, Associate Dean, 757-683-3520, Fax: 757-683-4076, E-mail: aardalan@odu.edu. *Interim Dean,* Dr. Bruce Rubin, 757-683-3520, Fax: 757-683-4076, E-mail: mbainfo@odu.edu.

College of Engineering and Technology Students: 217 full-time (40 women), 335 part-time (59 women); includes 73 minority (34 African Americans, 30 Asian Americans or Pacific Islanders, 8 Hispanic Americans, 1 Native American), 245 international. Average age 30. 468 applicants, 87% accepted. *Faculty:* 88 full-time (7 women), 28 part-time/adjunct (8 women). Expenses: Contact institution. *Financial support:* In 2001–02, 186 students received support, including 6 fellowships with full and partial tuition reimbursements available (averaging $9,000 per year), 140 research assistantships with full and partial tuition reimbursements available (averaging $12,100 per year), 20 teaching assistantships with full and partial tuition reimbursements available (averaging $9,000 per year); career-related internships or fieldwork, Federal Work-Study, institutionally sponsored loans, scholarships/grants, tuition waivers (partial), and unspecified assistantships also available. Support available to part-time students. Financial award applicants required to submit FAFSA. In 2001, 106 master's, 12 doctorates awarded. *Degree program information:* Part-time and evening/weekend programs available. Postbaccalaureate distance learning degree programs offered. Offers aerospace engineering (ME, MS, PhD); aerospace engineering mechanics (ME, MS, PhD); computer engineering (ME, MS); design manufacturing (ME); electrical engineering (ME, MS); electrical engineering and computer engineering (PhD); engineering (ME, MS, PhD); engineering and technology (ME, MEM, MS, PhD); engineering management (MEM, MS, PhD); engineering mechanics (ME, MS, PhD); environmental engineering (ME, MS, PhD); global engineering (ME); materials science and engineering (ME, MS); mechanical engineering (ME, MS, PhD); modeling and simulation (ME, MS, PhD); operations research and systems analysis (ME). *Application deadline:* Applications are processed on a rolling basis. *Application fee:* $30. Electronic applications accepted. *Application Contact:* Dr. Oktay Baysal, Associate Dean, 757-683-3789, Fax: 757-683-4898, E-mail: obaysal@odu.edu. *Dean,* Dr. William Swart, 757-683-3787, Fax: 757-683-4898, E-mail: wswart@odu.edu.

College of Health Sciences Students: 172 full-time (121 women), 146 part-time (123 women); includes 56 minority (38 African Americans, 11 Asian Americans or Pacific Islanders, 5 Hispanic Americans, 2 Native Americans), 9 international. Average age 35. 485 applicants, 53% accepted. *Faculty:* 49 full-time (39 women), 17 part-time/adjunct (12 women). Expenses: Contact institution. *Financial support:* In 2001–02, 220 students received support, including 12 research assistantships with tuition reimbursements available (averaging $5,000 per year), 3 teaching assistantships with tuition reimbursements available (averaging $4,000 per year); fellowships, career-related internships or fieldwork, scholarships/grants, tuition waivers (partial), and unspecified assistantships also available. Support available to part-time students. Financial award application deadline: 2/15; financial award applicants required to submit FAFSA. In 2001, 142 master's, 3 doctorates awarded. *Degree program information:* Part-time programs available. Postbaccalaureate distance learning degree programs offered (no on-campus study). Offers community health professions (MS); environmental health (MS); health care administration (MS); health sciences (MPH, MS, MSN, DPT, PhD); nursing (MSN); physical therapy (DPT); public health (MPH); urban services/urban health services (PhD); wellness and promotion (MS). *Application deadline:* Applications are processed on a rolling basis. *Application fee:* $30. Electronic applications accepted. *Dean,* Dr. Cheryl T. Samuels, 757-683-4960, Fax: 757-683-5674, E-mail: csamuels@odu.edu.

Program in Dental Hygiene Students: 3 full-time (all women), 7 part-time (all women); includes 3 minority (2 African Americans, 1 Native American), 2 international. Average age 34. 9 applicants, 78% accepted, 6 enrolled. *Faculty:* 9 full-time (8 women). Expenses: Contact institution. *Financial support:* In 2001–02, 3 students received support, including 1 fellowship (averaging $5,000 per year), 2 teaching assistantships with tuition reimbursements available (averaging $6,000 per year); career-related internships or fieldwork, scholarships/grants, tuition waivers (partial), and unspecified assistantships also available. Support available to part-time students. Financial award application deadline: 2/15; financial award applicants required to submit CSS PROFILE or FAFSA. In 2001, 1 degree awarded. *Degree program information:* Part-time programs available. Offers dental hygiene (MS). *Application deadline:* For fall admission, 7/1; for spring admission, 12/1. Applications are processed on a rolling basis. *Application fee:* $30. Electronic applications accepted. *Graduate Program Director,* Prof. Michele L. Darby, 757-683-5232, Fax: 757-683-5329, E-mail: dnthgpd@odu.edu or mdarby@odu.edu.

College of Sciences Students: 311 full-time (127 women), 227 part-time (95 women); includes 50 minority (23 African Americans, 14 Asian Americans or Pacific Islanders, 9 Hispanic Americans, 4 Native Americans), 241 international. Average age 29. 592 applicants, 51% accepted. *Faculty:* 159 full-time (38 women), 23 part-time/adjunct (16 women). Expenses: Contact institution. *Financial support:* In 2001–02, 3 fellowships (averaging $5,057 per year), 158 research assistantships with tuition reimbursements (averaging $9,532 per year), 101 teaching assistantships with tuition reimbursements (averaging $8,819 per year) were awarded. Career-related internships or fieldwork, scholarships/grants, and tuition waivers (partial) also available. Support available to part-time students. Financial award application deadline: 2/15; financial award applicants required to submit FAFSA. In 2001, 86 master's, 32 doctorates awarded. *Degree program information:* Part-time and evening/weekend programs available. Offers analytical chemistry (MS); biochemistry (MS); biology (MS); biomedical sciences (PhD); clinical chemistry (MS); clinical psychology (Psy D); computational and applied mathematics (MS, PhD); computer science (MS, PhD); ecological sciences (PhD); environmental chemistry (MS); geology (MS); industrial/organizational psychology (PhD); oceanography (MS, PhD); organic chemistry (MS); physical chemistry (MS); physics (MS, PhD); psychology (MS); sciences (MS, PhD, Psy D). *Application fee:* $30. Electronic applications accepted. *Application Contact:* Dr. Joseph H. Rule, Associate Dean, 757-683-4418, Fax: 757-683-3034, E-mail: jrule@odu.edu. *Dean,* Dr. Thomas L. Isenhour, 757-683-3274, Fax: 757-683-3034, E-mail: tisenhou@odu.edu.

Darden College of Education Students: 356 full-time (272 women), 950 part-time (657 women); includes 268 minority (207 African Americans, 21 Asian Americans or Pacific Islanders, 27 Hispanic Americans, 13 Native Americans), 24 international. Average age 35. 1,125 applicants, 72% accepted. *Faculty:* 81 full-time (35 women), 83 part-time/adjunct (46 women). Expenses: Contact institution. *Financial support:* In 2001–02, 4 fellowships (averaging $2,840 per year), 60 research assistantships with tuition reimbursements (averaging $6,674 per year), 25 teaching assistantships with tuition reimbursements (averaging $5,263 per year) were awarded. Career-related internships or fieldwork, Federal Work-Study, institutionally sponsored loans, scholarships/grants, and tuition waivers (partial) also available. Support available to part-time students. Financial award application deadline: 2/15; financial award applicants required to submit CSS PROFILE or FAFSA. In 2001, 647 master's, 6 doctorates, 4 other advanced degrees awarded. *Degree program information:* Part-time and evening/weekend programs available. Postbaccalaureate distance learning degree programs offered (no on-campus study). Offers administration (MS Ed); athletic training (MS Ed); biology (MS Ed); business and industry training (MS); chemistry (MS Ed); community agency counseling (MS Ed); community college teaching (MS); counseling (Ed S); curriculum and instruction (MS Ed); early childhood education (MS Ed); education (MS, MS Ed, PhD, Ed S); educational administration (Ed S); educational media (MS Ed); educational training (MS Ed); elementary education (MS Ed); English (MS Ed); exercise science and wellness (MS Ed); higher education (MS Ed, Ed S); instructional technology (MS Ed); library science (MS Ed); mathematics (MS Ed); middle and secondary teaching (MS); middle school education (MS Ed); physical education (MS Ed); principal preparation (MS Ed); reading education (MS Ed); recreation administration (MS Ed); school counseling (MS Ed); secondary education (MS Ed); social studies (MS Ed); special education (MS Ed); speech-language pathology (MS Ed); sports management (MS Ed); student development counseling in higher education (MS Ed); urban services/urban education concentration (PhD). *Application fee:* $30. Electronic applications accepted. *Dean,* Dr. William H. Graves, 757-683-3928, Fax: 757-683-5406, E-mail: wgraves@odu.edu.

See in-depth description on page 1017.

OLIVET COLLEGE, Olivet, MI 49076-9701

General Information Independent-religious, coed, comprehensive institution.

GRADUATE UNITS

Program in Education Offers education (MAT). Electronic applications accepted.

OLIVET NAZARENE UNIVERSITY, Bourbonnais, IL 60914-2271

General Information Independent-religious, coed, comprehensive institution. *Graduate housing:* Room and/or apartments available to single students; on-campus housing not available to married students. Housing application deadline: 8/15.

GRADUATE UNITS

Graduate School *Degree program information:* Part-time and evening/weekend programs available. Offers business administration (MBA); practical ministries (MPM).

Division of Education *Degree program information:* Evening/weekend programs available. Offers curriculum and instruction (MAE); elementary education (MAT); secondary education (MAT).

Division of Religion and Philosophy *Degree program information:* Part-time programs available. Offers biblical literature (MA); religion (MA); theology (MA).

Institute for Church Management *Degree program information:* Part-time programs available. Offers church management (MCM); pastoral counseling (MPC).

ORAL ROBERTS UNIVERSITY, Tulsa, OK 74171-0001

General Information Independent-religious, coed, comprehensive institution. *Enrollment:* 285 full-time matriculated graduate/professional students (114 women), 360 part-time matriculated graduate/professional students (204 women). *Enrollment by degree level:* 167 first professional, 282 master's, 196 doctoral. *Graduate faculty:* 33 full-time (5 women), 20 part-time/adjunct (5 women). *Tuition:* Full-time $6,288; part-time $262 per credit. *Required fees:* $360; $90 per term. Tuition and fees vary according to program. *Graduate housing:* Room and/or apartments available on a first-come, first-served basis to single students; on-campus housing not available to married students. Typical cost: $5,228 (including board). *Student services:* Campus employment opportunities, career counseling, disabled student services, exercise/wellness program, free psychological counseling, international student services, low-cost health insurance, teacher training. *Library facilities:* John D. Messick Resources Center plus 1 other. *Online resources:* library catalog, web page, access to other libraries' catalogs. *Collection:* 210,625 titles, 5,613 serial subscriptions, 23,149 audiovisual materials.

Computer facilities: 253 computers available on campus for general student use. A campuswide network can be accessed from student residence rooms and from off campus. Internet access is available. *Web address:* http://www.oru.edu/.

General Application Contact: 918-495-6236, Fax: 918-495-7965, E-mail: alsc@oru.edu.

GRADUATE UNITS

School of Business Students: 19 full-time (7 women), 31 part-time (20 women); includes 14 minority (13 African Americans, 1 Hispanic American), 10 international. 31 applicants, 90% accepted, 22 enrolled. *Faculty:* 7 full-time (1 woman), 3 part-time/adjunct (0 women). Expenses: Contact institution. *Financial support:* Scholarships/grants and unspecified assistantships available. Financial award application deadline: 6/1; financial award applicants required to submit FAFSA. In 2001, 20 degrees awarded. *Degree program information:* Part-time and evening/weekend programs available. Postbaccalaureate distance learning degree programs offered (minimal on-campus study). Offers accounting (MBA); finance (MBA); human resource management (M Man); international business (MBA); management (MBA); marketing (MBA); nonprofit organization (M Man). *Application deadline:* For fall admission, 7/1 (priority date); for spring admission, 12/1 (priority date). Applications are processed on a rolling basis. *Application fee:* $35. *Application Contact:* 918-495-6236, Fax: 918-495-7965, E-mail: alsc@oru.edu. *Dean,* Dr. David Dyson, 918-495-7040, Fax: 918-495-7316, E-mail: ddyson@oru.edu.

School of Education Students: 23 full-time (13 women), 207 part-time (139 women); includes 61 minority (48 African Americans, 1 Asian American or Pacific Islander, 10 Hispanic Americans, 2 Native Americans), 32 international. 140 applicants, 88% accepted, 118 enrolled. *Faculty:* 9 full-time (1 woman), 9 part-time/adjunct (4 women). Expenses: Contact institution. *Financial support:* Scholarships/grants and unspecified assistantships available. Financial award application deadline: 6/1; financial award applicants required to submit FAFSA. In 2001, 29 master's, 3 doctorates awarded. *Degree program information:* Part-time and evening/weekend programs available. Postbaccalaureate distance learning degree programs offered (minimal on-campus study). Offers Christian school administration (Ed D); Christian school administration (K-12) (MA Ed); Christian school administration (post-secondary) (MA Ed, Ed D); curriculum and instruction (MA Ed); early childhood education (MA Ed); public school administration (MA Ed); public school administration (K-12) (Ed D); public school teaching (MA Ed); teaching English as a second language (MA Ed). *Application deadline:* For fall admission, 7/1 (priority date); for spring admission, 12/1 (priority date). Applications are processed on a rolling basis. *Application fee:* $35. *Application Contact:* 918-495-6236, Fax: 918-495-7965, E-mail: alsc@oru.edu. *Dean,* Dr. David Hand, 918-495-7084, Fax: 918-495-6050, E-mail: dhand@oru.edu.

School of Theology and Missions Students: 243 full-time (94 women), 153 part-time (76 women); includes 144 minority (112 African Americans, 19 Asian Americans or Pacific Islanders, 12 Hispanic Americans, 1 Native American), 81 international. 200 applicants, 89% accepted, 127 enrolled. *Faculty:* 18 full-time (3 women), 8 part-time/adjunct (1 woman). Expenses: Contact institution. *Financial support:* In 2001–02, 18 teaching assistantships (averaging $3,600 per year) were awarded; scholarships/grants and employment assistantships also available. Financial award application deadline: 6/1; financial award applicants required to submit FAFSA. In 2001, 28 first professional degrees, 38 master's, 20 doctorates awarded. *Degree program information:* Part-time programs available. Postbaccalaureate distance learning degree programs offered (minimal on-campus study). Offers biblical literature (MA); Christian counseling (MA); Christian education (MA); divinity (M Div); missions (MA); practical theology (MA); theological/historical studies (MA); theology (D Min). *Application deadline:* For fall admission, 7/1 (priority date); for spring admission, 12/1 (priority date). Applications are processed on a rolling basis. *Application fee:* $35. *Application Contact:* 918-495-6236, Fax: 918-495-7965, E-mail: alsc@oru.edu. *Dean,* Dr. Thompson K. Mathew, 918-495-7016, Fax: 918-495-6259, E-mail: tmathew@oru.edu.

OREGON COLLEGE OF ORIENTAL MEDICINE, Portland, OR 97216

General Information Independent, coed, graduate-only institution. *Enrollment by degree level:* 201 master's. *Graduate faculty:* 11 full-time (5 women), 32 part-time/adjunct (20 women). *Tuition:* Full-time $9,858; part-time $5,872 per year. *Required fees:* $90; $10 per term. One-time fee: $50 full-time. *Graduate housing:* On-campus housing not available. *Student services:* Campus employment opportunities, campus safety program, low-cost health insurance, teacher training. *Library facilities:* Oregon College of Oriental Medicine Library. *Online resources:* library catalog, access to other libraries' catalogs. *Collection:* 1,375 titles, 65 serial subscriptions, 602 audiovisual materials.

Computer facilities: 2 computers available on campus for general student use. A campuswide network can be accessed. Internet access is available. *Web address:* http://www.ocom.edu/.

General Application Contact: Linda Powell, Admissions and Financial Aid Officer, 503-253-3443 Ext. 113, Fax: 503-253-2701, E-mail: lpowell@ocom.edu.

GRADUATE UNITS

Graduate Program in Acupuncture and Oriental Medicine Students: 154 full-time (109 women), 47 part-time (32 women); includes 23 minority (3 African Americans, 17 Asian Americans or Pacific Islanders, 1 Hispanic American, 2 Native Americans), 5 international. Average age 36. 118 applicants, 79% accepted, 71 enrolled. *Faculty:* 11 full-time (5 women), 32 part-time/adjunct (20 women). Expenses: Contact institution. *Financial support:* In 2001–02, 198 students received support. Federal Work-Study available. Support available to part-time students. Financial award applicants required to submit FAFSA. In 2001, 58 degrees awarded. *Degree program information:* Part-time programs available. Offers acupuncture and Oriental medicine (M Ac OM). *Application deadline:* For fall admission, 7/1 (priority date). Applications are processed on a rolling basis. *Application fee:* $50. *Application Contact:* Linda Powell, Admissions and Financial Aid Officer, 503-253-3443 Ext. 113, Fax: 503-253-2701, E-mail: lpowell@ocom.edu. *President*, Dr. Elizabeth A. Goldblatt, 503-253-3443 Ext. 111, Fax: 503-253-2701.

OREGON HEALTH & SCIENCE UNIVERSITY, Portland, OR 97239-3098

General Information State-related, coed, upper-level institution. *Graduate housing:* Room and/or apartments available to single students; on-campus housing not available to married students. *Research affiliation:* Oregon Regional Primate Research Center.

GRADUATE UNITS

School of Dentistry Offers dental materials (MS); dentistry (DMD, MS, Certificate); endodontics (MS, Certificate); oral molecular biology (MS); oral pathology (Certificate); orthodontics (MS, Certificate); periodontology (MS, Certificate). Electronic applications accepted.

School of Medicine *Degree program information:* Part-time programs available. Offers epidemiology and biostatistics (MPH); integrative biomedical sciences (PhD); medicine (MD, MPH, MS, PhD, Certificate).

Graduate Programs in Medicine *Degree program information:* Part-time programs available. Offers behavioral neuroscience (MS, PhD); biochemistry and molecular biology (PhD); cell and developmental biology (PhD); medical informatics (MS, Certificate); medicine (MS, PhD, Certificate); molecular and medical genetics (PhD); molecular microbiology and immunology (PhD); neuroscience (PhD); pharmacology (PhD); physiology (PhD).

School of Nursing *Degree program information:* Part-time programs available. Offers adult health and illness nursing (MS, Post Master's Certificate); adult nurse practitioner (MS, Post Master's Certificate); community health care systems (MS, Post Master's Certificate); families in health, illness, and transition (PhD); family nurse practitioner (MS, Post Master's Certificate); geriatric nurse practitioner (Post Master's Certificate); geriatric/adult nurse practitioner (MS); gerontological nursing (MS, PhD, Post Master's Certificate); mental health nursing (MS, Post Master's Certificate); nurse midwifery (MS, Post Master's Certificate); nursing (MPH, MS, PhD, Post Master's Certificate); pediatric nurse practitioner (MS, Post Master's Certificate); public health nursing (MPH); women's health care nurse practitioner (MS, Post Master's Certificate). Electronic applications accepted.

OREGON STATE UNIVERSITY, Corvallis, OR 97331

General Information State-supported, coed, university. CGS member. *Enrollment:* 2,543 full-time matriculated graduate/professional students (1,280 women), 936 part-time matriculated graduate/professional students (552 women). *Graduate faculty:* 1,429 full-time (548 women), 40 part-time/adjunct (21 women). *Tuition, area resident:* Full-time $15,933. Tuition, state resident: full-time $28,937. *Graduate housing:* Rooms and/or apartments available on a first-come, first-served basis to single and married students. Housing application deadline: 9/10. *Student services:* Campus employment opportunities, campus safety program, career counseling, child daycare facilities, disabled student services, exercise/wellness program, free psychological counseling, international student services, low-cost health insurance, multicultural affairs office. *Library facilities:* Valley Library. *Online resources:* library catalog, web page, access to other libraries' catalogs. *Collection:* 689,119 titles, 12,254 serial subscriptions, 6,225 audiovisual materials. *Research affiliation:* Molecular Probes, Inc. (microbiology), Merck and Company, Inc. (veterinary medicine), Ciba-Geigy Company (agriculture), Teledyne Wah Chang (chemistry), Pittsburgh Plate Glass (chemical engineering), Diamond Crystal Salt Company (agriculture).

Computer facilities: 2,251 computers available on campus for general student use. A campuswide network can be accessed from student residence rooms and from off campus. *Web address:* http://oregonstate.edu.

General Application Contact: Dr. Sally K. Francis, Dean of the Graduate School, Interim, 541-737-4881, Fax: 541-737-3313, E-mail: franciss@.orst.edu.

GRADUATE UNITS

College of Pharmacy Students: 240 full-time (151 women), 5 part-time (3 women); includes 95 minority (10 African Americans, 84 Asian Americans or Pacific Islanders, 1 Hispanic American), 25 international. Average age 27. *Faculty:* 37 full-time (20 women), 3 part-time/adjunct (2 women). Expenses: Contact institution. *Financial support:* Fellowships, research assistantships, teaching assistantships, career-related internships or fieldwork, Federal Work-Study, and institutionally sponsored loans available. Support available to part-time students. Financial award application deadline: 2/1. In 2001, 2 first professional degrees, 1 master's, 9 doctorates awarded. *Degree program information:* Part-time programs available. Offers pharmacy (Pharm D, MAIS, MS, PhD). *Application deadline:* For fall admission, 3/1. Applications are processed on a rolling basis. *Application fee:* $50. *Application Contact:* 541-737-5784, Fax: 541-737-3999. *Dean*, Dr. Wayne A. Kradjan, 541-737-5785, Fax: 541-737-3999, E-mail: wayne.kradjan@orst.edu.

College of Veterinary Medicine Students: 48 full-time (37 women), 29 part-time (20 women); includes 4 minority (2 Asian Americans or Pacific Islanders, 2 Hispanic Americans), 1 international. Average age 26. *Faculty:* 36 full-time (22 women). Expenses: Contact institution. *Financial support:* Fellowships, research assistantships, Federal Work-Study, institutionally sponsored loans, and scholarships/grants available. Support available to part-time students. Financial award application deadline: 2/1. In 2001, 34 first professional degrees, 1 master's awarded. *Degree program information:* Part-time programs available. Offers comparative veterinary medicine (PhD); microbiology (MS); pathology (MS); toxicology (MS); veterinary medicine (DVM, MS, PhD). DVM admissions open only to residents of Oregon and other states participating in the Western Interstate Commission for Higher Education (WICHE). *Application deadline:* For fall admission, 11/1. *Application fee:* $50. *Application Contact:* Dr. Linda L. Blythe, Associate Dean, 541-737-6945, Fax: 541-737-4245, E-mail: linda.blythe@orst.edu. *Dean*, Dr. Howard Gelberg, 541-737-2098, Fax: 541-737-4245.

Graduate School Students: 2,255 full-time (1,092 women), 902 part-time (529 women); includes 291 minority (36 African Americans, 172 Asian Americans or Pacific Islanders, 60 Hispanic Americans, 23 Native Americans), 802 international. Average age 31. *Faculty:* 1,374 full-time (524 women), 38 part-time/adjunct (20 women). Expenses: Contact institution. *Financial support:* Fellowships, research assistantships, teaching assistantships, career-related internships or fieldwork, Federal Work-Study, institutionally sponsored loans, and unspecified assistantships available. Support available to part-time students. Financial award application deadline: 2/1. In 2001, 590 master's, 203 doctorates awarded. *Degree program information:* Part-time programs available. Offers interdisciplinary studies (MAIS); plant physiology (MS, PhD). *Application fee:* $50. *Application Contact:* Stephen F. Massott, Assistant Director of Admissions and Orientation, 541-737-4411, Fax: 541-737-2482. *Dean*, Dr. Sally K. Francis, 541-737-4881, Fax: 541-737-3313, E-mail: franciss@orst.edu.

College of Agricultural Sciences Students: 373 full-time (175 women), 36 part-time (15 women); includes 15 minority (1 African American, 7 Asian Americans or Pacific Islanders, 6 Hispanic Americans, 1 Native American), 130 international. Average age 31. *Faculty:* 213 full-time (73 women), 8 part-time/adjunct (5 women). Expenses: Contact institution. *Financial support:* Fellowships, research assistantships, teaching assistantships, career-related internships or fieldwork, Federal Work-Study, and institutionally sponsored loans available. Support available to part-time students. Financial award application deadline: 2/1. In 2001, 51 master's, 28 doctorates awarded. *Degree program information:* Part-time programs available. Offers agricultural and resource economics (M Agr, MAIS, MS, PhD); agricultural education (M Agr, MAIS, MAT, MS); agricultural sciences (M Ag, M Agr, MA, MAIS, MAT, MS, PhD); agriculture (M Agr); animal science (M Agr, MAIS, MS, PhD); botany and plant pathology (MS, PhD); crop science (M Agr, MAIS, MS, PhD); economics (MS, PhD); environmental and molecular toxicology (MS); environmental soil science (MS, PhD); fisheries science (M Agr, MAIS, MS, PhD); food science and technology (M Agr, MAIS, MS, PhD); genetics (MA, MAIS, MS, PhD); horticulture (M Ag, MAIS, MS, PhD); marine science (MS, PhD); poultry science (M Agr, MAIS, MS, PhD); rangeland resources (M Agr, MAIS, MS, PhD); soil science (M Agr, MAIS, MS, PhD); toxicology (MS, PhD); wildlife science (MAIS, MS, PhD). *Application fee:* $50. *Application Contact:* Dr. Michael J. Burke, Associate Dean, 541-737-2211, Fax: 541-737-2256, E-mail: mike.burke@orst.edu. *Dean*, Dr. Thayne R. Dutson, 541-737-2331, Fax: 541-737-4574, E-mail: thayne.dutson@orst.edu.

College of Business Students: 60 full-time (24 women), 17 part-time (4 women); includes 3 minority (1 Asian American or Pacific Islander, 2 Hispanic Americans), 20 international. Average age 30. *Faculty:* 31 full-time (2 women), 4 part-time/adjunct (0 women). Expenses: Contact institution. *Financial support:* Fellowships, teaching assistantships, career-related internships or fieldwork, Federal Work-Study, and institutionally sponsored loans available. Financial award application deadline: 2/1. In 2001, 36 degrees awarded. *Degree program information:* Part-time programs available. Offers business (MAIS, MBA, Certificate). *Application deadline:* For fall admission, 3/15. Applications are processed on a rolling basis. *Application fee:* $50. *Application Contact:* Clara Horne, Head Adviser, 541-737-3716, Fax: 541-737-4890, E-mail: horne@bus.orst.edu. *Interim Dean*, Sabah Randhawa, 541-737-0732, Fax: 541-737-3033, E-mail: sabah.randhawa@orst.edu.

College of Engineering Students: 427 full-time (85 women), 69 part-time (5 women); includes 22 minority (1 African American, 16 Asian Americans or Pacific Islanders, 4 Hispanic Americans, 1 Native American), 332 international. Average age 28. *Faculty:* 108 full-time (12 women), 2 part-time/adjunct (1 woman). Expenses: Contact institution. *Financial support:* Fellowships, research assistantships, teaching assistantships, career-related internships or fieldwork, Federal Work-Study, institutionally sponsored loans, and instructorships available. Support available to part-time students. Financial award application deadline: 3/1. In 2001, 116 master's, 16 doctorates awarded. *Degree program information:* Part-time programs available. Offers bioengineering (M Agr, MAIS, MS, PhD); chemical engineering (MAIS, MS, PhD); civil engineering (MAIS, MS, PhD); computer science (MA, MAIS, MS, PhD); electrical and computer engineering (MAIS, MS, PhD); engineering (M Agr, M Eng, M Oc E, MA, MAIS, MS, PhD); industrial engineering (MAIS, MS, PhD); manufacturing engineering (M Eng); materials science (MAIS, MS); mechanical engineering (MS, PhD); nuclear engineering (MS, PhD); ocean engineering (M Oc E); radiation health physics (MS, PhD). *Application deadline:* Applications are processed on a rolling basis. *Application fee:* $50. *Application Contact:* Roy C. Rathja, Assistant Dean, 541-737-5236, Fax: 541-737-3124, E-mail: roy.rathja@orst.edu. *Dean*, Ronald L. Adams, 541-737-7722, Fax: 541-737-1805, E-mail: ronald.lynn.adams@orst.edu.

College of Forestry Students: 128 full-time (52 women), 6 part-time (2 women); includes 8 minority (1 African American, 5 Asian Americans or Pacific Islanders, 2 Hispanic Americans), 39 international. Average age 30. *Faculty:* 91 full-time (18 women), 1 part-time/adjunct (0 women). Expenses: Contact institution. *Financial support:* Fellowships, research assistantships, teaching assistantships, career-related internships or fieldwork, Federal Work-Study, institutionally sponsored loans, and unspecified assistantships available. Support available to part-time students. Financial award application deadline: 2/1. In 2001, 28 master's, 13 doctorates awarded. *Degree program information:* Part-time programs available. Offers economics (MS, PhD); forest engineering (MAIS, MF, MS, PhD); forest products (MAIS, MF, MS, PhD); forest resources (MAIS, MF, MS, PhD); forest science (MAIS, MF, MS, PhD); forestry (M Agr, MAIS, MF, MS, PhD); wood science and technology (MF, MS, PhD). *Application deadline:* Applications are processed on a rolling basis. *Application fee:* $50. *Application Contact:* Deborah J. Bird, Head Advisor, 541-737-2052, Fax: 541-737-8508, E-mail: birdd@for.orst.edu. *Dean*, Hal Salwasser, 541-737-1585, Fax: 541-737-2906, E-mail: salwassh@for.orst.edu.

College of Health and Human Sciences Students: 115 full-time (73 women), 26 part-time (17 women); includes 9 minority (1 African American, 4 Asian Americans or Pacific Islanders, 3 Hispanic Americans, 1 Native American), 19 international. Average age 31. *Faculty:* 34 full-time (15 women), 2 part-time/adjunct (1 woman). Expenses: Contact institution. *Financial support:* Fellowships, research assistantships, teaching assistantships, career-related internships or fieldwork, Federal Work-Study, and institutionally sponsored loans available. Support available to part-time students. Financial award application deadline:2/1. In 2001, 32 master's, 9 doctorates awarded. Offers environmental health management (MAIS, MS); health (MS, PhD); health and human sciences (MAIS, MAT, MPH, MS, PhD); health education (MAIS, MAT, MS); healthcare administration (MS); human performance (MAIS, MS, PhD); movement studies in disabilities (MAIS, MS); physical education (MAT); public health (MPH). *Application deadline:* Applications are processed on a rolling basis. *Application fee:* $50. *Application Contact:* Linda Johnson, Head Adviser, 541-737-3718, Fax: 541-737-4230, E-mail: linda.johnson@orst.edu. *Interim Dean*, Dr. Jeffery A. McCubbin, 541-737-5921, Fax: 541-737-4230, E-mail: jeff.mccubbin@orst.edu.

College of Home Economics Students: 43 full-time (40 women), 17 part-time (all women); includes 4 minority (3 Asian Americans or Pacific Islanders, 1 Hispanic American), 21 international. Average age 39. *Faculty:* 30 full-time (27 women). Expenses: Contact institution. *Financial support:* Fellowships, research assistantships, teaching assistantships, career-related internships or fieldwork, Federal Work-Study, and institutionally sponsored loans available. Support available to part-time students. Financial award application deadline:2/1. In 2001, 9 master's, 7 doctorates awarded. *Degree program information:* Part-time programs available. Offers apparel, interiors, housing, and merchandising (MA, MAIS, MS, PhD); gerontology (MAIS); home economics (MA, MAIS, MS, Ed D, PhD); human development and family studies (MS, PhD); nutrition and food management (MAIS, MS, PhD). *Application deadline:* Applications are processed on a rolling basis. *Application fee:* $50. *Dean*, Dr. Clara C. Pratt, 541-737-0941, E-mail: prattc@orst.edu.

College of Liberal Arts Students: 63 full-time (34 women), 8 part-time (7 women); includes 3 minority (1 African American, 1 Asian American or Pacific Islander, 1 Native American), 24 international. Average age 32. *Faculty:* 37 full-time (13 women). Expenses: Contact institution. *Financial support:* Fellowships, research assistantships, teaching assistantships, career-related internships or fieldwork, Federal Work-Study, and institutionally sponsored loans available. Support available to part-time students. Financial award application deadline:2/1. In 2001, 27 master's, 1 doctorate awarded. *Degree program information:* Part-time programs available. Offers anthropology (MAIS); applied anthropology (MA); economics (MA, MS, PhD); English (MA, MAIS); liberal arts (MA, MAIS, MAT, MS, PhD); music education (MAT). *Application deadline:* Applications are processed on a rolling basis. *Application fee:* $50. *Application Contact:* Polly Jeneva, Adviser, 541-737-6193, Fax: 541-737-2434, E-mail: polly.jeneva@orst.edu. *Dean*, Dr. Kay F. Schaffer, 541-737-4582, Fax: 541-737-2434, E-mail: kshaffer@orst.edu.

College of Oceanic and Atmospheric Sciences Students: 69 full-time (39 women), 6 part-time (2 women); includes 2 minority (1 Asian American or Pacific Islander, 1 Hispanic American), 17 international. Average age 30. *Faculty:* 69 full-time (15 women), 3 part-time/

adjunct (2 women). Expenses: Contact institution. *Financial support:* Fellowships, research assistantships, teaching assistantships, career-related internships or fieldwork, Federal Work-Study, and institutionally sponsored loans available. Support available to part-time students. Financial award application deadline: 2/1. In 2001, 20 master's, 6 doctorates awarded. Offers atmospheric sciences (MA, MS, PhD); geophysics (MA, MS, PhD); marine resource management (MA, MS); oceanography (MA, MS, PhD). *Application deadline:* For fall admission, 2/1 (priority date). Applications are processed on a rolling basis. *Application fee:* $50. *Application Contact:* Irma Delson, Assistant Director, Student Services, 541-737-5189, Fax: 541-737-2064, E-mail: student_adviser@oce.orst.edu. *Dean*, Mark R. Abbott, 541-737-4045, Fax: 541-737-2064, E-mail: mark@oce.orst.edu.

College of Science Students: 430 full-time (177 women), 27 part-time (9 women); includes 29 minority (1 African American, 19 Asian Americans or Pacific Islanders, 8 Hispanic Americans, 1 Native American), 113 international. Average age 30. *Faculty:* 177 full-time (49 women), 5 part-time/adjunct (2 women). Expenses: Contact institution. *Financial support:* Fellowships, research assistantships, teaching assistantships, career-related internships or fieldwork, Federal Work-Study, and institutionally sponsored loans available. Support available to part-time students. Financial award application deadline: 2/1. In 2001, 81 master's, 45 doctorates awarded. *Degree program information:* Part-time programs available. Offers advanced mathematics education (MAT); analytical chemistry (MS, PhD); applied statistics (MA, MS, PhD); biochemistry and biophysics (MA, MAIS, MS, PhD); biology education (MAT); biometry (MA, MS, PhD); chemistry (MA, MAIS); chemistry education (MAT); ecology (MA, MAIS, MS, PhD); entomology (M Agr, MA, MAIS, MS, PhD); environmental sciences (MS, PhD); environmental statistics (MA, MS, PhD); general science (MA, MS, PhD); genetics (MA, MAIS, MS, PhD); geography (MA, MAIS, MS, PhD); geology (MA, MAIS, MS, PhD); inorganic chemistry (MS, PhD); integrated science education (MAT); mathematical statistics (MA, MS, PhD); mathematics (MA, MAIS, MS, PhD); mathematics education (MA, MAT, MS, PhD); microbiology (M Agr, MA, MAIS, MS, PhD); molecular and cellular biology (MA, MAIS, MS, PhD); mycology (MA, MAIS, MS, PhD); nuclear and radiation chemistry (MS, PhD); operations research (MA, MAIS, MS); organic chemistry (MS, PhD); physical chemistry (MS, PhD); physics (MA, MS, PhD); physics education (MAT); plant pathology (MA, MAIS, MS, PhD); plant physiology (MA, MAIS, MS, PhD); science (M Agr, MA, MAIS, MAT, MS, PhD); science education (MA, MAT, MS, PhD); statistics (M Agr, MA, MS, PhD); structural botany (MA, MAIS, MS, PhD); systematics (MA, MAIS, MS, PhD); zoology (MA, MAIS, MS, PhD). *Application deadline:* Applications are processed on a rolling basis. *Application fee:* $50. *Application Contact:* Carolyn Brumley, Graduate Secretary, 541-737-6707, Fax: 541-737-2062, E-mail: carolyn.brumley@orst.edu. *Interim Dean*, Dr. Sherman H. Bloomer, 541-737-1218, Fax: 541-737-1009, E-mail: bloomers@geo.orst.edu.

School of Education Students: 96 full-time (74 women), 174 part-time (113 women); includes 38 minority (15 African Americans, 5 Asian Americans or Pacific Islanders, 15 Hispanic Americans, 3 Native Americans), 9 international. Average age 38. *Faculty:* 25 full-time (14 women), 4 part-time/adjunct (3 women). Expenses: Contact institution. *Financial support:* Fellowships, research assistantships, teaching assistantships, career-related internships or fieldwork, Federal Work-Study, and institutionally sponsored loans available. Support available to part-time students. Financial award application deadline: 2/1. In 2001, 127 master's, 21 doctorates awarded. *Degree program information:* Part-time programs available. Offers adult education (Ed M, MAIS); college student service administration (Ed M, MS); counseling (MS, PhD); education (Ed M, MAIS, MAT, MS, Ed D, PhD); elementary education (MAT); family and consumer sciences (MAT, MS); general education (Ed M, MAIS, MS, Ed D, PhD); professional technical education (MAT); teacher education (MAT). *Application fee:* $50. *Dean*, Dr. Sam Stern, 541-737-6392, Fax: 541-737-2040.

OTIS COLLEGE OF ART AND DESIGN, Los Angeles, CA 90045-9785

General Information Independent, coed, comprehensive institution. *Enrollment:* 31 full-time matriculated graduate/professional students (15 women), 7 part-time matriculated graduate/professional students (5 women). *Enrollment by degree level:* 38 master's. *Graduate faculty:* 3 full-time (1 woman), 14 part-time/adjunct (7 women). *Tuition:* Full-time $20,840; part-time $695 per credit. *Required fees:* $225 per semester. *Graduate housing:* On-campus housing not available. *Student services:* Campus employment opportunities, campus safety program, career counseling, international student services, low-cost health insurance, writing training. *Library facilities:* Millard Sheets Library. *Online resources:* library catalog, web page, access to other libraries' catalogs. *Collection:* 27,000 titles, 154 serial subscriptions, 2,000 audiovisual materials.

Computer facilities: 220 computers available on campus for general student use. A campuswide network can be accessed. Internet access, library on-line catalog are available. *Web address:* http://www.otis.edu/.

General Application Contact: Yvette Sobky, Senior Admissions Counselor, 310-665-6819, Fax: 310-665-6921, E-mail: ysobky@otis.edu.

GRADUATE UNITS

Program in Fine Arts Students: 20 full-time (8 women), 4 part-time (3 women); includes 6 minority (3 Asian Americans or Pacific Islanders, 3 Hispanic Americans), 1 international. Average age 33. 59 applicants, 37% accepted, 9 enrolled. *Faculty:* 2 full-time (1 woman), 9 part-time/adjunct (5 women). Expenses: Contact institution. *Financial support:* In 2001–02, 20 students received support. Career-related internships or fieldwork, Federal Work-Study, scholarships/grants, and tuition waivers (partial) available. Financial award application deadline: 2/15. In 2001, 7 degrees awarded. Offers new genres (MFA); painting (MFA); photography (MFA); sculpture (MFA). *Application deadline:* For fall admission, 4/15. *Application fee:* $40. Electronic applications accepted. *Application Contact:* Yvette Sobky, Senior Admissions Counselor, 310-665-6819, Fax: 310-665-6921, E-mail: ysobky@otis.edu. *Chair*, Roy Dowell, 310-665-6891, Fax: 310-665-6998, E-mail: grads@otis.edu.

Program in Writing and Critical Theory Students: 11 full-time (7 women), 3 part-time (2 women); includes 2 minority (1 African American, 1 Hispanic American), 1 international. Average age 33. 19 applicants, 89% accepted, 9 enrolled. *Faculty:* 1 full-time (0 women), 5 part-time/adjunct (2 women). Expenses: Contact institution. *Financial support:* Federal Work-Study, scholarships/grants, and tuition waivers (partial) available. Financial award application deadline: 3/1; financial award applicants required to submit FAFSA. Offers writing and critical theory (MFA). *Application deadline:* For fall admission, 4/15. *Application fee:* $40. Electronic applications accepted. *Application Contact:* Mike Rivas, Admissions Counselor, 310-665-6800, Fax: 310-665-6805, E-mail: otisart@otisart.edu. *Chair*, Paul Vangelisti, 310-665-6924, Fax: 310-665-6890.

OTTAWA UNIVERSITY, Ottawa, KS 66067-3399

General Information Independent-religious, coed, comprehensive institution. *Enrollment:* 50 full-time matriculated graduate/professional students (40 women), 340 part-time matriculated graduate/professional students (264 women). *Enrollment by degree level:* 390 master's. *Graduate faculty:* 7 full-time (2 women), 45 part-time/adjunct (30 women). *Graduate housing:* On-campus housing not available. *Library facilities:* Myers Library. *Collection:* 80,500 titles, 310 serial subscriptions.

Computer facilities: 71 computers available on campus for general student use. A campuswide network can be accessed from student residence rooms and from off campus. Internet access and online class registration are available. *Web address:* http://www.ottawa.edu/.

GRADUATE UNITS

Department of Human Services Average age 38. 17 applicants, 94% accepted. *Faculty:* 2 full-time (1 woman), 14 part-time/adjunct (7 women). Expenses: Contact institution. *Financial support:* Available to part-time students. Applicants required to submit FAFSA. In 2001, 21 degrees awarded. *Degree program information:* Part-time and evening/weekend programs available. Postbaccalaureate distance learning degree programs offered (minimal on-campus study). Offers human resources (MA). *Application deadline:* Applications are processed on a rolling basis. *Application fee:* $50. *Application Contact:* Karen Adams, Enrollment Manager, 913-451-1431, Fax: 913-451-0806, E-mail: adamsk@ottawa.edu. *Director of Graduate Studies-Kansas City*, Dr. W. A. Breytspraak, 913-451-1431, Fax: 913-451-0806, E-mail: breytspraak@ottawa.edu.

Graduate Studies-Phoenix Students: 50 full-time (40 women), 290 part-time (219 women); includes 35 minority (9 African Americans, 5 Asian Americans or Pacific Islanders, 17 Hispanic Americans, 4 Native Americans) Average age 39. *Faculty:* 5 full-time (1 woman), 31 part-time/adjunct (23 women). Expenses: Contact institution. *Financial support:* Career-related internships or fieldwork available. Support available to part-time students. Financial award applicants required to submit FAFSA. In 2001, 110 degrees awarded. *Degree program information:* Part-time programs available. Offers education (MA); human resources (MA); professional counseling (MA). *Application deadline:* For fall admission, 7/1 (priority date); for spring admission, 11/1. Applications are processed on a rolling basis. *Application fee:* $40. *Application Contact:* Jean Gray, Advisement Coordinator, 602-749-5151, Fax: 602-371-0035, E-mail: grayj@ottawa.edu. *Provost*, Dr. David Barnes, 602-371-0025, E-mail: barnesd@ottawa.edu.

OTTERBEIN COLLEGE, Westerville, OH 43081

General Information Independent-religious, coed, comprehensive institution. *Graduate housing:* On-campus housing not available. *Research affiliation:* Battelle Pacific Northwest Laboratories (research and development).

GRADUATE UNITS

Department of Business, Accounting and Economics Offers business, accounting and economics (MBA).

Department of Education *Degree program information:* Part-time and evening/weekend programs available. Offers education (MAE, MAT).

Program in Nursing Postbaccalaureate distance learning degree programs offered. Offers adult health care (MSN); adult health practitioner (Certificate); family nurse practitioner (Certificate); nurse service administration (MSN).

OUR LADY OF HOLY CROSS COLLEGE, New Orleans, LA 70131-7399

General Information Independent-religious, coed, comprehensive institution. *Enrollment:* 18 full-time matriculated graduate/professional students (16 women), 79 part-time matriculated graduate/professional students (55 women). *Enrollment by degree level:* 97 master's. *Graduate faculty:* 7 full-time (4 women), 8 part-time/adjunct (3 women). *Tuition:* Full-time $4,860; part-time $270 per semester hour. *Required fees:* $500; $250 per term. *Graduate housing:* On-campus housing not available. *Student services:* Career counseling, free psychological counseling, teacher training. *Library facilities:* Blaine Kern Library. *Online resources:* library catalog, web page. *Collection:* 85,404 titles, 970 serial subscriptions, 14,513 audiovisual materials.

Computer facilities: 65 computers available on campus for general student use. *Web address:* http://www.olhcc.edu/.

General Application Contact: Dr. Judith G. Miranti, Dean of Education, 504-394-7744 Ext. 214, Fax: 504-391-2421, E-mail: jmiranti@olhcc.edu.

GRADUATE UNITS

Program in Education and Counseling Students: 18 full-time (16 women), 79 part-time (55 women); includes 32 minority (25 African Americans, 2 Asian Americans or Pacific Islanders, 3 Hispanic Americans, 2 Native Americans) Average age 30. 20 applicants, 50% accepted. *Faculty:* 7 full-time (4 women), 8 part-time/adjunct (3 women). Expenses: Contact institution. *Financial support:* Federal Work-Study and tuition waivers (partial) available. Support available to part-time students. Financial award application deadline: 6/1. In 2001, 28 degrees awarded. *Degree program information:* Part-time and evening/weekend programs available. Offers administration and supervision (M Ed); curriculum and instruction (M Ed); marriage and family counseling (MA); school counseling (M Ed, MA). *Application deadline:* For fall admission, 9/1. *Application fee:* $20. *Application Contact:* Kristine Hatfield Kopecky, Dean of Student Affairs and Admissions, 504-394-7744 Ext. 185, Fax: 504-391-2421, E-mail: kkopecky@olhcc.edu. *Dean of Education*, Dr. Judith G. Miranti, 504-394-7744 Ext. 214, Fax: 504-391-2421, E-mail: jmiranti@olhcc.edu.

OUR LADY OF THE LAKE UNIVERSITY OF SAN ANTONIO, San Antonio, TX 78207-4689

General Information Independent-religious, coed, comprehensive institution. *Graduate housing:* Room and/or apartments available on a first-come, first-served basis to single students; on-campus housing not available to married students. Housing application deadline: 7/15.

GRADUATE UNITS

College of Arts and Sciences *Degree program information:* Part-time and evening/weekend programs available. Offers English (MA); English communication arts (MA); language and literature (MA).

School of Business *Degree program information:* Part-time and evening/weekend programs available. Offers general (MBA); health care management (MBA).

School of Education and Clinical Studies *Degree program information:* Part-time and evening/weekend programs available. Postbaccalaureate distance learning degree programs offered (minimal on-campus study). Offers administration/supervision (M Ed); communication and learning disorders (MA); counseling psychology (MS, Psy D); curriculum and instruction (M Ed); human sciences (MA); human sciences and sociology (MA); leadership studies (PhD); learning resources (M Ed); psychology (MS, Psy D); school counseling (MS); school supervision (M Ed); sociology (MA); special education (MA).

Worden School of Social Service *Degree program information:* Part-time programs available. Offers social service (MSW).

PACE UNIVERSITY, New York, NY 10038

General Information Independent, coed, university. CGS member. *Enrollment:* 858 full-time matriculated graduate/professional students (417 women), 1,568 part-time matriculated graduate/professional students (780 women). *Enrollment by degree level:* 2,255 master's, 115 doctoral, 56 other advanced degrees. *Graduate faculty:* 156 full-time, 141 part-time/adjunct. *Tuition:* Part-time $545 per credit. *Graduate housing:* Room and/or apartments available on a first-come, first-served basis to single students; on-campus housing not available to married students. *Student services:* Campus employment opportunities, career counseling, free psychological counseling, international student services, low-cost health insurance. *Library facilities:* Henry Birnbaum Library plus 3 others. *Online resources:* library catalog, web page, access to other libraries' catalogs. *Collection:* 786,132 titles, 2,637 serial subscriptions.

Computer facilities: 155 computers available on campus for general student use. A campuswide network can be accessed from student residence rooms and from off campus. *Web address:* http://www.pace.edu/.

General Application Contact: Joanna Broda, Director of Admissions, 212-346-1652, Fax: 212-346-1585, E-mail: gradnyc@pace.edu.

GRADUATE UNITS

Dyson College of Arts and Sciences Students: 100 full-time (88 women), 66 part-time (55 women); includes 25 minority (12 African Americans, 7 Asian Americans or Pacific Islanders, 5 Hispanic Americans, 1 Native American), 13 international. Average age 28. 262 applicants, 52% accepted, 55 enrolled. *Faculty:* 27 full-time, 56 part-time/adjunct. Expenses: Contact institution. *Financial support:* Research assistantships, teaching assistantships, career-related internships or fieldwork, Federal Work-Study, and tuition waivers (partial) available. Support available to part-time students. Financial award application deadline: 5/15; financial award applicants required to submit FAFSA. In 2001, 64 master's, 22 doctorates awarded. *Degree program information:* Part-time and evening/weekend programs available. Offers arts and sciences (MA, MS, MS Ed, Psy D); forensic science (MS); psychology (MA); publishing

Pace University (continued)

(MS); school-clinical child psychology (Psy D); school-community psychology (MS Ed, Psy D). *Application deadline:* Applications are processed on a rolling basis. *Application fee:* $65. Electronic applications accepted. *Application Contact:* Joanna Broda, Director of Admissions, 212-346-1652, Fax: 212-346-1585, E-mail: gradnyc@pace.edu. *Dean*, Dr. Gail Dinter-Gottlieb, 212-346-1517.

Lienhard School of Nursing Students: 16 full-time (13 women), 55 part-time (50 women); includes 27 minority (20 African Americans, 5 Asian Americans or Pacific Islanders, 2 Hispanic Americans), 1 international. Average age 33. 44 applicants, 82% accepted. Expenses: Contact institution. *Financial support:* Research assistantships, career-related internships or fieldwork, Federal Work-Study, and tuition waivers (partial) available. Support available to part-time students. Financial award applicants required to submit FAFSA. In 2001, 25 master's, 2 other advanced degrees awarded. *Degree program information:* Part-time and evening/weekend programs available. Offers nursing (MS, Advanced Certificate). *Application deadline:* For fall admission, 7/31 (priority date); for spring admission, 11/30. Applications are processed on a rolling basis. *Application fee:* $65. Electronic applications accepted. *Application Contact:* Richard Alvarez, Director of Admissions, 212-346-1531, Fax: 212-346-1585, E-mail: gradnyc@pace.edu. *Dean*, Dr. Harriet Feldman, 914-773-3341.

Lubin School of Business Students: 505 full-time (222 women), 704 part-time (304 women); includes 214 minority (66 African Americans, 115 Asian Americans or Pacific Islanders, 33 Hispanic Americans), 329 international. Average age 28. 1,155 applicants, 57% accepted, 298 enrolled. *Faculty:* 87 full-time, 42 part-time/adjunct. Expenses: Contact institution. *Financial support:* Research assistantships, career-related internships or fieldwork, Federal Work-Study, and tuition waivers (full and partial) available. Support available to part-time students. Financial award applicants required to submit FAFSA. In 2001, 391 master's, 4 doctorates, 4 other advanced degrees awarded. *Degree program information:* Part-time and evening/weekend programs available. Postbaccalaureate distance learning degree programs offered (minimal on-campus study). Offers banking and finance (MBA); business (MBA, MS, DPS, APC); corporate economic planning (MBA); corporate financial management (MBA); economics (MS); financial economics (MBA); financial management (MBA); health systems management (MBA); information systems (MBA); international business (MBA); international economics (MBA); investment management (MBA, MS); management (MBA); management science (MBA); managerial accounting (MBA); marketing management (MBA); marketing research (MBA); operations management (MBA); professional studies (DPS); public accounting (MBA, MS); taxation (MBA, MS). *Application deadline:* For fall admission, 7/31 (priority date); for spring admission, 11/30. Applications are processed on a rolling basis. *Application fee:* $65. Electronic applications accepted. *Application Contact:* Joanna Broda, Director of Admissions, 212-346-1652, Fax: 212-346-1585, E-mail: gradnyc@pace.edu. *Dean*, Dr. Arthur Centonze, 212-346-1963.

School of Computer Science and Information Systems Students: 210 full-time (70 women), 446 part-time (165 women); includes 129 minority (49 African Americans, 61 Asian Americans or Pacific Islanders, 19 Hispanic Americans), 197 international. Average age 28. 474 applicants, 72% accepted. *Faculty:* 23 full-time, 9 part-time/adjunct. Expenses: Contact institution. *Financial support:* Research assistantships, career-related internships or fieldwork available. Support available to part-time students. Financial award applicants required to submit FAFSA. In 2001, 112 master's, 6 other advanced degrees awarded. *Degree program information:* Part-time and evening/weekend programs available. Offers computer communications and networks (Certificate); computer science (MS); computing studies (DPS); information systems (MS); object-oriented programming (Certificate); telecommunications (MS, Certificate). *Application deadline:* For fall admission, 7/31 (priority date); for spring admission, 11/30. Applications are processed on a rolling basis. *Application fee:* $65. Electronic applications accepted. *Application Contact:* Joanna Broda, Director of Admissions, 212-346-1652, Fax: 212-346-1585, E-mail: gradnyc@pace.edu. *Dean*, Dr. Susan Merritt, 914-422-4375.

School of Education Students: 27 full-time (24 women), 297 part-time (206 women); includes 54 minority (29 African Americans, 8 Asian Americans or Pacific Islanders, 17 Hispanic Americans), 6 international. Average age 30. 89 applicants, 62% accepted. *Faculty:* 9 full-time, 12 part-time/adjunct. Expenses: Contact institution. *Financial support:* Research assistantships, career-related internships or fieldwork and Federal Work-Study available. Support available to part-time students. Financial award applicants required to submit FAFSA. In 2001, 27 master's, 14 other advanced degrees awarded. *Degree program information:* Part-time and evening/weekend programs available. Offers administration and supervision (MS Ed); curriculum and instruction (MS); education (MST); school business management (Certificate). *Application deadline:* For fall admission, 7/31 (priority date); for spring admission, 11/30. Applications are processed on a rolling basis. *Application fee:* $65. Electronic applications accepted. *Application Contact:* Joanna Broda, Director of Admissions, 212-346-1652, Fax: 212-346-1585, E-mail: gradnyc@pace.edu. *Dean*, Dr. Janet McDonald, 212-346-1512.

Announcement: Pace University offers a 36-credit master's program covering all aspects of publishing. Marketing principles and practices of publishing, professional editing, book and magazine production, magazine circulation, magazine advertising, sales, information systems, and subsidiary rights are some of the required courses. An internship or graduate seminar is also required. The program provides an opportunity to fulfill career ambitions in the industry.

See in-depth description on page 1019.

PACE UNIVERSITY, PLEASANTVILLE/BRIARCLIFF CAMPUS, Pleasantville, NY 10570

General Information Independent, coed, comprehensive institution. *Enrollment:* 25 full-time matriculated graduate/professional students (24 women), 106 part-time matriculated graduate/professional students (97 women). *Enrollment by degree level:* 115 master's, 9 other advanced degrees. *Graduate faculty:* 6 full-time (all women), 21 part-time/adjunct (13 women). *Tuition:* Full-time $13,080; part-time $545 per credit. Tuition and fees vary according to course load. *Graduate housing:* Room and/or apartments available on a first-come, first-served basis to single students; on-campus housing not available to married students. Typical cost: $6,370 per year. Room charges vary according to board plan, campus/location and housing facility selected. *Student services:* Campus employment opportunities, career counseling, free psychological counseling, international student services, low-cost health insurance. *Library facilities:* Mortola Library plus 3 others.

Computer facilities: 128 computers available on campus for general student use. A campuswide network can be accessed from student residence rooms and from off campus. *Web address:* http://www.pace.edu/.

General Application Contact: Joanna Broda, Director of Admissions, 914-422-4283, Fax: 914-422-4287, E-mail: gradwp@pace.edu.

GRADUATE UNITS

Lienhard School of Nursing Students: 25 full-time (24 women), 106 part-time (97 women); includes 34 minority (14 African Americans, 13 Asian Americans or Pacific Islanders, 7 Hispanic Americans), 2 international. Average age 35. 48 applicants, 81% accepted, 28 enrolled. *Faculty:* 6 full-time (all women), 21 part-time/adjunct (13 women). Expenses: Contact institution. *Financial support:* In 2001–02, 86 students received support, including 3 research assistantships; career-related internships or fieldwork, Federal Work-Study, and tuition waivers (partial) also available. Support available to part-time students. Financial award application deadline: 5/15; financial award applicants required to submit FAFSA. In 2001, 41 master's, 1 other advanced degree awarded. *Degree program information:* Part-time and evening/weekend programs available. Offers nursing (MS, Advanced Certificate). *Application deadline:* For fall admission, 7/31 (priority date); for spring admission, 11/30. Applications are processed on a rolling basis. *Application fee:* $65. Electronic applications accepted. *Application Contact:* Joanna Broda, Director of Admissions, 914-422-4283, Fax: 914-422-4287, E-mail: gradwp@pace.edu. *Dean*, Dr. Harriet Feldman, 914-773-3341.

PACE UNIVERSITY, WHITE PLAINS CAMPUS, White Plains, NY 10603

General Information Independent, coed, graduate-only institution. *Enrollment by degree level:* 1,116 master's, 57 doctoral, 4 other advanced degrees. *Graduate faculty:* 77 full-time, 83 part-time/adjunct. *Tuition:* Part-time $545 per credit. *Graduate housing:* Room and/or apartments available on a first-come, first-served basis to single students; on-campus housing not available to married students. *Student services:* Campus employment opportunities, career counseling, free psychological counseling, international student services, low-cost health insurance. *Collection:* 786,132 titles, 2,637 serial subscriptions.

Computer facilities: 68 computers available on campus for general student use. A campuswide network can be accessed. Internet access is available. *Web address:* http://www.pace.edu/.

General Application Contact: Joanna Broda, Director of Admissions, 914-422-4283, Fax: 914-422-4287, E-mail: gradwp@pace.edu.

GRADUATE UNITS

Dyson College of Arts and Sciences Students: 61 full-time (46 women), 100 part-time (69 women); includes 59 minority (40 African Americans, 3 Asian Americans or Pacific Islanders, 15 Hispanic Americans, 1 Native American), 6 international. Average age 28. 117 applicants, 69% accepted, 51 enrolled. *Faculty:* 18 full-time, 37 part-time/adjunct. Expenses: Contact institution. *Financial support:* Research assistantships, teaching assistantships, career-related internships or fieldwork, Federal Work-Study, and tuition waivers (partial) available. Support available to part-time students. Financial award applicants required to submit FAFSA. In 2001, 42 degrees awarded. *Degree program information:* Part-time and evening/weekend programs available. Offers arts and sciences (MPA, MS); counseling-substance abuse (MS); environmental science (MS); government management (MPA); health care administration (MPA); nonprofit management (MPA). *Application deadline:* For fall admission, 8/1 (priority date); for spring admission, 12/1 (priority date). Applications are processed on a rolling basis. *Application fee:* $65. Electronic applications accepted. *Application Contact:* Joanna Broda, Director of Admissions, 914-422-4283, Fax: 914-422-4287, E-mail: gradwp@pace.edu. *Dean*, Dr. Gail Dinter-Gottlieb, 212-346-1517.

Lubin School of Business Students: 87 full-time (42 women), 329 part-time (146 women); includes 69 minority (24 African Americans, 26 Asian Americans or Pacific Islanders, 17 Hispanic Americans, 2 Native Americans), 32 international. Average age 28. 233 applicants, 61% accepted, 90 enrolled. *Faculty:* 27 full-time, 15 part-time/adjunct. Expenses: Contact institution. *Financial support:* Research assistantships, career-related internships or fieldwork, Federal Work-Study, and tuition waivers (full and partial) available. Support available to part-time students. Financial award applicants required to submit FAFSA. In 2001, 125 degrees awarded. *Degree program information:* Part-time and evening/weekend programs available. Offers banking and finance (MBA); business (MBA, MS, APC); corporate economic planning (MBA); corporate financial management (MBA); economics (MS); financial economics (MBA); financial management (MBA); health systems management (MBA); information systems (MBA); international business (MBA); international economics (MBA); investment management (MBA, MS); management (MBA); management science (MBA, MS); managerial accounting (MBA); marketing management (MBA); marketing research (MBA); operations management (MBA); personal financial planning (MS); public accounting (MBA, MS); taxation (MBA, MS). *Application deadline:* For fall admission, 8/1 (priority date); for spring admission, 12/1 (priority date). Applications are processed on a rolling basis. *Application fee:* $65. Electronic applications accepted. *Application Contact:* Joanna Broda, Director of Admissions, 914-422-4283, Fax: 914-422-4287, E-mail: gradwp@pace.edu. *Dean*, Dr. Arthur Centonze, 212-346-1963.

School of Computer Science and Information Systems Students: 73 full-time (30 women), 307 part-time (117 women); includes 122 minority (37 African Americans, 60 Asian Americans or Pacific Islanders, 25 Hispanic Americans), 50 international. Average age 31. 262 applicants, 65% accepted, 117 enrolled. *Faculty:* 14 full-time, 6 part-time/adjunct. Expenses: Contact institution. *Financial support:* Research assistantships, career-related internships or fieldwork available. Support available to part-time students. Financial award applicants required to submit FAFSA. In 2001, 65 master's, 9 other advanced degrees awarded. *Degree program information:* Part-time and evening/weekend programs available. Offers computer communications and networks (Certificate); computer science (MS); computing studies (DPS); information systems (MS); object-oriented programming (Certificate); telecommunications (MS, Certificate). *Application deadline:* For fall admission, 8/1 (priority date); for spring admission, 12/1 (priority date). Applications are processed on a rolling basis. *Application fee:* $65. Electronic applications accepted. *Application Contact:* Joanna Broda, Director of Admissions, 914-422-4283, Fax: 914-422-4287, E-mail: gradwp@pace.edu. *Dean*, Dr. Susan Merritt, 914-422-4375.

School of Education Students: 44 full-time (36 women), 155 part-time (114 women); includes 23 minority (13 African Americans, 2 Asian Americans or Pacific Islanders, 8 Hispanic Americans), 3 international. Average age 31. 113 applicants, 73% accepted, 58 enrolled. *Faculty:* 18 full-time, 25 part-time/adjunct. Expenses: Contact institution. *Financial support:* Research assistantships, career-related internships or fieldwork and Federal Work-Study available. Support available to part-time students. Financial award applicants required to submit FAFSA. In 2001, 78 master's, 6 other advanced degrees awarded. *Degree program information:* Part-time and evening/weekend programs available. Offers administration and supervision (MS Ed); curriculum and instruction (MS); education (MST); school business management (Certificate). *Application deadline:* For fall admission, 8/1 (priority date); for spring admission, 12/1 (priority date). Applications are processed on a rolling basis. *Application fee:* $65. Electronic applications accepted. *Application Contact:* Joanna Broda, Director of Admissions, 914-422-4283, Fax: 914-422-4287, E-mail: gradwp@pace.edu. *Dean*, Dr. Janet McDonald, 212-346-1512.

School of Law Students: 426 full-time (260 women), 340 part-time (186 women); includes 129 minority (47 African Americans, 30 Asian Americans or Pacific Islanders, 52 Hispanic Americans), 18 international. Average age 26. 1,794 applicants, 46% accepted, 230 enrolled. *Faculty:* 37 full-time, 60 part-time/adjunct. Expenses: Contact institution. *Financial support:* Career-related internships or fieldwork, Federal Work-Study, institutionally sponsored loans, and scholarships/grants available. Support available to part-time students. Financial award application deadline: 2/1; financial award applicants required to submit FAFSA. In 2001, 214 first professional degrees, 17 master's awarded. *Degree program information:* Part-time and evening/weekend programs available. Offers comparative legal studies (LL M); environmental law (LL M, SJD); law (JD). *Application deadline:* For fall admission, 2/15 (priority date). Applications are processed on a rolling basis. *Application fee:* $55. Electronic applications accepted. *Application Contact:* Cathy Alexander, Director of Law Admissions, 914-422-4210, Fax: 914-422-4010, E-mail: calexander@law.pace.edu. *Dean*, David S. Cohen, 914-422-4205, E-mail: dcohen@law.pace.edu.

PACIFICA GRADUATE INSTITUTE, Carpinteria, CA 93013

General Information Proprietary, coed, graduate-only institution. *Enrollment by degree level:* 295 master's, 270 doctoral, 565 other advanced degrees. *Graduate faculty:* 30 full-time, 59 part-time/adjunct. *Tuition:* Full-time $13,900. *Graduate housing:* Rooms and/or apartments available to single and married students. Typical cost: $3,445 (including board) for single students; $3,445 (including board) for married students. Room and board charges vary according to housing facility selected. Housing application deadline: 8/15. *Student services:* Campus safety program, disabled student services, international student services, multicultural affairs office, writing training. *Library facilities:* Joseph Campbell and Marija Gimbutas Library plus 1 other. *Online resources:* library catalog, web page, access to other libraries' catalogs. *Collection:* 10,000 titles, 130 serial subscriptions, 250 audiovisual materials. *Research affiliation:* EBSCO—Elton B. Stevens Company (journal management), American Psychological Association (psychology-research), North California consortium of Psychology Libraries (psychology), Silverplatter Inc. (research technology), Ovid Technologies (research technology).

Computer facilities: 5 computers available on campus for general student use. A campuswide network can be accessed from off campus. Internet access is available. *Web address:* http://www.pacifica.edu/.

General Application Contact: Diane Huerta, Admissions Office, 805-969-3626 Ext. 128, Fax: 805-565-1932, E-mail: admissions@pacifica.edu.

GRADUATE UNITS

Graduate Programs Students: 545 full-time, 20 part-time. Average age 45. *Faculty:* 19 full-time, 50 part-time/adjunct. Expenses: Contact institution. *Financial support:* In 2001–02, 411 students received support. Scholarships/grants available. Financial award application deadline: 6/15; financial award applicants required to submit FAFSA. In 2001, 101 master's, 82 doctorates awarded. Offers clinical psychology (PhD); counseling psychology (MA); depth psychology (PhD); mythological studies (MA, PhD). *Application deadline:* For fall admission, 4/30 (priority date). *Application fee:* $60. *Application Contact:* Diane Huerta, Admissions Office, 805-969-3626 Ext. 128, Fax: 805-565-1932, E-mail: diane_huerta@pacifica.edu. *President,* Dr. Stephen Aizenstat, 805-969-3626 Ext. 102, Fax: 805-565-1932, E-mail: steve_aizenstat@pacifica.edu.

PACIFIC COLLEGE OF ORIENTAL MEDICINE, San Diego, CA 92108

General Information Proprietary, coed, graduate-only institution. *Graduate faculty:* 80. *Tuition:* Full-time $9,843. *Graduate housing:* On-campus housing not available. *Student services:* Campus employment opportunities. *Library facilities:* Reference Center. *Collection:* 2,587 titles, 52 serial subscriptions, 3,400 audiovisual materials. *Research affiliation:* National Institutes of Health (complementary and alternative medicine).

Computer facilities: 8 computers available on campus for general student use. A campuswide network can be accessed. Internet access is available. *Web address:* http://www.ormed.edu/.

General Application Contact: Jack Miller, President, 619-574-6909, Fax: 619-574-6641, E-mail: jmiller@ormed.edu.

GRADUATE UNITS

Graduate Program Students: 467. Average age 28. 90 applicants, 89% accepted, 60 enrolled. *Faculty:* 80. Expenses: Contact institution. *Financial support:* In 2001–02, 301 students received support. Career-related internships or fieldwork, Federal Work-Study, and scholarships/grants available. Support available to part-time students. Financial award applicants required to submit FAFSA. In 2001, 60 degrees awarded. *Degree program information:* Part-time and evening/weekend programs available. Offers Oriental medicine (MSTOM). *Application deadline:* Applications are processed on a rolling basis. *Application fee:* $50 ($100 for international students). *Application Contact:* Gina Rubbo, Admissions Counselor/Director of Outreach, 800-729-0941, Fax: 619-574-6641, E-mail: grubbo@ormed.edu. *President,* Jack Miller, 619-574-6909, Fax: 619-574-6641, E-mail: jmiller@ormed.edu.

PACIFIC COLLEGE OF ORIENTAL MEDICINE-CHICAGO, Chicago, IL 60613

General Information Proprietary, coed, graduate-only institution. *Graduate faculty:* 13. *Tuition:* Full-time $11,085. Tuition and fees vary according to campus/location. *Graduate housing:* On-campus housing not available. *Library facilities:* Reference Center. *Collection:* 300 titles, 30 audiovisual materials.

Computer facilities: 2 computers available on campus for general student use. A campuswide network can be accessed. Internet access is available. *Web address:* http://www.ormed.edu/.

General Application Contact: Jennifer Park, Admissions Counselor, 888-729-4811, Fax: 773-477-4109, E-mail: jpark@ormed.edu.

GRADUATE UNITS

Graduate Program Students: 60. Average age 37. 33 applicants, 91% accepted, 30 enrolled. *Faculty:* 13. Expenses: Contact institution. *Financial support:* In 2001–02, 26 students received support. Career-related internships or fieldwork, Federal Work-Study, and scholarships/grants available. Support available to part-time students. Financial award applicants required to submit FAFSA. *Degree program information:* Part-time and evening/weekend programs available. *Application deadline:* Applications are processed on a rolling basis. *Application fee:* $50 ($100 for international students). *Application Contact:* Jennifer Park, Admissions Counselor, 888-729-4811, Fax: 773-477-4109, E-mail: jpark@ormed.edu. *Chief Administration Officer,* Peter Stewart, 888-729-4811, Fax: 773-477-4109, E-mail: pstewart@ormed.edu.

PACIFIC COLLEGE OF ORIENTAL MEDICINE-NEW YORK, New York, NY 10010

General Information Proprietary, coed, graduate-only institution. *Graduate faculty:* 86. *Tuition:* Full-time $12,543. *Graduate housing:* On-campus housing not available. *Student services:* Campus employment opportunities. *Library facilities:* Reference Center. *Collection:* 2,843 serial subscriptions.

Computer facilities: 7 computers available on campus for general student use. A campuswide network can be accessed. Internet access is available. *Web address:* http://www.ormed.edu/.

General Application Contact: Alma Zengotita, Admissions Counselor, 800-729-3468, Fax: 212-982-6514, E-mail: azengotita@ormed.edu.

GRADUATE UNITS

Graduate Program Students: 435. Average age 30. 120 applicants, 79% accepted, 80 enrolled. *Faculty:* 86. Expenses: Contact institution. *Financial support:* In 2001–02, 273 students received support. Career-related internships or fieldwork, Federal Work-Study, and scholarships/grants available. Support available to part-time students. Financial award applicants required to submit FAFSA. In 2001, 82 degrees awarded. *Degree program information:* Part-time and evening/weekend programs available. Offers Oriental medicine (MSTOM). *Application deadline:* Applications are processed on a rolling basis. *Application fee:* $50 ($100 for international students). *Application Contact:* Alma Zengotita, Admissions Counselor, 800-729-3468, Fax: 212-982-6514, E-mail: azengotita@ormed.edu. *Chief Administrative Officer,* Reine Deming, 212-982-3456, Fax: 212-982-6514, E-mail: rdeming@ormed.edu.

PACIFIC GRADUATE SCHOOL OF PSYCHOLOGY, Palo Alto, CA 94303-4232

General Information Independent, coed, graduate-only institution. *Graduate housing:* On-campus housing not available.

GRADUATE UNITS

Distance Learning Program in Psychology Postbaccalaureate distance learning degree programs offered (no on-campus study). Offers psychology (MS).

Program in Clinical Psychology Offers clinical psychology (PhD, Psy D). Beginning Fall 2002, we have introduced the PGSP-Stanford Psy D Consortium.

PACIFIC LUTHERAN THEOLOGICAL SEMINARY, Berkeley, CA 94708-1597

General Information Independent-religious, coed, graduate-only institution. *Graduate faculty:* 15 full-time (4 women), 9 part-time/adjunct (1 woman). *Tuition:* Part-time $3,600 per semester. *Graduate housing:* Rooms and/or apartments available on a first-come, first-served basis to single and married students. Housing application deadline: 8/1. *Student services:* Campus employment opportunities, career counseling, international student services, multicultural affairs office. *Library facilities:* Flora Lamson Hewlett Library. *Online resources:* library catalog, access to other libraries' catalogs. *Collection:* 355,000 titles, 2,400 serial subscriptions.

Computer facilities: 5 computers available on campus for general student use. Internet access is available.

General Application Contact: Rev. John Goldstein, Director of Admissions, 510-524-5264, Fax: 510-524-2408, E-mail: admissions@plts.edu.

GRADUATE UNITS

Graduate and Professional Programs Students: 153 (95 women); includes 13 minority (3 African Americans, 6 Asian Americans or Pacific Islanders, 1 Hispanic American, 3 Native Americans) 10 international. 85 applicants, 80% accepted. *Faculty:* 15 full-time (4 women), 9 part-time/adjunct (1 woman). Expenses: Contact institution. *Financial support:* In 2001–02, 104 students received support; fellowships, career-related internships or fieldwork, Federal Work-Study, institutionally sponsored loans, and scholarships/grants available. Support available to part-time students. Financial award application deadline: 3/15; financial award applicants required to submit FAFSA. In 2001, 25 first professional degrees, 4 master's, 13 other advanced degrees awarded. *Degree program information:* Part-time programs available. Offers theology (M Div, MA, MTS, Certificate). *Application deadline:* For fall admission, 8/1 (priority date); for spring admission, 1/1 (priority date). Applications are processed on a rolling basis. *Application fee:* $35. *Application Contact:* Ardelle Hester, Registrar, 510-524-5264, Fax: 510-524-2408. *Academic Dean,* Dr. Michael Aune, 510-524-5264.

PACIFIC LUTHERAN UNIVERSITY, Tacoma, WA 98447

General Information Independent-religious, coed, comprehensive institution. *Enrollment:* 142 full-time matriculated graduate/professional students (82 women), 99 part-time matriculated graduate/professional students (54 women). *Enrollment by degree level:* 241 master's. *Graduate faculty:* 77. *Tuition:* Full-time $13,296; part-time $554 per credit. Tuition and fees vary according to course load and program. *Graduate housing:* Room and/or apartments available on a first-come, first-served basis to single students; on-campus housing not available to married students. Housing application deadline: 5/1. *Student services:* Campus employment opportunities, campus safety program, career counseling, disabled student services, free psychological counseling, international student services, low-cost health insurance, multicultural affairs office, teacher training. *Library facilities:* Mortvedt Library. *Online resources:* library catalog, web page. *Collection:* 365,021 titles, 2,186 serial subscriptions, 12,648 audiovisual materials.

Computer facilities: 200 computers available on campus for general student use. A campuswide network can be accessed from student residence rooms and from off campus. Internet access and online class registration are available. *Web address:* http://www.plu.edu/.

General Application Contact: Linda DuBay, Office of Admissions, 253-535-7151, Fax: 253-535-8320, E-mail: admissions@plu.edu.

GRADUATE UNITS

Division of Graduate Studies Students: 142 full-time (82 women), 98 part-time (54 women); includes 27 minority (6 African Americans, 15 Asian Americans or Pacific Islanders, 5 Hispanic Americans, 1 Native American), 21 international. Average age 32. 200 applicants, 78% accepted, 139 enrolled. *Faculty:* 77. Expenses: Contact institution. *Financial support:* Fellowships, research assistantships, career-related internships or fieldwork, Federal Work-Study, and scholarships/grants available. Support available to part-time students. Financial award application deadline: 3/1; financial award applicants required to submit FAFSA. In 2001, 136 degrees awarded. *Degree program information:* Part-time and evening/weekend programs available. *Application fee:* $35. *Application Contact:* Linda DuBay, Office of Admissions, 253-535-7151, Fax: 253-535-8320, E-mail: admissions@plu.edu. *Provost and Dean,* Dr. Paul Menzel, 253-535-7126, Fax: 253-535-8320, E-mail: provost@plu.edu.

Division of Social Sciences Students: 21 full-time (17 women), 19 part-time (13 women); includes 5 minority (2 African Americans, 2 Asian Americans or Pacific Islanders, 1 Hispanic American), 3 international. Average age 27. 35 applicants, 57% accepted, 18 enrolled. *Faculty:* 7. Expenses: Contact institution. *Financial support:* Research assistantships, career-related internships or fieldwork, Federal Work-Study, and scholarships/grants available. Financial award application deadline: 3/1. In 2001, 14 degrees awarded. Offers marriage and family therapy (MA); social sciences (MA). *Application deadline:* For fall admission, 1/31 (priority date). *Application fee:* $35. *Application Contact:* Linda DuBay, Office of Admissions, 253-535-7151, Fax: 253-535-8320, E-mail: admissions@plu.edu. *Chair,* Dr. David Huelsbeck, 253-535-7599.

School of Business Administration and Management Students: 70 full-time (23 women), 38 part-time (14 women); includes 11 minority (3 African Americans, 7 Asian Americans or Pacific Islanders, 1 Hispanic American), 15 international. Average age 32. 60 applicants, 75% accepted, 45 enrolled. *Faculty:* 11 full-time (1 woman). Expenses: Contact institution. *Financial support:* Fellowships, research assistantships, career-related internships or fieldwork, Federal Work-Study, and scholarships/grants available. Financial award application deadline: 3/1. In 2001, 50 degrees awarded. *Degree program information:* Part-time and evening/weekend programs available. Offers business administration (MBA). *Application deadline:* Applications are processed on a rolling basis. *Application fee:* $35. *Application Contact:* Catherine Pratt, Director, 253-535-7250, E-mail: prattca@plu.edu. *Dean,* Dr. Donald Bell, 253-535-7251.

School of Education Students: 39 full-time (31 women), 34 part-time (20 women); includes 10 minority (1 African American, 5 Asian Americans or Pacific Islanders, 3 Hispanic Americans, 1 Native American), 3 international. Average age 32. 88 applicants, 78% accepted, 64 enrolled. *Faculty:* 17 full-time (8 women), 1 (woman) part-time/adjunct. Expenses: Contact institution. *Financial support:* Fellowships, research assistantships, Federal Work-Study and scholarships/grants available. Financial award application deadline: 3/1. In 2001, 63 degrees awarded. *Degree program information:* Part-time and evening/weekend programs available. Offers classroom language and literacy focus (MA); early childhood (MA); education (MA); education administration (MA); elementary education (MA); kindergarten through twelfth grade (MA); language and literacy (MA); school library media (MA); secondary education (MA); teaching (MA). *Application deadline:* Applications are processed on a rolling basis. *Application fee:* $35. *Application Contact:* Linda DuBay, Office of Admissions, 253-535-7151, Fax: 253-535-8320, E-mail: admissions@plu.edu. *Dean,* Dr. Lynn Beck, 253-535-7272.

School of Nursing Students: 12 full-time (11 women), 7 part-time (all women); includes 1 minority (Asian American or Pacific Islander) Average age 42. 17 applicants, 88% accepted, 11 enrolled. *Faculty:* 8 full-time (all women), 2 part-time/adjunct (1 woman). Expenses: Contact institution. *Financial support:* Research assistantships, Federal Work-Study and scholarships/grants available. Financial award application deadline: 3/1. In 2001, 9 degrees awarded. *Degree program information:* Part-time and evening/weekend programs available. Offers client systems management (MSN); family nurse practitioner (MSN); health care systems management (MSN); nursing (MSN). *Application deadline:* For fall admission, 4/1 (priority date). Applications are processed on a rolling basis. *Application fee:* $35. *Application Contact:* Linda DuBay, Office of Admissions, 253-535-7151, Fax: 253-535-8320, E-mail: admissions@plu.edu. *Dean,* Dr. Terry Miller, 253-535-7672.

See in-depth description on page 1021.

PACIFIC OAKS COLLEGE, Pasadena, CA 91103

General Information Independent, coed, primarily women, upper-level institution. *Enrollment:* 89 full-time matriculated graduate/professional students (79 women), 451 part-time matriculated graduate/professional students (421 women). *Enrollment by degree level:* 540 master's. *Graduate faculty:* 27 full-time (22 women), 45 part-time/adjunct. *Tuition:* Full-time $10,450; part-time $550 per unit. *Required fees:* $30 per term. *Graduate housing:* On-campus housing not available. *Student services:* Campus employment opportunities, career counseling, disabled student services, international student services, teacher training. *Library facilities:* Andrew Norman Library. *Online resources:* library catalog. *Collection:* 18,451 titles, 106 serial subscriptions, 161 audiovisual materials. *Research affiliation:* Lactation Institute, California Department of Education (early childhood education), Los Angeles County Department of Education.

Computer facilities: 4 computers available on campus for general student use. A campuswide network can be accessed from off campus. Internet access, on-line class listings are available. *Web address:* http://www.pacificoaks.edu/.

General Application Contact: Marsha Franker, Director of Admissions, 626-397-1349, Fax: 626-577-6144, E-mail: admissions@pacificoaks.edu.

GRADUATE UNITS

Graduate School Students: 89 full-time (79 women), 451 part-time (421 women); includes 182 minority (54 African Americans, 28 Asian Americans or Pacific Islanders, 90 Hispanic Americans, 10 Native Americans), 2 international. Average age 38. 116 applicants, 90% accepted, 73 enrolled. *Faculty:* 27 full-time (22 women), 45 part-time/adjunct. Expenses: Contact institution. *Financial support:* Federal Work-Study and scholarships/grants available. Support available to part-time students. Financial award application deadline: 4/15; financial award applicants required to submit FAFSA. In 2001, 87 degrees awarded. *Degree program*

Pacific Oaks College (continued)

information: Part-time and evening/weekend programs available. Postbaccalaureate distance learning degree programs offered (minimal on-campus study). Offers human development (MA); marriage and family therapy (MA). *Application deadline:* For fall admission, 4/15 (priority date); for spring admission, 10/1 (priority date). Applications are processed on a rolling basis. *Application fee:* $55. *Application Contact:* Marsha Franker, Director of Admissions, 626-397-1349, Fax: 626-577-6144, E-mail: admissions@pacificoaks.edu.

PACIFIC SCHOOL OF RELIGION, Berkeley, CA 94709-1323

General Information Independent, coed, graduate-only institution. *Enrollment by degree level:* 169 master's, 30 doctoral, 16 other advanced degrees. *Graduate faculty:* 19 full-time (7 women), 28 part-time/adjunct (14 women). *Tuition:* Full-time $9,000; part-time $500 per unit. *Required fees:* $50; $50. *Graduate housing:* Rooms and/or apartments guaranteed to single and married students. Typical cost: $4,156 (including board) for single students; $6,129 per year ($6,269 including board) for married students. Housing application deadline: 4/1. *Student services:* Campus employment opportunities, career counseling, low-cost health insurance, writing training. *Library facilities:* Graduate Theological Union Library. *Online resources:* library catalog, web page. *Collection:* 600,000 titles, 2,227 serial subscriptions. *Research affiliation:* Center for Women and Religion (women's studies), Center for Ethics and Social Policy (business ethics), Pacific Asian American Center for Theology and Strategies (Asian-American advocacy), Disciples Seminary Foundation (theology), Swedenborgean House of Studies (theology), Bay Area Faith and Health Consortium (public health).

Computer facilities: 11 computers available on campus for general student use. A campuswide network can be accessed from off campus. Internet access is available. *Web address:* http://www.psr.edu/.

General Application Contact: Debra Mumford, Director of Admissions and Recruitment, 510-849-8231, Fax: 510-845-8948, E-mail: dmumford@psr.edu.

GRADUATE UNITS

Graduate and Professional Programs Students: 22 full-time (12 women), 4 part-time (3 women), 7 international. Average age 35. 125 applicants, 77% accepted, 86 enrolled. *Faculty:* 19 full-time (7 women), 28 part-time/adjunct (14 women). Expenses: Contact institution. *Financial support:* In 2001–02, 1 fellowship with tuition reimbursement (averaging $3,000 per year), 12 teaching assistantships with tuition reimbursements (averaging $2,200 per year) were awarded. Career-related internships or fieldwork, Federal Work-Study, and scholarships/grants also available. Support available to part-time students. Financial award application deadline: 3/1; financial award applicants required to submit FAFSA. In 2001, 53 first professional degrees, 63 master's, 7 doctorates, 1 other advanced degree awarded. *Degree program information:* Part-time programs available. *Application deadline:* For fall admission, 2/1 (priority date); for spring admission, 11/1. Applications are processed on a rolling basis. *Application fee:* $50. *Application Contact:* Debra Mumford, Director of Admissions and Recruitment, 510-849-8231, Fax: 510-845-8948, E-mail: dmumford@psr.edu. *President,* William McKinney, 510-849-8241, Fax: 510-849-8242, E-mail: wmckinney@psr.edu.

PACIFIC STATES UNIVERSITY, Los Angeles, CA 90006

General Information Independent, coed, comprehensive institution. *Enrollment:* 69 full-time matriculated graduate/professional students (33 women). *Enrollment by degree level:* 69 master's. *Graduate faculty:* 4 full-time (0 women), 14 part-time/adjunct (0 women). *Tuition:* Full-time $9,600. *Required fees:* $1,050. *Student services:* Campus employment opportunities, international student services. *Library facilities:* University Library plus 1 other. *Online resources:* library catalog, access to other libraries' catalogs. *Collection:* 15,000 titles, 108 serial subscriptions.

Computer facilities: 25 computers available on campus for general student use. *Web address:* http://www.psuca.edu/.

General Application Contact: Mai A. Diep, Registrar, 888-200-0383, Fax: 323-731-7276, E-mail: admission@psuca.edu.

GRADUATE UNITS

College of Business Students: 54 full-time (26 women); includes 52 Asian Americans or Pacific Islanders Average age 25. 35 applicants, 100% accepted. *Faculty:* 3 full-time (0 women), 12 part-time/adjunct (0 women). Expenses: Contact institution. *Financial support:* In 2001–02, 1 student received support; fellowships, research assistantships, teaching assistantships, scholarships/grants available. Financial award applicants required to submit FAFSA. In 2001, 40 degrees awarded. *Degree program information:* Part-time and evening/weekend programs available. Offers finance (MBA); international business (MBA); management of technology (MBA). *Application deadline:* For fall admission, 8/15 (priority date); for winter admission, 10/15 (priority date); for spring admission, 1/15 (priority date). Applications are processed on a rolling basis. *Application fee:* $100. Electronic applications accepted. *Application Contact:* Mai A. Diep, Registrar, 888-200-0383, Fax: 323-731-7276, E-mail: admission@psuca.edu. *Director,* Dr. Kamol Somvichian, 888-200-0383, Fax: 323-731-2383, E-mail: admission@psuca.edu.

College of Computer Science Students: 15 full-time (7 women); all minorities (all Asian Americans or Pacific Islanders) *Faculty:* 1 full-time (0 women), 2 part-time/adjunct (0 women). Expenses: Contact institution. *Financial support:* Applicants required to submit FAFSA. In 2001, 8 degrees awarded. *Degree program information:* Part-time and evening/weekend programs available. Offers computer science (MSCS). *Application deadline:* For fall admission, 8/15 (priority date); for winter admission, 10/15 (priority date); for spring admission, 1/15 (priority date). Applications are processed on a rolling basis. *Application fee:* $100. Electronic applications accepted. *Application Contact:* Mai A. Diep, Registrar, 888-200-0383, Fax: 323-731-7276, E-mail: admission@psuca.edu. *Dean,* Muyung Yoo, 888-200-0383, Fax: 323-731-7276, E-mail: admission@psuca.edu.

PACIFIC UNION COLLEGE, Angwin, CA 94508-9707

General Information Independent-religious, coed, comprehensive institution. *Enrollment:* 3 full-time matriculated graduate/professional students (2 women), 16 part-time matriculated graduate/professional students (15 women). *Enrollment by degree level:* 19 master's. *Graduate faculty:* 4 full-time (2 women), 1 (woman) part-time/adjunct. *Tuition:* Full-time $15,585; part-time $450 per unit. Tuition and fees vary according to course load and student's religious affiliation. *Graduate housing:* Rooms and/or apartments guaranteed to single students and available on a first-come, first-served basis to married students. Typical cost: $2,811 per year ($4,665 including board) for single students. Housing application deadline: 8/31. *Student services:* Campus employment opportunities, campus safety program, career counseling, child daycare facilities, disabled student services, exercise/wellness program, free psychological counseling, international student services, low-cost health insurance, teacher training, writing training. *Library facilities:* W. E. Nelson Memorial Library. *Online resources:* library catalog, web page, access to other libraries' catalogs. *Collection:* 240,213 titles, 930 serial subscriptions, 54,114 audiovisual materials.

Computer facilities: 134 computers available on campus for general student use. A campuswide network can be accessed from student residence rooms and from off campus. Internet access is available. *Web address:* http://www.puc.edu/.

General Application Contact: Marsha Crow, Credential Analyst, 707-965-6643, Fax: 707-965-6645, E-mail: mcrow@puc.edu.

GRADUATE UNITS

Department of Education Students: 3 full-time (2 women), 16 part-time (15 women); includes 2 minority (1 Asian American or Pacific Islander, 1 Hispanic American) Average age 29. 6 applicants, 100% accepted. *Faculty:* 4 full-time (2 women), 1 (woman) part-time/adjunct. Expenses: Contact institution. *Financial support:* In 2001–02, 2 students received support, including 2 teaching assistantships with full tuition reimbursements available (averaging $2,000 per year); Federal Work-Study and scholarships/grants also available. Support available to part-time students. Financial award application deadline: 3/1; financial award applicants required to submit FAFSA. In 2001, 4 degrees awarded. *Degree program information:* Part-time programs available. Offers Instructional Leadership (M Ed). *Application deadline:* For fall admission, 5/1 (priority date). Applications are processed on a rolling basis. Electronic applications accepted. *Application Contact:* Marsha Crow, Credential Analyst, 707-965-6643, Fax: 707-965-6645, E-mail: mcrow@puc.edu. *Chair,* Dr. Jean Buller, 707-965-7266, Fax: 707-965-6645, E-mail: jbuller@puc.edu.

PACIFIC UNIVERSITY, Forest Grove, OR 97116-1797

General Information Independent, coed, comprehensive institution. *Enrollment:* 924 full-time matriculated graduate/professional students (557 women), 281 part-time matriculated graduate/professional students (200 women). *Enrollment by degree level:* 360 first professional, 590 master's, 255 doctoral. *Graduate faculty:* 83 full-time (43 women), 105 part-time/adjunct (65 women). *Graduate housing:* Room and/or apartments available on a first-come, first-served basis to single students; on-campus housing not available to married students. Typical cost: $4,879 (including board). Room and board charges vary according to board plan. *Student services:* Campus employment opportunities, campus safety program, career counseling, disabled student services, free psychological counseling, international student services, low-cost health insurance. *Library facilities:* Scott Memorial Library. *Online resources:* library catalog, web page, access to other libraries' catalogs. *Collection:* 1,052 serial subscriptions, 1,026 audiovisual materials.

Computer facilities: 150 computers available on campus for general student use. A campuswide network can be accessed from student residence rooms and from off campus. Internet access is available. *Web address:* http://www.pacificu.edu/.

General Application Contact: Karen Dunston, Director of Graduate and Professional Admissions, 503-352-2218 Ext. 2321, E-mail: dunstonk@pacificu.edu.

GRADUATE UNITS

College of Optometry Students: 361 full-time (160 women). Average age 27. 367 applicants, 39% accepted. *Faculty:* 30 full-time (11 women), 15 part-time/adjunct (4 women). Expenses: Contact institution. *Financial support:* In 2001–02, 20 students received support; fellowships, teaching assistantships, career-related internships or fieldwork, Federal Work-Study, and scholarships/grants available. Support available to part-time students. Financial award applicants required to submit FAFSA. In 2001, 82 first professional degrees, 4 master's awarded. Offers clinical optometry (MS); optometry (OD, M Ed, MS). *Application deadline:* For fall admission, 12/1 (priority date). Applications are processed on a rolling basis. *Application fee:* $55. Electronic applications accepted. *Application Contact:* Ann Landstrom, Assistant Director of Admissions for Professional Programs, 503-352-2900, Fax: 503-352-2975, E-mail: landstra@pacificu.edu. *Dean,* Dr. Leland W. Carr, 503-359-6151, E-mail: carrl1@pacificu.edu.

School of Education Students: 199 full-time (146 women), 81 part-time (60 women). Average age 30. 170 applicants, 59% accepted. *Faculty:* 23 full-time (15 women), 18 part-time/adjunct (10 women). Expenses: Contact institution. *Financial support:* In 2001–02, 14 students received support. Career-related internships or fieldwork, institutionally sponsored loans, and scholarships/grants available. Support available to part-time students. Financial award application deadline: 5/1; financial award applicants required to submit FAFSA. In 2001, 161 degrees awarded. *Degree program information:* Part-time and evening/weekend programs available. Offers early childhood education (MAT); education (MAE); elementary education (MAT); high school education (MAT); middle school education (MAT); visual function in learning (M Ed). *Application deadline:* For fall admission, 3/15 (priority date); for spring admission, 10/15. Applications are processed on a rolling basis. *Application fee:* $35. Electronic applications accepted. *Application Contact:* Diana Watkins, Admissions Counselor, 503-352-2958, Fax: 503-352-2907, E-mail: teach@pacificu.edu. *Dean,* Dr. Willard Kniep, 503-359-2205.

School of Occupational Therapy Students: 44 full-time (40 women); includes 3 minority (1 African American, 2 Asian Americans or Pacific Islanders) Average age 26. 20 applicants, 65% accepted, 9 enrolled. *Faculty:* 5 full-time (4 women), 8 part-time/adjunct (all women). Expenses: Contact institution. *Financial support:* In 2001–02, 9 students received support. Career-related internships or fieldwork, Federal Work-Study, and scholarships/grants available. Support available to part-time students. Financial award applicants required to submit FAFSA. In 2001, 28 degrees awarded. Offers occupational therapy (MOT). *Application deadline:* For fall admission, 12/1 (priority date). Applications are processed on a rolling basis. *Application fee:* $55. Electronic applications accepted. *Application Contact:* Jon-Erik Larsen, Admissions Counselor, 503-352-2900, Fax: 503-352-2975, E-mail: admissions@pacificu.edu. *Interim Director,* Peggy L. Hanson, 503-352-2203, Fax: 503-352-2980, E-mail: hans1139@pacificu.edu.

School of Physical Therapy Students: 108 full-time (71 women); includes 12 minority (1 African American, 7 Asian Americans or Pacific Islanders, 2 Hispanic Americans, 2 Native Americans), 1 international. Average age 27. 155 applicants, 50% accepted, 36 enrolled. *Faculty:* 10 full-time (5 women), 3 part-time/adjunct (2 women). Expenses: Contact institution. *Financial support:* In 2001–02, 14 students received support. Career-related internships or fieldwork, Federal Work-Study, and scholarships/grants available. Financial award applicants required to submit FAFSA. Offers entry level (DPT); post-professional (DPT). *Application deadline:* For fall admission, 12/2. *Application fee:* $55. Electronic applications accepted. *Application Contact:* Jon-Erik Larsen, Admissions Counselor, 503-352-2900, Fax: 503-352-2975, E-mail: admissions@pacificu.edu. *Director,* Dr. Daiva A. Banaitis, 503-352-2846.

School of Physician Assistant Studies Students: 61 full-time (35 women), 1 part-time; includes 8 minority (6 Asian Americans or Pacific Islanders, 2 Hispanic Americans) Average age 29. 275 applicants, 15% accepted. *Faculty:* 5 full-time (2 women), 7 part-time/adjunct (1 woman). Expenses: Contact institution. *Financial support:* In 2001–02, 6 students received support. Career-related internships or fieldwork and Federal Work-Study available. Financial award applicants required to submit FAFSA. In 2001, 22 degrees awarded. Offers physician assistant studies (MHS, MS). *Application deadline:* For fall admission, 10/1. *Application fee:* $55. *Application Contact:* Karen Dunston, Director of Graduate and Professional Admissions, 503-352-2218 Ext. 2321, E-mail: dunstonk@pacificu.edu. *Director,* Christine Legler, 503-359-2898, Fax: 503-359-2977, E-mail: pa@pacificu.edu.

School of Professional Psychology Students: 166 full-time (125 women), 33 part-time (24 women); includes 24 minority (1 African American, 13 Asian Americans or Pacific Islanders, 9 Hispanic Americans, 1 Native American), 3 international. Average age 31. 175 applicants, 66% accepted, 65 enrolled. *Faculty:* 13 full-time (7 women), 19 part-time/adjunct (11 women). Expenses: Contact institution. *Financial support:* In 2001–02, 21 students received support, including 15 research assistantships (averaging $3,000 per year), 19 teaching assistantships; career-related internships or fieldwork, Federal Work-Study, scholarships/grants, and unspecified assistantships also available. Support available to part-time students. Financial award applicants required to submit FAFSA. In 2001, 41 master's, 19 doctorates awarded. *Degree program information:* Part-time programs available. Offers clinical psychology (Psy D); counseling psychology (MA). *Application deadline:* For fall admission, 1/10 (priority date); for winter admission, 3/15 (priority date). *Application fee:* $40. *Application Contact:* 503-359-2900, Fax: 503-359-2975, E-mail: admissions@pacificu.edu. *Dean,* Dr. Michel Hersen, 503-359-2240, Fax: 503-359-2314, E-mail: spp@pacificu.edu.

PALM BEACH ATLANTIC UNIVERSITY, West Palm Beach, FL 33416-4708

General Information Independent-religious, coed, comprehensive institution. *Enrollment:* 190 full-time matriculated graduate/professional students (128 women), 178 part-time matriculated graduate/professional students (108 women). *Enrollment by degree level:* 52 first professional, 316 master's. *Graduate faculty:* 25 full-time (7 women), 18 part-time/adjunct (13 women). *Tuition:* Part-time $290 per credit hour. *Graduate housing:* On-campus housing not available. *Student services:* Campus safety program, career counseling, exercise/wellness program, free psychological counseling, international student services, low-cost health insurance, teacher training. *Library facilities:* E. C. Blomeyer Library. *Online resources:* library catalog, web page, access to other libraries' catalogs. *Collection:* 81,016 titles, 2,144 serial subscriptions, 3,178 audiovisual materials.

Computer facilities: A campuswide network can be accessed from student residence rooms and from off campus. *Web address:* http://www.pbac.edu/.

General Application Contact: Carolanne M. Brown, Director of Graduate Admissions, 800-281-3466, Fax: 561-803-2115, E-mail: grad@pbac.edu.

GRADUATE UNITS

MacArthur School of Continuing Education Students: 3 full-time (all women), 33 part-time (20 women); includes 14 minority (11 African Americans, 1 Asian American or Pacific Islander, 2 Hispanic Americans) Average age 40. 31 applicants, 77% accepted, 16 enrolled. *Faculty:* 4 full-time (2 women), 1 part-time/adjunct (0 women). Expenses: Contact institution. *Financial support:* Tuition waivers (partial) available. Financial award applicants required to submit FAFSA. In 2001, 4 degrees awarded. Offers organizational leadership (MS). *Application deadline:* For fall admission, 7/15 (priority date); for spring admission, 11/15 (priority date). Applications are processed on a rolling basis. *Application fee:* $35. Electronic applications accepted. *Application Contact:* Carolanne M. Brown, Director of Graduate Admissions, 800-281-3466, Fax: 561-803-2115, E-mail: grad@pbac.edu. *Dean*, Dr. Gordon Eisenman, 561-803-2317, Fax: 561-803-2306.

Rinker School of Business Students: 13 full-time (2 women), 69 part-time (27 women); includes 14 minority (7 African Americans, 1 Asian American or Pacific Islander, 6 Hispanic Americans), 11 international. Average age 33. 86 applicants, 48% accepted, 36 enrolled. *Faculty:* 6 full-time (1 woman), 3 part-time/adjunct (1 woman). Expenses: Contact institution. *Financial support:* Career-related internships or fieldwork available. Support available to part-time students. Financial award applicants required to submit FAFSA. In 2001, 38 degrees awarded. *Degree program information:* Part-time and evening/weekend programs available. Offers business (MBA). *Application deadline:* For fall admission, 7/15 (priority date); for spring admission, 11/15 (priority date). Applications are processed on a rolling basis. *Application fee:* $35. Electronic applications accepted. *Application Contact:* Carolanne M. Brown, Director of Graduate Admissions, 800-281-3466, Fax: 561-803-2115, E-mail: grad@pbac.edu. *Acting Dean*, Dr. Bob Myers.

School of Education and Behavioral Studies Students: 129 full-time (102 women), 64 part-time (52 women); includes 46 minority (29 African Americans, 2 Asian Americans or Pacific Islanders, 14 Hispanic Americans, 1 Native American), 6 international. Average age 34. 118 applicants, 69% accepted, 65 enrolled. *Faculty:* 4 full-time (2 women), 7 part-time/adjunct (6 women). Expenses: Contact institution. *Financial support:* Available to part-time students. Applicants required to submit FAFSA. In 2001, 55 degrees awarded. Offers counseling psychology (MSCP); elementary education (M Ed). *Application deadline:* For fall admission, 7/15 (priority date); for spring admission, 11/15 (priority date). Applications are processed on a rolling basis. *Application fee:* $35. Electronic applications accepted. *Application Contact:* Carolanne M. Brown, Director of Graduate Admissions, 800-281-3466, Fax: 561-803-2115, E-mail: grad@pbac.edu. *Dean*, Dr. Dona Thornton, 561-803-2350, Fax: 561-803-2186, E-mail: thorntond@pbac.edu.

School of Ministry Students: 1 full-time (0 women), 3 part-time (1 woman); includes 1 minority (African American) Average age 40. 6 applicants, 0% accepted, 0 enrolled. *Faculty:* 7 full-time (0 women). Expenses: Contact institution. In 2001, 6 degrees awarded. Offers ministry (MA). *Application deadline:* For fall admission, 7/15 (priority date); for spring admission, 11/15 (priority date). Applications are processed on a rolling basis. *Application fee:* $35. Electronic applications accepted. *Application Contact:* Carolanne M. Brown, Director of Graduate Admissions, 800-281-3466, Fax: 561-803-2115, E-mail: grad@pbac.edu. *Vice President of Religious Life and Dean*, Dr. Kenneth L. Mahanes, 561-803-2540, Fax: 561-803-2587, E-mail: mahanesk@pbac.edu.

School of Pharmacy Students: 52 full-time (30 women); includes 18 minority (3 African Americans, 3 Asian Americans or Pacific Islanders, 12 Hispanic Americans) 124 applicants, 55% accepted, 52 enrolled. Expenses: Contact institution. Offers pharmacy (Pharm D). *Application fee:* $50. *Application Contact:* Carolanne M. Brown, Director of Graduate Admissions, 800-281-3466, Fax: 561-803-2115, E-mail: grad@pbac.edu. *Dean*, Dr. Scott Swigart, 561-803-2000, E-mail: swigarts@pbac.edu.

PALMER COLLEGE OF CHIROPRACTIC, Davenport, IA 52803-5287

General Information Independent, coed, comprehensive institution. *Enrollment:* 1,646 full-time matriculated graduate/professional students (486 women), 29 part-time matriculated graduate/professional students (12 women). *Enrollment by degree level:* 1,665 first professional, 10 master's. *Graduate faculty:* 88 full-time (22 women), 7 part-time/adjunct (2 women). *Tuition:* Part-time $225 per credit hour. Tuition and fees vary according to program and student level. *Graduate housing:* On-campus housing not available. *Student services:* Campus safety program, career counseling, disabled student services, exercise/wellness program, free psychological counseling, low-cost health insurance. *Library facilities:* D. D. Palmer Health Sciences Library. *Online resources:* library catalog, access to other libraries' catalogs. *Collection:* 51,445 titles, 894 serial subscriptions, 4,077 audiovisual materials.

Computer facilities: 75 computers available on campus for general student use. A campuswide network can be accessed from off campus. Internet access is available. *Web address:* http://www.palmer.edu/.

General Application Contact: Janet Zink, Graduate Studies Coordinator, 563-884-5741, Fax: 563-884-5226, E-mail: pcadmit@palmer.edu.

GRADUATE UNITS

Institute of Graduate Studies Students: 4 full-time (2 women), 6 part-time (3 women). Average age 40. 7 applicants, 71% accepted, 2 enrolled. *Faculty:* 2 full-time (0 women), 7 part-time/adjunct (2 women). Expenses: Contact institution. *Financial support:* In 2001–02, 5 students received support, including teaching assistantships with full and partial tuition reimbursements available (averaging $6,269 per year); research assistantships, Federal Work-Study, institutionally sponsored loans, tuition waivers (full), and stipends also available. Support available to part-time students. Financial award application deadline: 4/1; financial award applicants required to submit FAFSA. In 2001, 2 degrees awarded. Offers anatomy (MS). *Application deadline:* For fall admission, 9/1; for spring admission, 5/28. Applications are processed on a rolling basis. *Application fee:* $50. *Application Contact:* Janet Zink, Graduate Studies Coordinator, 563-884-5741, Fax: 563-884-5226, E-mail: pcadmit@palmer.edu. *Dean of Graduate and Undergraduate Studies*, Dr. Iftikhar H. Bhatti, 563-884-5741, Fax: 563-884-5226, E-mail: bhatti_i@palmer.edu.

Professional Program Students: 1,642 full-time (484 women), 23 part-time (9 women). *Faculty:* 86 full-time (22 women). Expenses: Contact institution. *Financial support:* Career-related internships or fieldwork, Federal Work-Study, institutionally sponsored loans, and tuition waivers (full and partial) available. Support available to part-time students. Financial award applicants required to submit FAFSA. In 2001, 441 degrees awarded. *Degree program information:* Part-time programs available. Offers chiropractic (DC). *Application deadline:* For fall admission, 10/1 (priority date); for spring admission, 2/1 (priority date). Applications are processed on a rolling basis. *Application fee:* $50. *Application Contact:* Dr. David Anderson, Director of Admissions, 563-884-5656, Fax: 563-884-5414, E-mail: pcadmit@palmer.edu. *Vice President for Academic Affairs*, Dr. Brian McAulay, 563-884-5466, Fax: 563-884-5624, E-mail: mcaulay_b@palmer.edu.

PALMER COLLEGE OF CHIROPRACTIC WEST, San Jose, CA 95134-1617

General Information Independent, coed, graduate-only institution. *Enrollment by degree level:* 470 first professional. *Graduate faculty:* 29 full-time (8 women), 44 part-time/adjunct (17 women). *Tuition:* Part-time $4,630 per quarter. One-time fee: $450 part-time. *Graduate housing:* On-campus housing not available. *Student services:* Campus employment opportunities, career counseling, free psychological counseling, international student services, low-cost health insurance. *Collection:* 7,800 titles, 185 serial subscriptions.

Computer facilities: 21 computers available on campus for general student use. A campuswide network can be accessed. Internet access is available. *Web address:* http://www.palmer.edu/.

General Application Contact: Dr. David Anderson, Director of Admissions, 408-944-6000, Fax: 408-944-6032, E-mail: pccw_admiss@palmer.edu.

GRADUATE UNITS

Professional Program *Degree program information:* Part-time programs available. Offers chiropractic (DC). Electronic applications accepted.

PARKER COLLEGE OF CHIROPRACTIC, Dallas, TX 75229-5668

General Information Independent, coed, graduate-only institution. *Graduate housing:* On-campus housing not available.

GRADUATE UNITS

First Professional Degree Program *Degree program information:* Part-time programs available. Offers chiropractic (DC). Electronic applications accepted.

PARK UNIVERSITY, Parkville, MO 64152-3795

General Information Independent, coed, comprehensive institution. *Graduate housing:* Room and/or apartments available to single students; on-campus housing not available to married students.

GRADUATE UNITS

Hauptmann School of Public Affairs Students: 31 full-time (16 women), 45 part-time (24 women); includes 28 minority (25 African Americans, 1 Asian American or Pacific Islander, 2 Hispanic Americans) Average age 30. 25 applicants, 80% accepted, 20 enrolled. *Faculty:* 1 full-time (0 women), 33 part-time/adjunct (12 women). Expenses: Contact institution. *Financial support:* In 2001–02, 30 students received support. Federal Work-Study, institutionally sponsored loans, scholarships/grants, health care benefits, and unspecified assistantships available. Support available to part-time students. Financial award application deadline: 8/1; financial award applicants required to submit FAFSA. In 2001, 19 degrees awarded. *Degree program information:* Part-time and evening/weekend programs available. Offers government/business relations (MPA); non-profit management (MPA); public management (MPA). *Application deadline:* For fall admission, 8/19; for spring admission, 1/13. Applications are processed on a rolling basis. *Application fee:* $50 ($100 for international students). *Application Contact:* Thomas E. Gee, Administrator, 816-421-1125 Ext. 236, Fax: 816-471-1658, E-mail: tgee@mail.park.edu. *Dean*, Dr. Jerzy Hauptmann, 816-421-1125 Ext. 236, Fax: 816-471-1658, E-mail: gspa@mail.park.edu.

Program in Business Administration Students: 90 full-time (50 women), 11 part-time (3 women); includes 26 minority (17 African Americans, 4 Asian Americans or Pacific Islanders, 5 Hispanic Americans), 2 international. Average age 30. 35 applicants, 66% accepted. *Faculty:* 5 full-time (1 woman), 4 part-time/adjunct (0 women). Expenses: Contact institution. *Financial support:* In 2001–02, 20 students received support. Application deadline: 4/1; In 2001, 11 degrees awarded. *Degree program information:* Part-time and evening/weekend programs available. Offers business administration (MBA). *Application deadline:* Applications are processed on a rolling basis. *Application fee:* $50 ($100 for international students). *Application Contact:* John L. Suter, Administrator, MBA Program, 816-584-6843 Ext. 6843, Fax: 816-741-5218, E-mail: mba@mail.park.edu. *Director*, Dr. Nicolas Koudou, 816-584-6291 Ext. 6291, Fax: 816-741-5218, E-mail: akoudou@mail.park.edu.

Program in Education *Degree program information:* Part-time and evening/weekend programs available. Offers education (M Ed).

PAYNE THEOLOGICAL SEMINARY, Wilberforce, OH 45384-3474

General Information Independent-religious, coed, primarily women, graduate-only institution. *Enrollment by degree level:* 67 first professional. *Graduate faculty:* 5 full-time (0 women), 8 part-time/adjunct (1 woman). *Tuition:* Full-time $3,528; part-time $147 per credit hour. One-time fee: $125. Tuition and fees vary according to course load. *Graduate housing:* Rooms and/or apartments available on a first-come, first-served basis to single and married students. Housing application deadline: 8/25. *Student services:* Campus employment opportunities, campus safety program, career counseling, disabled student services, exercise/wellness program, multicultural affairs office, teacher training, writing training. *Library facilities:* Reverdy C. Ransom Library. *Online resources:* library catalog, access to other libraries' catalogs. *Collection:* 33,000 titles, 67 serial subscriptions.

Computer facilities: 25 computers available on campus for general student use. A campuswide network can be accessed from student residence rooms and from off campus. Internet access is available. *Web address:* http://www.payne.edu/.

General Application Contact: Dr. Larry Darnell George, Academic Dean, 937-376-2946 Ext. 211, Fax: 937-376-2888, E-mail: ldgeorge@email.msn.com.

GRADUATE UNITS

Program in Theology Students: 40 full-time (24 women), 55 part-time (26 women). Average age 45. 34 applicants, 91% accepted, 24 enrolled. *Faculty:* 5 full-time (0 women), 8 part-time/adjunct (1 woman). Expenses: Contact institution. *Financial support:* In 2001–02, 21 students received support. Career-related internships or fieldwork and scholarships/grants available. Support available to part-time students. Financial award application deadline: 5/30; financial award applicants required to submit FAFSA. In 2001, 7 degrees awarded. *Degree program information:* Part-time and evening/weekend programs available. Offers theology (M Div). *Application deadline:* For fall admission, 6/15 (priority date); for spring admission, 12/31. Applications are processed on a rolling basis. *Application fee:* $50. *Academic Dean*, Dr. Larry Darnell George, 937-376-2946 Ext. 211, Fax: 937-376-2888, E-mail: ldgeorge@email.msn.com.

PENNSYLVANIA ACADEMY OF THE FINE ARTS, Philadelphia, PA 19102

General Information Independent, coed, graduate-only institution. *Enrollment by degree level:* 50 master's. *Graduate faculty:* 8 full-time (2 women), 13 part-time/adjunct (5 women). *Tuition:* Full-time $16,990. *Required fees:* $130. Tuition and fees vary according to degree level. *Graduate housing:* On-campus housing not available. *Student services:* Campus employment opportunities, campus safety program, free psychological counseling, international student services, low-cost health insurance. *Library facilities:* Pennsylvania Academy of the Fine Arts Library. *Collection:* 14,500 titles, 90 serial subscriptions, 206 audiovisual materials.

Computer facilities: 6 computers available on campus for general student use. Internet access is available. *Web address:* http://www.pafa.edu/.

General Application Contact: Angela Smith, Director of Admissions, 215-972-2047, Fax: 215-569-0153, E-mail: angela@pafa.org.

GRADUATE UNITS

Graduate School Students: 50 full-time (27 women); includes 7 minority (1 African American, 4 Asian Americans or Pacific Islanders, 2 Hispanic Americans) Average age 33. 100 applicants, 26% accepted. *Faculty:* 8 full-time (2 women), 13 part-time/adjunct (5 women). Expenses: Contact institution. *Financial support:* In 2001–02, 46 students received support. Federal Work-Study, institutionally sponsored loans, and scholarships/grants available. Financial award application deadline: 4/1; financial award applicants required to submit FAFSA. In 2001, 19 degrees awarded. Offers drawing (MFA, Certificate); painting (MFA, Certificate); printmaking (MFA, Certificate); sculpture (MFA, Certificate). *Application deadline:* For fall admission, 3/1. *Application fee:* $40. *Application Contact:* Angela Smith, Director of Admissions, 215-972-2047, Fax: 215-569-0153, E-mail: angela@pafa.org. *Chair of Graduate Programs*, Daniel D. Miller, 215-972-2027, Fax: 215-569-0153.

PENNSYLVANIA COLLEGE OF OPTOMETRY, Elkins Park, PA 19027-1598

General Information Independent, coed, graduate-only institution. *Enrollment by degree level:* 605 first professional, 81 master's, 159 doctoral. *Graduate faculty:* 46 full-time (23 women), 20 part-time/adjunct (9 women). *Tuition:* Full-time $23,300. *Required fees:* $120. Full-time tuition and fees vary according to degree level and program. *Graduate housing:* On-campus housing not available. *Student services:* Campus employment opportunities, campus safety program, career counseling, free psychological counseling, international student services, low-cost health insurance. *Library facilities:* Guard Cottét Library. *Online resources:*

Pennsylvania College of Optometry (continued)

library catalog, web page. *Collection:* 9,450 titles, 294 serial subscriptions, 1,155 audiovisual materials. *Research affiliation:* Dak Dak Technologies (photobiology), Charles River Laboratories (photobiology). *Web address:* http://www.pco.edu/.

General Application Contact: Robert E. Horne, Dean of Student Affairs, 215-780-1312, Fax: 215-780-1396, E-mail: rhorne@pco.edu.

GRADUATE UNITS

Graduate Studies in Vision Impairment Students: 5 full-time (4 women), 123 part-time (105 women); includes 26 minority (16 African Americans, 5 Asian Americans or Pacific Islanders, 5 Native Americans), 3 international. *Faculty:* 5 full-time (all women), 21 part-time/adjunct (13 women). Expenses: Contact institution. *Financial support:* Federal Work-Study and scholarships/grants available. Financial award applicants required to submit FAFSA. In 2001, 27 degrees awarded. *Degree program information:* Part-time programs available. Offers audiology (Au D); education of children and youth with visual and multiple impairments (M Ed, Certificate); low vision rehabilitation (MS, Certificate); orientation and mobility therapy (MS, Certificate); rehabilitation teaching (MS, Certificate). *Application deadline:* For fall admission, 6/1. Applications are processed on a rolling basis. *Application fee:* $50. *Application Contact:* Dr. Diane P. Wormsley, Recruitment Committee Chair, 215-780-1366, Fax: 215-780-1357, E-mail: dwormsley@pco.edu. *Associate Dean,* Dr. Kathleen M. Huebner, 215-780-1361, Fax: 215-780-1357, E-mail: kathyh@pco.edu.

Professional Program Students: 609 full-time (346 women), 236 part-time (176 women); includes 209 minority (37 African Americans, 149 Asian Americans or Pacific Islanders, 21 Hispanic Americans, 2 Native Americans), 29 international. Average age 23. 524 applicants, 56% accepted, 168 enrolled. *Faculty:* 40 full-time (19 women), 25 part-time/adjunct (12 women). Expenses: Contact institution. *Financial support:* In 2001–02, 550 students received support. Career-related internships or fieldwork, Federal Work-Study, institutionally sponsored loans, and scholarships/grants available. Financial award application deadline: 3/31; financial award applicants required to submit FAFSA. In 2001, 147 ODs awarded. Postbaccalaureate distance learning degree programs offered. Offers optometry (OD). *Application deadline:* For fall admission, 3/31 (priority date). Applications are processed on a rolling basis. *Application fee:* $50. *Application Contact:* Dr. James Caldwell, Director of Admissions, 215-780-1300, E-mail: jcaldwell@pco.edu. *Dean of Student Affairs,* Robert E. Horne, 215-780-1312, Fax: 215-780-1396, E-mail: rhorne@pco.edu.

THE PENNSYLVANIA STATE UNIVERSITY AT ERIE, THE BEHREND COLLEGE, Erie, PA 16563-0001

General Information State-related, coed, comprehensive institution. *Enrollment:* 148 matriculated graduate/professional students. Tuition, state resident: full-time $7,882; part-time $333 per credit. Tuition, nonresident: full-time $13,348; part-time $557 per credit. *Graduate housing:* Room and/or apartments available on a first-come, first-served basis to single students; on-campus housing not available to married students. *Student services:* Campus employment opportunities, campus safety program, career counseling, child daycare facilities, disabled student services, exercise/wellness program, free psychological counseling, international student services, low-cost health insurance, multicultural affairs office. *Collection:* 89,907 titles, 835 serial subscriptions, 2,838 audiovisual materials.

Computer facilities: 448 computers available on campus for general student use. A campuswide network can be accessed from student residence rooms and from off campus. Internet access and online class registration are available. *Web address:* http://www.pserie.psu.edu/.

General Application Contact: Ann Burbules, Admission Counselor, 814-898-6100, Fax: 814-898-6044, E-mail: amb29@psu.edu.

GRADUATE UNITS

Graduate Center Students: 148. Average age 32. Expenses: Contact institution. *Degree program information:* Part-time programs available. Offers business administration (MBA); manufacturing systems engineering (M Eng). *Application deadline:* For fall admission, 7/26. *Application fee:* $45. *Application Contact:* Mary Ellen Madigan, Director of Admissions and Financial Aid, 814-898-6100. *Interim Dean and Provost,* Dr. Jack Burke, 814-898-6160.

THE PENNSYLVANIA STATE UNIVERSITY GREAT VALLEY CAMPUS, Malvern, PA 19355-1488

General Information State-related, coed, graduate-only institution. *Graduate faculty:* 37 full-time (12 women), 77 part-time/adjunct (19 women). Tuition, state resident: part-time $415 per credit. Tuition, nonresident: part-time $680 per credit. Tuition and fees vary according to program. *Graduate housing:* On-campus housing not available. *Student services:* Campus employment opportunities, campus safety program, career counseling, international student services, low-cost health insurance. *Library facilities:* Great Valley Library. *Collection:* 31,719 titles, 380 serial subscriptions, 2,597 audiovisual materials.

Computer facilities: A campuswide network can be accessed from off campus. Internet access and online class registration are available. *Web address:* http://www.gv.psu.edu/.

General Application Contact: Dr. Kathy Mingioni, Assistant Director of Admissions, 610-648-3315, Fax: 610-725-5296, E-mail: kgm2@psu.edu.

GRADUATE UNITS

Graduate Studies and Continuing Education Students: 1,386. *Faculty:* 37 full-time (13 women), 78 part-time/adjunct (16 women). Expenses: Contact institution. *Financial support:* Research assistantships, Federal Work-Study available. Support available to part-time students. *Degree program information:* Part-time programs available. *Application fee:* $45. *Application Contact:* 610-648-3242, Fax: 610-889-1334. *Campus Executive Officer and Associate Dean,* Dr. William Milheim, 610-648-3379.

College of Education Students: 231. Expenses: Contact institution. Offers curriculum and instruction (M Ed); instructional systems (M Ed, MS); special education (M Ed, MS). *Application fee:* $45. *Application Contact:* 610-648-3242, Fax: 610-889-1334. *Interim Division Head,* Dr. Martin Sharp, 610-648-3286.

School of Graduate Professional Studies Students: 1,155. Expenses: Contact institution. Offers business administration (MBA); graduate professional studies (M Eng, MBA, MS, MSE, Post Master's Certificate); information science (MS); management (Post Master's Certificate); software engineering (MSE); systems engineering (M Eng). *Application fee:* $45. *Application Contact:* 610-648-3242, Fax: 610-889-1334.

THE PENNSYLVANIA STATE UNIVERSITY HARRISBURG CAMPUS OF THE CAPITAL COLLEGE, Middletown, PA 17057-4898

General Information State-related, coed, comprehensive institution. *Enrollment:* 1,293 matriculated graduate/professional students. Tuition, state resident: full-time $7,882; part-time $333 per credit. Tuition, nonresident: full-time $14,384; part-time $600 per credit. *Graduate housing:* Rooms and/or apartments available on a first-come, first-served basis to single and married students. *Student services:* Campus employment opportunities, campus safety program, career counseling, child daycare facilities, disabled student services, exercise/wellness program, free psychological counseling, international student services, low-cost health insurance, multicultural affairs office. *Collection:* 246,143 titles, 2,447 serial subscriptions, 5,373 audiovisual materials. *Research affiliation:* State Data Center.

Computer facilities: 132 computers available on campus for general student use. A campuswide network can be accessed from student residence rooms and from off campus. Internet access and online class registration are available. *Web address:* http://www.psu.edu/.

General Application Contact: Dr. Thomas Streveler, Director of Enrollment Services, 717-948-6250, Fax: 717-948-6325, E-mail: tis1@psu.edu.

GRADUATE UNITS

Graduate Center Students: 1,293. Average age 34. Expenses: Contact institution. *Financial support:* Career-related internships or fieldwork and Federal Work-Study available. Support available to part-time students. *Degree program information:* Part-time and evening/weekend programs available. *Application deadline:* For fall admission, 7/26. *Application fee:* $45. *Provost and Dean,* Dr. Madlyn L. Hanes, 717-948-6105.

School of Behavioral Sciences and Education Students: 596. Average age 33. Expenses: Contact institution. *Financial support:* Career-related internships or fieldwork available. *Degree program information:* Part-time and evening/weekend programs available. Offers adult education (D Ed); applied behavior analysis (MA); applied clinical psychology (MA); applied psychological research (MA); behavioral sciences and education (M Ed, MA, D Ed); community psychology and social change (MA); health education (M Ed); teaching and curriculum (M Ed); training and development (M Ed). *Application deadline:* For fall admission, 7/26. *Application fee:* $45. *Interim School Director,* Dr. Ernie Dishner, 717-948-6205.

School of Business Administration Students: 284. Average age 33. Expenses: Contact institution. Offers business administration (MBA, MSIS); information systems (MSIS). *Application deadline:* For fall admission, 7/26. *Application fee:* $45. *Director,* Dr. Mukund S. Kulkarni, 717-948-6141.

School of Humanities Students: 94. Average age 33. Expenses: Contact institution. *Financial support:* Career-related internships or fieldwork available. In 2001, 28 degrees awarded. *Degree program information:* Evening/weekend programs available. Offers American studies (MA); humanities (MA). *Application deadline:* For fall admission, 7/26. *Application fee:* $45. *Acting School Director,* Dr. Simon Bronnor, 717-948-6470.

School of Public Affairs Students: 185. Average age 33. Expenses: Contact institution. *Financial support:* Career-related internships or fieldwork available. *Degree program information:* Evening/weekend programs available. Offers health administration (MHA); public administration (MPA, PhD); public affairs (MHA, MPA, PhD). *Application deadline:* For fall admission, 7/26. *Application fee:* $45. *Director,* Dr. Steven A. Peterson, 717-948-6154.

School of Science, Engineering and Technology Students: 134. Average age 33. Expenses: Contact institution. *Degree program information:* Evening/weekend programs available. Offers computer science (MS); electrical engineering (M Eng); engineering science (M Eng); environmental pollution control (M Eng, MEPC, MS). *Application deadline:* For fall admission, 7/26. *Application fee:* $45. *Director,* Dr. Omid Ansary, 717-948-6353.

See in-depth description on page 1023.

THE PENNSYLVANIA STATE UNIVERSITY MILTON S. HERSHEY MEDICAL CENTER, Hershey, PA 17033-2360

General Information State-related, coed, graduate-only institution. *Enrollment by degree level:* 470 first professional. *Graduate faculty:* 571 full-time (141 women), 49 part-time/adjunct (29 women). Tuition, state resident: full-time $20,500. Tuition, nonresident: full-time $28,500. Full-time tuition and fees vary according to degree level. *Graduate housing:* Rooms and/or apartments available on a first-come, first-served basis to single students and available to married students. Typical cost: $5,310 per year for single students; $6,174 per year for married students. Room charges vary according to housing facility selected. *Student services:* Campus employment opportunities, campus safety program, career counseling, child daycare facilities, disabled student services, exercise/wellness program, free psychological counseling, international student services, low-cost health insurance. *Library facilities:* George T. Harrell Library. *Collection:* 105,325 titles, 2,147 serial subscriptions, 340 audiovisual materials. *Research affiliation:* Harrisburg Hospital, Polyclinic Medical Center, Geisinger Medical Center.

Computer facilities: A campuswide network can be accessed from student residence rooms and from off campus. Internet access and online class registration are available. *Web address:* http://www.collmed.psu.edu/.

General Application Contact: Dr. Eugene Rannels, Assistant Dean, 717-531-8892, Fax: 717-531-4139, E-mail: grad-hmc@psu.edu.

GRADUATE UNITS

College of Medicine Students: 470 full-time (232 women). Average age 25. Expenses: Contact institution. *Financial support:* Fellowships available. In 2001, 98 degrees awarded. Offers medicine (MD). *Application deadline:* For fall admission, 12/1. *Application fee:* $50. *Senior Vice President and Dean,* Dr. Darrell G. Kirch, 717-531-8521, Fax: 717-531-5351, E-mail: dkirch@psu.edu.

Graduate School Programs in the Biomedical Sciences Average age 25. 630 applicants, 14% accepted, 41 enrolled. Expenses: Contact institution. *Financial support:* In 2001–02, 33 fellowships (averaging $17,415 per year), 127 research assistantships with tuition reimbursements (averaging $17,415 per year) were awarded. Teaching assistantships with tuition reimbursements, scholarships/grants, health care benefits, tuition waivers (full), and unspecified assistantships also available. Financial award applicants required to submit FAFSA. Offers anatomy (MS, PhD); biochemistry and molecular biology (MS, PhD); bioengineering (MS, PhD); biomedical sciences (MS, PhD); cell and molecular biology (MS, PhD); genetics (MS, PhD); health evaluation sciences (MS); immunology (MS, PhD); integrative biosciences (MS, PhD); laboratory animal medicine (MS); microbiology (MS); microbiology/virology (PhD); molecular biology (PhD); neuroscience (MS, PhD); pharmacology (MS, PhD); physiology (MS, PhD). *Application deadline:* Applications are processed on a rolling basis. *Application fee:* $45. Electronic applications accepted. *Assistant Dean,* Dr. Eugene Rannels, 717-531-8892, Fax: 717-531-4139, E-mail: grad-hmc@psu.edu.

THE PENNSYLVANIA STATE UNIVERSITY UNIVERSITY PARK CAMPUS, State College, University Park, PA 16802-1503

General Information State-related, coed, university. CGS member. *Enrollment:* 6,289 matriculated graduate/professional students. *Graduate faculty:* 2,872. Tuition, state resident: full-time $7,882; part-time $333 per credit. Tuition, nonresident: full-time $16,142; part-time $673 per credit. *Required fees:* $124 per semester. *Graduate housing:* Rooms and/or apartments available on a first-come, first-served basis to single and married students. *Student services:* Campus employment opportunities, campus safety program, career counseling, child daycare facilities, disabled student services, exercise/wellness program, free psychological counseling, international student services, low-cost health insurance, multicultural affairs office. *Library facilities:* Pattee Library plus 7 others. *Online resources:* library catalog, web page, access to other libraries' catalogs. *Collection:* 2.8 million titles, 22,879 serial subscriptions, 684,067 audiovisual materials.

Computer facilities: 3,589 computers available on campus for general student use. A campuswide network can be accessed from student residence rooms and from off campus. Internet access and online class registration are available. *Web address:* http://www.psu.edu/.

General Application Contact: Cynthia Nicosia, Director of Graduate Enrollment Services, 814-865-1795, Fax: 814-863-4627.

GRADUATE UNITS

Graduate School Students: 6,289. Average age 30. *Faculty:* 2,872. Expenses: Contact institution. *Financial support:* Fellowships, research assistantships, teaching assistantships, Federal Work-Study, tuition waivers (full), and unspecified assistantships available. Support available to part-time students. *Degree program information:* Part-time programs available. Offers acoustics (M Eng, MS, PhD); bioengineering (MS, PhD); biotechnology (MS); ecology (MS, PhD); environmental pollution control (M Eng, MEPC, MS); genetics (MS, PhD); integrative biosciences (MS, PhD); mass communications (PhD); materials (MS, PhD); nutrition (M Ed, MS, PhD); physiology (MS, PhD); plant physiology (MS, PhD); quality and manufacturing management (MMM); science and biotechnology (MS). *Application fee:* $45. *Vice President, Research and Dean,* Dr. Eva J. Pell, 814-865-2516.

College of Agricultural Sciences Students: 209 full-time (104 women), 98 part-time (36 women). Expenses: Contact institution. Offers agricultural and extension education (M Ed,

MS, D Ed, PhD); agricultural sciences (M Agr, M Ed, MFR, MS, D Ed, PhD); agricultural, environmental and regional economics (M Agr, MS, PhD); agronomy (M Agr, MS, PhD); animal science (M Agr, MS, PhD); community and economic development (MS); entomology (M Agr, MS, PhD); food science (MS, PhD); forest resources (M Agr, MFR, MS, PhD); horticulture (M Agr, MS, PhD); pathobiology (MS, PhD); plant pathology (M Agr, MS, PhD); rural sociology (M Agr, MS, PhD); soil science (M Agr, MS, PhD); wildlife and fisheries sciences (M Agr, MFR, MS, PhD); youth and family education (M Ed). *Application fee:* $45. *Dean,* Dr. Robert D. Steele, 814-865-2541.

College of Arts and Architecture Students: 168 full-time (99 women), 44 part-time (29 women). Expenses: Contact institution. Offers architecture (MS); art (MA, MFA); art education (M Ed, MS, D Ed, PhD); art history (MA, PhD); arts and architecture (M Ed, M Mus, MA, MFA, MLA, MME, MS, D Ed, PhD); ceramics (MFA); composition/theory (M Mus); conducting (M Mus); drawing/painting (MFA); graphic design (MFA); landscape architecture (MLA); metals (MFA); music and music education (M Ed, M Mus, MA, MME, PhD); music education (M Ed, MME, PhD); music theory (MA); music theory and history (MA); musicology (MA); performance (M Mus); photography (MFA); piano pedagogy and performance (M Mus); printmaking (MFA); sculpture (MFA); theatre arts (MFA); voice performance and pedagogy (M Mus). *Application fee:* $45. *Dean,* Richard W. Durst, 814-865-2591.

College of Communications Students: 46 full-time (27 women), 19 part-time (6 women). Expenses: Contact institution. Offers communications (MA, PhD); mass communications (PhD); media studies (MA); telecommunications studies (MA). *Application deadline:* For fall admission, 3/30. *Application fee:* $45. *Dean,* Dr. Douglas Anderson, 814-863-1484.

College of Earth and Mineral Sciences Students: 332 full-time (89 women), 35 part-time (6 women). Expenses: Contact institution. *Financial support:* Fellowships, unspecified assistantships available. Offers ceramic science (MS, PhD); earth and mineral sciences (M Eng, MS, PhD); energy, environmental, and mineral economics (MS, PhD); fuel science (MS, PhD); geo-environmental engineering (MS, PhD); geochemistry (MS, PhD); geography (MS, PhD); geology (MS, PhD); geophysics (MS, PhD); metals science and engineering (MS, PhD); meteorology (MS, PhD); mineral engineering management (M Eng); mineral processing (MS, PhD); mining engineering (M Eng, MS, PhD); petroleum and natural gas engineering (MS, PhD); polymer science (MS, PhD). *Application fee:* $45. *Dean,* Dr. John A. Dutton, 814-865-6546.

College of Education Students: 500 full-time (331 women), 467 part-time (301 women). Expenses: Contact institution. Offers adult education (M Ed, D Ed); bilingual education (M Ed, MS, D Ed, PhD); counseling psychology (PhD); counselor education (M Ed, MS, D Ed); early childhood education (M Ed, MS, D Ed, PhD); education (M Ed, MA, MS, D Ed, PhD); educational administration (M Ed, MS, D Ed, PhD); educational psychology (MS, PhD); educational theory and policy (MA, PhD); elementary counseling (M Ed, MS); elementary education (M Ed, MS, D Ed, PhD); higher education (M Ed, D Ed, PhD); instructional systems (M Ed, MS, D Ed, PhD); language arts and reading (M Ed, MS, D Ed, PhD); school psychology (M Ed, MS, PhD); science education (M Ed, MS, D Ed, PhD); social studies education (MS, D Ed, PhD); special education (M Ed, MS, PhD); supervisor and curriculum development (M Ed, MS, D Ed, PhD); workforce education and development (M Ed, MS, D Ed, PhD). *Application fee:* $45. *Dean,* Dr. David Monk, 814-865-2526.

College of Engineering Students: 902 full-time (172 women), 276 part-time (37 women). Expenses: Contact institution. *Financial support:* Fellowships, research assistantships, teaching assistantships available. Offers aerospace engineering (M Eng, MS, PhD); agricultural engineering (MS, PhD); architectural engineering (M Eng, MAE, MS, PhD); chemical engineering (MS, PhD); civil engineering (M Eng, MS, PhD); computer science and engineering (M Eng, MS, PhD); electrical engineering (M Eng, MS, PhD); engineering (M Eng, MAE, MS, PhD); engineering mechanics (M Eng, MS); engineering science (MS); engineering science and mechanics (PhD); environmental engineering (M Eng, MS, PhD); industrial engineering (M Eng, MS, PhD); manufacturing engineering (M Eng); mechanical engineering (M Eng, MS, PhD); nuclear engineering (M Eng, MS, PhD); structural engineering (M Eng, MS, PhD); transportation and highway engineering (M Eng, MS, PhD); water resources engineering (M Eng, MS, PhD). *Application fee:* $45. *Dean,* Dr. David N. Wormley, 814-865-7537.

College of Health and Human Development Students: 286 full-time (203 women), 88 part-time (58 women). Expenses: Contact institution. Offers biobehavioral health (MS, PhD); communication disorders (M Ed, MS, PhD); health and human development (M Ed, MHA, MHRIM, MS, PhD); health policy and administration (MHA, MS, PhD); hotel, restaurant, and institutional management (MHRIM, MS, PhD); hotel, restaurant, and recreation management (M Ed, MHRIM, MS, PhD); human development and family studies (MS, PhD); human nutrition (M Ed); kinesiology (MS, PhD); leisure studies (M Ed, MS, PhD); nursing (MS, PhD); nutrition (MS, PhD). *Application fee:* $45. *Dean,* Dr. Raymond Coward, 814-865-1428.

College of Liberal Arts Students: 673 full-time (365 women), 173 part-time (105 women). Expenses: Contact institution. *Financial support:* Fellowships, research assistantships, teaching assistantships available. Offers anthropology (MA, PhD); applied linguistics (PhD); classical American philosophy (MA, PhD); clinical psychology (MS, PhD); cognitive psychology (MS, PhD); comparative literature (MA, PhD); contemporary European philosophy (MA, PhD); crime, law, and justice (MA, PhD); developmental psychology (MS, PhD); economics (MA, PhD); English (M Ed, MA, MFA, PhD); French (MA, PhD); German (M Ed, MA, PhD); history (M Ed, MA, PhD); history of philosophy (MA, PhD); industrial relations and human resources (MS); industrial/organizational psychology (MS, PhD); liberal arts (M Ed, MA, MFA, MS, PhD); linguistics and applied language studies (PhD); political science (MA, PhD); psychobiology (MS, PhD); Russian and comparative literature (MA); social psychology (MS, PhD); sociology (MA, PhD); Spanish (M Ed, MA, PhD); speech communication (MA, PhD); teaching English as a second language (MA). *Application fee:* $45. *Dean,* Dr. Susan Welch, 814-865-7691.

Eberly College of Science Students: 523 full-time (180 women), 75 part-time (24 women). Expenses: Contact institution. *Financial support:* Fellowships, research assistantships, teaching assistantships, tuition waivers (full) and unspecified assistantships available. Offers applied statistics (MAS); astronomy and astrophysics (MS, PhD); biochemistry, microbiology, and molecular biology (MS, PhD); biology (MS, PhD); cell and developmental biology (PhD); chemistry (MS, PhD); mathematics (M Ed, MA, D Ed, PhD); molecular evolutionary biology (MS, PhD); physics (M Ed, MS, D Ed, PhD); science (M Ed, MA, MAS, MS, D Ed, PhD); statistics (MA, MS, PhD). *Application fee:* $45. *Dean,* Dr. Daniel Larson, 814-865-9591.

The Mary Jean and Frank P. Smeal College of Business Administration Expenses: Contact institution. Offers accounting (MS, PhD); business administration (MBA, MS, PhD); business administration, executive (MBA); business logistics (MS); finance (MS); finance/insurance and real estate (PhD); insurance (MS); management and organization (PhD); management science and information systems (MS); management science/operations/logistics (PhD); marketing (MS); marketing and distribution (PhD); real estate (MS). *Application fee:* $45. *Dean,* Dr. Judy Olian, 814-863-0448.

School of Information Sciences and Technology Students: 11 full-time (6 women), 1 part-time. Expenses: Contact institution. Offers information sciences and technology (PhD). *Application fee:* $45. *Dean,* Dr. James Thomas, 814-865-8711.

See in-depth description on page 1025.

PEPPERDINE UNIVERSITY, Culver City, CA 90230-7615

General Information Independent-religious, coed, upper-level institution. *Enrollment by degree level:* 2,839 master's, 548 doctoral. *Graduate faculty:* 139 full-time (40 women), 145 part-time/adjunct (47 women). *Tuition:* Full-time $15,700; part-time $785 per unit. Tuition and fees vary according to degree level and program. *Graduate housing:* On-campus housing not available. *Student services:* Campus employment opportunities, career counseling, free psychological counseling, international student services, low-cost health insurance, teacher training. *Web address:* http://www.pepperdine.edu/.

General Application Contact: Admissions, 310-456-4392.

GRADUATE UNITS

Graduate School of Education and Psychology Students: 662 full-time (531 women), 923 part-time (648 women); includes 444 minority (164 African Americans, 112 Asian Americans or Pacific Islanders, 163 Hispanic Americans, 5 Native Americans), 26 international. Average age 35. 885 applicants, 71% accepted. *Faculty:* 61 full-time (26 women), 84 part-time/adjunct (32 women). Expenses: Contact institution. *Financial support:* Research assistantships, teaching assistantships, career-related internships or fieldwork, Federal Work-Study, institutionally sponsored loans, and scholarships/grants available. Support available to part-time students. Financial award application deadline: 7/1; financial award applicants required to submit FAFSA. In 2001, 632 master's, 66 doctorates awarded. *Degree program information:* Part-time and evening/weekend programs available. Postbaccalaureate distance learning degree programs offered (minimal on-campus study). Offers education and psychology (MA, MS, Ed D, Psy D). *Application deadline:* Applications are processed on a rolling basis. *Application fee:* $45. *Application Contact:* Admissions Adviser, 310-568-5609. *Dean,* Dr. Margaret J. Weber, 310-568-5600.

Division of Education Students: 407 full-time (322 women), 500 part-time (308 women); includes 277 minority (111 African Americans, 70 Asian Americans or Pacific Islanders, 95 Hispanic Americans, 1 Native American), 9 international. Average age 38. 466 applicants, 82% accepted. *Faculty:* 30 full-time (16 women), 28 part-time/adjunct (17 women). Expenses: Contact institution. *Financial support:* Research assistantships, teaching assistantships, career-related internships or fieldwork, institutionally sponsored loans, and scholarships/grants available. Support available to part-time students. Financial award application deadline: 7/1; financial award applicants required to submit FAFSA. In 2001, 388 master's, 44 doctorates awarded. *Degree program information:* Part-time and evening/weekend programs available. Postbaccalaureate distance learning degree programs offered (minimal on-campus study). Offers administration (MS); education (MA, MS, Ed D); educational leadership, administration, and policy (Ed D); educational technology (MA, Ed D); organization change (Ed D); organizational leadership (Ed D). *Application deadline:* Applications are processed on a rolling basis. *Application fee:* $45. *Application Contact:* Coordinator, 310-568-5600. *Associate Dean,* Dr. Terence Cannings, 310-568-5659.

Division of Psychology Students: 255 full-time (209 women), 423 part-time (340 women); includes 167 minority (53 African Americans, 42 Asian Americans or Pacific Islanders, 68 Hispanic Americans, 4 Native Americans), 17 international. Average age 33. 428 applicants, 54% accepted. *Faculty:* 31 full-time (13 women), 45 part-time/adjunct (24 women). Expenses: Contact institution. *Financial support:* Research assistantships, teaching assistantships, career-related internships or fieldwork and scholarships/grants available. Support available to part-time students. Financial award application deadline: 7/1; financial award applicants required to submit FAFSA. In 2001, 244 master's, 22 doctorates awarded. *Degree program information:* Part-time and evening/weekend programs available. Offers clinical psychology (MA); psychology (MA, Psy D). *Application deadline:* For fall admission, 2/1. Applications are processed on a rolling basis. *Application fee:* $55. *Application Contact:* Coordinator, 310-568-5605. *Associate Dean,* Dr. Cary Mitchell, 310-568-5600 Ext. 5650.

The Graziado School of Business and Management Students: 442 full-time (131 women), 1,360 part-time (551 women); includes 432 minority (84 African Americans, 216 Asian Americans or Pacific Islanders, 130 Hispanic Americans, 2 Native Americans), 54 international. Average age 35. 663 applicants, 68% accepted. *Faculty:* 78 full-time (14 women), 61 part-time/adjunct (15 women). Expenses: Contact institution. *Financial support:* Career-related internships or fieldwork, institutionally sponsored loans, scholarships/grants, and unspecified assistantships available. Support available to part-time students. Financial award applicants required to submit FAFSA. In 2001, 740 degrees awarded. *Degree program information:* Part-time and evening/weekend programs available. Offers business (MBA); executive business administration (MBAA); organizational development (MSOD); technology management (MSTM). *Application deadline:* For fall admission, 6/28. Applications are processed on a rolling basis. *Application fee:* $45. *Application Contact:* Darrell Eriksen, Director of Career Development and Student Recruitment, 310-568-5790. *Interim Dean,* Dr. William Larson, 310-568-5500, Fax: 310-568-5766.

See in-depth description on page 1027.

PEPPERDINE UNIVERSITY, Malibu, CA 90263-0002

General Information Independent-religious, coed, university. CGS member. *Enrollment:* 870 full-time matriculated graduate/professional students (406 women), 164 part-time matriculated graduate/professional students (69 women). *Enrollment by degree level:* 632 first professional, 402 master's. *Graduate faculty:* 75 full-time (18 women), 31 part-time/adjunct (10 women). *Tuition:* Full-time $15,700; part-time $785 per unit. Tuition and fees vary according to degree level and program. *Graduate housing:* Rooms and/or apartments guaranteed to single and married students. Typical cost: $5,920 per year for single students; $13,860 per year for married students. Room charges vary according to housing facility selected. *Student services:* Campus employment opportunities, career counseling, exercise/wellness program, free psychological counseling, international student services, low-cost health insurance, teacher training. *Library facilities:* Payson Library plus 2 others. *Collection:* 515,238 titles, 3,882 serial subscriptions.

Computer facilities: 292 computers available on campus for general student use. A campuswide network can be accessed from student residence rooms. *Web address:* http://www.pepperdine.edu/.

General Application Contact: Paul Long, Dean of Enrollment Management, 310-506-4392, Fax: 310-506-4861, E-mail: admission-seaver@pepperdine.edu.

GRADUATE UNITS

Malibu Graduate Business Programs Students: 166 full-time (69 women), 1 (woman) part-time; includes 42 minority (1 African American, 30 Asian Americans or Pacific Islanders, 10 Hispanic Americans, 1 Native American), 47 international. Average age 28. 385 applicants, 47% accepted. Expenses: Contact institution. *Financial support:* Career-related internships or fieldwork, institutionally sponsored loans, scholarships/grants, and unspecified assistantships available. Financial award application deadline: 6/1; financial award applicants required to submit FAFSA. In 2001, 102 degrees awarded. Offers business administration (MBA); international business (MIB). *Application deadline:* For fall admission, 6/28. Applications are processed on a rolling basis. *Application fee:* $45. *Application Contact:* Paul Pinckley, Executive Director, Recruitment and Career Development, 310-506-4100, Fax: 310-506-4126. *Associate Dean,* Dr. James A. Goodrich, 310-506-4100, Fax: 310-506-4126.

School of Law Students: 632 full-time (298 women), 36 part-time (16 women); includes 108 minority (32 African Americans, 38 Asian Americans or Pacific Islanders, 31 Hispanic Americans, 7 Native Americans), 14 international. Average age 31. 2,260 applicants, 39% accepted. *Faculty:* 38 full-time (8 women), 29 part-time/adjunct (10 women). Expenses: Contact institution. *Financial support:* Fellowships, research assistantships, teaching assistantships, career-related internships or fieldwork, Federal Work-Study, institutionally sponsored loans, and scholarships/grants available. Support available to part-time students. Financial award application deadline: 4/1; financial award applicants required to submit FAFSA. In 2001, 201 first professional degrees, 32 master's awarded. Offers dispute resolution (MDR); law (JD, MDR). *Application deadline:* For fall admission, 3/1. Applications are processed on a rolling basis. *Application fee:* $50. *Application Contact:* Shannon Phillips, Director of Admissions, 310-506-4631, Fax: 310-506-4266, E-mail: sphillip@pepperdine.edu. *Dean,* Dr. Richardson Lynn, 310-506-4611, Fax: 310-506-4266.

School of Public Policy Students: 56 full-time (28 women), 1 (woman) part-time; includes 9 minority (6 African Americans, 1 Asian American or Pacific Islander, 2 Hispanic Americans), 3 international. 76 applicants, 67% accepted. *Faculty:* 4 full-time (0 women), 2 part-time/adjunct (0 women). Expenses: Contact institution. *Financial support:* Research assistantships, teaching assistantships, institutionally sponsored loans and scholarships/grants available. Financial award application deadline: 5/1; financial award applicants required to submit FAFSA. In 2001, 15 degrees awarded. Offers public policy (MPP). *Application deadline:* For fall admission, 4/15. Applications are processed on a rolling basis. *Application fee:* $50. Electronic applications accepted. *Application Contact:* Melinda van Hemert, Director of Recruitment and Career Services, 310-506-7492, Fax: 310-506-7494. *Dean,* Dr. James Wilburn, 310-506-7490, Fax: 310-506-7494.

Seaver College Students: 16 full-time (11 women), 126 part-time (51 women); includes 25 minority (7 African Americans, 8 Asian Americans or Pacific Islanders, 10 Hispanic Americans), 3 international. Average age 32. 103 applicants, 72% accepted. *Faculty:* 33 full-time (10

Pepperdine University (continued)

women). Expenses: Contact institution. *Financial support:* Fellowships, research assistantships, teaching assistantships, career-related internships or fieldwork, Federal Work-Study, institutionally sponsored loans, scholarships/grants, and tuition waivers (partial) available. Support available to part-time students. Financial award application deadline: 2/15; financial award applicants required to submit FAFSA. In 2001, 23 degrees awarded. *Degree program information:* Part-time and evening/weekend programs available. Offers American studies (MA); communication (MA); history (MA); ministry (MS); religion (M Div, MA). *Application deadline:* For fall admission, 5/1. Applications are processed on a rolling basis. *Application fee:* $55. *Application Contact:* Paul Long, Dean of Enrollment Management, 310-506-4392, Fax: 310-506-4861, E-mail: admission-seaver@pepperdine.edu. *Dean,* Dr. David Baird, 310-506-4281.

PERU STATE COLLEGE, Peru, NE 68421

General Information State-supported, coed, comprehensive institution. *Enrollment:* 71 part-time matriculated graduate/professional students (50 women). *Enrollment by degree level:* 71 master's. *Graduate faculty:* 68 part-time/adjunct (42 women). *Graduate housing:* Rooms and/or apartments available to single and married students. *Student services:* Career counseling, child daycare facilities, disabled student services, low-cost health insurance. *Library facilities:* Peru State College Library. *Online resources:* web page. *Collection:* 177,373 titles, 232 serial subscriptions.

Computer facilities: 120 computers available on campus for general student use. A campuswide network can be accessed from student residence rooms. Internet access is available. *Web address:* http://www.peru.edu/.

General Application Contact: Dr. Korinne Tande, Dean, Graduate School, 402-872-2244, Fax: 402-872-2414, E-mail: ktande@oakmail.peru.edu.

GRADUATE UNITS

Graduate Studies *Faculty:* 68 part-time/adjunct (42 women). Expenses: Contact institution. In 2001, 27 degrees awarded. *Degree program information:* Part-time programs available. Offers education (MS Ed). *Application deadline:* Applications are processed on a rolling basis. *Application fee:* $10. *Dean, Graduate School,* Dr. Korinne Tande, 402-872-2244, Fax: 402-872-2414, E-mail: ktande@oakmail.peru.edu.

PFEIFFER UNIVERSITY, Misenheimer, NC 28109-0960

General Information Independent-religious, coed, comprehensive institution. *Enrollment:* 706 full-time matriculated graduate/professional students (406 women). *Enrollment by degree level:* 706 master's. *Graduate faculty:* 13 full-time (3 women), 28 part-time/adjunct (6 women). *Tuition:* Part-time $275 per credit hour. Tuition and fees vary according to campus/location. *Graduate housing:* On-campus housing not available. *Student services:* Campus employment opportunities, campus safety program, career counseling, international student services, writing training. *Library facilities:* Gustavus A. Pfeiffer Library. *Online resources:* library catalog, web page, access to other libraries' catalogs. *Collection:* 116,200 titles, 415 serial subscriptions, 2,349 audiovisual materials.

Computer facilities: 64 computers available on campus for general student use. Internet access is available. *Web address:* http://www.pfeiffer.edu/.

General Application Contact: Michael Utsman, Assistant Dean, 704-521-9116 Ext. 253, Fax: 704-521-8617.

GRADUATE UNITS

Program in Business Administration *Faculty:* 11 full-time (2 women), 8 part-time/adjunct (4 women). Expenses: Contact institution. *Financial support:* Unspecified assistantships available. Support available to part-time students. *Degree program information:* Part-time and evening/weekend programs available. Postbaccalaureate distance learning degree programs offered (minimal on-campus study). Offers business administration (MBA); organizational management (MS). *Application deadline:* For fall admission, 8/21. *Application fee:* $50. *Director of the MBA Program,* Dr. Robert Spear, 704-521-9116 Ext. 244, Fax: 704-521-8617, E-mail: rks@pfeiffer.edu.

School of Religion and Christian Education *Faculty:* 3 full-time (0 women), 1 part-time/adjunct (0 women). Expenses: Contact institution. *Degree program information:* Part-time and evening/weekend programs available. Offers religion, philosophy, and Christian education (MACE). *Application deadline:* For fall admission, 8/21 (priority date). Applications are processed on a rolling basis. *Application fee:* $50. *Coordinator,* Kay Kilbourne, 704-463-1360.

PHILADELPHIA BIBLICAL UNIVERSITY, Langhorne, PA 19047-2990

General Information Independent-religious, coed, comprehensive institution. *Enrollment:* 24 full-time matriculated graduate/professional students (11 women), 360 part-time matriculated graduate/professional students (197 women). *Enrollment by degree level:* 384 master's. *Graduate faculty:* 6 full-time (2 women), 23 part-time/adjunct (6 women). *Tuition:* Full-time $6,600; part-time $330 per credit. *Required fees:* $10. *Graduate housing:* On-campus housing not available. *Student services:* Campus employment opportunities, campus safety program, career counseling, disabled student services, exercise/wellness program, international student services, low-cost health insurance, multicultural affairs office, teacher training, writing training. *Library facilities:* Masland Learning Resource Center. *Online resources:* library catalog. *Collection:* 89,743 titles, 680 serial subscriptions, 13,272 audiovisual materials.

Computer facilities: 90 computers available on campus for general student use. A campuswide network can be accessed from student residence rooms and from off campus. Internet access is available. *Web address:* http://www.pbu.edu/.

General Application Contact: Jessica Martin, Senior Student Services Associate, 800-572-2472, Fax: 215-702-4359, E-mail: jmartin@pbu.edu.

GRADUATE UNITS

Graduate School Students: 24 full-time (11 women), 360 part-time (197 women); includes 108 minority (90 African Americans, 11 Asian Americans or Pacific Islanders, 7 Hispanic Americans), 28 international. Average age 38. 88 applicants, 95% accepted, 68 enrolled. *Faculty:* 6 full-time (2 women), 23 part-time/adjunct (6 women). Expenses: Contact institution. *Financial support:* In 2001–02, 203 students received support. Scholarships/grants available. Support available to part-time students. Financial award application deadline: 8/1. In 2001, 99 degrees awarded. *Degree program information:* Part-time and evening/weekend programs available. Offers Bible (MSB); Christian counseling (MSCC); educational leadership and administration (MS El); organizational leadership (MSOL); teacher education (MS Ed). *Application deadline:* Applications are processed on a rolling basis. *Application fee:* $25. *Application Contact:* Jessica Martin, Senior Student Services Associate, 800-572-2472, Fax: 215-702-4359, E-mail: jmartin@pbu.edu. *Associate Provost,* Dr. Kevin Huggins, 800-572-2472, Fax: 215-702-4359, E-mail: khuggins@pbu.edu.

PHILADELPHIA COLLEGE OF OSTEOPATHIC MEDICINE, Philadelphia, PA 19131-1694

General Information Independent, coed, graduate-only institution. *Enrollment by degree level:* 1,211 first professional, 197 master's, 217 doctoral. *Graduate faculty:* 71 full-time (24 women), 897 part-time/adjunct (106 women). *Tuition:* Part-time $441 per credit. *Required fees:* $250. Tuition and fees vary according to program. *Graduate housing:* On-campus housing not available. *Student services:* Campus safety program, career counseling, free psychological counseling, low-cost health insurance. *Library facilities:* O. J. Snyder Memorial Medical Library. *Online resources:* library catalog, web page, access to other libraries' catalogs. *Collection:* 32,000 titles, 700 serial subscriptions, 2,100 audiovisual materials. *Research affiliation:* Polyprobe, Inc. (molecular biology), Methodist Hospital (clinical pain studies).

Computer facilities: 75 computers available on campus for general student use. A campuswide network can be accessed from student residence rooms and from off campus. Internet access is available. *Web address:* http://www.pcom.edu/.

General Application Contact: Carol A. Fox, Associate Dean for Admissions and Enrollment Management, 215-871-6700, Fax: 215-871-6719, E-mail: admissions@pcom.edu.

GRADUATE UNITS

Graduate and Professional Programs Students: 1,425 full-time (739 women); includes 287 minority (104 African Americans, 137 Asian Americans or Pacific Islanders, 43 Hispanic Americans, 3 Native Americans) Average age 27. 4,209 applicants, 13% accepted. *Faculty:* 71 full-time (24 women), 897 part-time/adjunct (106 women). Expenses: Contact institution. *Financial support:* In 2001–02, 1,300 students received support; fellowships, research assistantships, career-related internships or fieldwork, Federal Work-Study, institutionally sponsored loans, and scholarships/grants available. Financial award application deadline: 4/15; financial award applicants required to submit FAFSA. In 2001, 240 first professional degrees, 10 master's, 5 doctorates awarded. Offers biomedical sciences (MS); clinical health psychology (MS); clinical psychology (Psy D); health sciences (MS); organizational leadership and development (MS); osteopathic medicine (DO, MS, Psy D). *Application deadline:* Applications are processed on a rolling basis. *Application fee:* $50. *Application Contact:* Carol A. Fox, Associate Dean for Admissions, 215-871-6700, Fax: 215-871-6719, E-mail: carolf@pcom.edu. *Associate Dean for Admissions and Enrollment Management,* Carol A. Fox, 215-871-6770, Fax: 215-871-6719, E-mail: carolf@pcom.edu.

PHILADELPHIA UNIVERSITY, Philadelphia, PA 19144-5497

General Information Independent, coed, comprehensive institution. *Enrollment:* 139 full-time matriculated graduate/professional students (88 women), 309 part-time matriculated graduate/professional students (197 women). *Enrollment by degree level:* 448 master's. *Graduate faculty:* 23 full-time (9 women), 57 part-time/adjunct (22 women). *Tuition:* Part-time $517 per credit. *Graduate housing:* On-campus housing not available. *Student services:* Campus employment opportunities, campus safety program, career counseling, disabled student services, free psychological counseling, international student services, low-cost health insurance. *Library facilities:* Paul J. Gutman Library. *Online resources:* library catalog, web page. *Collection:* 104,000 titles, 1,600 serial subscriptions, 37,650 audiovisual materials.

Computer facilities: 400 computers available on campus for general student use. A campuswide network can be accessed from student residence rooms and from off campus. Internet access, on-line registration for advanced workshops and seminars are available. *Web address:* http://www.philau.edu/.

General Application Contact: William H. Firman, Director of Graduate Admissions, 215-951-2943, Fax: 215-951-2907, E-mail: gradadm@philau.edu.

GRADUATE UNITS

School of Business Students: 48 full-time (23 women), 170 part-time (88 women); includes 30 minority (20 African Americans, 8 Asian Americans or Pacific Islanders, 2 Hispanic Americans), 26 international. 194 applicants, 69% accepted, 63 enrolled. *Faculty:* 15 full-time (3 women), 22 part-time/adjunct (6 women). Expenses: Contact institution. *Financial support:* In 2001–02, research assistantships with full tuition reimbursements (averaging $2,000 per year); career-related internships or fieldwork, Federal Work-Study, scholarships/grants, and unspecified assistantships also available. Support available to part-time students. Financial award applicants required to submit FAFSA. In 2001, 114 degrees awarded. *Degree program information:* Part-time and evening/weekend programs available. Postbaccalaureate distance learning degree programs offered (no on-campus study). Offers accounting (MBA); business (MBA, MS); business administration (MBA); finance (MBA); health care management (MBA); international business (MBA); marketing (MBA); taxation (MS). *Application deadline:* Applications are processed on a rolling basis. *Application fee:* $35. Electronic applications accepted. *Application Contact:* William H. Firman, Director of Graduate Admissions, 215-951-2943, Fax: 215-951-2907, E-mail: gradadm@philau.edu. *Dean,* Dr. Elmore Alexander, 215-951-2827, Fax: 215-951-2652, E-mail: alexandere@philau.edu.

School of Science and Health Students: 50 full-time (39 women), 119 part-time (91 women); includes 19 minority (15 African Americans, 4 Asian Americans or Pacific Islanders), 10 international. Average age 38. 275 applicants, 53% accepted, 95 enrolled. *Faculty:* 11 full-time (8 women), 21 part-time/adjunct (14 women). Expenses: Contact institution. *Financial support:* In 2001–02, research assistantships with full tuition reimbursements (averaging $2,000 per year); career-related internships or fieldwork, Federal Work-Study, and unspecified assistantships also available. Support available to part-time students. Financial award applicants required to submit FAFSA. In 2001, 67 degrees awarded. *Degree program information:* Part-time and evening/weekend programs available. Postbaccalaureate distance learning degree programs offered (minimal on-campus study). Offers instructional technology (MS); midwifery (MS); occupational therapy (MS); physician assistant studies (MS); science and health (MS). *Application deadline:* Applications are processed on a rolling basis. *Application fee:* $35. Electronic applications accepted. *Application Contact:* William H. Firman, Director of Graduate Admissions, 215-951-2943, Fax: 215-951-2907, E-mail: gradadm@philau.edu. *Dean,* Dr. William Brendley, 215-951-2874, Fax: 215-951-2615, E-mail: brendleyw@philau.edu.

School of Textiles and Materials Science Students: 41 full-time (26 women), 17 part-time (16 women); includes 5 minority (2 African Americans, 2 Asian Americans or Pacific Islanders, 1 Hispanic American), 31 international. Average age 28. 92 applicants, 67% accepted, 12 enrolled. *Faculty:* 18 full-time (4 women), 10 part-time/adjunct (5 women). Expenses: Contact institution. *Financial support:* In 2001–02, research assistantships with full tuition reimbursements (averaging $2,000 per year); career-related internships or fieldwork, Federal Work-Study, and unspecified assistantships also available. Support available to part-time students. Financial award applicants required to submit FAFSA. In 2001, 17 degrees awarded. *Degree program information:* Part-time programs available. Offers fashion-apparel studies (MS); textile design (MS); textile engineering (MS); textiles and materials science (MS). *Application deadline:* Applications are processed on a rolling basis. *Application fee:* $35. Electronic applications accepted. *Application Contact:* William H. Firman, Director of Graduate Admissions, 215-951-2943, Fax: 215-951-2907, E-mail: gradadm@philau.edu. *Dean of School of Textiles and Materials Technology,* Dr. David Brookstein, 215-951-2751, Fax: 215-951-2651, E-mail: brooksteind@philau.edu.

PHILLIPS GRADUATE INSTITUTE, Encino, CA 91316-1509

General Information Independent, coed, graduate-only institution. *Enrollment by degree level:* 384 master's. *Graduate faculty:* 13 full-time, 30 part-time/adjunct. *Tuition:* Part-time $550 per unit. *Graduate housing:* On-campus housing not available. *Student services:* Career counseling. *Online resources:* web page. *Collection:* 6,000 titles, 150 serial subscriptions.

Computer facilities: 3 computers available on campus for general student use. A campuswide network can be accessed from off campus. Internet access is available. *Web address:* http://www.pgi.edu/.

General Application Contact: Kim Bell, Assistant Director of Admission, 818-386-5639, Fax: 818-386-5699, E-mail: admit@pgi.edu.

GRADUATE UNITS

Program in Marriage and Family Therapy, Organizational Behavior and School Counseling Students: 384 full-time (311 women); includes 76 minority (21 African Americans, 17 Asian Americans or Pacific Islanders, 38 Hispanic Americans), 3 international. Average age 39. *Faculty:* 13 full-time, 30 part-time/adjunct. Expenses: Contact institution. *Financial support:* Tuition waivers (full and partial) available. Financial award application deadline: 8/15; financial award applicants required to submit FAFSA. In 2001, 117 degrees awarded. *Degree program information:* Evening/weekend programs available. Offers marital and family therapy (MA); organizational behavior (MA); school counseling (MA). *Application deadline:* For fall admission, 8/15 (priority date); for spring admission, 12/15. Applications are processed on a rolling basis. *Application fee:* $0. *Application Contact:* Kim Bell, Assistant Director of Admission, 818-386-5639, Fax: 818-386-5699, E-mail: admit@pgi.edu. *President,* Dr. Lisa Porche-Burke, 818-386-5650, Fax: 818-386-5699.

PHILLIPS THEOLOGICAL SEMINARY, Tulsa, OK 74116

General Information Independent-religious, coed, graduate-only institution. *Enrollment by degree level:* 107 first professional, 7 master's, 34 doctoral. *Graduate faculty:* 9 full-time (3 women), 11 part-time/adjunct (7 women). *Tuition:* Part-time $8,155 per degree program. *Graduate housing:* On-campus housing not available. *Student services:* Career counseling. *Library facilities:* Seminary Library. *Online resources:* web page. *Collection:* 124,550 titles, 419 serial subscriptions, 10,700 audiovisual materials.

Computer facilities: 3 computers available on campus for general student use. Internet access is available. *Web address:* http://www.ptstulsa.edu/.

General Application Contact: Rev. Myrna J. Jones, Director of Admissions, 918-610-8303, Fax: 918-610-8404, E-mail: myrna.jones@ptstulsa.edu.

GRADUATE UNITS

Phillips Theological Seminary *Degree program information:* Part-time programs available. Postbaccalaureate distance learning degree programs offered (minimal on-campus study). Offers parish ministry (D Min); pastoral counseling (D Min); practices of ministry (D Min); theology (M Div, MAMC, MTS, D Min).

PICOWER GRADUATE SCHOOL OF MOLECULAR MEDICINE, Manhasset, NY 11030

General Information Independent, coed, graduate-only institution. *Graduate housing:* On-campus housing not available.

GRADUATE UNITS

Program in Molecular Medicine Offers molecular medicine (PhD).

PIEDMONT BAPTIST COLLEGE, Winston-Salem, NC 27101-5197

General Information Independent-religious, coed, comprehensive institution. *Enrollment:* 3 full-time matriculated graduate/professional students (1 woman), 32 part-time matriculated graduate/professional students (2 women). *Enrollment by degree level:* 35 master's. *Graduate faculty:* 1 full-time (0 women), 8 part-time/adjunct (0 women). *Tuition:* Full-time $4,600; part-time $230 per credit hour. *Required fees:* $90 per term. *Graduate housing:* Rooms and/or apartments available on a first-come, first-served basis to single and married students. Typical cost: $1,480 per year ($3,700 including board) for single students. Housing application deadline: 5/1. *Student services:* Campus employment opportunities, campus safety program, career counseling, writing training. *Library facilities:* George Manuel Memorial Library. *Collection:* 50,000 titles, 204 serial subscriptions.

Computer facilities: 40 computers available on campus for general student use. A campuswide network can be accessed. *Web address:* http://www.pbc.edu/.

General Application Contact: Richard Whiteheart, Director of Admissions, 336-725-8344 Ext. 2326, Fax: 336-725-5522, E-mail: admissions@pbc.edu.

GRADUATE UNITS

Graduate Division Students: 3 full-time (1 woman), 32 part-time (2 women); includes 1 minority (Asian American or Pacific Islander) Average age 35. 12 applicants, 100% accepted. *Faculty:* 1 full-time (0 women), 8 part-time/adjunct (0 women). Expenses: Contact institution. *Financial support:* Career-related internships or fieldwork available. Support available to part-time students. Financial award applicants required to submit CSS PROFILE. In 2001, 7 degrees awarded. *Degree program information:* Part-time programs available. Postbaccalaureate distance learning degree programs offered (no on-campus study). Offers biblical studies (MBS); ministry (MM). *Application deadline:* For fall admission, 8/15 (priority date); for spring admission, 1/1. Applications are processed on a rolling basis. *Application fee:* $30. Electronic applications accepted. *Application Contact:* Patti Kurar, Admissions Director, 336-725-8344 Ext. 2327, Fax: 336-725-5522, E-mail: kurar@pbc.edu. *Graduate Dean,* Dr. Ron Minton, 336-725-8344, Fax: 336-725-5522, E-mail: mintonr@pbc.edu.

PIEDMONT COLLEGE, Demorest, GA 30535-0010

General Information Independent-religious, coed, comprehensive institution. *Enrollment:* 973 matriculated graduate/professional students (816 women). *Graduate faculty:* 77 full-time (40 women), 85 part-time/adjunct (38 women). *Tuition:* Part-time $230 per hour. *Graduate housing:* Room and/or apartments available to single students; on-campus housing not available to married students. Typical cost: $2,150 per year ($2,250 including board). Housing application deadline: 7/1. *Student services:* Campus employment opportunities, career counseling, disabled student services, exercise/wellness program, free psychological counseling, low-cost health insurance, teacher training, writing training. *Library facilities:* Arrendale Library. *Online resources:* library catalog, web page, access to other libraries' catalogs. *Collection:* 110,000 titles, 346 serial subscriptions, 474 audiovisual materials.

Computer facilities: 100 computers available on campus for general student use. A campuswide network can be accessed from student residence rooms and from off campus. Internet access, e-mail are available. *Web address:* http://www.piedmont.edu/.

General Application Contact: Carol E. Kokesh, Director of Graduate Studies, 706-778-8500 Ext. 1181, Fax: 706-776-6635, E-mail: ckokesh@piedmont.edu.

GRADUATE UNITS

Department of Social Sciences Students: 15 (8 women); includes 3 minority (2 African Americans, 1 Hispanic American) 2 international. 7 applicants, 86% accepted, 3 enrolled. *Faculty:* 3 full-time (1 woman), 2 part-time/adjunct (0 women). Expenses: Contact institution. *Financial support:* In 2001–02, 1 teaching assistantship with partial tuition reimbursement (averaging $5,000 per year) was awarded; career-related internships or fieldwork, Federal Work-Study, and institutionally sponsored loans also available. Support available to part-time students. In 2001, 15 degrees awarded. *Degree program information:* Part-time and evening/weekend programs available. Offers public administration (MPA). *Application deadline:* For fall admission, 7/15 (priority date); for spring admission, 12/1 (priority date). Applications are processed on a rolling basis. *Application fee:* $30. *Application Contact:* Carol E. Kokesh, Director of Graduate Studies, 706-778-8500 Ext. 1181, Fax: 706-776-6635, E-mail: ckokesh@piedmont.edu. *Chair,* Dr. Kenneth E. Melichar, 706-778-3000 Ext. 1264, Fax: 706-776-2811, E-mail: kmelichar@piedmont.edu.

Division of Education Students: 248 full-time (187 women), 695 part-time (612 women). 385 applicants, 84% accepted, 286 enrolled. *Faculty:* 18 full-time, 44 part-time/adjunct. Expenses: Contact institution. *Financial support:* In 2001–02, 4 teaching assistantships with partial tuition reimbursements (averaging $5,000 per year) were awarded; career-related internships or fieldwork, Federal Work-Study, and institutionally sponsored loans also available. Support available to part-time students. Financial award applicants required to submit FAFSA. In 2001, 428 degrees awarded. *Degree program information:* Part-time and evening/weekend programs available. Offers early childhood education (MA, MAT); instruction (Ed S); secondary education (MA, MAT). *Application deadline:* For fall admission, 7/15; for spring admission, 12/1. *Application fee:* $30. *Application Contact:* Carol E. Kokesh, Director of Graduate Studies, 706-778-8500 Ext. 1181, Fax: 706-776-6635, E-mail: ckokesh@piedmont.edu. *Dean, School of Education,* Dr. Jane McFerrin, 706-778-3000 Ext. 1201, Fax: 706-776-9608, E-mail: jmcferrin@piedmont.edu.

School of Business Students: 15 (9 women); includes 6 minority (5 African Americans, 1 Native American) 22 applicants, 95% accepted, 17 enrolled. Expenses: Contact institution. *Financial support:* In 2001–02, 1 teaching assistantship with partial tuition reimbursement (averaging $5,000 per year) was awarded Offers business (MBA). *Application fee:* $30. *Application Contact:* Carol E. Kokesh, Director of Graduate Studies, 706-778-8500 Ext. 1181, Fax: 706-776-6635, E-mail: ckokesh@piedmont.edu. *Dean,* Dr. William Piper, 706-778-3000 Ext. 1349, Fax: 706-776-2811, E-mail: bpiper@piedmont.edu.

PIKEVILLE COLLEGE, Pikeville, KY 41501

General Information Independent-religious, coed, comprehensive institution. *Enrollment:* 244 full-time matriculated graduate/professional students (83 women). *Enrollment by degree level:* 244 first professional. *Graduate faculty:* 21 full-time (7 women), 583 part-time/adjunct (82 women). *Tuition:* Full-time $25,000. *Graduate housing:* Room and/or apartments available on a first-come, first-served basis to married students; on-campus housing not available to single students. *Student services:* Child daycare facilities, free psychological counseling. *Library facilities:* Allara Library plus 1 other. *Online resources:* library catalog, web page, access to other libraries' catalogs. *Collection:* 60,052 titles, 3,234 serial subscriptions, 1,518 audiovisual materials.

Computer facilities: 170 computers available on campus for general student use. A campuswide network can be accessed from student residence rooms and from off campus. Internet access is available. *Web address:* http://www.pc.edu/.

General Application Contact: Stephen M. Payson, Associate Dean for Student Affairs, 606-218-5408, Fax: 606-218-5442, E-mail: spayson@pc.edu.

GRADUATE UNITS

School of Osteopathic Medicine Students: 244 full-time (83 women); includes 22 minority (2 African Americans, 17 Asian Americans or Pacific Islanders, 2 Hispanic Americans, 1 Native American) 1,469 applicants, 6% accepted, 63 enrolled. *Faculty:* 21 full-time (7 women), 583 part-time/adjunct (82 women). Expenses: Contact institution. *Financial support:* In 2001–02, 152 students received support, including 3 fellowships (averaging $25,000 per year); scholarships/grants also available. Financial award application deadline: 8/1; financial award applicants required to submit FAFSA. In 2001, 53 degrees awarded. Offers osteopathic medicine (DO). *Application deadline:* For fall admission, 2/1. Applications are processed on a rolling basis. *Application fee:* $75. *Application Contact:* Stephen M. Payson, Associate Dean for Student Affairs, 606-218-5408, Fax: 606-218-5442, E-mail: spayson@pc.edu. *Dean,* Dr. John A. Strosnider, 606-218-5411, Fax: 606-218-8442.

PITTSBURGH THEOLOGICAL SEMINARY, Pittsburgh, PA 15206-2596

General Information Independent-religious, coed, graduate-only institution. *Enrollment by degree level:* 182 first professional, 41 master's, 125 doctoral, 8 other advanced degrees. *Graduate faculty:* 23 full-time (5 women), 10 part-time/adjunct (3 women). *Tuition:* Full-time $5,994; part-time $242 per term. *Required fees:* $16 per term. Full-time tuition and fees vary according to course load. Part-time tuition and fees vary according to program. *Graduate housing:* Rooms and/or apartments available on a first-come, first-served basis to single and married students. Typical cost: $1,350 per year for single students. Room charges vary according to housing facility selected. Housing application deadline: 6/1. *Student services:* Campus employment opportunities, career counseling, child daycare facilities, disabled student services, exercise/wellness program, free psychological counseling, international student services, low-cost health insurance. *Library facilities:* Clifford E. Barbour Library. *Online resources:* library catalog, web page, access to other libraries' catalogs. *Collection:* 262,029 titles, 1,034 serial subscriptions, 10,681 audiovisual materials.

Computer facilities: 15 computers available on campus for general student use. A campuswide network can be accessed from off campus. Internet access is available. *Web address:* http://www.pts.edu/.

General Application Contact: Sherry Sparks, Director of Admissions, 412-362-5610 Ext. 2115, Fax: 412-363-3260, E-mail: sparks@pts.edu.

GRADUATE UNITS

Graduate and Professional Programs Students: 266 full-time (85 women), 90 part-time (49 women); includes 61 minority (53 African Americans, 8 Asian Americans or Pacific Islanders), 19 international. Average age 36. 121 applicants, 61% accepted, 66 enrolled. *Faculty:* 23 full-time (5 women), 10 part-time/adjunct (3 women). Expenses: Contact institution. *Financial support:* In 2001–02, 88 students received support. Career-related internships or fieldwork and scholarships/grants available. Financial award application deadline: 4/15; financial award applicants required to submit FAFSA. In 2001, 19 first professional degrees, 10 master's, 16 doctorates awarded. *Degree program information:* Part-time and evening/weekend programs available. Offers divinity (M Div); ministry (D Min); theology (MA, STM). *Application deadline:* For fall admission, 6/15 (priority date); for winter admission, 10/15 (priority date); for spring admission, 1/15 (priority date). Applications are processed on a rolling basis. *Application fee:* $25. *Application Contact:* Sherry Sparks, Director of Admissions, 412-362-5610 Ext. 2115, Fax: 412-363-3260, E-mail: sparks@pts.edu. *Dean,* Dr. John Wilson, 412-362-5610 Ext. 2118, Fax: 412-363-3260, E-mail: wilson@pts.edu.

PITTSBURG STATE UNIVERSITY, Pittsburg, KS 66762

General Information State-supported, coed, comprehensive institution. CGS member. *Enrollment:* 349 full-time matriculated graduate/professional students (185 women), 903 part-time matriculated graduate/professional students (599 women). *Graduate faculty:* 288 full-time (106 women), 77 part-time/adjunct (34 women). Tuition, state resident: full-time $2,676; part-time $114 per credit hour. Tuition, nonresident: full-time $6,778; part-time $285 per credit hour. *Graduate housing:* Rooms and/or apartments available to single and married students. Typical cost: $2,576 per year ($4,294 including board) for single students. *Student services:* Campus employment opportunities, campus safety program, career counseling, international student services, low-cost health insurance. *Library facilities:* Leonard H. Axe Library plus 2 others. *Online resources:* library catalog, web page, access to other libraries' catalogs. *Collection:* 290,798 titles, 1,368 serial subscriptions.

Computer facilities: 213 computers available on campus for general student use. A campuswide network can be accessed from student residence rooms and from off campus. Internet access and online class registration are available. *Web address:* http://www.pittstate.edu/.

General Application Contact: Marvene Darraugh, Administrative Officer, 620-235-4220, Fax: 620-235-4219, E-mail: mdarraug@pittstate.edu.

GRADUATE UNITS

Graduate School Students: 349 full-time (185 women), 903 part-time (599 women). *Faculty:* 288 full-time (106 women), 77 part-time/adjunct (34 women). Expenses: Contact institution. *Financial support:* In 2001–02, 78 teaching assistantships were awarded; research assistantships, career-related internships or fieldwork and Federal Work-Study also available. In 2001, 366 degrees awarded. *Application deadline:* Applications are processed on a rolling basis. *Application fee:* $0 ($40 for international students). *Application Contact:* Marvene Darraugh, Administrative Officer, 620-235-4220, Fax: 620-235-4219, E-mail: mdarraug@pittstate.edu. *Dean of Graduate Studies and Research,* Dr. Oliver Hensley, 620-235-4222, Fax: 620-235-4219.

College of Arts and Sciences Students: 97 full-time (61 women), 36 part-time (20 women). Expenses: Contact institution. *Financial support:* Research assistantships, teaching assistantships, career-related internships or fieldwork and Federal Work-Study available. Offers applied communication (MA); applied physics (MS); art education (MA); arts and sciences (MA, MM, MS, MSN); biology (MS); chemistry (MS); communication education (MA); English (MA); history (MA); instrumental music education (MM); mathematics (MS); music history/music literature (MM); nursing (MSN); performance (MM); physics (MS); professional physics (MS); social science (MS); studio art (MA); theatre (MA); theory and composition (MM); vocal music education (MM). *Application fee:* $0 ($40 for international students). *Application Contact:* Marvene Darraugh, Administrative Officer, 620-235-4220, Fax: 620-235-4219, E-mail: mdarraug@pittstate.edu. *Dean,* Dr. Lynette Olson, 620-235-4684.

College of Education Students: 83 full-time (53 women), 423 part-time (315 women). Expenses: Contact institution. *Financial support:* Teaching assistantships, career-related internships or fieldwork and Federal Work-Study available. Offers behavioral disorders (MS); classroom reading teacher (MS); community college and higher education (Ed S); counseling (MS); counselor education (MS); early childhood education (MS); education (MS, Ed S); educational leadership (MS); educational technology (MS); elementary education (MS); learning disabilities (MS); mentally retarded (MS); physical education (MS); psychology (MS); reading (MS); reading specialist (MS); school psychology (Ed S); secondary education (MS); special education teaching (MS). *Application fee:* $0 ($40 for international students). *Application Contact:* Marvene Darraugh, Administrative Officer, 620-235-4220, Fax: 620-235-4219, E-mail: mdarraug@pittstate.edu. *Dean,* Dr. Steve Scott, 620-235-4500.

College of Technology Students: 71 full-time (34 women), 77 part-time (27 women). Expenses: Contact institution. *Financial support:* Teaching assistantships, career-related internships or fieldwork and Federal Work-Study available. Offers engineering technology (MET); human resource development and technical teacher education (MS, Ed S); industrial

Pittsburg State University (continued)

education (Ed S); technology (MS); technology education (MS). *Application fee:* $0 ($40 for international students). *Application Contact:* Marvene Darraugh, Administrative Officer, 620-235-4220, Fax: 620-235-4219, E-mail: mdarraug@pittstate.edu. *Dean,* Dr. Tom Baldwin, 620-235-4365.

Kelce College of Business Students: 81 full-time (25 women), 20 part-time (12 women). Expenses: Contact institution. *Financial support:* Research assistantships, teaching assistantships, career-related internships or fieldwork and Federal Work-Study available. Financial award application deadline: 3/1. Offers accounting (MBA); business (MBA); general administration (MBA). *Application fee:* $0 ($40 for international students). *Application Contact:* Marvene Darraugh, Administrative Officer, 620-235-4220, Fax: 620-235-4219, E-mail: mdarraug@pittstate.edu. *Dean,* Dr. Ronald Clement, 620-235-4598.

PLATTSBURGH STATE UNIVERSITY OF NEW YORK, Plattsburgh, NY 12901-2681

General Information State-supported, coed, comprehensive institution. *Enrollment:* 279 full-time matriculated graduate/professional students (206 women), 367 part-time matriculated graduate/professional students (267 women). *Enrollment by degree level:* 564 master's, 82 other advanced degrees. *Graduate faculty:* 54 full-time (22 women), 1 part-time/adjunct (0 women). Tuition, state resident: part-time $213 per credit hour. Tuition, nonresident: part-time $351 per credit hour. *Graduate housing:* Room and/or apartments available on a first-come, first-served basis to single students; on-campus housing not available to married students. Typical cost: $3,330 per year ($5,580 including board). *Student services:* Campus employment opportunities, campus safety program, career counseling, child daycare facilities, disabled student services, free psychological counseling, international student services, low-cost health insurance, multicultural affairs office, teacher training, writing training. *Library facilities:* Feinberg Library. *Online resources:* library catalog, web page, access to other libraries' catalogs. *Collection:* 754,096 titles, 1,466 serial subscriptions, 23,329 audiovisual materials. *Research affiliation:* Miner Agricultural Research Institute (environmental science), New York State Sea Grant (environmental science).

Computer facilities: 366 computers available on campus for general student use. A campuswide network can be accessed from student residence rooms and from off campus. Internet access and online class registration are available. *Web address:* http://www.plattsburgh.edu/.

General Application Contact: Richard Higgins, Director of Graduate Admissions, 518-564-2040, Fax: 518-564-2045, E-mail: higginrj@splaub.cc.plattsburgh.edu.

GRADUATE UNITS

Center for Lifelong Learning Students: 17 full-time (9 women), 47 part-time (35 women); includes 5 minority (2 African Americans, 3 Hispanic Americans), 1 international. Average age 35. 27 applicants, 85% accepted. Expenses: Contact institution. *Financial support:* In 2001–02, 17 students received support. Federal Work-Study available. Support available to part-time students. Financial award application deadline: 4/15; financial award applicants required to submit FAFSA. In 2001, 25 degrees awarded. *Degree program information:* Part-time programs available. Postbaccalaureate distance learning degree programs offered (minimal on-campus study). Offers liberal studies (MA). *Application deadline:* For fall admission, 5/15 (priority date); for spring admission, 10/15 (priority date). Applications are processed on a rolling basis. *Application fee:* $50. *Application Contact:* Ann Prarie, Assistant for Continuing Education, 518-564-2050, Fax: 518-564-2052. *Director,* Dr. Janet Worthington, 518-564-2050.

Faculty of Arts and Science Students: 12 full-time (8 women), 5 part-time (all women); includes 1 minority (Hispanic American) Average age 24. Expenses: Contact institution. *Financial support:* Federal Work-Study available. Support available to part-time students. Financial award application deadline: 4/15; financial award applicants required to submit FAFSA. *Degree program information:* Part-time and evening/weekend programs available. Offers arts and science (MA, CAS); school psychology (MA, CAS). *Application deadline:* For fall admission, 3/1 (priority date). Applications are processed on a rolling basis. *Application fee:* $50. *Application Contact:* Richard Higgins, Director of Graduate Admissions, 518-564-2040, Fax: 518-564-2045, E-mail: higginrj@splaub.cc.plattsburgh.edu. *Dean,* Dr. Kathleen Lavoie, 518-564-3150.

Faculty of Professional Studies Students: 250 full-time (189 women), 315 part-time (227 women); includes 13 minority (4 African Americans, 3 Asian Americans or Pacific Islanders, 4 Hispanic Americans, 2 Native Americans), 3 international. 142 applicants, 76% accepted. Expenses: Contact institution. *Financial support:* In 2001–02, 139 students received support, including 1 teaching assistantship; research assistantships, career-related internships or fieldwork and Federal Work-Study also available. Support available to part-time students. Financial award application deadline: 4/15; financial award applicants required to submit FAFSA. In 2001, 209 master's, 10 other advanced degrees awarded. *Degree program information:* Part-time programs available. Offers biology 7-12 (MST); chemistry (MS Ed, MST); college/agency counseling (MS); curriculum and instruction (MS Ed); earth sciences 7-12 (MST); elementary education (MST); elementary education Pre K-6 (MS Ed); English 7-12 (MS Ed, MST); English 7-9 (MS Ed, MST); English Pre K-6 (MS Ed, MST); French 7-12 (MST); general science 7-9 (MS Ed, MST); general science Pre K-6 (MS Ed); general science Pre-K (MST); mathematics 7-12 (MST); mathematics 7-9 (MS Ed, MST); mathematics Pre K-6 (MS Ed, MST); physics 7-12 (MST); professional studies (MA, MS, MS Ed, MST, CAS); reading teacher (MS Ed); school administrator and supervisor (CAS); school counseling (MS Ed); school counselor (CAS); social studies 7-12 (MS Ed, MST); social studies 7-9 (MS Ed, MST); social studies Pre K-6 (MS Ed, MST); Spanish 7-12 (MST); special education (MS Ed); speech-language pathology (MA). *Application deadline:* Applications are processed on a rolling basis. *Application fee:* $50. *Dean,* Dr. Virginia Barker, 518-564-3066.

PLYMOUTH STATE COLLEGE, Plymouth, NH 03264-1595

General Information State-supported, coed, comprehensive institution. *Enrollment:* 36 full-time matriculated graduate/professional students (21 women), 276 part-time matriculated graduate/professional students (196 women). *Graduate faculty:* 73 full-time (33 women), 175 part-time/adjunct (84 women). Tuition, state resident: full-time $10,676; part-time $819 per course. Tuition, nonresident: full-time $11,484; part-time $894 per course. *Required fees:* $40 per semester. Tuition and fees vary according to program. *Graduate housing:* Rooms and/or apartments available on a first-come, first-served basis to single students and guaranteed to married students. Typical cost: $4,976 per year for single students; $4,976 per year for married students. Room charges vary according to housing facility selected. Housing application deadline: 5/1. *Student services:* Campus employment opportunities, campus safety program, career counseling, child daycare facilities, disabled student services, exercise/wellness program, free psychological counseling, grant writing training, teacher training, writing training. *Library facilities:* Lamson Library. *Online resources:* library catalog, web page, access to other libraries' catalogs. *Collection:* 243,717 titles, 1,065 serial subscriptions, 20,541 audiovisual materials.

Computer facilities: 500 computers available on campus for general student use. A campuswide network can be accessed from student residence rooms and from off campus. Internet access and online class registration are available. *Web address:* http://www.plymouth.edu/.

General Application Contact: Cheryl Baker, Education Coordinator, 603-535-2737, Fax: 603-535-2372, E-mail: forgrad@psc.plymouth.edu.

GRADUATE UNITS

Division of Graduate Studies, Continuing Education and Outreach Average age 36. 74 applicants, 84% accepted. Expenses: Contact institution. *Financial support:* In 2001–02, 1 fellowship with partial tuition reimbursement (averaging $10,000 per year), 17 teaching assistantships with full tuition reimbursements (averaging $4,000 per year) were awarded. Career-related internships or fieldwork, institutionally sponsored loans, scholarships/grants, tuition waivers (full), and unspecified assistantships also available. Support available to part-time students. Financial award applicants required to submit FAFSA. In 2001, 141 master's, 14 other advanced degrees awarded. *Degree program information:* Part-time and evening/weekend programs available. Postbaccalaureate distance learning degree programs offered (minimal on-campus study). Offers athletic training (M Ed); business (MBA); counselor education (M Ed); education (CAGS); educational leadership (M Ed); elementary and secondary education (M Ed); elementary education (teacher certification) K–8 (M Ed); elementary education (teacher certification) N–3 (M Ed); English education (M Ed); health education (M Ed); mathematics education (M Ed); reading and writing specialist (M Ed); secondary education (teacher certification) 7–12, K–12, 5–8 (M Ed); special education administration (M Ed); special education k-12 (M Ed). *Application deadline:* Applications are processed on a rolling basis. *Application fee:* $40 ($50 for international students).

POINT LOMA NAZARENE UNIVERSITY, San Diego, CA 92106-2899

General Information Independent-religious, coed, comprehensive institution. *Enrollment:* 272 full-time matriculated graduate/professional students (166 women), 256 part-time matriculated graduate/professional students (170 women). *Enrollment by degree level:* 382 master's, 146 other advanced degrees. *Graduate faculty:* 29 full-time (9 women), 44 part-time/adjunct (17 women). *Tuition:* Part-time $450 per unit. Tuition and fees vary according to program. *Graduate housing:* Rooms and/or apartments available to single students and available on a first-come, first-served basis to married students. Housing application deadline: 3/1. *Student services:* Campus employment opportunities, campus safety program, career counseling, disabled student services, free psychological counseling, international student services, low-cost health insurance, teacher training. *Library facilities:* Ryan Library. *Online resources:* library catalog, web page, access to other libraries' catalogs. *Collection:* 120,991 titles, 637 serial subscriptions, 7,449 audiovisual materials.

Computer facilities: 125 computers available on campus for general student use. A campuswide network can be accessed from student residence rooms and from off campus. *Web address:* http://www.ptloma.edu/.

General Application Contact: Dr. Darrel Falk, Associate Provost for Research and Dean of Graduate and Continuing Education, 619-849-2272, Fax: 619-849-7018, E-mail: dfalk@ptloma.edu.

GRADUATE UNITS

Graduate Programs Students: 272 full-time (166 women), 256 part-time (170 women); includes 166 minority (43 African Americans, 36 Asian Americans or Pacific Islanders, 84 Hispanic Americans, 3 Native Americans), 3 international. Average age 35. *Faculty:* 29 full-time (9 women), 44 part-time/adjunct (17 women). Expenses: Contact institution. *Financial support:* Career-related internships or fieldwork available. Support available to part-time students. Financial award application deadline: 4/10. In 2001, 52 degrees awarded. *Degree program information:* Part-time and evening/weekend programs available. Postbaccalaureate distance learning degree programs offered (minimal on-campus study). Offers business (MBA); education (MA, Ed S); religion (M Min, MA). *Application deadline:* For fall admission, 5/15 (priority date); for spring admission, 11/1. Applications are processed on a rolling basis. *Application fee:* $25. *Associate Provost for Research and Dean of Graduate and Continuing Education,* Dr. Darrel Falk, 619-849-2272, Fax: 619-849-7018, E-mail: dfalk@ptloma.edu.

POINT PARK COLLEGE, Pittsburgh, PA 15222-1984

General Information Independent, coed, comprehensive institution. *Enrollment:* 154 full-time matriculated graduate/professional students (78 women), 171 part-time matriculated graduate/professional students (99 women). *Enrollment by degree level:* 325 master's. *Graduate faculty:* 21 full-time, 39 part-time/adjunct. *Tuition:* Full-time $7,290; part-time $405 per credit. *Required fees:* $270; $15 per credit. *Graduate housing:* Rooms and/or apartments available on a first-come, first-served basis to single and married students. Typical cost: $2,964 per year ($5,948 including board) for single students; $2,964 per year ($5,948 including board) for married students. Housing application deadline: 7/31. *Student services:* Campus employment opportunities, career counseling, child daycare facilities, disabled student services, free psychological counseling, international student services. *Library facilities:* The Library Center. *Online resources:* library catalog, access to other libraries' catalogs. *Collection:* 269,192 titles, 681 serial subscriptions.

Computer facilities: 200 computers available on campus for general student use. A campuswide network can be accessed from student residence rooms and from off campus. Internet access is available. *Web address:* http://www.ppc.edu/.

General Application Contact: Kathryn B. Ballas, Director, Accelerated and Graduate Enrollment, 412-392-3812, Fax: 412-392-6164, E-mail: kballas@ppc.edu.

GRADUATE UNITS

Department of Business Students: 119 full-time (53 women), 91 part-time (47 women); includes 37 minority (30 African Americans, 4 Asian Americans or Pacific Islanders, 3 Hispanic Americans), 3 international. Average age 35. 203 applicants, 71% accepted, 99 enrolled. *Faculty:* 5 full-time, 21 part-time/adjunct. Expenses: Contact institution. *Financial support:* In 2001–02, 2 research assistantships with full tuition reimbursements (averaging $4,500 per year) were awarded; career-related internships or fieldwork and scholarships/grants also available. Support available to part-time students. Financial award application deadline: 5/1; financial award applicants required to submit FAFSA. In 2001, 121 degrees awarded. *Degree program information:* Part-time and evening/weekend programs available. Offers business (MBA). *Application deadline:* Applications are processed on a rolling basis. *Application fee:* $30. Electronic applications accepted. *Application Contact:* Kathryn B. Ballas, Director, Accelerated and Graduate Enrollment, 412-392-3812, Fax: 412-392-6164, E-mail: kballas@ppc.edu. *Assistant Chair,* Dr. William Breslove, 412-392-3944, Fax: 412-765-2570, E-mail: wbreslove@ppc.edu.

Department of Education and Community Services Students: 15 full-time (13 women), 31 part-time (23 women); includes 12 minority (all African Americans) Average age 38. 30 applicants, 80% accepted, 10 enrolled. *Faculty:* 6 full-time, 8 part-time/adjunct. Expenses: Contact institution. *Financial support:* In 2001–02, 2 research assistantships with full tuition reimbursements (averaging $4,500 per year) were awarded; career-related internships or fieldwork and scholarships/grants also available. Support available to part-time students. Financial award application deadline: 5/1; financial award applicants required to submit FAFSA. In 2001, 7 degrees awarded. *Degree program information:* Part-time and evening/weekend programs available. Offers curriculum and instruction (MA). *Application deadline:* Applications are processed on a rolling basis. *Application fee:* $30. Electronic applications accepted. *Application Contact:* Martin Paonessa, Associate Director, 412-392-3915, Fax: 412-392-6164, E-mail: mpaonessa@ppc.edu. *Program Director,* Dr. Christina R. Shorall, 412-392-3976, Fax: 412-392-3927, E-mail: cshorall@ppc.edu.

Department of Journalism and Mass Communications Students: 16 full-time (10 women), 34 part-time (27 women); includes 4 minority (3 African Americans, 1 Asian American or Pacific Islander) Average age 31. 57 applicants, 70% accepted, 23 enrolled. *Faculty:* 7 full-time, 9 part-time/adjunct. Expenses: Contact institution. *Financial support:* In 2001–02, 2 research assistantships with full tuition reimbursements (averaging $4,500 per year) were awarded; career-related internships or fieldwork and scholarships/grants also available. Support available to part-time students. Financial award application deadline: 5/1; financial award applicants required to submit FAFSA. In 2001, 10 degrees awarded. *Degree program information:* Part-time and evening/weekend programs available. Offers journalism and mass communications (MA). *Application deadline:* Applications are processed on a rolling basis. *Application fee:* $30. Electronic applications accepted. *Application Contact:* Kathryn B. Ballas, Director, Accelerated and Graduate Enrollment, 412-392-3812, Fax: 412-392-6164, E-mail: kballas@ppc.edu. *Director,* Dr. Dane Claussen, 412-392-3412, Fax: 412-392-3917, E-mail: dclaussen@ppc.edu.

POLYTECHNIC UNIVERSITY, BROOKLYN CAMPUS, Brooklyn, NY 11201-2990

General Information Independent, coed, university. CGS member. *Enrollment:* 453 full-time matriculated graduate/professional students (104 women), 583 part-time matriculated graduate/professional students (117 women). *Enrollment by degree level:* 913 master's, 116 doctoral, 7 other advanced degrees. *Graduate faculty:* 169 full-time (35 women), 164 part-time/adjunct (35 women). *Tuition:* Full-time $14,535; part-time $765 per credit. *Required fees:* $660; $150 per semester. *Graduate housing:* Room and/or apartments available on a first-come, first-served basis to single students; on-campus housing not available to married students. Typical cost: $4,050 (including board). Housing application deadline: 6/30. *Student services:* Campus employment opportunities, campus safety program, career counseling, international student services, low-cost health insurance. *Library facilities:* Bern Dibner Library. *Online resources:* library catalog, web page, access to other libraries' catalogs. *Collection:* 148,000 titles, 613 serial subscriptions, 235 audiovisual materials.

Computer facilities: 350 computers available on campus for general student use. A campuswide network can be accessed from off campus. Internet access is available. *Web address:* http://www.poly.edu/.

General Application Contact: Stacey Walters, Associate Dean for Admissions, 718-260-3200, Fax: 718-260-3446, E-mail: admitme@poly.edu.

GRADUATE UNITS

Department of Applied Mathematics *Degree program information:* Part-time and evening/weekend programs available. Offers mathematics (MS, PhD). Electronic applications accepted.

Department of Chemical Engineering, Chemistry and Materials Science *Degree program information:* Part-time and evening/weekend programs available. Offers chemical engineering (MS, PhD); chemistry (MS, PhD); materials chemistry (PhD); polymer science and engineering (MS). Electronic applications accepted.

Department of Civil and Environmental Engineering *Degree program information:* Part-time and evening/weekend programs available. Offers civil engineering (MS, PhD); environmental engineering (MS); environmental health science (MS); transportation management (MS); transportation planning and engineering (MS). Electronic applications accepted.

Department of Computer and Information Science *Degree program information:* Part-time and evening/weekend programs available. Offers computer science (MS, PhD); information systems engineering (MS). Electronic applications accepted.

Department of Electrical Engineering *Degree program information:* Part-time and evening/weekend programs available. Offers computer engineering (MS); electrical engineering (MS, PhD); electrophysics (MS); systems engineering (MS); telecommunication networks (MS). Electronic applications accepted.

Department of Humanities and Social Sciences *Degree program information:* Part-time and evening/weekend programs available. Offers environment behavior studies (MS); history of science (MS); specialized journalism (MS). Electronic applications accepted.

Department of Management *Degree program information:* Part-time and evening/weekend programs available. Offers financial engineering (MS); management (MS); management of technology (MS); operations management (MS); organizational behavior (MS); telecommunications and information management (MS). Electronic applications accepted.

Program in Physics *Degree program information:* Part-time and evening/weekend programs available. Offers physics (MS, PhD). Electronic applications accepted.

POLYTECHNIC UNIVERSITY, LONG ISLAND GRADUATE CENTER, Melville, NY 11747

General Information Independent, coed, graduate-only institution. *Enrollment:* 13 full-time matriculated graduate/professional students (4 women), 134 part-time matriculated graduate/professional students (24 women). *Enrollment by degree level:* 142 master's, 3 doctoral, 2 other advanced degrees. *Graduate faculty:* 169 full-time (35 women), 165 part-time/adjunct (36 women). *Tuition:* Full-time $14,535; part-time $765 per credit. *Required fees:* $660; $150 per semester. *Graduate housing:* On-campus housing not available. *Student services:* Campus employment opportunities, career counseling, international student services. *Web address:* http://www.poly.edu/li/.

General Application Contact: Stacey Walters, Associate Dean of Admissions, 718-260-3200, Fax: 718-260-3446, E-mail: admitme@poly.edu.

GRADUATE UNITS

Graduate Programs *Degree program information:* Part-time and evening/weekend programs available. Offers aeronautics and astronautics (MS); chemical engineering (MS, PhD); chemistry (MS, PhD); civil engineering (MS, PhD); computer engineering (MS); computer science (MS, PhD); distributed information systems engineering (MS); electrical engineering (MS, PhD); electrophysics (MS); environmental engineering (MS); financial engineering (MS); industrial engineering (MS); information systems engineering (MS); management (MS); manufacturing engineering (MS); mathematics (MS, PhD); mechanical engineering (MS, PhD); operations management (MS); organizational behavior (MS); systems engineering (MS); telecommunication networks (MS); transportation planning and engineering (MS). Electronic applications accepted.

Program in Physics Offers physics (MS, PhD). Electronic applications accepted.

POLYTECHNIC UNIVERSITY OF PUERTO RICO, Hato Rey, PR 00919

General Information Independent, coed, comprehensive institution. *Graduate housing:* On-campus housing not available.

POLYTECHNIC UNIVERSITY, WESTCHESTER GRADUATE CENTER, Hawthorne, NY 10532-1507

General Information Independent, coed, graduate-only institution. *Enrollment by degree level:* 157 master's, 1 doctoral, 1 other advanced degree. *Graduate faculty:* 169 full-time (35 women), 164 part-time/adjunct (35 women). *Tuition:* Full-time $13,770; part-time $765 per credit. *Required fees:* $660; $150 per term. *Graduate housing:* On-campus housing not available. *Student services:* Campus employment opportunities, career counseling, international student services.

Computer facilities: 30 computers available on campus for general student use. A campuswide network can be accessed from off campus. Internet access is available. *Web address:* http://west.poly.edu/~www/.

GRADUATE UNITS

Graduate Programs *Degree program information:* Part-time and evening/weekend programs available. Offers chemical engineering (MS); chemistry (MS); civil engineering (MS, PhD); computer engineering (MS); computer science (MS, PhD); electrical engineering (MS, PhD); electrophysics (MS); environmental engineering (MS); industrial engineering (MS); information systems engineering (MS); manufacturing engineering (MS); materials science (MS); systems engineering (MS); telecommunication networks (MS); transportation management (MS). Electronic applications accepted.

Division of Management *Degree program information:* Part-time and evening/weekend programs available. Offers financial engineering (MS); management (MS); operations management (MS); organizational behavior (MS). Electronic applications accepted.

PONCE SCHOOL OF MEDICINE, Ponce, PR 00732-7004

General Information Independent, coed, graduate-only institution. *Enrollment by degree level:* 240 first professional, 137 doctoral. *Graduate faculty:* 123 full-time (31 women), 210 part-time/adjunct (47 women). *Tuition:* Full-time $17,835. *Required fees:* $2,340. Full-time tuition and fees vary according to class time, course load, degree level, program and student level. *Graduate housing:* On-campus housing not available. *Student services:* Career counseling, free psychological counseling, low-cost health insurance. *Library facilities:* Fundación Angel Ramos Library. *Online resources:* library catalog, web page. *Collection:* 31,156 titles, 433 serial subscriptions, 27,870 audiovisual materials.

Computer facilities: 42 computers available on campus for general student use. A campuswide network can be accessed. Internet access is available. *Web address:* http://www.psm.edu/.

General Application Contact: Dr. Carmen Mercado, Assistant Dean of Admissions, 787-840-2575 Ext. 251, E-mail: cmercado@psm.edu.

GRADUATE UNITS

Professional Program Students: 240 full-time (95 women); includes 217 minority (11 Asian Americans or Pacific Islanders, 205 Hispanic Americans, 1 Native American), 3 international. Average age 25. 928 applicants, 16% accepted, 63 enrolled. *Faculty:* 118 full-time (29 women), 210 part-time/adjunct (47 women). Expenses: Contact institution. *Financial support:* In 2001–02, 95 students received support. Scholarships/grants available. Financial award applicants required to submit FAFSA. In 2001, 66 degrees awarded. Offers medicine (MD). *Application deadline:* For fall admission, 12/15 (priority date). Applications are processed on a rolling basis. *Application fee:* $100. *Application Contact:* Dr. Carmen Mercado, Assistant Dean of Admissions, 787-840-2575 Ext. 251, E-mail: cmercado@psm.edu. *President and Dean,* Dr. Manuel Martinez-Maldonado, 787-844-3710, Fax: 787-840-9756, E-mail: mmartinez@psm.edu.

Program in Clinical Psychology Students: 114 full-time (89 women); all minorities (all Hispanic Americans) Average age 30. 63 applicants, 65% accepted, 34 enrolled. *Faculty:* 5 full-time (2 women). Expenses: Contact institution. Offers clinical health psychology (Psy D); consultant psychology (Psy D); pediatric psychology (Psy D); psychotherapeutic interventions (Psy D). *Application deadline:* For fall admission, 3/30. Applications are processed on a rolling basis. *Application fee:* $100. *Application Contact:* Dr. Carmen Mercado, Assistant Dean of Admissions, 787-840-2575 Ext. 251, E-mail: cmercado@psm.edu. *Head,* Dr. José Pons, 787-840-2575, E-mail: jponspr@yahoo.com.

PONTIFICAL CATHOLIC UNIVERSITY OF PUERTO RICO, Ponce, PR 00717-0777

General Information Independent-religious, coed, university. *Enrollment:* 785 full-time matriculated graduate/professional students (441 women), 1,079 part-time matriculated graduate/professional students (728 women). *Enrollment by degree level:* 552 first professional, 1,001 master's, 305 doctoral, 5 other advanced degrees. *Graduate faculty:* 60 full-time (29 women), 55 part-time/adjunct (19 women). *Tuition:* Full-time $2,880; part-time $160 per credit. *Required fees:* $360. Tuition and fees vary according to degree level and program. *Graduate housing:* Room and/or apartments available to single students; on-campus housing not available to married students. Typical cost: $1,240 per year ($3,967 including board). Housing application deadline: 7/15. *Student services:* Campus employment opportunities, campus safety program, career counseling, child daycare facilities, disabled student services, free psychological counseling, international student services, low-cost health insurance. *Library facilities:* Encarnacion Valdes Library plus 1 other. *Online resources:* library catalog, web page, access to other libraries' catalogs. *Collection:* 48,580 serial subscriptions.

Computer facilities: 419 computers available on campus for general student use. A campuswide network can be accessed from off campus. Internet access is available. *Web address:* http://www.pucpr.edu/.

General Application Contact: Ana O. Bonilla, Director of Admissions, 787-841-2000 Ext. 1000, Fax: 787-840-4295.

GRADUATE UNITS

College of Arts and Humanities Students: 21 full-time (6 women), 19 part-time (13 women); all minorities (all Hispanic Americans) Average age 30. 15 applicants, 93% accepted, 13 enrolled. *Faculty:* 8 full-time (4 women). Expenses: Contact institution. *Financial support:* Federal Work-Study, institutionally sponsored loans, and tuition waivers (partial) available. Support available to part-time students. Financial award application deadline: 7/15. *Degree program information:* Part-time and evening/weekend programs available. Offers arts and humanities (MA); divinity (MA); hispanic studies (MA); history (MA). *Application deadline:* For fall admission, 4/30 (priority date). Applications are processed on a rolling basis. *Application fee:* $25. *Application Contact:* Ana O. Bonilla, Director of Admissions, 787-841-2000 Ext. 1000, Fax: 787-840-4295. *Chairperson,* Rev. Felix Lazaro, 787-841-2000 Ext. 1685.

College of Business Administration Students: 48 full-time (29 women), 249 part-time (148 women); all minorities (all Hispanic Americans) Average age 34. 148 applicants, 91% accepted, 122 enrolled. *Faculty:* 4 full-time (2 women), 3 part-time/adjunct (1 woman). Expenses: Contact institution. *Financial support:* Fellowships, Federal Work-Study and tuition waivers (partial) available. Support available to part-time students. Financial award application deadline: 7/15. In 2001, 41 degrees awarded. *Degree program information:* Part-time and evening/weekend programs available. Offers accounting (MBA); business administration (PhD); finance (MBA); human resources (MBA); merchandising (MBA); office administration (MBA). *Application deadline:* For fall admission, 4/30 (priority date). Applications are processed on a rolling basis. *Application fee:* $25. Electronic applications accepted. *Application Contact:* Ana O. Bonilla, Director of Admissions, 787-841-2000 Ext. 1000, Fax: 787-840-4295. *Chairperson,* Dr. Kenya Carrasquillo, 787-841-2000 Ext. 2511.

College of Education Students: 67 full-time (53 women), 255 part-time (193 women); all minorities (all Hispanic Americans) Average age 37. 158 applicants, 99% accepted, 109 enrolled. *Faculty:* 7 full-time (5 women), 8 part-time/adjunct (6 women). Expenses: Contact institution. *Financial support:* Fellowships, career-related internships or fieldwork, Federal Work-Study, and tuition waivers (partial) available. Support available to part-time students. Financial award application deadline: 7/15. In 2001, 25 degrees awarded. *Degree program information:* Part-time and evening/weekend programs available. Offers commercial education (MRE); curriculum instruction (M Ed); education (PhD); education-general (MRE); english as a second language (MRE); religious education (MA Ed); scholar psychology (MRE). *Application deadline:* For fall admission, 4/30 (priority date). Applications are processed on a rolling basis. *Application fee:* $25. Electronic applications accepted. *Application Contact:* Ana O. Bonilla, Director of Admissions, 787-841-2000 Ext. 1000, Fax: 787-840-4295. *Chairperson,* Dr. Myvian Zayas, 787-841-2000 Ext. 1742.

College of Sciences Students: 10 full-time (9 women), 50 part-time (38 women); all minorities (all Hispanic Americans) Average age 35. 26 applicants, 65% accepted. *Faculty:* 3 full-time (all women), 3 part-time/adjunct (1 woman). Expenses: Contact institution. *Financial support:* Fellowships, Federal Work-Study and tuition waivers (partial) available. Support available to part-time students. Financial award application deadline: 7/15. In 2001, 19 degrees awarded. *Degree program information:* Part-time and evening/weekend programs available. Offers chemistry (MS); medical-surgical nursing (MS); mental health and psychiatric nursing (MS); obstetric nursing (MS); sciences (MS). *Application deadline:* For fall admission, 4/30 (priority date). Applications are processed on a rolling basis. *Application fee:* $25. Electronic applications accepted. *Application Contact:* Ana O. Bonilla, Director of Admissions, 787-841-2000 Ext. 1000, Fax: 787-840-4295. *Dean,* Carmen Velázquez, 787-841-2000 Ext. 1495.

Institute of Graduate Studies in Behavioral Science and Community Affairs Students: 86 full-time (56 women), 394 part-time (266 women); all minorities (all Hispanic Americans) 141 applicants, 83% accepted, 104 enrolled. *Faculty:* 10 full-time (7 women), 17 part-time/adjunct (12 women). Expenses: Contact institution. *Financial support:* Federal Work-Study and tuition waivers (partial) available. Support available to part-time students. Financial award application deadline: 7/15. In 2001, 35 degrees awarded. *Degree program information:* Part-time and evening/weekend programs available. Offers clinical psychology (MS); clinical social work (MSW); criminology (MA); industrial psychology (MS); psychology (PhD); public administration (MA). *Application deadline:* For fall admission, 4/30 (priority date). Applications are processed on a rolling basis. *Application fee:* $50. Electronic applications accepted. *Application Contact:* Ana O. Bonilla, Director of Admissions, 787-841-2000 Ext. 1000, Fax: 787-840-4295. *Director,* Dr. Nilde Cordoline, 787-841-2000 Ext. 1024.

School of Law Students: 560 full-time (299 women), 6 part-time (4 women); all minorities (all Hispanic Americans) Average age 31. 484 applicants, 44% accepted. *Faculty:* 27 full-time (7 women), 20 part-time/adjunct (1 woman). Expenses: Contact institution. *Financial support:* Fellowships, Federal Work-Study available. Support available to part-time students. Financial award application deadline: 7/15. In 2001, 187 degrees awarded. *Degree program information:*

Pontifical Catholic University of Puerto Rico (continued)
Part-time and evening/weekend programs available. Offers law (JD). *Application deadline:* For fall admission, 4/30 (priority date). Applications are processed on a rolling basis. *Application fee:* $60. Electronic applications accepted. *Application Contact:* Ana O. Bonilla, Director of Admissions, 787-841-2000 Ext. 1000, Fax: 787-840-4295. *Dean*, Charles Cuprill, 787-841-2000 Ext. 1839.

PONTIFICAL COLLEGE JOSEPHINUM, Columbus, OH 43235-1498

General Information Independent-religious, coed, primarily men, comprehensive institution. *Enrollment:* 51 full-time matriculated graduate/professional students, 2 part-time matriculated graduate/professional students. *Enrollment by degree level:* 51 first professional, 2 master's. *Graduate faculty:* 16 full-time (3 women), 3 part-time/adjunct (0 women). *Tuition:* Full-time $11,720; part-time $488 per hour. *Required fees:* $600. *Graduate housing:* Room and/or apartments guaranteed to single students; on-campus housing not available to married students. Typical cost: $6,400 (including board). Housing application deadline: 8/15. *Student services:* Campus employment opportunities, free psychological counseling, international student services, low-cost health insurance. *Library facilities:* Wehrle Memorial Library. *Collection:* 124,742 titles, 520 serial subscriptions.

Computer facilities: 10 computers available on campus for general student use. A campuswide network can be accessed. *Web address:* http://www.pcj.edu/.

General Application Contact: Arminda Crawford, Admissions, 614-885-5585, Fax: 614-885-2307, E-mail: acrawford@pcj.edu.

GRADUATE UNITS

School of Theology Students: 51 full-time (0 women), 2 part-time; includes 1 minority (Asian American or Pacific Islander), 19 international. Average age 28. 23 applicants, 96% accepted, 22 enrolled. *Faculty:* 16 full-time (3 women), 3 part-time/adjunct (0 women). Expenses: Contact institution. *Financial support:* Career-related internships or fieldwork and Federal Work-Study available. Financial award application deadline: 8/15. In 2001, 14 first professional degrees, 6 master's awarded. *Degree program information:* Part-time programs available. Offers theology (M Div, MA). *Application deadline:* For fall admission, 8/15. Applications are processed on a rolling basis. *Application fee:* $35. *Application Contact:* Arminda Crawford, Admissions, 614-885-5585, Fax: 614-885-2307, E-mail: acrawfor@pcj.edu. *Vice Rector*, Rev. Brian Moore, 614-885-5585, Fax: 614-885-2307, E-mail: bmoore@pcj.edu.

PORTLAND STATE UNIVERSITY, Portland, OR 97207-0751

General Information State-supported, coed, university. CGS member. *Enrollment:* 1,636 full-time matriculated graduate/professional students (1,049 women), 1,560 part-time matriculated graduate/professional students (888 women). *Enrollment by degree level:* 2,806 master's, 390 doctoral. *Graduate faculty:* 590 full-time (237 women), 332 part-time/adjunct (158 women). *Graduate housing:* Rooms and/or apartments available on a first-come, first-served basis to single and married students. *Student services:* Campus employment opportunities, campus safety program, career counseling, child daycare facilities, disabled student services, free psychological counseling, international student services, low-cost health insurance, multicultural affairs office, teacher training. *Library facilities:* Branford P. Millar Library. *Online resources:* library catalog, web page, access to other libraries' catalogs. *Collection:* 1.8 million titles, 10,230 serial subscriptions, 127,925 audiovisual materials. *Research affiliation:* Tektronix (electrical engineering), Tri-County Metropolitan Transportation District of Oregon, City of Portland (civil engineering, urban planning), Intel Corporation (electronic cooling, engineering), Battelle Pacific Northwest Laboratories (computer science, geographic information systems, mechanical engineering, science education), Bonneville Power Administration (civil and mechanical engineering, geology, urban studies).

Computer facilities: 340 computers available on campus for general student use. A campuswide network can be accessed from student residence rooms and from off campus. Internet access and online class registration are available. *Web address:* http://www.pdx.edu/.

General Application Contact: Agnes A. Hoffman, Director of Admissions and Records, 503-725-3511, Fax: 503-725-4882, E-mail: hoffmana@pdx.edu.

GRADUATE UNITS

Graduate Studies Students: 1,636 full-time (1,049 women), 1,560 part-time (888 women); includes 316 minority (68 African Americans, 107 Asian Americans or Pacific Islanders, 112 Hispanic Americans, 29 Native Americans), 340 international. Average age 34. 2,667 applicants, 61% accepted. Expenses: Contact institution. *Financial support:* In 2001–02, 230 research assistantships with full tuition reimbursements (averaging $5,078 per year), 239 teaching assistantships with full tuition reimbursements (averaging $6,362 per year) were awarded. Fellowships, career-related internships or fieldwork, Federal Work-Study, and institutionally sponsored loans also available. Support available to part-time students. Financial award application deadline: 3/1; financial award applicants required to submit FAFSA. In 2001, 1,092 master's, 31 doctorates awarded. *Degree program information:* Part-time and evening/weekend programs available. Postbaccalaureate distance learning degree programs offered (minimal on-campus study). *Application deadline:* Applications are processed on a rolling basis. *Application fee:* $50. *Application Contact:* Agnes A. Hoffman, Director of Admissions and Records, 503-725-3511, Fax: 503-725-4882, E-mail: hoffmana@pdx.edu. *Vice Provost for Research and Dean*, Dr. William H. Feyerherm, 503-725-3423, Fax: 503-725-3416.

College of Engineering and Computer Science Students: 118 full-time (34 women), 161 part-time (35 women); includes 29 minority (3 African Americans, 19 Asian Americans or Pacific Islanders, 5 Hispanic Americans, 2 Native Americans), 142 international. Average age 31. 297 applicants, 67% accepted. *Faculty:* 53 full-time (6 women), 19 part-time/adjunct (3 women). Expenses: Contact institution. *Financial support:* In 2001–02, 18 research assistantships with full tuition reimbursements (averaging $6,292 per year), 11 teaching assistantships with full tuition reimbursements (averaging $6,752 per year) were awarded. Career-related internships or fieldwork, Federal Work-Study, and institutionally sponsored loans also available. Support available to part-time students. Financial award application deadline: 3/1; financial award applicants required to submit FAFSA. In 2001, 101 master's, 2 doctorates awarded. *Degree program information:* Part-time and evening/weekend programs available. Offers civil engineering (MS, PhD); computer science (MS); electrical and computer engineering (MS, PhD); engineering and computer science (M Eng, ME, MS, PhD, Certificate); engineering and technology management (M Eng, MS, PhD); manufacturing engineering (ME); mechanical engineering (MS, PhD); systems engineering (M Eng); systems engineering fundamentals (Certificate); systems science/anthropology (PhD); systems science/business administration (PhD); systems science/civil engineering (PhD); systems science/economics (PhD); systems science/engineering management (PhD); systems science/general (PhD); systems science/mathematical sciences (PhD); systems science/mechanical engineering (PhD); systems science/psychology (PhD); systems science/sociology (PhD). *Application deadline:* For fall admission, 3/1 (priority date). Applications are processed on a rolling basis. *Application fee:* $50. *Application Contact:* Alisia Walton, Administrative Assistant, 503-725-4631, Fax: 503-725-4298, E-mail: waltona@eas.pdx.edu. *Dean*, Dr. Robert D. Dryden, 503-725-4631, Fax: 503-725-4298, E-mail: drydenr@eas.pdx.edu.

College of Liberal Arts and Sciences Students: 456 full-time (291 women), 334 part-time (199 women); includes 53 minority (9 African Americans, 19 Asian Americans or Pacific Islanders, 22 Hispanic Americans, 3 Native Americans), 76 international. Average age 33. 584 applicants, 56% accepted. *Faculty:* 256 full-time (104 women), 85 part-time/adjunct (44 women). Expenses: Contact institution. *Financial support:* In 2001–02, 42 research assistantships with full tuition reimbursements (averaging $6,537 per year), 144 teaching assistantships with full tuition reimbursements (averaging $7,057 per year) were awarded. Career-related internships or fieldwork, Federal Work-Study, and institutionally sponsored loans also available. Support available to part-time students. Financial award application deadline: 3/1; financial award applicants required to submit FAFSA. In 2001, 178 master's, 6 doctorates awarded. *Degree program information:* Part-time and evening/weekend programs available. Offers anthropology (MA, PhD); applied economics (MA, MS); biology (MA, MS, PhD); chemistry (MA, MS, PhD); economics (PhD); English (MA, MAT); environmental management (MEM); environmental sciences/biology (PhD); environmental sciences/chemistry (PhD); environmental sciences/civil engineering (PhD); environmental sciences/economics (PhD); environmental sciences/geography (PhD); environmental sciences/geology (PhD); environmental sciences/physics (PhD); environmental studies (MS); foreign literature and language (MA); French (MA); general arts and letters education (MAT, MST); general economics (MA, MS); general science education (MAT, MST); general social science education (MAT, MST); general speech communication (MA, MS); geography (MA, MS, PhD); geology (MA, MS, PhD); German (MA); history (MA); liberal arts and sciences (MA, MAT, MEM, MS, MST, PhD); mathematical sciences (MA, MAT, MS, MST, PhD); mathematics education (PhD); physics (MA, MS, PhD); psychology (MA, MS, PhD); science/geology (MAT, MST); sociology (MA, MS, PhD); Spanish (MA); speech and hearing sciences (MA, MS); teaching English to speakers of other languages (MA). *Application deadline:* Applications are processed on a rolling basis. *Application fee:* $50. *Application Contact:* Sonia Rae, Dean's Assistant, 523-725-3514, Fax: 523-725-3693. *Dean*, Dr. Marvin Kaiser, 503-725-3514, Fax: 503-725-3693, E-mail: marvin@clas.pdx.edu.

College of Urban and Public Affairs Students: 183 full-time (99 women), 271 part-time (167 women); includes 45 minority (9 African Americans, 13 Asian Americans or Pacific Islanders, 16 Hispanic Americans, 7 Native Americans), 40 international. Average age 35. 231 applicants, 72% accepted. *Faculty:* 52 full-time (15 women), 58 part-time/adjunct (23 women). Expenses: Contact institution. *Financial support:* In 2001–02, 57 research assistantships with full tuition reimbursements (averaging $4,243 per year), 3 teaching assistantships with full tuition reimbursements (averaging $4,379 per year) were awarded. Fellowships, career-related internships or fieldwork, Federal Work-Study, and institutionally sponsored loans also available. Support available to part-time students. Financial award application deadline: 3/1; financial award applicants required to submit FAFSA. In 2001, 110 master's, 6 doctorates awarded. *Degree program information:* Part-time and evening/weekend programs available. Offers administration of justice (MS, PhD); gerontology (Certificate); government (MA, MAT, MPA, MPH, MS, MST, PhD); health administration (MPA, MPH); health administration and policy (MPH); health education (MA, MS); health education and health promotion (MPH); political science (MA, MAT, MS, MST, PhD); public administration (MPA); public administration and policy (PhD); urban and public affairs (MA, MAT, MPA, MPH, MS, MST, MURP, MUS, PhD, Certificate); urban and regional planning (MURP, PhD); urban studies (MUS, PhD); urban studies and planning (MURP, MUS, PhD, Certificate); urban studies: regional science (PhD). *Application fee:* $50. *Application Contact:* Rod Johnson, Office Specialist, 503-725-4044, Fax: 503-725-5199, E-mail: johnsonro@pdx.edu. *Dean*, Dr. Nohad A. Toulan, 503-725-4043, Fax: 503-725-5199, E-mail: nohad@upa.pdx.edu.

Graduate School of Social Work Students: 298 full-time (255 women), 63 part-time (47 women); includes 57 minority (21 African Americans, 16 Asian Americans or Pacific Islanders, 14 Hispanic Americans, 6 Native Americans), 4 international. Average age 35. 433 applicants, 49% accepted. *Faculty:* 33 full-time (24 women), 2 part-time/adjunct (1 woman). Expenses: Contact institution. *Financial support:* In 2001–02, 12 research assistantships with full tuition reimbursements (averaging $9,543 per year) were awarded; teaching assistantships, career-related internships or fieldwork, Federal Work-Study, and institutionally sponsored loans also available. Support available to part-time students. Financial award application deadline: 3/1; financial award applicants required to submit FAFSA. In 2001, 203 master's, 1 doctorate awarded. *Degree program information:* Part-time programs available. Offers social work (MSW); social work and social research (PhD). *Application deadline:* For fall admission, 3/1. *Application fee:* $50. *Application Contact:* Janet Putnam, Coordinator, 503-725-4712, Fax: 503-725-5545, E-mail: janet@ssw.pdx.edu. *Dean*, Dr. James Ward, 503-725-4712, Fax: 503-725-5545, E-mail: james@ssw.pdx.edu.

School of Business Administration Students: 122 full-time (55 women), 216 part-time (68 women); includes 26 minority (4 African Americans, 15 Asian Americans or Pacific Islanders, 6 Hispanic Americans, 1 Native American), 44 international. Average age 31. 313 applicants, 51% accepted. *Faculty:* 54 full-time (18 women), 24 part-time/adjunct (6 women). Expenses: Contact institution. *Financial support:* In 2001–02, 22 research assistantships with full tuition reimbursements (averaging $2,710 per year), 1 teaching assistantship with full tuition reimbursement (averaging $4,968 per year) were awarded. Career-related internships or fieldwork, Federal Work-Study, and institutionally sponsored loans also available. Support available to part-time students. Financial award application deadline: 3/1; financial award applicants required to submit FAFSA. In 2001, 171 degrees awarded. *Degree program information:* Part-time and evening/weekend programs available. Offers business administration (MBA, MIM, MSFA, PhD); financial analysis (MSFA); international management (MIM). *Application deadline:* Applications are processed on a rolling basis. *Application fee:* $50. *Application Contact:* Leslie Gilderson, Office Specialist, 503-725-3712, Fax: 503-725-5850, E-mail: gildersonl@sba.pdx.edu. *Interim Dean*, Dr. Scott Dawson, 503-725-3721, Fax: 503-725-5850, E-mail: scott@sba.pdx.edu.

School of Education Students: 358 full-time (262 women), 467 part-time (349 women); includes 96 minority (21 African Americans, 18 Asian Americans or Pacific Islanders, 49 Hispanic Americans, 8 Native Americans), 13 international. Average age 36. 678 applicants, 72% accepted. *Faculty:* 51 full-time (32 women), 46 part-time/adjunct (29 women). Expenses: Contact institution. *Financial support:* In 2001–02, 28 research assistantships with full tuition reimbursements (averaging $3,515 per year), 2 teaching assistantships with full tuition reimbursements (averaging $2,484 per year) were awarded. Career-related internships or fieldwork, Federal Work-Study, and institutionally sponsored loans also available. Support available to part-time students. Financial award application deadline: 3/1; financial award applicants required to submit FAFSA. In 2001, 312 master's, 8 doctorates awarded. *Degree program information:* Part-time and evening/weekend programs available. Offers counselor education (MA, MS); early childhood education (MA, MS); education (M Ed, MA, MS); educational administration (MA, MS); educational administration and leadership (MA, MS, Ed D); educational leadership/educational administration (Ed D); educational leadership/postsecondary adult and continuing education (Ed D); educational leadership: curriculum and instruction (Ed D); educational media/school librarianship (MA, MS); elementary education (M Ed, MAT, MST); postsecondary education (Ed D); reading (MA, MS); secondary education (M Ed, MAT, MST); special education (MA, MS). *Application fee:* $50. *Application Contact:* Mary MacKillep, Secretary, 503-725-4621, Fax: 503-725-5599, E-mail: marym@ed.pdx.edu. *Dean*, Dr. Phyllis Edmundson, 503-725-4621, Fax: 503-725-5399, E-mail: phyliss@ed.pdx.edu.

School of Fine and Performing Arts Students: 49 full-time (29 women), 17 part-time (12 women); includes 5 minority (1 African American, 3 Asian Americans or Pacific Islanders, 1 Hispanic American), 5 international. Average age 33. 61 applicants, 57% accepted. *Faculty:* 42 full-time (16 women), 34 part-time/adjunct (18 women). Expenses: Contact institution. *Financial support:* In 2001–02, 25 teaching assistantships with full tuition reimbursements (averaging $2,735 per year) were awarded; research assistantships with full tuition reimbursements, career-related internships or fieldwork, Federal Work-Study, and institutionally sponsored loans also available. Support available to part-time students. Financial award application deadline: 3/1; financial award applicants required to submit FAFSA. In 2001, 17 degrees awarded. *Degree program information:* Part-time programs available. Offers ceramics (MFA); conducting (MM); fine and performing arts (MA, MAT, MFA, MM, MST); music education (MAT, MST); painting (MFA); performance (MM); sculpture (MFA); theater arts (MA). *Application deadline:* Applications are processed on a rolling basis. *Application fee:* $50. *Application Contact:* Aaron Frehnmayer, Office Specialist, 503-725-3105, Fax: 503-725-3351, E-mail: frehmayera@pdx.edu. *Dean*, Dr. Robert Sylvester, 503-725-3105, Fax: 503-725-3351, E-mail: sylvesterr@pdx.edu.

PRAIRIE VIEW A&M UNIVERSITY, Prairie View, TX 77446-0188

General Information State-supported, coed, comprehensive institution. *Enrollment:* 439 full-time matriculated graduate/professional students (316 women), 853 part-time matriculated graduate/professional students (612 women). *Enrollment by degree level:* 1,292 master's. *Graduate faculty:* 129 full-time (35 women), 31 part-time/adjunct (10 women). Tuition, state resident: full-time $864; part-time $48 per credit hour. Tuition, nonresident: full-time $4,716;

part-time $262 per credit hour. *Required fees:* $1,324; $59 per credit hour. $131 per term. *Graduate housing:* Room and/or apartments available on a first-come, first-served basis to single students; on-campus housing not available to married students. Housing application deadline: 4/16. *Student services:* Campus employment opportunities, campus safety program, career counseling, disabled student services, exercise/wellness program, free psychological counseling, grant writing training, international student services, low-cost health insurance, multicultural affairs office, teacher training, writing training. *Library facilities:* John B. Coleman Library. *Online resources:* library catalog, web page, access to other libraries' catalogs. *Research affiliation:* Science and Engineering Alliance, NASA (space radiation on material systems and devices), Lawrence Livermore National Laboratory (engineering and sciences), Sandia National Laboratories (engineering and chemistry), U.S. Department of Defense (engineering), U.S. Department of Energy (engineering and sciences).

Computer facilities: 102 computers available on campus for general student use. *Web address:* http://www.pvamu.edu/.

General Application Contact: Dr. William H. Parker, Dean of the Graduate School, 936-857-2312, Fax: 936-857-4127, E-mail: william_parker@pvamu.edu.

GRADUATE UNITS

Graduate School Students: 439 full-time (316 women), 853 part-time (612 women); includes 1,034 minority (983 African Americans, 12 Asian Americans or Pacific Islanders, 36 Hispanic Americans, 3 Native Americans), 30 international. Average age 37. 600 applicants, 70% accepted. *Faculty:* 129 full-time (35 women), 31 part-time/adjunct (10 women). Expenses: Contact institution. *Financial support:* In 2001–02, 1,050 students received support, including 8 fellowships with tuition reimbursements available (averaging $12,000 per year), 10 research assistantships with tuition reimbursements available (averaging $15,000 per year); teaching assistantships, career-related internships or fieldwork, Federal Work-Study, institutionally sponsored loans, and tuition waivers (full and partial) also available. Support available to part-time students. Financial award application deadline: 4/1; financial award applicants required to submit FAFSA. In 2001, 402 degrees awarded. *Degree program information:* Part-time and evening/weekend programs available. Offers community development (MCD). *Application deadline:* Applications are processed on a rolling basis. *Application fee:* $50. *Application Contact:* Dr. Michael McFrazier, Graduate Admission Coordinator, 936-857-2315, Fax: 936-857-4521, E-mail: michael_mcfrazier@pvamu.edu. *Dean of the Graduate School,* Dr. William H. Parker, 936-857-2312, Fax: 936-857-4127, E-mail: william_parker@pvamu.edu.

College of Agriculture and Human Sciences Students: 45 full-time (28 women), 28 part-time (21 women); includes 63 minority (61 African Americans, 2 Asian Americans or Pacific Islanders), 6 international. Average age 35. 15 applicants, 100% accepted. *Faculty:* 15 full-time (5 women), 1 part-time/adjunct (0 women). Expenses: Contact institution. *Financial support:* In 2001–02, 10 research assistantships with tuition reimbursements (averaging $13,500 per year) were awarded; career-related internships or fieldwork, Federal Work-Study, and institutionally sponsored loans also available. Financial award application deadline: 4/1. In 2001, 20 degrees awarded. Offers agricultural economics (MS); animal sciences (MS); interdisciplinary human sciences (MS); marriage and family therapy (MS); soil science (MS). *Application deadline:* For fall admission, 10/2 (priority date); for spring admission, 2/19. Applications are processed on a rolling basis. *Application fee:* $25. *Dean,* Dr. Elizabeth Noel, 936-857-2996, Fax: 936-857-2998.

College of Arts and Sciences Students: 9 full-time (8 women), 17 part-time (14 women); includes 20 minority (all African Americans), 2 international. Average age 33. *Faculty:* 29 full-time (9 women), 10 part-time/adjunct (4 women). Expenses: Contact institution. *Financial support:* Teaching assistantships, career-related internships or fieldwork, Federal Work-Study, and institutionally sponsored loans available. Support available to part-time students. Financial award application deadline: 4/1. In 2001, 9 degrees awarded. *Degree program information:* Part-time and evening/weekend programs available. Offers arts and sciences (MA, MS); biology (MS); chemistry (MS); English (MA); mathematics (MS); sociology (MA). *Application deadline:* For fall admission, 10/2 (priority date); for spring admission, 2/19. Applications are processed on a rolling basis. *Application fee:* $25. *Dean,* Gerard Rambally, 936-857-4710, Fax: 936-857-2118, E-mail: gerald_rambally@pvamu.edu.

College of Business Students: 16 full-time (6 women), 70 part-time (39 women); includes 74 minority (69 African Americans, 1 Asian American or Pacific Islander, 3 Hispanic Americans, 1 Native American), 6 international. Average age 31. 61 applicants, 69% accepted, 35 enrolled. *Faculty:* 13 full-time (2 women), 1 part-time/adjunct (0 women). Expenses: Contact institution. *Financial support:* In 2001–02, 20 students received support; fellowships, research assistantships, teaching assistantships, Federal Work-Study and institutionally sponsored loans available. Financial award application deadline: 2/1. In 2001, 18 degrees awarded. *Degree program information:* Part-time and evening/weekend programs available. Offers general business administration (MBA). *Application deadline:* For fall admission, 7/1 (priority date); for spring admission, 11/1 (priority date). Applications are processed on a rolling basis. *Application fee:* $25. *Application Contact:* Peter Sutanto, Coordinator, 936-857-4310, Fax: 936-857-2797, E-mail: peter_sutanto@pvamu.edu. *Dean,* Dr. Munir Quddus, 936-857-4310, Fax: 936-857-2797, E-mail: munir_quddus@pvamu.edu.

College of Education Students: 312 full-time (244 women), 664 part-time (493 women); includes 778 minority (742 African Americans, 3 Asian Americans or Pacific Islanders, 31 Hispanic Americans, 2 Native Americans), 3 international. Average age 37. *Faculty:* 31 full-time (12 women), 15 part-time/adjunct (5 women). Expenses: Contact institution. *Financial support:* Career-related internships or fieldwork and Federal Work-Study available. Financial award application deadline: 4/1. In 2001, 334 degrees awarded. *Degree program information:* Part-time and evening/weekend programs available. Offers counseling (MA, MS Ed); curriculum and instruction (M Ed, MS Ed); education (M Ed, MA, MA Ed, MS Ed); health education (MA Ed, MS Ed); physical education (MA Ed, MS Ed); school administration (M Ed, MS Ed); school supervision (M Ed, MS Ed); special education (M Ed, MS Ed). *Application deadline:* For fall admission, 10/2 (priority date); for spring admission, 2/19. Applications are processed on a rolling basis. *Application fee:* $50. *Application Contact:* Dr. William H. Parker, Dean of the Graduate School, 936-857-2312, Fax: 936-857-4127, E-mail: william_parker@pvamu.edu. *Dean,* Dr. M. Paul Mehta, 936-857-3880, Fax: 936-857-2911.

College of Engineering Students: 13 full-time (3 women), 12 part-time (1 woman); includes 16 minority (10 African Americans, 6 Asian Americans or Pacific Islanders), 8 international. Average age 31. 16 applicants, 100% accepted, 8 enrolled. *Faculty:* 24 full-time (0 women), 1 part-time/adjunct (0 women). Expenses: Contact institution. *Financial support:* In 2001–02, 12 students received support, including 11 research assistantships (averaging $14,000 per year), 1 teaching assistantship (averaging $12,000 per year); career-related internships or fieldwork, Federal Work-Study, institutionally sponsored loans, and scholarships/grants also available. Support available to part-time students. Financial award application deadline: 4/1; financial award applicants required to submit FAFSA. In 2001, 15 degrees awarded. *Degree program information:* Part-time and evening/weekend programs available. Offers engineering (MS Engr). *Application deadline:* For fall admission, 7/1 (priority date); for spring admission, 11/1 (priority date). Applications are processed on a rolling basis. *Application fee:* $50. *Application Contact:* Dr. Shield B. Lin, Graduate Director, 936-857-4200, Fax: 936-857-4246, E-mail: shield_lin@pvamu.edu. *Dean,* Dr. Milton R. Bryant, 936-857-2211, Fax: 936-857-2222.

College of Nursing Students: 4 full-time (3 women), 21 part-time (20 women); includes 24 minority (all African Americans) Average age 37. 25 applicants, 40% accepted. *Faculty:* 4 full-time (3 women), 2 part-time/adjunct (1 woman). Expenses: Contact institution. *Financial support:* In 2001–02, 6 students received support. Scholarships/grants and traineeships available. Financial award application deadline: 4/1; financial award applicants required to submit FAFSA. In 2001, 5 degrees awarded. *Degree program information:* Part-time programs available. Offers nursing (MSN). *Application deadline:* For fall admission, 10/2 (priority date); for spring admission, 4/1 (priority date). Applications are processed on a rolling basis. *Application fee:* $50. *Application Contact:* Dr. Chloe Gaines, Associate Professor, 713-797-7017, Fax: 713-797-7012, E-mail: chloe_gaines@pvamu.edu. *Dean,* Dr. Betty N. Adams, 713-797-7009, Fax: 713-797-7013, E-mail: betty_adams@pvamu.edu.

School of Juvenile Justice and Psychology Students: 33 full-time (21 women), 41 part-time (24 women); includes 54 minority (52 African Americans, 2 Hispanic Americans), 5 international. Average age 34. 51 applicants, 45% accepted, 23 enrolled. *Faculty:* 12 full-time (4 women), 1 part-time/adjunct (0 women). Expenses: Contact institution. *Financial support:* In 2001–02, 12 students received support, including 5 research assistantships (averaging $16,000 per year), 3 teaching assistantships (averaging $16,000 per year); career-related internships or fieldwork and scholarships/grants also available. Financial award application deadline: 4/1. In 2001, 1 degree awarded. *Degree program information:* Part-time and evening/weekend programs available. Offers juvenile forensic psychology (MSJFP); juvenile justice (MSJJ, PhD). *Application deadline:* For fall admission, 4/1 (priority date); for spring admission, 11/1. Applications are processed on a rolling basis. *Application fee:* $50. *Application Contact:* Sandy Siegmund, Executive Secretary, Graduate Program, 936-857-4938, Fax: 936-857-4941, E-mail: sandy_siegmund@pvamu.edu. *Dean,* Dr. Elaine Rodney, 936-857-4938, Fax: 936-857-4941.

PRATT INSTITUTE, Brooklyn, NY 11205-3899

General Information Independent, coed, comprehensive institution. *Enrollment:* 875 full-time matriculated graduate/professional students (577 women), 459 part-time matriculated graduate/professional students (346 women). *Enrollment by degree level:* 1,334 master's. *Graduate faculty:* 46 full-time (14 women), 220 part-time/adjunct (95 women). *Tuition:* Full-time $19,248; part-time $802 per credit. *Graduate housing:* Room and/or apartments available to single students; on-campus housing not available to married students. Housing application deadline: 5/1. *Student services:* Campus employment opportunities, campus safety program, career counseling, free psychological counseling, international student services, low-cost health insurance. *Library facilities:* Pratt Institute Library. *Online resources:* library catalog, web page, access to other libraries' catalogs. *Collection:* 172,000 titles, 540 serial subscriptions, 2,851 audiovisual materials. *Research affiliation:* Ford Motor Company (transportation), The Procter & Gamble Company (product design), General Motors Corporation (transportation).

Computer facilities: 250 computers available on campus for general student use. A campuswide network can be accessed from student residence rooms and from off campus. Internet access and online class registration are available. *Web address:* http://www.pratt.edu/.

General Application Contact: Young Ha, Acting Director of Graduate Admissions, 718-636-3669, Fax: 718-636-3670, E-mail: yhah@pratt.edu.

GRADUATE UNITS

School of Architecture *Degree program information:* Part-time and evening/weekend programs available. Offers architecture (M Arch, MS, MSCRP, MSUD, MSUESM); city and regional planning (MSCRP); facilities management (MS); urban design (MSUD); urban environmental systems management (MSUESM). Electronic applications accepted.

School of Art and Design *Degree program information:* Part-time and evening/weekend programs available. Offers art and design (MFA, MID, MPS, MS); art and design education (MS); art history (MS); art therapy and creativity development (MPS); art therapy-special education (MPS); arts and cultural management (MPS); ceramics (MFA); communications design (MS); computer graphics design and interactive media (MFA); dance therapy (MPS); design management (MPS); industrial design (MID); interior design (MS); metals (MFA); new forms (MFA); package design (MS); painting (MFA); photography (MFA); printmaking (MFA); sculpture (MFA); theory and criticism (MS). Electronic applications accepted.

School of Information and Library Science *Degree program information:* Part-time and evening/weekend programs available. Offers information and library science (MS, Adv C). Electronic applications accepted.

PRESCOTT COLLEGE, Prescott, AZ 86301-2990

General Information Independent, coed, comprehensive institution. *Graduate housing:* On-campus housing not available.

GRADUATE UNITS

Graduate Programs *Degree program information:* Part-time programs available. Postbaccalaureate distance learning degree programs offered (minimal on-campus study). Offers adventure education/wilderness leadership (MA); agroecology (MA); bilingual education (MA); counseling and psychology (MA); ecopsychology (MA); education (MA); environmental education (MA); environmental studies (MA); humanities (MA); multicultural education (MA); Southwestern regional history (MA); sustainability (MA).

See in-depth description on page 1029.

PRINCETON THEOLOGICAL SEMINARY, Princeton, NJ 08542-0803

General Information Independent-religious, coed, graduate-only institution. *Enrollment by degree level:* 438 first professional, 56 master's, 233 doctoral. *Graduate faculty:* 51 full-time (13 women), 11 part-time/adjunct (1 woman). *Tuition:* Full-time $7,800. *Required fees:* $1,445. One-time fee: $175 full-time. *Graduate housing:* Rooms and/or apartments available on a first-come, first-served basis to single and married students. Typical cost: $2,030 per year ($5,830 including board) for single students; $2,030 per year ($5,830 including board) for married students. Room and board charges vary according to board plan and housing facility selected. *Student services:* Campus employment opportunities, campus safety program, child daycare facilities, free psychological counseling, international student services, low-cost health insurance, writing training. *Library facilities:* Robert E. Speer Library plus 3 others. *Online resources:* library catalog, web page. *Collection:* 477,364 titles, 3,954 serial subscriptions, 1,534 audiovisual materials. *Research affiliation:* Center of Theological Inquiry.

Computer facilities: 52 computers available on campus for general student use. A campuswide network can be accessed from student residence rooms and from off campus. Internet access is available. *Web address:* http://www.ptsem.edu/.

General Application Contact: Victor Aloyo, Director of Vocations, 609-688-1940, Fax: 609-497-7870, E-mail: victor.aloyo@ptsem.edu.

GRADUATE UNITS

Graduate and Professional Programs Students: 604 full-time (234 women), 123 part-time (31 women); includes 144 minority (68 African Americans, 57 Asian Americans or Pacific Islanders, 19 Hispanic Americans), 76 international. 410 applicants, 58% accepted, 154 enrolled. *Faculty:* 51 full-time (13 women), 11 part-time/adjunct (1 woman). Expenses: Contact institution. *Financial support:* Fellowships with full tuition reimbursements, research assistantships with full tuition reimbursements, teaching assistantships with full tuition reimbursements, career-related internships or fieldwork, Federal Work-Study, institutionally sponsored loans, scholarships/grants, and teaching fellowships available. In 2001, 139 first professional degrees, 51 master's, 29 doctorates awarded. *Degree program information:* Part-time programs available. Offers theology (M Div, MA, Th M, D Min, PhD). *Application deadline:* For spring admission, 3/1. Applications are processed on a rolling basis. *Application fee:* $35. *Application Contact:* Dr. Katharine D. Sakenfeld, Director of PhD Studies, 609-497-7818, Fax: 609-924-1970. *Dean of Academic Affairs,* Dr. James Armstrong, 609-497-7815.

PRINCETON UNIVERSITY, Princeton, NJ 08544-1019

General Information Independent, coed, university. CGS member. *Enrollment:* 1,728 full-time matriculated graduate/professional students (632 women). *Graduate faculty:* 709 full-time (166 women). *Graduate housing:* Rooms and/or apartments available to single and married students. Housing application deadline: 4/15. *Student services:* Campus employment opportunities, career counseling, child daycare facilities, free psychological counseling, international student services, low-cost health insurance, teacher training. *Library facilities:* Harvey S. Firestone Memorial Library plus 22 others. *Online resources:* library catalog, web page, access to other libraries' catalogs. *Collection:* 5.1 million titles, 34,348 serial subscriptions, 398,347 audiovisual materials. *Research affiliation:* Institute for Advanced Study, Brookhaven National Laboratory, Textile Research Laboratory.

Computer facilities: 500 computers available on campus for general student use. A campuswide network can be accessed from student residence rooms and from off campus. *Web address:* http://www.princeton.edu/.

Princeton University (continued)

General Application Contact: Barbara Basel, Director of Graduate Admission, 609-258-3034, Fax: 609-258-6180, E-mail: gsadmit@princeton.edu.

GRADUATE UNITS

Graduate School Offers African-American studies (PhD); ancient history (PhD); ancient Near Eastern studies (PhD); anthropology (PhD); applied and computational mathematics (PhD); archaeology (PhD); astrophysical sciences (PhD); atmospheric and oceanic sciences (PhD); biology (PhD); cell biology (PhD); chemistry (PhD); Chinese and Japanese art and archaeology (PhD); classical archaeology (PhD); classical philosophy (PhD); community college history teaching (PhD); comparative literature (PhD); composition (PhD); demography (PhD, Certificate); demography and public affairs (PhD); developmental biology (PhD); East Asian civilizations (PhD); East Asian studies (PhD); economics (PhD); economics and demography (PhD); English (PhD); environmental engineering and water resources (PhD); French (PhD); geological and geophysical sciences (PhD); Germanic languages and literatures (PhD); history (PhD); history of science (PhD); history, archaeology and religions of the ancient world (PhD); industrial chemistry (MS); Islamic studies (PhD); Latin American studies (PhD); mathematical physics (PhD); mathematics (PhD); modern Near Eastern studies (MA); molecular biology (PhD); molecular biophysics (PhD); musicology (PhD); neuroscience (PhD); philosophy (PhD); physics (PhD); physics and chemical physics (PhD); plasma physics (PhD); political philosophy (PhD); politics (PhD); polymer sciences and materials (MSE, PhD); psychology (PhD); religion (PhD); Slavic languages and literatures (PhD); sociology (PhD); sociology and demography (PhD); Spanish (PhD).

School of Architecture Offers architecture (M Arch, PhD).

School of Engineering and Applied Science Offers applied and computational mathematics (PhD); applied physics (M Eng, MSE, PhD); chemical engineering (M Eng, MSE, PhD); computational methods (M Eng, MSE); computer engineering (PhD); computer science (M Eng, MSE, PhD); dynamics and control systems (M Eng, MSE, PhD); electrical engineering (M Eng); electronic materials and devices (PhD); energy and environmental policy (M Eng, MSE, PhD); energy conversion, propulsion, and combustion (M Eng, MSE, PhD); engineering and applied science (M Eng, MSE, PhD); environmental engineering and water resources (PhD); financial engineering (M Eng); flight science and technology (M Eng, MSE, PhD); fluid mechanics (M Eng, MSE, PhD); information sciences and systems (PhD); mechanics, materials, and structures (M Eng, MSE, PhD); operations research and financial engineering (MSE, PhD); optoelectronics (PhD); plasma science and technology (MSE, PhD); polymer sciences and materials (MSE, PhD); statistics and operations research (MSE, PhD); transportation systems (MSE, PhD).

Woodrow Wilson School of Public and International Affairs Offers public affairs (MPA, MPA-URP, PhD); public affairs and urban and regional planning (MPA-URP, PhD); public and international affairs (MPA, MPA-URP, MPP, PhD).

THE PROTESTANT EPISCOPAL THEOLOGICAL SEMINARY IN VIRGINIA, Alexandria, VA 22304

General Information Independent-religious, coed, graduate-only institution. *Graduate housing:* Room and/or apartments available to single students; on-campus housing not available to married students.

GRADUATE UNITS

Graduate and Professional Programs *Degree program information:* Part-time programs available. Offers theology (M Div, MACE, MTS, D Min).

PROVIDENCE COLLEGE, Providence, RI 02918

General Information Independent-religious, coed, comprehensive institution. *Enrollment:* 75 full-time matriculated graduate/professional students (42 women), 416 part-time matriculated graduate/professional students (264 women). *Enrollment by degree level:* 491 master's. *Graduate faculty:* 53 full-time (19 women), 38 part-time/adjunct (16 women). *Tuition:* Part-time $236 per credit. *Graduate housing:* On-campus housing not available. *Student services:* Career counseling, disabled student services, international student services, multicultural affairs office, teacher training. *Library facilities:* Phillips Memorial Library. *Online resources:* library catalog, web page, access to other libraries' catalogs. *Collection:* 383,396 titles, 1,812 serial subscriptions, 981 audiovisual materials.

Computer facilities: 150 computers available on campus for general student use. A campuswide network can be accessed from student residence rooms and from off campus. Internet access is available. *Web address:* http://www.providence.edu/.

General Application Contact: Dr. Thomas F. Flaherty, Dean, 401-865-2247, Fax: 401-865-2057, E-mail: tflahert@providence.edu.

GRADUATE UNITS

Graduate School Students: 75 full-time (42 women), 416 part-time (264 women); includes 15 minority (6 African Americans, 6 Asian Americans or Pacific Islanders, 2 Hispanic Americans, 1 Native American) Average age 33. 101 applicants, 99% accepted. *Faculty:* 53 full-time (19 women), 38 part-time/adjunct (16 women). Expenses: Contact institution. *Financial support:* In 2001–02, 44 research assistantships with full tuition reimbursements (averaging $7,800 per year) were awarded; career-related internships or fieldwork, Federal Work-Study, institutionally sponsored loans, and unspecified assistantships also available. Support available to part-time students. Financial award applicants required to submit FAFSA. In 2001, 249 degrees awarded. *Degree program information:* Part-time and evening/weekend programs available. Offers administration (M Ed); biblical studies (MA); business administration (MBA); education literacy (M Ed); elementary administration (M Ed); guidance and counseling (M Ed); history (MA); mathematics (MAT); pastoral ministry (MA); religious education (MA); religious studies (MA); secondary administration (M Ed); special education (M Ed). *Application deadline:* For fall admission, 8/12 (priority date). Applications are processed on a rolling basis. *Application fee:* $55. *Dean,* Dr. Thomas F. Flaherty, 401-865-2247, Fax: 401-865-2057, E-mail: tflahert@providence.edu.

PROVIDENCE COLLEGE AND THEOLOGICAL SEMINARY, Otterburne, MB R0A 1G0, Canada

General Information Independent-religious, coed, comprehensive institution. *Graduate housing:* Rooms and/or apartments guaranteed to single students and available on a first-come, first-served basis to married students. Housing application deadline: 8/15.

GRADUATE UNITS

Theological Seminary *Degree program information:* Part-time programs available. Offers biblical studies (MA); Christian education (MA); counseling (MA); divinity (M Div); ministry (D Min); missions (MA); student development (MA); teaching English to speakers of other languages (Certificate); theology (MA).

PURCHASE COLLEGE, STATE UNIVERSITY OF NEW YORK, Purchase, NY 10577-1400

General Information State-supported, coed, comprehensive institution. *Enrollment:* 133 full-time matriculated graduate/professional students (70 women), 19 part-time matriculated graduate/professional students (13 women). *Enrollment by degree level:* 152 master's. *Graduate faculty:* 31 full-time (16 women), 66 part-time/adjunct (29 women). *Tuition:* Full-time $5,100. *Required fees:* $364. *Graduate housing:* Room and/or apartments available on a first-come, first-served basis to single students; on-campus housing not available to married students. *Student services:* Campus employment opportunities, campus safety program, career counseling, child daycare facilities, disabled student services, exercise/wellness program, free psychological counseling, international student services, low-cost health insurance. *Library facilities:* Purchase College Library. *Online resources:* library catalog, web page, access to other libraries' catalogs. *Collection:* 178,365 titles, 1,400 serial subscriptions, 102,302 audiovisual materials.

Computer facilities: 350 computers available on campus for general student use. A campuswide network can be accessed from student residence rooms and from off campus. Internet access, e-mail are available. *Web address:* http://www.purchase.edu/.

General Application Contact: Barbara Washington, Counselor, 914-251-6310, Fax: 914-251-6314, E-mail: admissn@purchase.edu.

GRADUATE UNITS

Conservatory of Dance Students: 9 full-time (6 women); includes 1 minority (African American), 6 international. Average age 30. 16 applicants, 38% accepted, 4 enrolled. *Faculty:* 3 full-time (2 women), 7 part-time/adjunct (4 women). Expenses: Contact institution. *Financial support:* Fellowships, teaching assistantships, Federal Work-Study, scholarships/grants, and tuition waivers (partial) available. Support available to part-time students. Financial award application deadline: 3/15; financial award applicants required to submit FAFSA. In 2001, 2 degrees awarded. Offers choreography (MFA); performance and pedagogy (MFA). *Application deadline:* For fall admission, 3/15 (priority date). Applications are processed on a rolling basis. *Application fee:* $35. Electronic applications accepted. *Application Contact:* Barbara Washington, Counselor, 914-251-6310, Fax: 914-251-6314, E-mail: admissn@purchase.edu. *Dean,* Carol Walker, 914-251-6800, Fax: 914-251-6806.

Conservatory of Music Students: 93 full-time (44 women), 11 part-time (6 women); includes 7 minority (1 African American, 4 Asian Americans or Pacific Islanders, 2 Hispanic Americans), 44 international. Average age 29. 88 applicants, 52% accepted, 46 enrolled. *Faculty:* 11 full-time (5 women), 39 part-time/adjunct (17 women). Expenses: Contact institution. *Financial support:* In 2001–02, 32 students received support; fellowships, teaching assistantships, career-related internships or fieldwork, Federal Work-Study, scholarships/grants, tuition waivers (partial), and minority fellowships available. Support available to part-time students. Financial award application deadline: 3/15; financial award applicants required to submit FAFSA. In 2001, 33 degrees awarded. Offers composition (MFA); instrumental (MFA); voice (MFA). *Application deadline:* For fall admission, 3/1. *Application fee:* $35. Electronic applications accepted. *Application Contact:* Barbara Washington, Counselor, 914-251-6310, Fax: 914-251-6314, E-mail: admissn@purchase.edu. *Dean,* Karl Kramer, 914-251-6700, Fax: 914-251-6739.

Conservatory of Theatre Arts and Film Students: 8 full-time (4 women), 2 international. Average age 27. 18 applicants, 39% accepted, 4 enrolled. *Faculty:* 2 full-time (0 women), 15 part-time/adjunct (5 women). Expenses: Contact institution. *Financial support:* In 2001–02, 7 students received support; fellowships, teaching assistantships, career-related internships or fieldwork, Federal Work-Study, scholarships/grants, tuition waivers (partial), and minority fellowships available. Support available to part-time students. Financial award application deadline: 3/15; financial award applicants required to submit FAFSA. In 2001, 4 degrees awarded. Offers theatre design (MFA); theatre technology (MFA). *Application deadline:* For fall admission, 3/1. *Application fee:* $35. Electronic applications accepted. *Application Contact:* Barbara Washington, Counselor, 914-251-6310, Fax: 914-251-6314, E-mail: admissn@purchase.edu. *Acting Dean,* Dan Hanessian, 914-251-6830, Fax: 914-251-6839.

Division of Humanities Students: 9 full-time (7 women), 7 part-time (all women), 4 international. Average age 37. 8 applicants, 100% accepted, 7 enrolled. *Faculty:* 3 full-time (all women), 2 part-time/adjunct (1 woman). Expenses: Contact institution. *Financial support:* In 2001–02, 1 student received support, including 1 fellowship (averaging $5,000 per year); Federal Work-Study, scholarships/grants, and tuition waivers (partial) also available. Support available to part-time students. Financial award application deadline: 3/15; financial award applicants required to submit FAFSA. Offers art history (MA). *Application deadline:* For fall admission, 3/15. *Application fee:* $35. *Application Contact:* Barbara Washington, Counselor, 914-251-6310, Fax: 914-251-6314, E-mail: admissn@purchase.edu. *Head,* Gari LaGuardia.

School of Art and Design Students: 14 full-time (9 women), 1 part-time. Average age 30. 69 applicants, 19% accepted, 5 enrolled. *Faculty:* 12 full-time (6 women), 3 part-time/adjunct (2 women). Expenses: Contact institution. *Financial support:* In 2001–02, 8 students received support; fellowships, teaching assistantships, Federal Work-Study, scholarships/grants, and tuition waivers (partial) available. Support available to part-time students. Financial award application deadline: 3/15; financial award applicants required to submit FAFSA. In 2001, 3 degrees awarded. Offers art and design (MFA). *Application deadline:* For fall admission, 3/1. Applications are processed on a rolling basis. *Application fee:* $35. Electronic applications accepted. *Application Contact:* Barbara Washington, Counselor, 914-251-6310, Fax: 914-251-6314, E-mail: admissn@purchase.edu. *Dean,* Kenneth Strickland, 914-251-6750, Fax: 914-251-6793, E-mail: strickl@brick.purchase.edu.

PURDUE UNIVERSITY, West Lafayette, IN 47907

General Information State-supported, coed, university. CGS member. *Enrollment:* 5,149 full-time matriculated graduate/professional students (2,161 women), 1,598 part-time matriculated graduate/professional students (599 women). *Enrollment by degree level:* 878 first professional, 2,860 master's, 3,006 doctoral, 3 other advanced degrees. *Graduate faculty:* 1,713 full-time (385 women), 106 part-time/adjunct (35 women). Tuition, state resident: full-time $4,164; part-time $149 per credit hour. Tuition, nonresident: full-time $13,872; part-time $458 per credit hour. Tuition and fees vary according to campus/location and program. *Graduate housing:* Rooms and/or apartments available on a first-come, first-served basis to single and married students. Typical cost: $6,120 (including board) for single students; $6,120 (including board) for married students. Room and board charges vary according to board plan and housing facility selected. Housing application deadline: 3/1. *Student services:* Campus employment opportunities, campus safety program, career counseling, disabled student services, exercise/wellness program, free psychological counseling, grant writing training, international student services, low-cost health insurance, multicultural affairs office, teacher training, writing training. *Library facilities:* Hicks Undergraduate Library plus 14 others. *Online resources:* library catalog, web page, access to other libraries' catalogs. *Collection:* 1.1 million titles, 18,635 serial subscriptions, 10,666 audiovisual materials.

Computer facilities: 2,100 computers available on campus for general student use. A campuswide network can be accessed from student residence rooms and from off campus. Internet access is available. *Web address:* http://www.purdue.edu/.

General Application Contact: Graduate School Admissions, 765-494-2600, Fax: 765-494-0136, E-mail: gradinfo@purdue.edu.

GRADUATE UNITS

Graduate School Students: 4,284 full-time (1,537 women), 1,585 part-time (590 women); includes 483 minority (181 African Americans, 164 Asian Americans or Pacific Islanders, 121 Hispanic Americans, 17 Native Americans), 2,579 international. Average age 29. ###### applicants, 34% accepted. *Faculty:* 1,713 full-time (385 women), 106 part-time/adjunct (35 women). Expenses: Contact institution. *Financial support:* Fellowships with tuition reimbursements, research assistantships with tuition reimbursements, teaching assistantships with tuition reimbursements, career-related internships or fieldwork, scholarships/grants, tuition waivers (full and partial), and instructorships available. Support available to part-time students. Financial award applicants required to submit FAFSA. In 2001, 1,353 master's, 445 doctorates awarded. *Degree program information:* Part-time and evening/weekend programs available. Postbaccalaureate distance learning degree programs offered (no on-campus study). Offers biochemistry and molecular biology (PhD); genetics (MS, PhD); neuroscience (PhD); plant biology (PhD). *Application fee:* $30. Electronic applications accepted. *Application Contact:* Graduate School Admissions, 765-494-2600, Fax: 765-494-0136, E-mail: gradinfo@purdue.edu. *Vice President for Research and Dean,* Dr. Gary E. Isom, 765-494-2604, Fax: 765-494-0136.

Krannert Graduate School of Management Students: 604 full-time (154 women), 45 part-time (12 women); includes 74 minority (28 African Americans, 34 Asian Americans or Pacific Islanders, 12 Hispanic Americans), 314 international. Average age 30. 2,763 applicants, 21% accepted. Expenses: Contact institution. *Financial support:* Fellowships, research assistantships, teaching assistantships, career-related internships or fieldwork available. Support available to part-time students. Financial award application deadline: 2/15; financial award applicants required to submit FAFSA. In 2001, 330 master's, 13 doctorates awarded. *Degree program information:* Evening/weekend programs available. Postbaccalaureate distance learning degree programs offered. Offers accounting (MS,

PhD); applied optimization (PhD); applied statistics (PhD); economics (MS, PhD); finance (MSM, PhD); general management (MSM); human resource management (MS); industrial administration (MSIA); management (EMS); management information systems (MSM, PhD); management science (MSM); marketing (MSM, PhD); operations management (MSM, PhD); organizational behavior and human resource management (PhD); quantitative methods (MSM, PhD); strategic management (MSM, PhD). *Application fee:* $30. Electronic applications accepted. *Dean,* Dr. R. A. Cosier, 765-494-4366.

School of Agriculture Students: 393 full-time (157 women), 55 part-time (20 women); includes 29 minority (13 African Americans, 6 Asian Americans or Pacific Islanders, 8 Hispanic Americans, 2 Native Americans), 186 international. Average age 29. 468 applicants, 34% accepted. Expenses: Contact institution. *Financial support:* Fellowships with tuition reimbursements, research assistantships with tuition reimbursements, teaching assistantships with tuition reimbursements, career-related internships or fieldwork and tuition waivers (partial) available. Support available to part-time students. Financial award applicants required to submit FAFSA. In 2001, 65 master's, 43 doctorates awarded. *Degree program information:* Part-time programs available. Offers agricultural economics (MS, PhD); agriculture (EMBA, M Agr, MS, MSF, PhD); agronomy (MS, PhD); animal sciences (MS, PhD); aquaculture, fisheries, aquatic science (MSF); aquaculture, fisheries, aquatic sciences (MS, PhD); biochemistry (MS, PhD); botany and plant pathology (MS, PhD); entomology (MS, PhD); food and agricultural business (EMBA); food science (MS, PhD); forest biology (MS, MSF, PhD); horticulture (M Agr, MS, PhD); natural resources and environmental policy (MS, MSF); natural resources environmental policy (PhD); outdoor recreation and tourism (MS, MSF, PhD); quantitative resource analysis (MS, MSF, PhD); wildlife science (MS, MSF, PhD); wood science and technology (MS, MSF, PhD). *Application fee:* $30. Electronic applications accepted. *Dean,* Dr. Victor L. Lechtenberg, 765-494-8392.

School of Consumer and Family Sciences Students: 115 full-time (90 women), 53 part-time (37 women); includes 14 minority (7 African Americans, 5 Asian Americans or Pacific Islanders, 2 Hispanic Americans), 74 international. Average age 30. 234 applicants, 47% accepted. *Faculty:* 70. Expenses: Contact institution. *Financial support:* Fellowships, research assistantships, teaching assistantships, career-related internships or fieldwork available. Support available to part-time students. Financial award applicants required to submit FAFSA. In 2001, 33 master's, 17 doctorates awarded. *Degree program information:* Part-time programs available. Offers consumer and family sciences (MS, PhD); consumer behavior (MS, PhD); developmental studies (MS, PhD); family and consumer economics (MS, PhD); family studies (MS, PhD); food sciences (MS, PhD); hospitality and tourism management (MS, PhD); marriage and family therapy (MS, PhD); nutrition (MS, PhD); retail management (MS, PhD); textile science (MS, PhD). *Application fee:* $30. Electronic applications accepted. *Dean,* Dr. Dennis A. Savaiano, 765-494-8210.

School of Education Students: 130 full-time (92 women), 269 part-time (156 women); includes 36 minority (24 African Americans, 3 Asian Americans or Pacific Islanders, 7 Hispanic Americans, 2 Native Americans), 56 international. Average age 35. 260 applicants, 65% accepted. *Faculty:* 60 full-time (28 women), 26 part-time/adjunct (15 women). Expenses: Contact institution. *Financial support:* Fellowships with full tuition reimbursements, research assistantships with full tuition reimbursements, teaching assistantships with full tuition reimbursements, career-related internships or fieldwork and tuition waivers (full) available. Support available to part-time students. Financial award application deadline: 3/1; financial award applicants required to submit FAFSA. In 2001, 85 master's, 28 doctorates, 5 other advanced degrees awarded. *Degree program information:* Part-time and evening/weekend programs available. Offers administration (MS Ed, PhD, Ed S); agricultural and extension education (PhD, Ed S); agriculture and extension education (MS, MS Ed); art education (PhD); consumer and family sciences and extension education (MS Ed, PhD, Ed S); counseling and development (MS Ed, PhD); curriculum studies (MS Ed, PhD, Ed S); education (MS, MS Ed, PhD, Ed S); education of the gifted (MS Ed); educational psychology (MS Ed, PhD); educational technology (MS Ed, PhD, Ed S); elementary education (MS Ed); foreign language education (MS Ed, PhD, Ed S); foundations of education (MS Ed, PhD); higher education administration (MS Ed, PhD); industrial technology (PhD, Ed S); language arts (MS Ed, PhD, Ed S); literacy (MS Ed, PhD, Ed S); mathematics/science education (MS, MS Ed, PhD, Ed S); social studies (MS Ed, PhD); social studies education (Ed S); special education (MS Ed, PhD); vocational/industrial education (MS Ed, PhD, Ed S); vocational/technical education (MS Ed, PhD, Ed S). *Application deadline:* For fall admission, 1/15; for spring admission, 9/15. *Application fee:* $30. Electronic applications accepted. *Interim Head,* Dr. J. L. Peters, 765-494-7935, Fax: 765-496-1622, E-mail: peters@purdue.edu.

School of Health Sciences Students: 16 full-time (6 women), 5 part-time (2 women); includes 3 minority (2 Asian Americans or Pacific Islanders, 1 Hispanic American), 6 international. Average age 32. 41 applicants, 39% accepted. *Faculty:* 7 full-time (1 woman). Expenses: Contact institution. *Financial support:* In 2001–02, 10 students received support, including 5 fellowships, 2 research assistantships, 3 teaching assistantships; career-related internships or fieldwork and traineeships also available. Support available to part-time students. Financial award applicants required to submit FAFSA. In 2001, 4 master's, 1 doctorate awarded. *Degree program information:* Part-time programs available. Offers environmental health (MS, PhD); health physics (MS, PhD); health sciences (MS, PhD); industrial hygiene (MS, PhD); medical physics (MS, PhD); toxicology (MS, PhD). *Application deadline:* Applications are processed on a rolling basis. *Application fee:* $30. Electronic applications accepted. *Application Contact:* Dr. Gary Carlson, Graduate Chairperson, 765-494-1412, Fax: 765-496-1377, E-mail: gcarlson@purdue.edu. *Head,* Dr. George A. Sandison, 765-494-7863, Fax: 765-496-1377, E-mail: sandison@purdue.edu.

School of Liberal Arts Students: 664 full-time (403 women), 298 part-time (178 women); includes 100 minority (37 African Americans, 22 Asian Americans or Pacific Islanders, 36 Hispanic Americans, 5 Native Americans), 212 international. Average age 30. 1,368 applicants, 38% accepted. Expenses: Contact institution. *Financial support:* Fellowships, research assistantships, teaching assistantships, career-related internships or fieldwork, scholarships/grants, and tuition waivers (full) available. Support available to part-time students. Financial award applicants required to submit FAFSA. In 2001, 168 master's, 86 doctorates awarded. *Degree program information:* Part-time and evening/weekend programs available. Offers American studies (MA, PhD); anthropology (MS, PhD); art and design (MA); audiology (MS, Au D, PhD); communication (MA, MS, PhD); comparative literature (MA, PhD); creative writing (MFA); exercise, human physiology of movement and sport (PhD); French (MA, MAT, PhD); French education (MAT); German (MA, MAT, PhD); German education (MAT); health and fitness (MS); health promotion (MS); health promotion and disease prevention (PhD); history (MA, PhD); liberal arts (MA, MAT, MFA, MS, Au D, PhD); linguistics (MS, PhD); literature (MA, PhD); movement and sport science (MS); pedagogy and administration (MS); pedagogy of physical activity and health (PhD); philosophy (MA, PhD); political science (MA, PhD); psychological sciences (PhD); psychology of sport and exercise, and motor behavior (PhD); sociology (MS, PhD); Spanish (MA, MAT, PhD); Spanish education (MAT); speech and hearing science (MS, PhD); speech-language pathology (MS, PhD); theatre (MA, MFA). *Application fee:* $30. Electronic applications accepted. *Dean,* Dr. Margaret M. Rowe, 765-494-3662.

School of Science Students: 643 full-time (197 women), 217 part-time (75 women); includes 77 minority (28 African Americans, 23 Asian Americans or Pacific Islanders, 25 Hispanic Americans, 1 Native American), 467 international. Average age 27. 1,789 applicants, 26% accepted. Expenses: Contact institution. *Financial support:* Fellowships with tuition reimbursements, research assistantships with tuition reimbursements, teaching assistantships with tuition reimbursements, career-related internships or fieldwork and tuition waivers (partial) available. Support available to part-time students. Financial award applicants required to submit FAFSA. In 2001, 127 master's, 108 doctorates awarded. *Degree program information:* Part-time programs available. Offers analytical chemistry (MS, PhD); applied statistics (MS); biochemistry (MS, PhD); biophysics (PhD); cell and developmental biology (PhD); chemical education (MS, PhD); computer sciences (MS, PhD); earth and atmospheric sciences (MS, PhD); ecology (MS, PhD); ecology, evolutionary and population biology (MS, PhD); evolutionary biology (MS, PhD); genetics (MS, PhD); inorganic chemistry (MS, PhD); mathematics (MS, PhD); microbiology (MS, PhD); molecular biology (PhD); neurobiology (MS, PhD); organic chemistry (MS, PhD); physical chemistry (MS, PhD); physics (MS, PhD); plant physiology (PhD); population biology (MS, PhD); science (MS, PhD); statistics (PhD); statistics and computer science (MS); statistics/computational finance (MS); theoretical statistics (MS). *Application fee:* $30. Electronic applications accepted. *Dean,* Dr. Harry A. Morrison, 765-494-1730.

School of Technology Students: 48 full-time (10 women), 55 part-time (16 women); includes 11 minority (3 African Americans, 6 Asian Americans or Pacific Islanders, 1 Hispanic American, 1 Native American), 18 international. Average age 29. 116 applicants, 41% accepted. *Faculty:* 92 full-time (14 women). Expenses: Contact institution. *Financial support:* In 2001–02, 37 teaching assistantships were awarded; fellowships Support available to part-time students. Financial award applicants required to submit FAFSA. In 2001, 53 degrees awarded. Postbaccalaureate distance learning degree programs offered. Offers technology (MS). *Application deadline:* For fall admission, 4/1 (priority date); for spring admission, 10/1. Applications are processed on a rolling basis. *Application fee:* $30. Electronic applications accepted. *Acting Dean,* Dr. Fred W. Emshousen, 765-494-2554.

Schools of Engineering Students: 1,275 full-time (179 women), 658 part-time (119 women); includes 166 minority (41 African Americans, 77 Asian Americans or Pacific Islanders, 44 Hispanic Americans, 4 Native Americans), 1,010 international. Average age 28. 3,973 applicants, 36% accepted, 568 enrolled. Expenses: Contact institution. *Financial support:* Fellowships, research assistantships, teaching assistantships, career-related internships or fieldwork available. Support available to part-time students. Financial award applicants required to submit FAFSA. In 2001, 399 master's, 142 doctorates awarded. *Degree program information:* Part-time and evening/weekend programs available. Postbaccalaureate distance learning degree programs offered (no on-campus study). Offers aeronautics and astronautics (MS, MSAAE, MSE, PhD); agricultural and biological engineering (MS, MSABE, MSE, PhD); biomedical engineering (MS Bm E, PhD); chemical engineering (MS, PhD); civil engineering (MS, MSCE, MSE, PhD); computer engineering (MS, PhD); continuing engineering education (MS, MSE); electrical engineering (MS, PhD); engineering (MS, MS Bm E, MS Met E, MSAAE, MSABE, MSCE, MSE, MSIE, MSME, MSNE, PhD); human factors in industrial engineering (MS, MSIE, PhD); manufacturing engineering (MS, MSIE, PhD); materials engineering (MS, MSE, PhD); mechanical engineering (MS, MSE, MSME, PhD); metallurgical engineering (MS Met E); nuclear engineering (MS, MSNE, PhD); operations research (MS, MSIE, PhD); systems engineering (MS, MSIE, PhD). *Application fee:* $30. Electronic applications accepted. *Dean,* Dr. Linda P. Katehi, 765-494-5345.

School of Pharmacy and Pharmacal Sciences Average age 24. Expenses: Contact institution. *Financial support:* Fellowships, research assistantships, teaching assistantships, career-related internships or fieldwork, Federal Work-Study, scholarships/grants, and traineeships available. Support available to part-time students. Financial award applicants required to submit FAFSA. *Degree program information:* Part-time programs available. Offers analytical medicinal chemistry (PhD); clinical pharmacy (MS, PhD); computational and biophysical medicinal chemistry (PhD); industrial and physical pharmacy (PhD); medicinal and bioorganic chemistry (PhD); medicinal biochemistry and molecular biology (PhD); medicinal chemistry and molecular pharmacology (MS, PhD); molecular pharmacology and toxicology (PhD); natural products and pharmacognosy (PhD); nuclear pharmacy (MS); pharmacy administration (MS, PhD); pharmacy and pharmacal sciences (Pharm D, MS, PhD); pharmacy practice (MS, PhD); radiopharmaceutical chemistry and nuclear pharmacy (PhD). *Application deadline:* Applications are processed on a rolling basis. *Application fee:* $30. Electronic applications accepted. *Application Contact:* Dr. G. M. Loudon, Associate Dean for Graduate Programs, 765-494-1362. *Dean,* Dr. Charles O. Rutledge, 765-494-1368.

School of Veterinary Medicine Students: 325 full-time (226 women), 2 part-time (both women); includes 25 minority (4 African Americans, 10 Asian Americans or Pacific Islanders, 11 Hispanic Americans), 19 international. *Faculty:* 77 full-time (19 women). Expenses: Contact institution. *Financial support:* In 2001–02, 7 fellowships, 18 research assistantships, 3 teaching assistantships were awarded. Career-related internships or fieldwork, Federal Work-Study, institutionally sponsored loans, scholarships/grants, and tuition waivers (full and partial) also available. Support available to part-time students. Financial award application deadline: 3/1; financial award applicants required to submit FAFSA. In 2001, 65 first professional degrees, 8 master's, 11 doctorates awarded. *Degree program information:* Part-time and evening/weekend programs available. Offers anatomy (MS, PhD); basic medical sciences (MS, PhD); biochemistry and molecular biology (MS, PhD); comparative epidemiology (MS, PhD); epidemiology (MS, PhD); immunology (MS, PhD); infectious diseases (MS, PhD); interdisciplinary genetics (PhD); microbiology (MS, PhD); molecular virology (MS, PhD); parasitology (MS, PhD); pathology (MS, PhD); pharmacology (MS, PhD); physiology (MS, PhD); public health (MS); toxicology (MS, PhD); veterinary anatomic pathology (MS, PhD); veterinary clinical pathology (MS, PhD); veterinary clinical sciences (MS, PhD); veterinary medicine (DVM, MS, PhD); veterinary pathobiology (MS, PhD); virology (MS, PhD). *Application Contact:* Denise A. Ottinger, Director, Student Services, 765-494-7893, Fax: 765-496-2891, E-mail: admissions@vet.purdue.edu. *Dean,* Dr. Alan H. Rebar, 765-494-7608.

PURDUE UNIVERSITY CALUMET, Hammond, IN 46323-2094

General Information State-supported, coed, comprehensive institution. *Graduate faculty:* 140. Tuition, state resident: part-time $141 per hour. Tuition, nonresident: part-time $321 per hour. *Required fees:* $7 per hour. *Graduate housing:* On-campus housing not available. *Student services:* Campus employment opportunities, campus safety program, career counseling, child daycare facilities, disabled student services, exercise/wellness program, free psychological counseling, international student services, low-cost health insurance, teacher training, writing training. *Library facilities:* Purdue Calumet Library. *Collection:* 215,830 titles, 1,736 serial subscriptions.

Computer facilities: 250 computers available on campus for general student use. A campuswide network can be accessed. Internet access is available. *Web address:* http://www.calumet.purdue.edu/.

General Application Contact: Dr. Daniel M. Dunn, Executive Dean, 219-989-2257.

GRADUATE UNITS

Graduate School *Degree program information:* Part-time and evening/weekend programs available.

School of Education Offers counseling and personnel services (MS Ed); educational administration (MS Ed); elementary education (MS Ed); instructional development (MS Ed); media sciences (MS Ed); secondary education (MS Ed).

School of Engineering, Mathematics, and Science *Degree program information:* Part-time programs available. Offers biology (MS); biology teaching (MS); engineering (MSE); engineering, mathematics, and science (MS, MSE); mathematics (MS).

School of Liberal Arts and Sciences *Degree program information:* Part-time programs available. Offers communication (MA); English (MA); history and political science (MA); liberal arts and sciences (MA, MS); marriage and family therapy (MS).

School of Management *Degree program information:* Part-time and evening/weekend programs available. Offers accountancy (M Acc); business administration (MBA). Electronic applications accepted.

School of Nursing *Degree program information:* Part-time programs available. Postbaccalaureate distance learning degree programs offered (minimal on-campus study). Offers nursing (MS). Electronic applications accepted.

PURDUE UNIVERSITY NORTH CENTRAL, Westville, IN 46391-9542

General Information State-supported, coed, comprehensive institution. *Enrollment:* 40 part-time matriculated graduate/professional students (31 women). *Enrollment by degree level:* 40 master's. *Graduate faculty:* 4 full-time (3 women), 2 part-time/adjunct (0 women). *Tuition:* Part-time $142 per credit hour. *Required fees:* $11 per credit hour. *Graduate housing:* On-campus housing not available. *Student services:* Career counseling, child daycare facilities, disabled student services, exercise/wellness program, free psychological counseling, low-cost health insurance, writing training. *Library facilities:* Purdue University North Central Library. *Online resources:* library catalog, web page, access to other libraries' catalogs. *Collection:* 88,156 titles, 417 serial subscriptions, 541 audiovisual materials.

Purdue University North Central (continued)

Computer facilities: 382 computers available on campus for general student use. A campuswide network can be accessed. *Web address:* http://www.purduenc.edu/.

General Application Contact: Dr. Cynthia J. Pulver-Fontaine, Acting Chair, 219-785-5322, Fax: 219-785-5516, E-mail: cpulver@purduenc.edu.

GRADUATE UNITS

Graduate Program in Education Average age 32. 5 applicants, 80% accepted. *Faculty:* 4 full-time (3 women), 2 part-time/adjunct (0 women). Expenses: Contact institution. In 2001, 4 degrees awarded. *Degree program information:* Part-time and evening/weekend programs available. Offers elementary education (MS Ed). *Application deadline:* For fall admission, 9/15; for winter admission, 1/15. Applications are processed on a rolling basis. *Application fee:* $30. *Acting Chair,* Dr. Cynthia J. Pulver-Fontaine, 219-785-5322, Fax: 219-785-5516, E-mail: cpulver@purduenc.edu.

QUEENS COLLEGE OF THE CITY UNIVERSITY OF NEW YORK, Flushing, NY 11367-1597

General Information State and locally supported, coed, comprehensive institution. CGS member. *Enrollment:* 303 full-time matriculated graduate/professional students (225 women), 3,181 part-time matriculated graduate/professional students (2,315 women). *Graduate faculty:* 495 full-time (172 women), 555 part-time/adjunct (269 women). Tuition, state resident: full-time $2,175; part-time $185 per credit. Tuition, nonresident: full-time $3,800; part-time $320 per credit. *Required fees:* $114; $57 per semester. Tuition and fees vary according to course load. *Graduate housing:* On-campus housing not available. *Student services:* Campus employment opportunities, career counseling, child daycare facilities, disabled student services, free psychological counseling, international student services, low-cost health insurance, multicultural affairs office, teacher training, writing training. *Library facilities:* Benjamin S. Rosenthal Library plus 1 other. *Online resources:* library catalog, web page, access to other libraries' catalogs. *Collection:* 3,439 serial subscriptions, 94,631 audiovisual materials. *Research affiliation:* Bellcore (physics), Brookhaven National Laboratory/SUNY Stony Brook (physics), Institute for Comparative and Environmental Toxicology (chemistry).

Computer facilities: 500 computers available on campus for general student use. A campuswide network can be accessed from off campus. Internet access is available. *Web address:* http://www.qc.edu/.

General Application Contact: Mario Caruso, Director of Graduate Admissions, 718-997-5200, Fax: 718-997-5193, E-mail: graduate_admissions@qc.edu.

GRADUATE UNITS

Division of Graduate Studies Students: 303 full-time (225 women), 3,181 part-time (2,315 women). Average age 26. 2,873 applicants, 69% accepted. *Faculty:* 495 full-time (172 women), 555 part-time/adjunct (269 women). Expenses: Contact institution. *Financial support:* Career-related internships or fieldwork, Federal Work-Study, institutionally sponsored loans, tuition waivers (partial), unspecified assistantships, and adjunct lectureships available. Support available to part-time students. Financial award application deadline: 4/1; financial award applicants required to submit FAFSA. In 2001, 1,125 master's, 93 other advanced degrees awarded. *Degree program information:* Part-time and evening/weekend programs available. *Application deadline:* Applications are processed on a rolling basis. *Application fee:* $40. *Application Contact:* Mario Caruso, Director of Graduate Admissions, 718-997-5200, Fax: 718-997-5193, E-mail: graduate_admissions@qc.edu. *Assistant to the Provost for Graduate Studies,* Dr. Robert Engel, 718-997-5191, Fax: 718-997-5493, E-mail: robert_engel@qc.edu.

Arts Division Students: 61 full-time (47 women), 219 part-time (130 women). Average age 26. 534 applicants, 47% accepted. *Faculty:* 134 full-time (46 women), 38 part-time/adjunct (17 women). Expenses: Contact institution. *Financial support:* Career-related internships or fieldwork, Federal Work-Study, institutionally sponsored loans, tuition waivers (partial), and adjunct lectureships available. Support available to part-time students. Financial award application deadline: 4/1; financial award applicants required to submit FAFSA. In 2001, 97 degrees awarded. *Degree program information:* Part-time and evening/weekend programs available. Offers applied linguistics (MA); art history (MA); arts (MA, MFA, MS Ed); creative writing (MA); English language and literature (MA); fine arts (MFA); French (MA); Italian (MA); media studies (MA); music (MA); Spanish (MA); speech pathology (MA); teaching English to speakers of other languages (MS Ed). *Application deadline:* Applications are processed on a rolling basis. *Application fee:* $40. *Application Contact:* Mario Caruso, Director of Graduate Admissions, 718-997-5200, Fax: 718-997-5193, E-mail: graduate_admissions@qc.edu. *Acting Dean,* Dr. Tamara Evans, 718-997-5790, E-mail: tamara_evans@qc.edu.

Division of Education Students: 159 full-time (126 women), 2,082 part-time (1,613 women). 1,950 applicants, 65% accepted. *Faculty:* 57 full-time (35 women), 123 part-time/adjunct (76 women). Expenses: Contact institution. *Financial support:* Career-related internships or fieldwork, Federal Work-Study, institutionally sponsored loans, and tuition waivers (partial) available. Support available to part-time students. Financial award application deadline: 4/1; financial award applicants required to submit FAFSA. In 2001, 650 master's, 93 ACs awarded. *Degree program information:* Part-time and evening/weekend programs available. Offers administration and supervision (AC); art (MS Ed); bilingual education (MS Ed); biology (MS Ed, AC); chemistry (MS Ed, AC); counselor education (MS Ed); earth sciences (MS Ed, AC); education (MS Ed, AC); elementary education (MS Ed, AC); English (MS Ed, AC); French (MS Ed, AC); Italian (MS Ed, AC); literacy (MS Ed); mathematics (MS Ed, AC); music (MS Ed, AC); physics (MS Ed, AC); school psychology (MS Ed, AC); social studies (MS Ed, AC); Spanish (MS Ed, AC); special education (MS Ed). *Application deadline:* For fall admission, 4/1; for spring admission, 11/1. Applications are processed on a rolling basis. *Application fee:* $40. *Application Contact:* Mario Caruso, Director of Graduate Admissions, 718-997-5200, Fax: 718-997-5193, E-mail: graduate_admissions@qc.edu. *Acting Dean,* Dr. Philip Anderson, 718-997-5220.

Mathematics and Natural Sciences Division Students: 45 full-time (24 women), 289 part-time (155 women). Average age 26. 481 applicants, 76% accepted. *Faculty:* 127 full-time (29 women). Expenses: Contact institution. *Financial support:* Career-related internships or fieldwork, Federal Work-Study, institutionally sponsored loans, tuition waivers (partial), unspecified assistantships, and adjunct lectureships available. Support available to part-time students. Financial award application deadline: 4/1; financial award applicants required to submit FAFSA. In 2001, 184 degrees awarded. *Degree program information:* Part-time and evening/weekend programs available. Offers biochemistry (MA); biology (MA); chemistry (MA); clinical behavioral applications in mental health settings (MA); computer science (MA); earth and environmental science (MA); home economics (MS Ed); mathematics (MA); mathematics and natural sciences (MA, MS Ed); physical education and exercise sciences (MS Ed); physics (MA); psychology (MA). *Application deadline:* For fall admission, 4/1; for spring admission, 11/1. Applications are processed on a rolling basis. *Application fee:* $40. *Application Contact:* Mario Caruso, Director of Graduate Admissions, 718-997-5200, Fax: 718-997-5193, E-mail: graduate_admissions@qc.edu. *Dean,* Dr. Thomas Strekas, 718-997-4105, E-mail: thomas_strekas@qc.edu.

Social Science Division Students: 38 full-time (28 women), 591 part-time (417 women). 371 applicants, 94% accepted. *Faculty:* 66 full-time (20 women), 23 part-time/adjunct (6 women). Expenses: Contact institution. *Financial support:* Career-related internships or fieldwork, Federal Work-Study, institutionally sponsored loans, and tuition waivers (partial) available. Support available to part-time students. Financial award application deadline: 4/1; financial award applicants required to submit FAFSA. In 2001, 194 degrees awarded. *Degree program information:* Part-time and evening/weekend programs available. Offers accounting (MS); history (MA); liberal studies (MALS); library and information studies (MLS, AC); social science (MA, MALS, MASS, MLS, MS, AC); social sciences (MASS); sociology (MA); urban studies (MA). *Application deadline:* For fall admission, 4/1; for spring admission, 11/1. Applications are processed on a rolling basis. *Application fee:* $40. *Application Contact:* Mario Caruso, Director of Graduate Admissions, 718-997-5200, Fax: 718-997-5193, E-mail: graduate_admissions@qc.edu. *Dean,* Dr. Donald Scott, 718-997-5210, E-mail: donald_scott@qc.edu.

See in-depth description on page 1031.

QUEEN'S UNIVERSITY AT KINGSTON, Kingston, ON K7L 3N6, Canada

General Information Province-supported, coed, university. CGS member. *Enrollment:* 1,690 full-time matriculated graduate/professional students (802 women), 422 part-time matriculated graduate/professional students (227 women). *Enrollment by degree level:* 1,281 master's, 783 doctoral. *Graduate faculty:* 682 full-time (190 women), 125 part-time/adjunct (36 women). *Tuition:* Full-time $3,506. *Graduate housing:* Rooms and/or apartments available to single students and available on a first-come, first-served basis to married students. Housing application deadline: 6/15. *Student services:* Campus employment opportunities, campus safety program, career counseling, child daycare facilities, disabled student services, exercise/wellness program, free psychological counseling, grant writing training, international student services, low-cost health insurance, teacher training, writing training. *Library facilities:* Joseph S. Stauffer Library plus 7 others. *Online resources:* library catalog, web page, access to other libraries' catalogs. *Collection:* 3.2 million titles, 10,825 serial subscriptions. *Research affiliation:* Centre for Research in Earth and Space Technology, Communications and Information Technology Ontario, Protein Engineering Network of Centres of Excellence, Intelligent Sensing for Innovative Structures, Canadian Bacterial Diseases Network.

Computer facilities: 400 computers available on campus for general student use. A campuswide network can be accessed from student residence rooms and from off campus. *Web address:* http://www.queensu.ca/.

General Application Contact: Monica Corbett, Registrar, School of Graduate Studies and Research, 613-533-6100, Fax: 613-533-6015.

GRADUATE UNITS

Faculty of Law Students: 7 full-time (5 women), 2 part-time (1 woman). 45 applicants, 36% accepted, 9 enrolled. *Faculty:* 24 full-time (9 women), 7 part-time/adjunct (5 women). Expenses: Contact institution. *Financial support:* In 2001–02, 6 students received support, including 4 fellowships; research assistantships, institutionally sponsored loans and scholarships/grants also available. Financial award application deadline: 2/1. In 2001, 10 degrees awarded. *Degree program information:* Part-time programs available. Offers law (LL B, LL M). *Application deadline:* For fall admission, 2/1 (priority date). *Application fee:* $70 Canadian dollars. *Application Contact:* Prof. A. Manson, Graduate Coordinator, 613-533-2220, Fax: 613-533-6509, E-mail: llm@qsilver.queensu.ca. *Dean,* Prof. A. Harvison-Young, 613-533-2220, Fax: 613-533-6611, E-mail: llb@qsilver.queensu.ca.

Queen's Theological College Students: 26 full-time (17 women), 40 part-time (24 women). 24 applicants, 67% accepted. *Faculty:* 14 full-time (4 women), 8 part-time/adjunct (3 women). Expenses: Contact institution. *Financial support:* In 2001–02, 26 students received support. Scholarships/grants available. Support available to part-time students. Financial award application deadline: 9/15. In 2001, 10 M Divs, 2 master's awarded. Offers theology (M Div, MTS). *Application deadline:* For fall admission, 4/15 (priority date). Applications are processed on a rolling basis. *Application fee:* $30 Canadian dollars. *Application Contact:* Cheryl O'Shea, Admissions Officer, 613-533-2109, Fax: 613-533-6879, E-mail: osheac@post.queensu.ca. *Principal,* Dr. Jean Stairs, 613-533-2109, Fax: 613-533-6879, E-mail: stairs@post.queensu.ca.

School of Business Students: 38 full-time (17 women), 4 part-time (2 women); includes 15 minority (14 Asian Americans or Pacific Islanders, 1 Hispanic American) Average age 26. 300 applicants, 17% accepted, 24 enrolled. *Faculty:* 40 full-time (10 women), 8 part-time/adjunct (0 women). Expenses: Contact institution. *Financial support:* In 2001–02, 33 students received support, including fellowships (averaging $8,000 per year), research assistantships (averaging $12,500 per year); teaching assistantships, institutionally sponsored loans and scholarships/grants also available. Financial award application deadline: 3/1. In 2001, 11 master's, 1 doctorate awarded. Offers business (M Sc, MBA, PhD); business administration (MBA); business administration for science and technology (MBA). *Application deadline:* For winter admission, 3/1 (priority date). Applications are processed on a rolling basis. *Application fee:* $70. *Application Contact:* Dr. Julian Barling, Information Contact, 613-533-2303, Fax: 613-533-6847, E-mail: phd@business.queensu.ca. *Dean,* Dr. Margot Northey, 613-533-2305.

School of Graduate Studies and Research Students: 1,615 full-time (764 women), 403 part-time (221 women). 4,594 applicants, 25% accepted. *Faculty:* 684 full-time (192 women), 125 part-time/adjunct (36 women). Expenses: Contact institution. *Financial support:* In 2001–02, 230 fellowships (averaging $8,000 per year), 551 research assistantships (averaging $5,333 per year), 948 teaching assistantships (averaging $3,899 per year) were awarded. Institutionally sponsored loans also available. Support available to part-time students. Financial award application deadline: 3/1. In 2001, 716 master's, 111 doctorates awarded. *Degree program information:* Part-time programs available. *Application deadline:* Applications are processed on a rolling basis. *Application fee:* $70 Canadian dollars. *Application Contact:* Sandra Howard-Ferreira, Senior Administrative Officer, 613-533-6100. *Dean,* Dr. Ulrich Scheck, 613-533-6100.

Faculty of Applied Science Students: 216 full-time (60 women), 45 part-time (4 women). *Faculty:* 77 full-time (8 women), 14 part-time/adjunct (0 women). Expenses: Contact institution. *Financial support:* Fellowships, research assistantships, teaching assistantships, institutionally sponsored loans available. Financial award application deadline: 3/1. In 2001, 59 master's, 15 doctorates awarded. *Degree program information:* Part-time programs available. Offers applied science (M Sc, M Sc Eng, PhD); chemical engineering (M Sc, M Sc Eng, PhD); civil engineering (M Sc, M Sc Eng, PhD); electrical and computer engineering (M Sc, M Sc Eng, PhD); mechanical engineering (M Sc, M Sc Eng, PhD); mining engineering (M Sc, M Sc Eng, PhD). *Application deadline:* Applications are processed on a rolling basis. *Application fee:* $60 Canadian dollars. Electronic applications accepted. *Application Contact:* Monica Corbett, Registrar, 613-533-6100, Fax: 613-533-6015. *Dean,* T. J. Harris, 613-533-2055.

Faculty of Arts and Sciences Students: 1,138 full-time (598 women), 344 part-time (213 women). *Faculty:* 550 full-time (159 women), 102 part-time/adjunct (30 women). Expenses: Contact institution. *Financial support:* Fellowships, research assistantships, teaching assistantships, institutionally sponsored loans available. Financial award application deadline: 3/1. In 2001, 249 master's, 115 doctorates awarded. *Degree program information:* Part-time programs available. Offers art conservation (MAC); art history (MA, PhD); arts and sciences (M Sc, M Sc Eng, MA, MAC, MTS, PhD); biology (M Sc, PhD); brain behavior and cognitive science (MA, PhD); chemistry (M Sc, PhD); classics, greek, latin (MA); clinical psychology (MA, PhD); computing and information science (M Sc, PhD); developmental psychology (MA, PhD); economics (MA, PhD); English language and literature (MA, PhD); experimental psychology (PhD); French studies (MA, PhD); geography (M Sc, MA, PhD); geological sciences and geological engineering (M Sc, M Sc Eng, PhD); German language and literature (MA, PhD); history (MA, PhD); mathematics (M Sc, M Sc Eng, PhD); philosophy (MA, PhD); physics (M Sc, M Sc Eng, PhD); political studies (MA, PhD); religious studies (MA); social personality psychology (MA, PhD); social psychology (PhD); sociology (MA, PhD); Spanish (MA); statistics (M Sc, M Sc Eng, PhD). *Application fee:* $70 Canadian dollars. Electronic applications accepted. *Dean,* Dr. R. A. Silverman, 613-533-2446, Fax: 613-533-2067.

Faculty of Education Students: 60 full-time (50 women), 88 part-time (58 women). 144 applicants, 47% accepted, 48 enrolled. *Faculty:* 42 full-time (22 women). Expenses: Contact institution. *Financial support:* In 2001–02, 6 fellowships (averaging $8,000 per year), 12 teaching assistantships (averaging $4,600 per year) were awarded. Research assistantships, institutionally sponsored loans also available. Financial award application deadline: 3/1. In 2001, 19 degrees awarded. *Degree program information:* Part-time programs available. Offers education (M Ed, PhD). *Application deadline:* 1/31. *Application fee:* $70 Canadian dollars. *Application Contact:* M. S. Sayers, Program Manager, 613-533-6206, Fax: 613-533-6584, E-mail: sayersm@educ.queensu.ca. *Dean,* Dr. R. Bruno-Jofré, 613-533-6210.

Faculty of Health Sciences Students: 279 full-time (131 women), 38 part-time (29 women). Average age 30. *Faculty:* 135 full-time (45 women), 34 part-time/adjunct (14 women).

Expenses: Contact institution. *Financial support:* Fellowships with partial tuition reimbursements, research assistantships, teaching assistantships, institutionally sponsored loans available. Financial award application deadline: 3/1. *Degree program information:* Part-time programs available. Offers anatomy and cell biology (M Sc, PhD); biochemistry (M Sc, PhD); epidemiology (M Sc); health sciences (M Sc, PhD); microbiology and immunology (M Sc, PhD); nursing (M Sc); pathology (M Sc, PhD); pharmacology and toxicology (M Sc, PhD); physiology (M Sc, PhD); rehabilitation therapy (M Sc, PhD). *Application deadline:* For fall admission, 9/1; for spring admission, 2/1. Applications are processed on a rolling basis. *Application fee:* $70 Canadian dollars. Electronic applications accepted. *Dean*, Dr. Barry T. Smith, 613-533-2544.

School of Industrial Relations Students: 30 full-time (22 women), 1 part-time. Average age 25. 97 applicants, 64% accepted, 30 enrolled. *Faculty:* 4 full-time (2 women), 1 (woman) part-time/adjunct. Expenses: Contact institution. *Financial support:* In 2001–02, 30 students received support, including 12 fellowships (averaging $8,000 per year); institutionally sponsored loans also available. Financial award application deadline: 3/1. In 2001, 31 degrees awarded. *Degree program information:* Part-time programs available. Offers industrial relations (MIR). *Application deadline:* For spring admission, 3/1 (priority date). Applications are processed on a rolling basis. *Application fee:* $70 Canadian dollars. *Application Contact:* Grier Owen, MIR Program Administrator, 613-533-6000 Ext. 77322, Fax: 613-533-2560, E-mail: go4@post.queensu.ca. *Director*, Dr. Carol Beatty, 613-533-6000 Ext. 77087, Fax: 613-533-2560, E-mail: beattyc@qsilver.queensu.ca.

School of Physical and Health Education Students: 32 full-time (18 women), 6 part-time (5 women). 28 applicants, 29% accepted. *Faculty:* 11 full-time (3 women). Expenses: Contact institution. *Financial support:* In 2001–02, 18 fellowships (averaging $8,000 per year), 8 research assistantships (averaging $5,000 per year), 20 teaching assistantships (averaging $2,000 per year) were awarded. Institutionally sponsored loans also available. Financial award application deadline: 3/1. In 2001, 11 master's, 1 doctorate awarded. *Degree program information:* Part-time programs available. Offers applied exercise science (PhD); biomechanics/ergonomics (M Sc); exercise physiology rehabilitation (M Sc); social psychology of sport and exercise rehabilitation (MA); sociology of sport (MA). *Application deadline:* For fall admission, 2/28 (priority date). *Application fee:* $70 Canadian dollars. Electronic applications accepted. *Application Contact:* Leisa McDonald, Administrative Assistant, 613-533-6000 Ext. 75214, Fax: 613-533-2009, E-mail: phegrad@post.queensu.ca. *Director*, Dr. Janice Deakin, 613-533-6601, Fax: 613-533-2009, E-mail: deakinj@post.queensu.ca.

School of Policy Studies Students: 39 full-time (21 women), 93 part-time (71 women). 250 applicants, 36% accepted, 70 enrolled. *Faculty:* 9 full-time (2 women), 12 part-time/adjunct (2 women). Expenses: Contact institution. *Financial support:* In 2001–02, 30 fellowships (averaging $6,500 per year) were awarded; career-related internships or fieldwork, Federal Work-Study, and institutionally sponsored loans also available. Financial award application deadline: 3/1. In 2001, 43 degrees awarded. *Degree program information:* Part-time programs available. Offers policy studies (MPA). *Application deadline:* For fall admission, 3/1 (priority date). Applications are processed on a rolling basis. *Application fee:* $70 Canadian dollars. *Application Contact:* Lynn Freeman, Program Coordinator, 613-533-2154, Fax: 613-533-2135, E-mail: policy@qsilver.queensu.ca. *Director*, Dr. K. G. Banting, 613-533-6555, Fax: 613-533-6606.

School of Urban and Regional Planning Students: 49 full-time (22 women), 13 part-time (9 women). 66 applicants, 70% accepted, 29 enrolled. *Faculty:* 6 full-time (1 woman), 2 part-time/adjunct (0 women). Expenses: Contact institution. *Financial support:* Fellowships, institutionally sponsored loans available. Financial award application deadline: 3/1. In 2001, 20 degrees awarded. *Degree program information:* Part-time programs available. Offers urban and regional planning (M Pl). *Application deadline:* For fall admission, 2/28 (priority date). *Application fee:* $70 Canadian dollars. *Application Contact:* Dr. A. Skaburskis, Graduate Coordinator, 613-533-6000 Ext. 77059, Fax: 613-533-6905, E-mail: skabursk@fred.surp.queensu.ca. *Director*, Dr. Hok-Lin Leung, 613-533-6000 Ext. 77062, Fax: 613-533-6905, E-mail: leungh@post.queensu.ca.

School of Medicine Students: 332 full-time. Expenses: Contact institution. *Financial support:* Institutionally sponsored loans and scholarships/grants available. Support available to part-time students. Offers medicine (MD). *Application deadline:* For fall admission, 10/15. Electronic applications accepted. *Vice Principal of Health Sciences and Dean*, Dr. David Walker, 613-533-2544.

QUEENS UNIVERSITY OF CHARLOTTE, Charlotte, NC 28274-0002

General Information Independent-religious, coed, comprehensive institution. *Enrollment:* 113 full-time matriculated graduate/professional students (62 women), 304 part-time matriculated graduate/professional students (176 women). *Enrollment by degree level:* 417 master's. *Graduate faculty:* 22 full-time (12 women), 9 part-time/adjunct (4 women). *Tuition:* Full-time $9,500. *Graduate housing:* On-campus housing not available. *Student services:* Campus safety program, international student services, teacher training. *Library facilities:* Everett Library plus 1 other. *Online resources:* library catalog, web page, access to other libraries' catalogs. *Collection:* 129,061 titles, 459 serial subscriptions, 1,365 audiovisual materials.

Computer facilities: 125 computers available on campus for general student use. A campuswide network can be accessed from student residence rooms. Internet access and online class registration are available. *Web address:* http://www.queens.edu/.

General Application Contact: Robert Mobley, Director of MBA Admissions, 704-337-2224, Fax: 704-337-2594.

GRADUATE UNITS

College of Arts and Sciences Students: 27 full-time (22 women). *Faculty:* 4 full-time (1 woman), 2 part-time/adjunct (1 woman). Expenses: Contact institution. Offers creative writing (MFA). *Application Contact:* Jennifer Matz, Information Contact, 704-337-2404. *Head*, Dr. Norris Frederick, 704-337-2577.

Hayworth College Students: 20 full-time (19 women), 115 part-time (105 women); includes 18 minority (13 African Americans, 1 Asian American or Pacific Islander, 3 Hispanic Americans, 1 Native American), 2 international. Average age 29. 95 applicants, 66% accepted. *Faculty:* 12 full-time (9 women), 6 part-time/adjunct (4 women). Expenses: Contact institution. *Financial support:* In 2001–02, 30 students received support, including 5 fellowships; institutionally sponsored loans also available. Support available to part-time students. Financial award applicants required to submit FAFSA. In 2001, 35 degrees awarded. *Degree program information:* Part-time and evening/weekend programs available. Offers elementary education (MAT); organizational communications (MA). *Application deadline:* Applications are processed on a rolling basis. *Application fee:* $25. Electronic applications accepted. *Application Contact:* James Mathis, Director of Admissions, 704-337-2314, Fax: 704-337-2415. *Dean*, Dr. Darrel Miller, 704-337-2574.

Division of Nursing 14 applicants, 79% accepted. *Faculty:* 4 full-time (all women), 2 part-time/adjunct (1 woman). Expenses: Contact institution. In 2001, 4 degrees awarded. Offers nursing management (MSN). *Application deadline:* Applications are processed on a rolling basis. *Application fee:* $25. Electronic applications accepted. *Application Contact:* Anne Duplessis, Director of Admissions, 704-337-2314, Fax: 704-337-2415. *Chair*, Dr. Joan McGill, 704-337-2295.

McColl School of Business Students: 68 full-time (23 women), 189 part-time (71 women); includes 26 minority (21 African Americans, 2 Asian Americans or Pacific Islanders, 2 Hispanic Americans, 1 Native American), 4 international. Average age 31. 105 applicants, 71% accepted. *Faculty:* 8 full-time (1 woman), 6 part-time/adjunct (2 women). Expenses: Contact institution. *Financial support:* In 2001–02, 40 fellowships were awarded; institutionally sponsored loans also available. Support available to part-time students. In 2001, 97 degrees awarded. *Degree program information:* Part-time and evening/weekend programs available. Offers business (EMBA, MBA). *Application deadline:* Applications are processed on a rolling basis. *Application fee:* $25. Electronic applications accepted. *Application Contact:* Katie M. Wireman, Director of MBA Admissions, 704-337-2224, Fax: 704-337-2594. *Head*, Peter Browning, 704-337-2234.

QUINCY UNIVERSITY, Quincy, IL 62301-2699

General Information Independent-religious, coed, comprehensive institution. *Enrollment:* 37 full-time matriculated graduate/professional students (16 women), 135 part-time matriculated graduate/professional students (95 women). *Enrollment by degree level:* 172 master's. *Graduate faculty:* 8 full-time (3 women), 5 part-time/adjunct (3 women). *Tuition:* Part-time $440 per semester hour. *Graduate housing:* On-campus housing not available. *Student services:* Campus safety program, career counseling, free psychological counseling, international student services, teacher training. *Library facilities:* Brenner Library. *Online resources:* library catalog, web page, access to other libraries' catalogs. *Collection:* 239,983 titles, 814 serial subscriptions, 4,383 audiovisual materials.

Computer facilities: 200 computers available on campus for general student use. A campuswide network can be accessed from student residence rooms and from off campus. Internet access and online class registration are available. *Web address:* http://www.quincy.edu/.

General Application Contact: Kevin Brown, Director of Admissions, 217-228-5210, Fax: 217-228-5648, E-mail: admissions@quincy.edu.

GRADUATE UNITS

Division of Business Students: 34 full-time (14 women), 14 part-time (2 women); includes 22 minority (1 African American, 21 Asian Americans or Pacific Islanders) *Faculty:* 6 full-time (3 women). Expenses: Contact institution. *Financial support:* In 2001–02, 9 students received support. Available to part-time students. Applicants required to submit FAFSA. In 2001, 68 degrees awarded. *Degree program information:* Part-time and evening/weekend programs available. Offers business (MBA). *Application fee:* $25. *Application Contact:* Kevin Brown, Director of Admissions, 217-228-5210, Fax: 217-228-5648, E-mail: admissions@quincy.edu. *Director, MBA Program*, Dr. Richard Magliari, 217-228-5394, E-mail: majliri@quincy.edu.

Division of Education Students: 3 full-time (2 women), 121 part-time (93 women); includes 1 minority (African American) *Faculty:* 2 full-time (0 women), 5 part-time/adjunct (3 women). Expenses: Contact institution. *Financial support:* In 2001–02, 44 students received support. Available to part-time students. Applicants required to submit FAFSA. In 2001, 18 degrees awarded. *Degree program information:* Part-time programs available. Offers education (MS Ed). *Application deadline:* Applications are processed on a rolling basis. *Application fee:* $25. *Application Contact:* Kevin Brown, Director of Admissions, 217-228-5210, Fax: 217-228-5648, E-mail: admissions@quincy.edu. *Chair*, Dr. Alice Mills, 217-228-5420.

QUINNIPIAC UNIVERSITY, Hamden, CT 06518-1940

General Information Independent, coed, comprehensive institution. *Enrollment:* 934 full-time matriculated graduate/professional students (549 women), 592 part-time matriculated graduate/professional students (313 women). *Enrollment by degree level:* 695 first professional, 831 master's. *Graduate faculty:* 89 full-time (38 women), 58 part-time/adjunct (23 women). *Tuition:* Part-time $450 per credit hour. *Required fees:* $25 per term. *Graduate housing:* On-campus housing not available. *Student services:* Campus employment opportunities, campus safety program, career counseling, exercise/wellness program, free psychological counseling, international student services, low-cost health insurance, multicultural affairs office. *Library facilities:* Arnold Bernhard Library plus 1 other. *Online resources:* library catalog, web page, access to other libraries' catalogs. *Collection:* 285,000 titles, 4,400 serial subscriptions.

Computer facilities: 200 computers available on campus for general student use. A campuswide network can be accessed from student residence rooms and from off campus. Internet access is available. *Web address:* http://www.quinnipiac.edu/.

General Application Contact: 800-462-1944, Fax: 203-582-3443, E-mail: graduate@quinnipiac.edu.

GRADUATE UNITS

College of Liberal Arts Students: 83 full-time (60 women), 11 part-time (5 women); includes 5 minority (1 African American, 1 Asian American or Pacific Islander, 3 Hispanic Americans), 2 international. Average age 27. 80 applicants, 83% accepted, 52 enrolled. *Faculty:* 13 full-time (7 women), 17 part-time/adjunct (9 women). Expenses: Contact institution. *Financial support:* Career-related internships or fieldwork, tuition waivers (partial), and unspecified assistantships available. Support available to part-time students. Financial award application deadline: 4/15; financial award applicants required to submit FAFSA. In 2001, 45 degrees awarded. *Degree program information:* Part-time programs available. Offers biology (MAT); chemistry (MAT); elementary school teaching (MAT); English (MAT); French (MAT); history/social studies (MAT); liberal arts (MAT); mathematics (MAT); physics (MAT); Spanish (MAT). *Application deadline:* For fall admission, 7/30 (priority date); for spring admission, 12/15 (priority date). Applications are processed on a rolling basis. *Application fee:* $45. Electronic applications accepted. *Application Contact:* 800-462-1944, Fax: 203-582-3443, E-mail: graduate@quinnipiac.edu. *Interim Dean*, Dr. Suzanne Hudd, 203-582-8730, Fax: 203-582-8709, E-mail: suzanne.hudd@quinnipiac.edu.

Lender School of Business Students: 53 full-time (26 women), 165 part-time (71 women); includes 11 minority (2 African Americans, 4 Asian Americans or Pacific Islanders, 5 Hispanic Americans), 9 international. Average age 27. 98 applicants, 82% accepted, 68 enrolled. *Faculty:* 33 full-time (8 women), 11 part-time/adjunct (3 women). Expenses: Contact institution. *Financial support:* In 2001–02, 6 research assistantships with tuition reimbursements were awarded; career-related internships or fieldwork also available. Support available to part-time students. Financial award application deadline: 4/15; financial award applicants required to submit FAFSA. In 2001, 63 degrees awarded. *Degree program information:* Part-time and evening/weekend programs available. Offers accounting (MBA); business (MBA, MHA, MS); computer information systems (MBA); economics (MBA); finance (MBA); health administration (MHA); health management (MBA); information systems (MS); international business (MBA); long-term care administration (MHA); management (MBA); marketing (MBA). *Application deadline:* For fall admission, 7/30 (priority date); for spring admission, 12/15. Applications are processed on a rolling basis. *Application fee:* $45. Electronic applications accepted. *Application Contact:* Louise Howe, Associate Director of Graduate Admissions and Financial Aid, 800-462-1944, Fax: 203-582-3443, E-mail: graduate@quinnipiac.edu. *Dean*, Dr. Phillip Frese, 203-582-8745, Fax: 203-582-8664, E-mail: phillip.frese@quinnipiac.edu.

School of Communications Students: 18 full-time (11 women), 41 part-time (23 women); includes 6 minority (3 African Americans, 2 Asian Americans or Pacific Islanders, 1 Hispanic American), 3 international. Average age 27. 67 applicants, 73% accepted, 42 enrolled. *Faculty:* 5 full-time (1 woman), 2 part-time/adjunct (0 women). Expenses: Contact institution. *Financial support:* In 2001–02, 1 fellowship with full tuition reimbursement was awarded; career-related internships or fieldwork and unspecified assistantships also available. Support available to part-time students. Financial award application deadline: 4/15; financial award applicants required to submit FAFSA. In 2001, 14 degrees awarded. *Degree program information:* Part-time and evening/weekend programs available. Offers communications (MS); e-media (MS); journalism (MS). *Application deadline:* For fall admission, 7/30 (priority date); for spring admission, 12/15 (priority date). Applications are processed on a rolling basis. *Application fee:* $45. Electronic applications accepted. *Application Contact:* Scott Farber, Director of Graduate Admissions, 800-462-1944, Fax: 203-582-3443, E-mail: graduate@quinnipiac.edu. *Dean*, Dr. Jarice Hanson, 203-582-8974, Fax: 203-582-5310, E-mail: jarice.hanson@quinnipiac.edu.

School of Health Sciences Students: 336 full-time (240 women), 124 part-time (104 women); includes 39 minority (7 African Americans, 20 Asian Americans or Pacific Islanders, 12 Hispanic Americans), 10 international. Average age 28. 569 applicants, 50% accepted, 207 enrolled. *Faculty:* 38 full-time (22 women), 28 part-time/adjunct (11 women). Expenses: Contact institution. *Financial support:* In 2001–02, 1 teaching assistantship was awarded; career-related internships or fieldwork and tuition waivers (partial) also available. Support available to part-time students. Financial award application deadline: 4/15; financial award applicants required to submit FAFSA. In 2001, 138 degrees awarded. *Degree program information:* Part-time and evening/weekend programs available. Offers advanced clinical practice (MSPT); biomedical sciences (MHS); forensic nursing (MSN); health sciences (MHS, MPT, MS, MSN, MSPT); laboratory management (MHS); microbiology (MHS); molecular and

Quinnipiac University (continued)

cell biology (MS); neurorehabilitation (MSPT); nurse practitioner-adult (MSN); nurse practitioner-family (MSN); orthopedic physical therapy (MSPT); pathologists' assistant (MHS); physical therapy (MPT); physician assistant (MHS). *Application fee:* $45. Electronic applications accepted. *Application Contact:* 800-462-1944, Fax: 203-582-3443, E-mail: graduate@quinnipiac.edu. *Dean,* Dr. Joseph Woods, 203-582-8674, Fax: 203-582-8706.

School of Law Students: 402 full-time (183 women), 283 part-time (130 women); includes 92 minority (41 African Americans, 12 Asian Americans or Pacific Islanders, 37 Hispanic Americans, 2 Native Americans) Average age 26. 1,999 applicants, 34% accepted, 188 enrolled. *Faculty:* 60 full-time (22 women), 66 part-time/adjunct (14 women). Expenses: Contact institution. *Financial support:* Fellowships, career-related internships or fieldwork, Federal Work-Study, and scholarships/grants available. Support available to part-time students. Financial award application deadline: 5/1; financial award applicants required to submit FAFSA. In 2001, 212 degrees awarded. *Degree program information:* Part-time and evening/weekend programs available. Offers law (JD). *Application deadline:* Applications are processed on a rolling basis. *Application fee:* $40. Electronic applications accepted. *Application Contact:* John J. Noonan, Dean of Admissions, 203-582-3400, Fax: 203-582-3339, E-mail: ladm@quinnipiac.edu. *Dean,* Brad Saxton, 203-582-3200, Fax: 203-582-3209, E-mail: ladm@quinnipiac.edu.

See in-depth description on page 1033.

RABBI ISAAC ELCHANAN THEOLOGICAL SEMINARY, New York, NY 10033-2807

General Information Independent-religious, men only, graduate-only institution. *Enrollment by degree level:* 291 other advanced degrees. *Graduate faculty:* 31 full-time (0 women), 22 part-time/adjunct (3 women). *Tuition:* Full-time $12,500. *Graduate housing:* Rooms and/or apartments guaranteed to single students and available on a first-come, first-served basis to married students. Typical cost: $4,750 per year for single students. Housing application deadline: 6/1. *Student services:* Campus employment opportunities, campus safety program, career counseling, free psychological counseling, international student services, low-cost health insurance, teacher training, writing training. *Library facilities:* Mendel Gottesman Library of Hebraica-Judaica plus 3 others. *Online resources:* library catalog. *Collection:* 491,816 titles, 1,347 serial subscriptions.

Computer facilities: 100 computers available on campus for general student use. A campuswide network can be accessed from student residence rooms and from off campus. Internet access is available. *Web address:* http://www.yu.edu/riets/.

General Application Contact: Rabbi Zevulun Charlop, Dean, 212-960-5344, Fax: 212-960-0061.

GRADUATE UNITS

Graduate Program Students: 286 full-time (0 women), 5 part-time. Average age 24. 60 applicants, 75% accepted. *Faculty:* 31 full-time (0 women), 22 part-time/adjunct (3 women). Expenses: Contact institution. *Financial support:* In 2001–02, 275 students received support, including 100 fellowships; career-related internships or fieldwork, institutionally sponsored loans, scholarships/grants, traineeships, and tuition waivers (full) also available. Financial award application deadline: 4/1. In 2001, 30 degrees awarded. Offers theology (Certificate of Advanced Ordination, Certificate of Ordination). *Application deadline:* For fall admission, 7/1 (priority date); for spring admission, 11/1 (priority date). *Application fee:* $10. *Application Contact:* Rabbi Chaim Bronstan, Administrator, 212-960-5344, Fax: 212-960-0061. *Dean,* Rabbi Zevulun Charlop, 212-960-5344, Fax: 212-960-0061.

RABBINICAL ACADEMY MESIVTA RABBI CHAIM BERLIN, Brooklyn, NY 11230-4715

General Information Independent-religious, men only, comprehensive institution. *Graduate housing:* Room and/or apartments available to single students; on-campus housing not available to married students. Housing application deadline: 9/30.

GRADUATE UNITS

School of Talmudic Law and Rabbinics Offers Talmudic law and rabbinics (Advanced Talmudic Degree, Second Talmudic Degree).

RABBINICAL COLLEGE BETH SHRAGA, Monsey, NY 10952-3035

General Information Independent-religious, men only, comprehensive institution.

GRADUATE UNITS

Graduate Programs Offers theology).

RABBINICAL COLLEGE BOBOVER YESHIVA B'NEI ZION, Brooklyn, NY 11219

General Information Independent-religious, men only, comprehensive institution. *Graduate housing:* Room and/or apartments available to single students; on-campus housing not available to married students.

GRADUATE UNITS

Graduate Programs Offers theology).

RABBINICAL COLLEGE CH'SAN SOFER, Brooklyn, NY 11204

General Information Independent-religious, men only, comprehensive institution.

GRADUATE UNITS

Graduate Programs Offers theology).

RABBINICAL COLLEGE OF LONG ISLAND, Long Beach, NY 11561-3305

General Information Independent-religious, men only, comprehensive institution.

GRADUATE UNITS

Graduate Programs Offers theology).

RABBINICAL SEMINARY M'KOR CHAIM, Brooklyn, NY 11219

General Information Independent-religious, men only, comprehensive institution.

GRADUATE UNITS

Graduate Programs Offers theology).

RABBINICAL SEMINARY OF AMERICA, Forest Hills, NY 11375

General Information Independent-religious, men only, comprehensive institution. *Graduate housing:* Room and/or apartments available to single students; on-campus housing not available to married students. Housing application deadline: 6/15.

GRADUATE UNITS

Graduate Programs Offers theology).

RADFORD UNIVERSITY, Radford, VA 24142

General Information State-supported, coed, comprehensive institution. CGS member. *Enrollment:* 400 full-time matriculated graduate/professional students (285 women), 471 part-time matriculated graduate/professional students (348 women). *Enrollment by degree level:* 852 master's, 19 other advanced degrees. *Graduate faculty:* 212 full-time (85 women), 18 part-time/adjunct (10 women). Tuition, state resident: full-time $2,564; part-time $167 per credit hour. Tuition, nonresident: full-time $6,314; part-time $323 per credit hour. *Required fees:* $1,440. *Graduate housing:* Room and/or apartments guaranteed to single students; on-campus housing not available to married students. Typical cost: $2,398 per year ($2,835 including board). Room and board charges vary according to board plan. Housing application deadline: 5/1. *Student services:* Campus employment opportunities, campus safety program, career counseling, child daycare facilities, disabled student services, exercise/wellness program, free psychological counseling, international student services, low-cost health insurance, teacher training, writing training. *Library facilities:* McConnell Library. *Online resources:* library catalog, web page, access to other libraries' catalogs. *Collection:* 527,789 titles, 14,914 audiovisual materials. *Research affiliation:* National Science Foundation (biology, physical science, mathematics), NASA (physical science), Department of Transportation (communications), State Government (communications, physical science, social science, business and management), Department of Defense (psychology), U.S. Army (computer science).

Computer facilities: 460 computers available on campus for general student use. A campuswide network can be accessed from student residence rooms and from off campus. Internet access is available. *Web address:* http://www.radford.edu/.

General Application Contact: Dr. Gary D. Ellerman, Interim Dean, 540-831-5431, Fax: 540-831-6061, E-mail: gellerma@radford.edu.

GRADUATE UNITS

Graduate College Students: 400 full-time (285 women), 471 part-time (348 women); includes 49 minority (30 African Americans, 11 Asian Americans or Pacific Islanders, 4 Hispanic Americans, 4 Native Americans), 28 international. Average age 31. 820 applicants, 62% accepted, 390 enrolled. *Faculty:* 212 full-time (85 women), 18 part-time/adjunct (10 women). Expenses: Contact institution. *Financial support:* In 2001–02, 632 students received support, including 47 fellowships with tuition reimbursements available (averaging $6,314 per year), 206 research assistantships (averaging $4,409 per year), 18 teaching assistantships with tuition reimbursements available (averaging $8,129 per year); career-related internships or fieldwork, Federal Work-Study, institutionally sponsored loans, and scholarships/grants also available. Financial award application deadline: 2/1; financial award applicants required to submit FAFSA. In 2001, 366 master's, 10 other advanced degrees awarded. *Degree program information:* Part-time programs available. Postbaccalaureate distance learning degree programs offered (minimal on-campus study). *Application deadline:* For fall admission, 2/1 (priority date); for spring admission, 10/1. Applications are processed on a rolling basis. *Application fee:* $25. Electronic applications accepted. *Application Contact:* Sharon D. Gunter, Graduate Admissions and Records Manager, 540-831-5431, Fax: 540-831-6061, E-mail: sgunter@radford.edu. *Interim Dean,* Dr. Gary D. Ellerman, 540-831-5431, Fax: 540-831-6061, E-mail: gellerma@radford.edu.

College of Arts and Sciences Students: 144 full-time (88 women), 79 part-time (53 women); includes 10 minority (2 African Americans, 5 Asian Americans or Pacific Islanders, 1 Hispanic American, 2 Native Americans), 5 international. Average age 27. 237 applicants, 80% accepted, 68 enrolled. *Faculty:* 91 full-time (26 women). Expenses: Contact institution. *Financial support:* In 2001–02, 155 students received support, including 25 fellowships with tuition reimbursements available (averaging $7,750 per year), 79 research assistantships (averaging $5,295 per year), 16 teaching assistantships with tuition reimbursements available (averaging $8,267 per year); career-related internships or fieldwork, Federal Work-Study, institutionally sponsored loans, and scholarships/grants also available. Financial award application deadline: 2/1; financial award applicants required to submit FAFSA. In 2001, 96 master's, 10 other advanced degrees awarded. *Degree program information:* Part-time programs available. Postbaccalaureate distance learning degree programs offered (minimal on-campus study). Offers arts and sciences (MA, MS, Ed S); clinical psychology (MA); corporate and professional communication (MS); counseling psychology (MA); criminal justice (MA, MS); engineering geosciences (MS); English (MA, MS); general psychology (MA, MS); industrial-organizational psychology (MA); school psychology (Ed S). *Application deadline:* For fall admission, 2/1 (priority date); for spring admission, 10/1. Applications are processed on a rolling basis. *Application fee:* $25. Electronic applications accepted. *Dean,* Dr. Ivan B. Liss, 540-831-5149, Fax: 540-831-5970, E-mail: iliss@radford.edu.

College of Business and Economics Students: 35 full-time (15 women), 56 part-time (31 women); includes 6 minority (1 African American, 3 Asian Americans or Pacific Islanders, 2 Hispanic Americans), 16 international. Average age 31. 75 applicants, 60% accepted, 23 enrolled. *Faculty:* 20 full-time (2 women), 1 part-time/adjunct (0 women). Expenses: Contact institution. *Financial support:* In 2001–02, 40 students received support, including 29 research assistantships (averaging $3,579 per year); fellowships with tuition reimbursements available, teaching assistantships with tuition reimbursements available, career-related internships or fieldwork, Federal Work-Study, institutionally sponsored loans, and scholarships/grants also available. Financial award application deadline: 2/1; financial award applicants required to submit FAFSA. In 2001, 51 degrees awarded. *Degree program information:* Part-time programs available. Postbaccalaureate distance learning degree programs offered (minimal on-campus study). Offers business administration (MBA); business and economics (MBA). *Application deadline:* For fall admission, 2/1 (priority date); for spring admission, 10/1. Applications are processed on a rolling basis. *Application fee:* $25. Electronic applications accepted. *Dean,* Dr. William A. Dempsey, 540-831-5187, Fax: 540-831-6103, E-mail: wdempsey@radford.edu.

College of Education and Human Development Students: 98 full-time (71 women), 218 part-time (166 women); includes 26 minority (21 African Americans, 2 Asian Americans or Pacific Islanders, 1 Hispanic American, 2 Native Americans) Average age 32. 155 applicants, 76% accepted, 83 enrolled. *Faculty:* 39 full-time (19 women), 9 part-time/adjunct (6 women). Expenses: Contact institution. *Financial support:* In 2001–02, 181 students received support, including 4 fellowships with tuition reimbursements available (averaging $6,820 per year), 43 research assistantships (averaging $5,441 per year), 1 teaching assistantship with tuition reimbursement available (averaging $8,680 per year); career-related internships or fieldwork, Federal Work-Study, institutionally sponsored loans, and scholarships/grants also available. Financial award application deadline: 2/1; financial award applicants required to submit FAFSA. In 2001, 115 degrees awarded. *Degree program information:* Part-time programs available. Postbaccalaureate distance learning degree programs offered (minimal on-campus study). Offers counselor education (MS); curriculum and instruction (MS); education and human development (MS); education of the emotionally disturbed (MS); educational leadership (MS); educational media (MS); learning disabilities (MS); mentally retarded (MS); reading (MS). *Application deadline:* For fall admission, 2/1 (priority date); for spring admission, 10/1. Applications are processed on a rolling basis. *Application fee:* $25. Electronic applications accepted. *Dean,* Dr. R. Paul Sale, 540-831-5439, Fax: 540-831-6053, E-mail: rsale@radford.edu.

College of Visual and Performing Arts Students: 20 full-time (13 women), 21 part-time (14 women), 7 international. Average age 33. 34 applicants, 56% accepted, 10 enrolled. *Faculty:* 26 full-time (9 women), 3 part-time/adjunct (1 woman). Expenses: Contact institution. *Financial support:* In 2001–02, 30 students received support, including 7 fellowships with tuition reimbursements available (averaging $4,405 per year), 9 research assistantships (averaging $4,457 per year), 2 teaching assistantships with tuition reimbursements available (averaging $5,580 per year); career-related internships or fieldwork, Federal Work-Study, institutionally sponsored loans, and scholarships/grants also available. Financial award application deadline: 2/1; financial award applicants required to submit FAFSA. In 2001, 15 degrees awarded. *Degree program information:* Part-time programs available. Postbaccalaureate distance learning degree programs offered (minimal on-campus study). Offers art (MFA); art education (MS); music (MA); music education (MS); visual and performing arts (MA, MFA, MS). *Application deadline:* For fall admission, 2/1 (priority date); for spring admission, 10/1. Applications are processed on a rolling basis. *Application fee:* $25. Electronic applications accepted. *Dean,* Dr. Joseph P. Scartelli, 540-831-5141, Fax: 540-831-6313, E-mail: jscartel@radford.edu.

Waldron College of Health and Human Services Students: 103 full-time (98 women), 97 part-time (84 women); includes 7 minority (6 African Americans, 1 Asian American or Pacific Islander) Average age 31. 154 applicants, 80% accepted, 71 enrolled. *Faculty:* 36 full-time (29 women), 9 part-time/adjunct (8 women). Expenses: Contact institution. *Financial support:* In 2001–02, 155 students received support, including 11 fellowships with tuition reimbursements available (averaging $3,808 per year), 46 research assistantships (averaging $3,404 per year); teaching assistantships with tuition reimbursements available, career-related internships or fieldwork, Federal Work-Study, institutionally sponsored loans, and scholarships/grants also available. Financial award application deadline: 2/1; financial award applicants required to submit FAFSA. In 2001, 89 degrees awarded. *Degree program* *information:* Part-time programs available. Postbaccalaureate distance learning degree programs offered (minimal on-campus study). Offers communication science and disorders (MA, MS); health and human services (MA, MS, MSN, MSW); nursing (MS, MSN); social work (MSW). *Application deadline:* For fall admission, 2/1 (priority date); for spring admission, 10/1. Applications are processed on a rolling basis. *Application fee:* $25. Electronic applications accepted. *Dean,* Dr. Stephen L. Heater, 540-831-7600, Fax: 540-831-6314, E-mail: sheater@radford.edu.

See in-depth description on page 1035.

RAMAPO COLLEGE OF NEW JERSEY, Mahwah, NJ 07430-1680

General Information State-supported, coed, comprehensive institution. *Graduate housing:* Rooms and/or apartments available on a first-come, first-served basis to single and married students. Housing application deadline: 6/15.

GRADUATE UNITS

Program in Liberal Studies *Degree program information:* Part-time and evening/weekend programs available. Offers liberal studies (MA).

RAND GRADUATE SCHOOL OF POLICY STUDIES, Santa Monica, CA 90407-2138

General Information Independent, coed, graduate-only institution. *Enrollment by degree level:* 69 doctoral. *Graduate faculty:* 55 part-time/adjunct (14 women). *Tuition:* Full-time $18,000. *Graduate housing:* On-campus housing not available. *Student services:* Campus employment opportunities, career counseling, free psychological counseling, grant writing training, international student services, low-cost health insurance. *Library facilities:* RAND Corporation Library. *Online resources:* library catalog, web page, access to other libraries' catalogs. *Collection:* 133,000 titles, 2,400 serial subscriptions.

Computer facilities: 69 computers available on campus for general student use. A campuswide network can be accessed from student residence rooms and from off campus. Internet access and online class registration are available. *Web address:* http://www.rgs.edu/.

General Application Contact: Marcy F. Agmon, Assistant Dean, 310-393-0411 Ext. 6419, Fax: 310-451-6978, E-mail: agmon@rgs.edu.

GRADUATE UNITS

Program in Policy Analysis Students: 69 full-time (21 women); includes 6 minority (1 African American, 4 Asian Americans or Pacific Islanders, 1 Hispanic American), 34 international. Average age 32. 92 applicants, 45% accepted, 20 enrolled. *Faculty:* 55 part-time/adjunct (14 women). Expenses: Contact institution. *Financial support:* In 2001–02, 69 fellowships, 69 research assistantships, 10 teaching assistantships (averaging $1,500 per year) were awarded. Career-related internships or fieldwork also available. In 2001, 5 degrees awarded. Offers policy analysis (PhD). *Application deadline:* For fall admission, 2/1 (priority date). *Application fee:* $50. Electronic applications accepted. *Application Contact:* Marcy F. Agmon, Assistant Dean, 310-393-0411 Ext. 6419, Fax: 310-451-6978, E-mail: agmon@rgs.edu. *Dean,* Dr. Robert Klitgaard, 310-393-0411 Ext. 7075, Fax: 310-451-6978, E-mail: robert_klitgaard@rgs.edu.

RECONSTRUCTIONIST RABBINICAL COLLEGE, Wyncote, PA 19095-1898

General Information Independent-religious, coed, graduate-only institution. *Enrollment by degree level:* 61 first professional, 11 master's. *Graduate faculty:* 7 full-time (4 women), 22 part-time/adjunct (10 women). *Tuition:* Full-time $8,600; part-time $1,350 per course. *Required fees:* $50. *Graduate housing:* On-campus housing not available. *Student services:* Campus employment opportunities, career counseling, disabled student services, international student services, low-cost health insurance, writing training. *Library facilities:* Mordecai M. Kaplan Library. *Online resources:* library catalog, access to other libraries' catalogs. *Collection:* 48,000 titles, 125 serial subscriptions, 50 audiovisual materials.

Computer facilities: 16 computers available on campus for general student use. A campuswide network can be accessed from off campus. Internet access, class materials are available. *Web address:* http://www.rrc.edu/.

General Application Contact: Rabbi Daniel Aronson, Dean of Admissions, 215-576-0800 Ext. 135, Fax: 215-576-6143, E-mail: daronson@rrc.edu.

GRADUATE UNITS

Graduate Program Students: 60 full-time (39 women), 12 part-time (5 women). Average age 32. 35 applicants, 46% accepted. *Faculty:* 7 full-time (4 women), 22 part-time/adjunct (10 women). Expenses: Contact institution. *Financial support:* In 2001–02, 44 students received support, including 4 fellowships with full tuition reimbursements available (averaging $7,500 per year), 1 research assistantship with partial tuition reimbursement available (averaging $2,000 per year), 5 teaching assistantships (averaging $2,000 per year); career-related internships or fieldwork, institutionally sponsored loans, and scholarships/grants also available. Financial award application deadline: 4/15; financial award applicants required to submit FAFSA. In 2001, 4 first professional degrees, 2 master's awarded. *Degree program information:* Part-time programs available. Offers rabbinical studies (MAHL, MAJS, DHL, Certificate). *Application deadline:* For spring admission, 4/30 (priority date). Applications are processed on a rolling basis. *Application fee:* $50. *Application Contact:* Rabbi Daniel Aronson, Dean of Admissions, 215-576-0800 Ext. 135, Fax: 215-576-6143, E-mail: daronson@rrc.edu. *President,* Rabbi Dan Ehrenkrantz, 215-576-0800 Ext. 129, Fax: 215-576-6143, E-mail: dehrenkrantz@rrc.edu.

REED COLLEGE, Portland, OR 97202-8199

General Information Independent, coed, comprehensive institution. *Enrollment:* 24 part-time matriculated graduate/professional students (12 women). *Enrollment by degree level:* 24 master's. *Graduate faculty:* 18. *Tuition:* Part-time $592 per credit. *Graduate housing:* On-campus housing not available. *Student services:* Campus employment opportunities, campus safety program, career counseling, disabled student services, free psychological counseling, writing training. *Library facilities:* Hauser Library plus 1 other. *Online resources:* library catalog, web page, access to other libraries' catalogs. *Collection:* 470,000 titles, 1,858 serial subscriptions, 15,485 audiovisual materials.

Computer facilities: 190 computers available on campus for general student use. A campuswide network can be accessed from student residence rooms and from off campus. Internet access and online class registration are available. *Web address:* http://www.reed.edu/.

General Application Contact: Barbara A. Amen, Director, 503-777-7259, Fax: 503-777-7581, E-mail: barbara.amen@reed.edu.

GRADUATE UNITS

Graduate Program in Liberal Studies Average age 35. 13 applicants, 77% accepted, 8 enrolled. *Faculty:* 18. Expenses: Contact institution. *Financial support:* In 2001–02, 6 students received support. Federal Work-Study and scholarships/grants available. Support available to part-time students. Financial award application deadline: 5/1; financial award applicants required to submit CSS PROFILE or FAFSA. In 2001, 2 degrees awarded. *Degree program information:* Part-time and evening/weekend programs available. Offers liberal studies (MALS). *Application deadline:* For fall admission, 7/1 (priority date); for spring admission, 12/1 (priority date). Applications are processed on a rolling basis. *Application fee:* $50. *Director,* Barbara A. Amen, 503-777-7259, Fax: 503-777-7581, E-mail: barbara.amen@reed.edu.

REFORMED PRESBYTERIAN THEOLOGICAL SEMINARY, Pittsburgh, PA 15208-2594

General Information Independent-religious, coed, primarily men, graduate-only institution. *Graduate housing:* Rooms and/or apartments available on a first-come, first-served basis to single and married students.

GRADUATE UNITS

Graduate and Professional Programs *Degree program information:* Part-time and evening/weekend programs available. Offers theology (M Div, MTS). Electronic applications accepted.

REFORMED THEOLOGICAL SEMINARY, Oviedo, FL 32765-7197

General Information Independent-religious, coed, primarily men, graduate-only institution. *Enrollment by degree level:* 150 first professional, 211 master's, 126 doctoral, 34 other advanced degrees. *Graduate faculty:* 16 full-time (0 women), 5 part-time/adjunct (0 women). *Tuition:* Part-time $250 per semester hour. *Required fees:* $40 per semester. Tuition and fees vary according to degree level. *Graduate housing:* Rooms and/or apartments available on a first-come, first-served basis to single students and available to married students. *Student services:* Campus employment opportunities, career counseling, free psychological counseling, international student services, low-cost health insurance, writing training. *Library facilities:* Reformed Theological Seminary Library. *Online resources:* library catalog. *Collection:* 70,000 titles, 330 serial subscriptions, 500 audiovisual materials.

Computer facilities: 4 computers available on campus for general student use. A campuswide network can be accessed from off campus. Internet access and online class registration are available. *Web address:* http://www.rts.edu/.

General Application Contact: David S. Kirkendall, Director of Admissions, 800-752-4382, Fax: 407-366-9425, E-mail: dkirkendall@rts.edu.

GRADUATE UNITS

Graduate Program Students: 521. *Faculty:* 21. Expenses: Contact institution. In 2001, 35 first professional degrees, 38 master's, 2 doctorates awarded. *Degree program information:* Part-time programs available. Postbaccalaureate distance learning degree programs offered (minimal on-campus study). Offers biblical studies (MA); Christian thought (MA); counseling (MA); ministry (D Min); religion (MA); theological studies (MA); theology (M Div, Th M). MA (religion) offered at Washington, D.C. campus site only. *Application deadline:* For fall admission, 5/21 (priority date); for winter admission, 10/3 (priority date); for spring admission, 11/5 (priority date). Applications are processed on a rolling basis. *Application fee:* $40. *Application Contact:* David S. Kirkendall, Director of Admissions, 800-752-4382, Fax: 407-366-9425, E-mail: dkirkendall@rts.edu. *President,* 407-366-9493, Fax: 407-366-9425.

REFORMED THEOLOGICAL SEMINARY, Bethesda, MD 20816-3342

General Information Independent-religious, coed, primarily men, graduate-only institution. *Enrollment by degree level:* 69 master's. *Graduate faculty:* 18 part-time/adjunct (0 women). *Tuition:* Full-time $7,000; part-time $250 per hour. *Graduate housing:* On-campus housing not available. *Student services:* Campus employment opportunities, career counseling, international student services, low-cost health insurance, writing training. *Library facilities:* Library Consortium. *Collection:* 400,000 titles, 100 serial subscriptions, 10,000 audiovisual materials.

Computer facilities: Online class registration is available. *Web address:* http://www.rts.edu/.

General Application Contact: Daniel C. Claire, Dean of Students/Director of Admissions, 800-639-0226, Fax: 301-320-9004, E-mail: dclaire@rts.edu.

GRADUATE UNITS

Graduate and Professional Programs Students: 3 full-time (0 women), 66 part-time (12 women); includes 15 minority (3 African Americans, 11 Asian Americans or Pacific Islanders, 1 Hispanic American) Average age 35. 74 applicants, 84% accepted. *Faculty:* 18 part-time/adjunct (0 women). Expenses: Contact institution. *Financial support:* In 2001–02, 50 students received support, including 5 fellowships (averaging $1,000 per year); institutionally sponsored loans, scholarships/grants, tuition waivers (partial), and unspecified assistantships also available. Support available to part-time students. Financial award application deadline: 6/15. *Degree program information:* Part-time and evening/weekend programs available. Offers religion (MA). *Application deadline:* Applications are processed on a rolling basis. *Application fee:* $35. *Application Contact:* Daniel C. Claire, Dean of Students/Director of Admissions, 800-639-0226, Fax: 301-320-9004, E-mail: dclaire@rts.edu. *Vice President,* Dr. Frank E. Young, 301-320-3434 Ext. 204, Fax: 301-320-9004, E-mail: fyoung@4thpres.org.

REFORMED THEOLOGICAL SEMINARY, Jackson, MS 39209-3099

General Information Independent-religious, coed, primarily men, graduate-only institution. *Enrollment by degree level:* 96 first professional, 96 master's, 12 doctoral, 3 other advanced degrees. *Graduate faculty:* 16 full-time (0 women), 16 part-time/adjunct (3 women). *Tuition:* Full-time $6,500; part-time $250 per hour. *Required fees:* $120. One-time fee: $120 part-time. Tuition and fees vary according to degree level. *Graduate housing:* Rooms and/or apartments available on a first-come, first-served basis to single and married students. Typical cost: $1,920 per year for single students; $4,620 per year for married students. *Student services:* Campus employment opportunities, low-cost health insurance. *Library facilities:* Main library plus 1 other. *Collection:* 109,269 titles, 640 serial subscriptions.

Computer facilities: 20 computers available on campus for general student use. A campuswide network can be accessed. Internet access and online class registration are available. *Web address:* http://www.rts.edu/.

General Application Contact: Brian Gault, Director of Admissions, 601-923-1600, Fax: 601-923-1654.

GRADUATE UNITS

Graduate and Professional Programs Students: 130 full-time (31 women), 77 part-time (26 women); includes 38 minority (25 African Americans, 9 Asian Americans or Pacific Islanders, 4 Hispanic Americans) *Faculty:* 16 full-time (0 women), 16 part-time/adjunct (3 women). Expenses: Contact institution. *Financial support:* Research assistantships, career-related internships or fieldwork, scholarships/grants, and tuition waivers (full and partial) available. Financial award application deadline: 5/1. In 2001, 24 first professional degrees, 26 master's, 59 doctorates awarded. Offers Bible, theology, and missions (Certificate); biblical studies (MA); Christian education (M Div, MA); counseling (M Div); divinity (M Div, Diploma); intercultural studies (PhD); marriage and family therapy (MA); ministry (D Min); missions (M Div, MA, D Min); New Testament (Th M); Old Testament (Th M); theological studies (MA); theology (Th M). *Application deadline:* Applications are processed on a rolling basis. *Application fee:* $25. *Application Contact:* Brian Gault, Director of Admissions, 601-923-1600, Fax: 601-923-1654. *Dean,* Dr. Allen Curry, 601-922-4988, Fax: 601-922-1153.

REFORMED THEOLOGICAL SEMINARY, Charlotte, NC 28226-6399

General Information Independent-religious, coed, primarily men, graduate-only institution. *Graduate housing:* On-campus housing not available.

GRADUATE UNITS

Graduate and Professional Programs *Degree program information:* Part-time programs available. Postbaccalaureate distance learning degree programs offered (minimal on-campus study). Offers biblical studies (M Div, MA); Christian education/youth ministry (M Div); counseling (M Div); ministry (D Min); missions (M Div, MA); theological studies (M Div, MA); worship (M Div).

REGENT COLLEGE, Vancouver, BC V6T 2E4, Canada

General Information Independent-religious, coed, graduate-only institution. *Graduate faculty:* 22 full-time (2 women), 15 part-time/adjunct (6 women). *Graduate tuition:* Tuition and fees charges are reported in Canadian dollars. *Tuition:* Part-time $320 Canadian dollars per credit. *Required fees:* $180 Canadian dollars; $35 Canadian dollars per semester. One-time fee: $177 Canadian dollars full-time. *Graduate housing:* On-campus housing not available. *Student services:* Campus employment opportunities, campus safety program, career counseling, disabled student services, international student services, low-cost health insurance, writing training. *Library facilities:* Regent-Carey Library. *Online resources:* library catalog, web

Regent College (continued)

page, access to other libraries' catalogs. *Collection:* 120,000 titles, 500 serial subscriptions, 2,000 audiovisual materials.

Computer facilities: 12 computers available on campus for general student use. A campuswide network can be accessed from off campus. *Web address:* http://www.regent-college.edu/.

General Application Contact: Roland Carelse-Borzel, Admissions Officer, 604-224-3245 Ext. 335, Fax: 604-224-3097, E-mail: admissions@regent-college.edu.

GRADUATE UNITS

Program in Theology Students: 188 full-time (56 women), 458 part-time (176 women). Average age 36. 228 applicants, 94% accepted. *Faculty:* 22 full-time (2 women), 15 part-time/adjunct (6 women). Expenses: Contact institution. *Financial support:* In 2001–02, 156 students received support, including 94 teaching assistantships (averaging $3,120 per year); career-related internships or fieldwork and scholarships/grants also available. Financial award application deadline: 4/1. In 2001, 49 M Divs, 76 master's, 79 other advanced degrees awarded. *Degree program information:* Part-time and evening/weekend programs available. Offers theology (M Div, MCS, Th M, Dip CS). *Application deadline:* For fall admission, 6/1 (priority date); for winter admission, 10/1 (priority date). Applications are processed on a rolling basis. *Application fee:* $50. *Application Contact:* Admissions Officer, 604-224-3245, Fax: 604-224-3097, E-mail: admissions@regent-college.edu. *President*, Dr. Rod J. Wilson, 604-224-3245, Fax: 604-222-2476, E-mail: presidentsoffice@regent-college.edu.

REGENT UNIVERSITY, Virginia Beach, VA 23464-9800

General Information Independent, coed, graduate-only institution. *Enrollment by degree level:* 600 first professional, 1,377 master's, 448 doctoral, 11 other advanced degrees. *Graduate faculty:* 90 full-time (17 women), 97 part-time/adjunct (47 women). *Tuition:* Part-time $500 per credit hour. *Required fees:* $50 per semester. *Graduate housing:* Rooms and/or apartments available on a first-come, first-served basis to single and married students. Housing application deadline: 8/30. *Student services:* Campus employment opportunities, career counseling, disabled student services, free psychological counseling, international student services, low-cost health insurance, teacher training, writing training. *Library facilities:* University Library plus 1 other. *Online resources:* library catalog, web page, access to other libraries' catalogs. *Collection:* 209,815 titles, 1,484 serial subscriptions, 12,840 audiovisual materials.

Computer facilities: 78 computers available on campus for general student use. A campuswide network can be accessed. Internet access and online class registration, Electronic Reference Center—University Library are available. *Web address:* http://www.regent.edu/.

General Application Contact: Alice Souter-Jones, Director, Central Enrollment Management, 800-373-5504, Fax: 757-226-4381, E-mail: admissions@regent.edu.

GRADUATE UNITS

Graduate School Students: 1,255 full-time (721 women), 1,434 part-time (707 women); includes 808 minority (590 African Americans, 109 Asian Americans or Pacific Islanders, 92 Hispanic Americans, 17 Native Americans), 208 international. Average age 36. 1,802 applicants, 83% accepted, 966 enrolled. *Faculty:* 90 full-time (17 women), 97 part-time/adjunct (47 women). Expenses: Contact institution. *Financial support:* In 2001–02, 1,865 students received support, including 16 fellowships with full and partial tuition reimbursements available (averaging $13,800 per year), 11 research assistantships (averaging $4,300 per year), 5 teaching assistantships (averaging $10,000 per year); career-related internships or fieldwork, scholarships/grants, and tuition waivers (full and partial) also available. Financial award application deadline: 9/1. In 2001, 156 first professional degrees, 389 master's, 41 doctorates, 2 other advanced degrees awarded. *Degree program information:* Part-time and evening/weekend programs available. Postbaccalaureate distance learning degree programs offered (minimal on-campus study). *Application deadline:* Applications are processed on a rolling basis. *Application fee:* $40. Electronic applications accepted. *Application Contact:* Alice Souter-Jones, Director, Central Enrollment Management, 800-373-5504, Fax: 757-226-4381, E-mail: admissions@regent.edu. *Vice President of Academic Affairs*, Dr. Barry E. Ryan, 757-226-4320, Fax: 757-226-4448, E-mail: rpacad@regent.edu.

Center for Leadership Studies Students: 339 (113 women); includes 95 minority (69 African Americans, 12 Asian Americans or Pacific Islanders, 11 Hispanic Americans, 3 Native Americans) 32 international. Average age 43. 237 applicants, 81% accepted, 123 enrolled. *Faculty:* 2 full-time (1 woman), 7 part-time/adjunct (2 women). Expenses: Contact institution. *Financial support:* In 2001–02, 192 students received support; fellowships with full and partial tuition reimbursements available, scholarships/grants available. Financial award application deadline: 9/1. In 2001, 6 master's, 13 doctorates awarded. *Degree program information:* Part-time programs available. Postbaccalaureate distance learning degree programs offered (minimal on-campus study). Offers leadership studies (Certificate); organizational leadership (MA, PhD); strategic leadership (DSL). *Application deadline:* For fall admission, 5/1 (priority date); for spring admission, 10/1 (priority date). Applications are processed on a rolling basis. *Application fee:* $100. *Application Contact:* Michael Hartsfield, Director of Admissions, 800-373-5504, Fax: 757-226-4381, E-mail: admissions@regent.edu. *Dean*, Dr. Kathaleen Reid-Martinez, 757-226-4022, Fax: 757-226-4448, E-mail: kathrei@regent.edu.

College of Communication and the Arts Students: 283 (165 women); includes 77 minority (54 African Americans, 5 Asian Americans or Pacific Islanders, 16 Hispanic Americans, 2 Native Americans) 4 international. Average age 35. 175 applicants, 92% accepted, 98 enrolled. *Faculty:* 18 full-time (1 woman), 8 part-time/adjunct (0 women). Expenses: Contact institution. *Financial support:* In 2001–02, 55 students received support, including 9 fellowships with full and partial tuition reimbursements available (averaging $10,000 per year); research assistantships, scholarships/grants also available. Financial award application deadline: 9/1; financial award applicants required to submit FAFSA. In 2001, 63 master's, 8 doctorates awarded. *Degree program information:* Part-time programs available. Postbaccalaureate distance learning degree programs offered (minimal on-campus study). Offers communication (MA, PhD); communication and the arts (MA, MFA, PhD); fine arts (MFA); journalism (MA). *Application deadline:* For fall admission, 3/1 (priority date); for spring admission, 10/1 (priority date). Applications are processed on a rolling basis. *Application fee:* $40. Electronic applications accepted. *Application Contact:* Vicki Glasscock, Director of Admissions for Communication, 800-373-5504, Fax: 757-226-4891, E-mail: admissions@regent.edu. *Dean*, Dr. William J. Brown, 757-226-4215, Fax: 757-226-4291, E-mail: willbro@regent.edu.

Robertson School of Government Students: 79 (40 women); includes 24 minority (19 African Americans, 2 Asian Americans or Pacific Islanders, 2 Hispanic Americans, 1 Native American) 3 international. Average age 32. 61 applicants, 90% accepted, 30 enrolled. *Faculty:* 8 full-time (1 woman), 6 part-time/adjunct (0 women). Expenses: Contact institution. *Financial support:* In 2001–02, 2 students received support; research assistantships available. Financial award application deadline: 9/1; financial award applicants required to submit FAFSA. In 2001, 29 degrees awarded. *Degree program information:* Part-time programs available. Offers public administration (MA); public management (MA); public policy (MA). *Application deadline:* For fall admission, 5/1 (priority date); for spring admission, 11/1 (priority date). Applications are processed on a rolling basis. *Application fee:* $40. Electronic applications accepted. *Application Contact:* B. Nathaniel Smith, Acting Manager of Admissions, 800-373-5504, Fax: 757-226-4381, E-mail: admissions@regent.edu. *Dean*, Dr. Kathaleen Reid-Martinez, 757-226-4022, Fax: 757-226-4448, E-mail: kathrei@regent.edu.

School of Business Students: 265 (99 women); includes 97 minority (67 African Americans, 17 Asian Americans or Pacific Islanders, 9 Hispanic Americans, 4 Native Americans) 8 international. Average age 34. 132 applicants, 99% accepted, 83 enrolled. *Faculty:* 9 full-time (0 women), 6 part-time/adjunct (4 women). Expenses: Contact institution. *Financial support:* In 2001–02, 27 students received support, including 1 fellowship with full and partial tuition reimbursement available (averaging $10,000 per year); research assistantships, career-related internships or fieldwork and scholarships/grants also available. Support available to part-time students. Financial award application deadline: 9/1; financial award applicants required to submit FAFSA. In 2001, 83 degrees awarded. *Degree program information:* Part-time and evening/weekend programs available. Postbaccalaureate distance learning degree programs offered (minimal on-campus study). Offers business administration (MBA); management (MA). *Application deadline:* For fall admission, 4/1 (priority date); for spring admission, 10/15 (priority date). Applications are processed on a rolling basis. *Application fee:* $40. *Application Contact:* Tom Stansbury, Enrollment Manager, 800-373-5504, Fax: 757-226-4381, E-mail: admissions@regent.edu. *Dean*, Dr. John E. Mulford, 757-226-4320, Fax: 757-226-4448, E-mail: johnmul@regent.edu.

School of Divinity Students: 348 (111 women); includes 117 minority (67 African Americans, 34 Asian Americans or Pacific Islanders, 16 Hispanic Americans) 18 international. Average age 39. 238 applicants, 79% accepted, 127 enrolled. *Faculty:* 12 full-time (1 woman), 4 part-time/adjunct (0 women). Expenses: Contact institution. *Financial support:* In 2001–02, 258 students received support. Career-related internships or fieldwork and scholarships/grants available. Support available to part-time students. Financial award application deadline: 9/1; financial award applicants required to submit FAFSA. In 2001, 11 first professional degrees, 29 master's, 25 doctorates awarded. *Degree program information:* Part-time programs available. Postbaccalaureate distance learning degree programs offered (minimal on-campus study). Offers biblical studies (MA); ministry (D Min); missiology (M Div, MA); practical theology (M Div, MA). *Application deadline:* For fall admission, 5/1 (priority date). Applications are processed on a rolling basis. *Application fee:* $65. *Application Contact:* Raymond P. Willis, Director of Admissions for Divinity, 800-373-5504, Fax: 757-226-4381, E-mail: admissions@regent.edu. *Dean*, Dr. Vinson Synan, 757-226-4414, Fax: 757-226-4597, E-mail: vinssyn@regent.edu.

School of Education Students: 549 (438 women); includes 174 minority (148 African Americans, 10 Asian Americans or Pacific Islanders, 15 Hispanic Americans, 1 Native American) 129 international. Average age 39. 385 applicants, 81% accepted, 205 enrolled. *Faculty:* 13 full-time (8 women), 34 part-time/adjunct (27 women). Expenses: Contact institution. *Financial support:* In 2001–02, 319 students received support; fellowships, career-related internships or fieldwork, scholarships/grants, and tuition waivers (full and partial) available. Support available to part-time students. Financial award application deadline: 9/1; financial award applicants required to submit FAFSA. In 2001, 121 degrees awarded. *Degree program information:* Part-time and evening/weekend programs available. Postbaccalaureate distance learning degree programs offered (minimal on-campus study). Offers education (M Ed, Ed D, CAGS). *Application deadline:* For fall admission, 4/1 (priority date); for spring admission, 10/15 (priority date). Applications are processed on a rolling basis. *Application fee:* $40. *Application Contact:* Cayti Strickland, Manager of Admissions, 800-373-5504, Fax: 757-226-4381, E-mail: admissions@regent.edu. *Dean*, Dr. Alan A. Arroyo, 757-226-4261, Fax: 757-226-4318, E-mail: alanarr@regent.edu.

School of Law Students: 553 (248 women); includes 125 minority (83 African Americans, 22 Asian Americans or Pacific Islanders, 16 Hispanic Americans, 4 Native Americans) 33 international. Average age 32. 470 applicants, 70% accepted, 208 enrolled. *Faculty:* 26 full-time (5 women), 31 part-time/adjunct (9 women). Expenses: Contact institution. *Financial support:* In 2001–02, 454 students received support. Scholarships/grants available. Support available to part-time students. Financial award application deadline: 9/1. In 2001, 114 first professional degrees, 31 master's awarded. *Degree program information:* Part-time and evening/weekend programs available. Postbaccalaureate distance learning degree programs offered (minimal on-campus study). Offers international taxation (LL M, MIT); law (JD). *Application deadline:* For fall admission, 3/1. Applications are processed on a rolling basis. *Application fee:* $40. *Application Contact:* Bonnie Creef, Director of Law Admissions, 757-226-4584, Fax: 757-226-4139, E-mail: lawschool@regent.edu. *Dean*, Jeffrey Brauch, 757-226-4040, Fax: 757-226-4329, E-mail: jeffbra@regent.edu.

School of Psychology and Counseling Students: 248 (200 women); includes 76 minority (62 African Americans, 6 Asian Americans or Pacific Islanders, 6 Hispanic Americans, 2 Native Americans) 4 international. Average age 34. 142 applicants, 85% accepted, 92 enrolled. *Faculty:* 11 full-time (3 women), 11 part-time/adjunct (5 women). Expenses: Contact institution. *Financial support:* In 2001–02, 185 students received support, including 6 teaching assistantships (averaging $10,000 per year); career-related internships or fieldwork and scholarships/grants also available. Support available to part-time students. Financial award application deadline: 9/1. In 2001, 59 master's, 3 doctorates awarded. *Degree program information:* Part-time programs available. Offers counseling (MA); counseling psychology (Psy D). *Application deadline:* For fall admission, 4/1 (priority date); for spring admission, 11/1 (priority date). Applications are processed on a rolling basis. *Application fee:* $40. *Application Contact:* Steve Bruce, Director of Admissions for Counseling, 800-373-5504, Fax: 757-226-4381, E-mail: admissions@regent.edu. *Dean*, Dr. Rosemarie Hughes, 757-226-4255, Fax: 757-226-4263, E-mail: rosehug@regent.edu.

Announcement: With faith as the foundation of its mission, Regent prepares leaders to have a positive impact on American society and the world. Regent offers predominantly graduate-level study. Regent's highly motivated students may choose to pursue degree programs on the main campus in Virginia Beach, at the Graduate Center in the northern Virginia/DC area, or online via the Worldwide Campus. The University has full SACS accreditation, the School of Law is accredited by the ABA, the School of Divinity is accredited by the Association of Theological Schools, and the master's programs in the School of Psychology and Counseling are accredited by the Council for Accreditation of Counseling and Related Educational Programs.

See in-depth description on page 1037.

REGIS COLLEGE, Toronto, ON M4Y 2R5, Canada

General Information Independent-religious, coed, graduate-only institution. *Enrollment by degree level:* 110 first professional, 23 master's, 26 doctoral, 36 other advanced degrees. *Graduate faculty:* 16 full-time (3 women), 9 part-time/adjunct (5 women). *International tuition:* $10,000 full-time. *Tuition, area resident:* Full-time $4,320. *Required fees:* $711. *Graduate housing:* On-campus housing not available. *Library facilities:* Regis College Library. *Online resources:* library catalog, access to other libraries' catalogs. *Collection:* 123,642 titles, 367 serial subscriptions, 108 audiovisual materials.

Computer facilities: 6 computers available on campus for general student use. A campuswide network can be accessed from off campus. Internet access and online class registration are available. *Web address:* http://www.utoronto.ca/regis/.

General Application Contact: Heather L. Gamester, Registrar, 416-922-5474, Fax: 416-922-2898, E-mail: regis.registrar@utoronto.ca.

GRADUATE UNITS

Graduate and Professional Programs Students: 89 full-time (36 women), 105 part-time (67 women); includes 39 minority (8 African Americans, 25 Asian Americans or Pacific Islanders, 6 Hispanic Americans), 12 international. Average age 46. 94 applicants, 77% accepted. *Faculty:* 16 full-time (3 women), 9 part-time/adjunct (5 women). Expenses: Contact institution. *Financial support:* In 2001–02, 27 students received support. Career-related internships or fieldwork and scholarships/grants available. Support available to part-time students. Financial award application deadline: 3/15. In 2001, 9 first professional degrees, 6 master's, 3 doctorates, 3 other advanced degrees awarded. Offers ministry (D Min); ministry and spirituality (MAMS); sacred theology (STM, STD, STL); theological study (MTS); theology (M Div, MA, Th M, PhD, Th D). *Application deadline:* For fall admission, 3/15 (priority date); for spring admission, 1/15. Applications are processed on a rolling basis. *Application fee:* $25. *Application Contact:* Heather L. Gamester, Registrar, 416-922-5474, Fax: 416-922-2898, E-mail: regis.registrar@utoronto.ca. *Dean*, Ronald A. Mercier, SJ, 416-922-5474, Fax: 416-922-2898, E-mail: ron.mercier@utoronto.ca.

REGIS COLLEGE, Weston, MA 02493

General Information Independent-religious, women only, comprehensive institution. *Enrollment:* 59 full-time matriculated graduate/professional students (55 women), 171 part-time matriculated graduate/professional students (166 women). *Enrollment by degree level:* 230 master's. *Graduate faculty:* 14 full-time (10 women), 17 part-time/adjunct (14 women). *Tuition:* Full-time $18,400; part-time $450 per credit hour. *Required fees:* $140; $35 per semester. *Graduate housing:* Room and/or apartments available to single students; on-campus housing not available to married students. *Student services:* Campus employment opportunities, campus safety program, career counseling, exercise/wellness program, low-cost health insurance, multicultural affairs office, teacher training. *Library facilities:* Regis College Library. *Online resources:* library catalog, web page, access to other libraries' catalogs. *Collection:* 133,565 titles, 968 serial subscriptions, 5,684 audiovisual materials. *Research affiliation:* Edith Nourse Rogers Veterans Administration Hospital (nursing).

Computer facilities: 133 computers available on campus for general student use. A campuswide network can be accessed from student residence rooms. Internet access is available. *Web address:* http://www.regiscollege.edu/.

General Application Contact: Patricia Andaloro, Associate Director of Admissions, 781-768-7188, Fax: 781-768-8339, E-mail: patricia.andaloro@regiscollege.edu.

GRADUATE UNITS

Department of Education Students: 1 (woman) full-time, 23 part-time (all women). Average age 30. *Faculty:* 3 full-time (all women), 4 part-time/adjunct (all women). Expenses: Contact institution. *Financial support:* In 2001–02, 3 students received support. Federal Work-Study and tuition waivers available. Support available to part-time students. Financial award application deadline: 3/1; financial award applicants required to submit FAFSA. In 2001, 7 degrees awarded. *Degree program information:* Part-time and evening/weekend programs available. Offers education (MAT). *Application deadline:* Applications are processed on a rolling basis. *Application fee:* $30. *Application Contact:* Patricia Andaloro, Associate Director of Admissions, 781-768-7188, Fax: 781-768-8339, E-mail: patricia.andaloro@regiscollege.edu. *Program Director,* Dr. Joanne Ruane Seltzer, 781-768-7008, Fax: 781-768-8339, E-mail: joanne.ruane@regiscollege.edu.

Department of Management and Leadership Average age 29. *Faculty:* 1 full-time (0 women), 2 part-time/adjunct (0 women). Expenses: Contact institution. *Degree program information:* Part-time and evening/weekend programs available. Offers leadership and organizational change (MS). *Application deadline:* Applications are processed on a rolling basis. *Application fee:* $30. *Application Contact:* Patricia Andaloro, Associate Director of Admissions, 781-768-7188, Fax: 781-768-8339, E-mail: patricia.andaloro@regiscollege.edu. *Chair,* Dr. Phillip F. Jutras, 781-768-7436, Fax: 781-768-7159, E-mail: phillip.jutras@regiscollege.edu.

Nursing Students: 57 full-time (53 women), 129 part-time (125 women); includes 19 minority (12 African Americans, 6 Asian Americans or Pacific Islanders, 1 Hispanic American) Average age 39. *Faculty:* 10 full-time (7 women), 11 part-time/adjunct (10 women). Expenses: Contact institution. *Financial support:* In 2001–02, 31 students received support, including 4 research assistantships (averaging $2,500 per year); Federal Work-Study, scholarships/grants, and traineeships also available. Support available to part-time students. Financial award application deadline: 3/1; financial award applicants required to submit FAFSA. In 2001, 47 master's, 1 other advanced degree awarded. *Degree program information:* Part-time and evening/weekend programs available. Offers nursing (MS, Certificate). *Application deadline:* Applications are processed on a rolling basis. *Application fee:* $30. *Application Contact:* Patricia Andaloro, Associate Director of Admissions, 781-768-7188, Fax: 781-768-8339, E-mail: patricia.andaloro@regiscollege.edu. *Chair,* Dr. Amy Anderson, 781-768-7090, Fax: 781-768-8339, E-mail: amy.anderson@regiscollege.edu.

REGIS UNIVERSITY, Denver, CO 80221-1099

General Information Independent-religious, coed, comprehensive institution. *Enrollment:* 3,500 matriculated graduate/professional students. *Graduate faculty:* 575. *Tuition:* Part-time $316 per credit hour. *Graduate housing:* On-campus housing not available. *Student services:* Campus employment opportunities, campus safety program, career counseling, disabled student services, exercise/wellness program, grant writing training, international student services, low-cost health insurance, teacher training, writing training. *Library facilities:* Dayton Memorial Library. *Online resources:* library catalog, web page, access to other libraries' catalogs. *Collection:* 430,514 titles, 7,850 serial subscriptions, 104,887 audiovisual materials.

Computer facilities: 300 computers available on campus for general student use. A campuswide network can be accessed from student residence rooms and from off campus. *Web address:* http://www.regis.edu/.

General Application Contact: 303-458-4080, Fax: 303-964-5538, E-mail: masters@regis.edu.

GRADUATE UNITS

Regis College Students: 75. Average age 35. 5 applicants, 100% accepted. *Faculty:* 8. Expenses: Contact institution. *Financial support:* Available to part-time students. Application deadline: 3/15; In 2001, 19 degrees awarded. *Degree program information:* Part-time and evening/weekend programs available. Offers education (MA). Offered at Northwest Denver Campus. *Application deadline:* Applications are processed on a rolling basis. *Application fee:* $75. *Application Contact:* Kathleen Nutting, Director, 303-458-4349, Fax: 303-964-5421, E-mail: knutting@regis.edu. *Dean,* Dr. Steve Doty, 303-458-4040.

School for Healthcare Professions Students: 203. Expenses: Contact institution. *Financial support:* Career-related internships or fieldwork and Federal Work-Study available. Offers healthcare professions (MSN, MSPT, DPT); nursing (MSN); physical therapy (DPT). *Application deadline:* Applications are processed on a rolling basis. *Application Contact:* Assistant to the Dean, 303-458-4174, Fax: 303-964-5533, E-mail: deastman@regis.edu. *Academic Dean,* Dr. Patricia Ladewig, 303-458-4174.

School for Professional Studies Students: 3,476 (1,747 women). Average age 35. *Faculty:* 575. Expenses: Contact institution. *Financial support:* In 2001–02, 12 fellowships were awarded; career-related internships or fieldwork and Federal Work-Study also available. Support available to part-time students. Financial award applicants required to submit FAFSA. In 2001, 630 degrees awarded. *Degree program information:* Part-time and evening/weekend programs available. Postbaccalaureate distance learning degree programs offered (no on-campus study). Offers accounting (MBA); adult learning, training and development (MLS, Certificate); business administration (MBA, Certificate); database technologies (MSCIT, Certificate); e-commerce engineering (MSCIT, Certificate); electronic commerce (MBA); executive international management (Certificate); executive leadership (Certificate); finance (MBA); international business (MBA, Certificate); language and communication (MLS); leadership (Certificate); licensed professional counselor (MLS); management of technology (MSCIT); market strategy (MBA); networking technologies (MSCIT); networking technology (Certificate); nonprofit management (MNM); object-oriented technologies (MSCIT); object-oriented technology (Certificate); operations management (MBA); organizational leadership (MSM); physicians practice (MBA, Certificate); program management (Certificate); project leadership and management (Certificate); psychology (MLS); resource development (Certificate); social science (MLS); strategic business (Certificate); strategic human resource (Certificate); technical communication (Certificate). *Application deadline:* Applications are processed on a rolling basis. *Application fee:* $75. Electronic applications accepted. *Application Contact:* 800-677-9270, Fax: 303-964-5538, E-mail: admarg@regis.edu. *Associate Dean,* Dr. Steve Berkshire, 303-458-4302, Fax: 303-964-5538.

Announcement: Founded in 1877, Regis University's academic programs combine the strength of the 125-year-old Jesuit tradition of excellence in teaching with the resources and expertise to meet the demands of a rapidly changing world. The result is an application-based education that is both cutting-edge and rooted in tradition.

See in-depth description on page 1039.

RENSSELAER AT HARTFORD, Hartford, CT 06120-2991

General Information Independent, coed, graduate-only institution. *Enrollment by degree level:* 1,550 master's. *Graduate faculty:* 37 full-time (8 women), 42 part-time/adjunct (2 women). *Tuition:* Full-time $11,700; part-time $650 per credit. *Graduate housing:* On-campus housing not available. *Student services:* Career counseling. *Library facilities:* Cole Library. *Online resources:* web page. *Collection:* 30,000 titles, 424 serial subscriptions.

Computer facilities: 125 computers available on campus for general student use. A campuswide network can be accessed. Internet access is available. *Web address:* http://www.rh.edu/.

General Application Contact: Rebecca Danchak, Director of Admissions, 860-548-2420, Fax: 860-548-7823, E-mail: rdanchak@rh.edu.

GRADUATE UNITS

Department of Computer and Information Science Students: 12 full-time (5 women), 364 part-time (79 women); includes 58 minority (3 African Americans, 46 Asian Americans or Pacific Islanders, 7 Hispanic Americans, 2 Native Americans), 47 international. Average age 31. 99 applicants, 69% accepted, 52 enrolled. *Faculty:* 7 full-time (2 women), 11 part-time/adjunct (1 woman). Expenses: Contact institution. *Financial support:* Research assistantships, tuition waivers (full and partial) and unspecified assistantships available. Support available to part-time students. Financial award applicants required to submit FAFSA. In 2001, 65 degrees awarded. *Degree program information:* Part-time and evening/weekend programs available. Offers computer science (MS); engineering science (MS). *Application deadline:* For fall admission, 8/6 (priority date). Applications are processed on a rolling basis. *Application fee:* $45. Electronic applications accepted. *Application Contact:* Rebecca Danchak, Director of Admissions, 860-548-2420, Fax: 860-548-7823, E-mail: rdanchak@rh.edu. *Chair,* James McKim, 860-548-2455, E-mail: jcm@rh.edu.

Department of Engineering Students: 2 full-time (0 women), 225 part-time (30 women). Average age 31. *Faculty:* 11 full-time (2 women), 34 part-time/adjunct (1 woman). Expenses: Contact institution. *Financial support:* Research assistantships, career-related internships or fieldwork, tuition waivers (full and partial), and unspecified assistantships available. Support available to part-time students. Financial award applicants required to submit FAFSA. In 2001, 66 degrees awarded. *Degree program information:* Part-time and evening/weekend programs available. Offers computer and systems engineering (ME); electrical engineering (MS); engineering (ME, MS); mechanical engineering (MS). *Application deadline:* For fall admission, 8/6 (priority date). Applications are processed on a rolling basis. *Application fee:* $45. *Application Contact:* Rebecca Danchak, Director of Admissions, 860-548-2420, Fax: 860-548-7823, E-mail: rdanchak@rh.edu. *Chair,* James McKim, 860-548-2455, E-mail: jcm@rh.edu.

Lally School of Management and Technology Students: 74 full-time (22 women), 873 part-time (283 women); includes 126 minority (40 African Americans, 56 Asian Americans or Pacific Islanders, 30 Hispanic Americans), 32 international. Average age 32. 336 applicants, 78% accepted, 142 enrolled. *Faculty:* 26 full-time (6 women), 8 part-time/adjunct (1 woman). Expenses: Contact institution. *Financial support:* Research assistantships, tuition waivers (full and partial) and unspecified assistantships available. Support available to part-time students. Financial award applicants required to submit FAFSA. In 2001, 420 degrees awarded. *Degree program information:* Part-time and evening/weekend programs available. Postbaccalaureate distance learning degree programs offered (no on-campus study). Offers management and technology (MBA, MS). *Application deadline:* For fall admission, 8/6 (priority date). Applications are processed on a rolling basis. *Application fee:* $45. *Application Contact:* Rebecca Danchak, Director of Admissions, 860-548-2420, Fax: 860-548-7823, E-mail: rdanchak@rh.edu. *Chair,* David Rainey, 860-548-7830, E-mail: dlrainey@rh.edu.

RENSSELAER POLYTECHNIC INSTITUTE, Troy, NY 12180-3590

General Information Independent, coed, university. CGS member. *Enrollment:* 1,499 full-time matriculated graduate/professional students (430 women), 964 part-time matriculated graduate/professional students (236 women). *Enrollment by degree level:* 1,658 master's, 805 doctoral. *Graduate faculty:* 370 full-time (58 women), 17 part-time/adjunct (5 women). *Tuition:* Full-time $26,400; part-time $1,320 per credit hour. *Required fees:* $1,437. *Graduate housing:* Rooms and/or apartments available on a first-come, first-served basis to single and married students. Typical cost: $8,553 (including board) for single students. *Student services:* Campus employment opportunities, campus safety program, career counseling, disabled student services, free psychological counseling, international student services, low-cost health insurance, multicultural affairs office, teacher training, writing training. *Library facilities:* Folsom Library plus 1 other. *Online resources:* library catalog, web page, access to other libraries' catalogs. *Collection:* 309,171 titles, 10,210 serial subscriptions, 91,435 audiovisual materials. *Research affiliation:* Lockheed Martin Corporation (chemistry, decision sciences, mathematics, mechanical engineering, environmental engineering, physics), National Science Foundation (biomedical engineering, materials engineering, mechanical engineering, nuclear engineering, mathematics), U.S. Department of Energy (architecture, mechanical engineering, nuclear engineering), New York State Energy Research and Development Authority (architecture, lighting), Semiconductor Research Corporation (chemical engineering, electrical engineering, materials engineering, physics), U.S. Environmental Protection Agency (biology, earth and environmental sciences).

Computer facilities: 500 computers available on campus for general student use. A campuswide network can be accessed from student residence rooms and from off campus. Internet access and online class registration are available. *Web address:* http://www.rpi.edu/.

General Application Contact: Teresa C. Duffy, Dean of Enrollment Management, 518-276-6216, Fax: 518-276-4072, E-mail: admissions@rpi.edu.

GRADUATE UNITS

Graduate School Students: 1,499 full-time (430 women), 964 part-time (236 women); includes 166 minority (33 African Americans, 84 Asian Americans or Pacific Islanders, 45 Hispanic Americans, 4 Native Americans), 785 international. Average age 27. 3,726 applicants, 36% accepted, 568 enrolled. *Faculty:* 370 full-time (58 women), 17 part-time/adjunct (5 women). Expenses: Contact institution. *Financial support:* Fellowships with full tuition reimbursements, research assistantships with full and partial tuition reimbursements, teaching assistantships with full and partial tuition reimbursements, career-related internships or fieldwork, institutionally sponsored loans, scholarships/grants, and tuition waivers (full and partial) available. Financial award applicants required to submit FAFSA. In 2001, 701 master's, 91 doctorates awarded. *Degree program information:* Part-time and evening/weekend programs available. Postbaccalaureate distance learning degree programs offered (no on-campus study). *Application deadline:* For fall admission, 1/15 (priority date). Applications are processed on a rolling basis. *Application fee:* $45. Electronic applications accepted. *Application Contact:* Teresa C. Duffy, Dean of Enrollment Management, 518-276-6216, Fax: 518-276-4072, E-mail: admissions@rpi.edu. *Dean of Graduate Education,* Dr. Thomas Apple, 518-276-3022, Fax: 518-276-8062, E-mail: applet@rpi.edu.

Lally School of Management and Technology Students: 404 full-time (62 women), 1,230 part-time (383 women); includes 139 minority (37 African Americans, 68 Asian Americans or Pacific Islanders, 33 Hispanic Americans, 1 Native American), 95 international. Average age 32. 659 applicants, 68% accepted, 274 enrolled. *Faculty:* 41 full-time (6 women), 2 part-time/adjunct (0 women). Expenses: Contact institution. *Financial support:* In 2001–02, 104 students received support; fellowships, research assistantships, teaching assistantships, career-related internships or fieldwork, institutionally sponsored loans, scholarships/grants, and tuition waivers (full and partial) available. Financial award application deadline: 1/15. In 2001, 692 master's, 3 doctorates awarded. *Degree program information:* Part-time and evening/weekend programs available. Postbaccalaureate distance learning degree programs offered (no on-campus study). Offers e-business (MBA, MS); environmental management and policy (MBA, MS); finance (MBA, MS); management (PhD); management and technology (MBA, MS, PhD); management information systems (MBA, MS); new product development and marketing (MBA); new production and operations research (MS); product development and marketing (MS); production and operations research (MBA); technological entrepreneurship (MBA, MS). *Application deadline:* For fall admission, 1/15 (priority date); for spring admission, 11/1 (priority date). Applications are processed on a rolling basis. *Application fee:* $45. Electronic applications accepted. *Application Contact:* Michele Martens, Manager of Enrollment Services, 518-276-6586, Fax: 518-276-2665, E-mail: martem@rpi.edu. *Interim Dean,* Dr. Robert A. Baron, 518-276-6586, Fax: 518-276-2665, E-mail: lallymba@rpi.edu.

School of Architecture Students: 75 full-time (36 women), 3 part-time (2 women); includes 4 minority (2 Asian Americans or Pacific Islanders, 2 Hispanic Americans), 10 international. 158 applicants, 48% accepted, 34 enrolled. *Faculty:* 29 full-time (6 women), 36 part-time/adjunct (11 women). Expenses: Contact institution. *Financial support:* In 2001–02, 2 fellowships with full tuition reimbursements (averaging $15,000 per year) were awarded; research assistantships, teaching assistantships with partial tuition reimbursements, career-

Rensselaer Polytechnic Institute (continued)

related internships or fieldwork, institutionally sponsored loans, scholarships/grants, and tuition waivers (partial) also available. Financial award application deadline: 2/1. *Degree program information:* Part-time and evening/weekend programs available. Offers architecture (M Arch); building conservation (MS); building science (MS); building sciences (MS); infomatics and architecture (MS); informatics and architecture (MS); lighting (MS). *Application deadline:* For fall admission, 1/15 (priority date). Applications are processed on a rolling basis. *Application fee:* $45. Electronic applications accepted. *Application Contact:* Lecia O'Dell, Admissions Coordinator, 518-276-8478, Fax: 518-276-3034, E-mail: odell@rpi.edu. *Director, Graduate Programs in Architecture*, Prof. Peter Parsons, 518-276-6876, Fax: 518-276-3034, E-mail: parsop@rpi.edu.

School of Engineering Students: 664 full-time (121 women), 481 part-time (90 women); includes 116 minority (38 African Americans, 52 Asian Americans or Pacific Islanders, 26 Hispanic Americans), 515 international. 2,438 applicants, 37% accepted, 409 enrolled. *Faculty:* 141 full-time (7 women), 30 part-time/adjunct (5 women). Expenses: Contact institution. *Financial support:* In 2001–02, fellowships with full tuition reimbursements (averaging $15,000 per year), research assistantships with full and partial tuition reimbursements (averaging $12,600 per year), teaching assistantships with full and partial tuition reimbursements (averaging $12,600 per year) were awarded. Career-related internships or fieldwork, institutionally sponsored loans, scholarships/grants, tuition waivers (full and partial), and unspecified assistantships also available. Financial award application deadline: 2/1; financial award applicants required to submit FAFSA. In 2001, 324 master's, 62 doctorates awarded. *Degree program information:* Part-time and evening/weekend programs available. Postbaccalaureate distance learning degree programs offered (no on-campus study). Offers aerospace engineering (M Eng, MS, D Eng, PhD); biomedical engineering (M Eng, MS, D Eng, PhD); ceramics and glass science (M Eng, MS, PhD); chemical engineering (M Eng, MS, D Eng, PhD); composites (M Eng, MS, PhD); computer and systems engineering (M Eng, MS, D Eng, PhD); decision sciences and engineering systems (PhD); electric power engineering (M Eng, MS, D Eng, PhD); electrical engineering (M Eng, MS, D Eng, PhD); electronic materials (M Eng, MS, PhD); engineering (M Eng, MS, D Eng, PhD); engineering physics (M Eng, D Eng, PhD); engineering science (MS, PhD); environmental engineering (M Eng, MS, D Eng, PhD); geotechnical engineering (M Eng, MS, D Eng, PhD); industrial and management engineering (M Eng, MS, PhD); manufacturing systems engineering (M Eng, MS, PhD); mechanical engineering (M Eng, MS, D Eng, PhD); mechanics (M Eng, MS, PhD); mechanics of composite materials and structures (M Eng, MS, D Eng, PhD); metallurgy (M Eng, MS, PhD); nuclear engineering (M Eng, MS, D Eng); nuclear engineering and science (PhD); operations research and statistics (M Eng, MS, PhD); polymers (M Eng, MS, PhD); structural engineering (M Eng, MS, D Eng, PhD); transportation engineering (M Eng, MS, D Eng, PhD). *Application deadline:* For fall admission, 1/15 (priority date). Applications are processed on a rolling basis. *Application fee:* $45. Electronic applications accepted. *Dean*, Dr. William A. Baeslack, 518-276-6298, Fax: 518-276-8788, E-mail: baeslack@rpi.edu.

School of Humanities and Social Sciences Students: 154 full-time (82 women), 27 part-time (16 women); includes 10 minority (2 African Americans, 4 Asian Americans or Pacific Islanders, 3 Hispanic Americans, 1 Native American), 33 international. 185 applicants, 52% accepted. *Faculty:* 63 full-time (20 women), 9 part-time/adjunct (4 women). Expenses: Contact institution. *Financial support:* Fellowships with full tuition reimbursements, research assistantships with full and partial tuition reimbursements, teaching assistantships with full and partial tuition reimbursements, career-related internships or fieldwork, institutionally sponsored loans, and tuition waivers (full and partial) available. Financial award application deadline: 2/1. In 2001, 39 master's, 7 doctorates awarded. *Degree program information:* Part-time and evening/weekend programs available. Postbaccalaureate distance learning degree programs offered (no on-campus study). Offers communication and rhetoric (MS, PhD); ecological economics (PhD); ecological economics, values, and policy (MS); economics (MS); electronic arts (MFA); human factors (MS); humanities and social sciences (MFA, MS, PhD); industrial-organizational psychology (MS); philosophy (MS); psychology (MS); science and technology studies (MS, PhD); technical communication (MS). *Application deadline:* For fall admission, 1/15 (priority date). Applications are processed on a rolling basis. *Application fee:* $45. Electronic applications accepted. *Application Contact:* Teresa C. Duffy, Dean of Enrollment Management, 518-276-6216, Fax: 518-276-4072, E-mail: admissions@rpi.edu. *Dean*, Dr. Faye Duchin, 518-276-6575, Fax: 518-276-4871, E-mail: largee@rpi.edu.

School of Science Students: 350 full-time (107 women), 54 part-time (13 women); includes 22 minority (12 African Americans, 7 Asian Americans or Pacific Islanders, 2 Hispanic Americans, 1 Native American), 207 international. 958 applicants, 16% accepted. *Faculty:* 107 full-time (21 women). Expenses: Contact institution. *Financial support:* Fellowships with full tuition reimbursements, research assistantships with full and partial tuition reimbursements, teaching assistantships with full and partial tuition reimbursements, career-related internships or fieldwork, institutionally sponsored loans, and tuition waivers (full and partial) available. Financial award application deadline: 2/1. In 2001, 145 master's, 32 doctorates awarded. *Degree program information:* Part-time and evening/weekend programs available. Postbaccalaureate distance learning degree programs offered (no on-campus study). Offers analytical chemistry (MS, PhD); applied mathematics (MS); applied science (MS); biochemistry (MS, PhD); bioinformatics (MS); biophysics (MS, PhD); cell biology (MS, PhD); computer science (MS, PhD); developmental biology (MS, PhD); environmental chemistry (MS, PhD); geochemistry (MS, PhD); geology (MS, PhD); geophysics (MS, PhD); hydrogeology (MS); information technology (MS); inorganic chemistry (MS, PhD); mathematics (MS, PhD); microbiology (MS, PhD); molecular biology (MS, PhD); multidisciplinary science (MS, PhD); natural sciences (MS); organic chemistry (MS, PhD); petrology (MS, PhD); physical chemistry (MS, PhD); physics (MS, PhD); planetary geology (MS, PhD); polymer chemistry (MS, PhD); science (MS, PhD); tectonics (MS, PhD). *Application deadline:* For fall admission, 1/15 (priority date). Applications are processed on a rolling basis. *Application fee:* $45. Electronic applications accepted. *Application Contact:* Teresa C. Duffy, Dean of Enrollment Management, 518-276-6216, Fax: 518-276-4072, E-mail: admissions@rpi.edu. *Dean, School of Science*, Dr. Joseph E. Flaherty, 518-276-2699, Fax: 518-276-2344, E-mail: flahej@rpi.edu.

See in-depth description on page 1041.

RESEARCH COLLEGE OF NURSING, Kansas City, MO 64132

General Information Independent, coed, primarily women, comprehensive institution. *Enrollment:* 19 part-time matriculated graduate/professional students (all women). *Enrollment by degree level:* 19 master's. *Graduate faculty:* 12 full-time (all women). *Tuition:* Part-time $325 per credit. *Required fees:* $25 per hour. Part-time tuition and fees vary according to course load. *Graduate housing:* Rooms and/or apartments available on a first-come, first-served basis to single and married students. Typical cost: $6,500 per year for single students; $6,500 per year for married students. Room charges vary according to housing facility selected. *Student services:* Campus safety program, child daycare facilities, disabled student services, low-cost health insurance, writing training. *Library facilities:* Greenlease Library. *Online resources:* library catalog, web page, access to other libraries' catalogs. *Collection:* 150,000 titles, 675 serial subscriptions.

Computer facilities: 125 computers available on campus for general student use. A campuswide network can be accessed from student residence rooms and from off campus. Internet access is available. *Web address:* http://www.researchcollege.edu/.

General Application Contact: Leslie Ann Mendenhall, Director of Transfer and Graduate Recruitment, 816-276-4733, Fax: 816-276-3526, E-mail: lamendenhall@healthmidwest.org.

GRADUATE UNITS

Nursing Program Average age 30. *Faculty:* 12 full-time (all women). Expenses: Contact institution. *Financial support:* Applicants required to submit FAFSA. In 2001, 5 degrees awarded. *Degree program information:* Part-time programs available. Offers family nurse practitioner (MSN). *Application deadline:* For spring admission, 10/1 (priority date). Applications are processed on a rolling basis. *Application fee:* $50. *Application Contact:* Leslie Ann Mendenhall, Director of Transfer and Graduate Recruitment, 816-276-4733, Fax: 816-276-3526, E-mail: lamendenhall@healthmidwest.org. *President and Dean*, Dr. Nancy O. De Basio, 816-276-4721, Fax: 816-276-3526, E-mail: nodebasio@healthmidwest.org.

RHODE ISLAND COLLEGE, Providence, RI 02908-1991

General Information State-supported, coed, comprehensive institution. CGS member. *Enrollment:* 268 full-time matriculated graduate/professional students (218 women), 507 part-time matriculated graduate/professional students (408 women). *Enrollment by degree level:* 693 master's, 38 doctoral, 44 other advanced degrees. *Graduate faculty:* 196 full-time (77 women), 39 part-time/adjunct (19 women). Tuition, state resident: full-time $3,060; part-time $170 per credit. Tuition, nonresident: full-time $6,390; part-time $355 per credit. *Graduate housing:* Room and/or apartments available on a first-come, first-served basis to single students; on-campus housing not available to married students. Typical cost: $2,983 per year ($5,946 including board). Housing application deadline: 4/1. *Student services:* Campus employment opportunities, career counseling, free psychological counseling, international student services, low-cost health insurance. *Library facilities:* Adams Library. *Online resources:* library catalog, web page, access to other libraries' catalogs. *Collection:* 368,891 titles, 1,766 serial subscriptions, 3,982 audiovisual materials.

Computer facilities: 350 computers available on campus for general student use. A campuswide network can be accessed from off campus. *Web address:* http://www.ric.edu/.

General Application Contact: Dean of Graduate Studies, 401-456-8700.

GRADUATE UNITS

School of Graduate Studies Students: 268 full-time (218 women), 507 part-time (408 women); includes 30 minority (9 African Americans, 6 Asian Americans or Pacific Islanders, 12 Hispanic Americans, 3 Native Americans) Average age 34. *Faculty:* 196 full-time (77 women), 39 part-time/adjunct (19 women). Expenses: Contact institution. *Financial support:* Fellowships, research assistantships, teaching assistantships, career-related internships or fieldwork, Federal Work-Study, traineeships, and tuition waivers (partial) available. Support available to part-time students. Financial award application deadline: 4/1; financial award applicants required to submit FAFSA. In 2001, 294 master's, 3 doctorates, 15 other advanced degrees awarded. *Degree program information:* Part-time and evening/weekend programs available. *Application deadline:* For fall admission, 4/1 (priority date); for spring admission, 11/1. Applications are processed on a rolling basis. *Application fee:* $25. *Dean*, 401-456-8700.

Center for Management and Technology Average age 34. *Faculty:* 6 full-time (3 women), 1 part-time/adjunct (0 women). Expenses: Contact institution. In 2001, 8 degrees awarded. Offers industrial technology (MS); management and technology (MP Ac, MS). *Director*, Dr. James Schweikart, 401-456-8009, E-mail: jschweikart@ric.edu.

Faculty of Arts and Sciences Students: 28 full-time (13 women), 34 part-time (17 women); includes 2 minority (1 Asian American or Pacific Islander, 1 Native American) Average age 33. *Faculty:* 137 full-time (52 women), 22 part-time/adjunct (8 women). Expenses: Contact institution. *Financial support:* Career-related internships or fieldwork available. Financial award application deadline: 4/1. In 2001, 46 degrees awarded. *Degree program information:* Part-time and evening/weekend programs available. Offers art education (MAT); art education and studio art (MA, MAT); art studio (MA); arts and sciences (MA, MAT, MFA, MM, CAGS); biology (MA, MAT); English (MA, MAT); French (MA, MAT); general science (MAT); history (MA, MAT); mathematics (MA, MAT, CAGS); music (MM); music education (MAT); physical science (MAT); psychology (MA); Spanish (MAT); theatre (MFA). *Application deadline:* For fall admission, 4/1. Applications are processed on a rolling basis. *Application fee:* $25. *Dean*, Dr. Richard R. Weiner, 401-456-8106, E-mail: rweiner@ric.edu.

Feinstein School of Education and Human Development Students: 116 full-time (95 women), 410 part-time (344 women). Average age 35. *Faculty:* 50 full-time (21 women), 16 part-time/adjunct (11 women). Expenses: Contact institution. *Financial support:* Fellowships, career-related internships or fieldwork available. Financial award application deadline: 4/1. In 2001, 180 master's, 3 doctorates, 15 other advanced degrees awarded. *Degree program information:* Part-time and evening/weekend programs available. Offers agency counseling (MA); bilingual/bicultural education (M Ed); counselor education (M Ed, CAGS); curriculum (CAGS); early childhood education (M Ed); education (PhD); education and human development (M Ed, MA, MAT, MS, PhD, CAGS); educational administration (M Ed, CAGS); educational psychology (MA); elementary education (M Ed, MAT); English as a second language (M Ed); health education (M Ed); reading education (M Ed, CAGS); school psychology (CAGS); secondary education (M Ed); special education (M Ed, CAGS); teaching of the handicapped (M Ed, CAGS); technology education (M Ed). *Application deadline:* For fall admission, 4/1. Applications are processed on a rolling basis. *Application fee:* $25. *Dean*, Dr. James A. Bucci, 401-456-8110, E-mail: jabucci@ric.edu.

School of Social Work Students: 121 full-time (107 women), 33 part-time (30 women); includes 12 minority (4 African Americans, 7 Hispanic Americans, 1 Native American) Average age 33. *Faculty:* 12 full-time (9 women), 12 part-time/adjunct (6 women). Expenses: Contact institution. *Financial support:* Career-related internships or fieldwork available. Financial award application deadline: 4/1. In 2001, 60 degrees awarded. *Degree program information:* Part-time programs available. Offers social work (MSW). *Application deadline:* For fall admission, 2/1. Applications are processed on a rolling basis. *Application fee:* $25. *Dean*, Dr. George Metrey, 401-456-8043, E-mail: gmetrey@ric.edu.

See in-depth description on page 1043.

RHODE ISLAND SCHOOL OF DESIGN, Providence, RI 02903-2784

General Information Independent, coed, comprehensive institution. *Enrollment:* 274 full-time matriculated graduate/professional students (165 women). *Enrollment by degree level:* 274 master's. *Graduate faculty:* 69 full-time (26 women), 80 part-time/adjunct (33 women). *Tuition:* Full-time $22,952. *Required fees:* $445. *Graduate housing:* Room and/or apartments available on a first-come, first-served basis to single students; on-campus housing not available to married students. Typical cost: $6,830 (including board). *Student services:* Campus employment opportunities, career counseling, free psychological counseling, international student services, low-cost health insurance. *Library facilities:* RISD Library. *Online resources:* library catalog. *Collection:* 95,161 titles, 423 serial subscriptions, 158,325 audiovisual materials.

Computer facilities: 300 computers available on campus for general student use. A campuswide network can be accessed from student residence rooms and from off campus. Internet access is available. *Web address:* http://www.risd.edu/.

General Application Contact: Edward Newhall, Director of Admissions, 401-454-6300, Fax: 401-454-6309, E-mail: admissions@risd.edu.

GRADUATE UNITS

Graduate Studies Students: 274 full-time (165 women); includes 29 minority (1 African American, 16 Asian Americans or Pacific Islanders, 9 Hispanic Americans, 3 Native Americans), 58 international. Average age 29. 1,308 applicants, 22% accepted. *Faculty:* 69 full-time (26 women), 80 part-time/adjunct (33 women). Expenses: Contact institution. *Financial support:* Fellowships, teaching assistantships, career-related internships or fieldwork, Federal Work-Study, institutionally sponsored loans, and scholarships/grants available. Financial award application deadline: 2/1; financial award applicants required to submit FAFSA. In 2001, 98 degrees awarded. Offers art education (MA, MAT). *Application deadline:* For fall admission, 2/1. *Application fee:* $45. *Application Contact:* Edward Newhall, Director of Admissions, 401-454-6300, Fax: 401-454-6309, E-mail: admissions@risd.edu. *Dean of Graduate Studies*, Nancy Friese, 401-454-6134, Fax: 401-454-6320, E-mail: nfriese@risd.edu.

Division of Architecture and Design Students: 164 full-time (94 women). Average age 29. 608 applicants, 32% accepted, 86 enrolled. *Faculty:* 40 full-time (14 women), 43 part-time/adjunct (12 women). Expenses: Contact institution. *Financial support:* Fellowships, teaching assistantships, career-related internships or fieldwork, Federal Work-Study, institutionally sponsored loans, and scholarships/grants available. Financial award application deadline: 2/1; financial award applicants required to submit FAFSA. In 2001, 84 degrees awarded. Offers architecture (M Arch); architecture and design (M Arch, MFA, MIA, MID, MLA); furniture design (MFA); graphic design (MFA); industrial design (MID); interior architecture (MIA); landscape architecture (MLA). *Application deadline:* For fall admission, 2/1. *Applica-*

tion fee: $45. *Application Contact:* Edward Newhall, Director of Admissions, 401-454-6300, Fax: 401-454-6309, E-mail: admissions@risd.edu. *Dean,* Dawn Barrett, 401-454-6283, Fax: 401-454-6320.

Division of Fine Arts Students: 93 full-time (57 women). Average age 29. 658 applicants, 11% accepted, 44 enrolled. *Faculty:* 27 full-time (12 women), 34 part-time/adjunct (19 women). Expenses: Contact institution. *Financial support:* Fellowships, teaching assistantships, Federal Work-Study and institutionally sponsored loans available. Financial award application deadline: 2/1; financial award applicants required to submit FAFSA. Offers ceramics (MFA); glass (MFA); jewelry and light metals (MFA); painting (MFA); photography (MFA); printmaking (MFA); sculpture (MFA); textiles (MFA). *Application deadline:* For fall admission, 2/1. *Application fee:* $45. *Application Contact:* Edward Newhall, Director of Admissions, 401-454-6300, Fax: 401-454-6309, E-mail: admissions@risd.edu. *Dean,* John Terry, 401-454-6235, Fax: 401-454-6233, E-mail: jterry@risd.edu.

RHODES COLLEGE, Memphis, TN 38112-1690

General Information Independent-religious, coed, comprehensive institution. *Enrollment:* 16 full-time matriculated graduate/professional students (12 women). *Enrollment by degree level:* 16 master's. *Graduate faculty:* 6 full-time (3 women), 3 part-time/adjunct (0 women). *Tuition:* Full-time $21,366. *Graduate housing:* Room and/or apartments available to single students; on-campus housing not available to married students. Housing application deadline: 3/1. *Student services:* Campus employment opportunities, campus safety program, career counseling, disabled student services, free psychological counseling, international student services, multicultural affairs office. *Library facilities:* Burrow Library plus 3 others. *Online resources:* library catalog, web page, access to other libraries' catalogs. *Collection:* 263,000 titles, 1,200 serial subscriptions, 96,000 audiovisual materials.

Computer facilities: 125 computers available on campus for general student use. A campuswide network can be accessed from student residence rooms and from off campus. *Web address:* http://www.rhodes.edu/.

General Application Contact: Dr. Pamela H. Church, Program Director, 901-843-3920, Fax: 901-843-3798, E-mail: church@rhodes.edu.

GRADUATE UNITS

Department of Economics/Business Administration Students: 16 full-time (12 women); includes 2 minority (both African Americans) Average age 22. *Faculty:* 6 full-time (3 women), 3 part-time/adjunct (0 women). Expenses: Contact institution. *Financial support:* In 2001–02, 16 students received support. Career-related internships or fieldwork and scholarships/grants available. Support available to part-time students. Financial award application deadline: 3/1; financial award applicants required to submit FAFSA. In 2001, 6 degrees awarded. *Degree program information:* Part-time programs available. Offers accounting (MS). *Application deadline:* For fall admission, 3/1. *Application fee:* $25. *Program Director,* Dr. Pamela H. Church, 901-843-3920, Fax: 901-843-3798, E-mail: church@rhodes.edu.

RICE UNIVERSITY, Houston, TX 77251-1892

General Information Independent, coed, university. CGS member. *Enrollment:* 1,657 full-time matriculated graduate/professional students (617 women), 106 part-time matriculated graduate/professional students (49 women). *Graduate faculty:* 434 full-time, 150 part-time/adjunct. *Tuition:* Full-time $17,300. *Required fees:* $250. *Graduate housing:* Rooms and/or apartments available on a first-come, first-served basis to single and married students. Housing application deadline: 7/15. *Student services:* Campus employment opportunities, campus safety program, career counseling, exercise/wellness program, free psychological counseling, international student services, low-cost health insurance, multicultural affairs office, teacher training. *Library facilities:* Fondren Library. *Online resources:* library catalog, web page, access to other libraries' catalogs. *Collection:* 2 million titles, 14,000 serial subscriptions. *Research affiliation:* Fermi National Accelerator Laboratory, Los Alamos National Laboratory, Brookhaven National Laboratory, Arecibo Observatory, Houston Area Research Center.

Computer facilities: 600 computers available on campus for general student use. A campuswide network can be accessed from student residence rooms and from off campus. Internet access is available. *Web address:* http://www.rice.edu/.

GRADUATE UNITS

Graduate Programs Students: 1,657 full-time (617 women), 106 part-time (49 women); includes 186 minority (39 African Americans, 88 Asian Americans or Pacific Islanders, 54 Hispanic Americans, 5 Native Americans), 586 international. 3,652 applicants, 17% accepted, 601 enrolled. *Faculty:* 434 full-time, 150 part-time/adjunct. Expenses: Contact institution. *Financial support:* Fellowships, research assistantships, teaching assistantships, career-related internships or fieldwork, Federal Work-Study, institutionally sponsored loans, scholarships/grants, and tuition waivers (full and partial) available. Financial award applicants required to submit CSS PROFILE or FAFSA. In 2001, 311 master's, 109 doctorates awarded. *Degree program information:* Part-time programs available. *Application fee:* $35. Electronic applications accepted. *Application Contact:* Susan Massey, Admissions and Enrollment Manager, 713-348-4002, Fax: 713-348-4806, E-mail: graduate@rice.edu. *Vice Provost for Research and Graduate Studies,* Jordan Konisky, 713-348-4002, Fax: 713-348-4806, E-mail: graduate@rice.edu.

George R. Brown School of Engineering Students: 385 full-time (96 women), 25 part-time (8 women); includes 48 minority (10 African Americans, 22 Asian Americans or Pacific Islanders, 15 Hispanic Americans, 1 Native American), 206 international. 1,668 applicants, 16% accepted, 138 enrolled. *Faculty:* 98 full-time, 27 part-time/adjunct. Expenses: Contact institution. *Financial support:* In 2001–02, 182 fellowships with full tuition reimbursements (averaging $18,856 per year), 212 research assistantships with full tuition reimbursements (averaging $18,703 per year), 18 teaching assistantships with full tuition reimbursements (averaging $18,072 per year) were awarded. Federal Work-Study and tuition waivers (full) also available. Financial award applicants required to submit FAFSA. In 2001, 65 master's, 51 doctorates awarded. *Degree program information:* Part-time programs available. Offers bioengineering (MS, PhD); biostatistics (PhD); chemical engineering (M Ch E, MS, PhD); circuits, controls, and communication systems (MS, PhD); civil engineering (MCE, MS, PhD); computational and applied mathematics (MA, MCAM, PhD); computational finance (PhD); computer science (MCS, MS, PhD); computer science and engineering (MS, PhD); computer science in bioinformatics (MCS); electrical engineering (MEE); engineering (M Ch E, M Stat, MA, MCAM, MCE, MCS, MEE, MEE, MES, MME, MMS, MS, PhD); environmental engineering (MEE, MES, MS, PhD); environmental science (MEE, MES, MS, PhD); lasers, microwaves, and solid-state electronics (MS, PhD); materials science (MMS, MS, PhD); mechanical engineering (MME, MS, PhD); statistics (M Stat, MA, PhD). *Application deadline:* For fall admission, 2/1 (priority date); for spring admission, 11/1. Applications are processed on a rolling basis. *Application fee:* $25. Electronic applications accepted. *Dean of Engineering,* C. Sidney Burrus, 713-348-4009, Fax: 713-348-5300, E-mail: grbsoe@rice.edu.

Jesse H. Jones Graduate School of Management Students: 323 full-time (117 women); includes 65 minority (18 African Americans, 29 Asian Americans or Pacific Islanders, 17 Hispanic Americans, 1 Native American), 80 international. Average age 27. 790 applicants, 37% accepted, 175 enrolled. *Faculty:* 45 full-time (11 women), 42 part-time/adjunct (8 women). Expenses: Contact institution. *Financial support:* In 2001–02, 210 students received support. Career-related internships or fieldwork, Federal Work-Study, institutionally sponsored loans, scholarships/grants, and tuition waivers (full and partial) available. Financial award application deadline: 6/1; financial award applicants required to submit FAFSA. In 2001, 148 degrees awarded. Offers business administration (MBA). *Application deadline:* For fall admission, 3/15. Applications are processed on a rolling basis. *Application fee:* $100. Electronic applications accepted. *Application Contact:* Peter E. Veruki, Executive Director of Career Planning and Admissions, 713-348-4918, Fax: 713-348-6147, E-mail: ricemba@rice.edu. *Dean,* Dr. Gilbert R. Whitaker, 713-348-4838.

School of Architecture Students: 78 full-time (33 women); includes 8 minority (1 African American, 5 Asian Americans or Pacific Islanders, 2 Hispanic Americans), 23 international. Average age 25. 357 applicants, 20% accepted, 38 enrolled. *Faculty:* 14 full-time (2 women), 25 part-time/adjunct (2 women). Expenses: Contact institution. *Financial support:* In 2001–02, 66 fellowships were awarded; Federal Work-Study also available. In 2001, 17 degrees awarded. Offers architecture (M Arch, D Arch); urban design (M Arch UD). *Application deadline:* For fall admission, 2/1 (priority date). *Application fee:* $25. *Application Contact:* Graduate Programs, 713-348-5202, Fax: 713-348-5277, E-mail: lerup@rice.edu. *Dean,* Lars Lerup, 713-348-4044, Fax: 713-348-5277, E-mail: lerup@rice.edu.

School of Humanities Students: 157 full-time (84 women). 452 applicants, 21% accepted. *Faculty:* 83 full-time, 23 part-time/adjunct. Expenses: Contact institution. *Financial support:* In 2001–02, 91 fellowships, 9 teaching assistantships with full tuition reimbursements were awarded. Federal Work-Study, institutionally sponsored loans, scholarships/grants, and tuition waivers (full and partial) also available. Financial award applicants required to submit CSS PROFILE or FAFSA. In 2001, 14 master's, 26 doctorates awarded. Offers education (MAT); English (MA, PhD); French studies (MA, PhD); history (MA, PhD); humanities (MA, MAT, PhD); linguistics (MA, PhD); philosophy (MA, PhD); religious studies (MA, PhD); Spanish (MA). *Application deadline:* For fall admission, 2/1. *Application fee:* $25. *Dean,* Gale Stokes, 713-348-4810.

School of Social Sciences Students: 129 full-time (70 women); includes 18 minority (3 African Americans, 7 Asian Americans or Pacific Islanders, 7 Hispanic Americans, 1 Native American), 52 international. 266 applicants, 12% accepted. *Faculty:* 64 full-time (12 women), 22 part-time/adjunct (14 women). Expenses: Contact institution. *Financial support:* In 2001–02, 87 students received support, including 70 fellowships, 9 research assistantships, 8 teaching assistantships; Federal Work-Study and tuition waivers (full and partial) also available. In 2001, 16 master's, 20 doctorates awarded. Offers anthropology (MA, PhD); economics (MA, PhD); industrial-organizational/social psychology (MA, PhD); political science (MA, PhD); psychology (MA, PhD); social sciences (MA, PhD). *Application deadline:* For fall admission, 2/1 (priority date); for spring admission, 11/1. Applications are processed on a rolling basis. *Application fee:* $25. *Dean,* Robert M. Stein, 713-527-4824.

Shepherd School of Music Students: 152 full-time (86 women), 14 part-time (2 women); includes 14 minority (5 African Americans, 5 Asian Americans or Pacific Islanders, 4 Hispanic Americans), 50 international. Average age 24. 360 applicants, 20% accepted, 63 enrolled. *Faculty:* 31 full-time (10 women), 23 part-time/adjunct (7 women). Expenses: Contact institution. *Financial support:* In 2001–02, 140 students received support, including 75 fellowships with full and partial tuition reimbursements available (averaging $2,000 per year), 3 teaching assistantships with full tuition reimbursements available (averaging $6,000 per year); Federal Work-Study, scholarships/grants, and tuition waivers (full and partial) also available. Financial award application deadline: 2/15. In 2001, 57 master's, 11 doctorates awarded. Offers composition (MM, DMA); conducting (MM); history (MM); performance (MM, DMA); theory (MM). *Application deadline:* For fall admission, 2/15; for winter admission, 10/15; for spring admission, 11/1. Applications are processed on a rolling basis. *Application fee:* $25. Electronic applications accepted. *Application Contact:* Christiane Denise Melancon, Graduate Coordinator, 713-348-2319, Fax: 713-348-5317, E-mail: melancon@rice.edu. *Dean,* Dr. Anne Schnoebelen, 713-348-4837, Fax: 713-348-5317.

Wiess School of Natural Sciences Students: 291 full-time (100 women); includes 94 minority (4 African Americans, 74 Asian Americans or Pacific Islanders, 16 Hispanic Americans), 109 international. *Faculty:* 116 full-time, 4 part-time/adjunct. Expenses: Contact institution. *Financial support:* In 2001–02, 126 fellowships (averaging $18,000 per year), 165 research assistantships (averaging $18,000 per year) were awarded. Federal Work-Study and tuition waivers (full and partial) also available. *Degree program information:* Part-time programs available. Offers applied physics (MS, PhD); biochemistry and cell biology (MA, PhD); chemistry (MA); earth science (MA, PhD); ecology and evolutionary biology (MA, PhD); energy exploration (MS); environmental analysis and decision-making (MS); inorganic chemistry (PhD); mathematics (MA, PhD); nanoscale physics (MS); natural sciences (MA, MS, PhD); organic chemistry (PhD); physical chemistry (PhD); physics (MA); physics and astronomy (MS, PhD). *Application deadline:* Applications are processed on a rolling basis. *Application fee:* $25. Electronic applications accepted. *Application Contact:* Rachel S. Miller, Assistant Dean, 713-348-6148, Fax: 713-348-6149, E-mail: gradinfo@rice.edu. *Dean of Natural Sciences,* Dr. Kathleen S. Matthews, 713-348-3350, Fax: 713-348-6149.

THE RICHARD STOCKTON COLLEGE OF NEW JERSEY, Pomona, NJ 08240-0195

General Information State-supported, coed, comprehensive institution. *Graduate housing:* Room and/or apartments available to single students. Housing application deadline: 4/1. *Research affiliation:* National Science Foundation (quantitative instruction), NASA–Goddard Space Flight Center (laser radar studies), Energy Foundation (geothermal transfer), Coastal Research Center (shoreline erosion), New Jersey American Water Company (radioactive contaminants), Bacharach Institute (holistic health).

GRADUATE UNITS

Graduate Programs *Degree program information:* Part-time programs available. Offers business studies (MBS); Holocaust and genocide studies (MA); instructional technology (MA); nursing (MSN); occupational therapy (MSOT); physical therapy (MPT). Electronic applications accepted.

RICHMOND, THE AMERICAN INTERNATIONAL UNIVERSITY IN LONDON, Richmond, Surrey TW10 6JP, United Kingdom

General Information Independent, coed, comprehensive institution. *Enrollment:* 39 full-time matriculated graduate/professional students (14 women). *Enrollment by degree level:* 39 master's. *Graduate faculty:* 24 full-time, 6 part-time/adjunct. *Graduate tuition:* Tuition charges are reported in British pounds. *Tuition:* Full-time 11,975 British pounds. *Graduate housing:* Room and/or apartments available on a first-come, first-served basis to single students; on-campus housing not available to married students. Housing application deadline: 7/30. *Student services:* Campus employment opportunities, campus safety program, free psychological counseling, international student services, low-cost health insurance. *Library facilities:* Taylor Library plus 2 others. *Online resources:* library catalog, access to other libraries' catalogs. *Collection:* 80,000 titles, 277 serial subscriptions.

Computer facilities: 400 computers available on campus for general student use. A campuswide network can be accessed from off campus. Internet access and online class registration are available. *Web address:* http://www.richmond.ac.uk/.

General Application Contact: Rick Doyle, Associate Director of Admissions, 207-368-8475, Fax: 207-376-0836, E-mail: grad@richmond.ac.uk.

GRADUATE UNITS

MBA Program Students: 28 full-time (5 women). Average age 25. 170 applicants, 51% accepted. Expenses: Contact institution. *Financial support:* Career-related internships or fieldwork, scholarships/grants, tuition waivers (partial), and unspecified assistantships available. Financial award application deadline: 7/20; financial award applicants required to submit FAFSA. In 2001, 31 degrees awarded. Offers business administration (MBA). *Application deadline:* For fall admission, 8/15 (priority date); for winter admission, 12/1 (priority date). Applications are processed on a rolling basis. *Application fee:* $35. Electronic applications accepted. *Application Contact:* Rick Doyle, Associate Director of Admissions, 207-368-8475, Fax: 207-376-0836, E-mail: grad@richmond.ac.uk. *Dean, School of Business,* Dr. Tereza Domal, 207-368-8488, Fax: 207-938-3037, E-mail: grad@richmond.ac.uk.

Program in Art History Students: 11 full-time (9 women). Average age 24. 22 applicants, 68% accepted. *Faculty:* 1 (woman) full-time, 1 (woman) part-time/adjunct. Expenses: Contact institution. *Financial support:* Career-related internships or fieldwork, scholarships/grants, and tuition waivers (partial) available. Support available to part-time students. Financial award application deadline: 6/30. In 2001, 6 degrees awarded. *Degree program information:* Part-time programs available. Offers art history (MA). *Application deadline:* For fall admission, 6/1 (priority date). *Application fee:* $35. Electronic applications accepted. *Application Contact:* Nancy Barrett, Director of Graduate Admissions, 207-368-8475, Fax: 207-376-0836, E-mail: grad@richmond.ac.uk. *Associate Director of Admissions,* Rick Doyle, 207-368-8475, Fax: 207-376-0836, E-mail: grad@richmond.ac.uk.

RIDER UNIVERSITY, Lawrenceville, NJ 08648-3001

General Information Independent, coed, comprehensive institution. *Enrollment:* 180 full-time matriculated graduate/professional students (126 women), 608 part-time matriculated graduate/professional students (399 women). *Enrollment by degree level:* 788 master's. *Graduate faculty:* 75 full-time, 63 part-time/adjunct. Tuition, state resident: part-time $365 per credit hour. *Required fees:* $200. Tuition and fees vary according to campus/location and program. *Graduate housing:* Room and/or apartments available on a first-come, first-served basis to single students; on-campus housing not available to married students. Typical cost: $5,000 per year ($8,390 including board) ; $2,500 per year for married students. Housing application deadline: 7/1. *Student services:* Campus employment opportunities, campus safety program, career counseling, disabled student services, exercise/wellness program, free psychological counseling, international student services, multicultural affairs office. *Library facilities:* Franklin F. Moore Library plus 1 other. *Online resources:* library catalog, web page, access to other libraries' catalogs. *Collection:* 394,308 titles, 2,763 serial subscriptions, 24,457 audiovisual materials.

Computer facilities: 403 computers available on campus for general student use. A campuswide network can be accessed from student residence rooms and from off campus. Internet access is available. *Web address:* http://www.rider.edu/.

General Application Contact: Dr. Christine Zelenak, Director of Graduate Admissions, 609-896-5036, Fax: 609-896-5261, E-mail: czelenak@rider.edu.

GRADUATE UNITS

College of Business Administration Students: 29 full-time (18 women), 196 part-time (93 women); includes 22 minority (4 African Americans, 11 Asian Americans or Pacific Islanders, 6 Hispanic Americans, 1 Native American), 2 international. Average age 32. 154 applicants, 57% accepted, 73 enrolled. *Faculty:* 24 full-time (8 women), 4 part-time/adjunct (1 woman). Expenses: Contact institution. *Financial support:* In 2001–02, 18 students received support, including 7 research assistantships with full tuition reimbursements available (averaging $11,730 per year); career-related internships or fieldwork, institutionally sponsored loans, and institutional work/study also available. Financial award application deadline: 4/1; financial award applicants required to submit FAFSA. In 2001, 91 degrees awarded. *Degree program information:* Part-time and evening/weekend programs available. Offers accountancy (M Acc); business administration (M Acc, MBA). *Application deadline:* For fall admission, 8/1 (priority date); for spring admission, 12/1. Applications are processed on a rolling basis. *Application fee:* $40. *Application Contact:* Dr. Christine Zelenak, Director of Graduate Admissions, 609-896-5036, Fax: 609-896-5261, E-mail: czelenak@rider.edu. *Associate Dean,* Thomas Charles Kelly, 609-896-5127, Fax: 609-896-5304, E-mail: kelly@rider.edu.

Department of Graduate Education and Human Services Students: 497 (364 women); includes 55 minority (44 African Americans, 6 Asian Americans or Pacific Islanders, 5 Hispanic Americans) Average age 36. 211 applicants, 50% accepted. *Faculty:* 15 full-time (7 women), 28 part-time/adjunct (15 women). Expenses: Contact institution. *Financial support:* In 2001–02, 20 students received support; research assistantships, career-related internships or fieldwork and Federal Work-Study available. Support available to part-time students. In 2001, 121 degrees awarded. *Degree program information:* Part-time and evening/weekend programs available. Offers business education (Certificate); counseling services (MA, Ed S); curriculum, instruction and supervision (MA); educational administration (MA); elementary education (Certificate); English education (Certificate); foreign language education (Certificate); graduate education and human services (MA, Certificate, Ed S); human services administration (MA); mathematics education (Certificate); reading/language arts (MA); science education (Certificate); social studies education (Certificate). *Application deadline:* For fall admission, 5/1 (priority date); for spring admission, 11/1 (priority date). Applications are processed on a rolling basis. *Application fee:* $35. *Application Contact:* Dr. Christine Zelenak, Director of Graduate Admissions, 609-896-5036, Fax: 609-896-5261, E-mail: czelenak@rider.edu. *Assistant Dean,* Dr. Jesse DeEsch, 609-896-5353, Fax: 609-896-5362, E-mail: deesch@rider.edu.

Westminster Choir College of Rider University Students: 90 full-time, 16 part-time; includes 8 minority (2 African Americans, 5 Asian Americans or Pacific Islanders, 1 Hispanic American), 36 international. *Faculty:* 35 full-time (11 women). Expenses: Contact institution. *Financial support:* In 2001–02, 54 students received support. Career-related internships or fieldwork, Federal Work-Study, and unspecified assistantships available. Support available to part-time students. Financial award application deadline: 3/1; financial award applicants required to submit FAFSA. In 2001, 95 degrees awarded. *Degree program information:* Part-time and evening/weekend programs available. Offers choral conducting (MM); composition (MM); music education (MM, MME); organ performance (MM); piano accompanying and coaching (MM); piano pedagogy and performance (MM); sacred music (MM); vocal pedagogy and performance (MM). *Application deadline:* Applications are processed on a rolling basis. *Application fee:* $40 ($50 for international students). *Application Contact:* Monica Thomas-Tritto, Admissions Office, 800-96-CHOIR, Fax: 609-921-2538, E-mail: wccadmission@rider.edu. *Associate Dean,* Dr. James Goldsworthy, 609-921-7100 Ext. 207, E-mail: goldswor@rider.edu.

RIVIER COLLEGE, Nashua, NH 03060-5086

General Information Independent-religious, coed, comprehensive institution. *Enrollment:* 88 full-time matriculated graduate/professional students (67 women), 459 part-time matriculated graduate/professional students (330 women). *Enrollment by degree level:* 547 master's. *Graduate faculty:* 27 full-time (13 women), 51 part-time/adjunct (24 women). *Tuition:* Part-time $360 per credit. *Required fees:* $25 per year. Part-time tuition and fees vary according to course level and course load. *Graduate housing:* On-campus housing not available. *Student services:* Career counseling, free psychological counseling, international student services, multicultural affairs office. *Library facilities:* Regina Library plus 1 other. *Online resources:* library catalog, web page. *Collection:* 105,000 titles, 1,802 serial subscriptions, 29,094 audiovisual materials.

Computer facilities: 93 computers available on campus for general student use. A campuswide network can be accessed from student residence rooms and from off campus. *Web address:* http://www.rivier.edu/.

General Application Contact: Diane Monahan, Director of Graduate Admissions, 603-897-8129, Fax: 603-897-8810, E-mail: gradadm@rivier.edu.

GRADUATE UNITS

School of Graduate Studies Students: 88 full-time (67 women), 459 part-time (330 women); includes 28 minority (5 African Americans, 13 Asian Americans or Pacific Islanders, 7 Hispanic Americans, 3 Native Americans), 41 international. Average age 37. *Faculty:* 27 full-time (13 women), 51 part-time/adjunct (24 women). Expenses: Contact institution. *Financial support:* Available to part-time students. Application deadline: 2/1; In 2001, 255 degrees awarded. *Degree program information:* Part-time and evening/weekend programs available. Offers arts and sciences (M Ed, MA, MAT, MBA, MS, CAGS); business administration (MBA); computer information systems (MS); computer science (MS); counseling and psychotherapy (MA); counselor education (M Ed); early childhood education (M Ed); educational administration (M Ed); elementary education (M Ed); English (MA, MAT); French (MAT); general education (M Ed); health care administration (MBA); human resources management (MS); information science (MS); learning disabilities (M Ed); mathematics (MAT); modern languages (MAT); nursing (MS); nursing education (MS); reading (M Ed); secondary education (M Ed); social studies education (MAT); Spanish (MAT); writing and literature (MA). *Application deadline:* Applications are processed on a rolling basis. *Application fee:* $25. Electronic applications accepted. *Application Contact:* Diane Monahan, Director of Graduate Admissions, 603-897-8129, Fax: 603-897-8810, E-mail: gradadm@rivier.edu. *Dean,* Dr. Albert DeCiccio, 603-888-1311, E-mail: ajohnson@rivier.edu.

See in-depth description on page 1045.

ROBERT MORRIS UNIVERSITY, Moon Township, PA 15108-1189

General Information Independent, coed, comprehensive institution. *Enrollment:* 906 part-time matriculated graduate/professional students (406 women). *Enrollment by degree level:* 861 master's, 45 doctoral. *Graduate faculty:* 25 full-time (3 women), 28 part-time/adjunct (6 women). *Tuition:* Part-time $410 per credit. Part-time tuition and fees vary according to degree level and program. *Graduate housing:* Room and/or apartments available on a first-come, first-served basis to single students; on-campus housing not available to married students. Typical cost: $3,900 per year ($6,580 including board). Room and board charges vary according to board plan and housing facility selected. Housing application deadline: 5/1. *Student services:* Campus employment opportunities, career counseling, disabled student services, international student services. *Library facilities:* Robert Morris College Library. *Online resources:* library catalog. *Collection:* 212,950 titles, 853 serial subscriptions, 3,165 audiovisual materials.

Computer facilities: 300 computers available on campus for general student use. A campuswide network can be accessed from off campus. Internet access and online class registration are available. *Web address:* http://www.rmu.edu/.

General Application Contact: Kellie Laurenzi, Director of Enrollment Services, 800-762-0097, Fax: 412-299-2425, E-mail: laurenzi@rmu.edu.

GRADUATE UNITS

Graduate Studies Average age 33. 478 applicants, 75% accepted, 276 enrolled. *Faculty:* 25 full-time (3 women), 28 part-time/adjunct (6 women). Expenses: Contact institution. *Financial support:* In 2001–02, 236 students received support. Federal Work-Study, institutionally sponsored loans, and unspecified assistantships available. Support available to part-time students. Financial award application deadline: 5/1; financial award applicants required to submit FAFSA. *Degree program information:* Part-time and evening/weekend programs available. Offers engineering management (MS); engineering, mathematics and science (MS). *Application deadline:* For fall admission, 8/1 (priority date). Applications are processed on a rolling basis. *Application fee:* $35. Electronic applications accepted. *Application Contact:* Kellie Laurenzi, Director of Enrollment Services, 800-762-0097, Fax: 412-299-2425, E-mail: laurenzi@rmu.edu. *Senior Vice President for Academic and Student Affairs,* Dr. William J. Katip, 412-262-8285, Fax: 412-604-2528.

School of Business 256 applicants, 75% accepted, 143 enrolled. *Faculty:* 18 full-time (3 women), 25 part-time/adjunct (15 women). Expenses: Contact institution. *Financial support:* Federal Work-Study, institutionally sponsored loans, and unspecified assistantships available. Support available to part-time students. Financial award application deadline: 5/1; financial award applicants required to submit FAFSA. In 2001, 197 degrees awarded. *Degree program information:* Part-time and evening/weekend programs available. Offers accounting (MS); business administration and management (MBA); finance (MS); nonprofit management (MS); sport management (MS); taxation (MS). *Application deadline:* For fall admission, 8/1 (priority date); for spring admission, 11/30 (priority date). Applications are processed on a rolling basis. *Application fee:* $35. Electronic applications accepted. *Application Contact:* Kellie Laurenzi, Director of Enrollment Services, 800-762-0097, Fax: 412-299-2425, E-mail: laurenzi@rmu.edu. *Dean,* Dr. Richard W. Stolz, 412-262-4882, Fax: 412-262-8494, E-mail: stolz@rmu.edu.

School of Communications and Information Systems 210 applicants, 73% accepted, 121 enrolled. Expenses: Contact institution. *Financial support:* Institutionally sponsored loans and unspecified assistantships available. Support available to part-time students. Financial award application deadline: 5/1. In 2001, 132 degrees awarded. *Degree program information:* Part-time and evening/weekend programs available. Offers business education (MS); communications and information systems (MS); information systems and communications (D Sc); information systems management (MS); instructional leadership (MS); Internet information systems (MS). *Application deadline:* For fall admission, 8/1 (priority date). Applications are processed on a rolling basis. *Application fee:* $35. Electronic applications accepted. *Application Contact:* Kellie Laurenzi, Director of Enrollment Services, 800-762-0097, Fax: 412-299-2425, E-mail: laurenzi@rmu.edu. *Dean,* Dr. David L. Jamison, 412-604-2591, Fax: 412-262-8483, E-mail: jamison@rmu.edu.

See in-depth description on page 1047.

ROBERTS WESLEYAN COLLEGE, Rochester, NY 14624-1997

General Information Independent-religious, coed, comprehensive institution. *Graduate housing:* Room and/or apartments available on a first-come, first-served basis to single students; on-campus housing not available to married students.

GRADUATE UNITS

Division of Business and Management *Degree program information:* Evening/weekend programs available. Offers business and management (MS); organizational management (MS).

Division of Social Work and Social Sciences Offers child and family services (MSW); physical and mental health services (MSW).

Division of Teacher Education *Degree program information:* Part-time and evening/weekend programs available. Offers teacher education (M Ed, Advanced Certificate).

ROCHESTER INSTITUTE OF TECHNOLOGY, Rochester, NY 14623-5698

General Information Independent, coed, comprehensive institution. CGS member. *Enrollment:* 1,011 full-time matriculated graduate/professional students (392 women), 1,140 part-time matriculated graduate/professional students (403 women). *Enrollment by degree level:* 2,100 master's, 33 doctoral, 18 other advanced degrees. *Tuition:* Full-time $20,928; part-time $587 per hour. *Required fees:* $162. Tuition and fees vary according to program. *Graduate housing:* Rooms and/or apartments available on a first-come, first-served basis to single and married students. Typical cost: $7,266 (including board) for single students; $7,266 (including board) for married students. Housing application deadline: 4/30. *Student services:* Campus employment opportunities, campus safety program, career counseling, child daycare facilities, disabled student services, free psychological counseling, international student services, low-cost health insurance, multicultural affairs office. *Library facilities:* Wallace Memorial Library. *Online resources:* library catalog, web page, access to other libraries' catalogs. *Collection:* 350,000 titles, 4,305 serial subscriptions, 8,215 audiovisual materials.

Computer facilities: 2,500 computers available on campus for general student use. A campuswide network can be accessed from student residence rooms and from off campus. Internet access and online class registration, student account information are available. *Web address:* http://www.rit.edu/.

General Application Contact: Diane Ellison, Director, Graduate Enrollment Services, 585-475-7284, Fax: 585-475-7464, E-mail: dmeges@rit.edu.

GRADUATE UNITS

Graduate Enrollment Services Students: 1,011 full-time (392 women), 1,140 part-time (403 women); includes 188 minority (49 African Americans, 89 Asian Americans or Pacific Islanders, 42 Hispanic Americans, 8 Native Americans), 720 international. 2,420 applicants, 68% accepted. Expenses: Contact institution. *Financial support:* Fellowships, research assistantships, teaching assistantships, career-related internships or fieldwork, Federal Work-Study, institutionally sponsored loans, scholarships/grants, tuition waivers (full and partial), and unspecified assistantships available. Support available to part-time students. In 2001, 734 master's, 3 doctorates, 40 other advanced degrees awarded. *Degree program information:* Part-time and evening/weekend programs available. *Application deadline:* For fall admission, 3/1 (priority date). Applications are processed on a rolling basis. *Application fee:* $50. Electronic applications accepted. *Director, Graduate Enrollment Services,* Diane Ellison, 585-475-7284, Fax: 585-475-7464, E-mail: dmeges@rit.edu.

College of Applied Science and Technology Students: 66 full-time (28 women), 203 part-time (102 women); includes 28 minority (16 African Americans, 4 Asian Americans or Pacific Islanders, 5 Hispanic Americans, 3 Native Americans), 67 international. 191 applicants, 80% accepted, 100 enrolled. Expenses: Contact institution. *Financial support:* Research assistantships, teaching assistantships, scholarships/grants and unspecified assistantships available. In 2001, 121 master's, 1 other advanced degree awarded. *Degree program information:* Part-time and evening/weekend programs available. Offers applied science and technology (MS, AC); computer integrated manufacturing (MS); cross-disciplinary professional studies (MS); environmental management (MS); health systems administration (MS, AC); health systems-finance (AC); hospitality-tourism management (MS); human resources development (MS); instructional technology (MS); integrated health systems (AC); multidisciplinary studies (MS, AC); packaging science (MS); service management (MS); technical information design (AC). *Application deadline:* For fall admission, 3/1 (priority date). Applications are processed on a rolling basis. *Application fee:* $50. Electronic applications accepted. *Dean,* Dr. Wiley McKinzie, 585-475-2369.

College of Business Students: 199 full-time (59 women), 180 part-time (62 women); includes 24 minority (8 African Americans, 11 Asian Americans or Pacific Islanders, 4 Hispanic Americans, 1 Native American), 101 international. 418 applicants, 67% accepted, 156 enrolled. Expenses: Contact institution. *Financial support:* Research assistantships, career-related internships or fieldwork and scholarships/grants available. Support available to part-time students. In 2001, 185 degrees awarded. *Degree program information:* Part-time and evening/weekend programs available. Offers accounting (MBA, MS); business (Exec MBA, MBA, MS); business administration (MBA); executive business administration (Exec MBA); finance (MS); international business (MS); manufacturing management and leadership (MS). *Application deadline:* For fall admission, 3/1 (priority date). Applications are processed on a rolling basis. *Application fee:* $50. *Dean,* Dr. Thomas D. Hopkins, 585-475-7042, E-mail: tdhbbu@rit.edu.

College of Engineering Students: 58 full-time (12 women), 137 part-time (28 women); includes 21 minority (5 African Americans, 8 Asian Americans or Pacific Islanders, 8 Hispanic Americans), 62 international. 543 applicants, 53% accepted, 72 enrolled. Expenses: Contact institution. *Financial support:* Fellowships, research assistantships, teaching assistantships, career-related internships or fieldwork, Federal Work-Study, institutionally sponsored loans, and tuition waivers (partial) available. Support available to part-time students. In 2001, 79 master's, 6 other advanced degrees awarded. *Degree program information:* Part-time and evening/weekend programs available. Offers applied statistics (MS); computer engineering (MS); electrical engineering (MSEE); engineering (ME, MS, MSEE, MSME, AC); engineering management (ME); industrial engineering (ME); manufacturing engineering (ME); mechanical engineering (MSME); microelectronic engineering (ME, MS); product development (MS); statistical quality (AC); systems engineering (ME). *Application deadline:* For fall admission, 3/1 (priority date). Applications are processed on a rolling basis. *Application fee:* $50. *Application Contact:* Dr. Richard Reeve, Associate Dean, 585-475-5382, E-mail: nrreie@rit.edu. *Dean,* Dr. Harvey Palmer, 585-475-2146.

College of Imaging Arts and Sciences Students: 259 full-time (132 women), 74 part-time (33 women); includes 30 minority (8 African Americans, 14 Asian Americans or Pacific Islanders, 7 Hispanic Americans, 1 Native American), 114 international. 432 applicants, 65% accepted, 158 enrolled. Expenses: Contact institution. *Financial support:* Fellowships, research assistantships, teaching assistantships, career-related internships or fieldwork, institutionally sponsored loans, tuition waivers (partial), and unspecified assistantships available. In 2001, 125 degrees awarded. *Degree program information:* Part-time programs available. Offers art education (MST); computer graphics design (MFA); crafts (MFA, MST); fine arts (MFA, MST); fine arts studio (MST); graphic arts publishing (MS); graphic arts systems (MS); graphic design (MFA, MST); imaging arts (MFA); imaging arts and sciences (MFA, MS, MST); industrial design (MFA, MST); interior design (MFA, MST); medical illustration (MFA); painting (MFA); printing technology (MS); printmaking (MFA). *Application deadline:* For fall admission, 3/1 (priority date). Applications are processed on a rolling basis. *Application fee:* $50. *Dean,* Dr. Joan Stone, 585-475-7249, E-mail: jbsntm@rit.edu.

College of Liberal Arts Students: 40 full-time (35 women), 7 part-time (all women); includes 3 minority (1 African American, 1 Asian American or Pacific Islander, 1 Hispanic American) 63 applicants, 57% accepted, 25 enrolled. Expenses: Contact institution. *Financial support:* Teaching assistantships available. In 2001, 30 master's, 18 other advanced degrees awarded. Offers communication (MS); communication and media technologies (MS); liberal arts (MS, AC); public policy (MS); school psychology (MS, AC); school psychology and deafness (AC). *Application deadline:* For fall admission, 3/1 (priority date). Applications are processed on a rolling basis. *Application fee:* $50. *Dean,* Dr. Andrew Moore, 585-475-2447, E-mail: ammgla@rit.edu.

College of Science Students: 56 full-time (23 women), 60 part-time (20 women); includes 10 minority (4 Asian Americans or Pacific Islanders, 6 Hispanic Americans), 39 international. 128 applicants, 66% accepted, 50 enrolled. Expenses: Contact institution. *Financial support:* Research assistantships, teaching assistantships, career-related internships or fieldwork, Federal Work-Study, institutionally sponsored loans, and tuition waivers (full and partial) available. Support available to part-time students. In 2001, 36 master's, 3 doctorates awarded. *Degree program information:* Part-time and evening/weekend programs available. Offers chemistry (MS); clinical chemistry (MS); color science (MS); imaging science (MS, PhD); industrial and applied mathematics (MS); materials science and engineering (MS); science (MS, PhD). *Application deadline:* For fall admission, 3/1 (priority date). Applications are processed on a rolling basis. *Application fee:* $50. *Interim Dean,* Dr. Ian Gatley, 585-475-2483, E-mail: ixgpci@rit.edu.

Golisano College of Computing and Information Sciences Students: 309 full-time (85 women), 432 part-time (132 women); includes 71 minority (11 African Americans, 47 Asian Americans or Pacific Islanders, 10 Hispanic Americans, 3 Native Americans), 334 international. 622 applicants, 75% accepted, 220 enrolled. Expenses: Contact institution. In 2001, 126 master's, 15 other advanced degrees awarded. Offers computer science (MS); computing and information sciences (MS, AC); information technology (MS); interactive multimedia development (AC); software development and management (MS). *Application deadline:* For fall admission, 3/1 (priority date). Applications are processed on a rolling basis. *Application fee:* $50. Electronic applications accepted. *Interim Dean,* Walter Wolf, 585-475-4786, E-mail: waw@cs.rit.edu.

National Technical Institute for the Deaf Students: 24 full-time (18 women), 10 part-time (9 women); includes 1 minority (Hispanic American), 3 international. 23 applicants, 100% accepted, 20 enrolled. Expenses: Contact institution. In 2001, 14 degrees awarded. Offers secondary education (MS). *Application deadline:* For fall admission, 3/1 (priority date). Applications are processed on a rolling basis. *Application fee:* $50. *Dean,* Dr. Alan Hurwitz, 585-475-6317, E-mail: alan_hurwitz@rit.edu.

See in-depth description on page 1049.

THE ROCKEFELLER UNIVERSITY, New York, NY 10021-6399

General Information Independent, coed, graduate-only institution. CGS member. *Enrollment by degree level:* 169 doctoral. *Graduate faculty:* 227 full-time (74 women), 195 part-time/adjunct (45 women). *Graduate housing:* Rooms and/or apartments guaranteed to single and married students. Typical cost: $4,000 per year for single students; $4,000 per year for married students. Housing application deadline: 6/1. *Student services:* Campus safety program, free psychological counseling, low-cost health insurance. *Library facilities:* Rockefeller University Library. *Online resources:* library catalog, web page, access to other libraries' catalogs. *Collection:* 115,098 titles, 480 serial subscriptions, 16 audiovisual materials.

Computer facilities: 18 computers available on campus for general student use. A campuswide network can be accessed from student residence rooms and from off campus. Internet access is available. *Web address:* http://www.rockefeller.edu/.

General Application Contact: Dr. Sidney Strickland, Dean of Graduate Studies, 212-327-8086, Fax: 212-327-8505, E-mail: phd@rockefeller.edu.

GRADUATE UNITS

Program in Biomedical Sciences Students: 169 full-time (83 women); includes 35 minority (5 African Americans, 23 Asian Americans or Pacific Islanders, 7 Hispanic Americans), 69 international. Average age 25. 550 applicants, 14% accepted. *Faculty:* 227 full-time (74 women), 195 part-time/adjunct (45 women). Expenses: Contact institution. *Financial support:* In 2001–02, 169 fellowships with full tuition reimbursements (averaging $22,000 per year) were awarded; institutionally sponsored loans, scholarships/grants, traineeships, and health care benefits also available. In 2001, 15 degrees awarded. Offers biomedical sciences (PhD). MD/PhD offered through the Tri-Institutional Program with Cornell University Medical College and Sloan-Kettering Institute. *Application deadline:* For fall admission, 1/1. *Application fee:* $60. *Application Contact:* Kristen Cullen, Admissions and Records Administrator, 212-327-8088, Fax: 212-327-8505, E-mail: cullenk@mail.rockefeller.edu. *Dean of Graduate Studies,* Dr. Sidney Strickland, 212-327-8086, Fax: 212-327-8505, E-mail: phd@mail.rockefeller.edu.

ROCKFORD COLLEGE, Rockford, IL 61108-2393

General Information Independent, coed, comprehensive institution. *Graduate housing:* Room and/or apartments available to single students; on-campus housing not available to married students.

GRADUATE UNITS

Graduate Studies *Degree program information:* Part-time and evening/weekend programs available. Offers art education (MAT); business administration (MBA); elementary education (MAT); English (MAT); history (MAT); learning disabilities (MAT); political science (MAT); reading (MAT); secondary education (MAT); social sciences (MAT).

ROCKHURST UNIVERSITY, Kansas City, MO 64110-2561

General Information Independent-religious, coed, comprehensive institution. CGS member. *Enrollment:* 211 full-time matriculated graduate/professional students (135 women), 508 part-time matriculated graduate/professional students (220 women). *Enrollment by degree level:* 719 master's. *Graduate faculty:* 53 full-time (24 women), 14 part-time/adjunct (8 women). *Tuition:* Full-time $7,380; part-time $410 per hour. *Required fees:* $15 per term. One-time fee: $40. *Graduate housing:* Room and/or apartments available on a first-come, first-served basis to single students; on-campus housing not available to married students. Typical cost: $6,050 (including board). Housing application deadline: 6/10. *Student services:* Campus employment opportunities, campus safety program, career counseling, free psychological counseling, international student services, multicultural affairs office. *Library facilities:* Greenlease Library. *Online resources:* library catalog, web page, access to other libraries' catalogs. *Collection:* 53,720 titles, 100 serial subscriptions, 2,730 audiovisual materials.

Computer facilities: 500 computers available on campus for general student use. A campuswide network can be accessed from student residence rooms and from off campus. Internet access is available. *Web address:* http://www.rockhurst.edu/.

General Application Contact: Director of Graduate Recruitment, 816-501-4100, Fax: 816-501-4241.

GRADUATE UNITS

College of Arts and Sciences Students: 123 full-time (106 women), 57 part-time (39 women); includes 17 minority (8 African Americans, 4 Asian Americans or Pacific Islanders, 4 Hispanic Americans, 1 Native American), 1 international. Average age 26. 165 applicants, 79% accepted, 74 enrolled. *Faculty:* 29 full-time (25 women), 7 part-time/adjunct (4 women). Expenses: Contact institution. *Financial support:* In 2001–02, 10 research assistantships, 20 teaching assistantships were awarded. Career-related internships or fieldwork, institutionally sponsored loans, and unspecified assistantships also available. Financial award application deadline: 4/1; financial award applicants required to submit FAFSA. In 2001, 73 degrees awarded. *Degree program information:* Part-time programs available. Offers arts and sciences (M Ed, MOT, MPT, MS); communication sciences and disorders (MS); occupational therapy education (MOT); physical therapy (MPT). *Application deadline:* Applications are processed on a rolling basis. *Application fee:* $25. Electronic applications accepted. *Application Contact:* Jyll Whiteman, Director of Graduate Recruitment, 816-501-4097, Fax: 816-501-4241, E-mail: jyll.whiteman@rockhurst.edu. *Dean,* Dr. William Haefele, 816-501-4075, Fax: 816-501-4169, E-mail: william.haefele@rockhurst.edu.

Division of Behavioral and Social Sciences Students: 1 (woman) full-time, 16 part-time (12 women); includes 5 minority (4 African Americans, 1 Asian American or Pacific Islander) Average age 28. *Faculty:* 4 full-time (3 women), 1 part-time/adjunct (0 women). Expenses: Contact institution. *Financial support:* Institutionally sponsored loans and scholarships/grants available. Financial award applicants required to submit FAFSA. *Degree program information:* Evening/weekend programs available. Offers behavioral and social sciences (M Ed); education (M Ed). *Application deadline:* Applications are processed on a rolling basis. *Application fee:* $25. *Application Contact:* Jyll Whiteman, Director of Graduate Recruitment, 816-501-4097, Fax: 816-501-4241, E-mail: jyll.whiteman@rockhurst.edu. *Head,* Dr. Marilyn Carroll, 816-510-4102.

Helzberg School of Management Students: 88 full-time (29 women), 426 part-time (169 women); includes 49 minority (21 African Americans, 16 Asian Americans or Pacific Islanders, 11 Hispanic Americans, 1 Native American), 11 international. Average age 31. 247 applicants, 78% accepted, 169 enrolled. *Faculty:* 29 full-time (6 women), 7 part-time/adjunct (2 women). Expenses: Contact institution. *Financial support:* Career-related internships or fieldwork available. Support available to part-time students. Financial award application deadline: 4/1; financial award applicants required to submit FAFSA. In 2001, 186 degrees awarded. *Degree program information:* Part-time and evening/weekend programs available. Postbaccalaureate distance learning degree programs offered (minimal on-campus study). Offers management (MBA). *Application deadline:* For fall admission, 7/25 (priority date); for spring admission, 12/15. Applications are processed on a rolling basis. *Application fee:* $0. *Application Contact:* Monna Finkle, Director of Graduate Recruitment, 816-501-4654, Fax: 816-501-4241, E-mail: monna.finkle@rockhurst.edu. *Interim Dean,* Dr. John Darling, 816-501-4201, Fax: 816-501-4650, E-mail: john.darling@rockhurst.edu.

ROGER WILLIAMS UNIVERSITY, Bristol, RI 02809

General Information Independent, coed, comprehensive institution. *Enrollment:* 234 full-time matriculated graduate/professional students, 131 part-time matriculated graduate/professional students. *Graduate faculty:* 23 full-time (8 women), 16 part-time/adjunct (7 women). *Tuition:* Part-time $740 per credit. *Graduate housing:* Rooms and/or apartments available on a first-come, first-served basis to single students and available to married students. *Student services:* Campus employment opportunities, campus safety program, career counseling, disabled student services, exercise/wellness program, low-cost health insurance, writing training. *Library facilities:* Roger Williams University Library plus 2 others. *Online resources:* library catalog, web page. *Collection:* 168,460 titles, 1,225 serial subscriptions, 60,694 audiovisual materials.

Computer facilities: 425 computers available on campus for general student use. A campuswide network can be accessed from student residence rooms and from off campus. Internet access, telephone registration are available. *Web address:* http://www.rwu.edu/.

General Application Contact: Michael W. Boylen, Director of Admissions, 401-254-4555, Fax: 401-254-4516, E-mail: admissions@law.rwu.edu.

GRADUATE UNITS

Ralph R. Papitto School of Law Students: 338 full-time (174 women), 132 part-time (68 women); includes 51 minority (26 African Americans, 15 Asian Americans or Pacific Islanders, 10 Hispanic Americans) Average age 28. 1,030 applicants, 65% accepted, 240 enrolled. *Faculty:* 28 full-time (13 women), 15 part-time/adjunct (3 women). Expenses: Contact institution. *Financial support:* In 2001–02, 248 students received support, including 26 research assistantships; career-related internships or fieldwork, institutionally sponsored loans, scholarships/grants, and tuition waivers (full and partial) also available. Support available to part-time students. Financial award application deadline: 5/15; financial award applicants required to submit FAFSA. In 2001, 97 degrees awarded. *Degree program information:* Part-time and evening/weekend programs available. Offers law (JD). *Application deadline:* For fall admission, 5/15 (priority date). Applications are processed on a rolling basis. *Application fee:* $60. Electronic applications accepted. *Application Contact:* Christel L. Ertel, Dean of Admissions, 401-254-4515, Fax: 401-254-4516, E-mail: certel@law.rwu.edu. *Interim Dean,* Bruce I. Kogan, 401-254-4502, E-mail: bkogan@law.rwu.edu.

ROLLINS COLLEGE, Winter Park, FL 32789-4499

General Information Independent, coed, comprehensive institution. *Enrollment:* 270 full-time matriculated graduate/professional students (118 women), 475 part-time matriculated graduate/professional students (317 women). *Enrollment by degree level:* 745 master's. *Tuition:* Part-time $226 per credit hour. *Graduate housing:* On-campus housing not available. *Student services:* Campus employment opportunities, campus safety program, career counseling, disabled student services, exercise/wellness program, free psychological counseling,

Rollins College (continued)

international student services, low-cost health insurance, multicultural affairs office. *Library facilities:* Olin Library. *Online resources:* library catalog, web page, access to other libraries' catalogs. *Collection:* 237,333 titles, 6,259 serial subscriptions, 4,853 audiovisual materials.

Computer facilities: 200 computers available on campus for general student use. A campuswide network can be accessed from student residence rooms and from off campus. Internet access is available. *Web address:* http://www.rollins.edu/.

General Application Contact: Information Contact, 407-646-2000.

GRADUATE UNITS

Crummer Graduate School of Business Students: 236 full-time (86 women), 148 part-time (52 women); includes 68 minority (16 African Americans, 21 Asian Americans or Pacific Islanders, 31 Hispanic Americans), 44 international. Average age 30. Expenses: Contact institution. *Financial support:* Fellowships, research assistantships, career-related internships or fieldwork, Federal Work-Study, scholarships/grants, and tuition waivers (full) available. In 2001, 171 degrees awarded. *Degree program information:* Part-time and evening/weekend programs available. Offers business (MBA). *Application deadline:* For fall admission, 4/1 (priority date); for spring admission, 12/1. Applications are processed on a rolling basis. *Application fee:* $50. *Application Contact:* Student Admissions Office, 407-646-2405, Fax: 407-646-1550. *Dean*, Dr. Craig M. McAllaster, 407-646-2249, Fax: 407-646-1550.

Hamilton Holt School Students: 34 full-time (32 women), 327 part-time (265 women); includes 44 minority (18 African Americans, 8 Asian Americans or Pacific Islanders, 16 Hispanic Americans, 2 Native Americans), 1 international. Average age 37. Expenses: Contact institution. *Financial support:* Teaching assistantships, institutionally sponsored loans and scholarships/grants available. Support available to part-time students. In 2001, 97 degrees awarded. *Degree program information:* Part-time and evening/weekend programs available. Offers corporate communications and technology (MA); elementary education (M Ed, MAT); human resources (MA); liberal studies (MLS); mental health counseling (MA); school counseling (MA); secondary education (MAT). *Application deadline:* Applications are processed on a rolling basis. *Application fee:* $50. *Application Contact:* Graduate Program Admission, 407-646-2232, Fax: 407-646-1551. *Dean*, Dr. Patricia A. Lancaster, 407-646-2232, Fax: 407-646-1551.

ROOSEVELT UNIVERSITY, Chicago, IL 60605-1394

General Information Independent, coed, comprehensive institution. *Enrollment:* 762 full-time matriculated graduate/professional students (486 women), 2,100 part-time matriculated graduate/professional students (1,416 women). *Enrollment by degree level:* 2,778 master's, 84 doctoral. *Graduate faculty:* 173 full-time (62 women), 295 part-time/adjunct (110 women). *Tuition:* Full-time $9,090; part-time $505 per credit hour. *Required fees:* $100 per term. *Graduate housing:* Room and/or apartments available to single students; on-campus housing not available to married students. Typical cost: $6,270 (including board). Room and board charges vary according to board plan. Housing application deadline: 7/1. *Student services:* Campus employment opportunities, campus safety program, career counseling, child daycare facilities, disabled student services, exercise/wellness program, free psychological counseling, international student services, low-cost health insurance, teacher training, writing training. *Library facilities:* Murray-Green Library plus 4 others. *Online resources:* library catalog, web page, access to other libraries' catalogs. *Collection:* 300,000 titles, 1,200 serial subscriptions, 21,000 audiovisual materials.

Computer facilities: 380 computers available on campus for general student use. A campuswide network can be accessed from off campus. Internet access and online class registration are available. *Web address:* http://www.roosevelt.edu/.

General Application Contact: Joanne Canyon-Heller, Coordinator of Graduate Admissions, 312-281-3250, Fax: 312-341-3523, E-mail: applyru@roosevelt.edu.

GRADUATE UNITS

Graduate Division Students: 762 full-time (486 women), 2,100 part-time (1,416 women); includes 922 minority (646 African Americans, 118 Asian Americans or Pacific Islanders, 150 Hispanic Americans, 8 Native Americans), 276 international. Average age 32. 1,623 applicants, 73% accepted, 787 enrolled. *Faculty:* 173 full-time (62 women), 295 part-time/adjunct (110 women). Expenses: Contact institution. *Financial support:* In 2001–02, 175 students received support; research assistantships, teaching assistantships, career-related internships or fieldwork, Federal Work-Study, scholarships/grants, tuition waivers (full and partial), and unspecified assistantships available. Support available to part-time students. Financial award application deadline: 5/1; financial award applicants required to submit FAFSA. In 2001, 848 master's, 14 doctorates awarded. *Degree program information:* Part-time and evening/weekend programs available. *Application deadline:* For fall admission, 6/1 (priority date); for spring admission, 12/1. Applications are processed on a rolling basis. *Application fee:* $25 ($35 for international students). *Application Contact:* Joanne Canyon-Heller, Coordinator of Graduate Admissions, 312-281-3250, Fax: 312-341-3523, E-mail: applyru@roosevelt.edu. *Associate Provost for Graduate Studies*, Dr. Brigitte Erbe, 312-341-3616, Fax: 312-341-2013, E-mail: berbe@roosevelt.edu.

College of Arts and Sciences Students: 1,097 (874 women); includes 379 minority (276 African Americans, 42 Asian Americans or Pacific Islanders, 57 Hispanic Americans, 4 Native Americans) 62 international. *Faculty:* 75 full-time, 100 part-time/adjunct. Expenses: Contact institution. *Financial support:* Research assistantships, teaching assistantships, career-related internships or fieldwork, Federal Work-Study, institutionally sponsored loans, scholarships/grants, and tuition waivers (full and partial) available. Support available to part-time students. Financial award application deadline: 2/15. In 2001, 78 degrees awarded. *Degree program information:* Part-time and evening/weekend programs available. Offers applied economics (MA); arts and sciences (MA, MFA, MPA, MS, MSC, MSIMC, MSJ, MST, Psy D); chemistry (MS); clinical professional psychology (MA); clinical psychology (MA, Psy D); communication (MSIMC, MSJ); computer science (MSC); computer science and telecommunications (MSC, MST); creative writing (MFA); economics (MA); English (MA); general psychology (MA); history (MA); industrial/organizational psychology (MA); integrated marketing communications (MSIMC); journalism (MSJ); liberal studies (MA, MFA); mathematical sciences (MS); policy studies (MA, MPA); political science (MA); public administration (MPA); science and mathematics (MS); sociology (MA); sociology-gerontology (MA); Spanish (MA); telecommunications (MST); women's studies (MA). *Application deadline:* For fall admission, 6/1 (priority date). Applications are processed on a rolling basis. *Application fee:* $25 ($35 for international students). *Application Contact:* Joanne Canyon-Heller, Coordinator of Graduate Admissions, 312-281-3250, Fax: 312-341-3523, E-mail: applyru@roosevelt.edu. *Dean*, Lynn Weiner, 312-341-2134.

College of Education Students: 153 full-time (109 women), 437 part-time (320 women); includes 206 minority (166 African Americans, 13 Asian Americans or Pacific Islanders, 26 Hispanic Americans, 1 Native American), 4 international. Expenses: Contact institution. *Financial support:* Federal Work-Study available. Support available to part-time students. Financial award application deadline: 2/15. In 2001, 145 master's, 22 doctorates awarded. *Degree program information:* Part-time and evening/weekend programs available. Offers early childhood education (MA); educational administration and supervision (MA, Ed D); elementary education (MA); guidance and counseling (MA); reading education (MA); secondary education (MA). *Application deadline:* For fall admission, 6/1 (priority date). Applications are processed on a rolling basis. *Application fee:* $25 ($35 for international students). *Application Contact:* Joanne Canyon-Heller, Coordinator of Graduate Admissions, 312-281-3250, Fax: 312-341-3523, E-mail: applyru@roosevelt.edu. *Dean*, Dr. George Lowery, 312-341-3700.

College of the Performing Arts Students: 50 full-time (30 women), 37 part-time (25 women); includes 13 minority (8 African Americans, 4 Asian Americans or Pacific Islanders, 1 Hispanic American), 34 international. *Faculty:* 25 full-time (12 women), 67 part-time/adjunct (28 women). Expenses: Contact institution. *Financial support:* Research assistantships, career-related internships or fieldwork, Federal Work-Study, scholarships/grants, and tuition waivers (full and partial) available. Support available to part-time students. In 2001, 30 degrees awarded. *Degree program information:* Part-time and evening/weekend programs available. Offers directing and dramaturgy (MFA); music (MM); music education (MM Ed); musical theatre (MFA); performing arts (MA, MFA, MM, MM Ed, Diploma); piano pedagogy (Diploma); theatre (MA, MFA); theatre-directing (MA); theatre-performance (MFA). *Application deadline:* For fall admission, 6/1 (priority date). Applications are processed on a rolling basis. *Application fee:* $25 ($35 for international students). *Application Contact:* Joanne Canyon-Heller, Coordinator of Graduate Admissions, 312-281-3250, Fax: 312-341-3523, E-mail: applyru@roosevelt.edu. *Head*, James Gundre, 312-341-3782.

Evelyn T. Stone University College Students: 23 full-time (16 women), 99 part-time (72 women); includes 32 minority (28 African Americans, 4 Asian Americans or Pacific Islanders), 5 international. *Faculty:* 5 full-time (2 women), 7 part-time/adjunct (5 women). Expenses: Contact institution. *Financial support:* Federal Work-Study available. Support available to part-time students. Financial award application deadline: 2/15. In 2001, 17 degrees awarded. *Degree program information:* Part-time and evening/weekend programs available. Offers general studies (MGS); hospitality management (MS); training and development (MA). *Application deadline:* For fall admission, 6/1 (priority date). Applications are processed on a rolling basis. *Application fee:* $25 ($35 for international students). *Application Contact:* Joanne Canyon-Heller, Coordinator of Graduate Admissions, 312-281-3250, Fax: 312-341-3523, E-mail: applyru@roosevelt.edu. *Dean*, Laura Evans, 312-281-3126.

Walter E. Heller College of Business Administration Students: 595 (295 women). Expenses: Contact institution. *Financial support:* Career-related internships or fieldwork, Federal Work-Study, and tuition waivers (partial) available. Support available to part-time students. Financial award application deadline: 2/15. In 2001, 107 degrees awarded. *Degree program information:* Part-time and evening/weekend programs available. Offers accounting (MSA); business administration (MBA, MSA, MSIB, MSIS); information systems (MSIS); international business (MSIB). *Application deadline:* For fall admission, 6/1 (priority date). Applications are processed on a rolling basis. *Application fee:* $25 ($35 for international students). *Application Contact:* Joanne Canyon-Heller, Coordinator of Graduate Admissions, 312-281-3250, Fax: 312-341-3523, E-mail: applyru@roosevelt.edu. *Acting Dean*, Thomas Head, 312-281-3254.

See in-depth description on page 1051.

ROSE-HULMAN INSTITUTE OF TECHNOLOGY, Terre Haute, IN 47803-3920

General Information Independent, coed, primarily men, comprehensive institution. *Enrollment:* 57 full-time matriculated graduate/professional students (11 women), 115 part-time matriculated graduate/professional students (9 women). *Enrollment by degree level:* 172 master's. *Graduate faculty:* 62 full-time (7 women), 4 part-time/adjunct (1 woman). *Tuition:* Full-time $21,792; part-time $615 per credit hour. *Required fees:* $405. *Graduate housing:* Room and/or apartments available on a first-come, first-served basis to single students; on-campus housing not available to married students. Typical cost: $3,360 per year ($6,039 including board). Housing application deadline: 4/15. *Student services:* Campus employment opportunities, career counseling, exercise/wellness program, international student services, low-cost health insurance. *Library facilities:* Logan Library. *Online resources:* library catalog, web page, access to other libraries' catalogs. *Collection:* 74,525 titles, 589 serial subscriptions, 325 audiovisual materials. *Research affiliation:* Eli Lilly & Company (life sciences).

Computer facilities: 100 computers available on campus for general student use. A campuswide network can be accessed from student residence rooms and from off campus. Internet access and online class registration are available. *Web address:* http://www.rose-hulman.edu/.

General Application Contact: Dr. Daniel J. Moore, Interim Associate Dean of the Faculty, 812-877-8110, Fax: 812-877-8061, E-mail: daniel.j.moore@rose-hulman.edu.

GRADUATE UNITS

Faculty of Engineering and Applied Sciences Students: 57 full-time (11 women), 115 part-time (9 women); includes 8 minority (1 African American, 7 Asian Americans or Pacific Islanders), 40 international. Average age 28. 90 applicants, 81% accepted, 55 enrolled. *Faculty:* 62 full-time (7 women), 4 part-time/adjunct (1 woman). Expenses: Contact institution. *Financial support:* In 2001–02, 68 students received support; fellowships with full and partial tuition reimbursements available, research assistantships with full and partial tuition reimbursements available, institutionally sponsored loans, scholarships/grants, and tuition waivers (full and partial) available. Financial award application deadline: 2/1. In 2001, 25 degrees awarded. *Degree program information:* Part-time and evening/weekend programs available. Postbaccalaureate distance learning degree programs offered (minimal on-campus study). Offers biomedical engineering (MS); chemical engineering (MS); electrical engineering (MS); engineering and applied sciences (MS); engineering management (MS); environmental engineering (MS); mechanical engineering (MS); optical engineering (MS). *Application deadline:* For fall admission, 2/1 (priority date). Applications are processed on a rolling basis. *Application fee:* $0. *Interim Associate Dean of the Faculty*, Dr. Daniel J. Moore, 812-877-8110, Fax: 812-877-8061, E-mail: daniel.j.moore@rose-hulman.edu.

ROSEMONT COLLEGE, Rosemont, PA 19010-1699

General Information Independent-religious, women only, comprehensive institution. *Enrollment:* 316 matriculated graduate/professional students (263 women). *Graduate faculty:* 48. *Tuition:* Part-time $470 per credit. One-time fee: $50 part-time. Tuition and fees vary according to program. *Graduate housing:* Room and/or apartments available to single students; on-campus housing not available to married students. Typical cost: $4,400 (including board). *Student services:* Campus employment opportunities, career counseling, free psychological counseling, international student services, teacher training, writing training. *Library facilities:* Kistler Library. *Online resources:* library catalog, web page, access to other libraries' catalogs. *Collection:* 154,000 titles, 736 serial subscriptions, 2,600 audiovisual materials.

Computer facilities: 90 computers available on campus for general student use. A campuswide network can be accessed from student residence rooms and from off campus. Internet access is available. *Web address:* http://www.rosemont.edu/.

General Application Contact: Karen Scales, Enrollment and Marketing Coordinator, 610-527-0200 Ext. 2187, Fax: 610-526-2964, E-mail: gradstudies@rosemont.edu.

GRADUATE UNITS

Graduate School Students: 316 (263 women). Average age 34. 60 applicants, 95% accepted. *Faculty:* 48. Expenses: Contact institution. *Financial support:* In 2001–02, 24 students received support. Career-related internships or fieldwork available. Support available to part-time students. Financial award applicants required to submit FAFSA. In 2001, 19 degrees awarded. *Degree program information:* Part-time and evening/weekend programs available. Offers arts/culture/project management (MS); business administration (MBA); criminal justice (MS); elementary certification (MA); English (MA); English and publishing (MA); human services (MA); middle school education (M Ed); not for profit (MS); school counseling (MA); technology in education (M Ed); training and leadership (MS). *Application deadline:* Applications are processed on a rolling basis. *Application fee:* $50. *Application Contact:* Karen Scales, Enrollment and Marketing Coordinator, 610-527-0200 Ext. 2187, Fax: 610-526-2964, E-mail: gradstudies@rosemont.edu. *Dean of Graduate Studies*, Dr. Debra Klinman, 610-527-0200 Ext. 2344, Fax: 610-526-2964, E-mail: dklinman@rosemont.edu.

See in-depth description on page 1053.

ROWAN UNIVERSITY, Glassboro, NJ 08028-1701

General Information State-supported, coed, comprehensive institution. CGS member. *Enrollment:* 150 full-time matriculated graduate/professional students (97 women), 685 part-time matriculated graduate/professional students (514 women). *Enrollment by degree level:* 790 master's, 45 doctoral. *Graduate faculty:* 88 full-time (36 women), 19 part-time/adjunct (7 women). Tuition, state resident: full-time $7,080; part-time $295 per semester hour. Tuition, nonresident: full-time $11,328; part-time $472 per semester hour. *Required fees:* $855; $39 per semester hour. Tuition and fees vary according to degree level. *Graduate housing:* On-campus housing not available. *Student services:* Campus employment opportunities, campus safety program, career counseling, child daycare facilities, disabled student services, exercise/wellness program, free psychological counseling, international student services, low-cost health insurance, multicultural affairs office, teacher training, writing training. *Library facilities:* Keith and Shirley Campbell Library plus 2 others. *Online resources:* library catalog, web page, access to other libraries' catalogs.

Computer facilities: 350 computers available on campus for general student use. A campuswide network can be accessed from student residence rooms and from off campus. Internet access is available. *Web address:* http://www.rowan.edu/.

General Application Contact: Dr. Jay Kuder, Dean, Graduate Studies, 856-256-4050, Fax: 856-256-4436, E-mail: kuder@rowan.edu.

GRADUATE UNITS

Graduate School Students: 150 full-time (97 women), 685 part-time (514 women); includes 111 minority (72 African Americans, 14 Asian Americans or Pacific Islanders, 20 Hispanic Americans, 5 Native Americans) Average age 35. 263 applicants, 71% accepted, 177 enrolled. *Faculty:* 88 full-time (36 women), 19 part-time/adjunct (7 women). Expenses: Contact institution. *Financial support:* In 2001–02, 97 students received support. Career-related internships or fieldwork, Federal Work-Study, and unspecified assistantships available. Support available to part-time students. In 2001, 251 master's, 3 doctorates awarded. *Degree program information:* Part-time and evening/weekend programs available. *Application deadline:* Applications are processed on a rolling basis. *Application fee:* $50. Electronic applications accepted. *Application Contact:* Dorie Gilchrist, Director of Graduate Admissions, 856-256-4054, Fax: 609-256-4436. *Dean,* Dr. Jay Kuder, 856-256-4050, Fax: 609-256-4436.

College of Business Students: 4 full-time (3 women), 36 part-time (9 women); includes 4 minority (3 Asian Americans or Pacific Islanders, 1 Native American) Average age 34. 18 applicants, 44% accepted, 7 enrolled. Expenses: Contact institution. *Financial support:* Federal Work-Study and unspecified assistantships available. Support available to part-time students. In 2001, 19 degrees awarded. *Degree program information:* Part-time and evening/weekend programs available. Offers accounting (MS); business (MBA, MS); business administration (MBA). *Application deadline:* Applications are processed on a rolling basis. *Application fee:* $50. Electronic applications accepted. *Dean,* Dr. Edward Schoen, 856-256-4025.

College of Communication Students: 23 full-time (13 women), 52 part-time (40 women); includes 8 minority (5 African Americans, 2 Asian Americans or Pacific Islanders, 1 Hispanic American) Average age 33. 30 applicants, 77% accepted, 23 enrolled. Expenses: Contact institution. *Financial support:* Career-related internships or fieldwork and unspecified assistantships available. Support available to part-time students. In 2001, 19 degrees awarded. *Degree program information:* Part-time and evening/weekend programs available. Offers public relations (MA); writing (MA). *Application deadline:* Applications are processed on a rolling basis. *Application fee:* $50. *Application Contact:* Dr. Donald Bagin, Adviser, 856-256-4332. *Dean,* Dr. George Thottam, 856-256-4290.

College of Education Students: 83 full-time (61 women), 552 part-time (439 women); includes 92 minority (67 African Americans, 6 Asian Americans or Pacific Islanders, 16 Hispanic Americans, 3 Native Americans) 177 applicants, 75% accepted, 126 enrolled. Expenses: Contact institution. *Financial support:* Career-related internships or fieldwork, Federal Work-Study, and unspecified assistantships available. Support available to part-time students. In 2001, 187 master's, 3 doctorates awarded. *Degree program information:* Part-time and evening/weekend programs available. Offers art education (MA); biological science education (MA); education (MA, MST, Ed D, Ed S); educational leadership (Ed D); elementary education (MA, MST); environmental education (MA); higher education administration (MA); learning disabilities (MA); mathematics education (MA); music education (MA); physical science education (MA); reading education (MA); school administration (MA); school administration-business administration (MA); school and public librarianship (MA); school psychology (MA, Ed S); science education (MA); special education (MA, MST); student personnel services (MA); subject matter teaching (MA); supervision and curriculum development (MA); teaching-secondary (MST). *Application deadline:* Applications are processed on a rolling basis. *Application fee:* $50. Electronic applications accepted. *Dean,* 856-256-4750.

College of Engineering Students: 14 full-time (1 woman), 7 part-time (1 woman); includes 2 minority (both Asian Americans or Pacific Islanders) Average age 28. 8 applicants, 50% accepted, 4 enrolled. Expenses: Contact institution. *Financial support:* Career-related internships or fieldwork, Federal Work-Study, and unspecified assistantships available. Support available to part-time students. In 2001, 9 degrees awarded. *Degree program information:* Part-time and evening/weekend programs available. Offers engineering (MS). *Application deadline:* Applications are processed on a rolling basis. *Application fee:* $50. Electronic applications accepted. *Application Contact:* Dr. T. R. Chandrupata, Program Adviser, 856-256-5342. *Dean,* Dr. Dianne Dorland, 856-256-5300.

College of Fine and Performing Arts Students: 4 full-time (2 women), 14 part-time (7 women); includes 1 minority (Asian American or Pacific Islander) Average age 37. 8 applicants, 75% accepted, 6 enrolled. Expenses: Contact institution. *Financial support:* Career-related internships or fieldwork, Federal Work-Study, and unspecified assistantships available. Support available to part-time students. In 2001, 3 degrees awarded. *Degree program information:* Part-time and evening/weekend programs available. Offers fine and performing arts (MA, MM); music (MM); theatre (MA). *Application deadline:* Applications are processed on a rolling basis. *Application fee:* $50. Electronic applications accepted. *Dean,* Dr. Donald Gephardt, 856-256-4550.

College of Liberal Arts and Sciences Students: 21 full-time (16 women), 20 part-time (15 women); includes 4 minority (3 Hispanic Americans, 1 Native American) Average age 31. 17 applicants, 65% accepted, 8 enrolled. Expenses: Contact institution. *Financial support:* Career-related internships or fieldwork, Federal Work-Study, and unspecified assistantships available. Support available to part-time students. In 2001, 14 degrees awarded. *Degree program information:* Part-time and evening/weekend programs available. Offers applied psychology (MA); liberal arts and sciences (MA); mathematics (MA). *Application deadline:* Applications are processed on a rolling basis. *Application fee:* $50. Electronic applications accepted. *Dean,* Dr. Jay Harper, 856-256-4850.

See in-depth description on page 1055.

ROYAL MILITARY COLLEGE OF CANADA, Kingston, ON K7K 7B4, Canada

General Information Federally supported, coed, comprehensive institution. *Enrollment:* 215 full-time matriculated graduate/professional students, 435 part-time matriculated graduate/professional students. *Enrollment by degree level:* 599 master's, 51 doctoral. *Graduate faculty:* 174 full-time, 25 part-time/adjunct. *Library facilities:* Massey Library plus 1 other. *Online resources:* library catalog, web page. *Collection:* 300,000 titles, 1,100 serial subscriptions, 2,510 audiovisual materials.

Computer facilities: A campuswide network can be accessed from student residence rooms and from off campus. Internet access is available. *Web address:* http://www.rmc.ca/.

General Application Contact: Peggy Murphy, Administrative Assistant, Graduate Studies, 613-541-6000 Ext. 6361, Fax: 613-542-8612, E-mail: murphy-p@rmc.ca.

GRADUATE UNITS

Division of Graduate Studies and Research Students: 599 full-time, 51 part-time. *Faculty:* 174 full-time, 25 part-time/adjunct. Expenses: Contact institution. *Financial support:* In 2001–02, 40 students received support, including 4 fellowships with full tuition reimbursements available (averaging $20,000 per year), 20 research assistantships with partial tuition reimbursements available (averaging $17,000 per year), 10 teaching assistantships with partial tuition reimbursements available (averaging $5,000 per year); tuition waivers (partial) also available. In 2001, 76 master's, 1 doctorate awarded. *Degree program information:* Part-time programs available. Postbaccalaureate distance learning degree programs offered (minimal on-campus study). Offers arts (MA, MBA, MDS); business administration (MBA); chemical engineering (M Eng, MA Sc, PhD); chemistry (M Sc, PhD); civil engineering (M Eng, MA Sc, PhD); computer engineering (M Eng, MA Sc, PhD); computer science (M Sc); defense management and policy (MA); defense studies (MDS); electrical engineering (M Eng, MA Sc, PhD); engineering (M Eng, M Sc, MA Sc, PhD); environmental engineering (M Eng, MA Sc, PhD); environmental science (M Sc, PhD); materials science (M Sc, PhD); mathematics (M Sc); mechanical engineering (M Eng, MA Sc, PhD); nuclear engineering (M Eng, MA Sc, PhD); nuclear science (M Sc, PhD); physics (M Sc); science (M Eng, M Sc, MA Sc, PhD); software engineering (M Eng, MA Sc, PhD); war studies (MA). *Application deadline:* For fall admission, 5/1 (priority date); for winter admission, 9/1 (priority date). Applications are processed on a rolling basis. Electronic applications accepted. *Application Contact:* Peggy Murphy, Administrative Assistant, Graduate Studies, 613-541-6000 Ext. 6361, Fax: 613-542-8612, E-mail: murphy-p@rmc.ca. *Dean,* Dr. R. D. Weir, 613-541-6000 Ext. 6612, Fax: 613-542-9489, E-mail: weir-r@rmc.ca.

ROYAL ROADS UNIVERSITY, Victoria, BC V9B 5Y2, Canada

General Information Province-supported, coed, upper-level institution. *Enrollment:* 1,647 full-time matriculated graduate/professional students (752 women). *Enrollment by degree level:* 1,647 master's. *Graduate faculty:* 11 full-time (3 women), 79 part-time/adjunct (31 women). *Graduate tuition:* Tuition and fees charges are reported in Canadian dollars. *International tuition:* $12,000 Canadian dollars full-time. Tuition, Canadian resident: full-time $8,000 Canadian dollars. *Required fees:* $600 Canadian dollars. Full-time tuition and fees vary according to program. *Graduate housing:* Room and/or apartments available on a first-come, first-served basis to single students; on-campus housing not available to married students. *Student services:* Career counseling, disabled student services, exercise/wellness program, free psychological counseling, international student services, multicultural affairs office. *Library facilities:* Learning Resource Centre plus 1 other. *Online resources:* library catalog, web page, access to other libraries' catalogs. *Collection:* 40,000 titles, 609 audiovisual materials.

Computer facilities: 100 computers available on campus for general student use. A campuswide network can be accessed from student residence rooms and from off campus. Internet access and online class registration are available. *Web address:* http://www.royalroads.ca/.

General Application Contact: Office of Learner Services and Registrar, 250-391-2505, Fax: 250-391-2522, E-mail: rruregistrar@royalroads.ca.

GRADUATE UNITS

Graduate Studies Students: 1,647 full-time (752 women). Average age 39. 1,201 applicants, 95% accepted. *Faculty:* 11 full-time (3 women), 79 part-time/adjunct (31 women). Expenses: Contact institution. *Financial support:* In 2001–02, 22 students received support. Federal Work-Study, institutionally sponsored loans, and scholarships/grants available. Support available to part-time students. In 2001, 292 degrees awarded. Postbaccalaureate distance learning degree programs offered (minimal on-campus study). Offers conflict analysis and management (MA); distributed learning (MA); environment and management (M Sc, MA); leadership and training (MA). *Application deadline:* Applications are processed on a rolling basis. *Application fee:* $50 ($100 for international students). Electronic applications accepted. *Application Contact:* Office of Learner Services and Registrar, 250-391-2505, Fax: 250-391-2522, E-mail: rruregistrar@royalroads.ca. *Vice President, Learning,* Dr. Ron Bordessa, 250-391-2545, Fax: 250-391-2538.

School of Business Students: 981 full-time (359 women). Average age 36. 829 applicants, 97% accepted. *Faculty:* 4 full-time (1 woman), 40 part-time/adjunct (16 women). Expenses: Contact institution. *Financial support:* In 2001–02, 15 students received support. Federal Work-Study, institutionally sponsored loans, and scholarships/grants available. Support available to part-time students. Financial award application deadline: 4/3. In 2001, 147 degrees awarded. Postbaccalaureate distance learning degree programs offered (minimal on-campus study). Offers digital technologies management (MBA); executive management (MBA); human resources management (MBA); public relations and communications management (MBA). *Application deadline:* For winter admission, 12/15 (priority date). Applications are processed on a rolling basis. *Application fee:* $50 ($100 for international students). Electronic applications accepted. *Application Contact:* Deborah Wickins, Manager, MBA Programs, 250-391-2647, Fax: 250-391-2610, E-mail: deborah.wickins@royalroads.ca. *Director,* Dr. Eric West, 250-391-2655, Fax: 250-391-2610, E-mail: eric.west@royalroads.ca.

RUSH UNIVERSITY, Chicago, IL 60612-3832

General Information Independent, coed, upper-level institution. CGS member. *Enrollment:* 676 full-time matriculated graduate/professional students (396 women), 445 part-time matriculated graduate/professional students (380 women). *Enrollment by degree level:* 487 first professional, 443 master's, 191 doctoral. *Graduate faculty:* 783 full-time, 387 part-time/adjunct. *Tuition:* Full-time $14,310; part-time $400 per hour. Tuition and fees vary according to program. *Graduate housing:* Rooms and/or apartments available on a first-come, first-served basis to single and married students. *Student services:* Career counseling, child daycare facilities, free psychological counseling, international student services, low-cost health insurance. *Library facilities:* Library of Rush University. *Online resources:* library catalog, web page. *Collection:* 120,042 titles, 1,992 serial subscriptions.

Computer facilities: 39 computers available on campus for general student use. A campuswide network can be accessed from student residence rooms and from off campus. Internet access is available. *Web address:* http://www.rushu.rush.edu/.

General Application Contact: Hicela Castruita Woods, Director, College Admissions Services, 312-942-7100, Fax: 312-942-2219, E-mail: hicela_castruita@rush.edu.

GRADUATE UNITS

College of Health Sciences Students: 144 full-time (118 women), 57 part-time (45 women); includes 37 minority (13 African Americans, 18 Asian Americans or Pacific Islanders, 6 Hispanic Americans), 14 international. Average age 27. 227 applicants, 33% accepted. *Faculty:* 130 full-time (89 women), 69 part-time/adjunct (30 women). Expenses: Contact institution. *Financial support:* In 2001–02, 129 students received support. Career-related internships or fieldwork, Federal Work-Study, institutionally sponsored loans, and scholarships/grants available. Support available to part-time students. Financial award application deadline: 4/15; financial award applicants required to submit FAFSA. In 2001, 5 degrees awarded. *Degree program information:* Part-time and evening/weekend programs available. Offers audiology (MS, Au D); clinical laboratory management (MS); clinical laboratory science (MS); clinical nutrition (MS); health sciences (MA, MS, Au D); health systems management (MS); healthcare ethics (MA); occupational therapy (MS); speech-language pathology (MS). *Application fee:* $40. Electronic applications accepted. *Application Contact:* Hicela Castruita Woods, Director, College Admissions Services, 312-942-7100, Fax: 312-942-2219, E-mail: hicela_castruita@rush.edu. *Dean,* Dr. John E. Trufant, 312-942-7120, Fax: 312-942-2100, E-mail: jtrufant@rushu.rush.edu.

College of Nursing Students: 43 full-time (29 women), 267 part-time (247 women); includes 59 minority (18 African Americans, 31 Asian Americans or Pacific Islanders, 9 Hispanic Americans, 1 Native American), 4 international. Average age 36. 187 applicants, 71% accepted. *Faculty:* 41 full-time (39 women), 45 part-time/adjunct (41 women). Expenses: Contact institution. *Financial support:* In 2001–02, 242 students received support, including 8 research assistantships (averaging $3,500 per year), 8 teaching assistantships with tuition reimbursements available (averaging $20,000 per year); fellowships, Federal Work-Study, institutionally sponsored loans, scholarships/grants, and traineeships also available. Support available to part-time students. Financial award applicants required to submit FAFSA. In 2001, 62 master's, 24 doctorates awarded. *Degree program information:* Part-time programs available. Postbaccalaureate distance learning degree programs offered (minimal on-campus study). Offers acute care nurse practitioner (MSN, DN Sc); adult nurse practitioner (MSN, DN Sc); adult/gerontological nurse practitioner (MSN, DN Sc); anesthesia nurse practitioner (MSN, DN Sc); critical care clinical specialist (MSN, DN Sc); family nurse practitioner (MSN); gerontological nurse practitioner (MSN, DN Sc); medical surgical clinical specialist (MSN, DN Sc); neonatal nurse practitioner (MSN, DN Sc); nursing (MSN, DN Sc); pediatric clinical nurse specialist (MSN, DN Sc); pediatric critical care nurse practitioner (MSN, DN Sc); pediatric nurse practitioner (MSN, DN Sc); psychiatric nurse practitioner (MSN, DN Sc); psychiatric/adult nurse practitioner (MSN, DN Sc); public health nursing (MSN, DN Sc); women's health clinical nurse specialist (MSN, DN Sc). *Application deadline:* For fall admission, 8/1; for winter admission, 11/15; for spring admission, 2/15. Applications are processed on a rolling basis. *Application fee:* $40. Electronic applications accepted. *Application Contact:* Hicela Castruita Woods, Director, College Admissions Services, 312-942-7100, Fax: 312-942-2219, E-mail: hicela_castruita@rush.edu. *Dean,* Dr. Kathleen Andreoli, 312-942-7117.

Rush University (continued)

Graduate College Students: 64 full-time (38 women), 18 part-time (9 women); includes 3 African Americans, 7 Asian Americans or Pacific Islanders, 1 Hispanic American, 29 international. Average age 31. 235 applicants, 13% accepted. *Faculty:* 67 full-time (12 women), 34 part-time/adjunct (3 women). Expenses: Contact institution. *Financial support:* In 2001–02, 64 students received support, including 7 fellowships with full tuition reimbursements available, 40 research assistantships with full tuition reimbursements available (averaging $14,000 per year); teaching assistantships, career-related internships or fieldwork, Federal Work-Study, institutionally sponsored loans, and tuition waivers (full and partial) also available. Support available to part-time students. Financial award applicants required to submit FAFSA. In 2001, 1 master's, 14 doctorates awarded. Offers anatomical sciences (MS, PhD); biochemistry (PhD); clinical research (MS); immunology (PhD); medical physics (MS, PhD); microbiology (PhD); pharmacology (MS, PhD); physiology (PhD); virology (PhD). *Application fee:* $40. *Application Contact:* Thyra Jackson, Coordinator of Admissions, 312-942-6247, Fax: 312-942-2100, E-mail: thyra_r_jackson@rush.edu. *Dean,* Dr. John E. Trufant, 312-942-6247, Fax: 312-942-2100, E-mail: jtrufant@rushu.rush.edu.

Rush Medical College Offers medicine (MD).

RUTGERS, THE STATE UNIVERSITY OF NEW JERSEY, CAMDEN, Camden, NJ 08102-1401

General Information State-supported, coed, university. *Enrollment:* 674 full-time matriculated graduate/professional students (321 women), 746 part-time matriculated graduate/professional students (357 women). *Graduate faculty:* 232 full-time (78 women), 152 part-time/adjunct (60 women). *Graduate housing:* Rooms and/or apartments available to single and married students. *Student services:* Campus employment opportunities, campus safety program, career counseling, child daycare facilities, disabled student services, free psychological counseling, low-cost health insurance, multicultural affairs office, teacher training. *Library facilities:* Paul Robeson Library plus 2 others. *Collection:* 3.8 million titles, 28,760 serial subscriptions.

Computer facilities: 184 computers available on campus for general student use. A campuswide network can be accessed from student residence rooms and from off campus. Internet access, online grade reports are available. *Web address:* http://camden-www.rutgers.edu/.

General Application Contact: Dr. Deborah B. Bowles, Director of Admissions, 856-225-6056, Fax: 856-225-6498.

GRADUATE UNITS

Graduate School Students: 73 full-time (41 women), 314 part-time (184 women). 452 applicants, 63% accepted. Expenses: Contact institution. *Financial support:* In 2001–02, 117 students received support, including 27 fellowships, 1 research assistantship with full tuition reimbursement available (averaging $16,500 per year), 16 teaching assistantships with full tuition reimbursements available (averaging $16,500 per year); career-related internships or fieldwork, Federal Work-Study, institutionally sponsored loans, scholarships/grants, and unspecified assistantships also available. Support available to part-time students. Financial award application deadline: 3/15; financial award applicants required to submit FAFSA. In 2001, 72 degrees awarded. *Degree program information:* Part-time and evening/weekend programs available. Offers American and public history (MA); biology (MS, MST); chemistry (MS); criminal justice (MA); English (MA); health care management and policy (MPA); international public service and development (MPA); liberal studies (MA); mathematics (MS); physical therapy (MPT); public management (MPA). *Application deadline:* Applications are processed on a rolling basis. *Application fee:* $50. Electronic applications accepted. *Application Contact:* Dr. Deborah B. Bowles, Director of Admissions, 856-225-6056, Fax: 856-225-6498. *Dean,* Dr. Margaret Marsh, 856-225-6097, Fax: 856-225-6495.

School of Business Students: 46 full-time (15 women), 230 part-time (85 women). Average age 29. 103 applicants, 83% accepted. Expenses: Contact institution. *Financial support:* In 2001–02, 25 students received support; fellowships with partial tuition reimbursements available available. Support available to part-time students. Financial award applicants required to submit FAFSA. In 2001, 42 degrees awarded. *Degree program information:* Part-time and evening/weekend programs available. Offers business (M Ac, MBA). *Application deadline:* For fall admission, 8/1 (priority date); for spring admission, 12/1. Applications are processed on a rolling basis. *Application fee:* $50. *Application Contact:* Izzet Kenis, MBA Director, 856-225-6216, Fax: 856-225-6231, E-mail: kenis@crab.rutgers.edu. *Dean,* Milton Leontiades, 856-225-6217, Fax: 856-225-6231.

School of Law Students: 555 full-time (265 women), 202 part-time (88 women). Average age 27. 1,910 applicants, 31% accepted. Expenses: Contact institution. *Financial support:* In 2001–02, 600 students received support. Career-related internships or fieldwork, Federal Work-Study, and scholarships/grants available. Support available to part-time students. Financial award application deadline: 4/1; financial award applicants required to submit FAFSA. In 2001, 228 degrees awarded. *Degree program information:* Part-time and evening/weekend programs available. Offers law (JD). *Application deadline:* For fall admission, 3/1 (priority date). Applications are processed on a rolling basis. *Application fee:* $50. Electronic applications accepted. *Application Contact:* Camille Spinello Andrews, Associate Dean of Enrollment, Law Admissions, 856-225-6102, Fax: 856-225-6537, E-mail: csa@crab.rutgers.edu. *Dean,* Rayman L. Solomon, 856-225-6191, Fax: 856-225-6487.

See in-depth description on page 1057.

RUTGERS, THE STATE UNIVERSITY OF NEW JERSEY, NEWARK, Newark, NJ 07102

General Information State-supported, coed, university. CGS member. *Enrollment:* 1,248 full-time matriculated graduate/professional students (589 women), 2,236 part-time matriculated graduate/professional students (1,059 women). *Graduate faculty:* 424 full-time (160 women), 184 part-time/adjunct (81 women). *Graduate housing:* Room and/or apartments available to single students; on-campus housing not available to married students. Housing application deadline: 5/15. *Student services:* Career counseling, free psychological counseling, low-cost health insurance. *Library facilities:* John Cotton Dana Library plus 4 others. *Collection:* 3.8 million titles, 28,760 serial subscriptions.

Computer facilities: 708 computers available on campus for general student use. A campuswide network can be accessed from student residence rooms and from off campus. Internet access, online grade reports are available. *Web address:* http://info.rutgers.edu/newark/.

General Application Contact: Bruce C. Neimeyer, Director of Admissions, 973-353-5205, Fax: 973-353-1440.

GRADUATE UNITS

Graduate School Students: 268 full-time (138 women), 907 part-time (591 women). 1,303 applicants, 53% accepted. Expenses: Contact institution. *Financial support:* In 2001–02, 53 fellowships with full tuition reimbursements (averaging $13,000 per year), 166 teaching assistantships with full tuition reimbursements (averaging $13,700 per year) were awarded. Research assistantships with full tuition reimbursements, tuition waivers (full and partial) and unspecified assistantships also available. In 2001, 150 master's, 57 doctorates awarded. *Degree program information:* Part-time and evening/weekend programs available. Offers accounting (PhD); accounting information systems (PhD); American political system (MA); analytical chemistry (MS, PhD); applied physics (MS, PhD); biochemistry (MS, PhD); biology (MS, PhD); cognitive neuroscience (PhD); cognitive science (PhD); computational biology (MS); computer information systems (PhD); criminal justice (PhD); English (MA); environmental geology (MS); finance (PhD); global affairs (PhD); health care administration (MPA); history (MA, MAT); human resources administration (MPA); information technology (PhD); inorganic chemistry (MS, PhD); integrated neuroscience (PhD); international business (PhD); international relations (MA); jazz history and research (MA); liberal studies (MALS); management science (PhD); marketing (PhD); mathematical sciences (PhD); organic chemistry (MS, PhD); organization management (PhD); perception (PhD); physical chemistry (MS, PhD); psychobiology (PhD); public administration (PhD); public management (MPA); public policy analysis (MPA); social cognition (PhD); urban systems (PhD); urban systems and issues (MPA). *Application deadline:* Applications are processed on a rolling basis. *Application fee:* $50. Electronic applications accepted. *Application Contact:* Bruce C. Neimeyer, Director of Admissions, 973-353-5205, Fax: 973-353-1440. *Associate Dean,* Dr. Gary Roth, 973-353-5834 Ext. 10, Fax: 973-353-1191, E-mail: garyroth@andromeda.rutgers.edu.

Center for Global Change and Governance 42 applicants, 71% accepted. Expenses: Contact institution. *Financial support:* In 2001–02, 3 teaching assistantships with full tuition reimbursements (averaging $13,700 per year) were awarded; career-related internships or fieldwork and institutionally sponsored loans also available. Financial award application deadline: 3/7; financial award applicants required to submit FAFSA. In 2001, 2 degrees awarded. *Degree program information:* Part-time and evening/weekend programs available. Offers global studies (MA); international studies (MS). *Application deadline:* For fall admission, 6/1 (priority date). Applications are processed on a rolling basis. *Application fee:* $50. Electronic applications accepted. *Director,* Prof. Richard Langhorne, 973-353-5585, Fax: 973-353-5074, E-mail: langhorn@andromeda.rutgers.edu.

College of Nursing 221 applicants, 71% accepted. Expenses: Contact institution. *Financial support:* In 2001–02, 4 fellowships (averaging $8,000 per year), 1 research assistantship, 4 teaching assistantships with full tuition reimbursements (averaging $13,700 per year) were awarded. Career-related internships or fieldwork, Federal Work-Study, institutionally sponsored loans, scholarships/grants, and traineeships also available. Financial award application deadline: 4/15. In 2001, 45 master's, 3 doctorates awarded. *Degree program information:* Part-time programs available. Offers nursing (MS); nursing research (PhD). *Application deadline:* For fall admission, 5/15. Applications are processed on a rolling basis. *Application fee:* $50. Electronic applications accepted. *Application Contact:* Dr. Elaine Dolinsky, Associate Dean for Student Life and Services, 973-353-5060 Ext. 611, Fax: 973-353-1277, E-mail: dolinsky@nursetech.rutgers.edu. *Program Director,* Dr. Joanne Stevenson, 973-353-5293 Ext. 606, Fax: 973-353-1277, E-mail: stevenson@nursetech.rutgers.edu.

Rutgers Business School: Graduate Programs-Newark/New Brunswick Students: 410 full-time (150 women), 1,106 part-time (371 women). Average age 28. 986 applicants, 51% accepted. Expenses: Contact institution. *Financial support:* In 2001–02, 215 students received support; fellowships with tuition reimbursements available, teaching assistantships with tuition reimbursements available, career-related internships or fieldwork, Federal Work-Study, institutionally sponsored loans, scholarships/grants, and tuition waivers (full and partial) available. Support available to part-time students. Financial award application deadline: 3/15; financial award applicants required to submit FAFSA. In 2001, 400 master's, 24 doctorates awarded. *Degree program information:* Part-time and evening/weekend programs available. Offers business (M Accy, MBA, MQF, PhD); finance and economics (MBA); international business (MBA); management science/computer information systems (MBA); marketing (MBA); organization management (MBA); professional accounting (MBA). *Application deadline:* For fall admission, 6/1; for spring admission, 11/15. Applications are processed on a rolling basis. *Application fee:* $50. Electronic applications accepted. *Application Contact:* Doris Holohan, Assistant Dean of Admissions, 973-353-1234, Fax: 973-353-1592, E-mail: admit@andromeda.rutgers.edu. *Dean, Faculty of Management,* Dr. Howard Tuckman, 973-353-5128, Fax: 973-353-1345, E-mail: htuckman@eudoramail.com.

School of Criminal Justice Students: 14 full-time (11 women), 42 part-time (22 women). Average age 35. 110 applicants, 39% accepted. Expenses: Contact institution. *Financial support:* In 2001–02, 27 students received support, including 17 fellowships, 13 teaching assistantships; research assistantships, career-related internships or fieldwork, Federal Work-Study, institutionally sponsored loans, and tuition waivers (full and partial) also available. Support available to part-time students. Financial award application deadline:3/1. In 2001, 22 master's, 3 doctorates awarded. *Degree program information:* Part-time and evening/weekend programs available. Offers criminal justice (MA, PhD). *Application deadline:* For fall admission, 3/1 (priority date); for spring admission, 12/1. Applications are processed on a rolling basis. *Application fee:* $50. Electronic applications accepted. *Application Contact:* Director of Admissions, 973-353-5205, Fax: 973-353-1440. *Director,* Dr. Leslie Kennedy, 973-353-5870, Fax: 973-353-5896.

School of Law Students: 556 full-time (240 women), 181 part-time (75 women). Average age 27. 2,001 applicants, 36% accepted. Expenses: Contact institution. *Financial support:* In 2001–02, 585 students received support, including 13 fellowships (averaging $3,800 per year), 20 research assistantships with partial tuition reimbursements available (averaging $1,900 per year), 23 teaching assistantships (averaging $750 per year); career-related internships or fieldwork, Federal Work-Study, and institutionally sponsored loans also available. Support available to part-time students. Financial award application deadline: 3/1; financial award applicants required to submit FAFSA. In 2001, 191 degrees awarded. *Degree program information:* Part-time and evening/weekend programs available. Offers law (JD). *Application deadline:* For fall admission, 3/15. Applications are processed on a rolling basis. *Application fee:* $50. *Application Contact:* Anita T. Walton, Director of Admissions, 973-353-5557, Fax: 973-353-1445, E-mail: awalton@andromeda.rutgers.edu. *Dean,* Stuart L. Deutsch, 973-353-5551, Fax: 973-353-1445.

See in-depth description on page 1059.

RUTGERS, THE STATE UNIVERSITY OF NEW JERSEY, NEW BRUNSWICK, New Brunswick, NJ 08901-1281

General Information State-supported, coed, university. CGS member. *Enrollment:* 2,792 full-time matriculated graduate/professional students (1,603 women), 4,507 part-time matriculated graduate/professional students (2,932 women). *Graduate faculty:* 1,906 full-time (624 women), 598 part-time/adjunct (297 women). *Graduate housing:* Rooms and/or apartments available to single and married students. *Student services:* Campus employment opportunities, career counseling, child daycare facilities, free psychological counseling, international student services, low-cost health insurance. *Library facilities:* Archibald S. Alexander Library plus 14 others. *Online resources:* library catalog, web page, access to other libraries' catalogs. *Collection:* 3.8 million titles, 28,760 serial subscriptions.

Computer facilities: 1,450 computers available on campus for general student use. A campuswide network can be accessed from student residence rooms and from off campus. Internet access, online grade reports are available. *Web address:* http://www.rutgers.edu/.

General Application Contact: Dr. Donald J. Taylor, Director of Graduate Admissions, 732-932-7711, Fax: 732-932-8231, E-mail: kdc@rci.rutgers.edu.

GRADUATE UNITS

Ernest Mario College of Pharmacy Average age 23. 163 applicants, 71% accepted. *Faculty:* 23 full-time (13 women), 9 part-time/adjunct (5 women). Expenses: Contact institution. *Financial support:* In 2001–02, 5 teaching assistantships with full tuition reimbursements were awarded; career-related internships or fieldwork, scholarships/grants, and tuition waivers (partial) also available. Financial award application deadline: 2/1. In 2001, 81 degrees awarded. *Degree program information:* Part-time programs available. Offers pharmacy (Pharm D). *Application deadline:* For fall admission, 2/1 (priority date); for spring admission, 12/1. Applications are processed on a rolling basis. *Application fee:* $50. *Director,* Dr. Joseph Barone, 732-445-5215 Ext. 418, Fax: 732-445-2533.

Edward J. Bloustein School of Planning and Public Policy Average age 28. 360 applicants, 61% accepted. Expenses: Contact institution. *Financial support:* In 2001–02, 110 students received support, including 15 fellowships with full and partial tuition reimbursements available (averaging $10,000 per year), 10 research assistantships with full tuition reimbursements available (averaging $14,000 per year), 22 teaching assistantships with full and partial tuition reimbursements available (averaging $14,000 per year); career-related internships or fieldwork, Federal Work-Study, institutionally sponsored loans, scholarships/grants, tuition waivers (full and partial), and unspecified assistantships also available. Financial award application deadline: 2/1; financial award applicants required to submit FAFSA. In 2001, 112 master's, 6 doctorates awarded. *Degree program information:* Part-time and evening/weekend programs available. Offers planning and public policy (MCRP, MCRS, MPAP, MPH, MPP, Dr PH, PhD); public health (MPH, Dr PH, PhD); public policy (MPAP, MPP); urban planning and policy development (MCRP, MCRS, PhD). *Application deadline:* For fall admission, 6/1 (priority date); for spring admission, 11/1 (priority date). *Application fee:* $50.

Electronic applications accepted. *Application Contact:* Stephen D. Weston, Coordinator, Student and Academic Services, 732-932-5475 Ext. 753, Fax: 732-935-1771, E-mail: sdweston@rci.rutgers.edu. *Dean,* James W. Hughes, 732-932-5475 Ext. 756.

Graduate School Students: 1,621 full-time (755 women), 1,475 part-time (947 women). 6,175 applicants, 26% accepted. Expenses: Contact institution. *Financial support:* In 2001–02, 627 fellowships with full tuition reimbursements (averaging $13,800 per year), 564 research assistantships with full tuition reimbursements (averaging $13,800 per year), 813 teaching assistantships with full tuition reimbursements (averaging $13,800 per year) were awarded. Career-related internships or fieldwork, Federal Work-Study, institutionally sponsored loans, scholarships/grants, traineeships, tuition waivers (full and partial), and unspecified assistantships also available. Support available to part-time students. Financial award applicants required to submit FAFSA. In 2001, 1,144 master's, 412 doctorates awarded. *Degree program information:* Part-time and evening/weekend programs available. Postbaccalaureate distance learning degree programs offered. Offers agricultural economics (MS); air resources (MS, PhD); American political institutions (PhD); analytical chemistry (MS, PhD); anthropology (MA, PhD); applied mathematics (MS, PhD); applied microbiology (MS, PhD); aquatic biology (MS, PhD); aquatic chemistry (MS, PhD); art history (MA, PhD); astronomy (MS, PhD); biochemistry (MS, PhD); biological chemistry (PhD); biomedical engineering (MS, PhD); biophysics (PhD); biopsychology and behavioral neuroscience (PhD); bioresource engineering (MS); cell biology (MS, PhD); cellular and molecular pharmacology (PhD); ceramic and materials science and engineering (MS, PhD); chemical and biochemical engineering (MS, PhD); chemistry and physics of aerosol and hydrosol systems (MS, PhD); chemistry education (MST); civil and environmental engineering (MS, PhD); classics (MA, MAT, PhD); clinical microbiology (MS, PhD); clinical psychology (PhD); cognitive psychology (PhD); communication and information studies (PhD); communications and solid-state electronics (MS, PhD); comparative literature (PhD); comparative politics (PhD); composition (MA, PhD); computational fluid dynamics (MS, PhD); computational molecular biology (PhD); computer engineering (MS, PhD); computer science (MS, PhD); condensed matter physics (MS, PhD); control systems (MS, PhD); design and dynamics (MS, PhD); developmental biology (MS, PhD); digital signal processing (MS, PhD); diplomatic history (PhD); direct intervention in interpersonal situations (PhD); early American history (PhD); early modern European history (PhD); ecology and evolution (MS, PhD); economics (MA, PhD); educational policy (PhD); educational psychology (PhD); elementary particle physics (MS, PhD); endocrine control of growth and metabolism (MS, PhD); entomology (MS, PhD); environmental chemistry (MS, PhD); environmental microbiology (MS, PhD); environmental toxicology (MS, PhD); exposure assessment (PhD); fluid mechanics (MS, PhD); food science (M Phil, MS, PhD); French (MA, PhD); French studies (MAT); geography (MA, MS, PhD); geological sciences (MS, PhD); German (PhD); global/comparative history (PhD); heat transfer (MS, PhD); history (PhD); history of technology, medicine, and science (PhD); horticulture (MS, PhD); immunology (MS, PhD); industrial and systems engineering (MS, PhD); industrial pharmacy (MS, PhD); industrial relations and human resources (MS, PhD); industrial-occupational toxicology (MS, PhD); inorganic chemistry (MS, PhD); interdisciplinary developmental psychology (PhD); interdisciplinary health psychology (PhD); intermediate energy nuclear physics (MS); international relations (PhD); Italian (MA); Italian history (PhD); Italian literature and literary criticism (MA, PhD); language, literature and civilization (MAT); Latin American history (PhD); linguistics (PhD); literacy education (PhD); literature (MA, PhD); literatures in English (PhD); manufacturing systems (MS); mathematics (MS, PhD); mathematics education (PhD); mechanics (MS, PhD); medicinal chemistry (MS, PhD); medieval history (PhD); microbial biochemistry (MS, PhD); modern American history (PhD); modern British history (PhD); modern European history (PhD); molecular and cell biology (PhD); molecular biology (MS, PhD); molecular biology and biochemistry (MS, PhD); molecular genetics (MS, PhD); museum studies (MA); music history (MA, PhD); nuclear physics (MS, PhD); nutrition of ruminant and nonruminant animals (MS, PhD); nutritional sciences (MS, PhD); nutritional toxicology (MS, PhD); oceanography (MS, PhD); operations research (PhD); organic chemistry (MS, PhD); pathology (MS, PhD); pharmaceutical chemistry (MS, PhD); pharmaceutical toxicology (MS, PhD); pharmaceutics (MS, PhD); philosophy (PhD); physical chemistry (MS, PhD); physical metallurgy (MS, PhD); physics (MST); physiology and neurobiology (PhD); plant ecology (MS, PhD); plant genetics (PhD); plant physiology (MS, PhD); political and cultural history (PhD); political economy (PhD); political theory (PhD); polymer science (MS, PhD); production and management (MS); public law (PhD); quality and productivity management (MS); quality and reliability engineering (MS); reproductive endocrinology and neuroendocrinology (MS, PhD); social policy analysis and administration (PhD); social psychology (PhD); social work (PhD); sociology (MA, PhD); solid mechanics (MS, PhD); Spanish (MA, MAT, PhD); Spanish-American literature (MA, PhD); statistics (MS, PhD); structure and plant groups (MS, PhD); surface science (PhD); theoretical physics (MS, PhD); translation (MA); virology (MS, PhD); water and wastewater treatment (MS, PhD); water resources (MS, PhD); women and politics (PhD); women's and gender studies (MA); women's history (PhD); women's studies (MA). *Application deadline:* Applications are processed on a rolling basis. *Application fee:* $50. *Application Contact:* Dr. Donald J. Taylor, Director of Graduate Admissions, 732-932-7711, Fax: 732-932-8231, E-mail: kdc@rci.rutgers.edu. *Dean of the Graduate School,* Dr. Richard Falk, 732-932-7896.

Eagleton Institute of Politics Average age 24. Expenses: Contact institution. *Financial support:* In 2001–02, 16 students received support; fellowships, research assistantships, career-related internships or fieldwork, Federal Work-Study, institutionally sponsored loans, and tuition waivers (full and partial) available. Financial award application deadline: 3/1. *Degree program information:* Part-time programs available. Offers politics (MS). *Application deadline:* For fall admission, 3/1. *Application fee:* $40. *Application Contact:* Christine Lenart, Administrative Assistant, 732-828-2210 Ext. 244, Fax: 732-932-6778, E-mail: clenart@rci.rutgers.edu. *Program Director,* Ruth B. Mandel, 732-932-9384, Fax: 732-932-6778.

Graduate School of Applied and Professional Psychology Students: 94 full-time (63 women), 111 part-time (89 women). Average age 29. 381 applicants, 9% accepted. Expenses: Contact institution. *Financial support:* In 2001–02, 48 fellowships with tuition reimbursements (averaging $6,500 per year), 6 research assistantships with tuition reimbursements (averaging $11,513 per year), 3 teaching assistantships with full tuition reimbursements (averaging $12,000 per year) were awarded. Career-related internships or fieldwork, Federal Work-Study, institutionally sponsored loans, scholarships/grants, traineeships, and unspecified assistantships also available. Support available to part-time students. Financial award application deadline: 1/15; financial award applicants required to submit FAFSA. In 2001, 25 master's, 25 doctorates awarded. Offers applied and professional psychology (Psy M, Psy D); clinical psychology (Psy M, Psy D); organizational psychology (Psy M, Psy D); school psychology (Psy M, Psy D). *Application deadline:* For fall admission, 1/5. *Application fee:* $50. Electronic applications accepted. *Application Contact:* M. Ruth Peters, Associate Dean, 732-445-6116, Fax: 732-445-4888, E-mail: mpeters@rci.rutgers.edu. *Dean,* Sandra L. Harris, 732-445-2186, Fax: 732-445-4888, E-mail: sharris@rci.rutgers.edu.

Graduate School of Education 824 applicants, 65% accepted. Expenses: Contact institution. *Financial support:* In 2001–02, 188 students received support, including 10 fellowships with full and partial tuition reimbursements available (averaging $2,508 per year), 14 research assistantships with full tuition reimbursements available (averaging $14,000 per year), 15 teaching assistantships with full tuition reimbursements available (averaging $14,000 per year); career-related internships or fieldwork, Federal Work-Study, institutionally sponsored loans, and scholarships/grants also available. Support available to part-time students. Financial award application deadline: 3/1; financial award applicants required to submit FAFSA. In 2001, 303 master's, 29 doctorates awarded. *Degree program information:* Part-time and evening/weekend programs available. Postbaccalaureate distance learning degree programs offered. Offers adult and continuing education (Ed M, Ed D); counseling psychology (Ed M); early childhood/elementary education (Ed M, Ed D); education (Ed M, Ed D, PhD, Ed S); education administration (Ed M); educational administration and supervision (Ed M, Ed D, Ed S); educational statistics and measurement (Ed M); English as a second language education (Ed M, Ed D); English education (Ed M); language education (Ed M, Ed D); learning cognition and development (Ed M); literacy education (Ed M, Ed D); mathematics education (Ed M, Ed D); reading education (Ed M); school business administration (Ed M); science education (Ed M, Ed D); social and philosophical foundations of education (Ed M, Ed D, Ed S); social studies education (Ed M, Ed D, Ed S); special education (Ed M); vocational-technical education (Ed M, Ed D, Ed S). *Application deadline:* For fall admission, 3/1; for spring admission, 11/1. *Application fee:* $50. Electronic applications accepted. *Application Contact:* Paul Elwood, Associate Dean, 732-932-7496 Ext. 8104, Fax: 732-932-8206, E-mail: pelwood@rci.rutgers.edu. *Dean,* Dr. Louise Cherry Wilkinson, 732-932-7496 Ext. 8117.

Mason Gross School of the Arts Students: 154 full-time (77 women), 96 part-time (59 women). Average age 28. 556 applicants, 24% accepted. Expenses: Contact institution. *Financial support:* Fellowships, teaching assistantships, career-related internships or fieldwork, Federal Work-Study, institutionally sponsored loans, and tuition waivers (full and partial) available. Support available to part-time students. *Degree program information:* Part-time programs available. Offers acting (MFA); arts (MFA, MM, DMA, AD); design (MFA); directing (MFA); music (MM, DMA, AD); playwriting (MFA); visual arts (MFA). *Application deadline:* Applications are processed on a rolling basis. *Application fee:* $50. *Application Contact:* Dr. Donald J. Taylor, Director of Graduate Admissions, 732-932-7711, Fax: 732-932-8231, E-mail: kdc@rci.rutgers.edu. *Dean,* George B. Stauffer, 732-932-9360 Ext. 507, Fax: 732-932-8794.

Programs in Engineering Expenses: Contact institution. Offers engineering (MS, PhD). Degrees offered through the Graduate School.

School of Communication, Information and Library Studies Students: 90 full-time (72 women), 303 part-time (242 women). Average age 32. 341 applicants, 65% accepted. Expenses: Contact institution. *Financial support:* Fellowships, research assistantships, teaching assistantships, career-related internships or fieldwork, Federal Work-Study, institutionally sponsored loans, and tuition waivers (full) available. Support available to part-time students. Financial award application deadline: 3/1; financial award applicants required to submit FAFSA. In 2001, 155 degrees awarded. *Degree program information:* Part-time programs available. Offers communication and information studies (MCIS); library and information science (MLS). *Application deadline:* For fall admission, 5/1; for spring admission, 11/1. Applications are processed on a rolling basis. *Application fee:* $50. *Application Contact:* Dr. Donald J. Taylor, Director of Graduate Admissions, 732-932-7711, Fax: 732-932-8231, E-mail: kdc@rci.rutgers.edu. *Dean,* Dr. Friedrich W. Gustav, 732-932-7500, Fax: 732-932-6916, E-mail: gusf@scils.rutgers.edu.

School of Management and Labor Relations Students: 77 full-time (46 women), 203 part-time (157 women). Average age 30. Expenses: Contact institution. *Financial support:* Fellowships, research assistantships with tuition reimbursements, teaching assistantships with tuition reimbursements, career-related internships or fieldwork, Federal Work-Study, and tuition waivers (full and partial) available. In 2001, 77 degrees awarded. *Degree program information:* Part-time and evening/weekend programs available. Offers human resource management (MHRM); labor and employment relations (MLER); management and labor relations (MHRM, MLER, PhD). *Application deadline:* Applications are processed on a rolling basis. *Application fee:* $50. Electronic applications accepted. *Dean,* Dr. John F. Burton, 732-445-5993, Fax: 732-445-4188, E-mail: jfburton@rci.rutgers.edu.

School of Social Work Students: 246 full-time (224 women), 597 part-time (515 women). Average age 32. 680 applicants, 36% accepted. Expenses: Contact institution. *Financial support:* Fellowships, research assistantships, teaching assistantships, career-related internships or fieldwork, Federal Work-Study, scholarships/grants, and traineeships available. Support available to part-time students. Financial award applicants required to submit FAFSA. In 2001, 288 degrees awarded. *Degree program information:* Part-time programs available. Offers social work (MSW, PhD). PhD offered through the Graduate School. *Application deadline:* For spring admission, 3/1 (priority date). Applications are processed on a rolling basis. *Application fee:* $50. Electronic applications accepted. *Application Contact:* Noah Hart, Acting Assistant Dean, 732-932-7126, Fax: 732-932-8181, E-mail: noahhart@rci.rutgers.edu. *Dean,* Mary Edna Davidson, 732-932-7253, Fax: 732-932-8181, E-mail: davidsn@rci.rutgers.edu.

RYERSON UNIVERSITY, Toronto, ON M5B 2K3, Canada

General Information Province-supported, coed, comprehensive institution.

GRADUATE UNITS

School of Graduate Studies

SACRED HEART MAJOR SEMINARY, Detroit, MI 48206-1799

General Information Independent-religious, coed, comprehensive institution. *Enrollment:* 41 full-time matriculated graduate/professional students, 87 part-time matriculated graduate/professional students (50 women). *Enrollment by degree level:* 41 first professional, 87 master's. *Graduate faculty:* 19 full-time (5 women), 6 part-time/adjunct (0 women). *Tuition:* Full-time $9,254; part-time $232 per credit. *Required fees:* $40; $20 per term. One-time fee: $30. *Graduate housing:* Room and/or apartments guaranteed to single students; on-campus housing not available to married students. Typical cost: $5,306 (including board). Housing application deadline: 8/1. *Student services:* Writing training. *Library facilities:* Szoka Library. *Collection:* 120,000 titles, 495 serial subscriptions.

Computer facilities: 8 computers available on campus for general student use.

General Application Contact: Fr. Patrick Halfpenny, Vice Rector, 313-883-8500, Fax: 313-868-6440.

GRADUATE UNITS

Graduate School of Theology Students: 41 full-time (0 women), 87 part-time (50 women); includes 19 minority (8 African Americans, 5 Asian Americans or Pacific Islanders, 4 Hispanic Americans, 2 Native Americans), 5 international. *Faculty:* 19 full-time (5 women), 6 part-time/adjunct (0 women). Expenses: Contact institution. *Financial support:* In 2001–02, 39 students received support. Institutionally sponsored loans and scholarships/grants available. Financial award application deadline: 4/1; financial award applicants required to submit FAFSA. In 2001, 7 first professional degrees, 13 master's awarded. *Degree program information:* Part-time and evening/weekend programs available. Offers pastoral studies (MAPS); theology (M Div, MA). *Application deadline:* For fall admission, 9/5; for winter admission, 12/20 (priority date). *Application fee:* $30. *Application Contact:* Dr. Peter Williamson, Assistant Dean, 313-883-8500, Fax: 313-868-6440. *Dean of Studies,* Rev. Steven Boguslawski, OP, 313-883-8500, Fax: 313-868-6440.

SACRED HEART SCHOOL OF THEOLOGY, Hales Corners, WI 53130-0429

General Information Independent-religious, coed, primarily men, graduate-only institution. *Enrollment by degree level:* 96 first professional, 17 master's. *Graduate faculty:* 33 full-time (10 women), 9 part-time/adjunct (5 women). *Tuition:* Part-time $325 per credit. *Required fees:* $125. One-time fee: $325. *Graduate housing:* Room and/or apartments guaranteed to single students; on-campus housing not available to married students. Typical cost: $6,600 (including board). *Student services:* Campus employment opportunities, career counseling, disabled student services, exercise/wellness program, free psychological counseling, international student services, multicultural affairs office, writing training. *Library facilities:* Leo Dehon Library. *Online resources:* library catalog, web page, access to other libraries' catalogs. *Collection:* 99,540 titles, 450 serial subscriptions, 16,404 audiovisual materials.

Computer facilities: 6 computers available on campus for general student use. A campuswide network can be accessed from student residence rooms and from off campus. Internet access is available. *Web address:* http://www.shst.edu.

General Application Contact: Rev. Thomas L. Knoebel, Director of Admissions, 414-425-8300 Ext. 6984, Fax: 414-529-6999, E-mail: tknoebel@shst.edu.

GRADUATE UNITS

Professional Program Students: 83 full-time (1 woman), 30 part-time (15 women); includes 21 minority (4 African Americans, 4 Asian Americans or Pacific Islanders, 13 Hispanic Americans), 1 international. Average age 44. 35 applicants, 94% accepted. *Faculty:* 33 full-time (10 women), 9 part-time/adjunct (5 women). Expenses: Contact institution. *Financial support:* In 2001–02, 6 students received support. Career-related internships or fieldwork and scholarships/grants available. Financial award application deadline: 9/30; financial award applicants required to submit FAFSA. In 2001, 24 first professional degrees, 7 master's awarded. *Degree program information:* Part-time programs available. Offers theology (M Div, MA).

Sacred Heart School of Theology (continued)

Application deadline: For fall admission, 8/25; for spring admission, 12/20. *Application fee:* $50. *Application Contact:* Rev. Thomas L. Knoebel, Director of Admissions, 414-425-8300 Ext. 6984, Fax: 414-529-6999, E-mail: tknoebel@shst.edu. *President/Rector,* Rev. James D. Brackin, SCJ, 414-425-8300 Ext. 6986, Fax: 414-529-6999, E-mail: jbrackin@shst.edu.

SACRED HEART UNIVERSITY, Fairfield, CT 06432-1000

General Information Independent-religious, coed, comprehensive institution. *Enrollment:* 420 full-time matriculated graduate/professional students (304 women), 1,402 part-time matriculated graduate/professional students (895 women). *Enrollment by degree level:* 1,822 master's. *Graduate faculty:* 153 full-time, 302 part-time/adjunct. *Tuition:* Full-time $16,128; part-time $435 per credit. *Required fees:* $285 per term. *Graduate housing:* Room and/or apartments available on a first-come, first-served basis to single students; on-campus housing not available to married students. Typical cost: $5,738 per year ($7,998 including board). *Student services:* Campus employment opportunities, campus safety program, career counseling, free psychological counseling, international student services, low-cost health insurance. *Library facilities:* Ryan-Matura Library. *Online resources:* library catalog, web page, access to other libraries' catalogs. *Collection:* 141,431 titles, 2,911 serial subscriptions, 11,594 audiovisual materials.

Computer facilities: 110 computers available on campus for general student use. A campuswide network can be accessed from student residence rooms and from off campus. Internet access and online class registration, Intranet are available. *Web address:* http://www.sacredheart.edu/.

General Application Contact: Alexis Haakonsen, Interim Dean of Graduate Admissions, 203-365-7619, Fax: 203-365-4732, E-mail: gradstudies@sacredheart.edu.

GRADUATE UNITS

Graduate Studies Students: 420 full-time (304 women), 1,402 part-time (895 women); includes 191 minority (71 African Americans, 70 Asian Americans or Pacific Islanders, 42 Hispanic Americans, 8 Native Americans), 30 international. Average age 31. 712 applicants, 57% accepted. Expenses: Contact institution. *Financial support:* Career-related internships or fieldwork, institutionally sponsored loans, traineeships, tuition waivers (partial), and unspecified assistantships available. Support available to part-time students. Financial award applicants required to submit FAFSA. In 2001, 497 degrees awarded. *Degree program information:* Part-time and evening/weekend programs available. Postbaccalaureate distance learning degree programs offered (minimal on-campus study). *Application deadline:* Applications are processed on a rolling basis. *Application fee:* $45 ($100 for international students). *Application Contact:* Alexis Haakonsen, Interim Director of Graduate Admissions, 203-365-7619, Fax: 203-365-4732, E-mail: gradstudies@sacredheart.edu.

College of Arts and Sciences Students: 16 full-time, 210 part-time; includes 64 minority (18 African Americans, 38 Asian Americans or Pacific Islanders, 6 Hispanic Americans, 2 Native Americans), 17 international. Average age 32. 95 applicants, 33% accepted. Expenses: Contact institution. *Financial support:* Career-related internships or fieldwork and unspecified assistantships available. Support available to part-time students. Financial award applicants required to submit FAFSA. In 2001, 13 degrees awarded. *Degree program information:* Part-time and evening/weekend programs available. Offers arts and sciences (MA, MS, CPS); chemistry (MS); computer science (MS, CPS); e-commerce (CPS); information technology (MS, CPS); multimedia (CPS); religious studies (MA). *Application deadline:* Applications are processed on a rolling basis. *Application fee:* $45 ($100 for international students). *Application Contact:* Alexis Haakonsen, Interim Director of Graduate Admissions, 203-365-7619, Fax: 203-365-4732, E-mail: gradstudies@sacredheart.edu. *Dean,* Dr. Claire Paolini, 203-396-8020.

College of Business Students: 38 full-time (20 women), 369 part-time (189 women); includes 74 minority (30 African Americans, 22 Asian Americans or Pacific Islanders, 20 Hispanic Americans, 2 Native Americans), 10 international. Average age 36. 122 applicants, 56% accepted. Expenses: Contact institution. *Financial support:* In 2001–02, 10 students received support. Career-related internships or fieldwork and unspecified assistantships available. Support available to part-time students. Financial award applicants required to submit FAFSA. In 2001, 147 degrees awarded. *Degree program information:* Part-time and evening/weekend programs available. Offers business administration (MBA); health care administration (MBA). *Application deadline:* Applications are processed on a rolling basis. *Application fee:* $45 ($100 for international students). *Application Contact:* Doug Pearson, Assistant Director of Graduate Admissions, 203-396-8259, Fax: 203-365-4732, E-mail: pearsond@sacredheart.edu. *Interim Director,* Dr. Mary Trefry, 203-371-7850, E-mail: trefrym@sacredheart.edu.

College of Education and Health Professions Students: 366 full-time (275 women), 823 part-time (624 women); includes 53 minority (23 African Americans, 9 Asian Americans or Pacific Islanders, 17 Hispanic Americans, 4 Native Americans), 3 international. Average age 32. 494 applicants, 62% accepted. Expenses: Contact institution. *Financial support:* Research assistantships, career-related internships or fieldwork, traineeships, tuition waivers (partial), and unspecified assistantships available. Support available to part-time students. Financial award applicants required to submit FAFSA. In 2001, 328 master's, 94 other advanced degrees awarded. *Degree program information:* Part-time and evening/weekend programs available. Offers administration (CAS); education (CAS); education and health professions (MAT, MOT, MSN, MSPT, CAS); elementary education (MAT); family nurse practitioner (MSN); occupational therapy (MOT); patient care services (MSN); physical therapy (MSPT); secondary education (MAT). *Application deadline:* Applications are processed on a rolling basis. *Application fee:* $45 ($100 for international students). *Application Contact:* Alexis Haakonsen, Interim Director of Graduate Admissions, 203-365-7619, Fax: 203-365-4732, E-mail: gradstudies@sacredheart.edu. *Dean,* Dr. Patricia Walker, 203-396-8024.

See in-depth description on page 1061.

SAGE GRADUATE SCHOOL, Troy, NY 12180-4115

General Information Independent, coed, graduate-only institution. *Enrollment by degree level:* 984 master's. *Graduate faculty:* 51 full-time (39 women), 21 part-time/adjunct (9 women). *Tuition:* Full-time $7,600. *Required fees:* $100. *Graduate housing:* Room and/or apartments available on a first-come, first-served basis to single students; on-campus housing not available to married students. Typical cost: $2,890 per year ($6,200 including board). Housing application deadline: 5/1. *Student services:* Career counseling, low-cost health insurance. *Library facilities:* James Wheelock Clark Library plus 1 other. *Online resources:* library catalog, web page. *Collection:* 373,106 titles, 1,057 serial subscriptions, 34,260 audiovisual materials. *Research affiliation:* Enlarged City School District of Troy (education), Albany Medical College (occupational therapy), Samaritan Hospital (nursing), Ellis Hospital (nursing), Samuel Stratton Veterans Administration Hospital (nursing).

Computer facilities: 286 computers available on campus for general student use. A campuswide network can be accessed from student residence rooms and from off campus. Internet access is available. *Web address:* http://www.sage.edu/.

General Application Contact: Melissa M. Robertson, Associate Director of Admissions, 518-244-6878, Fax: 518-244-6880, E-mail: sgsadm@sage.edu.

GRADUATE UNITS

Graduate School Students: 258 full-time (221 women), 726 part-time (569 women); includes 48 minority (26 African Americans, 10 Asian Americans or Pacific Islanders, 10 Hispanic Americans, 2 Native Americans) Average age 32. 321 applicants, 94% accepted, 223 enrolled. *Faculty:* 51 full-time (39 women), 21 part-time/adjunct (9 women). Expenses: Contact institution. *Financial support:* Research assistantships, career-related internships or fieldwork, scholarships/grants, and unspecified assistantships available. Support available to part-time students. Financial award application deadline: 3/1; financial award applicants required to submit FAFSA. In 2001, 328 degrees awarded. *Degree program information:* Part-time and evening/weekend programs available. Offers physical therapy (MS). *Application deadline:* Applications are processed on a rolling basis. *Application fee:* $40. *Application Contact:* Melissa M. Robertson, Associate Director of Admissions, 518-244-6878, Fax: 518-244-6880, E-mail: sgsadm@sage.edu. *Dean,* Dr. Connell G. Frazer, 518-244-2264, E-mail: frazec@sage.edu.

Division of Education Students: 105 full-time (93 women), 276 part-time (215 women); includes 11 minority (5 African Americans, 1 Asian American or Pacific Islander, 5 Hispanic Americans) Average age 30. 151 applicants, 98% accepted, 107 enrolled. *Faculty:* 13 full-time (6 women), 11 part-time/adjunct (6 women). Expenses: Contact institution. *Financial support:* Research assistantships, career-related internships or fieldwork, scholarships/grants, and unspecified assistantships available. Support available to part-time students. Financial award application deadline: 3/1; financial award applicants required to submit FAFSA. In 2001, 127 degrees awarded. *Degree program information:* Part-time and evening/weekend programs available. Offers biology (MAT); childhood education (MS Ed); childhood special education (MS Ed); English (MAT); guidance and counseling (MS, PMC); health education (MS); literacy (MS Ed); literacy/childhood special education (MS Ed); mathematics (MAT); school health education (MS); secondary education (MS Ed); social studies (MAT); teaching (MAT). *Application fee:* $40. *Application Contact:* Melissa M. Robertson, Associate Director of Admissions, 518-244-6878, Fax: 518-244-6880, E-mail: sgsadm@sage.edu. *Chair,* Dr. Kathleen Gormley, 518-244-2326, Fax: 518-244-2334, E-mail: gormlk@sage.edu.

Division of Management, Communications and Legal Studies Students: 28 full-time (20 women), 136 part-time (98 women); includes 11 minority (6 African Americans, 4 Asian Americans or Pacific Islanders, 1 Hispanic American) Average age 33. 55 applicants, 96% accepted, 43 enrolled. *Faculty:* 6 full-time (3 women), 6 part-time/adjunct (0 women). Expenses: Contact institution. *Financial support:* Research assistantships, career-related internships or fieldwork, scholarships/grants, and unspecified assistantships available. Support available to part-time students. Financial award application deadline: 3/1; financial award applicants required to submit FAFSA. In 2001, 66 degrees awarded. *Degree program information:* Part-time and evening/weekend programs available. Offers communications (MBA, MS); finance (MBA); gerontology (MS); health education (MS); human resources management (MBA); human services administration (MS); management (MS); management, communications and legal studies (MBA, MS); marketing (MBA); nutrition and dietetics (MS); public management (MS). *Application fee:* $40. *Application Contact:* Melissa M. Robertson, Associate Director of Admissions, 518-244-6878, Fax: 518-244-6880, E-mail: sgsadm@sage.edu. *Director,* Dr. Michael Hall, 518-292-1794, Fax: 518-292-5414, E-mail: hallm@sage.edu.

Division of Nursing Students: 34 full-time (28 women), 59 part-time (58 women); includes 3 minority (all African Americans) Average age 41. 15 applicants, 100% accepted, 11 enrolled. *Faculty:* 12 full-time (all women), 3 part-time/adjunct (2 women). Expenses: Contact institution. *Financial support:* Career-related internships or fieldwork, Federal Work-Study, scholarships/grants, and unspecified assistantships available. Financial award application deadline: 3/1; financial award applicants required to submit FAFSA. In 2001, 36 degrees awarded. *Degree program information:* Part-time and evening/weekend programs available. Offers adult health (MS); adult nurse practitioner (MS); community health nursing (MS); family nurse practitioner (MS); nursing (PMC); psychiatric–mental health nurse practitioner (MS); psychology mental health (MS). *Application fee:* $40. *Application Contact:* Melissa M. Robertson, Associate Director of Admissions, 518-244-6878, Fax: 518-244-6880, E-mail: sgsadm@sage.edu. *Director,* Dr. Glenda Kelman, 518-244-2384, E-mail: kelmag@sage.edu.

Division of Psychology Students: 19 full-time (17 women), 93 part-time (74 women); includes 8 minority (5 African Americans, 3 Hispanic Americans) Average age 32. 65 applicants, 85% accepted, 30 enrolled. *Faculty:* 9 full-time (all women), 1 (woman) part-time/adjunct. Expenses: Contact institution. *Financial support:* Career-related internships or fieldwork, scholarships/grants, and unspecified assistantships available. Support available to part-time students. Financial award application deadline: 3/1; financial award applicants required to submit FAFSA. In 2001, 17 degrees awarded. *Degree program information:* Part-time and evening/weekend programs available. Offers chemical dependence (MA); child care and children's services (MA); community counseling (MA); community health (MA); community psychology (MA); forensic psychology (MA); general psychology (MA); visual art therapy (MA). *Application fee:* $40. *Application Contact:* Melissa M. Robertson, Associate Director of Admissions, 518-244-6878, Fax: 518-244-6880, E-mail: sgsadm@sage.edu. *Director,* Dr. Sam Hill, 518-244-2227, Fax: 518-244-4545, E-mail: hills@sage.edu.

See in-depth description on page 1063.

SAGINAW VALLEY STATE UNIVERSITY, University Center, MI 48710

General Information State-supported, coed, comprehensive institution. *Enrollment:* 489 full-time matriculated graduate/professional students (338 women), 1,127 part-time matriculated graduate/professional students (818 women). *Enrollment by degree level:* 1,569 master's, 47 other advanced degrees. *Graduate faculty:* 108 full-time (48 women), 14 part-time/adjunct (8 women). Tuition, state resident: full-time $2,263; part-time $189 per credit. Tuition, nonresident: full-time $4,480; part-time $373 per credit. *Required fees:* $201; $17 per credit. *Graduate housing:* Rooms and/or apartments available on a first-come, first-served basis to single and married students. Typical cost: $4,175 per year ($5,200 including board) for single students; $4,175 per year ($5,200 including board) for married students. Room and board charges vary according to board plan, campus/location and housing facility selected. Housing application deadline: 6/5. *Student services:* Campus employment opportunities, career counseling, disabled student services, free psychological counseling, international student services, multicultural affairs office, writing training. *Library facilities:* Zahnow Library. *Online resources:* library catalog, web page, access to other libraries' catalogs. *Collection:* 3,119 serial subscriptions, 19,231 audiovisual materials. *Research affiliation:* Pharmacia and Upjohn Company, NASA, Dow and International Scholars, Center for Health Professions, Wickson-Nickless Distinguished Lectureship.

Computer facilities: 408 computers available on campus for general student use. A campuswide network can be accessed from off campus. Internet access is available. *Web address:* http://www.svsu.edu/.

General Application Contact: Barb Sageman, Director, Graduate Admissions, 989-249-1696, Fax: 989-790-0180, E-mail: gradadm@svsu.edu.

GRADUATE UNITS

College of Arts and Behavioral Sciences Students: 88 full-time (52 women), 69 part-time (45 women); includes 24 minority (16 African Americans, 3 Asian Americans or Pacific Islanders, 3 Hispanic Americans, 2 Native Americans), 34 international. Average age 33. 76 applicants, 82% accepted, 37 enrolled. *Faculty:* 16 full-time (3 women). Expenses: Contact institution. *Financial support:* Federal Work-Study available. Support available to part-time students. Financial award applicants required to submit FAFSA. In 2001, 35 degrees awarded. *Degree program information:* Part-time and evening/weekend programs available. Offers arts and behavioral sciences (MA); communication and multimedia (MA); leadership in public administration (MA). *Application deadline:* Applications are processed on a rolling basis. *Application fee:* $25. *Application Contact:* Barb Sageman, Director, Graduate Admissions, 989-249-1696, Fax: 989-790-0180, E-mail: gradadm@svsu.edu. *Dean,* Dr. Donald Bachand, 989-790-4062, E-mail: abs-dean@svsu.edu.

College of Business and Management Students: 39 full-time (17 women), 73 part-time (34 women); includes 6 minority (5 African Americans, 1 Asian American or Pacific Islander), 37 international. Average age 31. 45 applicants, 60% accepted, 19 enrolled. *Faculty:* 12 full-time (3 women). Expenses: Contact institution. *Financial support:* In 2001–02, 1 research assistantship with full tuition reimbursement (averaging $5,000 per year) was awarded; fellowships with partial tuition reimbursements, Federal Work-Study also available. Support available to part-time students. Financial award application deadline: 4/1; financial award applicants required to submit FAFSA. In 2001, 47 degrees awarded. *Degree program information:* Part-time and evening/weekend programs available. Offers business and management (MBA). *Application deadline:* Applications are processed on a rolling basis. *Application fee:* $25. *Application Contact:* Barb Sageman, Director, Graduate Admissions, 989-249-

1696, Fax: 989-790-0180, E-mail: gradadm@svsu.edu. *Dean*, Dr. Paul J. Useldіng, 989-790-4064, Fax: 989-249-1960, E-mail: cbmdean@svsu.edu.

College of Education Students: 309 full-time (230 women), 925 part-time (698 women); includes 43 minority (26 African Americans, 4 Asian Americans or Pacific Islanders, 10 Hispanic Americans, 3 Native Americans), 1 international. Average age 34. 474 applicants, 100% accepted, 175 enrolled. *Faculty:* 32 full-time (20 women). Expenses: Contact institution. *Financial support:* Federal Work-Study available. Support available to part-time students. Financial award applicants required to submit FAFSA. In 2001, 365 master's, 22 other advanced degrees awarded. *Degree program information:* Part-time and evening/weekend programs available. Postbaccalaureate distance learning degree programs offered (minimal on-campus study). Offers chief business officers (M Ed); early childhood education (MAT); education (M Ed, MAT, Ed S); education leadership (Ed S); educational administration and supervision (M Ed); elementary classroom teaching (MAT); learning and behavioral disorders (MAT); middle school (MAT); middle school classroom teaching (MAT); principalship (M Ed); reading (MAT); secondary classroom teaching (MAT); secondary school (MAT); superintendency (M Ed). *Application deadline:* Applications are processed on a rolling basis. *Application fee:* $25. *Application Contact:* Jeanne Chipman, Certification Officer, 989-790-4057, Fax: 989-790-4385, E-mail: jdc@svsu.edu. *Interim Dean*, Dr. Ken Wahl, 989-790-4058, Fax: 989-790-4385, E-mail: wahl@svsu.edu.

College of Science, Engineering, and Technology Students: 19 full-time (7 women), 23 part-time (5 women); includes 5 minority (3 African Americans, 1 Asian American or Pacific Islander, 1 Hispanic American), 5 international. Average age 33. 20 applicants, 75% accepted, 6 enrolled. *Faculty:* 11 full-time (1 woman). Expenses: Contact institution. *Financial support:* In 2001–02, 1 fellowship with partial tuition reimbursement, 1 research assistantship with full tuition reimbursement (averaging $2,500 per year) were awarded. Federal Work-Study also available. Support available to part-time students. Financial award application deadline: 4/1; financial award applicants required to submit FAFSA. In 2001, 10 degrees awarded. *Degree program information:* Part-time and evening/weekend programs available. Offers science, engineering, and technology (MS); technological processes (MS). *Application deadline:* Applications are processed on a rolling basis. *Application fee:* $25. *Application Contact:* Barb Sageman, Director, Graduate Admissions, 989-249-1696, Fax: 989-790-0180, E-mail: gradadm@svsu.edu. *Dean*, Dr. Thomas Kullgren, 989-790-4144, Fax: 989-790-2717, E-mail: kullgren@svsu.edu.

Crystal M. Lange College of Nursing and Health Sciences Students: 34 full-time (32 women), 37 part-time (36 women); includes 4 minority (2 African Americans, 1 Asian American or Pacific Islander, 1 Native American), 1 international. Average age 40. 19 applicants, 89% accepted, 11 enrolled. *Faculty:* 7 full-time (6 women). Expenses: Contact institution. *Financial support:* Fellowships with partial tuition reimbursements, research assistantships with full tuition reimbursements, Federal Work-Study available. Support available to part-time students. Financial award application deadline: 4/1; financial award applicants required to submit FAFSA. In 2001, 11 degrees awarded. *Degree program information:* Part-time and evening/weekend programs available. Offers client care management (MSN); clinical nurse specialist (MSN); nurse practitioner (MSN); nursing (MSN); nursing education (MSN). *Application deadline:* Applications are processed on a rolling basis. *Application fee:* $25. *Application Contact:* Barb Sageman, Director, Graduate Admissions, 989-249-1696, Fax: 989-790-0180, E-mail: gradadm@svsu.edu. *Dean*, Dr. Cheryl Easley, 989-790-4145, Fax: 989-790-1978.

ST. AMBROSE UNIVERSITY, Davenport, IA 52803-2898

General Information Independent-religious, coed, comprehensive institution. *Enrollment:* 325 full-time matriculated graduate/professional students (207 women), 695 part-time matriculated graduate/professional students (376 women). *Enrollment by degree level:* 996 master's, 24 doctoral. *Graduate faculty:* 63 full-time (19 women), 42 part-time/adjunct (19 women). *Tuition:* Full-time $8,280; part-time $456 per credit. One-time fee: $100. Tuition and fees vary according to degree level and program. *Graduate housing:* Room and/or apartments available on a first-come, first-served basis to single students; on-campus housing not available to married students. Typical cost: $2,420 per year ($5,340 including board). Room and board charges vary according to board plan and housing facility selected. Housing application deadline: 8/15. *Student services:* Campus employment opportunities, campus safety program, career counseling, child daycare facilities, disabled student services, free psychological counseling, international student services, teacher training, writing training. *Library facilities:* O'Keefe Library plus 1 other. *Online resources:* library catalog, web page, access to other libraries' catalogs. *Collection:* 198,391 titles, 3,261 serial subscriptions, 1,953 audiovisual materials.

Computer facilities: 190 computers available on campus for general student use. A campuswide network can be accessed from student residence rooms and from off campus. Internet access and online class registration, on-line course syllabi, class listings are available. *Web address:* http://www.sau.edu/.

General Application Contact: Suzanne Humphrey, Assistant Dean for Graduate Studies, 563-333-6308, Fax: 563-333-6243, E-mail: shumphrey@sau.edu.

GRADUATE UNITS

College of Arts and Sciences Students: 58 full-time (46 women), 73 part-time (41 women); includes 14 minority (7 African Americans, 1 Asian American or Pacific Islander, 6 Hispanic Americans), 1 international. Average age 38. 68 applicants, 93% accepted, 53 enrolled. *Faculty:* 12 full-time (4 women), 6 part-time/adjunct (4 women). Expenses: Contact institution. *Financial support:* In 2001–02, 96 students received support, including 2 research assistantships with partial tuition reimbursements available (averaging $2,000 per year); career-related internships or fieldwork, scholarships/grants, and tuition waivers (partial) also available. Support available to part-time students. Financial award application deadline: 8/15; financial award applicants required to submit FAFSA. In 2001, 35 degrees awarded. *Degree program information:* Part-time and evening/weekend programs available. Offers arts and sciences (MOL, MPS, MSW); leadership studies (MOL); pastoral studies (MPS); social work (MSW). *Application deadline:* For fall admission, 8/1 (priority date); for winter admission, 12/15 (priority date); for spring admission, 1/1 (priority date). Applications are processed on a rolling basis. *Application fee:* $25. Electronic applications accepted. *Application Contact:* Suzanne Humphrey, Assistant Dean for Graduate Studies, 563-333-6308, Fax: 563-333-6243, E-mail: shumphrey@sau.edu. *Dean*, Dr. Paul Koch, 563-333-6196, Fax: 563-333-6297, E-mail: pkoch@saunix.sau.edu.

College of Business Students: 136 full-time (61 women), 477 part-time (222 women); includes 34 minority (17 African Americans, 6 Asian Americans or Pacific Islanders, 11 Hispanic Americans), 15 international. Average age 34. 264 applicants, 97% accepted, 196 enrolled. *Faculty:* 28 full-time (4 women), 25 part-time/adjunct (6 women). Expenses: Contact institution. *Financial support:* In 2001–02, 453 students received support, including 18 research assistantships with partial tuition reimbursements available (averaging $2,736 per year); career-related internships or fieldwork, scholarships/grants, and tuition waivers (partial) also available. Support available to part-time students. Financial award application deadline: 3/15; financial award applicants required to submit FAFSA. In 2001, 159 master's awarded. *Degree program information:* Part-time and evening/weekend programs available. Offers accounting (M Ac); business (M Ac, MBA, MBAH, DBA); business administration (DBA); health care administration (MBAH); management generalist (MBA); technical management (MBA). *Application deadline:* For fall admission, 8/15 (priority date); for winter admission, 12/15; for spring admission, 1/1. Applications are processed on a rolling basis. *Application fee:* $25. Electronic applications accepted. *Dean*, Dr. Richard M. Dienesch, 563-333-6270, Fax: 563-333-6268.

College of Human Services Students: 131 full-time (101 women), 145 part-time (113 women); includes 6 minority (3 African Americans, 1 Asian American or Pacific Islander, 2 Hispanic Americans) Average age 30. 264 applicants, 87% accepted, 183 enrolled. *Faculty:* 23 full-time (11 women), 11 part-time/adjunct (9 women). Expenses: Contact institution. *Financial support:* In 2001–02, 218 students received support, including 20 research assistantships with partial tuition reimbursements available (averaging $2,280 per year); career-related internships or fieldwork, scholarships/grants, tuition waivers (full and partial), and unspecified assistantships also available. Support available to part-time students. Financial award application deadline: 3/15; financial award applicants required to submit FAFSA. In 2001, 46 degrees awarded. *Degree program information:* Part-time and evening/weekend programs available. Postbaccalaureate distance learning degree programs offered (no on-campus study). Offers criminal justice (MCJ); human services (M Ed, MCJ, MOT, MPT, MS, MSITM, DPT); information technology management (MSITM); juvenile justice (MCJ); occupational therapy (MOT); physical therapy (DPT); special education (M Ed). *Application deadline:* For fall admission, 8/15 (priority date); for winter admission, 12/15 (priority date); for spring admission, 1/1 (priority date). Applications are processed on a rolling basis. *Application fee:* $25. Electronic applications accepted. *Application Contact:* Suzanne Humphrey, Assistant Dean for Graduate Studies, 563-333-6308, Fax: 563-333-6243, E-mail: shumphrey@sau.edu. *Dean*, Dr. Daniel Bozik, 563-333-6137.

ST. ANDREW'S COLLEGE, Saskatoon, SK S7N 0W3, Canada

General Information Independent-religious, coed, graduate-only institution.

GRADUATE UNITS

Graduate Programs in Theology Offers theology (M Div, MPC, MTS, STM).

ST. ANDREW'S COLLEGE IN WINNIPEG, Winnipeg, MB R3T 2M7, Canada

General Information Independent-religious, coed, primarily men, graduate-only institution. *Graduate housing:* Rooms and/or apartments available to single and married students. Housing application deadline: 7/31.

GRADUATE UNITS

Graduate Programs Offers theology (M Div).

ST. AUGUSTINE'S SEMINARY OF TORONTO, Scarborough, ON M1M 1M3, Canada

General Information Independent-religious, coed, primarily men, graduate-only institution. *Enrollment by degree level:* 75 first professional, 75 master's. *Graduate faculty:* 12 full-time (4 women), 21 part-time/adjunct (8 women). *Graduate tuition:* Tuition and fees charges are reported in Canadian dollars. *Tuition:* Full-time $4,500 Canadian dollars; part-time $423 Canadian dollars per course. *Required fees:* $323 Canadian dollars; $8 Canadian dollars per course. $15 Canadian dollars per term. *Graduate housing:* On-campus housing not available. *Library facilities:* St. Augustine's Seminary Library. *Online resources:* library catalog, access to other libraries' catalogs. *Collection:* 35,406 titles, 203 serial subscriptions, 829 audiovisual materials.

Computer facilities: 2 computers available on campus for general student use. A campuswide network can be accessed from student residence rooms and from off campus. Internet access is available. *Web address:* http://www.staugustines.on.ca/.

General Application Contact: Theresa Mary Vicioso, Registrar/Administrative Assistant to the Dean of Studies, 416-261-7207 Ext. 230, Fax: 416-261-2529, E-mail: t.vicioso@utoronto.ca.

GRADUATE UNITS

Graduate and Professional Programs Students: 69 full-time (0 women), 81 part-time (19 women); includes 26 minority (4 African Americans, 19 Asian Americans or Pacific Islanders, 3 Hispanic Americans), 27 international. Average age 38. 53 applicants, 92% accepted. *Faculty:* 12 full-time (4 women), 21 part-time/adjunct (8 women). Expenses: Contact institution. In 2001, 9 first professional degrees, 13 master's awarded. *Degree program information:* Part-time and evening/weekend programs available. *Application deadline:* For fall admission, 7/15 (priority date); for winter admission, 11/15 (priority date); for spring admission, 4/15 (priority date). *Application fee:* $25 Canadian dollars. *Application Contact:* Theresa Mary Vicioso, Registrar/Administrative Assistant to the Dean of Studies, 416-261-7207 Ext. 230, Fax: 416-261-2529, E-mail: t.vicioso@utoronto.ca. *Dean of Studies*, 416-261-7207, Fax: 416-261-2529.

SAINT BERNARD'S SCHOOL OF THEOLOGY AND MINISTRY, Rochester, NY 14620-2545

General Information Independent-religious, coed, graduate-only institution. *Enrollment by degree level:* 17 first professional, 66 master's, 8 other advanced degrees. *Graduate faculty:* 6 full-time (3 women), 14 part-time/adjunct (3 women). *Tuition:* Part-time $1,020 per course. *Required fees:* $30 per semester. *Graduate housing:* Rooms and/or apartments available to single students and available on a first-come, first-served basis to married students. *Student services:* Writing training. *Library facilities:* Ambrose Swasey Library. *Online resources:* library catalog, access to other libraries' catalogs. *Collection:* 287,954 titles, 622 serial subscriptions, 3,620 audiovisual materials. *Research affiliation:* Colgate Rochester Divinity School.

Computer facilities: 13 computers available on campus for general student use. Internet access, word processing, scanning, image editing, chat utilities are available. *Web address:* http://www.stbernards.edu/.

General Application Contact: Thomas McDade Clay, Director of Admissions and Recruitment, 585-271-3657 Ext. 289, Fax: 585-271-2045, E-mail: tmcdadeclay@stbernards.edu.

ST. BONAVENTURE UNIVERSITY, St. Bonaventure, NY 14778-2284

General Information Independent-religious, coed, comprehensive institution. CGS member. *Enrollment:* 286 full-time matriculated graduate/professional students (196 women), 212 part-time matriculated graduate/professional students (139 women). *Enrollment by degree level:* 498 master's. *Graduate faculty:* 65 full-time (17 women), 28 part-time/adjunct (9 women). *Tuition:* Full-time $9,540; part-time $530 per credit hour. *Graduate housing:* Room and/or apartments available to single students; on-campus housing not available to married students. Housing application deadline: 3/19. *Student services:* Campus employment opportunities, career counseling, free psychological counseling, international student services, low-cost health insurance, teacher training. *Library facilities:* Friedsam Library. *Online resources:* library catalog, web page. *Collection:* 372,090 titles, 1,621 serial subscriptions, 6,186 audiovisual materials.

Computer facilities: 200 computers available on campus for general student use. A campuswide network can be accessed from student residence rooms and from off campus. Internet access and online class registration are available. *Web address:* http://www.sbu.edu/.

General Application Contact: Paula J. DeHaven, Secretary, School of Graduate Studies, 716-375-2021, Fax: 716-375-4015, E-mail: gradsch@sbu.edu.

GRADUATE UNITS

School of Graduate Studies Students: 286 full-time (196 women), 212 part-time (139 women); includes 19 minority (3 African Americans, 2 Asian Americans or Pacific Islanders, 7 Hispanic Americans, 7 Native Americans), 10 international. Average age 31. *Faculty:* 65 full-time (17 women), 28 part-time/adjunct (9 women). Expenses: Contact institution. *Financial support:* In 2001–02, 35 students received support; research assistantships with full tuition reimbursements available, career-related internships or fieldwork, Federal Work-Study, and tuition waivers (full and partial) available. Support available to part-time students. In 2001, 246 master's, 6 other advanced degrees awarded. *Degree program information:* Part-time and evening/weekend programs available. *Application deadline:* Applications are processed on a rolling basis. *Application Contact:* Paula J. DeHaven, Secretary, School of Graduate Studies, 716-375-2021, Fax: 716-375-4015, E-mail: gradsch@sbu.edu. *Dean*, Dr. David E. Cook, 716-375-2224, Fax: 716-375-7834, E-mail: dcook@sbu.edu.

School of Arts and Sciences Students: 4 full-time (2 women), 7 part-time (5 women), 1 international. Average age 34. 12 applicants, 92% accepted. *Faculty:* 24 full-time (7 women), 7 part-time/adjunct (2 women). Expenses: Contact institution. *Financial support:* Research assistantships, career-related internships or fieldwork, Federal Work-Study, and tuition waivers (full and partial) available. In 2001, 3 degrees awarded. *Degree program information:* Part-time and evening/weekend programs available. Offers arts and sciences (MA); English (MA). *Application deadline:* For fall admission, 8/1; for spring admission, 10/15

St. Bonaventure University (continued)

(priority date). Applications are processed on a rolling basis. *Application Contact:* Dr. David E. Cook, Dean of Graduate Studies, 716-375-2224, Fax: 716-375-7834, E-mail: dcook@sbu.edu. *Dean,* Dr. James White, 716-375-2028.

School of Business Students: 69 full-time (34 women), 56 part-time (24 women); includes 7 minority (1 African American, 2 Asian Americans or Pacific Islanders, 2 Hispanic Americans, 2 Native Americans), 1 international. Average age 32. 64 applicants, 97% accepted. *Faculty:* 19 full-time (3 women), 4 part-time/adjunct (1 woman). Expenses: Contact institution. *Financial support:* Research assistantships with full tuition reimbursements, career-related internships or fieldwork and Federal Work-Study available. Support available to part-time students. In 2001, 87 master's, 92 other advanced degrees awarded. *Degree program information:* Part-time and evening/weekend programs available. Offers accounting (Adv C); accounting and finance (MBA); finance (Adv C); management (Adv C); management and marketing (MBA); marketing (Adv C); professional leadership (Adv C). *Application deadline:* For fall admission, 7/1; for spring admission, 12/1. Applications are processed on a rolling basis. *Application Contact:* Brian C. McAllister, MBA Director, 716-375-2098, Fax: 716-375-2191, E-mail: bmac@sbu.edu. *Dean,* Dr. Michael J. Fischer, 716-375-2200.

School of Education Students: 205 full-time (159 women), 139 part-time (105 women); includes 6 minority (2 African Americans, 4 Hispanic Americans) Average age 30. 167 applicants, 89% accepted. *Faculty:* 18 full-time (8 women), 11 part-time/adjunct (4 women). Expenses: Contact institution. *Financial support:* In 2001–02, 8 students received support, including 5 research assistantships; career-related internships or fieldwork and Federal Work-Study also available. Support available to part-time students. In 2001, 149 master's, 10 other advanced degrees awarded. *Degree program information:* Part-time and evening/weekend programs available. Offers counseling education (Adv C); counseling education-agency (MS, MS Ed); counseling education-school (MS, MS Ed); education (MS, MS Ed, Adv C); educational leadership (MS Ed, Adv C); literacy (MS Ed). *Application deadline:* For fall admission, 8/1; for spring admission, 10/15 (priority date). Applications are processed on a rolling basis. *Application fee:* $35. *Dean,* Dr. Carol Anne Pierson, 716-375-2313, E-mail: cpierson@sbu.edu.

School of Franciscan Studies Students: 10 full-time (3 women), 8 part-time (5 women); includes 1 minority (Hispanic American), 8 international. Average age 41. 10 applicants, 100% accepted. *Faculty:* 5 full-time (1 woman), 7 part-time/adjunct (3 women). Expenses: Contact institution. *Financial support:* In 2001–02, 1 student received support, including 1 research assistantship; Federal Work-Study also available. Support available to part-time students. Financial award application deadline: 3/15. In 2001, 6 degrees awarded. *Degree program information:* Part-time programs available. Offers Franciscan studies (MA, Adv C). *Application deadline:* For fall admission, 8/1; for spring admission, 10/15 (priority date). Applications are processed on a rolling basis. *Application fee:* $35. *Application Contact:* Sr. Elise Saggau, OSF, Application Coordinator, 716-375-2160, Fax: 716-375-2156, E-mail: esaggau@sbu.edu. *Dean,* Sr. Margaret Carney, OSF, 716-375-2148, Fax: 716-375-2156, E-mail: mblastic@sbu.edu.

ST. CHARLES BORROMEO SEMINARY, OVERBROOK, Wynnewood, PA 19096

General Information Independent-religious, men only, comprehensive institution. *Enrollment:* 72 full-time matriculated graduate/professional students, 85 part-time matriculated graduate/professional students (45 women). *Enrollment by degree level:* 57 first professional, 100 master's. *Graduate faculty:* 12 full-time (1 woman), 15 part-time/adjunct (2 women). *Tuition:* Full-time $9,580; part-time $180 per credit. *Graduate housing:* Room and/or apartments guaranteed to single students; on-campus housing not available to married students. Typical cost: $6,020 (including board). Housing application deadline: 7/15. *Student services:* Campus employment opportunities, career counseling. *Library facilities:* Ryan Memorial Library. *Online resources:* web page. *Collection:* 130,485 titles, 564 serial subscriptions, 8,838 audiovisual materials.

Computer facilities: 48 computers available on campus for general student use. Internet access is available. *Web address:* http://www.scs.edu/.

General Application Contact: Rev. Christopher J. Schreck, Vice Rector, 610-785-6209, Fax: 610-667-9267, E-mail: vicerectorscs@adphila.org.

GRADUATE UNITS

Graduate and Professional Programs Students: 72 full-time (0 women), 85 part-time (45 women); includes 20 minority (6 African Americans, 6 Asian Americans or Pacific Islanders, 8 Hispanic Americans), 2 international. Average age 42. 83 applicants, 96% accepted. *Faculty:* 12 full-time (1 woman), 15 part-time/adjunct (2 women). Expenses: Contact institution. *Financial support:* Federal Work-Study and scholarships/grants available. In 2001, 22 first professional degrees, 34 master's awarded. *Degree program information:* Part-time programs available. Offers religious studies (MA); theology (M Div, STB, MA). *Application deadline:* For fall admission, 7/15. Applications are processed on a rolling basis. *Application fee:* $0. *Application Contact:* Rev. Christopher J. Schreck, Vice Rector, 610-785-6209, Fax: 610-667-9267, E-mail: vicerectorscs@adphila.org. *Rector and President,* Rev. Msgr. Michael F. Burbidge, 610-785-6200, Fax: 610-667-7635, E-mail: rectorscs@adphila.org.

ST. CLOUD STATE UNIVERSITY, St. Cloud, MN 56301-4498

General Information State-supported, coed, comprehensive institution. CGS member. *Enrollment:* 372 full-time matriculated graduate/professional students (225 women), 613 part-time matriculated graduate/professional students (393 women). *Graduate faculty:* 375 full-time (139 women), 49 part-time/adjunct (26 women). Tuition, state resident: part-time $156 per credit. Tuition, nonresident: part-time $244 per credit. *Required fees:* $20 per credit. *Graduate housing:* Room and/or apartments available on a first-come, first-served basis to single students; on-campus housing not available to married students. *Student services:* Campus employment opportunities, campus safety program, career counseling, child daycare facilities, international student services, low-cost health insurance, multicultural affairs office. *Library facilities:* Miller Learning Center. *Online resources:* library catalog, web page, access to other libraries' catalogs. *Collection:* 622,316 titles, 8,324 serial subscriptions, 28,148 audiovisual materials.

Computer facilities: 1,045 computers available on campus for general student use. A campuswide network can be accessed from student residence rooms and from off campus. Online class registration is available. *Web address:* http://www.stcloudstate.edu/.

General Application Contact: Dr. Dennis Nunes, Dean of Graduate Studies, 320-255-2113, Fax: 320-654-5371, E-mail: dlnunes@stcloudstate.edu.

GRADUATE UNITS

School of Graduate Studies Students: 372 full-time (225 women), 613 part-time (393 women); includes 108 minority (16 African Americans, 78 Asian Americans or Pacific Islanders, 6 Hispanic Americans, 8 Native Americans) 669 applicants, 74% accepted. *Faculty:* 375 full-time (139 women), 49 part-time/adjunct (26 women). Expenses: Contact institution. *Financial support:* Career-related internships or fieldwork, Federal Work-Study, and unspecified assistantships available. Financial award application deadline: 3/1. In 2001, 268 degrees awarded. *Degree program information:* Part-time programs available. *Application deadline:* Applications are processed on a rolling basis. *Application fee:* $35. *Application Contact:* Ann Anderson, Graduate Studies Office, 320-255-2113, Fax: 320-654-5371, E-mail: aeanderson@stcloudstate.edu. *Dean,* Dr. Dennis Nunes, 320-255-2113, Fax: 320-654-5371, E-mail: dlnunes@stcloudstate.edu.

College of Education Students: 183 full-time (114 women), 434 part-time (299 women); includes 31 minority (7 African Americans, 14 Asian Americans or Pacific Islanders, 4 Hispanic Americans, 6 Native Americans) 315 applicants, 97% accepted. *Faculty:* 98 full-time (46 women), 17 part-time/adjunct (13 women). Expenses: Contact institution. *Financial support:* Career-related internships or fieldwork, Federal Work-Study, and unspecified assistantships available. Financial award application deadline: 3/1. In 2001, 141 degrees awarded. Offers behavior analysis (MS); child and family studies (MS); college student development (MS); community counseling (MS); curriculum and instruction (MS); educable mentally handicapped (MS); education (MS, Spt); educational administration (MS); educational leadership and community psychology (Spt); emotionally disturbed (MS); exercise science (MS); gifted and talented (MS); information media (MS); learning disabled (MS); physical education (MS); rehabilitation counseling (MS); school counseling (MS); social responsibility (MS); special education (MS); sports management (MS); trainable mentally retarded (MS). *Application deadline:* Applications are processed on a rolling basis. *Application fee:* $35. *Application Contact:* Lindalou Krueger, Graduate Studies Office, 320-255-2113, Fax: 320-654-5371, E-mail: lekrueger@stcloudstate.edu. *Dean,* Dr. Joane McKay, 320-255-3023, Fax: 320-255-4237.

College of Fine Arts and Humanities Students: 82 full-time (65 women), 52 part-time (41 women); includes 17 minority (2 African Americans, 13 Asian Americans or Pacific Islanders, 1 Hispanic American, 1 Native American) 118 applicants, 75% accepted. *Faculty:* 75 full-time (34 women), 10 part-time/adjunct (all women). Expenses: Contact institution. *Financial support:* Federal Work-Study and unspecified assistantships available. Financial award application deadline: 3/1. In 2001, 43 degrees awarded. *Degree program information:* Part-time programs available. Offers art (MA); communication disorders (MS); conducting and literature (MM); English (MA, MS); fine arts and humanities (MA, MM, MS); mass communication (MS); music education (MM); piano pedagogy (MM); teaching English as a second language (MA). *Application fee:* $35. *Application Contact:* Lindalou Krueger, Graduate Studies Office, 320-255-2113, Fax: 320-654-5371, E-mail: lekrueger@stcloudstate.edu. *Dean,* Dr. Roland Specht-Jarvis, 320-255-3093, Fax: 320-255-4716.

College of Science and Engineering Students: 32 full-time (15 women), 21 part-time (13 women); includes 27 minority (2 African Americans, 24 Asian Americans or Pacific Islanders, 1 Native American) 90 applicants, 40% accepted. *Faculty:* 70 full-time (21 women), 3 part-time/adjunct (1 woman). Expenses: Contact institution. *Financial support:* Federal Work-Study and unspecified assistantships available. Financial award application deadline: 3/1. In 2001, 9 degrees awarded. Offers biological sciences (MA, MS); computer science (MS); electrical engineering (MS); environmental and technological studies (MS); mathematics (MS); mechanical engineering (MS); science and engineering (MA, MS). *Application fee:* $35. *Application Contact:* Lindalou Krueger, Graduate Studies Office, 320-255-2113, Fax: 320-654-5371, E-mail: lekrueger@stcloudstate.edu. *Dean,* Dr. A. I. Musah, 320-255-3909, Fax: 320-255-4262, E-mail: cose@stcloudstate.edu.

College of Social Sciences Students: 39 full-time (17 women), 48 part-time (18 women); includes 14 minority (5 African Americans, 8 Asian Americans or Pacific Islanders, 1 Hispanic American) 59 applicants, 58% accepted. *Faculty:* 67 full-time (20 women), 19 part-time/adjunct (2 women). Expenses: Contact institution. *Financial support:* Federal Work-Study and unspecified assistantships available. Financial award application deadline: 3/1. In 2001, 42 degrees awarded. *Degree program information:* Part-time programs available. Offers applied economics (MS); geography (MS); gerontology (MS); history (MA, MS); public and nonprofit institutions (MS); public safety executive leadership (MS); social sciences (MA, MS). *Application deadline:* Applications are processed on a rolling basis. *Application fee:* $35. *Application Contact:* Lindalou Krueger, Graduate Studies Office, 320-255-2113, Fax: 320-654-5371, E-mail: lekrueger@stcloudstate.edu. *Dean,* Dr. Richard Lewis, 320-255-4790.

G.R. Herberger College of Business Students: 36 full-time (14 women), 58 part-time (22 women); includes 18 minority (all Asian Americans or Pacific Islanders) 87 applicants, 37% accepted. *Faculty:* 65 full-time (18 women). Expenses: Contact institution. *Financial support:* Federal Work-Study and unspecified assistantships available. Financial award application deadline: 3/1. In 2001, 33 degrees awarded. *Degree program information:* Part-time programs available. Offers management and finance (MBA); marketing and general business (MBA). *Application deadline:* Applications are processed on a rolling basis. *Application fee:* $35. *Application Contact:* Lindalou Krueger, Graduate Studies Office, 320-255-2113, Fax: 320-654-5371, E-mail: lekrueger@stcloudstate.edu. *Graduate Director,* Dr. Michael Pesch, 320-255-3212.

ST. EDWARD'S UNIVERSITY, Austin, TX 78704-6489

General Information Independent-religious, coed, comprehensive institution. *Enrollment:* 130 full-time matriculated graduate/professional students (81 women), 633 part-time matriculated graduate/professional students (345 women). *Enrollment by degree level:* 763 master's. *Graduate faculty:* 16 full-time (6 women), 47 part-time/adjunct (15 women). *Tuition:* Full-time $7,974; part-time $443 per credit hour. *Graduate housing:* Room and/or apartments available on a first-come, first-served basis to single students; on-campus housing not available to married students. Typical cost: $5,118 (including board). Room and board charges vary according to housing facility selected. *Student services:* Campus employment opportunities, campus safety program, career counseling, disabled student services, free psychological counseling, international student services, low-cost health insurance. *Library facilities:* Scarborough–Phillips Library. *Online resources:* library catalog, web page, access to other libraries' catalogs. *Collection:* 107,231 titles, 4,122 serial subscriptions, 2,152 audiovisual materials.

Computer facilities: 288 computers available on campus for general student use. A campuswide network can be accessed from student residence rooms and from off campus. Internet access and online class registration are available. *Web address:* http://www.stedwards.edu/.

General Application Contact: Bridget Sowinski, Graduate Admissions Coordinator, 512-428-1061, Fax: 512-428-1032, E-mail: bridgets@admin.stewards.edu.

GRADUATE UNITS

College of Professional and Graduate Studies Students: 130 full-time (81 women), 633 part-time (345 women); includes 202 minority (48 African Americans, 45 Asian Americans or Pacific Islanders, 102 Hispanic Americans, 7 Native Americans), 68 international. Average age 33. 301 applicants, 78% accepted, 200 enrolled. *Faculty:* 16 full-time (6 women), 47 part-time/adjunct (15 women). Expenses: Contact institution. *Financial support:* In 2001–02, 271 students received support. Institutionally sponsored loans and scholarships/grants available. Support available to part-time students. Financial award application deadline: 4/15; financial award applicants required to submit FAFSA. In 2001, 234 degrees awarded. *Degree program information:* Part-time and evening/weekend programs available. Offers accounting (MBA); business management (MBA); computer information science (MS); conflict resolution (Certificate); counseling (MA); e-commerce (MBA, Certificate); entrepreneurship (MBA, Certificate); finance—general (MBA, Certificate); global business (MBA, Certificate); human resource management (MBA, Certificate); human services (MA); liberal arts (MLA); management information systems (MBA, Certificate); marketing (MBA, Certificate); nonprofit and association management (MBA, Certificate); operations management (MBA, Certificate); organizational leadership and ethics (MS); personal financial planner (MBA, Certificate); sports management (MBA, Certificate). *Application deadline:* For fall admission, 8/1; for spring admission, 12/1. Applications are processed on a rolling basis. *Application fee:* $30 ($50 for international students). Electronic applications accepted. *Application Contact:* Bridget Sowinski, Graduate Admissions Coordinator, 512-428-1061, Fax: 512-428-1032, E-mail: bridgets@admin.stewards.edu. *Vice President,* Dr. John Houghton, 512-448-8721, Fax: 512-464-8888, E-mail: johnh@admin.stedwards.edu.

SAINT FRANCIS SEMINARY, St. Francis, WI 53235-3795

General Information Independent-religious, coed, graduate-only institution. *Enrollment by degree level:* 30 first professional, 30 master's. *Graduate faculty:* 17 full-time (4 women), 8 part-time/adjunct (2 women). *Tuition:* Full-time $16,000; part-time $300 per credit. *Required fees:* $20 per credit. *Graduate housing:* Room and/or apartments available to single students; on-campus housing not available to married students. Housing application deadline: 7/15. *Student services:* Free psychological counseling, international student services, low-cost health insurance. *Library facilities:* Salzmann Library. *Online resources:* library catalog, web page, access to other libraries' catalogs. *Collection:* 85,718 titles, 450 serial subscriptions, 458 audiovisual materials.

Computer facilities: 9 computers available on campus for general student use. Internet access is available. *Web address:* http://www.sfs.edu.

General Application Contact: Dr. David A. Stosur, Academic Dean, 414-747-6430, Fax: 414-747-6442, E-mail: dstosur@sfs.edu.

GRADUATE UNITS

Graduate and Professional Programs Students: 20 full-time (3 women), 40 part-time (31 women); includes 4 minority (2 African Americans, 2 Hispanic Americans), 10 international. Average age 41. 24 applicants, 83% accepted. *Faculty:* 17 full-time (4 women), 8 part-time/adjunct (2 women). Expenses: Contact institution. *Financial support:* Career-related internships or fieldwork available. Support available to part-time students. In 2001, 4 first professional degrees, 7 master's awarded. *Degree program information:* Part-time programs available. Offers theology (M Div, MAPS). *Application deadline:* For fall admission, 7/15 (priority date); for spring admission, 11/20. *Application fee:* $25. *Application Contact:* Gary Pokorny, Director, Lay Formation Program, 414-747-6432, Fax: 414-747-6442, E-mail: gpokorny@sfs.edu. *Academic Dean*, Dr. David A. Stosur, 414-747-6430, Fax: 414-747-6442, E-mail: dstosur@sfs.edu.

SAINT FRANCIS UNIVERSITY, Loretto, PA 15940-0600

General Information Independent-religious, coed, comprehensive institution. *Enrollment:* 252 full-time matriculated graduate/professional students (192 women), 366 part-time matriculated graduate/professional students (207 women). *Enrollment by degree level:* 618 master's. *Graduate faculty:* 35 full-time (19 women), 58 part-time/adjunct (18 women). *Tuition:* Full-time $4,446; part-time $494 per credit. Tuition and fees vary according to course load and program. *Graduate housing:* Rooms and/or apartments available on a first-come, first-served basis to single and married students. Typical cost: $3,266 per year ($6,974 including board) for single students; $3,266 per year ($6,974 including board) for married students. Room and board charges vary according to board plan, campus/location and housing facility selected. *Student services:* Campus employment opportunities, campus safety program, career counseling, free psychological counseling, low-cost health insurance, multicultural affairs office, writing training. *Library facilities:* Pasquerella Library. *Online resources:* library catalog, web page, access to other libraries' catalogs. *Collection:* 155,143 titles, 975 serial subscriptions, 1,957 audiovisual materials.

Computer facilities: 60 computers available on campus for general student use. A campuswide network can be accessed from student residence rooms. *Web address:* http://www.francis.edu/.

General Application Contact: Dr. Peter Raymond Skoner, Assistant Vice President for Academic Affairs, 814-472-3085, Fax: 814-472-3365, E-mail: pskoner@francis.edu.

GRADUATE UNITS

Business Administration Program Students: 10 full-time (3 women), 134 part-time (57 women). Average age 33. 60 applicants. *Faculty:* 6 full-time (1 woman), 6 part-time/adjunct (2 women). Expenses: Contact institution. *Financial support:* In 2001–02, 10 students received support, including 10 research assistantships with full tuition reimbursements available; teaching assistantships with full tuition reimbursements available, career-related internships or fieldwork and Federal Work-Study also available. In 2001, 21 degrees awarded. *Degree program information:* Part-time programs available. Offers business administration (MBA). *Application deadline:* For fall admission, 8/1 (priority date); for spring admission, 12/1. Applications are processed on a rolling basis. *Application fee:* $30. *Application Contact:* Roxane Hogue, Administrative Assistant, 814-472-3087, Fax: 814-472-3174, E-mail: rhogue@sfcpa.edu. *Director*, Dr. Randy C. Frye, 814-472-3041, Fax: 814-472-3174, E-mail: rfrye@sfcpa.edu.

Department of Physical Therapy Students: 67 full-time (42 women). 4 applicants, 25% accepted, 0 enrolled. *Faculty:* 7 full-time (4 women), 2 part-time/adjunct (1 woman). Expenses: Contact institution. *Financial support:* In 2001–02, 8 teaching assistantships with partial tuition reimbursements were awarded Financial award applicants required to submit FAFSA. In 2001, 22 degrees awarded. Offers physical therapy (MPT). *Application deadline:* For winter admission, 1/15. *Application fee:* $30. Electronic applications accepted. *Application Contact:* Evan Lipp, Dean for Enrollment Management, 814-472-3100, Fax: 814-472-3335, E-mail: elipp@sfcpa.edu. *Associate Professor and Chair*, Dr. Edward M. Pisarski, 814-472-3123, Fax: 814-472-3140, E-mail: episarski@sfcpa.edu.

Department of Physician Assistant Sciences Students: 105 full-time (82 women); includes 6 minority (1 African American, 5 Asian Americans or Pacific Islanders) Average age 22. 162 applicants, 54% accepted, 55 enrolled. *Faculty:* 9 full-time (7 women), 3 part-time/adjunct (0 women). Expenses: Contact institution. *Financial support:* Applicants required to submit FAFSA. In 2001, 51 degrees awarded. Offers physician assistant sciences (MPAS). *Application deadline:* For fall admission, 11/30. *Application fee:* $30. Electronic applications accepted. *Application Contact:* Therese Schrift, Admissions Representative, 814-472-3106, Fax: 814-472-3335, E-mail: tschrift@francis.edu. *Chair*, Albert Simon, 814-472-3130, Fax: 814-472-3137, E-mail: bsimon@francis.edu.

Graduate School of Human Resource Management and Industrial Relations Students: 8 full-time (7 women), 118 part-time (81 women); includes 11 minority (8 African Americans, 1 Asian American or Pacific Islander, 2 Hispanic Americans) Average age 32. 29 applicants, 100% accepted. *Faculty:* 1 full-time (0 women), 31 part-time/adjunct (12 women). Expenses: Contact institution. *Financial support:* In 2001–02, 9 students received support, including 1 research assistantship (averaging $12,000 per year); fellowships with partial tuition reimbursements available, scholarships/grants, tuition waivers, and unspecified assistantships also available. Support available to part-time students. Financial award application deadline: 7/1. *Degree program information:* Part-time and evening/weekend programs available. Offers human resource management and industrial relations (MHRM). *Application deadline:* For fall admission, 8/1 (priority date); for spring admission, 12/1 (priority date). Applications are processed on a rolling basis. *Application fee:* $25. *Application Contact:* Sally Weber, Graduate School of HRM/IR Program Assistant, 814-472-3026, Fax: 814-472-3369, E-mail: hrir@francis.edu. *Director*, Dr. Philip Benham, 814-472-3026, Fax: 814-472-3369, E-mail: pbenham@francis.edu.

Medical Science Program Average age 25. 35 applicants, 100% accepted. *Faculty:* 1 full-time (0 women), 10 part-time/adjunct (1 woman). Expenses: Contact institution. *Financial support:* Teaching assistantships with full tuition reimbursements, career-related internships or fieldwork available. In 2001, 23 degrees awarded. *Degree program information:* Part-time and evening/weekend programs available. Postbaccalaureate distance learning degree programs offered (no on-campus study). Offers medical science (MMS). *Application deadline:* For fall admission, 9/1 (priority date); for spring admission, 1/1. Applications are processed on a rolling basis. *Application fee:* $50. *Director*, Dr. William Duryea, 814-472-3132, Fax: 814-472-3137, E-mail: bduryea@francis.edu.

Occupational Therapy Program Students: 37 full-time (35 women). Average age 24. 36 applicants, 100% accepted, 35 enrolled. *Faculty:* 6 full-time (3 women). Expenses: Contact institution. In 2001, 33 degrees awarded. Offers occupational therapy (MOT). *Application Contact:* Erin Mathes, Assistant Director of Admissions, 814-472-3110, Fax: 814-472-3335, E-mail: fcrouse@francis.edu. *Chair*, Donald Walkovich, 814-472-3899, E-mail: dwalkovich@francis.edu.

Program in Education Students: 1 (woman) full-time, 81 part-time (53 women). Average age 30. 22 applicants, 100% accepted, 22 enrolled. *Faculty:* 3 full-time (2 women), 10 part-time/adjunct (3 women). Expenses: Contact institution. *Financial support:* Research assistantships with full and partial tuition reimbursements, teaching assistantships with full and partial tuition reimbursements, career-related internships or fieldwork and unspecified assistantships available. In 2001, 22 degrees awarded. *Degree program information:* Part-time and evening/weekend programs available. Offers education (M Ed); leadership (M Ed). *Application deadline:* Applications are processed on a rolling basis. *Application fee:* $25. *Department Chair*, Dr. Elizabeth Gensante, 814-472-3058, Fax: 814-472-3864, E-mail: egensante@sfcpa.edu.

ST. FRANCIS XAVIER UNIVERSITY, Antigonish, NS B2G 2W5, Canada

General Information Independent-religious, coed, comprehensive institution. *Enrollment:* 84 full-time matriculated graduate/professional students (62 women), 118 part-time matriculated graduate/professional students (85 women). *Enrollment by degree level:* 202 master's. *Graduate faculty:* 24 full-time (3 women), 18 part-time/adjunct (8 women). *Tuition:* Full-time $4,600; part-time $980 per unit. *Required fees:* $157; $13 per unit. *Graduate housing:* Room and/or apartments available to single students; on-campus housing not available to married students. Typical cost: $5,495 (including board). Housing application deadline: 7/1. *Student services:* Campus employment opportunities, campus safety program, career counseling, child daycare facilities, disabled student services, exercise/wellness program, free psychological counseling, international student services, low-cost health insurance, writing training. *Library facilities:* Angus L. MacDonald Library plus 1 other. *Online resources:* library catalog, web page, access to other libraries' catalogs. *Collection:* 632,575 titles, 3,282 serial subscriptions, 6,598 audiovisual materials.

Computer facilities: 300 computers available on campus for general student use. A campuswide network can be accessed from student residence rooms and from off campus. Internet access and online class registration are available. *Web address:* http://www.stfx.ca/.

General Application Contact: Dr. Jim O. Taylor, Chair, Committee on Graduate Studies, 902-867-2135, Fax: 902-867-2329, E-mail: jtaylor@stfx.ca.

GRADUATE UNITS

Graduate Studies *Degree program information:* Part-time programs available. Postbaccalaureate distance learning degree programs offered (minimal on-campus study). Offers adult education (M Ad Ed); biology (M Sc); chemistry (M Sc); education (M Ed, Diploma); English (MAT); geology (M Sc); physics (M Sc).

ST. JOHN FISHER COLLEGE, Rochester, NY 14618-3597

General Information Independent-religious, coed, comprehensive institution. *Enrollment:* 116 full-time matriculated graduate/professional students (84 women), 464 part-time matriculated graduate/professional students (306 women). *Enrollment by degree level:* 580 master's. *Graduate faculty:* 34 full-time (17 women), 35 part-time/adjunct (17 women). *Tuition:* Part-time $465 per credit hour. *Graduate housing:* Room and/or apartments available on a first-come, first-served basis to single students; on-campus housing not available to married students. Housing application deadline: 8/1. *Student services:* Campus employment opportunities, campus safety program, career counseling, child daycare facilities, disabled student services, international student services, low-cost health insurance, teacher training. *Library facilities:* Charles V. Lavery Library plus 1 other. *Online resources:* library catalog, web page, access to other libraries' catalogs. *Collection:* 195,000 titles, 1,330 serial subscriptions, 27,666 audiovisual materials.

Computer facilities: 133 computers available on campus for general student use. A campuswide network can be accessed from student residence rooms and from off campus. Internet access and online class registration are available. *Web address:* http://www.sjfc.edu/.

General Application Contact: Scott Kelly, Director, Graduate Admissions, 585-385-8161, Fax: 585-385-8344, E-mail: kelly@sjfc.edu.

GRADUATE UNITS

Office of Academic Affairs Students: 116 full-time (84 women), 464 part-time (306 women); includes 54 minority (40 African Americans, 4 Asian Americans or Pacific Islanders, 9 Hispanic Americans, 1 Native American), 3 international. Average age 34. 243 applicants, 90% accepted. *Faculty:* 34 full-time (17 women), 35 part-time/adjunct (17 women). Expenses: Contact institution. *Financial support:* In 2001–02, 16 students received support. Federal Work-Study and scholarships/grants available. Financial award application deadline: 2/15; financial award applicants required to submit FAFSA. In 2001, 120 degrees awarded. *Degree program information:* Part-time and evening/weekend programs available. Offers childhood and adolescence (MS Ed); educational administration (MS Ed); family nurse practitioner (Certificate); human resources development (MS); human service administration (MS); international studies (MS); literacy (MS); management (MBA); mathematics/science/technology education (MS); nursing (MS); special education (MS); taxation (MS). *Application deadline:* For fall admission, 8/1; for spring admission, 11/15. *Application fee:* $30. *Application Contact:* Scott Kelly, Director, Graduate Admissions, 585-385-8161, Fax: 585-385-8344, E-mail: kelly@sjfc.edu. *Dean of Graduate and Undergraduate Studies*, Dr. David A. Pate, 585-385-7316, Fax: 585-385-8117, E-mail: pate@sjfc.edu.

ST. JOHN'S COLLEGE, Annapolis, MD 21404

General Information Independent, coed, comprehensive institution. *Graduate housing:* On-campus housing not available.

GRADUATE UNITS

Graduate Institute in Liberal Education Students: 61 full-time (26 women), 5 part-time (2 women); includes 4 minority (2 Asian Americans or Pacific Islanders, 1 Hispanic American, 1 Native American), 1 international. Average age 31. 31 applicants, 100% accepted. *Faculty:* 9 full-time (4 women), 7 part-time/adjunct (5 women). Expenses: Contact institution. *Financial support:* In 2001–02, 46 students received support. Scholarships/grants available. Financial award applicants required to submit FAFSA. In 2001, 30 degrees awarded. *Degree program information:* Evening/weekend programs available. Offers liberal arts (MA). *Application deadline:* Applications are processed on a rolling basis. *Application fee:* $0. *Application Contact:* Miriam L. Callahan-Hean, Graduate Admissions Administrator, 410-626-2541, Fax: 410-626-2880, E-mail: giadm@sjca.edu. *Director*, Dr. William Pastille, 410-626-2542, Fax: 410-626-2880.

ST. JOHN'S COLLEGE, Santa Fe, NM 87505-4599

General Information Independent, coed, comprehensive institution. *Enrollment:* 84 full-time matriculated graduate/professional students (41 women). *Enrollment by degree level:* 84 master's. *Graduate faculty:* 20 full-time (6 women). *Tuition:* Part-time $4,990 per term. Full-time tuition and fees vary according to program. *Graduate housing:* Rooms and/or apartments available on a first-come, first-served basis to single and married students. Typical cost: $2,172 (including board) for single students; $2,172 (including board) for married students. Room and board charges vary according to board plan. Housing application deadline: 4/1. *Student services:* Career counseling, free psychological counseling, low-cost health insurance. *Library facilities:* Meem Library. *Online resources:* library catalog, web page, access to other libraries' catalogs. *Collection:* 40,103 titles, 135 serial subscriptions.

Computer facilities: 20 computers available on campus for general student use. A campuswide network can be accessed. *Web address:* http://www.sjcsf.edu/.

General Application Contact: Jean-Paul Ruch, Assistant Director of Graduate Admissions, 505-984-6083, Fax: 505-984-6003, E-mail: giadmiss@mail.sjcsf.edu.

GRADUATE UNITS

Graduate Institute in Liberal Education Students: 84 full-time (41 women). Average age 34. 139 applicants, 63% accepted, 73 enrolled. *Faculty:* 20 full-time (6 women). Expenses: Contact institution. *Financial support:* Scholarships/grants available. Support available to part-time students. Financial award application deadline: 5/1; financial award applicants required to submit FAFSA. In 2001, 47 degrees awarded. *Degree program information:* Evening/weekend programs available. Offers Eastern classics (MA); liberal arts (MA); liberal education (MA). *Application deadline:* For fall admission, 4/15 (priority date). Applications are processed on a rolling basis. *Application fee:* $0. *Application Contact:* Jean-Paul Ruch, Assistant Director of Graduate Admissions, 505-984-6083, Fax: 505-984-6003, E-mail: giadmiss@mail.sjcsf.edu. *Director of Graduate Institute*, Frank Pagano, 505-984-6082, Fax: 505-984-6003, E-mail: gi@mail.sjcsf.edu.

ST. JOHN'S SEMINARY, Camarillo, CA 93012-2598

General Information Independent-religious, coed, primarily men, graduate-only institution. *Enrollment by degree level:* 65 first professional, 4 master's, 69 other advanced degrees. *Graduate faculty:* 24 full-time (4 women), 8 part-time/adjunct (4 women). *Tuition:* Full-time $9,000; part-time $300 per unit. *Required fees:* $250. *Graduate housing:* Room and/or apartments guaranteed to single students; on-campus housing not available to married students. Typical cost: $5,600 (including board). *Student services:* Campus employment opportunities, career counseling, free psychological counseling, international student services, low-cost health insurance. *Library facilities:* Edward Laurence Doheny Memorial Library plus 1 other. *Online resources:* library catalog, web page. *Collection:* 110,512 titles, 262 serial subscriptions, 2,730 audiovisual materials.

St. John's Seminary (continued)

Computer facilities: 20 computers available on campus for general student use. A campuswide network can be accessed from student residence rooms and from off campus. Internet access is available. *Web address:* http://www.stjohnsem.edu.

General Application Contact: Dr. Mark F. Fischer, Director of Admissions, 805-482-2755 Ext. 1063, Fax: 805-482-3470, E-mail: fischer@sjs-sc.org.

GRADUATE UNITS

Graduate and Professional Programs Students: 68 full-time (1 woman), 1 part-time; includes 37 minority (1 African American, 18 Asian Americans or Pacific Islanders, 18 Hispanic Americans), 12 international. Average age 33. 25 applicants, 84% accepted, 18 enrolled. *Faculty:* 24 full-time (4 women), 8 part-time/adjunct (4 women). Expenses: Contact institution. In 2001, 12 first professional degrees, 15 master's awarded. Offers divinity (M Div); theology (MA). *Application deadline:* For fall admission, 7/15 (priority date). Applications are processed on a rolling basis. *Application fee:* $0. *Application Contact:* Esmé M. Takahashi, Registrar, 805-482-2755 Ext. 1014, Fax: 805-482-3470, E-mail: registrar-sjs@sjs-sc.org. *Academic Dean,* Rev. Richard Benson, CM, 805-482-2755, Fax: 805-482-3470, E-mail: rbensoncm@sjs-sc.org.

SAINT JOHN'S SEMINARY, Brighton, MA 02135

General Information Independent-religious, coed, primarily men, graduate-only institution. *Enrollment by degree level:* 86 first professional, 73 master's. *Graduate faculty:* 11 full-time (1 woman), 16 part-time/adjunct (8 women). *Tuition:* Full-time $7,000; part-time $350 per credit. *Graduate housing:* Room and/or apartments guaranteed to single students; on-campus housing not available to married students. Typical cost: $4,000 (including board). Housing application deadline: 8/1. *Student services:* Campus employment opportunities, exercise/wellness program, free psychological counseling, international student services, low-cost health insurance. *Library facilities:* St. John's Seminary Library. *Collection:* 163,000 titles.

Computer facilities: Internet access and online class registration are available. *Web address:* http://www.sjs.edu/.

General Application Contact: Martin V. Grace, Registrar, 617-254-2610, Fax: 617-787-2336, E-mail: martin_grace@rcab.org.

GRADUATE UNITS

Graduate Programs Students: 100 full-time (16 women), 59 part-time (37 women). *Faculty:* 11 full-time (1 woman), 16 part-time/adjunct (8 women). Expenses: Contact institution. *Application deadline:* Applications are processed on a rolling basis. *Application fee:* $0. *Registrar,* Martin V. Grace, 617-254-2610, Fax: 617-787-2336, E-mail: martin_grace@rcab.org.

SAINT JOHN'S UNIVERSITY, Collegeville, MN 56321

General Information Independent-religious, coed, comprehensive institution. *Enrollment:* 75 full-time matriculated graduate/professional students (35 women), 76 part-time matriculated graduate/professional students (46 women). *Enrollment by degree level:* 151 master's. *Graduate faculty:* 9 full-time (4 women), 13 part-time/adjunct (1 woman). *Tuition:* Full-time $9,776; part-time $545 per credit. *Required fees:* $80. One-time fee: $80 part-time. Full-time tuition and fees vary according to program. Part-time tuition and fees vary according to course load. *Graduate housing:* Rooms and/or apartments available on a first-come, first-served basis to single and married students. Typical cost: $3,480 per year ($5,392 including board) for single students; $4,550 per year ($5,856 including board) for married students. Room and board charges vary according to board plan and housing facility selected. *Student services:* Campus employment opportunities, campus safety program, career counseling, exercise/wellness program, free psychological counseling, international student services, low-cost health insurance, multicultural affairs office, writing training. *Library facilities:* Alcuin Library plus 2 others. *Online resources:* library catalog, web page, access to other libraries' catalogs. *Collection:* 726,844 titles, 8,564 serial subscriptions, 18,824 audiovisual materials. *Research affiliation:* Hill Monastic Manuscript Library (monastic studies, liturgy, spirituality), Center for Ecumenical and Cultural Research, Arca Artium (visual and book arts).

Computer facilities: 350 computers available on campus for general student use. A campuswide network can be accessed from student residence rooms and from off campus. Internet access and online class registration are available. *Web address:* http://www.csbsju.edu/.

General Application Contact: Sr. Mary Beth Banken, OSB, Director of Enrollment, 320-363-2102, Fax: 320-363-3145, E-mail: mbanken@csbsju.edu.

GRADUATE UNITS

School of Theology and Seminary Students: 75 full-time (35 women), 76 part-time (46 women); includes 6 minority (5 Asian Americans or Pacific Islanders, 1 Hispanic American), 6 international. Average age 37. 68 applicants, 81% accepted, 49 enrolled. *Faculty:* 9 full-time (4 women), 13 part-time/adjunct (1 woman). Expenses: Contact institution. *Financial support:* In 2001–02, 121 students received support, including 10 fellowships (averaging $8,000 per year); research assistantships, career-related internships or fieldwork, Federal Work-Study, institutionally sponsored loans, scholarships/grants, and tuition waivers (full and partial) also available. Support available to part-time students. Financial award applicants required to submit CSS PROFILE or FAFSA. In 2001, 28 degrees awarded. *Degree program information:* Part-time programs available. Postbaccalaureate distance learning degree programs offered (no on-campus study). Offers divinity (M Div); liturgical music (MA); liturgical studies (MA); pastoral ministry (MA); theology (MA). *Application deadline:* Applications are processed on a rolling basis. *Application fee:* $25. Electronic applications accepted. *Application Contact:* Sr. Mary Beth Banken, OSB, Director of Enrollment, 320-363-2102, Fax: 320-363-3145, E-mail: mbanken@csbsju.edu. *Dean,* Dr. William J. Cahoy, 320-363-3182, Fax: 320-363-3145, E-mail: bcahoy@csbju.edu.

ST. JOHN'S UNIVERSITY, Jamaica, NY 11439

General Information Independent-religious, coed, university. CGS member. *Enrollment:* 1,388 full-time matriculated graduate/professional students (749 women), 2,396 part-time matriculated graduate/professional students (1,524 women). *Enrollment by degree level:* 1,015 first professional, 2,238 master's, 415 doctoral, 116 other advanced degrees. *Graduate faculty:* 563 full-time (183 women), 632 part-time/adjunct (387 women). *Tuition:* Full-time $14,520; part-time $605 per credit. *Required fees:* $150; $75 per term. Tuition and fees vary according to class time, course load, degree level, campus/location, program and student level. *Graduate housing:* Room and/or apartments available to single students; on-campus housing not available to married students. Typical cost: $5,800 per year. *Student services:* Campus employment opportunities, campus safety program, career counseling, disabled student services, exercise/wellness program, free psychological counseling, international student services, low-cost health insurance, writing training. *Library facilities:* St. John's University Library plus 2 others. *Online resources:* library catalog, web page, access to other libraries' catalogs. *Collection:* 5 million titles, 15,974 serial subscriptions, 22,095 audiovisual materials. *Research affiliation:* Booth Ferris (education and human services), William T. Grant Foundation (psychology), Ortho Biotech (clinical pharmacy practice), James Kemper Foundation (risk management), International Foundation for Ethical Research (pharmacy), Exhale Therapeutics (pharmacy).

Computer facilities: 950 computers available on campus for general student use. A campuswide network can be accessed from student residence rooms and from off campus. Internet access and online class registration, various software packages are available. *Web address:* http://www.stjohns.edu/.

General Application Contact: Matthew Whelan, Director, Office of Admission, 718-990-2000, Fax: 718-990-2096, E-mail: admissions@stjohns.edu.

GRADUATE UNITS

College of Pharmacy and Allied Health Professions Students: 76 full-time (37 women), 137 part-time (77 women); includes 40 minority (4 African Americans, 28 Asian Americans or Pacific Islanders, 8 Hispanic Americans), 86 international. Average age 29. 301 applicants, 59% accepted, 65 enrolled. *Faculty:* 52 full-time (20 women), 17 part-time/adjunct (5 women). Expenses: Contact institution. *Financial support:* Fellowships with full tuition reimbursements, research assistantships with full tuition reimbursements, career-related internships or fieldwork, scholarships/grants, and unspecified assistantships available. Support available to part-time students. Financial award application deadline: 3/1; financial award applicants required to submit FAFSA. In 2001, 16 first professional degrees, 29 master's, 2 doctorates awarded. *Degree program information:* Part-time and evening/weekend programs available. Offers clinical pharmacy (MS); cosmetic sciences (MS); industrial pharmacy (MS, PhD); medical technology (MS); medicinal chemistry (MS, PhD); pharmaceutical (MS); pharmaceutical sciences (MS, PhD); pharmacology (MS, PhD); pharmacotherapeutics (MS); pharmacy (Pharm D, MS, PhD); pharmacy administration (MS); pharmacy and allied health professions (Pharm D, MS, PhD); toxicology (MS, PhD). *Application deadline:* For spring admission, 10/1. Applications are processed on a rolling basis. *Application fee:* $40. *Application Contact:* Matthew Whelan, Director, Office of Admission, 718-990-2000, Fax: 718-990-2096, E-mail: admissions@stjohns.edu. *Dean,* Dr. Robert Mangione, 718-990-6411, Fax: 718-990-1871, E-mail: mangionr@stjohns.edu.

The Peter J. Tobin College of Business Students: 199 full-time (91 women), 560 part-time (224 women); includes 188 minority (67 African Americans, 71 Asian Americans or Pacific Islanders, 50 Hispanic Americans), 168 international. Average age 29. 569 applicants, 62% accepted, 185 enrolled. *Faculty:* 101 full-time (18 women), 43 part-time/adjunct (9 women). Expenses: Contact institution. *Financial support:* In 2001–02, 30 research assistantships with full tuition reimbursements (averaging $6,000 per year) were awarded; scholarships/grants also available. Support available to part-time students. Financial award application deadline: 3/1; financial award applicants required to submit FAFSA. In 2001, 322 master's, 3 other advanced degrees awarded. *Degree program information:* Part-time and evening/weekend programs available. Offers accounting (MBA, MS, Adv C); actuarial science (MS); business (MBA, MS, Adv C); computer information systems and decision sciences (MBA, Adv C); economics (MBA, Adv C); finance (MBA, Adv C); international business (MBA); management (MBA, Adv C); marketing (MBA, Adv C); risk management and insurance (MBA, MS); taxation (MBA, Adv C). *Application deadline:* Applications are processed on a rolling basis. *Application fee:* $40. Electronic applications accepted. *Application Contact:* Nicole T. Bryan, Assistant Dean, 718-990-2599, Fax: 718-990-5242, E-mail: admissions@stjohns.edu. *Dean,* Peter J. Tobin, 718-990-2030, Fax: 718-990-5727, E-mail: tobinp@stjohns.edu.

St. John's College of Liberal Arts and Sciences Students: 299 full-time (227 women), 498 part-time (337 women); includes 188 minority (68 African Americans, 43 Asian Americans or Pacific Islanders, 76 Hispanic Americans, 1 Native American), 78 international. Average age 31. 932 applicants, 43% accepted, 221 enrolled. *Faculty:* 243 full-time (69 women), 260 part-time/adjunct (106 women). Expenses: Contact institution. *Financial support:* In 2001–02, 61 fellowships with full and partial tuition reimbursements (averaging $7,500 per year), 45 research assistantships with full tuition reimbursements (averaging $5,000 per year), 10 teaching assistantships with full tuition reimbursements (averaging $7,500 per year) were awarded. Career-related internships or fieldwork, scholarships/grants, and unspecified assistantships also available. Support available to part-time students. Financial award application deadline: 3/1; financial award applicants required to submit FAFSA. In 2001, 190 master's, 21 doctorates, 2 other advanced degrees awarded. *Degree program information:* Part-time and evening/weekend programs available. Offers algebra (MA); analysis (MA); applied mathematics (MA); arts and sciences (M Div, MA, MLS, MS, DA, PhD, Psy D, APC, Adv C); biological sciences (MS, PhD); chemistry (MS); clinical psychology (MA, PhD); clinical psychology-child (MA, PhD); clinical psychology-general (MA, PhD); computer science (MA); English (MA, DA); general experimental psychology (MA); geometry-topology (MA); government and politics (MA); history (MA); international law and diplomacy (Adv C); library and information science (MLS, Adv C); logic and foundations (MA); modern world history (DA); pastoral ministry (Adv C); priestly studies (M Div); probability and statistics (MA); school psychology (MS, Psy D); sociology (MA); Spanish (MA); speech pathology and audiology (MA); theology (MA). *Application deadline:* Applications are processed on a rolling basis. *Application fee:* $40. *Application Contact:* Matthew Whelan, Director, Office of Admission, 718-990-2000, Fax: 718-990-2096, E-mail: admissions@stjohns.edu. *Acting Dean,* Dr. Jeffrey Fagen, 718-990-6068, Fax: 718-990-6593, E-mail: fagenj@stjohns.edu.

Institute of Asian Studies Students: 4 full-time (3 women), 9 part-time (7 women); includes 6 minority (5 Asian Americans or Pacific Islanders, 1 Hispanic American), 6 international. Average age 34. 11 applicants, 4 enrolled. *Faculty:* 1 (woman) full-time, 5 part-time/adjunct (4 women). Expenses: Contact institution. *Financial support:* Research assistantships with full tuition reimbursements, scholarships/grants available. Support available to part-time students. Financial award application deadline: 3/1; financial award applicants required to submit FAFSA. In 2001, 4 degrees awarded. *Degree program information:* Part-time and evening/weekend programs available. Offers Asian and African cultural studies (Adv C); Asian studies (Adv C); Chinese studies (MA, Adv C); East Asian culture studies (Adv C); East Asian studies (MA). *Application deadline:* Applications are processed on a rolling basis. *Application fee:* $40. *Application Contact:* Matthew Whelan, Director, Office of Admission, 718-990-2000, Fax: 718-990-2096, E-mail: admissions@stjohns.edu. *Director,* Dr. John Lin, 718-990-6582, E-mail: linj@stjohns.edu.

The School of Education Students: 86 full-time (62 women), 938 part-time (782 women); includes 196 minority (85 African Americans, 22 Asian Americans or Pacific Islanders, 88 Hispanic Americans, 1 Native American), 19 international. Average age 32. 581 applicants, 72% accepted, 252 enrolled. *Faculty:* 40 full-time (23 women), 63 part-time/adjunct (34 women). Expenses: Contact institution. *Financial support:* In 2001–02, 3 fellowships with full tuition reimbursements (averaging $10,000 per year), 14 research assistantships with full tuition reimbursements (averaging $5,000 per year) were awarded. Career-related internships or fieldwork and scholarships/grants also available. Support available to part-time students. Financial award application deadline: 3/1; financial award applicants required to submit FAFSA. In 2001, 338 master's, 22 doctorates, 32 other advanced degrees awarded. *Degree program information:* Part-time and evening/weekend programs available. Offers administration and supervision (MS Ed, Ed D, PD); bilingual school counseling (MS Ed); bilingual special education (MS Ed, PD); bilingual/multicultural education/teaching English to speakers of other languages (MS Ed); education (MS Ed, Ed D, PD); elementary education (MS Ed); instructional leadership (Ed D, PD); reading special education (MS Ed); reading specialist (MS Ed, PD); rehabilitation counseling (MS Ed, PD); school counseling (MS Ed, PD); secondary education (MS Ed); special education (MS Ed, PD); special education/bilingual special education/reading special education (MS Ed, PD); student development practice in higher education (MS Ed, PD). *Application deadline:* Applications are processed on a rolling basis. *Application fee:* $40. *Application Contact:* Kelly Ronayne, Assistant Dean, 718-990-2303, Fax: 718-990-6069, E-mail: admissions@stjohns.edu. *Dean,* Dr. Jerrold Ross, 718-990-1305, Fax: 718-990-6096, E-mail: rossj@stjohns.edu.

School of Law Students: 727 full-time (332 women), 220 part-time (89 women); includes 172 minority (51 African Americans, 64 Asian Americans or Pacific Islanders, 53 Hispanic Americans, 4 Native Americans), 9 international. Average age 27. 2,536 applicants, 36% accepted, 303 enrolled. *Faculty:* 44 full-time (12 women), 28 part-time/adjunct (6 women). Expenses: Contact institution. *Financial support:* In 2001–02, 921 students received support. Career-related internships or fieldwork and scholarships/grants available. Support available to part-time students. Financial award application deadline: 3/1; financial award applicants required to submit FAFSA. In 2001, 278 first professional degrees, 6 master's awarded. *Degree program information:* Part-time and evening/weekend programs available. Offers bankruptcy (LL M); law (JD). *Application deadline:* For fall admission, 3/1; for spring admission, 11/1. *Application fee:* $50. *Application Contact:* Robert Harrison, Assistant Dean and Director of Admissions, 718-990-2310, Fax: 718-591-1855, E-mail: harrisor@stjohns.edu. *Dean,* Joseph W. Bellacosa, 718-990-6601, Fax: 718-591-1855, E-mail: bellacoj@stjohns.edu.

See in-depth description on page 1065.

SAINT JOSEPH COLLEGE, West Hartford, CT 06117-2700

General Information Independent-religious, women only, comprehensive institution. *Enrollment:* 76 full-time matriculated graduate/professional students (65 women), 408 part-time matriculated graduate/professional students (372 women). *Enrollment by degree level:* 484 master's. *Graduate faculty:* 36 full-time (22 women), 28 part-time/adjunct (20 women). *Tuition:* Part-time $475 per credit hour. *Graduate housing:* On-campus housing not available. *Student services:* Campus employment opportunities, campus safety program, career counseling, child daycare facilities, disabled student services, exercise/wellness program, free psychological counseling, international student services, low-cost health insurance, multicultural affairs office, teacher training, writing training. *Library facilities:* Pope Pius XII Library plus 1 other. *Online resources:* library catalog, access to other libraries' catalogs. *Collection:* 164,283 titles, 605 serial subscriptions, 3,282 audiovisual materials.

Computer facilities: 150 computers available on campus for general student use. A campuswide network can be accessed from student residence rooms and from off campus. Internet access is available. *Web address:* http://www.sjc.edu/.

General Application Contact: Monica Gat, Graduate Recruiter, 860-231-5261, Fax: 860-231-8396, E-mail: mgat@sjc.edu.

GRADUATE UNITS

Graduate Division Students: 76 full-time (65 women), 408 part-time (372 women); includes 23 minority (19 African Americans, 1 Asian American or Pacific Islander, 3 Hispanic Americans), 2 international. Average age 33. *Faculty:* 36 full-time (22 women), 28 part-time/adjunct (20 women). Expenses: Contact institution. *Financial support:* Research assistantships with full and partial tuition reimbursements, career-related internships or fieldwork, traineeships, tuition waivers (partial), and unspecified assistantships available. Support available to part-time students. Financial award application deadline: 7/15; financial award applicants required to submit FAFSA. In 2001, 186 degrees awarded. *Degree program information:* Part-time and evening/weekend programs available. Postbaccalaureate distance learning degree programs offered. Offers biology (MS); biology/chemistry (MS); chemistry (MS); community counseling (MA); early childhood education (MA); education (MA); family health nurse practitioner (MS); family health nursing (MS); human development/gerontology (MA, Certificate); marriage and family therapy (MA); nursing (Post Master's Certificate); psychiatric/mental health nursing (MS); special education (MA); spirituality (Certificate). *Application deadline:* Applications are processed on a rolling basis. *Application fee:* $25. *Associate Dean,* Dr. Clark Hendley, 860-231-5261, Fax: 860-231-8396, E-mail: assocdean@sjc.edu.

SAINT JOSEPH'S COLLEGE, Rensselaer, IN 47978

General Information Independent-religious, coed, comprehensive institution. *Graduate housing:* Rooms and/or apartments available on a first-come, first-served basis to single students and available to married students. Housing application deadline: 6/20.

GRADUATE UNITS

Rensselaer Program of Church Music and Liturgy *Degree program information:* Part-time programs available. Offers music (MA); pastoral liturgy (Diploma). Offered during summer only.

SAINT JOSEPH'S COLLEGE, Standish, ME 04084-5263

General Information Independent-religious, coed, comprehensive institution. *Graduate housing:* On-campus housing not available.

GRADUATE UNITS

Department of Nursing *Degree program information:* Part-time programs available. Postbaccalaureate distance learning degree programs offered (minimal on-campus study). Offers nursing (MS). Offered only through faculty directed independent study. Electronic applications accepted.

Program in Health Services Administration *Degree program information:* Part-time programs available. Postbaccalaureate distance learning degree programs offered (minimal on-campus study). Offers health services administration (MHSA). Degree program is external; available only by correspondence. Electronic applications accepted.

Program in Pastoral Studies *Degree program information:* Part-time programs available. Postbaccalaureate distance learning degree programs offered (minimal on-campus study). Offers pastoral studies (MA). Electronic applications accepted.

Program in Teacher Education *Degree program information:* Part-time programs available. Postbaccalaureate distance learning degree programs offered (minimal on-campus study). Offers teacher education (MS). Electronic applications accepted.

ST. JOSEPH'S COLLEGE, SUFFOLK CAMPUS, Patchogue, NY 11772-2399

General Information Independent, coed, comprehensive institution. *Enrollment:* 57 part-time matriculated graduate/professional students (56 women). *Enrollment by degree level:* 57 master's. *Graduate faculty:* 7 full-time, 5 part-time/adjunct. *Tuition:* Part-time $423 per credit. *Graduate housing:* On-campus housing not available. *Student services:* Career counseling, disabled student services, exercise/wellness program, low-cost health insurance. *Library facilities:* Callahan Library. *Online resources:* library catalog. *Collection:* 65,530 titles, 514 serial subscriptions, 727 audiovisual materials.

Computer facilities: 85 computers available on campus for general student use. A campuswide network can be accessed from off campus. Internet access is available. *Web address:* http://www.sjcny.edu/.

General Application Contact: Marion E. Salgado, Director of Admissions, 631-447-3219, Fax: 631-447-1734.

GRADUATE UNITS

Infant/Toddler Therapeutic Education Major Average age 31. 53 applicants, 58% accepted. *Faculty:* 7 full-time, 5 part-time/adjunct. Expenses: Contact institution. *Financial support:* Student loans available. Financial award application deadline: 3/15; financial award applicants required to submit FAFSA. In 2001, 19 degrees awarded. *Degree program information:* Part-time and evening/weekend programs available. Offers infant/toddler therapeutic education (MA). *Application deadline:* For fall admission, 8/15 (priority date). Applications are processed on a rolling basis. *Application fee:* $25. *Application Contact:* Marion E. Salgado, Director of Admissions, 631-447-3219, Fax: 631-447-1734. *Co-Director,* Sr. Frances Carmody, 631-447-3307, Fax: 631-447-1734, E-mail: fcarmody@sjcny.edu.

ST. JOSEPH'S SEMINARY, Yonkers, NY 10704

General Information Independent-religious, coed, graduate-only institution. *Enrollment by degree level:* 41 first professional, 104 master's. *Graduate faculty:* 15 full-time (2 women), 35 part-time/adjunct (5 women). *Graduate housing:* Room and/or apartments available to single students; on-campus housing not available to married students. *Student services:* Free psychological counseling, low-cost health insurance. *Library facilities:* Corrigan Library. *Collection:* 74,770 titles, 16,242 serial subscriptions.

Computer facilities: 8 computers available on campus for general student use.

General Application Contact: Rev. Msgr. Francis J. McAree, STD, Rector, 914-968-6200, Fax: 914-376-2019.

GRADUATE UNITS

Institute of Religious Studies *Degree program information:* Part-time and evening/weekend programs available. Offers religious studies (MA). Housing not available for this program. Electronic applications accepted.

Professional Program Students: 43 full-time (0 women); includes 6 minority (3 African Americans, 1 Asian American or Pacific Islander, 2 Hispanic Americans), 2 international. Average age 22. 10 applicants, 100% accepted. *Faculty:* 14 full-time (2 women), 18 part-time/adjunct (2 women). Expenses: Contact institution. In 2001, 3 first professional degrees, 3 master's awarded. Offers divinity (M Div); theology (MA). *Application Contact:* Rev. Joseph R. Giandurco, JCD, Dean of Admissions, 914-968-6200, Fax: 914-376-2019. *Rector,* Rev. Msgr. Francis J. McAree, STD, 914-968-6200, Fax: 914-376-2019.

SAINT JOSEPH'S UNIVERSITY, Philadelphia, PA 19131-1395

General Information Independent-religious, coed, comprehensive institution. *Enrollment:* 417 full-time matriculated graduate/professional students (224 women), 2,306 part-time matriculated graduate/professional students (1,499 women). *Enrollment by degree level:* 2,723 master's. *Graduate faculty:* 108 full-time (33 women), 109 part-time/adjunct (43 women). *Tuition:* Part-time $550 per credit. Tuition and fees vary according to program. *Graduate housing:* On-campus housing not available. *Student services:* Campus employment opportunities, campus safety program, career counseling, disabled student services, free psychological counseling, low-cost health insurance, multicultural affairs office, teacher training, writing training. *Library facilities:* Francis A. Drexel Library plus 1 other. *Online resources:* library catalog, web page, access to other libraries' catalogs. *Collection:* 197,788 titles, 4,900 serial subscriptions, 3,457 audiovisual materials. *Research affiliation:* Bayer AG (biology), Mountain Top Technologies (early responders to distance learning).

Computer facilities: 180 computers available on campus for general student use. A campuswide network can be accessed from student residence rooms and from off campus. Internet access and online class registration are available. *Web address:* http://www.sju.edu/.

General Application Contact: Dr. Robert H. Palestini, Graduate Programs Office, 610-660-1289, Fax: 610-660-3230, E-mail: rpalesti@sju.edu.

GRADUATE UNITS

College of Arts and Sciences Students: 277 full-time (161 women), 1,227 part-time (860 women); includes 229 minority (189 African Americans, 23 Asian Americans or Pacific Islanders, 17 Hispanic Americans), 165 international. Average age 32. *Faculty:* 60 full-time (25 women), 81 part-time/adjunct (41 women). Expenses: Contact institution. *Financial support:* In 2001–02, 16 teaching assistantships with full and partial tuition reimbursements (averaging $4,000 per year) were awarded; research assistantships, career-related internships or fieldwork, Federal Work-Study, scholarships/grants, and unspecified assistantships also available. Support available to part-time students. Financial award applicants required to submit FAFSA. In 2001, 366 degrees awarded. *Degree program information:* Part-time and evening/weekend programs available. Offers arts and sciences (MA, MS, D Ed, Ed D, Certificate); biology (MA, MS); chemistry (MS); chemistry education (MS); computer science (MS); criminal justice (MS); education (MS, Certificate); educational leadership (D Ed); gerontological services (MS); health administration (MS); health education (MS); mathematics education (MS); nurse anesthesia (MS); professional education (MS); psychology (MS); reading (MS); secondary education (MS); special education (MS); training and development (MS). *Application deadline:* For fall admission, 7/15. *Application fee:* $35. *Graduate Programs Office,* Dr. Robert H. Palestini, 610-660-1289, Fax: 610-660-3230, E-mail: rpalesti@sju.edu.

Erivan K. Haub School of Business Students: 160 full-time (80 women), 2,775 part-time (1,515 women); includes 241 minority (98 African Americans, 102 Asian Americans or Pacific Islanders, 39 Hispanic Americans, 2 Native Americans), 38 international. Expenses: Contact institution. *Financial support:* In 2001–02, 8 research assistantships with tuition reimbursements (averaging $2,000 per year) were awarded; career-related internships or fieldwork, Federal Work-Study, institutionally sponsored loans, scholarships/grants, tuition waivers (partial), and unspecified assistantships also available. Support available to part-time students. Financial award applicants required to submit FAFSA. In 2001, 275 degrees awarded. *Degree program information:* Part-time and evening/weekend programs available. Offers accounting (MBA); business (EMBA, MBA, MS); business administration (EMBA); finance (MBA); financial services (MS); food marketing (MS); general business (MBA); health and medical services administration (MBA); human resource management (MS); information systems (MBA); international business (MBA); international marketing (MBA, MS); management (MBA); marketing (MBA); pharmaceutical marketing (MBA). *Application deadline:* For fall admission, 7/15; for spring admission, 11/15 (priority date). Applications are processed on a rolling basis. *Application fee:* $35. Electronic applications accepted. *Application Contact:* Adele C. Foley, Associate Dean, Director Graduate Business Programs, 610-660-1690, Fax: 610-660-1599, E-mail: afoley@sju.edu. *Dean,* Dr. Joseph DiAngelo, 610-660-1645, Fax: 610-660-1649, E-mail: jodiange@sju.edu.

See in-depth description on page 1067.

ST. LAWRENCE UNIVERSITY, Canton, NY 13617-1455

General Information Independent, coed, comprehensive institution. *Enrollment:* 14 full-time matriculated graduate/professional students (8 women), 70 part-time matriculated graduate/professional students (42 women). *Graduate faculty:* 8 full-time (4 women), 25 part-time/adjunct (14 women). *Tuition:* Part-time $515 per credit. *Graduate housing:* Room and/or apartments available on a first-come, first-served basis to single students; on-campus housing not available to married students. Housing application deadline: 4/1. *Student services:* Campus employment opportunities, campus safety program, career counseling, free psychological counseling, international student services, low-cost health insurance. *Library facilities:* Owen D. Young Library plus 1 other. *Online resources:* library catalog, web page, access to other libraries' catalogs. *Collection:* 509,348 titles, 2,014 serial subscriptions.

Computer facilities: 600 computers available on campus for general student use. A campuswide network can be accessed from student residence rooms and from off campus. Internet access, internships, shadowing programs are available. *Web address:* http://www.stlawu.edu/.

General Application Contact: Naomi S. Ten Eyck, Senior Secretary, 315-229-5861, Fax: 315-229-7423, E-mail: nteneyck@stlawu.edu.

GRADUATE UNITS

Department of Education Students: 14 full-time (8 women), 70 part-time (42 women). *Faculty:* 8 full-time (4 women), 25 part-time/adjunct (14 women). Expenses: Contact institution. *Financial support:* In 2001–02, 3 research assistantships with tuition reimbursements (averaging $12,120 per year), 1 teaching assistantship with tuition reimbursement (averaging $12,120 per year) were awarded. Career-related internships or fieldwork, Federal Work-Study, and tuition waivers (full) also available. Support available to part-time students. In 2001, 39 degrees awarded. *Degree program information:* Part-time and evening/weekend programs available. Offers counseling and human development (M Ed, CAS); education (Certificate); educational administration (M Ed, CAS); general studies (M Ed). *Application deadline:* Applications are processed on a rolling basis. *Application fee:* $0. *Application Contact:* Naomi S. Ten Eyck, Senior Secretary, 315-229-5861, Fax: 315-229-7423, E-mail: nteneyck@stlawu.edu. *Chair,* Dr. James Shuman, 315-229-5847, Fax: 315-229-7423, E-mail: jshuman@stlawu.edu.

SAINT LEO UNIVERSITY, Saint Leo, FL 33574-6665

General Information Independent-religious, coed, comprehensive institution. *Enrollment:* 198 full-time matriculated graduate/professional students (109 women), 29 part-time matriculated graduate/professional students (24 women). *Enrollment by degree level:* 227 master's. *Graduate faculty:* 3 full-time (0 women), 8 part-time/adjunct (4 women). *Tuition:* Full-time $5,040; part-time $280 per semester hour. Tuition and fees vary according to program. *Graduate housing:* On-campus housing not available. *Student services:* Campus employment opportunities, career counseling, disabled student services, exercise/wellness program, free psychological counseling, international student services, low-cost health insurance, multicultural affairs office. *Library facilities:* Cannon Memorial Library. *Online resources:* library catalog, web page, access to other libraries' catalogs. *Collection:* 103,938 titles, 750 serial subscriptions, 5,768 audiovisual materials. *Research affiliation:* American Jewish Committee (religion).

Computer facilities: 570 computers available on campus for general student use. A campuswide network can be accessed from student residence rooms and from off campus. Internet access is available. *Web address:* http://www.saintleo.edu/.

General Application Contact: Martin Smith, Director of Graduate Admission, 352-588-8236, Fax: 352-588-8205, E-mail: martin.smith@saintleo.edu.

GRADUATE UNITS

Graduate Business Studies Students: 142 full-time (62 women), 4 part-time; includes 68 minority (16 African Americans, 3 Asian Americans or Pacific Islanders, 47 Hispanic Americans, 2 Native Americans), 9 international. Average age 37. 117 applicants, 69% accepted, 58 enrolled. *Faculty:* 1 full-time (0 women), 4 part-time/adjunct (1 woman). Expenses: Contact institution. *Financial support:* In 2001–02, 56 students received support, including 2 research assistantships with tuition reimbursements available (averaging $6,000 per year); unspecified assistantships also available. Support available to part-time students. Financial award application deadline: 3/1; financial award applicants required to submit FAFSA. In 2001, 46

Saint Leo University (continued)

degrees awarded. *Degree program information:* Part-time and evening/weekend programs available. Offers business (MBA). *Application deadline:* For fall admission, 6/26 (priority date); for spring admission, 11/13 (priority date). Applications are processed on a rolling basis. *Application fee:* $45. Electronic applications accepted. *Application Contact:* Martin Smith, Director of Graduate Admission, 352-588-8236, Fax: 352-588-8205, E-mail: martin.smith@saintleo.edu. *Director*, Dr. T. Lynn Wilson, 352-588-8314, Fax: 352-588-8312, E-mail: lynn.wilson@saintleo.edu.

Graduate Studies in Education Students: 56 full-time (47 women), 25 part-time (24 women); includes 12 minority (8 African Americans, 4 Hispanic Americans) Average age 37. 67 applicants, 54% accepted, 32 enrolled. *Faculty:* 2 full-time (0 women), 4 part-time/adjunct (3 women). Expenses: Contact institution. *Financial support:* In 2001–02, 33 students received support, including 2 research assistantships with tuition reimbursements available (averaging $6,000 per year); career-related internships or fieldwork and unspecified assistantships also available. Support available to part-time students. Financial award application deadline: 3/1; financial award applicants required to submit FAFSA. In 2001, 41 degrees awarded. *Degree program information:* Part-time and evening/weekend programs available. Offers education (M Ed). *Application deadline:* For fall admission, 6/26 (priority date); for winter admission, 11/16 (priority date); for spring admission, 3/4 (priority date). Applications are processed on a rolling basis. *Application fee:* $45. Electronic applications accepted. *Application Contact:* Martin Smith, Director of Graduate Admission, 352-588-8236, Fax: 352-588-8205, E-mail: martin.smith@saintleo.edu. *Director*, Dr. Charles Hale, 352-588-8309, Fax: 352-588-8861, E-mail: charles.hale@saintleo.edu.

ST. LOUIS COLLEGE OF PHARMACY, St. Louis, MO 63110-1088

General Information Independent, coed, comprehensive institution. *Enrollment:* 66 full-time matriculated graduate/professional students (47 women), 6 part-time matriculated graduate/professional students (4 women). *Enrollment by degree level:* 68 first professional, 4 master's. *Graduate faculty:* 43 full-time (28 women), 4 part-time/adjunct (1 woman). *Tuition:* Full-time $17,000; part-time $735 per credit hour. *Required fees:* $120; $60 per semester. One-time fee: $120. *Graduate housing:* Rooms and/or apartments available on a first-come, first-served basis to single and married students. Typical cost: $5,364 (including board) for single students; $4,185 per year for married students. Housing application deadline: 5/1. *Student services:* Campus safety program, career counseling, disabled student services, exercise/wellness program, free psychological counseling, low-cost health insurance, writing training. *Library facilities:* O. J. Cloughly Alumni Library. *Online resources:* library catalog, web page, access to other libraries' catalogs. *Collection:* 56,636 titles, 282 serial subscriptions, 1,003 audiovisual materials.

Computer facilities: 80 computers available on campus for general student use. A campuswide network can be accessed from student residence rooms and from off campus. Internet access is available. *Web address:* http://www.stlcop.edu/.

General Application Contact: Penny Myers Bryant, Director of Admissions/Registrar, 314-367-8700 Ext. 1067, Fax: 314-367-2784, E-mail: pbryant@stlcop.edu.

GRADUATE UNITS

Professional Program in Pharmacy Students: 66 full-time (47 women), 2 part-time (both women); includes 17 minority (4 African Americans, 13 Asian Americans or Pacific Islanders), 1 international. Average age 24. 6 applicants, 33% accepted, 1 enrolled. *Faculty:* 43 full-time (28 women), 4 part-time/adjunct (1 woman). Expenses: Contact institution. *Financial support:* Scholarships/grants and health care benefits available. In 2001, 64 degrees awarded. Offers pharmacy (Pharm D). *Application deadline:* For fall admission, 2/1 (priority date). Applications are processed on a rolling basis. *Application fee:* $35. Electronic applications accepted. *Director of Admissions/Registrar*, Penny Myers Bryant, 314-367-8700 Ext. 1067, Fax: 314-367-2784, E-mail: pbryant@stlcop.edu.

Program in Pharmacy Administration Average age 35. 3 applicants, 100% accepted, 3 enrolled. *Faculty:* 3 full-time (0 women), 6 part-time/adjunct (2 women). Expenses: Contact institution. In 2001, 3 degrees awarded. *Degree program information:* Part-time and evening/weekend programs available. Postbaccalaureate distance learning degree programs offered (minimal on-campus study). Offers managed care pharmacy (MS); pharmacy administration (MS). *Application deadline:* For fall admission, 8/1 (priority date); for winter admission, 12/20 (priority date); for spring admission, 3/15 (priority date). Applications are processed on a rolling basis. *Application fee:* $35. *Application Contact:* Lois F. Dunaway, Division Secretary, 314-367-8700 Ext. 1746, Fax: 314-367-2784, E-mail: ldunaway@stlcop.edu. *Director of Graduate Studies*, Dr. Kenneth W. Schafermeyer, 314-367-8700 Ext. 1743, Fax: 314-367-2784, E-mail: kschafermeyer@stlcop.edu.

SAINT LOUIS UNIVERSITY, St. Louis, MO 63103-2097

General Information Independent-religious, coed, university. CGS member. *Enrollment:* 2,044 full-time matriculated graduate/professional students (1,124 women), 1,782 part-time matriculated graduate/professional students (1,095 women). *Enrollment by degree level:* 1,356 first professional, 1,597 master's, 836 doctoral, 38 other advanced degrees. *Graduate faculty:* 1,153 full-time (362 women), 1,522 part-time/adjunct (388 women). *Tuition:* Part-time $630 per credit hour. *Graduate housing:* Room and/or apartments available to single students. Housing application deadline: 6/1. *Student services:* Campus employment opportunities, campus safety program, career counseling, free psychological counseling, international student services, low-cost health insurance. *Library facilities:* Pius XII Memorial Library plus 3 others. *Online resources:* web page. *Collection:* 1.3 million titles, 14,724 serial subscriptions, 200,400 audiovisual materials. *Research affiliation:* National Center for Atmospheric Research (earth and atmospheric sciences), Argonne National Laboratory (energy/physics/chemistry/mathematics and computer science), Tropical Research Center (Belize), Small Business Administration (business, administration and entrepreneurship), Monsanto Chemical Corporation (chemistry), Missouri Botanical Garden (biology/plant science).

Computer facilities: 6,500 computers available on campus for general student use. A campuswide network can be accessed from student residence rooms and from off campus. Internet access and online class registration are available. *Web address:* http://www.slu.edu/.

General Application Contact: Dr. Marcia Buresch, Associate Dean of the Graduate School, 314-977-2240, Fax: 314-977-3943, E-mail: bureschm@slu.edu.

GRADUATE UNITS

Graduate School Students: 496 full-time (300 women), 1,274 part-time (801 women); includes 306 minority (196 African Americans, 59 Asian Americans or Pacific Islanders, 44 Hispanic Americans, 7 Native Americans), 143 international. 1,385 applicants, 54% accepted, 454 enrolled. *Faculty:* 474 full-time (162 women), 309 part-time/adjunct (152 women). Expenses: Contact institution. *Financial support:* In 2001–02, 1,029 students received support; fellowships with full tuition reimbursements available, research assistantships with full tuition reimbursements available, teaching assistantships, career-related internships or fieldwork, Federal Work-Study, institutionally sponsored loans, traineeships, tuition waivers (full and partial), and unspecified assistantships available. Support available to part-time students. Financial award application deadline: 4/1; financial award applicants required to submit FAFSA. In 2001, 294 master's, 137 doctorates, 7 other advanced degrees awarded. *Degree program information:* Part-time and evening/weekend programs available. Postbaccalaureate distance learning degree programs offered (minimal on-campus study). Offers advanced dental education (MS, MS(R)); aerospace engineering (MS, MS(R)); engineering and aviation (MS, MS(R)). *Application deadline:* Applications are processed on a rolling basis. *Application fee:* $40. *Application Contact:* Dr. Marcia Buresch, Associate Dean of the Graduate School, 314-977-2240, Fax: 314-977-3943, E-mail: bureschm@slu.edu. *Dean*, Dr. Donald G. Brennan, 314-977-2244, Fax: 314-977-3943.

Center for Health Care Ethics Students: 9 full-time (1 woman), 9 part-time (2 women); includes 2 minority (1 African American, 1 Asian American or Pacific Islander), 3 international. Average age 36. 7 applicants, 43% accepted, 2 enrolled. *Faculty:* 4 full-time (1 woman), 2 part-time/adjunct (1 woman). Expenses: Contact institution. *Financial support:* In 2001–02, 12 students received support; fellowships with full tuition reimbursements available, tuition waivers (full) and unspecified assistantships available. Financial award application deadline: 4/1; financial award applicants required to submit FAFSA. In 2001, 2 doctorates awarded. Offers health care ethics (PhD). *Application deadline:* For fall admission, 7/1; for spring admission, 11/1. Applications are processed on a rolling basis. *Application fee:* $40. *Application Contact:* Dr. Marcia Buresch, Associate Dean of the Graduate School, 314-977-2240, Fax: 314-977-3943, E-mail: bureschm@slu.edu. *Executive Director*, Rev. Gerard Magill, 314-977-6660, E-mail: magill@slu.edu.

College of Arts and Sciences Students: 156 full-time (75 women), 342 part-time (169 women); includes 64 minority (34 African Americans, 8 Asian Americans or Pacific Islanders, 21 Hispanic Americans, 1 Native American), 24 international. Average age 31. 435 applicants, 54% accepted, 117 enrolled. *Faculty:* 230 full-time (60 women), 60 part-time/adjunct (14 women). Expenses: Contact institution. *Financial support:* In 2001–02, 344 students received support, including 15 fellowships, 43 research assistantships, 104 teaching assistantships; career-related internships or fieldwork, Federal Work-Study, institutionally sponsored loans, tuition waivers (partial), and unspecified assistantships also available. Support available to part-time students. Financial award application deadline: 4/1; financial award applicants required to submit FAFSA. In 2001, 73 master's, 45 doctorates awarded. *Degree program information:* Part-time programs available. Offers American studies (MA, MA(R), PhD); applied experimental psychology (MS(R), PhD); arts and sciences (M Pr Met, MA, MA(R), MS, MS(R), PhD); biology (MS, MS(R), PhD); chemistry (MS, MS(R)); clinical psychology (MS(R), PhD); communication (MA, MA(R)); English (MA, MA(R), PhD); French (MA); geophysics (PhD); geoscience (MS, MS(R)); historical theology (MA, PhD); history (MA, MA(R), PhD); mathematics (MA, MA(R), PhD); meteorology (M Pr Met, MS(R), PhD); philosophy (MA, MA(R), PhD); Spanish (MA); theology (MA). *Application deadline:* For spring admission, 11/1. Applications are processed on a rolling basis. *Application fee:* $40. *Application Contact:* Dr. Marcia Buresch, Associate Dean of the Graduate School, 314-977-2240, Fax: 314-977-3943, E-mail: bureschm@slu.edu. *Dean*, Dr. Joseph Weixlmann, 314-977-2705, Fax: 314-977-3649, E-mail: weixlmj@slu.edu.

College of Public Service Students: 99 full-time (76 women), 490 part-time (318 women); includes 119 minority (99 African Americans, 11 Asian Americans or Pacific Islanders, 5 Hispanic Americans, 4 Native Americans), 9 international. Average age 38. 277 applicants, 74% accepted, 136 enrolled. *Faculty:* 49 full-time (26 women), 30 part-time/adjunct (20 women). Expenses: Contact institution. *Financial support:* In 2001–02, 184 students received support, including 5 fellowships, 5 research assistantships, 2 teaching assistantships; career-related internships or fieldwork, Federal Work-Study, traineeships, tuition waivers (partial), and unspecified assistantships also available. Financial award application deadline: 4/1; financial award applicants required to submit FAFSA. In 2001, 68 master's, 67 doctorates awarded. Offers communication sciences and disorders (MA, MA(R)); counseling and family therapy (PhD); curriculum and instruction (MA, Ed D, PhD); education (MAT); educational leadership (MA, Ed D, PhD, Ed S); foundations (MA, Ed D, PhD); higher education (MA, Ed D, PhD); human development counseling (MA); marriage and family therapy (Certificate); public administration (MAPA); public policy analysis (PhD); public service (MA, MA(R), MAPA, MAT, MAUA, MUPRED, Ed D, PhD, Certificate, Ed S); school counseling (MA); special education (MA); urban affairs (MAUA); urban planning and real estate development (MUPRED). *Application deadline:* Applications are processed on a rolling basis. *Application fee:* $40. *Application Contact:* Dr. Marcia Buresch, Associate Dean of the Graduate School, 314-977-2240, Fax: 314-977-3943, E-mail: bureschm@slu.edu. *Dean*, Dr. James F. Gilsinian, 314-977-3292, Fax: 314-977-3290, E-mail: gilsinanjf@slu.edu.

School of Allied Health Professions Students: 16 full-time (all women), 43 part-time (37 women); includes 6 minority (3 African Americans, 1 Asian American or Pacific Islander, 2 Hispanic Americans), 4 international. Average age 28. 23 applicants, 96% accepted, 17 enrolled. *Faculty:* 6 full-time (5 women), 5 part-time/adjunct (all women). Expenses: Contact institution. *Financial support:* In 2001–02, 25 students received support, including 6 teaching assistantships; career-related internships or fieldwork also available. Financial award application deadline: 4/1; financial award applicants required to submit FAFSA. In 2001, 7 degrees awarded. Offers allied health (MMS, MSPT); allied health professions (MMS, MOT, MS, MSPT); nutrition and dietetics (MS); physical therapy (MSPT); physician assistant (MMS). *Application deadline:* For fall admission, 7/1; for spring admission, 11/1. Applications are processed on a rolling basis. *Application fee:* $40. *Application Contact:* Dr. Marcia Buresch, Associate Dean of the Graduate School, 314-977-2240, Fax: 314-977-3943, E-mail: bureschm@slu.edu. *Interim Dean*, Dr. Joan Hrubetz, 314-577-8501, Fax: 314-577-8513, E-mail: hrubetz@slu.edu.

School of Nursing Students: 26 full-time (22 women), 194 part-time (183 women); includes 33 minority (16 African Americans, 7 Asian Americans or Pacific Islanders, 8 Hispanic Americans, 2 Native Americans), 5 international. Average age 40. 85 applicants, 86% accepted, 54 enrolled. *Faculty:* 29 full-time (28 women), 81 part-time/adjunct (73 women). Expenses: Contact institution. *Financial support:* In 2001–02, 62 students received support, including 9 research assistantships with tuition reimbursements available; fellowships, teaching assistantships, traineeships also available. Financial award application deadline: 4/1; financial award applicants required to submit FAFSA. In 2001, 34 master's, 7 doctorates, 7 other advanced degrees awarded. Postbaccalaureate distance learning degree programs offered (minimal on-campus study). Offers nursing (MSN, MSN(R), PhD, Certificate). *Application deadline:* For fall admission, 7/1; for spring admission, 11/1. Applications are processed on a rolling basis. *Application fee:* $40. *Application Contact:* Dr. Marcia Buresch, Associate Dean of the Graduate School, 314-977-2240, Fax: 314-977-3943, E-mail: bureschm@slu.edu. *Director*, Dr. Mary Ellen McSweeney, 314-577-8913, Fax: 314-577-8949, E-mail: mcsweem@slu.edu.

School of Public Health Students: 122 full-time (85 women), 103 part-time (56 women); includes 66 minority (40 African Americans, 21 Asian Americans or Pacific Islanders, 5 Hispanic Americans), 56 international. Average age 31. 230 applicants, 71% accepted, 86 enrolled. *Faculty:* 39 full-time (18 women), 86 part-time/adjunct (36 women). Expenses: Contact institution. *Financial support:* In 2001–02, 112 students received support, including 29 research assistantships with tuition reimbursements available; career-related internships or fieldwork and unspecified assistantships also available. Financial award application deadline: 4/1; financial award applicants required to submit FAFSA. In 2001, 83 master's, 5 doctorates awarded. Offers behavioral science in health education (MPH); biostatistics (MPH); biostatistics and epidemiology (MPH); community health (MPH); environmental and occupational health (MPH); environmental health and epidemiology (MPH); epidemiology (MPH); health management and policy (MHA); health management policy (MHA); health services research (PhD). *Application deadline:* Applications are processed on a rolling basis. *Application fee:* $40. *Application Contact:* Dr. Marcia Buresch, Associate Dean of the Graduate School, 314-977-2240, Fax: 314-977-3943, E-mail: bureschm@slu.edu. *Interim Dean*, Dr. William True, 314-977-8100, Fax: 314-977-8150, E-mail: true@slu.edu.

John Cook School of Business Students: 134 full-time (58 women), 147 part-time (54 women); includes 30 minority (12 African Americans, 12 Asian Americans or Pacific Islanders, 5 Hispanic Americans, 1 Native American), 44 international. Average age 28. 270 applicants, 63% accepted, 90 enrolled. *Faculty:* 85 full-time (17 women), 21 part-time/adjunct (8 women). Expenses: Contact institution. *Financial support:* In 2001–02, 102 students received support, including 1 research assistantship; fellowships, teaching assistantships, career-related internships or fieldwork and Federal Work-Study also available. Support available to part-time students. Financial award application deadline: 4/1; financial award applicants required to submit FAFSA. In 2001, 187 master's, 7 doctorates awarded. *Degree program information:* Part-time and evening/weekend programs available. Offers accounting (M Acct); business (EMIB, M Acct, M Dec S, M Fin, M Mgt, MA, MBA, MIB, MMIS, PhD); business administration (PhD); economics (MBA); executive international business (EMIB); finance (M Fin); international business and marketing (PhD). *Application deadline:* Applications are processed on a rolling basis. *Application fee:* $40. Electronic applications accepted. *Dean*, 314-977-3800, Fax: 314-977-1416, E-mail: mba@slu.edu.

School of Law Students: 544 full-time (254 women), 213 part-time (113 women); includes 94 minority (51 African Americans, 19 Asian Americans or Pacific Islanders, 20 Hispanic Americans, 4 Native Americans), 11 international. Average age 28. 1,390 applicants, 54% accepted, 274 enrolled. *Faculty:* 34 full-time (8 women), 31 part-time/adjunct (7 women). Expenses:

Contact institution. *Financial support:* In 2001–02, 368 students received support, including 30 fellowships; career-related internships or fieldwork, Federal Work-Study, and tuition waivers (partial) also available. Support available to part-time students. Financial award application deadline: 4/1; financial award applicants required to submit FAFSA. In 2001, 214 first professional degrees, 11 master's awarded. *Degree program information:* Part-time and evening/weekend programs available. Offers law (JD, LL M, Certificate). *Application deadline:* For fall admission, 3/1 (priority date). Applications are processed on a rolling basis. *Application fee:* $55. Electronic applications accepted. *Application Contact:* Michael J. Kolnik, Director of Admissions, 314-977-2800, E-mail: kolnikmj@slu.edu. *Dean*, Jeffrey E. Lewis, Fax: 314-977-3332.

School of Medicine Students: 610 full-time (286 women); includes 208 minority (71 African Americans, 118 Asian Americans or Pacific Islanders, 18 Hispanic Americans, 1 Native American), 1 international. Average age 25. 5,042 applicants, 8% accepted, 153 enrolled. *Faculty:* 520 full-time (149 women), 1,135 part-time/adjunct (203 women). Expenses: Contact institution. *Financial support:* In 2001–02, 266 students received support, including 12 fellowships, 6 research assistantships, 2 teaching assistantships; career-related internships or fieldwork, Federal Work-Study, institutionally sponsored loans, and tuition waivers (full and partial) also available. Support available to part-time students. Financial award application deadline: 4/1; financial award applicants required to submit FAFSA. In 2001, 141 degrees awarded. Offers anatomy (MS(R), PhD); biochemistry and molecular biology (PhD); medicine (MD, MS(R), PhD); molecular microbiology and immunology (PhD); neurobiology (PhD); pathology (PhD); pharmacological and physiological science (PhD). *Application deadline:* For winter admission, 12/15 (priority date). Applications are processed on a rolling basis. *Application fee:* $100. Electronic applications accepted. *Application Contact:* Dr. James Willmore, Dean of Admissions, 314-577-8205, Fax: 314-577-8214, E-mail: willmore@slu.edu. *Dean*, Dr. Patricia L. Monteleone, 314-577-8201, Fax: 314-577-8253, E-mail: montelpl@slu.edu.

School of Social Service Students: 123 full-time (109 women), 147 part-time (126 women); includes 54 minority (44 African Americans, 7 Asian Americans or Pacific Islanders, 2 Hispanic Americans, 1 Native American), 6 international. Average age 31. 141 applicants, 91% accepted, 93 enrolled. *Faculty:* 20 full-time (10 women), 22 part-time/adjunct (14 women). Expenses: Contact institution. *Financial support:* In 2001–02, 211 students received support. Career-related internships or fieldwork, Federal Work-Study, scholarships/grants, traineeships, tuition waivers (partial), and unspecified assistantships available. Support available to part-time students. Financial award application deadline: 3/1; financial award applicants required to submit FAFSA. In 2001, 109 degrees awarded. *Degree program information:* Part-time and evening/weekend programs available. Offers social service (MSW). *Application deadline:* For fall admission, 4/1 (priority date); for spring admission, 11/1 (priority date). Applications are processed on a rolling basis. *Application fee:* $40. *Application Contact:* Director of Admission, 314-977-2722, Fax: 314-977-2731. *Dean*, Dr. Susan C. Tebb, 314-977-3460, Fax: 314-977-2731, E-mail: tebbsc@slu.edu.

See in-depth description on page 1069.

SAINT MARTIN'S COLLEGE, Lacey, WA 98503-7500

General Information Independent-religious, coed, comprehensive institution. *Enrollment:* 194 full-time matriculated graduate/professional students (114 women), 88 part-time matriculated graduate/professional students (48 women). *Enrollment by degree level:* 282 master's. *Graduate faculty:* 20 full-time (10 women), 12 part-time/adjunct (3 women). *Tuition:* Part-time $519 per credit hour. *Required fees:* $180; $90 per semester. One-time fee: $125 full-time. *Graduate housing:* Rooms and/or apartments available on a first-come, first-served basis to single and married students. Typical cost: $1,672 per year ($4,926 including board) for single students; $1,972 per year ($4,926 including board) for married students. Housing application deadline: 4/1. *Student services:* Campus employment opportunities, campus safety program, career counseling, disabled student services, exercise/wellness program, free psychological counseling, international student services, low-cost health insurance, writing training. *Library facilities:* Saint Martin's College Library. *Online resources:* library catalog, web page, access to other libraries' catalogs. *Collection:* 84,220 titles, 852 serial subscriptions, 1,239 audiovisual materials.

Computer facilities: 110 computers available on campus for general student use. A campuswide network can be accessed from student residence rooms and from off campus. Internet access is available. *Web address:* http://www.stmartin.edu/.

General Application Contact: 360-438-4311.

GRADUATE UNITS

Graduate Programs Students: 194 full-time (114 women), 88 part-time (48 women); includes 44 minority (15 African Americans, 16 Asian Americans or Pacific Islanders, 8 Hispanic Americans, 5 Native Americans), 3 international. Average age 37. *Faculty:* 20 full-time (10 women), 12 part-time/adjunct (3 women). Expenses: Contact institution. *Financial support:* In 2001–02, 185 students received support; fellowships, research assistantships, career-related internships or fieldwork, Federal Work-Study, institutionally sponsored loans, scholarships/grants, and tuition waivers (partial) available. Support available to part-time students. Financial award application deadline: 3/1; financial award applicants required to submit FAFSA. In 2001, 108 degrees awarded. *Degree program information:* Part-time and evening/weekend programs available. Offers civil engineering (MCE); classroom leadership (M Ed); computers in education (M Ed); counseling and community psychology (MAC); counseling and guidance (M Ed); engineering management (M Eng Mgt); reading (M Ed); special education (M Ed); teaching (MIT). *Application deadline:* For fall admission, 7/1. Applications are processed on a rolling basis. *Application fee:* $35. *Vice President, Academic Affairs*, Dr. Jacqueline Johnson, 360-438-4310, Fax: 360-438-4591, E-mail: jjohnson@stmartin.edu.

Division of Economics and Business Administration Average age 28. *Faculty:* 7 full-time (0 women), 6 part-time/adjunct (1 woman). Expenses: Contact institution. *Financial support:* Career-related internships or fieldwork and scholarships/grants available. Support available to part-time students. Financial award application deadline: 3/1. In 2001, 27 degrees awarded. *Degree program information:* Part-time and evening/weekend programs available. Offers economics and business administration (MBA). *Application deadline:* Applications are processed on a rolling basis. *Application fee:* $35. *Application Contact:* Leslie Good, Administrative Assistant, 360-438-4512, Fax: 360-438-4522, E-mail: lgood@stmartin.edu. *Director*, Haldon D. Wilson, 360-438-4326, Fax: 360-438-4522, E-mail: hwilson@stmartin.edu.

SAINT MARY COLLEGE, Leavenworth, KS 66048-5082

General Information Independent-religious, coed, comprehensive institution. *Graduate housing:* On-campus housing not available.

GRADUATE UNITS

Graduate Programs *Degree program information:* Part-time and evening/weekend programs available. Postbaccalaureate distance learning degree programs offered (no on-campus study). Offers business administration (MBA); curriculum and instruction (MA); education (MA); management (MS); psychology (MA); teaching (MA). Electronic applications accepted.

SAINT MARY-OF-THE-WOODS COLLEGE, Saint Mary-of-the-Woods, IN 47876

General Information Independent-religious, women only, comprehensive institution. *Enrollment:* 1 (woman) full-time matriculated graduate/professional student, 116 part-time matriculated graduate/professional students (97 women). *Enrollment by degree level:* 117 master's. *Graduate faculty:* 8 full-time (4 women), 27 part-time/adjunct (23 women). *Tuition:* Part-time $350 per credit hour. *Graduate housing:* Rooms and/or apartments available to single and married students. *Student services:* Campus safety program, career counseling, child daycare facilities, disabled student services, international student services. *Library facilities:* College Library. *Online resources:* library catalog, access to other libraries' catalogs. *Collection:* 152,162 titles, 301 serial subscriptions, 522 audiovisual materials.

Computer facilities: 65 computers available on campus for general student use. A campuswide network can be accessed from student residence rooms and from off campus. Internet access is available. *Web address:* http://www.smwc.edu/.

General Application Contact: Gwen Hagemeyer, Director of Admissions, 812-535-5107, Fax: 812-535-4613, E-mail: mapt@smwc.edu.

GRADUATE UNITS

Interdisciplinary Program in Earth Literacy Students: 1 (woman) full-time, 31 part-time (29 women). Average age 43. 17 applicants, 100% accepted. *Faculty:* 11 part-time/adjunct (9 women). Expenses: Contact institution. *Financial support:* Career-related internships or fieldwork available. Financial award application deadline: 3/1; financial award applicants required to submit FAFSA. In 2001, 1 degree awarded. *Degree program information:* Part-time programs available. Postbaccalaureate distance learning degree programs offered (minimal on-campus study). Offers earth literacy (MA). *Application deadline:* Applications are processed on a rolling basis. *Application fee:* $35. Electronic applications accepted. *Director*, Mary Lou Dolan, 812-535-5160, Fax: 812-535-5127, E-mail: mldolan@smwc.edu.

Program in Art Therapy Average age 39. 20 applicants, 50% accepted, 3 enrolled. *Faculty:* 3 full-time (2 women), 6 part-time/adjunct (5 women). Expenses: Contact institution. *Financial support:* Scholarships/grants available. Financial award applicants required to submit FAFSA. *Degree program information:* Part-time and evening/weekend programs available. Postbaccalaureate distance learning degree programs offered (minimal on-campus study). Offers art therapy (MAT). *Application deadline:* For fall admission, 5/20 (priority date); for winter admission, 12/7 (priority date). *Application fee:* $35. Electronic applications accepted. *Director*, Kathy Jeanne Gotshall, 812-535-5162, Fax: 812-535-4613, E-mail: kgotshall@smwc.edu.

Program in Music Therapy Average age 32. 2 applicants, 100% accepted. *Faculty:* 3 full-time (2 women), 6 part-time/adjunct (5 women). Expenses: Contact institution. *Financial support:* In 2001–02, 2 students received support. In 2001, 2 degrees awarded. *Degree program information:* Part-time programs available. Postbaccalaureate distance learning degree programs offered (minimal on-campus study). Offers music therapy (MA). *Application deadline:* Applications are processed on a rolling basis. *Application fee:* $35. Electronic applications accepted. *Director*, Tracy Gay Richardson, 812-535-5154, Fax: 812-535-4613, E-mail: trichard@smwc.edu.

Program in Pastoral Theology Average age 45. 8 applicants, 100% accepted. *Faculty:* 2 full-time (0 women), 4 part-time/adjunct (all women). Expenses: Contact institution. *Financial support:* In 2001–02, 3 students received support. Scholarships/grants and tuition waivers (partial) available. Financial award applicants required to submit FAFSA. In 2001, 12 degrees awarded. *Degree program information:* Part-time and evening/weekend programs available. Postbaccalaureate distance learning degree programs offered (minimal on-campus study). Offers pastoral theology (MA). *Application deadline:* For fall admission, 8/1 (priority date); for winter admission, 12/1 (priority date); for spring admission, 4/1 (priority date). Applications are processed on a rolling basis. *Application fee:* $35. *Director, Graduate Program in Pastoral Theology*, Dr. Virginia Unverzagt, 812-535-5206, Fax: 812-535-4613, E-mail: vunverzagt@smwc.edu.

SAINT MARY'S COLLEGE OF CALIFORNIA, Moraga, CA 94556

General Information Independent-religious, coed, comprehensive institution. *Enrollment:* 501 full-time matriculated graduate/professional students (310 women), 565 part-time matriculated graduate/professional students (445 women). *Enrollment by degree level:* 1,066 master's. *Graduate faculty:* 42 full-time (26 women), 356 part-time/adjunct (250 women). *Tuition:* Full-time $10,416; part-time $496 per unit. Full-time tuition and fees vary according to course load and program. *Graduate housing:* On-campus housing not available. *Student services:* Campus employment opportunities, campus safety program, career counseling, disabled student services, international student services, low-cost health insurance, multicultural affairs office, teacher training. *Library facilities:* St. Albert Hall plus 1 other. *Online resources:* library catalog, web page, access to other libraries' catalogs. *Collection:* 153,576 titles, 1,066 serial subscriptions, 6,925 audiovisual materials.

Computer facilities: 250 computers available on campus for general student use. A campuswide network can be accessed from student residence rooms and from off campus. Internet access is available. *Web address:* http://www.stmarys-ca.edu/.

General Application Contact: Michael Beseda, Vice President, Enrollment Services, 925-631-4277, Fax: 925-376-8339, E-mail: mbeseda@stmarys-ca.edu.

GRADUATE UNITS

Graduate Business Programs Students: 162 full-time (66 women), 112 part-time (35 women); includes 59 minority (6 African Americans, 36 Asian Americans or Pacific Islanders, 17 Hispanic Americans) Average age 33. 152 applicants, 65% accepted, 73 enrolled. *Faculty:* 9 full-time (2 women), 20 part-time/adjunct (5 women). Expenses: Contact institution. *Financial support:* Career-related internships or fieldwork available. Support available to part-time students. Financial award application deadline: 3/2; financial award applicants required to submit FAFSA. In 2001, 89 degrees awarded. *Degree program information:* Part-time and evening/weekend programs available. Offers business administration (MBA); economics and business administration (MBA); executive business administration (MBA). *Application deadline:* Applications are processed on a rolling basis. *Application fee:* $50. *Application Contact:* Bob Peterson, Director of Admissions, 925-631-4505, Fax: 925-376-6521, E-mail: smcmba@stmarys-ca.edu. *Director*, Nelson Shelton, 925-631-4514, Fax: 925-376-6521, E-mail: smcmba@stmarys-ca.edu.

School of Education Students: 227 full-time (172 women), 278 part-time (258 women); includes 81 minority (20 African Americans, 19 Asian Americans or Pacific Islanders, 38 Hispanic Americans, 4 Native Americans), 13 international. Average age 31. 455 applicants, 89% accepted. *Faculty:* 33 full-time (28 women), 53 part-time/adjunct (38 women). Expenses: Contact institution. *Financial support:* In 2001–02, 44 students received support. Career-related internships or fieldwork and tuition waivers (partial) available. Support available to part-time students. Financial award application deadline: 2/15; financial award applicants required to submit FAFSA. In 2001, 52 degrees awarded. *Degree program information:* Part-time and evening/weekend programs available. Offers early childhood education and Montessori teacher training (M Ed, MA); education (M Ed, MA); educational leadership (MA); general counseling (MA); marital and family therapy (MA); reading leadership (MA); school counseling (MA); special education (M Ed, MA). *Application deadline:* Applications are processed on a rolling basis. *Application fee:* $50. *Application Contact:* Dr. Calla Bringolf, Coordinator, 925-631-4700, Fax: 925-376-8379, E-mail: soereq@stmarys-ca.edu. *Dean*, Dr. Nancy L. Sorenson, 925-631-4309, Fax: 925-376-8379, E-mail: nsorenson@stmarys-ca.edu.

School of Extended Education Average age 41. 16 applicants, 94% accepted. *Faculty:* 3 full-time (0 women), 26 part-time/adjunct (13 women). Expenses: Contact institution. *Financial support:* Available to part-time students. Applicants required to submit FAFSA. In 2001, 7 degrees awarded. *Degree program information:* Part-time and evening/weekend programs available. Offers extended education (MA, MS); leadership (MA); liberal studies (MA). *Application deadline:* For fall admission, 9/1 (priority date); for winter admission, 12/9; for spring admission, 2/26. Applications are processed on a rolling basis. *Application fee:* $50. *Application Contact:* Nancy A. Reggio, Director of Recruitment, 925-631-4547, Fax: 925-631-9869, E-mail: nreggio@stmarys-ca.edu. *Dean*, Dr. Dean Elias, 925-631-4477, Fax: 925-631-9214, E-mail: delias@stmarys-ca.edu.

School of Liberal Arts Students: 37 full-time (23 women), 73 part-time (20 women); includes 17 minority (8 African Americans, 3 Asian Americans or Pacific Islanders, 6 Hispanic Americans) Average age 26. *Faculty:* 11 full-time (5 women), 7 part-time/adjunct (2 women). Expenses: Contact institution. *Financial support:* Fellowships, teaching assistantships, career-related internships or fieldwork, institutionally sponsored loans, and tuition waivers (partial) available. Support available to part-time students. Financial award applicants required to submit FAFSA. In 2001, 40 degrees awarded. *Degree program information:* Part-time programs available. Offers creative writing (MFA); health, physical education and recreation (MA); liberal arts (MA, MFA). *Dean*, Francis Sweeney, 925-631-4443, Fax: 925-631-4490, E-mail: fsweeney@stmarys-ca.edu.

SAINT MARY SEMINARY AND GRADUATE SCHOOL OF THEOLOGY, Wickliffe, OH 44092-2527

General Information Independent-religious, coed, primarily men, graduate-only institution. *Enrollment by degree level:* 28 first professional, 38 master's, 17 doctoral, 25 other

Saint Mary Seminary and Graduate School of Theology (continued)

advanced degrees. *Graduate faculty:* 14 full-time (2 women), 10 part-time/adjunct (2 women). *Tuition:* Part-time $248 per credit hour. *Graduate housing:* Room and/or apartments available to single students; on-campus housing not available to married students. *Student services:* Exercise/wellness program, free psychological counseling, writing training. *Library facilities:* Joseph M. Bruening Library plus 1 other. *Collection:* 65,429 titles, 338 serial subscriptions, 881 audiovisual materials.

Computer facilities: 8 computers available on campus for general student use. A campuswide network can be accessed. Internet access is available. *Web address:* http://www.stmarysem.edu/.

General Application Contact: Rev. Thomas W. Tifft, President-Rector, 440-945-7600, Fax: 440-943-7377.

GRADUATE UNITS

School of Theology Students: 44 full-time, 64 part-time. Average age 32. 19 applicants, 79% accepted. *Faculty:* 14 full-time (2 women), 10 part-time/adjunct (2 women). Expenses: Contact institution. In 2001, 3 first professional degrees, 7 master's awarded. *Degree program information:* Part-time programs available. Offers theology (M Div, MA, D Min). *Application deadline:* For fall admission, 6/1. Applications are processed on a rolling basis. *Application fee:* $0. *Dean*, Rev. Mark A. Latcovich, 440-943-7600, Fax: 440-943-7577.

ST. MARY'S SEMINARY AND UNIVERSITY, Baltimore, MD 21210-1994

General Information Independent-religious, coed, primarily men, graduate-only institution. *Enrollment:* 88 full-time matriculated graduate/professional students (3 women), 61 part-time matriculated graduate/professional students (40 women). *Enrollment by degree level:* 88 first professional, 61 master's. *Graduate faculty:* 21 full-time (4 women), 37 part-time/adjunct (7 women). *Tuition:* Full-time $10,480; part-time $585 per course. *Required fees:* $35; $75 per term. One-time fee: $40 full-time. *Graduate housing:* Room and/or apartments guaranteed to single students; on-campus housing not available to married students. Typical cost: $3,360 per year ($8,290 including board). Housing application deadline: 8/15. *Student services:* Campus employment opportunities, international student services, low-cost health insurance. *Library facilities:* Knott Library. *Online resources:* library catalog, access to other libraries' catalogs. *Collection:* 148,261 titles, 376 serial subscriptions, 535 audiovisual materials.

Computer facilities: 30 computers available on campus for general student use. A campuswide network can be accessed from student residence rooms and from off campus. Internet access is available. *Web address:* http://www.stmarys.edu/.

General Application Contact: Rev. Timothy A. Kulbicki, OFM,CONV., Dean, School of Theology, 410-864-3601, Fax: 410-433-1384, E-mail: tkulbicki@stmarys.edu.

GRADUATE UNITS

Ecumenical Institute of Theology Students: 5 full-time (3 women), 56 part-time (40 women); includes 16 minority (all African Americans) Average age 49. 42 applicants, 86% accepted. *Faculty:* 1 full-time (0 women), 17 part-time/adjunct (4 women). Expenses: Contact institution. *Financial support:* In 2001–02, 40 students received support. Career-related internships or fieldwork and scholarships/grants available. Support available to part-time students. Financial award application deadline: 8/1. In 2001, 27 degrees awarded. *Degree program information:* Part-time and evening/weekend programs available. Offers church ministries (MA); theology (MA Th, Certificate). *Application deadline:* Applications are processed on a rolling basis. *Application Contact:* Zenaida Bench, Assistant to the Dean for Admissions and Academic Services, 410-864-4202, Fax: 410-864-4205, E-mail: zbench@stmarys.edu. *Dean*, Dr. Michael J. Gorman, 410-864-4201, Fax: 410-864-4205, E-mail: mgorman@stmarys.edu.

School of Theology Students: 83 full-time (0 women), 5 part-time; includes 22 minority (3 African Americans, 5 Asian Americans or Pacific Islanders, 14 Hispanic Americans) Average age 36. 23 applicants, 96% accepted. *Faculty:* 17 full-time (2 women), 8 part-time/adjunct (4 women). Expenses: Contact institution. In 2001, 9 first professional degrees, 4 master's, 13 other advanced degrees awarded. *Degree program information:* Part-time programs available. Offers theology (M Div, STB, MA Th, STD, STL). *Application deadline:* For fall admission, 9/1. *Application fee:* $40. *Application Contact:* Fr. Thomas Burke, Vice Rector, 410-864-3613, E-mail: tburke@stmary.edu. *Dean*, Rev. Timothy A. Kulbicki, OFM,CONV., 410-864-3601, Fax: 410-433-1384, E-mail: tkulbicki@stmarys.edu.

SAINT MARY'S UNIVERSITY, Halifax, NS B3H 3C3, Canada

General Information Province-supported, coed, comprehensive institution. *Graduate housing:* Rooms and/or apartments available on a first-come, first-served basis to single students and available to married students. Housing application deadline: 3/30.

GRADUATE UNITS

Faculty of Arts *Degree program information:* Part-time and evening/weekend programs available. Offers arts (MA); Atlantic Canada studies (MA); criminology (MA); history (MA); international development studies (MA); philosophy (MA); women's studies (MA).

Faculty of Commerce *Degree program information:* Part-time and evening/weekend programs available. Offers business administration (MBA); management (PhD).

Faculty of Science *Degree program information:* Part-time programs available. Offers applied psychology (M Sc); astronomy (M Sc); science (M Sc).

SAINT MARY'S UNIVERSITY OF MINNESOTA, Winona, MN 55987-1399

General Information Independent-religious, coed, comprehensive institution. *Enrollment:* 496 full-time matriculated graduate/professional students (317 women), 2,793 part-time matriculated graduate/professional students (1,978 women). *Enrollment by degree level:* 2,935 master's, 135 doctoral, 219 other advanced degrees. *Graduate faculty:* 26 full-time (18 women), 213 part-time/adjunct (90 women). *Tuition:* Full-time $4,230; part-time $235 per credit. One-time fee: $220. Tuition and fees vary according to degree level and program. *Graduate housing:* On-campus housing not available. *Student services:* Campus safety program, career counseling, disabled student services, free psychological counseling, international student services, writing training. *Library facilities:* Fitzgerald Library. *Online resources:* library catalog, web page, access to other libraries' catalogs. *Collection:* 160,712 titles, 1,650 serial subscriptions, 8,952 audiovisual materials.

Computer facilities: 356 computers available on campus for general student use. A campuswide network can be accessed from student residence rooms and from off campus. Internet access is available. *Web address:* http://www.smumn.edu/.

General Application Contact: Jim Stevens, Director of Admissions, 612-728-5207, Fax: 612-728-5121, E-mail: jstevens@smumn.edu.

GRADUATE UNITS

Graduate School *Degree program information:* Part-time and evening/weekend programs available. Postbaccalaureate distance learning degree programs offered (minimal on-campus study). Offers arts administration (MA); business (MS); counseling and psychological services (MA); criminal justice (MS); developmental disabilities (MA); education (MA); educational administration (MA); educational leadership (Ed D); human and health services administration (MA); human development (MA); management (MA); natural resources (MS); nurse anesthesia (MS); philanthropy and development (MA); public administration (MS); telecommunications (MS).

Institute of Pastoral Ministries *Degree program information:* Part-time programs available. Offers pastoral ministries (MA, Certificate).

ST. MARY'S UNIVERSITY OF SAN ANTONIO, San Antonio, TX 78228-8507

General Information Independent-religious, coed, comprehensive institution. *Enrollment:* 908 full-time matriculated graduate/professional students (470 women), 615 part-time matriculated graduate/professional students (298 women). *Enrollment by degree level:* 703 first professional, 758 master's, 62 doctoral. *Graduate faculty:* 208. *Tuition:* Full-time $8,190; part-time $455 per credit hour. *Required fees:* $375. *Graduate housing:* Room and/or apartments available on a first-come, first-served basis to single students; on-campus housing not available to married students. Typical cost: $3,380 per year ($5,535 including board). *Student services:* Campus employment opportunities, career counseling, free psychological counseling, low-cost health insurance. *Library facilities:* Academic Library plus 1 other. *Online resources:* library catalog, web page, access to other libraries' catalogs. *Collection:* 837,287 titles, 1,126 serial subscriptions, 3,104 audiovisual materials. *Research affiliation:* Southeast Research Consortium (behavioral science, biomedical engineering, social science).

Computer facilities: 100 computers available on campus for general student use. A campuswide network can be accessed from student residence rooms and from off campus. *Web address:* http://www.stmarytx.edu/.

General Application Contact: Dr. Ronald D. Merrell, Dean of the Graduate School, 210-436-3101, Fax: 210-431-2220, E-mail: gradsch@alvin.stmarytx.edu.

GRADUATE UNITS

Graduate School Students: 189 full-time (119 women), 518 part-time (226 women). *Faculty:* 43 full-time (14 women), 68 part-time/adjunct. Expenses: Contact institution. *Financial support:* Career-related internships or fieldwork, Federal Work-Study, institutionally sponsored loans, scholarships/grants, tuition waivers (full), and employer tuition benefit available. Financial award application deadline: 4/1; financial award applicants required to submit FAFSA. In 2001, 233 master's, 4 doctorates awarded. *Degree program information:* Part-time and evening/weekend programs available. Postbaccalaureate distance learning degree programs offered (minimal on-campus study). Offers Catholic principalship (Certificate); Catholic school administrators (Certificate); Catholic school leadership (MA); Catholic school teachers (Certificate); clinical psychology (MA, MS); communication studies (MA); community counseling (MA); computer information systems (MS); computer science (MS); counseling (PhD, Sp C); educational leadership (MA); electrical /computer engineering (MS); electrical engineering (MS); electrical/computer engineering (MS); engineering administration (MS); engineering computer applications (MS); engineering management (MS); engineering systems management (MS); English literature and language (MA); financial economics (MA); history (MA); industrial engineering (MS); industrial psychology (MA, MS); inter-American administration (MPA); international relations (MA); justice administration (MJA); Latin American and U.S. Latino history (MA); marriage and family relations (Certificate); marriage and family therapy (MA, PhD); mental health (MA); mental health and substance abuse counseling (Certificate); operations research (MS); pastoral ministry (MA); political communications and applied science (MA); political economy (MA); political science (MA); principalship (Certificate); principalship (mid-management) (Certificate); public management (MPA); reading (MA); school psychology (MA); software engineering (MS); speech communication (MA); substance abuse (MA); theology (MA). *Application deadline:* Applications are processed on a rolling basis. *Application fee:* $15. Electronic applications accepted. *Dean*, Dr. Ronald D. Merrell, 210-436-3101, Fax: 210-431-2220, E-mail: gradsch@alvin.stmarytx.edu.

School of Business Administration Students: 20 full-time (9 women), 117 part-time (49 women); includes 60 minority (2 African Americans, 5 Asian Americans or Pacific Islanders, 52 Hispanic Americans, 1 Native American), 4 international. Average age 29. *Faculty:* 17 full-time (2 women), 7 part-time/adjunct (1 woman). Expenses: Contact institution. *Financial support:* Research assistantships, Federal Work-Study and institutionally sponsored loans available. Financial award application deadline: 3/1. In 2001, 50 degrees awarded. *Degree program information:* Part-time and evening/weekend programs available. Postbaccalaureate distance learning degree programs offered (minimal on-campus study). Offers accounting (M Acc); finance (MBA); international business (MBA); management (MBA); taxation (M Acc). *Application deadline:* Applications are processed on a rolling basis. *Application fee:* $15. Electronic applications accepted. *Graduate Program Director*, Dr. Thomas Hamilton, 210-436-3708.

School of Law Students: 694 full-time (333 women), 9 part-time (2 women); includes 305 minority (24 African Americans, 12 Asian Americans or Pacific Islanders, 266 Hispanic Americans, 3 Native Americans), 6 international. Average age 25. *Faculty:* 46 full-time (16 women), 51 part-time/adjunct (17 women). Expenses: Contact institution. *Financial support:* In 2001–02, 59 research assistantships (averaging $1,000 per year), 35 teaching assistantships (averaging $1,250 per year) were awarded. Career-related internships or fieldwork, Federal Work-Study, and institutionally sponsored loans also available. Financial award application deadline: 2/15; financial award applicants required to submit FAFSA. In 2001, 222 degrees awarded. Offers law (JD). *Application deadline:* For fall admission, 3/1 (priority date). *Application fee:* $45. Electronic applications accepted. *Application Contact:* Dr. William Charles Wilson, Assistant Dean and Director of Admissions, 210-436-3523, Fax: 210-431-4202. *Dean*, Robert William Piatt, 210-436-3533, Fax: 210-436-3515.

SAINT MEINRAD SCHOOL OF THEOLOGY, Saint Meinrad, IN 47577

General Information Independent-religious, coed, primarily men, graduate-only institution. *Enrollment by degree level:* 81 first professional, 36 master's. *Graduate faculty:* 19 full-time (2 women), 10 part-time/adjunct (1 woman). *Tuition:* Full-time $12,095; part-time $300 per credit. *Required fees:* $275. *Graduate housing:* Room and/or apartments guaranteed to single students; on-campus housing not available to married students. Typical cost: $6,145 (including board). Housing application deadline: 8/1. *Student services:* Campus employment opportunities, campus safety program, exercise/wellness program, free psychological counseling, low-cost health insurance. *Library facilities:* Archabbey Library. *Online resources:* library catalog, access to other libraries' catalogs. *Collection:* 163,866 titles, 452 serial subscriptions, 3,918 audiovisual materials.

Computer facilities: 30 computers available on campus for general student use. A campuswide network can be accessed from student residence rooms and from off campus. Internet access is available. *Web address:* http://www.saintmeinrad.edu/.

General Application Contact: Rev. John Thomas, Director of Enrollment, 812-357-6206, Fax: 812-357-6462, E-mail: jthomas@saintmeinrad.edu.

GRADUATE UNITS

Professional Program Students: 81 full-time (0 women); includes 2 minority (1 African American, 1 Hispanic American), 9 international. Average age 33. 33 applicants, 100% accepted, 32 enrolled. *Faculty:* 19 full-time (2 women), 10 part-time/adjunct (1 woman). Expenses: Contact institution. *Financial support:* In 2001–02, 53 students received support. Career-related internships or fieldwork, Federal Work-Study, institutionally sponsored loans, and scholarships/grants available. Support available to part-time students. Financial award application deadline: 7/31; financial award applicants required to submit FAFSA. In 2001, 14 degrees awarded. Offers theology (M Div). *Application deadline:* For fall admission, 8/1 (priority date). Applications are processed on a rolling basis. *Application fee:* $0. *Application Contact:* Rev. John Thomas, Director of Enrollment, 812-357-6201, Fax: 812-357-6462, E-mail: jthomas@saintmeinrad.edu. *Academic Dean*, Dr. Tom Walters, 812-357-6620, Fax: 812-357-6792, E-mail: twalters@saintmeinrad.edu.

Program in Catholic Thought and Life Students: 1 (woman) full-time, 13 part-time (7 women); includes 1 minority (Hispanic American) *Faculty:* 19 full-time (2 women), 10 part-time/adjunct (1 woman). Expenses: Contact institution. *Financial support:* In 2001–02, 9 students received support. Federal Work-Study, institutionally sponsored loans, and scholarships/grants available. Support available to part-time students. Financial award application deadline: 7/31; financial award applicants required to submit FAFSA. In 2001, 18 degrees awarded. *Degree program information:* Part-time programs available. Offers Catholic thought and life (MA). *Application deadline:* For fall admission, 8/1 (priority date). Applications are processed on a rolling basis. *Application fee:* $0. *Application Contact:* Kyle Kramer, Associate Director of Enrollment, 812-357-6841, Fax: 812-357-6462, E-mail: kkramer@saintmeinrad.edu. *Associate Academic Dean and Lay Formation Dean*, Kyle Kramer, 812-357-6621, Fax: 812-357-6792, E-mail: dlebeau@saintmeinrad.edu.

Program in Theological Studies Students: 2 full-time (1 woman), 20 part-time (14 women). *Faculty:* 19 full-time (2 women), 10 part-time/adjunct (1 woman). Expenses: Contact institution. *Financial support:* In 2001–02, 15 students received support. Federal Work-Study, institutionally sponsored loans, and scholarships/grants available. Support available to part-time students. Financial award application deadline: 7/31; financial award applicants required to submit FAFSA. In 2001, 10 degrees awarded. *Degree program information:* Part-time programs available. Offers theological studies (MTS). *Application deadline:* For fall admission, 6/1 (priority date). Applications are processed on a rolling basis. *Application fee:* $0. *Application Contact:* Kyle Kramer, Associate Director of Enrollment, 812-357-6841, Fax: 812-357-6462, E-mail: kkramer@saintmeinrad.edu. *Associate Academic Dean and Lay Formation Dean,* Kyle Kramer, 812-357-6621, Fax: 812-357-6792, E-mail: dlebeau@saintmeinrad.edu.

SAINT MICHAEL'S COLLEGE, Colchester, VT 05439

General Information Independent-religious, coed, comprehensive institution. *Enrollment:* 98 full-time matriculated graduate/professional students (67 women), 549 part-time matriculated graduate/professional students (408 women). *Graduate faculty:* 20 full-time (10 women), 137 part-time/adjunct (77 women). *Tuition:* Full-time $8,280; part-time $345 per credit. *Graduate housing:* On-campus housing not available. *Student services:* Campus employment opportunities, campus safety program, career counseling, international student services. *Library facilities:* Durick Library. *Online resources:* library catalog, web page, access to other libraries' catalogs. *Collection:* 206,124 titles, 3,312 serial subscriptions, 6,195 audiovisual materials.

Computer facilities: 180 computers available on campus for general student use. A campuswide network can be accessed from student residence rooms and from off campus. Internet access is available. *Web address:* http://www.smcvt.edu/.

General Application Contact: Dee M. Goodrich, Director of Admissions and Marketing, Graduate Programs, 802-654-2251, Fax: 802-654-2591, E-mail: dggodrich@smcvt.edu.

GRADUATE UNITS

Graduate Programs *Degree program information:* Part-time and evening/weekend programs available. Offers administration (M Ed, CAGS); administration and management (MSA, CAMS); adult education (CAGS); arts in education (CAGS); clinical psychology (MA); curriculum and instruction (M Ed, CAGS); information technology (CAGS); reading (M Ed); self designed (M Ed); special education (M Ed, CAGS); teaching English as a second language (MATESL, CAS); technology (M Ed); theology (MA, CAS, Certificate).

ST. NORBERT COLLEGE, De Pere, WI 54115-2099

General Information Independent-religious, coed, comprehensive institution. *Enrollment:* 72 part-time matriculated graduate/professional students (65 women). *Enrollment by degree level:* 72 master's. *Graduate faculty:* 6 full-time, 35 part-time/adjunct. *Tuition:* Part-time $275 per credit hour. Part-time tuition and fees vary according to course load and program. *Graduate housing:* On-campus housing not available. *Student services:* Campus employment opportunities, campus safety program, career counseling, child daycare facilities, disabled student services, exercise/wellness program, free psychological counseling, international student services, low-cost health insurance, multicultural affairs office, teacher training, writing training. *Library facilities:* Todd Wehr Library. *Online resources:* library catalog, web page, access to other libraries' catalogs. *Collection:* 140,514 titles, 10,000 serial subscriptions, 7,625 audiovisual materials.

Computer facilities: 179 computers available on campus for general student use. A campuswide network can be accessed from student residence rooms and from off campus. Internet access and online class registration are available. *Web address:* http://www.snc.edu/.

General Application Contact: Dan Meyer, Dean of Admissions, 800-236-4878, Fax: 920-403-4072, E-mail: admit@mail.snc.edu.

GRADUATE UNITS

Program in Adaptive Education 14 applicants, 100% accepted, 14 enrolled. *Faculty:* 5 full-time, 26 part-time/adjunct. Expenses: Contact institution. *Financial support:* Career-related internships or fieldwork and tuition waivers (partial) available. Support available to part-time students. In 2001, 4 degrees awarded. *Degree program information:* Part-time programs available. Offers adaptive education (MS). *Application deadline:* Applications are processed on a rolling basis. *Application fee:* $0. Electronic applications accepted. *Director,* Barb Natelle, 920-403-3076, Fax: 920-403-4057, E-mail: adaped@mail.snc.edu.

Program in Education 31 applicants, 100% accepted, 28 enrolled. *Faculty:* 9 part-time/adjunct. Expenses: Contact institution. *Degree program information:* Part-time and evening/weekend programs available. Postbaccalaureate distance learning degree programs offered (minimal on-campus study). Offers education (MS). *Application deadline:* Applications are processed on a rolling basis. *Application fee:* $35. Electronic applications accepted. *Director, Master of Science in Education Program,* Dr. Yvonne Murnane, 920-403-3363, Fax: 920-403-4086, E-mail: mse@mail.snc.edu.

Program in Theological Studies (Masters) 5 applicants, 100% accepted. *Faculty:* 9 part-time/adjunct (1 woman). Expenses: Contact institution. *Financial support:* Scholarships/grants available. Support available to part-time students. Financial award application deadline: 5/15. In 2001, 4 degrees awarded. *Degree program information:* Part-time programs available. Offers theological studies (MTS). *Application deadline:* Applications are processed on a rolling basis. *Application fee:* $25. Electronic applications accepted. *Director,* Dr. Howard Ebert, 920-403-3956, Fax: 920-403-4086, E-mail: howard.ebert@snc.edu.

ST. PATRICK'S SEMINARY, Menlo Park, CA 94025-3596

General Information Independent-religious, coed, primarily men, graduate-only institution. *Enrollment by degree level:* 58 first professional, 32 master's. *Graduate faculty:* 15 full-time (3 women), 13 part-time/adjunct (4 women). *Tuition:* Full-time $8,500; part-time $300 per unit. *Required fees:* $550. One-time fee: $100 full-time. *Graduate housing:* Room and/or apartments guaranteed to single students; on-campus housing not available to married students. Typical cost: $7,200 (including board). Housing application deadline: 8/1. *Student services:* Campus employment opportunities, campus safety program, free psychological counseling, international student services, writing training. *Library facilities:* McKeon Memorial Library. *Online resources:* library catalog, web page. *Collection:* 108,277 titles, 320 serial subscriptions, 1,233 audiovisual materials.

Computer facilities: 8 computers available on campus for general student use. Internet access is available. *Web address:* http://www.stpatricksseminary.org/.

General Application Contact: Rev. Milton T. Walsh, Academic Dean, 650-325-5621 Ext. 28, Fax: 650-322-0097, E-mail: mwalsh@stpatricksseminary.org.

GRADUATE UNITS

School of Theology Students: 89 full-time (0 women), 1 part-time; includes 29 minority (21 Asian Americans or Pacific Islanders, 8 Hispanic Americans), 33 international. Average age 34. 36 applicants, 89% accepted. *Faculty:* 15 full-time (3 women), 13 part-time/adjunct (4 women). Expenses: Contact institution. *Financial support:* In 2001–02, 75 students received support. Tuition waivers (full) available. Financial award application deadline: 10/1. In 2001, 7 first professional degrees, 2 master's awarded. *Degree program information:* Part-time programs available. Offers theology (M Div, STB, MA). *Application deadline:* For fall admission, 6/30 (priority date). *Application Contact:* Rev. Gerald D. Coleman, President/Rector, 650-325-5621 Ext. 22, Fax: 650-322-0997, E-mail: info@www.stpatricksseminary.org. *Academic Vice-President and Provost,* Rev. Milton T. Walsh, 650-325-5621 Ext. 28, Fax: 650-322-0097, E-mail: mwalsh@stpatricksseminary.org.

SAINT PAUL SCHOOL OF THEOLOGY, Kansas City, MO 64127-2440

General Information Independent-religious, coed, graduate-only institution. *Graduate housing:* Rooms and/or apartments available to single and married students. Housing application deadline: 5/31.

GRADUATE UNITS

Graduate and Professional Programs *Degree program information:* Part-time programs available. Offers theology (M Div, MTS, D Min).

SAINT PAUL UNIVERSITY, Ottawa, ON K1S 1C4, Canada

General Information Province-supported, coed, university. *Graduate housing:* Room and/or apartments available to single students; on-campus housing not available to married students.

GRADUATE UNITS

Faculty of Canon Law Students: 53 full-time (15 women), 2 part-time (1 woman). Average age 40. 50 applicants, 54% accepted, 24 enrolled. *Faculty:* 10 full-time (2 women), 5 part-time/adjunct (0 women). Expenses: Contact institution. *Financial support:* In 2001–02, 7 students received support. Bursaries available. In 2001, 19 master's, 3 doctorates awarded. *Degree program information:* Part-time programs available. Offers canon law (MA, MCL, JCD, PhD, JCL). *Application deadline:* For fall admission, 9/15 (priority date). Applications are processed on a rolling basis. *Application fee:* $35. *Application Contact:* Beverly Ruth Kavanaugh, Administrative Secretary, 613-751-4018, Fax: 613-751-4036, E-mail: bkavanaugh@ustpaul.uottawa.ca. *Dean,* Dr. Roch Pagé, 613-751-4035, Fax: 613-751-4036, E-mail: rpage@ustpaul.uottawa.ca.

Faculty of Human Sciences Offers individual and/or marital/couple counseling (MA Past St); mission and interreligious studies (MA, Certificate); pastoral care in health care services (MA Past St); pastoral group work (MA Past St). Program offered in French and English.

Faculty of Theology Students: 58 full-time (14 women), 25 part-time (15 women). 41 applicants, 76% accepted, 30 enrolled. Expenses: Contact institution. In 2001, 13 master's, 6 doctorates, 15 other advanced degrees awarded. Offers theology (MA Th, MP Th, MRE, D Th, PhD, L Th). *Application deadline:* For fall admission, 6/15 (priority date); for winter admission, 10/15. Applications are processed on a rolling basis. *Application fee:* $35. *Application Contact:* Francine Forgues, Registrar, 613-236-1393 Ext. 2237, Fax: 613-782-3014, E-mail: fforgues@ustpaul.uottawa.ca. *Dean,* Dr. David Perrin, 613-236-1393 Ext. 2277, Fax: 613-751-4016, E-mail: dperrin@ustpaul.uottawa.ca.

SAINT PETER'S COLLEGE, Jersey City, NJ 07306-5997

General Information Independent-religious, coed, comprehensive institution. *Graduate housing:* On-campus housing not available.

GRADUATE UNITS

Graduate Programs in Education *Degree program information:* Part-time and evening/weekend programs available. Offers administration and supervision (MA); elementary teacher (Certificate); reading specialist (MA); supervisor of instruction (Certificate); teaching (MA, Certificate); urban education (MA).

MBA Programs *Degree program information:* Part-time and evening/weekend programs available. Offers finance (MBA); international business (MBA); management (MBA); management information systems (MBA); marketing (MBA).

Nursing Program *Degree program information:* Part-time and evening/weekend programs available. Offers nursing (MSN).

Program in Accountancy *Degree program information:* Part-time and evening/weekend programs available. Offers accountancy (MS, Certificate).

See in-depth description on page 1071.

ST. PETER'S SEMINARY, London, ON N6A 3Y1, Canada

General Information Independent-religious, men only, graduate-only institution.

GRADUATE UNITS

Department of Theology Offers theology (M Div).

SAINTS CYRIL AND METHODIUS SEMINARY, Orchard Lake, MI 48324

General Information Independent-religious, coed, graduate-only institution. *Enrollment by degree level:* 36 first professional, 51 master's. *Graduate faculty:* 18 full-time (10 women), 4 part-time/adjunct (1 woman). *Tuition:* Full-time $7,500; part-time $250 per credit hour. *Required fees:* $450 per semester. *Graduate housing:* Room and/or apartments guaranteed to single students; on-campus housing not available to married students. Typical cost: $3,184 per year ($7,428 including board). Housing application deadline: 7/1. *Student services:* Campus employment opportunities, career counseling, international student services. *Library facilities:* Alumni Memorial Library plus 1 other. *Online resources:* library catalog, web page. *Collection:* 81,483 titles, 341 serial subscriptions, 1,488 audiovisual materials.

Computer facilities: 10 computers available on campus for general student use. Internet access is available.

General Application Contact: Rev. Dariusz Dudzik, Director of Recruitment and Admissions, 248-683-0422, Fax: 248-738-6735, E-mail: sscyrilmethodiussem@earthlink.net.

GRADUATE UNITS

Graduate and Professional Programs Students: 31 full-time (2 women), 56 part-time (34 women); includes 4 minority (1 African American, 2 Asian Americans or Pacific Islanders, 1 Hispanic American), 26 international. Average age 40. 79 applicants, 15% accepted, 11 enrolled. *Faculty:* 18 full-time (10 women), 4 part-time/adjunct (1 woman). Expenses: Contact institution. In 2001, 9 first professional degrees, 7 master's awarded. Offers pastoral ministry (MAPM); religious education (MARE); theology (M Div, MA). *Application deadline:* Applications are processed on a rolling basis. *Application fee:* $40. *Application Contact:* Rev. Dariusz Dudzik, Director of Recruitment and Admissions, 248-683-0422, Fax: 248-738-6735, E-mail: sscyrilmethodiussem@earthlink.net. *Rector,* Rev. Msgr. Francis B. Koper, 248-683-0311, Fax: 248-738-6735, E-mail: sscyrilmethodiussem@earthlink.net.

ST. STEPHEN'S COLLEGE, Edmonton, AB T6G 2J6, Canada

General Information Independent-religious, coed, graduate-only institution. *Graduate housing:* On-campus housing not available.

GRADUATE UNITS

Programs in Theology *Degree program information:* Part-time and evening/weekend programs available. Postbaccalaureate distance learning degree programs offered (minimal on-campus study). Offers ministry (D Min); pastoral counseling (MA); social transformation ministry (MA); spirituality and liturgy (MA); theological studies (MTS); theology (M Th). Electronic applications accepted.

ST. THOMAS AQUINAS COLLEGE, Sparkill, NY 10976

General Information Independent, coed, comprehensive institution. *Enrollment:* 24 full-time matriculated graduate/professional students, 232 part-time matriculated graduate/professional students. *Graduate faculty:* 20 full-time (12 women), 16 part-time/adjunct (5 women). *Tuition:* Part-time $450 per credit. *Graduate housing:* On-campus housing not available. *Student services:* Career counseling, disabled student services, free psychological counseling, international student services, teacher training. *Library facilities:* Lougheed Library plus 1 other. *Online resources:* library catalog, access to other libraries' catalogs. *Collection:* 176,000 titles, 940 serial subscriptions. *Research affiliation:* Lederle Laboratories (science education), Lamont Doherty Laboratories (science education).

Computer facilities: 200 computers available on campus for general student use. A campuswide network can be accessed from student residence rooms and from off campus. Internet access is available. *Web address:* http://www.stac.edu/.

General Application Contact: Tracey Howard-Ubelhoer, Director of Admissions, 845-398-4102, Fax: 845-398-4224, E-mail: thoward@stac.edu.

GRADUATE UNITS

Division of Business Administration Students: 4 full-time, 81 part-time; includes 33 minority (6 African Americans, 25 Asian Americans or Pacific Islanders, 2 Hispanic Americans) Average age 28. 21 applicants, 95% accepted, 18 enrolled. *Faculty:* 11 full-time (5 women), 10 part-time/adjunct (2 women). Expenses: Contact institution. *Financial support:* Tuition waivers (partial) available. Support available to part-time students. Financial award applica-

St. Thomas Aquinas College (continued)

tion deadline: 2/15; financial award applicants required to submit FAFSA. In 2001, 19 degrees awarded. *Degree program information:* Part-time and evening/weekend programs available. Offers finance (MBA); management (MBA); marketing (MBA). *Application deadline:* Applications are processed on a rolling basis. *Application fee:* $30. Electronic applications accepted. *Application Contact:* Karen Gray, Director of Admissions, 845-398-4043, Fax: 845-359-8136, E-mail: kgray@stac.edu. *Chairperson*, Michael Murphy, 845-398-4113, Fax: 845-359-8136, E-mail: mmurphy@stac.edu.

Division of Teacher Education Students: 20 full-time (12 women), 151 part-time (103 women); includes 9 minority (2 Asian Americans or Pacific Islanders, 7 Hispanic Americans) Average age 28. 88 applicants, 63% accepted. *Faculty:* 9 full-time (7 women), 6 part-time/adjunct (3 women). Expenses: Contact institution. *Financial support:* Tuition waivers (partial) and unspecified assistantships available. Support available to part-time students. Financial award application deadline: 2/15; financial award applicants required to submit FAFSA. In 2001, 40 master's, 30 other advanced degrees awarded. *Degree program information:* Part-time and evening/weekend programs available. Offers adolescence education (MST); childhood and special education (MST); childhood education (MST); elementary education (MS Ed); reading (MS Ed, PMC); secondary education (MS Ed); special education (MS Ed, PMC). *Application deadline:* For fall admission, 7/31 (priority date); for spring admission, 12/1. Applications are processed on a rolling basis. *Application fee:* $30. Electronic applications accepted. *Application Contact:* Tracey Howard-Ubelhoer, Director of Admissions, 845-398-4102, Fax: 845-398-4224, E-mail: thoward@stac.edu. *Chairperson*, Dr. Meenakshi Gajria, 845-398-4150, Fax: 845-398-4224, E-mail: mgajria@stac.edu.

Announcement: Three graduate programs: MS Ed, MST, and MBA. The MS Ed is designed to enhance professional skills of those teaching or preparing to teach special education, elementary or secondary education, or reading. MS Ed requires 36 credits; students may opt to take program in 3 summers. A Master of Science in Teaching (MST) is also available for those who want teacher certification in childhood education, childhood and special education, and adolescent education. The MBA is designed with specializations in finance, management, or marketing, accommodating students who may be working full-time. All courses are offered on weekends. Information on MS Ed, MST, or MBA is available from the graduate admissions office at 845-398-4100.

ST. THOMAS UNIVERSITY, Miami, FL 33054-6459

General Information Independent-religious, coed, comprehensive institution. *Graduate housing:* Room and/or apartments available to single students; on-campus housing not available to married students. Housing application deadline: 7/1.

GRADUATE UNITS

School of Graduate Studies *Degree program information:* Part-time and evening/weekend programs available. Offers accounting (MBA); business administration (M Acc, MBA, Certificate); elementary education (MS); general management (MSM, Certificate); guidance and counseling (MS, Certificate); health management (MBA, MSM, Certificate); human resource management (MSM, Certificate); international business (MBA, MSM, Certificate); justice administration (MSM, Certificate); management (MBA); marriage and family therapy (MS); mental health counseling (MS); public management (MSM, Certificate); sports administration (MBA).

Institute of Pastoral Ministries *Degree program information:* Part-time and evening/weekend programs available. Offers pastoral ministries (MA, Certificate).

School of Law Postbaccalaureate distance learning degree programs offered (no on-campus study). Offers international human rights (LL M); international taxation (LL M); law (JD). Electronic applications accepted.

See in-depth description on page 1073.

SAINT VINCENT DE PAUL REGIONAL SEMINARY, Boynton Beach, FL 33436-4899

General Information Independent-religious, coed, primarily men, graduate-only institution. *Enrollment by degree level:* 83 first professional, 23 master's. *Graduate faculty:* 19 full-time (3 women), 10 part-time/adjunct (4 women). *Tuition:* Full-time $9,500; part-time $175 per credit. *Required fees:* $200. One-time fee: $15 part-time. *Graduate housing:* Room and/or apartments available to single students; on-campus housing not available to married students. Typical cost: $6,000 (including board). *Student services:* Low-cost health insurance, multicultural affairs office. *Library facilities:* Saint Vincent de Paul Seminary Library. *Online resources:* library catalog, web page. *Collection:* 59,000 titles, 440 serial subscriptions, 799 audiovisual materials.

Computer facilities: 17 computers available on campus for general student use. A campuswide network can be accessed.

General Application Contact: Rev. Stephen C. Bosso, Rector/President, 561-732-4424, Fax: 561-737-2205.

GRADUATE UNITS

Graduate and Professional Programs Students: 92 full-time (0 women), 14 part-time (7 women); includes 46 minority (1 African American, 6 Asian Americans or Pacific Islanders, 39 Hispanic Americans), 19 international. Average age 34. 34 applicants, 79% accepted, 27 enrolled. *Faculty:* 19 full-time (3 women), 10 part-time/adjunct (4 women). Expenses: Contact institution. *Financial support:* Career-related internships or fieldwork and tuition waivers (full and partial) available. Support available to part-time students. Financial award applicants required to submit FAFSA. In 2001, 10 first professional degrees, 2 master's awarded. *Degree program information:* Part-time programs available. Offers church history (MA Th); divinity (M Div); moral theology (MA Th); scripture (MA Th); systematic theology (MA Th). *Application deadline:* For fall admission, 7/1 (priority date). Applications are processed on a rolling basis. *Application fee:* $0. *Application Contact:* Rev. Stephen C. Bosso, Rector/President, 561-732-4424, Fax: 561-737-2205. *Academic Dean/Registrar*, Dr. Miguel Diaz, 561-732-4424 Ext. 161, Fax: 561-737-2205, E-mail: mhdiaz@svdp.edu.

SAINT VINCENT SEMINARY, Latrobe, PA 15650-2690

General Information Independent-religious, coed, primarily men, graduate-only institution. *Enrollment by degree level:* 54 first professional, 39 master's. *Graduate faculty:* 9 full-time (1 woman), 15 part-time/adjunct (4 women). *Tuition:* Part-time $427 per credit. *Required fees:* $10 per semester. *Graduate housing:* Room and/or apartments available to single students; on-campus housing not available to married students. Typical cost: $6,308 (including board). Housing application deadline: 8/1. *Student services:* Campus safety program, exercise/wellness program, low-cost health insurance, writing training. *Library facilities:* Saint Vincent College Library. *Online resources:* library catalog, access to other libraries' catalogs. *Collection:* 266,562 titles, 803 serial subscriptions, 2,984 audiovisual materials.

Computer facilities: 127 computers available on campus for general student use. A campuswide network can be accessed from student residence rooms and from off campus. Internet access is available. *Web address:* http://www.stvincent.edu/.

General Application Contact: Sr. Cecilia Murphy, RSM, Academic Dean, 724-539-9761 Ext. 2395, Fax: 724-532-5052, E-mail: cecilia.murphy@email.stvincent.edu.

GRADUATE UNITS

School of Theology Students: 81 full-time (1 woman), 12 part-time (4 women); includes 2 minority (1 Asian American or Pacific Islander, 1 Hispanic American), 18 international. Average age 26. *Faculty:* 9 full-time (1 woman), 15 part-time/adjunct (4 women). Expenses: Contact institution. *Financial support:* In 2001–02, 91 students received support. Scholarships/grants available. Support available to part-time students. Financial award application deadline: 8/1; financial award applicants required to submit FAFSA. In 2001, 14 first professional degrees, 12 master's awarded. *Degree program information:* Part-time programs available. Offers theology (M Div, MA). *Application deadline:* For fall admission, 8/1 (priority date). Applications are processed on a rolling basis. *Application fee:* $25. *Application Contact:* Sr. Cecilia Murphy, RSM, Academic Dean, 724-539-9761 Ext. 2395, Fax: 724-532-5052, E-mail: cecilia.murphy@email.stvincent.edu. *President/Rector*, Very Rev. Kurt Belsole, 724-537-4592, Fax: 724-532-5052, E-mail: kurt.belsole@email.stvincent.edu.

ST. VLADIMIR'S ORTHODOX THEOLOGICAL SEMINARY, Crestwood, NY 10707-1699

General Information Independent-religious, coed, primarily men, graduate-only institution. *Graduate housing:* Rooms and/or apartments available on a first-come, first-served basis to single and married students. Housing application deadline: 5/1.

GRADUATE UNITS

Graduate School of Theology *Degree program information:* Part-time programs available. Offers general theological studies (MA); liturgical music (MA); religious education (MA); theology (M Div, M Th, D Min). MA (general theological studies), M Div offered jointly with St. Nersess Seminary.

SAINT XAVIER UNIVERSITY, Chicago, IL 60655-3105

General Information Independent-religious, coed, comprehensive institution. *Enrollment:* 160 full-time matriculated graduate/professional students (119 women), 1,941 part-time matriculated graduate/professional students (1,557 women). *Graduate faculty:* 152. *Tuition:* Full-time $4,500; part-time $500 per credit. *Required fees:* $40 per term. *Graduate housing:* Room and/or apartments available on a first-come, first-served basis to single students; on-campus housing not available to married students. Typical cost: $3,408 per year ($5,974 including board). Housing application deadline: 8/15. *Student services:* Campus employment opportunities, career counseling, child daycare facilities, free psychological counseling, international student services, low-cost health insurance, teacher training. *Library facilities:* Byrne Memorial Library. *Online resources:* library catalog, web page, access to other libraries' catalogs. *Collection:* 123,325 titles, 2,199 serial subscriptions, 2,292 audiovisual materials. *Research affiliation:* Alexian Brothers Hospital, Holy Cross Hospital, Little Company of Mary Hospital, Mercy Center for Health Care Services.

Computer facilities: 261 computers available on campus for general student use. A campuswide network can be accessed from student residence rooms and from off campus. Internet access is available. *Web address:* http://www.sxu.edu/.

General Application Contact: Beth Gierach, Vice President of Enrollment Services, 773-298-3050, Fax: 773-298-3076, E-mail: gierach@sxu.edu.

GRADUATE UNITS

Graduate Studies Students: 160 full-time (119 women), 1,941 part-time (1,557 women); includes 318 minority (219 African Americans, 26 Asian Americans or Pacific Islanders, 70 Hispanic Americans, 3 Native Americans), 1 international. Average age 36. *Faculty:* 152. Expenses: Contact institution. *Financial support:* Research assistantships, teaching assistantships, career-related internships or fieldwork available. Support available to part-time students. Financial award applicants required to submit FAFSA. In 2001, 596 degrees awarded. *Degree program information:* Part-time and evening/weekend programs available. *Application deadline:* Applications are processed on a rolling basis. *Application fee:* $35. Electronic applications accepted. *Application Contact:* Beth Gierach, Managing Director of Admission, 773-298-3053, Fax: 773-298-3076, E-mail: gierach@sxu.edu. *Vice President of Academic Affairs*, 773-298-3194, Fax: 773-298-3002.

Graham School of Management Students: 28 full-time (14 women), 177 part-time (90 women); includes 45 minority (27 African Americans, 8 Asian Americans or Pacific Islanders, 10 Hispanic Americans), 1 international. Average age 35. *Faculty:* 27. Expenses: Contact institution. *Financial support:* Career-related internships or fieldwork available. Support available to part-time students. Financial award applicants required to submit FAFSA. In 2001, 61 degrees awarded. *Degree program information:* Part-time and evening/weekend programs available. Offers employee health benefits (Certificate); finance (MBA, MS); financial planning (MBA, Certificate); financial trading and practice (MBA, Certificate); generalist/administration (MBA); health administration (MBA, MS); managed care (Certificate); management (MBA, MS); marketing (MBA); public health (MPH); taxation (MBA). *Application deadline:* For fall admission, 8/15. Applications are processed on a rolling basis. *Application fee:* $35. Electronic applications accepted. *Application Contact:* Beth Gierach, Managing Director of Admission, 773-298-3053, Fax: 773-298-3076, E-mail: gierach@sxu.edu. *Dean*, Dr. John Eber, 773-298-3601, Fax: 773-298-3601, E-mail: eber@sxu.edu.

School of Arts and Sciences Students: 31 full-time (17 women), 132 part-time (68 women); includes 17 African Americans, 3 Hispanic Americans Average age 35. *Faculty:* 19. Expenses: Contact institution. *Financial support:* Research assistantships, teaching assistantships, career-related internships or fieldwork available. Support available to part-time students. Financial award applicants required to submit FAFSA. In 2001, 36 degrees awarded. *Degree program information:* Part-time and evening/weekend programs available. Offers adult counseling (Certificate); applied computer science in Internet information systems (MS); arts and sciences (MA, MS, CAS, Certificate); child/adolescent counseling (Certificate); core counseling (Certificate); counseling psychology (MA); English (CAS); literary studies (MA); speech-language pathology (MS); teaching of writing (MA); writing pedagogy (CAS). *Application deadline:* For fall admission, 8/15. *Application fee:* $35. *Application Contact:* Beth Gierach, Managing Director of Admission, 773-298-3053, Fax: 773-298-3076, E-mail: gierach@sxu.edu. *Dean*, Dr. Lawrence Frank, 773-298-3090, Fax: 773-779-9061, E-mail: lfrank@sxu.edu.

School of Education Students: 65 full-time (54 women), 1,457 part-time (1,234 women); includes 175 minority (129 African Americans, 9 Asian Americans or Pacific Islanders, 35 Hispanic Americans, 2 Native Americans) Average age 33. *Faculty:* 92. Expenses: Contact institution. *Financial support:* Career-related internships or fieldwork available. Support available to part-time students. Financial award applicants required to submit FAFSA. In 2001, 474 degrees awarded. *Degree program information:* Part-time and evening/weekend programs available. Offers curriculum and instruction (MA); early childhood education (MA); education (CAS); educational administration (MA); elementary education (MA); field-based education (MA); general educational studies (MA); individualized program (MA); learning disabilities (MA); reading (MA); secondary education (MA). *Application deadline:* For fall admission, 8/15 (priority date). Applications are processed on a rolling basis. *Application fee:* $35. *Application Contact:* Beth Gierach, Managing Director of Admission, 773-298-3053, Fax: 773-298-3076, E-mail: gierach@sxu.edu. *Dean*, Dr. Beverly Gulley, 773-298-3221, Fax: 773-779-9061, E-mail: gulley@sxu.edu.

School of Nursing Students: 36 full-time (34 women), 163 part-time (153 women); includes 73 minority (45 African Americans, 8 Asian Americans or Pacific Islanders, 19 Hispanic Americans, 1 Native American) Average age 35. *Faculty:* 11. Expenses: Contact institution. *Financial support:* Available to part-time students. Applicants required to submit FAFSA. In 2001, 36 degrees awarded. *Degree program information:* Part-time and evening/weekend programs available. Offers adult health clinical nurse specialist (MS); family nurse practitioner (MS, PMC); leadership in community health nursing (MS); psychiatric-mental health clinical nurse specialist (MS); psychiatric-mental health clinical specialist (PMC). MBA/MS offered in cooperation with the Graham School of Management. *Application deadline:* For fall admission, 2/15; for spring admission, 9/15. Applications are processed on a rolling basis. *Application fee:* $35. *Managing Director of Admission*, Beth Gierach, 773-298-3053, Fax: 773-298-3076, E-mail: gierach@sxu.edu.

SALEM COLLEGE, Winston-Salem, NC 27108-0548

General Information Independent-religious, women only, comprehensive institution. *Graduate housing:* On-campus housing not available.

GRADUATE UNITS

Department of Education *Degree program information:* Part-time and evening/weekend programs available. Offers early education and leadership (MAT); elementary education (MAT); language and literacy (M Ed); learning disabilities (MAT).

SALEM INTERNATIONAL UNIVERSITY, Salem, WV 26426-0500

General Information Independent, coed, comprehensive institution. *Enrollment:* 27 full-time matriculated graduate/professional students (20 women), 55 part-time matriculated graduate/

professional students (40 women). *Enrollment by degree level:* 82 master's. *Graduate faculty:* 3 full-time (2 women), 2 part-time/adjunct (0 women). *Tuition:* Part-time $170 per credit hour. *Required fees:* $5 per term. Full-time tuition and fees vary according to program. *Graduate housing:* Room and/or apartments available on a first-come, first-served basis to single students; on-campus housing not available to married students. Typical cost: $2,680 per year ($4,432 including board) ; $2,680 per year ($4,432 including board) for married students. *Student services:* Campus employment opportunities, career counseling, free psychological counseling, international student services, low-cost health insurance. *Library facilities:* Benedum Library. *Online resources:* library catalog. *Collection:* 179,096 titles, 625 serial subscriptions, 798 audiovisual materials.

Computer facilities: 79 computers available on campus for general student use. A campuswide network can be accessed from off campus. *Web address:* http://www.salemiu.edu/.

General Application Contact: William M. Martin, Director of Admissions, 304-782-5336, Fax: 304-782-5592, E-mail: admissions@salemiu.edu.

GRADUATE UNITS

Program in Bioscience Students: 5 full-time (1 woman), 4 international. Average age 27. 10 applicants, 50% accepted. *Faculty:* 2 full-time (1 woman). Expenses: Contact institution. *Financial support:* In 2001–02, 4 students received support, including 3 research assistantships with full tuition reimbursements available (averaging $7,200 per year); fellowships, teaching assistantships, career-related internships or fieldwork and tuition waivers (full) also available. Financial award application deadline: 4/15; financial award applicants required to submit FAFSA. Offers biotechnology/molecular biology (MS). *Application deadline:* Applications are processed on a rolling basis. *Application fee:* $25. Electronic applications accepted. *Application Contact:* William M. Martin, Director of Admissions, 304-782-5336, Fax: 304-782-5592, E-mail: admissions@salemiu.edu. *Director of Graduate Bioscience Program,* Dr. Patrick Lai, 304-782-5575, Fax: 304-782-5579, E-mail: bio@salemiu.edu.

Program in Education Students: 22 full-time (19 women), 55 part-time (40 women). Average age 41. 76 applicants, 89% accepted. *Faculty:* 1 (woman) full-time, 3 part-time/adjunct (2 women). Expenses: Contact institution. *Financial support:* Application deadline: 4/15; In 2001, 21 degrees awarded. *Degree program information:* Part-time and evening/weekend programs available. Offers elementary education (MA); equestrian education (MA); secondary education (MA). *Application deadline:* Applications are processed on a rolling basis. *Application fee:* $25. Electronic applications accepted. *Application Contact:* William M. Martin, Director of Admissions, 304-782-5336, Fax: 304-782-5592, E-mail: admissions@salemiu.edu. *Director of Graduate Program in Education,* Dr. Mary Harris-John, 304-782-5258, Fax: 304-782-5395, E-mail: meadows@salen.wvnet.edu.

SALEM STATE COLLEGE, Salem, MA 01970-5353

General Information State-supported, coed, comprehensive institution. CGS member. *Enrollment:* 249 full-time matriculated graduate/professional students (164 women), 1,151 part-time matriculated graduate/professional students (855 women). *Enrollment by degree level:* 1,400 master's. *Graduate faculty:* 13 full-time (10 women), 77 part-time/adjunct (16 women). *Graduate housing:* On-campus housing not available. *Student services:* Campus employment opportunities, campus safety program, career counseling, child daycare facilities, disabled student services, exercise/wellness program, free psychological counseling, international student services, low-cost health insurance, teacher training, writing training. *Library facilities:* Salem State College Library. *Collection:* 236,337 titles, 1,360 serial subscriptions.

Computer facilities: 150 computers available on campus for general student use. *Web address:* http://www.salemstate.edu/.

General Application Contact: Dr. Marion D. de B. Kilson, Dean of the Graduate School, 978-542-6323, Fax: 978-542-7023, E-mail: marion.kilson@salem.mass.edu.

GRADUATE UNITS

Graduate School Students: 249 full-time (164 women), 1,151 part-time (855 women). Average age 32. *Faculty:* 13 full-time (10 women), 77 part-time/adjunct (16 women). Expenses: Contact institution. *Financial support:* Fellowships with partial tuition reimbursements, research assistantships with full tuition reimbursements, career-related internships or fieldwork and Federal Work-Study available. Support available to part-time students. *Degree program information:* Part-time and evening/weekend programs available. Offers bilingual education (M Ed); business administration (MBA); chemistry (MAT); counseling and psychological services (MS); early childhood education (M Ed); education (CAGS); elementary education (M Ed); English (MA, MAT); English as a second language (MAT); geo-information science (MS); geography (MA, MAT); guidance and counseling (M Ed); history (MA, MAT); library media studies (M Ed); mathematics (MAT, MS); middle school education (M Ed); nursing (MSN); reading (M Ed); school administration (M Ed); secondary education (M Ed); social work (MSW); special education (M Ed); teaching English as a second language K–9 (M Ed); technology in education (M Ed). *Application deadline:* Applications are processed on a rolling basis. *Application fee:* $25. *Dean of the Graduate School,* Dr. Marion D. de B. Kilson, 978-542-6323, Fax: 978-542-7023, E-mail: marion.kilson@salem.mass.edu.

SALISBURY UNIVERSITY, Salisbury, MD 21801-6837

General Information State-supported, coed, comprehensive institution. *Enrollment:* 101 full-time matriculated graduate/professional students (62 women), 287 part-time matriculated graduate/professional students (213 women). *Enrollment by degree level:* 388 master's. *Graduate faculty:* 108 full-time (34 women). Tuition, state resident: full-time $6,272; part-time $174 per credit. Tuition, nonresident: full-time $12,988; part-time $355 per credit. *Required fees:* $4 per term. *Graduate housing:* On-campus housing not available. *Student services:* Campus employment opportunities, campus safety program, career counseling, disabled student services, free psychological counseling, international student services, multicultural affairs office. *Library facilities:* Blackwell Library plus 1 other. *Online resources:* library catalog, web page, access to other libraries' catalogs. *Collection:* 249,710 titles, 1,762 serial subscriptions, 10,663 audiovisual materials. *Research affiliation:* NASA (mathematics, physics).

Computer facilities: 200 computers available on campus for general student use. A campuswide network can be accessed from student residence rooms and from off campus. Internet access is available. *Web address:* http://www.salisbury.edu/.

General Application Contact: Jane H. Dané, Dean, Enrollment Management, 410-543-6161, Fax: 410-546-6016, E-mail: admissions@salisbury.edu.

GRADUATE UNITS

Graduate Division Students: 101 full-time (62 women), 287 part-time (213 women). Expenses: Contact institution. *Financial support:* Fellowships, research assistantships with full tuition reimbursements, teaching assistantships with full tuition reimbursements, career-related internships or fieldwork, institutionally sponsored loans, scholarships/grants, and unspecified assistantships available. Support available to part-time students. Financial award applicants required to submit FAFSA. In 2001, 145 degrees awarded. *Degree program information:* Part-time and evening/weekend programs available. Offers applied health physiology (MS); art (MAT); biology (MAT); business administration (MBA); business education (MAT); chemistry (MAT); composition, language and rhetoric (MA); early childhood education (M Ed); educational administration (M Ed); elementary education (M Ed); English (M Ed, MAT); French (MAT); geography (MAT); history (MA, MAT); literature (MA); mathematics (MAT); media and technology (MAT); music (MAT); nursing (MS); psychology (MAT); public school administration (MS Ed); reading education (MAT); science (MAT); secondary education (MAT); social studies (MAT); social work (MSW); Spanish (MAT); teaching English to speakers of other languages (MA). *Application deadline:* Applications are processed on a rolling basis. *Application fee:* $30. *Application Contact:* Jane H. Dané, Dean, Enrollment Management, 410-543-6161, Fax: 410-546-6016, E-mail: admissions@salisbury.edu.

SALVE REGINA UNIVERSITY, Newport, RI 02840-4192

General Information Independent-religious, coed, comprehensive institution. *Enrollment:* 30 full-time matriculated graduate/professional students (21 women), 294 part-time matriculated graduate/professional students (150 women). *Enrollment by degree level:* 267 master's, 57 doctoral. *Graduate faculty:* 54. *Tuition:* Full-time $5,400; part-time $300 per credit. *Required fees:* $330; $40 per term. Tuition and fees vary according to degree level. *Graduate housing:* On-campus housing not available. *Student services:* Campus employment opportunities, campus safety program, career counseling, free psychological counseling, multicultural affairs office. *Library facilities:* McKillop Library. *Online resources:* library catalog, web page, access to other libraries' catalogs. *Collection:* 105,262 titles, 783 serial subscriptions, 18,785 audiovisual materials.

Computer facilities: 163 computers available on campus for general student use. A campuswide network can be accessed from student residence rooms and from off campus. Internet access is available. *Web address:* http://www.salve.edu/.

General Application Contact: Karen E. Johnson, Graduate Admissions Counselor, 401-341-2153, Fax: 401-341-2973, E-mail: graduate_studies@salve.edu.

GRADUATE UNITS

Graduate School Students: 30 full-time (21 women), 294 part-time (150 women); includes 13 minority (6 African Americans, 5 Asian Americans or Pacific Islanders, 2 Hispanic Americans) Average age 38. 165 applicants, 55% accepted, 20 enrolled. *Faculty:* 54. Expenses: Contact institution. *Financial support:* Career-related internships or fieldwork and Federal Work-Study available. Support available to part-time students. Financial award application deadline: 3/1. In 2001, 98 master's, 3 doctorates, 4 other advanced degrees awarded. *Degree program information:* Part-time and evening/weekend programs available. Postbaccalaureate distance learning degree programs offered (minimal on-campus study). Offers administration of justice (MS); business administration (MBA, MS); health services administration (MS); holistic counseling (MA, CAGS); humanities (MA, PhD, CAGS); international relations (MA). *Application deadline:* Applications are processed on a rolling basis. *Application fee:* $50. Electronic applications accepted. *Application Contact:* Karen E. Johnson, Graduate Admissions Counselor, 401-341-2153, Fax: 401-341-2973, E-mail: graduate_studies@salve.edu. *Acting Director,* Dr. Theresa I. Madonna, 401-341-2222, Fax: 401-341-2973, E-mail: madonnat@salve.edu.

See in-depth description on page 1075.

SAMFORD UNIVERSITY, Birmingham, AL 35229-0002

General Information Independent-religious, coed, university. *Enrollment:* 1,239 full-time matriculated graduate/professional students (622 women), 223 part-time matriculated graduate/professional students (136 women). *Enrollment by degree level:* 1,095 first professional, 278 master's, 71 doctoral, 18 other advanced degrees. *Graduate faculty:* 110 full-time (37 women), 32 part-time/adjunct (7 women). *Tuition:* Full-time $383. *Graduate housing:* Room and/or apartments available on a first-come, first-served basis to married students; on-campus housing not available to single students. Housing application deadline: 7/31. *Student services:* Campus employment opportunities, campus safety program, career counseling, disabled student services, free psychological counseling, international student services, low-cost health insurance. *Library facilities:* Samford University Library plus 3 others. *Online resources:* library catalog, web page, access to other libraries' catalogs. *Collection:* 428,432 titles, 11,117 serial subscriptions, 12,857 audiovisual materials. *Research affiliation:* Alabama Marine Consortium, Amazon Center for Environmental Education and Research (Amazon environmental research).

Computer facilities: 350 computers available on campus for general student use. A campuswide network can be accessed from student residence rooms. *Web address:* http://www.samford.edu/.

General Application Contact: Dr. Phil Kimrey, Dean of Admissions and Financial Aid, 205-726-2871, Fax: 205-726-2171, E-mail: ppkimrey@samford.edu.

GRADUATE UNITS

Beeson School of Divinity Students: 195 full-time (42 women), 21 part-time (8 women); includes 31 minority (23 African Americans, 2 Asian Americans or Pacific Islanders, 6 Hispanic Americans) Average age 31. 94 applicants, 72% accepted, 53 enrolled. *Faculty:* 14 full-time (3 women), 3 part-time/adjunct (0 women). Expenses: Contact institution. *Financial support:* In 2001–02, 189 students received support. Scholarships/grants, tuition waivers (full and partial), and unspecified assistantships available. Financial award applicants required to submit FAFSA. In 2001, 41 first professional degrees, 5 master's, 7 doctorates awarded. *Degree program information:* Part-time programs available. Offers divinity (M Div, MTS, D Min). *Application deadline:* For fall admission, 3/1; for spring admission, 10/1. *Application fee:* $25. *Application Contact:* Kymberly C. Dale, Director of Admissions and Recruiting, 205-726-2066, Fax: 205-726-4120, E-mail: kcdale@samford.edu. *Dean,* Dr. Timothy George, 205-726-2632, E-mail: tfeorge@samford.edu.

Cumberland School of Law Students: 506 full-time (211 women), 4 part-time (2 women); includes 30 minority (20 African Americans, 6 Asian Americans or Pacific Islanders, 3 Hispanic Americans, 1 Native American) Average age 26. 879 applicants, 53% accepted, 168 enrolled. *Faculty:* 27 full-time (7 women), 17 part-time/adjunct (3 women). Expenses: Contact institution. *Financial support:* In 2001–02, 433 students received support; research assistantships, teaching assistantships, career-related internships or fieldwork, Federal Work-Study, institutionally sponsored loans, and scholarships/grants available. Financial award application deadline: 3/1; financial award applicants required to submit FAFSA. In 2001, 190 first professional degrees awarded. Offers law (JD, SJD). *Application deadline:* For fall admission, 2/28 (priority date). Applications are processed on a rolling basis. *Application fee:* $40. *Application Contact:* Mitzi S. Davis, Assistant Dean for Admissions, 205-726-2702, Fax: 205-726-2673, E-mail: msdavis@samford.edu. *Dean,* John L. Carroll, 205-726-2704, Fax: 205-726-4107, E-mail: jlcarrol@samford.edu.

Howard College of Arts and Sciences Students: 12 full-time (6 women), 15 part-time (9 women); includes 4 minority (all African Americans) Average age 31. 19 applicants, 95% accepted, 12 enrolled. *Faculty:* 3 full-time (0 women), 1 part-time/adjunct (0 women). Expenses: Contact institution. *Financial support:* In 2001–02, 13 students received support. In 2001, 17 degrees awarded. *Degree program information:* Part-time and evening/weekend programs available. Offers arts and sciences (MSEM). *Application deadline:* For fall admission, 8/30; for spring admission, 1/2. *Application fee:* $25. *Application Contact:* Dr. Ron Hunsinger, Head, 205-726-2944, Fax: 205-726-2479, E-mail: mhusin@samford.edu. *Dean,* Dr. David W. Chapman, 205-726-2771, Fax: 205-726-2279.

Ida V. Moffett School of Nursing Students: 49 full-time (43 women), 8 part-time (7 women); includes 10 minority (all African Americans) Average age 35. 32 applicants, 88% accepted, 13 enrolled. *Faculty:* 7 full-time (all women). Expenses: Contact institution. *Financial support:* In 2001–02, 47 students received support. Career-related internships or fieldwork, Federal Work-Study, and institutionally sponsored loans available. Financial award application deadline: 3/1; financial award applicants required to submit FAFSA. In 2001, 24 degrees awarded. *Degree program information:* Part-time programs available. Offers nursing (MSN). *Application deadline:* For fall admission, 8/1 (priority date); for spring admission, 1/2. Applications are processed on a rolling basis. *Application fee:* $25. *Application Contact:* Jan Paine, Director, 205-726-2746, Fax: 205-870-2219, E-mail: jgpaine@samford.edu. *Dean,* Dr. Nena F. Sanders, 205-726-2629, E-mail: nfsander@samford.edu.

McWhorter School of Pharmacy Students: 414 full-time (287 women), 6 part-time (3 women); includes 52 minority (25 African Americans, 25 Asian Americans or Pacific Islanders, 1 Hispanic American, 1 Native American) Average age 24. 184 applicants, 70% accepted, 101 enrolled. *Faculty:* 30 full-time (11 women), 1 part-time/adjunct (0 women). Expenses: Contact institution. *Financial support:* In 2001–02, 388 students received support. Career-related internships or fieldwork, Federal Work-Study, and institutionally sponsored loans available. Financial award application deadline: 5/2; financial award applicants required to submit FAFSA. In 2001, 113 degrees awarded. Postbaccalaureate distance learning degree programs offered (minimal on-campus study). Offers pharmacy (Pharm D). *Application deadline:* For fall admission, 4/1. Applications are processed on a rolling basis. *Application fee:* $25. *Application Contact:* C. Bruce Foster, Assistant Dean for Student/Alumni Affairs, 205-726-2053, Fax: 205-726-2759, E-mail: cbfoster@samford.edu. *Dean,* Dr. Joe Dean, 205-726-2820, Fax: 205-726-2759, E-mail: jodean@samford.edu.

School of Business Students: 44 full-time (19 women), 65 part-time (24 women); includes 8 minority (all African Americans) Average age 31. 90 applicants, 76% accepted, 37 enrolled.

Samford University (continued)

Faculty: 12 full-time (2 women), 1 (woman) part-time/adjunct. Expenses: Contact institution. *Financial support:* In 2001–02, 38 students received support. Career-related internships or fieldwork and institutionally sponsored loans available. Support available to part-time students. Financial award applicants required to submit FAFSA. In 2001, 67 degrees awarded. *Degree program information:* Part-time and evening/weekend programs available. Offers business (M Acc, MBA). *Application deadline:* For fall admission, 7/15 (priority date); for spring admission, 12/15. Applications are processed on a rolling basis. *Application fee:* $25. *Application Contact:* Francoise Horn, Director of Graduate Programs, 205-726-2931, Fax: 205-726-2540, E-mail: fhhorn@samford.edu. *Dean,* Dr. Carl W. Gooding, 205-726-2308, Fax: 205-726-2464, E-mail: cwgoodin@samford.edu.

School of Education Students: 13 full-time (all women), 104 part-time (83 women); includes 19 minority (17 African Americans, 1 Asian American or Pacific Islander, 1 Hispanic American) Average age 38. 95 applicants, 100% accepted, 56 enrolled. *Faculty:* 8 full-time (5 women), 6 part-time/adjunct (3 women). Expenses: Contact institution. *Financial support:* In 2001–02, 117 students received support; research assistantships, career-related internships or fieldwork, Federal Work-Study, and tuition waivers (partial) available. Support available to part-time students. Financial award applicants required to submit FAFSA. In 2001, 29 degrees awarded. *Degree program information:* Part-time programs available. Offers early childhood education (MS Ed, Ed S); educational administration (MS Ed, Ed D, Ed S); elementary education (MS Ed, Ed S); music education (MS Ed). *Application deadline:* Applications are processed on a rolling basis. *Application fee:* $25. *Application Contact:* Dr. Maurice Persall, Director, Graduate Office, 205-726-2019, E-mail: jmpersal@samford.edu. *Dean,* Dr. Ruth Ash, 205-726-2745, E-mail: rcash@samford.edu.

School of Music Students: 6 full-time (1 woman). Average age 24. 5 applicants, 20% accepted, 1 enrolled. *Faculty:* 9 full-time (2 women), 3 part-time/adjunct (0 women). Expenses: Contact institution. *Financial support:* In 2001–02, 6 students received support. Federal Work-Study, scholarships/grants, and tuition waivers (partial) available. Financial award application deadline: 9/1. In 2001, 1 degree awarded. *Degree program information:* Part-time programs available. Offers music (MM, MME). *Application deadline:* For fall admission, 9/1; for spring admission, 1/20. *Application fee:* $25. *Application Contact:* Dr. Paul Richardson, Assistant Dean for Graduate Studies, 205-726-2496, Fax: 205-726-2165. *Dean,* Dr. Milburn Price, 205-726-2165, E-mail: smprice@samford.edu.

SAM HOUSTON STATE UNIVERSITY, Huntsville, TX 77341

General Information State-supported, coed, comprehensive institution. *Enrollment:* 348 full-time matriculated graduate/professional students (208 women), 1,052 part-time matriculated graduate/professional students (759 women). *Enrollment by degree level:* 1,208 master's, 149 doctoral. *Tuition, area resident:* Part-time $69 per credit. Tuition, state resident: full-time $1,380; part-time $69 per credit. Tuition, nonresident: full-time $5,600; part-time $280 per credit. *Required fees:* $748. Tuition and fees vary according to course load. *Graduate housing:* Rooms and/or apartments available on a first-come, first-served basis to single and married students. Typical cost: $1,904 per year ($3,672 including board) for single students; $1,904 per year ($3,672 including board) for married students. Room and board charges vary according to housing facility selected. *Student services:* Campus employment opportunities, campus safety program, career counseling, child daycare facilities, disabled student services, free psychological counseling, international student services, multicultural affairs office. *Library facilities:* Newton Gresham Library. *Online resources:* library catalog, access to other libraries' catalogs. *Collection:* 1.8 million titles, 3,297 serial subscriptions, 18,427 audiovisual materials. *Research affiliation:* Texas Department of Corrections, Research Division, Texas Criminal Justice Division.

Computer facilities: 200 computers available on campus for general student use. A campuswide network can be accessed from off campus. Internet access is available. *Web address:* http://www.shsu.edu/.

General Application Contact: Dr. Don Bumpass, Director of Graduate Studies, 936-294-1971, Fax: 936-294-1271, E-mail: graduate@shsu.edu.

GRADUATE UNITS

College of Arts and Sciences Students: 99 full-time (57 women), 119 part-time (66 women); includes 9 minority (5 African Americans, 1 Asian American or Pacific Islander, 2 Hispanic Americans, 1 Native American), 37 international. Average age 32. Expenses: Contact institution. *Financial support:* Research assistantships, teaching assistantships, career-related internships or fieldwork, Federal Work-Study, institutionally sponsored loans, scholarships/grants, and tuition waivers (partial) available. Support available to part-time students. Financial award application deadline: 5/31; financial award applicants required to submit FAFSA. In 2001, 43 degrees awarded. *Degree program information:* Part-time and evening/weekend programs available. Offers applied music and literature (MM); art education (M Ed); arts and sciences (M Ed, MA, MFA, MM, MS); biological sciences (M Ed, MA, MS); ceramics (MA, MFA); chemistry (M Ed, MS); computing science (M Ed, MS); conducting (MM); dance (MFA); drawing (MA, MFA); elementary (M Ed); English (M Ed, MA); history (MA); instrumental (M Ed); jewelry (MA); Kodály pedagogy (MM); Kodaly pedagogy (M Ed); mathematics (M Ed, MA, MS); music education (M Ed); musicology (MM); painting (MA, MFA); performance (MM); physics (MS); political science (MA); printmaking (MA, MFA); sculpture (MA, MFA); social research (MA); sociology (MA); statistics (MS); studio art (MFA); theory and composition (MM); vocal (M Ed). *Application deadline:* For fall admission, 8/1; for spring admission, 12/1. Applications are processed on a rolling basis. *Application fee:* $20. Electronic applications accepted. *Dean,* Dr. Brian Chapman, 936-294-1401, Fax: 936-294-1598, E-mail: dca_ctb@shsu.edu.

College of Business Administration Students: 59 full-time (28 women), 127 part-time (66 women); includes 32 minority (9 African Americans, 9 Asian Americans or Pacific Islanders, 13 Hispanic Americans, 1 Native American), 8 international. Average age 31. Expenses: Contact institution. *Financial support:* Research assistantships, Federal Work-Study, institutionally sponsored loans, and unspecified assistantships available. Financial award application deadline: 5/31; financial award applicants required to submit FAFSA. In 2001, 67 degrees awarded. *Degree program information:* Part-time and evening/weekend programs available. Offers business administration (MBA). *Application deadline:* For fall admission, 8/1; for spring admission, 12/1. Applications are processed on a rolling basis. *Application fee:* $20. *Dean,* Dr. R. Dean Lewis, 936-294-1254.

College of Criminal Justice Students: 61 full-time (28 women), 84 part-time (41 women); includes 19 minority (8 African Americans, 1 Asian American or Pacific Islander, 8 Hispanic Americans, 2 Native Americans), 22 international. Average age 33. Expenses: Contact institution. *Financial support:* Fellowships, research assistantships, teaching assistantships, career-related internships or fieldwork, Federal Work-Study, institutionally sponsored loans, and unspecified assistantships available. Support available to part-time students. Financial award application deadline: 5/31; financial award applicants required to submit FAFSA. In 2001, 16 master's, 4 doctorates awarded. Offers criminal justice (MA, MS, PhD). *Application deadline:* For fall admission, 8/1; for spring admission, 12/1. Applications are processed on a rolling basis. *Application fee:* $20. *Application Contact:* Joann Davis, Administrative Assistant to Graduate Programs, 936-294-1647, Fax: 936-294-1653. *Dean,* Dr. Richard Ward, 936-294-1632.

College of Education and Applied Science Students: 129 full-time (95 women), 722 part-time (586 women); includes 122 minority (29 African Americans, 4 Asian Americans or Pacific Islanders, 88 Hispanic Americans, 1 Native American), 8 international. Average age 35. Expenses: Contact institution. *Financial support:* Research assistantships, teaching assistantships, career-related internships or fieldwork, Federal Work-Study, institutionally sponsored loans, and tuition waivers (partial) available. Support available to part-time students. Financial award application deadline: 5/31; financial award applicants required to submit FAFSA. In 2001, 245 master's, 12 doctorates awarded. *Degree program information:* Part-time and evening/weekend programs available. Offers agricultural business (MS); agricultural education (M Ed); agricultural mechanization (MS); agriculture (MS); bilingual education and English as a second language (Certificate); clinical psychology (MA); counseling (M Ed, MA); curriculum and instruction (Ed D); early childhood education (M Ed); education and applied science (M Ed, MA, MLS, MS, Ed D, PhD, Certificate); educational administration (M Ed, PhD); elementary education (M Ed, Certificate); forensic psychology (PhD); health and kinesiology (M Ed, MA); home economics (MA); industrial education (M Ed, MA); industrial technology (MA); library science (MLS); psychology (MA); reading (M Ed); school psychology (MA); secondary education (M Ed, MA, Certificate); special education (M Ed); supervision (M Ed); vocational education (M Ed, MS). *Application deadline:* For fall admission, 8/1; for spring admission, 12/1. *Application fee:* $20. *Acting Dean,* Dr. James Merchant, 936-294-1101, Fax: 936-294-1102, E-mail: edu_jnm@shsu.edu.

SAMRA UNIVERSITY OF ORIENTAL MEDICINE, Los Angeles, CA 90034

General Information Independent, coed, graduate-only institution. *Graduate faculty:* 10 full-time (5 women), 60 part-time/adjunct (30 women). *Tuition:* Full-time $18,000; part-time $325 per unit. *Graduate housing:* On-campus housing not available. *Student services:* Career counseling, exercise/wellness program, international student services, low-cost health insurance. *Library facilities:* Samra University Library plus 1 other. *Collection:* 4,000 titles, 50 serial subscriptions.

Computer facilities: 3 computers available on campus for general student use. Internet access is available. *Web address:* http://www.samra.edu/.

General Application Contact: Taula Jackson, Admissions Director, 310-202-6444 Ext. 104, Fax: 310-202-6007, E-mail: tjackson@samra.edu.

GRADUATE UNITS

Program in Oriental Medicine Students: 322 full-time, 138 part-time. *Faculty:* 10 full-time (5 women), 60 part-time/adjunct (30 women). Expenses: Contact institution. *Financial support:* Available to part-time students. *Degree program information:* Part-time and evening/weekend programs available. Offers Oriental medicine (MS). *Application deadline:* Applications are processed on a rolling basis. *Application fee:* $100. *Application Contact:* Taula Jackson, Admissions Director, 310-202-6444 Ext. 104, Fax: 310-202-6007, E-mail: tjackson@samra.edu. *Provost,* Dr. Katsuyuki P. Sakamoto, 310-202-6444 Ext. 113, Fax: 310-202-6004, E-mail: ksakamoto@samra.edu.

SAMUEL MERRITT COLLEGE, Oakland, CA 94609-3108

General Information Independent, coed, primarily women, comprehensive institution. *Graduate housing:* Room and/or apartments available to single students; on-campus housing not available to married students. *Research affiliation:* Summit Medical Center (nursing).

GRADUATE UNITS

Department of Occupational Therapy Offers occupational therapy (MOT).

Department of Physical Therapy Offers physical therapy (MPT, MSPT).

Department of Physician Assistant Studies Offers physician assistant studies (MPA).

School of Nursing *Degree program information:* Part-time and evening/weekend programs available. Offers case management (MSN); family nurse practitioner (MSN, Certificate); nurse anesthetist (MSN, Certificate); nursing (MSN).

SAN DIEGO STATE UNIVERSITY, San Diego, CA 92182

General Information State-supported, coed, university. CGS member. *Graduate housing:* Room and/or apartments available to single students; on-campus housing not available to married students. *Research affiliation:* Hubbs Sea World Research Institute, Naval Ocean Systems Center (engineering, computer science), Sony Electronics, Inc. (digital speech technology), San Diego Zoo (biology), Asian Pacific Center, Cubic Corporation (radio frequency communication systems and signal processing).

GRADUATE UNITS

Graduate and Research Affairs *Degree program information:* Part-time and evening/weekend programs available. Electronic applications accepted.

College of Arts and Letters *Degree program information:* Part-time and evening/weekend programs available. Offers anthropology (MA); arts and letters (MA, MFA, PhD, CAL); Asian studies (MA); creative writing (MFA); economics (MA); English (MA); French (MA); geography (MA, PhD); history (MA); Latin American studies (MA); liberal arts (MA); linguistics and Oriental languages (MA, CAL); philosophy (MA); political science (MA); sociology (MA); Spanish (MA); women's studies (MA).

College of Education *Degree program information:* Part-time and evening/weekend programs available. Offers counseling and school psychology (MS); education (MA, MS, PhD); educational administration and supervision (MA); educational technology (MA); elementary curriculum and instruction (MA); policy studies in language and cross cultural education (MA); reading education (MA); rehabilitation counseling (MS); secondary curriculum and instruction (MA); special education (MA).

College of Engineering *Degree program information:* Part-time and evening/weekend programs available. Offers aerospace engineering (MS); civil engineering (MS); electrical engineering (MS); engineering (MS, PhD); engineering mechanics (MS); engineering sciences and applied mechanics (PhD); flight dynamics (MS); fluid dynamics (MS); mechanical engineering (MS).

College of Health and Human Services *Degree program information:* Part-time and evening/weekend programs available. Offers communicative disorders (MA); environmental health (MPH, MS); epidemiology (MPH, PhD); health and human services (MA, MPH, MS, MSW, PhD); health promotion (MPH); health services administration (MPH); industrial hygiene (MS); language and communicative disorders (PhD); nursing (MS); social work (MSW); toxicology (MS).

College of Professional Studies and Fine Arts *Degree program information:* Part-time programs available. Offers advertising and public relations (MA); art history (MA); city planning (MCP); communication (MA); criminal justice administration (MPA); criminal justice and criminology (MS); critical-cultural studies (MA); drama (MA, MFA); exercise physiology (MA); interaction studies (MA); intercultural and international studies (MA); music and dance (MA, MM); new media studies (MA); news and information studies (MA); nutritional science (MS); physical education (MS); professional studies and fine arts (MA, MCP, MFA, MM, MPA, MS); public administration (MPA); studio arts (MA, MFA); telecommunications and media management (MA); television, film, and new media production (MA).

College of Sciences *Degree program information:* Part-time programs available. Offers applied mathematics (MS); astronomy (MS); biology (MA, MS); cell and molecular biology (PhD); chemistry (MA, MS, PhD); clinical psychology (MS, PhD); computer science (MS); ecology (PhD); geological sciences (MS); industrial and organizational psychology (MS); mathematics (MA); mathematics and science education (PhD); microbiology (MS); molecular biology (MA, MS); physics (MA, MS); program evaluation (MS); psychology (MA); radiological physics (MS); sciences (MA, MS, PhD); statistics (MS).

Graduate School of Business *Degree program information:* Part-time and evening/weekend programs available. Offers accountancy (MBA, MS); business (MBA, MS); business administration (MBA); finance (MBA, MS); human resources management (MS); information and decision systems (MBA, MS); international business (MBA, MS); management science (MS); marketing (MBA, MS); product operations management (MS). Electronic applications accepted.

Interdisciplinary Studies *Degree program information:* Part-time programs available. Offers interdisciplinary studies (MA, MS).

SAN FRANCISCO ART INSTITUTE, San Francisco, CA 94133

General Information Independent, coed, comprehensive institution. *Graduate housing:* On-campus housing not available.

GRADUATE UNITS

Graduate Program Offers filmmaking (MFA, Certificate); fine arts (MFA, Certificate); painting/drawing (MFA, Certificate); performance/video (MFA); photography (MFA, Certificate); printmaking (MFA, Certificate); sculpture/ceramic sculpture (MFA, Certificate).

SAN FRANCISCO CONSERVATORY OF MUSIC, San Francisco, CA 94122-4411

General Information Independent, coed, comprehensive institution. *Graduate housing:* On-campus housing not available.

GRADUATE UNITS

Graduate Division *Degree program information:* Part-time programs available. Offers chamber music (MM); classical guitar (MM); composition (MM); conducting (MM); keyboards (MM); orchestral instruments (MM); voice (MM).

SAN FRANCISCO STATE UNIVERSITY, San Francisco, CA 94132-1722

General Information State-supported, coed, comprehensive institution. CGS member. *Graduate housing:* Room and/or apartments available on a first-come, first-served basis to single students; on-campus housing not available to married students.

GRADUATE UNITS

Graduate Division *Degree program information:* Part-time and evening/weekend programs available.

College of Behavioral and Social Sciences *Degree program information:* Part-time and evening/weekend programs available. Offers anthropology (MA); behavioral and social sciences (MA, MPA, MS); economics (MA); geography (MA); history (MA); international relations (MA); nonprofit administration (MPA); policy analysis (MPA); political science (MA); psychology (MA, MS); public management (MPA); social science (MA); urban administration (MPA).

College of Business *Degree program information:* Part-time and evening/weekend programs available. Offers business (MBA, MS); business administration (MBA); taxation (MS).

College of Creative Arts *Degree program information:* Part-time and evening/weekend programs available. Offers art (MFA); art history (MA); broadcast and electronic communication arts (MA); cinema (MFA); cinema studies (MA); creative arts (MA, MFA, MM); industrial arts (MA); music (MA, MM); theatre arts (MA, MFA).

College of Education *Degree program information:* Part-time and evening/weekend programs available. Offers adult education (MA, AC); communicative disorders (MS); early childhood education (MA); education (MA, MS, Ed D, PhD, AC); educational administration (MA, AC); educational technology (MA); elementary education (MA); language and literacy education (MA); mathematics education (MA); secondary education (MA, AC); special education (MA, Ed D, PhD, AC); special interest (MA); training systems development (AC).

College of Ethnic Studies *Degree program information:* Part-time programs available. Offers ethnic studies (MA).

College of Health and Human Services *Degree program information:* Part-time programs available. Offers case management (MS); counseling (MS); ethnogerontology (MA); health and human services (MA, MPH, MS, MSW); health education (MPH); healthy aging (MA); home economics (MA); life-long learning (MA); long-term care administration (MA); marriage and family counseling (MS); marriage, family, and child counseling (MS); nursing administration (MS); nursing education (MS); physical education (MA); physical therapy (MS); recreation and leisure studies (MS); rehabilitation counseling (MS); social work education (MSW).

College of Humanities *Degree program information:* Part-time and evening/weekend programs available. Offers Chinese (MA); classics (MA); composition (MA, Certificate); creative writing (MA, MFA); English as a foreign/second language (MA); French (MA); German (MA); humanities (MA, MFA, Certificate); Italian (MA); Japanese (MA); linguistics (MA); literature (MA); museum studies (MA); philosophy (MA); Russian (MA); Spanish (MA); speech and communication studies (MA); teaching composition (Certificate); teaching critical thinking (Certificate); teaching post-secondary reading (Certificate); women's studies (MA); world and comparative literature (MA).

College of Science and Engineering *Degree program information:* Part-time programs available. Offers applied geosciences (MS); biomedical laboratory science (MS); cell and molecular biology (MA); chemistry (MS); computer science (MS); conservation biology (MA); ecology and systematic biology (MA); engineering (MS); marine biology (MA); mathematics (MA); microbiology (MA); physics and astrophysics (MS); physiology and behavioral biology (MA); science and engineering (MA, MS).

SAN FRANCISCO THEOLOGICAL SEMINARY, San Anselmo, CA 94960-2997

General Information Independent-religious, coed, graduate-only institution. *Graduate housing:* Rooms and/or apartments available on a first-come, first-served basis to single and married students. Housing application deadline: 5/1.

GRADUATE UNITS

Graduate and Professional Programs *Degree program information:* Part-time programs available. Offers theology (M Div, MA, MATS, D Min, PhD, Th D).

SAN JOAQUIN COLLEGE OF LAW, Clovis, CA 93612-1312

General Information Independent, coed, graduate-only institution. *Graduate housing:* On-campus housing not available.

GRADUATE UNITS

Law Program *Degree program information:* Part-time and evening/weekend programs available. Offers law (JD).

SAN JOSE STATE UNIVERSITY, San Jose, CA 95192-0001

General Information State-supported, coed, comprehensive institution. CGS member. *Enrollment:* 2,257 full-time matriculated graduate/professional students (1,594 women), 3,509 part-time matriculated graduate/professional students (2,117 women). *Enrollment by degree level:* 5,766 master's. *Graduate faculty:* 933 full-time (216 women), 488 part-time/adjunct (152 women). Tuition, nonresident: part-time $246 per unit. *Required fees:* $678 per semester. Tuition and fees vary according to course load. *Graduate housing:* Room and/or apartments available to single students; on-campus housing not available to married students. Housing application deadline: 6/1. *Student services:* Campus employment opportunities, campus safety program, career counseling, child daycare facilities, disabled student services, free psychological counseling, international student services, low-cost health insurance, teacher training. *Library facilities:* Robert D. Clark Library plus 1 other. *Online resources:* library catalog, web page, access to other libraries' catalogs. *Collection:* 1.1 million titles, 2,504 serial subscriptions, 37,146 audiovisual materials. *Research affiliation:* Moss Landing Marine Laboratories.

Computer facilities: 993 computers available on campus for general student use. A campuswide network can be accessed from student residence rooms and from off campus. Internet access and online class registration are available. *Web address:* http://www.sjsu.edu/.

General Application Contact: Dr. Nabil A. Ibrahim, Associate Vice President, 408-924-2480, Fax: 408-924-2477, E-mail: nibrahim@email.sjsu.edu.

GRADUATE UNITS

Graduate Studies Students: 2,257 full-time (1,594 women), 3,509 part-time (2,117 women); includes 2,270 minority (167 African Americans, 1,429 Asian Americans or Pacific Islanders, 636 Hispanic Americans, 38 Native Americans), 341 international. Average age 33. 5,124 applicants, 62% accepted. *Faculty:* 933 full-time (216 women), 488 part-time/adjunct (152 women). Expenses: Contact institution. *Financial support:* Fellowships, research assistantships, teaching assistantships, career-related internships or fieldwork, Federal Work-Study, institutionally sponsored loans, scholarships/grants, and tuition waivers (partial) available. Support available to part-time students. Financial award applicants required to submit FAFSA. In 2001, 1541 degrees awarded. *Degree program information:* Part-time and evening/weekend programs available. Postbaccalaureate distance learning degree programs offered (minimal on-campus study). Offers human factors/ergonomics (MS); interdisciplinary studies (MA, MS); library and information science (MLIS). *Application deadline:* For fall admission, 6/29; for spring admission, 11/30. Applications are processed on a rolling basis. *Application fee:* $59. Electronic applications accepted. *Application Contact:* 408-924-2480, Fax: 408-924-2477. *Associate Vice President*, Dr. Nabil A. Ibrahim, 408-924-2480, Fax: 408-924-2477, E-mail: nibrahim@email.sjsu.edu.

College of Applied Arts and Sciences Students: 204 full-time (158 women), 278 part-time (220 women); includes 145 minority (17 African Americans, 89 Asian Americans or Pacific Islanders, 37 Hispanic Americans, 2 Native Americans), 34 international. Average age 32. 477 applicants, 62% accepted. *Faculty:* 110 full-time (49 women), 38 part-time/adjunct (24 women). Expenses: Contact institution. *Financial support:* Fellowships, teaching assistantships, career-related internships or fieldwork, Federal Work-Study, institutionally sponsored loans, scholarships/grants, and tuition waivers (partial) available. Support available to part-time students. Financial award applicants required to submit FAFSA. In 2001, 122 degrees awarded. *Degree program information:* Part-time and evening/weekend programs available. Offers administration of justice (MS); applied arts and sciences (MA, MPH, MS, Certificate); community health nursing (MS); gerontology (MS); gerontology nurse practitioner (MS); health administration (Certificate); health science (MA); kinesiology (MA); mass communication (MS); nutritional science (MS); occupational therapy (MS); public health (MPH); recreation (MS). *Application deadline:* For fall admission, 6/29; for spring admission, 11/30. Applications are processed on a rolling basis. *Application fee:* $59. Electronic applications accepted. *Dean*, Dr. Michael Ego, 408-924-2900, Fax: 408-924-2901.

College of Business Students: 85 full-time (56 women), 214 part-time (89 women); includes 148 minority (1 African American, 129 Asian Americans or Pacific Islanders, 14 Hispanic Americans, 4 Native Americans), 27 international. Average age 32. 598 applicants, 50% accepted. *Faculty:* 95 full-time (4 women), 65 part-time/adjunct (10 women). Expenses: Contact institution. *Financial support:* Applicants required to submit FAFSA. In 2001, 250 degrees awarded. *Degree program information:* Part-time and evening/weekend programs available. Postbaccalaureate distance learning degree programs offered (minimal on-campus study). Offers accountancy (MS); business (MBA, MS); business administration, information management, and manufacturing management (MBA); taxation (MS); transportation management (MS). *Application deadline:* For fall admission, 6/29; for spring admission, 11/30. Applications are processed on a rolling basis. *Application fee:* $59. Electronic applications accepted. *Application Contact:* Dr. Lee Jerrell, Graduate Director, 408-924-3420, Fax: 408-924-3426. *Dean*, Dr. David Conroth, 408-924-3400, Fax: 408-924-3419.

College of Education Students: 373 full-time (295 women), 424 part-time (338 women); includes 255 minority (30 African Americans, 79 Asian Americans or Pacific Islanders, 137 Hispanic Americans, 9 Native Americans), 9 international. Average age 37. 491 applicants, 79% accepted. *Faculty:* 152 full-time (63 women), 73 part-time/adjunct (29 women). Expenses: Contact institution. *Financial support:* Career-related internships or fieldwork available. Financial award applicants required to submit FAFSA. In 2001, 342 degrees awarded. *Degree program information:* Evening/weekend programs available. Offers administration and higher education (MA); audiology (MA); child development (MA); counseling (MA); education (MA, Certificate); education for the hearing impaired (MA); education for the severely handicapped (MA); elementary education (MA); instructional technology (MA, Certificate); learning handicapped (MA); school business management (Certificate); secondary education (MA); special education (MA); speech pathology (MA). *Application deadline:* For fall admission, 6/29; for spring admission, 11/30. Applications are processed on a rolling basis. *Application fee:* $59. Electronic applications accepted. *Acting Dean*, Dr. Susan Myers, 408-924-3600, Fax: 408-924-3713.

College of Engineering Students: 300 full-time (145 women), 776 part-time (227 women); includes 682 minority (14 African Americans, 639 Asian Americans or Pacific Islanders, 27 Hispanic Americans, 2 Native Americans), 165 international. Average age 29. 771 applicants, 56% accepted. *Faculty:* 60 full-time (5 women), 82 part-time/adjunct (7 women). Expenses: Contact institution. *Financial support:* Teaching assistantships, career-related internships or fieldwork, Federal Work-Study, and institutionally sponsored loans available. Support available to part-time students. Financial award applicants required to submit FAFSA. In 2001, 237 degrees awarded. *Degree program information:* Part-time programs available. Offers aerospace engineering (MS); chemical engineering (MS); civil and environmental engineering (MS); computer engineering (MS); computer software (MS); computerized robots and computer applications (MS); electrical engineering (MS); engineering (MS); general engineering (MS); information and systems engineering (MS); materials engineering (MS); mechanical engineering (MS); microprocessors and microcomputers (MS); quality assurance (MS). *Application deadline:* For fall admission, 6/29; for spring admission, 11/30. Applications are processed on a rolling basis. *Application fee:* $59. Electronic applications accepted. *Dean*, Dr. Don Kirk, 408-924-3800, Fax: 408-924-3818.

College of Humanities and Arts Students: 155 full-time (91 women), 174 part-time (121 women); includes 79 minority (7 African Americans, 37 Asian Americans or Pacific Islanders, 34 Hispanic Americans, 1 Native American), 22 international. Average age 36. 266 applicants, 67% accepted. *Faculty:* 189 full-time (48 women), 85 part-time/adjunct (37 women). Expenses: Contact institution. *Financial support:* Applicants required to submit FAFSA. In 2001, 92 degrees awarded. Offers art education (MA); art history (MA); environmental design (MA); French (MA); graphic arts (MA); humanities and arts (MA, MFA, Certificate); industrial design (MA); interior design (MA); linguistics (MA, Certificate); literature (MA); music (MA); music performance (MA); philosophy (MA, Certificate); pictorial arts (MFA); plastic arts (MFA); Spanish (MA); teaching English as a second language (MA); technical writing (MA); textiles (MA); theatre arts (MA). *Application deadline:* For fall admission, 6/29; for spring admission, 11/30. Applications are processed on a rolling basis. *Application fee:* $59. Electronic applications accepted. *Acting Dean*, Dr. Carmen Sigler, 408-924-4300, Fax: 408-924-4365.

College of Science Students: 98 full-time (66 women), 236 part-time (125 women); includes 153 minority (4 African Americans, 138 Asian Americans or Pacific Islanders, 9 Hispanic Americans, 2 Native Americans), 45 international. Average age 31. 518 applicants, 27% accepted. *Faculty:* 156 full-time (19 women), 59 part-time/adjunct (15 women). Expenses: Contact institution. *Financial support:* Teaching assistantships, career-related internships or fieldwork, Federal Work-Study, and institutionally sponsored loans available. Support available to part-time students. Financial award applicants required to submit FAFSA. In 2001, 78 degrees awarded. *Degree program information:* Part-time and evening/weekend programs available. Offers analytical chemistry (MS); biochemistry (MS); biological sciences (MA, MS); chemistry (MA); computational physics (MS); computer science (MS); geology (MS); inorganic chemistry (MS); marine science (MS); mathematics (MA, MS); meteorology (MS); organic chemistry (MS); physical chemistry (MS); physics (MS); polymer chemistry (MS); radiochemistry (MS); science (MA, MS). *Application deadline:* For fall admission, 6/29; for spring admission, 11/30. Applications are processed on a rolling basis. *Application fee:* $59. Electronic applications accepted. *Dean*, Dr. Gerry Selter, 408-924-4800, Fax: 408-924-4815.

College of Social Sciences Students: 125 full-time (80 women), 211 part-time (117 women); includes 115 minority (17 African Americans, 45 Asian Americans or Pacific Islanders, 53 Hispanic Americans), 17 international. Average age 33. 381 applicants, 57% accepted. *Faculty:* 159 full-time (26 women), 76 part-time/adjunct (25 women). Expenses: Contact institution. *Financial support:* In 2001–02, 29 teaching assistantships were awarded; career-related internships or fieldwork, Federal Work-Study, institutionally sponsored loans, scholarships/grants, and tuition waivers (partial) also available. Support available to part-time students. Financial award applicants required to submit FAFSA. In 2001, 90 degrees awarded. *Degree program information:* Part-time and evening/weekend programs available. Offers applied economics (MA); clinical psychology (MS); counseling (MS); criminology (MA); economics (MA); environmental studies (MS); geography (MA); history (MA); industrial psychology (MS); public administration (MPA); research psychology (MA); social sciences (MA, MPA, MS); sociology (MA); speech communication (MA). *Application deadline:* For fall admission, 6/29; for spring admission, 11/30. Applications are processed on a rolling basis. *Application fee:* $59. Electronic applications accepted. *Dean*, Dr. Lela Noble, 408-924-5300, Fax: 408-924-5303.

San Jose State University (continued)

College of Social Work Students: 240 full-time (187 women), 108 part-time (66 women); includes 180 minority (30 African Americans, 38 Asian Americans or Pacific Islanders, 105 Hispanic Americans, 7 Native Americans), 10 international. Average age 32. 357 applicants, 59% accepted. *Faculty:* 12 full-time (2 women), 10 part-time/adjunct (5 women). Expenses: Contact institution. *Financial support:* Teaching assistantships, career-related internships or fieldwork, Federal Work-Study, and institutionally sponsored loans available. Financial award application deadline: 5/31; financial award applicants required to submit FAFSA. In 2001, 108 degrees awarded. *Degree program information:* Part-time programs available. Offers Mexican-American studies (MA); social work (MA, MSW, MUP); urban and regional planning (MUP). *Application deadline:* For fall admission, 6/29; for spring admission, 11/30. Applications are processed on a rolling basis. *Application fee:* $59. Electronic applications accepted. *Dean,* Dr. Sylvia Andrew, 408-924-5800, Fax: 408-924-5892.

SANTA BARBARA COLLEGE OF ORIENTAL MEDICINE, Santa Barbara, CA 93101

General Information Proprietary, coed, primarily women, graduate-only institution. *Enrollment by degree level:* 112 master's. *Graduate faculty:* 2 full-time (1 woman), 13 part-time/adjunct (9 women). *Tuition:* Full-time $8,700; part-time $155 per unit. *Required fees:* $25 per term. One-time fee: $175. Tuition and fees vary according to course load and program. *Graduate housing:* On-campus housing not available. *Student services:* Career counseling. *Library facilities:* Santa Barbara College of Oriental Medicine. *Collection:* 1,000 titles, 72 serial subscriptions.

Computer facilities: 2 computers available on campus for general student use. Internet access is available. *Web address:* http://www.sbcom.edu/.

General Application Contact: Amy Dowd, Admissions Assistant, 805-898-1180, Fax: 805-682-1864, E-mail: admissions@sbcom.edu.

GRADUATE UNITS

Program in Acupuncture and Oriental Medicine Students: 71 full-time (49 women), 41 part-time (29 women); includes 10 minority (1 African American, 5 Asian Americans or Pacific Islanders, 4 Hispanic Americans), 1 international. Average age 34. 52 applicants, 88% accepted, 42 enrolled. *Faculty:* 2 full-time (1 woman), 13 part-time/adjunct (9 women). Expenses: Contact institution. *Financial support:* In 2001–02, 67 students received support. Applicants required to submit FAFSA. In 2001, 17 degrees awarded. *Degree program information:* Part-time and evening/weekend programs available. Offers acupuncture and Oriental medicine (M Ac OM). *Application deadline:* For fall admission, 5/31 (priority date). Applications are processed on a rolling basis. *Application fee:* $75 ($100 for international students). *Application Contact:* Amy Dowd, Admissions Assistant, 805-898-1180, Fax: 805-682-1864, E-mail: admissions@sbcom.edu. *President,* JoAnn Tall, 805-898-1180.

SANTA CLARA UNIVERSITY, Santa Clara, CA 95053

General Information Independent-religious, coed, university. CGS member. *Enrollment:* 1,318 full-time matriculated graduate/professional students (683 women), 1,510 part-time matriculated graduate/professional students (609 women). *Enrollment by degree level:* 917 first professional, 1,656 master's, 18 doctoral, 237 other advanced degrees. *Graduate faculty:* 187 full-time (52 women), 114 part-time/adjunct (35 women). *Tuition:* Part-time $320 per unit. Tuition and fees vary according to class time, degree level, program and student level. *Graduate housing:* On-campus housing not available. *Student services:* Campus employment opportunities, campus safety program, career counseling, child daycare facilities, free psychological counseling, international student services, multicultural affairs office. *Library facilities:* Orradre Library plus 1 other. *Online resources:* library catalog, web page, access to other libraries' catalogs. *Collection:* 454,470 titles, 8,919 serial subscriptions, 12,570 audiovisual materials.

Computer facilities: 535 computers available on campus for general student use. A campuswide network can be accessed from student residence rooms and from off campus. *Web address:* http://www.scu.edu/.

General Application Contact: Richard J. Toomey, Dean, Enrollment Management, 408-554-4505, E-mail: rtoomey@scu.edu.

GRADUATE UNITS

College of Arts and Sciences Students: 2 full-time (1 woman), 41 part-time (26 women); includes 7 minority (1 African American, 2 Asian Americans or Pacific Islanders, 4 Hispanic Americans), 2 international. Average age 44. 16 applicants, 81% accepted. *Faculty:* 3 full-time (0 women), 3 part-time/adjunct (2 women). Expenses: Contact institution. *Financial support:* Fellowships, research assistantships, career-related internships or fieldwork, Federal Work-Study, and institutionally sponsored loans available. Support available to part-time students. Financial award application deadline: 3/1; financial award applicants required to submit FAFSA. In 2001, 17 degrees awarded. *Degree program information:* Part-time and evening/weekend programs available. Offers arts and sciences (MA); catechetics (MA); liturgical music (MA); pastoral liturgy (MA); spirituality (MA). *Application deadline:* For fall admission, 8/21; for winter admission, 11/20; for spring admission, 2/12. Applications are processed on a rolling basis. *Application fee:* $25. *Dean,* Dr. Peter A. Facione, 408-554-4455.

Division of Counseling Psychology and Education Students: 104 full-time (90 women), 241 part-time (201 women); includes 70 minority (8 African Americans, 31 Asian Americans or Pacific Islanders, 30 Hispanic Americans, 1 Native American), 12 international. Average age 36. 207 applicants, 79% accepted. *Faculty:* 13 full-time (7 women), 18 part-time/adjunct (11 women). Expenses: Contact institution. *Financial support:* Fellowships, teaching assistantships, career-related internships or fieldwork, Federal Work-Study, institutionally sponsored loans, and scholarships/grants available. Support available to part-time students. Financial award application deadline: 3/1; financial award applicants required to submit FAFSA. In 2001, 95 master's, 52 other advanced degrees awarded. *Degree program information:* Part-time and evening/weekend programs available. Offers counseling psychology (MA); counseling psychology and education (MA, Certificate); education (MA); educational administration (MA); health psychology (MA); marriage, family, and child counseling (MA); multiple subject teaching (Certificate); pastoral counseling (MA); single subject teaching (Certificate); special education (MA). *Application deadline:* For fall admission, 4/1; for winter admission, 11/1; for spring admission, 2/1. Applications are processed on a rolling basis. *Application fee:* $35. *Application Contact:* Helen Valine, Assistant to the Dean, 408-554-4656, Fax: 408-554-2392. *Administrator,* Dr. Peter A. Facione, 408-554-4455.

Leavey School of Business Students: 220 full-time (84 women), 698 part-time (228 women); includes 246 minority (12 African Americans, 204 Asian Americans or Pacific Islanders, 28 Hispanic Americans, 2 Native Americans), 241 international. Average age 32. 374 applicants, 71% accepted. *Faculty:* 82 full-time (16 women), 5 part-time/adjunct (0 women). Expenses: Contact institution. *Financial support:* Fellowships, research assistantships, career-related internships or fieldwork, Federal Work-Study, institutionally sponsored loans, and scholarships/grants available. Support available to part-time students. Financial award application deadline: 3/1; financial award applicants required to submit FAFSA. In 2001, 335 degrees awarded. *Degree program information:* Part-time and evening/weekend programs available. Offers business (EMBA, MBA); business administration (EMBA, MBA). *Application deadline:* For fall admission, 6/1; for winter admission, 9/1; for spring admission, 12/1. Applications are processed on a rolling basis. *Application fee:* $75 for international students. Electronic applications accepted. *Application Contact:* Elizabeth Ford, Assistant Dean of Admissions, 408-554-2752, Fax: 408-554-4571. *Dean,* Dr. Barry Posner, 408-554-4523.

School of Engineering Students: 146 full-time (67 women), 459 part-time (117 women); includes 206 minority (8 African Americans, 183 Asian Americans or Pacific Islanders, 15 Hispanic Americans), 253 international. Average age 30. 441 applicants, 49% accepted. *Faculty:* 42 full-time (11 women), 54 part-time/adjunct (4 women). Expenses: Contact institution. *Financial support:* Fellowships, research assistantships, teaching assistantships, career-related internships or fieldwork, Federal Work-Study, institutionally sponsored loans, and scholarships/grants available. Support available to part-time students. Financial award application deadline: 3/1; financial award applicants required to submit FAFSA. In 2001, 196 master's, 2 doctorates, 1 other advanced degree awarded. *Degree program information:* Part-time and evening/weekend programs available. Offers applied mathematics (MSAM); ASIC design and test (Certificate); civil engineering (MSCE); computer science and engineering (MSCSE, PhD); data storage technologies (Certificate); electrical engineering (MSEE, PhD, Engineer); engineering (MS, MSAM, MSCE, MSCSE, MSE, MSE Mgt, MSEE, MSME, PhD, Certificate, Engineer); engineering management (MSE Mgt); high performance computing (Certificate); mechanical engineering (MSME, PhD, Engineer); software engineering (MS, Certificate). *Application deadline:* For fall admission, 6/1; for spring admission, 1/1. Applications are processed on a rolling basis. *Application fee:* $45 ($55 for international students). Electronic applications accepted. *Application Contact:* Tina Samms, Assistant Director of Graduate Admissions, 408-554-4313, Fax: 408-554-5474, E-mail: engr-grad@scu.edu. *Dean,* Dr. Terry E. Shoup, 408-554-4600.

School of Law Students: 846 full-time (441 women), 71 part-time (37 women); includes 316 minority (22 African Americans, 211 Asian Americans or Pacific Islanders, 75 Hispanic Americans, 8 Native Americans), 33 international. Average age 28. 2,664 applicants, 62% accepted. *Faculty:* 47 full-time (18 women), 34 part-time/adjunct (18 women). Expenses: Contact institution. *Financial support:* Fellowships, research assistantships, career-related internships or fieldwork, Federal Work-Study, institutionally sponsored loans, and scholarships/grants available. Support available to part-time students. Financial award application deadline: 2/1; financial award applicants required to submit FAFSA. In 2001, 259 first professional degrees, 15 master's awarded. *Degree program information:* Part-time and evening/weekend programs available. Offers law (JD, LL M, Certificate). *Application deadline:* For fall admission, 3/1. *Application fee:* $50 ($60 for international students). *Application Contact:* Julia Yaffee, Director of Admissions, 408-554-4800, Fax: 408-554-7897. *Dean,* Mack Player, 408-554-4361.

SARAH LAWRENCE COLLEGE, Bronxville, NY 10708

General Information Independent, coed, comprehensive institution. CGS member. *Graduate housing:* Room and/or apartments available to single students; on-campus housing not available to married students. Housing application deadline: 7/1. *Research affiliation:* Columbia University Medical Center, New York University Medical Center, Albert Einstein College of Medicine of Yeshiva University, New York Hospital–Cornell Medical Center.

GRADUATE UNITS

Graduate Studies *Degree program information:* Part-time programs available. Offers art of teaching (MS Ed); child development (MA); dance (MA, MFA); health advocacy (MA, MPS); human genetics (MPS, MS); individualized study (MA); theater arts (MA, MFA); women's history (MA); writing (MFA).

See in-depth description on page 1077.

SAVANNAH COLLEGE OF ART AND DESIGN, Savannah, GA 31402-3146

General Information Independent, coed, comprehensive institution. *Enrollment:* 555 full-time matriculated graduate/professional students (272 women), 76 part-time matriculated graduate/professional students (33 women). *Enrollment by degree level:* 631 master's. *Graduate faculty:* 91 full-time (37 women), 9 part-time/adjunct (4 women). *Tuition:* Full-time $17,775; part-time $395 per credit hour. One-time fee: $500. *Graduate housing:* Room and/or apartments available to single students; on-campus housing not available to married students. Typical cost: $4,800 per year ($7,620 including board). Room and board charges vary according to housing facility selected. Housing application deadline: 4/1. *Student services:* Campus employment opportunities, campus safety program, career counseling, disabled student services, exercise/wellness program, international student services, multicultural affairs office, writing training. *Library facilities:* Savannah College of Art and Design Library plus 1 other. *Online resources:* library catalog, web page. *Collection:* 72,000 titles, 900 serial subscriptions, 2,100 audiovisual materials.

Computer facilities: 664 computers available on campus for general student use. A campuswide network can be accessed from student residence rooms and from off campus. Internet access and online class registration are available. *Web address:* http://www.scad.edu/.

General Application Contact: Darrell Tutchton, Director of Graduate and International Enrollment, 912-525-5961, Fax: 912-525-5985, E-mail: admissions@scad.edu.

GRADUATE UNITS

Graduate School Students: 555 full-time (272 women), 76 part-time (33 women); includes 61 minority (40 African Americans, 10 Asian Americans or Pacific Islanders, 10 Hispanic Americans, 1 Native American), 179 international. Average age 25. 654 applicants, 77% accepted. *Faculty:* 137 full-time (53 women), 6 part-time/adjunct (2 women). Expenses: Contact institution. *Financial support:* In 2001–02, 92 fellowships were awarded; career-related internships or fieldwork and Federal Work-Study also available. Financial award application deadline: 9/1; financial award applicants required to submit FAFSA. In 2001, 205 degrees awarded. *Degree program information:* Part-time programs available. Offers architectural history (MA, MFA); architecture (M Arch); art history (MA, MFA); computer art (MA, MFA); fashion (MA, MFA); fibers (MA, MFA); furniture design (MA, MFA); graphic design (MA, MFA); historic preservation (MA, MFA); illustration (MA, MFA); interior design (MA, MFA); media and performing arts (MA, MFA); metals and jewelry (MA, MFA); painting (MA, MFA); photography (MA, MFA); product design (MA, MFA); sequential art (MA, MFA); video/film (MA, MFA). *Application deadline:* For fall admission, 9/1 (priority date). Applications are processed on a rolling basis. *Application fee:* $50. Electronic applications accepted. *Application Contact:* Darrell Tutchton, Director of Graduate and International Enrollment, 912-525-5961, Fax: 912-525-5985, E-mail: admissions@scad.edu. *Dean of Graduate Studies,* Kathleen Marks, 912-525-5800, Fax: 912-525-5817, E-mail: kmarks@sead.edu.

SAVANNAH STATE UNIVERSITY, Savannah, GA 31404

General Information State-supported, coed, comprehensive institution. *Graduate housing:* On-campus housing not available.

GRADUATE UNITS

Program in Public Administration Offers public administration (MPA).

Program in Social Work Offers social work (MSW).

Program in Urban Studies *Degree program information:* Part-time programs available. Offers urban studies (MS).

SAYBROOK GRADUATE SCHOOL AND RESEARCH CENTER, San Francisco, CA 94133-4640

General Information Independent, coed, graduate-only institution. *Enrollment by degree level:* 76 master's, 316 doctoral. *Graduate faculty:* 20 full-time (6 women), 83 part-time/adjunct (29 women). *Tuition:* Full-time $13,800. *Required fees:* $2,000. One-time fee: $600 full-time. *Graduate housing:* On-campus housing not available. *Library facilities:* Library and Information Services plus 1 other. *Online resources:* library catalog, web page, access to other libraries' catalogs. *Collection:* 1,200 titles, 3,000 serial subscriptions, 20 audiovisual materials. *Research affiliation:* Rollo May Center for Humanistic Studies.

Computer facilities: A campuswide network can be accessed from off campus. Internet access and online class registration are available. *Web address:* http://www.saybrook.edu/.

General Application Contact: Mindy Myers, Vice President for Recruitment and Admissions, 800-825-4480, Fax: 415-433-9271, E-mail: mmyers@saybrook.edu.

GRADUATE UNITS

Program in Psychology, Human Science and Organizational Systems Students: 392 full-time (246 women); includes 63 minority (28 African Americans, 16 Asian Americans or Pacific Islanders, 14 Hispanic Americans, 5 Native Americans), 17 international. Average age 42. 280 applicants, 34% accepted. *Faculty:* 20 full-time (6 women), 83 part-time/adjunct (29 women). Expenses: Contact institution. *Financial support:* In 2001–02, 275 students received support. Scholarships/grants available. Financial award applicants required to submit FAFSA. In 2001, 9 master's, 35 doctorates awarded. Postbaccalaureate distance learning degree programs offered (minimal on-campus study). Offers human science (MA, PhD); organizational systems (MA, PhD); psychology (MA, PhD). *Application deadline:* For fall admission, 6/1 (priority date); for spring admission, 12/16 (priority date). Electronic applications accepted. *Application Contact:* Mindy Myers, Vice President for Recruitment and Admissions, 800-825-4480, Fax: 415-433-9271, E-mail: mmyers@saybrook.edu. *President,* Dr. Maureen O'Hara, 800-825-4480, Fax: 415-433-9271, E-mail: mohara@saybrook.edu.

SCHILLER INTERNATIONAL UNIVERSITY, 69121 Heidelberg, Germany

General Information Independent, coed, comprehensive institution. *Graduate housing:* Room and/or apartments available on a first-come, first-served basis to single students; on-campus housing not available to married students.

GRADUATE UNITS

MBA Program, Heidelberg, Germany *Degree program information:* Part-time and evening/weekend programs available. Offers international business (MBA, MIM).

SCHILLER INTERNATIONAL UNIVERSITY, 75015 Paris, France

General Information Independent, coed, comprehensive institution. *Graduate housing:* On-campus housing not available.

GRADUATE UNITS

MBA Program Paris, France *Degree program information:* Part-time and evening/weekend programs available. Offers international business (MBA); international relations and diplomacy (MA). Bilingual French/English MBA available for native French speakers.

SCHILLER INTERNATIONAL UNIVERSITY, 28015 Madrid, Spain

General Information Independent, coed, comprehensive institution. *Graduate housing:* On-campus housing not available.

GRADUATE UNITS

MBA Program, Madrid, Spain *Degree program information:* Part-time programs available. Offers international business (MBA). Electronic applications accepted.

SCHILLER INTERNATIONAL UNIVERSITY, Strasbourg, 6700, France

General Information Independent, coed, graduate-only institution. *Graduate housing:* Rooms and/or apartments available to single and married students.

GRADUATE UNITS

MBA Program, Strasbourg, France Campus *Degree program information:* Part-time and evening/weekend programs available. Offers international business (MBA).

SCHILLER INTERNATIONAL UNIVERSITY, London SE1 8TX, United Kingdom

General Information Independent, coed, comprehensive institution. *Graduate housing:* Rooms and/or apartments available on a first-come, first-served basis to single and married students.

GRADUATE UNITS

Graduate Programs, London *Degree program information:* Part-time and evening/weekend programs available. Offers international business (MBA); international hotel and tourism management (MA, MBA); international management (MIM); international relations and diplomacy (MA); management of information technology (MBA).

SCHILLER INTERNATIONAL UNIVERSITY, Dunedin, FL 34698-7532

General Information Independent, coed, comprehensive institution. *Graduate housing:* Room and/or apartments available to single students; on-campus housing not available to married students.

GRADUATE UNITS

MBA Programs, Florida *Degree program information:* Part-time and evening/weekend programs available. Offers international business (MBA); international hotel and tourism management (MBA).

SCHILLER INTERNATIONAL UNIVERSITY, AMERICAN COLLEGE OF SWITZERLAND, CH-1854 Leysin, Switzerland

General Information Independent, coed, comprehensive institution. *Graduate housing:* Room and/or apartments available to single students; on-campus housing not available to married students.

GRADUATE UNITS

MBA Program Offers international business (MBA).

THE SCHOLL COLLEGE OF PODIATRIC MEDICINE AT FINCH UNIVERSITY OF HEALTH SCIENCES/THE CHICAGO MEDICAL SCHOOL, North Chicago, IL 60064-3095

General Information Independent, coed, upper-level institution. *Enrollment:* 248 full-time matriculated graduate/professional students (93 women). *Enrollment by degree level:* 248 first professional. *Graduate faculty:* 17 full-time (4 women), 15 part-time/adjunct (4 women). *Tuition:* Full-time $22,200. *Graduate housing:* On-campus housing not available. *Student services:* Campus employment opportunities, campus safety program, career counseling, disabled student services, exercise/wellness program, free psychological counseling, international student services, low-cost health insurance, multicultural affairs office. *Online resources:* library catalog. *Collection:* 8,000 titles, 285 serial subscriptions.

Computer facilities: 12 computers available on campus for general student use. *Web address:* http://www.finchcms.edu/scholl/.

General Application Contact: Admissions Coordinator, 847-578-3000, E-mail: admiss@scholl.edu.

GRADUATE UNITS

Dr. William M. Scholl College of Podiatric Medicine Students: 248 full-time (93 women); includes 56 minority (15 African Americans, 31 Asian Americans or Pacific Islanders, 9 Hispanic Americans, 1 Native American), 6 international. Average age 26. 235 applicants, 57% accepted, 72 enrolled. *Faculty:* 17 full-time (4 women), 15 part-time/adjunct (4 women). Expenses: Contact institution. *Financial support:* In 2001–02, 225 students received support, including 55 fellowships (averaging $4,000 per year); Federal Work-Study and scholarships/grants also available. Support available to part-time students. Financial award application deadline: 5/1; financial award applicants required to submit FAFSA. In 2001, 100 degrees awarded. Offers podiatric medicine (DPM). *Application deadline:* For fall admission, 8/1 (priority date). Applications are processed on a rolling basis. *Application fee:* $50. Electronic applications accepted. *Application Contact:* Admissions Coordinator, 847-578-3000, E-mail: admiss@scholl.edu. *Dean,* Dr. Terence Albright, 847-578-3000.

SCHOOL FOR INTERNATIONAL TRAINING, Brattleboro, VT 05302-0676

General Information Independent, coed, graduate-only institution. *Enrollment by degree level:* 176 master's. *Graduate faculty:* 35 full-time (15 women), 19 part-time/adjunct (8 women). *Graduate housing:* Room and/or apartments available on a first-come, first-served basis to single students; on-campus housing not available to married students. Typical cost: $3,682 (including board). *Student services:* Campus employment opportunities, campus safety program, career counseling, exercise/wellness program, free psychological counseling, international student services, low-cost health insurance, teacher training, writing training. *Library facilities:* Donald B. Watt Library. *Collection:* 32,000 titles, 450 serial subscriptions.

Computer facilities: 42 computers available on campus for general student use. A campuswide network can be accessed from off campus. Internet access is available. *Web address:* http://www.sit.edu/.

General Application Contact: Kim Noble, Admissions Assistant, 802-257-7751 Ext. 3267, Fax: 802-258-3500, E-mail: admissions@sit.edu.

GRADUATE UNITS

Graduate Programs Students: 176 full-time (118 women). Average age 27. *Faculty:* 35 full-time (15 women), 19 part-time/adjunct (8 women). Expenses: Contact institution. *Financial support:* Career-related internships or fieldwork, Federal Work-Study, institutionally sponsored loans, and scholarships/grants available. Financial award application deadline: 4/1; financial award applicants required to submit FAFSA. Offers conflict transformation intercultural service, leadership and management (MA); endorsement in bilingual-multicultural education (MAT); English for speakers of other languages (MAT); French (MAT); intercultural relations (MA); international education (MA); non-governmental organization leadership and management (Postgraduate Diploma); organizational management (MS); Spanish (MAT); sustainable development (MA). *Application deadline:* Applications are processed on a rolling basis. *Application fee:* $45. *Application Contact:* Kim Noble, Admissions Assistant, 802-257-7751 Ext. 3267, Fax: 802-258-3500, E-mail: admissions@sit.edu. *President,* Jim Cramer, 802-257-7751.

See in-depth description on page 1079.

SCHOOL OF ADVANCED AIRPOWER STUDIES, Maxwell AFB, AL 36112-6424

General Information Federally supported, graduate-only institution.

GRADUATE UNITS

Program in Airpower Art and Science Offers airpower art and science (MA). Available to active duty military officers only.

SCHOOL OF THE ART INSTITUTE OF CHICAGO, Chicago, IL 60603-3103

General Information Independent, coed, comprehensive institution. *Graduate housing:* Room and/or apartments available on a first-come, first-served basis to single students; on-campus housing not available to married students. Housing application deadline: 3/21.

GRADUATE UNITS

Graduate Division *Degree program information:* Part-time programs available. Offers art and technology (MFA); art education (MAAE, Certificate); art history, theory, and criticism (MA, Certificate); art therapy (MAAT); arts administration (MAAA); ceramics (MFA); fiber (MFA); filmmaking (MFA); historic preservation (MSHP); interior architecture (MFA); painting and drawing (MFA); performance art (MFA); photography (MFA); printmaking (MFA); sculpture (MFA); video (MFA); visual communication (MFA); writing (MFA).

SCHOOL OF THE MUSEUM OF FINE ARTS, Boston, MA 02115

General Information Independent, coed, comprehensive institution. *Enrollment by degree level:* 89 master's. *Graduate faculty:* 53 full-time, 100 part-time/adjunct. *Tuition:* Full-time $20,208. *Required fees:* $482. *Graduate housing:* On-campus housing not available. *Student services:* Campus employment opportunities, career counseling, free psychological counseling, international student services. *Library facilities:* William Morris Hunt Memorial Library plus 1 other. *Online resources:* library catalog, web page, access to other libraries' catalogs. *Collection:* 657 serial subscriptions, 220 audiovisual materials.

Computer facilities: 46 computers available on campus for general student use. A campuswide network can be accessed from off campus. Internet access is available. *Web address:* http://www.smfa.edu/.

General Application Contact: John Williamson, Director of Enrollment and Student Services, 617-369-3626, Fax: 617-369-3679, E-mail: admissions@smfa.edu.

GRADUATE UNITS

Graduate Program Students: 89 full-time (59 women); includes 8 minority (6 Asian Americans or Pacific Islanders, 2 Hispanic Americans), 13 international. Average age 30. 280 applicants, 33% accepted, 35 enrolled. *Faculty:* 53 full-time, 100 part-time/adjunct. Expenses: Contact institution. *Financial support:* Teaching assistantships, Federal Work-Study and scholarships/grants available. Support available to part-time students. Financial award application deadline: 4/15; financial award applicants required to submit FAFSA. In 2001, 24 degrees awarded. Offers fine arts (MAT, MFA, Certificate). *Application deadline:* For fall admission, 1/15. *Application fee:* $50. *Application Contact:* John Williamson, Director of Enrollment and Student Services, 617-369-3626, Fax: 617-369-3679, E-mail: admissions@smfa.edu. *Dean/Deputy Director of Education,* Deborah H. Dluhy, 617-369-3611, Fax: 617-424-6271, E-mail: ddluhy@mfa.org.

SCHOOL OF VISUAL ARTS, New York, NY 10010-3994

General Information Proprietary, coed, comprehensive institution. *Enrollment:* 282 full-time matriculated graduate/professional students (160 women), 37 part-time matriculated graduate/professional students (20 women). *Enrollment by degree level:* 319 master's. *Graduate faculty:* 8 full-time (1 woman), 106 part-time/adjunct (38 women). *Tuition:* Full-time $18,400; part-time $650 per credit. *Required fees:* $500. *Graduate housing:* Room and/or apartments available on a first-come, first-served basis to single students; on-campus housing not available to married students. Typical cost: $2,500 per year ($7,000 including board). *Student services:* Campus employment opportunities, career counseling, international student services, low-cost health insurance. *Library facilities:* School of Visual Arts Library. *Online resources:* library catalog, access to other libraries' catalogs. *Collection:* 70,680 titles, 306 serial subscriptions, 1,600 audiovisual materials.

Computer facilities: 600 computers available on campus for general student use. A campuswide network can be accessed from off campus. *Web address:* http://www.schoolofvisualarts.edu/.

General Application Contact: Brenda Hanegan, Admissions Coordinator, 212-592-2106, Fax: 212-592-2116, E-mail: bhanegan@adm.schoolofvisualarts.edu.

GRADUATE UNITS

Graduate Programs Students: 282 full-time (160 women), 37 part-time (20 women); includes 25 minority (5 African Americans, 11 Asian Americans or Pacific Islanders, 9 Hispanic Americans), 123 international. Average age 28. 1,035 applicants, 25% accepted. *Faculty:* 8 full-time (1 woman), 106 part-time/adjunct (38 women). Expenses: Contact institution. *Financial support:* In 2001–02, 161 students received support. Career-related internships or fieldwork, scholarships/grants, and unspecified assistantships available. Financial award application deadline: 2/2; financial award applicants required to submit FAFSA. In 2001, 105 degrees awarded. Offers art therapy (MPS); computer art (MFA); design (MFA); illustration (MFA); painting (MFA); photography (MFA); printmaking (MFA); sculpture (MFA). *Application deadline:* For fall admission, 2/16. *Application fee:* $60 ($70 for international students). *Application Contact:* Brenda Hanegan, Admissions Coordinator, 212-592-2106, Fax: 212-592-2116, E-mail: bhanegan@adm.schoolofvisualarts.edu. *President,* David Rhodes, 212-592-2350, Fax: 212-260-7621, E-mail: davidrhodes@adm.schoolofvisualarts.edu.

See in-depth description on page 1081.

SCHREINER UNIVERSITY, Kerrville, TX 78028-5697

General Information Independent-religious, coed, comprehensive institution. *Enrollment:* 15 full-time matriculated graduate/professional students (8 women). *Enrollment by degree level:* 15 master's. *Graduate faculty:* 3 full-time (1 woman). *Tuition:* Part-time $243 per credit hour. *Graduate housing:* Rooms and/or apartments available on a first-come, first-served basis to single and married students. Typical cost: $3,244 per year ($6,936 including

Schreiner University (continued)

board) for single students; $4,850 per year for married students. Room and board charges vary according to board plan, campus/location and housing facility selected. Housing application deadline: 8/1. *Student services:* Campus employment opportunities, campus safety program, career counseling, disabled student services, exercise/wellness program, free psychological counseling, international student services, teacher training. *Library facilities:* W. M. Logan Library. *Online resources:* library catalog, web page. *Collection:* 73,335 titles, 702 serial subscriptions, 613 audiovisual materials.

Computer facilities: 62 computers available on campus for general student use. A campuswide network can be accessed from student residence rooms and from off campus. Internet access is available. *Web address:* http://www.schreiner.edu/.

General Application Contact: Dr. Jack E. Cockrill, Director of Graduate Program, 830-792-7445 Ext. 445, Fax: 830-792-7382, E-mail: jecockrill@schreiner.edu.

GRADUATE UNITS

Program in Education Students: 15 full-time (8 women); includes 4 minority (2 African Americans, 2 Hispanic Americans) Average age 40. 14 applicants, 43% accepted, 6 enrolled. *Faculty:* 3 full-time (1 woman). Expenses: Contact institution. *Financial support:* Application deadline: 8/1; In 2001, 27 degrees awarded. *Degree program information:* Evening/weekend programs available. Offers education (M Ed). *Application deadline:* For fall admission, 7/15 (priority date); for spring admission, 12/6 (priority date). Applications are processed on a rolling basis. *Application fee:* $25. Electronic applications accepted. *Application Contact:* Betty Lavonne Miller, Administrative Assistant, 830-792-7455 Ext. 455. *Director of Graduate Program,* Dr. Jack E. Cockrill, 830-792-7445 Ext. 445, Fax: 830-792-7382, E-mail: jecockrill@schreiner.edu.

THE SCRIPPS RESEARCH INSTITUTE, La Jolla, CA 92037

General Information Independent, coed, graduate-only institution. *Enrollment by degree level:* 150 doctoral. *Graduate faculty:* 97 full-time (13 women), 4 part-time/adjunct (1 woman). *Tuition:* Full-time $5,000. *Graduate housing:* On-campus housing not available. *Student services:* Campus employment opportunities, campus safety program, career counseling, child daycare facilities, exercise/wellness program, free psychological counseling, grant writing training, international student services, low-cost health insurance, multicultural affairs office, writing training. *Library facilities:* Kresge Library. *Online resources:* library catalog. *Collection:* 45,000 titles, 800 serial subscriptions.

Computer facilities: 257 computers available on campus for general student use. A campuswide network can be accessed from student residence rooms and from off campus. Internet access is available. *Web address:* http://www.scripps.edu/.

General Application Contact: Marylyn Rinaldi, Graduate Program Administrator, 858-784-8469, Fax: 858-784-2802, E-mail: mrinaldi@scripps.edu.

GRADUATE UNITS

Office of Graduate Studies Students: 151 full-time (45 women); includes 21 minority (3 African Americans, 14 Asian Americans or Pacific Islanders, 4 Hispanic Americans), 32 international. Average age 22. 370 applicants, 27% accepted, 39 enrolled. *Faculty:* 97 full-time (13 women), 4 part-time/adjunct (1 woman). Expenses: Contact institution. *Financial support:* Institutionally sponsored loans and stipends available. In 2001, 21 degrees awarded. Offers chemistry (PhD); macromolecular and cellular structure and chemistry (PhD). *Application deadline:* For fall admission, 1/1. *Application fee:* $0. *Application Contact:* Marylyn Rinaldi, Graduate Program Administrator, 858-784-8469, Fax: 858-784-2802, E-mail: mrinaldi@scripps.edu. *Dean,* Dr. Jeffery W. Kelly, 858-784-8469, Fax: 858-784-2801, E-mail: gradprgm@scripps.edu.

SEABURY-WESTERN THEOLOGICAL SEMINARY, Evanston, IL 60201-2976

General Information Independent-religious, coed, graduate-only institution. *Graduate housing:* Rooms and/or apartments available to single students and available on a first-come, first-served basis to married students. Housing application deadline: 5/30.

GRADUATE UNITS

School of Theology *Degree program information:* Part-time programs available. Offers Anglican ministries (D Min); congregational development (MTS, D Min); preaching (D Min); theological studies (MTS); theology (M Div, L Th). MTS and D Min (congregational development) offered in summer only.

SEATTLE INSTITUTE OF ORIENTAL MEDICINE, Seattle, WA 98115

General Information Private, coed, primarily women, graduate-only institution. *Graduate faculty:* 2 full-time (1 woman), 9 part-time/adjunct (3 women). *Tuition:* Full-time $12,000. *Graduate housing:* On-campus housing not available. *Student services:* Free psychological counseling, low-cost health insurance. *Library facilities:* SIOM Library. *Collection:* 450 titles, 20 serial subscriptions.

Computer facilities: 1 computer available on campus for general student use. Internet access is available. *Web address:* http://www.siom.com/.

General Application Contact: Dr. Paul D. Karsten, President, 206-517-4541, Fax: 206-526-1932, E-mail: pkarsten@siom.com.

GRADUATE UNITS

Graduate Program Students: 28 full-time (20 women); includes 1 minority (Asian American or Pacific Islander) Average age 37. 28 applicants, 71% accepted, 16 enrolled. *Faculty:* 2 full-time (1 woman), 9 part-time/adjunct (3 women). Expenses: Contact institution. In 2001, 10 degrees awarded. *Application deadline:* For fall admission, 2/15. Applications are processed on a rolling basis. *Application fee:* $50. *Application Contact:* Sue B. Wozniak, Registrar, 206-517-4541, Fax: 206-526-1932, E-mail: info@siom.com. *President,* Dr. Paul D. Karsten, 206-517-4541, Fax: 206-526-1932, E-mail: pkarsten@siom.com.

SEATTLE PACIFIC UNIVERSITY, Seattle, WA 98119-1997

General Information Independent-religious, coed, comprehensive institution. *Enrollment:* 219 full-time matriculated graduate/professional students (169 women), 443 part-time matriculated graduate/professional students (273 women). *Enrollment by degree level:* 500 master's, 162 doctoral. *Graduate faculty:* 45 full-time (18 women), 21 part-time/adjunct (9 women). *Tuition:* Part-time $300 per credit hour. Tuition and fees vary according to program. *Graduate housing:* Rooms and/or apartments available on a first-come, first-served basis to single and married students. Typical cost: $6,249 (including board) for single students. Room and board charges vary according to board plan and housing facility selected. Housing application deadline: 8/1. *Student services:* Campus employment opportunities, campus safety program, career counseling, disabled student services, exercise/wellness program, free psychological counseling, international student services, low-cost health insurance, multicultural affairs office, teacher training. *Library facilities:* Seattle Pacific University Library. *Online resources:* library catalog, web page, access to other libraries' catalogs. *Collection:* 141,712 titles, 1,192 serial subscriptions, 2,670 audiovisual materials. *Research affiliation:* Fred Hutchinson Cancer Research Center (cancer and tumors).

Computer facilities: 150 computers available on campus for general student use. A campuswide network can be accessed from student residence rooms and from off campus. Internet access and online class registration are available. *Web address:* http://www.spu.edu/.

General Application Contact: Dr. Les L. Steele, Dean of Graduate Studies, 206-281-2125, Fax: 206-281-2115, E-mail: ttrzyna@spu.edu.

GRADUATE UNITS

Graduate School Students: 219 full-time (169 women), 443 part-time (273 women); includes 75 minority (18 African Americans, 34 Asian Americans or Pacific Islanders, 18 Hispanic Americans, 5 Native Americans), 32 international. 231 applicants, 93% accepted, 187 enrolled. *Faculty:* 45 full-time (18 women), 21 part-time/adjunct (9 women). Expenses: Contact institution. *Financial support:* Research assistantships, teaching assistantships, career-related internships or fieldwork, traineeships, and unspecified assistantships available. Financial award applicants required to submit FAFSA. In 2001, 172 master's, 11 doctorates, 53 other advanced degrees awarded. *Degree program information:* Part-time and evening/weekend programs available. Postbaccalaureate distance learning degree programs offered (no on-campus study). *Application deadline:* Applications are processed on a rolling basis. *Vice President for Academic Affairs,* Dr. Les L. Steele, 206-281-2125, Fax: 206-281-2115, E-mail: lsteele@spu.edu.

College of Arts and Sciences Students: 53 (38 women); includes 6 minority (2 African Americans, 3 Asian Americans or Pacific Islanders, 1 Hispanic American) 1 international. Expenses: Contact institution. *Financial support:* Research assistantships, career-related internships or fieldwork and unspecified assistantships available. Financial award applicants required to submit FAFSA. In 2001, 21 degrees awarded. *Degree program information:* Part-time and evening/weekend programs available. Offers arts and sciences (MA, MS); physical education (MS); teaching English as a second language (MA). *Application deadline:* Applications are processed on a rolling basis. *Dean,* Dr. Joyce Erickson, 206-281-2165.

School of Business and Economics Students: 120 (48 women); includes 19 minority (1 African American, 15 Asian Americans or Pacific Islanders, 2 Hispanic Americans, 1 Native American) 25 international. Expenses: Contact institution. *Financial support:* In 2001–02, 5 students received support, including 2 research assistantships; career-related internships or fieldwork also available. Financial award applicants required to submit FAFSA. In 2001, 39 degrees awarded. *Degree program information:* Part-time and evening/weekend programs available. Offers business administration (MBA); business and economics (MBA, MS); information systems management (MS). *Application deadline:* For fall admission, 8/1 (priority date); for winter admission, 11/1; for spring admission, 2/1. Applications are processed on a rolling basis. *Application Contact:* Debbie Wysomierski, Assistant Graduate Director, 206-281-2753, Fax: 206-281-2733, E-mail: mba@spu.edu. *Graduate Director,* Gary Karns, 206-281-2753, Fax: 206-281-2733.

School of Education Students: 282 (184 women); includes 24 minority (6 African Americans, 9 Asian Americans or Pacific Islanders, 6 Hispanic Americans, 3 Native Americans) 1 international. Expenses: Contact institution. *Financial support:* In 2001–02, 5 research assistantships (averaging $4,500 per year) were awarded; career-related internships or fieldwork also available. Financial award applicants required to submit FAFSA. In 2001, 65 master's, 1 doctorate, 53 other advanced degrees awarded. *Degree program information:* Part-time and evening/weekend programs available. Offers education (M Ed, MAT, Ed D, Ed S); educational leadership (M Ed); reading/language arts education (M Ed); school counseling (M Ed); school psychology (Ed S); secondary teaching (MAT). *Application deadline:* Applications are processed on a rolling basis. *Application Contact:* Roger M. Long, Assistant to Dean for Graduate Programs, 206-281-2378, Fax: 206-281-2756, E-mail: rmlong@spu.edu. *Dean,* Dr. Bill Rowley, 206-281-2214.

School of Health Sciences Students: 30 (27 women); includes 4 minority (all Asian Americans or Pacific Islanders) 1 international. Expenses: Contact institution. *Financial support:* In 2001–02, 2 teaching assistantships were awarded; career-related internships or fieldwork and traineeships also available. Financial award applicants required to submit FAFSA. In 2001, 25 degrees awarded. *Degree program information:* Part-time and evening/weekend programs available. Offers health sciences (MSN, Certificate); nurse practitioner (Certificate); nursing leadership (MSN). *Application deadline:* For fall admission, 9/1 (priority date). Applications are processed on a rolling basis. *Application fee:* $50. *Application Contact:* Dr. Donna J. Allis, Director, 206-281-2649, Fax: 206-281-2767, E-mail: dallis@spu.edu. *Dean,* Dr. Lucille Kelley, 206-281-2608, Fax: 206-281-2767, E-mail: lkelley@spu.edu.

School of Psychology, Family and Community Students: 177 (145 women); includes 22 minority (9 African Americans, 3 Asian Americans or Pacific Islanders, 9 Hispanic Americans, 1 Native American) 4 international. Expenses: Contact institution. *Financial support:* Research assistantships, career-related internships or fieldwork and unspecified assistantships available. Financial award applicants required to submit FAFSA. In 2001, 22 master's, 10 doctorates awarded. *Degree program information:* Part-time programs available. Offers clinical psychology (PhD); marriage and family therapy (MS); psychology, family and community (MS, PhD). *Application Contact:* Kelley Unger, Program Manager, 206-281-2759, Fax: 206-281-2695, E-mail: kunger@spu.edu. *Chair,* Dr. Nathan Brown, 206-281-2987, E-mail: ncbrown@spu.edu.

SEATTLE UNIVERSITY, Seattle, WA 98122

General Information Independent-religious, coed, comprehensive institution. *Enrollment:* 1,175 full-time matriculated graduate/professional students (689 women), 1,409 part-time matriculated graduate/professional students (771 women). *Graduate faculty:* 179 full-time (88 women), 130 part-time/adjunct (59 women). *Tuition:* Full-time $7,740; part-time $430 per credit hour. Tuition and fees vary according to course load, degree level and program. *Graduate housing:* Room and/or apartments available on a first-come, first-served basis to single students; on-campus housing not available to married students. Typical cost: $2,220 per year ($6,318 including board). *Student services:* Campus employment opportunities, campus safety program, career counseling, disabled student services, exercise/wellness program, free psychological counseling, international student services, low-cost health insurance, multicultural affairs office, teacher training, writing training. *Library facilities:* Lemieux Library plus 1 other. *Online resources:* library catalog, web page, access to other libraries' catalogs. *Collection:* 502,438 titles, 6,504 serial subscriptions, 5,857 audiovisual materials.

Computer facilities: 401 computers available on campus for general student use. A campuswide network can be accessed from student residence rooms and from off campus. *Web address:* http://www.seattleu.edu/.

General Application Contact: Janet Shandley, Associate Dean of Graduate Admissions, 206-296-5900, Fax: 206-298-5656, E-mail: grad_admissions@seattleu.edu.

GRADUATE UNITS

Albers School of Business and Economics Students: 128 full-time (59 women), 493 part-time (187 women); includes 93 minority (4 African Americans, 76 Asian Americans or Pacific Islanders, 11 Hispanic Americans, 2 Native Americans), 79 international. Average age 32. 306 applicants, 73% accepted, 131 enrolled. *Faculty:* 46 full-time (14 women), 17 part-time/adjunct (4 women). Expenses: Contact institution. *Financial support:* Career-related internships or fieldwork, Federal Work-Study, and unspecified assistantships available. Support available to part-time students. Financial award applicants required to submit FAFSA. In 2001, 194 master's, 4 other advanced degrees awarded. *Degree program information:* Part-time and evening/weekend programs available. Offers business administration (MBA, Certificate); business and economics (MBA, MIB, MPAC, MSF, Certificate); finance (MSF, Certificate); international business (MIB, Certificate); professional accounting (MPAC). *Application deadline:* For fall admission, 8/20 (priority date); for winter admission, 11/20; for spring admission, 2/20. Applications are processed on a rolling basis. *Application fee:* $55. *Application Contact:* Janet Shandley, Associate Dean of Graduate Admissions, 206-296-5900, Fax: 206-298-5656, E-mail: grad_admissions@seattleu.edu. *Dean,* Dr. Joseph Phillips, 206-296-5700, Fax: 206-296-5795.

College of Arts and Sciences Students: 54 full-time (38 women), 110 part-time (70 women); includes 26 minority (11 African Americans, 9 Asian Americans or Pacific Islanders, 3 Hispanic Americans, 3 Native Americans), 5 international. Average age 35. 77 applicants, 66% accepted, 39 enrolled. *Faculty:* 14 full-time (5 women), 13 part-time/adjunct (5 women). Expenses: Contact institution. *Financial support:* Career-related internships or fieldwork and Federal Work-Study available. Support available to part-time students. Financial award applicants required to submit FAFSA. In 2001, 77 degrees awarded. Offers arts and sciences (MA Psych, MNPL, MPA); existential and phenomenological therapeutic psychology (MA Psych). *Application fee:* $55. *Application Contact:* Janet Shandley, Associate Dean of Graduate Admissions, 206-296-5900, Fax: 206-298-5656, E-mail: grad_admissions@seattleu.edu. *Dean,* Dr. Wallace Loh, 206-296-5300, E-mail: lohw@seattleu.edu.

Institute of Public Service Students: 17 full-time (15 women), 106 part-time (67 women); includes 23 minority (11 African Americans, 6 Asian Americans or Pacific Islanders, 3 Hispanic Americans, 3 Native Americans), 3 international. Average age 34. 26 applicants,

85% accepted, 16 enrolled. *Faculty:* 6 full-time (2 women), 9 part-time/adjunct (2 women). Expenses: Contact institution. *Financial support:* Career-related internships or fieldwork, Federal Work-Study, and unspecified assistantships available. Support available to part-time students. Financial award applicants required to submit FAFSA. In 2001, 62 degrees awarded. Offers public administration (MPA); public service (MNPL, MPA); social enterprise management and not-for-profit leadership (MNPL). *Application fee:* $55. *Application Contact:* Janet Shandley, Associate Dean of Graduate Admissions, 206-296-5900, Fax: 206-298-5656, E-mail: grad_admissions@seattleu.edu. *Director*, Dr. Russell Lidman, 206-296-5442, Fax: 206-296-5997, E-mail: lidmanr@seattleu.edu.

School of Education Students: 153 full-time (117 women), 353 part-time (269 women); includes 76 minority (20 African Americans, 28 Asian Americans or Pacific Islanders, 23 Hispanic Americans, 5 Native Americans), 17 international. Average age 35. 266 applicants, 73% accepted, 122 enrolled. *Faculty:* 30 full-time (16 women), 20 part-time/adjunct (10 women). Expenses: Contact institution. *Financial support:* Career-related internships or fieldwork, Federal Work-Study, and unspecified assistantships available. Support available to part-time students. Financial award applicants required to submit FAFSA. In 2001, 212 master's, 5 doctorates, 15 other advanced degrees awarded. *Degree program information:* Part-time and evening/weekend programs available. Offers adult education and training (M Ed, MA, Certificate); counseling (MA); curriculum and instruction (M Ed, MA, Certificate); education (M Ed, MA, MIT, Ed D, Certificate, Ed S); educational administration (M Ed, MA, Certificate, Ed S); educational diagnostics/school psychology (Ed S); educational leadership (Ed D); student development administration (M Ed, MA); teacher education (MIT); teaching English to speakers of other languages (M Ed, MA, Certificate). *Application fee:* $55. *Application Contact:* Janet Shandley, Associate Dean of Graduate Admissions, 206-296-5900, Fax: 206-298-5656, E-mail: grad_admissions@seattleu.edu. *Dean*, Dr. Sue Schmitt, 206-296-5760, E-mail: sschmitt@seattleu.edu.

School of Law Students: 765 full-time (426 women), 245 part-time (108 women); includes 191 minority (33 African Americans, 111 Asian Americans or Pacific Islanders, 34 Hispanic Americans, 13 Native Americans), 16 international. Average age 28. 1,379 applicants, 61% accepted, 345 enrolled. *Faculty:* 48 full-time (26 women), 40 part-time/adjunct (16 women). Expenses: Contact institution. *Financial support:* Career-related internships or fieldwork, Federal Work-Study, institutionally sponsored loans, and scholarships/grants available. Support available to part-time students. Financial award application deadline: 4/1; financial award applicants required to submit FAFSA. In 2001, 261 degrees awarded. *Degree program information:* Part-time and evening/weekend programs available. Offers law (JD). *Application deadline:* For fall admission, 4/1 (priority date). Applications are processed on a rolling basis. *Application fee:* $50. *Application Contact:* Carol T. Cochran, Director of Admissions, 206-398-4200, Fax: 206-398-4058, E-mail: ccochran@seattleu.edu. *Dean*, Rudolph Hasl, 206-398-4300, Fax: 206-398-4310, E-mail: hasl@seattleu.edu.

School of Nursing Students: 1 (woman) full-time, 18 part-time (15 women); includes 5 minority (1 African American, 4 Asian Americans or Pacific Islanders) Average age 38. 15 applicants, 80% accepted, 8 enrolled. *Faculty:* 21 full-time (19 women), 8 part-time/adjunct (all women). Expenses: Contact institution. *Financial support:* Fellowships, research assistantships, career-related internships or fieldwork and Federal Work-Study available. Support available to part-time students. Financial award applicants required to submit FAFSA. In 2001, 5 master's, 1 other advanced degree awarded. *Degree program information:* Part-time and evening/weekend programs available. Offers nursing (MSN, Certificate). *Application deadline:* For fall admission, 7/1. *Application fee:* $55. *Application Contact:* Janet Shandley, Associate Dean of Graduate Admissions, 206-296-5900, Fax: 206-298-5656, E-mail: grad_admissions@seattleu.edu. *Dean*, Dr. Mary Walker, 206-296-5676.

School of Science and Engineering Students: 8 full-time (3 women), 42 part-time (11 women); includes 9 minority (7 Asian Americans or Pacific Islanders, 1 Hispanic American, 1 Native American), 18 international. Average age 34. 29 applicants, 62% accepted, 10 enrolled. *Faculty:* 10 full-time (3 women), 5 part-time/adjunct (0 women). Expenses: Contact institution. *Financial support:* Career-related internships or fieldwork and Federal Work-Study available. Support available to part-time students. Financial award applicants required to submit FAFSA. In 2001, 25 degrees awarded. *Degree program information:* Part-time and evening/weekend programs available. Offers science and engineering (MSE); software engineering (MSE). *Application deadline:* For fall admission, 7/1. *Application fee:* $55. *Application Contact:* Janet Shandley, Associate Dean of Graduate Admissions, 206-296-5900, Fax: 206-298-5656, E-mail: grad_admissions@seattleu.edu. *Dean*, Dr. George Simmons, 206-296-5500, Fax: 206-296-2071.

School of Theology and Ministry Students: 66 full-time (45 women), 148 part-time (111 women); includes 22 minority (9 African Americans, 5 Asian Americans or Pacific Islanders, 5 Hispanic Americans, 3 Native Americans), 7 international. Average age 45. 78 applicants, 85% accepted, 61 enrolled. *Faculty:* 10 full-time (5 women), 27 part-time/adjunct (16 women). Expenses: Contact institution. *Financial support:* Career-related internships or fieldwork and Federal Work-Study available. Support available to part-time students. Financial award applicants required to submit FAFSA. In 2001, 10 first professional degrees, 35 master's, 2 other advanced degrees awarded. *Degree program information:* Part-time and evening/weekend programs available. Offers divinity (M Div); pastoral studies (MAPS); theology and ministry (M Div, MAPS, MATS, Certificate); transforming spirituality (MATS, Certificate). *Application deadline:* For fall admission, 7/1. *Application fee:* $55. *Application Contact:* Catherine Kehoe Fallon, Admissions Coordinator, 206-296-5333, Fax: 206-296-5329, E-mail: fallon@seattleu.edu. *Dean*, Dr. Patrick Howell, SJ, 206-296-5330, Fax: 206-296-5329.

See in-depth description on page 1083.

SEMINARY OF THE IMMACULATE CONCEPTION, Huntington, NY 11743-1696

General Information Independent-religious, coed, graduate-only institution. *Enrollment by degree level:* 37 first professional, 99 master's, 8 doctoral. *Graduate faculty:* 7 full-time (2 women), 15 part-time/adjunct (1 woman). *Tuition:* Full-time $12,000; part-time $350 per credit. *Required fees:* $1,320; $20 per semester. One-time fee: $100 full-time; $30 part-time. *Graduate housing:* Room and/or apartments available to single students; on-campus housing not available to married students. Housing application deadline: 8/30. *Student services:* Low-cost health insurance. *Online resources:* library catalog. *Collection:* 52,429 titles, 360 serial subscriptions, 825 audiovisual materials.

Computer facilities: 8 computers available on campus for general student use. A campuswide network can be accessed from student residence rooms. Internet access is available. *Web address:* http://www.icseminary.edu/.

General Application Contact: Rev. Robert J. Smith, Academic Dean, 631-423-0483 Ext. 130, Fax: 631-432-2346.

GRADUATE UNITS

School of Theology Students: 37 full-time (0 women), 107 part-time (65 women); includes 12 minority (5 African Americans, 3 Asian Americans or Pacific Islanders, 4 Hispanic Americans) Average age 32. 30 applicants, 90% accepted, 27 enrolled. *Faculty:* 7 full-time (2 women), 15 part-time/adjunct (1 woman). Expenses: Contact institution. *Financial support:* In 2001–02, 37 students received support. Available to part-time students. Applicants required to submit FAFSA. In 2001, 14 first professional degrees, 12 master's, 8 doctorates, 2 other advanced degrees awarded. *Degree program information:* Part-time and evening/weekend programs available. Offers theology (M Div, MA, D Min, Certificate). *Application deadline:* For fall admission, 8/30 (priority date); for spring admission, 1/20. Applications are processed on a rolling basis. *Application Contact:* Joan B. Innvar, Registrar, 631-423-0483 Ext. 112, Fax: 631-423-2346, E-mail: jinnvar@icseminary.edu. *Academic Dean*, Rev. Robert J. Smith, 631-423-0483 Ext. 130, Fax: 631-432-2346.

SETON HALL UNIVERSITY, South Orange, NJ 07079-2697

General Information Independent-religious, coed, university. CGS member. *Enrollment:* 1,619 full-time matriculated graduate/professional students (858 women), 2,162 part-time matriculated graduate/professional students (1,139 women). *Enrollment by degree level:* 1,210 first professional, 2,091 master's, 386 doctoral, 94 other advanced degrees. *Graduate faculty:* 379 full-time (165 women), 455 part-time/adjunct (177 women). *Tuition:* Full-time $10,818; part-time $601 per credit. *Required fees:* $610; $185 per term. Tuition and fees vary according to course load, program and student's religious affiliation. *Graduate housing:* Room and/or apartments available on a first-come, first-served basis to single students; on-campus housing not available to married students. Housing application deadline: 5/1. *Student services:* Campus employment opportunities, career counseling, disabled student services, exercise/wellness program, free psychological counseling, international student services, low-cost health insurance, teacher training. *Library facilities:* Walsh Library plus 1 other. *Online resources:* library catalog, web page, access to other libraries' catalogs. *Collection:* 385,000 titles, 2,271 serial subscriptions, 3,558 audiovisual materials.

Computer facilities: 500 computers available on campus for general student use. A campuswide network can be accessed from student residence rooms and from off campus. Internet access and online class registration are available. *Web address:* http://www.shu.edu/.

GRADUATE UNITS

College of Arts and Sciences *Degree program information:* Part-time and evening/weekend programs available. Offers analytical chemistry (MS, PhD); arts and sciences (MA, MHA, MPA, MS, PhD); Asian studies (MA); biochemistry (MS, PhD); biology (MS); chemistry (MS); corporate and public communication (MA); English (MA); French (MA); inorganic chemistry (MS, PhD); Jewish-Christian studies (MA); microbiology (MS); museum professions (MA); organic chemistry (MS, PhD); physical chemistry (MS, PhD); Spanish (MA).

Center for Public Service *Degree program information:* Part-time and evening/weekend programs available. Offers arts administration (MPA); criminal justice (MPA); health policy and management (MPA); healthcare administration (MHA); management of nonprofit organizations (MPA); public service administration and policy (MPA); religious organization management (MPA).

College of Education and Human Services Students: 253 full-time (156 women), 688 part-time (393 women); includes 110 minority (56 African Americans, 12 Asian Americans or Pacific Islanders, 40 Hispanic Americans, 2 Native Americans), 9 international. Average age 37. 360 applicants, 83% accepted, 206 enrolled. *Faculty:* 41 full-time (20 women), 114 part-time/adjunct (33 women). Expenses: Contact institution. *Financial support:* In 2001–02, 13 students received support; fellowships, research assistantships, career-related internships or fieldwork and institutionally sponsored loans available. Financial award application deadline: 2/1. In 2001, 253 master's, 61 doctorates, 27 other advanced degrees awarded. *Degree program information:* Part-time and evening/weekend programs available. Offers bilingual education (MA, Ed S); Catholic school leadership (MA); Catholic school teaching EPICS (MA); counseling psychology (PhD); counselor preparation (MA); education and human services (MA, MS, Ed D, Exec Ed D, PhD, Ed S); education media specialist (MA); elementary education (MA); English as a second language (MA, Ed S); higher education administration (PhD); human resource training and development (MA); instructional design (MA, Ed S); K–12 administration and supervision (Ed D, Exec Ed D, Ed S); marriage and family counseling (MS, PhD, Ed S); professional development (MA, Ed S); psychological studies (MA); school psychology (Ed S); secondary education (MA). *Application deadline:* Applications are processed on a rolling basis. *Application fee:* $50. Electronic applications accepted. *Application Contact:* Rev. Kevin M. Hanbury, Associate Dean, 973-761-9668, Fax: 973-275-2187, E-mail: hanburke@shu.edu.

College of Nursing *Degree program information:* Part-time programs available. Offers acute care nurse practitioner (MSN); adult nurse practitioner (MSN); advanced practice in acute care nursing (MSN); advanced practice in primary health care (MSN); gerontological nurse practitioner (MSN); nursing (MA, MSN); nursing administration (MSN); nursing case management (MSN); nursing education (MA); pediatric nurse practitioner (MSN); school nurse practitioner (MSN); women's health nurse practitioner (MSN).

Immaculate Conception Seminary School of Theology Students: 63 full-time (4 women), 76 part-time (21 women); includes 13 minority (1 African American, 8 Asian Americans or Pacific Islanders, 4 Hispanic Americans), 18 international. Average age 36. 76 applicants, 99% accepted, 63 enrolled. *Faculty:* 11 full-time (1 woman), 17 part-time/adjunct (2 women). Expenses: Contact institution. *Financial support:* Career-related internships or fieldwork, Federal Work-Study, scholarships/grants, and tuition waivers (partial) available. Support available to part-time students. Financial award applicants required to submit FAFSA. In 2001, 15 first professional degrees, 17 master's awarded. *Degree program information:* Part-time and evening/weekend programs available. Offers pastoral ministry (M Div, MA); theology (MA, Certificate). *Application deadline:* For fall admission, 8/1 (priority date); for spring admission, 12/15 (priority date). Applications are processed on a rolling basis. *Application fee:* $50. Electronic applications accepted. *Application Contact:* Rev. Anthony Ziccardi, SSL, Associate Dean, 973-761-9633, E-mail: theology@shu.edu. *Rector/Dean*, Rev. Msgr. Robert F. Coleman, 973-761-9016, Fax: 973-761-9577, E-mail: colemaro@shu.edu.

School of Diplomacy and International Relations Students: 80 full-time (48 women), 45 part-time (26 women); includes 34 minority (23 African Americans, 10 Asian Americans or Pacific Islanders, 1 Hispanic American), 21 international. Average age 26. 93 applicants, 85% accepted. *Faculty:* 4 full-time (1 woman), 14 part-time/adjunct (4 women). Expenses: Contact institution. *Financial support:* In 2001–02, 10 students received support, including 3 research assistantships with full and partial tuition reimbursements available (averaging $4,500 per year), 2 teaching assistantships (averaging $3,000 per year); career-related internships or fieldwork, Federal Work-Study, and unspecified assistantships also available. Support available to part-time students. Financial award application deadline: 4/15; financial award applicants required to submit FAFSA. In 2001, 12 degrees awarded. *Degree program information:* Part-time and evening/weekend programs available. Offers diplomacy and international relations (MA). *Application deadline:* For fall admission, 6/1 (priority date); for winter admission, 10/1 (priority date); for spring admission, 2/1 (priority date). Applications are processed on a rolling basis. *Application fee:* $50. *Application Contact:* David P. Giovanella, Director of Graduate Admissions, 973-275-2515, Fax: 973-275-2519, E-mail: diplomat@shu.edu. *Dean*, Clay Constantinou, 973-275-2515, Fax: 973-275-2519, E-mail: constacl@shu.edu.

School of Graduate Medical Education Students: 148 full-time (127 women), 43 part-time (33 women); includes 29 minority (11 African Americans, 11 Asian Americans or Pacific Islanders, 7 Hispanic Americans), 1 international. *Faculty:* 29 full-time (18 women), 83 part-time/adjunct (46 women). Expenses: Contact institution. *Financial support:* Federal Work-Study, institutionally sponsored loans, scholarships/grants, and unspecified assistantships available. *Degree program information:* Part-time and evening/weekend programs available. Offers athletic training (MS); audiology (Sc D); health sciences (MS, PhD); medical education (MS, DPT, PhD, Sc D); occupational therapy (MS); physician assistant (MS); post-professional physical therapy (DPT); professional physical therapy (DPT); speech-language pathology (MS). *Application deadline:* Applications are processed on a rolling basis. *Application fee:* $75. Electronic applications accepted. *Application Contact:* Deborah Ann Verederosa, Office of Graduate Medical Education, 973-761-7145, Fax: 973-275-2370, E-mail: gradmeded@shu.edu. *Dean*, Dr. John A. Paterson, 973-275-2800, Fax: 973-275-2370, E-mail: gradmeded@shu.edu.

School of Law Students: 784 full-time (385 women), 372 part-time (172 women); includes 251 minority (64 African Americans, 86 Asian Americans or Pacific Islanders, 97 Hispanic Americans, 4 Native Americans) Average age 27. 2,384 applicants, 43% accepted, 382 enrolled. *Faculty:* 58 full-time (21 women), 83 part-time/adjunct (22 women). Expenses: Contact institution. *Financial support:* In 2001–02, 706 students received support, including 61 research assistantships; career-related internships or fieldwork, Federal Work-Study, institutionally sponsored loans, and scholarships/grants also available. Support available to part-time students. Financial award application deadline: 4/19; financial award applicants required to submit FAFSA. In 2001, 320 first professional degrees, 4 master's awarded. *Degree program information:* Part-time and evening/weekend programs available. Offers law (JD, LL M, MSJ). *Application deadline:* For fall admission, 4/1. Applications are processed on a rolling basis. *Application fee:* $50. Electronic applications accepted. *Application Contact:* William Perez, Dean for Admissions and Financial Resource Management, 973-642-8747, Fax: 973-642-8876, E-mail: admitme@shu.edu. *Dean*, Patrick E. Hobbs, 973-642-8750, Fax: 973-642-8031, E-mail: hobbspat@shu.edu.

Seton Hall University (continued)

Stillman School of Business Students: 77 full-time (26 women), 445 part-time (166 women); includes 71 minority (22 African Americans, 33 Asian Americans or Pacific Islanders, 16 Hispanic Americans), 12 international. Average age 29. 332 applicants, 68% accepted. *Faculty:* 58 full-time (13 women), 36 part-time/adjunct (6 women). Expenses: Contact institution. *Financial support:* In 2001–02, 115 students received support, including research assistantships with full and partial tuition reimbursements available (averaging $5,400 per year); career-related internships or fieldwork, Federal Work-Study, scholarships/grants, health care benefits, and unspecified assistantships also available. Support available to part-time students. Financial award application deadline: 6/1; financial award applicants required to submit FAFSA. In 2001, 178 degrees awarded. *Degree program information:* Part-time and evening/weekend programs available. Offers accounting (MS, Post-Graduate Certificate); business (MBA, MS, Certificate, Post-Graduate Certificate); finance (Post-Graduate Certificate); information systems (Post-Graduate Certificate); international business (Post-Graduate Certificate); management (Post-Graduate Certificate); professional accounting (MS); sport management (Post-Graduate Certificate); taxation (Post-Graduate Certificate). *Application deadline:* For fall admission, 6/1 (priority date); for spring admission, 11/1 (priority date). Applications are processed on a rolling basis. *Application fee:* $75 ($100 for international students). Electronic applications accepted. *Application Contact:* Lorrie A. Dougherty, Director of Graduate Admissions and Career Development, 973-761-9220, Fax: 973-761-9208, E-mail: doughelo@shu.edu. *Dean*, Dr. Karen E. Boroff, 973-761-9013, Fax: 973-275-2465, E-mail: boroffka@shu.edu.

Center for Graduate Studies Students: 68 full-time (23 women), 333 part-time (124 women); includes 56 minority (16 African Americans, 29 Asian Americans or Pacific Islanders, 11 Hispanic Americans), 9 international. Average age 29. 275 applicants, 67% accepted, 106 enrolled. *Faculty:* 58 full-time (13 women), 36 part-time/adjunct (6 women). Expenses: Contact institution. *Financial support:* In 2001–02, 94 students received support, including research assistantships with full and partial tuition reimbursements available (averaging $5,400 per year); career-related internships or fieldwork, Federal Work-Study, scholarships/grants, health care benefits, and unspecified assistantships also available. Support available to part-time students. Financial award application deadline: 6/1; financial award applicants required to submit FAFSA. In 2001, 121 degrees awarded. *Degree program information:* Part-time and evening/weekend programs available. Offers accounting (MBA); business (Certificate); finance (MBA); financial institutions (MBA); healthcare management (MBA); information systems (MBA); international business (MBA); management (MBA); marketing (MBA); pharmaceutical management (MBA); sports management (MBA, Post-Graduate Certificate). *Application deadline:* For fall admission, 6/1 (priority date); for spring admission, 11/1 (priority date). Applications are processed on a rolling basis. *Application fee:* $75 ($100 for international students). Electronic applications accepted. *Application Contact:* Lorrie A. Dougherty, Director of Graduate Admissions and Career Development, 973-761-9220, Fax: 973-761-9208, E-mail: doughelo@shu.edu. *Associate Dean for Undergraduate and MBA Curricula*, Dr. Joyce A. Strawser, 973-761-9225, Fax: 973-761-9217, E-mail: strawsjo@shu.edu.

See in-depth description on page 1085.

SETON HILL UNIVERSITY, Greensburg, PA 15601

General Information Independent-religious, coed, primarily women, comprehensive institution. *Enrollment:* 63 full-time matriculated graduate/professional students (52 women), 180 part-time matriculated graduate/professional students (146 women). *Enrollment by degree level:* 243 master's. *Graduate faculty:* 20 full-time (9 women), 29 part-time/adjunct (17 women). *Tuition:* Full-time $10,800; part-time $400 per credit. *Required fees:* $80; $40 per semester. *Graduate housing:* Room and/or apartments guaranteed to single students; on-campus housing not available to married students. Typical cost: $5,450 (including board). Room and board charges vary according to board plan. Housing application deadline: 8/15. *Student services:* Campus employment opportunities, campus safety program, career counseling, child daycare facilities, disabled student services, free psychological counseling, grant writing training, international student services, multicultural affairs office, teacher training, writing training. *Library facilities:* Reeves Memorial Library. *Online resources:* library catalog. *Collection:* 83,354 titles, 501 serial subscriptions, 6,000 audiovisual materials.

Computer facilities: 260 computers available on campus for general student use. A campuswide network can be accessed from student residence rooms and from off campus. Internet access, e-mail are available. *Web address:* http://www.setonhill.edu/.

General Application Contact: Dana Sember, Program Advisor, 724-838-4283, Fax: 724-830-1294, E-mail: sember@setonhill.edu.

GRADUATE UNITS

Program in Art Therapy Students: 14 full-time (11 women), 11 part-time (all women); includes 2 minority (1 African American, 1 Asian American or Pacific Islander) Average age 36. 23 applicants, 96% accepted, 16 enrolled. *Faculty:* 2 full-time (1 woman), 2 part-time/adjunct (both women). Expenses: Contact institution. *Financial support:* Scholarships/grants and tuition waivers (partial) available. Support available to part-time students. Financial award application deadline: 8/15. In 2001, 6 degrees awarded. *Degree program information:* Part-time programs available. Offers art therapy (MA, Certificate). *Application deadline:* For fall admission, 8/15 (priority date); for spring admission, 12/15. Applications are processed on a rolling basis. *Application fee:* $30. Electronic applications accepted. *Application Contact:* Dana Sember, Program Advisor, 724-838-4283, Fax: 724-830-1294, E-mail: sember@setonhill.edu. *Director*, Nina Denninger, 724-830-1047, Fax: 724-830-1294, E-mail: denninger@setonhill.edu.

Program in Business Administration Students: 13 full-time (6 women), 30 part-time (20 women). Average age 33. 22 applicants, 86% accepted, 9 enrolled. *Faculty:* 3 full-time (1 woman), 9 part-time/adjunct (5 women). Expenses: Contact institution. *Financial support:* Scholarships/grants available. Support available to part-time students. Financial award application deadline: 8/15; financial award applicants required to submit FAFSA. In 2001, 35 degrees awarded. *Degree program information:* Evening/weekend programs available. Offers business administration (MBA). *Application deadline:* For fall admission, 8/15 (priority date); for spring admission, 12/15. Applications are processed on a rolling basis. *Application fee:* $30. Electronic applications accepted. *Application Contact:* Dana Sember, Program Advisor, 724-838-4283, Fax: 724-830-1294, E-mail: sember@setonhill.edu. *Director*, Mark Nolan, 724-830-1070, Fax: 724-830-1294, E-mail: nolan@setonhill.edu.

Program in Elementary Education Students: 13 full-time (12 women), 48 part-time (42 women). Average age 33. 26 applicants, 92% accepted, 20 enrolled. *Faculty:* 5 full-time (3 women), 6 part-time/adjunct (4 women). Expenses: Contact institution. *Financial support:* Scholarships/grants and tuition waivers (partial) available. Support available to part-time students. Financial award application deadline: 8/15; financial award applicants required to submit FAFSA. In 2001, 10 degrees awarded. *Degree program information:* Part-time and evening/weekend programs available. Offers elementary education (MA, Teaching Certificate). *Application deadline:* For fall admission, 8/15 (priority date); for spring admission, 12/15. Applications are processed on a rolling basis. *Application fee:* $30. Electronic applications accepted. *Application Contact:* Dana Sember, Program Advisor, 724-838-4283, Fax: 724-830-1294, E-mail: sember@setonhill.edu. *Director*, Dr. Terrance E. DePasquale, 724-838-4256, Fax: 724-830-1294, E-mail: depasqua@setonhill.edu.

Program in Marriage and Family Therapy Students: 13 full-time (all women), 24 part-time (18 women). Average age 32. 26 applicants, 81% accepted, 20 enrolled. *Faculty:* 3 full-time (2 women), 5 part-time/adjunct (2 women). Expenses: Contact institution. *Financial support:* Scholarships/grants available. Support available to part-time students. Financial award application deadline: 8/15; financial award applicants required to submit FAFSA. *Degree program information:* Part-time and evening/weekend programs available. Offers marriage and family therapy (MA). *Application deadline:* For fall admission, 8/15 (priority date); for spring admission, 12/15. Applications are processed on a rolling basis. *Application fee:* $30. Electronic applications accepted. *Application Contact:* Dana Sember, Program Advisor, 724-838-4283, Fax: 724-830-1294, E-mail: sember@setonhill.edu. *Director*, Dr. Tracey Laszloffy, 724-838-7816, E-mail: laszloffy@setonhill.edu.

Program in Special Education Students: 6 full-time (all women), 48 part-time (40 women). Average age 35. 15 applicants, 73% accepted, 9 enrolled. *Faculty:* 5 full-time (3 women), 6 part-time/adjunct (4 women). Expenses: Contact institution. *Financial support:* Scholarships/grants and tuition waivers (partial) available. Support available to part-time students. Financial award application deadline: 8/15; financial award applicants required to submit FAFSA. In 2001, 1 degree awarded. *Degree program information:* Part-time and evening/weekend programs available. Offers special education (MA, Teaching Certificate). *Application deadline:* For fall admission, 8/15 (priority date); for spring admission, 12/15. Applications are processed on a rolling basis. *Application fee:* $30. Electronic applications accepted. *Application Contact:* Dana Sember, Program Advisor, 724-838-4283, Fax: 724-830-1294, E-mail: sember@setonhill.edu. *Director*, Dr. Sondra Lettrich, 724-830-1010, Fax: 724-830-1294, E-mail: lettrich@setonhill.edu.

Program in Technologies Enhanced Learning Students: 3 full-time (all women), 19 part-time (15 women). Average age 35. 16 applicants, 88% accepted, 10 enrolled. *Faculty:* 2 full-time (1 woman), 1 (woman) part-time/adjunct. Expenses: Contact institution. *Financial support:* Scholarships/grants and tuition waivers (partial) available. Support available to part-time students. Financial award application deadline: 8/15; financial award applicants required to submit FAFSA. *Degree program information:* Part-time and evening/weekend programs available. *Application deadline:* For fall admission, 8/15 (priority date); for spring admission, 12/15. Applications are processed on a rolling basis. *Application fee:* $30. Electronic applications accepted. *Application Contact:* Dana Sember, Program Advisor, 724-838-4283, Fax: 724-830-1294, E-mail: sember@setonhill.edu. *Director*, Dr. Frank Klapak, 724-830-1064, Fax: 724-830-1294, E-mail: klapak@setonhill.edu.

Program in Writing Popular Fiction Average age 41. 12 applicants, 92% accepted, 9 enrolled. *Faculty:* 3 full-time (1 woman), 6 part-time/adjunct (3 women). Expenses: Contact institution. *Financial support:* Scholarships/grants and tuition waivers (partial) available. Support available to part-time students. Financial award application deadline: 8/15; financial award applicants required to submit FAFSA. *Degree program information:* Part-time programs available. Postbaccalaureate distance learning degree programs offered (minimal on-campus study). Offers writing popular fiction (MA). *Application deadline:* For fall admission, 6/1; for spring admission, 12/15. Applications are processed on a rolling basis. *Application fee:* $30. Electronic applications accepted. *Application Contact:* Dana Sember, Program Advisor, 724-838-4283, Fax: 724-830-1294, E-mail: sember@setonhill.edu. *Director*, Dr. Lee McClain, 724-830-1040, Fax: 724-830-1294, E-mail: tobin@setonhill.edu.

See in-depth description on page 1087.

SHASTA BIBLE COLLEGE, Redding, CA 96002

General Information Independent-religious, coed, comprehensive institution.

GRADUATE UNITS

Program in School/Church Administration

SHAW UNIVERSITY, Raleigh, NC 27601-2399

General Information Independent-religious, coed, comprehensive institution. *Enrollment:* 101 full-time matriculated graduate/professional students (47 women), 50 part-time matriculated graduate/professional students (30 women). *Enrollment by degree level:* 151 first professional. *Graduate faculty:* 6 full-time (0 women), 8 part-time/adjunct (2 women). *Tuition:* Full-time $4,950; part-time $275 per credit. *Required fees:* $532; $266 per semester. *Graduate housing:* Room and/or apartments available on a first-come, first-served basis to single students; on-campus housing not available to married students. Typical cost: $989 per year ($4,880 including board). *Student services:* Campus employment opportunities, campus safety program, career counseling, disabled student services, free psychological counseling, international student services, low-cost health insurance, teacher training, writing training. *Library facilities:* James E. Cheek Learning Resources Center. *Online resources:* library catalog, web page, access to other libraries' catalogs. *Collection:* 137,349 titles, 5,002 serial subscriptions, 435 audiovisual materials. *Research affiliation:* Old North State Medical Society (health and spirituality), The University of North Carolina at Chapel Hill (health disparities in the African American community), General Baptist State Convention (domestic violence prevention).

Computer facilities: 150 computers available on campus for general student use. A campuswide network can be accessed. Internet access and online class registration are available. *Web address:* http://www.shawuniversity.edu/.

General Application Contact: Rev. Linda W. Bryan, Assistant Dean, 919-546-8577, Fax: 919-546-8271, E-mail: lbryan@shawu.edu.

GRADUATE UNITS

Divinity School Students: 101 full-time (47 women), 50 part-time (30 women); includes 149 minority (148 African Americans, 1 Hispanic American) Average age 45. 84 applicants, 86% accepted, 49 enrolled. *Faculty:* 6 full-time (0 women), 8 part-time/adjunct (2 women). Expenses: Contact institution. *Financial support:* Federal Work-Study, scholarships/grants, and tuition waivers (full) available. Support available to part-time students. Financial award applicants required to submit FAFSA. In 2001, 22 degrees awarded. *Degree program information:* Part-time and evening/weekend programs available. Offers divinity (M Div). *Application deadline:* For fall admission, 7/30 (priority date); for spring admission, 11/30 (priority date). Applications are processed on a rolling basis. *Application fee:* $20 ($45 for international students). Electronic applications accepted. *Application Contact:* Rev. Linda W. Bryan, Assistant Dean, 919-546-8577, Fax: 919-546-8271, E-mail: lbryan@shawu.edu. *Dean*, Dr. James T. Robeson, 919-546-8570, Fax: 919-546-8271, E-mail: jtrob@shawu.edu.

SHENANDOAH UNIVERSITY, Winchester, VA 22601-5195

General Information Independent-religious, coed, comprehensive institution. *Enrollment:* 565 full-time matriculated graduate/professional students (390 women), 481 part-time matriculated graduate/professional students (312 women). *Enrollment by degree level:* 367 first professional, 589 master's, 81 doctoral, 9 other advanced degrees. *Graduate faculty:* 105 full-time (53 women), 44 part-time/adjunct (23 women). *Tuition:* Part-time $520 per credit hour. One-time fee: $500 full-time; $100 part-time. Tuition and fees vary according to campus/location, program and reciprocity agreements. *Graduate housing:* Rooms and/or apartments available on a first-come, first-served basis to single and married students. Typical cost: $6,400 (including board) for single students; $6,250 per year for married students. Room and board charges vary according to board plan. Housing application deadline: 7/15. *Student services:* Campus employment opportunities, campus safety program, career counseling, child daycare facilities, disabled student services, exercise/wellness program, free psychological counseling, international student services, low-cost health insurance. *Library facilities:* Alson H. Smith Jr. Library plus 1 other. *Online resources:* library catalog, web page, access to other libraries' catalogs. *Collection:* 117,800 titles, 9,160 serial subscriptions, 17,100 audiovisual materials. *Research affiliation:* Durell Institute of Monetary Science (education, research and public programs in finance, banking, and related disciplines).

Computer facilities: 170 computers available on campus for general student use. A campuswide network can be accessed from student residence rooms and from off campus. Internet access and online class registration are available. *Web address:* http://www.su.edu/.

General Application Contact: Michael Carpenter, Director of Admissions, 540-665-4581, Fax: 540-665-4627, E-mail: admit@su.edu.

GRADUATE UNITS

Byrd School of Business Students: 37 full-time (15 women), 26 part-time (6 women); includes 1 minority (Asian American or Pacific Islander), 23 international. Average age 32. 39 applicants, 100% accepted, 29 enrolled. *Faculty:* 9 full-time (1 woman), 5 part-time/adjunct (0 women). Expenses: Contact institution. *Financial support:* In 2001–02, 31 students received support, including 12 fellowships with partial tuition reimbursements available (averaging $1,464 per year), 1 teaching assistantship with partial tuition reimbursement available (averaging $1,000 per year); career-related internships or fieldwork and unspecified assistantships also available. Support available to part-time students. Financial award application deadline: 3/15; financial award applicants required to submit FAFSA. In 2001, 31 master's, 14 other advanced degrees awarded. *Degree program information:* Part-time and evening/weekend programs available. Offers business administration (MBA); health care management

(Certificate); information systems and computer technology (Certificate); public management (Certificate). *Application deadline:* For fall admission, 3/1 (priority date). Applications are processed on a rolling basis. *Application fee:* $30. Electronic applications accepted. *Application Contact:* Michael Carpenter, Director of Admissions, 540-665-4581, Fax: 540-665-4627, E-mail: admit@su.edu. *Dean,* Stan Harrison, 540-665-4572, Fax: 540-665-5437, E-mail: sharriso@su.edu.

Division of Nursing Students: 11 full-time (9 women), 12 part-time (11 women). Average age 36. 6 applicants, 100% accepted, 5 enrolled. *Faculty:* 7 full-time (all women), 3 part-time/adjunct (all women). Expenses: Contact institution. *Financial support:* In 2001–02, 19 students received support, including 2 teaching assistantships with partial tuition reimbursements available (averaging $2,000 per year) Support available to part-time students. Financial award application deadline: 3/15; financial award applicants required to submit FAFSA. In 2001, 13 degrees awarded. *Degree program information:* Part-time programs available. Offers family nurse practitioner (Certificate); nursing (MSN). *Application deadline:* For fall admission, 6/15 (priority date). Applications are processed on a rolling basis. *Application fee:* $30. Electronic applications accepted. *Application Contact:* Michael Carpenter, Director of Admissions, 540-665-4581, Fax: 540-665-4627, E-mail: admit@su.edu. *Director,* Dr. Sheila Sparks, 540-678-4381, Fax: 540-665-5519, E-mail: ssparks@su.edu.

Division of Occupational Therapy Students: 72 full-time (66 women), 1 (woman) part-time; includes 4 minority (all African Americans) Average age 27. 33 applicants, 97% accepted, 17 enrolled. *Faculty:* 6 full-time (5 women), 3 part-time/adjunct (2 women). Expenses: Contact institution. *Financial support:* In 2001–02, 71 students received support. Available to part-time students. Application deadline: 3/15; In 2001, 33 degrees awarded. Offers occupational therapy (MS). *Application deadline:* For fall admission, 3/1 (priority date). Applications are processed on a rolling basis. *Application fee:* $30. Electronic applications accepted. *Application Contact:* Michael Carpenter, Director of Admissions, 540-665-4581, Fax: 540-665-4627, E-mail: admit@su.edu. *Director,* Dr. Gretchen Stone, 540-665-5543, Fax: 540-665-5564, E-mail: gstone@su.edu.

Division of Physical Therapy Students: 81 full-time (58 women); includes 2 minority (1 African American, 1 Asian American or Pacific Islander) Average age 25. 34 applicants, 100% accepted, 20 enrolled. *Faculty:* 7 full-time (4 women). Expenses: Contact institution. *Financial support:* In 2001–02, 81 students received support. Available to part-time students. Application deadline: 3/15; Offers physical therapy (DPT). *Application deadline:* For fall admission, 2/1 (priority date). Applications are processed on a rolling basis. *Application fee:* $30. Electronic applications accepted. *Application Contact:* Michael Carpenter, Director of Admissions, 540-665-4581, Fax: 540-665-4627, E-mail: admit@su.edu. *Director,* Dr. Steven H. Tepper, 540-665-5528, Fax: 540-665-5530, E-mail: stepper@su.edu.

School of Arts and Sciences Students: 40 full-time (23 women), 244 part-time (177 women); includes 6 minority (4 African Americans, 1 Asian American or Pacific Islander, 1 Hispanic American), 14 international. Average age 37. 107 applicants, 100% accepted, 71 enrolled. *Faculty:* 10 full-time (4 women), 13 part-time/adjunct (6 women). Expenses: Contact institution. *Financial support:* In 2001–02, 33 students received support, including fellowships with partial tuition reimbursements available (averaging $2,030 per year); career-related internships or fieldwork and unspecified assistantships also available. Support available to part-time students. Financial award application deadline: 3/15; financial award applicants required to submit FAFSA. In 2001, 95 master's, 1 other advanced degree awarded. *Degree program information:* Part-time and evening/weekend programs available. Postbaccalaureate distance learning degree programs offered (minimal on-campus study). Offers administration and leadership (D Ed); advanced professional teaching English to speakers of other languages (Certificate); business education (Certificate); computer education (MSC); computer studies for educators (Certificate); education (MSE); elementary education (Certificate); middle school education (Certificate); professional studies (Certificate); professional teaching English to speakers of other languages (Certificate); secondary education (Certificate). *Application deadline:* For fall admission, 7/1 (priority date). Applications are processed on a rolling basis. *Application fee:* $30. Electronic applications accepted. *Application Contact:* Michael Carpenter, Director of Admissions, 540-665-4581, Fax: 540-665-4627, E-mail: admit@su.edu. *Dean,* Dr. Tracy Fitzsimmons, 540-665-4587, Fax: 540-665-4644, E-mail: tfitzsim@su.edu.

School of Pharmacy Students: 268 full-time (188 women), 99 part-time (58 women); includes 93 minority (40 African Americans, 44 Asian Americans or Pacific Islanders, 9 Hispanic Americans), 5 international. Average age 30. 198 applicants, 71% accepted, 91 enrolled. *Faculty:* 26 full-time (11 women), 12 part-time/adjunct (8 women). Expenses: Contact institution. *Financial support:* In 2001–02, 251 students received support. Scholarships/grants available. Financial award application deadline: 3/15; financial award applicants required to submit FAFSA. In 2001, 136 degrees awarded. *Degree program information:* Part-time programs available. Postbaccalaureate distance learning degree programs offered (minimal on-campus study). Offers pharmacy and non-traditional pharmacy (Pharm D). *Application deadline:* For fall admission, 3/15 (priority date). Applications are processed on a rolling basis. *Application fee:* $30. Electronic applications accepted. *Application Contact:* Michael Carpenter, Director of Admissions, 540-665-4581, Fax: 540-665-4627, E-mail: admit@su.edu. *Dean,* Dr. Alan McKay, 540-665-1280, Fax: 540-665-1283, E-mail: amckay@su.edu.

Shenandoah Conservatory Students: 38 full-time (18 women), 98 part-time (58 women); includes 6 minority (4 African Americans, 2 Hispanic Americans), 28 international. Average age 34. 51 applicants, 100% accepted, 35 enrolled. *Faculty:* 35 full-time (18 women), 7 part-time/adjunct (4 women). Expenses: Contact institution. *Financial support:* In 2001–02, fellowships with partial tuition reimbursements (averaging $1,756 per year), 28 teaching assistantships with partial tuition reimbursements (averaging $1,000 per year) were awarded. Career-related internships or fieldwork, scholarships/grants, and unspecified assistantships also available. Support available to part-time students. Financial award application deadline: 3/15; financial award applicants required to submit FAFSA. In 2001, 29 master's, 6 doctorates, 2 other advanced degrees awarded. *Degree program information:* Part-time and evening/weekend programs available. Offers arts administration (MS); church music (MM, Certificate); composition (MM); conducting (MM); dance accompanying (MM); dance choreography and performance (MFA); music education (MME, DMA); music therapy (MMT); pedagogy (MM); performance (MM, DMA); piano accompanying (MM). *Application deadline:* For fall admission, 7/1 (priority date). Applications are processed on a rolling basis. *Application fee:* $30. Electronic applications accepted. *Application Contact:* Michael Carpenter, Director of Admissions, 540-665-4581, Fax: 540-665-4627, E-mail: admit@su.edu. *Dean,* Dr. Charlotte A. Collins, 540-665-4600, Fax: 540-665-5402, E-mail: ccollins@su.edu.

SHERMAN COLLEGE OF STRAIGHT CHIROPRACTIC, Spartanburg, SC 29304-1452

General Information Independent, coed, graduate-only institution. *Enrollment by degree level:* 407 first professional. *Graduate faculty:* 26 full-time (11 women), 15 part-time/adjunct (5 women). *Tuition:* Full-time $18,500. *Graduate housing:* Rooms and/or apartments available to single and married students. *Student services:* Campus employment opportunities, campus safety program, career counseling, exercise/wellness program, free psychological counseling, international student services, low-cost health insurance. *Library facilities:* Tom and Mae Bahan Library. *Collection:* 13,154 titles, 165 serial subscriptions, 1,462 audiovisual materials. *Research affiliation:* Foundation for Chiropractic Education and Research, American Public Health Service (chiropractic research).

Computer facilities: 16 computers available on campus for general student use. A campuswide network can be accessed from off campus. Internet access is available. *Web address:* http://www.sherman.edu/.

General Application Contact: Lisa A. Hildebrand, Director of Admissions, 864-578-8770 Ext. 1222, Fax: 864-599-4860, E-mail: lhildebrand@sherman.edu.

GRADUATE UNITS

Professional Program Students: 373 full-time (130 women), 34 part-time (13 women); includes 36 minority (14 African Americans, 11 Asian Americans or Pacific Islanders, 10 Hispanic Americans, 1 Native American), 18 international. Average age 28. 96 applicants, 86% accepted. *Faculty:* 26 full-time (11 women), 15 part-time/adjunct (5 women). Expenses: Contact institution. *Financial support:* In 2001–02, 321 students received support. Career-related internships or fieldwork, Federal Work-Study, institutionally sponsored loans, and scholarships/grants available. Support available to part-time students. Financial award applicants required to submit FAFSA. In 2001, 102 degrees awarded. Offers chiropractic (DC). *Application deadline:* Applications are processed on a rolling basis. *Application fee:* $35. Electronic applications accepted. *Application Contact:* Susan Newlin, Vice President for Enrollment Management, 864-578-8770 Ext. 1223, Fax: 864-599-4860, E-mail: admissions@sherman.edu.

SHIPPENSBURG UNIVERSITY OF PENNSYLVANIA, Shippensburg, PA 17257-2299

General Information State-supported, coed, comprehensive institution. CGS member. *Enrollment:* 200 full-time matriculated graduate/professional students (121 women), 618 part-time matriculated graduate/professional students (373 women). *Enrollment by degree level:* 818 master's. *Graduate faculty:* 113 full-time (39 women), 19 part-time/adjunct (9 women). Tuition, state resident: full-time $4,600; part-time $256 per credit hour. Tuition, nonresident: full-time $7,554; part-time $420 per credit hour. *Required fees:* $290; $145 per semester. *Graduate housing:* On-campus housing not available. *Student services:* Campus employment opportunities, campus safety program, career counseling, child daycare facilities, disabled student services, free psychological counseling, international student services, low-cost health insurance, multicultural affairs office. *Library facilities:* Ezra Lehman Memorial Library plus 1 other. *Online resources:* library catalog, web page, access to other libraries' catalogs. *Collection:* 445,631 titles, 1,443 serial subscriptions, 15,383 audiovisual materials.

Computer facilities: 527 computers available on campus for general student use. A campuswide network can be accessed from student residence rooms and from off campus. Internet access, personal Web pages are available. *Web address:* http://www.ship.edu/.

General Application Contact: Renee Payne, Associate Dean of Graduate Admissions, 717-477-1231, Fax: 717-477-4016, E-mail: rmpayn@ship.edu.

GRADUATE UNITS

School of Graduate Studies and Research Students: 200 full-time (121 women), 618 part-time (373 women); includes 52 minority (37 African Americans, 5 Asian Americans or Pacific Islanders, 6 Hispanic Americans, 4 Native Americans), 37 international. Average age 32. 648 applicants, 66% accepted, 259 enrolled. *Faculty:* 113 full-time (39 women), 19 part-time/adjunct (9 women). Expenses: Contact institution. *Financial support:* In 2001–02, 161 research assistantships with full tuition reimbursements were awarded; career-related internships or fieldwork and unspecified assistantships also available. Support available to part-time students. Financial award application deadline: 3/1; financial award applicants required to submit FAFSA. In 2001, 274 degrees awarded. *Degree program information:* Part-time and evening/weekend programs available. Offers business (MBA). *Application deadline:* Applications are processed on a rolling basis. *Application fee:* $30. Electronic applications accepted. *Application Contact:* Renee Payne, Associate Dean of Graduate Admissions, 717-477-1231, Fax: 717-477-4016, E-mail: rmpayn@ship.edu. *Dean of Graduate Studies and Associate Provost,* Dr. James G. Coolsen, 717-477-1148, Fax: 717-477-4038, E-mail: jgcool@ship.edu.

College of Arts and Sciences Students: 107 full-time (48 women), 139 part-time (56 women); includes 13 minority (7 African Americans, 2 Asian Americans or Pacific Islanders, 1 Hispanic American, 3 Native Americans), 36 international. Average age 30. 216 applicants, 65% accepted, 58 enrolled. *Faculty:* 64 full-time (21 women), 3 part-time/adjunct (0 women). Expenses: Contact institution. *Financial support:* In 2001–02, 85 research assistantships with full tuition reimbursements were awarded; career-related internships or fieldwork and unspecified assistantships also available. Support available to part-time students. Financial award application deadline: 3/1; financial award applicants required to submit FAFSA. In 2001, 113 degrees awarded. *Degree program information:* Part-time and evening/weekend programs available. Offers applied history (MA); arts and sciences (MA, MPA, MS); biology (MS); communication studies (MS); computer science (MS); geoenvironmental studies (MS); information systems (MS); psychology (MS); public administration (MPA). *Application deadline:* Applications are processed on a rolling basis. *Application fee:* $30. Electronic applications accepted. *Application Contact:* Renee Payne, Associate Dean of Graduate Admissions, 717-477-1231, Fax: 717-477-4016, E-mail: rmpayn@ship.edu. *Dean,* Dr. Janet Gross, 717-477-1151, Fax: 717-477-4026, E-mail: jsgros@ship.edu.

College of Education and Human Services Students: 93 full-time (73 women), 479 part-time (317 women); includes 39 minority (30 African Americans, 3 Asian Americans or Pacific Islanders, 5 Hispanic Americans, 1 Native American), 1 international. Average age 32. 296 applicants, 51% accepted, 117 enrolled. *Faculty:* 30 full-time (14 women), 15 part-time/adjunct (9 women). Expenses: Contact institution. *Financial support:* In 2001–02, 74 research assistantships with full tuition reimbursements were awarded; career-related internships or fieldwork and unspecified assistantships also available. Support available to part-time students. Financial award application deadline: 3/1; financial award applicants required to submit FAFSA. In 2001, 161 degrees awarded. *Degree program information:* Part-time and evening/weekend programs available. Offers Adlerian studies (Certificate); administration of justice (MS); advanced study in counseling (Certificate); counseling (MS); curriculum and instruction (M Ed); education and human services (M Ed, MS, Certificate); educational administration (M Ed); elementary education (M Ed); guidance and counseling (M Ed); reading (M Ed); reading recovery teacher leader training (Certificate); special education (M Ed). *Application deadline:* Applications are processed on a rolling basis. *Application fee:* $30. Electronic applications accepted. *Application Contact:* Renee Payne, Associate Dean of Graduate Admissions, 717-477-1231, Fax: 717-477-4016, E-mail: rmpayn@ship.edu. *Dean,* Dr. Robert B. Bartos, 717-477-1373, Fax: 717-477-4012, E-mail: rbbart@ship.edu.

See in-depth description on page 1089.

SHORTER COLLEGE, Rome, GA 30165

General Information Independent-religious, coed, comprehensive institution. *Enrollment by degree level:* 52 master's. *Graduate faculty:* 7 full-time (1 woman), 1 part-time/adjunct (0 women). *Tuition:* Full-time $7,990; part-time $340 per credit hour. *Required fees:* $775. *Library facilities:* Livingston Library. *Online resources:* library catalog, web page, access to other libraries' catalogs. *Collection:* 82,597 titles, 612 serial subscriptions, 10,916 audiovisual materials.

Computer facilities: 100 computers available on campus for general student use. A campuswide network can be accessed from student residence rooms. Internet access, e-mail are available. *Web address:* http://www.shorter.edu/.

General Application Contact: Dr. Janet S. Jones, Dean, 770-989-5661, Fax: 770-951-9590, E-mail: jjones@shorter.edu.

GRADUATE UNITS

School of Professional Programs Students: 52 full-time (25 women); includes 21 minority (17 African Americans, 3 Asian Americans or Pacific Islanders, 1 Hispanic American) Average age 35. *Faculty:* 7 full-time (1 woman), 1 part-time/adjunct (0 women). Expenses: Contact institution. *Financial support:* Applicants required to submit FAFSA. In 2001, 12 degrees awarded. *Degree program information:* Part-time and evening/weekend programs available. *Application deadline:* Applications are processed on a rolling basis. *Application fee:* $30. *Dean,* Dr. Janet S. Jones, 770-989-5661, Fax: 770-951-9590, E-mail: jjones@shorter.edu.

SH'OR YOSHUV RABBINICAL COLLEGE, Far Rockaway, NY 11691-4002

General Information Independent-religious, men only, comprehensive institution.

SIENA HEIGHTS UNIVERSITY, Adrian, MI 49221-1796

General Information Independent-religious, coed, comprehensive institution. *Graduate housing:* Room and/or apartments available to single students; on-campus housing not available to married students. Housing application deadline: 4/1.

GRADUATE UNITS

Graduate Studies *Degree program information:* Part-time and evening/weekend programs available. Offers agency counseling (MA); curriculum and instruction (MA); early childhood education (MA); elementary education (MA); elementary education/reading (MA); human resource development (MA); middle school education (MA); Montessori education (MA); school counseling (MA); secondary education (MA); secondary education/reading (MA).

SIERRA NEVADA COLLEGE, Incline Village, NV 89451

General Information Independent, coed, comprehensive institution. *Graduate housing:* On-campus housing not available. *Research affiliation:* Kauffman Center for Entrepreneurial Leadership.

GRADUATE UNITS

Program in Teacher Education Offers elementary education (Certificate); secondary education (Certificate).

SILVER LAKE COLLEGE, Manitowoc, WI 54220-9319

General Information Independent-religious, coed, comprehensive institution. *Enrollment:* 128 full-time matriculated graduate/professional students (82 women), 273 part-time matriculated graduate/professional students (200 women). *Enrollment by degree level:* 401 master's. *Graduate faculty:* 5 full-time (all women), 46 part-time/adjunct (23 women). *Tuition:* Part-time $295 per credit. *Graduate housing:* Room and/or apartments available on a first-come, first-served basis to single students; on-campus housing not available to married students. Typical cost: $3,465 per year. *Student services:* Campus employment opportunities, campus safety program, career counseling, disabled student services, international student services, low-cost health insurance, teacher training, writing training. *Library facilities:* The Erma M. and Theodore M. Zigmunt Library. *Online resources:* library catalog, access to other libraries' catalogs. *Collection:* 64,668 titles, 306 serial subscriptions, 17,983 audiovisual materials.

Computer facilities: 50 computers available on campus for general student use. A campuswide network can be accessed from off campus. Internet access is available. *Web address:* http://www.sl.edu/.

General Application Contact: Lori Salm, Office Manager, Admissions, 920-686-6175, Fax: 920-684-7082, E-mail: lsalm@silver.sl.edu.

GRADUATE UNITS

Graduate Studies *Degree program information:* Part-time and evening/weekend programs available. Postbaccalaureate distance learning degree programs offered (minimal on-campus study). Offers administrative leadership (MA); management and organizational behavior (MS); music education (MM Ed); teacher leadership (MA). Electronic applications accepted.

SIMMONS COLLEGE, Boston, MA 02115

General Information Independent, women only, comprehensive institution. *Enrollment:* 650 full-time matriculated graduate/professional students (585 women), 1,462 part-time matriculated graduate/professional students (1,245 women). *Enrollment by degree level:* 2,065 master's, 47 doctoral. *Graduate faculty:* 119 full-time, 159 part-time/adjunct. *Graduate housing:* Room and/or apartments available on a first-come, first-served basis to single students; on-campus housing not available to married students. Housing application deadline: 7/15. *Student services:* Campus employment opportunities, campus safety program, career counseling, free psychological counseling, international student services, low-cost health insurance. *Library facilities:* Beatley Library plus 5 others. *Online resources:* library catalog, web page, access to other libraries' catalogs. *Collection:* 285,698 titles, 1,861 serial subscriptions, 5,725 audiovisual materials.

Computer facilities: 250 computers available on campus for general student use. A campuswide network can be accessed from student residence rooms and from off campus. Internet access is available. *Web address:* http://www.simmons.edu/.

General Application Contact: Director, Graduate Studies Admission, 617-521-2910, Fax: 617-521-3058, E-mail: gsa@simmons.edu.

GRADUATE UNITS

Competitive Intelligence Center *Degree program information:* Part-time and evening/weekend programs available. Offers competitive intelligence (Master in Competitive Intelligence). Electronic applications accepted.

Graduate School Students: 194 full-time (175 women), 569 part-time (467 women). Average age 28. 240 applicants, 79% accepted. *Faculty:* 50 full-time (39 women), 39 part-time/adjunct (22 women). Expenses: Contact institution. *Financial support:* In 2001–02, 257 students received support, including research assistantships (averaging $3,400 per year), teaching assistantships (averaging $3,400 per year); fellowships, career-related internships or fieldwork, Federal Work-Study, institutionally sponsored loans, scholarships/grants, tuition waivers (partial), and unspecified assistantships also available. Support available to part-time students. Financial award application deadline: 3/1; financial award applicants required to submit FAFSA. In 2001, 324 degrees awarded. *Degree program information:* Part-time programs available. *Application deadline:* Applications are processed on a rolling basis. *Application fee:* $35. Electronic applications accepted. *Application Contact:* Bryan E. Moody, Director, Graduate Enrollment Management and Admission, 617-521-2910, Fax: 617-521-3058, E-mail: gsa@simmons.edu. *Interim Dean,* Dr. Diane Raymond, 617-521-2910, Fax: 617-521-3058, E-mail: gsa@simmons.edu.

College of Arts and Sciences and Professional Studies Expenses: Contact institution. Offers arts and sciences and professional studies (MA, MAT, MS, MS Ed, CAGS, Ed S); assistive technology (MS Ed, Ed S); behavioral education (MS Ed, Ed S); children's literature (MA); communications management (MS); educational leadership (MS Ed, CAGS); elementary school education (MAT); English (MA); gender/cultural studies (MA); general purposes (CAGS); inclusion specialist (MS Ed); intensive special needs (MS Ed); language-based learning disabilities (MS Ed, Ed S); secondary education (MAT); Spanish (MA); special education (MS Ed, Ed S); special needs (MS Ed); teacher preparation (MAT); teaching English as a second language (MAT). *Application deadline:* Applications are processed on a rolling basis. *Application fee:* $35. Electronic applications accepted. *Application Contact:* Bryan E. Moody, Director, Graduate Enrollment Management and Admission, 617-521-2910, Fax: 617-521-3058, E-mail: gsa@simmons.edu.

Graduate School of Library and Information Science Students: 550. Average age 34. 307 applicants, 70% accepted, 141 enrolled. *Faculty:* 17 full-time (8 women), 29 part-time/adjunct (20 women). Expenses: Contact institution. *Financial support:* In 2001–02, 462 students received support, including 4 research assistantships (averaging $18,900 per year); teaching assistantships, career-related internships or fieldwork, Federal Work-Study, institutionally sponsored loans, scholarships/grants, and tuition waivers (full and partial) also available. Support available to part-time students. Financial award application deadline: 3/1; financial award applicants required to submit FAFSA. In 2001, 374 master's, 3 doctorates awarded. *Degree program information:* Part-time and evening/weekend programs available. Offers archives management (MS); competitive intelligence (MS, Certificate); library and information science (DA); school library media specialist (MS, Certificate). MS/DA and MS/MA offered jointly with Department of History. *Application deadline:* For fall admission, 7/1 (priority date); for spring admission, 11/1. Applications are processed on a rolling basis. *Application fee:* $35. Electronic applications accepted. *Application Contact:* Judith J. Beal, Director of Admissions, 617-521-2141, Fax: 617-521-3045, E-mail: judy.beal@simmons.edu. *Dean,* Dr. James Matarazzo, 617-521-2806, Fax: 617-521-3192, E-mail: matarazz@simmons.edu.

School for Health Studies Students: 303. Average age 28. 508 applicants, 41% accepted. *Faculty:* 51. Expenses: Contact institution. *Financial support:* In 2001–02, research assistantships (averaging $2,000 per year), teaching assistantships (averaging $2,000 per year) were awarded. Fellowships, Federal Work-Study, institutionally sponsored loans, scholarships/grants, traineeships, and unspecified assistantships also available. Support available to part-time students. Financial award application deadline: 3/1; financial award applicants required to submit FAFSA. In 2001, 219 master's, 19 other advanced degrees awarded. *Degree program information:* Part-time and evening/weekend programs available. Offers health care administration (MS, CAGS); health studies (MS, DPT, CAGS, Certificate); nutrition and health promotion (MS, Certificate); physical therapy (DPT); primary health care (MS, CAGS). *Application deadline:* For fall admission, 7/1; for spring admission, 11/1. Applications are processed on a rolling basis. *Application fee:* $50. Electronic applications accepted. *Application Contact:* Staff Assistant, 617-521-2650, Fax: 617-521-3137, E-mail: gshsadm@simmons.edu. *Dean,* Dr. Gerald P. Koocher, 617-521-2652, Fax: 617-521-3137.

School of Social Work Students: 278; includes 50 minority (23 African Americans, 9 Asian Americans or Pacific Islanders, 18 Hispanic Americans), 4 international. Average age 27. 397 applicants, 44% accepted, 175 enrolled. *Faculty:* 21 full-time (17 women), 56 part-time/adjunct (36 women). Expenses: Contact institution. *Financial support:* Fellowships, career-related internships or fieldwork, Federal Work-Study, institutionally sponsored loans, and tuition waivers (full) available. Support available to part-time students. Financial award application deadline: 3/1; financial award applicants required to submit FAFSA. In 2001, 225 master's, 3 doctorates awarded. *Degree program information:* Part-time programs available. Offers clinical social work (MSW, PhD). *Application deadline:* For fall admission, 12/15 (priority date); for winter admission, 2/15. *Application fee:* $45. *Application Contact:* Deborah Sheehan, Director of Admissions, 617-521-3920, Fax: 617-521-3980, E-mail: ssw@simmons.edu. *Dean,* Dr. Joseph M. Regan, 617-521-3900.

Simmons School of Management Students: 45 full-time (all women), 187 part-time (all women); includes 19 minority (11 African Americans, 3 Asian Americans or Pacific Islanders, 4 Hispanic Americans, 1 Native American), 18 international. Average age 32. 211 applicants, 68% accepted, 115 enrolled. *Faculty:* 19 full-time (15 women), 4 part-time/adjunct (all women). Expenses: Contact institution. *Financial support:* In 2001–02, 68 students received support. Institutionally sponsored loans and scholarships/grants available. Support available to part-time students. Financial award application deadline: 3/30; financial award applicants required to submit FAFSA. In 2001, 97 degrees awarded. *Degree program information:* Part-time and evening/weekend programs available. Offers management (MBA). *Application deadline:* For fall admission, 4/30 (priority date); for spring admission, 11/15 (priority date). Applications are processed on a rolling basis. *Application fee:* $75. Electronic applications accepted. *Application Contact:* Andrea Bruce, Director of Admissions/Marketing, 617-521-3840, Fax: 617-521-3880, E-mail: gsmadm@simmons.edu. *Dean,* Dr. Patricia O'Brien, 617-521-3817, Fax: 617-521-3881, E-mail: obrien@simmons.edu.

SIMON FRASER UNIVERSITY, Burnaby, BC V5A 1S6, Canada

General Information Province-supported, coed, university. *Enrollment:* 2,990 full-time matriculated graduate/professional students (2,032 women), 276 part-time matriculated graduate/professional students (193 women). *Enrollment by degree level:* 2,060 master's, 834 doctoral, 352 other advanced degrees. *Graduate faculty:* 624 full-time (152 women), 7 part-time/adjunct (2 women). *Graduate tuition:* Tuition charges are reported in Canadian dollars. *Tuition:* Part-time $948 Canadian dollars per unit. *Graduate housing:* Rooms and/or apartments available on a first-come, first-served basis to single and married students. Housing application deadline: 1/2. *Student services:* Campus employment opportunities, campus safety program, career counseling, child daycare facilities, disabled student services, exercise/wellness program, free psychological counseling, grant writing training, international student services, low-cost health insurance, teacher training, writing training. *Library facilities:* W. A. C. Bennett Library. *Online resources:* library catalog, web page, access to other libraries' catalogs. *Collection:* 1.6 million titles, 12,534 serial subscriptions, 58,674 audiovisual materials. *Research affiliation:* Bamfield Marine Research Station.

Computer facilities: 900 computers available on campus for general student use. A campuswide network can be accessed from off campus. Internet access and online class registration are available. *Web address:* http://www.sfu.ca/.

General Application Contact: Andrea J. Sator, Receptionist, 604-268-6568, Fax: 604-291-3080, E-mail: ajsator@sfu.ca.

GRADUATE UNITS

Graduate Studies Students: 1,668. Average age 35. *Faculty:* 624 full-time (152 women), 7 part-time/adjunct (2 women). Expenses: Contact institution. *Financial support:* In 2001–02, 456 fellowships were awarded; research assistantships, teaching assistantships, career-related internships or fieldwork, Federal Work-Study, institutionally sponsored loans, and scholarships/grants also available. Support available to part-time students. In 2001, 438 master's, 72 doctorates awarded. *Degree program information:* Part-time and evening/weekend programs available. Offers molecular biology and biochemistry (M Sc, PhD). *Application fee:* $55. *Dean,* Dr. Jonathan Driver, 604-291-4255, Fax: 604-291-3080.

Faculty of Applied Science Students: 411. *Faculty:* 103 full-time (17 women). Expenses: Contact institution. *Financial support:* In 2001–02, 124 fellowships were awarded; research assistantships, teaching assistantships, career-related internships or fieldwork, Federal Work-Study, and institutionally sponsored loans also available. In 2001, 59 master's, 14 doctorates awarded. Offers applied science (M Eng, M Sc, MA, MA Sc, MRM, PhD); communication (MA, PhD); computing science (M Sc, PhD); engineering science (M Eng, MA Sc, PhD); kinesiology (M Sc, PhD); resource and environmental management (MRM, PhD). *Application fee:* $55. *Dean,* R. G. Marteniuk, 604-291-4724, Fax: 604-291-5802.

Faculty of Arts Students: 740. *Faculty:* 303 full-time (93 women), 4 part-time/adjunct (2 women). Expenses: Contact institution. *Financial support:* In 2001–02, 168 fellowships were awarded; research assistantships, teaching assistantships In 2001, 103 master's, 29 doctorates awarded. *Degree program information:* Part-time and evening/weekend programs available. Offers anthropology (MA, PhD); archaeology (MA, PhD); arts (M Pub, M Sc, MA, MALS, MFA, PhD); contemporary arts (MFA); criminology (MA, PhD); economics (MA, PhD); English (MA, PhD); French (MA); geography (M Sc, MA, PhD); gerontology (MA); history (MA, PhD); Latin American studies (MA); liberal studies (MALS); linguistics (MA, PhD); philosophy (MA, PhD); political science (MA, PhD); psychology (MA, PhD); publishing (M Pub); sociology (MA, PhD); women's studies (MA). *Application fee:* $55. *Dean,* J. T. Pierce, 604-291-4414, Fax: 604-291-3033.

Faculty of Business Administration Students: 293 full-time (107 women). Average age 28. 286 applicants. *Faculty:* 60 full-time (18 women). Expenses: Contact institution. *Financial support:* In 2001–02, 41 fellowships (averaging $4,400 per year) were awarded; research assistantships with partial tuition reimbursements, teaching assistantships with partial tuition reimbursements, career-related internships or fieldwork and scholarships/grants also available. In 2001, 43 degrees awarded. Postbaccalaureate distance learning degree programs offered. Offers business administration (EMBA); decision support systems (MBA); international business (MBA); management, organization studies (MBA); marketing (MBA). *Application deadline:* For fall admission, 4/2; for winter admission, 10/1; for spring admission, 2/2. Applications are processed on a rolling basis. *Application fee:* $100. *Application Contact:* Program Assistant, 604-291-3047, Fax: 604-291-3404, E-mail: mba@sfu.ca. *Director,* Judy Zaichkowsky, 604-291-4493, Fax: 604-291-3404, E-mail: zaichkow@sfu.ca.

Faculty of Education Tuition charges are reported in Canadian dollars. Offers administrative leadership (M Ed, MA); curriculum and instruction (M Ed, M Sc, MA, PhD); education (M Ed, M Sc, MA, PhD); educational psychology (M Ed, MA, PhD); guidance and counseling (M Ed, MA).

Faculty of Science Students: 342. *Faculty:* 130 full-time (11 women), 2 part-time/adjunct (0 women). Expenses: Contact institution. *Financial support:* In 2001–02, 98 fellowships were awarded; research assistantships, teaching assistantships, career-related internships or fieldwork also available. In 2001, 48 master's, 25 doctorates awarded. *Degree program information:* Part-time programs available. Offers applied mathematics (M Sc, PhD); biological sciences (M Sc, PhD); biophysics (M Sc, PhD); chemical physics (M Sc, PhD); chemistry (M Sc, PhD); earth sciences (M Sc); environmental toxicology (Diploma); pest management (MPM); physics (M Sc, PhD); pure mathematics (M Sc, PhD); science (M Sc, MET, MPM, PhD, Diploma); statistics and actuarial science (M Sc, PhD). *Application fee:* $55. *Dean,* W. S. Davidson, 604-291-4590, Fax: 604-291-3424.

SIMPSON COLLEGE AND GRADUATE SCHOOL, Redding, CA 96003-8606

General Information Independent-religious, coed, comprehensive institution. *Enrollment:* 82 full-time matriculated graduate/professional students (54 women), 93 part-time matriculated graduate/professional students (50 women). *Enrollment by degree level:* 175 master's. *Graduate faculty:* 17 full-time (3 women), 9 part-time/adjunct (3 women). *Tuition:* Full-time $12,800; part-time $540 per credit hour. Tuition and fees vary according to program. *Graduate housing:* On-campus housing not available. *Student services:* Campus safety program, teacher training. *Library facilities:* Start-Kilgour Memorial Library. *Online resources:* library catalog, web page. *Collection:* 66,103 titles, 316 serial subscriptions, 1,139 audiovisual materials.

Computer facilities: 26 computers available on campus for general student use. A campuswide network can be accessed from student residence rooms and from off campus. Internet access is available. *Web address:* http://www.simpsonca.edu/.

General Application Contact: Christy L. Meadows, Director of Admissions and Enrollment Development, 530-226-4606, Fax: 530-226-4861, E-mail: cmeadows@simpsonca.edu.

GRADUATE UNITS

Graduate School Students: 82 full-time (54 women), 93 part-time (50 women). Average age 38. 49 applicants, 67% accepted. *Faculty:* 17 full-time (3 women), 9 part-time/adjunct (3 women). Expenses: Contact institution. *Financial support:* Career-related internships or fieldwork and tuition waivers (partial) available. Support available to part-time students. Financial award application deadline: 3/1; financial award applicants required to submit FAFSA. In 2001, 12 degrees awarded. *Degree program information:* Part-time and evening/weekend programs available. Offers Christian ministry (MA); education (MA); missiology (MA). *Application deadline:* For fall admission, 8/15 (priority date). Applications are processed on a rolling basis. *Application fee:* $20. Electronic applications accepted. *Application Contact:* Christy L. Meadows, Director of Admissions and Enrollment Development, 530-226-4606, Fax: 530-226-4861, E-mail: cmeadows@simpsonca.edu. *Vice President for Academic Affairs,* Dr. Judith Fortune, 530-224-5600, Fax: 530-224-2051.

SINTE GLESKA UNIVERSITY, Rosebud, SD 57570-0490

General Information Independent, coed, comprehensive institution. *Enrollment:* 20 part-time matriculated graduate/professional students (15 women). *Enrollment by degree level:* 20 master's. *Graduate faculty:* 1 full-time (0 women), 4 part-time/adjunct (3 women). *Tuition, area resident:* Part-time $87 per hour. *Required fees:* $88; $44 per semester. One-time fee: $25. *Graduate housing:* Rooms and/or apartments available on a first-come, first-served basis to single and married students. *Student services:* Campus employment opportunities, career counseling, child daycare facilities, free psychological counseling, grant writing training, teacher training. *Library facilities:* Sinte Gleska University Library. *Online resources:* library catalog. *Collection:* 25,000 titles, 80 serial subscriptions.

Computer facilities: 35 computers available on campus for general student use. A campuswide network can be accessed. Internet access is available. *Web address:* http://www.sinte.edu/.

General Application Contact: Dr. Archie Beauvais, Chair, Graduate Education Programs, 605-747-2263 Ext. 45, Fax: 605-747-4258, E-mail: abeaux@post.harvard.edu.

GRADUATE UNITS

Graduate Education Program Students: 20 full-time (15 women); includes 18 minority (all Native Americans) Average age 35. 5 applicants, 100% accepted. *Faculty:* 1 full-time (0 women), 4 part-time/adjunct (3 women). Expenses: Contact institution. In 2001, 2 degrees awarded. *Degree program information:* Part-time and evening/weekend programs available. Offers elementary education (M Ed). *Application deadline:* Applications are processed on a rolling basis. *Application fee:* $0. *Chair,* Dr. Archie Beauvais, 605-747-2263 Ext. 45, Fax: 605-747-4258, E-mail: abeaux@post.harvard.edu.

SKIDMORE COLLEGE, Saratoga Springs, NY 12866-1632

General Information Independent, coed, comprehensive institution. *Enrollment:* 51 part-time matriculated graduate/professional students (35 women). *Enrollment by degree level:* 51 master's. *Graduate faculty:* 78 full-time (38 women), 2 part-time/adjunct (0 women). *Tuition:* Full-time $5,200. *Graduate housing:* On-campus housing not available. *Student services:* Career counseling. *Library facilities:* Scribner Library. *Online resources:* library catalog, web page, access to other libraries' catalogs. *Collection:* 477,658 titles, 2,164 serial subscriptions, 130,040 audiovisual materials.

Computer facilities: 173 computers available on campus for general student use. A campuswide network can be accessed from student residence rooms and from off campus. Internet access is available. *Web address:* http://www.skidmore.edu/.

General Application Contact: Dr. David P. Glaser, Director, 518-580-5480, Fax: 518-580-5486, E-mail: dglaser@skidmore.edu.

GRADUATE UNITS

Liberal Studies Program Average age 42. 29 applicants, 48% accepted, 11 enrolled. *Faculty:* 78 full-time (38 women), 2 part-time/adjunct (0 women). Expenses: Contact institution. *Financial support:* Career-related internships or fieldwork available. Financial award applicants required to submit FAFSA. In 2001, 6 degrees awarded. *Degree program information:* Part-time programs available. Postbaccalaureate distance learning degree programs offered (minimal on-campus study). Offers liberal studies (MA). *Application deadline:* For fall admission, 7/1 (priority date); for spring admission, 10/1. Applications are processed on a rolling basis. *Application fee:* $50. *Application Contact:* Information Contact, 518-580-5480, Fax: 518-580-5486, E-mail: mals@skidmore.edu. *Director,* Dr. David P. Glaser, 518-580-5480, Fax: 518-580-5486, E-mail: dglaser@skidmore.edu.

SLIPPERY ROCK UNIVERSITY OF PENNSYLVANIA, Slippery Rock, PA 16057

General Information State-supported, coed, comprehensive institution. *Enrollment:* 322 full-time matriculated graduate/professional students (201 women), 324 part-time matriculated graduate/professional students (248 women). *Graduate faculty:* 67 full-time (33 women), 6 part-time/adjunct (4 women). Tuition, state resident: full-time $4,600; part-time $256 per credit. Tuition, nonresident: full-time $7,754; part-time $420 per credit. *Required fees:* $67 per credit. Tuition and fees vary according to course load and program. *Graduate housing:* Room and/or apartments available on a first-come, first-served basis to single students; on-campus housing not available to married students. Typical cost: $2,254 per year ($4,210 including board). Room and board charges vary according to board plan and housing facility selected. *Student services:* Campus employment opportunities, campus safety program, career counseling, child daycare facilities, disabled student services, exercise/wellness program, free psychological counseling, international student services, multicultural affairs office, writing training. *Library facilities:* Bailey Library. *Online resources:* library catalog, web page, access to other libraries' catalogs. *Collection:* 774,723 titles, 14,101 serial subscriptions, 86,686 audiovisual materials.

Computer facilities: 545 computers available on campus for general student use. A campuswide network can be accessed from student residence rooms and from off campus. Internet access and online class registration are available. *Web address:* http://www.sru.edu/.

General Application Contact: Dr. Duncan M. Sargent, Director of Graduate Studies, 724-738-2051 Ext. 2116, Fax: 724-738-2146, E-mail: graduate.studies@sru.edu.

GRADUATE UNITS

Graduate Studies Students: 322 full-time (201 women), 324 part-time (248 women); includes 25 minority (8 African Americans, 8 Asian Americans or Pacific Islanders, 5 Hispanic Americans, 4 Native Americans), 13 international. Average age 29. 348 applicants, 79% accepted, 142 enrolled. *Faculty:* 67 full-time (33 women), 6 part-time/adjunct (4 women). Expenses: Contact institution. *Financial support:* In 2001–02, 141 students received support, including 117 research assistantships with full and partial tuition reimbursements available (averaging $4,000 per year); career-related internships or fieldwork, Federal Work-Study, institutionally sponsored loans, scholarships/grants, and tuition waivers (full) also available. Support available to part-time students. Financial award application deadline: 5/1; financial award applicants required to submit FAFSA. In 2001, 126 master's, 46 doctorates awarded. *Degree program information:* Part-time and evening/weekend programs available. Postbaccalaureate distance learning degree programs offered (no on-campus study). *Application deadline:* For fall admission, 7/1; for spring admission, 11/1. Applications are processed on a rolling basis. *Application fee:* $25. Electronic applications accepted. *Director of Graduate Studies,* Dr. Duncan M. Sargent, 724-738-2051 Ext. 2116, Fax: 724-738-2146, E-mail: graduate.studies@sru.edu.

College of Humanities, Fine and Performing Arts Students: 22 full-time (8 women), 25 part-time (16 women); includes 3 minority (1 Asian American or Pacific Islander, 2 Hispanic Americans), 2 international. Average age 31. 27 applicants, 93% accepted. *Faculty:* 12 full-time (5 women). Expenses: Contact institution. *Financial support:* In 2001–02, 13 students received support, including research assistantships with full and partial tuition reimbursements available (averaging $4,000 per year); career-related internships or fieldwork and scholarships/grants also available. Support available to part-time students. Financial award application deadline: 5/1; financial award applicants required to submit FAFSA. In 2001, 9 degrees awarded. *Degree program information:* Part-time and evening/weekend programs available. Offers English (MA); history (MA); humanities, fine and performing arts (MA). *Application deadline:* For fall admission, 7/1; for spring admission, 11/1. Applications are processed on a rolling basis. *Application fee:* $25. Electronic applications accepted. *Application Contact:* Dr. Duncan M. Sargent, Director of Graduate Studies, 724-738-2051 Ext. 2116, Fax: 724-738-2146, E-mail: graduate.studies@sru.edu. *Dean,* Dr. William McKinney, 724-738-4863 Ext. 4866, Fax: 724-738-2188, E-mail: william.mckinney@sru.edu.

College of Business, Information, and Social Sciences Average age 33. 9 applicants, 33% accepted. *Faculty:* 3 full-time (1 woman). Expenses: Contact institution. *Financial support:* In 2001–02, research assistantships with full and partial tuition reimbursements (averaging $4,000 per year); career-related internships or fieldwork, Federal Work-Study, and scholarships/grants also available. Support available to part-time students. Financial award application deadline: 5/1; financial award applicants required to submit FAFSA. In 2001, 2 degrees awarded. *Degree program information:* Part-time programs available. Offers accounting (MS); business, information, and social sciences (MS). *Application deadline:* For fall admission, 7/1; for spring admission, 11/1. Applications are processed on a rolling basis. *Application fee:* $25. Electronic applications accepted. *Application Contact:* Dr. Duncan M. Sargent, Director of Graduate Studies, 724-738-2051 Ext. 2116, Fax: 724-738-2146, E-mail: graduate.studies@sru.edu. *Dean,* Dr. Frank V. Mastrianna, 724-738-2008, Fax: 724-738-4767, E-mail: frank.mastrianna@sru.edu.

College of Education Students: 165 full-time (110 women), 252 part-time (200 women); includes 15 minority (7 African Americans, 3 Asian Americans or Pacific Islanders, 3 Hispanic Americans, 2 Native Americans), 7 international. Average age 30. 206 applicants, 78% accepted. *Faculty:* 29 full-time (14 women), 3 part-time/adjunct (2 women). Expenses: Contact institution. *Financial support:* In 2001–02, 87 students received support, including research assistantships with full and partial tuition reimbursements available (averaging $4,000 per year); career-related internships or fieldwork, Federal Work-Study, and scholarships/grants also available. Support available to part-time students. Financial award application deadline: 5/1; financial award applicants required to submit FAFSA. In 2001, 97 degrees awarded. *Degree program information:* Part-time and evening/weekend programs available. Offers community counseling (MA); early childhood education (M Ed); education (M Ed, MA, MS); elementary guidance and counseling (M Ed); exercise and wellness promotion (MS); math/science (M Ed); reading (M Ed); secondary education in math/science (M Ed); secondary guidance and counseling (M Ed); special education (M Ed); sport management (MS); student personnel (MA). *Application deadline:* For fall admission, 7/1; for spring admission, 11/1. Applications are processed on a rolling basis. *Application fee:* $25. Electronic applications accepted. *Application Contact:* Dr. Duncan M. Sargent, Director of Graduate Studies, 724-738-2051 Ext. 2116, Fax: 724-738-2146, E-mail: graduate.studies@sru.edu. *Dean,* Dr. C. Jay Hertzog, 724-738-2007 Ext. 2685, Fax: 724-738-2880, E-mail: jay.hertzog@sru.edu.

College of Health, Environment, and Science Students: 134 full-time (82 women), 21 part-time (11 women); includes 6 minority (1 African American, 4 Asian Americans or Pacific Islanders, 1 Native American), 4 international. Average age 26. 240 applicants, 44% accepted. *Faculty:* 23 full-time (13 women), 3 part-time/adjunct (2 women). Expenses: Contact institution. *Financial support:* In 2001–02, 41 students received support, including research assistantships with full and partial tuition reimbursements available (averaging $4,000 per year); fellowships with full tuition reimbursements available, career-related internships or fieldwork, Federal Work-Study, institutionally sponsored loans, scholarships/grants, and unspecified assistantships also available. Support available to part-time students. Financial award application deadline: 5/1; financial award applicants required to submit FAFSA. In 2001, 14 master's, 46 doctorates awarded. *Degree program information:* Part-time and evening/weekend programs available. Offers environmental education (M Ed); health, environment, and science (M Ed, MS, MSN, DPT); nursing (MSN); physical therapy (DPT); resource management (MS); sustainable systems (MS). *Application deadline:* For fall admission, 7/1; for spring admission, 11/1. Applications are processed on a rolling basis. *Application fee:* $25. Electronic applications accepted. *Application Contact:* Dr. Duncan M. Sargent, Director of Graduate Studies, 724-738-2051 Ext. 2116, Fax: 724-738-2146, E-mail: graduate.studies@sru.edu. *Dean,* Dr. Jane Fulton, 724-738-4862 Ext. 2331, Fax: 724-738-2881, E-mail: jane.fulton@sru.edu.

See in-depth description on page 1091.

SMITH COLLEGE, Northampton, MA 01063

General Information Independent, women only, comprehensive institution. *Enrollment:* 419 full-time matriculated graduate/professional students (379 women), 14 part-time matriculated graduate/professional students (11 women). *Graduate faculty:* 295 full-time (147 women), 124 part-time/adjunct (84 women). *Tuition:* Full-time $24,550; part-time $770 per credit. *Graduate housing:* Room and/or apartments available on a first-come, first-served basis to single students; on-campus housing not available to married students. Typical cost: $4,310 per year. Housing application deadline: 5/1. *Student services:* Campus employment opportunities, campus safety program, career counseling, child daycare facilities, disabled student services, exercise/wellness program, international student services, low-cost health insurance, multicultural affairs office, teacher training, writing training. *Library facilities:* Neilson Library plus 3 others. *Online resources:* library catalog, web page, access to other libraries' catalogs. *Collection:* 1.2 million titles, 5,119 serial subscriptions, 62,517 audiovisual materials.

Computer facilities: 550 computers available on campus for general student use. A campuswide network can be accessed from student residence rooms and from off campus. Internet access and online class registration, e-mail are available. *Web address:* http://www.smith.edu/.

General Application Contact: Donald Siegel, Director, 413-585-3051, Fax: 413-585-3054, E-mail: gradstudy@smith.edu.

GRADUATE UNITS

Graduate Studies Students: 63 full-time (57 women), 14 part-time (11 women); includes 5 minority (all African Americans), 12 international. Average age 29. 131 applicants, 65% accepted. *Faculty:* 282 full-time (138 women), 18 part-time/adjunct (7 women). Expenses: Contact institution. *Financial support:* In 2001–02, 22 teaching assistantships with full tuition reimbursements (averaging $9,520 per year) were awarded; fellowships, research assistantships, career-related internships or fieldwork, institutionally sponsored loans, and scholarships/grants also available. Support available to part-time students. Financial award application deadline: 1/15; financial award applicants required to submit CSS PROFILE or FAFSA. In 2001, 59 degrees awarded. *Degree program information:* Part-time programs available. Offers biological sciences (MA, MAT, PhD); biological sciences education (MAT); chemistry (MAT); chemistry education (MAT); dance (MFA); education of the deaf (MED); elementary education (Ed M); English education (MAT); exercise and sport studies (MSESS); French education (MAT); French language and literature (MAT); geology education (MAT); history (MA, MAT); history education (MAT); Italian (MA); mathematics education (MAT); music (MA, MAT); physics education (MAT); playwriting (MFA); preschool education (Ed M); religion

Smith College (continued)

(MA); secondary education (MAT); Spanish education (MAT). *Application deadline:* For fall admission, 1/15; for spring admission, 12/1. *Application fee:* $50. *Director*, Donald Siegel, 413-585-3051, Fax: 413-585-3054, E-mail: gradstdy@smith.edu.

School for Social Work Students: 356 full-time (322 women); includes 50 minority (23 African Americans, 13 Asian Americans or Pacific Islanders, 13 Hispanic Americans, 1 Native American), 12 international. Average age 38. 328 applicants, 64% accepted. *Faculty:* 13 full-time (9 women), 106 part-time/adjunct (77 women). Expenses: Contact institution. *Financial support:* In 2001–02, 176 students received support. Institutionally sponsored loans and scholarships/grants available. Financial award application deadline: 5/15; financial award applicants required to submit FAFSA. In 2001, 107 master's, 9 doctorates awarded. Offers social work (MSW, PhD). *Application deadline:* For fall admission, 2/15. Applications are processed on a rolling basis. *Application fee:* $50. *Application Contact:* Irene Rodriguez Martin, Director of Enrollment Management and Continuing Education, 413-585-7960, Fax: 413-585-7994, E-mail: imartin@smith.edu. *Acting Dean*, Dr. Carolyn Jacobs, 413-585-7977, E-mail: cjacobs@smith.edu.

SONOMA STATE UNIVERSITY, Rohnert Park, CA 94928-3609

General Information State-supported, coed, comprehensive institution. *Enrollment:* 166 full-time matriculated graduate/professional students (125 women), 317 part-time matriculated graduate/professional students (232 women). *Enrollment by degree level:* 483 master's. *Graduate faculty:* 266. Tuition, nonresident: full-time $4,428; part-time $246 per unit. *Required fees:* $2,084; $727 per semester. *Graduate housing:* Room and/or apartments available on a first-come, first-served basis to single students; on-campus housing not available to married students. *Student services:* Campus employment opportunities, career counseling, child daycare facilities, disabled student services, exercise/wellness program, free psychological counseling, international student services. *Library facilities:* Jean and Charles Schultz Information Center. *Online resources:* library catalog, web page, access to other libraries' catalogs. *Collection:* 571,505 titles, 2,402 serial subscriptions, 7,951 audiovisual materials. *Research affiliation:* California Foreign Language Project, Department of Health and Human Services (nursing), North Bay International Studies Project, California Reading and Literature Project, Pathway to the Stars science, North Bay Math Project.

Computer facilities: 300 computers available on campus for general student use. A campuswide network can be accessed from student residence rooms and from off campus. Internet access is available. *Web address:* http://www.sonoma.edu/.

General Application Contact: Elaine Sundberg, Director, Graduate Studies, 707-664-2215, Fax: 707-664-4060, E-mail: elaine.sundberg@sonoma.edu.

GRADUATE UNITS

Institute of Interdisciplinary Studies/Special Major Students: 8 full-time (5 women), 18 part-time (14 women); includes 1 minority (Hispanic American) Average age 40. 11 applicants, 91% accepted, 5 enrolled. *Faculty:* 1 (woman) full-time, 1 part-time/adjunct (0 women). Expenses: Contact institution. *Financial support:* In 2001–02, 4 students received support. Career-related internships or fieldwork, Federal Work-Study, and institutionally sponsored loans available. Support available to part-time students. In 2001, 8 degrees awarded. *Degree program information:* Part-time programs available. Offers special major (MA, MS). *Application deadline:* For fall admission, 1/31; for spring admission, 10/31. *Application fee:* $55. *Contact*, Dr. Ellen Carlton, 707-664-3918, E-mail: ellen.carlton@sonoma.edu.

School of Arts and Humanities Students: 15 full-time (13 women), 24 part-time (18 women); includes 3 minority (2 Asian Americans or Pacific Islanders, 1 Hispanic American), 2 international. Average age 36. 17 applicants, 82% accepted, 8 enrolled. *Faculty:* 10 full-time (7 women), 29 part-time/adjunct (22 women). Expenses: Contact institution. *Financial support:* In 2001–02, 6 fellowships were awarded; career-related internships or fieldwork and Federal Work-Study also available. Support available to part-time students. Financial award application deadline: 3/2. In 2001, 17 degrees awarded. *Degree program information:* Part-time and evening/weekend programs available. Offers American literature (MA); arts and humanities (MA); creative writing (MA); English literature (MA); world literature (MA). *Application deadline:* For fall admission, 11/30 (priority date). *Application fee:* $55. *Application Contact:* Tim Wandling, Chair, 707-664-2140, E-mail: tim.wandling@sonoma.edu. *Dean*, Dr. William Babula, 707-664-2146, E-mail: william.babula@sonoma.edu.

School of Business and Economics Students: 6 full-time (3 women), 46 part-time (17 women); includes 3 minority (1 African American, 1 Asian American or Pacific Islander, 1 Hispanic American), 1 international. Average age 35. 41 applicants, 63% accepted, 14 enrolled. *Faculty:* 18 full-time (8 women), 18 part-time/adjunct (7 women). Expenses: Contact institution. *Financial support:* In 2001–02, 1 fellowship was awarded; career-related internships or fieldwork, Federal Work-Study, and institutionally sponsored loans also available. Support available to part-time students. Financial award application deadline: 3/2. In 2001, 10 degrees awarded. *Degree program information:* Part-time and evening/weekend programs available. Offers business administration (MBA); business and economics (MBA). *Application deadline:* For fall admission, 1/31 (priority date); for spring admission, 8/31. Applications are processed on a rolling basis. *Application fee:* $55. *Dean*, Dr. Ahmad Hosseini, 707-664-2220, E-mail: ahmad.hosseini@sonoma.edu.

School of Education Students: 29 full-time (22 women), 91 part-time (79 women); includes 11 minority (3 African Americans, 3 Asian Americans or Pacific Islanders, 5 Hispanic Americans) Average age 40. 22 applicants, 73% accepted, 13 enrolled. *Faculty:* 24 full-time (12 women), 43 part-time/adjunct (25 women). Expenses: Contact institution. *Financial support:* Fellowships, career-related internships or fieldwork and Federal Work-Study available. Support available to part-time students. Financial award application deadline: 3/2. *Degree program information:* Part-time and evening/weekend programs available. Offers culture (MA); curriculum and instruction (MA); early childhood and elementary education (MA); educatinal leadership (MA); education (MA); language (MA); reading (MA); special education (MA). *Application fee:* $55. *Dean*, Dr. Phyllis Fernlund, 707-664-2131, E-mail: phyllis.fernlund@sonoma.edu.

School of Science and Technology Students: 31 full-time (27 women), 58 part-time (44 women); includes 13 minority (3 African Americans, 9 Asian Americans or Pacific Islanders, 1 Hispanic American) Average age 38. 71 applicants, 77% accepted, 39 enrolled. *Faculty:* 28 full-time (14 women), 46 part-time/adjunct (29 women). Expenses: Contact institution. *Financial support:* Fellowships, research assistantships, teaching assistantships, career-related internships or fieldwork and Federal Work-Study available. Support available to part-time students. Financial award application deadline: 3/2. In 2001, 44 degrees awarded. *Degree program information:* Part-time programs available. Offers environmental biology (MA); family nurse practitioner (MS); general biology (MA); kinesiology (MA); natural sciences (MA, MS). *Application deadline:* For fall admission, 11/30. *Application fee:* $55. *Dean*, Dr. Saeid Rahimi, 707-664-2171, E-mail: saeid.rahimi@sonoma.edu.

School of Social Sciences Students: 77 full-time (55 women), 82 part-time (60 women); includes 31 minority (3 African Americans, 6 Asian Americans or Pacific Islanders, 20 Hispanic Americans, 2 Native Americans), 6 international. Average age 35. 97 applicants, 47% accepted, 38 enrolled. *Faculty:* 26 full-time (10 women), 22 part-time/adjunct (11 women). Expenses: Contact institution. *Financial support:* Career-related internships or fieldwork and Federal Work-Study available. Support available to part-time students. Financial award application deadline: 3/2. In 2001, 51 degrees awarded. *Degree program information:* Part-time and evening/weekend programs available. Offers counseling (MA); cultural resources management (MA); history (MA); marriage, family, and child counseling (MA); political science (MA); public administration (MPA); pupil personnel services (MA); social sciences (MA, MPA). *Application deadline:* For fall admission, 11/30. *Application fee:* $55. *Dean*, Dr. Elaine Leeder, 707-664-2112, E-mail: elaine.leeder@sonoma.edu.

SOUTH BAYLO UNIVERSITY, Anaheim, CA 92801-1701

General Information Independent, coed, graduate-only institution. *Enrollment by degree level:* 607 master's. *Graduate faculty:* 27 full-time (12 women), 59 part-time/adjunct (18 women). *Tuition:* Part-time $105 per quarter hour. *Required fees:* $65 per quarter. *Graduate housing:* On-campus housing not available. *Student services:* Campus employment opportunities, campus safety program, career counseling, free psychological counseling, international student services, multicultural affairs office, teacher training. *Library facilities:* Anaheim Library plus 1 other. *Online resources:* library catalog. *Collection:* 8,837 titles, 107 serial subscriptions, 585 audiovisual materials.

Computer facilities: 46 computers available on campus for general student use. A campuswide network can be accessed. Internet access and online class registration are available. *Web address:* http://www.southbaylo.edu/.

General Application Contact: Theodore Ahn, Director of Admission, 714-533-1495 Ext. 222, Fax: 714-533-6040.

GRADUATE UNITS

Program in Oriental Medicine and Acupuncture Students: 487 full-time, 120 part-time. Average age 28. 104 applicants, 94% accepted, 86 enrolled. *Faculty:* 27 full-time (12 women), 59 part-time/adjunct (18 women). Expenses: Contact institution. *Financial support:* In 2001–02, 293 students received support, including 6 fellowships with partial tuition reimbursements available (averaging $500 per year); Federal Work-Study and scholarships/grants also available. Support available to part-time students. Financial award applicants required to submit FAFSA. In 2001, 199 degrees awarded. *Degree program information:* Part-time and evening/weekend programs available. Offers Oriental medicine and acupuncture (MS). *Application deadline:* For fall admission, 10/1; for winter admission, 1/5; for spring admission, 4/2. Applications are processed on a rolling basis. *Application fee:* $100. Electronic applications accepted. *Application Contact:* Theodore Ahn, Director of Admission, 714-533-1495 Ext. 222, Fax: 714-533-6040. *Academic Dean*, Dr. Hong Feng, 714-533-1495 Ext. 225, Fax: 714-533-6040, E-mail: hfeng@southbaylo.edu.

SOUTH CAROLINA STATE UNIVERSITY, Orangeburg, SC 29117-0001

General Information State-supported, coed, comprehensive institution. CGS member. *Graduate housing:* Room and/or apartments available to married students; on-campus housing not available to single students.

GRADUATE UNITS

School of Graduate Studies *Degree program information:* Part-time and evening/weekend programs available.

School of Applied Professional Sciences *Degree program information:* Part-time and evening/weekend programs available. Offers applied professional sciences (MA, MS); individual and family development (MS); nutritional sciences (MS); rehabilitation counseling (MA); speech/language pathology (MA).

School of Business *Degree program information:* Part-time and evening/weekend programs available. Offers agribusiness (MS); agribusiness and economics (MS).

School of Education *Degree program information:* Part-time and evening/weekend programs available. Offers early childhood and special education (M Ed); early childhood education (MAT); education (M Ed, MAT, Ed D, Ed S); educational leadership (Ed D, Ed S); elementary counselor education (M Ed); elementary education (M Ed, MAT); engineering (MAT); general science (MAT); mathematics (MAT); secondary counselor education (M Ed); secondary education (M Ed); special education (M Ed); speech pathology (MAT).

SOUTH DAKOTA SCHOOL OF MINES AND TECHNOLOGY, Rapid City, SD 57701-3995

General Information State-supported, coed, university. CGS member. *Graduate housing:* Rooms and/or apartments available on a first-come, first-served basis to single students and available to married students. *Research affiliation:* CEA USA, Inc. (radium/nickel extraction), Black Hills Corporation (wind power), EG & G Idaho, Inc. (ground-probing radar), RE/SPEC, Inc. (preparation of new plant growth regulators), Homestake Mining Company (gold ore exploration and development), Horizons, Inc. (interferometric synthetic aperture radar).

GRADUATE UNITS

Graduate Division *Degree program information:* Part-time programs available. Offers atmospheric sciences (MS, PhD); atmospheric, environmental, and water resources (PhD); chemical engineering (PhD); chemistry (MS, PhD); civil engineering (MS, PhD); computer science (MS); electrical engineering (PhD); geology and geological engineering (MS, PhD); materials engineering and science (MS, PhD); mechanical engineering (PhD); metallurgical engineering (MS, PhD); paleontology (MS); physics (MS, PhD); technology management (MS). Electronic applications accepted.

See in-depth description on page 1093.

SOUTH DAKOTA STATE UNIVERSITY, Brookings, SD 57007

General Information State-supported, coed, university. CGS member. *Graduate housing:* Rooms and/or apartments available to single and married students. *Research affiliation:* Associated Western Universities, Inc.

GRADUATE UNITS

Graduate School *Degree program information:* Part-time and evening/weekend programs available.

College of Agriculture and Biological Sciences *Degree program information:* Part-time programs available. Offers agriculture and biological sciences (MS, PhD); agronomy (MS, PhD); animal science (MS, PhD); biological sciences (PhD); biology (MS); dairy science (MS, PhD); economics (MS); entomology (MS); microbiology (MS); plant pathology (MS); rural sociology (MS, PhD); wildlife and fisheries sciences (MS).

College of Arts and Science *Degree program information:* Part-time programs available. Offers analytical chemistry (MS, PhD); arts and science (MA, MS, PhD); biochemistry (MS, PhD); chemistry (MS, PhD); communication studies and theatre (MS); English (MA); geography (MS); health, physical education and recreation (MS); inorganic chemistry (MS, PhD); journalism (MS); organic chemistry (MS, PhD); physical chemistry (MS, PhD).

College of Education and Counseling *Degree program information:* Part-time programs available. Offers counseling and human resource development (MS); curriculum and instruction (M Ed); education and counseling (M Ed, MS); educational administration (M Ed).

College of Engineering *Degree program information:* Part-time programs available. Offers agricultural engineering (MS, PhD); atmospheric, environmental, and water resources (PhD); electrical engineering (MS); engineering (MS); industrial management (MS); mathematics (MS); mechanical engineering (MS); physics (MS).

College of Family and Consumer Sciences Offers family and consumer sciences (MS).

College of Nursing Offers nursing (MS).

College of Pharmacy Offers pharmaceutical sciences (MS); pharmacy (Pharm D, MS).

SOUTHEASTERN BAPTIST THEOLOGICAL SEMINARY, Wake Forest, NC 27588-1889

General Information Independent-religious, coed. *Enrollment:* 752 full-time matriculated graduate/professional students (66 women), 570 part-time matriculated graduate/professional students (118 women). *Enrollment by degree level:* 984 first professional, 217 master's, 121 doctoral, 1,322 other advanced degrees. *Graduate faculty:* 62 full-time (2 women), 13 part-time/adjunct (2 women). *Tuition:* Full-time $2,880; part-time $120 per hour. *Graduate housing:* Rooms and/or apartments available to single and married students. *Student services:* Campus employment opportunities, campus safety program, career counseling, child daycare facilities. *Collection:* 167,044 titles, 938 serial subscriptions.

Computer facilities: 7 computers available on campus for general student use. A campuswide network can be accessed. *Web address:* http://www.sebts.edu/.

General Application Contact: Jerry Yandell, Admissions Director, 919-761-2280, E-mail: jyandell@sabts.edu.

GRADUATE UNITS

Graduate and Professional Programs Offers advanced biblical studies (M Div); Christian education (M Div, MACE); Christian ethics (PhD); Christian ministry (M Div); Christian planting (M Div); church music (MACM); counseling (MACO); evangelism (PhD); language (M Div); ministry (D Min); New Testament (PhD); Old Testament (PhD); philosophy (PhD); theology (Th M, PhD); women's studies (M Div).

SOUTHEASTERN LOUISIANA UNIVERSITY, Hammond, LA 70402

General Information State-supported, coed, comprehensive institution. *Enrollment:* 357 full-time matriculated graduate/professional students (227 women), 693 part-time matriculated graduate/professional students (551 women). *Enrollment by degree level:* 1,050 master's. *Graduate faculty:* 149 full-time (68 women), 16 part-time/adjunct (8 women). *International tuition:* $6,573 full-time. Tuition, state resident: full-time $2,457. Tuition, nonresident: full-time $6,453. *Graduate housing:* Rooms and/or apartments available on a first-come, first-served basis to single and married students. Typical cost: $1,650 per year ($3,440 including board) for single students. Room and board charges vary according to board plan and housing facility selected. Housing application deadline: 7/15. *Student services:* Campus employment opportunities, campus safety program, career counseling, disabled student services, exercise/wellness program, free psychological counseling, international student services, low-cost health insurance, multicultural affairs office, teacher training, writing training. *Library facilities:* Sims Memorial Library. *Online resources:* library catalog, web page, access to other libraries' catalogs. *Collection:* 554,523 titles, 2,122 serial subscriptions, 48,081 audiovisual materials. *Research affiliation:* Dynamac (zoology), MECOM (environmental resources), Argonne National Laboratory (chemistry), St. Louis Zoo (zoology).

Computer facilities: 702 computers available on campus for general student use. A campuswide network can be accessed from off campus. Internet access and online class registration are available. *Web address:* http://www.selu.edu/.

General Application Contact: Josie Mercante, Associate Director of Admissions, 985-549-2066, Fax: 985-549-5632, E-mail: jmercante@selu.edu.

GRADUATE UNITS

College of Arts and Sciences Students: 53 full-time (35 women), 89 part-time (56 women); includes 14 minority (11 African Americans, 1 Asian American or Pacific Islander, 2 Hispanic Americans), 6 international. Average age 31. 81 applicants, 74% accepted, 43 enrolled. *Faculty:* 64 full-time (19 women), 6 part-time/adjunct (2 women). Expenses: Contact institution. *Financial support:* In 2001–02, 12 fellowships with full tuition reimbursements (averaging $2,450 per year), 20 research assistantships with full tuition reimbursements (averaging $2,200 per year), 22 teaching assistantships with full tuition reimbursements (averaging $2,200 per year) were awarded. Career-related internships or fieldwork, Federal Work-Study, and unspecified assistantships also available. Support available to part-time students. Financial award application deadline: 5/1; financial award applicants required to submit FAFSA. In 2001, 30 degrees awarded. *Degree program information:* Part-time programs available. Offers applied sociology (MS); arts and sciences (M Mus, MA, MS); biology (MS); English (MA); history (MA); music and dramatic arts (M Mus); organizational communications (MA); psychology (MA). *Application deadline:* For fall admission, 7/15 (priority date); for spring admission, 12/1 (priority date). Applications are processed on a rolling basis. *Application fee:* $20 ($30 for international students). Electronic applications accepted. *Application Contact:* Josie Mercante, Associate Director of Admissions, 985-549-2066, Fax: 985-549-5632, E-mail: jmercante@selu.edu. *Dean,* Dr. John S. Miller, 985-549-2101, Fax: 985-549-5014, E-mail: jsmiller@selu.edu.

College of Business and Technology Students: 155 full-time (74 women), 93 part-time (53 women); includes 31 minority (24 African Americans, 5 Asian Americans or Pacific Islanders, 2 Hispanic Americans), 63 international. Average age 28. 124 applicants, 69% accepted, 63 enrolled. *Faculty:* 26 full-time (5 women), 2 part-time/adjunct (0 women). Expenses: Contact institution. *Financial support:* In 2001–02, 12 research assistantships with full tuition reimbursements (averaging $2,200 per year) were awarded; career-related internships or fieldwork, Federal Work-Study, and unspecified assistantships also available. Support available to part-time students. Financial award application deadline: 5/1; financial award applicants required to submit FAFSA. In 2001, 94 degrees awarded. *Degree program information:* Part-time and evening/weekend programs available. Offers business and technology (MBA). *Application deadline:* For fall admission, 7/15 (priority date); for spring admission, 12/1 (priority date). Applications are processed on a rolling basis. *Application fee:* $20 ($30 for international students). Electronic applications accepted. *Application Contact:* Josie Mercante, Associate Director of Admissions, 985-549-2066, Fax: 985-549-5632, E-mail: jmercante@selu.edu. *Dean,* Dr. Michael Budden, 985-549-2258, Fax: 985-549-5038, E-mail: mbudden@selu.edu.

College of Education and Human Development Students: 68 full-time (54 women), 396 part-time (353 women); includes 78 minority (75 African Americans, 2 Hispanic Americans, 1 Native American), 3 international. Average age 35. 126 applicants, 78% accepted, 74 enrolled. *Faculty:* 35 full-time (27 women), 7 part-time/adjunct (5 women). Expenses: Contact institution. *Financial support:* In 2001–02, 4 research assistantships with full tuition reimbursements (averaging $2,200 per year), 1 teaching assistantship with full tuition reimbursement (averaging $2,200 per year) were awarded. Fellowships, career-related internships or fieldwork, Federal Work-Study, and unspecified assistantships also available. Support available to part-time students. Financial award application deadline: 5/1; financial award applicants required to submit FAFSA. In 2001, 115 degrees awarded. *Degree program information:* Part-time programs available. Offers administration and supervision (M Ed); counselor education (M Ed); curriculum and instruction (M Ed); education and human development (M Ed); special education (M Ed). *Application deadline:* For fall admission, 7/15 (priority date); for spring admission, 12/1 (priority date). Applications are processed on a rolling basis. *Application fee:* $20 ($30 for international students). Electronic applications accepted. *Application Contact:* Josie Mercante, Associate Director of Admissions, 985-549-2066, Fax: 985-549-5632, E-mail: jmercante@selu.edu. *Interim Dean,* Dr. Martha Head, 985-549-2217, Fax: 985-549-2070, E-mail: mhead@selu.edu.

College of Nursing and Health Sciences Students: 76 full-time (62 women), 101 part-time (82 women); includes 24 minority (18 African Americans, 5 Hispanic Americans, 1 Native American), 3 international. Average age 31. 108 applicants, 72% accepted, 56 enrolled. *Faculty:* 24 full-time (17 women), 1 (woman) part-time/adjunct. Expenses: Contact institution. *Financial support:* In 2001–02, 12 research assistantships with full tuition reimbursements (averaging $2,200 per year) were awarded; career-related internships or fieldwork, Federal Work-Study, and unspecified assistantships also available. Support available to part-time students. Financial award application deadline: 5/1; financial award applicants required to submit FAFSA. In 2001, 39 degrees awarded. *Degree program information:* Part-time programs available. Offers communication sciences and disorders (MS); kinesiology and health studies (MA); nursing (MSN); nursing and health sciences (MA, MS, MSN). *Application deadline:* For fall admission, 7/15 (priority date); for spring admission, 12/1 (priority date). Applications are processed on a rolling basis. *Application fee:* $20 ($30 for international students). Electronic applications accepted. *Application Contact:* Josie Mercante, Associate Director of Admissions, 985-549-2066, Fax: 985-549-5632, E-mail: jmercante@selu.edu. *Dean,* Dr. Donnie Booth, 985-549-5045, Fax: 985-549-5087, E-mail: dbooth@selu.edu.

SOUTHEASTERN OKLAHOMA STATE UNIVERSITY, Durant, OK 74701-0609

General Information State-supported, coed, comprehensive institution. *Graduate housing:* Rooms and/or apartments available on a first-come, first-served basis to single and married students. Housing application deadline: 8/1. *Research affiliation:* Oklahoma Small Business Development Center.

GRADUATE UNITS

Graduate School *Degree program information:* Part-time and evening/weekend programs available.

School of Arts and Sciences *Degree program information:* Part-time and evening/weekend programs available. Offers technology (MT).

School of Business *Degree program information:* Part-time and evening/weekend programs available. Offers business (MBA, MS).

School of Education *Degree program information:* Part-time and evening/weekend programs available. Offers educational administration (M Ed); educational instruction and leadership (M Ed); educational technology (M Ed); elementary education (M Ed); guidance and counseling (MBS); school counseling (M Ed); secondary education (M Ed).

SOUTHEASTERN UNIVERSITY, Washington, DC 20024-2788

General Information Independent, coed, comprehensive institution. *Enrollment:* 216 full-time matriculated graduate/professional students (118 women), 253 part-time matriculated graduate/professional students (167 women). *Enrollment by degree level:* 469 master's. *Graduate faculty:* 9 full-time (3 women), 34 part-time/adjunct (6 women). *Tuition:* Full-time $7,695; part-time $285 per credit hour. One-time fee: $45. *Graduate housing:* On-campus housing not available. *Student services:* Campus employment opportunities, career counseling, international student services. *Library facilities:* The Learning Resources Center plus 1 other. *Collection:* 32,000 titles, 200 serial subscriptions, 250 audiovisual materials.

Computer facilities: 137 computers available on campus for general student use. A campuswide network can be accessed from off campus. *Web address:* http://www.seu.edu/.

General Application Contact: Director of Admissions, 202-265-5343, Fax: 202-488-8093.

GRADUATE UNITS

College of Graduate Studies Students: 216 full-time (118 women), 253 part-time (167 women); includes 177 minority (155 African Americans, 18 Asian Americans or Pacific Islanders, 2 Hispanic Americans, 2 Native Americans), 281 international. Average age 33. 119 applicants, 91% accepted, 95 enrolled. *Faculty:* 9 full-time (3 women), 34 part-time/adjunct (6 women). Expenses: Contact institution. *Financial support:* In 2001–02, 87 students received support. Career-related internships or fieldwork, Federal Work-Study, and institutionally sponsored loans available. Support available to part-time students. Financial award application deadline: 8/21. In 2001, 285 degrees awarded. *Degree program information:* Part-time and evening/weekend programs available. Offers accounting (MBA); business (MBA, MPA, MS); computer science (MBA, MS); financial management (MBA); government program management (MPA); health services administration (MPA); international management (MBA); management (MBA); management information systems (MBA); marketing (MBA); public administration (MPA); taxation (MS). *Application deadline:* Applications are processed on a rolling basis. *Application fee:* $45. *Application Contact:* Director of Admissions, 202-265-5343, Fax: 202-488-8093. *Dean of Faculty and Academic Departments,* Dr. Elaine Heath, 202-488-8162, Fax: 202-488-8043.

See in-depth description on page 1095.

SOUTHEAST MISSOURI STATE UNIVERSITY, Cape Girardeau, MO 63701-4799

General Information State-supported, coed, comprehensive institution. CGS member. *Enrollment:* 210 full-time matriculated graduate/professional students (135 women), 622 part-time matriculated graduate/professional students (433 women). *Enrollment by degree level:* 321 master's, 11 doctoral, 500 other advanced degrees. *Graduate faculty:* 223 full-time (78 women). Tuition, state resident: full-time $1,242; part-time $138 per hour. Tuition, nonresident: full-time $2,268; part-time $252 per hour. *Graduate housing:* Room and/or apartments available on a first-come, first-served basis to single students; on-campus housing not available to married students. Typical cost: $2,960 per year ($4,842 including board). Room and board charges vary according to board plan and campus/location. *Student services:* Campus employment opportunities, campus safety program, career counseling, child daycare facilities, disabled student services, exercise/wellness program, free psychological counseling, international student services, low-cost health insurance, multicultural affairs office, teacher training, writing training. *Library facilities:* Kent Library. *Online resources:* library catalog, web page, access to other libraries' catalogs. *Collection:* 429,421 titles, 6,264 serial subscriptions, 7,955 audiovisual materials. *Research affiliation:* Gulf Coast Research Laboratory.

Computer facilities: 650 computers available on campus for general student use. A campuswide network can be accessed from student residence rooms and from off campus. Internet access and online class registration are available. *Web address:* http://www.semo.edu/.

General Application Contact: Dr. Phil Parette, Dean of the School of Graduate Studies and Research, 573-651-2192, Fax: 573-651-2001, E-mail: pparette@semo.edu.

GRADUATE UNITS

School of Graduate Studies and Research Students: 210 full-time (135 women), 622 part-time (433 women). Average age 35. 620 applicants, 85% accepted. *Faculty:* 223 full-time (78 women). Expenses: Contact institution. *Financial support:* In 2001–02, 399 students received support, including 1 fellowship (averaging $5,000 per year), 76 research assistantships with full tuition reimbursements available (averaging $6,100 per year), 50 teaching assistantships with full tuition reimbursements available (averaging $6,100 per year); career-related internships or fieldwork and Federal Work-Study also available. Financial award applicants required to submit FAFSA. In 2001, 223 master's, 20 other advanced degrees awarded. *Degree program information:* Part-time and evening/weekend programs available. Offers art education (MA); athletic administration (MSA); biology (MNS); business education (MA); chemistry (MNS); communication disorders (MA); community counseling (MA); criminal justice (MS); criminal justice administration (MSA); educational administration (MA, Ed D, Ed S); educational studies (MA); educational technology (MA); elementary education (MA); English (MA); exceptional child education (MA); geosciences (MNS); guidance and counseling (MA); health fitness administration (MSA); history (MA); human environmental studies (MA); human services administration (MSA); industrial management (MS); mathematics (MNS); middle level education (MA); music education (MME); nursing (MSN); nutrition and exercise science (MS); public administration (MSA); science education (MNS); social studies (MA); teaching English to speakers of other languages (MA). *Application deadline:* For spring admission, 11/21. Applications are processed on a rolling basis. *Application fee:* $20 ($100 for international students). *Application Contact:* Marsha L. Arant, Senior Administrative Assistant, 573-651-2192, Fax: 573-651-2001, E-mail: marant@semo.edu. *Dean,* Dr. Phil Parette, 573-651-2192, Fax: 573-651-2001, E-mail: pparette@semo.edu.

Harrison College of Business Students: 43 full-time (17 women), 46 part-time (19 women); includes 2 minority (both African Americans), 39 international. Average age 29. 73 applicants, 73% accepted. *Faculty:* 32 full-time (9 women). Expenses: Contact institution. *Financial support:* In 2001–02, 14 research assistantships with full tuition reimbursements (averaging $6,100 per year) were awarded In 2001, 29 degrees awarded. *Degree program information:* Part-time and evening/weekend programs available. Offers accounting (MBA); general management (MBA). *Application deadline:* For fall admission, 4/1 (priority date); for spring admission, 11/21. Applications are processed on a rolling basis. *Application fee:* $20 ($100 for international students). *Application Contact:* Marsha L. Arant, Office of Graduate Studies, 573-651-2192, Fax: 573-651-2001, E-mail: marant@semovm.semo.edu. *Director,* Kenneth Heischmidt, 573-651-5116, Fax: 573-651-5032, E-mail: kheischmidt@semo.edu.

SOUTHERN ADVENTIST UNIVERSITY, Collegedale, TN 37315-0370

General Information Independent-religious, coed, comprehensive institution. *Enrollment:* 57 full-time matriculated graduate/professional students (28 women), 194 part-time matriculated graduate/professional students (95 women). *Enrollment by degree level:* 251 master's. *Graduate faculty:* 24 full-time (7 women), 18 part-time/adjunct (5 women). *Tuition:* Full-time $5,580; part-time $310 per credit hour. *Graduate housing:* Rooms and/or apartments available on a first-come, first-served basis to single and married students. Typical cost: $4,600 (including board) for single students. *Student services:* Campus employment opportunities, campus safety program, career counseling, disabled student services, exercise/wellness program, free psychological counseling, international student services, low-cost health insurance, multi-

Southern Adventist University (continued)

cultural affairs office, teacher training, writing training. *Library facilities:* McKee Library. *Online resources:* library catalog, web page. *Collection:* 151,045 titles, 6,746 serial subscriptions, 3,606 audiovisual materials.

Computer facilities: 200 computers available on campus for general student use. A campuswide network can be accessed from student residence rooms and from off campus. Internet access is available. *Web address:* http://www.southern.edu/.

General Application Contact: Marc Grundy, Director of Admissions, 423-238-2843, Fax: 423-238-3005, E-mail: admissions@southern.edu.

GRADUATE UNITS

School of Business and Management Students: 7 full-time (3 women), 62 part-time (29 women); includes 8 minority (3 African Americans, 4 Asian Americans or Pacific Islanders, 1 Hispanic American), 1 international. Average age 35. 29 applicants, 97% accepted, 20 enrolled. *Faculty:* 4 full-time (0 women), 4 part-time/adjunct (0 women). Expenses: Contact institution. *Financial support:* In 2001–02, 4 students received support. Scholarships/grants available. Financial award application deadline: 9/1; financial award applicants required to submit FAFSA. In 2001, 14 degrees awarded. *Degree program information:* Part-time and evening/weekend programs available. Postbaccalaureate distance learning degree programs offered (no on-campus study). Offers accounting (MBA); administration (MS); health care administration (MBA); management (MBA). *Application deadline:* For fall admission, 8/15 (priority date); for winter admission, 1/1 (priority date); for spring admission, 5/1 (priority date). Applications are processed on a rolling basis. *Application fee:* $25. Electronic applications accepted. *Application Contact:* Linda Wilhelm, Admissions Coordinator, 423-238-2751, Fax: 423-238-3151, E-mail: lwilhelm@southern.edu. *Dean,* Don Van Ornam, 423-238-2750, Fax: 423-238-3151, E-mail: dvanorna@southern.edu.

School of Computing Students: 4 full-time (0 women), 5 part-time. Average age 26. 5 applicants, 60% accepted, 3 enrolled. *Faculty:* 1 full-time (0 women), 4 part-time/adjunct (0 women). Expenses: Contact institution. *Financial support:* In 2001–02, 5 students received support. Career-related internships or fieldwork and tuition waivers (partial) available. Financial award application deadline: 3/1; financial award applicants required to submit FAFSA. In 2001, 1 degree awarded. *Degree program information:* Part-time programs available. Offers computing (MSE). *Application deadline:* For fall admission, 3/1 (priority date); for winter admission, 10/1 (priority date). Applications are processed on a rolling basis. *Application fee:* $25. Electronic applications accepted. *Application Contact:* Darlene J. Williams, Application Coordinator, 423-238-2936, Fax: 423-238-2234, E-mail: mse@southern.edu. *Dean,* Dr. Jared Bruckner, 423-238-2935, Fax: 423-238-2234, E-mail: bruckner@southern.edu.

School of Education and Psychology Students: 46 full-time (25 women), 70 part-time (48 women); includes 23 minority (11 African Americans, 1 Asian American or Pacific Islander, 10 Hispanic Americans, 1 Native American), 2 international. Average age 36. 22 applicants, 91% accepted. *Faculty:* 11 full-time (7 women), 2 part-time/adjunct (1 woman). Expenses: Contact institution. *Financial support:* In 2001–02, 11 students received support, including 1 research assistantship; career-related internships or fieldwork, scholarships/grants, and tuition waivers (partial) also available. Support available to part-time students. Financial award application deadline: 4/1; financial award applicants required to submit FAFSA. In 2001, 29 degrees awarded. *Degree program information:* Part-time and evening/weekend programs available. Offers community counseling (MS); curriculum and instruction (MS Ed); educational administration and supervision (MS Ed); inclusive education (MS Ed); marriage and family therapy (MS); multiage/multigrade teaching (MS Ed); outdoor teacher education (MS Ed); school counseling (MS). *Application deadline:* Applications are processed on a rolling basis. *Application fee:* $25. Electronic applications accepted. *Application Contact:* Cathy Olson, Information Contact, 423-238-2765, Fax: 423-238-2468, E-mail: cjolson@southern.edu. *Dean,* Dr. Alberto dos Santos, 423-238-2779, Fax: 423-238-2468, E-mail: adossant@southern.edu.

School of Nursing Average age 39. 18 applicants, 100% accepted, 17 enrolled. *Faculty:* 6 part-time/adjunct (4 women). Expenses: Contact institution. *Degree program information:* Part-time and evening/weekend programs available. Offers adult nurse practitioner (MSN); family nurse practitioner (MSN); health care administration (MSN); nurse educator (MSN). *Application deadline:* Applications are processed on a rolling basis. *Application fee:* $25. Electronic applications accepted. *Application Contact:* Linda L. Marlowe, Admissions Coordinator, 423-238-2941, Fax: 423-238-3004, E-mail: lmarlowe@southern.edu. *Dean,* Dr. L. Phil Hunt, 423-238-2940, Fax: 423-238-3004, E-mail: phunt@southern.edu.

School of Religion Average age 36. 3 applicants, 100% accepted. *Faculty:* 8 full-time (0 women), 2 part-time/adjunct (0 women). Expenses: Contact institution. *Financial support:* In 2001–02, 1 student received support. Tuition waivers (full) available. Support available to part-time students. Financial award application deadline: 4/1; financial award applicants required to submit FAFSA. In 2001, 3 degrees awarded. *Degree program information:* Part-time programs available. Offers church leadership and management (MA); evangelism (MA); homiletics (MA); religious education (MA); religious studies (MA). Summer program only. *Application deadline:* For spring admission, 3/30 (priority date). Applications are processed on a rolling basis. *Application fee:* $25. *Application Contact:* Karen J. Arnold, Administrative Assistant, 423-238-2977, Fax: 423-238-3163, E-mail: karnold@southern.edu. *Dean,* Dr. Ron E. M. Clouzet, 423-238-2983, Fax: 423-238-3163, E-mail: clouzet@southern.edu.

SOUTHERN ARKANSAS UNIVERSITY–MAGNOLIA, Magnolia, AR 71753

General Information State-supported, coed, comprehensive institution. *Enrollment:* 24 full-time matriculated graduate/professional students (15 women), 93 part-time matriculated graduate/professional students (72 women). *Enrollment by degree level:* 117 master's. *Graduate faculty:* 35 full-time (16 women), 4 part-time/adjunct (3 women). Tuition, state resident: full-time $2,322; part-time $129 per hour. Tuition, nonresident: full-time $3,366; part-time $187 per hour. *Required fees:* $48; $1 per hour. $15 per semester. *Graduate housing:* Room and/or apartments available on a first-come, first-served basis to single students; on-campus housing not available to married students. Typical cost: $3,070 (including board). Housing application deadline: 6/1. *Student services:* Campus employment opportunities, campus safety program, career counseling, exercise/wellness program, free psychological counseling, international student services, low-cost health insurance, multicultural affairs office. *Library facilities:* Magale Library. *Online resources:* library catalog, web page. *Collection:* 1.1 million titles, 965 serial subscriptions, 9,877 audiovisual materials.

Computer facilities: 150 computers available on campus for general student use. A campuswide network can be accessed from off campus. Internet access is available. *Web address:* http://www.saumag.edu/.

General Application Contact: Dr. John R. Jones, Associate Dean, Graduate Studies, 870-235-4055, Fax: 870-235-5035, E-mail: jrjones@saumag.edu.

GRADUATE UNITS

Graduate Programs Students: 24 full-time (15 women), 93 part-time (72 women); includes 17 minority (15 African Americans, 1 Asian American or Pacific Islander, 1 Hispanic American), 1 international. 63 applicants, 38% accepted. *Faculty:* 35 full-time (16 women), 4 part-time/adjunct (3 women). Expenses: Contact institution. *Financial support:* In 2001–02, 70 students received support, including 35 research assistantships with full tuition reimbursements available (averaging $3,091 per year); career-related internships or fieldwork, Federal Work-Study, scholarships/grants, and unspecified assistantships also available. Financial award application deadline: 8/15; financial award applicants required to submit FAFSA. In 2001, 45 degrees awarded. *Degree program information:* Part-time programs available. Offers agency counseling (M Ed); education (M Ed); library media and information specialist (M Ed); teaching (MAT). *Application deadline:* For fall admission, 8/15. Applications are processed on a rolling basis. *Application fee:* $0. *Associate Dean, Graduate Studies,* Dr. John R. Jones, 870-235-4055, Fax: 870-235-5035, E-mail: jrjones@saumag.edu.

SOUTHERN BAPTIST THEOLOGICAL SEMINARY, Louisville, KY 40280-0004

General Information Independent-religious, coed, comprehensive institution. *Graduate housing:* Rooms and/or apartments available to single and married students.

GRADUATE UNITS

Billy Graham School of Missions, Evangelism, and Church Growth *Degree program information:* Part-time and evening/weekend programs available. Postbaccalaureate distance learning degree programs offered (minimal on-campus study). Offers Christian mission/world religion (PhD); evangelism/church growth (PhD); ministry (D Min); missiology (MA, D Miss); theology (Th M).

School of Christian Education and Leadership *Degree program information:* Part-time programs available. Postbaccalaureate distance learning degree programs offered (minimal on-campus study). Offers Christian education and leadership (M Div, MACE, Ed D, PhD).

School of Church Music and Worship Offers church music and worship (M Div, MCM, DMA, DMM).

School of Theology *Degree program information:* Part-time and evening/weekend programs available. Postbaccalaureate distance learning degree programs offered (minimal on-campus study). Offers theology (M Div, Th M, D Min, PhD).

SOUTHERN CALIFORNIA BIBLE COLLEGE & SEMINARY, El Cajon, CA 92019

General Information Independent-religious, comprehensive institution.

GRADUATE UNITS

Graduate and Professional Programs *Degree program information:* Part-time and evening/weekend programs available. Postbaccalaureate distance learning degree programs offered (no on-campus study). Offers biblical studies (MA); counseling psychology (MACP); religious studies (MRS); theology (M Div). Electronic applications accepted.

SOUTHERN CALIFORNIA COLLEGE OF OPTOMETRY, Fullerton, CA 92831-1615

General Information Independent, coed, graduate-only institution. *Enrollment by degree level:* 376 first professional. *Graduate faculty:* 40 full-time (12 women), 44 part-time/adjunct (13 women). *Tuition:* Full-time $21,150; part-time $590 per credit. *Required fees:* $90. One-time fee: $795 full-time. *Graduate housing:* On-campus housing not available. *Student services:* Campus employment opportunities, campus safety program, career counseling, exercise/wellness program, free psychological counseling, low-cost health insurance. *Library facilities:* M. B. Ketchum Memorial Library. *Online resources:* library catalog, web page. *Collection:* 10,427 titles, 300 serial subscriptions, 900 audiovisual materials. *Research affiliation:* Vistakon–Johnson & Johnson (contact lenses), Coopervision/Coast (contact lenses), Ciba Vision (contact lenses, education), Bausch & Lomb (contact lenses), Allergan (ophthalmic products), Royal Philips Electronics (display technology).

Computer facilities: 32 computers available on campus for general student use. A campuswide network can be accessed. Internet access is available. *Web address:* http://www.scco.edu/.

General Application Contact: Dr. Lorraine I. Voorhees, Dean of Student Affairs, 714-449-7445, Fax: 714-992-7878, E-mail: lvoorhees@scco.edu.

GRADUATE UNITS

Professional Program Students: 376 full-time (234 women); includes 239 minority (3 African Americans, 220 Asian Americans or Pacific Islanders, 15 Hispanic Americans, 1 Native American), 5 international. Average age 25. 433 applicants, 35% accepted. *Faculty:* 40 full-time (12 women), 44 part-time/adjunct (13 women). Expenses: Contact institution. *Financial support:* In 2001–02, 338 students received support, including 15 research assistantships, 42 teaching assistantships; career-related internships or fieldwork, Federal Work-Study, and institutionally sponsored loans also available. Financial award application deadline: 6/1; financial award applicants required to submit CSS PROFILE or FAFSA. In 2001, 95 degrees awarded. Offers optometry (OD). *Application deadline:* For fall admission, 3/15 (priority date). Applications are processed on a rolling basis. *Application fee:* $50. *Application Contact:* Dr. Lorraine I. Voorhees, Dean of Student Affairs, 714-449-7445, Fax: 714-992-7878, E-mail: lvoorhees@scco.edu. *Dean, Academic Affairs,* Dr. Morris S. Berman, 714-449-7455, Fax: 714-992-7878, E-mail: mberman@scco.edu.

SOUTHERN CALIFORNIA INSTITUTE OF ARCHITECTURE, Los Angeles, CA 90013

General Information Independent, coed, comprehensive institution. *Graduate housing:* On-campus housing not available.

GRADUATE UNITS

Graduate Program in Architecture Offers architecture design (M Arch).

SOUTHERN CALIFORNIA UNIVERSITY OF HEALTH SCIENCES, Whittier, CA 90609-1166

General Information Independent, coed, graduate-only institution. *Graduate housing:* On-campus housing not available. *Research affiliation:* RAND Corporation (appropriateness study, health insurance), University of California, Irvine–Medical Center (low back pain, complementary medicine), Veterans Administration Medical Center, University of California, Los Angeles–School of Medicine.

GRADUATE UNITS

College of Acupuncture and Oriental Medicine Offers acupuncture and Oriental medicine (MAOM).

Los Angeles College of Chiropractic Offers chiropractic (DC).

SOUTHERN CHRISTIAN UNIVERSITY, Montgomery, AL 36117

General Information Independent-religious, coed, comprehensive institution. *Enrollment:* 224 full-time matriculated graduate/professional students (86 women). *Enrollment by degree level:* 39 first professional, 153 master's, 32 doctoral. *Graduate faculty:* 43 full-time (5 women), 18 part-time/adjunct (8 women). *Tuition:* Full-time $7,020; part-time $390 per semester hour. *Required fees:* $1,600; $400 per semester. Tuition and fees vary according to course load. *Graduate housing:* On-campus housing not available. *Student services:* Campus employment opportunities, campus safety program, career counseling, disabled student services, free psychological counseling, low-cost health insurance. *Library facilities:* Southern Christian University Library. *Online resources:* library catalog, web page, access to other libraries' catalogs. *Collection:* 73,000 titles, 500 serial subscriptions.

Computer facilities: 5 computers available on campus for general student use. A campuswide network can be accessed from off campus. Internet access and online class registration are available. *Web address:* http://www.southernchristian.edu/.

General Application Contact: Becky Bagwell, Admissions Officer, 334-387-3877 Ext. 224, Fax: 334-387-3878, E-mail: beckybagwell@southernchristian.edu.

GRADUATE UNITS

Graduate and Professional Programs Students: 224 full-time (86 women); includes 69 minority (64 African Americans, 3 Asian Americans or Pacific Islanders, 2 Native Americans) Average age 35. *Faculty:* 43 full-time (5 women), 18 part-time/adjunct (8 women). Expenses: Contact institution. *Financial support:* Federal Work-Study and scholarships/grants available. Support available to part-time students. Financial award applicants required to submit FAFSA. In 2001, 8 first professional degrees, 29 master's, 3 doctorates awarded. *Degree program information:* Part-time and evening/weekend programs available. Postbaccalaureate distance learning degree programs offered (no on-campus study). Offers biblical studies (MA, D Min); Christian ministry (M Div); marriage and family therapy (M Div, D Min, PhD); ministerial leadership (MS); organizational leadership (MS); pastoral counseling (M Div, MS, PhD); practical theology (MA); professional counseling (M Div, PhD). *Application deadline:* For fall admission, 9/1 (priority date); for spring admission, 1/1 (priority date). Applications are processed on a rolling basis. *Application fee:* $50. Electronic applications accepted. *Application Contact:* Becky Bagwell, Admissions Officer, 334-387-3877 Ext. 224, Fax: 334-387-

3878, E-mail: beckybagwell@southernchristian.edu. *Director of Enrollment Management*, Rick Johnson, 800-351-4040 Ext. 213, Fax: 334-387-3878, E-mail: rickjohnson@southernchristian.edu.

SOUTHERN COLLEGE OF OPTOMETRY, Memphis, TN 38104-2222

General Information Independent, coed, graduate-only institution. *Enrollment by degree level:* 481 first professional. *Graduate faculty:* 43 full-time (10 women), 11 part-time/adjunct (3 women). Tuition, state resident: full-time $11,884. Tuition, nonresident: full-time $16,884. *Graduate housing:* On-campus housing not available. *Student services:* Campus employment opportunities, campus safety program, career counseling, international student services, low-cost health insurance, teacher training. *Library facilities:* SCO Library. *Online resources:* library catalog, web page. *Collection:* 20,735 titles, 170 serial subscriptions, 1,379 audiovisual materials.

Computer facilities: 37 computers available on campus for general student use. A campuswide network can be accessed from off campus. Internet access is available. *Web address:* http://www.sco.edu/.

General Application Contact: Joseph H. Hauser, Director of Records and Admissions, 901-722-3228, Fax: 901-722-3328, E-mail: jhauser@sco.edu.

GRADUATE UNITS

Professional Program Offers optometry (OD).

SOUTHERN CONNECTICUT STATE UNIVERSITY, New Haven, CT 06515-1355

General Information State-supported, coed, comprehensive institution. CGS member. *Enrollment:* 718 full-time matriculated graduate/professional students (538 women), 3,209 part-time matriculated graduate/professional students (2,393 women). *Enrollment by degree level:* 3,583 master's, 344 other advanced degrees. *Graduate faculty:* 343 full-time (134 women), 400 part-time/adjunct. *Graduate housing:* Room and/or apartments available on a first-come, first-served basis to single students; on-campus housing not available to married students. *Student services:* Campus employment opportunities, campus safety program, career counseling, child daycare facilities, disabled student services, exercise/wellness program, free psychological counseling, grant writing training, international student services, low-cost health insurance, multicultural affairs office, teacher training, writing training. *Library facilities:* Hilton C. Buley Library. *Online resources:* library catalog, web page, access to other libraries' catalogs. *Collection:* 495,660 titles, 3,549 serial subscriptions.

Computer facilities: 300 computers available on campus for general student use. A campuswide network can be accessed from student residence rooms and from off campus. Internet access is available. *Web address:* http://www.southernct.edu/.

General Application Contact: Jennifer Croffy, Assistant to the Dean, 203-392-5337, Fax: 203-392-5235, E-mail: croffy@southernct.edu.

GRADUATE UNITS

School of Graduate Studies Students: 718 full-time (538 women), 3,209 part-time (2,393 women); includes 303 minority (172 African Americans, 41 Asian Americans or Pacific Islanders, 89 Hispanic Americans, 1 Native American), 22 international. 3,116 applicants, 36% accepted. *Faculty:* 343 full-time (134 women), 400 part-time/adjunct. Expenses: Contact institution. *Financial support:* Fellowships, research assistantships, teaching assistantships, career-related internships or fieldwork available. Support available to part-time students. Financial award application deadline: 4/15; financial award applicants required to submit FAFSA. In 2001, 886 master's, 242 other advanced degrees awarded. *Degree program information:* Part-time and evening/weekend programs available. Postbaccalaureate distance learning degree programs offered (no on-campus study). *Application deadline:* Applications are processed on a rolling basis. *Application fee:* $40. *Application Contact:* Jennifer Croffy, Assistant to the Dean, 203-329-5337, Fax: 203-329-5235, E-mail: croffy@scsu.ctstate.edu. *Dean*, Dr. Sandra Holley, 203-392-5240, Fax: 203-392-5235, E-mail: holley@southernct.edu.

School of Arts and Sciences Students: 134 full-time, 431 part-time. 662 applicants, 31% accepted. *Faculty:* 44 full-time, 16 part-time/adjunct. Expenses: Contact institution. *Financial support:* Teaching assistantships, career-related internships or fieldwork available. In 2001, 132 degrees awarded. Offers art education (MS); arts and sciences (MA, MS, Diploma); biology (MS); biology for nurse anesthetists (MS); chemistry (MS); English (MA, MS); environmental education (MS); French (MA); history (MA, MS); mathematics (MS); multicultural-bilingual education/teaching English to speakers of other languages (MS); political science (MS); psychology (MA); Romance languages (MA); science education (MS, Diploma); sociology (MS); Spanish (MA); women's studies (MA). *Application fee:* $40. *Interim Dean*, Dr. Donna Jean Fredeen, 203-392-5468.

School of Business Students: 65 full-time (28 women), 9 part-time (5 women); includes 19 minority (16 African Americans, 3 Asian Americans or Pacific Islanders), 3 international. 65 applicants, 71% accepted. *Faculty:* 28 full-time (5 women). Expenses: Contact institution. *Financial support:* Application deadline: 4/15; In 2001, 36 degrees awarded. *Degree program information:* Evening/weekend programs available. Offers business (MBA); business administration (MBA). *Application deadline:* For fall admission, 7/1 (priority date). Applications are processed on a rolling basis. *Application fee:* $40. *Application Contact:* Dan Mitchell, Coordinator, 203-392-5881, Fax: 203-392-5988, E-mail: mitchell_d@southernct.edu. *Dean*, Dr. Kenneth L. Kraft, 203-392-5987, E-mail: kraft@southernct.edu.

School of Communication, Information and Library Science Students: 27 full-time (23 women), 175 part-time (149 women); includes 6 minority (5 African Americans, 1 Hispanic American), 1 international. 244 applicants, 32% accepted. *Faculty:* 6 full-time (4 women). Expenses: Contact institution. *Financial support:* Research assistantships available. Financial award application deadline: 4/15; financial award applicants required to submit FAFSA. In 2001, 76 master's, 2 other advanced degrees awarded. *Degree program information:* Part-time and evening/weekend programs available. Offers communication, information and library science (MLS, MS, Diploma); instructional technology (MS); library science (MLS); library/information studies (Diploma). *Application deadline:* For fall admission, 7/15 (priority date). Applications are processed on a rolling basis. *Application fee:* $40. *Dean*, Dr. Edward Harris, 203-392-5701.

School of Education Students: 1,618. *Faculty:* 56 full-time, 31 part-time/adjunct. Expenses: Contact institution. *Financial support:* Research assistantships, teaching assistantships, career-related internships or fieldwork available. *Degree program information:* Part-time programs available. Offers classroom teacher specialist (Diploma); community counseling (MS); counseling (Diploma); education (MS, MS Ed, Diploma); educational leadership (Diploma); elementary education (MS); foundational studies (Diploma); human performance (MS); physical education (MS); reading (MS, Diploma); research, measurement and quantitative analysis (MS); school counseling (MS); school health education (MS); school psychology (MS, Diploma); special education (MS Ed, Diploma); sport psychology (MS). *Application fee:* $40. *Dean*, Dr. Rodney Lane, 203-392-5900.

School of Health and Human Services Students: 275 full-time (240 women), 283 part-time (228 women); includes 74 minority (40 African Americans, 6 Asian Americans or Pacific Islanders, 28 Hispanic Americans), 3 international. *Faculty:* 35 full-time, 20 part-time/adjunct. Expenses: Contact institution. *Financial support:* Teaching assistantships, career-related internships or fieldwork available. Financial award application deadline: 4/15; financial award applicants required to submit FAFSA. In 2001, 175 degrees awarded. *Degree program information:* Part-time and evening/weekend programs available. Offers audiology (MS); health and human services (MFT, MPH, MS, MSN, MSW); marriage and family therapy (MFT); nursing administration (MSN); nursing education (MSN); public health (MPH); recreation and leisure studies (MS); social work (MSW); speech pathology (MS); urban studies (MS). *Application fee:* $40. *Dean*, Dr. Fay Miller, 203-392-6906.

Announcement: The University maintains a high standard of excellence in its programs and seeks to instill in its students a desire for continuing self-education and self-development. Each school of the University has developed its graduate programs in accordance with the highest national standards for the respective fields.

See in-depth description on page 1097.

SOUTHERN EVANGELICAL SEMINARY, Charlotte, NC 28270

General Information Independent-religious, graduate-only institution.

GRADUATE UNITS

Graduate School of Ministry and Missions Offers biblical studies (Certificate); Christian ministries (MACM); church ministry (Certificate); divinity (Certificate); theology (M Div).

Veritas Graduate School of Apologetics and Counter-Cult Ministry Offers apologetics (MA, Certificate); apologetics and counter-cults (M Min); ministry (Certificate).

SOUTHERN ILLINOIS UNIVERSITY CARBONDALE, Carbondale, IL 62901-6806

General Information State-supported, coed, university. CGS member. *Enrollment:* 2,178 full-time matriculated graduate/professional students (1,110 women), 2,618 part-time matriculated graduate/professional students (1,401 women). *Graduate faculty:* 1,074 full-time (262 women), 112 part-time/adjunct. Tuition, state resident: full-time $3,794; part-time $154 per hour. Tuition, nonresident: full-time $6,566; part-time $308 per hour. *Required fees:* $277 per hour. *Graduate housing:* Rooms and/or apartments available on a first-come, first-served basis to single and married students. *Student services:* Campus employment opportunities, campus safety program, career counseling, child daycare facilities, disabled student services, exercise/wellness program, free psychological counseling, grant writing training, international student services, low-cost health insurance, teacher training. *Library facilities:* Morris Library plus 1 other. *Online resources:* library catalog, web page, access to other libraries' catalogs. *Collection:* 4 million titles, 20,450 serial subscriptions, 365,392 audiovisual materials. *Research affiliation:* Argonne National Laboratory, NASA–Ames Research Center.

Computer facilities: 1,426 computers available on campus for general student use. A campuswide network can be accessed from student residence rooms and from off campus. Internet access and online class registration are available. *Web address:* http://www.siuc.edu.

General Application Contact: Associate Dean of the Graduate School, 618-536-7791.

GRADUATE UNITS

Graduate School Students: 1,478 full-time (776 women), 2,615 part-time (1,400 women); includes 533 minority (366 African Americans, 76 Asian Americans or Pacific Islanders, 68 Hispanic Americans, 23 Native Americans), 942 international. 1,798 applicants, 61% accepted. *Faculty:* 780 full-time (198 women), 14 part-time/adjunct (9 women). Expenses: Contact institution. *Financial support:* In 2001–02, 1,516 students received support, including 59 fellowships with full tuition reimbursements available, 536 research assistantships with full tuition reimbursements available, 980 teaching assistantships with full tuition reimbursements available; career-related internships or fieldwork, Federal Work-Study, institutionally sponsored loans, tuition waivers (full), and dissertation research awards, clinical assistantships also available. Support available to part-time students. In 2001, 820 master's, 119 doctorates awarded. *Degree program information:* Part-time programs available. *Application deadline:* Applications are processed on a rolling basis. *Application Contact:* Lu Lyons, Supervisor, Admissions, 618-453-4512, E-mail: llyons@siu.edu. *Acting Dean*, Dr. John Koropchak, 618-536-7791.

College of Agriculture Students: 75 full-time (33 women), 66 part-time (39 women); includes 7 minority (6 Hispanic Americans, 1 Native American), 14 international. 44 applicants, 66% accepted, 29 enrolled. *Faculty:* 51 full-time (8 women). Expenses: Contact institution. *Financial support:* In 2001–02, 35 students received support, including 31 research assistantships; fellowships, teaching assistantships, career-related internships or fieldwork, Federal Work-Study, institutionally sponsored loans, and tuition waivers (full) also available. Support available to part-time students. In 2001, 47 degrees awarded. *Degree program information:* Part-time programs available. Offers agribusiness economics (MS); agriculture (MS); animal science (MS); food and nutrition (MS); forestry (MS); horticultural science (MS); plant and soil science (MS). *Application deadline:* Applications are processed on a rolling basis. *Application fee:* $0. *Dean*, David Shoup.

College of Business and Administration Students: 177 full-time (94 women), 72 part-time (31 women); includes 24 minority (15 African Americans, 8 Asian Americans or Pacific Islanders, 1 Native American), 122 international. Average age 26. 220 applicants, 48% accepted. *Faculty:* 42 full-time (4 women). Expenses: Contact institution. *Financial support:* In 2001–02, 123 students received support, including 2 fellowships, 42 research assistantships, 49 teaching assistantships; Federal Work-Study, institutionally sponsored loans, and tuition waivers (full) also available. Support available to part-time students. In 2001, 148 master's, 9 doctorates awarded. *Degree program information:* Part-time programs available. Offers accountancy (M Acc, PhD); business administration (MBA, PhD). *Application deadline:* For fall admission, 6/15 (priority date). Applications are processed on a rolling basis. *Application fee:* $20. *Application Contact:* Barbara Humphrey, Administrative Aide, 618-453-3030, Fax: 618-453-7961, E-mail: barbh@siu.edu. *Dean*, Dan Worrell, 618-453-3328.

College of Education Students: 356 full-time (241 women), 661 part-time (456 women); includes 140 minority (111 African Americans, 11 Asian Americans or Pacific Islanders, 14 Hispanic Americans, 4 Native Americans), 128 international. Average age 34. 457 applicants, 61% accepted. *Faculty:* 175 full-time (74 women), 25 part-time/adjunct (6 women). Expenses: Contact institution. *Financial support:* In 2001–02, 306 students received support, including 8 fellowships, 115 research assistantships, 166 teaching assistantships; career-related internships or fieldwork, Federal Work-Study, institutionally sponsored loans, traineeships, tuition waivers (full), and unspecified assistantships also available. Support available to part-time students. In 2001, 324 master's, 36 doctorates awarded. *Degree program information:* Part-time programs available. Offers behavioral analysis and therapy (MS); communication disorders and sciences (MS); counselor education (MS Ed, PhD); curriculum and instruction (MS Ed, PhD); education (MS, MS Ed, MSW, PhD, Rh D); educational administration (MS Ed, PhD); educational psychology (MS Ed, PhD); health education (MS Ed, PhD); higher education (MS Ed); human learning and development (MS Ed); measurement and statistics (PhD); physical education (MS Ed); recreation (MS Ed); rehabilitation (Rh D); rehabilitation administration and services (MS); rehabilitation counseling (MS); social work (MSW); special education (MS Ed); workforce education and development (MS Ed, PhD). *Application fee:* $20. *Dean*, Dr. William A. Henk, 618-453-2415.

College of Engineering Students: 169 full-time (25 women), 109 part-time (25 women); includes 25 minority (11 African Americans, 10 Asian Americans or Pacific Islanders, 1 Hispanic American, 3 Native Americans), 174 international. 327 applicants, 32% accepted. *Faculty:* 55 full-time (3 women), 3 part-time/adjunct (0 women). Expenses: Contact institution. *Financial support:* In 2001–02, 112 students received support, including 1 fellowship, 58 research assistantships, 95 teaching assistantships; Federal Work-Study, institutionally sponsored loans, and tuition waivers (full) also available. Support available to part-time students. In 2001, 60 master's, 3 doctorates awarded. Offers civil engineering and mechanics (MS); electrical engineering (MS); electrical systems (PhD); engineering (MS, PhD); fossil energy (PhD); manufacturing systems (MS); mechanical engineering and energy processes (MS); mechanics (PhD); mining engineering (MS). *Application deadline:* Applications are processed on a rolling basis. *Application fee:* $20. *Application Contact:* Dr. James Evers, Associate Dean of Research and Graduate Programs, 618-453-4321, Fax: 618-453-4235, E-mail: evers@sysa.c_engri.siu.edu. *Dean*, Dr. George Swisher, 618-536-2368.

College of Liberal Arts Students: 665 full-time (340 women), 355 part-time (177 women); includes 106 minority (54 African Americans, 19 Asian Americans or Pacific Islanders, 27 Hispanic Americans, 6 Native Americans), 211 international. 676 applicants, 40% accepted. *Faculty:* 254 full-time (87 women), 8 part-time/adjunct (3 women). Expenses: Contact institution. *Financial support:* In 2001–02, 608 students received support, including 24 fellowships, 146 research assistantships, 325 teaching assistantships; career-related internships or fieldwork, Federal Work-Study, institutionally sponsored loans, scholarships/grants, and tuition waivers (full) also available. Support available to part-time students. In 2001, 160 master's, 48 doctorates awarded. *Degree program information:* Part-time programs available. Offers administration of justice (MA); anthropology (MA, PhD); applied linguistics (MA); ceramics (MFA); clinical psychology (MA, MS, PhD); composition (MA, PhD); composition and theory (MM); counseling psychology (MA, MS, PhD); creative

Southern Illinois University Carbondale (continued)

writing (MFA); drawing (MFA); economics (MA, MS, PhD); experimental psychology (MA, MS, PhD); fiber/weaving (MFA); foreign languages and literatures (MA); geography (MS, PhD); glass (MFA); history (MA, PhD); history and literature (MM); jewelry (MFA); liberal arts (MA, MFA, MM, MPA, MS, PhD); literature (MA, PhD); metals/blacksmithing (MFA); music education (MM); opera/music theater (MM); painting (MFA); performance (MM); philosophy (MA, PhD); piano pedagogy (MM); political science (MA, PhD); printmaking (MFA); public administration (MPA); rhetoric (MA, PhD); sculpture (MFA); sociology (MA, PhD); speech communication (MA, MS, PhD); speech/theater (PhD); teaching English as a second language (MA); theater (MFA). *Application deadline:* Applications are processed on a rolling basis. *Dean,* Dr. Shirley Scott Clay, 618-453-2466.

College of Mass Communication and Media Arts Students: 89 full-time (50 women), 85 part-time (40 women); includes 18 minority (11 African Americans, 5 Asian Americans or Pacific Islanders, 2 Hispanic Americans), 66 international. Average age 28. 156 applicants, 26% accepted. *Faculty:* 35 full-time (9 women), 2 part-time/adjunct (0 women). Expenses: Contact institution. *Financial support:* In 2001–02, 75 students received support; fellowships, research assistantships, teaching assistantships, career-related internships or fieldwork, Federal Work-Study, institutionally sponsored loans, and tuition waivers (full) available. Support available to part-time students. In 2001, 25 master's, 5 doctorates awarded. *Degree program information:* Part-time programs available. Offers mass communication and media arts (MA, MFA, PhD). *Application deadline:* Applications are processed on a rolling basis. *Application fee:* $20. *Director of Graduate Studies,* Dr. Thomas Johnson, 618-453-3279, E-mail: jschool@siu.edu.

College of Science Students: 243 full-time (91 women), 158 part-time (59 women); includes 22 minority (12 African Americans, 4 Asian Americans or Pacific Islanders, 2 Hispanic Americans, 4 Native Americans), 170 international. 562 applicants, 23% accepted. *Faculty:* 137 full-time (8 women), 2 part-time/adjunct (0 women). Expenses: Contact institution. *Financial support:* In 2001–02, 239 students received support, including 11 fellowships, 90 research assistantships, 160 teaching assistantships; career-related internships or fieldwork, Federal Work-Study, institutionally sponsored loans, scholarships/grants, and tuition waivers (full) also available. Support available to part-time students. In 2001, 52 master's, 15 doctorates awarded. *Degree program information:* Part-time programs available. Offers biological sciences (MS); chemistry and biochemistry (MS, PhD); computer science (MS); environmental resources and policy (PhD); geology (MS, PhD); mathematics (MA, MS, PhD); molecular biology, microbiology, and biochemistry (MS, PhD); physics (MS); plant biology (MS, PhD); science (MA, MS, PhD); statistics (MS); zoology (MS, PhD). *Application deadline:* Applications are processed on a rolling basis. *Application Contact:* William G. Dyer, Associate Dean, 618-536-6666. *Dean,* Jack Parker, 618-536-6666.

School of Law Students: 347 full-time (156 women), 3 part-time (1 woman); includes 28 minority (11 African Americans, 9 Asian Americans or Pacific Islanders, 7 Hispanic Americans, 1 Native American), 3 international. Average age 27. 592 applicants, 64% accepted. *Faculty:* 27 full-time (11 women), 10 part-time/adjunct (7 women). Expenses: Contact institution. *Financial support:* In 2001–02, 340 students received support. Career-related internships or fieldwork, Federal Work-Study, institutionally sponsored loans, and scholarships/grants available. Support available to part-time students. Financial award applicants required to submit FAFSA. In 2001, 127 degrees awarded. *Degree program information:* Part-time programs available. Offers law (JD). *Application deadline:* For fall admission, 3/1 (priority date). Applications are processed on a rolling basis. *Application fee:* $40. Electronic applications accepted. *Application Contact:* Michael P. Ruiz, Assistant Dean for Admissions and Student Affairs, 618-453-8858, Fax: 618-453-8769, E-mail: mikeruiz@siu.edu. *Dean,* Thomas F. Guernsey, 618-536-7711.

School of Medicine Students: 290 full-time (120 women). *Faculty:* 251 full-time (80 women), 22 part-time/adjunct (9 women). Expenses: Contact institution. *Financial support:* Fellowships, research assistantships, teaching assistantships, institutionally sponsored loans and tuition waivers (full) available. In 2001, 3 master's, 5 doctorates awarded. Offers medicine (MD, MS, PhD); pharmacology (MS, PhD); physiology (MS, PhD). *Dean and Provost,* Dr. Carl J. Getto, 217-782-3318.

Announcement: Southern Illinois University Carbondale has a diverse graduate program across all of its departments. Students can attain degrees at both master's and doctoral levels in a variety of areas and concentrations. Many graduates have gone on to leadership positions in their respective fields.

See in-depth description on page 1099.

SOUTHERN ILLINOIS UNIVERSITY EDWARDSVILLE, Edwardsville, IL 62026-0001

General Information State-supported, coed, comprehensive institution. CGS member. *Enrollment:* 859 full-time matriculated graduate/professional students (434 women), 1,436 part-time matriculated graduate/professional students (900 women). *Enrollment by degree level:* 199 first professional, 2,068 master's, 28 other advanced degrees. *Graduate faculty:* 523 full-time (198 women), 217 part-time/adjunct (133 women). Tuition, state resident: full-time $2,712; part-time $113 per credit hour. Tuition, nonresident: full-time $5,424; part-time $226 per credit hour. *Required fees:* $250; $125 per term. $125 per term. Tuition and fees vary according to course load, campus/location and reciprocity agreements. *Graduate housing:* Rooms and/or apartments available on a first-come, first-served basis to single and married students. Typical cost: $4,200 per year ($5,200 including board) for single students; $7,970 (including board) for married students. Room and board charges vary according to board plan, campus/location and housing facility selected. Housing application deadline: 5/1. *Student services:* Campus employment opportunities, campus safety program, career counseling, child daycare facilities, disabled student services, exercise/wellness program, free psychological counseling, grant writing training, international student services, low-cost health insurance, multicultural affairs office, teacher training, writing training. *Library facilities:* Lovejoy Library. *Online resources:* library catalog, web page, access to other libraries' catalogs. *Collection:* 763,443 titles, 12,174 serial subscriptions, 28,400 audiovisual materials.

Computer facilities: 550 computers available on campus for general student use. A campuswide network can be accessed from student residence rooms and from off campus. Internet access is available. *Web address:* http://www.siue.edu/.

General Application Contact: Dr. Stephen L. Hansen, Dean of Graduate Studies and Research, 618-650-3010, Fax: 618-650-3523, E-mail: shansen@siue.edu.

GRADUATE UNITS

Graduate Studies and Research Students: 660 full-time (364 women), 1,436 part-time (900 women); includes 186 minority (127 African Americans, 23 Asian Americans or Pacific Islanders, 27 Hispanic Americans, 9 Native Americans), 347 international. Average age 33. 1,731 applicants, 72% accepted, 722 enrolled. *Faculty:* 512 full-time (192 women), 120 part-time/adjunct (69 women). Expenses: Contact institution. *Financial support:* In 2001–02, 19 fellowships with full tuition reimbursements (averaging $7,533 per year), 75 research assistantships with full tuition reimbursements (averaging $7,633 per year), 117 teaching assistantships with full tuition reimbursements (averaging $7,533 per year) were awarded. Career-related internships or fieldwork, Federal Work-Study, institutionally sponsored loans, scholarships/grants, traineeships, tuition waivers (full), and unspecified assistantships also available. Support available to part-time students. Financial award application deadline: 3/1; financial award applicants required to submit FAFSA. In 2001, 681 master's, 5 other advanced degrees awarded. *Degree program information:* Part-time programs available. *Application deadline:* For fall admission, 7/20; for spring admission, 12/7. Applications are processed on a rolling basis. *Application fee:* $25. *Application Contact:* Linda Skelton, Staff Assistant, 618-650-2958, Fax: 618-650-3523, E-mail: lskelto@siue.edu. *Dean of Graduate Studies and Research,* Dr. Stephen L. Hansen, 618-650-3010, Fax: 618-650-3523, E-mail: shansen@siue.edu.

College of Arts and Sciences Students: 205 full-time (133 women), 342 part-time (198 women); includes 79 minority (59 African Americans, 7 Asian Americans or Pacific Islanders, 8 Hispanic Americans, 5 Native Americans), 50 international. Average age 33. 346 applicants, 71% accepted, 181 enrolled. *Faculty:* 252 full-time (89 women), 63 part-time/adjunct (32 women). Expenses: Contact institution. *Financial support:* In 2001–02, 10 fellowships with full tuition reimbursements, 10 research assistantships with full tuition reimbursements, 68 teaching assistantships with full tuition reimbursements were awarded. Career-related internships or fieldwork, Federal Work-Study, institutionally sponsored loans, scholarships/grants, traineeships, and unspecified assistantships also available. Support available to part-time students. Financial award application deadline: 3/1. In 2001, 132 degrees awarded. *Degree program information:* Part-time programs available. Offers American and English literature (MA); art therapy counseling (MA); arts and sciences (MA, MFA, MM, MPA, MS, MSW); biological sciences (MA, MS); ceramics (MFA); chemistry (MS); drawing (MFA); environmental sciences (MS); fiber/fabrics (MFA); geography (MA, MS); history (MA); mass communication (MS); mathematics and statistics (MS); music education (MM); music performance (MM); painting (MFA); physics (MS); printmaking (MFA); public administration (MPA); sculpture (MFA); social work (MSW); sociology (MA); speech communication (MA); teaching English as a second language (MA); teaching of writing (MA). *Application deadline:* For fall admission, 7/20; for spring admission, 12/7. Applications are processed on a rolling basis. *Application fee:* $25. *Dean,* Dr. M. Kent Neely, 618-650-5047, E-mail: kneely@siue.edu.

School of Business Students: 114 full-time (52 women), 229 part-time (104 women); includes 27 minority (17 African Americans, 4 Asian Americans or Pacific Islanders, 5 Hispanic Americans, 1 Native American), 79 international. Average age 33. 203 applicants, 89% accepted, 99 enrolled. *Faculty:* 65 full-time (14 women), 14 part-time/adjunct (6 women). Expenses: Contact institution. *Financial support:* In 2001–02, 1 fellowship with full tuition reimbursement, 18 research assistantships with full tuition reimbursements were awarded. Teaching assistantships with full tuition reimbursements, career-related internships or fieldwork, Federal Work-Study, institutionally sponsored loans, traineeships, and unspecified assistantships also available. Support available to part-time students. Financial award application deadline: 3/1; financial award applicants required to submit FAFSA. In 2001, 123 degrees awarded. *Degree program information:* Part-time programs available. Offers accountancy (MSA); business (MA, MBA, MMR, MS, MSA); business administration (MBA); e-business (MBA); economics and finance (MA, MS); management information systems (MBA); marketing research (MBA, MMR). *Application deadline:* For fall admission, 7/20; for spring admission, 12/7. *Application fee:* $25. *Application Contact:* Dr. Kathryn Martell, Associate Dean, 618-650-2485, E-mail: kmartel@siue.edu. *Dean,* Dr. M. Robert Carver, 618-650-3823, E-mail: bcarver@siue.edu.

School of Education Students: 146 full-time (124 women), 610 part-time (470 women); includes 60 minority (41 African Americans, 5 Asian Americans or Pacific Islanders, 12 Hispanic Americans, 2 Native Americans), 10 international. Average age 33. 347 applicants, 63% accepted, 155 enrolled. *Faculty:* 68 full-time (33 women), 31 part-time/adjunct (24 women). Expenses: Contact institution. *Financial support:* In 2001–02, 6 fellowships with full tuition reimbursements, 1 research assistantship with full tuition reimbursement, 10 teaching assistantships with full tuition reimbursements were awarded. Career-related internships or fieldwork, Federal Work-Study, institutionally sponsored loans, traineeships, and unspecified assistantships also available. Support available to part-time students. Financial award application deadline: 3/1; financial award applicants required to submit FAFSA. In 2001, 275 master's, 6 other advanced degrees awarded. *Degree program information:* Part-time programs available. Offers clinical adult (MS); community school (MS); education (MA, MS, MS Ed, Certificate, Ed S); educational administration and supervision (MS Ed, Ed S); elementary education (MS Ed); exercise physiology (Certificate); general academic (MA); industrial organizational (MS); instructional technology (MS Ed); kinesiology and health education (MS Ed); pedigogy/administration (Certificate); school psychology (Ed S); secondary education (MS Ed); special education and communication disorders (MS Ed); speech pathology (MS); sports and exercise behavior (Certificate). *Application deadline:* For fall admission, 7/20; for spring admission, 12/7. *Application fee:* $25. *Application Contact:* Dr. Lela DeToye, Associate Dean, 618-650-3358, E-mail: ldetoye@siue.edu. *Dean,* Dr. Elliott Lessen, 618-650-3350, E-mail: elessen@siue.edu.

School of Engineering Students: 145 full-time (24 women), 146 part-time (30 women); includes 10 minority (3 African Americans, 6 Asian Americans or Pacific Islanders, 1 Native American), 208 international. Average age 33. 336 applicants, 56% accepted, 80 enrolled. *Faculty:* 40 full-time (3 women), 9 part-time/adjunct (1 woman). Expenses: Contact institution. *Financial support:* In 2001–02, 11 research assistantships with full tuition reimbursements, 12 teaching assistantships with full tuition reimbursements were awarded. Fellowships with full tuition reimbursements, career-related internships or fieldwork, Federal Work-Study, institutionally sponsored loans, scholarships/grants, traineeships, and unspecified assistantships also available. Support available to part-time students. Financial award application deadline: 3/1; financial award applicants required to submit FAFSA. In 2001, 91 degrees awarded. *Degree program information:* Part-time programs available. Offers civil engineering (MS); computer information systems (MS); electrical engineering (MS); engineering (MS); mechanical engineering (MS). *Application deadline:* For fall admission, 7/20; for spring admission, 12/7. *Application fee:* $25. *Application Contact:* Dr. Jacob Van Roekel, Associate Dean, 618-650-2534, E-mail: jvanroe@siue.edu. *Dean,* Dr. Paul Seaburg, 618-650-2861, E-mail: pseabur@siue.edu.

School of Nursing Students: 50 full-time (31 women), 82 part-time (79 women); includes 10 minority (7 African Americans, 1 Asian American or Pacific Islander, 2 Hispanic Americans) Average age 33. 101 applicants, 83% accepted, 70 enrolled. *Faculty:* 38 full-time (36 women), 18 part-time/adjunct (17 women). Expenses: Contact institution. *Financial support:* In 2001–02, 2 fellowships with full tuition reimbursements were awarded; research assistantships, teaching assistantships, career-related internships or fieldwork, Federal Work-Study, institutionally sponsored loans, scholarships/grants, traineeships, and unspecified assistantships also available. Support available to part-time students. Financial award application deadline: 3/1; financial award applicants required to submit FAFSA. In 2001, 78 degrees awarded. Offers community health nursing (MS); medical-surgical nursing (MS); nurse anesthesia (MS); nurse practitioner nursing (MS); psychiatric nursing (MS). *Application deadline:* For fall admission, 7/20; for spring admission, 12/7. *Application fee:* $25. *Application Contact:* Dr. Wendy Nehring, Director, 618-650-3934, E-mail: wnehrin@siue.edu. *Dean,* Dr. Felissa Lashley, 618-650-3959, E-mail: flashle@siue.edu.

School of Dental Medicine Students: 194 full-time (68 women); includes 35 minority (8 African Americans, 20 Asian Americans or Pacific Islanders, 3 Hispanic Americans, 4 Native Americans), 1 international. Average age 25. 413 applicants, 26% accepted, 49 enrolled. *Faculty:* 36 full-time (8 women), 39 part-time/adjunct (14 women). Expenses: Contact institution. In 2001, 48 degrees awarded. Offers dental medicine (DMD). *Application deadline:* For fall admission, 3/1 (priority date). *Application fee:* $25. *Dean,* Dr. Patrick Ferrillo, 618-474-7120, E-mail: pferril@siue.edu.

See in-depth description on page 1101.

SOUTHERN METHODIST UNIVERSITY, Dallas, TX 75275

General Information Independent-religious, coed, university. CGS member. *Enrollment:* 1,095 full-time matriculated graduate/professional students, 2,595 part-time matriculated graduate/professional students. *Enrollment by degree level:* 1,093 first professional, 2,157 master's, 305 doctoral. *Graduate faculty:* 520 full-time. *Tuition:* Part-time $285 per credit hour. *Graduate housing:* Rooms and/or apartments available on a first-come, first-served basis to single students and available to married students. Housing application deadline: 5/31. *Student services:* Campus employment opportunities, campus safety program, career counseling, child daycare facilities, disabled student services, free psychological counseling, international student services, low-cost health insurance. *Library facilities:* Central University Library plus 7 others. *Online resources:* library catalog, web page, access to other libraries' catalogs. *Collection:* 3.1 million titles, 11,216 serial subscriptions. *Research affiliation:* Baylor Research Foundation, University of Texas Health Science Center.

Computer facilities: 409 computers available on campus for general student use. A campuswide network can be accessed from student residence rooms and from off campus. *Web address:* http://www. smu.edu/.

General Application Contact: Dr. U. Narayan Bhat, Dean of Research and Graduate Studies, 214-768-3268.

GRADUATE UNITS

Dedman College Students: 160 full-time (89 women), 455 part-time (288 women); includes 85 minority (24 African Americans, 18 Asian Americans or Pacific Islanders, 42 Hispanic Americans, 1 Native American), 86 international. Average age 31. 572 applicants, 46% accepted. *Faculty:* 241 full-time (72 women). Expenses: Contact institution. *Financial support:* Fellowships, research assistantships with full tuition reimbursements, teaching assistantships with full tuition reimbursements, career-related internships or fieldwork, Federal Work-Study, institutionally sponsored loans, scholarships/grants, and tuition waivers (full and partial) available. Support available to part-time students. Financial award applicants required to submit FAFSA. In 2001, 89 master's, 19 doctorates awarded. *Degree program information:* Part-time and evening/weekend programs available. Offers anthropology (MA, PhD); applied economics (MA); applied geophysics (MS); applied mathematics (MS); archaeology (MA, PhD); bilingual education (MBE); biological sciences (MA, MS, PhD); chemistry (MS); clinical and counseling psychology (MA); economics (MA, PhD); English (MA); exploration geophysics (MS); geology (MS, PhD); geophysics (MS, PhD); history (MA, PhD); Latin American studies (MA); liberal arts (MBE, MLA); mathematical sciences (PhD); medical anthropology (MA, PhD); medieval studies (MA); physics (MS, PhD); psychology (MA, PhD); religious studies (MA, PhD); statistical science (MS, PhD). *Application deadline:* Applications are processed on a rolling basis. *Application fee:* $50. *Dean,* Dr. Jasper Neel, 214-768-3212.

Dedman School of Law Students: 875 (398 women); includes 78 minority (12 African Americans, 34 Asian Americans or Pacific Islanders, 27 Hispanic Americans, 5 Native Americans) 34 international. Average age 26. 1,538 applicants, 42% accepted. *Faculty:* 39 full-time (13 women). Expenses: Contact institution. *Financial support:* Federal Work-Study and scholarships/grants available. Financial award application deadline: 2/1; financial award applicants required to submit FAFSA. In 2001, 230 first professional degrees, 60 master's awarded. Offers comparative and international law (LL M); law (JD, LL M, SJD); taxation (LL M). *Application deadline:* For fall admission, 2/15 (priority date). Applications are processed on a rolling basis. *Application fee:* $50. Electronic applications accepted. *Application Contact:* Lynn Bozalis, Assistant Dean for Admissions, 214-768-2550, Fax: 214-768-2549. *Dean,* John B. Attanasio, 214-768-8999, Fax: 214-768-2182, E-mail: jba@mail.smu.edu.

Edwin L. Cox School of Business Students: 988; includes 152 minority (36 African Americans, 71 Asian Americans or Pacific Islanders, 40 Hispanic Americans, 5 Native Americans), 115 international. Average age 31. 600 applicants, 33% accepted. *Faculty:* 71 full-time (18 women). Expenses: Contact institution. *Financial support:* In 2001–02, 70 fellowships (averaging $15,000 per year) were awarded; research assistantships, career-related internships or fieldwork, scholarships/grants, and tuition waivers (full and partial) also available. Support available to part-time students. Financial award application deadline: 3/1; financial award applicants required to submit FAFSA. In 2001, 375 degrees awarded. *Degree program information:* Part-time and evening/weekend programs available. Offers accounting (MSA); business (Exec MBA, MBA, MSA). *Application deadline:* For fall admission, 3/30 (priority date); for spring admission, 11/30 (priority date). Applications are processed on a rolling basis. *Application fee:* $50. Electronic applications accepted. *Application Contact:* Dr. Marci Armstrong, Director of MBA Admissions, 214-768-3920, Fax: 214-768-3956, E-mail: marmstro@mail.cox.smu.edu. *Dean,* Dr. Albert Neimi, 214-768-3012, Fax: 214-768-3713, E-mail: aneimi@mail.cox.smu.edu.

Meadows School of the Arts Students: 167 (104 women); includes 21 minority (12 African Americans, 5 Asian Americans or Pacific Islanders, 3 Hispanic Americans, 1 Native American) 19 international. Average age 28. 196 applicants, 51% accepted. *Faculty:* 88 full-time (32 women), 45 part-time/adjunct (13 women). Expenses: Contact institution. *Financial support:* Research assistantships, teaching assistantships, career-related internships or fieldwork, scholarships/grants, and unspecified assistantships available. Financial award application deadline: 3/1; financial award applicants required to submit FAFSA. In 2001, 66 degrees awarded. *Degree program information:* Part-time programs available. Offers acting (MFA); art history (MA); arts (MA, MFA, MM, MMT, MSM); choreographic theory and practice (MFA); conducting (MM); design (MFA); directing (MFA); music composition (MM); music education (MM); music history (MM); music theory (MM); music therapy (MMT); performance (MM); piano performance and pedagogy (MM); sacred music (MSM); studio art (MFA). *Application fee:* $50. *Application Contact:* Jean Cherry, Director of Graduate Admissions and Records, 214-768-3765, Fax: 214-768-3272, E-mail: jcherry@mail.smu.edu. *Dean,* Carole Brandt, 214-768-2880.

Center for Communication Arts Students: 7 full-time (5 women), 3 part-time (1 woman); includes 2 minority (both African Americans), 6 international. Average age 30. 8 applicants, 75% accepted. *Faculty:* 22 full-time (7 women). Expenses: Contact institution. *Financial support:* In 2001–02, 7 students received support, including teaching assistantships with full tuition reimbursements available (averaging $5,006 per year); career-related internships or fieldwork also available. Financial award application deadline: 3/1; financial award applicants required to submit FAFSA. In 2001, 1 degree awarded. *Degree program information:* Part-time programs available. Offers communication arts (MA). *Application deadline:* For fall admission, 3/1 (priority date). *Application fee:* $50. *Application Contact:* Jean Cherry, Director of Graduate Admissions and Records, 214-768-3765, Fax: 214-768-3272, E-mail: jcherry@mail.smu.edu. *Director,* Alan Albarran, 214-768-3607.

Division of Arts Administration and Corporate Communications Students: 15 full-time (13 women); includes 2 minority (1 African American, 1 Hispanic American) Average age 24. 18 applicants, 50% accepted, 8 enrolled. *Faculty:* 5 full-time (all women). Expenses: Contact institution. *Financial support:* In 2001–02, 12 students received support. Tuition waivers (partial) available. Financial award application deadline: 3/1; financial award applicants required to submit FAFSA. Offers arts administration and corporate communications). *Application deadline:* For fall admission, 2/1 (priority date). Applications are processed on a rolling basis. *Application fee:* $50. *Application Contact:* Jean Cherry, Director of Graduate Admissions and Records, 214-768-3765, Fax: 214-768-3272, E-mail: jcherry@mail.smu.edu. *Director,* Dr. Gregory Poggi, 214-768-3425.

Perkins School of Theology Students: 243 full-time (102 women), 261 part-time (136 women); includes 114 minority (79 African Americans, 17 Asian Americans or Pacific Islanders, 15 Hispanic Americans, 3 Native Americans), 14 international. Average age 39. 240 applicants, 75% accepted, 134 enrolled. *Faculty:* 35 full-time (11 women). Expenses: Contact institution. *Financial support:* In 2001–02, 324 students received support, including 3 fellowships (averaging $14,984 per year); career-related internships or fieldwork, Federal Work-Study, and scholarships/grants also available. Support available to part-time students. Financial award applicants required to submit FAFSA. In 2001, 70 first professional degrees, 5 master's, 15 doctorates awarded. *Degree program information:* Part-time programs available. Offers theology (M Div, MRE, MSM, MTS, D Min). *Application deadline:* For fall admission, 5/1 (priority date); for spring admission, 11/1 (priority date). Applications are processed on a rolling basis. *Application fee:* $30. *Application Contact:* Shonda Jones, Admissions, 214-768-2139, Fax: 214-768-4245, E-mail: shondaj@mail.smu.edu. *Dean,* Dr. William Lawrence, 214-768-2125.

School of Engineering Students: 795 (164 women); includes 223 minority (49 African Americans, 125 Asian Americans or Pacific Islanders, 47 Hispanic Americans, 2 Native Americans) 197 international. Average age 32. 777 applicants, 42% accepted. *Faculty:* 48 full-time (5 women). Expenses: Contact institution. *Financial support:* Fellowships, research assistantships, teaching assistantships, career-related internships or fieldwork, Federal Work-Study, institutionally sponsored loans, scholarships/grants, and tuition waivers (full and partial) available. Financial award applicants required to submit FAFSA. In 2001, 217 master's, 18 doctorates awarded. *Degree program information:* Part-time programs available. Post-baccalaureate distance learning degree programs offered (no on-campus study). Offers applied science (MS, PhD); civil engineering (MS); computer engineering (MS Cp E, PhD); computer science (MS, PhD); electrical engineering (MSEE, PhD); engineering (MS, MS Cp E, MSEE, MSEM, MSME, DE, PhD); engineering management (MSEM, DE); environmental engineering (MS); envrionmental systems management (MS); manufacturing systems management (MS); mechanical engineering (MSME, PhD); operations research (MS, PhD); software engineering (MS); systems engineering (MS); telecommunications (MS). *Application deadline:* For fall admission, 7/1; for spring admission, 11/15. Applications are processed on a rolling basis. *Application fee:* $30. *Application Contact:* Jim Dees, Director, Student Administration, 214-768-1456, Fax: 214-768-3845, E-mail: jdees@engr.smu.edu. *Dean,* Dr. Stephen A. Szygenda, 214-768-3051, Fax: 214-768-3845, E-mail: szygenda@engr.smu.edu.

See in-depth description on page 1103.

SOUTHERN NAZARENE UNIVERSITY, Bethany, OK 73008

General Information Independent-religious, coed, comprehensive institution. *Graduate housing:* Rooms and/or apartments available to single and married students. Housing application deadline: 8/1.

GRADUATE UNITS

Graduate College *Degree program information:* Part-time and evening/weekend programs available. Offers practical theology (M Min); theology (MA). Electronic applications accepted.

School of Business *Degree program information:* Part-time and evening/weekend programs available. Offers business (MBA, MS Mgt). Electronic applications accepted.

School of Education *Degree program information:* Part-time and evening/weekend programs available. Offers education (MA).

School of Psychology Offers counseling psychology (MSCP); marriage and family therapy (MA).

SOUTHERN NEW ENGLAND SCHOOL OF LAW, North Dartmouth, MA 02747-1252

General Information Independent, coed, graduate-only institution. *Enrollment by degree level:* 156 first professional. *Graduate faculty:* 10 full-time (4 women), 21 part-time/adjunct (3 women). *Tuition:* Full-time $17,986; part-time $644 per credit. *Required fees:* $375. *Graduate housing:* On-campus housing not available. *Student services:* Campus employment opportunities, career counseling, free psychological counseling, low-cost health insurance, writing training. *Library facilities:* Southern New England School of Law Library. *Online resources:* library catalog, web page. *Collection:* 48,225 titles, 1,100 serial subscriptions, 246 audiovisual materials.

Computer facilities: 23 computers available on campus for general student use. A campuswide network can be accessed. Internet access and online class registration, email, listservs, financial aid are available. *Web address:* http://www.snesl.edu/.

General Application Contact: Nancy Fitzsimmons Hebert, Director of Admissions, 508-998-9400, Fax: 508-998-9561, E-mail: nhebert@snesl.edu.

GRADUATE UNITS

Professional Program Students: 57 full-time (30 women), 99 part-time (55 women); includes 29 minority (23 African Americans, 3 Asian Americans or Pacific Islanders, 3 Hispanic Americans), 1 international. Average age 37. 174 applicants, 87% accepted, 63 enrolled. *Faculty:* 10 full-time (4 women), 21 part-time/adjunct (3 women). Expenses: Contact institution. *Financial support:* In 2001–02, 125 students received support, including 3 research assistantships (averaging $2,400 per year); scholarships/grants and tuition waivers (full and partial) also available. Support available to part-time students. Financial award application deadline: 6/30; financial award applicants required to submit FAFSA. In 2001, 36 degrees awarded. *Degree program information:* Part-time and evening/weekend programs available. Offers law (JD). *Application deadline:* For fall admission, 6/30. Applications are processed on a rolling basis. *Application fee:* $50. *Application Contact:* Nancy Fitzsimmons Hebert, Director of Admissions, 508-998-9400, Fax: 508-998-9561, E-mail: nhebert@snesl.edu. *Dean,* Robert V. Ward, 508-998-9600 Ext. 170, Fax: 508-998-9561, E-mail: rward@snesl.edu.

SOUTHERN NEW HAMPSHIRE UNIVERSITY, Manchester, NH 03106-1045

General Information Independent, coed, comprehensive institution. *Enrollment:* 441 full-time matriculated graduate/professional students (180 women), 1,443 part-time matriculated graduate/professional students (643 women). *Enrollment by degree level:* 1,765 master's, 25 doctoral. *Graduate faculty:* 31 full-time (5 women), 104 part-time/adjunct (28 women). *Tuition:* Full-time $11,340; part-time $1,260 per course. One-time fee: $540 full-time. Full-time tuition and fees vary according to course load, degree level and program. *Graduate housing:* Room and/or apartments available to single students; on-campus housing not available to married students. Typical cost: $6,036 per year ($9,396 including board). Room and board charges vary according to housing facility selected. *Student services:* Campus employment opportunities, campus safety program, career counseling, disabled student services, exercise/wellness program, free psychological counseling, international student services, low-cost health insurance, multicultural affairs office, teacher training. *Library facilities:* Harry A. B. and Gertrude C. Shapiro Library. *Online resources:* library catalog, web page. *Collection:* 1,943 audiovisual materials.

Computer facilities: 250 computers available on campus for general student use. A campuswide network can be accessed from student residence rooms and from off campus. *Web address:* http://www.snhu.edu/.

General Application Contact: Patricia Gerard, Assistant Dean, Academic Services, School of Business, 603-644-3102, Fax: 603-644-3144, E-mail: p.gerard@snhu.edu.

GRADUATE UNITS

School of Business, Graduate Programs Students: 441 full-time (180 women), 1,443 part-time (643 women). Average age 32. *Faculty:* 31 full-time (5 women), 104 part-time/adjunct (28 women). Expenses: Contact institution. *Financial support:* In 2001–02, 1 fellowship, 10 research assistantships were awarded. Career-related internships or fieldwork, Federal Work-Study, institutionally sponsored loans, and tuition waivers (partial) also available. Support available to part-time students. In 2001, 584 master's awarded. *Degree program information:* Part-time and evening/weekend programs available. Offers accounting (Certificate); artificial intelligence (Certificate); business (MBA, MS, DBA, PhD, Certificate); business administration (MBA); business education (MS); computer information systems (MS, Certificate); computer informations systems (Certificate); database management (Certificate); finance (Certificate); health administration (Certificate); human resource management (Certificate); international business (Certificate); marketing (Certificate); operations management (Certificate); school business administration (Certificate); taxation (Certificate); telecommunications and networking (Certificate); training and development (Certificate). *Application deadline:* Applications are processed on a rolling basis. *Application Contact:* Patricia Gerard, Assistant Dean, Academic Services, School of Business, 603-644-3102, Fax: 603-644-3144, E-mail: p.gerard@snhu.edu. *Dean,* Dr. Paul Schneiderman, 603-644-3102, Fax: 603-644-3144, E-mail: schneipa@snhc.edu.

School of Community Economic Development Students: 20 full-time (9 women), 74 part-time (37 women), 30 international. Average age 30. *Faculty:* 4 full-time (1 woman), 13 part-time/adjunct (7 women). Expenses: Contact institution. *Financial support:* In 2001–02, 1 research assistantship was awarded; Federal Work-Study also available. Support available to part-time students. In 2001, 45 degrees awarded. *Degree program information:* Part-time and evening/weekend programs available. Offers community economic development (MS, PhD). *Application deadline:* Applications are processed on a rolling basis. *Application fee:* $20. *Application Contact:* Patricia Gerard, Assistant Dean, Academic Services, School of Business, 603-644-3102, Fax: 603-644-3144, E-mail: p.gerard@snhu.edu. *Director,* Dr. Michael Swack, E-mail: mswack@minerva.snhc.edu.

SOUTHERN OREGON UNIVERSITY, Ashland, OR 97520

General Information State-supported, coed, comprehensive institution. *Enrollment:* 221 full-time matriculated graduate/professional students (143 women), 147 part-time matriculated graduate/professional students (96 women). *Graduate faculty:* 190 full-time (73 women), 137 part-time/adjunct (69 women). Tuition, state resident: full-time $5,184; part-time $192 per credit. Tuition, nonresident: full-time $9,828; part-time $364 per credit. *Required fees:* $927. One-time fee: $75 full-time. Full-time tuition and fees vary according to course load, program and reciprocity agreements. *Graduate housing:* Rooms and/or apartments available on a first-come, first-served basis to single and married students. Typical cost: $5,445 (including board) for single students. Room and board charges vary according to board plan. *Student services:* Campus employment opportunities, campus safety program, career counseling,

Southern Oregon University (continued)

child daycare facilities, disabled student services, exercise/wellness program, free psychological counseling, international student services, low-cost health insurance, multicultural affairs office, teacher training, writing training. *Library facilities:* Southern Oregon University Library. *Online resources:* library catalog, web page, access to other libraries' catalogs. *Collection:* 260,662 titles, 2,076 serial subscriptions, 38,483 audiovisual materials. *Research affiliation:* U.S. Forest Service (biology, ecology studies), U.S. Fish and Wildlife Service (forensics), Oregon Shakespeare Festival, Crater Lake National Park (scientific studies), Bureau of Land Management (ecological studies), Bear Creek Corporation (environmental studies).

Computer facilities: 400 computers available on campus for general student use. A campuswide network can be accessed. *Web address:* http://www.sou.edu/.

General Application Contact: Mara Affre, Director of Admissions and Records, 541-552-6411, Fax: 541-552-6329, E-mail: affrem@sou.edu.

GRADUATE UNITS

Graduate Office Students: 221 full-time (143 women), 147 part-time (96 women); includes 18 minority (1 African American, 3 Asian Americans or Pacific Islanders, 9 Hispanic Americans, 5 Native Americans), 7 international. Average age 35. 245 applicants, 94% accepted, 187 enrolled. *Faculty:* 190 full-time (73 women), 137 part-time/adjunct (69 women). Expenses: Contact institution. *Financial support:* Fellowships, career-related internships or fieldwork, Federal Work-Study, institutionally sponsored loans, scholarships/grants, and unspecified assistantships available. Support available to part-time students. In 2001, 247 degrees awarded. *Degree program information:* Part-time programs available. *Application deadline:* Applications are processed on a rolling basis. *Application fee:* $50. Electronic applications accepted. *Application Contact:* Mara Affre, Director of Admissions and Records, 541-552-6411, Fax: 541-552-6329, E-mail: affrem@sou.edu. *Dean,* Dr. John Laughlin, 541-552-6483, Fax: 541-552-6329, E-mail: laughlin@sou.edu.

School of Arts and Letters Students: 3 full-time (2 women), 1 international. Average age 35. 2 applicants, 100% accepted. Expenses: Contact institution. In 2001, 21 degrees awarded. Offers arts and letters (MA, MS); music (MA, MS). *Application deadline:* Applications are processed on a rolling basis. *Application fee:* $50. Electronic applications accepted. *Application Contact:* Max McKee, Director, American Band College, 541-482-5030, E-mail: maxmckee@jeffnet.org. *Dean,* Dr. Edwin Battistella, 541-552-6520.

School of Business Students: 16 full-time (7 women), 35 part-time (21 women); includes 3 minority (1 Asian American or Pacific Islander, 2 Native Americans), 3 international. Average age 35. 20 applicants, 80% accepted, 16 enrolled. *Faculty:* 16 full-time (5 women). Expenses: Contact institution. *Financial support:* Career-related internships or fieldwork, Federal Work-Study, institutionally sponsored loans, scholarships/grants, and unspecified assistantships available. Support available to part-time students. In 2001, 13 degrees awarded. Offers business (MA Ed, MIM, MS Ed). *Application deadline:* Applications are processed on a rolling basis. *Application fee:* $50. Electronic applications accepted. *Dean,* Dr. John Laughlin, 541-552-6483, Fax: 541-552-6329, E-mail: laughlin@sou.edu.

School of Sciences Students: 20 full-time (9 women), 13 part-time (5 women); includes 1 minority (Hispanic American), 8 international. Average age 35. 23 applicants, 48% accepted, 6 enrolled. *Faculty:* 46 full-time (9 women), 5 part-time/adjunct (3 women). Expenses: Contact institution. *Financial support:* In 2001–02, 5 teaching assistantships with tuition reimbursements (averaging $3,519 per year) were awarded; institutionally sponsored loans and unspecified assistantships also available. In 2001, 17 degrees awarded. *Degree program information:* Part-time programs available. Offers environmental education (MA, MS); mathematics/computer science (MA, MS); science (MA, MS). *Application deadline:* For fall admission, 4/15 (priority date); for winter admission, 10/15 (priority date); for spring admission, 1/15 (priority date). *Application fee:* $50. *Application Contact:* Susan Koralek, Administrative Assistant, 541-552-6474. *Dean,* Dr. Joseph Graf, 541-552-6474.

School of Social Science, Health and Physical Education Students: 174 full-time (122 women), 46 part-time (36 women); includes 11 minority (1 African American, 1 Asian American or Pacific Islander, 8 Hispanic Americans, 1 Native American) Average age 35. 162 applicants, 100% accepted, 123 enrolled. Expenses: Contact institution. *Financial support:* Fellowships available. In 2001, 170 degrees awarded. Offers applied psychology (MAP); elementary education (MA Ed, MS Ed); human service-organizational training and development (MA, MS); secondary education (MA Ed, MS Ed); social science (MA, MS); social science, health and physical education (MA, MA Ed, MAP, MAT, MS, MS Ed); teaching (MAT). *Application deadline:* For fall admission, 2/1. *Application fee:* $50. *Dean,* Dr. Kenneth Kempner, 541-552-6417, E-mail: kempner@sou.edu.

SOUTHERN POLYTECHNIC STATE UNIVERSITY, Marietta, GA 30060-2896

General Information State-supported, coed, comprehensive institution. *Enrollment:* 182 full-time matriculated graduate/professional students (91 women), 381 part-time matriculated graduate/professional students (146 women). *Enrollment by degree level:* 526 master's, 37 other advanced degrees. *Graduate faculty:* 3 full-time (0 women), 46 part-time/adjunct (7 women). Tuition, state resident: full-time $1,746; part-time $97 per credit. Tuition, nonresident: full-time $6,966; part-time $387 per credit. *Required fees:* $221 per term. *Graduate housing:* Room and/or apartments available on a first-come, first-served basis to single students; on-campus housing not available to married students. Typical cost: $4,308 (including board). Housing application deadline: 8/1. *Student services:* Campus employment opportunities, campus safety program, career counseling, disabled student services, exercise/wellness program, free psychological counseling, international student services, low-cost health insurance, multicultural affairs office. *Library facilities:* Lawrence V. Johnson Library. *Online resources:* library catalog, access to other libraries' catalogs. *Collection:* 194,302 titles, 1,415 serial subscriptions, 62 audiovisual materials.

Computer facilities: 500 computers available on campus for general student use. A campuswide network can be accessed from off campus. *Web address:* http://www.spsu.edu/.

General Application Contact: Virginia A. Head, Director of Admissions, 770-528-7281, Fax: 770-528-7292, E-mail: vhead@spsu.edu.

GRADUATE UNITS

School of Arts and Sciences Students: 14 full-time (10 women), 57 part-time (39 women); includes 19 minority (17 African Americans, 1 Asian American or Pacific Islander, 1 Hispanic American), 5 international. Average age 33. *Faculty:* 6 part-time/adjunct (2 women). Expenses: Contact institution. *Financial support:* Teaching assistantships, career-related internships or fieldwork, Federal Work-Study, scholarships/grants, and unspecified assistantships available. Support available to part-time students. Financial award application deadline: 5/1; financial award applicants required to submit FAFSA. In 2001, 32 degrees awarded. *Degree program information:* Part-time and evening/weekend programs available. Offers arts and sciences (MS); technical and professional communication (MS). *Application deadline:* For fall admission, 7/1 (priority date); for spring admission, 11/1. Applications are processed on a rolling basis. *Application fee:* $20. Electronic applications accepted. *Application Contact:* Virginia A. Head, Director of Admissions, 770-528-7281, Fax: 770-528-7292, E-mail: vhead@spsu.edu. *Acting Dean,* Dr. Alan Gabrielli, 770-528-7464, Fax: 770-528-5510, E-mail: agabriel@spsu.edu.

School of Engineering Technology and Management Students: 19 full-time (11 women), 129 part-time (36 women); includes 48 minority (36 African Americans, 7 Asian Americans or Pacific Islanders, 5 Hispanic Americans), 22 international. Average age 36. *Faculty:* 16 part-time/adjunct (2 women). Expenses: Contact institution. *Financial support:* Teaching assistantships, career-related internships or fieldwork, Federal Work-Study, scholarships/grants, and unspecified assistantships available. Support available to part-time students. Financial award application deadline: 5/1; financial award applicants required to submit FAFSA. In 2001, 40 degrees awarded. *Degree program information:* Part-time and evening/weekend programs available. Postbaccalaureate distance learning degree programs offered. Offers engineering technology (MS); management (MS); quality assurance (MS); technology (MS). *Application deadline:* For fall admission, 7/15 (priority date); for spring admission, 12/1. Applications are processed on a rolling basis. *Application fee:* $20. Electronic applications accepted. *Application Contact:* Virginia A. Head, Director of Admissions, 770-528-7281, Fax: 770-528-7292, E-mail: vhead@spsu.edu. *Dean,* Dr. Richard M. Aynsley, 770-528-7234, Fax: 770-528-7134, E-mail: raynsley@spsu.edu.

See in-depth description on page 1105.

SOUTHERN UNIVERSITY AND AGRICULTURAL AND MECHANICAL COLLEGE, Baton Rouge, LA 70813

General Information State-supported, coed, comprehensive institution. CGS member. *Enrollment:* 417 full-time matriculated graduate/professional students (289 women), 465 part-time matriculated graduate/professional students (346 women). *Enrollment by degree level:* 789 master's, 93 doctoral. *Graduate faculty:* 143 full-time (43 women), 3 part-time/adjunct (2 women). *International tuition:* $2,613 full-time. Tuition, state resident: full-time $1,323. Tuition, nonresident: full-time $2,583. Tuition and fees vary according to program. *Graduate housing:* Room and/or apartments available on a first-come, first-served basis to single students; on-campus housing not available to married students. Housing application deadline: 6/30. *Student services:* Campus employment opportunities, career counseling, disabled student services, exercise/wellness program, international student services, low-cost health insurance. *Library facilities:* John B. Cade Library plus 2 others. *Online resources:* library catalog, web page, access to other libraries' catalogs. *Collection:* 672,448 titles, 17,016 serial subscriptions, 27,620 audiovisual materials. *Research affiliation:* NASA (mechanical engineering), Michigan State University (language screening of African-Americans), University of Georgia at Athens (substance abuse prevention), University of Alabama (diabetes), NASA (drinking water remote sensing), Livingston Observatory (gravitational waves/cosmic gravity waves/black waves).

Computer facilities: 835 computers available on campus for general student use. A campuswide network can be accessed from student residence rooms and from off campus. Internet access and online class registration are available. *Web address:* http://www.subr.edu/.

General Application Contact: Eura B. Adams, Director of Graduate Admissions and Recruitment, 225-771-5390, Fax: 225-771-5723, E-mail: ebadams@hotmail.com.

GRADUATE UNITS

Graduate School Students: 417 full-time (289 women), 465 part-time (346 women); includes 785 minority (723 African Americans, 62 Asian Americans or Pacific Islanders), 20 international. Average age 34. 487 applicants, 100% accepted, 286 enrolled. *Faculty:* 143 full-time (43 women), 3 part-time/adjunct (2 women). Expenses: Contact institution. *Financial support:* In 2001–02, 24 research assistantships (averaging $7,000 per year), 4 teaching assistantships (averaging $7,000 per year) were awarded. Fellowships, career-related internships or fieldwork, Federal Work-Study, institutionally sponsored loans, and scholarships/grants also available. Financial award application deadline: 4/15; financial award applicants required to submit FAFSA. In 2001, 294 master's, 4 doctorates awarded. *Degree program information:* Part-time programs available. Offers science/mathematics education (PhD). *Application deadline:* For fall admission, 6/1 (priority date); for spring admission, 11/1. Applications are processed on a rolling basis. *Application fee:* $25. *Application Contact:* Eura B. Adams, Director of Graduate Admissions and Recruitment, 225-771-5390, Fax: 225-771-5723, E-mail: ebadams@hotmail.com. *Associate Vice Chancellor for Academic Affairs and Dean of Graduate Studies,* Dr. Kweku K. Bentil, 225-771-5390, Fax: 225-771-5723, E-mail: kbentil@aol.com.

College of Agricultural, Family and Consumer Sciences Students: 14 full-time (4 women), 10 part-time (4 women); includes 18 minority (11 African Americans, 7 Asian Americans or Pacific Islanders), 1 international. Average age 33. 7 applicants, 71% accepted. *Faculty:* 5 full-time (2 women). Expenses: Contact institution. *Financial support:* In 2001–02, 14 students received support, including 7 research assistantships (averaging $5,897 per year); scholarships/grants and tuition waivers (full) also available. Financial award application deadline: 4/15; financial award applicants required to submit FAFSA. In 2001, 5 degrees awarded. Offers urban forestry (MS). *Application deadline:* For fall admission, 6/1 (priority date); for spring admission, 11/1 (priority date). Applications are processed on a rolling basis. *Application fee:* $25. *Application Contact:* Dr. Daniel J. Collins, Director of Graduate Studies, 225-771-6292, Fax: 225-771-5134, E-mail: wmaude@bellsouth.net. *Dean and Research Director,* Dr. Kirkland E. Mellad, 225-771-3661, Fax: 225-771-5134, E-mail: kmellad@subr.edu.

College of Arts and Humanities Students: 30 full-time (16 women), 29 part-time (15 women); includes 57 minority (all African Americans) Average age 30. 13 applicants, 92% accepted. *Faculty:* 14 full-time (4 women). Expenses: Contact institution. *Financial support:* In 2001–02, 4 research assistantships (averaging $7,000 per year) were awarded; teaching assistantships, career-related internships or fieldwork, Federal Work-Study, institutionally sponsored loans, and scholarships/grants also available. Financial award application deadline: 4/15; financial award applicants required to submit FAFSA. In 2001, 18 degrees awarded. Offers arts and humanities (MA); mass communications (MA); social sciences (MA). *Application deadline:* For fall admission, 6/1 (priority date); for spring admission, 11/1. Applications are processed on a rolling basis. *Application fee:* $25. *Dean,* Dr. Richard Webb, 225-771-5260, Fax: 225-771-3696, E-mail: dick62442@aol.com.

College of Business Students: 3 full-time (all women), 5 part-time (all women); all minorities (7 African Americans, 1 Asian American or Pacific Islander) Average age 30. 10 applicants, 10% accepted. *Faculty:* 3 full-time (0 women). Expenses: Contact institution. *Financial support:* In 2001–02, 2 research assistantships (averaging $7,000 per year) were awarded Financial award application deadline: 4/15. In 2001, 6 degrees awarded. Offers accountancy (MPA); business (MPA). *Application deadline:* For fall admission, 6/1 (priority date); for spring admission, 11/1. Applications are processed on a rolling basis. *Application fee:* $25. *Application Contact:* Dr. Herbert Vessel, MPA Director, 225-771-5642, Fax: 225-771-5642. *Dean,* Dr. Donald Andrews, 225-771-5642, Fax: 225-771-5642.

College of Education Students: 101 full-time (82 women), 217 part-time (174 women); includes 293 minority (292 African Americans, 1 Asian American or Pacific Islander), 3 international. Average age 25. 113 applicants, 79% accepted. *Faculty:* 17 full-time (8 women). Expenses: Contact institution. *Financial support:* In 2001–02, 5 teaching assistantships were awarded Financial award application deadline: 4/15; financial award applicants required to submit FAFSA. In 2001, 106 degrees awarded. Offers administration and supervision (M Ed); counselor education (MA); education (M Ed, MA, MS); elementary education (M Ed); media (M Ed); mental health counseling (MA); secondary education (M Ed); therapeutic recreation (MS). *Application deadline:* For fall admission, 6/1 (priority date); for spring admission, 11/1. Applications are processed on a rolling basis. *Application fee:* $25. *Dean,* Dr. Ivory Toldson, 225-771-2290.

College of Sciences Students: 124 full-time (71 women), 64 part-time (37 women); includes 138 minority (133 African Americans, 5 Asian Americans or Pacific Islanders), 42 international. 61 applicants, 72% accepted. *Faculty:* 68 full-time (17 women), 1 part-time/adjunct (0 women). Expenses: Contact institution. *Financial support:* In 2001–02, 31 research assistantships (averaging $7,000 per year), 10 teaching assistantships (averaging $7,000 per year) were awarded. Fellowships, scholarships/grants also available. Financial award application deadline: 4/15; financial award applicants required to submit FAFSA. In 2001, 61 degrees awarded. *Degree program information:* Part-time programs available. Offers analytical chemistry (MS); biochemistry (MS); biology (MS); environmental sciences (MS); information systems (MS); inorganic chemistry (MS); mathematics (MS); micro/minicomputer architecture (MS); operating systems (MS); organic chemistry (MS); physical chemistry (MS); physics (MS); rehabilitation counseling (MS); sciences (MA, MS). *Application deadline:* For fall admission, 6/1 (priority date); for spring admission, 11/1. Applications are processed on a rolling basis. *Application fee:* $25. *Dean,* Dr. Robert Harvey Miller, 225-771-5170, Fax: 225-771-2013, E-mail: rhmillerjr@aol.com.

Institute for the Study and Rehabilitation of Exceptional Children and Youth Students: 52 full-time (46 women), 40 part-time (39 women); includes 76 minority (all African Americans), 1 international. Average age 31. *Faculty:* 6 full-time (5 women), 1 (woman) part-time/adjunct. Expenses: Contact institution. *Financial support:* In 2001–02, 4 students received support. Unspecified assistantships available. Financial award application deadline: 4/15. In 2001, 25 degrees awarded. *Degree program information:* Part-time and evening/weekend programs available. Offers study and rehabilitation of exceptional children and youth (M Ed, PhD). *Application deadline:* For fall admission, 6/1; for spring admission, 11/1.

Applications are processed on a rolling basis. *Application fee:* $25. *Departmental Liaison to the Office of the Dean,* Dr. Ordia Limar-Gee, 225-771-3950, Fax: 225-771-5652.

School of Public Policy and Urban Affairs Students: 79 full-time (53 women), 75 part-time (24 women); includes 136 minority (128 African Americans, 8 Asian Americans or Pacific Islanders), 6 international. Average age 32. 50 applicants, 80% accepted. *Faculty:* 5 full-time (2 women). Expenses: Contact institution. *Financial support:* In 2001–02, 6 fellowships with tuition reimbursements (averaging $12,000 per year), 30 research assistantships with partial tuition reimbursements (averaging $8,000 per year), 1 teaching assistantship with partial tuition reimbursement (averaging $14,000 per year) were awarded. Federal Work-Study, scholarships/grants, and tuition waivers (full) also available. Financial award application deadline: 4/15; financial award applicants required to submit FAFSA. In 2001, 48 master's, 4 doctorates awarded. Offers public administration (MPA); public policy (PhD); public policy and urban affairs (MA, MPA, PhD); social sciences (MA). *Application deadline:* For fall admission, 6/1; for spring admission, 11/1. Applications are processed on a rolling basis. *Application fee:* $25. *Application Contact:* Dr. Valentine Udah James, Director of PhD Program, 225-771-2034, Fax: 225-771-3105, E-mail: vjames@subr.edu. *Dean,* Dr. Damien Ejigiri, 225-771-3092.

School of Nursing Students: 14 full-time (11 women), 21 part-time (19 women); includes 26 minority (all African Americans) Average age 38. 10 applicants, 100% accepted, 10 enrolled. *Faculty:* 3 full-time (all women), 1 (woman) part-time/adjunct. Expenses: Contact institution. *Financial support:* In 2001–02, 10 students received support, including 2 fellowships with tuition reimbursements available (averaging $3,480 per year), 4 research assistantships (averaging $7,000 per year), 2 teaching assistantships (averaging $20,000 per year); Federal Work-Study, institutionally sponsored loans, scholarships/grants, traineeships, and unspecified assistantships also available. Financial award applicants required to submit FAFSA. In 2001, 15 degrees awarded. *Degree program information:* Part-time programs available. Offers educator/administrator (PhD); family health nursing (MSN); family nurse practitioner (PhD, Post Master's Certificate). *Application deadline:* For fall admission, 7/1; for spring admission, 11/1. Applications are processed on a rolling basis. *Application fee:* $25. *Application Contact:* Dr. Constance S. Hendricks, Graduate Nursing Programs Chair, 225-771-2663, Fax: 225-771-3547, E-mail: constancehendricks@suson.subr.edu. *Dean,* Dr. Janet Rami, 225-771-2166, Fax: 225-771-2641.

Southern University Law Center Offers law (JD).

SOUTHERN UNIVERSITY AT NEW ORLEANS, New Orleans, LA 70126-1009

General Information State-supported, coed, comprehensive institution. *Enrollment:* 140 full-time matriculated graduate/professional students (121 women), 101 part-time matriculated graduate/professional students (92 women). *Enrollment by degree level:* 241 master's. *Graduate faculty:* 21 full-time (13 women). *Tuition:* Part-time $623 per unit. Tuition and fees vary according to course load. *Graduate housing:* On-campus housing not available. *Student services:* Campus employment opportunities, campus safety program, career counseling. *Library facilities:* Leonard Washington Library.

Computer facilities: 100 computers available on campus for general student use. *Web address:* http://www.suno.edu/.

General Application Contact: James Donald Smith, Director of Student Affairs, 504-286-5376, Fax: 504-286-5387.

GRADUATE UNITS

School of Social Work Students: 140 full-time (121 women), 101 part-time (92 women); includes 190 minority (all African Americans) Average age 35. *Faculty:* 21 full-time (13 women). Expenses: Contact institution. *Financial support:* Fellowships, career-related internships or fieldwork and institutionally sponsored loans available. *Degree program information:* Part-time and evening/weekend programs available. Offers social work (MSW). *Application deadline:* For fall admission, 3/1. *Application fee:* $25. *Application Contact:* James Donald Smith, Director of Student Affairs, 504-286-5376, Fax: 504-286-5387. *Dean,* Mille M. Charles, 504-286-5376, Fax: 504-286-5387.

SOUTHERN UTAH UNIVERSITY, Cedar City, UT 84720-2498

General Information State-supported, coed, comprehensive institution. *Enrollment:* 47 full-time matriculated graduate/professional students (14 women), 164 part-time matriculated graduate/professional students (84 women). *Enrollment by degree level:* 211 master's. *Graduate faculty:* 41. Tuition, state resident: full-time $2,758; part-time $137 per credit hour. Tuition, nonresident: full-time $10,444; part-time $522 per credit hour. *Required fees:* $462. *Graduate housing:* Room and/or apartments available on a first-come, first-served basis to single students; on-campus housing not available to married students. Typical cost: $1,260 per year ($2,866 including board). *Student services:* Campus employment opportunities, campus safety program, career counseling, disabled student services, exercise/wellness program, free psychological counseling, international student services, low-cost health insurance, multicultural affairs office, teacher training. *Library facilities:* Southern Utah University Library. *Online resources:* library catalog, web page, access to other libraries' catalogs. *Collection:* 180,424 titles, 6,165 serial subscriptions, 13,352 audiovisual materials.

Computer facilities: 300 computers available on campus for general student use. A campuswide network can be accessed from student residence rooms and from off campus. *Web address:* http://www.suu.edu/.

General Application Contact: Dr. Carl Templin, Provost, 435-586-7704, Fax: 435-586-5475, E-mail: templin@suu.edu.

GRADUATE UNITS

College of Education Students: 18 full-time (12 women), 127 part-time (66 women); includes 4 minority (1 African American, 1 Asian American or Pacific Islander, 1 Hispanic American, 1 Native American) Average age 33. 44 applicants, 61% accepted. *Faculty:* 18 full-time (8 women), 6 part-time/adjunct (2 women). Expenses: Contact institution. *Financial support:* In 2001–02, 5 teaching assistantships with full tuition reimbursements (averaging $1,770 per year) were awarded; scholarships/grants also available. In 2001, 95 degrees awarded. *Degree program information:* Part-time programs available. Offers education (M Ed). *Application deadline:* Applications are processed on a rolling basis. *Application fee:* $30. *Associate Professor of Teacher Education,* Dr. Prent Klag, 435-586-7803, Fax: 435-865-8046, E-mail: klag@suu.edu.

School of Business Students: 33 full-time (6 women), 25 part-time (9 women). Average age 25. 46 applicants, 89% accepted. *Faculty:* 7 full-time (1 woman). Expenses: Contact institution. *Financial support:* In 2001–02, 9 research assistantships with full tuition reimbursements were awarded; career-related internships or fieldwork, institutionally sponsored loans, tuition waivers (full and partial), and unspecified assistantships also available. In 2001, 26 degrees awarded. *Degree program information:* Part-time programs available. Offers accounting (M Acc); business (M Acc, MBA). *Application deadline:* For fall admission, 8/1 (priority date). Applications are processed on a rolling basis. *Application fee:* $30. *Application Contact:* Paula Alger, Curriculum Coordinator and Adviser, 435-865-8157, Fax: 435-586-5493, E-mail: alger@suu.edu. *Provost,* Dr. Carl Templin, 435-586-7704, Fax: 435-586-5475, E-mail: templin@suu.edu.

SOUTHERN WESLEYAN UNIVERSITY, Central, SC 29630-1020

General Information Independent-religious, coed, comprehensive institution. *Enrollment:* 170 full-time matriculated graduate/professional students (100 women). *Enrollment by degree level:* 170 master's. *Graduate faculty:* 10 full-time (1 woman), 17 part-time/adjunct (3 women). *Tuition:* Full-time $6,840; part-time $190 per credit. *Required fees:* $83 per course. One-time fee: $80. *Graduate housing:* On-campus housing not available. *Student services:* Career counseling, disabled student services, free psychological counseling, writing training. *Library facilities:* Rickman Library. *Online resources:* library catalog, access to other libraries' catalogs. *Collection:* 79,628 titles, 520 serial subscriptions, 3,100 audiovisual materials.

Computer facilities: 60 computers available on campus for general student use. A campuswide network can be accessed from student residence rooms and from off campus. Internet access is available. *Web address:* http://www.swu.edu/.

General Application Contact: Dr. Tom Griffin, Associate Academic Vice President, 864-639-2453 Ext. 401, Fax: 864-639-4050, E-mail: tgriffin@swu.edu.

GRADUATE UNITS

Program in Christian Ministries Students: 16 full-time (2 women), 1 part-time; includes 4 minority (2 African Americans, 2 Hispanic Americans) *Faculty:* 6 full-time (1 woman). Expenses: Contact institution. *Financial support:* Tuition waivers (full) available. In 2001, 5 degrees awarded. *Degree program information:* Evening/weekend programs available. Offers Christian ministries (M Min). *Application deadline:* Applications are processed on a rolling basis. *Application fee:* $25. *Director,* Dr. Mari Gonlag, 864-644-5229, Fax: 864-644-5902, E-mail: mgonlag@swu.edu.

Program in Management Students: 151 full-time (98 women); includes 70 minority (63 African Americans, 6 Hispanic Americans, 1 Native American) Expenses: Contact institution. In 2001, 31 degrees awarded. *Degree program information:* Part-time and evening/weekend programs available. Offers management (MSM). *Application deadline:* Applications are processed on a rolling basis. *Application fee:* $25. *Vice President for Adult and Graduate Studies,* Dr. Tom Griffin, 864-644-5538, Fax: 864-644-5973, E-mail: tgriffin@swu.edu.

SOUTH TEXAS COLLEGE OF LAW, Houston, TX 77002-7000

General Information Independent, coed, graduate-only institution. *Enrollment by degree level:* 1,250 first professional. *Graduate faculty:* 55 full-time (17 women), 38 part-time/adjunct (7 women). *Tuition:* Full-time $17,100; part-time $11,400 per year. *Required fees:* $600; $300 per term. Tuition and fees vary according to course load. *Graduate housing:* Rooms and/or apartments available to single and married students. Typical cost: $7,418 (including board) for single students; $7,418 (including board) for married students. *Student services:* Campus employment opportunities, campus safety program, career counseling, disabled student services, international student services. *Library facilities:* The Fred Parks Law Library. *Online resources:* library catalog, web page, access to other libraries' catalogs. *Collection:* 214,935 titles, 4,427 serial subscriptions, 681 audiovisual materials.

Computer facilities: 90 computers available on campus for general student use. A campuswide network can be accessed from off campus. Internet access and online class registration, online class schedules, assignments, grades are available. *Web address:* http://www.stcl.edu/.

General Application Contact: Alicia K. Cramer, Assistant Dean of Admissions, 713-646-1810, Fax: 713-646-2906, E-mail: admissions@stcl.edu.

GRADUATE UNITS

Professional Program Students: 831 full-time (395 women), 419 part-time (219 women); includes 313 minority (80 African Americans, 78 Asian Americans or Pacific Islanders, 149 Hispanic Americans, 6 Native Americans), 3 international. Average age 29. 1,394 applicants, 67% accepted, 370 enrolled. *Faculty:* 55 full-time (17 women), 38 part-time/adjunct (7 women). Expenses: Contact institution. *Financial support:* In 2001–02, 1,141 students received support. Federal Work-Study, scholarships/grants, and tuition waivers (full and partial) available. Support available to part-time students. Financial award application deadline: 5/1; financial award applicants required to submit FAFSA. In 2001, 356 degrees awarded. *Degree program information:* Part-time and evening/weekend programs available. Offers law (JD). *Application deadline:* For fall admission, 2/25; for spring admission, 10/1. *Application fee:* $50. Electronic applications accepted. *Application Contact:* Alicia K. Cramer, Assistant Dean of Admissions, 713-646-1810, Fax: 713-646-2906, E-mail: admissions@stcl.edu. *President and Dean,* Frank T. Read, 713-646-1819, Fax: 713-646-2909, E-mail: tread@stcl.edu.

SOUTHWEST ACUPUNCTURE COLLEGE, Santa Fe, NM 87505

General Information Private, coed, primarily women, graduate-only institution. *Enrollment by degree level:* 263 master's. *Graduate faculty:* 20 full-time (9 women), 20 part-time/adjunct (12 women). *Tuition:* Part-time $13 per semester hour. *Required fees:* $200. One-time fee: $100 full-time. *Graduate housing:* On-campus housing not available. *Student services:* Campus employment opportunities. *Library facilities:* Southwest Acupuncture College Library. *Collection:* 5,843 titles, 132 serial subscriptions, 406 audiovisual materials.

Computer facilities: 2 computers available on campus for general student use. Internet access is available. *Web address:* http://www.acupuncturecollege.edu/.

General Application Contact: Dr. Lea A. Krier, Campus Director, 505-438-8884, Fax: 505-438-8883, E-mail: admin@acupuncturecollege.edu.

GRADUATE UNITS

Program in Oriental Medicine, Albuquerque Campus Students: 44 full-time (32 women); includes 7 minority (4 Asian Americans or Pacific Islanders, 3 Hispanic Americans), 2 international. Average age 36. 15 applicants, 100% accepted, 9 enrolled. *Faculty:* 8 full-time (1 woman), 3 part-time/adjunct (2 women). Expenses: Contact institution. *Financial support:* In 2001–02, 39 students received support. Scholarships/grants available. Financial award application deadline: 5/31; financial award applicants required to submit FAFSA. In 2001, 9 degrees awarded. *Degree program information:* Part-time programs available. Offers Oriental medicine (MS). *Application deadline:* For fall admission, 5/15 (priority date); for winter admission, 12/15 (priority date). Applications are processed on a rolling basis. *Application fee:* $50. Electronic applications accepted. *Application Contact:* Dr. Qijian Ye, Academic Dean, 505-888-8898, Fax: 505-888-1380, E-mail: abq@acupunctcollege.edu. *Administrative Director,* Pamela Jo Weber, 505-888-8898, Fax: 505-888-1380, E-mail: abq@acupuncturecollege.edu.

Program in Oriental Medicine, Boulder Campus Students: 122 full-time (81 women), 8 part-time (all women); includes 2 minority (both Asian Americans or Pacific Islanders), 3 international. Average age 34. 56 applicants, 73% accepted, 35 enrolled. *Faculty:* 9 full-time (3 women), 13 part-time/adjunct (8 women). Expenses: Contact institution. *Financial support:* In 2001–02, 104 students received support. Scholarships/grants available. Financial award application deadline: 5/31; financial award applicants required to submit FAFSA. In 2001, 42 degrees awarded. *Degree program information:* Part-time programs available. Offers Oriental medicine (MS). *Application deadline:* For fall admission, 5/15 (priority date); for winter admission, 12/15 (priority date). Applications are processed on a rolling basis. *Application fee:* $50. *Application Contact:* Melanie Crane, Academic Dean, 303-581-9955, Fax: 303-581-9944, E-mail: boulder@acupuncturecollege.edu. *Campus Director,* Valerie L. Hobbs, 303-581-9955, Fax: 303-581-9944, E-mail: boulder@acupuncturecollege.edu.

Program in Oriental Medicine, Santa Fe Campus Students: 79 full-time (53 women), 1 (woman) part-time; includes 2 minority (both Asian Americans or Pacific Islanders), 1 international. Average age 33. 25 applicants, 92% accepted, 21 enrolled. *Faculty:* 9 full-time (3 women), 11 part-time/adjunct (8 women). Expenses: Contact institution. *Financial support:* In 2001–02, 69 students received support. Scholarships/grants available. Financial award application deadline: 5/31; financial award applicants required to submit FAFSA. In 2001, 23 degrees awarded. *Degree program information:* Part-time programs available. Offers Oriental medicine (MS). *Application deadline:* For fall admission, 5/15 (priority date); for winter admission, 12/15 (priority date). Applications are processed on a rolling basis. *Application fee:* $50. *Application Contact:* Dr. Lea A. Krier, Campus Director, 505-438-8884, Fax: 505-438-8883, E-mail: admin@acupuncturecollege.edu. *Executive Director,* Dr. Skya Abbate, 505-438-8884, Fax: 505-438-8883, E-mail: admin@acupuncturecollege.edu.

SOUTHWEST BAPTIST UNIVERSITY, Bolivar, MO 65613-2597

General Information Independent-religious, coed, comprehensive institution. *Enrollment:* 352 full-time matriculated graduate/professional students (259 women), 498 part-time matriculated graduate/professional students (405 women). *Enrollment by degree level:* 850 master's. *Graduate faculty:* 18 full-time (6 women), 59 part-time/adjunct (24 women). *Tuition:* Part-time $130 per credit hour. *Required fees:* $85 per year. Tuition and fees vary according to campus/location and program. *Graduate housing:* Room and/or apartments available on a first-come, first-served basis to single students; on-campus housing not available to married students. *Student services:* Campus employment opportunities, campus safety program, career counseling, disabled student services, free psychological counseling, international student services, low-cost health insurance, teacher training. *Library facilities:*

Southwest Baptist University (continued)

Harriett K. Hutchens Library. *Online resources:* library catalog, web page. *Collection:* 108,128 titles, 2,518 serial subscriptions, 9,370 audiovisual materials.

Computer facilities: 130 computers available on campus for general student use. A campuswide network can be accessed from off campus. Internet access is available. *Web address:* http://www.sbuniv.edu/.

General Application Contact: Dr. Gordon Dutile, Provost, 417-328-1601, Fax: 417-328-1514, E-mail: gdutile@sbuniv.edu.

GRADUATE UNITS

Graduate Studies Students: 352 full-time (259 women), 498 part-time (405 women); includes 7 minority (3 African Americans, 1 Asian American or Pacific Islander, 1 Hispanic American, 2 Native Americans), 2 international. Average age 32. *Faculty:* 18 full-time (6 women), 59 part-time/adjunct (24 women). Expenses: Contact institution. *Financial support:* Teaching assistantships, career-related internships or fieldwork, institutionally sponsored loans, and tuition waivers (partial) available. Support available to part-time students. In 2001, 403 degrees awarded. *Degree program information:* Part-time and evening/weekend programs available. *Application deadline:* Applications are processed on a rolling basis. *Application fee:* $25. *Provost*, Dr. Gordon Dutile, 417-328-1601, Fax: 417-328-1514, E-mail: gdutile@sbuniv.edu.

College of Business and Computer Science Students: 19 full-time (11 women), 29 part-time (16 women); includes 2 minority (both African Americans), 1 international. Average age 30. 31 applicants, 81% accepted. *Faculty:* 7 full-time (2 women), 1 (woman) part-time/adjunct. Expenses: Contact institution. *Financial support:* In 2001–02, 2 students received support, including 1 research assistantship with full tuition reimbursement available (averaging $4,750 per year) *Degree program information:* Part-time and evening/weekend programs available. Offers administration (MBA); business (MBA); business and computer science (MBA). *Application deadline:* For fall admission, 8/1 (priority date); for spring admission, 1/1 (priority date). Applications are processed on a rolling basis. *Application fee:* $25. *Application Contact:* Ronda Middleton, Director of Graduate Studies in Business, 417-328-2000, Fax: 417-328-1887. *Dean*, Dr. David Whitlock, 417-328-1759, Fax: 417-328-1887, E-mail: dwhitloc@sbuniv.edu.

College of Science and Mathematics Students: 37 full-time (24 women); includes 2 minority (1 Asian American or Pacific Islander, 1 Native American) Average age 27. 23 applicants, 96% accepted, 19 enrolled. *Faculty:* 7 full-time (3 women), 1 (woman) part-time/adjunct. Expenses: Contact institution. *Financial support:* Research assistantships, unspecified assistantships available. In 2001, 27 degrees awarded. Offers physical therapy (MSPT); science and mathematics (MSPT). *Application deadline:* For winter admission, 1/6 (priority date); for spring admission, 4/1 (priority date). Applications are processed on a rolling basis. *Application fee:* $25. *Application Contact:* Rosalie Christian, Physical Therapy Administrative Assistant, 417-328-1906, E-mail: pt@sbuniv.edu. *Dean*, Dr. Gary Gray, 417-328-1659.

Lewis E. Schollian College of Education and Social Sciences Students: 296 full-time (224 women), 469 part-time (389 women); includes 3 minority (1 African American, 1 Hispanic American, 1 Native American), 1 international. Average age 32. 200 applicants, 100% accepted, 200 enrolled. *Faculty:* 4 full-time (1 woman), 57 part-time/adjunct (22 women). Expenses: Contact institution. *Financial support:* In 2001–02, 50 students received support; research assistantships, career-related internships or fieldwork and institutionally sponsored loans available. Support available to part-time students. Financial award application deadline: 6/1; financial award applicants required to submit FAFSA. In 2001, 303 degrees awarded. *Degree program information:* Part-time and evening/weekend programs available. Offers education (MS); education and social sciences (MS); educational administration (MS). *Application deadline:* Applications are processed on a rolling basis. *Application fee:* $25. *Application Contact:* Dr. Tom Hollis, Director, Graduate Studies in Education, 417-328-1737, Fax: 417-328-1719, E-mail: thollis@sbuniv.edu. *Dean*, Dr. John Wheeler, 417-328-1710, E-mail: jwheeler@sbuniv.edu.

SOUTHWEST COLLEGE OF NATUROPATHIC MEDICINE AND HEALTH SCIENCES, Tempe, AZ 85282

General Information Independent, coed, graduate-only institution. *Enrollment by degree level:* 275 doctoral. *Graduate faculty:* 14 full-time (5 women), 40 part-time/adjunct (18 women). *Tuition:* Part-time $19 per hour. Tuition and fees vary according to student level. *Graduate housing:* On-campus housing not available. *Student services:* Campus employment opportunities, career counseling, free psychological counseling, low-cost health insurance. *Library facilities:* Southwest College Library. *Online resources:* web page. *Collection:* 4,400 titles, 139 serial subscriptions. *Research affiliation:* Dolisos, Inc. (neutraceuticals), Springdale West Valley (nursing home), Elisa Act Biotechnologies, Inc. (analytical laboratory), Gaia Herbs, Inc. (neutraceuticals), Arthritis Health Clinic (patient-care physicians group).

Computer facilities: 9 computers available on campus for general student use. Internet access is available. *Web address:* http://www.scnm.edu/.

General Application Contact: Melissa A. Winquist, Director of Enrollment, 480-858-9100 Ext. 218, Fax: 480-858-9116, E-mail: admissions@scnm.edu.

GRADUATE UNITS

Program in Naturopathic Medicine Students: 263 full-time (195 women), 12 part-time (6 women); includes 48 minority (21 African Americans, 13 Asian Americans or Pacific Islanders, 11 Hispanic Americans, 3 Native Americans), 9 international. Average age 33. 189 applicants, 49% accepted, 62 enrolled. *Faculty:* 14 full-time (5 women), 40 part-time/adjunct (18 women). Expenses: Contact institution. *Financial support:* In 2001–02, 202 students received support. Available to part-time students. Applicants required to submit FAFSA. In 2001, 51 degrees awarded. Offers naturopathic medicine (ND). *Application deadline:* For fall admission, 8/1 (priority date); for spring admission, 2/1 (priority date). Applications are processed on a rolling basis. *Application fee:* $65 ($90 for international students). *Application Contact:* Melissa A. Winquist, Director of Enrollment, 480-858-9100 Ext. 218, Fax: 480-858-9116, E-mail: admissions@scnm.edu. *Director*, Dr. Kareen O'Brien, 480-858-9100, Fax: 480-858-9116.

SOUTHWESTERN ADVENTIST UNIVERSITY, Keene, TX 76059

General Information Independent-religious, coed, comprehensive institution. *Enrollment:* 6 full-time matriculated graduate/professional students (2 women), 22 part-time matriculated graduate/professional students (13 women). *Enrollment by degree level:* 28 master's. *Graduate faculty:* 8 full-time (2 women), 5 part-time/adjunct (0 women). *Tuition:* Full-time $2,790; part-time $310 per semester hour. *Graduate housing:* Rooms and/or apartments available on a first-come, first-served basis to single and married students. Typical cost: $4,778 (including board) for single students; $2,385 per year for married students. Housing application deadline: 8/31. *Student services:* Campus employment opportunities, career counseling, international student services, low-cost health insurance. *Library facilities:* Chan Shun Centennial Library. *Online resources:* library catalog, web page, access to other libraries' catalogs. *Collection:* 108,481 titles, 457 serial subscriptions.

Computer facilities: 50 computers available on campus for general student use. A campuswide network can be accessed from student residence rooms and from off campus. Internet access is available. *Web address:* http://www.swau.edu/.

General Application Contact: Laura Yanez, Graduate Secretary, 817-556-4724, Fax: 817-556-4744, E-mail: lauryane@swau.edu.

GRADUATE UNITS

Business Department, Graduate Program Students: 4 full-time (1 woman), 17 part-time (8 women); includes 7 minority (2 African Americans, 2 Asian Americans or Pacific Islanders, 3 Hispanic Americans), 11 international. Average age 28. 31 applicants, 77% accepted. *Faculty:* 4 full-time (1 woman), 4 part-time/adjunct (0 women). Expenses: Contact institution. In 2001, 6 degrees awarded. *Degree program information:* Part-time and evening/weekend programs available. Offers accounting (MBA). *Application deadline:* For fall admission, 8/24 (priority date); for spring admission, 12/28. Applications are processed on a rolling basis. *Application fee:* $0. *Application Contact:* Laura Yanez, Graduate Secretary, 817-556-4724, Fax: 817-556-4744, E-mail: lauryane@swau.edu. *Chair*, Dr. Allen Stembridge, 817-556-4771, Fax: 817-556-4744, E-mail: stem@swau.edu.

Education Department, Graduate Program Students: 2 full-time (1 woman), 5 part-time (all women). Average age 33. 5 applicants, 60% accepted. *Faculty:* 4 full-time (1 woman), 1 part-time/adjunct (0 women). Expenses: Contact institution. *Financial support:* Federal Work-Study and institutionally sponsored loans available. Support available to part-time students. Financial award application deadline: 5/1. In 2001, 2 degrees awarded. *Degree program information:* Part-time and evening/weekend programs available. Offers elementary education (M Ed). *Application deadline:* For fall admission, 8/24 (priority date); for spring admission, 12/28. Applications are processed on a rolling basis. *Application fee:* $0. *Application Contact:* Laura Yanez, Graduate Secretary, 817-556-4724, Fax: 817-556-4744, E-mail: lauryane@swau.edu. *Chair*, Dr. Randy Gilliam, 817-645-3921 Ext. 279, Fax: 817-556-4744, E-mail: gilliamr@swau.edu.

SOUTHWESTERN ASSEMBLIES OF GOD UNIVERSITY, Waxahachie, TX 75165-2397

General Information Independent-religious, coed, comprehensive institution. *Enrollment:* 21 full-time matriculated graduate/professional students (7 women), 33 part-time matriculated graduate/professional students (10 women). *Enrollment by degree level:* 54 master's. *Graduate faculty:* 40. *Tuition:* Part-time $260 per hour. *Graduate housing:* Room and/or apartments guaranteed to single students. *Library facilities:* P. C. Nelson Memorial Library plus 1 other. *Online resources:* web page. *Collection:* 110,000 titles, 600 serial subscriptions.

Computer facilities: 45 computers available on campus for general student use. A campuswide network can be accessed from off campus. Internet access is available. *Web address:* http://www.sagu.edu/.

General Application Contact: Eddie Davis, Senior Director, Enrollment Services, 972-937-4010 Ext. 1123, E-mail: edavis@sagu.edu.

GRADUATE UNITS

Thomas F. Harrison School of Graduate Studies Students: 21 full-time (7 women), 33 part-time (10 women); includes 9 minority (2 African Americans, 3 Asian Americans or Pacific Islanders, 4 Hispanic Americans) 43 applicants, 98% accepted. *Faculty:* 40. Expenses: Contact institution. *Financial support:* In 2001–02, 26 students received support. Federal Work-Study and scholarships/grants available. Financial award application deadline: 3/1; financial award applicants required to submit FAFSA. In 2001, 12 degrees awarded. *Degree program information:* Part-time and evening/weekend programs available. Postbaccalaureate distance learning degree programs offered (minimal on-campus study). Offers Bible and theology (MS); Christian school administration (MS); counseling psychology (MS); curriculum development (MS). *Application deadline:* For fall admission, 7/1 (priority date); for spring admission, 11/1 (priority date). Applications are processed on a rolling basis. *Application fee:* $50. Electronic applications accepted. *Application Contact:* Eddie Davis, Senior Director, Enrollment Services, 972-937-4010 Ext. 1123, E-mail: edavis@sagu.edu. *Dean*, Dr. Robert N. Harden, 972-937-4010 Ext. 2403, Fax: 972-923-2714, E-mail: rharden@sagu.edu.

SOUTHWESTERN BAPTIST THEOLOGICAL SEMINARY, Fort Worth, TX 76122-0000

General Information Independent-religious, coed, primarily men, graduate-only institution. *Enrollment by degree level:* 1,169 first professional, 1,062 master's, 401 doctoral, 93 other advanced degrees. *Graduate faculty:* 88 full-time, 81 part-time/adjunct. *Tuition:* Part-time $90 per hour. *Required fees:* $580; $275 per term. Tuition and fees vary according to degree level, campus/location, program and student's religious affiliation. *Graduate housing:* Rooms and/or apartments available on a first-come, first-served basis to single and married students. Typical cost: $1,485 per year for single students; $4,800 per year for married students. *Student services:* Campus employment opportunities, career counseling, child daycare facilities, free psychological counseling, international student services, low-cost health insurance. *Library facilities:* A. Webb Roberts Library plus 3 others. *Online resources:* library catalog, web page, access to other libraries' catalogs. *Collection:* 800,000 titles, 90,177 serial subscriptions, 24,300 audiovisual materials.

Computer facilities: 45 computers available on campus for general student use. A campuswide network can be accessed from off campus. Internet access is available. *Web address:* http://www.swbts.edu/.

General Application Contact: Judy Morris, Director of Admissions, 817-923-1921 Ext. 2700, Fax: 817-921-8758, E-mail: admissn@swbts.edu.

GRADUATE UNITS

School of Church Music Students: 166. Average age 33. 42 applicants, 64% accepted, 21 enrolled. *Faculty:* 20 full-time (3 women), 6 part-time/adjunct (4 women). Expenses: Contact institution. *Financial support:* In 2001–02, 166 students received support; teaching assistantships, career-related internships or fieldwork, institutionally sponsored loans, and scholarships/grants available. Support available to part-time students. Financial award application deadline: 11/1. In 2001, 43 master's awarded. *Degree program information:* Part-time programs available. Offers church music (M Div CM, MACM, MM, DMA, PhD). *Application deadline:* For fall admission, 7/1 (priority date); for spring admission, 11/1 (priority date). Applications are processed on a rolling basis. *Application fee:* $35. Electronic applications accepted. *Application Contact:* Judy Morris, Director of Admissions, 817-923-1921 Ext. 2700, Fax: 817-921-8758, E-mail: admissn@swbts.edu. *Dean*, Dr. Benjamin Harlan, 817-923-1921 Ext. 3111, Fax: 817-921-8762, E-mail: bharlan@swbts.edu.

School of Educational Ministries Students: 941. Average age 33. 258 applicants, 85% accepted, 178 enrolled. *Faculty:* 24 full-time (5 women), 13 part-time/adjunct (5 women). Expenses: Contact institution. *Financial support:* In 2001–02, 941 students received support; teaching assistantships, career-related internships or fieldwork, institutionally sponsored loans, scholarships/grants, and tuition waivers (partial) available. Support available to part-time students. Financial award application deadline: 11/1. In 2001, 263 master's, 8 doctorates awarded. *Degree program information:* Part-time and evening/weekend programs available. Offers educational ministries (MA Comm, MACCM, MACE, MACSE, MAMFC, PhD). *Application deadline:* For fall admission, 7/1 (priority date); for spring admission, 11/1 (priority date). Applications are processed on a rolling basis. *Application fee:* $35. Electronic applications accepted. *Application Contact:* Judy Morris, Director of Admissions, 817-923-1921 Ext. 2700, Fax: 817-921-8758, E-mail: admissn@swbts.edu. *Dean*, Dr. Daryl Eldridge, 817-923-1921 Ext. 2140, Fax: 817-921-8763, E-mail: dre@swbts.edu.

School of Theology Students: 1,618. Average age 33. 428 applicants, 80% accepted, 296 enrolled. *Faculty:* 34 full-time (1 woman), 54 part-time/adjunct (4 women). Expenses: Contact institution. *Financial support:* In 2001–02, 1,618 students received support; teaching assistantships, career-related internships or fieldwork, institutionally sponsored loans, scholarships/grants, and tuition waivers (partial) available. Support available to part-time students. Financial award application deadline: 11/1. In 2001, 200 first professional degrees, 13 master's, 51 doctorates awarded. *Degree program information:* Part-time and evening/weekend programs available. Offers theology (M Div, MA Missions, MA Th, Th M, D Min, PhD). *Application deadline:* For fall admission, 7/15 (priority date); for spring admission, 12/1 (priority date). Applications are processed on a rolling basis. *Application fee:* $35. Electronic applications accepted. *Application Contact:* Judy Morris, Director of Admissions, 817-923-1921 Ext. 2700, Fax: 817-921-8758, E-mail: admissn@swbts.edu. *Dean*, 817-923-1921, Fax: 817-921-8767.

SOUTHWESTERN CHRISTIAN UNIVERSITY, Bethany, OK 73008-0340

General Information Independent-religious, coed, comprehensive institution. *Enrollment:* 55 full-time matriculated graduate/professional students (10 women), 12 part-time matriculated graduate/professional students (2 women). *Enrollment by degree level:* 67 master's. *Graduate faculty:* 3 full-time (0 women), 13 part-time/adjunct (2 women). *Tuition:* Part-time $250 per semester hour. *Library facilities:* Springer Learning Center. *Collection:* 38,900 titles, 100 serial subscriptions.

Computer facilities: 13 computers available on campus for general student use. A campuswide network can be accessed. Internet access is available. *Web address:* http://www.sccm.edu/.

General Application Contact: Beverly Haug, Graduate School Secretary, 405-789-7661 Ext. 3447, Fax: 405-495-0078, E-mail: beverly@sccm.edu.

GRADUATE UNITS

Program in Ministry Students: 55 full-time (10 women), 12 part-time (2 women); includes 14 minority (12 African Americans, 1 Asian American or Pacific Islander, 1 Hispanic American) Average age 40. 38 applicants, 76% accepted. *Faculty:* 3 full-time (0 women), 13 part-time/adjunct (2 women). Expenses: Contact institution. *Financial support:* In 2001–02, 25 students received support. Scholarships/grants available. Support available to part-time students. Financial award applicants required to submit FAFSA. In 2001, 6 degrees awarded. *Degree program information:* Part-time programs available. Offers ministry (M Min). *Application deadline:* For fall admission, 8/1 (priority date); for spring admission, 12/1 (priority date). Applications are processed on a rolling basis. *Application fee:* $50. *Application Contact:* Beverly Haug, Graduate School Secretary, 405-789-7661 Ext. 3447, Fax: 405-495-0078, E-mail: beverly@sccm.edu. *Dean,* Dr. Garnet E. Pike, 405-789-7661 Ext. 3446, Fax: 405-789-7661, E-mail: garnet@sccm.edu.

SOUTHWESTERN COLLEGE, Winfield, KS 67156-2499

General Information Independent-religious, coed, comprehensive institution. *Enrollment:* 1 (woman) full-time matriculated graduate/professional student, 38 part-time matriculated graduate/professional students (27 women). *Enrollment by degree level:* 39 master's. *Graduate faculty:* 10 part-time/adjunct (5 women). *Tuition:* Full-time $2,640; part-time $220 per credit. *Graduate housing:* Rooms and/or apartments available on a first-come, first-served basis to single and married students. Typical cost: $990 per year ($2,290 including board) for single students; $990 per year ($2,290 including board) for married students. Housing application deadline: 6/1. *Student services:* Career counseling, disabled student services, teacher training. *Library facilities:* Memorial Library plus 1 other. *Online resources:* library catalog, web page, access to other libraries' catalogs. *Collection:* 75,000 titles, 300 serial subscriptions.

Computer facilities: 55 computers available on campus for general student use. A campuswide network can be accessed from student residence rooms and from off campus. Internet access is available. *Web address:* http://www.sckans.edu/.

General Application Contact: Victoria White, Director of Graduate Studies, 800-846-1543 Ext. 6115, Fax: 620-229-6341, E-mail: vwhite@sckans.edu.

GRADUATE UNITS

Center for Teaching Excellence Students: 1 (woman) full-time, 38 part-time (27 women); includes 1 minority (Hispanic American) Average age 33. 39 applicants, 100% accepted. *Faculty:* 10 part-time/adjunct (5 women). Expenses: Contact institution. *Financial support:* Institutionally sponsored loans available. Financial award application deadline: 4/1; financial award applicants required to submit FAFSA. In 2001, 1 degree awarded. *Degree program information:* Part-time and evening/weekend programs available. Postbaccalaureate distance learning degree programs offered (minimal on-campus study). Offers special education (M Ed). *Application deadline:* For fall admission, 8/24 (priority date); for spring admission, 1/24 (priority date). Applications are processed on a rolling basis. *Application fee:* $20. Electronic applications accepted. *Director of Graduate Studies,* Victoria White, 800-846-1543 Ext. 6115, Fax: 620-229-6341, E-mail: vwhite@sckans.edu.

SOUTHWESTERN COLLEGE, Santa Fe, NM 87502-4788

General Information Independent, coed, graduate-only institution. *Enrollment by degree level:* 125 master's. *Graduate faculty:* 5 full-time (4 women), 22 part-time/adjunct (15 women). *Tuition:* Full-time $11,760; part-time $245 per unit. *Graduate housing:* On-campus housing not available. *Student services:* Campus employment opportunities, campus safety program, career counseling. *Library facilities:* Quimby Memorial Library. *Collection:* 10,000 titles, 50 serial subscriptions, 200 audiovisual materials.

Computer facilities: 4 computers available on campus for general student use. A campuswide network can be accessed from off campus. Internet access is available. *Web address:* http://www.swc.edu/.

General Application Contact: Kristine Schmidt, Director of Admissions, 877-471-5756 Ext. 26, Fax: 877-471-4071, E-mail: admissions@swc.edu.

GRADUATE UNITS

Program in Art Therapy Students: 19 full-time (all women), 16 part-time (all women); includes 3 minority (1 Hispanic American, 2 Native Americans) Average age 41. 24 applicants, 100% accepted, 17 enrolled. *Faculty:* 5 full-time (4 women), 22 part-time/adjunct (15 women). Expenses: Contact institution. *Financial support:* In 2001–02, 25 students received support. Career-related internships or fieldwork, institutionally sponsored loans, and scholarships/grants available. Support available to part-time students. Financial award application deadline: 6/1; financial award applicants required to submit FAFSA. In 2001, 9 master's awarded. *Degree program information:* Part-time and evening/weekend programs available. Offers art therapy (MA, Certificate). *Application deadline:* For fall admission, 6/30 (priority date); for winter admission, 9/30 (priority date); for spring admission, 1/15 (priority date). Applications are processed on a rolling basis. *Application fee:* $50. *Application Contact:* Kristine Schmidt, Director of Admissions, 877-471-5756, Fax: 877-471-4071, E-mail: admissions@swc.edu. *Chair,* Kate Rogers, 877-471-5756 Ext. 15.

Program in Counseling Students: 27 full-time (18 women), 62 part-time (57 women); includes 3 minority (2 African Americans, 1 Hispanic American) Average age 41. 34 applicants, 100% accepted, 24 enrolled. *Faculty:* 5 full-time (4 women), 22 part-time/adjunct (15 women). Expenses: Contact institution. *Financial support:* In 2001–02, 46 students received support. Career-related internships or fieldwork, institutionally sponsored loans, and scholarships/grants available. Support available to part-time students. Financial award application deadline: 6/1; financial award applicants required to submit FAFSA. In 2001, 12 degrees awarded. *Degree program information:* Part-time and evening/weekend programs available. Offers counseling (MA); school counseling (Certificate). *Application deadline:* For fall admission, 6/30 (priority date); for winter admission, 9/30 (priority date); for spring admission, 1/15 (priority date). Applications are processed on a rolling basis. *Application fee:* $50. *Application Contact:* Kristine Schmidt, Director of Admissions, 505-471-5756 Ext. 26, Fax: 505-471-4071, E-mail: admissions@swc.edu. *Chair,* Dr. Pamela Bell, 877-471-5756 Ext. 13.

Program in Grief Counseling Average age 41. 25 applicants, 100% accepted, 25 enrolled. *Faculty:* 1 (woman) full-time. Expenses: Contact institution. In 2001, 11 degrees awarded. Offers grief counseling (Certificate). *Application deadline:* Applications are processed on a rolling basis. *Application fee:* $25. *Application Contact:* Kristine Schmidt, Director of Admissions, 877-471-5756, Fax: 877-471-4071, E-mail: admissions@swc.edu. *Director,* Dr. Janet Schreiber, 877-471-5756, Fax: 877-471-4071.

Program in Psychodrama and Action Methods Average age 41. 12 applicants, 100% accepted, 12 enrolled. *Faculty:* 1 (woman) part-time/adjunct. Expenses: Contact institution. Offers psychodrama and action methods (Certificate). *Application deadline:* Applications are processed on a rolling basis. *Application fee:* $25. *Application Contact:* Kristine Schmidt, Director of Admissions, 877-471-5756, Fax: 877-471-4071, E-mail: admissions@swc.edu. *Director,* Kate Cook, 877-471-5756, Fax: 877-471-4071.

See in-depth description on page 1107.

SOUTHWESTERN OKLAHOMA STATE UNIVERSITY, Weatherford, OK 73096-3098

General Information State-supported, coed, comprehensive institution. *Enrollment:* 369 full-time matriculated graduate/professional students (221 women), 241 part-time matriculated graduate/professional students (144 women). *Enrollment by degree level:* 330 first professional, 280 master's. *Graduate faculty:* 130 full-time (37 women). Tuition, state resident: part-time $70 per credit hour. Tuition, nonresident: part-time $162 per credit hour. *Required fees:* $7 per semester. *Graduate housing:* Rooms and/or apartments available on a first-come, first-served basis to single and married students. Typical cost: $1,860 per year for married students. Room charges vary according to board plan and housing facility selected. *Student services:* Campus employment opportunities, campus safety program, career counseling, disabled student services, exercise/wellness program, free psychological counseling, international student services, low-cost health insurance, teacher training. *Library facilities:* Al Harris Library. *Online resources:* library catalog, web page, access to other libraries' catalogs. *Collection:* 280,000 titles, 1,200 serial subscriptions, 872 audiovisual materials. *Research affiliation:* Gulf Coast Research Laboratory.

Computer facilities: 270 computers available on campus for general student use. A campuswide network can be accessed from off campus. Internet access is available. *Web address:* http://www.swosu.edu/.

General Application Contact: Dr. Gregory P. Moss, Dean, School of Education and Graduate Studies, 580-774-3285, Fax: 580-774-7043, E-mail: mossg@swosu.edu.

GRADUATE UNITS

Graduate School Students: 369 full-time (221 women), 241 part-time (144 women). Average age 35. 121 applicants, 44% accepted. *Faculty:* 131. Expenses: Contact institution. *Financial support:* Research assistantships, teaching assistantships, career-related internships or fieldwork, Federal Work-Study, institutionally sponsored loans, and tuition waivers (partial) available. Support available to part-time students. Financial award application deadline: 3/1; financial award applicants required to submit FAFSA. In 2001, 66 degrees awarded. *Degree program information:* Part-time and evening/weekend programs available. Postbaccalaureate distance learning degree programs offered (minimal on-campus study). *Application deadline:* Applications are processed on a rolling basis. *Application fee:* $15. *Dean, Education and Graduate Programs,* Dr. Gregory P. Moss, 580-774-3285, Fax: 580-774-7043, E-mail: mossg@swosu.edu.

School of Arts and Sciences Students: 12 full-time (5 women); includes 1 minority (Native American) 2 applicants, 100% accepted. *Faculty:* 12 full-time (2 women). Expenses: Contact institution. *Financial support:* Research assistantships, teaching assistantships, career-related internships or fieldwork, Federal Work-Study, institutionally sponsored loans, and tuition waivers (partial) available. Support available to part-time students. Financial award application deadline: 3/1; financial award applicants required to submit FAFSA. In 2001, 5 degrees awarded. *Degree program information:* Part-time programs available. Offers arts and sciences (MM); education (MM); performance (MM). *Application deadline:* Applications are processed on a rolling basis. *Application fee:* $15. *Application Contact:* Dr. Dan Dill, Associate Vice President for Academic Affairs and Dean of the Graduate School, 580-774-3769, Fax: 580-774-7101, E-mail: dilld@swosu.edu. *Dean,* Dr. Vilas Prabhu, 580-774-3704, E-mail: prabhuv@swosu.edu.

School of Business Students: 24 full-time (10 women); includes 1 minority (Asian American or Pacific Islander), 1 international. 5 applicants, 80% accepted. *Faculty:* 8 full-time (3 women). Expenses: Contact institution. *Financial support:* Research assistantships, teaching assistantships, Federal Work-Study, institutionally sponsored loans, and tuition waivers (partial) available. Support available to part-time students. Financial award application deadline: 3/1; financial award applicants required to submit FAFSA. In 2001, 10 degrees awarded. *Degree program information:* Part-time and evening/weekend programs available. Postbaccalaureate distance learning degree programs offered (minimal on-campus study). Offers business (MBA). MBA distance learning degree program offered to Oklahoma residents only. *Application deadline:* Applications are processed on a rolling basis. *Application fee:* $15. *Application Contact:* Dr. Dan Dill, Associate Vice President for Academic Affairs and Dean of the Graduate School, 580-774-3769, Fax: 580-774-7101, E-mail: dilld@swosu.edu. *Director,* Dr. Elizabeth Ferrell, 580-774-3040, E-mail: ferrelm@swosu.edu.

School of Education Students: 75 full-time (48 women), 183 part-time (117 women); includes 23 minority (6 African Americans, 2 Asian Americans or Pacific Islanders, 4 Hispanic Americans, 11 Native Americans), 1 international. 19 applicants, 100% accepted. *Faculty:* 85 full-time. Expenses: Contact institution. *Financial support:* Research assistantships, teaching assistantships, career-related internships or fieldwork, Federal Work-Study, institutionally sponsored loans, and tuition waivers (partial) available. Support available to part-time students. Financial award application deadline: 3/1; financial award applicants required to submit FAFSA. In 2001, 55 degrees awarded. *Degree program information:* Part-time and evening/weekend programs available. Postbaccalaureate distance learning degree programs offered (minimal on-campus study). Offers agency counseling (M Ed); art (M Ed); early childhood education (M Ed); education (M Ed); educational administration (M Ed); elementary education (M Ed); English (M Ed); health, physical education and recreation (M Ed); mathematics (M Ed); natural sciences (M Ed); psychometry (M Ed); school counseling (M Ed); social sciences (M Ed); special education (M Ed); technology (M Ed). *Application deadline:* Applications are processed on a rolling basis. *Application fee:* $15. *Application Contact:* Dr. Dan Dill, Associate Vice President for Academic Affairs and Dean of the Graduate School, 580-774-3769, Fax: 580-774-7101, E-mail: dilld@swosu.edu. *Dean, Education and Graduate Programs,* Dr. Gregory P. Moss, 580-774-3285, Fax: 580-774-7043, E-mail: mossg@swosu.edu.

School of Pharmacy Students: 232 full-time (134 women), 113 part-time (58 women); includes 57 minority (5 African Americans, 23 Asian Americans or Pacific Islanders, 3 Hispanic Americans, 26 Native Americans) 100 applicants, 34% accepted. *Faculty:* 12 full-time (1 woman), 20 part-time/adjunct (9 women). Expenses: Contact institution. Offers pharmacy (Pharm D). *Application deadline:* For fall admission, 2/1; for spring admission, 10/1. *Application Contact:* Susan Thiessen, Admissions Counselor, 580-774-3190, Fax: 580-774-7020, E-mail: thiess@swosu.edu. *Dean,* Dr. David Bergman, 580-774-3104, Fax: 580-774-7020, E-mail: bergmad@swosu.edu.

SOUTHWESTERN UNIVERSITY SCHOOL OF LAW, Los Angeles, CA 90005-3992

General Information Independent, coed, graduate-only institution. *Enrollment by degree level:* 879 first professional. *Graduate faculty:* 50 full-time (17 women), 38 part-time/adjunct (12 women). *Tuition:* Full-time $24,840; part-time $828 per unit. *Required fees:* $100; $100 per year. Tuition and fees vary according to course load and program. *Graduate housing:* On-campus housing not available. *Student services:* Campus employment opportunities, campus safety program, career counseling, free psychological counseling, writing training. *Online resources:* library catalog. *Collection:* 425,000 titles, 4,574 serial subscriptions.

Computer facilities: 85 computers available on campus for general student use. A campuswide network can be accessed from off campus. Internet access is available. *Web address:* http://www.swlaw.edu/.

General Application Contact: Anne Wilson, Director of Admissions, 213-738-6717, Fax: 213-383-1688, E-mail: admissions@swlaw.edu.

GRADUATE UNITS

Professional Program Students: 597 full-time (321 women), 282 part-time (140 women); includes 333 minority (58 African Americans, 154 Asian Americans or Pacific Islanders, 109 Hispanic Americans, 12 Native Americans), 8 international. Average age 27. 2,143 applicants, 47% accepted. *Faculty:* 50 full-time (17 women), 38 part-time/adjunct (12 women). Expenses: Contact institution. *Financial support:* Research assistantships, career-related internships or fieldwork, Federal Work-Study, institutionally sponsored loans, scholarships/grants, and tuition waivers (full and partial) available. Support available to part-time students. Financial award application deadline: 6/1; financial award applicants required to submit FAFSA. In 2001, 207 degrees awarded. *Degree program information:* Part-time and evening/weekend programs available. Offers entertainment and media law (LL M). *Application deadline:* For fall admission, 6/30. Applications are processed on a rolling basis. *Application fee:* $50. Electronic applications accepted. *Application Contact:* Anne Wilson, Director of Admissions, 213-738-6717, Fax: 213-383-1688, E-mail: admissions@swlaw.edu. *Dean,* Leigh H. Taylor, 213-738-6710, Fax: 213-383-1688.

SOUTHWEST MISSOURI STATE UNIVERSITY, Springfield, MO 65804-0094

General Information State-supported, coed, comprehensive institution. CGS member. *Enrollment:* 916 full-time matriculated graduate/professional students (547 women), 2,189 part-time matriculated graduate/professional students (1,478 women). *Graduate faculty:* 466 full-time (129 women), 54 part-time/adjunct (14 women). Tuition, state resident: full-time $2,286; part-time $127 per credit. Tuition, nonresident: full-time $4,572; part-time $254 per credit. *Required fees:* $151 per semester. Tuition and fees vary according to course level and program. *Graduate housing:* Rooms and/or apartments available to single and married students. Typical cost: $2,814 per year ($4,248 including board) for single students; $2,550 per year ($4,800 including board) for married students. Housing application deadline: 8/1. *Student services:* Campus employment opportunities, campus safety program, career counseling, child daycare facilities, disabled student services, exercise/wellness program, free psychological counseling, grant writing training, international student services, low-cost health insurance, multicultural affairs office, teacher training, writing training. *Library facilities:* Meyer Library plus 3 others. *Online resources:* library catalog, web page, access to other libraries' catalogs. *Collection:* 771,382 titles, 891,319 serial subscriptions, 32,773 audiovisual materials.

Computer facilities: 3,500 computers available on campus for general student use. A campuswide network can be accessed from student residence rooms and from off campus. *Web address:* http://www.smsu.edu/.

General Application Contact: Frank A. Einhellig, Associate Vice President for Academic Affairs and Dean, 417-836-5335, Fax: 417-836-6888, E-mail: fae942f@mail.smsu.edu.

GRADUATE UNITS

Graduate College Students: 771 full-time (449 women), 1,397 part-time (929 women); includes 78 minority (16 African Americans, 24 Asian Americans or Pacific Islanders, 13 Hispanic Americans, 25 Native Americans), 165 international. *Faculty:* 466 full-time (129 women), 54 part-time/adjunct (14 women). Expenses: Contact institution. *Financial support:* In 2001–02, 60 research assistantships with full tuition reimbursements (averaging $6,150 per year), 140 teaching assistantships with full tuition reimbursements (averaging $6,150 per year) were awarded. Career-related internships or fieldwork, Federal Work-Study, institutionally sponsored loans, scholarships/grants, tuition waivers (partial), and unspecified assistantships also available. Support available to part-time students. Financial award application deadline: 3/31; financial award applicants required to submit FAFSA. In 2001, 612 master's, 14 other advanced degrees awarded. *Degree program information:* Part-time and evening/weekend programs available. Postbaccalaureate distance learning degree programs offered. Offers community analysis (MSAS); environmental management (MSAS). *Application deadline:* For fall admission, 8/5 (priority date); for spring admission, 12/20 (priority date). Applications are processed on a rolling basis. *Application fee:* $25. Electronic applications accepted. *Application Contact:* Barbara L. Helvey, Administrative Assistant, 417-836-5335, Fax: 417-836-6888, E-mail: blh5695@smsu.edu. *Associate Vice President for Academic Affairs and Dean*, Frank A. Einhellig, 417-836-5335, Fax: 417-836-6888, E-mail: fae942f@mail.smsu.edu.

College of Arts and Letters Students: 50 full-time (33 women), 101 part-time (60 women); includes 5 minority (2 Asian Americans or Pacific Islanders, 3 Native Americans), 7 international. Average age 29. *Faculty:* 80 full-time (32 women). Expenses: Contact institution. *Financial support:* In 2001–02, research assistantships with full tuition reimbursements (averaging $6,150 per year), 61 teaching assistantships with full tuition reimbursements (averaging $6,150 per year) were awarded. Career-related internships or fieldwork, Federal Work-Study, institutionally sponsored loans, scholarships/grants, and unspecified assistantships also available. Support available to part-time students. Financial award application deadline: 3/31. In 2001, 56 degrees awarded. *Degree program information:* Part-time and evening/weekend programs available. Offers arts and letters (MA, MM, MS Ed); communication and mass media (MA, MS Ed); English (MS Ed); English and writing (MA); music (MM, MS Ed); theatre (MA). *Application deadline:* For fall admission, 8/5 (priority date); for spring admission, 12/20 (priority date). Applications are processed on a rolling basis. *Application fee:* $25. Electronic applications accepted. *Dean*, Dr. David O. Belcher, 417-836-4366, Fax: 417-836-6940, E-mail: dob458f@mail.smsu.edu.

College of Business Administration Students: 226 full-time (97 women), 185 part-time (74 women); includes 16 minority (2 African Americans, 8 Asian Americans or Pacific Islanders, 3 Hispanic Americans, 3 Native Americans), 106 international. Average age 25. *Faculty:* 83 full-time (16 women), 2 part-time/adjunct (0 women). Expenses: Contact institution. *Financial support:* In 2001–02, 4 research assistantships with full tuition reimbursements (averaging $6,150 per year), teaching assistantships with full tuition reimbursements (averaging $6,150 per year) were awarded. Career-related internships or fieldwork, Federal Work-Study, institutionally sponsored loans, scholarships/grants, tuition waivers (partial), and unspecified assistantships also available. Support available to part-time students. Financial award application deadline: 3/31. In 2001, 131 degrees awarded. *Degree program information:* Part-time and evening/weekend programs available. Postbaccalaureate distance learning degree programs offered (minimal on-campus study). Offers accountancy (M Acc); business administration (M Acc, MBA, MHA, MS, MS Ed); computer information systems (MS); computer science (MS); health administration (MHA). *Application deadline:* For fall admission, 8/5 (priority date); for spring admission, 12/20 (priority date). Applications are processed on a rolling basis. *Application fee:* $25. Electronic applications accepted. *Application Contact:* Dr. D. Michael Fields, Director, 417-836-5646, Fax: 417-836-4407, E-mail: dmf603f@smsu.edu. *Dean*, Dr. Ronald Bottin, 417-836-4408, Fax: 417-836-4407, E-mail: rrb639f@smsu.edu.

College of Education Students: 67 full-time (54 women), 857 part-time (633 women); includes 25 minority (5 African Americans, 3 Asian Americans or Pacific Islanders, 5 Hispanic Americans, 12 Native Americans), 8 international. *Faculty:* 41 full-time (23 women), 12 part-time/adjunct (7 women). Expenses: Contact institution. *Financial support:* In 2001–02, 12 research assistantships with full tuition reimbursements (averaging $6,150 per year), 1 teaching assistantship with full tuition reimbursement (averaging $6,150 per year) were awarded. Career-related internships or fieldwork, Federal Work-Study, institutionally sponsored loans, scholarships/grants, and unspecified assistantships also available. Support available to part-time students. Financial award application deadline: 3/31. In 2001, 199 degrees awarded. *Degree program information:* Part-time and evening/weekend programs available. Postbaccalaureate distance learning degree programs offered (minimal on-campus study). Offers counseling (MS); director of special education (Ed S); director of vocational education (Ed S); early education (MS Ed); education (MS, MS Ed, PhD, Ed S); educational administration (MS Ed, Ed S); educational leadership (PhD); elementary education (MS Ed); elementary principal (Ed S); instructional media technology (MS Ed); middle school education (MS Ed); reading education (MS Ed); secondary education (MS Ed); secondary principal (Ed S); special education (MS Ed); superintendent (Ed S); teacher education (MS Ed); vocational education (MS Ed). *Application deadline:* For fall admission, 8/5 (priority date); for spring admission, 12/20 (priority date). Applications are processed on a rolling basis. *Application fee:* $25. Electronic applications accepted. *Dean*, Dr. David L. Hough, 417-836-5254, Fax: 417-836-4884, E-mail: dah315f@smsu.edu.

College of Health and Human Services Students: 313 full-time (225 women), 96 part-time (81 women); includes 20 minority (3 African Americans, 8 Asian Americans or Pacific Islanders, 4 Hispanic Americans, 5 Native Americans), 15 international. Average age 24. *Faculty:* 82 full-time (36 women), 22 part-time/adjunct (3 women). Expenses: Contact institution. *Financial support:* In 2001–02, 11 research assistantships with full tuition reimbursements (averaging $6,150 per year), 23 teaching assistantships with full tuition reimbursements (averaging $6,150 per year) were awarded. Career-related internships or fieldwork, Federal Work-Study, institutionally sponsored loans, scholarships/grants, and unspecified assistantships also available. Support available to part-time students. Financial award application deadline: 3/31. In 2001, 119 degrees awarded. *Degree program information:* Part-time programs available. Offers cell and molecular biology (MS); communication sciences and disorders (MS); health and human services (MPH, MPT, MS, MS Ed, MSN, MSW); health promotion and wellness management (MS); health, physical education, and recreation (MS Ed); nurse anesthesia (MS); nursing (MSN); physical therapy (MPT); physician assistant studies (MS); psychology (MS, MS Ed); public health (MPH); social work (MSW). *Application deadline:* For fall admission, 8/5; for spring admission, 12/20. *Application fee:* $25. Electronic applications accepted. *Dean*, Dr. Jeanne L. Thomas, 417-836-4176, Fax: 417-836-6905.

College of Humanities and Public Affairs Students: 69 full-time (18 women), 53 part-time (19 women); includes 5 minority (1 African American, 3 Asian Americans or Pacific Islanders, 1 Native American), 18 international. Average age 33. *Faculty:* 64 full-time (8 women), 16 part-time/adjunct (3 women). Expenses: Contact institution. *Financial support:* In 2001–02, 33 research assistantships with full tuition reimbursements (averaging $6,150 per year), teaching assistantships with full tuition reimbursements (averaging $6,150 per year) were awarded. Career-related internships or fieldwork, Federal Work-Study, institutionally sponsored loans, scholarships/grants, tuition waivers (partial), and unspecified assistantships also available. Support available to part-time students. Financial award application deadline: 3/31; financial award applicants required to submit FAFSA. In 2001, 44 degrees awarded. *Degree program information:* Part-time and evening/weekend programs available. Offers defense and strategic studies (MS); history (MA, MS Ed); humanities and public affairs (MA, MIAA, MPA, MS, MS Ed); international affairs and administration (MIAA); public administration (MPA); religious studies (MS). *Application deadline:* For fall admission, 8/25 (priority date); for spring admission, 12/20. Applications are processed on a rolling basis. *Application fee:* $25. Electronic applications accepted. *Dean*, Dr. Lorene H. Stone, 417-836-5529, Fax: 417-836-8472.

College of Natural and Applied Sciences Students: 70 full-time (31 women), 42 part-time (20 women); includes 4 minority (1 African American, 1 Asian American or Pacific Islander, 1 Hispanic American, 1 Native American), 12 international. *Faculty:* 116 full-time (14 women), 2 part-time/adjunct (1 woman). Expenses: Contact institution. *Financial support:* In 2001–02, 4 research assistantships with full tuition reimbursements (averaging $6,150 per year), 55 teaching assistantships with full tuition reimbursements (averaging $6,150 per year) were awarded. Career-related internships or fieldwork, Federal Work-Study, scholarships/grants, and unspecified assistantships also available. Support available to part-time students. Financial award application deadline: 3/31. In 2001, 37 degrees awarded. *Degree program information:* Part-time and evening/weekend programs available. Offers agriculture (MS, MS Ed); biology (MS, MS Ed); biology education (MS); chemistry (MS); fruit science (MS); industrial management (MS Ed); materials science (MS); mathematics (MS); natural and applied sciences (MNAS, MS, MS Ed); plant science (MS); resource planning (MS). *Application deadline:* For fall admission, 8/5; for spring admission, 12/20. Applications are processed on a rolling basis. *Application fee:* $25. Electronic applications accepted. *Dean*, Dr. Lawrence E. Banks, 417-836-5249, Fax: 417-836-6934, E-mail: leb793f@smsu.edu.

See in-depth description on page 1109.

SOUTHWEST STATE UNIVERSITY, Marshall, MN 56258-1598

General Information State-supported, coed, comprehensive institution. *Graduate housing:* Room and/or apartments available to single students; on-campus housing not available to married students.

GRADUATE UNITS

Department of Business Administration Offers business administration (MS). Electronic applications accepted.

Department of Education Offers education (MS).

SOUTHWEST TEXAS STATE UNIVERSITY, San Marcos, TX 78666

General Information State-supported, coed, comprehensive institution. CGS member. *Enrollment:* 1,158 full-time matriculated graduate/professional students (786 women), 2,180 part-time matriculated graduate/professional students (1,458 women). *Enrollment by degree level:* 2,441 master's, 30 doctoral, 867 other advanced degrees. *Graduate faculty:* 276 full-time (118 women), 51 part-time/adjunct (22 women). Tuition, state resident: full-time $1,512; part-time $84 per credit hour. Tuition, nonresident: full-time $5,310; part-time $295 per credit hour. *Required fees:* $864; $29 per credit hour. $195 per term. Full-time tuition and fees vary according to course load. *Graduate housing:* Rooms and/or apartments available on a first-come, first-served basis to single and married students. Typical cost: $3,126 per year ($5,152 including board) for single students; $3,450 per year ($5,476 including board) for married students. Room and board charges vary according to board plan and housing facility selected. Housing application deadline: 7/1. *Student services:* Campus employment opportunities, campus safety program, career counseling, disabled student services, exercise/wellness program, free psychological counseling, international student services, low-cost health insurance, multicultural affairs office, teacher training. *Library facilities:* Alkek Library. *Online resources:* library catalog, web page, access to other libraries' catalogs. *Collection:* 710,223 titles, 6,252 serial subscriptions, 276,299 audiovisual materials. *Research affiliation:* Texas Research Institute (Austin, TX), International Consortium for the Environment, Texas Regional Institute for Environmental Studies, Texas Engineering Experiment Station.

Computer facilities: 731 computers available on campus for general student use. A campuswide network can be accessed from student residence rooms and from off campus. Internet access is available. *Web address:* http://www.swt.edu/.

General Application Contact: Dr. J. Michael Willoughby, Dean of the Graduate School, 512-245-2581, Fax: 512-245-8365, E-mail: gradcollege@swt.edu.

GRADUATE UNITS

Graduate School Students: 940 full-time (627 women), 1,531 part-time (1,014 women); includes 546 minority (143 African Americans, 62 Asian Americans or Pacific Islanders, 327 Hispanic Americans, 14 Native Americans), 216 international. Average age 32. 1,373 applicants, 73% accepted, 656 enrolled. *Faculty:* 276 full-time (118 women), 51 part-time/adjunct (22 women). Expenses: Contact institution. *Financial support:* In 2001–02, 1,282 students received support, including 88 research assistantships (averaging $10,574 per year), 56 teaching assistantships (averaging $11,149 per year); fellowships, career-related internships or fieldwork, Federal Work-Study, institutionally sponsored loans, scholarships/grants, unspecified assistantships, and laboratory instructorships, stipends also available. Support available to part-time students. Financial award application deadline: 4/1; financial award applicants required to submit FAFSA. In 2001, 754 master's, 3 doctorates awarded. *Degree program information:* Part-time and evening/weekend programs available. Offers interdisciplinary studies in applied sociology (MAIS); interdisciplinary studies in criminal justice (MSIS); interdisciplinary studies in education administration and psychological services (MAIS); interdisciplinary studies in elementary mathematics, science, and technology (MSIS); interdisciplinary studies in health, physical education, and recreation (MAIS, MSIS); interdisciplinary studies in liberal arts (MAIS); interdisciplinary studies in modern languages (MAIS); interdisciplinary studies in occupational education (MSIS); interdisciplinary studies in political science (MAIS); interdisciplinary studies in science (MSIS); international studies (MA). *Application deadline:* For fall admission, 6/15; for spring admission, 10/15. Applications are processed on a rolling basis. *Application fee:* $40 ($90 for international students). *Dean*, Dr. J. Michael Willoughby, 512-245-2581, Fax: 512-245-8365, E-mail: gradcollege@swt.edu.

College of Applied Arts Students: 21 full-time (14 women), 135 part-time (88 women); includes 58 minority (26 African Americans, 1 Asian American or Pacific Islander, 30 Hispanic Americans, 1 Native American), 1 international. Average age 37. 83 applicants, 82% accepted, 35 enrolled. *Faculty:* 23 full-time (15 women), 12 part-time/adjunct (8 women). Expenses: Contact institution. *Financial support:* In 2001–02, 1 research assistantship (averaging $8,530 per year), 13 teaching assistantships (averaging $7,380 per year) were awarded. Career-related internships or fieldwork, Federal Work-Study, and institutionally sponsored loans also available. Support available to part-time students. Financial award application deadline: 4/1; financial award applicants required to submit FAFSA. In 2001, 32 degrees awarded. *Degree program information:* Part-time and evening/weekend programs available. Offers agriculture education (M Ed); applied arts (M Ed, MS, MSCJ); criminal justice (MSCJ); family and child studies (MS). *Application deadline:* For fall admission, 6/15 (priority date); for spring admission, 10/15 (priority date). Applications are processed on a rolling basis. *Application fee:* $40 ($90 for international students). *Application Contact:* Dr. J. Michael Willoughby, Dean of the Graduate School, 512-245-2581, Fax: 512-245-8365, E-mail: gradcollege@swt.edu. *Dean,* Dr. Jaime Chahin, 512-245-3333, Fax: 512-245-3338, E-mail: tc03@swt.edu.

College of Business Administration Students: 119 full-time (58 women), 205 part-time (99 women); includes 52 minority (11 African Americans, 12 Asian Americans or Pacific Islanders, 27 Hispanic Americans, 2 Native Americans), 35 international. Average age 30. 144 applicants, 75% accepted, 63 enrolled. *Faculty:* 23 full-time (5 women), 2 part-time/adjunct (0 women). Expenses: Contact institution. *Financial support:* In 2001–02, 9 teaching assistantships (averaging $8,740 per year) were awarded; research assistantships, Federal Work-Study and institutionally sponsored loans also available. Support available to part-time students. Financial award application deadline: 4/1; financial award applicants required to submit FAFSA. In 2001, 123 degrees awarded. *Degree program information:* Part-time programs available. Offers accounting (M Acy); business administration (M Acy, MBA). *Application deadline:* For fall admission, 6/15 (priority date); for spring admission, 10/15 (priority date). Applications are processed on a rolling basis. *Application fee:* $40 ($90 for international students). *Application Contact:* Dr. J. Michael Willoughby, Dean of the Graduate School, 512-245-2581, Fax: 512-245-8365, E-mail: gradcollege@swt.edu. *Dean,* Dr. Denise Smart, 512-245-2311, Fax: 512-245-8375, E-mail: ds37@swt.edu.

College of Education Students: 223 full-time (184 women), 492 part-time (415 women); includes 146 minority (47 African Americans, 5 Asian Americans or Pacific Islanders, 94 Hispanic Americans), 10 international. Average age 33. 374 applicants, 78% accepted, 195 enrolled. *Faculty:* 53 full-time (32 women), 8 part-time/adjunct (6 women). Expenses: Contact institution. *Financial support:* In 2001–02, 9 research assistantships (averaging $8,705 per year), 23 teaching assistantships (averaging $8,320 per year) were awarded. Fellowships, career-related internships or fieldwork, Federal Work-Study, and institutionally sponsored loans also available. Support available to part-time students. Financial award application deadline: 4/1; financial award applicants required to submit FAFSA. In 2001, 244 degrees awarded. *Degree program information:* Part-time and evening/weekend programs available. Offers counseling and guidance (M Ed, MA); developmental education (MA); education (M Ed, MA, MS, MSRLS); educational administration (M Ed, MA); elementary education (M Ed, MA); elementary education-bilingual/bicultural (M Ed, MA); health and physical education (MA); health education (M Ed); management of vocational/technical education (M Ed); physical education (M Ed); professional counseling (MA); reading education (M Ed); recreation and leisure services (MSRLS); school psychology (MA); secondary education (M Ed, MA); special education (M Ed). *Application deadline:* For fall admission, 6/15 (priority date); for spring admission, 10/15 (priority date). Applications are processed on a rolling basis. *Application fee:* $40 ($90 for international students). *Application Contact:* Dr. J. Michael Willoughby, Dean of the Graduate School, 512-245-2581, Fax: 512-245-8365, E-mail: gradcollege@swt.edu. *Dean,* Dr. John Beck, 512-245-2150, Fax: 512-245-8345, E-mail: jb01@swt.edu.

College of Fine Arts and Communication Students: 53 full-time (35 women), 41 part-time (26 women); includes 22 minority (3 African Americans, 5 Asian Americans or Pacific Islanders, 13 Hispanic Americans, 1 Native American), 5 international. Average age 30. 62 applicants, 79% accepted, 34 enrolled. *Faculty:* 25 full-time (11 women), 3 part-time/adjunct (0 women). Expenses: Contact institution. *Financial support:* In 2001–02, 12 research assistantships (averaging $9,197 per year), 33 teaching assistantships (averaging $8,522 per year) were awarded. Career-related internships or fieldwork, Federal Work-Study, institutionally sponsored loans, scholarships/grants, and unspecified assistantships also available. Support available to part-time students. Financial award application deadline: 4/1; financial award applicants required to submit FAFSA. In 2001, 33 degrees awarded. *Degree program information:* Part-time and evening/weekend programs available. Offers fine arts and communication (MA, MM); mass communication (MA); music education (MM); music performance (MM); speech communication (MA); theatre arts (MA). *Application deadline:* For fall admission, 6/15 (priority date); for spring admission, 10/15 (priority date). Applications are processed on a rolling basis. *Application fee:* $40 ($90 for international students). *Application Contact:* Dr. J. Michael Willoughby, Dean of the Graduate School, 512-245-2581, Fax: 512-245-8365, E-mail: gradcollege@swt.edu. *Dean,* Dr. T. Richard Cheatham, 512-245-2308, Fax: 512-245-8334, E-mail: tc02@swt.edu.

College of Health Professions Students: 154 full-time (116 women), 155 part-time (125 women); includes 96 minority (23 African Americans, 7 Asian Americans or Pacific Islanders, 64 Hispanic Americans, 2 Native Americans), 8 international. Average age 30. 147 applicants, 65% accepted, 69 enrolled. *Faculty:* 30 full-time (21 women), 7 part-time/adjunct (4 women). Expenses: Contact institution. *Financial support:* In 2001–02, 6 research assistantships (averaging $9,633 per year), 13 teaching assistantships (averaging $6,314 per year) were awarded. Fellowships, career-related internships or fieldwork, Federal Work-Study, institutionally sponsored loans, scholarships/grants, and stipends also available. Support available to part-time students. Financial award application deadline: 4/1; financial award applicants required to submit FAFSA. In 2001, 112 degrees awarded. *Degree program information:* Part-time and evening/weekend programs available. Offers allied health research (MSHP); communication disorders (MA, MSCD); health human resources (MSHP); health professions (MA, MHA, MSCD, MSHP, MSPT, MSW); healthcare administration (MHA); physical therapy (MSPT); social work (MSW). *Application deadline:* For spring admission, 10/15 (priority date). *Application fee:* $40 ($90 for international students). *Application Contact:* Dr. J. Michael Willoughby, Dean of the Graduate School, 512-245-2581, Fax: 512-245-8365, E-mail: gradcollege@swt.edu. *Dean,* Dr. Rumaldo Z. Juarez, 512-245-3300, Fax: 512-245-3791, E-mail: rj05@swt.edu.

College of Liberal Arts Students: 158 full-time (107 women), 402 part-time (230 women); includes 123 minority (35 African Americans, 7 Asian Americans or Pacific Islanders, 75 Hispanic Americans, 6 Native Americans), 20 international. Average age 33. 321 applicants, 76% accepted, 167 enrolled. *Faculty:* 82 full-time (32 women), 12 part-time/adjunct (5 women). Expenses: Contact institution. *Financial support:* In 2001–02, 28 research assistantships (averaging $10,060 per year), 117 teaching assistantships (averaging $9,683 per year) were awarded. Fellowships, career-related internships or fieldwork, Federal Work-Study, institutionally sponsored loans, and scholarships/grants also available. Support available to part-time students. Financial award application deadline: 4/1; financial award applicants required to submit FAFSA. In 2001, 122 master's, 3 doctorates awarded. *Degree program information:* Part-time and evening/weekend programs available. Offers applied geography (MAG); cartography/geographic information systems (MAG); creative writing (MFA); environmental geography (PhD); environmental geography and geography education (PhD); geography (MAG); geography education (PhD); health psychology (MA); history (M Ed, MA); land/area studies (MAG); legal studies (MA); liberal arts (M Ed, MA, MAG, MAT, MFA, MPA, PhD); literature (MA); political science (M Ed, MA); political science education (M Ed); public administration (MPA); resource and environmental studies (MAG); sociology (MA); Spanish (MA, MAT); Spanish education (MAT); technical communication (MA). *Application deadline:* For fall admission, 6/15 (priority date); for spring admission, 10/15 (priority date). Applications are processed on a rolling basis. *Application fee:* $40 ($90 for international students). *Application Contact:* Dr. J. Michael Willoughby, Dean of the Graduate School, 512-245-2581, Fax: 512-245-8365, E-mail: gradcollege@swt.edu. *Dean,* Dr. Ann Marrie Ellis, 512-245-2317, Fax: 512-245-8291, E-mail: ae02@swt.edu.

College of Science Students: 214 full-time (114 women), 144 part-time (60 women); includes 57 minority (2 African Americans, 25 Asian Americans or Pacific Islanders, 29 Hispanic Americans, 1 Native American), 138 international. Average age 31. 239 applicants, 64% accepted, 93 enrolled. *Faculty:* 51 full-time (11 women), 1 part-time/adjunct (0 women). Expenses: Contact institution. *Financial support:* In 2001–02, 23 research assistantships (averaging $11,777 per year), 94 teaching assistantships (averaging $11,000 per year) were awarded. Career-related internships or fieldwork, Federal Work-Study, institutionally sponsored loans, and laboratory instructorships also available. Support available to part-time students. Financial award application deadline: 4/1; financial award applicants required to submit FAFSA. In 2001, 88 degrees awarded. *Degree program information:* Part-time and evening/weekend programs available. Offers aquatic biology (MS); biochemistry (MS); biology (M Ed, MA, MS); chemistry (M Ed, MA, MS); computer science (MA, MS); industrial technology (MST); mathematics (M Ed, MA, MS); physics (MA, MS); science (M Ed, MA, MS, MST); software engineering (MS). *Application deadline:* For fall admission, 6/15 (priority date); for spring admission, 10/15 (priority date). Applications are processed on a rolling basis. *Application fee:* $40 ($90 for international students). *Application Contact:* Dr. J. Michael Willoughby, Dean of the Graduate School, 512-245-2581, Fax: 512-245-8365, E-mail: gradcollege@swt.edu. *Dean,* Dr. Stanley C. Israel, 512-245-2119, Fax: 512-245-8095, E-mail: si02@swt.edu.

SPALDING UNIVERSITY, Louisville, KY 40203-2188

General Information Independent-religious, coed, comprehensive institution. CGS member. *Enrollment:* 218 full-time matriculated graduate/professional students (182 women), 364 part-time matriculated graduate/professional students (271 women). *Enrollment by degree level:* 347 master's, 235 doctoral. *Graduate faculty:* 39 full-time (24 women), 17 part-time/adjunct (9 women). *Tuition:* Full-time $6,000; part-time $400 per credit hour. *Required fees:* $96. *Graduate housing:* Room and/or apartments available to single students; on-campus housing not available to married students. Typical cost: $800 per year ($1,550 including board). Room and board charges vary according to board plan. Housing application deadline: 8/15. *Student services:* Campus employment opportunities, career counseling, free psychological counseling, international student services, low-cost health insurance, teacher training, writing training. *Library facilities:* Spalding Library. *Online resources:* library catalog, web page, access to other libraries' catalogs. *Collection:* 190,994 titles, 601 serial subscriptions, 14,864 audiovisual materials.

Computer facilities: 80 computers available on campus for general student use. A campuswide network can be accessed. Internet access is available. *Web address:* http://www.spalding.edu/.

General Application Contact: 502-585-7105, Fax: 502-585-7158, E-mail: gradadmissions@spalding.edu.

GRADUATE UNITS

Graduate Studies Students: 218 full-time (182 women), 364 part-time (271 women); includes 69 minority (52 African Americans, 8 Asian Americans or Pacific Islanders, 4 Hispanic Americans, 5 Native Americans), 58 international. Average age 36. 279 applicants, 60% accepted. *Faculty:* 39 full-time (24 women), 17 part-time/adjunct (9 women). Expenses: Contact institution. *Financial support:* In 2001–02, 280 students received support, including 40 research assistantships (averaging $3,600 per year); career-related internships or fieldwork, Federal Work-Study, scholarships/grants, and traineeships also available. Support available to part-time students. Financial award application deadline: 3/15; financial award applicants required to submit FAFSA. In 2001, 106 master's, 29 doctorates awarded. *Degree program information:* Part-time and evening/weekend programs available. *Application fee:* $30. *Application Contact:* Graduate Office, 502-585-7105, Fax: 502-585-7158, E-mail: gradadmissions@spalding.edu.

College of Arts and Sciences Students: 10. 7 applicants, 57% accepted. *Faculty:* 3 full-time (1 woman), 2 part-time/adjunct (both women). Expenses: Contact institution. *Financial support:* Research assistantships, Federal Work-Study and scholarships/grants available. Support available to part-time students. Financial award application deadline: 3/15; financial award applicants required to submit FAFSA. *Degree program information:* Part-time and evening/weekend programs available. Offers ministry studies (MA); religion and ministry (MA); religious studies (MA); writing (MFA). *Application deadline:* For fall admission, 8/15 (priority date); for spring admission, 12/15 (priority date). Applications are processed on a rolling basis. *Application fee:* $30. *Application Contact:* 502-585-7105, Fax: 502-585-7158, E-mail: gradadmissions@spalding.edu. *Dean,* Kathleen Nesbitt, 502-585-9911, Fax: 502-585-7158, E-mail: knesbitt@spalding.edu.

School of Education Students: 41 full-time (35 women), 188 part-time (139 women); includes 30 minority (21 African Americans, 5 Asian Americans or Pacific Islanders, 2 Hispanic Americans, 2 Native Americans), 42 international. 77 applicants, 83% accepted. *Faculty:* 10 full-time (8 women), 4 part-time/adjunct (2 women). Expenses: Contact institution. *Financial support:* In 2001–02, 105 students received support, including 9 research assistantships (averaging $1,500 per year); career-related internships or fieldwork, Federal Work-Study, and scholarships/grants also available. Support available to part-time students. Financial award application deadline: 3/15; financial award applicants required to submit FAFSA. In 2001, 44 master's, 8 doctorates awarded. *Degree program information:* Part-time and evening/weekend programs available. Offers 5–8 (MA, MAT); 9–12 (MA, MAT); education (MA, MAT, Ed D); guidance (MA); K–4 (MA, MAT); leadership education (Ed D); reading specialist (MA); school media librarianship (MA). *Application deadline:* For fall admission, 8/15 (priority date). Applications are processed on a rolling basis. *Application fee:* $30. *Application Contact:* 502-585-7105, Fax: 502-585-7158, E-mail: gradadmissions@spalding.edu. *Dean,* Dr. Betty Lindsey, 502-585-9911, Fax: 502-585-7158, E-mail: education@spalding4.win.net.

School of Nursing and Health Sciences Students: 15 full-time (13 women), 20 part-time (17 women); includes 5 minority (3 African Americans, 1 Asian American or Pacific Islander, 1 Hispanic American), 2 international. 29 applicants, 76% accepted. *Faculty:* 5 full-time (all women). Expenses: Contact institution. *Financial support:* In 2001–02, 35 students received support, including 1 research assistantship (averaging $2,800 per year); career-related internships or fieldwork, scholarships/grants, and traineeships also available. Support available to part-time students. Financial award application deadline: 3/15; financial award applicants required to submit FAFSA. In 2001, 28 degrees awarded. *Degree program information:* Part-time and evening/weekend programs available. Offers administration (MSN); family nurse practitioner (MSN). *Application deadline:* For fall admission, 8/15 (priority date); for spring admission, 12/15 (priority date). Applications are processed on a rolling basis. *Application fee:* $30. *Application Contact:* Graduate Office, 502-585-7105, Fax: 502-585-7158, E-mail: gradadmissions@spalding.edu. *Dean,* Dr. Cynthia Crabtree, 502-585-7125, Fax: 502-585-7158, E-mail: nursing@spalding10.win.net.

School of Psychology Students: 46 full-time (33 women), 86 part-time (64 women); includes 11 minority (6 African Americans, 2 Asian Americans or Pacific Islanders, 1 Hispanic American, 2 Native Americans), 8 international. 136 applicants, 40% accepted. *Faculty:* 8 full-time (3 women), 8 part-time/adjunct (3 women). Expenses: Contact institution. *Financial support:* In 2001–02, 28 research assistantships (averaging $4,100 per year) were awarded; career-related internships or fieldwork, Federal Work-Study, and scholarships/grants also available. Financial award application deadline: 3/15. In 2001, 8 master's, 21 doctorates awarded. *Degree program information:* Part-time programs available. Offers clinical psychology (MA, Psy D). *Application deadline:* For fall admission, 1/15. *Application fee:* $30. *Application Contact:* 502-585-1705, Fax: 502-585-7158, E-mail: gradadmissions@spalding.edu. *Dean,* Dr. Barbara Williams, 502-585-9911.

School of Social Work Students: 27 full-time (all women), 7 part-time (1 woman); includes 7 minority (6 African Americans, 1 Native American), 2 international. Average age 35. 30 applicants, 80% accepted. *Faculty:* 5 full-time (4 women), 4 part-time/adjunct (2 women). Expenses: Contact institution. *Financial support:* In 2001–02, 22 students received support, including 2 research assistantships (averaging $4,200 per year); career-related internships or fieldwork, Federal Work-Study, and scholarships/grants also available. Support available to part-time students. Financial award application deadline: 3/15; financial award applicants required to submit FAFSA. In 2001, 23 degrees awarded. *Degree program information:* Evening/weekend programs available. Offers social work (MSW). *Application deadline:* For fall admission, 4/1 (priority date). *Application fee:* $30. *Application Contact:* Graduate Office, 502-585-7105, Fax: 502-585-7158, E-mail: gradadmissions@spalding.edu. *Dean,* Dr. Helen Deines, 502-585-7183, Fax: 502-585-7158.

See in-depth description on page 1111.

SPERTUS INSTITUTE OF JEWISH STUDIES, Chicago, IL 60605-1901

General Information Independent, coed, graduate-only institution. *Enrollment by degree level:* 219 master's, 11 doctoral. *Graduate faculty:* 39 part-time/adjunct (16 women). *Tuition:* Part-time $200 per quarter hour. Tuition and fees vary according to degree level and program. *Graduate housing:* On-campus housing not available. *Student services:* Grant writing train-

Spertus Institute of Jewish Studies (continued)

ing, international student services, writing training. *Library facilities:* Asher Library. *Online resources:* library catalog, web page. *Collection:* 100,000 titles, 800 serial subscriptions.

Computer facilities: 4 computers available on campus for general student use. Internet access is available. *Web address:* http://www.spertus.edu/.

General Application Contact: Lisa Burnstein, Director of Student Services, 312-922-9012, Fax: 312-922-6406, E-mail: lisa@spertus.edu.

GRADUATE UNITS

Judaica Studies Graduate Programs Institute of Advanced Judaica Average age 30. 65 applicants, 78% accepted. *Faculty:* 39 part-time/adjunct (16 women). Expenses: Contact institution. *Financial support:* Scholarships/grants available. Support available to part-time students. Financial award applicants required to submit FAFSA. In 2001, 74 master's, 1 doctorate awarded. *Degree program information:* Part-time and evening/weekend programs available. Postbaccalaureate distance learning degree programs offered (minimal on-campus study). Offers human services administration (MSHSA); Jewish communal studies (MAJCS); Jewish education (MAJ Ed); Jewish studies (MAJS, MSJE, MSJS, DJS, DSJS); Judaica (MAJ Ed, MAJCS, MAJS, MSHSA, MSJE, MSJS, DJS, DSJS). *Application deadline:* Applications are processed on a rolling basis. *Application fee:* $50. *Application Contact:* Dr. Dean Bell, Dean, 312-922-9012, Fax: 312-922-6406, E-mail: college@spertus.edu. *Dean*, Dr. Dean Bell, 312-922-9012, Fax: 312-922-6406, E-mail: college@spertus.edu.

SPRING ARBOR UNIVERSITY, Spring Arbor, MI 49283-9799

General Information Independent-religious, coed, comprehensive institution. *Enrollment:* 266 full-time matriculated graduate/professional students (171 women), 177 part-time matriculated graduate/professional students (123 women). *Enrollment by degree level:* 443 master's. *Graduate faculty:* 11 full-time (3 women), 82 part-time/adjunct (30 women). *Tuition:* Part-time $289 per credit. *Required fees:* $216. *Graduate housing:* Rooms and/or apartments available to single students and available on a first-come, first-served basis to married students. *Student services:* Campus safety program. *Library facilities:* Hugh A. White Library plus 1 other. *Collection:* 84,225 titles, 5,120 audiovisual materials.

Computer facilities: 85 computers available on campus for general student use. Internet access is available. *Web address:* http://www.arbor.edu/.

General Application Contact: Jennifer DeBiasi, Admissions Representative, 517-750-6536, Fax: 517-750-6624, E-mail: falconer@arbor.edu.

GRADUATE UNITS

School of Adult Studies *Degree program information:* Evening/weekend programs available. Offers organizational management (MAOM).

School of Business and Management *Degree program information:* Part-time and evening/weekend programs available. Offers business and management (MBA).

School of Education Offers education (MAE). Electronic applications accepted.

SPRINGFIELD COLLEGE, Springfield, MA 01109-3797

General Information Independent, coed, comprehensive institution. *Enrollment:* 1,048 full-time matriculated graduate/professional students (700 women), 290 part-time matriculated graduate/professional students (201 women). *Enrollment by degree level:* 1,324 master's, 14 doctoral. *Graduate faculty:* 156 full-time (78 women), 98 part-time/adjunct (46 women). *Graduate housing:* Rooms and/or apartments available on a first-come, first-served basis to single and married students. *Student services:* Campus employment opportunities, campus safety program, career counseling, child daycare facilities, disabled student services, exercise/wellness program, free psychological counseling, international student services, low-cost health insurance, multicultural affairs office, teacher training, writing training. *Library facilities:* Babson Library. *Collection:* 125,000 titles, 850 serial subscriptions.

Computer facilities: 95 computers available on campus for general student use. A campuswide network can be accessed from student residence rooms and from off campus. Internet access is available. *Web address:* http://www.springfieldcollege.edu.

General Application Contact: Donald James Shaw, Director of Graduate Admissions, 413-748-3225, Fax: 413-748-3694, E-mail: donald_shaw_jr@spfldcol.edu.

GRADUATE UNITS

School of Graduate Studies Students: 1,048 full-time (700 women), 290 part-time (201 women); includes 333 minority (249 African Americans, 15 Asian Americans or Pacific Islanders, 65 Hispanic Americans, 4 Native Americans), 45 international. Average age 26. 1,200 applicants, 82% accepted. *Faculty:* 156 full-time (78 women), 98 part-time/adjunct (46 women). Expenses: Contact institution. *Financial support:* In 2001–02, 4 fellowships with partial tuition reimbursements, 99 teaching assistantships with partial tuition reimbursements were awarded. Career-related internships or fieldwork, Federal Work-Study, institutionally sponsored loans, scholarships/grants, traineeships, and tuition waivers (full and partial) also available. Financial award application deadline: 3/1; financial award applicants required to submit FAFSA. In 2001, 528 master's, 1 doctorate, 5 other advanced degrees awarded. *Degree program information:* Part-time and evening/weekend programs available. Offers adapted physical education (M Ed, MPE, MS, CAS); advanced level coaching (M Ed, MPE, MS, CAS); alcohol rehabilitation/substance abuse counseling (M Ed, MS, CAS); applied exercise science (M Ed, MPE, MS); art therapy (M Ed, MS, CAS); athletic administration (M Ed, MPE, MS, CAS); athletic counseling (M Ed, MS, CAS); biomechanics (M Ed, MPE, MS); clinical masters in physical education (M Ed, MPE, MS); counseling and secondary education (M Ed, MS); deaf counseling (M Ed, MS, CAS); developmental disabilities (M Ed, MS, CAS); education (M Ed, MS); exercise physiology (M Ed, MPE, MS); general counseling (M Ed, MS, CAS); general counseling and casework (M Ed, MS, CAS); general physical education (DPE); health care management (M Ed, MS); health promotion/wellness management (M Ed, MS, CAS); human services (MS); industrial/organizational psychology (MS, CAS); interdisciplinary studies (M Ed, MPE, MS); marriage and family therapy (M Ed, MS, CAS); mental health counseling (M Ed, MS, CAS); occupational therapy (M Ed, MS, CAS); outdoor recreational management (M Ed, MS); physical therapy (MS); psychiatric rehabilitation/mental health counseling (M Ed, MS, CAS); recreational management (M Ed, MS); school guidance and counseling (M Ed, MS, CAS); social work (MSW); special services (M Ed, MS, CAS); sport management (M Ed, MPE, MS, CAS); sport psychology (M Ed, MPE, MS, DPE, CAS); sport studies (M Ed, MPE, MS, CAS); sports injury prevention and management (M Ed, MPE, MS); student personnel in higher education (M Ed, MS, CAS); teaching and administration (M Ed, MPE, MS, CAS); therapeutic recreational management (M Ed, MS); vocational evaluation and work adjustment (M Ed, MS, CAS). *Application deadline:* Applications are processed on a rolling basis. *Application fee:* $40. Electronic applications accepted. *Application Contact:* Donald James Shaw, Director of Graduate Admissions, 413-748-3225, Fax: 413-748-3694, E-mail: donald_shaw_jr@spfldcol.edu. *Dean*, Dr. Betty L. Mann, 413-748-3125, Fax: 413-748-3764.

See in-depth description on page 1113.

SPRING HILL COLLEGE, Mobile, AL 36608-1791

General Information Independent-religious, coed, comprehensive institution. *Enrollment:* 20 full-time matriculated graduate/professional students (16 women), 219 part-time matriculated graduate/professional students (152 women). *Enrollment by degree level:* 239 master's. *Graduate faculty:* 20 full-time (6 women), 9 part-time/adjunct (3 women). *Tuition:* Part-time $195 per credit hour. Tuition and fees vary according to program. *Graduate housing:* On-campus housing not available. *Student services:* Career counseling, free psychological counseling, international student services, low-cost health insurance, multicultural affairs office, teacher training. *Library facilities:* Thomas Byrne Memorial Library. *Online resources:* library catalog, web page, access to other libraries' catalogs. *Collection:* 88,100 titles, 1,324 serial subscriptions, 336 audiovisual materials.

Computer facilities: 141 computers available on campus for general student use. A campuswide network can be accessed from student residence rooms and from off campus. Internet access is available. *Web address:* http://www.shc.edu/.

General Application Contact: Joyce Genz, Dean of Life Long Learning and Director of Graduate Programs, 251-380-3094, Fax: 251-460-2190, E-mail: grad@shc.edu.

GRADUATE UNITS

Graduate Programs Students: 20 full-time (16 women), 219 part-time (152 women); includes 35 minority (29 African Americans, 1 Asian American or Pacific Islander, 3 Hispanic Americans, 2 Native Americans), 2 international. Average age 41. *Faculty:* 20 full-time (6 women), 9 part-time/adjunct (3 women). Expenses: Contact institution. *Financial support:* In 2001–02, 126 students received support. Available to part-time students. Applicants required to submit FAFSA. In 2001, 62 degrees awarded. *Degree program information:* Part-time and evening/weekend programs available. Offers business administration (MBA); early childhood education (MAT, MS Ed); elementary education (MAT, MS Ed); liberal arts (MLA); secondary education (MAT, MS Ed); theology (MA, MPS, MTS). *Application deadline:* For fall admission, 8/1 (priority date); for spring admission, 12/1 (priority date). Applications are processed on a rolling basis. *Application fee:* $25. *Dean of Life Long Learning and Director of Graduate Programs*, Joyce Genz, 251-380-3094, Fax: 251-460-2190, E-mail: grad@shc.edu.

STANFORD UNIVERSITY, Stanford, CA 94305-9991

General Information Independent, coed, university. CGS member. *Enrollment:* 6,318 full-time matriculated graduate/professional students (2,293 women), 1,382 part-time matriculated graduate/professional students (472 women). *Enrollment by degree level:* 1,011 first professional, 3,004 master's, 3,685 doctoral. *Graduate faculty:* 1,670 full-time (342 women). *Graduate housing:* Rooms and/or apartments guaranteed to single and married students. Housing application deadline: 5/10. *Student services:* Campus employment opportunities, campus safety program, career counseling, child daycare facilities, disabled student services, exercise/wellness program, free psychological counseling, international student services, low-cost health insurance, multicultural affairs office, teacher training. *Library facilities:* Green Library plus 18 others. *Online resources:* library catalog, web page, access to other libraries' catalogs. *Collection:* 7 million titles, 44,504 serial subscriptions, 1.3 million audiovisual materials.

Computer facilities: 1,000 computers available on campus for general student use. A campuswide network can be accessed from student residence rooms and from off campus. Internet access and online class registration are available. *Web address:* http://www.stanford.edu/.

General Application Contact: Mary Lue Eiche, Graduate Admissions Support Section, 650-723-4291, Fax: 650-723-8371, E-mail: ck.gaa@forsythe.stanford.edu.

GRADUATE UNITS

Graduate School of Business Students: 806 full-time (293 women), 14 part-time (4 women); includes 190 minority (38 African Americans, 102 Asian Americans or Pacific Islanders, 42 Hispanic Americans, 8 Native Americans), 256 international. Average age 28. 6,109 applicants, 8% accepted. *Faculty:* 85 full-time (15 women). Expenses: Contact institution. In 2001, 394 master's, 23 doctorates awarded. Offers business (MBA, PhD). *Application fee:* $180. Electronic applications accepted. *Application Contact:* Information Contact, 650-723-2766, Fax: 650-725-7831, E-mail: mba@gsb.stanford.edu. *Dean*, Robert L. Joss, 650-723-1063, Fax: 650-723-1322, E-mail: joss_robert@gsb.stanford.edu.

Law School Students: 558 full-time (257 women), 35 part-time (13 women); includes 173 minority (43 African Americans, 50 Asian Americans or Pacific Islanders, 76 Hispanic Americans, 4 Native Americans), 63 international. Average age 27. 4,228 applicants, 13% accepted. *Faculty:* 42 full-time (8 women). Expenses: Contact institution. In 2001, 202 first professional degrees, 1 master's awarded. Offers law (JD, JSM, MLS, JSD). *Application deadline:* For fall admission, 2/1. *Application fee:* $65 ($80 for international students). Electronic applications accepted. *Application Contact:* Faye Deal, Director of Admissions, 650-723-0302, E-mail: law.admissions@stanford.edu. *Dean*, Kathleen M. Sullivan, 650-723-4455, Fax: 650-725-0253.

School of Earth Sciences Students: 184 full-time (60 women), 25 part-time (8 women); includes 7 minority (6 Asian Americans or Pacific Islanders, 1 Hispanic American), 113 international. Average age 27. 206 applicants, 32% accepted. *Faculty:* 44 full-time (6 women). Expenses: Contact institution. In 2001, 42 master's, 22 doctorates awarded. Offers earth sciences (MS, PhD, Eng); earth systems (MS); geological and environmental sciences (MS, PhD, Eng); geophysics (MS, PhD); petroleum engineering (MS, PhD, Eng). *Application deadline:* For fall admission, 1/15. *Application fee:* $65 ($80 for international students). Electronic applications accepted. *Dean*, Franklin M. Orr, 650-723-2750, Fax: 650-725-6566, E-mail: dean@pangea.stanford.edu.

School of Education Students: 286 full-time (194 women), 56 part-time (37 women); includes 98 minority (19 African Americans, 48 Asian Americans or Pacific Islanders, 28 Hispanic Americans, 3 Native Americans), 46 international. Average age 30. 483 applicants, 35% accepted. *Faculty:* 45 full-time (16 women). Expenses: Contact institution. In 2001, 148 master's, 32 doctorates awarded. Offers administration and policy analysis (Ed D, PhD); anthropology of education (PhD); art education (AM, PhD); child and adolescent development (PhD); counseling psychology (PhD); dance education (AM); economics of education (PhD); education (AM, Ed D, PhD); educational linguistics (PhD); educational psychology (PhD); English education (AM, PhD); evaluation (AM); general curriculum studies (AM, PhD); higher education (PhD); history of education (PhD); interdisciplinary studies (PhD); international comparative education (AM, PhD); international education administration and policy analysis (AM); languages education (AM); learning, design and technology (AM, PhD); mathematics education (AM, PhD); philosophy of education (PhD); policy analysis (AM); prospective principal's program (AM); science education (AM, PhD); social studies education (AM, PhD); sociology of education (PhD); symbolic systemis in education (PhD); teacher education (AM, PhD). *Application deadline:* For fall admission, 1/2. *Application fee:* $65 ($80 for international students). Electronic applications accepted. *Application Contact:* 650-723-4794. *Dean*, Deborah J. Stipek, 650-725-9090, Fax: 650-725-7412, E-mail: stipek@stanford.edu.

School of Engineering Students: 2,472 full-time (533 women), 574 part-time (107 women); includes 589 minority (65 African Americans, 439 Asian Americans or Pacific Islanders, 81 Hispanic Americans, 4 Native Americans), 1,401 international. Average age 26. 4,518 applicants, 39% accepted. *Faculty:* 219 full-time (19 women). Expenses: Contact institution. In 2001, 1,009 master's, 196 doctorates awarded. Offers aeronautics and astronautics (MS, PhD, Eng); biomechanical engineering (MS); chemical engineering (MS, PhD, Eng); civil and environmental engineering (MS, PhD, Eng); computer science (MS, PhD); electrical engineering (MS, PhD, Eng); engineering (MS, PhD, Eng); management science and engineering (MS, PhD); management science and engineering and electrical engineering (MS); manufacturing systems engineering (MS); materials science and engineering (MS, PhD, Eng); mechanical engineering (MS, PhD, Eng); product design (MS); scientific computing and computational mathematics (MS, PhD). *Application fee:* $65 ($80 for international students). Electronic applications accepted. *Application Contact:* 650-723-4291, E-mail: ck.gaa@stanford.edu. *Dean*, James D. Plummer, 650-723-3938, Fax: 650-723-8545, E-mail: plummer@ee.stanford.edu.

School of Humanities and Sciences Students: 1,532 full-time (676 women), 474 part-time (218 women); includes 364 minority (61 African Americans, 178 Asian Americans or Pacific Islanders, 106 Hispanic Americans, 19 Native Americans), 636 international. Average age 28. 4,529 applicants, 19% accepted. *Faculty:* 524 full-time (123 women). Expenses: Contact institution. In 2001, 406 master's, 241 doctorates awarded. Offers anthropological sciences (AM, MS, PhD); applied physics (MS, PhD); art (MFA, PhD); biological sciences (MS, PhD); biophysics (PhD); chemistry (PhD); Chinese (AM, PhD); classics (AM, PhD); communication theory and research (PhD); comparative literature (PhD); computer-based music theory and acoustics (AM, PhD); cultural and social anthropology (AM, PhD); documentary film and video (AM); drama (PhD); economics (PhD); English (AM, PhD); financial mathematics (MS); French (AM, PhD); German studies (AM, PhD); history (AM, PhD); humanities (AM); humanities and sciences (AM, MFA, MS, DMA, PhD); international policy studies (AM); Italian (AM, PhD); Japanese (AM, PhD); journalism (AM); linguistics (AM, PhD); mathematics (MS, PhD); modern thought and literature (PhD); music composition (AM, DMA); music history (AM); music, science, and technology (AM); musicology (PhD); philosophy (AM, PhD); physics (PhD); political science (AM, PhD); psychology (PhD); religious studies (AM, PhD); Russian

(AM); Slavic languages and literatures (PhD); sociology (PhD); Spanish (AM, PhD); statistics (MS, PhD). *Application fee:* $65 ($80 for international students). Electronic applications accepted. *Dean,* Malcolm R. Beasley, 650-725-1569, Fax: 650-723-3235, E-mail: beasley@stanford.edu.

Center for East Asian Studies Students: 20 full-time (10 women), 3 part-time; includes 5 minority (4 Asian Americans or Pacific Islanders, 1 Native American), 6 international. Average age 25. 55 applicants, 56% accepted. Expenses: Contact institution. *Financial support:* Research assistantships available. In 2001, 14 degrees awarded. Offers East Asian studies (AM). *Application deadline:* For fall admission, 1/4. *Application fee:* $65 ($80 for international students). Electronic applications accepted. *Application Contact:* Director of Graduate Admissions, 650-723-3362. *Director,* Jean Oi, 650-725-1418, Fax: 650-725-0597, E-mail: joi@stanford.edu.

Center for Latin American Studies Students: 12 full-time (7 women); includes 3 minority (2 Hispanic Americans, 1 Native American), 2 international. Average age 28. 28 applicants, 57% accepted. Expenses: Contact institution. In 2001, 14 degrees awarded. Offers Latin American studies (AM). *Application deadline:* For fall admission, 1/5. *Application fee:* $65 ($80 for international students). Electronic applications accepted. *Application Contact:* Graduate Program Administrator, 650-723-4444. *Director,* Terry L. Karl, 650-725-2012, Fax: 650-725-9255, E-mail: tkarl@stanford.edu.

Center for Russian and East European Studies Students: 6 full-time (4 women), 2 international. Average age 29. 7 applicants, 57% accepted. Expenses: Contact institution. In 2001, 5 degrees awarded. Offers Russian and East European studies (AM). *Application deadline:* For fall admission, 1/1. *Application fee:* $65 ($80 for international students). Electronic applications accepted. *Application Contact:* Graduate Program Administrator, 650-723-3568. *Director,* Nancy Kollman, 650-723-9475, Fax: 650-725-0597, E-mail: kollmann@leland.stanford.edu.

School of Medicine Students: 624 full-time (320 women), 190 part-time (84 women); includes 308 minority (42 African Americans, 200 Asian Americans or Pacific Islanders, 57 Hispanic Americans, 9 Native Americans), 53 international. Average age 27. 6,845 applicants, 5% accepted. *Faculty:* 674 full-time (154 women). Expenses: Contact institution. In 2001, 86 first professional degrees, 21 master's, 51 doctorates awarded. Offers medicine (MD, MS, PhD). *Application fee:* $65 ($80 for international students). Electronic applications accepted. *Application Contact:* Admissions Office, 650-723-6861. *Dean,* Philip A. Pizzo, 650-736-2889, E-mail: philip.pizzo@stanford.edu.

Graduate Programs in Medicine Students: 273 full-time (136 women), 96 part-time (42 women); includes 106 minority (15 African Americans, 74 Asian Americans or Pacific Islanders, 16 Hispanic Americans, 1 Native American), 43 international. Average age 27. 831 applicants, 14% accepted. *Faculty:* 81 full-time (24 women). Expenses: Contact institution. *Financial support:* Teaching assistantships available. In 2001, 21 master's, 51 doctorates awarded. Offers biochemistry (PhD); biomedical informatics (MS, PhD); cancer biology (PhD); developmental biology (PhD); epidemiology (MS, PhD); genetics (PhD); health services research (MS); immunology (PhD); medicine (MS, PhD); microbiology and immunology (PhD); molecular and cellular physiology (PhD); molecular pharmacology (PhD); neurosciences (PhD); structural biology (PhD). *Application deadline:* For fall admission, 12/15. *Application fee:* $65 ($80 for international students). Electronic applications accepted. *Application Contact:* Admissions Office, 650-723-2460, Fax: 650-725-7855.

STARR KING SCHOOL FOR THE MINISTRY, Berkeley, CA 94709-1209

General Information Independent-religious, coed, graduate-only institution. *Enrollment by degree level:* 58 first professional. *Graduate faculty:* 6 full-time, 8 part-time/adjunct. *Tuition:* Part-time $33,330 per degree program. *Graduate housing:* On-campus housing not available. *Student services:* Campus employment opportunities. *Library facilities:* Graduate Theological Union Library. *Web address:* http://www.sksm.edu/.

General Application Contact: Becky Leyser, Student Services Director, 510-845-6232 Ext. 114, Fax: 510-845-6273.

GRADUATE UNITS

Professional Program Students: 58 full-time (45 women). *Faculty:* 6 full-time, 8 part-time/adjunct. Expenses: Contact institution. *Financial support:* Career-related internships or fieldwork and Federal Work-Study available. Offers theology (M Div). *Application deadline:* For fall admission, 3/15. *Application fee:* $65. *Application Contact:* Becky Leyser, Student Services Director, 510-845-6232 Ext. 114, Fax: 510-845-6273. *Dean,* Ibrahim Farajajé, 510-845-6232 Ext. 105, Fax: 510-845-6273.

STATE UNIVERSITY OF NEW YORK AT ALBANY, Albany, NY 12222-0001

General Information State-supported, coed, university. CGS member. *Enrollment:* 2,357 full-time matriculated graduate/professional students (1,397 women), 2,073 part-time matriculated graduate/professional students (1,328 women). *Enrollment by degree level:* 2,688 master's, 1,620 doctoral, 124 other advanced degrees. *Graduate faculty:* 558 full-time, 328 part-time/adjunct. Tuition, state resident: full-time $2,550; part-time $213 per credit. Tuition, nonresident: full-time $4,208; part-time $351 per credit. *Required fees:* $470; $470 per year. *Graduate housing:* Rooms and/or apartments available on a first-come, first-served basis to single and married students. Typical cost: $2,043 (including board) for single students. Housing application deadline: 9/1. *Student services:* Campus employment opportunities, campus safety program, career counseling, child daycare facilities, disabled student services, free psychological counseling, grant writing training, international student services, low-cost health insurance, multicultural affairs office, teacher training, writing training. *Library facilities:* University Library plus 2 others. *Online resources:* library catalog, web page, access to other libraries' catalogs. *Collection:* 1.1 million titles, 16,103 serial subscriptions. *Research affiliation:* Woods Hole Oceanographic Institution, Wadsworth Laboratories, New York State Department of Health, IBM–Watson Research Laboratories, General Electric Corporate Research and Development Center, Naval Research Laboratories, Stanford Linear Accelerator Center.

Computer facilities: 500 computers available on campus for general student use. A campuswide network can be accessed from student residence rooms and from off campus. *Web address:* http://www.albany.edu/.

General Application Contact: Jeffrey Collins, Director, Graduate Admissions, 518-442-3980, Fax: 518-442-3922, E-mail: graduate@uamail.albany.edu.

GRADUATE UNITS

College of Arts and Sciences Students: 799 full-time (380 women), 480 part-time (255 women); includes 117 minority (38 African Americans, 22 Asian Americans or Pacific Islanders, 53 Hispanic Americans, 4 Native Americans), 302 international. Average age 32. 1,230 applicants, 54% accepted. Expenses: Contact institution. *Financial support:* Fellowships, research assistantships, teaching assistantships, career-related internships or fieldwork, Federal Work-Study, institutionally sponsored loans, and unspecified assistantships available. In 2001, 228 master's, 68 doctorates, 19 other advanced degrees awarded. *Degree program information:* Part-time and evening/weekend programs available. Offers African studies (MA); Afro-American studies (MA); anthropology (MA, PhD); art (MA, MFA); arts and sciences (MA, MFA, MRP, MS, DA, PhD, Certificate); atmospheric science (MS, PhD); biodiversity, conservation, and policy (MS); biopsychology (PhD); chemistry (MS, PhD); classics (MA); clinical psychology (PhD); communication (MA); computer science (MS, PhD); demography (Certificate); ecology, evolution, and behavior (MS, PhD); economics (MA, PhD, Certificate); English (MA, PhD); forensic molecular biology (MS); French (MA, PhD); general/experimental psychology (PhD); geographic information systems and spatial analysis (Certificate); geography (MA, Certificate); geology (MS, PhD); history (MA, PhD); humanistic studies (DA); industrial/organizational psychology (PhD); Italian (MA); Latin American and Caribbean studies (MA, Certificate); liberal studies (MA); mathematics (PhD); molecular, cellular, developmental, and neural biology (MS, PhD); philosophy (MA, PhD); physics (MS, PhD); psychology (MA); public history (Certificate); regional planning (MRP); Russian (MA, Certificate); Russian translation (Certificate); secondary teaching (MA); social/personality psychology (PhD); sociology (MA, PhD); sociology and communication (PhD); Spanish (MA, PhD); statistics (MA); theatre (MA); urban policy (Certificate); women's studies (MA). *Application deadline:* For spring admission, 11/1. *Application fee:* $50. *Application Contact:* Jeffrey Collins, Director, Graduate Admissions, 518-442-3980, Fax: 518-442-3922, E-mail: graduate@uamail.albany.edu. *Interim Dean,* V. Mark Durand, 518-442-4654.

Nelson A. Rockefeller College of Public Affairs and Policy Students: 175 full-time (88 women), 107 part-time (48 women); includes 36 minority (21 African Americans, 3 Asian Americans or Pacific Islanders, 12 Hispanic Americans), 59 international. Average age 32. 220 applicants, 71% accepted. Expenses: Contact institution. *Financial support:* Fellowships, research assistantships, teaching assistantships, career-related internships or fieldwork, Federal Work-Study, and institutionally sponsored loans available. Financial award application deadline: 2/1. In 2001, 71 master's, 5 doctorates, 7 other advanced degrees awarded. *Degree program information:* Part-time and evening/weekend programs available. Offers administrative behavior (PhD); comparative and development administration (MPA, PhD); human resources (MPA); legislative administration (MPA); planning and policy analysis (CAS); policy analysis (MPA); political science (MA, PhD); program analysis and evaluation (PhD); public affairs and policy (MA); public finance (MPA, PhD); public management (MPA, PhD). *Application deadline:* For fall admission, 7/1. *Application fee:* $50. *Application Contact:* Florance Bolton, Assistant to the Dean of Graduate Studies, 518-442-5200. *Dean,* Dr. Frank J. Thompson, 518-442-5244.

School of Business Students: 91 full-time (47 women), 28 part-time (18 women). Average age 32. 574 applicants, 54% accepted. Expenses: Contact institution. *Financial support:* Fellowships, research assistantships, career-related internships or fieldwork, Federal Work-Study, and minority fellowships available. In 2001, 216 degrees awarded. *Degree program information:* Part-time and evening/weekend programs available. Offers accounting (MS); business (MBA, MS, PhD); finance (MBA); human resource systems (MBA); management science and information systems (MBA); marketing (MBA); organizational studies (PhD); taxation (MS). *Application deadline:* Applications are processed on a rolling basis. *Application fee:* $50. *Application Contact:* Jeffrey Collins, Director, Graduate Admissions, 518-442-3980, Fax: 518-442-3922, E-mail: graduate@uamail.albany.edu. *Dean,* Richard Highfield, 518-442-4910.

School of Criminal Justice Students: 93 full-time (52 women), 63 part-time (38 women); includes 18 minority (11 African Americans, 2 Asian Americans or Pacific Islanders, 4 Hispanic Americans, 1 Native American), 21 international. Average age 32. 111 applicants, 63% accepted. Expenses: Contact institution. *Financial support:* Fellowships, research assistantships, teaching assistantships, career-related internships or fieldwork, Federal Work-Study, and institutionally sponsored loans available. Financial award application deadline: 4/1. In 2001, 36 master's, 6 doctorates awarded. *Degree program information:* Part-time and evening/weekend programs available. Offers criminal justice (MA, PhD). *Application deadline:* For fall admission, 7/1. *Application fee:* $50. *Dean,* James Acker, 518-442-5214.

School of Education Students: 459 full-time (328 women), 879 part-time (648 women); includes 92 minority (47 African Americans, 5 Asian Americans or Pacific Islanders, 40 Hispanic Americans), 48 international. Average age 32. 681 applicants, 64% accepted. Expenses: Contact institution. *Financial support:* Fellowships, career-related internships or fieldwork and Federal Work-Study available. In 2001, 422 master's, 35 doctorates, 35 other advanced degrees awarded. *Degree program information:* Part-time and evening/weekend programs available. Offers counseling psychology (MS, PhD, CAS); curriculum and instruction (MS, Ed D, CAS); curriculum planning and development (MA); education (MA, MS, Ed D, PhD, Psy D, CAS); educational administration (MS, PhD, CAS); educational communications (MS, CAS); educational psychology (Ed D); educational psychology and statistics (MS); measurements and evaluation (Ed D); reading (MS, Ed D, CAS); rehabilitation counseling (MS); school counselor (CAS); school psychology (Psy D, CAS); special education (MS); statistics and research design (Ed D). *Application fee:* $50. *Application Contact:* Sreeroopa Sarkar, Assistant to the Dean of Graduate Studies, 518-442-3980. *Interim Dean,* Susan Phillips, 518-442-4988.

School of Information Science and Policy Students: 127 full-time (96 women), 102 part-time (81 women); includes 8 minority (4 African Americans, 3 Hispanic Americans, 1 Native American), 29 international. Average age 35. 172 applicants, 76% accepted. Expenses: Contact institution. *Financial support:* Fellowships, Federal Work-Study available. Financial award application deadline: 4/1. In 2001, 81 master's, 5 doctorates awarded. *Degree program information:* Part-time and evening/weekend programs available. Offers information science (MS, PhD); information science and policy (CAS); library science (MLS). *Application deadline:* For fall admission, 7/1; for spring admission, 11/1. *Application fee:* $50. *Application Contact:* Florance Bolton, Assistant to the Dean of Graduate Studies, 518-442-5200. *Dean,* Philip Eppard, 518-442-5115.

School of Public Health Students: 177 full-time (104 women), 100 part-time (57 women); includes 29 minority (20 African Americans, 5 Asian Americans or Pacific Islanders, 3 Hispanic Americans, 1 Native American), 104 international. Average age 31. 308 applicants, 64% accepted. Expenses: Contact institution. *Financial support:* Fellowships, research assistantships available. In 2001, 78 master's, 13 doctorates awarded. Offers biochemistry, molecular biology, and genetics (MS, PhD); biometry and statistics (MS, PhD); cell and molecular structure (MS, PhD); environmental and occupational health (MS, PhD); environmental chemistry (MS, PhD); epidemiology (MS, PhD); health policy and management (MS); immunobiology and immunochemistry (MS, PhD); molecular pathogenesis (MS, PhD); neuroscience (MS, PhD); public health (MPH, MS, Dr PH, PhD); toxicology (MS, PhD). *Application fee:* $50. *Application Contact:* Jeffrey Collins, Director, Graduate Admissions, 518-442-3980, Fax: 518-442-3922, E-mail: graduate@uamail.albany.edu. *Interim Dean,* Dr. Peter Levin, 518-485-5500.

School of Social Welfare Students: 317 full-time (258 women), 151 part-time (125 women); includes 67 minority (35 African Americans, 6 Asian Americans or Pacific Islanders, 21 Hispanic Americans, 5 Native Americans), 10 international. Average age 34. 353 applicants, 84% accepted. Expenses: Contact institution. *Financial support:* Fellowships, career-related internships or fieldwork and Federal Work-Study available. Financial award application deadline: 2/15. In 2001, 156 master's, 7 doctorates awarded. *Degree program information:* Part-time and evening/weekend programs available. Offers social welfare (MSW, PhD). *Application deadline:* For fall admission, 2/15. *Application fee:* $50. *Application Contact:* Florance Bolton, Assistant to the Dean of Graduate Studies, 518-442-5200. *Dean,* Katharine Briar-Lawson, 518-442-5324.

See in-depth description on page 1115.

STATE UNIVERSITY OF NEW YORK AT BINGHAMTON, Binghamton, NY 13902-6000

General Information State-supported, coed, university. CGS member. *Enrollment:* 1,403 full-time matriculated graduate/professional students (634 women), 926 part-time matriculated graduate/professional students (489 women). *Enrollment by degree level:* 1,557 master's, 772 doctoral. *Graduate faculty:* 444 full-time (148 women), 208 part-time/adjunct (84 women). Tuition, state resident: full-time $5,100; part-time $213 per credit. Tuition, nonresident: full-time $8,416; part-time $351 per credit. *Required fees:* $811. *Graduate housing:* On-campus housing not available. *Student services:* Campus employment opportunities, career counseling, child daycare facilities, disabled student services, exercise/wellness program, free psychological counseling, grant writing training, international student services, low-cost health insurance, teacher training. *Library facilities:* Glenn G. Bartle Library plus 1 other. *Online resources:* library catalog, web page, access to other libraries' catalogs. *Collection:* 1.7 million titles, 9,196 serial subscriptions, 120,191 audiovisual materials. *Research affiliation:* IBM (engineering), Matco Company (engineering), Lockheed Martin Corporation (engineering, management, mathematics), Universal Instruments (engineering).

Computer facilities: 5,300 computers available on campus for general student use. A campuswide network can be accessed from student residence rooms and from off campus. Internet access and online class registration are available. *Web address:* http://www.binghamton.edu/.

General Application Contact: David G. Payne, Vice Provost and Dean of the Graduate School, 607-777-2070, Fax: 607-777-2501, E-mail: dpayne@binghamton.edu.

State University of New York at Binghamton (continued)

GRADUATE UNITS

Graduate School Students: 1,403 full-time (634 women), 926 part-time (489 women); includes 247 minority (83 African Americans, 92 Asian Americans or Pacific Islanders, 62 Hispanic Americans, 10 Native Americans), 682 international. Average age 31. 3,151 applicants, 53% accepted, 698 enrolled. *Faculty:* 444 full-time (148 women), 208 part-time/adjunct (84 women). Expenses: Contact institution. *Financial support:* In 2001–02, 1,169 students received support, including 138 fellowships with full tuition reimbursements available (averaging $6,332 per year), 188 research assistantships with full tuition reimbursements available (averaging $7,370 per year), 612 teaching assistantships with full tuition reimbursements available (averaging $8,074 per year); career-related internships or fieldwork, Federal Work-Study, institutionally sponsored loans, traineeships, tuition waivers (full and partial), and unspecified assistantships also available. Support available to part-time students. Financial award application deadline: 2/15; financial award applicants required to submit FAFSA. In 2001, 553 master's, 118 doctorates awarded. *Degree program information:* Part-time and evening/weekend programs available. Offers public administration (MPA). *Application deadline:* For fall admission, 4/5 (priority date); for spring admission, 11/1. Applications are processed on a rolling basis. *Application fee:* $60. Electronic applications accepted. *Application Contact:* Suzette Vandeburg, Assistant to the Dean of the Graduate School, 607-777-2239, Fax: 607-777-2501, E-mail: gradad@binghamton.edu. *Vice Provost and Dean of the Graduate School,* David G. Payne, 607-777-2070, Fax: 607-777-2501, E-mail: dpayne@binghamton.edu.

School of Arts and Sciences Students: 685 full-time (332 women), 410 part-time (228 women); includes 136 minority (46 African Americans, 37 Asian Americans or Pacific Islanders, 48 Hispanic Americans, 5 Native Americans), 280 international. Average age 32. 1,036 applicants, 47% accepted, 206 enrolled. *Faculty:* 301 full-time (92 women), 141 part-time/adjunct (55 women). Expenses: Contact institution. *Financial support:* In 2001–02, 590 students received support, including 84 fellowships with full tuition reimbursements available (averaging $7,850 per year), 64 research assistantships with full tuition reimbursements available (averaging $9,300 per year), 434 teaching assistantships with full tuition reimbursements available (averaging $8,527 per year); career-related internships or fieldwork, Federal Work-Study, institutionally sponsored loans, tuition waivers (full and partial), and unspecified assistantships also available. Support available to part-time students. Financial award application deadline: 2/15. In 2001, 130 master's, 103 doctorates awarded. *Degree program information:* Part-time and evening/weekend programs available. Offers analytical chemistry (PhD); anthropology (MA, PhD); applied physics (MS); art (MA, PhD); arts and sciences (MA, MM, MS, PhD, Certificate); behavioral neuroscience (MA, PhD); biological sciences (MA, PhD); chemistry (MA, MS); clinical psychology (MA, PhD); cognitive and behavioral science (MA, PhD); comparative literature (MA, PhD); computer science (MA, PhD); economics (MA, PhD); economics and finance (MA, PhD); English (MA, PhD); French (MA); geography (MA); geological sciences (MA, PhD); history (MA, PhD); inorganic chemistry (PhD); Italian (MA); music (MA, MM); organic chemistry (PhD); philosophy (MA, PhD); physical chemistry (PhD); physics (MA, MS); political science (MA, PhD); probability and statistics (MA, PhD); public policy (MA, PhD); sociology (MA, PhD); Spanish (MA, Certificate); theater (MA); translation (Certificate); translation research and instruction (Certificate). *Application deadline:* For fall admission, 4/15 (priority date); for spring admission, 11/1. Applications are processed on a rolling basis. Electronic applications accepted. *Dean,* Dr. Jean-Pierre Mileur, 607-777-2144.

School of Education and Human Development Students: 181 full-time (121 women), 208 part-time (162 women); includes 36 minority (17 African Americans, 8 Asian Americans or Pacific Islanders, 10 Hispanic Americans, 1 Native American), 9 international. Average age 33. 235 applicants, 74% accepted, 95 enrolled. *Faculty:* 23 full-time (14 women), 18 part-time/adjunct (13 women). Expenses: Contact institution. *Financial support:* In 2001–02, 70 students received support, including 14 fellowships with full tuition reimbursements available (averaging $6,866 per year), 6 research assistantships with full tuition reimbursements available (averaging $5,775 per year), 44 teaching assistantships with full tuition reimbursements available (averaging $5,880 per year); career-related internships or fieldwork, Federal Work-Study, institutionally sponsored loans, tuition waivers (full and partial), and unspecified assistantships also available. Support available to part-time students. Financial award application deadline: 2/15. In 2001, 130 master's, 3 doctorates awarded. *Degree program information:* Part-time and evening/weekend programs available. Offers biology education (MAT, MS Ed, MST); early childhood and elementary education (MS Ed); earth science education (MAT, MS Ed, MST); education and human development (MASS, MAT, MS Ed, MST, Ed D); educational theory and practice (Ed D); English education (MAT, MS Ed, MST); French education (MAT, MST); mathematical sciences education (MAT, MS Ed, MST); physics (MAT, MS Ed, MST); reading education (MS Ed); social science (MASS); social studies (MAT, MS Ed, MST); Spanish education (MAT, MST); special education (MS Ed). *Application deadline:* For fall admission, 4/15 (priority date); for spring admission, 11/1. Applications are processed on a rolling basis. Electronic applications accepted. *Dean,* Dr. Ernest Rose, 607-777-2833.

School of Management Students: 210 full-time (88 women), 58 part-time (17 women); includes 22 minority (5 African Americans, 14 Asian Americans or Pacific Islanders, 1 Hispanic American, 2 Native Americans), 108 international. Average age 29. 514 applicants, 52% accepted, 108 enrolled. *Faculty:* 38 full-time (8 women), 15 part-time/adjunct (2 women). Expenses: Contact institution. *Financial support:* In 2001–02, 44 students received support, including 1 fellowship with full tuition reimbursement available (averaging $8,700 per year), 39 teaching assistantships with full tuition reimbursements available (averaging $7,127 per year); research assistantships, career-related internships or fieldwork, Federal Work-Study, institutionally sponsored loans, tuition waivers (partial), and unspecified assistantships also available. Support available to part-time students. Financial award application deadline: 2/15. In 2001, 137 master's, 2 doctorates awarded. *Degree program information:* Part-time and evening/weekend programs available. Offers accounting (MS, PhD); business administration (MBA, PhD); health care professional executive (MBA); management (MBA, MS, PhD). *Application deadline:* For fall admission, 4/15 (priority date); for spring admission, 11/1. Applications are processed on a rolling basis. Electronic applications accepted. *Dean,* Dr. Upinder S. Dhillon, 607-777-2314.

School of Nursing Students: 50 full-time (46 women), 40 part-time (38 women); includes 7 minority (2 African Americans, 3 Asian Americans or Pacific Islanders, 1 Hispanic American, 1 Native American), 3 international. Average age 41. 33 applicants, 97% accepted, 13 enrolled. *Faculty:* 30 full-time (28 women), 9 part-time/adjunct (8 women). Expenses: Contact institution. *Financial support:* In 2001–02, 43 students received support, including 7 fellowships with partial tuition reimbursements available (averaging $7,743 per year), 3 research assistantships with full tuition reimbursements available (averaging $7,233 per year), 12 teaching assistantships with full tuition reimbursements available (averaging $6,325 per year); career-related internships or fieldwork, Federal Work-Study, institutionally sponsored loans, traineeships, tuition waivers (full and partial), and unspecified assistantships also available. Support available to part-time students. Financial award application deadline: 2/15. In 2001, 22 master's, 23 other advanced degrees awarded. *Degree program information:* Part-time and evening/weekend programs available. Offers nursing (MS, PhD, Certificate). *Application deadline:* For fall admission, 4/15 (priority date); for spring admission, 11/1. Applications are processed on a rolling basis. Electronic applications accepted. *Dean,* Dr. Mary Collins, 607-777-2354.

Thomas J. Watson School of Engineering and Applied Science Students: 277 full-time (47 women), 210 part-time (44 women); includes 46 minority (13 African Americans, 30 Asian Americans or Pacific Islanders, 2 Hispanic Americans, 1 Native American), 282 international. Average age 29. 1,055 applicants, 41% accepted, 105 enrolled. *Faculty:* 50 full-time (6 women), 24 part-time/adjunct (6 women). Expenses: Contact institution. *Financial support:* In 2001–02, 198 students received support, including 7 fellowships with full tuition reimbursements available (averaging $6,476 per year), 112 research assistantships with full tuition reimbursements available (averaging $6,360 per year), 80 teaching assistantships with full tuition reimbursements available (averaging $7,583 per year); career-related internships or fieldwork, Federal Work-Study, institutionally sponsored loans, tuition waivers (full and partial), and unspecified assistantships also available. Support available to part-time students. Financial award application deadline: 2/15. In 2001, 123 master's, 10 doctorates awarded. *Degree program information:* Part-time and evening/weekend programs available. Offers computer science (M Eng, MS, PhD); electrical engineering (M Eng, MS, PhD); engineering and applied science (M Eng, MS, MSAT, PhD); mechanical engineering (M Eng, MS, PhD); systems science and industrial engineering (M Eng, MS, MSAT, PhD). *Application deadline:* For fall admission, 4/15 (priority date); for spring admission, 11/1. Applications are processed on a rolling basis. Electronic applications accepted. *Dean,* Dr. Charles R. Westgate, 607-777-2871.

See in-depth description on page 1117.

STATE UNIVERSITY OF NEW YORK AT NEW PALTZ, New Paltz, NY 12561

General Information State-supported, coed, comprehensive institution. *Enrollment:* 349 full-time matriculated graduate/professional students (240 women), 1,310 part-time matriculated graduate/professional students (910 women). *Enrollment by degree level:* 1,509 master's, 150 other advanced degrees. *Graduate faculty:* 116 full-time, 90 part-time/adjunct. Tuition, state resident: full-time $5,100; part-time $213 per credit. Tuition, nonresident: full-time $8,416; part-time $351 per credit. *Required fees:* $624; $21 per credit. $60 per semester. *Graduate housing:* Room and/or apartments available on a first-come, first-served basis to single students; on-campus housing not available to married students. *Student services:* Campus employment opportunities, campus safety program, career counseling, child daycare facilities, free psychological counseling, low-cost health insurance. *Library facilities:* Sojourner Truth Library. *Online resources:* library catalog, web page. *Collection:* 524,000 titles, 4,950 serial subscriptions, 764 audiovisual materials.

Computer facilities: 600 computers available on campus for general student use. A campuswide network can be accessed from student residence rooms and from off campus. Internet access and online class registration, e-mail are available. *Web address:* http://www.newpaltz.edu/.

General Application Contact: Dr. Phyllis Freeman, Adviser, 845-257-3470.

GRADUATE UNITS

Graduate School Students: 349 full-time (240 women), 1,310 part-time (910 women); includes 151 minority (55 African Americans, 42 Asian Americans or Pacific Islanders, 48 Hispanic Americans, 6 Native Americans), 80 international. Average age 34. *Faculty:* 116 full-time (51 women), 90 part-time/adjunct. Expenses: Contact institution. *Financial support:* Research assistantships, teaching assistantships, career-related internships or fieldwork, Federal Work-Study, institutionally sponsored loans, and tuition waivers (full) available. Support available to part-time students. In 2001, 426 master's, 41 other advanced degrees awarded. *Degree program information:* Part-time and evening/weekend programs available. *Application deadline:* For fall admission, 3/15 (priority date). Applications are processed on a rolling basis. *Application fee:* $50. *Adviser,* Dr. Phyllis Freeman, 845-257-3470.

Faculty of Education Students: 207 full-time (147 women), 730 part-time (550 women); includes 67 minority (32 African Americans, 8 Asian Americans or Pacific Islanders, 24 Hispanic Americans, 3 Native Americans), 5 international. *Faculty:* 37 full-time (22 women), 64 part-time/adjunct. Expenses: Contact institution. *Financial support:* Teaching assistantships, career-related internships or fieldwork, Federal Work-Study, and institutionally sponsored loans available. In 2001, 291 master's, 42 other advanced degrees awarded. *Degree program information:* Part-time and evening/weekend programs available. Offers early childhood education (MS Ed); education (MAT, MPS, MS Ed, MST, CAS); educational administration (MS Ed, CAS); elementary education (MST); English as a second language (MS Ed); environmental education (MS Ed); general education (MS Ed); humanistic education (MPS); reading (MS Ed); secondary education (MAT, MS Ed); special education (MS Ed). *Application deadline:* For fall admission, 3/15 (priority date). Applications are processed on a rolling basis. *Application fee:* $50. *Dean,* Dr. Robert Michael, 845-257-2800.

Faculty of Fine and Performing Arts Students: 31 full-time (19 women), 36 part-time (32 women); includes 1 minority (Native American), 5 international. *Faculty:* 50 full-time (27 women), 39 part-time/adjunct. Expenses: Contact institution. *Financial support:* Research assistantships, teaching assistantships, Federal Work-Study and institutionally sponsored loans available. In 2001, 30 degrees awarded. *Degree program information:* Part-time and evening/weekend programs available. Offers art education (MS); ceramics (MA, MFA); fine and performing arts (MA, MFA, MS); metal (MA, MFA); painting (MA, MFA); photography (MA, MFA); piano pedagogy (MA, MFA); printmaking (MA, MFA); sculpture (MA, MFA). *Application deadline:* For fall admission, 3/15 (priority date). Applications are processed on a rolling basis. *Application fee:* $50. *Dean,* Dr. Patricia Phillips, 845-257-3860.

Faculty of Liberal Arts and Sciences Students: 73 full-time (50 women), 163 part-time (112 women); includes 26 minority (4 African Americans, 19 Asian Americans or Pacific Islanders, 2 Hispanic Americans, 1 Native American), 35 international. *Faculty:* 173 full-time (62 women), 173 part-time/adjunct. Expenses: Contact institution. *Financial support:* Research assistantships, teaching assistantships, career-related internships or fieldwork, Federal Work-Study, institutionally sponsored loans, and tuition waivers (full) available. In 2001, 88 degrees awarded. *Degree program information:* Part-time and evening/weekend programs available. Offers biology (MA, MAT, MS Ed); communication disorders (MS Ed); English (MA, MAT, MS Ed); gerontological nursing (MS); liberal arts and sciences (MA, MAT, MS, MS Ed); psychology (MA); sociology (MA). *Application deadline:* For fall admission, 3/15 (priority date). Applications are processed on a rolling basis. *Application fee:* $50. *Dean,* Dr. Gerald Benjamin, 845-257-3520.

School of Business Students: 32 full-time (16 women), 20 part-time (9 women); includes 11 minority (3 African Americans, 5 Asian Americans or Pacific Islanders, 3 Hispanic Americans), 17 international. Expenses: Contact institution. In 2001, 13 degrees awarded. Offers accounting (MBA); finance (MBA); international business (MBA); marketing (MBA). *Application deadline:* For fall admission, 3/15 (priority date). Applications are processed on a rolling basis. *Application fee:* $50. *Dean,* Dr. Hadi Salavitabar, 845-257-3720.

School of Physical Sciences and Engineering Expenses: Contact institution. Offers chemistry (MA, MAT, MS Ed); computer science (MS); electrical and computer engineering (MS); engineering (MA, MAT, MS, MS Ed); geological sciences (MA, MAT, MS Ed); mathematics (MA, MAT, MS Ed); physics (MS). *Application deadline:* For fall admission, 3/15 (priority date). Applications are processed on a rolling basis. *Application fee:* $50. John Harrington, 845-257-3728.

STATE UNIVERSITY OF NEW YORK AT OSWEGO, Oswego, NY 13126

General Information State-supported, coed, comprehensive institution. CGS member. *Enrollment:* 303 full-time matriculated graduate/professional students (207 women), 669 part-time matriculated graduate/professional students (448 women). *Enrollment by degree level:* 790 master's, 182 other advanced degrees. *Graduate faculty:* 75 full-time, 31 part-time/adjunct. Tuition, state resident: full-time $5,100; part-time $213 per credit. Tuition, nonresident: full-time $8,416; part-time $351 per credit. *Graduate housing:* Room and/or apartments available to single students; on-campus housing not available to married students. Typical cost: $5,290 per year ($8,096 including board). *Student services:* Campus employment opportunities, career counseling, child daycare facilities, disabled student services, exercise/wellness program, free psychological counseling, grant writing training, international student services, low-cost health insurance. *Library facilities:* Penfield Library plus 1 other. *Online resources:* library catalog, web page, access to other libraries' catalogs. *Collection:* 453,390 titles, 1,802 serial subscriptions, 36,749 audiovisual materials. *Research affiliation:* Sun Microsystems, Inc. (research and education), Alcan (research and education), World Wildlife Federation (research and education).

Computer facilities: 600 computers available on campus for general student use. A campuswide network can be accessed from student residence rooms and from off campus. Internet access and online class registration are available. *Web address:* http://www.oswego.edu/.

General Application Contact: Dr. Jack Y. Narayan, Dean of Graduate Studies, 315-312-3152, Fax: 315-312-3577, E-mail: narayan@oswego.edu.

GRADUATE UNITS

Graduate Studies Students: 303 full-time (207 women), 669 part-time (448 women); includes 42 minority (24 African Americans, 6 Asian Americans or Pacific Islanders, 8 Hispanic Americans, 4 Native Americans), 14 international. Average age 25. 742 applicants, 84% accepted. *Faculty:* 75 full-time, 31 part-time/adjunct. Expenses: Contact institution. *Financial support:* Research assistantships, teaching assistantships with full and partial tuition reimbursements, career-related internships or fieldwork, Federal Work-Study, institutionally sponsored loans, scholarships/grants, tuition waivers (partial), unspecified assistantships, and minority fellowships available. Support available to part-time students. Financial award application deadline: 4/1; financial award applicants required to submit FAFSA. In 2001, 328 master's, 40 other advanced degrees awarded. *Degree program information:* Part-time programs available. *Application deadline:* For fall admission, 2/1; for spring admission, 10/1. Applications are processed on a rolling basis. *Application fee:* $50. *Dean,* Dr. Jack Y. Narayan, 315-312-3152, Fax: 315-312-3577, E-mail: narayan@oswego.edu.

Division of Arts and Sciences Students: 17 full-time (7 women), 32 part-time (18 women); includes 2 minority (both African Americans), 1 international. Average age 25. 46 applicants, 85% accepted. *Faculty:* 33 full-time, 2 part-time/adjunct. Expenses: Contact institution. *Financial support:* In 2001–02, 10 teaching assistantships with full and partial tuition reimbursements were awarded; career-related internships or fieldwork, Federal Work-Study, institutionally sponsored loans, scholarships/grants, and tuition waivers (partial) also available. Support available to part-time students. Financial award application deadline: 4/1; financial award applicants required to submit FAFSA. In 2001, 17 degrees awarded. *Degree program information:* Part-time programs available. Offers art (MA); arts and sciences (MA, MS); chemistry (MS); English (MA); history (MA). *Application deadline:* For fall admission, 4/1; for spring admission, 10/1. Applications are processed on a rolling basis. *Application fee:* $50. *Application Contact:* Dr. Jack Y. Narayan, Dean of Graduate Studies, 315-312-3152, Fax: 315-312-3577, E-mail: narayan@oswego.edu. *Dean,* Dr. Sara Varhus, 315-312-2285.

School of Business Students: 36 full-time (17 women), 29 part-time (11 women); includes 5 minority (1 African American, 2 Asian Americans or Pacific Islanders, 2 Hispanic Americans), 13 international. Average age 32. 70 applicants, 83% accepted. *Faculty:* 11 full-time, 5 part-time/adjunct. Expenses: Contact institution. *Financial support:* In 2001–02, 1 teaching assistantship with partial tuition reimbursement was awarded; career-related internships or fieldwork, Federal Work-Study, institutionally sponsored loans, scholarships/grants, and tuition waivers (partial) also available. Support available to part-time students. Financial award application deadline: 4/1; financial award applicants required to submit FAFSA. In 2001, 40 degrees awarded. *Degree program information:* Part-time and evening/weekend programs available. Offers business (MBA); business administration (MBA). *Application deadline:* For fall admission, 4/1; for spring admission, 10/1. Applications are processed on a rolling basis. *Application fee:* $50. *Application Contact:* Dr. Charles Spector, Director, 315-312-2911, E-mail: spector@oswego.edu. *Dean,* Dr. Lanny A. Karns, 315-312-2272.

School of Education Students: 250 full-time (183 women), 608 part-time (419 women); includes 35 minority (21 African Americans, 4 Asian Americans or Pacific Islanders, 6 Hispanic Americans, 4 Native Americans) 626 applicants, 85% accepted. *Faculty:* 31 full-time, 24 part-time/adjunct. Expenses: Contact institution. *Financial support:* In 2001–02, 20 teaching assistantships with full and partial tuition reimbursements were awarded; research assistantships, career-related internships or fieldwork, Federal Work-Study, institutionally sponsored loans, tuition waivers (partial), and unspecified assistantships also available. Support available to part-time students. Financial award application deadline:4/1. In 2001, 271 master's, 40 other advanced degrees awarded. *Degree program information:* Part-time programs available. Offers art education (MAT); counseling services (MS, CAS); education (MAT, MS, MS Ed, CAS); elementary education (MS Ed); human services/counseling (MS); instructional administration (MS Ed, CAS); reading education (MS Ed); school psychology (MS, CAS); secondary education (MS Ed); special education (MS Ed); technology (MS Ed); vocational-technical education (MS Ed). *Application deadline:* For fall admission, 2/1; for spring admission, 10/1. *Application fee:* $50. *Dean,* Dr. Linda Markert, 315-312-2102.

STATE UNIVERSITY OF NEW YORK COLLEGE AT BROCKPORT, Brockport, NY 14420-2997

General Information State-supported, coed, comprehensive institution. *Enrollment:* 275 full-time matriculated graduate/professional students (194 women), 1,086 part-time matriculated graduate/professional students (680 women). *Enrollment by degree level:* 1,133 master's, 228 other advanced degrees. *Graduate faculty:* 139 full-time (56 women), 85 part-time/adjunct (38 women). Tuition, state resident: full-time $5,100; part-time $213 per credit. Tuition, nonresident: full-time $8,416; part-time $351 per credit. *Required fees:* $537; $23 per credit. *Graduate housing:* Room and/or apartments available on a first-come, first-served basis to single students; on-campus housing not available to married students. Typical cost: $3,740 per year ($6,200 including board). Housing application deadline: 7/1. *Student services:* Campus employment opportunities, campus safety program, career counseling, child daycare facilities, disabled student services, exercise/wellness program, free psychological counseling, grant writing training, international student services, low-cost health insurance, multicultural affairs office, teacher training, writing training. *Library facilities:* Drake Memorial Library. *Online resources:* library catalog, web page, access to other libraries' catalogs. *Collection:* 551,072 titles, 1,485 serial subscriptions, 37,292 audiovisual materials.

Computer facilities: 700 computers available on campus for general student use. A campuswide network can be accessed from student residence rooms and from off campus. Internet access is available. *Web address:* http://www.brockport.edu/.

General Application Contact: Sue A. Smithson, Graduate Admissions Secretary, 585-395-5465, Fax: 585-395-2515, E-mail: gradadmit@brockport.edu.

GRADUATE UNITS

School of Arts and Performance Students: 55 full-time (40 women), 84 part-time (26 women); includes 11 minority (10 African Americans, 1 Asian American or Pacific Islander), 5 international. Expenses: Contact institution. *Financial support:* In 2001–02, 19 teaching assistantships were awarded; fellowships, career-related internships or fieldwork, Federal Work-Study, scholarships/grants, and unspecified assistantships also available. Financial award application deadline: 3/15; financial award applicants required to submit FAFSA. In 2001, 51 degrees awarded. Offers arts and performance (MA, MFA, MS Ed); communication (MA); dance (MA, MFA); physical education (MS Ed); visual studies (MFA). *Application fee:* $50. *Dean,* Sharon Vasquez, 585-395-2350, E-mail: svasquez@brockport.edu.

School of Letters and Sciences Students: 58 full-time (38 women), 190 part-time (105 women); includes 16 minority (9 African Americans, 2 Asian Americans or Pacific Islanders, 4 Hispanic Americans, 1 Native American), 4 international. Average age 32. Expenses: Contact institution. *Financial support:* Fellowships, research assistantships, teaching assistantships, career-related internships or fieldwork, Federal Work-Study, scholarships/grants, and unspecified assistantships available. Financial award application deadline: 3/15; financial award applicants required to submit FAFSA. In 2001, 94 degrees awarded. *Degree program information:* Part-time and evening/weekend programs available. Offers biological sciences (MS); computational science (MS); English (MA); history (MA); letters and sciences (MA, MS); liberal studies (MA); mathematics (MA); psychology (MA). *Application fee:* $50. *Dean,* Dr. Michael Maggiotto, 585-395-2394.

School of Professions Students: 162 full-time (116 women), 812 part-time (549 women); includes 85 minority (58 African Americans, 5 Asian Americans or Pacific Islanders, 20 Hispanic Americans, 2 Native Americans), 4 international. Expenses: Contact institution. *Financial support:* In 2001–02, teaching assistantships with tuition reimbursements (averaging $6,000 per year); fellowships with tuition reimbursements, career-related internships or fieldwork, Federal Work-Study, scholarships/grants, traineeships, and unspecified assistantships also available. Support available to part-time students. Financial award application deadline: 3/15; financial award applicants required to submit FAFSA. In 2001, 261 master's, 106 other advanced degrees awarded. *Degree program information:* Part-time and evening/weekend programs available. Offers bilingual education (MS Ed); biology education (MS Ed); chemistry education (MS Ed); counselor education (MS Ed, CAS); earth science education (MS Ed); elementary education (MS Ed); English education (MS Ed); family nurse practitioner (MS, CAS); health science (MS Ed); mathematics education (MS Ed); physics education (MS Ed); public administration (MPA); reading (MS Ed); recreation and leisure studies (MS); school administration and supervision (MS Ed, CAS); school business administration (CAS); school district administration (CAS); secondary education (MS Ed); social studies education (MS Ed); social work (MSW); special education: childhood (MS Ed). *Application fee:* $50. *Dean,* Dr. Jospeh Mason, 585-395-2510, E-mail: jmason@brockport.edu.

See in-depth description on page 1119.

STATE UNIVERSITY OF NEW YORK COLLEGE AT BUFFALO, Buffalo, NY 14222-1095

General Information State-supported, coed, comprehensive institution. CGS member. *Enrollment:* 299 full-time matriculated graduate/professional students (233 women), 1,492 part-time matriculated graduate/professional students (1,047 women). *Graduate faculty:* 185 full-time (78 women), 73 part-time/adjunct (47 women). Tuition, state resident: full-time $5,100; part-time $226 per credit hour. Tuition, nonresident: full-time $8,416; part-time $351 per credit hour. *Graduate housing:* Room and/or apartments available on a first-come, first-served basis to single students; on-campus housing not available to married students. Housing application deadline: 8/15. *Student services:* Campus employment opportunities, campus safety program, career counseling, child daycare facilities, disabled student services, exercise/wellness program, free psychological counseling, grant writing training, international student services, low-cost health insurance, multicultural affairs office, teacher training, writing training. *Library facilities:* E. H. Butler Library. *Online resources:* library catalog, web page, access to other libraries' catalogs. *Collection:* 359,433 titles, 3,033 serial subscriptions, 17,824 audiovisual materials. *Research affiliation:* Roswell Park Memorial Institute, U.S. Fish and Wildlife Service (aquatic biology), Independent Health Corporation (community health), NYNEX (technology).

Computer facilities: 900 computers available on campus for general student use. A campuswide network can be accessed from student residence rooms and from off campus. Internet access is available. *Web address:* http://www.buffalostate.edu/.

General Application Contact: Graduate Studies and Research, 716-878-5601, Fax: 716-878-5630, E-mail: gradoffc@buffalostate.edu.

GRADUATE UNITS

Graduate Studies and Research Students: 299 full-time (233 women), 1,492 part-time (1,047 women); includes 173 minority (121 African Americans, 12 Asian Americans or Pacific Islanders, 33 Hispanic Americans, 7 Native Americans), 16 international. Average age 32. 796 applicants, 78% accepted. *Faculty:* 185 full-time (78 women), 73 part-time/adjunct (47 women). Expenses: Contact institution. *Financial support:* In 2001–02, 37 fellowships with full tuition reimbursements (averaging $7,000 per year), 85 research assistantships with partial tuition reimbursements (averaging $6,000 per year) were awarded. Teaching assistantships, career-related internships or fieldwork, Federal Work-Study, institutionally sponsored loans, scholarships/grants, tuition waivers (full and partial), and unspecified assistantships also available. Support available to part-time students. Financial award application deadline: 3/1; financial award applicants required to submit FAFSA. In 2001, 495 master's, 21 other advanced degrees awarded. *Degree program information:* Part-time and evening/weekend programs available. Offers multidisciplinary studies (MA, MS). *Application deadline:* For fall admission, 5/1 (priority date); for spring admission, 10/1 (priority date). Applications are processed on a rolling basis. *Application fee:* $50. *Application Contact:* Graduate Admissions Counselor, 716-878-5601, E-mail: gradoffc@buffalostate.edu. *Dean,* Dr. Richard S. Podemski, 716-878-5609, Fax: 716-878-5630, E-mail: podemsrs@buffalostate.edu.

Faculty of Applied Science and Education Students: 215 full-time (174 women), 1,041 part-time (791 women); includes 117 minority (83 African Americans, 6 Asian Americans or Pacific Islanders, 24 Hispanic Americans, 4 Native Americans), 12 international. Average age 34. 503 applicants, 78% accepted. *Faculty:* 97 full-time (34 women), 58 part-time/adjunct (40 women). Expenses: Contact institution. *Financial support:* In 2001–02, 27 fellowships with partial tuition reimbursements, 55 research assistantships with partial tuition reimbursements were awarded. Career-related internships or fieldwork, Federal Work-Study, scholarships/grants, tuition waivers (full and partial), and unspecified assistantships also available. Support available to part-time students. Financial award application deadline: 3/1. In 2001, 337 master's, 21 other advanced degrees awarded. *Degree program information:* Part-time and evening/weekend programs available. Offers adult education (MS); applied science and education (MPS, MS, MS Ed, CAS); business and marketing education (MS Ed); career and technical education (MS Ed); childhood education (MS Ed); creative studies (MS); criminal justice (MS); early childhood education (MS Ed); educational computing (MS Ed); educational leadership and facilitation (CAS); elementary and early secondary education (MS Ed); elementary education (MS Ed); English education (MS Ed); general science education (MS Ed); industrial technology (MS); literacy specialist (MPS, MS Ed); literacy specialist (ages 0 months-6 years) (MS Ed); literacy specialist (ages 5-12 years) (MPS); mathematics education (MS Ed); social studies education (MS Ed); special education (MS Ed); speech language pathology (MS Ed); student personnel administration (MS); teaching bilingual exceptional individuals (MS Ed); technology education (MS Ed). *Application deadline:* For fall admission, 5/1 (priority date); for spring admission, 10/1. *Application fee:* $50. *Dean,* Dr. Daniel King, 718-878-4214, Fax: 716-878-5301, E-mail: kingdl@buffalostate.edu.

Faculty of Arts and Humanities Students: 43 full-time (33 women), 157 part-time (105 women); includes 7 minority (4 African Americans, 2 Hispanic Americans, 1 Native American), 1 international. Average age 30. 104 applicants, 64% accepted. *Faculty:* 65 full-time (21 women), 4 part-time/adjunct (2 women). Expenses: Contact institution. *Financial support:* In 2001–02, 2 research assistantships with partial tuition reimbursements were awarded; fellowships with full tuition reimbursements, career-related internships or fieldwork, Federal Work-Study, and unspecified assistantships also available. Support available to part-time students. Financial award application deadline: 3/1. In 2001, 42 degrees awarded. *Degree program information:* Part-time and evening/weekend programs available. Offers art conservation (CAS); art education (MS Ed); arts and humanities (MA, MS Ed, CAS); conservation of historic works and art works (MA); English (MA); secondary education (MS Ed). *Application deadline:* For fall admission, 5/1 (priority date); for spring admission, 10/1 (priority date). *Application fee:* $50. *Dean,* Dr. Emile C. Netzhammer, 716-878-6326, Fax: 716-878-6914, E-mail: netzhaec@buffalostate.edu.

Faculty of Natural and Social Sciences Students: 17 full-time (10 women), 163 part-time (73 women); includes 15 minority (8 African Americans, 2 Asian Americans or Pacific Islanders, 3 Hispanic Americans, 2 Native Americans), 3 international. Average age 32. 73 applicants, 79% accepted. *Faculty:* 113 full-time (23 women), 12 part-time/adjunct (5 women). Expenses: Contact institution. *Financial support:* In 2001–02, 2 fellowships with full tuition reimbursements (averaging $7,000 per year), 28 research assistantships with partial tuition reimbursements (averaging $6,000 per year) were awarded. Teaching assistantships, career-related internships or fieldwork, Federal Work-Study, tuition waivers (full), and unspecified assistantships also available. Support available to part-time students. Financial award application deadline: 3/1. In 2001, 40 degrees awarded. *Degree program information:* Part-time and evening/weekend programs available. Offers applied economics (MA); biology (MA); chemistry (MA); history (MA); mathematics education (MS Ed); natural and social sciences (MA, MS Ed); secondary education (MS Ed). *Application deadline:* For fall admission, 5/1 (priority date); for spring admission, 10/1 (priority date). Applications are processed on a rolling basis. *Application fee:* $50. *Dean,* Dr. Lawrence G. Flood, 716-878-6434, Fax: 716-878-4009, E-mail: floodlg@buffalostate.edu.

STATE UNIVERSITY OF NEW YORK COLLEGE AT CORTLAND, Cortland, NY 13045

General Information State-supported, coed, comprehensive institution. *Enrollment:* 266 full-time matriculated graduate/professional students (166 women), 1,264 part-time matriculated graduate/professional students (873 women). *Enrollment by degree level:* 1,334 master's, 198 other advanced degrees. *Graduate faculty:* 62. *Graduate housing:* Room and/or apartments available to single students; on-campus housing not available to married students.

State University of New York College at Cortland (continued)
Student services: Campus employment opportunities, campus safety program, career counseling, child daycare facilities, disabled student services, exercise/wellness program, free psychological counseling, international student services, low-cost health insurance, teacher training, writing training. *Library facilities:* Memorial Library. *Online resources:* library catalog, web page, access to other libraries' catalogs. *Collection:* 396,222 titles, 2,744 serial subscriptions, 4,557 audiovisual materials.

Computer facilities: 832 computers available on campus for general student use. A campuswide network can be accessed from student residence rooms and from off campus. *Web address:* http://www.cortland.edu/.

General Application Contact: Mark Yacavone, Associate Director of Admissions, 607-753-4711, Fax: 607-753-5998, E-mail: marky@em.cortland.edu.

GRADUATE UNITS

Graduate Studies Students: 201 full-time (123 women), 996 part-time (688 women). 405 applicants, 82% accepted. *Faculty:* 62. Expenses: Contact institution. *Financial support:* In 2001–02, 4 fellowships were awarded; career-related internships or fieldwork, Federal Work-Study, tuition waivers (partial), and alumni assistantships also available. Support available to part-time students. Financial award applicants required to submit CSS PROFILE or FAFSA. In 2001, 334 master's, 57 other advanced degrees awarded. *Degree program information:* Part-time and evening/weekend programs available. Offers American civilization and culture (CAS). *Application deadline:* Applications are processed on a rolling basis. *Application fee:* $50. *Application Contact:* Mark Yacavone, Assistant Director of Admissions, 607-753-4711, Fax: 607-753-5998, E-mail: marky@em.cortland.edu.

Division of Arts and Sciences Students: 99 full-time (49 women), 98 part-time (41 women). 69 applicants, 87% accepted. Expenses: Contact institution. *Financial support:* Career-related internships or fieldwork, Federal Work-Study, tuition waivers (partial), and alumni assistantships available. Support available to part-time students. Financial award applicants required to submit CSS PROFILE or FAFSA. In 2001, 59 degrees awarded. *Degree program information:* Part-time and evening/weekend programs available. Offers arts and sciences (MA, MAT, MS Ed); biology (MAT, MS Ed); chemistry (MAT, MS Ed); earth science (MAT, MS Ed); English (MS Ed); French (MS Ed); history (MA, MS Ed); mathematics (MAT, MS Ed); physics (MAT, MS Ed); social studies (MS Ed); Spanish (MS Ed). *Application deadline:* Applications are processed on a rolling basis. *Application fee:* $50. *Application Contact:* Mark Yacavone, Assistant Director of Admissions, 607-753-4711, Fax: 607-753-5998, E-mail: marky@em.cortland.edu. *Dean,* Dr. John Ryder, 607-753-4312, E-mail: ryderj@cortland.edu.

Division of Professional Studies Students: 100 full-time (67 women), 840 part-time (602 women). Expenses: Contact institution. *Financial support:* In 2001–02, 4 fellowships were awarded; career-related internships or fieldwork, Federal Work-Study, tuition waivers (partial), and alumni assistantships also available. Support available to part-time students. Financial award application deadline: 3/31; financial award applicants required to submit CSS PROFILE or FAFSA. In 2001, 275 master's, 57 other advanced degrees awarded. *Degree program information:* Part-time and evening/weekend programs available. Offers childhood education (MST); elementary education (MS Ed); English education (MS Ed); general science education (MS Ed); health education (MS Ed); mathematics education (MS Ed); physical education (MS Ed); professional studies (MS, MS Ed, MST, CAS); reading (MS Ed); recreation education (MS, MS Ed); school administration and supervision (CAS); school business administrator (CAS); social studies education (MS Ed). *Application deadline:* Applications are processed on a rolling basis. *Application fee:* $50. *Application Contact:* Mark Yacavone, Assistant Director of Admissions, 607-753-4711, Fax: 607-753-5998, E-mail: marky@em.cortland.edu. *Dean,* Dr. Helen Giles-Gee, 607-753-2829, Fax: 607-753-5987, E-mail: gilesgeeh@cortland.edu.

STATE UNIVERSITY OF NEW YORK COLLEGE AT FREDONIA, Fredonia, NY 14063-1136

General Information State-supported, coed, comprehensive institution. *Enrollment:* 90 full-time matriculated graduate/professional students (72 women), 275 part-time matriculated graduate/professional students (200 women). *Enrollment by degree level:* 328 master's, 37 other advanced degrees. *Graduate faculty:* 40 full-time (12 women), 14 part-time/adjunct (9 women). *Tuition, area resident:* Part-time $213 per credit hour. Tuition, state resident: full-time $3,400; part-time $351 per credit hour. Tuition, nonresident: full-time $8,300. *Required fees:* $825; $30 per credit hour. *Graduate housing:* Room and/or apartments available on a first-come, first-served basis to single students; on-campus housing not available to married students. Typical cost: $3,270 per year ($5,600 including board). Housing application deadline: 7/15. *Student services:* Campus employment opportunities, campus safety program, career counseling, child daycare facilities, free psychological counseling, international student services, low-cost health insurance. *Library facilities:* Reed Library. *Online resources:* library catalog, web page, access to other libraries' catalogs. *Collection:* 396,000 titles, 2,270 serial subscriptions, 17,607 audiovisual materials.

Computer facilities: 500 computers available on campus for general student use. A campuswide network can be accessed from student residence rooms and from off campus. *Web address:* http://www.fredonia.edu/.

General Application Contact: Dr. Leonard E. Faulk, Dean of Graduate Studies, 716-673-3808, Fax: 716-673-3338, E-mail: leonard.faulk@fredonia.edu.

GRADUATE UNITS

Graduate Studies Students: 90 full-time (72 women), 275 part-time (200 women); includes 11 minority (4 African Americans, 1 Asian American or Pacific Islander, 5 Hispanic Americans, 1 Native American), 6 international. 245 applicants, 87% accepted. *Faculty:* 40 full-time (12 women), 14 part-time/adjunct (9 women). Expenses: Contact institution. *Financial support:* In 2001–02, 27 teaching assistantships with partial tuition reimbursements (averaging $5,570 per year) were awarded; research assistantships, career-related internships or fieldwork and tuition waivers (full and partial) also available. Support available to part-time students. Financial award application deadline: 3/15. In 2001, 138 master's, 6 other advanced degrees awarded. *Degree program information:* Part-time and evening/weekend programs available. Offers biology (MS, MS Ed); chemistry (MS, MS Ed); English (MA, MS Ed); mathematics (MS Ed); social sciences (MA, MS); speech pathology and audiology (MS, MS Ed). *Application deadline:* For fall admission, 8/5; for spring admission, 12/1. Applications are processed on a rolling basis. *Application fee:* $50. Electronic applications accepted. *Dean of Graduate Studies,* Dr. Leonard E. Faulk, 716-673-3808, Fax: 716-673-3338, E-mail: leonard.faulk@fredonia.edu.

School of Education Students: 31 full-time (27 women), 195 part-time (153 women); includes 4 minority (1 African American, 1 Asian American or Pacific Islander, 1 Hispanic American, 1 Native American) 119 applicants, 95% accepted. *Faculty:* 10 full-time (5 women), 7 part-time/adjunct (2 women). Expenses: Contact institution. *Financial support:* In 2001–02, 8 teaching assistantships with partial tuition reimbursements (averaging $5,570 per year) were awarded; research assistantships, career-related internships or fieldwork and tuition waivers (full and partial) also available. Support available to part-time students. Financial award application deadline: 3/15. In 2001, 68 master's, 6 CASs awarded. *Degree program information:* Part-time and evening/weekend programs available. Offers educational administration (CAS); elementary education (MS Ed); reading (MS Ed); secondary education (MS Ed). *Application deadline:* For fall admission, 8/5; for spring admission, 12/1. *Application fee:* $50. *Chair,* Dr. Julius Adams, 716-673-3311, E-mail: julius.adams@fredonia.edu.

School of Music Students: 9 full-time (4 women), 13 part-time (7 women), 1 international. 31 applicants, 90% accepted. *Faculty:* 9 full-time (2 women). Expenses: Contact institution. *Financial support:* In 2001–02, 6 teaching assistantships with partial tuition reimbursements (averaging $5,570 per year) were awarded; research assistantships, tuition waivers (full and partial) also available. Support available to part-time students. Financial award application deadline: 3/15. In 2001, 18 degrees awarded. *Degree program information:* Part-time and evening/weekend programs available. Offers music (MM); music education (MM). *Application deadline:* For fall admission, 8/5; for spring admission, 12/1. *Application fee:* $50. *Director,* Dr. Peter Schoenbach, 716-673-3151, E-mail: peter.schoenbach@fredonia.edu.

STATE UNIVERSITY OF NEW YORK COLLEGE AT GENESEO, Geneseo, NY 14454-1401

General Information State-supported, coed, comprehensive institution. *Enrollment:* 64 full-time matriculated graduate/professional students (61 women), 154 part-time matriculated graduate/professional students (132 women). *Enrollment by degree level:* 218 master's. *Graduate faculty:* 38 full-time (19 women), 12 part-time/adjunct (8 women). *Tuition, area resident:* Full-time $5,100; part-time $213 per credit hour. Tuition, nonresident: full-time $8,416; part-time $351 per credit hour. *Required fees:* $475; $20 per credit hour. Part-time tuition and fees vary according to course load. *Graduate housing:* On-campus housing not available. *Student services:* Campus employment opportunities, campus safety program, career counseling, disabled student services, exercise/wellness program, free psychological counseling, international student services, low-cost health insurance, multicultural affairs office, teacher training. *Library facilities:* Milne Library plus 1 other. *Online resources:* library catalog, web page. *Collection:* 502,537 titles, 2,284 serial subscriptions, 22,641 audiovisual materials. *Research affiliation:* Arecibo Observatory (astronomy), Rochester Laser Fusion Laboratory (nuclear physics), Great Lakes Research Consortium, National Technical Institute for the Deaf (communicative disorders), Eastman Kodak (physics), Delphi Automotive (engineering).

Computer facilities: 800 computers available on campus for general student use. A campuswide network can be accessed from student residence rooms and from off campus. Internet access and online class registration are available. *Web address:* http://www.geneseo.edu/.

General Application Contact: Dr. Thomas Greenfield, Dean of the College, 585-245-5546, Fax: 585-245-5005, E-mail: tag@geneseo.edu.

GRADUATE UNITS

Graduate Studies Students: 64 full-time (61 women), 154 part-time (132 women); includes 2 minority (1 Asian American or Pacific Islander, 1 Hispanic American) Average age 26. 137 applicants, 66% accepted, 76 enrolled. *Faculty:* 38 full-time (19 women), 12 part-time/adjunct (8 women). Expenses: Contact institution. *Financial support:* In 2001–02, 12 students received support, including 12 teaching assistantships (averaging $7,500 per year); fellowships, research assistantships, career-related internships or fieldwork, Federal Work-Study, and institutionally sponsored loans also available. Financial award application deadline: 4/1; financial award applicants required to submit FAFSA. In 2001, 103 degrees awarded. *Degree program information:* Part-time and evening/weekend programs available. Offers communicative disorders and sciences (MA). *Application deadline:* For fall admission, 6/1; for spring admission, 10/1. *Application fee:* $35. *Dean of the College,* Dr. Thomas Greenfield, 585-245-5546, Fax: 585-245-5005, E-mail: tag@geneseo.edu.

School of Education Students: 22 full-time (20 women), 154 part-time (132 women); includes 1 minority (Asian American or Pacific Islander) Average age 26. 58 applicants, 86% accepted, 50 enrolled. *Faculty:* 31 full-time (15 women), 8 part-time/adjunct (4 women). Expenses: Contact institution. *Financial support:* In 2001–02, 10 students received support, including 10 teaching assistantships (averaging $7,500 per year); fellowships, career-related internships or fieldwork, Federal Work-Study, and institutionally sponsored loans also available. Financial award application deadline: 4/1; financial award applicants required to submit FAFSA. In 2001, 92 degrees awarded. *Degree program information:* Part-time and evening/weekend programs available. Offers elementary education (MS Ed); reading (MPS, MS Ed); secondary education (MS Ed); special education (MS Ed). *Application deadline:* For fall admission, 6/1 (priority date); for spring admission, 10/1. *Application fee:* $35. *Interim Head,* Dr. Dennis Showers, 585-245-5558, Fax: 585-245-5220, E-mail: showers@geneseo.edu.

STATE UNIVERSITY OF NEW YORK COLLEGE AT ONEONTA, Oneonta, NY 13820-4015

General Information State-supported, coed, comprehensive institution. CGS member. *Enrollment:* 45 full-time matriculated graduate/professional students (34 women), 160 part-time matriculated graduate/professional students (130 women). *Enrollment by degree level:* 180 master's, 25 other advanced degrees. *Graduate faculty:* 144 part-time/adjunct. Tuition, state resident: full-time $5,100; part-time $213 per credit hour. Tuition, nonresident: full-time $8,416; part-time $351 per credit hour. *Required fees:* $616; $12 per credit hour. *Graduate housing:* Room and/or apartments available on a first-come, first-served basis to single students; on-campus housing not available to married students. *Student services:* Campus employment opportunities, campus safety program, career counseling, child daycare facilities, disabled student services, exercise/wellness program, free psychological counseling, grant writing training, international student services, low-cost health insurance, multicultural affairs office, teacher training, writing training. *Library facilities:* Milne Library. *Online resources:* library catalog, web page, access to other libraries' catalogs. *Collection:* 546,770 titles, 2,221 serial subscriptions, 33,865 audiovisual materials.

Computer facilities: 525 computers available on campus for general student use. A campuswide network can be accessed from student residence rooms and from off campus. Internet access and online class registration are available. *Web address:* http://www.oneonta.edu/.

General Application Contact: Dr. Carolyn Haessig, Director, 607-436-2523, Fax: 607-436-3084, E-mail: haessicj@oneonta.edu.

GRADUATE UNITS

Graduate Studies Students: 45 full-time (34 women), 160 part-time (130 women). 89 applicants, 46% accepted. Expenses: Contact institution. *Financial support:* Fellowships, teaching assistantships, Federal Work-Study available. In 2001, 73 master's, 8 other advanced degrees awarded. *Degree program information:* Part-time and evening/weekend programs available. Offers biology (MA); earth science (MA); history museum studies (MA). *Application deadline:* Applications are processed on a rolling basis. *Application fee:* $50. *Director,* Dr. Carolyn Haessig, 607-436-2523, Fax: 607-436-3084, E-mail: haessicj@oneonta.edu.

Division of Education Students: 11 full-time (8 women), 158 part-time (128 women). 42 applicants, 71% accepted, 23 enrolled. Expenses: Contact institution. In 2001, 60 master's, 8 other advanced degrees awarded. *Degree program information:* Part-time and evening/weekend programs available. Offers adolescent education (MS Ed); childhood education (MS Ed); community mental health (MS); educational psychology (MS, MS Ed, CAS); elementary and reading education (MS Ed); literacy education (MS Ed); marriage and family therapy (MS); school counselor K-12 (MS Ed, CAS). *Application deadline:* For fall admission, 3/25 (priority date); for spring admission, 10/1 (priority date). Applications are processed on a rolling basis. *Application fee:* $50. *Associate Dean,* Dr. Barbara Stoehr, 607-436-2541, Fax: 607-436-2554, E-mail: stoehrb@oneonta.edu.

STATE UNIVERSITY OF NEW YORK COLLEGE AT POTSDAM, Potsdam, NY 13676

General Information State-supported, coed, comprehensive institution. *Enrollment:* 437 full-time matriculated graduate/professional students (312 women), 340 part-time matriculated graduate/professional students (260 women). *Enrollment by degree level:* 777 master's. *Graduate faculty:* 48 full-time (11 women), 19 part-time/adjunct (7 women). *International tuition:* $9,031 full-time. Tuition, state resident: full-time $5,100; part-time $213 per credit. Tuition, nonresident: full-time $8,416; part-time $351 per credit hour. *Required fees:* $19 per credit. *Graduate housing:* Room and/or apartments guaranteed to single students; on-campus housing not available to married students. *Student services:* Campus employment opportunities, campus safety program, career counseling, child daycare facilities, disabled student services, exercise/wellness program, free psychological counseling, grant writing training, international student services, low-cost health insurance, multicultural affairs office, teacher training, writing training. *Library facilities:* F. W. Crumb Memorial Library plus 1 other. *Online resources:* library catalog, web page, access to other libraries' catalogs. *Collection:* 325,079 titles, 1,309 serial subscriptions, 19,134 audiovisual materials.

Computer facilities: 400 computers available on campus for general student use. A campuswide network can be accessed from student residence rooms and from off campus. Internet access and online class registration, Appletalk network are available. *Web address:* http://www.potsdam.edu/.

General Application Contact: Dr. William Amoriell, Dean of Education and Graduate Studies, 315-267-2515, Fax: 315-267-4802, E-mail: amoriewj@potsdam.edu.

GRADUATE UNITS

Crane School of Music Students: 29 full-time (8 women), 4 part-time (all women). *Faculty:* 12 full-time (4 women), 1 part-time/adjunct (0 women). Expenses: Contact institution. *Financial support:* Teaching assistantships with full tuition reimbursements, career-related internships or fieldwork, Federal Work-Study, and scholarships/grants available. Support available to part-time students. Financial award applicants required to submit FAFSA. *Degree program information:* Part-time programs available. Offers composition (MM); history and literature (MM); music education (MM); music theory (MM); performance (MM). *Application deadline:* Applications are processed on a rolling basis. *Application fee:* $50. *Application Contact:* Dr. William Amoriell, Dean of Education and Graduate Studies, 315-267-2515, Fax: 315-267-4802, E-mail: amoriewj@potsdam.edu. *Dean,* Dr. Alan Solomon, 315-267-2415, Fax: 315-267-2413, E-mail: solomon@postsdam.edu.

School of Arts and Sciences Students: 13 full-time (8 women), 8 part-time (7 women); includes 5 minority (2 African Americans, 1 Hispanic American, 2 Native Americans), 1 international. 5 applicants, 100% accepted. *Faculty:* 9 full-time (3 women), 2 part-time/adjunct (1 woman). Expenses: Contact institution. *Financial support:* Teaching assistantships with full tuition reimbursements, Federal Work-Study available. Support available to part-time students. Financial award application deadline: 3/1. *Degree program information:* Part-time and evening/weekend programs available. Offers arts and sciences (MA); English (MA); mathematics (MA). *Application deadline:* Applications are processed on a rolling basis. *Application fee:* $50. *Application Contact:* Dr. William Amoriell, Dean of Education and Graduate Studies, 315-267-2515, Fax: 315-267-4802, E-mail: amoriewj@potsdam.edu. *Dean,* Dr. Galen K. Pletcher, 315-267-2231, Fax: 315-267-3140, E-mail: pletchgk@potsdam.edu.

School of Education Students: 395 full-time (296 women), 327 part-time (248 women); includes 32 minority (12 African Americans, 6 Asian Americans or Pacific Islanders, 4 Hispanic Americans, 10 Native Americans), 149 international. *Faculty:* 27 full-time (4 women), 16 part-time/adjunct (6 women). Expenses: Contact institution. *Financial support:* Fellowships, teaching assistantships with full tuition reimbursements, career-related internships or fieldwork, Federal Work-Study, scholarships/grants, and tuition waivers (full) available. Support available to part-time students. Financial award application deadline: 3/1. *Degree program information:* Part-time and evening/weekend programs available. Postbaccalaureate distance learning degree programs offered (minimal on-campus study). Offers education (MS Ed, MST); educational technology (MS Ed); elementary education (MS Ed, MST); professional education (MS Ed); reading education (MS Ed); secondary education (MS Ed, MST); special education (MS Ed). *Application deadline:* Applications are processed on a rolling basis. *Application fee:* $50. *Dean of Education and Graduate Studies,* Dr. William Amoriell, 315-267-2515, Fax: 315-267-4802, E-mail: amoriewj@potsdam.edu.

STATE UNIVERSITY OF NEW YORK COLLEGE OF ENVIRONMENTAL SCIENCE AND FORESTRY, Syracuse, NY 13210-2779

General Information State-supported, coed, university. *Enrollment:* 289 full-time matriculated graduate/professional students (141 women), 215 part-time matriculated graduate/professional students (77 women). *Enrollment by degree level:* 307 master's, 197 doctoral. *Graduate faculty:* 131 full-time (28 women), 2 part-time/adjunct (both women). *Tuition, area resident:* Part-time $213 per credit hour. Tuition, state resident: full-time $5,100. Tuition, nonresident: full-time $8,416; part-time $351 per credit hour. *Required fees:* $250. One-time fee: $43 full-time. *Graduate housing:* Rooms and/or apartments available to single and married students. Housing application deadline: 5/1. *Student services:* Campus employment opportunities, campus safety program, career counseling, free psychological counseling, international student services, low-cost health insurance. *Library facilities:* F. Franklin Moon Library plus 1 other. *Online resources:* library catalog, access to other libraries' catalogs. *Collection:* 130,305 titles, 2,001 serial subscriptions, 732 audiovisual materials. *Research affiliation:* Northeast Forest Experiment Station, Great Lakes Research Consortium, Empire State Paper Research Associates, U.S. Department of Agriculture, Forest Service Cooperative Research Unit, National Park Service, NASA.

Computer facilities: 150 computers available on campus for general student use. A campuswide network can be accessed from student residence rooms and from off campus. Internet access and online class registration are available. *Web address:* http://www.esf.edu/.

General Application Contact: Dr. Robert H. Frey, Dean, Instruction and Graduate Studies, 315-470-6599, Fax: 315-470-6978, E-mail: esfgrad@esf.edu.

GRADUATE UNITS

Faculty of Chemistry Students: 28 full-time (7 women), 11 part-time (7 women); includes 1 minority (Native American), 18 international. Average age 29. 48 applicants, 81% accepted, 10 enrolled. *Faculty:* 16 full-time (1 woman). Expenses: Contact institution. *Financial support:* In 2001–02, 35 students received support, including 4 fellowships with full tuition reimbursements available (averaging $8,817 per year), 14 research assistantships with full tuition reimbursements available (averaging $11,250 per year), 17 teaching assistantships with full tuition reimbursements available (averaging $10,060 per year); Federal Work-Study, institutionally sponsored loans, scholarships/grants, health care benefits, and unspecified assistantships also available. Financial award applicants required to submit FAFSA. In 2001, 1 master's, 1 doctorate awarded. Offers biochemistry (MS, PhD); environmental and forest chemistry (MS, PhD); organic chemistry of natural products (MS, PhD); polymer chemistry (MS, PhD). *Application deadline:* For fall admission, 2/1 (priority date); for spring admission, 11/1. Applications are processed on a rolling basis. *Application fee:* $50. *Application Contact:* Dr. Robert H. Frey, Dean, Instruction and Graduate Studies, 315-470-6599, Fax: 315-470-6978, E-mail: esfgrad@esf.edu. *Chairperson,* Dr. John P. Hassett, 315-470-6827, Fax: 315-470-6856, E-mail: jphasset@syr.edu.

Faculty of Construction Management and Wood Products Engineering Students: 7 full-time (1 woman), 15 part-time (3 women), 8 international. Average age 36. 4 applicants, 100% accepted, 4 enrolled. *Faculty:* 8 full-time (0 women), 1 (woman) part-time/adjunct. Expenses: Contact institution. *Financial support:* In 2001–02, 8 students received support, including 2 fellowships with full tuition reimbursements available (averaging $8,817 per year), 3 research assistantships with full tuition reimbursements available (averaging $9,000 per year), 3 teaching assistantships with full tuition reimbursements available (averaging $8,817 per year); career-related internships or fieldwork, Federal Work-Study, institutionally sponsored loans, scholarships/grants, health care benefits, and unspecified assistantships also available. Financial award applicants required to submit FAFSA. In 2001, 3 master's, 3 doctorates awarded. Offers environmental and resources engineering (MPS, MS, PhD). *Application deadline:* For fall admission, 2/1 (priority date); for spring admission, 11/1 (priority date). Applications are processed on a rolling basis. *Application fee:* $50. *Application Contact:* Dr. Robert H. Frey, Dean, Instruction and Graduate Studies, 315-470-6599, Fax: 315-470-6879, E-mail: esfgrad@esf.edu. *Chair,* Dr. George H. Kyanka, 315-470-6835, Fax: 315-470-6879.

Faculty of Environmental and Forest Biology Students: 96 full-time (55 women), 52 part-time (19 women); includes 4 minority (1 Asian American or Pacific Islander, 2 Hispanic Americans, 1 Native American), 15 international. Average age 28. 83 applicants, 63% accepted, 32 enrolled. *Faculty:* 30 full-time (4 women). Expenses: Contact institution. *Financial support:* In 2001–02, 86 students received support, including 6 fellowships with full and partial tuition reimbursements available (averaging $8,045 per year), 57 research assistantships with full and partial tuition reimbursements available (averaging $9,000 per year), 23 teaching assistantships with full and partial tuition reimbursements available (averaging $8,817 per year); Federal Work-Study, institutionally sponsored loans, scholarships/grants, health care benefits, and unspecified assistantships also available. In 2001, 26 master's, 7 doctorates awarded. Offers chemical ecology (MPS, MS, PhD); conservation biology (MPS, MS, PhD); ecology (MPS, MS, PhD); entomology (MPS, MS, PhD); environmental interpretation (MPS, PhD); environmental physiology (MPS, MS, PhD); environmental interpretation (MS); fish and wildlife biology (MPS, MS, PhD); forest pathology and mycology (MPS, MS, PhD); plant science and biotechnology (MPS, MS, PhD). *Application deadline:* For fall admission, 2/1 (priority date); for spring admission, 11/1. Applications are processed on a rolling basis. *Application fee:* $50. *Application Contact:* Dr. Robert H. Frey, Dean, Instruction and Graduate Studies, 315-470-6599, Fax: 315-470-6978, E-mail: esfgrad@esf.edu. *Chairperson,* Dr. Neil H. Ringler, 315-470-6770, Fax: 315-470-6934, E-mail: neilringler@esf.edu.

Faculty of Environmental Resources and Forest Engineering Students: 15 full-time (5 women), 48 part-time (12 women); includes 3 minority (1 African American, 2 Asian Americans or Pacific Islanders), 8 international. Average age 33. 31 applicants, 71% accepted, 12 enrolled. *Faculty:* 7 full-time (1 woman). Expenses: Contact institution. *Financial support:* In 2001–02, 20 students received support, including 3 fellowships with full and partial tuition reimbursements available (averaging $8,817 per year), 12 research assistantships with full and partial tuition reimbursements available (averaging $9,000 per year), 5 teaching assistantships with full and partial tuition reimbursements available (averaging $8,817 per year); Federal Work-Study, institutionally sponsored loans, scholarships/grants, health care benefits, and unspecified assistantships also available. Financial award applicants required to submit FAFSA. In 2001, 6 degrees awarded. Offers environmental and resources engineering (MPS, MS, PhD). *Application deadline:* For fall admission, 2/1 (priority date); for spring admission, 11/1. Applications are processed on a rolling basis. *Application fee:* $50. *Application Contact:* Dr. Robert H. Frey, Dean, Instruction and Graduate Studies, 315-470-6599, Fax: 315-470-6978, E-mail: esfgrad@esf.edu. *Chairperson,* Dr. James M. Hassett, 315-470-6633, Fax: 315-470-6958, E-mail: jhassett@esf.edu.

Faculty of Environmental Studies Students: 44 full-time (29 women), 35 part-time (18 women); includes 4 minority (2 African Americans, 2 Hispanic Americans), 26 international. Average age 32. 74 applicants, 76% accepted, 21 enrolled. *Faculty:* 10 full-time (5 women), 1 (woman) part-time/adjunct. Expenses: Contact institution. *Financial support:* In 2001–02, 25 students received support, including 7 fellowships with full and partial tuition reimbursements available (averaging $8,817 per year), 6 research assistantships with full and partial tuition reimbursements available (averaging $9,000 per year), 12 teaching assistantships with full and partial tuition reimbursements available (averaging $8,817 per year); career-related internships or fieldwork, Federal Work-Study, institutionally sponsored loans, scholarships/grants, health care benefits, and unspecified assistantships also available. Support available to part-time students. Financial award applicants required to submit FAFSA. In 2001, 15 master's, 3 doctorates awarded. *Degree program information:* Part-time programs available. Offers environmental and community land planning (MPS, MS, PhD); environmental communication and information (MPS, MS, PhD); environmental policy and democratic processes (MPS, MS, PhD); environmental systems and risk management (MPS, MS, PhD); water and wetland resource studies (MPS, MS, PhD). *Application deadline:* For fall admission, 2/1 (priority date); for spring admission, 11/1. Applications are processed on a rolling basis. *Application fee:* $50. *Application Contact:* Dr. Robert H. Frey, Dean, Instruction and Graduate Studies, 315-470-6599, Fax: 315-470-6978, E-mail: esfgrad@esf.edu. *Chairperson,* Dr. Richard Smardon, 315-470-6636, Fax: 315-470-6915, E-mail: rsmardon@syr.edu.

Faculty of Forest and Natural Resources Management Students: 54 full-time (26 women), 39 part-time (10 women); includes 3 minority (1 African American, 1 Asian American or Pacific Islander, 1 Hispanic American), 23 international. Average age 31. 49 applicants, 94% accepted, 23 enrolled. *Faculty:* 28 full-time (5 women). Expenses: Contact institution. *Financial support:* In 2001–02, 43 students received support, including 6 fellowships with full and partial tuition reimbursements available (averaging $8,817 per year), 26 research assistantships with full and partial tuition reimbursements available (averaging $9,000 per year), 11 teaching assistantships with full and partial tuition reimbursements available (averaging $8,817 per year); career-related internships or fieldwork, Federal Work-Study, institutionally sponsored loans, scholarships/grants, health care benefits, and unspecified assistantships also available. Financial award applicants required to submit FAFSA. In 2001, 13 master's, 4 doctorates awarded. Offers environmental and natural resource policy (MS, PhD); environmental and natural resources policy (MPS); forest management and operations (MF); forestry ecosystems science and applications (MPS, MS, PhD); natural resources management (MPS, MS, PhD); quantitative methods in forest science (MPS, MS, PhD); recreation and resource management (MPS, MS, PhD); watershed management and forest hydrology (MPS, MS, PhD). *Application deadline:* For fall admission, 2/1 (priority date); for spring admission, 11/1. Applications are processed on a rolling basis. *Application fee:* $50. *Application Contact:* Dr. Robert H. Frey, Dean, Instruction and Graduate Studies, 315-470-6599, Fax: 315-470-6978, E-mail: esfgrad@esf.edu. *Chair,* Dr. William Bentley, 315-470-6514, Fax: 315-470-6535, E-mail: wbentley@esf.edu.

Faculty of Landscape Architecture Students: 35 full-time (15 women), 8 part-time (5 women); includes 1 minority (African American), 6 international. Average age 31. 43 applicants, 81% accepted, 16 enrolled. *Faculty:* 17 full-time (5 women). Expenses: Contact institution. *Financial support:* In 2001–02, 24 students received support, including 3 fellowships with full and partial tuition reimbursements available (averaging $8,817 per year), 3 research assistantships with full and partial tuition reimbursements available (averaging $9,000 per year), 8 teaching assistantships with full and partial tuition reimbursements available (averaging $8,817 per year); career-related internships or fieldwork and Federal Work-Study also available. Support available to part-time students. Financial award applicants required to submit FAFSA. In 2001, 14 degrees awarded. Offers cultural landscape studies and conservation (MLA, MS); ecological design and planning (MLA, MS); landscape and urban ecology (MLA, MS). *Application deadline:* For fall admission, 2/1 (priority date); for spring admission, 11/1. Applications are processed on a rolling basis. *Application fee:* $50. *Application Contact:* Dr. Robert H. Frey, Dean, Instruction and Graduate Studies, 315-470-6599, Fax: 315-470-6978, E-mail: esfgrad@esf.edu. *Chairperson,* Richard Hawks, 315-470-6544, Fax: 315-470-6540, E-mail: rshawks@esf.edu.

Faculty of Paper Science and Engineering Students: 7 full-time (3 women), 7 part-time (3 women), 11 international. 10 applicants, 80% accepted, 2 enrolled. *Faculty:* 7 full-time (0 women). Expenses: Contact institution. *Financial support:* In 2001–02, 12 students received support, including 2 fellowships with full tuition reimbursements available (averaging $8,817 per year), 8 research assistantships with full tuition reimbursements available (averaging $10,000 per year), 2 teaching assistantships with full tuition reimbursements available (averaging $8,817 per year); career-related internships or fieldwork, Federal Work-Study, institutionally sponsored loans, scholarships/grants, health care benefits, and unspecified assistantships also available. Support available to part-time students. Financial award applicants required to submit FAFSA. In 2001, 2 degrees awarded. Offers environmental and resources engineering (MS); environmental and resources engineering (PhD). *Application deadline:* For fall admission, 2/1 (priority date); for spring admission, 11/1 (priority date). Applications are processed on a rolling basis. *Application fee:* $50. *Application Contact:* Dr. Robert H. Frey, Dean, Instruction and Graduate Studies, 315-470-6599, Fax: 315-470-6978, E-mail: esfgrad@esf.edu. *Chair,* Dr. Thomas E. Amidon, 315-470-6524, Fax: 315-470-6945, E-mail: teamidon@syr.edu.

STATE UNIVERSITY OF NEW YORK COLLEGE OF OPTOMETRY, New York, NY 10036

General Information State-supported, coed, graduate-only institution. *Enrollment by degree level:* 282 first professional, 20 master's, 4 doctoral. *Graduate faculty:* 45 full-time (10 women), 102 part-time/adjunct (28 women). Tuition, state resident: full-time $10,842. Tuition, nonresident: full-time $21,942. *Required fees:* $181. Full-time tuition and fees vary according to program. *Graduate housing:* On-campus housing not available. *Student services:* Campus employment opportunities, campus safety program, career counseling, international student services, low-cost health insurance. *Library facilities:* Harold Kohn Visual Science Library. *Collection:* 3,600 titles, 400 serial subscriptions. *Research affiliation:* Schnurmacher Institute for Vision Research.

Computer facilities: 29 computers available on campus for general student use. A campuswide network can be accessed from off campus. Internet access is available. *Web address:* http://www.sunyopt.edu/.

State University of New York College of Optometry (continued)

General Application Contact: Dr. Edward Johnston, Vice President for Student Affairs and Director of Admissions, 212-780-5100, Fax: 212-780-5104, E-mail: johnston@sunyopt.edu.

GRADUATE UNITS

Graduate Programs Students: 11 full-time (8 women), 13 part-time (9 women); includes 5 minority (all Asian Americans or Pacific Islanders), 10 international. *Faculty:* 23 full-time (1 woman), 3 part-time/adjunct (all women). Expenses: Contact institution. *Financial support:* In 2001–02, 11 students received support, including 11 teaching assistantships with full tuition reimbursements available (averaging $15,000 per year); fellowships, research assistantships, Federal Work-Study, tuition waivers (full and partial), and unspecified assistantships also available. Financial award application deadline: 3/1. In 2001, 3 master's, 1 doctorate awarded. *Degree program information:* Part-time programs available. *Application deadline:* For fall admission, 3/1 (priority date). Applications are processed on a rolling basis. *Application fee:* $50. *Application Contact:* Debra Berger, Assistant to Associate Dean, 212-780-5044, Fax: 212-780-5009, E-mail: berger@sunyopt.edu. *Associate Dean*, Dr. Jerry Feldman, 212-780-5140, Fax: 212-780-5009, E-mail: jfeldman@sunyopt.edu.

Professional Program Students: 282 full-time (178 women); includes 107 minority (10 African Americans, 90 Asian Americans or Pacific Islanders, 7 Hispanic Americans), 18 international. Average age 24. 378 applicants, 37% accepted. *Faculty:* 45 full-time (10 women), 102 part-time/adjunct (28 women). Expenses: Contact institution. *Financial support:* In 2001–02, 220 students received support. Career-related internships or fieldwork, Federal Work-Study, tuition waivers (full and partial), and minority fellowships available. Financial award application deadline: 4/15. In 2001, 68 degrees awarded. Offers optometry (OD). *Application deadline:* For fall admission, 2/15 (priority date). Applications are processed on a rolling basis. *Application fee:* $75. *Vice President for Student Affairs and Director of Admissions*, Dr. Edward Johnston, 212-780-5100, Fax: 212-780-5104.

STATE UNIVERSITY OF NEW YORK EMPIRE STATE COLLEGE, Saratoga Springs, NY 12866-4391

General Information State-supported, coed, comprehensive institution. *Enrollment:* 29 full-time matriculated graduate/professional students (19 women), 285 part-time matriculated graduate/professional students (181 women). *Enrollment by degree level:* 314 master's. *Graduate faculty:* 6 full-time (2 women), 109 part-time/adjunct (45 women). Tuition, state resident: part-time $218 per credit hour. Tuition, nonresident: part-time $336 per credit hour. Tuition and fees vary according to program. *Graduate housing:* On-campus housing not available. *Student services:* Writing training. *Collection:* 5,300 titles, 209 serial subscriptions.

Computer facilities: 100 computers available on campus for general student use. A campuswide network can be accessed from off campus. Internet access and online class registration are available. *Web address:* http://www.esc.edu/.

General Application Contact: Cammie Baker Clancy, Assistant Director, 518-587-2100 Ext. 393, Fax: 518-587-9760, E-mail: cammie.baker-clancy@esc.edu.

GRADUATE UNITS

Graduate Studies Students: 29 full-time (19 women), 285 part-time (181 women). Average age 42. 200 applicants, 90% accepted. *Faculty:* 6 full-time (2 women), 109 part-time/adjunct (45 women). Expenses: Contact institution. *Financial support:* In 2001–02, 3 fellowships with full tuition reimbursements (averaging $2,800 per year) were awarded; career-related internships or fieldwork and Federal Work-Study also available. Support available to part-time students. Financial award application deadline: 7/1; financial award applicants required to submit FAFSA. In 2001, 98 degrees awarded. *Degree program information:* Part-time and evening/weekend programs available. Postbaccalaureate distance learning degree programs offered (minimal on-campus study). Offers business administration (MBA); business and policy studies (MA); labor and policy studies (MA); liberal studies (MA); social policy (MA). *Application deadline:* For fall admission, 7/1 (priority date); for spring admission, 12/1 (priority date). Applications are processed on a rolling basis. *Application fee:* $50. Electronic applications accepted. *Application Contact:* Cammie Baker Clancy, Assistant Director, 518-587-2100 Ext. 393, Fax: 518-587-9760, E-mail: cammie.baker-clancy@esc.edu. *Dean*, Dr. Robert Carey, 518-587-2100 Ext. 207, Fax: 518-587-9760, E-mail: robert.carey@esc.edu.

STATE UNIVERSITY OF NEW YORK HEALTH SCIENCE CENTER AT BROOKLYN, Brooklyn, NY 11203-2098

General Information State-supported, coed, upper-level institution. *Enrollment:* 932 full-time matriculated graduate/professional students (377 women), 132 part-time matriculated graduate/professional students (all women). *Enrollment by degree level:* 771 first professional, 88 doctoral. *Graduate faculty:* 119 full-time (28 women), 6 part-time/adjunct (all women). Tuition, state resident: full-time $5,100; part-time $213 per credit. Tuition, nonresident: full-time $8,416; part-time $351 per credit. *Required fees:* $150. *Graduate housing:* Rooms and/or apartments available to single and married students. Housing application deadline: 5/29. *Student services:* Campus employment opportunities, career counseling, child daycare facilities, free psychological counseling, low-cost health insurance. *Library facilities:* The Medical Research Library of Brooklyn. *Online resources:* library catalog, web page, access to other libraries' catalogs. *Collection:* 357,209 titles, 2,104 serial subscriptions, 812 audiovisual materials. *Research affiliation:* Staten Island Institute for Basic Research in Developmental Disabilities, Brooklyn Veterans Administration Medical Center.

Computer facilities: 183 computers available on campus for general student use. A campuswide network can be accessed from student residence rooms and from off campus. Internet access is available. *Web address:* http://www.downstate.edu/.

General Application Contact: Denise Sheares, Admissions Officer, 718-270-2738, Fax: 718-270-3378, E-mail: dsheares@downstate.edu.

GRADUATE UNITS

College of Medicine Students: 775 full-time (388 women). Average age 24. 2,750 applicants, 17% accepted, 188 enrolled. *Faculty:* 545 full-time, 155 part-time/adjunct. Expenses: Contact institution. *Financial support:* In 2001–02, 89 teaching assistantships with tuition reimbursements (averaging $17,000 per year) were awarded; career-related internships or fieldwork, Federal Work-Study, and tuition waivers (full and partial) also available. Support available to part-time students. Financial award application deadline: 5/1; financial award applicants required to submit FAFSA. In 2001, 193 degrees awarded. Offers medicine (MD). *Application deadline:* For fall admission, 2/1. Applications are processed on a rolling basis. *Application fee:* $65. *Application Contact:* Dr. Lorraine Terracina, Assistant Vice President Student Affairs and Dean of Students, 718-270-2446. *Dean*, Dr. Eugene B. Feigelson, 718-270-3776.

College of Nursing *Degree program information:* Part-time and evening/weekend programs available. Offers nurse anesthesia (MS); nurse practitioner (MS, Post Master's Certificate); nursing (MS).

MD/PhD Program

School of Graduate Studies Students: 81 full-time (34 women), 1 part-time; includes 16 minority (2 African Americans, 12 Asian Americans or Pacific Islanders, 2 Hispanic Americans), 47 international. Average age 30. 149 applicants, 17% accepted. *Faculty:* 115 full-time (24 women). Expenses: Contact institution. *Financial support:* Fellowships, research assistantships, teaching assistantships, career-related internships or fieldwork, Federal Work-Study, and tuition waivers (full and partial) available. In 2001, 6 degrees awarded. Offers anatomy and cell biology (PhD); biochemistry (PhD); biophysics (PhD); microbiology and immunology (PhD); neural and behavioral science (PhD); neural and behavioral sciences (PhD); pharmacology (PhD); physiology (PhD). *Application deadline:* For fall admission, 7/1. *Application fee:* $35. *Application Contact:* Denise Sheares, Admissions Officer, 718-270-2738, Fax: 718-270-3378, E-mail: dsheares@downstate.edu. *Dean*, Dr. Susan Schwartz-Giblin, 718-270-1155.

STATE UNIVERSITY OF NEW YORK INSTITUTE OF TECHNOLOGY AT UTICA/ROME, Utica, NY 13504-3050

General Information State-supported, coed, comprehensive institution. *Enrollment:* 117 full-time matriculated graduate/professional students (52 women), 270 part-time matriculated graduate/professional students (142 women). *Enrollment by degree level:* 377 master's, 10 other advanced degrees. *Graduate faculty:* 59 full-time (18 women), 8 part-time/adjunct (5 women). Tuition, state resident: full-time $5,100; part-time $213 per credit hour. Tuition, nonresident: full-time $8,416; part-time $351 per credit hour. *Required fees:* $525; $21 per credit hour. Tuition and fees vary according to course load. *Graduate housing:* Room and/or apartments available on a first-come, first-served basis to single students; on-campus housing not available to married students. Typical cost: $3,820 per year ($6,240 including board). Room and board charges vary according to board plan. *Student services:* Campus employment opportunities, campus safety program, career counseling, disabled student services, exercise/wellness program, free psychological counseling, international student services, low-cost health insurance, multicultural affairs office, writing training. *Library facilities:* SUNY Institute of Technology at Utica/Rome Library. *Online resources:* library catalog, web page, access to other libraries' catalogs. *Collection:* 193,682 titles, 1,090 serial subscriptions, 11,818 audiovisual materials. *Research affiliation:* Information Institute of Rome Air Force Research Lab (information technology research).

Computer facilities: 250 computers available on campus for general student use. A campuswide network can be accessed from student residence rooms and from off campus. Internet access and online class registration, various other software applications are available. *Web address:* http://www.sunyit.edu/.

General Application Contact: Marybeth Lyons, Director of Admissions, 315-792-7500, Fax: 315-792-7837, E-mail: smbl@sunyit.edu.

GRADUATE UNITS

School of Arts and Sciences Students: 3 full-time (2 women), 30 part-time (21 women); includes 4 minority (2 African Americans, 1 Asian American or Pacific Islander, 1 Hispanic American) Average age 34. 23 applicants, 83% accepted. *Faculty:* 11 full-time (2 women), 1 (woman) part-time/adjunct. Expenses: Contact institution. *Financial support:* In 2001–02, 1 student received support. Federal Work-Study, scholarships/grants, and unspecified assistantships available. Financial award applicants required to submit FAFSA. *Degree program information:* Part-time and evening/weekend programs available. Offers applied sociology (MS); information design and technology (MS). *Application deadline:* For fall admission, 6/15 (priority date). Applications are processed on a rolling basis. *Application fee:* $50. *Application Contact:* Marybeth Lyons, Director of Admissions, 315-792-7500, Fax: 315-792-7837, E-mail: smbl@sunyit.edu. *Dean*, Dr. Daniel J. Murphy, 315-792-7333, Fax: 315-792-7503, E-mail: murphy@sunyit.edu.

School of Information Systems and Engineering Technology Students: 52 full-time (12 women), 74 part-time (15 women); includes 8 minority (4 African Americans, 4 Asian Americans or Pacific Islanders), 41 international. Average age 32. 96 applicants, 88% accepted. *Faculty:* 20 full-time (3 women), 2 part-time/adjunct (0 women). Expenses: Contact institution. *Financial support:* In 2001–02, 39 students received support. Federal Work-Study, scholarships/grants, and unspecified assistantships available. Financial award applicants required to submit FAFSA. In 2001, 25 degrees awarded. *Degree program information:* Part-time and evening/weekend programs available. Offers advanced technology (MS); computer and information science (MS); telecommunications (MS). *Application deadline:* For fall admission, 6/15 (priority date). Applications are processed on a rolling basis. *Application fee:* $50. *Application Contact:* Marybeth Lyons, Director of Admissions, 315-792-7500, Fax: 315-792-7837, E-mail: smbl@sunyit.edu. *Dean*, Dr. Orlando Baiocchi, 315-792-7234, Fax: 315-792-7800, E-mail: baiocco@sunyit.edu.

School of Management Students: 44 full-time (23 women), 133 part-time (73 women); includes 11 minority (4 African Americans, 4 Asian Americans or Pacific Islanders, 3 Hispanic Americans), 7 international. Average age 35. 74 applicants, 85% accepted. *Faculty:* 17 full-time (2 women). Expenses: Contact institution. *Financial support:* In 2001–02, 16 students received support. Federal Work-Study, scholarships/grants, and unspecified assistantships available. Financial award applicants required to submit FAFSA. In 2001, 39 degrees awarded. *Degree program information:* Part-time and evening/weekend programs available. Postbaccalaureate distance learning degree programs offered (no on-campus study). Offers accountancy (MS); business management (MS); health services administration (MS). *Application deadline:* For fall admission, 6/15 (priority date). Applications are processed on a rolling basis. *Application fee:* $50. *Application Contact:* Marybeth Lyons, Director of Admissions, 315-792-7500, Fax: 315-792-7837, E-mail: smbl@sunyit.edu. *Dean*, Dr. Sanjay Varshney, 315-792-7429, Fax: 315-792-7138, E-mail: fsbv@sunyit.edu.

School of Nursing Students: 18 full-time (15 women), 33 part-time (all women); includes 1 minority (African American) Average age 41. 15 applicants, 40% accepted. *Faculty:* 11 full-time (all women), 5 part-time/adjunct (4 women). Expenses: Contact institution. *Financial support:* In 2001–02, 1 student received support. Federal Work-Study, scholarships/grants, and unspecified assistantships available. Financial award applicants required to submit FAFSA. In 2001, 32 degrees awarded. *Degree program information:* Part-time programs available. Offers adult nurse practitioner (MS, Certificate); family nurse practitioner (MS, Certificate); nursing administration (MS, CAS). *Application deadline:* For fall admission, 6/15 (priority date). Applications are processed on a rolling basis. *Application fee:* $50. *Application Contact:* Marybeth Lyons, Director of Admissions, 315-792-7500, Fax: 315-792-7837, E-mail: smbl@sunyit.edu. *Dean*, Dr. Jeannine Muldoon, 315-792-7295, Fax: 315-792-7555, E-mail: muldooj@dunyit.edu.

See in-depth description on page 1121.

STATE UNIVERSITY OF NEW YORK MARITIME COLLEGE, Throggs Neck, NY 10465-4198

General Information State-supported, coed, primarily men, comprehensive institution. *Graduate housing:* Room and/or apartments available to single students; on-campus housing not available to married students. *Research affiliation:* Port Authority of New York and New Jersey (transportation), Transportation Infrastructure Research Consortium, Transportation Research Board (maritime transportation).

GRADUATE UNITS

Program in Transportation Management *Degree program information:* Part-time and evening/weekend programs available. Offers transportation management (MS).

STATE UNIVERSITY OF NEW YORK UPSTATE MEDICAL UNIVERSITY, Syracuse, NY 13210-2334

General Information State-supported, coed, upper-level institution. CGS member. *Graduate housing:* Rooms and/or apartments available to single and married students. Housing application deadline: 8/1.

GRADUATE UNITS

College of Graduate Studies Offers anatomy and cell biology (MS, PhD); biochemistry and molecular biology (MS, PhD); cell and developmental biology (PhD); cell and molecular biology (PhD); microbiology and immunology (MS, PhD); neuroscience (PhD); pharmacology (MS, PhD); physiology (MS, PhD).

College of Health Professions Students: 85 full-time (56 women), 1 (woman) part-time; includes 12 minority (4 African Americans, 6 Asian Americans or Pacific Islanders, 2 Native Americans), 2 international. Average age 27. 99 applicants, 39% accepted, 25 enrolled. *Faculty:* 6 full-time (4 women), 3 part-time/adjunct (2 women). Expenses: Contact institution. *Financial support:* Federal Work-Study, institutionally sponsored loans, and scholarships/grants available. Support available to part-time students. Financial award application deadline: 3/1; financial award applicants required to submit FAFSA. In 2001, 31 degrees awarded. Offers health professions (MPT, MS); medical technology (MS); physical therapy (MPT). *Application deadline:* For fall admission, 1/15. Applications are processed on a rolling basis. *Application fee:* $30. *Application Contact:* Donna Vavonese, Associate Director of Admissions, 315-464-4570, Fax: 315-464-8867, E-mail: vavonesd@upstate.edu. *Dean,* Dr. Hugh W. Bonner, 315-464-6560, Fax: 315-464-4561.

College of Medicine Students: 640 full-time (270 women); includes 233 minority (52 African Americans, 156 Asian Americans or Pacific Islanders, 25 Hispanic Americans), 5 international. Average age 26. 2,445 applicants, 17% accepted, 156 enrolled. *Faculty:* 434 full-time (89 women), 154 part-time/adjunct (27 women). Expenses: Contact institution. *Financial support:* In 2001–02, 548 students received support. Career-related internships or fieldwork, Federal Work-Study, institutionally sponsored loans, scholarships/grants, and tuition waivers (full and partial) available. Support available to part-time students. Financial award application deadline: 3/1; financial award applicants required to submit FAFSA. In 2001, 151 degrees awarded. Offers medicine (MD). *Application deadline:* For fall admission, 12/1. Applications are processed on a rolling basis. *Application fee:* $60. *Application Contact:* Jennifer Welch, Director of Admissions, 315-464-4570, Fax: 315-464-8867, E-mail: welchj@upstate.edu. *Dean,* Dr. Michael Roizen, 315-464-4515.

College of Nursing Students: 14 full-time (all women), 55 part-time (53 women); includes 5 minority (3 African Americans, 1 Asian American or Pacific Islander, 1 Hispanic American) Average age 39. 39 applicants, 92% accepted, 25 enrolled. *Faculty:* 7 full-time (all women). Expenses: Contact institution. *Financial support:* In 2001–02, 17 students received support. Federal Work-Study, scholarships/grants, and traineeships available. Support available to part-time students. Financial award application deadline: 3/1; financial award applicants required to submit FAFSA. In 2001, 23 degrees awarded. *Degree program information:* Part-time programs available. Offers nursing (MS). *Application deadline:* For fall admission, 3/1 (priority date). Applications are processed on a rolling basis. *Application fee:* $40. *Application Contact:* Donna Vavonese, Associate Director of Admissions, 315-464-4570, Fax: 315-464-8867, E-mail: vavonesd@upstate.edu. *Dean,* Dr. Elvira Szigeti, 315-464-4276, Fax: 315-464-5168.

STATE UNIVERSITY OF WEST GEORGIA, Carrollton, GA 30118

General Information State-supported, coed, comprehensive institution. CGS member. *Enrollment:* 317 full-time matriculated graduate/professional students (214 women), 1,470 part-time matriculated graduate/professional students (1,156 women). *Enrollment by degree level:* 1,046 master's, 29 doctoral, 712 other advanced degrees. *Graduate faculty:* 246 full-time (92 women). Tuition, state resident: full-time $232; part-time $97 per credit hour. Tuition, nonresident: full-time $928; part-time $387 per credit hour. *Required fees:* $536; $14 per credit. $100 per semester. *Graduate housing:* Room and/or apartments available on a first-come, first-served basis to single students; on-campus housing not available to married students. Typical cost: $2,274 per year ($4,100 including board). Housing application deadline: 6/1. *Student services:* Campus employment opportunities, campus safety program, career counseling, child daycare facilities, disabled student services, exercise/wellness program, free psychological counseling, international student services, low-cost health insurance, multicultural affairs office, teacher training, writing training. *Library facilities:* Irvine Sullivan Ingram Library. *Online resources:* library catalog, web page, access to other libraries' catalogs. *Collection:* 292,883 titles, 2,095 serial subscriptions.

Computer facilities: A campuswide network can be accessed from student residence rooms and from off campus. Internet access and online class registration are available. *Web address:* http://www.westga.edu/.

General Application Contact: Dr. Jack O. Jenkins, Dean, Graduate School, 770-836-6419, Fax: 770-836-2301, E-mail: jjenkins@westga.edu.

GRADUATE UNITS

Graduate School Students: 317 full-time (214 women), 1,470 part-time (1,156 women); includes 365 minority (340 African Americans, 6 Asian Americans or Pacific Islanders, 17 Hispanic Americans, 2 Native Americans), 36 international. Average age 34. 806 applicants. *Faculty:* 246 full-time (92 women). Expenses: Contact institution. *Financial support:* In 2001–02, 120 research assistantships with partial tuition reimbursements (averaging $5,000 per year) were awarded; career-related internships or fieldwork, tuition waivers (partial), and unspecified assistantships also available. Support available to part-time students. Financial award applicants required to submit FAFSA. In 2001, 441 master's, 119 other advanced degrees awarded. *Degree program information:* Part-time and evening/weekend programs available. Postbaccalaureate distance learning degree programs offered (no on-campus study). *Application deadline:* For fall admission, 8/1 (priority date); for spring admission, 12/18. *Application fee:* $20. Electronic applications accepted. *Application Contact:* Cheryl Lynn Thomas, Director of Graduate Admissions, 770-836-6419, Fax: 770-830-2301, E-mail: gradsch@westga.edu. *Dean,* Dr. Jack O. Jenkins, 770-836-6419, Fax: 770-836-2301, E-mail: jjenkins@westga.edu.

College of Arts and Sciences Students: 95 full-time (59 women), 101 part-time (65 women); includes 35 minority (29 African Americans, 5 Hispanic Americans, 1 Native American), 7 international. Average age 31. *Faculty:* 138 full-time (47 women). Expenses: Contact institution. *Financial support:* In 2001–02, 40 research assistantships with full tuition reimbursements (averaging $6,000 per year) were awarded; career-related internships or fieldwork and unspecified assistantships also available. Support available to part-time students. Financial award applicants required to submit FAFSA. In 2001, 57 degrees awarded. *Degree program information:* Part-time programs available. Offers applied computer science (MS); art education (M Ed); arts and sciences (M Ed, M Mus, MA, MPA, MS); biology (MS); English language and literature (MA); gerontology (MA); history (MA); music (M Mus); music education (M Mus); music performance (M Mus); psychology (MA); public administration (MPA); rural and small town planning (MS); sociology (MA). *Application deadline:* For fall admission, 8/1 (priority date); for spring admission, 12/18. *Application fee:* $20. Electronic applications accepted. *Application Contact:* Dr. Jack O. Jenkins, Dean, Graduate School, 770-836-6419, Fax: 770-836-2301, E-mail: jjenkins@westga.edu. *Dean,* Dr. Richard G. Miller, 770-836-6405, Fax: 770-836-6791, E-mail: dmiller@westga.edu.

College of Education Students: 181 full-time (137 women), 1,292 part-time (1,034 women). Average age 34. *Faculty:* 71 full-time (39 women). Expenses: Contact institution. *Financial support:* In 2001–02, 46 research assistantships with partial tuition reimbursements (averaging $6,000 per year) were awarded; career-related internships or fieldwork and unspecified assistantships also available. Support available to part-time students. Financial award applicants required to submit FAFSA. In 2001, 341 master's, 119 other advanced degrees awarded. *Degree program information:* Part-time and evening/weekend programs available. Offers administration and supervision (M Ed, Ed S); art education (M Ed); business education (M Ed, Ed S); counseling and guidance (M Ed, Ed S); early childhood education (M Ed, Ed S); education (M Ed, Ed D, Ed S); French (M Ed); media (M Ed, Ed S); middle grades education (M Ed, Ed S); physical education (M Ed, Ed S); reading education (M Ed); school improvement (Ed D); secondary education—English (M Ed, Ed S); secondary education—foreign language (M Ed); secondary education—mathematics (M Ed, Ed S); secondary education—science (M Ed, Ed S); secondary education—social studies (M Ed, Ed S); Spanish (M Ed); special education-curriculum specialist (Ed S); special education-emotionally handicapped (M Ed, Ed S); special education-learning disabled (M Ed); special education-mentally handicapped (M Ed); speech-language pathology (M Ed). *Application deadline:* For fall admission, 8/1; for spring admission, 12/18. Applications are processed on a rolling basis. *Application fee:* $20. *Application Contact:* Dr. Jack O. Jenkins, Dean, Graduate School, 770-836-6419, Fax: 770-836-2301, E-mail: jjenkins@westga.edu. *Dean,* Dr. Kent Layton, 770-836-6570, Fax: 770-836-6729, E-mail: klayton@westga.edu.

Richards College of Business Students: 38 full-time (17 women), 34 part-time (19 women); includes 11 minority (10 African Americans, 1 Hispanic American), 28 international. Average age 27. *Faculty:* 34 full-time (6 women). Expenses: Contact institution. *Financial support:* In 2001–02, 10 students received support, including 10 research assistantships with full tuition reimbursements available (averaging $6,000 per year); career-related internships or fieldwork and tuition waivers (partial) also available. Financial award application deadline: 7/1; financial award applicants required to submit FAFSA. In 2001, 43 degrees awarded. *Degree program information:* Part-time and evening/weekend programs available. Offers accounting and finance (MP Acc); business (MBA, MP Acc); business administration (MBA). *Application deadline:* For fall admission, 8/1 (priority date); for spring admission, 12/1. *Application fee:* $20. Electronic applications accepted. *Application Contact:* Dr. Jack O. Jenkins, Dean, Graduate School, 770-836-6419, Fax: 770-836-2301, E-mail: jjenkins@westga.edu. *Dean,* Dr. Jack E. Johnson, 770-836-6467, Fax: 770-836-6774, E-mail: jjohnson@westga.edu.

STEPHEN F. AUSTIN STATE UNIVERSITY, Nacogdoches, TX 75962

General Information State-supported, coed, comprehensive institution. *Enrollment:* 464 full-time matriculated graduate/professional students (294 women), 804 part-time matriculated graduate/professional students (502 women). *Graduate faculty:* 347 full-time (119 women), 72 part-time/adjunct (15 women). Tuition, state resident: full-time $1,008; part-time $42 per credit. Tuition, nonresident: full-time $6,072; part-time $253 per credit. *Required fees:* $1,248; $52 per credit. Tuition and fees vary according to course load. *Graduate housing:* Rooms and/or apartments available on a first-come, first-served basis to single students and available to married students. Typical cost: $4,720 (including board) for single students; $3,600 per year for married students. Housing application deadline: 6/1. *Student services:* Campus employment opportunities, career counseling, disabled student services, exercise/wellness program, free psychological counseling, international student services, low-cost health insurance, multicultural affairs office. *Library facilities:* Ralph W. Steen Library. *Online resources:* library catalog, web page. *Collection:* 694,812 titles, 4,083 serial subscriptions, 48,902 audiovisual materials. *Research affiliation:* University Health Center at Tyler (biotechnology, environmental science).

Computer facilities: 800 computers available on campus for general student use. A campuswide network can be accessed from student residence rooms and from off campus. Internet access and online class registration are available. *Web address:* http://www.sfasu.edu/.

General Application Contact: Dr. David Jeffrey, Associate Vice President for Graduate Studies and Research, 936-468-2807, Fax: 936-468-1251, E-mail: gschool@titan.sfasu.edu.

GRADUATE UNITS

Graduate School Students: 464 full-time (294 women), 804 part-time (502 women); includes 176 minority (104 African Americans, 13 Asian Americans or Pacific Islanders, 45 Hispanic Americans, 14 Native Americans), 35 international. 588 applicants, 86% accepted. *Faculty:* 347 full-time (119 women), 72 part-time/adjunct (15 women). Expenses: Contact institution. *Financial support:* In 2001–02, research assistantships (averaging $6,700 per year), teaching assistantships (averaging $6,700 per year) were awarded. Fellowships, career-related internships or fieldwork, Federal Work-Study, institutionally sponsored loans, traineeships, and unspecified assistantships also available. Support available to part-time students. Financial award application deadline: 3/1. In 2001, 363 master's, 9 doctorates awarded. *Degree program information:* Part-time and evening/weekend programs available. *Application deadline:* For fall admission, 7/1 (priority date); for spring admission, 11/1 (priority date). Applications are processed on a rolling basis. *Application fee:* $25 ($50 for international students). Electronic applications accepted. *Associate Vice President for Graduate Studies and Research,* Dr. David Jeffrey, 936-468-2807, Fax: 936-468-1251, E-mail: gschool@titan.sfasu.edu.

College of Applied Arts and Science Students: 50 full-time (39 women), 37 part-time (22 women); includes 25 minority (17 African Americans, 1 Asian American or Pacific Islander, 5 Hispanic Americans, 2 Native Americans) Average age 26. 60 applicants, 92% accepted. *Faculty:* 19 full-time (7 women). Expenses: Contact institution. *Financial support:* In 2001–02, 2 research assistantships (averaging $6,600 per year), 13 teaching assistantships (averaging $6,633 per year) were awarded. Career-related internships or fieldwork, Federal Work-Study, and institutionally sponsored loans also available. Support available to part-time students. Financial award application deadline: 3/1. In 2001, 38 degrees awarded. *Degree program information:* Part-time programs available. Offers applied arts and science (MA, MIS, MSW); communication (MA); interdisciplinary studies (MIS); mass communication (MA); social work (MSW). *Application deadline:* Applications are processed on a rolling basis. *Application fee:* $25 ($50 for international students). *Dean,* Dr. James O. Standley, 936-468-4604.

College of Business Students: 48 full-time (22 women), 64 part-time (19 women); includes 18 minority (8 African Americans, 2 Asian Americans or Pacific Islanders, 7 Hispanic Americans, 1 Native American), 7 international. Average age 29. 71 applicants, 94% accepted. *Faculty:* 49 full-time (16 women). Expenses: Contact institution. *Financial support:* In 2001–02, 1 research assistantship (averaging $6,633 per year), 13 teaching assistantships (averaging $6,633 per year) were awarded. Federal Work-Study and institutionally sponsored loans also available. Support available to part-time students. Financial award application deadline: 3/1. In 2001, 33 degrees awarded. *Degree program information:* Part-time and evening/weekend programs available. Offers business (MBA); computer science (MS); management and marketing (MBA); professional accountancy (MPAC). *Application deadline:* Applications are processed on a rolling basis. *Application fee:* $0 ($50 for international students). *Dean,* Dr. Marlin C. Young, 409-468-3101.

College of Education Students: 183 full-time (142 women), 565 part-time (388 women); includes 93 minority (62 African Americans, 3 Asian Americans or Pacific Islanders, 23 Hispanic Americans, 5 Native Americans), 1 international. 300 applicants, 80% accepted. *Faculty:* 88 full-time (54 women), 3 part-time/adjunct (0 women). Expenses: Contact institution. *Financial support:* Research assistantships, teaching assistantships, career-related internships or fieldwork, Federal Work-Study, and institutionally sponsored loans available. Financial award application deadline: 3/1. In 2001, 184 master's, 6 doctorates awarded. *Degree program information:* Part-time and evening/weekend programs available. Offers agriculture (MS); counseling (MA); early childhood education (M Ed); education (M Ed, MA, MS, Ed D); educational leadership (Ed D); elementary education (M Ed); health education (M Ed); human sciences (MS); physical education (M Ed); school psychology (MA); secondary education (M Ed); special education (M Ed); speech pathology (MS). *Application deadline:* For fall admission, 3/1; for spring admission, 10/1. Applications are processed on a rolling basis. *Application fee:* $25 ($50 for international students). *Interim Dean,* Dr. Patsy Hallman, 936-468-2901.

College of Fine Arts Students: 32 full-time (16 women), 14 part-time (8 women); includes 5 minority (4 African Americans, 1 Hispanic American) 15 applicants, 87% accepted. *Faculty:* 37 full-time (6 women). Expenses: Contact institution. *Financial support:* Fellowships, research assistantships, teaching assistantships, Federal Work-Study, institutionally sponsored loans, and unspecified assistantships available. Financial award application deadline: 3/1. In 2001, 26 degrees awarded. *Degree program information:* Part-time programs available. Offers art (MA); design (MFA); drawing (MFA); fine arts (MA, MFA, MM); music (MA, MM); painting (MFA); sculpture (MFA). *Application deadline:* For fall admission, 8/1 (priority date); for spring admission, 12/1. Applications are processed on a rolling basis. *Application fee:* $0 ($50 for international students). *Interim Dean,* Dr. Richard Berry, 936-468-2801.

College of Forestry Students: 24 full-time (11 women), 20 part-time (7 women); includes 1 minority (Native American), 2 international. 15 applicants, 100% accepted. *Faculty:* 19 full-time (1 woman), 24 part-time/adjunct (3 women). Expenses: Contact institution. *Financial support:* In 2001–02, 26 research assistantships (averaging $13,000 per year), 6 teaching assistantships (averaging $6,633 per year) were awarded. Career-related internships or fieldwork and Federal Work-Study also available. Support available to part-time students. Financial award application deadline: 3/1. In 2001, 10 master's, 3 doctorates awarded. *Degree program information:* Part-time programs available. Offers forestry (MF, MSF, PhD). *Application deadline:* For fall admission, 8/1 (priority date); for spring admission, 12/15. Applications are processed on a rolling basis. *Application fee:* $25 ($50 for international students). *Dean,* Dr. Scott Beasley, 936-468-3304.

College of Liberal Arts Students: 50 full-time (25 women), 51 part-time (31 women); includes 21 minority (12 African Americans, 3 Asian Americans or Pacific Islanders, 6 Hispanic Americans), 2 international. 49 applicants, 94% accepted. *Faculty:* 52 full-time (20 women), 3 part-time/adjunct (0 women). Expenses: Contact institution. *Financial support:* In 2001–02, research assistantships (averaging $6,633 per year), teaching assistantships (averaging $6,633 per year) were awarded. Career-related internships or fieldwork, Federal Work-Study, institutionally sponsored loans, health care benefits, and unspecified assistantships also available. Support available to part-time students. Financial award application deadline: 3/1. In 2001, 22 degrees awarded. *Degree program information:* Part-time and

Stephen F. Austin State University (continued)

evening/weekend programs available. Offers English (MA); history (MA); liberal arts (MA, MPA); psychology (MA); public administration (MPA). *Application deadline:* For fall admission, 8/1 (priority date); for spring admission, 12/15. Applications are processed on a rolling basis. *Application fee:* $0 ($50 for international students). *Interim Dean*, Dr. Herbert Dean, 936-468-2803.

College of Sciences and Mathematics Students: 76 full-time (39 women), 31 part-time (12 women); includes 13 minority (4 Asian Americans or Pacific Islanders, 5 Hispanic Americans, 4 Native Americans), 23 international. 70 applicants, 96% accepted. *Faculty:* 59 full-time (10 women), 77 part-time/adjunct (22 women). Expenses: Contact institution. *Financial support:* Fellowships, research assistantships, teaching assistantships, Federal Work-Study, institutionally sponsored loans, and unspecified assistantships available. Support available to part-time students. Financial award application deadline: 3/1. In 2001, 47 degrees awarded. *Degree program information:* Part-time programs available. Offers biology (MS); biotechnology (MS); chemistry (MS); environmental science (MS); geology (MS, MSNS); mathematics (MS); mathematics education (MS); physics (MS); sciences and mathematics (MS, MSNS); statistics (MS). *Application deadline:* For fall admission, 8/1 (priority date); for spring admission, 12/15. Applications are processed on a rolling basis. *Application fee:* $0 ($50 for international students). *Dean*, Dr. Thomas Atchison, 936-468-2805.

STEPHENS COLLEGE, Columbia, MO 65215-0002

General Information Independent, women only, comprehensive institution. *Graduate housing:* On-campus housing not available.

GRADUATE UNITS

School of Graduate and Continuing Education *Degree program information:* Part-time programs available. Postbaccalaureate distance learning degree programs offered (minimal on-campus study). Offers business administration (MBA); education (M Ed); school counseling (M Ed). Electronic applications accepted.

STETSON UNIVERSITY, DeLand, FL 32723

General Information Independent, coed, comprehensive institution. *Enrollment:* 788 full-time matriculated graduate/professional students (440 women), 250 part-time matriculated graduate/professional students (145 women). *Enrollment by degree level:* 750 first professional, 288 master's. *Graduate faculty:* 64 full-time (22 women), 42 part-time/adjunct (15 women). *Tuition:* Part-time $430 per credit hour. Full-time tuition and fees vary according to program. *Graduate housing:* Rooms and/or apartments available to single and married students. *Student services:* Campus employment opportunities, campus safety program, career counseling, child daycare facilities, free psychological counseling, international student services, multicultural affairs office, teacher training. *Library facilities:* DuPont-Ball Library plus 2 others. *Online resources:* library catalog, web page, access to other libraries' catalogs. *Collection:* 347,628 titles, 4,747 serial subscriptions, 18,760 audiovisual materials.

Computer facilities: 262 computers available on campus for general student use. A campuswide network can be accessed from student residence rooms and from off campus. Internet access is available. *Web address:* http://www.stetson.edu/.

General Application Contact: Pat LeClaire, Office of Graduate Studies, 386-822-7075, Fax: 386-822-7388, E-mail: pat.leclaire@stetson.edu.

GRADUATE UNITS

College of Arts and Sciences Students: 35 full-time (32 women), 105 part-time (83 women); includes 24 minority (18 African Americans, 2 Asian Americans or Pacific Islanders, 4 Hispanic Americans), 1 international. Average age 35. Expenses: Contact institution. *Financial support:* Career-related internships or fieldwork, Federal Work-Study, institutionally sponsored loans, scholarships/grants, and tuition waivers (partial) available. Support available to part-time students. In 2001, 40 master's, 1 other advanced degree awarded. *Degree program information:* Part-time and evening/weekend programs available. Offers arts and sciences (M Ed, MA, MS, Ed S); career teaching (Ed S); education (MA); educational leadership (M Ed, Ed S); elementary education (M Ed); exceptional student education (M Ed); marriage and family therapy (MS); mental health counseling (MS); reading education (M Ed); school guidance and family consultation (MS); varying exceptionalities (M Ed). *Application deadline:* For fall admission, 3/1 (priority date); for spring admission, 11/1. Applications are processed on a rolling basis. *Application fee:* $25. *Application Contact:* Pat LeClaire, Office of Graduate Studies, 386-822-7075, Fax: 386-822-7388, E-mail: pat.leclaire@stetson.edu. *Dean*, Dr. Grady Ballenger, 386-822-7515.

Division of Humanities Average age 36. Expenses: Contact institution. In 2001, 1 degree awarded. Offers English (MA). *Application deadline:* For fall admission, 3/1 (priority date); for spring admission, 11/1. Applications are processed on a rolling basis. *Application fee:* $25. *Application Contact:* Pat LeClaire, Office of Graduate Studies, 386-822-7075, Fax: 386-822-7388, E-mail: pat.leclaire@stetson.edu.

College of Law Students: 727 full-time (400 women), 23 part-time (7 women); includes 109 minority (39 African Americans, 13 Asian Americans or Pacific Islanders, 53 Hispanic Americans, 4 Native Americans), 31 international. Average age 27. Expenses: Contact institution. *Financial support:* Research assistantships, teaching assistantships, career-related internships or fieldwork, institutionally sponsored loans, and scholarships/grants available. Financial award application deadline: 4/1; financial award applicants required to submit FAFSA. In 2001, 257 degrees awarded. Offers law (JD, LL M). *Application deadline:* For fall admission, 3/1 (priority date); for spring admission, 9/1. *Application fee:* $50. *Application Contact:* Pamela Coleman, Assistant Dean and Director of Admissions, 727-562-7802, E-mail: lawadmit@law.stetson.edu. *Dean*, Dr. W. Gary Vause, 727-562-7810.

School of Business Administration Students: 26 full-time (8 women), 122 part-time (55 women); includes 19 minority (5 African Americans, 5 Asian Americans or Pacific Islanders, 8 Hispanic Americans, 1 Native American), 12 international. Average age 28. Expenses: Contact institution. *Financial support:* In 2001–02, 3 research assistantships were awarded; Federal Work-Study and institutionally sponsored loans also available. Support available to part-time students. Financial award application deadline: 3/15. In 2001, 79 degrees awarded. *Degree program information:* Part-time and evening/weekend programs available. Offers accounting (M Acc); business administration (M Acc, MBA). *Application deadline:* For fall admission, 7/1. *Application fee:* $25. *Application Contact:* Jeanne Bosco, Administrative Assistant, 386-822-7410, Fax: 386-822-7413, E-mail: jbosco@stetson.edu. *Dean*, Dr. Paul Dasher, 386-822-7415.

STEVENS INSTITUTE OF TECHNOLOGY, Hoboken, NJ 07030

General Information Independent, coed, university. *Enrollment:* 433 full-time matriculated graduate/professional students (111 women), 2,210 part-time matriculated graduate/professional students (633 women). *Graduate faculty:* 104 full-time (8 women), 80 part-time/adjunct (9 women). *Tuition:* Full-time $13,950; part-time $775 per credit. *Required fees:* $180. One-time fee: $180 part-time. Full-time tuition and fees vary according to degree level and program. *Graduate housing:* Rooms and/or apartments available to single and married students. Typical cost: $6,330 per year for single students. *Student services:* Campus employment opportunities, campus safety program, career counseling, exercise/wellness program, free psychological counseling, international student services, low-cost health insurance, teacher training. *Library facilities:* S. C. Williams Library. *Online resources:* library catalog, web page, access to other libraries' catalogs. *Collection:* 59,489 titles, 162 serial subscriptions. *Research affiliation:* Polymer Processing Institute.

Computer facilities: 1,700 computers available on campus for general student use. A campuswide network can be accessed from student residence rooms and from off campus. Internet access and online class registration, online grade and account information are available. *Web address:* http://www.stevens-tech.edu/.

General Application Contact: Dr. Charles L. Suffel, Dean of the Graduate School, 201-216-5234, Fax: 201-216-8044, E-mail: csuffel@stevens-tech.edu.

GRADUATE UNITS

Graduate School *Degree program information:* Part-time and evening/weekend programs available. Postbaccalaureate distance learning degree programs offered (no on-campus study). Offers interdisciplinary sciences and engineering (M Eng, MS, PhD). Electronic applications accepted.

Charles V. Schaefer Jr. School of Engineering *Degree program information:* Part-time and evening/weekend programs available. Postbaccalaureate distance learning degree programs offered. Offers advanced manufacturing (Certificate); air pollution technology (Certificate); analysis of polymer processing methods (Certificate); biochemical engineering (M Eng, PhD, Engr); building energy systems (Certificate); civil engineering (M Eng, PhD, Certificate, Engr); coastal and ocean engineering (M Eng, PhD, Engr); computational methods in fluid mechanics and heat transfer (Certificate); computer and communications security (Certificate); computer and information engineering (M Eng, PhD, Engr); computer architecture and digital system design (M Eng, PhD, Engr); computer engineering (M Eng, PhD, Certificate, Engr); concurrent design management (M Eng); concurrent engineering (PhD, Certificate); construction accounting/estimating (Certificate); construction engineering (M Eng, PhD, Certificate, Engr); construction law/disputes (Certificate); construction management (MS); construction/quality management (Certificate); controls in aerospace and robotics (Certificate); design and production management (MS, Certificate); digital systems and VLSI design (Certificate); electrical engineering (M Eng, MS, PhD, Certificate, Engr); engineering (M Eng, MS, PhD, Certificate, Engr); environmental compatibility in engineering (Certificate); environmental engineering (M Eng, PhD, Certificate); environmental process (M Eng, PhD, Certificate); finite-element analysis (Certificate); fundamentals of modern chemical engineering (Certificate); geotechnical engineering (Certificate); geotechnical/geoenvironmental engineering (M Eng, PhD, Engr); groundwater and soil pollution control (M Eng, PhD, Certificate); image and signal processing (M Eng, PhD, Engr); information networks (Certificate); inland and coastal environmental hydrodynamics (M Eng, PhD, Certificate); integrated production design (Certificate); maritime systems (M Eng); materials engineering (M Eng, PhD); materials science (MS, PhD); mechanical engineering (M Eng, PhD, Engr); mechanism design (Certificate); ocean engineering (M Eng, PhD); polymer engineering (M Eng, PhD, Engr); polymer processing (Certificate); power generation (Certificate); process control (M Eng, PhD, Engr); process engineering (M Eng, PhD, Certificate, Engr); robotics and automation (M Eng, PhD, Engr); robotics and control (Certificate); robotics/control/instrumentation (M Eng, PhD, Engr); satellite communications engineering (Certificate); signal and image processing (M Eng, PhD, Engr); software engineering (M Eng, PhD, Engr); stress analysis and design (Certificate); structural analysis of materials (Certificate); structures (M Eng, PhD, Engr); surface modification of materials (Certificate); telecommunications engineering (M Eng, PhD, Engr); telecommunications management (MS, PhD, Certificate); vibration and noise control (Certificate); water quality (Certificate). Electronic applications accepted.

School of Applied Sciences and Liberal Arts *Degree program information:* Part-time and evening/weekend programs available. Offers advanced programming: theory, design and verification (Certificate); algebra (PhD); analysis (PhD); applied mathematics (MS, PhD); applied optics (Certificate); applied sciences and liberal arts (M Eng, MS, PhD, Certificate); applied statistics (MS, Certificate); artificial intelligence and robotics (MS, PhD); chemistry (MS, PhD, Certificate); computer and information systems (MS, PhD); computer architecture and digital system design (MS, PhD); database systems (Certificate); elements of computer science (Certificate); engineering physics (M Eng); information systems (MS, Certificate); mathematics (MS, PhD); network and graph theory (Certificate); physics (MS, PhD); software design (MS, PhD); software engineering (Certificate); surface physics (Certificate); theoretical computer science (MS, PhD, Certificate); wireless communications (Certificate). Electronic applications accepted.

Wesley J. Howe School of Technology Management *Degree program information:* Part-time and evening/weekend programs available. Postbaccalaureate distance learning degree programs offered. Offers computer science (MS); construction management (MS); design and production management (MS, Certificate); e-commerce (MS, Certificate); general management (MS); information management (MIM, MS, PhD, Certificate); management planning (MS); network planning and evaluation (MS, PhD); project management (MS, PhD, Certificate); technology applications in science education (Certificate); technology management (EMTM, MIM, MS, MTM, PhD, Certificate); technology management marketing (MS, PhD); telecommunications management (MS, Certificate). Electronic applications accepted.

See in-depth description on page 1123.

STONEHILL COLLEGE, Easton, MA 02357-5510

General Information Independent-religious, coed, comprehensive institution. *Enrollment:* 9 full-time matriculated graduate/professional students (8 women). *Enrollment by degree level:* 9 master's. *Graduate faculty:* 5 full-time (1 woman). *Tuition:* Full-time $18,550. *Graduate housing:* Room and/or apartments available on a first-come, first-served basis to single students; on-campus housing not available to married students. Typical cost: $8,492 (including board). Housing application deadline: 3/1. *Student services:* Campus employment opportunities, career counseling, disabled student services, exercise/wellness program, free psychological counseling, multicultural affairs office. *Library facilities:* Bartley MacPhaidin, C.S.C. Library plus 1 other. *Online resources:* library catalog, web page. *Collection:* 188,980 titles, 1,800 serial subscriptions, 4,335 audiovisual materials.

Computer facilities: 210 computers available on campus for general student use. A campuswide network can be accessed from student residence rooms and from off campus. Internet access, online class schedules, assignments, grades; student account are available. *Web address:* http://www.stonehill.edu/.

General Application Contact: Brian P. Murphy, Dean of Admissions and Enrollment, 508-565-1373, Fax: 508-565-1545, E-mail: admissions@stonehill.edu.

GRADUATE UNITS

Program in Accounting Students: 9 full-time (8 women). 12 applicants, 92% accepted, 9 enrolled. *Faculty:* 5 full-time (1 woman). Expenses: Contact institution. *Financial support:* In 2001–02, 8 students received support. Federal Work-Study and scholarships/grants available. Financial award application deadline: 3/1; financial award applicants required to submit FAFSA. In 2001, 12 degrees awarded. *Degree program information:* Part-time programs available. Offers accountancy (MSA). *Application deadline:* For fall admission, 3/1. *Application fee:* $50. *Application Contact:* Brian P. Murphy, Dean of Admissions and Enrollment, 508-565-1373, Fax: 508-565-1545, E-mail: admissions@stonehill.edu. *Chairperson*, Dr. Robert H. Carver, 508-565-1130, E-mail: rcarver@stonehill.edu.

STONY BROOK UNIVERSITY, STATE UNIVERSITY OF NEW YORK, Stony Brook, NY 11794

General Information State-supported, coed, university. CGS member. *Enrollment:* 3,111 full-time matriculated graduate/professional students (1,610 women), 2,983 part-time matriculated graduate/professional students (1,835 women). *Enrollment by degree level:* 582 first professional, 2,627 master's, 2,470 doctoral, 415 other advanced degrees. *Graduate faculty:* 1,145 full-time (315 women), 363 part-time/adjunct (132 women). Tuition, state resident: full-time $5,100; part-time $213 per credit. Tuition, nonresident: full-time $8,416; part-time $351 per credit. *Required fees:* $496. *Graduate housing:* Rooms and/or apartments available to single and married students. *Student services:* Campus employment opportunities, campus safety program, career counseling, child daycare facilities, disabled student services, exercise/wellness program, free psychological counseling, grant writing training, international student services, low-cost health insurance, multicultural affairs office, teacher training, writing training. *Library facilities:* Frank Melville, Jr. Building Library plus 7 others. *Online resources:* library catalog, web page, access to other libraries' catalogs. *Collection:* 1.9 million titles, 14,024 serial subscriptions. *Research affiliation:* Brookhaven National Laboratory, Cold Spring Harbor Laboratory, Winthrop University Hospital, Nassau County Medical Center, Veterans Affairs Medical Center (Northport, NY).

Computer facilities: 500 computers available on campus for general student use. A campuswide network can be accessed from student residence rooms and from off campus. Internet access and online class registration are available. *Web address:* http://www.stonybrook.edu/.

General Application Contact: Dr. Kent Marks, Director, Admissions and Records, 631-632-4723, Fax: 631-632-7243, E-mail: kent.marks@sunysb.edu.

GRADUATE UNITS

Graduate School Students: 1,692 full-time (736 women), 1,033 part-time (437 women); includes 305 minority (69 African Americans, 145 Asian Americans or Pacific Islanders, 89 Hispanic Americans, 2 Native Americans), 1,291 international. 4,496 applicants, 41% accepted. *Faculty:* 810 full-time (180 women), 59 part-time/adjunct (12 women). Expenses: Contact institution. *Financial support:* In 2001–02, 111 fellowships, 524 research assistantships, 1,012 teaching assistantships were awarded. Career-related internships or fieldwork, Federal Work-Study, institutionally sponsored loans, and tuition waivers (full) also available. In 2001, 473 master's, 210 doctorates, 1 other advanced degree awarded. *Degree program information:* Part-time and evening/weekend programs available. *Application fee:* $50. *Application Contact:* Dr. Kent Marks, Director, Admissions and Records, 631-632-4723, Fax: 631-632-7243, E-mail: kent.marks@sunysb.edu. *Dean,* Dr. Lawrence B. Martin, 631-632-7035, Fax: 631-632-7243.

College of Arts and Sciences Students: 1,112 full-time (541 women), 694 part-time (345 women); includes 211 minority (50 African Americans, 83 Asian Americans or Pacific Islanders, 76 Hispanic Americans, 2 Native Americans), 677 international. 2,596 applicants, 39% accepted. *Faculty:* 643 full-time (159 women), 37 part-time/adjunct (12 women). Expenses: Contact institution. *Financial support:* In 2001–02, 92 fellowships, 339 research assistantships, 752 teaching assistantships were awarded. Career-related internships or fieldwork and Federal Work-Study also available. In 2001, 252 master's, 166 doctorates awarded. *Degree program information:* Part-time and evening/weekend programs available. Offers anthropology (MA, PhD); art history and criticism (MA, PhD); arts and sciences (MA, MAPP, MAT, MFA, MM, MS, DA, DMA, PhD); astronomy (MS, PhD); biochemistry and molecular biology (PhD); biochemistry and structural biology (PhD); biological and biomedical sciences (PhD); biological sciences (MA); biopsychology (PhD); cellular and developmental biology (PhD); chemistry (MAT, MS, PhD); clinical psychology (PhD); dramaturgy (MFA); earth and space science (MS, PhD); earth and space sciences (MS, PhD); earth science (MAT); ecology and evolution (PhD); economics (MA, PhD); English (MA, MAT, PhD); experimental psychology (PhD); foreign languages (DA); French (MA, MAT, DA); genetics (PhD); German (MA, MAT, DA); Germanic languages and literatures (MA); Hispanic languages and literature (MA, DA, PhD); history (MA, MAT, PhD); immunology and pathology (PhD); Italian (MA, MAT, DA); linguistics (MA, PhD); mathematics (MA, PhD); molecular and cellular biology (MA, PhD); music (MA, PhD); music history, theory and composition (MA, PhD); music performance (MM, DMA); neurobiology and behavior (PhD); philosophy (MA, PhD); physics (MA, MAT, MS, PhD); psychology (MA); public policy (MAPP); Romance languages and literatures (MA); Russian (MAT, DA); Slavic languages and literatures (MA); social/health psychology (PhD); sociology (MA, PhD); studio art (MFA); teaching English to speakers of other languages (MA, DA); theatre (MA). *Application deadline:* For fall admission, 1/15. *Application fee:* $50. *Interim Dean,* Dr. Bob Libermann, 631-632-6999, Fax: 631-632-6900.

College of Engineering and Applied Sciences Students: 580 full-time (195 women), 339 part-time (92 women); includes 94 minority (19 African Americans, 62 Asian Americans or Pacific Islanders, 13 Hispanic Americans), 614 international. 1,714 applicants, 46% accepted. *Faculty:* 167 full-time (21 women), 22 part-time/adjunct (0 women). Expenses: Contact institution. *Financial support:* In 2001–02, 19 fellowships, 185 research assistantships, 260 teaching assistantships were awarded. Career-related internships or fieldwork also available. In 2001, 221 master's, 44 doctorates, 1 other advanced degree awarded. *Degree program information:* Part-time and evening/weekend programs available. Offers applied mathematics and statistics (MS, PhD); biomedical engineering (MS, PhD, Certificate); computer science (MS, PhD); educational computing (MS); electrical and computer engineering (MS, PhD); engineering and applied sciences (MBA, MS, PhD, Certificate); environmental and waste management (MS); industrial management (MS, Certificate); management and policy (MS); materials science and engineering (MS, PhD); mechanical engineering (MS, PhD); medical physics (PhD); software engineering (Certificate); technological systems management (MS); technology management (MBA, MS). *Application deadline:* For fall admission, 1/15. *Application fee:* $50. *Dean,* Dr. Yacov Shamash, 631-632-8380.

Institute for Terrestrial and Planetary Atmospheres Expenses: Contact institution. *Financial support:* Fellowships available. Offers terrestrial and planetary atmospheres (PhD). *Application deadline:* For fall admission, 3/1. *Application fee:* $50. *Director,* Minghua Zhang, 631-632-8318.

Marine Sciences Research Center Students: 85 full-time (48 women), 17 part-time (9 women); includes 5 minority (2 African Americans, 1 Asian American or Pacific Islander, 2 Hispanic Americans), 40 international. Average age 30. 98 applicants, 51% accepted. *Faculty:* 34 full-time (5 women), 1 (woman) part-time/adjunct. Expenses: Contact institution. *Financial support:* In 2001–02, 16 fellowships, 35 research assistantships, 28 teaching assistantships were awarded. Career-related internships or fieldwork and tuition waivers (full) also available. In 2001, 20 master's, 11 doctorates awarded. *Degree program information:* Evening/weekend programs available. Offers coastal oceanography (PhD); marine environmental sciences (MS); terrestrial and planetary atmospheres (PhD). *Application fee:* $50. *Application Contact:* Dr. Henry Bokuniewicz, Director, 631-632-8681, Fax: 631-632-8200, E-mail: hbokuniewicz@ccmail.sunysb.edu. *Dean and Director,* Dr. Marvin A. Geller, 631-632-8700, Fax: 631-632-8200.

Health Sciences Center Students: 1,096 full-time (690 women), 634 part-time (514 women); includes 468 minority (169 African Americans, 200 Asian Americans or Pacific Islanders, 88 Hispanic Americans, 11 Native Americans), 60 international. 4,330 applicants, 23% accepted. *Faculty:* 750. Expenses: Contact institution. *Financial support:* Fellowships, research assistantships, teaching assistantships, career-related internships or fieldwork, Federal Work-Study, institutionally sponsored loans, traineeships, and tuition waivers (full) available. Financial award applicants required to submit FAFSA. In 2001, 120 first professional degrees, 332 master's, 21 doctorates, 68 other advanced degrees awarded. *Degree program information:* Part-time programs available. Offers health sciences (DDS, MD, MS, MSW, PhD, Advanced Certificate, Certificate). *Application fee:* $50. *Dean and Vice President,* Dr. Norman H. Edelman, 631-444-2080, Fax: 631-444-6032.

School of Dental Medicine Students: 153 full-time (78 women), 20 part-time (9 women); includes 43 minority (1 African American, 37 Asian Americans or Pacific Islanders, 5 Hispanic Americans), 4 international. 981 applicants, 7% accepted. *Faculty:* 31 full-time (9 women), 40 part-time/adjunct (10 women). Expenses: Contact institution. *Financial support:* In 2001–02, 2 fellowships, 4 research assistantships, 1 teaching assistantship were awarded. Federal Work-Study also available. In 2001, 25 first professional degrees, 3 doctorates, 7 other advanced degrees awarded. Offers dental medicine (DDS); endodontics (Certificate); oral biology and pathology (PhD); orthodontics (Certificate); periodontics (Certificate). *Application deadline:* For fall admission, 1/15. *Application fee:* $75. *Application Contact:* Kim M. Lambiase, Director of Admissions, 631-632-8980, E-mail: klambias@epo.hsc.sunysb.edu. *Dean,* Dr. Barry R. Rifkin, 631-632-8950, Fax: 631-632-9105.

School of Health Technology and Management Students: 21 full-time (16 women), 67 part-time (39 women); includes 21 minority (7 African Americans, 11 Asian Americans or Pacific Islanders, 3 Hispanic Americans), 2 international. 82 applicants, 90% accepted. *Faculty:* 45 full-time, 2 part-time/adjunct. Expenses: Contact institution. *Financial support:* Career-related internships or fieldwork, Federal Work-Study, and institutionally sponsored loans available. Financial award application deadline: 3/15. In 2001, 26 master's, 29 other advanced degrees awarded. *Degree program information:* Part-time programs available. Offers community health (Advanced Certificate); health care management (Advanced Certificate); health care policy and management (MS). *Application deadline:* For fall admission, 1/15. *Application fee:* $50. *Application Contact:* Alan Leiken, Associate Dean for Graduate Studies, 631-444-3240, Fax: 631-444-7621. *Dean,* Dr. Craig A. Lehmann, 631-444-2251, Fax: 631-444-7621.

School of Medicine Students: 489 full-time (235 women), 49 part-time (22 women); includes 195 minority (40 African Americans, 126 Asian Americans or Pacific Islanders, 22 Hispanic Americans, 7 Native Americans), 26 international. 2,681 applicants, 11% accepted. *Faculty:* 504 full-time (150 women), 75 part-time/adjunct (32 women). Expenses: Contact institution. *Financial support:* In 2001–02, 33 fellowships, 63 research assistantships, 25 teaching assistantships were awarded. Career-related internships or fieldwork, Federal Work-Study, and tuition waivers (full) also available. In 2001, 95 first professional degrees, 18 doctorates awarded. Offers anatomical sciences (PhD); medicine (MD, PhD); molecular and cellular pharmacology (PhD); molecular microbiology (PhD); physiology and biophysics (PhD). *Application deadline:* For fall admission, 1/15. *Application Contact:* Dr. William Jungers, Chairman, Committee on Admissions, 631-444-2113, Fax: 631-444-6032, E-mail: admissions@dean.som.sunysb.edu. *Dean and Vice President,* Dr. Norman H. Edelman, 631-444-2080, Fax: 631-444-6032.

School of Nursing Students: 105 full-time (99 women), 462 part-time (417 women); includes 88 minority (43 African Americans, 22 Asian Americans or Pacific Islanders, 19 Hispanic Americans, 4 Native Americans), 23 international. Average age 30. 302 applicants, 90% accepted. *Faculty:* 26 full-time (24 women), 24 part-time/adjunct (21 women). Expenses: Contact institution. *Financial support:* Fellowships, research assistantships, teaching assistantships, career-related internships or fieldwork, Federal Work-Study, institutionally sponsored loans, and traineeships available. Financial award application deadline: 3/15. In 2001, 145 master's, 32 other advanced degrees awarded. Postbaccalaureate distance learning degree programs offered. Offers adult health nurse practitioner (Certificate); adult health/primary care nursing (MS); child health nurse practitioner (Certificate); child health nursing (MS); family nurse practitioner (MS, Certificate); gerontological nursing (MS); mental health nurse practitioner (Certificate); mental health/psychiatric nursing (MS); neonatal nurse practitioner (Certificate); neonatal nursing (MS); nurse-midwifery (MS, Certificate); nursing (MS, Certificate); perinatal/women's health nurse practitioner (Certificate); perinatal/women's health nursing (MS). *Application deadline:* For fall admission, 1/15. *Application fee:* $50. *Dean,* Dr. Lenora J. McClean, 631-444-3200, Fax: 631-444-3136.

School of Social Welfare Students: 328 full-time (262 women), 36 part-time (27 women); includes 121 minority (78 African Americans, 4 Asian Americans or Pacific Islanders, 39 Hispanic Americans), 5 international. Average age 35. 344 applicants, 84% accepted. *Faculty:* 17 full-time (10 women), 20 part-time/adjunct (12 women). Expenses: Contact institution. *Financial support:* In 2001–02, 1 fellowship, 15 teaching assistantships were awarded. Career-related internships or fieldwork, Federal Work-Study, and institutionally sponsored loans also available. Financial award applicants required to submit FAFSA. In 2001, 155 degrees awarded. *Degree program information:* Part-time programs available. Offers social welfare (PhD); social work (MSW). *Application fee:* $50. *Application Contact:* Kathy Albin, Admissions Director, 631-444-3141, Fax: 631-444-7565, E-mail: kathleen.albin@sunysb.edu. *Dean,* Dr. Frances L. Brisbane, 631-444-2138, Fax: 631-444-7565.

School of Professional Development and Continuing Studies Students: 240 full-time (133 women), 1,307 part-time (868 women); includes 101 minority (43 African Americans, 13 Asian Americans or Pacific Islanders, 43 Hispanic Americans, 2 Native Americans), 9 international. Average age 28. *Faculty:* 1 full-time, 101 part-time/adjunct. Expenses: Contact institution. *Financial support:* In 2001–02, 1 fellowship, 7 teaching assistantships were awarded. Research assistantships, career-related internships or fieldwork also available. Support available to part-time students. In 2001, 478 master's, 157 other advanced degrees awarded. *Degree program information:* Part-time and evening/weekend programs available. Postbaccalaureate distance learning degree programs offered. Offers art and philosophy (Certificate); biology 7-12 (MAT); chemistry-grade 7-12 (MAT); coaching (Certificate); computer integrated engineering (Certificate); cultural studies (Certificate); earth science-grade 7-12 (MAT); educational computing (Certificate); English-grade 7-12 (MAT); environmental/occupational health and safety (Certificate); French-grade 7-12 (MAT); German-grade 7-12 (MAT); human resource management (Certificate); industrial management (Certificate); information systems management (Certificate); Italian-grade 7-12 (MAT); liberal studies (MA); liberal studies online (MA); Long Island regional studies (Certificate); oceanic science (Certificate); operation research (Certificate); physics-grade 7-12 (MAT); Russian-grade 7-12 (MAT); school administration and supervision (Certificate); school district administration (Certificate); social science and the professions (MPS); social studies 7-12 (MAT); waste management (Certificate); women's studies (Certificate). *Application deadline:* Applications are processed on a rolling basis. *Application fee:* $50. *Application Contact:* Sandra Romansky, Director of Admissions and Advisement, 631-632-7050, Fax: 631-632-9046, E-mail: sandra.romansky@sunysb.edu. *Dean,* Dr. Paul J. Edelson, 631-632-7052, Fax: 631-632-9046, E-mail: paul.edelson@sunysb.edu.

See in-depth description on page 1125.

STRATFORD UNIVERSITY, Falls Church, VA 22043

General Information Proprietary, coed.

STRAYER UNIVERSITY, Washington, DC 20005-2603

General Information Proprietary, coed, comprehensive institution. CGS member. *Enrollment:* 1,225 full-time matriculated graduate/professional students (616 women), 1,052 part-time matriculated graduate/professional students (567 women). *Enrollment by degree level:* 2,277 master's. *Graduate faculty:* 61 full-time (7 women), 51 part-time/adjunct (17 women). *Tuition:* Full-time $7,958; part-time $1,323 per credit. *Graduate housing:* On-campus housing not available. *Student services:* Campus employment opportunities, career counseling, international student services, low-cost health insurance. *Library facilities:* Wilkes Library plus 13 others. *Online resources:* library catalog, web page. *Collection:* 29,500 titles, 460 serial subscriptions, 1,350 audiovisual materials.

Computer facilities: 1,000 computers available on campus for general student use. A campuswide network can be accessed. Internet access and online class registration are available. *Web address:* http://www.strayer.edu/.

General Application Contact: Melvin Z. Menns, Administrative Dean, Region I, 202-408-2400, Fax: 202-289-1831, E-mail: mzm@strayer.edu.

GRADUATE UNITS

Graduate School Students: 1,225 full-time (616 women), 1,052 part-time (567 women); includes 474 minority (229 African Americans, 159 Asian Americans or Pacific Islanders, 77 Hispanic Americans, 9 Native Americans), 473 international. Average age 35. *Faculty:* 61 full-time (7 women), 51 part-time/adjunct (17 women). Expenses: Contact institution. *Financial support:* Federal Work-Study and institutionally sponsored loans available. Support available to part-time students. Financial award applicants required to submit FAFSA. In 2001, 205 degrees awarded. *Degree program information:* Part-time and evening/weekend programs available. Postbaccalaureate distance learning degree programs offered (minimal on-campus study). Offers business administration (MBA). *Application deadline:* For fall admission, 9/24 (priority date); for winter admission, 1/7 (priority date); for spring admission, 4/1 (priority date). Applications are processed on a rolling basis. *Application fee:* $25. Electronic applications accepted. *Application Contact:* Melvin Z. Menns, Administrative Dean, Region I, 202-408-2400, Fax: 202-289-1831, E-mail: mzm@strayer.edu. *Director of Graduate Studies,* Dr. Joel O. Nwagbaraocha, 202-408-2400, Fax: 202-289-1820, E-mail: jon@strayer.edu.

SUFFOLK UNIVERSITY, Boston, MA 02108-2770

General Information Independent, coed, comprehensive institution. *Enrollment:* 1,402 full-time matriculated graduate/professional students (767 women), 2,058 part-time matriculated graduate/professional students (1,040 women). *Enrollment by degree level:* 1,678 first professional, 1,720 master's, 62 doctoral. *Graduate faculty:* 187 full-time, 173 part-time/adjunct. *Tuition:* Full-time $12,888; part-time $1,191 per year. Tuition and fees vary according to degree level and program. *Graduate housing:* On-campus housing not available. *Student services:* Campus employment opportunities, campus safety program, career counseling, disabled student services, exercise/wellness program, free psychological counseling, grant writing training, international student services, low-cost health insurance, multicultural affairs office, teacher training, writing training. *Library facilities:* Mildred Sawyer Library plus 3 others. *Online resources:* library catalog, web page, access to other libraries' catalogs. *Collection:* 279,000 titles, 6,900 serial subscriptions, 16,000 audiovisual materials.

Suffolk University (continued)

Computer facilities: 300 computers available on campus for general student use. A campuswide network can be accessed from student residence rooms and from off campus. Internet access is available. *Web address:* http://www.suffolk.edu/.

General Application Contact: Judith Reynolds, Director of Graduate Admissions, 617-573-8302, Fax: 617-523-0116, E-mail: grad.admission@suffolk.edu.

GRADUATE UNITS

College of Arts and Sciences Students: 148 full-time (103 women), 276 part-time (200 women); includes 39 minority (21 African Americans, 7 Asian Americans or Pacific Islanders, 11 Hispanic Americans), 63 international. Average age 29. 389 applicants, 73% accepted, 127 enrolled. *Faculty:* 59 full-time, 31 part-time/adjunct. Expenses: Contact institution. *Financial support:* In 2001–02, 220 students received support, including 63 fellowships with full and partial tuition reimbursements available (averaging $7,828 per year); career-related internships or fieldwork, Federal Work-Study, institutionally sponsored loans, scholarships/grants, and unspecified assistantships also available. Support available to part-time students. Financial award application deadline: 3/15; financial award applicants required to submit FAFSA. In 2001, 134 master's, 6 doctorates, 3 other advanced degrees awarded. *Degree program information:* Part-time and evening/weekend programs available. Offers adult and organizational learning (MS, CAGS); arts and sciences (M Ed, MA, MS, MSEP, MSIE, PhD, CAGS); clinical-developmental psychology (PhD); communication (MA); computer science (MS); counseling and human relations (M Ed, MS, CAGS); criminal justice); economic policy (MSEP); educational administration (M Ed); foundations of education (M Ed, CAGS); higher education administration (M Ed, CAGS); human resources (MS, CAGS); instructional design (CAGS); international economics (MSIE); leadership (CAGS); mental health counseling (MS); organizational development (CAGS); organizational learning (CAGS); political science (MS); school counseling (M Ed); secondary school teaching (MS). *Application deadline:* For fall admission, 6/15 (priority date); for spring admission, 11/15 (priority date). Applications are processed on a rolling basis. *Application fee:* $35. *Application Contact:* Judith Reynolds, Director of Graduate Admissions, 617-573-8302, Fax: 617-523-0116, E-mail: grad.admission@suffolk.edu. *Dean,* Dr. Michael Ronayne, 617-573-8265, Fax: 617-573-8513, E-mail: mronayne@suffolk.edu.

New England School of Art and Design Students: 23 full-time (21 women), 29 part-time (all women); includes 2 minority (1 African American, 1 Hispanic American), 10 international. Average age 31. 28 applicants, 86% accepted, 18 enrolled. *Faculty:* 3 full-time (1 woman), 3 part-time/adjunct (1 woman). Expenses: Contact institution. *Financial support:* In 2001–02, 18 students received support, including 7 fellowships with partial tuition reimbursements available (averaging $3,460 per year) Financial award application deadline: 3/15. *Degree program information:* Part-time and evening/weekend programs available. Offers interior design (MA). *Application deadline:* For fall admission, 6/15 (priority date); for spring admission, 11/15 (priority date). Applications are processed on a rolling basis. *Application fee:* $35. *Application Contact:* Judith Reynolds, Director of Graduate Admissions, 617-573-8302, Fax: 617-523-0116, E-mail: grad.admission@suffolk.edu. *Program Director,* Karen Clark, 617-573-8785, Fax: 617-536-0461, E-mail: kclarke@suffolk.edu.

Law School Students: 857 full-time, 849 part-time; includes 178 minority (73 African Americans, 60 Asian Americans or Pacific Islanders, 42 Hispanic Americans, 3 Native Americans) Average age 25. *Faculty:* 60 full-time (10 women), 90 part-time/adjunct (22 women). Expenses: Contact institution. *Financial support:* In 2001–02, 796 students received support; research assistantships, career-related internships or fieldwork, Federal Work-Study, institutionally sponsored loans, and scholarships/grants available. Support available to part-time students. Financial award application deadline: 3/1. In 2001, 494 degrees awarded. *Degree program information:* Part-time and evening/weekend programs available. Offers civil litigation (JD); financial services (JD); health care/biotechnology law (JD); intellectual property law (JD). *Application deadline:* For fall admission, 3/1 (priority date). Applications are processed on a rolling basis. *Application fee:* $50. Electronic applications accepted. *Dean of Admissions,* Gail N. Ellis, 617-573-8144, Fax: 617-523-1317, E-mail: gellis@suffolk.edu.

Sawyer School of Management Students: 231 full-time (111 women), 981 part-time (454 women); includes 79 minority (30 African Americans, 32 Asian Americans or Pacific Islanders, 14 Hispanic Americans, 3 Native Americans), 173 international. Average age 32. 785 applicants, 81% accepted, 384 enrolled. *Faculty:* 68 full-time (18 women), 52 part-time/adjunct (16 women). Expenses: Contact institution. *Financial support:* In 2001–02, 374 students received support, including 86 fellowships with partial tuition reimbursements available (averaging $4,895 per year); career-related internships or fieldwork, Federal Work-Study, and institutionally sponsored loans also available. Support available to part-time students. Financial award application deadline: 3/15; financial award applicants required to submit FAFSA. In 2001, 435 degrees awarded. *Degree program information:* Part-time and evening/weekend programs available. Offers accounting (MSA, GDPA); banking and financial services (MS); business administration (MBA, APC); disability studies (MPA); executive business administration (EMBA); finance (MSF); health administration (MHA, MPA); management (EMBA, M Ph M, MBA, MBAH, MHA, MPA, MS, MSA, MSF, MST, APC, CASPA, GDPA); nonprofit management (MPA); public administration (CASPA); public finance and human resources (MPA); state and local government (MPA); taxation (MST). *Application deadline:* For fall admission, 6/15 (priority date); for spring admission, 11/15. Applications are processed on a rolling basis. *Application fee:* $50. *Application Contact:* Judith Reynolds, Director of Graduate Admissions, 617-573-8302, Fax: 617-523-0116, E-mail: grad.admission@suffolk.edu. *Associate Dean,* Dr. C. Richard Torrisi, 617-573-8088, Fax: 617-573-8704, E-mail: rtorrisi@suffolk.edu.

Visionaries Institute of Suffolk University Students: 20 full-time (14 women), 8 part-time (7 women); includes 3 minority (1 African American, 1 Asian American or Pacific Islander, 1 Hispanic American) Average age 36. 42 applicants, 98% accepted, 31 enrolled. Expenses: Contact institution. *Financial support:* In 2001–02, 17 students received support, including 5 fellowships (averaging $4,120 per year) Financial award application deadline: 3/15; financial award applicants required to submit FAFSA. In 2001, 3 degrees awarded. *Application deadline:* For fall admission, 6/15; for spring admission, 11/15 (priority date). Applications are processed on a rolling basis. *Application fee:* $50. *Application Contact:* Judith Reynolds, Director of Graduate Admissions, 617-573-8302, Fax: 617-523-0116, E-mail: grad.admission@suffolk.edu. *Director,* Dr. Michael Lavin, 413-229-0350, Fax: 413-229-9970, E-mail: institute@visionaries.org.

SULLIVAN UNIVERSITY, Louisville, KY 40205

General Information Proprietary, coed, comprehensive institution.

GRADUATE UNITS

School of Business Offers business (MBA).

SUL ROSS STATE UNIVERSITY, Alpine, TX 79832

General Information State-supported, coed, comprehensive institution. *Enrollment:* 184 full-time matriculated graduate/professional students (105 women), 620 part-time matriculated graduate/professional students (394 women). *Enrollment by degree level:* 804 master's. *Graduate faculty:* 58 full-time (15 women), 8 part-time/adjunct (3 women). Tuition, state resident: part-time $64 per semester hour. Tuition, nonresident: part-time $275 per semester hour. *Required fees:* $71; $32 per semester hour. *Graduate housing:* Rooms and/or apartments available to single and married students. *Student services:* Campus employment opportunities, campus safety program, career counseling, exercise/wellness program, free psychological counseling, teacher training, writing training. *Library facilities:* Bryan Wildenthal Memorial Library. *Online resources:* library catalog, web page, access to other libraries' catalogs. *Collection:* 262,466 titles. *Research affiliation:* Chihuahuan Desert Research Institute (biology, geology), Big Bend National Park (biology, geology).

Computer facilities: 200 computers available on campus for general student use. A campuswide network can be accessed from student residence rooms and from off campus. Internet access is available. *Web address:* http://www.sulross.edu/.

General Application Contact: Robert Cullins, Dean of Admissions and Records, 915-837-8050, Fax: 915-837-8431, E-mail: rcullins@sulross.edu.

GRADUATE UNITS

Division of Agricultural and Natural Resource Science Students: 20 full-time (4 women), 17 part-time (6 women); includes 8 minority (1 Asian American or Pacific Islander, 7 Hispanic Americans) Average age 32. 11 applicants. *Faculty:* 7 full-time (0 women), 2 part-time/adjunct (0 women). Expenses: Contact institution. *Financial support:* Research assistantships, teaching assistantships, career-related internships or fieldwork, Federal Work-Study, and institutionally sponsored loans available. Support available to part-time students. Financial award application deadline: 5/1; financial award applicants required to submit FAFSA. In 2001, 11 degrees awarded. *Degree program information:* Part-time programs available. Offers agricultural and natural resource science (M Ag, MS); animal science (M Ag, MS); range and wildlife management (M Ag, MS). *Application deadline:* Applications are processed on a rolling basis. *Application fee:* $0 ($50 for international students). *Director,* Dr. Robert Kinucan, 915-837-8200, Fax: 915-837-8046.

Rio Grande College of Sul Ross State University Students: 45 full-time (36 women), 255 part-time (168 women); includes 218 minority (2 African Americans, 215 Hispanic Americans, 1 Native American), 1 international. Average age 36. *Faculty:* 16 full-time (2 women), 2 part-time/adjunct (1 woman). Expenses: Contact institution. *Financial support:* Career-related internships or fieldwork, Federal Work-Study, and institutionally sponsored loans available. Support available to part-time students. Financial award application deadline: 5/1; financial award applicants required to submit FAFSA. In 2001, 47 degrees awarded. *Degree program information:* Part-time and evening/weekend programs available. Offers business administration (MBA); teacher education (M Ed). *Application deadline:* Applications are processed on a rolling basis. *Application fee:* $0 ($50 for international students). *Dean,* Dr. Frank Abbott, 512-278-3339, Fax: 512-278-3330.

School of Arts and Sciences Students: 42 full-time (24 women), 45 part-time (22 women); includes 23 minority (3 African Americans, 1 Asian American or Pacific Islander, 18 Hispanic Americans, 1 Native American) Average age 36. Expenses: Contact institution. *Financial support:* Research assistantships, teaching assistantships, career-related internships or fieldwork, Federal Work-Study, and institutionally sponsored loans available. Support available to part-time students. Financial award application deadline: 5/1; financial award applicants required to submit FAFSA. In 2001, 26 degrees awarded. *Degree program information:* Part-time and evening/weekend programs available. Offers art education (M Ed); art history (M Ed); arts and sciences (M Ed, MA, MS); biology (MS); English (MA); geology and chemistry (MS); history (MA); political science (MA); psychology (MA); public administration (MA); studio art (M Ed). *Application deadline:* Applications are processed on a rolling basis. *Application fee:* $0 ($50 for international students). *Dean,* Dr. Bruce Glasrud, 915-837-8369.

School of Professional Studies Students: 72 full-time (39 women), 242 part-time (159 women); includes 146 minority (5 African Americans, 141 Hispanic Americans), 9 international. Average age 37. *Faculty:* 17. Expenses: Contact institution. *Financial support:* Teaching assistantships, career-related internships or fieldwork, Federal Work-Study, and institutionally sponsored loans available. Support available to part-time students. Financial award application deadline: 5/1; financial award applicants required to submit FAFSA. In 2001, 159 degrees awarded. *Degree program information:* Part-time and evening/weekend programs available. Offers bilingual education (M Ed); counseling (M Ed); criminal justice (MS); educational diagnostics (M Ed); elementary education (M Ed); industrial arts (M Ed); international trade (MBA); management (MBA); physical education (M Ed); professional studies (M Ed, MBA, MS); reading specialist (M Ed); school administration (M Ed); secondary education (M Ed); supervision (M Ed). *Application fee:* $0 ($50 for international students). *Dean,* Dr. Chet Sample, 915-837-8134.

SUNBRIDGE COLLEGE, Spring Valley, NY 10977

General Information Independent, graduate-only institution. *Graduate housing:* Room and/or apartments available on a first-come, first-served basis to single students; on-campus housing not available to married students.

GRADUATE UNITS

Programs in Education *Degree program information:* Part-time programs available. Offers Waldorf early childhood education (MS Ed); Waldorf elementary school education (MS Ed).

SYRACUSE UNIVERSITY, Syracuse, NY 13244-0003

General Information Independent, coed, university. CGS member. *Enrollment:* 2,929 full-time matriculated graduate/professional students (1,510 women), 2,084 part-time matriculated graduate/professional students (1,092 women). *Enrollment by degree level:* 767 first professional, 3,046 master's, 1,132 doctoral, 68 other advanced degrees. *Tuition:* Full-time $15,528; part-time $647 per credit. *Required fees:* $420; $38 per term. Tuition and fees vary according to program. *Graduate housing:* Rooms and/or apartments available on a first-come, first-served basis to single and married students. Typical cost: $5,930 per year for single students; $6,290 per year for married students. Room charges vary according to housing facility selected. Housing application deadline: 6/1. *Student services:* Campus employment opportunities, campus safety program, career counseling, child daycare facilities, disabled student services, exercise/wellness program, free psychological counseling, grant writing training, international student services, low-cost health insurance, multicultural affairs office, teacher training, writing training. *Library facilities:* E. S. Bird Library plus 6 others. *Online resources:* library catalog, web page, access to other libraries' catalogs. *Collection:* 3 million titles, 12,000 serial subscriptions, 763,000 audiovisual materials. *Research affiliation:* State University of New York Health Science Center at Syracuse, State University of New York Science Center at Syracuse.

Computer facilities: 1,200 computers available on campus for general student use. A campuswide network can be accessed from student residence rooms and from off campus. Internet access and online class registration, online services, networked client and server computing are available. *Web address:* http://www.syracuse.edu/.

General Application Contact: The Graduate Enrollment Management Center, 315-443-4492, E-mail: grad@gwmail.syr.edu.

GRADUATE UNITS

College of Law Students: 756 full-time (355 women), 7 part-time (3 women); includes 140 minority (52 African Americans, 51 Asian Americans or Pacific Islanders, 33 Hispanic Americans, 4 Native Americans), 29 international. Average age 25. *Faculty:* 51 full-time (20 women), 46 part-time/adjunct (7 women). Expenses: Contact institution. *Financial support:* In 2001–02, 630 students received support; fellowships, research assistantships, teaching assistantships, career-related internships or fieldwork, Federal Work-Study, institutionally sponsored loans, scholarships/grants, and tuition waivers (full and partial) available. Support available to part-time students. Financial award application deadline: 2/1; financial award applicants required to submit FAFSA. In 2001, 255 degrees awarded. *Degree program information:* Part-time programs available. Offers law (JD). *Application deadline:* For fall admission, 4/1 (priority date). Applications are processed on a rolling basis. *Application fee:* $50. *Application Contact:* Anikka Laubenstein, Director of Admissions, 315-443-1962, Fax: 315-443-9568, E-mail: admissions@law.syr.edu. *Dean,* Hannah Arterian, 315-443-2524, Fax: 315-443-4213.

Graduate School Students: 2,392 full-time (1,272 women), 2,022 part-time (1,010 women). Average age 32. 6,300 applicants, 40% accepted. *Faculty:* 830 full-time, 565 part-time/adjunct. Expenses: Contact institution. *Financial support:* Fellowships, research assistantships, teaching assistantships, career-related internships or fieldwork, Federal Work-Study, institutionally sponsored loans, scholarships/grants, tuition waivers (partial), and administrative assistantships available. Support available to part-time students. In 2001, 1,849 master's, 120 doctorates awarded. *Degree program information:* Part-time and evening/weekend programs available. Postbaccalaureate distance learning degree programs offered. *Application fee:* $50. *Acting Dean,* Dr. John Mercer, 315-443-5012.

College of Arts and Sciences Students: 486 full-time (264 women), 76 part-time (43 women). Average age 30. 899 applicants, 28% accepted. *Faculty:* 235. Expenses: Contact institution. *Financial support:* Fellowships, research assistantships, teaching assistantships, career-related internships or fieldwork, Federal Work-Study, scholarships/grants, and tuition waivers (partial) available. In 2001, 83 master's, 36 doctorates awarded. *Degree program information:* Part-time programs available. Offers applied statistics (MS); art history (MA); arts and sciences (MA, MFA, MS, PhD, CAS); biology (MS, PhD); biophysics (PhD); chemistry (MS, PhD); classics (MA); clinical psychology (MA, MS, PhD); college science teaching (PhD); composition and cultural rhetoric (PhD); creative writing (MFA); English (PhD); experimental psychology (MA, MS, PhD); French language, literature and culture (MA); geology (MA, MS, PhD); hydrogeology (MS); linguistic studies (MA); literature and critical theory (MA); mathematics (MS, PhD); mathematics education (MS, PhD); philosophy (MA, PhD); physics (MS, PhD); psychology (MA, MS, PhD); religion (MA, PhD); school psychology (PhD); social psychology (PhD); Spanish language, literature and culture (MA); structural biology, biochemistry and biophysics (PhD); women's studies (CAS). *Application deadline:* Applications are processed on a rolling basis. *Application fee:* $50. *Dean,* Dr. Cathryn Newton, 315-443-3949.

College of Human Services and Health Professions Students: 242 full-time (218 women), 140 part-time (122 women). Average age 33. 219 applicants, 70% accepted. *Faculty:* 40 full-time (25 women), 19 part-time/adjunct (11 women). Expenses: Contact institution. *Financial support:* Fellowships, research assistantships, teaching assistantships, career-related internships or fieldwork, Federal Work-Study, scholarships/grants, tuition waivers (partial), and unspecified assistantships available. Financial award application deadline: 1/15; financial award applicants required to submit FAFSA. *Degree program information:* Part-time and evening/weekend programs available. Offers child and family studies (MA, MS, PhD); human services and health professions (MA, MS, MSW, PhD); marriage and family therapy (MA, PhD); nursing (MS); nutrition science and food management (MA, MS); social work (MSW). *Application deadline:* For fall admission, 1/15 (priority date); for spring admission, 11/1. *Application fee:* $50. Electronic applications accepted. *Application Contact:* Linda M. Littlejohn, Assistant Dean, Enrollment Management, 315-443-5555, Fax: 315-443-2562, E-mail: inquire@hshp.syr.edu. *Dean,* Dr. William Pollard, 315-443-5582.

College of Visual and Performing Arts Students: 117 full-time (80 women), 63 part-time (39 women); includes 4 minority (all Hispanic Americans), 18 international. Average age 33. 518 applicants, 40% accepted. *Faculty:* 103 full-time, 72 part-time/adjunct. Expenses: Contact institution. *Financial support:* In 2001–02, 103 students received support, including 8 fellowships with full tuition reimbursements available (averaging $13,000 per year), 34 research assistantships with full and partial tuition reimbursements available (averaging $8,610 per year), 59 teaching assistantships with full and partial tuition reimbursements available (averaging $8,610 per year); Federal Work-Study, tuition waivers (partial), and unspecified assistantships also available. Financial award application deadline: 3/1. In 2001, 74 degrees awarded. *Degree program information:* Part-time and evening/weekend programs available. Postbaccalaureate distance learning degree programs offered (minimal on-campus study). Offers advertising design (MFA); art and design (MA, MFA); art photography process (MFA); ceramics (MFA); cinema/drama (MFA); computer graphics (MFA); consumer studies (MA, MS); drama (MA, MFA); fashion design (MA); fiber structure interlocking (MFA); film-art/drama (MFA); illustration (MFA); metalsmithing (MFA); museum studies (MA); music composition (M Mus); organ (M Mus); painting (MFA); percussion (M Mus); piano (M Mus); printmaking (MFA); sculpture (MFA); speech communication (MA, MS); strings (M Mus); textile design (MS); theory (M Mus); video research (MFA); visual and performing arts (M Mus, MA, MFA, MS); voice (M Mus); wind instruments (M Mus). *Application deadline:* For spring admission, 3/1 (priority date). Applications are processed on a rolling basis. *Application fee:* $50. Electronic applications accepted. *Application Contact:* Arthur Jensen, Assistant Dean, 315-443-3089, E-mail: adjensen@syr.edu. *Dean,* Carole Brozozowski, 315-443-5888.

L. C. Smith College of Engineering and Computer Science Students: 614 full-time (66 women), 222 part-time (27 women); includes 18 minority (5 African Americans, 13 Asian Americans or Pacific Islanders), 569 international. Average age 29. 979 applicants, 85% accepted, 297 enrolled. *Faculty:* 27 full-time (3 women), 15 part-time/adjunct (1 woman). Expenses: Contact institution. *Financial support:* In 2001–02, 16 fellowships with full tuition reimbursements (averaging $13,680 per year), 101 research assistantships with full tuition reimbursements (averaging $11,000 per year), 71 teaching assistantships with full tuition reimbursements (averaging $11,000 per year) were awarded. Federal Work-Study and tuition waivers (partial) also available. Financial award application deadline: 1/10. In 2001, 215 master's, 15 doctorates awarded. *Degree program information:* Part-time and evening/weekend programs available. Offers aerospace engineering (MS, PhD); bioengineering (ME, MS, PhD); chemical engineering (MS, PhD); civil engineering (MS, PhD); computer and information science (MS, PhD); computer engineering (MS, PhD, CE); computer science (MS); electrical engineering (MS, PhD, EE); engineering and computer science (ME, MS, PhD, CE, EE); engineering management (MS); environmental engineering (MS); environmental engineering science (MS); hydrogeology (MS); manufacturing engineering (MS); mechanical engineering (MS, PhD); mechanical systems (ME); neuroscience (MS, PhD); solid-state science and technology (MS, PhD); systems and information science (MS). *Application deadline:* Applications are processed on a rolling basis. *Application fee:* $50. *Application Contact:* Dr. Eric F. Spina, Associate Dean, 315-443-3604, Fax: 315-443-4936, E-mail: efspina@syr.edu. *Dean,* Dr. Edward Bogucz, 315-443-4341, Fax: 315-443-4936, E-mail: bogucz@syr.edu.

Maxwell School of Citizenship and Public Affairs Students: 513 full-time (288 women), 272 part-time (107 women); includes 70 minority (31 African Americans, 14 Asian Americans or Pacific Islanders, 16 Hispanic Americans, 9 Native Americans), 215 international. Average age 33. 657 applicants, 51% accepted. *Faculty:* 150 full-time, 6 part-time/adjunct. Expenses: Contact institution. *Financial support:* In 2001–02, 164 students received support, including fellowships with full tuition reimbursements available (averaging $12,000 per year), research assistantships with full tuition reimbursements available (averaging $10,600 per year), teaching assistantships with full tuition reimbursements available (averaging $10,600 per year); career-related internships or fieldwork, Federal Work-Study, tuition waivers (partial), and unspecified assistantships also available. Financial award application deadline: 2/15. In 2001, 256 master's, 27 doctorates awarded. *Degree program information:* Part-time and evening/weekend programs available. Offers anthropology (MA, PhD); citizenship and public affairs (MA, MPA, MS Sc, PhD, CAS); economics (MA, PhD); geography (MA, PhD); health services management and policy (CAS); history (MA, PhD); international relations (MA); political science (MA, PhD); public administration (MA, MPA, PhD); social sciences (MS Sc, PhD); sociology (MA, PhD). *Application deadline:* For fall admission, 2/15 (priority date). Applications are processed on a rolling basis. *Application fee:* $50. Electronic applications accepted. *Dean,* John Palmer, 315-443-3641.

School of Architecture Students: 60 full-time (15 women), 4 part-time (2 women); includes 5 minority (2 African Americans, 2 Asian Americans or Pacific Islanders, 1 Hispanic American), 23 international. Average age 26. 161 applicants, 46% accepted. *Faculty:* 33. Expenses: Contact institution. *Financial support:* Fellowships, teaching assistantships, Federal Work-Study, scholarships/grants, tuition waivers (partial), and unspecified assistantships available. In 2001, 35 degrees awarded. Offers architecture (M Arch). *Application deadline:* Applications are processed on a rolling basis. *Application fee:* $50. *Application Contact:* Arthur McDonald, Graduate Program Director, 315-443-1041, Fax: 315-443-5082, E-mail: awmcdona@syr.edu. *Dean,* Bruce Abbey, 315-443-2255.

School of Education Students: 564 full-time (417 women), 180 part-time (143 women). 593 applicants, 75% accepted, 247 enrolled. *Faculty:* 62 full-time (18 women), 2 part-time/adjunct (1 woman). Expenses: Contact institution. *Financial support:* Fellowships, research assistantships, teaching assistantships, career-related internships or fieldwork, Federal Work-Study, institutionally sponsored loans, and unspecified assistantships available. Support available to part-time students. In 2001, 231 master's, 24 doctorates awarded. *Degree program information:* Part-time and evening/weekend programs available. Postbaccalaureate distance learning degree programs offered (minimal on-campus study). Offers art education (MS, CAS); audiology and speech pathology (MS, PhD); counselor education (MS, Ed D, PhD, CAS); cultural foundations of education (MS, PhD, CAS); educating infants and young children with special needs (MS); education (M Mu, MS, Ed D, PhD, CAS); educational leadership (MS, Ed D, PhD, CAS); elementary education (MS, CAS); English education (MS, Ed D, PhD, CAS); exercise science (MS, CAS); higher education (MS, Ed D, PhD, CAS); instructional design, development, and evaluation (MS, Ed D, PhD, CAS); learning disabilities (MS); mathematics education (MS, Ed D, PhD, CAS); music education (M Mu, MS); reading and language arts (MS, Ed D, PhD, CAS); rehabilitation counseling (MS, Ed D, PhD); science education (MS, Ed D, PhD, CAS); social studies education (MS, CAS); special education (emotional disorders and severe disabilities) (MS, Ed D, PhD); teaching and curriculum (MS, Ed D, PhD, CAS). *Application deadline:* For fall admission, 2/1 (priority date). Applications are processed on a rolling basis. *Application fee:* $50. Electronic applications accepted. *Application Contact:* Graduate Admission Recruiter, 315-443-2505, Fax: 315-443-5732, E-mail: gradrcrt@gwmail.syr.edu. *Interim Dean,* Dr. Corinne Smith, 315-443-2506, Fax: 315-443-5732.

School of Information Studies Students: 97 full-time (42 women), 341 part-time (189 women); includes 30 minority (12 African Americans, 9 Asian Americans or Pacific Islanders, 7 Hispanic Americans, 2 Native Americans), 173 international. Average age 35. *Faculty:* 33 full-time (12 women), 42 part-time/adjunct (12 women). Expenses: Contact institution. *Financial support:* Fellowships, research assistantships, teaching assistantships, career-related internships or fieldwork, Federal Work-Study, and tuition waivers (partial) available. In 2001, 272 master's, 1 doctorate awarded. *Degree program information:* Part-time and evening/weekend programs available. Postbaccalaureate distance learning degree programs offered (minimal on-campus study). Offers information and library science (MLS, CAS); information management (MS); information transfer (PhD); telecommunications and network management (MS). *Application deadline:* For fall admission, 2/15 (priority date); for spring admission, 11/1. *Application fee:* $50. Electronic applications accepted. *Dean,* Dr. Raymond F. von Dran, 315-443-2911.

School of Management Students: 475. Average age 32. 597 applicants, 56% accepted. *Faculty:* 57 full-time, 24 part-time/adjunct. Expenses: Contact institution. *Financial support:* Fellowships, research assistantships, teaching assistantships, Federal Work-Study and tuition waivers (partial) available. In 2001, 194 degrees awarded. *Degree program information:* Part-time and evening/weekend programs available. Offers accounting (PhD); business administration (MBA, PhD); finance (MBA, MS, PhD); management (MBA, MS, MS Acct, PhD); management information systems (PhD); managerial statistics (PhD); marketing (PhD); operations management (PhD); organizational behavior (PhD); strategy and human resources (PhD); supply chain management (PhD). *Application fee:* $50. *Application Contact:* Carol Swanberg, Director of Graduate Students Admissions, 315-443-3850. *Dean,* George Burman, 315-443-3751.

S. I. Newhouse School of Public Communications Students: 185 full-time (110 women). *Faculty:* 39 full-time (13 women), 18 part-time/adjunct (7 women). Expenses: Contact institution. *Financial support:* In 2001–02, fellowships with tuition reimbursements (averaging $13,000 per year), research assistantships with tuition reimbursements (averaging $8,320 per year), teaching assistantships with tuition reimbursements (averaging $8,320 per year) were awarded. Career-related internships or fieldwork, Federal Work-Study, scholarships/grants, and tuition waivers (partial) also available. Support available to part-time students. Financial award application deadline: 2/10; financial award applicants required to submit FAFSA. In 2001, 106 master's, 4 doctorates awarded. Postbaccalaureate distance learning degree programs offered (minimal on-campus study). Offers advertising (MA); broadcast journalism (MS); communications management (MS); magazine, newspaper and online journalism (MA); mass communications (PhD); media management (MS); media studies (MA); new media (MS); photography (MS); public communications (MA, MS, PhD); public relations (MA, MS); television-radio-film (MA). *Application deadline:* For fall admission, 2/10. *Application fee:* $50. Electronic applications accepted. *Application Contact:* Graduate Admissions, 315-443-4039, Fax: 315-443-3946, E-mail: pcgrad@syr.edu. *Dean,* David M. Rubin, 315-443-2302, Fax: 315-443-3946, E-mail: newhouse@syr.edu.

TAI HSUAN FOUNDATION: COLLEGE OF ACUPUNCTURE AND HERBAL MEDICINE, Honolulu, HI 96828

General Information Independent, coed, graduate-only institution. *Graduate housing:* On-campus housing not available.

GRADUATE UNITS

Program in Acupuncture and Oriental Medicine *Degree program information:* Part-time and evening/weekend programs available. Offers acupuncture and Oriental medicine (M Ac OM).

TAI SOPHIA INSTITUTE, Laurel, MD 20723

General Information Independent, coed, primarily women, graduate-only institution. *Enrollment by degree level:* 250 master's. *Graduate faculty:* 22 full-time (13 women), 44 part-time/adjunct (34 women). *Tuition:* Full-time $10,000. Tuition and fees vary according to course load and program. *Graduate housing:* On-campus housing not available. *Student services:* Campus employment opportunities, free psychological counseling, international student services, low-cost health insurance. *Library facilities:* Tai Sophia Library. *Online resources:* library catalog, access to other libraries' catalogs. *Collection:* 8,000 titles, 100 serial subscriptions, 1,000 audiovisual materials. *Research affiliation:* Maryland State Department of Public Safety and Corrections (acupuncture detox services).

Computer facilities: 14 computers available on campus for general student use. A campuswide network can be accessed. Internet access is available. *Web address:* http://www.tai.edu/.

General Application Contact: Lisa Connelly-Duggan, Director of Admissions, 800-735-2968 Ext. 647, Fax: 410-997-5011, E-mail: admissions@tai.edu.

TALMUDICAL ACADEMY OF NEW JERSEY, Adelphia, NJ 07710

General Information Independent-religious, men only, comprehensive institution.

GRADUATE UNITS

Graduate Program

TALMUDIC COLLEGE OF FLORIDA, Miami Beach, FL 33139

General Information Independent-religious, men only, comprehensive institution. *Enrollment:* 16 full-time matriculated graduate/professional students. *Graduate faculty:* 4 full-time (0 women), 4 part-time/adjunct (0 women). *Tuition:* Full-time $6,500. *Graduate housing:* Rooms and/or apartments available on a first-come, first-served basis to single and married students. Typical cost: $4,300 (including board) for single students. *Student services:* Campus employment opportunities, campus safety program, career counseling, international student services, teacher training. *Collection:* 23,000 titles.

Computer facilities: 14 computers available on campus for general student use.

General Application Contact: Rabbi Ira Hill, Administrator, 305-534-7050, Fax: 305-534-8444, E-mail: ryhill@bellsouth.net.

GRADUATE UNITS

Program in Talmudic Law Students: 16 full-time (0 women); includes 2 minority (both Hispanic Americans), 1 international. Average age 22. 10 applicants, 100% accepted, 10 enrolled. *Faculty:* 4 full-time (0 women), 4 part-time/adjunct (0 women). Expenses: Contact institution. *Financial support:* In 2001–02, 10 fellowships with partial tuition reimbursements, 3 research assistantships with partial tuition reimbursements, 2 teaching assistantships with partial tuition reimbursements were awarded. Federal Work-Study also available. Support available to part-time students. Financial award application deadline: 4/15. In 2001, 3 master's awarded. Offers Talmudic law (Master of Talmudic Law, Doctor of Talmudic Law). *Application deadline:* Applications are processed on a rolling basis. *Application fee:* $200. *Application Contact:* Rabbi Milton Simon, Registrar, 305-534-7050, Fax: 305-534-8444. *Administrator,* Rabbi Ira Hill, 305-534-7050, Fax: 305-534-8444, E-mail: ryhill@bellsouth.net.

TARLETON STATE UNIVERSITY, Stephenville, TX 76402

General Information State-supported, coed, comprehensive institution. *Graduate housing:* Rooms and/or apartments available to single and married students.

GRADUATE UNITS

College of Graduate Studies *Degree program information:* Part-time and evening/weekend programs available. Postbaccalaureate distance learning degree programs offered (minimal on-campus study). Electronic applications accepted.

Tarleton State University (continued)

College of Agriculture and Human Sciences *Degree program information:* Part-time and evening/weekend programs available. Postbaccalaureate distance learning degree programs offered (minimal on-campus study). Offers agriculture (MS).

College of Business Administration *Degree program information:* Part-time and evening/weekend programs available. Postbaccalaureate distance learning degree programs offered (minimal on-campus study). Offers business administration (MBA); computer and information systems (MS).

College of Education *Degree program information:* Part-time and evening/weekend programs available. Postbaccalaureate distance learning degree programs offered (minimal on-campus study). Offers counseling (M Ed); counseling and psychology (M Ed); counseling psychology (M Ed); curriculum and instruction (M Ed); education (M Ed, Certificate); educational administration (M Ed, Certificate); educational psychology (M Ed); health and physical education (M Ed, Certificate); reading (Certificate); secondary education (M Ed, Certificate); special education (Certificate).

College of Sciences and Technology *Degree program information:* Part-time and evening/weekend programs available. Postbaccalaureate distance learning degree programs offered (minimal on-campus study). Offers arts and sciences (MA, MCJ, MS); biological sciences (MS); English and languages (MA); environmental science (MS); history (MA); mathematics (MA); political science (MA); social work, sociology, and criminal justice (MCJ).

TAYLOR UNIVERSITY COLLEGE AND SEMINARY, Edmonton, AB T6J 4T3, Canada

General Information Independent-religious, coed, comprehensive institution. *Graduate housing:* Rooms and/or apartments available on a first-come, first-served basis to single students and available to married students. Housing application deadline: 8/1.

GRADUATE UNITS

Graduate and Professional Programs *Degree program information:* Part-time programs available. Offers theology (M Div, MTS).

TEACHERS COLLEGE COLUMBIA UNIVERSITY, New York, NY 10027-6696

General Information Independent, coed, graduate-only institution. *Enrollment by degree level:* 2,771 master's, 1,757 doctoral, 607 other advanced degrees. *Graduate faculty:* 140 full-time (78 women), 227 part-time/adjunct. *Tuition:* Full-time $19,080; part-time $780 per unit. *Required fees:* $170 per semester. *Graduate housing:* Rooms and/or apartments available on a first-come, first-served basis to single and married students. Typical cost: $2,635 per year ($14,400 including board) for single students; $5,845 per year ($19,500 including board) for married students. Housing application deadline: 2/1. *Student services:* Campus employment opportunities, career counseling, child daycare facilities, disabled student services, exercise/wellness program, free psychological counseling, grant writing training, international student services, low-cost health insurance, writing training. *Library facilities:* Milbank Memorial Library. *Online resources:* library catalog, web page, access to other libraries' catalogs. *Collection:* 611,826 titles, 2,723 serial subscriptions, 10,282 audiovisual materials.

Computer facilities: 169 computers available on campus for general student use. A campuswide network can be accessed from student residence rooms and from off campus. Internet access and online class registration are available. *Web address:* http://www.tc.columbia.edu/.

General Application Contact: Christine Souders, Director of Admissions, 212-678-3083, Fax: 212-678-4171.

GRADUATE UNITS

Graduate Faculty of Education Students: 1,005 full-time (818 women), 4,130 part-time (3,189 women); includes 1,340 minority (536 African Americans, 466 Asian Americans or Pacific Islanders, 328 Hispanic Americans, 10 Native Americans), 616 international. Average age 34. 3,559 applicants, 67% accepted, 1027 enrolled. *Faculty:* 140 full-time (78 women), 227 part-time/adjunct. Expenses: Contact institution. *Financial support:* Fellowships, research assistantships, teaching assistantships, career-related internships or fieldwork, Federal Work-Study, institutionally sponsored loans, traineeships, tuition waivers (full and partial), and unspecified assistantships available. Support available to part-time students. Financial award application deadline: 2/1. In 2001, 1,462 master's, 201 doctorates awarded. *Degree program information:* Part-time and evening/weekend programs available. Offers administration and supervision in special education (Ed M, MA, Ed D, PhD); adult education (MA, Ed D); anthropology (Ed M, MA, Ed D, PhD); applied educational psychology—school psychology (Ed M, MA, Ed D, PhD); applied linguistics (Ed M, MA, Ed D); applied physiology (Ed M, MA, MS, Ed D); art and art education (Ed M, MA, Ed D, Ed DCT); arts administration (MA); audiology (Ed M, MS, Ed D, PhD); behavioral disorders (MA, Ed D, PhD); bilingual and bicultural education (MA); blind and visual impairment (MA, Ed D); clinical psychology (MA, PhD); college teaching and academic leadership (Ed D); communications (Ed M, MA, Ed D); comparative and international education (Ed M, MA, Ed D, PhD); computing in education (MA); counseling psychology (Ed M, Ed D, PhD); curriculum and teaching (Ed M, MA, Ed D); curriculum and teaching in physical education (Ed M, MA, Ed D); dance and dance education (MA); developmental psychology (MA, Ed D, PhD); early childhood education (Ed M, MA, Ed D); early childhood special education (Ed M, MA); economics and education (Ed M, MA, Ed D, PhD); education (Ed M, MA, MS, Ed D, Ed DCT, PhD); educational administration (Ed M, MA, Ed D, PhD); educational media/instructional technology (Ed M, MA, Ed D); educational psychology-human cognition and learning (Ed M, MA, Ed D, PhD); elementary/childhood education, preservice (MA); giftedness (MA, Ed D); health education (MA, MS, Ed D); hearing impairment (MA, Ed D); higher education (Ed M, MA, Ed D, PhD); history and education (Ed M, MA, Ed D, PhD); inquiry in educational administration (Ed D); interdisciplinary studies (Ed M, MA, Ed D); international educational development (Ed M, MA, Ed D, PhD); learning disabilities (Ed M, MA, Ed D); mathematics education (Ed M, MA, MS, Ed D, Ed DCT, PhD); measurement, evaluation, and statistics (MA, MS, Ed D, PhD); mental retardation (MA, Ed D, PhD); motor learning (Ed M, MA, Ed D); music and music education (Ed M, MA, Ed D, Ed DCT); neuroscience and education (Ed M); nurse executive (Ed M, MA, Ed D); nursing, professional role (Ed M, MA, Ed D); nutrition and education (Ed M, MS, Ed D); nutrition education (Ed M, MS, Ed D); nutrition education and public health nutrition (Ed M, MS, Ed D); organizational psychology (MA, Ed D, PhD); philosophy and education (Ed M, MA, Ed D, PhD); physical disabilities (MA, Ed D, PhD); politics and education (Ed M, MA, Ed D, PhD); reading specialist (MA); reading/learning disability (Ed M); religion and education (Ed M, MA, Ed D); research in special education (Ed D); science education (Ed M, MA, MS, Ed D, Ed DCT, PhD); social and organizational psychology (MA, Ed D, PhD); social psychology (Ed D, PhD); social studies education (Ed M, MA, Ed D, PhD); sociology and education (Ed M, MA, Ed D, PhD); special education administration and supervision, instructional practice (Ed M, MA, Ed D); speech-language pathology (Ed M, MS, Ed D, PhD); student personnel administration (Ed M, MA, Ed D); teaching English to speakers of other languages (Ed M, MA, Ed D); teaching of English and English education (Ed M, MA, Ed D, PhD); teaching of Spanish (Ed M, MA, Ed D, Ed DCT, PhD). *Application fee:* $50. *Application Contact:* Christine Souders, Director of Admissions, 212-678-3083, Fax: 212-678-4171. *President,* Arthur Levine, 212-678-3050.

TÉLÉ-UNIVERSITÉ, Québec, QC G1K 9H5, Canada

General Information Province-supported, coed, comprehensive institution. *Graduate housing:* On-campus housing not available.

GRADUATE UNITS

Graduate Programs *Degree program information:* Part-time programs available. Offers computer science (PhD); corporate finance (MS); distance learning (MS).

TELSHE YESHIVA–CHICAGO, Chicago, IL 60625-5598

General Information Independent-religious, men only, comprehensive institution.

TEMPLE BAPTIST SEMINARY, Chattanooga, TN 37404-3530

General Information Independent-religious, coed, primarily men, graduate-only institution. *Enrollment by degree level:* 69 first professional, 92 master's, 33 doctoral, 14 other advanced degrees. *Graduate faculty:* 4 full-time (0 women), 7 part-time/adjunct (0 women). *Tuition:* Part-time $170 per credit hour. *Required fees:* $50 per semester. *Graduate housing:* On-campus housing not available. *Student services:* Campus safety program, career counseling, international student services, low-cost health insurance. *Library facilities:* Cierpke Memorial Library. *Collection:* 118,770 titles, 300 serial subscriptions.

Computer facilities: 90 computers available on campus for general student use. A campuswide network can be accessed from off campus. Internet access is available. *Web address:* http://www.templebaptistseminary.edu/.

General Application Contact: Paulette M. Trachian, Admissions Secretary, 423-493-4221, Fax: 423-493-4471, E-mail: tbsinfo@templebaptistseminary.edu.

GRADUATE UNITS

Program in Theology *Degree program information:* Part-time and evening/weekend programs available. Postbaccalaureate distance learning degree programs offered (minimal on-campus study). Offers theology (M Div, MABS, MM, MRE, D Min).

TEMPLE UNIVERSITY, Philadelphia, PA 19122-6096

General Information State-related, coed, university. CGS member. *Enrollment:* 5,096 full-time matriculated graduate/professional students (2,585 women), 3,642 part-time matriculated graduate/professional students (2,118 women). *Graduate faculty:* 833 full-time (287 women). Tuition, state resident: full-time $8,487; part-time $369 per credit hour. Tuition, nonresident: full-time $12,282; part-time $534 per credit hour. *Required fees:* $350. Tuition and fees vary according to course load, program and reciprocity agreements. *Graduate housing:* Rooms and/or apartments available on a first-come, first-served basis to single and married students. Housing application deadline: 5/1. *Student services:* Campus employment opportunities, campus safety program, career counseling, disabled student services, exercise/wellness program, free psychological counseling, international student services, low-cost health insurance, multicultural affairs office, teacher training, writing training. *Library facilities:* Paley Library plus 11 others. *Online resources:* library catalog, web page, access to other libraries' catalogs. *Collection:* 5.1 million titles, 16,755 serial subscriptions, 10.1 million audiovisual materials.

Computer facilities: 2,000 computers available on campus for general student use. A campuswide network can be accessed from student residence rooms and from off campus. Internet access and online class registration, student account and grade information are available. *Web address:* http://www.temple.edu/.

General Application Contact: Monica Reid, Head, 215-204-1380, Fax: 215-204-8781, E-mail: reidm@mail.temple.edu.

GRADUATE UNITS

Graduate School *Degree program information:* Part-time and evening/weekend programs available. Electronic applications accepted.

College of Education *Degree program information:* Part-time and evening/weekend programs available. Offers adult and organizational development (Ed M); counseling psychology (Ed M, PhD); early childhood education and elementary education (MS); education (Ed M, MS, Ed D, PhD); educational administration (Ed M, Ed D); educational psychology (Ed M, PhD); kinesiology (PhD); math/science education (Ed D); physical education (Ed M); reading and language education (MS, Ed D); school psychology (Ed M, PhD); secondary education (MS); special education (MS); urban education (Ed M, Ed D); vocational education (MS). Electronic applications accepted.

College of Liberal Arts *Degree program information:* Part-time and evening/weekend programs available. Offers African-American studies (MA, PhD); anthropology (MA, PhD); clinical psychology (PhD); cognitive psychology (PhD); creative writing (MA); criminal justice (MA, PhD); developmental psychology (PhD); English (MA, PhD); experimental psychology (PhD); geography (MA); history (MA, PhD); liberal arts (MA, MLA, PhD); philosophy (MA, PhD); political science (MA, PhD); religion (MA, PhD); social and organizational psychology (PhD); sociology (MA, PhD); Spanish (MA, PhD); urban studies (MA). Electronic applications accepted.

College of Science and Technology *Degree program information:* Part-time and evening/weekend programs available. Offers applied and computational mathematics (MA, PhD); biology (MA, PhD); chemistry (MA, PhD); civil and environmental engineering (MSE); computer and information sciences (MS, PhD); electrical and computer engineering (MSE); engineering (PhD); environmental health (MS); environmental health sciences (MS); geology (MA); mechanical engineering (MSE); physics (MA, PhD); pure mathematics (MA, PhD); science and technology (MA, MS, MSE, PhD).

Esther Boyer College of Music *Degree program information:* Part-time and evening/weekend programs available. Offers composition (MM, DMA); dance (M Ed, MFA, PhD); music (M Ed, MFA, MM, MMT, DMA, PhD); music education (MM, PhD); music history (MM); music performance (MM, DMA); music theory (MM); music therapy (MMT, PhD).

Fox School of Business and Management Students: 1,158. Average age 32. 1,277 applicants, 50% accepted. *Faculty:* 132 full-time (26 women), 26 part-time/adjunct (4 women). Expenses: Contact institution. *Financial support:* In 2001–02, 3 fellowships with full and partial tuition reimbursements (averaging $11,500 per year), 38 research assistantships with full and partial tuition reimbursements (averaging $11,500 per year), 15 teaching assistantships with full and partial tuition reimbursements (averaging $11,500 per year) were awarded. Career-related internships or fieldwork, Federal Work-Study, institutionally sponsored loans, scholarships/grants, and tuition waivers (full and partial) also available. Financial award applicants required to submit FAFSA. In 2001, 436 master's, 14 doctorates awarded. *Degree program information:* Part-time and evening/weekend programs available. Postbaccalaureate distance learning degree programs offered (minimal on-campus study). Offers accounting (MBA, MS, PhD); actuarial science (MS); business administration (EMBA, MBA); business and management (EMBA, IMBA, MA, MBA, MS, PhD); e-business (MBA, MS); economics (MA, MBA, PhD); finance (MBA, MS, PhD); general and strategic management (MBA, PhD); healthcare financial management (MS); healthcare management (MBA, PhD); human resource administration (MBA, MS, PhD); international business (IMBA); international business administration (IMBA, PhD); management information systems (MBA, MS, PhD); management science/operations management (MBA, MS); management science/operations research (MBA, PhD); marketing (MBA, MS, PhD); Philadelphia (EMBA); risk management and insurance (MBA); risk, insurance, and health-care management (PhD); statistics (MBA, MS, PhD); Tokyo (EMBA); tourism (PhD). *Application deadline:* Applications are processed on a rolling basis. *Application fee:* $40. Electronic applications accepted. *Application Contact:* Natale Butto, Director of Graduate Admissions, 215-204-7678, Fax: 215-204-8300, E-mail: butto@sbm.temple.edu. *Dean,* Dr. M. Moshe Porat, 215-204-7676.

School of Communications and Theater *Degree program information:* Part-time and evening/weekend programs available. Offers acting (MFA); broadcasting, telecommunications and mass media (MA); communications and theater (MA, MFA, MJ, PhD); design (MFA); directing (MFA); film and media arts (MFA); journalism (MJ); mass media and communication (PhD). Electronic applications accepted.

School of Social Administration *Degree program information:* Part-time and evening/weekend programs available. Offers community health education (MPH); health studies (PhD); public health (MPH); school health education (Ed M); social administration (Ed M, MPH, MSW, PhD); social work (MSW); therapeutic recreation (Ed M). Electronic applications accepted.

School of Tourism and Hospitality Management *Degree program information:* Part-time and evening/weekend programs available. Offers sport and recreation administration (Ed M); tourism and hospitality management (Ed M, MTHM).

Tyler School of Art *Degree program information:* Part-time and evening/weekend programs available. Offers art (M Ed, MA, MFA, PhD); art education (M Ed); art history (MA, PhD);

ceramics (MFA); fibers (MFA); glass (MFA); metalworking (MFA); painting/drawing (MFA); photography (MFA); printmaking (MFA); sculpture (MFA); visual design (MFA). Electronic applications accepted.

Health Sciences Center *Degree program information:* Part-time and evening/weekend programs available. Offers advanced education in general dentistry (Certificate); dentistry (DMD, MS, Certificate); endodontology (Certificate); health sciences (DMD, DPM, MD, Pharm D, MA, MPT, MS, MSN, PhD, Certificate); oral and maxillofacial surgery (Certificate); oral biology (MS); orthodontics (Certificate); periodontology (Certificate); prosthodontics (Certificate).

College of Allied Health Professions Students: 251 full-time (196 women), 221 part-time (175 women); includes 116 minority (71 African Americans, 25 Asian Americans or Pacific Islanders, 20 Hispanic Americans) Average age 25. 400 applicants, 47% accepted, 126 enrolled. *Faculty:* 39 full-time (30 women). Expenses: Contact institution. *Financial support:* In 2001–02, 14 students received support, including 14 teaching assistantships with full tuition reimbursements available (averaging $10,650 per year); fellowships, research assistantships, career-related internships or fieldwork, Federal Work-Study, institutionally sponsored loans, traineeships, and tuition waivers (partial) also available. Support available to part-time students. In 2001, 116 master's, 13 doctorates awarded. *Degree program information:* Part-time and evening/weekend programs available. Postbaccalaureate distance learning degree programs offered (minimal on-campus study). Offers allied health professions (MA, MPT, MS, MSN, PhD); applied communication (MA); communication sciences (PhD); linguistics (MA); nursing (MSN); occupational therapy (MS); physical therapy (MPT, MS, PhD); speech, language, and hearing (MA). *Application fee:* $40. *Associate Dean*, Dr. Donna Weiss, 215-707-4812, Fax: 215-707-7819, E-mail: donna.weiss@temple.edu.

School of Medicine Offers anatomy and cell biology (PhD); biochemistry (MS, PhD); medicine (MD, MS, PhD); microbiology and immunology (MS, PhD); molecular biology and genetics (PhD); pathology and laboratory medicine (PhD); pharmacology (MS, PhD); physiology (MS, PhD). Electronic applications accepted.

School of Pharmacy *Degree program information:* Part-time and evening/weekend programs available. Postbaccalaureate distance learning degree programs offered (minimal on-campus study). Offers medicinal and pharmaceutical chemistry (MS, PhD); pharmaceutics (MS, PhD); pharmacy (Pharm D, MS, PhD); quality assurance/regulatory affairs (MS).

School of Podiatric Medicine Students: 298 full-time (121 women); includes 88 minority (33 African Americans, 45 Asian Americans or Pacific Islanders, 9 Hispanic Americans, 1 Native American) Average age 26. 240 applicants, 60% accepted, 66 enrolled. *Faculty:* 23 full-time. Expenses: Contact institution. *Financial support:* Career-related internships or fieldwork, Federal Work-Study, institutionally sponsored loans, and scholarships/grants available. Financial award application deadline: 6/30; financial award applicants required to submit FAFSA. In 2001, 87 degrees awarded. Offers podiatric medicine (DPM). *Application deadline:* For fall admission, 8/15. Applications are processed on a rolling basis. *Application fee:* $95. *Application Contact:* David E. Martin, Director of Student Affairs, 215-625-5448, Fax: 215-627-2815, E-mail: dmartin@tuspm.temple.edu. *Dean*, Dr. John A. Mattiacci, 215-625-5400, Fax: 215-629-1929, E-mail: jmattiacci@tuspm.temple.edu.

James E. Beasley School of Law Students: 783 full-time (390 women), 291 part-time (138 women); includes 207 minority (93 African Americans, 66 Asian Americans or Pacific Islanders, 44 Hispanic Americans, 4 Native Americans), 11 international. Average age 26. 3,225 applicants, 40% accepted, 345 enrolled. *Faculty:* 61 full-time (20 women), 155 part-time/adjunct (43 women). Expenses: Contact institution. *Financial support:* In 2001–02, 863 students received support, including research assistantships (averaging $4,300 per year), teaching assistantships (averaging $4,300 per year); Federal Work-Study, scholarships/grants, tuition waivers (full and partial), and unspecified assistantships also available. Support available to part-time students. Financial award application deadline: 3/1; financial award applicants required to submit FAFSA. In 2001, 322 first professional degrees, 127 master's awarded. *Degree program information:* Part-time and evening/weekend programs available. Offers law (JD); taxation (LL M); transnational law (LL M); trial advocacy (LL M). *Application deadline:* For fall admission, 3/1. Applications are processed on a rolling basis. *Application fee:* $50. Electronic applications accepted. *Application Contact:* Marylouise C. Esten, Assistant Dean for Admissions, Financial Aid, and Student Affairs, 800-560-1428, Fax: 215-204-1185, E-mail: lawadmis@blue.temple.edu. *Dean*, Robert J. Reinstein, 215-204-7863, Fax: 215-204-1185, E-mail: law@astro.ocis.temple.edu.

Announcement: Located in the fifth-largest city in the United States, Temple University is as diverse academically as it is culturally. With nearly 30,000 students, Temple offers 57 doctoral and 124 master's programs that range from fine arts and sciences to professional degrees. These programs are housed in selective schools and are immersed in the cultural wealth of a comprehensive university.

See in-depth description on page 1127.

TENNESSEE STATE UNIVERSITY, Nashville, TN 37209-1561

General Information State-supported, coed, comprehensive institution. CGS member. *Enrollment:* 494 full-time matriculated graduate/professional students (335 women), 1,111 part-time matriculated graduate/professional students (756 women). *Graduate faculty:* 208 full-time (62 women), 35 part-time/adjunct (15 women). Tuition, state resident: full-time $3,884; part-time $247 per hour. Tuition, nonresident: full-time $10,356; part-time $517 per hour. *Graduate housing:* Rooms and/or apartments available on a first-come, first-served basis to single and married students. Typical cost: $2,380 per year ($3,940 including board) for single students. Housing application deadline: 8/1. *Student services:* Campus employment opportunities, campus safety program, career counseling, child daycare facilities, disabled student services, free psychological counseling, international student services, low-cost health insurance, teacher training, writing training. *Library facilities:* Martha M. Brown/Lois H. Daniel Library plus 1 other. *Online resources:* library catalog, web page. *Collection:* 580,650 titles, 23,668 audiovisual materials. *Research affiliation:* Bill Wilkerson Speech and Hearing Center, Meharry Medical Center, U.S. Army Corps of Engineers.

Computer facilities: 320 computers available on campus for general student use. A campuswide network can be accessed from student residence rooms and from off campus. *Web address:* http://www.tnstate.edu/.

General Application Contact: Dr. Helen Barrett, Dean of the Graduate School, 615-963-5901, Fax: 615-963-5963, E-mail: hbarrett@picard.tnstate.edu.

GRADUATE UNITS

Graduate School Students: 494 full-time (335 women), 1,111 part-time (756 women); includes 776 minority (707 African Americans, 48 Asian Americans or Pacific Islanders, 18 Hispanic Americans, 3 Native Americans), 105 international. Average age 27. 828 applicants, 86% accepted. *Faculty:* 208 full-time (62 women), 35 part-time/adjunct (15 women). Expenses: Contact institution. *Financial support:* In 2001–02, 60 students received support, including 6 fellowships (averaging $17,772 per year), 37 research assistantships, 39 teaching assistantships; career-related internships or fieldwork, institutionally sponsored loans, scholarships/grants, and unspecified assistantships also available. Support available to part-time students. Financial award applicants required to submit FAFSA. In 2001, 387 master's, 53 doctorates awarded. *Degree program information:* Part-time and evening/weekend programs available. *Application deadline:* Applications are processed on a rolling basis. *Application fee:* $15. Electronic applications accepted. *Application Contact:* Coordinator of Admissions, 615-963-5962. *Dean*, Dr. Helen Barrett, 615-963-5901, Fax: 615-963-5963, E-mail: hbarrett@picard.tnstate.edu.

College of Arts and Sciences Students: 67 full-time (41 women), 56 part-time (37 women); includes 83 minority (75 African Americans, 8 Asian Americans or Pacific Islanders) Average age 27. 79 applicants, 91% accepted. *Faculty:* 48 full-time (13 women). Expenses: Contact institution. *Financial support:* In 2001–02, 8 research assistantships, 19 teaching assistantships were awarded. Fellowships, unspecified assistantships also available. Support available to part-time students. In 2001, 37 degrees awarded. *Degree program information:* Part-time and evening/weekend programs available. Offers arts and sciences (MA, MCJ, MS, PhD); biological sciences (MS, PhD); chemistry (MS); criminal justice (MCJ); English (MA); mathematics (MS); music education (MS). *Application deadline:* Applications are processed on a rolling basis. *Application fee:* $15. Electronic applications accepted. *Dean*, Dr. William Lawson, 615-963-7519, E-mail: wlawson@tnstate.edu.

College of Business Students: 35 full-time (22 women), 48 part-time (26 women); includes 61 minority (44 African Americans, 17 Asian Americans or Pacific Islanders) Average age 30. 122 applicants, 83% accepted. *Faculty:* 25 full-time (4 women), 1 part-time/adjunct. Expenses: Contact institution. *Financial support:* In 2001–02, 6 research assistantships (averaging $17,772 per year) were awarded In 2001, 19 degrees awarded. *Degree program information:* Part-time and evening/weekend programs available. Offers business (MBA). *Application deadline:* Applications are processed on a rolling basis. *Application fee:* $15. *Application Contact:* G. Bruce Hartmann, Coordinator, 615-963-7145, Fax: 615-963-7139. *Dean*, Dr. Tilden J. Curry, 615-963-7121, Fax: 615-963-7139.

College of Education Students: 193 full-time (139 women), 436 part-time (312 women); includes 320 minority (303 African Americans, 12 Asian Americans or Pacific Islanders, 3 Hispanic Americans, 2 Native Americans) 397 applicants, 82% accepted. *Faculty:* 44 full-time (18 women), 19 part-time/adjunct (10 women). Expenses: Contact institution. *Financial support:* In 2001–02, 6 fellowships (averaging $17,772 per year), 8 research assistantships (averaging $20,772 per year), 10 teaching assistantships (averaging $26,318 per year) were awarded. Career-related internships or fieldwork and institutionally sponsored loans also available. Support available to part-time students. Financial award application deadline: 5/1; financial award applicants required to submit FAFSA. In 2001, 238 master's, 36 doctorates awarded. *Degree program information:* Part-time and evening/weekend programs available. Offers counseling and guidance (MS); counseling psychology (PhD); curriculum and instruction (Ed D); curriculum planning (Ed D); education (M Ed, MA Ed, MS, Ed D, PhD); educational administration (M Ed, MA Ed, Ed D); elementary education (M Ed, MA Ed, Ed D); human performance and sports science (MA Ed); psychology (MS, PhD); school psychology (MS, PhD); special education (M Ed, MA Ed, Ed D). *Application deadline:* Applications are processed on a rolling basis. *Application fee:* $15. *Application Contact:* Dr. Helen Barrett, Dean of the Graduate School, 615-963-5901, Fax: 615-963-5963, E-mail: hbarrett@picard.tnstate.edu. *Dean*, Dr. Franklin Jones, 615-963-5451.

College of Engineering and Technology Students: 30 full-time (10 women), 28 part-time (5 women); includes 48 minority (21 African Americans, 24 Asian Americans or Pacific Islanders, 3 Hispanic Americans) Average age 27. 92 applicants, 88% accepted. *Faculty:* 20 full-time (0 women), 5 part-time/adjunct (0 women). Expenses: Contact institution. *Financial support:* In 2001–02, 7 research assistantships (averaging $13,646 per year), 6 teaching assistantships (averaging $16,665 per year) were awarded. Financial award application deadline: 4/30. In 2001, 14 degrees awarded. *Degree program information:* Part-time and evening/weekend programs available. Offers engineering and technology (ME). *Application deadline:* Applications are processed on a rolling basis. *Application fee:* $15. Electronic applications accepted. *Application Contact:* Dr. Mohan J. Malkani, Associate Dean, 615-963-5400, Fax: 615-963-5397, E-mail: malkani@harpo.tnstate.edu. *Dean*, Dr. Decatur B. Rogers, 615-963-5409, Fax: 615-963-5397.

Institute of Government Students: 16 full-time (12 women), 46 part-time (26 women); includes 30 minority (27 African Americans, 3 Asian Americans or Pacific Islanders) Average age 39. 31 applicants, 87% accepted. *Faculty:* 6 full-time (1 woman), 2 part-time/adjunct (1 woman). Expenses: Contact institution. *Financial support:* In 2001–02, 3 research assistantships (averaging $6,741 per year) were awarded Support available to part-time students. In 2001, 14 degrees awarded. *Degree program information:* Part-time and evening/weekend programs available. Offers public administration (MPA, PhD). *Application deadline:* Applications are processed on a rolling basis. *Application fee:* $15. Electronic applications accepted. *Application Contact:* Dr. Harry W. Fuchs, Coordinator of Graduate Studies, 615-963-7249, Fax: 615-963-7245, E-mail: hfuchs@picard.tnstate.edu. *Director*, Dr. Ann-Marie Rizzo, 615-963-7244, Fax: 615-963-7245, E-mail: arizzo@picard.tnstate.edu.

School of Agriculture and Family Services Students: 5 full-time (3 women), 15 part-time (8 women); includes 17 minority (16 African Americans, 1 Hispanic American) Average age 35. 10 applicants, 60% accepted. *Faculty:* 8 full-time (5 women), 5 part-time/adjunct (1 woman). Expenses: Contact institution. *Financial support:* In 2001–02, 2 research assistantships (averaging $5,924 per year), 1 teaching assistantship (averaging $2,962 per year) were awarded. In 2001, 5 degrees awarded. *Degree program information:* Part-time and evening/weekend programs available. Offers agriculture and family services (MS). *Application deadline:* Applications are processed on a rolling basis. *Application fee:* $15. Electronic applications accepted. *Dean*, Dr. Troy Wakefield, 615-963-7620, E-mail: twakefield@picard.tnstate.edu.

School of Allied Health Professions Students: 22 full-time (20 women), 14 part-time (12 women); includes 12 minority (all African Americans) Average age 25. 71 applicants, 94% accepted. *Faculty:* 10 full-time (7 women), 4 part-time/adjunct (3 women). Expenses: Contact institution. *Financial support:* In 2001–02, 3 research assistantships (averaging $7,405 per year), 1 teaching assistantship (averaging $2,962 per year) were awarded. Fellowships, scholarships/grants also available. Financial award application deadline: 3/15. In 2001, 22 degrees awarded. *Degree program information:* Part-time and evening/weekend programs available. Offers allied health professions (M Ed). *Application deadline:* Applications are processed on a rolling basis. *Application fee:* $15. Electronic applications accepted. *Application Contact:* Dr. Harold R. Mitchell, Head, Department of Speech Pathology and Audiology, 615-963-7009, Fax: 615-963-7119. *Interim Head*, Dr. P. Burch-Sims, 615-963-5927, Fax: 615-963-5926.

School of Nursing Students: 16 full-time (14 women), 11 part-time (10 women); includes 15 minority (all African Americans) 20 applicants, 40% accepted. Expenses: Contact institution. *Financial support:* In 2001–02, 2 teaching assistantships (averaging $5,924 per year) were awarded In 2001, 10 degrees awarded. Offers nursing (MS). *Application deadline:* Applications are processed on a rolling basis. *Application fee:* $15. *Dean*, Dr. Yvonne Stringfield, 615-963-5254.

TENNESSEE TECHNOLOGICAL UNIVERSITY, Cookeville, TN 38505

General Information State-supported, coed, university. CGS member. *Enrollment:* 384 full-time matriculated graduate/professional students (136 women), 857 part-time matriculated graduate/professional students (632 women). *Graduate faculty:* 341 full-time (62 women). Tuition, state resident: full-time $4,000; part-time $215 per hour. Tuition, nonresident: full-time $10,500; part-time $495 per hour. *Required fees:* $1,971 per semester. *Graduate housing:* Rooms and/or apartments available to single and married students. Typical cost: $2,000 per year ($4,000 including board) for single students; $2,700 per year ($5,500 including board) for married students. Housing application deadline: 6/1. *Student services:* Campus employment opportunities, campus safety program, career counseling, child daycare facilities, disabled student services, exercise/wellness program, free psychological counseling, international student services, low-cost health insurance, teacher training. *Library facilities:* University Library. *Online resources:* library catalog, web page, access to other libraries' catalogs. *Collection:* 593,431 titles, 3,752 serial subscriptions, 17,695 audiovisual materials. *Research affiliation:* Center for Excellence in Teacher Evaluation, Appalachian Center for Crafts, Center of Excellence in Water Resources, Center of Excellence in Manufacturing Resources, Center of Excellence in Electric Power.

Computer facilities: 407 computers available on campus for general student use. A campuswide network can be accessed from student residence rooms and from off campus. Internet access and online class registration are available. *Web address:* http://www.tntech.edu/.

General Application Contact: Dr. Francis O. Otuonye, Associate Vice President for Research and Graduate Studies, 931-372-3233, Fax: 931-372-3497, E-mail: fotuonye@tntech.edu.

GRADUATE UNITS

Graduate School Students: 384 full-time (136 women), 857 part-time (632 women); includes 197 minority (51 African Americans, 138 Asian Americans or Pacific Islanders, 6 Hispanic Americans, 2 Native Americans) Average age 27. 1,493 applicants, 58% accepted. *Faculty:* 341 full-time (62 women). Expenses: Contact institution. *Financial support:* In 2001–02, 34 fellowships (averaging $8,000 per year), 167 research assistantships (averaging $6,973 per

Tennessee Technological University (continued)

year), 88 teaching assistantships (averaging $6,213 per year) were awarded. Career-related internships or fieldwork and Federal Work-Study also available. Support available to part-time students. Financial award application deadline: 4/1. In 2001, 395 master's, 5 doctorates, 102 other advanced degrees awarded. *Degree program information:* Part-time and evening/weekend programs available. *Application deadline:* For fall admission, 3/1 (priority date); for spring admission, 8/1. *Application fee:* $25 ($30 for international students). Electronic applications accepted. *Associate Vice President for Research and Graduate Studies,* Dr. Francis O. Otuonye, 931-372-3233, Fax: 931-372-3497, E-mail: fotuonye@tntech.edu.

College of Arts and Sciences Students: 53 full-time (14 women), 15 part-time (8 women); includes 17 minority (1 African American, 15 Asian Americans or Pacific Islanders, 1 Hispanic American) Average age 27. 75 applicants, 41% accepted. *Faculty:* 78 full-time (15 women). Expenses: Contact institution. *Financial support:* In 2001–02, 22 research assistantships (averaging $7,600 per year), 31 teaching assistantships (averaging $6,630 per year) were awarded. Fellowships, career-related internships or fieldwork also available. Support available to part-time students. Financial award application deadline: 4/1. In 2001, 19 degrees awarded. *Degree program information:* Part-time programs available. Offers arts and sciences (MA, MS, PhD); chemistry (MS); English (MA); environmental biology (MS); environmental sciences (PhD); fish, game, and wildlife management (MS); mathematics (MS). *Application deadline:* For fall admission, 3/1 (priority date); for spring admission, 8/1. *Application fee:* $25 ($30 for international students). Electronic applications accepted. *Application Contact:* Dr. Francis O. Otuonye, Associate Vice President for Research and Graduate Studies, 931-372-3233, Fax: 931-372-3497, E-mail: fotuonye@tntech.edu. *Dean,* Dr. Jack Armistead, 931-372-3118, Fax: 931-372-6142, E-mail: jarmistead@tntech.edu.

College of Business Administration Students: 68 full-time (17 women), 52 part-time (27 women); includes 9 minority (4 African Americans, 3 Asian Americans or Pacific Islanders, 2 Hispanic Americans) Average age 25. 72 applicants, 56% accepted. *Faculty:* 28 full-time (5 women). Expenses: Contact institution. *Financial support:* In 2001–02, 3 fellowships (averaging $10,000 per year), 42 research assistantships (averaging $4,000 per year), teaching assistantships (averaging $4,000 per year) were awarded. Support available to part-time students. Financial award application deadline: 4/1. In 2001, 46 degrees awarded. *Degree program information:* Part-time and evening/weekend programs available. Offers business administration (MBA). *Application deadline:* For fall admission, 3/1 (priority date); for spring admission, 8/1. *Application fee:* $25 ($30 for international students). *Application Contact:* Dr. Francis O. Otuonye, Associate Vice President for Research and Graduate Studies, 931-372-3233, Fax: 931-372-3497, E-mail: fotuonye@tntech.edu. *Director,* Dr. Virginia Moore, 931-372-3600, Fax: 931-372-6249, E-mail: vmoore@tntech.edu.

College of Education Students: 126 full-time (89 women), 753 part-time (591 women); includes 48 minority (42 African Americans, 1 Asian American or Pacific Islander, 3 Hispanic Americans, 2 Native Americans) Average age 27. 381 applicants, 90% accepted. *Faculty:* 58 full-time (16 women). Expenses: Contact institution. *Financial support:* In 2001–02, 30 fellowships (averaging $8,000 per year), 12 research assistantships (averaging $4,000 per year), 28 teaching assistantships (averaging $4,000 per year) were awarded. Career-related internships or fieldwork also available. Support available to part-time students. Financial award application deadline: 4/1. In 2001, 273 master's, 103 other advanced degrees awarded. *Degree program information:* Part-time and evening/weekend programs available. Offers curriculum (MA, Ed S); early childhood education (MA, Ed S); education (MA, PhD, Certificate, Ed S); educational psychology (MA, Ed S); educational psychology and student personnel (MA, Ed S); elementary education (MA, Ed S); exceptional learning (PhD); health and physical education (MA); instructional leadership (MA, Ed S); library science (MA); reading (MA, Ed S); secondary education (MA, Ed S); special education (MA, Ed S). *Application deadline:* For fall admission, 3/1 (priority date); for spring admission, 8/1. *Application fee:* $25 ($30 for international students). Electronic applications accepted. *Application Contact:* Dr. Francis O. Otuonye, Associate Vice President for Research and Graduate Studies, 931-372-3233, Fax: 931-372-3497, E-mail: fotuonye@tntech.edu. *Dean,* Dr. Darrell Garber, 931-372-3124, Fax: 931-372-6319, E-mail: dgarber@tntech.edu.

College of Engineering Students: 131 full-time (14 women), 43 part-time (9 women); includes 123 minority (4 African Americans, 119 Asian Americans or Pacific Islanders) Average age 28. 965 applicants, 47% accepted. *Faculty:* 76 full-time (2 women). Expenses: Contact institution. *Financial support:* In 2001–02, 1 fellowship (averaging $10,000 per year), 91 research assistantships (averaging $9,293 per year), 29 teaching assistantships (averaging $7,223 per year) were awarded. Career-related internships or fieldwork also available. Support available to part-time students. Financial award application deadline: 4/1. In 2001, 57 master's, 5 doctorates awarded. *Degree program information:* Part-time programs available. Offers chemical engineering (MS, PhD); civil engineering (MS, PhD); electrical engineering (MS, PhD); engineering (MS, PhD); industrial engineering (MS, PhD); mechanical engineering (MS, PhD). *Application deadline:* For fall admission, 3/1 (priority date); for spring admission, 8/1. *Application fee:* $25 ($30 for international students). *Application Contact:* Dr. Francis O. Otuonye, Associate Vice President for Research and Graduate Studies, 931-372-3233, Fax: 931-372-3497, E-mail: fotuonye@tntech.edu. *Dean,* Dr. Glen Johnson, 931-372-3172, Fax: 931-372-6172.

TENNESSEE TEMPLE UNIVERSITY, Chattanooga, TN 37404-3587

General Information Independent-religious, coed, comprehensive institution. *Graduate housing:* Rooms and/or apartments available to single students and available on a first-come, first-served basis to married students. Housing application deadline: 6/1.

GRADUATE UNITS

Graduate Studies Division *Degree program information:* Part-time programs available. Offers curriculum and instruction (MS); educational administration and supervision (MS).

TEXAS A&M INTERNATIONAL UNIVERSITY, Laredo, TX 78041-1900

General Information State-supported, coed, comprehensive institution. *Enrollment:* 116 full-time matriculated graduate/professional students (47 women), 648 part-time matriculated graduate/professional students (370 women). *Enrollment by degree level:* 764 master's. *Graduate faculty:* 62 full-time (15 women), 3 part-time/adjunct (1 woman). Tuition, state resident: full-time $1,536; part-time $64 per credit. Tuition, nonresident: full-time $6,600; part-time $275 per credit. *Required fees:* $594; $9 per credit. $33 per term. One-time fee: $10 part-time. *Graduate housing:* Rooms and/or apartments available on a first-come, first-served basis to single and married students. Typical cost: $3,120 per year for single students; $3,120 per year for married students. *Student services:* Campus employment opportunities, campus safety program, career counseling, child daycare facilities, disabled student services, exercise/wellness program, free psychological counseling, international student services, low-cost health insurance, multicultural affairs office, teacher training, writing training. *Library facilities:* Sue and Radcliff Killam Library. *Online resources:* library catalog, web page. *Collection:* 166,951 titles, 8,492 serial subscriptions, 1,040 audiovisual materials.

Computer facilities: 200 computers available on campus for general student use. A campuswide network can be accessed from off campus. *Web address:* http://www.tamiu.edu/.

General Application Contact: Maria R. Rosillo, Director of Admissions, 956-326-2200, Fax: 956-326-2199, E-mail: enroll@tamiu.edu.

GRADUATE UNITS

Division of Graduate Studies Students: 116 full-time (47 women), 648 part-time (370 women). Average age 33. 411 applicants, 68% accepted, 184 enrolled. *Faculty:* 62 full-time (15 women), 3 part-time/adjunct (1 woman). Expenses: Contact institution. *Financial support:* In 2001–02, 238 students received support, including 40 fellowships with partial tuition reimbursements available; Federal Work-Study, institutionally sponsored loans, and scholarships/grants also available. Support available to part-time students. Financial award application deadline: 11/1; financial award applicants required to submit FAFSA. In 2001, 177 degrees awarded. *Degree program information:* Part-time and evening/weekend programs available. Offers biology (MAIS); mathematics (MAIS); science and technology (MAIS). *Application deadline:* For fall admission, 7/15 (priority date); for spring admission, 11/12 (priority date). Applications are processed on a rolling basis. *Application fee:* $0. *Application Contact:* Veronica Gonzalez, Director of Enrollment Management and School Relations, 956-326-2270, Fax: 956-326-2269, E-mail: enroll@tamiu.edu. *Dean,* Dr. Jerry Thompson, 956-326-2240, Fax: 956-326-2239, E-mail: jthompson@tamiu.edu.

College of Arts and Humanities Students: 15 full-time (8 women), 130 part-time (68 women); includes 123 minority (2 Asian Americans or Pacific Islanders, 121 Hispanic Americans), 4 international. Average age 30. *Faculty:* 24 full-time (8 women). Expenses: Contact institution. *Financial support:* Federal Work-Study and institutionally sponsored loans available. Support available to part-time students. Financial award application deadline: 11/1; financial award applicants required to submit FAFSA. In 2001, 37 degrees awarded. *Degree program information:* Part-time and evening/weekend programs available. Offers arts and humanities (MA, MPAD, MSCJ); counseling psychology (MA); criminal justice (MSCJ); English (MA); history (MA); political science (MA); public administration (MPAD); sociology (MA); Spanish (MA). *Application deadline:* For fall admission, 7/15 (priority date); for spring admission, 11/12. Applications are processed on a rolling basis. *Application fee:* $0. *Application Contact:* Veronica Gonzalez, Director of Enrollment Management and School Relations, 956-326-2270, Fax: 956-326-2269, E-mail: enroll@tamiu.edu. *Interim Dean,* Dr. Nasser Momayezi, 956-326-2460, Fax: 956-326-2459, E-mail: nmomayezi@tamiu.edu.

College of Business Administration Students: 81 full-time (26 women), 181 part-time (66 women); includes 129 minority (2 Asian Americans or Pacific Islanders, 127 Hispanic Americans), 114 international. Average age 30. *Faculty:* 18 full-time (2 women), 2 part-time/adjunct (0 women). Expenses: Contact institution. *Financial support:* In 2001–02, 40 fellowships were awarded; Federal Work-Study and institutionally sponsored loans also available. Support available to part-time students. Financial award application deadline: 11/1; financial award applicants required to submit FAFSA. In 2001, 98 degrees awarded. *Degree program information:* Part-time and evening/weekend programs available. Offers business administration (MBA, MPA, MSIS); information systems (MSIS); international banking (MBA); international trade (MBA); professional accountancy (MPA). *Application deadline:* For fall admission, 7/15 (priority date); for spring admission, 11/12. Applications are processed on a rolling basis. *Application fee:* $0. *Application Contact:* David Jones, Director of Graduate Student Services, 956-326-2771, Fax: 956-326-2459, E-mail: coba@tamiu.edu. *Dean,* Dr. John P. Kohl, 956-326-2480, Fax: 210-326-2479, E-mail: jkohl@tamiu.edu.

College of Education Students: 8 full-time (6 women), 333 part-time (232 women); includes 305 minority (4 African Americans, 1 Asian American or Pacific Islander, 298 Hispanic Americans, 2 Native Americans), 5 international. Average age 30. *Faculty:* 15 full-time (5 women), 1 (woman) part-time/adjunct. Expenses: Contact institution. *Financial support:* Fellowships, Federal Work-Study and institutionally sponsored loans available. Support available to part-time students. Financial award application deadline: 11/1; financial award applicants required to submit FAFSA. In 2001, 38 degrees awarded. *Degree program information:* Part-time and evening/weekend programs available. Offers administration (MS Ed); bilingual education (MS Ed); counseling education (MS Ed); curriculum and instruction (MS); early childhood education (MS Ed); reading (MS Ed); special education (MS). *Application deadline:* For fall admission, 7/15 (priority date); for spring admission, 11/12. Applications are processed on a rolling basis. *Application fee:* $0. *Application Contact:* Veronica Gonzalez, Director of Enrollment Management and School Relations, 956-326-2270, Fax: 956-326-2269, E-mail: enroll@tamiu.edu. *Interim Dean,* Dr. Rosa Maria Vida, 956-326-2420, Fax: 956-326-2419, E-mail: rmvida@tamiu.edu.

TEXAS A&M UNIVERSITY, College Station, TX 77843

General Information State-supported, coed, university. CGS member. *Enrollment:* 7,556 matriculated graduate/professional students (2,973 women). *Enrollment by degree level:* 497 first professional, 4,158 master's, 2,901 doctoral. *Graduate faculty:* 2,611. Tuition, state resident: full-time $11,872. Tuition, nonresident: full-time $17,892. *Graduate housing:* Room and/or apartments available to married students; on-campus housing not available to single students. *Student services:* Campus employment opportunities, campus safety program, career counseling, child daycare facilities, disabled student services, exercise/wellness program, free psychological counseling, grant writing training, international student services, low-cost health insurance, multicultural affairs office, teacher training, writing training. *Library facilities:* Sterling C. Evans Library plus 4 others. *Online resources:* library catalog, web page, access to other libraries' catalogs. *Collection:* 1.5 million titles, 26,625 serial subscriptions, 253,951 audiovisual materials. *Research affiliation:* Houston Advanced Research Center, Scott and White Clinic (human medicine), Texas Engineering Experiment Station (engineering systems), Texas Transportation Institute (highway safety), Texas Agricultural Extension Service.

Computer facilities: 1,500 computers available on campus for general student use. A campuswide network can be accessed from student residence rooms and from off campus. *Web address:* http://www.tamu.edu/.

General Application Contact: Graduate Admissions, 979-845-1044, E-mail: admissions@tamu.edu.

GRADUATE UNITS

College of Agriculture and Life Sciences Students: 1,112 (478 women). Average age 29. *Faculty:* 670. Expenses: Contact institution. *Financial support:* Fellowships, research assistantships, teaching assistantships, career-related internships or fieldwork, Federal Work-Study, institutionally sponsored loans, scholarships/grants, tuition waivers (partial), and unspecified assistantships available. Support available to part-time students. Financial award applicants required to submit FAFSA. *Degree program information:* Part-time programs available. Offers agricultural chemistry (M Agr); agricultural economics (MAB, MS, PhD); agricultural education (M Ed, MS, Ed D, PhD); agriculture (M Agr, MAD); agriculture and life sciences (M Agr, M Ed, M Eng, MAB, MAD, MS, Ed D, PhD); agronomy (M Agr, MS, PhD); animal breeding (MS, PhD); animal science (M Agr, MS, PhD); biochemistry (MS, PhD); biological and agricultural engineering (M Agr, M Eng, MS, PhD); biophysics (MS); dairy science (M Agr, MS); entomology (M Agr, MS, PhD); food science and technology (M Agr, MS, PhD); forestry (MS, PhD); genetics (MS, PhD); horticulture (PhD); horticulture and floriculture (M Agr, MS); molecular and environmental plant sciences (MS, PhD); natural resource development (M Agr); natural resources development (M Agr); nutrition (MS, PhD); physiology of reproduction (MS, PhD); plant breeding (MS, PhD); plant pathology (MS, PhD); plant protection (M Agr); poultry science (M Agr, MS, PhD); rangeland ecology and management (M Agr, MS, PhD); recreation and resources development (M Agr); recreation, park, and tourism sciences (MS, PhD); soil science (MS, PhD); wildlife and fisheries sciences (M Agr, MS, PhD). *Application deadline:* Applications are processed on a rolling basis. *Application fee:* $50 ($75 for international students). Electronic applications accepted. *Dean,* Dr. Edward A. Hiler, 979-845-4747.

Faculty of Genetics Students: 44 full-time (23 women), 5 part-time (2 women). Average age 29. 77 applicants, 19% accepted. *Faculty:* 61. Expenses: Contact institution. *Financial support:* Fellowships, research assistantships, teaching assistantships available. Financial award application deadline: 4/15; financial award applicants required to submit FAFSA. In 2001, 1 degree awarded. Offers genetics (MS, PhD). Program composed of members from 4 colleges and 14 departments. *Application deadline:* For fall admission, 4/15 (priority date). Applications are processed on a rolling basis. *Application fee:* $50 ($75 for international students). Electronic applications accepted. *Application Contact:* Linda Fisher, Administrative Assistant, 979-845-6848, Fax: 979-845-9274. *Chair,* Dr. Linda Guarino, 979-845-1013.

College of Architecture Students: 417 (136 women); includes 33 minority (6 African Americans, 9 Asian Americans or Pacific Islanders, 17 Hispanic Americans, 1 Native American) 208 international. Average age 29. 444 applicants, 63% accepted, 140 enrolled. *Faculty:* 88 full-time (12 women), 20 part-time/adjunct (5 women). Expenses: Contact institution. *Financial support:* Fellowships, research assistantships, teaching assistantships, career-related internships or fieldwork, Federal Work-Study, institutionally sponsored loans, and unspecified assistantships available. Financial award applicants required to submit FAFSA. In 2001, 87 master's, 3 doctorates awarded. Offers architectural design (M Arch); architectural history and preservation (M Arch); architecture (MS, PhD); construction management (MS); health facilities planning and design (M Arch); interior architecture (M Arch); landscape architecture (MLA); management in architecture (M Arch); urban and regional science (PhD); urban planning (MUP); visualization sciences (MS). *Application deadline:* For fall admission, 2/1 (priority date). Applications are processed on a rolling basis. *Application fee:* $50 ($75 for international students). *Application Contact:* 979-845-6582, Fax: 979-845-4491. *Dean,* J. Thomas Regan, 979-845-1221, Fax: 979-845-4491.

College of Education Students: 996 (677 women). Average age 36. *Faculty:* 171. Expenses: Contact institution. *Financial support:* In 2001–02, fellowships with partial tuition reimbursements (averaging $12,000 per year), research assistantships with partial tuition reimbursements (averaging $10,000 per year), teaching assistantships with partial tuition reimbursements (averaging $10,000 per year) were awarded. Career-related internships or fieldwork, Federal Work-Study, institutionally sponsored loans, scholarships/grants, tuition waivers (partial), and unspecified assistantships also available. Financial award applicants required to submit FAFSA. *Degree program information:* Part-time and evening/weekend programs available. Postbaccalaureate distance learning degree programs offered (no on-campus study). Offers bilingual education (M Ed, MS, PhD); counseling (MS); counseling psychology (PhD); curriculum development (M Ed, MS, Ed D, PhD); education (M Ed, MS, Ed D, PhD); educational administration and human resource development (M Ed, MS, Ed D, PhD); educational technology (M Ed); gifted and talented education (M Ed, MS); health education (M Ed, MS, PhD); intelligence, creativity, and giftedness (PhD); kinesiology (M Ed, MS, Ed D, PhD); learning, development, and instruction (M Ed, MS, PhD); licensing specialist in school psychology (MS); math/science (M Ed, MS, Ed D, PhD); physical education (M Ed, Ed D); reading (M Ed, MS, Ed D, PhD); research, measurement and statistics (MS); research, measurement, and statistics (M Ed, PhD); school counseling (M Ed); school psychology (PhD); social foundation (M Ed, MS, Ed D, PhD); special education (M Ed, PhD). *Application fee:* $50 ($75 for international students). Electronic applications accepted. *Application Contact:* Becky Carr, Assistant Dean, 979-845-5311, Fax: 979-845-6129, E-mail: bcarr@tamu.edu. *Dean,* Jane Conoley, 979-845-5311.

College of Engineering Students: 1,976 (328 women); includes 82 minority (18 African Americans, 30 Asian Americans or Pacific Islanders, 34 Hispanic Americans) 1,550 international. 4,692 applicants, 36% accepted, 515 enrolled. *Faculty:* 437. Expenses: Contact institution. *Financial support:* Fellowships, research assistantships, teaching assistantships, career-related internships or fieldwork, institutionally sponsored loans, scholarships/grants, health care benefits, and unspecified assistantships available. Financial award applicants required to submit FAFSA. In 2001, 434 master's, 128 doctorates awarded. *Degree program information:* Part-time programs available. Postbaccalaureate distance learning degree programs offered (minimal on-campus study). Offers aerospace engineering (M Eng, MS, PhD); biomedical engineering (M Eng, MS, D Eng, PhD); chemical engineering (M Eng, MS, PhD); computer engineering (MCE, MS, PhD); computer science (MCS, MS, PhD); construction engineering and project management (M Eng, MS, D Eng, PhD); electrical engineering (M Eng, MS, PhD); engineering (M Eng, MCE, MCS, MID, MS, D Eng, DE, PhD); engineering mechanics (M Eng, MS, PhD); environmental engineering (M Eng, MS, D Eng, PhD); geotechnical engineering (M Eng, MS, D Eng, PhD); health physics (MS); health physics/radiological health (MS); hydraulic engineering (M Eng, MS, PhD); hydrology (M Eng, MS, PhD); industrial engineering (M Eng, MS, D Eng, PhD); industrial hygiene (MS); materials engineering (M Eng, MS, D Eng, PhD); mechanical engineering (M Eng, MS, D Eng, PhD); nuclear engineering (M Eng, MS, PhD); ocean engineering (M Eng, MS, D Eng, PhD); petroleum engineering (M Eng, MS, D Eng, PhD); public works engineering and management (M Eng, MS, PhD); safety engineering (MS); structural engineering and structural mechanics (M Eng, MS, D Eng, PhD); transportation engineering (M Eng, MS, D Eng, PhD); water resources engineering (M Eng, MS, D Eng, PhD). *Application fee:* $50 ($75 for international students). Electronic applications accepted. *Application Contact:* Karen Butler-Purry, Assistant Dean, 979-845-7200, Fax: 979-847-8654, E-mail: eapo@tamu.edu. *Dean,* C. Roland Haden, 979-845-7203, Fax: 979-845-8986, E-mail: r-haden@tamu.edu.

College of Geosciences Students: 229 full-time, 60 part-time; includes 10 minority (3 Asian Americans or Pacific Islanders, 6 Hispanic Americans, 1 Native American), 103 international. Average age 30. 221 applicants, 48% accepted, 60 enrolled. *Faculty:* 80 full-time (7 women), 5 part-time/adjunct (0 women). Expenses: Contact institution. *Financial support:* In 2001–02, 54 students received support, including 12 fellowships with partial tuition reimbursements available; research assistantships, teaching assistantships, career-related internships or fieldwork, Federal Work-Study, institutionally sponsored loans, scholarships/grants, health care benefits, tuition waivers (partial), unspecified assistantships, and foreign government supports also available. Financial award application deadline: 3/1; financial award applicants required to submit FAFSA. In 2001, 65 master's, 22 doctorates awarded. *Degree program information:* Part-time programs available. Offers atmospheric sciences (MS, PhD); geography (MS, PhD); geology and geophysics (MS, PhD); geosciences (MGS, MS, PhD); oceanography (MS, PhD). *Application deadline:* For fall admission, 3/1 (priority date); for spring admission, 12/1. Applications are processed on a rolling basis. *Application fee:* $50 ($75 for international students). Electronic applications accepted. *Dean,* Dr. David B. Prior, 979-845-3651, Fax: 979-845-0056, E-mail: dprior@ocean.tamu.edu.

College of Liberal Arts Students: 704 (321 women); includes 67 minority (10 African Americans, 10 Asian Americans or Pacific Islanders, 45 Hispanic Americans, 2 Native Americans) 154 international. 887 applicants, 41% accepted. *Faculty:* 336 full-time (90 women), 56 part-time/adjunct (26 women). Expenses: Contact institution. *Financial support:* In 2001–02, 21 fellowships (averaging $14,000 per year), 286 research assistantships with partial tuition reimbursements (averaging $10,385 per year), 137 teaching assistantships with partial tuition reimbursements (averaging $11,090 per year) were awarded. Career-related internships or fieldwork, Federal Work-Study, institutionally sponsored loans, unspecified assistantships, and assistant lecturer positions also available. Financial award applicants required to submit FAFSA. In 2001, 66 master's, 38 doctorates awarded. *Degree program information:* Part-time programs available. Offers anthropology (MA, PhD); clinical psychology (MS, PhD); economics (MS, PhD); English (MA, PhD); general psychology (MS, PhD); history (MA, PhD); industrial/organizational psychology (MS, PhD); liberal arts (MA, MS, PhD); philosophy (MA, PhD); political science (MA, PhD); science and technology journalism (MS); sociology (MS, PhD); Spanish (MA); speech communication (MA, PhD). *Application fee:* $50 ($75 for international students). Electronic applications accepted. *Application Contact:* Dr. Larry J. Oliver, Associate Dean, 979-845-8541, Fax: 979-845-5164, E-mail: l-oliver@tamu.edu. *Dean,* Dr. Charles A. Johnson, 979-845-5141, Fax: 979-845-5164, E-mail: cjohnson@tamu.edu.

College of Science Students: 606. 973 applicants, 28% accepted. *Faculty:* 252 full-time (32 women), 32 part-time/adjunct (11 women). Expenses: Contact institution. *Financial support:* Fellowships, research assistantships, teaching assistantships, career-related internships or fieldwork, institutionally sponsored loans, and scholarships/grants available. Financial award applicants required to submit FAFSA. In 2001, 36 master's, 55 doctorates awarded. *Degree program information:* Part-time programs available. Offers applied physics (PhD); biology (MS, PhD); botany (MS, PhD); chemistry (MS, PhD); mathematics (MS, PhD); microbial genetics and genomics (PhD); microbiology (MS, PhD); molecular and cell biology (PhD); physics (MS, PhD); science (MS, PhD); statistics (MS, PhD); zoology (MS, PhD). *Application fee:* $75 for international students. *Application Contact:* James C. Holste, Associate Dean for Graduate Studies, 979-845-7362, Fax: 979-845-6077, E-mail: j-holste@tamu.edu. *Dean,* H. Joseph Newton, 979-845-7361, Fax: 979-845-6077.

College of Veterinary Medicine Students: 639 (405 women); includes 58 minority (3 African Americans, 20 Asian Americans or Pacific Islanders, 31 Hispanic Americans, 4 Native Americans) *Faculty:* 165 full-time, 54 part-time/adjunct. Expenses: Contact institution. *Financial support:* Fellowships, research assistantships, teaching assistantships, career-related internships or fieldwork, Federal Work-Study, institutionally sponsored loans, tuition waivers (partial), and clinical associateships available. Support available to part-time students. Financial award applicants required to submit FAFSA. In 2001, 124 first professional degrees, 41 master's, 104 doctorates awarded. *Degree program information:* Part-time programs available. Offers anatomy (MS, PhD); epidemiology (MS); genetics (MS, PhD); physiology (MS, PhD); reproductive biology (PhD); toxicology (MS, PhD); veterinary anatomy and public health (MS, PhD); veterinary clinical science (MS); veterinary large animal medicine and surgery (MS, PhD); veterinary medical science (MS); veterinary medicine (DVM, MS, PhD); veterinary microbiology (MS, PhD); veterinary parasitology (MS); veterinary pathology (MS, PhD); veterinary physiology and pharmacology (MS, PhD); veterinary public health (MS); veterinary small animal medicine and surgery (MS). *Dean,* Dr. H. Richard Adams, 979-845-5051, Fax: 979-845-5088.

George Bush School of Government and Public Service Students: 47 full-time (22 women); includes 8 minority (3 African Americans, 1 Asian American or Pacific Islander, 4 Hispanic Americans), 3 international. Average age 24. 97 applicants, 26% accepted. *Faculty:* 5 full-time (0 women), 19 part-time/adjunct (5 women). Expenses: Contact institution. *Financial support:* In 2001–02, 27 fellowships with partial tuition reimbursements (averaging $15,000 per year), 10 research assistantships with partial tuition reimbursements (averaging $11,000 per year) were awarded. Career-related internships or fieldwork, Federal Work-Study, and institutionally sponsored loans also available. Financial award application deadline: 2/1; financial award applicants required to submit FAFSA. In 2001, 1 degree awarded. Offers government and public service (MA, MPSA); international affairs (MA). *Application deadline:* For fall admission, 1/31 (priority date). *Application fee:* $50 ($75 for international students). *Application Contact:* Reigen Smith, Recruitment/Placement Officer, 979-458-4767, Fax: 979-845-4155, E-mail: admissions@bushschool.tamu.edu. *Dean,* Richard A. Chilcoat, 979-862-8007, Fax: 979-845-4155, E-mail: bushschool@tamu.edu.

Intercollegiate Faculty in Nutrition Students: 41 full-time (35 women), 23 part-time (14 women); includes 5 minority (2 Asian Americans or Pacific Islanders, 3 Hispanic Americans), 9 international. 7 applicants, 14% accepted. *Faculty:* 41 full-time (8 women), 9 part-time/adjunct (8 women). Expenses: Contact institution. *Financial support:* Fellowships, research assistantships, teaching assistantships available. Financial award application deadline: 4/1; financial award applicants required to submit FAFSA. In 2001, 8 master's, 4 doctorates awarded. *Degree program information:* Part-time programs available. Offers nutrition (MS, PhD). *Application deadline:* Applications are processed on a rolling basis. *Application fee:* $50 ($75 for international students). *Application Contact:* Fara D. Goodwyn, Chair, 979-845-1735, Fax: 979-862-2378, E-mail: chapkin@acs.tamu.edu. *Chair,* Dr. Robert S. Chapkin, 979-845-1735, Fax: 979-862-2378, E-mail: chapkin@acs.tamu.edu.

Interdisciplinary Faculty in Toxicology Students: 45 full-time (21 women); includes 6 minority (1 African American, 3 Asian Americans or Pacific Islanders, 2 Hispanic Americans), 15 international. Average age 25. 34 applicants, 35% accepted, 8 enrolled. *Faculty:* 63 full-time (12 women), 4 part-time/adjunct (2 women). Expenses: Contact institution. *Financial support:* In 2001–02, 8 fellowships with partial tuition reimbursements (averaging $17,500 per year), 37 research assistantships (averaging $15,000 per year) were awarded. Federal Work-Study, institutionally sponsored loans, scholarships/grants, traineeships, health care benefits, and unspecified assistantships also available. Financial award application deadline: 3/1; financial award applicants required to submit FAFSA. In 2001, 8 degrees awarded. Offers toxicology (MS, PhD). Program composed of faculty members from 7 colleges and 21 departments. *Application deadline:* For fall admission, 2/1 (priority date); for spring admission, 8/1. Applications are processed on a rolling basis. *Application fee:* $50 ($75 for international students). Electronic applications accepted. *Application Contact:* Kimberly D. Daniel, Program Assistant, 979-845-5529, Fax: 979-862-4929, E-mail: tox@cvm.tamu.edu. *Chair,* Dr. Timothy D. Phillips, 979-845-5529, Fax: 979-862-4929, E-mail: tphillips@cvm.tamu.edu.

Interdisciplinary Faculty of Biotechnology Students: 11 full-time (6 women); includes 5 minority (1 African American, 4 Asian Americans or Pacific Islanders) Average age 25. 20 applicants, 55% accepted, 11 enrolled. *Faculty:* 49 full-time. Expenses: Contact institution. *Financial support:* Fellowships, research assistantships, scholarships/grants available. Financial award applicants required to submit FAFSA. In 2001, 5 degrees awarded. Offers biotechnology (MBIOT). Program begins in Summer term. *Application fee:* $50 ($75 for international students). Electronic applications accepted. *Application Contact:* Jeannine Kantz, Program Coordinator, 979-862-4935, Fax: 979-862-4790, E-mail: jkantz@tamu.edu. *Head,* Dr. Jorge Piedrahita, 979-845-0732, Fax: 979-862-4790.

Mays Business School Students: 869 (346 women). Average age 28. *Faculty:* 137 full-time. Expenses: Contact institution. *Financial support:* In 2001–02, 235 students received support; fellowships, research assistantships, teaching assistantships, career-related internships or fieldwork, Federal Work-Study, and institutionally sponsored loans available. Financial award application deadline: 2/1. In 2001, 414 master's, 17 doctorates awarded. Offers accounting (MS, PhD); business (EMBA, MBA, MLERE, MS, MSHRM, PhD); business administration (EMBA, MBA); finance (MS, PhD); human resource management (MSHRM); land economics and real estate (MLERE); management (MS, MSHRM, PhD); management information systems (MS, PhD); marketing (MS, PhD). *Application deadline:* Applications are processed on a rolling basis. *Application fee:* $50 ($75 for international students). Electronic applications accepted. *Application Contact:* Dr. Dan H. Robertson, Director, MBA Program, 979-845-4714, Fax: 979-862-2393, E-mail: maysmba@tamu.edu. *Dean,* Dr. Jerry R. Strawser, 979-845-4711.

TEXAS A&M UNIVERSITY–COMMERCE, Commerce, TX 75429-3011

General Information State-supported, coed, university. CGS member. *Enrollment:* 704 full-time matriculated graduate/professional students (343 women), 2,782 part-time matriculated graduate/professional students (1,912 women). *Enrollment by degree level:* 3,228 master's, 258 doctoral. *Graduate faculty:* 137 full-time (35 women), 26 part-time/adjunct (16 women). *International tuition:* $7,285 full-time. Tuition, state resident: full-time $2,221. *Graduate housing:* Rooms and/or apartments available on a first-come, first-served basis to single and married students. Typical cost: $1,385 per year for single students; $1,385 per year for married students. Room charges vary according to housing facility selected. *Student services:* Campus employment opportunities, career counseling, child daycare facilities, disabled student services, exercise/wellness program, free psychological counseling, grant writing training, international student services, low-cost health insurance, teacher training, writing training. *Library facilities:* Gee Library. *Online resources:* library catalog, web page, access to other libraries' catalogs. *Collection:* 2.7 million titles, 1,779 serial subscriptions, 44,492 audiovisual materials. *Research affiliation:* A&M–Commerce Regional Division of Texas Engineering Experiment Station.

Computer facilities: 405 computers available on campus for general student use. A campuswide network can be accessed from student residence rooms and from off campus. Internet access and online class registration are available. *Web address:* http://www.tamu-commerce.edu/.

General Application Contact: Tammi Higginbotham, Graduate Admissions Adviser, 843-886-5167, Fax: 843-886-5165, E-mail: tammi_higginbotham@tamu-commerce.edu.

GRADUATE UNITS

Graduate School Students: 704 full-time (343 women), 2,782 part-time (1,912 women); includes 837 minority (592 African Americans, 52 Asian Americans or Pacific Islanders, 157 Hispanic Americans, 36 Native Americans), 359 international. 1,663 applicants, 93% accepted. *Faculty:* 137 full-time (35 women), 26 part-time/adjunct (16 women). Expenses: Contact institution. *Financial support:* In 2001–02, research assistantships (averaging $7,875 per year), teaching assistantships (averaging $7,875 per year) were awarded. Career-related internships or fieldwork, Federal Work-Study, institutionally sponsored loans, and scholarships/grants also available. Financial award application deadline: 5/1; financial award applicants required to submit FAFSA. In 2001, 586 master's, 37 doctorates awarded. *Degree program information:* Part-time programs available. *Application deadline:* For fall admission, 6/1 (priority date); for spring admission, 11/1 (priority date). Applications are processed on a rolling basis. *Application fee:* $0 ($25 for international students). Electronic applications accepted. *Application Contact:* Tammi Higginbotham, Graduate Admissions Adviser, 843-886-5167, Fax: 843-886-5165, E-mail: tammi_higginbotham@tamu-commerce.edu. *Dean,* Dr. Mathew Kanjirathinkal, 903-886-5163, Fax: 903-886-5165, E-mail: mathew_kanjirathinkal@tamu-commerce.edu.

College of Arts and Sciences Students: 289 full-time (95 women), 292 part-time (154 women); includes 70 minority (31 African Americans, 13 Asian Americans or Pacific Islanders, 20 Hispanic Americans, 6 Native Americans), 230 international. 118 applicants, 95% accepted. *Faculty:* 62 full-time (12 women), 5 part-time/adjunct (1 woman). Expenses:

Texas A&M University–Commerce (continued)

Contact institution. *Financial support:* In 2001–02, research assistantships (averaging $7,875 per year), teaching assistantships (averaging $7,875 per year) were awarded. Federal Work-Study, institutionally sponsored loans, and scholarships/grants also available. Financial award application deadline: 5/1; financial award applicants required to submit FAFSA. In 2001, 103 master's, 1 doctorate awarded. *Degree program information:* Part-time programs available. Offers agricultural education (M Ed, MS); agricultural sciences (M Ed, MS); art (MA, MS); art history (MA); arts and sciences (M Ed, MA, MFA, MM, MS, MSW, Ed D, PhD); biological and earth sciences (M Ed, MS); chemistry (M Ed, MS); college teaching of English (PhD); computer science (MS); English (MA, MS); fine arts (MFA); history (MA, MS); mathematics (MA, MS); music (MA, MS); music composition (MA, MM); music education (MA, MM, MS); music literature (MA); music performance (MA, MM); music theory (MA, MM); physics (M Ed, MS); social sciences (M Ed, MS); social work (MSW); sociology (MA, MS); Spanish (MA); studio art (MA); theatre (MA, MS). *Application deadline:* For fall admission, 6/1 (priority date); for spring admission, 11/1 (priority date). Applications are processed on a rolling basis. *Application fee:* $0 ($25 for international students). Electronic applications accepted. *Application Contact:* Tammi Higginbotham, Graduate Admissions Adviser, 843-886-5167, Fax: 843-886-5165, E-mail: tammi_higginbotham@tamu-commerce.edu. *Dean,* Dr. Finnie Murray, 903-886-5175, Fax: 903-886-5199, E-mail: finnie_murray@tamu-commerce.edu.

College of Business and Technology Students: 94 full-time (36 women), 143 part-time (56 women); includes 50 minority (29 African Americans, 7 Asian Americans or Pacific Islanders, 13 Hispanic Americans, 1 Native American), 80 international. Average age 36. 51 applicants, 96% accepted. *Faculty:* 20 full-time (2 women), 2 part-time/adjunct (0 women). Expenses: Contact institution. *Financial support:* In 2001–02, research assistantships (averaging $7,875 per year), teaching assistantships (averaging $7,875 per year) were awarded. Federal Work-Study, institutionally sponsored loans, and scholarships/grants also available. Financial award application deadline: 5/1; financial award applicants required to submit FAFSA. In 2001, 101 degrees awarded. *Degree program information:* Part-time programs available. Offers business administration (MBA); business and technology (MA, MBA, MS); economics (MA, MS); industry and technology (MS). *Application deadline:* For fall admission, 6/1 (priority date); for spring admission, 11/1 (priority date). Applications are processed on a rolling basis. *Application fee:* $0 ($25 for international students). Electronic applications accepted. *Application Contact:* Tammi Higginbotham, Graduate Admissions Adviser, 843-886-5167, Fax: 843-886-5165, E-mail: tammi_higginbotham@tamu-commerce.edu. *Graduate Admissions Adviser,* Harold Langford, 903-886-5167, Fax: 903-886-5165, E-mail: hal_langford@tamu-commerce.edu.

College of Education Students: 276 full-time (193 women), 1,355 part-time (1,002 women); includes 324 minority (235 African Americans, 9 Asian Americans or Pacific Islanders, 67 Hispanic Americans, 13 Native Americans), 21 international. Average age 36. *Faculty:* 53 full-time (21 women), 19 part-time/adjunct (15 women). Expenses: Contact institution. *Financial support:* In 2001–02, research assistantships (averaging $7,875 per year), teaching assistantships (averaging $7,875 per year) were awarded. Career-related internships or fieldwork, Federal Work-Study, institutionally sponsored loans, and scholarships/grants also available. Financial award application deadline: 5/1; financial award applicants required to submit FAFSA. In 2001, 381 master's, 36 doctorates awarded. *Degree program information:* Part-time programs available. Offers counseling (M Ed, MS, Ed D); early childhood education (M Ed, MA, MS); education (M Ed, MA, MS, Ed D, PhD); educational administration (M Ed, MS, Ed D); educational psychology (PhD); elementary education (M Ed, MS); health and physical education (M Ed, MS); higher education (MS); learning technology and information systems (M Ed, MS); psychology (MA, MS); reading (M Ed, MA, MS); secondary education (M Ed, MA, MS); special education (M Ed, MA, MS); supervision of curriculum and instruction: elementary education (Ed D); supervision of curriculum and instruction: higher education (PhD); training and development (MS); vocational/technical education (M Ed, MA, MS). *Application deadline:* For fall admission, 6/1 (priority date); for spring admission, 11/1 (priority date). Applications are processed on a rolling basis. *Application fee:* $0 ($25 for international students). Electronic applications accepted. *Application Contact:* Tammi Higginbotham, Graduate Admissions Adviser, 843-886-5167, Fax: 843-886-5165, E-mail: tammi_higginbotham@tamu-commerce.edu. *Interim Dean,* Dr. Jerry Hutton, 903-886-5181.

See in-depth description on page 1129.

TEXAS A&M UNIVERSITY–CORPUS CHRISTI, Corpus Christi, TX 78412-5503

General Information State-supported, coed, comprehensive institution. *Graduate housing:* Room and/or apartments available on a first-come, first-served basis to single students; on-campus housing not available to married students. Housing application deadline: 5/1. *Research affiliation:* Center for Environmental Studies and Services, Early Childhood Development Center, Center for Coastal Studies.

GRADUATE UNITS

Graduate Programs *Degree program information:* Part-time and evening/weekend programs available. Postbaccalaureate distance learning degree programs offered (minimal on-campus study). Electronic applications accepted.

College of Arts and Humanities *Degree program information:* Part-time and evening/weekend programs available. Offers English (MA); interdisciplinary studies (MA); liberal arts (MA, MPA); psychology (MA); public administration (MPA). Electronic applications accepted.

College of Business Administration *Degree program information:* Part-time and evening/weekend programs available. Offers accounting (M Acc); management (MBA). Electronic applications accepted.

College of Education *Degree program information:* Part-time and evening/weekend programs available. Offers curriculum and instruction (MS); educational administration (MS); educational administration and supervision (MS); educational leadership (Ed D); elementary education (MS); guidance and counseling (MS); occupational education (MS); secondary education (MS); special education (MS). Electronic applications accepted.

College of Science and Technology *Degree program information:* Part-time and evening/weekend programs available. Offers biology (MS); computer science (MS); environmental sciences (MS); mariculture (MS); mathematics (MS); nursing administration (MSN); science and technology (MS, MSN). Electronic applications accepted.

TEXAS A&M UNIVERSITY–KINGSVILLE, Kingsville, TX 78363

General Information State-supported, coed, university. *Enrollment:* 426 full-time matriculated graduate/professional students (202 women), 719 part-time matriculated graduate/professional students (441 women). *Graduate faculty:* 120 full-time (21 women), 26 part-time/adjunct (7 women). Tuition, state resident: part-time $42 per hour. Tuition, nonresident: part-time $253 per hour. *Required fees:* $56 per hour. One-time fee: $46 part-time. Tuition and fees vary according to program. *Graduate housing:* Rooms and/or apartments available on a first-come, first-served basis to single students and available to married students. Housing application deadline: 8/1. *Student services:* Campus employment opportunities, campus safety program, career counseling, child daycare facilities, disabled student services, exercise/wellness program, free psychological counseling, international student services, low-cost health insurance. *Library facilities:* James C. Jernigan Library. *Online resources:* library catalog, access to other libraries' catalogs. *Collection:* 358,466 titles, 2,304 serial subscriptions, 3,224 audiovisual materials. *Research affiliation:* Gas Research Institute (engineering), U.S. Filters (engineering), Texas A&M University (biology), University of Texas Health Science Center–Houston (biology), University of Texas Health Science Center–San Antonio (biology), Institute of Biosciences and Technology (biology).

Computer facilities: 600 computers available on campus for general student use. A campuswide network can be accessed from student residence rooms and from off campus. *Web address:* http://www.tamuk.edu/.

General Application Contact: Dr. Alberto M. Olivares, Dean, College of Graduate Studies, 361-593-2808, Fax: 361-593-3412.

GRADUATE UNITS

College of Graduate Studies Students: 426 full-time (202 women), 719 part-time (441 women); includes 527 minority (27 African Americans, 11 Asian Americans or Pacific Islanders, 488 Hispanic Americans, 1 Native American), 278 international. Average age 34. *Faculty:* 120 full-time (21 women), 26 part-time/adjunct (7 women). Expenses: Contact institution. *Financial support:* Fellowships, research assistantships, teaching assistantships, career-related internships or fieldwork, Federal Work-Study, institutionally sponsored loans, scholarships/grants, tuition waivers (partial), and unspecified assistantships available. Support available to part-time students. Financial award application deadline: 5/15; financial award applicants required to submit FAFSA. In 2001, 330 master's, 9 doctorates awarded. *Degree program information:* Part-time and evening/weekend programs available. Postbaccalaureate distance learning degree programs offered (minimal on-campus study). *Application deadline:* For fall admission, 6/1; for spring admission, 11/15. Applications are processed on a rolling basis. *Application fee:* $15 ($25 for international students). *Dean,* Dr. Alberto M. Olivares, 361-593-2808, Fax: 361-593-3412.

College of Agriculture and Home Economics Students: 52 full-time (25 women), 41 part-time (27 women); includes 22 minority (1 African American, 21 Hispanic Americans), 15 international. Average age 29. *Faculty:* 9 full-time (3 women), 7 part-time/adjunct (1 woman). Expenses: Contact institution. *Financial support:* Fellowships, research assistantships, teaching assistantships, career-related internships or fieldwork and Federal Work-Study available. Support available to part-time students. Financial award application deadline: 5/15. In 2001, 21 master's, 4 doctorates awarded. *Degree program information:* Part-time and evening/weekend programs available. Offers agribusiness (MS); agricultural education (MS); agriculture and home economics (MS, PhD); animal sciences (MS); human sciences (MS); plant and soil sciences (MS); range and wildlife management (MS); wildlife science (PhD). *Application deadline:* For fall admission, 6/1; for spring admission, 11/15. Applications are processed on a rolling basis. *Application fee:* $15 ($25 for international students). *Application Contact:* Dr. Ray Broglie, Graduate Coordinator, 361-593-3711. *Dean,* Dr. Ron Rosati, 361-593-3712.

College of Arts and Sciences Students: 81 full-time (57 women), 114 part-time (81 women); includes 107 minority (6 African Americans, 1 Asian American or Pacific Islander, 100 Hispanic Americans), 16 international. Average age 33. *Faculty:* 49 full-time (8 women), 7 part-time/adjunct (1 woman). Expenses: Contact institution. *Financial support:* Fellowships, research assistantships, teaching assistantships, career-related internships or fieldwork, Federal Work-Study, institutionally sponsored loans, and tuition waivers (partial) available. Support available to part-time students. Financial award application deadline: 5/15. In 2001, 58 degrees awarded. *Degree program information:* Part-time and evening/weekend programs available. Offers applied geology (MS); art (MA, MS); arts and sciences (MA, MM, MS); biology (MS); chemistry (MS); communication (MS); English (MA, MS); gerontology (MS); history and political science (MA, MS); mathematics (MS); music education (MM); psychology (MA, MS); sociology (MA, MS); Spanish (MA). *Application deadline:* For fall admission, 6/1; for spring admission, 11/15. Applications are processed on a rolling basis. *Application fee:* $15 ($25 for international students). *Application Contact:* Director of Admissions, 361-593-2315. *Dean,* Dr. Mary Mattingly, 361-593-2761.

College of Business Administration Students: 21 full-time (14 women), 15 part-time (11 women); includes 15 minority (1 Asian American or Pacific Islander, 14 Hispanic Americans), 16 international. Average age 27. *Faculty:* 12 full-time (1 woman). Expenses: Contact institution. *Financial support:* Federal Work-Study available. Support available to part-time students. Financial award application deadline: 5/15. In 2001, 19 degrees awarded. *Degree program information:* Part-time and evening/weekend programs available. Offers business administration (MBA, MS). *Application deadline:* For fall admission, 6/1; for spring admission, 11/15. Applications are processed on a rolling basis. *Application fee:* $15 ($25 for international students). *Graduate Coordinator,* Dr. Darvin Hoffman, 361-593-3802.

College of Education Students: 130 full-time (88 women), 469 part-time (315 women); includes 358 minority (19 African Americans, 6 Asian Americans or Pacific Islanders, 332 Hispanic Americans, 1 Native American), 43 international. Average age 38. *Faculty:* 21 full-time (7 women), 16 part-time/adjunct (5 women). Expenses: Contact institution. *Financial support:* Fellowships, teaching assistantships, Federal Work-Study, institutionally sponsored loans, scholarships/grants, and tuition waivers (partial) available. Support available to part-time students. Financial award application deadline: 5/15. In 2001, 163 master's, 5 doctorates awarded. *Degree program information:* Part-time and evening/weekend programs available. Offers adult education (M Ed); bilingual education (MA, MS, Ed D); early childhood education (M Ed); education (M Ed, MA, MS, Ed D, PhD); elementary education (MA, MS); English as a second language (M Ed); guidance and counseling (MA, MS); health and kinesiology (MA, MS); higher education administration leadership (PhD); reading (MS); school administration (MA, MS, Ed D); secondary education (MA, MS); special education (M Ed); supervision (MA, MS). *Application deadline:* For fall admission, 6/1; for spring admission, 11/15. Applications are processed on a rolling basis. *Application fee:* $15 ($25 for international students). *Dean,* Dr. Fred Litton, 361-593-2801.

College of Engineering Students: 142 full-time (18 women), 80 part-time (7 women); includes 25 minority (1 African American, 3 Asian Americans or Pacific Islanders, 21 Hispanic Americans), 188 international. Average age 26. *Faculty:* 25 full-time (3 women). Expenses: Contact institution. *Financial support:* Fellowships, research assistantships, teaching assistantships, career-related internships or fieldwork, Federal Work-Study, institutionally sponsored loans, tuition waivers (partial), and unspecified assistantships available. Support available to part-time students. Financial award application deadline: 5/15. In 2001, 69 degrees awarded. *Degree program information:* Part-time and evening/weekend programs available. Offers chemical engineering (ME, MS); civil engineering (ME, MS); computer science (MS); electrical engineering (ME, MS); engineering (ME, MS); environmental engineering (ME, MS); industrial engineering (ME, MS); mechanical engineering (ME, MS); natural gas engineering (ME, MS). *Application deadline:* For fall admission, 6/1; for spring admission, 11/15. Applications are processed on a rolling basis. *Application fee:* $15 ($25 for international students). *Dean,* Dr. Phil V. Compton, 361-593-2001.

See in-depth description on page 1131.

TEXAS A&M UNIVERSITY SYSTEM HEALTH SCIENCE CENTER, College Station, Bryan, TX 77802

General Information State-supported, coed, upper-level institution. *Enrollment:* 1,032 matriculated graduate/professional students (541 women). *Enrollment by degree level:* 626 first professional, 175 master's, 93 doctoral, 78 other advanced degrees. *Graduate faculty:* 57 full-time (13 women), 48 part-time/adjunct (17 women). Tuition, state resident: part-time $84 per credit hour. Tuition, nonresident: part-time $253 per credit hour. *Required fees:* $12 per credit hour. $135 per semester. *Graduate housing:* On-campus housing not available. *Student services:* Campus employment opportunities, career counseling, exercise/wellness program, free psychological counseling, low-cost health insurance, multicultural affairs office. *Library facilities:* Baylor Hospital. *Web address:* http://tamushsc.tamu.edu/.

General Application Contact: Dr. John Quarles, Dean for Graduate School of Biomedical Sciences, 979-845-0370, Fax: 979-845-6509, E-mail: quarles@medicine.tamu.edu.

GRADUATE UNITS

Baylor College of Dentistry Offers dentistry (DDS, MD, MS, PhD, Certificate).

Graduate Division *Degree program information:* Part-time programs available. Offers biomaterials science (MS); biomedical sciences (MS, PhD); dental hygiene (MS); endodontics (MS, PhD, Certificate); health professions education (MS); oral and maxillofacial pathology (MS, PhD, Certificate); oral and maxillofacial surgery (MD, Certificate); oral biology (MS, PhD); orthodontics (MS, Certificate); pediatric dentistry (MS, Certificate); periodontics (MS, Certificate); prosthodontics (MS, Certificate).

College of Medicine Students: 276 full-time (149 women); includes 101 minority (3 African Americans, 84 Asian Americans or Pacific Islanders, 13 Hispanic Americans, 1 Native American) Average age 25. 1,806 applicants, 5% accepted, 69 enrolled. *Faculty:* 771 full-time (134 women), 64 part-time/adjunct (12 women). Expenses: Contact institution. *Financial support:* In 2001–02, 2 fellowships, 26 research assistantships were awarded. Teaching assistantships, institutionally sponsored loans and scholarships/grants also available. Financial award applicants required to submit FAFSA. Offers medicine (PhD). *Application deadline:* For fall admission, 10/15. *Application fee:* $45. *Application Contact:* Filomeno G. Maldonado, Assistant Dean of Admissions, 979-845-7743, Fax: 979-845-5533. *Interim Dean,* Dr. Roderick E. McCallum, 979-845-3431, Fax: 979-847-8663, E-mail: rmccallum@tamu.edu.

Graduate School of Biomedical Sciences Students: 60 full-time (27 women), 24 part-time (14 women); includes 17 minority (2 African Americans, 5 Asian Americans or Pacific Islanders, 9 Hispanic Americans, 1 Native American), 23 international. Average age 28. 220 applicants, 12% accepted, 15 enrolled. *Faculty:* 57 full-time (13 women), 48 part-time/adjunct (17 women). Expenses: Contact institution. *Financial support:* In 2001–02, 26 research assistantships (averaging $17,600 per year) were awarded; fellowships, teaching assistantships, institutionally sponsored loans also available. Financial award applicants required to submit FAFSA. In 2001, 3 degrees awarded. Offers human anatomy and medical neurobiology (PhD); immunology (PhD); medical biochemistry and genetics (PhD); medical microbiology and immunology (PhD); medical pharmacology and toxicology (PhD); medical physiology (PhD); microbiology (PhD); molecular biology (PhD); molecular pathology (PhD); neuroscience (PhD); pathology and laboratory medicine (PhD); virology (PhD). *Application deadline:* For fall admission, 2/1 (priority date). Applications are processed on a rolling basis. *Application fee:* $50 ($75 for international students). *Dean for Graduate School of Biomedical Sciences,* Dr. John Quarles, 979-845-0370, Fax: 979-845-6509, E-mail: quarles@medicine.tamu.edu.

Institute of Biosciences and Technology Students: 17 full-time (9 women); includes 7 minority (1 African American, 2 Asian Americans or Pacific Islanders, 3 Hispanic Americans, 1 Native American), 8 international. Average age 30. 5 applicants, 100% accepted. *Faculty:* 9 full-time (0 women), 7 part-time/adjunct (0 women). Expenses: Contact institution. *Financial support:* In 2001–02, research assistantships (averaging $18,500 per year); fellowships, unspecified assistantships also available. Offers medical sciences (PhD). Degree awarded by the Graduate School for Biomedical Sciences. *Application deadline:* For fall admission, 3/1 (priority date); for winter admission, 6/1 (priority date); for spring admission, 8/1 (priority date). Applications are processed on a rolling basis. *Application fee:* $50 ($75 for international students). *Application Contact:* Dr. Richard R. Sinden, Graduate Program Director, 713-677-7716, Fax: 713-677-7725, E-mail: gradprog@ibt.tamu.edu. *Director,* Dr. Richard Finnell, 713-677-7716, Fax: 713-677-7725, E-mail: rfinell@ibt.tamu.edu.

School of Rural Public Health Students: 43 full-time (27 women), 118 part-time (76 women); includes 63 minority (13 African Americans, 13 Asian Americans or Pacific Islanders, 37 Hispanic Americans), 1 international. Average age 32. 162 applicants, 83% accepted, 118 enrolled. *Faculty:* 16 full-time (7 women), 4 part-time/adjunct (1 woman). Expenses: Contact institution. *Financial support:* In 2001–02, research assistantships (averaging $10,800 per year) In 2001, 10 degrees awarded. *Degree program information:* Part-time programs available. Postbaccalaureate distance learning degree programs offered (no on-campus study). Offers environmental/occupational health (MPH); epidemiology/biostatistics (MPH); health policy/management (MPH); social and behavioral health (MPH). *Application deadline:* For fall admission, 8/27; for spring admission, 1/14. Applications are processed on a rolling basis. *Application fee:* $35 ($75 for international students). Electronic applications accepted. *Application Contact:* Dr. James Robinson, Professor/Special Advisor to the Dean, 409-845-2387, Fax: 409-862-8371, E-mail: jrobinson@medicine.tamu.edu. *Dean,* Dr. Ciro V. Sumaya.

TEXAS A&M UNIVERSITY–TEXARKANA, Texarkana, TX 75505-5518

General Information State-supported, coed, upper-level institution. *Enrollment:* 47 full-time matriculated graduate/professional students (30 women), 200 part-time matriculated graduate/professional students (144 women). *Enrollment by degree level:* 247 master's. *Graduate faculty:* 29 full-time (12 women), 4 part-time/adjunct (2 women). Tuition, state resident: part-time $84 per semester hour. Tuition, nonresident: part-time $295 per semester hour. *Required fees:* $13 per semester hour. *Graduate housing:* On-campus housing not available. *Student services:* Campus employment opportunities, career counseling, disabled student services, low-cost health insurance, teacher training, writing training. *Library facilities:* John F. Moss Library plus 1 other. *Online resources:* library catalog, web page. *Collection:* 325,388 titles, 164,250 serial subscriptions, 3,620 audiovisual materials.

Computer facilities: 170 computers available on campus for general student use. A campuswide network can be accessed from off campus. Internet access and online class registration are available. *Web address:* http://www.tamut.edu/.

General Application Contact: Patricia E. Black, Director of Admissions and Registrar, 903-223-3068, Fax: 903-223-3140, E-mail: pat.black@tamut.edu.

GRADUATE UNITS

Graduate School Students: 47 full-time (30 women), 200 part-time (144 women); includes 30 minority (22 African Americans, 6 Hispanic Americans, 2 Native Americans), 1 international. Average age 32. 130 applicants, 77% accepted, 92 enrolled. *Faculty:* 29 full-time (12 women), 4 part-time/adjunct (2 women). Expenses: Contact institution. *Financial support:* Career-related internships or fieldwork and scholarships/grants available. Financial award application deadline: 3/1; financial award applicants required to submit FAFSA. In 2001, 98 degrees awarded. *Degree program information:* Part-time and evening/weekend programs available. *Application deadline:* Applications are processed on a rolling basis. *Application fee:* $0 ($25 for international students). Electronic applications accepted. *Application Contact:* Patricia E. Black, Director of Admissions and Registrar, 903-223-3068, Fax: 903-223-3140, E-mail: pat.black@tamut.edu. *Vice President for Academic Affairs,* Dr. John Johnson, 903-223-3003.

College of Arts and Sciences and Education Students: 129. *Faculty:* 16 full-time (8 women), 3 part-time/adjunct (1 woman). Expenses: Contact institution. *Financial support:* Career-related internships or fieldwork and scholarships/grants available. Financial award applicants required to submit FAFSA. In 2001, 37 degrees awarded. *Degree program information:* Part-time and evening/weekend programs available. Offers adult education (MS); educational administration (M Ed); elementary education (M Ed, MA, MS); interdisciplinary studies (MA, MS); secondary education (M Ed, MA, MS); special education (M Ed, MA, MS). *Application deadline:* For fall admission, 7/15 (priority date); for spring admission, 12/1 (priority date). Applications are processed on a rolling basis. *Application fee:* $0 ($25 for international students). Electronic applications accepted. *Application Contact:* Patricia E. Black, Director of Admissions and Registrar, 903-223-3068, Fax: 903-223-3140, E-mail: pat.black@tamut.edu. *Dean,* Dr. Gene Mueller, 903-223-3136, E-mail: gene.mueller@tamut.edu.

College of Business and Behavioral Sciences Students: 118. Average age 32. *Faculty:* 13 full-time (4 women), 1 (woman) part-time/adjunct. Expenses: Contact institution. *Financial support:* Career-related internships or fieldwork and scholarships/grants available. Financial award application deadline: 3/1; financial award applicants required to submit FAFSA. In 2001, 33 degrees awarded. *Degree program information:* Part-time and evening/weekend programs available. Offers accounting (MSA); business administration (MBA, MS); counseling psychology (MS). *Application deadline:* For fall admission, 7/15 (priority date); for spring admission, 12/1 (priority date). Applications are processed on a rolling basis. *Application fee:* $0 ($25 for international students). Electronic applications accepted. *Application Contact:* Patricia E. Black, Director of Admissions and Registrar, 903-223-3068, Fax: 903-223-3140, E-mail: pat.black@tamut.edu. *Dean,* Dr. Alfred Ntoko, 903-223-3106, E-mail: alfred.ntoko@tamut.edu.

TEXAS CHIROPRACTIC COLLEGE, Pasadena, TX 77505-1699

General Information Independent, coed, upper-level institution. *Enrollment:* 397 full-time matriculated graduate/professional students (116 women), 1 part-time matriculated graduate/professional student. *Enrollment by degree level:* 398 first professional. *Graduate faculty:* 33 full-time (10 women), 2 part-time/adjunct (0 women). *Tuition:* Full-time $15,750; part-time $438 per hour. *Required fees:* $255; $85 per trimester. One-time fee: $125. *Graduate housing:* On-campus housing not available. *Student services:* Campus employment opportunities, career counseling, exercise/wellness program, free psychological counseling, international student services, low-cost health insurance. *Library facilities:* Mae Hilty Memorial Library. *Collection:* 10,500 titles, 160 serial subscriptions. *Web address:* http://www.txchiro.edu/.

General Application Contact: Dr. Alvin Richard, Director of Recruitment, 281-998-6016, Fax: 281-991-4871, E-mail: rcooper@txchiro.edu.

GRADUATE UNITS

Professional Program Students: 397 full-time (116 women), 1 part-time; includes 144 minority (42 African Americans, 45 Asian Americans or Pacific Islanders, 56 Hispanic Americans, 1 Native American), 6 international. Average age 30. 100 applicants, 54% accepted. *Faculty:* 33 full-time (10 women), 2 part-time/adjunct (0 women). Expenses: Contact institution. *Financial support:* Career-related internships or fieldwork, Federal Work-Study, institutionally sponsored loans, and tuition waivers (partial) available. Support available to part-time students. Financial award application deadline: 4/15; financial award applicants required to submit FAFSA. In 2001, 109 degrees awarded. *Degree program information:* Part-time programs available. Offers chiropractic (DC). *Application deadline:* For fall admission, 9/1 (priority date); for spring admission, 12/1. Applications are processed on a rolling basis. *Application fee:* $50. *President,* Dr. Shelby Elliott, 281-487-1170, Fax: 281-487-0329, E-mail: selliott@txchiro.edu.

TEXAS CHRISTIAN UNIVERSITY, Fort Worth, TX 76129-0002

General Information Independent-religious, coed, university. CGS member. *Enrollment:* 500 full-time matriculated graduate/professional students (243 women), 669 part-time matriculated graduate/professional students (381 women). *Enrollment by degree level:* 170 first professional, 786 master's, 169 doctoral, 44 other advanced degrees. *Graduate faculty:* 288. *Tuition:* Full-time $8,190; part-time $455 per credit hour. *Required fees:* $1,760. *Graduate housing:* Rooms and/or apartments available to single and married students. *Student services:* Campus employment opportunities, campus safety program, career counseling, disabled student services, exercise/wellness program, free psychological counseling, international student services, low-cost health insurance, multicultural affairs office, teacher training. *Library facilities:* Mary Couts Burnett Library. *Online resources:* library catalog, web page, access to other libraries' catalogs. *Collection:* 1.3 million titles, 4,734 serial subscriptions, 55,702 audiovisual materials. *Research affiliation:* Intel Corporation (hands-on science projects), Technispan, LLC (microfabricated gas chromatograph), Sid Richardson Carbon Company (structures of carbon black), Presby Corporation.

Computer facilities: 4,225 computers available on campus for general student use. A campuswide network can be accessed from student residence rooms and from off campus. Internet access and online class registration are available. *Web address:* http://www.tcu.edu/.

GRADUATE UNITS

AddRan College of Humanities and Social Sciences Students: 23 full-time (13 women), 62 part-time (38 women); includes 7 minority (1 African American, 1 Asian American or Pacific Islander, 5 Hispanic Americans), 7 international. Expenses: Contact institution. *Financial support:* Unspecified assistantships available. Financial award application deadline: 3/1. *Degree program information:* Part-time and evening/weekend programs available. Offers economics (MA); English (MA, PhD); history (MA, PhD); humanities and social sciences (MA, PhD). *Application deadline:* For fall admission, 3/1; for spring admission, 12/1. Applications are processed on a rolling basis. *Application fee:* $0. *Dean,* Dr. Mary Volcansek, 817-257-7160.

Brite Divinity School Students: 142 full-time (67 women), 113 part-time (57 women); includes 34 minority (26 African Americans, 2 Asian Americans or Pacific Islanders, 2 Hispanic Americans, 4 Native Americans), 6 international. 99 applicants, 88% accepted. Expenses: Contact institution. *Financial support:* Career-related internships or fieldwork and unspecified assistantships available. Financial award application deadline: 3/1. In 2001, 30 first professional degrees, 10 master's, 3 doctorates awarded. *Degree program information:* Part-time and evening/weekend programs available. Offers Biblical interpretation (PhD); Christian service (MACS); divinity (M Div); homiletics (D Min); pastoral theology and pastoral counseling (D Min, PhD); theological studies (MTS, CTS); theology (Th M). *Application deadline:* For fall admission, 3/1; for spring admission, 12/1. Applications are processed on a rolling basis. *Application fee:* $0. *Application Contact:* Dr. J. Stanley Hagadone, Director of Admissions, 817-921-7804, E-mail: j.hagadone@tcu.edu. *President,* Dr. Leo Perdue, 817-257-7575, E-mail: l.perdue@tcu.edu.

College of Communication Students: 21 full-time (18 women), 18 part-time (9 women); includes 9 minority (5 African Americans, 1 Asian American or Pacific Islander, 3 Hispanic Americans), 5 international. Expenses: Contact institution. *Financial support:* Unspecified assistantships available. Financial award application deadline: 3/1. In 2001, 40 degrees awarded. *Degree program information:* Part-time and evening/weekend programs available. Offers advertising/public relations (MS); communication (MA, MS); journalism and mass communication (MS); media arts (MA); speech communication (MS). *Application deadline:* For fall admission, 3/1; for spring admission, 12/1. Applications are processed on a rolling basis. *Application fee:* $0. *Application Contact:* Dr. John Burton, Director of Graduate Studies, 817-257-7603, Fax: 817-257-7703, E-mail: j.burton@tcu.edu. *Dean,* Dr. William T. Slater, 817-257-5918, E-mail: w.slater@tcu.edu.

College of Fine Arts Students: 26 full-time (17 women), 15 part-time (9 women); includes 5 minority (2 African Americans, 2 Hispanic Americans, 1 Native American), 17 international. Expenses: Contact institution. *Financial support:* Application deadline: 3/1. *Degree program information:* Part-time and evening/weekend programs available. Offers art history (MA); ballet (MFA); ballet/modern dance (MFA); fine arts (M Mus, MA, MFA, MM Ed); modern dance (MFA); studio art (MFA). *Application deadline:* For fall admission, 3/1; for spring admission, 12/1. Applications are processed on a rolling basis. *Application fee:* $0. *Dean,* Dr. Scott Sullivan, 817-257-7601.

School of Music Students: 14 full-time (7 women), 15 part-time (9 women); includes 1 minority (Hispanic American), 16 international. Expenses: Contact institution. *Financial support:* Unspecified assistantships available. Financial award application deadline: 3/1. In 2001, 15 degrees awarded. *Degree program information:* Part-time and evening/weekend programs available. Offers conducting (M Mus); instrumental performance (M Mus); music education (MM Ed); musicology (M Mus); piano pedagogy (M Mus); theory/composition (M Mus); vocal performance (M Mus). *Application deadline:* For fall admission, 3/1; for spring admission, 12/1. Applications are processed on a rolling basis. *Application fee:* $0. *Application Contact:* Dr. Joseph Butler, Associate Dean, College of Fine Arts, E-mail: j.butler@tcu.edu. *Director,* Dr. Richard Gipson, 817-257-7602.

College of Health and Human Sciences Students: 22 full-time (13 women), 33 part-time (29 women); includes 13 minority (3 African Americans, 1 Asian American or Pacific Islander, 8 Hispanic Americans, 1 Native American), 4 international. Expenses: Contact institution. *Financial support:* Application deadline: 3/1. *Degree program information:* Part-time and evening/weekend programs available. Offers health and human sciences (MS, MSN); kinesiology (MS); nursing (MSN); speech-language pathology (MS). *Application deadline:* For fall admission, 3/1; for spring admission, 12/1. Applications are processed on a rolling basis. *Application fee:* $0. *Dean,* Dr. Rhonda Keen-Payne, 817-257-7621.

College of Science and Engineering Students: 28 full-time (20 women), 66 part-time (33 women); includes 9 minority (2 African Americans, 2 Asian Americans or Pacific Islanders, 4 Hispanic Americans, 1 Native American), 24 international. Expenses: Contact institution. *Financial support:* Fellowships, teaching assistantships, unspecified assistantships available. Financial award application deadline: 3/1. In 2001, 29 master's, 30 doctorates awarded. *Degree program information:* Part-time and evening/weekend programs available. Offers biology (MA, MS); chemistry (MA, MS, PhD); environmental sciences (MS); geology (MS); mathematics (MAT); physics (MA, MS, PhD); psychology (MA, MS, PhD); science and engineering (MA, MAT, MS, PhD). *Application deadline:* For fall admission, 3/1; for spring admission, 12/1. Applications are processed on a rolling basis. *Application fee:* $0. *Dean,* Dr. Michael McCracken, 817-257-7727, E-mail: m.mccracken@tcu.edu.

Graduate Studies and Research Students: 15 full-time (10 women), 82 part-time (53 women); includes 21 minority (8 African Americans, 5 Asian Americans or Pacific Islanders, 7 Hispanic Americans, 1 Native American), 5 international. Expenses: Contact institution. *Financial support:* Application deadline: 3/1. In 2001, 34 degrees awarded. *Degree program information:*

Texas Christian University (continued)

Part-time and evening/weekend programs available. Offers liberal arts (MLA). *Application deadline:* For fall admission, 3/1; for spring admission, 12/1. Applications are processed on a rolling basis. *Application fee:* $0. *Application Contact:* Information Contact, 817-257-6290, E-mail: d.coerver@tcu.edu. *Director*, Dr. Don Coerver, 817-257-6290, E-mail: d.coerver@tcu.edu.

School of Education Students: 36 full-time (29 women), 159 part-time (124 women); includes 46 minority (28 African Americans, 16 Hispanic Americans, 2 Native Americans), 10 international. *Faculty:* 21. Expenses: Contact institution. *Financial support:* Career-related internships or fieldwork and unspecified assistantships available. Financial award application deadline: 3/1. In 2001, 55 degrees awarded. *Degree program information:* Part-time and evening/weekend programs available. Offers counseling (M Ed); education (M Ed, Ed D, Certificate); education leadership (Ed D); educational administration (M Ed); educational foundations (M Ed); elementary education (M Ed, Certificate); secondary education (M Ed, Certificate); special education (M Ed). *Application deadline:* For fall admission, 3/1; for spring admission, 12/1. Applications are processed on a rolling basis. *Application fee:* $0. *Application Contact:* Dr. Sherrie Reynolds, Director of Graduate Studies, 817-257-7661, E-mail: s.reynolds@tcu.edu. *Dean*, Dr. Sam Deitz, 817-257-7663, E-mail: s.deitz@tcu.edu.

TEXAS COLLEGE OF TRADITIONAL CHINESE MEDICINE, Austin, TX 78704

General Information Private, coed, graduate-only institution.

GRADUATE UNITS

Program in Oriental Medicine *Degree program information:* Part-time and evening/weekend programs available. Offers Oriental medicine (MSOM). Electronic applications accepted.

TEXAS SOUTHERN UNIVERSITY, Houston, TX 77004-4584

General Information State-supported, coed, university. CGS member. *Enrollment:* 971 full-time matriculated graduate/professional students (517 women), 427 part-time matriculated graduate/professional students (285 women). *Enrollment by degree level:* 750 first professional, 634 master's, 14 doctoral. *Graduate faculty:* 128 full-time (48 women), 43 part-time/adjunct (14 women). Tuition, state resident: full-time $1,188. Tuition, nonresident: full-time $4,644. *Required fees:* $900. Tuition and fees vary according to degree level. *Graduate housing:* Room and/or apartments available to single students; on-campus housing not available to married students. Typical cost: $4,116 (including board). Housing application deadline: 7/15. *Student services:* Career counseling, free psychological counseling. *Library facilities:* Robert J. Terry Library plus 2 others. *Online resources:* library catalog, access to other libraries' catalogs. *Collection:* 473,499 titles, 1,715 serial subscriptions. *Research affiliation:* Houston Advanced Research Center, Texas Space Grant Consortium, Lockheed Missile Company, Inc.

Computer facilities: 410 computers available on campus for general student use. A campuswide network can be accessed. Internet access is available. *Web address:* http://www.tsu.edu/.

General Application Contact: Dr. Joseph Jones, Dean of the Graduate School, 713-313-7232, Fax: 713-639-1876.

GRADUATE UNITS

College of Pharmacy and Health Sciences Students: 110 full-time (67 women), 28 part-time (13 women); includes 122 minority (89 African Americans, 19 Asian Americans or Pacific Islanders, 13 Hispanic Americans, 1 Native American), 8 international. Average age 28. 260 applicants, 42% accepted, 109 enrolled. *Faculty:* 13 full-time (4 women), 3 part-time/adjunct (1 woman). Expenses: Contact institution. *Financial support:* Fellowships, teaching assistantships, career-related internships or fieldwork, scholarships/grants, and tuition waivers (partial) available. In 2001, 92 degrees awarded. Postbaccalaureate distance learning degree programs offered. Offers pharmacy and health sciences (Pharm D). *Application deadline:* For fall admission, 2/15. *Application fee:* $50 ($75 for international students). *Application Contact:* LaJoy Kay, Head, 713-313-1880. *Dean*, Dr. Barbara Hayes, 713-313-7164, Fax: 713-313-1091.

Graduate School Students: 249 full-time (145 women), 399 part-time (272 women); includes 576 minority (542 African Americans, 16 Asian Americans or Pacific Islanders, 18 Hispanic Americans), 38 international. 517 applicants, 82% accepted, 172 enrolled. *Faculty:* 80 full-time (29 women), 24 part-time/adjunct (9 women). Expenses: Contact institution. *Financial support:* Fellowships, research assistantships, teaching assistantships, career-related internships or fieldwork, Federal Work-Study, institutionally sponsored loans, scholarships/grants, tuition waivers (partial), and unspecified assistantships available. In 2001, 165 master's, 16 doctorates awarded. *Degree program information:* Part-time and evening/weekend programs available. *Application deadline:* For fall admission, 7/15 (priority date). Applications are processed on a rolling basis. *Application fee:* $35 ($75 for international students). *Dean*, Dr. Joseph Jones, 713-313-7232, Fax: 713-639-1876.

College of Education Students: 100 full-time (68 women), 237 part-time (176 women); includes 298 minority (281 African Americans, 4 Asian Americans or Pacific Islanders, 13 Hispanic Americans), 8 international. *Faculty:* 19 full-time (7 women), 4 part-time/adjunct (3 women). Expenses: Contact institution. *Financial support:* Fellowships, research assistantships, teaching assistantships, career-related internships or fieldwork, Federal Work-Study, and institutionally sponsored loans available. Financial award application deadline: 5/1. In 2001, 60 master's, 14 doctorates awarded. *Degree program information:* Part-time and evening/weekend programs available. Offers bilingual education (M Ed); business education (M Ed); counseling (M Ed, Ed D); counseling education (Ed D); curriculum, instruction, and urban education (Ed D); early childhood education (M Ed); education (M Ed, MS, Ed D); educational administration (M Ed, Ed D); elementary education (M Ed); health education (MS); higher education administration (Ed D); mid-management superintending (Ed D); physical education (MS); reading education (M Ed); research education and certification (Ed D); research education and education (Ed D); secondary education (M Ed); special education (M Ed). *Application deadline:* For fall admission, 7/15 (priority date). Applications are processed on a rolling basis. *Application fee:* $35 ($75 for international students). *Dean*, Dr. Jay Cummings, 713-313-7343.

College of Liberal Arts and Behavioral Sciences Students: 51 full-time (31 women), 54 part-time (42 women). Average age 32. 26 applicants, 69% accepted. *Faculty:* 23 full-time (13 women), 3 part-time/adjunct (all women). Expenses: Contact institution. *Financial support:* Fellowships, research assistantships, teaching assistantships, career-related internships or fieldwork, Federal Work-Study, and institutionally sponsored loans available. Financial award application deadline: 5/1. In 2001, 35 degrees awarded. *Degree program information:* Part-time and evening/weekend programs available. Offers city planning (MCP); English (MA, MS); history (MA); human services and consumer sciences (MS); humanities, fine arts and social sciences (MA, MCP, MPA, MS); journalism (MA); music (MA); public administration (MPA); sociology (MA); speech communications (MA); telecommunications (MA). *Application deadline:* For fall admission, 7/15 (priority date). Applications are processed on a rolling basis. *Application fee:* $35 ($75 for international students). *Acting Dean*, Dr. Merline Pitre, 713-313-7210, E-mail: pitre_mx@tsu.edu.

Jesse H. Jones School of Business Students: 33 full-time (19 women), 29 part-time (17 women); includes 53 minority (46 African Americans, 3 Asian Americans or Pacific Islanders, 4 Hispanic Americans), 8 international. Average age 30. 114 applicants, 51% accepted. *Faculty:* 11 full-time (4 women), 5 part-time/adjunct (1 woman). Expenses: Contact institution. *Financial support:* In 2001–02, 6 research assistantships were awarded Financial award application deadline: 5/1. In 2001, 42 degrees awarded. *Degree program information:* Part-time and evening/weekend programs available. Offers business (MBA); business administration (MBA). *Application deadline:* For fall admission, 7/15 (priority date); for spring admission, 11/15. Applications are processed on a rolling basis. *Application fee:* $35 ($75 for international students). *Application Contact:* Bobbie J. Richardson, Executive Secretary, 713-313-7309, Fax: 713-313-7705, E-mail: richardson_bj@tsu.edu. *Dean*, Dr. Joseph Boyd, 713-313-7215, Fax: 713-313-7701.

School of Science and Technology Students: 45 full-time (15 women), 53 part-time (21 women); includes 80 minority (72 African Americans, 7 Asian Americans or Pacific Islanders, 1 Hispanic American), 16 international. Average age 26. *Faculty:* 20 full-time (3 women), 12 part-time/adjunct (2 women). Expenses: Contact institution. *Financial support:* Fellowships, research assistantships, teaching assistantships, career-related internships or fieldwork, Federal Work-Study, institutionally sponsored loans, scholarships/grants, tuition waivers (partial), and unspecified assistantships available. Financial award application deadline: 5/1. In 2001, 19 master's, 2 doctorates awarded. *Degree program information:* Part-time and evening/weekend programs available. Offers biology (MS); chemistry (MS); constructional technology (M Ed); educational technology (M Ed); environmental toxicology (MS, PhD); mathematics (MA, MS); science and technology (M Ed, MA, MS, PhD); transportation (MS). *Application deadline:* For fall admission, 7/15 (priority date). Applications are processed on a rolling basis. *Application fee:* $35 ($75 for international students). *Dean*, Dr. Daniel Davis, 713-313-7007, E-mail: davis_dx@tsu.edu.

Thurgood Marshall School of Law Students: 612 full-time (305 women); includes 513 minority (391 African Americans, 19 Asian Americans or Pacific Islanders, 101 Hispanic Americans, 2 Native Americans), 1 international. 1,213 applicants, 44% accepted, 250 enrolled. *Faculty:* 35 full-time (15 women), 16 part-time/adjunct (4 women). Expenses: Contact institution. *Financial support:* In 2001–02, 612 students received support, including 24 research assistantships (averaging $4,500 per year); fellowships, career-related internships or fieldwork, Federal Work-Study, institutionally sponsored loans, scholarships/grants, and tuition waivers (partial) also available. Financial award application deadline: 5/1; financial award applicants required to submit FAFSA. In 2001, 176 degrees awarded. Offers law (JD). *Application deadline:* For fall admission, 4/1 (priority date). Applications are processed on a rolling basis. *Application fee:* $50. Electronic applications accepted. *Application Contact:* Edward Rene, Director of Admissions, 713-313-7115 Ext. 1004, Fax: 713-313-1049, E-mail: erene@tsulaw.edu. *Dean*, John C. Brittain, 713-313-1076, Fax: 713-313-1049, E-mail: jbrittain@tsulaw.edu.

See in-depth description on page 1133.

TEXAS TECH UNIVERSITY, Lubbock, TX 79409

General Information State-supported, coed, university. CGS member. *Enrollment:* 2,913 full-time matriculated graduate/professional students (1,244 women), 1,391 part-time matriculated graduate/professional students (770 women). *Enrollment by degree level:* 663 first professional, 1,844 master's, 1,064 doctoral, 733 other advanced degrees. *Graduate faculty:* 692 full-time (173 women), 49 part-time/adjunct (15 women). Tuition, state resident: full-time $1,926; part-time $107 per credit hour. Tuition, nonresident: full-time $5,724; part-time $318 per credit hour. *Required fees:* $779; $737 per year. Tuition and fees vary according to course level, course load and program. *Graduate housing:* Room and/or apartments available on a first-come, first-served basis to single students; on-campus housing not available to married students. Typical cost: $2,887 per year ($5,337 including board). Housing application deadline: 6/1. *Student services:* Campus employment opportunities, campus safety program, career counseling, child daycare facilities, disabled student services, exercise/wellness program, free psychological counseling, international student services, low-cost health insurance, multicultural affairs office, teacher training, writing training. *Library facilities:* Texas Tech Library plus 3 others. *Online resources:* library catalog, web page, access to other libraries' catalogs. *Collection:* 4.2 million titles, 27,054 serial subscriptions, 80,953 audiovisual materials. *Research affiliation:* Supachill USA (cryobiology).

Computer facilities: 2,000 computers available on campus for general student use. A campuswide network can be accessed from student residence rooms and from off campus. Internet access and online class registration are available. *Web address:* http://www.ttu.edu/.

General Application Contact: Judith S. Toyama, Assistant Dean of Graduate Admissions and Recruitment, 806-742-2787, Fax: 806-742-4038, E-mail: gradschool@ttu.edu.

GRADUATE UNITS

Graduate School Students: 2,257 full-time (944 women), 1,384 part-time (767 women); includes 434 minority (85 African Americans, 61 Asian Americans or Pacific Islanders, 271 Hispanic Americans, 17 Native Americans), 744 international. Average age 32. 2,767 applicants, 51% accepted, 873 enrolled. *Faculty:* 692 full-time (173 women), 49 part-time/adjunct (15 women). Expenses: Contact institution. *Financial support:* In 2001–02, 2,505 students received support, including 200 fellowships with partial tuition reimbursements available (averaging $3,200 per year), 661 research assistantships with partial tuition reimbursements available (averaging $9,906 per year), 760 teaching assistantships with partial tuition reimbursements available (averaging $10,448 per year); career-related internships or fieldwork, Federal Work-Study, institutionally sponsored loans, and scholarships/grants also available. Support available to part-time students. Financial award application deadline: 5/1; financial award applicants required to submit FAFSA. In 2001, 775 master's, 138 doctorates, 201 other advanced degrees awarded. *Degree program information:* Part-time and evening/weekend programs available. Postbaccalaureate distance learning degree programs offered. Offers art (MFA); art education (MAE); composition (DMA); conducting (DMA); fine arts (MFA, PhD); heritage management (MA); interdisciplinary studies (MA, MS); museum science (MA); music education (MM Ed); music history and literature (MM); music performance (MM); music theory (MM); performance (DMA); piano pedagogy (DMA); theatre arts (MA, MFA); visual and performing arts (MA, MAE, MFA, MM, MM Ed, DMA, PhD). *Application deadline:* Applications are processed on a rolling basis. *Application fee:* $25 ($50 for international students). Electronic applications accepted. *Application Contact:* Rosa Gallegos, Coordinator of Graduate School Recruitment, 806-742-2787, Fax: 806-742-4038, E-mail: gradschool@ttu.edu. *Dean*, Dr. Ronald Anderson, 806-742-2787, Fax: 806-742-4038, E-mail: gradschool@hu.edu.

College of Agricultural Sciences and Natural Resources Students: 147 full-time (38 women), 63 part-time (23 women); includes 6 minority (1 Asian American or Pacific Islander, 4 Hispanic Americans, 1 Native American), 37 international. Average age 30. 92 applicants, 54% accepted, 32 enrolled. *Faculty:* 58 full-time (6 women), 4 part-time/adjunct (1 woman). Expenses: Contact institution. *Financial support:* In 2001–02, 123 research assistantships with partial tuition reimbursements (averaging $9,757 per year), 15 teaching assistantships with partial tuition reimbursements (averaging $10,496 per year) were awarded. Fellowships, career-related internships or fieldwork, Federal Work-Study, and institutionally sponsored loans also available. Support available to part-time students. Financial award application deadline: 5/1; financial award applicants required to submit FAFSA. In 2001, 35 master's, 15 doctorates awarded. *Degree program information:* Part-time and evening/weekend programs available. Offers agricultural and applied economics (MS, PhD); agricultural education (MS, Ed D); agricultural sciences and natural resources (M Agr, MLA, MS, Ed D, PhD); agriculture (M Agr); agronomy (PhD); animal science (MS, PhD); crop science (MS); entomology (MS); fishery science (MS, PhD); food technology (MS); horticulture (MS); landscape architecture (MLA); range science (MS, PhD); soil science (MS); wildlife science (MS, PhD). *Application deadline:* Applications are processed on a rolling basis. *Application fee:* $25 ($50 for international students). Electronic applications accepted. *Application Contact:* Graduate Adviser, 806-742-2808, Fax: 806-742-2836. *Dean*, Dr. John R. Abernathy, 806-742-2808, Fax: 806-742-2836.

College of Architecture Students: 121 full-time (26 women), 19 part-time (7 women); includes 26 minority (2 African Americans, 3 Asian Americans or Pacific Islanders, 20 Hispanic Americans, 1 Native American), 9 international. Average age 26. 58 applicants, 67% accepted, 30 enrolled. *Faculty:* 19 full-time (4 women), 2 part-time/adjunct (1 woman). Expenses: Contact institution. *Financial support:* In 2001–02, 56 students received support, including 20 research assistantships with partial tuition reimbursements available (averaging $8,805 per year), 2 teaching assistantships with partial tuition reimbursements available (averaging $12,000 per year); fellowships, career-related internships or fieldwork, Federal Work-Study, and institutionally sponsored loans also available. Support available to part-time students. Financial award application deadline: 5/1; financial award applicants required to submit FAFSA. In 2001, 52 master's, 2 doctorates awarded. *Degree program information:* Part-time programs available. Offers architecture (M Arch, MS, PhD); land-use planning, management, and design (PhD). *Application deadline:* Applications are processed on a rolling basis. *Application fee:* $25 ($50 for international students). Electronic applications accepted. *Dean*, Dr. Andrew Vernooy, 806-742-3136, Fax: 806-742-2855.

College of Arts and Sciences Students: 800 full-time (388 women), 294 part-time (147 women); includes 124 minority (23 African Americans, 19 Asian Americans or Pacific

Islanders, 78 Hispanic Americans, 4 Native Americans), 207 international. Average age 31. 638 applicants, 56% accepted, 214 enrolled. *Faculty:* 344 full-time (88 women), 20 part-time/adjunct (6 women). Expenses: Contact institution. *Financial support:* In 2001–02, 651 students received support, including 125 research assistantships with partial tuition reimbursements available (averaging $11,147 per year), 574 teaching assistantships with partial tuition reimbursements available (averaging $10,770 per year); fellowships, career-related internships or fieldwork, Federal Work-Study, and institutionally sponsored loans also available. Support available to part-time students. Financial award application deadline: 5/1; financial award applicants required to submit FAFSA. In 2001, 232 master's, 66 doctorates awarded. *Degree program information:* Part-time and evening/weekend programs available. Offers anthropology (MA); applied linguistics (MA); applied physics (MS, PhD); arts and sciences (MA, MPA, MS, PhD); atmospheric sciences (MS); biology (MS, PhD); biotechnology (MS); chemistry (MS, PhD); classics (MA); clinical psychology (PhD); communication studies (MA); counseling psychology (PhD); economics (MA, PhD); English (MA, PhD); environmental toxicology (MS, PhD); exercise physiology (PhD); general experimental (MA, PhD); geoscience (MS, PhD); German (MA); history (MA, PhD); mass communications (MA); mathematics (MA, MS, PhD); microbiology (MS); philosophy (MA); physical education (MS); physics (MS, PhD); political science (MA, PhD); public administration (MPA); Romance languages-French (MA); Romance languages-Spanish (MA); sociology (MA); Spanish (PhD); sports health (MS); statistics (MS); technical communication (MA); technical communication and rhetoric (PhD); zoology (MS, PhD). *Application deadline:* Applications are processed on a rolling basis. *Application fee:* $25 ($50 for international students). Electronic applications accepted. *Dean,* Dr. Jane L. Winer, 806-742-3833, Fax: 806-742-3893.

College of Education Students: 255 full-time (178 women), 363 part-time (225 women); includes 115 minority (23 African Americans, 8 Asian Americans or Pacific Islanders, 82 Hispanic Americans, 2 Native Americans), 27 international. Average age 35. 260 applicants, 77% accepted, 99 enrolled. *Faculty:* 39 full-time (19 women), 4 part-time/adjunct (2 women). Expenses: Contact institution. *Financial support:* In 2001–02, 397 students received support, including 33 research assistantships with partial tuition reimbursements available (averaging $9,465 per year), 8 teaching assistantships with partial tuition reimbursements available (averaging $9,450 per year); fellowships, career-related internships or fieldwork, Federal Work-Study, and institutionally sponsored loans also available. Support available to part-time students. Financial award application deadline: 5/1; financial award applicants required to submit FAFSA. In 2001, 104 master's, 22 doctorates awarded. *Degree program information:* Part-time programs available. Offers bilingual education (M Ed); business education (M Ed); counselor (Certificate); counselor education (M Ed, Ed D); curriculum and instruction (M Ed, Ed D); early childhood education (M Ed); education (M Ed, Ed D, Certificate); education diagnostician (Certificate); educational leadership (M Ed, Ed D); educational psychology (M Ed, Ed D); elementary education (M Ed); gifted and talented (Certificate); higher education (M Ed, Ed D); information processing technologist (Certificate); instructional technology (M Ed, Ed D); instructional technology-distance education (M Ed); language and literacy education (M Ed); principal (Certificate); secondary education (M Ed); special education (M Ed, Ed D); special education counselor (Certificate); superintendent (Certificate); supervision (M Ed); visually handicapped (Certificate). *Application deadline:* Applications are processed on a rolling basis. *Application fee:* $25 ($50 for international students). Electronic applications accepted. *Dean,* Dr. Gerald Skoog, 806-742-2377, Fax: 806-742-2179.

College of Engineering Students: 341 full-time (53 women), 88 part-time (17 women); includes 20 minority (2 African Americans, 3 Asian Americans or Pacific Islanders, 14 Hispanic Americans, 1 Native American), 284 international. Average age 28. 980 applicants, 33% accepted, 121 enrolled. *Faculty:* 91 full-time (8 women), 4 part-time/adjunct (0 women). Expenses: Contact institution. *Financial support:* In 2001–02, 188 research assistantships with partial tuition reimbursements (averaging $10,087 per year), 36 teaching assistantships with partial tuition reimbursements (averaging $10,027 per year) were awarded. Fellowships, career-related internships or fieldwork, Federal Work-Study, and institutionally sponsored loans also available. Support available to part-time students. Financial award application deadline: 5/1; financial award applicants required to submit FAFSA. In 2001, 107 master's, 15 doctorates awarded. *Degree program information:* Part-time programs available. Offers chemical engineering (MS Ch E, PhD); civil engineering (MSCE, PhD); computer science (MS, PhD); electrical and computer engineering (MSEE, PhD); engineering (M Engr, M Env E, MS, MS Ch E, MS Pet E, MSCE, MSEE, MSETM, MSIE, MSME, MSSEM, PhD); environmental engineering (M Env E); environmental technology and management (MSETM); industrial engineering (MSIE, PhD); mechanical engineering (MSME, PhD); petroleum engineering (MS Pet E, PhD); software engineering (MS); systems and engineering management (MSSEM). *Application deadline:* Applications are processed on a rolling basis. *Application fee:* $25 ($50 for international students). Electronic applications accepted. *Application Contact:* Graduate Adviser, 806-742-3451, Fax: 806-742-3493. *Dean,* Dr. William M. Marcy, 806-742-3451, Fax: 806-742-3493.

College of Human Sciences Students: 124 full-time (90 women), 63 part-time (42 women); includes 17 minority (9 African Americans, 1 Asian American or Pacific Islander, 7 Hispanic Americans), 46 international. Average age 32. 102 applicants, 65% accepted, 31 enrolled. *Faculty:* 49 full-time (29 women), 4 part-time/adjunct (all women). Expenses: Contact institution. *Financial support:* In 2001–02, 132 students received support, including 56 research assistantships with partial tuition reimbursements available (averaging $10,045 per year), 48 teaching assistantships with partial tuition reimbursements available (averaging $9,707 per year); career-related internships or fieldwork, Federal Work-Study, institutionally sponsored loans, and scholarships/grants also available. Support available to part-time students. Financial award application deadline: 5/1; financial award applicants required to submit FAFSA. In 2001, 35 master's, 9 doctorates awarded. *Degree program information:* Part-time programs available. Postbaccalaureate distance learning degree programs offered (minimal on-campus study). Offers environmental design (MS); environmental design and consumer economics (PhD); family and consumer sciences education (MS, PhD); family financial planing (MS); food and nutrition (MS, PhD); human development and family studies (MS, PhD); human sciences (MS, PhD); marriage and family therapy (MS, PhD); restaurant, hotel, and institutional management (MS). *Application deadline:* Applications are processed on a rolling basis. *Application fee:* $25 ($50 for international students). Electronic applications accepted. *Application Contact:* Dr. Steven M. Harris, Associate Dean, 806-742-3031, Fax: 806-742-1849, E-mail: sharris@HS.ttu.edu. *Interim Dean,* Linda Hoover, 806-742-3031, Fax: 806-742-1849.

Jerry S. Rawls College of Business Administration Students: 353 full-time (115 women), 58 part-time (25 women); includes 38 minority (7 African Americans, 15 Asian Americans or Pacific Islanders, 15 Hispanic Americans, 1 Native American), 109 international. Average age 30. 367 applicants, 47% accepted, 102 enrolled. *Faculty:* 64 full-time (4 women). Expenses: Contact institution. *Financial support:* In 2001–02, 130 students received support, including 46 research assistantships (averaging $5,500 per year), 34 teaching assistantships (averaging $14,816 per year); fellowships, career-related internships or fieldwork, Federal Work-Study, scholarships/grants, health care benefits, and unspecified assistantships also available. Financial award applicants required to submit FAFSA. In 2001, 180 master's, 9 doctorates awarded. *Degree program information:* Part-time and evening/weekend programs available. Offers accounting (PhD); accounting information systems (MS Acct); accounting information systems assurance (MS Acct); accounting information systems design control (MS Acct); agricultural business (MBA); audit/financial reporting (MS Acct); business administration (MBA, MS, MS Acct, MSA, MSBA, PhD, Certificate); business statistics (MSBA, PhD); controllership (MS Acct); e-business (MBA); entrepreneurial family studies (MBA); entrepreneurial skills (MBA); finance (MBA); general business (MBA); global entrepreneurship (MBA); health operations management controllership (MSA); health organization management (MBA, Certificate); health organization management/controllership (MSA); high performance management (MBA); home health organization management (MS); international business (MBA); management (PhD); management information systems (MBA, MS, MSBA, PhD); marketing (MBA, MSBA, PhD); production and operations management (MSBA, PhD); taxation (MS Acct); telecommunications (MSBA). *Application deadline:* For fall admission, 3/1 (priority date); for spring admission, 9/1 (priority date). Applications are processed on a rolling basis. *Application fee:* $25 ($50 for international students). Electronic applications accepted. *Application Contact:* Janet L. Hubbert, Director, Graduate Services Center, 806-742-3184, Fax: 806-742-3958, E-mail: bagrad@ba.ttu.edu. *Senior Executive Associate Dean,* Dr. R. Stephen Sears, 806-742-0632, Fax: 806-742-1092, E-mail: ssears@ba.ttu.edu.

School of Law Students: 656 full-time (300 women), 7 part-time (3 women); includes 85 minority (16 African Americans, 5 Asian Americans or Pacific Islanders, 59 Hispanic Americans, 5 Native Americans), 2 international. Average age 26. 1,127 applicants, 49% accepted, 233 enrolled. *Faculty:* 31 full-time (10 women), 7 part-time/adjunct (1 woman). Expenses: Contact institution. *Financial support:* In 2001–02, 575 students received support, including 22 research assistantships with partial tuition reimbursements available (averaging $9,045 per year), 1 teaching assistantship with partial tuition reimbursement available (averaging $12,000 per year); fellowships, career-related internships or fieldwork, Federal Work-Study, and institutionally sponsored loans also available. Financial award application deadline: 5/1; financial award applicants required to submit FAFSA. In 2001, 201 degrees awarded. Offers law (JD). *Application deadline:* For fall admission, 2/1 (priority date). Applications are processed on a rolling basis. *Application fee:* $25. *Application Contact:* Graduate Adviser, 806-742-3793, Fax: 806-742-1629. *Interim Dean,* James Eissinger, 806-742-3793, Fax: 803-742-1629.

See in-depth description on page 1135.

TEXAS TECH UNIVERSITY HEALTH SCIENCES CENTER, Lubbock, TX 79430

General Information State-supported, coed, graduate-only institution. *Graduate housing:* On-campus housing not available.

GRADUATE UNITS

Graduate School of Biomedical Sciences Offers anatomy/cell biology (MS, PhD); biomedical sciences (MS, PhD); health services research (MS); medical biochemistry (MS, PhD); medical microbiology (MS, PhD); pharmaceutical sciences (MS, PhD); pharmacology (MS, PhD); physiology (MS, PhD). Electronic applications accepted.

Program in Biotechnology Offers biotechnology (MS). Offered jointly with the General Academic Campus of TTU (science/agriculture track).

School of Allied Health Students: 353 full-time (252 women), 15 part-time (7 women); includes 27 minority (3 African Americans, 2 Asian Americans or Pacific Islanders, 20 Hispanic Americans, 2 Native Americans), 1 international. Average age 24. 254 applicants, 65% accepted. *Faculty:* 47 full-time (23 women). Expenses: Contact institution. *Financial support:* Fellowships, research assistantships, teaching assistantships, career-related internships or fieldwork, institutionally sponsored loans, scholarships/grants, and tuition waivers (full) available. Financial award application deadline: 9/1; financial award applicants required to submit FAFSA. In 2001, 101 degrees awarded. Offers allied health (MAT, MOT, MPAS, MPT, MS, MSMP, MVR, Au D); athletic training (MAT); communication disorders (MS, Au D); molecular pathology (MSMP); occupational therapy (MOT); physical therapy (MPT); physician assistant studies (MPAS); vocational rehabilitation (MVR). *Application fee:* $35. *Application Contact:* Carey E. Woodward, Director of Admissions and Student Affairs, 806-743-3220, Fax: 806-743-3249, E-mail: carey.woodward@ttuhsc.edu. *Dean,* Dr. Paul P. Brooke, 806-743-3247, Fax: 806-743-3249, E-mail: alhpb@ttuhsc.edu.

School of Medicine Offers medicine (MD). Open only to residents of Texas, eastern New Mexico, and southwestern Oklahoma.

School of Nursing Students: 9 full-time (all women), 64 part-time (57 women); includes 4 minority (3 Hispanic Americans, 1 Native American), 3 international. Average age 41. 20 applicants, 85% accepted. *Faculty:* 18 full-time (all women). Expenses: Contact institution. *Financial support:* In 2001–02, 9 students received support. Institutionally sponsored loans, scholarships/grants, and traineeships available. Support available to part-time students. Financial award application deadline: 12/1; financial award applicants required to submit FAFSA. In 2001, 12 degrees awarded. *Degree program information:* Part-time programs available. Postbaccalaureate distance learning degree programs offered (minimal on-campus study). Offers acute care nurse practitioner (MSN, Certificate); administration (MSN); community health (MSN); education (MSN); family nurse practitioner (MSN, Certificate); gerontics (MSN); pediatric nurse practitioner (MSN, Certificate). *Application deadline:* For fall admission, 7/15 (priority date); for spring admission, 11/15 (priority date). Applications are processed on a rolling basis. *Application fee:* $40 ($90 for international students). *Application Contact:* Dr. Barbara A. Johnston, Associate Dean for Graduate Programs, 806-743-3055, Fax: 806-743-1622, E-mail: barbara.johnston@ttuhsc.edu. *Dean,* Dr. Alexia E. Green, 806-743-2738, Fax: 806-743-1622, E-mail: alexia.green@ttuhsc.edu.

TEXAS WESLEYAN UNIVERSITY, Fort Worth, TX 76105-1536

General Information Independent-religious, coed, comprehensive institution. *Enrollment:* 651 full-time matriculated graduate/professional students (324 women), 574 part-time matriculated graduate/professional students (365 women). *Enrollment by degree level:* 638 first professional, 587 master's. *Graduate faculty:* 37 full-time (11 women), 40 part-time/adjunct (13 women). *Tuition:* Part-time $250 per semester hour. *Required fees:* $720. Tuition and fees vary according to program. *Graduate housing:* Room and/or apartments available on a first-come, first-served basis to single students; on-campus housing not available to married students. Typical cost: $3,990 (including board). *Student services:* Campus employment opportunities, career counseling, free psychological counseling, international student services, low-cost health insurance, teacher training, writing training. *Library facilities:* Eunice and James L. West Library plus 1 other. *Online resources:* library catalog. *Collection:* 192,044 titles, 632 serial subscriptions, 5,302 audiovisual materials.

Computer facilities: 65 computers available on campus for general student use. A campuswide network can be accessed. Internet access is available. *Web address:* http://www.txwesleyan.edu/.

General Application Contact: Terri Evans, Director of Transfer/Graduate Admissions, 817-531-4458, Fax: 817-531-4231, E-mail: evanst@txwes.edu.

GRADUATE UNITS

Graduate Programs Students: 309 full-time (135 women), 278 part-time (218 women); includes 113 minority (53 African Americans, 6 Asian Americans or Pacific Islanders, 47 Hispanic Americans, 7 Native Americans), 9 international. Average age 32. 372 applicants, 60% accepted, 181 enrolled. *Faculty:* 26 full-time (9 women), 17 part-time/adjunct (6 women). Expenses: Contact institution. *Financial support:* Fellowships with full and partial tuition reimbursements, teaching assistantships, career-related internships or fieldwork, Federal Work-Study, institutionally sponsored loans, scholarships/grants, and tuition waivers (full and partial) available. Support available to part-time students. Financial award application deadline: 3/15; financial award applicants required to submit FAFSA. In 2001, 144 degrees awarded. *Degree program information:* Part-time and evening/weekend programs available. Postbaccalaureate distance learning degree programs offered (no on-campus study). Offers business administration (MBA); education (MA Ed, MAT, MS Ed); nurse anesthesia (MHS, MSNA). *Application deadline:* Applications are processed on a rolling basis. *Application fee:* $50 for international students. Electronic applications accepted. *Application Contact:* Terri Evans, Director of Transfer/Graduate Admissions, 817-531-4458, Fax: 817-531-4231, E-mail: transfer@txwes.edu. *Interim Provost,* Dr. Allen Henderson, 817-531-4405.

School of Law Students: 342 full-time (189 women), 296 part-time (147 women); includes 133 minority (58 African Americans, 16 Asian Americans or Pacific Islanders, 49 Hispanic Americans, 10 Native Americans), 2 international. Average age 29. *Faculty:* 25 full-time (8 women), 28 part-time/adjunct (11 women). Expenses: Contact institution. *Financial support:* Career-related internships or fieldwork, scholarships/grants, and tuition waivers (full and partial) available. Support available to part-time students. Financial award application deadline: 3/15; financial award applicants required to submit FAFSA. In 2001, 111 degrees awarded. *Degree program information:* Part-time and evening/weekend programs available. Offers law (JD). *Application deadline:* For fall admission, 5/1 (priority date). Applications are processed on a rolling basis. *Application fee:* $50. Electronic applications accepted. *Application Contact:* Sonel Y. Shropshire, Assistant Dean/Director of Admissions, 817-212-4045, Fax: 817-212-

Texas Wesleyan University (continued)

4002, E-mail: law_admissions@law.txwes.edu. *Dean*, Richard L. Gershon, 817-212-4000, Fax: 817-212-4199.

TEXAS WOMAN'S UNIVERSITY, Denton, TX 76201

General Information State-supported, coed, primarily women, university. CGS member. *Enrollment:* 1,016 full-time matriculated graduate/professional students (923 women), 2,507 part-time matriculated graduate/professional students (2,163 women). *Enrollment by degree level:* 3,012 master's, 511 doctoral. *Graduate faculty:* 284 full-time (206 women), 23 part-time/adjunct (17 women). Tuition, state resident: part-time $90 per semester hour. Tuition, nonresident: part-time $303 per semester hour. *Required fees:* $24 per credit hour. $79 per semester. *Graduate housing:* Rooms and/or apartments available on a first-come, first-served basis to single students and available to married students. *Student services:* Campus employment opportunities, campus safety program, career counseling, child daycare facilities, disabled student services, exercise/wellness program, free psychological counseling, grant writing training, international student services, low-cost health insurance, multicultural affairs office, teacher training, writing training. *Library facilities:* Blagg-Huey Library. *Online resources:* library catalog, web page. *Collection:* 559,116 titles, 8,287 serial subscriptions, 84,120 audiovisual materials.

Computer facilities: 332 computers available on campus for general student use. A campuswide network can be accessed from student residence rooms and from off campus. Internet access is available. *Web address:* http://www.twu.edu/.

General Application Contact: Dr. Michael H. Droge, Dean for Graduate Studies and Research, 940-898-3415, Fax: 940-898-3412, E-mail: mdroge@twu.edu.

GRADUATE UNITS

Graduate Studies and Research Students: 1,016 full-time (923 women), 2,507 part-time (2,163 women); includes 893 minority (400 African Americans, 137 Asian Americans or Pacific Islanders, 340 Hispanic Americans, 16 Native Americans), 141 international. Average age 34. 1,265 applicants, 49% accepted. *Faculty:* 284 full-time (206 women), 23 part-time/adjunct (17 women). Expenses: Contact institution. *Financial support:* In 2001–02, 1,535 students received support, including 103 teaching assistantships (averaging $8,514 per year); fellowships, research assistantships, career-related internships or fieldwork, Federal Work-Study, institutionally sponsored loans, scholarships/grants, traineeships, tuition waivers (full and partial), and unspecified assistantships also available. Support available to part-time students. Financial award applicants required to submit CSS PROFILE. In 2001, 650 master's, 86 doctorates awarded. *Degree program information:* Part-time and evening/weekend programs available. Postbaccalaureate distance learning degree programs offered. *Application deadline:* Applications are processed on a rolling basis. *Application fee:* $30. Electronic applications accepted. *Application Contact:* Holly Kiser, Graduate Admissions Coordinator, 940-898-3188, Fax: 940-898-3081, E-mail: hkiser@twu.edu. *Dean for Graduate Studies and Research*, Dr. Michael H. Droge, 940-898-3415, Fax: 940-898-3412, E-mail: mdroge@twu.edu.

College of Arts and Sciences Students: 179 full-time (171 women), 366 part-time (309 women); includes 95 minority (46 African Americans, 16 Asian Americans or Pacific Islanders, 30 Hispanic Americans, 3 Native Americans), 40 international. Average age 35. 390 applicants, 65% accepted. *Faculty:* 97 full-time (56 women), 12 part-time/adjunct (7 women). Expenses: Contact institution. *Financial support:* In 2001–02, 19 fellowships, 26 research assistantships (averaging $7,000 per year), 95 teaching assistantships (averaging $8,000 per year) were awarded. Career-related internships or fieldwork, Federal Work-Study, institutionally sponsored loans, scholarships/grants, tuition waivers (partial), and unspecified assistantships also available. Support available to part-time students. In 2001, 80 master's, 17 doctorates awarded. *Degree program information:* Part-time and evening/weekend programs available. Offers art (MA, MFA); arts and sciences (MA, MBA, MFA, MS, PhD); biology (MS); biology teaching (MS); business administration (MBA); chemistry (MS); chemistry teaching (MS); counseling psychology (MA, PhD); dance (MA, MFA, PhD); drama (MA); English (MA); government (MA); history (MA); mathematics (MA, MS); mathematics teaching (MS); molecular biology (PhD); music (MA); rhetoric (PhD); school psychology (MA, PhD); science teaching (MS); sociology (MA, PhD); women's studies (MA). *Application fee:* $30. *Interim Dean*, Dr. Richard Rodean, 940-898-3326, Fax: 940-898-3366, E-mail: rrodean@twu.edu.

College of Health Sciences Students: 282 full-time (266 women), 281 part-time (235 women); includes 139 minority (49 African Americans, 30 Asian Americans or Pacific Islanders, 59 Hispanic Americans, 1 Native American), 28 international. Average age 33. *Faculty:* 56 full-time (39 women), 7 part-time/adjunct (all women). Expenses: Contact institution. *Financial support:* In 2001–02, 17 fellowships, 21 research assistantships, 45 teaching assistantships were awarded. Career-related internships or fieldwork, Federal Work-Study, institutionally sponsored loans, scholarships/grants, and tuition waivers (partial) also available. Support available to part-time students. In 2001, 104 master's, 21 doctorates awarded. *Degree program information:* Part-time and evening/weekend programs available. Postbaccalaureate distance learning degree programs offered. Offers education of the deaf (MS); exercise and sports nutrition (MS); food science (MS); health care administration (MHA); health sciences (MHA, MS, Ed D, PhD); health studies (MS, Ed D, PhD); institutional administration (MS); kinesiology (MS, PhD); nutrition (MS, PhD); speech-language pathology (MS). *Application fee:* $30. *Dean*, Dr. Jean Pyfer, 940-898-2852, Fax: 940-898-2853, E-mail: jpyfer@twu.edu.

College of Nursing Students: 68 full-time (63 women), 336 part-time (321 women); includes 108 minority (52 African Americans, 28 Asian Americans or Pacific Islanders, 24 Hispanic Americans, 4 Native Americans), 7 international. Average age 39. *Faculty:* 36 full-time (all women). Expenses: Contact institution. *Financial support:* In 2001–02, 16 students received support, including 4 research assistantships (averaging $10,818 per year), 4 teaching assistantships (averaging $10,818 per year); traineeships also available. Financial award application deadline: 4/1. In 2001, 74 master's, 18 doctorates awarded. *Degree program information:* Part-time programs available. Postbaccalaureate distance learning degree programs offered. Offers adult health nurse (MS); adult health nurse practitioner (MS); child health (MS); community health nursing (MS); family nurse practitioner (MS); mental health nursing (MS); nursing (PhD); pediatric nurse practitioner (MS); women's health nurse (MS); women's health nurse practitioner (MS). *Application deadline:* Applications are processed on a rolling basis. *Application fee:* $30. *Dean*, Dr. Carolyn S. Gunning, 940-898-2401, Fax: 940-898-2437, E-mail: cgunning@twu.edu.

College of Professional Education Students: 141 full-time (124 women), 1,294 part-time (1,108 women); includes 454 minority (235 African Americans, 17 Asian Americans or Pacific Islanders, 197 Hispanic Americans, 5 Native Americans), 32 international. Average age 36. *Faculty:* 48 full-time (35 women), 4 part-time/adjunct (3 women). Expenses: Contact institution. *Financial support:* In 2001–02, 30 fellowships, 7 research assistantships, 4 teaching assistantships were awarded. Career-related internships or fieldwork, Federal Work-Study, institutionally sponsored loans, tuition waivers (partial), and graders also available. Support available to part-time students. In 2001, 197 master's, 23 doctorates awarded. *Degree program information:* Part-time and evening/weekend programs available. Offers administration (M Ed, MA); child development (MS, PhD); counseling and development (MS); early childhood education (M Ed, MA, MS, Ed D); elementary education (M Ed, MA); family studies (MS, PhD); family therapy (MS, PhD); library science (MA, MLS, PhD); professional education (M Ed, MA, MLS, MS, Ed D, PhD); reading education (M Ed, MA, MS, Ed D, PhD); special education (M Ed, MA, PhD); supervision (MA). *Application fee:* $30. *Dean*, Dr. Keith Swigger, 940-898-2202, Fax: 940-898-2611, E-mail: kswigger@twu.edu.

School of Occupational Therapy Students: 176 full-time (164 women), 36 part-time (34 women); includes 38 minority (12 African Americans, 14 Asian Americans or Pacific Islanders, 10 Hispanic Americans, 2 Native Americans), 11 international. Average age 29. 80 applicants, 75% accepted. *Faculty:* 23 full-time (22 women). Expenses: Contact institution. *Financial support:* In 2001–02, 10 research assistantships with partial tuition reimbursements, 4 teaching assistantships with partial tuition reimbursements were awarded. Career-related internships or fieldwork, Federal Work-Study, institutionally sponsored loans, and unspecified assistantships also available. Support available to part-time students. Financial award application deadline: 4/1. In 2001, 112 master's, 5 doctorates awarded. *Degree program information:* Part-time and evening/weekend programs available. Postbaccalaureate distance learning degree programs offered. Offers occupational therapy (MA, MOT, PhD). *Application deadline:* For fall admission, 11/15 (priority date); for spring admission, 7/15. Applications are processed on a rolling basis. *Application fee:* $100. *Interim Dean*, Dr. Sally Schultz, 940-898-2801, Fax: 940-898-2806, E-mail: sschultz@twu.edu.

School of Physical Therapy Students: 168 full-time (134 women), 188 part-time (150 women); includes 59 minority (6 African Americans, 32 Asian Americans or Pacific Islanders, 20 Hispanic Americans, 1 Native American), 23 international. Average age 29. 223 applicants, 58% accepted. *Faculty:* 24 full-time (18 women). Expenses: Contact institution. *Financial support:* In 2001–02, 178 students received support, including 7 research assistantships (averaging $16,140 per year), 2 teaching assistantships (averaging $12,546 per year); career-related internships or fieldwork, Federal Work-Study, and institutionally sponsored loans also available. Support available to part-time students. Financial award application deadline: 4/1. In 2001, 83 master's, 7 doctorates awarded. *Degree program information:* Part-time and evening/weekend programs available. Offers physical therapy (MS, PhD). *Application deadline:* For fall admission, 11/1 (priority date). Applications are processed on a rolling basis. *Application fee:* $100. *Application Contact:* Information Contact, 940-898-2460, Fax: 940-898-2486. *Dean*, Dr. Carolyn K. Rozier, 940-898-2460, Fax: 940-898-2486, E-mail: crozier@twu.edu.

See in-depth description on page 1137.

THOMAS COLLEGE, Waterville, ME 04901-5097

General Information Independent, coed, comprehensive institution. *Graduate housing:* On-campus housing not available.

GRADUATE UNITS

Graduate School *Degree program information:* Part-time and evening/weekend programs available. Offers business (MBA); computer technology education (MS); human resource management (MBA); taxation (MS).

THOMAS EDISON STATE COLLEGE, Trenton, NJ 08608-1176

General Information State-supported, coed, comprehensive institution. *Enrollment:* 183 part-time matriculated graduate/professional students (80 women). *Enrollment by degree level:* 183 master's. *Graduate faculty:* 28 part-time/adjunct (11 women). Tuition, state resident: part-time $298 per credit. Tuition, nonresident: part-time $298 per credit. *Graduate housing:* On-campus housing not available.

Computer facilities: A campuswide network can be accessed from off campus. Internet access and online class registration are available. *Web address:* http://www.tesc.edu/.

General Application Contact: Gregg Dye, Coordinator of Graduate Advising, 800-442-8372, Fax: 609-633-8593, E-mail: graduatestudies@tesc.edu.

GRADUATE UNITS

Graduate Studies Average age 42. 117 applicants, 79 enrolled. *Faculty:* 28 part-time/adjunct (11 women). Expenses: Contact institution. *Financial support:* Applicants required to submit FAFSA. In 2001, 39 degrees awarded. *Degree program information:* Part-time programs available. Offers insurance (MSM); leadership (MSM); liberal studies (MAPS); management (MSM); project management (MSM); substance abuse (MSM). *Application deadline:* For fall admission, 7/1 (priority date); for winter admission, 11/1 (priority date); for spring admission, 3/1 (priority date). Applications are processed on a rolling basis. *Application fee:* $75. Electronic applications accepted. *Application Contact:* Gregg Dye, Coordinator of Graduate Advising, 800-442-8372, Fax: 609-633-8593, E-mail: graduatestudies@tesc.edu. *Dean of Graduate Studies/Associate Vice President of New Program Development*, Dr. Sonja Eveslage, 800-442-8372, Fax: 609-633-8593, E-mail: graduatestudies@tesc.edu.

See in-depth description on page 1139.

THOMAS JEFFERSON SCHOOL OF LAW, San Diego, CA 92110-2905

General Information Independent, coed, graduate-only institution. *Enrollment by degree level:* 611 first professional. *Graduate faculty:* 26 full-time (13 women), 30 part-time/adjunct (9 women). *Tuition:* Full-time $22,180; part-time $13,960 per year. *Required fees:* $75 per semester. Tuition and fees vary according to course load. *Graduate housing:* On-campus housing not available. *Student services:* Campus employment opportunities, career counseling, disabled student services, free psychological counseling, low-cost health insurance. *Library facilities:* Thomas Jefferson School of Law Library. *Online resources:* library catalog, web page, access to other libraries' catalogs. *Collection:* 105,524 titles, 2,934 serial subscriptions, 1,016 audiovisual materials.

Computer facilities: 46 computers available on campus for general student use. A campuswide network can be accessed from student residence rooms and from off campus. Internet access is available. *Web address:* http://www.tjsl.edu/.

General Application Contact: Jennifer M. Keller, Assistant Dean of Admissions and Registrar, 619-297-9700 Ext. 1472, Fax: 619-294-4713, E-mail: jkeller@tjsl.edu.

GRADUATE UNITS

Professional Program Students: 423 full-time (187 women), 188 part-time (72 women); includes 139 minority (22 African Americans, 46 Asian Americans or Pacific Islanders, 70 Hispanic Americans, 1 Native American), 1 international. Average age 28. 1,522 applicants, 69% accepted. *Faculty:* 26 full-time (13 women), 30 part-time/adjunct (9 women). Expenses: Contact institution. *Financial support:* Research assistantships, teaching assistantships, career-related internships or fieldwork, Federal Work-Study, institutionally sponsored loans, scholarships/grants, and tuition waivers available. Support available to part-time students. Financial award application deadline: 4/23; financial award applicants required to submit FAFSA. In 2001, 154 degrees awarded. *Degree program information:* Part-time and evening/weekend programs available. Offers law (JD). *Application deadline:* For fall admission, 8/25 (priority date); for spring admission, 1/25 (priority date). Applications are processed on a rolling basis. *Application fee:* $35. Electronic applications accepted. *Application Contact:* Jennifer M. Keller, Assistant Dean of Admissions and Registrar, 619-297-9700 Ext. 1472, Fax: 619-294-4713, E-mail: jkeller@tjsl.edu. *Dean*, Kenneth J. Vandevelde, 619-297-9700 Ext. 1404, E-mail: kennethv@tjsl.edu.

THOMAS JEFFERSON UNIVERSITY, Philadelphia, PA 19107

General Information Independent, coed, upper-level institution. CGS member. *Enrollment:* 1,135 full-time matriculated graduate/professional students (553 women), 341 part-time matriculated graduate/professional students (249 women). *Enrollment by degree level:* 899 first professional, 446 master's, 122 doctoral, 9 other advanced degrees. *Graduate faculty:* 197 full-time (36 women), 11 part-time/adjunct (2 women). *Tuition:* Full-time $13,440. Tuition and fees vary according to degree level and program. *Graduate housing:* Rooms and/or apartments available to single and married students. *Student services:* Campus employment opportunities, campus safety program, career counseling, child daycare facilities, exercise/wellness program, free psychological counseling, international student services, low-cost health insurance, multicultural affairs office. *Library facilities:* Scott Memorial Library plus 1 other. *Online resources:* web page. *Collection:* 170,000 titles, 2,290 serial subscriptions. *Research affiliation:* Wills Eye Hospital, Veterans Administration Hospital, A. I. Dupont Institute, Lankenau Center for Medical Research, University of Delaware (chemical engineering and computer science), Fox Chase Cancer Center.

Computer facilities: 100 computers available on campus for general student use. A campuswide network can be accessed from off campus. *Web address:* http://www.tju.edu/jchp.

General Application Contact: Jessie F. Pervall, Director of Admissions, 215-503-0155, Fax: 215-503-3433, E-mail: jessie.pervall@mail.tju.edu.

GRADUATE UNITS

College of Graduate Studies Students: 236 full-time (139 women), 341 part-time (249 women); includes 106 minority (43 African Americans, 46 Asian Americans or Pacific Islanders, 13 Hispanic Americans, 4 Native Americans), 28 international. Average age 29. 465 applicants, 55% accepted, 199 enrolled. *Faculty:* 208. Expenses: Contact institution. *Financial support:* In 2001–02, 187 students received support, including 135 fellowships with full tuition reimbursements available; research assistantships, Federal Work-Study, institutionally sponsored loans, traineeships, and training grants also available. Support available to part-time students. Financial award application deadline: 5/1; financial award applicants required to submit FAFSA. In 2001, 142 master's, 15 doctorates awarded. *Degree program information:* Part-time and evening/weekend programs available. Postbaccalaureate distance learning degree programs offered (no on-campus study). Offers biochemistry and molecular biology (PhD); biomedical chemistry (MS); cell and tissue engineering (PhD); clinical research, public health, and research management (Certificate); developmental biology and teratology (MS, PhD); genetics (PhD); immunology (PhD); interdisciplinary biomedical sciences (PhD); laboratory sciences (MS); microbiology (MS); microbiology and molecular virology (PhD); molecular pharmacology and structural biology (PhD); nursing (MS); occupational therapy (MS); pathology and cell biology (PhD); pharmacology (MS); physical therapy (MS); physiology (PhD). *Application deadline:* For fall admission, 3/1 (priority date). Applications are processed on a rolling basis. *Application fee:* $40. Electronic applications accepted. *Application Contact:* Jessie F. Pervall, Director of Admissions, 215-503-0155, Fax: 215-503-3433, E-mail: jessie.pervall@mail.tju.edu. *Dean*, Dr. Jussi J. Saukkonen, 215-503-8986, Fax: 215-503-6690.

Jefferson Medical College Students: 899 full-time (414 women); includes 238 minority (22 African Americans, 192 Asian Americans or Pacific Islanders, 20 Hispanic Americans, 4 Native Americans), 4 international. 5,732 applicants, 8% accepted. *Faculty:* 689 full-time (167 women), 42 part-time/adjunct (11 women). Expenses: Contact institution. *Financial support:* In 2001–02, 650 students received support. Federal Work-Study and institutionally sponsored loans available. Financial award application deadline: 3/1; financial award applicants required to submit FAFSA. In 2001, 211 degrees awarded. Offers medicine (MD). *Application deadline:* For fall admission, 11/15 (priority date). *Application fee:* $65. Electronic applications accepted. *Application Contact:* Dr. Clara Callahan, Associate Dean for Admissions, 215-955-6983, Fax: 215-923-6939, E-mail: clara.callahan@mail.tju.edu. *Senior Vice President and Dean for Academic Affairs*, Dr. Thomas J. Nasca, 215-955-6980, Fax: 215-923-6939.

Kimmel Cancer Institute *Faculty:* 57 full-time (8 women), 1 part-time/adjunct (0 women). Expenses: Contact institution. *Financial support:* Fellowships available. Financial award application deadline: 3/1. Offers genetics (PhD); immunology (PhD); microbiology and molecular virology (PhD); molecular pharmacology and structural biology (PhD). *Application deadline:* For fall admission, 3/1 (priority date). Applications are processed on a rolling basis. Electronic applications accepted. *Application Contact:* Joanne Balitzky, Graduate Coordinator, 215-503-6687, Fax: 215-503-0622, E-mail: joanne.balitzky@mail.tju.edu. *Director*, Dr. Carlo M. Croce, 215-503-4645.

THOMAS M. COOLEY LAW SCHOOL, Lansing, MI 48901-3038

General Information Independent, coed, graduate-only institution. *Enrollment by degree level:* 1,819 first professional. *Graduate faculty:* 60 full-time (21 women), 95 part-time/adjunct (33 women). *Tuition:* Full-time $19,980; part-time $682 per credit. *Required fees:* $20 per term. Tuition and fees vary according to course load. *Graduate housing:* On-campus housing not available. *Student services:* Campus employment opportunities, career counseling, disabled student services, multicultural affairs office, writing training. *Library facilities:* Thomas M. Cooley Law School Library plus 5 others. *Online resources:* library catalog, web page. *Collection:* 177,232 titles, 4,226 serial subscriptions, 1,331 audiovisual materials.

Computer facilities: 124 computers available on campus for general student use. A campuswide network can be accessed from off campus. Internet access is available. *Web address:* http://www.cooley.edu/.

General Application Contact: Stephanie Gregg, Dean of Admissions, 517-371-5140, Fax: 517-334-5718, E-mail: greggs@cooley.edu.

GRADUATE UNITS

Professional Program Students: 389 full-time (189 women), 1,430 part-time (695 women); includes 638 minority (409 African Americans, 100 Asian Americans or Pacific Islanders, 118 Hispanic Americans, 11 Native Americans), 37 international. Average age 26. 3,128 applicants, 74% accepted, 915 enrolled. *Faculty:* 60 full-time (21 women), 95 part-time/adjunct (33 women). Expenses: Contact institution. *Financial support:* In 2001–02, 1,456 students received support, including 29 research assistantships with tuition reimbursements available, 39 teaching assistantships with tuition reimbursements available; fellowships with tuition reimbursements available, career-related internships or fieldwork, Federal Work-Study, and scholarships/grants also available. Support available to part-time students. Financial award applicants required to submit FAFSA. In 2001, 419 degrees awarded. *Degree program information:* Part-time and evening/weekend programs available. Offers law (JD). *Application deadline:* Applications are processed on a rolling basis. *Application fee:* $0. *Application Contact:* Stephanie Gregg, Dean of Admissions, 517-371-5140, Fax: 517-334-5718, E-mail: greggs@cooley.edu.

THOMAS MORE COLLEGE, Crestview Hills, KY 41017-3495

General Information Independent-religious, coed, comprehensive institution. *Enrollment:* 133 full-time matriculated graduate/professional students (57 women). *Enrollment by degree level:* 133 master's. *Graduate faculty:* 13 full-time (3 women), 6 part-time/adjunct (2 women). *Tuition:* Full-time $8,010. *Required fees:* $840. One-time fee: $100 full-time. *Graduate housing:* On-campus housing not available. *Student services:* Career counseling, free psychological counseling, international student services. *Library facilities:* Thomas More Library. *Online resources:* web page. *Collection:* 131,694 titles, 571 serial subscriptions, 1,756 audiovisual materials.

Computer facilities: 100 computers available on campus for general student use. A campuswide network can be accessed from student residence rooms and from off campus. *Web address:* http://www.thomasmore.edu/.

General Application Contact: Tony Hayes, Director of Lifelong Learning, 859-344-3604, Fax: 859-344-3342, E-mail: tony.hayes@thomasmore.edu.

GRADUATE UNITS

Program in Business Administration Students: 133 full-time (57 women); includes 18 minority (12 African Americans, 2 Asian Americans or Pacific Islanders, 4 Hispanic Americans) Average age 33. 48 applicants, 85% accepted, 38 enrolled. *Faculty:* 13 full-time (3 women), 6 part-time/adjunct (2 women). Expenses: Contact institution. *Financial support:* Fellowships, research assistantships, teaching assistantships, institutionally sponsored loans available. Financial award applicants required to submit FAFSA. In 2001, 79 degrees awarded. *Degree program information:* Evening/weekend programs available. Offers business administration (MBA). *Application deadline:* Applications are processed on a rolling basis. *Application fee:* $15. Electronic applications accepted. *Application Contact:* Tony Hayes, Director of Lifelong Learning, 859-344-3604, Fax: 859-344-3342, E-mail: tony.hayes@thomasmore.edu. *Director of Lifelong Learning*, Tony Hayes, 859-344-3604, Fax: 859-344-3342, E-mail: tony.hayes@thomasmore.edu.

THOMAS UNIVERSITY, Thomasville, GA 31792-7499

General Information Independent, coed, comprehensive institution. *Enrollment:* 35 full-time matriculated graduate/professional students (21 women), 46 part-time matriculated graduate/professional students (31 women). *Enrollment by degree level:* 81 master's. *Graduate faculty:* 7 full-time (2 women). *Tuition:* Full-time $4,950; part-time $3,300 per year. *Required fees:* $93 per term. Tuition and fees vary according to course load. *Graduate housing:* Rooms and/or apartments available on a first-come, first-served basis to single and married students. Typical cost: $2,400 per year for single students. Housing application deadline: 8/1. *Student services:* Campus employment opportunities, disabled student services. *Library facilities:* Thomas University Library. *Online resources:* library catalog. *Collection:* 42,749 titles, 449 serial subscriptions, 546 audiovisual materials.

Computer facilities: 50 computers available on campus for general student use. A campuswide network can be accessed. *Web address:* http://www.thomasu.edu/.

General Application Contact: Lourena Maxwell, Recruiter, 229-226-1621, Fax: 229-227-6919, E-mail: lmaxwell@thomasu.edu.

GRADUATE UNITS

Department of Business Administration Students: 12 full-time (4 women), 6 part-time (3 women). Average age 37. 7 applicants, 71% accepted. *Faculty:* 4 full-time (1 woman). Expenses: Contact institution. In 2001, 10 degrees awarded. Offers business administration (MBA). *Application deadline:* Applications are processed on a rolling basis. *Application fee:* $50 ($75 for international students). *Application Contact:* Lourena Maxwell, Recruiter, 229-226-1621, Fax: 229-227-6919, E-mail: lmaxwell@thomasu.edu. *Assistant Professor*, Dr. Lee Washington, 229-226-1621, Fax: 229-226-1653, E-mail: lwashington@thomasu.edu.

Department of Rehabilitation Counseling Students: 23 full-time (17 women), 40 part-time (28 women). Average age 33. 6 applicants, 83% accepted. *Faculty:* 3 full-time (1 woman). Expenses: Contact institution. Offers rehabilitation counseling (MRC). *Application deadline:* Applications are processed on a rolling basis. *Application fee:* $50 ($75 for international students). *Application Contact:* Lourena Maxwell, Recruiter, 229-226-1621, Fax: 229-227-6919, E-mail: lmaxwell@thomasu.edu. *Chair of Human Services Division*, Dr. Shirley Chandler.

THUNDERBIRD, THE AMERICAN GRADUATE SCHOOL OF INTERNATIONAL MANAGEMENT, Glendale, AZ 85306-3236

General Information Independent, coed, graduate-only institution. *Enrollment by degree level:* 1,517 master's. *Graduate faculty:* 65 full-time (21 women), 26 part-time/adjunct (9 women). *Tuition:* Part-time $12,600 per term. *Graduate housing:* Room and/or apartments available on a first-come, first-served basis to single students; on-campus housing not available to married students. Typical cost: $4,200 per year ($5,700 including board). Housing application deadline: 2/1. *Student services:* Campus employment opportunities, campus safety program, career counseling, international student services, low-cost health insurance. *Library facilities:* The Merle A. Hinrichs International Business Information Centre plus 1 other. *Online resources:* library catalog, web page, access to other libraries' catalogs. *Collection:* 70,000 titles, 1,600 serial subscriptions, 1,757 audiovisual materials. *Research affiliation:* Wiley (publishing).

Computer facilities: 150 computers available on campus for general student use. A campuswide network can be accessed from student residence rooms and from off campus. Internet access, My Thunderbird Online, campus intranet are available. *Web address:* http://www.t-bird.edu/.

General Application Contact: Judy Johnson, Director of Admissions, 602-978-7210, Fax: 602-439-5432, E-mail: johnsonj@t-bird.edu.

GRADUATE UNITS

Graduate Programs Students: 1,517. Average age 29. 1,126 applicants, 78% accepted, 410 enrolled. *Faculty:* 65 full-time (21 women), 26 part-time/adjunct (9 women). Expenses: Contact institution. *Financial support:* In 2001–02, 329 students received support. Federal Work-Study, scholarships/grants, and tuition waivers (partial) available. Support available to part-time students. Financial award application deadline: 2/15; financial award applicants required to submit FAFSA. In 2001, 770 degrees awarded. Offers executive development (EMBA); executive education (EMBA, MIMLA); international management (EMBA, MBA, MIM, MIMLA); international management for Latin America (MIMLA). MIM/MBA offered jointly with Arizona State University, Case Western Reserve University, Drury College, University of Arizona, University of Colorado at Denver, University of Florida, University of Houston, and ESADE in Barcelona, Spain. *Application deadline:* Applications are processed on a rolling basis. *Application fee:* $125. Electronic applications accepted. *Application Contact:* Judy Johnson, Director of Admissions, 602-978-7210, Fax: 602-439-5432, E-mail: johnsonj@t-bird.edu. *Dean of Faculty and Programs*, Dr. David Bowen, 602-978-7037, Fax: 602-547-1356, E-mail: bowend@t-bird.edu.

TIFFIN UNIVERSITY, Tiffin, OH 44883-2161

General Information Independent, coed, comprehensive institution. *Enrollment:* 216 part-time matriculated graduate/professional students (121 women). *Enrollment by degree level:* 216 master's. *Graduate faculty:* 26 full-time (10 women), 26 part-time/adjunct (10 women). *Tuition:* Full-time $8,400; part-time $525 per credit hour. Tuition and fees vary according to course load. *Graduate housing:* Room and/or apartments available on a first-come, first-served basis to single students; on-campus housing not available to married students. Typical cost: $5,700 (including board). Room and board charges vary according to board plan and housing facility selected. Housing application deadline: 8/1. *Student services:* Campus employment opportunities, career counseling, exercise/wellness program, free psychological counseling, international student services, low-cost health insurance. *Library facilities:* Pfeiffer Library. *Online resources:* library catalog, access to other libraries' catalogs. *Collection:* 28,042 titles, 250 serial subscriptions, 497 audiovisual materials.

Computer facilities: 60 computers available on campus for general student use. A campuswide network can be accessed from student residence rooms and from off campus. Internet access and online class registration are available. *Web address:* http://www.tiffin.edu/.

General Application Contact: Richard A. Geyer, Director of Graduate Admissions, 800-968-6446 Ext. 3310, Fax: 419-443-5002, E-mail: geyerra@tiffin.edu.

GRADUATE UNITS

Master of Business Administration Program Students: 119 full-time (60 women), 66 part-time (32 women); includes 19 minority (10 African Americans, 6 Asian Americans or Pacific Islanders, 3 Hispanic Americans), 7 international. Average age 29. 72 applicants, 89% accepted. *Faculty:* 14 full-time (5 women), 10 part-time/adjunct (3 women). Expenses: Contact institution. *Financial support:* In 2001–02, 88 students received support. Available to part-time students. Application deadline: 7/31; In 2001, 48 degrees awarded. *Degree program information:* Part-time and evening/weekend programs available. Postbaccalaureate distance learning degree programs offered (minimal on-campus study). Offers business administration (MBA). *Application deadline:* For fall admission, 8/10 (priority date); for spring admission, 1/5. Applications are processed on a rolling basis. *Application fee:* $50. Electronic applications accepted. *Application Contact:* Richard A. Geyer, Director of Graduate Admissions, 800-968-6446 Ext. 3310, Fax: 419-443-5002, E-mail: geyerra@tiffin.edu. *Dean of the School of Graduate Studies*, Dr. Shawn P. Daly, 419-448-3404, Fax: 419-443-5002, E-mail: sdaly@tiffin.edu.

Master of Criminal Justice Program Students: 60 full-time (33 women), 6 part-time (all women); includes 29 African Americans Average age 29. 94 applicants, 78% accepted. *Faculty:* 7 full-time (1 woman), 6 part-time/adjunct (0 women). Expenses: Contact institution. *Financial support:* In 2001–02, 34 students received support. Available to part-time students. Application deadline: 7/31; In 2001, 48 degrees awarded. *Degree program information:* Part-time and evening/weekend programs available. Postbaccalaureate distance learning degree programs offered. Offers criminal justice (MCJ). *Application deadline:* For fall admission, 8/10 (priority date); for spring admission, 1/5 (priority date). Applications are processed on a rolling basis. *Application fee:* $50. Electronic applications accepted. *Application Contact:* Richard A. Geyer, Director of Graduate Admissions, 800-968-6446 Ext. 3310, Fax: 419-443-5002, E-mail: geyerra@tiffin.edu. *Dean of the School of Graduate Studies*, Dr. Shawn P. Daly, 419-448-3404, Fax: 419-443-5002, E-mail: sdaly@tiffin.edu.

See in-depth description on page 1141.

TORONTO SCHOOL OF THEOLOGY, Toronto, ON M5S 2C3, Canada

General Information Independent-religious, coed, graduate-only institution. *Enrollment by degree level:* 629 first professional, 71 master's, 203 doctoral, 23 other advanced degrees. *Graduate faculty:* 106 full-time (27 women), 123 part-time/adjunct (31 women). *Graduate tuition:* Tuition and fees charges are reported in Canadian dollars. Tuition, province resident: part-time $403 Canadian dollars per course. Tuition, Canadian resident: part-time $1,000

Toronto School of Theology (continued)

Canadian dollars per course. *Required fees:* $131 Canadian dollars per year. Tuition and fees vary according to degree level, program and student level. *Graduate housing:* On-campus housing not available. *Student services:* Career counseling, child daycare facilities, disabled student services, free psychological counseling, international student services, low-cost health insurance, writing training. *Library facilities:* Robarts Library plus 6 others. *Collection:* 802,000 titles, 1,640 serial subscriptions. *Web address:* http://www.tst.edu/.

General Application Contact: Sofia Kirschner, Registrar, 416-978-4040, Fax: 416-978-7821, E-mail: registrar.tst@utoronto.ca.

GRADUATE UNITS

Graduate Programs Students: 514 full-time (209 women), 412 part-time (231 women). Average age 40. *Faculty:* 106 full-time (27 women), 123 part-time/adjunct (31 women). Expenses: Contact institution. *Financial support:* Career-related internships or fieldwork available. In 2001, 144 first professional degrees, 12 master's, 23 doctorates awarded. Offers theology (M Div, M Rel, MA, MAMS, MPS, MRE, MTS, Th M, D Min, PhD, Th D). Federation of seven Toronto-area theological colleges; basic degrees offered through the member colleges co-jointly with the University of Toronto. *Application deadline:* For fall admission, 1/15 (priority date). *Application fee:* $60. *Application Contact:* Prof. Michael G. Steinhauser, Director for Advanced Degree Programs, 416-978-4039, Fax: 416-978-7821, E-mail: m.steinhauser@utoronto.ca. *Director,* Dr. David Neelands, 416-978-4039, Fax: 416-978-7821, E-mail: d.neelands@utoronto.ca.

TOURO COLLEGE, New York, NY 10010

General Information Independent, coed, comprehensive institution. *Enrollment:* 978 full-time matriculated graduate/professional students (515 women), 953 part-time matriculated graduate/professional students (628 women). *Graduate faculty:* 84 full-time, 137 part-time/adjunct. *Student services:* Career counseling, free psychological counseling, low-cost health insurance. *Collection:* 534,280 titles, 4,715 serial subscriptions.

Computer facilities: 350 computers available on campus for general student use. *Web address:* http://www.touro.edu/.

GRADUATE UNITS

Barry Z. Levine School of Health Sciences Offers biomedical sciences (MS); health information management (Certificate); occupational therapy (MS); physical therapy (MS).

Jacob D. Fuchsberg Law Center *Degree program information:* Part-time and evening/weekend programs available. Offers law (JD); U.S. law for foreign lawyers (LL M).

School of Jewish Studies *Degree program information:* Part-time programs available. Offers Jewish studies (MA).

TOURO UNIVERSITY COLLEGE OF OSTEOPATHIC MEDICINE, Vallejo, CA 94592

General Information Independent, coed, graduate-only institution.

GRADUATE UNITS

Professional Program

TOWSON UNIVERSITY, Towson, MD 21252-0001

General Information State-supported, coed, comprehensive institution. CGS member. *Enrollment:* 706 full-time matriculated graduate/professional students (501 women), 2,315 part-time matriculated graduate/professional students (1,757 women). *Enrollment by degree level:* 2,982 master's, 17 doctoral, 22 other advanced degrees. Tuition, state resident: part-time $211 per credit. Tuition, nonresident: part-time $435 per credit. *Required fees:* $52 per credit. *Graduate housing:* Rooms and/or apartments available to single students and available on a first-come, first-served basis to married students. *Student services:* Campus employment opportunities, campus safety program, career counseling, child daycare facilities, disabled student services, exercise/wellness program, free psychological counseling, grant writing training, international student services, low-cost health insurance, multicultural affairs office, teacher training, writing training. *Library facilities:* Cook Library. *Online resources:* library catalog, web page, access to other libraries' catalogs. *Collection:* 363,430 titles, 2,227 serial subscriptions.

Computer facilities: 1,013 computers available on campus for general student use. A campuswide network can be accessed from student residence rooms and from off campus. Internet access is available. *Web address:* http://www.towson.edu/.

General Application Contact: 410-704-2501, Fax: 410-704-4675, E-mail: grads@towson.edu.

GRADUATE UNITS

Graduate School Students: 706 full-time (501 women), 2,315 part-time (1,757 women); includes 651 minority (550 African Americans, 65 Asian Americans or Pacific Islanders, 27 Hispanic Americans, 9 Native Americans), 206 international. Average age 31. Expenses: Contact institution. *Financial support:* Fellowships with full and partial tuition reimbursements, research assistantships with full and partial tuition reimbursements, teaching assistantships with full and partial tuition reimbursements, career-related internships or fieldwork, Federal Work-Study, and unspecified assistantships available. Support available to part-time students. Financial award application deadline: 4/1; financial award applicants required to submit FAFSA. In 2001, 657 master's, 25 other advanced degrees awarded. *Degree program information:* Part-time and evening/weekend programs available. Offers administration and supervision (Certificate); allied health professions (MS); applied and industrial mathematics (MS); applied gerontology (MS); applied information technology (MS); art education (M Ed); audiology (Au D); biology (MS); clinical psychology (MA); clinician-administrator transition (Certificate); communications management (MS); computer science (MS); counseling psychology (MA); Dalcroze (Certificate); early childhood education (M Ed); elementary education (M Ed); environmental science (MS, Certificate); experimental psychology (MA); geography and environmental planning (MA); human resource development (MS); humanities (MA); information security and assurance (Certificate); information systems management (Certificate); instructional technology (MS); interdisciplinary theatre (Certificate); Internet application development (Certificate); internet application development (Certificate); Kodály (Certificate); liberal and professional studies (MA); management and leadership development (Certificate); mathematics education (MS); music education (MS); music performance (MM); networking technologies (Certificate); nursing (MS, Certificate); occupational science (Sc D); occupational therapy (MS); Orff (Certificate); physician assistant studies (MS); professional writing (MS); psychology (MA); reading education (M Ed); school psychology (MA, CAS); secondary education (M Ed); social science (MS); software engineering (Certificate); speech-language pathology (MS); strategic public relations and integrated communications (Certificate); studio arts (MFA); teaching (MAT); theatre (MFA); women's studies (MS). *Application fee:* $40. Electronic applications accepted. *Application Contact:* 410-704-2501, Fax: 410-704-4675, E-mail: grads@towson.edu. *Dean of Graduate Education and Research,* Dr. Jin Gong, 410-704-2501, E-mail: jgong@towson.edu.

See in-depth description on page 1143.

TRENT UNIVERSITY, Peterborough, ON K9J 7B8, Canada

General Information Province-supported, coed, comprehensive institution. *Graduate housing:* Room and/or apartments available to single students; on-campus housing not available to married students. Housing application deadline: 7/10. *Research affiliation:* Watershed Science Centre (watershed studies), Ontario Power Generation, Inc. (acid rain deposition), Enbridge Consumers Gas (ozone depletion), Forensics Laboratory (DNA testing).

GRADUATE UNITS

Graduate Studies *Degree program information:* Part-time programs available. Offers anthropology (MA); applications of modeling in the natural and social sciences (MA); biology (M Sc, PhD); Canadian studies and native studies (MA); chemistry (M Sc); computer studies (M Sc); environmental and resource studies (M Sc, PhD); geography (M Sc, PhD); methodologies for the study of Western history and culture (MA); native studies (PhD); physics (M Sc).

TREVECCA NAZARENE UNIVERSITY, Nashville, TN 37210-2877

General Information Independent-religious, coed, comprehensive institution. *Enrollment:* 652 matriculated graduate/professional students. *Graduate faculty:* 16 full-time (8 women), 38 part-time/adjunct (14 women). *Tuition:* Part-time $270 per credit. Tuition and fees vary according to program. *Graduate housing:* Rooms and/or apartments available to single and married students. Housing application deadline: 6/15. *Student services:* Career counseling, free psychological counseling. *Library facilities:* Mackey Library. *Online resources:* library catalog, web page, access to other libraries' catalogs. *Collection:* 102,419 titles, 2,353 serial subscriptions, 3,731 audiovisual materials.

Computer facilities: 200 computers available on campus for general student use. A campuswide network can be accessed from student residence rooms and from off campus. Internet access is available. *Web address:* http://www.trevecca.edu/.

General Application Contact: Dr. Stephen M. Pusey, Vice President of Academic Affairs, 615-248-1258, Fax: 615-248-7728, E-mail: spusey@trevecca.edu.

GRADUATE UNITS

Graduate Division Students: 573 full-time (399 women), 87 part-time (52 women); includes 116 minority (104 African Americans, 3 Asian Americans or Pacific Islanders, 5 Hispanic Americans, 4 Native Americans), 5 international. Average age 36. 387 applicants, 64% accepted. *Faculty:* 16 full-time (8 women), 38 part-time/adjunct (14 women). Expenses: Contact institution. *Financial support:* Applicants required to submit FAFSA. In 2001, 297 master's, 21 doctorates awarded. *Degree program information:* Part-time and evening/weekend programs available. *Vice President of Academic Affairs,* Dr. Stephen M. Pusey, 615-248-1258, Fax: 615-248-7728, E-mail: spusey@trevecca.edu.

Division of Natural and Applied Sciences Students: 59 full-time (42 women); includes 1 Asian American or Pacific Islander, 1 international. Average age 27. 122 applicants, 27% accepted. *Faculty:* 4 full-time (1 woman), 2 part-time/adjunct (both women). Expenses: Contact institution. *Financial support:* Applicants required to submit FAFSA. In 2001, 33 degrees awarded. Offers natural and applied sciences (MS); physician assistant (MS). *Application deadline:* For fall admission, 12/1. *Application fee:* $45. *Application Contact:* Admissions Coordinator, 615-248-1621, Fax: 615-248-1622, E-mail: admissions_pa@trevecca.edu. *Division Chair,* Dr. Mike Moredock, 615-248-1261, Fax: 615-248-1622, E-mail: mmoredock@trevecca.edu.

Division of Social and Behavioral Sciences Students: 143. Average age 42. 45 applicants, 87% accepted. *Faculty:* 2 full-time (0 women), 14 part-time/adjunct (6 women). Expenses: Contact institution. *Financial support:* Career-related internships or fieldwork available. Financial award applicants required to submit FAFSA. In 2001, 35 degrees awarded. *Degree program information:* Part-time and evening/weekend programs available. Offers counseling (MA); counseling psychology (MA); marriage and family therapy (MMFT). *Application deadline:* For fall admission, 8/31; for spring admission, 1/18. Applications are processed on a rolling basis. *Application fee:* $25. *Application Contact:* Joyce Houk, Division of Social and Behavior Sciences, 615-248-1417, Fax: 615-248-1366, E-mail: admissions_psy@trevecca.edu. *Division Chair,* Dr. Peter Wilson, 615-248-1417, Fax: 615-248-1366, E-mail: pwilson@trevecca.edu.

School of Business and Management Students: 82 full-time (47 women); includes 38 minority (35 African Americans, 2 Hispanic Americans, 1 Native American), 1 international. Average age 35. 61 applicants, 46% accepted. *Faculty:* 2 part-time/adjunct (0 women). Expenses: Contact institution. *Financial support:* Applicants required to submit FAFSA. In 2001, 44 degrees awarded. *Degree program information:* Evening/weekend programs available. Offers business administration (MBA); business and management (MBA, MSM); management (MSM). *Application deadline:* For fall admission, 8/31; for spring admission, 1/18. Applications are processed on a rolling basis. *Application fee:* $25. *Application Contact:* Jon Burch, Assistant Director-Admissions and Student Services, 615-248-1535, E-mail: admissions_masm@trevecca.edu. *Dean,* Dr. Jim Hiatt, 615-248-1256, Fax: 615-248-7728, E-mail: jhiatt@trevecca.edu.

School of Education Students: 326. Average age 38. 130 applicants, 93% accepted. *Faculty:* 10 full-time (7 women), 18 part-time/adjunct (6 women). Expenses: Contact institution. *Financial support:* Applicants required to submit FAFSA. In 2001, 177 master's, 21 doctorates awarded. *Degree program information:* Part-time and evening/weekend programs available. Offers educational leadership (M Ed); instructional effectiveness (M Ed); library and information science (MLI Sc); professional practice (D Ed); professional practics (D Ed). *Application deadline:* For fall admission, 8/31; for spring admission, 1/18. Applications are processed on a rolling basis. *Application fee:* $25. *Application Contact:* Jerry Doyle, Admissions Office, 615-248-1201, Fax: 615-248-1597, E-mail: admissions_ged@trevecca.edu. *Dean,* Dr. Melvin Welch, 615-248-1201, Fax: 615-248-1597, E-mail: mwelch@trevecca.edu.

School of Religion and Philosophy Students: 25 full-time (6 women), 17 part-time (3 women); includes 1 minority (African American), 1 international. Average age 30. 29 applicants, 93% accepted. *Faculty:* 6 full-time (0 women), 2 part-time/adjunct (0 women). Expenses: Contact institution. *Financial support:* Applicants required to submit FAFSA. In 2001, 8 degrees awarded. *Degree program information:* Part-time programs available. Offers religion and philosophy (MA); religious studies (MA). *Application deadline:* For fall admission, 8/31; for spring admission, 1/18. Applications are processed on a rolling basis. *Application fee:* $25. *Application Contact:* Sherry Crutchfield, Secretary for the Department of Religion and Philosophy, 615-248-1378, Fax: 615-248-7417, E-mail: admissions_rel@trevecca.edu. *Dean,* Dr. Tim Green, 615-248-1378, Fax: 615-248-7728, E-mail: tgreen@trevecca.edu.

TRINITY COLLEGE, Hartford, CT 06106-3100

General Information Independent, coed, comprehensive institution. *Enrollment:* 9 full-time matriculated graduate/professional students (4 women), 176 part-time matriculated graduate/professional students (86 women). *Enrollment by degree level:* 185 master's. *Graduate faculty:* 14 full-time (8 women), 6 part-time/adjunct (0 women). *Tuition:* Part-time $900 per course. *Required fees:* $25 per term. *Graduate housing:* On-campus housing not available. *Student services:* Campus safety program, career counseling, child daycare facilities, disabled student services, exercise/wellness program, free psychological counseling, multicultural affairs office, writing training. *Library facilities:* Trinity College Library plus 2 others. *Online resources:* library catalog, web page, access to other libraries' catalogs. *Collection:* 962,703 titles, 3,492 serial subscriptions, 228,596 audiovisual materials.

Computer facilities: 315 computers available on campus for general student use. A campuswide network can be accessed from student residence rooms and from off campus. Internet access and online class registration, e-mail, Web pages are available. *Web address:* http://www.trincoll.edu/.

General Application Contact: Marilyn Brazil, Program Manager for Graduate Studies, 860-297-2527, Fax: 860-297-2529, E-mail: marilyn.brazil@mail.trincoll.edu.

GRADUATE UNITS

Graduate Programs Students: 9 full-time (4 women), 176 part-time (86 women); includes 24 minority (15 African Americans, 3 Asian Americans or Pacific Islanders, 6 Hispanic Americans) Average age 38. *Faculty:* 14 full-time (8 women), 6 part-time/adjunct (0 women). Expenses: Contact institution. *Financial support:* In 2001–02, 20 students received support, including 20 fellowships with partial tuition reimbursements available (averaging $9,000 per year); scholarships/grants and tuition waivers (full) also available. Support available to part-time students. Financial award application deadline: 4/1; financial award applicants required to submit FAFSA. In 2001, 26 degrees awarded. *Degree program information:* Part-time and evening/weekend programs available. Offers American studies (MA); economics (MA); English (MA); history (MA); public policy studies (MA). *Application deadline:* For fall admission, 4/1; for spring admission, 11/1. *Application fee:* $50. Electronic applications accepted. *Application Contact:* Marilyn Brazil, Program Manager for Graduate Studies, 860-297-2527, Fax: 860-297-2529, E-mail: marilyn.brazil@mail.trincoll.edu. *Director,* Dr. Nancy Birch Wagner, 860-297-2527, Fax: 860-297-2529, E-mail: grad_studies@trincoll.edu.

TRINITY COLLEGE, Washington, DC 20017-1094

General Information Independent-religious, women only, comprehensive institution. *Enrollment:* 74 full-time matriculated graduate/professional students (66 women), 351 part-time matriculated graduate/professional students (294 women). *Enrollment by degree level:* 425 master's. *Graduate faculty:* 15 full-time (11 women), 50 part-time/adjunct (40 women). *Tuition:* Full-time $9,180; part-time $510 per credit. *Required fees:* $60; $30 per semester. Tuition and fees vary according to program. *Graduate housing:* Room and/or apartments available on a first-come, first-served basis to single students; on-campus housing not available to married students. Typical cost: $3,100 per year ($6,970 including board). *Student services:* Campus employment opportunities, campus safety program, career counseling, child daycare facilities, disabled student services, exercise/wellness program, free psychological counseling, international student services, low-cost health insurance, teacher training, writing training. *Library facilities:* Sister Helen Sheehan Library plus 1 other. *Online resources:* library catalog, web page, access to other libraries' catalogs. *Collection:* 210,285 titles, 537 serial subscriptions, 14,411 audiovisual materials.

Computer facilities: 80 computers available on campus for general student use. A campuswide network can be accessed from student residence rooms and from off campus. Internet access and online class registration are available. *Web address:* http://www.trinitydc.edu/.

General Application Contact: Idenne Russell, Director of Graduate Admissions, 202-884-9400, Fax: 202-884-9229, E-mail: russelli@trinitydc.edu.

GRADUATE UNITS

School of Education Students: 61 full-time (54 women), 300 part-time (245 women). *Faculty:* 11 full-time (9 women), 39 part-time/adjunct (34 women). Expenses: Contact institution. *Financial support:* Career-related internships or fieldwork, Federal Work-Study, and unspecified assistantships available. Support available to part-time students. Financial award applicants required to submit FAFSA. *Degree program information:* Part-time and evening/weekend programs available. Offers counseling (MA); curriculum and instruction (M Ed); early childhood (MAT); educational administration (MAT, MSA); elementary education (MAT); English as a second language (MAT); secondary education (MAT); special education (MAT). *Application deadline:* For fall admission, 4/1 (priority date); for winter and spring admission, 11/1 (priority date). Applications are processed on a rolling basis. *Application fee:* $35. *Application Contact:* Tomicula Williams, Director of Graduate Admissions for School of Education, 202-884-9400, Fax: 202-884-9229, E-mail: williamsts@trinitydc.edu. *Dean,* Dr. Suellen Harris, 202-884-9504, Fax: 202-884-9506, E-mail: harrissu@trinitydc.edu.

School of Professional Studies Students: 13 full-time (12 women), 51 part-time (49 women). *Faculty:* 5 full-time (3 women), 10 part-time/adjunct (5 women). Expenses: Contact institution. *Financial support:* Fellowships with full tuition reimbursements, career-related internships or fieldwork, institutionally sponsored loans, and traineeships available. Support available to part-time students. Financial award applicants required to submit FAFSA. *Degree program information:* Part-time and evening/weekend programs available. Offers business administration (MBA); communication (MA); human resources management (MSA); Information assurance (MS); non-profit management (MSA); organizational development (MSA); public community health (MSA). *Application deadline:* For fall admission, 4/1 (priority date); for winter and spring admission, 11/1 (priority date). Applications are processed on a rolling basis. *Application fee:* $35. *Application Contact:* Susan Scully, Director, Student Recruitment, 202-884-9628, E-mail: scullys@trinitydc.edu. *Vice President for Academic Affairs,* Dr. Robert M. Preston, 202-884-9214, Fax: 202-884-9229, E-mail: prestonr@trinitydc.edu.

See in-depth description on page 1145.

TRINITY EPISCOPAL SCHOOL FOR MINISTRY, Ambridge, PA 15003-2397

General Information Independent-religious, coed, graduate-only institution. *Graduate faculty:* 13 full-time (1 woman), 6 part-time/adjunct (3 women). *Tuition:* Part-time $200 per credit hour. *Required fees:* $355. *Graduate housing:* Rooms and/or apartments available on a first-come, first-served basis to single and married students. *Student services:* Career counseling, free psychological counseling, international student services, low-cost health insurance, writing training. *Online resources:* library catalog, web page, access to other libraries' catalogs. *Collection:* 75,000 titles, 425 serial subscriptions, 2,000 audiovisual materials.

Computer facilities: 10 computers available on campus for general student use. A campuswide network can be accessed. Internet access is available. *Web address:* http://www.tesm.edu/.

General Application Contact: Pam Stephens, Director of Admissions, 724-266-3838, Fax: 724-266-4517, E-mail: pamstephens@tesm.edu.

GRADUATE UNITS

Professional Program Students: 79 full-time (17 women), 20 part-time (8 women). Average age 37. *Faculty:* 13 full-time (1 woman), 6 part-time/adjunct (3 women). Expenses: Contact institution. *Financial support:* In 2001–02, 35 students received support. Career-related internships or fieldwork and scholarships/grants available. Financial award application deadline: 6/1; financial award applicants required to submit FAFSA. In 2001, 28 degrees awarded. *Degree program information:* Part-time programs available. Offers divinity (M Div); ministry (D Min); mission and evangelism (MAME); religion (MAR); theology (Diploma). *Application deadline:* For fall admission, 8/1 (priority date). Applications are processed on a rolling basis. *Application fee:* $25. *Application Contact:* Pam Stephens, Director of Admissions, 724-266-3838, Fax: 724-266-4617, E-mail: pamstephens@tesm.edu. *Dean and President,* Rev. Dr. Peter C. Moore, 724-266-3838, Fax: 724-266-4617.

TRINITY INTERNATIONAL UNIVERSITY, Deerfield, IL 60015-1284

General Information Independent-religious, coed, university. *Enrollment:* 508 full-time matriculated graduate/professional students (89 women), 460 part-time matriculated graduate/professional students (103 women). *Enrollment by degree level:* 360 first professional, 608 master's. *Graduate faculty:* 41 full-time (2 women), 38 part-time/adjunct (3 women). *Tuition:* Full-time $10,440; part-time $522 per credit. Part-time tuition and fees vary according to course load and degree level. *Graduate housing:* Rooms and/or apartments available on a first-come, first-served basis to single students and available to married students. Typical cost: $2,030 per year ($4,610 including board) for single students; $4,680 per year for married students. Room and board charges vary according to board plan and housing facility selected. *Student services:* Campus employment opportunities, career counseling, child daycare facilities, disabled student services, exercise/wellness program, international student services, low-cost health insurance, multicultural affairs office. *Library facilities:* Rolfing Memorial Library. *Online resources:* library catalog, web page, access to other libraries' catalogs. *Collection:* 154,051 titles, 1,438 serial subscriptions, 3,888 audiovisual materials.

Computer facilities: 80 computers available on campus for general student use. A campuswide network can be accessed from student residence rooms and from off campus. Internet access is available. *Web address:* http://www.tiu.edu/.

General Application Contact: Ken Botton, Director of Admissions, 800-345-8337, Fax: 847-317-8097, E-mail: kbotton@tiu.edu.

GRADUATE UNITS

Trinity Evangelical Divinity School *Degree program information:* Part-time programs available. Postbaccalaureate distance learning degree programs offered (minimal on-campus study). Offers biblical studies (Certificate); biblical, historical and theological studies (M Div); bioethics for the chaplaincy (D Min); children's ministries (MA); Christian thought (MA); church history (Th M); counseling ministries (MA); cultural studies (M Div); educational leadership (M Div); educational studies (PhD); evangelism (MA); general studies (MAR); intercultural studies (PhD); interdisciplinary studies (M Div); leadership and management (D Min); missiology (D Min); missions (M Div, MA); missions and evangelism (Th M); New Testament (MA, Th M); Old Testament (MA, Th M); pastoral and general church ministries (M Div); pastoral care (D Min); pastoral counseling (Th M); pastoral ministry (D Min); practical theology (Th M); preaching (D Min); systematics (Th M); theological studies (PhD); urban ministry (MAR); youth ministries (MA). Electronic applications accepted.

Trinity Graduate School *Degree program information:* Part-time and evening/weekend programs available. Postbaccalaureate distance learning degree programs offered (minimal on-campus study). Offers bioethics (M Div, MA, PhD); counseling psychology (MA, Psy D); faith and culture (M Div, MA, PhD). Electronic applications accepted.

Trinity Law School Offers law (JD).

TRINITY INTERNATIONAL UNIVERSITY, SOUTH FLORIDA CAMPUS, Miami, FL 33132-1996

General Information Independent-religious, coed, graduate-only institution. *Graduate housing:* On-campus housing not available.

GRADUATE UNITS

Program in Counseling Psychology Offers counseling psychology (MA).

Program in Religion Offers religion (MA).

TRINITY LUTHERAN SEMINARY, Columbus, OH 43209-2334

General Information Independent-religious, coed, graduate-only institution. *Enrollment by degree level:* 167 first professional, 47 master's. *Graduate faculty:* 23 full-time (7 women), 12 part-time/adjunct (2 women). *Tuition:* Full-time $9,460; part-time $220 per credit hour. *Required fees:* $444; $113 per term. *Graduate housing:* Rooms and/or apartments available on a first-come, first-served basis to single and married students. Typical cost: $2,367 per year for single students; $4,185 per year for married students. Housing application deadline: 5/15. *Student services:* Campus employment opportunities, child daycare facilities, international student services, low-cost health insurance, writing training. *Library facilities:* Hamma Library. *Online resources:* library catalog, web page, access to other libraries' catalogs. *Collection:* 131,500 titles, 653 serial subscriptions, 5,149 audiovisual materials. *Research affiliation:* American School of Oriental Research (archaeology).

Computer facilities: 10 computers available on campus for general student use. A campuswide network can be accessed from student residence rooms and from off campus. Internet access is available. *Web address:* http://www.trinitylutheranseminary.edu/.

General Application Contact: Stacey Anderson, Director of Admissions, 614-235-4136, Fax: 614-238-0263, E-mail: sanderson@trinitylutheranseminary.

GRADUATE UNITS

Graduate and Professional Programs Students: 130 full-time (64 women), 84 part-time (49 women); includes 15 minority (12 African Americans, 2 Asian Americans or Pacific Islanders, 1 Hispanic American), 2 international. Average age 34. 95 applicants, 75% accepted. *Faculty:* 23 full-time (7 women), 12 part-time/adjunct (2 women). Expenses: Contact institution. *Financial support:* In 2001–02, 102 students received support. Career-related internships or fieldwork, Federal Work-Study, institutionally sponsored loans, and scholarships/grants available. Support available to part-time students. Financial award application deadline: 5/1; financial award applicants required to submit FAFSA. In 2001, 44 first professional degrees, 18 master's awarded. *Degree program information:* Part-time programs available. Offers church music (MA); divinity (M Div); lay ministry (MA); sacred theology (STM); theological studies (MTS). *Application deadline:* For fall admission, 4/15 (priority date). Applications are processed on a rolling basis. *Application fee:* $25. *Application Contact:* Stacey Anderson, Director of Admissions, 614-235-4136, Fax: 614-238-0263, E-mail: sanderson@trinitylutheranseminary.edu. *Dean,* Dr. Donald L. Huber, 614-235-4136, Fax: 614-238-0263, E-mail: dhuber@trinitylutheranseminary.edu.

TRINITY UNIVERSITY, San Antonio, TX 78212-7200

General Information Independent-religious, coed, comprehensive institution. CGS member. *Enrollment:* 110 full-time matriculated graduate/professional students (73 women), 96 part-time matriculated graduate/professional students (55 women). *Enrollment by degree level:* 206 master's. *Graduate faculty:* 22 full-time (10 women), 23 part-time/adjunct (9 women). *Tuition:* Full-time $16,410; part-time $684 per credit hour. *Required fees:* $6 per credit hour. *Graduate housing:* On-campus housing not available. *Student services:* Campus employment opportunities, campus safety program, career counseling, disabled student services, free psychological counseling, international student services. *Library facilities:* Elizabeth Huth Coates Library. *Online resources:* library catalog, web page, access to other libraries' catalogs. *Collection:* 871,081 titles, 3,450 serial subscriptions, 61,179 audiovisual materials.

Computer facilities: 100 computers available on campus for general student use. A campuswide network can be accessed from student residence rooms and from off campus. Internet access is available. *Web address:* http://www.trinity.edu/.

General Application Contact: Dr. Mary E. Stefl, Dean, 210-999-7521, Fax: 210-999-7522, E-mail: mstefl@trinity.edu.

GRADUATE UNITS

Division of Behavioral and Administrative Studies Students: 110 full-time (73 women), 96 part-time (55 women); includes 53 minority (7 African Americans, 13 Asian Americans or Pacific Islanders, 32 Hispanic Americans, 1 Native American), 2 international. Average age 29. *Faculty:* 22 full-time (10 women), 23 part-time/adjunct (9 women). Expenses: Contact institution. *Financial support:* In 2001–02, 163 students received support; fellowships, research assistantships, teaching assistantships, career-related internships or fieldwork, Federal Work-Study, institutionally sponsored loans, scholarships/grants, and unspecified assistantships available. Support available to part-time students. Financial award application deadline: 4/1. In 2001, 117 degrees awarded. *Degree program information:* Part-time and evening/weekend programs available. Offers accounting (MS); behavioral and administrative studies (M Ed, MA, MAT, MS); educational administration (M Ed); health care administration (MS); school psychology (MA); teacher education (MAT). *Application deadline:* For fall admission, 4/1. *Application fee:* $40. *Dean,* Dr. Mary E. Stefl, 210-999-7521, Fax: 210-999-7522, E-mail: mstefl@trinity.edu.

TRINITY WESTERN UNIVERSITY, Langley, BC V2Y 1Y1, Canada

General Information Independent-religious, coed, comprehensive institution. *Enrollment by degree level:* 446 master's. *Graduate faculty:* 40 full-time (3 women), 44 part-time/adjunct (10 women). *Graduate tuition:* Tuition charges are reported in Canadian dollars. *Tuition:* Part-time $395 Canadian dollars per semester hour. Part-time tuition and fees vary according to program. *Graduate housing:* Rooms and/or apartments available to single and married students. Housing application deadline: 7/6. *Student services:* Campus employment opportunities, campus safety program, career counseling, free psychological counseling, international student services, low-cost health insurance. *Library facilities:* Norma Marion Alloway Library. *Online resources:* library catalog, web page, access to other libraries' catalogs. *Collection:* 115,626 titles, 2,316 serial subscriptions, 3,002 audiovisual materials. *Research affiliation:* Department of National Defense (polymers), Department of Wildlife (weeds).

Computer facilities: 50 computers available on campus for general student use. A campuswide network can be accessed from student residence rooms and from off campus. Internet access is available. *Web address:* http://www.twu.ca/.

General Application Contact: Vic Cornish, Director, Graduate Admissions, 604-513-2121 Ext. 5130, Fax: 604-513-2061, E-mail: vic.cornish@twu.ca.

GRADUATE UNITS

ACT Seminaries Students: 99 full-time, 181 part-time. Average age 35. *Faculty:* 21. Expenses: Contact institution. *Financial support:* Research assistantships, career-related internships or fieldwork, Federal Work-Study, and institutionally sponsored loans available. Financial award application deadline: 3/1; financial award applicants required to submit FAFSA. In 2001, 69 degrees awarded. *Degree program information:* Part-time programs available. Offers christian studies (MA); church ministries (MA); cross cultural ministries (MA); theology (M Div, M Th, MC, MLE, MTS). *Application deadline:* Applications are processed on a rolling basis. *Application fee:* $40. *Application Contact:* Dr. Arnie Friesen, Director of Admissions, 604-513-2044,

Trinity Western University (continued)

Fax: 604-513-2045, E-mail: afriesen@twu.ca. *Principal,* Dr. Phil Zylla, 604-588-7531 Ext. 3825, Fax: 604-513-2045, E-mail: phil.zylla@twu.edu.

Program in Administrative Leadership Students: 43 full-time (22 women). 35 applicants, 74% accepted. *Faculty:* 2 full-time (0 women), 18 part-time/adjunct (4 women). Expenses: Contact institution. *Financial support:* Research assistantships, teaching assistantships available. In 2001, 25 degrees awarded. Postbaccalaureate distance learning degree programs offered (minimal on-campus study). Offers administrative leadership (MA). *Application deadline:* For spring admission, 2/15 (priority date). Applications are processed on a rolling basis. *Application fee:* $35. *Application Contact:* Vic Cornish, Director, Graduate Admissions, 604-513-2121 Ext. 5130, Fax: 604-513-2061, E-mail: vic.cornish@twu.ca. *Director,* Dr. Don Page, 604-888-7511 Ext. 3336, Fax: 604-513-2042, E-mail: page@twu.ca.

Program in Biblical Studies 8 applicants, 100% accepted. *Faculty:* 7 full-time (0 women), 5 part-time/adjunct (0 women). Expenses: Contact institution. *Financial support:* In 2001–02, 12 students received support, including research assistantships (averaging $1,500 per year), teaching assistantships (averaging $1,500 per year); institutionally sponsored loans and scholarships/grants also available. Financial award application deadline: 4/1; financial award applicants required to submit FAFSA. In 2001, 2 degrees awarded. *Degree program information:* Part-time programs available. Offers biblical studies (MA). *Application deadline:* For fall admission, 5/1; for spring admission, 11/1. Applications are processed on a rolling basis. *Application fee:* $35 Canadian dollars. *Application Contact:* Vic Cornish, Director, Graduate Admissions, 604-888-7511 Ext. 3130, Fax: 604-513-2061, E-mail: vic.cornish@twu.edu. *Director,* Dr. Peter Flint, 604-888-2511 Ext. 3117, Fax: 604-513-2094, E-mail: flint@twu.ca.

Program in Counseling Psychology Students: 33 full-time, 45 part-time. Average age 27. *Faculty:* 9 full-time (2 women), 12 part-time/adjunct (5 women). Expenses: Contact institution. *Financial support:* Research assistantships, teaching assistantships available. In 2001, 10 degrees awarded. *Degree program information:* Part-time programs available. Offers counseling psychology (MA). *Application deadline:* For fall admission, 4/1 (priority date); for spring admission, 11/15 (priority date). *Application fee:* $35 Canadian dollars. *Application Contact:* Vic Cornish, Director, Graduate Admissions, 604-888-7511 Ext. 3130, Fax: 604-513-2061, E-mail: vic.cornish@twu.edu. *Director,* Dr. Marvin McDonald, 604-888-7511 Ext. 3223, Fax: 604-513-2010, E-mail: mcdonald@twu.edu.

Program in Religion, Culture and Ethics Students: 12 full-time, 1 part-time. Average age 26. 10 applicants, 100% accepted. *Faculty:* 1 full-time (0 women), 9 part-time/adjunct (1 woman). Expenses: Contact institution. *Financial support:* Research assistantships, teaching assistantships, institutionally sponsored loans and scholarships/grants available. Financial award application deadline: 3/1; financial award applicants required to submit FAFSA. In 2001, 1 degree awarded. *Degree program information:* Part-time programs available. Offers religion, culture and ethics (MA). *Application deadline:* For fall admission, 5/1; for spring admission, 11/1. *Application fee:* $35 Canadian dollars. *Application Contact:* Vic Cornish, Director, Graduate Admissions, 604-513-2121 Ext. 5130, Fax: 604-513-2061, E-mail: vic.cornish@twu.ca. *Director,* Dr. Phillip Wiebe, 604-888-7511 Ext. 3334, Fax: 604-513-2010, E-mail: pwiebe@twu.ca.

TRI STATE COLLEGE OF ACUPUNCTURE, New York, NY 10011

General Information Independent, coed, graduate-only institution. *Graduate faculty:* 31 part-time/adjunct (20 women). *Tuition:* Full-time $12,000. *Required fees:* $400. *Graduate housing:* On-campus housing not available. *Library facilities:* TSCA Library. *Collection:* 600 titles, 400 serial subscriptions. *Web address:* http://www.tsca.edu/.

General Application Contact: 212-242-2255, Fax: 212-242-2920, E-mail: tscacupuncture@aol.com.

GRADUATE UNITS

Program in Acupuncture Students: 128 full-time (79 women), 24 part-time (14 women). Average age 40. 79 applicants, 90% accepted, 49 enrolled. *Faculty:* 31 part-time/adjunct (20 women). Expenses: Contact institution. *Financial support:* In 2001–02, 90 students received support. Application deadline: 7/15; In 2001, 45 degrees awarded. *Degree program information:* Evening/weekend programs available. Offers acupuncture (MS); traditional Chinese herbology (Certificate). *Application deadline:* For fall admission, 6/15 (priority date). Applications are processed on a rolling basis. *Application fee:* $50.

TROY STATE UNIVERSITY, Troy, AL 36082

General Information State-supported, coed, comprehensive institution. *Graduate housing:* Rooms and/or apartments available to single and married students. Housing application deadline: 7/31. *Research affiliation:* Georgia-Pacific Corporation (chemistry).

GRADUATE UNITS

Graduate School *Degree program information:* Part-time and evening/weekend programs available. Electronic applications accepted.

College of Arts and Sciences *Degree program information:* Part-time and evening/weekend programs available. Offers administration of criminal justice (MS); arts and sciences (MS); corrections (MS); environmental analysis and management (MS); international relations (MS); police administration (MS); public administration (MS). Electronic applications accepted.

College of Health and Human Services *Degree program information:* Part-time and evening/weekend programs available. Offers health and human services (MS); nursing (MS). Electronic applications accepted.

School of Education *Degree program information:* Part-time and evening/weekend programs available. Offers counseling and human development (MS); counselor education (MS); early childhood education (MS, Ed S); education (MS, Ed S); educational leadership/administration (MS); elementary education (MS, Ed S); emotional conflict (MS); foundations of education (MS); guidance services (MS); learning disabilities (MS); mental retardation (MS); mild learning handicapped (MS, Ed S); N–12 education (MS, Ed S); secondary education (MS, Ed S). Electronic applications accepted.

University College *Degree program information:* Part-time and evening/weekend programs available. Offers business administration (MBA); management (MS); personnel management (MS). Electronic applications accepted.

TROY STATE UNIVERSITY DOTHAN, Dothan, AL 36304-0368

General Information State-supported, coed, comprehensive institution. *Enrollment:* 76 full-time matriculated graduate/professional students (57 women), 280 part-time matriculated graduate/professional students (201 women). *Enrollment by degree level:* 323 master's, 33 other advanced degrees. *Graduate faculty:* 52 full-time (18 women), 9 part-time/adjunct (2 women). Tuition, state resident: part-time $138 per credit hour. Tuition, nonresident: part-time $276 per credit hour. *Required fees:* $64 per semester. *Graduate housing:* On-campus housing not available. *Student services:* Campus employment opportunities, campus safety program, career counseling, disabled student services, international student services, low-cost health insurance, writing training. *Library facilities:* Troy State University Dotham Library. *Online resources:* library catalog, web page, access to other libraries' catalogs. *Collection:* 100,223 titles, 609 serial subscriptions, 13,879 audiovisual materials.

Computer facilities: 150 computers available on campus for general student use. A campuswide network can be accessed. Internet access is available. *Web address:* http://www.tsud.edu/.

General Application Contact: Reta Cordell, Director of Admissions and Records, 334-983-6556 Ext. 228, Fax: 334-983-6322, E-mail: rcordell@tsud.edu.

GRADUATE UNITS

Graduate School Students: 76 full-time (57 women), 280 part-time (201 women); includes 56 minority (46 African Americans, 3 Asian Americans or Pacific Islanders, 6 Hispanic Americans, 1 Native American) Average age 35. 119 applicants, 67% accepted, 64 enrolled. *Faculty:* 52 full-time (18 women), 9 part-time/adjunct (2 women). Expenses: Contact institution. *Financial support:* Federal Work-Study and scholarships/grants available. Support available to part-time students. Financial award applicants required to submit FAFSA. In 2001, 117 master's, 12 other advanced degrees awarded. *Degree program information:* Part-time and evening/weekend programs available. *Application deadline:* For fall admission, 7/20; for spring admission, 12/1. Applications are processed on a rolling basis. *Application fee:* $20. Electronic applications accepted. *Application Contact:* Reta Cordell, Director of Admissions and Records, 334-983-6556 Ext. 228, Fax: 334-983-6322, E-mail: rcordell@tsud.edu. *Executive Vice President,* Dr. Barbara Alford, 334-983-6556 Ext. 220, Fax: 334-983-6322, E-mail: balford@tsud.edu.

College of Arts and Sciences Students: 2 full-time (0 women), 37 part-time (21 women); includes 7 minority (5 African Americans, 2 Hispanic Americans) Average age 38. 24 applicants, 63% accepted, 3 enrolled. *Faculty:* 21 full-time (7 women), 2 part-time/adjunct (0 women). Expenses: Contact institution. *Financial support:* Federal Work-Study and scholarships/grants available. Support available to part-time students. Financial award applicants required to submit FAFSA. *Degree program information:* Part-time and evening/weekend programs available. Offers arts and sciences (MS); history and political sciences (MS). *Application deadline:* For fall admission, 7/20; for spring admission, 12/1. Applications are processed on a rolling basis. *Application fee:* $20. *Application Contact:* Reta Cordell, Director of Admissions and Records, 334-983-6556 Ext. 228, Fax: 334-983-6322, E-mail: rcordell@tsud.edu. *Dean,* Dr. Alan Belsches, 334-983-6556 Ext. 390.

College of Business Administration Students: 18 full-time (13 women), 49 part-time (31 women); includes 9 minority (8 African Americans, 1 Asian American or Pacific Islander) Average age 34. 27 applicants, 59% accepted, 15 enrolled. *Faculty:* 17 full-time (3 women), 1 part-time/adjunct (0 women). Expenses: Contact institution. *Financial support:* Federal Work-Study and scholarships/grants available. Support available to part-time students. Financial award applicants required to submit FAFSA. In 2001, 37 degrees awarded. *Degree program information:* Part-time and evening/weekend programs available. Offers accounting (MBA, MS); business (MBA, MS); business education (MS); business law (MS); computer information systems (MS); general business (MBA); human resource management (MBA, MS). *Application deadline:* For fall admission, 7/20; for spring admission, 12/1. Applications are processed on a rolling basis. *Application fee:* $20. *Application Contact:* Reta Cordell, Director of Admissions and Records, 334-983-6556 Ext. 228, Fax: 334-983-6322, E-mail: rcordell@tsud.edu. *Dean,* Dr. Adair Gilbert, 334-983-6556 Ext. 264.

College of Education Students: 56 full-time (44 women), 194 part-time (149 women); includes 40 minority (33 African Americans, 2 Asian Americans or Pacific Islanders, 4 Hispanic Americans, 1 Native American) Average age 35. 68 applicants, 72% accepted, 46 enrolled. *Faculty:* 14 full-time (8 women), 6 part-time/adjunct (2 women). Expenses: Contact institution. *Financial support:* Federal Work-Study and scholarships/grants available. Support available to part-time students. Financial award applicants required to submit FAFSA. In 2001, 80 master's, 12 other advanced degrees awarded. *Degree program information:* Part-time and evening/weekend programs available. Offers counseling and psychology (MS, Ed S); curriculum and instruction (MS, Ed S); education (MS, MS Ed, Ed S); leadership, foundations, and technology (MS, Ed S). *Application deadline:* For fall admission, 7/20; for spring admission, 12/1. Applications are processed on a rolling basis. *Application fee:* $20. *Application Contact:* Reta Cordell, Director of Admissions and Records, 334-983-6556 Ext. 228, Fax: 334-983-6322, E-mail: rcordell@tsud.edu. *Dean,* Dr. Cynthia Lumpkin, 334-983-6556 Ext. 360.

TROY STATE UNIVERSITY MONTGOMERY, Montgomery, AL 36103-4419

General Information State-supported, coed, comprehensive institution. Tuition, state resident: full-time $2,286; part-time $127 per semester hour. Tuition, nonresident: full-time $4,572; part-time $254 per semester hour. *Required fees:* $30 per term. Tuition and fees vary according to program. *Graduate housing:* On-campus housing not available. *Student services:* Campus employment opportunities, campus safety program, career counseling, low-cost health insurance. *Library facilities:* Troy State University Montgomery Library. *Online resources:* library catalog, web page, access to other libraries' catalogs. *Collection:* 34,864 titles, 476 serial subscriptions, 9,194 audiovisual materials.

Computer facilities: 190 computers available on campus for general student use. A campuswide network can be accessed from off campus. Internet access and online class registration are available. *Web address:* http://www.tsum.edu/.

General Application Contact: Dr. Kimberly A. Combs, Interim Dean of Graduate Division, 334-241-9581, Fax: 334-241-9586, E-mail: kcombs@tsum.edu.

GRADUATE UNITS

Graduate Programs Students: 411. Average age 35. Expenses: Contact institution. In 2001, 191 master's, 3 other advanced degrees awarded. *Degree program information:* Part-time and evening/weekend programs available. *Application deadline:* Applications are processed on a rolling basis. *Application fee:* $30. Electronic applications accepted. *Interim Dean of Graduate Division,* Dr. Kimberly A. Combs, 334-241-9581, Fax: 334-241-9586, E-mail: kcombs@tsum.edu.

Division of Business Students: 231. Expenses: Contact institution. In 2001, 110 degrees awarded. *Degree program information:* Part-time and evening/weekend programs available. Offers business administration (MBA); computer and information science (MS); human resources management (MS); management (MS). *Application deadline:* Applications are processed on a rolling basis. *Application fee:* $30. Electronic applications accepted. *Acting Dean,* Dr. Jimmy Simpson, 334-241-9717, Fax: 334-241-9734, E-mail: jsimpson@tsum.edu.

Division of Counseling, Education, and Psychology Students: 190. Expenses: Contact institution. In 2001, 81 master's, 3 other advanced degrees awarded. *Degree program information:* Part-time and evening/weekend programs available. Offers adult education (MS); counseling (MS, Ed S); counseling and human development (MS, Ed S); elementary education (MS); general education administration (Ed S); teaching (MA). *Application deadline:* Applications are processed on a rolling basis. *Application fee:* $30. Electronic applications accepted. *Interim Dean,* Dr. Chris Randall, 334-241-9594, Fax: 334-241-9586.

TRUMAN STATE UNIVERSITY, Kirksville, MO 63501-4221

General Information State-supported, coed, comprehensive institution. CGS member. *Enrollment:* 193 full-time matriculated graduate/professional students (133 women), 15 part-time matriculated graduate/professional students (12 women). *Enrollment by degree level:* 208 master's. *Graduate faculty:* 151. Tuition, state resident: full-time $4,072. Tuition, nonresident: full-time $7,412. *Required fees:* $30. *Graduate housing:* Rooms and/or apartments available on a first-come, first-served basis to single and married students. Housing application deadline: 5/1. *Student services:* Campus employment opportunities, campus safety program, career counseling, child daycare facilities, disabled student services, exercise/wellness program, free psychological counseling, grant writing training, international student services, low-cost health insurance, multicultural affairs office, writing training. *Library facilities:* Pickler Memorial Library plus 1 other. *Online resources:* library catalog, web page, access to other libraries' catalogs. *Collection:* 472,652 titles, 3,665 serial subscriptions, 33,694 audiovisual materials. *Research affiliation:* Gulf Coast Research Laboratory (marine science), Kirksville College of Osteopathic Medicine (biology).

Computer facilities: 769 computers available on campus for general student use. A campuswide network can be accessed from student residence rooms and from off campus. Internet access is available. *Web address:* http://www.truman.edu/.

General Application Contact: Crista Chappell, Graduate Office Secretary, 660-785-4109, Fax: 660-785-7460, E-mail: gradinfo@truman.edu.

GRADUATE UNITS

Graduate School Students: 193 full-time (133 women), 15 part-time (12 women); includes 9 minority (3 African Americans, 2 Asian Americans or Pacific Islanders, 4 Hispanic Americans), 7 international. *Faculty:* 151. Expenses: Contact institution. *Financial support:* Fellowships, research assistantships with tuition reimbursements, teaching assistantships with tuition reimbursements, career-related internships or fieldwork, Federal Work-Study, and institutionally sponsored loans available. Financial award application deadline: 5/1; financial award applicants required to submit FAFSA. In 2001, 105 degrees awarded. *Application deadline:* For fall admission, 6/15 (priority date); for spring admission, 11/1 (priority date). Applications are processed on a rolling basis. *Application fee:* $0. *Application Contact:* Crista Chappell, Graduate Office Secretary, 660-785-4109, Fax: 660-785-7460, E-mail: gradinfo@truman.edu. *Dean of Graduate Studies,* Dr. Maria Di Stefano, 660-785-4109, Fax: 660-785-7460, E-mail: mdistefa@truman.edu.

Division of Business and Accountancy Students: 26 full-time (8 women), 1 (woman) part-time; includes 2 minority (1 African American, 1 Asian American or Pacific Islander), 4 international. 18 applicants, 100% accepted. Expenses: Contact institution. *Financial support:* Research assistantships with tuition reimbursements, teaching assistantships with tuition reimbursements, career-related internships or fieldwork and Federal Work-Study available. Financial award application deadline: 5/1; financial award applicants required to submit FAFSA. In 2001, 9 degrees awarded. Offers accounting (M Ac). *Application deadline:* For fall admission, 6/15; for spring admission, 11/1. Applications are processed on a rolling basis. *Application fee:* $0. *Application Contact:* Crista Chappell, Graduate Office Secretary, 660-785-4109, Fax: 660-785-7460, E-mail: gradinfo@truman.edu. *Coordinator,* Dr. Jeffrey Romine, 660-785-4375, Fax: 660-785-7471, E-mail: jromine@truman.edu.

Division of Education Students: 109 full-time (85 women), 5 part-time (3 women); includes 3 minority (1 African American, 2 Hispanic Americans) Expenses: Contact institution. *Financial support:* Fellowships with tuition reimbursements, research assistantships with tuition reimbursements, career-related internships or fieldwork and Federal Work-Study available. Financial award application deadline: 5/1; financial award applicants required to submit FAFSA. In 2001, 66 degrees awarded. Offers education (MAE). *Application deadline:* For fall admission, 2/15; for spring admission, 9/15. *Application fee:* $0. *Application Contact:* Crista Chappell, Graduate Office Secretary, 660-785-4109, Fax: 660-785-7460, E-mail: gradinfo@truman.edu. *Head,* Dr. Sam Minner, 660-785-4383, Fax: 660-785-4393.

Division of Fine Arts Students: 3 full-time (2 women). 4 applicants, 75% accepted. Expenses: Contact institution. *Financial support:* Research assistantships with tuition reimbursements, teaching assistantships with tuition reimbursements, career-related internships or fieldwork and Federal Work-Study available. Financial award application deadline: 5/1; financial award applicants required to submit FAFSA. In 2001, 2 degrees awarded. Offers music (MA). *Application deadline:* For fall admission, 6/15 (priority date); for spring admission, 11/1 (priority date). Applications are processed on a rolling basis. *Application fee:* $0. *Application Contact:* Crista Chappell, Graduate Office Secretary, 660-785-4109, Fax: 660-785-7460, E-mail: gradinfo@truman.edu. *Head,* Robert Jones, 660-785-4417, Fax: 660-785-7463, E-mail: fa01@academic.truman.edu.

Division of Human Potential and Performance Students: 14 full-time (all women), 2 part-time (both women). 35 applicants, 80% accepted. Expenses: Contact institution. *Financial support:* Fellowships, career-related internships or fieldwork and Federal Work-Study available. Financial award application deadline: 5/1; financial award applicants required to submit FAFSA. In 2001, 10 degrees awarded. Offers communication disorders (MA). *Application deadline:* For fall admission, 6/15 (priority date); for spring admission, 11/1. Applications are processed on a rolling basis. *Application fee:* $0. *Application Contact:* Crista Chappell, Graduate Office Secretary, 660-785-4109, Fax: 660-785-7460, E-mail: gradinfo@truman.edu.

Division of Language and Literature Students: 17 full-time (12 women); includes 1 minority (Asian American or Pacific Islander) 12 applicants, 100% accepted. Expenses: Contact institution. *Financial support:* Research assistantships with tuition reimbursements, teaching assistantships with tuition reimbursements, career-related internships or fieldwork and Federal Work-Study available. Financial award application deadline: 5/1; financial award applicants required to submit FAFSA. In 2001, 7 degrees awarded. Offers English (MA). *Application deadline:* For fall admission, 6/15 (priority date); for spring admission, 11/1 (priority date). Applications are processed on a rolling basis. *Application fee:* $0. *Application Contact:* Crista Chappell, Graduate Office Secretary, 660-785-4109, Fax: 660-785-7460, E-mail: gradinfo@truman.edu. *Head,* Dr. Heinz Woehlk, 660-785-4481, Fax: 660-785-7486, E-mail: heinz@academic.truman.edu.

Division of Science Students: 7 full-time (4 women), 3 international. 6 applicants, 67% accepted. Expenses: Contact institution. *Financial support:* Research assistantships with tuition reimbursements, teaching assistantships with tuition reimbursements, career-related internships or fieldwork and Federal Work-Study available. Financial award application deadline: 5/1; financial award applicants required to submit FAFSA. In 2001, 3 degrees awarded. Offers biology (MS). *Application deadline:* For fall admission, 6/15 (priority date); for spring admission, 11/1. Applications are processed on a rolling basis. *Application fee:* $0. *Application Contact:* Crista Chappell, Graduate Office Secretary, 660-785-4109, Fax: 660-785-7460, E-mail: gradinfo@truman.edu. *Head,* Dr. Scott Ellis, 660-785-4597, Fax: 660-785-4045, E-mail: sellis@truman.edu.

Division of Social Science Students: 17 full-time (8 women), 7 part-time (6 women); includes 4 minority (1 African American, 3 Hispanic Americans) 24 applicants, 58% accepted. Expenses: Contact institution. *Financial support:* Research assistantships with tuition reimbursements, teaching assistantships with tuition reimbursements, career-related internships or fieldwork and Federal Work-Study available. Financial award application deadline: 5/1; financial award applicants required to submit FAFSA. In 2001, 9 degrees awarded. Offers counseling (MA); history (MA). *Application deadline:* For fall admission, 6/15 (priority date); for spring admission, 11/1. Applications are processed on a rolling basis. *Application fee:* $0. *Application Contact:* Crista Chappell, Graduate Office Secretary, 660-785-4109, Fax: 660-785-7460, E-mail: gradinfo@truman.edu. *Head,* Dr. Seymour Patterson, 660-785-4636, Fax: 660-785-4337, E-mail: spatters@truman.edu.

See in-depth description on page 1147.

TUFTS UNIVERSITY, Medford, MA 02155

General Information Independent, coed, university. CGS member. *Enrollment:* 3,434 full-time matriculated graduate/professional students (1,946 women), 842 part-time matriculated graduate/professional students (469 women). *Enrollment by degree level:* 1,636 first professional, 2,640 master's. *Graduate faculty:* 679 full-time (262 women), 424 part-time/adjunct (182 women). *Tuition:* Full-time $26,853. Full-time tuition and fees vary according to program. *Graduate housing:* Room and/or apartments available on a first-come, first-served basis to single students; on-campus housing not available to married students. Typical cost: $4,900 per year. *Student services:* Campus employment opportunities, campus safety program, career counseling, child daycare facilities, disabled student services, exercise/wellness program, free psychological counseling, international student services, low-cost health insurance, multicultural affairs office, teacher training, writing training. *Library facilities:* Tisch Library plus 1 other. *Online resources:* library catalog, web page, access to other libraries' catalogs. *Collection:* 1.6 million titles, 5,329 serial subscriptions, 32,200 audiovisual materials.

Computer facilities: 254 computers available on campus for general student use. A campuswide network can be accessed from student residence rooms and from off campus. Internet access and online class registration are available. *Web address:* http://www.tufts.edu/.

General Application Contact: Darla Pires, Admissions Coordinator, 617-627-2750.

GRADUATE UNITS

Division of Graduate and Continuing Studies and Research *Degree program information:* Part-time and evening/weekend programs available. Offers bioengineering (Certificate); biotechnology (Certificate); biotechnology engineering (Certificate); community environmental studies (Certificate); computer science (Certificate); computer science minor (Certificate); electro-optics technology (Certificate); environmental management (Certificate); epidemiology (Certificate); human-computer interaction (Certificate); management of community organizations (Certificate); manufacturing engineering (Certificate); microwave and wireless engineering (Certificate); museum studies (Certificate); occupational therapy (Certificate); premedical studies (Certificate); program evaluation (Certificate).

Graduate School of Arts and Sciences Students: 1,332 (785 women). Average age 29. 1,603 applicants, 52% accepted. *Faculty:* 304 full-time, 216 part-time/adjunct. Expenses: Contact institution. *Financial support:* Fellowships with full and partial tuition reimbursements, research assistantships with full and partial tuition reimbursements, teaching assistantships with full and partial tuition reimbursements, career-related internships or fieldwork, Federal Work-Study, scholarships/grants, and tuition waivers (full and partial) available. Support available to part-time students. Financial award applicants required to submit FAFSA. In 2001, 330 master's, 39 doctorates awarded. *Degree program information:* Part-time and evening/weekend programs available. Offers analytical chemistry (MS, PhD); applied developmental psychology (PhD); art history (MA); arts and sciences (MA, MAT, ME, MFA, MS, MSEM, PhD, CAGS); biology (MS, PhD); bioorganic chemistry (MS, PhD); chemical and biochemical engineering (ME, MS, PhD); child development (MA, CAGS); civil engineering (MS, PhD); classical archaeology (MA); classics (MA); community development (MA); computer science (MS, PhD); dance (MA, PhD); drama (MA); dramatic literature and criticism (PhD); early childhood education (MAT); economics (MA); education (CAGS); electrical engineering (MS, PhD); elementary education (MAT); engineering (ME, MS, MSEM, PhD); engineering management (MSEM); English (MA, PhD); environmental chemistry (MS, PhD); environmental engineering (MS, PhD); environmental policy (MA); ethnomusicology (MA); French (MA); German (MA); health and human welfare (MA); history (MA, PhD); housing policy (MA); human factors (MS); inorganic chemistry (MS, PhD); international environment/development policy (MA); mathematics (MA, MS, PhD); mechanical engineering (ME, MS, PhD); middle and secondary education (MA, MAT); music history and literature (MA); music theory and composition (MA); occupational therapy (MA, MS); organic chemistry (MS, PhD); philosophy (MA); physical chemistry (MS, PhD); physics (MS, PhD); psychology (MS, PhD); public policy and citizen participation (MA); school psychology (MA, CAGS); secondary education (MA); studio art (MFA); theater history (PhD). *Application deadline:* Applications are processed on a rolling basis. *Application fee:* $50. Electronic applications accepted. *Application Contact:* Gretchen Inman, Administrative Director, 617-627-3395, Fax: 617-627-3016, E-mail: gsas@infonet.tufts.edu. *Dean,* Robin Kanarek, 617-627-3395, Fax: 617-627-3016.

Fletcher School of Law and Diplomacy Students: 427 full-time (224 women); includes 45 minority (14 African Americans, 24 Asian Americans or Pacific Islanders, 7 Hispanic Americans), 210 international. Average age 28. 1,158 applicants, 41% accepted, 158 enrolled. *Faculty:* 29 full-time (5 women), 40 part-time/adjunct (11 women). Expenses: Contact institution. *Financial support:* In 2001–02, 221 students received support, including 221 fellowships (averaging $7,000 per year); research assistantships, teaching assistantships, career-related internships or fieldwork, Federal Work-Study, institutionally sponsored loans, and scholarships/grants also available. Financial award application deadline: 1/15; financial award applicants required to submit FAFSA. In 2001, 192 master's, 11 doctorates awarded. Postbaccalaureate distance learning degree programs offered (minimal on-campus study). Offers law and diplomacy (MA, MAHA, MALD, PhD). *Application deadline:* For fall admission, 1/15; for spring admission, 10/15. *Application fee:* $50. Electronic applications accepted. *Application Contact:* Laurie A. Hurley, Director of Admissions and Financial Aid, 617-627-3040, Fax: 617-627-3712, E-mail: fletcheradmissions@tufts.edu. *Dean,* Stephen W. Bosworth, 617-627-3050, Fax: 617-627-3712.

Sackler School of Graduate Biomedical Sciences Students: 212 full-time (124 women), 2 part-time (both women); includes 25 minority (3 African Americans, 13 Asian Americans or Pacific Islanders, 9 Hispanic Americans), 53 international. 887 applicants, 13% accepted. *Faculty:* 139 full-time (40 women). Expenses: Contact institution. *Financial support:* In 2001–02, research assistantships with full tuition reimbursements (averaging $19,456 per year); fellowships with full tuition reimbursements, career-related internships or fieldwork, scholarships/grants, and tuition waivers (full and partial) also available. Financial award applicants required to submit FAFSA. In 2001, 3 master's, 37 doctorates awarded. Offers biochemistry (PhD); biomedical sciences (MS, PhD); cell, molecular and developmental biology (PhD); cellular and molecular physiology (PhD); genetics (PhD); immunology (PhD); microbiology (PhD); molecular biology (PhD); molecular microbiology (PhD); neuroscience (PhD); pharmacology and experimental therapeutics (PhD). *Application deadline:* For fall admission, 1/15 (priority date). Applications are processed on a rolling basis. *Application fee:* $50. *Application Contact:* Staff Assistant, 617-636-6767, Fax: 617-636-0375, E-mail: sackler-school@tufts.edu. *Dean,* Dr. Louis Lasagna, 617-636-6767.

Division of Clinical Care Research Students: 19 full-time (4 women), 4 part-time (2 women); includes 9 minority (3 African Americans, 6 Asian Americans or Pacific Islanders) Average age 34. 10 applicants, 100% accepted, 10 enrolled. *Faculty:* 10 full-time (4 women), 1 part-time/adjunct (0 women). Expenses: Contact institution. *Financial support:* In 2001–02, 3 fellowships with full tuition reimbursements (averaging $44,000 per year) were awarded In 2001, 5 degrees awarded. *Degree program information:* Part-time programs available. Offers clinical care research (MS, PhD). *Application deadline:* For winter admission, 1/5 (priority date). Applications are processed on a rolling basis. *Application fee:* $45. *Program Director,* Dr. Harry P. Selker, 617-636-5009, Fax: 617-636-8023, E-mail: hselker@lifespan.org.

School of Dental Medicine Offers dental medicine (DMD, MS, Certificate); dentistry (Certificate).

School of Medicine 9,187 applicants, 6% accepted. Expenses: Contact institution. *Financial support:* Career-related internships or fieldwork, Federal Work-Study, and institutionally sponsored loans available. Support available to part-time students. Financial award applicants required to submit FAFSA. In 2001, 158 first professional degrees, 59 master's awarded. *Degree program information:* Part-time and evening/weekend programs available. Offers education and policy (MS); health communication (MS); medicine (MD, MPH, MS); pain research (MS); public health (MPH). *Application Contact:* Thomas Slavin, Director of Admissions, 617-636-6571. *Dean,* Dr. John Harrington, 617-636-6565.

School of Nutrition Science and Policy *Degree program information:* Part-time programs available. Offers nutrition (MS, PhD). Electronic applications accepted.

School of Veterinary Medicine Students: 305 full-time. Average age 29. 723 applicants, 80 enrolled. *Faculty:* 82 full-time, 148 part-time/adjunct. Expenses: Contact institution. *Financial support:* Career-related internships or fieldwork, Federal Work-Study, institutionally sponsored loans, scholarships/grants, and institutional aid awards available. Financial award application deadline: 3/15. In 2001, 75 first professional degrees, 8 master's awarded. Offers animals and public policy (MS); comparative biomedical sciences (PhD); veterinary medicine (DVM, MS, PhD). *Application deadline:* For fall admission, 12/1. *Application fee:* $60. Electronic applications accepted. *Application Contact:* Rebecca Russo, Director of Admissions, 508-839-7920, Fax: 508-839-2953, E-mail: rebecca.russo@tufts.edu. *Dean,* Dr. Philip Kosch, 508-839-5302, Fax: 508-839-2953.

See in-depth description on page 1149.

TULANE UNIVERSITY, New Orleans, LA 70118-5669

General Information Independent, coed, university. CGS member. *Enrollment:* 4,179 full-time matriculated graduate/professional students (2,129 women), 680 part-time matriculated graduate/professional students (286 women). *Enrollment by degree level:* 2,172 first professional, 1,850 master's. *Graduate faculty:* 958 full-time, 322 part-time/adjunct. *Tuition:* Full-time $24,675. *Required fees:* $2,210. *Graduate housing:* Rooms and/or apartments available on a first-come, first-served basis to single and married students. Typical cost: $4,128 per year ($7,128 including board) for single students; $4,128 per year ($7,128 including board) for married students. Housing application deadline: 3/24. *Student services:* Campus safety program, career counseling, child daycare facilities, exercise/wellness program, free psychological counseling, international student services, low-cost health insurance, multicultural affairs office. *Library facilities:* Howard Tilton Memorial Library plus 8 others. *Online resources:* library catalog, web page. *Collection:* 1.3 million titles, 15,286 serial subscriptions, 83,774 audiovisual materials. *Research affiliation:* U.S.–Japan Cooperative Biomedical Research Laboratories (neuroendocrinology, diabetes), Center for Legal Studies on Intergovernmental Relations (legal aspects of public policy issues), Energy Spatial Analysis Research Laboratory.

Computer facilities: A campuswide network can be accessed from student residence rooms and from off campus. *Web address:* http://www.tulane.edu/.

General Application Contact: Dr. Michael Herman, Dean, 504-865-5100, Fax: 504-865-5274, E-mail: mherman@tulane.edu.

GRADUATE UNITS

A. B. Freeman School of Business Students: 186 full-time, 294 part-time; includes 51 minority (27 African Americans, 9 Asian Americans or Pacific Islanders, 14 Hispanic Americans,

Tulane University (continued)

1 Native American), 210 international. 450 applicants, 53% accepted. *Faculty:* 60 full-time (9 women), 16 part-time/adjunct (4 women). Expenses: Contact institution. *Financial support:* Fellowships, research assistantships, teaching assistantships, career-related internships or fieldwork, Federal Work-Study, tuition waivers (full and partial), and unspecified assistantships available. Support available to part-time students. Financial award application deadline: 4/15; financial award applicants required to submit FAFSA. In 2001, 200 master's, 2 doctorates awarded. *Degree program information:* Part-time and evening/weekend programs available. Offers business (EMBA, M Acct, MBA, PhD). *Application deadline:* For fall admission, 5/1; for spring admission, 12/1. Applications are processed on a rolling basis. *Application fee:* $40 ($50 for international students). *Application Contact:* John C. Silbernagel, Assistant Dean for Admissions and Financial Aid, 504-865-5410, Fax: 504-865-6770, E-mail: freeman.admissions@tulane.edu. *Dean,* Dr. James W. McFarland, 504-865-5407, Fax: 504-865-5491.

Graduate School Students: 892 full-time, 63 part-time; includes 132 minority (60 African Americans, 29 Asian Americans or Pacific Islanders, 41 Hispanic Americans, 2 Native Americans), 192 international. 1,453 applicants, 32% accepted. *Faculty:* 370. Expenses: Contact institution. *Financial support:* Fellowships, research assistantships, teaching assistantships, career-related internships or fieldwork, Federal Work-Study, institutionally sponsored loans, and tuition waivers (full and partial) available. Financial award application deadline:2/1. In 2001, 102 master's, 72 doctorates awarded. *Degree program information:* Part-time programs available. Offers anthropology (MA, MS, PhD); applied development (MA, PhD); applied mathematics (MS); art (MFA); art history (MA); biology (MS, PhD); chemistry (MS, PhD); civic and cultural management (MA); classical studies (MA); economics (MA, PhD); English (MA, PhD); French and Italian (MA, PhD); geology (MS, PhD); history (MA, PhD); liberal arts (MLA); mathematics (MS, PhD); music (MA, MFA); paleontology (PhD); philosophy (MA, PhD); physics (MS, PhD); political science (MA, PhD); psychology (MS, PhD); sociology (MA, MAD, PhD); Spanish and Portuguese (MA, PhD); statistics (MS); theatre and dance (MFA). *Application deadline:* For fall admission, 2/1. *Application fee:* $45. Electronic applications accepted. *Application Contact:* Kay D. Orriu, Assistant Dean, 504-865-5100, Fax: 504-865-5274. *Dean,* Dr. Michael Herman, 504-865-5100, Fax: 504-865-5274, E-mail: mherman@tulane.edu.

Roger Thayer Stone Center for Latin American Studies Offers Latin American studies (MA, PhD).

School of Architecture Students: 22 full-time, 13 part-time. *Faculty:* 21. Expenses: Contact institution. *Financial support:* In 2001–02, 24 students received support, including 1 fellowship; Federal Work-Study and scholarships/grants also available. Support available to part-time students. Financial award application deadline: 2/1; financial award applicants required to submit FAFSA. In 2001, 12 degrees awarded. *Degree program information:* Part-time programs available. Offers architecture (M Arch, MPS). *Application deadline:* For fall admission, 2/15. *Application fee:* $35. *Application Contact:* Peggy M. Vitry, Director of Academic Affairs, 504-865-5389, Fax: 504-862-8798, E-mail: pvitry@mailhost.tcs.tulane.edu. *Dean,* Don Gatzke, 504-865-5389, Fax: 504-862-8798, E-mail: gatzke@mailhost.tcs.tulane.edu.

School of Engineering 533 applicants, 22% accepted. *Faculty:* 55 full-time, 1 part-time/adjunct. Expenses: Contact institution. *Financial support:* Fellowships, research assistantships, teaching assistantships, career-related internships or fieldwork, Federal Work-Study, institutionally sponsored loans, and tuition waivers (full and partial) available. Financial award application deadline: 2/1. In 2001, 38 master's, 13 doctorates awarded. *Degree program information:* Part-time programs available. Offers biomedical engineering (MS, MSE, PhD, Sc D); chemical engineering (MS, MSE, PhD, Sc D); civil and environmental engineering (MS, MSE, PhD, Sc D); computer science (MS, MSCS, PhD, Sc D); electrical engineering (MS, MSE, PhD, Sc D); engineering (MS, MSCS, MSE, PhD, Sc D); mechanical engineering (MS, MSE, PhD, Sc D). MS and PhD offered through the Graduate School. *Application fee:* $35. *Application Contact:* Dr. E. Michaelides, Associate Dean, 504-865-5764. *Acting Dean,* Dr. Nicholas Altiero, 504-865-5766, Fax: 504-862-8747.

School of Law Students: 1,025; includes 8 minority (3 African Americans, 5 Hispanic Americans), 69 international. Average age 25. 3,013 applicants, 47% accepted. *Faculty:* 53 full-time (12 women), 105 part-time/adjunct (18 women). Expenses: Contact institution. *Financial support:* In 2001–02, 3 fellowships with full and partial tuition reimbursements were awarded; career-related internships or fieldwork, Federal Work-Study, institutionally sponsored loans, scholarships/grants, and tuition waivers (full and partial) also available. Financial award application deadline: 2/15; financial award applicants required to submit FAFSA. In 2001, 292 first professional degrees, 62 master's awarded. Offers admiralty (LL M); energy and environment (LL M); international and comparative law (LL M); law (JD, LL M, SJD). *Application deadline:* For fall admission, 3/15 (priority date). Applications are processed on a rolling basis. *Application fee:* $50. Electronic applications accepted. *Application Contact:* Susan Krinsky, Associate Dean, 504-865-5930, Fax: 504-865-6710, E-mail: skrinsky@law.tulane.edu. *Dean,* Lawrence Ponoroff, 504-865-5938, E-mail: lponoroff@law.tulane.edu.

School of Medicine Students: 606 (260 women); includes 137 minority (35 African Americans, 83 Asian Americans or Pacific Islanders, 14 Hispanic Americans, 5 Native Americans) 10 international. *Faculty:* 429 full-time, 31 part-time/adjunct. Expenses: Contact institution. *Financial support:* Fellowships, research assistantships, teaching assistantships, career-related internships or fieldwork, Federal Work-Study, and institutionally sponsored loans available. Financial award application deadline: 2/1. In 2001, 157 first professional degrees, 4 master's, 25 doctorates awarded. Offers medicine (MD, MPHTM, MS, MSPH, PhD, Sc D, Diploma). *Application Contact:* Information Contact, 504-588-5187. *Dean,* Dr. Paul Whelton, 504-588-5462.

Graduate Programs in Medicine Offers biochemistry (MS, PhD); clinical tropical medicine and travelers health (Diploma); human genetics (MS, PhD); medicine (MPHTM, MS, MSPH, PhD, Sc D, Diploma); microbiology and immunology (MS, PhD); molecular and cellular biology (PhD); neuroscience (MS, PhD); parasitology (MS, MSPH, PhD, Sc D); pharmacology (MS, PhD); physiology (MS, PhD); public health and tropical medicine (MPHTM); structural and cellular biology (MS, PhD).

School of Public Health and Tropical Medicine Students: 653 full-time, 246 part-time; includes 255 minority (170 African Americans, 49 Asian Americans or Pacific Islanders, 27 Hispanic Americans, 9 Native Americans), 166 international. Average age 33. 830 applicants, 88% accepted. *Faculty:* 101. Expenses: Contact institution. *Financial support:* Fellowships, research assistantships, teaching assistantships, Federal Work-Study, institutionally sponsored loans, scholarships/grants, and traineeships available. Support available to part-time students. Financial award application deadline: 2/1; financial award applicants required to submit FAFSA. In 2001, 400 master's, 20 doctorates awarded. *Degree program information:* Part-time and evening/weekend programs available. Postbaccalaureate distance learning degree programs offered (no on-campus study). Offers biostatistics (MS, MSPH, PhD, Sc D); environmental health sciences (MPH, MSPH, Sc D); epidemiology (MPH, MS, Dr PH, PhD); health communication/education (MPH); health systems management (MHA, MMM, MPH, Dr PH); international health and development (MADH, MPH, Dr PH); maternal and child health (MPH, Dr PH); nutrition (MPH); population studies (MPH); public health and tropical medicine (MADH, MHA, MMM, MPH, MPHTM, MS, MSPH, Dr PH, PhD, Sc D, Diploma). MS, MADH, PhD offered through the Graduate School. *Application deadline:* Applications are processed on a rolling basis. *Application fee:* $40. Electronic applications accepted. *Application Contact:* Jeffrey T. Johnson, Director of Admissions, 504-588-5387, Fax: 504-584-1667, E-mail: jeff@tulane.edu. *Dean,* Dr. Ann C. Anderson, 504-588-5397, Fax: 504-588-5718.

School of Social Work Students: 128 full-time, 31 part-time; includes 52 minority (45 African Americans, 1 Asian American or Pacific Islander, 5 Hispanic Americans, 1 Native American), 2 international. 186 applicants, 81% accepted. *Faculty:* 19 full-time (14 women), 37 part-time/adjunct (22 women). Expenses: Contact institution. *Financial support:* Fellowships, Federal Work-Study available. Financial award applicants required to submit FAFSA. In 2001, 80 master's, 2 doctorates awarded. *Degree program information:* Part-time programs available. Offers social work (MSW, PhD). *Application deadline:* For fall admission, 3/31 (priority date). Applications are processed on a rolling basis. *Application fee:* $25. Electronic applications accepted. *Application Contact:* Gail Brown, Admissions Coordinator, 504-865-5314, Fax: 504-862-8727. *Dean,* Dr. Ronald Marks, 504-865-5314, Fax: 504-862-8727.

See in-depth description on page 1151.

TUSCULUM COLLEGE, Greeneville, TN 37743-9997

General Information Independent-religious, coed, comprehensive institution. *Enrollment:* 237 full-time matriculated graduate/professional students (172 women). *Enrollment by degree level:* 237 master's. *Graduate faculty:* 20 full-time (10 women), 15 part-time/adjunct (6 women). *Tuition:* Full-time $6,000. *Graduate housing:* On-campus housing not available. *Student services:* Campus safety program, career counseling, international student services. *Library facilities:* Albert Columbus Tate Library plus 2 others. *Online resources:* library catalog, web page, access to other libraries' catalogs. *Collection:* 68,573 titles, 1,000 serial subscriptions, 832 audiovisual materials.

Computer facilities: 60 computers available on campus for general student use. A campuswide network can be accessed from student residence rooms and from off campus. Internet access is available. *Web address:* http://www.tusculum.edu/.

General Application Contact: Information Contact, 423-693-1177 Ext. 330, Fax: 423-638-5181.

GRADUATE UNITS

Graduate School Students: 237 full-time (172 women); includes 17 minority (13 African Americans, 1 Asian American or Pacific Islander, 2 Hispanic Americans, 1 Native American) *Faculty:* 20 full-time (10 women), 15 part-time/adjunct (6 women). Expenses: Contact institution. In 2001, 162 degrees awarded. *Degree program information:* Evening/weekend programs available. Offers adult education (MA Ed); K–12 (MA Ed); organizational management (MAOM). *Application deadline:* Applications are processed on a rolling basis. *Application fee:* $0. *Application Contact:* Don Stout, Executive Director of Professional Studies, 423-636-7330 Ext. 612, Fax: 423-638-5181. *Dean,* Dr. Denise Wood, 865-693-1177, Fax: 423-638-5181.

TUSKEGEE UNIVERSITY, Tuskegee, AL 36088

General Information Independent, coed, comprehensive institution. *Enrollment:* 313 full-time matriculated graduate/professional students (199 women), 57 part-time matriculated graduate/professional students (22 women). *Enrollment by degree level:* 226 first professional, 132 master's, 12 doctoral. *Graduate faculty:* 112 full-time (17 women), 11 part-time/adjunct (5 women). *Tuition:* Full-time $5,163; part-time $612 per credit hour. *Graduate housing:* Rooms and/or apartments available to single and married students. Housing application deadline: 5/1. *Student services:* Campus safety program, career counseling, child daycare facilities, free psychological counseling, international student services, low-cost health insurance. *Library facilities:* Hollis B. Frissell Library plus 3 others. *Online resources:* library catalog. *Collection:* 623,824 titles, 81,157 serial subscriptions.

Computer facilities: 1,000 computers available on campus for general student use. A campuswide network can be accessed from student residence rooms and from off campus. Internet access and online class registration are available. *Web address:* http://www.tusk.edu/.

General Application Contact: William E. Mathis, Director of Admissions, 334-727-8580.

GRADUATE UNITS

Graduate Programs Students: 313 full-time (199 women), 57 part-time (22 women); includes 261 African Americans, 2 Asian Americans or Pacific Islanders, 6 Hispanic Americans, 46 international. Average age 24. 394 applicants, 49% accepted. *Faculty:* 112 full-time (17 women), 11 part-time/adjunct (5 women). Expenses: Contact institution. *Financial support:* Fellowships, research assistantships, teaching assistantships, career-related internships or fieldwork, Federal Work-Study, institutionally sponsored loans, and scholarships/grants available. Support available to part-time students. Financial award application deadline: 4/15. In 2001, 54 first professional degrees, 30 master's awarded. *Degree program information:* Part-time programs available. *Application deadline:* For fall admission, 7/15. Applications are processed on a rolling basis. *Application fee:* $25 ($35 for international students). *Application Contact:* William E. Mathis, Director of Admissions, 334-727-8580. *Provost,* Dr. William L. Lester, 334-727-8164.

College of Agricultural, Environmental and Natural Sciences Students: 37 full-time (25 women), 16 part-time (7 women); includes 49 minority (48 African Americans, 1 Asian American or Pacific Islander), 4 international. Average age 24. 31 applicants, 90% accepted. *Faculty:* 26 full-time (12 women), 1 part-time/adjunct (0 women). Expenses: Contact institution. *Financial support:* Fellowships, research assistantships, teaching assistantships, career-related internships or fieldwork, Federal Work-Study, and institutionally sponsored loans available. Support available to part-time students. Financial award application deadline: 4/15. In 2001, 9 degrees awarded. Offers agricultural and resource economics (MS); agricultural, environmental and natural sciences (MS); animal and poultry sciences (MS); biology (MS); chemistry (MS); environmental sciences (MS); food and nutritional sciences (MS); plant and soil sciences (MS). *Application deadline:* For fall admission, 7/15. Applications are processed on a rolling basis. *Application fee:* $25 ($35 for international students). *Dean,* Dr. Walter A. Hill, 334-727-8157.

College of Engineering, Architecture and Physical Sciences Students: 27 full-time (3 women), 20 part-time (3 women); includes 20 minority (19 African Americans, 1 Asian American or Pacific Islander), 25 international. Average age 24. 104 applicants, 59% accepted. *Faculty:* 19 full-time (0 women). Expenses: Contact institution. *Financial support:* Fellowships, research assistantships, teaching assistantships, career-related internships or fieldwork, Federal Work-Study, and institutionally sponsored loans available. Support available to part-time students. Financial award application deadline: 4/15. In 2001, 17 degrees awarded. Offers electrical engineering (MSEE); engineering, architecture and physical sciences (MSEE, MSME, PhD); material science engineering (PhD); mechanical engineering (MSME). *Application deadline:* For fall admission, 7/15. Applications are processed on a rolling basis. *Application fee:* $25 ($35 for international students). *Acting Dean,* Dr. Legand L. Burge, 334-727-8356.

College of Liberal Arts and Education Average age 24. 128 applicants, 66% accepted. Expenses: Contact institution. *Financial support:* Fellowships, research assistantships, teaching assistantships, career-related internships or fieldwork, Federal Work-Study, institutionally sponsored loans, and scholarships/grants available. Support available to part-time students. Financial award application deadline: 4/15. In 2001, 4 degrees awarded. Offers general science education (M Ed); liberal arts and education (M Ed). *Application deadline:* For fall admission, 7/15. Applications are processed on a rolling basis. *Application fee:* $25 ($35 for international students). *Interim Dean,* Dr. Benjamin Benford, 334-727-8561, Fax: 334-724-4196.

College of Veterinary Medicine and Allied Health Students: 243 full-time (167 women), 14 part-time (6 women); includes 183 African Americans, 6 Hispanic Americans, 16 international. Average age 25. 279 applicants, 27% accepted. *Faculty:* 62 full-time (6 women). Expenses: Contact institution. *Financial support:* Fellowships, research assistantships, teaching assistantships, career-related internships or fieldwork, Federal Work-Study, institutionally sponsored loans, and scholarships/grants available. Support available to part-time students. Financial award application deadline: 4/15. In 2001, 54 first professional degrees, 4 master's awarded. Offers veterinary medicine (DVM, MS); veterinary medicine and allied health (DVM, MS). *Application deadline:* For fall admission, 7/15. Applications are processed on a rolling basis. *Application fee:* $25 ($35 for international students). *Dean,* Dr. Alfonza Atkinson, 334-727-8174, Fax: 334-727-8177.

TYNDALE COLLEGE & SEMINARY, Toronto, ON M2M 4B3, Canada

General Information Independent-religious, coed, comprehensive institution. *Graduate housing:* Room and/or apartments available to single students; on-campus housing not available to married students. Housing application deadline: 6/25.

GRADUATE UNITS

Graduate Programs *Degree program information:* Part-time programs available. Offers theology (M Div, MTS).

UNIFICATION THEOLOGICAL SEMINARY, Barrytown, NY 12571

General Information Independent-religious, coed, primarily men, graduate-only institution. *Enrollment by degree level:* 16 first professional, 90 master's. *Graduate faculty:* 6 full-time (1 woman), 14 part-time/adjunct (5 women). *Tuition:* Full-time $6,300; part-time $175 per semester hour. *Required fees:* $75 per term. Tuition and fees vary according to course load and campus/location. *Graduate housing:* Rooms and/or apartments guaranteed to single students and available on a first-come, first-served basis to married students. Typical cost: $1,650 per year ($3,150 including board) for single students; $4,500 per year for married students. Room and board charges vary according to housing facility selected. *Student services:* Campus employment opportunities, international student services. *Library facilities:* Unification Theological Seminary Library. *Online resources:* library catalog. *Collection:* 56,000 titles, 200 serial subscriptions, 636 audiovisual materials.

Computer facilities: 11 computers available on campus for general student use. Internet access is available. *Web address:* http://www.uts.edu/.

General Application Contact: Tessa Hodson, Director of Admissions, 845-752-3015, Fax: 845-752-3016, E-mail: admissions@uts.edu.

GRADUATE UNITS

Graduate Program Students: 72 full-time (12 women), 34 part-time (11 women); includes 41 minority (21 African Americans, 15 Asian Americans or Pacific Islanders, 4 Hispanic Americans, 1 Native American), 59 international. Average age 38. 121 applicants, 81% accepted, 52 enrolled. *Faculty:* 6 full-time (1 woman), 14 part-time/adjunct (5 women). Expenses: Contact institution. *Financial support:* In 2001–02, 3 students received support. Career-related internships or fieldwork, institutionally sponsored loans, scholarships/grants, and tuition waivers (partial) available. In 2001, 11 first professional degrees, 25 master's awarded. *Degree program information:* Part-time programs available. Offers theology (M Div, MRE). *Application deadline:* For fall admission, 8/15 (priority date); for winter admission, 12/15 (priority date); for spring admission, 3/15 (priority date). Applications are processed on a rolling basis. *Application fee:* $0. *Application Contact:* Tessa Hodson, Director of Admissions, 845-752-3015, Fax: 845-752-3016, E-mail: admissions@uts.edu. *Academic Dean,* Dr. Andrew WIlson, 845-752-3082, Fax: 845-752-3014, E-mail: wilson@uts.edu.

UNIFORMED SERVICES UNIVERSITY OF THE HEALTH SCIENCES, Bethesda, MD 20814-4799

General Information Federally supported, coed, graduate-only institution. *Graduate faculty:* 347 full-time (113 women), 3,765 part-time/adjunct (741 women). *Graduate tuition:* Tuition waived. *Graduate housing:* On-campus housing not available. *Student services:* Grant writing training, multicultural affairs office. *Library facilities:* Learning Resource Center. *Online resources:* library catalog, web page, access to other libraries' catalogs. *Collection:* 522,672 titles, 3,200 serial subscriptions. *Research affiliation:* U.S. Armed Forces Radiobiology Research Institute, National Institutes of Health, National Library of Medicine, Walter Reed Army Institute of Research, Armed Forces Institute of Pathology.

Computer facilities: 40 computers available on campus for general student use. A campuswide network can be accessed from off campus. Internet access is available. *Web address:* http://www.usuhs.mil/.

General Application Contact: Janet M. Anastasi, Graduate Program Coordinator, 301-295-3913, Fax: 301-295-6772, E-mail: janastasi@usuhs.mil.

GRADUATE UNITS

Graduate School of Nursing Tuition waived. Postbaccalaureate distance learning degree programs offered (no on-campus study). Offers nurse anesthesia (MSN); nurse practitioner (MSN); nursing (MSN). Available to military officers only. Electronic applications accepted.

School of Medicine Students: 817 full-time (242 women), 67 part-time (24 women); includes 163 minority (27 African Americans, 93 Asian Americans or Pacific Islanders, 31 Hispanic Americans, 12 Native Americans), 2 international. Average age 26. 1,989 applicants, 4% accepted, 227 enrolled. *Faculty:* 347 full-time (113 women), 3,765 part-time/adjunct (741 women). Expenses: Contact institution. *Financial support:* In 2001–02, fellowships with full tuition reimbursements (averaging $17,000 per year), research assistantships with full tuition reimbursements (averaging $17,000 per year) were awarded. Career-related internships or fieldwork and tuition waivers (full) also available. In 2001, 165 first professional degrees, 33 master's, 13 doctorates awarded. Offers medicine (MD, MMH, MPH, MS, MSPH, MTMH, Dr PH, PhD). *Application deadline:* Applications are processed on a rolling basis. *Application fee:* $0. *Application Contact:* Janet M. Anastasi, Graduate Program Coordinator, 301-295-3913, Fax: 301-295-6772, E-mail: janastasi@usuhs.mil. *President,* Dr. James A. Zimble, 301-295-3013, E-mail: jzimble@usuhs.mil.

Division of Basic Medical Sciences Students: 134 full-time (67 women), 25 part-time (8 women); includes 20 minority (7 African Americans, 9 Asian Americans or Pacific Islanders, 2 Hispanic Americans, 2 Native Americans), 2 international. Average age 26. 224 applicants, 36% accepted, 60 enrolled. *Faculty:* 407 full-time (113 women), 3,765 part-time/adjunct (741 women). Expenses: Contact institution. *Financial support:* In 2001–02, fellowships with full tuition reimbursements (averaging $17,000 per year), research assistantships with full tuition reimbursements (averaging $17,000 per year) were awarded. Career-related internships or fieldwork and tuition waivers (full) also available. In 2001, 33 master's, 13 doctorates awarded. Offers anatomy, physiology and genetics (PhD); applied human biology (MS, PhD); aviation medicine (MS); biochemistry (PhD); cell biology, developmental biology, and neurobiology (PhD); clinical psychology (PhD); emerging infectious diseases (PhD); environmental health science (PhD); medical and clinical psychology (PhD); medical history (MMH); medical psychology (PhD); medical zoology (PhD); microbiology and immunology (PhD); military and emergency medicine (MS, PhD); molecular and cell biology (PhD); molecular pathobiology (PhD); neuroscience (PhD); pathology (PhD); pharmacology (PhD); preventive medicine/biometrics (MPH, MSPH, MTMH, Dr PH, PhD); public health (MPH, MSPH, Dr PH); tropical medicine and hygiene (MTMH); undersea medicine (MS, PhD). *Application deadline:* For fall admission, 1/15 (priority date). Applications are processed on a rolling basis. *Application fee:* $0. *Application Contact:* Janet M. Anastasi, Graduate Program Coordinator, 301-295-3913, Fax: 301-295-6772, E-mail: janastasi@usuhs.mil. *Director,* Dr. Cinda J. Helke, 301-295-3238, E-mail: chelke@usuhs.mil.

UNION COLLEGE, Barbourville, KY 40906-1499

General Information Independent-religious, coed, comprehensive institution. *Enrollment:* 5 full-time matriculated graduate/professional students, 250 part-time matriculated graduate/professional students. *Graduate faculty:* 6 full-time (1 woman), 18 part-time/adjunct (1 woman). *Tuition:* Full-time $11,720; part-time $225 per hour. *Graduate housing:* Rooms and/or apartments available to single and married students. Typical cost: $7,060 (including board) for single students. *Student services:* Campus employment opportunities, career counseling, low-cost health insurance. *Library facilities:* Weeks-Townsend Memorial Library plus 1 other. *Online resources:* library catalog, web page, access to other libraries' catalogs. *Collection:* 105,210 titles, 2,469 serial subscriptions, 5,004 audiovisual materials.

Computer facilities: 100 computers available on campus for general student use. A campuswide network can be accessed from student residence rooms and from off campus. Internet access is available. *Web address:* http://www.unionky.edu/.

General Application Contact: Dr. William E. Bernhardt, Dean of Graduate Academic Affairs, 606-546-1210, Fax: 606-546-1330, E-mail: webern@unionky.edu.

GRADUATE UNITS

Graduate Programs Students: 5 full-time, 250 part-time; includes 3 minority (all African Americans) *Faculty:* 24 full-time, 5 part-time/adjunct. Expenses: Contact institution. In 2001, 80 degrees awarded. *Degree program information:* Part-time and evening/weekend programs available. Offers elementary education (MA); elementary principalship (Certificate); health (MA Ed); health and physical education (MA); middle grades (MA); middle grades principalship (Certificate); music education (MA); principalship (MA); reading specialist (MA); secondary education (MA); secondary school principalship (Certificate); special education (MA); supervisor of instruction (Certificate). *Application deadline:* Applications are processed on a rolling basis. *Application fee:* $15. *Dean of Graduate Academic Affairs,* Dr. William E. Bernhardt, 606-546-1210, Fax: 606-546-1330, E-mail: webern@unionky.edu.

UNION COLLEGE, Schenectady, NY 12308-2311

General Information Independent, coed, comprehensive institution. *Enrollment:* 137 full-time matriculated graduate/professional students (67 women), 90 part-time matriculated graduate/professional students (36 women). *Enrollment by degree level:* 227 master's. *Graduate faculty:* 11 full-time, 19 part-time/adjunct. *Tuition:* Part-time $1,620 per course. *Graduate housing:* On-campus housing not available. *Student services:* Campus safety program, career counseling, free psychological counseling, low-cost health insurance, teacher training. *Library facilities:* Schaffer Library. *Online resources:* library catalog, web page, access to other libraries' catalogs. *Collection:* 287,293 titles, 6,826 serial subscriptions, 7,429 audiovisual materials. *Research affiliation:* Fairchild Foundation (mathematics), Research Corporation (physics), General Electric (mechanical engineering), Schering Plough (chemistry), AT&T (mechanical engineering), Dreyfus Foundation (chemistry).

Computer facilities: 320 computers available on campus for general student use. A campuswide network can be accessed from student residence rooms and from off campus. Internet access is available. *Web address:* http://www.union.edu/.

General Application Contact: Rhonda Sheehan, Coordinator of Recruiting and Admissions, 518-388-6238, Fax: 518-388-6754, E-mail: sheehanr@union.edu.

GRADUATE UNITS

Center for Graduate Education and Special Programs Students: 137 full-time (67 women), 90 part-time (36 women); includes 5 minority (2 African Americans, 3 Asian Americans or Pacific Islanders), 24 international. Average age 31. 107 applicants, 92% accepted, 62 enrolled. *Faculty:* 11 full-time, 19 part-time/adjunct. Expenses: Contact institution. *Financial support:* Research assistantships, career-related internships or fieldwork, scholarships/grants, health care benefits, and tuition waivers (partial) available. Support available to part-time students. In 2001, 139 degrees awarded. *Degree program information:* Part-time and evening/weekend programs available. Offers biology (MAT); chemistry (MAT); earth science (MAT); English (MAT); French (MAT); general science (MAT); German (MAT); Latin (MAT); mathematics (MAT); mathematics/computer science (MS); natural sciences (MS); physical sciences (MS); physics (MAT); social studies (MAT); Spanish (MAT). *Application deadline:* Applications are processed on a rolling basis. *Application fee:* $50. *Application Contact:* Rhonda Sheehan, Coordinator of Recruiting and Admissions, 518-388-6238, Fax: 518-388-6754, E-mail: sheehanr@union.edu. *Dean,* Dr. Susan Lehrman, 518-388-6597, Fax: 518-388-6754, E-mail: lehrmans@union.edu.

Center for Clinical Bioethics and Leadership Average age 48. 5 applicants, 60% accepted, 2 enrolled. Expenses: Contact institution. *Financial support:* Health care benefits available. In 2001, 4 degrees awarded. *Degree program information:* Part-time and evening/weekend programs available. Offers bioethics (MS); leadership in health management (MS). *Application deadline:* For spring admission, 5/1. *Application fee:* $50. *Application Contact:* Rhonda Sheehan, Coordinator of Recruiting and Admissions, 518-388-6238, Fax: 518-388-6754, E-mail: sheehanr@union.edu. *Director,* Dr. Robert B. Baker, 518-388-6215, E-mail: bakerr@union.edu.

Division of Engineering and Computer Science Students: 11 full-time (3 women), 32 part-time (4 women); includes 1 minority (African American), 5 international. Average age 32. 8 applicants, 100% accepted, 6 enrolled. Expenses: Contact institution. *Financial support:* Research assistantships, health care benefits available. Support available to part-time students. In 2001, 21 degrees awarded. *Degree program information:* Part-time and evening/weekend programs available. Offers computer science (MS); electrical engineering (MS); engineering and computer science (MS); mechanical engineering (MS). *Application deadline:* Applications are processed on a rolling basis. *Application fee:* $50. *Application Contact:* Rhonda Sheehan, Coordinator of Recruiting and Admissions, 518-388-6238, Fax: 518-388-6754, E-mail: sheehanr@union.edu.

Graduate Management Institute Students: 79 full-time (33 women), 39 part-time (18 women); includes 4 minority (1 African American, 3 Asian Americans or Pacific Islanders), 16 international. Average age 30. 67 applicants, 93% accepted, 42 enrolled. Expenses: Contact institution. *Financial support:* Research assistantships, career-related internships or fieldwork, scholarships/grants, health care benefits, and tuition waivers (partial) available. In 2001, 63 degrees awarded. *Degree program information:* Part-time and evening/weekend programs available. Offers business administration (MBA); health systems administration (MBA). *Application deadline:* Applications are processed on a rolling basis. *Application fee:* $50. *Application Contact:* Rhonda Sheehan, Coordinator of Recruiting and Admissions, 518-388-6238, Fax: 518-388-6754, E-mail: sheehanr@union.edu. *Director,* Dr. Susan Lehrman, 518-388-6597, Fax: 518-388-6754, E-mail: lehrmans@union.edu.

UNION INSTITUTE & UNIVERSITY, Cincinnati, OH 45206-1925

General Information Independent, coed, university. *Enrollment:* 1,113 full-time matriculated graduate/professional students (684 women). *Graduate faculty:* 61 full-time (35 women), 81 part-time/adjunct (41 women). *Tuition:* Full-time $9,392. Full-time tuition and fees vary according to degree level and program. *Graduate housing:* On-campus housing not available. *Student services:* Disabled student services, writing training. *Online resources:* library catalog, web page, access to other libraries' catalogs. *Collection:* 4,500 titles, 18 audiovisual materials.

Computer facilities: 18 computers available on campus for general student use. A campuswide network can be accessed from off campus. Internet access is available. *Web address:* http://www.tui.edu/.

General Application Contact: Lisa Schrenger, Director of Admissions, 800-486-3116, Fax: 513-861-0779, E-mail: admissions@tui.edu.

GRADUATE UNITS

School of Interdisciplinary Arts and Sciences Students: 972 full-time (598 women); includes 281 minority (215 African Americans, 16 Asian Americans or Pacific Islanders, 33 Hispanic Americans, 17 Native Americans), 28 international. Average age 48. *Faculty:* 56 full-time (26 women), 26 part-time/adjunct (9 women). Expenses: Contact institution. *Financial support:* In 2001–02, 637 students received support. Federal Work-Study available. Financial award application deadline: 5/1; financial award applicants required to submit FAFSA. In 2001, 168 degrees awarded. Offers interdisciplinary studies (PhD). Individually designed, interdisciplinary programs. *Application deadline:* Applications are processed on a rolling basis. *Application fee:* $50. *Application Contact:* Lisa Schrenger, Director of Admissions, 800-486-3116, Fax: 513-861-0779, E-mail: admissions@tui.edu. *Vice President and Dean, Graduate Studies,* Dr. Richard Green, 513-861-6400 Ext. 1133, E-mail: rgreen@tui.edu.

School of Professional Psychology Students: 141 full-time (86 women); includes 24 minority (17 African Americans, 4 Asian Americans or Pacific Islanders, 3 Hispanic Americans), 1 international. Average age 46. *Faculty:* 56 full-time (26 women), 26 part-time/adjunct (9 women). Expenses: Contact institution. *Financial support:* In 2001–02, 83 students received support. Federal Work-Study, scholarships/grants, and tuition waivers available. Financial award application deadline: 5/1; financial award applicants required to submit FAFSA. In 2001, 26 degrees awarded. Offers clinical psychology (PhD). *Application deadline:* Applications are processed on a rolling basis. *Application fee:* $50. *Application Contact:* Director of Admissions, 800-486-3116, Fax: 513-861-0779, E-mail: admissions@tui.edu. *Vice President and Dean, Graduate Studies,* Dr. Richard Green, 513-861-6400 Ext. 1133, E-mail: rgreen@tui.edu.

UNION THEOLOGICAL SEMINARY AND PRESBYTERIAN SCHOOL OF CHRISTIAN EDUCATION, Richmond, VA 23227-4597

General Information Independent-religious, coed, graduate-only institution. *Graduate faculty:* 28 full-time (7 women), 21 part-time/adjunct (9 women). *Tuition:* Full-time $6,750; part-time $675 per credit. *Required fees:* $50. Full-time tuition and fees vary according to course load, degree level and program. *Graduate housing:* Rooms and/or apartments available on a first-come, first-served basis to single and married students. Typical cost: $2,044 (including board) for single students; $2,094 (including board) for married students. Room and board charges vary according to campus/location and housing facility selected. *Student services:* Campus employment opportunities, campus safety program, career counseling, free psychologi-

Union Theological Seminary and Presbyterian School of Christian Education (continued)

cal counseling, international student services, writing training. *Library facilities:* William Smith Morton Library. *Online resources:* library catalog, web page. *Collection:* 315,000 titles, 1,416 serial subscriptions.

Computer facilities: 10 computers available on campus for general student use. A campuswide network can be accessed. Internet access is available. *Web address:* http://www.union-psce.edu/.

General Application Contact: Rev. James W. Dale, Director of Admissions, 804-355-0671 Ext. 222, Fax: 804-355-3919, E-mail: jdale@union-psce.edu.

GRADUATE UNITS

School of Christian Education Students: 228 full-time (140 women); includes 41 minority (28 African Americans, 13 Asian Americans or Pacific Islanders), 18 international. Average age 36. 54 applicants, 54% accepted. *Faculty:* 7 full-time (3 women), 4 part-time/adjunct (2 women). Expenses: Contact institution. *Financial support:* In 2001–02, 67 students received support; fellowships, teaching assistantships, career-related internships or fieldwork and institutionally sponsored loans available. Financial award application deadline: 8/1; financial award applicants required to submit FAFSA. In 2001, 32 master's, 3 doctorates awarded. *Degree program information:* Part-time and evening/weekend programs available. Postbaccalaureate distance learning degree programs offered (minimal on-campus study). Offers Christian education (MA, Ed D, Ed S). *Application deadline:* For fall admission, 7/1; for winter admission, 9/1; for spring admission, 12/1. Applications are processed on a rolling basis. *Application fee:* $45. *Application Contact:* Rev. James W. Dale, Director of Admissions, 804-355-0671 Ext. 222, Fax: 804-355-3919, E-mail: jdale@union-psce.edu. *Dean of Education Faculty,* Dr. James A. Brashler, 804-254-8047, Fax: 804-355-3919, E-mail: jbrashler@union-psce.edu.

School of Theological Studies Students: 238 full-time (90 women), 12 part-time (5 women); includes 26 minority (15 African Americans, 11 Asian Americans or Pacific Islanders), 27 international. Average age 36. 257 applicants, 42% accepted. *Faculty:* 21 full-time (4 women), 18 part-time/adjunct (7 women). Expenses: Contact institution. *Financial support:* In 2001–02, 139 students received support; fellowships, teaching assistantships, career-related internships or fieldwork and institutionally sponsored loans available. Financial award application deadline: 6/1; financial award applicants required to submit FAFSA. In 2001, 45 master's, 20 doctorates awarded. Offers theological studies (M Div, Th M, D Min, PhD). *Application deadline:* For fall admission, 7/1; for spring admission, 12/1. Applications are processed on a rolling basis. *Application fee:* $45. *Application Contact:* Rev. James W. Dale, Director of Admissions, 804-355-0671 Ext. 222, Fax: 804-355-3919, E-mail: jdale@union-psce.edu. *Dean of Theology Faculty,* Dr. John T. Carroll, 804-355-0671, Fax: 804-355-3919, E-mail: jcarroll@union-psce.edu.

UNION THEOLOGICAL SEMINARY IN THE CITY OF NEW YORK, New York, NY 10027-5710

General Information Independent-religious, coed, graduate-only institution. *Graduate housing:* Rooms and/or apartments available on a first-come, first-served basis to single and married students. Housing application deadline: 5/15.

GRADUATE UNITS

Graduate and Professional Programs *Degree program information:* Part-time programs available. Offers theology (M Div, MA, STM, Ed D, PhD).

UNION UNIVERSITY, Jackson, TN 38305-3697

General Information Independent-religious, coed, comprehensive institution. *Enrollment:* 506 full-time matriculated graduate/professional students (333 women), 73 part-time matriculated graduate/professional students (59 women). *Graduate faculty:* 69. *Tuition:* Part-time $220 per semester hour. *Graduate housing:* Rooms and/or apartments available on a first-come, first-served basis to single and married students. *Student services:* Campus employment opportunities, campus safety program, career counseling, exercise/wellness program, free psychological counseling, international student services, teacher training. *Library facilities:* Emma Waters Summar Library. *Online resources:* library catalog, web page, access to other libraries' catalogs. *Collection:* 135,877 titles, 4,655 serial subscriptions, 11,526 audiovisual materials.

Computer facilities: 236 computers available on campus for general student use. A campuswide network can be accessed from student residence rooms and from off campus. Internet access is available. *Web address:* http://www.uu.edu/.

General Application Contact: Robbie Graves, Director of Enrollment Services, 731-661-5008, Fax: 731-661-5017, E-mail: rgraves@uu.edu.

GRADUATE UNITS

McAfee School of Business Administration Students: 277. Average age 32. *Faculty:* 9 full-time, 5 part-time/adjunct. Expenses: Contact institution. *Financial support:* Application deadline: 2/15; In 2001, 100 degrees awarded. *Degree program information:* Evening/weekend programs available. Offers business administration (MBA). Also available at Germantown campus. *Application deadline:* For fall admission, 6/1 (priority date); for spring admission, 1/15 (priority date). Applications are processed on a rolling basis. *Application fee:* $25 ($50 for international students). *Application Contact:* Barbara A. Perry, MBA Director, 731-661-5363, Fax: 731-661-5105, E-mail: bperry@uu.edu. *Interim Dean,* Dr. Walton Padelford, 731-661-5362, Fax: 731-661-5101, E-mail: wpadelfo@uu.edu.

School of Education and Human Studies Students: 270 (233 women). Average age 32. *Faculty:* 15 full-time (9 women), 16 part-time/adjunct (11 women). Expenses: Contact institution. *Financial support:* In 2001–02, 117 students received support. Application deadline: 2/15; In 2001, 77 master's, 58 other advanced degrees awarded. *Degree program information:* Part-time and evening/weekend programs available. Offers education (M Ed, MA Ed); education administration generalist (Ed S); educational supervision (Ed S). M Ed also available at Germantown campus. *Application deadline:* Applications are processed on a rolling basis. *Application fee:* $25 ($50 for international students). *Application Contact:* Helen F. Butler, Coordinator of Programs, 731-661-5374, Fax: 731-661-5063, E-mail: hbutler@uu.edu. *Dean,* Dr. Tom Rosebrough, 731-661-5372, Fax: 731-661-5063, E-mail: trosebro@uu.edu.

UNITED STATES ARMY COMMAND AND GENERAL STAFF COLLEGE, Fort Leavenworth, KS 66027-1352

General Information Federally supported, coed, primarily men, graduate-only institution. *Graduate housing:* Rooms and/or apartments available to single and married students.

GRADUATE UNITS

Graduate Program Offers military art and science (MMAS). Only career military officers are selected to attend United States Army Command and General Staff College.

UNITED STATES INTERNATIONAL UNIVERSITY, Nairobi, Kenya

General Information Independent, coed, comprehensive institution. *Graduate housing:* Room and/or apartments available to single students. Housing application deadline: 2/9.

GRADUATE UNITS

College of Business Administration Offers finance (MBA, MIBA); integrated studies (MBA, MIBA); management and organizational development (MS); marketing (MBA, MIBA).

UNITED STATES SPORTS ACADEMY, Daphne, AL 36526-7055

General Information Independent, coed, graduate-only institution. *Enrollment by degree level:* 538 master's, 75 doctoral. *Graduate faculty:* 8 full-time (1 woman), 23 part-time/adjunct (3 women). *Tuition:* Full-time $12,375; part-time $375 per semester hour. *Required fees:* $750. Tuition and fees vary according to course load and degree level. *Graduate housing:* On-campus housing not available. *Student services:* Campus employment opportunities, campus safety program, career counseling, exercise/wellness program, free psychological counseling, international student services, low-cost health insurance. *Library facilities:* Academy Library. *Online resources:* web page. *Collection:* 3,998 titles, 232 serial subscriptions, 1,058 audiovisual materials.

Computer facilities: 12 computers available on campus for general student use. A campuswide network can be accessed. Internet access is available. *Web address:* http://www.ussa.edu/.

General Application Contact: Ron Dickerson, Dean of Student Services, 251-626-3303 Ext. 147, Fax: 251-625-1035, E-mail: rdicker@ussa.edu.

GRADUATE UNITS

Graduate Programs Students: 102 full-time (45 women), 147 part-time (37 women); includes 32 minority (21 African Americans, 5 Asian Americans or Pacific Islanders, 6 Hispanic Americans), 8 international. Average age 30. 120 applicants, 94% accepted. *Faculty:* 8 full-time (1 woman), 23 part-time/adjunct (3 women). Expenses: Contact institution. *Financial support:* In 2001–02, 2 research assistantships with full tuition reimbursements (averaging $10,000 per year) were awarded; career-related internships or fieldwork, Federal Work-Study, scholarships/grants, and service assistantships also available. Support available to part-time students. Financial award application deadline: 8/15; financial award applicants required to submit FAFSA. In 2001, 89 master's, 2 doctorates awarded. *Degree program information:* Part-time programs available. Postbaccalaureate distance learning degree programs offered (minimal on-campus study). Offers health and fitness management (MSS); recreation management (MSS); sport art (MSS); sport coaching (MSS); sport management (MSS, DSM, Ed D); sport studies (MSS); sports medicine (MSS). *Application deadline:* Applications are processed on a rolling basis. *Application fee:* $50 ($125 for international students). Electronic applications accepted. *Application Contact:* Ron Dickerson, Dean of Student Services, 251-626-3303 Ext. 147, Fax: 251-625-1035, E-mail: rdicker@ussa.edu. *Vice President of Academic Affairs,* Dr. Cynthia E. Ryder, 251-626-3303 Ext. 127, Fax: 251-626-1149, E-mail: ceryder@ussa.edu.

UNITED TALMUDICAL SEMINARY, Brooklyn, NY 11211-7900

General Information Independent-religious, men only, comprehensive institution.

UNITED THEOLOGICAL SEMINARY, Dayton, OH 45406-4599

General Information Independent-religious, coed, graduate-only institution. *Enrollment by degree level:* 142 first professional, 47 master's, 133 doctoral. *Graduate faculty:* 23 full-time (10 women), 11 part-time/adjunct (4 women). *Tuition:* Full-time $3,420; part-time $356 per semester hour. *Graduate housing:* Rooms and/or apartments available on a first-come, first-served basis to single and married students. *Student services:* Campus employment opportunities, disabled student services, international student services. *Library facilities:* Memorial Library. *Collection:* 140,349 titles, 517 serial subscriptions, 8,062 audiovisual materials.

Computer facilities: 10 computers available on campus for general student use. A campuswide network can be accessed. Internet access is available. *Web address:* http://www.united.edu/.

General Application Contact: Betty J. Stutler, Director of Admissions, 937-278-5817 Ext. 185, Fax: 937-278-1218, E-mail: utsadmis@united.edu.

GRADUATE UNITS

Graduate and Professional Programs Students: 288 full-time (109 women), 34 part-time (17 women); includes 119 minority (109 African Americans, 9 Asian Americans or Pacific Islanders, 1 Hispanic American), 19 international. *Faculty:* 23 full-time (10 women), 11 part-time/adjunct (4 women). Expenses: Contact institution. *Financial support:* In 2001–02, 137 students received support. Career-related internships or fieldwork, Federal Work-Study, scholarships/grants, and tuition waivers (partial) available. Financial award application deadline: 6/1; financial award applicants required to submit CSS PROFILE or FAFSA. In 2001, 34 first professional degrees, 16 master's, 42 doctorates awarded. *Degree program information:* Part-time and evening/weekend programs available. Postbaccalaureate distance learning degree programs offered (minimal on-campus study). Offers theology (M Div, MARC, MASM, MATS, D Min). *Application deadline:* For fall admission, 7/15 (priority date); for spring admission, 1/15. Applications are processed on a rolling basis. *Application fee:* $40. Electronic applications accepted. *Director of Admissions,* Betty J. Stutler, 937-278-5817 Ext. 185, Fax: 937-278-1218, E-mail: utsadmis@united.edu.

UNITED THEOLOGICAL SEMINARY OF THE TWIN CITIES, New Brighton, MN 55112-2598

General Information Independent-religious, coed, graduate-only institution. *Enrollment by degree level:* 91 first professional, 48 master's, 25 doctoral, 57 other advanced degrees. *Graduate faculty:* 12 full-time (7 women), 16 part-time/adjunct (11 women). *Tuition:* Full-time $8,340. *Graduate housing:* Rooms and/or apartments available on a first-come, first-served basis to single and married students. Housing application deadline: 4/1. *Student services:* Campus employment opportunities, career counseling, free psychological counseling, international student services, multicultural affairs office, writing training. *Library facilities:* Spencer Library. *Online resources:* library catalog, access to other libraries' catalogs. *Collection:* 81,000 titles, 300 serial subscriptions.

Computer facilities: 6 computers available on campus for general student use. A campuswide network can be accessed from off campus. Internet access is available. *Web address:* http://www.unitedseminary-mn.org/.

General Application Contact: Sandy Casmey, Director of Admissions, 651-633-4311 Ext. 107, Fax: 651-633-4315, E-mail: scasmey@unitedseminary-mn.org.

GRADUATE UNITS

Graduate and Professional Programs Students: 80 full-time, 141 part-time; includes 11 minority (7 African Americans, 2 Asian Americans or Pacific Islanders, 2 Hispanic Americans), 2 international. Average age 46. *Faculty:* 12 full-time (7 women), 16 part-time/adjunct (11 women). Expenses: Contact institution. *Financial support:* In 2001–02, 110 students received support. Career-related internships or fieldwork, institutionally sponsored loans, and scholarships/grants available. Support available to part-time students. Financial award application deadline: 5/1; financial award applicants required to submit FAFSA. In 2001, 29 first professional degrees, 9 master's, 3 doctorates, 1 other advanced degree awarded. *Degree program information:* Part-time programs available. Offers advanced theological studies (Diploma); Indian ministry (Diploma); ministry (D Min); religion and theology (MA); religious leadership (MARL); theology (M Div); theology and the arts (MA); women's studies (MA). *Application deadline:* For fall admission, 8/1 (priority date); for winter admission, 12/1 (priority date); for spring admission, 1/1 (priority date). Applications are processed on a rolling basis. *Application fee:* $40. *Application Contact:* Sandy Casmey, Director of Admissions, 651-633-4311 Ext. 107, Fax: 651-633-4315, E-mail: scasmey@unitedseminary-mn.org. *Dean,* Dr. Richard D. Weis, 651-633-4311, Fax: 651-633-4315, E-mail: rweis@unitedseminary-mn.org.

UNIVERSIDAD CENTRAL DEL CARIBE, Bayamón, PR 00960-6032

General Information Independent, coed, graduate-only institution. *Graduate housing:* On-campus housing not available.

GRADUATE UNITS

Professional Program Offers medicine (MD).

UNIVERSIDAD DE LAS AMERICAS, A.C., Mexico City, 06700, Mexico

General Information Independent, comprehensive institution.

GRADUATE UNITS

Program in Business Administration Offers finance (MBA); marketing research (MBA); production and quality (MBA).

Program in Education Offers education (M Ed).

Program in International Organizations and Institutions Offers international organizations and institutions (MA).

Program in Psychology Offers family therapy (MA).

UNIVERSIDAD DE LAS AMÉRICAS–PUEBLA, 72820 Puebla, Mexico

General Information Independent, coed, comprehensive institution. CGS member. *Graduate housing:* On-campus housing not available. *Research affiliation:* Laboratorios Clínicos de Puebla (clinical analysis), Degussa Corporation (mechanical engineering), Petroleos Mexicanos (business administration), Institute Mexicano del Petroleo (chemical engineering).

GRADUATE UNITS

Division of Graduate Studies *Degree program information:* Part-time and evening/weekend programs available.

School of Business Administration *Degree program information:* Part-time and evening/weekend programs available. Offers business administration (MBA); finance (M Adm).

School of Engineering *Degree program information:* Part-time and evening/weekend programs available. Offers chemical engineering (MS); computer science (MS); construction management (M Adm); electronic engineering (MS); engineering (M Adm, MS); food technology (MS); industrial engineering (MS); production management (M Adm).

School of Humanities *Degree program information:* Part-time and evening/weekend programs available. Offers humanities (MA); information design (MA); linguistics (MA); literature (MA).

School of Sciences *Degree program information:* Part-time and evening/weekend programs available. Offers clinical analysis (MS); sciences (MS).

School of Social Sciences *Degree program information:* Part-time and evening/weekend programs available. Offers American studies (MA); anthropology (MA); archaeology (MA); economics (MA); education (MA); finance (M Adm); psychology (MA); social sciences (M Adm, MA).

UNIVERSIDAD DEL TURABO, Turabo, PR 00778-3030

General Information Independent, coed, comprehensive institution. *Graduate housing:* On-campus housing not available.

GRADUATE UNITS

Graduate Programs *Degree program information:* Part-time and evening/weekend programs available. Offers accounting (MBA); bilingual education (MA); criminal justice studies (MPA); education administration and supervision (MA); environmental studies (MES); human resources (MBA); human services administration (MPA); logistics and materials management (MBA); management (MBA); marketing (MBA); school libraries administration (MA); special education (MA); teaching English as a second language (MA).

UNIVERSIDAD METROPOLITANA, Río Piedras, PR 00928-1150

General Information Independent, coed, comprehensive institution. *Graduate housing:* On-campus housing not available. *Research affiliation:* Berkeley National Laboratories (bioremediation), University Consortium of Atmospheric Research (computer science, atmospheric science), University of Colorado at Boulder (computer science, biology), University of Puerto Rico (physics, chemistry), University of Utah (computational chemistry), Howard University (computational chemistry).

GRADUATE UNITS

Graduate Programs in Education *Degree program information:* Part-time and evening/weekend programs available. Offers curriculum and teaching (MA); educational administration and supervision (MA); environmental education (MA); fitness management (MA); managing leisure services (MA); pre-school centers administration (MA); pre-school education (MA); special education (MA); teaching of physical education (MA). Electronic applications accepted.

School of Business Administration *Degree program information:* Part-time and evening/weekend programs available. Offers accounting (MBA); management (MBA); marketing (MBA). Electronic applications accepted.

School of Environmental Affairs Offers conservation and management of natural resources (MEM); environmental affairs (MEM); environmental planning (MEM); environmental risk and assessment management (MEM). Electronic applications accepted.

UNIVERSITÉ DE MONCTON, Moncton, NB E1A 3E9, Canada

General Information Province-supported, coed, comprehensive institution. *Enrollment:* 401 full-time matriculated graduate/professional students (250 women), 119 part-time matriculated graduate/professional students (60 women). *Enrollment by degree level:* 108 first professional, 404 master's, 8 doctoral. *Graduate faculty:* 257 full-time (64 women), 4 part-time/adjunct (0 women). *Graduate tuition:* Tuition charges are reported in Canadian dollars. *International tuition:* $6,000 Canadian dollars full-time. *Tuition, area resident:* Full-time $3,505 Canadian dollars; part-time $200 Canadian dollars per credit. Tuition, Canadian resident: part-time $220 Canadian dollars per credit. *Graduate housing:* Rooms and/or apartments available on a first-come, first-served basis to single and married students. Typical cost: $3,000 Canadian dollars per year ($4,600 Canadian dollars including board) for single students; $3,200 Canadian dollars per year for married students. Room and board charges vary according to board plan, campus/location and housing facility selected. *Student services:* Campus employment opportunities, career counseling, child daycare facilities, exercise/wellness program, free psychological counseling, international student services, low-cost health insurance, teacher training. *Library facilities:* Bibliothèque Champlain plus 2 others. *Online resources:* library catalog, web page, access to other libraries' catalogs. *Collection:* 789,046 titles, 2,059 serial subscriptions, 28,818 audiovisual materials.

Computer facilities: 900 computers available on campus for general student use. A campuswide network can be accessed from student residence rooms and from off campus. Internet access is available. *Web address:* http://www.umoncton.ca/.

General Application Contact: Dr. Truong Vo-Van, Dean, Faculty of Graduate Studies and Research, 506-858-4310, Fax: 506-858-4279, E-mail: vovant@umoncton.ca.

GRADUATE UNITS

Faculty of Administration Students: 59 full-time (29 women), 85 part-time (40 women). Average age 32. 105 applicants, 63% accepted, 39 enrolled. *Faculty:* 10 full-time (1 woman), 2 part-time/adjunct (0 women). Expenses: Contact institution. *Financial support:* In 2001–02, 15 students received support, including 8 fellowships; teaching assistantships, career-related internships or fieldwork and institutionally sponsored loans also available. Support available to part-time students. Financial award application deadline: 5/30. In 2001, 25 degrees awarded. *Degree program information:* Part-time programs available. Postbaccalaureate distance learning degree programs offered (no on-campus study). Offers administration (MBA). *Application deadline:* For fall admission, 6/1. *Application fee:* $30. *Application Contact:* Nicole Savoie, Conseillière à l'admission, 506-858-4115, Fax: 506-858-4544, E-mail: savoien@umoncton.ca. *Dean*, Gaston LeBlanc, 506-858-4205, Fax: 506-858-4093, E-mail: leblanga@umoncton.ca.

Faculty of Arts Tuition charges are reported in Canadian dollars. *Degree program information:* Part-time programs available. Offers arts (M Fr, MA, PhD); French (M Fr, MA, PhD); history (MA). Electronic applications accepted.

Faculty of Education Tuition charges are reported in Canadian dollars. *Degree program information:* Part-time programs available. Offers education (M Ed, MA Ed).

Graduate Studies in Education Tuition charges are reported in Canadian dollars. *Degree program information:* Part-time programs available. Offers educational psychology (M Ed, MA Ed); guidance (M Ed, MA Ed); school administration (M Ed, MA Ed); teaching (M Ed, MA Ed).

Faculty of Law Students: 103 full-time (68 women). Average age 27. 87 applicants, 53% accepted, 34 enrolled. *Faculty:* 13 full-time (4 women), 2 part-time/adjunct (0 women). Expenses: Contact institution. *Financial support:* In 2001–02, 56 fellowships (averaging $2,700 per year) were awarded; career-related internships or fieldwork also available. Financial award application deadline: 10/31. In 2001, 20 degrees awarded. Offers law (LL B, LL M, Diploma). Programs offered exclusively in French. *Application deadline:* For fall admission, 3/31 (priority date). Applications are processed on a rolling basis. *Application fee:* $39. *Application Contact:* Andréa Boudreau Ouellet, Associate Dean, 506-863-2121, Fax: 506-858-4534, E-mail: boudrea@umoncton.ca. *Dean*, Serge Rousselle, 506-858-4560, Fax: 506-858-4534, E-mail: rousses@umoncton.ca.

Faculty of Science Students: 51 full-time (17 women); includes 13 minority (10 African Americans, 3 Asian Americans or Pacific Islanders), 10 international. Average age 24. *Faculty:* 35 full-time (6 women). Expenses: Contact institution. *Financial support:* Fellowships, research assistantships, teaching assistantships, institutionally sponsored loans available. In 2001, 3 master's, 16 other advanced degrees awarded. *Degree program information:* Part-time programs available. Offers biochemistry (M Sc); biology (M Sc); chemistry (M Sc); information technology (M Sc, Certificate, Diploma); mathematics (M Sc); physics and astronomy (M Sc); science (M Sc, Certificate, Diploma). *Application deadline:* For fall admission, 6/1 (priority date); for winter admission, 11/15 (priority date). Applications are processed on a rolling basis. *Application fee:* $39. Electronic applications accepted. *Dean*, Dr. Charles Bourque, 506-858-4301, Fax: 506-858-4541, E-mail: bourquch@umoncton.ca.

Faculty of Social Sciences Tuition charges are reported in Canadian dollars. *Degree program information:* Part-time and evening/weekend programs available. Offers economics (MA); psychology (MA Ps); public administration (MPA); social sciences (MA, MA Ps, MPA, MSS).

School of Social Work Tuition charges are reported in Canadian dollars. Offers social work (MSS).

School of Engineering Tuition charges are reported in Canadian dollars. Offers civil engineering (M Sc A); electrical engineering (M Sc A); industrial engineering (M Sc A); mechanical engineering (M Sc A).

School of Food Science, Nutrition and Family Studies Students: 11 full-time (10 women), 1 part-time. Average age 25. 3 applicants, 33% accepted. *Faculty:* 7 full-time (5 women). Expenses: Contact institution. *Financial support:* In 2001–02, 1 fellowship, 2 research assistantships were awarded. Career-related internships or fieldwork and scholarships/grants also available. Financial award application deadline: 5/23. In 2001, 4 degrees awarded. *Degree program information:* Part-time programs available. Offers family studies (M Sc); foods/nutrition (M Sc). *Application deadline:* For fall admission, 6/1 (priority date); for winter admission, 11/15 (priority date); for spring admission, 3/31 (priority date). Applications are processed on a rolling basis. *Application fee:* $35. *Director*, Lita Villalon, 506-858-4003, Fax: 506-858-4540, E-mail: villall@umoncton.ca.

UNIVERSITÉ DE MONTRÉAL, Montréal, QC H3C 3J7, Canada

General Information Independent, coed, university. CGS member. *Enrollment:* 6,453 full-time matriculated graduate/professional students (3,715 women), 1,808 part-time matriculated graduate/professional students (1,233 women). *Graduate faculty:* 1,180 full-time, 133 part-time/adjunct. *Graduate tuition:* Tuition charges are reported in Canadian dollars. *Tuition:* Part-time $920 Canadian dollars per term. Tuition and fees vary according to degree level. *Graduate housing:* Room and/or apartments available to single students; on-campus housing not available to married students. Housing application deadline: 2/1. *Student services:* Campus safety program, career counseling, child daycare facilities, disabled student services, exercise/wellness program, free psychological counseling, international student services, low-cost health insurance. *Library facilities:* Main library plus 18 others. *Online resources:* library catalog, web page. *Collection:* 15,300 serial subscriptions, 164,079 audiovisual materials. *Research affiliation:* Institut Universitaire de gériatric de Montréal (gérontologie clinique et gériatric neurosciences cognitives, soins et services, nutrition et les troubles sensoriels), Institut de Cardiologie de Montréal (cardiologie, médicine et chirurgie cardiovasculaires, prévention et réadaption), Institut de recherches cliniques de Montréal (bioéthique, cancer, chimie bioorganique, génétique, hématolgie, immunologie, neurosciences et endocrinologie, systeme cardiovasculaire), Centre de Recherche de L'Hôpital Sacré-Coeur (maladies cardiovasculaires, maladies rénales, maladies respiratoires, neurobiologie psychiatrique et troubles du sommeil et traumatologie), Centre Hospitalier Universitaire Mère-Enfant de l'Hôpital Sainte-Justine (pédiatric, urgentologie pédiatrique et périnatalogie).

Computer facilities: 600 computers available on campus for general student use. A campuswide network can be accessed from student residence rooms and from off campus. Internet access is available. *Web address:* http://www.umontreal.ca/.

General Application Contact: Kathleen Lennon, Admissions Office in the Faculty of Graduate Studies, 514-343-6426, Fax: 514-343-2252, E-mail: fes-admission@fes.umontreal.ca.

GRADUATE UNITS

Faculty of Dentistry Students: 28 full-time (15 women). 67 applicants, 10% accepted, 7 enrolled. *Faculty:* 44. Expenses: Contact institution. In 2001, 81 first professional degrees, 2 master's, 11 other advanced degrees awarded. Offers dentistry (DMD, M Sc, Certificate); multidisciplinary residency (Certificate); oral and dental sciences (M Sc); orthodontics (M Sc, Certificate); pediatric dentistry (M Sc, Certificate); prosthodontics rehabilitation (M Sc); stomatology residency (Certificate). *Application deadline:* For fall admission, 10/1. *Application fee:* $30. Electronic applications accepted. *Application Contact:* Dr. Antonio Nanci, Associate Dean for Research, 514-343-5846, Fax: 514-343-2233. *Dean*, Dr. Claude Lamarche, 514-343-6005, Fax: 514-343-2233.

Faculty of Graduate Studies Students: 2,976 full-time (1,588 women), 268 part-time (176 women). 266 applicants, 54% accepted, 128 enrolled. Expenses: Contact institution. *Financial support:* Fellowships, research assistantships, teaching assistantships, career-related internships or fieldwork, Federal Work-Study, institutionally sponsored loans, and tuition waivers (full and partial) available. Support available to part-time students. In 2001, 40 master's, 15 doctorates, 26 other advanced degrees awarded. *Degree program information:* Part-time programs available. Offers administration (DESS); applied human sciences (PhD); bioethics (MA, DESS); environment and prevention (DESS); ergonomics (DESS); human movement sciences (M Sc, PhD); molecular biology (M Sc, PhD); museum studies-museology (MA); physical activity and health promotion (DESS); sport and fitness management (M Sc); toxicology and risk analysis (DESS). *Application deadline:* For fall and spring admission, 2/1 (priority date); for winter admission, 11/1 (priority date). *Application fee:* $30. Electronic applications accepted. *Application Contact:* Kathleen Lennon, Admissions Office, 514-343-6426, Fax: 514-343-2252, E-mail: fes-admission@fes.umontreal.ca. *Dean*, Louis Maheu, 514-343-6537, Fax: 514-343-2252.

Faculty of Arts and Sciences Students: 2,908 full-time (1,558 women), 266 part-time (176 women). 2,639 applicants, 38% accepted, 866 enrolled. *Faculty:* 567. Expenses: Contact institution. *Financial support:* Fellowships, research assistantships, teaching assistantships, career-related internships or fieldwork, Federal Work-Study, institutionally sponsored loans, and tuition waivers (full and partial) available. Support available to part-time students. In 2001, 551 master's, 124 doctorates, 42 other advanced degrees awarded. *Degree program information:* Part-time programs available. Offers anthropology (M Sc, PhD); art history (MA, PhD); arts and sciences (M Ps, M Sc, MA, MBSI, PhD, DESS); biological sciences (M Sc, PhD); chemistry (M Sc, PhD); communications (M Sc, PhD); comparative literature (MA); computer systems (M Sc, PhD); criminology (M Sc, PhD); demography (M Sc, PhD); economics (M Sc, PhD); English (MA, PhD); film studies (MA); French studies (MA, PhD); geography (M Sc, PhD, DESS); German (MA, PhD); Hispanic studies (MA, PhD); history (MA, PhD); industrial relations (M Sc, PhD); information and library science (MBSI); information science (PhD); linguistics and traduction (MA, PhD); literature (PhD); mathematics (M Sc, PhD); philosophy (MA, PhD); physics (M Sc, PhD);

Université de Montréal (continued)

political science (M Sc, PhD); psychoeducation (M Sc); psychology (M Ps, M Sc, PhD); social work (M Sc); sociology (M Sc, PhD); statistics (M Sc, PhD). *Application deadline:* For fall and spring admission, 2/1 (priority date); for winter admission, 11/1 (priority date). *Application fee:* $30. Electronic applications accepted. *Dean,* Hubert Joseph, 514-343-6262, Fax: 514-343-2185.

Faculty of Education Students: 294 full-time (200 women), 731 part-time (550 women). 446 applicants, 70% accepted, 273 enrolled. *Faculty:* 78. Expenses: Contact institution. *Financial support:* Fellowships, research assistantships, teaching assistantships available. In 2001, 109 master's, 24 doctorates, 65 other advanced degrees awarded. *Degree program information:* Part-time and evening/weekend programs available. Offers didactics (M Ed, MA, PhD, DESS); education (M Ed, MA, PhD, DESS); education and educational administration (M Ed, MA, PhD, DESS); psychopedagogy and andragogy (M Ed, MA, PhD, DESS). *Application deadline:* For fall and spring admission, 2/1 (priority date); for winter admission, 11/1 (priority date). *Application fee:* $30. Electronic applications accepted. *Application Contact:* Manon Théoêt, Graduate Chairman and Vice Dean, 514-343-7491, Fax: 514-343-7276. *Dean,* Gisèle Painchaud, 514-343-6658, Fax: 514-343-7276.

Faculty of Environmental Design and Planning Students: 221 full-time (104 women), 48 part-time (19 women). 227 applicants, 49% accepted, 97 enrolled. *Faculty:* 57. Expenses: Contact institution. In 2001, 35 master's, 2 doctorates, 6 other advanced degrees awarded. Offers environmental design and planning (M Sc A, M Urb, PhD, DESS). *Application deadline:* For fall and spring admission, 2/1 (priority date); for winter admission, 11/1 (priority date). *Application fee:* $30. Electronic applications accepted. *Application Contact:* Jacques Fisette, Vice Dean, 514-343-6499, Fax: 514-343-2183. *Dean,* Irène Cinq-Mars, 514-343-6001, Fax: 514-343-2183.

Faculty of Music Students: 173 full-time (98 women). 165 applicants, 56% accepted, 81 enrolled. *Faculty:* 34. Expenses: Contact institution. In 2001, 39 master's, 5 doctorates, 8 other advanced degrees awarded. Offers composition (M Mus, D Mus); musicology and ethnomusicology (MA, PhD); orchestra conducting (M Mus, D Mus); orchestral repertoire (DESS); performance interpretation (DESS); voice and instruments interpretation (M Mus, D Mus). *Application deadline:* For fall and spring admission, 2/1 (priority date); for winter admission, 11/1 (priority date). *Application fee:* $30. Electronic applications accepted. *Application Contact:* Lise Daoust, Vice Dean, 514-343-7998, Fax: 514-343-5727. *Dean,* Rejean Poirier, 514-343-6429, Fax: 514-343-5727.

Faculty of Nursing Students: 96 full-time (82 women), 106 part-time (100 women). 125 applicants, 54% accepted, 63 enrolled. *Faculty:* 33. Expenses: Contact institution. *Financial support:* Fellowships, research assistantships, teaching assistantships, career-related internships or fieldwork, Federal Work-Study, and institutionally sponsored loans available. In 2001, 15 master's, 4 doctorates, 6 other advanced degrees awarded. *Degree program information:* Part-time programs available. Offers nursing (M Sc, PhD, DESS). *Application deadline:* For fall and spring admission, 2/1 (priority date); for winter admission, 11/1 (priority date). Applications are processed on a rolling basis. *Application fee:* $30. Electronic applications accepted. *Application Contact:* Jacinthe Pepin, Vice Dean of Studies, 514-343-6178, Fax: 514-343-2306, E-mail: jacinthe.pepin@umontreal.ca. *Dean,* Christine Colin, 514-343-6436, Fax: 514-343-2306.

Faculty of Theology Students: 78 full-time (31 women), 53 part-time (28 women). 53 applicants, 79% accepted, 37 enrolled. *Faculty:* 18. Expenses: Contact institution. *Financial support:* Research assistantships, teaching assistantships, institutionally sponsored loans and tuition waivers (partial) available. In 2001, 17 master's, 4 doctorates awarded. Offers biblical studies (MA, PhD); pastoral studies (MA, PhD, DESS); religious studies (PhD); theological studies (MA, D Th, PhD, L Th); theology (MA, D Th, PhD, DESS, L Th). *Application deadline:* For fall and spring admission, 2/1 (priority date); for winter admission, 11/1 (priority date). *Application fee:* $30. Electronic applications accepted. *Application Contact:* Jean DuHaime, Vice Dean of Graduate Studies, 514-343-6840, Fax: 514-343-5738. *Dean,* Jean-Marc Charron, 514-343-7160, Fax: 514-343-5738.

Faculty of Law Students: 236 full-time (139 women), 76 part-time (37 women). 407 applicants, 44% accepted, 146 enrolled. *Faculty:* 56. Expenses: Contact institution. *Financial support:* Fellowships, research assistantships, teaching assistantships available. In 2001, 279 LL Bs, 40 master's, 3 doctorates, 85 other advanced degrees awarded. *Degree program information:* Part-time programs available. Offers law (LL B, LL M, LL D, DDN, DESS). *Application deadline:* For fall and spring admission, 2/1 (priority date); for winter admission, 11/1 (priority date). *Application fee:* $30. Electronic applications accepted. *Application Contact:* Louise Rolland, Graduate Chair, 514-343-7202, Fax: 514-343-2030. *Dean,* Jacques Frémont, 514-343-7583, Fax: 514-343-2199.

Faculty of Medicine Students: 1,678 full-time (1,050 women), 269 part-time (141 women). *Faculty:* 303. Expenses: Contact institution. *Financial support:* Fellowships, research assistantships, teaching assistantships, career-related internships or fieldwork, institutionally sponsored loans, and tuition waivers (full) available. In 2001, 321 first professional degrees, 219 master's, 46 doctorates, 12 other advanced degrees awarded. Offers anesthesia-resuscitation (DESS); audiology and speech pathology (MOA); biochemistry (M Sc, PhD, DEPD); biomedical engineering (M Sc A, PhD); biomedical sciences (M Sc, PhD); biophysics and molecular physiology (M Sc, PhD); clinical biochemistry (DEPD); communal and public health (M Sc, PhD, DESS); community health (M Sc, PhD, DESS); environmental and occupational health (M Sc, DESS); family medicine (DESS); family medicine and emergency (DESS); health administration (M Sc); medical biochemistry (DESS); medicine (DESS); microbiology and immunology (M Sc, PhD); microbiology and infectious diseases (DESS); neurological sciences (M Sc, PhD); nuclear medicine (DESS); nutrition (M Sc, PhD); obstetrics and gynecology (DESS); ophthalmology (DESS); pathology (DESS); pathology and cellular biology (M Sc, PhD); pediatrics (DESS); pharmacology (M Sc, PhD); physiology (M Sc, PhD); specialized studies (DES); speech-language pathology and audiology (MOA); surgery (DESS); virology (PhD); virology and immunology (PhD). *Application deadline:* For fall and spring admission, 2/1 (priority date); for winter admission, 11/1 (priority date). *Application fee:* $30. Electronic applications accepted. *Application Contact:* Dr. Laurent Descarries, Vice Dean of Studies, 514-343-6300, Fax: 514-343-5751, E-mail: descarries@umontreal.ca. *Dean,* Patrick Vinay, 514-343-6351, Fax: 514-343-5850.

Faculty of Pharmacy Students: 130 full-time (89 women), 80 part-time (59 women). 147 applicants, 61% accepted, 82 enrolled. *Faculty:* 22. Expenses: Contact institution. *Financial support:* Fellowships, teaching assistantships, career-related internships or fieldwork, Federal Work-Study, and institutionally sponsored loans available. In 2001, 42 master's, 4 doctorates awarded. *Degree program information:* Part-time programs available. Offers hospital pharmacy (M Sc); pharmacy (M Sc, PhD). *Application deadline:* For fall and spring admission, 2/1 (priority date); for winter admission, 11/1 (priority date). *Application fee:* $30. Electronic applications accepted. *Application Contact:* Huy Ong, Vice Dean, 514-343-6467, Fax: 514-343-2102. *Dean,* Jacques Turgeon, 514-343-6440, Fax: 514-343-2102.

Faculty of Veterinary Medicine Students: 121 full-time (68 women), 16 part-time (6 women). 55 applicants, 40% accepted, 20 enrolled. *Faculty:* 77. Expenses: Contact institution. *Financial support:* Research assistantships, teaching assistantships, career-related internships or fieldwork and scholarships/grants available. In 2001, 72 first professional degrees, 16 master's, 32 doctorates, 22 other advanced degrees awarded. Offers veterinary medicine (DVM, M Sc, DES, PhD, Certificate, DESS). *Application deadline:* For fall and spring admission, 2/1 (priority date); for winter admission, 11/1 (priority date). *Application fee:* $30. Electronic applications accepted. *Application Contact:* Dr. Diane Blais, Associate Dean, Student Affairs, 450-773-8521 Ext. 8273, Fax: 450-778-8132, E-mail: saefmv@medvet.umontreal.ca. *Dean,* Raymond Roy, 450-773-8521 Ext. 8246, Fax: 450-778-8101, E-mail: raymond.s.roy@umontreal.ca.

School of Optometry Students: 26 full-time (19 women), 4 part-time (2 women). 17 applicants, 53% accepted, 9 enrolled. *Faculty:* 17. Expenses: Contact institution. *Financial support:* Research assistantships, teaching assistantships, career-related internships or fieldwork available. Support available to part-time students. In 2001, 42 first professional degrees, 5 master's, 6 other advanced degrees awarded. *Degree program information:* Part-time programs available. Offers optometry (OD, M Sc, DESS); physiological optics (M Sc). *Application deadline:* For fall and spring admission, 2/1 (priority date); for winter admission, 11/1 (priority date). *Application fee:* $30. Electronic applications accepted. *Application Contact:* Micheline Cohen, Chairperson, 514-343-6325, Fax: 514-343-2382, E-mail: micheline.cohen@umontreal.ca. *Director,* Dr. Pierre Simonet, 514-343-6948, Fax: 514-343-2382, E-mail: pierre.simonet@umontreal.ca.

UNIVERSITÉ DE SHERBROOKE, Sherbrooke, QC J1K 2R1, Canada

General Information Independent, coed, university. *Graduate housing:* Room and/or apartments available to single students; on-campus housing not available to married students. Housing application deadline: 6/1. *Research affiliation:* Société de Microélectronique Industrielle.

GRADUATE UNITS

Faculty of Administration *Degree program information:* Part-time and evening/weekend programs available. Offers accounting (M Sc); administration (EMBA, M Sc, M Tax, MBA, DBA, Diploma); business administration (EMBA, MBA, DBA, Diploma); finance (M Sc); international business (M Sc); management information systems (M Sc); marketing (M Sc); organizational change and intervention (M Sc); taxation (M Tax, Diploma).

Faculty of Education *Degree program information:* Part-time and evening/weekend programs available. Offers adult education training (Diploma); counseling (M Ed); education (M Ed, MA, Diploma); elementary education (M Ed, Diploma); postsecondary education training (M Ed, Diploma); school administration (M Ed); sciences of education (MA); special education (M Ed, Diploma).

Faculty of Engineering Students: 217 full-time (39 women), 227 part-time (53 women), 130 international. 141 applicants, 44% accepted. *Faculty:* 63 full-time (3 women). Expenses: Contact institution. In 2001, 59 master's, 13 doctorates awarded. *Degree program information:* Part-time programs available. Offers chemical engineering (M Sc A, PhD); civil engineering (M Sc A, PhD); electrical engineering (M Sc A, PhD); engineering (M Eng, M Eng Mgt, M Env, M Sc A, PhD); engineering management (M Eng); environment (M Env); mechanical engineering (M Sc A, PhD). *Application deadline:* Applications are processed on a rolling basis. *Application fee:* $30 Canadian dollars. Electronic applications accepted. *Application Contact:* Roland Leduc, Assistant Dean, Research, 819-821-8000 Ext. 3110, Fax: 819-821-6994, E-mail: roland.leduc@courrier.usherb.ca. *Dean,* Richard J. Marceau, 819-821-7111, Fax: 819-821-7903, E-mail: richard.marceau@courrier.usherb.ca.

Faculty of Law Students: 549 full-time (323 women), 138 part-time (42 women); includes 23 minority (14 African Americans, 3 Asian Americans or Pacific Islanders, 5 Hispanic Americans, 1 Native American), 1 international. Average age 24. 731 applicants, 87% accepted, 607 enrolled. *Faculty:* 30 full-time (11 women), 77 part-time/adjunct (44 women). Expenses: Contact institution. *Financial support:* In 2001–02, 41 fellowships (averaging $1,000 per year), 7 research assistantships (averaging $5,224 per year), 13 teaching assistantships were awarded. Career-related internships or fieldwork also available. In 2001, 12 master's awarded. *Degree program information:* Part-time programs available. Offers alternative dispute resolution (Diploma); health law (LL M, Diploma); law (LL D); legal management (Diploma); notarial law (DDN); transitional law (Diploma). *Application deadline:* For fall admission, 3/1. *Application fee:* $30. Electronic applications accepted. *Application Contact:* Nathalie Vezina, Associate Dean, 819-821-8000, Fax: 819-821-7578, E-mail: nvezina@droit.usherb.ca. *Dean,* Louis Marquis, 819-821-7511, Fax: 819-821-7578, E-mail: louis.marquis@droit.usherb.ca.

Faculty of Letters and Human Sciences *Degree program information:* Part-time programs available. Offers comparative Canadian literature (MA, PhD); economics (MA); French literature (MA, PhD); geography and remote sensing (M Sc, PhD); gerontology (MA); history (MA); letters and human sciences (M Psych, M Sc, MA, MSS, PhD, Diploma); linguistics (MA); lit&erature de création (MA, PhD); philosophy (MA); social service (MSS); theatre (MA).

Institute of Management and Development of Cooperatives Offers management and development of cooperatives (MA, Diploma).

Faculty of Medicine *Degree program information:* Part-time programs available. Offers biochemistry (M Sc, PhD); cell biology (M Sc, PhD); clinical science (M Sc, PhD); immunology (M Sc, PhD); medicine (MD, M Sc, PhD); microbiology (M Sc, PhD); pharmacology (M Sc, PhD); physiology (biophysics) (M Sc, PhD); radiobiology (M Sc, PhD). Electronic applications accepted.

Faculty of Physical Education *Degree program information:* Part-time programs available. Offers kinanthropology (M Sc); physical activity (Diploma); physical education (M Sc, Diploma).

Faculty of Sciences Offers biology (M Sc, PhD); chemistry (M Sc, PhD); environment (M Env); gestion de l'environement (Diploma); mathematics and informatics (M Sc, PhD); physics (M Sc, PhD); sciences (M Env, M Sc, PhD, Diploma).

Faculty of Theology, Ethics and Philosophy *Degree program information:* Part-time and evening/weekend programs available. Postbaccalaureate distance learning degree programs offered. Offers applied ethics (Diploma); human science of religions (MA); intercultural training (Diploma); philosophy (MA, PhD); spiritual anthropology (Diploma); theology (MA, PhD, Diploma).

UNIVERSITÉ DU QUÉBEC À CHICOUTIMI, Chicoutimi, QC G7H 2B1, Canada

General Information Province-supported, coed, university. *Graduate housing:* Room and/or apartments available to single students; on-campus housing not available to married students.

GRADUATE UNITS

Graduate Programs *Degree program information:* Part-time programs available. Offers didactics of French-mother tongue (Diploma); earth sciences (M Sc A); education (M Ed, MA, PhD); engineering (M Sc A, PhD); ethics (Diploma); fine arts (MA); genetics (M Sc); linguistics (MA); literary studies (MA); mineral resources (PhD); project management (M Sc); regional studies (MA); renewable resources (M Sc); small and medium-sized organization management (M Sc); theology (pastoral studies) (MA, PhD).

UNIVERSITÉ DU QUÉBEC EN OUTAOUAIS, Hull, QC J8X 3X7, Canada

General Information Province-supported, coed, comprehensive institution. *Graduate faculty:* 14. *Graduate tuition:* Tuition charges are reported in Canadian dollars. *International tuition:* $5,598 Canadian dollars full-time. *Tuition, area resident:* Part-time $155 Canadian dollars per credit. Tuition, province resident: full-time $1,800 Canadian dollars. Tuition, Canadian resident: full-time $3,114 Canadian dollars; part-time $225 Canadian dollars per credit. *Graduate housing:* Room and/or apartments available on a first-come, first-served basis to single students; on-campus housing not available to married students. Typical cost: $3,375 Canadian dollars per year. *Student services:* Campus employment opportunities, career counseling, international student services. *Online resources:* library catalog, web page. *Collection:* 169,289 titles, 4,458 serial subscriptions.

Computer facilities: 120 computers available on campus for general student use. A campuswide network can be accessed from off campus. Internet access is available. *Web address:* http://www.uquebec.ca/.

General Application Contact: Richard Bérubé, Registrar, 819-773-1849, Fax: 819-773-1835, E-mail: richard_berube@uqah.uquebec.ca.

GRADUATE UNITS

Graduate Programs Students: 125 full-time (75 women), 659 part-time (389 women), 6 international. 525 applicants, 78% accepted. *Faculty:* 14. Expenses: Contact institution. *Financial support:* Fellowships, research assistantships, teaching assistantships available. In 2001, 80 master's, 21 other advanced degrees awarded. *Degree program information:* Part-time programs available. Offers accounting (Diploma); adult education (Diploma); computer network (M Sc, Diploma); education (M Ed, MA, PhD, Diploma); industrial relations (M Sc, MA); nursing (M Sc, Diploma); project management (M Sc, MA, Diploma); psycho-education (M Ed, MA); regional development (MA); social work (MA). *Application deadline:* For fall admission, 8/21. *Application fee:* $30 Canadian dollars. *Application Contact:* Richard Bérubé,

Registrar, 819-773-1849, Fax: 819-773-1835, E-mail: richard_berube@uqah.uquebec.ca. *Dean*, Daniel Pelletier, 819-595-3985, Fax: 819-595-3924, E-mail: daniel_pelletier@uqah.uqubec.ca.

UNIVERSITÉ DU QUÉBEC À MONTRÉAL, Montréal, QC H3C 3P8, Canada

General Information Province-supported, coed, university. CGS member. *Graduate housing:* Room and/or apartments available to single students; on-campus housing not available to married students. *Research affiliation:* Labopharm, Inc. (pharmacology), Hydro-Québec (environmental sciences), Bell (computer sciences), Microcréatif (computer sciences), University Corporation for Atmospheric Resources.

GRADUATE UNITS

Graduate Programs *Degree program information:* Part-time programs available. Offers accounting (M Sc, MPA, Diploma); actuarial sciences (Diploma); art history (PhD); art studies (MA); atmospheric sciences (M Sc); biology (M Sc, PhD); business administration (MBA); business administration (research) (MBA); chemistry (M Sc); communications (MA, PhD); dance (MA); death (Diploma); dramatic arts (MA); economics (M Sc, PhD); education (M Ed, MA, PhD); education of the environmental sciences (Diploma); environmental sciences (M Sc, PhD); ergonomics in occupational health and safety (Diploma); finance (Diploma); fine arts (MA); geographical information systems (Diploma); geography (M Sc); geology-research (M Sc); history (MA, PhD); human movement studies (M Sc); linguistics (MA, PhD); literary studies (MA, PhD); management consultant (Diploma); management information systems (M Sc, M Sc A); mathematics (M Sc, PhD); meteorology (PhD, Diploma); mineral resources (PhD); museology (MA); non-renewable resources (DESS); philosophy (MA, PhD); political science (MA, PhD); project management (MGP, Diploma); psychology (D Ps, PhD); religious sciences (MA, PhD); semiology (PhD); sexology (MA); social and labor law (LL M); social intervention (MA); sociology (MA, PhD); study and practices of the arts (PhD); urban analysis and management (MA); urban studies (PhD).

UNIVERSITÉ DU QUÉBEC À RIMOUSKI, Rimouski, QC G5L 3A1, Canada

General Information Province-supported, coed, comprehensive institution. *Graduate housing:* Room and/or apartments available to single students; on-campus housing not available to married students.

GRADUATE UNITS

Graduate Programs *Degree program information:* Part-time programs available. Offers education (M Ed, MA, PhD); ethics (MA); literary studies (MA); management of marine resources (M Sc); oceanography (M Sc, PhD); project management (M Sc); regional development (MA); regional public administration (Diploma); wildlife resources management (M Sc, Diploma).

UNIVERSITÉ DU QUÉBEC À TROIS-RIVIÈRES, Trois-Rivières, QC G9A 5H7, Canada

General Information Province-supported, coed, university. *Enrollment:* 761 full-time matriculated graduate/professional students (415 women), 472 part-time matriculated graduate/professional students (211 women). *Graduate faculty:* 1,180. *Tuition:* Part-time $1,200 per term. *Graduate housing:* Room and/or apartments available to single students; on-campus housing not available to married students. Housing application deadline: 2/1. *Student services:* Campus employment opportunities, campus safety program, career counseling, child daycare facilities, disabled student services, exercise/wellness program, free psychological counseling, international student services. *Library facilities:* Main library plus 1 other. *Online resources:* library catalog, web page, access to other libraries' catalogs. *Collection:* 464,338 titles.

Computer facilities: 200 computers available on campus for general student use. A campuswide network can be accessed from student residence rooms and from off campus. Internet access is available. *Web address:* http://www.uqtr.ca/.

General Application Contact: Jean Bois, Admissions Officer, 819-376-5011 Ext. 2591, Fax: 819-376-5210, E-mail: jean_bois@uqtr.ca.

GRADUATE UNITS

Graduate Programs Students: 761 full-time (415 women), 472 part-time (211 women). Expenses: Contact institution. *Financial support:* Fellowships, research assistantships, teaching assistantships available. *Degree program information:* Part-time programs available. Offers accounting science (DESS); biophysics and cellular biology (M Sc, PhD); business administration (DBA); chemistry (M Sc); education (M Ed, MA, DESS); educational administration (PhD); electrical engineering (M Sc A, PhD); energy sciences (M Sc, PhD); environmental sciences (M Sc, PhD); finance and economic finance (DESS); industrial engineering (M Sc, DESS); labor relations (DESS); leisure, culture and tourism sciences (MA, DESS); literary studies (MA); management of small and medium-sized enterprises and their environment (M Sc); mathematics and computer science (M Sc); nursing sciences (M Sc, DESS); philosophy (MA, PhD); physical education (M Sc); project management (M Sc, MGP, DESS); psychoeducation (M Ed); psychology (MA, PhD); pulp and paper engineering (M Sc A, PhD); Quebec studies (MA, PhD). *Application deadline:* For fall admission, 2/1. *Application fee:* $30. *Application Contact:* Jean Bois, Admissions Officer, 819-376-5011 Ext. 2591, Fax: 819-376-5210, E-mail: jean_bois@uqtr.ca. *Dean*, Alain Maire, 819-376-5119 Ext. 2131, Fax: 819-376-5228, E-mail: alain_maire@uqtr.uquebec.ca.

UNIVERSITÉ DU QUÉBEC, ÉCOLE DE TECHNOLOGIE SUPÉRIEURE, Montréal, QC H3C 1K3, Canada

General Information Province-supported, coed, primarily men, comprehensive institution. *Enrollment:* 175 full-time matriculated graduate/professional students (20 women), 228 part-time matriculated graduate/professional students (30 women). *Enrollment by degree level:* 280 master's, 70 doctoral, 53 other advanced degrees. *Graduate tuition:* Tuition charges are reported in Canadian dollars. *Tuition, area resident:* Part-time $56 Canadian dollars per credit. Tuition, province resident: part-time $127 Canadian dollars per credit. Tuition, Canadian resident: part-time $249 Canadian dollars per credit. Tuition and fees vary according to degree level. *Graduate housing:* Rooms and/or apartments available on a first-come, first-served basis to single and married students. *Student services:* Campus employment opportunities, free psychological counseling, international student services. *Online resources:* library catalog, web page, access to other libraries' catalogs. *Collection:* 44,195 titles, 630 serial subscriptions. *Web address:* http://www.uquebec.ca/.

General Application Contact: Francine Gamache, Registrar, 514-396-8885, Fax: 514-396-8831, E-mail: francine.gamache@etsmtl.ca.

GRADUATE UNITS

Graduate Programs Students: 175 full-time (20 women), 228 part-time (30 women). 171 applicants, 81% accepted, 67 enrolled. Expenses: Contact institution. *Financial support:* Fellowships, research assistantships, teaching assistantships available. In 2001, 52 master's, 3 doctorates, 3 other advanced degrees awarded. Offers engineering (M Eng, PhD, Diploma). *Application fee:* $30. *Application Contact:* Francine Gamache, Registrar, 514-396-8885, Fax: 514-396-8831, E-mail: francine.gamache@etsmtl.ca. *Head*, Christian Lardinois, E-mail: clardinois@info.etsmtl.ca.

UNIVERSITÉ DU QUÉBEC, ÉCOLE NATIONALE D'ADMINISTRATION PUBLIQUE, Quebec, QC G1K 9E5, Canada

General Information Province-supported, coed, graduate-only institution. *Enrollment by degree level:* 449 master's, 14 doctoral, 662 other advanced degrees. *Graduate faculty:* 50. *Graduate tuition:* Tuition charges are reported in Canadian dollars. *International tuition:* $4,542 Canadian dollars full-time. Tuition, province resident: full-time $1,884 Canadian dollars; part-time $225 Canadian dollars. Tuition, Canadian resident: full-time $2,037 Canadian dollars. *Graduate housing:* On-campus housing not available. *Student services:* International student services. *Online resources:* library catalog, web page, access to other libraries' catalogs. *Collection:* 93,489 titles, 21,507 serial subscriptions, 354 audiovisual materials.

Computer facilities: A campuswide network can be accessed. *Web address:* http://www.enap.uquebec.ca/.

General Application Contact: Robert Brulotte, Registrar, 418-641-3000 Ext. 6267, Fax: 418-641-3055, E-mail: robert_brulotte@enap.uquebec.ca.

GRADUATE UNITS

Graduate Program in Public Administration 1,338 applicants, 84% accepted. Expenses: Contact institution. *Financial support:* Fellowships, research assistantships, teaching assistantships available. In 2001, 208 master's, 69 other advanced degrees awarded. *Degree program information:* Part-time programs available. Offers international administration (MAP, Diploma); public administration (MAGU, MAP, Diploma); regional public administration (Diploma); urban analysis and management (MAGU). *Application deadline:* For fall admission, 4/1. *Application fee:* $30. *Application Contact:* Robert Brulotte, Registrar, 418-641-3000 Ext. 6267, Fax: 418-641-3055, E-mail: robert_brulotte@enap.uquebec.ca. *Dean*, Luc Bernier, 418-641-3000 Ext. 6230, Fax: 418-657-2620, E-mail: luc_bernier@enap.uquebec.ca.

UNIVERSITÉ DU QUÉBEC EN ABITIBI-TÉMISCAMINGUE, Rouyn-Noranda, QC J9X 5E4, Canada

General Information Province-supported, coed, comprehensive institution. *Enrollment:* 3 full-time matriculated graduate/professional students (2 women), 50 part-time matriculated graduate/professional students (19 women). *Graduate faculty:* 75. *Graduate tuition:* Tuition charges are reported in Canadian dollars. *International tuition:* $9,356 Canadian dollars full-time. Tuition, province resident: full-time $1,856 Canadian dollars. Tuition, Canadian resident: full-time $3,900 Canadian dollars. *Graduate housing:* Room and/or apartments available on a first-come, first-served basis to single students; on-campus housing not available to married students. Typical cost: $600 Canadian dollars per year. Room charges vary according to campus/location and housing facility selected. Housing application deadline: 3/1. *Student services:* Campus employment opportunities, career counseling, child daycare facilities, disabled student services, exercise/wellness program, free psychological counseling, international student services, multicultural affairs office, writing training. *Online resources:* library catalog, web page, access to other libraries' catalogs. *Collection:* 135,882 titles, 302 serial subscriptions.

Computer facilities: 85 computers available on campus for general student use. A campuswide network can be accessed from off campus. Internet access is available. *Web address:* http://www.uqat.ca/.

General Application Contact: Denis Verret, Registrar, 819-762-0971 Ext. 2210, Fax: 819-797-4727, E-mail: denis.verret@uqat.ca.

GRADUATE UNITS

Graduate Programs Students: 3 full-time (2 women), 50 part-time (19 women). 12 applicants, 42% accepted. Expenses: Contact institution. *Financial support:* Fellowships, research assistantships, teaching assistantships available. In 2001, 5 degrees awarded. *Degree program information:* Part-time programs available. Offers business administration (MBA); education (M Ed, MA, PhD); organization management (M Sc); project management (M Sc). *Application deadline:* For fall admission, 4/1. *Application fee:* $30. *Application Contact:* Denis Verret, Registrar, 819-762-0971 Ext. 2210, Fax: 819-797-4727, E-mail: denis.verret@uqat.ca. *Research and Academic Vice Rector*, Johanne Jean, 819-762-0971 Ext. 2256, Fax: 819-797-4727.

UNIVERSITÉ DU QUÉBEC, INSTITUT NATIONAL DE LA RECHERCHE SCIENTIFIQUE, Ste-Foy, QC G1V 4C7, Canada

General Information Province-supported, coed, graduate-only institution. *Graduate housing:* On-campus housing not available.

GRADUATE UNITS

Graduate Programs *Degree program information:* Part-time programs available.

Research Center—Earth *Degree program information:* Part-time programs available. Offers earth sciences (M Sc, PhD); earth sciences-environmental technologies (M Sc).

Research Center—Energy and Materials *Degree program information:* Part-time programs available. Offers energy and materials science (M Sc, PhD).

Research Center—INRS—Institut Armand-Frappier—Human Health *Degree program information:* Part-time programs available. Offers experimental health sciences (M Sc); virologie et immunologie (M Sc, PhD).

Research Center—INRS—Institut Armand-Frappier—Microbiology and Biotechnology *Degree program information:* Part-time programs available. Offers applied microbiology (M Sc); biology (PhD).

Research Center—Telecommunications *Degree program information:* Part-time programs available. Offers information technology (M Sc, Diploma); software engineering (M Sc); telecommunications (M Sc, PhD).

Research Center—Urbanization-Culture and Society *Degree program information:* Part-time programs available. Offers socioeconomic studies of inner city rehabilitation (Diploma); urban studies (MA, PhD).

Research Center—Water *Degree program information:* Part-time programs available. Offers water sciences (M Sc, PhD).

UNIVERSITÉ LAVAL, Québec, QC G1K 7P4, Canada

General Information Independent, coed, university. CGS member. *Enrollment:* 5,134 full-time matriculated graduate/professional students (2,638 women), 2,611 part-time matriculated graduate/professional students (1,542 women). *Enrollment by degree level:* 791 first professional, 4,154 master's, 1,709 doctoral, 1,091 other advanced degrees. *Graduate faculty:* 1,424 full-time (333 women), 20 part-time/adjunct (1 woman). *Graduate tuition:* Tuition charges are reported in Canadian dollars. *International tuition:* $9,030 Canadian dollars full-time. *Tuition, area resident:* Full-time $1,830 Canadian dollars. Tuition, province resident: part-time $62 Canadian dollars per credit. Tuition, Canadian resident: full-time $4,020 Canadian dollars. Full-time tuition and fees vary according to degree level. *Graduate housing:* Room and/or apartments available on a first-come, first-served basis to single students; on-campus housing not available to married students. Typical cost: $1,594 Canadian dollars per year ($5,333 Canadian dollars including board). Housing application deadline: 2/15. *Student services:* Campus employment opportunities, campus safety program, career counseling, child daycare facilities, disabled student services, exercise/wellness program, free psychological counseling, international student services, multicultural affairs office, teacher training, writing training. *Library facilities:* Bibliothéque Générale plus 2 others. *Online resources:* library catalog, web page. *Collection:* 2.2 million titles, 13,655 serial subscriptions, 19,700 audiovisual materials. *Research affiliation:* Centre Hospitalier Universitaire de Québec (biomedical research), Institut National d'optique (optics and photonics), Centre de Développement de la Geomatique (applied geomatics), Institut Maurice-Lamontagne (oceanography), Forintek Canada (forestry and wood processing).

Computer facilities: 7,000 computers available on campus for general student use. A campuswide network can be accessed from student residence rooms and from off campus. Internet access is available. *Web address:* http://www.ulaval.ca/.

General Application Contact: Mme. Rachele Tremblay, Registrar, 418-656-3080, Fax: 418-656-5216, E-mail: reg@reg.ulaval.ca.

GRADUATE UNITS

Faculty of Administrative Sciences Students: 529 full-time (232 women), 599 part-time (277 women), 210 international. Average age 30. 1,713 applicants, 52% accepted, 517 enrolled. *Faculty:* 80. Expenses: Contact institution. In 2001, 242 master's, 5 doctorates, 57 other advanced degrees awarded. Offers accounting (MBA); administrative sciences (M Sc, MBA, PhD, Diploma); administrative studies (M Sc, PhD); agri-food management (MBA); electronic business (MBA, Diploma); factory management and logistics (MBA); finance (MBA); financial engineering (M Sc); firm management (MBA); information technology management (MBA); international management (MBA); management (MBA); management accounting (MBA, Diploma); marketing (MBA); modelization and organizational decision (MBA); occupational

Université Laval (continued)

health and safety management (MBA); organizations management and development (Diploma); pharmacy management (MBA); public accountancy (MBA, Diploma). *Application deadline:* For fall and spring admission, 2/1 (priority date); for winter admission, 9/1 (priority date). Applications are processed on a rolling basis. *Application fee:* $30. Electronic applications accepted. *Dean,* Bernard Garnier, 418-656-2131 Ext. 2216, Fax: 418-656-2624, E-mail: bernard.garnier@fsa.ulaval.ca.

Faculty of Agricultural and Food Sciences Students: 294 full-time (163 women), 63 part-time (35 women), 96 international. Average age 29. 389 applicants, 41% accepted, 63 enrolled. *Faculty:* 110. Expenses: Contact institution. In 2001, 60 master's, 17 doctorates, 5 other advanced degrees awarded. Offers agri-food engineering (M Sc); agricultural and food sciences (M Sc, PhD, Diploma); agricultural economics (M Sc); agricultural microbiology (M Sc, PhD); animal sciences (M Sc, PhD); consumer sciences (Diploma); food sciences and technology (M Sc, PhD); integrated rural development (Diploma); nutrition (M Sc, PhD); plant biology (M Sc, PhD, Diploma); soils and environment science (M Sc); soils and environment science (PhD). *Application deadline:* For fall and spring admission, 2/1 (priority date); for winter admission, 9/1 (priority date). Applications are processed on a rolling basis. *Application fee:* $30. Electronic applications accepted. *Dean,* Jean-Claude Dufour, 418-656-2131 Ext. 3496, Fax: 418-656-7806, E-mail: jean-claude.dufour@eac.ulaval.ca.

Faculty of Architecture, Planning and Visual Arts Students: 151 full-time (68 women), 26 part-time (13 women), 38 international. Average age 28. 277 applicants, 55% accepted, 85 enrolled. *Faculty:* 40. Expenses: Contact institution. In 2001, 73 master's, 1 doctorate awarded. Offers architecture, planning and visual arts (M Arch, MA, MATDR, PhD); planning and regional development (MATDR, PhD). *Application deadline:* For fall and spring admission, 2/1 (priority date); for winter admission, 9/1 (priority date). Applications are processed on a rolling basis. *Application fee:* $30 Canadian dollars. Electronic applications accepted. *Interim Director,* Claude Dubé, 418-656-2131 Ext. 2546, Fax: 418-656-3325, E-mail: claude.dube@faaav.ulaval.ca.

School of Architecture Students: 43 full-time (18 women), 9 part-time (4 women), 10 international. Average age 25. 79 applicants, 61% accepted, 36 enrolled. *Faculty:* 16. Expenses: Contact institution. In 2001, 11 degrees awarded. Offers architecture (M Arch). *Application deadline:* For fall and spring admission, 2/1 (priority date); for winter admission, 9/1 (priority date). Applications are processed on a rolling basis. *Application fee:* $30. Electronic applications accepted. *Director,* Emilien Vachon, 418-656-2131 Ext. 5019, Fax: 418-656-2785, E-mail: faaav@faaav.ulaval.ca.

School of Visual Arts Students: 40 full-time (23 women), 7 part-time (5 women), 4 international. 61 applicants, 49% accepted, 22 enrolled. *Faculty:* 17. Expenses: Contact institution. In 2001, 29 degrees awarded. Offers graphic design and multimedia (MA); visual arts (MA). *Application deadline:* For fall and spring admission, 2/1 (priority date); for winter admission, 9/1 (priority date). Applications are processed on a rolling basis. *Application fee:* $30 Canadian dollars. Electronic applications accepted. *Interim Director,* Claude Dubé, 418-656-2131 Ext. 2546, Fax: 418-656-3325, E-mail: claude.dube@faaav.ulaval.ca.

Faculty of Dentistry Students: 201 full-time (108 women), 23 part-time (9 women), 2 international. Average age 24. 332 applicants, 20% accepted, 54 enrolled. *Faculty:* 30. Expenses: Contact institution. In 2001, 46 first professional degrees, 2 master's, 5 other advanced degrees awarded. Offers buccal and maxillofacial surgery (DESS); dentistry (DMD, M Sc, DESS); endodontics (DESS); gerodontology (DESS); multidisciplinary dentistry (DESS); periodontics (DESS). *Application deadline:* Applications are processed on a rolling basis. *Application fee:* $30. Electronic applications accepted. *Dean,* Diane Lachapelle, 418-656-2131 Ext. 7532, Fax: 418-656-2720, E-mail: fmd@fmd.ulaval.ca.

Faculty of Education Students: 315 full-time (224 women), 484 part-time (397 women), 35 international. Average age 32. 474 applicants, 72% accepted, 248 enrolled. *Faculty:* 100. Expenses: Contact institution. *Financial support:* Fellowships available. In 2001, 141 master's, 20 doctorates, 29 other advanced degrees awarded. Offers didactics (MA, PhD); education (M Sc, MA, PhD, Diploma); educational administration and evaluation (MA, PhD); educational pedagogy (Diploma); educational practice (Diploma); educational psychology (MA, PhD); educational supervision (Diploma); orientation sciences (MA, PhD); pedagogy management and development (Diploma); physical education (M Sc, PhD); school adaptation (Diploma); small groups animation (Diploma); teaching technology (MA, PhD). *Application deadline:* For fall and spring admission, 2/1 (priority date); for winter admission, 9/1 (priority date). Applications are processed on a rolling basis. *Application fee:* $30. Electronic applications accepted. *Dean,* Jean-Claude Gagnon, 418-656-2131 Ext. 2059, Fax: 418-656-2731, E-mail: jean-claude.gagnon@fse.ulaval.ca.

Faculty of Forestry and Geomatics Students: 153 full-time (51 women), 20 part-time (6 women), 49 international. Average age 30. 151 applicants, 54% accepted, 42 enrolled. *Faculty:* 47. Expenses: Contact institution. In 2001, 43 master's, 10 doctorates awarded. Offers agroforestry (M Sc); forestry and geomatics (M Sc, PhD); forestry sciences (M Sc, PhD); geomatics sciences (M Sc, PhD); wood sciences (M Sc, PhD). *Application deadline:* For fall and spring admission, 2/1 (priority date); for winter admission, 9/1 (priority date). Applications are processed on a rolling basis. *Application fee:* $30 Canadian dollars. Electronic applications accepted. *Dean,* Denis Brière, 418-656-2131 Ext. 7907, Fax: 418-656-3177, E-mail: ffg@ffg.ulaval.ca.

Faculty of Law Students: 94 full-time (47 women), 49 part-time (28 women), 27 international. Average age 32. 193 applicants, 43% accepted, 35 enrolled. *Faculty:* 46. Expenses: Contact institution. In 2001, 23 master's, 3 doctorates, 12 other advanced degrees awarded. Offers international and transnational law (Diploma); law (LL M, LL D); law of business (Diploma); notarial law (Diploma). *Application deadline:* For fall and spring admission, 2/1 (priority date); for winter admission, 9/1 (priority date). Applications are processed on a rolling basis. *Application fee:* $30 Canadian dollars. Electronic applications accepted. *Dean,* Pierre Lemieux, 418-656-2131 Ext. 3511, Fax: 418-656-7714, E-mail: fd@fd.ulaval.ca.

Faculty of Letters Students: 560 full-time (339 women), 262 part-time (187 women), 95 international. Average age 30. 594 applicants, 71% accepted, 241 enrolled. *Faculty:* 163. Expenses: Contact institution. In 2001, 99 master's, 27 doctorates, 12 other advanced degrees awarded. Offers ancient civilization (PhD); ancient civilization (MA); archaeology (MA, PhD); art history (MA, PhD); English literatures (MA, PhD); ethnology of French-speaking people in North America (MA, PhD); French and Québec literature (MA, PhD); French studies (MA); geographical sciences (M Sc Geogr, PhD); geography (M Sc Geogr, PhD); history (MA, PhD); international journalism (Diploma); letters (M Sc Geogr, MA, PhD, Diploma); linguistics (MA, PhD); literature and the screen and stage (MA, PhD); museology (Diploma); public communication (MA); public relations (Diploma); Spanish literature (MA, PhD); terminology and translation (MA, Diploma). *Application deadline:* For fall and spring admission, 2/1 (priority date); for winter admission, 9/1 (priority date). Applications are processed on a rolling basis. *Application fee:* $30 Canadian dollars. Electronic applications accepted. *Director,* Jacques Mathieu, 418-656-2131 Ext. 5197, Fax: 418-656-3603, E-mail: jacques.mathieu@hst.ulaval.ca.

Faculty of Medicine Students: 1,081 full-time (660 women), 164 part-time (99 women), 70 international. Average age 25. 1,795 applicants, 31% accepted, 322 enrolled. *Faculty:* 302. Expenses: Contact institution. *Financial support:* Fellowships available. In 2001, 113 first professional degrees, 113 master's, 36 doctorates, 10 other advanced degrees awarded. Offers accident prevention and occupational health and safety management (Diploma); anatomy and physiology (M Sc, PhD); anatomy–pathology (DESS); anesthesia–resuscitation (DESS); cardiology (DESS); care of older people (Diploma); cellular and molecular biology (M Sc, PhD); community health (M Sc, PhD, DESS); dermatology (DESS); diagnostic radiology (DESS); emergency medicine (Diploma); epidemiology (M Sc, PhD); experimental medicine (M Sc, PhD); family medicine (DESS); general surgery (DESS); geriatrics (DESS); hematology (DESS); internal medicine (DESS); kinesiology (M Sc, PhD); maternal and fetal medicine (Diploma); medical biochemistry (DESS); medical microbiology and infectious diseases (DESS); medical oncology (DESS); medicine (MD, M Sc, PhD, DESS, Diploma); microbiology-immunology (M Sc, PhD); nephrology (DESS); neurobiology (M Sc, PhD); neurology (DESS); neurosurgery (DESS); obstretics and gynecology (DESS); ophthalmology (DESS); orthopedic surgery (DESS); oto-rhino-laryngology (DESS); pallative medicine (Diploma); pediatrics (DESS); physiology-endocrinology (M Sc, PhD); psychiatry (DESS); pulmonary medicine (DESS); radiology–oncology (DESS); speech therapy (M Sc); urology (DESS). *Application deadline:* For fall and spring admission, 2/1 (priority date); for winter admission, 9/1 (priority date). Applications are processed on a rolling basis. *Application fee:* $30 Canadian dollars. Electronic applications accepted. *Dean,* Marc Desmeules, 418-656-2131 Ext. 2301, Fax: 418-656-5062, E-mail: marc.desmeules@fmed.ulaval.ca.

Faculty of Music Students: 41 full-time (22 women), 25 part-time (12 women), 3 international. Average age 28. 35 applicants, 89% accepted, 25 enrolled. *Faculty:* 22. Expenses: Contact institution. In 2001, 11 master's awarded. Offers composition (M Mus); instrumental didactics (M Mus); interpretation (M Mus); music (PhD); music education (M Mus); musicology (M Mus). *Application deadline:* For fall and spring admission, 2/1 (priority date); for winter admission, 9/1 (priority date). Applications are processed on a rolling basis. *Application fee:* $30. Electronic applications accepted. *Dean,* Raymond Ringuette, 418-656-2131 Ext. 3321, Fax: 418-656-7365, E-mail: mus@mus.ulaval.ca.

Faculty of Nursing Students: 7 full-time (5 women), 51 part-time (44 women). Average age 34. 41 applicants, 83% accepted, 24 enrolled. *Faculty:* 18. Expenses: Contact institution. In 2001, 12 master's, 3 other advanced degrees awarded. Offers nursing (M Sc, Diploma). *Application deadline:* For fall and spring admission, 2/1 (priority date); for winter admission, 9/1 (priority date). Applications are processed on a rolling basis. *Application fee:* $30. Electronic applications accepted. *Dean,* Linda Lepage, 418-656-2131 Ext. 3366, Fax: 418-656-7747, E-mail: fsi@fsi.ulaval.ca.

Faculty of Pharmacy Students: 41 full-time (28 women), 87 part-time (64 women), 4 international. Average age 30. 49 applicants, 67% accepted, 25 enrolled. *Faculty:* 17. Expenses: Contact institution. In 2001, 30 master's, 6 doctorates, 6 other advanced degrees awarded. Offers community pharmacy (Diploma); hospital pharmacy (M Sc); pharmacy (M Sc, PhD, Diploma). *Application deadline:* For fall and spring admission, 2/1 (priority date); for winter admission, 9/1 (priority date). Applications are processed on a rolling basis. *Application fee:* $30. Electronic applications accepted. *Dean,* Monique Richer, 418-656-2131 Ext. 5639, Fax: 418-656-2305, E-mail: pha@pha.ulaval.ca.

Faculty of Philosophy Students: 82 full-time (21 women), 32 part-time (7 women), 5 international. Average age 32. 60 applicants, 85% accepted, 23 enrolled. *Faculty:* 18. Expenses: Contact institution. In 2001, 18 master's, 5 doctorates awarded. Offers philosophy (MA, PhD). *Application deadline:* For fall and spring admission, 2/1 (priority date); for winter admission, 9/1 (priority date). Applications are processed on a rolling basis. *Application fee:* $30. Electronic applications accepted. *Dean,* Jean-Marc Narbonne, 418-656-2131 Ext. 2642, Fax: 418-656-7267, E-mail: jean-marc.narbonne@fp.ulaval.ca.

Faculty of Sciences and Engineering Students: 764 full-time (208 women), 141 part-time (27 women), 238 international. Average age 28. 921 applicants, 39% accepted, 204 enrolled. *Faculty:* 249. Expenses: Contact institution. In 2001, 173 master's, 44 doctorates, 12 other advanced degrees awarded. Offers aerospace engineering (M Sc); biochemistry (M Sc, PhD); biology (M Sc, PhD); chemical engineering (M Sc, PhD); chemistry (M Sc, PhD); civil engineering (M Sc, PhD); computer science (M Sc, PhD); earth sciences (M Sc, PhD); electrical engineering (M Sc, PhD); geology (M Sc, PhD); industrial engineering (Diploma); mathematics (M Sc, PhD); mechanical engineering (M Sc, PhD); metallurgical engineering (M Sc, PhD); microbiology (M Sc, PhD); mining engineering (M Sc, PhD); oceanography (PhD); physics (M Sc, PhD); sciences and engineering (M Sc, PhD, Diploma); software engineering (Diploma); statistics (M Sc); technological entrepreneurship (Diploma); urban infrastructure engineering (Diploma). *Application deadline:* For fall and spring admission, 2/1 (priority date); for winter admission, 9/1 (priority date). Applications are processed on a rolling basis. *Application fee:* $30. Electronic applications accepted. *Dean,* Pierre Moreau, 418-656-2131 Ext. 2354, Fax: 418-656-5902, E-mail: pierre.moreau@fsg.ulaval.ca.

Faculty of Social Sciences Students: 612 full-time (368 women), 321 part-time (218 women), 85 international. Average age 29. 1,040 applicants, 55% accepted, 274 enrolled. *Faculty:* 179. Expenses: Contact institution. In 2001, 229 master's, 37 doctorates, 3 other advanced degrees awarded. Offers anthropology (MA, PhD); clinical psychology (PhD); economics (MA, PhD); feminist studies (Diploma); industrial relations (MA, PhD); political science (MA, PhD); politics analysis (MA); psychology (PhD); social sciences (M Ps, M Serv Soc, MA, PhD, Diploma); social work (PhD); sociology (MA, PhD). *Application deadline:* For fall and spring admission, 2/1 (priority date); for winter admission, 9/1 (priority date). Applications are processed on a rolling basis. *Application fee:* $30 Canadian dollars. Electronic applications accepted. *Dean,* Claude Beauchamp, 418-656-2131 Ext. 2615, Fax: 418-656-2114, E-mail: fss@fss.ulaval.ca.

School of Psychology Students: 97 full-time (77 women), 97 part-time (79 women). 282 applicants, 49% accepted, 75 enrolled. *Faculty:* 35. Expenses: Contact institution. In 2001, 106 degrees awarded. Offers psychology (M Ps, MA). *Application deadline:* For fall and spring admission, 2/1 (priority date); for winter admission, 9/1 (priority date). Applications are processed on a rolling basis. *Application fee:* $30. Electronic applications accepted. *Director,* François Y. Doré, 418-656-2131 Ext. 5383, Fax: 418-656-3646, E-mail: psy@psy.ulaval.ca.

School of Social Work Students: 72 full-time (56 women), 82 part-time (65 women). 113 applicants, 68% accepted, 45 enrolled. *Faculty:* 26. Expenses: Contact institution. In 2001, 27 degrees awarded. Offers social work (M Serv Soc). *Application deadline:* For fall and spring admission, 2/1 (priority date); for winter admission, 9/1 (priority date). Applications are processed on a rolling basis. *Application fee:* $30. Electronic applications accepted. *Director,* Marie Simard, 418-656-2131 Ext. 2371, Fax: 418-656-3567, E-mail: fss@fss.ulaval.ca.

Faculty of Theology and Religious Sciences Students: 94 full-time (28 women), 49 part-time (14 women), 13 international. Average age 39. 100 applicants, 91% accepted, 60 enrolled. *Faculty:* 23. Expenses: Contact institution. In 2001, 11 master's, 5 doctorates awarded. Offers applied ethics (Diploma); human sciences of religion (MA, PhD); practical theology (D Th P); theology (MA, PhD); theology and religious sciences (MA, D Th P, PhD, Diploma). *Application deadline:* For fall and spring admission, 2/1 (priority date); for winter admission, 9/1 (priority date). Applications are processed on a rolling basis. *Application fee:* $30. Electronic applications accepted. *Dean,* Marc Pelchat, 418-656-2131 Ext. 7823, Fax: 418-656-3273, E-mail: marc.pelchat@ftsr.ulaval.ca.

Québec Institute for Advanced International Studies Students: 75 full-time (39 women), 27 part-time (13 women), 11 international. Average age 25. 166 applicants, 45% accepted, 40 enrolled. Expenses: Contact institution. In 2001, 24 degrees awarded. Offers advanced international studies (MA); international relations (MA). *Application deadline:* For fall and spring admission, 2/1 (priority date); for winter admission, 9/1 (priority date). Applications are processed on a rolling basis. *Application fee:* $30. Electronic applications accepted. *Director,* Louis Bélanger, 418-656-2131 Ext. 7071, Fax: 418-656-3634, E-mail: hei@hei.ulaval.ca.

See in-depth description on page 1153.

UNIVERSITY AT BUFFALO, THE STATE UNIVERSITY OF NEW YORK, Buffalo, NY 14260

General Information State-supported, coed, university. CGS member. *Enrollment:* 6,007 full-time matriculated graduate/professional students (2,858 women), 2,121 part-time matriculated graduate/professional students (1,243 women). *Enrollment by degree level:* 1,929 first professional, 3,802 master's, 2,304 doctoral, 93 other advanced degrees. *Graduate faculty:* 1,195 full-time (347 women), 694 part-time/adjunct (258 women). Tuition, state resident: full-time $6,118. Tuition, nonresident: full-time $9,434. *Graduate housing:* Rooms and/or apartments available on a first-come, first-served basis to single students and available to married students. Housing application deadline: 5/1. *Student services:* Campus employment opportunities, campus safety program, career counseling, child daycare facilities, disabled student services, exercise/wellness program, free psychological counseling, international student services, low-cost health insurance, multicultural affairs office, teacher training, writing training. *Library facilities:* Lockwood Library plus 7 others. *Online resources:* library catalog, web page, access to other libraries' catalogs. *Collection:* 3.2 million titles, 26,444 serial subscriptions, 157,596 audiovisual materials. *Research affiliation:* Roswell Park

Cancer Institute, Calspan–UB Research Center, Veterans Administration Medical Center, Hauptman-Woodward Medical Research Institute, Kaleida Health.

Computer facilities: 1,800 computers available on campus for general student use. A campuswide network can be accessed from student residence rooms and from off campus. Internet access and online class registration are available. *Web address:* http://www.buffalo.edu/.

General Application Contact: Katherine Gerstle Ferguson, Associate Vice Provost, 716-645-5908, Fax: 716-645-6998, E-mail: kgfergus@buffalo.edu.

GRADUATE UNITS

Graduate School Students: 6,007 full-time (2,858 women), 2,121 part-time (1,243 women). *Faculty:* 1,195 full-time (347 women), 694 part-time/adjunct (258 women). Expenses: Contact institution. *Financial support:* Fellowships with full and partial tuition reimbursements, research assistantships with full and partial tuition reimbursements, teaching assistantships with full and partial tuition reimbursements, career-related internships or fieldwork, Federal Work-Study, institutionally sponsored loans, scholarships/grants, traineeships, tuition waivers (full and partial), unspecified assistantships, and stipends available. Support available to part-time students. Financial award applicants required to submit FAFSA. In 2001, 466 first professional degrees, 1,537 master's, 288 doctorates, 32 other advanced degrees awarded. *Degree program information:* Part-time and evening/weekend programs available. Postbaccalaureate distance learning degree programs offered. Offers biomedical sciences (MS, PhD); cellular and molecular biology (PhD); experimental pathology (PhD); immunology (PhD); molecular and cellular biophysics (MS, PhD); molecular pharmacology and cancer therapeutics (PhD); natural and biomedical sciences (MS). *Application deadline:* Applications are processed on a rolling basis. Electronic applications accepted. *Application Contact:* Katherine Gerstle Ferguson, Associate Vice Provost, 716-645-5908, Fax: 716-645-6998, E-mail: kgfergus@buffalo.edu. *Associate Provost and Executive Director of the Graduate School,* Dr. Myron A. Thompson, 716-645-6227, Fax: 716-645-6142, E-mail: gradschl@buffalo.edu.

College of Arts and Sciences Students: 1,325 full-time (616 women), 396 part-time (173 women); includes 135 minority (39 African Americans, 36 Asian Americans or Pacific Islanders, 50 Hispanic Americans, 10 Native Americans), 557 international. Average age 29. *Faculty:* 435 full-time (112 women), 128 part-time/adjunct (65 women). Expenses: Contact institution. *Financial support:* Fellowships with full and partial tuition reimbursements, research assistantships with full tuition reimbursements, teaching assistantships with full tuition reimbursements, career-related internships or fieldwork, Federal Work-Study, institutionally sponsored loans, scholarships/grants, tuition waivers (full and partial), and unspecified assistantships available. Support available to part-time students. Financial award applicants required to submit FAFSA. In 2001, 283 master's, 110 doctorates, 6 other advanced degrees awarded. *Degree program information:* Part-time programs available. Offers American studies (MA, PhD); anthropology (MA, PhD); art (MFA); art history (MA); arts and sciences (MA, MFA, MM, MS, Au D, PhD, Certificate); audiology (Au D); behavioral neuroscience (PhD); biological sciences (MA, MS, PhD); chemistry (MA, PhD); classics (MA, PhD); clinical psychology (PhD); cognitive psychology (PhD); communicative disorders and sciences (MA, PhD); comparative literature (MA, PhD); economics (MA, PhD); English (MA, PhD); financial economics (Certificate); French (MA, PhD); general psychology (MA); geographic information science (Certificate); geography (MA, PhD); geology (MA, MS, PhD); health services (Certificate); historical musicology and music theory (PhD); history (MA, PhD); humanities (MA); information and Internet economics (Certificate); international economics (Certificate); law and regulation (Certificate); linguistics (MA, PhD); mathematics (MA, PhD); media study (MFA); medicinal chemistry (MS, PhD); music composition (MA, PhD); music history (MA); music performance (MM); music theory (MA); natural science (MS); philosophy (MA, PhD); physics (MS, PhD); political science (MA, PhD); social sciences (MS); social-personality (PhD); sociology (MA, PhD); Spanish (MA, PhD); urban and regional economics (Certificate). *Application deadline:* Applications are processed on a rolling basis. *Application fee:* $35. Electronic applications accepted. *Application Contact:* Dr. Munroe Eagles, Associate Dean, 716-645-2711, Fax: 716-645-3888, E-mail: eagles@ascu.buffalo.edu. *Interim Dean,* Dr. Charles Stinger, 716-645-2711, Fax: 716-645-3888, E-mail: cas-dean@ascu.buffalo.edu.

Graduate School of Education Students: 532 full-time (399 women), 659 part-time (483 women); includes 133 minority (68 African Americans, 16 Asian Americans or Pacific Islanders, 45 Hispanic Americans, 4 Native Americans), 95 international. *Faculty:* 67 full-time (35 women), 37 part-time/adjunct (28 women). Expenses: Contact institution. *Financial support:* Fellowships with full tuition reimbursements, research assistantships with full tuition reimbursements, teaching assistantships with full tuition reimbursements, career-related internships or fieldwork, Federal Work-Study, institutionally sponsored loans, tuition waivers (full and partial), and unspecified assistantships available. Financial award applicants required to submit FAFSA. In 2001, 264 master's, 67 doctorates, 26 other advanced degrees awarded. *Degree program information:* Part-time programs available. Postbaccalaureate distance learning degree programs offered (minimal on-campus study). Offers bilingual education (Ed M); biology (Ed M); chemistry (Ed M); counseling school psychology (PhD); counselor education (PhD); Earth science (Ed M); education (Ed M, MA, MM, MS, Ed D, PhD, Certificate); educational administration (Ed M, Ed D, PhD); educational psychology (MA, PhD); elementary education (Ed M, Ed D, PhD); English (Ed M); English education (Ed D, PhD); foreign and second language education (PhD); French (Ed M); general education (Ed M); German (Ed M); higher education (PhD); Italian (Ed M); Latin (Ed M); mathematics (Ed M); mathematics education (Ed D, PhD); music education (MM, Certificate); physics (Ed M); reading education (Ed D, PhD); reading teacher (Ed M); rehabilitation counseling (MS); Russian (Ed M); school administrator and supervisor (Certificate); school counseling (Ed M, Certificate); school psychology (MA); science education (PhD); secondary education (Certificate); social foundations (PhD); social studies (Ed M); Spanish (Ed M); special education (PhD); specialist in education administration (Certificate); teaching English to Speakers of Other Languages (Ed M). *Application deadline:* Applications are processed on a rolling basis. *Application fee:* $50. *Dean,* Mary H. Gresham, 716-645-6640, Fax: 716-645-2479.

School of Architecture and Planning Students: 178 full-time (61 women), 40 part-time (8 women); includes 27 minority (14 African Americans, 5 Asian Americans or Pacific Islanders, 7 Hispanic Americans, 1 Native American), 47 international. Average age 25. 200 applicants, 75% accepted. *Faculty:* 28 full-time (8 women), 18 part-time/adjunct (4 women). Expenses: Contact institution. *Financial support:* Fellowships with full tuition reimbursements, research assistantships with full tuition reimbursements, teaching assistantships with full and partial tuition reimbursements, career-related internships or fieldwork, Federal Work-Study, institutionally sponsored loans, scholarships/grants, traineeships, tuition waivers (full and partial), and unspecified assistantships available. Support available to part-time students. Financial award applicants required to submit FAFSA. In 2001, 74 degrees awarded. *Degree program information:* Part-time programs available. Offers architecture (M Arch); architecture and planning (M Arch, MUP); planning (MUP). *Application deadline:* Applications are processed on a rolling basis. *Application fee:* $35. Electronic applications accepted. *Interim Dean,* Dr. Kenneth J. Levy, 716-829-3485 Ext. 121, Fax: 716-829-2297.

School of Dental Medicine Students: 394 full-time (115 women), 14 part-time (5 women); includes 89 minority (5 African Americans, 78 Asian Americans or Pacific Islanders, 6 Hispanic Americans), 63 international. Average age 24. 1,378 applicants, 16% accepted, 136 enrolled. *Faculty:* 71 full-time (20 women), 116 part-time/adjunct (30 women). Expenses: Contact institution. *Financial support:* In 2001–02, 396 students received support; fellowships with full and partial tuition reimbursements available, research assistantships with full and partial tuition reimbursements available, teaching assistantships with full and partial tuition reimbursements available, career-related internships or fieldwork, Federal Work-Study, institutionally sponsored loans, scholarships/grants, traineeships, tuition waivers (full and partial), and unspecified assistantships available. Financial award applicants required to submit FAFSA. In 2001, 78 first professional degrees, 8 master's, 2 doctorates awarded. *Degree program information:* Part-time programs available. Offers advanced education in general dentistry (Certificate); biomaterials (MS); combined prosthodontics (Certificate); dental medicine (DDS, MS, PhD, Certificate); endodontics (Certificate); esthetic dentistry (Certificate); oral and maxillofacial pathology (Certificate); oral and maxillofacial surgery (Certificate); oral biology (PhD); oral sciences (MS); orthodontics (MS, Certificate); pediatric dentistry (Certificate); periodontics (Certificate); temporomandibular disorders and oralfacial pain (Certificate). *Application deadline:* Applications are processed on a rolling basis. *Application fee:* $35. Electronic applications accepted. *Application Contact:* Dr. Robert Joynt, Director of Admissions, 716-829-2839, Fax: 716-833-3517, E-mail: joynt@buffalo.edu. *Dean,* Dr. Richard N. Buchanan, 716-829-2836, Fax: 716-833-3517, E-mail: rb26@buffalo.edu.

School of Engineering and Applied Sciences Students: 637 full-time (110 women), 220 part-time (39 women); includes 42 minority (10 African Americans, 26 Asian Americans or Pacific Islanders, 4 Hispanic Americans, 2 Native Americans), 602 international. Average age 25. 2,307 applicants, 59% accepted, 357 enrolled. *Faculty:* 124 full-time (12 women), 30 part-time/adjunct (4 women). Expenses: Contact institution. *Financial support:* In 2001–02, 22 fellowships with full tuition reimbursements (averaging $16,000 per year), 210 research assistantships with full and partial tuition reimbursements (averaging $14,000 per year), 180 teaching assistantships with full tuition reimbursements (averaging $10,700 per year) were awarded. Career-related internships or fieldwork, Federal Work-Study, institutionally sponsored loans, scholarships/grants, tuition waivers (full and partial), and unspecified assistantships also available. Support available to part-time students. Financial award applicants required to submit FAFSA. In 2001, 250 master's, 59 doctorates awarded. *Degree program information:* Part-time and evening/weekend programs available. Postbaccalaureate distance learning degree programs offered (minimal on-campus study). Offers aerospace engineering (M Eng, MS, PhD); chemical engineering (M Eng, MS, PhD); civil engineering (M Eng, MS, PhD); computer science (MS, PhD); electrical engineering (M Eng, MS, PhD); engineering and applied sciences (M Eng, MS, PhD); engineering science (MS); industrial engineering (M Eng, MS, PhD); mechanical engineering (M Eng, MS, PhD). *Application deadline:* Applications are processed on a rolling basis. *Application fee:* $35. Electronic applications accepted. *Application Contact:* Dr. Andres Soom, Associate Dean, 716-645-2772, Fax: 716-645-2495, E-mail: soom@eng.buffalo.edu. *Dean,* Dr. Mark H. Karwan, 716-645-2771, Fax: 716-645-2495.

School of Health Related Professions Students: 95 full-time (65 women), 37 part-time (31 women); includes 13 minority (4 African Americans, 8 Asian Americans or Pacific Islanders, 1 Native American), 37 international. Average age 28. *Faculty:* 42 full-time (24 women), 29 part-time/adjunct (25 women). Expenses: Contact institution. *Financial support:* In 2001–02, 15 fellowships with full tuition reimbursements (averaging $2,500 per year), 3 research assistantships with full tuition reimbursements (averaging $15,000 per year), 18 teaching assistantships with full tuition reimbursements (averaging $8,500 per year) were awarded. Career-related internships or fieldwork, Federal Work-Study, institutionally sponsored loans, scholarships/grants, tuition waivers (full and partial), and unspecified assistantships also available. Financial award applicants required to submit FAFSA. In 2001, 21 master's, 2 doctorates awarded. *Degree program information:* Part-time programs available. Offers exercise science (MS, PhD); health related professions (MS, DPT, PhD, Certificate); medical technology (MS); nutrition (MS); occupational therapy (MS); physical therapy (DPT); rehabilitation science (PhD). *Application fee:* $35. *Application Contact:* Dr. Dale R. Fish, Associate Dean, 716-829-3434 Ext. 272, Fax: 716-829-2034, E-mail: dfish@buffalo.edu. *Dean,* Dr. Maurizio Trevisan, 716-829-3434 Ext. 411, Fax: 716-829-2034, E-mail: trevisan@buffalo.edu.

School of Informatics Students: 164 full-time (117 women), 182 part-time (141 women); includes 22 minority (10 African Americans, 9 Asian Americans or Pacific Islanders, 2 Hispanic Americans, 1 Native American), 48 international. *Faculty:* 19 full-time (6 women), 2 part-time/adjunct (1 woman). Expenses: Contact institution. In 2001, 122 master's, 4 doctorates awarded. Offers communication (MA, PhD); informatics (MA, MLS, PhD, Certificate); library and information studies (MLS, PhD, Certificate). *Dean,* Dr. W. David Penniman, 716-645-6481, Fax: 716-645-3775, E-mail: penniman@buffalo.edu.

School of Law Students: 727 full-time (356 women), 6 part-time (3 women); includes 119 minority (59 African Americans, 23 Asian Americans or Pacific Islanders, 31 Hispanic Americans, 6 Native Americans), 15 international. Average age 25. 1,225 applicants, 40% accepted. *Faculty:* 56 full-time (22 women), 32 part-time/adjunct (8 women). Expenses: Contact institution. *Financial support:* In 2001–02, 637 students received support, including 29 fellowships with full tuition reimbursements available (averaging $10,000 per year); research assistantships, Federal Work-Study, institutionally sponsored loans, tuition waivers (full and partial), and unspecified assistantships also available. Financial award application deadline: 3/1; financial award applicants required to submit FAFSA. In 2001, 218 degrees awarded. Offers law (JD, LL M). *Application deadline:* For fall admission, 3/15 (priority date). Applications are processed on a rolling basis. *Application fee:* $50. Electronic applications accepted. *Application Contact:* Jack D. Cox, Associate Dean and Director of Admissions and Financial Aid, 716-645-6233, Fax: 716-645-6676, E-mail: law-admissions@buffalo.edu. *Dean,* R. Nils Olsen, 716-645-2052, Fax: 716-645-5968, E-mail: law-deans@buffalo.edu.

School of Management Students: 520 full-time (152 women), 160 part-time (51 women); includes 21 minority (4 African Americans, 15 Asian Americans or Pacific Islanders, 1 Hispanic American, 1 Native American), 340 international. Average age 27. 1,256 applicants, 41% accepted, 445 enrolled. *Faculty:* 59 full-time (11 women), 5 part-time/adjunct (0 women). Expenses: Contact institution. *Financial support:* In 2001–02, 188 students received support, including 17 fellowships with full tuition reimbursements available (averaging $7,070 per year), 21 research assistantships with full tuition reimbursements available (averaging $12,300 per year), 19 teaching assistantships with full tuition reimbursements available (averaging $7,200 per year); career-related internships or fieldwork, Federal Work-Study, institutionally sponsored loans, scholarships/grants, and unspecified assistantships also available. Financial award application deadline: 2/15; financial award applicants required to submit FAFSA. In 2001, 316 master's, 3 doctorates awarded. *Degree program information:* Part-time and evening/weekend programs available. Offers accounting (MS); management (MBA, PhD); management information systems (MS); supply chains and operations management (MS). *Application deadline:* For fall admission, 7/1. Applications are processed on a rolling basis. *Application fee:* $50. Electronic applications accepted. *Application Contact:* David W. Frasier, Administrative Director of the MBA Program and Assistant Dean, 716-645-3204, Fax: 716-645-2341, E-mail: davidf@buffalo.edu. *Dean,* Jerry M. Newman, 716-645-3221, Fax: 716-645-5926, E-mail: jmnewman@buffalo.edu.

School of Medicine and Biomedical Sciences Students: 734 full-time (379 women), 61 part-time (34 women); includes 116 minority (27 African Americans, 69 Asian Americans or Pacific Islanders, 18 Hispanic Americans, 2 Native Americans), 75 international. Average age 25. 2,340 applicants, 9% accepted. *Faculty:* 182 full-time (34 women), 251 part-time/adjunct (62 women). Expenses: Contact institution. *Financial support:* In 2001–02, fellowships with full tuition reimbursements (averaging $20,000 per year), research assistantships with full tuition reimbursements (averaging $17,000 per year), teaching assistantships with full tuition reimbursements (averaging $17,000 per year) were awarded. Career-related internships or fieldwork, Federal Work-Study, institutionally sponsored loans, scholarships/grants, traineeships, health care benefits, tuition waivers (full and partial), and unspecified assistantships also available. Financial award application deadline: 2/1; financial award applicants required to submit FAFSA. In 2001, 123 first professional degrees, 15 master's, 27 doctorates awarded. *Degree program information:* Part-time programs available. Offers anatomical sciences (MA, PhD); biochemical pharmacology (MS); biochemistry (MA, PhD); biophysical sciences (MS, PhD); epidemiology (MS); epidemiology and community health (PhD); medicine (MD); medicine and biomedical sciences (MD, MA, MPH, MS, PhD); microbiology (MA, PhD); pathology (MA, PhD); pharmacology (MA, PhD); physiology (MA, PhD); public health (MPH). *Application deadline:* For fall admission, 2/1 (priority date). Applications are processed on a rolling basis. *Application fee:* $35. Electronic applications accepted. *Application Contact:* Elizabeth A. Hayden, Staff Associate, 716-829-3398, Fax: 716-829-2437, E-mail: ehayden@buffalo.edu. *Dean and Vice President for Health Affairs,* Dr. Michael E. Bernadino, 716-829-3955, Fax: 716-829-3395, E-mail: mbernard@buffalo.edu.

School of Nursing Students: 103 full-time (92 women), 77 part-time (69 women); includes 16 minority (7 African Americans, 6 Asian Americans or Pacific Islanders, 3 Hispanic Americans), 18 international. Average age 28. 125 applicants, 86% accepted, 64 enrolled. *Faculty:* 34 full-time (29 women), 12 part-time/adjunct (all women). Expenses: Contact

University at Buffalo, The State University of New York (continued)

institution. *Financial support:* In 2001–02, 73 students received support, including 2 fellowships with full tuition reimbursements available (averaging $15,000 per year), 1 research assistantship with full tuition reimbursement available, 12 teaching assistantships with full tuition reimbursements available (averaging $8,746 per year); Federal Work-Study, scholarships/grants, traineeships, tuition waivers (partial), unspecified assistantships, and Federal traineeships also available. Financial award application deadline: 3/15; financial award applicants required to submit FAFSA. In 2001, 34 master's, 3 doctorates awarded. *Degree program information:* Part-time programs available. Offers acute care nurse practitioner (MS, Certificate); adult health nursing (Certificate); adult health nursing-nurse practitioner (MS); child health nursing-nurse practitioner (MS); family nursing (Certificate); family nursing-nurse practitioner (MS); geriatric nurse practitioner (MS, Certificate); maternal and women's health nursing (Certificate); maternal and women's health nursing-nurse practitioner (MS); nurse anesthetist (MS); nursing (DNS); pediatric nurse practitioner (Certificate); psychiatric and mental health nursing (Certificate). *Application deadline:* For fall admission, 5/1 (priority date); for spring admission, 10/15. Applications are processed on a rolling basis. *Application fee:* $50. Electronic applications accepted. *Application Contact:* Dr. Elaine Cusker, Assistant Dean, 716-829-3314, Fax: 716-829-2021, E-mail: ecusker@buffalo.edu. *Dean*, Dr. Mecca S. Cranley, 716-829-2533, Fax: 716-829-2566, E-mail: mcranley@buffalo.edu.

School of Pharmacy and Pharmaceutical Sciences Students: 298 full-time (185 women), 21 part-time (6 women); includes 68 minority (13 African Americans, 52 Asian Americans or Pacific Islanders, 3 Hispanic Americans), 43 international. Average age 26. 327 applicants, 36% accepted, 119 enrolled. *Faculty:* 32 full-time (9 women), 12 part-time/adjunct (7 women). Expenses: Contact institution. *Financial support:* Fellowships with full tuition reimbursements, research assistantships with full tuition reimbursements, teaching assistantships with tuition reimbursements, Federal Work-Study, institutionally sponsored loans, tuition waivers (full and partial), and unspecified assistantships available. Financial award application deadline: 2/28; financial award applicants required to submit FAFSA. In 2001, 47 first professional degrees, 4 master's, 2 doctorates awarded. *Degree program information:* Part-time programs available. Offers pharmaceutical sciences (MS, PhD); pharmacy (Pharm D); pharmacy and pharmaceutical sciences (Pharm D, MS, PhD). *Application deadline:* Applications are processed on a rolling basis. *Application fee:* $35. Electronic applications accepted. *Dean*, Dr. Wayne K. Anderson, 716-645-2823, Fax: 716-645-3688.

School of Social Work Students: 162 full-time (138 women), 212 part-time (183 women); includes 65 minority (34 African Americans, 5 Asian Americans or Pacific Islanders, 19 Hispanic Americans, 7 Native Americans), 8 international. Average age 32. 239 applicants, 86% accepted, 151 enrolled. *Faculty:* 20 full-time (15 women), 4 part-time/adjunct (all women). Expenses: Contact institution. *Financial support:* In 2001–02, 5 research assistantships with tuition reimbursements (averaging $15,000 per year), 6 teaching assistantships with tuition reimbursements (averaging $15,000 per year) were awarded. Fellowships with tuition reimbursements, career-related internships or fieldwork, Federal Work-Study, institutionally sponsored loans, scholarships/grants, tuition waivers (partial), and unspecified assistantships also available. Support available to part-time students. Financial award application deadline: 2/1; financial award applicants required to submit FAFSA. In 2001, 130 master's, 1 doctorate awarded. *Degree program information:* Part-time programs available. Offers social work (MSW, PhD). MSW available in Buffalo, Rochester, Jamestown, and Corning, New York. *Application deadline:* For fall admission, 3/1 (priority date). Applications are processed on a rolling basis. *Application fee:* $50. Electronic applications accepted. *Application Contact:* Ann Still, Admissions Secretary, 716-645-3381 Ext. 246, Fax: 716-645-3456, E-mail: amls@acsu.buffalo.edu. *Dean*, Dr. Lawrence Shulman, 716-645-3381 Ext. 221, Fax: 716-645-3883.

See in-depth description on page 1155.

UNIVERSITY COLLEGE OF CAPE BRETON, Sydney, NS B1P 6L2, Canada

General Information Province-supported, coed, comprehensive institution. *Graduate housing:* Room and/or apartments available on a first-come, first-served basis to single students; on-campus housing not available to married students. *Research affiliation:* Advanced Glazing, Limited (transparent insulation), Atlantic Geomatics (computer networking and software development), Dynagen Industrial Mine Technology (mining industry equipment), Fortress Louisbourg National Historic Park (museum/heritage projects), Sable Offshore Energy, Inc. (petroleum resources), North Atlantic Islands Programme (small-scale manufacturing, tourism, export of knowledge-based services).

GRADUATE UNITS

Program in Extension and Community Affairs *Degree program information:* Part-time and evening/weekend programs available. Postbaccalaureate distance learning degree programs offered (no on-campus study). Electronic applications accepted.

School of Business Offers community economic development (MBA).

UNIVERSITY OF ADVANCING TECHNOLOGY, Tempe, AZ 85283-1042

General Information Proprietary, coed, comprehensive institution. *Enrollment:* 16 full-time matriculated graduate/professional students (2 women). *Enrollment by degree level:* 16 master's. *Graduate faculty:* 11 full-time (3 women), 3 part-time/adjunct (0 women). *Tuition:* Full-time $4,824; part-time $402 per credit. *Student services:* Campus employment opportunities. *Library facilities:* University of Advancing Computer Technology Library. *Online resources:* web page.

Computer facilities: 190 computers available on campus for general student use. A campuswide network can be accessed from off campus. Internet access and online class registration are available. *Web address:* http://www.uat.edu/.

General Application Contact: Dr. Elana Michelson, Admissions Office, 800-658-5744, Fax: 602-383-8222, E-mail: fbutler@uact.edu.

GRADUATE UNITS

Program in Technology Students: 16 full-time (2 women). Average age 25. *Faculty:* 11 full-time (3 women), 3 part-time/adjunct (0 women). Expenses: Contact institution. In 2001, 3 degrees awarded. Offers technology (MS). *Application deadline:* For fall admission, 8/15 (priority date); for winter admission, 12/15 (priority date); for spring admission, 4/1 (priority date). *Application Contact:* Information Contact, 800-658-5744, Fax: 602-383-8222.

THE UNIVERSITY OF AKRON, Akron, OH 44325-0001

General Information State-supported, coed, university. CGS member. *Enrollment:* 2,158 full-time matriculated graduate/professional students (1,096 women), 1,970 part-time matriculated graduate/professional students (1,203 women). *Enrollment by degree level:* 583 first professional, 2,753 master's, 606 doctoral, 186 other advanced degrees. *Graduate faculty:* 545 full-time (178 women), 372 part-time/adjunct (172 women). Tuition, state resident: full-time $6,562; part-time $219 per credit. Tuition, nonresident: full-time $9,027; part-time $383 per credit. *Required fees:* $272; $11 per credit. Tuition and fees vary according to course load. *Graduate housing:* Room and/or apartments available on a first-come, first-served basis to single students; on-campus housing not available to married students. *Student services:* Campus employment opportunities, campus safety program, career counseling, child daycare facilities, disabled student services, free psychological counseling, international student services, multicultural affairs office, writing training. *Library facilities:* Bierce Library plus 3 others. *Online resources:* library catalog, web page, access to other libraries' catalogs. *Collection:* 742,213 titles, 6,087 serial subscriptions, 39,773 audiovisual materials. *Research affiliation:* Akron Children's Medical Center (communicative disorders, biomedical research, early childhood education), Akron City Hospital (biomedical engineering, cardiovascular research), Cleveland Clinic (cardiovascular research), Edison Polymer Innovation Corporation, Edwin Shaw Hospital (rehabilitation).

Computer facilities: 1,200 computers available on campus for general student use. A campuswide network can be accessed from student residence rooms and from off campus. Internet access and online class registration are available. *Web address:* http://www.uakron.edu/.

General Application Contact: Dr. Lathardus Goggins, Associate Dean of the Graduate School, 330-972-7663, Fax: 330-972-6475, E-mail: lgoggin@uakron.edu.

GRADUATE UNITS

Graduate School Students: 1,591 full-time (834 women), 1,954 part-time (1,191 women); includes 359 minority (269 African Americans, 38 Asian Americans or Pacific Islanders, 38 Hispanic Americans, 14 Native Americans), 629 international. Average age 33. 1,218 applicants, 85% accepted. *Faculty:* 545 full-time (178 women), 372 part-time/adjunct (172 women). Expenses: Contact institution. *Financial support:* In 2001–02, 1,461 students received support, including 26 fellowships with full tuition reimbursements available, 454 research assistantships with full tuition reimbursements available, 512 teaching assistantships with full tuition reimbursements available; career-related internships or fieldwork, Federal Work-Study, institutionally sponsored loans, scholarships/grants, tuition waivers (full and partial), unspecified assistantships, and administrative assistantships also available. Support available to part-time students. In 2001, 945 master's, 121 doctorates awarded. *Degree program information:* Part-time and evening/weekend programs available. *Application deadline:* Applications are processed on a rolling basis. *Application fee:* $40 ($50 for international students). *Application Contact:* Dr. Lathardus Goggins, Associate Dean of the Graduate School, 330-972-7663, Fax: 330-972-6475, E-mail: lgoggin@uakron.edu. *Vice President for Research and Dean of the Graduate School*, Dr. George R. Newkome, 330-972-6458, Fax: 330-972-2413, E-mail: newkome@uakron.edu.

Buchtel College of Arts and Sciences Students: 442 full-time (218 women), 243 part-time (119 women); includes 80 minority (56 African Americans, 9 Asian Americans or Pacific Islanders, 13 Hispanic Americans, 2 Native Americans), 166 international. Average age 31. 463 applicants, 71% accepted, 185 enrolled. *Faculty:* 224 full-time (57 women), 76 part-time/adjunct (24 women). Expenses: Contact institution. *Financial support:* In 2001–02, 436 students received support, including 6 fellowships with full tuition reimbursements available, 74 research assistantships with full tuition reimbursements available, 295 teaching assistantships with full tuition reimbursements available; career-related internships or fieldwork, Federal Work-Study, institutionally sponsored loans, scholarships/grants, tuition waivers (full and partial), unspecified assistantships, and administrative assistantships also available. Support available to part-time students. In 2001, 196 master's, 32 doctorates awarded. *Degree program information:* Part-time and evening/weekend programs available. Offers applied cognitive aging (MA, PhD); applied mathematics (MS); applied politics (MA); arts and sciences (MA, MPA, MS, PhD); biology (MS); chemistry (MS, PhD); computer science (MS); counseling psychology (MA); earth science (MS); economics (MA); English (MA); geography (MS); geology (MS); geophysics (MS); history (MA, PhD); industrial/organizational psychology (MA, PhD); labor and industrial relations (MA); mathematics (MS); physics (MS); political science (MA); psychology (MA, PhD); public administration (MPA); sociology (MA, PhD); Spanish (MA); statistics (MS); urban planning (MA, PhD); urban studies (MA, PhD); urban studies and public affairs (PhD). *Application deadline:* Applications are processed on a rolling basis. *Application fee:* $40 ($50 for international students). *Dean*, Dr. Roger Creel, 330-972-7882, E-mail: rcreel@uakron.edu.

College of Business Administration Students: 154 full-time (73 women), 333 part-time (125 women); includes 30 minority (15 African Americans, 10 Asian Americans or Pacific Islanders, 3 Hispanic Americans, 2 Native Americans), 96 international. Average age 31. 229 applicants, 86% accepted, 107 enrolled. *Faculty:* 64 full-time (10 women), 37 part-time/adjunct (3 women). Expenses: Contact institution. *Financial support:* In 2001–02, 91 students received support, including 54 research assistantships with full tuition reimbursements available, 3 teaching assistantships with full tuition reimbursements available; fellowships with full tuition reimbursements available, career-related internships or fieldwork, Federal Work-Study, tuition waivers (full), and administrative assistantships also available. Financial award application deadline: 4/30. In 2001, 158 degrees awarded. *Degree program information:* Part-time and evening/weekend programs available. Offers accountancy (MS); accounting (MBA); business administration (MBA, MS, MT); electronic business (MBA); entrepreneurship (MBA); finance (MBA); international business (MBA); management (MBA); management of technology (MBA); management-human resources (MS); management-information systems (MS); marketing (MBA); quality management (MBA); taxation (MT). *Application deadline:* For fall admission, 8/15. Applications are processed on a rolling basis. *Application fee:* $40 ($50 for international students). *Application Contact:* Dr. James Divoky, Director of Graduate Business Programs, 330-972-7032, Fax: 330-972-6588, E-mail: jdivoky@uakron.edu. *Dean*, Dr. Stephen F. Hallam, 330-972-7442, E-mail: hallam@uakron.edu.

College of Education Students: 261 full-time (192 women), 890 part-time (647 women); includes 150 minority (128 African Americans, 6 Asian Americans or Pacific Islanders, 9 Hispanic Americans, 7 Native Americans), 18 international. Average age 35. 224 applicants, 81% accepted, 132 enrolled. *Faculty:* 56 full-time (33 women), 143 part-time/adjunct (85 women). Expenses: Contact institution. *Financial support:* In 2001–02, 163 students received support, including 52 research assistantships with full tuition reimbursements available, 19 teaching assistantships with full tuition reimbursements available; fellowships with full tuition reimbursements available, career-related internships or fieldwork, Federal Work-Study, tuition waivers (full), and unspecified assistantships also available. In 2001, 346 master's, 28 doctorates awarded. *Degree program information:* Part-time programs available. Offers administrative specialist (MA, MS); athletic training/sports medicine (MA, MS); classroom guidance for teachers (MA, MS); community counseling (MA, MS); counseling psychology (PhD); education (MA, MS, Ed D, PhD); educational administration (MA, MS, Ed D); elementary education (MA, MS, PhD); elementary education with certification (MS); elementary school counseling (MA); exercise physiology/adult fitness (MA, MS); guidance and counseling (PhD); higher education administration (MA, MS); marriage and family therapy (MA, MS); outdoor education (MA); physical education K–12 (MS); principalship (MA, MS); school psychology (MS); secondary education (MA, MS, PhD); secondary education with certification (MS); secondary school counseling (MA); special education (MA, MS); sports science/coaching (MA); superintendent (MA, MS); technical education (MS); technical education teaching (MS); technical education training (MS). *Application deadline:* For fall admission, 8/15. Applications are processed on a rolling basis. *Application fee:* $25 ($50 for international students). *Interim Dean*, Dr. Elizabeth Stroble, 330-972-7680, E-mail: estroble@uakron.edu.

College of Engineering Students: 178 full-time (33 women), 102 part-time (16 women); includes 8 minority (2 African Americans, 2 Asian Americans or Pacific Islanders, 3 Hispanic Americans, 1 Native American), 167 international. Average age 29. 263 applicants, 74% accepted, 60 enrolled. *Faculty:* 54 full-time (6 women), 26 part-time/adjunct (0 women). Expenses: Contact institution. *Financial support:* In 2001–02, 183 students received support, including 52 research assistantships with full tuition reimbursements available, 90 teaching assistantships with full tuition reimbursements available; fellowships with full tuition reimbursements available, career-related internships or fieldwork, Federal Work-Study, and tuition waivers (full) also available. Financial award application deadline: 3/1. In 2001, 71 master's, 21 doctorates awarded. *Degree program information:* Part-time and evening/weekend programs available. Offers biomedical engineering (MS); chemical engineering (MS, PhD); civil engineering (MS, PhD); electrical engineering (MS, PhD); engineering (MS, PhD); engineering (management specialization) (MS); engineering (polymer specialization) (MS); engineering-applied mathematics (PhD); mechanical engineering (MS, PhD). *Application deadline:* Applications are processed on a rolling basis. *Application fee:* $40 ($50 for international students). *Interim Dean*, Dr. S. Graham Kelly, 330-972-6978, E-mail: sgraham@uakron.edu.

College of Fine and Applied Arts Students: 261 full-time (213 women), 114 part-time (89 women); includes 57 minority (48 African Americans, 2 Asian Americans or Pacific Islanders, 6 Hispanic Americans, 1 Native American), 15 international. Average age 31. 259 applicants, 87% accepted, 151 enrolled. *Faculty:* 85 full-time (45 women), 69 part-time/adjunct (47 women). Expenses: Contact institution. *Financial support:* In 2001–02, 224 students received support, including 35 research assistantships with full tuition reimbursements available, 103 teaching assistantships with full tuition reimbursements available; fellowships with full tuition reimbursements available, career-related internships or fieldwork, Federal Work-Study, institutionally sponsored loans, tuition waivers (partial), and unspecified assistantships also available. Support available to part-time students. In 2001, 112 degrees awarded. *Degree program information:* Part-time and evening/weekend programs available. Offers arts administration (MA); audiology (MA); child development (MA); child life (MA); clothing, textiles and interiors (MA); communication (MA); composition (MM); family development (MA); fine and applied arts (MA, MM, MS); food science (MA); music education (MM); music history and literature (MM); music technology (MM); nutrition and dietetics (MS); performance (MM); social work (MS); speech-language pathology (MA); theatre arts (MA); theory (MM). *Application deadline:* Applications are processed on a rolling basis. *Application fee:* $40 ($50 for international students). *Dean,* Dr. Mark Auburn, 330-972-7543, E-mail: auburn@uakron.edu.

College of Nursing Students: 90 full-time (56 women), 92 part-time (76 women); includes 14 minority (10 African Americans, 3 Asian Americans or Pacific Islanders, 1 Native American), 1 international. Average age 35. 52 applicants, 85% accepted, 34 enrolled. *Faculty:* 30 full-time (all women), 12 part-time/adjunct (11 women). Expenses: Contact institution. *Financial support:* In 2001–02, 65 students received support, including 19 fellowships with full tuition reimbursements available, 14 research assistantships with full tuition reimbursements available, 2 teaching assistantships with full tuition reimbursements available; career-related internships or fieldwork, Federal Work-Study, and tuition waivers (full) also available. Financial award application deadline: 5/15. In 2001, 42 degrees awarded. *Degree program information:* Part-time programs available. Offers nursing (MSN, PhD); public health (MPH). *Application deadline:* For fall admission, 8/15. Applications are processed on a rolling basis. *Application fee:* $40 ($50 for international students). *Application Contact:* Dr. Kathleen M. Ross-Alaolmolki, Coordinator, 330-972-5936, E-mail: kross-alaolmolki@uakron.edu. *Dean,* Dr. Cynthia F. Capers, 330-972-7552, E-mail: capers@uakron.edu.

College of Polymer Science and Polymer Engineering Students: 196 full-time (43 women), 24 part-time (7 women); includes 6 minority (2 African Americans, 3 Asian Americans or Pacific Islanders, 1 Hispanic American), 157 international. Average age 29. 168 applicants, 59% accepted, 61 enrolled. *Faculty:* 29 full-time (2 women), 9 part-time/adjunct (2 women). Expenses: Contact institution. *Financial support:* In 2001–02, 213 students received support, including 1 fellowship with full tuition reimbursement available, 173 research assistantships with full tuition reimbursements available; teaching assistantships with full tuition reimbursements available, scholarships/grants and tuition waivers (full) also available. In 2001, 20 master's, 40 doctorates awarded. *Degree program information:* Part-time and evening/weekend programs available. Offers polymer engineering (MS, PhD); polymer science (MS, PhD). *Application deadline:* Applications are processed on a rolling basis. *Application fee:* $40 ($50 for international students). *Dean,* Dr. Frank Kelley, 330-972-7500, E-mail: fkelley@uakron.edu.

School of Law Students: 368 full-time (169 women), 215 part-time (105 women); includes 60 minority (39 African Americans, 12 Asian Americans or Pacific Islanders, 8 Hispanic Americans, 1 Native American), 3 international. Average age 27. *Faculty:* 28 full-time (10 women), 16 part-time/adjunct (4 women). Expenses: Contact institution. *Financial support:* In 2001–02, 310 students received support. Career-related internships or fieldwork, scholarships/grants, and tuition waivers (full and partial) available. Support available to part-time students. Financial award application deadline: 5/1; financial award applicants required to submit FAFSA. In 2001, 144 degrees awarded. *Degree program information:* Part-time and evening/weekend programs available. Offers law (JD). *Application deadline:* For fall admission, 3/1 (priority date). *Application fee:* $40. Electronic applications accepted. *Application Contact:* Lauri S. File, Director of Admissions and Financial Assistance and Assistant to the Dean, 330-972-7331, Fax: 330-258-2343, E-mail: lfile@uakron.edu. *Dean,* Richard L. Aynes, 330-972-7331, Fax: 330-258-2343, E-mail: raynes@uakron.edu.

See in-depth description on page 1157.

THE UNIVERSITY OF ALABAMA, Tuscaloosa, AL 35487

General Information State-supported, coed, university. CGS member. *Enrollment:* 2,601 full-time matriculated graduate/professional students (1,267 women), 1,328 part-time matriculated graduate/professional students (862 women). *Enrollment by degree level:* 589 first professional, 2,369 master's, 971 doctoral. *Graduate faculty:* 795 full-time (239 women), 77 part-time/adjunct (34 women). Tuition, state resident: full-time $3,292; part-time $183 per credit hour. Tuition, nonresident: full-time $8,912; part-time $495 per credit hour. Tuition and fees vary according to course load, campus/location and program. *Graduate housing:* Rooms and/or apartments guaranteed to single students and available on a first-come, first-served basis to married students. Typical cost: $2,560 per year ($4,110 including board) for single students. Room and board charges vary according to board plan and housing facility selected. Housing application deadline: 3/1. *Student services:* Campus employment opportunities, campus safety program, career counseling, child daycare facilities, disabled student services, exercise/wellness program, free psychological counseling, grant writing training, international student services, low-cost health insurance, multicultural affairs office, teacher training, writing training. *Library facilities:* Amelia Gayle Gorgas Library plus 8 others. *Online resources:* library catalog, web page, access to other libraries' catalogs. *Collection:* 3.4 million titles, 17,788 serial subscriptions, 480,498 audiovisual materials. *Research affiliation:* Ford Foundation (communication research), Argonne National Laboratory (fuel cell, materials), DuPont (chemistry), March of Dimes Birth Defects Foundation (biological), National Storage Industry Consortium (magnetic information).

Computer facilities: 1,450 computers available on campus for general student use. A campuswide network can be accessed from student residence rooms and from off campus. Internet access is available. *Web address:* http://www.ua.edu/.

General Application Contact: Libby Williams, Admissions Supervisor, 205-348-5921, Fax: 205-348-0400, E-mail: lwilliams@aalan.ua.edu.

GRADUATE UNITS

Graduate School Students: 2,601 full-time (1,267 women), 1,328 part-time (862 women); includes 448 minority (345 African Americans, 35 Asian Americans or Pacific Islanders, 43 Hispanic Americans, 25 Native Americans), 513 international. Average age 28. 4,854 applicants, 38% accepted, 1343 enrolled. *Faculty:* 795 full-time (239 women), 77 part-time/adjunct (34 women). Expenses: Contact institution. *Financial support:* Fellowships with full and partial tuition reimbursements, research assistantships with full and partial tuition reimbursements, teaching assistantships with full and partial tuition reimbursements, career-related internships or fieldwork, Federal Work-Study, institutionally sponsored loans, scholarships/grants, traineeships, tuition waivers (full and partial), and unspecified assistantships available. Support available to part-time students. In 2001, 1,117 master's, 173 doctorates, 61 other advanced degrees awarded. *Degree program information:* Part-time and evening/weekend programs available. Postbaccalaureate distance learning degree programs offered. Offers nursing (MSN). *Application deadline:* Applications are processed on a rolling basis. *Application fee:* $25. Electronic applications accepted. *Application Contact:* Libby Williams, Admissions Supervisor, 205-348-5921, Fax: 205-348-0400, E-mail: lwilliams@aalan.ua.edu. *Dean,* Dr. Ronald Rogers, 205-348-5921, Fax: 205-348-0400, E-mail: rrogers@aalan.ua.edu.

College of Arts and Sciences Students: 723 full-time (340 women), 192 part-time (81 women); includes 94 minority (60 African Americans, 9 Asian Americans or Pacific Islanders, 18 Hispanic Americans, 7 Native Americans), 140 international. Average age 29. 1,069 applicants, 32% accepted, 222 enrolled. *Faculty:* 339 full-time (82 women), 11 part-time/adjunct (5 women). Expenses: Contact institution. *Financial support:* Fellowships with full tuition reimbursements, research assistantships with full tuition reimbursements, teaching assistantships with full and partial tuition reimbursements, career-related internships or fieldwork, Federal Work-Study, institutionally sponsored loans, scholarships/grants, tuition waivers (full and partial), and unspecified assistantships available. Support available to part-time students. Financial award applicants required to submit FAFSA. In 2001, 189 master's, 69 doctorates awarded. *Degree program information:* Part-time programs available. Postbaccalaureate distance learning degree programs offered. Offers acting (MFA); administration (DMA); American studies (MA); anthropology (MA); applied linguistics (PhD); applied mathematics (PhD); art history (MA); arts and sciences (MA, MFA, MM, MPA, MS, MSCJ, DMA, DPA, Ed D, PhD, Certificate, Ed S); audiology (MS); biological sciences (MS, PhD); chemistry (MS, PhD); clinical psychology (PhD); cognitive psychology (PhD); composition (DMA); costume design (MFA); creative writing (MFA); criminal justice (MSCJ); directing (MFA); French (MA, PhD); French and Spanish (PhD); general psychology (MA); geography (MS); geological sciences (MS, PhD); German (MA); history (MA, PhD); Latin American studies (MA, Certificate); literature (MA, PhD); mathematics (MA); music education (Ed D, Ed S); musicology (MM); performance (MM, DMA); physics (MS, PhD); playwriting/dramaturgy (MFA); political science (MA, MPA, PhD); public administration (MPA, DPA); pure mathematics (PhD); rhetoric and composition (MA, PhD); Romance languages (MA, PhD); scene design/technical production (MFA); Spanish (MA, PhD); speech-language pathology (MS); stage management (MFA); studio art (MA, MFA); theatre (MFA); theatre management/administration (MFA); theory and criticism (MA); women's studies (MA). *Application fee:* $25. Electronic applications accepted. *Application Contact:* Libby Williams, Admissions Supervisor, 205-348-5921, Fax: 205-348-0400, E-mail: lwilliams@aalan.ua.edu. *Dean,* Dr. Robert D. Olin, 205-348-7007, Fax: 205-348-0272, E-mail: olin@as.ua.edu.

College of Communication and Information Sciences Students: 131 full-time (95 women), 135 part-time (115 women); includes 27 minority (22 African Americans, 2 Asian Americans or Pacific Islanders, 2 Hispanic Americans, 1 Native American), 18 international. Average age 32. 235 applicants, 52% accepted, 84 enrolled. *Faculty:* 42 full-time (13 women), 3 part-time/adjunct (1 woman). Expenses: Contact institution. *Financial support:* In 2001–02, 78 students received support, including 3 fellowships with tuition reimbursements available (averaging $10,000 per year), 34 research assistantships with tuition reimbursements available (averaging $9,000 per year), 38 teaching assistantships with tuition reimbursements available (averaging $8,560 per year); career-related internships or fieldwork, Federal Work-Study, and institutionally sponsored loans also available. Financial award application deadline: 2/15. In 2001, 134 master's, 9 doctorates, 2 other advanced degrees awarded. Offers advertising and public relations (MA); book arts (MFA); communication and information sciences (MA, MFA, MLIS, PhD, Ed S); communication studies (MA); journalism (MA, PhD); library and information studies (MLIS, PhD, Ed S); telecommunication and film (MA). *Application deadline:* For fall admission, 2/15 (priority date); for spring admission, 11/1 (priority date). Applications are processed on a rolling basis. *Application fee:* $25. Electronic applications accepted. *Application Contact:* Diane Shaddix, Information Contact, 205-348-8593, Fax: 205-348-6774, E-mail: dshaddix@bama.ua.edu. *Dean,* Dr. E. Culpepper Clark, 205-348-5520, Fax: 205-348-3836, E-mail: cclark@ccom.ua.edu.

College of Education Students: 271 full-time (195 women), 484 part-time (353 women); includes 92 minority (76 African Americans, 4 Asian Americans or Pacific Islanders, 7 Hispanic Americans, 5 Native Americans), 21 international. Average age 34. 407 applicants, 58% accepted, 190 enrolled. *Faculty:* 68 full-time (35 women), 6 part-time/adjunct (5 women). Expenses: Contact institution. *Financial support:* In 2001–02, research assistantships with full tuition reimbursements (averaging $8,426 per year); fellowships, teaching assistantships with full tuition reimbursements, career-related internships or fieldwork, Federal Work-Study, institutionally sponsored loans, and scholarships/grants also available. Financial award applicants required to submit FAFSA. In 2001, 302 master's, 47 doctorates, 59 other advanced degrees awarded. *Degree program information:* Part-time and evening/weekend programs available. Postbaccalaureate distance learning degree programs offered (minimal on-campus study). Offers education (MA, Ed D, PhD, Ed S); educational leadership, policy, and technology studies (MA, Ed D, PhD, Ed S); educational studies in psychology, research methodology, and counseling (MA, Ed D, PhD, Ed S); elementary education (MA, Ed D, PhD, Ed S); kinesiology (MA, PhD); music education (MA, Ed D, PhD, Ed S); secondary curriculum, teaching and learning (MA, Ed D, PhD, Ed S); teacher education (MA, Ed D, PhD, Ed S). *Application deadline:* For fall admission, 7/1; for spring admission, 11/17. Applications are processed on a rolling basis. *Application fee:* $25. *Dean,* Dr. John Dolly, 205-348-6052, Fax: 205-348-6873, E-mail: jdolly@bamaed.ua.edu.

College of Engineering Students: 252 full-time (40 women), 100 part-time (11 women); includes 18 minority (9 African Americans, 4 Asian Americans or Pacific Islanders, 4 Hispanic Americans, 1 Native American), 232 international. Average age 28. 889 applicants, 25% accepted, 100 enrolled. *Faculty:* 96 full-time (9 women), 3 part-time/adjunct (0 women). Expenses: Contact institution. *Financial support:* In 2001–02, 188 students received support, including 7 fellowships with full tuition reimbursements available, 117 research assistantships with full tuition reimbursements available (averaging $10,269 per year), 71 teaching assistantships with full tuition reimbursements available (averaging $10,319 per year); career-related internships or fieldwork, Federal Work-Study, and institutionally sponsored loans also available. In 2001, 83 master's, 19 doctorates awarded. *Degree program information:* Part-time and evening/weekend programs available. Postbaccalaureate distance learning degree programs offered. Offers aerospace engineering and mechanics (MSAE, MSESM, PhD); chemical engineering (MS Ch E, PhD); civil engineering (MSCE, PhD); computer science (MSCS, PhD); electrical engineering (MSEE, PhD); engineering (MS Ch E, MS Met E, MSAE, MSCE, MSCS, MSE, MSEE, MSESM, MSIE, MSME, PhD); environmental engineering (MSE); industrial engineering (MSE, MSIE); materials science (PhD); mechanical engineering (MSME, PhD); metallurgical and materials engineering (MS Met E, PhD). *Application deadline:* Applications are processed on a rolling basis. *Application fee:* $25. Electronic applications accepted. *Application Contact:* Ronald Rogers, Assistant Vice President for Academic Affairs and Dean, Graduate School, 205-348-8280, Fax: 205-348-0400, E-mail: rrogers@aalan.ua.edu. *Dean,* Dr. Timothy J. Greene, 205-348-6405, Fax: 205-348-8573, E-mail: tgreene@coe.eng.ua.edu.

College of Human Environmental Sciences Students: 75 full-time (54 women), 62 part-time (47 women); includes 24 minority (20 African Americans, 3 Hispanic Americans, 1 Native American), 3 international. Average age 30. 127 applicants, 75% accepted, 76 enrolled. *Faculty:* 37 full-time (23 women), 3 part-time/adjunct (all women). Expenses: Contact institution. *Financial support:* In 2001–02, 1 fellowship with tuition reimbursement (averaging $10,000 per year), 10 research assistantships with full tuition reimbursements (averaging $8,100 per year), 11 teaching assistantships with full tuition reimbursements (averaging $8,100 per year) were awarded. Career-related internships or fieldwork, Federal Work-Study, institutionally sponsored loans, and scholarships/grants also available. In 2001, 80 master's, 4 doctorates awarded. *Degree program information:* Part-time and evening/weekend programs available. Postbaccalaureate distance learning degree programs offered (no on-campus study). Offers clothing, textiles, and interior design (MSHES); consumer sciences (MSHES); health education and promotion (PhD); health studies (MA); human development and family studies (MSHES); human environmental sciences (MA, MSHES, PhD); human nutrition and hospitality management (MSHES). *Application deadline:* For fall admission, 7/6. Applications are processed on a rolling basis. *Application fee:* $25. *Dean and Acting Head,* Dr. Judy L. Bonner, 205-348-6250, Fax: 205-348-3789, E-mail: jbonne@ches.ua.edu.

The Manderson Graduate School of Business Students: 326 full-time (130 women), 24 part-time (12 women); includes 20 minority (15 African Americans, 5 Asian Americans or Pacific Islanders), 70 international. Average age 26. 595 applicants, 38% accepted, 175 enrolled. *Faculty:* 88 full-time (12 women), 3 part-time/adjunct (0 women). Expenses: Contact institution. *Financial support:* In 2001–02, 20 fellowships with full and partial tuition reimbursements, 77 research assistantships with full and partial tuition reimbursements, 57 teaching assistantships with full and partial tuition reimbursements were awarded. Career-related internships or fieldwork, Federal Work-Study, institutionally sponsored loans, and scholarships/grants also available. Support available to part-time students. In 2001, 199 master's, 18 doctorates awarded. *Degree program information:* Evening/weekend programs available. Offers accounting (M Acc, PhD); applied statistics (MS, PhD); banking and finance (MA, MSC, PhD); business (Exec MBA, M Acc, MA, MBA, MS, MSC, MTA, PhD); economics (MA, MSC, PhD); management science (MA, MBA, MSC, PhD); marketing (MA, PhD); marketing and management (MSC); tax accounting (MTA). *Application deadline:* Applications are processed on a rolling basis. Electronic applications accepted. *Application Contact:* Missy Brazil, Coordinator of Graduate Recruiting/Admissions, 205-348-6517, Fax: 205-348-4504, E-mail: mbrazil@cba.ua.edu. *Dean,* Dr. Joseph Barry Mason, 205-348-7443, E-mail: jbmason@cba.ua.edu.

School of Social Work Students: 181 full-time (152 women), 35 part-time (30 women); includes 52 minority (47 African Americans, 1 Asian American or Pacific Islander, 2 Hispanic Americans, 2 Native Americans), 8 international. Average age 30. 110 applicants, 72%

The University of Alabama (continued)

accepted, 50 enrolled. *Faculty:* 18 full-time (10 women), 10 part-time/adjunct (6 women). Expenses: Contact institution. *Financial support:* In 2001–02, 25 fellowships (averaging $7,500 per year), 6 research assistantships with partial tuition reimbursements (averaging $8,414 per year), 6 teaching assistantships with partial tuition reimbursements (averaging $8,414 per year) were awarded. Career-related internships or fieldwork, Federal Work-Study, scholarships/grants, traineeships, tuition waivers (partial), and unspecified assistantships also available. Financial award application deadline: 2/1. In 2001, 106 master's, 4 doctorates awarded. Postbaccalaureate distance learning degree programs offered. Offers social work (MSW, PhD). *Application deadline:* For fall admission, 2/1 (priority date). *Application fee:* $25. Electronic applications accepted. *Application Contact:* Dr. Ginny Raymond, Associate Dean, 205-348-3943, Fax: 205-348-9419, E-mail: graymond@sw.ua.edu. *Dean,* Dr. James P. Adams, 205-348-3924, Fax: 205-348-9419, E-mail: jadams@sw.ua.edu.

School of Law Students: 532 full-time (208 women), 1 (woman) part-time; includes 54 minority (37 African Americans, 7 Asian Americans or Pacific Islanders, 4 Hispanic Americans, 6 Native Americans), 11 international. Average age 25. 1,050 applicants, 17% accepted, 177 enrolled. *Faculty:* 34 full-time (9 women), 23 part-time/adjunct (3 women). Expenses: Contact institution. *Financial support:* In 2001–02, 377 students received support, including 54 research assistantships; career-related internships or fieldwork, Federal Work-Study, institutionally sponsored loans, and tuition waivers (full and partial) also available. Financial award application deadline: 5/15. In 2001, 170 first professional degrees, 6 master's awarded. Postbaccalaureate distance learning degree programs offered (no on-campus study). Offers law (JD, LL M, LL M in Tax). *Application deadline:* For fall admission, 3/1. Applications are processed on a rolling basis. *Application fee:* $25. *Application Contact:* Betty McGinley, Admissions Coordinator, 205-348-5440, Fax: 205-348-3917, E-mail: admissions@law.ua.edu. *Dean,* Kenneth C. Randall, 205-348-5117, Fax: 205-348-3917, E-mail: kcrandal@law.ua.edu.

THE UNIVERSITY OF ALABAMA AT BIRMINGHAM, Birmingham, AL 35294

General Information State-supported, coed, university. CGS member. *Enrollment:* 3,166 full-time matriculated graduate/professional students (1,614 women), 886 part-time matriculated graduate/professional students (582 women). *Enrollment by degree level:* 979 first professional, 2,095 master's, 876 doctoral, 102 other advanced degrees. Tuition, state resident: full-time $3,058. Tuition, nonresident: full-time $5,746. Tuition and fees vary according to course load, degree level and program. *Graduate housing:* Rooms and/or apartments available to single and married students. *Student services:* Campus employment opportunities, campus safety program, career counseling, child daycare facilities, disabled student services, exercise/wellness program, free psychological counseling, international student services, low-cost health insurance, multicultural affairs office, teacher training. *Library facilities:* Mervyn Sterne Library plus 1 other. *Online resources:* library catalog, web page, access to other libraries' catalogs. *Collection:* 5,288 serial subscriptions, 37,366 audiovisual materials. *Research affiliation:* Southern Research Institute.

Computer facilities: 400 computers available on campus for general student use. A campuswide network can be accessed from off campus. Internet access and online class registration are available. *Web address:* http://www.uab.edu/.

General Application Contact: Julie Bryant, Director of Graduate Admissions, 205-934-8227, Fax: 205-934-8413, E-mail: jbryant@uab.edu.

GRADUATE UNITS

Graduate School Students: 1,860 full-time (1,013 women), 1,348 part-time (879 women); includes 575 minority (448 African Americans, 86 Asian Americans or Pacific Islanders, 27 Hispanic Americans, 14 Native Americans), 527 international. Average age 31. 4,295 applicants, 65% accepted. Expenses: Contact institution. *Financial support:* Fellowships, research assistantships, teaching assistantships, career-related internships or fieldwork, Federal Work-Study, institutionally sponsored loans, scholarships/grants, traineeships, tuition waivers (full and partial), and unspecified assistantships available. Support available to part-time students. Financial award applicants required to submit FAFSA. In 2001, 1,073 master's, 108 doctorates, 31 other advanced degrees awarded. *Degree program information:* Part-time and evening/weekend programs available. Offers basic medical sciences (MSBMS); biochemistry (PhD); biochemistry and molecular genetics (PhD); biophysical sciences (PhD); cell biology (PhD); medical genetics (PhD); microbiology (PhD); neurobiology (PhD); neuroscience (PhD); pathology (PhD); pharmacology (PhD); pharmacology and toxicology (PhD); physiology and biophysics (PhD); toxicology (PhD). *Application deadline:* Applications are processed on a rolling basis. *Application fee:* $35 ($60 for international students). Electronic applications accepted. *Application Contact:* Julie Bryant, Director of Graduate Admissions, 205-934-8227, Fax: 205-934-8413, E-mail: jbryant@uab.edu. *Dean,* Dr. Joan F. Lorden, 205-934-8227, Fax: 205-975-7189.

Graduate School of Management Students: 152 full-time (64 women), 210 part-time (81 women); includes 46 minority (34 African Americans, 11 Asian Americans or Pacific Islanders, 1 Hispanic American), 25 international. Average age 29. 361 applicants, 76% accepted. Expenses: Contact institution. *Financial support:* Fellowships, career-related internships or fieldwork available. In 2001, 159 degrees awarded. Offers management (M Acct, MBA, PhD). *Application deadline:* Applications are processed on a rolling basis. *Application fee:* $35 ($60 for international students). Electronic applications accepted. *Application Contact:* Director, 205-934-8817. *Dean,* Dr. Robert E. Holmes, 205-934-8800, Fax: 205-934-8886, E-mail: holmesr@uab.edu.

School of Arts and Humanities Students: 16 full-time (10 women), 27 part-time (21 women); includes 2 minority (1 African American, 1 Hispanic American), 1 international. Average age 33. 38 applicants, 76% accepted. Expenses: Contact institution. *Financial support:* In 2001–02, 3 teaching assistantships (averaging $9,500 per year) were awarded; research assistantships, career-related internships or fieldwork, Federal Work-Study, and tuition waivers (partial) also available. Support available to part-time students. In 2001, 9 degrees awarded. Offers art history (MA); arts and humanities (MA); English (MA). *Application deadline:* Applications are processed on a rolling basis. *Application fee:* $35 ($60 for international students). Electronic applications accepted. *Dean,* Bert Brouwer, 205-934-2290, E-mail: bbrouwer@uab.edu.

School of Education Students: 179 full-time (148 women), 585 part-time (475 women); includes 202 minority (187 African Americans, 6 Asian Americans or Pacific Islanders, 5 Hispanic Americans, 4 Native Americans), 10 international. Average age 34. 760 applicants, 82% accepted. Expenses: Contact institution. *Financial support:* Fellowships, career-related internships or fieldwork and Federal Work-Study available. Support available to part-time students. In 2001, 327 master's, 9 doctorates, 31 other advanced degrees awarded. *Degree program information:* Part-time and evening/weekend programs available. Offers agency counseling (MA); allied health sciences (MA Ed); arts education (MA Ed); counseling (MA, MA Ed); curriculum and instruction (Ed S); early childhood education (MA Ed, PhD); education (MA, MA Ed, Ed D, PhD, Ed S); educational leadership (MA Ed, Ed D, PhD, Ed S); elementary education (MA Ed); health education (MA Ed); health education/health promotion (MA Ed); high school education (MA Ed); marriage and family counseling (MA); physical education (MA Ed); rehabilitation counseling (MA); school counseling (MA); school psychology (MA Ed); special education (MA Ed). *Application deadline:* Applications are processed on a rolling basis. *Application fee:* $35 ($60 for international students). Electronic applications accepted. *Dean,* Dr. Michael J. Froning, 205-934-5363, Fax: 205-934-4963.

School of Engineering Students: 142 full-time (30 women), 110 part-time (19 women); includes 30 minority (19 African Americans, 9 Asian Americans or Pacific Islanders, 2 Hispanic Americans), 120 international. Average age 28. 667 applicants, 62% accepted. Expenses: Contact institution. *Financial support:* Fellowships with full tuition reimbursements, research assistantships with full tuition reimbursements, career-related internships or fieldwork, Federal Work-Study, institutionally sponsored loans, and tuition waivers (full and partial) available. Support available to part-time students. In 2001, 50 master's, 9 doctorates awarded. *Degree program information:* Evening/weekend programs available. Offers biomedical engineering (MSBME, PhD); civil and environmental engineering (MSCE, PhD); electrical and computer engineering (MSEE, PhD); engineering (MS Mt E, MSBME, MSCE, MSEE, MSME, PhD); materials engineering (MS Mt E, PhD); materials science (PhD); mechanical engineering (MSME, PhD). *Application deadline:* Applications are processed on a rolling basis. *Application fee:* $35 ($60 for international students). Electronic applications accepted. *Dean,* Dr. Linda C. Lucas, 205-934-8420, Fax: 205-975-4919.

School of Health Related Professions Students: 449 full-time (277 women), 81 part-time (49 women); includes 70 minority (49 African Americans, 10 Asian Americans or Pacific Islanders, 5 Hispanic Americans, 6 Native Americans), 31 international. Average age 30. 588 applicants, 66% accepted. Expenses: Contact institution. *Financial support:* Fellowships, research assistantships, teaching assistantships, career-related internships or fieldwork, Federal Work-Study, institutionally sponsored loans, scholarships/grants, traineeships, and unspecified assistantships available. Support available to part-time students. In 2001, 184 master's, 2 doctorates awarded. *Degree program information:* Part-time programs available. Offers administration-health services (PhD); clinical laboratory science (MSCLS); clinical nutrition (MS); clinical nutrition and dietetics (MS, Certificate); critical care (MNA); dietetic internship (Certificate); health administration (MSHA); health informatics (MS); health related professions (MNA, MS, MSCLS, MSHA, PhD, Certificate); nurse anesthesia (MNA); nutrition sciences (PhD); occupational therapy (MS); physical therapy (MS). *Application fee:* $35 ($60 for international students). Electronic applications accepted. *Dean,* Dr. Harold P. Jones, 205-934-5149, Fax: 205-934-2412, E-mail: jonesh@uab.edu.

School of Natural Sciences and Mathematics Students: 146 full-time (43 women), 45 part-time (16 women); includes 18 minority (4 African Americans, 11 Asian Americans or Pacific Islanders, 3 Hispanic Americans), 98 international. Average age 28. 593 applicants, 42% accepted. Expenses: Contact institution. *Financial support:* Fellowships with tuition reimbursements, research assistantships with tuition reimbursements, teaching assistantships with tuition reimbursements, career-related internships or fieldwork, Federal Work-Study, institutionally sponsored loans, tuition waivers (full and partial), and unspecified assistantships available. Support available to part-time students. Financial award applicants required to submit FAFSA. In 2001, 49 master's, 8 doctorates awarded. Offers applied mathematics (PhD); biology (MS, PhD); chemistry (MS, PhD); computer and information sciences (MS, PhD); mathematics (MS); natural sciences and mathematics (MS, PhD); physics (MS, PhD). *Application deadline:* Applications are processed on a rolling basis. *Application fee:* $35 ($60 for international students). Electronic applications accepted. *Dean,* Dr. James B. McClintock, 205-934-5102, E-mail: mcclinto@uab.edu.

School of Nursing Students: 55 full-time (54 women), 126 part-time (120 women); includes 43 minority (38 African Americans, 2 Asian Americans or Pacific Islanders, 1 Hispanic American, 2 Native Americans), 15 international. Average age 36. 73 applicants, 70% accepted. Expenses: Contact institution. *Financial support:* In 2001–02, 3 fellowships (averaging $12,833 per year), 1 research assistantship, teaching assistantships (averaging $6,760 per year) were awarded. Federal Work-Study also available. Support available to part-time students. In 2001, 92 master's, 5 doctorates awarded. Offers nursing (MSN, PhD). *Application deadline:* Applications are processed on a rolling basis. *Application fee:* $35 ($60 for international students). Electronic applications accepted. *Application Contact:* Dr. Lynda L. Harrison, Associate for Graduate Studies, 205-934-6787. *Dean,* Dr. Rachel Z. Booth, 205-934-5360.

School of Public Health Students: 240 full-time (132 women), 108 part-time (63 women); includes 79 minority (59 African Americans, 16 Asian Americans or Pacific Islanders, 2 Hispanic Americans, 2 Native Americans), 106 international. 557 applicants, 50% accepted. Expenses: Contact institution. *Financial support:* In 2001–02, 115 students received support; fellowships, career-related internships or fieldwork, Federal Work-Study, scholarships/grants, and unspecified assistantships available. Support available to part-time students. Financial award application deadline: 2/15. In 2001, 141 master's, 13 doctorates awarded. *Degree program information:* Part-time programs available. Offers biomathematics (MS, PhD); biostatistics (MS, PhD); environmental health (PhD); environmental toxicology (PhD); epidemiology (PhD); health care organization and policy (MPH, MSPH); health education promotion (PhD); health education/promotion (PhD); industrial hygiene (PhD); maternal and child health (MSPH); public health (MPH, MS, MSPH, PhD). *Application deadline:* Applications are processed on a rolling basis. *Application fee:* $35 ($60 for international students). Electronic applications accepted. *Application Contact:* Nancy O. Pinson, Coordinator of Student Admissions, 205-934-4993, Fax: 205-975-5484. *Dean,* Dr. Max Michael, 205-975-7742, Fax: 205-975-5484, E-mail: maxm@uab.edu.

School of Social and Behavioral Sciences Students: 116 full-time (77 women), 48 part-time (31 women); includes 32 minority (28 African Americans, 1 Asian American or Pacific Islander, 3 Hispanic Americans), 5 international. Average age 30. 438 applicants, 34% accepted. Expenses: Contact institution. *Financial support:* Fellowships, research assistantships, teaching assistantships, career-related internships or fieldwork, Federal Work-Study, and institutionally sponsored loans available. Support available to part-time students. In 2001, 53 master's, 10 doctorates awarded. *Degree program information:* Part-time and evening/weekend programs available. Offers anthropology (MA); behavioral neuroscience (PhD); clinical psychology (PhD); criminal justice (MSCJ); developmental psychology (PhD); forensic science (MSFS); history (MA); medical psychology (PhD); medical sociology (PhD); psychology (MA, PhD); public administration (MPA); social and behavioral sciences (MA, MPA, MSCJ, MSFS, PhD); sociology (MA). *Application deadline:* Applications are processed on a rolling basis. *Application fee:* $35 ($60 for international students). Electronic applications accepted. *Dean,* Dr. Tennant S. McWilliams, 205-934-5643, Fax: 205-934-5643, E-mail: tsm@uab.edu.

School of Dentistry Students: 229 full-time (75 women); includes 28 minority (10 African Americans, 13 Asian Americans or Pacific Islanders, 2 Hispanic Americans, 3 Native Americans), 3 international. Average age 25. 428 applicants, 15% accepted, 56 enrolled. Expenses: Contact institution. *Financial support:* Fellowships, Federal Work-Study available. In 2001, 54 degrees awarded. Offers dentistry (DMD, MS, MSBMS, PhD); dentistry and oral biology (MS). *Application deadline:* For fall admission, 2/15. *Application fee:* $145. Electronic applications accepted. *Application Contact:* Dr. Steven J. Filler, Director of Dentistry Admissions, 205-934-5424, Fax: 205-975-6519, E-mail: sfiller@uab.edu. *Dean,* Dr. Mary Lynne Capilouto, 205-934-4720, Fax: 205-934-9283, E-mail: mlcap@uab.edu.

School of Medicine Students: 590 full-time (252 women); includes 150 minority (50 African Americans, 85 Asian Americans or Pacific Islanders, 8 Hispanic Americans, 7 Native Americans) Average age 25. 1,477 applicants, 15% accepted, 160 enrolled. Expenses: Contact institution. *Financial support:* Fellowships, career-related internships or fieldwork available. Financial award application deadline: 5/1; financial award applicants required to submit FAFSA. In 2001, 153 degrees awarded. Offers medicine (MD, MSBMS, PhD). *Application deadline:* For fall admission, 11/1. *Application fee:* $65. Electronic applications accepted. *Application Contact:* Dr. George S. Hand, Assistant Dean for Admissions, 205-934-2333, Fax: 205-934-8724, E-mail: ghand@uab.edu. *Vice President/Dean, School of Medicine,* Dr. William B. Deal, 205-934-1111, Fax: 205-934-0333, E-mail: wdeal@uab.edu.

School of Optometry Students: 156 full-time (88 women); includes 28 minority (7 African Americans, 19 Asian Americans or Pacific Islanders, 2 Hispanic Americans), 3 international. Average age 26. 209 applicants, 29% accepted. *Faculty:* 34 full-time, 5 part-time/adjunct. Expenses: Contact institution. *Financial support:* In 2001–02, 137 students received support. Federal Work-Study available. Financial award application deadline: 5/1; financial award applicants required to submit FAFSA. In 2001, 39 degrees awarded. Offers optometry (OD, MS, PhD); vision science (MS, PhD). *Application deadline:* Applications are processed on a rolling basis. *Application fee:* $40. *Application Contact:* Edith C. Jones, Director, Optometry Student Affairs, 205-934-6150, Fax: 205-934-6758, E-mail: ejones@uab.edu. *Interim Dean,* Dr. Jimmy D. Bartlett, 205-934-4488, Fax: 205-975-7052, E-mail: optometrydean@uab.edu.

See in-depth description on page 1159.

THE UNIVERSITY OF ALABAMA IN HUNTSVILLE, Huntsville, AL 35899

General Information State-supported, coed, university. CGS member. *Enrollment:* 459 full-time matriculated graduate/professional students (179 women), 701 part-time matriculated graduate/professional students (293 women). *Enrollment by degree level:* 891 master's, 260 doctoral, 9 other advanced degrees. *Graduate faculty:* 223 full-time (59 women), 28 part-time/adjunct (5 women). *Tuition, area resident:* Part-time $175 per hour. Tuition, state resident: full-time $4,408. Tuition, nonresident: full-time $9,054; part-time $361 per hour. *Graduate housing:* Rooms and/or apartments available on a first-come, first-served basis to single and married students. Typical cost: $4,920 per year ($6,220 including board) for single students; $4,920 per year for married students. Housing application deadline: 6/15. *Student services:* Campus employment opportunities, campus safety program, career counseling, child daycare facilities, disabled student services, free psychological counseling, international student services, low-cost health insurance, multicultural affairs office, writing training. *Library facilities:* University of Alabama in Huntsville Library. *Online resources:* library catalog, web page, access to other libraries' catalogs. *Collection:* 627,132 titles, 1,668 serial subscriptions, 2,677 audiovisual materials. *Research affiliation:* NASA–Marshall Space Flight Center (space science, earth science, information technology, materials science, optical science), Department of Defense/U.S. Army Aviation & Missile Command (missile research, development and engineering and manufacturing technology).

Computer facilities: 520 computers available on campus for general student use. A campuswide network can be accessed from student residence rooms and from off campus. Internet access and online class registration are available. *Web address:* http://www.uah.edu/.

General Application Contact: Dr. Gordon Emslie, Dean of Graduate Studies, 256-824-6002, Fax: 256-824-6349, E-mail: emslieg@email.uah.edu.

GRADUATE UNITS

School of Graduate Studies Students: 459 full-time (179 women), 701 part-time (293 women); includes 139 minority (77 African Americans, 41 Asian Americans or Pacific Islanders, 11 Hispanic Americans, 10 Native Americans), 256 international. Average age 33. 1,091 applicants, 67% accepted, 436 enrolled. *Faculty:* 220 full-time (58 women), 28 part-time/adjunct (5 women). Expenses: Contact institution. *Financial support:* In 2001–02, 344 students received support, including 66 fellowships with full and partial tuition reimbursements available (averaging $1,641 per year), 131 research assistantships with full and partial tuition reimbursements available (averaging $9,893 per year), 129 teaching assistantships with full and partial tuition reimbursements available (averaging $7,555 per year); career-related internships or fieldwork, Federal Work-Study, institutionally sponsored loans, scholarships/grants, and tuition waivers (full and partial) also available. Support available to part-time students. Financial award application deadline: 4/1; financial award applicants required to submit FAFSA. In 2001, 311 master's, 30 doctorates, 12 other advanced degrees awarded. *Degree program information:* Part-time and evening/weekend programs available. Postbaccalaureate distance learning degree programs offered (no on-campus study). Offers optical science and engineering (PhD). *Application deadline:* For fall admission, 7/24 (priority date); for spring admission, 11/15 (priority date). Applications are processed on a rolling basis. *Application fee:* $35. *Dean,* Dr. Gordon Emslie, 256-824-6002, Fax: 256-824-6349, E-mail: emslieg@email.uah.edu.

College of Administrative Science Students: 35 full-time (14 women), 150 part-time (55 women); includes 16 minority (8 African Americans, 6 Asian Americans or Pacific Islanders, 2 Native Americans), 22 international. Average age 33. 104 applicants, 89% accepted, 84 enrolled. *Faculty:* 27 full-time (5 women), 3 part-time/adjunct (1 woman). Expenses: Contact institution. *Financial support:* In 2001–02, 11 students received support, including 11 teaching assistantships with full and partial tuition reimbursements available (averaging $3,600 per year); fellowships with full and partial tuition reimbursements available, research assistantships with full and partial tuition reimbursements available, career-related internships or fieldwork, Federal Work-Study, institutionally sponsored loans, scholarships/grants, health care benefits, and tuition waivers (full and partial) also available. Support available to part-time students. Financial award application deadline: 4/1; financial award applicants required to submit FAFSA. In 2001, 40 master's, 6 other advanced degrees awarded. *Degree program information:* Part-time and evening/weekend programs available. Offers accounting (M Acc, Certificate); administrative science (M Acc, MS, MSM, MSMIS, Certificate); management (MS); management information systems (MSMIS). *Application deadline:* For fall admission, 7/24 (priority date); for spring admission, 11/15 (priority date). Applications are processed on a rolling basis. *Application fee:* $35. *Application Contact:* Dr. Daniel Sherman, Assistant Dean, 256-824-6024, Fax: 256-824-7571, E-mail: msmprog@email.uah.edu. *Dean,* Dr. C. David Billings, 256-824-6735, Fax: 256-824-6328, E-mail: billind@email.uah.edu.

College of Engineering Students: 179 full-time (32 women), 268 part-time (60 women); includes 45 minority (22 African Americans, 18 Asian Americans or Pacific Islanders, 4 Hispanic Americans, 1 Native American), 117 international. Average age 34. 584 applicants, 49% accepted, 137 enrolled. *Faculty:* 57 full-time (6 women), 8 part-time/adjunct (0 women). Expenses: Contact institution. *Financial support:* In 2001–02, 118 students received support, including 3 fellowships with full and partial tuition reimbursements available (averaging $13,000 per year), 66 research assistantships with full and partial tuition reimbursements available (averaging $9,304 per year), 47 teaching assistantships with full and partial tuition reimbursements available (averaging $7,834 per year); career-related internships or fieldwork, Federal Work-Study, institutionally sponsored loans, scholarships/grants, health care benefits, and tuition waivers (full and partial) also available. Support available to part-time students. Financial award application deadline: 4/1; financial award applicants required to submit FAFSA. In 2001, 83 master's, 19 doctorates awarded. *Degree program information:* Part-time and evening/weekend programs available. Postbaccalaureate distance learning degree programs offered (no on-campus study). Offers aerospace engineering (MSE); biotechnology science and engineering (PhD); chemical engineering (MSE); civil and environmental engineering (MSE); computer engineering (PhD); electrical and computer engineering (MSE); electrical engineering (PhD); engineering (MSE, MSOR, PhD); industrial engineering (MSE, PhD); mechanical engineering (MSE, PhD); operations research (MSOR); optical science and engineering (PhD). *Application deadline:* For fall admission, 7/24 (priority date); for spring admission, 11/15 (priority date). Applications are processed on a rolling basis. *Application fee:* $35. *Dean,* Dr. Jorge Aunon, 256-824-6474, Fax: 256-824-6843, E-mail: aunon@eb.uah.edu.

College of Liberal Arts Students: 30 full-time (22 women), 52 part-time (41 women); includes 18 minority (10 African Americans, 3 Asian Americans or Pacific Islanders, 3 Hispanic Americans, 2 Native Americans), 1 international. Average age 33. 59 applicants, 95% accepted, 34 enrolled. *Faculty:* 43 full-time (23 women), 4 part-time/adjunct (1 woman). Expenses: Contact institution. *Financial support:* In 2001–02, 21 students received support, including 3 research assistantships with full and partial tuition reimbursements available (averaging $7,473 per year), 9 teaching assistantships with full and partial tuition reimbursements available (averaging $7,400 per year); fellowships with full and partial tuition reimbursements available, career-related internships or fieldwork, Federal Work-Study, institutionally sponsored loans, scholarships/grants, health care benefits, and tuition waivers (full and partial) also available. Support available to part-time students. Financial award application deadline: 4/1; financial award applicants required to submit FAFSA. In 2001, 33 degrees awarded. *Degree program information:* Part-time and evening/weekend programs available. Offers English (MA); history (MA); liberal arts (MA, Certificate); psychology (MA); public affairs (MA); teaching of English to speakers of other languages (Certificate); technical communications (Certificate). *Application deadline:* For fall admission, 7/24 (priority date); for spring admission, 11/15 (priority date). Applications are processed on a rolling basis. *Application fee:* $35. *Dean,* Dr. Sue Kirkpatrick, 256-824-6200, Fax: 256-824-6949, E-mail: kirkpas@email.uah.edu.

College of Nursing Students: 56 full-time (49 women), 115 part-time (101 women); includes 29 minority (21 African Americans, 2 Asian Americans or Pacific Islanders, 2 Hispanic Americans, 4 Native Americans), 3 international. Average age 36. 107 applicants, 93% accepted, 67 enrolled. *Faculty:* 16 full-time (all women), 2 part-time/adjunct (1 woman). Expenses: Contact institution. *Financial support:* In 2001–02, 68 students received support, including 63 fellowships with full and partial tuition reimbursements available (averaging $1,641 per year), 5 teaching assistantships with full and partial tuition reimbursements available (averaging $7,544 per year); research assistantships, career-related internships or fieldwork, Federal Work-Study, institutionally sponsored loans, scholarships/grants, traineeships, health care benefits, tuition waivers (full and partial), and unspecified assistantships also available. Support available to part-time students. Financial award application deadline: 4/1; financial award applicants required to submit FAFSA. In 2001, 78 master's, 6 other advanced degrees awarded. *Degree program information:* Part-time and evening/weekend programs available. Offers family nurse practitioner (Certificate); nursing (MSN). *Application deadline:* For fall admission, 7/24 (priority date); for spring admission, 11/15 (priority date). Applications are processed on a rolling basis. *Application fee:* $35. *Application Contact:* Lavon Wilson, Director of Student Affairs, 256-824-6742, Fax: 256-824-6026, E-mail: wilson@email.uah.edu. *Dean,* Dr. Fay Raines, 256-824-6345, Fax: 256-824-6026, E-mail: rainesc@email.uah.edu.

College of Science Students: 159 full-time (62 women), 116 part-time (36 women); includes 31 minority (16 African Americans, 12 Asian Americans or Pacific Islanders, 2 Hispanic Americans, 1 Native American), 113 international. Average age 31. 227 applicants, 82% accepted, 107 enrolled. *Faculty:* 80 full-time (9 women), 8 part-time/adjunct (2 women). Expenses: Contact institution. *Financial support:* In 2001–02, 128 students received support, including 62 research assistantships with full and partial tuition reimbursements available (averaging $10,639 per year), 57 teaching assistantships with full and partial tuition reimbursements available (averaging $8,114 per year); fellowships with full and partial tuition reimbursements available, career-related internships or fieldwork, Federal Work-Study, institutionally sponsored loans, scholarships/grants, health care benefits, tuition waivers (full and partial), and unspecified assistantships also available. Support available to part-time students. Financial award application deadline: 4/1; financial award applicants required to submit FAFSA. In 2001, 77 master's, 11 doctorates awarded. *Degree program information:* Part-time and evening/weekend programs available. Offers applied mathematics (PhD); atmospheric and environmental science (MS, PhD); biological sciences (MS); chemistry (MS); computer science (MS, PhD); materials science (MS, PhD); mathematics (MA, MS); physics (MS, PhD); science (MA, MS, PhD, Certificate); software engineering (Certificate). *Application deadline:* For fall admission, 7/24 (priority date); for spring admission, 11/15 (priority date). Applications are processed on a rolling basis. *Application fee:* $35. *Dean,* Dr. Jack Fix, 256-824-6605, Fax: 256-824-6819, E-mail: fixj@email.uah.edu.

UNIVERSITY OF ALASKA ANCHORAGE, Anchorage, AK 99508-8060

General Information State-supported, coed, comprehensive institution. CGS member. *Graduate housing:* Room and/or apartments available on a first-come, first-served basis to single students; on-campus housing not available to married students. Housing application deadline: 6/15. *Research affiliation:* Alaska Small Business Development Center, Alaska Hospital and Medical Center, Providence Hospital, Municipality of Anchorage.

GRADUATE UNITS

College of Arts and Sciences *Degree program information:* Part-time programs available. Offers arts and sciences (MA, MFA, MS); biological sciences (MS); clinical psychology (MS); creative writing and literary arts (MFA); English (MA); interdisciplinary studies (MA, MS).

College of Business and Public Policy *Degree program information:* Part-time and evening/weekend programs available. Offers business administration (MBA); business and public policy (MBA, MPA); public administration (MPA).

College of Health, Education, and Social Welfare *Degree program information:* Part-time and evening/weekend programs available. Offers health, education, and social welfare (M Ed, MAT, MS, MSW, Certificate); substance abuse disorders (Certificate).

School of Education *Degree program information:* Part-time programs available. Offers adult education (M Ed); counseling and guidance (M Ed); education (M Ed, MAT); educational leadership (M Ed); master teacher (M Ed); special education (M Ed); teaching (MAT).

School of Nursing *Degree program information:* Part-time and evening/weekend programs available. Offers nursing and health science (MS).

School of Social Work Offers social work (MSW).

Community and Technical College *Degree program information:* Part-time programs available. Offers vocational education (MS).

School of Engineering *Degree program information:* Part-time and evening/weekend programs available. Offers arctic engineering (MS); civil engineering (MCE, MS); engineering (MCE, MS); engineering management (MS); environmental quality engineering (MS); environmental quality science (MS); science management (MS).

UNIVERSITY OF ALASKA FAIRBANKS, Fairbanks, AK 99775-7480

General Information State-supported, coed, university. CGS member. *Enrollment:* 526 full-time matriculated graduate/professional students (263 women), 306 part-time matriculated graduate/professional students (180 women). *Enrollment by degree level:* 627 master's, 170 doctoral, 35 other advanced degrees. *Graduate faculty:* 507 full-time (160 women), 261 part-time/adjunct (136 women). Tuition, state resident: full-time $4,272; part-time $178 per credit. Tuition, nonresident: full-time $8,328; part-time $347 per credit. *Required fees:* $960; $60 per term. Part-time tuition and fees vary according to course load. *Graduate housing:* Rooms and/or apartments available on a first-come, first-served basis to single and married students. Typical cost: $2,500 per year ($4,760 including board) for single students; $5,085 per year ($7,345 including board) for married students. Room and board charges vary according to board plan and housing facility selected. Housing application deadline: 3/15. *Student services:* Campus employment opportunities, campus safety program, career counseling, child daycare facilities, disabled student services, exercise/wellness program, free psychological counseling, grant writing training, international student services, low-cost health insurance, multicultural affairs office, teacher training, writing training. *Library facilities:* Rasmuson Library plus 8 others. *Online resources:* library catalog, web page, access to other libraries' catalogs. *Collection:* 586,421 titles, 6,825 serial subscriptions, 662,500 audiovisual materials. *Research affiliation:* Alaska Cooperative Fishery and Wildlife Research Unit, Institute of Northern Forestry.

Computer facilities: 500 computers available on campus for general student use. A campuswide network can be accessed from student residence rooms and from off campus. Internet access is available. *Web address:* http://www.uaf.edu/.

General Application Contact: Nancy Dix, Interim Director of Admissions, 907-474-7500, Fax: 907-474-5379, E-mail: fyapply@uaf.edu.

GRADUATE UNITS

Graduate School Students: 6 full-time (3 women), 11 part-time (6 women); includes 1 minority (Native American), 8 international. Average age 37. 14 applicants, 79% accepted, 10 enrolled. *Faculty:* 1 (woman) full-time. Expenses: Contact institution. *Financial support:* In 2001–02, fellowships with tuition reimbursements (averaging $10,000 per year), research assistantships with full tuition reimbursements (averaging $10,000 per year), teaching assistantships with full tuition reimbursements (averaging $10,000 per year) were awarded. Career-related internships or fieldwork, Federal Work-Study, institutionally sponsored loans, and scholarships/grants also available. Financial award applicants required to submit FAFSA. In 2001, 8 master's, 4 doctorates awarded. *Degree program information:* Part-time programs available. *Application deadline:* For fall admission, 4/1; for spring admission, 11/1. Applications are processed on a rolling basis. *Application fee:* $35. Electronic applications accepted. *Application Contact:* Elke Richmond, Coordinator of Graduate Student Services, 907-474-7186, Fax: 907-474-7225, E-mail: fnkc@uaf.edu. *Dean,* Dr. Joe Kan, 907-474-7431, Fax: 907-474-7225.

College of Liberal Arts Students: 113 full-time (66 women), 69 part-time (41 women); includes 23 minority (2 African Americans, 2 Asian Americans or Pacific Islanders, 2 Hispanic Americans, 17 Native Americans), 15 international. Average age 36. 179 applicants, 62% accepted, 75 enrolled. *Faculty:* 155 full-time (70 women), 167 part-time/adjunct (94 women). Expenses: Contact institution. *Financial support:* In 2001–02, fellowships with tuition reimbursements (averaging $10,000 per year); research assistantships with tuition reimbursements, teaching assistantships with tuition reimbursements, career-related internships or fieldwork, Federal Work-Study, institutionally sponsored loans, and scholarships/

University of Alaska Fairbanks (continued)

grants also available. In 2001, 24 master's, 1 doctorate awarded. *Degree program information:* Part-time programs available. Offers administration of justice (MA); Alaskan ethnomusicology (MA); anthropology (MA, PhD); art (MA, MFA); community psychology (MA); creative writing (MFA); English (MA); journalism (MA); liberal arts (MA, MAT, MFA, PhD); music (MAT); music education (MA); music history (MA); music theory (MA); Northern studies (MA, PhD); performance (MA). *Application deadline:* Applications are processed on a rolling basis. *Application fee:* $35. Electronic applications accepted. *Application Contact:* Office of Admissions, 907-474-7500. *Interim Dean,* Dr. John Leipzig, 907-474-7231.

College of Rural Alaska Students: 7 full-time (5 women), 17 part-time (10 women); includes 20 minority (1 Asian American or Pacific Islander, 19 Native Americans) Average age 46. 11 applicants, 91% accepted, 9 enrolled. *Faculty:* 64 full-time (27 women), 35 part-time/adjunct (24 women). Expenses: Contact institution. *Financial support:* Federal Work-Study and scholarships/grants available. Offers Alaska native and rural development (MS, PhD). *Application deadline:* For fall admission, 4/1; for spring admission, 11/1. *Application fee:* $35. *Executive Dean,* Dr. Joseph Bernice, 907-474-7143.

College of Science, Engineering and Mathematics Students: 199 full-time (70 women), 62 part-time (26 women); includes 14 minority (5 African Americans, 7 Asian Americans or Pacific Islanders, 1 Hispanic American, 1 Native American), 74 international. Average age 32. 245 applicants, 52% accepted, 85 enrolled. *Faculty:* 160 full-time (28 women), 36 part-time/adjunct (5 women). Expenses: Contact institution. *Financial support:* In 2001–02, fellowships (averaging $10,000 per year), research assistantships (averaging $12,000 per year), teaching assistantships (averaging $12,000 per year) were awarded. Career-related internships or fieldwork, Federal Work-Study, institutionally sponsored loans, and scholarships/grants also available. In 2001, 50 master's, 17 doctorates awarded. *Degree program information:* Part-time programs available. Offers arctic engineering (MS); atmospheric science (MS, PhD); biochemistry (MS, PhD); biological sciences (MAT, MS, PhD); chemistry (MA, MAT, MS); civil engineering (MCE, MS); computer science (MS); electrical engineering (MEE, MS); environmental quality engineering (MS); environmental quality science (MS); geology (MS, PhD); geophysics (MS, PhD); geoscience (MAT); mathematics (MAT, MS, PhD); mechanical engineering (MS); physics (MS, PhD); science, engineering and mathematics (MA, MAT, MCE, MEE, MS, PhD); space physics (MS, PhD); statistics (MS); wildlife biology and management (MS, PhD). *Application deadline:* For fall admission, 4/1; for spring admission, 11/1. Applications are processed on a rolling basis. *Application fee:* $35. *Dean,* Dr. David Woodall, 907-474-7941.

School of Education Students: 64 full-time (46 women), 64 part-time (52 women); includes 18 minority (4 African Americans, 1 Asian American or Pacific Islander, 1 Hispanic American, 12 Native Americans), 1 international. Average age 39. 98 applicants, 72% accepted, 51 enrolled. *Faculty:* 18 full-time (12 women), 12 part-time/adjunct (11 women). Expenses: Contact institution. *Financial support:* In 2001–02, fellowships with tuition reimbursements (averaging $10,000 per year); research assistantships with tuition reimbursements, teaching assistantships with tuition reimbursements, career-related internships or fieldwork, Federal Work-Study, and scholarships/grants also available. In 2001, 12 degrees awarded. Offers cross-cultural education (M Ed, Ed S); curriculum and instruction (M Ed); educational administration (M Ed); guidance and counseling (M Ed); language and literature (M Ed). *Application deadline:* For fall admission, 4/1; for spring admission, 10/1. *Application fee:* $35. *Director,* Dr. Roger Norris-Tull, 907-474-6670.

School of Fisheries and Ocean Sciences Students: 68 full-time (41 women), 32 part-time (18 women); includes 5 minority (all Asian Americans or Pacific Islanders), 15 international. Average age 33. 59 applicants, 63% accepted, 27 enrolled. *Faculty:* 46 full-time (9 women), 2 part-time/adjunct (1 woman). Expenses: Contact institution. *Financial support:* In 2001–02, fellowships (averaging $10,000 per year), research assistantships with tuition reimbursements (averaging $12,000 per year), teaching assistantships with tuition reimbursements (averaging $12,000 per year) were awarded. Federal Work-Study and scholarships/grants also available. In 2001, 9 master's, 4 doctorates awarded. Offers fisheries (MS, PhD); fisheries and ocean sciences (MS, PhD); marine biology (MS); oceanography (MS, PhD). *Application deadline:* For fall admission, 4/1 (priority date); for spring admission, 11/1. Applications are processed on a rolling basis. *Application fee:* $35. *Dean,* Dr. Vera Alexander, 907-474-7531.

School of Management Students: 26 full-time (16 women), 24 part-time (14 women); includes 4 minority (2 Asian Americans or Pacific Islanders, 2 Native Americans), 6 international. Average age 33. 30 applicants, 57% accepted, 13 enrolled. Expenses: Contact institution. *Financial support:* In 2001–02, fellowships with tuition reimbursements (averaging $10,000 per year); research assistantships with tuition reimbursements, teaching assistantships with tuition reimbursements, career-related internships or fieldwork, Federal Work-Study, and scholarships/grants also available. In 2001, 19 degrees awarded. *Degree program information:* Part-time programs available. Offers capital markets (MBA); general management (MBA); management (MBA, MS); resource economics (MS). *Application deadline:* For fall admission, 4/1; for spring admission, 11/1. Applications are processed on a rolling basis. *Application fee:* $35. *Application Contact:* Dr. Harikumar Sankaram, Director, MBA Program, 907-474-6534. *Dean,* Dr. James Collins, 907-474-7461.

School of Mineral Engineering Students: 9 full-time (0 women), 1 part-time, 7 international. Average age 30. 23 applicants, 43% accepted, 5 enrolled. *Faculty:* 15 full-time (0 women), 1 part-time/adjunct (0 women). Expenses: Contact institution. *Financial support:* In 2001–02, fellowships with tuition reimbursements (averaging $10,000 per year); research assistantships with tuition reimbursements, teaching assistantships with tuition reimbursements, career-related internships or fieldwork, Federal Work-Study, and scholarships/grants also available. In 2001, 3 degrees awarded. *Degree program information:* Part-time programs available. Offers geological engineering (MS, EM); mineral engineering (MS, EM); mineral preparation engineering (MS); mining engineering (MS, EM); petroleum engineering (MS). *Application deadline:* For fall admission, 4/1; for spring admission, 11/1. Applications are processed on a rolling basis. *Application fee:* $35. *Head,* Dr. Sukumar Bandopadhyay, 907-474-7366.

School of Agriculture and Land Resources Management Students: 17 full-time (7 women), 11 part-time (8 women); includes 2 minority (1 Asian American or Pacific Islander, 1 Native American), 5 international. Average age 32. 22 applicants, 41% accepted, 8 enrolled. *Faculty:* 22 full-time (8 women), 1 (woman) part-time/adjunct. Expenses: Contact institution. *Financial support:* In 2001–02, fellowships with tuition reimbursements (averaging $10,000 per year); research assistantships with tuition reimbursements, teaching assistantships with tuition reimbursements, career-related internships or fieldwork, Federal Work-Study, and scholarships/grants also available. *Degree program information:* Part-time programs available. Offers natural resource management (MS). *Application deadline:* For fall admission, 4/1; for spring admission, 11/1. Applications are processed on a rolling basis. *Application fee:* $35. *Application Contact:* Barbara Pierson, Recruitment Coordinator, 907-474-5276. *Interim Dean,* Dr. Carol Lewis, 907-474-7083.

UNIVERSITY OF ALASKA SOUTHEAST, Juneau, AK 99801

General Information State-supported, coed, comprehensive institution. *Enrollment:* 40 full-time matriculated graduate/professional students (23 women), 64 part-time matriculated graduate/professional students (44 women). *Enrollment by degree level:* 73 master's, 31 other advanced degrees. *Graduate faculty:* 12 full-time (6 women), 8 part-time/adjunct (5 women). Tuition, state resident: part-time $178 per credit hour. Tuition, nonresident: part-time $374 per credit hour. *Required fees:* $6 per credit hour. $100 per semester. *Graduate housing:* Rooms and/or apartments available on a first-come, first-served basis to single and married students. Typical cost: $3,000 per year ($5,430 including board) for single students. Housing application deadline: 5/1. *Student services:* Campus employment opportunities, career counseling, disabled student services, international student services, low-cost health insurance, writing training. *Library facilities:* Egan Memorial Library. *Online resources:* library catalog, web page, access to other libraries' catalogs. *Collection:* 102,171 titles, 1,500 serial subscriptions. *Research affiliation:* National Park Service, National Marine Fisheries Services, National Oceanic and Atmospheric Administration, National Science Foundation, Alaska Department of Fish and Game, Alaska Department of Education.

Computer facilities: 75 computers available on campus for general student use. A campuswide network can be accessed from student residence rooms and from off campus. Internet access is available. *Web address:* http://www.jun.alaska.edu/.

General Application Contact: Greg Wagner, Recruiter, 907-465-6239, Fax: 907-465-6365, E-mail: greg.wagner@uas.alaska.edu.

GRADUATE UNITS

Graduate Programs Students: 40 full-time (23 women), 64 part-time (44 women); includes 6 minority (2 Asian Americans or Pacific Islanders, 4 Native Americans), 5 international. Average age 36. *Faculty:* 12 full-time (6 women), 8 part-time/adjunct (5 women). Expenses: Contact institution. *Financial support:* Federal Work-Study, scholarships/grants, and tuition waivers (full and partial) available. Support available to part-time students. Financial award applicants required to submit FAFSA. In 2001, 43 degrees awarded. *Degree program information:* Part-time and evening/weekend programs available. Postbaccalaureate distance learning degree programs offered (minimal on-campus study). Offers early childhood education (M Ed); educational technology (M Ed); elementary education (M Ed, MAT); public administration (MPA); secondary education (M Ed, MAT). *Application deadline:* Applications are processed on a rolling basis. Electronic applications accepted. *Application Contact:* Greg Wagner, Recruiter, 907-465-6239, Fax: 907-465-6365, E-mail: greg.wagner@uas.alaska.edu. *Vice Chancellor for Academic Affairs,* Dr. Roberta Stell, 907-465-6472, E-mail: roberta.stell@ucs.alaska.edu.

UNIVERSITY OF ALBERTA, Edmonton, AB T6G 2E1, Canada

General Information Province-supported, coed, university. CGS member. *Enrollment:* 3,071 full-time matriculated graduate/professional students (1,454 women), 1,942 part-time matriculated graduate/professional students (1,148 women). *International tuition:* $5,474 full-time. Tuition, province resident: full-time $2,737. *Graduate housing:* Rooms and/or apartments available on a first-come, first-served basis to single students and available to married students. *Student services:* Campus employment opportunities, campus safety program, career counseling, child daycare facilities, disabled student services, exercise/wellness program, free psychological counseling, grant writing training, international student services, teacher training, writing training. *Library facilities:* Cameron Library plus 10 others. *Online resources:* library catalog, web page, access to other libraries' catalogs. *Collection:* 5.3 million titles, 26,000 serial subscriptions.

Computer facilities: 721 computers available on campus for general student use. A campuswide network can be accessed from student residence rooms and from off campus. Internet access, e-mail are available. *Web address:* http://www.ualberta.ca/.

GRADUATE UNITS

Faculty of Graduate Studies and Research Students: 3,071 full-time (1,454 women), 1,942 part-time (1,148 women). Expenses: Contact institution. *Financial support:* In 2001–02, 2,400 fellowships, 425 research assistantships, 875 teaching assistantships were awarded. Career-related internships or fieldwork, institutionally sponsored loans, and scholarships/grants also available. Support available to part-time students. In 2001, 468 master's, 292 doctorates awarded. *Degree program information:* Part-time and evening/weekend programs available. Offers accounting (PhD); administration of post secondary education (Ed D); administration of postsecondary education (M Ed, PhD); adult and higher education (M Ed); agricultural economics (M Ag, M Sc, PhD); agricultural, food and nutritional science (M Ag, M Eng, M Sc, PhD); agroforestry (M Ag, M Sc, MF); ancient history (PhD); anthropology (MA, PhD); applied linguistics (Germanic, Romance, Slavic) (MA); applied mathematics (M Sc, PhD); applied music (M Mus); astrophysics (M Sc, PhD); biostatistics (M Sc); business administration (Exec MBA); chemical engineering (M Eng, M Sc, PhD); chemistry (M Sc, PhD); Chinese literature (MA); choral conducting (M Mus); classical archaeology (MA, PhD); classical literature (PhD); classics (MA); communications (M Eng, M Sc, PhD); composition (M Mus); computer engineering (M Eng, M Sc, PhD); computing science (M Sc, PhD); condensed matter (M Sc, PhD); conservation biology (M Sc, PhD); construction engineering and management (M Eng, M Sc, PhD); counseling psychology (M Ed, PhD); criminal justice (MA); demography (MA, PhD); design (MFA); directing (MFA); drama (MA); drawing (MFA); earth and atmospheric sciences (M Sc, MA, PhD); East Asian interdisciplinary studies (MA); economics (MA, PhD); economics and finance (MA); educational administration and leadership (M Ed, Ed D, PhD, Postgraduate Diploma); educational psychology (M Ed, PhD); electromagnetics (M Eng, M Sc, PhD); elementary education (M Ed, Ed D, PhD); engineering management (M Eng); English (MA, PhD); environmental and natural resource economics (PhD); environmental biology and ecology (M Sc, PhD); environmental engineering (M Eng, M Sc, PhD); environmental science (M Sc, PhD); ethnomusicology (MA); experimental phonetics (M Sc, PhD); family ecology and practice (M Sc, PhD); finance (PhD); First Nations education (M Ed, PhD); forest biology and management (M Sc, PhD); forest economics (M Ag, M Sc, PhD); French language, literatures and linguistics (PhD); French language, literatures, and linguistics (MA); geoenvironmental engineering (M Eng, M Sc, PhD); geophysics (M Sc, PhD); geotechnical engineering (M Sc); geotechnical engineering (M Eng, PhD); Germanic languages, literatures and linguistics (PhD); Germanic languages, literatures, and linguistics (MA); history (MA, PhD); history of art, design, and visual culture (MA); history of education (PhD); human resources/industrial relations (PhD); industrial design (M Des); instructional technology (M Ed); international and global education (M Ed, PhD); international business (MBA); Italian studies (MA); Japanese literature (MA); land reclamation and remediation (M Sc, PhD); leisure and sport management (MBA); library and information studies (MLIS); management science (PhD); marketing (PhD); materials engineering (M Eng, M Sc, PhD); mathematical finance (M Sc); mathematical physics (M Sc, PhD); mathematics (M Sc, PhD); mechanical engineering (M Eng, M Sc, PhD); medical physics (M Sc, PhD); microbiology and biotechnology (M Sc, PhD); mining engineering (M Eng, M Sc, PhD); molecular biology and genetics (M Sc, PhD); music (PhD); music theory (MA); musicology (MA); nanotechnology and microdevices (M Eng, M Sc, PhD); natural resources and energy (MBA); neurolinguistics (M Sc, PhD); occupational therapy (M Sc); organ (D Mus); organizational analysis (PhD); painting (MFA); petroleum engineering (M Eng, M Sc, PhD); pharmacology (M Sc, PhD); philosophy (MA, PhD); philosophy of education (PhD); physical therapy (M Sc); physiology and cell biology (M Sc, PhD); piano (D Mus); plant biology (M Sc, PhD); political science (MA, PhD); power/power electronics (M Eng, M Sc, PhD); printmaking (MFA); process control (M Eng, M Sc, PhD); protected areas and wildlands management (M Sc, PhD); psycholinguistics (M Sc, PhD); psychology (M Sc, MA, PhD); rural sociology (M Ag, M Sc); school counseling (M Ed); school psychology (M Ed, PhD); sculpture (MFA); secondary education (M Ed, Ed D, PhD); Slavic languages and literatures (Russian, Ukrainian) (MA, PhD); Slavic linguistics (Russian, Ukrainian) (MA, PhD); social and cultural education (M Ed, PhD); sociology (MA, PhD); sociology of education (PhD); soil science (M Ag, M Sc, PhD); Spanish and Latin American studies (MA, PhD); special education (M Ed, PhD); special education-deafness studies (M Ed); speech production and perception (M Sc, PhD); speech-language pathology (M Sc, MSLP); statistics (M Sc, PhD, Postgraduate Diploma); structural engineering (M Eng, M Sc, PhD); subatomic physics (M Sc, PhD); systematics and evolution (M Sc, PhD); systems (M Eng, M Sc, PhD); teaching English as a second language (M Ed); technology commercialization (MBA); textiles and clothing (M Sc, MA, PhD); Ukrainian folklore (MA, PhD); visual communication design (M Des); water and land resources (M Ag, M Sc, PhD); water resources (M Eng, M Sc, PhD); welding (M Eng); wildlife ecology and management (M Sc, PhD). *Application fee:* $0. *Dean,* Dr. M. T. Dale, 780-492-3499, Fax: 403-492-0692.

Centre for Health Promotion Studies Students: 20 full-time (17 women), 78 part-time (72 women). 77 applicants, 25% accepted. *Faculty:* 1 (woman) full-time, 15 part-time/adjunct (10 women). Expenses: Contact institution. *Financial support:* In 2001–02, 14 students received support, including 9 fellowships with partial tuition reimbursements available, 14 research assistantships; career-related internships or fieldwork and scholarships/grants also available. In 2001, 9 master's, 4 other advanced degrees awarded. *Degree program information:* Part-time programs available. Postbaccalaureate distance learning degree programs offered (minimal on-campus study). Offers health promotion studies (M Sc, Postgraduate Diploma). *Application deadline:* For fall admission, 3/31 (priority date). *Graduate Coordinator,* Dr. Helen M. Madill, 780-492-9437, Fax: 780-492-9579, E-mail: helen.madill@ualberta.ca.

Faculte Saint Jean Students: 4 full-time (2 women), 64 part-time (50 women). Average age 30. 25 applicants, 92% accepted. *Faculty:* 9 full-time (7 women). Expenses: Contact institution. *Financial support:* In 2001–02, 3 fellowships (averaging $9,000 per year), 1 research assistantship with tuition reimbursement were awarded. Teaching assistantships, scholarships/grants also available. In 2001, 9 degrees awarded. *Degree program information:* Part-time and evening/weekend programs available. Postbaccalaureate distance learning degree programs offered (minimal on-campus study). Offers education (M Ed). *Application deadline:* Applications are processed on a rolling basis. *Application fee:* $0. *Application Contact:* Lise Desbiens, Department Office, 403-465-8703, Fax: 403-465-8760, E-mail: ldesbien@gpu.srv.ualberta.ca. *Graduate Coordinator,* Dr. Yvette Mahe, 780-465-8770, Fax: 403-465-8760.

Faculty of Nursing Students: 33 full-time (all women), 89 part-time (84 women). 52 applicants, 79% accepted, 36 enrolled. *Faculty:* 48 full-time (47 women). Expenses: Contact institution. *Financial support:* In 2001–02, 10 fellowships with partial tuition reimbursements (averaging $14,989 per year), 38 research assistantships with partial tuition reimbursements (averaging $4,552 per year), 12 teaching assistantships with partial tuition reimbursements (averaging $2,920 per year) were awarded. Institutionally sponsored loans and research grants, tuition scholarships also available. In 2001, 10 master's, 5 doctorates awarded. *Degree program information:* Part-time programs available. Offers nursing (MN, PhD). *Application deadline:* For fall admission, 6/30 (priority date). Applications are processed on a rolling basis. *Application Contact:* Elaine Carswell, Administrative Assistant, 403-492-6251, Fax: 403-492-2551, E-mail: elaine.carswell@ualberta.ca. *Assistant Dean,* Dr. Joanne Olson, 780-492-4567, Fax: 403-492-2551.

Faculty of Pharmacy and Pharmaceutical Sciences Students: 28 full-time (7 women), 25 part-time (14 women), 14 international. Average age 30. 562 applicants, 2% accepted, 11 enrolled. Expenses: Contact institution. *Financial support:* In 2001–02, 13 students received support, including 1 fellowship, 6 teaching assistantships; tuition waivers (partial) also available. In 2001, 3 master's, 5 doctorates awarded. Offers pharmacy and pharmaceutical sciences (M Pharm, M Sc, PhD). *Application deadline:* For fall admission, 5/1. Applications are processed on a rolling basis. Electronic applications accepted. *Application Contact:* Dr. Edward E. Knaus, Director of Graduate Affairs, 780-492-5993, Fax: 780-492-1217. *Dean,* Dr. F. M. Pasutto, 780-492-0204.

Faculty of Physical Education and Recreation Students: 60 full-time (34 women), 55 part-time (28 women), 10 international. 69 applicants, 36% accepted. *Faculty:* 30 full-time (10 women). Expenses: Contact institution. *Financial support:* In 2001–02, 63 students received support, including 28 research assistantships, 35 teaching assistantships; career-related internships or fieldwork and scholarships/grants also available. Support available to part-time students. In 2001, 13 master's, 7 doctorates awarded. *Degree program information:* Part-time programs available. Offers physical education (M Sc); recreation and physical education (MA, PhD). *Application deadline:* For fall admission, 1/1 (priority date). Applications are processed on a rolling basis. *Application Contact:* Anne Jordan, Department Office, 403-492-3198, Fax: 403-492-2364, E-mail: ajordan@per.ualberta.ca. *Assistant Dean,* Dr. D. D. Shogan, 780-492-3198, Fax: 403-492-2364.

Faculty of Rehabilitation Medicine Students: 12 full-time (7 women), 1 (woman) part-time. Average age 32. 4 applicants, 75% accepted. *Faculty:* 21 full-time (13 women), 3 part-time/adjunct (0 women). Expenses: Contact institution. *Financial support:* In 2001–02, 1 fellowship (averaging $13,000 per year), 7 research assistantships (averaging $2,721 per year), 1 teaching assistantship (averaging $2,535 per year) were awarded. Institutionally sponsored loans, scholarships/grants, and traineeships also available. Financial award application deadline: 1/14. In 2001, 2 degrees awarded. Offers rehabilitation medicine (PhD). *Application deadline:* For fall admission, 5/15; for winter admission, 10/15. Applications are processed on a rolling basis. *Application fee:* $0. *Application Contact:* Kathleen Dean, Administrative Assistant, Graduate Studies, 780-492-1595, Fax: 780-492-1626, E-mail: kathleen.dean@ualberta.ca. *Associate Dean,* Dr. P. Hagler, 780-492-1595, Fax: 780-492-1626, E-mail: paul.hagler@ualberta.ca.

Faculty of Law *Degree program information:* Part-time programs available. Offers law (LL B, LL M, Postgraduate Diploma). Electronic applications accepted.

Faculty of Medicine and Dentistry Students: 516 full-time (252 women), 2 part-time (both women). 1,100 applicants, 11% accepted, 125 enrolled. *Faculty:* 375 full-time, 320 part-time/adjunct. Expenses: Contact institution. *Financial support:* Fellowships, research assistantships, teaching assistantships, career-related internships or fieldwork, institutionally sponsored loans, scholarships/grants, tuition waivers (full and partial), and tuition bursaries available. Support available to part-time students. In 2001, 103 degrees awarded. Offers dental hygiene (Certificate); dental sciences (M Sc, PhD); dentistry (DDS); medical sciences (PhD); medicine and dentistry (DDS, M Sc, MPH, PhD, Certificate, Postgraduate Diploma); oral biology (M Sc); orthodontics (M Sc, PhD). *Application deadline:* For fall admission, 11/1. *Application fee:* $60. Electronic applications accepted. *Application Contact:* Marlene Healey, Administrator of Admissions, 780-492-9525, Fax: 780-492-9531, E-mail: marlene.healey@ualberta.ca. *Dean,* Dr. D. Lorne J. Tyrrell, 780-492-9728, Fax: 780-492-7303.

Graduate Programs in Medicine Students: 371 full-time (173 women), 95 part-time (61 women). Expenses: Contact institution. *Financial support:* Fellowships, research assistantships, teaching assistantships, career-related internships or fieldwork, institutionally sponsored loans, scholarships/grants, tuition waivers (full and partial), and tuition bursaries available. Support available to part-time students. In 2001, 40 master's, 29 doctorates awarded. *Degree program information:* Part-time programs available. Offers anesthesiology and pain medicine (M Sc); biochemistry (M Sc, PhD); biomedical engineering (M Sc); cell biology (M Sc, PhD); clinical epidemiology (M Sc); environmental health (M Sc, PhD); epidemiology (M Sc, PhD); health policy and management (MPH, PhD); health policy research (MPH); health services administration (Postgraduate Diploma); medical genetics (M Sc, PhD); medical microbiology and immunology (M Sc, PhD); medical sciences (M Sc, PhD); medical sciences/ophthalmology (M Sc, PhD); medicine (M Sc); neuroscience (M Sc, PhD); obstetrics and gynecology (M Sc); occupational health (M Sc); pediatrics (M Sc, PhD); physiology (M Sc, PhD); population health (M Sc, PhD); psychiatry (M Sc, PhD); radiology and diagnostic imaging (M Sc); surgery (M Sc, PhD). *Application deadline:* Applications are processed on a rolling basis. *Application fee:* $0. *Application Contact:* Janis Davis, Administrative Secretary, 780-492-9721, Fax: 780-492-7303, E-mail: janis.davis@ualberta.ca. *Research Administration Officer,* Colleen Iwanicka, 780-492-9720, Fax: 780-492-7303, E-mail: colleen.iwanicka@ualberta.ca.

THE UNIVERSITY OF ARIZONA, Tucson, AZ 85721

General Information State-supported, coed, university. CGS member. *Enrollment:* 4,674 full-time matriculated graduate/professional students (2,233 women), 3,383 part-time matriculated graduate/professional students (1,865 women). *Enrollment by degree level:* 897 first professional, 3,072 master's, 3,053 doctoral. *Graduate faculty:* 1,392 full-time (362 women), 103 part-time/adjunct (32 women). Tuition, state resident: full-time $2,490; part-time $436 per unit. Tuition, nonresident: full-time $10,300; part-time $436 per unit. Full-time tuition and fees vary according to degree level and program. *Graduate housing:* Room and/or apartments available on a first-come, first-served basis to single students; on-campus housing not available to married students. Housing application deadline: 5/1. *Student services:* Campus employment opportunities, campus safety program, career counseling, child daycare facilities, disabled student services, exercise/wellness program, free psychological counseling, grant writing training, international student services, low-cost health insurance, multicultural affairs office, teacher training, writing training. *Library facilities:* University of Arizona Main Library plus 5 others. *Online resources:* library catalog, web page, access to other libraries' catalogs. *Collection:* 4.7 million titles, 26,908 serial subscriptions, 49,171 audiovisual materials. *Research affiliation:* Argonne National Laboratory (physics), Kitt Peak National Observatory (astronomy), National Center for Atmospheric Research (atmospheric physics), Smithsonian Astrophysical Observatory (astronomy), Research Corporation (astronomy).

Computer facilities: 1,750 computers available on campus for general student use. A campuswide network can be accessed from student residence rooms and from off campus. Internet access is available. *Web address:* http://www.arizona.edu/.

General Application Contact: Graduate Admissions Office, 520-621-3132, Fax: 520-621-7112, E-mail: gradadm@grad.arizona.edu.

GRADUATE UNITS

College of Medicine *Degree program information:* Part-time programs available. Offers biochemistry (MS, PhD); cell biology and anatomy (PhD); medicine (MD, MPH, MS, PhD); microbiology and immunology (MS, PhD); public health (MPH). MD program open only to state residents.

Graduate College Students: 4,290 full-time (1,905 women), 2,032 part-time (1,149 women); includes 785 minority (101 African Americans, 184 Asian Americans or Pacific Islanders, 406 Hispanic Americans, 94 Native Americans), 1,240 international. Average age 32. 7,497 applicants, 36% accepted. *Faculty:* 1,368 full-time (325 women), 75 part-time/adjunct (16 women). Expenses: Contact institution. *Financial support:* Fellowships, research assistantships, teaching assistantships, career-related internships or fieldwork, Federal Work-Study, institutionally sponsored loans, scholarships/grants, and tuition waivers (full and partial) available. Support available to part-time students. In 2001, 374 doctorates, 6 other advanced degrees awarded. *Degree program information:* Part-time and evening/weekend programs available. Offers American Indian studies (MA); applied mathematics (MS, PMS, PhD); arid land resource sciences (PhD); cancer biology (PhD); comparative cultural and literary studies (MA, PhD); dietetics (MS); epidemiology (MS, PhD); epidermalogical nutrition/public health nutrition (PhD); genetics (MS, PhD); gerontological studies (MS, Certificate); human/clinical nutrition (PhD); insect science (PhD); mathematical sciences (PMS); molecular nutrition (PhD); neuroscience (PhD); nutritional biochemistry (MS, PhD); nutritional sciences (PhD); pharmacology and toxicology (PhD); physiological sciences (PhD); planning (MS); public health (MPH); second language acquisition and teaching (PhD). *Application fee:* $35. *Application Contact:* General Information, 520-621-3471, Fax: 520-621-7112, E-mail: gradadm@grad.arizona.edu. *Dean,* Gary Pivo.

College of Agriculture and Life Sciences *Degree program information:* Part-time programs available. Offers agricultural and biosystems engineering (MS, PhD); agricultural and resource economics (MS); agricultural education (M Ag Ed, MS); agriculture and life sciences (M Ag Ed, MHE Ed, ML Arch, MS, PhD); animal sciences (MS, PhD); dietetics (MS); entomology (MS, PhD); family and consumer sciences (MS); family studies and human development (PhD); forest-watershed management (MS, PhD); nutritional sciences (MS); pathobiology (MS, PhD); plant pathology (MS, PhD); plant sciences (MS, PhD); range management (MS, PhD); renewable natural resources (ML Arch, MS, PhD); retailing and consumer sciences (MS, PhD); soil, water and environmental science (MS, PhD); wildlife and fisheries science (MS, PhD).

College of Architecture, Planning and Landscape Architecture Students: 113 full-time (54 women), 33 part-time (18 women); includes 14 minority (3 Asian Americans or Pacific Islanders, 11 Hispanic Americans), 46 international. Average age 33. 159 applicants, 62% accepted, 65 enrolled. *Faculty:* 23. Expenses: Contact institution. *Financial support:* Fellowships, research assistantships, teaching assistantships, career-related internships or fieldwork, Federal Work-Study, tuition waivers (full), and unspecified assistantships available. In 2001, 23 degrees awarded. *Degree program information:* Part-time programs available. Offers architecture (M Arch); landscape architecture (ML Arch); planning (MS). *Application deadline:* Applications are processed on a rolling basis. *Application fee:* $45. *Application Contact:* Susan K.E. Moody, Assistant Dean, 520-621-6751, Fax: 520-621-8700, E-mail: skemoody@u.arizona.edu. *Dean,* Dr. Richard Eribes, 520-621-6751.

College of Business and Public Administration *Degree program information:* Part-time and evening/weekend programs available. Offers accounting (M Ac); business administration (MBA); business and public administration (M Ac, MA, MBA, MPA, MS, PhD); economics (MA, PhD); finance (MS); management (PhD); management and policy (MS); management information systems (MS); marketing (MS, PhD); public administration (MPA); public administration and policy (PhD).

College of Education Students: 567 full-time (429 women), 289 part-time (195 women); includes 218 minority (33 African Americans, 27 Asian Americans or Pacific Islanders, 127 Hispanic Americans, 31 Native Americans), 74 international. Average age 38. 410 applicants, 68% accepted, 181 enrolled. *Faculty:* 65 full-time (28 women), 35 part-time/adjunct (25 women). Expenses: Contact institution. *Financial support:* Fellowships, research assistantships, teaching assistantships, career-related internships or fieldwork, Federal Work-Study, institutionally sponsored loans, scholarships/grants, and tuition waivers (full and partial) available. In 2001, 195 master's, 35 doctorates, 4 other advanced degrees awarded. *Degree program information:* Part-time programs available. Offers bilingual education (M Ed); bilingual/multicultural education (MA); education (M Ed, MA, MS, MT, Ed D, PhD, Ed S); educational leadership (Ed D, Ed S); educational psychology (MA, PhD); elementary education (MT, Ed D); higher education (MA, PhD); language, reading and culture (MA, Ed D, PhD, Ed S); school counseling (M Ed); secondary education (MT, Ed D, Ed S); special education, rehabilitation and school psychology (M Ed, MA, MS, Ed D, PhD, Ed S); teaching and teacher education (M Ed, MA, Ed D, PhD). *Application deadline:* Applications are processed on a rolling basis. *Application fee:* $45. *Dean,* Dr. John Taylor, 520-621-1461, Fax: 520-621-9271.

College of Engineering and Mines Students: 631 full-time (121 women), 167 part-time (37 women); includes 67 minority (5 African Americans, 31 Asian Americans or Pacific Islanders, 24 Hispanic Americans, 7 Native Americans), 475 international. Average age 29. 1,412 applicants, 49% accepted, 227 enrolled. *Faculty:* 243. Expenses: Contact institution. *Financial support:* Fellowships, research assistantships, teaching assistantships, institutionally sponsored loans and scholarships/grants available. In 2001, 123 master's, 44 doctorates awarded. *Degree program information:* Part-time programs available. Offers aerospace engineering (MS, PhD); chemical engineering (MS, PhD); civil engineering (MS, PhD); electrical and computer engineering (M Eng, MS, PhD); engineering and mines (M Eng, MS, PhD); engineering mechanics (MS, PhD); environmental engineering (MS, PhD); geological and geophysical engineering (MS, PhD); hydrology (MS, PhD); industrial engineering (MS); materials science and engineering (MS, PhD); mechanical engineering (MS, PhD); mining engineering (PhD); nuclear engineering (MS, PhD); reliability and quality engineering (MS); systems and industrial engineering (PhD); systems engineering (MS); water resource administration (MS, PhD). *Application fee:* $35. *Dean,* Dr. Thomas W. Peterson, 520-621-6594, Fax: 520-621-2232, E-mail: peterson@erc.arizona.edu.

College of Fine Arts *Degree program information:* Part-time programs available. Offers art (studio) (MFA); art education (MA); art history (MA); composition (MM, A Mus D); conducting (MM, A Mus D); fine arts (MA, MFA, MM, A Mus D, PhD); history and theory of art (PhD); media arts (MA); music education (MM, PhD); music theory (MM, PhD); musicology (MM); performance (MM, A Mus D); theatre arts (MA, MFA).

College of Humanities Students: 299 full-time (191 women), 54 part-time (31 women); includes 53 minority (7 African Americans, 7 Asian Americans or Pacific Islanders, 36 Hispanic Americans, 3 Native Americans), 66 international. Average age 33. 483 applicants, 35% accepted, 89 enrolled. *Faculty:* 168. Expenses: Contact institution. *Financial support:* Fellowships, research assistantships, teaching assistantships, career-related internships or fieldwork, Federal Work-Study, institutionally sponsored loans, scholarships/grants, and tuition waivers (full and partial) available. Support available to part-time students. In 2001, 88 master's, 16 doctorates awarded. *Degree program information:* Part-time programs available. Offers classics (MA); creative writing (MFA); East Asian studies (MA, PhD); English (MA, PhD); English language/linguistics (MA); French (M Ed, MA, PhD); German (MA); humanities (M Ed, MA, MFA, PhD); rhetoric, composition and teaching of English (PhD); Russian (M Ed, MA); Spanish (M Ed, MA, PhD). *Application fee:* $35. *Dean,* Dr. Charles M. Tatum, 520-621-1044, Fax: 520-621-5594.

College of Nursing Students: 70 full-time (61 women), 39 part-time (37 women); includes 17 minority (1 African American, 3 Asian Americans or Pacific Islanders, 13 Hispanic Americans), 9 international. Average age 43. 48 applicants, 88% accepted, 31 enrolled. *Faculty:* 28 full-time (all women). Expenses: Contact institution. *Financial support:* In 2001–02, 44 students received support, including 13 fellowships with full tuition reimbursements available (averaging $4,317 per year), 23 research assistantships with partial tuition reimbursements available (averaging $6,761 per year); teaching assistantships, career-related internships or fieldwork, institutionally sponsored loans, scholarships/grants, traineeships, and tuition waivers (full) also available. Financial award application deadline: 7/1. In 2001, 19 master's, 7 doctorates awarded. *Degree program information:* Part-time programs available. Offers nursing (MS, PhD). *Application deadline:* For fall admission, 4/1. Applications are processed on a rolling basis. *Application fee:* $45. *Application Contact:* Vickie L. Radoye, Assistant Dean, Student Affairs, 520-626-3808, Fax: 520-626-6424, E-mail:

The University of Arizona (continued)

vradoye@nursing.arizona.edu. *Dean,* Dr. Marjorie A. Isenberg, 520-626-6152, E-mail: misenberg@nursing.arizona.edu.

College of Pharmacy *Degree program information:* Part-time programs available. Offers pharmaceutical sciences (MS, PhD); pharmacology and toxicology (MS, PhD); pharmacy (Pharm D, MS, PhD).

College of Science Students: 622 full-time (256 women), 79 part-time (26 women); includes 47 minority (7 African Americans, 17 Asian Americans or Pacific Islanders, 19 Hispanic Americans, 4 Native Americans), 242 international. Average age 28. 1,227 applicants, 28% accepted, 207 enrolled. *Faculty:* 372. Expenses: Contact institution. *Financial support:* Fellowships, research assistantships, teaching assistantships, career-related internships or fieldwork, Federal Work-Study, institutionally sponsored loans, scholarships/grants, and tuition waivers (full and partial) available. Support available to part-time students. In 2001, 100 master's, 49 doctorates awarded. *Degree program information:* Part-time programs available. Offers applied and industrial physics (MS); applied biosciences (MS); astronomy (MS, PhD); atmospheric sciences (MS, PhD); chemistry (MA, MS, PhD); computer science (MS, PhD); ecology and evolutionary biology (MS, PhD); geosciences (MS, PhD); mathematical sciences (MS); mathematics (M Ed, MA, MS, PhD); molecular and cellular biology (MS, PhD); physics (M Ed, MS, PhD); planetary sciences/lunar and planetary laboratory (MS, PhD); science (M Ed, MA, MS, PhD); speech and hearing sciences (MS, PhD); statistics (MS, PhD). *Application fee:* $35. *Application Contact:* General Information, 520-621-3471, Fax: 520-621-7112. *Dean,* Dr. Joaquin Ruiz.

College of Social and Behavioral Sciences *Degree program information:* Part-time and evening/weekend programs available. Offers anthropology (MA, PhD); communication (MA, PhD); geography (MA, PhD); history (M Ed, MA, PhD); journalism (MA); Latin American studies (MA); library science (MA, PhD); linguistics (MA, PhD); Near Eastern studies (MA, PhD); philosophy (MA, PhD); political science (MA, PhD); psychology (PhD); social and behavioral sciences (M Ed, MA, PhD); sociology (MA, PhD); women's studies (MA).

James E. Rogers College of Law Students: 503 full-time (257 women). Average age 26. 1,870 applicants, 23% accepted, 162 enrolled. *Faculty:* 30 full-time (13 women), 55 part-time/adjunct (23 women). Expenses: Contact institution. *Financial support:* In 2001–02, 357 students received support, including fellowships (averaging $3,250 per year); career-related internships or fieldwork, Federal Work-Study, institutionally sponsored loans, scholarships/grants, and tuition waivers (full and partial) also available. Financial award application deadline: 3/1; financial award applicants required to submit FAFSA. In 2001, 152 first professional degrees, 14 master's awarded. Offers international indigenous peoples' rights and policy (LL M); international trade law (LL M); law (JD). *Application deadline:* For fall admission, 2/15. Applications are processed on a rolling basis. *Application fee:* $50. Electronic applications accepted. *Application Contact:* Terry Sue Holpert, Assistant Dean for Admissions, 520-621-3477, Fax: 520-621-9140, E-mail: holpert@law.arizona.edu. *Dean,* Toni M. Massaro, 520-621-1498, Fax: 520-621-9140, E-mail: massaro@law.arizona.edu.

Optical Sciences Center Students: 146 full-time (21 women), 30 part-time (8 women); includes 16 minority (2 African Americans, 7 Asian Americans or Pacific Islanders, 7 Hispanic Americans), 48 international. Average age 30. 182 applicants, 31% accepted, 53 enrolled. *Faculty:* 52. Expenses: Contact institution. *Financial support:* Fellowships, research assistantships, teaching assistantships, scholarships/grants available. In 2001, 31 master's, 18 doctorates awarded. *Degree program information:* Part-time programs available. Offers optical sciences (MS, PhD). *Application deadline:* For fall admission, 3/1. Applications are processed on a rolling basis. *Application fee:* $45. *Application Contact:* Dr. Richard L. Shoemaker, Associate Director, Academic Affairs, 520-621-2825, Fax: 520-621-6778, E-mail: shoemaker@optics.arizona.edu. *Director,* Dr. James Wyant, 520-621-6997, Fax: 520-621-9613, E-mail: lbrunette@optics.arizona.edu.

UNIVERSITY OF ARKANSAS, Fayetteville, AR 72701-1201

General Information State-supported, coed, university. CGS member. *Enrollment:* 2,757 full-time matriculated graduate/professional students (1,319 women). *Enrollment by degree level:* 373 first professional, 1,669 master's, 706 doctoral, 9 other advanced degrees. *Graduate faculty:* 659 full-time (163 women), 5 part-time/adjunct (1 woman). Tuition, state resident: full-time $3,553; part-time $197 per credit. Tuition, nonresident: full-time $8,411; part-time $467 per credit. *Required fees:* $42 per credit. Tuition and fees vary according to course load and program. *Graduate housing:* Rooms and/or apartments available on a first-come, first-served basis to single and married students. Typical cost: $3,554 (including board) for single students; $4,032 (including board) for married students. Room and board charges vary according to board plan, campus/location and housing facility selected. *Student services:* Campus employment opportunities, campus safety program, career counseling, disabled student services, exercise/wellness program, free psychological counseling, international student services, low-cost health insurance, multicultural affairs office, teacher training, writing training. *Library facilities:* David W. Mullins Library plus 5 others. *Online resources:* library catalog, web page, access to other libraries' catalogs. *Collection:* 643,468 titles, 15,431 serial subscriptions, 26,673 audiovisual materials. *Research affiliation:* Oak Ridge Associated Universities, Southern Regional Education Board Uncommon Facilities Program, Southeastern Universities Research Association, Southern Regional Education Board, National Minority Graduate Feeder Project, Science Coalition.

Computer facilities: 1,415 computers available on campus for general student use. A campuswide network can be accessed from student residence rooms and from off campus. Internet access is available. *Web address:* http://www.uark.edu/.

General Application Contact: Regina Jeweicka, Information Contact, 479-575-6629, Fax: 479-575-5908, E-mail: gradinfo@cavern.uark.edu.

GRADUATE UNITS

Graduate School Students: 1,481 full-time (720 women), 885 part-time (427 women); includes 280 minority (156 African Americans, 40 Asian Americans or Pacific Islanders, 38 Hispanic Americans, 46 Native Americans), 489 international. 1,282 applicants, 84% accepted. Expenses: Contact institution. *Financial support:* In 2001–02, 160 fellowships, 361 research assistantships, 546 teaching assistantships with full tuition reimbursements were awarded. Career-related internships or fieldwork, Federal Work-Study, institutionally sponsored loans, scholarships/grants, traineeships, and unspecified assistantships also available. Support available to part-time students. Financial award application deadline: 4/1; financial award applicants required to submit FAFSA. In 2001, 742 master's, 86 doctorates, 8 other advanced degrees awarded. *Degree program information:* Part-time programs available. Postbaccalaureate distance learning degree programs offered (no on-campus study). Offers cell and molecular biology (MS, PhD); microelectronics and photonics (MS, PhD); public policy (PhD). *Application fee:* $40 ($50 for international students). *Application Contact:* Sandy Bramlet, Administrative Assistant, 479-575-5903, Fax: 501-575-5908, E-mail: bramlet@uark.edu. *Associate Dean,* Dr. Patricia R. Koski, 479-575-4401, E-mail: gradinfo@cavern.uark.edu.

College of Education and Health Professions Students: 355 full-time (267 women), 325 part-time (224 women); includes 106 minority (75 African Americans, 4 Asian Americans or Pacific Islanders, 14 Hispanic Americans, 13 Native Americans), 37 international. 247 applicants, 98% accepted. Expenses: Contact institution. *Financial support:* In 2001–02, 2 fellowships, 17 research assistantships, 72 teaching assistantships were awarded. Career-related internships or fieldwork and Federal Work-Study also available. Support available to part-time students. Financial award application deadline: 4/1; financial award applicants required to submit FAFSA. In 2001, 266 master's, 30 doctorates, 8 other advanced degrees awarded. Offers adult education (M Ed, Ed D, Ed S); childhood education (MAT); communication disorders (MS); counseling education (MS, PhD, Ed S); curriculum and instruction (PhD); education (M Ed, Ed D, Ed S); education and health professions (M Ed, MAT, MS, Ed D, PhD, Ed S); educational administration (M Ed, Ed D, Ed S); educational technology (M Ed); elementary education (M Ed, Ed S); health science (MS, PhD); higher education (M Ed, Ed D, Ed S); kinesiology (MS, PhD); middle-level education (MAT); physical education (M Ed, MAT); recreation (M Ed, Ed D); rehabilitation (MS, PhD); secondary education (M Ed, MAT, Ed S); special education (M Ed, MAT); vocational education (M Ed, MAT, Ed D, Ed S). *Application fee:* $40 ($50 for international students). *Associate Dean,* M. Reed Greenwood, 479-575-3208.

College of Engineering Students: 182 full-time (38 women), 144 part-time (32 women); includes 42 minority (23 African Americans, 11 Asian Americans or Pacific Islanders, 5 Hispanic Americans, 3 Native Americans), 149 international. 254 applicants, 85% accepted. Expenses: Contact institution. *Financial support:* In 2001–02, 97 research assistantships, 74 teaching assistantships were awarded. Fellowships, career-related internships or fieldwork and Federal Work-Study also available. Support available to part-time students. Financial award application deadline: 4/1; financial award applicants required to submit FAFSA. In 2001, 120 master's, 7 doctorates awarded. Offers biological and agricultural engineering (MSBAE, MSE, PhD); chemical engineering (MS Ch E, MSE, PhD); civil engineering (MSCE, MSE, PhD); computer systems engineering (MSCSE, MSE, PhD); electrical engineering (MSEE, PhD); engineering (MS, MS Ch E, MS En E, MS Tc E, MSBAE, MSCE, MSCSE, MSE, MSEE, MSIE, MSME, MSOR, MSTE, PhD); environmental engineering (MS En E, MSE); industrial engineering (MSE, MSIE, PhD); mechanical engineering (MSE, MSME, PhD); operations management (MS); operations research (MSE, MSOR); telecommunications engineering (MS Tc E); transportation engineering (MSE, MSTE). *Application fee:* $40 ($50 for international students). *Dean,* Dr. Otto Loewer, 479-575-3054.

Dale Bumpers College of Agricultural, Food and Life Sciences Students: 176 full-time (69 women), 120 part-time (50 women); includes 122 minority (19 African Americans, 34 Asian Americans or Pacific Islanders, 2 Hispanic Americans, 67 Native Americans), 85 international. 145 applicants, 75% accepted. Expenses: Contact institution. *Financial support:* In 2001–02, 24 fellowships, 163 research assistantships, 21 teaching assistantships were awarded. Career-related internships or fieldwork, Federal Work-Study, scholarships/grants, and unspecified assistantships also available. Support available to part-time students. Financial award application deadline: 4/1; financial award applicants required to submit FAFSA. In 2001, 67 master's, 12 doctorates awarded. Offers agricultural and extension education (MS); agricultural economics (MS); agricultural education (MAT); agricultural, food and life sciences (MAT, MS, PhD); agronomy (MS, PhD); animal science (MS, PhD); entomology (MS, PhD); food science (MS, PhD); general agriculture (MS); horticulture (MS); human environmental sciences (MS); plant pathology (MS); plant science (PhD); poultry science (MS, PhD). *Application fee:* $40 ($50 for international students). *Dean,* Dr. Greg Weideman, 479-575-2252.

J. William Fulbright College of Arts and Sciences Students: 551 full-time (265 women), 87 part-time (72 women); includes 53 minority (16 African Americans, 10 Asian Americans or Pacific Islanders, 13 Hispanic Americans, 14 Native Americans), 133 international. 398 applicants, 82% accepted. Expenses: Contact institution. *Financial support:* In 2001–02, 64 fellowships, 101 research assistantships, 398 teaching assistantships with full tuition reimbursements were awarded. Career-related internships or fieldwork, Federal Work-Study, institutionally sponsored loans, and traineeships also available. Support available to part-time students. Financial award application deadline: 4/1; financial award applicants required to submit FAFSA. In 2001, 160 master's, 26 doctorates awarded. Offers anthropology (MA); applied physics (MS); art (MFA); arts and sciences (MA, MFA, MM, MPA, MS, PhD); biology (MA, MS, PhD); chemistry (MS, PhD); communication (MA); comparative literature (MA, PhD); computer science (MS, PhD); creative writing (MFA); drama (MA, MFA); English (MA, PhD); environmental dynamics (PhD); French (MA); geography (MA); geology (MS); German (MA); history (MA, PhD); journalism (MA); mathematics (MS, PhD); music (MM); philosophy (MA, PhD); physics (MA, MS, PhD); political science (MA); psychology (MA, PhD); public administration (MPA); secondary mathematics (MA); sociology (MA); Spanish (MA); statistics (MS); translation (MFA). *Application fee:* $40 ($50 for international students). *Dean,* Dr. Randall Woods, 479-575-4801.

Sam M. Walton College of Business Administration Students: 157 full-time (59 women), 87 part-time (38 women); includes 27 minority (12 African Americans, 8 Asian Americans or Pacific Islanders, 2 Hispanic Americans, 5 Native Americans), 56 international. 130 applicants, 85% accepted. Expenses: Contact institution. *Financial support:* In 2001–02, 9 fellowships were awarded; research assistantships, teaching assistantships, career-related internships or fieldwork and Federal Work-Study also available. Support available to part-time students. Financial award application deadline: 4/1; financial award applicants required to submit FAFSA. In 2001, 91 master's, 11 doctorates awarded. Offers accounting (M Acc); business administration (M Acc, MA, MBA, MIS, MTLM, PhD); economics (MA, PhD); information systems (MIS); transportation and logistics management (MTLM). *Application fee:* $40 ($50 for international students). *Dean,* Dr. Doyle Williams, 479-575-5949.

School of Law Students: 373 full-time (164 women); includes 62 minority (29 African Americans, 10 Asian Americans or Pacific Islanders, 8 Hispanic Americans, 15 Native Americans), 4 international. 591 applicants, 54% accepted. *Faculty:* 34 full-time (13 women), 15 part-time/adjunct (2 women). Expenses: Contact institution. *Financial support:* In 2001–02, 105 students received support, including 11 fellowships (averaging $4,680 per year), 7 research assistantships with full tuition reimbursements available (averaging $15,358 per year); career-related internships or fieldwork, Federal Work-Study, and scholarships/grants also available. Support available to part-time students. Financial award application deadline: 4/1; financial award applicants required to submit FAFSA. In 2001, 106 first professional degrees, 5 master's awarded. Offers agricultural law (LL M); law (JD). *Application deadline:* For fall admission, 4/1. Applications are processed on a rolling basis. *Application fee:* $0. *Application Contact:* James K. Miller, Associate Dean for Students, 479-575-3102. *Dean,* Robert Moberly, 479-575-5601.

UNIVERSITY OF ARKANSAS AT LITTLE ROCK, Little Rock, AR 72204-1099

General Information State-supported, coed, university. CGS member. *Enrollment:* 881 full-time matriculated graduate/professional students (513 women), 1,253 part-time matriculated graduate/professional students (915 women). *Enrollment by degree level:* 376 first professional, 1,288 master's, 214 doctoral, 256 other advanced degrees. *Graduate faculty:* 345 full-time (196 women). Tuition, state resident: full-time $3,006; part-time $107 per credit. Tuition, nonresident: full-time $6,012; part-time $357 per credit. *Required fees:* $22 per credit. Tuition and fees vary according to program. *Graduate housing:* Room and/or apartments available on a first-come, first-served basis to single students; on-campus housing not available to married students. *Student services:* Campus employment opportunities, campus safety program, career counseling, disabled student services, free psychological counseling, international student services, low-cost health insurance, writing training. *Library facilities:* Ottenheimer Library plus 1 other. *Online resources:* library catalog, access to other libraries' catalogs. *Collection:* 3,998 serial subscriptions.

Computer facilities: 500 computers available on campus for general student use. A campuswide network can be accessed from off campus. Internet access is available. *Web address:* http://www.ualr.edu/.

General Application Contact: Dr. Richard Hanson, Dean of the Graduate School, 501-569-3206, Fax: 501-569-3039, E-mail: rhhanson@ualr.edu.

GRADUATE UNITS

Graduate School *Degree program information:* Part-time and evening/weekend programs available. Postbaccalaureate distance learning degree programs offered. Electronic applications accepted.

College of Arts, Humanities, and Social Science *Degree program information:* Part-time and evening/weekend programs available. Offers applied psychology (MAP); art education (MA); art history (MA); arts, humanities, and social science (MA, MALS, MAP); expository writing (MA); liberal studies (MALS); public history (MA); studio art (MA); technical writing (MA).

College of Business Administration *Degree program information:* Part-time and evening/weekend programs available. Offers business administration (MBA).

College of Education *Degree program information:* Part-time and evening/weekend programs available. Offers adult education (M Ed); counselor education (M Ed); early childhood education (M Ed, Ed S); early childhood special education (M Ed); education (M Ed, MA, Ed D, Ed S); education of hearing impaired children (M Ed); educational administration (M Ed, Ed D, Ed S); educational administration and supervision (M Ed,

Ed D, Ed S); higher education administration (Ed D); instructional resources (M Ed); middle childhood education (M Ed, Ed S); reading (M Ed, Ed S); rehabilitation for the blind (MA); school counseling (M Ed); secondary education (M Ed); special education (M Ed); teaching of the mildly disabled student (M Ed); teaching persons with severe disabilities (M Ed); teaching the gifted and talented (M Ed); teaching the visually impaired child (M Ed).

College of Information Science and Systems Engineering *Degree program information:* Part-time and evening/weekend programs available. Offers computer science (MS); information science and systems engineering (MA, MS, PhD); instrumental sciences (MS, PhD).

College of Professional Studies *Degree program information:* Part-time and evening/weekend programs available. Offers applied gerontology (CG); clinical social work (MSW); criminal justice (MA); gerontology (MA); health services administration (MHSA); interpersonal communications (MA); journalism (MA); organizational communications (MA); professional studies (MA, MHSA, MPA, MSW, CG); public administration (MPA); social program administration (MSW); social work (MA, MSW, CG).

College of Science and Mathematics Offers applied mathematics (MS); chemistry (MA, MS); science and mathematics (MA, MS).

William H. Bowen School of Law Students: 234 full-time (113 women), 141 part-time (59 women); includes 35 minority (21 African Americans, 3 Asian Americans or Pacific Islanders, 9 Hispanic Americans, 2 Native Americans), 4 international. Average age 27. 430 applicants, 59% accepted, 135 enrolled. *Faculty:* 28 full-time (12 women), 24 part-time/adjunct (8 women). Expenses: Contact institution. *Financial support:* In 2001–02, 296 students received support, including 25 research assistantships (averaging $1,250 per year); career-related internships or fieldwork, Federal Work-Study, scholarships/grants, and tuition waivers (partial) also available. Support available to part-time students. Financial award application deadline: 3/1; financial award applicants required to submit FAFSA. In 2001, 127 degrees awarded. *Degree program information:* Part-time and evening/weekend programs available. Offers law (JD). *Application deadline:* For fall admission, 5/1. Applications are processed on a rolling basis. *Application fee:* $40. *Application Contact:* Jean M. Probasco, Director of Admissions and Registrar, 501-324-9939, Fax: 501-324-9433, E-mail: jmprobasco@ualr.edu. *Dean,* Charles W. Goldner, 501-324-9434, Fax: 501-324-9433, E-mail: cwgoldner@ualr.edu.

UNIVERSITY OF ARKANSAS AT MONTICELLO, Monticello, AR 71656

General Information State-supported, coed, comprehensive institution. *Graduate housing:* Rooms and/or apartments guaranteed to single students and available on a first-come, first-served basis to married students. Housing application deadline: 8/15.

GRADUATE UNITS

School of Education *Degree program information:* Part-time and evening/weekend programs available. Offers elementary education (M Ed); secondary education (M Ed).

School of Forest Resources *Degree program information:* Part-time programs available. Offers forest resources (MS).

UNIVERSITY OF ARKANSAS AT PINE BLUFF, Pine Bluff, AR 71601-2799

General Information State-supported, coed, comprehensive institution. *Graduate housing:* Rooms and/or apartments available to single and married students. Housing application deadline: 8/1.

GRADUATE UNITS

Program in Education *Degree program information:* Part-time and evening/weekend programs available. Offers elementary education (M Ed); secondary education (M Ed).

UNIVERSITY OF ARKANSAS FOR MEDICAL SCIENCES, Little Rock, AR 72205-7199

General Information State-supported, coed, upper-level institution. *Enrollment:* 1,240 matriculated graduate/professional students (650 women). *Graduate faculty:* 146 full-time (23 women), 27 part-time/adjunct (4 women). Tuition, state resident: part-time $1,860 per semester. Tuition, nonresident: part-time $4,000 per semester. Tuition and fees vary according to program. *Graduate housing:* Rooms and/or apartments available to single and married students. *Student services:* Campus employment opportunities, campus safety program, child daycare facilities, low-cost health insurance. *Library facilities:* Medical Sciences Library. *Online resources:* library catalog, web page. *Collection:* 183,975 titles, 1,567 serial subscriptions. *Research affiliation:* National Center for Toxicological Research, Veterans Administration Hospital, Oak Ridge Associated Universities, Arkansas Children's Hospital.

Computer facilities: A campuswide network can be accessed from student residence rooms and from off campus. Internet access is available. *Web address:* http://www.uams.edu/.

General Application Contact: Paul Carter, Assistant to the Vice Chancellor for Academic Affairs, 501-686-5454, Fax: 501-686-5661, E-mail: carterpaulv@uams.edu.

GRADUATE UNITS

College of Medicine Students: 570 (190 women); includes 79 minority (28 African Americans, 43 Asian Americans or Pacific Islanders, 7 Hispanic Americans, 1 Native American) Expenses: Contact institution. *Financial support:* In 2001–02, 95 research assistantships were awarded; fellowships, teaching assistantships, Federal Work-Study and unspecified assistantships also available. Support available to part-time students. Offers medicine (MD, MS, PhD). *Application Contact:* Tom South, Director of Student Admissions, 501-686-5354. *Interim Dean,* Dr. John P. Shock, 501-686-5350.

Graduate Programs in Medicine Students: 77 full-time (28 women), 28 part-time (13 women). Expenses: Contact institution. *Financial support:* In 2001–02, 95 research assistantships were awarded; fellowships, teaching assistantships, unspecified assistantships also available. Support available to part-time students. Offers anatomy and neurobiology (MS, PhD); biochemistry and molecular biology (MS, PhD); medicine (MS, PhD); microbiology and immunology (MS, PhD); occupational and environmental health (MS); pathology (MS); pharmacology (MS, PhD); physiology and biophysics (MS, PhD); toxicology (MS, PhD). *Application fee:* $0. *Application Contact:* Paul Carter, Assistant to the Vice Chancellor for Academic Affairs, 501-686-5454. *Dean, Graduate School,* Dr. Michael A. Jennings, 501-686-5454.

College of Pharmacy Students: 312 full-time (183 women); includes 25 minority (16 African Americans, 8 Asian Americans or Pacific Islanders, 1 Hispanic American) Expenses: Contact institution. *Financial support:* In 2001–02, 5 research assistantships were awarded Support available to part-time students. In 2001, 140 first professional degrees, 1 master's awarded. Offers pharmacy (Pharm D, MS). *Application fee:* $0. *Application Contact:* Dr. Kim Light, Information Contact, 501-686-5557. *Dean,* Dr. L. D. Milne, 501-686-5557.

Graduate School Students: 180 full-time (121 women), 249 part-time (208 women); includes 60 minority (30 African Americans, 25 Asian Americans or Pacific Islanders, 1 Hispanic American, 4 Native Americans), 26 international. *Faculty:* 219 full-time (63 women), 52 part-time/adjunct (12 women). Expenses: Contact institution. *Financial support:* In 2001–02, 131 research assistantships were awarded; career-related internships or fieldwork, Federal Work-Study, and traineeships also available. Support available to part-time students. In 2001, 93 master's, 26 doctorates awarded. *Degree program information:* Part-time programs available. Offers clinical nutrition (MS); communicative disorders (MS). *Application fee:* $0. *Interim Dean,* Dr. Michael L. Jennings, 501-686-5454.

College of Nursing Students: 12 full-time (10 women), 150 part-time (138 women). *Faculty:* 26 full-time (23 women), 8 part-time/adjunct (7 women). Expenses: Contact institution. *Financial support:* Career-related internships or fieldwork and traineeships available. Support available to part-time students. In 2001, 57 master's, 2 doctorates awarded. *Degree program information:* Part-time programs available. Offers nursing (MN Sc, PhD). *Application fee:* $0. *Application Contact:* Dr. Pegge L. Bell, Information Contact, 501-686-7997. *Dean,* Dr. Linda C. Hodges, 501-686-5374.

UNIVERSITY OF BALTIMORE, Baltimore, MD 21201-5779

General Information State-supported, coed, upper-level institution. *Enrollment:* 1,353 full-time matriculated graduate/professional students (704 women), 997 part-time matriculated graduate/professional students (597 women). *Graduate faculty:* 214 full-time (63 women), 161 part-time/adjunct (48 women). Tuition, state resident: full-time $5,508; part-time $306 per credit. Tuition, nonresident: full-time $8,352; part-time $464 per credit. *Required fees:* $37 per credit. $60 per semester. Tuition and fees vary according to course load and degree level. *Graduate housing:* On-campus housing not available. *Student services:* Campus employment opportunities, career counseling, disabled student services, international student services, low-cost health insurance, multicultural affairs office. *Library facilities:* Langsdale Library plus 1 other. *Online resources:* library catalog, web page, access to other libraries' catalogs. *Collection:* 258,747 titles, 10,738 serial subscriptions, 883 audiovisual materials.

Computer facilities: 135 computers available on campus for general student use. A campuswide network can be accessed from off campus. Internet access is available. *Web address:* http://www.ubalt.edu/.

General Application Contact: Jeffrey Zavrotny, Assistant Director of Admissions, 410-837-4777, Fax: 410-837-4793, E-mail: jzavrotny@ubalt.edu.

GRADUATE UNITS

Graduate School Students: 499 full-time (260 women), 963 part-time (580 women); includes 443 minority (376 African Americans, 44 Asian Americans or Pacific Islanders, 19 Hispanic Americans, 4 Native Americans), 187 international. Average age 32. 968 applicants, 76% accepted. *Faculty:* 166 full-time (56 women), 176 part-time/adjunct (53 women). Expenses: Contact institution. *Financial support:* In 2001–02, 257 students received support, including 73 research assistantships; fellowships, career-related internships or fieldwork, Federal Work-Study, and scholarships/grants also available. Support available to part-time students. Financial award application deadline: 4/1; financial award applicants required to submit FAFSA. In 2001, 498 master's, 1 doctorate awarded. *Degree program information:* Part-time and evening/weekend programs available. Postbaccalaureate distance learning degree programs offered (no on-campus study). *Application deadline:* For fall admission, 7/15 (priority date); for spring admission, 12/15. Applications are processed on a rolling basis. *Application fee:* $30. Electronic applications accepted. *Application Contact:* Jeffrey Zavrotny, Assistant Director of Admissions, 410-837-4777, Fax: 410-837-4793, E-mail: jzavrotny@ubalt.edu. *Provost,* Ronald Legon, 410-837-4244, Fax: 410-837-4249.

College of Liberal Arts Students: 201 full-time (138 women), 592 part-time (397 women); includes 316 minority (290 African Americans, 9 Asian Americans or Pacific Islanders, 14 Hispanic Americans, 3 Native Americans), 28 international. Average age 33. 469 applicants, 83% accepted. *Faculty:* 56 full-time (25 women), 31 part-time/adjunct (12 women). Expenses: Contact institution. *Financial support:* In 2001–02, 35 research assistantships were awarded; fellowships, career-related internships or fieldwork and Federal Work-Study also available. Support available to part-time students. Financial award application deadline: 4/1; financial award applicants required to submit FAFSA. In 2001, 194 master's, 1 doctorate awarded. *Degree program information:* Part-time and evening/weekend programs available. Offers applied assessment and consulting (Psy D); applied psychology (MS); communications design (DCD); counseling (MS); criminal justice (MS); government and public administration (MPA, DPA); human services administration (MS); industrial and organizational psychology (MS); interaction design and information architecture (MS); legal and ethical studies (MA); liberal arts (MA, MPA, MS, DCD, DPA, Psy D); negotiations and conflict management (MS); publications design (MA). *Application deadline:* For fall admission, 7/15 (priority date); for spring admission, 12/15. Applications are processed on a rolling basis. *Application fee:* $30. Electronic applications accepted. *Application Contact:* Jeffrey Zavrotny, Assistant Director of Admissions, 410-837-4777, Fax: 410-837-4793, E-mail: jzavrotny@ubalt.edu. *Dean,* Dr. Carl Stenberg, 410-837-5359.

School of Business Students: 298 full-time (122 women), 371 part-time (183 women); includes 124 minority (86 African Americans, 35 Asian Americans or Pacific Islanders, 2 Hispanic Americans, 1 Native American), 159 international. Average age 31. 499 applicants, 69% accepted. *Faculty:* 54 full-time (11 women), 36 part-time/adjunct (6 women). Expenses: Contact institution. *Financial support:* Fellowships, research assistantships, career-related internships or fieldwork and Federal Work-Study available. Support available to part-time students. Financial award application deadline: 4/1; financial award applicants required to submit FAFSA. In 2001, 292 degrees awarded. *Degree program information:* Part-time and evening/weekend programs available. Postbaccalaureate distance learning degree programs offered (no on-campus study). Offers accounting (MS); business (MBA, MS); business administration (MBA); business/management information systems (MS); business/marketing and venturing (MS); finance (MS); taxation (MS). *Application deadline:* For fall admission, 7/15 (priority date); for spring admission, 12/15. Applications are processed on a rolling basis. *Application fee:* $30. Electronic applications accepted. *Application Contact:* Jeffrey Zavrotny, Assistant Director of Admissions, 410-837-4777, Fax: 410-837-4793, E-mail: jzavrotny@ubalt.edu. *Interim Dean,* Dr. Dan Gerlowski, 410-837-4955.

School of Law *Degree program information:* Part-time and evening/weekend programs available. Offers law (JD); taxation (LL M). Electronic applications accepted.

UNIVERSITY OF BRIDGEPORT, Bridgeport, CT 06601

General Information Independent, coed, comprehensive institution. CGS member. *Enrollment:* 1,060 full-time matriculated graduate/professional students (482 women), 1,088 part-time matriculated graduate/professional students (630 women). *Enrollment by degree level:* 199 first professional, 1,742 master's, 170 doctoral, 37 other advanced degrees. *Graduate faculty:* 84 full-time (15 women), 218 part-time/adjunct (80 women). *Tuition:* Part-time $385 per credit hour. *Required fees:* $50 per term. Tuition and fees vary according to degree level and program. *Graduate housing:* Room and/or apartments guaranteed to single students; on-campus housing not available to married students. Typical cost: $3,980 per year ($7,500 including board). *Student services:* Campus employment opportunities, campus safety program, career counseling, disabled student services, exercise/wellness program, free psychological counseling, international student services, low-cost health insurance, multicultural affairs office, teacher training. *Library facilities:* Wahlstrom Library. *Online resources:* library catalog, web page, access to other libraries' catalogs. *Collection:* 272,430 titles, 2,117 serial subscriptions, 5,485 audiovisual materials. *Research affiliation:* Burndy Library, Marine Biology Station (Hummingbird Cay, Bahamas), Connecticut Medicine Research Consortia.

Computer facilities: 350 computers available on campus for general student use. A campuswide network can be accessed from student residence rooms and from off campus. *Web address:* http://www.bridgeport.edu/.

General Application Contact: Barbara L. Maryak, Dean of Admissions, 203-576-4552, Fax: 203-576-4941, E-mail: admit@bridgeport.edu.

GRADUATE UNITS

College of Chiropractic Students: 198 full-time (65 women), 1 (woman) part-time; includes 33 minority (7 African Americans, 12 Asian Americans or Pacific Islanders, 14 Hispanic Americans), 13 international. Average age 29. 123 applicants, 59% accepted, 29 enrolled. *Faculty:* 18 full-time (4 women), 32 part-time/adjunct (16 women). Expenses: Contact institution. *Financial support:* In 2001–02, 195 students received support. Federal Work-Study and institutionally sponsored loans available. Support available to part-time students. Financial award application deadline: 6/1; financial award applicants required to submit FAFSA. In 2001, 60 degrees awarded. Offers acupuncture (MS); chiropractic (DC). *Application deadline:* For fall admission, 3/1 (priority date); for spring admission, 7/1. Applications are processed on a rolling basis. *Application fee:* $75. Electronic applications accepted. *Application Contact:* Jennifer Boutin, Admissions Coordinator, 203-576-4348, Fax: 203-576-4941, E-mail: chiro@bridgeport.edu. *Dean,* Dr. Francis A. Zolli, 203-576-4279.

College of Naturopathic Medicine Students: 103 full-time (62 women), 5 part-time (4 women); includes 28 minority (12 African Americans, 10 Asian Americans or Pacific Islanders, 4 Hispanic Americans, 2 Native Americans), 2 international. Average age 34. 74 applicants, 66% accepted, 28 enrolled. *Faculty:* 4 full-time (0 women), 20 part-time/adjunct (10 women). Expenses: Contact institution. *Financial support:* In 2001–02, 80 students received support. Federal Work-Study, institutionally sponsored loans, and scholarships/grants available. Financial

University of Bridgeport (continued)

award application deadline: 4/1; financial award applicants required to submit FAFSA. In 2001, 3 degrees awarded. Offers naturopathic medicine (ND). *Application deadline:* For fall admission, 8/1 (priority date); for spring admission, 12/1. Applications are processed on a rolling basis. Electronic applications accepted. *Application Contact:* Miriam Madwed, Director of Admissions, 203-576-4108, Fax: 203-576-4107, E-mail: natmed@bridgeport.edu. *Dean,* Dr. Peter Allen Martin, 203-576-4110.

Division of Allied Health Technology Students: 19 full-time (15 women), 131 part-time (87 women); includes 12 minority (7 African Americans, 1 Asian American or Pacific Islander, 4 Hispanic Americans), 15 international. Average age 36. 180 applicants, 78% accepted, 39 enrolled. *Faculty:* 1 (woman) full-time, 6 part-time/adjunct (3 women). Expenses: Contact institution. *Financial support:* In 2001–02, 33 students received support. Available to part-time students. Application deadline: 6/1; In 2001, 38 degrees awarded. *Degree program information:* Part-time and evening/weekend programs available. Postbaccalaureate distance learning degree programs offered (no on-campus study). Offers allied health technology (MS). *Application deadline:* For fall admission, 8/1 (priority date); for spring admission, 12/1 (priority date). Applications are processed on a rolling basis. *Application fee:* $25 ($35 for international students). Electronic applications accepted. *Director,* Dr. Blonnie Y. Thompson, 203-576-4667.

Human Nutrition Institute Students: 19 full-time (15 women), 131 part-time (87 women). Average age 36. 180 applicants, 78% accepted, 39 enrolled. *Faculty:* 1 (woman) full-time, 6 part-time/adjunct (3 women). Expenses: Contact institution. *Financial support:* In 2001–02, 33 students received support. Available to part-time students. Application deadline: 6/1; In 2001, 38 degrees awarded. *Degree program information:* Part-time and evening/weekend programs available. Postbaccalaureate distance learning degree programs offered (no on-campus study). Offers human nutrition (MS). *Application deadline:* For fall admission, 8/1 (priority date); for spring admission, 12/1 (priority date). Applications are processed on a rolling basis. *Application fee:* $25 ($35 for international students). Electronic applications accepted. *Director, Division of Allied Health Technology,* Dr. Blonnie Y. Thompson, 203-576-4667.

School of Business Students: 172 full-time (63 women), 121 part-time (48 women); includes 25 minority (8 African Americans, 10 Asian Americans or Pacific Islanders, 7 Hispanic Americans), 230 international. Average age 29. 368 applicants, 77% accepted, 86 enrolled. *Faculty:* 12 full-time (0 women), 21 part-time/adjunct (7 women). Expenses: Contact institution. *Financial support:* In 2001–02, 69 students received support; fellowships, research assistantships, teaching assistantships, career-related internships or fieldwork, Federal Work-Study, institutionally sponsored loans, and tuition waivers (partial) available. Support available to part-time students. Financial award application deadline: 6/1; financial award applicants required to submit FAFSA. In 2001, 76 degrees awarded. *Degree program information:* Part-time and evening/weekend programs available. Postbaccalaureate distance learning degree programs offered (minimal on-campus study). Offers business (MBA, MS); business administration (MBA). *Application deadline:* For fall admission, 8/1 (priority date); for spring admission, 12/1 (priority date). Applications are processed on a rolling basis. *Application fee:* $25 ($35 for international students). Electronic applications accepted. *Application Contact:* Diane Richardson, MBA Director, 203-576-4368, Fax: 203-576-4388, E-mail: mba@bridgeport.edu. *Director,* Dr. Glenn A. Bassett, 203-576-4384.

School of Education and Human Resources Students: 305 full-time (234 women), 476 part-time (368 women); includes 112 minority (81 African Americans, 6 Asian Americans or Pacific Islanders, 24 Hispanic Americans, 1 Native American), 54 international. Average age 35. 444 applicants, 85% accepted, 279 enrolled. *Faculty:* 14 full-time (3 women), 63 part-time/adjunct (30 women). Expenses: Contact institution. *Financial support:* In 2001–02, 330 students received support; fellowships, research assistantships, teaching assistantships, career-related internships or fieldwork, Federal Work-Study, and institutionally sponsored loans available. Support available to part-time students. Financial award application deadline: 6/1; financial award applicants required to submit FAFSA. In 2001, 206 master's, 1 doctorate, 6 other advanced degrees awarded. *Degree program information:* Part-time and evening/weekend programs available. Offers education and human resources (MS, Ed D, Diploma). *Application deadline:* For fall admission, 8/1 (priority date); for spring admission, 12/1 (priority date). Applications are processed on a rolling basis. *Application fee:* $25 ($35 for international students). Electronic applications accepted. *Dean,* Dr. James J. Ritchie, 203-576-4192, Fax: 203-576-4102, E-mail: ritchie@bridgeport.edu.

Division of Counseling and Human Resources Students: 11 full-time (8 women), 76 part-time (70 women); includes 42 minority (33 African Americans, 2 Asian Americans or Pacific Islanders, 7 Hispanic Americans), 5 international. Average age 35. 64 applicants, 83% accepted, 28 enrolled. *Faculty:* 4 full-time (1 woman), 9 part-time/adjunct (4 women). Expenses: Contact institution. *Financial support:* In 2001–02, 27 students received support; fellowships, research assistantships, teaching assistantships, career-related internships or fieldwork, Federal Work-Study, and institutionally sponsored loans available. Support available to part-time students. Financial award application deadline: 6/1; financial award applicants required to submit FAFSA. In 2001, 11 degrees awarded. *Degree program information:* Part-time and evening/weekend programs available. Offers community agency counseling (MS); human resource development and counseling (MS). *Application deadline:* For fall admission, 8/1 (priority date); for spring admission, 12/1 (priority date). Applications are processed on a rolling basis. *Application fee:* $25 ($35 for international students). Electronic applications accepted. *Director,* Dr. Joseph E. Nechasek, 203-576-4175, Fax: 203-576-4102, E-mail: nechasek@bridgeport.edu.

Division of Education Students: 294 full-time (226 women), 400 part-time (298 women); includes 70 minority (48 African Americans, 4 Asian Americans or Pacific Islanders, 17 Hispanic Americans, 1 Native American), 49 international. Average age 35. 380 applicants, 85% accepted, 251 enrolled. *Faculty:* 10 full-time (2 women), 54 part-time/adjunct (26 women). Expenses: Contact institution. *Financial support:* In 2001–02, 303 students received support; fellowships, research assistantships, teaching assistantships, career-related internships or fieldwork, Federal Work-Study, and institutionally sponsored loans available. Support available to part-time students. Financial award application deadline: 6/1; financial award applicants required to submit FAFSA. In 2001, 195 master's, 1 doctorate, 6 other advanced degrees awarded. *Degree program information:* Part-time and evening/weekend programs available. Offers computer specialist (MS, Diploma); early childhood education (MS, Diploma); education (MS); educational management (Ed D, Diploma); elementary education (MS, Diploma); international education (MS, Diploma); reading specialist (MS, Diploma); secondary education (MS, Diploma). *Application deadline:* For fall admission, 8/1 (priority date); for spring admission, 12/1 (priority date). Applications are processed on a rolling basis. *Application fee:* $25 ($35 for international students). Electronic applications accepted. *Associate Dean,* Dr. Allen P. Cook, 203-576-4206, Fax: 203-576-4200, E-mail: acook@bridgeport.edu.

School of Engineering Students: 263 full-time (43 women), 354 part-time (122 women); includes 40 minority (4 African Americans, 27 Asian Americans or Pacific Islanders, 1 Hispanic American, 8 Native Americans), 567 international. Average age 28. 1,209 applicants, 80% accepted, 159 enrolled. *Faculty:* 11 full-time (0 women), 15 part-time/adjunct (0 women). Expenses: Contact institution. *Financial support:* In 2001–02, 76 students received support; fellowships, research assistantships, teaching assistantships, career-related internships or fieldwork, Federal Work-Study, institutionally sponsored loans, and tuition waivers (partial) available. Support available to part-time students. Financial award application deadline: 6/1; financial award applicants required to submit FAFSA. In 2001, 121 degrees awarded. *Degree program information:* Part-time and evening/weekend programs available. Offers computer engineering (MS); computer science (MS); electrical engineering (MS); engineering and design (MS); mechanical engineering (MS); technology management (MS). *Application deadline:* For fall admission, 8/1 (priority date); for spring admission, 12/1 (priority date). Applications are processed on a rolling basis. *Application fee:* $25 ($35 for international students). Electronic applications accepted. *Director,* Dr. Tarek M. Sobh, 203-576-4111, Fax: 203-576-4766, E-mail: sobh@bridgeport.edu.

See in-depth description on page 1161.

THE UNIVERSITY OF BRITISH COLUMBIA, Vancouver, BC V6T 1Z1, Canada

General Information Province-supported, coed, university. *Enrollment:* 6,656 matriculated graduate/professional students (3,697 women). *Enrollment by degree level:* 5,563 master's, 1,093 doctoral. *Graduate faculty:* 2,280. *International tuition:* $7,000 full-time. Tuition, province resident: full-time $2,657. *Graduate housing:* Rooms and/or apartments available on a first-come, first-served basis to single students and available to married students. Housing application deadline: 3/1. *Student services:* Campus employment opportunities, campus safety program, career counseling, child daycare facilities, disabled student services, exercise/wellness program, free psychological counseling, international student services, low-cost health insurance, teacher training. *Library facilities:* Walter C. Koerner Library plus 16 others. *Online resources:* library catalog, web page, access to other libraries' catalogs. *Collection:* 3.9 million titles, 25,966 serial subscriptions. *Research affiliation:* Forintek Canada (forest technology), British Columbia Research (chemical and biological science technology), Pacific Biological Station (Nanaimo) (fisheries and oceanography), Pacific Environment Institute, Pulp and Paper Research Institute of Canada (pulp and paper research), National Research Council of Canada Institute of Machinery Research (machinery research).

Computer facilities: 1,100 computers available on campus for general student use. A campuswide network can be accessed from student residence rooms and from off campus. *Web address:* http://www.ubc.ca/.

General Application Contact: Katriona MacDonald, Director, Student Academic Services, 604-822-2934, Fax: 604-822-5802, E-mail: graduate@interchange.ubc.ca.

GRADUATE UNITS

Faculty of Arts Expenses: Contact institution. *Financial support:* Fellowships, research assistantships, teaching assistantships, career-related internships or fieldwork, Federal Work-Study, institutionally sponsored loans, scholarships/grants, tuition waivers (full and partial), unspecified assistantships, and federal awards available. Support available to part-time students. *Degree program information:* Part-time programs available. Offers anthropology (MA, PhD); art history (MA, PhD); arts (M Mus, M Sc, MA, MAS, MFA, MJ, MLIS, MSW, DMA, PhD, CAS); Asian studies (MA, PhD); biopsychology (MA, PhD); Central, Eastern and Northern European studies (MA, PhD); classical archaeology (MA); classics (MA, PhD); clinical psychology (MA, PhD); cognitive science (MA, PhD); comparative literature (MA, PhD); creative writing (MFA); developmental psychology (MA, PhD); economics (MA, PhD); English (MA, PhD); environmental psychology (MA, PhD); film and video production (MFA); film studies (MA, MFA); forensic psychology (MA, PhD); French (MA, PhD); geography (M Sc, MA, PhD); history (MA, PhD); linguistics (MA, PhD); perception psychology (MA, PhD); philosophy (MA, PhD); political science (MA, PhD); psychometrics (MA, PhD); religious studies (MA); social/personality psychology (MA, PhD); sociology (MA, PhD); Spanish (MA, PhD); theatre (MA, MFA, PhD); theatre design (MFA); theatre directing (MFA); visual arts (MFA). *Application fee:* $65 Canadian dollars. Electronic applications accepted. *Dean Pro-Tem,* Dr. Anne Martin-Matthews, 604-822-3751, Fax: 604-822-6096, E-mail: oertwig@arts.ubc.ca.

The School of Journalism Students: 41 full-time (22 women); includes 15 minority (14 Asian Americans or Pacific Islanders, 1 Hispanic American) 150 applicants, 17% accepted. *Faculty:* 3 full-time (2 women), 6 part-time/adjunct (3 women). Expenses: Contact institution. *Financial support:* In 2001–02, 4 students received support, including 4 fellowships (averaging $12,000 per year); career-related internships or fieldwork also available. Financial award application deadline: 12/15. In 2001, 18 degrees awarded. Offers journalism (MJ). *Application deadline:* For fall admission, 1/15. *Application fee:* $65. *Application Contact:* Sim Lee, Assistant to the Director, 604-822-6688, Fax: 604-822-6707, E-mail: journal@interchange.ubc.ca. *Director,* Prof. Donna Logan, 604-822-6688, Fax: 604-822-6707, E-mail: dlogan@interchange.ubc.ca.

School of Library, Archival and Information Studies Students: 42 full-time (35 women), 53 part-time (43 women). Average age 30. 128 applicants, 73% accepted, 71 enrolled. *Faculty:* 8 full-time (5 women), 12 part-time/adjunct (9 women). Expenses: Contact institution. *Financial support:* In 2001–02, 3 fellowships (averaging $16,000 per year), 10 research assistantships, 2 teaching assistantships were awarded. Federal Work-Study, scholarships/grants, and unspecified assistantships also available. In 2001, 53 degrees awarded. *Degree program information:* Part-time programs available. Offers archival studies (MAS, CAS); archival studies/library and information studies (MLIS, CAS); children's literature (MA). *Application deadline:* For fall admission, 2/1; for winter admission, 5/1; for spring admission, 12/1. Applications are processed on a rolling basis. *Application fee:* $65 Canadian dollars. Electronic applications accepted. *Application Contact:* Dr. Richard L. Hopkins, Graduate Admissions Officer, 604-822-2404, Fax: 604-822-6006, E-mail: slais.admissions@ubc.ca. *Director,* Dr. Ken Haycock, 604-822-2404, Fax: 604-822-6006, E-mail: ken@ubc.ca.

School of Music Students: 102 full-time (68 women), 1 (woman) part-time; includes 23 minority (2 African Americans, 19 Asian Americans or Pacific Islanders, 2 Hispanic Americans), 12 international. Average age 24. 95 applicants, 31% accepted. *Faculty:* 27 full-time (4 women), 52 part-time/adjunct (19 women). Expenses: Contact institution. *Financial support:* In 2001–02, 63 students received support, including 13 fellowships with partial tuition reimbursements available (averaging $16,000 per year), 38 teaching assistantships (averaging $4,000 per year); institutionally sponsored loans and scholarships/grants also available. Financial award application deadline: 2/28. In 2001, 12 master's awarded. *Degree program information:* Part-time programs available. Offers music (M Mus, MA, DMA, PhD). *Application deadline:* For fall admission, 2/28 (priority date). Applications are processed on a rolling basis. *Application fee:* $65 Canadian dollars. *Application Contact:* Graduate Admissions Officer, 604-822-2079, Fax: 604-822-4884, E-mail: isabelm@interchange.ubc.ca. *Director,* Jesse Read, 604-822-2079, Fax: 604-822-4884, E-mail: readjes@interchange.ubc.ca.

School of Social Work and Family Studies Students: 25 full-time (22 women), 10 part-time (8 women); includes 6 minority (5 Asian Americans or Pacific Islanders, 1 Native American) Average age 34. 75 applicants, 47% accepted. *Faculty:* 17 full-time (8 women), 1 part-time/adjunct (0 women). Expenses: Contact institution. *Financial support:* In 2001–02, 1 fellowship (averaging $15,000 per year), 6 research assistantships (averaging $2,000 per year), 12 teaching assistantships (averaging $2,000 per year) were awarded. Career-related internships or fieldwork, Federal Work-Study, and institutionally sponsored loans also available. Financial award application deadline: 6/30. In 2001, 42 degrees awarded. *Degree program information:* Part-time programs available. Postbaccalaureate distance learning degree programs offered (no on-campus study). Offers family studies (MA); social work (MSW). *Application deadline:* For fall admission, 1/2. *Application fee:* $65 Canadian dollars. Electronic applications accepted. *Application Contact:* Alina Yuhymets, Academic Adviser, 604-822-4119, Fax: 604-822-8656, E-mail: yuhymets@interchange.ubc.ca. *Director,* Graham Riches, 604-822-0782, Fax: 604-822-8656.

Faculty of Dentistry Students: 30 full-time (19 women), 5 part-time (4 women); includes 6 minority (all Asian Americans or Pacific Islanders), 5 international. Average age 25. 51 applicants, 20% accepted, 10 enrolled. *Faculty:* 32 full-time (7 women), 3 part-time/adjunct (1 woman). Expenses: Contact institution. *Financial support:* In 2001–02, 11 students received support, including 3 fellowships with partial tuition reimbursements available (averaging $24,000 per year), 2 research assistantships with partial tuition reimbursements available (averaging $16,000 per year), 6 teaching assistantships with partial tuition reimbursements available (averaging $800 per year); career-related internships or fieldwork, Federal Work-Study, scholarships/grants, tuition waivers (partial), and unspecified assistantships also available. Financial award application deadline: 12/5. In 2001, 1 first professional degree, 2 master's, 1 doctorate awarded. *Degree program information:* Part-time programs available. Offers dental science (M Sc); dentistry (DMD, M Sc, PhD, Certificate, Diploma); oral biology (PhD); periodontics (Diploma). *Application deadline:* For spring admission, 3/31. Applications are processed on a rolling basis. *Application fee:* $65. Electronic applications accepted. *Application Contact:* Viki Koulouris, Admissions Coordinator, 604-822-4486, Fax: 604-822-3562, E-mail: vickybk@interchange.ubc.ca. *Dean,* Dr. E. H. K. Yen, 604-822-5773, Fax: 604-822-4532.

Faculty of Graduate Studies Students: 6,656 (3,697 women). 8,147 applicants, 42% accepted. *Faculty:* 1,959. Expenses: Contact institution. *Financial support:* Fellowships, research assistantships, teaching assistantships, career-related internships or fieldwork, Federal Work-Study, institutionally sponsored loans, and tuition waivers (full and partial) available. In 2001, 276 degrees awarded. *Degree program information:* Part-time and evening/weekend programs available. Offers genetics (M Sc, PhD); resource management and environmental studies (M Sc, MA, PhD). *Application fee:* $65. Electronic applications accepted. *Application Contact:* Katriona MacDonald, Director, Student Academic Services, 604-822-2934, Fax: 604-822-5802, E-mail: graduate@interchange.ubc.ca. *Dean*, Dr. Frieda Granot, 604-822-2848, Fax: 604-822-5802.

Faculty of Agricultural Sciences Students: 221 full-time (149 women), 54 international. Average age 24. 226 applicants, 32% accepted, 45 enrolled. *Faculty:* 54 full-time (14 women), 10 part-time/adjunct (4 women). Expenses: Contact institution. *Financial support:* In 2001–02, 91 students received support, including 91 fellowships with partial tuition reimbursements available (averaging $9,104 per year), 49 research assistantships with partial tuition reimbursements available (averaging $14,000 per year), 87 teaching assistantships with partial tuition reimbursements available (averaging $2,200 per year); career-related internships or fieldwork, Federal Work-Study, institutionally sponsored loans, scholarships/grants, and tuition waivers (partial) also available. In 2001, 11 master's, 3 doctorates awarded. Offers agricultural economics (M Sc); agricultural sciences (M Sc, MASLA, MLA, PhD); animal science (M Sc, PhD); food science (M Sc, PhD); human nutrition (M Sc, PhD); landscape architecture (MASLA, MLA); plant science (M Sc, PhD); soil science (M Sc, PhD). *Application deadline:* For fall admission, 4/30; for winter admission, 8/31; for spring admission, 12/31. Applications are processed on a rolling basis. *Application fee:* $65 Canadian dollars. Electronic applications accepted. *Application Contact:* Joyce Tom, Research/Graduate Programs Manager, 604-822-4593, Fax: 604-822-4400, E-mail: gradapp@interchange.ubc.ca. *Associate Dean, Research/Graduate Programs*, Dr. James Robert Thompson, 604-822-4593, Fax: 604-822-4400, E-mail: gradapp@interchange.ubc.ca.

Faculty of Applied Science *Degree program information:* Part-time and evening/weekend programs available. Offers applied science (M Arch, M Eng, M Sc, MA Sc, MASA, MSN, MSS, PhD); architecture (M Arch, MASA); chemical engineering (M Eng, MA Sc, PhD); civil engineering (M Eng, MA Sc, PhD); electrical and computer engineering (M Eng, MA Sc, PhD); integrated computer systems research (MSS); materials and metallurgy (M Sc, PhD); mechanical engineering (M Eng, MA Sc, PhD); metals and materials engineering (M Eng, MA Sc, PhD); mining and mineral process engineering (M Eng, MA Sc, PhD); nursing (MSN, PhD); pulp and paper engineering (M Eng).

Faculty of Commerce and Business Administration Students: 387. *Faculty:* 95 full-time (6 women), 19 part-time/adjunct (3 women). Expenses: Contact institution. *Financial support:* Fellowships with full tuition reimbursements, research assistantships with full tuition reimbursements, teaching assistantships with full tuition reimbursements, career-related internships or fieldwork, Federal Work-Study, institutionally sponsored loans, and scholarships/grants available. In 2001, 130 master's, 10 doctorates awarded. Offers accounting (PhD); business administration (M Sc, MBA); commerce and business administration (M Sc, MBA, PhD); finance (M Sc, PhD); management information systems (M Sc, PhD); management science (M Sc, PhD); marketing (PhD); organizational behavior (PhD); policy analysis and strategy (PhD); transport and logistics (M Sc); urban land economics (M Sc, PhD). *Application deadline:* Applications are processed on a rolling basis. Electronic applications accepted. *Application Contact:* Wendy H. Ma, Associate Director, Masters' Programs, 604-822-8422, Fax: 604-822-9030, E-mail: masters.programs@commerce.ubc.ca. *Dean*, Dr. Daniel F. Muzyka, 604-822-8555.

Faculty of Education *Degree program information:* Part-time and evening/weekend programs available. Offers adult education (M Ed, MA); art education (M Ed, MA, PhD); business education (M Ed, MA); counseling psychology (M Ed, MA, PhD, Diploma); curriculum and instruction (M Ed, MA, PhD); early childhood education (M Ed, MA); education (M Ed, M Sc, MA, MHK, Ed D, PhD, Diploma); educational administration (M Ed, MA); educational leadership and policy (Ed D); educational psychology (M Ed); educational studies (M Ed, MA, PhD); English education (M Ed, MA, PhD); higher education (M Ed, MA); home economics education (M Ed, MA, PhD); human kinetics (M Sc, MA, MHK, PhD); human learning, development and instruction (MA, PhD); library education (M Ed, MA, PhD); math education (M Ed, MA, PhD); measurement and evaluation and research methodology (M Ed); measurement, evaluation and research methodology (MA); measurement, evaluation, and research methodology (PhD); modern language education (M Ed, MA, PhD); music education (M Ed, MA, PhD); physical education (M Ed, MA); reading education (M Ed, MA, Ed D, PhD); school psychology (M Ed, MA, PhD); science education (M Ed, MA, PhD); social studies education (M Ed, MA, PhD); special education (M Ed, MA, PhD, Diploma); teaching English as a second language (M Ed, MA, PhD); technical studies education (M Ed, MA, PhD). Electronic applications accepted.

Faculty of Forestry Students: 202 full-time (77 women), 76 international. 157 applicants, 20% accepted, 31 enrolled. *Faculty:* 55 full-time (7 women). Expenses: Contact institution. *Financial support:* In 2001–02, 50 fellowships (averaging $15,890 per year), 125 research assistantships (averaging $10,149 per year), 87 teaching assistantships (averaging $3,689 per year) were awarded. Scholarships/grants and tuition waivers (partial) also available. In 2001, 35 master's, 23 doctorates awarded. *Degree program information:* Part-time programs available. Offers forestry (M Sc, MA Sc, MF, PhD). *Application deadline:* For fall admission, 3/31; for spring admission, 10/1. Applications are processed on a rolling basis. *Application fee:* $65 Canadian dollars. Electronic applications accepted. *Application Contact:* Hiltrud Vogler, Graduate Secretary, 604-822-6177, Fax: 604-822-8645, E-mail: gradfor@interchange.ubc.ca. *Associate Dean, Graduate Studies and Research*, Dr. John McLean, 604-822-3360, Fax: 604-822-8645, E-mail: mclean@interchange.ubc.ca.

Faculty of Law *Degree program information:* Part-time programs available. Offers law (LL M, PhD). Electronic applications accepted.

Faculty of Pharmaceutical Sciences Offers pharmaceutical sciences (Pharm D, M Sc, PhD); pharmacy (Pharm D). Electronic applications accepted.

Faculty of Science Expenses: Contact institution. *Financial support:* Fellowships, research assistantships, teaching assistantships, career-related internships or fieldwork, Federal Work-Study, institutionally sponsored loans, and tuition waivers (partial) available. *Degree program information:* Part-time programs available. Offers atmospheric science (M Sc, PhD); botany (M Sc, PhD); chemistry (M Sc, PhD); computer science (M Sc, PhD); engineering physics (MA Sc); geological engineering (M Eng, MA Sc, PhD); geological sciences (M Sc, PhD); geophysics (M Sc, MA Sc, PhD); mathematics (M Sc, MA, PhD); microbiology and immunology (M Sc, PhD); oceanography (M Sc, PhD); physics (M Sc, PhD); science (M Eng, M Sc, MA, MA Sc, PhD); statistics (M Sc, PhD); zoology (M Sc, PhD). *Application fee:* $60. Electronic applications accepted. *Dean*, Dr. B. C. McBride, 604-822-3820, Fax: 604-822-5558.

Institute of Applied Mathematics Offers applied mathematics (M Sc, PhD).

Institute of Asian Research *Degree program information:* Part-time programs available. Offers Asian research (MAPPS). Electronic applications accepted.

School of Community and Regional Planning Students: 116 full-time (78 women), 3 part-time (1 woman), 15 international. Average age 28. 119 applicants, 47% accepted, 30 enrolled. *Faculty:* 10 full-time (4 women). Expenses: Contact institution. *Financial support:* In 2001–02, 12 fellowships with partial tuition reimbursements (averaging $16,000 per year) were awarded; research assistantships, teaching assistantships, career-related internships or fieldwork, Federal Work-Study, institutionally sponsored loans, and research travel bursaries also available. Financial award application deadline: 9/28. In 2001, 25 master's, 3 doctorates awarded. *Degree program information:* Part-time programs available. Offers community and regional planning (M Sc P, MAP, PhD). *Application deadline:* For fall admission, 1/15. *Application fee:* $65. Electronic applications accepted. *Application Contact:* Patti Toporowski, Secretary, 604-822-4422, Fax: 604-822-3787, E-mail: ptop@interchange.ubc.ca. *Director*, Anthony H. J. Dorcey, 604-822-5725, Fax: 604-822-3787, E-mail: dorcey@interchange.ubc.ca.

School of Occupational and Environmental Hygiene Students: 15 full-time (13 women), 5 part-time (1 woman); includes 8 minority (all Asian Americans or Pacific Islanders), 1 international. Average age 25. 26 applicants, 46% accepted, 7 enrolled. *Faculty:* 4 full-time (1 woman), 22 part-time/adjunct (9 women). Expenses: Contact institution. *Financial support:* In 2001–02, 1 fellowship (averaging $8,000 per year), 4 research assistantships (averaging $16,000 per year), 6 teaching assistantships (averaging $2,300 per year) were awarded. Career-related internships or fieldwork and institutionally sponsored loans also available. In 2001, 8 degrees awarded. *Degree program information:* Part-time programs available. Offers occupational and environmental hygiene (M Sc, PhD). *Application deadline:* For fall admission, 3/31. *Application fee:* $60. Electronic applications accepted. *Application Contact:* Dr. Kay Teschke, Graduate Adviser, 604-822-9595, Fax: 604-822-9588, E-mail: teschke@interchg.ubc.ca. *Director*, Dr. Murray Hodgson, 604-822-9595, Fax: 604-822-9588, E-mail: hodgson@mech.ubc.ca.

Faculty of Medicine *Degree program information:* Part-time programs available. Offers experimental pathology (M Sc, PhD); medicine (MD, M Sc, MH Sc, MHA, PhD). Open only to Canadian residents.

Graduate Programs in Medicine *Degree program information:* Part-time programs available. Offers anatomy (M Sc, PhD); audiology and speech sciences (M Sc, PhD); biochemistry and molecular biology (M Sc, PhD); clinical epidemiology (MH Sc); community health (MH Sc); epidemiology/clinical epidemiology (M Sc, PhD); experimental medicine (M Sc, PhD); health administration (MHA); health services research (M Sc, PhD); medical genetics (M Sc, PhD); medicine (M Sc, MH Sc, MHA, PhD); neuroscience (M Sc, PhD); occupational and environmental health (M Sc, PhD); occupational health (MH Sc); pharmacology and therapeutics (M Sc, PhD); physiology (M Sc, PhD); rehabilitation sciences (M Sc); reproductive and developmental sciences (M Sc, PhD); surgery (M Sc).

UNIVERSITY OF CALGARY, Calgary, AB T2N 1N4, Canada

General Information Province-supported, coed, university. CGS member. *Enrollment:* 5,218 matriculated graduate/professional students. *Graduate faculty:* 425. *Graduate tuition:* Tuition and fees charges are reported in Canadian dollars. *International tuition:* $8,750 Canadian dollars full-time. *Tuition, area resident:* Full-time $4,375 Canadian dollars; part-time $1,094 Canadian dollars per course. *Required fees:* $400 Canadian dollars; $35 Canadian dollars per term. *Graduate housing:* Rooms and/or apartments available on a first-come, first-served basis to single and married students. Housing application deadline: 3/31. *Student services:* Campus employment opportunities, campus safety program, career counseling, child daycare facilities, disabled student services, exercise/wellness program, free psychological counseling, grant writing training, international student services, low-cost health insurance, multicultural affairs office. *Library facilities:* MacKimmie Library plus 4 others. *Online resources:* library catalog, web page, access to other libraries' catalogs. *Collection:* 2.3 million titles, 14,776 serial subscriptions, 111,445 audiovisual materials. *Research affiliation:* Alta Telecommunications Research Centre, Alberta Sulphur Research, Calgary Society for Students with Learning Difficulties, Canadian Institute of Resources Law, Canadian Music Centre, Canadian Energy Research Institute.

Computer facilities: 1,000 computers available on campus for general student use. A campuswide network can be accessed from student residence rooms and from off campus. Internet access and online class registration are available. *Web address:* http://www.ucalgary.ca/.

General Application Contact: Robert L. Mansell, Dean of the Faculty of Graduate Studies, 403-220-6356, Fax: 403-289-7635.

GRADUATE UNITS

Faculty of Environmental Design Students: 258 full-time (121 women), 9 part-time (3 women). Average age 30. 221 applicants, 44% accepted, 52 enrolled. *Faculty:* 26 full-time (5 women), 43 part-time/adjunct (7 women). Expenses: Contact institution. *Financial support:* In 2001–02, 1 fellowship, 57 research assistantships, 9 teaching assistantships were awarded. Career-related internships or fieldwork and scholarships/grants also available. In 2001, 51 degrees awarded. Offers architecture (M Arch); environmental design (M Env Des, PhD); environmental science (M Env Des); industrial design (M Env Des); planning (M Env Des). *Application deadline:* For fall admission, 2/1. *Application fee:* $60. *Application Contact:* D. McInnes, Admissions Officer, 403-220-3630, Fax: 403-284-4399, E-mail: info@evds.ucalgary.ca. *Dean*, Dr. M. M. Tyler, 403-220-6606, Fax: 403-284-4399.

Faculty of Graduate Studies Students: 2,917 full-time (1,408 women), 1,149 part-time (643 women). Average age 33. Expenses: Contact institution. *Financial support:* In 2001–02, fellowships with partial tuition reimbursements (averaging $500 per year), research assistantships with partial tuition reimbursements (averaging $3,950 per year) were awarded. Teaching assistantships with partial tuition reimbursements, career-related internships or fieldwork, institutionally sponsored loans, and tuition waivers (full and partial) also available. Financial award application deadline: 2/1. In 2001, 654 master's, 116 doctorates awarded. *Degree program information:* Part-time and evening/weekend programs available. Postbaccalaureate distance learning degree programs offered (minimal on-campus study). Offers resources and the environment (M Sc, MA, PhD). *Application fee:* $60. *Application Contact:* Martha A. Stroud, Senior Communications and Projects Officer, 403-220-4932, Fax: 403-282-5262, E-mail: mstroud@ucalgary.ca. *Dean of the Faculty of Graduate Studies*, Robert L. Mansell, 403-220-6108, Fax: 403-282-5262.

Faculty of Communication and Culture Students: 47 full-time (37 women), 27 part-time (17 women); includes 3 minority (1 African American, 2 Asian Americans or Pacific Islanders), 1 international. Average age 31. 150 applicants, 19% accepted. *Faculty:* 6 full-time (2 women), 5 part-time/adjunct (2 women). Expenses: Contact institution. *Financial support:* In 2001–02, 24 students received support; research assistantships, teaching assistantships, scholarships/grants available. Financial award application deadline: 2/1. In 2001, 10 degrees awarded. *Degree program information:* Part-time and evening/weekend programs available. Offers communication and culture (MA, MCS, PhD). *Application deadline:* For fall admission, 2/1. *Application fee:* $60. *Application Contact:* Sylvia Mills, Graduate Programs Administrator, 403-220-7592, Fax: 403-210-8164, E-mail: smills@ucalgary.ca. *Director*, Dr. David Mitchell, 403-220-6460, Fax: 403-210-8164, E-mail: mitchell@ucalgary.ca.

Faculty of Continuing Education 70 applicants, 69% accepted. *Faculty:* 8 full-time (3 women), 22 part-time/adjunct (13 women). Expenses: Contact institution. *Financial support:* Bursaries available. In 2001, 7 degrees awarded. *Degree program information:* Part-time programs available. Postbaccalaureate distance learning degree programs offered (minimal on-campus study). Offers learning in the workplace (MCE). Program offered on campus in spring and summer sessions only. Program offered by computer conferencing in fall and winter sessions. *Application deadline:* For spring admission, 12/1. *Application fee:* $60. *Application Contact:* S. Hutton, Program Director, 403-220-5988, Fax: 403-284-3948, E-mail: shutton@ucalgary.ca. *Dean*, Dr. T. P. Keenan, 403-220-5429, Fax: 403-284-3948, E-mail: keenan@ucalgary.ca.

Faculty of Education Students: 369 full-time, 338 part-time. *Faculty:* 63 full-time, 37 part-time/adjunct. Expenses: Contact institution. *Financial support:* In 2001–02, 10 students received support, including research assistantships (averaging $3,920 per year); fellowships, teaching assistantships, career-related internships or fieldwork and scholarships/grants also available. *Degree program information:* Part-time and evening/weekend programs available. Postbaccalaureate distance learning degree programs offered (minimal on-campus study). Offers adult, community and higher education (M Ed, MA, Ed D, PhD); community rehabilitation and disability studies (M Ed, M Sc, Ed D, PhD); counseling psychology (M Ed, M Sc, PhD); curriculum, teaching and learning (M Ed, M Sc, MA, Ed D, PhD); education (M Ed, M Sc, MA, Ed D, PhD); educational contexts (M Ed, MA, Ed D, PhD); educational leadership (M Ed, MA, Ed D, PhD); educational technology (M Ed, M Sc, MA, Ed D, PhD); human development and learning (M Ed, M Sc, PhD); school psychology (M Ed, M Sc, PhD); special education (M Ed, M Sc, PhD); teaching English as a second language (M Ed). *Application fee:* $60. *Dean*, Dr. Annette LaGrange, 403-220-5627, Fax: 403-282-5849, E-mail: avlagran@ucalgary.ca.

Faculty of Engineering Students: 338 full-time (72 women), 108 part-time (21 women). Average age 25. 2,400 applicants, 5% accepted. *Faculty:* 106 full-time (9 women), 31 part-time/adjunct (0 women). Expenses: Contact institution. *Financial support:* In 2001–02, 59 fellowships, 21 research assistantships, 96 teaching assistantships were awarded. Career-related internships or fieldwork, institutionally sponsored loans, scholarships/grants, and unspecified assistantships also available. In 2001, 75 master's, 24 doctorates awarded. *Degree program information:* Part-time and evening/weekend programs available. Offers biomedical engineering (M Eng, M Sc, PhD); chemical and petroleum engineering

University of Calgary (continued)

(M Eng, M Sc, PhD); civil engineering (M Eng, M Sc, MPM, PhD); electrical and computer engineering (M Eng, M Sc, PhD); engineering (M Eng, M Sc, MPM, PhD); geomatics engineering (M Eng, M Sc, PhD); mechanical engineering (M Eng, M Sc, PhD). *Application deadline:* Applications are processed on a rolling basis. *Dean*, Dr. S. C. Wirasinghe, 403-220-5731, Fax: 403-284-3697, E-mail: wirasing@ucalgary.ca.

Faculty of Fine Arts Students: 58 full-time (33 women). 84 applicants, 35% accepted. *Faculty:* 35 full-time (8 women). Expenses: Contact institution. *Financial support:* In 2001–02, 35 students received support; fellowships, research assistantships, teaching assistantships, institutionally sponsored loans, scholarships/grants, and tuition waivers (partial) available. In 2001, 23 degrees awarded. Offers art (MFA); design/technical (MFA); directing (MFA); drama (PhD); fine arts (M Mus, MA, MFA, PhD); music (M Mus, MA, PhD); theatre studies (MFA). *Application deadline:* Applications are processed on a rolling basis. *Application fee:* $60. Electronic applications accepted. *Dean*, A. Calvert, 403-220-5498, Fax: 403-282-6925.

Faculty of Humanities Expenses: Contact institution. *Financial support:* Fellowships, research assistantships, teaching assistantships, institutionally sponsored loans, scholarships/grants, and research scholarships, summer teaching available. *Degree program information:* Part-time and evening/weekend programs available. Offers English (MA, PhD); French (MA, PhD); German (MA); Greek and Roman studies (MA); humanities (MA, PhD); philosophy (MA, PhD); religious studies (MA, PhD); Spanish (MA). *Application deadline:* Applications are processed on a rolling basis. Electronic applications accepted. *Dean*, Dr. Pierre-Yves Mocquais, 403-220-5044, Fax: 403-284-0848, E-mail: macquais@ucalgary.ca.

Faculty of Kinesiology Students: 51 full-time (22 women); includes 3 Asian Americans or Pacific Islanders Average age 26. 41 applicants, 73% accepted, 23 enrolled. *Faculty:* 39 full-time (13 women), 28 part-time/adjunct (8 women). Expenses: Contact institution. *Financial support:* In 2001–02, 21 students received support, including 3 research assistantships, 18 teaching assistantships; career-related internships or fieldwork and unspecified assistantships also available. Financial award application deadline: 3/31. In 2001, 10 degrees awarded. Offers biomedical engineering (M Sc, PhD); kinesiology (M Kin, M Sc, PhD). *Application deadline:* For fall admission, 3/31. *Application fee:* $60. *Application Contact:* Marion Benaschak, Graduate Program Administrator, 403-220-5183, Fax: 403-220-0105, E-mail: benascha@ucalgary.ca. *Associate Dean*, Dr. Warren Veale, 403-220-5183, Fax: 403-220-0105, E-mail: veale@ucalgary.ca.

Faculty of Nursing Students: 73 full-time (71 women), 30 part-time (29 women). Average age 30. 57 applicants, 60% accepted. *Faculty:* 45 full-time (43 women), 107 part-time/adjunct (100 women). Expenses: Contact institution. *Financial support:* In 2001–02, 7 teaching assistantships (averaging $6,458 per year) were awarded; institutionally sponsored loans and scholarships/grants also available. Support available to part-time students. In 2001, 19 master's, 1 doctorate awarded. *Degree program information:* Part-time programs available. Offers nursing (MN, PhD). *Application deadline:* For fall admission, 2/1. *Application fee:* $60. Electronic applications accepted. *Application Contact:* Pat Jolly, Graduate Programs Administrator, 403-220-6241, Fax: 403-284-4803, E-mail: pjolly@ucalgary.ca. *Associate Dean, Research and Graduate Programs*, Dr. Florence Myrick, 403-220-4630, Fax: 403-284-4803, E-mail: mareimer@ucalgary.ca.

Faculty of Science Students: 400 full-time (153 women), 32 part-time (8 women). 419 applicants, 33% accepted. *Faculty:* 181 full-time (14 women), 24 part-time/adjunct (3 women). Expenses: Contact institution. *Financial support:* Fellowships, research assistantships, teaching assistantships, career-related internships or fieldwork, institutionally sponsored loans, scholarships/grants, and research scholarships available. In 2001, 55 master's, 34 doctorates awarded. *Degree program information:* Part-time programs available. Offers analytical chemistry (M Sc, PhD); applied chemistry (M Sc, PhD); biological sciences (M Sc, PhD); computer science (M Sc, PhD); geology (M Sc, PhD); geophysics (M Sc, PhD); inorganic chemistry (M Sc, PhD); mathematics and statistics (M Sc, PhD); organic chemistry (M Sc, PhD); physical chemistry (M Sc, PhD); physics and astronomy (M Sc, PhD); polymer chemistry (M Sc, PhD); science (M Sc, PhD); software engineering (M Sc); theoretical chemistry (M Sc, PhD). *Application deadline:* Applications are processed on a rolling basis. *Application fee:* $60. *Dean*, P. M. Boorman, 403-220-6286.

Faculty of Social Sciences Students: 356 full-time (196 women), 24 part-time (9 women). 486 applicants, 32% accepted. *Faculty:* 173 full-time (50 women), 12 part-time/adjunct (6 women). Expenses: Contact institution. *Financial support:* Fellowships, research assistantships, teaching assistantships, career-related internships or fieldwork, institutionally sponsored loans, and unspecified assistantships available. *Degree program information:* Part-time and evening/weekend programs available. Offers anthropology (MA, PhD); archaeology (MA, PhD); clinical psychology (M Sc, PhD); economics (M Ec, MA, PhD); geography (M Sc, MA, MGIS, PhD); history (MA, PhD); linguistics (MA, PhD); political science (MA, PhD); psychology (M Sc, PhD); social sciences (M Ec, M Sc, MA, MGIS, PhD); sociology (MA, PhD). *Application deadline:* Applications are processed on a rolling basis. *Application fee:* $60. *Dean*, S. J. Randall, 403-220-5400, Fax: 403-282-8606.

Faculty of Social Work Tuition and fees charges are reported in Canadian dollars. Offers social work (MSW, PhD).

Haskayne School of Business Students: 192 full-time (77 women), 339 part-time (130 women); includes 58 minority (1 African American, 52 Asian Americans or Pacific Islanders, 5 Hispanic Americans), 3 international. Average age 32. 412 applicants, 53% accepted, 172 enrolled. *Faculty:* 71 full-time (19 women), 44 part-time/adjunct (18 women). Expenses: Contact institution. *Financial support:* In 2001–02, 44 students received support, including 30 research assistantships (averaging $3,900 per year), 10 teaching assistantships (averaging $3,250 per year); fellowships with partial tuition reimbursements available, scholarships/grants also available. Financial award application deadline: 2/1. In 2001, 204 master's, 5 doctorates awarded. *Degree program information:* Part-time and evening/weekend programs available. Offers business (EMBA, MBA, PhD); business administration (EMBA, MBA); management (PhD). *Application deadline:* For fall admission, 5/1. Applications are processed on a rolling basis. *Application fee:* $38. Electronic applications accepted. *Application Contact:* Penny O'Hearn, Administrative Assistant, 403-220-3808, Fax: 403-282-0095, E-mail: pohearn@mgmt.ucalgary.ca. *Dean*, Dr. David M. Saunders, 403-220-5689, Fax: 403-282-0095.

Faculty of Law Students: 226 full-time (127 women), 10 part-time (8 women). Average age 29. 663 applicants, 11% accepted, 71 enrolled. *Faculty:* 18 full-time (8 women), 23 part-time/adjunct (8 women). Expenses: Contact institution. *Financial support:* In 2001–02, 2 research assistantships (averaging $3,920 per year) were awarded; scholarships/grants and study awards also available. Financial award application deadline: 2/1. In 2001, 64 LL Bs, 1 master's awarded. Offers law (LL B, LL M). *Application deadline:* For fall admission, 2/1. *Application fee:* $60. *Application Contact:* Karen Argento, Admissions and Student Affairs Officer, 403-220-8154, Fax: 403-282-8325, E-mail: kargento@ucalgary.ca. *Dean*, Prof. Patricia Hughes, 403-220-7116, Fax: 403-282-8325, E-mail: phughes@ucalgary.ca.

Faculty of Medicine Students: 640 full-time (334 women), 9 part-time (4 women). Average age 27. 1,559 applicants, 13% accepted. *Faculty:* 293 full-time (35 women), 22 part-time/adjunct (1 woman). Expenses: Contact institution. *Financial support:* Fellowships, research assistantships, teaching assistantships, career-related internships or fieldwork, scholarships/grants, and tuition waivers (full and partial) available. In 2001, 73 first professional degrees, 34 master's, 25 doctorates awarded. *Degree program information:* Part-time programs available. Offers biochemistry and molecular biology (M Sc, PhD); biomedical technology (MBT); cardiovascular and respiratory sciences (M Sc, PhD); community health sciences (M Sc, MCM, PhD); gastrointestinal sciences (M Sc, PhD); medical science (M Sc, PhD); medicine (MD, M Sc, MBT, MCM, PhD); microbiology and infectious diseases (M Sc, PhD); neuroscience (M Sc, PhD). *Application deadline:* Applications are processed on a rolling basis. Electronic applications accepted. *Dean*, Dr. D. G. Gall, 403-220-6843.

UNIVERSITY OF CALIFORNIA, BERKELEY, Berkeley, CA 94720-1500

General Information State-supported, coed, university. CGS member. *Enrollment:* 8,625 matriculated graduate/professional students (3,880 women). *Graduate faculty:* 1,500. Tuition, nonresident: full-time $10,704. *Required fees:* $4,349. *Graduate housing:* Rooms and/or apartments available to single and married students. *Student services:* Campus employment opportunities, campus safety program, career counseling, child daycare facilities, disabled student services, exercise/wellness program, free psychological counseling, grant writing training, international student services, low-cost health insurance, multicultural affairs office. *Library facilities:* Doe Library plus 30 others. *Online resources:* library catalog, web page, access to other libraries' catalogs. *Collection:* 12.3 million titles, 139,455 serial subscriptions, 83,367 audiovisual materials.

Computer facilities: 600 computers available on campus for general student use. A campuswide network can be accessed from student residence rooms and from off campus. Internet access and online class registration are available. *Web address:* http://www.berkeley.edu/.

General Application Contact: 510-642-7405.

GRADUATE UNITS

Graduate Division Average age 26. Expenses: Contact institution. *Financial support:* Fellowships, research assistantships, teaching assistantships, career-related internships or fieldwork, Federal Work-Study, institutionally sponsored loans, and tuition waivers (full and partial) available. Support available to part-time students. Financial award applicants required to submit FAFSA. *Degree program information:* Part-time and evening/weekend programs available. Offers ancient history and Mediterranean archaeology (MA, PhD); applied science and technology (PhD); Asian studies (PhD); bioengineering (PhD); biophysics (MA, PhD); Buddhist studies (PhD); comparative biochemistry (PhD); demography (MA, PhD); East Asian studies (MA); endocrinology (MA, PhD); energy and resources (MA, MS, PhD); ethnic studies (PhD); folklore (MA); French (PhD); international and area studies (MA); Italian (PhD); Latin American studies (MA, PhD); logic and the methodology of science (PhD); microbiology (PhD); molecular and biochemical nutrition (PhD); neuroscience (PhD); Northeast Asian studies (MA); ocean engineering (M Eng, MS, D Eng, PhD); performance studies (PhD, C Phil); range management (MS); sociology and demography (PhD); South Asian studies (MA); Southeast Asian studies (MA); Spanish (PhD); vision science (MS, PhD); wood science and technology (MS, PhD). *Application fee:* $60. *Application Contact:* 510-642-7405. *Vice Chancellor for Research and Dean*, Dr. Joseph Cerny.

College of Chemistry Students: 454 full-time (143 women); includes 91 minority (8 African Americans, 68 Asian Americans or Pacific Islanders, 14 Hispanic Americans, 1 Native American), 57 international. *Faculty:* 51 full-time (5 women), 3 part-time/adjunct (1 woman). Expenses: Contact institution. *Financial support:* Fellowships with tuition reimbursements, research assistantships with tuition reimbursements, teaching assistantships with tuition reimbursements, institutionally sponsored loans available. Financial award applicants required to submit FAFSA. In 2001, 12 master's, 60 doctorates awarded. Offers chemical engineering (MS, PhD); chemistry (MS, PhD). *Application fee:* $60. *Application Contact:* Dr. Judith P. Klinman, Chairman, 510-643-9057, Fax: 510-642-9675, E-mail: chemgrad@cchem.berkeley.edu. *Dean*, Dr. Clayton H. Heathcock, 510-642-5060.

College of Engineering Offers ceramic sciences and engineering (M Eng, MS, D Eng, PhD); computer science (MS, PhD); construction engineering and management (M Eng, MS, D Eng, PhD); electrical engineering (M Eng, MS, D Eng, PhD); engineering (M Eng, MS, D Eng, PhD); engineering geoscience (M Eng, MS, D Eng, PhD); environmental quality and environmental water resources engineering (M Eng, MS, D Eng, PhD); geotechnical engineering (M Eng, MS, D Eng, PhD); industrial engineering and operations research (M Eng, MS, D Eng, PhD); materials engineering (M Eng, MS, D Eng, PhD); mechanical engineering (M Eng, MS, D Eng, PhD); mineral engineering (M Eng, MS, D Eng, PhD); nuclear engineering (M Eng, MS, PhD); petroleum engineering (M Eng, MS, D Eng, PhD); physical metallurgy (M Eng, MS, D Eng, PhD); structural engineering, mechanics and materials (M Eng, MS, D Eng, PhD); transportation engineering (M Eng, MS, D Eng, PhD).

College of Environmental Design Offers architecture (M Arch); building science and urban design (MS, PhD); city and regional planning (MCP, PhD); design (MA); design theories and methods (MS, PhD); environmental design (M Arch, MA, MCP, MLA, MS, MUD, PhD); environmental design in developing countries (MS, PhD); environmental planning (MLA, PhD); history of architecture and urban design (MS, PhD); landscape architecture (MLA); landscape design and site planning (MLA); social basis of architecture and urban design (MS, PhD); structures and construction (MS, PhD); the building process (MS, PhD); urban and community design (MLA); urban design (MUD).

College of Letters and Science Offers African American studies (PhD); anthropology (PhD); applied mathematics (PhD); art practice (MFA); astrophysics (PhD); Chinese language (PhD); classical archaeology (MA, PhD); classics (MA, PhD); comparative literature (MA, PhD); composition (MA, PhD); Czech (MA, PhD); economics (PhD); endocrinology (PhD); English (PhD); ethnomusicology (MA, PhD); French (PhD); geography (PhD); geology (MA, MS, PhD); geophysics (MA, MS, PhD); German (MA, PhD); Greek (MA); Hindi-Urdu (MA, PhD); Hispanic languages and literatures (MA, PhD); history (PhD, C Phil); history of art (PhD); integrative biology (PhD); Italian studies (MA, PhD); Japanese language (PhD); Latin (MA); letters and science (MA, MFA, MS, PhD, C Phil); linguistics (MA, PhD); Malay-Indonesian (MA, PhD); mathematics (MA, PhD, C Phil); medical anthropology (PhD); molecular and cell biology (PhD); musicology (MA, PhD); Near Eastern religions (PhD); Near Eastern studies (MA, PhD, C Phil); philosophy (PhD); physics (PhD); Polish (MA, PhD); political science (PhD); psychology (PhD); rhetoric (PhD); Russian (MA, PhD); Sanskrit (MA, PhD); Scandinavian languages and literatures (MA, PhD); Serbo-Croatian (MA, PhD); sociology (MA, PhD); South Asian civilization (MA); statistics (MA, PhD); Tamil (MA, PhD). Electronic applications accepted.

College of Natural Resources Offers agricultural and environmental chemistry (MS, PhD); agricultural and resource economics and policy (PhD); environmental science, policy, and management (MS, PhD); forestry (MF); natural resources (MA, MF, MS, PhD); plant biology (PhD); range management (MS).

Graduate School of Journalism Students: 111 full-time (74 women); includes 34 minority (14 African Americans, 10 Asian Americans or Pacific Islanders, 10 Hispanic Americans), 11 international. Average age 27. 310 applicants, 30% accepted, 59 enrolled. *Faculty:* 15 full-time (5 women), 2 part-time/adjunct (1 woman). Expenses: Contact institution. *Financial support:* In 2001–02, 45 students received support; fellowships, research assistantships, teaching assistantships, career-related internships or fieldwork, Federal Work-Study, institutionally sponsored loans, scholarships/grants, and tuition waivers (full and partial) available. Financial award application deadline: 12/16; financial award applicants required to submit FAFSA. In 2001, 51 degrees awarded. Offers journalism (MJ). *Application deadline:* For fall admission, 12/16. *Application fee:* $60. *Application Contact:* Michele Rabin, Director of Admissions, 510-642-3383, Fax: 510-643-9136, E-mail: applysoj@uclink.berkeley.edu. *Dean*, Orville Schell, 510-642-3394.

Graduate School of Public Policy Offers public policy (MPP, PhD).

Haas School of Business Students: 608 full-time (169 women), 343 part-time (85 women); includes 165 minority (12 African Americans, 132 Asian Americans or Pacific Islanders, 21 Hispanic Americans), 358 international. Average age 28. *Faculty:* 70 full-time (14 women), 67 part-time/adjunct (11 women). Expenses: Contact institution. *Financial support:* Fellowships, research assistantships, teaching assistantships, career-related internships or fieldwork, Federal Work-Study, institutionally sponsored loans, scholarships/grants, and tuition waivers (full) available. Support available to part-time students. Financial award application deadline: 3/2; financial award applicants required to submit FAFSA. In 2001, 359 master's, 13 doctorates awarded. *Degree program information:* Part-time and evening/weekend programs available. Offers accounting (PhD); business (MBA, MFE, PhD, MBA/MFE); business administration (MBA); business administration and financial engineering (MBA/MFE); business administrator (MBA); business and public policy (PhD); finance (PhD); financial engineering (MFE); marketing (PhD); organizational behavior and industrial relations (PhD); real estate (PhD). *Application fee:* $60. *Application Contact:* MBA Admissions Office, 510-642-1405, Fax: 510-643-6659, E-mail: mbaadms@haas.berkeley.edu. *Dean*, Benjamin E. Hermalin, 510-643-9690, Fax: 510-642-9128, E-mail: hermalin@haas.berkeley.edu.

School of Education Offers advanced reading and language leadership (MA); developmental teacher education (MA); education (MA, Ed D, PhD, Certificate); education in mathematics, science, and technology (MA, PhD); education with a multiple subject credential (MA); education/single subject teaching: mathematics (MA); education/single subject teaching: science (MA); educational leadership (Ed D); English (Certificate); human development and education (MA, PhD); language, literacy, and culture (MA, Ed D, PhD); policy (MA); policy research (PhD); program evaluation and assessment (Ed D); quantitative methods in education (PhD); school psychology (PhD); science and mathematics (PhD); science and mathematics education (MA); social and cultural analysis and social theory (MA, PhD); special education (PhD).

School of Information Management and Systems Offers information management and systems (MIMS, PhD).

School of Public Health Offers biostatistics (MPH); environmental health sciences (MPH, MS, PhD); epidemiology (MPH, MS, PhD); epidemiology/biostatistics (MPH); health and medical sciences (MS); health and social behavior (MPH); health policy and management (MPH); health services and policy analysis (PhD); infectious diseases (MPH, MS, PhD); infectious diseases and immunity (PhD); interdisciplinary (MPH); maternal and child health (MPH); public health (MA, MPH, MS, Dr PH, PhD); public health nutrition (MPH).

School of Social Welfare Students: 222 full-time (187 women); includes 68 minority (16 African Americans, 23 Asian Americans or Pacific Islanders, 22 Hispanic Americans, 7 Native Americans), 7 international. Average age 28. 438 applicants, 34% accepted, 98 enrolled. Expenses: Contact institution. *Financial support:* Fellowships, research assistantships with partial tuition reimbursements, teaching assistantships with partial tuition reimbursements, career-related internships or fieldwork, Federal Work-Study, scholarships/grants, traineeships, health care benefits, and unspecified assistantships available. Financial award application deadline: 12/15; financial award applicants required to submit FAFSA. In 2001, 94 master's, 7 doctorates awarded. Offers social welfare (MSW, PhD). *Application deadline:* Applications are processed on a rolling basis. *Application fee:* $60. *Application Contact:* Rafael Herrera, Director of Admissions, 510-642-9042, Fax: 510-643-6126, E-mail: socwelf@uclink4.berkeley.edu. *Dean*, Dr. James Midgley, 510-642-5039.

School of Law Students: 957 full-time (573 women); includes 233 minority (32 African Americans, 141 Asian Americans or Pacific Islanders, 56 Hispanic Americans, 4 Native Americans), 37 international. Average age 24. 5,632 applicants, 16% accepted, 299 enrolled. *Faculty:* 69 full-time (25 women), 95 part-time/adjunct (31 women). Expenses: Contact institution. *Financial support:* In 2001–02, 903 students received support, including 9 fellowships with partial tuition reimbursements available (averaging $7,778 per year), 38 research assistantships with partial tuition reimbursements available (averaging $7,841 per year), 25 teaching assistantships with full and partial tuition reimbursements available (averaging $8,276 per year); career-related internships or fieldwork, Federal Work-Study, institutionally sponsored loans, scholarships/grants, health care benefits, tuition waivers (partial), and unspecified assistantships also available. Support available to part-time students. Financial award application deadline: 3/2; financial award applicants required to submit FAFSA. In 2001, 282 first professional degrees, 29 master's, 5 doctorates awarded. Offers jurisprudence and social policy (PhD); law (JD, LL M, JSD). *Application deadline:* For fall admission, 2/1. Applications are processed on a rolling basis. *Application fee:* $65. *Application Contact:* Edward Tom, Director of Admissions, 510-642-2274, Fax: 510-643-6222, E-mail: admissions@law.berkeley.edu. *Dean*, John P. Dwyer, 510-642-6483, Fax: 510-642-9893.

School of Optometry Students: 230 full-time (145 women). Average age 24. 191 applicants, 31% accepted. *Faculty:* 26 full-time (5 women), 111 part-time/adjunct (25 women). Expenses: Contact institution. *Financial support:* Career-related internships or fieldwork, Federal Work-Study, institutionally sponsored loans, and scholarships/grants available. Financial award application deadline: 3/2; financial award applicants required to submit FAFSA. In 2001, 56 degrees awarded. Offers optometry (OD). *Application deadline:* For fall admission, 12/31. *Application fee:* $60. *Application Contact:* Dr. Alberto Ledesma, Student Affairs Officer, 510-642-9537, Fax: 510-643-5109, E-mail: ucbso@spectacle.berkeley.edu. *Dean*, Dr. Dennis M. Levi, 510-642-3414, Fax: 510-642-7806, E-mail: dlevi@spectacle.berkeley.edu.

UNIVERSITY OF CALIFORNIA, DAVIS, Davis, CA 95616

General Information State-supported, coed, university. CGS member. *Enrollment:* 4,890 full-time matriculated graduate/professional students (2,527 women), 9 part-time matriculated graduate/professional students (3 women). *Graduate faculty:* 1,371 full-time, 231 part-time/adjunct. Tuition, state resident: full-time $4,831. Tuition, nonresident: full-time $15,725. *Graduate housing:* Rooms and/or apartments available to single and married students. Housing application deadline: 4/1. *Student services:* Campus employment opportunities, campus safety program, career counseling, child daycare facilities, disabled student services, exercise/wellness program, free psychological counseling, grant writing training, international student services, low-cost health insurance, multicultural affairs office, teacher training, writing training. *Library facilities:* Peter J. Shields Library plus 5 others. *Online resources:* library catalog, web page, access to other libraries' catalogs. *Collection:* 2.9 million titles, 45,665 serial subscriptions.

Computer facilities: 600 computers available on campus for general student use. A campuswide network can be accessed from student residence rooms and from off campus. Internet access, software packages are available. *Web address:* http://www.ucdavis.edu/.

General Application Contact: 530-752-2772.

GRADUATE UNITS

Graduate School of Management Students: 130 full-time (51 women), 2 part-time (1 woman); includes 23 minority (1 African American, 19 Asian Americans or Pacific Islanders, 2 Hispanic Americans, 1 Native American), 11 international. Average age 29. 449 applicants, 29% accepted. *Faculty:* 23 full-time (4 women), 23 part-time/adjunct (2 women). Expenses: Contact institution. *Financial support:* In 2001–02, 81 students received support; research assistantships with partial tuition reimbursements available, teaching assistantships with partial tuition reimbursements available, career-related internships or fieldwork, Federal Work-Study, institutionally sponsored loans, scholarships/grants, health care benefits, tuition waivers (full), and unspecified assistantships available. Support available to part-time students. Financial award application deadline: 3/1; financial award applicants required to submit FAFSA. In 2001, 125 degrees awarded. *Degree program information:* Part-time programs available. Offers management (MBA). *Application deadline:* For fall admission, 12/1 (priority date). Applications are processed on a rolling basis. *Application fee:* $60. Electronic applications accepted. *Application Contact:* Holly Bishop-Green, Associate Director, Admissions and Student Services, 530-752-7363, Fax: 530-752-2924, E-mail: hbbishopgreen@ucdavis.edu. *Dean*, Robert H. Smiley, 530-752-7366, Fax: 530-752-2924.

Graduate Studies Students: 3,374 full-time (1,609 women), 9 part-time (3 women); includes 539 minority (49 African Americans, 328 Asian Americans or Pacific Islanders, 132 Hispanic Americans, 30 Native Americans), 806 international. Average age 29. 6,074 applicants, 42% accepted, 1011 enrolled. Expenses: Contact institution. *Financial support:* In 2001–02, 2,889 students received support, including 1,240 fellowships with full and partial tuition reimbursements available (averaging $5,739 per year), 1,484 research assistantships with full and partial tuition reimbursements available (averaging $9,446 per year), 1,052 teaching assistantships with partial tuition reimbursements available (averaging $13,186 per year); career-related internships or fieldwork, Federal Work-Study, institutionally sponsored loans, scholarships/grants, traineeships, and tuition waivers (full and partial) also available. Support available to part-time students. Financial award application deadline: 1/15; financial award applicants required to submit FAFSA. In 2001, 495 master's, 346 doctorates awarded. *Degree program information:* Part-time programs available. Offers acting (MFA); agricultural and environmental chemistry (MS, PhD); agricultural and resource economics (MS, PhD); animal behavior (MS, PhD); animal science (MAM, MS); anthropology (MA, PhD); applied linguistics (MA); applied mathematics (MS, PhD); art (MFA); art history (MA); atmospheric sciences (MS, PhD); avian sciences (MS); biochemistry and molecular biology (MS, PhD); biophysics (MS, PhD); cell and developmental biology (PhD); chemistry (MS, PhD); child development (MS); community development (MS); comparative literature (PhD); comparative pathology (MS, PhD); composition (MA, PhD); conducting (MA, PhD); creative writing (MA); cultural studies (MA, PhD); dramatic art (PhD); ecology (MS, PhD); economics (MA, PhD); education (Ed D); English (MA, PhD); entomology (MS, PhD); epidemiology (MS, PhD); exercise science (MS); food science (MS, PhD); French (PhD); genetics (MS, PhD); geography (MA, PhD); geology (MS, PhD); German (MA, PhD); history (MA, PhD); horticulture and agronomy (MS); human development (PhD); hydrologic sciences (MS, PhD); immunology (MS, PhD); instructional studies (PhD); international agricultural development (MS); linguistics (MA); mathematics (MA, MAT, PhD); medical informatics (MS); microbiology (MS, PhD); molecular, cellular and integrative physiology (MS, PhD); musicology (MA, PhD); Native American studies (MA, PhD); neuroscience (PhD); nutrition (MS, PhD); pharmacology/toxicology (MS, PhD); philosophy (MA, PhD); physics (MS, PhD); plant biology (MS, PhD); plant pathology (MS, PhD); plant protection and pest management (MS); political science (MA, PhD); population biology (PhD); psychological studies (PhD); psychology (PhD); sociocultural studies (PhD); sociology (MA, PhD); soil science (MS, PhD); Spanish (MA, PhD); statistics (MS, PhD); textile arts and costume design (MFA); textiles (MS). *Application deadline:* Applications are processed on a rolling basis. *Application fee:* $60. Electronic applications accepted. *Application Contact:* Dr. Lisa S. Webb, Assistant Dean of Students, 530-752-2119, Fax: 530-752-6622, E-mail: lswebb@ucdavis.edu. *Dean*, Christina González, 530-752-0650, Fax: 530-752-6222.

College of Engineering Students: 756 full-time (194 women), 4 part-time; includes 141 minority (9 African Americans, 112 Asian Americans or Pacific Islanders, 18 Hispanic Americans, 2 Native Americans), 257 international. Average age 29. 1,960 applicants, 39% accepted, 223 enrolled. *Faculty:* 231 full-time, 9 part-time/adjunct. Expenses: Contact institution. *Financial support:* In 2001–02, 579 students received support, including 204 fellowships with full and partial tuition reimbursements available (averaging $5,561 per year), 367 research assistantships with full and partial tuition reimbursements available (averaging $9,650 per year), 149 teaching assistantships with partial tuition reimbursements available (averaging $11,582 per year); career-related internships or fieldwork, Federal Work-Study, institutionally sponsored loans, scholarships/grants, and tuition waivers (full and partial) also available. Support available to part-time students. Financial award application deadline: 1/15; financial award applicants required to submit FAFSA. In 2001, 141 master's, 70 doctorates awarded. *Degree program information:* Part-time programs available. Offers aeronautical engineering (M Engr, MS, D Engr, PhD, Certificate); applied science (MS, PhD); biological and agricultural engineering (M Engr, MS, D Engr, PhD); biomedical engineering (MS, PhD); chemical engineering (MS, PhD); civil and environmental engineering (M Engr, MS, D Engr, PhD, Certificate); computer science (MS, PhD); electrical and computer engineering (MS, PhD); engineering (M Engr, MS, D Engr, PhD, Certificate); materials science (MS, PhD, Certificate); mechanical engineering (M Engr, MS, D Engr, PhD, Certificate); transportation, technology and policy (MS, PhD). *Application deadline:* Applications are processed on a rolling basis. *Application fee:* $60. Electronic applications accepted. *Application Contact:* Donna Davies, Information Contact, 530-752-0592, Fax: 530-752-8058, E-mail: dedavies@ucdavis.edu. *Interim Dean*, Dr. Zuhair A. Munir, 530-752-0554.

School of Law Students: 552 full-time (312 women); includes 169 minority (14 African Americans, 108 Asian Americans or Pacific Islanders, 45 Hispanic Americans, 2 Native Americans), 15 international. Average age 25. 2,779 applicants, 31% accepted, 214 enrolled. *Faculty:* 32 full-time (10 women), 28 part-time/adjunct (11 women). Expenses: Contact institution. *Financial support:* In 2001–02, 475 students received support, including 13 research assistantships with partial tuition reimbursements available, 18 teaching assistantships with partial tuition reimbursements available; Federal Work-Study, institutionally sponsored loans, scholarships/grants, and health care benefits also available. Financial award application deadline: 3/2; financial award applicants required to submit FAFSA. In 2001, 164 first professional degrees, 13 master's awarded. Offers law (JD, LL M). *Application deadline:* For fall admission, 2/1. Applications are processed on a rolling basis. *Application fee:* $60. Electronic applications accepted. *Application Contact:* Sharon Pinkney, Director, Admissions, 530-752-6477, Fax: 530-752-4704, E-mail: lawadmissions@ucdavis.edu. *Dean*, Rex R. Perschbacher, 530-752-0243, Fax: 530-752-4704, E-mail: rrperschbacher@ucdavis.edu.

School of Medicine Students: 406 full-time (203 women); includes 190 minority (12 African Americans, 138 Asian Americans or Pacific Islanders, 37 Hispanic Americans, 3 Native Americans) Average age 26. 4,231 applicants, 12% accepted. *Faculty:* 508 full-time (129 women), 64 part-time/adjunct (22 women). Expenses: Contact institution. *Financial support:* In 2001–02, 360 students received support, including 16 fellowships with full tuition reimbursements available (averaging $17,000 per year), 6 research assistantships with full tuition reimbursements available (averaging $4,230 per year), 6 teaching assistantships with partial tuition reimbursements available (averaging $2,265 per year); institutionally sponsored loans and scholarships/grants also available. Financial award application deadline: 3/2; financial award applicants required to submit FAFSA. In 2001, 93 degrees awarded. Offers medicine (MD, MA). *Application deadline:* For fall admission, 11/1. Applications are processed on a rolling basis. *Application fee:* $60. *Application Contact:* Edward D. Dagang, Director of Admissions, 530-752-2717, Fax: 916-752-2376, E-mail: medadmsinfo@ucdavis.edu. *Dean*, Dr. Joseph Silva, 530-752-0321.

School of Veterinary Medicine Offers veterinary medicine (DVM, MPVM, Certificate). Electronic applications accepted.

See in-depth description on page 1163.

UNIVERSITY OF CALIFORNIA, HASTINGS COLLEGE OF THE LAW, San Francisco, CA 94102-4978

General Information State-supported, coed, graduate-only institution. *Enrollment by degree level:* 1,252 first professional. *Graduate faculty:* 46 full-time (11 women), 88 part-time/adjunct (28 women). Tuition, state resident: full-time $10,175. Tuition, nonresident: full-time $19,661. *Required fees:* $1,234. *Graduate housing:* Rooms and/or apartments available on a first-come, first-served basis to single and married students. Typical cost: $7,200 per year for single students; $7,200 per year for married students. Room charges vary according to housing facility selected. *Student services:* Campus employment opportunities, campus safety program, career counseling, disabled student services, free psychological counseling, international student services, low-cost health insurance, writing training. *Library facilities:* Hastings Law Library. *Online resources:* library catalog, web page. *Collection:* 413,468 titles, 8,036 serial subscriptions, 3,205 audiovisual materials.

Computer facilities: 143 computers available on campus for general student use. A campuswide network can be accessed from student residence rooms and from off campus. Internet access is available. *Web address:* http://www.uchastings.edu/.

General Application Contact: Akira Shiroma, Director of Admissions, 415-565-4623, Fax: 415-565-4863, E-mail: admiss@uchastings.edu.

GRADUATE UNITS

Graduate Program Students: 1,252 full-time (658 women); includes 410 minority (39 African Americans, 272 Asian Americans or Pacific Islanders, 92 Hispanic Americans, 7 Native Americans), 4 international. Average age 27. 4,800 applicants, 31% accepted. *Faculty:* 46 full-time (11 women), 88 part-time/adjunct (28 women). Expenses: Contact institution. *Financial support:* In 2001–02, 1,063 students received support. Career-related internships or fieldwork, Federal Work-Study, institutionally sponsored loans, and scholarships/grants available. Support available to part-time students. Financial award application deadline: 3/1; financial award applicants required to submit FAFSA. In 2001, 351 degrees awarded. Offers law (JD, LL M). *Application deadline:* For fall admission, 3/1. Applications are processed on a rolling basis. *Application fee:* $60. Electronic applications accepted. *Application Contact:* Akira Shiroma, Director of Admissions, 415-565-4623, Fax: 415-565-4863, E-mail: admiss@uchastings.edu. *Chancellor and Dean*, Mary Kay Kane, 415-565-4700, Fax: 415-565-4702.

UNIVERSITY OF CALIFORNIA, IRVINE, Irvine, CA 92697

General Information State-supported, coed, university. CGS member. *Enrollment:* 3,286 full-time matriculated graduate/professional students (1,282 women), 112 part-time matriculated graduate/professional students (27 women). *Graduate faculty:* 870. Tuition, nonresident: full-time $10,704. *Required fees:* $8,396. Tuition and fees vary according to course load, program and student level. *Graduate housing:* Rooms and/or apartments available on a first-come, first-served basis to single and married students. Typical cost: $2,850 per year ($6,500 including board) for single students; $5,350 per year for married students. *Student services:* Campus employment opportunities, campus safety program, career counseling,

University of California, Irvine (continued)
child daycare facilities, disabled student services, exercise/wellness program, free psychological counseling, grant writing training, international student services, low-cost health insurance, multicultural affairs office, teacher training, writing training. *Library facilities:* Main Library plus 1 other. *Online resources:* library catalog, web page, access to other libraries' catalogs. *Collection:* 2.4 million titles, 19,287 serial subscriptions, 88,308 audiovisual materials.

Computer facilities: 500 computers available on campus for general student use. A campuswide network can be accessed from student residence rooms and from off campus. Internet access and online class registration are available. *Web address:* http://www.uci.edu/.

General Application Contact: 949-824-4611, Fax: 949-824-2095, E-mail: ogsfront@uci.edu.

GRADUATE UNITS

College of Medicine Students: 483 full-time (225 women), 1 part-time; includes 71 minority (8 African Americans, 24 Asian Americans or Pacific Islanders, 39 Hispanic Americans), 11 international. Average age 27. 118 applicants, 19% accepted, 8 enrolled. *Faculty:* 164. Expenses: Contact institution. *Financial support:* Fellowships, research assistantships, teaching assistantships, career-related internships or fieldwork, institutionally sponsored loans, and tuition waivers (full and partial) available. Financial award application deadline: 3/2; financial award applicants required to submit FAFSA. In 2001, 83 first professional degrees, 7 master's, 13 doctorates awarded. Offers medicine (MD, MS, PhD). *Application fee:* $60. Electronic applications accepted. *Application Contact:* Peggy Harvey-Lee, Director of Admissions, 949-824-5388. *Dean,* Dr. Thomas Cesario, 949-824-5926.

Graduate Programs in Medicine Students: 105 full-time (52 women), 1 (woman) part-time; includes 35 minority (24 Asian Americans or Pacific Islanders, 11 Hispanic Americans), 11 international. 118 applicants, 19% accepted, 8 enrolled. *Faculty:* 78. Expenses: Contact institution. *Financial support:* Fellowships, research assistantships, teaching assistantships, career-related internships or fieldwork, institutionally sponsored loans, and tuition waivers (full and partial) available. Financial award application deadline: 3/2; financial award applicants required to submit FAFSA. In 2001, 7 master's, 13 doctorates awarded. Offers biological sciences (MS, PhD); environmental toxicology (MS, PhD); genetic counseling (MS); medicine (MS, PhD); pharmacology and toxicology (MS, PhD). *Application deadline:* For fall and spring admission, 1/15; for winter admission, 10/15. Applications are processed on a rolling basis. *Application fee:* $60. Electronic applications accepted. *Application Contact:* Peggy Harvey-Lee, Director of Admissions, 949-824-5388.

Office of Research and Graduate Studies Students: 2,803 full-time (1,057 women), 111 part-time (27 women); includes 593 minority (29 African Americans, 400 Asian Americans or Pacific Islanders, 159 Hispanic Americans, 5 Native Americans), 478 international. Average age 31. 5,883 applicants, 35% accepted, 1027 enrolled. *Faculty:* 706. Expenses: Contact institution. *Financial support:* Fellowships with full and partial tuition reimbursements, research assistantships with full tuition reimbursements, teaching assistantships with full and partial tuition reimbursements, career-related internships or fieldwork, Federal Work-Study, institutionally sponsored loans, scholarships/grants, tuition waivers (full and partial), and unspecified assistantships available. Support available to part-time students. Financial award application deadline: 3/2; financial award applicants required to submit FAFSA. In 2001, 601 master's, 110 doctorates awarded. *Degree program information:* Part-time and evening/weekend programs available. Offers educational administration (Ed D); elementary and secondary education (MA); information and computer science (MS, PhD). *Application deadline:* For fall and spring admission, 1/15; for winter admission, 10/15. *Application fee:* $60. Electronic applications accepted. *Application Contact:* 949-824-4611, Fax: 949-824-9096, E-mail: ogsfront@uci.edu. *Vice Chancellor for Research and Dean of Graduate Studies,* Dr. William Parker, 949-824-5796, Fax: 949-824-2095, E-mail: whparker@uci.edu.

Graduate School of Management Students: 811 full-time (219 women), 8 part-time; includes 96 minority (7 African Americans, 73 Asian Americans or Pacific Islanders, 15 Hispanic Americans, 1 Native American), 71 international. 1,405 applicants, 43% accepted, 350 enrolled. *Faculty:* 40. Expenses: Contact institution. *Financial support:* In 2001–02, 320 students received support, including 61 fellowships with partial tuition reimbursements available (averaging $6,000 per year), 25 research assistantships with partial tuition reimbursements available (averaging $6,000 per year), 65 teaching assistantships with partial tuition reimbursements available (averaging $13,329 per year); career-related internships or fieldwork, Federal Work-Study, institutionally sponsored loans, scholarships/grants, tuition waivers (full), and unspecified assistantships also available. Support available to part-time students. Financial award application deadline: 3/2; financial award applicants required to submit FAFSA. In 2001, 354 master's, 1 doctorate awarded. *Degree program information:* Part-time and evening/weekend programs available. Offers management (MBA, PhD). *Application deadline:* For fall admission, 12/1 (priority date); for spring admission, 5/1. Applications are processed on a rolling basis. *Application fee:* $75. Electronic applications accepted. *Application Contact:* 949-824-4622, Fax: 949-824-2944, E-mail: gsm-mba@uci.edu. *Dean,* David H. Blake, 949-824-8470, Fax: 949-824-8469.

School of Biological Sciences Students: 182 full-time (107 women), 1 (woman) part-time; includes 58 minority (1 African American, 40 Asian Americans or Pacific Islanders, 17 Hispanic Americans), 20 international. Average age 27. 398 applicants, 39% accepted, 75 enrolled. *Faculty:* 80. Expenses: Contact institution. *Financial support:* Fellowships with full tuition reimbursements, research assistantships with full tuition reimbursements, teaching assistantships with full tuition reimbursements, career-related internships or fieldwork, institutionally sponsored loans, scholarships/grants, and tuition waivers (full and partial) available. Financial award application deadline: 3/2; financial award applicants required to submit FAFSA. In 2001, 1 master's, 7 doctorates awarded. Offers biological science (MS); biological sciences (MS, PhD); neurobiology and behavior (MS). *Application deadline:* For fall and spring admission, 1/15; for winter admission, 10/15. Applications are processed on a rolling basis. *Application fee:* $60. Electronic applications accepted. *Application Contact:* Kimberly McKinney, Administrator, 949-824-8145, Fax: 949-824-7407, E-mail: gp-mbgb@uci.edu. *Dean,* Dr. Susan V. Bryant, 949-824-5316.

School of Engineering Students: 346 full-time (69 women), 57 part-time (6 women); includes 97 minority (2 African Americans, 82 Asian Americans or Pacific Islanders, 13 Hispanic Americans), 161 international. Average age 29. 991 applicants, 35% accepted, 155 enrolled. *Faculty:* 77. Expenses: Contact institution. *Financial support:* In 2001–02, 45 fellowships with tuition reimbursements (averaging $1,250 per year), 119 research assistantships with tuition reimbursements (averaging $1,120 per year), 38 teaching assistantships with tuition reimbursements (averaging $1,480 per year) were awarded. Institutionally sponsored loans and tuition waivers (full and partial) also available. Financial award application deadline: 3/2; financial award applicants required to submit FAFSA. In 2001, 69 master's, 20 doctorates awarded. *Degree program information:* Part-time programs available. Offers biomedical engineering (MS, PhD); chemical and biochemical engineering (MS, PhD); civil engineering (MS, PhD); computer networks and distributed computing (MS, PhD); computer systems and software (MS, PhD); electrical engineering (MS, PhD); engineering (MS, PhD); environmental engineering (MS, PhD); material science (MS); mechanical and aerospace engineering (MS, PhD). *Application deadline:* For fall and spring admission, 1/15 (priority date); for winter admission, 10/15 (priority date). Applications are processed on a rolling basis. *Application fee:* $60. Electronic applications accepted. *Application Contact:* John Sommerhauser, Graduate Counselor, 949-824-6475, Fax: 949-824-3440, E-mail: jdsommer@uci.edu. *Dean,* Dr. Nicolaos G. Alexopoulos, 949-824-6002, Fax: 949-824-7966, E-mail: alfios@uci.edu.

School of Humanities Students: 354 full-time (193 women), 4 part-time (1 woman); includes 92 minority (3 African Americans, 42 Asian Americans or Pacific Islanders, 46 Hispanic Americans, 1 Native American), 16 international. Average age 31. 754 applicants, 21% accepted, 80 enrolled. *Faculty:* 146. Expenses: Contact institution. *Financial support:* Fellowships with full and partial tuition reimbursements, research assistantships with full tuition reimbursements, teaching assistantships with full and partial tuition reimbursements, institutionally sponsored loans and tuition waivers (full and partial) available. Financial award application deadline: 3/2; financial award applicants required to submit FAFSA. In 2001, 38 master's, 22 doctorates awarded. Offers art history (MA, PhD); Chinese (MA, PhD); classics (MA, PhD); comparative literature (MA, PhD); East Asian cultures (MA, PhD); English (MA, PhD); French (MA, PhD); German (MA, PhD); history (MA, PhD); humanities (MA, MAT, MFA, PhD); Japanese (MA, PhD); philosophy (MA, PhD); Spanish (MA, MAT, PhD); visual studies (PhD); writing (MFA). *Application deadline:* For fall and spring admission, 1/15; for winter admission, 10/15. Applications are processed on a rolling basis. *Application fee:* $60. Electronic applications accepted. *Dean,* Karen Lawrence, 949-824-5131, Fax: 949-824-2379, E-mail: krlawren@uci.edu.

School of Physical Sciences Students: 298 full-time (76 women), 3 part-time; includes 57 minority (2 African Americans, 37 Asian Americans or Pacific Islanders, 17 Hispanic Americans, 1 Native American), 48 international. Average age 27. 502 applicants, 58% accepted, 104 enrolled. *Faculty:* 110. Expenses: Contact institution. *Financial support:* Fellowships, research assistantships, teaching assistantships, career-related internships or fieldwork, institutionally sponsored loans, and tuition waivers (full and partial) available. Financial award application deadline: 3/2; financial award applicants required to submit FAFSA. In 2001, 18 master's, 28 doctorates awarded. Offers chemical and material physics (MS, PhD); chemistry (MS, PhD); chemistry and material physics (PhD); earth system science (MS, PhD); mathematics (MS, PhD); physical sciences (MS, PhD); physics (MS, PhD). *Application deadline:* For fall and spring admission, 1/15 (priority date); for winter admission, 10/15 (priority date). Applications are processed on a rolling basis. *Application fee:* $60. Electronic applications accepted. *Application Contact:* Robert Doedens, Associate Dean, 949-824-6507, Fax: 949-824-2261, E-mail: rjdoeden@uci.edu. *Dean,* Ronald Stern, 949-824-6022, Fax: 949-824-2261, E-mail: rstern@uci.edu.

School of Social Ecology Students: 151 full-time (97 women), 1 part-time; includes 35 minority (1 African American, 18 Asian Americans or Pacific Islanders, 15 Hispanic Americans, 1 Native American), 5 international. Average age 31. 217 applicants, 41% accepted, 38 enrolled. *Faculty:* 56. Expenses: Contact institution. *Financial support:* Fellowships, research assistantships, teaching assistantships, institutionally sponsored loans and tuition waivers (full and partial) available. Financial award application deadline: 3/2; financial award applicants required to submit FAFSA. In 2001, 12 master's, 5 doctorates awarded. Offers criminology, law and society (PhD); environmental analysis and design (PhD); health psychology (PhD); human development (PhD); social ecology (PhD); urban and regional planning (MURP, PhD). *Application deadline:* For fall and spring admission, 1/15 (priority date); for winter admission, 10/15 (priority date). Applications are processed on a rolling basis. *Application fee:* $60. Electronic applications accepted. *Application Contact:* Jeanne Haynes, Academic Counselor, 949-824-5917, Fax: 949-824-2056, E-mail: jhaynes@uci.edu. *Dean,* C. Ronald Huff, 949-824-6094, Fax: 949-824-1845, E-mail: rhuff@uci.edu.

School of Social Sciences Students: 238 full-time (126 women), 4 part-time (2 women); includes 49 minority (4 African Americans, 28 Asian Americans or Pacific Islanders, 16 Hispanic Americans, 1 Native American), 45 international. Average age 32. 419 applicants, 35% accepted, 56 enrolled. *Faculty:* 103. Expenses: Contact institution. *Financial support:* Fellowships, research assistantships, teaching assistantships, institutionally sponsored loans and tuition waivers (full and partial) available. Financial award application deadline: 3/2; financial award applicants required to submit FAFSA. In 2001, 27 master's, 20 doctorates awarded. Offers anthropology (MA, PhD); demographic and social analysis (MA); economics (MA, PhD); linguistics (MA, PhD); logic and philosophy of science (PhD); mathematical behavioral sciences (MA, PhD); political psychology (PhD); political sciences (PhD); psychology (PhD); public choice (MA, PhD); social networks (PhD); social networks-social science (MA); social science (MA, PhD); social sciences (MA, PhD); sociology and social relations-social science (MA, PhD); transportation economics (MA, PhD); transportation science (MA, PhD). *Application deadline:* For fall and spring admission, 1/15 (priority date); for winter admission, 10/15 (priority date). Applications are processed on a rolling basis. *Application fee:* $60. Electronic applications accepted. *Application Contact:* Ivonne Maldonado, Graduate Counselor, 949-824-4074, Fax: 949-824-3548, E-mail: immaldon@uci.edu. *Dean,* William Schonfeld, 949-824-6801.

School of the Arts Students: 119 full-time (69 women), 4 part-time (all women); includes 24 minority (4 African Americans, 11 Asian Americans or Pacific Islanders, 9 Hispanic Americans), 7 international. Average age 29. 343 applicants, 17% accepted, 52 enrolled. *Faculty:* 46. Expenses: Contact institution. *Financial support:* Fellowships, teaching assistantships, institutionally sponsored loans and tuition waivers (full and partial) available. Financial award application deadline: 3/2; financial award applicants required to submit FAFSA. In 2001, 43 degrees awarded. Offers accounting (MFA); acting (MFA); arts (MFA, PhD); choral conducting (MFA); composition and technology (MFA); dance (MFA); design and stage management (MFA); directing (MFA); drama and theatre (PhD); guitar/lute performance (MFA); instrument performance (MFA); jazz composition (MFA); jazz instrumental performance (MFA); piano performance (MFA); studio art (MFA); vocal performance (MFA). *Application deadline:* For fall and spring admission, 1/15; for winter admission, 10/15. Applications are processed on a rolling basis. *Application fee:* $60. Electronic applications accepted. *Application Contact:* Rose May Verrico, Arts Office of Student Affairs, 949-824-2252, Fax: 949-824-2450, E-mail: rmverric@uci.edu. *Dean,* Jill Beck, 949-824-6612, Fax: 949-824-2450, E-mail: jillbeck@uci.edu.

UNIVERSITY OF CALIFORNIA, LOS ANGELES, Los Angeles, CA 90095

General Information State-supported, coed, university. CGS member. *Enrollment:* 8,618 full-time matriculated graduate/professional students (4,099 women). Tuition, nonresident: full-time $10,244. *Required fees:* $3,609. Full-time tuition and fees vary according to program. *Graduate housing:* Rooms and/or apartments available to single and married students. Housing application deadline: 5/15. *Student services:* Campus employment opportunities, campus safety program, career counseling, child daycare facilities, disabled student services, free psychological counseling, international student services, low-cost health insurance, multicultural affairs office. *Library facilities:* University Research Library plus 13 others. *Online resources:* library catalog, web page, access to other libraries' catalogs. *Collection:* 7.5 million titles, 93,854 serial subscriptions, 4.6 million audiovisual materials.

Computer facilities: A campuswide network can be accessed from student residence rooms and from off campus. *Web address:* http://www.ucla.edu/.

General Application Contact: Graduate Admissions, 310-825-1711.

GRADUATE UNITS

Graduate Division Students: 8,618 full-time (4,099 women); includes 2,239 minority (298 African Americans, 1,245 Asian Americans or Pacific Islanders, 652 Hispanic Americans, 44 Native Americans), 1,735 international. ###### applicants, 29% accepted, 2754 enrolled. Expenses: Contact institution. *Financial support:* Fellowships, research assistantships, teaching assistantships, career-related internships or fieldwork, Federal Work-Study, institutionally sponsored loans, scholarships/grants, and tuition waivers (full and partial) available. Support available to part-time students. Financial award application deadline: 3/1; financial award applicants required to submit FAFSA. *Degree program information:* Part-time programs available. Offers East Asian studies (MA). *Application fee:* $60. Electronic applications accepted. *Application Contact:* Graduate Admissions, 310-825-1711. *Dean,* Dr. Claudia Mitchell-Kernan, 310-825-4383.

College of Letters and Science Students: 2,599 full-time (1,236 women); includes 577 minority (73 African Americans, 311 Asian Americans or Pacific Islanders, 169 Hispanic Americans, 24 Native Americans), 528 international. 4,305 applicants, 33% accepted, 525 enrolled. Expenses: Contact institution. *Financial support:* Fellowships, research assistantships, teaching assistantships, Federal Work-Study, institutionally sponsored loans, scholarships/grants, and tuition waivers (full and partial) available. Financial award application deadline: 3/1. Offers African studies (MA); Afro-American studies (MA); American Indian studies (MA); anthropology (MA, PhD); applied linguistics (PhD); applied linguistics and teaching English as a second language (MA); archaeology (MA, PhD); art history (MA, PhD); Asian-American studies (MA); astronomy (MAT, MS, PhD); atmospheric sciences (MS, PhD); biochemistry and molecular biology (MS, PhD); biology (MA, PhD); chemistry (MS, PhD); classics (MA, PhD); comparative literature (MA, PhD); East Asian languages and cultures (MA, PhD); economics (MA, PhD); English (MA, PhD); French and Francophone studies (MA, PhD); geochemistry (MS, PhD); geography (MA, PhD); geology (MS, PhD); geophysics and space physics (MS, PhD); German (MA); Germanic languages (MA, PhD);

Greek (MA); Hispanic languages and literature (PhD); history (MA, PhD); Indo-European studies (PhD); Islamic studies (MA, PhD); Italian (MA, PhD); Latin (MA); Latin American studies (MA); letters and science (MA, MAT, MS, PhD, Certificate); linguistics (MA, PhD); mathematics (MA, MAT, PhD); microbiology, immunology and molecular genetics (PhD); molecular and cellular life sciences (PhD); molecular biology (PhD); molecular, cellular and integrative physiology (PhD); musicology (MA, PhD); Near Eastern languages and cultures (MA, PhD); philosophy (MA, PhD); physics (MAT, MS, PhD); physics education (MAT); physiological science (MS, PhD); plant molecular biology (PhD); political science (MA, PhD); Portuguese (MA); psychology (MA, PhD); Romance linguistics and literature (MA, PhD); Scandinavian (MA, PhD); Slavic languages and literatures (MA, PhD); sociology (MA, PhD); Spanish (MA); statistics (MS, PhD); women's studies (MS, PhD). *Application fee:* $60. Electronic applications accepted. *Application Contact:* Graduate Division Admissions Office, 310-825-1711. *Provost,* Dr. Brian P. Copenhaver, 310-825-4286.

Graduate School of Education and Information Studies Students: 772 full-time (584 women); includes 298 minority (47 African Americans, 106 Asian Americans or Pacific Islanders, 143 Hispanic Americans, 2 Native Americans), 50 international. 927 applicants, 56% accepted, 319 enrolled. *Faculty:* 53. Expenses: Contact institution. *Financial support:* In 2001–02, 503 students received support, including 218 fellowships, 309 research assistantships, 55 teaching assistantships; career-related internships or fieldwork, Federal Work-Study, institutionally sponsored loans, scholarships/grants, and tuition waivers (full and partial) also available. Support available to part-time students. Financial award application deadline: 3/1; financial award applicants required to submit FAFSA. In 2001, 138 master's, 33 doctorates awarded. *Degree program information:* Part-time programs available. Offers archival studies (MLIS); education (M Ed, MA, Ed D, PhD); education and information studies (M Ed, MA, MLIS, Ed D, PhD, Certificate); educational leadership (Ed D); informatics (MLIS); library and information science (PhD, Certificate); library studies (MLIS); special education (PhD). *Application deadline:* For fall admission, 12/15. *Application fee:* $60. Electronic applications accepted. *Application Contact:* Departmental Office, 310-825-8326, E-mail: nobody@bert.gse.ucla.edu. *Interim Dean,* Dr. Herold Levine, 310-825-8326.

John E. Anderson Graduate School of Management *Degree program information:* Part-time programs available. Offers management (MBA, MS, PhD).

School of Engineering and Applied Science Students: 1,165 full-time (210 women); includes 324 minority (10 African Americans, 285 Asian Americans or Pacific Islanders, 29 Hispanic Americans), 576 international. 2,873 applicants, 37% accepted, 362 enrolled. *Faculty:* 135 full-time, 105 part-time/adjunct. Expenses: Contact institution. *Financial support:* In 2001–02, 215 fellowships, 662 research assistantships, 416 teaching assistantships were awarded. Career-related internships or fieldwork, Federal Work-Study, institutionally sponsored loans, and tuition waivers (full and partial) also available. Financial award applicants required to submit FAFSA. In 2001, 191 master's, 91 doctorates awarded. Offers aerospace engineering (MS, PhD); biomedical engineering (MS, PhD); ceramics engineering (MS, PhD); chemical engineering (MS, PhD); computer science (MS, PhD); electrical engineering (MS, PhD); engineering and applied science (MS, PhD); environmental engineering (MS, PhD); geotechnical engineering (MS, PhD); manufacturing engineering (MS); mechanical engineering (MS, PhD); metallurgy (MS, PhD); operations research (MS, PhD); structures (MS, PhD); water resource systems engineering (MS, PhD). *Application fee:* $60. Electronic applications accepted. *Application Contact:* Diane Golomb, Student Affairs Officer, 310-825-1704, Fax: 310-825-2473, E-mail: diane@ea.ucla.edu. *Associate Dean, Academic and Student Affairs,* Dr. Stephen E. Jacobsen, 310-825-1704.

School of Nursing Students: 264 full-time (254 women); includes 89 minority (19 African Americans, 38 Asian Americans or Pacific Islanders, 29 Hispanic Americans, 3 Native Americans), 2 international. 205 applicants, 75% accepted, 116 enrolled. Expenses: Contact institution. *Financial support:* In 2001–02, 232 students received support, including 194 fellowships, 29 research assistantships, 21 teaching assistantships; Federal Work-Study, institutionally sponsored loans, scholarships/grants, and tuition waivers (full and partial) also available. Financial award application deadline: 3/1. In 2001, 127 master's, 3 doctorates awarded. Offers nursing (MSN, PhD). *Application deadline:* For fall admission, 2/1. *Application fee:* $60. Electronic applications accepted. *Application Contact:* Departmental Office, 310-825-7181, E-mail: sonsaff@sonnet.ucla.edu. *Dean,* Marie J. Cowan, 310-825-7181.

School of Public Health Students: 565 full-time (396 women); includes 170 minority (29 African Americans, 97 Asian Americans or Pacific Islanders, 41 Hispanic Americans, 3 Native Americans), 118 international. 801 applicants, 57% accepted, 214 enrolled. *Faculty:* 53. Expenses: Contact institution. *Financial support:* In 2001–02, 483 students received support, including 308 fellowships, 23 research assistantships, 63 teaching assistantships; career-related internships or fieldwork, Federal Work-Study, institutionally sponsored loans, scholarships/grants, and tuition waivers (full and partial) also available. Financial award application deadline: 3/1. In 2001, 143 master's, 5 doctorates awarded. Offers biostatistics (MS, PhD); environmental health sciences (MS, PhD); environmental science and engineering (D Env); epidemiology (MS, PhD); health services (MS, PhD); molecular toxicology (PhD); public health (MS, PhD); public health for health professionals (MPH). *Application deadline:* For fall admission, 12/15. *Application fee:* $60. Electronic applications accepted. *Application Contact:* Departmental Office, 310-825-5524, E-mail: request@admin.ph.ucla.edu. *Dean,* Dr. Linda Rosenstock, 310-825-5524.

School of Public Policy and Social Research Students: 436 full-time (319 women); includes 162 minority (27 African Americans, 53 Asian Americans or Pacific Islanders, 81 Hispanic Americans, 1 Native American), 41 international. 858 applicants, 51% accepted, 137 enrolled. Expenses: Contact institution. *Financial support:* In 2001–02, 365 students received support, including 185 fellowships, 82 research assistantships, 42 teaching assistantships; career-related internships or fieldwork, Federal Work-Study, institutionally sponsored loans, scholarships/grants, and tuition waivers (full and partial) also available. Financial award application deadline: 3/1. Offers public policy (MPP); public policy and social research (MA, MPP, MSW, PhD); social welfare (MSW, PhD); urban planning (MA, PhD). *Application fee:* $60. Electronic applications accepted. *Application Contact:* Departmental Office, 310-206-3148. *Dean,* Barbara Nelson, 310-825-3792.

School of the Arts and Architecture Students: 416 full-time (210 women); includes 87 minority (15 African Americans, 41 Asian Americans or Pacific Islanders, 27 Hispanic Americans, 4 Native Americans), 80 international. 1,542 applicants, 20% accepted, 144 enrolled. Expenses: Contact institution. *Financial support:* In 2001–02, 365 students received support, including 217 fellowships, 16 research assistantships; teaching assistantships, Federal Work-Study, institutionally sponsored loans, scholarships/grants, and tuition waivers (full and partial) also available. Financial award application deadline: 3/1. In 2001, 128 master's, 15 doctorates awarded. Offers architecture and urban design (M Arch, MA, PhD); art (MA, MFA); arts and architecture (M Arch, MA, MFA, MM, DMA, PhD); composition (MA, PhD); culture and performance (MA, PhD); dance (MA, MFA); design/media arts (MFA); ethnomusicology (MA, PhD); performance (MM, DMA). *Application fee:* $60. Electronic applications accepted. *Application Contact:* Departmental Office, 310-825-0525. *Dean,* Dr. Daniel Neuman, 310-206-8504.

School of Theater, Film and Television Students: 370 full-time (188 women); includes 91 minority (21 African Americans, 33 Asian Americans or Pacific Islanders, 35 Hispanic Americans, 2 Native Americans), 38 international. 1,168 applicants, 13% accepted, 106 enrolled. Expenses: Contact institution. *Financial support:* Fellowships with full and partial tuition reimbursements, research assistantships with partial tuition reimbursements, teaching assistantships with partial tuition reimbursements, career-related internships or fieldwork, Federal Work-Study, institutionally sponsored loans, scholarships/grants, traineeships, tuition waivers (full and partial), and unspecified assistantships available. Financial award application deadline: 3/1. In 2001, 68 master's, 5 doctorates awarded. Offers film and television (MA, MFA, PhD); film, television, and digital media (MA, MFA, PhD); theater (MFA, PhD). *Application fee:* $60. Electronic applications accepted. *Application Contact:* Departmental Office, 310-206-8441, E-mail: fdesk103@emeinitz.ucla.edu. *Dean,* Robert Rosen, 310-825-5761.

School of Dentistry Students: 367 full-time (164 women); includes 100 minority (7 African Americans, 90 Asian Americans or Pacific Islanders, 3 Hispanic Americans), 9 international. 1,248 applicants, 11% accepted, 87 enrolled. Expenses: Contact institution. *Financial support:* In 2001–02, 11 fellowships, 7 teaching assistantships were awarded. Research assistantships, Federal Work-Study, institutionally sponsored loans, and tuition waivers (full and partial) also available. Financial award application deadline: 3/1. In 2001, 93 first professional degrees, 9 master's, 4 doctorates awarded. Offers dentistry (DDS, MS, PhD, Certificate); oral biology (MS, PhD). *Application deadline:* For fall admission, 1/15. *Application fee:* $60. *Application Contact:* Departmental Office, 310-825-7354. *Dean,* Dr. No-Hee Park, 310-825-6401.

School of Law Students: 944 full-time (497 women); includes 230 minority (19 African Americans, 138 Asian Americans or Pacific Islanders, 70 Hispanic Americans, 3 Native Americans), 24 international. 5,303 applicants, 20% accepted, 353 enrolled. *Faculty:* 50. Expenses: Contact institution. *Financial support:* In 2001–02, 868 students received support, including 6 research assistantships, 10 teaching assistantships; fellowships, career-related internships or fieldwork, Federal Work-Study, institutionally sponsored loans, and tuition waivers (full and partial) also available. Financial award application deadline: 3/1. In 2001, 293 first professional degrees, 14 master's awarded. Offers law (JD, LL M). *Application fee:* $60. *Application Contact:* Admissions Office, 310-825-2080. *Dean,* Dr. Jonathan Varat, 310-825-4841.

School of Medicine Students: 1,071 full-time (521 women). 5,952 applicants, 5% accepted. Expenses: Contact institution. *Financial support:* In 2001–02, 267 fellowships, 1 research assistantship, 5 teaching assistantships were awarded. Career-related internships or fieldwork, Federal Work-Study, institutionally sponsored loans, scholarships/grants, and tuition waivers (full and partial) also available. In 2001, 141 degrees awarded. Offers medicine (MD, MA, MS, PhD). *Application fee:* $60. *Application Contact:* Admissions Office, 310-825-6081. *Dean/Provost,* Dr. Gerald S. Levey, 310-825-6081.

Graduate Programs in Medicine Students: 488 full-time (234 women). 327 applicants, 21% accepted. Expenses: Contact institution. *Financial support:* In 2001–02, 267 fellowships, 1 research assistantship, 5 teaching assistantships were awarded. Career-related internships or fieldwork, Federal Work-Study, institutionally sponsored loans, scholarships/grants, and tuition waivers (full and partial) also available. Financial award application deadline: 3/1. Offers anatomy and cell biology (PhD); biological chemistry (MS, PhD); biomathematics (MS, PhD); biomedical physics (MS, PhD); clinical research (MS); experimental pathology (MS, PhD); human genetics (MS, PhD); medicine (MA, MS, PhD); microbiology, immunology and molecular genetics (MS, PhD); molecular and medical pharmacology (MS, PhD); molecular, cell and developmental biology (MA, PhD); neuroscience (PhD); physiology (MS, PhD). *Application fee:* $60. *Application Contact:* School of Medicine Admissions Office, 310-825-6081. *Associate Dean,* Dr. David I. Meyer.

UNIVERSITY OF CALIFORNIA, RIVERSIDE, Riverside, CA 92521-0102

General Information State-supported, coed, university. CGS member. *Enrollment:* 1,509 full-time matriculated graduate/professional students (714 women), 31 part-time matriculated graduate/professional students (11 women). *Enrollment by degree level:* 443 master's, 1,091 doctoral. *Graduate faculty:* 510 full-time (123 women). Tuition, state resident: full-time $5,001. Tuition, nonresident: full-time $15,897. *Graduate housing:* Rooms and/or apartments available on a first-come, first-served basis to single and married students. Housing application deadline: 6/1. *Student services:* Campus safety program, career counseling, child daycare facilities, disabled student services, exercise/wellness program, free psychological counseling, international student services, low-cost health insurance, multicultural affairs office, teacher training, writing training. *Library facilities:* Tomas Rivera Library plus 6 others. *Online resources:* library catalog, web page, access to other libraries' catalogs. *Collection:* 2 million titles, 19,294 serial subscriptions, 48,489 audiovisual materials. *Research affiliation:* Lawrence Livermore National Laboratory (archaeology), J. Paul Getty Museum (art history), U.S. Salinity Laboratory (environmental sciences, biochemistry), National Synchrotron Light Source (chemistry, physics), Los Alamos National Laboratory (botany and plant sciences, chemistry, earth sciences, physics), Fermi National Accelerator Laboratory (physics).

Computer facilities: 600 computers available on campus for general student use. A campuswide network can be accessed from student residence rooms and from off campus. Internet access and online class registration are available. *Web address:* http://www.ucr.edu/.

General Application Contact: Graduate Admissions, 909-787-3313, Fax: 909-787-2238, E-mail: grdadmis@ucrac1.ucr.edu.

GRADUATE UNITS

Graduate Division Students: 1,509 full-time (714 women), 31 part-time (11 women); includes 253 minority (26 African Americans, 109 Asian Americans or Pacific Islanders, 110 Hispanic Americans, 8 Native Americans), 492 international. Average age 31. 2,833 applicants, 37% accepted. *Faculty:* 470 full-time (110 women). Expenses: Contact institution. *Financial support:* In 2001–02, fellowships with full and partial tuition reimbursements (averaging $12,000 per year), research assistantships with full and partial tuition reimbursements (averaging $17,128 per year), teaching assistantships with full and partial tuition reimbursements (averaging $14,145 per year) were awarded. Career-related internships or fieldwork, Federal Work-Study, institutionally sponsored loans, scholarships/grants, tuition waivers (full and partial), and readerships also available. Financial award applicants required to submit FAFSA. In 2001, 232 master's, 108 doctorates awarded. *Degree program information:* Part-time and evening/weekend programs available. Offers anthropology (MA, MS, PhD); applied mathematics (MS); applied statistics (PhD); archival management (MA); art history (MA); biochemistry and molecular biology (MS, PhD); biology (MS, PhD); biomedical sciences (PhD); botany (MS, PhD); botany (plant genetics) (PhD); cell, molecular, and developmental biology (MS, PhD); chemical and environmental engineering (MS, PhD); chemistry (MS, PhD); classics (MA, PhD); comparative literature (MA, PhD); computer science (MS, PhD); creative writing and writing for the performing arts (MFA); dance (MFA); dance history and theory (PhD); economics (MA, PhD); electrical engineering (MS, PhD); English (MA, PhD); entomology (MS, PhD); environmental sciences (MS, PhD); environmental toxicology (MS, PhD); genomics and bioinformatics (PhD); geological sciences (MS, PhD); historic preservation (MA); history (MA, PhD); mathematics (MA, MS, PhD); microbiology (MS, PhD); molecular genetics, evolutionary and population genetics (PhD); museum curatorship (MA); music (MA); neuroscience (PhD); philosophy (MA, PhD); physics (MS, PhD); plant biology (PhD); plant biology (plant genetics) (PhD); plant pathology (MS, PhD); plant science (MS); political science (MA, PhD); psychology (PhD); sociology (PhD); soil and water sciences (MS, PhD); statistics (MS). *Application deadline:* For fall admission, 5/1; for winter admission, 2/1; for spring admission, 12/1. Applications are processed on a rolling basis. *Application fee:* $40. Electronic applications accepted. *Application Contact:* Graduate Admissions, 909-787-3313, Fax: 909-787-2238, E-mail: grdadmis@ucrac1.ucr.edu. *Dean,* Dr. Neal Schiller, 909-787-3313, Fax: 909-787-2238.

A. Gary Anderson Graduate School of Management Students: 133 full-time (66 women), 14 part-time (1 woman); includes 30 minority (4 African Americans, 21 Asian Americans or Pacific Islanders, 5 Hispanic Americans), 82 international. Average age 27. Expenses: Contact institution. *Financial support:* Fellowships, research assistantships, teaching assistantships, career-related internships or fieldwork, Federal Work-Study, institutionally sponsored loans, scholarships/grants, and tuition waivers (full) available. Financial award application deadline: 2/1; financial award applicants required to submit FAFSA. In 2001, 73 degrees awarded. *Degree program information:* Part-time and evening/weekend programs available. Offers management (MBA). *Application deadline:* For fall admission, 5/1; for winter admission, 9/1; for spring admission, 12/1. Applications are processed on a rolling basis. *Application fee:* $40. *Application Contact:* Charlotte Weber, Assistant Dean, 909-787-4551, Fax: 909-787-3970, E-mail: mba@agsmmail.ucr.edu. *Dean,* Donald Dye.

Graduate School of Education Students: 169 full-time (122 women), 3 part-time; includes 43 minority (5 African Americans, 10 Asian Americans or Pacific Islanders, 26 Hispanic Americans, 2 Native Americans), 1 international. Average age 34. 173 applicants, 48% accepted, 68 enrolled. *Faculty:* 20 full-time (6 women), 27 part-time/adjunct (20 women). Expenses: Contact institution. *Financial support:* Fellowships with full and partial tuition reimbursements, research assistantships with full and partial tuition reimbursements, teaching assistantships with full and partial tuition reimbursements, career-related internships or fieldwork, Federal Work-Study, institutionally sponsored loans, and tuition waivers (full and

University of California, Riverside (continued)

partial) available. Financial award application deadline: 2/1; financial award applicants required to submit FAFSA. In 2001, 16 master's, 6 doctorates awarded. Offers education (M Ed, MA, PhD). *Application deadline:* For fall admission, 5/1; for winter admission, 9/1; for spring admission, 12/1. Applications are processed on a rolling basis. *Application fee:* $40. Electronic applications accepted. *Application Contact:* Dr. Sharon Duffy, Graduate Adviser, 909-787-5990, Fax: 909-787-3942, E-mail: edgrad@ucr.edu. *Dean,* Dr. Robert Calfee, 909-787-5802, Fax: 909-787-3942, E-mail: robert.calfee@ucr.edu.

Spanish Studies Students: 17 full-time (9 women), 1 (woman) part-time; includes 2 minority (both Hispanic Americans), 5 international. Average age 30. 19 applicants, 53% accepted, 6 enrolled. *Faculty:* 7 full-time (3 women), 8 part-time/adjunct (5 women). Expenses: Contact institution. *Financial support:* In 2001–02, teaching assistantships with tuition reimbursements (averaging $14,000 per year); fellowships, career-related internships or fieldwork, Federal Work-Study, institutionally sponsored loans, and tuition waivers (full and partial) also available. Financial award application deadline: 1/5; financial award applicants required to submit FAFSA. In 2001, 1 master's, 1 doctorate awarded. *Degree program information:* Part-time programs available. Offers Spanish (MA, PhD). *Application deadline:* For fall admission, 1/5; for winter admission, 9/1; for spring admission, 12/1. Applications are processed on a rolling basis. *Application fee:* $40. *Application Contact:* Dr. James Parr, Graduate Adviser, 909-787-3746 Ext. 1210, Fax: 909-787-2294, E-mail: clhsgrad@ucr.edu. *Chair,* Dr. William Megenney, E-mail: william.megenney@ucr.edu.

UNIVERSITY OF CALIFORNIA, SAN DIEGO, La Jolla, CA 92093

General Information State-supported, coed, university. CGS member. *Enrollment:* 3,575 matriculated graduate/professional students (1,436 women). *Graduate faculty:* 1,800. Tuition, nonresident: full-time $10,434. *Required fees:* $4,883. *Graduate housing:* Rooms and/or apartments available to single and married students. Typical cost: $8,000 (including board) for single students; $10,000 (including board) for married students. *Student services:* Campus employment opportunities, campus safety program, career counseling, child daycare facilities, disabled student services, free psychological counseling, grant writing training, international student services, low-cost health insurance, multicultural affairs office, teacher training. *Library facilities:* Geisel Library plus 7 others. *Online resources:* library catalog, web page, access to other libraries' catalogs. *Collection:* 2.6 million titles, 25,000 serial subscriptions, 87,625 audiovisual materials. *Research affiliation:* Salk Institute, Veterans Administration Medical Center, Scripps Clinic and Research Foundation, La Jolla Institute.

Computer facilities: 1,020 computers available on campus for general student use. A campuswide network can be accessed from student residence rooms and from off campus. Internet access and online class registration, e-mail are available. *Web address:* http://www.ucsd.edu/.

General Application Contact: Graduate Admissions Office, 858-534-1193.

GRADUATE UNITS

Graduate Studies and Research Students: 3,090 (1,227 women). 8,018 applicants, 30% accepted, 1046 enrolled. *Faculty:* 1,100. Expenses: Contact institution. *Financial support:* Fellowships with full and partial tuition reimbursements, research assistantships with full and partial tuition reimbursements, teaching assistantships with partial tuition reimbursements, career-related internships or fieldwork, institutionally sponsored loans, scholarships/grants, and traineeships available. Support available to part-time students. Financial award applicants required to submit CSS PROFILE or FAFSA. In 2001, 442 master's, 285 doctorates awarded. Offers acting (MFA); aerospace engineering (MS, PhD); anthropology (PhD); applied mathematics (MA); applied mechanics (MS, PhD); applied ocean science (MS, PhD); applied physics (MS, PhD); bilingual education (MA); bioengineering (M Eng, MS, PhD); bioinformatics (PhD); biological oceanography (MS, PhD); biophysics (MS, PhD); chemical engineering (MS, PhD); chemistry (MS, PhD); clinical psychology (PhD); cognitive science (PhD); cognitive science/anthropology (PhD); cognitive science/communication (PhD); cognitive science/computer science and engineering (PhD); cognitive science/linguistics (PhD); cognitive science/neuroscience (PhD); cognitive science/philosophy (PhD); cognitive science/psychology (PhD); cognitive science/sociology (PhD); communication (MA, PhD); communication theory and systems (MS, PhD); comparative literature (MA, PhD); computer engineering (MS, PhD); computer science (MS, PhD); curriculum design (MA); design (MFA); directing (MFA); drama and theatre (PhD); economics (PhD); economics and international affairs (PhD); electrical engineering (M Eng); electronic circuits and systems (MS, PhD); engineering physics (MS, PhD); ethnic studies (PhD); French literature (MA, PhD); geochemistry and marine chemistry (MS, PhD); German literature (MA, PhD); history (MA, PhD); intelligent systems, robotics and control (MS, PhD); Judaic studies (MA); language and communicative disorders (PhD); Latin American studies (MA); linguistics (PhD); literature (PhD); literatures in English (MA, PhD); marine biology (MS, PhD); materials science (MS, PhD); mathematics (MA, PhD); mathematics and science education (PhD); mechanical engineering (MS, PhD); music (MA, DMA, PhD); philosophy (PhD); photonics (MS, PhD); physical oceanography and geological sciences (MS, PhD); physics (MS, PhD); physics/materials physics (MS); playwriting (MFA); political science (PhD); political science and international affairs (PhD); psychology (PhD); public health and epidemiology (PhD); science studies (PhD); signal and image processing (MS, PhD); sociology (PhD); Spanish literature (MA, PhD); stage management (MFA); statistics (MS); structural engineering (MS, PhD); teacher education (M Ed); theatre (PhD); visual arts (MFA). *Application fee:* $40. Electronic applications accepted. *Application Contact:* 858-534-1193. *Dean,* Richard Attiyeh, 858-534-3555.

Division of Biology Students: 196 (88 women). 374 applicants, 41% accepted, 57 enrolled. *Faculty:* 97. Expenses: Contact institution. *Financial support:* Tuition waivers (full) and stipends available. In 2001, 28 master's, 40 doctorates awarded. Offers biochemistry (PhD); biology (MS); cell and developmental biology (PhD); computational neurobiology (PhD); ecology, behavior, and evolution (PhD); genetics and molecular biology (PhD); immunology, virology, and cancer biology (PhD); molecular and cellular biology (PhD); neurobiology (PhD); plant molecular biology (PhD); signal transduction (PhD). Offered in association with the Salk Institute. *Application deadline:* For fall admission, 1/4. *Application fee:* $40. Electronic applications accepted. *Application Contact:* Biology Graduate Admissions Committee, 858-534-3835, E-mail: gradprog@biology.ucsd.edu. *Dean,* Dr. Eduardo Macagno.

Graduate School of International Relations and Pacific Studies Students: 204 full-time (105 women); includes 44 minority (31 Asian Americans or Pacific Islanders, 13 Hispanic Americans), 86 international. Average age 27. 384 applicants, 61% accepted. *Faculty:* 24 full-time (3 women), 31 part-time/adjunct (12 women). Expenses: Contact institution. *Financial support:* In 2001–02, 120 students received support, including 20 fellowships with full and partial tuition reimbursements available (averaging $6,387 per year), 11 research assistantships with partial tuition reimbursements available, 65 teaching assistantships with partial tuition reimbursements available; career-related internships or fieldwork, institutionally sponsored loans, and tuition waivers (full and partial) also available. Support available to part-time students. Financial award application deadline: 3/2; financial award applicants required to submit FAFSA. In 2001, 87 master's, 1 doctorate awarded. *Degree program information:* Part-time programs available. Offers economics and international affairs (PhD); Pacific international affairs (MPIA); political science and international affairs (PhD). *Application deadline:* For fall admission, 2/15 (priority date). Applications are processed on a rolling basis. *Application fee:* $40. Electronic applications accepted. *Application Contact:* Jori J. Cincotta, Director of Admissions, 858-534-5914, Fax: 858-534-1135, E-mail: irps-apply@ucsd.edu. *Dean,* Peter Cowhey, 858-534-1946, Fax: 858-534-3939.

School of Medicine Students: 485 (209 women). *Faculty:* 700. Expenses: Contact institution. Offers medicine (MD, PhD); molecular pathology (PhD); neurosciences (PhD). *Application fee:* $40. *Application Contact:* 858-534-3880.

Graduate Studies in Biomedical Sciences Students: 242. 247 applicants, 25% accepted, 24 enrolled. *Faculty:* 108. Expenses: Contact institution. *Financial support:* Fellowships, research assistantships, stipends available. In 2001, 13 degrees awarded. Offers cell and molecular biology (PhD); molecular pathology (PhD); neuroscience (PhD); pharmacology (PhD); physiology (PhD); regulatory biology (PhD). *Application deadline:* For fall admission, 1/6. *Application fee:* $40. Electronic applications accepted. *Application Contact:* Gina Butcher, Coordinator, 858-534-3982. *Chair,* Jeff Esko, 858-822-1100.

UNIVERSITY OF CALIFORNIA, SAN FRANCISCO, San Francisco, CA 94143

General Information State-supported, coed, graduate-only institution. CGS member. *Graduate faculty:* 1,592. *Graduate housing:* Rooms and/or apartments available to single and married students. *Student services:* Campus employment opportunities, campus safety program, child daycare facilities, free psychological counseling, international student services, low-cost health insurance. *Collection:* 691,041 titles, 5,408 serial subscriptions. *Web address:* http://www.ucsf.edu/.

General Application Contact: Dr. Clifford Attkisson, Dean of Graduate Studies, 415-476-2310.

GRADUATE UNITS

Graduate Division Students: 917 full-time (627 women), 10 part-time (9 women); includes 228 minority (24 African Americans, 146 Asian Americans or Pacific Islanders, 53 Hispanic Americans, 5 Native Americans), 76 international. 1,879 applicants, 22% accepted. *Faculty:* 400. Expenses: Contact institution. *Financial support:* Fellowships, research assistantships, teaching assistantships, career-related internships or fieldwork, Federal Work-Study, institutionally sponsored loans, and tuition waivers (full and partial) available. Support available to part-time students. Financial award applicants required to submit FAFSA. In 2001, 208 master's, 120 doctorates awarded. *Degree program information:* Part-time programs available. Offers anatomy (PhD); biochemistry and molecular biology (PhD); bioengineering (PhD); biophysics (PhD); cell biology (PhD); developmental biology (PhD); endocrinology (PhD); experimental pathology (PhD); genetics (PhD); history of health sciences (MA, PhD); medical anthropology (PhD); microbiology and immunology (PhD); neuroscience (PhD); oral biology (MS, PhD); physical therapy (MPT); physiology (PhD). *Application fee:* $40. *Dean of Graduate Studies,* Dr. Clifford Attkisson, 415-476-2310.

School of Nursing Students: 426 (388 women); includes 117 minority (14 African Americans, 71 Asian Americans or Pacific Islanders, 31 Hispanic Americans, 1 Native American) Expenses: Contact institution. *Financial support:* Fellowships, career-related internships or fieldwork and Federal Work-Study available. Support available to part-time students. Offers nursing (MS, PhD); sociology (PhD). *Application deadline:* For fall admission, 3/1. *Application fee:* $40. *Application Contact:* Jeff Kilmer, Director, Office of Student and Curriculum Services, 415-476-1435. *Dean,* Jane S. Norbeck, 415-476-1805.

School of Dentistry Offers dentistry (DDS).

School of Medicine Students: 605 full-time (327 women); includes 298 minority (36 African Americans, 196 Asian Americans or Pacific Islanders, 61 Hispanic Americans, 5 Native Americans) Average age 24. 4,832 applicants, 5% accepted, 141 enrolled. *Faculty:* 1,460. Expenses: Contact institution. *Financial support:* In 2001–02, 502 students received support. Federal Work-Study, institutionally sponsored loans, scholarships/grants, and tuition waivers (partial) available. Financial award application deadline: 2/1; financial award applicants required to submit FAFSA. In 2001, 142 degrees awarded. Offers medicine (MD). *Application deadline:* For fall admission, 11/1. Applications are processed on a rolling basis. *Application fee:* $60. Electronic applications accepted. *Application Contact:* Kathleen Ryan, Admissions Officer, 415-476-4044, Fax: 415-476-5490. *Dean,* Dr. Haile T. Debas, 415-476-2342, Fax: 415-476-0689, E-mail: hdebas@medsch.ucsf.edu.

School of Pharmacy Students: 584 full-time (410 women); includes 377 minority (9 African Americans, 342 Asian Americans or Pacific Islanders, 26 Hispanic Americans), 13 international. Average age 27. 734 applicants, 23% accepted, 134 enrolled. *Faculty:* 67 full-time (27 women), 8 part-time/adjunct (3 women). Expenses: Contact institution. *Financial support:* In 2001–02, 451 students received support; fellowships, research assistantships, teaching assistantships, career-related internships or fieldwork, Federal Work-Study, institutionally sponsored loans, scholarships/grants, traineeships, and tuition waivers (full) available. Financial award applicants required to submit FAFSA. In 2001, 118 first professional degrees, 1 master's, 10 doctorates awarded. Offers biological and medical informatics (MS, PhD); chemistry and chemical biology (PhD); pharmaceutical sciences and pharmacogenomics (PhD); pharmacy (Pharm D, MS, PhD). *Application fee:* $60. *Application Contact:* James C. Betbeze, Admissions Coordinator, 415-476-2732, Fax: 415-476-6805, E-mail: jcb@itsa.ucsf.edu. *Dean,* Mary Anne Koda Kimble, 415-476-1225, Fax: 415-476-0688, E-mail: deansop@itsa.ucsf.edu.

UNIVERSITY OF CALIFORNIA, SANTA BARBARA, Santa Barbara, CA 93106

General Information State-supported, coed, university. CGS member. *Graduate housing:* Rooms and/or apartments available to single and married students. *Research affiliation:* National Institute for Theoretical Physics, Center for Black Studies (ethnic studies), Jorge de Sena Center for Portuguese Studies, Center for Quantum Electronic Structures (engineering), David Simonett Center for Spatial Analysis, Center for Theater, Education and Research.

GRADUATE UNITS

Graduate Division Electronic applications accepted.

College of Engineering Offers chemical engineering (MS, PhD); computer science (MS, PhD); electrical and computer engineering (MS, PhD); engineering (MS, PhD); materials (MS, PhD); mechanical and environmental engineering (MS, PhD). Electronic applications accepted.

College of Letters and Sciences Offers anthropology (MA, PhD); applied mathematics (MA); art history (MA, PhD); art studio (MFA); biochemistry and molecular biology (PhD); chemistry and biochemistry (MA, MS, PhD); classics (MA, PhD); communication (PhD); comparative literature (MA, PhD); dramatic art (MA, PhD); East Asian languages and cultural studies (MA); ecology, evolution, and marine biology (MA, PhD); economics (MA, PhD); English (PhD); French (MA, PhD); geography (MA, PhD); geological sciences (MA, PhD); geophysics (MS); Germanic languages and literature (MA, PhD); Hispanic languages and literature (PhD); history (MA, PhD); humanities and fine arts (MA, MFA, MM, DMA, PhD); Latin American and Iberian studies (MA); letters and science (MA, MFA, MM, MS, DMA, PhD); linguistics (PhD); marine science (MS, PhD); mathematics (MA, PhD); mathematics, life, and physical sciences (MA, MS, PhD); molecular, cellular, and developmental biology (MA, PhD); music (MA, MM, DMA, PhD); performance (MM, DMA); philosophy (PhD); physics (PhD); political science (MA, PhD); Portuguese (MA); psychology (MA, PhD); religious studies (MA, PhD); social science (MA, PhD); sociology (MA, PhD); Spanish (MA); statistics and applied probability (MA, PhD). Electronic applications accepted.

Donald Bren School of Environmental Science and Management Offers environmental science and management (MESM, PhD). Electronic applications accepted.

Graduate School of Education Offers clinical/school/counseling psychology (M Ed, PhD); education (M Ed, MA, PhD); school psychology (M Ed). Electronic applications accepted.

UNIVERSITY OF CALIFORNIA, SANTA CRUZ, Santa Cruz, CA 95064

General Information State-supported, coed, university. CGS member. *Enrollment:* 1,168 full-time matriculated graduate/professional students (615 women). *Enrollment by degree level:* 320 master's, 816 doctoral, 32 other advanced degrees. *Graduate faculty:* 486 full-time (168 women). *Tuition:* Full-time $19,857. *Graduate housing:* Rooms and/or apartments available to single and married students. *Student services:* Campus employment opportunities, campus safety program, career counseling, child daycare facilities, disabled student services, exercise/wellness program, free psychological counseling, international student services, low-cost health insurance, teacher training. *Library facilities:* McHenry Library plus 9 others. *Online resources:* library catalog, web page, access to other libraries' catalogs. *Collection:* 1.2 million titles, 10,004 serial subscriptions, 500,000 audiovisual materials. *Research affiliation:* Stanford Linear Accelerator Center, Fermi National Accelerator Laboratory, Lawrence Livermore National Laboratory, Scripps Institution of Oceanography (earth sciences), University of Texas Marine Science Institute (earth sciences).

Computer facilities: 200 computers available on campus for general student use. A campuswide network can be accessed from student residence rooms and from off campus. Internet access is available. *Web address:* http://www.ucsc.edu/.

General Application Contact: Diana J. Dean, Graduate Admissions, 831-459-2301.

GRADUATE UNITS

Division of Graduate Studies Students: 1,168 full-time (615 women); includes 212 minority (18 African Americans, 98 Asian Americans or Pacific Islanders, 82 Hispanic Americans, 14 Native Americans), 204 international. 2,825 applicants, 37% accepted. *Faculty:* 486 full-time (168 women). Expenses: Contact institution. *Financial support:* Fellowships, research assistantships, teaching assistantships, career-related internships or fieldwork, Federal Work-Study, institutionally sponsored loans, and tuition waivers (full and partial) available. Financial award applicants required to submit FAFSA. In 2001, 168 master's, 85 doctorates, 24 other advanced degrees awarded. Offers arts (MA, Certificate); computer engineering (MS, PhD); computer science (MS, PhD); electrical engineering (MS, PhD); engineering (MS, PhD); music (MA); theater arts (Certificate). *Application fee:* $40. Electronic applications accepted. *Application Contact:* Diana J. Dean, Graduate Admissions, 831-459-2301. *Provost, Dean of Graduate Studies*, Dr. Frank Talanantes, 831-459-4108, Fax: 831-459-4843.

Division of Humanities Students: 177 full-time (114 women); includes 39 minority (5 African Americans, 20 Asian Americans or Pacific Islanders, 11 Hispanic Americans, 3 Native Americans), 14 international. 463 applicants, 20% accepted. *Faculty:* 77 full-time. Expenses: Contact institution. *Financial support:* Fellowships, research assistantships, teaching assistantships, career-related internships or fieldwork, Federal Work-Study, and institutionally sponsored loans available. In 2001, 23 master's, 13 doctorates awarded. Offers history (PhD); history of consciousness (PhD); humanities (MA, PhD); linguistics (MA, PhD); literature (MA, PhD). *Application fee:* $40. Electronic applications accepted. *Application Contact:* Graduate Admissions, 831-459-2301. *Dean*, Dr. Wlad Godzich, 831-459-2696.

Division of Natural Sciences Students: 376 full-time (183 women); includes 45 minority (6 African Americans, 19 Asian Americans or Pacific Islanders, 18 Hispanic Americans, 2 Native Americans), 42 international. 744 applicants, 35% accepted. *Faculty:* 152 full-time. Expenses: Contact institution. *Financial support:* Fellowships, research assistantships, teaching assistantships, career-related internships or fieldwork, Federal Work-Study, and institutionally sponsored loans available. In 2001, 52 master's, 53 doctorates, 18 other advanced degrees awarded. Offers applied mathematics (MA, PhD); astronomy and astrophysics (PhD); chemistry (MS, PhD); earth sciences (MS, PhD); ecology and evolutionary biology (MA, PhD); environmental toxicology (MS, PhD); marine sciences (MS); mathematics (MA, PhD); molecular, cellular, and developmental biology (MA, PhD); natural sciences (MA, MS, PhD, Certificate); ocean sciences (PhD); physics (MS, PhD); science communication (Certificate). *Application fee:* $40. *Application Contact:* Graduate Admissions, 831-459-2301. *Dean*, Dr. David Kliger, 831-459-2931.

Division of Social Sciences Students: 380 full-time (247 women); includes 93 minority (5 African Americans, 32 Asian Americans or Pacific Islanders, 47 Hispanic Americans, 9 Native Americans), 45 international. 628 applicants, 32% accepted. *Faculty:* 99 full-time. Expenses: Contact institution. *Financial support:* Fellowships, research assistantships, teaching assistantships, career-related internships or fieldwork, Federal Work-Study, institutionally sponsored loans, and tuition waivers (partial) available. In 2001, 83 master's, 17 doctorates awarded. Offers anthropology (MA, PhD); applied economics (MS); developmental psychology (PhD); education (MA, Certificate); environmental studies (PhD); experimental psychology (PhD); international economics (PhD); politics (PhD); social psychology (PhD); social sciences (MA, MS, PhD, Certificate); sociology (PhD). *Application fee:* $40. *Application Contact:* Graduate Admissions, 831-459-2301. *Dean*, Martin Chemers, 831-459-2855.

UNIVERSITY OF CENTRAL ARKANSAS, Conway, AR 72035-0001

General Information State-supported, coed, comprehensive institution. CGS member. *Enrollment:* 417 full-time matriculated graduate/professional students (298 women), 529 part-time matriculated graduate/professional students (421 women). *Enrollment by degree level:* 819 master's, 79 doctoral, 48 other advanced degrees. *Graduate faculty:* 177. Tuition, state resident: full-time $3,303; part-time $184 per hour. Tuition, nonresident: full-time $5,922; part-time $329 per hour. *Required fees:* $68; $24 per semester. *Graduate housing:* Rooms and/or apartments available on a first-come, first-served basis to single and married students. Typical cost: $2,486 per year ($4,000 including board) for single students; $2,486 per year ($4,000 including board) for married students. Housing application deadline: 7/1. *Student services:* Campus employment opportunities, campus safety program, career counseling, disabled student services, exercise/wellness program, free psychological counseling, grant writing training, international student services, low-cost health insurance, multicultural affairs office, teacher training, writing training. *Library facilities:* Torreyson Library. *Online resources:* library catalog, web page, access to other libraries' catalogs. *Collection:* 414,709 titles, 2,561 serial subscriptions. *Research affiliation:* Acxiom Corporation (computer science technology), Southwestern Bell (technology), Texas Instruments (mathematics education), Conway Corporation (art), American Writing Project (writing).

Computer facilities: 500 computers available on campus for general student use. A campuswide network can be accessed from student residence rooms and from off campus. Internet access is available. *Web address:* http://www.uca.edu/.

General Application Contact: Dr. Elaine M. McNiece, Associate Provost and Dean of the Graduate School, 501-450-3124, Fax: 501-450-5066, E-mail: elainem@mail.uca.edu.

GRADUATE UNITS

Graduate School Students: 417 full-time (298 women), 529 part-time (421 women); includes 109 minority (89 African Americans, 5 Asian Americans or Pacific Islanders, 3 Hispanic Americans, 12 Native Americans), 20 international. Average age 31. *Faculty:* 177. Expenses: Contact institution. *Financial support:* In 2001–02, 40 fellowships with full tuition reimbursements (averaging $6,000 per year), 114 research assistantships with partial tuition reimbursements (averaging $6,000 per year), 6 teaching assistantships with partial tuition reimbursements (averaging $9,000 per year) were awarded. Career-related internships or fieldwork, Federal Work-Study, scholarships/grants, traineeships, tuition waivers (partial), and unspecified assistantships also available. Support available to part-time students. Financial award application deadline: 2/15. In 2001, 336 degrees awarded. *Degree program information:* Part-time programs available. *Application deadline:* For fall admission, 3/1 (priority date); for spring admission, 10/1 (priority date). Applications are processed on a rolling basis. *Application fee:* $25 ($40 for international students). *Application Contact:* Roberta Hicks, Secretary, 504-450-3124, Fax: 504-450-5066, E-mail: rhicks@mail.uca.edu. *Associate Provost*, Dr. Elaine M. McNiece, 501-450-3124, Fax: 501-450-5066, E-mail: elainem@mail.uca.edu.

College of Education Students: 61 full-time (52 women), 197 part-time (188 women); includes 36 minority (35 African Americans, 1 Native American), 2 international. *Faculty:* 32. Expenses: Contact institution. *Financial support:* In 2001–02, 56 students received support, including 14 research assistantships with partial tuition reimbursements available (averaging $5,700 per year); career-related internships or fieldwork, Federal Work-Study, scholarships/grants, tuition waivers (partial), and unspecified assistantships also available. Financial award application deadline: 2/15. In 2001, 101 degrees awarded. *Degree program information:* Part-time programs available. Offers business education (MSE); community service counseling (MS); counseling psychology (MS); early childhood education (MSE); early childhood special education (MSE); education (MS, MSE, PhD); education media and library science (MS); elementary education (MSE); elementary education for the gifted (MSE); elementary school counseling (MS); mildly handicapped (MSE); moderately/profoundly handicapped (MSE); reading education (MSE); school counseling (MS); school psychology (MS, PhD); secondary school counseling (MS); seriously emotionally disturbed (MSE); special education (MSE); student personnel services in higher education (MS). *Application deadline:* For fall admission, 3/1 (priority date); for spring admission, 10/1 (priority date). Applications are processed on a rolling basis. *Application fee:* $25 ($40 for international students). *Application Contact:* Jane Douglas, Co-Admissions Secretary, 501-450-5064, Fax: 501-450-5066, E-mail: janed@ecom.uca.edu. *Dean*, Dr. Jane McHaney, 501-450-3175.

College of Fine Arts and Communication Students: 6 full-time (2 women), 6 part-time (4 women); includes 1 minority (Asian American or Pacific Islander), 1 international. *Faculty:* 13. Expenses: Contact institution. *Financial support:* In 2001–02, 7 students received support, including 6 research assistantships with partial tuition reimbursements available (averaging $5,700 per year); Federal Work-Study, scholarships/grants, tuition waivers (partial), and unspecified assistantships also available. Financial award application deadline: 2/15. In 2001, 3 degrees awarded. *Degree program information:* Part-time programs available. Offers choral conducting (MM); fine arts and communication (MM); instrumental conducting (MM); music education (MM); music theory (MM); performance (MM). *Application deadline:* For fall admission, 3/1 (priority date); for spring admission, 10/1 (priority date). Applications are processed on a rolling basis. *Application fee:* $25 ($40 for international students). *Application Contact:* Jane Douglas, Co-Admissions Secretary, 501-450-5064, Fax: 501-450-5066, E-mail: janed@ecom.uca.edu. *Dean*, Dr. Robert G. Everding, 501-450-3167, Fax: 501-450-5678, E-mail: everding@mail.uca.edu.

College of Health and Applied Sciences Students: 260 full-time (197 women), 125 part-time (104 women); includes 32 minority (19 African Americans, 4 Asian Americans or Pacific Islanders, 1 Hispanic American, 8 Native Americans), 2 international. *Faculty:* 46. Expenses: Contact institution. *Financial support:* In 2001–02, 230 students received support, including 27 fellowships with full tuition reimbursements available (averaging $6,000 per year), 38 research assistantships with full and partial tuition reimbursements available (averaging $6,000 per year); career-related internships or fieldwork, Federal Work-Study, scholarships/grants, traineeships, tuition waivers (partial), and unspecified assistantships also available. Support available to part-time students. Financial award application deadline: 2/15. In 2001, 132 degrees awarded. Offers family and consumer sciences (MS); health and applied sciences (MS, MSN, DPT, PhD); health education (MS); health systems (MS); kinesiology (MS); nursing (MSN); occupational therapy (MS); physical therapy (MS, DPT, PhD); speech-language pathology (MS). *Application deadline:* For fall admission, 3/1 (priority date); for spring admission, 10/1. Applications are processed on a rolling basis. *Application fee:* $25 ($40 for international students). *Application Contact:* Nancy Gage, Co-Admissions Secretary, 501-450-3124, Fax: 501-450-5066, E-mail: nancyg@ecom.uca.edu. *Dean*, Dr. Neil Hattlestad, 501-450-3122, Fax: 501-450-5503, E-mail: neilh@mail.uca.edu.

College of Liberal Arts Students: 20 full-time (10 women), 19 part-time (11 women); includes 1 minority (African American), 1 international. *Faculty:* 27. Expenses: Contact institution. *Financial support:* In 2001–02, 17 students received support, including 7 research assistantships with partial tuition reimbursements available (averaging $5,700 per year), 1 teaching assistantship with partial tuition reimbursement available (averaging $5,700 per year); Federal Work-Study, scholarships/grants, and unspecified assistantships also available. Financial award application deadline: 2/15. In 2001, 7 degrees awarded. *Degree program information:* Part-time programs available. Offers English (MA); foreign languages (MSE); history (MA); liberal arts (MA, MSE). *Application deadline:* For fall admission, 3/1 (priority date); for spring admission, 10/1 (priority date). Applications are processed on a rolling basis. *Application fee:* $25 ($40 for international students). *Application Contact:* Jane Douglas, Co-Admissions Secretary, 501-450-5064, Fax: 501-450-5066, E-mail: janed@ecom.uca.edu. *Dean*, Maurice Lee, 501-450-3167, Fax: 501-450-5185, E-mail: mauricel@mail.uca.edu.

College of Natural Sciences and Math Students: 10 full-time (8 women), 9 part-time (8 women); includes 2 minority (1 African American, 1 Asian American or Pacific Islander), 2 international. *Faculty:* 33. Expenses: Contact institution. *Financial support:* In 2001–02, 6 research assistantships with partial tuition reimbursements (averaging $8,000 per year), 9 teaching assistantships with partial tuition reimbursements (averaging $8,500 per year) were awarded. Career-related internships or fieldwork, Federal Work-Study, and unspecified assistantships also available. Financial award application deadline: 2/15. In 2001, 8 degrees awarded. *Degree program information:* Part-time programs available. Offers biological science (MS); mathematics (MA); natural sciences and math (MA, MS). *Application deadline:* For fall admission, 3/1 (priority date); for spring admission, 10/1 (priority date). Applications are processed on a rolling basis. *Application fee:* $25 ($40 for international students). *Application Contact:* Nancy Gage, Co-Admissions Secretary, 501-450-3124, Fax: 501-450-5066, E-mail: nancyg@ecom.uca.edu. *Dean*, Dr. Ron Toll, 501-450-3199, Fax: 501-450-5084.

Graduate School of Management, Leadership, and Administration Students: 42 full-time (17 women), 73 part-time (34 women); includes 27 minority (22 African Americans, 2 Hispanic Americans, 3 Native Americans), 10 international. *Faculty:* 21. Expenses: Contact institution. *Financial support:* In 2001–02, 42 students received support, including 13 research assistantships with partial tuition reimbursements available (averaging $5,700 per year); career-related internships or fieldwork, Federal Work-Study, scholarships/grants, tuition waivers, and unspecified assistantships also available. Financial award application deadline: 2/15. In 2001, 60 degrees awarded. *Degree program information:* Part-time programs available. Offers business administration (IMBA, MBA); educational leadership (Ed S); elementary school leadership (MSE); management, leadership and administration (IMBA, MBA, MSE, Ed S); secondary school leadership (MSE). *Application deadline:* For fall admission, 3/1 (priority date); for spring admission, 10/1. Applications are processed on a rolling basis. *Application fee:* $25 ($40 for international students). *Application Contact:* Jane Douglas, Co-Admissions Secretary, 501-450-5064, Fax: 501-450-5066, E-mail: janed@ecom.uca.edu. *Associate Dean*, Dr. Ira Saltz, 501-450-5303, Fax: 501-450-5302, E-mail: iras@mail.uca.edu.

UNIVERSITY OF CENTRAL FLORIDA, Orlando, FL 32816

General Information State-supported, coed, university. CGS member. *Enrollment:* 2,105 full-time matriculated graduate/professional students (1,212 women), 2,806 part-time matriculated graduate/professional students (1,587 women). *Enrollment by degree level:* 3,931 master's, 858 doctoral, 122 other advanced degrees. *Graduate faculty:* 795 full-time (298 women), 413 part-time/adjunct (207 women). Tuition, state resident: part-time $162 per hour. Tuition, nonresident: part-time $569 per hour. *Graduate housing:* Room and/or apartments available on a first-come, first-served basis to single students; on-campus housing not available to married students. Typical cost: $3,300 per year ($5,670 including board). Room and board charges vary according to housing facility selected. Housing application deadline: 3/1. *Student services:* Campus employment opportunities, career counseling, child daycare facilities, disabled student services, exercise/wellness program, free psychological counseling, international student services, low-cost health insurance, multicultural affairs office. *Library facilities:* University Library. *Online resources:* library catalog, web page, access to other libraries' catalogs. *Collection:* 865,527 titles, 7,423 serial subscriptions, 29,966 audiovisual materials. *Research affiliation:* Agere Systems, Inc., Lockheed Martin Corporation, Geltech Inc., Siemens Westinghouse, Boeing, Honeywell Space System.

Computer facilities: 1,191 computers available on campus for general student use. A campuswide network can be accessed from student residence rooms and from off campus. Internet access and online class registration are available. *Web address:* http://www.ucf.edu/.

General Application Contact: Dr. Patricia Bishop, Vice Provost and Dean of Graduate Studies, 407-823-2766, Fax: 407-823-3299, E-mail: graduate@mail.ucf.edu.

GRADUATE UNITS

College of Arts and Sciences Students: 364 full-time (224 women), 408 part-time (235 women); includes 151 minority (41 African Americans, 25 Asian Americans or Pacific Islanders, 82 Hispanic Americans, 3 Native Americans), 40 international. Average age 32. 695 applicants, 54% accepted, 248 enrolled. *Faculty:* 300 full-time (104 women), 136 part-time/adjunct (70 women). Expenses: Contact institution. *Financial support:* In 2001–02, 158 fellowships with partial tuition reimbursements (averaging $3,250 per year), 389 research assistantships with partial tuition reimbursements (averaging $3,032 per year), 352 teaching assistantships with partial tuition reimbursements (averaging $4,185 per year) were awarded. Career-related internships or fieldwork, Federal Work-Study, institutionally sponsored loans, tuition waivers (partial), and unspecified assistantships also available. Financial award application deadline: 3/1; financial award applicants required to submit FAFSA. In 2001, 146 master's, 12 doctorates awarded. *Degree program information:* Part-time and evening/weekend programs available. Offers applied sociology (MA); arts and sciences (MA, MALS, MFA, MS,

University of Central Florida (continued)

PhD, Certificate); biological sciences (MS); clinical psychology (MA, MS, PhD); conservation biology (Certificate); creative writing (MA); domestic violence (Certificate); foreign languages (MA, Certificate); gender studies (Certificate); history (MA); human factors psychology (PhD); industrial chemistry (MS); industrial/organizational psychology (MS, PhD); liberal studies (MALS); literature (MA); mathematical science (MS); mathematics (PhD); Mayan studies (Certificate); physics (MS, PhD); political science (MA); professional writing (Certificate); Spanish (MA); statistical computing (MS); teaching English as a second language (MA, Certificate); technical writing (MA); theater (MFA). *Application fee:* $20. Electronic applications accepted. *Application Contact:* Ben Morgan, Associate Dean and Graduate Coordinator, 407-823-0218, E-mail: morgan@mail.ucf.edu. *Dean,* K. L. Seidel, 407-823-2251, E-mail: seidel@mail.ucf.edu.

School of Communication Students: 28 full-time (20 women), 38 part-time (26 women); includes 12 minority (5 African Americans, 3 Asian Americans or Pacific Islanders, 4 Hispanic Americans), 5 international. Average age 29. 44 applicants, 68% accepted, 19 enrolled. *Faculty:* 36 full-time (12 women), 27 part-time/adjunct (11 women). Expenses: Contact institution. *Financial support:* In 2001–02, 13 fellowships with partial tuition reimbursements (averaging $3,058 per year), 29 research assistantships with partial tuition reimbursements (averaging $2,474 per year), 10 teaching assistantships with partial tuition reimbursements (averaging $3,060 per year) were awarded. Career-related internships or fieldwork, Federal Work-Study, institutionally sponsored loans, tuition waivers (partial), and unspecified assistantships also available. Financial award application deadline: 3/1; financial award applicants required to submit FAFSA. In 2001, 19 degrees awarded. *Degree program information:* Part-time and evening/weekend programs available. Offers communication (MA). *Application deadline:* For fall admission, 7/15; for spring admission, 12/7. *Application fee:* $20. Electronic applications accepted. *Application Contact:* Dr. B. Pryor, Coordinator, 407-823-2681, Fax: 407-823-6360, E-mail: apryor@pegasus.cc.ucf.edu. *Chair,* Dr. M. D. Meeske, 407-823-2683, Fax: 407-823-5216, E-mail: meeske@ucf1vm.cc.ucf.edu.

College of Business Administration Students: 250 full-time (113 women), 533 part-time (244 women); includes 138 minority (27 African Americans, 53 Asian Americans or Pacific Islanders, 54 Hispanic Americans, 4 Native Americans), 50 international. Average age 30. 548 applicants, 58% accepted, 227 enrolled. *Faculty:* 118 full-time (39 women), 43 part-time/adjunct (15 women). Expenses: Contact institution. *Financial support:* In 2001–02, 49 fellowships with partial tuition reimbursements (averaging $3,153 per year), 258 research assistantships with partial tuition reimbursements (averaging $2,889 per year), 50 teaching assistantships with partial tuition reimbursements (averaging $6,332 per year) were awarded. Career-related internships or fieldwork, Federal Work-Study, institutionally sponsored loans, tuition waivers (partial), and unspecified assistantships also available. Financial award application deadline: 3/1; financial award applicants required to submit FAFSA. In 2001, 224 degrees awarded. *Degree program information:* Part-time and evening/weekend programs available. Offers business administration (MBA); economics (MAAE); finance (PhD); management (PhD); marketing (PhD); taxation (MST). *Application deadline:* For spring admission, 11/1 (priority date). *Application fee:* $20. Electronic applications accepted. *Application Contact:* Dr. Robert L. Ford, Assistant Dean, 407-823-2385, Fax: 407-823-6206, E-mail: robert.ford@bus.ucf.edu. *Acting Dean,* Dr. Thomas Keon, 407-823-2183, E-mail: thomas.keon@bus.ucf.edu.

School of Accounting Students: 19 full-time (7 women), 50 part-time (28 women); includes 11 minority (3 African Americans, 3 Asian Americans or Pacific Islanders, 5 Hispanic Americans) Average age 32. 67 applicants, 69% accepted, 26 enrolled. *Faculty:* 23 full-time (11 women), 14 part-time/adjunct (5 women). Expenses: Contact institution. *Financial support:* In 2001–02, 5 fellowships with partial tuition reimbursements (averaging $4,600 per year), 17 research assistantships with partial tuition reimbursements (averaging $3,004 per year) were awarded. Teaching assistantships with partial tuition reimbursements, career-related internships or fieldwork, Federal Work-Study, institutionally sponsored loans, tuition waivers (partial), and unspecified assistantships also available. Financial award application deadline: 3/1; financial award applicants required to submit FAFSA. In 2001, 18 degrees awarded. *Degree program information:* Part-time and evening/weekend programs available. Offers accounting (MS). *Application deadline:* For fall admission, 6/15 (priority date); for spring admission, 11/1 (priority date). *Application fee:* $20. Electronic applications accepted. *Application Contact:* Dr. Linda Savage, Graduate Adviser, 407-823-5661, Fax: 407-823-6206, E-mail: linda.savage@bus.ucf.edu. *Director,* Dr. Andrew J. Judd, 407-823-2876, E-mail: andrew.judd@bus.ucf.edu.

College of Education Students: 398 full-time (312 women), 749 part-time (608 women); includes 180 minority (79 African Americans, 25 Asian Americans or Pacific Islanders, 70 Hispanic Americans, 6 Native Americans), 13 international. Average age 35. 475 applicants, 67% accepted, 252 enrolled. *Faculty:* 99 full-time (57 women), 83 part-time/adjunct (64 women). Expenses: Contact institution. *Financial support:* In 2001–02, 146 fellowships with partial tuition reimbursements (averaging $3,177 per year), 296 research assistantships with partial tuition reimbursements (averaging $2,580 per year), 29 teaching assistantships with partial tuition reimbursements (averaging $2,968 per year) were awarded. Career-related internships or fieldwork, Federal Work-Study, institutionally sponsored loans, tuition waivers (partial), and unspecified assistantships also available. Financial award application deadline: 3/1; financial award applicants required to submit FAFSA. In 2001, 282 master's, 35 doctorates, 24 other advanced degrees awarded. *Degree program information:* Part-time and evening/weekend programs available. Offers art education (M Ed, MA); counselor education (M Ed, MA, PhD); curriculum and instruction (Ed D); early childhood education (M Ed, MA); education (PhD); educational leadership (M Ed, MA, Ed D, Ed S); educational media (M Ed); educational studies (M Ed, MA, Ed S); educational technology (MA); elementary education (M Ed, MA, PhD); English language arts education (M Ed, MA); exceptional education (M Ed, MA, PhD); instructional systems (MA); instructional technology (PhD); mathematics education (M Ed, MA, PhD); music education (M Ed, MA); physical education-exercise physiology (M Ed, MA); pre-kindergarten handicapped endorsement (Certificate); reading education (M Ed, MA); school psychology (Ed S); science education (M Ed, MA); social science education (M Ed, MA); vocational education (M Ed, MA); world studies education (Certificate); writing education (Certificate). *Application fee:* $20. Electronic applications accepted. *Dean,* Dr. Sandra Robinson, 407-823-5529.

College of Engineering and Computer Sciences Students: 450 full-time (92 women), 522 part-time (116 women); includes 215 minority (37 African Americans, 105 Asian Americans or Pacific Islanders, 69 Hispanic Americans, 4 Native Americans), 379 international. Average age 29. 1,432 applicants, 65% accepted, 317 enrolled. *Faculty:* 117 full-time (13 women), 40 part-time/adjunct (4 women). Expenses: Contact institution. *Financial support:* In 2001–02, 156 fellowships with partial tuition reimbursements (averaging $4,015 per year), 1,041 research assistantships with partial tuition reimbursements (averaging $3,221 per year), 285 teaching assistantships with partial tuition reimbursements (averaging $3,673 per year) were awarded. Career-related internships or fieldwork, Federal Work-Study, institutionally sponsored loans, tuition waivers (partial), and unspecified assistantships also available. Financial award application deadline: 3/1; financial award applicants required to submit FAFSA. In 2001, 232 master's, 41 doctorates awarded. *Degree program information:* Part-time and evening/weekend programs available. Offers aerospace engineering (MSAE); air pollution control (Certificate); applied operations research (Certificate); CAD/CAM technology (Certificate); civil engineering (MS, MSCE, PhD, Certificate); computational methods in mechanics (Certificate); computer science (MS, PhD); computer-integrated manufacturing (MS); design for usability (Certificate); drinking water treatment (Certificate); engineering (MS, MS Cp E, MS Env E, MSAE, MSCE, MSEE, MSIE, MSME, MSMSE, PhD, Certificate); engineering management (MS); environmental engineering (MS, MS Env E, PhD, Certificate); geotechnical engineering (Certificate); hazardous waste management (Certificate); HVAC engineering (Certificate); industrial engineering (MSIE); industrial engineering and management systems (PhD); industrial ergonomics and safety (Certificate); launch/spacecraft vehicle processing (Certificate); materials characterization (Certificate); materials failure analysis (Certificate); materials science and engineering (MSMSE, PhD); mechanical engineering (MSME, PhD, Certificate); operations research (MS); product assurance engineering (MS); project engineering (Certificate); quality assurance (Certificate); simulation systems (MS); structural engineering (Certificate); surface water modeling (Certificate); systems simulations for engineers (Certificate); thermofluids (MSME, PhD); training simulation (Certificate); transportation engineering (Certificate); wastewater treatment (Certificate). *Application deadline:* For fall admission, 7/15; for spring admission, 12/1. *Application fee:* $20. Electronic applications accepted. *Application Contact:* Dr. Issa Batarseh, Graduate Coordinator, 407-823-0185, E-mail: batarseh@pegasus.cc.ucf.edu. *Dean,* Dr. Martin Wanielista, 407-823-2156, E-mail: wanielis@ucf1vm.cc.ucf.edu.

School of Electrical Engineering and Computer Science Students: 133 full-time (31 women), 155 part-time (28 women); includes 69 minority (10 African Americans, 46 Asian Americans or Pacific Islanders, 12 Hispanic Americans, 1 Native American), 130 international. Average age 29. 509 applicants, 57% accepted, 86 enrolled. Expenses: Contact institution. *Financial support:* In 2001–02, 57 fellowships with partial tuition reimbursements (averaging $3,727 per year), research assistantships with partial tuition reimbursements (averaging $2,995 per year), teaching assistantships with partial tuition reimbursements (averaging $2,286 per year) were awarded. Career-related internships or fieldwork, Federal Work-Study, institutionally sponsored loans, tuition waivers (partial), and unspecified assistantships also available. Financial award application deadline: 3/1; financial award applicants required to submit FAFSA. In 2001, 83 master's, 17 doctorates awarded. *Degree program information:* Part-time and evening/weekend programs available. Offers antennas and propagation (Certificate); communications systems (Certificate); computer engineering (MS Cp E, PhD, Certificate); digital signal processing (Certificate); electrical engineering (MSEE, PhD, Certificate); electronic circuits (Certificate). *Application deadline:* For fall admission, 7/15 (priority date); for spring admission, 12/1 (priority date). *Application fee:* $20. Electronic applications accepted. *Application Contact:* Dr. Michael Georgiopoulos, Coordinator, 407-823-5338, E-mail: michaelg@pegasus.cc.ucf.edu. *Chair,* Dr. Erol Gelenbe, 407-823-2311, Fax: 407-823-5419, E-mail: erol@cs.ucf.edu.

College of Health and Public Affairs Students: 568 full-time (444 women), 504 part-time (337 women); includes 229 minority (107 African Americans, 20 Asian Americans or Pacific Islanders, 99 Hispanic Americans, 3 Native Americans), 11 international. Average age 32. 613 applicants, 81% accepted, 332 enrolled. *Faculty:* 145 full-time (83 women), 111 part-time/adjunct (54 women). Expenses: Contact institution. *Financial support:* In 2001–02, 131 fellowships with partial tuition reimbursements (averaging $2,710 per year), 165 research assistantships with partial tuition reimbursements (averaging $2,695 per year), 161 teaching assistantships with partial tuition reimbursements (averaging $2,343 per year) were awarded. Career-related internships or fieldwork, Federal Work-Study, institutionally sponsored loans, traineeships, tuition waivers (partial), and unspecified assistantships also available. Financial award application deadline: 3/1; financial award applicants required to submit FAFSA. In 2001, 368 degrees awarded. *Degree program information:* Part-time and evening/weekend programs available. Offers communicative disorders (MA); crime analysis (Certificate); criminal justice (MS); gerontology (Certificate); health and public affairs (MA, MPA, MS, MSN, MSW, PhD, Certificate); health care information systems (Certificate); health services administration (MS); managed care (Certificate); medical group management (Certificate); microbiology (MS); molecular biology (MS); non-profit management (Certificate); physical therapy (MS); public administration (MPA, Certificate); public affairs (PhD); risk quality management (Certificate); social work (MSW). *Application fee:* $20. Electronic applications accepted. *Application Contact:* Joyce Dorner, Assistant Dean and Graduate Coordinator, 407-823-0205, E-mail: jdorner@pegasus.cc.ucf.edu. *Dean,* Dr. Belinda R. McCarthy, 407-823-2604, E-mail: mccarthy@mail.ucf.edu.

School of Nursing Students: 26 full-time (23 women), 78 part-time (73 women); includes 15 minority (7 African Americans, 3 Asian Americans or Pacific Islanders, 5 Hispanic Americans) Average age 40. 48 applicants, 85% accepted, 38 enrolled. *Faculty:* 30 full-time (all women), 17 part-time/adjunct (all women). Expenses: Contact institution. *Financial support:* In 2001–02, 35 students received support, including 33 fellowships with partial tuition reimbursements available (averaging $1,545 per year), 7 research assistantships with partial tuition reimbursements available (averaging $1,301 per year), 12 teaching assistantships with partial tuition reimbursements available (averaging $1,605 per year); career-related internships or fieldwork, Federal Work-Study, institutionally sponsored loans, traineeships, and unspecified assistantships also available. Financial award application deadline: 3/1; financial award applicants required to submit FAFSA. In 2001, 21 degrees awarded. *Degree program information:* Part-time and evening/weekend programs available. Offers adult practitioner (MSN); family practitioner (MSN); nursing (MSN); nursing and health profession education (MSN). *Application deadline:* For fall admission, 2/15; for spring admission, 9/15. *Application fee:* $20. Electronic applications accepted. *Application Contact:* Dr. Mary Lou Sole, Coordinator, 407-823-2744, Fax: 407-823-5675, E-mail: msole@pegasus.cc.ucf.edu. *Chair,* E. Stullenbarger, 407-823-2744, E-mail: estullen@pegasus.cc.ucf.edu.

School of Optics Students: 50 full-time (12 women), 29 part-time (3 women); includes 9 minority (5 Asian Americans or Pacific Islanders, 4 Hispanic Americans), 43 international. Average age 28. 99 applicants, 41% accepted, 24 enrolled. *Faculty:* 16 full-time (2 women). Expenses: Contact institution. *Financial support:* In 2001–02, 58 fellowships with partial tuition reimbursements (averaging $3,848 per year), 199 research assistantships with partial tuition reimbursements (averaging $3,586 per year) were awarded. Teaching assistantships with partial tuition reimbursements, career-related internships or fieldwork, Federal Work-Study, institutionally sponsored loans, tuition waivers (partial), and unspecified assistantships also available. Financial award application deadline: 3/1; financial award applicants required to submit FAFSA. In 2001, 14 master's, 1 doctorate awarded. *Degree program information:* Part-time and evening/weekend programs available. Offers applied optics (Certificate); lasers (Certificate); optical communication (Certificate); optics (MS, PhD). *Application deadline:* For fall admission, 2/1 (priority date); for spring admission, 12/1. *Application fee:* $20. Electronic applications accepted. *Application Contact:* Dr. Jim Moharam, Coordinator, 407-823-6833, E-mail: moharam@creol.ucf.edu. *Director,* Dr. Eric W. Van Stryland, 407-823-6814, E-mail: cwvs@mail.creol.ucf.edu.

See in-depth description on page 1165.

UNIVERSITY OF CENTRAL OKLAHOMA, Edmond, OK 73034-5209

General Information State-supported, coed, comprehensive institution. CGS member. *Graduate housing:* Rooms and/or apartments available on a first-come, first-served basis to single and married students. Housing application deadline: 7/1. *Research affiliation:* U.S. Department of Agriculture–Agricultural Research Service (grazing lands), National Geographic Society (global positioning system education).

GRADUATE UNITS

College of Graduate Studies and Research *Degree program information:* Part-time and evening/weekend programs available. Electronic applications accepted.

College of Arts, Media, and Design *Degree program information:* Part-time programs available. Offers arts, media, and design (MFA, MM); design and interior design (MFA); music education (MM); performance (MM).

College of Business Administration *Degree program information:* Part-time programs available. Offers business administration (MBA). Electronic applications accepted.

College of Education *Degree program information:* Part-time programs available. Offers adult education (M Ed); community services (M Ed); counseling psychology (MS); early childhood education (M Ed); education (M Ed, MA, MS); elementary education (M Ed); family and child studies (MS); family and consumer science education (MS); general education (M Ed); gerontology (M Ed); guidance and counseling (M Ed); instructional media (M Ed); interior design (MS); nutrition-food management (MS); professional health occupations (M Ed); psychology (MA); reading (M Ed); school administration (M Ed); secondary education (M Ed); special education (M Ed); speech-language pathology (M Ed).

College of Liberal Arts *Degree program information:* Part-time programs available. Offers composition skills (MA); contemporary literature (MA); creative writing (MA); criminal justice management and administration (MA); history (MA); international affairs (MA); liberal arts (MA); museum studies (MA); political science (MA); social studies teaching (MA); Southwestern studies (MA); teaching English as a second language (MA); traditional studies (MA); urban affairs (MA).

College of Mathematics and Science *Degree program information:* Part-time programs available. Offers applied mathematical sciences (MS); biology (MS); chemistry (MS); industrial and applied physics (MS); mathematics and science (MS).

UNIVERSITY OF CHARLESTON, Charleston, WV 25304-1099

General Information Independent, coed, comprehensive institution. *Graduate housing:* Room and/or apartments available to single students; on-campus housing not available to married students.

GRADUATE UNITS

Jones-Benedum Division of Business *Degree program information:* Part-time and evening/weekend programs available. Offers business (MBA, MHRM); business administration (MBA); human resource management (MHRM).

UNIVERSITY OF CHICAGO, Chicago, IL 60637-1513

General Information Independent, coed, university. CGS member. *Enrollment:* 6,534 full-time matriculated graduate/professional students (2,769 women), 2,355 part-time matriculated graduate/professional students (726 women). *Enrollment by degree level:* 1,076 first professional, 4,553 master's, 3,260 doctoral. *Graduate faculty:* 2,110 full-time (593 women), 773 part-time/adjunct (250 women). *Tuition:* Full-time $16,548. *Graduate housing:* Rooms and/or apartments available on a first-come, first-served basis to single students and available to married students. Typical cost: $5,200 per year for single students; $6,300 per year for married students. Room charges vary according to campus/location and housing facility selected. *Student services:* Campus employment opportunities, campus safety program, career counseling, disabled student services, exercise/wellness program, free psychological counseling, international student services, low-cost health insurance, teacher training, writing training. *Library facilities:* Joseph Regenstein Library plus 8 others. *Online resources:* library catalog, web page. *Collection:* 5.8 million titles, 47,000 serial subscriptions. *Research affiliation:* Argonne National Laboratory (energy, materials), Fermilab (high-energy physics), McDonald Observatory (astronomy), Field Museum of Natural History (archaeology, zoology), Smithsonian Tropical Research Institute (biology), National Opinion Research Center (social science).

Computer facilities: 1,000 computers available on campus for general student use. A campuswide network can be accessed from student residence rooms and from off campus. *Web address:* http://www.uchicago.edu/.

General Application Contact: Kathy Skipper, Manager, Office of Graduate Affairs, 773-702-7813, Fax: 773-702-1194, E-mail: graduate-affairs-admissions@uchicago.edu.

GRADUATE UNITS

Divinity School Students: 320 full-time (140 women); includes 29 minority (15 African Americans, 8 Asian Americans or Pacific Islanders, 6 Hispanic Americans), 15 international. 300 applicants, 47% accepted. *Faculty:* 30 full-time (10 women). Expenses: Contact institution. *Financial support:* In 2001–02, 320 students received support; fellowships with full and partial tuition reimbursements available, career-related internships or fieldwork, Federal Work-Study, institutionally sponsored loans, and tuition waivers (full and partial) available. Support available to part-time students. Financial award application deadline: 1/5; financial award applicants required to submit FAFSA. In 2001, 14 first professional degrees, 36 master's, 29 doctorates awarded. *Degree program information:* Part-time programs available. Offers divinity (M Div, AM, AMRS, PhD). *Application deadline:* For fall admission, 1/5. *Application fee:* $45 ($55 for international students). Electronic applications accepted. *Application Contact:* Winnifred Fallers Sullivan, Dean of Students, 773-702-8217, Fax: 773-834-4581, E-mail: wsulliva@uchicago.edu. *Dean,* Dr. Richard A. Rosengarten, 773-702-8221, E-mail: raroseng@midway.uchicago.edu.

Division of Social Sciences Students: 1,324. Expenses: Contact institution. *Financial support:* Fellowships, research assistantships, teaching assistantships, Federal Work-Study and institutionally sponsored loans available. Financial award application deadline: 12/28; financial award applicants required to submit FAFSA. Offers anthropology (PhD); economics (PhD); history (PhD); human development (PhD); international relations (AM); Latin American and Caribbean studies (AM); Middle Eastern studies (AM); political science (PhD); psychology (PhD); social sciences (AM, PhD); social thought (PhD); sociology (PhD). *Application deadline:* For fall admission, 12/28. *Application fee:* $55. Electronic applications accepted. *Application Contact:* Office of the Dean of Students, 773-702-8415. *Acting Dean,* Prof. John Lucy.

Division of the Biological Sciences Students: 337 full-time (160 women); includes 62 minority (12 African Americans, 39 Asian Americans or Pacific Islanders, 11 Hispanic Americans), 54 international. Average age 25. *Faculty:* 458 full-time (99 women), 18 part-time/adjunct (8 women). Expenses: Contact institution. *Financial support:* In 2001–02, 333 students received support, including fellowships with full tuition reimbursements available (averaging $22,754 per year), research assistantships with full tuition reimbursements available (averaging $22,754 per year); institutionally sponsored loans, scholarships/grants, and traineeships also available. In 2001, 17 master's, 39 doctorates awarded. Offers biochemistry and molecular biology (PhD); biological sciences (MS, PhD); cancer biology (PhD); cell physiology (PhD); cellular and molecular physiology (PhD); cellular differentiation (PhD); computational neurobiology (PhD); developmental biology (PhD); developmental endocrinology (PhD); developmental genetics (PhD); developmental neurobiology (PhD); ecology and evolution (PhD); evolutionary biology (PhD); functional and evolutionary biology (PhD); gene expression (PhD); genetics (PhD); health studies (MS); human genetics (PhD); human nutrition and nutritional biology (PhD); immunology (PhD); medical physics (PhD); microbiology (PhD); molecular genetics and cell biology (PhD); neurobiology (PhD); neurobiology, pharmacology and physiology (PhD); ophthalmology and visual science (PhD); organismal biology and anatomy (PhD); pathology (PhD); pharmacological and physiological sciences (PhD). *Application deadline:* For fall admission, 1/5 (priority date). Applications are processed on a rolling basis. *Application fee:* $55. Electronic applications accepted. *Application Contact:* Parag M. Shah, Administrator, Graduate Affairs, 773-702-5853, Fax: 773-834-1618, E-mail: pshah@bsd.uchicago.edu. *Dean,* Dr. James Madara, 773-702-9000.

Division of the Humanities Students: 1,196 full-time (615 women), 8 part-time (5 women); includes 119 minority (25 African Americans, 59 Asian Americans or Pacific Islanders, 33 Hispanic Americans, 2 Native Americans), 244 international. 1,409 applicants, 66% accepted. *Faculty:* 188. Expenses: Contact institution. *Financial support:* Fellowships, teaching assistantships, career-related internships or fieldwork, Federal Work-Study, institutionally sponsored loans, and tuition waivers (full and partial) available. Financial award application deadline: 12/28; financial award applicants required to submit FAFSA. In 2001, 168 master's, 57 doctorates awarded. Offers ancient Mediterranean world (AM, PhD); ancient philosophy (AM, PhD); anthropology and linguistics (PhD); art history (AM, PhD); cinema and media studies (AM, PhD); classical archaeology (AM, PhD); classical languages and literatures (AM, PhD); comparative literature (AM, PhD); conceptual and historical studies of science (AM, PhD); East Asian languages and civilizations (AM, PhD); English language and literature (AM, PhD); French (AM, PhD); general studies in the humanities (AM); Germanic languages and literatures (AM, PhD); history of culture (AM, PhD); humanities (AM, MFA, PhD); Italian (AM, PhD); Jewish history and culture (AM, PhD); Jewish studies (AM); linguistics (AM, PhD); music (AM, PhD); Near Eastern languages and civilizations (AM, PhD); New Testament and early Christian culture (AM, PhD); philosophy (AM, PhD); Slavic languages and literatures (AM, PhD); South Asian languages and civilizations (AM, PhD); Spanish (AM, PhD); visual arts (MFA). *Application deadline:* For fall admission, 12/28. *Application fee:* $55. *Dean of Students,* Thomas B. Thuerer, 773-702-8498.

Division of the Physical Sciences Students: 533 full-time (135 women), 60 part-time (21 women). Average age 26. *Faculty:* 173 full-time (7 women), 9 part-time/adjunct (1 woman). Expenses: Contact institution. *Financial support:* Fellowships, research assistantships, teaching assistantships, career-related internships or fieldwork, Federal Work-Study, institutionally sponsored loans, and training grants available. Support available to part-time students. Financial award applicants required to submit FAFSA. In 2001, 99 master's, 76 doctorates awarded. Offers applied mathematics (SM, PhD); astronomy and astrophysics (SM, PhD); atmospheric sciences (SM, PhD); chemistry (SM, PhD); computer science (SM, PhD); earth sciences (SM, PhD); financial mathematics (MS); mathematics (SM, PhD); paleobiology (PhD); physical sciences (MS, SM, PhD); physics (SM, PhD); planetary and space sciences (SM, PhD); statistics (SM, PhD). *Application fee:* $55. Electronic applications accepted. *Application Contact:* Richard Hefley, Dean of Students, 773-702-8789. *Dean,* David Oxtoby, 773-702-7950.

Executive MBA Program Asia Average age 36. *Faculty:* 124 full-time, 50 part-time/adjunct. Expenses: Contact institution. Offers international business administration (MBA). *Application deadline:* For winter admission, 2/1; for spring admission, 5/1. *Application Contact:* Ria Sugita, Assistant Director, Marketing, 65-835-6482, Fax: 65-835-6483, E-mail: singapore.inquiries@gsb.uchicago.edu. *Managing Director,* Beth Bader, 656-835-6482, Fax: 656-835-6483, E-mail: singapore.inquiries@gsb.uchicago.edu.

Graduate Program in Health Administration and Policy Offers health administration and policy (AM, MBA, MPP, Certificate).

Graduate School of Business Students: 1,169 full-time (278 women), 1,891 part-time (395 women); includes 190 minority (38 African Americans, 128 Asian Americans or Pacific Islanders, 24 Hispanic Americans), 346 international. Average age 29. 4,175 applicants, 44% accepted, 1279 enrolled. *Faculty:* 124 full-time, 50 part-time/adjunct. Expenses: Contact institution. *Financial support:* Career-related internships or fieldwork, Federal Work-Study, institutionally sponsored loans, and scholarships/grants available. Support available to part-time students. Financial award applicants required to submit FAFSA. In 2001, 1097 degrees awarded. *Degree program information:* Part-time and evening/weekend programs available. Offers business (MBA); business administration (MBA); international business administration (MBA). *Application deadline:* For fall admission, 11/30 (priority date); for winter admission, 1/18; for spring admission, 3/22. Applications are processed on a rolling basis. *Application fee:* $175. Electronic applications accepted. *Application Contact:* Don Martin, Associate Dean of Enrollment Management, 773-702-7369, Fax: 773-702-9085, E-mail: admissions@gsb.uchicago.edu. *Dean,* Edward A. Snyder, 773-702-6680.

The Irving B. Harris Graduate School of Public Policy Studies *Degree program information:* Part-time programs available. Offers environmental science and policy (MS); public policy studies (AM, MPP, PhD).

The Law School Students: 596 full-time (247 women); includes 157 minority (24 African Americans, 68 Asian Americans or Pacific Islanders, 59 Hispanic Americans, 6 Native Americans), 3 international. Average age 24. 3,859 applicants, 19% accepted. *Faculty:* 59 full-time, 56 part-time/adjunct. Expenses: Contact institution. *Financial support:* In 2001–02, 328 students received support, including 13 fellowships with partial tuition reimbursements available; career-related internships or fieldwork, institutionally sponsored loans, and scholarships/grants also available. Financial award application deadline: 3/15; financial award applicants required to submit FAFSA. In 2001, 193 first professional degrees, 51 master's, 1 doctorate awarded. Offers law (JD, LL M, MCL, DCL, JSD). *Application deadline:* For fall admission, 2/1 (priority date). Applications are processed on a rolling basis. *Application fee:* $60. *Application Contact:* Genita Robinson, Dean of Admissions, 773-702-9484, Fax: 773-834-0942, E-mail: admissions@law.uchicago.edu. *Dean,* Saul Levmore, 773-702-9494, Fax: 773-834-4409.

Pritzker School of Medicine Students: 417 full-time (216 women); includes 155 minority (48 African Americans, 92 Asian Americans or Pacific Islanders, 15 Hispanic Americans), 8 international. Average age 24. 6,517 applicants, 4% accepted, 104 enrolled. *Faculty:* 888 full-time. Expenses: Contact institution. *Financial support:* In 2001–02, 350 students received support, including 10 fellowships with full tuition reimbursements available (averaging $20,500 per year), 75 teaching assistantships; career-related internships or fieldwork, Federal Work-Study, institutionally sponsored loans, and scholarships/grants also available. Financial award application deadline: 4/1; financial award applicants required to submit FAFSA. In 2001, 104 degrees awarded. Offers medicine (MD). *Application deadline:* For fall admission, 10/15. Applications are processed on a rolling basis. *Application fee:* $60. *Application Contact:* 773-702-1937, Fax: 773-834-5412, E-mail: admissions@pritzker.bsd.uchicago.edu. *Dean,* Dr. Robert Madera, 773-702-9000.

School of Social Service Administration Students: 313 full-time (260 women), 117 part-time (88 women); includes 134 minority (69 African Americans, 23 Asian Americans or Pacific Islanders, 40 Hispanic Americans, 2 Native Americans), 6 international. 525 applicants, 36% accepted, 173 enrolled. *Faculty:* 31 full-time (17 women), 51 part-time/adjunct (36 women). Expenses: Contact institution. *Financial support:* In 2001–02, 415 students received support; fellowships, research assistantships with full tuition reimbursements available, teaching assistantships, career-related internships or fieldwork, Federal Work-Study, institutionally sponsored loans, and scholarships/grants available. Support available to part-time students. Financial award application deadline: 4/15; financial award applicants required to submit FAFSA. In 2001, 142 master's, 10 doctorates awarded. *Degree program information:* Part-time and evening/weekend programs available. Offers social service administration (PhD); social work (AM). *Application deadline:* For fall admission, 4/1 (priority date). Applications are processed on a rolling basis. *Application fee:* $60 ($70 for international students). Electronic applications accepted. *Application Contact:* Madeleine Metzler, Director of Admissions, 773-702-1492, Fax: 773-702-0874, E-mail: mmetzler@uchicago.edu. *Dean, School of Social Service Administration,* Edward F. Lawlor, 773-834-3618, Fax: 773-702-1979, E-mail: e-lawlor@uchicago.edu.

UNIVERSITY OF CINCINNATI, Cincinnati, OH 45221

General Information State-supported, coed, university. CGS member. *Enrollment:* 3,743 full-time matriculated graduate/professional students (2,011 women), 1,685 part-time matriculated graduate/professional students (919 women). Tuition, state resident: part-time $2,698 per quarter. Tuition, nonresident: part-time $4,977 per quarter. *Graduate housing:* Rooms and/or apartments available on a first-come, first-served basis to single and married students. Housing application deadline: 7/1. *Student services:* Campus employment opportunities, campus safety program, career counseling, child daycare facilities, disabled student services, exercise/wellness program, free psychological counseling, grant writing training, international student services, low-cost health insurance, multicultural affairs office, teacher training. *Library facilities:* Langsam Library plus 7 others. *Online resources:* library catalog, web page, access to other libraries' catalogs. *Collection:* 16,363 serial subscriptions, 48,757 audiovisual materials.

Computer facilities: 325 computers available on campus for general student use. A campuswide network can be accessed from student residence rooms and from off campus. *Web address:* http://www.uc.edu/.

General Application Contact: Dr. Howard Jackson, Vice President and University Dean, 513-556-2872, Fax: 513-556-0128, E-mail: howard.jackson@uc.edu.

GRADUATE UNITS

College of Law Students: 366 full-time (201 women); includes 64 minority (33 African Americans, 16 Asian Americans or Pacific Islanders, 14 Hispanic Americans, 1 Native American), 1 international. Average age 24. 1,124 applicants, 36% accepted, 97 enrolled. *Faculty:* 31 full-time (15 women), 60 part-time/adjunct (14 women). Expenses: Contact institution. *Financial support:* In 2001–02, 300 students received support, including 202 fellowships (averaging $5,226 per year), 74 research assistantships; career-related internships or fieldwork, Federal Work-Study, scholarships/grants, tuition waivers (full and partial), and unspecified assistantships also available. Financial award application deadline: 4/1; financial award applicants required to submit FAFSA. In 2001, 128 degrees awarded. Offers law (JD). *Application deadline:* For fall admission, 4/1 (priority date). Applications are processed on a rolling basis. *Application fee:* $35. Electronic applications accepted. *Application Contact:* Al Watson, Assistant Dean and Director of Admissions, 513-556-0077, Fax: 513-556-2391, E-mail: al.watson@uc.edu. *Dean,* Dr. Joseph P. Tomain, 513-556-0121, Fax: 513-556-5550, E-mail: joseph.tomain@uc.edu.

Division of Research and Advanced Studies Students: 3,743 full-time (2,011 women), 1,685 part-time (919 women); includes 1,403 minority (299 African Americans, 998 Asian Americans or Pacific Islanders, 90 Hispanic Americans, 16 Native Americans), 482 international. 7,205 applicants, 37% accepted. Expenses: Contact institution. *Financial support:* Fellowships, research assistantships, teaching assistantships, career-related internships or fieldwork, Federal Work-Study, institutionally sponsored loans, scholarships/grants, tuition waivers (partial), and unspecified assistantships available. In 2001, 1,305 master's, 266 doctorates awarded.

University of Cincinnati (continued)

Degree program information: Part-time and evening/weekend programs available. Electronic applications accepted. *Application Contact:* Barbara Patterson, Receptionist, 513-556-4341, Fax: 513-556-0128, E-mail: barb.patterson@uc.edu. *Vice President and University Dean,* Dr. Howard Jackson, 513-556-2872, Fax: 513-556-0128, E-mail: howard.jackson@uc.edu.

College-Conservatory of Music Students: 430 full-time (240 women), 260 part-time (120 women); includes 50 minority (14 African Americans, 17 Asian Americans or Pacific Islanders, 16 Hispanic Americans, 3 Native Americans), 203 international. 906 applicants, 31% accepted, 204 enrolled. *Faculty:* 91 full-time (26 women), 45 part-time/adjunct (20 women). Expenses: Contact institution. *Financial support:* In 2001–02, 149 teaching assistantships with full tuition reimbursements (averaging $5,744 per year) were awarded; fellowships, research assistantships, career-related internships or fieldwork, Federal Work-Study, scholarships/grants, tuition waivers (full and partial), and unspecified assistantships also available. In 2001, 103 master's, 21 doctorates, 11 other advanced degrees awarded. Offers arts administration (MA); choral conducting (MM, DMA); composition (MM, DMA); directing (MFA); keyboard studies (MM, DMA, AD); music (MA, MFA, MM, DMA, PhD, AD); music education (MM); music history (MM); music theory (MM, PhD); musicology (PhD); orchestral conducting (MM, DMA); performance (MM, DMA, AD); theater design and production (MFA); theater performance (MFA); wind conducting (MM, DMA). *Application deadline:* For fall admission, 2/1. Applications are processed on a rolling basis. *Application fee:* $80. Electronic applications accepted. *Application Contact:* Paul R. Hillner, Assistant Dean for Admissions and Student Services, 513-556-5462, Fax: 513-556-1028, E-mail: paul.hillner@uc.edu. *Dean,* Douglas A. Lowry, 513-556-3737, Fax: 513-556-0202, E-mail: douglas.lowry@uc.edu.

College of Allied Health Sciences Students: 104 full-time (91 women), 58 part-time (55 women). 500 applicants, 27% accepted. *Faculty:* 33 full-time (27 women). Expenses: Contact institution. *Financial support:* Fellowships, career-related internships or fieldwork, tuition waivers (full), and unspecified assistantships available. Support available to part-time students. Financial award application deadline: 5/1. In 2001, 65 master's, 5 doctorates awarded. *Degree program information:* Part-time programs available. Offers allied health sciences (MA, MPT, MS, PhD); blood transfusion medicine (MS); communication sciences and disorders (MA, PhD); medical genetics (MS); nutrition science (MS); rehabilitation science (MPT). *Application deadline:* For winter admission, 2/1. *Application fee:* $30. *Application Contact:* Gilbert R. Hageman, Associate Dean, 513-558-7495, Fax: 513-556-7494, E-mail: gilbert.hageman@uc.edu. *Dean,* Dr. Elizabeth King, 513-558-7495, Fax: 513-558-7494.

College of Business Administration Expenses: Contact institution. *Financial support:* Fellowships, research assistantships, teaching assistantships, tuition waivers (partial) and unspecified assistantships available. Financial award application deadline: 2/15. *Degree program information:* Part-time and evening/weekend programs available. Offers accounting (MBA, PhD); business administration (MBA, MS, PhD); finance (MBA, PhD); information systems (MBA, PhD); international business (MBA); management (MBA, PhD); marketing (MBA, PhD); operations management (MBA, PhD); quantitative analysis (MBA, MS, PhD); real estate (MBA). *Application fee:* $30. *Application Contact:* Ralph Katerberg, Associate Dean, 513-556-7003, Fax: 513-556-4891, E-mail: ralph.katerberg@uc.edu. *Dean,* Dr. Frederick Russ, 513-556-7001, Fax: 513-556-4891, E-mail: frederick.russ@uc.edu.

College of Design, Architecture, Art and Planning Students: 176 full-time, 56 part-time. 255 applicants, 59% accepted, 105 enrolled. *Faculty:* 33 full-time. Expenses: Contact institution. *Financial support:* Fellowships, career-related internships or fieldwork, Federal Work-Study, tuition waivers (full), and unspecified assistantships available. Support available to part-time students. In 2001, 60 degrees awarded. *Degree program information:* Part-time programs available. Offers architecture (M Arch, MS Arch); art education (MA); art history (MA); community planning (MCP); design, architecture, art and planning (M Arch, M Des, MA, MCP, MFA, MS Arch); fashion design (M Des); fine arts (MFA); graphic design (M Des); industrial design (M Des); interior design (M Des); planning (MCP). *Application deadline:* For fall admission, 2/1. *Application fee:* $30. *Application Contact:* Dr. Ann Marie Borys, Associate Dean, 513-556-0232, Fax: 513-556-3288. *Dean,* Dr. Judith Smith Koroscik, 513-556-1204, Fax: 513-556-3288, E-mail: judith.koroscik@uc.edu.

College of Education Students: 436 full-time (319 women), 353 part-time (264 women). 940 applicants, 32% accepted, 275 enrolled. *Faculty:* 99 full-time. Expenses: Contact institution. *Financial support:* In 2001–02, 22 fellowships with full tuition reimbursements, 43 research assistantships with full tuition reimbursements, 43 teaching assistantships with full tuition reimbursements were awarded. Career-related internships or fieldwork, tuition waivers (partial), and unspecified assistantships also available. Support available to part-time students. Financial award application deadline: 2/1. In 2001, 231 master's, 36 doctorates awarded. *Degree program information:* Part-time programs available. Offers community health (M Ed); counselor education (Ed D, CAGS); criminal justice (MS, PhD); curriculum and instruction (M Ed, Ed D); early childhood education (M Ed); education (M Ed, MA, MS, Ed D, PhD, CAGS, Ed S); educational administration (M Ed, Ed S); educational foundations (M Ed, Ed D); educational studies (M Ed, Ed D, Ed S); elementary education (M Ed); health promotion and education (M Ed); human services (M Ed, MA, Ed D, PhD, CAGS); mental health (MA); reading/literacy (M Ed, Ed D); school counseling (M Ed); school psychology (M Ed, PhD); secondary education (M Ed); special education (M Ed, Ed D); urban educational leadership (Ed D). *Application deadline:* For fall admission, 2/1 (priority date). Applications are processed on a rolling basis. *Application fee:* $30. Electronic applications accepted. *Application Contact:* Dr. Donald Wagner, Director, Graduate Programs, 513-556-3857, Fax: 513-556-2483, E-mail: donald.wagner@uc.edu. *Dean,* Dr. Lawrence Johnson, 513-556-2338, Fax: 513-556-2483, E-mail: lawrence.johnson@uc.edu.

College of Engineering Students: 775 full-time (127 women), 251 part-time (46 women); includes 71 minority (23 African Americans, 38 Asian Americans or Pacific Islanders, 10 Hispanic Americans), 684 international. 2,085 applicants, 33% accepted. *Faculty:* 110 full-time. Expenses: Contact institution. *Financial support:* Fellowships, research assistantships, teaching assistantships, career-related internships or fieldwork, tuition waivers (full), and unspecified assistantships available. Support available to part-time students. Financial award application deadline: 2/1. In 2001, 252 master's, 59 doctorates awarded. *Degree program information:* Part-time and evening/weekend programs available. Offers aerospace engineering (MS, PhD); ceramic science and engineering (MS, PhD); chemical engineering (MS, PhD); civil engineering (MS, PhD); computer engineering (MS); computer science (MS); computer science and engineering (PhD); electrical engineering (MS, PhD); engineering (MS, PhD); environmental engineering (MS, PhD); environmental sciences (MS, PhD); health physics (MS); industrial engineering (MS, PhD); materials science and engineering (MS, PhD); mechanical engineering (MS, PhD); metallurgical engineering (MS, PhD); nuclear engineering (MS, PhD); polymer science and engineering (MS, PhD). *Application deadline:* For fall admission, 2/1 (priority date). *Application fee:* $40. *Dean,* Dr. Stephen T. Kowel, 513-556-2933, Fax: 513-556-3626.

College of Medicine Students: 1,000. Expenses: Contact institution. *Financial support:* Fellowships with full tuition reimbursements, research assistantships with full tuition reimbursements, career-related internships or fieldwork, institutionally sponsored loans, and tuition waivers (partial) available. Financial award application deadline: 5/1. In 2001, 154 first professional degrees, 36 master's, 29 doctorates awarded. Offers anatomy (PhD); biophysics (PhD); cell and molecular biology (PhD); cell biophysics (PhD); environmental and industrial hygiene (MS); environmental and occupational medicine (MS); environmental health (PhD); environmental hygiene science and engineering (MS, PhD); epidemiology and biostatistics (MS); medicine (MD, MS, D Sc, PhD); molecular and cellular pathophysiology (D Sc); molecular and developmental biology (MS, PhD); molecular genetics, biochemistry and microbiology (MS, PhD); neurobiology (PhD); neuroscience (PhD); occupational safety (MS); pathology (PhD); pharmacology (PhD); physiology (PhD); radiology sciences (MS); teratology (MS, PhD); toxicology (MS, PhD). *Application deadline:* Applications are processed on a rolling basis. Electronic applications accepted. *Application Contact:* Bridgette Harrison, Director, Graduate Affairs, 513-558-5625, E-mail: bridgette.harrison@uc.edu. *Dean,* Dr. John Hutton, 513-558-7334, Fax: 513-558-1165, E-mail: john.hutton@uc.edu.

College of Nursing Students: 156 full-time (136 women), 85 part-time (70 women); includes 25 minority (8 African Americans, 14 Asian Americans or Pacific Islanders, 2 Hispanic Americans, 1 Native American), 9 international. Average age 34. 140 applicants, 48% accepted, 50 enrolled. *Faculty:* 39 full-time (all women), 7 part-time/adjunct (all women). Expenses: Contact institution. *Financial support:* In 2001–02, 144 students received support, including 11 research assistantships with tuition reimbursements available (averaging $9,057 per year), 4 teaching assistantships with tuition reimbursements available (averaging $9,057 per year); institutionally sponsored loans, scholarships/grants, traineeships, and tuition waivers (full and partial) also available. Support available to part-time students. Financial award application deadline: 1/1; financial award applicants required to submit FAFSA. In 2001, 93 master's, 4 doctorates awarded. *Degree program information:* Part-time programs available. Offers adult health nursing (MSN); community health nursing (MSN); nurse anesthesia (MSN); nurse midwifery (MSN); nurse practitioner studies (MSN); nursing (PhD); nursing administration (MSN); occupational health (MSN); parent/child nursing (MSN); psychiatric nursing (MSN); woman's health (MSN). *Application deadline:* For fall admission, 1/1 (priority date). Applications are processed on a rolling basis. *Application fee:* $30. *Application Contact:* Loren Carter, Program Coordinator, 513-558-5072, Fax: 513-558-7523, E-mail: loren.carter@uc.edu. *Dean,* Dr. Andrea Lindell, 513-558-5500, Fax: 513-558-9030, E-mail: andrea.lindell@uc.edu.

College of Pharmacy *Degree program information:* Part-time programs available. Offers pharmaceutical sciences (MS, PhD); pharmacy (Pharm D, MS, PhD); pharmacy practice (Pharm D).

McMicken College of Arts and Sciences Students: 723 full-time (379 women), 298 part-time (156 women); includes 100 minority (40 African Americans, 39 Asian Americans or Pacific Islanders, 19 Hispanic Americans, 2 Native Americans), 249 international. 1,009 applicants, 24% accepted. *Faculty:* 262 full-time. Expenses: Contact institution. *Financial support:* Fellowships with tuition reimbursements, research assistantships with tuition reimbursements, teaching assistantships with tuition reimbursements available. In 2001, 201 master's, 70 doctorates awarded. *Degree program information:* Part-time and evening/weekend programs available. Offers analytical chemistry (MS, PhD); anthropology (MA); applied economics (MA); applied mathematics (MS, PhD); arts and sciences (MA, MALER, MAT, MS, PhD, Certificate); biochemistry (MS, PhD); biological sciences (MS, PhD); classics (MA, PhD); clinical psychology (PhD); communication (MA); English (MA, PhD); experimental psychology (PhD); French (MA, PhD); geography (MA, PhD); geology (MS, PhD); Germanic languages and literature (MA, MAT, PhD); history (MA, MAT, PhD); inorganic chemistry (MS, PhD); interdisciplinary studies (PhD); labor and employment relations (MALER); mathematics education (MAT); organic chemistry (MS, PhD); philosophy (MA, PhD); physical chemistry (MS, PhD); physics (MS, PhD); political science (MA, PhD); polymer chemistry (MS, PhD); pure mathematics (MS, PhD); sociology (MA, PhD); Spanish (MA, PhD); statistics (MS, PhD); women's studies (MA, Certificate). *Application deadline:* For fall admission, 2/1. *Application Contact:* Joseph Scanio, Associate Dean, 513-556-5870, Fax: 513-556-0142, E-mail: joseph.scanio@uc.edu. *Dean,* Dr. Karen Gould, 513-556-5858, Fax: 513-556-0142, E-mail: karen.gould@uc.edu.

School of Social Work Expenses: Contact institution. *Financial support:* Fellowships, career-related internships or fieldwork, tuition waivers (partial), and unspecified assistantships available. Financial award application deadline: 5/1. *Degree program information:* Part-time programs available. Offers social work (MSW). *Application deadline:* For fall admission, 2/1. *Application fee:* $30. Electronic applications accepted. *Application Contact:* Gerald Bostwick, Graduate Program Director, 513-556-4624, Fax: 513-556-2077, E-mail: gerald.bostwick@uc.edu. *Director,* Dr. Philip Jackson, 513-556-4615, Fax: 513-556-2077, E-mail: philip.jackson@uc.edu.

UNIVERSITY OF COLORADO AT BOULDER, Boulder, CO 80309

General Information State-supported, coed, university. CGS member. *Enrollment:* 3,463 full-time matriculated graduate/professional students (1,609 women), 910 part-time matriculated graduate/professional students (449 women). *Graduate faculty:* 1,004 full-time (279 women). Tuition, state resident: full-time $3,474. Tuition, nonresident: full-time $16,624. *Graduate housing:* Rooms and/or apartments available to single and married students. *Student services:* Campus employment opportunities, campus safety program, career counseling, child daycare facilities, free psychological counseling, international student services, low-cost health insurance. *Library facilities:* Norlin Library plus 5 others. *Online resources:* library catalog, web page, access to other libraries' catalogs. *Collection:* 2.7 million titles, 14,772 serial subscriptions, 60,202 audiovisual materials. *Research affiliation:* National Center for Atmospheric Research, National Institute of Standards and Technology, National Oceanic and Atmospheric Administration, U.S. West Advanced Technologies, NASA.

Computer facilities: 1,700 computers available on campus for general student use. A campuswide network can be accessed from student residence rooms and from off campus. Internet access and online class registration, standard and academic software, student government voting are available. *Web address:* http://www.colorado.edu/.

General Application Contact: Office of Graduate Studies, E-mail: gradinfo@colorado.edu.

GRADUATE UNITS

Graduate School Students: 2,741 full-time (1,278 women), 893 part-time (445 women); includes 328 minority (34 African Americans, 130 Asian Americans or Pacific Islanders, 144 Hispanic Americans, 20 Native Americans), 676 international. Average age 30. 2,954 applicants, 68% accepted. *Faculty:* 910 full-time (259 women). Expenses: Contact institution. *Financial support:* In 2001–02, 405 fellowships with full tuition reimbursements (averaging $3,137 per year), 474 research assistantships with full tuition reimbursements (averaging $16,024 per year), 909 teaching assistantships with full tuition reimbursements (averaging $14,741 per year) were awarded. Career-related internships or fieldwork, Federal Work-Study, institutionally sponsored loans, scholarships/grants, traineeships, tuition waivers (full and partial), and unspecified assistantships also available. Support available to part-time students. Financial award applicants required to submit FAFSA. In 2001, 866 master's, 250 doctorates awarded. *Degree program information:* Part-time programs available. Postbaccalaureate distance learning degree programs offered. Offers museum (MS); museum and field studies (MBS). *Application fee:* $50 ($60 for international students). Electronic applications accepted. *Dean,* Carol Lynch, 303-492-7401, Fax: 303-492-5777, E-mail: gradinfo@colorado.edu.

College of Arts and Sciences Students: 1,460 full-time (745 women), 487 part-time (243 women); includes 168 minority (17 African Americans, 61 Asian Americans or Pacific Islanders, 76 Hispanic Americans, 14 Native Americans), 266 international. Average age 30. 1,223 applicants, 73% accepted. *Faculty:* 695 full-time (207 women). Expenses: Contact institution. *Financial support:* In 2001–02, 262 fellowships with full tuition reimbursements (averaging $2,620 per year), 256 research assistantships with full tuition reimbursements (averaging $16,068 per year), 708 teaching assistantships with full tuition reimbursements (averaging $15,144 per year) were awarded. Career-related internships or fieldwork, Federal Work-Study, institutionally sponsored loans, scholarships/grants, traineeships, tuition waivers (full), and unspecified assistantships also available. Support available to part-time students. In 2001, 293 master's, 164 doctorates awarded. *Degree program information:* Part-time programs available. Offers animal behavior (MA, PhD); anthropology (MA, PhD); applied mathematics (MS, PhD); aquatic biology (MA, PhD); art history (MA); arts and sciences (MA, MFA, MS, PhD); astrophysical and geophysical fluid dynamics (MS, PhD); astrophysics (MS, PhD); audiology (MA, PhD); behavioral genetics (MA, PhD); biochemistry (PhD); cellular structure and function (MA, PhD); chemical physics (PhD); chemistry (MS, PhD); Chinese (MA); classics (MA, PhD); communication (MA, PhD); comparative literature (MA, PhD); dance (MFA); developmental biology (MA, PhD); drawing (MFA); ecology (MA, PhD); economics (MA, PhD); English literature (MA, PhD); French (MA, PhD); geography (MA, PhD); geology (MS, PhD); geophysics (PhD); German (MA); history (MA, PhD); international affairs (MA); Japanese (MA); kinesiology (PhD); linguistics (MA, PhD); liquid crystal science and technology (PhD); mathematical physics (PhD); mathematics (MA, MS, PhD); medical physics (PhD); microbiology (MA, PhD); molecular biology (MA, PhD); neurobiology (MA, PhD); optical sciences and engineering (PhD); painting (MFA); philosophy (MA, PhD); photography (MFA); physical education (MS); physics (MS, PhD); plant and animal physiology (MA, PhD); plant and animal systematics (MA, PhD); plasma physics (MS, PhD); political science (MA, PhD); population biology (MA, PhD); population genetics

(MA, PhD); printmaking (MFA); psychology (MA, PhD); public policy analysis (MA); religious studies (MA); sculpture (MFA); sociology (MA, PhD); Spanish (MA, PhD); speech-language pathology (MA, PhD); theatre (MA, PhD). *Application fee:* $50 ($60 for international students). Electronic applications accepted. *Dean*, Todd T. Gleeson, 303-492-7294, E-mail: gleeson@stripe.colorado.edu.

College of Engineering and Applied Science Students: 786 full-time (188 women), 196 part-time (45 women); includes 95 minority (11 African Americans, 54 Asian Americans or Pacific Islanders, 28 Hispanic Americans, 2 Native Americans), 366 international. Average age 29. 1,184 applicants, 56% accepted. *Faculty:* 156 full-time (17 women). Expenses: Contact institution. *Financial support:* In 2001–02, 93 fellowships with full tuition reimbursements (averaging $4,765 per year), 190 research assistantships with full tuition reimbursements (averaging $16,271 per year), 89 teaching assistantships with full tuition reimbursements (averaging $15,839 per year) were awarded. Career-related internships or fieldwork, scholarships/grants, traineeships, and tuition waivers (full) also available. In 2001, 369 master's, 63 doctorates awarded. *Degree program information:* Part-time programs available. Postbaccalaureate distance learning degree programs offered. Offers aerospace engineering sciences (ME, MS, PhD); building systems (MS, PhD); chemical engineering (ME, MS, PhD); computer science (ME, MS, PhD); construction engineering and management (MS, PhD); electrical engineering (ME, MS, PhD); engineering and applied science (ME, MS, PhD); engineering management (ME); environmental engineering (MS, PhD); geoenvironmental engineering (MS, PhD); geotechnical engineering (MS, PhD); mechanical engineering (ME, MS, PhD); structural engineering (MS, PhD); telecommunications (ME, MS); water resource engineering (MS, PhD). *Application fee:* $50 ($60 for international students). Electronic applications accepted. *Dean*, Ross Corotis, 303-492-7006, Fax: 303-492-2199, E-mail: corotis@colorado.edu.

College of Music Students: 165 full-time (90 women), 38 part-time (19 women); includes 17 minority (11 Asian Americans or Pacific Islanders, 5 Hispanic Americans, 1 Native American), 24 international. Average age 31. 138 applicants, 87% accepted. *Faculty:* 55 full-time (14 women). Expenses: Contact institution. *Financial support:* In 2001–02, 15 fellowships (averaging $2,408 per year), 58 teaching assistantships (averaging $9,045 per year) were awarded. Tuition waivers (full) also available. Financial award application deadline: 3/1. In 2001, 36 master's, 10 doctorates awarded. Offers church music (M Mus); composition (M Mus, D Mus A); conducting (M Mus, D Mus A); music education (M Mus Ed, PhD); music literature (M Mus); musicology (PhD); pedagogy (M Mus, D Mus A); performance (M Mus, D Mus A). *Application deadline:* For fall admission, 3/1 (priority date). Applications are processed on a rolling basis. *Application fee:* $50 ($60 for international students). *Application Contact:* Information Contact, 303-492-2207, Fax: 303-492-5619. *Dean*, Daniel P. Sher, 303-492-7505, Fax: 303-492-5619, E-mail: daniel.sher@colorado.edu.

School of Education Students: 205 full-time (169 women), 157 part-time (131 women); includes 37 minority (4 African Americans, 3 Asian Americans or Pacific Islanders, 28 Hispanic Americans, 2 Native Americans), 3 international. Average age 32. 251 applicants, 88% accepted. *Faculty:* 26 full-time (12 women). Expenses: Contact institution. *Financial support:* In 2001–02, 20 fellowships (averaging $3,194 per year), 19 research assistantships (averaging $11,888 per year), 32 teaching assistantships (averaging $13,369 per year) were awarded. Career-related internships or fieldwork, Federal Work-Study, scholarships/grants, and tuition waivers (full and partial) also available. Support available to part-time students. Financial award application deadline: 2/1. In 2001, 136 master's, 9 doctorates awarded. *Degree program information:* Part-time programs available. Offers education (MA, PhD); educational and psychological studies (MA, PhD); instruction and curriculum (MA, PhD); research and evaluation methodologies (PhD); social multicultural and bilingual foundations (MA, PhD). *Application deadline:* For fall admission, 2/1 (priority date); for spring admission, 8/1. *Application fee:* $50 ($60 for international students). *Application Contact:* Jenny Dittenhofer, Graduate Program Assistant, 303-375-0096, Fax: 303-492-5839, E-mail: jennifer.dittenhofer@colorado.edu. *Interim Dean*, Lorrie Shepard, 303-492-6937, Fax: 303-492-7090, E-mail: lorrie.shepard@colorado.edu.

School of Journalism and Mass Communication Students: 103 full-time (70 women), 13 part-time (5 women); includes 9 minority (2 African Americans, 1 Asian American or Pacific Islander, 5 Hispanic Americans, 1 Native American), 17 international. Average age 32. 144 applicants, 73% accepted. *Faculty:* 18 full-time (9 women). Expenses: Contact institution. *Financial support:* In 2001–02, 10 fellowships (averaging $2,595 per year), 9 research assistantships with tuition reimbursements (averaging $18,279 per year), 21 teaching assistantships with tuition reimbursements (averaging $13,866 per year) were awarded. Institutionally sponsored loans and unspecified assistantships also available. Financial award application deadline: 3/1. In 2001, 22 master's, 3 doctorates awarded. *Degree program information:* Part-time programs available. Offers communication (PhD); integrated marketing communications (MA); mass communication research (MA); media studies (PhD); newsgathering (MA). *Application deadline:* For fall admission, 3/1. Applications are processed on a rolling basis. *Application fee:* $50 ($60 for international students). *Application Contact:* Ruth Bracey, Graduate Program Assistant, 303-492-5008, Fax: 303-492-0969. *Director, Graduate Program*, Robert Trager, 303-492-0502, Fax: 303-492-0969, E-mail: trager@spot.colorado.edu.

Leeds School of Business Students: 234 full-time (70 women), 17 part-time (4 women); includes 27 minority (4 African Americans, 16 Asian Americans or Pacific Islanders, 6 Hispanic Americans, 1 Native American), 40 international. Average age 31. 182 applicants, 64% accepted. *Faculty:* 61 full-time (11 women). Expenses: Contact institution. *Financial support:* In 2001–02, 21 fellowships (averaging $3,931 per year), 9 research assistantships (averaging $23,035 per year), 12 teaching assistantships (averaging $21,181 per year) were awarded. Career-related internships or fieldwork, Federal Work-Study, scholarships/grants, and unspecified assistantships also available. Financial award application deadline: 3/1. In 2001, 127 master's, 6 doctorates awarded. *Degree program information:* Part-time and evening/weekend programs available. Offers accounting (MS); business administration (MBA, PhD); business self designed (MBA); entrepreneurship (MBA); finance (MBA, PhD); marketing (MBA, PhD); operations management (MBA); organization management (MBA, PhD); real estate (MBA); taxation (MS); technology and innovation management (MBA). *Application deadline:* For fall admission, 3/1 (priority date). Applications are processed on a rolling basis. *Application fee:* $50 ($60 for international students). Electronic applications accepted. *Application Contact:* Diane Dimeff, Assistant Director, Admissions, 303-492-3537, Fax: 303-492-1727, E-mail: busgrad@spot.colorado.edu. *Dean*, Steven Manaster, 303-492-1809, Fax: 303-492-7676.

School of Law Students: 488 full-time (261 women); includes 87 minority (23 African Americans, 24 Asian Americans or Pacific Islanders, 33 Hispanic Americans, 7 Native Americans), 1 international. Average age 27. 2,236 applicants, 27% accepted. *Faculty:* 33 full-time (9 women). Expenses: Contact institution. *Financial support:* In 2001–02, 3 research assistantships (averaging $468 per year), 13 teaching assistantships (averaging $2,453 per year) were awarded. Fellowships, Federal Work-Study and institutionally sponsored loans also available. Financial award application deadline: 3/1; financial award applicants required to submit FAFSA. Offers law (JD). *Application deadline:* For fall admission, 2/15. Applications are processed on a rolling basis. *Application fee:* $50 ($60 for international students). *Application Contact:* Clarice Jonez, Graduate Program Assistant, 303-492-3825, Fax: 303-492-2542, E-mail: clarice.jonez@colorado.edu. *Dean*, Harold H. Bruff, 303-492-8047, Fax: 303-492-1757, E-mail: harold.bruff@colorado.edu.

UNIVERSITY OF COLORADO AT COLORADO SPRINGS, Colorado Springs, CO 80933-7150

General Information State-supported, coed, comprehensive institution. *Enrollment:* 1,238 matriculated graduate/professional students. *Enrollment by degree level:* 1,194 master's, 33 doctoral. *Graduate faculty:* 121 full-time (39 women), 53 part-time/adjunct (32 women). Tuition, state resident: full-time $2,900; part-time $174 per credit. Tuition, nonresident: full-time $9,961; part-time $591 per credit. *Required fees:* $14 per credit. $141 per semester. Tuition and fees vary according to course load, program and student level. *Graduate housing:* Room and/or apartments available on a first-come, first-served basis to single students; on-campus housing not available to married students. Typical cost: $5,896 (including board). *Student services:* Campus employment opportunities, campus safety program, career counseling, child daycare facilities, disabled student services, exercise/wellness program, free psychological counseling, international student services, low-cost health insurance, multicultural affairs office, teacher training, writing training. *Library facilities:* University of Colorado at Colorado Springs Kraemer Family Library. *Online resources:* library catalog, web page, access to other libraries' catalogs. *Collection:* 380,948 titles, 2,171 serial subscriptions, 5,055 audiovisual materials. *Research affiliation:* Symetrix (ferroelectronics), Colorado Vintage Companies (radon mitigation), Omegatech (genetics).

Computer facilities: 350 computers available on campus for general student use. A campuswide network can be accessed from student residence rooms and from off campus. *Web address:* http://www.uccs.edu/.

General Application Contact: Information Contact, 719-262-3417, Fax: 719-262-3037, E-mail: gradschl@uccs.edu.

GRADUATE UNITS

Beth-El College of Nursing Students: 49 full-time (42 women), 48 part-time (45 women); includes 14 minority (1 African American, 2 Asian Americans or Pacific Islanders, 9 Hispanic Americans, 2 Native Americans) Average age 41. *Faculty:* 9 full-time (8 women), 2 part-time/adjunct (both women). Expenses: Contact institution. *Financial support:* In 2001–02, 1 student received support; fellowships, career-related internships or fieldwork, Federal Work-Study, and institutionally sponsored loans available. Support available to part-time students. In 2001, 17 degrees awarded. *Degree program information:* Part-time programs available. Postbaccalaureate distance learning degree programs offered (minimal on-campus study). Offers adult health nurse practitioner and clinical specialist (MSN); family practitioner (MSN); neonatal nurse practitioner and clinical specialist (MSN). *Application deadline:* For fall admission, 2/15 (priority date); for spring admission, 10/15. *Application fee:* $60 ($75 for international students). Electronic applications accepted. *Chair*, Barbara Joyce-Nagata, 719-262-4430, Fax: 719-262-4416, E-mail: bnagata@mail.uccs.edu.

Graduate School Students: 531 full-time (318 women), 247 part-time (131 women); includes 103 minority (31 African Americans, 23 Asian Americans or Pacific Islanders, 44 Hispanic Americans, 5 Native Americans), 22 international. Average age 35. *Faculty:* 92 full-time (27 women), 39 part-time/adjunct (27 women). Expenses: Contact institution. *Financial support:* Fellowships, research assistantships, teaching assistantships, career-related internships or fieldwork, Federal Work-Study, and institutionally sponsored loans available. Support available to part-time students. Financial award applicants required to submit FAFSA. In 2001, 234 master's, 1 doctorate awarded. *Degree program information:* Part-time and evening/weekend programs available. *Application deadline:* Applications are processed on a rolling basis. *Application fee:* $60 ($75 for international students). *Application Contact:* Information Contact, 719-262-3417, Fax: 719-262-3037, E-mail: gradschl@uccs.edu. *Dean*, Dr. David Schmidt, 719-262-3044, Fax: 719-262-3067.

College of Education Students: 302 full-time (216 women), 102 part-time (76 women); includes 57 minority (23 African Americans, 5 Asian Americans or Pacific Islanders, 26 Hispanic Americans, 3 Native Americans) Average age 36. *Faculty:* 18 full-time (10 women), 26 part-time/adjunct (20 women). Expenses: Contact institution. *Financial support:* Fellowships, career-related internships or fieldwork and Federal Work-Study available. In 2001, 134 degrees awarded. *Degree program information:* Part-time and evening/weekend programs available. Offers counseling and human services (MA); curriculum and instruction (MA); educational administration (MA); educational leadership (MA); special education (MA). *Application deadline:* Applications are processed on a rolling basis. *Application fee:* $60 ($75 for international students). *Application Contact:* Connie Wroten, Professional Assistant, 719-262-4102, Fax: 719-262-4110, E-mail: cwroten@uccs.edu. *Dean*, Dr. David E. Nelson, 719-262-4111, Fax: 719-262-4110, E-mail: denelson@uccs.edu.

College of Engineering and Applied Science Students: 129 full-time (34 women), 93 part-time (15 women); includes 21 minority (2 African Americans, 13 Asian Americans or Pacific Islanders, 6 Hispanic Americans), 21 international. Average age 33. *Faculty:* 30 full-time (1 woman), 10 part-time/adjunct (4 women). Expenses: Contact institution. *Financial support:* Fellowships, research assistantships, teaching assistantships, career-related internships or fieldwork and Federal Work-Study available. In 2001, 56 master's, 1 doctorate awarded. *Degree program information:* Part-time and evening/weekend programs available. Offers applied mathematics (MS); computer science (MS, PhD); electrical engineering (MS, PhD); engineering and applied science (ME, MS, PhD); engineering management (ME); information operations (ME); manufacturing (ME); mechanical engineering (MS); software engineering (ME); space operations (ME). *Application deadline:* Applications are processed on a rolling basis. *Application fee:* $60 ($75 for international students). *Dean*, Dr. John Trapp, 719-262-3246, Fax: 719-262-3542, E-mail: jtrapp@uccs.edu.

College of Letters, Arts and Sciences Students: 100 full-time (68 women), 52 part-time (40 women); includes 25 minority (6 African Americans, 5 Asian Americans or Pacific Islanders, 12 Hispanic Americans, 2 Native Americans), 1 international. Average age 33. *Faculty:* 44 full-time (16 women), 3 part-time/adjunct (all women). Expenses: Contact institution. *Financial support:* Fellowships, research assistantships, teaching assistantships, career-related internships or fieldwork, Federal Work-Study, and institutionally sponsored loans available. Support available to part-time students. Financial award applicants required to submit FAFSA. In 2001, 44 degrees awarded. *Degree program information:* Part-time and evening/weekend programs available. Offers basic science (MBS); communications (MA); history (MA); letters, arts and sciences (MA, MBS, MS); physics (MBS, MS); psychology (MA); sociology (MA). *Application deadline:* Applications are processed on a rolling basis. *Dean*, Dr. Thomas M. Christensen, 719-262-4550, Fax: 719-262-3023, E-mail: tchriste@mail.uccs.edu.

Graduate School of Business Administration Students: 219 full-time (75 women), 71 part-time (34 women); includes 28 minority (4 African Americans, 12 Asian Americans or Pacific Islanders, 12 Hispanic Americans), 12 international. Average age 32. *Faculty:* 16 full-time (3 women), 5 part-time/adjunct (0 women). Expenses: Contact institution. *Financial support:* Career-related internships or fieldwork, Federal Work-Study, and institutionally sponsored loans available. Support available to part-time students. Financial award applicants required to submit FAFSA. In 2001, 170 degrees awarded. *Degree program information:* Part-time and evening/weekend programs available. Offers accounting (MBA); finance (MBA); information systems (MBA); marketing (MBA); organizational management (MBA); production management (MBA). *Application deadline:* For fall admission, 6/1; for spring admission, 11/1. *Application fee:* $60 ($75 for international students). *Application Contact:* Maureen Cathey, Adviser, 719-262-3408, Fax: 719-262-3100, E-mail: busadvsr@uccs.edu. *Dean*, Dr. Joseph Rallo, 719-262-3113, Fax: 719-262-3494, E-mail: jrallo@uccs.edu.

Graduate School of Public Affairs Students: 34 full-time (23 women), 39 part-time (20 women); includes 11 minority (3 Asian Americans or Pacific Islanders, 6 Hispanic Americans, 2 Native Americans) Average age 37. 8 applicants, 100% accepted. *Faculty:* 4 full-time (1 woman), 7 part-time/adjunct (3 women). Expenses: Contact institution. *Financial support:* Career-related internships or fieldwork and Federal Work-Study available. Support available to part-time students. In 2001, 22 degrees awarded. *Degree program information:* Part-time and evening/weekend programs available. Offers criminal justice (MCJ); public administration (MPA). *Application deadline:* For fall admission, 6/1 (priority date); for spring admission, 11/1. Applications are processed on a rolling basis. *Application fee:* $60 ($75 for international students). *Application Contact:* Mary Lou Kartis, Program Assistant, 719-262-4182, Fax: 719-262-4183, E-mail: mkartis@uccs.edu. *Dean*, Dr. Kathleen Beatty, 719-262-4103, Fax: 719-262-4183, E-mail: kbeatty@carbon.cudenver.edu.

UNIVERSITY OF COLORADO AT DENVER, Denver, CO 80217-3364

General Information State-supported, coed, university. CGS member. *Enrollment:* 1,471 full-time matriculated graduate/professional students (825 women), 2,665 part-time matriculated graduate/professional students (1,506 women). *Enrollment by degree level:* 3,824 master's, 257 doctoral, 55 other advanced degrees. *Graduate faculty:* 347 full-time (121 women). Tuition, state resident: full-time $3,284; part-time $198 per credit hour. Tuition, nonresident: full-time $13,380; part-time $802 per credit hour. *Required fees:* $444; $222 per semester. *Graduate housing:* On-campus housing not available. *Student services:* Campus employment opportunities, campus safety program, career counseling, child daycare facilities, disabled

University of Colorado at Denver (continued)

student services, exercise/wellness program, free psychological counseling, international student services, low-cost health insurance, teacher training, writing training. *Library facilities:* Auraria Library. *Online resources:* library catalog, web page, access to other libraries' catalogs. *Collection:* 555,794 titles, 4,364 serial subscriptions, 15,720 audiovisual materials.

Computer facilities: 577 computers available on campus for general student use. A campuswide network can be accessed from off campus. Internet access and online class registration are available. *Web address:* http://www.cudenver.edu/.

General Application Contact: Annette Beck, Program Specialist, 303-556-2663, Fax: 303-556-2164, E-mail: abeck@castle.cudenver.edu.

GRADUATE UNITS

College of Architecture and Planning Students: 316 full-time (132 women), 84 part-time (44 women); includes 30 minority (4 African Americans, 8 Asian Americans or Pacific Islanders, 16 Hispanic Americans, 2 Native Americans), 52 international. Average age 30. 328 applicants, 50% accepted, 124 enrolled. *Faculty:* 31 full-time (7 women). Expenses: Contact institution. *Financial support:* In 2001–02, 1 fellowship with partial tuition reimbursement, 11 research assistantships, 1 teaching assistantship (averaging $1,050 per year) were awarded. Career-related internships or fieldwork, Federal Work-Study, institutionally sponsored loans, scholarships/grants, and tuition waivers (full and partial) also available. Support available to part-time students. Financial award application deadline: 3/1; financial award applicants required to submit FAFSA. In 2001, 140 degrees awarded. *Degree program information:* Part-time programs available. Offers architecture (M Arch); architecture and planning (M Arch, MLA, MUD, MURP, PhD); design and planning (PhD); landscape architecture (MLA); urban and regional planning (MURP); urban design (MUD). *Application deadline:* For fall admission, 3/15; for spring admission, 10/1. *Application fee:* $50 ($60 for international students). *Application Contact:* Heather Zertuche, Administrative Assistant 2, 303-556-3382, Fax: 303-556-3687, E-mail: a&p-grad-info@carbon.cudenver.edu. *Dean*, Patricia O'Leary, 303-556-3382, Fax: 303-556-3687.

Graduate School Students: 820 full-time (593 women), 1,716 part-time (1,195 women); includes 343 minority (58 African Americans, 93 Asian Americans or Pacific Islanders, 169 Hispanic Americans, 23 Native Americans), 126 international. Average age 33. 1,970 applicants, 73% accepted, 847 enrolled. *Faculty:* 347 full-time (121 women). Expenses: Contact institution. *Financial support:* Fellowships, research assistantships, teaching assistantships, career-related internships or fieldwork and Federal Work-Study available. Financial award applicants required to submit FAFSA. In 2001, 1,483 master's, 32 doctorates, 32 other advanced degrees awarded. *Degree program information:* Part-time and evening/weekend programs available. *Application deadline:* Applications are processed on a rolling basis. *Application fee:* $50 ($60 for international students). Electronic applications accepted. *Application Contact:* Lisa Atencio, Assistant to the Dean, 303-352-3701, Fax: 303-352-3215, E-mail: latencio@carbon.cudenver.edu. *Interim Vice Chancellor for Academic and Student Affairs*, Mark Gelernter, 303-556-2550, Fax: 303-556-2164.

College of Engineering and Applied Science Students: 46 full-time (18 women), 260 part-time (119 women); includes 57 minority (8 African Americans, 32 Asian Americans or Pacific Islanders, 14 Hispanic Americans, 3 Native Americans), 52 international. Average age 33. 195 applicants, 72% accepted, 75 enrolled. *Faculty:* 39 full-time (7 women). Expenses: Contact institution. *Financial support:* Research assistantships, teaching assistantships, career-related internships or fieldwork and Federal Work-Study available. Financial award application deadline: 3/1; financial award applicants required to submit FAFSA. In 2001, 84 master's, 2 doctorates awarded. *Degree program information:* Part-time and evening/weekend programs available. Offers civil engineering (MS, PhD); computer science (MS); electrical engineering (MS); engineering (ME); engineering and applied science (ME, MS, PhD); mechanical engineering (MS). *Application deadline:* Applications are processed on a rolling basis. *Application fee:* $50 ($60 for international students). Electronic applications accepted. *Application Contact:* Judith Stalnaker, Associate Dean, 303-556-8405, Fax: 303-556-2368, E-mail: judy.stalnaker@cudenver.edu. *Chair*, Peter Jenkins, 303-556-2871, Fax: 303-556-2511, E-mail: pjenkins@cse.cudenver.edu.

College of Liberal Arts and Sciences Students: 187 full-time (109 women), 359 part-time (199 women); includes 70 minority (18 African Americans, 19 Asian Americans or Pacific Islanders, 27 Hispanic Americans, 6 Native Americans), 67 international. Average age 35. 253 applicants, 70% accepted, 113 enrolled. *Faculty:* 153 full-time (58 women). Expenses: Contact institution. *Financial support:* Fellowships, research assistantships, teaching assistantships, career-related internships or fieldwork and Federal Work-Study available. Financial award application deadline: 3/1; financial award applicants required to submit FAFSA. In 2001, 139 master's, 6 doctorates awarded. *Degree program information:* Part-time and evening/weekend programs available. Offers anthropology (MA); applied mathematics (MS, PhD); basic science (MBS); biology (MA); chemistry (MS); communication (MA); economics (MA); environmental science (MS); health and behavioral science (PhD); history (MA); humanities (MH); liberal arts and sciences (MA, MBS, MH, MS, MSS, PhD); literature (MA); political science (MA); psychology (MA); social sciences (MSS); sociology (MA); teaching English as a second language (MA); teaching of writing (MA); technical communication (MS). *Application deadline:* Applications are processed on a rolling basis. *Application fee:* $50 ($60 for international students). Electronic applications accepted. *Application Contact:* Jana Everett, Associate Dean, 303-556-3513, Fax: 303-556-4681, E-mail: jana.everett@cudenver.edu. *Dean*, Jim Smith, 303-556-2557, Fax: 303-556-4861.

Graduate School of Business Administration Students: 417 full-time (178 women), 883 part-time (355 women); includes 150 minority (35 African Americans, 67 Asian Americans or Pacific Islanders, 43 Hispanic Americans, 5 Native Americans), 206 international. Average age 33. 637 applicants, 81% accepted, 277 enrolled. *Faculty:* 62 full-time (17 women). Expenses: Contact institution. *Financial support:* In 2001–02, 290 students received support, including 75 research assistantships; career-related internships or fieldwork, Federal Work-Study, institutionally sponsored loans, scholarships/grants, traineeships, and tuition waivers (partial) also available. Support available to part-time students. Financial award applicants required to submit CSS PROFILE or FAFSA. In 2001, 558 degrees awarded. *Degree program information:* Part-time and evening/weekend programs available. Postbaccalaureate distance learning degree programs offered (minimal on-campus study). Offers accounting (MS); business administration (Exec MBA, Exec MS, MBA, MS, MSIB); finance (MS); health administration (Exec MBA, MS); information systems management (MS); international business (MSIB); management (MS); marketing (MS). *Application deadline:* Applications are processed on a rolling basis. Electronic applications accepted. *Application Contact:* Ken Bettenhausen, Associate Dean, 303-556-5803, Fax: 303-556-5914, E-mail: kbettenh@cudenver.edu. *Dean*, Jean Claude Bosch, 303-556-6804, Fax: 303-556-5899, E-mail: jbosch@castle.cudenver.edu.

Graduate School of Public Affairs Students: 77 full-time (46 women), 275 part-time (166 women); includes 58 minority (21 African Americans, 7 Asian Americans or Pacific Islanders, 22 Hispanic Americans, 8 Native Americans), 35 international. Average age 35. 211 applicants, 78% accepted, 88 enrolled. *Faculty:* 14 full-time (5 women). Expenses: Contact institution. *Financial support:* In 2001–02, 50 fellowships with partial tuition reimbursements (averaging $500 per year), 20 research assistantships with partial tuition reimbursements (averaging $500 per year), 13 teaching assistantships with partial tuition reimbursements (averaging $1,000 per year) were awarded. Career-related internships or fieldwork, Federal Work-Study, and institutionally sponsored loans also available. Support available to part-time students. Financial award application deadline: 4/1. In 2001, 99 master's, 6 doctorates awarded. *Degree program information:* Part-time and evening/weekend programs available. Postbaccalaureate distance learning degree programs offered. Offers criminal justice (MCJ); public administration (Exec MPA, MPA, PhD); public affairs (Exec MPA, MCJ, MPA, PhD). *Application fee:* $50 ($60 for international students). *Application Contact:* Antoinette Sandoval, Student Service Specialist, 303-556-5970, Fax: 303-556-5971, E-mail: asandoval@castle.cudenver.edu. *Dean*, Kathleen Beatty, 303-556-5974, Fax: 303-556-5971, E-mail: kbeatty@carbon.cudenver.edu.

School of Education Students: 587 full-time (466 women), 1,097 part-time (877 women); includes 216 minority (32 African Americans, 42 Asian Americans or Pacific Islanders, 128 Hispanic Americans, 14 Native Americans), 17 international. Average age 35. 332 applicants, 81% accepted, 165 enrolled. *Faculty:* 48 full-time (27 women). Expenses: Contact institution. *Financial support:* Fellowships, research assistantships, teaching assistantships, Federal Work-Study available. Financial award applicants required to submit FAFSA. In 2001, 463 master's, 18 doctorates, 32 other advanced degrees awarded. *Degree program information:* Part-time and evening/weekend programs available. Offers administration, supervision, and curriculum development (MA); counseling psychology and counselor education (MA); curriculum and instruction (MA); education (MA, PhD, Ed S); educational administration, curriculum and supervision (Ed S); educational psychology (MA); initial professional teacher education (MA); leadership and innovation (PhD); professional learning and advancement (MA, Ed S). *Application deadline:* For fall admission, 4/15; for spring admission, 9/15. Applications are processed on a rolling basis. *Application fee:* $50 ($60 for international students). Electronic applications accepted. *Application Contact:* Sue Green, Program Assistant, 303-556-2717, Fax: 303-556-4479. *Acting Dean*, Lynn Rhodes, 303-556-2844, Fax: 303-556-4479, E-mail: lynn_rhodes@ceo.cudenver.edu.

UNIVERSITY OF COLORADO HEALTH SCIENCES CENTER, Denver, CO 80262

General Information State-supported, coed, upper-level institution. CGS member. *Enrollment:* 1,792 matriculated graduate/professional students. *Graduate faculty:* 1,110 full-time. Tuition, state resident: part-time $170 per unit. Tuition, nonresident: part-time $391 per unit. *Graduate housing:* On-campus housing not available. *Student services:* Campus employment opportunities, campus safety program, career counseling, disabled student services, exercise/wellness program, free psychological counseling, low-cost health insurance, multicultural affairs office. *Library facilities:* Denison Library plus 1 other. *Online resources:* library catalog, web page, access to other libraries' catalogs. *Collection:* 250,000 titles, 1,650 serial subscriptions. *Research affiliation:* National Jewish Center (immunology, molecular biology).

Computer facilities: 36 computers available on campus for general student use. A campuswide network can be accessed from off campus. Internet access and online class registration are available. *Web address:* http://www.uchsc.edu/.

General Application Contact: Dr. David Sorenson, Director, Student and Administrative Services and Admissions, 303-315-7676, Fax: 303-315-3358.

GRADUATE UNITS

Graduate School Students: 823. Average age 30. 1,056 applicants, 32% accepted. Expenses: Contact institution. *Financial support:* Fellowships, research assistantships, teaching assistantships, career-related internships or fieldwork, Federal Work-Study, and institutionally sponsored loans available. Support available to part-time students. Financial award application deadline: 3/15. In 2001, 131 master's, 24 doctorates awarded. *Degree program information:* Part-time programs available. Offers child health associate/physician assistant (MS); nursing (MS, PhD); pharmaceutical sciences (PhD); physical therapy (MS); public health (MSPH); toxicology (PhD). *Application fee:* $50. *Application Contact:* Frances Osterberg, Director of Admissions and Student Support, 303-315-7928. *Dean*, Dr. John Freed, 303-315-6446.

Programs in Biological Sciences Average age 29. 43 applicants, 12 enrolled. Expenses: Contact institution. *Financial support:* Fellowships, research assistantships, teaching assistantships, career-related internships or fieldwork, Federal Work-Study, institutionally sponsored loans, and traineeships available. Support available to part-time students. Offers analytic health sciences (PhD); biochemistry (PhD); biological sciences (MS, PhD); biometrics (MS); biophysics and genetics (PhD); cell and developmental biology (PhD); cellular and molecular physiology (PhD); clinical science (PhD); experimental pathology (PhD); genetic counseling (MS); immunology (PhD); medical physics (MS, PhD); microbiology (PhD); molecular biology (PhD); neuroscience (PhD); pharmacology (PhD). *Application fee:* $50. *Application Contact:* Frances Osterberg, Director of Admissions and Student Support, 303-315-7928. *Head*, Dr. Steven Anderson, 303-315-4787.

School of Dentistry Students: 143 full-time (56 women); includes 24 minority (1 African American, 12 Asian Americans or Pacific Islanders, 9 Hispanic Americans, 2 Native Americans) Average age 26. 695 applicants, 5% accepted. *Faculty:* 52 full-time. Expenses: Contact institution. *Financial support:* Federal Work-Study and institutionally sponsored loans available. Financial award application deadline: 3/15. In 2001, 37 degrees awarded. Offers dentistry (DDS, M Ed). *Application deadline:* For fall admission, 1/1. *Application fee:* $50. *Application Contact:* Dr. Randy L. Kluender, Assistant Dean for Admissions and Student Affairs, 303-315-7259. *Dean*, Howard Landesman, 303-315-8773.

School of Medicine Students: 524 full-time (263 women), 22 part-time (11 women); includes 112 minority (16 African Americans, 52 Asian Americans or Pacific Islanders, 40 Hispanic Americans, 4 Native Americans), 1 international. Average age 28. 2,148 applicants, 127 enrolled. *Faculty:* 923 full-time. Expenses: Contact institution. *Financial support:* Fellowships, research assistantships, teaching assistantships, career-related internships or fieldwork, Federal Work-Study, and institutionally sponsored loans available. Support available to part-time students. In 2001, 123 degrees awarded. Offers medicine (MD). *Application fee:* $70. *Application Contact:* Dr. Maureen Garrity, Associate Dean for Admissions, 303-315-7361. *Dean*, Dr. Richard Krugman, 303-315-7565.

School of Nursing Students: 44 full-time, 9 part-time. Average age 33. *Faculty:* 93 full-time. Expenses: Contact institution. *Financial support:* Fellowships, research assistantships, teaching assistantships, career-related internships or fieldwork, Federal Work-Study, and institutionally sponsored loans available. Support available to part-time students. Financial award application deadline: 3/15. *Degree program information:* Part-time programs available. Offers nursing (MS, ND, PhD). *Application Contact:* Chris Muller, Director of Admissions and Student Support, 303-315-0933. *Interim Dean*, Patricia Moritz, 303-315-8542.

School of Pharmacy Students: 215 full-time (162 women), 2 part-time (both women); includes 99 minority (19 African Americans, 53 Asian Americans or Pacific Islanders, 23 Hispanic Americans, 4 Native Americans), 5 international. Average age 27. 320 applicants, 110 enrolled. *Faculty:* 39 full-time. Expenses: Contact institution. *Financial support:* Fellowships, research assistantships, teaching assistantships, career-related internships or fieldwork, Federal Work-Study, and institutionally sponsored loans available. Support available to part-time students. In 2001, 112 degrees awarded. Offers pharmacy (Pharm D). *Application deadline:* For fall admission, 12/1. *Application Contact:* Dr. Carol Balmer, Director, 303-315-7709. *Dean*, Louis Diamond, 303-315-5055.

UNIVERSITY OF CONNECTICUT, Storrs, CT 06269

General Information State-supported, coed, university. CGS member. *Graduate housing:* Room and/or apartments available to single students; on-campus housing not available to married students. Housing application deadline: 4/1. *Research affiliation:* Haskins Laboratories, U.S. Navy–Submarine Medical Research Laboratory.

GRADUATE UNITS

Graduate School *Degree program information:* Part-time and evening/weekend programs available. Offers biomedical science (PhD); dental science (M Dent Sc); public health (MPH).

College of Agriculture and Natural Resources Offers agricultural and resource economics (MS, PhD); agriculture and natural resources (MS, PhD); animal science (MS, PhD); natural resources: land, water, and air (MS); nutritional sciences (MS, PhD); pathobiology (MS, PhD); plant and soil sciences (MS, PhD).

College of Liberal Arts and Sciences Offers African studies (MA); anthropology (MA, PhD); behavioral neuroscience (PhD); biochemistry (MS, PhD); biophysics (MS, PhD); biopsychology (PhD); biotechnology (MS); botany (MS, PhD); cell and developmental biology (MS, PhD); chemistry (MS, PhD); clinical psychology (PhD); cognition/instruction psychology (PhD); communication (MA); communication processes and marketing communication (PhD); comparative literature and cultural studies (MA, PhD); developmental psychobiology (MS, PhD); developmental psychology (PhD); ecological psychology (PhD); ecology (MS, PhD); ecology and evolutionary biology (MS, PhD); economics (MA, PhD); English (MA, PhD); entomology (MS, PhD); French (MA, PhD); general experimental psychology (PhD); genetics (MS, PhD); geography (MS, PhD); geology (MS, PhD); geophysics (MS, PhD); German (MA, PhD); history (MA, PhD); industrial and organizational psychology (PhD); international studies (MA); interpersonal communication (MA); Italian (MA, PhD); language psychology (PhD); Latin American studies (MA); liberal arts and sciences (MA,

MPA, MS, PhD); linguistics (MA, PhD); mass communication (MA); mathematics (MS, PhD); medieval studies (MA, PhD); microbiology (MS, PhD); molecular and cell biology (MS, PhD); neurobiology (MS, PhD); nonverbal communication (MA); oceanography (MS, PhD); organizational communication (MA); philosophy (MA, PhD); physics (MS, PhD); physiology (MS, PhD); physiology and neurobiology (MS, PhD); plant molecular and cell biology (MS, PhD); political science (MA, PhD); public affairs (MPA); Slavic and East European studies (MA); social psychology (PhD); sociology (MA, PhD); Spanish (MA, PhD); speech, language, and hearing (MA, PhD); statistics (MS, PhD); systematics (MS, PhD); Western European studies (MA); zoology (MS, PhD).

School of Allied Health Professions Offers allied health professions (MS).

School of Business Offers accounting (MBA, PhD); finance (PhD); general business administration (MBA); health care management (MBA); human resources management (MBA); management (MBA, PhD); marketing (MBA, PhD).

School of Education Offers adult and vocational education (MA, PhD); bilingual and bicultural education (MA, PhD); cognition and instruction (PhD); counseling psychology (MA, PhD); curriculum and instruction (MA, PhD); education (MA, PhD); educational administration (MA, PhD); educational psychology (MA, PhD); educational studies (MA, PhD); elementary education (MA, PhD); English education (MA, PhD); evaluation and measurement (MA, PhD); foreign languages education (MA, PhD); gifted and talented (MA, PhD); history and social science education (MA, PhD); instructional media and technology (MA, PhD); leisure science (MA, PhD); mathematics education (MA, PhD); professional higher education administration (MA, PhD); reading education (MA, PhD); school psychology (MA, PhD); science education (MA, PhD); secondary education (MA, PhD); special education (MA, PhD); sport science (MA, PhD).

School of Engineering Offers aerospace engineering (MS, PhD); applied mechanics (PhD); artificial intelligence (MS, PhD); biological engineering (MS); biomedical engineering (MS, PhD); chemical engineering (MS, PhD); chemistry (MS, PhD); civil engineering (MS, PhD); computer architecture (MS, PhD); computer science (MS, PhD); control and communication systems (MS, PhD); electromagnetics and physical electronics (MS, PhD); engineering (MS, PhD); environmental engineering (MS, PhD); fluid dynamics (PhD); material science (MS, PhD); mechanical engineering (MS, PhD); metallurgy (MS, PhD); ocean engineering (MS, PhD); operating systems (MS, PhD); polymer science (MS, PhD); robotics (MS, PhD); software engineering (MS, PhD).

School of Family Studies Offers family studies (MA, MS, PhD); human development and family relations (MA, PhD).

School of Fine Arts Offers art and art history (MFA); composition (M Mus); conducting (M Mus, DMA); dramatic arts (MA, MFA); fine arts (M Mus, MA, MFA, DMA, PhD); historical musicology (MA); music education (M Mus, PhD); music theory and history (PhD); performance (M Mus, DMA); psychomusicology (PhD); theory (MA).

School of Nursing Offers nurse education (MS); nursing (PhD); nursing management (MS).

School of Pharmacy Offers medicinal chemistry (MS, PhD); pharmaceutics (MS, PhD); pharmacology and toxicology (MS, PhD); pharmacy (MS, PhD).

School of Social Work Offers social work (MSW).

School of Law *Degree program information:* Part-time and evening/weekend programs available. Offers law (JD). Electronic applications accepted.

See in-depth description on page 1167.

UNIVERSITY OF CONNECTICUT HEALTH CENTER, Farmington, CT 06030

General Information State-supported, coed, graduate-only institution. *Enrollment by degree level:* 471 first professional, 222 master's, 147 doctoral, 55 other advanced degrees. *Graduate faculty:* 538. Tuition, state resident: full-time $5,272; part-time $293 per credit. Tuition, nonresident: full-time $13,696; part-time $761 per credit. *Required fees:* $1,070; $206 per semester. Full-time tuition and fees vary according to degree level, program and reciprocity agreements. *Graduate housing:* On-campus housing not available. *Student services:* Career counseling, free psychological counseling, low-cost health insurance. *Library facilities:* Lyman Maynard Stowe Library. *Online resources:* library catalog, web page, access to other libraries' catalogs. *Collection:* 186,500 titles, 2,330 serial subscriptions, 3,600 audiovisual materials.

Computer facilities: A campuswide network can be accessed from off campus. Internet access is available. *Web address:* http://www.uchc.edu/.

General Application Contact: Dr. Keat Sanford, Assistant Dean and Director, 860-679-3874, Fax: 860-679-1282, E-mail: sanford@nso1.uchc.edu.

GRADUATE UNITS

Graduate School Students: 183 full-time (107 women), 186 part-time (120 women); includes 52 minority (28 African Americans, 13 Asian Americans or Pacific Islanders, 9 Hispanic Americans, 2 Native Americans), 76 international. Average age 25. *Faculty:* 150. Expenses: Contact institution. *Financial support:* In 2001–02, research assistantships (averaging $20,000 per year); fellowships, teaching assistantships In 2001, 48 master's, 20 doctorates awarded. *Degree program information:* Part-time and evening/weekend programs available. Offers biomedical sciences); dental science (MDS); public health (MPH). *Application deadline:* For fall admission, 1/1 (priority date); for spring admission, 10/1. Applications are processed on a rolling basis. *Application fee:* $40 ($45 for international students). *Application Contact:* Dr. Keat Sanford, Assistant Dean and Director, 860-679-3874, Fax: 860-679-1282, E-mail: sanford@nso1.uchc.edu. *Associate Dean of the Graduate School,* Dr. Gerald Maxwell, 860-679-3523, Fax: 860-679-1274, E-mail: maxwell@neuron.uchc.edu.

Programs in Biomedical Sciences Students: 121 full-time (67 women); includes 10 minority (4 African Americans, 4 Asian Americans or Pacific Islanders, 2 Hispanic Americans), 59 international. Average age 27. *Faculty:* 100. Expenses: Contact institution. *Financial support:* In 2001–02, 20 research assistantships (averaging $20,000 per year) were awarded; teaching assistantships, Federal Work-Study also available. In 2001, 10 doctorates awarded. *Degree program information:* Part-time and evening/weekend programs available. Offers biomedical sciences (PhD); cell biology (PhD); cellular and molecular pharmacology (PhD); developmental biology (PhD); genetics, molecular biology, and biochemistry (PhD); immunology (PhD); neuroscience (PhD); oral biology); skeletal, craniofacial and oral biology (PhD). *Application deadline:* For fall admission, 1/1 (priority date); for spring admission, 10/1. Applications are processed on a rolling basis. *Application fee:* $40 ($45 for international students). *Application Contact:* Dr. Keat Sanford, Assistant Dean and Director, 860-679-3874, Fax: 860-679-1282, E-mail: sanford@nso1.uchc.edu.

School of Dental Medicine Students: 208 full-time (84 women), 1 part-time; includes 43 minority (6 African Americans, 23 Asian Americans or Pacific Islanders, 14 Hispanic Americans), 12 international. Average age 25. *Faculty:* 35 full-time (5 women). Expenses: Contact institution. *Financial support:* In 2001–02, research assistantships (averaging $20,000 per year); fellowships, teaching assistantships, Federal Work-Study and institutionally sponsored loans also available. Financial award applicants required to submit FAFSA. In 2001, 38 degrees awarded. Offers dental medicine (DMD, Certificate). *Application deadline:* For fall admission, 2/1. Applications are processed on a rolling basis. *Application fee:* $60. *Application Contact:* Michelle Toucey, Information Contact, 860-679-2175, Fax: 860-679-1899, E-mail: toucey@nso.uchc.edu. *Dean,* Dr. Peter J. Robinson, 860-679-2808, Fax: 860-679-1330, E-mail: probinson@nso.uchc.edu.

School of Medicine Students: 314 full-time (160 women), 2 part-time; includes 84 minority (32 African Americans, 36 Asian Americans or Pacific Islanders, 13 Hispanic Americans, 3 Native Americans), 2 international. Average age 24. 2,200 applicants, 7% accepted. Expenses: Contact institution. *Financial support:* In 2001–02, 250 students received support. Institutionally sponsored loans and tuition waivers (partial) available. Financial award application deadline: 4/1; financial award applicants required to submit FAFSA. In 2001, 76 degrees awarded. Offers medicine (MD). *Application deadline:* For fall admission, 12/15. Applications are processed on a rolling basis. *Application fee:* $75. *Application Contact:* Dr. Keat Sanford, Assistant Dean and Director, 860-679-3874, Fax: 860-679-1282, E-mail: sanford@nso1.uchc.edu. *Dean,* Dr. Peter J. Deckers, 860-679-2413, Fax: 860-679-1282.

UNIVERSITY OF DALLAS, Irving, TX 75062-4736

General Information Independent-religious, coed, university. *Enrollment:* 393 full-time matriculated graduate/professional students (162 women), 1,791 part-time matriculated graduate/professional students (714 women). *Enrollment by degree level:* 2,131 master's, 53 doctoral. *Graduate faculty:* 104 full-time (34 women), 90 part-time/adjunct. *Tuition:* Full-time $3,807; part-time $423 per credit. *Graduate housing:* Rooms and/or apartments available to single students and available on a first-come, first-served basis to married students. Typical cost: $6,044 (including board) for single students. Housing application deadline: 4/24. *Student services:* Campus employment opportunities, campus safety program, career counseling, international student services. *Library facilities:* William A. Blakley Library. *Online resources:* library catalog. *Collection:* 192,468 titles, 1,819 serial subscriptions, 1,223 audiovisual materials.

Computer facilities: 70 computers available on campus for general student use. A campuswide network can be accessed from student residence rooms and from off campus. *Web address:* http://www.udallas.edu/.

General Application Contact: Graduate Coordinator, 972-721-5106, Fax: 972-721-5280, E-mail: graduate@acad.udallas.edu.

GRADUATE UNITS

Braniff Graduate School of Liberal Arts Students: 70 full-time (25 women), 161 part-time (74 women); includes 24 minority (4 African Americans, 4 Asian Americans or Pacific Islanders, 16 Hispanic Americans), 12 international. Average age 39. 130 applicants, 75% accepted. *Faculty:* 23 full-time (2 women), 14 part-time/adjunct (1 woman). Expenses: Contact institution. *Financial support:* In 2001–02, 163 students received support; fellowships, research assistantships, scholarships/grants, tuition waivers (partial), and tuition remissions available. Financial award application deadline: 2/15; financial award applicants required to submit FAFSA. In 2001, 94 master's, 8 doctorates awarded. *Degree program information:* Part-time and evening/weekend programs available. Postbaccalaureate distance learning degree programs offered. Offers American studies (MAS); art (MA, MFA); English (M Eng, MA); humanities (M Hum, MA); liberal arts (M Eng, M Hum, M Pol, M Psych, M Th, MA, MAS, MCSL, MFA, MPM, MTS, PhD); philosophy (MA); politics (M Pol, MA); psychology (M Psych, MA); theology (M Th, MA). *Application deadline:* For fall admission, 2/15 (priority date); for spring admission, 11/15. Applications are processed on a rolling basis. *Application fee:* $40. *Application Contact:* Graduate Coordinator, 972-721-5106, Fax: 972-721-5280, E-mail: graduate@acad.udallas.edu. *Dean,* Dr. David Sweet, 972-721-5288, Fax: 972-721-5280, E-mail: dsweet@udallas.edu.

Institute for Religious and Pastoral Studies Students: 43 (15 women). Average age 45. 2 applicants, 100% accepted, 0 enrolled. *Faculty:* 1 full-time (0 women), 9 part-time/adjunct (1 woman). Expenses: Contact institution. *Financial support:* Scholarships/grants, tuition waivers (partial), and tuition remissions available. Financial award application deadline: 2/15. In 2001, 52 degrees awarded. *Degree program information:* Part-time and evening/weekend programs available. Postbaccalaureate distance learning degree programs offered (no on-campus study). Offers religious and pastoral studies (MCSL, MPM, MTS). *Application deadline:* For fall admission, 6/15 (priority date); for spring admission, 11/15. *Application fee:* $40. *Application Contact:* Program Coordinator, 972-721-5105, Fax: 972-721-4076, E-mail: IRPS@acad.udallas.edu. *Director,* Dr. Brian Schmisek, 972-721-4068, Fax: 972-721-4076, E-mail: schmisek@acad.udallas.edu.

Institute of Philosophic Studies Students: 26 full-time (5 women), 27 part-time (12 women); includes 4 minority (1 African American, 1 Asian American or Pacific Islander, 2 Hispanic Americans), 4 international. Average age 31. 33 applicants, 55% accepted. *Faculty:* 12 full-time (1 woman), 4 part-time/adjunct (1 woman). Expenses: Contact institution. *Financial support:* Research assistantships, tuition waivers and tuition remissions available. Financial award application deadline: 2/15. In 2001, 8 degrees awarded. Offers literature (PhD); philosophy (PhD); politics (PhD). *Application deadline:* For fall admission, 2/15 (priority date); for spring admission, 11/15. Applications are processed on a rolling basis. *Application fee:* $40. *Application Contact:* Graduate Coordinator, 972-721-5106, Fax: 972-721-5280, E-mail: graduate@udallas.edu.

Graduate School of Management Students: 323 full-time (137 women), 1,630 part-time (640 women); includes 535 minority (238 African Americans, 145 Asian Americans or Pacific Islanders, 143 Hispanic Americans, 9 Native Americans), 480 international. Average age 34. 837 applicants, 64% accepted, 400 enrolled. *Faculty:* 26 full-time (5 women), 85 part-time/adjunct (18 women). Expenses: Contact institution. *Financial support:* Scholarships/grants, tuition waivers (partial), and unspecified assistantships available. Financial award application deadline: 2/15; financial award applicants required to submit FAFSA. In 2001, 555 degrees awarded. *Degree program information:* Part-time programs available. Postbaccalaureate distance learning degree programs offered (no on-campus study). Offers corporate finance (MBA, MM); e-commerce (MBA, MM); engineering management (MBA, MM); entrepreneurship (MBA, MM); financial services (MBA, MM); global management (MBA, MM); health services management (MBA, MM); human resources management (MBA, MM); information assurance (MBA, MM); information technology (MBA, MM); management (MBA); marketing management (MBA, MM); sports and entertainment management (MBA, MM); supply chain management (MBA, MM); telecommunications management (MBA, MM). *Application deadline:* For fall admission, 8/6 (priority date); for spring admission, 12/8. Applications are processed on a rolling basis. *Application fee:* $50. Electronic applications accepted. *Application Contact:* Roxanne Del Rio, Director of Graduate Admissions, 972-721-5198, Fax: 972-721-4009, E-mail: admiss@gsm.udallas.edu. *Dean,* Dr. H. Gene Swanson, 972-721-5008, Fax: 972-721-5130.

UNIVERSITY OF DAYTON, Dayton, OH 45469-1300

General Information Independent-religious, coed, university. CGS member. *Enrollment:* 1,527 full-time matriculated graduate/professional students (763 women), 1,560 part-time matriculated graduate/professional students (1,025 women). *Enrollment by degree level:* 423 first professional, 2,536 master's, 128 doctoral. *Graduate faculty:* 282 full-time, 427 part-time/adjunct. *Tuition:* Full-time $5,436; part-time $453 per credit hour. *Required fees:* $50; $25 per term. *Graduate housing:* On-campus housing not available. *Student services:* Campus employment opportunities, campus safety program, career counseling, child daycare facilities, disabled student services, free psychological counseling, international student services, low-cost health insurance. *Library facilities:* Roesch Library plus 1 other. *Online resources:* library catalog, web page, access to other libraries' catalogs. *Collection:* 948,677 titles, 4,196 serial subscriptions, 2,108 audiovisual materials. *Research affiliation:* Edison Materials Technology Center, IT Alliance, National Composite Center, Air Force Research Laboratories, Advanced Integrated Manufacturing Center, Ohio Aerospace Institute.

Computer facilities: 550 computers available on campus for general student use. A campuswide network can be accessed from student residence rooms and from off campus. Internet access and online class registration are available. *Web address:* http://www.udayton.edu/.

General Application Contact: Nancy A. Wilson, Assistant to the Vice President for Graduate Studies and Research, 937-229-2390, Fax: 937-229-4545.

GRADUATE UNITS

Graduate School Students: 1,527 full-time (763 women), 1,560 part-time (1,025 women); includes 259 minority (161 African Americans, 39 Asian Americans or Pacific Islanders, 53 Hispanic Americans, 6 Native Americans), 150 international. Average age 33. Expenses: Contact institution. *Financial support:* Fellowships, research assistantships, teaching assistantships with full tuition reimbursements, career-related internships or fieldwork, Federal Work-Study, institutionally sponsored loans, scholarships/grants, traineeships, tuition waivers (full and partial), and unspecified assistantships available. Support available to part-time students. Financial award applicants required to submit FAFSA. In 2001, 842 master's, 37 doctorates awarded. *Degree program information:* Part-time and evening/weekend programs available. *Application deadline:* Applications are processed on a rolling basis. *Application fee:* $30. Electronic applications accepted. *Application Contact:* Nancy A. Wilson, Assistant to the Vice President for Graduate Studies and Research, 937-229-2390, Fax: 937-229-4545. *Vice President for Graduate Studies and Research and Dean,* Dr. Gordon A. Sargent, 937-229-2390, Fax: 937-229-4545.

University of Dayton (continued)

College of Arts and Sciences Students: 112 full-time (73 women), 188 part-time (100 women). *Faculty:* 101 full-time (34 women), 31 part-time/adjunct (12 women). Expenses: Contact institution. *Financial support:* Fellowships, research assistantships, teaching assistantships with full tuition reimbursements, career-related internships or fieldwork, Federal Work-Study, institutionally sponsored loans, scholarships/grants, traineeships, tuition waivers (full), and unspecified assistantships available. Support available to part-time students. In 2001, 80 master's, 1 doctorate awarded. *Degree program information:* Part-time and evening/weekend programs available. Postbaccalaureate distance learning degree programs offered (minimal on-campus study). Offers applied mathematics (MS); arts and sciences (MA, MCS, MPA, MS, PhD); biology (MS, PhD); chemistry (MS); clinical psychology (MA); communication (MA); computer science (MCS); English (MA); general psychology (MA); human factors and research (MA); pastoral ministry (MA); public administration (MPA); theological studies (MA); theology (PhD). *Application deadline:* Applications are processed on a rolling basis. *Application fee:* $30. Electronic applications accepted. *Dean,* Dr. Paul J. Morman, 937-229-2601, Fax: 937-229-2615.

School of Business Administration Students: 91 full-time (54 women), 339 part-time (129 women). Average age 29. 367 applicants, 80% accepted, 235 enrolled. *Faculty:* 38. Expenses: Contact institution. *Financial support:* In 2001–02, 17 fellowships with partial tuition reimbursements, 16 research assistantships with full tuition reimbursements were awarded. Career-related internships or fieldwork, scholarships/grants, and unspecified assistantships also available. Support available to part-time students. Financial award application deadline: 3/31; financial award applicants required to submit FAFSA. In 2001, 171 degrees awarded. *Degree program information:* Part-time and evening/weekend programs available. Offers business administration (MBA). *Application deadline:* For fall admission, 8/15 (priority date); for spring admission, 12/15 (priority date). Applications are processed on a rolling basis. *Application fee:* $0. Electronic applications accepted. *Application Contact:* Janice M. Glynn, Associate Dean and Director, MBA Program, 937-229-3733, Fax: 937-229-3882, E-mail: mba@udayton.edu. *Dean,* Dr. Sam Gould, 937-229-3731, Fax: 937-229-3301.

School of Education and Allied Professions Students: 69 full-time (58 women), 1,347 part-time (993 women). Average age 33. 707 applicants, 92% accepted. *Faculty:* 64 full-time (32 women), 115 part-time/adjunct (53 women). Expenses: Contact institution. *Financial support:* In 2001–02, 19 research assistantships (averaging $6,100 per year) were awarded; career-related internships or fieldwork, Federal Work-Study, and institutionally sponsored loans also available. Support available to part-time students. In 2001, 545 master's, 13 doctorates awarded. *Degree program information:* Part-time and evening/weekend programs available. Offers adolescent/young adult (MS Ed); art education (MS Ed); college student personnel (MS Ed); community counseling (MS Ed); early childhood education (MS Ed); education and allied professions (MS Ed, PhD, Ed S); educational leadership (MS Ed, PhD); exercise sports science (MS Ed); higher education administration (MS Ed); human development services (MS Ed); inclusive early childhood (MS Ed); interdisciplinary education (MS Ed); intervention specialist education, mild/moderate (MS Ed); literacy (MS Ed); middle childhood (MS Ed); physical education (MS Ed); school counseling (MS Ed); school psychology (MS Ed); teacher as child/youth development specialist (MS Ed); teacher as leader (MS Ed); technology in education (MS Ed). *Application deadline:* Applications are processed on a rolling basis. *Application fee:* $30. Electronic applications accepted. *Application Contact:* Dr. C. Daniel Raisch, Associate Dean of Administration, 937-229-3146, Fax: 937-229-3199, E-mail: dan.raisch@notes.udayton.edu. *Dean,* Dr. Thomas J. Lasley, 937-229-3146, Fax: 937-229-3199, E-mail: thomas.lasley@notes.udayton.edu.

School of Engineering Students: 215 full-time (42 women), 146 part-time (31 women); includes 43 minority (16 African Americans, 10 Asian Americans or Pacific Islanders, 17 Hispanic Americans), 91 international. Average age 24. *Faculty:* 54 full-time (1 woman), 53 part-time/adjunct (3 women). Expenses: Contact institution. *Financial support:* In 2001–02, 3 fellowships with full tuition reimbursements (averaging $18,000 per year), 76 research assistantships with full tuition reimbursements (averaging $13,500 per year), 9 teaching assistantships with full tuition reimbursements (averaging $10,000 per year) were awarded. Career-related internships or fieldwork, institutionally sponsored loans, and tuition waivers (full and partial) also available. In 2001, 86 master's, 25 doctorates awarded. *Degree program information:* Part-time and evening/weekend programs available. Offers aerospace engineering (MSAE, DE, PhD); chemical engineering (MS Ch E); electrical and computer engineering (MSEE, DE, PhD); electro-optics (MSEO, PhD); engineering (MS Ch E, MS Mat E, MSAE, MSCE, MSE, MSEE, MSEM, MSEM, MSEO, MSME, MSMS, DE, PhD); engineering management (MSEM); engineering mechanics (MSEM); environmental engineering (MSCE); management science (MSMS); materials engineering (MS Mat E, DE, PhD); mechanical engineering (MSME, DE, PhD); soil mechanics (MSCE); structural engineering (MSCE); transport engineering (MSCE). *Application deadline:* For fall admission, 8/1 (priority date). Applications are processed on a rolling basis. *Application fee:* $30. Electronic applications accepted. *Application Contact:* Dr. Donald L. Moon, Associate Dean, 937-229-2241, Fax: 937-229-2471, E-mail: dmoon@notes.udayton.edu. *Dean,* Dr. Blake Cherrington, 937-229-2736, Fax: 937-229-2756.

School of Law Students: 424 full-time (173 women); includes 66 minority (30 African Americans, 12 Asian Americans or Pacific Islanders, 20 Hispanic Americans, 4 Native Americans), 2 international. Average age 25. 1,340 applicants, 64% accepted. *Faculty:* 28 full-time (10 women), 33 part-time/adjunct (6 women). Expenses: Contact institution. *Financial support:* Career-related internships or fieldwork, scholarships/grants, and tuition waivers (full and partial) available. Financial award application deadline: 3/1; financial award applicants required to submit FAFSA. In 2001, 151 degrees awarded. Offers law (JD). *Application deadline:* For fall admission, 5/1 (priority date). Applications are processed on a rolling basis. *Application fee:* $50. Electronic applications accepted. *Application Contact:* Janet L. Hein, Director of Admissions and Financial Aid, 937-229-3555, Fax: 937-229-2469, E-mail: lawinfo@udayton.edu. *Dean,* Lisa A. Kloppenberg, 937-229-3795, Fax: 937-229-4769.

See in-depth description on page 1169.

UNIVERSITY OF DELAWARE, Newark, DE 19716

General Information State-related, coed, university. CGS member. *Enrollment:* 2,171 full-time matriculated graduate/professional students (1,049 women), 771 part-time matriculated graduate/professional students (415 women). *Enrollment by degree level:* 1,960 master's, 982 doctoral. *Graduate faculty:* 1,030 full-time (348 women), 24 part-time/adjunct (16 women). Tuition, state resident: full-time $4,770; part-time $265 per credit. Tuition, nonresident: full-time $13,860; part-time $770 per credit. *Required fees:* $414. *Graduate housing:* Rooms and/or apartments available to single and married students. Typical cost: $3,000 per year ($5,500 including board) for single students. Housing application deadline: 3/15. *Student services:* Campus employment opportunities, campus safety program, career counseling, disabled student services, exercise/wellness program, free psychological counseling, international student services, low-cost health insurance, multicultural affairs office, teacher training, writing training. *Library facilities:* Hugh Morris Library plus 3 others. *Online resources:* library catalog, web page. *Collection:* 2.4 million titles, 12,633 serial subscriptions, 12,746 audiovisual materials. *Research affiliation:* Hagley Museum, Winterthur Museum, Longwood Gardens, Bartol Research Foundation.

Computer facilities: 900 computers available on campus for general student use. A campuswide network can be accessed from student residence rooms and from off campus. *Web address:* http://www.udel.edu/.

General Application Contact: Mary Martin, Assistant Provost for Graduate Studies, 302-831-8916, Fax: 302-831-8745, E-mail: marym@udel.edu.

GRADUATE UNITS

College of Agriculture and Natural Resources Students: 125 full-time (63 women), 15 part-time (5 women); includes 6 minority (2 African Americans, 4 Asian Americans or Pacific Islanders), 43 international. Average age 28. 227 applicants, 31% accepted, 49 enrolled. *Faculty:* 79 full-time (14 women), 1 part-time/adjunct (0 women). Expenses: Contact institution. *Financial support:* In 2001–02, 100 students received support, including 14 fellowships with full tuition reimbursements available (averaging $14,355 per year), 47 research assistantships with full tuition reimbursements available (averaging $12,625 per year), 17 teaching assistantships with full tuition reimbursements available (averaging $11,185 per year); career-related internships or fieldwork, Federal Work-Study, institutionally sponsored loans, and tuition waivers (full) also available. In 2001, 37 master's, 7 doctorates awarded. *Degree program information:* Part-time programs available. Offers agricultural economics (MS); agriculture and natural resources (MS, PhD); animal sciences (MS, PhD); entomology and applied ecology (MS, PhD); food sciences (MS); horticulture (MS); operations research (MS, PhD); plant and soil sciences (MS, PhD); statistics (MS). *Application fee:* $50. Electronic applications accepted. *Acting Dean,* Dr. Robin Morgan, 302-831-2501.

College of Arts and Science Students: 971 full-time (500 women), 93 part-time (44 women); includes 91 minority (25 African Americans, 29 Asian Americans or Pacific Islanders, 31 Hispanic Americans, 6 Native Americans), 249 international. Average age 29. 2,071 applicants, 34% accepted, 325 enrolled. *Faculty:* 529 full-time (176 women), 10 part-time/adjunct (7 women). Expenses: Contact institution. *Financial support:* In 2001–02, 625 students received support, including 134 fellowships with full tuition reimbursements available (averaging $12,135 per year), 140 research assistantships with full tuition reimbursements available (averaging $13,058 per year), 299 teaching assistantships with full tuition reimbursements available (averaging $11,900 per year); career-related internships or fieldwork, Federal Work-Study, institutionally sponsored loans, and tuition waivers (full and partial) also available. In 2001, 199 master's, 76 doctorates awarded. *Degree program information:* Part-time and evening/weekend programs available. Offers acting (MFA); applied mathematics (MA, MS, PhD); art (MA, MFA); art history (MA, PhD); arts and science (MA, MALS, MFA, MM, MPT, MS, PhD, Certificate); behavioral neuroscience (PhD); biochemistry (MA, MS, PhD); biotechnology (MS, PhD); cell and extracellular matrix biology (MS, PhD); cell and systems physiology (MS, PhD); chemistry (MA, MS, PhD); climatology (PhD); clinical psychology (PhD); cognitive psychology (PhD); communication (MA); computer and information sciences (MS, PhD); criminology (MA, PhD); early American culture (MA); ecology and evolution (MS, PhD); English education (MA); English literature (MA); foreign language pedagogy (MA); French (MA); geography (MA, MS); geology (MS, PhD); German (MA); history (MA, PhD); international relations (MA); liberal studies (MALS); linguistics (MA, PhD); literature (PhD); mathematics (MA, MS, PhD); microbiology (MS, PhD); molecular biology and genetics (MS, PhD); museum studies (Certificate); music education (MM); neuroscience and biology (PhD); neuroscience and psychology (PhD); performance (MM); physical therapy (MPT); physics and astronomy (MS, PhD); plant biology (MS, PhD); political science (MA, PhD); practicing art conservation (MS); social psychology (PhD); sociology (MA, PhD); Spanish (MA); stage management (MFA); technical production (MFA). *Application fee:* $50. Electronic applications accepted. *Acting Dean,* Dr. Mark W. Huddleston, 302-831-2793, Fax: 302-831-6398, E-mail: mwh@udel.edu.

College of Business and Economics Students: 207 full-time (86 women), 232 part-time (73 women); includes 37 minority (18 African Americans, 15 Asian Americans or Pacific Islanders, 4 Hispanic Americans), 98 international. Average age 31. 553 applicants, 66% accepted, 226 enrolled. *Faculty:* 99 full-time (24 women). Expenses: Contact institution. *Financial support:* In 2001–02, 123 students received support, including 2 fellowships (averaging $10,440 per year), 30 research assistantships (averaging $6,432 per year), 21 teaching assistantships (averaging $10,440 per year); career-related internships or fieldwork, Federal Work-Study, scholarships/grants, tuition waivers (full and partial), and unspecified assistantships also available. Financial award application deadline: 2/1. In 2001, 178 master's, 3 doctorates awarded. *Degree program information:* Part-time and evening/weekend programs available. Offers accounting (MS); business administration (MBA); business and economics (MA, MBA, MS, PhD); economics (MA, MS, PhD); economics for educators (MA); information systems and technology management (MS). *Application deadline:* For fall admission, 5/1; for spring admission, 11/1. Applications are processed on a rolling basis. *Application fee:* $50. Electronic applications accepted. *Application Contact:* Ronald T. Sibert, Director, MBA Programs, 302-831-2221, Fax: 302-831-3329, E-mail: sibertr@be.udel.edu. *Dean,* Michael J. Ginzberg, 302-831-2551.

College of Engineering Students: 379 full-time (93 women), 66 part-time (13 women); includes 25 minority (9 African Americans, 9 Asian Americans or Pacific Islanders, 7 Hispanic Americans), 247 international. Average age 27. 1,441 applicants, 24% accepted, 141 enrolled. *Faculty:* 82 full-time (5 women). Expenses: Contact institution. *Financial support:* In 2001–02, 304 students received support, including 16 fellowships with full tuition reimbursements available (averaging $14,000 per year), 216 research assistantships with full tuition reimbursements available (averaging $16,040 per year), 42 teaching assistantships with full tuition reimbursements available (averaging $14,400 per year); career-related internships or fieldwork, Federal Work-Study, and institutionally sponsored loans also available. Support available to part-time students. Financial award applicants required to submit FAFSA. In 2001, 47 master's, 38 doctorates awarded. *Degree program information:* Part-time and evening/weekend programs available. Postbaccalaureate distance learning degree programs offered (minimal on-campus study). Offers biomechanics and movement science (MS, PhD); chemical engineering (M Ch E, PhD); electrical and computer engineering (MEE, PhD); engineering (M Ch E, MAS, MCE, MEE, MEM, MMSE, MS, MSME, PhD); environmental engineering (MAS, MCE, PhD); geotechnical engineering (MAS, MCE, PhD); materials science and engineering (MMSE, PhD); mechanical engineering (MEM, MSME, PhD); ocean engineering (MAS, MCE, PhD); railroad engineering (MAS, MCE, PhD); structural engineering (MAS, MCE, PhD); transportation engineering (MAS, MCE, PhD); water resource engineering (MAS, MCE, PhD). *Application fee:* $50. Electronic applications accepted. *Dean,* Dr. Eric W. Kaler, 302-831-8017, Fax: 302-831-8179, E-mail: kaler@udel.edu.

College of Health and Nursing Sciences Students: 77 full-time (53 women), 76 part-time (67 women); includes 13 minority (9 African Americans, 4 Asian Americans or Pacific Islanders), 9 international. Average age 31. 72 applicants, 64% accepted, 39 enrolled. *Faculty:* 68 full-time (45 women), 10 part-time/adjunct (9 women). Expenses: Contact institution. *Financial support:* In 2001–02, 42 students received support, including 4 fellowships with full tuition reimbursements available (averaging $12,375 per year), 15 research assistantships with full tuition reimbursements available (averaging $11,000 per year), 12 teaching assistantships with full tuition reimbursements available (averaging $11,000 per year); career-related internships or fieldwork, Federal Work-Study, institutionally sponsored loans, and tuition waivers (full and partial) also available. Support available to part-time students. In 2001, 48 master's, 3 doctorates awarded. *Degree program information:* Part-time and evening/weekend programs available. Offers adult nurse practitioner (MSN, PMC); biomechanics (MS); cardiopulmonary clinical nurse specialist (MSN, PMC); cardiopulmonary clinical nurse specialist/adult nurse practitioner (MSN, PMC); exercise physiology (MS); family nurse practitioner (MSN, PMC); general human nutrition (MS); gerontology clinical nurse specialist (MSN, PMC); gerontology clinical nurse specialist geriatric nurse practitioner (PMC); gerontology clinical nurse specialist/geriatric nurse practitioner (MSN); health and nursing sciences (MS, MSN, PhD, PMC); health promotion (MS); health services administration (MSN, PMC); nursing of children clinical nurse specialist (MSN, PMC); nursing of children clinical nurse specialist/pediatric nurse practitioner (MSN, PMC); oncology/immune deficiency clinical nurse specialist (MSN, PMC); oncology/immune deficiency clinical nurse specialist/adult nurse practitioner (MSN, PMC); perinatal/women's health clinical nurse specialist (MSN, PMC); perinatal/women's health clinical nurse specialist/women's health nurse practitioner (MSN, PMC); psychiatric nursing clinical nurse specialist (MSN, PMC). *Application deadline:* For fall admission, 7/1. *Application fee:* $50. Electronic applications accepted. *Dean,* Dr. Betty J. Paulanka, 302-831-8370, Fax: 302-831-2382, E-mail: betty.paulanka@mvs.udel.edu.

College of Human Services, Education and Public Policy Students: 316 full-time (205 women), 287 part-time (213 women). Average age 31. 630 applicants, 48% accepted, 238 enrolled. *Faculty:* 138 full-time (81 women), 3 part-time/adjunct (0 women). Expenses: Contact institution. *Financial support:* In 2001–02, 259 students received support, including 11 fellowships with full tuition reimbursements available (averaging $11,000 per year), 159 research assistantships with full tuition reimbursements available (averaging $11,100 per year), 44 teaching assistantships with full tuition reimbursements available (averaging $11,000 per year); career-related internships or fieldwork, Federal Work-Study, institutionally sponsored loans, and tuition waivers (partial) also available. In 2001, 180 master's, 26 doctorates awarded. *Degree program information:* Part-time and evening/weekend programs available. Offers college counseling (M Ed); family studies (PhD); human services, education and public policy (M Ed, MA, MI, MPA, MS, Ed D, PhD); individual and family studies (MS); student affairs practice in higher education (M Ed). *Application deadline:* For fall admission, 3/1; for spring admission, 9/1. Applications are processed on a rolling basis. *Application fee:* $50. Electronic applications accepted. *Dean*, Dr. Daniel Rich, 302-831-2396, Fax: 302-831-4605, E-mail: drich@udel.edu.

Center for Energy and Environmental Policy Students: 20 full-time (8 women), 2 part-time (both women); includes 1 minority (Asian American or Pacific Islander), 11 international. Average age 28. 74 applicants, 28% accepted, 11 enrolled. *Faculty:* 6 full-time (1 woman), 5 part-time/adjunct (1 woman). Expenses: Contact institution. *Financial support:* In 2001–02, 14 students received support, including 2 fellowships with tuition reimbursements available (averaging $11,000 per year), 9 research assistantships with tuition reimbursements available (averaging $11,000 per year), 1 teaching assistantship with full tuition reimbursement available (averaging $11,000 per year); career-related internships or fieldwork, Federal Work-Study, and tuition waivers (full) also available. Financial award application deadline: 3/1. In 2001, 4 master's, 1 doctorate awarded. Offers environmental and energy policy (MS, PhD); urban affairs and public policy (MA, PhD). *Application deadline:* For spring admission, 3/1. *Application fee:* $50. *Application Contact:* Terri Brower, Staff Assistant, 302-831-8405, Fax: 302-831-3098, E-mail: tbrower@udel.edu. *Director*, Dr. John Byrne, 302-831-8405, Fax: 302-831-3098, E-mail: jbbyrne@udel.edu.

School of Education Students: 99 full-time (71 women), 233 part-time (177 women); includes 36 minority (27 African Americans, 3 Asian Americans or Pacific Islanders, 5 Hispanic Americans, 1 Native American), 9 international. 317 applicants, 65% accepted. *Faculty:* 45 full-time (23 women), 1 part-time/adjunct (0 women). Expenses: Contact institution. *Financial support:* In 2001–02, 65 students received support, including 2 fellowships with full tuition reimbursements available (averaging $11,000 per year), 28 research assistantships with full tuition reimbursements available (averaging $11,200 per year), 19 teaching assistantships with full tuition reimbursements available (averaging $11,000 per year); career-related internships or fieldwork, Federal Work-Study, tuition waivers (partial), and unspecified assistantships also available. Financial award application deadline: 3/1. In 2001, 77 master's, 19 doctorates awarded. *Degree program information:* Part-time and evening/weekend programs available. Offers cognition and instruction (MA); cognition, development, and instruction (PhD); curriculum and instruction (M Ed, PhD); educational leadership (M Ed, Ed D); educational policy (MA, PhD); English as a second language/bilingualism (MA); exceptional children (M Ed); exceptionality (PhD); instruction (MI); measurements, statistics, and evaluation (MA, PhD); school counseling (M Ed); school psychology (MA); secondary education (M Ed). *Application deadline:* For fall admission, 7/1; for spring admission, 1/15. Applications are processed on a rolling basis. *Application fee:* $50. *Application Contact:* Dr. Gail S. Rys, Assistant Director, 302-831-1165, Fax: 302-831-4421, E-mail: gailrys@udel.edu. *Director*, Dr. Christopher M. Clark, 302-831-2573, Fax: 302-831-4421, E-mail: cmclark@udel.edu.

School of Urban Affairs and Public Policy Students: 168 full-time (96 women), 41 part-time (24 women); includes 37 minority (29 African Americans, 2 Asian Americans or Pacific Islanders, 4 Hispanic Americans, 2 Native Americans), 42 international. Average age 33. 192 applicants, 36% accepted. *Faculty:* 28 full-time (9 women), 1 (woman) part-time/adjunct. Expenses: Contact institution. *Financial support:* In 2001–02, 123 students received support, including 7 fellowships with full tuition reimbursements available (averaging $11,000 per year), 107 research assistantships with full tuition reimbursements available (averaging $11,000 per year), 5 teaching assistantships with full tuition reimbursements available (averaging $11,000 per year); career-related internships or fieldwork, Federal Work-Study, institutionally sponsored loans, tuition waivers (full), and stipends also available. Financial award application deadline: 2/1. In 2001, 50 master's, 5 doctorates awarded. *Degree program information:* Part-time and evening/weekend programs available. Offers community development and nonprofit leadership (MA); energy and environmental policy (MA); governance, planning and management (PhD); historic preservation (MA); public administration (MPA); social and urban policy (PhD); technology, environment and society (PhD); urban affairs and public policy (MA, MPA, PhD). *Application deadline:* For fall admission, 2/1; for spring admission, 12/1. *Application fee:* $50. Electronic applications accepted. *Application Contact:* Linda C. Boyd, Administrative Coordinator, 302-831-8289, Fax: 302-831-3587, E-mail: lcboyd@udel.edu. *Director*, Dr. Jeffrey A. Raffel, 302-831-8289, Fax: 302-831-3587, E-mail: raffel@udel.edu.

College of Marine Studies Students: 96 full-time (49 women), 2 part-time; includes 8 minority (2 African Americans, 2 Asian Americans or Pacific Islanders, 4 Hispanic Americans), 25 international. Average age 29. 123 applicants, 32% accepted, 22 enrolled. *Faculty:* 35 full-time (3 women). Expenses: Contact institution. *Financial support:* In 2001–02, 68 students received support, including 17 fellowships with full tuition reimbursements available (averaging $12,000 per year), 54 research assistantships with full tuition reimbursements available (averaging $12,000 per year), 1 teaching assistantship with full tuition reimbursement available (averaging $13,500 per year); career-related internships or fieldwork, Federal Work-Study, and tuition waivers (full and partial) also available. Financial award application deadline: 3/1. In 2001, 9 master's, 8 doctorates awarded. Offers marine policy (MS); marine studies (MS); oceanography (MS). *Application deadline:* For fall admission, 3/1; for spring admission, 10/1. Applications are processed on a rolling basis. *Application fee:* $50. Electronic applications accepted. *Application Contact:* Dr. Doris Manship, Coordinator, 302-645-4226, E-mail: dmanship@udel.edu. *Dean*, Dr. Carolyn A. Thoroughgood, 302-831-2841.

Delaware Biotechnology Institute Offers biotechnology (PhD).

See in-depth description on page 1171.

UNIVERSITY OF DENVER, Denver, CO 80208

General Information Independent, coed, university. CGS member. *Enrollment:* 4,903 matriculated graduate/professional students. *Graduate faculty:* 978. *Tuition:* Full-time $21,456. *Graduate housing:* Rooms and/or apartments available to single and married students. *Student services:* Campus employment opportunities, campus safety program, career counseling, disabled student services, exercise/wellness program, free psychological counseling, international student services, low-cost health insurance, multicultural affairs office. *Library facilities:* Penrose Library. *Online resources:* library catalog, web page, access to other libraries' catalogs. *Collection:* 1.3 million titles, 5,788 serial subscriptions, 1,736 audiovisual materials. *Research affiliation:* National Center for Atmospheric Research (infrared measurements).

Computer facilities: 750 computers available on campus for general student use. A campuswide network can be accessed from student residence rooms and from off campus. *Web address:* http://www.du.edu/.

General Application Contact: 360-871-2706.

GRADUATE UNITS

College of Education Students: 392 (312 women); includes 47 minority (10 African Americans, 11 Asian Americans or Pacific Islanders, 23 Hispanic Americans, 3 Native Americans) 12 international. Average age 31. 352 applicants, 68% accepted. *Faculty:* 25 full-time (16 women), 1 (woman) part-time/adjunct. Expenses: Contact institution. *Financial support:* In 2001–02, 92 students received support, including 7 fellowships with full and partial tuition reimbursements available, 1 research assistantship with full and partial tuition reimbursement available (averaging $7,785 per year), 19 teaching assistantships with full and partial tuition reimbursements available (averaging $7,677 per year); career-related internships or fieldwork, Federal Work-Study, institutionally sponsored loans, and scholarships/grants also available. Support available to part-time students. Financial award application deadline: 3/1; financial award applicants required to submit FAFSA. In 2001, 71 master's, 27 doctorates awarded. *Degree program information:* Part-time and evening/weekend programs available. Postbaccalaureate distance learning degree programs offered (no on-campus study). Offers counseling psychology (MA, PhD); curriculum and instruction (MA, PhD); educational psychology (MA, PhD, Ed S); higher education and adult studies (MA, PhD); school administration (PhD). *Application deadline:* For fall admission, 1/1. Applications are processed on a rolling basis. *Application fee:* $45. Electronic applications accepted. *Application Contact:* Linda McCarthy, Contact, 303-871-2509. *Dean*, Dr. Virginia Maloney, 303-871-3828.

College of Law Students: 1,379 (717 women). 1,926 applicants, 76% accepted. *Faculty:* 54 full-time (17 women), 1 part-time/adjunct. Expenses: Contact institution. *Financial support:* In 2001–02, 702 students received support; research assistantships with full and partial tuition reimbursements available, career-related internships or fieldwork, Federal Work-Study, institutionally sponsored loans, and legal research assistantships, tutorships available. Support available to part-time students. Financial award application deadline: 2/15; financial award applicants required to submit FAFSA. *Degree program information:* Part-time and evening/weekend programs available. Offers American and corporate law (LL M); law (JD, LL M, MRLS, MSLA, MT); legal administration (MSLA); natural resources law (LL M, MRLS); taxation (LL M, MT). *Application deadline:* For fall admission, 5/1. Applications are processed on a rolling basis. *Application fee:* $45. *Application Contact:* Forrest Stanford, Director of Admissions, 303-871-6135, Fax: 303-871-6378. *Dean*, Mary E. Ricketson, 303-871-6000.

Daniels College of Business Students: 839 (330 women). Average age 28. 920 applicants, 78% accepted. Expenses: Contact institution. *Financial support:* In 2001–02, 260 students received support, including 25 teaching assistantships with full and partial tuition reimbursements available (averaging $6,219 per year); research assistantships with full and partial tuition reimbursements available, career-related internships or fieldwork, Federal Work-Study, institutionally sponsored loans, and scholarships/grants also available. Support available to part-time students. Financial award application deadline: 2/15; financial award applicants required to submit FAFSA. *Degree program information:* Part-time and evening/weekend programs available. Offers business (M Acc, MBA, MIM, MRECM, MS, MSF, MSIT, MSM, MSMC, MSMGEN, MSRTM); business administration (MBA); education management (MSM); finance (MBA, MS, MSF); health care management (MSM); information technology and electronic commerce (MBA, MIM, MSIT); international business/management (MIM); management and communications (MSMC); management and general engineering (MSMGEN); management and telecommunications (MSMC); marketing (MBA, MIM); public health management (MSM); resort and tourism management (MS, MSRTM); sports management (MSM). *Application deadline:* Applications are processed on a rolling basis. *Application fee:* $50. *Application Contact:* Jan Johnson, Executive Director, Student Services, 303-871-3416, Fax: 303-871-4466, E-mail: dcb@du.edu. *Dean*, James R. Griesemer, 303-871-3354.

School of Accountancy Students: 31 (15 women); includes 3 minority (all Asian Americans or Pacific Islanders) 10 international. Average age 30. 38 applicants, 76% accepted. *Faculty:* 13 full-time (2 women). Expenses: Contact institution. *Financial support:* In 2001–02, 9 students received support, including 2 teaching assistantships with full and partial tuition reimbursements available (averaging $6,165 per year); research assistantships with full and partial tuition reimbursements available, career-related internships or fieldwork, Federal Work-Study, institutionally sponsored loans, and scholarships/grants also available. Support available to part-time students. Financial award application deadline: 2/15; financial award applicants required to submit FAFSA. In 2001, 38 degrees awarded. *Degree program information:* Part-time and evening/weekend programs available. Offers accountancy (M Acc); accounting (MBA). *Application deadline:* For fall admission, 5/1 (priority date); for spring admission, 1/1. Applications are processed on a rolling basis. *Application fee:* $50. *Application Contact:* Abby Davidson, Executive Director, Student Services, 303-871-3414, Fax: 303-871-4466, E-mail: dcb@du.edu. *Director*, Dr. Ronald Kucic, 303-871-2017.

School of Real Estate and Construction Management Students: 1 (woman) Average age 27. *Faculty:* 4 full-time (0 women). Expenses: Contact institution. *Financial support:* In 2001–02, 1 teaching assistantship with full and partial tuition reimbursement (averaging $6,201 per year) was awarded; research assistantships with full and partial tuition reimbursements, career-related internships or fieldwork, Federal Work-Study, institutionally sponsored loans, and scholarships/grants also available. Support available to part-time students. Financial award application deadline: 2/15; financial award applicants required to submit FAFSA. In 2001, 3 degrees awarded. *Degree program information:* Part-time programs available. Offers real estate (MBA). *Application deadline:* For fall admission, 5/1 (priority date); for spring admission, 1/1. Applications are processed on a rolling basis. *Application fee:* $50. *Application Contact:* Celeste Fredrico, Executive Director, Student Services, 303-871-3379, Fax: 303-871-4466, E-mail: dcb@du.edu. *Director*, Dr. Mark Levine, 303-871-2142.

Graduate School of International Studies Students: 209 (112 women); includes 22 minority (7 African Americans, 4 Asian Americans or Pacific Islanders, 11 Hispanic Americans) 48 international. Average age 27. 470 applicants, 73% accepted. *Faculty:* 21 full-time (4 women), 1 part-time/adjunct (0 women). Expenses: Contact institution. *Financial support:* In 2001–02, 116 students received support, including 3 fellowships with full and partial tuition reimbursements available, 1 research assistantship with full and partial tuition reimbursement available (averaging $6,003 per year), 2 teaching assistantships with full and partial tuition reimbursements available (averaging $9,518 per year); career-related internships or fieldwork, Federal Work-Study, institutionally sponsored loans, and research and teaching internships, language/dissertation/travel grants also available. Support available to part-time students. Financial award application deadline: 2/15; financial award applicants required to submit FAFSA. In 2001, 99 master's, 9 doctorates awarded. *Degree program information:* Part-time and evening/weekend programs available. Offers international studies (MA, MIM, PhD). *Application deadline:* For fall admission, 2/15 (priority date); for spring admission, 1/15. *Application fee:* $50 ($45 for international students). *Application Contact:* Andrew Burns, Director of Admissions and Student Affairs, 303-871-2544, Fax: 303-871-2456, E-mail: gsisadm@du.edu. *Dean*, Dr. Tom Farer, 303-871-2539.

Graduate School of Professional Psychology Students: 138 (114 women); includes 24 minority (3 African Americans, 10 Asian Americans or Pacific Islanders, 10 Hispanic Americans, 1 Native American) 1 international. 320 applicants, 31% accepted. *Faculty:* 6 full-time (3 women), 9 part-time/adjunct (4 women). Expenses: Contact institution. *Financial support:* In 2001–02, 61 students received support, including 5 fellowships with full and partial tuition reimbursements available, 1 research assistantship with full and partial tuition reimbursement available (averaging $2,322 per year), 5 teaching assistantships with full and partial tuition reimbursements available (averaging $6,957 per year); career-related internships or fieldwork, Federal Work-Study, institutionally sponsored loans, scholarships/grants, and clinical assistantships also available. Support available to part-time students. Financial award application deadline: 3/1; financial award applicants required to submit FAFSA. In 2001, 31 degrees awarded. Offers clinical psychology (Psy D). *Application deadline:* For fall admission, 1/6. *Application fee:* $45. *Application Contact:* Samara Ferber, Admissions Coordinator, 303-871-3873, Fax: 303-871-4220. *Dean*, Dr. Peter Buirski, 303-871-2382.

Graduate School of Social Work Students: 256 (230 women); includes 38 minority (11 African Americans, 5 Asian Americans or Pacific Islanders, 18 Hispanic Americans, 4 Native Americans) 7 international. Average age 34. 353 applicants, 86% accepted. *Faculty:* 22 full-time (14 women). Expenses: Contact institution. *Financial support:* In 2001–02, 230 students received support, including 6 fellowships with full and partial tuition reimbursements available, 3 research assistantships with full and partial tuition reimbursements available (averaging $8,199 per year), 6 teaching assistantships with full and partial tuition reimbursements available (averaging $8,199 per year); career-related internships or fieldwork, Federal Work-Study, institutionally sponsored loans, scholarships/grants, and tuition waivers (partial) also available. Support available to part-time students. Financial award application deadline: 2/1; financial award applicants required to submit FAFSA. In 2001, 179 master's, 7 doctorates awarded. *Degree program information:* Part-time and evening/weekend programs available. Offers social work (MSW, PhD). *Application deadline:* For fall admission, 5/1. Applications are processed on a rolling basis. *Application fee:* $50. *Application Contact:* Melodie Rahimi, Assistant Director, Graduate Admissions, 303-871-2841, Fax: 303-871-2845. *Dean*, Dr. Christian Molidor, 303-871-4652.

Graduate Studies Students: 446. Expenses: Contact institution. *Financial support:* In 2001–02, 225 students received support, including 23 fellowships with full and partial tuition reimbursements available, 19 research assistantships with full and partial tuition reimbursements available (averaging $10,809 per year), 163 teaching assistantships with full and partial tuition reimbursements available (averaging $8,739 per year); career-related internships or fieldwork, Federal Work-Study, institutionally sponsored loans, and scholarships/grants also available. Support available to part-time students. Financial award applicants required to submit FAFSA. *Degree program information:* Part-time and evening/weekend programs available. Offers international and intercultural communication (MA). *Application deadline:* Applications are processed on a rolling basis. *Application Contact:* Karen Fennel,

University of Denver (continued)

Graduate Studies Executive Assistant, 303-871-2706, Fax: 303-871-4566. *Vice Provost,* Dr. Sarah Nelson, 303-871-2706.

Faculty of Arts and Humanities/Social Sciences Students: 176. Expenses: Contact institution. *Financial support:* In 2001–02, 104 students received support, including 13 fellowships with full and partial tuition reimbursements available, 7 research assistantships with full and partial tuition reimbursements available (averaging $9,153 per year), 82 teaching assistantships with full and partial tuition reimbursements available (averaging $7,416 per year); career-related internships or fieldwork, Federal Work-Study, institutionally sponsored loans, and scholarships/grants also available. Support available to part-time students. Financial award applicants required to submit FAFSA. *Degree program information:* Part-time programs available. Offers anthropology (MA); art history (MA); art history/museum studies (MA); arts and humanities/social sciences (MA, MFA, PhD); composition (MA); conducting (MA); economics (MA); English (MA, PhD); French (MA); German (MA); history (MA); Judaic studies (MA); music education (MA); music history and literature (MA); Orff-Schulwerk (MA); performance (MA); philosophy (MA); piano pedagogy (MA); psychology (PhD); religious studies (MA, PhD); Spanish (MA); studio art (MFA); Suzuki pedagogy (MA); theory (MA). *Application deadline:* Applications are processed on a rolling basis. *Application fee:* $45. *Dean,* Dr. Gregg Kvistad, 303-871-4449.

Faculty of Natural Sciences, Mathematics and Engineering Students: 150. Expenses: Contact institution. *Financial support:* In 2001–02, 63 students received support, including 10 fellowships with full and partial tuition reimbursements available, 8 research assistantships with full and partial tuition reimbursements available (averaging $11,880 per year), 53 teaching assistantships with full and partial tuition reimbursements available (averaging $12,102 per year); career-related internships or fieldwork, Federal Work-Study, institutionally sponsored loans, and scholarships/grants also available. Support available to part-time students. Financial award application deadline: 3/1; financial award applicants required to submit FAFSA. *Degree program information:* Part-time and evening/weekend programs available. Offers applied mathematics (MA, MS); biological sciences (MS, PhD); chemistry (MA, MS, PhD); computer science (MS); computer science and engineering (MS); electrical engineering (MS); geography (MA, PhD); management and general engineering (MSMGEN); materials science (PhD); mathematics and computer science (PhD); mechanical engineering (MS); natural sciences, mathematics and engineering (MA, MS, MSMGEN, PhD); physics and astronomy (MS, PhD). *Application deadline:* Applications are processed on a rolling basis. *Application fee:* $45. *Application Contact:* Helen Cahill, Assistant to Dean, 303-871-4003. *Interim Dean,* Dr. James Fogleman, 303-871-2693.

School of Communication Students: 103 (67 women); includes 9 minority (2 African Americans, 4 Asian Americans or Pacific Islanders, 3 Hispanic Americans) 12 international. 245 applicants, 64% accepted. *Faculty:* 21 full-time (9 women). Expenses: Contact institution. *Financial support:* In 2001–02, 53 students received support, including 1 fellowship with full and partial tuition reimbursement available, 18 teaching assistantships with full and partial tuition reimbursements available (averaging $9,135 per year); research assistantships with full and partial tuition reimbursements available, career-related internships or fieldwork, Federal Work-Study, institutionally sponsored loans, and scholarships/grants also available. Support available to part-time students. In 2001, 25 master's, 4 doctorates awarded. *Degree program information:* Part-time programs available. Offers advertising management (MS); communication (MA, MS, PhD); digital media studies (MA); human communication studies (MA, PhD); mass communications (MA); public relations (MS); video production (MA). *Application deadline:* Applications are processed on a rolling basis. *Application fee:* $45. *Application Contact:* Lindsay Wilbanks, Information Contact, 303-871-2166. *Chairperson,* Dr. Margaret Thompson, 303-871-3947.

University College Students: 1,244 (618 women); includes 177 minority (65 African Americans, 53 Asian Americans or Pacific Islanders, 54 Hispanic Americans, 5 Native Americans) 76 international. 54 applicants, 85% accepted. *Faculty:* 167 part-time/adjunct (52 women). Expenses: Contact institution. *Financial support:* In 2001–02, 174 students received support. In 2001, 274 degrees awarded. *Degree program information:* Part-time and evening/weekend programs available. Postbaccalaureate distance learning degree programs offered (no on-campus study). Offers applied communication (MSS); computer information systems (MCIS); environmental policy and management (MEPM); healthcare systems (MHS); liberal studies (MLS); library and information services (MLIS); public health (MPH); technology management (MoTM); telecommunications (MTEL). *Application deadline:* For fall admission, 7/15 (priority date); for winter admission, 10/14 (priority date); for spring admission, 2/10 (priority date). Applications are processed on a rolling basis. *Application fee:* $25. *Application Contact:* Cindy Kraft, Admission Coordinator, 303-871-3969, Fax: 303-871-3303. *Dean,* Mike Bloom, 303-871-3141.

See in-depth descriptions on pages 1173 and 1175.

UNIVERSITY OF DETROIT MERCY, Detroit, MI 48219-0900

General Information Independent-religious, coed, university. *Enrollment:* 875 full-time matriculated graduate/professional students (413 women), 1,256 part-time matriculated graduate/professional students (661 women). *Enrollment by degree level:* 672 first professional, 1,354 master's, 59 doctoral, 46 other advanced degrees. *Graduate faculty:* 175. *Tuition:* Full-time $10,620; part-time $590 per credit hour. *Required fees:* $400; $590 per credit hour. Tuition and fees vary according to program. *Graduate housing:* Rooms and/or apartments available to single and married students. Typical cost: $3,760 per year ($6,090 including board) for single students. *Student services:* Campus employment opportunities, campus safety program, career counseling, international student services, low-cost health insurance, teacher training. *Library facilities:* McNichols Campus Library plus 3 others. *Online resources:* library catalog, web page, access to other libraries' catalogs. *Collection:* 9,340 serial subscriptions, 32,053 audiovisual materials.

Computer facilities: 250 computers available on campus for general student use. A campuswide network can be accessed from student residence rooms and from off campus. Internet access is available. *Web address:* http://www.udmercy.edu/.

General Application Contact: Michael Joseph, Vice President, Enrollment Management, 313-993-1245.

GRADUATE UNITS

College of Business Administration Students: 89 full-time (28 women), 317 part-time (129 women); includes 105 minority (78 African Americans, 21 Asian Americans or Pacific Islanders, 4 Hispanic Americans, 2 Native Americans), 110 international. Average age 32. *Faculty:* 23 full-time (5 women). Expenses: Contact institution. *Financial support:* Research assistantships, career-related internships or fieldwork, Federal Work-Study, institutionally sponsored loans, and unspecified assistantships available. Support available to part-time students. Financial award application deadline: 8/1. In 2001, 168 degrees awarded. *Degree program information:* Part-time and evening/weekend programs available. Offers business administration (MBA, MSCIS); computer information systems (MSCIS). *Application deadline:* For fall admission, 8/1 (priority date). Applications are processed on a rolling basis. *Application fee:* $30 ($50 for international students). *Application Contact:* Dr. Bahman Mirshab, Associate Dean, Graduate Business Programs, 313-993-1202, Fax: 313-993-1052, E-mail: mba@udmercy.edu. *Dean,* Dr. Gary Giamartino, 313-993-1204, Fax: 313-993-1052.

College of Engineering and Science Students: 74 full-time (16 women), 227 part-time (50 women); includes 50 minority (30 African Americans, 13 Asian Americans or Pacific Islanders, 5 Hispanic Americans, 2 Native Americans), 109 international. Average age 31. *Faculty:* 40 full-time (11 women). Expenses: Contact institution. *Financial support:* Fellowships, teaching assistantships, career-related internships or fieldwork and Federal Work-Study available. In 2001, 132 master's, 2 doctorates awarded. *Degree program information:* Part-time and evening/weekend programs available. Offers automotive engineering (DE); chemical engineering (ME, DE); civil and environmental engineering (ME); computer science (MSCS); electrical engineering (ME, DE); elementary mathematics education (MATM); engineering and science (M Eng Mgt, MATM, ME, MS, MSCS, DE); engineering management (M Eng Mgt); junior high mathematics education (MATM); macromolecular chemistry (MS); manufacturing engineering (DE); mechanical engineering (ME, DE); polymer engineering (ME); secondary mathematics education (MATM); teaching of mathematics (MATM). *Application deadline:* For fall admission, 8/1 (priority date). Applications are processed on a rolling basis. *Application fee:* $30 ($50 for international students). *Dean,* Dr. Leo Hanifin, 313-993-1216, Fax: 313-993-1187, E-mail: hanifinl@udmercy.edu.

College of Health Professions Students: 95 full-time (70 women), 144 part-time (108 women); includes 46 minority (36 African Americans, 8 Asian Americans or Pacific Islanders, 2 Hispanic Americans), 4 international. Average age 35. *Faculty:* 15 full-time. Expenses: Contact institution. *Financial support:* Institutionally sponsored loans and tuition waivers (partial) available. Support available to part-time students. Financial award applicants required to submit FAFSA. In 2001, 67 master's, 1 other advanced degree awarded. Offers family nurse practitioner (MSN, Certificate); health professions (MS, MSN, Certificate); health services administration (MS); health systems management (MSN); nurse anesthesiology (MS); physician assistant (MS). *Application fee:* $30 ($50 for international students). *Dean,* Dr. Suzanne Mellon, 313-993-6055, Fax: 313-993-6175.

College of Liberal Arts and Education Students: 96 full-time (77 women), 371 part-time (277 women); includes 221 minority (204 African Americans, 9 Asian Americans or Pacific Islanders, 2 Hispanic Americans, 6 Native Americans), 8 international. Average age 35. *Faculty:* 46 full-time (26 women). Expenses: Contact institution. *Financial support:* Fellowships, career-related internships or fieldwork and Federal Work-Study available. In 2001, 134 master's, 7 doctorates, 16 other advanced degrees awarded. *Degree program information:* Part-time and evening/weekend programs available. Offers addiction counseling (MA); addiction studies (Certificate); clinical psychology (MA, PhD); community counseling (MA); counseling and addiction studies (MA, Certificate); criminal justice (MA); curriculum and instruction (MA); early childhood education (MA); educational administration (MA); emotionally impaired (MA); industrial/organizational psychology (MA); learning disabilities (MA); liberal arts and education (MA, MALS, MS, PhD, Certificate, Spec); liberal studies (MALS); religious studies (MA); school counseling (MA); school psychology (Spec); security administration (MS); special education (MA); teaching and learning (MA). *Application deadline:* For fall admission, 8/1 (priority date). Applications are processed on a rolling basis. *Application fee:* $30 ($50 for international students). *Dean,* Fr. John Staudenmaier, SJ, 313-993-1287, Fax: 313-993-1266, E-mail: liberalarts@udmercy.edu.

School of Dentistry Students: 313 full-time (125 women), 5 part-time (2 women); includes 52 minority (15 African Americans, 29 Asian Americans or Pacific Islanders, 5 Hispanic Americans, 3 Native Americans), 65 international. Average age 26. *Faculty:* 45 full-time (15 women). Expenses: Contact institution. *Financial support:* Career-related internships or fieldwork, Federal Work-Study, and stipends available. Financial award application deadline: 4/15. In 2001, 76 first professional degrees, 8 master's, 7 other advanced degrees awarded. Offers dentistry (DDS, MS, Certificate); endodontics (MS, Certificate); orthodontics (MS, Certificate). *Application fee:* $50. *Application Contact:* Karin LaRose-Neil, Associate Director, Dental Admissions, 313-494-6650, Fax: 313-494-6659. *Dean,* Dr. H. Robert Steiman, 313-446-1806, Fax: 313-446-1918.

School of Law Students: 196 full-time (95 women), 177 part-time (87 women); includes 57 minority (39 African Americans, 11 Asian Americans or Pacific Islanders, 6 Hispanic Americans, 1 Native American), 28 international. Average age 27. *Faculty:* 22 full-time (8 women). Expenses: Contact institution. *Financial support:* Career-related internships or fieldwork, Federal Work-Study, and institutionally sponsored loans available. Support available to part-time students. In 2001, 267 degrees awarded. *Degree program information:* Part-time programs available. Offers law (JD). *Application deadline:* For fall admission, 4/15. *Application fee:* $50. *Application Contact:* Kathleen H. Caprio, Assistant Dean, 313-596-0287, Fax: 313-993-0280, E-mail: capriok@udmercy.edu. *Dean,* Mark C. Gordon, 313-596-0200.

UNIVERSITY OF DUBUQUE, Dubuque, IA 52001-5099

General Information Independent-religious, coed, comprehensive institution. *Enrollment:* 192 full-time matriculated graduate/professional students (66 women), 120 part-time matriculated graduate/professional students (61 women). *Enrollment by degree level:* 139 first professional, 129 master's, 44 doctoral. *Graduate faculty:* 21 full-time (6 women), 12 part-time/adjunct (4 women). *Tuition:* Part-time $385 per credit hour. *Graduate housing:* Rooms and/or apartments available on a first-come, first-served basis to single students and available to married students. Typical cost: $3,900 per year for single students; $5,400 per year for married students. *Student services:* Campus employment opportunities, career counseling, exercise/wellness program, international student services, low-cost health insurance, multicultural affairs office, teacher training. *Library facilities:* Charles C. Myer's Library. *Online resources:* library catalog, web page, access to other libraries' catalogs. *Collection:* 139,513 titles, 700 serial subscriptions, 525 audiovisual materials.

Computer facilities: 100 computers available on campus for general student use. A campuswide network can be accessed from off campus. Internet access, intranet are available. *Web address:* http://www.dbq.edu/.

General Application Contact: Dr. Rodney Foth, Associate Dean for Academic Affairs, 563-589-3205, E-mail: rfoth@dbq.edu.

GRADUATE UNITS

Program in Business Administration *Degree program information:* Part-time and evening/weekend programs available. Offers aviation management (MBA); business administration (MBA); finance (MBA); quality management (MBA). Electronic applications accepted.

Program in Communication *Degree program information:* Part-time and evening/weekend programs available. Offers communication (MA).

Theological Seminary Students: 166 full-time (51 women), 2 part-time (1 woman); includes 5 minority (2 African Americans, 1 Hispanic American, 2 Native Americans), 35 international. Average age 34. 93 applicants, 82% accepted, 67 enrolled. *Faculty:* 10 full-time (4 women), 2 part-time/adjunct (both women). Expenses: Contact institution. *Financial support:* In 2001–02, 114 students received support, including 114 fellowships (averaging $6,440 per year); career-related internships or fieldwork, Federal Work-Study, institutionally sponsored loans, scholarships/grants, and tuition waivers (full and partial) also available. Support available to part-time students. Financial award application deadline: 6/1; financial award applicants required to submit FAFSA. In 2001, 38 first professional degrees, 7 master's, 28 doctorates awarded. Offers theology (M Div, MAR, D Min). *Application deadline:* For fall admission, 8/1 (priority date); for winter admission, 11/1 (priority date); for spring admission, 12/31 (priority date). Applications are processed on a rolling basis. *Application fee:* $30. *Application Contact:* Donna F. Warhover, Director of Seminary Admissions, 319-589-3112, Fax: 319-589-3110, E-mail: udtsadms@dbq.edu. *Dean,* Dr. Bradley Longfield, 319-589-3112, Fax: 319-589-3110, E-mail: blongfie@dbq.edu.

UNIVERSITY OF EVANSVILLE, Evansville, IN 47722-0002

General Information Independent-religious, coed, comprehensive institution. *Graduate housing:* On-campus housing not available. *Research affiliation:* Indiana Higher Education Television Services.

GRADUATE UNITS

Graduate Programs *Degree program information:* Part-time and evening/weekend programs available.

College of Education and Health Sciences *Degree program information:* Part-time and evening/weekend programs available. Offers education (MA, MS, MS Coun); nursing (MS).

THE UNIVERSITY OF FINDLAY, Findlay, OH 45840-3653

General Information Independent-religious, coed, comprehensive institution. CGS member. *Enrollment:* 404 full-time matriculated graduate/professional students (227 women), 800 part-time matriculated graduate/professional students (487 women). *Enrollment by degree level:* 1,204 master's. *Tuition:* Part-time $335 per semester hour. *Required fees:* $15 per term. Tuition and fees vary according to program. *Graduate housing:* Room and/or apartments available to single students; on-campus housing not available to married students. *Student services:* Campus employment opportunities, campus safety program, career counseling, disabled student services, exercise/wellness program, free psychological counseling, grant writing training, international student services, low-cost health insurance, teacher training. *Library facilities:* Shafer Library. *Online resources:* library catalog, access to other libraries' catalogs. *Collection:* 135,000 titles, 1,050 serial subscriptions, 2,000 audiovisual materials. *Research affiliation:* Department of Housing and Urban Development (bioterrorism), American Association of Family and Consumer Sciences (intergenerational research), Retirement Research Foundation (occupational therapy), Ohio State University Research Foundation (occupational therapy), U.S. Department of Health and Human Services, Centers for Disease Control and Prevention (biological terrorism).

Computer facilities: 200 computers available on campus for general student use. A campuswide network can be accessed from student residence rooms and from off campus. Internet access is available. *Web address:* http://www.findlay.edu/.

General Application Contact: Nancy Leatherman, Administrative Assistant to the VP for Academic Affairs, 419-434-4553, Fax: 419-434-4822.

GRADUATE UNITS

Graduate Studies Students: 404 full-time (227 women), 800 part-time (487 women); includes 213 minority (20 African Americans, 185 Asian Americans or Pacific Islanders, 5 Hispanic Americans, 3 Native Americans), 23 international. Average age 35. Expenses: Contact institution. *Financial support:* In 2001–02, 8 students received support, including 8 teaching assistantships with full tuition reimbursements available (averaging $6,000 per year); unspecified assistantships also available. Financial award application deadline: 4/1; financial award applicants required to submit FAFSA. In 2001, 300 degrees awarded. *Degree program information:* Part-time and evening/weekend programs available. Offers administration (MA Ed); early childhood (MA Ed); elementary education (MA Ed); professional studies (MA, MA Ed, MBA, MOT, MPT, MS, MSEM); special education (MA Ed); technology (MA Ed). *Application deadline:* Applications are processed on a rolling basis. *Application fee:* $25 ($0 for international students). Electronic applications accepted. *Application Contact:* Nancy Leatherman, Administrative Assistant to the VP for Academic Affairs, 419-434-4553, Fax: 419-434-4822.

College of Liberal Arts Students: 79. Expenses: Contact institution. *Financial support:* In 2001–02, 1 student received support, including 1 teaching assistantship with full tuition reimbursement available (averaging $6,000 per year) Financial award application deadline: 4/1; financial award applicants required to submit FAFSA. In 2001, 38 degrees awarded. *Degree program information:* Part-time and evening/weekend programs available. Postbaccalaureate distance learning degree programs offered (minimal on-campus study). Offers bilingual and multicultural education (MA); liberal arts (MA); teaching English to speakers of other languages (MA). *Application deadline:* Applications are processed on a rolling basis. *Application fee:* $25 ($0 for international students). Electronic applications accepted. *Dean,* Dr. Dale R. Brougher, 419-434-4729, Fax: 419-434-4822.

College of Science Students: 125. Expenses: Contact institution. *Financial support:* Unspecified assistantships available. Financial award application deadline: 4/1. In 2001, 30 degrees awarded. *Degree program information:* Part-time and evening/weekend programs available. Postbaccalaureate distance learning degree programs offered (minimal on-campus study). Offers occupational therapy (MOT); physical therapy (MPT); science (MOT, MPT, MS, MSEM). *Application deadline:* Applications are processed on a rolling basis. *Application fee:* $25 ($0 for international students). Electronic applications accepted. *Application Contact:* Randy Van Dyne, Director, Environmental Management, 419-434-5747. *Dean,* Dr. Luke Bartolomeo, 419-434-4869.

MBA Program Students: 473. Expenses: Contact institution. *Financial support:* In 2001–02, 1 student received support, including 1 teaching assistantship with full tuition reimbursement available (averaging $6,000 per year); unspecified assistantships also available. Financial award application deadline: 4/1; financial award applicants required to submit FAFSA. In 2001, 131 degrees awarded. *Degree program information:* Part-time and evening/weekend programs available. Postbaccalaureate distance learning degree programs offered (minimal on-campus study). Offers financial management (MBA); human resource management (MBA); international management (MBA); management (MBA); marketing (MBA); public management (MBA). *Application deadline:* Applications are processed on a rolling basis. *Application fee:* $25 ($0 for international students). Electronic applications accepted. *Application Contact:* Dr. Ahmed I. El-Zayaty, Professor of Business, 419-434-4897, Fax: 419-434-4822. *Dean,* Dr. Theodore C. Alex, 419-434-4704, Fax: 419-434-4822.

UNIVERSITY OF FLORIDA, Gainesville, FL 32611

General Information State-supported, coed, university. CGS member. *Enrollment:* 7,003 full-time matriculated graduate/professional students (3,163 women), 1,868 part-time matriculated graduate/professional students (916 women). *Graduate faculty:* 2,850 full-time (628 women). Tuition, state resident: part-time $164 per hour. Tuition, nonresident: part-time $571 per hour. Tuition and fees vary according to course level and program. *Graduate housing:* Rooms and/or apartments available on a first-come, first-served basis to single and married students. Typical cost: $1,393 per year for single students; $3,480 per year for married students. Room charges vary according to board plan, campus/location and housing facility selected. *Student services:* Campus employment opportunities, campus safety program, career counseling, child daycare facilities, disabled student services, exercise/wellness program, free psychological counseling, grant writing training, international student services, low-cost health insurance, multicultural affairs office, teacher training, writing training. *Library facilities:* George A. Smathers Library plus 15 others. *Online resources:* library catalog, web page, access to other libraries' catalogs. *Collection:* 5 million titles, 28,103 serial subscriptions, 36,078 audiovisual materials. *Research affiliation:* Los Alamos National Laboratory (high magnetic field research), National Center for Automated Information Research (law and business data), Oracle Corporation (database management), IBM (information infrastructure), Association of Universities for Research in Astronomy (Gemini multinational telescope).

Computer facilities: 447 computers available on campus for general student use. A campuswide network can be accessed from student residence rooms and from off campus. *Web address:* http://www.ufl.edu/.

General Application Contact: Information Contact, 352-392-3261.

GRADUATE UNITS

College of Dentistry Students: 365 full-time (140 women); includes 100 minority (8 African Americans, 33 Asian Americans or Pacific Islanders, 58 Hispanic Americans, 1 Native American), 4 international. Average age 29. 1,220 applicants, 12% accepted. *Faculty:* 106 full-time (19 women), 38 part-time/adjunct (8 women). Expenses: Contact institution. *Financial support:* In 2001–02, 303 students received support. Federal Work-Study, institutionally sponsored loans, and scholarships/grants available. Financial award applicants required to submit FAFSA. In 2001, 78 first professional degrees, 6 master's, 23 other advanced degrees awarded. Offers dentistry (DMD); endodontics (MS, Certificate); foreign trained dentistry (Certificate); orthodontics (MS, Certificate); periodontics (MS, Certificate); prosthodontics (MS, Certificate). *Application deadline:* For fall admission, 10/15. *Application fee:* $20. *Application Contact:* Dr. Venita Sposetti, Assistant Dean for Admissions and Financial Aid, 352-392-4866, Fax: 352-846-0311, E-mail: sposetti@dental.ufl.edu. *Dean,* Dr. Frank A. Catalanotto, 352-392-2911, Fax: 352-392-3070, E-mail: catalano@dental.ufl.edu.

College of Medicine Students: 687 full-time (334 women), 21 part-time (13 women); includes 215 minority (41 African Americans, 111 Asian Americans or Pacific Islanders, 58 Hispanic Americans, 5 Native Americans), 51 international. Average age 27. *Faculty:* 1,080. Expenses: Contact institution. *Financial support:* In 2001–02, 423 students received support, including 32 fellowships, 208 research assistantships; teaching assistantships, institutionally sponsored loans, scholarships/grants, and traineeships also available. Financial award application deadline: 4/1; financial award applicants required to submit FAFSA. In 2001, 117 first professional degrees, 13 master's, 22 doctorates awarded. Offers medicine (MD, MPAS, MPH, MS, PhD); physician assistant studies (MPAS). *Application fee:* $20. Electronic applications accepted. *Application Contact:* Dr. Wayne McCormack, Associate Dean of Graduate Education, 352-392-5461, Fax: 352-846-3466, E-mail: idp@dean.med.ufl.edu. *Vice President and Dean,* Dr. Kenneth I. Berns, 352-392-5397.

Interdisciplinary Program in Biomedical Sciences Students: 244 full-time (109 women), 21 part-time (13 women); includes 37 minority (6 African Americans, 18 Asian Americans or Pacific Islanders, 13 Hispanic Americans), 51 international. 260 applicants, 43% accepted, 50 enrolled. *Faculty:* 250. Expenses: Contact institution. *Financial support:* In 2001–02, research assistantships with full tuition reimbursements (averaging $18,000 per year); fellowships with full tuition reimbursements, teaching assistantships, institutionally sponsored loans, traineeships, health care benefits, and unspecified assistantships also available. In 2001, 13 master's, 22 doctorates awarded. Offers anatomy and cell biology (PhD); biochemistry and molecular biology (MS, PhD); biomedical sciences (MS, PhD); clinical chemistry (MS); clinical investigation (MS); genetics (PhD); immunology and microbiology (PhD); immunology and molecular pathology (PhD); molecular cell biology (PhD); molecular genetics and microbiology (MS, PhD); neuroscience (MS, PhD); oral biology (PhD); pharmacology and therapeutics (PhD); physiology and functional genomics (PhD); physiology and pharmacology (PhD). *Application deadline:* For fall admission, 2/15. *Application fee:* $20. Electronic applications accepted. *Application Contact:* Dr. Wayne McCormack, Associate Dean of Graduate Education, 352-392-5461, Fax: 352-846-3466, E-mail: idp@dean.med.ufl.edu. *Associate Dean of Graduate Education,* Dr. Wayne McCormack, 352-392-5461, Fax: 352-846-3466, E-mail: idp@dean.med.ufl.edu.

College of Pharmacy *Degree program information:* Part-time programs available. Postbaccalaureate distance learning degree programs offered (no on-campus study). Offers medicinal chemistry (MSP, PhD); pharmaceutics (MSP, PhD); pharmacodynamics (MSP, PhD); pharmacology (PhD); pharmacy (MSP, PhD); pharmacy health care administration (MS, MSP, PhD). Electronic applications accepted.

College of Veterinary Medicine *Degree program information:* Part-time programs available. Offers forensic toxicology (Certificate); veterinary medical science (MS, PhD); veterinary medicine (DVM, MS, PhD, Certificate).

Fredric G. Levin College of Law *Degree program information:* Part-time programs available. Offers comparative law (LL M CL); law (JD, LL M, LL M CL, LL M T, SJD); taxation (LL M T). Electronic applications accepted.

Graduate School *Degree program information:* Part-time programs available. Electronic applications accepted.

College of Agricultural and Life Sciences Students: 807 full-time (362 women); includes 92 minority (23 African Americans, 19 Asian Americans or Pacific Islanders, 42 Hispanic Americans, 8 Native Americans), 219 international. *Faculty:* 727. Expenses: Contact institution. *Financial support:* In 2001–02, 390 students received support, including 22 fellowships with tuition reimbursements available; research assistantships with tuition reimbursements available, teaching assistantships with tuition reimbursements available, career-related internships or fieldwork, Federal Work-Study, institutionally sponsored loans, and unspecified assistantships also available. Support available to part-time students. In 2001, 152 master's, 64 doctorates awarded. *Degree program information:* Part-time programs available. Offers agribusiness (MAB); agricultural education and communication (M Ag, MS, PhD); agriculture and life sciences (M Ag, MAB, MFAS, MFRC, MS, DPM, PhD); agronomy (MS, PhD); animal sciences (M Ag, MS, PhD); cell biology (MS, PhD); entomology and nematology (MS, PhD); environmental horticulture (MS, PhD); fisheries and aquatic science (MFAS, MS, PhD); food and resource economics (M Ag, MS, PhD); food science and human nutrition (MS, PhD); forest resources and conservation (MFRC, MS, PhD); fruit crops (MS, PhD); microbiology (MS, PhD); microbiology and cell science (M Ag); plant molecular and cellular biology (MS, PhD); plant pathology (MS, PhD); soil and water science (M Ag, MS, PhD); vegetable crops and crop science (MS, PhD); wildlife ecology (MS, PhD). *Application deadline:* Applications are processed on a rolling basis. *Application fee:* $20. Electronic applications accepted. *Application Contact:* Dr. E. Jane Luzar, Associate Dean for Academic Programs, 352-392-2251, Fax: 352-392-8988, E-mail: ejluzar@mail.ifas.ufl.edu. *Dean,* Dr. Jimmy G. Cheek, 352-392-1961, Fax: 352-392-8988, E-mail: jgcheek@mail.ifas.ufl.edu.

College of Design, Construction and Planning *Degree program information:* Part-time programs available. Offers building construction (MBC, MICM, MSBC); design, construction and planning (M Arch, MAURP, MBC, MICM, MID, MLA, MS, MSAS, MSBC, PhD); interior design (MID); landscape architecture (MLA, MS); urban and regional planning (MAURP). Electronic applications accepted.

College of Education *Degree program information:* Part-time programs available. Offers bilingual education (M Ed, MAE, Ed D, PhD, Ed S); computer education (M Ed, MAE, Ed D, PhD, Ed S); curriculum and instructional leadership (Ed D, PhD, Ed S); early childhood education (M Ed, MAE, Ed D, PhD, Ed S); economics education (M Ed, MAE, Ed D, PhD, Ed S); education (M Ed, MAE, Ed D, PhD, Ed S); educational administration (M Ed, MAE, Ed D, PhD, Ed S); educational leadership (PhD); educational psychology (M Ed, MAE, Ed D, PhD, Ed S); elementary education (M Ed, MAE, Ed D, PhD, Ed S); English education (M Ed, MAE, Ed D, PhD, Ed S); foreign language education (M Ed, MAE, Ed D, PhD, Ed S); higher education (Ed D, PhD, Ed S); marriage and family counseling (M Ed, Ed D, PhD, Ed S); mathematics education (M Ed, MAE, Ed D, PhD, Ed S); media and instructional design (M Ed, MAE, Ed D, PhD, Ed S); mental health counseling (M Ed, Ed D, PhD, Ed S); middle school education (M Ed, MAE, Ed D, PhD, Ed S); reading and language arts (M Ed, MAE, Ed D, PhD, Ed S); school counseling and guidance (M Ed, Ed D, Ed S); school psychology (MAE, Ed D, PhD, Ed S); science education (M Ed, MAE, Ed D, PhD, Ed S); secondary education (M Ed, MAE, Ed D, PhD, Ed S); social studies education (M Ed, MAE, Ed D, PhD, Ed S); special education (M Ed, MAE, Ed D, PhD, Ed S); statistics, measurement and evaluation methodology (Ed S); statistics, measurement, and evaluation methodology (M Ed, MAE, Ed D, PhD); student counseling and guidance (PhD); student personnel services in higher education (M Ed, Ed D, PhD, Ed S). Electronic applications accepted.

College of Engineering *Degree program information:* Part-time programs available. Offers aerospace engineering (ME, MS, PhD, Certificate, Engr); agricultural and biological engineering (ME, MS, PhD, Engr); agricultural operations management (MS, PhD); biomedical engineering (ME, MS, PhD, Certificate, Engr); ceramic science and engineering (ME, MS, PhD, Engr); chemical engineering (ME, MS, PhD, Engr); civil engineering (MCE, ME, MS, PhD, Engr); coastal and oceanographic engineering (ME, MS, PhD, Engr); computer and information science and engineering (ME); computer organization (MS, PhD, Engr); electrical and computer engineering (ME, MS, PhD, Engr); engineering (MCE, ME, MS, PhD, Certificate, Engr); engineering management (ME, MS); engineering physics (ME, MS, PhD, Engr); engineering science and engineering mechanics (ME, MS, PhD, Engr); environmental engineering sciences (ME, MS, PhD, Engr); facilities layout decision support systems energy (PhD); health physics (MS, PhD); health systems (ME, MS); industrial engineering (PhD, Engr); information systems (MS, PhD, Engr); manufacturing systems engineering (ME, MS, PhD, Certificate); materials science and engineering (ME, MS, PhD, Certificate, Engr); mechanical engineering (ME, MS, PhD, Certificate, Engr); medical physics (MS, PhD); metallurgical and materials engineering (ME, MS, PhD, Engr); metallurgical engineering (ME, MS, PhD, Engr); nuclear engineering sciences (ME, PhD, Engr); nuclear sciences engineering (MS); operations research (ME, MS, PhD, Engr); polymer science and engineering (ME, MS, PhD, Engr); production planning and control engineering management (PhD); quality and reliability assurance (ME, MS); software systems (MS, PhD, Engr); systems engineering (PhD, Engr). Electronic applications accepted.

College of Fine Arts *Degree program information:* Part-time programs available. Offers art (MFA); art education (MA); art history (MA); fine arts (MA, MFA, MM, PhD); museology (MA); music (MA, MM, PhD); music education (MM, PhD); theatre and dance (MFA). Electronic applications accepted.

College of Health and Human Performance *Degree program information:* Part-time programs available. Offers athletics training/sport medicine (PhD); biomechanics (PhD); exercise and sport science (MESS, MSESS, PhD); exercise physiology (PhD); health and human performance (MESS, MHSE, MPH, MSESS, MSHSE, MSRS, PhD); health behavior (PhD); health science education (MHSE, MSHSE, PhD); motor learning control (PhD); natural resource recreation (PhD); public health (MPH); recreation (MSRS); recreation, parks and tourism (PhD); sport and exercise psychology (PhD); therapeutic recreation (PhD); tourism (PhD). Electronic applications accepted.

College of Health Professions *Degree program information:* Part-time programs available. Offers audiology (Au D); clinical and health psychology (PhD); health administration (EMHA, MHA); health professions (EMHA, MHA, MHS, MPH, MPT, Au D, PhD); health services research (PhD); occupational therapy (MHS); physical therapy (MPT); rehabilitation counseling (MHS); rehabilitation sciences (PhD). Electronic applications accepted.

College of Journalism and Communications *Degree program information:* Part-time programs available. Offers advertising (MAMC, PhD); documentary (MAMC); international

University of Florida (continued)
communication (MAMC); journalism (MAMC, PhD); mass communication (MAMC); political communication (MAMC); public relations (MAMC, PhD); sports communication (MAMC); telecommunication (MAMC, PhD). Electronic applications accepted.

College of Liberal Arts and Sciences *Degree program information:* Part-time programs available. Offers African studies (Certificate); anthropology (MA, MAT, PhD); applied mathematics (MS, PhD); astronomy (MS, PhD); botany (M Ag, MS, PhD); botany education (MST); chemistry (MS, MST, PhD); classical studies (MA, PhD); communication sciences and disorders (MA, PhD); creative writing (MFA); English (MA, PhD); French (MA, MAT, PhD); geography (MA, MAT, MS, MST, PhD); geology (MS, PhD); geology education (MST); German (MA, PhD); history (MA, PhD); international development policy (MA); international relations (MA, MAT, PhD); Latin American studies (MA, MAT, Certificate); liberal arts and sciences (M Ag, M Stat, MA, MAT, MFA, MS, MS Stat, MST, Au D, PhD, Certificate); linguistics (MA, MAT, PhD); mathematics (MA, MS, PhD); mathematics teaching (MAT, MST); philosophy (MA, MAT, PhD); physics (MS, PhD); physics education (MST); political campaigning (MA, Certificate); political science (MA, MAT, PhD); psychology (MA, MAT, MS, MST, PhD); public affairs (MA, Certificate); religion (MA); sociology (MA, PhD); Spanish (MA, PhD); statistics (M Stat, MS Stat, PhD); teaching English as a second language (Certificate); zoology (MS, MST, PhD). Electronic applications accepted.

College of Natural Resources and Environment Offers interdisciplinary ecology (MS, PhD); natural resources and environment (MS, PhD). Electronic applications accepted.

College of Nursing *Degree program information:* Part-time programs available. Offers nursing (MS Nsg, PhD). Electronic applications accepted.

Graduate Engineering and Research Center (GERC) *Degree program information:* Part-time programs available. Postbaccalaureate distance learning degree programs offered. Offers aerospace engineering (ME, MS, PhD, Engr); electrical and computer engineering (ME, MS, PhD, Engr); engineering mechanics (ME, MS, PhD, Engr); industrial and systems engineering (ME, MS, PhD, Engr). Electronic applications accepted.

Warrington College of Business Administration *Degree program information:* Part-time programs available. Offers accounting (M Acc, PhD); business administration (M Acc, MA, MAIB, MBA, MS, MSM, PhD); decision and information sciences (MA, MS, PhD); economics (MA, MS, PhD); finance (PhD); finance, real estate and urban analysis (MA); human resources management (PhD); international business (MAIB); management (MA, MS, PhD); marketing (MA, MS, PhD); strategy (PhD). Electronic applications accepted.

See in-depth description on page 1177.

UNIVERSITY OF GEORGIA, Athens, GA 30602

General Information State-supported, coed, university. CGS member. *Enrollment:* 3,714 full-time matriculated graduate/professional students (2,009 women), 1,859 part-time matriculated graduate/professional students (1,264 women). *Graduate faculty:* 1,520 full-time (416 women). Tuition, state resident: full-time $2,376; part-time $132 per credit hour. Tuition, nonresident: full-time $9,504; part-time $528 per credit hour. *Required fees:* $236 per semester. *Graduate housing:* Rooms and/or apartments available to single and married students. *Student services:* Career counseling, free psychological counseling. *Library facilities:* Ilah Dunlap Little Memorial Library plus 2 others. *Online resources:* library catalog, web page, access to other libraries' catalogs. *Collection:* 3.8 million titles, 54,366 serial subscriptions, 201,184 audiovisual materials. *Research affiliation:* Organization for Tropical Studies, Russell Research Laboratory, Southeast Water Laboratory, Skidaway Institute of Oceanography.

Computer facilities: 2,500 computers available on campus for general student use. A campuswide network can be accessed from student residence rooms and from off campus. Internet access and online class registration, e-mail, Web pages are available. *Web address:* http://www.uga.edu/.

General Application Contact: Dr. Jan Sandor, Director of Graduate Admissions, 706-542-1739, Fax: 706-542-9480, E-mail: gradadm@uga.edu.

GRADUATE UNITS

College of Pharmacy Students: 440. 237 applicants, 6% accepted. *Faculty:* 40 full-time (8 women). Expenses: Contact institution. *Financial support:* Fellowships, research assistantships, teaching assistantships, career-related internships or fieldwork, Federal Work-Study, institutionally sponsored loans, tuition waivers, and unspecified assistantships available. Support available to part-time students. Financial award application deadline: 2/15. In 2001, 5 master's, 14 doctorates awarded. Offers experimental therapeutics (PhD); experimental therapeutics (MS); medicinal chemistry (MS, PhD); pharmaceutics (MS, PhD); pharmacology (MS, PhD); pharmacy (Pharm D, MS, PhD); pharmacy care administration (MS, PhD); toxicology (MS, PhD). *Application deadline:* For fall admission, 7/1 (priority date); for spring admission, 11/15. *Application fee:* $30. Electronic applications accepted. *Dean,* Dr. Svein Oie, 706-542-1914, Fax: 706-542-5269, E-mail: soie@mail.rx.uga.edu.

College of Veterinary Medicine Students: 406 full-time (262 women), 15 part-time (12 women). 101 applicants, 22% accepted. Expenses: Contact institution. *Financial support:* Fellowships, research assistantships, teaching assistantships, Federal Work-Study, scholarships/grants, and unspecified assistantships available. Financial award applicants required to submit FAFSA. In 2001, 10 master's, 3 doctorates awarded. Offers avian medicine (MAM); medical microbiology (MS, PhD); medical microbiology and parasitology (MS, PhD); parasitology (MS, PhD); pathology (MS, PhD); pharmacology (MS, PhD); physiology (MS, PhD); physiology and pharmacology (MS, PhD); toxicology (MS, PhD); veterinary anatomy (MS); veterinary anatomy and radiology (MS); veterinary medicine (DVM, MAM, MS, PhD). *Application deadline:* For fall admission, 7/1 (priority date); for spring admission, 11/15. *Application fee:* $30. Electronic applications accepted. *Dean,* Dr. Keith W. Prasse, 706-542-3461, Fax: 706-542-8254, E-mail: prassek@vet.uga.edu.

Graduate School Students: 3,714 full-time (2,009 women), 1,859 part-time (1,264 women); includes 493 minority (336 African Americans, 76 Asian Americans or Pacific Islanders, 71 Hispanic Americans, 10 Native Americans), 1,023 international. 6,912 applicants, 34% accepted. *Faculty:* 1,495 full-time (396 women). Expenses: Contact institution. *Financial support:* Fellowships, research assistantships, teaching assistantships, career-related internships or fieldwork, Federal Work-Study, institutionally sponsored loans, and unspecified assistantships available. Support available to part-time students. In 2001, 1,220 master's, 376 doctorates, 60 other advanced degrees awarded. *Degree program information:* Part-time programs available. *Application deadline:* For fall admission, 7/1 (priority date); for spring admission, 11/15. *Application fee:* $30. Electronic applications accepted. *Application Contact:* Dr. Jan Sandor, Director of Graduate Admissions, 706-542-1739, Fax: 706-542-9480, E-mail: gradadm@uga.edu. *Dean,* Dr. Maureen Grasso, 706-542-4788.

College of Agricultural and Environmental Sciences Students: 287 full-time (139 women), 73 part-time (32 women); includes 19 minority (13 African Americans, 4 Asian Americans or Pacific Islanders, 2 Hispanic Americans), 131 international. 368 applicants, 34% accepted. *Faculty:* 237 full-time (23 women). Expenses: Contact institution. *Financial support:* Fellowships, research assistantships, teaching assistantships, career-related internships or fieldwork and unspecified assistantships available. In 2001, 54 master's, 22 doctorates awarded. Offers agricultural and environmental sciences (MA Ext, MAE, MCCS, MFT, MPPPM, MS, PhD); agricultural economics (MAE, MS, PhD); agricultural engineering (MS); agricultural extension (MA Ext); agronomy (MS, PhD); animal and dairy science (PhD); animal nutrition (PhD); animal science (MS); biological and agricultural engineering (PhD); biological engineering (MS); crop and soil sciences (MCCS); dairy science (MS); entomology (MS, PhD); environmental economics (MS); environmental health (MS); food science (MS, PhD); food technology (MFT); horticulture (MS, PhD); plant pathology (MS, PhD); plant protection and pest management (MPPPM); poultry science (MS, PhD); toxicology (MS, PhD). *Application deadline:* For fall admission, 7/1 (priority date); for spring admission, 11/15. *Application fee:* $30. Electronic applications accepted. *Dean,* Dr. Gale A. Buchanan, 706-542-3924, Fax: 706-542-0803, E-mail: caesdean@uga.edu.

College of Arts and Sciences Students: 1,441 full-time (718 women), 321 part-time (173 women); includes 104 minority (54 African Americans, 25 Asian Americans or Pacific Islanders, 23 Hispanic Americans, 2 Native Americans), 445 international. 2,729 applicants, 30% accepted. *Faculty:* 678 full-time (168 women). Expenses: Contact institution. *Financial support:* Fellowships, research assistantships, teaching assistantships, Federal Work-Study, institutionally sponsored loans, and unspecified assistantships available. In 2001, 242 master's, 161 doctorates awarded. Offers analytical chemistry (MS, PhD); anthropology (MA, PhD); applied mathematical science (MAMS); art (MFA, PhD); art history (MA); artificial intelligence (MS); arts and sciences (MA, MAMS, MAT, MFA, MM, MPA, MS, DMA, DPA, PhD); biochemistry and molecular biology (MS, PhD); botany (MS, PhD); cellular biology (MS, PhD); classics (MA); comparative literature (MA, PhD); computer science (MS, PhD); conservation ecology and sustainable development (MS); drama (MFA, PhD); ecology (MS, PhD); English (MA, MAT, PhD); French (MA, MAT); genetics (MS, PhD); geography (MA, MS, PhD); geology (MS, PhD); German (MA); Greek (MA); history (MA, PhD); inorganic chemistry (MS, PhD); Latin (MA); linguistics (MA, PhD); marine sciences (MS, PhD); mathematics (MA, PhD); microbiology (MS, PhD); music (MA, MM, DMA, PhD); organic chemistry (MS, PhD); philosophy (MA, PhD); physical chemistry (MS, PhD); physics (MS, PhD); political science (MA, PhD); psychology (MS, PhD); public administration (MPA, DPA); religion (MA); Romance languages (MA, MAT, PhD); sociology (MA, PhD); Spanish (MA, MAT); speech communication (MA, PhD); statistics (MS, PhD). *Application deadline:* For fall admission, 7/1 (priority date); for spring admission, 11/15. *Application fee:* $30. Electronic applications accepted. *Dean,* Dr. Wyatt W. Anderson, 706-542-3400, Fax: 706-542-3422, E-mail: wyatt@franklin.uga.edu.

College of Education Students: 817 full-time (543 women), 1,252 part-time (930 women); includes 226 minority (178 African Americans, 19 Asian Americans or Pacific Islanders, 25 Hispanic Americans, 4 Native Americans), 139 international. 1,655 applicants, 45% accepted. *Faculty:* 201 full-time (95 women). Expenses: Contact institution. *Financial support:* Fellowships, research assistantships, teaching assistantships, unspecified assistantships available. In 2001, 443 master's, 130 doctorates, 60 other advanced degrees awarded. Offers adult education (M Ed, MA, Ed D, PhD, Ed S); agricultural education (M Ed); art education (MA Ed, Ed D, Ed S); business education (M Ed); college student affairs administration (M Ed); communication sciences and disorders (M Ed, MA, PhD, Ed S); computer-based education (M Ed); counseling and student personnel services (PhD); counseling psychology (PhD); early childhood education (M Ed, PhD, Ed S); education (MA); education of the gifted (Ed D); educational leadership (M Ed, MA, Ed D, Ed S); educational psychology (M Ed, MA, PhD); elementary and middle school education (M Ed, PhD, Ed S); elementary education (PhD); English education (M Ed, Ed S); exercise science (M Ed, Ed D, PhD); family and consumer sciences education (M Ed); guidance and counseling (M Ed); health and human performance (M Ed, MA, Ed D, PhD, Ed S); health promotion and behavior (PhD); health promotion and behavior and safety education (M Ed); higher education (Ed D, PhD); human resource and organization development (M Ed); human resources and organization development (M Ed); instructional technology (M Ed, PhD, Ed S); language education (PhD); marketing education (M Ed); mathematics education (M Ed, Ed D, PhD, Ed S); middle school education (M Ed, PhD, Ed S); music education (MM Ed, Ed D, Ed S); occupational studies (M Ed, Ed D, PhD, Ed S); physical education and sport studies (M Ed, MA, Ed D, PhD, Ed S); reading education (M Ed, MA, Ed D, PhD, Ed S); recreation and leisure studies (M Ed, MA, Ed D); safety education (Ed S); school psychology and school psychometry (Ed S); science education (M Ed, Ed D, PhD, Ed S); social foundations of education (PhD); social science education (M Ed, Ed D, PhD); special education (M Ed, MA, Ed D, PhD, Ed S); teaching additional languages (M Ed, Ed S); technological studies (M Ed). *Application deadline:* For fall admission, 7/1 (priority date); for spring admission, 11/15. *Application fee:* $30. Electronic applications accepted. *Dean,* Dr. Louis A. Castenell, 706-542-6446, Fax: 706-542-0360, E-mail: lcastene@coe.uga.edu.

College of Family and Consumer Sciences Students: 99 full-time (72 women), 22 part-time (17 women); includes 15 minority (9 African Americans, 2 Asian Americans or Pacific Islanders, 4 Hispanic Americans), 38 international. 157 applicants, 33% accepted. *Faculty:* 56 full-time (33 women). Expenses: Contact institution. *Financial support:* Fellowships, research assistantships, teaching assistantships, unspecified assistantships available. In 2001, 20 master's, 17 doctorates awarded. Offers child and family development (MFCS, MS, PhD); family and consumer sciences (MFCS, MS, PhD); foods and nutrition (MFCS, MS, PhD); housing and consumer economics (MS, PhD); textiles, merchandising, and interiors (MS, PhD). *Application deadline:* For fall admission, 7/1 (priority date); for spring admission, 11/15. *Application fee:* $30. Electronic applications accepted. *Dean,* Dr. Sharon Y. Nickols, 706-542-4860, Fax: 706-542-4862, E-mail: snickols@fcs.uga.edu.

School of Environmental Design Students: 70 full-time (39 women), 11 part-time (7 women); includes 1 minority (Native American), 3 international. 90 applicants, 42% accepted. *Faculty:* 13 full-time (1 woman). Expenses: Contact institution. *Financial support:* Fellowships, research assistantships, teaching assistantships, unspecified assistantships available. In 2001, 20 degrees awarded. Offers environmental design (MHP, MLA); historic preservation (MHP); landscape architecture (MLA). *Application deadline:* For fall admission, 7/1 (priority date); for spring admission, 11/15. *Application fee:* $30. Electronic applications accepted. *Dean,* John F. Crowley, 706-542-1365, Fax: 706-542-4485, E-mail: jcrowley@arches.uga.edu.

School of Forest Resources Students: 108 full-time (35 women), 17 part-time (9 women); includes 6 minority (3 African Americans, 3 Asian Americans or Pacific Islanders), 24 international. 79 applicants, 58% accepted. *Faculty:* 44 full-time (4 women). Expenses: Contact institution. *Financial support:* Fellowships, research assistantships, teaching assistantships, unspecified assistantships available. In 2001, 24 master's, 5 doctorates awarded. Offers forest resources (MFR, MS, PhD). *Application deadline:* For fall admission, 7/1 (priority date); for spring admission, 11/15. *Application fee:* $30. Electronic applications accepted. *Application Contact:* Dr. Scott A. Merkle, Graduate Coordinator, 706-542-1183, Fax: 706-542-6112, E-mail: smerkle@smokey.forestry.uga.edu. *Dean,* Dr. Arnett C. Mace, 706-542-4741, Fax: 706-542-2281, E-mail: amace@smokey.forestry.uga.edu.

School of Journalism and Mass Communication Students: 83 full-time (44 women), 26 part-time (18 women); includes 11 minority (9 African Americans, 2 Hispanic Americans), 28 international. 300 applicants, 24% accepted. *Faculty:* 30 full-time (13 women). Expenses: Contact institution. *Financial support:* Fellowships, research assistantships, teaching assistantships, unspecified assistantships available. In 2001, 39 master's, 3 doctorates awarded. Offers journalism and mass communication (MA); mass communication (MMC, PhD). *Application deadline:* For fall admission, 7/1 (priority date); for spring admission, 11/15. *Application fee:* $30. Electronic applications accepted. *Application Contact:* Dr. Leonard N. Reid, Graduate Coordinator, 706-542-5040, Fax: 706-542-2183, E-mail: lnreid@uga.edu. *Dean,* John Soloski, 706-542-1704, Fax: 706-542-3113.

School of Social Work Students: 233 full-time (208 women), 43 part-time (32 women); includes 49 minority (38 African Americans, 3 Asian Americans or Pacific Islanders, 6 Hispanic Americans, 2 Native Americans), 12 international. 260 applicants, 53% accepted. *Faculty:* 19 full-time (9 women). Expenses: Contact institution. *Financial support:* Fellowships, research assistantships, teaching assistantships, unspecified assistantships available. In 2001, 99 master's, 5 doctorates awarded. Offers nonprofit organizations (MA); social work (MSW, PhD). *Application deadline:* For fall admission, 7/1 (priority date); for spring admission, 11/15. *Application fee:* $30. Electronic applications accepted. *Application Contact:* Dr. Larry Nackerud, Graduate Coordinator, 706-542-5422, Fax: 706-542-5429, E-mail: nackerud@uga.edu. *Dean,* Dr. Bonnie L. Yegidis, 706-542-5424, Fax: 706-542-3845.

Terry College of Business Students: 426 full-time (146 women), 64 part-time (27 women); includes 42 minority (18 African Americans, 16 Asian Americans or Pacific Islanders, 7 Hispanic Americans, 1 Native American), 113 international. 825 applicants, 29% accepted. *Faculty:* 100 full-time (18 women). Expenses: Contact institution. *Financial support:* Fellowships, research assistantships, teaching assistantships, unspecified assistantships available. In 2001, 239 master's, 16 doctorates awarded. Offers accounting (M Acc); business (M Acc, MA, MBA, MIT, MMR, PhD); business administration (MA, MBA, PhD); economics (MA, PhD); marketing research (MMR). *Application deadline:* For fall admission, 7/1 (priority date); for spring admission, 11/15. *Application fee:* $30. Electronic applications accepted. *Application Contact:* Dr. Melvin R. Crask, Graduate Coordinator, 706-542-1709, Fax: 706-542-5351, E-mail: mcrask@terry.uga.edu. *Dean,* Dr. P. George Benson, 706-542-8100, Fax: 706-542-3835, E-mail: gbenson@terry.uga.edu.

School of Law Expenses: Contact institution. *Financial support:* Fellowships, research assistantships, teaching assistantships, Federal Work-Study, institutionally sponsored loans, tuition waivers (partial), and unspecified assistantships available. Financial award application deadline: 1/31. In 2001, 25 degrees awarded. Offers law (JD, LL M). *Application deadline:* For fall admission, 7/1 (priority date); for spring admission, 11/15. *Application fee:* $30. Electronic applications accepted. *Application Contact:* Giles Kennedy, Director of Law Admissions, 706-542-7060. *Dean,* David E. Shipley, 706-542-7140, Fax: 706-542-5556, E-mail: shipley@uga.edu.

See in-depth description on page 1179.

UNIVERSITY OF GREAT FALLS, Great Falls, MT 59405

General Information Independent-religious, coed, comprehensive institution. *Enrollment:* 41 full-time matriculated graduate/professional students (30 women), 85 part-time matriculated graduate/professional students (63 women). *Enrollment by degree level:* 126 master's. *Graduate faculty:* 10 full-time (8 women), 12 part-time/adjunct (7 women). *Tuition:* Part-time $440 per credit. One-time fee: $35 full-time. *Graduate housing:* Rooms and/or apartments available on a first-come, first-served basis to single and married students. Typical cost: $2,100 per year ($5,100 including board) for single students; $2,920 per year ($3,790 including board) for married students. Room and board charges vary according to board plan, campus/location and housing facility selected. Housing application deadline: 5/1. *Student services:* Campus employment opportunities, campus safety program, career counseling, child daycare facilities, disabled student services, exercise/wellness program, free psychological counseling, grant writing training, international student services, low-cost health insurance, teacher training. *Library facilities:* University of Great Falls Library. *Online resources:* library catalog, web page. *Collection:* 76,517 titles, 563 serial subscriptions, 4,069 audiovisual materials.

Computer facilities: 75 computers available on campus for general student use. A campuswide network can be accessed. Internet access is available. *Web address:* http://www.ugf.edu/.

General Application Contact: Dr. Deborah J. Kottel, Dean of Graduate Studies Division, 406-791-5339, Fax: 406-791-5990, E-mail: dkottel@ugf.edu.

GRADUATE UNITS

Graduate Studies Division Students: 41 full-time (30 women), 85 part-time (63 women); includes 19 minority (2 African Americans, 1 Hispanic American, 16 Native Americans) Average age 37. 62 applicants, 77% accepted. *Faculty:* 10 full-time (8 women), 12 part-time/adjunct (7 women). Expenses: Contact institution. *Financial support:* In 2001–02, 123 students received support, including 2 fellowships (averaging $2,000 per year), 10 research assistantships (averaging $2,000 per year); career-related internships or fieldwork, Federal Work-Study, institutionally sponsored loans, and scholarships/grants also available. Support available to part-time students. Financial award application deadline: 3/1; financial award applicants required to submit FAFSA. In 2001, 44 degrees awarded. *Degree program information:* Part-time and evening/weekend programs available. Postbaccalaureate distance learning degree programs offered (no on-campus study). Offers addictions counseling (MAC); chemical dependent services (MHSA); counseling psychology (MSC); criminal justice administration (MCJ); curriculum and instruction (MAT); elementary education (M Ed, MAT); family services (MHSA); guidance and counseling (M Ed); information systems (MIS); marriage and family counseling (MSC); secondary education (MAT). *Application deadline:* For fall admission, 8/15 (priority date); for winter admission, 11/15 (priority date); for spring admission, 12/15 (priority date). Applications are processed on a rolling basis. *Application fee:* $35. *Dean,* Dr. Deborah J. Kottel, 406-791-5339, Fax: 406-791-5990, E-mail: dkottel@ugf.edu.

UNIVERSITY OF GUAM, Mangilao, GU 96923

General Information Territory-supported, coed, comprehensive institution. *Graduate housing:* Room and/or apartments available on a first-come, first-served basis to single students; on-campus housing not available to married students. *Research affiliation:* Bernice Pauahi Bishop Museum (science, cultural preservation), Pilar Project, Inc. (salvage of artifacts, archaeology).

GRADUATE UNITS

Graduate School and Research *Degree program information:* Part-time programs available.

College of Arts and Sciences *Degree program information:* Part-time programs available. Offers arts and sciences (MA, MS); ceramics (MA); environmental science (MS); graphics (MA); Micronesian studies (MA); painting (MA); tropical marine biology (MS).

College of Business and Public Administration *Degree program information:* Part-time programs available. Offers business administration (MBA); business and public administration (MBA, MPA); public administration (MPA).

College of Education *Degree program information:* Part-time programs available. Offers administration and supervision (M Ed); counseling (MA); education (M Ed, MA); instructional leadership (MA); language and literacy (M Ed); secondary education (M Ed); special education (M Ed); teaching English to speakers of other languages (M Ed).

UNIVERSITY OF GUELPH, Guelph, ON N1G 2W1, Canada

General Information Province-supported, coed, university. *Enrollment:* 1,636 full-time matriculated graduate/professional students, 105 part-time matriculated graduate/professional students. *Enrollment by degree level:* 1,190 master's, 534 doctoral, 17 other advanced degrees. *Graduate faculty:* 700. *Graduate tuition:* Tuition charges are reported in Canadian dollars. *International tuition:* $7,500 Canadian dollars full-time. *Tuition, area resident:* Full-time $5,000 Canadian dollars. *Graduate housing:* Rooms and/or apartments available to single and married students. Typical cost: $4,500 Canadian dollars per year ($9,000 Canadian dollars including board) for single students; $6,000 Canadian dollars per year ($10,500 Canadian dollars including board) for married students. Housing application deadline: 6/1. *Student services:* Campus employment opportunities, campus safety program, career counseling, child daycare facilities, disabled student services, exercise/wellness program, free psychological counseling, grant writing training, international student services, low-cost health insurance, multicultural affairs office, teacher training, writing training. *Library facilities:* McLaughlin Library plus 1 other. *Online resources:* library catalog, web page, access to other libraries' catalogs. *Collection:* 2.1 million titles, 7,294 serial subscriptions, 16,437 audiovisual materials.

Computer facilities: 1,200 computers available on campus for general student use. A campuswide network can be accessed from student residence rooms and from off campus. Internet access is available. *Web address:* http://www.uoguelph.ca/.

General Application Contact: Chris Goody, Graduate Admissions Officer, 519-824-4120 Ext. 6736, Fax: 519-766-0143, E-mail: cgoody@registrar.uoguelph.ca.

GRADUATE UNITS

Graduate Program Services Students: 1,636 full-time, 105 part-time. *Faculty:* 700. Expenses: Contact institution. *Financial support:* Fellowships with full tuition reimbursements, research assistantships, teaching assistantships with full tuition reimbursements, career-related internships or fieldwork, Federal Work-Study, institutionally sponsored loans, scholarships/grants, tuition waivers (full), unspecified assistantships, and bursaries available. Support available to part-time students. *Degree program information:* Part-time and evening/weekend programs available. Postbaccalaureate distance learning degree programs offered (minimal on-campus study). Offers agribusiness (Exec MBA); agribusiness management (MBA); aquaculture (M Sc); biophysics (M Sc, PhD); English (MA); food safety and quality assurance (M Sc); history (MA, PhD); rural studies (PhD); toxicology (M Sc, PhD). *Application fee:* $75. Electronic applications accepted. *Application Contact:* Chris Goody, Graduate Admissions Officer, 519-824-4120 Ext. 6736, Fax: 519-766-0143, E-mail: cgoody@registrar.uoguelph.ca. *Dean,* Dr. I. Heathcote, 519-824-4120 Ext. 2441, E-mail: iheathc@registrar.uoguelph.ca.

Collaborative International Development Studies Students: 42 full-time (36 women), 2 part-time (1 woman); includes 12 minority (2 African Americans, 7 Asian Americans or Pacific Islanders, 3 Hispanic Americans), 11 international. *Faculty:* 62 full-time (14 women). Expenses: Contact institution. *Financial support:* Fellowships, research assistantships, teaching assistantships available. In 2001, 17 degrees awarded. Offers international development studies (M Sc, MA, MBA). MA offered in cooperation with the Departments of Agricultural Economics and Business, Animal and Poultry Science, Economics, Geography, History, Land Resource Science, Philosophy, Political Science, Rural Extension Studies, Rural Planning and Development, and Program in English. *Application fee:* $60. *Graduate Coordinator,* Dr. Sally Anne Humphries, 519-824-4120 Ext. 3542, Fax: 519-837-9561, E-mail: shumphri@uoguelph.ca.

College of Arts Tuition charges are reported in Canadian dollars. *Degree program information:* Part-time programs available. Offers arts (MA, MFA, PhD); drama (MA); English (MA); history (MA, PhD); philosophy (MA, PhD); studio art (MFA).

College of Biological Science Students: 36 full-time (14 women); includes 1 African American, 6 Asian Americans or Pacific Islanders, 1 Hispanic American 21 applicants, 19% accepted, 4 enrolled. *Faculty:* 14 full-time (2 women), 6 part-time/adjunct (1 woman). Expenses: Contact institution. *Financial support:* In 2001–02, 108 research assistantships (averaging $12,000 per year), 58 teaching assistantships (averaging $2,717 per year) were awarded. Scholarships/grants also available. In 2001, 4 master's, 4 doctorates awarded. *Degree program information:* Part-time programs available. Offers biological science (M Sc, PhD); botany (M Sc, PhD); microbiology (M Sc, PhD); molecular biology and genetics (M Sc, PhD); nutritional sciences (M Sc, PhD); zoology (M Sc, PhD). *Application deadline:* Applications are processed on a rolling basis. *Application fee:* $75. *Dean,* 519-824-4120 Ext. 6102.

College of Physical and Engineering Science Tuition charges are reported in Canadian dollars. *Degree program information:* Part-time programs available. Offers applied computer science (M Sc); applied mathematics (PhD); applied statistics (PhD); biochemistry (M Sc, PhD); biological engineering (M Eng, M Sc, PhD); chemistry (M Sc, PhD); computer science (M Sc); engineering systems and computing (M Sc, PhD); environmental engineering (M Eng, M Sc, PhD); mathematics and statistics (M Sc); physical and engineering science (M Eng, M Sc, PhD); physics (M Sc, PhD); water resources engineering (M Eng, M Sc, PhD).

College of Social and Applied Human Sciences Students: 294 full-time (213 women), 9 part-time (6 women). *Faculty:* 139 full-time (43 women). Expenses: Contact institution. *Financial support:* Fellowships with partial tuition reimbursements, research assistantships, teaching assistantships, career-related internships or fieldwork, scholarships/grants, tuition waivers (full), and bursaries available. Support available to part-time students. In 2001, 128 master's, 13 doctorates awarded. *Degree program information:* Part-time programs available. Offers anthropology (MA); applied developmental psychology (PhD); applied nutrition (MAN); applied social psychology (PhD); consumer studies (M Sc); economics (MA, PhD); family relations and human development (M Sc, PhD); general and experimental psychology (MA); geography (M Sc, MA, PhD); hospitality and tourism (MBA); industrial/organizational psychology (MA, PhD); political science (MA); social and applied human sciences (M Sc, MA, MAN, MBA, PhD); sociology (MA). *Application fee:* $60. *Dean,* Alun E. Joseph, 519-824-4120 Ext. 2400, E-mail: ajoseph@uoguelph.ca.

Ontario Agricultural College Students: 554 full-time (278 women), 56 part-time (22 women). Expenses: Contact institution. *Financial support:* Fellowships, research assistantships, teaching assistantships, scholarships/grants and unspecified assistantships available. Support available to part-time students. In 2001, 116 master's, 35 doctorates awarded. *Degree program information:* Part-time programs available. Postbaccalaureate distance learning degree programs offered (minimal on-campus study). Offers agricultural economics (M Sc, PhD); agriculture (M Sc, MLA, PhD); animal science (M Sc, PhD); atmospheric science (M Sc, PhD); environmental management (M Sc, PhD); food science (M Sc, PhD); land science (M Sc, PhD); landscape architecture (MLA); landscape architecture/rural planning and development (M Sc); plant agriculture (M Sc, PhD); plant protection (M Sc, PhD); poultry science (M Sc, PhD); resource and environmental economics (PhD); rural extension studies (M Sc); rural studies (PhD). *Application fee:* $60. *Dean,* Dr. Craig J. Pearson, 519-824-4120 Ext. 2285, Fax: 519-766-1425, E-mail: cpearson@oac.uoguelph.ca.

School of Rural Planning and Development Students: 80 full-time (48 women), 6 part-time (3 women), 19 international. 82 applicants, 57% accepted, 35 enrolled. *Faculty:* 8 full-time (1 woman), 5 part-time/adjunct (1 woman). Expenses: Contact institution. *Financial support:* In 2001–02, 50 students received support, including 35 research assistantships (averaging $2,700 per year), 9 teaching assistantships (averaging $3,000 per year); career-related internships or fieldwork, Federal Work-Study, institutionally sponsored loans, scholarships/grants, and unspecified assistantships also available. In 2001, 30 master's, 1 doctorate, 5 other advanced degrees awarded. *Degree program information:* Part-time programs available. Offers international rural development planning (Diploma); international rural planning and development (M Sc); rural planning and development in Canada (M Sc); rural studies (PhD). M Sc (international rural planning and development, rural planning and development in Canada) offered in cooperation with Departments of Agricultural Economics and Business, Geography, Land Resource Science, and others by arrangement. *Application deadline:* Applications are processed on a rolling basis. *Application fee:* $75. Electronic applications accepted. *Application Contact:* Dr. F. H. Cummings, Graduate Coordinator, 519-824-4120 Ext. 3637, Fax: 519-767-1692, E-mail: hcumming@rpd.uoguelph.ca. *Director of the SEDRD,* Dr. John E. FitzGibbon, 519-824-4120 Ext. 6784, Fax: 519-767-1692, E-mail: jfitzgib@oac.uoguelph.ca.

Ontario Veterinary College Tuition charges are reported in Canadian dollars. Offers anatomic pathology (DV Sc, Diploma); anesthesiology (M Sc, DV Sc); biomedical sciences (M Sc, DV Sc, PhD); cardiology (Diploma); clinical pathology (Diploma); clinical studies (M Sc, DV Sc, Diploma); comparative pathology (M Sc, PhD); emergency/critical care (Diploma); epidemiology (M Sc, DV Sc, PhD); immunology (M Sc, PhD); laboratory animal science (DV Sc); medicine (M Sc, DV Sc); morphology (M Sc, DV Sc, PhD); neurology (M Sc, DV Sc); ophthalmology (M Sc, DV Sc); pathobiology (M Sc, DV Sc, PhD, Diploma); pathology (M Sc, PhD, Diploma); pharmacology (M Sc, DV Sc, PhD); physiology (M Sc, DV Sc, PhD); population medicine (M Sc, DV Sc, PhD, Diploma); preventive medicine (M Sc, DV Sc); surgery (M Sc, DV Sc); theriogenology (M Sc, DV Sc); toxicology (M Sc, DV Sc, PhD); veterinary infectious diseases (M Sc, PhD); veterinary medicine (M Sc, DV Sc, PhD, Diploma); zoo animal/wildlife medicine (DV Sc).

UNIVERSITY OF HARTFORD, West Hartford, CT 06117-1599

General Information Independent, coed, comprehensive institution. CGS member. *Enrollment:* 466 full-time matriculated graduate/professional students (269 women), 790 part-time matriculated graduate/professional students (489 women). *Enrollment by degree level:* 942 master's, 248 doctoral, 28 other advanced degrees. *Graduate faculty:* 119 full-time (42 women), 89 part-time/adjunct (35 women). *Tuition:* Part-time $300 per credit hour. *Graduate housing:* Room and/or apartments available to single students; on-campus housing not available to married students. *Student services:* Campus employment opportunities, career counseling, disabled student services, free psychological counseling, international student services, low-cost health insurance, multicultural affairs office. *Library facilities:* Mortenson Library. *Online resources:* library catalog, web page. *Collection:* 522,640 titles, 3,131 serial subscriptions, 29,096 audiovisual materials. *Research affiliation:* Studio Arts Center International (Florence, Italy).

Computer facilities: 380 computers available on campus for general student use. A campuswide network can be accessed from student residence rooms and from off campus. *Web address:* http://www.hartford.edu/.

General Application Contact: Kellie Richard Westenfeld, Assistant Director of Graduate Admissions, 860-768-4371, Fax: 860-768-5160, E-mail: westenfel@mail.hartford.edu.

GRADUATE UNITS

Barney School of Business Students: 119 full-time (46 women), 244 part-time (101 women); includes 18 minority (11 African Americans, 5 Asian Americans or Pacific Islanders, 2 Hispanic Americans), 69 international. Average age 30. 258 applicants, 56% accepted. *Faculty:* 25 full-time (6 women), 14 part-time/adjunct (4 women). Expenses: Contact institution. *Financial support:* Fellowships, research assistantships, career-related internships or fieldwork and institutionally sponsored loans available. Support available to part-time students. Financial award application deadline: 5/1. In 2001, 166 degrees awarded. *Degree program information:* Part-time and evening/weekend programs available. Offers accounting (MSAT); accounting and taxation (MSAT); business (EMBA, MBA, MSAT); business administration (EMBA, MBA); taxation (MSAT). *Application deadline:* For fall admission, 7/1 (priority date); for spring

University of Hartford (continued)

admission, 12/1. Applications are processed on a rolling basis. *Application fee:* $35 ($50 for international students). Electronic applications accepted. *Application Contact:* Claire Silverstein, Associate Director, 860-768-4444, Fax: 860-768-4821, E-mail: barney@mail.hartford.edu. *Dean*, Corine T. Norgaard, 860-768-4243, Fax: 860-768-4198, E-mail: norgaard@mail.hartford.edu.

College of Arts and Sciences Students: 150 full-time (118 women), 129 part-time (99 women); includes 17 minority (6 African Americans, 7 Asian Americans or Pacific Islanders, 4 Hispanic Americans), 11 international. Average age 30. 258 applicants, 62% accepted. *Faculty:* 21 full-time (6 women), 24 part-time/adjunct (13 women). Expenses: Contact institution. *Financial support:* Fellowships, research assistantships, teaching assistantships, career-related internships or fieldwork, Federal Work-Study, and tuition waivers (partial) available. Support available to part-time students. Financial award application deadline: 6/1; financial award applicants required to submit FAFSA. In 2001, 78 master's, 24 doctorates awarded. *Degree program information:* Part-time and evening/weekend programs available. Offers arts and sciences (MA, MS, Psy D); biology (MS); clinical practices (MA); communication (MA); general experimental psychology (MA); neuroscience (MS); school psychology (MS). *Application deadline:* Applications are processed on a rolling basis. *Application fee:* $40 ($55 for international students). Electronic applications accepted. *Application Contact:* Kellie Richard Westenfeld, Assistant Director of Graduate Admissions, 860-768-4371, Fax: 860-768-5160, E-mail: westenfel@mail.hartford.edu. *Dean*, Dr. Edward Gray, 860-768-4103, Fax: 860-768-5043, E-mail: edtgray@mail.hartford.edu.

Graduate Institute of Professional Psychology Students: 89 full-time (72 women), 75 part-time (58 women); includes 15 minority (5 African Americans, 7 Asian Americans or Pacific Islanders, 3 Hispanic Americans), 4 international. Average age 30. 130 applicants, 53% accepted. *Faculty:* 4 full-time (1 woman), 12 part-time/adjunct (8 women). Expenses: Contact institution. *Financial support:* In 2001–02, 35 students received support, including 16 fellowships (averaging $2,000 per year), 3 research assistantships (averaging $3,100 per year), 16 teaching assistantships (averaging $3,100 per year); career-related internships or fieldwork and Federal Work-Study also available. Support available to part-time students. Financial award application deadline: 6/1; financial award applicants required to submit FAFSA. In 2001, 24 degrees awarded. Offers clinical psychology (Psy D). *Application deadline:* For fall admission, 1/15 (priority date). Applications are processed on a rolling basis. *Application fee:* $40 ($55 for international students). Electronic applications accepted. *Application Contact:* Robert D'Angelo, Program Administrator, 860-520-1151, Fax: 860-520-1156, E-mail: dangelo@mail.hartford.edu. *Director*, Dr. David L. Singer, 860-520-1151, Fax: 860-520-1156, E-mail: dasinger@mail.hartford.edu.

College of Education, Nursing, and Health Professions Students: 62 full-time (43 women), 315 part-time (256 women); includes 14 minority (9 African Americans, 3 Asian Americans or Pacific Islanders, 2 Hispanic Americans), 1 international. Average age 37. 93 applicants, 52% accepted. *Faculty:* 16 full-time (14 women), 18 part-time/adjunct (10 women). Expenses: Contact institution. *Financial support:* Unspecified assistantships and student loans available. Financial award application deadline: 6/1; financial award applicants required to submit FAFSA. In 2001, 139 master's, 6 doctorates, 15 other advanced degrees awarded. *Degree program information:* Part-time and evening/weekend programs available. Offers administration and supervision (CAGS, Sixth Year Certificate); community public health nursing (MSN); counseling (M Ed, MS, Sixth Year Certificate); early childhood education (M Ed); education, nursing, and health professions (M Ed, MS, MSN, MSN-OB, MSPT, Ed D, CAGS, Sixth Year Certificate); educational computing and technology (M Ed); educational leadership (Ed D); elementary education (M Ed); nursing education (MSN); nursing management (MSN); nursing/organizational behavior (MSN-OB); physical therapy (MS). *Application deadline:* Applications are processed on a rolling basis. *Application fee:* $40 ($55 for international students). Electronic applications accepted. *Application Contact:* Susan Brown, Assistant Dean/Academic Services, 860-768-4692, Fax: 860-768-5043, E-mail: brown@mail.hartford.edu. *Dean*, Dr. Dorothy A. Zeiser, 860-768-4649, Fax: 860-768-5043.

College of Engineering Students: 35 full-time (0 women), 66 part-time (12 women); includes 5 minority (1 African American, 2 Asian Americans or Pacific Islanders, 2 Hispanic Americans), 43 international. Average age 30. 118 applicants, 73% accepted. *Faculty:* 8 full-time (1 woman), 6 part-time/adjunct (0 women). Expenses: Contact institution. *Financial support:* In 2001–02, 20 students received support, including research assistantships (averaging $5,000 per year); Federal Work-Study and unspecified assistantships also available. Support available to part-time students. Financial award application deadline: 6/1; financial award applicants required to submit FAFSA. In 2001, 9 degrees awarded. *Degree program information:* Part-time and evening/weekend programs available. Offers engineering (M Eng). *Application deadline:* Applications are processed on a rolling basis. *Application fee:* $40 ($55 for international students). Electronic applications accepted. *Application Contact:* Laurie Granstrand, Manager of Student Services, 860-768-4858, E-mail: granstran@mail.hartford.edu. *Dean*, Alan Hadad, 860-768-4112, Fax: 860-768-5073, E-mail: hadad@mail.hartford.edu.

Hartford Art School Students: 13 full-time (11 women), 3 part-time (all women), 1 international. Average age 35. 32 applicants, 25% accepted. *Faculty:* 7 full-time (1 woman), 2 part-time/adjunct (both women). Expenses: Contact institution. *Financial support:* In 2001–02, 10 fellowships (averaging $6,000 per year) were awarded; Federal Work-Study also available. Support available to part-time students. Financial award application deadline: 6/1; financial award applicants required to submit FAFSA. In 2001, 4 degrees awarded. *Degree program information:* Part-time programs available. Offers art (MFA). *Application deadline:* For fall admission, 2/1 (priority date). Applications are processed on a rolling basis. *Application fee:* $40 ($55 for international students). Electronic applications accepted. *Application Contact:* Kellie Richard Westenfeld, Assistant Director of Graduate Admissions, 860-768-4371, Fax: 860-768-5160, E-mail: westenfel@mail.hartford.edu. *Associate Dean*, Tom Bradley, 860-768-4396, Fax: 860-768-5296.

Hartt School of Music Students: 87 full-time (51 women), 27 part-time (14 women); includes 3 minority (all Hispanic Americans), 42 international. Average age 28. 173 applicants, 55% accepted. *Faculty:* 35 full-time (4 women), 25 part-time/adjunct (6 women). Expenses: Contact institution. *Financial support:* Fellowships, teaching assistantships, Federal Work-Study available. Support available to part-time students. Financial award application deadline: 6/1; financial award applicants required to submit FAFSA. In 2001, 45 master's, 4 doctorates, 1 other advanced degree awarded. *Degree program information:* Part-time programs available. Offers choral conducting (MM Ed); composition (MM, DMA, Artist Diploma, Diploma); conducting (MM, DMA, Artist Diploma, Diploma); early childhood education (MM Ed); instrumental conducting (MM Ed); Kodály (MM Ed); music (CAGS); music education (DMA, PhD); music history (MM); music theory (MM); pedagogy (MM Ed); performance (MM, MM Ed, DMA, Artist Diploma, Diploma); research (MM Ed); technology (MM Ed). *Application deadline:* For fall admission, 4/1 (priority date). Applications are processed on a rolling basis. *Application fee:* $40 ($55 for international students). Electronic applications accepted. *Application Contact:* Dr. Amy Becher, Director of Admissions, 860-768-4115, Fax: 860-768-4441, E-mail: becher@mail.hartford.edu. *Dean*, Dr. Malcolm Morrison, 860-768-4468, E-mail: morrison@mail.hartford.edu.

UNIVERSITY OF HAWAII AT HILO, Hilo, HI 96720-4091

General Information State-supported, coed, comprehensive institution.

GRADUATE UNITS

Program in China-US Relations

UNIVERSITY OF HAWAII AT MANOA, Honolulu, HI 96822

General Information State-supported, coed, university. CGS member. *Enrollment:* 2,128 matriculated graduate/professional students. *Graduate faculty:* 1,320 full-time (356 women), 192 part-time/adjunct (28 women). Tuition, state resident: full-time $2,160; part-time $1,980 per year. Tuition, nonresident: full-time $5,190; part-time $4,829 per year. *Graduate housing:* Rooms and/or apartments available on a first-come, first-served basis to single and married students. Typical cost: $3,200 per year ($4,700 including board) for single students; $3,800 per year ($10,600 including board) for married students. Housing application deadline: 3/30. *Student services:* Campus employment opportunities, career counseling, child daycare facilities, disabled student services, exercise/wellness program, free psychological counseling, international student services, low-cost health insurance, multicultural affairs office. *Library facilities:* Hamilton Library plus 6 others. *Online resources:* library catalog, web page, access to other libraries' catalogs. *Collection:* 3.1 million titles, 26,767 serial subscriptions, 47,992 audiovisual materials. *Research affiliation:* Bernice Pauahi Bishop Museum (anthropology, zoology), Hawaiian Volcano Observatory (geology, geophysics), Honolulu Academy of Arts, East-West Center (communication, geography, economics), U.S. Geological Survey, Hawaii Sugar Planters' Association.

Computer facilities: 1,000 computers available on campus for general student use. A campuswide network can be accessed from student residence rooms and from off campus. Internet access, telephone registration are available. *Web address:* http://www.uhm.hawaii.edu/.

General Application Contact: Kenneth Tokuno, Interim Assistant Dean, 808-956-8950, Fax: 808-956-4261, E-mail: ken@admin.grad.hawaii.edu.

GRADUATE UNITS

Graduate Division Students: 1,683. 3,687 applicants, 52% accepted. *Faculty:* 2,484 full-time (585 women). Expenses: Contact institution. *Financial support:* In 2001–02, 432 research assistantships with full tuition reimbursements (averaging $16,255 per year), 383 teaching assistantships with full tuition reimbursements (averaging $13,490 per year) were awarded. Fellowships, career-related internships or fieldwork, Federal Work-Study, institutionally sponsored loans, scholarships/grants, and tuition waivers (full and partial) also available. Support available to part-time students. Financial award applicants required to submit FAFSA. In 2001, 963 master's, 160 doctorates awarded. *Degree program information:* Part-time and evening/weekend programs available. Offers cell, molecular, and neurosciences (MS, PhD); ecology, evolution and conservation biology (MS, PhD); marine biology (MS, PhD). *Application fee:* $25 ($50 for international students). *Application Contact:* Kenneth Tokuno, Interim Assistant Dean, 808-956-8950, Fax: 808-956-4261, E-mail: ken@admin.grad.hawaii.edu. *Interim Vice Chancellor for Research and Graduate Education*, Dr. Ed A. Laws, 808-956-7651, Fax: 808-956-8061, E-mail: laws@hawaii.edu.

College of Arts and Sciences Students: 1,235 full-time (674 women), 589 part-time (327 women). 1,793 applicants, 63% accepted. *Faculty:* 481 full-time (80 women), 13 part-time/adjunct (1 woman). Expenses: Contact institution. *Financial support:* Fellowships, research assistantships, teaching assistantships, career-related internships or fieldwork, Federal Work-Study, institutionally sponsored loans, scholarships/grants, and tuition waivers (full and partial) available. Support available to part-time students. Financial award applicants required to submit CSS PROFILE or FAFSA. In 2001, 305 master's, 100 doctorates awarded. *Degree program information:* Part-time and evening/weekend programs available. Offers advanced library and information science (Certificate); American studies (MA, PhD); anthropology (MA, PhD); art (MA); art history (MA); arts and humanities (M Mus, MA, MFA, PhD); arts and sciences (M Mus, MA, MFA, MLI Sc, MLIS, MPA, MS, MURP, PhD, Certificate); Asian and Asian-Western theatre (PhD); botany (MS, PhD); chemistry (MS, PhD); classics (MA); clinical psychology (PhD); communication (MA); communication and information science (PhD); community and culture (MA, PhD); community planning and social policy (MURP); computer science (PhD); dance (MA, MFA); dance and theatre (PhD); East Asian languages and literature (MA, PhD); economics (MA, PhD); English (MA, PhD); English as a second language (MA); environmental planning and management (MURP); French (MA); geography (MA, PhD); German (MA); history (MA, PhD); information and computer sciences (MS); land use and infrastructure planning (MURP); language, linguistics and literature (MA, PhD); library and information science (MLI Sc, MLIS, PhD, Certificate); linguistics (MA, PhD); mathematics (MA, PhD); microbiology (MS, PhD); music (M Mus, MA, PhD); natural sciences (MA, MLI Sc, MLIS, MS, PhD, Certificate); philosophy (MA, PhD); physics and astronomy (MS, PhD); political science (MA, PhD); psychology (MA, PhD); public administration (MPA, Certificate); religion (MA); second language acquisition (PhD); social sciences (MA, MPA, MURP, PhD, Certificate); sociology (MA, PhD); Spanish (MA); speech (MA); theatre (MA, MFA); urban and regional planning in Asia and Pacific (MURP); visual arts (MFA); zoology (MS, PhD). *Application fee:* $25 ($50 for international students). *Application Contact:* Kenneth Tokuno, Interim Assistant Dean, 808-956-8950, Fax: 808-956-4261, E-mail: ken@admin.grad.hawaii.edu.

College of Business Administration Students: 198 full-time (76 women), 172 part-time (76 women); includes 3 African Americans, 170 Asian Americans or Pacific Islanders, 5 Hispanic Americans *Faculty:* 46 full-time (7 women). Expenses: Contact institution. *Financial support:* In 2001–02, 8 research assistantships (averaging $16,189 per year), 3 teaching assistantships (averaging $14,382 per year) were awarded. Career-related internships or fieldwork, Federal Work-Study, and tuition waivers (full) also available. Support available to part-time students. *Degree program information:* Part-time and evening/weekend programs available. Offers accountancy (M Acc); business administration (EMBA, MBA); China focused business administration (EMBA); executive business administration (EMBA); international management (PhD); Japan focused business administration (EMBA). *Application fee:* $25 ($50 for international students). *Application Contact:* Marsha Anderson, Assistant Dean for Student Academic Services, 808-956-8266, Fax: 808-956-9890, E-mail: osas@busadm.cba.hawaii.edu. *Dean*, David McClain, 808-956-8377.

College of Education Students: 256 full-time (175 women), 485 part-time (346 women). 437 applicants, 76% accepted. *Faculty:* 147 full-time (71 women), 43 part-time/adjunct (19 women). Expenses: Contact institution. *Financial support:* In 2001–02, 17 research assistantships (averaging $15,556 per year), 12 teaching assistantships (averaging $13,751 per year) were awarded. Fellowships, career-related internships or fieldwork, Federal Work-Study, institutionally sponsored loans, and tuition waivers (full and partial) also available. Support available to part-time students. In 2001, 235 master's, 9 doctorates awarded. *Degree program information:* Part-time and evening/weekend programs available. Offers counselor education (M Ed); curriculum and instruction (PhD); education (M Ed, M Ed T, MS, PhD); education in teaching (M Ed T); educational administration (M Ed, PhD); educational foundations (M Ed, PhD); educational policy studies (PhD); educational psychology (M Ed, PhD); educational technology (M Ed); elementary education (M Ed); exceptionalities (PhD); kinesiology and leisure science (MS); secondary education (M Ed); special education (M Ed). *Application fee:* $25 ($50 for international students). *Dean*, Dr. Randy A. Hitz, 808-956-7703, Fax: 808-956-3106, E-mail: hitz@hawaii.edu.

College of Engineering Students: 97 full-time (23 women), 44 part-time (9 women). 182 applicants, 85% accepted. *Faculty:* 59 full-time (4 women), 14 part-time/adjunct (0 women). Expenses: Contact institution. *Financial support:* In 2001–02, 51 research assistantships (averaging $15,177 per year), 12 teaching assistantships (averaging $13,249 per year) were awarded. Fellowships, career-related internships or fieldwork, Federal Work-Study, and tuition waivers (full and partial) also available. Financial award applicants required to submit FAFSA. In 2001, 40 master's, 6 doctorates awarded. *Degree program information:* Part-time programs available. Offers civil engineering (MS, PhD); electrical engineering (MS, PhD); engineering (MS, PhD); mechanical engineering (MS, PhD). *Application deadline:* Applications are processed on a rolling basis. *Application fee:* $25 ($50 for international students). *Dean*, Dr. Wai-Fah Chen, 808-956-7727, Fax: 808-956-2291.

College of Health Sciences and Social Welfare Students: 203 full-time (175 women), 98 part-time (77 women). 479 applicants, 40% accepted. *Faculty:* 120 full-time (67 women). Expenses: Contact institution. *Financial support:* In 2001–02, 7 research assistantships with full and partial tuition reimbursements (averaging $15,306 per year), 1 teaching assistantship ($12,786 per year) were awarded. Fellowships with full and partial tuition reimbursements, career-related internships or fieldwork, Federal Work-Study, institutionally sponsored loans, traineeships, and tuition waivers (full) also available. Support available to part-time students. In 2001, 120 master's, 3 doctorates awarded. *Degree program information:* Part-time programs available. Offers clinical nurse specialist (MS); health sciences and social welfare (MS, MSW, PhD, Certificate); nurse practitioner (MS); nursing (PhD, Certificate); nursing administration (MS); social welfare (PhD); social work (MSW). *Application fee:* $25 ($50 for international students). *Application Contact:* Kenneth Tokuno, Interim Assistant Dean, 808-956-8950, Fax: 808-956-4261, E-mail: ken@admin.grad.hawaii.edu.

College of Tropical Agriculture and Human Resources 160 applicants, 71% accepted. *Faculty:* 103 full-time (14 women), 101 part-time/adjunct (13 women). Expenses: Contact institution. *Financial support:* In 2001–02, 44 research assistantships (averaging $15,743 per year), 21 teaching assistantships (averaging $12,985 per year) were awarded. Fellowships, career-related internships or fieldwork, Federal Work-Study, institutionally sponsored loans, tuition waivers (full and partial), and unspecified assistantships also available. In 2001, 15 master's, 12 doctorates awarded. *Degree program information:* Part-time programs available. Offers agricultural and resource economics (MS, PhD); agronomy and soil sciences (MS, PhD); animal sciences (MS); biosystems engineering (MS); botanical sciences (MS, PhD); entomology (MS, PhD); food science (MS); horticulture (MS, PhD); human nutrition, food and animal sciences (MS); molecular biosystems and bioengineering (MS, PhD); nutritional science (MS); plant pathology (MS, PhD); tropical agriculture and human resources (MS, PhD). *Application deadline:* For fall admission, 3/1; for spring admission, 9/1. *Application fee:* $25 ($50 for international students). *Dean,* Dr. Andrew Hashimoto, 808-956-8234, Fax: 808-956-9105, E-mail: dean@ctahr.hawaii.edu.

School of Architecture Students: 10 full-time (5 women), 2 part-time; includes 2 Asian Americans or Pacific Islanders Average age 31. 59 applicants, 58% accepted, 17 enrolled. *Faculty:* 11 full-time (4 women). Expenses: Contact institution. *Financial support:* In 2001–02, 1 research assistantship (averaging $15,558 per year), 3 teaching assistantships (averaging $12,786 per year) were awarded. Tuition waivers (full) also available. Offers architecture (D Arch). *Application deadline:* For fall admission, 2/1 (priority date); for spring admission, 9/1. *Application fee:* $25 ($50 for international students). *Application Contact:* Gordon Tyau, Graduate Field Chairperson, 808-956-3506, Fax: 808-956-7778, E-mail: gordonc@hawaii.edu. *Dean,* W. H. Raymond Yeh, 808-956-7225.

School of Hawaiian, Asian and Pacific Studies Students: 109 full-time (46 women), 31 part-time (19 women). 111 applicants, 86% accepted. *Faculty:* 42 full-time (14 women), 95 part-time/adjunct (22 women). Expenses: Contact institution. *Financial support:* In 2001–02, 1 research assistantship (averaging $14,958 per year), 3 teaching assistantships (averaging $12,786 per year) were awarded. Fellowships, career-related internships or fieldwork, Federal Work-Study, and tuition waivers (full) also available. In 2001, 33 degrees awarded. Offers Asian studies (MA); Pacific Island studies (MA). *Dean,* Willa Tanabe, 808-956-8922, Fax: 808-956-6345, E-mail: wjtanabe@hawaii.edu.

School of Ocean and Earth Science and Technology Students: 147 full-time (61 women), 19 part-time (9 women). 245 applicants, 49% accepted. *Faculty:* 79 full-time (9 women), 98 part-time/adjunct (11 women). Expenses: Contact institution. *Financial support:* In 2001–02, 106 research assistantships (averaging $17,664 per year), 16 teaching assistantships (averaging $16,112 per year) were awarded. Fellowships, career-related internships or fieldwork, Federal Work-Study, institutionally sponsored loans, and tuition waivers (full and partial) also available. Financial award applicants required to submit FAFSA. In 2001, 16 master's, 7 doctorates awarded. *Degree program information:* Part-time programs available. Offers high-pressure geophysics and geochemistry (MS, PhD); hydrogeology and engineering geology (MS, PhD); marine geology and geophysics (MS, PhD); meteorology (MS, PhD); ocean and earth science and technology (MS, PhD); ocean and resources engineering (MS, PhD); oceanography (MS, PhD); planetary geosciences and remote sensing (MS, PhD); seismology and solid-earth geophysics (MS, PhD); volcanology, petrology, and geochemistry (MS, PhD). *Application fee:* $25 ($50 for international students). *Dean,* C. Barry Raleigh, 808-956-6182, Fax: 808-956-9152.

School of Travel Industry Management Students: 17 full-time (14 women), 3 part-time (all women); includes 4 minority (all Asian Americans or Pacific Islanders), 11 international. Average age 28. 45 applicants, 44% accepted, 10 enrolled. *Faculty:* 8 full-time (3 women), 1 part-time/adjunct (0 women). Expenses: Contact institution. *Financial support:* Research assistantships, teaching assistantships, career-related internships or fieldwork, Federal Work-Study, scholarships/grants, tuition waivers (full), and student assistantships available. Financial award application deadline: 3/1. In 2001, 7 degrees awarded. *Degree program information:* Part-time programs available. Offers travel industry management (MS). *Application deadline:* For fall admission, 3/1; for spring admission, 10/1. Applications are processed on a rolling basis. *Application fee:* $25 ($50 for international students). Electronic applications accepted. *Application Contact:* Dr. Juanita C. Liu, Graduate Chair, 808-956-6610, Fax: 808-956-5378, E-mail: liujuani@hawaii.edu. *Interim Dean,* Dr. Pauline J. Sheldon, 808-956-7166, Fax: 808-956-5378, E-mail: psheldon@hawaii.edu.

John A. Burns School of Medicine Students: 415 full-time (235 women), 30 part-time (19 women). Average age 28. 1,452 applicants, 20% accepted. *Faculty:* 153 full-time (28 women), 11 part-time/adjunct (5 women). Expenses: Contact institution. *Financial support:* In 2001–02, 32 research assistantships (averaging $16,034 per year), 3 teaching assistantships (averaging $12,914 per year) were awarded. Fellowships, career-related internships or fieldwork, Federal Work-Study, institutionally sponsored loans, and tuition waivers (full and partial) also available. Support available to part-time students. Financial award applicants required to submit FAFSA. In 2001, 54 first professional degrees, 106 master's, 17 doctorates awarded. *Degree program information:* Part-time programs available. Offers medicine (MD, MPH, MS, PhD); public health sciences and epidemiology (MPH, MS). *Application fee:* $25 ($50 for international students). *Dean,* Dr. Edwin C. Cadman, 808-956-8287, Fax: 808-956-5506.

Graduate Programs in Biomedical Sciences Students: 136 full-time (103 women), 22 part-time (14 women). Average age 31. 178 applicants, 69% accepted. *Faculty:* 57 full-time (13 women), 8 part-time/adjunct (2 women). Expenses: Contact institution. *Financial support:* In 2001–02, 16 research assistantships (averaging $16,004 per year) were awarded; fellowships, teaching assistantships, career-related internships or fieldwork, Federal Work-Study, institutionally sponsored loans, and tuition waivers (full and partial) also available. Support available to part-time students. In 2001, 24 master's, 10 doctorates awarded. *Degree program information:* Part-time programs available. Offers biochemistry (MS, PhD); biomedical sciences (MS, PhD); biophysics (MS, PhD); genetics and molecular biology (MS, PhD); pharmacology (MS, PhD); physiology (MS, PhD); reproductive biology (PhD); speech pathology and audiology (MS); tropical medicine (MS, PhD). *Application fee:* $25 ($50 for international students). *Application Contact:* Martin Rayner, Graduate Chair, 808-956-7269, Fax: 808-956-9530, E-mail: martin@pbrc.hawaii.edu.

William S. Richardson School of Law Offers law (JD).

THE UNIVERSITY OF HEALTH SCIENCES, Kansas City, MO 64106-1453

General Information Independent, coed, primarily men, graduate-only institution. *Enrollment by degree level:* 890 first professional. *Graduate faculty:* 51 full-time (16 women), 181 part-time/adjunct (25 women). *Tuition:* Full-time $29,440. *Required fees:* $60. *Graduate housing:* On-campus housing not available. *Student services:* Campus employment opportunities, campus safety program, career counseling, free psychological counseling. *Library facilities:* The University of Health Sciences Library. *Online resources:* library catalog, web page, access to other libraries' catalogs. *Collection:* 94,010 titles, 270 serial subscriptions, 7,301 audiovisual materials. *Research affiliation:* Glaxo Welcome (asthma), Glaxo Welcome (chronic obstructive pulmonary disease), Bristol-Myers Squibb (community acquired pneumonia).

Computer facilities: 102 computers available on campus for general student use. A campuswide network can be accessed. Internet access is available. *Web address:* http://www.uhs.edu/.

General Application Contact: Minnie Marrs, Admissions Director, 816-283-2339, Fax: 816-283-2484, E-mail: mmarrs@uhs.edu.

GRADUATE UNITS

College of Osteopathic Medicine Students: 890 full-time (363 women); includes 105 minority (7 African Americans, 75 Asian Americans or Pacific Islanders, 16 Hispanic Americans, 7 Native Americans), 6 international. Average age 26. 2,262 applicants, 21% accepted, 250 enrolled. *Faculty:* 51 full-time (16 women), 181 part-time/adjunct (25 women). Expenses: Contact institution. *Financial support:* In 2001–02, 52 students received support; fellowships with full tuition reimbursements available, career-related internships or fieldwork, institutionally sponsored loans, and scholarships/grants available. Financial award application deadline: 4/1; financial award applicants required to submit FAFSA. In 2001, 208 degrees awarded. Offers osteopathic medicine (DO). *Application deadline:* For fall admission, 2/1. Applications are processed on a rolling basis. *Application fee:* $50. *Application Contact:* Minnie Marrs, Admissions Director, 816-283-2339, Fax: 816-283-2484, E-mail: mmarrs@uhs.edu. *Vice President for Academic Affairs and Dean,* Dr. James M. Carl, 816-283-2308, Fax: 816-283-2303, E-mail: jcarl@uhs.edu.

UNIVERSITY OF HOUSTON, Houston, TX 77204

General Information State-supported, coed, university. CGS member. *Enrollment:* 4,276 full-time matriculated graduate/professional students (2,202 women), 2,800 part-time matriculated graduate/professional students (1,532 women). *Enrollment by degree level:* 1,768 first professional, 3,944 master's, 1,364 doctoral. *Graduate faculty:* 588 full-time (142 women), 337 part-time/adjunct (126 women). Tuition, state resident: full-time $1,512. Tuition, nonresident: full-time $5,310. *Required fees:* $1,308. Tuition and fees vary according to program. *Graduate housing:* Rooms and/or apartments available on a first-come, first-served basis to single students and available to married students. Housing application deadline: 3/1. *Student services:* Campus employment opportunities, campus safety program, career counseling, child daycare facilities, disabled student services, exercise/wellness program, free psychological counseling, international student services, low-cost health insurance, teacher training, writing training. *Library facilities:* M.D. Anderson Library plus 5 others. *Online resources:* library catalog, web page, access to other libraries' catalogs. *Collection:* 2.1 million titles, 15,203 serial subscriptions, 13,385 audiovisual materials.

Computer facilities: 825 computers available on campus for general student use. A campuswide network can be accessed from student residence rooms and from off campus. Internet access and online class registration are available. *Web address:* http://www.uh.edu/.

General Application Contact: Adrianna Higgins, Director of Admissions, 713-743-1010, Fax: 713-743-9653, E-mail: admissions@uh.edu.

GRADUATE UNITS

College of Architecture Students: 53 full-time (26 women), 8 part-time (4 women); includes 10 minority (4 African Americans, 1 Asian American or Pacific Islander, 4 Hispanic Americans, 1 Native American), 21 international. Average age 29. 120 applicants, 38% accepted. *Faculty:* 1 full-time (0 women), 19 part-time/adjunct (1 woman). Expenses: Contact institution. *Financial support:* In 2001–02, 18 teaching assistantships were awarded; fellowships, research assistantships, career-related internships or fieldwork, Federal Work-Study, institutionally sponsored loans, and tuition waivers (partial) also available. Financial award application deadline: 3/1. In 2001, 15 degrees awarded. Offers architecture (M Arch). *Application deadline:* For fall admission, 2/1 (priority date); for spring admission, 10/1. Applications are processed on a rolling basis. *Application fee:* $10 ($75 for international students). *Application Contact:* Thomas M. Colbert, Director of Graduate Studies, 713-743-2400, Fax: 713-743-2358, E-mail: colbert@bayou.uh.edu. *Dean,* Joseph Mashburn, 713-743-2400, Fax: 713-743-2358.

College of Education Students: 268 full-time (219 women), 879 part-time (670 women); includes 362 minority (147 African Americans, 47 Asian Americans or Pacific Islanders, 158 Hispanic Americans, 10 Native Americans), 33 international. Average age 37. *Faculty:* 74 full-time (34 women), 40 part-time/adjunct (27 women). Expenses: Contact institution. *Financial support:* In 2001–02, 3 research assistantships, 43 teaching assistantships were awarded. Career-related internships or fieldwork, Federal Work-Study, and institutionally sponsored loans also available. Support available to part-time students. Financial award applicants required to submit FAFSA. In 2001, 308 master's, 77 doctorates awarded. *Degree program information:* Part-time and evening/weekend programs available. Offers allied health (M Ed, Ed D); art education (M Ed); bilingual education (M Ed); counseling psychology (M Ed, PhD); curriculum and instruction (Ed D); early childhood education (M Ed); education (M Ed, MS, Ed D, PhD); education of the gifted (M Ed); educational administration (M Ed, Ed D); educational psychology (M Ed); educational psychology and individual differences (PhD); elementary education (M Ed); exercise science (MS); health education (M Ed); higher education (M Ed); historical, social, and cultural foundations of education (M Ed, Ed D); mathematics education (M Ed); physical education (M Ed, Ed D); reading and language arts education (M Ed); science education (M Ed); second language education (M Ed); secondary education (M Ed); social studies education (M Ed); special education (M Ed, Ed D); teaching (M Ed). *Application fee:* $35 ($75 for international students). *Dean,* Robert K. Wimpelberg, 713-743-5001, Fax: 713-743-9870.

College of Liberal Arts and Social Sciences Students: 575 full-time (352 women), 358 part-time (214 women); includes 184 minority (34 African Americans, 48 Asian Americans or Pacific Islanders, 96 Hispanic Americans, 6 Native Americans), 104 international. Average age 33. 688 applicants, 35% accepted. *Faculty:* 139 full-time (48 women), 36 part-time/adjunct (21 women). Expenses: Contact institution. *Financial support:* Fellowships, research assistantships, teaching assistantships, career-related internships or fieldwork, Federal Work-Study, institutionally sponsored loans, scholarships/grants, and tuition waivers (full and partial) available. Support available to part-time students. Financial award applicants required to submit FAFSA. In 2001, 177 master's, 55 doctorates awarded. *Degree program information:* Part-time and evening/weekend programs available. Postbaccalaureate distance learning degree programs offered. Offers anthropology (MA); applied English linguistics (MA); clinical psychology (PhD); economics (MA, PhD); English and American literature (MA, PhD); French (MA); graphic communications (MFA); history (MA, PhD); industrial/organizational psychology (PhD); interior design (MFA); liberal arts and social sciences (MA, MFA, MM, DMA, PhD); literature and creative writing (MA, MFA, PhD); painting (MFA); philosophy (MA); photography (MFA); political science (MA, PhD); public history (MA); sculpture (MFA); social psychology (PhD); sociology (MA); Spanish (MA, PhD); speech language pathology (MA). *Application Contact:* Debra Frazier, Graduate Analyst, 713-743-2991, Fax: 713-743-2990. *Dean,* Dr. W. Andrew Achenbaum, 713-743-2992, Fax: 713-743-2990.

Moores School of Music Students: 88 full-time (49 women), 40 part-time (23 women); includes 16 minority (1 African American, 10 Asian Americans or Pacific Islanders, 4 Hispanic Americans, 1 Native American), 36 international. Average age 31. *Faculty:* 25 full-time (4 women), 27 part-time/adjunct (9 women). Expenses: Contact institution. *Financial support:* Fellowships, teaching assistantships, Federal Work-Study, institutionally sponsored loans, scholarships/grants, and tuition waivers (partial) available. Financial award application deadline: 3/31. In 2001, 26 master's, 9 doctorates awarded. *Degree program information:* Part-time programs available. Offers accompanying (MM); applied music (MM); composition (MM, DMA); conducting (DMA); music education (MM, DMA); music literature (MM); music performance and pedagogy (MM); music theory (MM); performance (DMA). *Application deadline:* For fall admission, 7/1 (priority date). Applications are processed on a rolling basis. *Application fee:* $0 ($75 for international students). *Application Contact:* Howard Pollack, Director of Graduate Studies, 713-743-3314, Fax: 713-743-3166. *Director,* David Ashley White, 713-743-3009, Fax: 713-743-3166.

School of Communication Students: 23 full-time (17 women), 33 part-time (29 women); includes 11 minority (3 African Americans, 2 Asian Americans or Pacific Islanders, 4 Hispanic Americans, 2 Native Americans), 9 international. Average age 31. 47 applicants, 23% accepted. *Faculty:* 8 full-time (2 women), 2 part-time/adjunct (0 women). Expenses: Contact institution. *Financial support:* In 2001–02, teaching assistantships (averaging $8,651 per year); career-related internships or fieldwork and institutionally sponsored loans also available. Financial award application deadline: 7/15. In 2001, 12 degrees awarded. *Degree program information:* Part-time and evening/weekend programs available. Offers mass communication studies (MA); public relations studies (MA); speech communication (MA). *Application deadline:* For fall admission, 7/3 (priority date). Applications are processed on a rolling basis. *Application fee:* $25 ($75 for international students). *Application Contact:* Angela Parrish, Graduate Coordinator, 713-743-2873, Fax: 713-743-2876, E-mail: aparrish@bayou.uh.edu. *Chairperson,* Garth Jowett, 713-743-3002, Fax: 713-743-2876.

School of Theatre Students: 30 full-time (19 women), 10 part-time (5 women); includes 7 minority (4 African Americans, 1 Asian American or Pacific Islander, 2 Hispanic Americans) Average age 33. 23 applicants, 83% accepted. *Faculty:* 9 full-time (4 women). Expenses: Contact institution. *Financial support:* In 2001–02, 3 teaching assistantships were awarded; career-related internships or fieldwork, Federal Work-Study, and institutionally sponsored loans also available. In 2001, 9 degrees awarded. *Degree program information:* Part-time programs available. Offers theatre (MA, MFA). *Application fee:* $25. *Director,* Sidney Berger, 713-743-3003, Fax: 713-749-1420, E-mail: sberger@uh.edu.

University of Houston (continued)

College of Natural Sciences and Mathematics Students: 525 full-time (176 women), 194 part-time (63 women); includes 86 minority (14 African Americans, 54 Asian Americans or Pacific Islanders, 17 Hispanic Americans, 1 Native American), 477 international. Average age 30. *Faculty:* 113 full-time (11 women), 13 part-time/adjunct (3 women). Expenses: Contact institution. *Financial support:* Fellowships, research assistantships, teaching assistantships, career-related internships or fieldwork, Federal Work-Study, institutionally sponsored loans, scholarships/grants, and tuition waivers (full and partial) available. Support available to part-time students. Financial award applicants required to submit FAFSA. In 2001, 120 master's, 40 doctorates awarded. *Degree program information:* Part-time and evening/weekend programs available. Postbaccalaureate distance learning degree programs offered. Offers applied mathematics (MSAM); biochemistry (MS, PhD); biology (MS, PhD); chemistry (MS, PhD); computer science (MS, PhD); geology (MS, PhD); geophysics (MS, PhD); mathematics (MSM, PhD); natural sciences and mathematics (MS, MSAM, MSM, PhD); physics (MS, PhD). *Application deadline:* Applications are processed on a rolling basis. Electronic applications accepted. *Dean,* Dr. John L. Bear, 713-743-2620.

College of Optometry Students: 396 full-time (241 women), 12 part-time (6 women); includes 213 minority (11 African Americans, 155 Asian Americans or Pacific Islanders, 46 Hispanic Americans, 1 Native American), 20 international. Average age 26. 305 applicants, 35% accepted. *Faculty:* 45 full-time (14 women), 37 part-time/adjunct (22 women). Expenses: Contact institution. *Financial support:* Fellowships with full tuition reimbursements, research assistantships with full tuition reimbursements, teaching assistantships with full tuition reimbursements, career-related internships or fieldwork, Federal Work-Study, and institutionally sponsored loans available. Support available to part-time students. In 2001, 99 first professional degrees, 3 master's awarded. Offers optometry (OD); physiological optics/vision science (MS Phys Op, PhD). *Application deadline:* Applications are processed on a rolling basis. *Application Contact:* Paul Pease, Director, Student Affairs and Admission, 713-743-2040, Fax: 713-743-2046, E-mail: ppease@uh.edu. *Dean,* Jerald Strickland, 713-743-1899, Fax: 713-743-0965, E-mail: strickland@uh.edu.

College of Pharmacy Students: 430 full-time (300 women), 45 part-time (31 women); includes 294 minority (35 African Americans, 220 Asian Americans or Pacific Islanders, 35 Hispanic Americans, 4 Native Americans), 35 international. Average age 26. *Faculty:* 34 full-time (17 women), 4 part-time/adjunct (3 women). Expenses: Contact institution. *Financial support:* In 2001–02, research assistantships with full tuition reimbursements (averaging $14,500 per year), teaching assistantships with full tuition reimbursements (averaging $14,500 per year) were awarded. Institutionally sponsored loans also available. Support available to part-time students. Financial award application deadline: 4/1. In 2001, 94 first professional degrees, 1 master's awarded. *Degree program information:* Part-time programs available. Offers hospital pharmacy (MSPHR); medical chemistry and pharmacology (MS); pharmaceutics (MS, PhD); pharmacology (MS, PhD); pharmacy (Pharm D); pharmacy administration (MSPHR). *Application deadline:* For spring admission, 3/1. Applications are processed on a rolling basis. *Application fee:* $25 ($75 for international students). *Application Contact:* Shara Zatopek, Assistant Dean for Admissions, 713-743-1262. *Dean,* Dr. M. F. Lokhandwala, 713-743-1253.

College of Technology Students: 36 full-time (17 women), 60 part-time (21 women); includes 28 minority (16 African Americans, 4 Asian Americans or Pacific Islanders, 8 Hispanic Americans), 17 international. Average age 35. 33 applicants, 82% accepted. *Faculty:* 11 full-time (5 women), 13 part-time/adjunct (4 women). Expenses: Contact institution. *Financial support:* Fellowships, research assistantships, teaching assistantships, career-related internships or fieldwork, Federal Work-Study, and institutionally sponsored loans available. Support available to part-time students. In 2001, 25 degrees awarded. *Degree program information:* Part-time and evening/weekend programs available. Offers construction management (MT); manufacturing systems (MT); microcomputer systems (MT); occupational technology (MSOT). *Application deadline:* For fall admission, 7/1; for spring admission, 11/1. *Application fee:* $35 ($110 for international students). *Application Contact:* Holly Rosenthal, Graduate Academic Adviser, 713-743-4098, Fax: 713-743-4032, E-mail: hrosenthal@uh.edu. *Dean,* Uma G. Gupta, 713-743-4032, Fax: 713-743-4032.

Conrad N. Hilton College of Hotel and Restaurant Management Students: 56 full-time (37 women), 6 part-time (4 women); includes 4 minority (2 African Americans, 2 Asian Americans or Pacific Islanders), 44 international. Average age 28. 77 applicants, 52% accepted. *Faculty:* 9 full-time (4 women), 9 part-time/adjunct (1 woman). Expenses: Contact institution. *Financial support:* In 2001–02, 2 fellowships with partial tuition reimbursements, 12 research assistantships with partial tuition reimbursements were awarded. Teaching assistantships, career-related internships or fieldwork, Federal Work-Study, institutionally sponsored loans, and tuition waivers (partial) also available. Support available to part-time students. In 2001, 27 degrees awarded. *Degree program information:* Part-time and evening/weekend programs available. Postbaccalaureate distance learning degree programs offered (minimal on-campus study). Offers hotel and restaurant management (MHM). *Application deadline:* For fall admission, 5/1; for spring admission, 10/1. Applications are processed on a rolling basis. *Application fee:* $25 ($75 for international students). Electronic applications accepted. *Application Contact:* Lilian Sutawan-Binns, Program Manager, 713-743-2457, Fax: 713-743-2591, E-mail: lbinns@uh.edu. *Interim Dean,* Dr. Agnes DeFranco, 713-743-4234, Fax: 713-743-2498.

C. T. Bauer College of Business Students: 575 full-time (207 women), 536 part-time (195 women); includes 248 minority (43 African Americans, 138 Asian Americans or Pacific Islanders, 64 Hispanic Americans, 3 Native Americans), 231 international. Average age 31. 346 applicants, 58% accepted. *Faculty:* 44 full-time (7 women), 30 part-time/adjunct (5 women). Expenses: Contact institution. *Financial support:* In 2001–02, research assistantships (averaging $7,200 per year), teaching assistantships (averaging $7,200 per year) were awarded. Career-related internships or fieldwork, Federal Work-Study, and institutionally sponsored loans also available. Support available to part-time students. Financial award application deadline: 3/1; financial award applicants required to submit FAFSA. In 2001, 453 master's, 5 doctorates awarded. *Degree program information:* Part-time and evening/weekend programs available. Offers accountancy (MS Accy); accounting (PhD); business (MBA, MS, MS Accy, MS Admin, PhD); decision and information sciences (MBA, PhD); finance (MS, PhD); management (PhD); marketing and entrepreneurship (PhD). *Application deadline:* For fall admission, 5/1; for spring admission, 10/1. Applications are processed on a rolling basis. *Application fee:* $75 ($150 for international students). *Application Contact:* Andrew Wayne Edwards, Office of Student Services, 713-743-4852, Fax: 713-743-4942, E-mail: aedwards@uh.edu. *Dean,* Dr. Arthur Warga, 713-743-4604, Fax: 713-743-4622.

Cullen College of Engineering Students: 392 full-time (87 women), 255 part-time (56 women); includes 107 minority (21 African Americans, 50 Asian Americans or Pacific Islanders, 36 Hispanic Americans), 355 international. Average age 29. 1,042 applicants, 46% accepted. *Faculty:* 85 full-time (5 women), 9 part-time/adjunct (0 women). Expenses: Contact institution. *Financial support:* In 2001–02, 290 fellowships with partial tuition reimbursements (averaging $1,440 per year), 198 research assistantships with partial tuition reimbursements (averaging $13,200 per year), 82 teaching assistantships with partial tuition reimbursements (averaging $12,000 per year) were awarded. Career-related internships or fieldwork, Federal Work-Study, institutionally sponsored loans, scholarships/grants, and tuition waivers (partial) also available. In 2001, 144 master's, 25 doctorates awarded. *Degree program information:* Part-time and evening/weekend programs available. Offers aerospace engineering (MS, PhD); biomedical engineering (MS); chemical engineering (M Ch E, MS Ch E, PhD); civil and environmental engineering (MCE, MS Env E, MSCE, PhD); computer and systems engineering (MS, PhD); electrical and computer engineering (MEE, MSEE, PhD); engineering (M Ch E, MCE, MEE, MIE, MME, MS, MS Ch E, MS Env E, MSCE, MSEE, MSIE, MSME, PhD); environmental engineering (MS, PhD); industrial engineering (MIE, MSIE, PhD); materials engineering (MS, PhD); mechanical engineering (MME, MSME); petroleum engineering (MS). *Application deadline:* Applications are processed on a rolling basis. *Application fee:* $25 ($75 for international students). *Application Contact:* Dr. Earl Joseph Charlson, Associate Dean, Graduate Programs, 713-743-4200, Fax: 713-743-4205, E-mail: jcharlson@uh.edu. *Dean,* Dr. Raymond W. Flumerfelt, 713-743-4207, Fax: 713-743-4214, E-mail: rwf@uh.edu.

Graduate School of Social Work Students: 178 full-time (157 women), 183 part-time (154 women); includes 166 minority (98 African Americans, 11 Asian Americans or Pacific Islanders, 57 Hispanic Americans), 6 international. Average age 35. 227 applicants, 72% accepted. *Faculty:* 16 full-time (8 women), 21 part-time/adjunct (15 women). Expenses: Contact institution. *Financial support:* In 2001–02, 9 fellowships with tuition reimbursements (averaging $8,000 per year), 1 research assistantship with tuition reimbursement (averaging $8,000 per year) were awarded. Career-related internships or fieldwork, Federal Work-Study, institutionally sponsored loans, and unspecified assistantships also available. Financial award application deadline: 4/1; financial award applicants required to submit FAFSA. In 2001, 95 master's, 2 doctorates awarded. *Degree program information:* Part-time programs available. Offers social work (MSW, PhD). *Application deadline:* For fall admission, 3/1 (priority date). Applications are processed on a rolling basis. *Application fee:* $50 ($125 for international students). *Application Contact:* Colen Skinner, Admissions Office, 713-743-8078, Fax: 713-743-8149, E-mail: cskinner@mail.uh.edu. *Dean,* Dr. Ira C. Colby, 713-743-8085, Fax: 713-743-3267, E-mail: icolby@uh.edu.

Law Center Students: 792 full-time (383 women), 264 part-time (114 women); includes 197 minority (37 African Americans, 67 Asian Americans or Pacific Islanders, 90 Hispanic Americans, 3 Native Americans), 31 international. Average age 29. 2,349 applicants, 35% accepted. *Faculty:* 34 full-time (8 women), 55 part-time/adjunct (16 women). Expenses: Contact institution. *Financial support:* In 2001–02, 691 students received support, including 1 research assistantship with partial tuition reimbursement available; career-related internships or fieldwork, Federal Work-Study, institutionally sponsored loans, and scholarships/grants also available. Support available to part-time students. Financial award application deadline: 4/1; financial award applicants required to submit FAFSA. In 2001, 337 first professional degrees, 49 master's awarded. *Degree program information:* Part-time and evening/weekend programs available. Offers law (JD, LL M). *Application deadline:* For fall admission, 2/15 (priority date). Applications are processed on a rolling basis. *Application fee:* $50 ($75 for international students). Electronic applications accepted. *Application Contact:* Sondra B. Tennessee, Assistant Dean for Admissions, 713-743-2181. *Dean,* Nancy B. Rapoport, 713-743-2100, Fax: 713-743-2122.

UNIVERSITY OF HOUSTON–CLEAR LAKE, Houston, TX 77058-1098

General Information State-supported, coed, upper-level institution. CGS member. *Enrollment:* 1,122 full-time matriculated graduate/professional students (654 women), 2,488 part-time matriculated graduate/professional students (1,469 women). *Enrollment by degree level:* 3,610 master's. *Graduate faculty:* 256. Tuition, state resident: full-time $2,016; part-time $84 per credit hour. Tuition, nonresident: full-time $6,072; part-time $253 per credit hour. Tuition and fees vary according to course load. *Graduate housing:* On-campus housing not available. *Student services:* Campus employment opportunities, campus safety program, career counseling, disabled student services, free psychological counseling, international student services, low-cost health insurance, multicultural affairs office, teacher training, writing training. *Library facilities:* Neumann Library. *Online resources:* library catalog, access to other libraries' catalogs. *Collection:* 650,000 titles, 2,000 serial subscriptions. *Research affiliation:* NASA–Johnson Space Center.

Computer facilities: 383 computers available on campus for general student use. A campuswide network can be accessed from off campus. Internet access and online class registration are available. *Web address:* http://www.cl.uh.edu/.

General Application Contact: John F. Smith, Executive Director of Enrollment Services, 281-283-2540, Fax: 281-283-2530, E-mail: smithjohnf@cl.uh.edu.

GRADUATE UNITS

School of Business and Public Administration Students: 422 full-time, 554 part-time; includes 250 minority (55 African Americans, 132 Asian Americans or Pacific Islanders, 63 Hispanic Americans), 212 international. Average age 31. Expenses: Contact institution. *Financial support:* Teaching assistantships, career-related internships or fieldwork, Federal Work-Study, institutionally sponsored loans, and scholarships/grants available. Support available to part-time students. Financial award application deadline: 5/1. In 2001, 275 degrees awarded. *Degree program information:* Part-time and evening/weekend programs available. Offers accounting (MS); administration of health services (MS); business administration (MBA); business and public administration (MA, MBA, MHA, MS); environmental management (MS); finance (MS); healthcare administration (MHA); human resource management (MA); public management (MA). *Application deadline:* For fall admission, 8/1; for spring admission, 12/1. Applications are processed on a rolling basis. *Application fee:* $30 ($70 for international students). Electronic applications accepted. *Application Contact:* Dr. Joan Bruno, Associate Dean, 281-283-3107, E-mail: bruno@cl.uh.edu. *Dean,* Dr. William Theodore Cummings, 281-283-3102, Fax: 281-283-3951, E-mail: cummings@cl.uh.edu.

School of Education Students: 206 full-time, 854 part-time; includes 271 minority (118 African Americans, 19 Asian Americans or Pacific Islanders, 132 Hispanic Americans, 2 Native Americans), 7 international. Average age 36. Expenses: Contact institution. *Financial support:* Career-related internships or fieldwork, Federal Work-Study, institutionally sponsored loans, and scholarships/grants available. Support available to part-time students. Financial award application deadline: 5/1. In 2001, 207 degrees awarded. *Degree program information:* Part-time and evening/weekend programs available. Offers counseling (MS); curriculum and instruction (MS); early childhood education (MS); education (MS); educational management (MS); instructional technology (MS); learning resources (MS); multicultural studies (MS); reading (MS). *Application deadline:* For fall admission, 7/1; for spring admission, 10/1. Applications are processed on a rolling basis. *Application fee:* $30 ($70 for international students). Electronic applications accepted. *Application Contact:* Dr. James M. Sherrill, Associate Dean, 281-283-3620, Fax: 281-283-3599, E-mail: sherrill@cl.uh.edu. *Dean,* Dr. Dennis Spuck, 281-283-3501, Fax: 281-283-3599, E-mail: spuck@cl.uh.edu.

School of Human Sciences and Humanities Students: 236 full-time, 587 part-time; includes 248 minority (131 African Americans, 21 Asian Americans or Pacific Islanders, 89 Hispanic Americans, 7 Native Americans), 20 international. Average age 36. Expenses: Contact institution. *Financial support:* Research assistantships, teaching assistantships, career-related internships or fieldwork, Federal Work-Study, institutionally sponsored loans, and scholarships/grants available. Support available to part-time students. Financial award application deadline: 5/1. In 2001, 190 degrees awarded. *Degree program information:* Part-time and evening/weekend programs available. Offers behavioral sciences (MA); clinical psychology (MA); cross-cultural studies (MA); family therapy (MA); fitness and human performance (MA); history (MA); human sciences and humanities (MA, MS); humanities (MA); literature (MA); school psychology (MA); studies of the future (MS). *Application deadline:* For fall admission, 7/1; for spring admission, 10/1. Applications are processed on a rolling basis. *Application fee:* $30 ($70 for international students). *Interim Dean,* Dr. Emily Sutter, 281-283-3301.

School of Natural and Applied Sciences Students: 247 full-time, 339 part-time; includes 150 minority (17 African Americans, 104 Asian Americans or Pacific Islanders, 28 Hispanic Americans, 1 Native American), 235 international. Average age 32. Expenses: Contact institution. *Financial support:* Research assistantships, teaching assistantships, career-related internships or fieldwork, Federal Work-Study, institutionally sponsored loans, and scholarships/grants available. Support available to part-time students. Financial award application deadline: 5/1. In 2001, 168 degrees awarded. *Degree program information:* Part-time and evening/weekend programs available. Offers biological sciences (MS); chemistry (MS); computer engineering (MS); computer information systems (MA); computer science (MS); environmental science (MS); mathematical sciences (MS); natural and applied sciences (MA, MS); physical science (MS); software engineering (MS); statistics (MS). *Application deadline:* For fall admission, 8/1; for spring admission, 12/1. Applications are processed on a rolling basis. *Application fee:* $30 ($70 for international students). *Application Contact:* Dr. Robert Ferebee, Associate Dean, 281-283-3700, Fax: 281-283-3707, E-mail: ferebee@cl.uh.edu. *Dean,* Dr. Charles McKay, 281-283-3703, Fax: 281-283-3707, E-mail: mckay@uhcl4.cl.uh.edu.

See in-depth description on page 1181.

UNIVERSITY OF HOUSTON–VICTORIA, Victoria, TX 77901-4450

General Information State-supported, coed, upper-level institution. *Enrollment:* 202 full-time matriculated graduate/professional students (127 women), 833 part-time matriculated graduate/professional students (545 women). *Enrollment by degree level:* 1,035 master's. *Graduate faculty:* 48 full-time (18 women). Tuition, state resident: full-time $1,368; part-time $76 per semester. Tuition, nonresident: full-time $4,554. Tuition and fees vary according to course load. *Graduate housing:* On-campus housing not available. *Student services:* Campus employment opportunities, career counseling, international student services. *Library facilities:* VC/UHV Library plus 1 other. *Online resources:* library catalog, web page, access to other libraries' catalogs. *Collection:* 202,484 titles, 1,051 serial subscriptions, 7,477 audiovisual materials.

Computer facilities: 150 computers available on campus for general student use. A campuswide network can be accessed from off campus. Internet access and online class registration are available. *Web address:* http://www.vic.uh.edu/.

General Application Contact: Minnie Urbano, Enrollment Management and Recruitment Coordinator, 361-570-4135, E-mail: murbanom@jade.vic.uh.edu.

GRADUATE UNITS

School of Arts and Sciences Students: 26 full-time (19 women), 57 part-time (41 women); includes 23 minority (5 African Americans, 9 Asian Americans or Pacific Islanders, 9 Hispanic Americans), 1 international. Average age 37. *Faculty:* 13 full-time (4 women). Expenses: Contact institution. *Financial support:* In 2001–02, research assistantships with partial tuition reimbursements (averaging $2,000 per year), teaching assistantships with partial tuition reimbursements (averaging $2,000 per year) were awarded. Career-related internships or fieldwork and Federal Work-Study also available. Support available to part-time students. Financial award application deadline: 4/15. In 2001, 18 degrees awarded. *Degree program information:* Part-time and evening/weekend programs available. Postbaccalaureate distance learning degree programs offered (no on-campus study). Offers arts and sciences (MA, MAIS); interdisciplinary studies (MAIS); psychology (MA). *Application deadline:* Applications are processed on a rolling basis. *Application fee:* $0. *Dean,* Dr. Dan Jaeckle, 361-570-4200, Fax: 351-570-4229, E-mail: jaeckled@cobalt.vic.uh.edu.

School of Business Administration Students: 124 full-time (65 women), 419 part-time (209 women); includes 294 minority (107 African Americans, 136 Asian Americans or Pacific Islanders, 51 Hispanic Americans), 3 international. Average age 33. *Faculty:* 17 full-time (2 women). Expenses: Contact institution. *Financial support:* In 2001–02, research assistantships with partial tuition reimbursements (averaging $2,000 per year), teaching assistantships with partial tuition reimbursements (averaging $2,000 per year) were awarded. Career-related internships or fieldwork and Federal Work-Study also available. Support available to part-time students. Financial award application deadline: 4/15. In 2001, 59 degrees awarded. *Degree program information:* Part-time and evening/weekend programs available. Postbaccalaureate distance learning degree programs offered (no on-campus study). Offers business administration (MBA). *Application deadline:* Applications are processed on a rolling basis. *Application fee:* $0. *Dean,* Charles Bullock, 361-570-4230, Fax: 361-570-4229, E-mail: bullockc@cobalt.vic.uh.edu.

School of Education Students: 51 full-time (42 women), 358 part-time (296 women); includes 136 minority (80 African Americans, 44 Hispanic Americans, 12 Native Americans), 1 international. Average age 38. *Faculty:* 18 full-time (12 women). Expenses: Contact institution. *Financial support:* In 2001–02, research assistantships with partial tuition reimbursements (averaging $2,000 per year), teaching assistantships with partial tuition reimbursements (averaging $2,000 per year) were awarded. Career-related internships or fieldwork and Federal Work-Study also available. Support available to part-time students. Financial award application deadline: 4/15. In 2001, 84 degrees awarded. *Degree program information:* Part-time and evening/weekend programs available. Postbaccalaureate distance learning degree programs offered (no on-campus study). Offers education (M Ed). *Application deadline:* Applications are processed on a rolling basis. *Application fee:* $0. *Dean,* Dr. Mary Natividad, 361-570-4260, Fax: 361-570-4257.

UNIVERSITY OF IDAHO, Moscow, ID 83844-2282

General Information State-supported, coed, university. CGS member. *Enrollment:* 1,163 full-time matriculated graduate/professional students (469 women), 1,240 part-time matriculated graduate/professional students (573 women). *Enrollment by degree level:* 302 first professional, 1,633 master's, 423 doctoral, 45 other advanced degrees. *Graduate faculty:* 599. Tuition, state resident: full-time $1,613. Tuition, nonresident: full-time $3,000. *Graduate housing:* Rooms and/or apartments available on a first-come, first-served basis to single and married students. *Student services:* Campus employment opportunities, campus safety program, career counseling, child daycare facilities, disabled student services, exercise/wellness program, free psychological counseling, grant writing training, international student services, low-cost health insurance, multicultural affairs office, writing training. *Library facilities:* University of Idaho Library plus 1 other. *Online resources:* library catalog, web page, access to other libraries' catalogs. *Collection:* 1.4 million titles, 14,230 serial subscriptions, 8,717 audiovisual materials. *Research affiliation:* Inland Northwest Research Alliance (INRA), Idaho Nuclear Environmental Engineering Laboratory, Battelle Pacific Northwest Laboratories, Snake River Conservation Research Center, Idaho Research Foundation, Idaho Mining and Materials Resources Research Institute.

Computer facilities: 750 computers available on campus for general student use. A campuswide network can be accessed from student residence rooms and from off campus. Internet access and online class registration are available. *Web address:* http://www.its.uidaho.edu/uihome/.

General Application Contact: Dr. Roger P. Wallins, Associate Dean of the College of Graduate Studies, 208-885-6243, Fax: 208-885-6198, E-mail: uigrad@uidaho.edu.

GRADUATE UNITS

College of Graduate Studies Students: 888 full-time (377 women), 1,229 part-time (572 women); includes 107 minority (7 African Americans, 39 Asian Americans or Pacific Islanders, 43 Hispanic Americans, 18 Native Americans), 275 international. Average age 35. 1,475 applicants, 58% accepted. *Faculty:* 718 full-time (193 women), 83 part-time/adjunct (39 women). Expenses: Contact institution. *Financial support:* In 2001–02, 282 research assistantships (averaging $8,968 per year), 319 teaching assistantships (averaging $5,263 per year) were awarded. Fellowships, career-related internships or fieldwork, Federal Work-Study, institutionally sponsored loans, scholarships/grants, and tuition waivers (full and partial) also available. Support available to part-time students. Financial award application deadline: 2/15. In 2001, 464 master's, 79 doctorates, 43 other advanced degrees awarded. *Application deadline:* For fall admission, 8/1; for spring admission, 12/15. Applications are processed on a rolling basis. *Application fee:* $35 ($45 for international students). *Application Contact:* Dr. Roger P. Wallins, Associate Dean, 208-885-6243, Fax: 208-885-6198, E-mail: uigrad@uidaho.edu. *Dean,* Dr. Charles R. Hatch, 208-885-6651, Fax: 208-885-6226, E-mail: crhatch@uidaho.edu.

College of Agriculture Students: 94 full-time (41 women), 49 part-time (18 women); includes 7 minority (3 Asian Americans or Pacific Islanders, 4 Hispanic Americans), 34 international. 126 applicants, 46% accepted. *Faculty:* 69 full-time (13 women). Expenses: Contact institution. *Financial support:* In 2001–02, 52 research assistantships (averaging $10,392 per year), 26 teaching assistantships (averaging $9,897 per year) were awarded. Career-related internships or fieldwork and Federal Work-Study also available. Support available to part-time students. Financial award application deadline: 2/15. In 2001, 38 master's, 11 doctorates awarded. Offers agricultural and extension education (MS); agricultural economics (MS); agriculture (M Engr, MS, PhD); animal physiology (PhD); biochemistry (MS, PhD); biological and agricultural engineering (M Engr, MS, PhD); entomology (MS, PhD); food science (MS); home economics (MS); microbiology (MS, PhD); microbiology, molecular biology and biochemistry (MS, PhD); plant protection (MS, PhD); plant science (MS, PhD); soil science (MS, PhD); veterinary science (MS). *Application deadline:* For fall admission, 8/1; for spring admission, 12/15. *Application fee:* $35 ($45 for international students). *Dean,* Dr. Larry Branen, 208-885-6681.

College of Art and Architecture Students: 62 full-time (20 women), 8 part-time (6 women); includes 7 minority (4 Asian Americans or Pacific Islanders, 3 Hispanic Americans), 3 international. 81 applicants, 68% accepted. *Faculty:* 26 full-time (8 women), 17 part-time/adjunct (9 women). Expenses: Contact institution. *Financial support:* In 2001–02, 29 teaching assistantships (averaging $2,507 per year) were awarded; research assistantships, Federal Work-Study also available. Support available to part-time students. Financial award application deadline: 2/15. In 2001, 46 degrees awarded. Offers architecture (M Arch, MA); art (MFA); art and architecture (M Arch, MA, MAT, MFA, MS); art education (MAT); landscape architecture (MS). *Application deadline:* For fall admission, 8/1; for spring admission, 12/15. *Application fee:* $35 ($45 for international students). *Application Contact:* Glenda Gardiner, Management Assistant, 208-885-7963, Fax: 208-885-9428, E-mail: art_arch@uidaho.edu.

College of Business and Economics Students: 18 full-time (10 women), 7 part-time (3 women), 13 international. 33 applicants, 70% accepted. *Faculty:* 12 full-time (3 women), 2 part-time/adjunct (1 woman). Expenses: Contact institution. *Financial support:* In 2001–02, 5 teaching assistantships (averaging $4,802 per year) were awarded; research assistantships, Federal Work-Study and scholarships/grants also available. Support available to part-time students. Financial award application deadline: 2/15. In 2001, 7 degrees awarded. Offers accounting (M Acct); business and economics (M Acct, MS); economics (MS). *Application deadline:* For fall admission, 8/1; for spring admission, 12/15. *Application fee:* $35 ($45 for international students). *Dean,* Dr. Byron Dangerfield, 208-885-6478.

College of Education Students: 179 full-time (104 women), 626 part-time (392 women); includes 43 minority (3 African Americans, 10 Asian Americans or Pacific Islanders, 22 Hispanic Americans, 8 Native Americans), 17 international. 131 applicants, 63% accepted. *Faculty:* 53 full-time (26 women), 4 part-time/adjunct (2 women). Expenses: Contact institution. *Financial support:* In 2001–02, 23 teaching assistantships (averaging $7,861 per year) were awarded; Federal Work-Study also available. Support available to part-time students. Financial award application deadline: 2/15. In 2001, 173 master's, 28 doctorates, 45 other advanced degrees awarded. Offers adult education (M Ed, MS, Ed D, PhD); business education (M Ed); counseling and human services (M Ed, MS, Ed D, PhD, CHSS); education (MAT, Ed D, PhD, Ed S); education administration (M Ed, MS, Ed D, PhD, EAS); educational administration (M Ed); elementary education (M Ed); industrial technology education (M Ed, MS, Ed D, PhD); physical education (M Ed, MS, PhD); professional-technical education (M Ed, Ed D, PhD, Ed Sp PTE); recreation (MS); school psychology (SPS); secondary education (M Ed, MS); special education (M Ed, MS, Sp Ed S); teacher education (MAT, Ed S); vocational education (MS). *Application deadline:* For fall admission, 8/1; for spring admission, 12/15. *Application fee:* $35 ($45 for international students). *Dean,* Dr. Dale Gentry, 208-885-6773.

College of Engineering Students: 106 full-time (28 women), 236 part-time (23 women); includes 26 minority (1 African American, 15 Asian Americans or Pacific Islanders, 7 Hispanic Americans, 3 Native Americans), 91 international. 390 applicants, 57% accepted. *Faculty:* 69 full-time (5 women), 6 part-time/adjunct (1 woman). Expenses: Contact institution. *Financial support:* In 2001–02, 34 research assistantships (averaging $5,157 per year), 38 teaching assistantships (averaging $3,387 per year) were awarded. Fellowships, career-related internships or fieldwork and Federal Work-Study also available. Support available to part-time students. Financial award application deadline: 2/15. In 2001, 55 master's, 4 doctorates awarded. Offers chemical engineering (M Engr, MS, PhD); civil engineering (M Engr, MS, PhD); computer engineering (M Engr, MS); computer science (MS, PhD); electrical engineering (M Engr, MS, PhD); engineering (M Engr, MS, PhD); environmental engineering (M Engr, MS); mechanical engineering (M Engr, MS, PhD); nuclear engineering (M Engr, MS, PhD); systems engineering (M Engr). *Application deadline:* For fall admission, 8/1; for spring admission, 12/15. *Application fee:* $35 ($45 for international students). *Dean,* Dr. David E. Thompson, 208-885-6479.

College of Letters and Science Students: 237 full-time (107 women), 152 part-time (79 women); includes 13 minority (3 African Americans, 4 Asian Americans or Pacific Islanders, 2 Hispanic Americans, 4 Native Americans), 66 international. 340 applicants, 60% accepted. *Faculty:* 171 full-time (52 women), 39 part-time/adjunct (24 women). Expenses: Contact institution. *Financial support:* In 2001–02, 26 research assistantships (averaging $10,095 per year), 138 teaching assistantships (averaging $5,089 per year) were awarded. Fellowships, Federal Work-Study also available. Support available to part-time students. Financial award application deadline: 2/15. In 2001, 78 master's, 21 doctorates awarded. Offers anthropology (MA); biological sciences (M Nat Sci); botany (MS, PhD); chemistry (MS, PhD); chemistry education (MAT); creative writing (MFA); English (MA, MAT); English education (MAT); environmental science (MS); French (MAT); history (MA, PhD); history education (MAT); interdisciplinary studies (MA, MS); letters and science (M Mus, M Nat Sci, MA, MAT, MFA, MPA, MS, PhD); mathematics (MAT, MS, PhD); mathematics education (MAT); music (M Mus, MA); physics (MS, PhD); physics education (MAT); political science (MA, PhD); psychology (MS); public administration (MPA); Spanish (MAT); statistics (MS); teaching English as a second language (MA); theatre arts (MFA); waste management (MS); zoology (MS, PhD). *Application deadline:* For fall admission, 8/1; for spring admission, 12/15. *Application fee:* $35 ($45 for international students). *Dean,* Dr. Kurt O. Olsson, 208-885-7885.

College of Mines and Earth Resources Students: 52 full-time (15 women), 66 part-time (13 women); includes 4 minority (2 Asian Americans or Pacific Islanders, 2 Native Americans), 18 international. 85 applicants, 51% accepted. *Faculty:* 30 full-time (4 women), 2 part-time/adjunct (0 women). Expenses: Contact institution. *Financial support:* In 2001–02, 19 research assistantships (averaging $3,931 per year), 21 teaching assistantships (averaging $2,589 per year) were awarded. Fellowships, career-related internships or fieldwork and Federal Work-Study also available. Support available to part-time students. Financial award application deadline: 2/15. In 2001, 22 master's, 3 doctorates awarded. Offers geography (MS, PhD); geography education (MAT); geological engineering (MS); geology (MS, PhD); geophysics (MS); hydrology (MS); metallurgical engineering (MS, PhD); metallurgy (MS); metallurgy engineering (MS); mines and earth resources (MAT, MS, PhD); mining engineering (MS, PhD); mining engineering: metallurgy (PhD). *Application deadline:* For fall admission, 8/1; for spring admission, 12/15. *Application fee:* $35 ($45 for international students). *Dean,* Dr. Earl H. Bennett, 208-885-6195.

College of Natural Resources Students: 124 full-time (46 women), 85 part-time (38 women); includes 6 minority (1 Asian American or Pacific Islander, 4 Hispanic Americans, 1 Native American), 33 international. 123 applicants, 48% accepted. *Faculty:* 47 full-time (7 women), 3 part-time/adjunct (1 woman). Expenses: Contact institution. *Financial support:* In 2001–02, 66 research assistantships (averaging $10,704 per year), 24 teaching assistantships (averaging $3,792 per year) were awarded. Fellowships, Federal Work-Study also available. Support available to part-time students. Financial award application deadline: 2/15. In 2001, 44 master's, 9 doctorates awarded. Offers fish and wildlife resources (MS); fish, game, and wildlife management (MS); fishery resources (MS, PhD); forest products (MS, PhD); forest resources (MS, PhD); forestry, wildlife, and range sciences (PhD); fsh, game, and wildlife management (PhD); natural resource management (MS, PhD); range science (MS, PhD); rangeland ecology and management (MS, PhD); recreation and park management (MS, PhD); wildlife resources (MS, PhD). *Application deadline:* For fall admission, 8/1; for spring admission, 12/15. *Application fee:* $35 ($45 for international students). *Application Contact:* Dr. Ali Moslemi, Graduate Coordinator, 208-885-6126. *Dean,* 208-885-6442, Fax: 208-885-6226.

College of Law Students: 275 full-time (92 women), 11 part-time (1 woman); includes 17 minority (2 African Americans, 6 Asian Americans or Pacific Islanders, 6 Hispanic Americans, 3 Native Americans) Average age 29. 464 applicants, 64% accepted. *Faculty:* 16 full-time (7 women), 1 part-time/adjunct (0 women). Expenses: Contact institution. *Financial support:* Career-related internships or fieldwork, Federal Work-Study, and institutionally sponsored loans available. Financial award application deadline: 2/15. In 2001, 100 degrees awarded. Offers law (JD). *Application deadline:* For fall admission, 2/1. *Application fee:* $35 ($45 for international students). *Dean,* John A. Miller, 208-885-6208.

See in-depth description on page 1183.

UNIVERSITY OF ILLINOIS AT CHICAGO, Chicago, IL 60607-7128

General Information State-supported, coed, university. CGS member. *Enrollment:* 5,405 full-time matriculated graduate/professional students, 2,738 part-time matriculated graduate/professional students. *Graduate faculty:* 1,319 full-time (326 women), 94 part-time/adjunct (15 women). Tuition, state resident: full-time $3,060. Tuition, nonresident: full-time $6,688. *Graduate housing:* Room and/or apartments available on a first-come, first-served basis to single

University of Illinois at Chicago (continued)

students; on-campus housing not available to married students. Typical cost: $4,654 per year ($6,258 including board). Housing application deadline: 3/1. *Student services:* Campus employment opportunities, campus safety program, career counseling, child daycare facilities, disabled student services, exercise/wellness program, free psychological counseling, international student services, low-cost health insurance, multicultural affairs office, writing training. *Library facilities:* University Library plus 8 others. *Online resources:* library catalog, web page, access to other libraries' catalogs. *Collection:* 2.1 million titles, 20,875 serial subscriptions, 27,856 audiovisual materials. *Research affiliation:* U.S. Department of Energy National Laboratories (physics, environment, computational science), National Surgical Adjuvant Breast and Bowel Project (prevention of breast cancer), Chicago Manufacturing Technology Extension Center (manufacturing research and development, industrial research), Eastern Cooperative Oncology Group (clinical cancer research).

Computer facilities: 600 computers available on campus for general student use. A campuswide network can be accessed from student residence rooms and from off campus. *Web address:* http://www.uic.edu/.

General Application Contact: Jackie Perry, Graduate College Receptionist, 312-413-2550, Fax: 312-413-0185, E-mail: gradcoll@uic.edu.

GRADUATE UNITS

College of Dentistry Students: 306 full-time (105 women), 2 part-time; includes 83 minority (4 African Americans, 64 Asian Americans or Pacific Islanders, 14 Hispanic Americans, 1 Native American), 19 international. 1,565 applicants, 8% accepted. Expenses: Contact institution. *Financial support:* Fellowships, research assistantships, teaching assistantships available. In 2001, 71 first professional degrees, 8 master's awarded. Offers dentistry (DDS, MS); oral sciences (MS). *Application fee:* $40 ($50 for international students). *Acting Dean*, Dale W. Eisenmann, 312-996-1040, Fax: 312-996-1022.

College of Medicine Students: 1,318 full-time (527 women), 20 part-time (8 women); includes 674 minority (117 African Americans, 409 Asian Americans or Pacific Islanders, 140 Hispanic Americans, 8 Native Americans) 6,895 applicants, 5% accepted. Expenses: Contact institution. *Financial support:* Fellowships, research assistantships, teaching assistantships, career-related internships or fieldwork, institutionally sponsored loans, and tuition waivers (full) available. In 2001, 297 first professional degrees, 12 master's, 25 doctorates awarded. *Degree program information:* Part-time programs available. Offers anatomy and cell biology (MS, PhD); biochemistry and molecular biology (MS, PhD); genetics (PhD); health professions education (MHPE); medicine (MD, MHPE, MS, PhD); microbiology and immunology (PhD); molecular genetics (PhD); pathology (MS, PhD); pharmacology (PhD); physiology and biophysics (MS, PhD); surgery (MS). *Application fee:* $40 ($50 for international students). *Dean*, Gerald S. Moss, 312-996-3500.

College of Pharmacy Students: 729 full-time (507 women), 51 part-time (28 women); includes 348 minority (39 African Americans, 279 Asian Americans or Pacific Islanders, 30 Hispanic Americans), 98 international. Expenses: Contact institution. *Financial support:* Fellowships, research assistantships, teaching assistantships, career-related internships or fieldwork, institutionally sponsored loans, and tuition waivers (full) available. In 2001, 152 first professional degrees, 21 master's, 17 doctorates awarded. Offers forensic science (MS); medicinal chemistry (MS, PhD); pharmaceutics (MS, PhD); pharmacodynamics (MS, PhD); pharmacognosy (MS, PhD); pharmacy (Pharm D, MS, PhD); pharmacy administration (MS, PhD). *Application fee:* $40 ($50 for international students). *Dean*, Rosalie Sagraves, 312-996-7240.

Center for Pharmaceutical Biotechnology Expenses: Contact institution.

Graduate College Students: 3,097 full-time (1,649 women), 2,518 part-time (1,495 women); includes 1,115 minority (429 African Americans, 308 Asian Americans or Pacific Islanders, 368 Hispanic Americans, 10 Native Americans), 1,610 international. Average age 31. 8,356 applicants, 35% accepted, 1638 enrolled. *Faculty:* 1,319 full-time (326 women), 94 part-time/adjunct (15 women). Expenses: Contact institution. *Financial support:* In 2001–02, 2,152 students received support; fellowships with full tuition reimbursements available, research assistantships with full tuition reimbursements available, teaching assistantships with full tuition reimbursements available, career-related internships or fieldwork, Federal Work-Study, institutionally sponsored loans, traineeships, tuition waivers (full and partial), and unspecified assistantships available. Support available to part-time students. Financial award application deadline: 3/1; financial award applicants required to submit FAFSA. In 2001, 1,597 master's, 195 doctorates awarded. *Degree program information:* Part-time and evening/weekend programs available. Offers neuroscience (PhD). *Application deadline:* For fall admission, 6/1; for spring admission, 11/1. *Application fee:* $40 ($50 for international students). *Application Contact:* Receptionist, 312-413-2550, E-mail: gradcoll@uic.edu. *Dean*, Dr. Clark Hulse, 312-413-2550.

College of Architecture and Art Students: 221 full-time, 38 part-time; includes 35 minority (9 African Americans, 12 Asian Americans or Pacific Islanders, 13 Hispanic Americans, 1 Native American), 45 international. Average age 23. 562 applicants, 41% accepted, 124 enrolled. *Faculty:* 81 full-time (17 women), 2 part-time/adjunct (0 women). Expenses: Contact institution. *Financial support:* In 2001–02, 126 students received support; fellowships with full tuition reimbursements available, research assistantships with full tuition reimbursements available, teaching assistantships with full tuition reimbursements available, career-related internships or fieldwork, Federal Work-Study, institutionally sponsored loans, and tuition waivers (full) available. Support available to part-time students. Financial award application deadline: 3/1. In 2001, 69 degrees awarded. *Degree program information:* Part-time and evening/weekend programs available. Offers architecture (M Arch); architecture and art (M Arch, MA, MFA, PhD); art history (MA, PhD); art therapy (MA); electronic visualization (MFA); film animation (MFA); graphic design (MFA); industrial design (MFA); photography (MFA); studio arts (MFA); theatre (MA). *Application deadline:* For fall admission, 6/1; for spring admission, 8/1. Applications are processed on a rolling basis. *Application fee:* $40 ($50 for international students). Electronic applications accepted. *Dean*, Dr. Judith Kirshner, 312-996-5611.

College of Applied Health Sciences Students: 120 full-time (103 women), 104 part-time (76 women); includes 45 minority (10 African Americans, 23 Asian Americans or Pacific Islanders, 10 Hispanic Americans, 2 Native Americans), 30 international. Average age 30. 214 applicants, 50% accepted, 82 enrolled. *Faculty:* 43 full-time (26 women), 8 part-time/adjunct (5 women). Expenses: Contact institution. *Financial support:* In 2001–02, 126 students received support; fellowships with full tuition reimbursements available, research assistantships with full tuition reimbursements available, teaching assistantships with full tuition reimbursements available, career-related internships or fieldwork, Federal Work-Study, institutionally sponsored loans, traineeships, and tuition waivers (full and partial) available. Financial award application deadline: 3/1; financial award applicants required to submit FAFSA. In 2001, 64 master's, 2 doctorates awarded. *Degree program information:* Part-time programs available. Offers associated health professions (MAMS, MS, PhD); biomedical visualization (MAMS); disability and human development (MS); disability studies (PhD); human nutrition and dietetics (MS, PhD); kinesiology (MS); medical laboratory sciences (MS); occupational therapy (MS); physical therapy (MS). *Application deadline:* For fall admission, 6/1. Applications are processed on a rolling basis. *Application fee:* $40 ($50 for international students). Electronic applications accepted. *Dean*, 312-996-6697.

College of Business Administration Students: 410 full-time (195 women), 285 part-time (113 women); includes 124 minority (37 African Americans, 57 Asian Americans or Pacific Islanders, 29 Hispanic Americans, 1 Native American), 283 international. Average age 30. 1,083 applicants, 48% accepted, 256 enrolled. *Faculty:* 82 full-time (18 women), 39 part-time/adjunct (5 women). Expenses: Contact institution. *Financial support:* In 2001–02, 150 students received support; fellowships with full tuition reimbursements available, research assistantships with full tuition reimbursements available, teaching assistantships with full tuition reimbursements available, career-related internships or fieldwork, Federal Work-Study, institutionally sponsored loans, and tuition waivers (full) available. Support available to part-time students. Financial award application deadline: 3/1; financial award applicants required to submit FAFSA. In 2001, 359 master's, 9 doctorates awarded. *Degree program information:* Part-time and evening/weekend programs available. Offers accounting (MS); business administration (MBA); business economics (PhD); economics (MA, PhD); finance (PhD); human resource management (PhD); human resources management (PhD); management information systems (MS, PhD); marketing (PhD); public policy analysis (PhD). *Application deadline:* For fall admission, 6/1; for spring admission, 11/1. Electronic applications accepted. *Acting Dean*, Wim Wiewiel, 312-996-2671, E-mail: wim@uic.edu.

College of Education Students: 137 full-time (101 women), 437 part-time (345 women); includes 199 minority (61 African Americans, 25 Asian Americans or Pacific Islanders, 113 Hispanic Americans), 10 international. Average age 30. 376 applicants, 56% accepted, 125 enrolled. *Faculty:* 39 full-time (14 women). Expenses: Contact institution. *Financial support:* In 2001–02, 73 students received support; fellowships with full tuition reimbursements available, research assistantships with full tuition reimbursements available, teaching assistantships with full tuition reimbursements available, career-related internships or fieldwork, institutionally sponsored loans, traineeships, and tuition waivers (full) available. Financial award application deadline: 3/1; financial award applicants required to submit FAFSA. In 2001, 172 master's, 14 doctorates awarded. *Degree program information:* Part-time and evening/weekend programs available. Offers curriculum and instruction (PhD); education (M Ed, PhD); educational policy and administration (PhD); instructional leadership (M Ed); leadership and administration (M Ed); special education (M Ed, PhD). *Application deadline:* For fall admission, 6/1. Applications are processed on a rolling basis. *Application fee:* $40 ($50 for international students). Electronic applications accepted. *Dean*, Connie Bridge, 312-413-2405.

College of Engineering Students: 547 full-time (128 women), 400 part-time (80 women); includes 111 minority (26 African Americans, 67 Asian Americans or Pacific Islanders, 18 Hispanic Americans), 615 international. Average age 27. 2,584 applicants, 23% accepted, 263 enrolled. *Faculty:* 85 full-time (1 woman). Expenses: Contact institution. *Financial support:* In 2001–02, 469 students received support; fellowships with full tuition reimbursements available, research assistantships with full tuition reimbursements available, teaching assistantships with full tuition reimbursements available, career-related internships or fieldwork, Federal Work-Study, and tuition waivers (full) available. Financial award application deadline: 3/1; financial award applicants required to submit FAFSA. In 2001, 244 master's, 31 doctorates awarded. *Degree program information:* Part-time and evening/weekend programs available. Offers bioengineering (MS, PhD); chemical engineering (MS, PhD); civil and materials engineering (MS, PhD); computer science and engineering (MS, PhD); electrical engineering (MS, PhD); engineering (MS, PhD); industrial engineering (MS); industrial engineering and operations research (PhD); mechanical engineering (MS, PhD). *Application deadline:* For fall admission, 6/1. Applications are processed on a rolling basis. *Application fee:* $40 ($50 for international students). Electronic applications accepted. *Dean*, Lawrence A. Kennedy, 312-996-2400.

College of Liberal Arts and Sciences Students: 792 full-time (384 women), 421 part-time (229 women); includes 190 minority (65 African Americans, 51 Asian Americans or Pacific Islanders, 71 Hispanic Americans, 3 Native Americans), 339 international. Average age 31. 1,474 applicants, 35% accepted, 291 enrolled. Expenses: Contact institution. *Financial support:* In 2001–02, 770 students received support; fellowships with full tuition reimbursements available, research assistantships with full tuition reimbursements available, teaching assistantships with full tuition reimbursements available, career-related internships or fieldwork, Federal Work-Study, institutionally sponsored loans, traineeships, and tuition waivers (full) available. Support available to part-time students. Financial award application deadline: 3/1; financial award applicants required to submit FAFSA. In 2001, 247 master's, 66 doctorates awarded. *Degree program information:* Part-time and evening/weekend programs available. Offers anthropology (MA, PhD); applied linguistics (teaching English as a second language) (MA); applied mathematics (MS, DA, PhD); cell and developmental biology (PhD); chemistry (MS, PhD); communication (MA); computer science (MS, DA, PhD); criminal justice (MA); crystallography (MS, PhD); ecology and evolution (MS, DA, PhD); English (MA, PhD); environmental and urban geography (MA); environmental geology (MS, PhD); environmental studies (MA); French (MA); genetics and development (PhD); geochemistry (MS, PhD); geology (MS, PhD); geomorphology (MS, PhD); geophysics (MS, PhD); geotechnical engineering and geosciences (PhD); Germanic studies (MA, PhD); Hispanic studies (MA, PhD); history (MA, MAT, PhD); hydrogeology (MS, PhD); language, literacy, and rhetoric (PhD); liberal arts and sciences (MA, MAT, MS, MST, DA, PhD); linguistics (MA); low-temperature and organic geochemistry (MS, PhD); mass communication (MA); mineralogy (MS, PhD); molecular biology (MS, PhD); neurobiology (MS, PhD); paleoclimatology (MS, PhD); paleontology (MS, PhD); petrology (MS, PhD); philosophy (MA, PhD); physics (MS, PhD); plant biology (MS, DA, PhD); political science (MA); probability and statistics (MS, DA, PhD); psychology (PhD); public policy analysis (PhD); pure mathematics (MS, DA, PhD); quaternary geology (MS, PhD); sedimentology (MS, PhD); Slavic languages and literatures (PhD); Slavic studies (MA); sociology (MA, PhD); teaching of mathematics (MST); urban geography (MA); water resources (MS, PhD). *Application deadline:* For fall admission, 6/1; for spring admission, 11/1. Applications are processed on a rolling basis. *Application fee:* $40 ($50 for international students). Electronic applications accepted. *Dean*, Stanley Fish.

College of Nursing Students: 86 full-time (83 women), 247 part-time (237 women); includes 47 minority (14 African Americans, 20 Asian Americans or Pacific Islanders, 13 Hispanic Americans), 18 international. Average age 38. 167 applicants, 66% accepted, 86 enrolled. *Faculty:* 63 full-time (61 women), 9 part-time/adjunct (8 women). Expenses: Contact institution. *Financial support:* In 2001–02, 46 students received support; fellowships with full tuition reimbursements available, research assistantships with full tuition reimbursements available, teaching assistantships with full tuition reimbursements available, career-related internships or fieldwork, Federal Work-Study, institutionally sponsored loans, traineeships, and tuition waivers (full and partial) available. Financial award application deadline: 3/1; financial award applicants required to submit FAFSA. In 2001, 93 master's, 6 doctorates awarded. *Degree program information:* Part-time programs available. Offers maternity nursing/nurse midwifery (MS); medical-surgical nursing (MS); mental health nursing (MS); nursing (MS, PhD); nursing administration studies (MS); nursing research (PhD); pediatric nursing (MS); perinatal nursing (MS); public health nursing (MS). *Application deadline:* For fall admission, 5/15; for spring admission, 10/15. *Application fee:* $40 ($50 for international students). Electronic applications accepted. *Application Contact:* Kathleen Knafl, Director of Graduate Studies, 312-996-2159. *Dean*, Dr. Joyce Johnson, 312-996-7924, E-mail: joycej@uic.edu.

College of Urban Planning and Public Affairs Students: 106 full-time (59 women), 157 part-time (81 women); includes 86 minority (51 African Americans, 7 Asian Americans or Pacific Islanders, 28 Hispanic Americans), 21 international. Average age 33. 255 applicants, 53% accepted, 83 enrolled. Expenses: Contact institution. *Financial support:* In 2001–02, 70 students received support; fellowships with full tuition reimbursements available, research assistantships with full tuition reimbursements available, teaching assistantships with full tuition reimbursements available, career-related internships or fieldwork, Federal Work-Study, and tuition waivers (full) available. Financial award application deadline: 3/1; financial award applicants required to submit FAFSA. In 2001, 64 master's, 6 doctorates awarded. *Degree program information:* Part-time and evening/weekend programs available. Offers public administration (MPA, PhD); public policy analysis (PhD); urban planning and policy (MUPP); urban planning and public affairs (MPA, MUPP, PhD). *Application deadline:* For fall admission, 6/1; for spring admission, 11/1. Applications are processed on a rolling basis. *Application fee:* $40 ($50 for international students). Electronic applications accepted. *Acting Dean*, Wim Wiewiel, 312-996-2671, E-mail: wim@uic.edu.

Jane Addams College of Social Work Students: 299 full-time (253 women), 225 part-time (191 women); includes 194 minority (126 African Americans, 21 Asian Americans or Pacific Islanders, 46 Hispanic Americans, 1 Native American), 4 international. Average age 32. 626 applicants, 38% accepted, 206 enrolled. *Faculty:* 28 full-time (15 women). Expenses: Contact institution. *Financial support:* In 2001–02, 44 students received support; fellowships with full tuition reimbursements available, research assistantships with full tuition reimbursements available, teaching assistantships with full tuition reimbursements available, Federal Work-Study and tuition waivers (full) available. Financial award applicants required to submit FAFSA. In 2001, 212 master's, 7 doctorates awarded. *Degree program information:* Part-time programs available. Offers social work (MSW, PhD). *Application deadline:* For fall admission, 2/1. *Application fee:* $40 ($50 for international students).

Electronic applications accepted. *Application Contact:* Barbara Bergstrom, Director of Admissions, 312-996-3218. *Dean,* C. F. Hairston, 312-996-3219.

School of Public Health Students: 50 full-time (40 women), 81 part-time (55 women); includes 31 minority (11 African Americans, 10 Asian Americans or Pacific Islanders, 10 Hispanic Americans), 31 international. Average age 35. 146 applicants, 29% accepted, 21 enrolled. *Faculty:* 46 full-time (13 women), 4 part-time/adjunct (0 women). Expenses: Contact institution. *Financial support:* In 2001–02, 54 students received support; fellowships with full tuition reimbursements available, research assistantships with full tuition reimbursements available, teaching assistantships with full tuition reimbursements available, career-related internships or fieldwork, Federal Work-Study, institutionally sponsored loans, traineeships, and tuition waivers (full) available. Support available to part-time students. Financial award application deadline: 3/1; financial award applicants required to submit FAFSA. In 2001, 18 master's, 9 doctorates awarded. *Degree program information:* Part-time programs available. Offers biostatistics (MS, PhD); community health sciences (MPH, MS, Dr PH, PhD); environmental and occupational health sciences (MPH, MS, Dr PH, PhD); epidemiology and biostatistics (MPH, MS, Dr PH, PhD); health resources management (MPH, MS, Dr PH, PhD). *Application deadline:* For fall admission, 6/1; for spring admission, 11/1. *Application fee:* $40 ($50 for international students). Electronic applications accepted. *Application Contact:* Dr. Sylvia Furner, Director of Graduate Studies, 312-996-9849. *Dean,* Dr. Susan Scrimshaw, 312-996-6620.

UNIVERSITY OF ILLINOIS AT SPRINGFIELD, Springfield, IL 62703-5404

General Information State-supported, coed, upper-level institution. CGS member. *Enrollment:* 406 full-time matriculated graduate/professional students (225 women), 1,582 part-time matriculated graduate/professional students (899 women). *Enrollment by degree level:* 1,547 master's, 24 doctoral. *Graduate faculty:* 170 full-time (66 women), 82 part-time/adjunct (36 women). Tuition, state resident: full-time $2,680. Tuition, nonresident: full-time $8,064. *Required fees:* $626. One-time fee: $626. *Graduate housing:* Rooms and/or apartments available to single and married students. Typical cost: $2,720 per year for single students; $2,720 per year for married students. Housing application deadline: 7/15. *Student services:* Campus employment opportunities, campus safety program, career counseling, child daycare facilities, exercise/wellness program, free psychological counseling, international student services, low-cost health insurance. *Library facilities:* Brookens Library. *Online resources:* library catalog, web page. *Collection:* 39,536 audiovisual materials. *Research affiliation:* Interuniversity Consortium for Political and Social Research, Illinois Vocational Curriculum Center/East Central Network for Curriculum Coordination, Convocom (interactive telecommunications network), Springfield Project–Communication Outreach–Partner Center (education–social services).

Computer facilities: 160 computers available on campus for general student use. A campuswide network can be accessed from student residence rooms and from off campus. Internet access is available. *Web address:* http://www.uis.edu/.

General Application Contact: 217-206-6626, Fax: 217-206-6720.

GRADUATE UNITS

Graduate Programs Students: 406 full-time (225 women), 1,582 part-time (899 women); includes 245 minority (168 African Americans, 42 Asian Americans or Pacific Islanders, 30 Hispanic Americans, 5 Native Americans), 149 international. Average age 35. 1,117 applicants, 78% accepted, 476 enrolled. *Faculty:* 108 full-time (35 women), 56 part-time/adjunct (20 women). Expenses: Contact institution. *Financial support:* In 2001–02, 629 students received support, including fellowships with full and partial tuition reimbursements available (averaging $10,000 per year), 142 research assistantships with full and partial tuition reimbursements available (averaging $6,300 per year); career-related internships or fieldwork, Federal Work-Study, scholarships/grants, tuition waivers (partial), and unspecified assistantships also available. Support available to part-time students. Financial award application deadline: 6/1; financial award applicants required to submit FAFSA. In 2001, 350 degrees awarded. *Degree program information:* Part-time and evening/weekend programs available. *Application deadline:* Applications are processed on a rolling basis. *Application fee:* $0. *Provost/Vice Chancellor for Academic Affairs,* Dr. Michael Charey, 217-206-6614.

College of Business and Management Students: 105 full-time (50 women), 297 part-time (124 women); includes 48 minority (24 African Americans, 17 Asian Americans or Pacific Islanders, 7 Hispanic Americans), 48 international. Average age 34. 277 applicants, 73% accepted, 112 enrolled. *Faculty:* 26 full-time (6 women), 11 part-time/adjunct (1 woman). Expenses: Contact institution. *Financial support:* In 2001–02, 111 students received support, including 18 research assistantships (averaging $6,300 per year); career-related internships or fieldwork, Federal Work-Study, scholarships/grants, tuition waivers (partial), and unspecified assistantships also available. Support available to part-time students. Financial award application deadline: 6/1; financial award applicants required to submit FAFSA. In 2001, 58 degrees awarded. *Degree program information:* Part-time and evening/weekend programs available. Offers accountancy (MA); business administration (MBA); business and management (MA, MBA); economics (MA); management information systems (MA). *Application deadline:* Applications are processed on a rolling basis. *Application fee:* $0. *Dean,* Dr. Paul McDevitt, 217-206-6534.

College of Education and Human Services Students: 61 full-time (45 women), 391 part-time (281 women); includes 51 minority (45 African Americans, 2 Asian Americans or Pacific Islanders, 3 Hispanic Americans, 1 Native American), 2 international. Average age 49. 243 applicants, 93% accepted, 150 enrolled. *Faculty:* 18 full-time (7 women), 12 part-time/adjunct (8 women). Expenses: Contact institution. *Financial support:* In 2001–02, 116 students received support, including 14 research assistantships with full and partial tuition reimbursements available (averaging $6,300 per year); career-related internships or fieldwork, Federal Work-Study, scholarships/grants, tuition waivers (partial), and unspecified assistantships also available. Support available to part-time students. Financial award application deadline: 6/1; financial award applicants required to submit FAFSA. In 2001, 63 degrees awarded. *Degree program information:* Part-time and evening/weekend programs available. Offers alcoholism and substance abuse (MA); child and family studies (MA); education and human services (MA, MPH); educational leadership (MA); gerontology (MA); human development counseling (MA); social services administration (MA). *Application deadline:* Applications are processed on a rolling basis. *Application fee:* $0. *Dean,* Dr. Larry Stonecipher, 217-206-7815.

College of Liberal Arts and Sciences Students: 115 full-time (52 women), 282 part-time (153 women); includes 32 minority (15 African Americans, 8 Asian Americans or Pacific Islanders, 7 Hispanic Americans, 2 Native Americans), 74 international. Average age 35. 326 applicants, 72% accepted, 107 enrolled. *Faculty:* 34 full-time (13 women), 17 part-time/adjunct (7 women). Expenses: Contact institution. *Financial support:* In 2001–02, 200 students received support, including 60 research assistantships with full and partial tuition reimbursements available (averaging $6,300 per year); career-related internships or fieldwork, Federal Work-Study, scholarships/grants, tuition waivers (partial), and unspecified assistantships also available. Support available to part-time students. Financial award application deadline: 6/1; financial award applicants required to submit FAFSA. In 2001, 101 degrees awarded. *Degree program information:* Part-time and evening/weekend programs available. Offers arts and sciences (MA); biology (MA); communication (MA); computer science (MA); English (MA); individual option (MA); public history (MA). *Application deadline:* Applications are processed on a rolling basis. *Application fee:* $0. *Dean,* William Bloemer, 217-206-6512.

College of Public Affairs and Administration Students: 113 full-time (72 women), 232 part-time (128 women); includes 65 minority (54 African Americans, 6 Asian Americans or Pacific Islanders, 4 Hispanic Americans, 1 Native American), 19 international. Average age 36. 271 applicants, 76% accepted, 107 enrolled. *Faculty:* 30 full-time (9 women), 16 part-time/adjunct (4 women). Expenses: Contact institution. *Financial support:* In 2001–02, 190 students received support, including 50 research assistantships with full and partial tuition reimbursements available (averaging $6,300 per year); career-related internships or fieldwork, Federal Work-Study, scholarships/grants, tuition waivers (partial), and unspecified assistantships also available. Support available to part-time students. Financial award application deadline: 6/1; financial award applicants required to submit FAFSA. In 2001, 128 degrees awarded. *Degree program information:* Part-time and evening/weekend programs available. Offers environmental studies (MA); legal studies (MA); political studies (MA); public administration (MPA, DPA); public affairs and administration (MA, MPA, MPH, DPA); public affairs reporting (MA); public health (MPH). *Application deadline:* Applications are processed on a rolling basis. *Application fee:* $0. *Dean,* Glen Cope, 217-206-6523.

See in-depth description on page 1185.

UNIVERSITY OF ILLINOIS AT URBANA–CHAMPAIGN, Champaign, IL 61820

General Information State-supported, coed, university. CGS member. *Enrollment:* 8,109 full-time matriculated graduate/professional students (3,593 women). *Graduate faculty:* 1,727 full-time, 131 part-time/adjunct. Tuition, state resident: part-time $3,227 per degree program. Tuition, nonresident: part-time $7,169 per degree program. Tuition and fees vary according to program. *Graduate housing:* Rooms and/or apartments available to single and married students. *Student services:* Campus employment opportunities, campus safety program, career counseling, disabled student services, exercise/wellness program, free psychological counseling, international student services, low-cost health insurance, multicultural affairs office, teacher training. *Library facilities:* University Library plus 40 others. *Online resources:* library catalog, web page, access to other libraries' catalogs. *Collection:* 9.5 million titles, 90,962 serial subscriptions, 868,538 audiovisual materials. *Research affiliation:* National Center for Atmospheric Research, Fermi National Accelerator Laboratory, Sandia National Laboratories, Midwest Universities Research Association.

Computer facilities: 3,000 computers available on campus for general student use. A campuswide network can be accessed from student residence rooms and from off campus. Internet access and online class registration are available. *Web address:* http://www.uiuc.edu/.

General Application Contact: Richard Wheeler, Dean, 217-333-6715, Fax: 217-333-8019, E-mail: rpw@uiuc.edu.

GRADUATE UNITS

College of Law Students: 32 full-time (11 women), 30 international. 264 applicants, 14% accepted. *Faculty:* 35 full-time (11 women), 12 part-time/adjunct (9 women). Expenses: Contact institution. *Financial support:* In 2001–02, 1 fellowship, 1 research assistantship were awarded. Teaching assistantships, tuition waivers (full and partial) also available. In 2001, 28 master's, 1 doctorate awarded. Offers law (JD, LL M, MCL, JSD). *Application deadline:* For fall admission, 3/15. Applications are processed on a rolling basis. *Application fee:* $40 ($50 for international students). Electronic applications accepted. *Application Contact:* Maggie Austin, Admissions Director, 217-244-6415, Fax: 217-244-1478, E-mail: maustin@uiuc.edu. *Dean,* Thomas M. Mengler, 217-333-9857, Fax: 217-244-1478, E-mail: tmengler@uiuc.edu.

College of Veterinary Medicine Students: 94 full-time (47 women); includes 5 minority (3 Asian Americans or Pacific Islanders, 2 Hispanic Americans), 30 international. 434 applicants, 32% accepted. *Faculty:* 75 full-time (26 women), 4 part-time/adjunct (3 women). Expenses: Contact institution. *Financial support:* In 2001–02, 48 fellowships, 22 research assistantships, 8 teaching assistantships were awarded. Career-related internships or fieldwork, Federal Work-Study, and tuition waivers (full and partial) also available. In 2001, 10 master's, 8 doctorates awarded. *Degree program information:* Part-time programs available. Postbaccalaureate distance learning degree programs offered (minimal on-campus study). Offers veterinary biosciences (MS, PhD); veterinary clinical medicine (MS, PhD); veterinary medicine (DVM, MS, PhD); veterinary pathobiology (MS, PhD). *Application fee:* $40 ($50 for international students). Electronic applications accepted. *Dean,* Herbert Whiteley, 217-333-2760, Fax: 217-333-4628, E-mail: hwhitele@uiuc.edu.

Graduate College Students: 7,940 full-time (3,518 women); includes 787 minority (243 African Americans, 355 Asian Americans or Pacific Islanders, 176 Hispanic Americans, 13 Native Americans), 3,103 international. ###### applicants, 21% accepted. *Faculty:* 1,772 full-time, 137 part-time/adjunct. Expenses: Contact institution. *Financial support:* In 2001–02, 786 fellowships, 2,769 research assistantships, 2,009 teaching assistantships were awarded. Career-related internships or fieldwork, Federal Work-Study, institutionally sponsored loans, scholarships/grants, traineeships, and tuition waivers (full and partial) also available. Support available to part-time students. Financial award applicants required to submit FAFSA. In 2001, 1,921 master's, 654 doctorates awarded. Postbaccalaureate distance learning degree programs offered. Offers medical scholars). *Application deadline:* Applications are processed on a rolling basis. *Application fee:* $40 ($50 for international students). Electronic applications accepted. *Application Contact:* Lamar Riley Murphy, Assistant Dean, 217-244-9488, Fax: 217-333-8019, E-mail: lmurphy@uiuc.edu. *Dean,* Richard Wheeler, 217-333-6715, Fax: 217-333-8019, E-mail: rpw@uiuc.edu.

College of Agricultural, Consumer and Environmental Sciences Students: 552 full-time (283 women); includes 33 minority (12 African Americans, 9 Asian Americans or Pacific Islanders, 11 Hispanic Americans, 1 Native American), 188 international. 593 applicants, 26% accepted. *Faculty:* 228 full-time, 15 part-time/adjunct. Expenses: Contact institution. *Financial support:* In 2001–02, 87 fellowships, 332 research assistantships, 74 teaching assistantships were awarded. Career-related internships or fieldwork and tuition waivers (full and partial) also available. Financial award application deadline: 2/15. In 2001, 120 master's, 48 doctorates awarded. Offers agricultural and consumer economics (MS, PhD); agricultural engineering (MS, PhD); agricultural, consumer and environmental sciences (AM, MS, PhD); animal sciences (MS, PhD); crop sciences (MS, PhD); extension education (MS); food science and human nutrition (MS, PhD); human and community development (AM, MS, PhD); natural resources and environmental science (MS, PhD); nutritional sciences (MS, PhD). *Application deadline:* Applications are processed on a rolling basis. *Application fee:* $40 ($50 for international students). Electronic applications accepted. *Application Contact:* Rebecca J. McBride, Assistant Dean, 217-333-3380, Fax: 217-244-6537, E-mail: l_foste@uiuc.edu. *Interim Dean,* Robert A. Easter, 217-333-0460, Fax: 217-244-2911, E-mail: r_easter@uiuc.edu.

College of Applied Life Studies Students: 214 full-time (135 women); includes 16 minority (9 African Americans, 3 Asian Americans or Pacific Islanders, 4 Hispanic Americans), 40 international. 367 applicants, 22% accepted. *Faculty:* 45 full-time, 2 part-time/adjunct. Expenses: Contact institution. *Financial support:* In 2001–02, 10 fellowships, 70 research assistantships, 68 teaching assistantships were awarded. Career-related internships or fieldwork, Federal Work-Study, institutionally sponsored loans, and tuition waivers (full and partial) also available. Financial award application deadline: 2/15. In 2001, 72 master's, 19 doctorates awarded. Offers applied life studies (AM, MS, MSPH, MST, PhD); community health (MSPH, PhD); kinesiology (MS, MST, PhD); leisure studies (MS, PhD); rehabilitation (MS); rehabilitation education services (MS); speech and hearing science (AM, MS, PhD). *Application deadline:* Applications are processed on a rolling basis. *Application fee:* $40 ($50 for international students). Electronic applications accepted. *Application Contact:* Sherry Polson, Secretary, 217-333-2131, Fax: 217-333-0404, E-mail: slpolson@uiuc.edu. *Director of Graduate Studies,* Tanya Gallagher, 217-333-2131, Fax: 217-333-0404, E-mail: tmgallag@uiuc.edu.

College of Commerce and Business Administration Students: 631 full-time (236 women); includes 25 minority (2 African Americans, 19 Asian Americans or Pacific Islanders, 3 Hispanic Americans, 1 Native American), 442 international. 657 applicants, 29% accepted. *Faculty:* 116 full-time, 16 part-time/adjunct. Expenses: Contact institution. *Financial support:* In 2001–02, 11 fellowships, 30 research assistantships, 137 teaching assistantships were awarded. Career-related internships or fieldwork and tuition waivers (full and partial) also available. Financial award application deadline: 2/15. In 2001, 191 master's, 36 doctorates awarded. Offers accountancy (MAS, MS, MSA, PhD); business administration (MBA, MSBA, PhD); commerce and business administration (MAS, MBA, MS, MSA, MSBA, PhD); economics (MS, PhD); finance (MS, PhD). *Application deadline:* Applications are processed on a rolling basis. *Application fee:* $40 ($50 for international students). Electronic applications accepted. *Application Contact:* J. E. Miller, Secretary, 217-333-4240, Fax: 217-244-7969, E-mail: j-miller@uiuc.edu. *Dean,* Avijit Ghosh, 217-333-2747, Fax: 217-244-3118, E-mail: ghosha@uiuc.edu.

University of Illinois at Urbana–Champaign (continued)

College of Communications Students: 85 full-time (59 women); includes 15 minority (6 African Americans, 4 Asian Americans or Pacific Islanders, 4 Hispanic Americans, 1 Native American), 28 international. 361 applicants, 10% accepted. *Faculty:* 36 full-time. Expenses: Contact institution. *Financial support:* In 2001–02, 11 fellowships, 30 research assistantships, 35 teaching assistantships were awarded. Career-related internships or fieldwork, Federal Work-Study, institutionally sponsored loans, and tuition waivers (full and partial) also available. In 2001, 32 master's, 1 doctorate awarded. Offers advertising (MS); communications (PhD); journalism (MS). *Application deadline:* Applications are processed on a rolling basis. *Application fee:* $40 ($50 for international students). Electronic applications accepted. *Application Contact:* Rhonda Kornegay, Administrative Aide, 217-333-2350, Fax: 217-333-9882, E-mail: rhonda@uiuc.edu. *Dean,* Kim B. Rotzoll, 217-333-2350, Fax: 217-333-9882, E-mail: krotzoll@uiuc.edu.

College of Education Students: 753 full-time (523 women); includes 142 minority (83 African Americans, 27 Asian Americans or Pacific Islanders, 30 Hispanic Americans, 2 Native Americans), 190 international. 758 applicants, 32% accepted. *Faculty:* 90 full-time, 9 part-time/adjunct. Expenses: Contact institution. *Financial support:* In 2001–02, 123 fellowships, 182 research assistantships, 118 teaching assistantships were awarded. Career-related internships or fieldwork, Federal Work-Study, and tuition waivers (full and partial) also available. In 2001, 173 master's, 72 doctorates awarded. Offers curriculum and instruction (AM, Ed M, MS, Ed D, PhD, AC); education (AM, Ed M, MS, Ed D, PhD, AC); education, organization and leadership (AM, Ed M, MS, Ed D, PhD, AC); educational policy studies (AM, Ed M, MS, Ed D, PhD, AC); educational psychology (AM, Ed M, MS, Ed D, PhD, AC); human resource education (AM, Ed M, MS, Ed D, PhD, AC); special education (AM, Ed M, MS, Ed D, PhD, AC). *Application deadline:* Applications are processed on a rolling basis. *Application fee:* $40 ($50 for international students). Electronic applications accepted. *Application Contact:* Anita Althaus, Administrative Secretary, 217-333-0964, Fax: 217-333-5847, E-mail: aalthaus@uiuc.edu. *Dean,* Susan A. Fowler, 217-333-0960, Fax: 217-333-5847.

College of Engineering Students: 2,069 full-time (323 women); includes 190 minority (11 African Americans, 141 Asian Americans or Pacific Islanders, 33 Hispanic Americans, 5 Native Americans), 1,134 international. 5,093 applicants, 17% accepted. *Faculty:* 360 full-time, 21 part-time/adjunct. Expenses: Contact institution. *Financial support:* In 2001–02, 126 fellowships, 1,215 research assistantships, 395 teaching assistantships were awarded. Federal Work-Study, institutionally sponsored loans, scholarships/grants, and tuition waivers (full and partial) also available. In 2001, 471 master's, 215 doctorates awarded. Postbaccalaureate distance learning degree programs offered. Offers aeronautical and astronautical engineering (MS, PhD); civil engineering (MS, PhD); computer engineering (MS, PhD); computer science (MCS, MS, MST, PhD); electrical engineering (MS, PhD); engineering (MCS, MS, MST, PhD); environmental engineering (MS, PhD); environmental engineering and environmental science (MS, PhD); environmental science (MS, PhD); health physics (MS, PhD); industrial engineering (MS, PhD); materials science and engineering (MS, PhD); mechanical engineering (MS, PhD); nuclear engineering (MS, PhD); physics (MS, PhD); systems engineering and engineering design (MS); theoretical and applied mechanics (MS, PhD). *Application deadline:* Applications are processed on a rolling basis. *Application fee:* $40 ($50 for international students). Electronic applications accepted. *Dean,* Dr. David E. Daniel, 217-333-2150, Fax: 217-333-5847, E-mail: dedaniel@uiuc.edu.

College of Fine and Applied Arts Students: 814 full-time (446 women); includes 70 minority (24 African Americans, 25 Asian Americans or Pacific Islanders, 21 Hispanic Americans), 243 international. 1,201 applicants, 25% accepted. *Faculty:* 176 full-time, 36 part-time/adjunct. Expenses: Contact institution. *Financial support:* In 2001–02, 70 fellowships, 178 research assistantships, 254 teaching assistantships were awarded. Career-related internships or fieldwork and tuition waivers (full and partial) also available. Financial award application deadline: 2/15. In 2001, 178 master's, 29 doctorates awarded. Offers architecture (M Arch); art and design (AM, MFA, Ed D, PhD); art education (AM, Ed D); art history (AM, PhD); dance (AM); fine and applied arts (AM, M Arch, M Mus, MFA, MLA, MS, MUP, DMA, Ed D, PhD); industrial design (MFA); landscape architecture (MLA); music (M Mus, MS, DMA, Ed D, PhD); regional planning (PhD); studio arts (MFA); theatre (AM, MFA, PhD); urban and regional planning (MUP). *Application deadline:* Applications are processed on a rolling basis. *Application fee:* $40 ($50 for international students). Electronic applications accepted. *Dean,* Kathleen F. Conlin, 217-333-1660, Fax: 217-244-8381, E-mail: kconlin@uiuc.edu.

College of Liberal Arts and Sciences Students: 2,098 full-time (958 women); includes 204 minority (41 African Americans, 114 Asian Americans or Pacific Islanders, 47 Hispanic Americans, 2 Native Americans), 764 international. 3,503 applicants, 15% accepted. *Faculty:* 679 full-time, 36 part-time/adjunct. Expenses: Contact institution. *Financial support:* In 2001–02, 249 fellowships, 522 research assistantships, 892 teaching assistantships were awarded. Career-related internships or fieldwork, Federal Work-Study, institutionally sponsored loans, traineeships, and tuition waivers (full and partial) also available. In 2001, 285 master's, 229 doctorates awarded. Offers African studies (AM); animal biology (PhD); anthropology (AM, PhD); applied mathematics (MS); applied measurement (MS); astronomy (MS, PhD); atmospheric science (MS, PhD); biochemistry (MS, PhD); biological psychology (AM, PhD); biophysics and computational biology (PhD); cell and structural biology (PhD); chemical engineering (MS, PhD); chemistry (MS, PhD); classics (AM, PhD); clinical psychology (AM, PhD); cognitive psychology (AM, PhD); comparative literature (AM, MAT, PhD); demography (AM, PhD); developmental psychology (AM, PhD); earth sciences (MS, PhD); East Asian languages and cultures (AM, PhD); ecology and evolutionary biology (PhD); engineering psychology (MS); English (AM, PhD); English as an international language (AM); entomology (MS, PhD); French (AM, MAT, PhD); geochemistry (MS, PhD); geography (AM, MS, PhD); geology (MS, PhD); geophysics (MS, PhD); Germanic languages and literatures (AM, MAT, PhD); history (AM, PhD); insect pest management (MS); integrative biology (MS, PhD); Italian (AM, PhD); Latin American and Caribbean studies (AM); liberal arts and sciences (AM, MAT, MS, PhD); linguistics (AM, PhD); mathematics (MS, PhD); microbiology (MS, PhD); molecular and cellular biology (MS, PhD); molecular and integrative physiology (MS, PhD); neuroscience (PhD); personnel psychology (MS); philosophy (AM, PhD); plant biology (MS, PhD); political science (AM, PhD); quantitative psychology (AM, PhD); Russian (AM, MAT, PhD); Russian and East European studies (AM); Slavic languages and literatures (AM, MAT, PhD); social-personality-organizational (AM, PhD); sociology (AM, PhD); Spanish (MAT); speech communication (AM, MAT, PhD); statistics (MS, PhD); teaching of mathematics (MS); visual cognition and human performance (AM, PhD). *Application fee:* $40 ($50 for international students). Electronic applications accepted. *Dean,* Jesse Delia, 217-333-1350, Fax: 217-333-9142, E-mail: j-delia@uiuc.edu.

Graduate School of Library and Information Science Students: 321 full-time (243 women); includes 22 minority (12 African Americans, 4 Asian Americans or Pacific Islanders, 6 Hispanic Americans), 45 international. Average age 31. 354 applicants, 38% accepted. *Faculty:* 16 full-time, 2 part-time/adjunct. Expenses: Contact institution. *Financial support:* In 2001–02, 38 fellowships, 151 research assistantships, 16 teaching assistantships were awarded. Tuition waivers (full and partial) also available. Financial award application deadline: 2/1. In 2001, 162 master's, 3 doctorates awarded. Offers library and information science (MS, PhD, CAS). *Application deadline:* For fall admission, 6/1 (priority date); for spring admission, 10/1. Applications are processed on a rolling basis. *Application fee:* $40 ($50 for international students). Electronic applications accepted. *Application Contact:* Carol DeVoss, Officer, 217-333-7197, Fax: 217-244-3302, E-mail: devoss@uiuc.edu. *Interim Dean,* Dr. Linda Smith, 217-333-3281, Fax: 217-244-3102, E-mail: lcsmith@uiuc.edu.

Institute of Labor and Industrial Relations Students: 145 full-time (94 women); includes 30 minority (17 African Americans, 8 Asian Americans or Pacific Islanders, 4 Hispanic Americans, 1 Native American), 13 international. Average age 25. 225 applicants, 30% accepted. *Faculty:* 12 full-time. Expenses: Contact institution. *Financial support:* In 2001–02, 36 fellowships, 23 research assistantships, 12 teaching assistantships were awarded. Career-related internships or fieldwork, Federal Work-Study, scholarships/grants, and tuition waivers (full) also available. Support available to part-time students. Financial award application deadline: 2/1. In 2001, 79 degrees awarded. *Degree program information:* Part-time programs available. Offers human resources (MHRIR, PhD); labor and industrial relations (MHRIR, PhD). *Application deadline:* For fall admission, 2/1; for spring admission, 11/1. *Application fee:* $40 ($50 for international students). Electronic applications accepted. *Application Contact:* Elizabeth Barker, Staff Associate, 217-333-2381, Fax: 217-244-9290, E-mail: e-barker@uiuc.edu. *Director,* Dr. Peter Feuille, 217-333-1480, Fax: 217-244-9290, E-mail: feuille@uiuc.edu.

School of Social Work Students: 249 full-time (211 women); includes 39 minority (25 African Americans, 1 Asian American or Pacific Islander, 13 Hispanic Americans), 16 international. 181 applicants, 29% accepted. *Faculty:* 14 full-time. Expenses: Contact institution. *Financial support:* In 2001–02, 25 fellowships, 36 research assistantships, 8 teaching assistantships were awarded. Career-related internships or fieldwork and tuition waivers (full and partial) also available. Financial award application deadline: 2/15. In 2001, 158 master's, 2 doctorates awarded. Offers social work (MSW, PhD). *Application deadline:* For fall admission, 2/1. Applications are processed on a rolling basis. *Application fee:* $40 ($50 for international students). *Application Contact:* Michele Winfrey, Secretary, 217-244-5244, Fax: 217-244-5220, E-mail: mwinfrey@uiuc.edu. *Dean,* Jill Doner Kagle, 217-333-2260, Fax: 217-244-5220, E-mail: j-kagle@uiuc.edu.

UNIVERSITY OF INDIANAPOLIS, Indianapolis, IN 46227-3697

General Information Independent-religious, coed, comprehensive institution. *Enrollment:* 292 full-time matriculated graduate/professional students (202 women), 540 part-time matriculated graduate/professional students (328 women). *Graduate faculty:* 15 full-time (10 women), 79 part-time/adjunct (29 women). *Tuition:* Part-time $260 per credit hour. Tuition and fees vary according to degree level. *Graduate housing:* Rooms and/or apartments available to single and married students. Housing application deadline: 5/15. *Student services:* Campus employment opportunities, career counseling, free psychological counseling, international student services, low-cost health insurance. *Library facilities:* Krannert Memorial Library. *Online resources:* library catalog, web page, access to other libraries' catalogs. *Collection:* 168,247 titles, 1,001 serial subscriptions, 8,152 audiovisual materials. *Research affiliation:* Methodist Hospital of Indiana (head injury in children).

Computer facilities: 218 computers available on campus for general student use. A campuswide network can be accessed from student residence rooms and from off campus. Internet access is available. *Web address:* http://www.uindy.edu/.

General Application Contact: Dr. Mary C. Moore, Associate Provost, 317-788-3390, Fax: 317-788-6152, E-mail: moore@uindy.edu.

GRADUATE UNITS

Graduate School Students: 292 full-time (202 women), 540 part-time (328 women); includes 15 minority (2 African Americans, 12 Asian Americans or Pacific Islanders, 1 Hispanic American), 20 international. Average age 32. 549 applicants, 32% accepted. *Faculty:* 15 full-time (10 women), 79 part-time/adjunct (29 women). Expenses: Contact institution. *Financial support:* Teaching assistantships, career-related internships or fieldwork, Federal Work-Study, tuition waivers (full and partial), and unspecified assistantships available. Financial award application deadline: 5/1; financial award applicants required to submit FAFSA. In 2001, 245 degrees awarded. *Degree program information:* Part-time and evening/weekend programs available. Offers accounting (M Acc); business administration (MBA). *Associate Provost,* Dr. Mary C. Moore, 317-788-3390, Fax: 317-788-6152, E-mail: moore@uindy.edu.

College of Arts and Sciences Students: 14 full-time (11 women), 31 part-time (15 women). *Faculty:* 18. Expenses: Contact institution. *Financial support:* Teaching assistantships, Federal Work-Study available. Financial award application deadline: 5/1; financial award applicants required to submit FAFSA. In 2001, 13 degrees awarded. *Degree program information:* Part-time and evening/weekend programs available. Offers applied sociology (MA); art (MA); arts and sciences (MA, MS); biology (MS); English language and literature (MA); history (MA). *Application deadline:* Applications are processed on a rolling basis. *Application fee:* $30. *Interim Dean,* Dr. David L. Anderson, 317-788-3222, Fax: 317-788-3480, E-mail: anderson@uindy.edu.

Krannert School of Physical Therapy Students: 101 full-time (73 women), 204 part-time (156 women); includes 2 minority (1 African American, 1 Hispanic American), 1 international. Average age 30. 309 applicants, 13% accepted. *Faculty:* 8 full-time (6 women), 35 part-time/adjunct (14 women). Expenses: Contact institution. *Financial support:* Teaching assistantships, career-related internships or fieldwork, Federal Work-Study, tuition waivers (full and partial), and unspecified assistantships available. Financial award application deadline: 5/1; financial award applicants required to submit FAFSA. In 2001, 99 degrees awarded. *Degree program information:* Part-time and evening/weekend programs available. Offers physical therapy (MHS, MS, DHS, DPT). *Application deadline:* For fall admission, 12/1. *Application fee:* $50. *Dean,* Dr. Elizabeth Domholdt, 317-788-3501, Fax: 317-788-3300.

School of Education Average age 35. 17 applicants, 100% accepted. *Faculty:* 15 part-time/adjunct (6 women). Expenses: Contact institution. *Financial support:* Federal Work-Study available. Financial award application deadline: 5/1; financial award applicants required to submit FAFSA. In 2001, 3 degrees awarded. *Degree program information:* Part-time and evening/weekend programs available. Offers art education (MAT); biology (MAT); chemistry (MAT); earth sciences (MAT); education (MA, MAT); elementary education (MA); English (MAT); French (MAT); math (MAT); physical education (MAT); physics (MAT); secondary education (MA); social studies (MAT); Spanish (MAT). *Application deadline:* Applications are processed on a rolling basis. *Application fee:* $30. *Dean,* Dr. E. Lynne Weisenbach, 317-788-3446, Fax: 317-788-3300, E-mail: weisenbach@uindy.edu.

School of Occupational Therapy Students: 99 full-time (88 women), 55 part-time (49 women). Average age 32. 97 applicants, 44% accepted. *Faculty:* 4 full-time (all women), 2 part-time/adjunct (both women). Expenses: Contact institution. *Financial support:* Career-related internships or fieldwork, Federal Work-Study, tuition waivers (full and partial), and unspecified assistantships available. Financial award application deadline: 5/1; financial award applicants required to submit FAFSA. In 2001, 35 degrees awarded. *Degree program information:* Part-time and evening/weekend programs available. Offers occupational therapy (MS). *Application deadline:* For fall admission, 1/2. *Application fee:* $50. *Dean,* Dr. Penelope Moyers, 317-788-3266, Fax: 317-788-3275, E-mail: moyers@uindy.edu.

School of Psychological Sciences Expenses: Contact institution. Offers psychological sciences (MA, Psy D). *Dean,* Dr. John McIlvried, 317-788-3247, Fax: 317-788-3480, E-mail: jmcilvried@uindy.edu.

THE UNIVERSITY OF IOWA, Iowa City, IA 52242-1316

General Information State-supported, coed, university. CGS member. *Enrollment:* 5,578 full-time matriculated graduate/professional students (2,728 women), 2,827 part-time matriculated graduate/professional students (1,400 women). *Enrollment by degree level:* 3,846 first professional, 2,229 master's, 2,305 doctoral, 25 other advanced degrees. *Graduate faculty:* 1,630 full-time (439 women), 77 part-time/adjunct (18 women). Tuition, state resident: full-time $3,702; part-time $206 per semester hour. Tuition, nonresident: full-time $11,924; part-time $206 per semester hour. *Required fees:* $101 per semester. Tuition and fees vary according to course load and program. *Graduate housing:* Rooms and/or apartments available on a first-come, first-served basis to single and married students. Typical cost: $3,189 per year ($5,539 including board) for single students; $4,152 per year for married students. Room and board charges vary according to board plan and housing facility selected. *Student services:* Campus employment opportunities, campus safety program, career counseling, child daycare facilities, disabled student services, exercise/wellness program, free psychological counseling, international student services, low-cost health insurance, multicultural affairs office, teacher training, writing training. *Library facilities:* Main Library plus 12 others. *Online resources:* library catalog, web page, access to other libraries' catalogs. *Collection:* 4 million titles, 44,644 serial subscriptions, 267,192 audiovisual materials.

Computer facilities: 1,200 computers available on campus for general student use. A campuswide network can be accessed from student residence rooms and from off campus. Internet access and online class registration, online degree process, grades, financial aid summary are available. *Web address:* http://www.uiowa.edu/.

General Application Contact: Betty Wood, Assistant Director of Admissions, 319-335-1525, Fax: 319-335-1535, E-mail: admissions@uiowa.edu.

GRADUATE UNITS

College of Dentistry Students: 370 full-time (144 women), 3 part-time (all women); includes 46 minority (10 African Americans, 13 Asian Americans or Pacific Islanders, 19 Hispanic Americans, 4 Native Americans), 28 international. *Faculty:* 82 full-time (24 women), 77 part-time/adjunct (15 women). Expenses: Contact institution. *Financial support:* Research assistantships, teaching assistantships, awards available. Financial award applicants required to submit FAFSA. In 2001, 72 first professional degrees, 16 master's, 22 other advanced degrees awarded. Offers dental public health (MS); dentistry (DDS, MS, PhD, Certificate); endodontics (MS, Certificate); operative dentistry (MS, Certificate); oral and maxillofacial pathology (Certificate); oral and maxillofacial radiology (Certificate); oral and maxillofacial surgery (MS, Certificate); oral pathology, radiology and medicine (MS, Certificate); oral science (MS, PhD); orthodontics (MS, Certificate); pediatric dentistry (MS, Certificate); periodontics (MS, Certificate); preventive and community dentistry (MS); prosthodontics (MS, Certificate); stomatology (MS). *Application fee:* $30 ($50 for international students). *Application Contact:* Dr. Yvonne Chalkley, Associate Dean for Student Affairs and Curriculum, 319-335-7157, Fax: 319-335-7155, E-mail: yvonne_chalkley@uiowa.edu. *Dean,* Dr. David C. Johnsen, 319-335-9650, Fax: 319-335-7155, E-mail: david-johnsen@uiowa.edu.

College of Law Students: 708 full-time (334 women); includes 103 minority (37 African Americans, 34 Asian Americans or Pacific Islanders, 22 Hispanic Americans, 10 Native Americans), 16 international. 1,273 applicants, 42% accepted, 245 enrolled. *Faculty:* 44 full-time (14 women), 41 part-time/adjunct (7 women). Expenses: Contact institution. *Financial support:* In 2001–02, 641 students received support, including 102 fellowships with full tuition reimbursements available, 125 research assistantships with partial tuition reimbursements available (averaging $1,653 per year); career-related internships or fieldwork, Federal Work-Study, institutionally sponsored loans, scholarships/grants, health care benefits, and tuition waivers (full and partial) also available. Financial award applicants required to submit FAFSA. In 2001, 202 first professional degrees, 11 master's awarded. Offers law (JD, LL M). *Application deadline:* For fall admission, 2/1. Applications are processed on a rolling basis. *Application fee:* $30 ($50 for international students). Electronic applications accepted. *Application Contact:* Patricia Cain, Acting Associate Dean, Admissions, 319-335-9905, Fax: 319-335-9019, E-mail: law-admissions@uiowa.edu. *Dean,* N. William Hines, 319-335-9034, Fax: 319-335-9019, E-mail: n-hines@uiowa.edu.

College of Medicine Average age 22. 3,338 applicants, 9% accepted. *Faculty:* 744 full-time (171 women), 506 part-time/adjunct (106 women). Expenses: Contact institution. *Financial support:* Fellowships, research assistantships, teaching assistantships, career-related internships or fieldwork, Federal Work-Study, institutionally sponsored loans, scholarships/grants, and tuition waivers (full and partial) available. Support available to part-time students. Financial award applicants required to submit FAFSA. In 2001, 182 first professional degrees, 99 master's, 56 doctorates awarded. *Degree program information:* Part-time programs available. Offers biosciences (PhD); medicine (MD, MA, MHA, MPAS, MPH, MPT, MS, PhD); translational biomedical research (MS, PhD). *Application fee:* $30. Electronic applications accepted. *Dean, College of Medicine, and Vice President for Statewide Health Services,* Dr. Robert P. Kelch, 319-335-8064, Fax: 319-335-8336, E-mail: robert-kelch@uiowa.edu.

Graduate Programs in Medicine Expenses: Contact institution. *Financial support:* Fellowships, research assistantships, teaching assistantships, career-related internships or fieldwork, Federal Work-Study, institutionally sponsored loans, and tuition waivers (full and partial) available. Support available to part-time students. Financial award applicants required to submit FAFSA. In 2001, 115 master's, 57 doctorates awarded. *Degree program information:* Part-time programs available. Offers anatomy and cell biology (PhD); biochemistry (MS, PhD); free radical and radiation biology (MS, PhD); general microbiology and microbial physiology (MS, PhD); immunology (MS, PhD); medicine (MA, MHA, MPAS, MPH, MPT, MS, PhD); microbial genetics (MS, PhD); pathogenic bacteriology (MS, PhD); pathology (MS); pharmacology (MS, PhD); physical therapy (MA, MPT); physician assistant (MPAS); physiology and biophysics (PhD); physiology and biophysiology (MS); rehabilitation science (PhD); virology (MS, PhD). *Application fee:* $30 ($50 for international students). Electronic applications accepted.

College of Pharmacy Expenses: Contact institution. *Financial support:* Fellowships, research assistantships, teaching assistantships available. Offers pharmacy (Pharm D, MS, PhD). *Dean,* Jordan Cohen, 319-335-8794, Fax: 319-353-5594.

Graduate College Students: 2,483 full-time (1,387 women), 2,076 part-time (1,171 women); includes 376 minority (121 African Americans, 107 Asian Americans or Pacific Islanders, 121 Hispanic Americans, 27 Native Americans), 1,120 international. Average age 29. 7,969 applicants, 38% accepted, 1681 enrolled. *Faculty:* 1,630 full-time (439 women), 77 part-time/adjunct (18 women). Expenses: Contact institution. *Financial support:* In 2001–02, 251 fellowships, 1,166 research assistantships, 1,464 teaching assistantships were awarded. Career-related internships or fieldwork, Federal Work-Study, and institutionally sponsored loans also available. Support available to part-time students. Financial award applicants required to submit FAFSA. In 2001, 1,281 master's, 304 doctorates, 17 other advanced degrees awarded. *Degree program information:* Part-time and evening/weekend programs available. Offers applied mathematical and computational sciences (PhD); genetics (PhD); immunology (PhD); molecular biology (PhD); neuroscience (PhD); second language acquisition (PhD); urban and regional planning (MA, MS). *Application fee:* $30 ($50 for international students). Electronic applications accepted. *Application Contact:* Betty Wood, Assistant Director of Admissions, 319-335-1525, Fax: 319-335-1535, E-mail: admissions@uiowa.edu. *Interim Dean,* Dr. John C. Keller, 319-335-2144, Fax: 319-335-2806.

College of Education Students: 289 full-time (210 women), 399 part-time (272 women); includes 84 minority (43 African Americans, 17 Asian Americans or Pacific Islanders, 20 Hispanic Americans, 4 Native Americans), 83 international. 410 applicants, 51% accepted, 108 enrolled. *Faculty:* 88 full-time, 4 part-time/adjunct. Expenses: Contact institution. *Financial support:* In 2001–02, 13 fellowships, 128 research assistantships, 104 teaching assistantships were awarded. Career-related internships or fieldwork, Federal Work-Study, institutionally sponsored loans, and unspecified assistantships also available. Financial award applicants required to submit FAFSA. In 2001, 128 master's, 36 doctorates, 5 other advanced degrees awarded. Offers art education (MA, MAT, PhD); counselor education (MA, PhD); curiculum and supervision (PhD); curriculum and supervision (MA, PhD); curriculum supervision (MA); developmental reading (MA); early childhood and elementary education (MA, PhD); early childhood education (MA); education (MA, MAT, PhD, Ed S); educational administration (MA, PhD, Ed S); elementary education (PhD); English education (MAT, PhD); foreign language education (MA, MAT); foreign language/ESL education (PhD); higher education (MA, PhD, Ed S); instructional design and technology (MA, PhD, Ed S); language, literature and culture (MA, PhD); music education (MA, PhD); psychological and quantitative foundations (MA, PhD, Ed S); rehabilitation counseling (MA, PhD); secondary education (MA, MAT, PhD); social foundations (MA, PhD); social studies (MA, PhD); special education (MA, PhD). *Application fee:* $30 ($50 for international students). Electronic applications accepted. *Dean,* Sondra Bowman Damico, 319-335-5380, Fax: 319-335-5359.

College of Engineering Students: 192 full-time (48 women), 146 part-time (30 women); includes 13 minority (4 African Americans, 6 Asian Americans or Pacific Islanders, 3 Hispanic Americans), 216 international. Average age 28. 893 applicants, 38% accepted, 90 enrolled. *Faculty:* 81 full-time (5 women), 13 part-time/adjunct (0 women). Expenses: Contact institution. *Financial support:* In 2001–02, 5 fellowships, 133 research assistantships, 80 teaching assistantships were awarded. Financial award applicants required to submit FAFSA. In 2001, 65 master's, 23 doctorates awarded. Offers biomedical engineering (MS, PhD); chemical and biochemical engineering (MS, PhD); civil and environmental engineering (MS, PhD); electrical and computer engineering (MS, PhD); engineering (MS, PhD); engineering design and manufacturing (MS, PhD); ergonomics (MS, PhD); information and engineering management (MS, PhD); mechanical engineering (MS, PhD); operations research (MS, PhD); quality engineering (MS, PhD). *Application fee:* $30 ($50 for international students). Electronic applications accepted. *Dean,* Dr. P. Barry Butler, 319-335-5766, Fax: 319-335-6086, E-mail: patrick-butler@uiowa.edu.

College of Liberal Arts and Sciences Students: 1,243 full-time (686 women), 1,035 part-time (565 women); includes 189 minority (54 African Americans, 46 Asian Americans or Pacific Islanders, 69 Hispanic Americans, 20 Native Americans), 556 international. 3,959 applicants, 29% accepted, 569 enrolled. *Faculty:* 729 full-time, 57 part-time/adjunct. Expenses: Contact institution. *Financial support:* In 2001–02, 180 fellowships, 392 research assistantships, 1,107 teaching assistantships were awarded. Career-related internships or fieldwork, Federal Work-Study, institutionally sponsored loans, and unspecified assistantships also available. Support available to part-time students. Financial award applicants required to submit FAFSA. In 2001, 487 master's, 151 doctorates awarded. *Degree program information:* Part-time programs available. Offers African American world studies (MA); American studies (MA, PhD); anthropology (MA, PhD); art (MA, MFA); art history (MA, PhD); Asian civilizations (MA); astronomy (MS); bibliography (PhD); biological sciences (MS, PhD); chemistry (MS, PhD); classics (MA, PhD); communication and mass communication (MA); communication research (MA, PhD); comparative literature (MA, PhD); comparative literature translation (MFA); computer science (MCS, MS, PhD); dance (MFA); development support communication (MA); English (MFA, PhD); exercise science (MS, PhD); expository writing (MA); film and video production (MA, MFA); film studies (MA, PhD); French (MA, PhD); geography (MA, PhD); geoscience (MS, PhD); German (MA, PhD); history (MA, PhD); leisure studies (MA); liberal arts (MA, MCS, MFA, MS, MSW, DMA, PhD); linguistics (MA, PhD); literary criticism (PhD); literary history (PhD); literary studies (MA); mass communication (PhD); mathematics (MS, PhD); music (MA, MFA, DMA, PhD); neural and behavioral sciences (PhD); nonfiction writing (MFA); pedagogy (PhD); philosophy (MA, PhD); physical education (PhD); physical education and sports studies (MA, PhD); physics (MS, PhD); political science (MA, PhD); professional journalism (MA); psychology (MA, PhD); religion (MA, PhD); rhetorical studies (MA, PhD); rhetorical theory and stylistics (PhD); science education (MS, PhD); social work (MSW, PhD); sociology (MA, PhD); Spanish and Portuguese (MA, PhD); speech and hearing science (PhD); speech pathology and audiology (MA); statistics and actuarial science (MS, PhD); theatre arts (MFA); women's studies (PhD); writer's workshop (MFA); writing (PhD). *Application fee:* $30 ($50 for international students). Electronic applications accepted. *Dean,* Linda Maxson, 319-335-2611, Fax: 319-335-3755.

College of Nursing Students: 74 full-time (62 women), 91 part-time (83 women); includes 7 minority (2 Asian Americans or Pacific Islanders, 4 Hispanic Americans, 1 Native American), 14 international. 65 applicants, 74% accepted, 36 enrolled. *Faculty:* 35 full-time, 4 part-time/adjunct. Expenses: Contact institution. *Financial support:* In 2001–02, 3 fellowships, 20 research assistantships, 19 teaching assistantships were awarded. Financial award applicants required to submit FAFSA. In 2001, 42 master's, 6 doctorates awarded. Offers nursing (MSN, PhD). *Application deadline:* For fall admission, 2/1; for spring admission, 10/1. *Application fee:* $30 ($50 for international students). Electronic applications accepted. *Dean,* Melanie Dreher, 319-335-7018, Fax: 319-335-9990.

College of Public Health Students: 104 full-time (56 women), 48 part-time (33 women); includes 16 minority (5 African Americans, 8 Asian Americans or Pacific Islanders, 3 Hispanic Americans), 35 international. 253 applicants, 52% accepted, 48 enrolled. *Faculty:* 41 full-time. Expenses: Contact institution. *Financial support:* In 2001–02, 1 fellowship, 64 research assistantships, 5 teaching assistantships were awarded. Financial award applicants required to submit FAFSA. In 2001, 41 master's, 11 doctorates awarded. Offers biostatistics (MS, PhD); epidemiology (MS, PhD); health management and policy (MHA, PhD); occupational and environmental health (MS, PhD); preventive medicine and environmental health (MPH, MS, PhD); public health (MHA, MPH, MS, PhD). *Application deadline:* Applications are processed on a rolling basis. *Application fee:* $30 ($50 for international students). Electronic applications accepted. *Dean,* Dr. James A. Merchant, 319-335-9627, Fax: 319-335-9200, E-mail: james-merchant@uiowa.edu.

Henry B. Tippie College of Business Students: 452 full-time (181 women), 574 part-time (175 women); includes 192 minority (11 African Americans, 167 Asian Americans or Pacific Islanders, 13 Hispanic Americans, 1 Native American), 144 international. Average age 30. 833 applicants, 26% accepted. *Faculty:* 106 full-time (22 women), 42 part-time/adjunct (14 women). Expenses: Contact institution. *Financial support:* Fellowships, research assistantships, teaching assistantships, career-related internships or fieldwork, Federal Work-Study, scholarships/grants, and tuition waivers (full and partial) available. Support available to part-time students. Financial award applicants required to submit FAFSA. In 2001, 254 master's, 16 doctorates awarded. *Degree program information:* Part-time and evening/weekend programs available. Offers accountancy (M Ac); business (M Ac, MA, MBA, PhD); business administration (PhD); economics (PhD); finance (PhD); management); management sciences (PhD); marketing (PhD). *Application fee:* $30 ($50 for international students). *Dean,* Prof. Gary C. Fethke, 319-335-0866, Fax: 319-335-0860, E-mail: gary-fethke@uiowa.edu.

School of Library and Information Science Students: 40 full-time (32 women), 41 part-time (35 women); includes 4 minority (3 Asian Americans or Pacific Islanders, 1 Native American), 6 international. 46 applicants, 70% accepted, 13 enrolled. *Faculty:* 4 full-time. Expenses: Contact institution. *Financial support:* In 2001–02, 12 research assistantships, 7 teaching assistantships were awarded. Financial award applicants required to submit FAFSA. In 2001, 27 degrees awarded. Offers library and information science (MA). *Application deadline:* For fall admission, 3/1 (priority date); for spring admission, 10/1 (priority date). *Application fee:* $30 ($50 for international students). Electronic applications accepted. *Director,* Joseph Kearney, 319-335-5707.

UNIVERSITY OF JUDAISM, Bel Air, CA 90077-1599

General Information Independent-religious, coed, comprehensive institution. *Graduate housing:* Rooms and/or apartments available to single and married students. Housing application deadline: 6/1.

GRADUATE UNITS

Graduate School *Degree program information:* Part-time and evening/weekend programs available.

David Lieber School of Graduate Studies *Degree program information:* Part-time and evening/weekend programs available. Offers general nonprofit administration (MBA); Jewish nonprofit administration (MBA).

Fingerhut School of Education Offers behavioral psychology (MA, MS); education (MA, MA Ed, MS).

Ziegler School of Rabbinic Studies Offers rabbinic studies (MARS).

UNIVERSITY OF KANSAS, Lawrence, KS 66045

General Information State-supported, coed, university. CGS member. *Enrollment:* 4,271 full-time matriculated graduate/professional students (2,253 women), 2,532 part-time matriculated graduate/professional students (1,393 women). *Enrollment by degree level:* 1,193 first professional, 3,768 master's, 1,805 doctoral, 37 other advanced degrees. *Graduate faculty:* 1,479. Tuition, state resident: full-time $2,722; part-time $113 per credit. Tuition, nonresident: full-time $8,586; part-time $358 per credit. *Required fees:* $551; $46 per credit. Tuition and fees vary according to campus/location, program and reciprocity agreements. *Graduate housing:* Rooms and/or apartments available on a first-come, first-served basis to single and married students. Typical cost: $4,348 (including board) for single students; $2,790 per year for married students. Housing application deadline: 2/15. *Student services:* Campus employment opportunities, campus safety program, career counseling, child daycare facilities, disabled student services, exercise/wellness program, free psychological counseling, grant writing training, international student services, low-cost health insurance, multicultural affairs office, teacher training, writing training. *Library facilities:* Watson Library plus 11 others. *Online resources:* library catalog, web page, access to other libraries' catalogs. *Collection:* 4.4 million titles, 32,722 serial subscriptions, 48,554 audiovisual materials. *Research affiliation:* Casey Family Program (education/disabilities research), Kansas Health Foundation (medical research), Kauffman Foundation (social welfare), American Heart Association (medical research), Biostratum, Inc. (medical research), Robert Wood Johnson Foundation (public health).

University of Kansas (continued)

Computer facilities: 938 computers available on campus for general student use. A campuswide network can be accessed from student residence rooms and from off campus. Internet access is available. *Web address:* http://www.ku.edu/.

General Application Contact: 785-864-4141, Fax: 785-864-4555.

GRADUATE UNITS

Graduate School Students: 2,792 full-time (1,472 women), 2,480 part-time (1,349 women); includes 394 minority (114 African Americans, 108 Asian Americans or Pacific Islanders, 116 Hispanic Americans, 56 Native Americans), 1,000 international. Average age 31. 3,890 applicants, 42% accepted, 1118 enrolled. *Faculty:* 1,208. Expenses: Contact institution. *Financial support:* In 2001–02, 617 research assistantships with partial tuition reimbursements (averaging $10,725 per year), 910 teaching assistantships with full and partial tuition reimbursements (averaging $9,948 per year) were awarded. Fellowships with full and partial tuition reimbursements, career-related internships or fieldwork, Federal Work-Study, institutionally sponsored loans, and scholarships/grants also available. Support available to part-time students. Financial award applicants required to submit FAFSA. In 2001, 1,061 master's, 231 doctorates, 8 other advanced degrees awarded. *Degree program information:* Part-time and evening/weekend programs available. Postbaccalaureate distance learning degree programs offered. Electronic applications accepted. *Dean*, Diana Carlin, 785-864-4141, Fax: 785-864-4555, E-mail: graduate@ku.edu.

College of Liberal Arts and Sciences Students: 1,148 full-time (628 women), 601 part-time (328 women); includes 148 minority (42 African Americans, 30 Asian Americans or Pacific Islanders, 49 Hispanic Americans, 27 Native Americans), 350 international. Average age 31. 1,318 applicants, 36% accepted, 328 enrolled. *Faculty:* 595. Expenses: Contact institution. *Financial support:* Fellowships, research assistantships with partial tuition reimbursements, teaching assistantships with full and partial tuition reimbursements, career-related internships or fieldwork, Federal Work-Study, and institutionally sponsored loans available. Support available to part-time students. Financial award applicants required to submit FAFSA. In 2001, 260 master's, 121 doctorates awarded. *Degree program information:* Part-time and evening/weekend programs available. Offers American studies (MA, PhD); anthropology (MA, PhD); applied mathematics and statistics (MA, PhD); audiology (PhD); biochemistry and biophysics (MA, PhD); biological sciences (MA, PhD); biology (MA, PhD); botany (MA, PhD); chemistry (MS, PhD); child language (MA, PhD); classics (MA); clinical child psychology (MA, PhD); communication studies (MA, PhD); computational physics and astronomy (MS); developmental and child psychology (PhD); early childhood education (MA, PhD); East Asian languages and cultures (MA); economics (MA, PhD); English (MA, PhD); entomology (MA, PhD); French (MA, PhD); geography (MA, PhD); geology (MS, PhD); German (MA, PhD); gerontology (MA, PhD); historical administration and museum studies (MHAMS); history (MA, PhD); history of art (MA, PhD); human development (MA, MHD); indigenous nations studies (MA); international studies (MA); Latin American studies (MA); liberal arts and sciences (MA, MHAMS, MHD, MPA, MS, PhD); linguistics (MA, PhD); mathematics (MA, PhD); microbiology (MA, PhD); molecular, cellular, and developmental biology (MA, PhD); philosophy (MA, PhD); physics (MS, PhD); political science (MA, PhD); psychology (MA, PhD); public administration (MPA); religious studies (MA); Russian and East European studies (MA); Slavic languages and literatures (MA, PhD); sociology (MA, PhD); Spanish (MA, PhD); speech-language pathology (MA); speech-languagge pathology (PhD); systematics and ecology (MA, PhD); theatre and film (MA, PhD). *Application fee:* $35. *Application Contact:* Kathy Mason, Director, 785-864-3696, Fax: 785-864-5331, E-mail: kathy@clasmain.clas.ukans.edu. *Dean*, Kim Wilcox, 785-864-3661, Fax: 785-864-5331.

School of Architecture and Urban Design Students: 90 full-time (35 women), 33 part-time (13 women); includes 11 minority (4 African Americans, 3 Asian Americans or Pacific Islanders, 3 Hispanic Americans, 1 Native American), 19 international. Average age 29. 103 applicants, 54% accepted, 35 enrolled. *Faculty:* 29. Expenses: Contact institution. *Financial support:* In 2001–02, 32 fellowships (averaging $1,500 per year), 2 research assistantships with partial tuition reimbursements (averaging $8,702 per year), 10 teaching assistantships with full and partial tuition reimbursements (averaging $10,080 per year) were awarded. Career-related internships or fieldwork also available. In 2001, 25 degrees awarded. *Degree program information:* Part-time programs available. Offers architecture (M Arch); architecture and urban design (M Arch, MUP); urban planning (MUP). *Application deadline:* For fall admission, 3/1. *Application fee:* $40. Electronic applications accepted. *Dean*, John Gaunt, 785-864-4281.

School of Business Students: 226 full-time (69 women), 346 part-time (100 women); includes 31 minority (8 African Americans, 12 Asian Americans or Pacific Islanders, 8 Hispanic Americans, 3 Native Americans), 90 international. Average age 29. 373 applicants, 46% accepted, 159 enrolled. *Faculty:* 48. Expenses: Contact institution. *Financial support:* In 2001–02, 20 research assistantships with partial tuition reimbursements (averaging $8,974 per year), 19 teaching assistantships with full and partial tuition reimbursements (averaging $7,915 per year) were awarded. Fellowships, career-related internships or fieldwork and Federal Work-Study also available. In 2001, 237 master's, 2 doctorates awarded. *Degree program information:* Part-time and evening/weekend programs available. Offers accounting and information systems (MAIS, PhD); business (MAIS, MBA, MS, MSBIS, PhD); business administration (MBA, MS). *Application deadline:* For fall admission, 4/1; for spring admission, 10/1. Applications are processed on a rolling basis. *Application fee:* $60. Electronic applications accepted. *Application Contact:* Student Advising Center, 785-864-4254, Fax: 785-864-5328, E-mail: bschoolgrad@ku.edu. *Dean*, William L. Fuerst, 785-864-3795, Fax: 785-864-5328, E-mail: bschoolgrad@ku.edu.

School of Education Students: 468 full-time (314 women), 754 part-time (535 women); includes 94 minority (30 African Americans, 21 Asian Americans or Pacific Islanders, 29 Hispanic Americans, 14 Native Americans), 106 international. Average age 33. 482 applicants, 67% accepted, 250 enrolled. *Faculty:* 86. Expenses: Contact institution. *Financial support:* Fellowships, research assistantships with partial tuition reimbursements, teaching assistantships with full and partial tuition reimbursements, career-related internships or fieldwork available. In 2001, 324 master's, 67 doctorates, 8 other advanced degrees awarded. *Degree program information:* Part-time programs available. Offers counseling psychology (MS, PhD); curriculum and instruction (MA, MS Ed, Ed D, PhD); education (MA, MS, MS Ed, Ed D, PhD, Ed S); education administration (MS Ed); educational policy and leadership (Ed D, PhD); educational psychology and research (MS Ed, PhD); foundations (MS Ed, Ed D, PhD); higher education (MS Ed, Ed D, PhD); physical education (MS Ed, Ed D, PhD); school administration (Ed D, PhD); school psychology (PhD, Ed S); special education (MS Ed, Ed D, PhD). *Application fee:* $35. Electronic applications accepted. *Application Contact:* Mary Ann Williams, Graduate Admissions Coordinator, 785-864-4510, Fax: 785-864-3566, E-mail: mwilliam@ku.edu. *Dean*, Angela Lumpkin, 785-864-4297.

School of Engineering Students: 303 full-time (50 women), 332 part-time (59 women); includes 39 minority (6 African Americans, 21 Asian Americans or Pacific Islanders, 8 Hispanic Americans, 4 Native Americans), 300 international. Average age 29. 1,103 applicants, 31% accepted, 141 enrolled. *Faculty:* 99. Expenses: Contact institution. *Financial support:* Fellowships, research assistantships with partial tuition reimbursements, teaching assistantships with full and partial tuition reimbursements, career-related internships or fieldwork and Federal Work-Study available. In 2001, 132 master's, 16 doctorates awarded. *Degree program information:* Part-time and evening/weekend programs available. Postbaccalaureate distance learning degree programs offered (no on-campus study). Offers aerospace engineering (ME, MS, DE, PhD); architectural engineering (MS); chemical engineering (MS); chemical/petroleum engineering (PhD); civil engineering (MCE, MS, DE, PhD); computer engineering (MS); computer science (MS, PhD); construction management (MCM); electrical engineering (MS, DE, PhD); engineering (MCE, MCM, ME, MS, DE, PhD); engineering management (MS); environmental engineering (MS, PhD); environmental science (MS, PhD); mechanical engineering (MS, DE, PhD); petroleum engineering (MS); water resources engineering (MS); water resources science (MS). *Application deadline:* Applications are processed on a rolling basis. *Application fee:* $40. *Application Contact:* Robb Sorem, Associate Dean, 785-864-2983, Fax: 785-864-5445, E-mail: sorem@ku.edu. *Dean*, Stuart R. Bell, 785-864-3881, E-mail: kuengr@ku.edu.

School of Fine Arts Students: 145 full-time (96 women), 66 part-time (42 women); includes 5 minority (1 African American, 4 Hispanic Americans), 59 international. Average age 29. 171 applicants, 52% accepted, 61 enrolled. *Faculty:* 102. Expenses: Contact institution. *Financial support:* Fellowships, research assistantships, teaching assistantships available. In 2001, 39 master's, 11 doctorates awarded. Offers art (MFA); church music (MM, DMA); composition (MM, DMA); conducting (MM, DMA); design (MFA); fine arts (MA, MFA, MM, MME, DMA, PhD); music education (PhD); music education and music therapy (MME, PhD); music theory (MM, PhD); musicology (MM, PhD); opera (MM); performance (MM, DMA); visual arts education (MA). *Application fee:* $35. *Dean*, Toni-Marie Montgomery, 785-864-3421, Fax: 785-864-5387.

School of Journalism and Mass Communications Students: 16 full-time (10 women), 56 part-time (40 women); includes 3 minority (2 African Americans, 1 Hispanic American), 5 international. Average age 31. 58 applicants, 55% accepted, 17 enrolled. *Faculty:* 24. Expenses: Contact institution. *Financial support:* In 2001–02, 8 students received support, including 1 teaching assistantship with full and partial tuition reimbursement available; fellowships, research assistantships, career-related internships or fieldwork also available. Support available to part-time students. Financial award application deadline:3/1. In 2001, 24 degrees awarded. *Degree program information:* Part-time programs available. Offers journalism (MS). *Application deadline:* For fall admission, 3/15. *Application fee:* $25. *Application Contact:* Cindy Nesvarba, Information Contact, 785-864-7649, Fax: 785-864-5318, E-mail: cnesvarb@valcon.cc.ukans.edu. *Dean*, James Gentry, 785-864-4755, Fax: 785-864-5318.

School of Pharmacy Students: 87 full-time (43 women), 9 part-time (5 women); includes 10 minority (2 African Americans, 5 Asian Americans or Pacific Islanders, 3 Hispanic Americans), 32 international. Average age 27. 84 applicants, 27% accepted, 16 enrolled. *Faculty:* 41. Expenses: Contact institution. *Financial support:* Fellowships, research assistantships with partial tuition reimbursements, teaching assistantships with full and partial tuition reimbursements, career-related internships or fieldwork and scholarships/grants available. In 2001, 20 master's, 13 doctorates awarded. *Degree program information:* Part-time and evening/weekend programs available. Offers medicinal chemistry (MS, PhD); pharmaceutical chemistry (MS, PhD); pharmacology (MS, PhD); pharmacy (MS, PhD); pharmacy practice (MS); toxicology (MS, PhD). *Application fee:* $30. *Dean*, Jack E. Fincham, 785-864-3591.

Graduate Studies Medical Center Students: 298 full-time (214 women), 268 part-time (211 women); includes 49 minority (17 African Americans, 16 Asian Americans or Pacific Islanders, 11 Hispanic Americans, 5 Native Americans), 39 international. Average age 32. 359 applicants, 40% accepted. *Faculty:* 235 full-time (100 women), 36 part-time/adjunct (27 women). Expenses: Contact institution. *Financial support:* In 2001–02, 31 research assistantships with partial tuition reimbursements, 57 teaching assistantships with full and partial tuition reimbursements were awarded. Fellowships, career-related internships or fieldwork, Federal Work-Study, institutionally sponsored loans, and traineeships also available. Support available to part-time students. Financial award application deadline: 3/30; financial award applicants required to submit FAFSA. In 2001, 179 master's, 17 doctorates awarded. *Degree program information:* Part-time and evening/weekend programs available. Postbaccalaureate distance learning degree programs offered (minimal on-campus study). Offers anatomy and cell biology (MA, PhD); biochemistry and molecular biology (MS, PhD); biomedical sciences (MA, MPH, MS, PhD); health policy and management (MHSA); microbiology, molecular genetics and immunology (PhD); molecular and integrative physiology (MS, PhD); pathology and laboratory medicine (MA, PhD); pharmacology (MS, PhD); preventive medicine (MPH); toxicology (MS, PhD). Electronic applications accepted. *Application Contact:* Karen Stanze, Director of Graduate Studies, 913-588-1238, Fax: 913-588-5242, E-mail: kstanze@kumc.edu. *Vice Chancellor for Academic Affairs and Dean of Graduate Studies*, Dr. Allen Rawitch, 913-588-1258, Fax: 913-588-5242, E-mail: arawitch@kumc.edu.

School of Allied Health Students: 203 full-time (140 women), 29 part-time (26 women); includes 18 minority (2 African Americans, 7 Asian Americans or Pacific Islanders, 5 Hispanic Americans, 4 Native Americans), 6 international. Average age 28. *Faculty:* 39 full-time (24 women), 12 part-time/adjunct (all women). Expenses: Contact institution. *Financial support:* Fellowships, research assistantships, teaching assistantships, career-related internships or fieldwork, Federal Work-Study, institutionally sponsored loans, and traineeships available. Support available to part-time students. Financial award application deadline: 3/30; financial award applicants required to submit FAFSA. In 2001, 80 degrees awarded. *Degree program information:* Part-time programs available. Offers allied health (MA, MS, PhD); audiology (MA, PhD); dietetics and nutrition (MS); education of the deaf (MS); nurse anesthesia education (MS); occupational therapy education (MS); physical therapy education (MS); speech and hearing science (PhD); speech-language pathology (MA, PhD). *Application fee:* $25. Electronic applications accepted. *Application Contact:* Moffett Ferguson, Student Affairs Coordinator, 913-588-5235, Fax: 913-588-5254, E-mail: mfergus@kumc.edu. *Dean*, Dr. Karen L. Miller, 913-588-5235, Fax: 913-588-5254.

School of Nursing Students: 42 full-time (all women), 118 part-time (113 women); includes 11 minority (7 African Americans, 2 Asian Americans or Pacific Islanders, 2 Hispanic Americans), 3 international. Average age 38. *Faculty:* 40 full-time (39 women), 13 part-time/adjunct (12 women). Expenses: Contact institution. *Financial support:* In 2001–02, 37 students received support, including 13 teaching assistantships with full and partial tuition reimbursements available; research assistantships, career-related internships or fieldwork, Federal Work-Study, institutionally sponsored loans, and traineeships also available. Support available to part-time students. Financial award application deadline: 3/30; financial award applicants required to submit FAFSA. In 2001, 47 master's, 8 doctorates awarded. *Degree program information:* Part-time programs available. Postbaccalaureate distance learning degree programs offered (minimal on-campus study). Offers nursing (MS, PhD). *Application deadline:* For fall admission, 4/1; for winter admission, 7/1; for spring admission, 9/1. *Application fee:* $25. *Application Contact:* Dr. Rita Clifford, Associate Dean, Student Affairs, 913-588-1619, Fax: 913-588-1615, E-mail: soninfo@kumc.edu. *Dean*, Dr. Karen L. Miller, 913-588-1619, Fax: 913-588-1615.

School of Law Students: 516 full-time (216 women); includes 50 minority (14 African Americans, 13 Asian Americans or Pacific Islanders, 16 Hispanic Americans, 7 Native Americans), 4 international. Average age 26. 682 applicants, 46% accepted, 125 enrolled. *Faculty:* 50 full-time (10 women), 14 part-time/adjunct (3 women). Expenses: Contact institution. *Financial support:* In 2001–02, 250 students received support, including 187 fellowships (averaging $3,700 per year), 56 research assistantships, 7 teaching assistantships with partial tuition reimbursements available; career-related internships or fieldwork, Federal Work-Study, institutionally sponsored loans, and scholarships/grants also available. Financial award application deadline: 3/1; financial award applicants required to submit FAFSA. In 2001, 159 degrees awarded. Offers law (JD). *Application deadline:* For fall admission, 3/15. Applications are processed on a rolling basis. *Application fee:* $40. Electronic applications accepted. *Application Contact:* Rachel Reitz, Director of Admissions, 866-220-3654, E-mail: admitlaw@ku.edu. *Dean*, Stephen R. McAllister, 785-864-4550, Fax: 785-864-5054, E-mail: stever@ku.edu.

School of Medicine Students: 711 full-time (325 women); includes 151 minority (43 African Americans, 69 Asian Americans or Pacific Islanders, 31 Hispanic Americans, 8 Native Americans) Average age 26. *Faculty:* 320 full-time (103 women), 101 part-time/adjunct (26 women). Expenses: Contact institution. *Financial support:* In 2001–02, 595 students received support. Career-related internships or fieldwork, Federal Work-Study, and institutionally sponsored loans available. Support available to part-time students. Financial award application deadline: 3/30; financial award applicants required to submit FAFSA. In 2001, 159 degrees awarded. Offers medicine (MD). *Application deadline:* For fall admission, 10/15. Applications are processed on a rolling basis. *Application Contact:* Peggy M. Heinen, Admissions Coordinator, 913-588-5283, Fax: 913-588-5259, E-mail: pheinen@kumc.edu. *Executive Dean*, Dr. Deborah Powell, 913-588-5287, Fax: 913-588-5259.

School of Social Welfare Students: 311 full-time (268 women), 70 part-time (60 women); includes 39 minority (21 African Americans, 4 Asian Americans or Pacific Islanders, 6 Hispanic Americans, 8 Native Americans), 5 international. Average age 33. 198 applicants, 58% accepted, 111 enrolled. *Faculty:* 30. Expenses: Contact institution. *Financial support:* In 2001–02, 24 research assistantships with partial tuition reimbursements (averaging $13,313 per year), 9 teaching assistantships with full and partial tuition reimbursements (averaging $11,506 per year) were awarded. Fellowships, Federal Work-Study, scholarships/grants, and tuition waivers (partial) also available. Support available to part-time students. Financial award applicants required to submit FAFSA. In 2001, 184 master's, 1 doctorate awarded. Offers social welfare (MSW, PhD). *Application deadline:* For fall admission, 2/15; for spring admission, 5/1 (priority date). Applications are processed on a rolling basis. *Application fee:* $25. *Application Contact:* Becky Hofer, Director of Admissions, 785-864-4720, Fax: 785-864-5277, E-mail: bhofer@ku.edu. *Dean*, Ann Weick, 785-864-4720, Fax: 785-864-5277, E-mail: annw@ku.edu.

UNIVERSITY OF KENTUCKY, Lexington, KY 40506-0032

General Information State-supported, coed, university. CGS member. *Enrollment:* 3,780 full-time matriculated graduate/professional students (1,883 women), 2,752 part-time matriculated graduate/professional students (1,615 women). *Enrollment by degree level:* 1,385 first professional, 2,680 master's, 1,754 doctoral, 46 other advanced degrees. *Graduate faculty:* 1,373 full-time (305 women), 140 part-time/adjunct (11 women). Tuition, state resident: full-time $4,075; part-time $213 per credit hour. Tuition, nonresident: full-time $11,295; part-time $614 per credit hour. *Graduate housing:* Rooms and/or apartments available to single and married students. *Student services:* Campus employment opportunities, career counseling, child daycare facilities, exercise/wellness program, free psychological counseling, international student services, low-cost health insurance. *Library facilities:* William T. Young Library plus 15 others. *Online resources:* library catalog, web page, access to other libraries' catalogs. *Collection:* 2.9 million titles, 29,850 serial subscriptions, 78,136 audiovisual materials. *Research affiliation:* National Drug Addiction Center (drug abuse and prevention), National Institute of Occupational Health and Safety (environmental health), Oak Ridge National Laboratory (nuclear physics), Continuous Electron Beam Accelerator Facility (high-energy physics), Battelle Pacific Northwest Laboratories (environmental sciences).

Computer facilities: 1,400 computers available on campus for general student use. A campuswide network can be accessed from student residence rooms and from off campus. Internet access and online class registration, various software packages are available. *Web address:* http://www.uky.edu/.

General Application Contact: Dr. Constance L. Wood, Associate Dean, 606-257-4613, Fax: 606-323-1928.

GRADUATE UNITS

College of Dentistry Students: 234 full-time (87 women); includes 33 minority (7 African Americans, 13 Asian Americans or Pacific Islanders, 12 Hispanic Americans, 1 Native American), 2 international. Average age 24. 834 applicants, 8% accepted, 50 enrolled. *Faculty:* 60 full-time (13 women), 53 part-time/adjunct (13 women). Expenses: Contact institution. *Financial support:* In 2001–02, 176 students received support, including 4 fellowships, 7 research assistantships (averaging $1,000 per year), 8 teaching assistantships (averaging $1,881 per year); career-related internships or fieldwork, Federal Work-Study, institutionally sponsored loans, and scholarships/grants also available. Support available to part-time students. Financial award application deadline: 4/1; financial award applicants required to submit FAFSA. In 2001, 45 first professional degrees, 5 master's awarded. Offers dentistry (DMD, MS). *Application deadline:* For fall admission, 11/1 (priority date); for winter admission, 2/1. Applications are processed on a rolling basis. *Application fee:* $25. *Application Contact:* Robert E. Mathews, Associate Director of Admissions and Student Affairs, 859-323-6071, Fax: 859-323-1042, E-mail: rmathews@uky.edu. *Dean*, Dr. Leon A. Assael, 859-323-5786, Fax: 859-323-1042.

College of Law Students: 379 full-time (166 women); includes 20 minority (17 African Americans, 2 Hispanic Americans, 1 Native American), 1 international. Average age 23. 881 applicants, 39% accepted. *Faculty:* 29 full-time (9 women), 22 part-time/adjunct (8 women). Expenses: Contact institution. *Financial support:* In 2001–02, 261 students received support, including 160 fellowships (averaging $2,500 per year); career-related internships or fieldwork, Federal Work-Study, and scholarships/grants also available. Support available to part-time students. Financial award application deadline: 4/1; financial award applicants required to submit FAFSA. In 2001, 139 degrees awarded. Offers law (JD). *Application deadline:* For fall admission, 3/1 (priority date). Applications are processed on a rolling basis. *Application fee:* $35. *Application Contact:* Drusilla V. Bakert, Associate Dean, 859-257-6770, Fax: 859-323-1061, E-mail: dbakert@pop.uky.edu. *Dean*, Alla W. Vestal, 859-257-1678, Fax: 859-323-1061.

College of Medicine Students: 371 full-time (162 women); includes 52 minority (21 African Americans, 28 Asian Americans or Pacific Islanders, 3 Hispanic Americans), 1 international. Average age 23. *Faculty:* 545 full-time (132 women), 64 part-time/adjunct (25 women). Expenses: Contact institution. *Financial support:* Fellowships, research assistantships, teaching assistantships, career-related internships or fieldwork, Federal Work-Study, and institutionally sponsored loans available. Financial award applicants required to submit FAFSA. In 2001, 94 degrees awarded. Offers medicine (MD, MPH). *Application deadline:* For fall admission, 11/1. Applications are processed on a rolling basis. *Application fee:* $30. *Head*, Kimberly Scott.

College of Pharmacy Students: 383 full-time (223 women), 134 part-time (85 women). Average age 24. 365 applicants, 33% accepted. *Faculty:* 62 full-time (17 women), 22 part-time/adjunct (13 women). Expenses: Contact institution. *Financial support:* In 2001–02, 364 students received support, including 7 fellowships with partial tuition reimbursements available (averaging $16,500 per year), 25 research assistantships with partial tuition reimbursements available (averaging $16,500 per year), 28 teaching assistantships with partial tuition reimbursements available (averaging $16,500 per year); career-related internships or fieldwork, Federal Work-Study, institutionally sponsored loans, and scholarships/grants also available. Support available to part-time students. Financial award applicants required to submit FAFSA. In 2001, 77 first professional degrees, 2 master's, 7 doctorates awarded. *Degree program information:* Part-time programs available. Postbaccalaureate distance learning degree programs offered. Offers pharmaceutical sciences (MS, PhD); pharmacy (Pharm D, MS, PhD). *Application deadline:* Applications are processed on a rolling basis. *Application Contact:* Susan Cox, College of Pharmacy Admissions, 859-257-5303, Fax: 859-257-7297, E-mail: scox2@uky.edu. *Dean*, Dr. Kenneth B. Roberts, 859-323-7601, Fax: 859-257-7297, E-mail: krobe2@pop.uky.edu.

Graduate School Students: 3,100 full-time (1,635 women), 1,464 part-time (905 women); includes 334 minority (225 African Americans, 68 Asian Americans or Pacific Islanders, 29 Hispanic Americans, 12 Native Americans), 874 international. 5,210 applicants, 61% accepted. *Faculty:* 1,918 full-time (456 women). Expenses: Contact institution. *Financial support:* In 2001–02, 294 fellowships, 846 research assistantships, 770 teaching assistantships were awarded. Career-related internships or fieldwork, Federal Work-Study, institutionally sponsored loans, tuition waivers (partial), and unspecified assistantships also available. Support available to part-time students. In 2001, 1,042 master's, 219 doctorates, 13 other advanced degrees awarded. *Degree program information:* Part-time and evening/weekend programs available. Offers anatomy and neurobiology (PhD); biomedical engineering (MSBE, PhD); dentistry (MS); gerontology (PhD); health administration (MHA); integrated biomedical sciences (MPH, MS, Dr PH, PhD); medical science (MS); medicine (MS); microbiology and immunology (PhD); molecular and biomedical pharmacology (PhD); molecular and cellular biochemistry (PhD); nutritional sciences (PhD); physiology (PhD); public administration (MPA, PhD); public health (MPH, Dr PH); toxicology (MS, PhD). *Application fee:* $30 ($35 for international students). *Application Contact:* Dr. Jeannine Blackwell, Associate Dean, 859-257-4905, Fax: 859-323-1928. *Acting Dean*, Dr. Douglas Kalika, 606-257-1759, Fax: 606-323-1928.

College of Architecture Students: 20 full-time (13 women), 11 part-time (7 women). 23 applicants, 91% accepted. *Faculty:* 9 full-time (3 women). Expenses: Contact institution. *Financial support:* In 2001–02, 9 research assistantships were awarded In 2001, 2 degrees awarded. Offers architecture (MHP); historic preservation (MHP). *Application deadline:* For fall admission, 7/19. *Application fee:* $30 ($35 for international students). *Application Contact:* Dr. Jeannine Blackwell, Associate Dean, 606-257-4613, Fax: 606-257-1928. *Dean*, Dr. David Mohney.

College of Communications and Information Studies Students: 105 full-time (72 women), 156 part-time (133 women); includes 14 minority (9 African Americans, 3 Asian Americans or Pacific Islanders, 1 Hispanic American, 1 Native American), 14 international. 172 applicants, 63% accepted. *Faculty:* 31 full-time (6 women). Expenses: Contact institution. *Financial support:* In 2001–02, 9 fellowships, 37 research assistantships, 28 teaching assistantships were awarded. Career-related internships or fieldwork, Federal Work-Study, institutionally sponsored loans, and unspecified assistantships also available. Support available to part-time students. In 2001, 82 master's, 7 doctorates awarded. *Degree program information:* Part-time programs available. Offers communication (MA, PhD); communications and information studies (MA, MSLS, PhD); library science (MA, MSLS). *Application fee:* $30 ($35 for international students). *Application Contact:* Dr. Jeannine Blackwell, Associate Dean, 859-257-4905, Fax: 859-323-1928. *Dean*, Dr. David Johnson, 859-257-3874.

College of Human Environmental Sciences Students: 49 full-time (41 women), 14 part-time (12 women); includes 8 minority (7 African Americans, 1 Native American), 3 international. 55 applicants, 53% accepted. *Faculty:* 46 full-time (36 women). Expenses: Contact institution. *Financial support:* In 2001–02, 2 fellowships, 10 research assistantships, 17 teaching assistantships were awarded. Federal Work-Study, institutionally sponsored loans, and unspecified assistantships also available. Support available to part-time students. In 2001, 25 degrees awarded. Offers family studies, human development, and resource management (MSFAM, PhD); hospitality and food science (MS); human environment: interior design, merchandising, and textiles (MAIDM, MSIDM); human environmental sciences (MAIDM, MS, MSFAM, MSIDM, PhD). *Application deadline:* Applications are processed on a rolling basis. *Application fee:* $30 ($35 for international students). *Application Contact:* Dr. Jeannine Blackwell, Associate Dean, 859-257-4905, Fax: 859-323-1928. *Dean*, Dr. Retia Scott Walker, 859-257-2878.

College of Nursing Students: 59 full-time (50 women), 91 part-time (85 women); includes 2 minority (1 African American, 1 Native American), 12 international. 81 applicants, 78% accepted. *Faculty:* 21 full-time (all women). Expenses: Contact institution. *Financial support:* In 2001–02, 1 fellowship, 10 research assistantships, 12 teaching assistantships were awarded. Federal Work-Study and institutionally sponsored loans also available. Support available to part-time students. Financial award application deadline: 3/1. In 2001, 29 master's, 1 doctorate awarded. Offers nursing (MSN, PhD). *Application deadline:* For fall admission, 3/1. Applications are processed on a rolling basis. *Application fee:* $30 ($35 for international students). *Application Contact:* Dr. Jeannine Blackwell, Associate Dean, 859-257-4905, Fax: 859-323-1928. *Dean*, Dr. Carolyn Williams, 859-323-6533.

College of Social Work Students: 202 full-time (166 women), 66 part-time (51 women); includes 25 minority (22 African Americans, 1 Asian American or Pacific Islander, 2 Hispanic Americans), 1 international. 192 applicants, 80% accepted. *Faculty:* 24 full-time (16 women). Expenses: Contact institution. *Financial support:* In 2001–02, 1 fellowship, 13 research assistantships, 16 teaching assistantships were awarded. Career-related internships or fieldwork, institutionally sponsored loans, and unspecified assistantships also available. Support available to part-time students. In 2001, 97 degrees awarded. Offers social work (MSW, PhD). *Application deadline:* For fall admission, 4/15. Applications are processed on a rolling basis. *Application fee:* $30 ($35 for international students). *Application Contact:* Dr. Jeannine Blackwell, Associate Dean, 859-257-4905, Fax: 859-323-1928. *Dean*, Dr. Kay Hoffman, 859-257-6654.

Graduate School Programs from the College of Agriculture Students: 177 full-time (83 women), 31 part-time (15 women); includes 6 minority (4 African Americans, 1 Hispanic American, 1 Native American), 65 international. 139 applicants, 45% accepted. *Faculty:* 186 full-time (19 women). Expenses: Contact institution. *Financial support:* In 2001–02, 26 fellowships, 152 research assistantships, 4 teaching assistantships were awarded. Career-related internships or fieldwork, Federal Work-Study, institutionally sponsored loans, and unspecified assistantships also available. Support available to part-time students. In 2001, 47 master's, 29 doctorates awarded. *Degree program information:* Part-time programs available. Offers agricultural economics (MS, PhD); agriculture (MS, MS Ag, MSFOR, PhD); animal sciences (MS, PhD); crop science (MS, MS Ag, PhD); entomology (MS, PhD); forestry (MSFOR); plant and soil science (MS); plant pathology (MS, PhD); plant physiology (PhD); soil science (PhD); veterinary science (MS, PhD). *Application deadline:* For fall admission, 7/19. *Application fee:* $30 ($35 for international students). *Application Contact:* Dr. Jeannine Blackwell, Associate Dean, 859-257-4905, Fax: 859-323-1928. *Dean*, Dr. M. Scott Smith, 859-257-4772.

Graduate School Programs from the College of Allied Health Students: 212 full-time (155 women), 14 part-time (12 women); includes 11 minority (7 African Americans, 3 Asian Americans or Pacific Islanders, 1 Hispanic American), 5 international. 164 applicants, 78% accepted. *Faculty:* 56 full-time (28 women). Expenses: Contact institution. *Financial support:* In 2001–02, 3 fellowships, 2 research assistantships were awarded. Teaching assistantships, career-related internships or fieldwork, Federal Work-Study, and institutionally sponsored loans also available. Support available to part-time students. In 2001, 96 degrees awarded. *Degree program information:* Part-time programs available. Offers allied health (MS, MSCD, MSHP, MSPAS, MSPT, MSRMP, DS, PhD); clinical sciences (MS, DS); communication disorders (MSCD); health physics (MSHP); physical therapy (MSPT); physician assistant studies (MSPAS); radiological medical physics (MSRMP); rehabilitation sciences (PhD). *Application deadline:* For fall admission, 7/19. Applications are processed on a rolling basis. *Application fee:* $30 ($35 for international students). *Application Contact:* Dr. Jeannine Blackwell, Associate Dean, 859-257-4905, Fax: 859-323-1928. *Dean*, Dr. Thomas Robinson, 859-323-1100 Ext. 235.

Graduate School Programs from the College of Arts and Sciences Students: 717 full-time (345 women), 181 part-time (90 women); includes 64 minority (40 African Americans, 10 Asian Americans or Pacific Islanders, 13 Hispanic Americans, 1 Native American), 193 international. 871 applicants, 51% accepted. *Faculty:* 438 full-time (97 women). Expenses: Contact institution. *Financial support:* In 2001–02, 97 fellowships, 141 research assistantships, 430 teaching assistantships were awarded. Career-related internships or fieldwork, Federal Work-Study, institutionally sponsored loans, and unspecified assistantships also available. Support available to part-time students. In 2001, 115 master's, 79 doctorates awarded. *Degree program information:* Part-time programs available. Offers anthropology (MA, PhD); arts and sciences (MA, MS, MS Ag, PhD); biological sciences (MS, PhD); chemistry (MS, PhD); classical languages and literatures (MA); English (MA, PhD); French (MA); geography (MA, PhD); geology (MS, PhD); German (MA); history (MA, PhD); mathematics (MA, MS, PhD); philosophy (MA, PhD); physics and astronomy (MS, PhD); political science (MA, PhD); psychology (MA, PhD); sociology (MA, MS Ag, PhD); Spanish (MA, PhD); statistics (MS, PhD). *Application fee:* $30 ($35 for international students). *Application Contact:* Dr. Jeannine Blackwell, Associate Dean, 859-257-4905, Fax: 859-323-1928. *Dean*, Dr. Howard Grotch, 859-257-5821.

Graduate School Programs from the College of Business and Economics Students: 230 full-time (88 women), 130 part-time (36 women); includes 36 minority (23 African Americans, 12 Asian Americans or Pacific Islanders, 1 Hispanic American), 53 international. 469 applicants, 56% accepted. *Faculty:* 78 full-time (12 women). Expenses: Contact institution. *Financial support:* In 2001–02, 22 fellowships, 12 research assistantships, 36 teaching assistantships were awarded. Career-related internships or fieldwork, Federal Work-Study, institutionally sponsored loans, and unspecified assistantships also available. Support available to part-time students. In 2001, 108 master's, 24 doctorates awarded. *Degree program information:* Part-time and evening/weekend programs available. Offers accounting (MSACC); business administration (MBA, PhD); business and economics (MBA, MS, MSACC, PhD); economics (MS, PhD). *Application deadline:* For fall admission, 7/19. Applications are processed on a rolling basis. *Application fee:* $30 ($35 for international students). *Application Contact:* Dr. Jeannine Blackwell, Associate Dean, 859-257-4905, Fax: 859-323-1928. *Dean*, Dr. Richard Furst, 859-257-8939.

Graduate School Programs from the College of Education Students: 338 full-time (227 women), 472 part-time (346 women); includes 88 minority (72 African Americans, 7 Asian Americans or Pacific Islanders, 4 Hispanic Americans, 5 Native Americans), 20 international. 587 applicants, 65% accepted. *Faculty:* 130 full-time (61 women). Expenses: Contact institution. *Financial support:* In 2001–02, 10 fellowships, 36 research assistantships, 71 teaching assistantships were awarded. Career-related internships or fieldwork, Federal Work-Study, institutionally sponsored loans, and unspecified assistantships also available. Support available to part-time students. In 2001, 211 master's, 33 doctorates, 13 other

University of Kentucky (continued)

advanced degrees awarded. *Degree program information:* Part-time and evening/weekend programs available. Offers administration and supervision (M Ed, Ed D, Ed S); clinical and college teaching (MS Ed); curriculum and instruction (Ed D); education (M Ed, MA Ed, MRC, MS, MS Ed, MSVE, Ed D, PhD, Ed S); educational and counseling psychology (MA Ed, MS Ed, Ed D, PhD, Ed S); educational policy studies and evaluation (MS Ed, Ed D, PhD); exercise science (PhD); instruction and administration (Ed D); kinesiology (MS, Ed D); rehabilitation counseling (MRC); special education (MA Ed, MS Ed, Ed D, Ed S); vocational education (MA Ed, MS Ed, MSVE, Ed D, Ed S). *Application deadline:* Applications are processed on a rolling basis. *Application fee:* $30 ($35 for international students). *Application Contact:* Dr. Jeannine Blackwell, Associate Dean, 859-257-4905, Fax: 859-323-1928. *Dean,* Dr. James Cibulka, 859-257-2813.

Graduate School Programs from the College of Engineering Students: 424 full-time (96 women), 101 part-time (13 women); includes 14 minority (2 African Americans, 11 Asian Americans or Pacific Islanders, 1 Hispanic American), 342 international. 1,118 applicants, 56% accepted. *Faculty:* 179 full-time (18 women). Expenses: Contact institution. *Financial support:* In 2001–02, 24 fellowships, 202 research assistantships, 82 teaching assistantships were awarded. Career-related internships or fieldwork, Federal Work-Study, and institutionally sponsored loans also available. Support available to part-time students. In 2001, 121 master's, 10 doctorates awarded. *Degree program information:* Part-time programs available. Offers biosystems and agricultural engineering (MSAE, PhD); chemical engineering (MS Ch E, PhD); civil engineering (MCE, MSCE, PhD); computer science (MS, PhD); electrical engineering (MSEE, PhD); engineering (M Eng, MCE, MME, MS, MS Ch E, MS Min, MSAE, MSCE, MSEE, MSEM, MSMAE, MSME, MSMSE, PhD); manufacturing systems engineering (MSMSE); materials science (MSMAE, PhD); mechanical engineering (MSME, PhD); mining engineering (MME, MS Min, PhD). *Application deadline:* For fall admission, 7/19. Applications are processed on a rolling basis. *Application fee:* $30 ($35 for international students). *Application Contact:* Dr. Jeannine Blackwell, Associate Dean, 859-257-4905, Fax: 859-323-1928. *Dean,* Dr. Thomas W. Lester, 859-257-1687.

Graduate School Programs from the College of Fine Arts Students: 112 full-time (59 women), 24 part-time (30 women); includes 11 minority (8 African Americans, 1 Asian American or Pacific Islander, 2 Hispanic Americans), 7 international. 88 applicants, 64% accepted. *Faculty:* 59 full-time (18 women). Expenses: Contact institution. *Financial support:* In 2001–02, 11 fellowships, 14 research assistantships, 38 teaching assistantships were awarded. Federal Work-Study and institutionally sponsored loans also available. Support available to part-time students. In 2001, 27 master's, 4 doctorates awarded. *Degree program information:* Part-time and evening/weekend programs available. Offers art education (MA); art history (MA); art studio (MFA); fine arts (MA, MFA, MM, DMA, PhD); music (MA, MM, DMA, PhD); theatre (MA). *Application deadline:* Applications are processed on a rolling basis. *Application fee:* $30 ($35 for international students). *Application Contact:* Dr. Jeannine Blackwell, Associate Dean, 859-257-4905, Fax: 859-323-1928. *Dean,* Dr. Robert Shay, 859-257-1707.

Patterson School of Diplomacy and International Commerce Students: 49 full-time (23 women), 5 part-time (4 women); includes 1 minority (Asian American or Pacific Islander), 8 international. 58 applicants, 67% accepted. *Faculty:* 6 full-time (0 women). Expenses: Contact institution. *Financial support:* In 2001–02, 7 fellowships, 2 research assistantships, 4 teaching assistantships were awarded. Federal Work-Study, institutionally sponsored loans, and unspecified assistantships also available. In 2001, 24 degrees awarded. Offers diplomacy and international commerce (MA). *Application deadline:* For fall admission, 2/1. *Application fee:* $30 ($35 for international students). *Application Contact:* Dr. Jeannine Blackwell, Associate Dean, 859-257-4905, Fax: 859-323-1928. *Director of Graduate Studies,* Dr. John D. Stempel, 859-257-4666, Fax: 859-257-4676, E-mail: psdstem@ukcc.uky.edu.

UNIVERSITY OF LA VERNE, La Verne, CA 91750-4443

General Information Independent, coed, university. *Enrollment:* 1,166 full-time matriculated graduate/professional students (749 women), 1,648 part-time matriculated graduate/professional students (1,028 women). *Enrollment by degree level:* 1,780 master's, 506 doctoral, 530 other advanced degrees. *Graduate faculty:* 57 full-time (28 women), 247 part-time/adjunct (109 women). *Tuition:* Full-time $4,410; part-time $245 per unit. *Required fees:* $60. Tuition and fees vary according to course load, degree level, campus/location and program. *Graduate housing:* On-campus housing not available. *Student services:* Campus employment opportunities, campus safety program, career counseling, disabled student services, free psychological counseling, international student services, low-cost health insurance, teacher training. *Library facilities:* Wilson Library plus 1 other. *Online resources:* library catalog, web page, access to other libraries' catalogs. *Collection:* 215,000 titles, 3,600 serial subscriptions. *Research affiliation:* Presbyterian Intercommunity Hospital, Riverside Community Hospital, San Antonio Community Hospital, Methodist Hospital of Southern California, Southern California Healthcare Systems, Huntington Memorial Hospital (health services management).

Computer facilities: 150 computers available on campus for general student use. A campuswide network can be accessed from student residence rooms and from off campus. Internet access, on-line grade information are available. *Web address:* http://www.ulv.edu/.

General Application Contact: Jo Nell Baker, Director, Graduate Admissions and Academic Services, 909-593-3511 Ext. 4504, Fax: 909-392-2761, E-mail: bakerj@ulv.edu.

GRADUATE UNITS

College of Arts and Sciences Students: 56 full-time (49 women), 52 part-time (41 women); includes 53 minority (10 African Americans, 8 Asian Americans or Pacific Islanders, 34 Hispanic Americans, 1 Native American), 1 international. Average age 34. *Faculty:* 9 full-time (5 women), 15 part-time/adjunct (9 women). Expenses: Contact institution. *Financial support:* In 2001–02, 74 students received support, including 1 fellowship (averaging $4,980 per year), 16 research assistantships (averaging $1,894 per year); career-related internships or fieldwork, institutionally sponsored loans, and scholarships/grants also available. Financial award application deadline: 3/2. In 2001, 16 degrees awarded. *Degree program information:* Part-time programs available. Offers arts and sciences (MS, Psy D); clinical-community psychology (Psy D); counseling (MS); counseling in higher education (MS); general counseling (MS); gerontology (MS); marriage, family and child counseling (MS); psychology (Psy D). *Application deadline:* Applications are processed on a rolling basis. *Application Contact:* Jo Nell Baker, Director, Graduate Admissions and Academic Services, 909-593-3511 Ext. 4504, Fax: 909-392-2761, E-mail: bakerj@ulv.edu. *Dean,* Dr. John Gingrich, 909-593-3511 Ext. 4186, E-mail: gingrich@ulv.edu.

College of Law *Degree program information:* Part-time and evening/weekend programs available. Offers law (JD). Also available at San Fernando Valley Campus, Woodland Hills, CA 91367. Contact Julius Walecki, Director of Admissions, 818-883-0529.

School of Business and Global Studies Students: 81 full-time (39 women), 222 part-time (102 women); includes 76 minority (21 African Americans, 25 Asian Americans or Pacific Islanders, 29 Hispanic Americans, 1 Native American), 158 international. Average age 30. *Faculty:* 9 full-time (1 woman), 14 part-time/adjunct (2 women). Expenses: Contact institution. *Financial support:* In 2001–02, 58 students received support, including 10 research assistantships (averaging $1,139 per year); fellowships, institutionally sponsored loans and scholarships/grants also available. Financial award application deadline: 3/1; financial award applicants required to submit FAFSA. In 2001, 131 degrees awarded. *Degree program information:* Part-time and evening/weekend programs available. Offers accounting (MBA); business and global studies (MBA, MBA-EP, MBIT, MS); business organizational management (MS); executive management (MBA-EP); finance (MBA, MBA-EP); health services management (MBA); information technology (MBA, MBA-EP); international business (MBA, MBA-EP); leadership (MBA-EP); managed care (MBA); management (MBA, MBA-EP); marketing (MBA, MBA-EP). *Application deadline:* Applications are processed on a rolling basis. *Application fee:* $40. *Application Contact:* Dr. Julius Walecki, Marketing Director, 909-593-3511 Ext. 4192, Fax: 909-392-2761, E-mail: waleckij@ulv.edu. *Interim Dean,* Verne Orr, 909-539-3511 Ext. 4216, Fax: 909-392-2704, E-mail: orrv@ulv.edu.

School of Continuing Education Students: 660 full-time (417 women), 619 part-time (357 women); includes 425 minority (128 African Americans, 69 Asian Americans or Pacific Islanders, 209 Hispanic Americans, 19 Native Americans) Average age 37. *Faculty:* 129 part-time/adjunct (47 women). Expenses: Contact institution. *Financial support:* In 2001–02, 396 students received support, including 58 fellowships (averaging $2,589 per year); Federal Work-Study and institutionally sponsored loans also available. Support available to part-time students. Financial award application deadline: 3/2; financial award applicants required to submit FAFSA. In 2001, 549 degrees awarded. *Degree program information:* Part-time programs available. Offers advanced teaching (M Ed); business (MBA-EP); continuing education (M Ed, MBA-EP, MHA, MS, Credential); cross cultural language and academic development (Credential); educational management (M Ed); health administration (MHA); leadership and management (MS); multiple subject (Credential); reading (M Ed); school counseling (MS); single subject (Credential). *Application deadline:* Applications are processed on a rolling basis. *Application fee:* $40. *Dean,* Dr. James C. Manolis, 909-985-0944, Fax: 909-981-8695, E-mail: manolisj@ulv.edu.

School of Education and Organizational Leadership Students: 319 full-time (218 women), 616 part-time (447 women); includes 307 minority (75 African Americans, 40 Asian Americans or Pacific Islanders, 186 Hispanic Americans, 6 Native Americans), 3 international. Average age 37. *Faculty:* 29 full-time (18 women), 73 part-time/adjunct (45 women). Expenses: Contact institution. *Financial support:* In 2001–02, 416 students received support, including 65 fellowships (averaging $3,406 per year), 36 research assistantships (averaging $1,001 per year); institutionally sponsored loans and scholarships/grants also available. Financial award application deadline: 3/2; financial award applicants required to submit FAFSA. In 2001, 140 master's, 2 doctorates awarded. *Degree program information:* Part-time programs available. Offers advanced teaching skills (M Ed); child development (MS); child development/child life (MS); child life (MS); education (M Ed); education (special emphasis) (M Ed); education and organizational leadership (M Ed, MS, Ed D, Credential); educational management (M Ed, Credential); leadership and management (MS); organizational leadership (Ed D); preliminary administrative services (Credential); professional administrative services (Credential); pupil personnel services (Credential); reading (M Ed, Credential); reading and language arts specialist (Credential); school counseling (MS, Credential); teacher education (Credential). *Application deadline:* Applications are processed on a rolling basis. *Application Contact:* Jo Nell Baker, Director, Graduate Admissions and Academic Services, 909-593-3511 Ext. 4504, Fax: 909-392-2761, E-mail: bakerj@ulv.edu. *Dean,* Dr. Leonard Pellicer, 909-593-3511 Ext. 4647, E-mail: pellicer@ulv.edu.

School of Public Affairs and Health Administration Students: 50 full-time (26 women), 139 part-time (81 women); includes 91 minority (45 African Americans, 19 Asian Americans or Pacific Islanders, 24 Hispanic Americans, 3 Native Americans), 14 international. Average age 42. *Faculty:* 10 full-time (4 women), 16 part-time/adjunct (6 women). Expenses: Contact institution. *Financial support:* In 2001–02, 75 students received support, including 1 fellowship (averaging $1,020 per year), 3 research assistantships (averaging $2,591 per year); institutionally sponsored loans also available. Financial award application deadline: 3/2; financial award applicants required to submit FAFSA. In 2001, 46 master's, 1 doctorate awarded. *Degree program information:* Part-time programs available. Offers business administration (MS); counseling (MS); gerontology (MS); gerontology administration (MS); health administration (MHA); health services management (MS); healthcare information management (MHA); managed care (MHA); public administration (MS); public affairs and health administration (MHA, MPA, MS, DPA). *Application deadline:* Applications are processed on a rolling basis. *Application fee:* $35. *Application Contact:* Jo Nell Baker, Director, Graduate Admissions and Academic Services, 909-593-3511 Ext. 4504, Fax: 909-392-2761, E-mail: bakerj@ulv.edu. *Dean,* Dr. Jack W. Meek, 909-593-3511 Ext. 4941, Fax: 909-596-5860, E-mail: meekj@ulv.edu.

THE UNIVERSITY OF LETHBRIDGE, Lethbridge, AB T1K 3M4, Canada

General Information Province-supported, coed, comprehensive institution. *Enrollment:* 100 full-time matriculated graduate/professional students, 192 part-time matriculated graduate/professional students. *Graduate faculty:* 250. *Graduate tuition:* Tuition charges are reported in Canadian dollars. *Tuition:* Full-time $2,208 Canadian dollars. Full-time tuition and fees vary according to program. *Graduate housing:* Rooms and/or apartments available on a first-come, first-served basis to single and married students. Typical cost: $4,749 Canadian dollars per year ($8,127 Canadian dollars including board) for single students; $7,560 Canadian dollars per year ($16,005 Canadian dollars including board) for married students. Housing application deadline: 4/1. *Student services:* Campus employment opportunities, campus safety program, career counseling, disabled student services, exercise/wellness program, free psychological counseling, international student services, low-cost health insurance, multicultural affairs office, teacher training, writing training. *Library facilities:* The University of Lethbridge Library. *Online resources:* library catalog, web page, access to other libraries' catalogs. *Collection:* 484,657 titles, 3,331 audiovisual materials. *Research affiliation:* National Sciences and Engineering Research Council, Social Sciences and Humanities Research Council, Alberta Heritage Fund (medical research), Federal Research Council (medical research), Alberta Advanced Education (post-secondary education), Alberta Agriculture (biology, botany, chemistry).

Computer facilities: 550 computers available on campus for general student use. A campuswide network can be accessed from student residence rooms and from off campus. Internet access and online class registration are available. *Web address:* http://www.uleth.ca/.

General Application Contact: Kathy Schrage, Administrative Assistant, School of Graduate Studies, 403-329-2121, Fax: 403-329-2097, E-mail: schrage@uleth.ca.

GRADUATE UNITS

Faculty of Education Average age 39. Expenses: Contact institution. *Financial support:* Research assistantships, teaching assistantships, career-related internships or fieldwork, scholarships/grants, health care benefits, and unspecified assistantships available. *Degree program information:* Part-time and evening/weekend programs available. Postbaccalaureate distance learning degree programs offered (minimal on-campus study). Offers education (Diploma). *Application deadline:* For fall admission, 6/1; for spring admission, 11/1. *Application fee:* $60 Canadian dollars. Electronic applications accepted. *Application Contact:* Dr. Kris Magnusson, Assistant Dean, Graduate Studies, 403-329-2425, Fax: 403-329-2252, E-mail: inquires@uleth.ca. *Dean, Faculty of Education,* Dr. Jane O'Dea, 403-329-2251, Fax: 403-329-2252, E-mail: inquires@uleth.ca.

School of Graduate Studies Students: 97 full-time, 190 part-time. Average age 39. 35 applicants, 100% accepted, 35 enrolled. *Faculty:* 250. Expenses: Contact institution. *Financial support:* Fellowships, research assistantships, teaching assistantships, scholarships/grants, health care benefits, and unspecified assistantships available. In 2001, 40 degrees awarded. *Degree program information:* Part-time and evening/weekend programs available. Offers accounting (MScM); agricultural biotechnology (M Sc); agricultural studies (M Sc, MA); anthropology (MA); archaeology (MA); art (MA); biochemistry (M Sc); biological sciences (M Sc); Canadian studies (MA); chemistry (M Sc); computer science (M Sc); counseling psychology (M Ed); dramatic arts (MA); economics (MA); English (MA); environmental science (M Sc); exercise science (M Sc); finance (MScM); French (MA); French/German (MA); French/Spanish (MA); general education (M Ed); general management (MScM); geography (M Sc, MA); German (MA); health sciences (M Sc, MA); history (MA); human resources/management and industrial relations (MScM); information systems (MScM); international management (MScM); kinesiology (M Sc, MA); management (M Sc, MA); marketing (MScM); mathematics (M Sc); music (MA); Native American studies (MA, MScM); neuroscience (M Sc, PhD); nursing (M Sc); philosophy (MA); physics (M Sc); political science (MA); psychology (M Sc, MA); religious studies (MA); sociology (MA); urban and regional studies (MA). *Application fee:* $60 Canadian dollars. *Application Contact:* Kathy Schrage, Administrative Assistant, Office of the Academic Vice President, 403-329-2121, Fax: 403-329-2097, E-mail: inquiries@uleth.ca. *Dean, School of Graduate Studies,* Dr. Shamsul Alam, 403-329-2121, Fax: 403-329-2097, E-mail: inquiries@uleth.ca.

UNIVERSITY OF LOUISIANA AT LAFAYETTE, Lafayette, LA 70504

General Information State-supported, coed, university. CGS member. *Enrollment:* 724 full-time matriculated graduate/professional students (325 women), 460 part-time matriculated graduate/professional students (278 women). *Enrollment by degree level:* 938 master's, 246 doctoral. *Graduate faculty:* 310 full-time (94 women). *International tuition:* $9,018 full-time. Tuition, state resident: full-time $2,317; part-time $79 per credit. Tuition, nonresident: full-time $8,882; part-time $369 per credit. *Graduate housing:* Rooms and/or apartments available on a first-come, first-served basis to single and married students. Typical cost: $2,886 (including board) for single students. *Student services:* Campus employment opportunities, campus safety program, career counseling, child daycare facilities, disabled student services, free psychological counseling, international student services, low-cost health insurance. *Library facilities:* Edith Garland Dupre Library. *Online resources:* library catalog, web page. *Collection:* 425,034 titles, 5,174 serial subscriptions, 5,755 audiovisual materials. *Research affiliation:* National Wetlands Research Center (biology, wetlands restoration), Louisiana Universities Marine Consortium (marine biology), U.S. Fish and Wildlife Service (ecology), Army Corps of Engineers (wetlands), U.S. Geological Survey, U.S. Department of Agriculture.

Computer facilities: 548 computers available on campus for general student use. A campuswide network can be accessed from off campus. Internet access and online class registration are available. *Web address:* http://www.louisiana.edu/.

General Application Contact: Dr. C. E. Palmer, Director, 337-482-6965, Fax: 337-482-6195, E-mail: palmer@louisiana.edu.

GRADUATE UNITS

Graduate School Students: 724 full-time (325 women), 460 part-time (278 women); includes 75 minority (50 African Americans, 11 Asian Americans or Pacific Islanders, 11 Hispanic Americans, 3 Native Americans), 391 international. Average age 31. 1,957 applicants, 66% accepted, 638 enrolled. *Faculty:* 310 full-time (94 women). Expenses: Contact institution. *Financial support:* In 2001–02, 50 fellowships with full tuition reimbursements (averaging $13,179 per year), 174 research assistantships with full tuition reimbursements (averaging $6,189 per year), 117 teaching assistantships with full tuition reimbursements (averaging $8,948 per year) were awarded. Career-related internships or fieldwork, Federal Work-Study, institutionally sponsored loans, scholarships/grants, and tuition waivers (full) also available. Support available to part-time students. In 2001, 343 master's, 36 doctorates awarded. *Degree program information:* Part-time and evening/weekend programs available. *Application deadline:* For fall admission, 5/15. *Application fee:* $20 ($30 for international students). *Director,* Dr. C. E. Palmer, 337-482-6965, Fax: 337-482-6195, E-mail: palmer@louisiana.edu.

College of Applied Life Sciences Students: 5 full-time (3 women), 17 part-time (15 women); includes 1 minority (African American) 14 applicants, 57% accepted, 6 enrolled. *Faculty:* 9 full-time (3 women). Expenses: Contact institution. *Financial support:* In 2001–02, 5 research assistantships with full tuition reimbursements (averaging $5,500 per year) were awarded; fellowships, teaching assistantships, Federal Work-Study also available. Financial award application deadline: 5/1. In 2001, 4 degrees awarded. *Degree program information:* Part-time programs available. Offers applied life sciences (MS); human resources (MS). *Application deadline:* For fall admission, 5/15. *Application fee:* $20 ($30 for international students). *Dean,* Dr. Linda Vincent, 337-482-6967.

College of Business Administration Students: 84 full-time (37 women), 86 part-time (36 women); includes 14 minority (10 African Americans, 3 Asian Americans or Pacific Islanders, 1 Hispanic American), 21 international. 150 applicants, 63% accepted. *Faculty:* 30 full-time (5 women). Expenses: Contact institution. *Financial support:* In 2001–02, 15 research assistantships with full tuition reimbursements (averaging $5,500 per year) were awarded; fellowships, Federal Work-Study and tuition waivers (full) also available. Support available to part-time students. Financial award application deadline: 5/1. In 2001, 59 degrees awarded. *Degree program information:* Part-time programs available. Offers business administration (MBA); health care administration (MBA); health care certification (MBA). *Application deadline:* For fall admission, 5/15. *Application fee:* $20 ($30 for international students). *Application Contact:* Dr. Joel Authenent, Graduate Coordinator, 337-482-6119. *Dean,* Dr. Michael Fronmueller, 337-482-6491.

College of Education Students: 29 full-time (24 women), 151 part-time (130 women); includes 18 minority (14 African Americans, 1 Asian American or Pacific Islander, 3 Hispanic Americans), 1 international. 93 applicants, 76% accepted, 49 enrolled. *Faculty:* 33 full-time (23 women). Expenses: Contact institution. *Financial support:* In 2001–02, 14 research assistantships with full tuition reimbursements (averaging $5,500 per year) were awarded; fellowships, teaching assistantships, Federal Work-Study also available. Financial award application deadline: 5/1. In 2001, 60 degrees awarded. *Degree program information:* Part-time programs available. Offers administration and supervision (M Ed); curriculum and instruction (M Ed); education (M Ed); education of the gifted (M Ed); guidance and counseling (M Ed). *Application deadline:* For fall admission, 5/15. *Application fee:* $20 ($30 for international students). *Acting Dean,* Dr. Gerald B. Carlson, 337-482-6678.

College of Engineering Students: 147 full-time (31 women), 48 part-time (7 women); includes 6 minority (5 African Americans, 1 Asian American or Pacific Islander), 148 international. 537 applicants, 56% accepted, 68 enrolled. *Faculty:* 56 full-time (5 women). Expenses: Contact institution. *Financial support:* In 2001–02, 5 fellowships with full tuition reimbursements (averaging $13,900 per year), 51 research assistantships with full tuition reimbursements (averaging $6,412 per year), 23 teaching assistantships with full tuition reimbursements (averaging $6,868 per year) were awarded. Federal Work-Study and tuition waivers (full and partial) also available. Support available to part-time students. In 2001, 53 master's, 5 doctorates awarded. *Degree program information:* Part-time and evening/weekend programs available. Offers chemical engineering (MSE); civil engineering (MSE); computer engineering (MS, PhD); computer science (MS, PhD); engineering (MS, MSE, MSET, MSTC, PhD); engineering management (MSET); mechanical engineering (MSE); petroleum engineering (MSE); telecommunications (MSTC). *Application deadline:* For fall admission, 5/15. *Application fee:* $20 ($30 for international students). *Dean,* Dr. Anthony B. Ponter, 337-482-6685.

College of Liberal Arts Students: 193 full-time (138 women), 84 part-time (58 women); includes 27 minority (16 African Americans, 4 Asian Americans or Pacific Islanders, 4 Hispanic Americans, 3 Native Americans), 24 international. 216 applicants, 68% accepted, 87 enrolled. *Faculty:* 97 full-time (32 women). Expenses: Contact institution. *Financial support:* In 2001–02, 28 fellowships with full tuition reimbursements (averaging $12,178 per year), 45 research assistantships with full tuition reimbursements (averaging $5,500 per year), 57 teaching assistantships with full tuition reimbursements (averaging $9,210 per year) were awarded. Career-related internships or fieldwork and Federal Work-Study also available. Support available to part-time students. Financial award application deadline: 5/1. In 2001, 77 master's, 15 doctorates awarded. *Degree program information:* Part-time programs available. Offers British and American literature (MA); communicative disorders (MS, PhD); creative writing (PhD); francophone studies (PhD); French (MA); history and geography (MA); liberal arts (MA, MS, PhD); literature (PhD); mass communications (MS); psychology (MS); rehabilitation counseling (MS); rhetoric (PhD). *Application deadline:* For fall admission, 5/15. *Application fee:* $20 ($30 for international students). *Dean,* Dr. A. David Barry, 337-482-6219.

College of Nursing Students: 11 full-time (8 women), 16 part-time (14 women); includes 2 minority (1 African American, 1 Hispanic American) 11 applicants, 82% accepted, 7 enrolled. *Faculty:* 14 full-time (12 women). Expenses: Contact institution. In 2001, 3 degrees awarded. Offers nursing (MSN). *Application deadline:* For fall admission, 5/15. *Application fee:* $20 ($30 for international students). *Application Contact:* Dr. Carolyn P. Delahoussaye, Graduate Coordinator, 337-482-5617. *Dean,* Dr. Gail Poirrier, 337-482-6808.

College of Sciences Students: 242 full-time (78 women), 54 part-time (16 women). 630 applicants, 57% accepted, 92 enrolled. *Faculty:* 89 full-time (14 women). Expenses: Contact institution. *Financial support:* In 2001–02, 17 fellowships with full tuition reimbursements (averaging $14,617 per year), 32 research assistantships with full tuition reimbursements (averaging $7,792 per year), 37 teaching assistantships with full tuition reimbursements (averaging $9,837 per year) were awarded. Federal Work-Study, institutionally sponsored loans, and tuition waivers (full) also available. Support available to part-time students. In 2001, 80 master's, 16 doctorates awarded. *Degree program information:* Part-time programs available. Offers applied physics (MS); biology (MS); cognitive science (PhD); computer science (MS); environmental and evolutionary biology (PhD); geology (MS); mathematics (MS, PhD); physics (MS); sciences (MS, PhD). *Application deadline:* For fall admission, 5/15. *Application fee:* $20 ($30 for international students). *Acting Dean,* Dr. Bradd D. Clark, 337-482-6986.

College of the Arts Students: 14 full-time (6 women), 5 part-time (3 women), 1 international. 10 applicants, 90% accepted, 7 enrolled. *Faculty:* 19 full-time (6 women). Expenses: Contact institution. *Financial support:* In 2001–02, 12 research assistantships with full tuition reimbursements (averaging $5,500 per year) were awarded; Federal Work-Study also available. Financial award application deadline: 5/1. In 2001, 7 degrees awarded. Offers architecture (M Arch); arts (M Arch, MM); conducting (MM); pedagogy (MM); vocal and instrumental performance (MM). *Application deadline:* For fall admission, 5/15. *Application fee:* $20 ($30 for international students). *Dean,* H. Gordon Brooks, 318-482-6224.

UNIVERSITY OF LOUISIANA AT MONROE, Monroe, LA 71209-0001

General Information State-supported, coed, university. *Graduate housing:* Room and/or apartments available on a first-come, first-served basis to single students; on-campus housing not available to married students. Housing application deadline: 7/28. *Research affiliation:* National Center for Toxicological Research, U.S. Army Corps of Engineers (toxicology, environmental science).

GRADUATE UNITS

Graduate Studies and Research *Degree program information:* Part-time and evening/weekend programs available.

College of Allied Health and Rehabilitation Professions Offers allied health and rehabilitation professions (MA); communicative disorders (MA).

College of Business Administration *Degree program information:* Part-time and evening/weekend programs available. Offers business administration (MBA).

College of Education and Human Development *Degree program information:* Part-time and evening/weekend programs available. Offers administration and supervision (M Ed, Ed S); counseling (M Ed, Ed S); curriculum and instruction (Ed D, Ed S); education (M Ed, MA, MS, Ed D, PhD, Ed S, SSP); educational leadership (Ed D); elementary education (M Ed, Ed S); English education (M Ed); health and human performance (M Ed, MS); marriage and family therapy (MA, PhD); psychology (MS); reading (M Ed); school psychology (SSP); secondary education (M Ed, Ed S); special education (M Ed); substance abuse counseling (MA).

College of Liberal Arts *Degree program information:* Part-time and evening/weekend programs available. Offers communication (MA); criminal justice (MA); English (MA); gerontological studies (CGS); gerontology (MA); history (MA); liberal arts (MA, MM, CGS); music (MM).

College of Pharmacy Offers pharmaceutical sciences (MS); pharmacy (PhD); pharmacy and health sciences (Pharm D, MS, PhD).

College of Pure and Applied Sciences Offers biology (MS); chemistry (MS); geosciences (MS); pure and applied sciences (MS).

UNIVERSITY OF LOUISVILLE, Louisville, KY 40292-0001

General Information State-supported, coed, university. CGS member. *Enrollment:* 3,221 full-time matriculated graduate/professional students (1,649 women), 2,272 part-time matriculated graduate/professional students (1,325 women). *Enrollment by degree level:* 1,271 first professional, 3,526 master's, 696 doctoral. *Graduate faculty:* 1,300 full-time (422 women), 511 part-time/adjunct (231 women). Tuition, state resident: full-time $4,134. Tuition, nonresident: full-time $11,486. *Graduate housing:* Rooms and/or apartments available to single and married students. *Student services:* Campus employment opportunities, campus safety program, career counseling, child daycare facilities, disabled student services, exercise/wellness program, free psychological counseling, grant writing training, international student services, low-cost health insurance, multicultural affairs office. *Library facilities:* William F. Ekstrom Library plus 5 others. *Online resources:* library catalog, web page. *Collection:* 969,925 titles, 13,333 serial subscriptions. *Research affiliation:* Oak Ridge National Laboratory, Argonne National Laboratory.

Computer facilities: 250 computers available on campus for general student use. A campuswide network can be accessed from student residence rooms and from off campus. Internet access is available. *Web address:* http://www.louisville.edu/.

General Application Contact: Jenny L. Sawyer, Information Contact, 502-852-3101, Fax: 502-852-3111, E-mail: gradadm@louisville.edu.

GRADUATE UNITS

Graduate School Students: 1,648 full-time (903 women), 2,186 part-time (1,262 women). Average age 33. Expenses: Contact institution. *Financial support:* Fellowships with full tuition reimbursements, research assistantships with full tuition reimbursements, teaching assistantships with full and partial tuition reimbursements, career-related internships or fieldwork, Federal Work-Study, institutionally sponsored loans, scholarships/grants, traineeships, tuition waivers (partial), and unspecified assistantships available. *Degree program information:* Part-time and evening/weekend programs available. *Application deadline:* Applications are processed on a rolling basis. *Application fee:* $25. Electronic applications accepted. *Application Contact:* Libby Sklare, Director of Admissions, 502-852-3101, Fax: 502-852-6536, E-mail: gradadm@louisville.edu. *Dean,* Dr. Ronald M. Atlas, 502-852-8371, Fax: 502-852-6616, E-mail: r.atlas@louisville.edu.

College of Arts and Sciences Students: 343 full-time (189 women), 265 part-time (147 women); includes 68 minority (41 African Americans, 12 Asian Americans or Pacific Islanders, 11 Hispanic Americans, 4 Native Americans), 76 international. Average age 34. *Faculty:* 314 full-time (119 women), 152 part-time/adjunct (73 women). Expenses: Contact institution. *Financial support:* Fellowships with full tuition reimbursements, research assistantships with full tuition reimbursements, teaching assistantships with full tuition reimbursements, career-related internships or fieldwork, institutionally sponsored loans, scholarships/grants, tuition waivers (partial), and unspecified assistantships available. In 2001, 119 master's, 27 doctorates awarded. *Degree program information:* Part-time and evening/weekend programs available. Offers analytical chemistry (MS, PhD); art (MA); art history (MA, PhD); arts and sciences (MA, MFA, MS, PhD); biology (MS); chemical physics (PhD); clinical psychology (PhD); creative art (MA); English (MA); English literature (MA); English rhetoric and composition (PhD); environmental biology (PhD); experimental psychology (PhD); French (MA); history (MA); humanities (MA); inorganic chemistry (MS, PhD); justice administration (MS); mathematics (MA); organic chemistry (MS, PhD); Pan-African studies (MA); performance (MFA); philosophy (MA); physical chemistry (MS, PhD); physics (MS); political science (MA); production (MFA); psychology (MA); sociology (MA); Spanish (MA); theatre arts (MA). *Application deadline:* Applications are processed on a rolling basis. *Application fee:* $25. *Dean,* James F. Brennan, 502-852-6490, Fax: 502-852-6888, E-mail: jfbren01@gwise.louisville.edu.

College of Business and Public Administration Students: 249 full-time (85 women), 390 part-time (147 women); includes 48 minority (26 African Americans, 17 Asian Americans or Pacific Islanders, 5 Hispanic Americans), 200 international. Average age 31. *Faculty:* 81 full-time (14 women), 38 part-time/adjunct (11 women). Expenses: Contact institution. *Financial support:* In 2001–02, 27 research assistantships with full tuition reimbursements (averaging $9,200 per year) were awarded; unspecified assistantships also available. In 2001, 267 master's, 4 doctorates awarded. *Degree program information:* Part-time programs available. Offers accountancy (MAC); business and public administration (MA, MAC, MBA, MPA, MUP, PhD); labor and public management (MPA); management (MBA); public administration (MPA); public policy and administration (MPA); systems science (MA); urban and public affairs (PhD); urban and regional development (MPA); urban planning (MUP). *Application deadline:* Applications are processed on a rolling basis. *Application*

University of Louisville (continued)

fee: $25. *Dean,* Dr. Robert L. Taylor, 508-852-6443, Fax: 502-852-7557, E-mail: robert.l.taylor@louisville.edu.

College of Education and Human Development Students: 485 full-time (346 women), 936 part-time (722 women); includes 140 minority (109 African Americans, 16 Asian Americans or Pacific Islanders, 11 Hispanic Americans, 4 Native Americans), 80 international. Average age 35. *Faculty:* 85 full-time (42 women), 76 part-time/adjunct (48 women). Expenses: Contact institution. *Financial support:* In 2001–02, 38 students received support, including 3 fellowships with full tuition reimbursements available (averaging $6,723 per year), 27 research assistantships with full tuition reimbursements available (averaging $12,000 per year), 9 teaching assistantships with full tuition reimbursements available (averaging $12,000 per year); career-related internships or fieldwork, Federal Work-Study, and scholarships/grants also available. In 2001, 501 master's, 19 doctorates, 3 other advanced degrees awarded. *Degree program information:* Part-time and evening/weekend programs available. Offers administration and higher education (M Ed, Ed D, Ed S); art education (MAT); college student personnel services (M Ed); community counseling (M Ed); counseling and personnel services (M Ed, Ed D); counseling psychology (M Ed, Ed D); early childhood education (M Ed); early elementary education (M Ed, MAT); education and human development (M Ed, MA, MAT, MS, Ed D, Ed S); educational administration (M Ed, Ed D, Ed S); evaluation (M Ed); exercise physiology (MS); expressive therapies (MA); foreign language education (MAT); higher education (MA); human resource education (M Ed); instructional technology (M Ed); interdisciplinary early childhood education (M Ed); middle school education (M Ed, MAT); music education (MAT); physical education (M Ed, MAT); reading education (M Ed); school counseling (M Ed); secondary education (M Ed, MAT); special education (M Ed); sport administration (MS). *Application deadline:* Applications are processed on a rolling basis. *Application fee:* $25. Electronic applications accepted. *Dean,* Dr. Douglas Simpson, 502-852-6411, Fax: 502-852-0726, E-mail: d.simpson@louisville.edu.

Interdisciplinary Studies Students: 4 full-time (1 woman), 6 part-time (all women); includes 2 minority (1 African American, 1 Hispanic American) Average age 40. Expenses: Contact institution. In 2001, 3 degrees awarded. Offers interdisciplinary studies (MA, MS). *Application deadline:* Applications are processed on a rolling basis. *Application fee:* $25. *Dean of Graduate School,* Dr. Ronald M. Atlas, 502-852-8371, Fax: 502-852-6616, E-mail: r.atlas@louisville.edu.

Raymond A. Kent School of Social Work Students: 215 full-time (171 women), 123 part-time (82 women); includes 45 minority (36 African Americans, 2 Asian Americans or Pacific Islanders, 2 Hispanic Americans, 5 Native Americans), 4 international. Average age 34. *Faculty:* 24 full-time (14 women), 29 part-time/adjunct (18 women). Expenses: Contact institution. *Financial support:* Research assistantships with full tuition reimbursements, tuition waivers (full) available. Financial award application deadline: 4/1. In 2001, 139 master's, 1 doctorate awarded. Offers social work (MSSW, PhD). *Application deadline:* Applications are processed on a rolling basis. *Application fee:* $25. *Dean,* Dr. Terry Singer, 502-852-6402, Fax: 502-852-0422, E-mail: terry.singer@louisville.edu.

School of Music Students: 42 full-time (14 women), 14 part-time (7 women); includes 4 minority (3 African Americans, 1 Hispanic American), 9 international. Average age 31. *Faculty:* 30 full-time (9 women), 43 part-time/adjunct (19 women). Expenses: Contact institution. *Financial support:* Fellowships with full tuition reimbursements, teaching assistantships with full and partial tuition reimbursements, scholarships/grants and unspecified assistantships available. In 2001, 13 degrees awarded. *Degree program information:* Part-time programs available. Offers music education (MAT, MME); music history (MM, PhD); music literature (PhD); music performance (MM); music theory and composition (MM); musicology (PhD). *Application deadline:* For fall admission, 3/15 (priority date). Applications are processed on a rolling basis. *Application fee:* $25. *Application Contact:* Mary P. Emrich, Admissions Officer, 502-852-1623, Fax: 502-852-0520, E-mail: mary.emrich@louisville.edu. *Dean,* Dr. Herbert L. Koerselman, 502-852-6907, Fax: 502-852-1874, E-mail: koerselman@louisville.edu.

School of Nursing Students: 22 full-time (all women), 92 part-time (88 women); includes 14 minority (6 African Americans, 3 Asian Americans or Pacific Islanders, 5 Hispanic Americans), 1 international. Average age 37. *Faculty:* 28 full-time (all women), 17 part-time/adjunct (15 women). Expenses: Contact institution. *Financial support:* In 2001–02, 1 research assistantship with full tuition reimbursement (averaging $10,800 per year) was awarded; institutionally sponsored loans, scholarships/grants, and traineeships also available. Financial award application deadline: 4/15; financial award applicants required to submit FAFSA. In 2001, 24 degrees awarded. *Degree program information:* Part-time programs available. Offers nursing (MSN). *Application deadline:* For fall admission, 5/1 (priority date); for spring admission, 10/1 (priority date). Applications are processed on a rolling basis. *Application fee:* $25. *Application Contact:* Dr. Cynthia A. McCurren, Associate Dean for Academic Affairs, 502-852-5366, Fax: 502-852-8783, E-mail: camccu01@gwise.louisville.edu. *Dean,* Dr. Mary H. Mundt, 502-852-5366, Fax: 502-852-8783, E-mail: mhmund01@gwise.louisville.edu.

Speed Scientific School Students: 288 full-time (75 women), 360 part-time (63 women); includes 60 minority (20 African Americans, 30 Asian Americans or Pacific Islanders, 9 Hispanic Americans, 1 Native American), 267 international. Average age 29. *Faculty:* 87 full-time (9 women), 18 part-time/adjunct (1 woman). Expenses: Contact institution. *Financial support:* In 2001–02, 19 fellowships with full tuition reimbursements (averaging $18,000 per year), 51 research assistantships with full tuition reimbursements (averaging $14,700 per year), 34 teaching assistantships with full tuition reimbursements (averaging $15,150 per year) were awarded. Federal Work-Study and scholarships/grants also available. In 2001, 205 master's, 4 doctorates awarded. *Degree program information:* Part-time programs available. Offers chemical engineering (M Eng, MS, PhD); civil and environmental engineering (M Eng, MS, PhD); computer engineering and computer science (M Eng, MS); computer science (MS); computer science and engineering (PhD); electrical and computer engineering (M Eng, MS); engineering (M Eng, MS, PhD); engineering management (M Eng); industrial engineering (M Eng, MS, PhD); mechanical engineering (M Eng, MS). *Application deadline:* Applications are processed on a rolling basis. *Application fee:* $25. Electronic applications accepted. *Application Contact:* Dr. Mickey R. Wilhelm, Associate Dean, 502-852-08002, Fax: 502-852-1577, E-mail: wilhelm@louisville.edu. *Dean,* Dr. Thomas R. Hanley, 502-852-6281, Fax: 502-852-7033, E-mail: trhanl01@gwise.louisville.edu.

Louis D. Brandeis School of Law Students: 281 full-time (135 women), 102 part-time (48 women); includes 32 minority (23 African Americans, 6 Asian Americans or Pacific Islanders, 2 Hispanic Americans, 1 Native American), 5 international. Average age 26. 796 applicants, 34% accepted, 129 enrolled. *Faculty:* 33 full-time (12 women), 8 part-time/adjunct (2 women). Expenses: Contact institution. *Financial support:* In 2001–02, 200 students received support; fellowships, research assistantships, teaching assistantships, career-related internships or fieldwork, Federal Work-Study, scholarships/grants, and tuition waivers (partial) available. Support available to part-time students. Financial award application deadline: 6/1; financial award applicants required to submit FAFSA. In 2001, 96 degrees awarded. *Degree program information:* Part-time and evening/weekend programs available. Offers law (JD). *Application deadline:* For fall admission, 3/1 (priority date). Applications are processed on a rolling basis. *Application fee:* $40. Electronic applications accepted. *Application Contact:* Connie C. Shumake, Dean of Admissions, 502-852-6364, Fax: 502-852-0862, E-mail: lawadmissions@louisville.edu. *Dean,* Laura Rothstein, 502-852-6879, Fax: 502-852-0862.

School of Dentistry Students: 339 full-time (110 women), 4 part-time; includes 30 minority (7 African Americans, 17 Asian Americans or Pacific Islanders, 2 Hispanic Americans, 4 Native Americans), 8 international. Average age 26. *Faculty:* 55 full-time (12 women), 69 part-time/adjunct (16 women). Expenses: Contact institution. In 2001, 67 first professional degrees, 10 master's awarded. Offers dentistry (DMD, MS); oral biology (MS). *Application fee:* $10. *Application Contact:* Dr. Anne Wells, Associate Dean for Student Affairs and Admissions, 502-852-5081, Fax: 502-852-1210, E-mail: a0well01@gwise.louisville.edu. *Dean,* Dr. John N. Williams, 502-852-5293, Fax: 502-852-7163, E-mail: john.williams@louisville.edu.

School of Medicine Students: 770 full-time (398 women), 82 part-time (60 women); includes 130 minority (60 African Americans, 58 Asian Americans or Pacific Islanders, 8 Hispanic Americans, 4 Native Americans), 74 international. Average age 29. *Faculty:* 574 full-time (168 women), 63 part-time/adjunct (26 women). Expenses: Contact institution. *Financial support:* Fellowships with full tuition reimbursements, research assistantships with full tuition reimbursements, teaching assistantships with full tuition reimbursements, career-related internships or fieldwork, institutionally sponsored loans, scholarships/grants, traineeships, tuition waivers (full and partial), and unspecified assistantships available. In 2001, 145 first professional degrees, 37 master's, 10 doctorates awarded. Offers audiology (Au D); biostatistics-decision science (MS); clinical investigation (Certificate); communicative disorders (MS); epidemiology: clinical investigation services (MS, PhD); medicine (MD, MS, Au D, PhD, Certificate); ophthalmology and visual sciences (PhD). *Application deadline:* For fall admission, 1/15. Applications are processed on a rolling basis. *Application fee:* $25. *Application Contact:* Director of Admissions, 502-8525193, Fax: 502-8526849. *Dean,* Dr. Joel A. Kaplan, 502-852-5184, Fax: 502-852-6849, E-mail: joel.kaplan@louisville.edu.

Integrated Programs in Biomedical Sciences Students: 140 full-time (64 women), 20 part-time (10 women); includes 15 minority (5 African Americans, 9 Asian Americans or Pacific Islanders, 1 Hispanic American), 64 international. Average age 29. Expenses: Contact institution. *Financial support:* Fellowships with full tuition reimbursements, research assistantships with full tuition reimbursements, teaching assistantships with full tuition reimbursements, career-related internships or fieldwork, institutionally sponsored loans, scholarships/grants, traineeships, tuition waivers (full and partial), and unspecified assistantships available. In 2001, 18 master's, 9 doctorates awarded. Offers anatomical sciences and neurobiology (MS, PhD); biochemistry and molecular biology (MS, PhD); biomedical sciences (MS, PhD); microbiology and immunology (MS, PhD); pharmacology and toxicology (MS, PhD); physiology and biophysics (MS, PhD). *Application deadline:* For fall admission, 1/15. *Director,* Dr. Nigel G. F. Cooper, 502-852-4480, Fax: 502-852-1465, E-mail: nigelcooper@louisville.edu.

See in-depth description on page 1187.

UNIVERSITY OF MAINE, Orono, ME 04469

General Information State-supported, coed, university. CGS member. *Enrollment:* 924 full-time matriculated graduate/professional students (551 women), 651 part-time matriculated graduate/professional students (410 women). *Enrollment by degree level:* 1,175 master's, 314 doctoral, 86 other advanced degrees. *Graduate faculty:* 650. Tuition, state resident: full-time $3,780; part-time $210 per credit hour. Tuition, nonresident: full-time $10,782; part-time $599 per credit hour. *Required fees:* $9.5 per credit hour. $32 per semester. Tuition and fees vary according to reciprocity agreements. *Graduate housing:* Rooms and/or apartments available on a first-come, first-served basis to single and married students. Typical cost: $5,728 (including board) for single students. Housing application deadline: 8/1. *Student services:* Campus employment opportunities, campus safety program, career counseling, child daycare facilities, disabled student services, exercise/wellness program, free psychological counseling, grant writing training, international student services, low-cost health insurance, multicultural affairs office, teacher training, writing training. *Library facilities:* Fogler Library. *Online resources:* library catalog, web page, access to other libraries' catalogs. *Collection:* 854,000 titles, 16,700 serial subscriptions, 25,000 audiovisual materials. *Research affiliation:* Jackson Laboratory (medical genetics), Bigelow Laboratories for Ocean Sciences (marine science), Mount Desert Island Biological Laboratory (marine molecular biology), Sensor Research Development Corporation (electrical sensors), Maine Medical Center Research Institute (clinical medicine).

Computer facilities: 520 computers available on campus for general student use. A campuswide network can be accessed from student residence rooms and from off campus. Internet access and online class registration, on-line grade information, e-mail are available. *Web address:* http://www.umaine.edu/.

General Application Contact: Scott G. Delcourt, Director of the Graduate School, 207-581-3218, Fax: 207-581-3232, E-mail: graduate@maine.edu.

GRADUATE UNITS

Graduate School Students: 924 full-time (551 women), 651 part-time (410 women); includes 52 minority (12 African Americans, 12 Asian Americans or Pacific Islanders, 8 Hispanic Americans, 20 Native Americans), 173 international. Average age 29. 1,294 applicants, 54% accepted, 408 enrolled. *Faculty:* 650. Expenses: Contact institution. *Financial support:* In 2001–02, 30 fellowships with tuition reimbursements (averaging $15,000 per year), 250 research assistantships with tuition reimbursements (averaging $12,000 per year), 250 teaching assistantships with tuition reimbursements (averaging $11,500 per year) were awarded. Career-related internships or fieldwork, Federal Work-Study, institutionally sponsored loans, scholarships/grants, tuition waivers (full and partial), and unspecified assistantships also available. Support available to part-time students. Financial award application deadline: 3/1; financial award applicants required to submit FAFSA. In 2001, 401 master's, 33 doctorates, 25 other advanced degrees awarded. *Degree program information:* Part-time and evening/weekend programs available. Offers information systems (MS); interdisciplinary studies (PhD); liberal studies (MA). *Application deadline:* Applications are processed on a rolling basis. *Application fee:* $50. Electronic applications accepted. *Director of the Graduate School,* Scott G. Delcourt, 207-581-3218, Fax: 207-581-3232, E-mail: graduate@maine.edu.

College of Business, Public Policy and Health Students: 169 full-time (115 women), 62 part-time (34 women); includes 13 minority (4 African Americans, 1 Asian American or Pacific Islander, 2 Hispanic Americans, 6 Native Americans), 18 international. 152 applicants, 76% accepted, 78 enrolled. Expenses: Contact institution. *Financial support:* Research assistantships with tuition reimbursements, teaching assistantships with tuition reimbursements, career-related internships or fieldwork, Federal Work-Study, institutionally sponsored loans, scholarships/grants, tuition waivers (full and partial), and unspecified assistantships available. Support available to part-time students. Financial award application deadline:3/1. In 2001, 73 degrees awarded. *Degree program information:* Part-time and evening/weekend programs available. Offers accounting (MS); business administration (MBA); business, public policy and health (MBA, MPA, MS, MSW, CAS); nursing (MS, CAS); public administration (MPA); social work (MSW). *Application deadline:* Applications are processed on a rolling basis. *Application fee:* $50. Electronic applications accepted. *Application Contact:* Scott G. Delcourt, Director of the Graduate School, 207-581-3218, Fax: 207-581-3232, E-mail: graduate@maine.edu. *Dean,* Dr. Daniel E. Innis, 207-581-1968, Fax: 207-581-1930.

College of Education and Human Development Students: 230 full-time (164 women), 368 part-time (262 women); includes 14 minority (4 African Americans, 4 Asian Americans or Pacific Islanders, 1 Hispanic American, 5 Native Americans), 3 international. 216 applicants, 84% accepted, 146 enrolled. *Faculty:* 34 full-time, 3 part-time/adjunct. Expenses: Contact institution. *Financial support:* In 2001–02, 2 research assistantships with tuition reimbursements (averaging $9,010 per year), 19 teaching assistantships with tuition reimbursements (averaging $9,010 per year) were awarded. Career-related internships or fieldwork, Federal Work-Study, institutionally sponsored loans, and unspecified assistantships also available. Support available to part-time students. Financial award application deadline: 3/1. In 2001, 177 master's, 6 doctorates, 25 other advanced degrees awarded. *Degree program information:* Part-time and evening/weekend programs available. Offers counselor education (M Ed, MA, MS, CAS); educational leadership (M Ed, Ed D, CAS); elementary education (M Ed, MAT, MS, CAS); higher education (M Ed, MA, MS, Ed D, CAS); human development (MS); human development and family studies (MS); instructional technology (M Ed); kinesiology and physical education (M Ed, MS); literacy education (M Ed, MA, MS, Ed D, CAS); science education (M Ed, MS, CAS); secondary education (M Ed, MA, MAT, MS, CAS); social studies education (M Ed, MA, MS, CAS); special education (M Ed, CAS). *Application deadline:* For fall admission, 2/1 (priority date). Applications are processed on a rolling basis. *Application fee:* $50. Electronic applications accepted. *Application Contact:* Scott G. Delcourt, Director of the Graduate School, 207-581-3218, Fax: 207-581-3232, E-mail: graduate@maine.edu. *Dean,* Dr. Robert A. Cobb, 207-581-2441, Fax: 207-581-2423.

College of Engineering Students: 99 full-time (22 women), 31 part-time (4 women); includes 3 minority (2 Hispanic Americans, 1 Native American), 53 international. 142 applicants, 48% accepted, 29 enrolled. *Faculty:* 55. Expenses: Contact institution. *Financial support:* Fellowships, research assistantships with tuition reimbursements, teaching assistantships with tuition reimbursements, Federal Work-Study, institutionally sponsored loans, scholarships/grants, and tuition waivers (full and partial) available. Financial award application deadline: 3/1. In 2001, 30 master's, 6 doctorates awarded. *Degree program information:* Part-time programs available. Offers biological engineering (MS); chemical and biological engineering (MS, PhD); chemical engineering (MS, PhD); civil engineering (MS, PhD); computer engineering (MS); electrical engineering (MS, PhD); engineering (MS, PhD); mechanical engineering (MS, PhD); spatial information science and engineering (MS, PhD). *Application deadline:* For fall admission, 2/1 (priority date). Applications are processed on a rolling basis. *Application fee:* $50. Electronic applications accepted. *Application Contact:* Scott G. Delcourt, Director of the Graduate School, 207-581-3218, Fax: 207-581-3232, E-mail: graduate@maine.edu. *Dean,* Dr. Larryl K. Matthews, 207-581-2216, Fax: 207-581-2220.

College of Liberal Arts and Sciences Students: 186 full-time (108 women), 81 part-time (46 women); includes 11 minority (2 African Americans, 4 Asian Americans or Pacific Islanders, 1 Hispanic American, 4 Native Americans), 50 international. 401 applicants, 49% accepted, 89 enrolled. Expenses: Contact institution. *Financial support:* Fellowships with tuition reimbursements, research assistantships with tuition reimbursements, teaching assistantships with tuition reimbursements, career-related internships or fieldwork, Federal Work-Study, institutionally sponsored loans, scholarships/grants, and tuition waivers (full and partial) available. Support available to part-time students. Financial award application deadline: 3/1. In 2001, 60 master's, 7 doctorates awarded. *Degree program information:* Part-time and evening/weekend programs available. Offers chemistry (MS, PhD); clinical psychology (PhD); communication (MA); communication sciences and disorders (MA); computer science (MS, PhD); developmental psychology (MA); economics (MA); engineering physics (M Eng); English (MA); experimental psychology (MA, PhD); financial economics (MA); French (MA, MAT); history (MA, PhD); liberal arts and sciences (M Eng, MA, MAT, MM, MS, PhD); mathematics (MA); music (MM); physics (MS, PhD); social psychology (MA); theatre (MA). *Application deadline:* For fall admission, 2/1 (priority date). Applications are processed on a rolling basis. *Application fee:* $50. Electronic applications accepted. *Application Contact:* Scott G. Delcourt, Director of the Graduate School, 207-581-3218, Fax: 207-581-3232, E-mail: graduate@maine.edu. *Dean,* Dr. Rebecca Eilers, 207-581-1927, Fax: 207-581-1947.

College of Natural Sciences, Forestry, and Agriculture Students: 217 full-time (131 women), 80 part-time (46 women); includes 8 minority (2 African Americans, 3 Asian Americans or Pacific Islanders, 1 Hispanic American, 2 Native Americans), 46 international. 369 applicants, 33% accepted, 58 enrolled. Expenses: Contact institution. *Financial support:* Fellowships, research assistantships, teaching assistantships, career-related internships or fieldwork, Federal Work-Study, institutionally sponsored loans, scholarships/grants, tuition waivers (full and partial), and unspecified assistantships available. Support available to part-time students. Financial award application deadline: 3/1. In 2001, 52 master's, 12 doctorates awarded. *Degree program information:* Part-time and evening/weekend programs available. Offers animal sciences (MPS, MS); biochemistry (MPS, MS); biochemistry and molecular biology (PhD); biological sciences (PhD); botany and plant pathology (MS); ecology and environmental science (MS, PhD); ecology and environmental sciences (MS, PhD); entomology (MS); food and nutritional sciences (PhD); food science and human nutrition (MS); forest resources (PhD); forestry (MF, MS); geological sciences (MS, PhD); horticulture (MS); marine biology (MS, PhD); marine policy (MS); microbiology (MPS, MS, PhD); natural sciences, forestry, and agriculture (MF, MPS, MS, MWC, PhD); oceanography (MS, PhD); plant science (PhD); plant, soil, and environmental sciences (MS); resource economics and policy (MS); resource utilization (MS); wildlife conservation (MWC); wildlife ecology (MS, PhD); zoology (MS, PhD). *Application deadline:* For fall admission, 2/1 (priority date). Applications are processed on a rolling basis. *Application fee:* $50. Electronic applications accepted. *Application Contact:* Scott G. Delcourt, Director of the Graduate School, 207-581-3218, Fax: 207-581-3232, E-mail: graduate@maine.edu. *Dean,* Dr. G. Bruce Wiersma, 207-581-3202, Fax: 207-581-3207.

Institute for Quaternary Studies Students: 5 full-time (2 women), 5 part-time (2 women), 2 international. 5 applicants, 80% accepted, 3 enrolled. *Faculty:* 13 full-time (2 women). Expenses: Contact institution. *Financial support:* In 2001–02, 6 research assistantships with tuition reimbursements (averaging $14,800 per year) were awarded; tuition waivers (full and partial) also available. Financial award application deadline: 3/1. In 2001, 3 degrees awarded. *Degree program information:* Part-time programs available. Offers quaternary studies (MS). *Application deadline:* For fall admission, 2/1 (priority date). Applications are processed on a rolling basis. *Application fee:* $50. Electronic applications accepted. *Application Contact:* Scott G. Delcourt, Director of the Graduate School, 207-581-3218, Fax: 207-581-3232, E-mail: graduate@maine.edu. *Director,* Dr. George Jacobson, 207-581-2190, Fax: 207-581-1203.

UNIVERSITY OF MANITOBA, Winnipeg, MB R3T 2N2, Canada

General Information Province-supported, coed, university. *Graduate housing:* Rooms and/or apartments available to single and married students. *Research affiliation:* Canada Department of Agriculture Research Station, Freshwater Institute, Atomic Energy of Canada, Manitoba Department of Mines, Resources, and Environmental Management, Northern Scientific Training Program (Northern studies), Taiga Biological Research Trust.

GRADUATE UNITS

Faculty of Dentistry Students: 22 full-time (4 women). *Faculty:* 28 full-time (6 women), 84 part-time/adjunct (5 women). Expenses: Contact institution. *Financial support:* In 2001–02, 1 student received support, including 1 fellowship (averaging $11,000 per year), 1 research assistantship; career-related internships or fieldwork and institutionally sponsored loans also available. Financial award application deadline: 6/30. In 2001, 24 first professional degrees, 4 master's, 1 doctorate awarded. Offers dental diagnostic and surgical sciences (M Dent); dental materials (M Sc); dentistry (DMD, M Dent, M Sc, PhD); oral and maxillofacial surgery (M Dent); oral biology (M Sc, PhD); orthodontics (M Sc); periodontology (M Dent); preventive dental science (M Sc); restorative dentistry (M Sc). *Application deadline:* For fall admission, 9/1. *Application fee:* $50 Canadian dollars. *Application Contact:* Dr. Norman Fleming, Associate Dean (Research), 204-789-3794, Fax: 204-789-3913, E-mail: nfleming@ms.umanitoba.ca. *Dean,* Dr. J. deVries, 204-789-3249, Fax: 204-888-4113, E-mail: devriesj@umanitoba.ca.

Faculty of Graduate Studies *Degree program information:* Part-time programs available. Offers interdisciplinary studies (M Sc, MA, PhD, Diploma); public administration (MA, MPA).

Faculty of Agriculture Offers agricultural economics and farm management (M Sc, PhD); agriculture (M Sc, PhD); animal science (M Sc, PhD); entomology (M Sc, PhD); food science (M Sc); horticulture (M Sc, PhD); soil science (M Sc, PhD).

Faculty of Architecture Offers architecture (M Arch, M Land Arch, MCP); city planning (MCP); landscape architecture (M Land Arch).

Faculty of Arts Offers anthropology (MA); arts (MA, PhD); classics (MA); clinical psychology (PhD); economics (MA, PhD); English (MA, PhD); French and Spanish (MA, PhD); geography (MA, PhD); German and Slavic studies (MA); history (MA, PhD); Icelandic studies (MA); linguistics (MA, PhD); philosophy (MA); political studies (MA); psychology (MA, PhD); religion (MA, PhD); sociology (MA).

Faculty of Education Offers art education (M Ed); counselor education (M Ed); curriculum studies (M Ed); drama education (M Ed); early childhood education (M Ed); education (M Ed); educational administration (M Ed); educational foundations (M Ed); educational technology (M Ed); English as a second language (M Ed); French as a second language (M Ed); health education (M Ed); home economics education (M Ed); industrial/vocational/business education (M Ed); instructional design and evaluation (M Ed); language arts (M Ed); mathematics education (M Ed); modern languages (M Ed); music education (M Ed); physical education (M Ed); postsecondary education (M Ed); reading (M Ed); science education (M Ed); social studies education (M Ed); special education (M Ed).

Faculty of Engineering Offers agricultural engineering (M Eng, M Sc, PhD); civil engineering (M Eng, M Sc, PhD); electrical and computer engineering (M Eng, M Sc, PhD); engineering (M Eng, M Sc, PhD); mechanical and industrial engineering (M Eng, M Sc, PhD).

Faculty of Human Ecology Offers clothing and textiles (M Sc); family studies (M Sc); foods and nutrition (M Sc, PhD); human ecology (M Sc, PhD).

Faculty of Management Offers accounting (MBA); actuarial mathematics and operational research (M Sc, MA); finance (MBA); management (M Sc, MA, MBA); marketing (MBA); personnel/industrial relations (MBA).

Faculty of Music Offers music (M Mus).

Faculty of Nursing Offers nursing (MN).

Faculty of Pharmacy Offers pharmacy (M Sc, PhD).

Faculty of Physical Education and Recreation Studies Offers physical education and recreation studies (M Sc).

Faculty of Science Offers applied mathematics (M Sc); botany (M Sc, PhD); chemistry (M Sc, PhD); computer science (M Sc, PhD); geology (M Sc, PhD); geophysics (M Sc, PhD); mathematics (M Sc, MA, PhD); microbiology (M Sc, PhD); physics (M Sc, PhD); science (M Sc, MA, PhD); statistics (M Sc, PhD); zoology (M Sc, PhD).

Faculty of Social Work Offers social work (MSW).

Natural Resources Institute Offers natural resources management (MNRM).

Faculty of Law *Degree program information:* Part-time programs available. Offers interdisciplinary studies (MA); law (LL M).

Faculty of Medicine *Degree program information:* Part-time programs available. Offers medicine (M Sc, PhD). Electronic applications accepted.

Graduate Programs in Medicine *Degree program information:* Part-time programs available. Offers biochemistry and medical genetics (M Sc, PhD); community health sciences (M Sc, PhD); human anatomy and cell science (M Sc, PhD); immunology (M Sc, PhD); medical microbiology (M Sc, PhD); medicine (M Sc, PhD); pathology (M Sc); pediatrics (M Sc); pharmacology and therapeutics (M Sc, PhD); physiology (M Sc, PhD); psychiatry (M Sc); rehabilitation (M Sc); surgery (M Sc).

St. John's College *Faculty:* 2 full-time (0 women), 1 part-time/adjunct (0 women). Expenses: Contact institution. *Financial support:* Fellowships, research assistantships, career-related internships or fieldwork and institutionally sponsored loans available. Support available to part-time students. In 2001, 1 degree awarded. Offers theology (M Div). *Application deadline:* For fall admission, 5/1 (priority date). *Application fee:* $50. *Application Contact:* Erin McShane, Registrar, 204-474-8520, Fax: 204-474-7610, E-mail: kolodiee@cc.umanitoba.ca. *Dean of Theology,* Rev. John K. Stafford, 204-474-8543, Fax: 204-474-7610, E-mail: j_stafford@umanitoba.ca.

Faculty of Theology *Faculty:* 2 full-time (0 women), 1 part-time/adjunct (0 women). Expenses: Contact institution. *Financial support:* Fellowships, institutionally sponsored loans available. Support available to part-time students. In 2001, 1 degree awarded. Offers theology (M Div). *Application deadline:* For fall admission, 5/1 (priority date). *Application fee:* $50. *Application Contact:* Erin McShane, Registrar, 204-474-8520, Fax: 204-474-7610, E-mail: kolodiee@cc.umanitoba.ca.

UNIVERSITY OF MARY, Bismarck, ND 58504-9652

General Information Independent-religious, coed, comprehensive institution. *Enrollment:* 233 full-time matriculated graduate/professional students (119 women), 423 part-time matriculated graduate/professional students (341 women). *Enrollment by degree level:* 656 master's. *Graduate faculty:* 19 full-time (13 women), 144 part-time/adjunct (67 women). *Tuition:* Part-time $290 per credit hour. *Required fees:* $3 per credit hour. *Graduate housing:* Room and/or apartments available on a first-come, first-served basis to single students; on-campus housing not available to married students. Housing application deadline: 7/15. *Student services:* Campus employment opportunities, career counseling, exercise/wellness program, free psychological counseling. *Library facilities:* University of Mary Library. *Collection:* 55,000 titles, 550 serial subscriptions.

Computer facilities: A campuswide network can be accessed. Internet access is available. *Web address:* http://www.umary.edu/.

General Application Contact: Dr. Randy G. Krieg, Director of Graduate Studies, 701-255-7500, Fax: 701-255-7687, E-mail: rkrieg@umary.edu.

GRADUATE UNITS

Department of Occupational Therapy Students: 67 full-time (64 women), 8 part-time (all women). 30 applicants, 57% accepted, 16 enrolled. *Faculty:* 6 full-time (5 women), 6 part-time/adjunct (4 women). Expenses: Contact institution. *Financial support:* In 2001–02, 2 teaching assistantships with full tuition reimbursements (averaging $2,500 per year) were awarded; career-related internships or fieldwork, Federal Work-Study, institutionally sponsored loans, scholarships/grants, and unspecified assistantships also available. Support available to part-time students. Financial award applicants required to submit FAFSA. Postbaccalaureate distance learning degree programs offered (minimal on-campus study). Offers occupational therapy (MS). *Application deadline:* For spring admission, 6/15 (priority date). Applications are processed on a rolling basis. *Application fee:* $25. Electronic applications accepted. *Application Contact:* Dr. Randy G. Krieg, Director of Graduate Studies, 701-255-7500, Fax: 701-255-7687, E-mail: rkrieg@umary.edu. *Director,* Stacie Lynn Iken, 701-255-7500 Ext. 535, Fax: 701-255-7687, E-mail: ikensl@umary.edu.

Division of Nursing Students: 34 full-time (32 women), 9 part-time (7 women); includes 1 minority (Native American) Average age 30. 11 applicants, 82% accepted, 9 enrolled. *Faculty:* 3 full-time (all women), 8 part-time/adjunct (4 women). Expenses: Contact institution. *Financial support:* In 2001–02, 14 fellowships with partial tuition reimbursements, 3 teaching assistantships with partial tuition reimbursements were awarded. Institutionally sponsored loans also available. Support available to part-time students. Financial award application deadline: 7/1. In 2001, 20 degrees awarded. *Degree program information:* Part-time and evening/weekend programs available. Postbaccalaureate distance learning degree programs offered (minimal on-campus study). Offers family nurse practitioner (MSN); nursing education (MSN). *Application deadline:* For fall admission, 4/15 (priority date). Applications are processed on a rolling basis. *Application fee:* $40. Electronic applications accepted. *Application Contact:* Dr. Randy G. Krieg, Director of Graduate Studies, 701-255-7500, Fax: 701-255-7687, E-mail: rkrieg@umary.edu. *Chair,* Sr. Mariah Dietz, 701-255-7500 Ext. 435, Fax: 701-255-7687, E-mail: mdietz@umary.edu.

Program in Education Students: 7 full-time (5 women), 78 part-time (58 women); includes 12 minority (all Native Americans) Average age 30. *Faculty:* 5 full-time (4 women), 10 part-time/adjunct (6 women). Expenses: Contact institution. *Financial support:* In 2001–02, 1 teaching assistantship was awarded; career-related internships or fieldwork also available. Support available to part-time students. Financial award application deadline: 8/1; financial award applicants required to submit FAFSA. In 2001, 21 degrees awarded. *Degree program information:* Part-time programs available. Offers elementary education (MS Ed); elementary education administration (MS Ed); higher education (MS Ed); secondary education administration (MS Ed); secondary teaching (MS Ed); special education (MS Ed). *Application deadline:* For fall admission, 8/1; for spring admission, 12/1. *Application fee:* $40. *Application Contact:* Dr. Randy G. Krieg, Director of Graduate Studies, 701-255-7500, Fax: 701-255-7687, E-mail: rkrieg@umary.edu. *Director,* Dr. Ramona Klein, 701-255-7500, E-mail: raklein@umary.edu.

Program in Management Students: 181 full-time (95 women). *Faculty:* 44 part-time/adjunct (15 women). Expenses: Contact institution. *Financial support:* Career-related internships or fieldwork available. Support available to part-time students. Financial award application deadline: 8/1; financial award applicants required to submit FAFSA. In 2001, 107 degrees awarded. *Degree program information:* Part-time and evening/weekend programs available. Offers management (M Mgmt). *Application deadline:* Applications are processed on a rolling basis. *Application fee:* $40. *Application Contact:* Dr. Randy G. Krieg, Director of Graduate Studies, 701-255-7500, Fax: 701-255-7687, E-mail: rkrieg@umary.edu. *Vice President of Enrollment Services,* David Herringer, 701-255-7500.

Program in Physical Therapy Students: 44 full-time (30 women). 49 applicants, 41% accepted. Expenses: Contact institution. *Financial support:* Teaching assistantships, career-related internships or fieldwork available. In 2001, 20 degrees awarded. Offers physical therapy (MPT). Applications must be requested in writing. *Application deadline:* For fall admission, 3/1. Applications are processed on a rolling basis. *Application fee:* $40. *Applica-*

University of Mary (continued)

tion Contact: Elaine Strand, Program/Records Secretary, 701-255-7500 Ext. 514, Fax: 701-255-7687, E-mail: mparker@umary.edu. *Program Director,* Michael Gary Parker, 701-255-7500, Fax: 701-255-7687.

UNIVERSITY OF MARY HARDIN-BAYLOR, Belton, TX 76513

General Information Independent-religious, coed, comprehensive institution. *Enrollment:* 40 full-time matriculated graduate/professional students (30 women), 146 part-time matriculated graduate/professional students (113 women). *Enrollment by degree level:* 186 master's. *Graduate faculty:* 45 full-time (13 women), 9 part-time/adjunct (3 women). *Tuition:* Full-time $5,940; part-time $330 per credit hour. *Required fees:* $554; $28 per credit hour. One-time fee: $40 part-time. *Graduate housing:* Room and/or apartments available on a first-come, first-served basis to single students; on-campus housing not available to married students. Typical cost: $6,039 (including board). Room and board charges vary according to board plan and housing facility selected. *Student services:* Career counseling, free psychological counseling, teacher training. *Library facilities:* Townsend Memorial Library. *Online resources:* library catalog, web page, access to other libraries' catalogs. *Collection:* 116,678 titles, 1,724 serial subscriptions, 6,382 audiovisual materials.

Computer facilities: 221 computers available on campus for general student use. A campuswide network can be accessed from student residence rooms. Internet access is available. *Web address:* http://www.umhb.edu/.

General Application Contact: Robbin Steen, Director, Graduate Enrollment, 254-295-4517, Fax: 254-295-5049, E-mail: rsteen@umhb.edu.

GRADUATE UNITS

Program in Health Services Management Students: 8 full-time (6 women), 53 part-time (42 women); includes 21 minority (16 African Americans, 1 Asian American or Pacific Islander, 3 Hispanic Americans, 1 Native American) 14 applicants, 93% accepted, 13 enrolled. *Faculty:* 4 full-time (2 women), 4 part-time/adjunct (1 woman). Expenses: Contact institution. *Financial support:* Career-related internships or fieldwork and scholarship for some active duty military personnel available. Support available to part-time students. Financial award application deadline: 6/1. In 2001, 34 degrees awarded. *Degree program information:* Part-time and evening/weekend programs available. Offers health services management (MHSM). *Application deadline:* For fall admission, 6/1 (priority date); for spring admission, 11/1 (priority date). Applications are processed on a rolling basis. *Application fee:* $35 ($135 for international students). *Chair,* Dr. Mary Anne Franklin, 254-295-4558, Fax: 254-933-3300, E-mail: mfranklin@umhb.edu.

School of Business Students: 13 full-time (10 women), 33 part-time (18 women); includes 4 minority (3 African Americans, 1 Asian American or Pacific Islander), 2 international. 15 applicants, 100% accepted, 14 enrolled. *Faculty:* 13 full-time (2 women). Expenses: Contact institution. *Financial support:* Scholarship for some active duty military personnel only available. Support available to part-time students. Financial award application deadline: 6/1. In 2001, 11 degrees awarded. *Degree program information:* Part-time and evening/weekend programs available. Offers business (MBA, MSIS). *Application deadline:* For fall admission, 6/1 (priority date); for spring admission, 11/1. Applications are processed on a rolling basis. *Application fee:* $35 ($135 for international students). *Application Contact:* Dr. Bert Moquin, Director, Graduate Studies in Business, 254-295-4143, E-mail: bmoquin@umhb.edu. *Dean,* Dr. James King, 254-295-4644, Fax: 254-295-4535, E-mail: jking@umhb.edu.

Graduate Studies in Business 5 applicants, 100% accepted, 5 enrolled. *Faculty:* 5 full-time (0 women). Expenses: Contact institution. *Financial support:* Scholarship for some active duty military personnel only available. *Degree program information:* Part-time and evening/weekend programs available. Offers information systems (MSIS). *Application deadline:* For fall admission, 6/1 (priority date); for spring admission, 11/1. Applications are processed on a rolling basis. *Application fee:* $35 ($135 for international students). *Director, Graduate Studies in Business,* Dr. Bert Moquin, 254-295-4143, E-mail: bmoquin@umhb.edu.

School of Education Students: 4 full-time (2 women), 42 part-time (40 women); includes 10 minority (6 African Americans, 4 Hispanic Americans) 19 applicants, 100% accepted, 17 enrolled. *Faculty:* 6 full-time (2 women), 4 part-time/adjunct (2 women). Expenses: Contact institution. *Financial support:* Scholarship for some active duty military personnel available. Support available to part-time students. Financial award application deadline: 6/1. In 2001, 13 degrees awarded. *Degree program information:* Part-time and evening/weekend programs available. Offers educational administration (M Ed); educational psychology (M Ed); general studies (M Ed); reading education (M Ed). *Application deadline:* For fall admission, 6/1 (priority date); for spring admission, 11/1. Applications are processed on a rolling basis. *Application fee:* $35 ($135 for international students). *Dean,* Dr. Clarence E. Ham, 254-295-4573, Fax: 254-295-4480, E-mail: ham@tenet.edu.

School of Sciences and Humanities Students: 15 full-time (12 women), 18 part-time (13 women); includes 11 minority (5 African Americans, 1 Asian American or Pacific Islander, 4 Hispanic Americans, 1 Native American) 14 applicants, 100% accepted, 14 enrolled. *Faculty:* 9 full-time (4 women), 3 part-time/adjunct (1 woman). Expenses: Contact institution. *Financial support:* In 2001–02, 1 student received support. Career-related internships or fieldwork and scholarship for some active duty military personnel available. Support available to part-time students. In 2001, 10 degrees awarded. *Degree program information:* Part-time and evening/weekend programs available. Offers counseling (MA); psychology (MA); sciences and humanities (MA, MTS); theological studies (MTS). *Application deadline:* For fall admission, 6/1 (priority date); for spring admission, 11/1. Applications are processed on a rolling basis. *Application fee:* $35 ($135 for international students). *Application Contact:* Dr. Raylene B. Statz, Graduate Director, 254-295-4548. *Dean,* Dr. Darrell G. Watson, 254-295-4537.

UNIVERSITY OF MARYLAND, Baltimore, MD 21201-1627

General Information State-supported, coed, graduate-only institution. CGS member. *Enrollment by degree level:* 2,485 first professional, 1,661 master's, 445 doctoral, 68 other advanced degrees. *Graduate faculty:* 1,329 full-time (526 women), 361 part-time/adjunct (160 women). Tuition, state resident: part-time $281 per credit. Tuition, nonresident: part-time $503 per credit. Tuition and fees vary according to class time, course load, degree level and program. *Graduate housing:* Rooms and/or apartments available on a first-come, first-served basis to single and married students. Typical cost: $4,160 per year for single students; $7,344 per year for married students. Room charges vary according to housing facility selected. Housing application deadline: 2/18. *Student services:* Campus employment opportunities, campus safety program, career counseling, disabled student services, exercise/wellness program, free psychological counseling, grant writing training, international student services, low-cost health insurance, multicultural affairs office, writing training. *Library facilities:* Health Sciences and Human Services Library plus 2 others. *Online resources:* library catalog, web page, access to other libraries' catalogs. *Collection:* 362,352 titles, 2,609 serial subscriptions.

Computer facilities: A campuswide network can be accessed from student residence rooms and from off campus. Internet access is available. *Web address:* http://www.umaryland.edu/.

General Application Contact: Keith T. Brooks, Director, Graduate Admissions and Records, 410-706-7131, Fax: 410-706-3473, E-mail: kbrooks@umaryland.edu.

GRADUATE UNITS

Graduate School Students: 624 full-time, 525 part-time; includes 252 minority (151 African Americans, 81 Asian Americans or Pacific Islanders, 20 Hispanic Americans), 18 international. 828 applicants, 56% accepted, 299 enrolled. Expenses: Contact institution. *Financial support:* Fellowships with full tuition reimbursements, research assistantships with full tuition reimbursements, teaching assistantships with partial tuition reimbursements, career-related internships or fieldwork, Federal Work-Study, institutionally sponsored loans, scholarships/grants, traineeships, tuition waivers (full), and unspecified assistantships available. Support available to part-time students. In 2001, 262 master's, 72 doctorates awarded. *Degree program information:* Part-time and evening/weekend programs available. Offers dental hygiene (MS); marine-estuarine-environmental sciences (MS, PhD); medical and research technology (MS); oral and craniofacial biological sciences (MS, PhD); oral biology (MS); oral pathology (MS, PhD); pharmaceutical sciences (PhD); pharmacy administration (PhD); pharmacy practice and science (PhD); social work (MSW, PhD). *Application deadline:* Applications are processed on a rolling basis. *Application fee:* $50. Electronic applications accepted. *Application Contact:* Keith T. Brooks, Director, Graduate Admissions and Enrollment Services, 410-706-7131, Fax: 410-706-3473, E-mail: kbrooks@umaryland.edu. *Vice President for Academic Affairs and Dean,* Dr. Malinda B. Orlin, 410-706-1850, Fax: 410-706-0234, E-mail: mborlin@umaryland.edu.

Graduate Programs in Medicine Students: 251 full-time, 43 part-time; includes 46 minority (18 African Americans, 28 Asian Americans or Pacific Islanders), 62 international. 350 applicants, 42% accepted, 90 enrolled. *Faculty:* 212. Expenses: Contact institution. *Financial support:* Fellowships, research assistantships, teaching assistantships, career-related internships or fieldwork and unspecified assistantships available. Support available to part-time students. Financial award application deadline: 2/15. In 2001, 28 master's, 33 doctorates awarded. *Degree program information:* Part-time and evening/weekend programs available. Offers anatomy and neurobiology (MS, PhD); applied professional ethics-medicine (MA); biochemistry (PhD); epidemiology and preventive medicine (MS, PhD); human genetics (MS, PhD); medical pathology (PhD); medicine (MA, MS, DPT, PhD); membrane biology (PhD); microbiology and immunology (MS, PhD); molecular and cell biology (PhD); neuroscience (PhD); neuroscience and cognitive sciences (MS, PhD); pathology (MS); pharmacology (PhD); pharmacology and experimental therapeutics (MS); physical and rehabilitation science (PhD); physical therapy (DPT); physiology (PhD); reproductive endocrinology (PhD); toxicology (MS, PhD). *Application fee:* $50. *Application Contact:* Vice President for Graduate Studies and Research, 410-706-2537. *Dean and Vice President for Medical Affairs,* Dr. Donald E. Wilson, 410-706-7411, Fax: 410-706-0235, E-mail: deanmed@som.umaryland.edu.

School of Nursing Students: 216 full-time, 294 part-time; includes 136 minority (87 African Americans, 37 Asian Americans or Pacific Islanders, 12 Hispanic Americans), 6 international. Average age 33. 219 applicants, 77% accepted, 119 enrolled. *Faculty:* 49. Expenses: Contact institution. *Financial support:* Fellowships, research assistantships, teaching assistantships, career-related internships or fieldwork and traineeships available. Support available to part-time students. Financial award application deadline: 2/15. In 2001, 221 master's, 13 doctorates awarded. *Degree program information:* Part-time programs available. Offers community health nursing (MS); direct nursing (PhD); gerontological nursing (MS); indirect nursing (PhD); maternal-child nursing (MS); medical-surgical nursing (MS); nursing (PhD); nursing administration (MS); nursing education (MS); nursing health policy (MS); primary care nursing (MS); psychiatric nursing (MS). *Application fee:* $50. *Application Contact:* Assistant Dean for Student Affairs, 410-706-0501, Fax: 410-706-7238. *Dean,* Dr. Barbara Heller, 410-706-6741, Fax: 410-706-4231, E-mail: heller@son.umaryland.edu.

Professional Program in Dentistry Students: 387 full-time (159 women); includes 126 minority (23 African Americans, 92 Asian Americans or Pacific Islanders, 10 Hispanic Americans, 1 Native American), 14 international. Average age 24. 1,339 applicants, 7% accepted, 97 enrolled. *Faculty:* 117 full-time (24 women), 98 part-time/adjunct (21 women). Expenses: Contact institution. *Financial support:* In 2001–02, 6 research assistantships with tuition reimbursements (averaging $18,500 per year) were awarded; career-related internships or fieldwork, Federal Work-Study, institutionally sponsored loans, scholarships/grants, and unspecified assistantships also available. Financial award application deadline: 2/15; financial award applicants required to submit FAFSA. In 2001, 91 degrees awarded. Offers dentistry (DDS). *Application deadline:* For fall admission, 1/15. Applications are processed on a rolling basis. *Application fee:* $60. *Application Contact:* Dr. Margaret Wilson, Associate Dean for Admissions and Student Affairs, 410-706-7472, Fax: 410-706-0945. *Dean,* Dr. Richard R. Ranney, 410-706-7461, Fax: 410-706-0406, E-mail: eranney@dental.umaryland.edu.

Professional Program in Medicine Students: 579 full-time (302 women); includes 193 minority (73 African Americans, 111 Asian Americans or Pacific Islanders, 9 Hispanic Americans) 3,185 applicants, 9% accepted. *Faculty:* 991 full-time (333 women), 175 part-time/adjunct. Expenses: Contact institution. *Financial support:* In 2001–02, research assistantships with full tuition reimbursements (averaging $15,000 per year); fellowships with full tuition reimbursements, Federal Work-Study, institutionally sponsored loans, and scholarships/grants also available. Financial award application deadline: 3/15. In 2001, 141 degrees awarded. Offers medicine (MD). *Application deadline:* For fall admission, 11/1. Applications are processed on a rolling basis. *Application fee:* $50. *Application Contact:* Dr. Milford M. Foxwell, Associate Dean for Admissions, 410-706-7478, Fax: 410-706-0467, E-mail: mfoxwell@som.umaryland.edu. *Dean and Vice President for Medical Affairs,* Dr. Donald E. Wilson, 410-706-7411, Fax: 410-706-0235, E-mail: deanmed@som.umaryland.edu.

Professional Program in Pharmacy Students: 422 full-time (297 women), 1 (woman) part-time; includes 225 minority (73 African Americans, 144 Asian Americans or Pacific Islanders, 6 Hispanic Americans, 2 Native Americans), 29 international. Average age 29. 424 applicants, 38% accepted, 131 enrolled. *Faculty:* 74 full-time, 436 part-time/adjunct. Expenses: Contact institution. *Financial support:* In 2001–02, 367 students received support. Career-related internships or fieldwork, Federal Work-Study, institutionally sponsored loans, and scholarships/grants available. Support available to part-time students. Financial award application deadline: 2/15; financial award applicants required to submit FAFSA. In 2001, 97 degrees awarded. Offers pharmacy (Pharm D). *Application deadline:* For fall admission, 3/1. Applications are processed on a rolling basis. *Application fee:* $60. *Application Contact:* Kimberly Mantelli, Recruitment Coordinator, 410-706-7653, Fax: 410-706-2158, E-mail: kmantell@rx.umaryland.edu. *Associate Dean for Student Affairs,* Dr. Robert S. Beardsley, 410-706-7587, Fax: 410-706-2158, E-mail: rbeardsl@rx.umaryland.edu.

School of Law Students: 717 full-time (420 women), 236 part-time (116 women); includes 217 minority (115 African Americans, 77 Asian Americans or Pacific Islanders, 22 Hispanic Americans, 3 Native Americans), 11 international. Average age 26. 2,718 applicants, 37% accepted, 364 enrolled. *Faculty:* 58 full-time (22 women), 38 part-time/adjunct (10 women). Expenses: Contact institution. *Financial support:* Federal Work-Study, institutionally sponsored loans, scholarships/grants, and unspecified assistantships available. Support available to part-time students. Financial award application deadline: 3/1; financial award applicants required to submit FAFSA. In 2001, 237 degrees awarded. *Degree program information:* Part-time and evening/weekend programs available. Offers law (JD). *Application deadline:* For fall admission, 3/1 (priority date). Applications are processed on a rolling basis. *Application fee:* $60. Electronic applications accepted. *Application Contact:* Patricia A. Scott, Director of Admissions, 410-706-3492, Fax: 410-706-4045, E-mail: admissions@law.umaryland.edu. *Dean and Marjorie Cook Professor of Law,* Karen H. Rothenberg, 410-706-3492, Fax: 410-706-4045.

See in-depth description on page 1189.

UNIVERSITY OF MARYLAND, BALTIMORE COUNTY, Baltimore, MD 21250-5398

General Information State-supported, coed, university. CGS member. *Graduate housing:* Room and/or apartments available on a first-come, first-served basis to single students; on-campus housing not available to married students. Housing application deadline: 3/15. *Research affiliation:* Ciena Corporation (computer science and electrical engineering), Aether Systems, Inc. (computer science and electrical engineering), Maryland Industrial Partnerships Program (mechanical engineering), Bechtel Nevada Corp. (computer science and electrical engineering), Raycorp, Inc. (computer science and electrical engineering), Sci Applications International (computer science and electrical engineering).

GRADUATE UNITS

Graduate School *Degree program information:* Part-time and evening/weekend programs available. Offers administration, planning, and policy (MS); applied and professional ethics (MA, Certificate); applied behavioral analysis (MA); applied developmental psychology (PhD); applied mathematics (MS, PhD); applied molecular biology (MS); applied physics (MS, PhD); applied sociology (MA, Certificate); atmospheric physics (MS, PhD); biochemistry (PhD); biological sciences (MS, PhD); biomedical and biobehavioral aspects of aging (PhD); chemistry (PhD); early childhood education (MA); economic policy analysis (MA); education (MA, MS);

elementary education (MA); English as a second language/bilingual education (MA); epidemiology of aging (PhD); French (MA); German (MA); historical studies (MA); imaging and digital arts (MFA); information systems (MS, PhD); instructional systems development (MA); language, literacy, and culture (PhD); law and social policy of aging (PhD); literacy, language and culture (PhD); marine-estuarine-environmental sciences (MS, PhD); medical sociology (MA); modern languages and linguistics (MA); molecular and cell biology (PhD); neuroscience (PhD); neurosciences and cognitive sciences (MS, PhD); policy sciences (MPS, PhD); post-baccalaureate teacher education (MA); preventive medicine and epidemiology (MS); psychology/human services (MA, PhD); Russian (MA); secondary education (MA); social and behavioral aspects of aging (PhD); Spanish (MA); statistics (MS, PhD); training systems (MA). Electronic applications accepted.

College of Engineering Students: 229 full-time (65 women), 103 part-time (26 women); includes 39 minority (18 African Americans, 14 Asian Americans or Pacific Islanders, 3 Hispanic Americans, 4 Native Americans), 212 international. 665 applicants, 36% accepted, 120 enrolled. *Faculty:* 53 full-time (6 women), 5 part-time/adjunct (1 woman). Expenses: Contact institution. *Financial support:* In 2001–02, 4 fellowships with full tuition reimbursements (averaging $20,294 per year), 93 research assistantships with full tuition reimbursements (averaging $13,373 per year), 77 teaching assistantships with full tuition reimbursements (averaging $11,102 per year) were awarded. Financial award application deadline: 3/1; financial award applicants required to submit FAFSA. In 2001, 63 master's, 16 doctorates awarded. *Degree program information:* Part-time and evening/weekend programs available. Offers chemical and biochemical engineering (MS, PhD); computer science (MS, PhD); electrical engineering (MS, PhD); engineering (MS, PhD); engineering management (MS); mechanical engineering (MS, PhD). *Application deadline:* For fall admission, 7/1; for spring admission, 12/1. Applications are processed on a rolling basis. *Application fee:* $45. Electronic applications accepted. *Dean,* Dr. Shlomo Carmi, 410-455-3270, Fax: 410-455-3559, E-mail: carmi@umbc.edu.

See in-depth description on page 1191.

UNIVERSITY OF MARYLAND, COLLEGE PARK, College Park, MD 20742

General Information State-supported, coed, university. CGS member. *Enrollment:* 5,544 full-time matriculated graduate/professional students (2,587 women), 3,669 part-time matriculated graduate/professional students (1,915 women). *Enrollment by degree level:* 120 first professional, 4,300 master's, 4,030 doctoral, 463 other advanced degrees. *Graduate faculty:* 2,749 full-time (943 women), 842 part-time/adjunct (320 women). Tuition, state resident: part-time $289 per credit hour. Tuition, nonresident: part-time $448 per credit hour. One-time fee: $436 part-time. Full-time tuition and fees vary according to course load, campus/location and program. *Graduate housing:* Rooms and/or apartments available on a first-come, first-served basis to single and married students. Typical cost: $8,778 per year for single students; $8,778 per year for married students. Room charges vary according to housing facility selected. *Student services:* Campus employment opportunities, campus safety program, career counseling, child daycare facilities, disabled student services, exercise/wellness program, free psychological counseling, international student services, low-cost health insurance, multicultural affairs office. *Library facilities:* McKeldin Library plus 6 others. *Online resources:* library catalog, web page, access to other libraries' catalogs. *Collection:* 2.9 million titles, 32,290 serial subscriptions, 244,336 audiovisual materials. *Research affiliation:* Federal-National Rotorcraft Technology Center (aerodynamics), Lockheed-Sanders (advanced sensors), Semiconductor Research, Inc. (semiconductors), Northrop Grumman Corporation (computer science), ITT, Inc. (computer science).

Computer facilities: 899 computers available on campus for general student use. A campuswide network can be accessed from student residence rooms and from off campus. Internet access and online class registration, student account information, financial aid summary are available. *Web address:* http://www.maryland.edu/.

General Application Contact: Trudy Lindsey, Director, Graduate Admissions and Records, 301-405-6991, Fax: 301-314-9305, E-mail: grschool@deans.umd.edu.

GRADUATE UNITS

Graduate Studies and Research Students: 5,544 full-time (2,587 women), 3,669 part-time (1,915 women); includes 1,428 minority (713 African Americans, 466 Asian Americans or Pacific Islanders, 217 Hispanic Americans, 32 Native Americans), 2,566 international. Average age 30. ###### applicants, 32% accepted, 2838 enrolled. *Faculty:* 2,749 full-time (943 women), 842 part-time/adjunct (320 women). Expenses: Contact institution. *Financial support:* In 2001–02, 5,755 students received support, including 412 fellowships with full tuition reimbursements available (averaging $9,990 per year), 1,220 research assistantships with tuition reimbursements available (averaging $14,916 per year), 2,472 teaching assistantships with tuition reimbursements available (averaging $11,970 per year); career-related internships or fieldwork, Federal Work-Study, institutionally sponsored loans, and scholarships/grants also available. Support available to part-time students. Financial award applicants required to submit FAFSA. In 2001, 28 first professional degrees, 1,657 master's, 430 doctorates, 3 other advanced degrees awarded. *Degree program information:* Part-time and evening/weekend programs available. Postbaccalaureate distance learning degree programs offered (no on-campus study). Offers neurosciences and cognitive sciences (PhD). *Application deadline:* Applications are processed on a rolling basis. *Application fee:* $50 ($70 for international students). Electronic applications accepted. *Application Contact:* Trudy Lindsey, Director, Graduate Admissions and Records, 301-405-6991, Fax: 301-314-9305, E-mail: grschool@deans.umd.edu. *Dean,* Dr. J. Dennis O'Connor, 301-405-4175, Fax: 301-314-9305.

A. James Clark School of Engineering Students: 857 full-time (154 women), 569 part-time (119 women); includes 159 minority (65 African Americans, 71 Asian Americans or Pacific Islanders, 22 Hispanic Americans, 1 Native American), 830 international. 2,938 applicants, 23% accepted, 391 enrolled. *Faculty:* 310 full-time (39 women), 92 part-time/adjunct (8 women). Expenses: Contact institution. *Financial support:* In 2001–02, 46 fellowships (averaging $11,832 per year), 509 research assistantships (averaging $14,390 per year), 178 teaching assistantships (averaging $13,313 per year) were awarded. Career-related internships or fieldwork, Federal Work-Study, institutionally sponsored loans, and scholarships/grants also available. Support available to part-time students. Financial award applicants required to submit FAFSA. In 2001, 314 master's, 93 doctorates awarded. *Degree program information:* Part-time and evening/weekend programs available. Postbaccalaureate distance learning degree programs offered. Offers aerospace engineering (M Eng); chemical engineering (M Eng); civil and environmental engineering (M Eng, MS, PhD); civil engineering (M Eng); electrical and computer engineering (M Eng, MS, PhD); electrical engineering (M Eng, MS, PhD); electronic packaging and reliability (MS, PhD); engineering (M Eng, ME, MS, PhD); fire protection engineering (M Eng); manufacturing and design (MS, PhD); materials science and engineering (M Eng, MS, PhD); mechanical engineering (M Eng); mechanics and materials (MS, PhD); nuclear engineering (ME, MS, PhD); reliability engineering (M Eng, MS, PhD); systems engineering (M Eng); telecommunications (MS); thermal and fluid sciences (MS, PhD). *Application deadline:* Applications are processed on a rolling basis. *Application fee:* $50 ($70 for international students). Electronic applications accepted. *Application Contact:* Trudy Lindsey, Director, Graduate Admissions and Records, 301-405-6991, Fax: 301-314-9305, E-mail: grschool@deans.umd.edu. *Dean,* Dr. Nariman Farvardin, 301-405-3868, Fax: 301-314-9281, E-mail: farvar@eng.umd.edu.

College of Agriculture and Natural Resources Students: 288 full-time (198 women), 98 part-time (46 women); includes 34 minority (19 African Americans, 11 Asian Americans or Pacific Islanders, 2 Hispanic Americans, 2 Native Americans), 111 international. 340 applicants, 37% accepted, 89 enrolled. *Faculty:* 372 full-time (143 women), 34 part-time/adjunct (20 women). Expenses: Contact institution. *Financial support:* In 2001–02, 11 fellowships with full tuition reimbursements (averaging $12,229 per year), 129 research assistantships with tuition reimbursements (averaging $17,024 per year), 47 teaching assistantships with tuition reimbursements (averaging $13,388 per year) were awarded. Career-related internships or fieldwork, Federal Work-Study, and scholarships/grants also available. Support available to part-time students. Financial award applicants required to submit FAFSA. In 2001, 28 first professional degrees, 35 master's, 18 doctorates awarded. *Degree program information:* Part-time and evening/weekend programs available. Offers agriculture and natural resources (DVM, MS, PhD); agriculture economics (MS, PhD); agronomy (MS, PhD); animal sciences (MS, PhD); biological resources engineering (MS, PhD); food science (MS, PhD); horticulture (MS, PhD); natural resource science (MS, PhD); nutrition (MS, PhD); poultry science (MS, PhD); resource economics (MS, PhD); veterinary medical sciences (PhD); veterinary medicine (DVM, PhD). *Application deadline:* Applications are processed on a rolling basis. *Application fee:* $50 ($70 for international students). Electronic applications accepted. *Application Contact:* Trudy Lindsey, Director, Graduate Admissions and Records, 301-405-6991, Fax: 301-314-9305, E-mail: grschool@deans.umd.edu. *Dean,* Dr. Thomas Fretz, 301-405-2072, Fax: 301-314-9146, E-mail: tf43@umail.umd.edu.

College of Arts and Humanities Students: 771 full-time (475 women), 428 part-time (262 women); includes 179 minority (80 African Americans, 57 Asian Americans or Pacific Islanders, 34 Hispanic Americans, 8 Native Americans), 252 international. 1,680 applicants, 39% accepted, 348 enrolled. *Faculty:* 382 full-time (168 women), 206 part-time/adjunct (98 women). Expenses: Contact institution. *Financial support:* In 2001–02, 62 fellowships with full tuition reimbursements (averaging $11,654 per year), 9 research assistantships with tuition reimbursements (averaging $13,282 per year), 534 teaching assistantships with tuition reimbursements (averaging $11,371 per year) were awarded. Career-related internships or fieldwork, Federal Work-Study, and scholarships/grants also available. Support available to part-time students. Financial award applicants required to submit FAFSA. In 2001, 152 master's, 64 doctorates awarded. *Degree program information:* Part-time and evening/weekend programs available. Offers American studies (MA, PhD); art (MFA); art history (MA, PhD); arts and humanities (M Ed, MA, MFA, MM, DMA, Ed D, PhD); classics (MA); communications (MA, PhD); comparative literature (MA, PhD); creative writing (MA, PhD); dance (MFA); English language and literature (MA, PhD); foreign languages and literatures (MA, PhD); French language and literature (MA, PhD); Germanic language and literature (MA, PhD); history (MA, PhD); linguistics (MA, PhD); modern French studies (PhD); music (M Ed, MA, MM, DMA, Ed D, PhD); philosophy (MA, PhD); Russian (MA); Russian language and literature (MA); Spanish (MA, PhD); theatre (MA, MFA, PhD); women's studies (MA, PhD). *Application deadline:* Applications are processed on a rolling basis. *Application fee:* $50 ($70 for international students). Electronic applications accepted. *Application Contact:* Trudy Lindsey, Director, Graduate Admissions and Records, 301-405-6991, Fax: 301-314-9305, E-mail: grschool@deans.umd.edu. *Dean,* Dr. James Harris, 301-405-2095, Fax: 301-314-9148, E-mail: jharris@deans.umd.edu.

College of Behavioral and Social Sciences Students: 563 full-time (327 women), 252 part-time (131 women); includes 135 minority (74 African Americans, 28 Asian Americans or Pacific Islanders, 31 Hispanic Americans, 2 Native Americans), 202 international. 1,909 applicants, 26% accepted, 221 enrolled. *Faculty:* 432 full-time (178 women), 86 part-time/adjunct (48 women). Expenses: Contact institution. *Financial support:* In 2001–02, 64 fellowships with full tuition reimbursements (averaging $10,725 per year), 37 research assistantships with tuition reimbursements (averaging $13,152 per year), 435 teaching assistantships with tuition reimbursements (averaging $11,632 per year) were awarded. Career-related internships or fieldwork, Federal Work-Study, and scholarships/grants also available. Support available to part-time students. Financial award applicants required to submit FAFSA. In 2001, 145 master's, 69 doctorates awarded. *Degree program information:* Part-time and evening/weekend programs available. Offers American politics (MA, PhD); applied anthropology (MAA); audiology (MA, PhD); behavioral and social sciences (MA, MAA, MS, PhD); clinical psychology (PhD); comparative politics (MA, PhD); criminology and criminal justice (MA, PhD); developmental psychology (PhD); economics (MA, PhD); experimental psychology (PhD); geography (MA, PhD); industrial psychology (MA, MS, PhD); international relations (MA, PhD); language pathology (MA, PhD); political economy (MA, PhD); political theory (MA, PhD); social psychology (PhD); sociology (MA, PhD); speech (MA, PhD); survey methodology (MS, PhD). *Application deadline:* Applications are processed on a rolling basis. *Application fee:* $50 ($70 for international students). Electronic applications accepted. *Application Contact:* Trudy Lindsey, Director, Graduate Admissions and Records, 301-405-6991, Fax: 301-314-9305, E-mail: grschool@deans.umd.edu. *Dean,* Dr. Irwin L. Goldstein, 301-405-1690, Fax: 301-314-9086, E-mail: irv@bsos.umd.edu.

College of Computer, Mathematical and Physical Sciences Students: 559 full-time (128 women), 203 part-time (54 women); includes 67 minority (26 African Americans, 22 Asian Americans or Pacific Islanders, 16 Hispanic Americans, 3 Native Americans), 399 international. 1,740 applicants, 27% accepted, 168 enrolled. *Faculty:* 447 full-time (66 women), 126 part-time/adjunct (20 women). Expenses: Contact institution. *Financial support:* In 2001–02, 64 fellowships with tuition reimbursements (averaging $10,410 per year), 362 research assistantships with tuition reimbursements (averaging $15,213 per year), 310 teaching assistantships with tuition reimbursements (averaging $13,492 per year) were awarded. Career-related internships or fieldwork, Federal Work-Study, and scholarships/grants also available. Support available to part-time students. Financial award applicants required to submit FAFSA. In 2001, 97 master's, 68 doctorates awarded. *Degree program information:* Part-time and evening/weekend programs available. Postbaccalaureate distance learning degree programs offered. Offers applied mathematics (MS, PhD); astronomy (MS, PhD); chemical physics (MS, PhD); computer science (MS, PhD); computer, mathematical and physical sciences (MA, MS, MSWE, PhD); geology (MS, PhD); mathematical statistics (MA, PhD); mathematics (MA, PhD); meteorology (MS, PhD); physics (MS, PhD); software engineering (MS, MSWE). *Application deadline:* Applications are processed on a rolling basis. *Application fee:* $50 ($70 for international students). Electronic applications accepted. *Application Contact:* Trudy Lindsey, Director, Graduate Admissions and Records, 301-405-6991, Fax: 301-314-9305, E-mail: grschool@deans.umd.edu. *Dean,* Dr. Stephen Halperin, 301-405-2316, Fax: 301-405-9377, E-mail: shalper@deans.umd.edu.

College of Education Students: 412 full-time (326 women), 679 part-time (537 women); includes 272 minority (165 African Americans, 58 Asian Americans or Pacific Islanders, 41 Hispanic Americans, 8 Native Americans), 75 international. 917 applicants, 39% accepted, 199 enrolled. *Faculty:* 131 full-time (83 women), 68 part-time/adjunct (50 women). Expenses: Contact institution. *Financial support:* In 2001–02, 37 fellowships with full tuition reimbursements (averaging $9,141 per year), 45 research assistantships with tuition reimbursements (averaging $14,359 per year), 102 teaching assistantships with tuition reimbursements (averaging $12,647 per year) were awarded. Career-related internships or fieldwork, Federal Work-Study, and scholarships/grants also available. Support available to part-time students. Financial award applicants required to submit FAFSA. In 2001, 170 master's, 45 doctorates, 3 other advanced degrees awarded. *Degree program information:* Part-time and evening/weekend programs available. Postbaccalaureate distance learning degree programs offered. Offers college student personnel (M Ed, MA); college student personnel administration (PhD); community counseling (CAGS); community/career counseling (M Ed, MA); counseling and personnel services (M Ed, MA, PhD); counseling psychology (PhD); counselor education (PhD); curriculum and educational communications (M Ed, MA, Ed D, PhD); early childhood/elementary education (M Ed, MA, Ed D, PhD, CAGS); education (M Ed, MA, Ed D, PhD, CAGS); human development (M Ed, MA, Ed D, PhD, CAGS); measurement (MA, PhD); program evaluation (MA, PhD); reading (M Ed, MA, PhD, CAGS); rehabilitation counseling (M Ed, MA); school counseling (M Ed, MA); school psychology (M Ed, MA, PhD); secondary education (M Ed, MA, Ed D, PhD, CAGS); social foundations of education (M Ed, MA, Ed D, PhD, CAGS); special education (M Ed, MA, Ed D, PhD, CAGS); statistics (MA, PhD); teaching English to speakers of other languages (M Ed). *Application deadline:* Applications are processed on a rolling basis. *Application fee:* $50 ($70 for international students). Electronic applications accepted. *Application Contact:* Trudy Lindsey, Director, Graduate Admissions and Records, 301-405-6991, Fax: 301-314-9305, E-mail: grschool@deans.umd.edu. *Dean,* Dr. Edna Szymanski, 301-405-2334, Fax: 301-314-9890, E-mail: ednas@deans.umd.edu.

College of Health and Human Performance Students: 127 full-time (79 women), 79 part-time (60 women); includes 42 minority (23 African Americans, 11 Asian Americans or Pacific Islanders, 6 Hispanic Americans, 2 Native Americans), 28 international. 246 applicants, 37% accepted, 51 enrolled. *Faculty:* 73 full-time (36 women), 30 part-time/adjunct (17 women). Expenses: Contact institution. *Financial support:* In 2001–02, 17 fellowships with full tuition reimbursements (averaging $10,679 per year), 19 research assistantships with

University of Maryland, College Park (continued)

tuition reimbursements (averaging $12,942 per year), 64 teaching assistantships with tuition reimbursements (averaging $11,841 per year) were awarded. Career-related internships or fieldwork, Federal Work-Study, and scholarships/grants also available. Support available to part-time students. Financial award applicants required to submit FAFSA. In 2001, 40 master's, 8 doctorates awarded. *Degree program information:* Part-time and evening/weekend programs available. Offers community health (MPH); family studies (MS, PhD); health and human performance (MA, MPH, MS, Ed D, PhD); health education (MA, Ed D, PhD); kinesiology (MA, PhD); marriage and family therapy (MS). *Application deadline:* Applications are processed on a rolling basis. *Application fee:* $50 ($70 for international students). Electronic applications accepted. *Application Contact:* Trudy Lindsey, Director, Graduate Admissions and Records, 301-405-6991, Fax: 301-314-9305, E-mail: grschool@deans.umd.edu. *Interim Dean,* Dr. Jerry Wrenn, 301-405-1362, Fax: 301-405-8397, E-mail: jwrenn@hlhp.umd.edu.

College of Information Studies Students: 136 full-time (114 women), 143 part-time (109 women); includes 36 minority (20 African Americans, 12 Asian Americans or Pacific Islanders, 2 Hispanic Americans, 2 Native Americans), 14 international. 209 applicants, 54% accepted, 73 enrolled. *Faculty:* 11 full-time (6 women), 13 part-time/adjunct (6 women). Expenses: Contact institution. *Financial support:* In 2001–02, 8 fellowships with full tuition reimbursements (averaging $5,963 per year), 21 teaching assistantships with tuition reimbursements (averaging $10,575 per year) were awarded. Career-related internships or fieldwork, Federal Work-Study, scholarships/grants, and tuition waivers (full and partial) also available. Support available to part-time students. Financial award application deadline: 2/1; financial award applicants required to submit FAFSA. In 2001, 111 master's, 1 doctorate awarded. *Degree program information:* Part-time and evening/weekend programs available. Offers information studies (MLS, PhD). *Application deadline:* For fall admission, 4/1; for spring admission, 11/1. Applications are processed on a rolling basis. *Application fee:* $50 ($70 for international students). Electronic applications accepted. *Application Contact:* Trudy Lindsey, Director, Graduate Admissions and Records, 301-405-6991, Fax: 301-314-9305, E-mail: grschool@deans.umd.edu. *Acting Dean,* Dr. Bruce Dearstyne, 301-405-2033, Fax: 301-314-9145, E-mail: ap57@umail.umd.edu.

College of Life Sciences Students: 409 full-time (224 women), 172 part-time (79 women); includes 43 minority (13 African Americans, 19 Asian Americans or Pacific Islanders, 10 Hispanic Americans, 1 Native American), 159 international. 827 applicants, 23% accepted, 125 enrolled. *Faculty:* 250 full-time (88 women), 36 part-time/adjunct (16 women). Expenses: Contact institution. *Financial support:* In 2001–02, 41 fellowships with full tuition reimbursements (averaging $8,114 per year), 99 research assistantships with tuition reimbursements (averaging $15,467 per year), 200 teaching assistantships with tuition reimbursements (averaging $13,634 per year) were awarded. Career-related internships or fieldwork, Federal Work-Study, and scholarships/grants also available. Support available to part-time students. Financial award applicants required to submit FAFSA. In 2001, 61 master's, 42 doctorates awarded. *Degree program information:* Part-time and evening/weekend programs available. Offers analytical chemistry (MS, PhD); behavior, ecology, evolution, and systematics (MS, PhD); biochemistry (MS, PhD); biology (MS, PhD); biophysics (MS); cell biology and molecular genetics (MS, PhD); chemistry (MS, PhD); entomology (MS, PhD); inorganic chemistry (MS, PhD); life sciences (MLS, MS, PhD); marine-estuarine-environmental sciences (MS, PhD); microbiology (MS, PhD); molecular and cell biology (PhD); organic chemistry (MS, PhD); physical chemistry (MS, PhD); plant biology (MS, PhD); sustainable development and conservation biology (MS); toxicology (MS, PhD); zoology (MS, PhD). *Application deadline:* Applications are processed on a rolling basis. *Application fee:* $50 ($70 for international students). Electronic applications accepted. *Application Contact:* Trudy Lindsey, Director, Graduate Admissions and Records, 301-405-6991, Fax: 301-314-9305, E-mail: grschool@deans.umd.edu. *Dean,* Dr. Norman M. Allewell, 301-405-2071, Fax: 301-314-9949, E-mail: allewell@deans.umd.edu.

Phillip Merrill College of Journalism Students: 45 full-time (32 women), 25 part-time (10 women); includes 18 minority (12 African Americans, 6 Asian Americans or Pacific Islanders), 4 international. 135 applicants, 38% accepted, 22 enrolled. *Faculty:* 28 full-time (11 women), 18 part-time/adjunct (3 women). Expenses: Contact institution. *Financial support:* In 2001–02, 32 fellowships with full tuition reimbursements (averaging $6,800 per year), 10 teaching assistantships with tuition reimbursements (averaging $11,666 per year) were awarded. Research assistantships with tuition reimbursements, career-related internships or fieldwork, Federal Work-Study, and scholarships/grants also available. Support available to part-time students. Financial award applicants required to submit FAFSA. In 2001, 23 degrees awarded. *Degree program information:* Part-time and evening/weekend programs available. Offers advertising (MA, PhD); broadcast journalism (MA, PhD); international communication (MA, PhD); journalism (MA); journalism education (MA, PhD); mass communication (PhD); mass communication research (MA, PhD); political communication (MA, PhD); public affairs reporting (MA, PhD); public communication (MA, PhD); public relations (MA, PhD); science communication (MA, PhD). *Application deadline:* For fall admission, 3/1; for spring admission, 11/1. Applications are processed on a rolling basis. *Application fee:* $50 ($70 for international students). Electronic applications accepted. *Application Contact:* Trudy Lindsey, Director, Graduate Admissions and Records, 301-405-6991, Fax: 301-314-9305, E-mail: grschool@deans.umd.edu. *Dean,* Thomas Kunkel, 301-405-2383, Fax: 301-314-1978, E-mail: tkunkel@jmail.umd.edu.

Robert H. Smith School of Business Students: 1,057 full-time (352 women), 228 part-time (64 women); includes 204 minority (69 African Americans, 113 Asian Americans or Pacific Islanders, 21 Hispanic Americans, 1 Native American), 357 international. 2,841 applicants, 30% accepted, 622 enrolled. *Faculty:* 104 full-time (17 women), 47 part-time/adjunct (9 women). Expenses: Contact institution. *Financial support:* In 2001–02, 16 fellowships with full tuition reimbursements (averaging $10,198 per year), 3 research assistantships with tuition reimbursements (averaging $14,120 per year), 261 teaching assistantships with tuition reimbursements (averaging $8,405 per year) were awarded. Federal Work-Study and scholarships/grants also available. Support available to part-time students. Financial award applicants required to submit FAFSA. In 2001, 423 master's, 6 doctorates awarded. *Degree program information:* Part-time and evening/weekend programs available. Postbaccalaureate distance learning degree programs offered. Offers business (MBA, MS, PhD); business administration (MBA); business and management (MS, PhD). *Application deadline:* For fall admission, 5/15. Applications are processed on a rolling basis. *Application fee:* $50 ($70 for international students). *Application Contact:* Trudy Lindsey, Director, Graduate Admissions and Records, 301-405-6991, Fax: 301-314-9305, E-mail: grschool@deans.umd.edu. *Dean,* Dr. Howard Frank, 301-405-2308, Fax: 301-314-9120, E-mail: hfrank@rhsmith.umd.edu.

School of Architecture Students: 118 full-time (67 women), 26 part-time (21 women); includes 25 minority (14 African Americans, 8 Asian Americans or Pacific Islanders, 3 Hispanic Americans), 14 international. 255 applicants, 37% accepted, 50 enrolled. *Faculty:* 23 full-time (4 women), 11 part-time/adjunct (4 women). Expenses: Contact institution. *Financial support:* In 2001–02, 4 fellowships with full tuition reimbursements (averaging $8,016 per year), 1 research assistantship with tuition reimbursement (averaging $12,044 per year), 70 teaching assistantships with tuition reimbursements (averaging $7,792 per year) were awarded. Career-related internships or fieldwork, Federal Work-Study, and scholarships/grants also available. Support available to part-time students. Financial award applicants required to submit FAFSA. In 2001, 43 degrees awarded. *Degree program information:* Part-time and evening/weekend programs available. Offers architecture (M Arch, MA, MCP); community planning (MCP). *Application deadline:* Applications are processed on a rolling basis. *Application fee:* $50 ($70 for international students). Electronic applications accepted. *Application Contact:* Trudy Lindsey, Director, Graduate Admissions and Records, 301-405-6991, Fax: 301-314-9305, E-mail: grschool@deans.umd.edu. *Dean,* Steven Hurtt, 301-405-6283, Fax: 301-314-9583, E-mail: shurtt@deans.umd.edu.

School of Public Affairs Students: 116 full-time (63 women), 81 part-time (41 women); includes 43 minority (30 African Americans, 8 Asian Americans or Pacific Islanders, 5 Hispanic Americans), 33 international. 345 applicants, 46% accepted, 72 enrolled. *Faculty:* 28 full-time (5 women), 15 part-time/adjunct (4 women). Expenses: Contact institution. *Financial support:* In 2001–02, 4 fellowships with full tuition reimbursements (averaging $10,001 per year), 1 research assistantship with tuition reimbursement (averaging $6,022 per year), 26 teaching assistantships with tuition reimbursements (averaging $8,974 per year) were awarded. Federal Work-Study and scholarships/grants also available. Support available to part-time students. Financial award applicants required to submit FAFSA. In 2001, 41 master's, 3 doctorates awarded. *Degree program information:* Part-time and evening/weekend programs available. Postbaccalaureate distance learning degree programs offered. Offers policy studies (PhD); public affairs (MPM, MPP, PhD); public management (MPM); public policy (MPP). *Application deadline:* Applications are processed on a rolling basis. *Application fee:* $50 ($70 for international students). Electronic applications accepted. *Application Contact:* Trudy Lindsey, Director, Graduate Admissions and Records, 301-405-6991, Fax: 301-314-9305, E-mail: grschool@deans.umd.edu. *Dean,* Dr. Susan C. Schwab, 301-405-6429, Fax: 301-403-4675.

UNIVERSITY OF MARYLAND EASTERN SHORE, Princess Anne, MD 21853-1299

General Information State-supported, coed, university. CGS member. *Enrollment:* 241 matriculated graduate/professional students (160 women). *Graduate faculty:* 107. *Graduate housing:* Room and/or apartments available on a first-come, first-served basis to single students; on-campus housing not available to married students. Housing application deadline: 6/15. *Student services:* Campus employment opportunities, campus safety program, career counseling, child daycare facilities, disabled student services, exercise/wellness program, free psychological counseling, grant writing training, international student services, teacher training, writing training. *Library facilities:* Frederick Douglass Library. *Online resources:* library catalog, web page, access to other libraries' catalogs. *Collection:* 150,000 titles, 1,260 serial subscriptions.

Computer facilities: 120 computers available on campus for general student use. A campuswide network can be accessed. *Web address:* http://www.umes.edu/.

General Application Contact: Terrance L. Hicks, Admissions and Advisement Coordinator, 410-651-8626, Fax: 410-651-7571, E-mail: thicks@mail.umes.edu.

GRADUATE UNITS

Graduate Programs *Degree program information:* Part-time programs available. Offers agriculture education and extension (MS); applied computer science (MS); career and technology education (M Ed); food and agricultural sciences (MS); guidance and counseling (M Ed); marine estuarine (MS, PhD); marine-estuarine-environmental sciences (MS, PhD); physical therapy (MPT); special education (M Ed); teaching (MAT); toxicology (MS, PhD). Electronic applications accepted.

See in-depth description on page 1193.

UNIVERSITY OF MARYLAND UNIVERSITY COLLEGE, Adelphi, MD 20783

General Information State-supported, coed, comprehensive institution. CGS member. *Enrollment:* 289 full-time matriculated graduate/professional students (158 women), 5,824 part-time matriculated graduate/professional students (2,854 women). *Enrollment by degree level:* 6,060 master's, 53 doctoral. *Graduate faculty:* 40 full-time (11 women), 111 part-time/adjunct (18 women). Tuition, state resident: full-time $5,418; part-time $301 per credit hour. Tuition, nonresident: full-time $8,892; part-time $494 per credit hour. *Graduate housing:* On-campus housing not available. *Student services:* Campus employment opportunities, career counseling, disabled student services, international student services, writing training. *Library facilities:* Information and Library Services plus 1 other. *Online resources:* library catalog, web page, access to other libraries' catalogs. *Collection:* 4,623 titles, 65 serial subscriptions.

Computer facilities: 375 computers available on campus for general student use. A campuswide network can be accessed from off campus. *Web address:* http://www.umuc.edu/.

General Application Contact: Coordinator, Graduate Admissions, 301-985-7155, Fax: 301-985-7175, E-mail: gradinfo@nova.wmuc.edu.

GRADUATE UNITS

Graduate School of Management and Technology Students: 289 full-time (158 women), 5,824 part-time (2,854 women); includes 2,430 minority (1,790 African Americans, 412 Asian Americans or Pacific Islanders, 196 Hispanic Americans, 32 Native Americans), 333 international. Average age 36. 1,899 applicants, 98% accepted. *Faculty:* 40 full-time (11 women), 111 part-time/adjunct (18 women). Expenses: Contact institution. *Financial support:* Federal Work-Study and scholarships/grants available. Support available to part-time students. Financial award application deadline: 6/1; financial award applicants required to submit FAFSA. In 2001, 762 degrees awarded. *Degree program information:* Part-time and evening/weekend programs available. Postbaccalaureate distance learning degree programs offered (no on-campus study). Offers accounting and financial management (MS); biotechnology studies (MS); business administration (Exec MBA, MBA); computer systems management (Exec MS, MS); distance education (MDE); education (M Ed); electronic commerce (MS); environmental management (MS); information technology (Exec MS, MS); international management (Exec MIM, MIM); management (MS, DM); management and technology (Exec MBA, Exec MIM, Exec MS, M Ed, M Sw E, MA, MBA, MDE, MIM, MS, DM); software engineering (M Sw E); teaching (MA); technology management (Exec MS, MS); telecommunications management (Exec MS, MS). Offered evenings and weekends only. *Application deadline:* Applications are processed on a rolling basis. *Application fee:* $50. Electronic applications accepted. *Application Contact:* Coordinator, Graduate Admissions, 301-985-7155, Fax: 301-985-7175, E-mail: gradinfo@nova.umuc.edu. *Acting Associate Vice President and Dean of Graduate Studies,* Dr. Christina A. Hannah, 301-985-7040, Fax: 301-985-4611, E-mail: channah@polaris.umuc.edu.

UNIVERSITY OF MASSACHUSETTS AMHERST, Amherst, MA 01003

General Information State-supported, coed, university. CGS member. *Enrollment:* 2,260 full-time matriculated graduate/professional students (1,211 women), 2,198 part-time matriculated graduate/professional students (1,117 women). *Graduate faculty:* 1,159 full-time (287 women). Tuition, state resident: full-time $1,980; part-time $110 per credit. Tuition, nonresident: full-time $7,456; part-time $414 per credit. *Required fees:* $4,112. One-time fee: $115 full-time. *Graduate housing:* Rooms and/or apartments available on a first-come, first-served basis to single and married students. Typical cost: $2,836 per year ($4,988 including board) for single students; $5,728 per year ($8,118 including board) for married students. Housing application deadline: 7/15. *Student services:* Campus employment opportunities, campus safety program, career counseling, child daycare facilities, disabled student services, free psychological counseling, grant writing training, international student services, low-cost health insurance. *Library facilities:* W. E. B. Du Bois Library plus 3 others. *Online resources:* library catalog, web page, access to other libraries' catalogs. *Collection:* 3 million titles, 15,362 serial subscriptions, 16,420 audiovisual materials.

Computer facilities: A campuswide network can be accessed from student residence rooms and from off campus. On-line course and grade information available. *Web address:* http://www.umass.edu/.

General Application Contact: Jean Ames, Supervisor of Admissions, 413-545-0721, Fax: 413-577-0010, E-mail: gradapp@resgs.umass.edu.

GRADUATE UNITS

Graduate School Students: 2,260 full-time (1,211 women), 2,198 part-time (1,117 women); includes 473 minority (157 African Americans, 145 Asian Americans or Pacific Islanders, 151 Hispanic Americans, 20 Native Americans), 1,214 international. Average age 32. 8,669 applicants, 28% accepted. *Faculty:* 1,159 full-time (287 women), 130 part-time/adjunct (59 women). Expenses: Contact institution. *Financial support:* In 2001–02, 858 fellowships with full tuition reimbursements (averaging $5,266 per year), 1,794 research assistantships with full tuition reimbursements (averaging $8,973 per year), 1,686 teaching assistantships with full tuition reimbursements (averaging $8,555 per year) were awarded. Career-related internships or fieldwork, Federal Work-Study, institutionally sponsored loans, scholarships/grants, traineeships, tuition waivers (full), and unspecified assistantships also available. Support available to part-time students. In 2001, 989 master's, 261 doctorates awarded. *Degree program information:* Part-time and evening/weekend programs available. Postbaccalaureate distance learning degree programs offered. Offers interdisciplinary studies (MS, PhD); neuroscience and behavior (MS, PhD); organismic and evolutionary biology (MS, PhD); plant biology (MS, PhD). *Application deadline:* Applications are processed on a rolling basis. *Application fee:* $40 ($50 for international students). *Application Contact:* Robert M. Swasey, Graduate Registrar, 413-545-0721, Fax: 413-577-0010, E-mail: rswasey@resgs.umass.edu. *Dean,* Dr. James F. Walker, 413-545-5271, Fax: 413-545-3754.

College of Engineering Students: 242 full-time (64 women), 206 part-time (32 women); includes 25 minority (2 African Americans, 14 Asian Americans or Pacific Islanders, 7 Hispanic Americans, 2 Native Americans), 266 international. Average age 28. 1,741 applicants, 20% accepted. *Faculty:* 86 full-time (8 women). Expenses: Contact institution. *Financial support:* In 2001–02, 93 fellowships with full tuition reimbursements (averaging $8,272 per year), 328 research assistantships with full tuition reimbursements (averaging $11,839 per year), 81 teaching assistantships with full tuition reimbursements (averaging $5,551 per year) were awarded. Career-related internships or fieldwork, Federal Work-Study, scholarships/grants, traineeships, and unspecified assistantships also available. Support available to part-time students. Financial award application deadline: 2/1. In 2001, 105 master's, 29 doctorates awarded. *Degree program information:* Part-time and evening/weekend programs available. Offers chemical engineering (MS, PhD); civil engineering (MS, PhD); electrical and computer engineering (MS, PhD); engineering (MS, PhD); engineering management (MS); environmental engineering (MS); industrial engineering and operations research (MS, PhD); manufacturing engineering (MS); mechanical engineering (MS, PhD). *Application deadline:* Applications are processed on a rolling basis. *Application fee:* $40 ($50 for international students). *Dean,* Dr. Joseph I. Goldstein, 413-545-0300, Fax: 413-545-0724, E-mail: jigo@ecs.umass.edu.

College of Food and Natural Resources Students: 259 full-time (134 women), 167 part-time (83 women); includes 24 minority (10 African Americans, 7 Asian Americans or Pacific Islanders, 7 Hispanic Americans), 133 international. Average age 29. 610 applicants, 37% accepted. *Faculty:* 150 full-time (25 women). Expenses: Contact institution. *Financial support:* In 2001–02, 1 fellowship with full tuition reimbursement (averaging $947 per year), 253 research assistantships with full tuition reimbursements (averaging $7,195 per year), 145 teaching assistantships with full tuition reimbursements (averaging $6,466 per year) were awarded. Career-related internships or fieldwork, Federal Work-Study, scholarships/grants, traineeships, and unspecified assistantships also available. Support available to part-time students. Financial award application deadline: 2/1. In 2001, 111 master's, 28 doctorates awarded. *Degree program information:* Part-time programs available. Offers entomology (MS, PhD); food and natural resources (MLA, MRP, MS, PhD); food science (MS, PhD); forestry and wood technology (MS, PhD); hotel, restaurant, and travel administration (MS); landscape architecture (MLA); mammalian and avian biology (MS, PhD); microbiology (MS, PhD); plant science (PhD); regional planning (MRP, PhD); resource economics (MS, PhD); soil science (MS, PhD); sport studies (MS, PhD); wildlife and fisheries conservation (MS, PhD). *Application deadline:* For fall admission, 2/1 (priority date). Applications are processed on a rolling basis. *Application fee:* $40 ($50 for international students). *Director,* Dr. Cleve Willis, 413-545-2491, Fax: 413-545-5853, E-mail: willis@resecon.umass.edu.

College of Humanities and Fine Arts Students: 407 full-time (232 women), 288 part-time (187 women); includes 94 minority (35 African Americans, 22 Asian Americans or Pacific Islanders, 34 Hispanic Americans, 3 Native Americans), 131 international. Average age 31. 1,210 applicants, 30% accepted. *Faculty:* 258 full-time (79 women). Expenses: Contact institution. *Financial support:* In 2001–02, 75 research assistantships with full tuition reimbursements (averaging $5,094 per year), 480 teaching assistantships with full tuition reimbursements (averaging $9,144 per year) were awarded. Fellowships with full tuition reimbursements, career-related internships or fieldwork, Federal Work-Study, scholarships/grants, traineeships, and unspecified assistantships also available. Support available to part-time students. In 2001, 136 master's, 37 doctorates awarded. *Degree program information:* Part-time programs available. Postbaccalaureate distance learning degree programs offered. Offers Afro-American studies (MA, PhD); ancient history (MA); art (MA, MFA, MS); art education (MA); art history (MA); British Empire history (MA); Chinese (MA); comparative literature (MA, PhD); creative writing (MFA); English and American literature (MA, PhD); European (medieval and modern) history (MA); European medieval and modern history (PhD); French and Francophone studies (MA, MAT); Germanic languages and literatures (MA, PhD); Hispanic literatures and linguistics (MA, MAT, PhD); humanities and fine arts (MA, MAT, MFA, MM, MS, PhD); interior design (MS); Islamic history (MA); Italian studies (MAT); Japanese (MA); Latin American history (MA, PhD); Latin and classical humanities (MAT); linguistics (MA, PhD); modern global history (MA); music (MM, PhD); philosophy (MA, PhD); public history (MA); science and technology history (MA); studio art (MFA); theater (MFA); U.S. history (MA, PhD). *Application deadline:* Applications are processed on a rolling basis. *Application fee:* $40 ($50 for international students). *Dean,* Dr. Lee Edwards, 413-545-4169, Fax: 413-545-4171, E-mail: lee.edwards@cas.umass.edu.

College of Natural Sciences and Mathematics Students: 362 full-time (137 women), 343 part-time (103 women); includes 39 minority (5 African Americans, 26 Asian Americans or Pacific Islanders, 7 Hispanic Americans, 1 Native American), 339 international. Average age 28. 2,269 applicants, 21% accepted. *Faculty:* 339 full-time (60 women). Expenses: Contact institution. *Financial support:* In 2001–02, 97 fellowships with full tuition reimbursements (averaging $8,451 per year), 483 research assistantships with full tuition reimbursements (averaging $11,057 per year), 240 teaching assistantships with full tuition reimbursements (averaging $7,992 per year) were awarded. Career-related internships or fieldwork, Federal Work-Study, scholarships/grants, traineeships, and unspecified assistantships also available. Support available to part-time students. In 2001, 102 master's, 56 doctorates awarded. *Degree program information:* Part-time programs available. Postbaccalaureate distance learning degree programs offered. Offers applied mathematics (MS); astronomy (MS, PhD); biochemistry (MS, PhD); biological chemistry (PhD); biology (MA, MS, PhD); cell and developmental biology (PhD); chemistry (MS, PhD); computer science (MS, PhD); geography (MS); geology (MS, PhD); geosciences (PhD); mathematics and statistics (MS, PhD); natural sciences and mathematics (MA, MS, PhD); physics (MS, PhD); polymer science and engineering (MS, PhD). *Application deadline:* Applications are processed on a rolling basis. *Application fee:* $40 ($50 for international students). *Dean,* Dr. Leon Osterweil, 413-545-1785, Fax: 413-545-4171, E-mail: ljo@nsm.umass.edu.

College of Social and Behavioral Sciences Students: 285 full-time (168 women), 287 part-time (153 women); includes 83 minority (24 African Americans, 20 Asian Americans or Pacific Islanders, 35 Hispanic Americans, 4 Native Americans), 113 international. Average age 31. 1,193 applicants, 20% accepted. *Faculty:* 164 full-time (51 women). Expenses: Contact institution. *Financial support:* In 2001–02, 135 fellowships with full tuition reimbursements (averaging $6,928 per year), 169 research assistantships with full tuition reimbursements (averaging $6,713 per year), 270 teaching assistantships with full tuition reimbursements (averaging $9,212 per year) were awarded. Career-related internships or fieldwork, Federal Work-Study, scholarships/grants, traineeships, and unspecified assistantships also available. Support available to part-time students. In 2001, 82 master's, 40 doctorates awarded. *Degree program information:* Part-time programs available. Offers anthropology (MA, PhD); clinical psychology (MS, PhD); communication (MA, PhD); economics (MA, PhD); labor studies (MS); political science (MA, PhD); public policy and administration (MPA); social and behavioral sciences (MA, MPA, MS, PhD); sociology (MA, PhD). *Application deadline:* Applications are processed on a rolling basis. *Application fee:* $40 ($50 for international students). *Dean,* Dr. Glen Gordon, 413-545-4173, Fax: 413-545-4171, E-mail: ggordon@polsci.umass.edu.

Isenberg School of Management Students: 100 full-time (54 women), 245 part-time (93 women); includes 26 minority (5 African Americans, 13 Asian Americans or Pacific Islanders, 6 Hispanic Americans, 2 Native Americans), 50 international. Average age 33. 378 applicants, 40% accepted. *Faculty:* 50 full-time (9 women). Expenses: Contact institution. *Financial support:* In 2001–02, 19 fellowships with full tuition reimbursements (averaging $8,187 per year), 54 research assistantships with full tuition reimbursements (averaging $7,618 per year), 66 teaching assistantships with full tuition reimbursements (averaging $10,875 per year) were awarded. Career-related internships or fieldwork, Federal Work-Study, scholarships/grants, traineeships, and unspecified assistantships also available. Support available to part-time students. Financial award application deadline: 2/1. In 2001, 98 master's, 9 doctorates awarded. *Degree program information:* Part-time and evening/weekend programs available. Offers business administration (PMBA); management (MBA, MS, PMBA, PhD). *Application deadline:* For fall admission, 2/1 (priority date). Applications are processed on a rolling basis. *Application fee:* $40 ($50 for international students). *Application Contact:* Anthony Butterfield, Director, 413-545-5580, Fax: 413-545-3858, E-mail: dabutter@mgmt.umass.edu.

School of Education Students: 343 full-time (245 women), 478 part-time (334 women); includes 139 minority (63 African Americans, 22 Asian Americans or Pacific Islanders, 48 Hispanic Americans, 6 Native Americans), 104 international. Average age 35. 534 applicants, 59% accepted. *Faculty:* 67 full-time (27 women). Expenses: Contact institution. *Financial support:* In 2001–02, 123 fellowships with full tuition reimbursements (averaging $6,990 per year), 151 research assistantships with full tuition reimbursements (averaging $6,670 per year), 167 teaching assistantships with full tuition reimbursements (averaging $7,341 per year) were awarded. Career-related internships or fieldwork, Federal Work-Study, scholarships/grants, traineeships, and unspecified assistantships also available. Support available to part-time students. Financial award application deadline: 1/15. In 2001, 219 master's, 45 doctorates awarded. *Degree program information:* Part-time programs available. Offers cultural diversity and curriculum reform (M Ed, Ed D, CAGS); early childhood education and development (M Ed, Ed D, CAGS); education (M Ed, Ed D, PhD, CAGS); educational administration (M Ed, Ed D, CAGS); elementary teacher education (M Ed, Ed D, CAGS); higher education (M Ed, Ed D, CAGS); international education (M Ed, Ed D, CAGS); mathematics, science, and instructional technology (M Ed, Ed D, CAGS); physical education teacher education (M Ed, Ed D, CAGS); reading and writing (M Ed, Ed D, CAGS); research and evaluation methods (M Ed, Ed D, CAGS); school psychology (PhD); school psychology and school counseling (M Ed, Ed D, CAGS); science education (Ed D); secondary teacher education (M Ed, Ed D, CAGS); social justice education (M Ed, Ed D, CAGS); special education (M Ed, Ed D, CAGS). *Application deadline:* For fall admission, 1/15. Applications are processed on a rolling basis. *Application fee:* $40 ($50 for international students). *Application Contact:* Nancy I. Kaminski, Administrator to Dean, 413-545-0234, Fax: 413-545-4240, E-mail: kaminski@educ.umass.edu. *Dean,* Dr. Bailey Jackson, 413-545-0233, Fax: 413-545-4240, E-mail: bailey.jackson@educ.umass.edu.

School of Nursing Students: 30 full-time (25 women), 39 part-time (35 women); includes 3 minority (1 African American, 1 Asian American or Pacific Islander, 1 Hispanic American), 2 international. Average age 44. 26 applicants, 73% accepted. *Faculty:* 13 full-time (all women). Expenses: Contact institution. *Financial support:* In 2001–02, 46 fellowships with full tuition reimbursements (averaging $1,941 per year), 2 research assistantships with full tuition reimbursements (averaging $3,952 per year), 14 teaching assistantships with full tuition reimbursements (averaging $3,444 per year) were awarded. Career-related internships or fieldwork, Federal Work-Study, scholarships/grants, traineeships, tuition waivers (full), and unspecified assistantships also available. Support available to part-time students. Financial award application deadline: 2/1. In 2001, 27 master's, 4 doctorates awarded. *Degree program information:* Part-time programs available. Offers nursing (MS, PhD). *Application deadline:* For fall admission, 2/1 (priority date); for spring admission, 10/1. Applications are processed on a rolling basis. *Application fee:* $40 ($50 for international students). *Dean,* Dr. Eileen T. Breslin, 413-545-5092, Fax: 413-545-0086, E-mail: breslin@nursing.umass.edu.

School of Public Health and Health Sciences Students: 176 full-time (120 women), 115 part-time (82 women); includes 27 minority (9 African Americans, 14 Asian Americans or Pacific Islanders, 3 Hispanic Americans, 1 Native American), 64 international. Average age 29. 566 applicants, 51% accepted. *Faculty:* 32 full-time (15 women). Expenses: Contact institution. *Financial support:* In 2001–02, 37 fellowships with full tuition reimbursements (averaging $6,468 per year), 96 research assistantships with full tuition reimbursements (averaging $7,003 per year), 66 teaching assistantships with full tuition reimbursements (averaging $5,536 per year) were awarded. Career-related internships or fieldwork, Federal Work-Study, scholarships/grants, traineeships, tuition waivers (full), and unspecified assistantships also available. Support available to part-time students. Financial award application deadline: 2/1. In 2001, 103 master's, 7 doctorates awarded. *Degree program information:* Part-time programs available. Offers communication disorders (MA, PhD); exercise science (MS, PhD); nutrition (MS); public health (MPH, MS, PhD); public health and health sciences (MA, MPH, MS, PhD). *Application deadline:* For fall admission, 2/1 (priority date); for spring admission, 10/1. Applications are processed on a rolling basis. *Application fee:* $40 ($50 for international students). *Dean,* Dr. Stephen Gelhbach, 413-545-6883, Fax: 413-545-1264, E-mail: gehlbach@schoolph.umass.edu.

See in-depth description on page 1195.

UNIVERSITY OF MASSACHUSETTS BOSTON, Boston, MA 02125-3393

General Information State-supported, coed, university. CGS member. *Graduate housing:* On-campus housing not available. *Research affiliation:* John F. Kennedy Presidential Library (twentieth century history and politics).

GRADUATE UNITS

Office of Graduate Studies and Research *Degree program information:* Part-time and evening/weekend programs available. Postbaccalaureate distance learning degree programs offered. Offers public affairs (MS); public policy (PhD).

College of Arts and Sciences *Degree program information:* Part-time and evening/weekend programs available. Offers American studies (MA); applied physics (MS); applied sociology (MA); archival methods (MA); arts (MA, PhD); arts and sciences (MA, MS, PhD); bilingual education (MA); biology (MS); biotechnology and biomedical science (MS); chemistry (MS); clinical psychology (PhD); computer science (MS, PhD); English (MA); English as a second language (MA); environmental biology (PhD); environmental sciences (MS); environmental, coastal and ocean sciences (PhD); foreign language pedagogy (MA); historical archaeology (MA); history (MA); sciences (MS, PhD).

College of Management *Degree program information:* Part-time and evening/weekend programs available. Offers business administration (MBA); management (MBA).

College of Nursing and Health Sciences *Degree program information:* Part-time and evening/weekend programs available. Offers nursing (MS, PhD).

College of Public and Community Service *Degree program information:* Part-time and evening/weekend programs available. Offers dispute resolution (MA, Certificate); gerontology (PhD); human services (MS); public and community service (MA, MS, PhD, Certificate).

Division of Continuing Education *Degree program information:* Part-time and evening/weekend programs available. Offers continuing education (Certificate); women in politics and government (Certificate).

Graduate College of Education *Degree program information:* Part-time and evening/weekend programs available. Offers counseling (M Ed, CAGS); critical and creative thinking (MA, Certificate); education (M Ed, Ed D); educational administration (M Ed, CAGS); elementary and secondary education/certification (M Ed); higher education administration (Ed D); instructional design (M Ed); school psychology (M Ed, CAGS); special education (M Ed); teacher certification (M Ed); urban school leadership (Ed D).

See in-depth description on page 1197.

UNIVERSITY OF MASSACHUSETTS DARTMOUTH, North Dartmouth, MA 02747-2300

General Information State-supported, coed, comprehensive institution. *Enrollment:* 269 full-time matriculated graduate/professional students (117 women), 346 part-time matriculated graduate/professional students (218 women). *Enrollment by degree level:* 590 master's, 23 doctoral, 2 other advanced degrees. *Graduate faculty:* 250 full-time (73 women), 78 part-time/adjunct (37 women). Tuition, state resident: full-time $2,071; part-time $86 per credit. Tuition, nonresident: full-time $8,099; part-time $337 per credit. Part-time tuition and fees vary

University of Massachusetts Dartmouth (continued)

according to course load and reciprocity agreements. *Graduate housing:* Room and/or apartments available on a first-come, first-served basis to single students; on-campus housing not available to married students. Typical cost: $3,544 per year. Room charges vary according to board plan and housing facility selected. *Student services:* Campus employment opportunities, campus safety program, career counseling, child daycare facilities, disabled student services, exercise/wellness program, free psychological counseling, grant writing training, international student services, low-cost health insurance, multicultural affairs office, teacher training, writing training. *Library facilities:* University of Massachusetts Dartmouth Library. *Online resources:* library catalog, web page, access to other libraries' catalogs. *Collection:* 288,189 titles, 2,925 serial subscriptions, 12,980 audiovisual materials. *Research affiliation:* Harvard University (marine science), Marine Biological Laboratory, Woods Hole Oceanographic Institution (marine sciences), Technical Education Research Center (mathematics), Massachusetts Institute of Technology (textiles).

Computer facilities: 368 computers available on campus for general student use. A campuswide network can be accessed from student residence rooms and from off campus. Internet access and online class registration are available. *Web address:* http://www.umassd.edu/.

General Application Contact: Maria E. Lomba, Graduate Admissions Officer, 508-999-8604, Fax: 508-999-8183, E-mail: graduate@umassd.edu.

GRADUATE UNITS

Graduate School Students: 269 full-time (117 women), 346 part-time (218 women); includes 15 minority (2 African Americans, 7 Asian Americans or Pacific Islanders, 5 Hispanic Americans, 1 Native American), 230 international. Average age 31. 711 applicants, 74% accepted, 187 enrolled. *Faculty:* 247 full-time (84 women), 82 part-time/adjunct (41 women). Expenses: Contact institution. *Financial support:* In 2001–02, 85 research assistantships with full tuition reimbursements (averaging $7,163 per year), 110 teaching assistantships with full tuition reimbursements (averaging $6,357 per year) were awarded. Career-related internships or fieldwork, Federal Work-Study, scholarships/grants, and unspecified assistantships also available. Support available to part-time students. Financial award application deadline: 3/1; financial award applicants required to submit FAFSA. In 2001, 165 master's, 3 doctorates awarded. *Degree program information:* Part-time programs available. *Application deadline:* Applications are processed on a rolling basis. *Application fee:* $25 ($45 for international students). *Application Contact:* Maria E. Lomba, Graduate Admissions Officer, 508-999-8604, Fax: 508-999-8183, E-mail: graduate@umassd.edu. *Associate Vice Chancellor for Academic Affairs/Graduate Studies,* Dr. Richard J. Panofsky, 508-999-8029, Fax: 508-999-8183, E-mail: rpanofsky@umassd.edu.

Charlton College of Business Students: 40 full-time (22 women), 40 part-time (15 women); includes 2 minority (1 Asian American or Pacific Islander, 1 Hispanic American), 35 international. Average age 29. 75 applicants, 83% accepted, 32 enrolled. *Faculty:* 38 full-time (10 women), 7 part-time/adjunct (3 women). Expenses: Contact institution. *Financial support:* In 2001–02, 1 teaching assistantship with full tuition reimbursement (averaging $2,500 per year) was awarded; research assistantships with full tuition reimbursements, Federal Work-Study and unspecified assistantships also available. Support available to part-time students. Financial award application deadline: 3/1; financial award applicants required to submit FAFSA. In 2001, 40 degrees awarded. *Degree program information:* Part-time programs available. Offers business (MBA); business administration (MBA). *Application deadline:* For fall admission, 6/1; for spring admission, 10/1. *Application fee:* $25 ($45 for international students). *Application Contact:* Maria E. Lomba, Graduate Admissions Officer, 508-999-8604, Fax: 508-999-8183, E-mail: graduate@umassd.edu. *Dean,* Dr. Ronald D. McNeil, 508-999-8432, Fax: 508-999-8776, E-mail: rmcneil@umassd.edu.

College of Arts and Sciences Students: 33 full-time (24 women), 130 part-time (98 women); includes 6 minority (1 African American, 3 Asian Americans or Pacific Islanders, 1 Hispanic American, 1 Native American), 13 international. Average age 33. 105 applicants, 71% accepted, 48 enrolled. *Faculty:* 81 full-time (25 women), 40 part-time/adjunct (19 women). Expenses: Contact institution. *Financial support:* In 2001–02, 6 research assistantships with full tuition reimbursements (averaging $9,334 per year), 41 teaching assistantships with full tuition reimbursements (averaging $10,128 per year) were awarded. Career-related internships or fieldwork, Federal Work-Study, and unspecified assistantships also available. Support available to part-time students. Financial award application deadline: 3/1; financial award applicants required to submit FAFSA. In 2001, 33 degrees awarded. *Degree program information:* Part-time programs available. Offers arts and sciences (MA, MAT, MS); biology (MS); chemistry (MS); clinical psychology (MA); general psychology (MA); marine biology (MS); professional writing (MA); teaching (MAT). *Application fee:* $25 ($45 for international students). *Application Contact:* Maria E. Lomba, Graduate Admissions Officer, 508-999-8604, Fax: 508-999-8183, E-mail: graduate@umassd.edu. *Dean,* Dr. Michael Steinman, 508-999-8200, Fax: 508-999-8183, E-mail: msteinman@umassd.edu.

College of Engineering Students: 147 full-time (30 women), 73 part-time (19 women); includes 4 minority (1 African American, 1 Asian American or Pacific Islander, 2 Hispanic Americans), 172 international. Average age 28. 423 applicants, 74% accepted, 68 enrolled. *Faculty:* 63 full-time (6 women), 10 part-time/adjunct (2 women). Expenses: Contact institution. *Financial support:* In 2001–02, 74 research assistantships with full tuition reimbursements (averaging $7,315 per year), 40 teaching assistantships with full tuition reimbursements (averaging $5,864 per year) were awarded. Federal Work-Study and unspecified assistantships also available. Support available to part-time students. Financial award application deadline: 3/1; financial award applicants required to submit FAFSA. In 2001, 54 master's, 3 doctorates awarded. *Degree program information:* Part-time programs available. Offers computer engineering (MS, Certificate); computer science (MS, Certificate); electrical engineering (MS, PhD, Certificate); engineering (MS, PhD, Certificate); mechanical engineering (MS); physics (MS); textile chemistry (MS); textile technology (MS). *Application deadline:* For fall admission, 4/20; for spring admission, 11/15. Applications are processed on a rolling basis. *Application fee:* $25 ($45 for international students). *Application Contact:* Maria E. Lomba, Graduate Admissions Officer, 508-999-8604, Fax: 508-999-8183, E-mail: graduate@umassd.edu. *Dean,* Dr. Farhad Azadivar, 508-999-8539, Fax: 508-999-9137, E-mail: fazadivar@umassd.edu.

College of Nursing Students: 2 full-time (both women), 63 part-time (59 women); includes 3 minority (2 Asian Americans or Pacific Islanders, 1 Hispanic American) Average age 41. 17 applicants, 100% accepted, 10 enrolled. *Faculty:* 26 full-time (all women), 12 part-time/adjunct (all women). Expenses: Contact institution. *Financial support:* In 2001–02, 4 research assistantships with full tuition reimbursements (averaging $1,875 per year), 5 teaching assistantships with full tuition reimbursements (averaging $1,500 per year) were awarded. Federal Work-Study, scholarships/grants, and unspecified assistantships also available. Support available to part-time students. Financial award application deadline: 3/1; financial award applicants required to submit FAFSA. In 2001, 13 degrees awarded. *Degree program information:* Part-time programs available. Offers nursing (MS, PMC). *Application deadline:* For fall admission, 4/20; for spring admission, 11/15. *Application fee:* $25 ($45 for international students). *Application Contact:* Maria E. Lomba, Graduate Admissions Officer, 508-999-8604, Fax: 508-999-8183, E-mail: graduate@umassd.edu. *Dean,* Dr. Elisabeth Pennington, 508-999-8586, Fax: 508-999-9127, E-mail: epennington@umassd.edu.

College of Visual and Performing Arts Students: 52 full-time (39 women), 35 part-time (27 women), 10 international. Average age 32. 91 applicants, 62% accepted, 29 enrolled. *Faculty:* 39 full-time (17 women), 13 part-time/adjunct (5 women). Expenses: Contact institution. *Financial support:* In 2001–02, 1 research assistantship with full tuition reimbursement (averaging $4,000 per year), 23 teaching assistantships with full tuition reimbursements (averaging $1,717 per year) were awarded. Federal Work-Study and unspecified assistantships also available. Support available to part-time students. Financial award application deadline: 3/1; financial award applicants required to submit FAFSA. In 2001, 25 degrees awarded. *Degree program information:* Part-time programs available. Offers art education (MAE); artisanry (MFA); fine arts (MFA); visual and performing arts (MAE, MFA); visual design (MFA). *Application deadline:* Applications are processed on a rolling basis. *Application fee:* $25 ($45 for international students). *Application Contact:* Maria E. Lomba, Graduate Admissions Officer, 508-999-8604, Fax: 508-999-8183, E-mail: graduate@umassd.edu. *Dean,* Dr. John C. Laughton, 508-999-8564, Fax: 508-999-9126, E-mail: jlaughton@umassd.edu.

See in-depth description on page 1199.

UNIVERSITY OF MASSACHUSETTS LOWELL, Lowell, MA 01854-2881

General Information State-supported, coed, university. CGS member. *Graduate housing:* Rooms and/or apartments available on a first-come, first-served basis to single students and available to married students. Housing application deadline: 4/1.

GRADUATE UNITS

Graduate School *Degree program information:* Part-time and evening/weekend programs available. Electronic applications accepted.

College of Arts and Sciences *Degree program information:* Part-time and evening/weekend programs available. Offers applied mathematics (MS); applied mechanics (PhD); applied physics (MS, PhD); arts and sciences (MA, MM, MMS, MS, MS Eng, PhD, Sc D); biochemistry (PhD); biological sciences (MS); biotechnology (MS); chemistry (MS, PhD); community and social psychology (MA); computational mathematics (PhD); computer science (MS, PhD, Sc D); criminal justice (MA); energy engineering (PhD); environmental studies (PhD); mathematics (MS); music education (MM); music theory (MM); performance (MM); physics (MS, PhD); polymer sciences (MS, PhD); radiological sciences and protection (MS, PhD); regional economic and social development (MS); sound recording technology (MMS).

College of Education *Degree program information:* Part-time and evening/weekend programs available. Offers curriculum and instruction (M Ed, Ed D, CAGS); education (M Ed, Ed D, CAGS); educational administration (M Ed, Ed D, CAGS); language arts and literacy (Ed D); leadership in schooling (Ed D); math and science education (Ed D); reading and language (M Ed, Ed D, CAGS).

College of Health Professions *Degree program information:* Part-time programs available. Offers administration of nursing services (PhD); adult psychiatric nursing (MS); advanced practice (MS); clinical laboratory studies (MS); family and community health nursing (MS); gerontological nursing (MS); health professions (MS, PhD); health promotion (PhD); health services administration (MS); occupational health nursing (MS); physical therapy (MS).

College of Management *Degree program information:* Part-time and evening/weekend programs available. Offers business administration (MBA); management (MBA, MMS); manufacturing management (MMS).

James B. Francis College of Engineering *Degree program information:* Part-time and evening/weekend programs available. Offers chemical engineering (MS Eng); chemistry (PhD); civil engineering (MS Eng); computer engineering (MS Eng, D Eng); electrical engineering (MS Eng, D Eng); energy engineering (MS Eng); engineering (MS, MS Eng, D Eng, PhD, Sc D); environmental studies (MS Eng); mechanical engineering (MS Eng, D Eng); plastics engineering (MS Eng, D Eng); systems engineering (MS Eng, D Eng); work environment (MS, Sc D).

See in-depth description on page 1201.

UNIVERSITY OF MASSACHUSETTS WORCESTER, Worcester, MA 01655-0115

General Information State-supported, coed, graduate-only institution. CGS member. *Enrollment by degree level:* 411 first professional, 52 master's, 219 doctoral, 4 other advanced degrees. *Graduate faculty:* 806 full-time (238 women), 109 part-time/adjunct (83 women). Tuition, state resident: full-time $2,640. Tuition, nonresident: full-time $9,856. *Required fees:* $1,338. *Graduate housing:* On-campus housing not available. *Student services:* Career counseling, child daycare facilities, free psychological counseling, international student services, low-cost health insurance. *Library facilities:* Lamar Soutter Library. *Online resources:* library catalog, web page. *Collection:* 270,000 titles, 1,935 serial subscriptions, 950 audiovisual materials. *Research affiliation:* Worcester Polytechnic Institute (biomedical engineering).

Computer facilities: 69 computers available on campus for general student use. A campuswide network can be accessed from off campus. Internet access is available. *Web address:* http://www.umass.edu/.

General Application Contact: Dr. Jane Cronin, Director of Admissions, 508-856-2303, Fax: 508-856-3629.

GRADUATE UNITS

Graduate School of Biomedical Sciences Students: 208 full-time (117 women); includes 11 minority (1 African American, 6 Asian Americans or Pacific Islanders, 3 Hispanic Americans, 1 Native American), 68 international. Average age 28. 307 applicants, 37% accepted, 52 enrolled. *Faculty:* 207 full-time (37 women). Expenses: Contact institution. *Financial support:* In 2001–02, 90 fellowships with full tuition reimbursements (averaging $19,000 per year), 116 research assistantships with full tuition reimbursements (averaging $19,000 per year) were awarded. Institutionally sponsored loans, tuition waivers (full), and unspecified assistantships also available. In 2001, 21 doctorates awarded. Offers biochemistry and molecular pharmacology (PhD); biomedical engineering and medical physics (PhD); biomedical sciences (PhD); cell biology (PhD); cellular and molecular physiology (PhD); medical sciences (PhD); neuroscience (PhD). *Application deadline:* For fall admission, 1/1 (priority date). Applications are processed on a rolling basis. *Application fee:* $25 ($50 for international students). *Application Contact:* Michael Cole, Director of Admissions and Recruitment, 508-856-4779, Fax: 508-856-3659, E-mail: michael.cole@umassmed.edu. *Dean,* Dr. Thomas B. Miller, 508-856-4135, E-mail: gsbs@umassmed.edu.

Graduate School of Nursing *Degree program information:* Part-time programs available. Offers adult acute/critical care (MS, Certificate); adult ambulatory/community care (MS, Certificate); adult nurse practitioner (MS); family nurse practitioner (Certificate); nursing (PhD).

Medical School Students: 411 full-time (214 women); includes 62 minority (12 African Americans, 40 Asian Americans or Pacific Islanders, 10 Hispanic Americans) Average age 27. 613 applicants, 25% accepted, 100 enrolled. *Faculty:* 806 full-time (238 women), 109 part-time/adjunct (83 women). Expenses: Contact institution. *Financial support:* In 2001–02, 316 students received support. Federal Work-Study, institutionally sponsored loans, scholarships/grants, and tuition waivers (partial) available. Financial award applicants required to submit CSS PROFILE or FAFSA. In 2001, 94 degrees awarded. Offers medicine (MD). *Application deadline:* For fall admission, 12/15. *Application fee:* $75. *Application Contact:* Dr. Jane Cronin, Director of Admissions, 508-856-2303, Fax: 508-856-3629. *Dean,* Dr. Aaron Lazare, 508-856-0011.

UNIVERSITY OF MEDICINE AND DENTISTRY OF NEW JERSEY, Newark, NJ 07107-3001

General Information State-supported, coed, graduate-only institution. CGS member. *Enrollment:* 3,215 full-time matriculated graduate/professional students (1,607 women), 472 part-time matriculated graduate/professional students (355 women). *Enrollment by degree level:* 1,961 first professional, 993 master's, 649 doctoral, 84 other advanced degrees. *Graduate faculty:* 1,865 full-time (669 women), 381 part-time/adjunct (161 women). Tuition, state resident: part-time $292 per credit. Tuition, nonresident: part-time $440 per credit. Full-time tuition and fees vary according to degree level, program and student level. *Graduate housing:* On-campus housing not available. *Student services:* Campus employment opportunities, campus safety program, career counseling, child daycare facilities, exercise/wellness program, free psychological counseling, international student services, low-cost health insurance. *Online resources:* library catalog, web page, access to other libraries' catalogs. *Collection:* 222,580 titles, 2,322 serial subscriptions, 4,234 audiovisual materials. *Research affiliation:* Coriell Institute for Medical Research (cancer and human development), Center for Advanced Biotechnology in Medicine (biotechnology), International Center for

Public Health (public health), Kessler Institute for Physical Rehabilitation (physical rehabilitation), Center for Applied Genomics (genomics).

Computer facilities: 234 computers available on campus for general student use. A campuswide network can be accessed from off campus. Internet access, distance learning, continuing education are available. *Web address:* http://www.umdnj.edu/.

GRADUATE UNITS

Graduate School of Biomedical Sciences Students: 704 full-time (347 women), 45 part-time (25 women); includes 387 minority (37 African Americans, 295 Asian Americans or Pacific Islanders, 55 Hispanic Americans) 255 applicants, 39% accepted. Expenses: Contact institution. *Financial support:* Fellowships, research assistantships, teaching assistantships, career-related internships or fieldwork, Federal Work-Study, institutionally sponsored loans, traineeships, and tuition waivers (full and partial) available. Financial award application deadline: 5/1. In 2001, 61 master's, 67 doctorates awarded. Offers biochemistry and molecular biology (MS, PhD); biomedical engineering (MS, PhD); biomedical sciences (MS, PhD); cell and developmental biology (MS, PhD); cell biology (MS, PhD); cell biology and molecular medicine (MS, PhD); cellular and molecular pharmacology (MS, PhD); developmental biology (MS, PhD); environmental toxicology (MS, PhD); experimental pathology (MS, PhD); immunology (MS); industrial-occupational toxicology (MS, PhD); microbiology and molecular genetics (MS, PhD); molecular genetics and microbiology (MS, PhD); neuroscience and cell biology (MS, PhD); neurosciences (MS, PhD); nutritional toxicology (MS, PhD); oral biology (MS); pathology and laboratory medicine (MS, PhD); pharmaceutical toxicology (MS, PhD); pharmacology (PhD); pharmacology and physiology (MS, PhD); physiology and neurobiology (MS, PhD); toxicology (MS, PhD). *Application deadline:* For spring admission, 10/1. Applications are processed on a rolling basis. *Application fee:* $40. *Acting Dean,* Dr. Henry E. Brezenoff, 973-972-5333, Fax: 973-972-7148, E-mail: hbrezeno@umdnj.edu.

New Jersey Dental School Students: 355 full-time (167 women); includes 119 minority (22 African Americans, 74 Asian Americans or Pacific Islanders, 23 Hispanic Americans) 825 applicants, 10% accepted. *Faculty:* 94 full-time (23 women), 108 part-time/adjunct (18 women). Expenses: Contact institution. *Financial support:* Fellowships, research assistantships, teaching assistantships, Federal Work-Study and institutionally sponsored loans available. Financial award application deadline: 5/1. In 2001, 81 first professional degrees, 19 other advanced degrees awarded. Offers advanced education in general dentistry (Certificate); dentistry (DMD); endodontics (Certificate); general practice residency (Certificate); oral and maxillofacial surgery (Certificate); oral biology (MS); oral medicine (Certificate); orthodontics (Certificate); pediatric dentistry (Certificate); periodontics (Certificate); prosthodontics (Certificate). *Application deadline:* For fall admission, 2/1. Applications are processed on a rolling basis. *Application fee:* $75. *Application Contact:* Dr. Zia Shey, Chairperson, 973-972-5065, Fax: 973-972-0309, E-mail: shey@umdnj.edu. *Dean,* Dr. Cecile A. Feldman, 973-972-4633, Fax: 973-972-3689.

New Jersey Medical School Students: 698 full-time (296 women); includes 372 minority (67 African Americans, 230 Asian Americans or Pacific Islanders, 75 Hispanic Americans) 2,403 applicants, 7% accepted. *Faculty:* 694 full-time (239 women), 77 part-time/adjunct (26 women). Expenses: Contact institution. *Financial support:* Fellowships, research assistantships, teaching assistantships, Federal Work-Study and institutionally sponsored loans available. Financial award application deadline: 5/1. In 2001, 168 degrees awarded. Offers medicine (MD). *Application deadline:* For fall admission, 12/1. Applications are processed on a rolling basis. *Application fee:* $75. *Application Contact:* Betty Taylor, Director of Admissions, 973-972-4631, Fax: 973-972-7986, E-mail: btaylor@umdnj.edu. Dr. Russell T Joffe, 973-972-4538, Fax: 973-972-7104.

Robert Wood Johnson Medical School Students: 634 full-time (279 women); includes 313 minority (79 African Americans, 196 Asian Americans or Pacific Islanders, 37 Hispanic Americans, 1 Native American) 2,218 applicants, 7% accepted. *Faculty:* 725 full-time (223 women), 140 part-time/adjunct (74 women). Expenses: Contact institution. *Financial support:* Fellowships, research assistantships, teaching assistantships, career-related internships or fieldwork, Federal Work-Study, institutionally sponsored loans, and tuition waivers (partial) available. Support available to part-time students. Financial award application deadline: 5/1; financial award applicants required to submit FAFSA. In 2001, 145 degrees awarded. *Degree program information:* Part-time and evening/weekend programs available. Offers environmental sciences (PhD); health care management (MS); medicine (MD, MS, PhD). *Application deadline:* For fall admission, 2/1. Applications are processed on a rolling basis. *Application fee:* $75. *Application Contact:* Dr. David Seiden, Associate Dean for Student Affairs, 732-235-4576, Fax: 732-235-5078, E-mail: seiden@umdnj.edu. *Dean,* Dr. Harold L. Paz, 732-235-6300, Fax: 732-235-6315.

School of Health Related Professions Students: 417 full-time (288 women), 270 part-time (179 women); includes 257 minority (68 African Americans, 149 Asian Americans or Pacific Islanders, 40 Hispanic Americans) 1,160 applicants, 43% accepted. *Faculty:* 116 full-time (83 women), 22 part-time/adjunct (18 women). Expenses: Contact institution. *Financial support:* Fellowships, research assistantships, teaching assistantships, Federal Work-Study and institutionally sponsored loans available. Financial award application deadline: 5/1. In 2001, 212 degrees awarded. *Degree program information:* Part-time programs available. Offers biomedical informatics (MS, PhD); cardiopulmonary sciences (PhD); clinical laboratory sciences (PhD); clinical nutrition (MS); clinical systems (MS, Certificate); dietetic internship (Certificate); health professions education (MA, MS); health related professions (MA, MPT, MS, MSHS, DPT, PhD, Certificate); health sciences (MSHS, PhD); healthcare informatics (Certificate); instructional design and technologies (MA); interdisciplinary studies (PhD); nurse midwifery (Certificate); nutrition science (PhD); organizational change (MA); physical therapy (MPT, MS, DPT, PhD); physical therapy/movement science (PhD); physician assistant (MS); psychiatric rehabilitation (MS, PhD); rehabilitation counseling (MS); vocational rehabilitation (MS). *Application deadline:* For fall admission, 6/1 (priority date); for spring admission, 10/1 (priority date). Applications are processed on a rolling basis. *Application fee:* $35. *Application Contact:* Dr. Laura B. Nelson, Associate Dean of Academic and Student Services, 973-972-5454, Fax: 973-972-7028, E-mail: shrp.adm@umdnj.edu. *Dean,* Dr. David M. Gibson, 973-972-4276, Fax: 973-972-7028.

School of Nursing Students: 33 full-time (24 women), 161 part-time (141 women); includes 78 minority (32 African Americans, 41 Asian Americans or Pacific Islanders, 5 Hispanic Americans) 329 applicants, 73% accepted. *Faculty:* 38 full-time (32 women), 2 part-time/adjunct (both women). Expenses: Contact institution. *Financial support:* Teaching assistantships, institutionally sponsored loans and scholarships/grants available. Support available to part-time students. Financial award application deadline: 5/1. In 2001, 49 master's, 1 other advanced degree awarded. *Degree program information:* Part-time programs available. Offers adult health (MSN); adult occupational health (MSN); advanced nursing practice (MSN, Certificate); family nurse practitioner (MSN); nurse anesthesia (MSN); nursing (MSN); nursing informatics (MSN); women's health practitioner (MSN). *Application deadline:* For fall admission, 4/15; for spring admission, 10/15. Applications are processed on a rolling basis. *Application fee:* $30. *Application Contact:* Joan Shields, Manager, Enrollment and Student Services, 973-972-5447, Fax: 973-972-7453, E-mail: shieldjo@umdnj.edu. *Dean,* Dr. Frances Ward, 973-972-4322, Fax: 973-972-3225.

School of Osteopathic Medicine Students: 322 full-time (163 women); includes 147 minority (45 African Americans, 74 Asian Americans or Pacific Islanders, 28 Hispanic Americans) 1,719 applicants, 5% accepted. *Faculty:* 169 full-time (53 women), 25 part-time/adjunct (18 women). Expenses: Contact institution. *Financial support:* Fellowships, research assistantships, teaching assistantships, career-related internships or fieldwork, Federal Work-Study, and institutionally sponsored loans available. Financial award application deadline: 5/1. In 2001, 68 degrees awarded. Offers osteopathic medicine (DO). *Application deadline:* For fall admission, 3/15. Applications are processed on a rolling basis. *Application fee:* $75. *Application Contact:* Dr. Warren S. Wallace, Associate Dean for Admissions, 856-566-7050, Fax: 856-566-6895, E-mail: wallacwa@umdnj.edu. *Dean,* Dr. Frederick J. Humphrey, 856-566-6998, Fax: 856-566-6865, E-mail: humphrey@umdnj.edu.

School of Public Health Students: 85 full-time (64 women), 216 part-time (152 women); includes 148 minority (55 African Americans, 69 Asian Americans or Pacific Islanders, 24 Hispanic Americans) 262 applicants, 46% accepted. Expenses: Contact institution. *Financial support:* In 2001–02, 21 students received support; fellowships, teaching assistantships, career-related internships or fieldwork available. Support available to part-time students. In 2001, 50 master's, 2 doctorates awarded. *Degree program information:* Part-time and evening/weekend programs available. Offers public health (MPH, Dr PH, PhD). *Application deadline:* For fall admission, 3/15; for spring admission, 11/1. *Application fee:* $45. *Application Contact:* Tina Greco, Administrative Manager, 732-445-0199, Fax: 732-445-0917, E-mail: tgreco@eohsi.rutgers.edu. *Interim Dean,* Dr. Audrey R. Gotsch, 732-235-9752, Fax: 732-445-0122, E-mail: gotsch@umdnj.edu.

THE UNIVERSITY OF MEMPHIS, Memphis, TN 38152

General Information State-supported, coed, university. CGS member. *Enrollment:* 2,242 full-time matriculated graduate/professional students (1,165 women), 2,478 part-time matriculated graduate/professional students (1,540 women). *Enrollment by degree level:* 413 first professional, 2,463 master's, 706 doctoral. *Graduate faculty:* 516 full-time (156 women), 63 part-time/adjunct (28 women). Tuition, state resident: full-time $2,026. Tuition, nonresident: full-time $4,528. *Graduate housing:* Rooms and/or apartments available on a first-come, first-served basis to single students and available to married students. Typical cost: $2,000 per year ($3,801 including board) for single students. *Student services:* Campus employment opportunities, campus safety program, career counseling, child daycare facilities, disabled student services, exercise/wellness program, free psychological counseling, grant writing training, international student services, low-cost health insurance, multicultural affairs office, teacher training, writing training. *Library facilities:* McWherter Library plus 6 others. *Online resources:* library catalog, web page, access to other libraries' catalogs. *Collection:* 10,578 serial subscriptions. *Research affiliation:* Gulf Coast Research Laboratory, St. Jude Children's Research Hospital, Oak Ridge National Laboratory, Federal Express.

Computer facilities: 2,000 computers available on campus for general student use. A campuswide network can be accessed from off campus. Internet access and online class registration are available. *Web address:* http://www.memphis.edu/.

General Application Contact: Dr. Dianne Horgan, Associate Dean of Graduate School, 901-678-2531, Fax: 901-678-3003, E-mail: gradsch@memphis.edu.

GRADUATE UNITS

Cecil C. Humphreys School of Law Students: 387 full-time (172 women), 34 part-time (24 women); includes 63 minority (55 African Americans, 4 Asian Americans or Pacific Islanders, 1 Hispanic American, 3 Native Americans) Average age 26. 771 applicants, 42% accepted, 146 enrolled. *Faculty:* 23 full-time (7 women), 34 part-time/adjunct (10 women). Expenses: Contact institution. *Financial support:* In 2001–02, 320 students received support, including 21 fellowships with full tuition reimbursements available (averaging $3,000 per year), 15 research assistantships with full tuition reimbursements available (averaging $2,000 per year); career-related internships or fieldwork, Federal Work-Study, and scholarships/grants also available. Support available to part-time students. Financial award application deadline: 4/1; financial award applicants required to submit FAFSA. In 2001, 161 degrees awarded. *Degree program information:* Part-time programs available. Offers law (JD). *Application deadline:* For fall admission, 2/15 (priority date). Applications are processed on a rolling basis. *Application fee:* $25. Electronic applications accepted. *Application Contact:* Dr. Sue Ann McClellan, Assistant Dean for Law Admissions, 901-678-5403, Fax: 901-678-5210, E-mail: smcclell@memphis.edu. *Dean,* Donald J. Polden, 901-678-2421, Fax: 901-678-5210, E-mail: djpolden@memphis.edu.

Graduate School Students: 2,242 full-time (1,165 women), 2,478 part-time (1,540 women); includes 1,211 minority (1,071 African Americans, 104 Asian Americans or Pacific Islanders, 28 Hispanic Americans, 8 Native Americans), 678 international. Average age 32. 4,236 applicants, 60% accepted. *Faculty:* 516 full-time (156 women), 63 part-time/adjunct (28 women). Expenses: Contact institution. *Financial support:* In 2001–02, 794 students received support, including 10 fellowships with full tuition reimbursements available (averaging $11,000 per year), 130 research assistantships with full tuition reimbursements available (averaging $4,770 per year), 213 teaching assistantships with full tuition reimbursements available (averaging $7,160 per year); career-related internships or fieldwork, Federal Work-Study, institutionally sponsored loans, scholarships/grants, and unspecified assistantships also available. Support available to part-time students. Financial award applicants required to submit CSS PROFILE. In 2001, 947 master's, 92 doctorates awarded. *Degree program information:* Part-time and evening/weekend programs available. Postbaccalaureate distance learning degree programs offered. *Application deadline:* Applications are processed on a rolling basis. *Application fee:* $25 ($50 for international students). Electronic applications accepted. *Associate Dean of Graduate School,* Dr. Dianne Horgan, 901-678-2531, Fax: 901-678-3003, E-mail: gradsch@memphis.edu.

College of Arts and Sciences Students: 542 full-time (284 women), 281 part-time (155 women); includes 134 minority (109 African Americans, 15 Asian Americans or Pacific Islanders, 6 Hispanic Americans, 4 Native Americans), 189 international. Average age 31. 917 applicants, 39% accepted. *Faculty:* 272 full-time (67 women), 151 part-time/adjunct (44 women). Expenses: Contact institution. *Financial support:* In 2001–02, 366 research assistantships with full tuition reimbursements, 515 teaching assistantships with full tuition reimbursements were awarded. Fellowships with full tuition reimbursements, career-related internships or fieldwork, Federal Work-Study, institutionally sponsored loans, scholarships/grants, and tuition waivers (full and partial) also available. Financial award applicants required to submit CSS PROFILE. In 2001, 214 master's, 32 doctorates awarded. *Degree program information:* Part-time and evening/weekend programs available. Offers anthropology (MA); applied mathematics (MS); applied statistics (PhD); arts and sciences (MA, MCRP, MFA, MHA, MPA, MS, PhD); bioinformatics (MS); biology (MS, PhD); chemistry (MS, PhD); city and regional planning (MCRP); clinical psychology (PhD); computer science (PhD); computer sciences (MS); creative writing (MFA); criminology and criminal justice (MA); earth sciences (PhD); English (MA); experimental psychology (PhD); French (MA); geography (MA, MS); geology (MS); geophysics (MS); health administration (MHA); health services administration (MPA); history (MA, PhD); human resources administration (MPA); mathematics (MS, PhD); non-profit administration (MPA); philosophy (MA, PhD); physics (MS); political science (MA); psychology (MS); public administration (MPA); school psychology (MA, PhD); sociology (MA); Spanish (MA); statistics (MS, PhD); urban affairs and public policy (MA, MCRP, MHA, MPA); urban management and planning (MPA); writing and language studies (PhD). *Application deadline:* Applications are processed on a rolling basis. *Application fee:* $25 ($50 for international students). *Interim Dean,* Dr. Henry A. Kurtz, 901-678-3067, Fax: 901-678-4831, E-mail: hkurtz@memphis.edu.

College of Communication and Fine Arts *Degree program information:* Part-time programs available. Postbaccalaureate distance learning degree programs offered (no on-campus study). Offers applied music (M Mu); art history (MA); ceramics (MFA); communication (MA); communication and fine arts (M Mu, MA, MFA, DMA, PhD); communication arts (PhD); composition (DMA); Egyptian art and archaeology (MA); film and video production (MA); general art history (MA); general journalism (MA); graphic design (MFA); interior design (MFA); journalism administration (MA); music education (M Mu, DMA); music history (M Mu); music theory (M Mu); musicology (PhD); Orff-Schulwerk (M Mu); painting (MFA); performance (DMA); piano pedagogy (M Mu); printmaking/photography (MFA); sacred music (M Mu, DMA); sculpture (MFA); Suzuki pedagogy-piano (M Mu); theatre (MFA).

College of Education Students: 320 full-time (240 women), 676 part-time (496 women); includes 305 minority (286 African Americans, 11 Asian Americans or Pacific Islanders, 7 Hispanic Americans, 1 Native American), 25 international. Average age 35. 513 applicants, 58% accepted. *Faculty:* 87 full-time (47 women), 109 part-time/adjunct (80 women). Expenses: Contact institution. *Financial support:* In 2001–02, 68 research assistantships with tuition reimbursements, 12 teaching assistantships with tuition reimbursements were awarded. Career-related internships or fieldwork, scholarships/grants, tuition waivers (partial), and community assistantships also available. In 2001, 280 master's, 34 doctorates, 11 other advanced degrees awarded. *Degree program information:* Part-time and evening/weekend programs available. Offers adult education (Ed D); clinical nutrition (MS); community education (Ed D); consumer science and education (MS); counseling and personnel services (MS, Ed D); counseling psychology (PhD); early childhood education (MAT, MS, Ed D); education (Ed S); educational leadership (Ed D); educational psychology and research (MS, Ed D, PhD); elementary education (MAT); exercise and sport science (MS);

The University of Memphis (continued)

health promotion (MS); higher education (Ed D); instruction and curriculum (MS, Ed D); instruction design and technology (MS, Ed D); leadership (MS); policy studies (Ed D); reading (MS, Ed D); school administration and supervision (MS); secondary education (MAT); special education (MAT, MS, Ed D); sport and leisure commerce (MS). *Application deadline:* Applications are processed on a rolling basis. *Application fee:* $25 ($50 for international students). *Application Contact:* Dr. Karen Weddle-West, Assistant Dean of Graduate Studies, 901-678-2352, Fax: 901-678-4778, E-mail: weddle.karen@coe.memphis.edu. *Interim Dean,* Dr. John W. Schifani, 901-678-4265.

Fogelman College of Business and Economics Students: 343 full-time (150 women), 302 part-time (114 women); includes 89 minority (67 African Americans, 18 Asian Americans or Pacific Islanders, 3 Hispanic Americans, 1 Native American), 176 international. Average age 30. 535 applicants, 65% accepted. *Faculty:* 86 full-time (15 women), 7 part-time/adjunct (2 women). Expenses: Contact institution. *Financial support:* In 2001–02, 191 students received support, including 77 research assistantships with tuition reimbursements available, 56 teaching assistantships with tuition reimbursements available; career-related internships or fieldwork, scholarships/grants, and unspecified assistantships also available. Financial award application deadline: 3/1. In 2001, 289 master's, 12 doctorates awarded. *Degree program information:* Part-time programs available. Offers accounting (MBA, MS, PhD); accounting systems (MS); business and economics (MA, MBA, MS, PhD); economics (MBA, PhD); executive business administration (MBA); finance (PhD); finance, insurance, and real estate (MBA, MS); international business administration (MBA); management (MBA, MS, PhD); management information systems (MBA, MS); management information systems and decision sciences (PhD); management science (MBA); marketing (MBA, MS, PhD); real estate development (MS); taxation (MS). *Application deadline:* For fall admission, 8/1; for spring admission, 12/1. *Application fee:* $25 ($50 for international students). *Application Contact:* Dr. Coy A. Jones, Interim Associate Dean for Academic Programs, 901-678-4649, Fax: 901-678-4705, E-mail: fcbegp@memphis.edu. *Dean,* Dr. John J. Pepin, 901-678-2432, Fax: 901-678-3759, E-mail: jjpepin@memphis.edu.

Herff College of Engineering *Degree program information:* Part-time programs available. Offers architectural technology (MS); automatic control systems (MS); biomedical engineering (MS, PhD); biomedical systems (MS); civil engineering (PhD); communications and propagation systems (MS); design and mechanical engineering (MS); electrical engineering (PhD); electronics engineering technology (MS); energy systems (MS); engineering (MS, PhD); engineering computer systems (MS); environmental engineering (MS); foundation engineering (MS); industrial and systems engineering (MS); manufacturing engineering technology (MS); mechanical engineering (PhD); mechanical systems (MS); power systems (MS); structural engineering (MS); transportation engineering (MS); water resources engineering (MS). Electronic applications accepted.

School of Audiology and Speech-Language Pathology *Degree program information:* Part-time programs available. Offers audiology and speech-language pathology (MA, Au D, PhD).

See in-depth description on page 1203.

UNIVERSITY OF MIAMI, Coral Gables, FL 33124

General Information Independent, coed, university. CGS member. *Enrollment:* 4,269 full-time matriculated graduate/professional students (2,071 women), 808 part-time matriculated graduate/professional students (524 women). *Enrollment by degree level:* 1,834 first professional, 2,177 master's, 852 doctoral, 214 other advanced degrees. *Graduate faculty:* 1,130 full-time (259 women), 6 part-time/adjunct (1 woman). *Tuition:* Part-time $960 per credit hour. *Required fees:* $85 per semester. Tuition and fees vary according to program. *Graduate housing:* Room and/or apartments available to single students; on-campus housing not available to married students. *Student services:* Campus employment opportunities, campus safety program, career counseling, child daycare facilities, disabled student services, exercise/wellness program, free psychological counseling, grant writing training, international student services, low-cost health insurance, multicultural affairs office, writing training. *Library facilities:* Otto G. Richter Library plus 6 others. *Online resources:* library catalog, web page. *Collection:* 1.3 million titles, 17,155 serial subscriptions, 109,633 audiovisual materials. *Research affiliation:* National Center for Atmospheric Research, Organization for Tropical Studies.

Computer facilities: 2,000 computers available on campus for general student use. A campuswide network can be accessed from student residence rooms and from off campus. Internet access and online class registration, online student account and grade information are available. *Web address:* http://www.miami.edu/.

General Application Contact: Office of Graduate Studies, 305-284-4154.

GRADUATE UNITS

Graduate School Students: 2,489 full-time (1,207 women), 550 part-time (372 women); includes 929 minority (199 African Americans, 74 Asian Americans or Pacific Islanders, 652 Hispanic Americans, 4 Native Americans), 696 international. Average age 31. 3,871 applicants, 47% accepted. *Faculty:* 680 full-time (148 women), 1 (woman) part-time/adjunct. Expenses: Contact institution. *Financial support:* Fellowships with tuition reimbursements, research assistantships with tuition reimbursements, teaching assistantships with tuition reimbursements, career-related internships or fieldwork, Federal Work-Study, institutionally sponsored loans, scholarships/grants, traineeships, tuition waivers (full and partial), and unspecified assistantships available. Support available to part-time students. Financial award applicants required to submit FAFSA. In 2001, 1,074 master's, 142 doctorates awarded. *Degree program information:* Part-time and evening/weekend programs available. Postbaccalaureate distance learning degree programs offered. *Application fee:* $50. Electronic applications accepted. *Dean,* Dr. Steven G. Ullmann, 305-284-4154, Fax: 305-284-5441, E-mail: graduateschool@miami.edu.

College of Arts and Sciences Students: 409 full-time (217 women), 69 part-time (46 women); includes 118 minority (23 African Americans, 13 Asian Americans or Pacific Islanders, 82 Hispanic Americans), 110 international. Average age 32. 626 applicants, 35% accepted, 125 enrolled. *Faculty:* 216 full-time (60 women). Expenses: Contact institution. *Financial support:* In 2001–02, 294 students received support, including 75 research assistantships with tuition reimbursements available (averaging $14,000 per year), 254 teaching assistantships with tuition reimbursements available (averaging $12,000 per year); fellowships with tuition reimbursements available, traineeships and unspecified assistantships also available. Financial award applicants required to submit FAFSA. In 2001, 69 master's, 36 doctorates awarded. *Degree program information:* Part-time and evening/weekend programs available. Postbaccalaureate distance learning degree programs offered. Offers applied developmental psychology (PhD); art history (MA); arts and sciences (MA, MALS, MFA, MS, DA, PhD); behavioral neuroscience (PhD); biology (MS, PhD); ceramics/glass (MFA); chemistry (MS); clinical psychology (PhD); computer science (MS); English (MA, MFA, PhD); French (PhD); genetics and evolution (MS, PhD); graphic design/multimedia (MFA); health psychology (PhD); history (MA, PhD); inorganic chemistry (PhD); liberal studies (MALS); mathematics (MA, MS, DA, PhD); organic chemistry (PhD); painting (MFA); philosophy (MA, MALS, PhD); photography/digital imaging (MFA); physical chemistry (PhD); physics (MS, DA, PhD); printmaking (MFA); psychology (MS); sculpture (MFA); sociology (MA, PhD); Spanish (PhD); tropical biology, ecology, and behavior (MS, PhD). *Application fee:* $50. Electronic applications accepted. *Application Contact:* Dr. Charles Mallery, Associate Dean, 305-284-3188, Fax: 305-284-4686, E-mail: gradadmin@mail.as.miami.edu. *Interim Dean,* Dr. Daniel L. Pals, 305-284-4117, Fax: 305-284-4686, E-mail: gradadmin@mail.as.miami.edu.

College of Engineering Students: 132 full-time (25 women), 11 part-time (3 women). Average age 28. 228 applicants, 82% accepted. *Faculty:* 43 full-time (2 women), 33 part-time/adjunct (2 women). Expenses: Contact institution. *Financial support:* In 2001–02, 53 students received support, including 7 fellowships with tuition reimbursements available (averaging $29,140 per year), 38 research assistantships with tuition reimbursements available (averaging $23,457 per year), 23 teaching assistantships with tuition reimbursements available (averaging $34,374 per year); career-related internships or fieldwork, Federal Work-Study, institutionally sponsored loans, scholarships/grants, tuition waivers (partial), and unspecified assistantships also available. Support available to part-time students. Financial award application deadline: 2/1; financial award applicants required to submit FAFSA. In 2001, 51 master's, 15 doctorates awarded. *Degree program information:* Part-time and evening/weekend programs available. Offers architectural engineering (MSAE); biomedical engineering (MSBE, PhD); civil engineering (MSCE, DA, PhD); electrical and computer engineering (MSECE, PhD); engineering (MS, MSAE, MSBE, MSCE, MSECE, MSEVH, MSIE, MSME, MSOES, DA, PhD); environmental health and safety (MS, MSEVH, MSOES); ergonomics (PhD); industrial engineering (MSIE, PhD); management of technology (MS); mechanical engineering (MS, MSME, DA, PhD); occupational ergonomics and safety (MSOES). *Application deadline:* Applications are processed on a rolling basis. *Application fee:* $50. *Application Contact:* Thomas D. Waite, Associate Dean, 305-284-2408, Fax: 305-284-2885, E-mail: twaite@miami.edu. *Dean,* Dr. M. Lewis Temares, 305-284-2404, Fax: 305-284-4792, E-mail: mtemares@miami.edu.

Rosenstiel School of Marine and Atmospheric Science Students: 158 full-time (72 women), 4 part-time (2 women); includes 12 minority (3 African Americans, 1 Asian American or Pacific Islander, 6 Hispanic Americans, 2 Native Americans), 57 international. Average age 30. 232 applicants, 31% accepted, 43 enrolled. *Faculty:* 99 full-time (17 women), 90 part-time/adjunct (10 women). Expenses: Contact institution. *Financial support:* In 2001–02, 126 students received support, including 18 fellowships with tuition reimbursements available (averaging $18,000 per year), 76 research assistantships with tuition reimbursements available (averaging $18,000 per year), 32 teaching assistantships with tuition reimbursements available (averaging $18,000 per year); career-related internships or fieldwork, Federal Work-Study, institutionally sponsored loans, and scholarships/grants also available. Financial award application deadline: 3/1; financial award applicants required to submit FAFSA. In 2001, 16 master's, 13 doctorates awarded. *Degree program information:* Part-time programs available. Offers applied marine physics (MS, PhD); marine affairs (MA, MS); marine and atmospheric chemistry (MS, PhD); marine and atmospheric science (MA, MS, PhD); marine biology and fisheries (MS, PhD); marine geology and geophysics (MS, PhD); ocean engineering (MS). *Application deadline:* For fall admission, 1/1 (priority date). Applications are processed on a rolling basis. *Application fee:* $50. Electronic applications accepted. *Application Contact:* Dr. Frank Millero, Associate Dean, 305-361-4155, Fax: 305-361-4771, E-mail: gso@rsmas.miami.edu. *Dean,* Dr. Otis Brown, 305-361-4000.

School of Architecture Students: 50 full-time (26 women); includes 20 minority (2 Asian Americans or Pacific Islanders, 18 Hispanic Americans), 6 international. Average age 26. 124 applicants, 49% accepted. *Faculty:* 23 full-time (2 women), 1 part-time/adjunct (0 women). Expenses: Contact institution. *Financial support:* Research assistantships, teaching assistantships, career-related internships or fieldwork, Federal Work-Study, institutionally sponsored loans, scholarships/grants, tuition waivers (partial), and unspecified assistantships available. Support available to part-time students. Financial award application deadline: 2/1; financial award applicants required to submit FAFSA. In 2001, 21 degrees awarded. Offers architecture (M Arch); computing in design (M Arch); suburb and town design (M Arch). *Application deadline:* For fall admission, 3/1 (priority date). Applications are processed on a rolling basis. *Application fee:* $50. *Application Contact:* Jude Alexander, Coordinator, 305-284-3060, Fax: 305-284-6879, E-mail: jalexander@miami.edu.

School of Business Administration Students: 853 full-time (321 women), 174 part-time (69 women); includes 555 minority (106 African Americans, 96 Asian Americans or Pacific Islanders, 353 Hispanic Americans) Average age 26. 652 applicants, 55% accepted, 190 enrolled. *Faculty:* 83 full-time (20 women), 15 part-time/adjunct (8 women). Expenses: Contact institution. *Financial support:* Fellowships, research assistantships, career-related internships or fieldwork, Federal Work-Study, institutionally sponsored loans, scholarships/grants, tuition waivers (partial), and unspecified assistantships available. Support available to part-time students. Financial award application deadline: 3/1. In 2001, 549 degrees awarded. *Degree program information:* Part-time and evening/weekend programs available. Offers accounting (MBA); business administration (Exec MBA, MA, MBA, MP Acc, MPA, MS, MS Tax, PhD, Certificate); computer information systems (MS); economic development (MA, PhD); financial economics (PhD); human resource economics (MA, PhD); international economics (MA, PhD); management science (MS, PhD); political science (MPA); professional accounting (MP Acc); taxation (MS Tax); telecommunications management (Certificate). *Application deadline:* For fall admission, 7/31; for spring admission, 12/31. Applications are processed on a rolling basis. *Application fee:* $50. Electronic applications accepted. *Application Contact:* Ania Nozewnik-Green, Director, Graduate Business Recruiting and Admissions, 305-284-4607, Fax: 305-284-1878, E-mail: mba@miami.edu. *Vice Dean,* Dr. Harold W. Berkman, 305-284-2510, Fax: 305-284-5905.

School of Communication Students: 104 full-time (62 women), 17 part-time (14 women); includes 39 minority (14 African Americans, 1 Asian American or Pacific Islander, 24 Hispanic Americans), 19 international. Average age 25. 257 applicants, 61% accepted, 64 enrolled. *Faculty:* 31. Expenses: Contact institution. *Financial support:* In 2001–02, 1 fellowship with full tuition reimbursement, 33 research assistantships with partial tuition reimbursements, 4 teaching assistantships with full tuition reimbursements were awarded. Federal Work-Study, institutionally sponsored loans, scholarships/grants, tuition waivers (partial), and unspecified assistantships also available. Financial award application deadline: 3/1; financial award applicants required to submit FAFSA. In 2001, 51 degrees awarded. *Degree program information:* Part-time programs available. Offers communication (PhD); communication studies (MA); film studies (MA); motion pictures (MFA); print journalism (MA); public relations (MA); television broadcast journalism (MA). *Application deadline:* For fall admission, 3/1 (priority date). Applications are processed on a rolling basis. *Application fee:* $50. Electronic applications accepted. *Application Contact:* Dr. John Chase Soliday, Director of Graduate Studies, 305-284-2219, Fax: 305-284-5205, E-mail: jsoliday@miami.edu. *Dean,* Edward J. Pfister, 305-284-2265.

School of Education Students: 196 full-time (149 women), 262 part-time (231 women); includes 198 minority (67 African Americans, 11 Asian Americans or Pacific Islanders, 119 Hispanic Americans, 1 Native American), 59 international. Average age 30. 400 applicants, 66% accepted. *Faculty:* 49 full-time (25 women), 55 part-time/adjunct (38 women). Expenses: Contact institution. *Financial support:* In 2001–02, 54 students received support, including 33 research assistantships (averaging $6,450 per year), 21 teaching assistantships (averaging $8,150 per year); fellowships, career-related internships or fieldwork, Federal Work-Study, institutionally sponsored loans, tuition waivers (full and partial), and unspecified assistantships also available. Support available to part-time students. Financial award application deadline: 3/1. In 2001, 136 master's, 26 doctorates awarded. *Degree program information:* Part-time and evening/weekend programs available. Offers bilingual and bicultural counseling (Certificate); counseling (MS Ed, Certificate); counseling psychology (PhD); early childhood special education (MS Ed, Ed S); education (MS Ed, PhD, Certificate, Ed S); educational research and evaluation (MS Ed); educational research/exercise physiology (PhD); elementary education (MS Ed, Ed S); emotional handicaps/learning disabilities (MS Ed, Ed S); exercise physiology (MS Ed, PhD); higher education/enrollment management (MS Ed); marriage and family therapy (MS Ed); mathematics/science resource (MS Ed, Ed S); mental health counseling (MS Ed); pre-K through primary education (MS Ed, Ed S); reading (PhD); reading and learning disabilities (MS Ed, Ed S); research and evaluation (MS Ed); special education (PhD); sports administration (MS Ed); sports medicine (MS Ed); teaching and learning (PhD); teaching English to speakers of other languages (MS Ed, PhD, Ed S). *Application deadline:* Applications are processed on a rolling basis. *Application fee:* $50. Electronic applications accepted. *Application Contact:* Karen Boss, Graduate Studies Coordinator, 305-284-2167, Fax: 305-284-3003, E-mail: kboss@miami.edu. *Dean,* Dr. Samuel Yarger, 305-284-3505, Fax: 305-284-3003, E-mail: syarger@umiami.ir.miami.edu.

School of International Studies Students: 92 full-time (55 women), 24 part-time (12 women); includes 34 minority (6 African Americans, 28 Hispanic Americans), 33 international. Average age 34. 115 applicants, 80% accepted, 40 enrolled. *Faculty:* 18 full-time (2 women), 6 part-time/adjunct (3 women). Expenses: Contact institution. *Financial support:* In 2001–02, fellowships with tuition reimbursements (averaging $17,000 per year), research assistantships with tuition reimbursements (averaging $11,000 per year), teaching assistantships with tuition reimbursements (averaging $11,000 per year) were awarded. Federal Work-Study, institutionally sponsored loans, and tuition waivers (partial) also available. Support available to part-time students. Financial award application deadline: 2/1. In 2001, 20 master's, 5 doctorates awarded. *Degree program information:* Part-time programs available. Offers international studies (MA, PhD). *Application deadline:* For fall admission, 5/15 (priority date); for spring admission, 11/15. Applications are processed on a rolling basis. *Application fee:* $50. *Application Contact:* Steven Ralph, Coordinator of Student Services, 305-284-3117, Fax: 305-284-4406, E-mail: sisdmissions@miami.edu.

School of Music Students: 197 full-time (86 women), 26 part-time (10 women); includes 61 minority (5 African Americans, 27 Asian Americans or Pacific Islanders, 29 Hispanic Americans) Average age 30. 174 applicants, 64% accepted. *Faculty:* 57 full-time (7 women), 55 part-time/adjunct (16 women). Expenses: Contact institution. *Financial support:* In 2001–02, 2 fellowships with full tuition reimbursements, 55 teaching assistantships with full tuition reimbursements (averaging $7,400 per year) were awarded. Career-related internships or fieldwork, Federal Work-Study, and tuition waivers (full and partial) also available. Financial award application deadline: 3/1. In 2001, 39 master's, 14 doctorates awarded. Offers accompanying and chamber music (MM, DMA); choral conducting (MM, DMA); composition (MM, DMA); electronic music (MM); instrumental conducting (MM, DMA); instrumental performance (MM, DMA); jazz composition (DMA); jazz pedagogy (MM); jazz performance (MM, DMA); keyboard performance and pedagogy (MM, DMA); media writing and production (MM); multiple woodwinds (MM, DMA); music (MM, MS, DMA, PhD, Spec M); music business and entertainment industries (MM); music education (MM, PhD, Spec M); music engineering (MS); music therapy (MM); musicology (MM); piano performance (MM, DMA); studio jazz writing (MM); vocal performance (MM, DMA). *Application deadline:* For fall admission, 3/15 (priority date). Applications are processed on a rolling basis. *Application fee:* $65. Electronic applications accepted. *Application Contact:* Dr. Edward Paul Asmus, Associate Dean for Graduate Studies, 305-284-2241, Fax: 305-284-6475, E-mail: ed.asmus@miami.edu. *Dean,* Dr. James William Hipp, 305-284-2241, Fax: 305-284-6475.

School of Nursing Students: 32 full-time (31 women), 32 part-time (all women); includes 34 minority (15 African Americans, 3 Asian Americans or Pacific Islanders, 16 Hispanic Americans) Average age 39. 64 applicants, 47% accepted. *Faculty:* 21 full-time (20 women), 1 (woman) part-time/adjunct. Expenses: Contact institution. *Financial support:* In 2001–02, 15 students received support, including 6 research assistantships, 8 teaching assistantships; fellowships, Federal Work-Study, institutionally sponsored loans, scholarships/grants, and unspecified assistantships also available. Support available to part-time students. Financial award application deadline: 3/1; financial award applicants required to submit FAFSA. In 2001, 17 master's, 1 doctorate awarded. *Degree program information:* Part-time programs available. Offers community health nursing (MSN); nursing (PhD); primary health care (MSN). *Application deadline:* For fall admission, 3/1 (priority date); for spring admission, 10/1 (priority date). Applications are processed on a rolling basis. *Application fee:* $50. Electronic applications accepted. *Application Contact:* Kim Nguyen, Student Services Coordinator, 305-284-4325, Fax: 305-284-4827, E-mail: knguyen@miami.edu. *Dean,* Dr. Diane Horner, 305-284-2107, Fax: 305-667-3787, E-mail: dhorner@miami.edu.

School of Law Students: 1,047 full-time (482 women), 136 part-time (64 women); includes 353 minority (93 African Americans, 45 Asian Americans or Pacific Islanders, 208 Hispanic Americans, 7 Native Americans), 69 international. Average age 26. 3,286 applicants, 48% accepted. *Faculty:* 51 full-time (15 women), 102 part-time/adjunct (24 women). Expenses: Contact institution. *Financial support:* In 2001–02, 1,049 students received support, including 7 research assistantships (averaging $13,800 per year); career-related internships or fieldwork, Federal Work-Study, institutionally sponsored loans, scholarships/grants, and unspecified assistantships also available. Support available to part-time students. Financial award application deadline: 3/1; financial award applicants required to submit FAFSA. In 2001, 292 first professional degrees, 101 master's awarded. *Degree program information:* Evening/weekend programs available. Offers comparative law (LL M); estate planning (LL M); inter-American law (LL M); international law (LL M); law (JD); ocean and coastal law (LL M); real property development (LL M); taxation (LL M). *Application deadline:* For fall admission, 3/8 (priority date). Applications are processed on a rolling basis. *Application fee:* $50. Electronic applications accepted. *Application Contact:* Therese Lambert, Director of Student Recruiting, 305-284-6746, Fax: 305-284-3084. *Assistant Dean of Admissions,* Michael Goodnight, E-mail: mgoodnig@law.miami.edu.

School of Medicine Students: 923 full-time (523 women); includes 333 minority (68 African Americans, 106 Asian Americans or Pacific Islanders, 157 Hispanic Americans, 2 Native Americans), 60 international. Expenses: Contact institution. *Financial support:* Fellowships, research assistantships, teaching assistantships, career-related internships or fieldwork, Federal Work-Study, institutionally sponsored loans, scholarships/grants, traineeships, tuition waivers (full and partial), and graduate administrative assistantships available. Support available to part-time students. Financial award applicants required to submit FAFSA. In 2001, 150 first professional degrees, 76 master's, 12 doctorates awarded. *Degree program information:* Part-time and evening/weekend programs available. Offers medicine (MD, MPH, MS, MSPH, MSPT, DPT, PhD). *Application deadline:* Applications are processed on a rolling basis. Electronic applications accepted. *Application Contact:* Admissions Office, 305-243-6791, Fax: 305-243-6548, E-mail: miami-md@mednet.med.miami.edu. *Vice President for Medical Affairs and Dean,* Dr. John Clarkson, 305-243-6548.

Graduate Programs in Medicine Students: 339 full-time (212 women); includes 88 minority (26 African Americans, 16 Asian Americans or Pacific Islanders, 44 Hispanic Americans, 2 Native Americans), 60 international. *Faculty:* 136 full-time (36 women). Expenses: Contact institution. *Financial support:* Fellowships, research assistantships, teaching assistantships, career-related internships or fieldwork, Federal Work-Study, institutionally sponsored loans, and tuition waivers (full and partial) available. Support available to part-time students. In 2001, 76 master's, 12 doctorates awarded. *Degree program information:* Part-time and evening/weekend programs available. Offers biochemistry and molecular biology (PhD); biomedical studies (PhD); epidemiology (PhD); medicine (MPH, MS, MSPH, MSPT, DPT, PhD); microbiology and immunology (PhD); molecular and cellular pharmacology (PhD); molecular cell and developmental biology (PhD); neuroscience (PhD); physical therapy (MS, MSPT, DPT, PhD); physiology and biophysics (PhD); public health (MPH, MSPH). *Application deadline:* Applications are processed on a rolling basis. *Application fee:* $50. Electronic applications accepted. *Application Contact:* Sara A. Sauceda, Executive Secretary, 305-243-1094, Fax: 305-243-3593, E-mail: ssauceda@miami.edu. *Associate Dean for Graduate Studies,* Dr. Richard J. Bookman, 305-243-6406, Fax: 305-243-3593, E-mail: biomedgrad@miami.edu.

See in-depth description on page 1205.

UNIVERSITY OF MICHIGAN, Ann Arbor, MI 48109

General Information State-supported, coed, university. CGS member. *Graduate housing:* Rooms and/or apartments available on a first-come, first-served basis to single and married students. *Research affiliation:* Freer Art Gallery, McGraw-Hill Observatory.

GRADUATE UNITS

College of Pharmacy Offers medicinal chemistry (MS, PhD); pharmaceutical chemistry (computational) (MS, PhD); pharmaceutics (MS, PhD); pharmacy (Pharm D, MS, PhD); pharmacy administration (MS, PhD).

Horace H. Rackham School of Graduate Studies Students: 5,954; includes 938 minority (334 African Americans, 367 Asian Americans or Pacific Islanders, 210 Hispanic Americans, 27 Native Americans), 1,687 international. ###### applicants, 33% accepted. *Faculty:* 3,349. Expenses: Contact institution. *Financial support:* Fellowships with full tuition reimbursements, research assistantships with full tuition reimbursements, teaching assistantships with full tuition reimbursements, career-related internships or fieldwork, Federal Work-Study, institutionally sponsored loans, scholarships/grants, traineeships, tuition waivers (full and partial), and unspecified assistantships available. Support available to part-time students. In 2001, 636 doctorates, 24 other advanced degrees awarded. *Degree program information:* Part-time programs available. Offers American culture (AM, PhD); bioinformatics (MS, PhD); biophysics (PhD); education and psychology (PhD); English and education (PhD); mechanical engineering (MSE, PhD); medical and biological illustration (MFA); medicinal chemistry (PhD); modern Middle Eastern and North African studies (AM); neuroscience (PhD); survey methodology (MS, PhD, CGS). *Application deadline:* Applications are processed on a rolling basis. *Application Contact:* Admissions Office, 734-764-8129. *Dean of the Graduate School and Vice Provost for Academic Affairs-Graduate Studies,* Earl Lewis, 734-764-4400.

College of Engineering Students: 1,916 full-time (391 women), 359 part-time (68 women); includes 270 minority (66 African Americans, 157 Asian Americans or Pacific Islanders, 40 Hispanic Americans, 7 Native Americans), 1,109 international. Average age 26. 5,182 applicants, 34% accepted, 683 enrolled. *Faculty:* 309 full-time (30 women). Expenses: Contact institution. *Financial support:* In 2001–02, 244 fellowships with full tuition reimbursements (averaging $20,200 per year), 838 research assistantships with full tuition reimbursements (averaging $20,200 per year), 216 teaching assistantships with full tuition reimbursements (averaging $13,468 per year) were awarded. Career-related internships or fieldwork, Federal Work-Study, institutionally sponsored loans, scholarships/grants, traineeships, tuition waivers (full and partial), and unspecified assistantships also available. Support available to part-time students. Financial award applicants required to submit FAFSA. In 2001, 581 master's, 184 doctorates awarded. *Degree program information:* Part-time programs available. Postbaccalaureate distance learning degree programs offered. Offers aerospace engineering (M Eng, MS, MSE, PhD, Aerospace E); applied physics (PhD); atmospheric and space sciences (MS, PhD); atmospheric, oceanic and space sciences (MS, PhD); automotive engineering (M Eng); biomedical engineering (MS, MSE, PhD); chemical engineering (MSE, PhD, Ch E); civil engineering (MSE, PhD, CE); computer science and engineering (MS, MSE, PhD); concurrent marine design (M Eng); construction engineering and management (MSE); electrical and computer engineering (MS, MSE, PhD); electrical engineering (MS, PhD); engineering (M Eng, MS, MSE, D Eng, PhD, Aerospace E, App ME, CE, Certificate, Ch E, EE, IOE, Mar Eng, Nav Arch, Nuc E); environmental engineering (MSE, PhD); financial engineering (MS); industrial and operations engineering (MS, MSE, PhD, IOE); integrated microsystems (M Eng); macromolecular science and engineering (MS, PhD); manufacturing (M Eng, D Eng); materials science and engineering (MS, PhD); naval architecture and marine engineering (MS, MSE, PhD, Mar Eng, Nav Arch); nuclear engineering (Nuc E); nuclear engineering and radiological sciences (PhD); nuclear science (MS, PhD); oceanography: physical (MS, PhD); pharmaceutical engineering (M Eng); plastics engineering (M Eng); remote sensing and geoinformation (M Eng); space and planetary physics (PhD); space systems (M Eng); systems science and engineering (MS, MSE, PhD). *Application deadline:* Applications are processed on a rolling basis. Electronic applications accepted. *Application Contact:* James Bean, Associate Dean, Graduate Education, 734-647-7009, Fax: 734-647-7045. *Dean,* Stephen W. Director, 734-647-7010, Fax: 734-647-7009.

College of Literature, Science, and the Arts *Degree program information:* Part-time programs available. Offers analytical chemistry (PhD); ancient Israel/Hebrew Bible (AM, PhD); anthropology (AM, PhD); anthropology and history (PhD); applied economics (AM); applied statistics (AM); Arabic (AM, PhD); Armenian (AM, PhD); Asian languages and cultures (MA, PhD); astronomy (MS, PhD); biology (MS, PhD); biopsychology (PhD); chemical biology (PhD); Chinese studies (AM); classical art and archaeology (PhD); classical studies (PhD); clinical psychology (PhD); cognition and perception (PhD); communication studies (PhD); comparative literature (PhD); creative writing (MFA); Czech (AM, PhD); developmental psychology (PhD); early Christian studies (AM, PhD); ecology and evolutionary biology (MS, PhD); economics (AM, PhD); English and education (PhD); English and women's studies (PhD); English language and literature (PhD); film and video studies (Certificate); French (PhD); general linguistics (PhD); geology (MS, PhD); German (AM, PhD); Greek (AM); Hebrew (AM, PhD); history (PhD); history and women's studies (PhD); history of art (PhD); inorganic chemistry (PhD); Islamic studies (AM, PhD); Japanese studies (AM); Latin (AM); linguistics and Germanic languages and literatures (PhD); linguistics and Romance languages and literatures (PhD); linguistics and Slavic languages and literatures (PhD); literature, science, and the arts (AM, MA, MAT, MFA, MS, PhD, Certificate); mass communication (PhD); material chemistry (PhD); mathematics (AM, MS, PhD); Mesopotamian and ancient Near Eastern studies (AM, PhD); mineralogy (MS, PhD); molecular, cellular, and developmental biology (MS, PhD); oceanography: marine geology and geochemistry (MS, PhD); organic chemistry (PhD); organizational psychology (PhD); Persian (AM, PhD); personality psychology (PhD); philosophy (AM, PhD); physical chemistry (PhD); physics (MS, PhD); plant biology (MS); Polish (AM, PhD); political science (AM, PhD); psychology and women's studies (PhD); public policy and sociology (PhD); Romance linguistics (PhD); Russian (AM, PhD); Russian and East European studies (AM, Certificate); Serbo-Croatian (AM, PhD); Slavic linguistics (AM, PhD); social psychology (PhD); social work and economics (PhD); social work and political science (PhD); social work and sociology (PhD); sociology (PhD); South Asian studies (AM); Southeast Asian studies (AM); Spanish (PhD); statistics (AM, PhD); teaching Latin (MAT); teaching of Arabic as a foreign Language (AM); Turkish (AM, PhD); Ukrainian (AM, PhD); women's studies (Certificate).

Division of Kinesiology Students: 37 full-time (21 women); includes 8 minority (7 Asian Americans or Pacific Islanders, 1 Hispanic American), 2 international. 69 applicants, 57% accepted, 20 enrolled. *Faculty:* 18 full-time (6 women), 1 (woman) part-time/adjunct. Expenses: Contact institution. *Financial support:* Fellowships with tuition reimbursements, teaching assistantships with tuition reimbursements, Federal Work-Study, scholarships/grants, health care benefits, and unspecified assistantships available. Financial award application deadline: 2/1. In 2001, 9 degrees awarded. Offers kinesiology (AM, MS, PhD). *Application deadline:* For fall admission, 2/1 (priority date). Applications are processed on a rolling basis. *Application fee:* $55. Electronic applications accepted. *Application Contact:* Carrie Stein, Student Services Associate, 734-764-1343, Fax: 734-936-1925, E-mail: steinc@umich.edu. *Dean,* Dr. Beverly D. Ulrich.

Gerald R. Ford School of Public Policy Students: 148 full-time (80 women); includes 26 minority (12 African Americans, 7 Asian Americans or Pacific Islanders, 7 Hispanic Americans), 14 international. Average age 27. 500 applicants, 50% accepted, 80 enrolled. *Faculty:* 34 full-time (13 women), 10 part-time/adjunct (1 woman). Expenses: Contact institution. *Financial support:* In 2001–02, 100 students received support, including 60 fellowships, 28 teaching assistantships; career-related internships or fieldwork also available. Financial award application deadline: 2/15; financial award applicants required to submit FAFSA. In 2001, 67 degrees awarded. Offers public policy (MPA, MPP, PhD). *Application deadline:* For fall admission, 1/15 (priority date). *Application fee:* $55. *Application Contact:* Trey Williams, Director of Student Services, 734-764-0453, Fax: 734-763-9181, E-mail: trey@umich.edu. *Dean,* Dr. Rebecca M. Blank, 734-764-3490, Fax: 734-763-9181, E-mail: blank@umich.edu.

School of Art and Design Students: 45 full-time (26 women); includes 10 minority (2 African Americans, 5 Asian Americans or Pacific Islanders, 3 Hispanic Americans), 1 international. Average age 27. 120 applicants, 27% accepted, 14 enrolled. *Faculty:* 29 full-time, 41 part-time/adjunct. Expenses: Contact institution. *Financial support:* In 2001–02, 11 fellowships with full and partial tuition reimbursements, 1 research assistantship with full and partial tuition reimbursement, 19 teaching assistantships with full and partial tuition reimbursements were awarded. Federal Work-Study and tuition waivers (partial) also available. Support available to part-time students. Financial award application deadline: 3/15. In 2001, 22 degrees awarded. *Degree program information:* Part-time programs available. Offers art and design (AM, MFA); biomedical visualization (MFA). *Application fee:* $55. *Application Contact:* Sherri Smith, Associate Dean for Graduate Studies, 734-764-0397, Fax: 734-936-0469, E-mail: grackle@umich.edu. *Dean,* Bryan Rogers, 734-764-0397, Fax: 734-936-0469, E-mail: soad.dean@umich.edu.

School of Education Students: 376 full-time (249 women), 52 part-time (37 women); includes 95 minority (41 African Americans, 20 Asian Americans or Pacific Islanders, 29 Hispanic Americans, 5 Native Americans), 36 international. 607 applicants, 66% accepted, 196 enrolled. *Faculty:* 68 full-time (33 women), 6 part-time/adjunct (all women). Expenses: Contact institution. *Financial support:* In 2001–02, 807 fellowships (averaging $6,500 per year), 228 research assistantships with full tuition reimbursements (averaging $6,182 per year), 102 teaching assistantships with full tuition reimbursements (averaging $6,208 per year) were awarded. Career-related internships or fieldwork, Federal Work-Study, institutionally sponsored loans, scholarships/grants, tuition waivers (full and partial), unspecified assistantships, and hourly appointments also available. Support available to part-time students. Financial award applicants required to submit FAFSA. In 2001, 153 master's, 26 doctorates awarded. *Degree program information:* Part-time programs available. Offers

University of Michigan (continued)

academic affairs and student development (PhD); community college administration (AM); curriculum development (AM); early childhood education (AM, PhD); education (AM, MS, PhD); educational administration and policy (PhD); educational foundation, administration, policy, and research methods (AM); educational foundations and policy (PhD); educational technology (PhD); elementary education (AM, MS, PhD); English education (AM); higher education (AM); individually designed concentration (PhD); learning technologies (AM, MS); literacy, language, and culture (AM, PhD); mathematics education (AM, MS, PhD); organizational behavior and management (PhD); public policy (PhD); public policy in postsecondary education (AM); research, evaluation, and assessment (PhD); science education (AM, MS, PhD); secondary education (AM, MS, PhD); social studies education (AM); special education (PhD); student development, support, and academic affairs (AM); teacher education (PhD). *Application fee:* $55. Electronic applications accepted. *Application Contact:* 734-764-7563, Fax: 734-763-1495, E-mail: ed.grad.admit@umich.edu. *Dean,* Karen Wixson, 734-764-9470, Fax: 734-763-1229.

School of Information *Degree program information:* Part-time programs available. Offers archives and records management (MS); human-computer interaction (MS); information (PhD); information economics, management and policy (MS); library and information services (MS).

School of Nursing Students: 114 full-time (105 women), 149 part-time (139 women); includes 18 minority (8 African Americans, 7 Asian Americans or Pacific Islanders, 2 Hispanic Americans, 1 Native American), 20 international. 185 applicants, 35% accepted, 63 enrolled. *Faculty:* 39 full-time (37 women), 7 part-time/adjunct (6 women). Expenses: Contact institution. *Financial support:* In 2001–02, 187 students received support, including 15 research assistantships with full and partial tuition reimbursements available, 28 teaching assistantships with full tuition reimbursements available; fellowships with full and partial tuition reimbursements available, Federal Work-Study, institutionally sponsored loans, scholarships/grants, traineeships, and tuition waivers (partial) also available. Support available to part-time students. In 2001, 59 master's, 10 doctorates awarded. *Degree program information:* Part-time programs available. Offers acute care pediatric (MS); adult acute care nurse practitioner (MS); adult primary care/adult nurse practitioner (MS); community care/home care (MS); community health nursing (MS); family nurse practitioner (MS); gerontology nurse practitioner (MS); gerontology nursing (MS); infant, child, adolescent health nurse practitioner (MS); medical-surgical nursing (MS); nurse midwifery (MS); nurse practitioner (MS); nursing (MS, PhD, Certificate); nursing business and health systems (MS); occupational health nursing (MS); parent-child nursing (MS); psychiatric mental health nurse practitioner (MS); psychiatric mental health nursing (MS). *Application deadline:* For fall admission, 2/1 (priority date); for winter admission, 5/1 (priority date); for spring admission, 11/1 (priority date). Applications are processed on a rolling basis. *Application fee:* $55. Electronic applications accepted. *Application Contact:* Dr. Ada Sue Hinshaw, Dean, 734-764-9454, Fax: 734-936-3644. *Dean,* Dr. Ada Sue Hinshaw, 734-764-9454, Fax: 734-936-3644.

Law School Students: 1,098 (471 women); includes 251 minority (87 African Americans, 104 Asian Americans or Pacific Islanders, 43 Hispanic Americans, 17 Native Americans) 2 international. 4,022 applicants, 29% accepted. *Faculty:* 72 full-time (18 women). Expenses: Contact institution. *Financial support:* Fellowships, career-related internships or fieldwork and Federal Work-Study available. Support available to part-time students. Financial award applicants required to submit FAFSA. Offers comparative law (MCL); law (JD, LL M, SJD). *Application deadline:* For fall admission, 2/15. Applications are processed on a rolling basis. *Application fee:* $60. *Application Contact:* Sarah C. Zearfoss, Assistant Dean and Director of Admissions, 734-764-0537, Fax: 734-647-3218, E-mail: law.jd.admissions@umich.edu. *Dean,* Jeffrey S. Lehman, 734-764-1358.

Medical School Students: 347 full-time (167 women), 2 part-time (1 woman); includes 77 minority (19 African Americans, 44 Asian Americans or Pacific Islanders, 12 Hispanic Americans, 2 Native Americans), 37 international. 576 applicants, 28% accepted. *Faculty:* 270. Expenses: Contact institution. *Financial support:* In 2001–02, 205 fellowships with full tuition reimbursements (averaging $17,500 per year), 121 research assistantships with full tuition reimbursements (averaging $17,500 per year), 8 teaching assistantships with full tuition reimbursements (averaging $17,500 per year) were awarded. Career-related internships or fieldwork, Federal Work-Study, institutionally sponsored loans, and tuition waivers (full) also available. Support available to part-time students. *Degree program information:* Part-time programs available. Offers biological chemistry (PhD); biomedical sciences (MS, PhD); cell and developmental biology (PhD); cellular and molecular biology (PhD); human genetics (MS, PhD); immunology (PhD); medicine (MD, MS, PhD); microbiology and immunology (PhD); pathology (PhD); pharmacology (PhD); physiology (PhD). MS and PhD offered through the Horace H. Rackham School of Graduate Studies. *Application deadline:* For fall admission, 1/5. *Application fee:* $55. Electronic applications accepted. *Dean,* Dr. Allen S. Lichter, E-mail: alichter@umich.edu.

School of Business Administration Offers business (M Acc, MBA, PhD); business administration (M Acc, MBA, PhD). Electronic applications accepted.

School of Dentistry *Degree program information:* Part-time programs available. Offers dentistry (DDS, MS, PhD, Certificate). Electronic applications accepted.

School of Music Students: 249 full-time (117 women); includes 37 minority (10 African Americans, 23 Asian Americans or Pacific Islanders, 4 Hispanic Americans), 38 international. 720 applicants, 34% accepted. *Faculty:* 84 full-time (25 women), 34 part-time/adjunct (10 women). Expenses: Contact institution. *Financial support:* Fellowships, teaching assistantships, career-related internships or fieldwork, Federal Work-Study, institutionally sponsored loans, and scholarships/grants available. Financial award application deadline: 2/1; financial award applicants required to submit FAFSA. In 2001, 76 master's, 26 doctorates awarded. Offers composition (AM, A Mus D); composition and theory (PhD); conducting (A Mus D); design (MFA); modern dance performance and choreography (MFA); music (AM, MFA, MM, A Mus D, PhD); music education (PhD); musicology (AM, PhD); performance (A Mus D); theatre (PhD); theory (AM, PhD). AM, MFA, A Mus D, and PhD offered through the Horace H. Rackham School of Graduate Studies. *Application deadline:* For fall admission, 12/1; for winter admission, 9/15. Applications are processed on a rolling basis. *Application fee:* $55. *Application Contact:* Laura J. Strozeski, Senior Admissions Counselor, 734-764-0593, Fax: 734-763-5097, E-mail: music.admissions@umich.edu. *Dean,* Karen L. Wolff, 734-764-0590, Fax: 734-763-5097.

School of Natural Resources and Environment Offers industrial ecology (Certificate); landscape architecture (MLA, PhD); natural resources and environment (PhD); resource ecology and management (MS, PhD); resource policy and behavior (MS, PhD); spatial analysis (Certificate). MLA, MS, PhD, and JD/MS offered through the Horace H. Rackham School of Graduate Studies. Electronic applications accepted.

School of Public Health Expenses: Contact institution. *Financial support:* Fellowships, research assistantships, teaching assistantships, career-related internships or fieldwork, Federal Work-Study, and scholarships/grants available. Support available to part-time students. Financial award application deadline: 3/1. *Degree program information:* Part-time and evening/weekend programs available. Offers biostatistics (MPH, MS, PhD); clinical research design and statistical analysis (MS); dental public health (MPH); environmental health (MPH, MS, Dr PH, PhD); epidemiologic science (PhD); epidemiology (MPH, Dr PH); health behavior and health education (MPH, PhD); health management and policy (MHSA, MPH); health services organization and policy (PhD); hospital and molecular epidemiology (MPH); human nutrition (MPH, MS); industrial hygiene (MS, PhD); international health (MPH); occupational health (MPH, MS, PhD); occupational medicine (MPH); public health (MHSA, MPH, MS, Dr PH, PhD); toxicology (MPH, MS, PhD). MS, PhD, MPH/AM, and MPH/MS offered through the Horace H. Rackham School of Graduate Studies. *Application deadline:* For fall admission, 3/1 (priority date). Applications are processed on a rolling basis. *Application fee:* $55. *Dean,* Noreen M. Clark, 734-764-5425.

School of Social Work Students: 568 full-time (502 women), 18 part-time (15 women); includes 128 minority (72 African Americans, 29 Asian Americans or Pacific Islanders, 22 Hispanic Americans, 5 Native Americans), 22 international. Average age 29. 698 applicants, 84% accepted, 340 enrolled. *Faculty:* 53 full-time (26 women), 58 part-time/adjunct (37 women). Expenses: Contact institution. *Financial support:* Career-related internships or fieldwork, Federal Work-Study, scholarships/grants, and traineeships available. Financial award applicants required to submit FAFSA. In 2001, 279 degrees awarded. Offers social work (MSW, PhD); social work and social science (PhD). PhD offered through the Horace H. Rackham School of Graduate Studies. *Application deadline:* For fall admission, 3/1 (priority date). Applications are processed on a rolling basis. *Application fee:* $50. Electronic applications accepted. *Application Contact:* Timothy Colenback, Assistant Dean of Student Services, 734-764-3309, Fax: 734-936-1961, E-mail: timot@umich.edu. *Dean,* Paula Allen-Meares, 734-764-5347, Fax: 734-764-9954, E-mail: pameares@umich.edu.

Taubman College of Architecture and Urban Planning *Degree program information:* Part-time programs available. Offers architecture (M Arch, M Sc, PhD); architecture and urban planning (M Arch, M Sc, MUD, MUP, PhD, Certificate); gaming/simulation studies (Certificate); urban design (MUD); urban planning (MUP); urban, technological, and environmental planning (PhD).

UNIVERSITY OF MICHIGAN–DEARBORN, Dearborn, MI 48128-1491

General Information State-supported, coed, comprehensive institution. *Enrollment:* 103 full-time matriculated graduate/professional students (35 women), 1,715 part-time matriculated graduate/professional students (672 women). *Enrollment by degree level:* 1,818 master's. *Graduate faculty:* 456. Tuition, state resident: part-time $300 per credit hour. Tuition, nonresident: part-time $756 per credit hour. *Required fees:* $90 per semester. Tuition and fees vary according to course level, course load and program. *Graduate housing:* On-campus housing not available. *Student services:* Campus employment opportunities, campus safety program, career counseling, child daycare facilities, disabled student services, exercise/wellness program, free psychological counseling, grant writing training, international student services, low-cost health insurance, multicultural affairs office, teacher training, writing training. *Library facilities:* Mardigian Library. *Online resources:* library catalog, web page, access to other libraries' catalogs. *Collection:* 214,909 titles, 1,244 serial subscriptions, 3,241 audiovisual materials.

Computer facilities: 350 computers available on campus for general student use. A campuswide network can be accessed from off campus. Internet access is available. *Web address:* http://www.umd.umich.edu/.

General Application Contact: Vivian J. Ladd, Graduate Coordinator, 313-593-1494, Fax: 313-436-9156, E-mail: umdgrad@umd.umich.edu.

GRADUATE UNITS

College of Arts, Sciences, and Letters Average age 35. 30 applicants, 90% accepted, 23 enrolled. *Faculty:* 161 full-time (61 women), 112 part-time/adjunct (41 women). Expenses: Contact institution. *Financial support:* Federal Work-Study and scholarships/grants available. Support available to part-time students. Financial award application deadline: 4/1; financial award applicants required to submit FAFSA. In 2001, 7 degrees awarded. *Degree program information:* Part-time and evening/weekend programs available. Offers applied and computational mathematics (MS); arts, sciences, and letters (MA, MS); environmental science (MS); liberal studies (MA). *Application deadline:* For fall admission, 8/1 (priority date); for winter admission, 12/1 (priority date); for spring admission, 4/1. Applications are processed on a rolling basis. *Application fee:* $55. Electronic applications accepted. *Application Contact:* Carol Ligienza, Administrative Assistant, 313-593-1183, Fax: 313-593-5552, E-mail: caslgrad@umd.umich.edu. *Dean,* Dr. Paul Wong, 313-593-5490, Fax: 313-593-5552, E-mail: paulwong@umd.umich.edu.

College of Engineering and Computer Science Students: 44 full-time (11 women), 741 part-time (151 women); includes 164 minority (22 African Americans, 111 Asian Americans or Pacific Islanders, 30 Hispanic Americans, 1 Native American) Average age 30. 440 applicants, 68% accepted, 102 enrolled. *Faculty:* 53 full-time (3 women), 30 part-time/adjunct (6 women). Expenses: Contact institution. *Financial support:* Fellowships, research assistantships, teaching assistantships, Federal Work-Study available. Financial award application deadline: 4/1; financial award applicants required to submit FAFSA. In 2001, 229 degrees awarded. *Degree program information:* Part-time and evening/weekend programs available. Offers automotive systems engineering (MSE); computer and information science (MS); computer engineering (MSE); electrical engineering (MSE); engineering (MS, MSE, D Eng); engineering management (MS); industrial and systems engineering (MSE); information systems and technology (MS); manufacturing systems engineering (MSE, D Eng); mechanical engineering (MSE); software engineering (MS). *Application deadline:* For fall admission, 6/15; for winter admission, 12/1; for spring admission, 2/15. Applications are processed on a rolling basis. *Application fee:* $55. Electronic applications accepted. *Application Contact:* Dr. Kashev Varde, Associate Dean, 313-593-5117, Fax: 313-593-9967, E-mail: varde@umich.edu. *Dean,* Dr. Subrata Sengupta, 313-593-5290, Fax: 313-593-9967, E-mail: razal@umich.edu.

School of Education Students: 17 full-time (11 women), 472 part-time (385 women); includes 73 minority (60 African Americans, 3 Asian Americans or Pacific Islanders, 7 Hispanic Americans, 3 Native Americans), 1 international. Average age 32. 129 applicants, 87% accepted, 108 enrolled. *Faculty:* 25 full-time (15 women), 41 part-time/adjunct (33 women). Expenses: Contact institution. *Financial support:* Career-related internships or fieldwork and Federal Work-Study available. Support available to part-time students. Financial award application deadline: 4/1; financial award applicants required to submit FAFSA. In 2001, 113 degrees awarded. *Degree program information:* Part-time and evening/weekend programs available. Offers adult instruction and performance technology (MA); education (MA); emotional impairments endorsement (M Ed); inclusion specialist (M Ed); learning disabilities endorsement (M Ed); public administration (MPA); teaching (MA). *Application deadline:* For fall admission, 8/1; for winter admission, 12/1; for spring admission, 4/1. Applications are processed on a rolling basis. *Application fee:* $30. Electronic applications accepted. *Application Contact:* Graduate Secretary, 313-593-5091. *Dean,* Dr. John Poster, 313-593-5435, E-mail: jposter@umd.umich.edu.

School of Management Students: 31 full-time (6 women), 400 part-time (119 women); includes 78 minority (19 African Americans, 45 Asian Americans or Pacific Islanders, 12 Hispanic Americans, 2 Native Americans) Average age 31. 154 applicants, 62% accepted, 77 enrolled. *Faculty:* 28 full-time (6 women), 6 part-time/adjunct (1 woman). Expenses: Contact institution. *Financial support:* Career-related internships or fieldwork, Federal Work-Study, and scholarships/grants available. Support available to part-time students. Financial award application deadline: 4/1; financial award applicants required to submit FAFSA. In 2001, 91 degrees awarded. *Degree program information:* Part-time and evening/weekend programs available. Postbaccalaureate distance learning degree programs offered (no on-campus study). Offers management (MBA, MSA, MSF). *Application deadline:* For fall admission, 8/1 (priority date); for winter admission, 12/1 (priority date); for spring admission, 4/1. Applications are processed on a rolling basis. *Application fee:* $55. *Application Contact:* Janet McIntire, Graduate Associate, 313-593-5460, Fax: 313-593-4071, E-mail: gradbusiness@umd.umich.edu. *Dean,* Dr. Gary Waissi, 313-593-5248, Fax: 313-593-4071, E-mail: gwaissi@umd.umich.edu.

See in-depth description on page 1207.

UNIVERSITY OF MICHIGAN–FLINT, Flint, MI 48502-1950

General Information State-supported, coed, comprehensive institution. *Enrollment:* 92 full-time matriculated graduate/professional students (54 women), 426 part-time matriculated graduate/professional students (229 women). *Enrollment by degree level:* 518 master's. *Tuition, area resident:* Part-time $386 per credit. Tuition, nonresident: full-time $6,950; part-time $386 per credit. *Required fees:* $113 per term. Full-time tuition and fees vary according to program. Part-time tuition and fees vary according to course load. *Graduate housing:* On-campus housing not available. *Student services:* Campus employment opportunities, campus safety program, career counseling, disabled student services, exercise/wellness program, free psychological counseling, low-cost health insurance, teacher training, writing training. *Library facilities:* Frances Willson Thompson Library. *Online resources:* library catalog, web page, access to other libraries' catalogs. *Collection:* 194,772 titles, 1,215 serial subscriptions, 22,278 audiovisual materials.

Computer facilities: 160 computers available on campus for general student use. A campuswide network can be accessed from off campus. Internet access and online class registration are available. *Web address:* http://www.flint.umich.edu/.

General Application Contact: Ann Briggs, Administrative Associate, 810-762-3171, Fax: 810-766-6789, E-mail: ahb@umich.edu.

GRADUATE UNITS

Graduate Programs Students: 12 full-time (5 women), 81 part-time (49 women). Average age 36. 20 applicants, 85% accepted. *Faculty:* 19 full-time (4 women). Expenses: Contact institution. *Financial support:* In 2001–02, 4 fellowships were awarded; career-related internships or fieldwork, Federal Work-Study, and scholarships/grants also available. Support available to part-time students. Financial award application deadline: 4/1. In 2001, 27 degrees awarded. *Degree program information:* Part-time and evening/weekend programs available. Offers American culture (MLS); public administration (MPA). *Application deadline:* For fall admission, 7/15; for winter admission, 11/15; for spring admission, 3/15. *Application fee:* $55. *Application Contact:* Ann Briggs, Administrative Associate, 810-762-3171, Fax: 810-766-6789, E-mail: ahb@umich.edu. *Associate Provost and Dean of Graduate Programs,* Dr. Vahid Lotfi, 810-762-3171, Fax: 810-766-6789, E-mail: vahidl@umich.edu.

School of Education and Human Services Expenses: Contact institution. Offers early childhood education (MA); education (M Ed). *Interim Dean,* Dr. Marian Kugler.

School of Health Professions and Studies Students: 59 full-time (37 women), 51 part-time (44 women); includes 15 minority (9 African Americans, 4 Asian Americans or Pacific Islanders, 1 Hispanic American, 1 Native American) 111 applicants, 50% accepted. *Faculty:* 21 full-time (14 women), 46 part-time/adjunct (21 women). Expenses: Contact institution. *Financial support:* Fellowships, career-related internships or fieldwork, Federal Work-Study, scholarships/grants, and traineeships available. Support available to part-time students. Financial award application deadline: 4/1. In 2001, 45 degrees awarded. *Degree program information:* Part-time and evening/weekend programs available. Offers anesthesia (MSA); health education (MS); health professions and studies (MPT, MS, MSA, MSN); nursing (MSN); physical therapy (MPT). *Dean,* Dr. Augustine D. Agho, 810-237-6503, Fax: 810-237-6532, E-mail: aagho@umflint.edu.

School of Management Average age 33. 72 applicants, 85% accepted, 55 enrolled. *Faculty:* 15 full-time (4 women), 8 part-time/adjunct (2 women). Expenses: Contact institution. *Financial support:* In 2001–02, 2 students received support. Federal Work-Study and scholarships/grants available. Support available to part-time students. Financial award application deadline: 3/15; financial award applicants required to submit FAFSA. In 2001, 70 degrees awarded. *Degree program information:* Part-time programs available. Postbaccalaureate distance learning degree programs offered (minimal on-campus study). Offers management (MBA). *Application deadline:* For fall admission, 7/1 (priority date); for winter admission, 11/1 (priority date). Applications are processed on a rolling basis. *Application fee:* $50. *Application Contact:* Janet M. McIntire, Coordinator of MBA Admissions and Student Services, 810-762-3163, Fax: 810-762-0736, E-mail: jmcintir@umflint.edu. *Dean,* Dr. Fred E. Williams, 810-762-3160, Fax: 810-762-3282, E-mail: tedwill@umflint.edu.

UNIVERSITY OF MINNESOTA, DULUTH, Duluth, MN 55812-2496

General Information State-supported, coed, comprehensive institution. *Enrollment:* 388 full-time matriculated graduate/professional students (248 women), 167 part-time matriculated graduate/professional students (98 women). *Enrollment by degree level:* 106 first professional, 449 master's. *Graduate faculty:* 195 full-time (55 women), 54 part-time/adjunct (21 women). Tuition, state resident: full-time $2,932; part-time $489 per credit. Tuition, nonresident: full-time $5,758; part-time $960 per credit. Tuition and fees vary according to course load. *Graduate housing:* Room and/or apartments available to single students; on-campus housing not available to married students. Typical cost: $3,250 per year ($5,014 including board). Housing application deadline: 3/1. *Student services:* Campus employment opportunities, career counseling, child daycare facilities, disabled student services, exercise/wellness program, free psychological counseling, grant writing training, international student services, low-cost health insurance, multicultural affairs office, teacher training. *Library facilities:* University of Minnesota Duluth Library plus 1 other. *Online resources:* library catalog, web page, access to other libraries' catalogs. *Collection;* 614,367 titles, 4,500 serial subscriptions, 13,000 audiovisual materials. *Research affiliation:* Environmental Protection Agency Environmental Research Laboratory (aquatic biology), Minnesota Geological Survey, Northeastern Minnesota National Historical Center (local history), U.S. Forest Service, Northcentral Forest Experiment Station.

Computer facilities: 525 computers available on campus for general student use. A campuswide network can be accessed from student residence rooms and from off campus. Internet access and online class registration are available. *Web address:* http://www.d.umn.edu/.

General Application Contact: Dr. Stephen C. Hedman, Associate Graduate Dean, 218-726-7523, Fax: 218-726-6970, E-mail: grad@d.umn.edu.

GRADUATE UNITS

Graduate School Students: 242 full-time (153 women), 96 part-time (53 women); includes 27 minority (1 African American, 12 Asian Americans or Pacific Islanders, 14 Native Americans), 63 international. Average age 29. 381 applicants, 73% accepted. *Faculty:* 195 full-time (55 women), 54 part-time/adjunct (21 women). Expenses: Contact institution. *Financial support:* In 2001–02, 185 students received support, including 52 fellowships with full tuition reimbursements available, 31 research assistantships with full tuition reimbursements available, 102 teaching assistantships with full tuition reimbursements available; career-related internships or fieldwork, Federal Work-Study, institutionally sponsored loans, scholarships/grants, traineeships, tuition waivers (full and partial), and unspecified assistantships also available. Support available to part-time students. Financial award applicants required to submit FAFSA. In 2001, 129 degrees awarded. *Degree program information:* Part-time and evening/weekend programs available. Postbaccalaureate distance learning degree programs offered (minimal on-campus study). Offers toxicology (MS, PhD). *Application deadline:* For fall admission, 7/15. Applications are processed on a rolling basis. *Application fee:* $50 ($55 for international students). *Associate Graduate Dean,* Dr. Stephen C. Hedman, 218-726-7523, Fax: 218-726-6970, E-mail: grad@d.umn.edu.

College of Education and Human Service Professions Students: 80 full-time (71 women), 21 part-time (19 women); includes 14 minority (2 Asian Americans or Pacific Islanders, 12 Native Americans), 4 international. Average age 30. 132 applicants, 78% accepted, 43 enrolled. *Faculty:* 15 full-time (11 women), 8 part-time/adjunct (6 women). Expenses: Contact institution. *Financial support:* In 2001–02, 44 students received support, including 34 fellowships with full and partial tuition reimbursements available (averaging $2,195 per year), 5 research assistantships (averaging $6,500 per year), 5 teaching assistantships with full tuition reimbursements available (averaging $6,500 per year); career-related internships or fieldwork, Federal Work-Study, institutionally sponsored loans, scholarships/grants, traineeships, and tuition waivers (full and partial) also available. Support available to part-time students. Financial award application deadline: 1/15. In 2001, 49 degrees awarded. *Degree program information:* Part-time and evening/weekend programs available. Postbaccalaureate distance learning degree programs offered (minimal on-campus study). Offers communication sciences and disorders (MA); education and human service professions (MA, MSW); social work (MSW). M Ed offered independently of the Graduate School. *Application fee:* $50 ($55 for international students). *Dean,* Dr. Paul Deputy, 218-726-7131, Fax: 218-726-7073.

College of Liberal Arts Students: 16 full-time (13 women), 12 part-time (9 women); includes 2 minority (1 African American, 1 Native American), 2 international. Average age 36. 25 applicants, 76% accepted, 14 enrolled. *Faculty:* 20 full-time (9 women), 22 part-time/adjunct (6 women). Expenses: Contact institution. *Financial support:* In 2001–02, 19 students received support, including 10 fellowships (averaging $1,773 per year), 9 teaching assistantships with full tuition reimbursements available (averaging $8,950 per year); career-related internships or fieldwork, Federal Work-Study, institutionally sponsored loans, and tuition waivers (full and partial) also available. Support available to part-time students. Financial award application deadline: 4/15; financial award applicants required to submit FAFSA. In 2001, 7 degrees awarded. *Degree program information:* Part-time programs available. Offers English (MA); liberal arts (MA, MLS); sociology/anthropology (MLS). *Application deadline:* For fall admission, 7/15; for spring admission, 11/15. Applications are processed on a rolling basis. *Application fee:* $50 ($55 for international students). *Dean,* Dr. Linda Krug, 218-726-8981, Fax: 218-726-6386.

College of Science and Engineering Students: 134 full-time (63 women), 24 part-time (4 women); includes 10 minority (9 Asian Americans or Pacific Islanders, 1 Native American), 56 international. Average age 26. 201 applicants, 68% accepted. *Faculty:* 102 full-time (19 women), 21 part-time/adjunct (7 women). Expenses: Contact institution. *Financial support:* In 2001–02, 108 students received support, including 1 fellowship with full tuition reimbursement available, 20 research assistantships with full tuition reimbursements available, 87 teaching assistantships with full tuition reimbursements available; career-related internships or fieldwork, Federal Work-Study, institutionally sponsored loans, scholarships/grants, traineeships, tuition waivers (full and partial), and unspecified assistantships also available. Support available to part-time students. In 2001, 55 degrees awarded. *Degree program information:* Part-time and evening/weekend programs available. Postbaccalaureate distance learning degree programs offered (minimal on-campus study). Offers applied and computational mathematics (MS); biology (MS); chemistry (MS); computer science (MS); engineering management (MS); environmental health and safety (MEHS); geological sciences (MS); physics (MS); science and engineering (MEHS, MS). *Application deadline:* For fall admission, 7/15. Applications are processed on a rolling basis. *Application fee:* $50 ($55 for international students). *Dean,* Dr. James Riehl, 218-726-7971.

School of Business and Economics Students: 6 full-time (2 women), 30 part-time (17 women); includes 1 minority (Asian American or Pacific Islander), 1 international. Average age 31. 15 applicants, 80% accepted. *Faculty:* 28 full-time (4 women). Expenses: Contact institution. *Financial support:* In 2001–02, 6 students received support, including 6 research assistantships with full and partial tuition reimbursements available (averaging $10,000 per year); career-related internships or fieldwork, Federal Work-Study, and institutionally sponsored loans also available. Support available to part-time students. Financial award applicants required to submit FAFSA. In 2001, 16 degrees awarded. *Degree program information:* Part-time and evening/weekend programs available. Offers business administration (MBA); business and economics (MBA). *Application deadline:* For fall admission, 7/15; for spring admission, 11/15. Applications are processed on a rolling basis. *Application fee:* $50 ($55 for international students). *Dean,* Kjell Knudsen, 218-726-7288.

School of Fine Arts Students: 6 full-time (4 women), 9 part-time (4 women). Average age 24. 8 applicants, 75% accepted, 3 enrolled. *Faculty:* 30 full-time (12 women), 3 part-time/adjunct (2 women). Expenses: Contact institution. *Financial support:* In 2001–02, 8 students received support, including 7 fellowships with full tuition reimbursements available, 1 teaching assistantship with full tuition reimbursement available; career-related internships or fieldwork, Federal Work-Study, institutionally sponsored loans, and scholarships/grants also available. In 2001, 2 degrees awarded. *Degree program information:* Part-time programs available. Offers fine arts (MFA, MM); graphic design (MFA); music education (MM); performance (MM). *Application deadline:* For fall admission, 7/15; for spring admission, 11/15. Applications are processed on a rolling basis. *Application fee:* $50 ($55 for international students). *Acting Dean,* Patricia Dennis, 218-726-7261, Fax: 218-726-6969, E-mail: sfa@d.umn.edu.

School of Medicine Students: 111 full-time (48 women), 3 part-time. Average age 25. 979 applicants, 8% accepted. *Faculty:* 40 full-time (9 women). Expenses: Contact institution. *Financial support:* In 2001–02, 93 students received support; fellowships, research assistantships, teaching assistantships, career-related internships or fieldwork, Federal Work-Study, institutionally sponsored loans, and scholarships/grants available. Support available to part-time students. Financial award applicants required to submit FAFSA. *Degree program information:* Part-time programs available. Offers anatomy and cell biology (MS, PhD); biochemistry and molecular biology (MS, PhD); medical microbiology and immunology (MS, PhD); medicine (MD, MS, PhD); pharmacology (MS, PhD); physiology (MS, PhD). *Application deadline:* Applications are processed on a rolling basis. *Application Contact:* Lillian A. Repesh, Associate Dean for Admissions and Student Affairs, 218-726-8511, Fax: 218-726-6235, E-mail: lrepesh@d.umn.edu. *Dean,* Dr. Richard J. Ziegler, 218-726-7572.

UNIVERSITY OF MINNESOTA, TWIN CITIES CAMPUS, Minneapolis, MN 55455-0213

General Information State-supported, coed, university. CGS member. *Enrollment:* 7,916 matriculated graduate/professional students (4,095 women). *Enrollment by degree level:* 3,863 master's, 4,053 doctoral. *Graduate faculty:* 2,235. Tuition, state resident: full-time $2,932; part-time $489 per credit. Tuition, nonresident: full-time $5,758; part-time $960 per credit. Part-time tuition and fees vary according to course load, program and reciprocity agreements. *Graduate housing:* Rooms and/or apartments available on a first-come, first-served basis to single and married students. Typical cost: $5,100 per year for single students; $4,350 per year for married students. Room charges vary according to board plan and housing facility selected. *Student services:* Campus employment opportunities, campus safety program, career counseling, child daycare facilities, disabled student services, exercise/wellness program, free psychological counseling, grant writing training, international student services, low-cost health insurance, multicultural affairs office, teacher training, writing training. *Library facilities:* Wilson Library plus 17 others. *Online resources:* library catalog, web page, access to other libraries' catalogs. *Collection:* 5.6 million titles, 46,989 serial subscriptions, 1.2 million audiovisual materials.

Computer facilities: A campuswide network can be accessed from student residence rooms and from off campus. E-mail available. *Web address:* http://www.umn.edu/tc/.

General Application Contact: Dr. Christine Maziar, Vice President for Research and Dean of the Graduate School, 612-625-3394, Fax: 612-626-7431.

GRADUATE UNITS

Carlson School of Management Students: 660 full-time (274 women), 1,199 part-time (418 women); includes 164 minority (52 African Americans, 91 Asian Americans or Pacific Islanders, 19 Hispanic Americans, 2 Native Americans), 168 international. Average age 30. *Faculty:* 114 full-time (18 women), 40 part-time/adjunct (7 women). Expenses: Contact institution. *Financial support:* In 2001–02, 2 fellowships with full and partial tuition reimbursements (averaging $5,500 per year), research assistantships with full tuition reimbursements (averaging $10,000 per year) were awarded. Teaching assistantships with full and partial tuition reimbursements, career-related internships or fieldwork, Federal Work-Study, institutionally sponsored loans, and tuition waivers (full and partial) also available. Support available to part-time students. Financial award application deadline: 4/1; financial award applicants required to submit FAFSA. In 2001, 556 master's, 21 doctorates awarded. *Degree program information:* Part-time and evening/weekend programs available. Offers accounting (MBA, PhD); business administration (MBA, PhD); business taxation (MBT); e-business (MBA); entrepreneurship (MBA); finance (MBA, PhD); healthcare management (MBA, MHA, PhD); human resources and industrial relations (MA, PhD); information and decision sciences (MBA, PhD); international business (MBA); management (EMBA, MA, MBA, MBT, MHA, MS, MSMOT, PhD); marketing and logistics management (MBA, PhD); operations and management science (MBA, PhD); strategic management and organization (MBA, PhD); supply chain management (MBA). Electronic applications accepted. *Dean,* Dr. Lawrence Benveniste, 612-625-0027, Fax: 612-624-6374, E-mail: carlsondean@csom.umn.edu.

College of Pharmacy *Degree program information:* Part-time programs available. Offers medicinal chemistry (MS, PhD); pharmaceutics (MS, PhD); pharmacy (Pharm D, MS, PhD); social and administrative pharmacy (MS, PhD).

College of Veterinary Medicine Expenses: Contact institution. *Financial support:* Fellowships, research assistantships, teaching assistantships, career-related internships or fieldwork and Federal Work-Study available. Support available to part-time students. Financial award applicants required to submit FAFSA. In 2001, 74 degrees awarded. *Degree program information:* Part-time programs available. Offers molecular veterinary biosciences (MS, PhD); veterinary medicine (DVM, MS, PhD). Electronic applications accepted. *Interim Dean,* Dr. Jeffrey Klausner, 612-624-6244, Fax: 612-624-8753.

Graduate School Students: 7,916 (4,095 women) 2,356 international. ###### applicants, 40% accepted. *Faculty:* 2,235. Expenses: Contact institution. *Financial support:* Fellowships

University of Minnesota, Twin Cities Campus (continued)
with full tuition reimbursements, research assistantships with full and partial tuition reimbursements, teaching assistantships with full and partial tuition reimbursements, career-related internships or fieldwork, Federal Work-Study, institutionally sponsored loans, scholarships/grants, traineeships, health care benefits, tuition waivers (full and partial), and unspecified assistantships available. Support available to part-time students. Financial award applicants required to submit CSS PROFILE or FAFSA. In 2001, 1,383 master's, 638 doctorates awarded. *Degree program information:* Part-time and evening/weekend programs available. Postbaccalaureate distance learning degree programs offered (minimal on-campus study). Offers biophysical sciences and medical physics (MS, PhD); genetic counseling (MS); health informatics (MS, PhD); molecular, cellular, developmental biology and genetics (PhD); neuroscience (MS, PhD); pharmacology (MS, PhD); scientific computation (MS, PhD). *Application deadline:* For fall admission, 6/15; for spring admission, 10/15. Applications are processed on a rolling basis. *Application fee:* $50 ($55 for international students). Electronic applications accepted. *Application Contact:* Office of Admissions, 612-625-3014, Fax: 612-625-6002. *Vice President for Research and Dean*, Dr. Christine Maziar, 612-625-3394, Fax: 612-626-7431.

College of Agricultural, Food, and Environmental Sciences Students: 241 full-time (136 women), 209 part-time (123 women); includes 92 minority (14 African Americans, 64 Asian Americans or Pacific Islanders, 14 Hispanic Americans) Average age 32. 526 applicants, 42% accepted, 129 enrolled. Expenses: Contact institution. *Financial support:* Fellowships, research assistantships, teaching assistantships, career-related internships or fieldwork, Federal Work-Study, institutionally sponsored loans, and tuition waivers (full) available. Support available to part-time students. In 2001, 71 master's, 51 doctorates awarded. *Degree program information:* Part-time and evening/weekend programs available. Offers agricultural and applied economics (MS, PhD); agricultural, food, and environmental sciences (MA, MBAE, MS, MSBAE, PhD); animal science (MS, PhD); applied plant sciences (MS, PhD); biosystems and agricultural engineering (MBAE, MSBAE, PhD); entomology (MS, PhD); food science (MS, PhD); horticultural science (MA, MS, PhD); microbial ecology (MS, PhD); nutrition (MS, PhD); plant pathology (MS, PhD); rhetoric and scientific and technical communication (MA, PhD); scientific and technical communication (MS); soil, water, and climate (MS, PhD). *Application fee:* $50 ($55 for international students). *Application Contact:* Steve Gillard, Information Contact, 612-625-6792. *Dean*, Dr. Charles C. Muscoplat, 612-624-5387.

College of Architecture and Landscape Architecture Offers architecture (M Arch); architecture and landscape architecture (M Arch, MLA, MS); landscape architecture (MLA, MS).

College of Biological Sciences Expenses: Contact institution. *Financial support:* Fellowships with full tuition reimbursements, research assistantships with full tuition reimbursements, teaching assistantships with full tuition reimbursements, career-related internships or fieldwork, Federal Work-Study, institutionally sponsored loans, scholarships/grants, traineeships, and tuition waivers (full and partial) available. Financial award applicants required to submit FAFSA. *Degree program information:* Part-time programs available. Offers biological science (MBS); biological sciences (MBS, MS, PhD); ecology, animal behavior, and evolution (MS, PhD); plant biology (MS, PhD). *Application fee:* $50 ($55 for international students). Electronic applications accepted. *Dean*, Dr. Robert Elde, 612-624-2244, Fax: 612-624-2785.

College of Education and Human Development Students: 1,324 full-time (957 women), 761 part-time (506 women); includes 182 minority (78 African Americans, 52 Asian Americans or Pacific Islanders, 34 Hispanic Americans, 18 Native Americans), 197 international. Average age 33. 513 applicants, 53% accepted, 178 enrolled. *Faculty:* 128 full-time (51 women). Expenses: Contact institution. *Financial support:* In 2001–02, 510 students received support, including 60 fellowships (averaging $5,175 per year), 196 research assistantships with full tuition reimbursements available (averaging $12,100 per year), 135 teaching assistantships with full tuition reimbursements available (averaging $12,100 per year); scholarships/grants and tuition waivers (partial) also available. Financial award applicants required to submit FAFSA. In 2001, 1,000 master's, 107 doctorates, 8 other advanced degrees awarded. *Degree program information:* Part-time programs available. Offers adapted physical education (MA, PhD); adult education (M Ed, MA, Ed D, PhD, Certificate); agricultural, food and environmental education (M Ed, MA, Ed D, PhD); art education (M Ed, MA, PhD); biomechanics (MA); biomechanics and neural control (PhD); business and industry education (M Ed, MA, Ed D, PhD); business education (M Ed); child psychology (MA, PhD); childrens literature (M Ed, MA, PhD); coaching (Certificate); comparative and international development education (MA, PhD); counseling and student personnel psychology (MA, PhD, Ed S); developmental adapted physical education (M Ed); disability policy and services (Certificate); early childhood education (M Ed, MA, PhD); education and human development (M Ed, MA, Ed D, PhD, Certificate, Ed S); educational administration (MA, Ed D, PhD); educational psychology (PhD); elementary education (M Ed, MA, PhD); English education (MA, PhD); environmental education (M Ed); evaluation studies (MA, PhD); exercise physiology (MA, PhD); family education (M Ed, MA, Ed D, PhD); higher education (MA, PhD); human factors/ergonomics (MA, PhD); human resource development (M Ed, MA, Ed D, PhD, Certificate); instructional systems and technology (M Ed, MA, PhD); interdisciplinary focus (M Ed); international/comparative sport (MA, PhD); kinesiology (M Ed, MA, PhD); language arts (MA, PhD); leisure services/management (MA, PhD); literacy education (MA); marketing education (M Ed); mathematics education (MA, PhD); motor development (MA, PhD); motor learning/control (MA, PhD); outdoor education/recreation (MA, PhD); physical education (M Ed); post-secondary administration (Ed D); postsecondary administration (Ed D); psychological foundations of education (MA, PhD, Ed S); reading education (MA, PhD); recreation, park, and leisure studies (M Ed, MA, PhD); school psychology (MA, PhD, Ed S); school-to-work (Certificate); science education (MA, PhD); second languages and cultures education (MA, PhD); social studies education (MA, PhD); special education (M Ed, MA, PhD, Ed S); sport and exercise science (M Ed); sport management (M Ed, MA, PhD); sport psychology (MA, PhD); sport sociology (MA, PhD); staff development (Certificate); talent development and gifted education (Certificate); teacher leadership (M Ed); teaching (M Ed); technical education (Certificate); technology education (M Ed, MA); therapeutic recreation (MA, PhD); work, community, and family education (M Ed, MA, Ed D, PhD); writing education (M Ed, MA, PhD); youth development leadership (M Ed). *Application fee:* $50. *Application Contact:* Dr. Mary Bents, Assistant Dean, 612-625-6501, Fax: 612-626-1580, E-mail: spsinfo@umn.edu. *Dean*, Dr. Steven Yussen, 612-626-9252, Fax: 612-626-7496, E-mail: syussen@umn.edu.

College of Human Ecology *Degree program information:* Part-time and evening/weekend programs available. Postbaccalaureate distance learning degree programs offered. Offers design, housing, and apparel (MA, MFA, MS, PhD); family social science (MA, PhD); human ecology (MA, MFA, MS, MSW, PhD); social work (MSW, PhD).

College of Liberal Arts Expenses: Contact institution. *Financial support:* Fellowships, research assistantships, teaching assistantships, career-related internships or fieldwork, Federal Work-Study, institutionally sponsored loans, and tuition waivers (full and partial) available. Support available to part-time students. Financial award applicants required to submit CSS PROFILE or FAFSA. *Degree program information:* Part-time and evening/weekend programs available. Offers American studies (PhD); ancient and medieval art and archaeology (MA, PhD); anthropology (MA, PhD); art (MFA); art history (MA, PhD); audiology (MA, PhD); biological psychopathology (PhD); classics (MA, PhD); clinical psychology (PhD); cognitive and biological psychology (PhD); communication studies (MA, PhD); comparative literature (MA, PhD); comparative studies in discourse and society (MA, PhD); counseling psychology (PhD); design technology (MFA); differential psychology/behavior genetics (PhD); directing (MFA); East Asian studies (MA); economics (PhD); English (MA, MFA, PhD); French (MA, PhD); geographic information science (MGIS); geography (MA, PhD); Germanic studies: German and Scandinavian (PhD); Germanic studies: German track (MA, PhD); Germanic studies: medieval (MA, PhD); Germanic studies: Scandinavian track (MA); Germanic studies: teaching German (MA); Greek (MA, PhD); health journalism (MA); hearing science (PhD); Hispanic and Luso-Brazilian literatures and linguistics (PhD); Hispanic linguistics (MA); history (MA, PhD); industrial/organizational psychology (PhD); Italian (MA); Latin (MA, PhD); liberal arts (MA, MFA, MGIS, MM, MS, DMA, PhD); linguistics (MA, PhD); mass communication (MA, PhD); music (MA, MM, DMA, PhD); personality research (PhD); philosophy (MA, PhD); political science (MA, PhD); Portuguese (MA); psychometric methods (MA, PhD); Russian area studies (MA); school psychology (PhD); social psychology (PhD); sociology (MA, PhD); Spanish (MA); speech science (PhD); speech-language pathology (MA, PhD); statistics (MS, PhD); theater arts and dance (PhD). Electronic applications accepted. *Dean*, Steven J. Rosenstone, 612-624-2535, Fax: 612-624-6839, E-mail: sjr@mailbox.mail.umn.edu.

College of Natural Resources Students: 121 full-time (53 women), 26 part-time (12 women); includes 10 minority (2 African Americans, 5 Asian Americans or Pacific Islanders, 3 Hispanic Americans), 26 international. 159 applicants, 33% accepted, 27 enrolled. *Faculty:* 50 full-time (11 women), 67 part-time/adjunct (5 women). Expenses: Contact institution. *Financial support:* In 2001–02, 10 fellowships with full tuition reimbursements (averaging $12,000 per year), 74 research assistantships with full and partial tuition reimbursements, 16 teaching assistantships were awarded. Tuition waivers (partial) also available. In 2001, 22 master's, 7 doctorates awarded. *Degree program information:* Part-time programs available. Offers conservation biology (MS, PhD); fisheries (MS, PhD); forestry (MF, MS, PhD); natural resources (MF, MS, PhD); wildlife conservation (MS, PhD). *Application deadline:* For fall admission, 1/1 (priority date). *Application fee:* $50 ($55 for international students). *Application Contact:* Kathleen A. Walter, Assistant for Graduate Studies, 612-624-2748, Fax: 612-624-6282, E-mail: kwalter@forestry.umn.edu. *Dean*, Dr. Alfred Sullivan, 612-624-1234.

Hubert H. Humphrey Institute of Public Affairs *Degree program information:* Part-time programs available. Offers advanced policy analysis methods (MPP); economic and community development (MPP); economic development (MURP); environmental and ecological planning (MURP); foreign policy (MPP); housing, social planning, and community development (MURP); land use and human settlements (MURP); landscape and urban design (MURP); planning process design and implementation (MURP); public affairs (MPA, MPP, MS, MURP, PhD/MPP); public and nonprofit leadership and management (MPP); science, technology, and environmental policy (MS); social policy (MPP); transportation planning (MURP); women and public policy (MPP). Electronic applications accepted.

Institute of Technology *Degree program information:* Part-time and evening/weekend programs available. Postbaccalaureate distance learning degree programs offered (minimal on-campus study). Offers aerospace engineering (M Aero E, MS, PhD); astronomy (MS, PhD); astrophysics (MS, PhD); biomedical engineering (MS, PhD); chemical engineering (M Ch E, MS Ch E, PhD); chemistry (MS, PhD); civil engineering (MCE, MS, PhD); computer and information sciences (MCIS, MS, PhD); computer engineering (M Comp E, MS); electrical and computer engineering (MEE, MSEE, PhD); geological engineering (M Geo E, MS, PhD); geology (MS, PhD); geophysics (MS, PhD); history of science and technology (MA, PhD); industrial engineering (MSIE, PhD); infrastructure systems engineering (MS); management of technology (MSMOT); materials science and engineering (M Mat SE, MS Mat SE, PhD); mathematics (MS, PhD); mechanical engineering (MSME, PhD); mechanics (MS, PhD); physics (MS, PhD); software engineering (MS); technology (M Aero E, M Ch E, M Comp E, M Geo E, M Mat SE, MA, MCE, MCIS, MEE, MS, MS Ch E, MS Mat SE, MSEE, MSIE, MSME, MSMOT, PhD). Electronic applications accepted.

School of Nursing Students: 120 full-time, 157 part-time. Average age 37. 220 applicants, 76% accepted. *Faculty:* 80. Expenses: Contact institution. *Financial support:* Fellowships, research assistantships, teaching assistantships, career-related internships or fieldwork and traineeships available. In 2001, 87 master's, 7 doctorates awarded. *Degree program information:* Part-time programs available. Postbaccalaureate distance learning degree programs offered (minimal on-campus study). Offers adolescent nursing (MS); adult health clinical nurse specialist (MS); advanced clinical specialist in gerontology (MS); children with special health care needs (MS); family nurse practitioner (MS); gerontology nurse practitioner (MS); midwifery (MS); nursing (MS, PhD); nursing education (MS); nursing management (MS); oncology nursing (MS); pediatric clinical nurse specialist (MS); pediatric nurse practitioner (MS); psychiatric mental health clinical nurse specialist (MS); public health nursing (MS); school nursing (MS). *Application deadline:* Applications are processed on a rolling basis. *Application fee:* $50 ($55 for international students). *Application Contact:* Jennifer Rosand, Nursing Recruiter, 612-624-4454, Fax: 612-624-3174, E-mail: rosan003@umn.edu. *Dean*, Sandra Edwardson, 612-624-4454, Fax: 612-626-2359.

Law School Students: 742 full-time (358 women); includes 110 minority (17 African Americans, 70 Asian Americans or Pacific Islanders, 17 Hispanic Americans, 6 Native Americans), 65 international. Average age 26. 1,926 applicants, 34% accepted, 235 enrolled. *Faculty:* 44 full-time (14 women), 110 part-time/adjunct (41 women). Expenses: Contact institution. *Financial support:* In 2001–02, 580 students received support; fellowships, research assistantships, teaching assistantships, career-related internships or fieldwork, Federal Work-Study, institutionally sponsored loans, scholarships/grants, and tuition waivers (partial) available. Financial award application deadline: 3/15; financial award applicants required to submit FAFSA. In 2001, 239 first professional degrees, 38 master's awarded. Offers law (JD, LL M). *Application deadline:* For fall admission, 3/1. Applications are processed on a rolling basis. *Application fee:* $50. Electronic applications accepted. *Application Contact:* Collins B. Byrd, Director of Admissions, 612-625-5005, Fax: 612-625-2011, E-mail: umnlsadm@umn.edu. *Dean*, E. Thomas Sullivan, 612-625-1000.

Medical School Students: 813 full-time (383 women); includes 132 minority (12 African Americans, 86 Asian Americans or Pacific Islanders, 16 Hispanic Americans, 18 Native Americans), 8 international. *Faculty:* 1,323 full-time. Expenses: Contact institution. *Financial support:* Fellowships, research assistantships, teaching assistantships, career-related internships or fieldwork, Federal Work-Study, institutionally sponsored loans, and tuition waivers (full and partial) available. *Degree program information:* Part-time and evening/weekend programs available. Offers medicine (MD, MA, MS, PhD). *Application Contact:* Information Contact, 612-625-7977.

Graduate Programs in Medicine Expenses: Contact institution. *Financial support:* Fellowships, research assistantships, teaching assistantships, career-related internships or fieldwork, Federal Work-Study, institutionally sponsored loans, and tuition waivers (full and partial) available. *Degree program information:* Part-time and evening/weekend programs available. Offers biochemistry, molecular biology and biophysics (PhD); cellular and integrative physiology (MS, PhD); clinical laboratory sciences (MS); experimental surgery (MS); history of medicine (MA, PhD); medicine (MA, MS, PhD); microbial engineering (MS); microbiology, immunology and cancer biology (PhD); otolaryngology (MS, PhD); physical therapy (MS); rehabilitation science (PhD); surgery (MS, PhD). *Application Contact:* Information Contact, 612-625-7977.

School of Dentistry Expenses: Contact institution. *Financial support:* Fellowships, research assistantships, teaching assistantships available. Offers dentistry (DDS, MS, PhD); endodontics (MS); oral biology (MS, PhD); oral health services for older adults (MS); orthodontics (MS); pediatric dentistry (MS); periodontology (MS); prosthodontics (MS); temporal mandibular joint (MS). *Dean*, Dr. Peter J. Polverini, 612-625-9982, Fax: 612-626-2654, E-mail: neovas@umn.edu.

School of Public Health Students: 251 full-time, 174 part-time. Average age 29. 559 applicants, 63% accepted. *Faculty:* 87 full-time, 15 part-time/adjunct. Expenses: Contact institution. *Financial support:* Fellowships with partial tuition reimbursements, research assistantships with partial tuition reimbursements, teaching assistantships with partial tuition reimbursements, career-related internships or fieldwork, Federal Work-Study, institutionally sponsored loans, scholarships/grants, traineeships, and tuition waivers (partial) available. Financial award applicants required to submit FAFSA. In 2001, 121 master's, 16 doctorates awarded. *Degree program information:* Part-time programs available. Postbaccalaureate distance learning degree programs offered (minimal on-campus study). Offers biostatistics (MPH, MS, PhD); clinical research (MS); community health education (MPH); environmental and occupational epidemiology (MPH, MS, PhD); environmental chemistry (MS, PhD); environmental health policy (MPH, MS, PhD); environmental microbiology (MPH, MS, PhD); environmental toxicology (MPH, MS, PhD); epidemiology (MPH, PhD); health services research, policy, and administration (MS, PhD); industrial hygiene (MPH, MS, PhD); maternal and child health (MPH); occupational health nursing (MPH, MS, PhD); occupational medicine (MPH); public health (MA, MPH, MS, PhD, Certificate); public health administration (MPH); public health nutrition (MPH); public health practice (MPH, Certificate). *Application deadline:* Applications are processed on a rolling basis. *Application fee:* $50 ($75 for international students). *Application Contact:* Student Services Center, 800-774-8636, Fax: 612-624-4498, E-mail: sph-ssc@tc.umn.edu. *Dean,* Dr. Mark P. Becker, 612-624-6669, Fax: 612-626-6931.

UNIVERSITY OF MISSISSIPPI, Oxford, University, MS 38677

General Information State-supported, coed, university. CGS member. *Enrollment:* 1,595 full-time matriculated graduate/professional students (748 women), 388 part-time matriculated graduate/professional students (242 women). *Enrollment by degree level:* 612 first professional, 839 master's, 492 doctoral, 40 other advanced degrees. *Graduate faculty:* 491 full-time (159 women). Tuition, state resident: full-time $3,626; part-time $202 per hour. Tuition, nonresident: full-time $8,172; part-time $454 per hour. *Graduate housing:* Rooms and/or apartments available to single and married students. Typical cost: $1,750 per year ($5,200 including board) for single students; $1,750 per year ($5,200 including board) for married students. *Student services:* Campus employment opportunities, campus safety program, career counseling, free psychological counseling, international student services, low-cost health insurance, teacher training. *Library facilities:* J. D. Williams Library plus 3 others. *Online resources:* library catalog, web page, access to other libraries' catalogs. *Collection:* 951,259 titles, 8,495 serial subscriptions, 143,717 audiovisual materials. *Research affiliation:* Oak Ridge Associated Universities, Gulf Coast Research Laboratory, Mississippi–Alabama Sea Grant Consortium, Mississippi Research Consortium, Water Resources Research Institute, Southeastern Universities Research Association.

Computer facilities: 3,500 computers available on campus for general student use. A campuswide network can be accessed from student residence rooms and from off campus. *Web address:* http://www.olemiss.edu/.

General Application Contact: Dr. Donald R. Cole, Associate Dean of Graduate School, 662-915-7474, Fax: 662-915-7577, E-mail: dcole@sunset.backbone.olemiss.edu.

GRADUATE UNITS

Graduate School Students: 1,118 full-time (552 women), 387 part-time (241 women); includes 224 minority (187 African Americans, 23 Asian Americans or Pacific Islanders, 6 Hispanic Americans, 8 Native Americans), 283 international. *Faculty:* 465. Expenses: Contact institution. *Financial support:* Fellowships, research assistantships, teaching assistantships, career-related internships or fieldwork, Federal Work-Study, institutionally sponsored loans, tuition waivers (full), and unspecified assistantships available. Financial award application deadline: 3/1. In 2001, 208 first professional degrees, 477 master's, 92 doctorates, 17 other advanced degrees awarded. *Degree program information:* Part-time programs available. Offers applied sciences (MA, MS, PhD); communicative disorders (MS); exercise science (MA, MS); exercise science and leisure management (PhD); leisure management (MA); wellness (MS). *Application deadline:* For fall admission, 8/1. Applications are processed on a rolling basis. *Application fee:* $0 ($25 for international students). *Application Contact:* Dr. Donald R. Cole, Associate Dean, 662-915-7474, Fax: 662-915-7577, E-mail: dcole@sunset.backbone.olemiss.edu. *Acting Dean,* Dr. Maurice Eftink, 662-915-7474, E-mail: eftink@olemiss.edu.

College of Liberal Arts Students: 363 full-time (176 women), 85 part-time (44 women); includes 57 minority (45 African Americans, 5 Asian Americans or Pacific Islanders, 2 Hispanic Americans, 5 Native Americans), 36 international. *Faculty:* 249. Expenses: Contact institution. *Financial support:* Fellowships, research assistantships, teaching assistantships, career-related internships or fieldwork, Federal Work-Study, institutionally sponsored loans, and unspecified assistantships available. Financial award application deadline: 3/1. In 2001, 75 master's, 36 doctorates awarded. *Degree program information:* Part-time programs available. Offers anthropology (MA); art education (MA); art history (MA); biology (MS, PhD); chemistry (MS, DA, PhD); classics (MA); clinical psychology (PhD); English (MA, DA, PhD); experimental psychology (PhD); fine arts (MFA); French (MA); German (MA); history (MA, PhD); journalism (MA); liberal arts (MA, MFA, MM, MS, MSS, DA, PhD); mathematics (MA, MS, PhD); music (MM, DA); philosophy (MA); physics (MA, MS, PhD); political science (MA, PhD); psychology (MA); sociology (MA, MSS); Southern studies (MA); Spanish (MA); theatre arts (MFA). *Application deadline:* For fall admission, 8/1. Applications are processed on a rolling basis. *Application fee:* $0 ($25 for international students). *Dean,* Dr. Glenn Hopkins, 662-915-7177, Fax: 662-915-5792.

School of Accountancy Students: 63 full-time (28 women), 7 part-time (3 women); includes 1 minority (African American), 4 international. *Faculty:* 13. Expenses: Contact institution. *Financial support:* Application deadline: 3/1. In 2001, 60 master's, 2 doctorates awarded. Offers accountancy (M Acc, PhD); taxation accounting (M Tax). *Application deadline:* For fall admission, 8/1. Applications are processed on a rolling basis. *Application fee:* $0 ($25 for international students). *Dean,* Dr. James W. Davis, 662-915-7468, Fax: 662-915-7483, E-mail: acdavis@olemiss.edu.

School of Business Administration Students: 132 full-time (46 women), 26 part-time (6 women); includes 13 minority (8 African Americans, 3 Asian Americans or Pacific Islanders, 1 Hispanic American, 1 Native American), 55 international. *Faculty:* 59. Expenses: Contact institution. *Financial support:* Fellowships, career-related internships or fieldwork, tuition waivers (full), and unspecified assistantships available. Financial award application deadline: 3/1. In 2001, 57 master's, 3 doctorates awarded. Offers business administration (MBA); economics (MA, PhD); systems management (MS). *Application deadline:* For fall admission, 8/1. Applications are processed on a rolling basis. *Application fee:* $0 ($25 for international students). *Dean,* Dr. N. Keith Womer, 662-915-5820, Fax: 662-915-5821, E-mail: kwomer@olemiss.edu.

School of Education Students: 154 full-time (111 women), 235 part-time (177 women); includes 112 minority (106 African Americans, 3 Asian Americans or Pacific Islanders, 1 Hispanic American, 2 Native Americans), 12 international. *Faculty:* 39. Expenses: Contact institution. *Financial support:* Application deadline: 3/1. In 2001, 210 master's, 29 doctorates, 17 other advanced degrees awarded. Offers counselor education (M Ed, PhD, Specialist); curriculum and instruction (M Ed, Ed D, Ed S); education (PhD); educational leadership (PhD); educational leadership and counselor education (M Ed, MA, Ed D, Ed S); higher education/student personnel (MA); secondary education (MA). *Application deadline:* For fall admission, 8/1. Applications are processed on a rolling basis. *Application fee:* $0 ($25 for international students). *Acting Dean,* Dr. James Chambless, 662-915-7063, Fax: 662-915-7249, E-mail: jchamble@olemiss.edu.

School of Engineering Students: 160 full-time (37 women), 17 part-time (3 women); includes 9 minority (7 African Americans, 2 Asian Americans or Pacific Islanders), 132 international. *Faculty:* 45 full-time (4 women). Expenses: Contact institution. *Financial support:* Application deadline: 3/1. In 2001, 37 master's, 6 doctorates awarded. Offers engineering science (MS, PhD). *Application deadline:* For fall admission, 8/1. Applications are processed on a rolling basis. *Application fee:* $0 ($25 for international students). *Dean,* Dr. Kai-Fong Lee, 662-915-7407, Fax: 662-915-1287, E-mail: engineer@olemiss.edu.

School of Pharmacy Students: 201 full-time (122 women), 4 part-time; includes 14 African Americans, 9 Asian Americans or Pacific Islanders, 44 international. *Faculty:* 43. Expenses: Contact institution. *Financial support:* Application deadline: 3/1. In 2001, 74 first professional degrees, 8 master's, 9 doctorates awarded. Offers medicinal chemistry (MS, PhD); pharmaceutics (MS, PhD); pharmacognosy (MS, PhD); pharmacology (MS, PhD); pharmacy (Pharm D, MS, PhD); pharmacy administration (MS, PhD); toxicology (PhD). *Application deadline:* For fall admission, 8/1. Applications are processed on a rolling basis. *Application fee:* $0 ($25 for international students). *Dean,* Dr. Barbara G. Wells, 662-915-7265, Fax: 662-915-5704, E-mail: pharmacy@olemiss.edu.

School of Law Students: 477 full-time (196 women), 1 (woman) part-time; includes 57 minority (48 African Americans, 2 Asian Americans or Pacific Islanders, 4 Hispanic Americans, 3 Native Americans), 2 international. Average age 24. *Faculty:* 26. Expenses: Contact institution. *Financial support:* Fellowships, research assistantships, teaching assistantships, career-related internships or fieldwork, Federal Work-Study, and institutionally sponsored loans available. Support available to part-time students. Financial award application deadline: 3/1. In 2001, 134 degrees awarded. Offers law (JD). *Application deadline:* For fall admission, 3/1. *Application fee:* $0 ($25 for international students). *Application Contact:* Barbara Vinson, Coordinator of Admissions, 662-915-7361. *Dean,* Dr. Samuel Davis, 662-915-6900, Fax: 662-915-5313, E-mail: smdavis@olemiss.edu.

UNIVERSITY OF MISSISSIPPI MEDICAL CENTER, Jackson, MS 39216-4505

General Information State-supported, coed, upper-level institution. *Enrollment:* 779 matriculated graduate/professional students (341 women). *Enrollment by degree level:* 564 first professional, 56 master's, 157 doctoral, 2 other advanced degrees. *Graduate faculty:* 528 full-time, 1,729 part-time/adjunct. *Tuition:* Part-time $158 per credit. Full-time tuition and fees vary according to degree level and program. *Graduate housing:* Rooms and/or apartments available on a first-come, first-served basis to single and married students. *Student services:* Campus employment opportunities, campus safety program, career counseling, disabled student services, exercise/wellness program, free psychological counseling, international student services, low-cost health insurance, multicultural affairs office. *Library facilities:* Rowland Medical Library. *Online resources:* library catalog, web page, access to other libraries' catalogs. *Collection:* 244,460 titles, 2,371 serial subscriptions, 17,084 audiovisual materials. *Research affiliation:* Gulf Coast Research Laboratory (microbiology), Oak Ridge National Laboratory (physiology, biomedical engineering), Catfish Genetics Research Unit (immunology), NASA–Stennis Space Center (imaging technology).

Computer facilities: 120 computers available on campus for general student use. A campuswide network can be accessed from off campus. Internet access is available. *Web address:* http://umc.edu/.

General Application Contact: Barbara M. Westerfield, Director, Student Records and Registrar, 601-984-1080, Fax: 601-984-1079, E-mail: bwesterfield@registrar.unsmed.edu.

GRADUATE UNITS

School of Dentistry Students: 119 full-time (35 women); includes 7 minority (4 African Americans, 2 Asian Americans or Pacific Islanders, 1 Hispanic American) Average age 25. 89 applicants, 35% accepted, 30 enrolled. *Faculty:* 44 full-time, 199 part-time/adjunct. Expenses: Contact institution. *Financial support:* Institutionally sponsored loans and scholarships/grants available. Financial award application deadline: 4/1. In 2001, 23 degrees awarded. Offers dentistry (DMD). *Application deadline:* For fall admission, 12/1. Applications are processed on a rolling basis. *Application fee:* $10. *Application Contact:* Dr. Billy M. Bishop, Director, Student Services and Records, 601-984-1080, Fax: 601-984-1079, E-mail: bbishop@registrar.umsmed.edu. *Interim Dean,* Dr. Willie J. Hill, 601-984-6000, Fax: 601-984-6014, E-mail: dentistry@sod.umsmed.edu.

School of Graduate Studies in the Health Sciences Students: 213; includes 33 minority (all African Americans), 53 international. Average age 28. 121 applicants, 46% accepted, 48 enrolled. Expenses: Contact institution. *Financial support:* In 2001–02, 71 research assistantships (averaging $16,234 per year) were awarded In 2001, 31 master's, 9 doctorates awarded. Offers anatomy (MS, PhD); biochemistry (MS, PhD); health sciences (MPT, MS, MSN, PhD); maternal-fetal medicine (MS); microbiology (MS, PhD); pathology (MS, PhD); pharmacology (MS, PhD); physiology and biophysics (MS, PhD); preventive medicine (MS, PhD); toxicology (MS, PhD). *Application deadline:* Applications are processed on a rolling basis. *Application fee:* $10. *Application Contact:* Barbara M. Westerfield, Director, Student Records and Registrar, 601-984-1080, Fax: 601-984-1079, E-mail: bwesterfield@registrar.unsmed.edu. *Dean,* Dr. I. K. Ho, 601-984-1600, Fax: 601-984-1637, E-mail: iho@pharmacology.umsmed.edu.

School of Health Related Professions Students: 48 full-time, 28 part-time; includes 13 minority (12 African Americans, 1 Asian American or Pacific Islander) 67 applicants, 64% accepted, 28 enrolled. Expenses: Contact institution. *Financial support:* Institutionally sponsored loans and scholarships/grants available. Support available to part-time students. Financial award application deadline: 4/1; financial award applicants required to submit FAFSA. In 2001, 39 master's, 4 doctorates awarded. *Degree program information:* Part-time programs available. Offers clinical health sciences (MS, PhD); health related professions (MPT, MS, PhD); physical therapy (MPT). *Application deadline:* Applications are processed on a rolling basis. *Application fee:* $10. *Application Contact:* Dr. David G. Fowler, Director, 601-984-6309, Fax: 601-984-6344, E-mail: dfowler@shrp.umsmed.edu. *Dean,* Dr. J. Maurice Mahan, 601-984-6300, Fax: 601-984-6344, E-mail: mmahan@shrp.umsmed.edu.

School of Nursing Students: 72 (62 women); includes 10 minority (9 African Americans, 1 Asian American or Pacific Islander) Average age 35. 59 applicants, 47% accepted, 23 enrolled. *Faculty:* 20 full-time (18 women), 4 part-time/adjunct (2 women). Expenses: Contact institution. *Financial support:* In 2001–02, 59 students received support. Institutionally sponsored loans and traineeships available. Support available to part-time students. Financial award application deadline: 4/1. In 2001, 22 master's, 1 doctorate awarded. *Degree program information:* Part-time and evening/weekend programs available. Offers nursing (MSN, PhD). *Application deadline:* For fall admission, 12/15 (priority date). *Application fee:* $10. Electronic applications accepted. *Application Contact:* Dr. Ola Allen, Associate Dean for Academic Affairs, 601-984-6256, Fax: 601-815-5957, E-mail: oallen@son.umsmed.edu. *Interim Dean,* Dr. Barbara Rogers, 601-984-6220, Fax: 601-984-6214, E-mail: brogers@son.umsmed.edu.

School of Medicine Students: 397 full-time (143 women); includes 41 minority (20 African Americans, 21 Asian Americans or Pacific Islanders) Average age 24. 517 applicants, 22% accepted, 100 enrolled. *Faculty:* 474 full-time, 996 part-time/adjunct. Expenses: Contact institution. *Financial support:* In 2001–02, 374 students received support. Institutionally sponsored loans and scholarships/grants available. Financial award application deadline:4/1. In 2001, 85 degrees awarded. Offers medicine (MD). *Application deadline:* For fall admission, 9/15; for winter admission, 12/1. Applications are processed on a rolling basis. *Application fee:* $10. *Application Contact:* Dr. Steven T. Case, Associate Dean for Medical School Admissions, 601-984-5010, Fax: 601-984-5008, E-mail: admitmd@som.umsmed.edu. *Dean,* Dr. A. Wallace Conerly, 601-984-1010.

UNIVERSITY OF MISSOURI–COLUMBIA, Columbia, MO 65211

General Information State-supported, coed, university. CGS member. *Enrollment:* 3,331 full-time matriculated graduate/professional students (1,694 women), 1,905 part-time matriculated graduate/professional students (1,037 women). *Enrollment by degree level:* 1,162 first professional, 2,360 master's, 1,670 doctoral, 44 other advanced degrees. *Graduate faculty:* 1,518 full-time (433 women), 49 part-time/adjunct (25 women). Tuition, state resident: part-time $179 per credit hour. Tuition, nonresident: part-time $539 per credit hour. *Required fees:* $122 per semester. Tuition and fees vary according to program. *Graduate housing:* Rooms and/or apartments available on a first-come, first-served basis to single and married students. Housing application deadline: 10/1. *Student services:* Campus employment opportunities, campus safety program, career counseling, child daycare facilities, disabled student services, exercise/wellness program, free psychological counseling, grant writing training, international student services, low-cost health insurance, multicultural affairs office, teacher training, writing training. *Library facilities:* Ellis Library plus 11 others. *Online resources:* library catalog, web page, access to other libraries' catalogs. *Collection:* 4.7 million titles, 20,524 serial subscriptions.

Computer facilities: 1,150 computers available on campus for general student use. A campuswide network can be accessed from student residence rooms and from off campus. Internet access and online class registration, telephone registration are available. *Web address:* http://www.missouri.edu/.

General Application Contact: Stephanie White-Thorn, Admissions, 573-882-3292.

GRADUATE UNITS

College of Veterinary Medicine Students: 260 full-time (181 women), 45 part-time (30 women); includes 19 minority (5 African Americans, 9 Asian Americans or Pacific Islanders, 3 Hispanic Americans, 2 Native Americans), 18 international. *Faculty:* 87 full-time (21 women), 1 (woman) part-time/adjunct. Expenses: Contact institution. *Financial support:* Fellowships, research assistantships, teaching assistantships, career-related internships or fieldwork, institutionally sponsored loans, and tuition waivers (full and partial) available. Support available to part-time students. In 2001, 62 first professional degrees, 4 master's, 6 doctorates awarded. Offers laboratory animal medicine (MS); pathobiology (MS, PhD); veterinary biomedical sciences (MS); veterinary clinical sciences (MS); veterinary medicine (DVM, MS). *Application Contact:* Dr. Gerald M. Buening, Associate Dean for Research and Postdoctoral

University of Missouri–Columbia (continued)

Studies, 573-882-2655, Fax: 573-884-5044, E-mail: bueningg@missouri.edu. *Dean,* Dr. Joe Kornegay, 573-882-3768, Fax: 573-884-5044, E-mail: kornegayj@missouri.edu.

Graduate School Students: 2,209 full-time (1,146 women), 1,864 part-time (1,012 women); includes 325 minority (170 African Americans, 63 Asian Americans or Pacific Islanders, 77 Hispanic Americans, 15 Native Americans), 1,002 international. *Faculty:* 1,518 full-time (433 women), 49 part-time/adjunct (25 women). Expenses: Contact institution. *Financial support:* Fellowships with full and partial tuition reimbursements, research assistantships with full and partial tuition reimbursements, teaching assistantships with full and partial tuition reimbursements, career-related internships or fieldwork, institutionally sponsored loans, scholarships/grants, traineeships, and tuition waivers (full and partial) available. Support available to part-time students. In 2001, 899 master's, 274 doctorates, 50 other advanced degrees awarded. *Degree program information:* Part-time and evening/weekend programs available. Offers dispute resolution (LL M); health administration (MHA); health informatics (MHA); health services management (MHA). *Application deadline:* Applications are processed on a rolling basis. *Application fee:* $25 ($50 for international students). *Dean,* Dr. Suzanne Ortega, 573-882-9576, E-mail: ortegas@missouri.edu.

College of Agriculture, Food and Natural Resources Students: 217 full-time (95 women), 154 part-time (56 women); includes 23 minority (15 African Americans, 1 Asian American or Pacific Islander, 6 Hispanic Americans, 1 Native American), 126 international. 66 applicants, 53% accepted. *Faculty:* 188 full-time (32 women), 3 part-time/adjunct (2 women). Expenses: Contact institution. *Financial support:* Fellowships, research assistantships, teaching assistantships, institutionally sponsored loans available. In 2001, 35 master's, 25 doctorates awarded. *Degree program information:* Part-time programs available. Offers agricultural economics (MS, PhD); agriculture, food and natural resources (MS, PhD); agronomy (MS, PhD); animal sciences (MS, PhD); entomology (MS, PhD); food science (MS, PhD); foods and food systems management (MS); horticulture (MS, PhD); human nutrition (MS); nutrition (MS, PhD); plant pathology and microbiology (MS, PhD); rural sociology (MS, PhD). *Application deadline:* Applications are processed on a rolling basis. *Application fee:* $25 ($50 for international students). *Dean,* Dr. Thomas T. Payne, 573-882-3846, E-mail: paynet@missouri.edu.

College of Arts and Sciences Students: 993; includes 81 minority (42 African Americans, 18 Asian Americans or Pacific Islanders, 17 Hispanic Americans, 4 Native Americans), 246 international. *Faculty:* 470 full-time (135 women), 8 part-time/adjunct (6 women). Expenses: Contact institution. *Financial support:* Fellowships, research assistantships, teaching assistantships, career-related internships or fieldwork, institutionally sponsored loans, and tuition waivers (full and partial) available. In 2001, 107 master's, 95 doctorates awarded. *Degree program information:* Part-time programs available. Offers analytical chemistry (MS, PhD); anthropology (MA, PhD); applied mathematics (MS); art (MFA); art history and archaeology (MA, PhD); arts and sciences (MA, MFA, MM, MS, MST, PhD); biological sciences (MA, PhD); classical studies (MA, PhD); communication (MA, PhD); economics (MA, PhD); English (MA, PhD); French (MA, PhD); genetics (PhD); geography (MA); geological sciences (MS, PhD); German (MA); history (MA, PhD); inorganic chemistry (MS, PhD); literature (MA); mathematics (MA, MST, PhD); music (MA, MM); organic chemistry (MS, PhD); philosophy (MA, PhD); physical chemistry (MS, PhD); physics (MS, PhD); political science (MA, PhD); psychological sciences (MA, MS, PhD); religious studies (MA); sociology (MA, PhD); Spanish (MA, PhD); statistics (MA, PhD); teaching (MA); theatre (MA, PhD). *Application deadline:* Applications are processed on a rolling basis. *Application fee:* $25 ($50 for international students). *Dean,* Dr. Richard Schwartz, 573-882-4421.

College of Business Students: 223 full-time (94 women), 70 part-time (46 women); includes 14 minority (10 African Americans, 2 Asian Americans or Pacific Islanders, 2 Hispanic Americans), 65 international. 176 applicants, 37% accepted. *Faculty:* 52 full-time (12 women). Expenses: Contact institution. *Financial support:* Fellowships, research assistantships, teaching assistantships, institutionally sponsored loans available. In 2001, 138 master's, 11 doctorates awarded. *Degree program information:* Part-time programs available. Offers accountancy (M Acc, PhD); business (MBA, PhD); business and public administration (M Acc, MBA, MPA, PhD). *Application deadline:* Applications are processed on a rolling basis. *Application fee:* $25 ($50 for international students). *Dean,* Dr. Bruce Walker, 573-882-6688.

College of Education Students: 376 full-time (255 women), 575 part-time (359 women); includes 78 minority (50 African Americans, 10 Asian Americans or Pacific Islanders, 12 Hispanic Americans, 6 Native Americans), 132 international. 131 applicants, 85% accepted. *Faculty:* 84 full-time (36 women). Expenses: Contact institution. *Financial support:* Fellowships, research assistantships, teaching assistantships, institutionally sponsored loans and scholarships/grants available. In 2001, 203 master's, 73 doctorates, 41 other advanced degrees awarded. *Degree program information:* Part-time and evening/weekend programs available. Offers early childhood and elementary education (M Ed, MA, Ed D, PhD, Ed S); education (M Ed, MA, Ed D, PhD, Ed S); education administration (M Ed, MA, Ed D, PhD, Ed S); educational and counseling psychology (M Ed, MA, PhD, Ed S); educational technology (M Ed, Ed S); higher and adult education (M Ed, MA, Ed D, PhD, Ed S); information science and learning technology (PhD); library science (MA); middle and secondary education (M Ed, MA, Ed D, PhD, Ed S). *Application deadline:* Applications are processed on a rolling basis. *Application fee:* $25 ($50 for international students). *Dean,* Dr. Richard Andrews, 573-882-8524, E-mail: andrewsr@missouri.edu.

College of Engineering Students: 228 full-time (53 women), 133 part-time (25 women); includes 28 minority (7 African Americans, 8 Asian Americans or Pacific Islanders, 13 Hispanic Americans), 248 international. 614 applicants, 53% accepted. *Faculty:* 103 full-time (9 women), 1 (woman) part-time/adjunct. Expenses: Contact institution. *Financial support:* Fellowships, research assistantships, teaching assistantships, institutionally sponsored loans available. In 2001, 78 master's, 13 doctorates awarded. *Degree program information:* Part-time programs available. Offers agricultural engineering (MS); biological engineering (MS, PhD); chemical engineering (MS, PhD); civil engineering (MS, PhD); computer engineering and computer science (MS, PhD); electrical and computer engineering (MS, PhD); engineering (MS, PhD); environmental engineering (MS, PhD); geotechnical engineering (MS, PhD); industrial and manufacturing systems engineering (MS, PhD); mechanical and aerospace engineering (MS, PhD); nuclear engineering (MS, PhD); structural engineering (MS, PhD); transportation and highway engineering (MS); water resources (MS, PhD). *Application deadline:* Applications are processed on a rolling basis. *Application fee:* $25 ($50 for international students). *Dean,* Dr. James Thompson, 573-882-4375, E-mail: thompsonje@missouri.edu.

College of Human Environmental Science Students: 45 full-time (34 women), 32 part-time (21 women); includes 5 minority (4 African Americans, 1 Hispanic American), 18 international. 93 applicants, 44% accepted. *Faculty:* 40 full-time (24 women), 2 part-time/adjunct (both women). Expenses: Contact institution. *Financial support:* Fellowships, research assistantships, teaching assistantships, institutionally sponsored loans available. In 2001, 28 master's, 10 doctorates awarded. *Degree program information:* Part-time programs available. Offers consumer and family economics (MS); environmental design (MA, MS); exercise physiology (PhD); exercise science (MA); food science (MS, PhD); foods and food systems management (MS); human development and family studies (MA, MS, PhD); human environmental science (MA, MS, PhD); human nutrition (MS); textiles and apparel management (MA, MS). *Application deadline:* Applications are processed on a rolling basis. *Application fee:* $25 ($50 for international students). *Dean,* Dr. Bea Smith, 573-882-6227, E-mail: beasmith@missouri.edu.

Graduate School of Public Affairs Students: 16 full-time (9 women), 31 part-time (16 women); includes 6 minority (4 African Americans, 2 Hispanic Americans), 1 international. *Faculty:* 8 full-time (3 women). Expenses: Contact institution. *Financial support:* Fellowships, research assistantships, teaching assistantships, institutionally sponsored loans available. In 2001, 31 degrees awarded. Offers public affairs (MPA). *Application deadline:* For fall admission, 2/15 (priority date). Applications are processed on a rolling basis. *Application fee:* $25 ($50 for international students). *Director of Graduate Studies,* Lisa Zanetti, 573-884-0953, E-mail: zanettil@missouri.edu.

School of Journalism Students: 146 full-time (86 women), 39 part-time (22 women); includes 24 minority (9 African Americans, 8 Asian Americans or Pacific Islanders, 5 Hispanic Americans, 2 Native Americans), 57 international. 235 applicants, 48% accepted. *Faculty:* 56 full-time (23 women). Expenses: Contact institution. *Financial support:* Fellowships, research assistantships, teaching assistantships, career-related internships or fieldwork and institutionally sponsored loans available. In 2001, 73 master's, 9 doctorates awarded. *Degree program information:* Part-time programs available. Offers journalism (MA, PhD). *Application deadline:* For fall admission, 2/1 (priority date); for winter admission, 9/1 (priority date). Applications are processed on a rolling basis. *Application fee:* $25 ($50 for international students). *Director of Graduate Studies,* Dr. Esther Thorson, 573-882-4852, E-mail: thorsone@missouri.edu.

School of Natural Resources Students: 50 full-time (18 women), 62 part-time (29 women); includes 8 minority (4 African Americans, 1 Asian American or Pacific Islander, 3 Hispanic Americans), 22 international. 40 applicants, 28% accepted. *Faculty:* 35 full-time (4 women). Expenses: Contact institution. *Financial support:* Fellowships, research assistantships, teaching assistantships, institutionally sponsored loans and scholarships/grants available. In 2001, 18 master's, 7 doctorates awarded. *Degree program information:* Part-time programs available. Offers atmospheric sciences (MS, PhD); fisheries and wildlife (MS, PhD); forestry (MS, PhD); natural resources (MS, PhD); parks, recreation and tourism (MS); soil sciences (MS, PhD). *Application deadline:* Applications are processed on a rolling basis. *Application fee:* $25 ($50 for international students). *Director,* Dr. A. R. Vogt, 573-882-6446, E-mail: vogta@missouri.edu.

School of Social Work Students: 92 full-time (82 women), 73 part-time (61 women); includes 15 minority (8 African Americans, 1 Asian American or Pacific Islander, 5 Hispanic Americans, 1 Native American), 2 international. 61 applicants, 48% accepted. *Faculty:* 17 full-time (11 women). Expenses: Contact institution. *Financial support:* Fellowships, research assistantships, teaching assistantships, institutionally sponsored loans available. In 2001, 57 degrees awarded. *Degree program information:* Part-time programs available. Offers social work (MSW). *Application deadline:* For fall admission, 1/15 (priority date). Applications are processed on a rolling basis. *Application fee:* $25 ($50 for international students). *Director of Graduate Studies,* Dr. Michael Kelly, 573-882-0922, E-mail: kellym@missouri.edu.

Sinclair School of Nursing Students: 15 full-time (13 women), 67 part-time (59 women); includes 5 minority (4 African Americans, 1 Hispanic American), 9 international. 17 applicants, 88% accepted. *Faculty:* 26 full-time (25 women). Expenses: Contact institution. *Financial support:* Fellowships, research assistantships, teaching assistantships, career-related internships or fieldwork, institutionally sponsored loans, traineeships, and tuition waivers (full) available. In 2001, 29 master's, 5 doctorates awarded. *Degree program information:* Part-time programs available. Offers nursing (MS, PhD). *Application deadline:* For fall admission, 2/1 (priority date). Applications are processed on a rolling basis. *Application fee:* $25 ($50 for international students). *Associate Dean,* Dr. Rose Porter, 573-882-0278, E-mail: porterr@missouri.edu.

School of Health Professions Students: 72 full-time (61 women), 3 part-time (all women); includes 4 minority (2 African Americans, 1 Asian American or Pacific Islander, 1 Hispanic American) *Faculty:* 11 full-time (7 women). Expenses: Contact institution. *Financial support:* Fellowships, research assistantships, teaching assistantships, institutionally sponsored loans available. In 2001, 60 degrees awarded. Offers communication science and disorders (MHS); health professions (MHS, MPT); physical therapy (MPT). *Application deadline:* For fall admission, 3/1 (priority date). Applications are processed on a rolling basis. *Application fee:* $25 ($50 for international students). *Dean,* Dr. Richard Oliver, 573-882-8013, E-mail: oliverr@health.missouri.edu.

School of Law Students: 516 full-time (202 women), 20 part-time (11 women); includes 55 minority (33 African Americans, 10 Asian Americans or Pacific Islanders, 8 Hispanic Americans, 4 Native Americans) Average age 25. 727 applicants, 57% accepted. *Faculty:* 34 full-time (11 women). Expenses: Contact institution. *Financial support:* In 2001–02, 478 students received support; fellowships, Federal Work-Study and institutionally sponsored loans available. Financial award application deadline: 3/1; financial award applicants required to submit FAFSA. In 2001, 156 degrees awarded. Offers law (JD, LL M). *Application deadline:* For fall admission, 3/1 (priority date). Applications are processed on a rolling basis. *Application fee:* $40. *Dean,* Dr. R. Lawrence Dessem, 573-882-6478, E-mail: dessemrl@law.missouri.edu.

School of Medicine Students: 439 full-time (198 women), 34 part-time (12 women); includes 54 minority (14 African Americans, 35 Asian Americans or Pacific Islanders, 4 Hispanic Americans, 1 Native American), 36 international. *Faculty:* 289 full-time (66 women), 34 part-time/adjunct (17 women). Expenses: Contact institution. *Financial support:* Fellowships, research assistantships, teaching assistantships, career-related internships or fieldwork, institutionally sponsored loans, and scholarships/grants available. Support available to part-time students. Financial award applicants required to submit FAFSA. In 2001, 96 first professional degrees, 5 master's, 14 doctorates awarded. *Degree program information:* Part-time programs available. Offers biochemistry (MS, PhD); family and community medicine (MSPH); medicine (MD, MA, MS, MSPH, PhD); molecular microbiology and immunology (MS, PhD); pharmacology (MS, PhD); physiology (MS, PhD). *Application deadline:* Applications are processed on a rolling basis. *Application Contact:* Dr. William Altemeier, Associate Dean for Students, 573-882-3490, E-mail: altemeierw@missouri.edu. *Dean,* Dr. William Crist, 573-884-8733, E-mail: cristwm@missouri.edu.

UNIVERSITY OF MISSOURI–KANSAS CITY, Kansas City, MO 64110-2499

General Information State-supported, coed, university. CGS member. *Enrollment:* 2,310 full-time matriculated graduate/professional students (1,190 women), 2,297 part-time matriculated graduate/professional students (1,456 women). *Graduate faculty:* 478. Tuition, state resident: part-time $233 per credit hour. Tuition, nonresident: part-time $623 per credit hour. Tuition and fees vary according to course load. *Graduate housing:* Room and/or apartments available to single students; on-campus housing not available to married students. *Student services:* Campus employment opportunities, campus safety program, career counseling, child daycare facilities, disabled student services, exercise/wellness program, free psychological counseling, international student services, multicultural affairs office, writing training. *Library facilities:* Miller-Nichols Library plus 3 others. *Online resources:* library catalog, web page, access to other libraries' catalogs. *Collection:* 1.6 million titles, 12,472 serial subscriptions, 363,933 audiovisual materials. *Research affiliation:* Midwest Research Institute, Veterans Administration Hospital, Truman Medical Center, Children's Mercy Hospital, United Telecommunications (computer science), St. Luke's Hospital.

Computer facilities: 400 computers available on campus for general student use. A campuswide network can be accessed from student residence rooms and from off campus. Internet access and online class registration are available. *Web address:* http://www.umkc.edu/.

General Application Contact: Mel Tyler, Director of Admissions, 816-235-1111.

GRADUATE UNITS

College of Arts and Sciences Students: 442. Average age 33. Expenses: Contact institution. *Financial support:* Fellowships with partial tuition reimbursements, research assistantships with full and partial tuition reimbursements, teaching assistantships with full and partial tuition reimbursements, career-related internships or fieldwork, Federal Work-Study, institutionally sponsored loans, scholarships/grants, and tuition waivers (full and partial) available. Support available to part-time students. Financial award applicants required to submit FAFSA. In 2001, 141 degrees awarded. *Degree program information:* Part-time and evening/weekend programs available. Offers acting (MFA); analytical chemistry (MS, PhD); art history (MA, PhD); arts and sciences (MA, MFA, MS, PhD); communication studies (MA); community psychology (PhD); criminal justice and criminology (MS); design technology (MFA); economics (MA, PhD); English (MA, PhD); geosciences (PhD); history (MA, PhD); inorganic chemistry (MS, PhD); liberal studies (MA); mathematics and statistics (MA, MS, PhD); organic chemistry (MS, PhD); physical chemistry (MS, PhD); physics (MS, PhD); political science (MA, PhD); polymer chemistry (MS, PhD); psychology (MA, PhD); Romance languages and literatures (MA); social work (MS); sociology (MA, PhD); studio art (MA); theatre (MA); urban environmental geology (MS). *Application fee:* $25. *Dean,* Dr. Bryan LeBeau, 816-235-1136.

Conservatory of Music Students: 94 full-time (52 women), 98 part-time (54 women); includes 19 minority (11 African Americans, 3 Asian Americans or Pacific Islanders, 3 Hispanic Americans, 2 Native Americans), 47 international. Average age 31. *Faculty:* 50 full-time (20 women), 20 part-time/adjunct (11 women). Expenses: Contact institution. *Financial support:* In 2001–02, 12 fellowships with tuition reimbursements (averaging $7,000 per year), 23 research assistantships with tuition reimbursements (averaging $4,500 per year), 17 teaching assistantships with tuition reimbursements (averaging $4,500 per year) were awarded. Career-related internships or fieldwork, Federal Work-Study, institutionally sponsored loans, and tuition waivers (partial) also available. Support available to part-time students. In 2001, 40 master's, 20 doctorates awarded. *Degree program information:* Part-time programs available. Offers composition (MM, DMA); conducting (MM, DMA); music (MA); music education (MME, PhD); music history and literature (MM); music theory (MM); performance (MM, DMA). *Application deadline:* For fall admission, 3/10 (priority date); for winter admission, 1/5 (priority date). *Application fee:* $25. *Application Contact:* James Elswick, Coordinator for Admissions, 816-235-2932, Fax: 816-235-5264, E-mail: cadmissions@umkc.edu. *Dean*, Dr. Randall Pembrook, 816-235-2731, Fax: 816-235-5265.

School of Biological Sciences Average age 30. *Faculty:* 37 full-time (11 women), 1 (woman) part-time/adjunct. Expenses: Contact institution. *Financial support:* In 2001–02, 23 research assistantships with full tuition reimbursements (averaging $16,000 per year), 12 teaching assistantships with full tuition reimbursements (averaging $16,000 per year) were awarded. Fellowships with full tuition reimbursements, Federal Work-Study, institutionally sponsored loans, scholarships/grants, tuition waivers (full and partial), and unspecified assistantships also available. Support available to part-time students. In 2001, 13 degrees awarded. *Degree program information:* Part-time and evening/weekend programs available. Offers biology (MA); cell biology and biophysics (PhD); cellular and molecular biology (MS, PhD); molecular biology and biochemistry (PhD). *Application deadline:* Applications are processed on a rolling basis. *Application fee:* $25. *Application Contact:* Dorothy M. Stringer, Graduate Programs Office, 816-235-2352, Fax: 816-235-5158, E-mail: stringerd@umkc.edu. *Interim Dean*, Dr. William Morgan, 816-235-1388, Fax: 816-235-5158.

School of Business and Public Administration Students: 185 full-time (86 women), 405 part-time (201 women); includes 61 minority (31 African Americans, 18 Asian Americans or Pacific Islanders, 9 Hispanic Americans, 3 Native Americans), 109 international. Average age 31. 421 applicants, 57% accepted. *Faculty:* 37 full-time (8 women), 18 part-time/adjunct (8 women). Expenses: Contact institution. *Financial support:* Fellowships, research assistantships, teaching assistantships, career-related internships or fieldwork, Federal Work-Study, institutionally sponsored loans, scholarships/grants, and tuition waivers (full and partial) available. Support available to part-time students. Financial award applicants required to submit FAFSA. In 2001, 252 degrees awarded. *Degree program information:* Part-time and evening/weekend programs available. Offers accounting (MS); business administration (MBA); business and public administration (MBA, MPA, MS, PhD). *Application deadline:* For fall admission, 5/1 (priority date); for winter admission, 10/1 (priority date). Applications are processed on a rolling basis. *Application fee:* $25. *Application Contact:* 816-235-1111. *Interim Dean*, Dr. Lanny E. Solomon, 816-235-2201.

L. P. Cookingham Institute of Public Affairs Students: 33 full-time (25 women), 70 part-time (49 women); includes 18 minority (16 African Americans, 2 Hispanic Americans), 7 international. Average age 34. 60 applicants, 95% accepted. *Faculty:* 7 full-time (0 women), 6 part-time/adjunct (1 woman). Expenses: Contact institution. *Financial support:* Fellowships, research assistantships, career-related internships or fieldwork, Federal Work-Study, institutionally sponsored loans, scholarships/grants, and tuition waivers (full and partial) available. Support available to part-time students. Financial award applicants required to submit FAFSA. In 2001, 43 degrees awarded. *Degree program information:* Part-time and evening/weekend programs available. Offers public affairs (MPA, PhD). PhD offered through the School of Graduate Studies. *Application deadline:* For fall admission, 5/1 (priority date); for winter admission, 10/1 (priority date). Applications are processed on a rolling basis. *Application fee:* $25. *Application Contact:* 816-235-1111. *Director*, Dr. Robert Herman, 816-235-2338.

School of Dentistry Students: 387 full-time (143 women), 56 part-time (21 women); includes 91 minority (16 African Americans, 55 Asian Americans or Pacific Islanders, 19 Hispanic Americans, 1 Native American), 42 international. Average age 26. *Faculty:* 147 full-time (40 women), 76 part-time/adjunct (15 women). Expenses: Contact institution. *Financial support:* Research assistantships, career-related internships or fieldwork, Federal Work-Study, institutionally sponsored loans, and tuition waivers (full and partial) available. Support available to part-time students. Financial award applicants required to submit FAFSA. In 2001, 65 first professional degrees, 4 master's, 19 other advanced degrees awarded. Offers advanced education in dentistry (Graduate Dental Certificate); dental hygiene education (MS); dental specialties (Graduate Dental Certificate); dentistry (DDS, MS, PhD, Graduate Dental Certificate); diagnostic sciences (Graduate Dental Certificate); oral and maxillofacial surgery (Graduate Dental Certificate); oral biology (MS, PhD); orthodontics and dentofacial orthopedics (Graduate Dental Certificate); pediatric dentistry (Graduate Dental Certificate); periodontics (Graduate Dental Certificate); prosthodontics (Graduate Dental Certificate). *Application fee:* $25. *Application Contact:* 816-235-2080. *Dean*, Dr. Michael Reed, 816-235-2010.

School of Education Students: 188 full-time (138 women), 641 part-time (491 women). Average age 35. *Faculty:* 46 full-time (21 women). Expenses: Contact institution. *Financial support:* In 2001–02, 292 students received support; fellowships, research assistantships, teaching assistantships, career-related internships or fieldwork, Federal Work-Study, institutionally sponsored loans, and tuition waivers (full and partial) available. Support available to part-time students. In 2001, 197 master's, 6 doctorates, 36 other advanced degrees awarded. *Degree program information:* Part-time and evening/weekend programs available. Offers counseling and guidance (MA, Ed S); counseling psychology (PhD); curriculum and instruction (MA, Ed S); education (PhD); education research and psychology (MA); reading education (MA, Ed S); special education (MA); urban leadership and policy studies (MA, PhD, Ed S). *Application fee:* $25. *Application Contact:* Gail Metcalf Schartel, Manager of Student Services, 816-235-2887, Fax: 816-235-5270, E-mail: scharteg@smtpgate.umkc.edu. *Interim Dean*, Dr. John E. Cleek, 816-235-2236, Fax: 816-235-5270.

School of Graduate Studies Students: 91 full-time (39 women), 232 part-time (100 women); includes 20 minority (11 African Americans, 3 Asian Americans or Pacific Islanders, 2 Hispanic Americans, 4 Native Americans), 103 international. Average age 38. 191 applicants, 44% accepted. *Faculty:* 370 full-time (118 women). Expenses: Contact institution. *Financial support:* In 2001–02, 21 fellowships with partial tuition reimbursements (averaging $7,800 per year), 30 research assistantships with partial tuition reimbursements (averaging $7,600 per year), 40 teaching assistantships with partial tuition reimbursements (averaging $7,600 per year) were awarded. Career-related internships or fieldwork, Federal Work-Study, and tuition waivers (partial) also available. Support available to part-time students. In 2001, 42 degrees awarded. Offers interdisciplinary studies (PhD). Students select two or more subjects. *Application deadline:* For fall admission, 2/1 (priority date); for spring admission, 9/1. Applications are processed on a rolling basis. *Application fee:* $25.

School of Interdisciplinary Computing and Engineering Students: 105 full-time (37 women), 103 part-time (27 women); includes 12 minority (3 African Americans, 8 Asian Americans or Pacific Islanders, 1 Hispanic American), 171 international. Average age 29. *Faculty:* 26 full-time (3 women), 18 part-time/adjunct (1 woman). Expenses: Contact institution. *Financial support:* In 2001–02, 15 research assistantships, 15 teaching assistantships were awarded. Career-related internships or fieldwork, Federal Work-Study, institutionally sponsored loans, and tuition waivers (partial) also available. Support available to part-time students. Financial award application deadline: 3/1. In 2001, 37 degrees awarded. *Degree program information:* Part-time programs available. Offers computer networking (MS, PhD); software engineering (MS); telecommunications networking (MS, PhD). PhD offered through the School of Graduate Studies. *Application deadline:* For fall admission, 3/1 (priority date); for spring admission, 10/1. Applications are processed on a rolling basis. *Application fee:* $25. *Dean*, Dr. William Osbourne, 816-235-1193, Fax: 816-235-5159.

School of Law Students: 457 full-time (225 women), 38 part-time (22 women). Average age 28. 696 applicants, 65% accepted. *Faculty:* 27 full-time (10 women), 1 part-time/adjunct (0 women). Expenses: Contact institution. *Financial support:* In 2001–02, 435 students received support, including 1 fellowship with partial tuition reimbursement available (averaging $1,500 per year), 25 research assistantships (averaging $1,000 per year), 35 teaching assistantships with partial tuition reimbursements available (averaging $1,350 per year); career-related internships or fieldwork, Federal Work-Study, institutionally sponsored loans, scholarships/grants, and tuition waivers (full and partial) also available. Support available to part-time students. In 2001, 146 first professional degrees, 9 master's awarded. *Degree program information:* Part-time programs available. Offers general (LL M); law (JD, LL M); taxation (LL M). *Application deadline:* For fall admission, 4/1 (priority date). Applications are processed on a rolling basis. *Application fee:* $25. *Application Contact:* Jean Klosterman, Director of Admissions, 816-325-2373, Fax: 816-235-5276, E-mail: klostermanj@umkc.edu. *Dean*, Dr. Burnele Powell, 816-235-1644, Fax: 816-235-5276.

School of Medicine Students: 347 full-time (197 women). Average age 22. 680 applicants, 23% accepted. *Faculty:* 543 full-time (170 women), 824 part-time/adjunct (117 women). Expenses: Contact institution. *Financial support:* Career-related internships or fieldwork, Federal Work-Study, institutionally sponsored loans, scholarships/grants, and tuition waivers (partial) available. Support available to part-time students. Financial award application deadline: 3/15; financial award applicants required to submit FAFSA. In 2001, 92 degrees awarded. Offers medicine (MD). *Application deadline:* For fall admission, 12/1. Applications are processed on a rolling basis. *Application fee:* $25. *Application Contact:* Janet Elrod, Selection Administrative Assistant, 816-235-1870, Fax: 816-235-5277, E-mail: elrodjk@umkc.edu. *Interim Dean*, Dr. Betty Drees, 816-235-1808.

School of Nursing Students: 30 full-time (29 women), 237 part-time (224 women). Average age 37. 105 applicants, 97% accepted. *Faculty:* 17 full-time (15 women), 40 part-time/adjunct (all women). Expenses: Contact institution. *Financial support:* In 2001–02, 30 students received support; fellowships, teaching assistantships, career-related internships or fieldwork, Federal Work-Study, institutionally sponsored loans, and tuition waivers (full and partial) available. Support available to part-time students. Financial award application deadline: 6/30. In 2001, 66 degrees awarded. *Degree program information:* Part-time programs available. Offers adult clinical nurse specialist (MSN); family nurse practitioner (MSN); neonatal nurse practitioner (MSN); nurse administrator (MSN); nurse educator (MSN); nursing (PhD); pediatric nurse practitioner (MSN). *Application deadline:* For fall admission, 2/1 (priority date); for spring admission, 9/15 (priority date). *Application fee:* $25. *Application Contact:* Brenda Riggs, Student Services Assistant, 816-235-1710, Fax: 816-235-1701, E-mail: riggsb@umkc.edu. *Dean*, Dr. Nancy Mills, 816-235-1700, Fax: 816-235-1701.

School of Pharmacy Average age 27. *Faculty:* 27 full-time (6 women), 1 part-time/adjunct (0 women). Expenses: Contact institution. *Financial support:* In 2001–02, 2 fellowships, 30 research assistantships, 24 teaching assistantships were awarded. Career-related internships or fieldwork, Federal Work-Study, institutionally sponsored loans, and tuition waivers (full and partial) also available. Financial award application deadline: 3/15. In 2001, 55 first professional degrees, 5 master's awarded. *Degree program information:* Part-time programs available. Postbaccalaureate distance learning degree programs offered (minimal on-campus study). Offers pharmaceutical sciences (MS); pharmacy (Pharm D, MS). *Application deadline:* For fall admission, 3/1; for spring admission, 10/1. *Application fee:* $25. Electronic applications accepted. *Application Contact:* Shelly M. Janasz, Manager, Student Services, 816-235-1613, Fax: 816-235-5190, E-mail: sjanasz@cctr.umkc.edu. *Dean*, Dr. Robert W. Piepho, 816-235-1609, Fax: 816-235-5190.

See in-depth description on page 1209.

UNIVERSITY OF MISSOURI–ROLLA, Rolla, MO 65409-0910

General Information State-supported, coed, university. *Graduate housing:* Rooms and/or apartments available on a first-come, first-served basis to single and married students.

GRADUATE UNITS

Graduate School *Degree program information:* Part-time and evening/weekend programs available. Electronic applications accepted.

College of Arts and Sciences *Degree program information:* Part-time programs available. Offers applied mathematics (MS); arts and sciences (MS, MST, PhD); chemistry (MS, PhD); chemistry education (MST); computer science (MS, PhD); mathematics (MST, PhD); mathematics education (MST); physics (MS, PhD). Electronic applications accepted.

School of Engineering *Degree program information:* Part-time and evening/weekend programs available. Offers aerospace engineering (MS, PhD); chemical engineering (MS, PhD); civil engineering (MS, PhD); computer engineering (MS, DE, PhD); construction engineering (MS, DE, PhD); electrical engineering (MS, DE, PhD); engineering (M Eng, MS, DE, PhD); engineering management (MS, PhD); engineering mechanics (MS, PhD); environmental engineering (MS); fluid mechanics (MS, DE, PhD); geotechnical engineering (MS, DE, PhD); hydrology and hydraulic engineering (MS, DE, PhD); manufacturing engineering (M Eng, MS); mechanical engineering (MS, DE, PhD); sanitary engineering and environmental health (MS, DE, PhD); structural analysis and design (MS, DE, PhD); structural materials (MS); structural methods (DE, PhD); systems engineering (MS). Electronic applications accepted.

School of Mines and Metallurgy *Degree program information:* Part-time programs available. Offers ceramic engineering (MS, PhD); geochemistry (MS, PhD); geological engineering (MS, DE, PhD); geology (MS, PhD); geophysics (MS, PhD); groundwater and environmental geology (MS, PhD); metallurgical engineering (MS, PhD); mines and metallurgy (MS, DE, PhD); mining engineering (MS, DE, PhD); nuclear engineering (MS, DE, PhD); petroleum engineering (MS, DE, PhD). Electronic applications accepted.

UNIVERSITY OF MISSOURI–ST. LOUIS, St. Louis, MO 63121-4499

General Information State-supported, coed, university. CGS member. *Enrollment:* 528 full-time matriculated graduate/professional students (338 women), 1,950 part-time matriculated graduate/professional students (1,312 women). *Enrollment by degree level:* 2,090 master's, 388 doctoral. *Graduate faculty:* 407. Tuition, state resident: part-time $231 per credit hour. Tuition, nonresident: part-time $621 per credit hour. *Graduate housing:* Rooms and/or apartments available on a first-come, first-served basis to single and married students. Housing application deadline: 7/1. *Student services:* Campus employment opportunities, campus safety program, career counseling, child daycare facilities, disabled student services, exercise/wellness program, free psychological counseling, grant writing training, international student services, low-cost health insurance, multicultural affairs office. *Library facilities:* Thomas Jefferson Library plus 2 others. *Online resources:* library catalog, web page, access to other libraries' catalogs. *Collection:* 1.1 million titles, 3,807 serial subscriptions, 3,871 audiovisual materials.

Computer facilities: 750 computers available on campus for general student use. A campuswide network can be accessed from student residence rooms and from off campus. Internet access is available. *Web address:* http://www.umsl.edu/.

General Application Contact: Graduate Admissions, 314-516-5458, Fax: 314-516-5310, E-mail: gradadm@umsl.edu.

GRADUATE UNITS

Graduate School Students: 528 full-time (338 women), 1,950 part-time (1,312 women); includes 356 minority (264 African Americans, 62 Asian Americans or Pacific Islanders, 22 Hispanic Americans, 8 Native Americans), 239 international. Average age 30. *Faculty:* 406. Expenses: Contact institution. *Financial support:* In 2001–02, 15 fellowships with full tuition reimbursements (averaging $12,667 per year), 140 research assistantships with full tuition reimbursements (averaging $10,651 per year), 135 teaching assistantships with full tuition reimbursements (averaging $11,086 per year) were awarded. Career-related internships or fieldwork, Federal Work-Study, and institutionally sponsored loans also available. Support available to part-time students. Financial award applicants required to submit FAFSA. In 2001, 513 master's, 32 doctorates awarded. *Degree program information:* Part-time and evening/weekend programs available. Offers gerontological social work (Certificate); gerontology (MS, Certificate); health policy (MPPA); nonprofit organization management (MPPA); nonprofit organization management and leadership (Certificate); public policy analysis (MPPA); public policy processes (MPPA); public sector human resources management (MPPA). *Applica-*

University of Missouri–St. Louis (continued)

tion fee: $25 ($40 for international students). Electronic applications accepted. *Application Contact:* Graduate Admissions, 314-516-5458, Fax: 314-516-5310, E-mail: gradadm@umsl.edu. *Interim Associate Vice Chancellor for Research and Dean,* Dr. Nasser Arshadi, 314-516-5898, Fax: 314-516-6759.

College of Arts and Sciences Students: 845; includes 119 minority (68 African Americans, 32 Asian Americans or Pacific Islanders, 15 Hispanic Americans, 4 Native Americans), 133 international. *Faculty:* 275. Expenses: Contact institution. *Financial support:* In 2001–02, 15 fellowships with full and partial tuition reimbursements (averaging $12,667 per year), 77 research assistantships with full and partial tuition reimbursements (averaging $11,513 per year), 117 teaching assistantships with full and partial tuition reimbursements (averaging $10,933 per year) were awarded. Career-related internships or fieldwork and Federal Work-Study also available. Support available to part-time students. In 2001, 121 master's, 21 doctorates awarded. *Degree program information:* Part-time and evening/weekend programs available. Offers advanced social perspective (MA); American literature (MA); American politics (MA); applied mathematics (MA, PhD); applied physics (MS); arts and sciences (MA, MFA, MME, MS, MSW, PhD, Certificate); astrophysics (MS); biology (MS, PhD); biotechnology (Certificate); chemistry (MS, PhD); clinical psychology (PhD); clinical psychology respecialization (Certificate); communication (MA); community conflict intervention (MA); comparative politics (MA); computer science (MS); creative writing (MFA); criminology and criminal justice (MA, PhD); English (MA); English literature (MA); experimental psychology (PhD); general economics (MA); general psychology (MA); historical agencies (MA); industrial/organizational (PhD); international politics (MA); international studies (Certificate); linguistics (MA); managerial economics (Certificate); museum studies (MA, Certificate); music education (MME); philosophy (MA); physics (PhD); political process and behavior (MA); political science (PhD); program design and evaluation research (MA); public administration and public policy (MA); social policy planning and administration (MA); social work (MSW); telecommunications science (Certificate); tropical biology and conservation (Certificate); urban and regional politics (MA); women's and gender studies (Certificate). *Application deadline:* Applications are processed on a rolling basis. *Application fee:* $25 ($40 for international students). Electronic applications accepted. *Application Contact:* Graduate Admissions, 314-516-5458, Fax: 314-516-5310, E-mail: gradadm@umsl.edu. *Dean,* Dr. Mark Burkholder, 314-516-5501.

College of Business Administration Students: 117 full-time (63 women), 288 part-time (107 women); includes 27 minority (12 African Americans, 14 Asian Americans or Pacific Islanders, 1 Hispanic American), 75 international. *Faculty:* 40. Expenses: Contact institution. *Financial support:* In 2001–02, 19 research assistantships with full and partial tuition reimbursements (averaging $7,958 per year), 3 teaching assistantships with full and partial tuition reimbursements (averaging $7,800 per year) were awarded. Career-related internships or fieldwork, Federal Work-Study, and institutionally sponsored loans also available. Support available to part-time students. Financial award application deadline: 4/1; financial award applicants required to submit FAFSA. In 2001, 109 degrees awarded. *Degree program information:* Part-time and evening/weekend programs available. Offers accounting (MBA); business administration (Certificate); corporate accounting (M Acc); electronic commerce (Certificate); finance (MBA); human resource management (Certificate); information resources management (Certificate); management (MBA); management information systems (PhD, Certificate); marketing (MBA); marketing management (Certificate); public sector accounting (M Acc); quantitative management science (MBA); taxation (M Acc, Certificate); telecommunications management (Certificate). *Application deadline:* For fall admission, 7/1 (priority date); for spring admission, 11/1 (priority date). Applications are processed on a rolling basis. *Application fee:* $25 ($40 for international students). Electronic applications accepted. *Application Contact:* Jeff Headtke, Graduate Admissions, 314-516-6928, Fax: 314-516-5310, E-mail: gradadm@umsl.edu. *Director of Graduate Studies,* Dr. Thomas Eyssell, 314-516-5885, Fax: 314-516-6420, E-mail: mba@umslvma.umsl.edu.

College of Nursing Students: 20 full-time (17 women), 219 part-time (208 women); includes 19 minority (14 African Americans, 4 Asian Americans or Pacific Islanders, 1 Hispanic American), 3 international. *Faculty:* 21. Expenses: Contact institution. *Financial support:* In 2001–02, 5 research assistantships with full and partial tuition reimbursements (averaging $10,080 per year) were awarded; teaching assistantships with full and partial tuition reimbursements In 2001, 29 master's, 5 doctorates awarded. Offers nursing (MSN, PhD). *Application deadline:* For fall admission, 7/1 (priority date); for spring admission, 10/1. Applications are processed on a rolling basis. *Application fee:* $25 ($40 for international students). Electronic applications accepted. *Application Contact:* Clara Jackson, Graduate Admissions Counselor, 314-516-6946, Fax: 314-516-5310, E-mail: gradadm@umsl.edu. *Interim Dean,* Dr. Connie Koch, 314-516-6066.

School of Education Students: 106 full-time (79 women), 784 part-time (614 women); includes 170 minority (152 African Americans, 11 Asian Americans or Pacific Islanders, 3 Hispanic Americans, 4 Native Americans), 17 international. *Faculty:* 59. Expenses: Contact institution. *Financial support:* In 2001–02, 27 research assistantships with full tuition reimbursements (averaging $11,215 per year), 6 teaching assistantships with full tuition reimbursements (averaging $12,600 per year) were awarded. Support available to part-time students. In 2001, 263 master's, 8 doctorates awarded. *Degree program information:* Part-time and evening/weekend programs available. Offers adult education (M Ed, Ed D, PhD); community education (M Ed); counseling (Ed D, PhD); curriculum and instruction (M Ed, Ed D, PhD); early childhood special education (M Ed); education (M Ed, Ed D, PhD); educational psychology, research, and evaluation (M Ed, Ed D, PhD); elementary administration (M Ed); elementary reading (M Ed, Ed D, PhD); elementary school counseling (M Ed); emotionally disturbed education (M Ed); general counseling (M Ed); higher education administration (Ed D, PhD); learning disabilities (M Ed); mentally retarded education (M Ed); reading (M Ed, Ed D, PhD); secondary administration (M Ed); secondary school counseling (M Ed). *Application deadline:* Applications are processed on a rolling basis. *Application fee:* $25 ($40 for international students). Electronic applications accepted. *Application Contact:* Clara Jackson, Graduate Admissions Counselor, 314-516-6946, Fax: 314-516-5310, E-mail: gradadm@umsl.edu. *Director of Graduate Studies,* Dr. Kathleen Haywood, 314-516-5483, Fax: 314-516-5227, E-mail: kathleen_haywood@umsl.edu.

School of Optometry Students: 167 full-time, 2 part-time; includes 24 minority (6 African Americans, 15 Asian Americans or Pacific Islanders, 1 Hispanic American, 2 Native Americans), 2 international. Average age 24. 255 applicants, 19% accepted, 44 enrolled. *Faculty:* 20 full-time (4 women), 10 part-time/adjunct (3 women). Expenses: Contact institution. *Financial support:* Fellowships with tuition reimbursements, research assistantships with partial tuition reimbursements, teaching assistantships, Federal Work-Study, institutionally sponsored loans, and tuition waivers (partial) available. Support available to part-time students. Financial award applicants required to submit FAFSA. In 2001, 42 first professional degrees, 1 master's awarded. Offers optometry (OD, MS, PhD); physiological optics (MS, PhD). *Application deadline:* For fall admission, 3/15. Applications are processed on a rolling basis. *Application fee:* $50. Electronic applications accepted. *Application Contact:* Dr. Edward S. Bennett, Director, Student Services, 314-516-6263, Fax: 514-516-6708, E-mail: optstudaff@umsl.edu. *Interim Dean,* Dr. Larry J. Davis, 514-516-5606, Fax: 314-516-6708, E-mail: opstudaff@umsl.edu.

See in-depth description on page 1211.

UNIVERSITY OF MOBILE, Mobile, AL 36663-0220

General Information Independent-religious, coed, comprehensive institution. *Enrollment:* 23 full-time matriculated graduate/professional students (18 women), 161 part-time matriculated graduate/professional students (115 women). *Enrollment by degree level:* 184 master's. *Graduate faculty:* 28 full-time (15 women), 36 part-time/adjunct (17 women). *Tuition:* Full-time $3,582; part-time $199 per semester hour. *Graduate housing:* Room and/or apartments available on a first-come, first-served basis to single students; on-campus housing not available to married students. Typical cost: $4,850 (including board). Housing application deadline: 8/15. *Student services:* Campus employment opportunities, career counseling, free psychological counseling, international student services, low-cost health insurance. *Library facilities:* J. L. Bedsole Library plus 2 others. *Online resources:* library catalog. *Collection:* 100,250 titles, 1,043 serial subscriptions, 2,222 audiovisual materials.

Computer facilities: 100 computers available on campus for general student use. A campuswide network can be accessed from off campus. Internet access is available. *Web address:* http://www.umobile.edu/.

General Application Contact: Dr. Kaye F. Brown, Dean, Graduate Programs and Director of Institutional Effectiveness, 251-442-2289, Fax: 251-442-2523, E-mail: kayebrown@free.umobile.edu.

GRADUATE UNITS

Graduate Programs Students: 23 full-time (18 women), 161 part-time (115 women); includes 55 minority (54 African Americans, 1 Hispanic American) Average age 36. *Faculty:* 28 full-time (15 women), 36 part-time/adjunct (17 women). Expenses: Contact institution. *Financial support:* Fellowships, Federal Work-Study available. Support available to part-time students. Financial award application deadline: 8/1. In 2001, 49 degrees awarded. *Degree program information:* Part-time and evening/weekend programs available. Offers biblical/theological studies (MA); business administration (MBA); marriage and family counseling (MA); nursing (MSN); teacher education (MA). *Application deadline:* For fall admission, 8/3 (priority date). Applications are processed on a rolling basis. *Application fee:* $40 ($50 for international students). *Dean,* Dr. Kaye F. Brown, 251-442-2289, Fax: 251-442-2523, E-mail: kayebrown@free.umobile.edu.

THE UNIVERSITY OF MONTANA–MISSOULA, Missoula, MT 59812-0002

General Information State-supported, coed, university. CGS member. *Enrollment:* 738 full-time matriculated graduate/professional students (376 women), 558 part-time matriculated graduate/professional students (275 women). *Enrollment by degree level:* 16 first professional, 1,050 master's, 272 doctoral. *Graduate faculty:* 539 full-time (180 women), 109 part-time/adjunct (51 women). Tuition, state resident: full-time $2,482; part-time $1,700 per year. Tuition, nonresident: full-time $7,372; part-time $5,000 per year. *Required fees:* $1,900. Tuition and fees vary according to degree level. *Graduate housing:* Rooms and/or apartments available on a first-come, first-served basis to single and married students. *Student services:* Campus employment opportunities, campus safety program, career counseling, child daycare facilities, disabled student services, exercise/wellness program, free psychological counseling, grant writing training, international student services, low-cost health insurance, multicultural affairs office, teacher training, writing training. *Library facilities:* Maureen and Mike Mansfield Library plus 2 others. *Online resources:* library catalog, web page, access to other libraries' catalogs. *Collection:* 570,287 titles, 6,248 serial subscriptions, 118,190 audiovisual materials. *Research affiliation:* Arthur Carhart National Wilderness Training Center (environmental), Nature Center at Ft. Missoula Museum (environmental), World Trade Center (business), Rocky Mountain National Laboratories (medical), Community Hospital Medical Center (medical), Aldo Leopold Wilderness Institute (forestry).

Computer facilities: 545 computers available on campus for general student use. A campuswide network can be accessed from student residence rooms and from off campus. Internet access and online class registration are available. *Web address:* http://www.umt.edu/.

General Application Contact: Dr. David A. Strobel, Dean of the Graduate School, 406-243-2572, Fax: 406-243-4593, E-mail: dstrobel@msp.umt.edu.

GRADUATE UNITS

Graduate School Students: 738 full-time (376 women), 558 part-time (275 women); includes 68 minority (5 African Americans, 16 Asian Americans or Pacific Islanders, 7 Hispanic Americans, 40 Native Americans), 100 international. 1,039 applicants, 54% accepted, 293 enrolled. *Faculty:* 539 full-time (180 women), 109 part-time/adjunct (51 women). Expenses: Contact institution. *Financial support:* In 2001–02, 40 fellowships (averaging $2,000 per year), 250 research assistantships, 250 teaching assistantships with full tuition reimbursements were awarded. Career-related internships or fieldwork, Federal Work-Study, scholarships/grants, and unspecified assistantships also available. Financial award application deadline: 3/1; financial award applicants required to submit FAFSA. In 2001, 396 master's, 27 doctorates awarded. *Degree program information:* Part-time programs available. Offers individual interdisciplinary programs (IIP) (PhD); interdisciplinary studies (MIS). *Application fee:* $45. *Application Contact:* Information Contact, E-mail: gradschl@mso.umt.edu. *Dean of the Graduate School,* Dr. David A. Strobel, 406-243-2572, Fax: 406-243-4593, E-mail: dstrobel@msp.umt.edu.

College of Arts and Sciences Students: 383 full-time (178 women), 225 part-time (130 women); includes 79 minority (4 African Americans, 30 Asian Americans or Pacific Islanders, 2 Hispanic Americans, 43 Native Americans) 662 applicants, 31% accepted. *Faculty:* 275 full-time (52 women), 15 part-time/adjunct (2 women). Expenses: Contact institution. *Financial support:* Fellowships, research assistantships, teaching assistantships with tuition reimbursements, career-related internships or fieldwork, Federal Work-Study, institutionally sponsored loans, scholarships/grants, tuition waivers (full and partial), and unspecified assistantships available. Support available to part-time students. Financial award application deadline: 3/1; financial award applicants required to submit FAFSA. In 2001, 179 master's, 22 doctorates, 9 other advanced degrees awarded. *Degree program information:* Part-time programs available. Offers animal behavior (PhD); arts and sciences (MA, MFA, MPA, MS, MST, PhD, Ed S); chemistry (MS, PhD); chemistry teaching (MST); clinical psychology (PhD); communication studies (MA); computer science (MS); creative writing (MFA); criminology (MA); cultural heritage (MA); developmental psychology (PhD); economics (MA); English literature (MA); English teaching (MA); environmental studies (MS); experimental psychology (PhD); fiction (MFA); French (MA); geography (MA); geology (MS, PhD); German (MA); history (MA); linguistics (MA); mathematics (MA, PhD); nonfiction (MFA); poetry (MFA); political science (MA); public administration (MPA); rural and environmental change (MA); school psychology (MA, Ed S); Spanish (MA); teaching ethics (MA). *Application fee:* $45. *Dean,* Dr. Thomas Storch, 406-243-2632.

Division of Biological Sciences Students: 48 full-time (22 women), 30 part-time (13 women); includes 2 minority (both Native Americans), 7 international. 72 applicants, 42% accepted, 21 enrolled. *Faculty:* 39 full-time (4 women). Expenses: Contact institution. *Financial support:* In 2001–02, 30 research assistantships with full tuition reimbursements (averaging $14,000 per year), 25 teaching assistantships with full tuition reimbursements (averaging $14,000 per year) were awarded. Federal Work-Study and unspecified assistantships also available. Financial award application deadline: 3/1; financial award applicants required to submit FAFSA. In 2001, 4 master's, 4 doctorates awarded. Offers biochemistry and microbiology (MS, PhD); biological sciences (MS, PhD); organismal biology and ecology (MS, PhD). *Application deadline:* For fall admission, 2/1 (priority date). Applications are processed on a rolling basis. *Application fee:* $45. *Application Contact:* Janean Clark, Graduate Programs Secretary, 406-243-5222, Fax: 406-243-4184, E-mail: jmclark@selway.umt.edu. *Associate Dean,* Dr. Don Christian, 406-243-5122.

School of Education Students: 76 full-time (47 women), 164 part-time (77 women); includes 17 minority (2 African Americans, 6 Asian Americans or Pacific Islanders, 1 Hispanic American, 8 Native Americans), 7 international. Average age 30. 61 applicants, 89% accepted. *Faculty:* 29 full-time (16 women), 4 part-time/adjunct (1 woman). Expenses: Contact institution. *Financial support:* Teaching assistantships with full tuition reimbursements, career-related internships or fieldwork, Federal Work-Study, and institutionally sponsored loans available. Financial award application deadline: 3/1; financial award applicants required to submit FAFSA. In 2001, 40 master's, 11 doctorates awarded. *Degree program information:* Part-time programs available. Offers counselor education (M Ed, MA, Ed D, Ed S); curriculum and instruction (M Ed, MA, Ed D); education (M Ed, MA, MS, Ed D, Ed S); exercise and performance psychology (MS); exercise science (MS); health promotion (MS); school administration and supervision (M Ed, Ed D, Ed S). *Application fee:* $45. *Dean,* Dr. Don Robson, 406-243-4911.

School of Fine Arts Students: 48 full-time (26 women), 6 part-time (4 women), 3 international. 23 applicants, 100% accepted, 14 enrolled. *Faculty:* 48 full-time (21 women). Expenses: Contact institution. *Financial support:* In 2001–02, 11 teaching assistantships with full tuition reimbursements (averaging $8,665 per year) were awarded; Federal Work-Study, tuition waivers (full), and unspecified assistantships also available. Financial award application deadline: 3/1; financial award applicants required to submit FAFSA. In 2001, 25 degrees awarded. Offers fine arts (MA, MFA); music (MM). *Application deadline:* Applications are processed on a rolling basis. *Application fee:* $45. *Dean,* Dr. Shirley Howell, 406-243-4970.

School of Forestry Students: 81 full-time (31 women), 51 part-time (18 women); includes 3 minority (all African Americans), 19 international. 63 applicants, 94% accepted. *Faculty:* 34 full-time (4 women). Expenses: Contact institution. *Financial support:* In 2001–02, 25 research assistantships with tuition reimbursements (averaging $9,400 per year), 12 teaching assistantships with full tuition reimbursements (averaging $9,400 per year) were awarded. Fellowships, career-related internships or fieldwork, Federal Work-Study, and institutionally sponsored loans also available. Financial award application deadline: 3/1; financial award applicants required to submit FAFSA. In 2001, 22 master's, 5 doctorates awarded. Offers ecosystem management (MEM); fish and wildlife biology (PhD); forestry (MEM, MS, PhD); recreation management (MS); resource conservation (MS); wildlife biology (MS). *Application deadline:* For fall admission, 1/31; for spring admission, 8/31. Applications are processed on a rolling basis. *Application fee:* $45. *Application Contact:* Dr. Don Potts, Associate Dean, 406-243-5521, Fax: 406-243-4845, E-mail: dpotts@forestry.unit.edu. *Dean,* Dr. Perry Brown, 406-243-5521, Fax: 406-243-4845, E-mail: pbrown@forestry.umt.edu.

School of Journalism Offers journalism (MA).

School of Pharmacy and Allied Health Sciences Students: 78 full-time (45 women), 1 part-time; includes 8 minority (4 Asian Americans or Pacific Islanders, 2 Hispanic Americans, 2 Native Americans) Average age 25. 237 applicants, 17% accepted, 41 enrolled. *Faculty:* 27 full-time (5 women), 3 part-time/adjunct (2 women). Expenses: Contact institution. *Financial support:* In 2001–02, 4 teaching assistantships with full and partial tuition reimbursements (averaging $17,000 per year) were awarded; career-related internships or fieldwork, Federal Work-Study, institutionally sponsored loans, scholarships/grants, and tuition waivers (full and partial) also available. Financial award applicants required to submit FAFSA. In 2001, 33 master's, 1 doctorate awarded. Offers pharmaceutical sciences (MS); pharmacology (PhD); pharmacy and allied health sciences (MS, DPT, PhD); physical therapy (MS, DPT). *Application deadline:* For fall admission, 3/1; for winter admission, 1/15 (priority date). Applications are processed on a rolling basis. Electronic applications accepted. *Application Contact:* Dr. Vernon R. Grund, Chair, Pharmaceutical Sciences, 406-243-4765, Fax: 406-243-4353, E-mail: grund@selway.umt.edu. *Dean,* Dr. David Forbes, 406-243-4621.

School of Business Administration *Degree program information:* Part-time and evening/weekend programs available. Postbaccalaureate distance learning degree programs offered. Offers accounting and finance (M Acct); business (MBA); business administration (M Acct, MBA).

School of Law Students: 253 full-time (106 women); includes 22 minority (1 African American, 3 Asian Americans or Pacific Islanders, 6 Hispanic Americans, 12 Native Americans), 4 international. Average age 28. 409 applicants, 56% accepted. *Faculty:* 15 full-time (7 women), 14 part-time/adjunct (6 women). Expenses: Contact institution. *Financial support:* In 2001–02, 220 students received support, including 22 research assistantships, 16 teaching assistantships with partial tuition reimbursements available (averaging $2,640 per year); career-related internships or fieldwork, Federal Work-Study, institutionally sponsored loans, scholarships/grants, and tuition waivers (partial) also available. Financial award application deadline: 3/1; financial award applicants required to submit FAFSA. In 2001, 69 degrees awarded. Offers law (JD). *Application deadline:* For fall admission, 3/15. Applications are processed on a rolling basis. *Application fee:* $60. *Application Contact:* Heidi Fanslow, Admissions Office, 406-243-2698, Fax: 406-243-2576, E-mail: hid314@selway.umt.edu. *Dean,* E. Edwin Eck, 406-243-4311, Fax: 406-243-2576, E-mail: eck@selway.umt.edu.

See in-depth description on page 1213.

UNIVERSITY OF MONTEVALLO, Montevallo, AL 35115

General Information State-supported, coed, comprehensive institution. *Graduate housing:* Room and/or apartments available to single students; on-campus housing not available to married students.

GRADUATE UNITS

College of Arts and Sciences *Degree program information:* Part-time and evening/weekend programs available. Offers arts and sciences (MA, MS); English (MA); speech pathology and audiology (MS).

College of Education *Degree program information:* Part-time and evening/weekend programs available. Offers early childhood education (M Ed); education (M Ed, Ed S); educational administration (M Ed, Ed S); elementary education (M Ed); guidance and counseling (M Ed); secondary education (M Ed, Ed S); teacher leader (Ed S).

College of Fine Arts *Degree program information:* Part-time programs available. Offers fine arts (MM); music (MM).

UNIVERSITY OF NEBRASKA AT KEARNEY, Kearney, NE 68849-0001

General Information State-supported, coed, comprehensive institution. CGS member. *Enrollment:* 133 full-time matriculated graduate/professional students (99 women), 467 part-time matriculated graduate/professional students (306 women). *Enrollment by degree level:* 524 master's, 76 other advanced degrees. *Graduate faculty:* 96 full-time (38 women). Tuition, state resident: part-time $102 per hour. Tuition, nonresident: part-time $201 per hour. *Required fees:* $12 per hour. *Graduate housing:* Rooms and/or apartments available on a first-come, first-served basis to single and married students. *Student services:* Campus employment opportunities, campus safety program, career counseling, disabled student services, exercise/wellness program, free psychological counseling, grant writing training, international student services, low-cost health insurance, multicultural affairs office, teacher training, writing training. *Library facilities:* Calvin T. Ryan Library. *Online resources:* library catalog, web page, access to other libraries' catalogs. *Collection:* 320,915 titles, 1,657 serial subscriptions, 75,881 audiovisual materials.

Computer facilities: 277 computers available on campus for general student use. A campuswide network can be accessed from student residence rooms and from off campus. Internet access and online class registration, online grade reports are available. *Web address:* http://www.unk.edu/.

General Application Contact: Dr. Kenneth Nikels, Graduate Dean, 308-865-8500, Fax: 308-865-8837, E-mail: nikelsk@unk.edu.

GRADUATE UNITS

College of Graduate Study Students: 133 full-time (99 women), 467 part-time (306 women); includes 10 minority (2 African Americans, 1 Asian American or Pacific Islander, 5 Hispanic Americans, 2 Native Americans), 25 international. 234 applicants, 94% accepted. *Faculty:* 96 full-time (38 women). Expenses: Contact institution. *Financial support:* In 2001–02, 29 research assistantships with full tuition reimbursements (averaging $5,694 per year), 36 teaching assistantships with full tuition reimbursements (averaging $5,694 per year) were awarded. Career-related internships or fieldwork, scholarships/grants, and unspecified assistantships also available. Support available to part-time students. Financial award application deadline: 3/1; financial award applicants required to submit FAFSA. In 2001, 200 master's, 18 other advanced degrees awarded. *Degree program information:* Part-time and evening/weekend programs available. *Application fee:* $35. *Application Contact:* Linda Johnson, Coordinator of Graduate Admissions, 308-865-8841, Fax: 308-865-8837, E-mail: johnsonli@unk.edu. *Dean,* Dr. Kenneth Nikels, 308-865-8500, Fax: 308-865-8837, E-mail: nikelsk@unk.edu.

College of Business and Technology Students: 18 full-time (9 women), 37 part-time (18 women), 11 international. 28 applicants, 82% accepted. *Faculty:* 23 full-time (6 women). Expenses: Contact institution. *Financial support:* In 2001–02, 8 research assistantships with full tuition reimbursements (averaging $5,694 per year) were awarded; career-related internships or fieldwork and scholarships/grants also available. Support available to part-time students. Financial award application deadline: 3/1; financial award applicants required to submit FAFSA. In 2001, 21 degrees awarded. *Degree program information:* Part-time and evening/weekend programs available. Offers business administration (MBA); business and technology (MBA). *Application deadline:* For fall admission, 8/1 (priority date); for spring admission, 12/15 (priority date). Applications are processed on a rolling basis. *Application fee:* $35. Electronic applications accepted. *Dean,* Dr. Kathleen Smith, 308-865-8342, E-mail: smithk@unk.edu.

College of Education Students: 101 full-time (85 women), 396 part-time (267 women); includes 10 minority (2 African Americans, 1 Asian American or Pacific Islander, 5 Hispanic Americans, 2 Native Americans), 12 international. 181 applicants, 95% accepted. *Faculty:* 28 full-time (14 women). Expenses: Contact institution. *Financial support:* In 2001–02, 19 research assistantships with full tuition reimbursements (averaging $5,694 per year), 17 teaching assistantships with full tuition reimbursements (averaging $5,694 per year) were awarded. Career-related internships or fieldwork, scholarships/grants, and unspecified assistantships also available. Support available to part-time students. Financial award application deadline: 3/1; financial award applicants required to submit FAFSA. In 2001, 163 master's, 18 other advanced degrees awarded. *Degree program information:* Part-time and evening/weekend programs available. Offers adapted physical education (MA Ed); counseling (MS Ed, Ed S); curriculum and instruction (MS Ed); early childhood education (MA Ed); early childhood special education (MA Ed); education (MA Ed, MS Ed, Ed S); education of behaviorally disordered (MA Ed); education of the gifted and talented (MA Ed); educational administration (MA Ed, Ed S); elementary education (MA Ed); exercise science (MA Ed); instructional technology (MS Ed); master teacher (MA Ed); middle school education (MA Ed); mild/moderate handicapped (MA Ed); reading education (MA Ed); school psychology (Ed S); special education (MA Ed); specific learning disabilities (MA Ed); speech pathology (MS Ed); supervisor of educational media (MA Ed). *Application deadline:* Applications are processed on a rolling basis. *Application fee:* $35. Electronic applications accepted. *Dean,* Dr. Marilyn Hadley, 308-865-8502, Fax: 308-865-8099, E-mail: hadleym@unk.edu.

College of Fine Arts and Humanities Students: 5 full-time (2 women), 21 part-time (15 women), 2 international. 14 applicants, 100% accepted. *Faculty:* 33 full-time (13 women). Expenses: Contact institution. *Financial support:* In 2001–02, 11 teaching assistantships with full tuition reimbursements (averaging $5,694 per year) were awarded; career-related internships or fieldwork also available. Support available to part-time students. Financial award application deadline: 3/1; financial award applicants required to submit FAFSA. In 2001, 11 degrees awarded. *Degree program information:* Part-time and evening/weekend programs available. Offers art education (MA Ed); English (MA); fine arts and humanities (MA, MA Ed); French (MA Ed); German (MA Ed); music education (MA Ed); Spanish (MA Ed). *Application deadline:* For fall admission, 8/1 (priority date); for spring admission, 12/15. Applications are processed on a rolling basis. *Application fee:* $35. Electronic applications accepted. *Dean,* Dr. Rodney Miller, 308-865-8521, E-mail: millerre@unk.edu.

College of Natural and Social Sciences Students: 9 full-time (3 women), 13 part-time (6 women). 11 applicants, 100% accepted. *Faculty:* 15 full-time (6 women). Expenses: Contact institution. *Financial support:* In 2001–02, 2 research assistantships with full tuition reimbursements (averaging $5,694 per year), 8 teaching assistantships with full tuition reimbursements (averaging $5,694 per year) were awarded. Career-related internships or fieldwork and scholarships/grants also available. Support available to part-time students. Financial award application deadline: 3/1; financial award applicants required to submit FAFSA. In 2001, 5 degrees awarded. *Degree program information:* Part-time and evening/weekend programs available. Offers biology (MS); history (MA); natural and social sciences (MA, MS, MS Ed); science education (MS Ed). *Application deadline:* For fall admission, 8/1 (priority date); for spring admission, 12/15 (priority date). Applications are processed on a rolling basis. *Application fee:* $35. Electronic applications accepted. *Dean,* Dr. Michael Schuyler, 308-865-8518.

Announcement: The University of Nebraska at Kearney is a regional, comprehensive university that places special emphasis on recruiting a diverse group of talented students. Graduate assistantships and degree programs are available in art, biology, business administration (MBA), community counseling, curriculum and instruction, educational administration, elementary education, English, exercise science, history, instructional technology, modern languages, physical education, school counseling, school psychology, science teaching, special education, and speech/language pathology. Financial support is available for student research and for travel to professional conferences. Contact the University for further information (telephone: 800-717-7881, toll-free; e-mail: gradstudies@unk.edu; WWW: http://www.unk.edu/acad/gradstudies).

UNIVERSITY OF NEBRASKA AT OMAHA, Omaha, NE 68182

General Information State-supported, coed, university. CGS member. *Enrollment:* 642 full-time matriculated graduate/professional students (373 women), 1,826 part-time matriculated graduate/professional students (1,151 women). *Enrollment by degree level:* 2,366 master's, 87 doctoral, 15 other advanced degrees. *Graduate faculty:* 288 full-time (85 women). Tuition, state resident: part-time $116 per credit hour. Tuition, nonresident: part-time $291 per credit hour. *Required fees:* $13 per credit hour. $4 per semester. One-time fee: $52 part-time. *Graduate housing:* Room and/or apartments available on a first-come, first-served basis to single students; on-campus housing not available to married students. *Student services:* Campus employment opportunities, campus safety program, career counseling, child daycare facilities, disabled student services, exercise/wellness program, free psychological counseling, grant writing training, international student services, low-cost health insurance, multicultural affairs office, teacher training, writing training. *Library facilities:* University Library. *Online resources:* web page. *Collection:* 750,000 titles, 3,200 serial subscriptions, 7,000 audiovisual materials.

Computer facilities: 64 computers available on campus for general student use. A campuswide network can be accessed from student residence rooms and from off campus. Internet access and online class registration are available. *Web address:* http://www.unomaha.edu/.

General Application Contact: Penny Harmoney, Manager, Graduate Studies, 402-554-2341, Fax: 402-554-3143, E-mail: graduate@unomaha.edu.

GRADUATE UNITS

Graduate Studies and Research Students: 642 full-time (373 women), 1,826 part-time (1,151 women); includes 177 minority (100 African Americans, 36 Asian Americans or Pacific Islanders, 34 Hispanic Americans, 7 Native Americans), 243 international. Average age 32. 1,285 applicants, 68% accepted, 702 enrolled. *Faculty:* 288 full-time (85 women). Expenses: Contact institution. *Financial support:* In 2001–02, 1,039 students received support; fellowships, research assistantships, teaching assistantships, career-related internships or fieldwork, Federal Work-Study, institutionally sponsored loans, tuition waivers (partial), and unspecified assistantships available. Support available to part-time students. Financial award application deadline: 3/1; financial award applicants required to submit FAFSA. In 2001, 646 master's, 14 doctorates, 13 other advanced degrees awarded. *Degree program information:* Part-time and evening/weekend programs available. Postbaccalaureate distance learning degree programs offered (no on-campus study). *Application deadline:* Applications are processed on a rolling basis. *Application fee:* $35. Electronic applications accepted. *Application Contact:* Penny Harmoney, Manager, Graduate Studies, 402-554-2341, Fax: 402-554-3143, E-mail: graduate@unomaha.edu. *Vice Chancellor of Academic Affairs and Dean for Graduate Studies,* Dr. Derek Hodgson, 402-554-2341.

College of Arts and Sciences Students: 83 full-time (50 women), 223 part-time (133 women); includes 19 minority (8 African Americans, 4 Asian Americans or Pacific Islanders, 6 Hispanic Americans, 1 Native American), 13 international. Average age 32. 224 applicants, 71% accepted, 124 enrolled. *Faculty:* 117 full-time (32 women). Expenses: Contact institution. *Financial support:* In 2001–02, 188 students received support; fellowships, research assistantships, teaching assistantships, career-related internships or fieldwork, Federal Work-Study, institutionally sponsored loans, scholarships/grants, tuition waivers (partial), and unspecified assistantships available. Support available to part-time students. Financial award application deadline: 3/1; financial award applicants required to submit FAFSA. In 2001, 72 master's, 4 other advanced degrees awarded. *Degree program information:* Part-time programs available. Offers arts and sciences (MA, MAT, MS, PhD, Certificate, Ed S);

University of Nebraska at Omaha (continued)

biology (MA, MS); communication (MA); developmental psychobiology (PhD); English (MA, Certificate); experimental child psychology (PhD); geographic information science (Certificate); geography (MA); history (MA); industrial/organizational psychology (MS, PhD); mathematics (MA, MAT, MS); political science (MS); psychology (MA); school psychology (MS, Ed S); sociology (MA). *Application deadline:* For fall admission, 3/1 (priority date); for spring admission, 10/1 (priority date). Applications are processed on a rolling basis. *Application fee:* $35. Electronic applications accepted. *Dean,* Dr. Shelton Hendricks, 402-554-2338.

College of Business Administration Students: 136 full-time (59 women), 325 part-time (139 women); includes 18 minority (8 African Americans, 8 Asian Americans or Pacific Islanders, 2 Hispanic Americans), 53 international. Average age 31. 277 applicants, 50% accepted, 122 enrolled. *Faculty:* 38 full-time (6 women). Expenses: Contact institution. *Financial support:* In 2001–02, 144 students received support; fellowships, research assistantships, career-related internships or fieldwork, Federal Work-Study, institutionally sponsored loans, scholarships/grants, tuition waivers (partial), and unspecified assistantships available. Support available to part-time students. Financial award application deadline: 3/1; financial award applicants required to submit FAFSA. In 2001, 134 degrees awarded. *Degree program information:* Part-time and evening/weekend programs available. Offers accounting (M Acc); business administration (EMBA, M Acc, MA, MBA, MS); economics (MA, MS). *Application deadline:* For fall admission, 7/1 (priority date); for spring admission, 12/1 (priority date). Applications are processed on a rolling basis. *Application fee:* $35. Electronic applications accepted. *Application Contact:* Lex Kaczmarek, Director, 402-554-2303. *Dean,* Dr. Stan Hille, 402-554-3458.

College of Education Students: 131 full-time (94 women), 747 part-time (575 women); includes 61 minority (41 African Americans, 8 Asian Americans or Pacific Islanders, 12 Hispanic Americans), 13 international. Average age 33. 305 applicants, 71% accepted, 180 enrolled. *Faculty:* 52 full-time (21 women). Expenses: Contact institution. *Financial support:* In 2001–02, 323 students received support; fellowships, research assistantships, teaching assistantships, career-related internships or fieldwork, Federal Work-Study, institutionally sponsored loans, scholarships/grants, tuition waivers (full), and unspecified assistantships available. Support available to part-time students. Financial award application deadline: 3/1; financial award applicants required to submit FAFSA. In 2001, 253 master's, 10 doctorates, 13 other advanced degrees awarded. *Degree program information:* Part-time and evening/weekend programs available. Offers community counseling (MA, MS); counseling gerontology (MA, MS); education (MA, MS, Ed D, Certificate, Ed S); educational administration and supervision (MS, Ed D, Ed S); elementary education (MA, MS); health, physical education, and recreation (MA, MS); instruction in urban schools (Certificate); instructional technology (Certificate); reading education (MS); school counseling-elementary (MA, MS); school counseling-secondary (MA, MS); secondary education (MA, MS); special education (MS); speech-language pathology (MA, MS); student affairs practice in higher education (MA, MS). *Application deadline:* For fall admission, 3/1 (priority date); for spring admission, 10/1 (priority date). Applications are processed on a rolling basis. *Application fee:* $35. *Dean,* Dr. John Christensen, 402-554-2719.

College of Fine Arts Students: 15 full-time (11 women), 18 part-time (11 women); includes 4 minority (3 African Americans, 1 Native American), 4 international. Average age 34. 20 applicants, 80% accepted, 14 enrolled. *Faculty:* 14 full-time (5 women). Expenses: Contact institution. *Financial support:* In 2001–02, 18 students received support, including 9 research assistantships; fellowships, career-related internships or fieldwork, Federal Work-Study, institutionally sponsored loans, traineeships, tuition waivers (full), and unspecified assistantships also available. Support available to part-time students. Financial award application deadline: 3/1; financial award applicants required to submit FAFSA. In 2001, 11 degrees awarded. *Degree program information:* Part-time and evening/weekend programs available. Offers fine arts (MA, MM); music (MM); theatre (MA). *Application deadline:* For fall admission, 7/1 (priority date); for spring admission, 12/1 (priority date). Applications are processed on a rolling basis. *Application fee:* $35. Electronic applications accepted. *Dean,* Dr. Karen White, 402-554-2231.

College of Information Science and Technology Students: 129 full-time (42 women), 184 part-time (62 women); includes 24 minority (8 African Americans, 12 Asian Americans or Pacific Islanders, 3 Hispanic Americans, 1 Native American), 146 international. Average age 34. 205 applicants, 72% accepted, 92 enrolled. *Faculty:* 20 full-time (3 women). Expenses: Contact institution. *Financial support:* In 2001–02, 118 students received support; fellowships, research assistantships, teaching assistantships, career-related internships or fieldwork, Federal Work-Study, institutionally sponsored loans, scholarships/grants, tuition waivers (full), and unspecified assistantships available. In 2001, 50 degrees awarded. *Degree program information:* Part-time and evening/weekend programs available. Offers computer science (MA, MS); information science and technology (MA, MS); management information systems (MS). *Application deadline:* For fall admission, 7/1 (priority date); for spring admission, 12/1 (priority date). Applications are processed on a rolling basis. *Application fee:* $35. Electronic applications accepted. *Dean,* Dr. David Hinton, 402-554-2276.

College of Public Affairs and Community Service Students: 148 full-time (117 women), 329 part-time (231 women); includes 51 minority (32 African Americans, 4 Asian Americans or Pacific Islanders, 11 Hispanic Americans, 4 Native Americans), 14 international. Average age 32. 304 applicants, 65% accepted, 170 enrolled. *Faculty:* 47 full-time (18 women). Expenses: Contact institution. *Financial support:* In 2001–02, 248 students received support, including 28 research assistantships; fellowships, teaching assistantships, career-related internships or fieldwork, Federal Work-Study, institutionally sponsored loans, scholarships/grants, tuition waivers (partial), and unspecified assistantships also available. Support available to part-time students. Financial award application deadline: 3/1; financial award applicants required to submit FAFSA. In 2001, 120 master's, 4 doctorates awarded. *Degree program information:* Part-time and evening/weekend programs available. Postbaccalaureate distance learning degree programs offered (no on-campus study). Offers criminal justice (MA, MS, PhD); gerontology (MA, Certificate); public administration (MPA, PhD); public affairs and community service (MA, MPA, MS, MSW, PhD, Certificate); social work (MSW). *Application deadline:* Applications are processed on a rolling basis. *Application fee:* $35. Electronic applications accepted. *Chairperson,* Dr. Burton J. Reed, 402-554-2625.

UNIVERSITY OF NEBRASKA–LINCOLN, Lincoln, NE 68588

General Information State-supported, coed, university. CGS member. *Enrollment:* 2,351 full-time matriculated graduate/professional students, 1,355 part-time matriculated graduate/professional students. *Enrollment by degree level:* 470 first professional, 1,790 master's, 1,501 doctoral, 24 other advanced degrees. *Graduate faculty:* 1,288. Tuition, state resident: full-time $2,412; part-time $134 per credit. Tuition, nonresident: full-time $6,223; part-time $346 per credit. Tuition and fees vary according to course load. *Graduate housing:* Rooms and/or apartments available on a first-come, first-served basis to single students and available to married students. Typical cost: $5,365 (including board) for single students; $4,800 per year for married students. Housing application deadline: 7/1. *Student services:* Campus employment opportunities, campus safety program, career counseling, child daycare facilities, disabled student services, exercise/wellness program, free psychological counseling, grant writing training, international student services, low-cost health insurance, multicultural affairs office, teacher training, writing training. *Library facilities:* Love Memorial Library plus 10 others. *Online resources:* library catalog, web page, access to other libraries' catalogs. *Collection:* 1.2 million titles, 20,234 serial subscriptions, 46,995 audiovisual materials. *Research affiliation:* U.S. Meat Animal Research Center.

Computer facilities: 500 computers available on campus for general student use. A campuswide network can be accessed from student residence rooms and from off campus. Internet access is available. *Web address:* http://www.unl.edu/.

General Application Contact: Dr. Prem Paul, Vice Chancellor for Research and Dean of Graduate Studies, 402-472-2875, Fax: 402-472-0589, E-mail: grad_admissions@unl.edu.

GRADUATE UNITS

College of Law Students: 392 full-time, 7 part-time; includes 27 minority (6 African Americans, 11 Asian Americans or Pacific Islanders, 10 Hispanic Americans), 4 international. 551 applicants, 61% accepted, 152 enrolled. *Faculty:* 22. Expenses: Contact institution. *Financial support:* In 2001–02, 1 fellowship, 3 research assistantships were awarded. Teaching assistantships, career-related internships or fieldwork, Federal Work-Study, institutionally sponsored loans, and tuition waivers (full) also available. In 2001, 122 degrees awarded. Offers law (JD, MLS); legal studies (MLS). *Application deadline:* For fall admission, 3/1. *Application fee:* $35. Electronic applications accepted. *Application Contact:* Glenda Pierce, Assistant Dean, 402-472-2161, Fax: 402-472-5185. *Dean,* Steven Willborn, 402-472-2161.

Graduate College Students: 1,959 full-time (954 women), 1,348 part-time (712 women); includes 226 minority (81 African Americans, 59 Asian Americans or Pacific Islanders, 69 Hispanic Americans, 17 Native Americans), 867 international. Average age 33. 3,017 applicants, 36% accepted, 609 enrolled. *Faculty:* 1,266. Expenses: Contact institution. *Financial support:* In 2001–02, 128 fellowships with full tuition reimbursements, 649 research assistantships with full tuition reimbursements, 472 teaching assistantships were awarded. Career-related internships or fieldwork, Federal Work-Study, health care benefits, and unspecified assistantships also available. Support available to part-time students. In 2001, 683 master's, 207 doctorates, 10 other advanced degrees awarded. *Degree program information:* Part-time and evening/weekend programs available. Postbaccalaureate distance learning degree programs offered. Offers museum studies (MA, MS); survey research and methodology (MS); toxicology (MS, PhD). *Application fee:* $35. Electronic applications accepted. *Application Contact:* Ginny Gross, Director of Graduate Admissions, 402-472-2878, Fax: 402-472-0589, E-mail: grad_admissions@unl.edu. *Vice Chancellor for Research and Dean of Graduate Studies,* Dr. Prem Paul, 402-472-2875, Fax: 402-472-0589, E-mail: grad_admissions@unl.edu.

College of Agricultural Sciences and Natural Resources Students: 435 (196 women); includes 17 minority (6 African Americans, 3 Asian Americans or Pacific Islanders, 7 Hispanic Americans, 1 Native American) 175 international. Average age 31. 321 applicants, 29% accepted, 63 enrolled. *Faculty:* 333. Expenses: Contact institution. *Financial support:* In 2001–02, 11 fellowships, 160 research assistantships, 27 teaching assistantships were awarded. Career-related internships or fieldwork, Federal Work-Study, health care benefits, and unspecified assistantships also available. Support available to part-time students. Financial award application deadline: 2/15. In 2001, 81 master's, 35 doctorates awarded. Offers agricultural economics (MS, PhD); agricultural leadership, education and communication (MS); agricultural sciences and natural resources (M Ag, MA, MS, PhD); agriculture (M Ag); agronomy (MS, PhD); animal science (MS, PhD); biochemistry (MS, PhD); biometry (MS); entomology (MS, PhD); food science and technology (MS, PhD); horticulture (MS, PhD); mechanized systems management (MS); natural resource sciences (MS); nutrition (MS, PhD); veterinary and biomedical sciences (MS, PhD). *Application fee:* $35. Electronic applications accepted. *Interim Dean,* Dr. Steven S. Waller, 402-472-2201.

College of Architecture Students: 130 (45 women); includes 10 minority (4 African Americans, 3 Asian Americans or Pacific Islanders, 1 Hispanic American, 2 Native Americans) 16 international. Average age 29. *Faculty:* 37. Expenses: Contact institution. *Financial support:* In 2001–02, 9 fellowships, 12 research assistantships, 18 teaching assistantships were awarded. Federal Work-Study also available. Support available to part-time students. Financial award application deadline: 2/15. In 2001, 35 degrees awarded. Offers architecture (M Arch, MS); community and regional planning (MCRP). *Application deadline:* For fall admission, 2/1. *Application fee:* $35. Electronic applications accepted. *Dean,* Wayne Drummond, 402-472-3592, Fax: 402-472-3806.

College of Arts and Sciences Students: 978 (460 women); includes 83 minority (22 African Americans, 20 Asian Americans or Pacific Islanders, 35 Hispanic Americans, 6 Native Americans) 298 international. Average age 32. 1,074 applicants, 34% accepted, 199 enrolled. *Faculty:* 405. Expenses: Contact institution. *Financial support:* In 2001–02, 36 fellowships, 199 research assistantships, 283 teaching assistantships were awarded. Federal Work-Study, health care benefits, and unspecified assistantships also available. Support available to part-time students. In 2001, 136 master's, 87 doctorates awarded. Offers analytical chemistry (PhD); anthropology (MA); arts and sciences (M Sc T, MA, MAT, MS, PhD); astronomy (MS, PhD); biological sciences (MA, MS, PhD); chemistry (MS); classics and religious studies (MA); communication studies and theatre arts (PhD); communications studies (MA); computer engineering (PhD); computer science (MS, PhD); English (MA, PhD); French (MA, PhD); geography (MA, PhD); geosciences (MS, PhD); German (MA, PhD); history (MA, PhD); inorganic chemistry (PhD); mathematics and statistics (M Sc T, MA, MAT, MS, PhD); organic chemistry (PhD); philosophy (MA, PhD); physical chemistry (PhD); physics (MS, PhD); political science (MA, PhD); psychology (MA, PhD); sociology (MA, PhD); Spanish (MA, PhD). *Application fee:* $35. Electronic applications accepted. *Dean,* Dr. Richard Hoffman, 402-472-2891, Fax: 402-472-1123.

College of Business Administration Students: 315 (109 women); includes 6 minority (2 African Americans, 2 Asian Americans or Pacific Islanders, 1 Hispanic American, 1 Native American) 98 international. Average age 32. 275 applicants, 34% accepted, 56 enrolled. *Faculty:* 64. Expenses: Contact institution. *Financial support:* In 2001–02, 30 fellowships, 38 research assistantships, 46 teaching assistantships were awarded. Federal Work-Study and health care benefits also available. Support available to part-time students. Financial award application deadline: 2/15. In 2001, 121 master's, 14 doctorates awarded. *Degree program information:* Part-time and evening/weekend programs available. Offers accountancy (PhD); actuarial science (MS); business (MA, MBA, PhD); business administration (MA, MBA, MPA, MS, PhD); economics (MA, PhD); finance (MA, PhD); management (MA, PhD); marketing (MA, PhD). *Application fee:* $35. Electronic applications accepted. *Dean,* Cynthia H. Milligan, 402-472-9500, Fax: 402-472-5180, E-mail: gradadv@cbamail.unl.edu.

College of Engineering and Technology Students: 315 (63 women); includes 14 minority (3 African Americans, 7 Asian Americans or Pacific Islanders, 4 Hispanic Americans) 196 international. Average age 30. 736 applicants, 29% accepted, 75 enrolled. *Faculty:* 143. Expenses: Contact institution. *Financial support:* In 2001–02, 3 fellowships with full tuition reimbursements, 146 research assistantships with full tuition reimbursements, 30 teaching assistantships were awarded. Federal Work-Study also available. Support available to part-time students. Financial award application deadline: 2/15. In 2001, 83 master's, 10 doctorates awarded. Offers agricultural and biological systems engineering (MS); agricultural science (MS); chemical engineering (MS); civil engineering (MS); electrical engineering (MS); engineering (PhD); engineering and technology (M Eng, MS, PhD); engineering mechanics (MS); environmental engineering (MS); industrial and management systems engineering (MS); manufacturing systems engineering (MS); mechanical engineering (MS). *Application fee:* $35. Electronic applications accepted. *Dean,* Dr. David H. Allen, 402-472-3181, Fax: 402-472-7792.

College of Fine and Performing Arts Students: 130 (71 women); includes 8 minority (3 African Americans, 2 Asian Americans or Pacific Islanders, 3 Hispanic Americans) 7 international. Average age 30. 129 applicants, 42% accepted, 37 enrolled. *Faculty:* 85. Expenses: Contact institution. *Financial support:* In 2001–02, 9 fellowships, 9 research assistantships, 27 teaching assistantships were awarded. Federal Work-Study and health care benefits also available. Support available to part-time students. Financial award application deadline: 2/15. In 2001, 24 master's, 2 doctorates awarded. Offers art and art history (MFA); fine and performing arts (MFA, MM, DMA); music (MM, DMA); theatre arts (MFA). *Application fee:* $35. Electronic applications accepted. *Dean,* Dr. Giacomo Oliva, 402-472-9339, Fax: 402-472-9353.

College of Human Resources and Family Sciences Students: 99 (91 women); includes 8 minority (4 African Americans, 3 Asian Americans or Pacific Islanders, 1 Hispanic American) 11 international. Average age 34. 63 applicants, 38% accepted, 12 enrolled. *Faculty:* 49. Expenses: Contact institution. *Financial support:* In 2001–02, 6 fellowships, 17 research assistantships, 7 teaching assistantships were awarded. Federal Work-Study, health care benefits, and unspecified assistantships also available. Financial award application deadline: 2/15. In 2001, 16 degrees awarded. Offers family and consumer sciences (MS); human resources and family sciences (PhD); nutritional science and dietetics (MS); textiles, clothing and design (MA, MS). *Application fee:* $35. Electronic applications accepted. *Dean,* Dr. Marjorie J. Kostelnik, 402-472-2911.

College of Journalism and Mass Communications Students: 58 (36 women); includes 4 minority (2 African Americans, 1 Asian American or Pacific Islander, 1 Hispanic American) 5 international. Average age 33. 33 applicants, 55% accepted, 15 enrolled. *Faculty:*

28. Expenses: Contact institution. *Financial support:* In 2001–02, 2 fellowships, 8 research assistantships were awarded. Teaching assistantships, Federal Work-Study, health care benefits, and unspecified assistantships also available. Financial award application deadline: 2/15. In 2001, 16 degrees awarded. Postbaccalaureate distance learning degree programs offered (no on-campus study). Offers journalism and mass communications (MA). *Application deadline:* For fall admission, 3/1 (priority date). Applications are processed on a rolling basis. *Application fee:* $35. Electronic applications accepted. *Dean*, Dr. Will Norton, 402-472-3041.

Teachers College Students: 852 (569 women); includes 76 minority (35 African Americans, 19 Asian Americans or Pacific Islanders, 16 Hispanic Americans, 6 Native Americans) 54 international. Average age 36. 297 applicants, 50% accepted, 114 enrolled. *Faculty:* 106. Expenses: Contact institution. *Financial support:* In 2001–02, 21 fellowships, 55 research assistantships, 33 teaching assistantships were awarded. Federal Work-Study, health care benefits, and unspecified assistantships also available. Support available to part-time students. Financial award application deadline: 2/15. In 2001, 161 master's, 59 doctorates, 10 other advanced degrees awarded. Offers administration, curriculum and instruction (Ed D, PhD); community and human resources (Ed D, PhD); curriculum and instruction (M Ed, MA, MST, Ed S); education (M Ed, MA, MPE, MS, MST, Ed D, PhD, Certificate, Ed S); educational administration (M Ed, MA, Ed D, Certificate); educational psychology (MA, Ed S); health, physical education, and recreation (M Ed, MPE); psychological and cultural studies (Ed D, PhD); special education (M Ed, MA); special education and communication disorders (Ed S); speech-language pathology and audiology (MS). *Application fee:* $35. Electronic applications accepted. *Dean*, Dr. James P. O'Hanlon, 402-472-5400.

See in-depth description on page 1215.

UNIVERSITY OF NEBRASKA MEDICAL CENTER, Omaha, NE 68198

General Information State-supported, coed, upper-level institution. CGS member. *Enrollment:* 1,339 full-time matriculated graduate/professional students (717 women), 237 part-time matriculated graduate/professional students (209 women). *Graduate faculty:* 360 full-time (100 women), 66 part-time/adjunct (18 women). Tuition, state resident: part-time $134 per semester hour. Tuition, nonresident: part-time $346 per semester hour. Tuition and fees vary according to course level and program. *Graduate housing:* On-campus housing not available. *Student services:* Campus employment opportunities, campus safety program, child daycare facilities, disabled student services, exercise/wellness program, free psychological counseling, international student services, low-cost health insurance, multicultural affairs office. *Library facilities:* McGoogan Medical Library plus 1 other. *Online resources:* library catalog, web page. *Collection:* 247,434 titles, 1,741 serial subscriptions, 849 audiovisual materials.

Computer facilities: 65 computers available on campus for general student use. A campuswide network can be accessed from off campus. Internet access, various software packages are available. *Web address:* http://www.unmc.edu/.

General Application Contact: Jeanne Ferbrache, Director Academic Records, 402-559-7262.

GRADUATE UNITS

College of Dentistry Students: 172 full-time (54 women), 3 part-time (2 women). 533 applicants, 11% accepted, 46 enrolled. *Faculty:* 58 full-time (12 women), 41 part-time/adjunct (7 women). Expenses: Contact institution. *Financial support:* Career-related internships or fieldwork, Federal Work-Study, institutionally sponsored loans, and stipends available. Support available to part-time students. Financial award application deadline: 3/1; financial award applicants required to submit FAFSA. In 2001, 43 degrees awarded. *Degree program information:* Part-time programs available. Offers dentistry (DDS, Certificate). *Application deadline:* For fall admission, 12/1 (priority date); for spring admission, 2/1. *Application fee:* $50. *Application Contact:* Glenda Canfield, Admissions Secretary, 402-472-1363, Fax: 402-472-5290, E-mail: gmcanfie@unmc.edu. *Dean*, Dr. John W. Reinhardt, 402-472-1344.

College of Medicine Offers medicine (MD).

College of Pharmacy Offers pharmacy (Pharm D).

Graduate Studies Students: 195 full-time (125 women), 223 part-time (199 women); includes 18 minority (10 African Americans, 3 Asian Americans or Pacific Islanders, 4 Hispanic Americans, 1 Native American), 66 international. 263 applicants, 50% accepted. *Faculty:* 360 full-time (100 women), 66 part-time/adjunct (18 women). Expenses: Contact institution. *Financial support:* In 2001–02, 6 fellowships with tuition reimbursements (averaging $16,500 per year), 20 research assistantships with tuition reimbursements (averaging $16,500 per year), teaching assistantships with tuition reimbursements (averaging $16,500 per year) were awarded. Career-related internships or fieldwork, institutionally sponsored loans, scholarships/grants, traineeships, tuition waivers (full), and unspecified assistantships also available. Support available to part-time students. In 2001, 56 master's, 26 doctorates awarded. *Degree program information:* Part-time programs available. Offers biochemistry and molecular biology (MS, PhD); cell biology and anatomy (MS, PhD); medical sciences (MS, PhD); nursing (MSN, PhD); pathology and microbiology (MS, PhD); pharmaceutical sciences (MS, PhD); pharmacology (MS, PhD); physiology (PhD); public health (MS); toxicology (MS, PhD). *Application deadline:* Applications are processed on a rolling basis. *Application fee:* $35. *Application Contact:* Jeanne Ferbrache, Director Academic Records, 402-559-7262. *Dean, Graduate Studies*, Dr. William O. Berndt, 402-559-5130, E-mail: wberndt@unmc.edu.

School of Allied Health Professions Offers allied health professions (MPA, MPT); physical therapy education (MPT); physician assistant education (MPA).

UNIVERSITY OF NEVADA, LAS VEGAS, Las Vegas, NV 89154-9900

General Information State-supported, coed, university. CGS member. *Enrollment:* 1,369 full-time matriculated graduate/professional students (779 women), 1,797 part-time matriculated graduate/professional students (1,128 women). *Enrollment by degree level:* 438 first professional, 2,418 master's, 310 doctoral. *Graduate faculty:* 856 full-time (255 women), 12 part-time/adjunct (6 women). Tuition, state resident: full-time $1,926; part-time $107 per credit. Tuition, nonresident: full-time $9,376; part-time $220 per credit. Tuition and fees vary according to course load. *Graduate housing:* Room and/or apartments available on a first-come, first-served basis to single students; on-campus housing not available to married students. Typical cost: $1,939 per year ($2,866 including board). Room and board charges vary according to board plan. *Student services:* Campus employment opportunities, campus safety program, career counseling, child daycare facilities, disabled student services, free psychological counseling, grant writing training, international student services, low-cost health insurance, multicultural affairs office, teacher training, writing training. *Library facilities:* James R. Dickinson Library. *Online resources:* library catalog, web page, access to other libraries' catalogs. *Collection:* 1.2 million titles, 356,176 serial subscriptions, 119,593 audiovisual materials. *Research affiliation:* Associated Western Universities, Inc..

Computer facilities: 1,100 computers available on campus for general student use. A campuswide network can be accessed from student residence rooms and from off campus. Internet access and online class registration are available. *Web address:* http://www.unlv.edu/.

General Application Contact: Dr. Paul Ferguson, Dean, Graduate College, 702-895-0946, Fax: 702-895-4180.

GRADUATE UNITS

Graduate College Students: 1,128 full-time (657 women), 1,600 part-time (1,035 women); includes 394 minority (139 African Americans, 115 Asian Americans or Pacific Islanders, 124 Hispanic Americans, 16 Native Americans), 201 international. Average age 26. 1,457 applicants, 63% accepted, 707 enrolled. *Faculty:* 830 full-time (243 women). Expenses: Contact institution. *Financial support:* In 2001–02, 426 students received support, including 6 fellowships with full tuition reimbursements available (averaging $14,500 per year), 165 research assistantships with full and partial tuition reimbursements available (averaging $10,070 per year), 351 teaching assistantships with partial tuition reimbursements available (averaging $11,000 per year); career-related internships or fieldwork, Federal Work-Study, institutionally sponsored loans, scholarships/grants, tuition waivers (full), and unspecified assistantships also available. Support available to part-time students. Financial award application deadline: 3/1. In 2001, 747 master's, 32 doctorates awarded. *Degree program information:* Part-time and evening/weekend programs available. *Application deadline:* Applications are processed on a rolling basis. *Application fee:* $40 ($55 for international students). *Application Contact:* Janine Barrett, Systems Analyst, 702-895-3346, Fax: 702-895-4180. *Dean, Graduate College*, Dr. Paul Ferguson, 702-895-4391, Fax: 702-895-4180.

College of Business Students: 102 full-time (39 women), 101 part-time (38 women); includes 19 minority (4 African Americans, 12 Asian Americans or Pacific Islanders, 3 Hispanic Americans), 30 international. 141 applicants, 52% accepted, 64 enrolled. *Faculty:* 74 full-time (8 women). Expenses: Contact institution. *Financial support:* In 2001–02, 9 research assistantships with partial tuition reimbursements (averaging $10,000 per year), 13 teaching assistantships with partial tuition reimbursements (averaging $10,000 per year) were awarded. Career-related internships or fieldwork also available. Financial award application deadline: 3/1. In 2001, 48 degrees awarded. *Degree program information:* Part-time and evening/weekend programs available. Offers accounting (MS); business (MA, MBA, MS); business administration (MBA); economics (MA). *Application deadline:* Applications are processed on a rolling basis. *Application fee:* $40 ($55 for international students). *Application Contact:* Graduate College Admissions Evaluator, 702-895-3320, Fax: 702-895-4180, E-mail: gradcollege@ccmail.nevada.edu. *Dean*, Dr. Richard Flaherty, 702-895-3362.

College of Education Students: 327 full-time (245 women), 886 part-time (678 women); includes 187 minority (76 African Americans, 40 Asian Americans or Pacific Islanders, 62 Hispanic Americans, 9 Native Americans), 19 international. 434 applicants, 79% accepted, 282 enrolled. *Faculty:* 146 full-time (71 women). Expenses: Contact institution. *Financial support:* In 2001–02, 34 research assistantships with partial tuition reimbursements (averaging $11,000 per year), 31 teaching assistantships with partial tuition reimbursements (averaging $11,000 per year) were awarded. Financial award application deadline: 3/1. In 2001, 392 master's, 19 doctorates awarded. *Degree program information:* Part-time and evening/weekend programs available. Offers assessment and evaluation techniques for the exceptional (Ed D); education (M Ed, MS, Ed D, PhD, Ed S); educational administration (M Ed, Ed D, PhD, Ed S); educational computing and technology (M Ed, MS); educational leadership (MS); educational psychology (M Ed, MS, PhD); emotional disturbance (Ed D); English/language arts (M Ed, MS); general elementary curriculum (M Ed, MS); general secondary education (M Ed, MS); general special education (Ed D); health promotion (M Ed); instructional and curricular studies (Ed D, PhD, Ed S); language and literacy education (M Ed, MS); learning disabilities (Ed D); library science and audiovisual education (M Ed, MS); mathematics education (M Ed, MS); mental retardation (Ed D); middle school education (M Ed, MS); postsecondary education (M Ed, MS); school psychology (Ed S); special education (M Ed, MS, PhD, Ed S); teaching English as a second language (M Ed, MS); vocational education (M Ed, MS). *Application fee:* $40 ($55 for international students). *Application Contact:* Graduate College Admissions Evaluator, 702-895-3320, E-mail: gradcollege@ccmail.nevada.edu. *Dean*, Dr. Gene Hall, 702-895-3374.

College of Fine Arts Students: 122 full-time (41 women), 39 part-time (16 women); includes 23 minority (5 African Americans, 8 Asian Americans or Pacific Islanders, 8 Hispanic Americans, 2 Native Americans), 15 international. 150 applicants, 69% accepted, 74 enrolled. *Faculty:* 84 full-time (22 women). Expenses: Contact institution. *Financial support:* In 2001–02, 1 research assistantship with partial tuition reimbursement (averaging $10,000 per year), 52 teaching assistantships with partial tuition reimbursements (averaging $11,000 per year) were awarded. Financial award application deadline: 3/1. In 2001, 48 degrees awarded. *Degree program information:* Part-time programs available. Offers acting (MA); applied music (performance) (MM); architecture (M Arch); art (MFA); composition/theory (MM); dance (MM); design and technical (MA); directing (MA); fine arts (M Arch, MA, MFA, MM, DMA); music education (MM); performance studies (DMA); playwriting (MA); screenwriting (MFA); theatre arts (MFA). *Application fee:* $40 ($55 for international students). *Dean*, Dr. Jeffrey Koep, 702-895-4210.

College of Health Sciences Students: 88 full-time (45 women), 30 part-time (20 women); includes 15 minority (2 African Americans, 9 Asian Americans or Pacific Islanders, 4 Hispanic Americans), 1 international. 79 applicants, 66% accepted, 41 enrolled. *Faculty:* 50 full-time (24 women). Expenses: Contact institution. *Financial support:* In 2001–02, 6 research assistantships with partial tuition reimbursements (averaging $10,000 per year), 20 teaching assistantships with partial tuition reimbursements (averaging $10,000 per year) were awarded. Financial award application deadline: 3/1. In 2001, 48 degrees awarded. *Degree program information:* Part-time programs available. Offers exercise physiology (MS); family nurse practitioner (MS); geriatric nurse practitioner (MS); health physics (MS); health sciences (MS); kinesiology (MS); pediatric nurse practitioner (MS); physical therapy (MS). *Application deadline:* Applications are processed on a rolling basis. *Application fee:* $40 ($55 for international students). *Application Contact:* Graduate College Admissions Evaluator, 702-895-3320, Fax: 702-895-4180, E-mail: gradcollege@ccmail.nevada.edu. *Dean*, Dr. Carolyn Sabo, 702-895-3693.

College of Liberal Arts Students: 133 full-time (88 women), 163 part-time (93 women); includes 35 minority (10 African Americans, 6 Asian Americans or Pacific Islanders, 18 Hispanic Americans, 1 Native American), 7 international. 196 applicants, 55% accepted, 79 enrolled. *Faculty:* 143 full-time (41 women). Expenses: Contact institution. *Financial support:* In 2001–02, 11 research assistantships with full and partial tuition reimbursements (averaging $11,000 per year), 92 teaching assistantships with partial tuition reimbursements (averaging $11,000 per year) were awarded. Institutionally sponsored loans also available. Support available to part-time students. Financial award application deadline:3/1. In 2001, 41 master's, 4 doctorates awarded. *Degree program information:* Part-time programs available. Offers anthropology (MA, PhD); clinical psychology (PhD); creative writing (MFA); English (PhD); English and American literature (MA); ethics and policy studies (MA); experimental psychology (PhD); French (MA); general psychology (MA); history (MA, PhD); language studies (MA); liberal arts (MA, MFA, PhD); political science (MA); sociology (MA, PhD); Spanish (MA); writing (MA). *Application fee:* $40 ($55 for international students). *Application Contact:* Graduate College Admissions Evaluator, 702-895-3320, Fax: 702-895-4180, E-mail: gradcollege@ccmail.nevada.edu. *Dean*, Dr. James Frey, 702-895-3401.

College of Science Students: 75 full-time (34 women), 82 part-time (39 women); includes 13 minority (1 African American, 9 Asian Americans or Pacific Islanders, 3 Hispanic Americans), 19 international. 91 applicants, 60% accepted, 38 enrolled. *Faculty:* 132 full-time (31 women). Expenses: Contact institution. *Financial support:* In 2001–02, 19 research assistantships with full tuition reimbursements (averaging $9,410 per year), 74 teaching assistantships with partial tuition reimbursements (averaging $11,000 per year) were awarded. Unspecified assistantships also available. Financial award application deadline: 3/1. In 2001, 20 master's, 3 doctorates awarded. *Degree program information:* Part-time programs available. Offers applied mathematics (MS); applied statistics (MS); biochemistry (MS); biological sciences (MS, PhD); chemistry (MS); geoscience (MS, PhD); physics (MS, PhD); pure mathematics (MS); science (MA, MS, PhD); water resources management (MS). *Application deadline:* Applications are processed on a rolling basis. *Application fee:* $40 ($55 for international students). *Application Contact:* Graduate College Admissions Evaluator, 702-895-3320, Fax: 702-895-4180, E-mail: gradcollege@ccmail.nevada.edu. *Interim Chair*, Dr. Fred Bachhuber, 702-895-3567.

Greenspun College of Urban Affairs Students: 149 full-time (110 women), 176 part-time (111 women); includes 71 minority (34 African Americans, 13 Asian Americans or Pacific Islanders, 21 Hispanic Americans, 3 Native Americans), 8 international. 125 applicants, 62% accepted, 61 enrolled. *Faculty:* 86 full-time (32 women). Expenses: Contact institution. *Financial support:* In 2001–02, 8 research assistantships (averaging $9,867 per year), 21 teaching assistantships with partial tuition reimbursements (averaging $10,000 per year) were awarded. Financial award application deadline: 3/1. In 2001, 95 master's, 1 doctorate awarded. *Degree program information:* Part-time and evening/weekend programs available. Offers community agency counseling (MS); criminal justice (MA); environmental science (MS, PhD); marriage and family counseling (MS); mass communications (MA); public administration (MPA); rehabilitation counseling (MS); social work (MSW); urban affairs (MA, MPA, MS, MSW, PhD). *Application fee:* $40 ($55 for international students).

University of Nevada, Las Vegas (continued)

Application Contact: Graduate College Admissions Evaluator, 702-895-3320, Fax: 702-895-4180, E-mail: gradcollege@ccmail.nevada.edu. *Dean,* Dr. Martha Watson, 702-895-3291.

Howard R. Hughes College of Engineering Students: 80 full-time (23 women), 87 part-time (23 women); includes 20 minority (4 African Americans, 13 Asian Americans or Pacific Islanders, 3 Hispanic Americans), 73 international. 137 applicants, 50% accepted, 44 enrolled. *Faculty:* 72 full-time (2 women). Expenses: Contact institution. *Financial support:* In 2001–02, 47 research assistantships with full and partial tuition reimbursements (averaging $8,354 per year), 48 teaching assistantships with partial tuition reimbursements (averaging $11,000 per year) were awarded. Fellowships, tuition waivers (full) also available. Financial award application deadline: 3/1. In 2001, 34 master's, 3 doctorates awarded. *Degree program information:* Part-time programs available. Offers civil and environmental engineering (MSE, PhD); computer science (MS, PhD); electrical and computer engineering (MSE, PhD); engineering (MS, MSE, PhD); mechanical engineering (MSE, PhD). *Application deadline:* For fall admission, 6/15; for spring admission, 11/15. *Application fee:* $40 ($55 for international students). *Application Contact:* Graduate College Admissions Evaluator, 702-895-3320, Fax: 702-895-4180, E-mail: gradcollege@ccmail.nevada.edu. *Interim Dean,* Dr. Darrell Pepper, 702-895-3699.

William F. Harrah College of Hotel Administration Students: 52 full-time (32 women), 36 part-time (17 women); includes 11 minority (3 African Americans, 5 Asian Americans or Pacific Islanders, 2 Hispanic Americans, 1 Native American), 29 international. 104 applicants, 31% accepted, 24 enrolled. *Faculty:* 43 full-time (12 women). Expenses: Contact institution. *Financial support:* In 2001–02, 30 research assistantships with partial tuition reimbursements (averaging $11,000 per year) were awarded; teaching assistantships with partial tuition reimbursements available. Financial award application deadline: 3/1. In 2001, 21 master's, 2 doctorates awarded. *Degree program information:* Part-time programs available. Offers hospitality administration (MHA, PhD); hotel administration (MS); leisure studies (MS). *Application deadline:* For fall admission, 6/15; for spring admission, 11/15. Applications are processed on a rolling basis. *Application fee:* $40 ($55 for international students). *Application Contact:* Graduate College Admissions Evaluator, 702-895-3320, Fax: 702-895-4180, E-mail: gradcollege@ccmail.nevada.edu. *Dean,* Dr. Stuart Mann, 702-895-3308.

William S. Boyd School of Law Students: 241 full-time (122 women), 197 part-time (93 women); includes 85 minority (16 African Americans, 18 Asian Americans or Pacific Islanders, 39 Hispanic Americans, 12 Native Americans) 770 applicants, 31% accepted, 142 enrolled. *Faculty:* 26 full-time (12 women), 12 part-time/adjunct (6 women). Expenses: Contact institution. *Financial support:* In 2001–02, 300 students received support. Career-related internships or fieldwork and scholarships/grants available. Support available to part-time students. Financial award application deadline: 2/1; financial award applicants required to submit FAFSA. In 2001, 89 degrees awarded. *Degree program information:* Part-time and evening/weekend programs available. Offers law (JD). *Application deadline:* For fall admission, 3/15 (priority date). Applications are processed on a rolling basis. *Application fee:* $40. Electronic applications accepted. *Application Contact:* Frank D. Durand, Assistant Dean, Admissions and Financial Aid, 702-895-3671, Fax: 702-895-1095, E-mail: fdurand@ccmail.nevada.edu. *Dean,* Richard J, Morgan, 702-895-3671, Fax: 702-895-1095, E-mail: morgan@ccmail.nevada.edu.

See in-depth description on page 1217.

UNIVERSITY OF NEVADA, RENO, Reno, NV 89557

General Information State-supported, coed, university. CGS member. *Enrollment:* 1,481 full-time matriculated graduate/professional students (802 women), 494 part-time matriculated graduate/professional students (290 women). *Graduate faculty:* 574 full-time (177 women), 76 part-time/adjunct (25 women). Tuition, state resident: full-time $2,067; part-time $108 per credit. Tuition, nonresident: full-time $9,282; part-time $109 per credit. *Required fees:* $57 per semester. Tuition and fees vary according to course load. *Graduate housing:* Rooms and/or apartments available to single and married students. Typical cost: $6,805 (including board) for single students; $6,805 (including board) for married students. *Student services:* Campus employment opportunities, campus safety program, career counseling, child daycare facilities, disabled student services, exercise/wellness program, free psychological counseling, grant writing training, international student services, low-cost health insurance, multicultural affairs office, teacher training, writing training. *Library facilities:* Getchell Library plus 5 others. *Online resources:* library catalog, web page, access to other libraries' catalogs. *Collection:* 1 million titles, 10,499 serial subscriptions, 446,434 audiovisual materials.

Computer facilities: 150 computers available on campus for general student use. A campuswide network can be accessed from student residence rooms and from off campus. *Web address:* http://www.unr.edu/.

General Application Contact: John C. Green, Admissions and Registrar Specialist, 775-784-6869, Fax: 775-784-6064, E-mail: gradschool@unr.edu.

GRADUATE UNITS

Graduate School Students: 1,481 full-time (802 women), 494 part-time (290 women); includes 179 minority (12 African Americans, 64 Asian Americans or Pacific Islanders, 84 Hispanic Americans, 19 Native Americans), 327 international. Average age 34. *Faculty:* 716. Expenses: Contact institution. *Financial support:* In 2001–02, 423 research assistantships with tuition reimbursements (averaging $10,000 per year), 485 teaching assistantships with tuition reimbursements (averaging $10,000 per year) were awarded. Fellowships with tuition reimbursements, career-related internships or fieldwork, Federal Work-Study, institutionally sponsored loans, tuition waivers (full and partial), and unspecified assistantships also available. Support available to part-time students. Financial award application deadline: 3/1. In 2001, 402 master's, 58 doctorates, 7 other advanced degrees awarded. *Degree program information:* Part-time and evening/weekend programs available. Offers atmospheric sciences (MS, PhD); biochemistry (MS, PhD); cell and molecular biology (MS, PhD); ecology, evolution, and conservation biology (PhD); environmental sciences and health (MS, PhD); hydrogeology (MS, PhD); hydrology (MS, PhD); judicial studies (MJS); land use planning (MS). *Application deadline:* For fall admission, 3/1 (priority date); for spring admission, 11/1. Applications are processed on a rolling basis. *Application fee:* $40. Electronic applications accepted. *Application Contact:* John C. Green, Associate Dean, 702-784-6869, Fax: 702-784-6064, E-mail: gradschool@unr.edu. *Associate Dean of the Graduate School,* Dr. Linda Brinkley, 775-327-2363, Fax: 775-784-6064, E-mail: read@unr.nevada.edu.

College of Agriculture, Biotechnology and Natural Resources Students: 32 full-time (17 women), 11 part-time (6 women); includes 1 minority (Hispanic American), 4 international. Average age 32. *Faculty:* 38. Expenses: Contact institution. *Financial support:* In 2001–02, 4 teaching assistantships were awarded; research assistantships, Federal Work-Study and institutionally sponsored loans also available. Financial award application deadline: 3/1. In 2001, 18 degrees awarded. Offers agriculture (MS); animal science (MS); environmental and natural resource science (MS); resource and applied economics (MS). *Application deadline:* For fall admission, 3/1 (priority date). Applications are processed on a rolling basis. *Application fee:* $40. *Dean,* Dr. David Trawley, 775-784-1660.

College of Arts and Science Students: 415 full-time (221 women), 173 part-time (115 women); includes 57 minority (4 African Americans, 12 Asian Americans or Pacific Islanders, 37 Hispanic Americans, 4 Native Americans), 76 international. Average age 33. *Faculty:* 243. Expenses: Contact institution. *Financial support:* In 2001–02, 112 research assistantships, 182 teaching assistantships were awarded. Fellowships, Federal Work-Study, institutionally sponsored loans, tuition waivers (full), and unspecified assistantships also available. Financial award application deadline: 3/1. In 2001, 81 master's, 25 doctorates awarded. *Degree program information:* Part-time and evening/weekend programs available. Offers anthropology (MA, PhD); arts and science (MA, MATE, MATM, MM, MPA, MS, PhD); Basque studies (PhD); biology (MS); chemical physics (PhD); chemistry (MS, PhD); English (MA, MATE, PhD); French (MA); geography (MS); German (MA); history (MA, PhD); mathematics (MS); music (MA, MM); philosophy (MA); physics (MS, PhD); political science (MA, PhD); psychology (MA, PhD); public administration (MPA); social psychology (PhD); sociology (MA); Spanish (MA); speech communications (MA); teaching mathematics (MATM). *Application fee:* $40. *Dean,* Dr. Robert W. Mead, 775-784-6155.

College of Business Administration Students: 121 full-time (42 women), 44 part-time (17 women); includes 18 minority (8 Asian Americans or Pacific Islanders, 8 Hispanic Americans, 2 Native Americans), 12 international. Average age 33. *Faculty:* 47. Expenses: Contact institution. *Financial support:* In 2001–02, 7 research assistantships with tuition reimbursements, 1 teaching assistantship with tuition reimbursement were awarded. Federal Work-Study, institutionally sponsored loans, tuition waivers (full), and unspecified assistantships also available. Financial award application deadline: 3/1. In 2001, 36 degrees awarded. *Degree program information:* Part-time and evening/weekend programs available. Offers accounting (M Acc); business administration (M Acc, MA, MBA, MS); economics (MA, MS). *Application deadline:* For fall admission, 2/1 (priority date); for spring admission, 11/1. Applications are processed on a rolling basis. *Application fee:* $40. *Application Contact:* Dr. Brent Bowman, Associate Dean, 775-784-4912, E-mail: bowman@unr.edu. *Dean,* Dr. H. Michael Reed, 775-784-4912.

College of Education Students: 355 full-time (269 women), 141 part-time (106 women); includes 49 minority (6 African Americans, 11 Asian Americans or Pacific Islanders, 24 Hispanic Americans, 8 Native Americans), 23 international. Average age 37. *Faculty:* 57. Expenses: Contact institution. *Financial support:* In 2001–02, 27 research assistantships with tuition reimbursements, 9 teaching assistantships with tuition reimbursements were awarded. Federal Work-Study, institutionally sponsored loans, and unspecified assistantships also available. Financial award application deadline: 3/1. In 2001, 9 doctorates, 7 other advanced degrees awarded. Offers counseling and educational psychology (M Ed, MA, MS, Ed D, PhD, Ed S); curriculum and instruction (Ed D, PhD, Ed S); education (M Ed, MA, MS, Ed D, PhD, Ed S); educational leadership (M Ed, MA, MS, Ed D, PhD, Ed S); elementary education (M Ed, MA, MS); secondary education (M Ed, MA, MS); special education (M Ed, MA, MS); teaching English as a second language (MA). *Application fee:* $40. *Dean,* Dr. William E. Sparkman, 775-784-4345.

College of Engineering Students: 158 full-time (37 women), 44 part-time (5 women); includes 18 minority (15 Asian Americans or Pacific Islanders, 3 Hispanic Americans), 117 international. Average age 29. *Faculty:* 48. Expenses: Contact institution. *Financial support:* In 2001–02, 50 research assistantships, 32 teaching assistantships were awarded. Fellowships, Federal Work-Study, institutionally sponsored loans, and tuition waivers (full) also available. Financial award application deadline: 3/1. In 2001, 45 master's, 5 doctorates awarded. Offers civil engineering (MS, PhD); computer engineering (MS, PhD); computer science (MS); electrical engineering (MS, PhD); engineering (MS, PhD); mechanical engineering (MS, PhD). *Application deadline:* For fall admission, 3/1 (priority date). Applications are processed on a rolling basis. *Application fee:* $40. *Dean,* Dr. Theodore Batchman, 775-784-6925.

College of Human and Community Sciences Students: 93 full-time (71 women), 23 part-time (20 women); includes 13 minority (2 African Americans, 5 Asian Americans or Pacific Islanders, 4 Hispanic Americans, 2 Native Americans), 5 international. Average age 34. *Faculty:* 54. Expenses: Contact institution. *Financial support:* In 2001–02, 25 research assistantships with tuition reimbursements, 2 teaching assistantships with tuition reimbursements were awarded. Federal Work-Study, institutionally sponsored loans, tuition waivers (full), and unspecified assistantships also available. Financial award application deadline: 3/1. In 2001, 42 degrees awarded. *Degree program information:* Part-time and evening/weekend programs available. Offers health ecology (MS); human and community sciences (MPH, MS, MSW); human development and family studies (MS); nursing (MS); nutrition (MS); public health (MPH); social work (MSW). *Application fee:* $40. *Dean,* Dr. Jean L. Perry, 702-784-6975.

Donald W. Reynolds School of Journalism Students: 12 full-time (8 women), 3 part-time (2 women); includes 2 minority (both Asian Americans or Pacific Islanders), 2 international. Average age 31. *Faculty:* 4. Expenses: Contact institution. *Financial support:* In 2001–02, 6 research assistantships were awarded; teaching assistantships, Federal Work-Study and institutionally sponsored loans also available. Financial award application deadline: 3/1. In 2001, 3 degrees awarded. Offers journalism (MA). *Application deadline:* For fall admission, 4/15 (priority date); for spring admission, 12/1. Applications are processed on a rolling basis. *Application fee:* $40. *Application Contact:* Jennifer Green, Graduate Program Director, 775-784-4191. *Dean,* Dr. Joann Lee, 775-784-6531.

Mackay School of Mines Students: 83 full-time (20 women), 15 part-time (1 woman); includes 5 minority (2 Asian Americans or Pacific Islanders, 2 Hispanic Americans, 1 Native American), 38 international. Average age 31. *Faculty:* 51. Expenses: Contact institution. *Financial support:* In 2001–02, 23 research assistantships, 10 teaching assistantships were awarded. Fellowships, career-related internships or fieldwork, Federal Work-Study, institutionally sponsored loans, and tuition waivers (full and partial) also available. Financial award application deadline: 3/1. In 2001, 15 master's, 5 doctorates awarded. *Degree program information:* Part-time programs available. Offers chemical engineering (MS, PhD); geochemistry (MS, PhD); geological engineering (MS, Geol E); geology (MS, PhD); geophysics (MS, PhD); metallurgical engineering (MS, PhD, Met E); mines (MS, PhD, EM, Geol E, Met E); mining engineering (MS, EM). *Application deadline:* For fall admission, 3/1 (priority date). Applications are processed on a rolling basis. *Application fee:* $40. *Dean,* Dr. Jane Long, 775-784-6987.

School of Medicine Expenses: Contact institution. *Financial support:* Fellowships, research assistantships, teaching assistantships, Federal Work-Study and institutionally sponsored loans available. Support available to part-time students. Financial award application deadline: 3/1. Offers medicine (MD, MS, PhD). *Application deadline:* Applications are processed on a rolling basis. *Dean,* Dr. Stephen McFarlane, 775-784-6001.

Graduate Programs in Medicine Students: 47 full-time (33 women), 3 part-time (2 women); includes 2 minority (1 Asian American or Pacific Islander, 1 Hispanic American), 5 international. Average age 29. *Faculty:* 5. Expenses: Contact institution. *Financial support:* Fellowships, research assistantships, teaching assistantships, Federal Work-Study available. Support available to part-time students. Financial award application deadline: 3/1. In 2001, 19 master's, 2 doctorates awarded. Offers biomedical engineering (MS, PhD); cellular and molecular pharmacology and physiology (MS, PhD); medicine (MS, PhD); speech pathology (PhD); speech pathology and audiology (MS). *Application deadline:* For fall admission, 3/1. Applications are processed on a rolling basis. *Application fee:* $40. *Associate Dean of the Graduate School,* Dr. Linda Brinkley, 775-327-2363, Fax: 775-784-6064, E-mail: read@unr.nevada.edu.

UNIVERSITY OF NEW BRUNSWICK FREDERICTON, Fredericton, NB E3B 5A3, Canada

General Information Province-supported, coed, university. *Graduate housing:* Rooms and/or apartments available to single and married students. Housing application deadline: 8/1.

GRADUATE UNITS

Faculty of Law Students: 231 full-time (125 women). Average age 24. 623 applicants, 30% accepted, 80 enrolled. Expenses: Contact institution. *Financial support:* Scholarships/grants available. Offers law (LL B). *Application deadline:* For fall admission, 3/1. Applications are processed on a rolling basis. *Application fee:* $50. *Application Contact:* Robin Dickson, Admissions Officer, 506-453-4693, Fax: 506-453-4604, E-mail: rjd@unb.ca. *Dean,* Anne Warner La Forest, 506-453-4627, Fax: 506-453-4604, E-mail: laforest@unb.ca.

School of Graduate Studies *Degree program information:* Part-time programs available.

Faculty of Administration *Degree program information:* Part-time programs available. Offers administration (MBA, MPA).

Faculty of Arts *Degree program information:* Part-time programs available. Offers anthropology (MA); arts (MA, PhD, Diploma); classics (MA); economics (MA); English (MA, PhD); French (MA); German and Russian (MA); history (MA, PhD); North American studies (MA); philosophy (MA); political science (MA); psychology (PhD); sociology (MA, PhD); Spanish (MA).

Faculty of Education *Degree program information:* Part-time programs available. Offers adult education (M Ed); curriculum and instruction (M Ed); education (M Ed); educational administration (M Ed); educational psychology (M Ed); guidance and counseling (M Ed); special education (M Ed); vocational education (M Ed).

Faculty of Engineering *Degree program information:* Part-time programs available. Offers applied mechanics (M Eng, M Sc E, PhD); chemical engineering (M Eng, M Sc E, PhD); computer science (M Sc CS, PhD); construction engineering and management (M Eng, M Sc E, PhD); electrical and computer engineering (M Eng, M Sc E, PhD); engineering (M Eng, M Sc CS, M Sc E, PhD, Diploma); environmental engineering (M Eng, M Sc E, PhD); geotechnical engineering (M Eng, M Sc E, PhD); groundwater/hydrology (M Eng, M Sc E, PhD); land information management (Diploma); mapping, charting and geodesy (Diploma); materials (M Eng, M Sc E, PhD); mechanical engineering (M Eng, M Sc E, PhD); pavements (M Eng, M Sc E, PhD); structures (M Eng, M Sc E, PhD); surveying engineering (M Eng, M Sc E, PhD); transportation (M Eng, M Sc E, PhD).

Faculty of Forestry and Environmental Management *Degree program information:* Part-time programs available. Offers ecological foundations of forest management (PhD); forest engineering (M Sc FE, MFE); forest resources (M Sc F, MF, PhD).

Faculty of Kinesiology *Degree program information:* Part-time programs available. Offers exercise and sport science (M Sc); sport and recreation administration (MA). Electronic applications accepted.

Faculty of Science *Degree program information:* Part-time programs available. Offers biology (M Sc, PhD); chemistry (M Sc, PhD); geology (M Sc, PhD); mathematics and statistics (M Sc, PhD); physics (M Sc, PhD); science (M Sc, PhD).

UNIVERSITY OF NEW BRUNSWICK SAINT JOHN, Saint John, NB E2L 4L5, Canada

General Information Province-supported, coed, comprehensive institution. *Enrollment by degree level:* 110 master's, 16 doctoral. *Graduate faculty:* 27 full-time (5 women). *Graduate tuition:* Tuition and fees charges are reported in Canadian dollars. *International tuition:* $7,115 Canadian dollars full-time. Tuition, Canadian resident: full-time $4,005 Canadian dollars; part-time $667 Canadian dollars per term. *Required fees:* $226 Canadian dollars; $472 Canadian dollars per course. Tuition and fees vary according to program. *Graduate housing:* Rooms and/or apartments available on a first-come, first-served basis to single and married students. Housing application deadline: 3/31. *Student services:* Campus employment opportunities, campus safety program, career counseling, disabled student services, exercise/wellness program, free psychological counseling, grant writing training, international student services, low-cost health insurance, teacher training, writing training. *Library facilities:* Ward Chipman Library. *Online resources:* library catalog, web page, access to other libraries' catalogs. *Collection:* 155,500 titles, 700 serial subscriptions.

Computer facilities: 100 computers available on campus for general student use. A campuswide network can be accessed from student residence rooms and from off campus. Internet access and online class registration are available. *Web address:* http://www.unb.ca/.

General Application Contact: Dr. Jack M. Terhune, Associate Dean of Graduate Studies, 506-648-5633, Fax: 506-648-5528, E-mail: graduate@unbsj.ca.

GRADUATE UNITS

Faculty of Arts Students: 5 full-time (all women), 3 part-time (2 women). Average age 23. 4 applicants, 50% accepted, 1 enrolled. *Faculty:* 8 full-time (1 woman). Expenses: Contact institution. *Financial support:* In 2001–02, 4 students received support, including 2 research assistantships (averaging $2,550 per year), 2 teaching assistantships (averaging $3,600 per year); fellowships, unspecified assistantships also available. Support available to part-time students. Financial award application deadline: 2/1. Offers psychology (MA). *Application deadline:* For fall admission, 2/1. *Application fee:* $50. Electronic applications accepted. *Application Contact:* Dr. Murray Goddard, Director of Graduate Studies, 506-648-5640, Fax: 506-648-5780, E-mail: graduate@unbsj.ca. *Chair of Psychology,* Dr. Alexander Wilson, 506-648-5640, Fax: 506-648-5780, E-mail: graduate@unbsj.ca.

Faculty of Business Students: 39 full-time (18 women), 20 part-time (6 women); includes 17 minority (15 Asian Americans or Pacific Islanders, 2 Hispanic Americans) Average age 26. 101 applicants, 59% accepted, 27 enrolled. *Faculty:* 10 full-time (2 women). Expenses: Contact institution. *Financial support:* In 2001–02, 3 students received support; fellowships, research assistantships, teaching assistantships, career-related internships or fieldwork and scholarships/grants available. In 2001, 35 degrees awarded. *Degree program information:* Part-time programs available. Offers administration (MBA); electronic commerce (MBA); international business (MBA). *Application deadline:* For fall admission, 5/15. *Application fee:* $100. *Application Contact:* Dr. Jack M. Terhune, Associate Dean of Graduate Studies, 506-648-5633, Fax: 506-648-5528, E-mail: graduate@unbsj.ca. *Director,* Dr. Frances Amatucci.

Faculty of Science, Applied Science and Engineering Students: 41 full-time (23 women), 6 part-time (4 women); includes 4 minority (2 Asian Americans or Pacific Islanders, 2 Hispanic Americans) Average age 23. *Faculty:* 9 full-time (2 women). Expenses: Contact institution. *Financial support:* In 2001–02, research assistantships (averaging $2,550 per year), teaching assistantships (averaging $3,600 per year) were awarded. Scholarships/grants and unspecified assistantships also available. In 2001, 2 master's, 1 doctorate awarded. *Degree program information:* Part-time programs available. Offers science, applied science and engineering (M Sc, PhD). *Application deadline:* For fall admission, 2/15. *Application fee:* $50 Canadian dollars. *Application Contact:* Dr. Tillmann Benfey, Director, Graduate Studies, 506-453-4583, Fax: 506-453-3583, E-mail: biology@unb.ca. *Professor of Biology,* Dr. Katherine Frego, 506-648-5565, E-mail: sjbiol@unbsj.ca.

UNIVERSITY OF NEW ENGLAND, Biddeford, ME 04005-9526

General Information Independent, coed, comprehensive institution. *Enrollment:* 1,009 full-time matriculated graduate/professional students (637 women), 436 part-time matriculated graduate/professional students (352 women). *Enrollment by degree level:* 456 first professional, 989 master's. *Graduate faculty:* 53 full-time (29 women), 84 part-time/adjunct (40 women). *Tuition:* Full-time $13,440; part-time $420 per credit. *Required fees:* $240. *Graduate housing:* Rooms and/or apartments available on a first-come, first-served basis to single students and available to married students. Typical cost: $6,770 (including board) for single students. Housing application deadline: 4/15. *Student services:* Campus employment opportunities, campus safety program, career counseling, child daycare facilities, free psychological counseling, international student services, low-cost health insurance. *Library facilities:* Ketchum Library plus 1 other. *Online resources:* library catalog, web page, access to other libraries' catalogs. *Collection:* 46,030 titles, 1,210 serial subscriptions, 9,536 audiovisual materials. *Research affiliation:* Bigelow Laboratories for Ocean Sciences.

Computer facilities: 76 computers available on campus for general student use. A campuswide network can be accessed from off campus. Internet access is available. *Web address:* http://www.une.edu/.

General Application Contact: Patricia T. Cribby, Dean of Admissions and Enrollment Management, 207-283-0171 Ext. 2297, Fax: 207-294-5900, E-mail: jshea@une.edu.

GRADUATE UNITS

College of Arts and Sciences Students: 258 full-time (200 women), 340 part-time (273 women); includes 13 minority (3 African Americans, 3 Asian Americans or Pacific Islanders, 5 Hispanic Americans, 2 Native Americans), 1 international. Average age 36. 303 applicants, 67% accepted. *Faculty:* 14 full-time (11 women), 9 part-time/adjunct (8 women). Expenses: Contact institution. *Financial support:* Available to part-time students. Application deadline: 5/1; In 2001, 187 degrees awarded. *Degree program information:* Part-time programs available. Postbaccalaureate distance learning degree programs offered. Offers arts and sciences (MS Ed, MSOT); education (MS Ed); occupational therapy (MSOT). *Application deadline:* Applications are processed on a rolling basis. *Application fee:* $40. *Application Contact:* Patricia T. Cribby, Dean of Admissions and Enrollment Management, 207-283-0171 Ext. 2297, Fax: 207-294-5900, E-mail: jshea@une.edu. *Director,* Jacque Carter, 207-283-0171 Ext. 2371, Fax: 207-797-7225, E-mail: jcarter@une.edu.

College of Health Professions Students: 289 full-time (205 women), 77 part-time (68 women); includes 14 minority (3 African Americans, 5 Asian Americans or Pacific Islanders, 5 Hispanic Americans, 1 Native American) Average age 34. 436 applicants, 46% accepted. *Faculty:* 25 full-time (13 women), 32 part-time/adjunct (17 women). Expenses: Contact institution. *Financial support:* Career-related internships or fieldwork and Federal Work-Study available. Support available to part-time students. Financial award application deadline: 5/1; financial award applicants required to submit FAFSA. In 2001, 163 degrees awarded. *Degree program information:* Part-time programs available. Postbaccalaureate distance learning degree programs offered (minimal on-campus study). Offers health professions (MPA, MS, MSPT, MSW); nurse anesthesia (MS); physical therapy (MSPT); physician assistant (MPA); social work (MSW). *Application deadline:* Applications are processed on a rolling basis. *Application fee:* $40. *Application Contact:* Patricia T. Cribby, Dean of Admissions and Enrollment Management, 207-283-0171 Ext. 2297, Fax: 207-294-5900, E-mail: jshea@une.edu. *Dean,* Dr. Vernon Moore, 207-283-0171 Ext. 2566, Fax: 207-282-6379, E-mail: vmoore@une.edu.

College of Osteopathic Medicine Students: 456 full-time (228 women); includes 37 minority (2 African Americans, 33 Asian Americans or Pacific Islanders, 2 Hispanic Americans), 1 international. Average age 28. 663 applicants, 28% accepted. *Faculty:* 16 full-time (5 women), 25 part-time/adjunct (7 women). Expenses: Contact institution. *Financial support:* In 2001–02, fellowships (averaging $10,407 per year); institutionally sponsored loans and tuition waivers (partial) also available. Support available to part-time students. Financial award application deadline: 5/1; financial award applicants required to submit FAFSA. In 2001, 112 degrees awarded. Offers osteopathic medicine (DO). *Application deadline:* For fall admission, 3/1. *Application fee:* $55. *Application Contact:* Patricia T. Cribby, Dean of Admissions and Enrollment Management, 207-283-0171 Ext. 2297, Fax: 207-294-5900, E-mail: jshea@une.edu. *Dean,* Dr. Stephen Shannon, 207-283-0171 Ext. 2340, Fax: 207-878-2434.

UNIVERSITY OF NEW HAMPSHIRE, Durham, NH 03824

General Information State-supported, coed, university. CGS member. *Enrollment:* 875 full-time matriculated graduate/professional students (508 women), 1,129 part-time matriculated graduate/professional students (616 women). *Enrollment by degree level:* 1,552 master's, 429 doctoral, 23 other advanced degrees. *Graduate faculty:* 636 full-time. Tuition, state resident: full-time $6,300; part-time $350 per credit. Tuition, nonresident: full-time $15,720; part-time $643 per credit. *Required fees:* $560; $280 per term. One-time fee: $15 part-time. Tuition and fees vary according to course load. *Graduate housing:* Rooms and/or apartments available on a first-come, first-served basis to single and married students. Typical cost: $3,646 per year ($5,910 including board) for single students; $3,646 per year ($5,910 including board) for married students. Room and board charges vary according to board plan and housing facility selected. Housing application deadline: 7/15. *Student services:* Campus employment opportunities, campus safety program, career counseling, child daycare facilities, disabled student services, free psychological counseling, international student services, low-cost health insurance, multicultural affairs office. *Library facilities:* Dimond Library plus 4 others. *Online resources:* library catalog, web page, access to other libraries' catalogs. *Collection:* 856,939 titles, 9,200 serial subscriptions, 22,761 audiovisual materials.

Computer facilities: 380 computers available on campus for general student use. A campuswide network can be accessed from student residence rooms and from off campus. Internet access and online class registration are available. *Web address:* http://www.unh.edu/.

General Application Contact: Graduate Admissions Office, 603-862-3000, Fax: 603-862-0275, E-mail: grad.school@unh.edu.

GRADUATE UNITS

Graduate School Students: 875 full-time (508 women), 1,129 part-time (616 women); includes 66 minority (16 African Americans, 23 Asian Americans or Pacific Islanders, 19 Hispanic Americans, 8 Native Americans), 242 international. Average age 29. 1,519 applicants, 73% accepted, 535 enrolled. *Faculty:* 636 full-time. Expenses: Contact institution. *Financial support:* In 2001–02, 37 fellowships, 194 research assistantships, 392 teaching assistantships were awarded. Career-related internships or fieldwork, Federal Work-Study, scholarships/grants, and tuition waivers (full and partial) also available. Support available to part-time students. Financial award application deadline: 2/15; financial award applicants required to submit FAFSA. In 2001, 605 master's, 54 doctorates, 5 other advanced degrees awarded. *Degree program information:* Part-time and evening/weekend programs available. Offers college teaching (MST); environmental education (MS); natural resources (PhD). *Application deadline:* For fall admission, 4/1 (priority date); for winter admission, 12/1 (priority date). Applications are processed on a rolling basis. *Application fee:* $50. Electronic applications accepted. *Application Contact:* 603-862-3000, Fax: 603-862-0275, E-mail: grad.school@unh.edu. *Associate Dean,* Dr. Harry J. Richards, 603-862-3000, Fax: 603-862-0275, E-mail: harry.richards@unh.edu.

College of Engineering and Physical Sciences Students: 176 full-time (47 women), 228 part-time (60 women); includes 15 minority (4 African Americans, 10 Asian Americans or Pacific Islanders, 1 Hispanic American), 161 international. Average age 30. 356 applicants, 78% accepted, 88 enrolled. *Faculty:* 178 full-time. Expenses: Contact institution. *Financial support:* In 2001–02, 4 fellowships, 116 research assistantships, 122 teaching assistantships were awarded. Career-related internships or fieldwork, Federal Work-Study, scholarships/grants, and tuition waivers (full and partial) also available. Support available to part-time students. Financial award application deadline: 2/15; financial award applicants required to submit FAFSA. In 2001, 78 master's, 19 doctorates awarded. *Degree program information:* Part-time and evening/weekend programs available. Offers applied mathematics (MS); chemical engineering (MS, PhD); chemistry (MS, MST, PhD); civil engineering (MS, PhD); computer science (MS, PhD); earth sciences (MS, PhD); electrical engineering (MS, PhD); engineering and physical sciences (MS, MST, PhD); hydrology (MS); materials science (MS, PhD); mathematics (MS, MST, PhD); mathematics education (PhD); mechanical engineering (MS, PhD); ocean engineering (MS, PhD); ocean mapping (MS); physics (MS, PhD); statistics (MS); systems design (PhD). *Application deadline:* For fall admission, 4/1 (priority date); for winter admission, 12/1 (priority date). Applications are processed on a rolling basis. *Application fee:* $50. Electronic applications accepted. *Dean,* Dr. Arthur Greenberg, 603-862-1781.

College of Liberal Arts Students: 293 full-time (203 women), 480 part-time (333 women). Average age 34. 476 applicants, 75% accepted, 192 enrolled. *Faculty:* 188 full-time. Expenses: Contact institution. *Financial support:* In 2001–02, 8 fellowships, 4 research assistantships, 128 teaching assistantships were awarded. Career-related internships or fieldwork, Federal Work-Study, scholarships/grants, and tuition waivers (full and partial) also available. Support available to part-time students. Financial award application deadline: 2/15. In 2001, 275 master's, 19 doctorates, 5 other advanced degrees awarded. *Degree program information:* Part-time programs available. Offers adult and occupational education (MAOE); counseling (M Ed, MA); early childhood education (M Ed); education (PhD); educational administration (M Ed, CAGS); elementary education (M Ed, MAT); English (PhD); English education (MST); history (MA, PhD); language and linguistics (MA); liberal arts (M Ed, MA, MALS, MAOE, MAT, MFA, MPA, MST, PhD, CAGS); liberal studies (MALS); literacy and schooling (PhD); literature (MA); museum studies (MA); music education (MA); music history (MA); painting (MFA); political science (MA); psychology (PhD); public administration (MPA); reading (M Ed); secondary education (M Ed, MAT); sociology (MA, PhD); Spanish (MA); special education (M Ed); teacher leadership (M Ed); writing (MA). *Application deadline:* For fall and spring admission, 4/1; for winter admission, 12/1. Applications are processed on a rolling basis. *Application fee:* $50. Electronic applications accepted. *Dean,* Dr. Marilyn Hoskin, 603-862-2062.

College of Life Sciences and Agriculture Students: 105 full-time (63 women), 115 part-time (62 women); includes 5 minority (3 African Americans, 1 Asian American or Pacific Islander, 1 Hispanic American), 32 international. Average age 34. 178 applicants, 51% accepted, 56 enrolled. *Faculty:* 175 full-time. Expenses: Contact institution. *Financial support:* In 2001–02, 8 fellowships, 65 research assistantships, 76 teaching assistantships were awarded. Career-related internships or fieldwork, Federal Work-Study, scholarships/grants, and tuition waivers (full and partial) also available. Support available to part-time students. Financial award application deadline: 2/15. In 2001, 44 master's, 10 doctorates awarded. *Degree program information:* Part-time programs available. Offers animal and nutritional sciences (PhD); animal science (MS); biochemistry and molecular biology (MS, PhD); environmental conservation (MS); forestry (MS); genetics (MS, PhD); life sciences and agriculture (MS, PhD); microbiology (MS, PhD); nutritional sciences (MS); plant biology (MS, PhD); resource administration (MS); resource economics (MS); soil science (MS); water resources management (MS); wildlife (MS); zoology (MS, PhD). *Application deadline:*

University of New Hampshire (continued)

For fall admission, 4/1. Applications are processed on a rolling basis. *Application fee:* $50. Electronic applications accepted. *Dean,* Dr. Andrew Rosenberg, 603-862-1450.

School of Health and Human Services Students: 181 full-time (156 women), 129 part-time (109 women); includes 9 minority (1 African American, 2 Asian Americans or Pacific Islanders, 3 Hispanic Americans, 3 Native Americans), 4 international. Average age 34. 289 applicants, 73% accepted, 106 enrolled. *Faculty:* 71 full-time. Expenses: Contact institution. *Financial support:* In 2001–02, 16 fellowships, 34 teaching assistantships were awarded. Research assistantships, career-related internships or fieldwork, Federal Work-Study, scholarships/grants, and tuition waivers (full and partial) also available. Support available to part-time students. Financial award application deadline: 2/15. In 2001, 138 degrees awarded. *Degree program information:* Part-time and evening/weekend programs available. Offers communication sciences and disorders (MS, MST); family studies (MS); health and human services (MPH, MS, MST, MSW); kinesiology (MS); marriage and family therapy (MS); nursing (MS); occupational therapy (MS); public health: ecology (MPH); public health: nursing (MPH); public health: policy and management (MPH); social work (MSW). *Application deadline:* For fall admission, 4/1 (priority date); for winter admission, 12/1 (priority date). Applications are processed on a rolling basis. *Application fee:* $50. Electronic applications accepted. *Dean,* Dr. James McCarthy, 603-862-1178.

Whittemore School of Business and Economics Students: 90 full-time (27 women), 158 part-time (45 women); includes 14 minority (2 African Americans, 6 Asian Americans or Pacific Islanders, 5 Hispanic Americans, 1 Native American), 28 international. Average age 34. 204 applicants, 76% accepted, 85 enrolled. *Faculty:* 51 full-time. Expenses: Contact institution. *Financial support:* In 2001–02, 29 teaching assistantships were awarded; fellowships, research assistantships, career-related internships or fieldwork, Federal Work-Study, scholarships/grants, and tuition waivers (full and partial) also available. Support available to part-time students. Financial award application deadline: 2/15. In 2001, 69 master's, 1 doctorate awarded. *Degree program information:* Part-time and evening/weekend programs available. Offers accounting (MS); business administration (MBA); business and economics (MA, MBA, MS, PhD); economics (MA, PhD); executive business administration (MBA); health management (MBA). *Application deadline:* For fall admission, 4/1; for winter admission, 12/1. Applications are processed on a rolling basis. *Application fee:* $50. Electronic applications accepted. *Dean,* Dr. Steve Bolander, 603-862-1981.

See in-depth description on page 1219.

UNIVERSITY OF NEW HAVEN, West Haven, CT 06516-1916

General Information Independent, coed, comprehensive institution. CGS member. *Enrollment:* 625 full-time matriculated graduate/professional students (342 women), 1,137 part-time matriculated graduate/professional students (538 women). *Enrollment by degree level:* 1,762 master's. *Graduate faculty:* 150 full-time, 100 part-time/adjunct. *Tuition:* Full-time $12,015; part-time $445 per credit hour. *Required fees:* $30. One-time fee: $100 full-time. *Graduate housing:* On-campus housing not available. *Student services:* Campus employment opportunities, campus safety program, career counseling, disabled student services, free psychological counseling, international student services, low-cost health insurance, multicultural affairs office, writing training. *Library facilities:* Marvin K. Peterson Library. *Online resources:* library catalog, web page, access to other libraries' catalogs. *Collection:* 313,385 titles, 2,261 serial subscriptions, 601 audiovisual materials.

Computer facilities: 800 computers available on campus for general student use. A campuswide network can be accessed from student residence rooms and from off campus. Internet access, e-mail are available. *Web address:* http://www.newhaven.edu/.

General Application Contact: Pam Sommers, Director of Graduate Admissions, 203-932-7448, Fax: 203-932-7137, E-mail: gradinfo@charger.newhaven.edu.

GRADUATE UNITS

Graduate School Students: 625 full-time (342 women), 1,137 part-time (538 women); includes 175 minority (92 African Americans, 49 Asian Americans or Pacific Islanders, 30 Hispanic Americans, 4 Native Americans), 246 international. 1,064 applicants, 69% accepted, 557 enrolled. *Faculty:* 150 full-time, 100 part-time/adjunct. Expenses: Contact institution. *Financial support:* Fellowships, research assistantships, teaching assistantships, career-related internships or fieldwork, Federal Work-Study, and unspecified assistantships available. Support available to part-time students. Financial award application deadline: 5/1; financial award applicants required to submit FAFSA. In 2001, 681 degrees awarded. *Degree program information:* Part-time and evening/weekend programs available. *Application deadline:* Applications are processed on a rolling basis. *Application fee:* $50. *Application Contact:* Pam Sommers, Director of Graduate Admissions, 203-932-7448, Fax: 203-932-7137, E-mail: gradinfo@charger.newhaven.edu. *Associate Provost and Dean of Graduate Studies,* Dr. Ira Kleinfeld, 203-932-7063.

College of Arts and Sciences Students: 182 full-time (143 women), 329 part-time (225 women); includes 46 minority (22 African Americans, 16 Asian Americans or Pacific Islanders, 6 Hispanic Americans, 2 Native Americans), 15 international. Expenses: Contact institution. *Financial support:* Career-related internships or fieldwork, Federal Work-Study, and unspecified assistantships available. Support available to part-time students. Financial award application deadline: 5/1; financial award applicants required to submit FAFSA. In 2001, 223 degrees awarded. *Degree program information:* Part-time and evening/weekend programs available. Offers arts and sciences (MA, MS, Certificate); cellular and molecular biology (MS); community psychology (MA, Certificate); education (MS); environmental sciences (MS); executive tourism and hospitality (MS); hotel, restaurant, tourism and dietetics administration (MS); human nutrition (MS); industrial and organizational psychology (MA, Certificate); tourism and hospitality management (MS). *Application deadline:* Applications are processed on a rolling basis. *Application fee:* $50. *Dean,* Dr. Nancy Carriuolo, 203-932-7257.

School of Business Students: 294 full-time (123 women), 442 part-time (204 women); includes 80 minority (51 African Americans, 15 Asian Americans or Pacific Islanders, 13 Hispanic Americans, 1 Native American), 114 international. Expenses: Contact institution. *Financial support:* Career-related internships or fieldwork and Federal Work-Study available. Support available to part-time students. Financial award application deadline: 5/1; financial award applicants required to submit FAFSA. In 2001, 279 degrees awarded. *Degree program information:* Part-time and evening/weekend programs available. Offers accounting (MBA); business (EMBA, MBA, MPA, MS); business administration (EMBA, MBA); business policy and strategy (MBA); corporate taxation (MS); finance (MBA); finance and financial services (MS); financial accounting (MS); health care administration (MS); health care management (MBA, MPA); human resources management (MBA); industrial relations (MS); international business (MBA); managerial accounting (MS); marketing (MBA); personnel and labor relations (MPA); public relations (MBA); public taxation (MS); sports management (MBA); taxation (MS); technology management (MBA). *Application deadline:* Applications are processed on a rolling basis. *Application fee:* $50. *Dean,* Dr. Zeljan Suster, 203-932-7115.

School of Engineering and Applied Science Students: 71 full-time (28 women), 218 part-time (48 women); includes 19 minority (4 African Americans, 13 Asian Americans or Pacific Islanders, 2 Hispanic Americans), 110 international. Expenses: Contact institution. *Financial support:* Federal Work-Study available. Support available to part-time students. Financial award application deadline: 5/1; financial award applicants required to submit FAFSA. In 2001, 80 degrees awarded. *Degree program information:* Part-time and evening/weekend programs available. Offers applications software (MS); civil engineering design (Certificate); electrical engineering (MSEE); engineering and applied science (MS, MSEE, MSIE, MSME, Certificate); environmental engineering (MS); industrial engineering (MSIE); logistics (Certificate); management information systems (MS); mechanical engineering (MSME); operations research (MS); systems software (MS). *Application deadline:* Applications are processed on a rolling basis. *Application fee:* $50. *Dean,* Dr. Zulma Turo-Ramos, 203-932-7167.

School of Public Safety and Professional Studies Students: 78 full-time (48 women), 135 part-time (55 women); includes 27 minority (15 African Americans, 2 Asian Americans or Pacific Islanders, 9 Hispanic Americans, 1 Native American), 7 international. Expenses: Contact institution. *Financial support:* Career-related internships or fieldwork and Federal Work-Study available. Support available to part-time students. Financial award application deadline: 5/1; financial award applicants required to submit FAFSA. In 2001, 86 degrees awarded. *Degree program information:* Part-time and evening/weekend programs available. Offers advanced investigation (MS); aviation science (MS); correctional counseling (MS); criminal justice management (MS); criminalistics (MS); fire science (MS); forensic science (MS); industrial hygiene (MS); occupational safety and health management (MS); public safety and professional studies (MS); security management (MS). *Application deadline:* Applications are processed on a rolling basis. *Application fee:* $50. *Dean,* Dr. Thomas Johnson, 203-932-7260.

See in-depth description on page 1221.

UNIVERSITY OF NEW MEXICO, Albuquerque, NM 87131-2039

General Information State-supported, coed, university. CGS member. *Enrollment:* 3,476 full-time matriculated graduate/professional students (1,920 women), 1,905 part-time matriculated graduate/professional students (1,120 women). *Enrollment by degree level:* 988 first professional, 2,038 master's, 1,212 doctoral, 23 other advanced degrees. *Graduate faculty:* 1,421 full-time (532 women), 533 part-time/adjunct (250 women). Tuition, state resident: full-time $2,771; part-time $115 per credit hour. Tuition, nonresident: full-time $11,207; part-time $467 per credit hour. *Required fees:* $570; $24 per credit hour. Part-time tuition and fees vary according to course load and program. *Graduate housing:* Rooms and/or apartments available on a first-come, first-served basis to single and married students. Typical cost: $3,604 per year ($5,624 including board) for single students. *Student services:* Campus employment opportunities, campus safety program, career counseling, child daycare facilities, disabled student services, exercise/wellness program, free psychological counseling, international student services, low-cost health insurance, teacher training. *Library facilities:* Zimmerman Library plus 7 others. *Online resources:* library catalog, web page, access to other libraries' catalogs. *Collection:* 2.3 million titles, 309,043 serial subscriptions, 3.8 million audiovisual materials. *Research affiliation:* Sandia National Laboratories, Los Alamos National Laboratory, Lovelace Respiratory Research Institute, Phillips Laboratory.

Computer facilities: 382 computers available on campus for general student use. A campuswide network can be accessed from student residence rooms and from off campus. Internet access and online class registration are available. *Web address:* http://www.unm.edu/.

General Application Contact: Elizabeth Zawahri, Student Admissions Coordinator, 505-277-7401, Fax: 505-277-7405.

GRADUATE UNITS

Graduate School Students: 2,324 full-time (1,262 women), 1,600 part-time (984 women); includes 912 minority (73 African Americans, 94 Asian Americans or Pacific Islanders, 624 Hispanic Americans, 121 Native Americans), 555 international. Average age 36. 2,761 applicants, 52% accepted, 681 enrolled. *Faculty:* 844 full-time (322 women), 385 part-time/adjunct (189 women). Expenses: Contact institution. *Financial support:* In 2001–02, 2,067 students received support; fellowships, research assistantships, teaching assistantships, tuition waivers (full and partial) and project assistantships, residencies available. Financial award application deadline: 3/1; financial award applicants required to submit FAFSA. In 2001, 833 master's, 203 doctorates awarded. *Degree program information:* Part-time and evening/weekend programs available. Postbaccalaureate distance learning degree programs offered. Offers pharmaceutical sciences (MS, PhD); pharmacy (Pharm D, MS, PhD); water resources (MWR). *Application fee:* $40. *Application Contact:* Elizabeth Zawahri, Student Admissions Coordinator, 505-277-7401, Fax: 505-277-7405, E-mail: lzawahri@unm.edu. *Dean of the Graduate School,* Dr. Teresita E. Aguilar, 505-277-2711, Fax: 505-277-7405.

College of Arts and Sciences Students: 977 full-time (548 women), 379 part-time (215 women); includes 238 minority (20 African Americans, 25 Asian Americans or Pacific Islanders, 170 Hispanic Americans, 23 Native Americans), 187 international. Average age 35. 973 applicants, 53% accepted, 229 enrolled. *Faculty:* 411 full-time (144 women), 141 part-time/adjunct (63 women). Expenses: Contact institution. *Financial support:* In 2001–02, 867 students received support; fellowships, research assistantships, teaching assistantships, scholarships/grants, health care benefits, tuition waivers (full and partial), and unspecified assistantships available. Financial award application deadline: 3/1; financial award applicants required to submit FAFSA. In 2001, 198 master's, 113 doctorates awarded. *Degree program information:* Part-time and evening/weekend programs available. Offers American studies (MA, PhD); anthropology (MA, MS, PhD); arts and sciences (MA, MS, PhD); biology (MS, PhD); chemistry (MS, PhD); clinical psychology (MS, PhD); communication (MA, PhD); comparative literature and cultural studies (MA); earth and planetary sciences (MS, PhD); economics (MA, PhD); English (MA, PhD); French (MA); French studies (PhD); geography (MS); German studies (MA); history (MA, PhD); Latin American studies (MA, PhD); linguistics (MA, PhD); mathematics (MS, PhD); optical sciences (PhD); philosophy (MA, PhD); physics (MS, PhD); political science (MA, PhD); Portuguese (MA); psychology (MS, PhD); sociology (MA, PhD); Spanish (MA); Spanish and Portuguese (PhD); speech and hearing sciences (MS); statistics (MS, PhD). *Application fee:* $40. *Application Contact:* Vicki Hall, Academic Administrator III, 505-277-6131, Fax: 505-277-0351, E-mail: vhall@unm.edu. *Dean,* Dr. Reed Way Dasenbrock, 505-277-3046, Fax: 505-277-0351, E-mail: rdasenbr@unm.edu.

College of Education Students: 477 full-time (359 women), 682 part-time (507 women); includes 404 minority (66 African Americans, 27 Asian Americans or Pacific Islanders, 253 Hispanic Americans, 58 Native Americans), 44 international. Average age 40. 231 applicants, 65% accepted, 100 enrolled. *Faculty:* 117 full-time (76 women), 81 part-time/adjunct (53 women). Expenses: Contact institution. *Financial support:* In 2001–02, 514 students received support. Tuition waivers (full and partial) available. Financial award application deadline: 3/1; financial award applicants required to submit FAFSA. In 2001, 325 master's, 61 doctorates awarded. *Degree program information:* Part-time and evening/weekend programs available. Offers art education (MA); counselor education (MA, PhD); education (MA, MS, Ed D, PhD, EDSPC); educational leadership (MA, Ed D, EDSPC); educational leadership and organizational learning (MA, Ed D, PhD, EDSPC); educational linguistics (Ed D, PhD); educational psychology (MA, PhD); educational specialities (MA, Ed D, PhD, EDSPC); educational thought and sociocultural studies (MA, Ed D, PhD); elementary education (MA); family studies (MA, PhD); health education (MS); health, physical education and recreation (Ed D); health, physical education, and recreation (PhD); individual, family, and community education (MA, MS, PhD); language, literacy, and sociocultural studies (MA, Ed D, PhD); multicultural teacher and childhood education (Ed D, PhD, EDSPC); nutrition (MS); organizational learning and instructional technologies (MA, PhD, EDSPC); physical education (MS); physical performance and development (MA, MS, Ed D, PhD, EDSPC); recreation (MA, EDSPC); secondary education (MA); special education (MA, Ed D, PhD, EDSPC). *Application fee:* $40. *Dean,* Dr. Viola E. Florez Tighe, 505-277-7267, Fax: 505-277-8427, E-mail: vflorez@unm.edu.

College of Fine Arts Students: 110 full-time (64 women), 71 part-time (36 women); includes 31 minority (4 African Americans, 5 Asian Americans or Pacific Islanders, 17 Hispanic Americans, 5 Native Americans), 10 international. Average age 33. 246 applicants, 42% accepted, 61 enrolled. *Faculty:* 72 full-time (29 women), 71 part-time/adjunct (46 women). Expenses: Contact institution. *Financial support:* In 2001–02, 144 students received support. Health care benefits and unspecified assistantships available. Financial award application deadline: 3/1; financial award applicants required to submit FAFSA. In 2001, 34 master's, 3 doctorates awarded. *Degree program information:* Part-time programs available. Offers art history (MA, PhD); dramatic writing (MFA); fine arts (M Mu, MA, MFA, PhD); music (M Mu); studio arts (MFA); theater and dance (MA). *Application fee:* $40. Dr. James S. Moy, 505-277-2111, Fax: 505-277-0708.

College of Nursing Students: 43 full-time (38 women), 40 part-time (38 women); includes 17 minority (3 Asian Americans or Pacific Islanders, 14 Hispanic Americans), 5 international. Average age 40. 35 applicants, 86% accepted, 25 enrolled. *Faculty:* 32 full-time (27 women), 9 part-time/adjunct (all women). Expenses: Contact institution. *Financial support:* In 2001–02, 34 students received support, including 2 research assistantships with partial tuition reimbursements available (averaging $5,000 per year), 4 teaching assistantships with partial tuition reimbursements available (averaging $5,000 per year); scholarships/

grants, traineeships, health care benefits, and tuition waivers (full) also available. Financial award application deadline: 3/1; financial award applicants required to submit FAFSA. In 2001, 72 master's awarded. *Degree program information:* Part-time programs available. Offers nursing (MSN, EDSPC). *Application deadline:* For fall admission, 6/15; for spring admission, 10/15. *Application fee:* $40. *Application Contact:* Martha A. Frederick, Student Program Advisor, 505-272-0849, Fax: 505-272-3970, E-mail: mfrederick@salud.unm.edu. *Dean*, Dr. Sandra Ferketich, 505-272-6284, Fax: 505-272-3970, E-mail: sferketich@salud.unm.edu.

Robert O. Anderson Graduate School of Management Students: 245 full-time (105 women), 186 part-time (77 women); includes 101 minority (8 African Americans, 20 Asian Americans or Pacific Islanders, 67 Hispanic Americans, 6 Native Americans), 29 international. Average age 31. 146 applicants, 63% accepted, 71 enrolled. *Faculty:* 49 full-time (15 women), 37 part-time/adjunct (10 women). Expenses: Contact institution. *Financial support:* In 2001–02, 75 students received support, including 12 fellowships (averaging $2,000 per year), 60 research assistantships with partial tuition reimbursements available (averaging $5,000 per year), 3 teaching assistantships with partial tuition reimbursements available (averaging $5,000 per year); career-related internships or fieldwork, Federal Work-Study, scholarships/grants, health care benefits, and unspecified assistantships also available. In 2001, 130 degrees awarded. *Degree program information:* Part-time and evening/weekend programs available. Offers accounting (M Acc, MBA); financial management (MBA); financial, international and technology management (MBA); general management (MBA); human resources management (MBA); international management (MBA); international management in Latin America (MBA); management information systems (MBA); management of technology (MBA); marketing management (MBA); marketing, information and decision sciences (MBA); operations and management science (MBA); organizational studies (MBA); policy and planning (MBA); tax accounting (MBA). *Application deadline:* For fall admission, 6/1 (priority date); for spring admission, 11/1 (priority date). Applications are processed on a rolling basis. *Application fee:* $40. *Application Contact:* Loyola Chastain, MBA Manager, 505-277-3147, Fax: 505-277-9356, E-mail: chastain@mgt.unm.edu. *Dean*, Dr. Howard L. Smith, 505-277-6471, Fax: 505-277-7108, E-mail: smith@mgt.unm.edu/.

School of Architecture and Planning Students: 139 full-time (58 women), 56 part-time (29 women); includes 54 minority (4 African Americans, 2 Asian Americans or Pacific Islanders, 39 Hispanic Americans, 9 Native Americans), 9 international. Average age 33. 113 applicants, 87% accepted, 52 enrolled. *Faculty:* 21 full-time (5 women), 19 part-time/adjunct (7 women). Expenses: Contact institution. *Financial support:* In 2001–02, 121 students received support. Health care benefits available. Financial award application deadline: 3/1; financial award applicants required to submit FAFSA. In 2001, 43 degrees awarded. *Degree program information:* Part-time programs available. Offers architecture (M Arch); architecture and planning (M Arch, MCRP, MLA); community and regional planning (MCRP); landscape architecture (MLA). *Application fee:* $40. *Application Contact:* Lois A. Kennedy, Senior Academic Adviser, 505-277-4847, Fax: 505-277-0076, E-mail: loisk@unm.edu. *Dean*, Dr. Roger L. Schluntz, 505-277-2879, Fax: 505-277-0076, E-mail: schluntz@unm.edu.

School of Engineering Students: 381 full-time (73 women), 182 part-time (40 women); includes 83 minority (5 African Americans, 22 Asian Americans or Pacific Islanders, 49 Hispanic Americans, 7 Native Americans), 269 international. Average age 32. 952 applicants, 46% accepted, 143 enrolled. *Faculty:* 105 full-time (10 women), 47 part-time/adjunct (4 women). Expenses: Contact institution. *Financial support:* In 2001–02, 207 students received support. Application deadline: 3/1; In 2001, 97 master's, 21 doctorates awarded. *Degree program information:* Part-time and evening/weekend programs available. Offers chemical engineering (MS); civil engineering (MS); computer science (MS, PhD); electrical engineering (MS); engineering (PhD); hazardous waste engineering (MEHWE); manufacturing engineering (MEME); mechanical engineering (MS); nuclear engineering (MS); optical sciences (PhD). *Application deadline:* Applications are processed on a rolling basis. *Application fee:* $40. *Dean*, Dr. Joseph L. Cecchi, 505-277-5431, Fax: 505-277-5433, E-mail: cecchi@unm.edu.

School of Public Administration Students: 39 full-time (25 women), 115 part-time (78 women); includes 63 minority (4 African Americans, 2 Asian Americans or Pacific Islanders, 49 Hispanic Americans, 8 Native Americans), 10 international. Average age 38. 43 applicants, 88% accepted, 29 enrolled. *Faculty:* 5 full-time (3 women), 3 part-time/adjunct (1 woman). Expenses: Contact institution. *Financial support:* In 2001–02, 38 students received support. Health care benefits available. Financial award application deadline: 3/1; financial award applicants required to submit FAFSA. In 2001, 39 degrees awarded. *Degree program information:* Part-time and evening/weekend programs available. Postbaccalaureate distance learning degree programs offered (no on-campus study). Offers public administration (MPA). *Application deadline:* For fall admission, 7/15; for spring admission, 11/15. *Application fee:* $40. *Application Contact:* Roberta Lopez, Department Administrator I, 505-277-1092, Fax: 505-277-2529, E-mail: lopez@unm.edu. *Director*, Dr. Thomas Zane Reeves, 505-277-3312, Fax: 505-277-2529, E-mail: tzane@unm.edu.

School of Law Students: 330 full-time (195 women); includes 116 minority (10 African Americans, 8 Asian Americans or Pacific Islanders, 76 Hispanic Americans, 22 Native Americans) Average age 30. 650 applicants, 39% accepted, 110 enrolled. *Faculty:* 34 full-time (16 women), 29 part-time/adjunct (9 women). Expenses: Contact institution. *Financial support:* Career-related internships or fieldwork, Federal Work-Study, and scholarships/grants available. Financial award application deadline: 3/1; financial award applicants required to submit FAFSA. In 2001, 106 degrees awarded. Offers law (JD). *Application deadline:* For fall admission, 2/15 (priority date). Applications are processed on a rolling basis. *Application fee:* $40. Electronic applications accepted. *Application Contact:* Susan L. Mitchell, Director of Admissions and Financial Aid, 505-277-0959, Fax: 505-277-9958, E-mail: mitchell@law.unm.edu. *Dean*, Robert J. Desiderio, 505-277-2146, Fax: 505-277-1597, E-mail: desiderior@law.unm.edu.

School of Medicine Students: 784 full-time (460 women), 118 part-time (68 women); includes 401 minority (14 African Americans, 123 Asian Americans or Pacific Islanders, 222 Hispanic Americans, 42 Native Americans), 17 international. Average age 28. 828 applicants, 11% accepted, 75 enrolled. *Faculty:* 486 full-time (157 women), 83 part-time/adjunct (54 women). Expenses: Contact institution. *Financial support:* In 2001–02, 260 students received support. Scholarships/grants available. Financial award application deadline: 5/1; financial award applicants required to submit FAFSA. In 2001, 67 degrees awarded. Offers biochemistry and molecular biology (MS, PhD); cell biology and physiology (MS, PhD); medicine (MD, Pharm D, MOT, MPH, MPT, MS, PhD); molecular genetics and microbiology (MS, PhD); neuroscience (MS, PhD); occupational therapy (MOT); pathology (MS, PhD); physical therapy (MPT); public health (MPH); toxicology (MS, PhD). *Application deadline:* For fall admission, 11/15. *Application fee:* $50. Electronic applications accepted. *Application Contact:* Dr. Roger Radloff, Assistant Dean for Admissions, 505-272-3414, Fax: 505-272-8239. *Dean*, Dr. Paul B. Roth, 505-272-2321.

See in-depth description on page 1223.

UNIVERSITY OF NEW ORLEANS, New Orleans, LA 70148

General Information State-supported, coed, university. CGS member. *Enrollment:* 1,365 full-time matriculated graduate/professional students (764 women), 2,105 part-time matriculated graduate/professional students (1,408 women). *Graduate faculty:* 184 full-time (56 women), 33 part-time/adjunct (13 women). Tuition, state resident: full-time $2,748; part-time $435 per credit. Tuition, nonresident: full-time $9,792; part-time $1,773 per credit. *Graduate housing:* Rooms and/or apartments available on a first-come, first-served basis to single students and available to married students. Typical cost: $3,900 (including board) for single students. Room and board charges vary according to housing facility selected. *Student services:* Campus employment opportunities, campus safety program, career counseling, child daycare facilities, disabled student services, free psychological counseling, international student services, low-cost health insurance. *Library facilities:* Earl K. Long Library. *Online resources:* library catalog, web page, access to other libraries' catalogs. *Collection:* 864,442 titles, 3,909 serial subscriptions, 123,120 audiovisual materials. *Research affiliation:* M. Rosenblatt & Sons, Inc. (engineering), Applied Research Lab-Penn State University (engineering), Almaden Research Center-IBM (chemistry), TJ Watson Research Center-IBM (chemistry), Band, Lavis & Associates, Inc. (engineering), John C. Stennis Space Center (acoustics, computer science).

Computer facilities: 1,084 computers available on campus for general student use. A campuswide network can be accessed from student residence rooms and from off campus. Internet access is available. *Web address:* http://www.uno.edu/.

General Application Contact: Dr. Robert Cashner, Dean, Graduate School, 504-280-6836, Fax: 504-280-6298, E-mail: gradsch@uno.edu.

GRADUATE UNITS

Graduate School Students: 1,365 full-time (764 women), 2,105 part-time (1,408 women); includes 884 minority (670 African Americans, 81 Asian Americans or Pacific Islanders, 120 Hispanic Americans, 13 Native Americans), 445 international. Average age 34. 2,717 applicants, 62% accepted, 944 enrolled. *Faculty:* 184 full-time (56 women), 33 part-time/adjunct (13 women). Expenses: Contact institution. *Financial support:* Fellowships, research assistantships, teaching assistantships, career-related internships or fieldwork, Federal Work-Study, institutionally sponsored loans, scholarships/grants, tuition waivers (full and partial), and unspecified assistantships available. Financial award applicants required to submit FAFSA. In 2001, 753 master's, 55 doctorates awarded. *Degree program information:* Part-time and evening/weekend programs available. *Application deadline:* Applications are processed on a rolling basis. *Application fee:* $20. Electronic applications accepted. *Dean*, Dr. Robert Cashner, 504-280-6836, Fax: 504-280-6298, E-mail: rcashner@uno.edu.

College of Business Administration Students: 472 full-time (261 women), 532 part-time (273 women); includes 249 minority (179 African Americans, 32 Asian Americans or Pacific Islanders, 36 Hispanic Americans, 2 Native Americans), 167 international. Average age 31. 766 applicants, 64% accepted, 323 enrolled. *Faculty:* 29 full-time (6 women), 7 part-time/adjunct (1 woman). Expenses: Contact institution. *Financial support:* Fellowships, research assistantships, teaching assistantships, Federal Work-Study available. Financial award applicants required to submit FAFSA. In 2001, 292 master's, 3 doctorates awarded. *Degree program information:* Part-time and evening/weekend programs available. Offers accounting (MS); business administration (MBA, MS, PhD); financial economics (PhD); health care management (MS); taxation (MS). *Application deadline:* For fall admission, 7/1 (priority date); for spring admission, 11/15 (priority date). Applications are processed on a rolling basis. *Application fee:* $20. Electronic applications accepted. *Application Contact:* Dr. Paul Hensel, Associate Dean, 504-280-6393, E-mail: phensel@uno.edu. *Dean*, Dr. Tim Ryan, 504-280-6954, Fax: 504-280-6958, E-mail: tpryan@uno.edu.

College of Education Students: 276 full-time (224 women), 1,113 part-time (918 women); includes 439 minority (371 African Americans, 17 Asian Americans or Pacific Islanders, 48 Hispanic Americans, 3 Native Americans), 18 international. Average age 36. 379 applicants, 88% accepted, 182 enrolled. *Faculty:* 33 full-time (19 women), 19 part-time/adjunct (12 women). Expenses: Contact institution. *Financial support:* Fellowships, research assistantships, teaching assistantships, career-related internships or fieldwork, institutionally sponsored loans, scholarships/grants, and tuition waivers (partial) available. Financial award applicants required to submit FAFSA. In 2001, 251 master's, 27 doctorates awarded. *Degree program information:* Evening/weekend programs available. Offers adapted physical education (MA); counselor education (M Ed, PhD, Certificate); curriculum and instruction (M Ed, PhD, Certificate); education (M Ed, MA, PhD, Certificate); educational leadership and foundations (M Ed, PhD, Certificate); exercise physiology (MA); gerontology (Certificate); health and physical education (Certificate); physical education (M Ed); science, pedagogy and coaching sport management (MA); special education (M Ed, PhD, Certificate). *Application deadline:* For fall admission, 7/1 (priority date); for spring admission, 11/15 (priority date). Applications are processed on a rolling basis. *Application fee:* $20. Electronic applications accepted. *Application Contact:* Dr. Jay Miller, Associate Dean, 504-280-6253, Fax: 504-280-5588, E-mail: jhmse@uno.edu. *Chairperson*, Dr. James Meza, 504-280-6719, Fax: 504-280-6065, E-mail: jmeza@uno.edu.

College of Engineering Students: 116 full-time (30 women), 97 part-time (26 women). Average age 29. 510 applicants, 39% accepted, 45 enrolled. *Faculty:* 17 full-time (2 women), 4 part-time/adjunct (0 women). Expenses: Contact institution. *Financial support:* Fellowships, research assistantships, teaching assistantships, institutionally sponsored loans available. Financial award applicants required to submit FAFSA. In 2001, 52 master's, 6 doctorates awarded. *Degree program information:* Part-time and evening/weekend programs available. Offers civil engineering (MS); electrical engineering (MS); engineering (MS, PhD, Certificate); engineering and applied sciences (PhD); engineering management (MS, Certificate); mechanical engineering (MS); naval architecture and marine engineering (MS). *Application deadline:* For fall admission, 7/1 (priority date). Applications are processed on a rolling basis. *Application fee:* $20. Electronic applications accepted. *Application Contact:* Dr. Paul Chirlian, Associate Director, 504-280-5504, Fax: 504-280-7413, E-mail: pchirlia@uno.edu. *Dean*, Dr. John N. Crisp, 504-280-6825, Fax: 504-280-7413, E-mail: jcrisp@uno.edu.

College of Liberal Arts Students: 185 full-time (100 women), 233 part-time (128 women); includes 68 minority (44 African Americans, 6 Asian Americans or Pacific Islanders, 16 Hispanic Americans, 2 Native Americans), 35 international. Average age 33. 313 applicants, 50% accepted, 99 enrolled. *Faculty:* 50 full-time (18 women), 3 part-time/adjunct (0 women). Expenses: Contact institution. *Financial support:* Fellowships, research assistantships, teaching assistantships, career-related internships or fieldwork, Federal Work-Study, institutionally sponsored loans, and tuition waivers (full and partial) available. Financial award applicants required to submit FAFSA. In 2001, 95 master's, 4 doctorates awarded. *Degree program information:* Part-time and evening/weekend programs available. Offers applied sociology (MA); archives and records administration (MA); arts administration (MA); communications (MA, MFA); creative writing (MFA); drama (MFA); English (MA); geography (MA); graphic design (MFA); graphics (MFA); history (MA); international relations (MA); liberal arts (MA, MFA, MM, PhD); music (MM); painting (MFA); photography (MFA); political science (MA, PhD); Romance languages (MA); sculpture (MFA); sociology (MA). *Application deadline:* For fall admission, 7/1 (priority date); for spring admission, 11/15 (priority date). Applications are processed on a rolling basis. *Application fee:* $20. Electronic applications accepted. *Application Contact:* Dr. Merrill Johnson, Associate Dean, 504-280-6408, E-mail: mljohso@uno.edu. *Associate Dean*, Fredrick P. Barton, 504-280-6267, Fax: 504-280-6468, E-mail: fbarton@uno.edu.

College of Sciences Students: 207 full-time (100 women), 91 part-time (31 women); includes 61 minority (33 African Americans, 18 Asian Americans or Pacific Islanders, 10 Hispanic Americans), 108 international. Average age 29. 341 applicants, 47% accepted, 71 enrolled. *Faculty:* 47 full-time (8 women). Expenses: Contact institution. *Financial support:* Fellowships, research assistantships, teaching assistantships, career-related internships or fieldwork, Federal Work-Study, institutionally sponsored loans, and unspecified assistantships available. Financial award applicants required to submit FAFSA. In 2001, 46 master's, 11 doctorates awarded. *Degree program information:* Part-time and evening/weekend programs available. Offers applied physics (MS); applied psychology (PhD); biological sciences (MS); chemistry (MS, PhD); computer science (MS); conservation biology (PhD); geology (MS); geophysics (MS); mathematics (MS); physics (MS); psychology (MS); science teaching (MA); sciences (MA, MS, PhD). *Application deadline:* For fall admission, 7/1 (priority date); for spring admission, 11/15 (priority date). Applications are processed on a rolling basis. *Application fee:* $20. Electronic applications accepted. *Application Contact:* Dr. Steve Stevenson, Associate Dean, 504-280-6783, Fax: 504-280-7483, E-mail: mmsteven@uno.edu. *Dean*, Dr. Joe King, 504-280-6563, Fax: 504-280-7483, E-mail: jmking@uno.edu.

College of Urban and Public Affairs Students: 64 full-time (39 women), 84 part-time (42 women); includes 47 minority (38 African Americans, 2 Asian Americans or Pacific Islanders, 4 Hispanic Americans, 3 Native Americans), 7 international. Average age 35. 83 applicants, 46% accepted, 17 enrolled. *Faculty:* 8 full-time (3 women). Expenses: Contact institution. *Financial support:* Research assistantships, career-related internships or fieldwork available. Financial award applicants required to submit FAFSA. In 2001, 14 master's, 4 doctorates awarded. *Degree program information:* Part-time and evening/weekend programs available. Offers public administration and policy (MPA); urban and public affairs (MPA, MS, MURP, PhD); urban and regional planning (MURP); urban studies (MS, PhD). *Application deadline:* For fall admission, 7/1 (priority date); for spring admission, 11/15 (priority date). Applications are processed on a rolling basis. *Application fee:* $20.

University of New Orleans (continued)

Electronic applications accepted. *Dean,* Dr. Robert K. Whelan, 504-280-6592, E-mail: rkwhelan@uno.edu.

UNIVERSITY OF NORTH ALABAMA, Florence, AL 35632-0001

General Information State-supported, coed, comprehensive institution. *Enrollment:* 115 full-time matriculated graduate/professional students (74 women), 459 part-time matriculated graduate/professional students (298 women). *Enrollment by degree level:* 564 master's, 10 other advanced degrees. *Graduate faculty:* 49 part-time/adjunct (12 women). Tuition, state resident: full-time $2,214; part-time $123 per credit hour. Tuition, nonresident: full-time $4,428; part-time $246 per credit hour. *Required fees:* $176; $7 per credit hour. *Graduate housing:* Rooms and/or apartments available on a first-come, first-served basis to single students and available to married students. *Student services:* Campus employment opportunities, career counseling, child daycare facilities, exercise/wellness program, grant writing training, international student services, multicultural affairs office. *Library facilities:* Collier Library. *Online resources:* library catalog, web page, access to other libraries' catalogs. *Collection:* 343,468 titles, 1,792 serial subscriptions, 8,945 audiovisual materials.

Computer facilities: 500 computers available on campus for general student use. A campuswide network can be accessed from student residence rooms and from off campus. Internet access is available. *Web address:* http://www.una.edu/.

General Application Contact: Kim Mauldin, Director of Admissions, 256-765-4221, Fax: 256-765-4329, E-mail: kmauldin@unanov.una.edu.

GRADUATE UNITS

College of Arts and Sciences Students: 18 full-time (13 women), 27 part-time (15 women); includes 5 minority (3 African Americans, 2 Native Americans), 1 international. Average age 30. *Faculty:* 9 part-time/adjunct (3 women). Expenses: Contact institution. In 2001, 13 degrees awarded. *Degree program information:* Part-time and evening/weekend programs available. Offers arts and sciences (MAEN, MSCJ); criminal justice (MSCJ); English (MAEN). *Application deadline:* For fall admission, 7/1 (priority date); for spring admission, 12/1. Applications are processed on a rolling basis. *Application fee:* $25. *Application Contact:* Dr. Sue Wilson, Dean of Enrollment Management, 256-765-4316. *Dean,* Dr. Elliot Pood, 256-765-4288.

College of Business Students: 40 full-time (20 women), 88 part-time (38 women); includes 25 minority (8 African Americans, 16 Asian Americans or Pacific Islanders, 1 Native American), 6 international. Average age 32. *Faculty:* 17 part-time/adjunct (3 women). Expenses: Contact institution. *Financial support:* Federal Work-Study available. Support available to part-time students. Financial award application deadline: 4/1. In 2001, 79 degrees awarded. *Degree program information:* Part-time and evening/weekend programs available. Offers business (MBA). *Application deadline:* For fall admission, 7/1 (priority date); for spring admission, 12/1. Applications are processed on a rolling basis. *Application fee:* $25. *Application Contact:* Dr. Sue Wilson, Dean of Enrollment Management, 256-765-4316. *Dean,* Dr. Kerry Gatlin, 256-765-4261.

College of Education Students: 57 full-time (41 women), 344 part-time (245 women); includes 22 minority (18 African Americans, 3 Hispanic Americans, 1 Native American) Average age 33. *Faculty:* 18 part-time/adjunct (8 women). Expenses: Contact institution. *Financial support:* Federal Work-Study available. Support available to part-time students. Financial award application deadline: 4/1. In 2001, 165 master's, 18 other advanced degrees awarded. *Degree program information:* Part-time and evening/weekend programs available. Offers counseling (MA, MA Ed); early childhood education (MA Ed); education (MA, MA Ed, Ed S); education leadership (Ed S); elementary education (MA Ed, Ed S); learning disabilities (MA Ed); mentally retarded (MA Ed); mild learning handicapped (MA Ed); non-school-based counseling (MA); non-school-based teaching (MA); principalship (MA Ed); principalship, superintendency, and supervision of instruction (MA Ed); secondary education (MA Ed); special education (MA Ed); superintendency (MA Ed); supervision of instruction (MA Ed). *Application deadline:* For fall admission, 7/1 (priority date); for spring admission, 12/1. Applications are processed on a rolling basis. *Application fee:* $25. *Application Contact:* Dr. Sue Wilson, Dean of Enrollment Management, 256-765-4316. *Dean,* Dr. Fred L. Hattabaugh, 256-765-4252.

THE UNIVERSITY OF NORTH CAROLINA AT ASHEVILLE, Asheville, NC 28804-3299

General Information State-supported, coed, comprehensive institution. *Enrollment:* 2 full-time matriculated graduate/professional students (1 woman), 26 part-time matriculated graduate/professional students (15 women). *Enrollment by degree level:* 28 master's. *Graduate faculty:* 11 full-time (3 women), 1 part-time/adjunct (0 women). Tuition, state resident: full-time $1,248. Tuition, nonresident: full-time $8,812. *Required fees:* $1,300. *Graduate housing:* On-campus housing not available. *Student services:* Campus employment opportunities, career counseling, disabled student services, exercise/wellness program, free psychological counseling, international student services, low-cost health insurance, multicultural affairs office, writing training. *Library facilities:* D. Hidden Ramsey Library. *Online resources:* library catalog, web page, access to other libraries' catalogs. *Collection:* 252,601 titles, 2,313 serial subscriptions, 8,855 audiovisual materials.

Computer facilities: 300 computers available on campus for general student use. A campuswide network can be accessed from student residence rooms and from off campus. Internet access and online class registration, online grade reports are available. *Web address:* http://www.unca.edu/.

General Application Contact: Dr. Ted Uldricks, Director, MLA Program, 828-251-6620, Fax: 828-251-6614, E-mail: uldricks@unca.edu.

GRADUATE UNITS

Graduate Studies Students: 2 full-time (1 woman), 26 part-time (15 women); includes 4 minority (1 African American, 1 Asian American or Pacific Islander, 2 Hispanic Americans), 1 international. Average age 45. 7 applicants, 100% accepted. *Faculty:* 11 full-time (3 women), 1 part-time/adjunct (0 women). Expenses: Contact institution. *Financial support:* Federal Work-Study and institutionally sponsored loans available. Support available to part-time students. Financial award application deadline: 5/1; financial award applicants required to submit FAFSA. In 2001, 12 degrees awarded. *Degree program information:* Part-time and evening/weekend programs available. *Application deadline:* For fall admission, 7/1 (priority date); for spring admission, 12/1. Applications are processed on a rolling basis. *Application fee:* $50. *Director,* Dr. Ted Uldricks, 828-251-6620, Fax: 828-251-6614, E-mail: uldricks@unca.edu.

THE UNIVERSITY OF NORTH CAROLINA AT CHAPEL HILL, Chapel Hill, NC 27599

General Information State-supported, coed, university. CGS member. *Enrollment:* 9,636 full-time matriculated graduate/professional students (5,575 women). *Enrollment by degree level:* 2,172 first professional, 4,238 master's, 2,791 doctoral. *Graduate faculty:* 1,810 full-time (470 women), 613 part-time/adjunct (329 women). Tuition, state resident: full-time $2,864. Tuition, nonresident: full-time $12,030. *Graduate housing:* Rooms and/or apartments available to single and married students. *Student services:* Campus employment opportunities, campus safety program, career counseling, child daycare facilities, disabled student services, exercise/wellness program, free psychological counseling, grant writing training, international student services, low-cost health insurance, multicultural affairs office, teacher training, writing training. *Library facilities:* Davis Library plus 14 others. *Online resources:* library catalog, web page, access to other libraries' catalogs. *Collection:* 4.9 million titles, 44,023 serial subscriptions, 176,445 audiovisual materials. *Research affiliation:* Centers for Disease Control, Research Triangle Institute, Triangle Universities Nuclear Laboratory.

Computer facilities: 540 computers available on campus for general student use. A campuswide network can be accessed from student residence rooms and from off campus. Internet access and online class registration, on-line grade reports are available. *Web address:* http://www.unc.edu/.

General Application Contact: Peggy O. Berryhill, Director of Admissions and Student Records, 919-962-1538.

GRADUATE UNITS

Graduate School Students: 3,322 full-time (2,068 women), 2,187 part-time (1,206 women). Average age 28. ###### applicants, 29% accepted. Expenses: Contact institution. *Financial support:* In 2001–02, 500 fellowships with full and partial tuition reimbursements, 1,162 research assistantships with full and partial tuition reimbursements, 986 teaching assistantships with full and partial tuition reimbursements were awarded. Career-related internships or fieldwork, Federal Work-Study, institutionally sponsored loans, scholarships/grants, traineeships, tuition waivers (full), and unspecified assistantships also available. Support available to part-time students. Financial award applicants required to submit FAFSA. In 2001, 1,472 master's, 378 doctorates awarded. *Degree program information:* Part-time programs available. Postbaccalaureate distance learning degree programs offered (minimal on-campus study). Offers materials science (MS, PhD); public policy (PhD); Russian and east European studies (MA); toxicology (MS, PhD). *Application deadline:* Applications are processed on a rolling basis. Electronic applications accepted. *Application Contact:* Peggy O. Berryhill, Director of Admissions and Student Records, 919-962-1538. *Dean,* Dr. Linda Dykstra, 919-962-3521.

College of Arts and Sciences Students: 2,118 full-time (1,036 women), 53 part-time (23 women). 5,014 applicants, 24% accepted. *Faculty:* 659. Expenses: Contact institution. *Financial support:* Fellowships, research assistantships, teaching assistantships, career-related internships or fieldwork, Federal Work-Study, and unspecified assistantships available. Financial award application deadline: 3/1. In 2001, 340 master's, 196 doctorates awarded. *Degree program information:* Part-time programs available. Offers acting (MFA); anthropology (MA, PhD); art history (MA, PhD); arts and sciences (MA, MFA, MPA, MRP, MS, MSRA, PhD, Certificate); athletic training (MA); biological psychology (PhD); botany (MA, MS, PhD); cell biology, development, and physiology (MA, MS, PhD); chemistry (MA, MS, PhD); city and regional planning (MRP); classical archaeology (MA, PhD); classics (MA, PhD); clinical psychology (PhD); cognitive psychology (PhD); communication studies (MA, PhD); comparative literature (MA, PhD); computer science (MS, PhD); costume production (MFA); developmental psychology (PhD); ecology (MA, MS, PhD); ecology and behavior (MA, MS, PhD); economics (MS, PhD); English (MA, PhD); exercise physiology (MA); folklore (MA); French (MA, PhD); genetics and molecular biology (MA, MS, PhD); geography (MA, PhD); geological sciences (MS, PhD); history (MA, PhD); Italian (MA, PhD); Latin American studies (Certificate); linguistics (MA, PhD); literature and Linguistics (MA); Literaure and Linguistics (PhD); marine sciences (MS, PhD); mathematics (MA, MS, PhD); morphology, systematics, and evolution (MA, MS, PhD); music (MA, PhD); operations research (MS, PhD); philosophy (MA, PhD); physics (MS, PhD); planning (PhD); Polish literature (PhD); political science (MA, PhD); Portuguese (MA, PhD); public administration (MPA); public policy analysis (PhD); quantitative psychology (PhD); recreation and leisure studies (MSRA); religious studies (MA, PhD); Romance languages (MA, PhD); Romance philology (MA, PhD); Russian literature (MA, PhD); Serbo-Croatian literature (PhD); Slavic linguistics (MA, PhD); social psychology (PhD); sociology (MA, PhD); Spanish (MA, PhD); sport administration (MA); statistics (MS, PhD); studio art (MFA); technical production (MFA); trans-Atlantic studies (MA). *Application deadline:* For fall admission, 1/1 (priority date). Applications are processed on a rolling basis. *Application fee:* $55. Electronic applications accepted. *Application Contact:* Peggy O. Berryhill, Director of Admissions and Student Records, 919-962-1538.

School of Education *Degree program information:* Part-time programs available. Offers culture, curriculum and change (PhD); curriculum and instruction (MA, Ed D); early childhood, family, and literacy studies (PhD); early intervention and family support (M Ed); education (M Ed, MA, MAT, MSA, Ed D, PhD); educational leadership (Ed D); educational psychology (M Ed, MA); elementary education (M Ed); English (MAT); French (MAT); German (MAT); Japanese (MAT); Latin (MAT); learning disabilities (M Ed); mathematics (MAT); music (MAT); psychological studies in education (PhD); school administration (MSA); school counseling (M Ed, MA); school psychology (M Ed, MA, PhD); science (MAT); secondary education (MAT); social studies/social science (MAT); Spanish (MAT); special education (M Ed, MA). Electronic applications accepted.

School of Information and Library Science Students: 189 full-time (142 women), 63 part-time (40 women); includes 29 minority (12 African Americans, 14 Asian Americans or Pacific Islanders, 3 Hispanic Americans), 33 international. Average age 30. 281 applicants, 58% accepted, 88 enrolled. *Faculty:* 17 full-time (9 women), 20 part-time/adjunct (10 women). Expenses: Contact institution. *Financial support:* In 2001–02, 54 fellowships with full tuition reimbursements, 69 research assistantships with full tuition reimbursements (averaging $10,000 per year), 10 teaching assistantships with full tuition reimbursements (averaging $14,000 per year) were awarded. Career-related internships or fieldwork, Federal Work-Study, institutionally sponsored loans, health care benefits, and unspecified assistantships also available. Financial award application deadline: 1/1; financial award applicants required to submit FAFSA. In 2001, 80 master's, 3 doctorates, 1 other advanced degree awarded. *Degree program information:* Part-time programs available. Offers information and library science (MSIS, MSLS, PhD, CAS). *Application deadline:* For fall admission, 1/1 (priority date); for spring admission, 10/15. Applications are processed on a rolling basis. *Application fee:* $60. Electronic applications accepted. *Application Contact:* Lucia Zonn, Student Services Manager, 919-962-8366, Fax: 919-962-8071, E-mail: info@ils.unc.edu. *Dean,* Dr. Joanne Gard Marshall, 919-962-8366, Fax: 919-962-8071, E-mail: info@ils.unc.edu.

School of Journalism and Mass Communication *Degree program information:* Part-time programs available. Offers mass communication (MA, PhD). Electronic applications accepted.

School of Public Health Students: 1,132 full-time (795 women); includes 334 minority (97 African Americans, 199 Asian Americans or Pacific Islanders, 35 Hispanic Americans, 3 Native Americans) Average age 28. 1,532 applicants, 44% accepted, 407 enrolled. *Faculty:* 207 full-time (87 women), 333 part-time/adjunct. Expenses: Contact institution. *Financial support:* In 2001–02, 546 students received support, including 163 fellowships with full and partial tuition reimbursements available (averaging $10,008 per year), 261 research assistantships with partial tuition reimbursements available (averaging $9,795 per year), 122 teaching assistantships with partial tuition reimbursements available (averaging $1,800 per year); career-related internships or fieldwork, Federal Work-Study, institutionally sponsored loans, scholarships/grants, traineeships, and unspecified assistantships also available. Support available to part-time students. Financial award application deadline: 1/1; financial award applicants required to submit FAFSA. In 2001, 284 master's, 59 doctorates awarded. *Degree program information:* Part-time programs available. Postbaccalaureate distance learning degree programs offered (minimal on-campus study). Offers air, radiation and industrial hygiene (MPH, MS, MSEE, MSPH, PhD); aquatic and atmospheric sciences (MPH, MS, MSPH, PhD); biostatistics (MPH, MS, Dr PH, PhD); environmental engineering (MPH, MS, MSEE, MSPH, PhD); environmental health sciences (MPH, MS, MSPH, PhD); environmental management and policy (MPH, MS, MSPH, PhD); epidemiology (MPH, MSPH, Dr PH, PhD); health behavior and health education (MPH, Dr PH, PhD); health care and prevention (MPH); health policy and administration (MHA, MPH, MSPH, Dr PH, PhD); leadership (MPH, Dr PH); maternal and child health (MPH, MSPH, Dr PH, PhD); nutrition (MPH, Dr PH, PhD); nutritional biochemistry (MS); occupational health nursing (MPH); professional practice program (MPH); public health (MHA, MPH, MS, MSEE, MSPH, Dr PH, PhD); public health nursing (MPH). *Application deadline:* For fall admission, 1/1. Applications are processed on a rolling basis. *Application fee:* $60. Electronic applications accepted. *Application Contact:* Aundra N. Shields, Associate Dean for Students, 919-966-2499, Fax: 919-966-6352, E-mail: student.affairs@sph.unc.edu. *Dean,* Dr. William L. Roper, 919-966-3215, Fax: 919-966-7678, E-mail: bill_roper@unc.edu.

School of Social Work Students: 246 full-time (203 women), 108 part-time (97 women); includes 64 minority (39 African Americans, 8 Asian Americans or Pacific Islanders, 12 Hispanic Americans, 5 Native Americans), 4 international. Average age 30. 437 applicants, 51% accepted, 152 enrolled. *Faculty:* 32 full-time (17 women), 25 part-time/adjunct (15 women). Expenses: Contact institution. *Financial support:* In 2001–02, 316 students received support, including 3 fellowships with full tuition reimbursements available (averaging $7,500 per year), 40 research assistantships with full tuition reimbursements available (averaging $9,000 per year); teaching assistantships with full tuition reimbursements available, career-related internships or fieldwork, Federal Work-Study, institutionally sponsored loans, scholarships/grants, and unspecified assistantships also available. Support available to part-time students. Financial award application deadline: 2/15; financial award applicants required to submit FAFSA. In 2001, 106 master's, 2 doctorates awarded. *Degree program information:* Part-time programs available. Offers social work (MSW, PhD). *Application deadline:* For fall admission, 1/1 (priority date). Applications are processed on a rolling basis. *Application fee:* $60. Electronic applications accepted. *Application Contact:* Prof. Dorothy N. Gamble, Assistant Dean for Student Services, 919-962-6446, Fax: 919-843-8562, E-mail: dee_gamble@unc.edu. *Interim Dean*, Dr. Jack Richman, 919-962-5650, Fax: 919-962-0890, E-mail: jrichman@email.unc.edu.

Kenan-Flagler Business School Students: 807 full-time. *Faculty:* 93 full-time. Expenses: Contact institution. *Financial support:* Fellowships, research assistantships, teaching assistantships, career-related internships or fieldwork and institutionally sponsored loans available. Support available to part-time students. Financial award application deadline: 3/1; financial award applicants required to submit FAFSA. *Degree program information:* Evening/weekend programs available. Postbaccalaureate distance learning degree programs offered (minimal on-campus study). Offers accounting (PhD); business (MAC, MBA, PhD); business administration (MBA, PhD); finance (PhD); marketing (PhD); operations management (PhD); organizational behavior (PhD); strategy (PhD). *Application deadline:* Applications are processed on a rolling basis. Electronic applications accepted. *Application Contact:* Programs Office and Information, 919-962-8301. *Dean*, Robert S. Sullivan, 919-962-3232, Fax: 919-962-1300.

School of Dentistry Students: 385 full-time (177 women); includes 85 minority (26 African Americans, 46 Asian Americans or Pacific Islanders, 9 Hispanic Americans, 4 Native Americans) Average age 26. 1,638 applicants, 9% accepted. *Faculty:* 84 full-time. Expenses: Contact institution. *Financial support:* Fellowships, research assistantships, teaching assistantships, Federal Work-Study, institutionally sponsored loans, and scholarships/grants available. Financial award application deadline: 3/1; financial award applicants required to submit FAFSA. In 2001, 78 first professional degrees, 16 master's, 4 doctorates awarded. Offers dentistry (DDS, MS); oral biology (PhD); oral epidemiology (PhD). Electronic applications accepted. *Application Contact:* Dr. William David Brunson, Assistant Dean of Predoctoral Education, 919-966-4565, Fax: 919-966-7007. *Dean*, Dr. John Stamm, 919-966-2731, Fax: 919-966-4049.

School of Law Students: 786 full-time (389 women); includes 127 minority (66 African Americans, 33 Asian Americans or Pacific Islanders, 21 Hispanic Americans, 7 Native Americans) Average age 25. 2,161 applicants, 24% accepted. *Faculty:* 48 full-time (21 women), 48 part-time/adjunct (21 women). Expenses: Contact institution. *Financial support:* In 2001–02, 541 students received support, including 40 research assistantships (averaging $2,100 per year); career-related internships or fieldwork, Federal Work-Study, and scholarships/grants also available. Financial award application deadline: 3/1; financial award applicants required to submit FAFSA. In 2001, 222 degrees awarded. Offers law (JD). *Application deadline:* For fall admission, 2/1. Applications are processed on a rolling basis. *Application fee:* $60. Electronic applications accepted. *Application Contact:* Victoria Taylor Carter, Assistant Dean for Admissions, 919-962-5109, Fax: 919-843-7939, E-mail: law_admission@unc.edu. *Dean*, Gene R. Nichol, 919-962-4417, Fax: 919-962-1170.

School of Medicine Offers allied health sciences (MS, Au D, PhD); biochemistry and biophysics (MS, PhD); biomedical engineering (MS, PhD); cell and developmental biology (PhD); cell and molecular physiology (PhD); experimental pathology (PhD); genetics and molecular biology (MS, PhD); human movement science (PhD); immunology (MS, PhD); medicine (MD, MPT, MS, Au D, PhD); microbiology (MS, PhD); microbiology and immunology (MS, PhD); neurobiology (PhD); occupational science (MS); pathology and laboratory medicine (PhD); pharmacology (PhD); physical therapy (MS); rehabilitation psychology and counseling (MS, PhD); speech and hearing sciences (MS, Au D, PhD). Electronic applications accepted.

School of Nursing *Degree program information:* Part-time programs available. Offers nursing (MSN, PhD).

School of Pharmacy Students: 63 full-time (26 women), 4 part-time (1 woman); includes 9 minority (5 African Americans, 3 Asian Americans or Pacific Islanders, 1 Hispanic American), 24 international. Average age 28. 138 applicants, 19% accepted. *Faculty:* 40 full-time (10 women), 23 part-time/adjunct (5 women). Expenses: Contact institution. *Financial support:* In 2001–02, 51 students received support, including 6 fellowships with full tuition reimbursements available (averaging $16,000 per year), 22 research assistantships with full tuition reimbursements available (averaging $16,000 per year), 24 teaching assistantships with full tuition reimbursements available (averaging $16,000 per year); career-related internships or fieldwork, Federal Work-Study, institutionally sponsored loans, and scholarships/grants also available. Financial award application deadline: 3/1. In 2001, 3 master's, 6 doctorates awarded. *Degree program information:* Part-time programs available. Postbaccalaureate distance learning degree programs offered (minimal on-campus study). Offers pharmacy (MS, PhD). *Application deadline:* For fall admission, 4/1; for spring admission, 10/15. Applications are processed on a rolling basis. *Application fee:* $60. Electronic applications accepted. *Application Contact:* Sherrie E. Settle, Director, Graduate Education, 919-962-0013, Fax: 919-966-6919, E-mail: sherrie_settle@unc.edu. *Dean*, Dr. William H. Campbell, 919-966-1122, Fax: 919-966-6919, E-mail: william_campbell@unc.edu.

See in-depth description on page 1225.

THE UNIVERSITY OF NORTH CAROLINA AT CHARLOTTE, Charlotte, NC 28223-0001

General Information State-supported, coed, university. CGS member. *Enrollment:* 830 full-time matriculated graduate/professional students (434 women), 1,611 part-time matriculated graduate/professional students (951 women). *Enrollment by degree level:* 2,234 master's, 207 doctoral. *Graduate faculty:* 484 full-time (152 women), 148 part-time/adjunct (48 women). Tuition, state resident: full-time $1,483; part-time $371 per year. Tuition, nonresident: full-time $9,850; part-time $2,463 per year. *Required fees:* $1,043; $277 per year. Tuition and fees vary according to course load. *Graduate housing:* Room and/or apartments available on a first-come, first-served basis to single students; on-campus housing not available to married students. Typical cost: $3,080 per year ($5,480 including board). Room and board charges vary according to board plan and housing facility selected. *Student services:* Campus employment opportunities, campus safety program, career counseling, disabled student services, free psychological counseling, international student services. *Library facilities:* J. Murrey Atkins Library. *Online resources:* library catalog, web page, access to other libraries' catalogs. *Collection:* 874,834 titles, 39,918 audiovisual materials.

Computer facilities: 750 computers available on campus for general student use. A campuswide network can be accessed from student residence rooms and from off campus. Internet access and online class registration are available. *Web address:* http://www.uncc.edu/.

General Application Contact: Dr. Thomas L. Reynolds, Interim Dean, 687-547-3366, Fax: 687-547-3279, E-mail: gradadm@email.uncc.edu.

GRADUATE UNITS

Graduate School Students: 830 full-time (434 women), 1,611 part-time (951 women); includes 353 minority (269 African Americans, 58 Asian Americans or Pacific Islanders, 21 Hispanic Americans, 5 Native Americans), 363 international. Average age 31. 2,122 applicants, 69% accepted, 855 enrolled. *Faculty:* 484 full-time (152 women), 148 part-time/adjunct (48 women). Expenses: Contact institution. *Financial support:* In 2001–02, 2,000 students received support, including 19 fellowships (averaging $3,040 per year), 109 research assistantships, 254 teaching assistantships; career-related internships or fieldwork, Federal Work-Study, institutionally sponsored loans, scholarships/grants, traineeships, and unspecified assistantships also available. Support available to part-time students. Financial award application deadline: 4/1; financial award applicants required to submit FAFSA. In 2001, 565 master's, 24 doctorates awarded. *Degree program information:* Part-time and evening/weekend programs available. Postbaccalaureate distance learning degree programs offered (no on-campus study). *Application deadline:* Applications are processed on a rolling basis. *Application fee:* $35. Electronic applications accepted. *Application Contact:* Kathy Barringer, Director of Graduate Admissions, 704-687-3366, Fax: 704-687-3279, E-mail: gradadm@email.uncc.edu. *Interim Dean*, Dr. Thomas L. Reynolds, 687-547-3366, Fax: 687-547-3279, E-mail: gradadm@email.uncc.edu.

Belk College of Business Administration Students: 106 full-time (35 women), 322 part-time (116 women); includes 49 minority (29 African Americans, 12 Asian Americans or Pacific Islanders, 8 Hispanic Americans), 61 international. Average age 30. 288 applicants, 77% accepted, 154 enrolled. *Faculty:* 60 full-time (12 women), 6 part-time/adjunct (1 woman). Expenses: Contact institution. *Financial support:* In 2001–02, 18 teaching assistantships were awarded; fellowships, research assistantships, career-related internships or fieldwork, Federal Work-Study, institutionally sponsored loans, scholarships/grants, and unspecified assistantships also available. Support available to part-time students. Financial award application deadline: 4/1; financial award applicants required to submit FAFSA. In 2001, 129 degrees awarded. *Degree program information:* Part-time and evening/weekend programs available. Offers accounting (M Acc); business administration (M Acc, MBA, MS); economics (MS). *Application deadline:* For fall admission, 7/15; for spring admission, 11/15. Applications are processed on a rolling basis. *Application fee:* $35. Electronic applications accepted. *Application Contact:* Kathy Barringer, Director of Graduate Admissions, 704-687-3366, Fax: 704-687-3279, E-mail: gradadm@email.uncc.edu. *Dean*, Dr. Claude C. Lilly, 704-687-2165, Fax: 704-687-4014, E-mail: cclilly@email.uncc.edu.

College of Architecture Students: 23 full-time (7 women), 4 part-time (2 women); includes 3 minority (1 African American, 1 Asian American or Pacific Islander, 1 Hispanic American), 1 international. Average age 28. 32 applicants, 63% accepted, 10 enrolled. *Faculty:* 22 full-time (6 women). Expenses: Contact institution. *Financial support:* In 2001–02, 1 fellowship (averaging $500 per year), 4 teaching assistantships were awarded. Research assistantships, career-related internships or fieldwork, Federal Work-Study, institutionally sponsored loans, scholarships/grants, and unspecified assistantships also available. Support available to part-time students. Financial award application deadline: 4/1; financial award applicants required to submit FAFSA. In 2001, 10 degrees awarded. Offers architecture (M Arch). *Application deadline:* For fall admission, 2/15. *Application fee:* $35. Electronic applications accepted. *Application Contact:* Kathy Barringer, Director of Graduate Admissions, 704-687-3366, Fax: 704-687-3279, E-mail: gradadm@email.uncc.edu. *Chair of Instruction*, Ken Lambla, 704-687-2358, Fax: 704-687-3353, E-mail: kalambla@email.uncc.edu.

College of Arts and Sciences Students: 211 full-time (135 women), 406 part-time (252 women); includes 89 minority (67 African Americans, 16 Asian Americans or Pacific Islanders, 4 Hispanic Americans, 2 Native Americans), 45 international. Average age 30. 469 applicants, 62% accepted, 213 enrolled. *Faculty:* 249 full-time (75 women), 76 part-time/adjunct (19 women). Expenses: Contact institution. *Financial support:* In 2001–02, 9 fellowships (averaging $3,500 per year), 27 research assistantships, 134 teaching assistantships were awarded. Career-related internships or fieldwork, Federal Work-Study, institutionally sponsored loans, scholarships/grants, and unspecified assistantships also available. Support available to part-time students. Financial award application deadline: 4/1; financial award applicants required to submit FAFSA. In 2001, 112 master's, 2 doctorates awarded. *Degree program information:* Part-time and evening/weekend programs available. Offers applied mathematics (MS, PhD); applied physics (MS); applied statistics (MS); arts and sciences (MA, MPA, MS, MSW, PhD); biology (MA, MS, PhD); chemistry (MS); communication studies (MA); community/clinical psychology (MA); criminal justice (MS); earth sciences (MS); English (MA); English education (MA); geography (MA); gerontology (MA); history (MA); industrial/organizational psychology (MA); liberal studies (MA); mathematics education (MA); political science (MPA); psychology (MA); public policy (PhD); social work (MSW); sociology (MA); Spanish (MA). *Application deadline:* Applications are processed on a rolling basis. *Application fee:* $35. Electronic applications accepted. *Application Contact:* Kathy Barringer, Director of Graduate Admissions, 704-687-3366, Fax: 704-687-3279, E-mail: gradadm@email.uncc.edu. *Dean*, Dr. Schley R. Lyons, 704-687-4303, Fax: 704-687-3228, E-mail: srlyons@email.uncc.edu.

College of Education Students: 181 full-time (139 women), 485 part-time (399 women); includes 121 minority (113 African Americans, 3 Asian Americans or Pacific Islanders, 4 Hispanic Americans, 1 Native American), 9 international. Average age 35. 367 applicants, 81% accepted, 250 enrolled. *Faculty:* 61 full-time (35 women), 24 part-time/adjunct (19 women). Expenses: Contact institution. *Financial support:* In 2001–02, 8 fellowships (averaging $2,719 per year), 10 research assistantships, 13 teaching assistantships were awarded. Career-related internships or fieldwork, Federal Work-Study, institutionally sponsored loans, scholarships/grants, and unspecified assistantships also available. Support available to part-time students. Financial award application deadline: 4/1; financial award applicants required to submit FAFSA. In 2001, 143 master's, 11 doctorates awarded. *Degree program information:* Part-time and evening/weekend programs available. Postbaccalaureate distance learning degree programs offered (no on-campus study). Offers child and family studies (M Ed); community and school counseling (MA); counseling (PhD); curriculum and supervision (M Ed); education (M Ed, MA, MSA, Ed D, PhD, CAS); educational administration (CAS); educational leadership (Ed D); elementary education (M Ed); instructional systems technology (M Ed); middle school and secondary education (M Ed); reading, language and literacy (M Ed); school administration (MSA); special education (M Ed, PhD); teaching English as a seconf language (M Ed). *Application deadline:* For fall admission, 7/15; for spring admission, 11/15. Applications are processed on a rolling basis. *Application fee:* $35. Electronic applications accepted. *Application Contact:* Kathy Barringer, Director of Graduate Admissions, 704-687-3366, Fax: 704-687-3279, E-mail: gradadm@email.uncc.edu. *Dean*, Dr. Mary Lynne Calhoun, 704-687-4707, Fax: 704-687-4705, E-mail: mlcalhou@email.uncc.edu.

College of Information Technology Students: 122 full-time (40 women), 90 part-time (32 women); includes 22 minority (9 African Americans, 12 Asian Americans or Pacific Islanders, 1 Hispanic American), 135 international. Average age 28. 382 applicants, 66% accepted, 89 enrolled. *Faculty:* 17 full-time (2 women), 15 part-time/adjunct (2 women). Expenses: Contact institution. *Financial support:* In 2001–02, 8 research assistantships, 25 teaching assistantships were awarded. Fellowships, career-related internships or fieldwork, Federal Work-Study, institutionally sponsored loans, scholarships/grants, and unspecified assistantships also available. Support available to part-time students. Financial award application deadline: 4/1; financial award applicants required to submit FAFSA. In 2001, 59 master's, 2 doctorates awarded. Offers computer science (MS); information technology (MS, PhD). *Application deadline:* For fall admission, 7/15; for spring admission, 11/15. Applications are processed on a rolling basis. *Application fee:* $35. Electronic applications accepted. *Application Contact:* Kathy Barringer, Director of Graduate Admissions, 704-687-3366, Fax: 704-687-3279, E-mail: gradadm@email.uncc.edu. *Dean*, Dr. Mirsad Hadzikadic, 704-687-3119, Fax: 704-687-6979, E-mail: mirsad@email.uncc.edu.

College of Nursing and Health Professions Students: 68 full-time (54 women), 169 part-time (132 women); includes 42 minority (34 African Americans, 4 Asian Americans or Pacific Islanders, 2 Hispanic Americans, 2 Native Americans), 2 international. Average age 34. 183 applicants, 45% accepted, 58 enrolled. *Faculty:* 25 full-time (20 women), 2 part-time/adjunct (both women). Expenses: Contact institution. *Financial support:* In 2001–02, 4 research assistantships, 7 teaching assistantships were awarded. Fellowships, career-related internships or fieldwork, Federal Work-Study, institutionally sponsored loans, scholarships/grants, traineeships, and unspecified assistantships also available. Support available to part-time students. Financial award application deadline: 4/1; financial award applicants required to submit FAFSA. In 2001, 72 degrees awarded. *Degree program information:* Part-time and evening/weekend programs available. Postbaccalaureate distance learning degree programs offered (no on-campus study). Offers adult health nursing (MSN); family and community nursing (MSN); health administration (MHA); health promotion (MS); nursing and health professions (MHA, MS, MSN). *Application deadline:* For fall admission, 7/15; for spring admission, 11/15. Applications are processed on a rolling basis. *Application fee:* $35. Electronic applications accepted. *Application Contact:* Kathy Barringer, Director of Graduate Admissions, 704-687-3366, Fax: 704-687-3279, E-mail: gradadm@email.uncc.edu. *Dean*, Dr. Sue M. Bishop, 704-687-4650, Fax: 704-687-3180, E-mail: isbishop@email.uncc.edu.

The William States Lee College of Engineering Students: 119 full-time (24 women), 135 part-time (18 women); includes 27 minority (16 African Americans, 10 Asian Americans or Pacific Islanders, 1 Hispanic American), 110 international. Average age 28. 401 applicants, 74% accepted, 81 enrolled. *Faculty:* 50 full-time (2 women), 12 part-time/adjunct (0 women).

The University of North Carolina at Charlotte (continued)

Expenses: Contact institution. *Financial support:* In 2001–02, 1 fellowship (averaging $4,000 per year), 57 research assistantships, 45 teaching assistantships were awarded. Career-related internships or fieldwork, Federal Work-Study, institutionally sponsored loans, scholarships/grants, and unspecified assistantships also available. Support available to part-time students. Financial award application deadline: 4/1; financial award applicants required to submit FAFSA. In 2001, 40 master's, 9 doctorates awarded. *Degree program information:* Part-time and evening/weekend programs available. Offers civil engineering (MSCE); electrical and computer engineering (MSEE, PhD); engineering (ME, MS, MSCE, MSE, MSEE, MSME, PhD); engineering management (MS); mechanical engineering and engineering science (MS, MSME, PhD). *Application deadline:* For fall admission, 7/15; for spring admission, 11/15. Applications are processed on a rolling basis. *Application fee:* $35. Electronic applications accepted. *Application Contact:* Kathy Barringer, Director of Graduate Admissions, 704-687-3366, Fax: 704-687-3279, E-mail: gradadm@email.uncc.edu. *Dean,* Dr. Robert E. Johnson, 704-687-2301, Fax: 704-687-2352, E-mail: robejohn@email.uncc.edu.

THE UNIVERSITY OF NORTH CAROLINA AT GREENSBORO, Greensboro, NC 27412-5001

General Information State-supported, coed, university. CGS member. *Enrollment:* 1,108 full-time matriculated graduate/professional students (799 women), 1,859 part-time matriculated graduate/professional students (1,251 women). *Enrollment by degree level:* 2,033 master's, 473 doctoral, 461 other advanced degrees. *Graduate faculty:* 511 full-time (221 women), 35 part-time/adjunct (10 women). Tuition, state resident: part-time $344 per course. Tuition, nonresident: part-time $2,457 per course. *Graduate housing:* Room and/or apartments available to single students; on-campus housing not available to married students. Housing application deadline: 5/15. *Student services:* Campus employment opportunities, campus safety program, career counseling, child daycare facilities, disabled student services, exercise/wellness program, free psychological counseling, grant writing training, international student services, low-cost health insurance, multicultural affairs office, writing training. *Library facilities:* Jackson Library plus 1 other. *Online resources:* library catalog, web page. *Collection:* 914,914 titles, 5,317 serial subscriptions. *Research affiliation:* Moses Cone Memorial Hospital, North Carolina Zoological Park, North Carolina Baptist Hospital.

Computer facilities: 400 computers available on campus for general student use. A campuswide network can be accessed from student residence rooms and from off campus. Internet access and online class registration are available. *Web address:* http://www.uncg.edu/.

General Application Contact: Dr. James Lynch, Director of Graduate Recruitment and Information Services, 336-334-4881, Fax: 336-334-4424, E-mail: jmlynch@office.uncg.edu.

GRADUATE UNITS

Graduate School Students: 1,108 full-time (799 women), 1,859 part-time (1,251 women); includes 457 minority (347 African Americans, 54 Asian Americans or Pacific Islanders, 41 Hispanic Americans, 15 Native Americans), 171 international. 3,423 applicants, 53% accepted, 1089 enrolled. *Faculty:* 511 full-time (221 women), 35 part-time/adjunct (10 women). Expenses: Contact institution. *Financial support:* In 2001–02, 838 students received support; fellowships, research assistantships, teaching assistantships, career-related internships or fieldwork, Federal Work-Study, institutionally sponsored loans, traineeships, and unspecified assistantships available. Support available to part-time students. Financial award application deadline: 3/1; financial award applicants required to submit FAFSA. In 2001, 807 master's, 68 doctorates, 6 other advanced degrees awarded. *Degree program information:* Part-time and evening/weekend programs available. Postbaccalaureate distance learning degree programs offered (minimal on-campus study). Offers genetic counseling (MS); gerontology (MS); liberal studies (MALS). *Application fee:* $35. *Application Contact:* Dr. James Lynch, Director of Graduate Recruitment and Information Services, 336-334-4881, Fax: 336-334-4424. *Dean,* Dr. Brad Bartel, 336-334-5596, Fax: 336-334-4424, E-mail: b_bartel@office.uncg.edu.

College of Arts and Sciences Students: 258 full-time (160 women), 338 part-time (207 women); includes 92 minority (68 African Americans, 8 Asian Americans or Pacific Islanders, 12 Hispanic Americans, 4 Native Americans), 24 international. 768 applicants, 31% accepted, 192 enrolled. *Faculty:* 237 full-time (81 women), 17 part-time/adjunct (2 women). Expenses: Contact institution. *Financial support:* In 2001–02, 7 fellowships with full tuition reimbursements (averaging $8,214 per year), 163 research assistantships with full tuition reimbursements (averaging $6,826 per year), 124 teaching assistantships with full tuition reimbursements (averaging $6,763 per year) were awarded. Unspecified assistantships also available. In 2001, 143 master's, 17 doctorates awarded. *Degree program information:* Part-time programs available. Offers acting (MFA); art (M Ed); arts and sciences (M Ed, MA, MFA, MPA, MS, PhD, Certificate); biology (M Ed, MS); chemistry (M Ed, MS); clinical psychology (MA, PhD); cognitive psychology (MA, PhD); communication studies (M Ed, MA); computer science (MA); creative writing (MFA); developmental psychology (MA, PhD); directing (MFA); drama (M Ed, MFA); English (M Ed, MA, PhD, Certificate); French (M Ed, MA); geography (MA); historic preservation (Certificate); history (M Ed, MA); Latin (M Ed); mathematical science (M Ed, MA); museum studies (Certificate); nonprofit management (Certificate); political science (MA); public affairs (MPA, Certificate); social psychology (MA, PhD); sociology (MA); Spanish (M Ed, MA); studio arts (MFA); technical writing (Certificate); theater design (MFA); theater education (M Ed); theater for youth (MFA); women's studies (Certificate). *Application fee:* $35. *Application Contact:* Dr. James Lynch, Director of Graduate Recruitment and Information Services, 336-334-4881, Fax: 336-334-4424. *Dean,* Walter Beale, 336-334-5241, Fax: 336-334-4260, E-mail: whbeale@hamlet.uncg.edu.

Joseph M. Bryan School of Business and Economics Students: 113 full-time (62 women), 278 part-time (117 women); includes 41 minority (27 African Americans, 12 Asian Americans or Pacific Islanders, 2 Hispanic Americans), 79 international. 358 applicants, 56% accepted, 155 enrolled. *Faculty:* 51 full-time (7 women), 2 part-time/adjunct (0 women). Expenses: Contact institution. *Financial support:* In 2001–02, 83 research assistantships with full tuition reimbursements (averaging $4,260 per year) were awarded; fellowships with full tuition reimbursements, teaching assistantships, career-related internships or fieldwork, Federal Work-Study, scholarships/grants, traineeships, and unspecified assistantships also available. Support available to part-time students. In 2001, 132 degrees awarded. *Degree program information:* Part-time programs available. Offers accounting (MS); applied economics (MA); business administration (MBA, Certificate); business and economics (MA, MBA, MS, Certificate); information systems and operations management (MS); international business administration (Certificate). *Application deadline:* For fall admission, 7/1 (priority date); for spring admission, 11/1. Applications are processed on a rolling basis. *Application fee:* $35. *Application Contact:* Dr. James Lynch, Director of Graduate Recruitment and Information Services, 336-334-4881, Fax: 336-334-4424. *Dean,* James K. Weeks, 336-334-5338, Fax: 336-334-4044, E-mail: jim_weeks@uncg.edu.

School of Education Students: 243 full-time (197 women), 511 part-time (410 women); includes 102 minority (80 African Americans, 10 Asian Americans or Pacific Islanders, 9 Hispanic Americans, 3 Native Americans), 14 international. 615 applicants, 41% accepted, 208 enrolled. *Faculty:* 51 full-time (26 women), 5 part-time/adjunct (3 women). Expenses: Contact institution. *Financial support:* In 2001–02, 10 fellowships with full tuition reimbursements (averaging $8,550 per year), 159 research assistantships with full tuition reimbursements (averaging $3,956 per year), 45 teaching assistantships with full tuition reimbursements (averaging $5,483 per year) were awarded. Career-related internships or fieldwork, institutionally sponsored loans, and unspecified assistantships also available. In 2001, 255 master's, 31 doctorates, 6 other advanced degrees awarded. *Degree program information:* Part-time and evening/weekend programs available. Offers counseling and development (MS, Ed D, PhD); cross categorical (M Ed); curriculum and instruction (M Ed); curriculum and teaching (PhD); deaf education (M Ed, MA); education (M Ed, MA, MLIS, MS, MS/Ed S, MSA, Ed D, PhD, Ed S, PMC); educational leadership (Ed D, PhD, Ed S); educational research, measurement and evaluation (M Ed, PhD); gerontological counseling (PMC); higher education (M Ed, Ed S); interdisciplinary studies in preschool education (M Ed); library and information studies (MLIS); marriage and family counseling (PMC); school administration (MSA); school counseling (PMC); special education (M Ed); supervision (M Ed). *Application fee:* $35. *Application Contact:* Dr. James Lynch, Director of Graduate Recruitment and Information Services, 336-334-4881, Fax: 336-334-4424. *Dean,* Dr. David Armstrong, 336-334-3403, Fax: 336-334-4120, E-mail: david.armstrong@uncg.edu.

School of Health and Human Performance Students: 153 full-time (133 women), 95 part-time (76 women); includes 42 minority (31 African Americans, 7 Asian Americans or Pacific Islanders, 2 Hispanic Americans, 2 Native Americans), 13 international. 397 applicants, 41% accepted, 92 enrolled. *Faculty:* 53 full-time (32 women), 1 (woman) part-time/adjunct. Expenses: Contact institution. *Financial support:* In 2001–02, 5 fellowships with full tuition reimbursements (averaging $5,200 per year), 41 research assistantships with full tuition reimbursements (averaging $5,155 per year), 45 teaching assistantships with full tuition reimbursements (averaging $7,443 per year) were awarded. Unspecified assistantships also available. In 2001, 69 master's, 9 doctorates awarded. Offers dance (MA, MFA); exercise and sports science (M Ed, MS, Ed D, PhD); health and human performance (M Ed, MA, MFA, MPH, MS, Ed D, PhD); parks and recreation management (MS); public health education (MPH); speech pathology and audiology (MA). *Application deadline:* For fall admission, 2/15 (priority date). *Application fee:* $35. *Application Contact:* Dr. James Lynch, Director of Graduate Recruitment and Information Services, 336-334-4881, Fax: 336-334-4424. *Dean,* David Perrin, 336-334-5744, Fax: 336-334-3238, E-mail: dhperrin@uncg.edu.

School of Human Environmental Sciences Students: 126 full-time (111 women), 64 part-time (55 women); includes 43 minority (38 African Americans, 2 Asian Americans or Pacific Islanders, 2 Hispanic Americans, 1 Native American), 29 international. 229 applicants, 52% accepted, 80 enrolled. *Faculty:* 42 full-time (30 women), 2 part-time/adjunct (0 women). Expenses: Contact institution. *Financial support:* In 2001–02, 6 fellowships with full tuition reimbursements (averaging $6,333 per year), 74 research assistantships with full tuition reimbursements (averaging $7,072 per year), 8 teaching assistantships with full tuition reimbursements (averaging $6,672 per year) were awarded. Unspecified assistantships also available. In 2001, 56 master's, 7 doctorates awarded. Offers housing and interior design (MS); human development and family studies (M Ed, MS, PhD); human environmental sciences (M Ed, MS, MSW, PhD); human nutrition (M Ed, MS, PhD); social work (MSW); textile products design and marketing (M Ed, MS, PhD). *Application fee:* $35. *Application Contact:* Dr. James Lynch, Director of Graduate Recruitment and Information Services, 336-334-4881, Fax: 336-334-4424. *Dean,* Laura S. Sims, 336-334-5980, Fax: 336-334-5089, E-mail: laura_sims@uncg.edu.

School of Music Students: 76 full-time (37 women), 84 part-time (42 women); includes 12 minority (10 African Americans, 1 Asian American or Pacific Islander, 1 Hispanic American), 6 international. 132 applicants, 46% accepted, 47 enrolled. *Faculty:* 43 full-time (12 women), 4 part-time/adjunct (1 woman). Expenses: Contact institution. *Financial support:* In 2001–02, 4 fellowships with full tuition reimbursements (averaging $9,125 per year), 20 research assistantships with full tuition reimbursements (averaging $3,098 per year), 52 teaching assistantships with full tuition reimbursements (averaging $4,294 per year) were awarded. Unspecified assistantships also available. In 2001, 32 master's, 4 doctorates awarded. Offers composition (MM); education (MM); music education (PhD); performance (MM, DMA). *Application deadline:* For fall admission, 3/1. *Application fee:* $35. *Application Contact:* Dr. James Lynch, Director of Graduate Recruitment and Information Services, 336-334-4881, Fax: 336-334-4424. *Dean,* Dr. John J. Deal, 336-334-5789, Fax: 336-334-5497, E-mail: jjdeal@uncg.edu.

School of Nursing Students: 96 full-time (65 women), 143 part-time (121 women). 168 applicants, 79% accepted, 58 enrolled. *Faculty:* 28 full-time (all women), 4 part-time/adjunct (3 women). Expenses: Contact institution. *Financial support:* In 2001–02, 20 research assistantships with full tuition reimbursements (averaging $4,209 per year) were awarded; career-related internships or fieldwork, Federal Work-Study, scholarships/grants, and traineeships also available. Support available to part-time students. In 2001, 107 degrees awarded. Offers administration of nursing in health agencies (MSN); gerontological nurse practitioner (PMC); nurse anesthesia (MSN, PMC). *Application fee:* $35. *Application Contact:* Dr. James Lynch, Director of Graduate Recruitment and Information Services, 336-334-4881, Fax: 336-334-4424. *Dean,* Dr. Lynne Pearcey, 336-334-5010, Fax: 336-334-3628, E-mail: l_pearce@uncg.edu.

See in-depth description on page 1227.

THE UNIVERSITY OF NORTH CAROLINA AT PEMBROKE, Pembroke, NC 28372-1510

General Information State-supported, coed, comprehensive institution. *Enrollment:* 48 full-time matriculated graduate/professional students (24 women), 379 part-time matriculated graduate/professional students (262 women). *Enrollment by degree level:* 427 master's. *Graduate faculty:* 27 full-time (9 women), 2 part-time/adjunct (1 woman). Tuition, state resident: full-time $1,022. Tuition, nonresident: full-time $8,292. Tuition and fees vary according to campus/location. *Graduate housing:* Room and/or apartments available to single students; on-campus housing not available to married students. Typical cost: $3,680 (including board). Room and board charges vary according to housing facility selected. Housing application deadline: 4/15. *Student services:* Career counseling, disabled student services, exercise/wellness program, free psychological counseling, international student services, low-cost health insurance, multicultural affairs office. *Library facilities:* Sampson-Livermore Library. *Online resources:* library catalog, web page, access to other libraries' catalogs. *Collection:* 296,080 titles, 1,471 serial subscriptions, 1,806 audiovisual materials.

Computer facilities: 367 computers available on campus for general student use. A campuswide network can be accessed from student residence rooms and from off campus. Internet access is available. *Web address:* http://www.uncp.edu/.

General Application Contact: Dr. Kathleen C. Hilton, Dean, 910-521-6271, Fax: 910-521-6497, E-mail: kathleen.hilton@uncp.edu.

GRADUATE UNITS

Graduate Studies Students: 48 full-time (24 women), 379 part-time (262 women); includes 90 minority (40 African Americans, 6 Asian Americans or Pacific Islanders, 2 Hispanic Americans, 42 Native Americans), 1 international. Average age 34. *Faculty:* 27 full-time (9 women), 2 part-time/adjunct (1 woman). Expenses: Contact institution. *Financial support:* In 2001–02, 25 research assistantships with full tuition reimbursements (averaging $6,000 per year) were awarded; career-related internships or fieldwork and unspecified assistantships also available. Support available to part-time students. Financial award application deadline: 4/15; financial award applicants required to submit FAFSA. In 2001, 82 degrees awarded. *Degree program information:* Part-time and evening/weekend programs available. Offers art education (MA Ed); business administration (MBA); English education (MA); mathematics education (MA Ed); physical education (MA Ed); public management (MS); school counseling (MA); science education (MA Ed); service agency counseling (MA); social sciences education (MA Ed); social studies education (MA Ed). *Application deadline:* For fall admission, 7/15 (priority date); for spring admission, 12/1 (priority date). Applications are processed on a rolling basis. *Application fee:* $40. *Dean,* Dr. Kathleen C. Hilton, 910-521-6271, Fax: 910-521-6497, E-mail: kathleen.hilton@uncp.edu.

School of Education Students: 1 (woman) full-time, 87 part-time (70 women); includes 18 minority (6 African Americans, 2 Asian Americans or Pacific Islanders, 10 Native Americans) Average age 36. *Faculty:* 8 full-time (2 women), 1 part-time/adjunct (0 women). Expenses: Contact institution. *Financial support:* Career-related internships or fieldwork and unspecified assistantships available. Support available to part-time students. Financial award application deadline: 4/15. In 2001, 46 degrees awarded. *Degree program information:* Part-time and evening/weekend programs available. Offers educational administration and supervision (MA Ed); elementary education (MA Ed); middle grades education (MA Ed); reading education (MA Ed); school administration (MSA). *Application deadline:* For fall admission, 7/15 (priority date); for spring admission, 12/1 (priority date). Applications are processed on a rolling basis. *Application fee:* $40. *Application Contact:* Dr. Kathleen C. Hilton, Dean, 910-521-6271, Fax: 910-521-6497, E-mail: kathleen.hilton@uncp.edu. *Dean,* Dr. Zoe W. Locklear, 910-521-6221, E-mail: zoe.locklear@uncp.edu.

THE UNIVERSITY OF NORTH CAROLINA AT WILMINGTON, Wilmington, NC 28403-3297

General Information State-supported, coed, comprehensive institution. CGS member. *Enrollment:* 191 full-time matriculated graduate/professional students (122 women), 467 part-time matriculated graduate/professional students (292 women). *Enrollment by degree level:* 658 master's. *Graduate faculty:* 139 full-time (50 women), 24 part-time/adjunct (10 women). Tuition, state resident: full-time $2,675. Tuition, nonresident: full-time $10,936. *Graduate housing:* Room and/or apartments available on a first-come, first-served basis to single students; on-campus housing not available to married students. Housing application deadline: 3/31. *Student services:* Campus employment opportunities, career counseling, free psychological counseling, international student services, low-cost health insurance. *Library facilities:* William M. Randall Library. *Online resources:* library catalog, web page, access to other libraries' catalogs. *Collection:* 852,937 titles, 4,304 serial subscriptions, 51,202 audiovisual materials.

Computer facilities: 778 computers available on campus for general student use. A campuswide network can be accessed from student residence rooms and from off campus. Internet access and online class registration are available. *Web address:* http://www.uncwil.edu/.

General Application Contact: Dr. Neil F. Hadley, Dean, Graduate School, 910-962-4117, Fax: 910-962-3787, E-mail: hadleyn@uncwil.edu.

GRADUATE UNITS

College of Arts and Sciences Students: 100 full-time (61 women), 285 part-time (172 women); includes 20 minority (12 African Americans, 3 Asian Americans or Pacific Islanders, 5 Hispanic Americans), 19 international. Average age 31. 391 applicants, 36% accepted, 135 enrolled. *Faculty:* 105 full-time (33 women), 18 part-time/adjunct (7 women). Expenses: Contact institution. *Financial support:* In 2001–02, 110 teaching assistantships were awarded; career-related internships or fieldwork and Federal Work-Study also available. Support available to part-time students. Financial award application deadline: 3/15. In 2001, 80 degrees awarded. *Degree program information:* Part-time programs available. Offers arts and sciences (MA, MALS, MFA, MS); biology (MS); chemistry (MS); creative writing (MFA); English (MA); geology (MS); history (MA); liberal studies (MALS); marine biology (MS); mathematical sciences (MA, MS); psychology (MA). *Application deadline:* Applications are processed on a rolling basis. *Application fee:* $45. *Application Contact:* Dr. Neil F. Hadley, Dean, Graduate School, 910-962-4117, Fax: 910-962-3787, E-mail: hadleyn@uncwil.edu. *Dean,* Dr. JoAnn Seiple, 910-962-3111.

School of Business Students: 41 full-time (20 women), 67 part-time (23 women); includes 6 minority (4 African Americans, 2 Asian Americans or Pacific Islanders), 2 international. Average age 32. 166 applicants, 49% accepted, 77 enrolled. *Faculty:* 11 full-time (2 women). Expenses: Contact institution. *Financial support:* In 2001–02, 25 teaching assistantships were awarded; career-related internships or fieldwork, Federal Work-Study, and unspecified assistantships also available. Support available to part-time students. Financial award application deadline: 3/15. In 2001, 107 degrees awarded. *Degree program information:* Part-time and evening/weekend programs available. Offers accountancy (MSA); business (MBA, MSA); business administration (MBA). *Application deadline:* Applications are processed on a rolling basis. *Application fee:* $45. *Application Contact:* Dr. Neil F. Hadley, Dean, Graduate School, 910-962-4117, Fax: 910-962-3787, E-mail: hadleyn@uncwil.edu. *Dean,* Dr. Lawrence Clark, 910-962-3501, E-mail: clarkl@uncwil.edu.

School of Education Students: 42 full-time (33 women), 98 part-time (83 women); includes 18 minority (14 African Americans, 2 Asian Americans or Pacific Islanders, 2 Native Americans) Average age 37. 111 applicants, 59% accepted, 51 enrolled. *Faculty:* 17 full-time (10 women), 5 part-time/adjunct (2 women). Expenses: Contact institution. *Financial support:* In 2001–02, 12 teaching assistantships were awarded; career-related internships or fieldwork, Federal Work-Study, and unspecified assistantships also available. Support available to part-time students. Financial award application deadline: 3/15. In 2001, 37 degrees awarded. *Degree program information:* Part-time and evening/weekend programs available. Offers curricular/instruction supervisor (M Ed); education (M Ed, MAT, MS, MSA); educational administration and supervision (M Ed); elementary education (M Ed); instructional technology (MS); middle grades education (M Ed); reading education (M Ed); school administration (MSA); secondary education (M Ed); special education (M Ed); teaching (MAT). *Application deadline:* For fall admission, 6/1. Applications are processed on a rolling basis. *Application fee:* $45. *Application Contact:* Dr. Neil F. Hadley, Dean, Graduate School, 910-962-4117, Fax: 910-962-3787, E-mail: hadleyn@uncwil.edu. *Dean,* Dr. Cathy L. Barlow, 910-962-3354, E-mail: barlowc@uncwil.edu.

School of Nursing Students: 8 full-time (all women), 17 part-time (14 women); includes 3 minority (all African Americans), 2 international. 12 applicants, 83% accepted, 10 enrolled. *Faculty:* 6 full-time (5 women), 1 (woman) part-time/adjunct. Expenses: Contact institution. *Financial support:* In 2001–02, 2 teaching assistantships were awarded In 2001, 12 degrees awarded. Offers nursing (MSN). *Application deadline:* For fall admission, 3/1. Applications are processed on a rolling basis. *Application fee:* $45. Electronic applications accepted. *Application Contact:* Dr. Neil F. Hadley, Dean, Graduate School, 910-962-4117, Fax: 910-962-3787, E-mail: hadleyn@uncwil.edu. *Dean,* Dr. Virginia W. Adams, 910-962-3784, E-mail: adamsv@uncwil.edu.

UNIVERSITY OF NORTH DAKOTA, Grand Forks, ND 58202

General Information State-supported, coed, university. CGS member. *Enrollment:* 2,089 matriculated graduate/professional students. *Graduate faculty:* 691. Tuition, state resident: full-time $3,298. Tuition, nonresident: full-time $7,998. *Graduate housing:* Rooms and/or apartments available on a first-come, first-served basis to single students and available to married students. *Student services:* Campus employment opportunities, campus safety program, career counseling, child daycare facilities, disabled student services, free psychological counseling, grant writing training, international student services, low-cost health insurance, multicultural affairs office, writing training. *Library facilities:* Chester Fritz Library plus 2 others. *Online resources:* library catalog, web page, access to other libraries' catalogs. *Collection:* 658,957 titles, 10,438 serial subscriptions, 14,306 audiovisual materials. *Research affiliation:* North Dakota Geological Survey, U.S. Department of Agriculture–Human Nutrition Laboratory, Neuropsychiatric Research Institute (neurosciences).

Computer facilities: 951 computers available on campus for general student use. A campuswide network can be accessed from student residence rooms and from off campus. Internet access is available. *Web address:* http://www.und.edu/.

General Application Contact: Kristin A. Ellwanger, Admissions Officer, 701-777-2945, Fax: 701-777-3619, E-mail: gradschool@mail.und.nodak.edu.

GRADUATE UNITS

Graduate School Students: 293 full-time (178 women), 1,264 part-time (700 women). Average age 34. 641 applicants, 75% accepted, 308 enrolled. *Faculty:* 396 full-time (111 women), 18 part-time/adjunct (2 women). Expenses: Contact institution. *Financial support:* In 2001–02, 476 students received support, including 73 research assistantships with full tuition reimbursements available (averaging $9,600 per year), 262 teaching assistantships with full tuition reimbursements available (averaging $9,600 per year); fellowships, career-related internships or fieldwork, Federal Work-Study, institutionally sponsored loans, scholarships/grants, traineeships, tuition waivers (full and partial), and unspecified assistantships also available. Support available to part-time students. Financial award application deadline: 3/15; financial award applicants required to submit FAFSA. In 2001, 380 master's, 32 doctorates, 2 other advanced degrees awarded. *Degree program information:* Part-time and evening/weekend programs available. Postbaccalaureate distance learning degree programs offered (minimal on-campus study). *Application deadline:* For fall admission, 3/15 (priority date); for spring admission, 10/15 (priority date). Applications are processed on a rolling basis. *Application fee:* $30. *Application Contact:* Kristin Ellwanger, Admissions Officer, 701-777-2945, Fax: 701-777-3619, E-mail: undgrad@mail.und.nodak.edu. *Dean,* Dr. Joseph N. Benoit, 701-777-2786, Fax: 701-777-3619, E-mail: j_benoit@mail.und.nodak.edu.

College of Arts and Sciences Students: 75 full-time (48 women), 212 part-time (108 women). 197 applicants, 57% accepted, 68 enrolled. *Faculty:* 167 full-time (40 women). Expenses: Contact institution. *Financial support:* In 2001–02, 207 students received support, including 26 research assistantships with full tuition reimbursements available (averaging $10,424 per year), 162 teaching assistantships with full tuition reimbursements available (averaging $9,723 per year); fellowships, career-related internships or fieldwork, Federal Work-Study, institutionally sponsored loans, scholarships/grants, tuition waivers (full and partial), and unspecified assistantships also available. Support available to part-time students. Financial award application deadline: 3/15; financial award applicants required to submit FAFSA. In 2001, 78 master's, 15 doctorates awarded. *Degree program information:* Part-time programs available. Offers arts and sciences (M Ed, M Mus, MA, MFA, MS, DA, PhD); botany (MS, PhD); chemistry (MS, PhD); clinical psychology (PhD); communication (MA, PhD); communication sciences and disorders (PhD); ecology (MS, PhD); English (MA, PhD); entomology (MS, PhD); environmental biology (MS, PhD); experimental psychology (PhD); fisheries/wildlife (MS, PhD); genetics (MS, PhD); geography (MA, MS); history (MA, DA); linguistics (MA); mathematics (M Ed, MS); music (M Mus); music education (M Mus); physics (MS, PhD); psychology (MA); sociology (MA); speech-language pathology (MS); theatre arts (MA); visual arts (MFA); zoology (MS, PhD). *Application deadline:* Applications are processed on a rolling basis. *Application fee:* $30. *Dean,* Dr. Albert J. Fivizzani, 701-777-2749, Fax: 701-777-4397, E-mail: albert_fivizzani@und.nodak.edu.

College of Business and Public Administration Students: 25 full-time (10 women), 129 part-time (54 women). 58 applicants, 97% accepted, 43 enrolled. *Faculty:* 35 full-time (9 women). Expenses: Contact institution. *Financial support:* In 2001–02, 38 students received support, including 25 teaching assistantships with full tuition reimbursements available (averaging $9,270 per year); fellowships, research assistantships with full tuition reimbursements available, Federal Work-Study, institutionally sponsored loans, scholarships/grants, tuition waivers (full and partial), and unspecified assistantships also available. Support available to part-time students. Financial award application deadline: 3/15; financial award applicants required to submit FAFSA. In 2001, 36 degrees awarded. *Degree program information:* Part-time and evening/weekend programs available. Postbaccalaureate distance learning degree programs offered. Offers business administration (MBA); business and public administration (MBA, MPA, MS); industrial technology (MS); public administration (MPA). *Application deadline:* For fall admission, 3/1 (priority date); for spring admission, 10/15 (priority date). Applications are processed on a rolling basis. *Application fee:* $30. *Dean,* Dr. Dennis J. Elbert, 701-777-2135, Fax: 701-777-5099, E-mail: dennis_elbert@mail.und.nodak.edu.

College of Education and Human Development Students: 68 full-time (47 women), 407 part-time (286 women). 113 applicants, 79% accepted, 69 enrolled. *Faculty:* 51 full-time (25 women). Expenses: Contact institution. *Financial support:* In 2001–02, 108 students received support, including 21 research assistantships with full tuition reimbursements available (averaging $9,270 per year), 28 teaching assistantships with full tuition reimbursements available (averaging $9,570 per year); fellowships, career-related internships or fieldwork, Federal Work-Study, institutionally sponsored loans, scholarships/grants, tuition waivers (full and partial), and unspecified assistantships also available. Support available to part-time students. Financial award application deadline: 3/15; financial award applicants required to submit FAFSA. In 2001, 125 master's, 10 doctorates, 2 other advanced degrees awarded. *Degree program information:* Part-time and evening/weekend programs available. Postbaccalaureate distance learning degree programs offered (minimal on-campus study). Offers counseling (MA); counseling psychology (PhD); early childhood education (MS); education and human development (M Ed, MA, MS, MSW, Ed D, PhD, Specialist); education/general studies (MS); educational leadership (M Ed, MS, Ed D, PhD, Specialist); elementary education (Ed D, PhD); instructional design and technology (M Ed, MS); kinesiology (MS); measurement and statistics (Ed D, PhD); reading education (M Ed, MS); secondary education (Ed D, PhD); social work (MSW); special education (M Ed, MS, Ed D, PhD). *Application deadline:* For fall admission, 2/1 (priority date); for spring admission, 9/15 (priority date). Applications are processed on a rolling basis. *Application fee:* $30. *Dean,* Dr. Dan R. Rice, 701-777-4255, Fax: 701-777-4393, E-mail: dan_rice@mail.und.nodak.edu.

College of Nursing Students: 39 full-time (31 women), 36 part-time (30 women). 53 applicants, 47% accepted, 22 enrolled. *Faculty:* 14 full-time (13 women). Expenses: Contact institution. *Financial support:* In 2001–02, 13 students received support, including 2 research assistantships (averaging $11,397 per year), 6 teaching assistantships with full tuition reimbursements available (averaging $11,397 per year); fellowships, Federal Work-Study, institutionally sponsored loans, scholarships/grants, traineeships, and tuition waivers (full and partial) also available. Support available to part-time students. Financial award application deadline: 3/15; financial award applicants required to submit FAFSA. In 2001, 20 degrees awarded. *Degree program information:* Part-time programs available. Postbaccalaureate distance learning degree programs offered (minimal on-campus study). Offers nursing (MS). *Application deadline:* For fall admission, 12/15. Applications are processed on a rolling basis. *Application fee:* $30. *Application Contact:* Maura Erickson, Administrative Secretary, 701-777-4552, Fax: 701-777-4096, E-mail: maura_erickson@mail.und.nodak.edu. *Director,* Dr. Ginny W. Guido, 701-777-4552, Fax: 701-777-4096, E-mail: ginny_guido@mail.und.nodak.edu.

John D. Odegard School of Aerospace Sciences Students: 11 full-time (3 women), 164 part-time (41 women). 67 applicants, 93% accepted, 29 enrolled. *Faculty:* 23 full-time (1 woman). Expenses: Contact institution. *Financial support:* In 2001–02, 33 students received support, including 16 research assistantships with full tuition reimbursements available (averaging $9,270 per year), 17 teaching assistantships with full tuition reimbursements available (averaging $9,270 per year); fellowships, career-related internships or fieldwork, Federal Work-Study, institutionally sponsored loans, scholarships/grants, tuition waivers (full and partial), and unspecified assistantships also available. Support available to part-time students. Financial award application deadline: 3/15; financial award applicants required to submit FAFSA. In 2001, 50 degrees awarded. *Degree program information:* Part-time programs available. Postbaccalaureate distance learning degree programs offered (minimal on-campus study). Offers aerospace sciences (MS); atmospheric sciences (MS); aviation (MS); computer science (MS); space studies (MS). *Application deadline:* For fall admission, 3/1 (priority date); for spring admission, 10/15 (priority date). Applications are processed on a rolling basis. *Application fee:* $30. *Dean,* Bruce A. Smith, 701-777-2791, Fax: 701-777-3016, E-mail: bsmith@aero.und.nodak.edu.

School of Engineering and Mines Students: 20 full-time (2 women), 33 part-time (5 women). 71 applicants, 89% accepted, 15 enrolled. *Faculty:* 40 full-time (0 women). Expenses: Contact institution. *Financial support:* In 2001–02, 34 students received support, including 28 research assistantships with full tuition reimbursements available (averaging $10,100 per year), 29 teaching assistantships with full tuition reimbursements available (averaging $10,100 per year); fellowships, career-related internships or fieldwork, Federal Work-Study, institutionally sponsored loans, scholarships/grants, tuition waivers (full and partial), and unspecified assistantships also available. Support available to part-time students. Financial award application deadline: 3/15; financial award applicants required to submit FAFSA. In 2001, 14 master's, 2 doctorates awarded. *Degree program information:* Part-time programs available. Offers chemical engineering (M Engr, MS); civil engineering (M Engr); electrical engineering (M Engr, MS); energy engineering (PhD); engineering and mines (M Engr, MA, MS, PhD); geology (MA, MS, PhD); mechanical engineering (M Engr, MS); sanitary engineering (M Engr). *Application deadline:* For fall admission, 3/1 (priority date); for spring admission, 10/15 (priority date). Applications are processed on a rolling basis. *Application fee:* $30. *Dean,* Dr. John L. Watson, 701-777-3411, Fax: 701-777-4838, E-mail: john_watson@mail.und.nodak.edu.

School of Law Students: 199 full-time (92 women), 1 part-time; includes 15 minority (1 African American, 2 Asian Americans or Pacific Islanders, 1 Hispanic American, 11 Native Americans), 12 international. 216 applicants, 66% accepted. *Faculty:* 13 full-time (4 women), 8 part-time/adjunct (3 women). Expenses: Contact institution. *Financial support:* In 2001–02, 4 teaching assistantships with full tuition reimbursements were awarded; career-related internships or fieldwork, Federal Work-Study, scholarships/grants, and tuition waivers (full and partial) also available. Financial award application deadline: 4/15; financial award applicants required to submit FAFSA. In 2001, 68 degrees awarded. Offers law (JD). *Application deadline:* For fall admission, 4/1 (priority date). Applications are processed on a rolling basis. *Application fee:* $35. *Application Contact:* Linda Kohoutek, Admissions and Records Officer,

University of North Dakota (continued)

701-777-2104, Fax: 701-777-2217, E-mail: linda.kohoutek@thor.law.und.nodak.edu. *Dean*, W. Jeremy Davis, 701-777-2104.

School of Medicine Students: 279 full-time (141 women), 53 part-time (31 women). *Faculty:* 165 full-time (28 women), 91 part-time/adjunct. Expenses: Contact institution. *Financial support:* In 2001–02, 34 students received support, including 14 research assistantships, 20 teaching assistantships; fellowships, Federal Work-Study, institutionally sponsored loans, and tuition waivers (full and partial) also available. Support available to part-time students. Financial award applicants required to submit FAFSA. In 2001, 50 first professional degrees, 61 master's, 9 doctorates awarded. Postbaccalaureate distance learning degree programs offered (minimal on-campus study). Offers anatomy (MS, PhD); biochemistry (MS, PhD); clinical laboratory science (MS); medicine (MD, MOT, MPAS, MPT, MS, DPT, PhD); microbiology and immunology (MS, PhD); occupational therapy (MOT); pharmacology (MS, PhD); physical therapy (MPT, DPT); physician assistant (MPAS); physiology (MS, PhD). *Application Contact:* Judy L. DeMers, Associate Dean, Student Affairs and Admissions, 701-777-4221, Fax: 701-777-4942. *Dean*, Dr. H. David Wilson, 701-777-2514, Fax: 701-777-3527, E-mail: hdwilson@medicine.nodak.edu.

UNIVERSITY OF NORTHERN BRITISH COLUMBIA, Prince George, BC V2N 4Z9, Canada

General Information Province-supported, comprehensive institution. *Enrollment by degree level:* 360 master's, 12 doctoral. *Graduate tuition:* Tuition charges are reported in Canadian dollars. *International tuition:* $4,697 Canadian dollars full-time. Tuition, province resident: full-time $1,708 Canadian dollars. Tuition, Canadian resident: part-time $451 Canadian dollars per semester. Tuition and fees vary according to program. *Graduate housing:* Room and/or apartments available on a first-come, first-served basis to single students; on-campus housing not available to married students. Typical cost: $1,646 Canadian dollars per year. Room charges vary according to housing facility selected. Housing application deadline: 2/15. *Student services:* Campus employment opportunities, campus safety program, career counseling, child daycare facilities, disabled student services, exercise/wellness program, grant writing training, international student services, low-cost health insurance, teacher training, writing training. *Research affiliation:* Mountain Equipment Coop (macro lichen species), Canadian Forest Products (silviculture practices), Environmental Protection Agency (Asian dust conference), District of Tumbler Ridge (community survey), West Fraser Mills (forestry). *Web address:* http://www.unbc.ca/.

General Application Contact: Susan Deevy, Graduate Studies Officer, 250-960-6336, Fax: 250-960-6330, E-mail: deevys@unbc.ca.

GRADUATE UNITS

Office of Graduate Studies Students: 200 full-time (133 women), 172 part-time (121 women). 277 applicants, 52% accepted. Expenses: Contact institution. *Financial support:* In 2001–02, 98 students received support, including 3 fellowships (averaging $2,000 per year), research assistantships (averaging $12,000 per year), 60 teaching assistantships (averaging $8,000 per year); career-related internships or fieldwork, Federal Work-Study, institutionally sponsored loans, and scholarships/grants also available. Support available to part-time students. Financial award application deadline: 2/15. In 2001, 81 degrees awarded. *Degree program information:* Part-time and evening/weekend programs available. Postbaccalaureate distance learning degree programs offered (no on-campus study). *Application deadline:* For fall and spring admission, 2/15; for winter admission, 9/15. Applications are processed on a rolling basis. *Application fee:* $35. Electronic applications accepted. *Application Contact:* Susan Deevy, Graduate Studies Officer, 250-960-6336, Fax: 250-960-6330, E-mail: deevys@unbc.ca. *Dean of Graduate Studies*, Dr. Robert W. Tait, 250-960-5726, Fax: 250-960-5362, E-mail: tait@unbc.ca.

UNIVERSITY OF NORTHERN COLORADO, Greeley, CO 80639

General Information State-supported, coed, university. CGS member. *Enrollment:* 1,004 full-time matriculated graduate/professional students (696 women), 423 part-time matriculated graduate/professional students (289 women). *Enrollment by degree level:* 1,102 master's, 282 doctoral, 43 other advanced degrees. *Graduate faculty:* 211 full-time (85 women). Tuition, state resident: full-time $2,549; part-time $546 per credit hour. Tuition, nonresident: full-time $10,459; part-time $581 per credit hour. *Required fees:* $631; $85 per year. Part-time tuition and fees vary according to course load. *Graduate housing:* Rooms and/or apartments available to single students and available on a first-come, first-served basis to married students. Typical cost: $2,450 per year ($5,240 including board) for single students; $2,450 per year ($5,240 including board) for married students. Room and board charges vary according to board plan, campus/location and housing facility selected. Housing application deadline: 5/30. *Student services:* Campus employment opportunities, campus safety program, career counseling, child daycare facilities, disabled student services, exercise/wellness program, free psychological counseling, international student services, low-cost health insurance, multicultural affairs office, teacher training. *Library facilities:* James A. Michener Library plus 2 others. *Online resources:* library catalog, web page, access to other libraries' catalogs. *Collection:* 711,965 titles, 3,219 serial subscriptions, 40,224 audiovisual materials.

Computer facilities: 1,100 computers available on campus for general student use. A campuswide network can be accessed from student residence rooms and from off campus. Internet access and online class registration are available. *Web address:* http://www.unco.edu/.

General Application Contact: Dorothy Eckas, Graduate Student Adviser, 970-351-1806, Fax: 970-351-2371, E-mail: dorothy.eckas@unco.edu.

GRADUATE UNITS

Graduate School Students: 1,004 full-time (696 women), 423 part-time (289 women); includes 114 minority (11 African Americans, 31 Asian Americans or Pacific Islanders, 62 Hispanic Americans, 10 Native Americans), 80 international. Average age 32. 969 applicants, 72% accepted. *Faculty:* 211 full-time (85 women). Expenses: Contact institution. *Financial support:* In 2001–02, 837 students received support, including 175 fellowships (averaging $1,327 per year), 156 research assistantships (averaging $8,787 per year), 101 teaching assistantships (averaging $8,213 per year); career-related internships or fieldwork, Federal Work-Study, institutionally sponsored loans, tuition waivers (partial), and unspecified assistantships also available. Support available to part-time students. Financial award application deadline: 3/1. In 2001, 638 master's, 69 doctorates, 12 other advanced degrees awarded. *Degree program information:* Part-time and evening/weekend programs available. Postbaccalaureate distance learning degree programs offered (minimal on-campus study). Offers interdisciplinary education (MA); interdisciplinary studies (MA, MS, DA, Ed D, Ed S). *Application deadline:* Applications are processed on a rolling basis. *Application fee:* $35. *Application Contact:* Dorothy Eckas, Graduate Student Adviser, 970-351-1806, Fax: 970-351-2371, E-mail: dorothy.eckas@unco.edu. *Associate Vice President for Research and Dean of the Graduate School*, Dr. Allen Huang, 970-351-2817, Fax: 970-351-2371.

College of Arts and Sciences Students: 137 full-time (84 women), 33 part-time (15 women); includes 15 minority (1 African American, 5 Asian Americans or Pacific Islanders, 7 Hispanic Americans, 2 Native Americans), 6 international. Average age 30. 112 applicants, 72% accepted. *Faculty:* 99 full-time (34 women). Expenses: Contact institution. *Financial support:* In 2001–02, 135 students received support, including 38 fellowships (averaging $735 per year), 43 research assistantships (averaging $8,971 per year), 54 teaching assistantships (averaging $9,008 per year); unspecified assistantships also available. Financial award application deadline: 3/1. In 2001, 67 master's, 8 doctorates awarded. Offers arts and sciences (MA, PhD); biological education (PhD); biological sciences (MA); chemical education (MA, PhD); chemical research (MA); communication (MA); earth sciences (MA); educational mathematics (MA, PhD); English (MA); history (MA); mathematics (MA, PhD); psychology (MA); sociology (MA); Spanish (MA). *Application deadline:* Applications are processed on a rolling basis. *Application fee:* $35. *Dean*, Dr. Sandra Flake, 970-351-2707.

College of Education Students: 524 full-time (398 women), 312 part-time (217 women); includes 66 minority (5 African Americans, 17 Asian Americans or Pacific Islanders, 39 Hispanic Americans, 5 Native Americans), 39 international. Average age 34. 469 applicants, 68% accepted. *Faculty:* 49 full-time (21 women). Expenses: Contact institution. *Financial support:* In 2001–02, 411 students received support, including 77 fellowships (averaging $1,542 per year), 67 research assistantships (averaging $9,890 per year), 15 teaching assistantships (averaging $8,569 per year); unspecified assistantships also available. Financial award application deadline: 3/1. In 2001, 389 master's, 44 doctorates, 12 other advanced degrees awarded. *Degree program information:* Part-time programs available. Offers agency counseling (MA); applied statistics and research methods (MS, PhD); counseling psychology (Psy D); counselor education (Ed D); counselor education and counseling psychology (MA, Ed D, Psy D); early childhood education (MA); education (MA, MS, Ed D, PhD, Psy D, Ed S); education of gifted (MA); educational leadership (MA, Ed D, Ed S); educational media (MA); educational psychology (MA, PhD); educational technology (MA, PhD); elementary education (MA, Ed D); elementary school counseling (MA); higher education and student affairs leadership (PhD); reading education (MA); school psychology (PhD, Ed S); secondary and postsecondary school counseling (MA); special education (MA, Ed D). *Application deadline:* Applications are processed on a rolling basis. *Application fee:* $35. *Dean*, Dr. Eugene Sheehan, 970-351-2817.

College of Health and Human Sciences Students: 258 full-time (179 women), 64 part-time (48 women); includes 27 minority (3 African Americans, 7 Asian Americans or Pacific Islanders, 14 Hispanic Americans, 3 Native Americans), 24 international. Average age 30. 317 applicants, 80% accepted. *Faculty:* 33 full-time (21 women). Expenses: Contact institution. *Financial support:* In 2001–02, 209 students received support, including 44 fellowships (averaging $1,256 per year), 26 research assistantships (averaging $7,766 per year), 13 teaching assistantships (averaging $7,737 per year); unspecified assistantships also available. Financial award application deadline: 3/1. In 2001, 140 master's, 9 doctorates awarded. Offers communication disorders (MA); community health (MPH); family nurse practitioner (MS); gerontology (MA); health and human sciences (MA, MPH, MS, Ed D, PhD); kinesiology and physical education (MA, Ed D); nursing education (MS); rehabilitation counseling (MA, PhD). *Application deadline:* Applications are processed on a rolling basis. *Application fee:* $35. *Dean*, Dr. Vincent Scalia, 970-351-2877.

College of Performing and Visual Arts Students: 83 full-time (33 women), 12 part-time (7 women); includes 5 minority (2 African Americans, 2 Asian Americans or Pacific Islanders, 1 Hispanic American), 10 international. Average age 31. 70 applicants, 61% accepted. *Faculty:* 30 full-time (9 women). Expenses: Contact institution. *Financial support:* In 2001–02, 79 students received support, including 16 fellowships (averaging $1,895 per year), 20 research assistantships (averaging $6,025 per year), 18 teaching assistantships (averaging $5,592 per year); unspecified assistantships also available. Financial award application deadline: 3/1. In 2001, 28 master's, 8 doctorates awarded. Offers music (MM, MME, DA); performing and visual arts (MA, MM, MME, DA); visual arts (MA). *Application deadline:* Applications are processed on a rolling basis. *Application fee:* $35. *Dean*, Dr. Kathleen Rountree, 970-351-2194.

See in-depth description on page 1229.

UNIVERSITY OF NORTHERN IOWA, Cedar Falls, IA 50614

General Information State-supported, coed, comprehensive institution. CGS member. *Enrollment:* 540 full-time matriculated graduate/professional students (351 women), 652 part-time matriculated graduate/professional students (453 women). *Enrollment by degree level:* 1,096 master's, 86 doctoral, 10 other advanced degrees. *Graduate faculty:* 536 full-time (199 women), 8 part-time/adjunct (3 women). Tuition, state resident: full-time $3,704; part-time $206 per credit hour. Tuition, nonresident: full-time $9,122; part-time $501 per credit hour. *Required fees:* $324; $108 per semester. Part-time tuition and fees vary according to course load. *Graduate housing:* Rooms and/or apartments available to single and married students. Typical cost: $4,410 (including board) for single students. Room and board charges vary according to board plan and housing facility selected. *Student services:* Campus employment opportunities, campus safety program, career counseling, child daycare facilities, disabled student services, exercise/wellness program, free psychological counseling, grant writing training, international student services, low-cost health insurance, multicultural affairs office. *Library facilities:* Rod Library plus 1 other. *Online resources:* library catalog, web page, access to other libraries' catalogs. *Collection:* 731,256 titles, 6,781 serial subscriptions, 18,452 audiovisual materials.

Computer facilities: 884 computers available on campus for general student use. A campuswide network can be accessed from student residence rooms and from off campus. Internet access and online class registration, course registration, student account and grade information are available. *Web address:* http://www.uni.edu/.

General Application Contact: Dr. John W. Somervill, Graduate Dean, 319-273-2748, Fax: 319-273-2243, E-mail: john.somervill@uni.edu.

GRADUATE UNITS

Graduate College Students: 540 full-time (351 women), 652 part-time (453 women); includes 89 minority (63 African Americans, 10 Asian Americans or Pacific Islanders, 14 Hispanic Americans, 2 Native Americans), 152 international. Average age 33. 714 applicants, 81% accepted. *Faculty:* 536 full-time (199 women), 8 part-time/adjunct (3 women). Expenses: Contact institution. *Financial support:* Fellowships, research assistantships, teaching assistantships, career-related internships or fieldwork, Federal Work-Study, institutionally sponsored loans, scholarships/grants, tuition waivers (full and partial), and unspecified assistantships available. Support available to part-time students. Financial award application deadline: 3/1. In 2001, 383 master's, 13 doctorates, 3 other advanced degrees awarded. *Degree program information:* Part-time and evening/weekend programs available. Offers public policy (MPP); women's studies (MA). *Application deadline:* Applications are processed on a rolling basis. *Application fee:* $20 ($50 for international students). *Application Contact:* Dr. Vivian R. Jackson, Associate Dean for Student Services, 319-273-2748, Fax: 319-273-2243, E-mail: vivian.jackson@uni.edu. *Dean*, Dr. John W. Somervill, 319-273-2748, Fax: 319-273-2243, E-mail: john.somervill@uni.edu.

College of Business Administration Students: 37 full-time (12 women), 20 part-time (6 women); includes 2 minority (both Asian Americans or Pacific Islanders), 13 international. 61 applicants, 74% accepted. *Faculty:* 55 full-time (10 women), 1 (woman) part-time/adjunct. Expenses: Contact institution. *Financial support:* Career-related internships or fieldwork, Federal Work-Study, scholarships/grants, and tuition waivers (full and partial) available. Support available to part-time students. Financial award application deadline:3/1. In 2001, 55 degrees awarded. *Degree program information:* Part-time and evening/weekend programs available. Offers accounting (M Acc); business administration (M Acc, MBA). *Application deadline:* For fall admission, 8/1 (priority date). Applications are processed on a rolling basis. *Application fee:* $20 ($50 for international students). *Interim Dean*, Dr. Farzad Moussavi, 319-273-6240, Fax: 319-273-2922, E-mail: farzad.moussavi@uni.edu.

College of Education Students: 177 full-time (125 women), 443 part-time (332 women); includes 47 minority (36 African Americans, 2 Asian Americans or Pacific Islanders, 7 Hispanic Americans, 2 Native Americans), 44 international. 279 applicants, 88% accepted. *Faculty:* 127 full-time (67 women), 2 part-time/adjunct (1 woman). Expenses: Contact institution. *Financial support:* Career-related internships or fieldwork, Federal Work-Study, institutionally sponsored loans, scholarships/grants, and tuition waivers (full and partial) available. Support available to part-time students. Financial award application deadline:3/1. In 2001, 163 master's, 2 doctorates, 3 other advanced degrees awarded. *Degree program information:* Part-time and evening/weekend programs available. Offers communication and training technology (MA); counseling (MA, MAE, Ed D); curriculum and instruction (MAE, Ed D); early childhood education (MAE); education (MA, MAE, Ed D, Ed S); education of the gifted (MAE); educational administration (Ed D); educational leadership (MAE, Ed D); educational media (MA); educational psychology (MAE); educational technology (MA); elementary education (MAE); elementary principal (MAE); elementary reading and language arts (MAE); health education (MA); leisure services (MA); middle school/junior high education (MAE); physical education (MA); postsecondary education (MAE); program administration (MA); reading (MAE); reading education (MAE); school counseling (MAE); school library media studies (MA); school psychology (Ed S); scientific basis of physical education (MA); secondary principal (MAE); secondary reading (MAE); special education (MAE); student affairs (MAE); teaching/coaching (MA); youth/human services administration (MA). *Application deadline:* For fall admission, 8/1 (priority date). Applications are processed on a rolling basis. *Application fee:* $20 ($50 for international students). *Dean*, Dr. Thomas J. Switzer, 319-273-2717, Fax: 319-273-2607, E-mail: thomas.switzer@uni.edu.

College of Humanities and Fine Arts Students: 161 full-time (126 women), 91 part-time (72 women); includes 14 minority (9 African Americans, 1 Asian American or Pacific Islander, 4 Hispanic Americans), 53 international. 187 applicants, 75% accepted. *Faculty:* 134 full-time (60 women), 4 part-time/adjunct (1 woman). Expenses: Contact institution. *Financial support:* Career-related internships or fieldwork, Federal Work-Study, scholarships/grants, and tuition waivers (full and partial) available. Support available to part-time students. Financial award application deadline: 3/1. In 2001, 111 degrees awarded. *Degree program information:* Part-time and evening/weekend programs available. Offers art (MA); art education (MA); audiology (MA); communication studies (MA); composition (MM); conducting (MM); English (MA); French (MA); German (MA); humanities and fine arts (MA, MM); jazz pedagogy (MM); music (MA); music education (MM); music history (MM); performance (MM); piano performance and pedagogy (MM); Spanish (MA); speech pathology (MA); teaching English to speakers of other languages (MA); teaching English to speakers of other languages/French (MA); teaching English to speakers of other languages/German (MA); teaching English to speakers of other languages/Spanish (MA); theatre (MA); two languages (MA). *Application deadline:* For fall admission, 8/1 (priority date). Applications are processed on a rolling basis. *Application fee:* $20 ($50 for international students). *Dean*, Dr. James F. Lubker, 319-273-2725, Fax: 319-273-2731, E-mail: james.lubker@uni.edu.

College of Natural Sciences Students: 58 full-time (15 women), 78 part-time (35 women); includes 5 minority (1 African American, 4 Asian Americans or Pacific Islanders), 32 international. 76 applicants, 78% accepted. *Faculty:* 111 full-time (24 women). Expenses: Contact institution. *Financial support:* Teaching assistantships, career-related internships or fieldwork, Federal Work-Study, scholarships/grants, and tuition waivers (full and partial) available. Support available to part-time students. Financial award application deadline:3/1. In 2001, 34 master's, 11 doctorates awarded. *Degree program information:* Part-time and evening/weekend programs available. Offers biology (MA, MS); chemistry (MA, MS); computer science (MA, MS); environmental science/technology (MS); industrial technology (MA, DIT); mathematics (MA); mathematics for middle grades (MA); natural sciences (MA, MS, DIT, SP); science (MA); science education (MA, SP). *Application deadline:* For fall admission, 8/1 (priority date). Applications are processed on a rolling basis. *Application fee:* $20 ($50 for international students). *Dean*, Dr. Kichoon Yang, 319-273-2585, Fax: 319-273-2893, E-mail: kichoon.yang@uni.edu.

College of Social and Behavioral Sciences Students: 83 full-time (57 women), 13 part-time (6 women); includes 12 minority (10 African Americans, 2 Hispanic Americans), 6 international. 87 applicants, 79% accepted. *Faculty:* 109 full-time (38 women), 1 part-time/adjunct (0 women). Expenses: Contact institution. *Financial support:* Career-related internships or fieldwork, Federal Work-Study, scholarships/grants, and tuition waivers (full and partial) available. Support available to part-time students. Financial award application deadline: 3/1. In 2001, 15 degrees awarded. *Degree program information:* Part-time and evening/weekend programs available. Offers geography (MA); history (MA); political science (MA); psychology (MA); social and behavioral sciences (MA, MSW); social work (MSW); sociology (MA). *Application deadline:* For fall admission, 8/1 (priority date). Applications are processed on a rolling basis. *Application fee:* $20 ($50 for international students). *Dean*, Dr. Julia E. Wallace, 319-273-2221, Fax: 319-273-2222, E-mail: julia.wallace@uni.edu.

UNIVERSITY OF NORTH FLORIDA, Jacksonville, FL 32224-2645

General Information State-supported, coed, comprehensive institution. *Enrollment:* 473 full-time matriculated graduate/professional students (305 women), 1,070 part-time matriculated graduate/professional students (677 women). *Enrollment by degree level:* 1,436 master's, 107 doctoral. *Graduate faculty:* 280 full-time (109 women). Tuition, state resident: full-time $2,411; part-time $134 per credit hour. Tuition, nonresident: full-time $9,391; part-time $522 per credit hour. *Required fees:* $670; $37 per credit hour. *Graduate housing:* Rooms and/or apartments available on a first-come, first-served basis to single and married students. Typical cost: $3,160 per year ($5,420 including board) for single students; $3,160 per year ($5,420 including board) for married students. Housing application deadline: 7/1. *Student services:* Campus employment opportunities, campus safety program, career counseling, child daycare facilities, disabled student services, exercise/wellness program, free psychological counseling, international student services, low-cost health insurance, multicultural affairs office, teacher training, writing training. *Library facilities:* Thomas G. Carpenter Library. *Online resources:* library catalog, web page, access to other libraries' catalogs. *Collection:* 704,799 titles, 3,000 serial subscriptions, 60,776 audiovisual materials.

Computer facilities: 700 computers available on campus for general student use. A campuswide network can be accessed from student residence rooms and from off campus. Internet access and online class registration, applications software are available. *Web address:* http://www.unf.edu/.

General Application Contact: Jim Owen, Assistant Director of Graduate Studies, 904-620-1360, Fax: 904-620-1362, E-mail: graduatestudies@unf.edu.

GRADUATE UNITS

College of Arts and Sciences Students: 76 full-time (53 women), 143 part-time (83 women); includes 30 minority (21 African Americans, 4 Asian Americans or Pacific Islanders, 4 Hispanic Americans, 1 Native American), 4 international. Average age 33. 224 applicants, 39% accepted, 55 enrolled. *Faculty:* 113 full-time (34 women). Expenses: Contact institution. *Financial support:* In 2001–02, 118 students received support, including 14 teaching assistantships (averaging $3,887 per year); research assistantships, career-related internships or fieldwork, Federal Work-Study, scholarships/grants, and tuition waivers (partial) also available. Support available to part-time students. Financial award application deadline: 4/1; financial award applicants required to submit FAFSA. In 2001, 65 degrees awarded. *Degree program information:* Part-time and evening/weekend programs available. Offers arts and sciences (MA, MAC, MPA, MS, MSCJ); counseling psychology (MAC); criminal justice (MSCJ); English (MA); general psychology (MA); history (MA); mathematical sciences (MS); public administration (MPA); statistics (MS). *Application deadline:* For fall admission, 7/6 (priority date); for winter admission, 11/2 (priority date); for spring admission, 3/10 (priority date). Applications are processed on a rolling basis. *Application fee:* $20. Electronic applications accepted. *Application Contact:* Dr. John Kemppainen, Director of Student Services, 904-620-2530, E-mail: jkemppai@unf.edu. *Dean*, Dr. Mark E. Workman, 904-620-2560, Fax: 904-620-2929, E-mail: hcamp@unf.edu.

College of Business Administration Students: 162 full-time (76 women), 347 part-time (152 women); includes 89 minority (36 African Americans, 24 Asian Americans or Pacific Islanders, 25 Hispanic Americans, 4 Native Americans), 31 international. Average age 30. 338 applicants, 59% accepted, 146 enrolled. *Faculty:* 51 full-time (10 women). Expenses: Contact institution. *Financial support:* In 2001–02, 151 students received support, including 1 research assistantship; fellowships, career-related internships or fieldwork, Federal Work-Study, scholarships/grants, and tuition waivers (partial) also available. Support available to part-time students. Financial award application deadline: 4/1; financial award applicants required to submit FAFSA. In 2001, 171 degrees awarded. *Degree program information:* Part-time and evening/weekend programs available. Offers accounting (M Acct); business administration (MBA); human resource management (MHRM). *Application deadline:* For fall admission, 7/6 (priority date); for winter admission, 11/2 (priority date); for spring admission, 3/10 (priority date). Applications are processed on a rolling basis. *Application fee:* $20. Electronic applications accepted. *Application Contact:* Dr. Jeffrey E. Michelman, Associate Dean and Director of Graduate Programs, 904-620-2590, E-mail: jmichelm@unf.edu. *Dean*, Dr. Earle C. Traynham, 904-620-2590, E-mail: etraynha@unf.edu.

College of Computer Sciences and Engineering Students: 11 full-time (7 women), 33 part-time (12 women); includes 11 minority (1 African American, 9 Asian Americans or Pacific Islanders, 1 Hispanic American), 4 international. Average age 33. 66 applicants, 27% accepted, 11 enrolled. *Faculty:* 18 full-time (2 women). Expenses: Contact institution. *Financial support:* In 2001–02, 14 students received support, including 3 teaching assistantships (averaging $4,992 per year); Federal Work-Study and tuition waivers (partial) also available. Support available to part-time students. Financial award application deadline: 4/1; financial award applicants required to submit FAFSA. In 2001, 9 degrees awarded. *Degree program information:* Part-time programs available. Offers computer and information sciences (MS). *Application deadline:* For fall admission, 7/6 (priority date); for winter admission, 11/2 (priority date); for spring admission, 3/10 (priority date). Applications are processed on a rolling basis. *Application fee:* $20. Electronic applications accepted. *Application Contact:* Dr. Charles Winton, Director of Graduate Studies, 904-620-2985, E-mail: cwinton@unf.edu. *Dean*, Dr. Neal Coulter, 904-620-1350, E-mail: ncoulter@unf.edu.

College of Education Students: 95 full-time (82 women), 448 part-time (357 women); includes 114 minority (81 African Americans, 10 Asian Americans or Pacific Islanders, 18 Hispanic Americans, 5 Native Americans), 1 international. Average age 37. 291 applicants, 47% accepted, 110 enrolled. *Faculty:* 61 full-time (35 women). Expenses: Contact institution. *Financial support:* In 2001–02, 251 students received support, including 2 research assistantships (averaging $1,934 per year); career-related internships or fieldwork, Federal Work-Study, scholarships/grants, and tuition waivers (partial) also available. Support available to part-time students. Financial award application deadline: 4/1; financial award applicants required to submit FAFSA. In 2001, 219 master's, 6 doctorates awarded. *Degree program information:* Part-time and evening/weekend programs available. Offers administration (M Ed); counselor education (M Ed); education (M Ed, Ed D); educational leadership (M Ed, Ed D); special education (M Ed). *Application deadline:* For fall admission, 7/6 (priority date); for winter admission, 11/2 (priority date); for spring admission, 3/10 (priority date). Applications are processed on a rolling basis. *Application fee:* $20. Electronic applications accepted. *Application Contact:* Dr. John Kemppainen, Director of Student Services, 904-620-2530, E-mail: jkemppai@unf.edu. *Director of Student Services*, Dr. John Kemppainen, 904-620-2530, E-mail: jkemppai@unf.edu.

Division of Curriculum and Instruction Students: 21 full-time (18 women), 133 part-time (123 women); includes 19 minority (9 African Americans, 1 Asian American or Pacific Islander, 8 Hispanic Americans, 1 Native American) Average age 37. 72 applicants, 38% accepted, 15 enrolled. *Faculty:* 33 full-time (19 women). Expenses: Contact institution. *Financial support:* In 2001–02, 55 students received support. Career-related internships or fieldwork, Federal Work-Study, and tuition waivers (partial) available. Support available to part-time students. Financial award application deadline: 4/1; financial award applicants required to submit FAFSA. In 2001, 101 degrees awarded. *Degree program information:* Part-time and evening/weekend programs available. Offers elementary education (M Ed); mathematics education (M Ed); music education (M Ed); science education (M Ed); secondary education (M Ed). *Application deadline:* For fall admission, 7/6 (priority date); for winter admission, 11/2 (priority date); for spring admission, 3/10 (priority date). Applications are processed on a rolling basis. *Application fee:* $20. Electronic applications accepted. *Application Contact:* Dr. John Kemppainen, Director of Student Services, 904-620-2530, E-mail: jkemppai@unf.edu. *Chair*, Dr. Phillip S. Riner, 904-620-2610, E-mail: priner@unf.edu.

College of Health Students: 129 full-time (87 women), 89 part-time (63 women); includes 44 minority (22 African Americans, 8 Asian Americans or Pacific Islanders, 12 Hispanic Americans, 2 Native Americans), 1 international. Average age 32. 217 applicants, 52% accepted, 54 enrolled. *Faculty:* 37 full-time (28 women). Expenses: Contact institution. *Financial support:* In 2001–02, 110 students received support, including 2 research assistantships (averaging $2,553 per year); career-related internships or fieldwork, Federal Work-Study, scholarships/grants, and tuition waivers (partial) also available. Support available to part-time students. Financial award application deadline: 4/1; financial award applicants required to submit FAFSA. In 2001, 94 degrees awarded. *Degree program information:* Part-time and evening/weekend programs available. Offers addictions counseling (MSH); advanced practice nursing (MSN); aging studies (Certificate); community health (MPH); employee health services (MSH); family nurse practitioner (Certificate); health (MHA, MPH, MPT, MSH, MSN, Certificate); health administration (MHA); health care administration (MSH); human ecology and nutrition (MSH); human performance (MSH); physical therapy (MPT). *Application deadline:* For fall admission, 7/6 (priority date); for winter admission, 11/2 (priority date); for spring admission, 3/10 (priority date). Applications are processed on a rolling basis. *Application fee:* $20. Electronic applications accepted. *Dean*, Dr. Pamela Chally, 904-620-2810, E-mail: pchally@unf.edu.

UNIVERSITY OF NORTH TEXAS, Denton, TX 76203

General Information State-supported, coed, university. CGS member. *Enrollment:* 2,175 full-time matriculated graduate/professional students (1,206 women), 4,008 part-time matriculated graduate/professional students (2,577 women). *Graduate faculty:* 870. Tuition, state resident: part-time $1,861 per hour. Tuition, nonresident: part-time $319 per hour. *Required fees:* $88; $21 per hour. *Graduate housing:* Rooms and/or apartments available on a first-come, first-served basis to single and married students. *Student services:* Campus employment opportunities, campus safety program, career counseling, child daycare facilities, disabled student services, exercise/wellness program, free psychological counseling, international student services, low-cost health insurance, multicultural affairs office, teacher training. *Library facilities:* Willis Library plus 4 others. *Online resources:* library catalog, web page, access to other libraries' catalogs. *Collection:* 1.8 million titles, 12,243 serial subscriptions, 63,338 audiovisual materials. *Research affiliation:* Oak Ridge National Laboratory (physics), North Texas Research Institute (physical and natural sciences), IBM (information systems), Miles Laboratories (environmental studies), Geo-Centers, Inc. (applied chemistry), Texas Instruments, Inc. (physics).

Computer facilities: 2,006 computers available on campus for general student use. A campuswide network can be accessed from student residence rooms and from off campus. *Web address:* http://www.unt.edu/.

General Application Contact: Dr. C. Neal Tate, Dean, 940-565-2383, Fax: 940-565-2141, E-mail: ntate@unt.edu.

GRADUATE UNITS

Robert B. Toulouse School of Graduate Studies Students: 2,175 full-time (1,206 women), 4,008 part-time (2,577 women); includes 858 minority (324 African Americans, 156 Asian Americans or Pacific Islanders, 332 Hispanic Americans, 46 Native Americans), 840 international. 3,866 applicants, 67% accepted. *Faculty:* 870. Expenses: Contact institution. *Financial support:* Fellowships, research assistantships, teaching assistantships, career-related internships or fieldwork, Federal Work-Study, institutionally sponsored loans, scholarships/grants, tuition waivers (full and partial), unspecified assistantships, and library assistantships available. Support available to part-time students. Financial award applicants required to submit FAFSA. In 2001, 1,147 master's, 159 doctorates awarded. *Degree program information:* Part-time and evening/weekend programs available. Postbaccalaureate distance learning degree programs offered. *Application deadline:* For fall admission, 6/16; for spring admission, 11/16. Applications are processed on a rolling basis. *Application fee:* $25 ($50 for international students). *Application Contact:* Dr. Sandra L. Terrell, Associate Dean, 940-565-2383, Fax: 940-565-2141, E-mail: terrell@unt.edu. *Dean*, Dr. C. Neal Tate, 940-565-2383, Fax: 940-565-2141, E-mail: ntate@unt.edu.

College of Arts and Sciences Students: 1,405. Average age 27. *Faculty:* 387. Expenses: Contact institution. *Financial support:* Fellowships, research assistantships, teaching assistantships, career-related internships or fieldwork, Federal Work-Study, institutionally sponsored loans, tuition waivers (partial), and unspecified assistantships available. Support available to part-time students. In 2001, 261 master's, 59 doctorates awarded. *Degree program information:* Part-time and evening/weekend programs available. Offers arts and sciences (MA, MJ, MS, PhD); biochemistry (MS, PhD); biology (MA, MS, PhD); chemistry (MS, PhD); clinical psychology (PhD); communication studies (MA, MS); computer sciences (MA, MS, PhD); counseling psychology (MA, MS, PhD); drama (MA, MS); economic research (MS); economics (MA); engineering technology (MS); English (MA, PhD); environmental science (MS, PhD); experimental psychology (MA, MS, PhD); French (MA); geography (MS); health psychology and behavioral medicine (PhD); history (MA, MS, PhD); industrial psychology (MA, MS); journalism (MA, MJ); labor and industrial relations (MS); materials science (MS, PhD); mathematics (MA, MS, PhD); molecular biology (MA, MS, PhD); philosophy and religion studies (MA); physics (MA, MS, PhD); political science (MA, MS, PhD); psychology (MA, MS, PhD); radio/television/film (MA, MS); school psychology (MA, MS, PhD); Spanish (MA); speech-language pathology/audiology (MA, MS). *Application fee:*

University of North Texas (continued)

$25 ($50 for international students). *Dean*, Dr. Warren Burggren, 940-565-2497, Fax: 940-565-4517.

College of Business Administration Students: 503. Average age 31. *Faculty:* 108.Expenses: Contact institution. *Financial support:* Fellowships, research assistantships, teaching assistantships, career-related internships or fieldwork, Federal Work-Study, and institutionally sponsored loans available. In 2001, 134 master's, 6 doctorates awarded. *Degree program information:* Part-time and evening/weekend programs available. Offers marketing and logistics (MBA, PhD); accounting (MS, PhD); administrative management (MBA); banking (MBA, PhD); business administration (MBA, MS, PhD); finance (MBA, PhD); information systems (MBA, PhD); insurance (MBA); management (MBA); management science (MBA, PhD); organization theory and policy (PhD); personnel and industrial relations (MBA, PhD); production/operations management (MBA, PhD); real estate (MBA). *Application deadline:* For fall admission, 7/17. Applications are processed on a rolling basis. *Application fee:* $25 ($50 for international students). *Application Contact:* Denise Galubenski, Counselor, 940-565-3027. *Dean*, Dr. Jared E. Hazleton, 940-565-2110.

College of Education Students: 1,715. *Faculty:* 122. Expenses: Contact institution. *Financial support:* Fellowships, research assistantships, teaching assistantships, career-related internships or fieldwork, Federal Work-Study, institutionally sponsored loans, and tuition waivers (partial) available. Support available to part-time students. Financial award application deadline: 4/1. In 2001, 364 master's, 54 doctorates awarded. *Degree program information:* Part-time and evening/weekend programs available. Offers applied technology and training development (M Ed, MS, Ed D, PhD, Certificate); community health (MS); computer education and cognitive systems (MS); counseling and student services (M Ed, MS, PhD); counselor education (M Ed, MS, PhD); curriculum and instruction (Ed D, PhD); development and family studies (MS); early childhood education (M Ed, MS, PhD); education (M Ed, MS, Ed D, PhD, Certificate); educational administration (M Ed, Ed D, PhD); educational research (PhD); elementary education (M Ed, MS); elementary school supervision (M Ed); health promotion (MS); higher education (Ed D, PhD); kinesiology (MS); reading (M Ed, MS, Ed D, PhD); recreation and leisure studies (MS, Certificate); school health (MS); secondary education (M Ed, MS); secondary school supervision (M Ed); special education (M Ed, MS, PhD); special subject supervision (M Ed); vocational counselor (Certificate). *Application deadline:* For fall admission, 7/17. *Application fee:* $25 ($50 for international students). *Application Contact:* Dr. John Williamson, Director of Student Services, 940-565-2736, Fax: 940-565-2728, E-mail: wllmsn@coe.unt.edu. *Dean*, Dr. Jean Keller, 940-565-2231, Fax: 940-565-4415.

College of Music Students: 479. Average age 26. *Faculty:* 96. Expenses: Contact institution. *Financial support:* Fellowships, research assistantships, teaching assistantships, career-related internships or fieldwork, Federal Work-Study, institutionally sponsored loans, and scholarships/grants available. Financial award application deadline: 4/1. In 2001, 78 master's, 16 doctorates awarded. Offers composition (MM, DMA, PhD); jazz studies (MM); music (MA); music education (MM, MME, PhD); music theory (MM, PhD); musicology (MM, PhD); performance (MM, DMA). *Application deadline:* For fall admission, 7/17. *Application fee:* $25 ($50 for international students). *Application Contact:* Dr. Edward Baird, Graduate Adviser, 940-565-3733, Fax: 940-565-2002, E-mail: ebaird@music.unt.edu. *Dean*, Dr. James Scott, 940-565-2791, Fax: 940-565-2002.

Interdisciplinary Studies Students: 16. Expenses: Contact institution. *Financial support:* Career-related internships or fieldwork, Federal Work-Study, and institutionally sponsored loans available. Financial award application deadline: 4/1. In 2001, 13 degrees awarded. *Degree program information:* Part-time programs available. Offers information science (PhD); interdisciplinary studies (MA, MS). *Application deadline:* For fall admission, 7/17. *Application fee:* $25 ($50 for international students). *Application Contact:* Dr. Sandra L. Terrell, Associate Dean, 940-565-2383, Fax: 940-565-2141, E-mail: terrell@unt.edu. *Head*, Donna Hughes, 940-565-2383, Fax: 940-565-2141, E-mail: hughesd@unt.edu.

School of Community Service Students: 406. Average age 28. *Faculty:* 69. Expenses: Contact institution. *Financial support:* Fellowships, research assistantships, teaching assistantships, career-related internships or fieldwork, Federal Work-Study, institutionally sponsored loans, scholarships/grants, and tuition waivers (full and partial) available. Support available to part-time students. Financial award applicants required to submit FAFSA. In 2001, 101 master's, 8 doctorates awarded. *Degree program information:* Part-time and evening/weekend programs available. Offers administration of aging organizations (MA, MS); administration of retirement facilities (MA, MS); aging (MA, MS, Certificate); applied economics (MS); behavior analysis (MS); community service (MA, MPA, MS, PhD, Certificate); public administration (MPA); rehabilitation counseling (MS); rehabilitation studies (MS); sociology (MA, MS, PhD); vocational evaluation (MS); work adjustment services (MS). *Application deadline:* For fall admission, 7/17. Applications are processed on a rolling basis. *Application fee:* $25 ($50 for international students). *Interim Dean*, Dr. David W. Hartman, 940-565-2239.

School of Library and Information Sciences Students: 73 full-time (61 women), 324 part-time (277 women); includes 47 minority (17 African Americans, 5 Asian Americans or Pacific Islanders, 22 Hispanic Americans, 3 Native Americans), 6 international. Average age 37. *Faculty:* 14. Expenses: Contact institution. *Financial support:* Fellowships, research assistantships, teaching assistantships, career-related internships or fieldwork, Federal Work-Study, institutionally sponsored loans, and library assistantships available. Financial award application deadline: 4/1. In 2001, 118 master's, 16 doctorates awarded. *Degree program information:* Part-time and evening/weekend programs available. Offers information science (MS, PhD); library science (MS). *Application deadline:* For fall admission, 7/17; for spring admission, 11/30. Applications are processed on a rolling basis. *Application fee:* $25 ($50 for international students). *Application Contact:* Dr. Herman Totten, Graduate Adviser, 940-565-2445, Fax: 940-565-3110, E-mail: totten@lis.admin.unt.edu. *Dean*, Dr. Philip M. Turner, 940-565-2445, Fax: 940-565-3110, E-mail: turner@lis.admin.unt.edu.

School of Merchandising and Hospitality Management Students: 27. *Faculty:* 21. Expenses: Contact institution. *Financial support:* Fellowships, research assistantships, teaching assistantships, career-related internships or fieldwork, Federal Work-Study, and institutionally sponsored loans available. Financial award application deadline: 4/1. In 2001, 5 degrees awarded. *Degree program information:* Part-time programs available. Offers hotel/restaurant management (MS); merchandising and fabric analytics (MS). *Application deadline:* For fall admission, 7/17. *Application fee:* $25 ($50 for international students). *Application Contact:* Dr. Richard Tas, Graduate Adviser, 940-565-2436, Fax: 940-565-4348, E-mail: tas@smhm.cmm.unt.edu. *Interim Dean*, Dr. Judith C. Forney, 940-565-2436, Fax: 940-565-4348, E-mail: forney@smhm.cmm.unt.edu.

School of Visual Arts Students: 103. Average age 27. *Faculty:* 50. Expenses: Contact institution. *Financial support:* Fellowships, teaching assistantships, career-related internships or fieldwork, Federal Work-Study, and institutionally sponsored loans available. Support available to part-time students. Financial award application deadline: 4/1. In 2001, 25 degrees awarded. *Degree program information:* Part-time programs available. Offers art (PhD); art education (MA, MFA, PhD); art history (MA, MFA); ceramics (MFA); communication design (MFA); fashion design (MFA); fibers (MFA); interior design (MFA); metalsmithing and jewelry (MFA); painting and drawing (MFA); photography (MFA); printmaking (MFA); sculpture (MFA). *Application deadline:* For fall admission, 7/17 (priority date); for spring admission, 10/1. Applications are processed on a rolling basis. *Application fee:* $25 ($50 for international students). *Application Contact:* Dr. Diane Taylor, Graduate Adviser, 940-565-4004, Fax: 940-565-4717, E-mail: dtaylor@art.unt.edu. *Dean*, Dr. D. Jack Davis, 940-565-2855, Fax: 940-565-4717, E-mail: davis@art.unt.edu.

See in-depth description on page 1231.

UNIVERSITY OF NORTH TEXAS HEALTH SCIENCE CENTER AT FORT WORTH, Fort Worth, TX 76107-2699

General Information State-supported, coed, graduate-only institution. CGS member. *Enrollment by degree level:* 465 first professional, 248 master's, 92 doctoral. *Graduate faculty:* 219 full-time (53 women), 25 part-time/adjunct (3 women). Tuition, state resident: full-time $6,550; part-time $858 per year. Tuition, nonresident: full-time $19,650; part-time $3,633 per year. *Required fees:* $1,300; $473 per year. Tuition and fees vary according to program. *Graduate housing:* On-campus housing not available. *Student services:* Campus employment opportunities, campus safety program, career counseling, disabled student services, exercise/wellness program, free psychological counseling, grant writing training, international student services, low-cost health insurance, multicultural affairs office. *Library facilities:* Gibson D. Lewis Health Sciences Library. *Online resources:* library catalog, web page. *Collection:* 222,414 titles, 3,868 serial subscriptions, 13,012 audiovisual materials. *Research affiliation:* Botanical Research Institutions of Texas, Genelink (familial DNA depository), Ethnobotanical Product Investigation Consortium (natural plant products), My-tech, Inc. (cardiovascular research), Myogen, Inc. (cardiac research), Novopharm, Inc. (gene control).

Computer facilities: A campuswide network can be accessed from off campus. Internet access is available. *Web address:* http://www.hsc.unt.edu/.

GRADUATE UNITS

Graduate School of Biomedical Sciences Students: 101 full-time (61 women), 35 part-time (19 women); includes 36 minority (13 African Americans, 7 Asian Americans or Pacific Islanders, 16 Hispanic Americans), 32 international. Average age 29. 90 applicants, 84% accepted, 42 enrolled. *Faculty:* 68 full-time (11 women), 7 part-time/adjunct (0 women). Expenses: Contact institution. *Financial support:* In 2001–02, 80 research assistantships (averaging $16,000 per year) were awarded; fellowships, teaching assistantships, career-related internships or fieldwork, Federal Work-Study, institutionally sponsored loans, scholarships/grants, and traineeships also available. Support available to part-time students. Financial award application deadline: 4/1; financial award applicants required to submit FAFSA. In 2001, 11 master's, 13 doctorates awarded. Offers anatomy and cell biology (MS, PhD); biochemistry and molecular biology (MS, PhD); biomedical sciences (MS, PhD); biotechnology (MS); forensic genetics (MS); integrative physiology (MS, PhD); medical science (MS); microbiology and immunology (MS, PhD); pharmacology (MS, PhD); science education (MS). *Application deadline:* For fall admission, 5/1; for spring admission, 11/1. Applications are processed on a rolling basis. *Application fee:* $25 ($50 for international students). *Application Contact:* Carla Lee, Director of Graduate Admissions and Services, 817-735-2560, Fax: 817-735-0243, E-mail: gsbs@hsc.unt.edu. *Dean*, Dr. Thomas Yorio, 817-735-2560, Fax: 817-735-0243, E-mail: yoriot@hsc.unt.edu.

School of Public Health Students: 69 full-time (38 women), 88 part-time (50 women); includes 53 minority (23 African Americans, 13 Asian Americans or Pacific Islanders, 15 Hispanic Americans, 2 Native Americans), 28 international. Average age 32. 121 applicants, 93% accepted, 69 enrolled. *Faculty:* 26 full-time (6 women). Expenses: Contact institution. *Financial support:* In 2001–02, 9 research assistantships with partial tuition reimbursements (averaging $16,000 per year), 2 teaching assistantships (averaging $8,100 per year) were awarded. Fellowships, Federal Work-Study, institutionally sponsored loans, and scholarships/grants also available. Support available to part-time students. Financial award application deadline: 4/1; financial award applicants required to submit FAFSA. In 2001, 48 degrees awarded. *Degree program information:* Part-time and evening/weekend programs available. Offers biostatistics (MPH); community health (MPH); disease control and prevention (Dr PH); environmental health (MPH); epidemiology (MPH); health behavior (MPH); health policy and management (MPH, Dr PH). *Application deadline:* For fall admission, 6/1; for spring admission, 11/1. Applications are processed on a rolling basis. *Application fee:* $25 ($50 for international students). Electronic applications accepted. *Application Contact:* Thomas Moorman, Director of Student Affairs, 817-735-0302, Fax: 817-735-0324, E-mail: tmoorman@hsc.unt.edu. *Dean*, Dr. Fernando Treviño, 817-735-2401, Fax: 817-735-0243, E-mail: sph@hsc.unt.edu.

Texas College of Osteopathic Medicine Students: 465 full-time (228 women); includes 176 minority (6 African Americans, 138 Asian Americans or Pacific Islanders, 31 Hispanic Americans, 1 Native American) Average age 27. 1,152 applicants, 13% accepted, 119 enrolled. *Faculty:* 184 full-time (37 women), 23 part-time/adjunct (5 women). Expenses: Contact institution. *Financial support:* In 2001–02, 415 students received support, including 4 research assistantships (averaging $10,440 per year), 7 teaching assistantships with tuition reimbursements available (averaging $10,440 per year); career-related internships or fieldwork, Federal Work-Study, institutionally sponsored loans, scholarships/grants, and tuition waivers (full) also available. Financial award applicants required to submit FAFSA. In 2001, 107 degrees awarded. Offers osteopathic medicine (DO); physician assistant studies (MPAS). *Application Contact:* Jane Anderson, Director of Admissions, 817-735-2204, Fax: 817-735-2225. *Dean*, Dr. Marc B. Hahn, 817-735-2416, Fax: 817-735-2486.

UNIVERSITY OF NOTRE DAME, Notre Dame, IN 46556

General Information Independent-religious, coed, university. CGS member. *Enrollment:* 1,404 full-time matriculated graduate/professional students (536 women), 53 part-time matriculated graduate/professional students (20 women). *Enrollment by degree level:* 41 first professional, 365 master's, 1,051 doctoral. *Graduate faculty:* 702 full-time (145 women), 102 part-time/adjunct (23 women). *Tuition:* Full-time $24,220; part-time $1,346 per credit hour. *Required fees:* $155. *Graduate housing:* Rooms and/or apartments available on a first-come, first-served basis to single and married students. Typical cost: $3,097 per year ($4,257 including board) for single students; $3,231 per year ($4,391 including board) for married students. Room and board charges vary according to housing facility selected. Housing application deadline: 5/1. *Student services:* Campus employment opportunities, campus safety program, career counseling, child daycare facilities, disabled student services, exercise/wellness program, free psychological counseling, grant writing training, international student services, low-cost health insurance, multicultural affairs office, teacher training, writing training. *Library facilities:* University Libraries of Notre Dame plus 8 others. *Online resources:* library catalog, web page, access to other libraries' catalogs. *Collection:* 2.6 million titles, 19,100 serial subscriptions, 18,416 audiovisual materials. *Research affiliation:* Argonne National Laboratory, Fermi National Accelerator Laboratory, Brookhaven National Laboratory, Lilly Endowment, Lockheed Martin Corporation, Jet Propulsion Laboratory.

Computer facilities: 880 computers available on campus for general student use. A campuswide network can be accessed from student residence rooms and from off campus. Internet access is available. *Web address:* http://www.nd.edu/.

General Application Contact: Dr. Terrence J. Akai, Director of Graduate Admissions, 574-631-7706, Fax: 574-631-4183, E-mail: gradad@nd.edu.

GRADUATE UNITS

Graduate School Students: 1,526 full-time (595 women), 25 part-time (11 women); includes 148 minority (33 African Americans, 44 Asian Americans or Pacific Islanders, 64 Hispanic Americans, 7 Native Americans), 504 international. 3,699 applicants, 23% accepted, 494 enrolled. *Faculty:* 589 full-time (119 women), 60 part-time/adjunct (15 women). Expenses: Contact institution. *Financial support:* In 2001–02, 1,486 students received support, including 558 fellowships with full tuition reimbursements available (averaging $15,000 per year), 282 research assistantships with full tuition reimbursements available (averaging $12,300 per year), 461 teaching assistantships with full tuition reimbursements available (averaging $11,950 per year); career-related internships or fieldwork, institutionally sponsored loans, scholarships/grants, traineeships, tuition waivers (full and partial), and unspecified assistantships also available. Support available to part-time students. In 2001, 16 first professional degrees, 300 master's, 124 doctorates awarded. *Degree program information:* Part-time programs available. *Application deadline:* Applications are processed on a rolling basis. *Application fee:* $50. Electronic applications accepted. *Application Contact:* Dr. Terrence J. Akai, Director of Graduate Admissions, 574-631-7706, Fax: 574-631-4183, E-mail: gradad@nd.edu. *Vice President for Graduate Studies and Research*, Dr. Jeffrey C. Kantor, 574-631-6291, Fax: 574-631-4183, E-mail: gradsch@nd.edu.

College of Arts and Letters Students: 875 full-time (400 women), 10 part-time (5 women); includes 114 minority (24 African Americans, 32 Asian Americans or Pacific Islanders, 54 Hispanic Americans, 4 Native Americans), 137 international. 1,900 applicants, 22% accepted, 297 enrolled. *Faculty:* 330 full-time (93 women), 45 part-time/adjunct (14 women). Expenses: Contact institution. *Financial support:* In 2001–02, 838 students received support, including 399 fellowships with full tuition reimbursements available (averaging $14,000 per year), 52 research assistantships with full tuition reimbursements available (averaging $10,800 per year), 252 teaching assistantships with full tuition reimbursements available (averaging $10,800 per year); career-related internships or fieldwork, scholarships/grants, and tuition waivers (full and partial) also available. Support available to part-time students. In 2001, 16 first professional degrees, 146 master's, 66 doctorates awarded. *Degree program information:* Part-time programs available. Offers art history (MA); arts and letters (M Div, M Ed, MA, MFA, MM, MMS, MTS, PhD); ceramics (MFA); cognitive psychology (PhD); counseling psychology (PhD); creative writing (MFA); design (MFA); developmental psychology (PhD); early Christian studies (MA); economics (MA, PhD); educational initiatives (M Ed); English (MA, PhD); French and Francophone studies (MA); German (MA); graphic design (MFA); history (MA, PhD); history and philosophy of science (MA, PhD); humanities (M Div, MA, MFA, MM, MMS, MTS, PhD); Iberian and Latin American studies (MA); industrial design (MFA); international peace studies (MA); Italian studies (MA); literature (PhD); medieval studies (MMS, PhD); music (MA, MM); painting (MFA); philosophy (PhD); photography (MFA); political science (PhD); printmaking (MFA); quantitative psychology (PhD); Romance literatures (MA); sculpture (MFA); social science (M Ed, MA, PhD); sociology (PhD); studio art (MFA); theology (M Div, MA, MTS, PhD). *Application deadline:* Applications are processed on a rolling basis. *Application fee:* $50. *Application Contact:* Dr. Terrence J. Akai, Director of Graduate Admissions, 574-631-7706, Fax: 574-631-4183, E-mail: gradad@nd.edu. *Dean,* Dr. Mark W. Roche, 574-631-7085.

College of Engineering Students: 321 full-time (79 women), 11 part-time (3 women); includes 18 minority (6 African Americans, 7 Asian Americans or Pacific Islanders, 3 Hispanic Americans, 2 Native Americans), 204 international. Average age 25. 826 applicants, 27% accepted, 97 enrolled. *Faculty:* 97 full-time (4 women), 7 part-time/adjunct (1 woman). Expenses: Contact institution. *Financial support:* In 2001–02, 323 students received support, including 92 fellowships with full tuition reimbursements available (averaging $18,800 per year), 156 research assistantships with full tuition reimbursements available (averaging $19,500 per year), 49 teaching assistantships with full tuition reimbursements available (averaging $18,300 per year); scholarships/grants, tuition waivers (full), and unspecified assistantships also available. Financial award application deadline: 2/1. In 2001, 62 master's, 18 doctorates awarded. *Degree program information:* Part-time programs available. Offers aerospace and mechanical engineering (PhD); aerospace engineering (MS); bioengineering (MS); chemical engineering (MS, PhD); civil engineering (MS); civil engineering and geological sciences (PhD); computer science and engineering (MS, PhD); electrical engineering (MS, PhD); engineering (ME, MEME, MS, PhD); environmental engineering (MS); geological sciences (MS); mechanical engineering (MEME, MS). *Application deadline:* For fall admission, 2/1 (priority date). Applications are processed on a rolling basis. *Application fee:* $50. Electronic applications accepted. *Application Contact:* Dr. Terrence J. Akai, Director of Graduate Admissions, 574-631-7706, Fax: 574-631-4183, E-mail: gradad@nd.edu. *Dean,* Dr. Frank P. Incropera, 574-631-5534, Fax: 574-631-8007, E-mail: incropera.1@nd.edu.

College of Science Students: 315 full-time (110 women), 3 part-time (all women); includes 14 minority (2 African Americans, 4 Asian Americans or Pacific Islanders, 7 Hispanic Americans, 1 Native American), 156 international. 904 applicants, 24% accepted, 90 enrolled. *Faculty:* 145 full-time (20 women), 6 part-time/adjunct (0 women). Expenses: Contact institution. *Financial support:* In 2001–02, 310 students received support, including 52 fellowships with full tuition reimbursements available (averaging $18,000 per year), 74 research assistantships with full tuition reimbursements available (averaging $14,100 per year), 160 teaching assistantships with full tuition reimbursements available (averaging $14,100 per year); traineeships and tuition waivers (full) also available. Financial award application deadline: 2/1. In 2001, 20 master's, 40 doctorates awarded. Offers aquatic ecology, evolution and environmental biology (MS, PhD); biochemistry (MS, PhD); cellular and molecular biology (MS, PhD); genetics (MS, PhD); inorganic chemistry (MS, PhD); mathematics (MSAM, PhD); organic chemistry (MS, PhD); physical chemistry (MS, PhD); physics (PhD); physiology (MS, PhD); science (MS, MSAM, PhD); vector biology and parasitology (MS, PhD). *Application deadline:* For fall admission, 2/1 (priority date). Applications are processed on a rolling basis. *Application fee:* $50. Electronic applications accepted. *Application Contact:* Dr. Terrence J. Akai, Director of Graduate Admissions, 574-631-7706, Fax: 574-631-4183, E-mail: gradad@nd.edu. *Dean,* Dr. Francis J. Castellino, 574-631-6456, E-mail: castellino.1@nd.edu.

School of Architecture Students: 15 full-time (6 women), 1 part-time; includes 2 minority (1 African American, 1 Asian American or Pacific Islander), 7 international. 69 applicants, 22% accepted, 10 enrolled. *Faculty:* 17 full-time (2 women), 2 part-time/adjunct (0 women). Expenses: Contact institution. *Financial support:* In 2001–02, 15 students received support, including 15 fellowships with full tuition reimbursements available (averaging $12,500 per year); research assistantships, teaching assistantships, institutionally sponsored loans and tuition waivers (full) also available. Financial award application deadline: 2/1. In 2001, 3 degrees awarded. Offers architecture (M Arch). *Application deadline:* For fall admission, 2/1 (priority date). Applications are processed on a rolling basis. *Application fee:* $50. Electronic applications accepted. *Application Contact:* Dr. Terrence J. Akai, Director of Graduate Admissions, 574-631-7706, Fax: 574-631-4183, E-mail: gradad@nd.edu. *Director of Graduate Studies,* Norman Crowe, 574-631-6137, Fax: 574-631-8486, E-mail: stein.12@nd.edu.

Law School Students: 528 full-time (223 women); includes 99 minority (17 African Americans, 37 Asian Americans or Pacific Islanders, 39 Hispanic Americans, 6 Native Americans), 7 international. Average age 24. 1,904 applicants, 32% accepted, 173 enrolled. *Faculty:* 35 full-time (9 women), 29 part-time/adjunct (5 women). Expenses: Contact institution. *Financial support:* In 2001–02, 289 students received support, including 289 fellowships (averaging $10,000 per year), 20 research assistantships (averaging $3,000 per year), 10 teaching assistantships (averaging $6,000 per year); career-related internships or fieldwork, Federal Work-Study, and institutionally sponsored loans also available. Financial award application deadline: 3/1; financial award applicants required to submit FAFSA. In 2001, 186 first professional degrees, 24 master's, 1 doctorate awarded. Offers human rights (LL M, JSD); international and comparative law (LL M); law (JD). *Application deadline:* For fall admission, 3/1. Applications are processed on a rolling basis. *Application fee:* $55. Electronic applications accepted. *Application Contact:* 574-631-6626, Fax: 574-631-3980, E-mail: lawadmit@nd.edu. *Dean,* Patricia A. O'Hara, 574-631-6789, Fax: 574-631-8400, E-mail: o'hara.3@nd.edu.

Mendoza College of Business Students: 554 full-time (138 women), 1 (woman) part-time; includes 62 minority (21 African Americans, 14 Asian Americans or Pacific Islanders, 23 Hispanic Americans, 4 Native Americans), 112 international. Average age 28. 1,274 applicants, 35% accepted, 295 enrolled. *Faculty:* 78 full-time (17 women), 13 part-time/adjunct (3 women). Expenses: Contact institution. *Financial support:* In 2001–02, 306 students received support, including 217 fellowships with full and partial tuition reimbursements available; career-related internships or fieldwork, Federal Work-Study, institutionally sponsored loans, scholarships/grants, tuition waivers (full and partial), and unspecified assistantships also available. Financial award applicants required to submit FAFSA. In 2001, 308 degrees awarded. *Degree program information:* Part-time and evening/weekend programs available. Postbaccalaureate distance learning degree programs offered (minimal on-campus study). Offers accountancy (MS); business (EMBA, MBA, MS); business administration (MBA); executive business administration (EMBA). *Application deadline:* Applications are processed on a rolling basis. Electronic applications accepted. *Dean,* Dr. Carolyn Y. Woo, 574-631-7236, Fax: 574-631-4825, E-mail: woo.5@nd.edu.

See in-depth description on page 1233.

UNIVERSITY OF OKLAHOMA, Norman, OK 73019-0390

General Information State-supported, coed, university. CGS member. *Enrollment:* 2,975 full-time matriculated graduate/professional students (1,423 women), 3,263 part-time matriculated graduate/professional students (1,796 women). *Enrollment by degree level:* 518 first professional, 1,526 master's, 1,146 doctoral, 48 other advanced degrees. *Graduate faculty:* 794 full-time (209 women), 101 part-time/adjunct (29 women). Tuition, state resident: full-time $2,208; part-time $92 per credit hour. Tuition, nonresident: part-time $297 per credit hour. Tuition and fees vary according to course level, course load and program. *Graduate housing:* Rooms and/or apartments available to single and married students. Typical cost: $5,162 (including board) for single students; $5,162 (including board) for married students. *Student services:* Campus employment opportunities, campus safety program, career counseling, child daycare facilities, disabled student services, free psychological counseling, international student services, low-cost health insurance, writing training. *Library facilities:* Bizzell Memorial Library plus 7 others. *Online resources:* library catalog, web page, access to other libraries' catalogs. *Collection:* 3.7 million titles, 15,833 serial subscriptions, 4,388 audiovisual materials. *Research affiliation:* Oklahoma Climatological Survey, National Severe Storms Laboratory, Oklahoma Geological Survey, Federal Aviation Administration Aeronautical Center.

Computer facilities: 600 computers available on campus for general student use. A campuswide network can be accessed from student residence rooms and from off campus. Internet access and online class registration are available. *Web address:* http://www.ou.edu/.

General Application Contact: Patricia Lynch, Acting Director of Admissions, 405-325-2251, Fax: 405-325-7124, E-mail: plynch@ou.edu.

GRADUATE UNITS

College of Law Students: 509 full-time (227 women), 13 part-time (4 women); includes 63 minority (13 African Americans, 6 Asian Americans or Pacific Islanders, 7 Hispanic Americans, 37 Native Americans), 1 international. Average age 27. 319 applicants, 55% accepted, 98 enrolled. *Faculty:* 3 full-time (1 woman), 1 part-time/adjunct (0 women). Expenses: Contact institution. *Financial support:* In 2001–02, 409 students received support. Career-related internships or fieldwork, Federal Work-Study, institutionally sponsored loans, scholarships/grants, and tuition waivers (full and partial) available. Support available to part-time students. Financial award application deadline: 3/1. In 2001, 190 degrees awarded. Offers law (JD). *Application deadline:* For fall admission, 3/15. Applications are processed on a rolling basis. *Application fee:* $50. Electronic applications accepted. *Application Contact:* Kathie Madden, Admissions Coordinator, 405-325-4728, Fax: 405-325-0502, E-mail: kmadden@ou.edu. *Dean,* Dr. Andrew M. Coats, 405-325-4699.

Graduate College Students: 2,409 full-time (1,141 women), 3,046 part-time (1,684 women); includes 1,085 minority (532 African Americans, 182 Asian Americans or Pacific Islanders, 178 Hispanic Americans, 193 Native Americans), 833 international. Average age 31. 2,384 applicants, 77% accepted, 1080 enrolled. *Faculty:* 791 full-time (208 women), 100 part-time/adjunct (29 women). Expenses: Contact institution. *Financial support:* In 2001–02, 1,201 students received support, including 65 fellowships with partial tuition reimbursements available, 557 research assistantships with full and partial tuition reimbursements available (averaging $10,893 per year), 684 teaching assistantships with full and partial tuition reimbursements available (averaging $10,290 per year); career-related internships or fieldwork, Federal Work-Study, institutionally sponsored loans, scholarships/grants, traineeships, health care benefits, tuition waivers (full and partial), and unspecified assistantships also available. Support available to part-time students. Financial award applicants required to submit FAFSA. In 2001, 1,463 master's, 159 doctorates, 6 other advanced degrees awarded. *Degree program information:* Part-time and evening/weekend programs available. Offers interdisciplinary studies (MA, MS, PhD). *Application fee:* $25 ($50 for international students). *Application Contact:* Ann Parker, Coordinator of Graduate Admissions, 405-325-7124, Fax: 405-325-6029. *Dean,* Lee William, 405-325-3811, Fax: 405-325-5346, E-mail: lwilliam@ou.edu.

College of Architecture Students: 57 full-time (27 women), 39 part-time (17 women); includes 9 minority (1 African American, 1 Asian American or Pacific Islander, 1 Hispanic American, 6 Native Americans), 36 international. 89 applicants, 72% accepted, 28 enrolled. *Faculty:* 31 full-time (9 women). Expenses: Contact institution. *Financial support:* In 2001–02, 28 students received support, including 8 research assistantships with partial tuition reimbursements available (averaging $9,373 per year), 11 teaching assistantships with partial tuition reimbursements available (averaging $9,349 per year); career-related internships or fieldwork, Federal Work-Study, scholarships/grants, and tuition waivers (partial) also available. Support available to part-time students. Financial award applicants required to submit FAFSA. In 2001, 22 degrees awarded. *Degree program information:* Part-time programs available. Offers architecture (M Arch, MLA, MRCP, MS); construction science (MS); landscape architecture (MLA); regional and city planning (MRCP). *Application deadline:* For fall admission, 6/1 (priority date). Applications are processed on a rolling basis. *Application fee:* $25 ($50 for international students). *Dean,* Bob G. Fillpot, 405-325-2444.

College of Arts and Sciences Students: 1,086 full-time (605 women), 1,769 part-time (1,046 women); includes 724 minority (395 African Americans, 116 Asian Americans or Pacific Islanders, 101 Hispanic Americans, 112 Native Americans), 174 international. 1,041 applicants, 79% accepted, 557 enrolled. *Faculty:* 357 full-time (98 women), 43 part-time/adjunct (10 women). Expenses: Contact institution. *Financial support:* In 2001–02, 685 students received support, including 41 fellowships (averaging $4,725 per year), 157 research assistantships with full and partial tuition reimbursements available (averaging $11,465 per year), 368 teaching assistantships with full and partial tuition reimbursements available (averaging $11,389 per year); career-related internships or fieldwork, Federal Work-Study, institutionally sponsored loans, scholarships/grants, traineeships, tuition waivers (full and partial), and unspecified assistantships also available. Support available to part-time students. In 2001, 915 master's, 77 doctorates awarded. *Degree program information:* Part-time and evening/weekend programs available. Offers anthropology (MA, PhD); arts and sciences (M Nat Sci, MA, MHR, MLIS, MNS, MPA, MS, MSW, PhD, Certificate); astrophysics (MS, PhD); botany (M Nat Sci, MS, PhD); chemistry and biochemistry (MS, PhD); communication (MA, PhD); economics (MA, PhD); English (MA, PhD); French (MA, PhD); German (MA); health and exercise science (MS); history (MA, PhD); history of science (MA, PhD); human relations (MHR); international studies (MA); library and information studies (MLIS, Certificate); mathematics (MA, MS, PhD); microbiology (M Nat Sci, MS, PhD); natural science (MNS); philosophy (MA, PhD); physics (MS, PhD); political science (MA, PhD); psychology (MS, PhD); public administration (MPA); social work (MSW); sociology (MA, PhD); Spanish (MA, PhD); sport management (MS); zoology (M Nat Sci, MS, PhD). *Application fee:* $25 ($50 for international students). *Dean,* Dr. Paul B. Bell, 405-325-2077.

College of Education Students: 296 full-time (210 women), 528 part-time (353 women); includes 176 minority (83 African Americans, 19 Asian Americans or Pacific Islanders, 32 Hispanic Americans, 42 Native Americans), 19 international. 169 applicants, 81% accepted, 106 enrolled. *Faculty:* 53 full-time (29 women), 20 part-time/adjunct (13 women). Expenses: Contact institution. *Financial support:* In 2001–02, 161 students received support, including 2 fellowships (averaging $2,200 per year), 49 research assistantships with partial tuition reimbursements available (averaging $9,895 per year), 23 teaching assistantships with partial tuition reimbursements available (averaging $10,182 per year); career-related internships or fieldwork, Federal Work-Study, institutionally sponsored loans, and tuition waivers (full and partial) also available. Support available to part-time students. Financial award applicants required to submit FAFSA. In 2001, 195 master's, 28 doctorates, 3 other advanced degrees awarded. *Degree program information:* Part-time and evening/weekend programs available. Offers adult and higher education (M Ed, PhD); community counseling (M Ed); counseling psychology (PhD); education (Certificate); educational administration, curriculum and supervision (PhD); educational administration, curriculum and supervision (M Ed, Ed D); historical, philosophical, and social foundations of education (M Ed, Ed D, PhD); instructional leadership and academic curriculum (M Ed, PhD); instructional psychology (M Ed, PhD); special education (M Ed, PhD). *Application fee:* $25 ($50 for international students). *Application Contact:* Barbi DeLong, Graduate Program Assistant, 405-325-2357. *Dean,* Dr. Joan Karen Smith, 405-325-1081.

College of Engineering Students: 456 full-time (86 women), 182 part-time (30 women); includes 37 minority (7 African Americans, 15 Asian Americans or Pacific Islanders, 8 Hispanic Americans, 7 Native Americans), 457 international. 534 applicants, 82% accepted, 158 enrolled. *Faculty:* 91 full-time (9 women), 6 part-time/adjunct (1 woman). Expenses: Contact institution. *Financial support:* In 2001–02, 5 fellowships (averaging $5,000 per year), 216 research assistantships with partial tuition reimbursements (averaging $10,257 per year), 97 teaching assistantships with partial tuition reimbursements (averaging $9,815 per year) were awarded. Career-related internships or fieldwork, Federal Work-Study, institutionally sponsored loans, and tuition waivers (full and partial) also available. Support available to part-time students. Financial award applicants required to submit FAFSA. In 2001, 159 master's, 27 doctorates awarded. *Degree program information:* Part-time and evening/weekend programs available. Offers aerospace engineering (MS, PhD); air

University of Oklahoma (continued)
(M Env Sc); chemical engineering (MS, PhD); civil engineering (MS, PhD); computer science (MS, PhD); electrical and computer engineering (MS, PhD); engineering (M Env Sc, MS, D Engr, PhD); engineering physics (MS, PhD); environmental engineering (MS); environmental science (M Env Sc, PhD); geotechnical engineering (MS); groundwater management (M Env Sc); hazardous solid waste (M Env Sc); industrial engineering (MS, PhD); mechanical engineering (MS, PhD); natural gas engineering and management (MS); occupational safety and health (M Env Sc); petroleum and geological engineering (MS, PhD); process design (M Env Sc); structures (MS); transportation (MS); water quality resources (M Env Sc). *Application fee:* $25 ($50 for international students). *Dean,* Dr. Arthur Porter, 405-325-2621.

College of Fine Arts Students: 127 full-time (77 women), 82 part-time (42 women); includes 23 minority (6 African Americans, 5 Asian Americans or Pacific Islanders, 5 Hispanic Americans, 7 Native Americans), 29 international. 89 applicants, 67% accepted, 38 enrolled. *Faculty:* 88 full-time (26 women), 5 part-time/adjunct (2 women). Expenses: Contact institution. *Financial support:* In 2001–02, 3 fellowships (averaging $4,000 per year), 10 research assistantships with partial tuition reimbursements (averaging $8,077 per year), 84 teaching assistantships with partial tuition reimbursements (averaging $8,753 per year) were awarded. Federal Work-Study, institutionally sponsored loans, and tuition waivers (partial) also available. Financial award application deadline: 4/7; financial award applicants required to submit FAFSA. In 2001, 23 master's, 14 doctorates awarded. *Degree program information:* Part-time programs available. Offers art (MA, MFA); art history (MA); ceramics (MFA); choreography (MFA); drama (MA, MFA); film and video (MFA); fine arts (M Mus, M Mus Ed, MA, MFA, DMA, PhD); music (M Mus); music education (M Mus Ed, PhD); painting and drawing (MFA); performance and composition (DMA); photography (MFA); printmaking (MFA); sculpture (MFA); visual communications (MFA). *Application fee:* $25 ($50 for international students). *Dean,* Marvin Lamb, 405-325-7370, Fax: 405-325-1667.

College of Geosciences Students: 120 full-time (36 women), 51 part-time (16 women); includes 6 minority (2 African Americans, 1 Asian American or Pacific Islander, 1 Hispanic American, 2 Native Americans), 47 international. 95 applicants, 59% accepted, 40 enrolled. *Faculty:* 55 full-time (3 women), 14 part-time/adjunct (1 woman). Expenses: Contact institution. *Financial support:* In 2001–02, 11 fellowships (averaging $4,682 per year), 67 research assistantships with partial tuition reimbursements (averaging $12,198 per year), 43 teaching assistantships with partial tuition reimbursements (averaging $13,350 per year) were awarded. Career-related internships or fieldwork, Federal Work-Study, institutionally sponsored loans, scholarships/grants, tuition waivers (partial), and unspecified assistantships also available. Support available to part-time students. Financial award application deadline: 2/1; financial award applicants required to submit FAFSA. In 2001, 23 master's, 9 doctorates awarded. Offers geography (MA, PhD); geology (MS, PhD); geophysics (MS); geosciences (MA, MS, MS Metr, PhD); meteorology (MS Metr, PhD). *Application deadline:* For fall admission, 2/1 (priority date). Applications are processed on a rolling basis. *Application fee:* $25 ($50 for international students). *Dean,* Dr. John T. Snow, 405-325-3101, Fax: 405-325-3148, E-mail: jsnow@ou.edu.

College of Liberal Studies Students: 6 full-time (5 women), 49 part-time (26 women); includes 9 minority (3 African Americans, 4 Hispanic Americans, 2 Native Americans) 23 applicants, 100% accepted, 12 enrolled. *Faculty:* 1 part-time/adjunct (0 women). Expenses: Contact institution. *Financial support:* In 2001–02, 15 students received support. Career-related internships or fieldwork, institutionally sponsored loans, and tuition waivers available. Support available to part-time students. Financial award applicants required to submit FAFSA. In 2001, 10 degrees awarded. *Degree program information:* Part-time programs available. Postbaccalaureate distance learning degree programs offered (minimal on-campus study). Offers liberal studies (MLS). *Application deadline:* For fall admission, 6/1 (priority date). Applications are processed on a rolling basis. *Application fee:* $25 ($50 for international students). *Application Contact:* Nancee Morris, Coordinator, 405-325-1061, Fax: 405-325-7132, E-mail: cls@ou.edu. *Dean,* Dr. James Pappas, 405-325-1061, Fax: 405-325-7132, E-mail: jpappas@ou.edu.

Gaylord College of Journalism and Mass Communication Students: 21 full-time (10 women), 24 part-time (19 women); includes 5 minority (3 Asian Americans or Pacific Islanders, 2 Native Americans), 5 international. 11 applicants, 82% accepted, 9 enrolled. *Faculty:* 20 full-time (3 women). Expenses: Contact institution. *Financial support:* In 2001–02, 14 students received support, including 1 research assistantship with partial tuition reimbursement available (averaging $10,800 per year), 11 teaching assistantships with partial tuition reimbursements available (averaging $9,009 per year); career-related internships or fieldwork, Federal Work-Study, scholarships/grants, health care benefits, tuition waivers (partial), and unspecified assistantships also available. Support available to part-time students. Financial award application deadline: 3/15; financial award applicants required to submit FAFSA. In 2001, 5 degrees awarded. *Degree program information:* Part-time programs available. Offers advertising (MA); broadcasting and electronic media (MA); newspaper (MA); professional writing (MA); public relations (MA). *Application deadline:* For fall admission, 7/1; for spring admission, 11/1. *Application fee:* $25. *Application Contact:* David Craig, Director of Graduate Studies, 405-325-5206, Fax: 405-325-7565, E-mail: dcraig@ou.edu. *Dean,* Charles Self, 405-325-2721, Fax: 405-325-7565, E-mail: cself@ou.edu.

Michael F. Price College of Business Students: 169 full-time (55 women), 118 part-time (46 women); includes 32 minority (10 African Americans, 9 Asian Americans or Pacific Islanders, 8 Hispanic Americans, 5 Native Americans), 54 international. 251 applicants, 55% accepted, 86 enrolled. *Faculty:* 49 full-time (10 women), 7 part-time/adjunct (0 women). Expenses: Contact institution. *Financial support:* In 2001–02, 77 students received support, including 3 fellowships (averaging $5,000 per year), 36 research assistantships with partial tuition reimbursements available (averaging $12,562 per year), 28 teaching assistantships with partial tuition reimbursements available (averaging $13,056 per year); career-related internships or fieldwork, scholarships/grants, tuition waivers (full and partial), and unspecified assistantships also available. Financial award applicants required to submit FAFSA. In 2001, 111 master's, 4 doctorates awarded. *Degree program information:* Part-time and evening/weekend programs available. Offers accounting (M Acc); business administration (MBA, PhD); management information systems (MS). *Application deadline:* For fall admission, 4/1; for spring admission, 11/1. Applications are processed on a rolling basis. *Application fee:* $25 ($50 for international students). *Application Contact:* Alice Watkins, Associate Director of Graduate Programs, 405-325-4090, Fax: 405-325-7753, E-mail: awatkins@ou.edu. *Dean,* Dr. Dennis Logue, 405-325-3612, Fax: 405-325-2096.

See in-depth description on page 1235.

UNIVERSITY OF OKLAHOMA HEALTH SCIENCES CENTER, Oklahoma City, OK 73190

General Information State-supported, coed, upper-level institution. CGS member. *Enrollment:* 1,228 full-time matriculated graduate/professional students (633 women), 421 part-time matriculated graduate/professional students (311 women). *Enrollment by degree level:* 850 first professional, 565 master's, 135 doctoral. *Graduate faculty:* 508 full-time (140 women), 306 part-time/adjunct (132 women). Tuition, state resident: part-time $92 per credit hour. Tuition, nonresident: part-time $296 per credit hour. *Graduate housing:* On-campus housing not available. *Student services:* Campus employment opportunities, campus safety program, career counseling, exercise/wellness program, free psychological counseling, grant writing training, international student services, low-cost health insurance, multicultural affairs office, writing training. *Library facilities:* Robert M. Bird Health Sciences Library. *Collection:* 234,000 titles, 2,658 serial subscriptions. *Research affiliation:* Dean A. McGee Eye Institute (ophthalmology), Oklahoma Medical Research Foundation, University of Oklahoma Medical Center, Veterans Administration Medical Center (clinical and applied medicine), Oklahoma Children's Memorial Hospital (pediatrics).

Computer facilities: 120 computers available on campus for general student use. A campuswide network can be accessed from off campus. Internet access is available. *Web address:* http://www.ouhsc.edu/.

General Application Contact: Dr. O. Ray Kling, Dean of the Graduate College, 405-271-2085, Fax: 405-271-1155, E-mail: ray-kling@ouhsc.edu.

GRADUATE UNITS

College of Dentistry Students: 228 full-time (63 women); includes 56 minority (2 African Americans, 25 Asian Americans or Pacific Islanders, 3 Hispanic Americans, 26 Native Americans), 8 international. Average age 28. 815 applicants, 7% accepted. *Faculty:* 47 full-time (8 women), 76 part-time/adjunct (8 women). Expenses: Contact institution. *Financial support:* Institutionally sponsored loans and tuition waivers (full) available. In 2001, 46 first professional degrees, 7 master's awarded. Offers dentistry (DDS, MS); orthodontics (MS); periodontics (MS). *Application deadline:* Applications are processed on a rolling basis. *Application fee:* $25 ($50 for international students). *Application Contact:* Dr. Robert C. Miller, Associate Dean for Student Affairs, 405-271-3530, Fax: 405-271-3423, E-mail: robert-miller@ouhsc.edu. *Dean,* Dr. Stephen K. Young, 405-271-5444, Fax: 405-271-3423, E-mail: stephen-young@ouhsc.edu.

College of Medicine Students: 615 full-time (245 women), 53 part-time (20 women); includes 133 minority (8 African Americans, 61 Asian Americans or Pacific Islanders, 14 Hispanic Americans, 50 Native Americans), 57 international. Average age 25. 1,100 applicants, 18% accepted. *Faculty:* 148 full-time (28 women), 44 part-time/adjunct (19 women). Expenses: Contact institution. *Financial support:* Fellowships, research assistantships, teaching assistantships, career-related internships or fieldwork, Federal Work-Study, institutionally sponsored loans, and tuition waivers (full and partial) available. Support available to part-time students. In 2001, 144 first professional degrees, 25 master's awarded. *Degree program information:* Part-time programs available. Offers biochemistry (MS, PhD); biochemistry and molecular biology (MS, PhD); biological psychology (MS, PhD); cell biology (MS, PhD); immunology (MS, PhD); medical radiation physics (MS, PhD); medical sciences (MS); medicine (MD, MS, PhD); microbiology (MS, PhD); microbiology and immunology (MS, PhD); molecular biology (MS, PhD); molecular medicine (PhD); neuroscience (MS, PhD); pathology (PhD); physiology (MS, PhD); psychiatry and behavioral sciences (MS, PhD); radiological sciences (MS, PhD). *Application fee:* $25 ($50 for international students). *Executive Dean,* Dr. Jerry Vannatta, 405-271-2265, E-mail: jerry-vannatta@ouhsc.edu.

College of Pharmacy Students: 398 full-time (231 women), 2 part-time (1 woman); includes 114 minority (16 African Americans, 47 Asian Americans or Pacific Islanders, 7 Hispanic Americans, 44 Native Americans), 14 international. 35 applicants, 6% accepted. *Faculty:* 24 full-time (5 women), 8 part-time/adjunct (3 women). Expenses: Contact institution. *Financial support:* Fellowships, research assistantships, teaching assistantships, career-related internships or fieldwork and institutionally sponsored loans available. In 2001, 144 first professional degrees, 2 doctorates awarded. Offers pharmacy (Pharm D, MS, PhD). *Application fee:* $25 ($50 for international students). *Application Contact:* Dr. Keith Swanson, Director of Student Services, 405-271-6598, E-mail: keith-swanson@ouhsc.edu. *Dean,* Dr. Carl K. Buckner, 405-271-6484, Fax: 405-271-3830, E-mail: carl-buckner@ouhsc.edu.

Graduate College Students: 245 full-time (173 women), 421 part-time (311 women); includes 136 minority (33 African Americans, 27 Asian Americans or Pacific Islanders, 11 Hispanic Americans, 65 Native Americans), 82 international. Average age 23. 700 applicants, 51% accepted. *Faculty:* 289 full-time (99 women), 178 part-time/adjunct (102 women). Expenses: Contact institution. *Financial support:* Fellowships, research assistantships, teaching assistantships, career-related internships or fieldwork, Federal Work-Study, institutionally sponsored loans, scholarships/grants, traineeships, and tuition waivers (full and partial) available. Support available to part-time students. In 2001, 23 degrees awarded. *Degree program information:* Part-time and evening/weekend programs available. *Application fee:* $25 ($50 for international students). *Application Contact:* Robin Howell, Assistant to Dean for Graduate Affairs, 405-271-2085 Ext. 48832, Fax: 405-271-1155, E-mail: robin-howell@ouhsc.edu. *Dean,* Dr. O. Ray Kling, 405-271-2085, Fax: 405-271-1155, E-mail: ray-kling@ouhsc.edu.

College of Allied Health Students: 57 full-time (56 women), 30 part-time (27 women); includes 9 minority (1 African American, 2 Asian Americans or Pacific Islanders, 6 Native Americans), 4 international. Average age 23. 134 applicants, 59% accepted. *Faculty:* 44 full-time (23 women), 27 part-time/adjunct (22 women). Expenses: Contact institution. *Financial support:* Fellowships, career-related internships or fieldwork, Federal Work-Study, institutionally sponsored loans, and traineeships available. Support available to part-time students. In 2001, 36 master's, 1 doctorate awarded. *Degree program information:* Part-time programs available. Offers allied health (MS, PhD, Certificate); allied health sciences (PhD); audiology (MS, PhD); communication sciences and disorders (Certificate); education of the deaf (MS); nutritional sciences (MS); rehabilitation sciences (MS); speech-language pathology (MS, PhD). *Application deadline:* For fall admission, 7/1 (priority date); for spring admission, 12/1. *Application fee:* $25 ($50 for international students). *Application Contact:* Dr. Jan Womack, Associate Dean, Academic and Student Affairs, 405-271-6588, Fax: 405-271-3120, E-mail: jan-womack@ouhsc.edu. *Dean,* Dr. Carole Sullivan, 405-271-2288, Fax: 405-271-1190, E-mail: carole-sullivan@ouhsc.edu.

College of Nursing Students: 53 full-time (49 women), 164 part-time (154 women); includes 48 minority (11 African Americans, 6 Asian Americans or Pacific Islanders, 4 Hispanic Americans, 27 Native Americans), 5 international. 91 applicants, 73% accepted, 54 enrolled. *Faculty:* 29 full-time (27 women), 34 part-time/adjunct (all women). Expenses: Contact institution. *Financial support:* Research assistantships, teaching assistantships, institutionally sponsored loans, scholarships/grants, and traineeships available. Support available to part-time students. Financial award application deadline: 8/1. In 2001, 65 degrees awarded. *Degree program information:* Part-time programs available. Offers nursing (MS). *Application deadline:* For fall admission, 1/15. Applications are processed on a rolling basis. *Application fee:* $25 ($50 for international students). *Application Contact:* Dr. Francene Weatherby, Information Contact, 405-271-2420, Fax: 405-271-3443, E-mail: francene-weatherby@ouhsc.edu. *Dean,* Dr. Patricia Forni, 405-271-2420, E-mail: patricia-forni@ouhsc.edu.

College of Public Health Students: 105 full-time (52 women), 172 part-time (109 women); includes 72 minority (21 African Americans, 13 Asian Americans or Pacific Islanders, 7 Hispanic Americans, 31 Native Americans), 46 international. Average age 36. 240 applicants, 62% accepted. *Faculty:* 44 full-time (16 women), 65 part-time/adjunct (24 women). Expenses: Contact institution. *Financial support:* Fellowships, research assistantships, career-related internships or fieldwork, Federal Work-Study, institutionally sponsored loans, traineeships, and tuition waivers (partial) available. Support available to part-time students. Financial award application deadline: 5/1. In 2001, 73 master's, 4 doctorates awarded. *Degree program information:* Part-time programs available. Offers biostatistics (MPH, MS, Dr PH, PhD); epidemiology (MPH, MS, Dr PH, PhD); health administration and policy (MHA, MPH, MS, Dr PH, PhD); health promotion sciences (MPH, MS, Dr PH, PhD); occupational and environmental health (MPH, MS, Dr PH, PhD); public health (MHA, MPH, MS, Dr PH, PhD). *Application deadline:* For fall admission, 7/1; for spring admission, 12/1. Applications are processed on a rolling basis. *Application fee:* $25 ($50 for international students). *Application Contact:* Sheryl Semler, Information Contact, 405-271-2308, E-mail: sheryl-semler@ouhsc.edu. *Dean,* Dr. Gary Raskob, 405-271-2232.

UNIVERSITY OF OREGON, Eugene, OR 97403

General Information State-supported, coed, university. CGS member. *Enrollment:* 3,398 full-time matriculated graduate/professional students (1,726 women), 1,028 part-time matriculated graduate/professional students (608 women). *Enrollment by degree level:* 511 first professional, 1,599 master's, 1,028 doctoral. *Graduate faculty:* 715 full-time (273 women), 188 part-time/adjunct (106 women). Tuition, state resident: full-time $4,968; part-time $501 per credit hour. Tuition, nonresident: full-time $8,400; part-time $691 per credit hour. *Graduate housing:* Rooms and/or apartments available to single and married students. *Student services:* Campus employment opportunities, campus safety program, career counseling, child daycare facilities, disabled student services, exercise/wellness program, free psychological counseling, grant writing training, international student services, low-cost health insurance, multicultural affairs office, teacher training, writing training. *Library facilities:* Knight Library plus 5 others. *Online resources:* library catalog, web page, access to other libraries' catalogs. *Collection:* 2.4 million titles, 15,898 serial subscriptions, 65,560 audiovisual materials. *Research affiliation:* Oregon Research Institute, Decision Research, Battelle Pacific

Northwest Laboratories, National Renewable Energy Laboratory, Stanford Linear Accelerator Center, Naval Research Laboratories.

Computer facilities: 1,250 computers available on campus for general student use. A campuswide network can be accessed from student residence rooms and from off campus. Internet access and online class registration are available. *Web address:* http://www.uoregon.edu/.

General Application Contact: 541-346-5129, E-mail: gradsch@oregon.uoregon.edu.

GRADUATE UNITS

Graduate School Students: 2,879 full-time (1,493 women), 1,009 part-time (600 women); includes 361 minority (39 African Americans, 155 Asian Americans or Pacific Islanders, 114 Hispanic Americans, 53 Native Americans), 514 international. Average age 30. 3,891 applicants, 34% accepted. *Faculty:* 715 full-time (273 women), 188 part-time/adjunct (106 women). Expenses: Contact institution. *Financial support:* In 2001–02, 1,194 teaching assistantships were awarded; fellowships, research assistantships, career-related internships or fieldwork, Federal Work-Study, institutionally sponsored loans, and tuition waivers (full) also available. Support available to part-time students. Financial award applicants required to submit FAFSA. In 2001, 795 master's, 169 doctorates awarded. *Degree program information:* Part-time and evening/weekend programs available. Offers applied information management (MS). *Application fee:* $50. *Associate Dean,* Marian Friestad, 541-346-5129.

Charles H. Lundquist College of Business Students: 246 full-time (71 women), 4 part-time (1 woman); includes 22 minority (1 African American, 15 Asian Americans or Pacific Islanders, 6 Hispanic Americans), 66 international. 348 applicants, 56% accepted. *Faculty:* 44 full-time (4 women), 5 part-time/adjunct (3 women). Expenses: Contact institution. *Financial support:* In 2001–02, 63 teaching assistantships were awarded; fellowships, research assistantships, career-related internships or fieldwork, Federal Work-Study, and institutionally sponsored loans also available. Support available to part-time students. In 2001, 128 master's, 6 doctorates awarded. *Degree program information:* Part-time and evening/weekend programs available. Offers accounting (M Actg, PhD); business (M Actg, MA, MBA, MS, PhD); decision sciences (MA, MS, PhD); finance (PhD); management (PhD); management: general business (MBA); marketing (PhD). *Application fee:* $50. *Application Contact:* Laura Balaty, Admissions Contact, 541-346-3306, E-mail: lbalaty@oregon.uoregon.edu. *Dean,* Philip J. Romero, 541-346-3300.

College of Arts and Sciences Students: 1,034 full-time (512 women), 124 part-time (65 women); includes 88 minority (10 African Americans, 30 Asian Americans or Pacific Islanders, 29 Hispanic Americans, 19 Native Americans), 258 international. 1,501 applicants, 30% accepted. *Faculty:* 418 full-time (140 women), 78 part-time/adjunct (36 women). Expenses: Contact institution. *Financial support:* In 2001–02, 787 teaching assistantships were awarded; fellowships, research assistantships, career-related internships or fieldwork, Federal Work-Study, and institutionally sponsored loans also available. Support available to part-time students. Financial award applicants required to submit FAFSA. In 2001, 246 master's, 113 doctorates awarded. *Degree program information:* Part-time and evening/weekend programs available. Offers anthropology (MA, MS, PhD); arts and sciences (MA, MFA, MS, MSE, PhD); Asian studies (MA); biochemistry (MA, MS, PhD); chemistry (MA, MS, PhD); Chinese (MA, PhD); classical civilization (MA); classics (MA); clinical psychology (PhD); cognitive psychology (MA, MS, PhD); comparative literature (MA, PhD); computer and information science (MA, MS, MSE, PhD); creative writing (MFA); developmental psychology (MA, MS, PhD); ecology and evolution (MA, MS, PhD); economics (MA, MS, PhD); English (MA, PhD); environmental studies (MA, MS); exercise and movement science (MS, PhD); French (MA); geography (MA, MS, PhD); geological sciences (MA, MS, PhD); Germanic languages and literatures (MA, PhD); Greek (MA); history (MA, PhD); independent study: folklore (MA, MS); international studies (MA); Italian (MA); Japanese (MA, PhD); Latin (MA); linguistics (MA, PhD); marine biology (MA, MS, PhD); mathematics (MA, MS, PhD); molecular, cellular and genetic biology (PhD); neuroscience and development (PhD); philosophy (MA, PhD); physics (MA, MS, PhD); physiological psychology (MA, MS, PhD); political science (MA, MS, PhD); psychology (MA, MS, PhD); Romance languages (MA, PhD); Russian and East European Studies (MA); social/personality psychology (MA, MS, PhD); sociology (MA, MS, PhD); Spanish (MA); theater arts (MA, MFA, MS, PhD). *Application fee:* $50. *Dean,* Joe Stone, 541-346-3902.

College of Education Students: 485 full-time (354 women), 246 part-time (156 women); includes 82 minority (14 African Americans, 22 Asian Americans or Pacific Islanders, 32 Hispanic Americans, 14 Native Americans), 90 international. 404 applicants, 44% accepted. *Faculty:* 107 full-time (70 women), 76 part-time/adjunct (55 women). Expenses: Contact institution. *Financial support:* In 2001–02, 86 teaching assistantships were awarded; fellowships, research assistantships, career-related internships or fieldwork, Federal Work-Study, institutionally sponsored loans, and tuition waivers (full) also available. In 2001, 225 master's, 25 doctorates awarded. *Degree program information:* Part-time programs available. Offers education (M Ed, MA, MS, D Ed, PhD). *Application fee:* $50. *Application Contact:* Ron Tuomi, Admissions Contact, 541-346-3528, Fax: 541-346-5818. *Dean,* Martin J. Kaufman, 541-346-3405.

School of Architecture and Allied Arts Students: 410 full-time (213 women), 49 part-time (33 women); includes 30 minority (11 Asian Americans or Pacific Islanders, 15 Hispanic Americans, 4 Native Americans), 50 international. 401 applicants, 55% accepted. *Faculty:* 69 full-time (31 women), 19 part-time/adjunct (8 women). Expenses: Contact institution. *Financial support:* In 2001–02, 119 teaching assistantships were awarded; fellowships, research assistantships, career-related internships or fieldwork, Federal Work-Study, and institutionally sponsored loans also available. Support available to part-time students. In 2001, 152 master's, 1 doctorate awarded. *Degree program information:* Part-time and evening/weekend programs available. Offers architecture (M Arch); architecture and allied arts (M Arch, MA, MCRP, MFA, MI Arch, MLA, MPA, MS, PhD); art history (MA, PhD); arts management (MA, MS); community and regional planning (MCRP); fine and applied arts (MFA); historic preservation (MS); interior architecture (MI Arch); landscape architecture (MLA); public affairs (MPA); public policy and management (MA, MS). *Application fee:* $50. *Dean,* Robert Melnick, 541-346-3631.

School of Journalism and Communication Students: 47 full-time (29 women), 10 part-time (6 women); includes 7 minority (3 Asian Americans or Pacific Islanders, 3 Hispanic Americans, 1 Native American), 13 international. 23 applicants, 87% accepted. *Faculty:* 16 full-time (7 women), 1 (woman) part-time/adjunct. Expenses: Contact institution. *Financial support:* In 2001–02, 37 teaching assistantships were awarded; career-related internships or fieldwork, Federal Work-Study, institutionally sponsored loans, and scholarships/grants also available. Financial award application deadline: 3/31. In 2001, 13 master's, 5 doctorates awarded. *Degree program information:* Part-time programs available. Offers journalism (MA, MS, PhD). *Application fee:* $50. *Application Contact:* Petra Hagen, Graduate Secretary, 541-346-2136. *Dean,* Timothy W. Gleason, 541-346-3738.

School of Music Students: 114 full-time (65 women), 23 part-time (12 women); includes 13 minority (1 African American, 8 Asian Americans or Pacific Islanders, 3 Hispanic Americans, 1 Native American), 20 international. 69 applicants, 87% accepted. *Faculty:* 34 full-time (11 women), 5 part-time/adjunct (2 women). Expenses: Contact institution. *Financial support:* In 2001–02, 75 teaching assistantships were awarded; career-related internships or fieldwork, Federal Work-Study, institutionally sponsored loans, and scholarships/grants also available. In 2001, 18 master's, 6 doctorates awarded. *Degree program information:* Part-time programs available. Offers composition (M Mus, DMA, PhD); conducting (M Mus); dance (MA, MS); jazz studies (M Mus); music (MA); music education (M Mus, DMA, PhD); music history (PhD); music theory (PhD); performance (M Mus, DMA); piano pedagogy (M Mus). *Application fee:* $50. *Application Contact:* Jill Michelle Cosart, Admissions Contact, 541-346-5664. *Dean,* Anne Dhu McLucas, 541-346-3761.

School of Law Students: 519 full-time (233 women), 19 part-time (8 women); includes 62 minority (8 African Americans, 29 Asian Americans or Pacific Islanders, 16 Hispanic Americans, 9 Native Americans), 3 international. 1,174 applicants, 53% accepted. *Faculty:* 27 full-time (10 women), 4 part-time/adjunct (1 woman). Expenses: Contact institution. *Financial support:* In 2001–02, 27 teaching assistantships were awarded; career-related internships or fieldwork, Federal Work-Study, institutionally sponsored loans, and tuition waivers (partial) also available. Financial award application deadline: 2/1; financial award applicants required to submit FAFSA. In 2001, 149 degrees awarded. Offers law (JD). *Application deadline:* For fall admission, 2/15 (priority date). *Application fee:* $50. *Application Contact:* Teresa Specht, Information Contact, Office of Admissions, 541-346-1810, Fax: 541-346-1564, E-mail: tspect@law.uoregon.edu. *Dean,* Rennard Strickland, 541-346-3852, Fax: 541-346-1564.

UNIVERSITY OF OTTAWA, Ottawa, ON K1N 6N5, Canada

General Information Province-supported, coed, university. CGS member. *Graduate housing:* Rooms and/or apartments available to single and married students. Housing application deadline: 6/30. *Research affiliation:* St. Jean Photochemicals Québec, Shipley Company (specialty chemicals for microchip manufacturing), Apoptogen, Inc. (genetic treatments), Bell Canada (high-speed data transmission, Internet), Nortel (high-speed data transmission, Internet).

GRADUATE UNITS

Faculty of Graduate and Postdoctoral Studies *Degree program information:* Part-time and evening/weekend programs available.

Faculty of Administration *Degree program information:* Part-time and evening/weekend programs available. Offers administration (EMBA, IMBA, M Sc, M Sys Sc, MBA, MHA, Certificate); business administration (MBA, Certificate); executive business administration (EMBA); health administration (MHA); international management (IMBA); systems science (M Sc, M Sys Sc, Certificate).

Faculty of Arts *Degree program information:* Part-time and evening/weekend programs available. Offers arts (M Mus, M Sc, MA, PhD, Diploma); classics and religious studies (MA, PhD); English (MA, PhD); geography (M Sc, MA, PhD); history (MA, PhD); interpreting (Diploma); legal translation (Diploma); lettres Françaises (MA, PhD); linguistics (MA, PhD); music (M Mus, MA); philosophy (MA, PhD); Spanish (MA, PhD); Spanish translation (Diploma); translation (MA); translation studies (PhD).

Faculty of Education Offers education (M Ed, MA Ed, PhD).

Faculty of Engineering Offers chemical engineering (M Eng, MA Sc, PhD); civil engineering (M Eng, MA Sc, PhD); computer science (MCS, PhD, Certificate); electrical and computer engineering (M Eng, MA Sc, PhD, Certificate); engineering (M Eng, MA Sc, MCS, PhD, Certificate); engineering management (M Eng, Certificate); mechanical and aerospace engineering (M Eng, MA Sc, PhD).

Faculty of Health Sciences *Degree program information:* Part-time and evening/weekend programs available. Offers health (M Sc); health sciences (M Sc, MA, PhD); human kinetics (MA); nursing (M Sc); population health (PhD).

Faculty of Law *Degree program information:* Part-time and evening/weekend programs available. Offers law (LL M, LL D); legislative drafting, legal drafting and legislation (Diploma).

Faculty of Medicine Offers biochemistry (M Sc, PhD); cellular and molecular medicine (M Sc, PhD); epidemiology and community medicine (M Sc); medicine (M Sc, PhD); microbiology and immunology (M Sc, PhD).

Faculty of Science *Degree program information:* Part-time and evening/weekend programs available. Offers biology (M Sc, PhD); chemistry (M Sc, PhD); earth sciences (M Sc, PhD); mathematics and statistics (M Sc, PhD); physics (M Sc, PhD); science (M Sc, PhD).

Faculty of Social Sciences *Degree program information:* Part-time and evening/weekend programs available. Offers Canadian studies (PhD); criminology (MA, MCA); economics (MA, PhD); English (PhD); geography (PhD); history (PhD); lettres Françaises (PhD); linguistics (PhD); philosophy (PhD); political science (PhD); psychology (PhD); religious studies (PhD); social sciences (MA, MCA, MSS, PhD); social work (MSS); sociology (MA); translation studies (PhD).

Institute of Women's Studies Offers criminology (MA, MCA); education (MA); English (MA); history (MA); human kinetics (MA); law (LL M); lettres françaises (MA); nursing (M Sc); pastoral studies (MA); political science (MA); religious studies (MA); sociology (MA).

UNIVERSITY OF PENNSYLVANIA, Philadelphia, PA 19104

General Information Independent, coed, university. CGS member. *Enrollment:* 8,254 full-time matriculated graduate/professional students (3,999 women), 1,638 part-time matriculated graduate/professional students (821 women). *Enrollment by degree level:* 2,286 first professional, 4,401 master's, 3,100 doctoral, 105 other advanced degrees. *Graduate faculty:* 2,251 full-time (549 women), 4,082 part-time/adjunct (1,467 women). *Tuition:* Part-time $12,875 per semester. *Graduate housing:* Rooms and/or apartments available to single and married students. Housing application deadline: 4/1. *Student services:* Campus safety program, career counseling, disabled student services, free psychological counseling, international student services, low-cost health insurance. *Library facilities:* Van Pelt-Dietrich Library plus 13 others. *Online resources:* library catalog, web page. *Collection:* 4.9 million titles, 35,543 serial subscriptions. *Research affiliation:* National Health Care Management Center, University City Science Center, Monell Chemical Senses Center, Wistar Institute of Anatomy and Biology, Academy of Natural Sciences, Children's Hospital of Philadelphia.

Computer facilities: 1,000 computers available on campus for general student use. A campuswide network can be accessed from student residence rooms and from off campus. Internet access and online class registration are available. *Web address:* http://www.upenn.edu/.

General Application Contact: Patricia Rea, Admissions Assistant, 215-898-5720, E-mail: grad-admis@sas.upenn.edu.

GRADUATE UNITS

Annenberg School for Communication Offers communication (MAC, PhD).

Fels Center of Government *Degree program information:* Part-time and evening/weekend programs available. Offers government (MGA).

Graduate School of Education *Degree program information:* Part-time programs available. Offers counseling psychology (MS Ed); early childhood education (MS Ed); education (MS Ed, Ed D, PhD); education, culture, and society (MS Ed, Ed D, PhD); educational leadership (MS Ed, Ed D, PhD); educational linguistics (PhD); educational policy and leadership (MS Ed, Ed D, PhD); elementary education (MS Ed); higher education (MS Ed, Ed D, PhD); human development (MS Ed, PhD); human sexuality education (MS Ed, Ed D, PhD); intercultural communication (MS Ed); language in education (MS Ed, Ed D, PhD); policy research, evaluation, and measurement (MS Ed, PhD); psychological services (MS Ed); reading, writing, and literacy (MS Ed, Ed D, PhD); school, community, and clinical child psychology (PhD); secondary education (MS Ed); teaching English to speakers of other languages (MS Ed).

Graduate School of Fine Arts *Degree program information:* Part-time programs available. Offers architecture (M Arch); city and regional planning (MCP, PhD, Certificate); conservation and heritage management (Certificate); fine arts (M Arch, MCP, MFA, MLA, MS, PhD, Certificate); historic conservation (Certificate); historic preservation (MS); landscape architecture and regional planning (MLA); landscape studies (Certificate); real estate design and development (Certificate); urban design (Certificate). Electronic applications accepted.

Law School Students: 843 full-time (417 women), 12 part-time (4 women); includes 198 minority (76 African Americans, 63 Asian Americans or Pacific Islanders, 57 Hispanic Americans, 2 Native Americans), 133 international. Average age 24. 3,700 applicants, 24% accepted. *Faculty:* 68 full-time (15 women), 53 part-time/adjunct (18 women). Expenses: Contact institution. *Financial support:* In 2001–02, 584 students received support, including 21 teaching assistantships (averaging $1,750 per year); fellowships, research assistantships, career-related internships or fieldwork, Federal Work-Study, institutionally sponsored loans, and scholarships/grants also available. Financial award application deadline: 3/1; financial award applicants required to submit FAFSA. In 2001, 268 first professional degrees, 67 master's, 3 doctorates awarded. Offers law (JD, LL CM, LL M, SJD). *Application deadline:* For fall admission, 3/1. Applications are processed on a rolling basis. *Application fee:* $70. Electronic applications accepted. *Application Contact:* Janice L. Austin, Assistant Dean of Admissions, 215-898-7743, Fax: 215-573-2025, E-mail: admissions@law.upenn.edu. *Dean,* Michael A. Fitts, 215-898-7061, Fax: 215-573-2025.

School of Arts and Sciences *Degree program information:* Part-time and evening/weekend programs available. Offers American civilization (AM, PhD); ancient history (AM, PhD); anthropology (AM, MS, PhD); art and archaeology of the Mediterranean world (AM, PhD);

University of Pennsylvania (continued)

arts and sciences (AM, MA, MBA, MS, PhD); Asian and Middle Eastern studies (AM, PhD); bioethics); cell, molecular, and developmental biology (PhD); chemistry (MS, PhD); classical studies (AM, PhD); comparative literature (AM, PhD); demography (AM, PhD); ecology and population biology (PhD); economics (AM, PhD); English (AM, PhD); folklore and folklife (AM, PhD); French (AM, PhD); geology (MS, PhD); Germanic languages (AM, PhD); history (AM, PhD); history and sociology of science (AM, PhD); history of art (AM, PhD); Italian (AM, PhD); linguistics (AM, PhD); literary theory (AM, PhD); mathematics (AM, PhD); music (AM, PhD); neurobiology/physiology and behavior (PhD); organizational dynamics (MS); philosophy (AM, PhD); physics (PhD); plant science (PhD); political science (AM, PhD); psychology (PhD); religious studies (PhD); sociology (AM, PhD); South Asian regional studies (AM, PhD); Spanish (AM, PhD). Electronic applications accepted.

Joseph H. Lauder Institute of Management and International Studies Students: 112 full-time (31 women); includes 14 minority (2 African Americans, 10 Asian Americans or Pacific Islanders, 2 Hispanic Americans), 45 international. Average age 28. 230 applicants, 35% accepted. Expenses: Contact institution. *Financial support:* Fellowships with tuition reimbursements, career-related internships or fieldwork and scholarships/grants available. Financial award application deadline: 1/9. In 2001, 45 degrees awarded. Offers international studies (MA). Applications made concurrently and separately to Lauder Institute and Wharton MBA program. *Application deadline:* For fall admission, 10/24; for winter admission, 1/9. Electronic applications accepted. *Application Contact:* Roxanne L. Rawson, Director of Admissions, 215-898-1215, Fax: 215-898-2067, E-mail: lauderinfo@wharton.upenn.edu. *Director*, Dr. Richard J. Herring, 215-898-1215.

School of Dental Medicine Students: 445 full-time (207 women); includes 179 minority (27 African Americans, 130 Asian Americans or Pacific Islanders, 21 Hispanic Americans, 1 Native American) Average age 24. 1,378 applicants, 21% accepted, 94 enrolled. *Faculty:* 71 full-time (12 women), 169 part-time/adjunct (28 women). Expenses: Contact institution. *Financial support:* In 2001–02, 232 students received support. Federal Work-Study, institutionally sponsored loans, and scholarships/grants available. Financial award application deadline: 6/1; financial award applicants required to submit FAFSA. In 2001, 124 degrees awarded. Offers dental medicine (DMD). *Application deadline:* For fall admission, 1/15. Applications are processed on a rolling basis. *Application fee:* $50. *Application Contact:* Corky Cacas, Director of Admissions, 215-898-8943, Fax: 215-898-5243, E-mail: cacas@pobox.upenn.edu. *Dean*, Dr. Raymond Fonseca, 215-898-8941, Fax: 215-898-5243.

School of Engineering and Applied Science *Degree program information:* Part-time and evening/weekend programs available. Offers applied mechanics (MSE, PhD); bioengineering (MSE, PhD); biotechnology (MS); chemical engineering (MSE, PhD); computer and information science (MCIT, MSE, PhD); electrical engineering (MSE, PhD); engineering and applied science (MCIT, MS, MSE, PhD, AC); environmental resources engineering (MSE); environmental/resources engineering (PhD); management of technology (MSE, AC); materials science and engineering (MSE, PhD); mechanical engineering (MSE, PhD); systems engineering (MSE, PhD); technology and public policy (MSE, PhD); telecommunications and networking (MSE); transportation (MSE, PhD). Electronic applications accepted.

School of Medicine Students: 1,734 full-time (801 women), 13 part-time (5 women). Average age 24. 5,543 applicants, 5% accepted. *Faculty:* 1,990 full-time (582 women), 996 part-time/adjunct (300 women). Expenses: Contact institution. *Financial support:* Fellowships, research assistantships, teaching assistantships, career-related internships or fieldwork, Federal Work-Study, institutionally sponsored loans, scholarships/grants, and unspecified assistantships available. Financial award application deadline: 1/2; financial award applicants required to submit FAFSA. In 2001, 158 first professional degrees, 23 master's, 72 doctorates awarded. *Degree program information:* Part-time programs available. Offers medicine (MD, MS, MSCE, PhD). *Application deadline:* Applications are processed on a rolling basis. *Application fee:* $65. Electronic applications accepted. *Application Contact:* Gaye Sheffler, Director, Admissions, 215-898-8001, Fax: 215-898-0833, E-mail: sheffler@mail.med.upenn.edu. *Dean*, Dr. Arthur M. Rubenstein, 215-898-6796, Fax: 215-573-2030, E-mail: amrdean@mail.med.upenn.edu.

Biomedical Graduate Studies Students: 490 full-time (237 women). 962 applicants, 19% accepted, 68 enrolled. *Faculty:* 533. Expenses: Contact institution. *Financial support:* In 2001–02, 419 students received support, including 325 fellowships, 154 research assistantships; teaching assistantships, institutionally sponsored loans, scholarships/grants, and unspecified assistantships also available. Financial award application deadline: 1/2. In 2001, 12 master's, 64 doctorates awarded. *Degree program information:* Part-time programs available. Offers biochemistry and molecular biophysics (PhD); biomedical studies (MS, PhD); biostatistics (MS, PhD); cell biology and physiology (PhD); cell growth and cancer (PhD); developmental biology (PhD); gene therapy (PhD); genetics and gene regulation (PhD); immunology (PhD); microbiology (PhD); microbiology and virology (PhD); neuroscience (PhD); parasitology (PhD); pharmacology (PhD). *Application deadline:* For fall admission, 1/2 (priority date). Applications are processed on a rolling basis. *Application fee:* $65. Electronic applications accepted. *Application Contact:* Suzanne Hakanen, Graduate Coordinator, 215-898-1030, Fax: 215-898-2671, E-mail: shakanen@mail.med.upenn.edu. *Director*, Dr. Michael E. Selzer, 215-898-1030.

Center for Clinical Epidemiology and Biostatistics Students: 44 full-time (21 women), 10 part-time (4 women); includes 11 minority (3 African Americans, 8 Asian Americans or Pacific Islanders) Average age 30. 38 applicants, 74% accepted. *Faculty:* 43 full-time (14 women), 60 part-time/adjunct (16 women). Expenses: Contact institution. *Financial support:* In 2001–02, 54 students received support, including 25 fellowships with full and partial tuition reimbursements available; career-related internships or fieldwork, scholarships/grants, unspecified assistantships, and faculty/staff benefits for partial tuition coverage also available. Financial award application deadline: 1/15. In 2001, 16 master's, 1 doctorate awarded. *Degree program information:* Part-time programs available. Offers clinical epidemiology (MSCE); epidemiology (PhD). PhD offered through the School of Arts and Sciences. *Application deadline:* For fall admission, 1/15 (priority date). Applications are processed on a rolling basis. *Application fee:* $0. *Application Contact:* Marsha Covitz, Program Coordinator, 215-573-2382, Fax: 215-573-5315, E-mail: mcovitz@cceb.med.upenn.edu. *Chair*, Dr. Brian L. Strom, 215-898-2368, Fax: 215-573-5315, E-mail: bstrom@cceb.med.upenn.edu.

School of Nursing *Degree program information:* Part-time programs available. Postbaccalaureate distance learning degree programs offered. Offers acute care nurse practitioner (MSN); administration/consulting (MSN); adult and special populations (MSN); adult oncology advanced practice nurse (MSN); adult/gerontological nurse practitioner (MSN); child and family (MSN); family health nurse practitioner (MSN, Certificate); geropsychiatrics (MSN); health care of women nurse practitioner (MSN); health leadership (MSN); neonatal nurse practitioner (MSN); nurse midwifery (MSN); nursing (MSN, PhD, Certificate); nursing and health care administration (MSN, PhD); pediatric acute/chronic care nurse practitioner (MSN); pediatric critical care nurse practitioner (MSN); pediatric nurse practitioner (MSN); pediatric oncology nurse practitioner (MSN); perinatal advanced practice nurse specialist (MSN); primary care (MSN). Electronic applications accepted.

School of Social Work Students: 164 full-time (148 women), 90 part-time (78 women); includes 72 minority (53 African Americans, 10 Asian Americans or Pacific Islanders, 7 Hispanic Americans, 2 Native Americans), 10 international. Average age 30. 308 applicants, 80% accepted, 126 enrolled. *Faculty:* 19 full-time (10 women), 33 part-time/adjunct (22 women). Expenses: Contact institution. *Financial support:* In 2001–02, 169 students received support. Career-related internships or fieldwork, Federal Work-Study, institutionally sponsored loans, scholarships/grants, and unspecified assistantships available. Support available to part-time students. Financial award application deadline: 4/15; financial award applicants required to submit FAFSA. In 2001, 134 master's, 9 doctorates awarded. Offers social welfare (PhD); social work (MSW, PhD). *Application deadline:* For fall admission, 3/31. Applications are processed on a rolling basis. *Application fee:* $65. Electronic applications accepted. *Application Contact:* Mary C. Mazzola, Director of Admissions and Recruitment, 215-898-5550, Fax: 215-573-2099, E-mail: admissions@ssw.upenn.edu. *Interim Dean*, Dr. Richard J. Gelles, 215-898-5541, Fax: 215-573-2099, E-mail: gelles@ssw.upenn.edu.

School of Veterinary Medicine Students: 441 full-time (311 women); includes 36 minority (1 African American, 25 Asian Americans or Pacific Islanders, 10 Hispanic Americans), 8 international. Average age 27. 1,300 applicants, 13% accepted. *Faculty:* 230 full-time, 5 part-time/adjunct. Expenses: Contact institution. *Financial support:* Career-related internships or fieldwork, Federal Work-Study, and institutionally sponsored loans available. In 2001, 101 degrees awarded. Offers veterinary medicine (VMD). *Application deadline:* For fall admission, 10/1. *Application fee:* $0. *Application Contact:* Malcolm Keiter, Director of Admissions, 215-898-5434, Fax: 215-573-8653. *Dean*, Dr. Alan M. Kelly, 215-898-8841, Fax: 215-573-8837, E-mail: vetdean@vet.upenn.edu.

Wharton School Students: 1,958 full-time (547 women), 110 part-time (28 women); includes 264 minority (69 African Americans, 153 Asian Americans or Pacific Islanders, 41 Hispanic Americans, 1 Native American), 819 international. Average age 28. *Faculty:* 214 full-time (32 women), 63 part-time/adjunct (10 women). Expenses: Contact institution. *Financial support:* In 2001–02, 1,150 students received support; fellowships with tuition reimbursements available, research assistantships with full tuition reimbursements available, teaching assistantships with full and partial tuition reimbursements available, career-related internships or fieldwork, Federal Work-Study, and institutionally sponsored loans available. Financial award application deadline: 2/1; financial award applicants required to submit FAFSA. In 2001, 867 master's, 20 doctorates awarded. *Degree program information:* Evening/weekend programs available. Offers accounting (AM, MBA, PhD); business (AM, MBA, MS, PhD); business and public policy (AM, MBA, PhD); finance (MBA, PhD); health care systems (AM, MBA, PhD); insurance and risk management (AM, MBA, PhD); management (MBA, PhD); marketing (MBA, PhD); operations and information management (MBA, MS, PhD); operations and information management operations research (PhD); real estate (MBA, PhD); statistics (AM, MBA, PhD). *Application fee:* $160. Electronic applications accepted. *Chairman*, Dr. Patrick T. Harker, 215-898-4715, Fax: 215-898-3664, E-mail: harker@opim.wharton.upenn.edu.

Wharton Executive MBA Division Students: 241 full-time (47 women), 33 part-time (7 women); includes 1 minority (Asian American or Pacific Islander), 4 international. Average age 34. *Faculty:* 199 full-time (32 women), 78 part-time/adjunct (10 women). Expenses: Contact institution. *Financial support:* In 2001–02, 6 students received support, including 5 fellowships; institutionally sponsored loans also available. Financial award application deadline: 4/30. In 2001, 97 degrees awarded. *Degree program information:* Evening/weekend programs available. Offers business administration (MBA). *Application deadline:* For fall admission, 2/1 (priority date). *Application fee:* $125. *Application Contact:* Catherine Molony, Senior Associate Director and Director of Admissions, 215-898-5887, Fax: 215-898-2598. *Director*, Dr. Howard Kaufold, 215-898-5887, Fax: 215-898-2598.

Wharton MBA Division Students: 1,561 full-time (457 women), 45 part-time (10 women); includes 251 minority (67 African Americans, 143 Asian Americans or Pacific Islanders, 40 Hispanic Americans, 1 Native American), 692 international. Average age 28. 7,382 applicants, 14% accepted. *Faculty:* 199 full-time (32 women), 78 part-time/adjunct (10 women). Expenses: Contact institution. *Financial support:* In 2001–02, 40 fellowships (averaging $10,000 per year) were awarded; research assistantships, teaching assistantships, career-related internships or fieldwork, Federal Work-Study, and institutionally sponsored loans also available. Financial award application deadline: 6/1; financial award applicants required to submit FAFSA. In 2001, 766 degrees awarded. Offers business administration (MBA). *Application deadline:* Applications are processed on a rolling basis. *Application fee:* $140. Electronic applications accepted. *Application Contact:* Rosemaria Martinelli, Director of Admissions and Financial Aid, 215-898-6183, Fax: 215-898-0120, E-mail: mba.admissions@wharton.upenn.edu. *Vice Dean*, Anjani Jain, 215-898-7604.

See in-depth description on page 1237.

UNIVERSITY OF PHOENIX-ATLANTA CAMPUS, Atlanta, GA 30328

General Information Proprietary, coed, comprehensive institution.

GRADUATE UNITS

College of Graduate Business and Management

College of Nursing and Health Care Systems

UNIVERSITY OF PHOENIX–BOSTON CAMPUS, Braintree, MA 02184-4949

General Information Proprietary, coed, comprehensive institution. *Tuition:* Full-time $10,560; part-time $440 per credit. *Graduate housing:* On-campus housing not available. *Web address:* http://www.phoenix.edu/.

General Application Contact: 781-843-0844, Fax: 781-843-8646.

GRADUATE UNITS

College of Graduate Business and Management Expenses: Contact institution. *Financial support:* Applicants required to submit FAFSA. *Degree program information:* Evening/weekend programs available. Postbaccalaureate distance learning degree programs offered (no on-campus study). Offers administration (MBA); global management (MBA); technology management (MBA). *Application deadline:* Applications are processed on a rolling basis. *Dean*, Dr. Brian Lindquist, 480-537-1221, E-mail: brian.lindquist@phoenix.edu.

UNIVERSITY OF PHOENIX-CHICAGO CAMPUS, Schaumburg, IL 60173-4399

General Information Proprietary, coed, comprehensive institution. *Tuition:* Full-time $9,792; part-time $408 per credit. *Graduate housing:* On-campus housing not available. *Web address:* http://www.phoenix.edu/.

General Application Contact: Campus Information Center, 847-413-1922, Fax: 847-413-8706.

GRADUATE UNITS

College of Graduate Business and Management Expenses: Contact institution. *Financial support:* Applicants required to submit FAFSA. *Degree program information:* Evening/weekend programs available. Postbaccalaureate distance learning degree programs offered (no on-campus study). Offers administration (MBA); e-business (MBA); organizational management (MAOM). *Application deadline:* Applications are processed on a rolling basis. *Application fee:* $85. *Dean*, Dr. Brian Lindquist, 480-557-1221, E-mail: brian.lindquist@phoenix.edu.

UNIVERSITY OF PHOENIX–COLORADO CAMPUS, Lone Tree, CO 80124-5453

General Information Proprietary, coed, comprehensive institution. *Enrollment:* 1,071 full-time matriculated graduate/professional students, 45 part-time matriculated graduate/professional students. *Graduate faculty:* 11 full-time, 393 part-time/adjunct. *Tuition:* Full-time $7,788; part-time $325 per credit. *Graduate housing:* On-campus housing not available. *Student services:* Campus safety program. *Library facilities:* University Library. *Online resources:* library catalog, web page. *Collection:* 17.5 million titles, 9,000 serial subscriptions.

Computer facilities: A campuswide network can be accessed from off campus. Internet access is available. *Web address:* http://www.phoenix.edu/.

General Application Contact: 303-694-9093, Fax: 303-662-0911.

GRADUATE UNITS

College of Education Students: 362 full-time. Average age 33. Expenses: Contact institution. *Financial support:* Applicants required to submit FAFSA. In 2001, 226 degrees awarded. *Degree program information:* Evening/weekend programs available. Postbaccalaureate distance learning degree programs offered (no on-campus study). Offers education (MA Ed). *Application deadline:* Applications are processed on a rolling basis. *Application fee:* $85. *Associate Dean*, Dr. Marla LaRue, 480-557-1218, E-mail: marla.larue@phoenix.edu.

College of Graduate Business and Management Students: 633 full-time. Average age 33. Expenses: Contact institution. *Financial support:* Applicants required to submit FAFSA. In

2001, 237 degrees awarded. *Degree program information:* Evening/weekend programs available. Postbaccalaureate distance learning degree programs offered (no on-campus study). Offers business administration (MBA); e-business (MBA); organizational management (MAOM); technology management (MBA). *Application deadline:* Applications are processed on a rolling basis. *Application fee:* $85. *Dean*, Dr. Brian Lindquist, 480-557-1221, E-mail: brian.lindquist@phoenix.edu.

College of Health Care Sciences and Nursing Students: 13 full-time. Average age 33. Expenses: Contact institution. *Financial support:* Applicants required to submit FAFSA. In 2001, 22 degrees awarded. *Degree program information:* Evening/weekend programs available. Postbaccalaureate distance learning degree programs offered (no on-campus study). Offers healthcare sciences and nursing (MSN). *Application deadline:* Applications are processed on a rolling basis. *Application fee:* $85. *Dean*, Dr. Catherine Garner, 480-557-1751, E-mail: catherine.garner@phoenix.edu.

College of Information Systems and Technology Students: 63 full-time, 45 part-time. Average age 33. Expenses: Contact institution. *Financial support:* Applicants required to submit FAFSA. In 2001, 30 degrees awarded. *Degree program information:* Evening/weekend programs available. Postbaccalaureate distance learning degree programs offered (no on-campus study). Offers information systems and technology (MSCIS). *Application deadline:* Applications are processed on a rolling basis. *Application fee:* $85. *Dean*, Dr. Adam Honea, 480-557-1659, E-mail: adam.honea@phoenix.edu.

UNIVERSITY OF PHOENIX–DALLAS CAMPUS, Dallas, TX 75251

General Information Proprietary, coed, comprehensive institution. *Enrollment:* 200 full-time matriculated graduate/professional students. *Enrollment by degree level:* 200 master's. *Graduate faculty:* 4 full-time, 43 part-time/adjunct. *Tuition:* Full-time $8,808; part-time $367 per credit. *Graduate housing:* On-campus housing not available. *Web address:* http://www.phoenix.edu/.

General Application Contact: Campus Information Center, 972-385-1055, Fax: 972-385-1700.

GRADUATE UNITS

College of Graduate Business and Management Students: 200 full-time. *Faculty:* 4 full-time, 43 part-time/adjunct. Expenses: Contact institution. *Financial support:* Applicants required to submit FAFSA. *Degree program information:* Evening/weekend programs available. Postbaccalaureate distance learning degree programs offered (no on-campus study). Offers administration (MBA); e-business (MBA); organizational management (MAOM). *Application deadline:* Applications are processed on a rolling basis. *Application fee:* $85. *Application Contact:* Campus Information Center, 972-385-1055, Fax: 972-385-1700. *Dean*, Dr. Brian Lindquist, 480-557-1221, E-mail: brian.lindquist@phoenix.edu.

UNIVERSITY OF PHOENIX–FORT LAUDERDALE CAMPUS, Fort Lauderdale, FL 33324-1393

General Information Proprietary, coed, comprehensive institution. *Enrollment:* 473 full-time matriculated graduate/professional students, 20 part-time matriculated graduate/professional students. *Graduate faculty:* 3 full-time, 97 part-time/adjunct. *Tuition:* Full-time $7,320; part-time $305 per credit. *Graduate housing:* On-campus housing not available. *Student services:* Campus safety program. *Library facilities:* University Library. *Online resources:* library catalog, web page. *Collection:* 17.5 million titles, 9,000 serial subscriptions.

Computer facilities: A campuswide network can be accessed from off campus. Internet access is available. *Web address:* http://www.phoenix.edu/.

General Application Contact: 954-832-5503, Fax: 954-382-5304.

GRADUATE UNITS

College of Graduate Business and Management Students: 309 full-time. Average age 35. Expenses: Contact institution. *Financial support:* Applicants required to submit FAFSA. In 2001, 65 degrees awarded. *Degree program information:* Evening/weekend programs available. Postbaccalaureate distance learning degree programs offered (no on-campus study). Offers business administration (MBA); health care management (MBA); organizational management (MAOM); technology management (MBA). *Application deadline:* Applications are processed on a rolling basis. *Application fee:* $85. *Application Contact:* Campus Information Center, 954-382-5303, Fax: 954-382-5304. *Dean*, Dr. Brian Lindquist, 480-557-1221, E-mail: brian.lindquist@phoenix.edu.

College of Health Care Sciences and Nursing Students: 42 full-time. Average age 35. Expenses: Contact institution. *Financial support:* Applicants required to submit FAFSA. In 2001, 46 degrees awarded. *Degree program information:* Evening/weekend programs available. Postbaccalaureate distance learning degree programs offered (no on-campus study). Offers healthcare sciences and nursing (MSN). *Application deadline:* Applications are processed on a rolling basis. *Application fee:* $85. *Application Contact:* 954-382-5303, Fax: 954-382-5303. *Dean*, Dr. Catherine Garner, 480-557-1751, E-mail: catherine.garner@phoenix.edu.

College of Information Systems and Technology Students: 44 full-time, 20 part-time. Average age 35. Expenses: Contact institution. *Financial support:* Applicants required to submit FAFSA. *Degree program information:* Evening/weekend programs available. Postbaccalaureate distance learning degree programs offered (no on-campus study). Offers information systems and technology (MSCIS). *Application deadline:* Applications are processed on a rolling basis. *Application fee:* $85. *Application Contact:* 954-382-5303, Fax: 954-382-5304. *Dean*, Dr. Adam Honea, 480-557-1659, E-mail: adam.honea@phoenix.edu.

UNIVERSITY OF PHOENIX–HAWAII CAMPUS, Honolulu, HI 96813-4317

General Information Proprietary, coed, comprehensive institution. *Enrollment:* 306 full-time matriculated graduate/professional students, 291 part-time matriculated graduate/professional students. *Enrollment by degree level:* 306 master's, 291 other advanced degrees. *Graduate faculty:* 8 full-time, 205 part-time/adjunct. *Tuition:* Full-time $8,784; part-time $366 per credit. *Graduate housing:* On-campus housing not available. *Student services:* Campus safety program. *Library facilities:* University Library. *Online resources:* library catalog, web page. *Collection:* 17.5 million titles, 9,000 serial subscriptions.

Computer facilities: A campuswide network can be accessed from off campus. Internet access is available. *Web address:* http://www.phoenix.edu/.

General Application Contact: Campus Information Center, 808-536-2686, Fax: 808-536-3848.

GRADUATE UNITS

College of Counseling and Human Services Students: 77 full-time. Average age 35. Expenses: Contact institution. *Financial support:* Applicants required to submit FAFSA. *Degree program information:* Evening/weekend programs available. Postbaccalaureate distance learning degree programs offered (no on-campus study). Offers community counseling (MC); marriage and family therapy (MC). *Application deadline:* Applications are processed on a rolling basis. *Application fee:* $85. *Application Contact:* Campus Information Center, 808-536-2686, Fax: 808-536-3848. *Dean*, Dr. Patrick Romine, 480-557-1074, E-mail: patrick.romine@phoenix.edu.

College of Education Students: 72 full-time, 173 part-time. Average age 35. Expenses: Contact institution. *Financial support:* Applicants required to submit FAFSA. In 2001, 13 degrees awarded. *Degree program information:* Evening/weekend programs available. Postbaccalaureate distance learning degree programs offered (no on-campus study). Offers educational counseling (MA Ed); secondary education (Certificate); special education 1 (Certificate); special education 2 (Certificate); special education for mild to moderate disabilities 1 (MA Ed); special education for mild to moderate disabilities 2 (MA Ed). *Application deadline:* Applications are processed on a rolling basis. *Application fee:* $85. *Application Contact:* Campus Information Center, 580-536-2686, Fax: 808-536-3848. *Associate Dean*, Dr. Marla LaRue, 480-557-1309, E-mail: marla.larue@phoenix.edu.

College of Graduate Business and Management Students: 164 full-time. Average age 35. Expenses: Contact institution. *Financial support:* Applicants required to submit FAFSA. In 2001, 60 degrees awarded. *Degree program information:* Evening/weekend programs available. Postbaccalaureate distance learning degree programs offered (no on-campus study). Offers business administration (MBA); e-business (MBA); health care management (MBA); organizational management (MAOM). *Application deadline:* Applications are processed on a rolling basis. *Application fee:* $85. *Application Contact:* Campus Information Center, 808-536-2686, Fax: 808-536-3848, E-mail: brian.lindquist@phoenix.edu. *Dean*, Dr. Brian Lindquist, 480-557-1221, E-mail: brian.lindquist@phoenix.edu.

College of Health Care Sciences and Nursing Students: 40 full-time. Average age 35. Expenses: Contact institution. *Financial support:* Applicants required to submit FAFSA. In 2001, 25 degrees awarded. *Degree program information:* Evening/weekend programs available. Postbaccalaureate distance learning degree programs offered (no on-campus study). Offers family nurse practitioner (MSN); nursing (MSN). *Application deadline:* Applications are processed on a rolling basis. *Application fee:* $85. *Application Contact:* Campus Information Center, 808-536-2686, Fax: 808-536-3848. *Dean*, Dr. Catherine Garner, 480-557-1751, E-mail: catherine.gainer@phoenix.edu.

College of Information Systems and Technology Students: 13 full-time, 46 part-time. Average age 35. Expenses: Contact institution. *Financial support:* Applicants required to submit FAFSA. In 2001, 14 degrees awarded. *Degree program information:* Evening/weekend programs available. Postbaccalaureate distance learning degree programs offered (no on-campus study). Offers information systems and technology (MSCIS). *Application deadline:* Applications are processed on a rolling basis. *Application fee:* $85. *Application Contact:* Campus Information Center, 808-536-2686, Fax: 808-536-3848. *Dean*, Dr. Adam Honea, 480-557-1659, E-mail: adam.honea@phoenix.edu.

UNIVERSITY OF PHOENIX–HOUSTON CAMPUS, Houston, TX 77079

General Information Proprietary, coed, comprehensive institution. *Enrollment:* 198 full-time matriculated graduate/professional students. *Enrollment by degree level:* 198 master's. *Graduate faculty:* 4 full-time, 37 part-time/adjunct. *Tuition:* Full-time $8,808; part-time $367 per credit. *Graduate housing:* On-campus housing not available. *Web address:* http://www.phoenix.edu/.

General Application Contact: 713-465-9966, Fax: 713-465-2686.

GRADUATE UNITS

College of Graduate Business and Management Students: 198 full-time. *Faculty:* 4 full-time, 37 part-time/adjunct. Expenses: Contact institution. *Financial support:* Applicants required to submit FAFSA. *Degree program information:* Evening/weekend programs available. Postbaccalaureate distance learning degree programs offered (no on-campus study). Offers administration (MBA); e-business (MBA); organizational management (MAOM). *Application deadline:* Applications are processed on a rolling basis. *Application fee:* $85. *Application Contact:* 713-465-9966, Fax: 713-465-2686. *Dean*, Dr. Brian Lindquist, 480-557-1221, E-mail: brian.lindquist@phoenix.edu.

UNIVERSITY OF PHOENIX-IDAHO CAMPUS, Meridian, ID 83642-3014

General Information Proprietary, coed, comprehensive institution. *Graduate faculty:* 6. *Tuition:* Full-time $7,080; part-time $295 per credit. *Graduate housing:* On-campus housing not available. *Web address:* http://www.phoenix.edu/.

General Application Contact: 208-888-1505, Fax: 208-888-4775.

GRADUATE UNITS

College of Graduate Business and Management Students: 34. *Faculty:* 6. Expenses: Contact institution. *Financial support:* Applicants required to submit FAFSA. *Degree program information:* Evening/weekend programs available. Postbaccalaureate distance learning degree programs offered (no on-campus study). *Application deadline:* Applications are processed on a rolling basis. *Application fee:* $85. *Dean*, Dr. Brian Lindquist, 480-557-1221, E-mail: brian.lindquist@phoenix.edu.

UNIVERSITY OF PHOENIX–JACKSONVILLE CAMPUS, Jacksonville, FL 32216-0959

General Information Proprietary, coed, comprehensive institution. *Enrollment:* 421 full-time matriculated graduate/professional students, 25 part-time matriculated graduate/professional students. *Enrollment by degree level:* 421 master's, 25 other advanced degrees. *Graduate faculty:* 6 full-time, 131 part-time/adjunct. *Tuition:* Full-time $7,320; part-time $305 per credit. *Graduate housing:* On-campus housing not available. *Student services:* Campus safety program. *Library facilities:* University Library. *Online resources:* library catalog, web page. *Collection:* 17.5 million titles, 9,000 serial subscriptions.

Computer facilities: A campuswide network can be accessed from off campus. Internet access is available. *Web address:* http://www.phoenix.edu/.

General Application Contact: 904-636-6645, Fax: 904-636-0998.

GRADUATE UNITS

College of Graduate Business and Management Students: 343 full-time. Average age 35. Expenses: Contact institution. *Financial support:* Applicants required to submit FAFSA. In 2001, 65 degrees awarded. *Degree program information:* Evening/weekend programs available. Postbaccalaureate distance learning degree programs offered (no on-campus study). Offers business administration (MBA); health care management (MBA); organizational management (MAOM); technology management (MBA). *Application deadline:* Applications are processed on a rolling basis. *Application fee:* $85. *Application Contact:* 904-636-6645, Fax: 904-636-0998. *Dean*, Dr. Brian Lindquist, 480-557-1221, E-mail: brian.lindquist@phoenix.edu.

College of Health Care and Nursing Students: 41 full-time. Average age 35. Expenses: Contact institution. *Financial support:* Applicants required to submit FAFSA. In 2001, 24 degrees awarded. *Degree program information:* Evening/weekend programs available. Postbaccalaureate distance learning degree programs offered. Offers healthcare and nursing (MSN). *Application deadline:* Applications are processed on a rolling basis. *Application fee:* $85. *Application Contact:* 904-636-6645, Fax: 904-636-0998. *Dean*, Dr. Catherine Garner, 480-557-1751, E-mail: catherine.garner@phoenix.edu.

College of Information Systems and Technology Students: 37 full-time, 25 part-time. Average age 35. Expenses: Contact institution. *Financial support:* Applicants required to submit FAFSA. In 2001, 13 degrees awarded. *Degree program information:* Evening/weekend programs available. Postbaccalaureate distance learning degree programs offered (no on-campus study). Offers information systems and technology (MSCIS). *Application deadline:* Applications are processed on a rolling basis. *Application fee:* $85. *Application Contact:* 904-636-6645, Fax: 904-636-0998. *Dean*, Dr. Adam Honea, 480-557-1659, E-mail: adam.honea@phoenix.edu.

UNIVERSITY OF PHOENIX-KANSAS CITY CAMPUS, Kansas City, MO 64131-4517

General Information Proprietary, coed, comprehensive institution. *Tuition:* Full-time $9,120; part-time $380 per credit. *Graduate housing:* On-campus housing not available. *Web address:* http://www.phoenix.edu/.

General Application Contact: Campus Information Center, 816-943-9600, Fax: 816-943-6675.

GRADUATE UNITS

College of Graduate Business and Management Expenses: Contact institution. *Financial support:* Applicants required to submit FAFSA. *Degree program information:* Evening/weekend programs available. Postbaccalaureate distance learning degree programs offered (no on-campus study). Offers administration (MBA); e-business (MBA); organizational management (MAOM). *Application deadline:* Applications are processed on a rolling basis. *Application fee:* $85. *Dean*, Dr. Brian Lindquist, 480-557-1221, E-mail: brian.lindquist@phoenix.edu.

UNIVERSITY OF PHOENIX–LOUISIANA CAMPUS, Metairie, LA 70001-2082

General Information Proprietary, coed, comprehensive institution. *Enrollment:* 557 full-time matriculated graduate/professional students, 30 part-time matriculated graduate/professional students. *Graduate faculty:* 7 full-time, 188 part-time/adjunct. *Tuition:* Full-time $6,552; part-time $273 per credit. *Required fees:* $273 per credit. *Graduate housing:* On-campus housing not available. *Student services:* Campus safety program. *Library facilities:* University Library. *Online resources:* library catalog, web page. *Collection:* 17.5 million titles, 9,000 serial subscriptions.

Computer facilities: A campuswide network can be accessed from off campus. Internet access is available. *Web address:* http://www.phoenix.edu/.

General Application Contact: Campus Information Center, 504-461-8852, Fax: 504-464-6373.

GRADUATE UNITS

College of Education Average age 34. Expenses: Contact institution. *Financial support:* Applicants required to submit FAFSA. In 2001, 8 degrees awarded. *Degree program information:* Evening/weekend programs available. Postbaccalaureate distance learning degree programs offered (no on-campus study). Offers curriculum and instruction (MA Ed); curriculum and technology (MA Ed). *Application deadline:* Applications are processed on a rolling basis. *Application fee:* $85. *Application Contact:* Campus Information Center, 504-461-8852, Fax: 504-464-0373. *Associate Dean*, Dr. Marla LaRue, E-mail: marla.larue@phoenix.edu.

College of Graduate Business and Management Students: 549 full-time. Average age 34. Expenses: Contact institution. *Financial support:* Applicants required to submit FAFSA. In 2001, 113 degrees awarded. *Degree program information:* Evening/weekend programs available. Offers business administration (MBA); e-business (MBA); health care management (MBA); organizational management (MAOM); technology management (MBA). *Application deadline:* Applications are processed on a rolling basis. *Application fee:* $85. *Dean*, Dr. Brian Lindquist, 480-557-1221, E-mail: brian.lindquist@phoenix.edu.

College of Health Care Sciences and Nursing Students: 8 full-time. Expenses: Contact institution. *Financial support:* Applicants required to submit FAFSA. In 2001, 69 degrees awarded. *Degree program information:* Evening/weekend programs available. Postbaccalaureate distance learning degree programs offered (no on-campus study). Offers health care sciences and nursing (MSN). *Application deadline:* Applications are processed on a rolling basis. *Application fee:* $85. *Dean*, Dr. Catherine Garner, 480-557-1751, E-mail: catherine.garner@phoenix.edu.

UNIVERSITY OF PHOENIX–MARYLAND CAMPUS, Columbia, MD 21045-5424

General Information Proprietary, coed, comprehensive institution. *Enrollment:* 348 full-time matriculated graduate/professional students. *Enrollment by degree level:* 348 master's. *Graduate faculty:* 7 full-time, 145 part-time/adjunct. *Tuition:* Full-time $9,960; part-time $415 per credit. *Graduate housing:* On-campus housing not available. *Student services:* Campus safety program. *Library facilities:* University Library. *Online resources:* library catalog, web page. *Collection:* 17.5 million titles, 9,000 serial subscriptions.

Computer facilities: A campuswide network can be accessed from off campus. Internet access is available. *Web address:* http://www.phoenix.edu/.

General Application Contact: 410-536-7144.

GRADUATE UNITS

College of Graduate Business and Management Students: 321 full-time. Average age 35. Expenses: Contact institution. *Financial support:* Applicants required to submit FAFSA. In 2001, 6 degrees awarded. *Degree program information:* Evening/weekend programs available. Postbaccalaureate distance learning degree programs offered (no on-campus study). Offers business administration (MBA); global management (MBA); organizational management (MAOM); technology management (MBA). *Application deadline:* Applications are processed on a rolling basis. *Application fee:* $85. *Dean*, Dr. Brian Lindquist, 480-557-1221, E-mail: brian.lindquist@phoenix.edu.

College of Information Systems and Technology Students: 27 full-time. Average age 34. Expenses: Contact institution. *Financial support:* Applicants required to submit FAFSA. *Degree program information:* Evening/weekend programs available. Postbaccalaureate distance learning degree programs offered (no on-campus study). Offers information systems and technology (MSCIS). *Application deadline:* Applications are processed on a rolling basis. *Application fee:* $85. *Dean*, Dr. Adam Honea, 480-537-1659, E-mail: adam.honea@phoenix.edu.

UNIVERSITY OF PHOENIX–METRO DETROIT CAMPUS, Troy, MI 48098-2623

General Information Proprietary, coed, comprehensive institution. *Enrollment:* 791 full-time matriculated graduate/professional students, 42 part-time matriculated graduate/professional students. *Graduate faculty:* 13 full-time, 350 part-time/adjunct. *Tuition:* Full-time $9,120; part-time $380 per credit. Full-time tuition and fees vary according to program. *Graduate housing:* On-campus housing not available. *Student services:* Campus safety program. *Library facilities:* University Library. *Online resources:* library catalog, web page. *Collection:* 17.5 million titles, 9,000 serial subscriptions.

Computer facilities: A campuswide network can be accessed from off campus. Internet access is available. *Web address:* http://www.phoenix.edu/.

General Application Contact: 800-834-2438.

GRADUATE UNITS

College of Graduate Business and Management Students: 712 full-time. Expenses: Contact institution. *Financial support:* Applicants required to submit FAFSA. In 2001, 197 degrees awarded. *Degree program information:* Evening/weekend programs available. Postbaccalaureate distance learning degree programs offered (no on-campus study). Offers business administration (MBA); global management (MBA); health care management (MBA); organizational management (MAOM); technology management (MBA). *Application deadline:* Applications are processed on a rolling basis. *Application fee:* $85. *Dean*, Dr. Brian Lindquist, 480-557-1221, E-mail: brian.lindquist@phoenix.edu.

College of Health Care Sciences and Nursing Students: 13 full-time. Average age 35. Expenses: Contact institution. *Financial support:* Applicants required to submit FAFSA. In 2001, 52 degrees awarded. *Degree program information:* Evening/weekend programs available. Postbaccalaureate distance learning degree programs offered (no on-campus study). Offers health care sciences and nursing (MSN). *Application deadline:* Applications are processed on a rolling basis. *Application fee:* $85. *Dean*, Dr. Catherine Garner, 480-557-1751, E-mail: catherine.garner@phoenix.edu.

College of Information Systems and Technology Students: 63 full-time. Average age 35. Expenses: Contact institution. *Financial support:* Applicants required to submit FAFSA. In 2001, 43 degrees awarded. *Degree program information:* Evening/weekend programs available. Postbaccalaureate distance learning degree programs offered (no on-campus study). Offers Information systems and technology (MSCIS). *Application deadline:* Applications are processed on a rolling basis. *Application fee:* $85. *Dean*, Dr. Adam Honea, 480-557-1659, E-mail: adam.honea@phoenix.edu.

UNIVERSITY OF PHOENIX–NEVADA CAMPUS, Las Vegas, NV 89106-3797

General Information Proprietary, coed, comprehensive institution. *Enrollment:* 945 full-time matriculated graduate/professional students, 116 part-time matriculated graduate/professional students. *Graduate faculty:* 14 full-time, 246 part-time/adjunct. *Tuition:* Full-time $7,272; part-time $303 per credit. Full-time tuition and fees vary according to program. *Graduate housing:* On-campus housing not available. *Student services:* Campus safety program. *Library facilities:* University Library. *Online resources:* library catalog, web page. *Collection:* 17.5 million titles, 9,000 serial subscriptions.

Computer facilities: A campuswide network can be accessed from off campus. Internet access is available. *Web address:* http://www.phoenix.edu/.

General Application Contact: 702-638-7249, Fax: 702-638-8035.

GRADUATE UNITS

College of Computer Information Systems and Technology Students: 44 full-time, 94 part-time. Average age 35. Expenses: Contact institution. *Financial support:* Applicants required to submit FAFSA. *Degree program information:* Evening/weekend programs available. Postbaccalaureate distance learning degree programs offered (no on-campus study). Offers computer information systems and technology (MSCIS). *Application deadline:* Applications are processed on a rolling basis. *Application fee:* $85. *Application Contact:* 702-638-7249, Fax: 702-638-8035. *Dean*, Dr. Adam Honea, 480-557-1659, E-mail: adam.honea@phoenix.edu.

College of Education Students: 475 full-time. Expenses: Contact institution. *Financial support:* Applicants required to submit FAFSA. In 2001, 181 degrees awarded. *Degree program information:* Evening/weekend programs available. Postbaccalaureate distance learning degree programs offered. Offers administration and supervision (MA Ed); educational counseling (MA Ed). *Application deadline:* Applications are processed on a rolling basis. *Application fee:* $85. *Application Contact:* 702-638-7249, Fax: 702-638-8085. *Associate Dean*, Dr. Marla LaRue, 480-557-1218, E-mail: marla.larue@phoenix.edu.

College of Graduate Business and Management Students: 614 full-time. Average age 35. Expenses: Contact institution. *Financial support:* Applicants required to submit FAFSA. In 2001, 162 degrees awarded. *Degree program information:* Evening/weekend programs available. Postbaccalaureate distance learning degree programs offered (no on-campus study). Offers business administration (MBA); organizational management (MAOM). *Application deadline:* Applications are processed on a rolling basis. *Application fee:* $85. *Application Contact:* 702-638-7249, Fax: 702-638-8035. *Dean*, Dr. Brian Lindquist, 480-557-1221, E-mail: brian.lindquest@phoenix.edu.

UNIVERSITY OF PHOENIX–NEW MEXICO CAMPUS, Albuquerque, NM 87109-4645

General Information Proprietary, coed, comprehensive institution. *Enrollment:* 907 full-time matriculated graduate/professional students, 54 part-time matriculated graduate/professional students. *Graduate faculty:* 15 full-time, 344 part-time/adjunct. *Tuition:* Full-time $7,336; part-time $306 per credit. Full-time tuition and fees vary according to program. *Graduate housing:* On-campus housing not available. *Student services:* Campus safety program. *Library facilities:* University Library. *Online resources:* library catalog, web page. *Collection:* 17.5 million titles, 9,000 serial subscriptions.

Computer facilities: A campuswide network can be accessed from off campus. Internet access is available. *Web address:* http://www.phoenix.edu/.

General Application Contact: 505-821-4800.

GRADUATE UNITS

College of Counseling and Human Services Students: 34 full-time. Average age 34. Expenses: Contact institution. *Financial support:* Applicants required to submit FAFSA. In 2001, 16 degrees awarded. *Degree program information:* Evening/weekend programs available. Postbaccalaureate distance learning degree programs offered (no on-campus study). Offers marriage and family therapy (MC); mental health counseling (MC). *Application deadline:* Applications are processed on a rolling basis. *Application fee:* $85. *Dean*, Dr. Patrick Romine, 480-557-1074, E-mail: patrick.romine@phoenix.edu.

College of Education Students: 8 full-time. Average age 35. Expenses: Contact institution. *Financial support:* Applicants required to submit FAFSA. In 2001, 9 degrees awarded. *Degree program information:* Evening/weekend programs available. Postbaccalaureate distance learning degree programs offered (no on-campus study). Offers education (MA Ed). *Application deadline:* Applications are processed on a rolling basis. *Application fee:* $85. *Associate Dean*, Dr. Marla LaRue, 480-557-1218, E-mail: marla.larue@phoenix.edu.

College of Graduate Business and Management Students: 699 full-time. Expenses: Contact institution. *Financial support:* Applicants required to submit FAFSA. In 2001, 290 degrees awarded. *Degree program information:* Evening/weekend programs available. Postbaccalaureate distance learning degree programs offered (no on-campus study). Offers business administration (MBA); global management (MBA); health care management (MBA); organizational management (MAOM); technology management (MBA). *Application deadline:* Applications are processed on a rolling basis. *Application fee:* $85. *Dean*, Dr. Brian Lindquist, 480-557-1221, E-mail: brian.lindquist@phoenix.edu.

College of Health Care Sciences and Nursing Students: 40 full-time. Average age 35. Expenses: Contact institution. *Financial support:* Applicants required to submit FAFSA. In 2001, 36 degrees awarded. *Degree program information:* Evening/weekend programs available. Postbaccalaureate distance learning degree programs offered (no on-campus study). Offers healthcare and nursing sciences (MSN). *Application deadline:* Applications are processed on a rolling basis. *Application fee:* $85. *Dean*, Dr. Catherine Garner, 480-557-1751, E-mail: catherine.garner@phoenix.edu.

College of Information Systems and Technology Students: 126 full-time, 54 part-time. Average age 35. Expenses: Contact institution. *Financial support:* Applicants required to submit FAFSA. In 2001, 68 degrees awarded. *Degree program information:* Evening/weekend programs available. Postbaccalaureate distance learning degree programs offered (no on-campus study). Offers information systems and technology (MSCIS). *Application deadline:* Applications are processed on a rolling basis. *Application fee:* $85. *Dean*, Dr. Adam Honea, 480-557-1659, E-mail: adam.honea@phoenix.edu.

UNIVERSITY OF PHOENIX–NORTHERN CALIFORNIA CAMPUS, Pleasanton, CA 94588-3677

General Information Proprietary, coed, comprehensive institution. *Enrollment:* 1,112 full-time matriculated graduate/professional students, 36 part-time matriculated graduate/professional students. *Graduate faculty:* 15 full-time, 737 part-time/adjunct. *Tuition:* Full-time $9,504; part-time $396 per credit. *Graduate housing:* On-campus housing not available. *Student services:* Campus safety program. *Library facilities:* University Library. *Online resources:* library catalog, web page. *Collection:* 17.5 million titles, 9,000 serial subscriptions.

Computer facilities: A campuswide network can be accessed from off campus. Internet access is available. *Web address:* http://www.phoenix.edu/.

General Application Contact: 408-435-8500, Fax: 408-435-8250.

GRADUATE UNITS

College of Education Average age 35. Expenses: Contact institution. *Financial support:* Applicants required to submit FAFSA. *Degree program information:* Evening/weekend programs available. Postbaccalaureate distance learning degree programs offered (no on-campus study). Offers curriculum and instruction (MA Ed); curriculum and technology (MA Ed). *Application deadline:* Applications are processed on a rolling basis. *Application fee:* $85. *Application Contact:* 408-435-8500, Fax: 408-435-8250. *Associate Dean*, Dr. Marla LaRue, 480-557-1218, E-mail: marla.larue@phoenix.edu.

College of Graduate Business and Management Students: 1,023 full-time. Average age 35. Expenses: Contact institution. *Financial support:* Applicants required to submit FAFSA. In 2001, 378 degrees awarded. *Degree program information:* Evening/weekend programs available. Postbaccalaureate distance learning degree programs offered (no on-campus study). Offers business administration (MBA); global management (MBA); health care management (MBA); organizational management (MAOM); technology management (MBA). *Application deadline:* Applications are processed on a rolling basis. *Application fee:* $85. *Application Contact:* 408-435-8500, Fax: 408-435-8250. *Dean*, Dr. Brian Lindquist, 408-557-1221, E-mail: brian.lindquist@phoenix.edu.

College of Health Care Sciences and Nursing Students: 22 full-time. Average age 35. Expenses: Contact institution. *Financial support:* Applicants required to submit FAFSA. In 2001, 25 degrees awarded. *Degree program information:* Evening/weekend programs available. Postbaccalaureate distance learning degree programs offered (no on-campus study). Offers health care sciences and nursing (MSN). *Application deadline:* Applications are processed on a rolling basis. *Application fee:* $85. *Application Contact:* 408-435-8500, Fax: 408-435-8250. *Dean*, Dr. Catherine Garner, 480-557-1727, E-mail: catherine.garner@phoenix.edu.

College of Information Systems and Technology Students: 67 full-time. Average age 35. Expenses: Contact institution. *Financial support:* Applicants required to submit FAFSA. *Degree program information:* Evening/weekend programs available. Postbaccalaureate distance learning degree programs offered (no on-campus study). Offers information systems and technology (MSCIS). *Application fee:* $85. *Application Contact:* 408-435-8500, Fax: 408-435-8250. *Dean*, Dr. Adam Honea, 480-557-1659, E-mail: adam.honea@phoenix.edu.

UNIVERSITY OF PHOENIX–OHIO CAMPUS, Independence, OH 44131-2194

General Information Proprietary, coed, comprehensive institution. *Enrollment:* 139 full-time matriculated graduate/professional students. *Enrollment by degree level:* 139 master's. *Graduate faculty:* 7 full-time, 70 part-time/adjunct. *Tuition:* Full-time $10,080; part-time $420 per credit. *Graduate housing:* On-campus housing not available. *Student services:* Campus safety program. *Library facilities:* University Library. *Online resources:* library catalog, web page. *Collection:* 17.5 million titles, 9,000 serial subscriptions.

Computer facilities: A campuswide network can be accessed from off campus. Internet access is available. *Web address:* http://www.phoenix.edu/.

General Application Contact: 216-447-8807, Fax: 216-447-9144.

GRADUATE UNITS

College of Graduate Business and Management Expenses: Contact institution. *Financial support:* Applicants required to submit FAFSA. *Degree program information:* Evening/weekend programs available. Postbaccalaureate distance learning degree programs offered (no on-campus study). Offers business administration (MBA); e-business (MBA); global management (MBA). *Application deadline:* Applications are processed on a rolling basis. *Application fee:* $85. *Application Contact:* 216-447-8807, Fax: 216-447-9144. *Dean*, Dr. Brian Lindquist, 480-557-1221, E-mail: brian.lindquist@phoenix.edu.

College of Information Systems and Technology Expenses: Contact institution. *Financial support:* Applicants required to submit FAFSA. *Degree program information:* Evening/weekend programs available. Postbaccalaureate distance learning degree programs offered (no on-campus study). Offers information systems and technology (MSCIS). *Application deadline:* Applications are processed on a rolling basis. *Application fee:* $85. *Application Contact:* 216-447-8807, Fax: 216-447-9144. *Dean*, Dr. Adam Honea, 480-557-1659, E-mail: adam.honea@phoenix.edu.

UNIVERSITY OF PHOENIX–OKLAHOMA CITY CAMPUS, Oklahoma City, OK 73116

General Information Proprietary, coed, comprehensive institution. *Enrollment:* 107 full-time matriculated graduate/professional students. *Graduate faculty:* 7 full-time, 106 part-time/adjunct. *Tuition:* Full-time $8,040; part-time $335 per credit. *Graduate housing:* On-campus housing not available. *Student services:* Campus safety program. *Library facilities:* University Library. *Online resources:* library catalog, web page. *Collection:* 17.5 million titles, 9,000 serial subscriptions.

Computer facilities: A campuswide network can be accessed from off campus. Internet access is available. *Web address:* http://www.phoenix.edu/.

General Application Contact: 405-842-8007, Fax: 405-841-3386.

GRADUATE UNITS

College of Graduate Business and Management Students: 103 full-time. Average age 35. Expenses: Contact institution. *Financial support:* Applicants required to submit FAFSA. In 2001, 45 degrees awarded. *Degree program information:* Evening/weekend programs available. Postbaccalaureate distance learning degree programs offered (no on-campus study). Offers business administration (MBA); e-business (MBA); organizational management (MAOM). *Application deadline:* Applications are processed on a rolling basis. *Application fee:* $85. *Application Contact:* 405-842-8007, Fax: 405-841-3386. *Dean*, Dr. Brian Lindquist, 480-557-1221, E-mail: brian.lindquist@phoenix.edu.

College of Information Systems and Technology Students: 4 full-time. Average age 35. Expenses: Contact institution. *Financial support:* Applicants required to submit FAFSA. *Degree program information:* Evening/weekend programs available. Postbaccalaureate distance learning degree programs offered (no on-campus study). Offers information systems and technology (MSCIS). *Application deadline:* Applications are processed on a rolling basis. *Application fee:* $85. *Application Contact:* 405-842-8007, Fax: 405-841-3386. *Dean*, Dr. Adam Honea, 480-557-1659, E-mail: adam.honea@phoenix.edu.

UNIVERSITY OF PHOENIX ONLINE CAMPUS, Phoenix, AZ 85040-1958

General Information Proprietary, coed, comprehensive institution.

GRADUATE UNITS

College of Graduate Business and Management

College of Nursing and Healthcare Sciences

UNIVERSITY OF PHOENIX–OREGON CAMPUS, Portland, OR 97223-8368

General Information Proprietary, coed, comprehensive institution. *Enrollment:* 244 full-time matriculated graduate/professional students. *Graduate faculty:* 10 full-time, 245 part-time/adjunct. *Tuition:* Full-time $7,800; part-time $325 per credit. *Graduate housing:* On-campus housing not available. *Student services:* Campus safety program. *Library facilities:* University Library. *Online resources:* library catalog, web page. *Collection:* 17.5 million titles, 9,000 serial subscriptions.

Computer facilities: A campuswide network can be accessed from off campus. Internet access is available. *Web address:* http://www.phoenix.edu/.

General Application Contact: 503-403-2900, Fax: 503-670-0614.

GRADUATE UNITS

College of Graduate Business and Management Students: 239 full-time. Average age 36. Expenses: Contact institution. *Financial support:* Applicants required to submit FAFSA. In 2001, 86 degrees awarded. *Degree program information:* Evening/weekend programs available. Postbaccalaureate distance learning degree programs offered (no on-campus study). Offers business administration (MBA); organizational management (MAOM); technology management (MBA). *Application deadline:* Applications are processed on a rolling basis. *Application fee:* $85. *Dean*, Dr. Brian Lindquist, 480-557-1221, E-mail: brian.lindquist@phoenix.edu.

UNIVERSITY OF PHOENIX–ORLANDO CAMPUS, Maitland, FL 32751

General Information Proprietary, coed, comprehensive institution. *Enrollment:* 462 full-time matriculated graduate/professional students, 22 part-time matriculated graduate/professional students. *Graduate faculty:* 9 full-time, 140 part-time/adjunct. *Tuition:* Full-time $7,320; part-time $305 per credit. *Graduate housing:* On-campus housing not available. *Student services:* Campus safety program. *Library facilities:* University Library. *Online resources:* library catalog, web page. *Collection:* 17.5 million titles, 9,000 serial subscriptions.

Computer facilities: A campuswide network can be accessed from off campus. Internet access is available. *Web address:* http://www.phoenix.edu/.

General Application Contact: 407-667-0555, Fax: 407-667-0560.

GRADUATE UNITS

College of Graduate Business and Management Students: 349 full-time. Average age 35. Expenses: Contact institution. In 2001, 114 degrees awarded. *Degree program information:* Evening/weekend programs available. Postbaccalaureate distance learning degree programs offered (no on-campus study). Offers business administration (MBA); health care management (MBA); organizational management (MAOM); technology management (MBA). *Application deadline:* Applications are processed on a rolling basis. *Application fee:* $85. *Dean*, Dr. Brian Lindquist, 480-557-1221, E-mail: brian.lindquist@phoenix.edu.

College of Health Care Sciences and Nursing Students: 62 full-time. Average age 35. Expenses: Contact institution. *Financial support:* Applicants required to submit FAFSA. In 2001, 32 degrees awarded. *Degree program information:* Evening/weekend programs available. Postbaccalaureate distance learning degree programs offered (no on-campus study). Offers healthcare and nursing (MSN). *Application deadline:* Applications are processed on a rolling basis. *Application fee:* $85. *Dean*, Dr. Catherine Garner, 480-557-1751, E-mail: catherine.garner@phoenix.edu.

College of Information Systems and Technology Students: 61 full-time, 22 part-time. Average age 35. Expenses: Contact institution. *Financial support:* Applicants required to submit FAFSA. In 2001, 36 degrees awarded. *Degree program information:* Evening/weekend programs available. Postbaccalaureate distance learning degree programs offered (no on-campus study). Offers information systems and technology (MSCIS). *Application deadline:* Applications are processed on a rolling basis. *Application fee:* $85. *Dean*, Dr. Adam Honea, 480-557-1659, E-mail: adam.honea@phoenix.edu.

UNIVERSITY OF PHOENIX–PHILADELPHIA CAMPUS, Wayne, PA 19087-2121

General Information Proprietary, coed, comprehensive institution. *Enrollment:* 303 full-time matriculated graduate/professional students. *Enrollment by degree level:* 133 master's. *Graduate faculty:* 8 full-time, 117 part-time/adjunct. *Tuition:* Full-time $8,040; part-time $335 per credit. *Graduate housing:* On-campus housing not available. *Student services:* Campus safety program. *Library facilities:* University Library. *Online resources:* library catalog, web page. *Collection:* 17.5 million titles, 9,000 serial subscriptions.

Computer facilities: A campuswide network can be accessed from off campus. Internet access is available. *Web address:* http://www.phoenix.edu/.

General Application Contact: 610-989-0880, Fax: 610-989-0881.

GRADUATE UNITS

College of Graduate Business and Management Students: 303 full-time. Average age 35. Expenses: Contact institution. *Financial support:* Applicants required to submit FAFSA. *Degree program information:* Evening/weekend programs available. Postbaccalaureate distance learning degree programs offered (no on-campus study). Offers business administration (MBA); global management (MBA); technology management (MBA). *Application deadline:* Applications are processed on a rolling basis. *Application fee:* $85. *Application Contact:* 610-984-0880, Fax: 610-989-0881. *Dean*, Dr. Brian Lindquist, 480-557-1221, E-mail: brian.lindquist@phoenix.edu.

UNIVERSITY OF PHOENIX–PHOENIX CAMPUS, Phoenix, AZ 85040-1958

General Information Proprietary, coed, comprehensive institution. CGS member. *Enrollment:* 2,685 full-time matriculated graduate/professional students, 493 part-time matriculated graduate/professional students. *Graduate faculty:* 28 full-time, 838 part-time/adjunct. *Tuition:* Full-time $7,680; part-time $320 per credit. Full-time tuition and fees vary according to campus/location and program. *Graduate housing:* On-campus housing not available. *Student services:* Campus safety program. *Library facilities:* University Library. *Online resources:* library catalog, web page. *Collection:* 17.5 million titles, 9,000 serial subscriptions.

Computer facilities: A campuswide network can be accessed from off campus. Internet access is available. *Web address:* http://www.phoenix.edu/.

General Application Contact: 480-966-7400.

GRADUATE UNITS

College of Counseling and Human Services Students: 241 full-time. Average age 33. Expenses: Contact institution. *Financial support:* Applicants required to submit FAFSA. In 2001, 70 degrees awarded. *Degree program information:* Evening/weekend programs available. Postbaccalaureate distance learning degree programs offered (no on-campus study). Offers community counseling (MC); marriage, family, and child therapy (MC); mental health counseling (MC). *Application deadline:* Applications are processed on a rolling basis. *Application fee:* $85. *Application Contact:* 480-966-7400. *Dean*, Dr. Patrick Romine, 480-557-1074 Ext. 1074, E-mail: patrick.romine@phoenix.edu.

College of Education Students: 437 full-time, 417 part-time. Average age 33. Expenses: Contact institution. *Financial support:* Applicants required to submit FAFSA. In 2001, 120 degrees awarded. *Degree program information:* Evening/weekend programs available. Postbaccalaureate distance learning degree programs offered (no on-campus study). Offers administration and supervision (MA Ed); diverse learner (MA Ed); educational counseling (MA Ed); English as a second language (MA Ed). *Application deadline:* Applications are processed on a rolling basis. *Application fee:* $85. *Application Contact:* 480-966-7400. *Associate Dean*, Dr. Marla LaRue, 480-557-1218, E-mail: marla.larue@phoenix.edu.

College of Graduate Business and Management Students: 1,751 full-time. Average age 33. Expenses: Contact institution. *Financial support:* Applicants required to submit FAFSA. In 2001, 635 degrees awarded. *Degree program information:* Evening/weekend programs available. Postbaccalaureate distance learning degree programs offered (no on-campus study). Offers business administration (MBA); global management (MBA); health care management (MBA); organizational management (MAOM); technology management (MBA). *Application deadline:* Applications are processed on a rolling basis. *Application fee:* $85. *Application Contact:* 602-966-7400. *Dean*, Dr. Brian Lindquist, 480-557-1221, E-mail: brian.lindquist@apollogrp.edu.

College of Information Systems and Technology Students: 95 full-time, 76 part-time. Average age 33. Expenses: Contact institution. *Financial support:* Applicants required to submit FAFSA. In 2001, 111 degrees awarded. *Degree program information:* Evening/weekend programs available. Postbaccalaureate distance learning degree programs offered (no on-campus study). Offers information systems and technology (MSCIS). *Application deadline:* Applications are processed on a rolling basis. *Application fee:* $85. *Application Contact:* 480-966-7400. *Dean*, Dr. Adam Honea, 480-557-1659, E-mail: adam.honea@phoenix.edu.

Health Care Sciences and Nursing Students: 161 full-time. Average age 33. Expenses: Contact institution. *Financial support:* Applicants required to submit FAFSA. In 2001, 41 degrees awarded. *Degree program information:* Evening/weekend programs available. Postbaccalaureate distance learning degree programs offered (no on-campus study). Offers nurse practitioner (MSN); nursing administration (MSN). *Application deadline:* Applications are processed on a rolling basis. *Application fee:* $85. *Application Contact:* 480-966-7400. *Dean*, Dr. Catherine Garner, 480-557-1751, E-mail: catherine.garner@phoenix.edu.

UNIVERSITY OF PHOENIX–PITTSBURGH CAMPUS, Pittsburgh, PA 15276

General Information Proprietary, coed, comprehensive institution. *Enrollment:* 110 full-time matriculated graduate/professional students. *Graduate faculty:* 7 full-time. *Graduate housing:* On-campus housing not available. *Student services:* Campus safety program. *Library facilities:* University Library. *Online resources:* library catalog, web page. *Collection:* 17.5 million titles, 9,000 serial subscriptions.

University of Phoenix–Pittsburgh Campus (continued)

Computer facilities: A campuswide network can be accessed from off campus. Internet access is available. *Web address:* http://www.phoenix.edu/.

General Application Contact: 412-747-9000, Fax: 412-747-0676.

GRADUATE UNITS

College of Graduate Business and Management Students: 110 full-time. *Faculty:* 7 full-time. Expenses: Contact institution. *Financial support:* Applicants required to submit FAFSA. *Degree program information:* Evening/weekend programs available. Postbaccalaureate distance learning degree programs offered (no on-campus study). Offers business administration (MBA); organizational management (MAOM); technology management (MBA). *Application deadline:* Applications are processed on a rolling basis. *Application fee:* $85. *Application Contact:* 412-747-9000, Fax: 412-747-0676. *Dean,* Dr. Brian Lindquist, 480-557-1221, E-mail: brian.lindquist@phoenix.edu.

UNIVERSITY OF PHOENIX–PUERTO RICO CAMPUS, Guaynabo, PR 00970-3870

General Information Proprietary, coed, comprehensive institution. *Enrollment:* 1,619 full-time matriculated graduate/professional students. *Graduate faculty:* 10 full-time, 127 part-time/adjunct. *Tuition:* Full-time $4,800; part-time $200 per credit. *Graduate housing:* On-campus housing not available. *Student services:* Campus safety program. *Library facilities:* University Library. *Online resources:* library catalog, web page. *Collection:* 17.5 million titles, 9,000 serial subscriptions.

Computer facilities: A campuswide network can be accessed from off campus. Internet access is available. *Web address:* http://www.phoenix.edu/.

General Application Contact: 787-731-5400, Fax: 787-731-1510.

GRADUATE UNITS

College of Counseling and Human Services Students: 227 full-time. Average age 34. Expenses: Contact institution. *Financial support:* Applicants required to submit FAFSA. In 2001, 19 degrees awarded. *Degree program information:* Evening/weekend programs available. Postbaccalaureate distance learning degree programs offered (no on-campus study). Offers counseling and human services (MC). *Application deadline:* Applications are processed on a rolling basis. *Application fee:* $85. *Application Contact:* 787-731-5400, Fax: 787-731-1510. *Dean,* Dr. Patrick Romine, 480-557-1074, E-mail: patrick.romine@phoenix.edu.

College of Education Students: 439 full-time. Average age 34. Expenses: Contact institution. *Financial support:* Applicants required to submit FAFSA. In 2001, 266 degrees awarded. *Degree program information:* Evening/weekend programs available. Postbaccalaureate distance learning degree programs offered (no on-campus study). Offers education (MA Ed). *Application deadline:* Applications are processed on a rolling basis. *Application fee:* $85. *Application Contact:* 787-731-5400, Fax: 787-731-1510. *Associate Dean,* Dr. Marla LaRue, 480-557-1218, E-mail: marla.larue@phoenix.edu.

College of Graduate Business and Management Students: 953 full-time. Average age 34. Expenses: Contact institution. *Financial support:* Applicants required to submit FAFSA. In 2001, 187 degrees awarded. *Degree program information:* Evening/weekend programs available. Postbaccalaureate distance learning degree programs offered (no on-campus study). Offers business and management (MAOM, MBA). *Application deadline:* Applications are processed on a rolling basis. *Application fee:* $85. *Application Contact:* 787-931-5400, Fax: 787-931-1510. *Dean,* Dr. Brian Lindquist, 480-557-1221, E-mail: brian.lindquist@phoenix.edu.

UNIVERSITY OF PHOENIX–SACRAMENTO CAMPUS, Sacramento, CA 95833-3632

General Information Proprietary, coed, comprehensive institution. *Enrollment:* 689 full-time matriculated graduate/professional students, 31 part-time matriculated graduate/professional students. *Graduate faculty:* 12 full-time, 364 part-time/adjunct. *Tuition:* Full-time $9,720; part-time $405 per credit. Full-time tuition and fees vary according to program. *Graduate housing:* On-campus housing not available. *Student services:* Campus safety program. *Library facilities:* University Library. *Online resources:* library catalog, web page. *Collection:* 17.5 million titles, 9,000 serial subscriptions.

Computer facilities: A campuswide network can be accessed from off campus. Internet access is available. *Web address:* http://www.phoenix.edu/.

General Application Contact: 916-923-2107, Fax: 916-923-3914.

GRADUATE UNITS

College of Counseling and Human Services Students: 109 full-time. Average age 34. Expenses: Contact institution. *Financial support:* Applicants required to submit FAFSA. In 2001, 46 degrees awarded. *Degree program information:* Evening/weekend programs available. Postbaccalaureate distance learning degree programs offered (no on-campus study). Offers marriage, family and child counseling (MC). *Application deadline:* Applications are processed on a rolling basis. *Application fee:* $85. *Dean,* Dr. Patrick Romine, 480-557-1074, E-mail: patrick.romine@phoenix.edu.

College of Graduate Business and Management Students: 414 full-time. Average age 34. Expenses: Contact institution. *Financial support:* Applicants required to submit FAFSA. In 2001, 81 degrees awarded. *Degree program information:* Evening/weekend programs available. Postbaccalaureate distance learning degree programs offered (no on-campus study). Offers business administration (MBA); e-business (MBA); organizational management (MAOM). *Application deadline:* Applications are processed on a rolling basis. *Application fee:* $85. *Dean,* Dr. Brian Lindquist, 480-557-1221, E-mail: brian.lindquist@phoenix.edu.

College of Health Care Sciences and Nursing Students: 87 full-time. Average age 34. Expenses: Contact institution. *Financial support:* Applicants required to submit FAFSA. In 2001, 29 degrees awarded. *Degree program information:* Evening/weekend programs available. Postbaccalaureate distance learning degree programs offered. Offers family nurse practitioner (MSN); nursing (MSN). *Application deadline:* Applications are processed on a rolling basis. *Application fee:* $85. *Application Contact:* 916-923-2107, Fax: 916-923-3914. *Dean,* Dr. Catherine Garner, 480-557-1751, E-mail: catherine.garner@phoenix.edu.

College of Information Systems and Technology Students: 60 full-time, 9 part-time. Average age 34. Expenses: Contact institution. *Financial support:* Applicants required to submit FAFSA. In 2001, 2 degrees awarded. *Degree program information:* Evening/weekend programs available. Postbaccalaureate distance learning degree programs offered (no on-campus study). Offers information systems and technology (MSCIS). *Application deadline:* Applications are processed on a rolling basis. *Application fee:* $85. *Dean,* Dr. Adam Honea, 480-557-1659, E-mail: adam.honea@phoenix.edu.

UNIVERSITY OF PHOENIX–ST. LOUIS CAMPUS, St. Louis, MO 63043

General Information Proprietary, coed, comprehensive institution. *Enrollment:* 59 full-time matriculated graduate/professional students. *Enrollment by degree level:* 59 master's. *Graduate faculty:* 7 full-time, 62 part-time/adjunct. *Tuition:* Full-time $9,120; part-time $380 per credit. *Graduate housing:* On-campus housing not available. *Student services:* Campus safety program. *Library facilities:* University Library. *Online resources:* library catalog, web page. *Collection:* 17.5 million titles, 9,000 serial subscriptions.

Computer facilities: A campuswide network can be accessed from off campus. Internet access is available. *Web address:* http://www.phoenix.edu/.

General Application Contact: Campus Information Center, 314-298-9755.

GRADUATE UNITS

College of Graduate Business and Management Students: 59 full-time. Average age 34. Expenses: Contact institution. Offers business administration (MBA); e-business (MBA-EB); organizational management (MAOM). *Dean,* Dr. Brian Lindquist, 480-557-1221, E-mail: brian.lindquist@phoenix.edu.

UNIVERSITY OF PHOENIX–SAN DIEGO CAMPUS, San Diego, CA 92130-2092

General Information Proprietary, coed, comprehensive institution. *Enrollment:* 1,071 full-time matriculated graduate/professional students, 96 part-time matriculated graduate/professional students. *Graduate faculty:* 11 full-time, 450 part-time/adjunct. *Tuition:* Full-time $8,808; part-time $367 per credit. *Graduate housing:* On-campus housing not available. *Student services:* Campus safety program. *Library facilities:* University Library. *Online resources:* library catalog, web page. *Collection:* 17.5 million titles, 9,000 serial subscriptions.

Computer facilities: A campuswide network can be accessed from off campus. Internet access is available. *Web address:* http://www.phoenix.edu/.

General Application Contact: 888-UOP-INFO.

GRADUATE UNITS

College of Counseling and Human Services Students: 133 full-time. Average age 34. Expenses: Contact institution. *Financial support:* Applicants required to submit FAFSA. In 2001, 30 degrees awarded. *Degree program information:* Evening/weekend programs available. Postbaccalaureate distance learning degree programs offered (no on-campus study). Offers marriage, family and child counseling (MC). *Application deadline:* Applications are processed on a rolling basis. *Application fee:* $85. *Application Contact:* Campus Information Center, 880-UOP-INFO. *Dean,* Dr. Patrick Romine, 480-557-1074, E-mail: patrick.romine@phoenix.edu.

College of Graduate Business and Management Students: 822 full-time. Average age 34. Expenses: Contact institution. *Financial support:* Applicants required to submit FAFSA. In 2001, 209 degrees awarded. *Degree program information:* Evening/weekend programs available. Postbaccalaureate distance learning degree programs offered (no on-campus study). Offers business administration (MBA); global management (MBA); health care management (MBA); organizational management (MAOM); technology management (MBA). *Application deadline:* Applications are processed on a rolling basis. *Application fee:* $85. *Application Contact:* Campus Information Center, 888-UOP-INFO. *Dean,* Dr. Brian Lindquist, 480-557-1221, E-mail: brian.lindquist@phoenix.edu.

College of Health Care Sciences and Nursing Students: 39 full-time. Average age 34. Expenses: Contact institution. *Financial support:* Applicants required to submit FAFSA. In 2001, 26 degrees awarded. *Degree program information:* Evening/weekend programs available. Postbaccalaureate distance learning degree programs offered (no on-campus study). Offers healthcare and nursing (MSN). *Application deadline:* Applications are processed on a rolling basis. *Application fee:* $85. *Application Contact:* 888-UOP-INFO. *Dean,* Dr. Catherine Garner, 480-557-1751, E-mail: catherine.garner@phoenix.edu.

College of Information Systems and Technology Students: 69 full-time, 39 part-time. Average age 34. Expenses: Contact institution. *Financial support:* Applicants required to submit FAFSA. In 2001, 64 degrees awarded. *Degree program information:* Evening/weekend programs available. Postbaccalaureate distance learning degree programs offered (no on-campus study). Offers information systems and technology (MSCIS). *Application deadline:* Applications are processed on a rolling basis. *Application fee:* $85. *Application Contact:* 888-UOP-INFO. *Dean,* Dr. Adam Honea, 480-557-1659, E-mail: adam.honea@phoenix.edu.

UNIVERSITY OF PHOENIX–SOUTHERN ARIZONA CAMPUS, Tucson, AZ 85712

General Information Proprietary, coed, comprehensive institution. *Enrollment:* 769 full-time matriculated graduate/professional students, 35 part-time matriculated graduate/professional students. *Graduate faculty:* 11 full-time, 364 part-time/adjunct. *Tuition:* Full-time $6,456; part-time $269 per credit. *Graduate housing:* On-campus housing not available. *Student services:* Campus safety program. *Library facilities:* University Library. *Online resources:* library catalog, web page. *Collection:* 17.5 million titles, 9,000 serial subscriptions.

Computer facilities: A campuswide network can be accessed from off campus. Internet access is available. *Web address:* http://www.phoenix.edu/.

General Application Contact: 520-881-6512, Fax: 520-795-6179.

GRADUATE UNITS

College of Counseling and Human Services Students: 74 full-time. Average age 34. Expenses: Contact institution. *Financial support:* Applicants required to submit FAFSA. In 2001, 30 degrees awarded. *Degree program information:* Evening/weekend programs available. Postbaccalaureate distance learning degree programs offered (no on-campus study). Offers counseling and human services (MC). *Application deadline:* Applications are processed on a rolling basis. *Application fee:* $85. *Application Contact:* 520-881-6512, Fax: 520-795-6177. *Dean,* Dr. Patrick Romine, 480-557-1074, E-mail: patrick.romine@phoenix.edu.

College of Education Students: 27 full-time, 240 part-time. Average age 34. Expenses: Contact institution. *Financial support:* Applicants required to submit FAFSA. In 2001, 26 degrees awarded. *Degree program information:* Evening/weekend programs available. Postbaccalaureate distance learning degree programs offered (no on-campus study). Offers education (MA Ed). *Application deadline:* Applications are processed on a rolling basis. *Application fee:* $85. *Application Contact:* 520-881-6512, Fax: 520-795-6177. *Dean,* Dr. Marla LaRue, 480-557-1218, E-mail: marla.larue@phoenix.edu.

College of Graduate Business and Management Students: 448 full-time. Average age 34. Expenses: Contact institution. *Financial support:* Applicants required to submit FAFSA. In 2001, 188 degrees awarded. *Degree program information:* Evening/weekend programs available. Postbaccalaureate distance learning degree programs offered (no on-campus study). Offers business administration (MBA); global management (MBA); health care management (MBA); organizational management (MAOM); technology management (MBA). *Application deadline:* Applications are processed on a rolling basis. *Application fee:* $85. *Application Contact:* 520-881-6512, Fax: 520-795-6177. *Dean,* Dr. Brian Lindquist, 480-557-1221, E-mail: brian.lindquist@phoenix.edu.

College of Health Care Sciences and Nursing Students: 24 full-time. Average age 34. Expenses: Contact institution. *Financial support:* Applicants required to submit FAFSA. In 2001, 10 degrees awarded. *Degree program information:* Evening/weekend programs available. Postbaccalaureate distance learning degree programs offered (no on-campus study). Offers healthcare and nursing (MSN). *Application deadline:* Applications are processed on a rolling basis. *Application fee:* $85. *Application Contact:* 520-881-6512, Fax: 520-795-6177. *Dean,* Dr. Catherine Garner, 480-557-1751, E-mail: catherine.garner@phoenix.edu.

College of Information Systems and Technology Students: 123 full-time, 35 part-time. Average age 34. Expenses: Contact institution. *Financial support:* Applicants required to submit FAFSA. In 2001, 59 degrees awarded. *Degree program information:* Evening/weekend programs available. Postbaccalaureate distance learning degree programs offered (no on-campus study). Offers information systems and technology (MSCIS). *Application deadline:* Applications are processed on a rolling basis. *Application fee:* $85. *Application Contact:* 520-881-6512, Fax: 520-795-6177. *Dean,* Adam Honea, 480-557-1659, E-mail: adam.honea@phoenix.edu.

UNIVERSITY OF PHOENIX–SOUTHERN CALIFORNIA CAMPUS, Fountain Valley, CA 92708-6027

General Information Proprietary, coed, comprehensive institution. *Enrollment:* 1,584 full-time matriculated graduate/professional students, 361 part-time matriculated graduate/professional students. *Graduate faculty:* 19 full-time, 909 part-time/adjunct. *Tuition:* Full-time $9,696; part-time $404 per credit. *Graduate housing:* On-campus housing not available. *Student services:* Campus safety program. *Library facilities:* University Library. *Online resources:* library catalog, web page. *Collection:* 17.5 million titles, 9,000 serial subscriptions.

Computer facilities: A campuswide network can be accessed from off campus. Internet access is available. *Web address:* http://www.phoenix.edu/.

General Application Contact: 714-378-1878, Fax: 714-378-5856.

GRADUATE UNITS

College of Education Students: 76 full-time, 308 part-time. Average age 35. Expenses: Contact institution. *Financial support:* Applicants required to submit FAFSA. *Degree program information:* Evening/weekend programs available. Postbaccalaureate distance learning degree programs offered (no on-campus study). Offers curriculum and instruction (MA Ed); curriculum and technology (MA Ed). *Application deadline:* Applications are processed on a rolling basis. *Application fee:* $85. *Application Contact:* 714-378-1878, Fax: 714-378-5856. *Dean*, Dr. Marla LaRue, 480-557-1218, E-mail: marla.larue@phoenix.edu.

College of Graduate Business and Management Students: 1,415 full-time. Average age 35. Expenses: Contact institution. *Financial support:* Applicants required to submit FAFSA. In 2001, 413 degrees awarded. *Degree program information:* Evening/weekend programs available. Postbaccalaureate distance learning degree programs offered (no on-campus study). Offers business administration (MBA); health care management (MBA); organizational management (MAOM); technology management (MBA). *Application deadline:* Applications are processed on a rolling basis. *Application fee:* $85. *Application Contact:* 714-378-1878, Fax: 714-378-5856. *Dean*, Dr. Brian Lindquist, 480-557-1221, E-mail: brian.lindquist@phoenix.edu.

College of Health Care Sciences and Nursing Students: 93 full-time. Average age 35. Expenses: Contact institution. *Financial support:* Applicants required to submit FAFSA. In 2001, 78 degrees awarded. *Degree program information:* Evening/weekend programs available. Postbaccalaureate distance learning degree programs offered (no on-campus study). Offers family nurse practitioner (MSN); nursing (MSN). *Application deadline:* Applications are processed on a rolling basis. *Application fee:* $85. *Application Contact:* 714-398-1878, Fax: 714-378-5856. *Dean*, Dr. Catherine Garner, 480-557-1751, E-mail: catherine.garner@phoenix.edu.

UNIVERSITY OF PHOENIX–SOUTHERN COLORADO CAMPUS, Colorado Springs, CO 80919-2335

General Information Proprietary, coed, comprehensive institution. *Enrollment:* 269 full-time matriculated graduate/professional students, 18 part-time matriculated graduate/professional students. *Graduate faculty:* 8 full-time, 165 part-time/adjunct. *Tuition:* Full-time $7,698; part-time $321 per credit. Full-time tuition and fees vary according to program. *Graduate housing:* On-campus housing not available. *Student services:* Campus safety program. *Library facilities:* University Library. *Online resources:* library catalog, web page. *Collection:* 17.5 million titles, 9,000 serial subscriptions.

Computer facilities: A campuswide network can be accessed from off campus. Internet access is available. *Web address:* http://www.phoenix.edu/.

General Application Contact: 719-599-5282, Fax: 719-599-7973.

GRADUATE UNITS

College of Education Students: 83 full-time. Average age 34. Expenses: Contact institution. *Financial support:* Applicants required to submit FAFSA. *Degree program information:* Evening/weekend programs available. Postbaccalaureate distance learning degree programs offered (no on-campus study). Offers education (MA Ed). *Application fee:* $85. *Associate Dean*, Dr. Marla LaRue, 480-552-1218, E-mail: marla.larue@phoenix.edu.

College of Graduate Business and Management Students: 130 full-time. Average age 34. Expenses: Contact institution. *Financial support:* Applicants required to submit FAFSA. *Degree program information:* Evening/weekend programs available. Postbaccalaureate distance learning degree programs offered (no on-campus study). Offers business administration (MBA); organizational management (MAOM); technology management (MBA). *Application deadline:* Applications are processed on a rolling basis. *Application fee:* $85. *Dean*, Dr. Brian Lindquist, 480-557-1221, E-mail: brian.lindquist@phoenix.edu.

College of Health Care Sciences and Nursing Students: 14 full-time. Average age 35. Expenses: Contact institution. *Financial support:* Applicants required to submit FAFSA. *Degree program information:* Evening/weekend programs available. Postbaccalaureate distance learning degree programs offered (no on-campus study). Offers healthcare sciences and nursing (MSN). *Application deadline:* Applications are processed on a rolling basis. *Application fee:* $85. *Dean*, Dr. Catherine Garner, 480-557-1751, E-mail: catherine.garner@phoenix.edu.

College of Information Systems and Technology Students: 23 full-time, 18 part-time. Average age 34. Expenses: Contact institution. *Financial support:* Applicants required to submit FAFSA. *Degree program information:* Evening/weekend programs available. Postbaccalaureate distance learning degree programs offered (no on-campus study). Offers information systems and technology (MSCIS). *Application deadline:* Applications are processed on a rolling basis. *Application fee:* $85. *Dean*, Dr. Adam Honea, 480-557-1659, E-mail: adam.honea@phoenix.edu.

UNIVERSITY OF PHOENIX–TAMPA CAMPUS, Tampa, FL 33637-1920

General Information Proprietary, coed, comprehensive institution. *Enrollment:* 548 full-time matriculated graduate/professional students. *Graduate faculty:* 8 full-time, 199 part-time/adjunct. *Tuition:* Full-time $7,320; part-time $305 per credit. *Graduate housing:* On-campus housing not available. *Student services:* Campus safety program. *Library facilities:* University Library. *Online resources:* library catalog, web page. *Collection:* 17.5 million titles, 9,000 serial subscriptions.

Computer facilities: A campuswide network can be accessed from off campus. Internet access is available. *Web address:* http://www.phoenix.edu/.

General Application Contact: 813-626-7911, Fax: 813-630-9377.

GRADUATE UNITS

College of Graduate Business and Management Students: 409 full-time. Average age 35. Expenses: Contact institution. *Financial support:* Applicants required to submit FAFSA. In 2001, 97 degrees awarded. *Degree program information:* Evening/weekend programs available. Postbaccalaureate distance learning degree programs offered (no on-campus study). Offers business administration (MBA); health care management (MBA); organizational management (MAOM); technology management (MBA). *Application deadline:* Applications are processed on a rolling basis. *Application fee:* $85. *Application Contact:* 813-626-7911, Fax: 813-630-9377. *Dean*, Dr. Brian Lindquist, 480-557-1221, E-mail: brian.lindquist@phoenix.edu.

College of Health Care Sciences and Nursing Students: 24 full-time. Expenses: Contact institution. *Financial support:* Applicants required to submit FAFSA. In 2001, 32 degrees awarded. *Degree program information:* Evening/weekend programs available. Postbaccalaureate distance learning degree programs offered (no on-campus study). Offers healthcare sciences and nursing (MSN). *Application deadline:* Applications are processed on a rolling basis. *Application fee:* $85. *Application Contact:* 813-626-7911, Fax: 813-630-9377. *Dean*, Dr. Catherine Garner, 480-557-1751, E-mail: catherine.garner@phoenix.edu.

College of Information Systems and Technology Students: 57 full-time, 58 part-time. Average age 35. Expenses: Contact institution. *Financial support:* Applicants required to submit FAFSA. In 2001, 38 degrees awarded. *Degree program information:* Evening/weekend programs available. Postbaccalaureate distance learning degree programs offered (no on-campus study). Offers information systems and technology (MSCIS). *Application deadline:* Applications are processed on a rolling basis. *Application fee:* $85. *Application Contact:* 813-626-7911, Fax: 813-630-9377. *Dean*, Dr. Adam Honea, 480-557-1659, E-mail: adam.honea@phoenix.edu.

UNIVERSITY OF PHOENIX–TULSA CAMPUS, Tulsa, OK 74146-3801

General Information Proprietary, coed, comprehensive institution. *Enrollment:* 190 full-time matriculated graduate/professional students, 21 part-time matriculated graduate/professional students. *Graduate faculty:* 8 full-time, 146 part-time/adjunct. *Tuition:* Full-time $8,040; part-time $335 per credit. *Graduate housing:* On-campus housing not available. *Student services:* Campus safety program. *Library facilities:* University Library. *Online resources:* library catalog, web page. *Collection:* 17.5 million titles, 9,000 serial subscriptions.

Computer facilities: A campuswide network can be accessed from off campus. Internet access is available. *Web address:* http://www.phoenix.edu/.

General Application Contact: 918-622-4877, Fax: 618-622-4981.

GRADUATE UNITS

College of Graduate Business and Management Students: 149 full-time. Average age 33. Expenses: Contact institution. *Financial support:* Applicants required to submit FAFSA. In 2001, 51 degrees awarded. *Degree program information:* Evening/weekend programs available. Postbaccalaureate distance learning degree programs offered (no on-campus study). Offers business administration (MBA); e-business (MBA); health care management (MBA); organizational management (MAOM). *Application deadline:* Applications are processed on a rolling basis. *Application fee:* $85. *Application Contact:* 918-622-4877, Fax: 918-622-4981. *Dean*, Dr. Brian Lindquist, 480-557-1221, E-mail: brian.lindquist@phoenix.edu.

College of Information Systems and Technology Students: 41 full-time, 21 part-time. Average age 33. Expenses: Contact institution. *Financial support:* Applicants required to submit FAFSA. *Degree program information:* Evening/weekend programs available. Postbaccalaureate distance learning degree programs offered (no on-campus study). Offers information systems and technology (MCSE, MSCIS). *Application deadline:* Applications are processed on a rolling basis. *Application fee:* $85. *Application Contact:* 918-622-4877, Fax: 918-622-4981. *Dean*, Dr. Adam Honea, 480-557-1659, E-mail: adam.honea@phoenix.edu.

UNIVERSITY OF PHOENIX–UTAH CAMPUS, Salt Lake City, UT 84123-4617

General Information Proprietary, coed, comprehensive institution. *Enrollment:* 1,044 full-time matriculated graduate/professional students. *Graduate faculty:* 14 full-time, 329 part-time/adjunct. *Tuition:* Full-time $7,315; part-time $305 per credit. Full-time tuition and fees vary according to program. *Graduate housing:* On-campus housing not available. *Student services:* Campus safety program. *Library facilities:* University Library. *Online resources:* library catalog, web page. *Collection:* 17.5 million titles, 9,000 serial subscriptions.

Computer facilities: A campuswide network can be accessed from off campus. Internet access is available. *Web address:* http://www.phoenix.edu/.

General Application Contact: 801-263-1444, Fax: 801-269-9766.

GRADUATE UNITS

College of Counseling and Human Services Students: 176 full-time. Average age 35. Expenses: Contact institution. *Financial support:* Applicants required to submit FAFSA. In 2001, 50 degrees awarded. *Degree program information:* Evening/weekend programs available. Postbaccalaureate distance learning degree programs offered (no on-campus study). Offers counseling and human services (MC). *Application deadline:* Applications are processed on a rolling basis. *Application fee:* $85. *Dean*, Dr. Patrick Romine, 480-557-1074, E-mail: patrick.romine@phoenix.edu.

College of Education Students: 317 full-time. Average age 35. Expenses: Contact institution. *Financial support:* Applicants required to submit FAFSA. In 2001, 136 degrees awarded. *Degree program information:* Evening/weekend programs available. Postbaccalaureate distance learning degree programs offered (no on-campus study). Offers education (MA Ed). *Application deadline:* Applications are processed on a rolling basis. *Application fee:* $85. *Associate Dean*, Dr. Marla LaRue, 480-557-1218, E-mail: marla.larue@phoenix.edu.

College of Graduate Business and Management Students: 470 full-time. Average age 35. Expenses: Contact institution. *Financial support:* Applicants required to submit FAFSA. In 2001, 181 degrees awarded. *Degree program information:* Evening/weekend programs available. Postbaccalaureate distance learning degree programs offered (no on-campus study). Offers business administration (MBA); global management (MBA); organizational management (MAOM). *Application deadline:* Applications are processed on a rolling basis. *Application fee:* $85. *Dean*, Dr. Brian Lindquist, 480-557-1221, E-mail: brian.lindquist@phoenix.edu.

College of Health Care Sciences and Nursing Students: 42 full-time. Average age 35. Expenses: Contact institution. *Financial support:* Applicants required to submit FAFSA. In 2001, 9 degrees awarded. *Degree program information:* Evening/weekend programs available. Postbaccalaureate distance learning degree programs offered (no on-campus study). Offers nursing (MSN). *Application deadline:* Applications are processed on a rolling basis. *Application fee:* $85. *Dean*, Dr. Catherine Garner, 480-557-1751, E-mail: catherine.garner@phoenix.edu.

College of Information Systems and Technology Students: 74 full-time. Average age 35. Expenses: Contact institution. *Financial support:* Applicants required to submit FAFSA. In 2001, 28 degrees awarded. *Degree program information:* Evening/weekend programs available. Postbaccalaureate distance learning degree programs offered (no on-campus study). Offers information systems and technology (MSCIS). *Application deadline:* Applications are processed on a rolling basis. *Application fee:* $85. *Dean*, Dr. Adam Honea, 480-557-1659, E-mail: adam.honea@phoenix.edu.

UNIVERSITY OF PHOENIX-VANCOUVER CAMPUS, Burnaby, BC V5C 6G9, Canada

General Information Proprietary, coed, comprehensive institution. *Enrollment:* 126 full-time matriculated graduate/professional students. *Graduate faculty:* 28. *Tuition:* Full-time $9,840; part-time $410 per credit. Full-time tuition and fees vary according to program. *Graduate housing:* On-campus housing not available. *Student services:* Campus safety program. *Library facilities:* University Library. *Online resources:* library catalog, web page. *Collection:* 17.5 million titles, 9,000 serial subscriptions.

Computer facilities: A campuswide network can be accessed from off campus. Internet access is available. *Web address:* http://www.phoenix.edu/.

General Application Contact: Campus Information Center, 604-205-6999.

GRADUATE UNITS

College of Education Students: 18 full-time. Average age 35. *Faculty:* 24 part-time/adjunct. Expenses: Contact institution. *Degree program information:* Evening/weekend programs available. Postbaccalaureate distance learning degree programs offered (no on-campus study). Offers curriculum and instruction (MA Ed). *Application deadline:* Applications are processed on a rolling basis. *Application fee:* $85. *Associate Dean*, Dr. Marla Larue, 480-557-1218, E-mail: marla.larue@phoenix.edu.

College of Graduate Business and Management Students: 106 full-time. Average age 35. Expenses: Contact institution. In 2001, 30 degrees awarded. *Degree program information:* Evening/weekend programs available. Postbaccalaureate distance learning degree programs offered (no on-campus study). Offers business administration (MBA); organizational management (MAOM). *Application deadline:* Applications are processed on a rolling basis. *Application fee:* $85. *Dean*, Dr. Brian Lindquist, 480-557-1221, E-mail: brian.lindquist@phoenix.edu.

UNIVERSITY OF PHOENIX–WASHINGTON CAMPUS, Seattle, WA 98188-7500

General Information Proprietary, coed, comprehensive institution. *Enrollment:* 356 full-time matriculated graduate/professional students. *Enrollment by degree level:* 356 master's. *Graduate faculty:* 9 full-time, 267 part-time/adjunct. *Tuition:* Full-time $7,848; part-time $327 per credit. *Graduate housing:* On-campus housing not available. *Student services:* Campus safety program. *Library facilities:* University Library. *Online resources:* library catalog, web page. *Collection:* 17.5 million titles, 9,000 serial subscriptions.

Computer facilities: A campuswide network can be accessed from off campus. Internet access is available. *Web address:* http://www.phoenix.edu/.

General Application Contact: 877-877-4867.

University of Phoenix–Washington Campus (continued)

GRADUATE UNITS

College of Graduate Business and Management Students: 356 full-time. Average age 33. Expenses: Contact institution. *Financial support:* Applicants required to submit FAFSA. In 2001, 75 degrees awarded. *Degree program information:* Evening/weekend programs available. Postbaccalaureate distance learning degree programs offered (no on-campus study). Offers business administration (MBA); organizational management (MAOM); technology management (MBA). *Application deadline:* Applications are processed on a rolling basis. *Application fee:* $85. *Dean,* Dr. Brian Lindquist, 480-557-1221, E-mail: brian.lindquist@phoenix.edu.

UNIVERSITY OF PHOENIX–WEST MICHIGAN CAMPUS, Grand Rapids, MI 49544-1683

General Information Proprietary, coed, comprehensive institution. *Enrollment:* 156 full-time matriculated graduate/professional students. *Enrollment by degree level:* 156 master's. *Graduate faculty:* 6 full-time, 83 part-time/adjunct. *Tuition:* Full-time $9,120; part-time $380 per credit. *Graduate housing:* On-campus housing not available. *Student services:* Campus safety program. *Library facilities:* University Library. *Online resources:* library catalog, web page. *Collection:* 17.5 million titles, 9,000 serial subscriptions.

Computer facilities: A campuswide network can be accessed from off campus. Internet access is available. *Web address:* http://www.phoenix.edu/.

General Application Contact: 888-345-9699.

GRADUATE UNITS

College of Graduate Business and Management Students: 68 full-time. Average age 34. Expenses: Contact institution. *Financial support:* Applicants required to submit FAFSA. *Degree program information:* Evening/weekend programs available. Postbaccalaureate distance learning degree programs offered (no on-campus study). Offers business administration (MBA); e-business (MBA); health care management (MBA); organizational management (MAOM); technology management (MBA). *Application deadline:* Applications are processed on a rolling basis. *Application fee:* $85. *Dean,* Dr. Brian Lindquist, 480-557-1221, E-mail: brian.lindquist@phoenix.edu.

College of Health Care Sciences and Nursing Students: 24 full-time. Average age 34. Expenses: Contact institution. *Financial support:* Applicants required to submit FAFSA. *Degree program information:* Evening/weekend programs available. Postbaccalaureate distance learning degree programs offered (no on-campus study). Offers health care sciences and nursing (MSN). *Application deadline:* Applications are processed on a rolling basis. *Application fee:* $85. *Dean,* Dr. Catherine Garner, 480-557-1751, E-mail: catherine.garner@phoenix.edu.

UNIVERSITY OF PHOENIX-WISCONSIN CAMPUS, Brookfield, WI 53005

General Information Proprietary, coed, comprehensive institution.

GRADUATE UNITS

College of Graduate Business and Management

UNIVERSITY OF PITTSBURGH, Pittsburgh, PA 15260

General Information State-related, coed, university. CGS member. *Enrollment:* 6,057 full-time matriculated graduate/professional students (3,089 women), 2,860 part-time matriculated graduate/professional students (1,687 women). *Enrollment by degree level:* 1,867 first professional, 7,045 master's. *Graduate faculty:* 3,253 full-time (1,079 women), 664 part-time/adjunct (324 women). Tuition, state resident: full-time $9,410; part-time $385 per credit. Tuition, nonresident: full-time $19,376; part-time $797 per credit. *Required fees:* $480; $90 per term. Tuition and fees vary according to program. *Graduate housing:* Rooms and/or apartments available to single and married students. *Student services:* Campus employment opportunities, campus safety program, career counseling, child daycare facilities, disabled student services, exercise/wellness program, free psychological counseling, international student services, low-cost health insurance. *Library facilities:* Hillman Library plus 26 others. *Online resources:* library catalog, web page, access to other libraries' catalogs. *Collection:* 3.6 million titles, 22,058 serial subscriptions, 926,142 audiovisual materials. *Research affiliation:* Oak Ridge Associated Universities, Ben Franklin Technology Center of Western Pennsylvania.

Computer facilities: 600 computers available on campus for general student use. A campuswide network can be accessed from student residence rooms and from off campus. Internet access and online class registration, on-line class listings are available. *Web address:* http://www.pitt.edu/.

GRADUATE UNITS

Center for Neuroscience Students: 75 full-time (34 women); includes 8 minority (5 Asian Americans or Pacific Islanders, 3 Hispanic Americans), 20 international. Average age 26. 132 applicants, 26% accepted, 15 enrolled. *Faculty:* 74 full-time (16 women). Expenses: Contact institution. *Financial support:* In 2001–02, 22 fellowships with full tuition reimbursements, 47 research assistantships with full tuition reimbursements, 6 teaching assistantships with full tuition reimbursements were awarded. Scholarships/grants, traineeships, and tuition waivers (full) also available. In 2001, 5 doctorates awarded. Offers neurobiology (PhD); neuroscience (PhD). *Application deadline:* For fall admission, 1/2 (priority date). *Application fee:* $40. Electronic applications accepted. *Application Contact:* Joan M. Blaney, Administrator, 412-624-5043, Fax: 412-624-9198, E-mail: jblaney@pitt.edu. *Co-Director, Graduate Program,* Dr. J. Patrick Card, 412-624-5043, Fax: 412-624-9188, E-mail: card@bns.pitt.edu.

Faculty of Arts and Sciences Students: 1,476. *Faculty:* 696. Expenses: Contact institution. *Financial support:* In 2001–02, 795 students received support; fellowships with full tuition reimbursements available, research assistantships with full tuition reimbursements available, teaching assistantships with full and partial tuition reimbursements available, career-related internships or fieldwork, Federal Work-Study, institutionally sponsored loans, scholarships/grants, traineeships, health care benefits, tuition waivers (full and partial), and unspecified assistantships available. Support available to part-time students. Financial award applicants required to submit FAFSA. In 2001, 147 master's, 113 doctorates, 19 other advanced degrees awarded. *Degree program information:* Part-time programs available. Offers anthropology (MA, PhD); applied mathematics (MA, MS); applied statistics (MA, MS); arts and sciences (MA, MFA, MS, PM Sc, PhD, Certificate); astronomy (MS, PhD); bioethics (MA); chemistry (MS, PhD); classics (MA, PhD); communication (MA, PhD); computer science (MS, PhD); cultural and critical studies (PhD); East Asian studies (MA); ecology and evolution (MS, PhD); English (MA); French (MA, PhD); geographical information systems (PM Sc); geology and planetary science (MS, PhD); Germanic languages and literatures (MA, PhD); Hispanic languages and literatures (MA, PhD); history (MA, PhD); history and philosophy of science (MA, PhD); history of art and architecture (MA, PhD); intelligent systems (MS, PhD); Italian (MA); linguistics (MA, PhD); mathematics (MA, MS, PhD); molecular biophysics (PhD); molecular, cellular, and developmental biology (PhD); music (MA, PhD); performance pedagogy (MFA); philosophy (MA, PhD); physics (MS, PhD); political science (MA, PhD); psychology (MS, PhD); religion (PhD); religious studies (MA); Slavic languages and literatures (MA, PhD); sociology (MA, PhD); statistics (MA, MS, PhD); teaching English as another language (MA, Certificate); theatre and performance studies (MA, PhD); women's studies (Certificate); writing (MFA). *Application deadline:* Applications are processed on a rolling basis. *Application fee:* $40. Electronic applications accepted. *Application Contact:* Elspeth Wissner, Administrative Secretary, 412-624-6094, Fax: 412-624-6855, E-mail: wissner@fcas.pitt.edu. *Associate Dean, Graduate Studies and Research,* Dr. Steven Husted, 412-624-6094, Fax: 412-624-6855, E-mail: husted@fcas.pitt.edu.

Center for Latin American Studies Students: 150 full-time (89 women), 18 part-time (11 women); includes 15 minority (6 African Americans, 9 Hispanic Americans), 89 international. *Faculty:* 122 full-time (31 women), 16 part-time/adjunct (7 women). Expenses: Contact institution. *Financial support:* In 2001–02, 32 students received support, including 16 fellowships; career-related internships or fieldwork, scholarships/grants, tuition waivers (full and partial), and unspecified assistantships also available. Support available to part-time students. Financial award application deadline: 2/28. In 2001, 19 degrees awarded. Offers Latin American studies (Certificate). Students must be enrolled in a separate degree granting program to attain the Certificate. *Application deadline:* Applications are processed on a rolling basis. *Application Contact:* Shirley A. Kregar, Associate Director for Academic Affairs, 412-648-7396, Fax: 412-648-2199, E-mail: kregar@ucis.pitt.edu. *Director,* Kathleen M. DeWalt, 412-648-7391, Fax: 412-648-2199, E-mail: kmdewalt@ucis.pitt.edu.

Department of Economics Students: 40 full-time (11 women), 2 part-time (1 woman). Average age 28. 385 applicants, 7% accepted, 11 enrolled. *Faculty:* 20 full-time (3 women), 2 part-time/adjunct (both women). Expenses: Contact institution. *Financial support:* In 2001–02, 7 fellowships with full tuition reimbursements (averaging $12,465 per year), 4 research assistantships with full tuition reimbursements (averaging $12,465 per year), 27 teaching assistantships with full tuition reimbursements (averaging $11,980 per year) were awarded. Career-related internships or fieldwork, Federal Work-Study, institutionally sponsored loans, scholarships/grants, traineeships, health care benefits, tuition waivers (full and partial), and unspecified assistantships also available. Support available to part-time students. Financial award application deadline: 2/1; financial award applicants required to submit FAFSA. In 2001, 4 master's, 2 doctorates awarded. *Degree program information:* Part-time programs available. Offers economics (MA, PhD). *Application deadline:* For fall admission, 2/1 (priority date). Applications are processed on a rolling basis. *Application fee:* $40. *Application Contact:* Terri Waters, Administrative/Graduate Secretary, 412-648-1399, Fax: 412-648-1793, E-mail: tmw40@pitt.edu. *Department Chair,* Dr. Jean-François Richard, 412-648-2821, Fax: 412-648-1793, E-mail: fantin@pitt.edu.

Graduate School of Public and International Affairs Students: 290 full-time (159 women), 107 part-time (62 women); includes 51 minority (39 African Americans, 6 Asian Americans or Pacific Islanders, 6 Hispanic Americans), 105 international. Average age 25. 512 applicants, 71% accepted, 161 enrolled. *Faculty:* 32 full-time (8 women), 12 part-time/adjunct (9 women). Expenses: Contact institution. *Financial support:* In 2001–02, 112 students received support, including 31 fellowships (averaging $17,000 per year), 1 research assistantship (averaging $21,500 per year), 5 teaching assistantships (averaging $7,700 per year); career-related internships or fieldwork, scholarships/grants, tuition waivers (full and partial), unspecified assistantships, and graduate student assistantships also available. Financial award application deadline: 2/1. In 2001, 144 master's, 4 doctorates awarded. *Degree program information:* Part-time programs available. Offers criminal justice (MPPM); development planning (MPPM); environmental management and policy (MPPM); international development (MPPM); international political economy (MPPM); international security studies (MPPM); management of non profit organizations (MPPM); metropolitan management and regional development (MPPM); personnel and labor relations (MPPM); policy analysis and evaluation (MPPM); public and international affairs (MID, MPA, MPIA, MPPM, PhD). *Application deadline:* For fall and spring admission, 3/1 (priority date); for winter admission, 10/1. Applications are processed on a rolling basis. *Application fee:* $40. Electronic applications accepted. *Application Contact:* Elizabeth Barthen-Braunsdorf, Assistant Director of Admissions, 412-648-7643, Fax: 412-648-7641, E-mail: barthen@bitch.gspia.pitt.edu. *Dean,* Dr. Carolyn Ban, 412-648-7662, Fax: 412-648-2605, E-mail: cban@birch.gspia.pitt.edu.

Division of International Development Students: 56 full-time (39 women), 8 part-time (7 women); includes 12 minority (7 African Americans, 4 Asian Americans or Pacific Islanders, 1 Hispanic American), 21 international. Average age 26. 114 applicants, 82% accepted, 35 enrolled. *Faculty:* 32 full-time (8 women), 12 part-time/adjunct (9 women). Expenses: Contact institution. *Financial support:* In 2001–02, 15 students received support, including 3 fellowships (averaging $20,260 per year), 3 research assistantships; career-related internships or fieldwork, scholarships/grants, tuition waivers (full and partial), and unspecified assistantships also available. Financial award application deadline: 2/1. In 2001, 27 degrees awarded. *Degree program information:* Part-time programs available. Offers development planning and environmental sustainability (MPIA); governmental organizations and civil society (MPIA). *Application deadline:* For fall admission, 3/1 (priority date); for spring admission, 10/1 (priority date). Applications are processed on a rolling basis. *Application fee:* $40. Electronic applications accepted. *Application Contact:* Maureen O'Malley, Admissions Counselor, 412-648-7646, Fax: 412-648-7641, E-mail: pronobis@birch.gspia.pitt.edu. *Director, International Development Division,* Dr. Paul J. Nelson, 412-648-7645, Fax: 412-648-2605, E-mail: pjnelson@birch.gspia.pitt.edu.

Division of Public and Urban Affairs Students: 59 full-time (37 women), 21 part-time (15 women); includes 12 minority (all African Americans), 8 international. Average age 27. 115 applicants, 67% accepted, 38 enrolled. *Faculty:* 32 full-time (8 women), 12 part-time/adjunct (9 women). Expenses: Contact institution. *Financial support:* In 2001–02, 36 students received support. In 2001, 19 degrees awarded. Offers policy research and analysis (MPA); public and urban affairs (MPA); public management and policy (MPA); urban and regional affairs (MPA). *Application Contact:* Maureen O'Malley, Admissions Counselor, 412-648-7646, Fax: 412-648-7641, E-mail: pronobis@birch.gspia.pitt.edu. *Director, Public and Urban Affairs Division,* Dr. Stephen Farber, 412-648-7602, Fax: 412-648-2605, E-mail: eofarb@birch.gspia.pitt.edu.

Doctoral Program in Public and International Affairs Students: 60 full-time (17 women), 12 part-time (4 women); includes 4 minority (2 African Americans, 1 Asian American or Pacific Islander, 1 Hispanic American), 45 international. Average age 30. 81 applicants, 41% accepted, 14 enrolled. *Faculty:* 32 full-time (8 women), 12 part-time/adjunct (9 women). Expenses: Contact institution. *Financial support:* In 2001–02, 15 students received support, including 12 fellowships (averaging $21,500 per year), 1 research assistantship (averaging $21,500 per year), 5 teaching assistantships (averaging $7,700 per year); career-related internships or fieldwork, scholarships/grants, unspecified assistantships, and graduate student assistantships also available. Financial award application deadline: 2/1. In 2001, 3 degrees awarded. *Degree program information:* Part-time programs available. Offers development studies (PhD); foreign and security policy (PhD); international political economy (PhD); public administration (PhD); public policy (PhD). *Application deadline:* For fall admission, 3/1 (priority date). Applications are processed on a rolling basis. *Application fee:* $40. Electronic applications accepted. *Application Contact:* Elizabeth Barthen-Braunsdorf, Assistant Director of Admissions, 412-648-7643, Fax: 412-648-7641, E-mail: barthen@bitch.gspia.pitt.edu. *Doctoral Program Coordinator,* Dr. William F. Matlack, 412-648-7604, E-mail: wfm@birch.gspia.pitt.edu.

International Affairs Division Students: 93 full-time (54 women), 12 part-time (7 women); includes 11 minority (7 African Americans, 1 Asian American or Pacific Islander, 3 Hispanic Americans), 28 international. Average age 23. 166 applicants, 79% accepted, 55 enrolled. *Faculty:* 32 full-time (8 women), 12 part-time/adjunct (9 women). Expenses: Contact institution. *Financial support:* In 2001–02, 44 students received support, including 9 fellowships (averaging $14,240 per year); career-related internships or fieldwork, scholarships/grants, tuition waivers (full and partial), and unspecified assistantships also available. Financial award application deadline: 2/1. In 2001, 52 degrees awarded. *Degree program information:* Part-time and evening/weekend programs available. Offers global political economy (MPIA); security and intelligence studies (MPIA). *Application deadline:* For fall admission, 3/1 (priority date); for spring admission, 10/1 (priority date). Applications are processed on a rolling basis. *Application fee:* $40. Electronic applications accepted. *Application Contact:* Elizabeth Barthen-Braunsdorf, Assistant Director of Admissions, 412-648-7643, Fax: 412-648-7641, E-mail: barthen@bitch.gspia.pitt.edu. *Director, International Affairs Division,* Dr. Martin Staniland, 412-648-7656, Fax: 412-648-2605, E-mail: mstan@birch.gspia.pitt.edu.

Graduate School of Public Health Students: 296 full-time (218 women), 267 part-time (168 women). 602 applicants, 41% accepted, 196 enrolled. *Faculty:* 110 full-time (44 women), 7 part-time/adjunct (5 women). Expenses: Contact institution. *Financial support:* In 2001–02, 150 students received support, including 130 research assistantships with full tuition reimbursements available (averaging $17,000 per year), 5 teaching assistantships with full tuition reimbursements available (averaging $17,000 per year); fellowships with full tuition reimbursements available, career-related internships or fieldwork, Federal Work-Study, institutionally sponsored loans, scholarships/grants, traineeships, tuition waivers (partial), and unspecified assistantships also available. Support available to part-time students. Financial award applicants required to submit CSS PROFILE or FAFSA. In 2001, 101 master's, 15 doctorates awarded. *Degree program information:* Part-time programs available. Offers behavioral and community health services (MHPE, MPH); biostatistics (MPH, MS, Dr PH, PhD); environmental and occupational health (MPH, MS, PhD); epidemiology (MPH, MS, Dr PH, PhD); genetic counseling (MS); health administration (MHA); health services administration (Dr PH); human genetics (MS, PhD); infectious diseases and microbiology (MPH, MS, Dr PH, PhD); Latin American studies (Certificate); non-profit organization (Certificate); occupational medicine (MPH); public health (MHA, MHPE, MPH, MS, Dr PH, PhD, Certificate); public health/aging (Certificate); radiation health (MS, Certificate). *Application deadline:* Applications are processed on a rolling basis. *Application fee:* $50 ($60 for international students). Electronic applications accepted. *Application Contact:* 412-624-5200, Fax: 412-624-3755, E-mail: stuaff@gsphedean.gsph.pitt.edu. *Dean*, Dr. Bernard D. Goldstein, 412-624-3001, Fax: 412-624-1020, E-mail: goldstein@gsphdean.gsph.pitt.edu.

Joseph M. Katz Graduate School of Business Students: 357 full-time (84 women), 531 part-time (157 women); includes 113 minority (31 African Americans, 67 Asian Americans or Pacific Islanders, 15 Hispanic Americans), 95 international. *Faculty:* 73 full-time (15 women), 23 part-time/adjunct (5 women). Expenses: Contact institution. *Financial support:* Fellowships with tuition reimbursements, research assistantships with tuition reimbursements, teaching assistantships with tuition reimbursements, Federal Work-Study, institutionally sponsored loans, scholarships/grants, tuition waivers (full and partial), and unspecified assistantships available. Financial award applicants required to submit FAFSA. In 2001, 371 master's, 9 doctorates awarded. *Degree program information:* Part-time and evening/weekend programs available. Offers business (EMBA, MBA, MHA, MS, PhD); business administration (MBA, PhD); international business (MBA); international business administration (MBA); management of information systems (MS). *Application deadline:* Applications are processed on a rolling basis. Electronic applications accepted. *Dean*, Dr. Frederick W. Winter, 412-648-1561, Fax: 412-648-1552, E-mail: rickwinter@katz.business.pitt.edu.

School of Dental Medicine Students: 364 full-time (130 women); includes 83 minority (14 African Americans, 47 Asian Americans or Pacific Islanders, 21 Hispanic Americans, 1 Native American), 32 international. 1,768 applicants, 12% accepted. *Faculty:* 96 full-time (29 women), 155 part-time/adjunct (28 women). Expenses: Contact institution. *Financial support:* In 2001–02, 320 students received support; fellowships, Federal Work-Study, institutionally sponsored loans, scholarships/grants, and unspecified assistantships available. Financial award applicants required to submit FAFSA. In 2001, 80 first professional degrees, 11 master's awarded. Offers anesthesiology (Certificate); dental medicine (DMD, MD, MDS, MS, Certificate); endodontics (Certificate); oral and maxillofacial surgery (MD, Certificate); orthodontics (MDS, Certificate); pediatric dentistry (Certificate); periodontics (Certificate); prosthodontics (Certificate). Electronic applications accepted. *Application Contact:* Recruitment/Financial Aid Officer, 412-648-8437, Fax: 412-383-7316. *Dean*, Dr. Thomas W. Braun, 412-648-8900, Fax: 412-648-8219, E-mail: twb3@pitt.edu.

School of Education Students: 360 full-time (260 women), 734 part-time (500 women); includes 109 minority (88 African Americans, 8 Asian Americans or Pacific Islanders, 13 Hispanic Americans), 111 international. 741 applicants, 69% accepted, 382 enrolled. *Faculty:* 63 full-time (27 women), 6 part-time/adjunct (3 women). Expenses: Contact institution. *Financial support:* In 2001–02, 30 fellowships (averaging $2,500 per year), 40 research assistantships with partial tuition reimbursements (averaging $8,000 per year), 22 teaching assistantships with partial tuition reimbursements (averaging $8,000 per year) were awarded. Career-related internships or fieldwork, Federal Work-Study, traineeships, tuition waivers (partial), and unspecified assistantships also available. Support available to part-time students. Financial award applicants required to submit FAFSA. In 2001, 275 master's, 69 doctorates awarded. *Degree program information:* Part-time and evening/weekend programs available. Offers child development (MS); cognitive studies (PhD); deaf and hard of hearing (M Ed); developmental movement (MS); early childhood education (M Ed); early education of disabled students (M Ed); education (M Ed, MA, MAT, MHPE, MS, Ed D, PhD); education of students with mental and physical disabilities (M Ed); education of the visually impaired (M Ed); educational and developmental psychology (PhD); educational leadership development (M Ed, Ed D); elementary education (M Ed, MAT); English/communications education (M Ed, MAT, Ed D, PhD); exercise physiology (MS, PhD); foreign languages education (M Ed, MA, MAT, Ed D, PhD); general special education (M Ed); health promotion and education (MHPE); higher education (M Ed, Ed D); international development education (MA, PhD); international developmental education (M Ed); mathematics education (M Ed, MAT, Ed D); movement science (MS, PhD); reading education (M Ed, Ed D, PhD); research methodology (M Ed, MA, PhD); school leadership development (M Ed, Ed D); science education (M Ed, MAT, MS, Ed D); secondary education (M Ed, MA, MAT, MS, Ed D, PhD); social and comparative analysis (M Ed, MA, PhD); social studies education (M Ed, MAT, Ed D, PhD); social, philosophical, and historical foundations of education (M Ed, MA, PhD); special education (M Ed, Ed D, PhD). *Application deadline:* For fall admission, 2/1 (priority date). Applications are processed on a rolling basis. *Application fee:* $40. Electronic applications accepted. *Application Contact:* Jackie Harden, Manager, 412-648-2230, Fax: 412-648-1899, E-mail: soeinfo@pitt.edu. *Dean*, Dr. Alan Lesgold, 412-648-1773, Fax: 412-648-1825, E-mail: al@pitt.edu.

School of Engineering Students: 309 full-time (70 women), 203 part-time (31 women); includes 37 minority (12 African Americans, 20 Asian Americans or Pacific Islanders, 5 Hispanic Americans), 198 international. 1,180 applicants, 40% accepted, 132 enrolled. *Faculty:* 89 full-time (7 women), 25 part-time/adjunct (0 women). Expenses: Contact institution. *Financial support:* In 2001–02, 226 students received support, including 11 fellowships with full tuition reimbursements available (averaging $20,074 per year), 162 research assistantships with full tuition reimbursements available (averaging $18,118 per year), 53 teaching assistantships with full tuition reimbursements available (averaging $18,244 per year); scholarships/grants, traineeships, and tuition waivers (full and partial) also available. Financial award application deadline: 2/15. In 2001, 100 master's, 43 doctorates awarded. *Degree program information:* Part-time and evening/weekend programs available. Postbaccalaureate distance learning degree programs offered (no on-campus study). Offers bioengineering (MSBENG, PhD); chemical engineering (MS Ch E, PhD); civil and environmental engineering (MSCEE, PhD); electrical engineering (MSEE, PhD); engineering (MS Ch E, MS Met E, MSBENG, MSCEE, MSEE, MSIE, MSME, MSMSE, MSMfSE, MSPE, PhD, Certificate); industrial engineering (MSIE, PhD); manufacturing systems engineering (MSMfSE); materials science and engineering (MSMSE, PhD); mechanical engineering (MSME, PhD); metallurgical engineering (MS Met E, PhD); petroleum engineering (MSPE). *Application deadline:* For fall admission, 8/1 (priority date); for spring admission, 12/1 (priority date). Applications are processed on a rolling basis. *Application fee:* $40. *Application Contact:* 412-624-9800, Fax: 412-624-9808, E-mail: admin@engrng.pitt.edu. *Dean*, Dr. Gerald D. Holder, 412-624-9811, Fax: 412-624-0412, E-mail: holder@engrng.pitt.edu.

School of Health and Rehabilitation Sciences Students: 235 full-time (170 women), 85 part-time (56 women). 462 applicants, 27% accepted. *Faculty:* 71 full-time (43 women), 7 part-time/adjunct (5 women). Expenses: Contact institution. *Financial support:* In 2001–02, 35 research assistantships with partial tuition reimbursements (averaging $20,830 per year), 32 teaching assistantships with full tuition reimbursements (averaging $12,133 per year) were awarded. Fellowships with full tuition reimbursements, career-related internships or fieldwork, Federal Work-Study, institutionally sponsored loans, scholarships/grants, traineeships, and unspecified assistantships also available. Support available to part-time students. Financial award applicants required to submit FAFSA. In 2001, 106 master's, 2 doctorates awarded. *Degree program information:* Part-time and evening/weekend programs available. Offers communication science and disorders (MA, MS, PhD); health and rehabilitation sciences (MS); physical therapy (MPT); rehabilitation engineering (Certificate); rehabilitation science (PhD); rehabilitation technology (Certificate); rehabilitation technology service delivery (Certificate); sports medicine (MS). *Application deadline:* Applications are processed on a rolling basis. *Application fee:* $40. *Application Contact:* Shameem Gangjee, Director of Admissions, 412-383-6557, Fax: 412-383-6535, E-mail: shrsadmi+@pitt.edu. *Dean*, Dr. Clifford Brubaker, 412-647-1260, Fax: 412-647-1255, E-mail: cliffb+@pitt.edu.

School of Information Sciences *Degree program information:* Part-time and evening/weekend programs available. Offers information science (MSIS, PhD, Certificate); information sciences (MLIS, MSIS, MST, PhD, Certificate); library and information science (MLIS, PhD, Certificate); telecommunications (MST, Certificate).

School of Law Students: 766 full-time (366 women), 1 (woman) part-time; includes 72 minority (37 African Americans, 25 Asian Americans or Pacific Islanders, 9 Hispanic Americans, 1 Native American), 13 international. 1,490 applicants, 52% accepted, 294 enrolled. *Faculty:* 40 full-time (14 women), 1 part-time/adjunct (0 women). Expenses: Contact institution. *Financial support:* In 2001–02, 240 students received support, including 13 fellowships (averaging $1,200 per year), 36 research assistantships (averaging $4,760 per year); career-related internships or fieldwork, Federal Work-Study, scholarships/grants, and unspecified assistantships also available. Financial award applicants required to submit FAFSA. In 2001, 210 first professional degrees, 15 master's awarded. Offers business law (MSL); civil litigation (Certificate); constitutional law (MSL); criminal justice (MSL); dispute resolution (MSL); education law (MSL); elder and estate planning law (MSL); employment and labor law (MSL); environment and real estate law (MSL); environmental law (Certificate); family law (MSL); general law and jurisprudence (MSL); health law (MSL); intellectual property and cyber law (MSL); intellectual property and technology law (Certificate); international and comparative law (LL M, MSL); international law (Certificate); law (JD, LL M, MA, MSL, Certificate); personal injury and civil litigation (MSL); regulatory law (MSL); self-designed (MSL). *Application deadline:* For fall admission, 3/1. Applications are processed on a rolling basis. *Application fee:* $50. Electronic applications accepted. *Application Contact:* Fredi G. Miller, Assistant Dean, 412-648-1414, Fax: 412-648-2647, E-mail: miller@law.pitt.edu. *Dean*, David J. Herring, 412-648-1401, Fax: 412-648-2647, E-mail: herring@law.pitt.edu.

School of Medicine Students: 839. *Faculty:* 2,041. Expenses: Contact institution. *Financial support:* Fellowships with full tuition reimbursements, research assistantships with full tuition reimbursements, teaching assistantships with full tuition reimbursements, Federal Work-Study, institutionally sponsored loans, scholarships/grants, traineeships, health care benefits, and unspecified assistantships available. Financial award applicants required to submit FAFSA. *Degree program information:* Part-time programs available. Postbaccalaureate distance learning degree programs offered (minimal on-campus study). Offers biochemistry and molecular genetics (MS, PhD); biomedical informatics (MS, PhD, Certificate); biomedical sciences (PhD); cell biology and molecular physiology (MS, PhD); cellular and molecular pathology (MS, PhD); clinical research (MS, Certificate); immunology (MS, PhD); medical education (MS, Certificate); medicine (MD, MS, PhD, Certificate); molecular pharmacology (PhD); molecular virology and microbiology (MS, PhD); neurobiology (MS, PhD). *Application deadline:* Applications are processed on a rolling basis. *Application fee:* $40. Electronic applications accepted. *Application Contact:* Graduate Studies Administrator, 412-648-8957, Fax: 412-648-1236, E-mail: biomed_phd@fs1.dean-med.pitt.edu. *Dean*, Dr. Arthur S. Levine, 412-648-8975, Fax: 412-648-1236, E-mail: alevine@fs1.dean-med.pitt.edu.

School of Nursing Students: 138 full-time (98 women), 165 part-time (148 women); includes 12 minority (8 African Americans, 3 Asian Americans or Pacific Islanders, 1 Hispanic American), 2 international. Average age 36. 151 applicants, 60% accepted, 80 enrolled. *Faculty:* 71 full-time (65 women), 194 part-time/adjunct (176 women). Expenses: Contact institution. *Financial support:* In 2001–02, 1 fellowship, 33 research assistantships, 15 teaching assistantships were awarded. Career-related internships or fieldwork, Federal Work-Study, institutionally sponsored loans, scholarships/grants, and traineeships also available. Support available to part-time students. Financial award applicants required to submit FAFSA. In 2001, 83 master's, 9 doctorates awarded. *Degree program information:* Part-time programs available. Offers acute care nurse practitioner (MSN); administration (MSN); adult nurse practitioner (MSN); anesthesia nursing (MSN); family nurse practitioner (MSN); informatics (MSN); medical/surgical clinical nurse specialist (MSN); nursing (MSN, PhD); nursing education (MSN); pediatric nurse practitioner (MSN); psychiatric and mental health clinical nurse specialist (MSN); psychiatric primary care nurse practitioner (MSN); research (MSN). *Application deadline:* Applications are processed on a rolling basis. *Application fee:* $40. *Dean*, Dr. Jacqueline Dunbar-Jacob, 412-624-2400, Fax: 412-624-2401, E-mail: nursao+@pitt.edu.

School of Pharmacy Students: 360 full-time (228 women), 5 part-time (3 women). 234 applicants, 43% accepted. *Faculty:* 78 full-time (35 women), 72 part-time/adjunct (35 women). Expenses: Contact institution. *Financial support:* In 2001–02, 160 students received support, including 15 teaching assistantships with full tuition reimbursements available (averaging $11,520 per year); career-related internships or fieldwork, Federal Work-Study, institutionally sponsored loans, and scholarships/grants also available. Financial award application deadline: 9/1. In 2001, 77 first professional degrees, 3 doctorates awarded. Offers pharmaceutical sciences (MS, PhD); pharmacy (Pharm D, MS, PhD). *Application fee:* $40. *Application Contact:* Anna M. Stracci, Director of Student Affairs, 412-648-8579, Fax: 412-648-1086. *Interim Dean*, Dr. Patricia D. Kroboth, 412-624-3270, Fax: 412-648-1086.

School of Social Work Students: 350 full-time (300 women), 237 part-time (195 women); includes 85 minority (83 African Americans, 1 Hispanic American, 1 Native American), 19 international. Average age 31. 417 applicants, 54% accepted, 218 enrolled. *Faculty:* 16 full-time (7 women), 45 part-time/adjunct (32 women). Expenses: Contact institution. *Financial support:* In 2001–02, 79 students received support, including 4 research assistantships with full tuition reimbursements available (averaging $9,780 per year), 2 teaching assistantships with full tuition reimbursements available (averaging $11,980 per year); fellowships, career-related internships or fieldwork, institutionally sponsored loans, scholarships/grants, traineeships, tuition waivers, and unspecified assistantships also available. Financial award application deadline: 6/1; financial award applicants required to submit FAFSA. In 2001, 171 master's, 4 doctorates, 1 other advanced degree awarded. *Degree program information:* Part-time programs available. Postbaccalaureate distance learning degree programs offered (no on-campus study). Offers employee assistance (Certificate); employee assistance programs (Certificate); family and marital therapy (Certificate); gerontology (Certificate); social work (MSW, PhD, Certificate). *Application deadline:* For fall admission, 3/31. Applications are processed on a rolling basis. *Application fee:* $40. *Application Contact:* Dr. Grady H. Roberts, Associate Dean of Admissions, 412-624-6346, Fax: 412-624-6323. *Dean*, Dr. Larry E. Davis, 412-624-6304, Fax: 412-624-6323, E-mail: ledavis@pitt.edu.

See in-depth description on page 1239.

UNIVERSITY OF PORTLAND, Portland, OR 97203-5798

General Information Independent-religious, coed, comprehensive institution. *Enrollment:* 135 full-time matriculated graduate/professional students (72 women), 302 part-time matriculated graduate/professional students (188 women). *Enrollment by degree level:* 437 master's. *Graduate faculty:* 84 full-time (26 women), 11 part-time/adjunct (5 women). *Tuition:* Part-time $600 per semester hour. Tuition and fees vary according to program. *Graduate housing:* Room and/or apartments available to single students; on-campus housing not available to married students. Housing application deadline: 7/1. *Student services:* Campus employment opportunities, campus safety program, career counseling, disabled student services, exercise/wellness program, free psychological counseling, international student services, low-cost health insurance, multicultural affairs office, teacher training, writing training. *Library facilities:* Wilson M. Clark Library plus 1 other. *Online resources:* library catalog, web page, access to other libraries' catalogs. *Collection:* 1,446 serial subscriptions, 7,827 audiovisual materials. *Research affiliation:* Oregon Graduate Institute of Science and Technology (applied engineering, applied physics), Kaiser Center Health Resources, Portland Area Nursing Consortium.

Computer facilities: 200 computers available on campus for general student use. A campuswide network can be accessed from student residence rooms and from off campus. Internet access is available. *Web address:* http://www.up.edu/.

General Application Contact: Dr. Patricia L. Chadwick, Assistant to the Academic Vice President and Dean of the Graduate School, 503-943-7107, Fax: 503-943-7178, E-mail: chadwick@up.edu.

GRADUATE UNITS

Graduate School Average age 35. 422 applicants, 80% accepted. *Faculty:* 84 full-time (26 women), 11 part-time/adjunct (5 women). Expenses: Contact institution. *Financial support:* Career-related internships or fieldwork, Federal Work-Study, and institutionally sponsored loans available. Support available to part-time students. Financial award application deadline: 3/15. In 2001, 211 degrees awarded. *Degree program information:* Part-time and evening/weekend programs available. Postbaccalaureate distance learning degree programs offered (minimal on-campus study). *Application deadline:* Applications are processed on a rolling basis. *Application fee:* $45. *Application Contact:* Marilyn Walker, Administrative Assistant, 503-943-7107, Fax: 503-943-7178, E-mail: walker@up.edu. *Assistant to the Academic Vice*

University of Portland (continued)

President and Dean of the Graduate School, Dr. Patricia L. Chadwick, 503-943-7107, Fax: 503-943-7178, E-mail: chadwick@up.edu.

College of Arts and Sciences Students: 8 full-time (5 women), 26 part-time (14 women). 35 applicants, 46% accepted. *Faculty:* 14 full-time (3 women), 1 part-time/adjunct (0 women). Expenses: Contact institution. *Financial support:* Teaching assistantships, career-related internships or fieldwork, Federal Work-Study, institutionally sponsored loans, and tuition waivers (partial) available. Support available to part-time students. Financial award application deadline: 3/15. In 2001, 14 degrees awarded. *Degree program information:* Part-time and evening/weekend programs available. Offers arts and sciences (MA, MFA, MS); communication studies (MA); drama (MFA); management communication (MS); music (MA); pastoral ministry (MA). *Application deadline:* For fall admission, 8/1 (priority date); for spring admission, 12/1. Applications are processed on a rolling basis. *Application fee:* $45. *Dean*, Dr. Marlene Moore, 503-943-7221, E-mail: moorem@up.edu.

Dr. Robert B. Pamplin, Jr. School of Business Students: 65 full-time (25 women), 82 part-time (34 women). 112 applicants, 83% accepted. *Faculty:* 24 full-time (5 women). Expenses: Contact institution. *Financial support:* Federal Work-Study, institutionally sponsored loans, and tuition waivers (partial) available. Support available to part-time students. Financial award application deadline: 3/15. In 2001, 51 degrees awarded. *Degree program information:* Part-time and evening/weekend programs available. Offers business (MBA). *Application deadline:* For fall admission, 8/1 (priority date); for spring admission, 12/1. Applications are processed on a rolling basis. *Application fee:* $45. *Application Contact:* Dr. Todd M. Shank, Graduate Program Director, 503-283-7226 Ext. 7279, E-mail: shank@up.edu. *Dean*, Dr. Larry Lewis, 503-943-7224.

Multnomah School of Engineering Students: 2 full-time (0 women), 1 part-time. 27 applicants, 63% accepted. *Faculty:* 16 full-time (0 women). Expenses: Contact institution. *Financial support:* Teaching assistantships, career-related internships or fieldwork, Federal Work-Study, and institutionally sponsored loans available. Support available to part-time students. Financial award application deadline: 3/15. In 2001, 5 degrees awarded. *Degree program information:* Part-time and evening/weekend programs available. Offers engineering (ME). *Application deadline:* For fall admission, 8/1 (priority date); for spring admission, 12/1. Applications are processed on a rolling basis. *Application fee:* $45. *Application Contact:* Dr. Khalid Khan, Graduate Program Director, 503-943-7276, E-mail: khan@up.edu. *Dean*, Dr. Zia Yamayee, 503-943-7314.

School of Education Students: 59 full-time (41 women), 150 part-time (101 women). 224 applicants, 85% accepted. *Faculty:* 19 full-time (8 women), 10 part-time/adjunct (5 women). Expenses: Contact institution. *Financial support:* Federal Work-Study and institutionally sponsored loans available. Support available to part-time students. Financial award application deadline: 3/15. In 2001, 136 degrees awarded. *Degree program information:* Part-time and evening/weekend programs available. Offers early childhood education (M Ed, MA, MAT); education (M Ed, MA, MAT); religious education (M Ed, MA); secondary education (M Ed, MA, MAT); special education (M Ed, MA). M Ed also available through the Graduate Outreach Program for teachers residing in the Oregon and Washington State areas. *Application deadline:* For fall admission, 8/1 (priority date); for spring admission, 12/1. Applications are processed on a rolling basis. *Application fee:* $45. *Dean*, Dr. Maria Ciriello, OP, 503-943-7135, Fax: 503-943-8042, E-mail: ciriello@up.edu.

School of Nursing Students: 1 (woman) full-time, 43 part-time (39 women). 24 applicants, 83% accepted. *Faculty:* 11 full-time (10 women). Expenses: Contact institution. *Financial support:* Fellowships, research assistantships, institutionally sponsored loans available. Support available to part-time students. Financial award application deadline: 3/15. In 2001, 5 degrees awarded. *Degree program information:* Part-time and evening/weekend programs available. Postbaccalaureate distance learning degree programs offered (minimal on-campus study). Offers family nurse practitioner (Post Master's Certificate); leadership in health care systems (Post Master's Certificate); nursing (MS); nursing education (Post Master's Certificate). *Application deadline:* Applications are processed on a rolling basis. *Application fee:* $45. *Dean*, Dr. Terry Misener, 503-943-7211, Fax: 503-943-7399, E-mail: misener@up.edu.

UNIVERSITY OF PRINCE EDWARD ISLAND, Charlottetown, PE C1A 4P3, Canada

General Information Province-supported, coed, comprehensive institution. *Graduate housing:* Rooms and/or apartments available on a first-come, first-served basis to single and married students. *Research affiliation:* Agriculture Canada Research Station, Diagnostic Chemicals, Ltd., Canadian Food Inspection Agency, AquaHealth.

GRADUATE UNITS

Atlantic Veterinary College *Degree program information:* Part-time programs available. Offers anatomy (M Sc, PhD); bacteriology (M Sc, PhD); clinical pharmacology (M Sc, PhD); clinical sciences (M Sc, PhD); epidemiology (M Sc, PhD); fish health (M Sc, PhD); food animal nutrition (M Sc, PhD); immunology (M Sc, PhD); microanatomy (M Sc, PhD); parasitology (M Sc, PhD); pathology (M Sc, PhD); pharmacology (M Sc, PhD); physiology (M Sc, PhD); toxicology (M Sc, PhD); veterinary medicine (DVM, M Sc, PhD); virology (M Sc, PhD).

UNIVERSITY OF PUERTO RICO, MAYAGÜEZ CAMPUS, Mayagüez, PR 00681-9000

General Information Commonwealth-supported, coed, university. CGS member. *Graduate housing:* Room and/or apartments available to married students; on-campus housing not available to single students. *Research affiliation:* Tropical Agriculture Research Station, Corporation for the Development and Administration of Marine Resources of Puerto Rico.

GRADUATE UNITS

Graduate Studies *Degree program information:* Part-time and evening/weekend programs available.

College of Agricultural Sciences *Degree program information:* Part-time programs available. Offers agricultural economics (MS); agricultural education (MS); agricultural extension (MS); agricultural sciences (MS); animal industry (MS); crop protection (MS); crops (MS); food technology (MS); horticulture (MS); soils (MS).

College of Arts and Sciences *Degree program information:* Part-time programs available. Offers applied mathematics (MS); arts and sciences (MA, MMS, MS, PhD); biological oceanography (MMS, PhD); biology (MS); chemical oceanography (MMS, PhD); chemistry (MS); computational sciences (MS); English (MA); geological oceanography (MMS, PhD); geology (MS); Hispanic studies (MA); physical oceanography (MMS, PhD); physics (MS); pure mathematics (MS); statistics (MS).

College of Business Administration *Degree program information:* Part-time and evening/weekend programs available. Offers business administration (MBA).

College of Engineering *Degree program information:* Part-time programs available. Offers chemical engineering (M Ch E, MS); civil engineering (MCE, MS, PhD); computer engineering (M Co E, MS); electrical engineering (MEE, MS); engineering (M Ch E, M Co E, MCE, MEE, MME, MMSE, MS, PhD); industrial engineering (MMSE); mechanical engineering (MME, MS).

UNIVERSITY OF PUERTO RICO, MEDICAL SCIENCES CAMPUS, San Juan, PR 00936-5067

General Information Commonwealth-supported, coed, primarily women, upper-level institution. *Graduate housing:* On-campus housing not available. *Research affiliation:* University of Kentucky Lexington (biomedical and clinical clinical research campus), National Institute of Deafness and Other Communications Disorders (biomedical and clinical research), National Institute of Health (biomedical and clinical research).

GRADUATE UNITS

College of Health Related Professions Students: 61 full-time (60 women), 62 part-time (51 women); all minorities (all Hispanic Americans) Average age 25. 147 applicants, 33% accepted, 44 enrolled. *Faculty:* 15 full-time (12 women), 18 part-time/adjunct (13 women). Expenses: Contact institution. *Financial support:* In 2001–02, 40 students received support, including 16 research assistantships with full tuition reimbursements available (averaging $7,000 per year), 5 teaching assistantships with full tuition reimbursements available (averaging $7,000 per year); career-related internships or fieldwork, Federal Work-Study, institutionally sponsored loans, and tuition waivers (partial) also available. Financial award application deadline: 4/30. In 2001, 38 degrees awarded. *Degree program information:* Part-time and evening/weekend programs available. Offers audiology (MS); clinical laboratory science (MS); health information management (MS); health related professions (MS); speech-language pathology (MS). *Application deadline:* For fall admission, 2/15 (priority date). Applications are processed on a rolling basis. *Application fee:* $25. *Application Contact:* Genoveva Ruiz, Student Affairs Office Director, 787-758-2525 Ext. 4000. *Dean*, Dr. Estela S. Estapé, 787-758-2525 Ext. 3209, Fax: 787-764-1760, E-mail: estelaestape@cprs.rem.upr.edu.

Graduate School of Public Health *Degree program information:* Part-time and evening/weekend programs available. Offers biostatistics (MPH); demography (MS); developmental disabilities-early intervention (Certificate); environmental health (MS, Dr PH); epidemiology (MPH, MS); evaluation research of health systems (MS); gerontology (MPH, Certificate); health education (MPHE); health science nutrition (MS); health services administration (MHSA); industrial hygiene (MS); mother and child health (MPH); nurse midwifery (MPH, Certificate); public health (MPH).

School of Dentistry Students: 190 full-time (91 women), 10 part-time (6 women). Average age 23. 206 applicants, 21% accepted, 40 enrolled. *Faculty:* 86 full-time (37 women), 23 part-time/adjunct (7 women). Expenses: Contact institution. *Financial support:* Research assistantships, teaching assistantships, Federal Work-Study, institutionally sponsored loans, tuition waivers (partial), and stipends available. In 2001, 48 DMDs, 17 other advanced degrees awarded. Offers dentistry (Certificate); general dentistry (MSD); oral and maxillofacial surgery (MSD); orthodontics (MSD); pediatric dentistry (MSD); prosthodontics (MSD). *Application deadline:* For fall admission, 12/15. *Application fee:* $15. *Application Contact:* Dr. Darrel F. Hillman, Assistant Dean, 787-758-2525 Ext. 1113, Fax: 787-751-0990, E-mail: dhillman@coqui.net. *Acting Dean*, Dr. Angel R. Pagan, 787-758-2525 Ext. 1105, Fax: 787-751-0990.

School of Medicine Students: 447 full-time (212 women); all minorities (all Hispanic Americans) 1,030 applicants, 14% accepted. *Faculty:* 330 full-time, 139 part-time/adjunct. Expenses: Contact institution. *Financial support:* Fellowships, research assistantships, teaching assistantships, career-related internships or fieldwork, Federal Work-Study, institutionally sponsored loans, and tuition waivers (full and partial) available. Support available to part-time students. In 2001, 102 degrees awarded. Offers medicine (MD, MS, PhD). *Application fee:* $15. *Application Contact:* Dr. Gladys González Navarrete, Assistant Dean for Student Affairs, 787-758-2525 Ext. 1810, Fax: 787-764-5740. *Dean*, Dr. Francisco Joglar, 787-758-2525 Ext. 1801.

Division of Graduate Studies Students: 59 full-time (33 women); all minorities (all Hispanic Americans) Average age 23. *Faculty:* 57 full-time (18 women). Expenses: Contact institution. *Financial support:* Fellowships, research assistantships, teaching assistantships, career-related internships or fieldwork, Federal Work-Study, institutionally sponsored loans, and tuition waivers (full and partial) available. Support available to part-time students. Financial award application deadline: 4/30. In 2001, 2 master's, 11 doctorates awarded. Offers anatomy (MS, PhD); biochemistry (MS, PhD); biomedical sciences (MS, PhD); medical zoology (MS, PhD); microbiology and medical zoology (MS, PhD); pharmacology and toxicology (MS, PhD); physiology (MS, PhD). *Application deadline:* For fall admission, 2/15. *Application fee:* $15. *Application Contact:* Julia M. Prado-Otero, Administrator Graduate Program, 787-758-2525 Ext. 7017, Fax: 787-767-8693, E-mail: jprado@rcm.upr.edu. *Associate Dean for Biomedical Sciences and Director Graduate Studies*, Dr. Walter I. Silva, 787-758-2525 Ext. 1831, Fax: 787-767-8693, E-mail: wsilva@rcm.upr.edu.

School of Nursing Students: 90 full-time (77 women), 77 part-time (62 women); all minorities (all Hispanic Americans) Average age 33. 52 applicants, 88% accepted, 36 enrolled. *Faculty:* 10 full-time (all women), 13 part-time/adjunct (9 women). Expenses: Contact institution. *Financial support:* In 2001–02, 76 students received support, including 6 research assistantships with full tuition reimbursements available (averaging $7,000 per year), 6 teaching assistantships with full tuition reimbursements available (averaging $7,000 per year); Federal Work-Study, scholarships/grants, traineeships, tuition waivers (full), and unspecified assistantships also available. Financial award application deadline: 6/30. In 2001, 60 degrees awarded. *Degree program information:* Evening/weekend programs available. Offers anesthesia (MSN); clinical specialist (MSN); nursing administration (MSN); nursing education (MSN). *Application deadline:* For fall admission, 3/21 (priority date). *Application fee:* $25. *Application Contact:* Rebecca Alberti, Director Graduate Department, 787-758-2525 Ext. 3105, Fax: 787-281-0721, E-mail: ecrouch@rcm.upr.edu. *Dean*, María E. Rosa, 787-758-2525 Ext. 2100, Fax: 787-281-0721, E-mail: mrosa@rcm.upr.edu.

School of Pharmacy Students: 74 full-time (60 women), 7 part-time (6 women); all minorities (1 Asian American or Pacific Islander, 80 Hispanic Americans) Average age 25. 110 applicants, 52% accepted. *Faculty:* 29 full-time (20 women), 3 part-time/adjunct (0 women). Expenses: Contact institution. *Financial support:* In 2001–02, 5 fellowships with partial tuition reimbursements, 10 research assistantships with full tuition reimbursements, 5 teaching assistantships with full tuition reimbursements were awarded. Career-related internships or fieldwork, Federal Work-Study, institutionally sponsored loans, scholarships/grants, and unspecified assistantships also available. In 2001, 2 degrees awarded. *Degree program information:* Part-time and evening/weekend programs available. Offers industrial pharmacy (MS); medicinal chemistry (MS); pharmaceutical sciences (MS); pharmacy (Pharm D). *Application deadline:* For fall admission, 2/15. *Application fee:* $15. *Application Contact:* Miriam Vélez, Assistant Dean of Student Affairs, 787-758-2525 Ext. 5407, Fax: 787-751-5680, E-mail: mivelez@rcm.upr.edu. *Assistant Dean for Graduate Affairs*, Dr. Ilia Oquendo, 787-758-2525 Ext. 5427, Fax: 787-751-5680, E-mail: ioquendo@rcm.upr.edu.

UNIVERSITY OF PUERTO RICO, RÍO PIEDRAS, San Juan, PR 00931

General Information Commonwealth-supported, coed, university. CGS member. *Enrollment:* 1,899 full-time matriculated graduate/professional students (1,270 women), 1,875 part-time matriculated graduate/professional students (1,241 women). *Enrollment by degree level:* 658 first professional, 2,478 master's, 587 doctoral, 51 other advanced degrees. *Graduate faculty:* 1,124 full-time (592 women), 748 part-time/adjunct (411 women). Tuition, commonwealth resident: full-time $1,200; part-time $70 per credit. Tuition, nonresident: full-time $3,500; part-time $219 per credit. *Required fees:* $70; $35 per semester. *Graduate housing:* Room and/or apartments available to single students; on-campus housing not available to married students. Typical cost: $4,180 (including board). Housing application deadline: 6/15. *Student services:* Campus employment opportunities, campus safety program, career counseling, child daycare facilities, free psychological counseling, low-cost health insurance. *Library facilities:* Jose M. Lazaro Library plus 10 others. *Online resources:* library catalog, access to other libraries' catalogs. *Collection:* 1.8 million titles, 5,599 serial subscriptions, 5,599 audiovisual materials. *Research affiliation:* National Laboratory for Ionospheric and Astrophysical Studies, Energetic and Environmental Center of Puerto Rico.

Computer facilities: 170 computers available on campus for general student use. A campuswide network can be accessed from student residence rooms. *Web address:* http://upracd.upr.clu.edu:9090/.

General Application Contact: Cruz B. Valentin-Arbelo, Admission Office Director, 787-764-0000 Ext. 5653.

GRADUATE UNITS

College of Education Students: 197 full-time (153 women), 370 part-time (310 women); includes 566 minority (all Hispanic Americans) Average age 44. 273 applicants, 61% accepted. Expenses: Contact institution. *Financial support:* Fellowships, research assistantships, teaching assistantships, career-related internships or fieldwork, Federal Work-Study, institutionally sponsored loans, and tuition waivers (partial) available. Financial award application deadline: 5/31. In 2001, 34 master's, 22 doctorates awarded. *Degree program information:* Part-time programs available. Offers biology education (M Ed); chemistry education (M Ed); child education (M Ed); curriculum and teaching (Ed D); education (M Ed, Ed D); educational research and evaluation (M Ed); English education (M Ed); family ecology and nutrition (M Ed); guidance and counseling (M Ed, Ed D); history education (M Ed); mathematics education (M Ed); physics education (M Ed); school administration and supervision (M Ed, Ed D); secondary education (M Ed); Spanish education (M Ed); special education (M Ed). *Application deadline:* For fall admission, 2/1. *Application fee:* $17. *Application Contact:* Juanita Rodríguez-Colón, Director of Graduate Education, 787-764-0000 Ext. 4368, Fax: 787-763-4130. *Dean*, Dr. María A. Irizarry, 787-764-0000 Ext. 2607, Fax: 787-763-4130.

College of Humanities Students: 229 full-time (149 women), 300 part-time (184 women); includes 520 minority (1 African American, 518 Hispanic Americans, 1 Native American), 8 international. Average age 44. 209 applicants, 69% accepted. Expenses: Contact institution. *Financial support:* Fellowships, research assistantships, teaching assistantships, Federal Work-Study, institutionally sponsored loans, and tuition waivers (partial) available. Financial award application deadline: 5/31. In 2001, 23 master's, 8 doctorates awarded. *Degree program information:* Part-time and evening/weekend programs available. Offers comparative literature (MA); English (MA); Hispanic studies (MA, PhD); history (MA, PhD); humanities (MA, PhD, Certificate); linguistics (MA); philosophy (MA); translation (MA, Certificate). *Application deadline:* For fall admission, 2/1. *Application fee:* $17. *Application Contact:* Samuel Pérez, Auxiliary Dean of Student Affairs, 787-764-0000 Ext. 3600, Fax: 787-763-5879. *Acting Dean*, Dr. José Luis Vega, 787-764-0000 Ext. 3525, Fax: 787-763-5879.

College of Social Sciences Students: 457 full-time (358 women), 455 part-time (322 women); includes 810 minority (all Hispanic Americans) Average age 22. 274 applicants, 62% accepted. Expenses: Contact institution. *Financial support:* Fellowships, research assistantships, teaching assistantships, career-related internships or fieldwork, Federal Work-Study, institutionally sponsored loans, and tuition waivers (partial) available. Financial award application deadline: 5/31. In 2001, 102 master's, 17 doctorates awarded. *Degree program information:* Part-time and evening/weekend programs available. Offers economics (MA); psychology (MA, PhD); social sciences (MA, MPA, MRC, MSW, PhD); sociology (MA). *Application deadline:* For fall admission, 2/1. *Application fee:* $17. *Application Contact:* Mildred Cordero, Auxiliary Dean of Student Affairs. *Acting Dean*, Dr. Carlos Severino-Valdés, 787-767-2040, Fax: 787-763-5599.

Beatriz Lassalle Graduate School of Social Work Students: 129 full-time (111 women), 34 part-time (27 women); all minorities (all Hispanic Americans) 61 applicants, 100% accepted. Expenses: Contact institution. *Financial support:* Fellowships, research assistantships, teaching assistantships, career-related internships or fieldwork, Federal Work-Study, institutionally sponsored loans, and tuition waivers (partial) available. Financial award application deadline: 5/31. In 2001, 38 degrees awarded. Offers social work (MSW). *Application deadline:* For fall admission, 2/1. *Application fee:* $17. *Application Contact:* Gladys N. Hernández, Student Affairs Officer, 787-764-0000 Ext. 5831, Fax: 787-763-3725. *Acting Chairperson*, Dr. Norma Rodriguez, 787-764-0000 Ext. 4256, Fax: 787-763-3725.

Graduate School of Rehabilitation Counseling Students: 93 full-time (80 women), 7 part-time (6 women); all minorities (all Hispanic Americans) *Faculty:* 8. Expenses: Contact institution. *Financial support:* Fellowships, research assistantships, teaching assistantships, career-related internships or fieldwork, Federal Work-Study, institutionally sponsored loans, and tuition waivers (partial) available. Financial award application deadline: 5/31. In 2001, 8 degrees awarded. *Degree program information:* Part-time and evening/weekend programs available. Offers rehabilitation counseling (MRC). *Application deadline:* For fall admission, 2/1. *Application fee:* $17. *Application Contact:* Luz M. Rivera, Administrative Officer, 787-764-0000 Ext. 2177, Fax: 787-764-0000 Ext. 1212. *Interim Chairperson*, Dr. Marilyn Mendoza-Lugo, 787-764-0000 Ext. 4206, Fax: 787-764-0000 Ext. 1212.

School of Public Administration Students: 53 full-time (39 women), 239 part-time (172 women); includes 291 minority (all Hispanic Americans) Expenses: Contact institution. *Financial support:* Fellowships, research assistantships, teaching assistantships, Federal Work-Study, institutionally sponsored loans, and tuition waivers (partial) available. Financial award application deadline: 5/31. In 2001, 41 degrees awarded. *Degree program information:* Part-time and evening/weekend programs available. Offers public administration (MPA). *Application deadline:* For fall admission, 2/1. *Application fee:* $17. *Chairperson*, José A. Punsoda-Días, 787-764-0000 Ext. 2097, Fax: 787-763-7510.

Faculty of Natural Sciences Students: 191 full-time (109 women), 128 part-time (52 women); includes 310 minority (1 African American, 290 Hispanic Americans, 19 Native Americans), 2 international. Average age 27. 127 applicants, 52% accepted. Expenses: Contact institution. *Financial support:* Fellowships, research assistantships, teaching assistantships, Federal Work-Study, institutionally sponsored loans, and tuition waivers (partial) available. Financial award application deadline: 5/31. In 2001, 17 master's, 27 doctorates awarded. *Degree program information:* Part-time and evening/weekend programs available. Offers applied physics (MS); biology (MS, PhD); chemistry (MS, PhD); mathematics (MS); natural sciences (MS, PhD); physics (MS); physics-chemical (PhD). *Application deadline:* For fall admission, 2/1. *Application fee:* $17. *Acting Dean*, Dr. Brad R. Weinner, 787-763-5101.

Graduate School of Business Administration Students: 131 full-time (83 women), 227 part-time (133 women); includes 356 minority (all Hispanic Americans), 1 international. Average age 26. 200 applicants, 61% accepted. *Faculty:* 9. Expenses: Contact institution. *Financial support:* Fellowships, research assistantships, teaching assistantships, Federal Work-Study, institutionally sponsored loans, and tuition waivers (partial) available. Financial award application deadline: 5/31. In 2001, 39 degrees awarded. *Degree program information:* Part-time and evening/weekend programs available. Offers business administration (MBA, PhD). *Application deadline:* For fall admission, 2/1. *Application fee:* $17. *Application Contact:* Dr. Carmen González, Student Affairs Officer, 787-764-0000 Ext. 4142, Fax: 787-763-6944. *Coordinator*, Dr. Jorge Ayala, 787-751-7410 Ext. 4141, Fax: 787-763-6944, E-mail: jayala@rrpac.upr.clu.edu.

Graduate School of Librarianship Students: 36 full-time (30 women), 99 part-time (70 women); all minorities (all Hispanic Americans) Average age 29. 49 applicants, 61% accepted. *Faculty:* 9. Expenses: Contact institution. *Financial support:* Fellowships, research assistantships, teaching assistantships, Federal Work-Study, institutionally sponsored loans, and tuition waivers (partial) available. Financial award application deadline: 5/31. In 2001, 20 degrees awarded. *Degree program information:* Part-time and evening/weekend programs available. Offers librarianship (Post-Graduate Certificate); librarianship and information services (MLS). *Application deadline:* For fall admission, 2/1. *Application fee:* $17. *Application Contact:* Migdalia Dávila, Student Affairs Officer, 787-764-0000 Ext. 5827, Fax: 787-764-2311. *Director*, Dr. Consuelo Figueras-Alvarez, 787-764-0000 Ext. 5207, Fax: 787-764-2311.

Graduate School of Planning Students: 47 full-time (30 women), 83 part-time (42 women); all minorities (all Hispanic Americans) Average age 27. 66 applicants, 9% accepted. *Faculty:* 10. Expenses: Contact institution. *Financial support:* Fellowships, research assistantships, teaching assistantships, Federal Work-Study, institutionally sponsored loans, and tuition waivers (partial) available. Financial award application deadline: 5/31. In 2001, 12 degrees awarded. *Degree program information:* Part-time and evening/weekend programs available. Offers planning (MP). *Application deadline:* For fall admission, 2/1. *Application fee:* $17. *Application Contact:* Raquel Rodríguez, Student Affairs Officer, 787-764-0000 Ext. 3182, Fax: 787-763-5375. *Director*, Dr. Elías R. R. Gutierrez, 787-764-0000 Ext. 5010, Fax: 787-763-5375, E-mail: nvega@rrpac.upr.clu.edu.

School of Architecture Students: 42 full-time (19 women), 22 part-time (9 women); all minorities (all Hispanic Americans) Average age 22. 31 applicants, 81% accepted. *Faculty:* 20. Expenses: Contact institution. *Financial support:* Fellowships, research assistantships, teaching assistantships, Federal Work-Study, institutionally sponsored loans, and tuition waivers (partial) available. Financial award application deadline: 5/31. In 2001, 13 degrees awarded. *Degree program information:* Part-time and evening/weekend programs available. Offers architecture (M Arch). *Application deadline:* For fall admission, 2/1. *Application fee:* $45. *Application Contact:* Bety Pastrana, Secretary, 787-764-0000 Ext. 3449, Fax: 787-763-5377. *Dean*, Dr. John B. Hertz, 809-763-2101 Ext. 2102.

School of Law Students: 517 full-time (296 women), 141 part-time (87 women); includes 150 minority (all Hispanic Americans), 1 international. Average age 22. 829 applicants, 30% accepted. Expenses: Contact institution. *Financial support:* Fellowships, research assistantships, teaching assistantships, career-related internships or fieldwork, Federal Work-Study, institutionally sponsored loans, and tuition waivers (partial) available. Financial award application deadline: 5/31. *Degree program information:* Part-time and evening/weekend programs available. Offers law (JD). *Application deadline:* For fall admission, 2/1. *Application fee:* $17. *Application Contact:* Lic. Inés Nieves, Admissions Officer, 787-764-2675 Ext. 3843, Fax: 787-764-2675. *Dean*, Efrén Rivera-Ramos, 787-764-2680 Ext. 3829, Fax: 787-764-2765.

School of Public Communication Students: 22 full-time (18 women), 39 part-time (26 women); all minorities (all Hispanic Americans) Average age 26. 63 applicants, 41% accepted. Expenses: Contact institution. *Financial support:* Fellowships, research assistantships, teaching assistantships, Federal Work-Study, institutionally sponsored loans, and tuition waivers (partial) available. Financial award application deadline: 5/31. In 2001, 8 degrees awarded. *Degree program information:* Part-time and evening/weekend programs available. Offers public communication (MA). *Application deadline:* For fall admission, 2/1. *Application fee:* $17. *Application Contact:* Hector Sepilveda, Student Affairs Coordinator, 787-764-0000 Ext. 5043, Fax: 787-763-5390, E-mail: hsepulve@rrpac.upr.clu.edu. *Chairperson*, Dr. Eliseo Colón, 787-764-0000 Ext. 5042, Fax: 787-763-5390.

UNIVERSITY OF PUGET SOUND, Tacoma, WA 98416

General Information Independent, coed, comprehensive institution. *Enrollment:* 162 full-time matriculated graduate/professional students (121 women), 45 part-time matriculated graduate/professional students (33 women). *Enrollment by degree level:* 207 master's. *Graduate faculty:* 26 full-time (16 women), 22 part-time/adjunct (18 women). *Tuition:* Full-time $16,920; part-time $2,820 per unit. Tuition and fees vary according to course load. *Graduate housing:* On-campus housing not available. *Student services:* Campus employment opportunities, campus safety program, career counseling, disabled student services, exercise/wellness program, free psychological counseling, international student services, low-cost health insurance, multicultural affairs office, teacher training, writing training. *Library facilities:* Collins Memorial Library. *Online resources:* library catalog, web page, access to other libraries' catalogs. *Collection:* 326,438 titles, 4,510 serial subscriptions, 15,846 audiovisual materials. *Research affiliation:* Education Development Corporation (education), Educational Inquiries (education).

Computer facilities: 180 computers available on campus for general student use. A campuswide network can be accessed from student residence rooms and from off campus. Internet access is available. *Web address:* http://www.ups.edu/.

General Application Contact: Dr. George H. Mills, Vice President for Enrollment, 253-879-3211, Fax: 253-879-3993, E-mail: admission@ups.edu.

GRADUATE UNITS

Graduate Studies Students: 162 full-time (121 women), 45 part-time (33 women); includes 43 minority (4 African Americans, 27 Asian Americans or Pacific Islanders, 7 Hispanic Americans, 5 Native Americans), 1 international. Average age 29. 264 applicants, 75% accepted, 101 enrolled. *Faculty:* 26 full-time (16 women), 22 part-time/adjunct (18 women). Expenses: Contact institution. *Financial support:* In 2001–02, 62 students received support, including 41 fellowships (averaging $5,284 per year), 1 teaching assistantship with tuition reimbursement available (averaging $6,405 per year); career-related internships or fieldwork, scholarships/grants, and tuition waivers (full) also available. Support available to part-time students. Financial award application deadline: 1/31; financial award applicants required to submit FAFSA. In 2001, 123 degrees awarded. *Degree program information:* Part-time programs available. *Application deadline:* Applications are processed on a rolling basis. Electronic applications accepted. *Application Contact:* Dr. George H. Mills, Vice President for Enrollment, 253-879-3211, Fax: 253-879-3993, E-mail: admission@ups.edu. *Associate Dean*, Dr. John M. Finney, 253-879-3207.

School of Education Students: 65 full-time (49 women), 26 part-time (17 women); includes 16 minority (2 African Americans, 8 Asian Americans or Pacific Islanders, 4 Hispanic Americans, 2 Native Americans) Average age 31. 129 applicants, 84% accepted, 68 enrolled. *Faculty:* 13 full-time (9 women), 3 part-time/adjunct (all women). Expenses: Contact institution. *Financial support:* In 2001–02, 21 students received support, including 16 fellowships (averaging $6,344 per year), 1 teaching assistantship with tuition reimbursement available (averaging $6,405 per year); career-related internships or fieldwork, scholarships/grants, and tuition waivers (full) also available. Support available to part-time students. Financial award application deadline: 1/31; financial award applicants required to submit FAFSA. In 2001, 74 degrees awarded. *Degree program information:* Part-time programs available. Offers counselor education (M Ed); education (M Ed, MAT); educational administration (M Ed); elementary education (MAT); improvement of instruction (M Ed); middle school education (MAT); pastoral counseling (M Ed); secondary education (MAT). *Application deadline:* For fall admission, 3/1 (priority date). Applications are processed on a rolling basis. Electronic applications accepted. *Application Contact:* Dr. George H. Mills, Vice President for Enrollment, 253-879-3211, Fax: 253-879-3993, E-mail: admission@ups.edu. *Dean*, Dr. Carol Merz, 253-879-3377.

School of Occupational and Physical Therapy Students: 97 full-time (72 women), 19 part-time (16 women); includes 27 minority (2 African Americans, 19 Asian Americans or Pacific Islanders, 3 Hispanic Americans, 3 Native Americans), 1 international. Average age 27. 135 applicants, 66% accepted, 33 enrolled. *Faculty:* 13 full-time (7 women), 19 part-time/adjunct (15 women). Expenses: Contact institution. *Financial support:* In 2001–02, 41 students received support, including 5 fellowships (averaging $4,606 per year); career-related internships or fieldwork and scholarships/grants also available. Support available to part-time students. Financial award application deadline: 1/31; financial award applicants required to submit FAFSA. In 2001, 17 master's, 32 doctorates awarded. Offers occupational and physical therapy (MOT, MSOT, DPT); occupational therapy (MOT, MSOT); physical therapy (DPT). *Application deadline:* For fall admission, 1/15 (priority date). Applications are processed on a rolling basis. Electronic applications accepted. *Application Contact:* Dr. George H. Mills, Vice President for Enrollment, 253-879-3211, Fax: 253-879-3993, E-mail: admission@ups.edu. *Head*, 253-879-3281.

UNIVERSITY OF REDLANDS, Redlands, CA 92373-0999

General Information Independent, coed, comprehensive institution. *Graduate housing:* Rooms and/or apartments available on a first-come, first-served basis to single students and available to married students. Housing application deadline: 8/19. *Research affiliation:* Environmental Systems Research Institute (geographic information systems).

GRADUATE UNITS

Graduate Studies Offers communicative disorders (MS). Electronic applications accepted.

School of Music Offers music (MM). Electronic applications accepted.

School of Business *Degree program information:* Evening/weekend programs available. Offers administrative services (MA); business administration (MBA); curriculum and instruction (MA); management and business (MAHRM, MBA); management and human resources (MAHRM); pupil personnel services (MA). Electronic applications accepted.

UNIVERSITY OF REGINA, Regina, SK S4S 0A2, Canada

General Information Province-supported, coed, university. *Enrollment:* 258 full-time matriculated graduate/professional students (139 women), 741 part-time matriculated graduate/professional students (413 women). *Graduate faculty:* 358 full-time (109 women), 72 part-time/adjunct (5 women). *Graduate tuition:* Tuition charges are reported in Canadian dollars. *Tuition:* Full-time $2,273 Canadian dollars. *Graduate housing:* Room and/or apartments available on a first-come, first-served basis to single students; on-campus housing not available to married students. *Student services:* Campus employment opportunities, campus safety program, career counseling, child daycare facilities, disabled student services, exercise/wellness program, free psychological counseling, international student services, low-cost health insurance, multicultural affairs office, teacher training, writing training. *Library facilities:* Dr. John Archer Library plus 6 others. *Collection:* 2.3 million titles. *Research affiliation:* Institute for Robotics and Intelligent Systems (knowledge-based systems, artificial intelligence), TR Labs (telecommunications), Jefferson Laboratory/Southeastern Universities Research Association, Inc. (electromagnetic physics), Tri-University Meson Facility (physics and particle masses), Micronet (microelectronic devices, circuits, systems), Petroleum Technology Research Center (greenhouse gas remediation).

University of Regina (continued)

Computer facilities: 150 computers available on campus for general student use. A campuswide network can be accessed from student residence rooms and from off campus. Internet access is available. *Web address:* http://www.uregina.ca/.

General Application Contact: Dr. Dave Malloy, Faculty of Graduate Studies and Research Office, 306-585-4161, Fax: 306-585-4893, E-mail: grad.studies@uregina.ca.

GRADUATE UNITS

Faculty of Graduate Studies and Research Students: 258 full-time (139 women), 741 part-time (413 women). 733 applicants, 53% accepted. *Faculty:* 358 full-time (109 women), 72 part-time/adjunct (5 women). Expenses: Contact institution. *Financial support:* In 2001–02, 265 students received support, including 143 fellowships, 115 teaching assistantships; research assistantships, career-related internships or fieldwork, institutionally sponsored loans, and scholarships/grants also available. Financial award application deadline: 6/15. In 2001, 177 master's, 7 doctorates, 7 other advanced degrees awarded. *Degree program information:* Part-time and evening/weekend programs available. Offers anthropology (MA); Indian studies (MA); individual studies (M Eng, M Sc, MA, MA Sc, PhD); linguistics (MA); philosophy (MA). *Application deadline:* For fall admission, 3/15 (priority date); for winter admission, 7/15 (priority date); for spring admission, 9/15 (priority date). Applications are processed on a rolling basis. *Application fee:* $60. *Application Contact:* Dr. Dave Malloy, Assistant Dean, 306-585-5185, Fax: 306-585-4893, E-mail: dave.malloy@uregina.ca. *Dean,* Rod Kelln, 306-585-5185, Fax: 306-585-4893, E-mail: rod.kelln@uregina.ca.

Faculty of Administration Students: 5 full-time (3 women), 72 part-time (33 women). 62 applicants, 69% accepted. *Faculty:* 30 full-time (8 women), 3 part-time/adjunct (0 women). Expenses: Contact institution. *Financial support:* In 2001–02, 6 students received support, including 1 fellowship, 2 research assistantships, 2 teaching assistantships; scholarships/grants also available. Financial award application deadline: 6/15. In 2001, 17 degrees awarded. *Degree program information:* Part-time and evening/weekend programs available. Offers administration (MBA, MHRM, MPA); business administration (MBA); human resources management (MHRM); public administration (MPA). *Application deadline:* Applications are processed on a rolling basis. *Application fee:* $60. *Application Contact:* Dr. Jason Vogelsang, Academic Advisor, 306-585-4011, Fax: 306-585-4805, E-mail: jason.vogelsang@uregina.ca. *Dean,* G. Garven, 306-585-4435, Fax: 306-585-4805, E-mail: garnet.garven@uregina.ca.

Faculty of Arts Students: 91 full-time (57 women), 102 part-time (59 women). 124 applicants, 60% accepted. *Faculty:* 140 full-time (39 women), 22 part-time/adjunct (1 woman). Expenses: Contact institution. *Financial support:* In 2001–02, 83 students received support, including 49 fellowships, 45 teaching assistantships; research assistantships, career-related internships or fieldwork and scholarships/grants also available. Financial award application deadline: 6/15. In 2001, 41 degrees awarded. *Degree program information:* Part-time programs available. Offers anthropology (MA); arts (M Eng, M Sc, MA, MA Sc, PhD); Canadian plains studies (MA, PhD); economics (MA); English (MA, PhD); French (MA); geography (M Sc, MA); history (MA); Indian studies (MA); individual studies (M Eng, M Sc, MA, MA Sc, PhD); political science (MA); psychology (MA, PhD); religious studies (MA); social studies (MA); sociology (MA). *Application deadline:* Applications are processed on a rolling basis. *Application fee:* $60. *Dean,* Dr. Murray Knuttila, 306-585-4895, Fax: 306-585-4815, E-mail: murray.knuttila@uregina.ca.

Faculty of Education Students: 29 full-time (25 women), 310 part-time (216 women). 102 applicants, 88% accepted. *Faculty:* 46 full-time (26 women), 2 part-time/adjunct (1 woman). Expenses: Contact institution. *Financial support:* In 2001–02, 22 students received support, including 13 fellowships, 8 teaching assistantships; research assistantships, career-related internships or fieldwork and scholarships/grants also available. Financial award application deadline: 6/15. In 2001, 61 master's, 1 doctorate awarded. *Degree program information:* Part-time programs available. Offers curriculum and instruction (M Ed); education (M Ed, MHRD, MVT Ed, PhD, Diploma); educational administration (M Ed, Diploma); educational psychology (M Ed, PhD, Diploma); human resources development (MHRD); vocational/technical education (MVT Ed, Diploma). *Application deadline:* For fall and spring admission, 2/15; for winter admission, 10/15. *Application fee:* $60. *Application Contact:* Vicki Minhinnick, Program Office Coordinator, 306-585-4506, Fax: 306-585-5387, E-mail: vicki.minhinnick@uregina.ca. *Dean,* Dr. M. McKinnon, 306-585-4816, Fax: 306-585-5387, E-mail: margaret.mckinnon@uregina.ca.

Faculty of Engineering Students: 36 full-time (7 women), 86 part-time (10 women). 222 applicants, 43% accepted. *Faculty:* 22 full-time (3 women), 17 part-time/adjunct (0 women). Expenses: Contact institution. *Financial support:* In 2001–02, 33 students received support, including 23 fellowships, 19 teaching assistantships; research assistantships, career-related internships or fieldwork and scholarships/grants also available. Financial award application deadline: 6/15. In 2001, 18 master's, 2 doctorates awarded. Offers advanced manufacturing and processing (M Sc, MA Sc); Canadian plains studies (MA, PhD); electronic systems engineering (M Eng, MA Sc, PhD); engineering (M Eng, M Sc, MA, MA Sc, PhD); environmental systems engineering (M Eng, MA Sc, PhD); industrial systems engineering (M Eng, MA Sc, PhD); petroleum systems engineering (M Eng, MA Sc, PhD). *Application deadline:* Applications are processed on a rolling basis. *Application fee:* $60. *Acting Dean,* Dr. P. Tontiwachwuthikul, 306-585-4159, Fax: 306-585-4855, E-mail: paitoon.tontiwachwuthikul@uregina.ca.

Faculty of Fine Arts Students: 11 full-time (7 women), 8 part-time (5 women). 16 applicants, 63% accepted. *Faculty:* 19 full-time (10 women). Expenses: Contact institution. *Financial support:* In 2001–02, 13 students received support, including 5 fellowships, 3 teaching assistantships; research assistantships, scholarships/grants also available. Financial award application deadline: 6/15. In 2001, 8 degrees awarded. *Degree program information:* Part-time programs available. Offers fine arts (M Mus, MA, MFA); music (M Mus); music theory (MA); musicology (MA); visual arts (MFA). *Application deadline:* For fall admission, 3/15. *Application fee:* $60. *Dean,* Kathryn Laurin, 306-585-5711, Fax: 306-585-5780, E-mail: laurinka@max.cc.uregina.ca.

Faculty of Kinesiology and Health Studies Students: 6 full-time (5 women), 12 part-time (4 women). 9 applicants, 89% accepted. *Faculty:* 12 full-time (4 women), 10 part-time/adjunct (1 woman). Expenses: Contact institution. *Financial support:* In 2001–02, 5 fellowships, 2 teaching assistantships were awarded. Research assistantships, scholarships/grants also available. In 2001, 1 degree awarded. Offers kinesiology and health studies (M Sc); physical activity studies (M Sc). *Application deadline:* Applications are processed on a rolling basis. *Application fee:* $60. *Dean,* Dr. C. Chamberlin, 306-585-4876, Fax: 306-585-4854.

Faculty of Science Students: 58 full-time (16 women), 75 part-time (27 women). 147 applicants, 30% accepted. *Faculty:* 73 full-time (10 women), 15 part-time/adjunct (2 women). Expenses: Contact institution. *Financial support:* In 2001–02, 76 students received support, including 40 fellowships, 31 research assistantships, 32 teaching assistantships; career-related internships or fieldwork and scholarships/grants also available. Financial award application deadline: 6/15. In 2001, 22 master's, 4 doctorates awarded. *Degree program information:* Part-time programs available. Offers analytical chemistry (M Sc, PhD); biochemistry (M Sc, PhD); biology (M Sc, PhD); computer science (M Sc, PhD); geology (M Sc); inorganic chemistry (M Sc, PhD); mathematics (M Sc, MA, PhD); organic chemistry (M Sc, PhD); physical chemistry (M Sc, PhD); physics (M Sc, PhD); science (M Sc, MA, PhD); statistics (M Sc, MA). *Application deadline:* Applications are processed on a rolling basis. *Application fee:* $60. *Dean,* Dr. K. Bergman, 306-585-4143, Fax: 306-585-4894.

Faculty of Social Work Students: 22 full-time (19 women), 76 part-time (59 women). 51 applicants, 53% accepted. *Faculty:* 16 full-time (9 women), 3 part-time/adjunct (0 women). Expenses: Contact institution. *Financial support:* In 2001–02, 14 students received support, including 7 fellowships, 4 teaching assistantships; research assistantships, career-related internships or fieldwork and scholarships/grants also available. Financial award application deadline: 6/15. In 2001, 9 degrees awarded. *Degree program information:* Part-time programs available. Offers social work (MSW). *Application deadline:* For fall admission, 2/15. *Application fee:* $60. *Application Contact:* Dr. Gloria Geller, Graduate Coordinator, 306-585-4549, Fax: 306-585-4872, E-mail: gloria.geller@uregina.ca. *Dean,* Dr. Michael MacLean, 306-585-4563, Fax: 306-585-4872, E-mail: michael.maclean@uregina.ca.

UNIVERSITY OF RHODE ISLAND, Kingston, RI 02881

General Information State-supported, coed, university. CGS member. *Enrollment:* 1,452 full-time matriculated graduate/professional students (861 women), 2,233 part-time matriculated graduate/professional students (1,427 women). *Graduate faculty:* 672 full-time (230 women), 10 part-time/adjunct (6 women). Tuition, state resident: full-time $3,756; part-time $209 per credit. Tuition, nonresident: full-time $10,774; part-time $599 per credit. *Required fees:* $1,586; $76 per credit. $76 per credit. One-time fee: $60 full-time. *Graduate housing:* Rooms and/or apartments available on a first-come, first-served basis to single and married students. *Student services:* Campus employment opportunities, campus safety program, career counseling, disabled student services, free psychological counseling, international student services, low-cost health insurance, multicultural affairs office. *Library facilities:* University Library plus 1 other. *Online resources:* library catalog, web page. *Collection:* 783,237 titles, 7,966 serial subscriptions, 9,510 audiovisual materials.

Computer facilities: 552 computers available on campus for general student use. A campuswide network can be accessed from off campus. *Web address:* http://www.uri.edu.

General Application Contact: Harold D. Bibb, Associate Dean of the Graduate School, 401-874-2262, Fax: 401-874-5491.

GRADUATE UNITS

Graduate School *Faculty:* 659 full-time (213 women), 10 part-time/adjunct (7 women). Expenses: Contact institution. *Financial support:* In 2001–02, 29 fellowships, 342 research assistantships, 385 teaching assistantships were awarded. Career-related internships or fieldwork, Federal Work-Study, institutionally sponsored loans, and tuition waivers (full and partial) also available. Support available to part-time students. In 2001, 73 first professional degrees, 491 master's, 95 doctorates awarded. *Degree program information:* Part-time and evening/weekend programs available. *Application deadline:* For fall admission, 4/15 (priority date). Applications are processed on a rolling basis. *Application fee:* $35. *Vice Provost for Graduate Studies, Research and Outreach,* Janett Trubatah, 401-874-4467.

Alan Shawn Feinstein College of Continuing Education Expenses: Contact institution. Offers clinical laboratory sciences (MS); continuing education (Exec MBA, MS). *Application deadline:* For fall admission, 4/15 (priority date). Applications are processed on a rolling basis. *Application fee:* $35. *Vice Provost,* John McCray, 401-277-5070.

College of Arts and Sciences Expenses: Contact institution. *Financial support:* Fellowships, research assistantships, teaching assistantships available. Offers arts and sciences (MA, MM, MMA, MPA, MS, PhD, Certificate); biochemistry (MS, PhD); botany (MS, PhD); chemistry (MS, PhD); clinical psychology (PhD); computer science and statistics (MS, PhD); English (MA, PhD); experimental psychology (PhD); French (MA); geology (MS); history (MA); international development studies (Certificate); marine affairs (MA, MMA); mathematics (MS, PhD); microbiology (MS, PhD); music (MM); philosophy (MA); physics (MS, PhD); political science (MA); public policy and administration (MPA); school psychology (MS, PhD); Spanish (MA); zoology (MS, PhD). *Application deadline:* Applications are processed on a rolling basis. *Application fee:* $35. *Dean,* Winifed Brownell, 401-874-2566.

College of Business Administration Expenses: Contact institution. *Financial support:* Unspecified assistantships available. In 2001, 86 master's, 1 doctorate awarded. Offers accounting (MS); applied mathematics (PhD); finance (MBA); international business (MBA); international sports management (MBA); management (MBA); management science (MBA); marketing (MBA). *Application deadline:* For fall admission, 4/15 (priority date). Applications are processed on a rolling basis. *Application fee:* $35. *Application Contact:* Dr. Laura Beauvais, Director of Graduate Programs, 401-874-2377. *Dean,* Dr. Edward Mazze, 401-874-2337.

College of Engineering Expenses: Contact institution. *Financial support:* Research assistantships, teaching assistantships, tuition waivers (full) available. *Degree program information:* Part-time programs available. Offers chemical engineering (MS, PhD); design/systems (MS, PhD); electrical and computer engineering (MS, PhD); engineering (MS, PhD); environmental engineering (MS, PhD); fluid mechanics (MS, PhD); geotechnical engineering (MS, PhD); industrial engineering (MS); manufacturing engineering (MS); ocean engineering (MS, PhD); solid mechanics (MS, PhD); structural engineering (MS, PhD); thermal sciences (MS, PhD); transportation engineering (MS, PhD). *Application deadline:* For fall admission, 4/15 (priority date). Applications are processed on a rolling basis. *Application fee:* $35. *Application Contact:* Dr. David Shao, Associate Dean, 401-874-2186. *Interim Dean,* Arun Shukla, 401-874-2186.

College of Human Science and Services Expenses: Contact institution. *Financial support:* Career-related internships or fieldwork available. *Degree program information:* Evening/weekend programs available. Offers adult education (MA); communicative disorders (MA, MS); elementary education (MA); guidance and counseling (MS); health (MS); home economics education (MS); human science and services (MA, MS); marriage and family therapy (MS); physical education (MS); physical therapy (MS); reading (MA); recreation (MS); secondary education (MA); textiles, fashion merchandising and design (MS). *Application deadline:* For fall admission, 4/15 (priority date); for spring admission, 11/15. Applications are processed on a rolling basis. *Application fee:* $35. *Interim Dean,* W. Lynn McKinney, 401-874-2244.

College of Nursing Expenses: Contact institution. In 2001, 34 master's, 5 doctorates awarded. Offers nursing (PhD); nursing service administration (MS); teaching of nursing (MS). *Application deadline:* For fall admission, 4/15. *Application fee:* $35. *Dean,* Dayle Joseph, 401-874-2766.

College of Pharmacy Expenses: Contact institution. In 2001, 64 first professional degrees, 7 master's, 2 doctorates awarded. Offers medicinal chemistry (MS, PhD); pharmaceutics (MS, PhD); pharmacognosy (MS, PhD); pharmacology and toxicology (MS, PhD); pharmacy (Pharm D, MS, PhD); pharmacy administration (MS). *Application deadline:* For fall admission, 4/15. *Application fee:* $35. *Dean,* Donald Letendre, 401-874-2761.

College of the Environment and Life Sciences Expenses: Contact institution. *Financial support:* Fellowships, research assistantships, tuition waivers (full and partial) available. *Degree program information:* Part-time programs available. Offers animal science (MS); community planning and area development (MCP); entomology (MS, PhD); environment and life sciences (MCP, MS, PhD); food and nutrition science (MS, PhD); food science and technology, nutrition and dietetics (MS, PhD); plant pathology (MS, PhD); plant pathology-entomology (MS, PhD); plant science (MS, PhD); resource economics and marine resources (MS, PhD). *Application deadline:* For fall admission, 4/15 (priority date). Applications are processed on a rolling basis. *Application fee:* $35. *Dean,* Jeffrey Seemann, 401-874-2474.

Graduate Library School Expenses: Contact institution. In 2001, 64 degrees awarded. Offers library science (MLIS). *Application deadline:* For fall admission, 4/15 (priority date). Applications are processed on a rolling basis. *Application fee:* $35. *Director,* Dr. W. Michael Havener, 401-874-2947.

Graduate School of Oceanography Expenses: Contact institution. In 2001, 4 master's, 10 doctorates awarded. Offers oceanography (MS, PhD). *Application deadline:* For fall admission, 4/15 (priority date). Applications are processed on a rolling basis. *Application fee:* $35. *Dean,* David Farmer, 401-874-6222.

Labor Research Center Average age 32. Expenses: Contact institution. *Financial support:* Fellowships, research assistantships, teaching assistantships, career-related internships or fieldwork, Federal Work-Study, institutionally sponsored loans, and tuition waivers (full and partial) available. Support available to part-time students. In 2001, 4 degrees awarded. *Degree program information:* Part-time and evening/weekend programs available. Offers labor and industrial relations (MS). *Application deadline:* For fall admission, 4/15 (priority date); for spring admission, 11/15. Applications are processed on a rolling basis. *Application fee:* $35. *Director,* Dr. Terry Thomason, 401-874-2239.

UNIVERSITY OF RICHMOND, Richmond, University of Richmond, VA 23173

General Information Independent, coed, comprehensive institution. *Enrollment:* 509 full-time matriculated graduate/professional students (241 women), 171 part-time matriculated graduate/professional students (67 women). *Enrollment by degree level:* 612 first professional, 58 master's. *Graduate faculty:* 172 full-time (43 women), 72 part-time/adjunct (26 women). *Tuition:* Full-time $22,360; part-time $385 per credit hour. *Graduate housing:* On-campus housing not available. *Student services:* Campus employment opportunities, campus safety program, career counseling, exercise/wellness program, free psychological counseling, international student services, low-cost health insurance, multicultural affairs office, writing training. *Library facilities:* Boatwright Memorial Library plus 4 others. *Online resources:* library catalog, web page, access to other libraries' catalogs. *Collection:* 716,677 titles, 3,579 serial subscriptions, 24,916 audiovisual materials.

Computer facilities: 500 computers available on campus for general student use. A campuswide network can be accessed from student residence rooms and from off campus. *Web address:* http://www.richmond.edu/.

General Application Contact: Dr. Dona J. Hickey, Director of the Graduate School, 804-289-8417, Fax: 804-289-8818, E-mail: bgriffin@richmond.edu.

GRADUATE UNITS

Graduate School Students: 21 full-time (10 women), 45 part-time (29 women). Average age 28. 89 applicants, 37% accepted, 27 enrolled. *Faculty:* 105 full-time (30 women), 8 part-time/adjunct (4 women). Expenses: Contact institution. *Financial support:* In 2001–02, 24 students received support; fellowships, research assistantships, teaching assistantships, career-related internships or fieldwork, Federal Work-Study, institutionally sponsored loans, tuition waivers (partial), unspecified assistantships, and tuition awards available. Financial award application deadline: 3/15; financial award applicants required to submit FAFSA. In 2001, 19 degrees awarded. *Degree program information:* Part-time and evening/weekend programs available. Offers biology (MS); English (MA); history (MA); liberal arts (MLA); psychology (MA). *Application deadline:* For fall admission, 3/15 (priority date); for spring admission, 11/15 (priority date). *Application fee:* $30. *Application Contact:* Suzanne V. Blyer, Administrative Assistant, 804-289-8417, Fax: 804-289-8818, E-mail: asgrad@richmond.edu. *Director,* Dr. Dona J. Hickey, 804-289-8417, Fax: 804-289-8818, E-mail: dhickey@richmond.edu.

The Robins School of Business Average age 29. 128 applicants, 78% accepted, 79 enrolled. *Faculty:* 44 full-time (7 women), 12 part-time/adjunct (4 women). Expenses: Contact institution. *Financial support:* In 2001–02, 30 students received support, including 6 research assistantships with tuition reimbursements available Support available to part-time students. Financial award applicants required to submit FAFSA. In 2001, 59 master's awarded. *Degree program information:* Part-time and evening/weekend programs available. Offers business (MBA); business administration (MBA). *Application deadline:* For fall admission, 5/1. *Application fee:* $50. *Application Contact:* Dr. Carol M. Laurence, Associate Dean for Graduate Business Studies, 804-289-8553, Fax: 804-287-6544, E-mail: claurence@richmond.edu. *Dean,* Dr. Karen Newman, 804-289-8550, Fax: 804-287-6544, E-mail: knewman@richmond.edu.

School of Law Offers law (JD). Electronic applications accepted.

See in-depth description on page 1241.

UNIVERSITY OF RIO GRANDE, Rio Grande, OH 45674

General Information Independent, coed, comprehensive institution. *Graduate housing:* On-campus housing not available.

GRADUATE UNITS

Graduate School *Degree program information:* Part-time and evening/weekend programs available. Offers classroom teaching (M Ed).

UNIVERSITY OF ROCHESTER, Rochester, NY 14627-0250

General Information Independent, coed, university. CGS member. *Enrollment:* 2,520 full-time matriculated graduate/professional students (1,045 women), 1,166 part-time matriculated graduate/professional students (663 women). *Enrollment by degree level:* 418 first professional, 1,318 master's, 1,465 doctoral, 573 other advanced degrees. *Graduate faculty:* 1,983. *Tuition:* Part-time $755 per credit hour. *Required fees:* $755 per credit hour. *Graduate housing:* Rooms and/or apartments available to single students and available on a first-come, first-served basis to married students. Housing application deadline: 6/2. *Student services:* Campus employment opportunities, campus safety program, career counseling, disabled student services, free psychological counseling, international student services, low-cost health insurance. *Library facilities:* Rush Rhees Library plus 5 others. *Online resources:* library catalog, web page, access to other libraries' catalogs. *Collection:* 3 million titles, 11,254 serial subscriptions, 78,600 audiovisual materials. *Research affiliation:* Brookhaven National Laboratory, Fermi National Accelerator Laboratory, Argonne National Laboratory, Lawrence Livermore National Laboratory, Los Alamos National Laboratory, Numeous corporations (Biomedical).

Computer facilities: 260 computers available on campus for general student use. A campuswide network can be accessed from student residence rooms and from off campus. *Web address:* http://www.rochester.edu/.

GRADUATE UNITS

The College, Arts and Sciences Students: 646 full-time (246 women), 23 part-time (16 women); includes 49 minority (17 African Americans, 14 Asian Americans or Pacific Islanders, 16 Hispanic Americans, 2 Native Americans), 295 international. 2,742 applicants, 16% accepted, 156 enrolled. *Faculty:* 234. Expenses: Contact institution. *Financial support:* Fellowships, research assistantships, teaching assistantships, tuition waivers (full and partial) available. Financial award application deadline: 2/1. In 2001, 113 master's, 74 doctorates awarded. *Degree program information:* Part-time programs available. Offers arts and sciences (MA, MS, PhD); biology (MS, PhD); brain and cognitive sciences (MS, PhD); chemistry (MS, PhD); clinical psychology (PhD); computer science (MS, PhD); developmental psychology (PhD); economics (MA, PhD); English (MA, PhD); geological sciences (MS, PhD); history (MA, PhD); mathematics (MA, MS, PhD); philosophy (MA, PhD); physics (MA, MS, PhD); physics and astronomy (PhD); political science (MA, PhD); psychology (MA); social-personality psychology (PhD); visual and cultural studies (MA, PhD). *Application deadline:* For fall admission, 2/1 (priority date). *Application fee:* $25. Electronic applications accepted. *Vice Provost and Dean of the Faculty,* Thomas LeBlanc, 585-273-5000.

The College, School of Engineering and Applied Sciences Students: 212 full-time (41 women), 26 part-time (7 women); includes 17 minority (4 African Americans, 8 Asian Americans or Pacific Islanders, 5 Hispanic Americans), 120 international. 980 applicants, 13% accepted, 59 enrolled. *Faculty:* 53. Expenses: Contact institution. *Financial support:* Fellowships, research assistantships, teaching assistantships, tuition waivers (full and partial) available. Financial award application deadline: 2/1. In 2001, 44 master's, 23 doctorates awarded. *Degree program information:* Part-time programs available. Offers biomedical engineering (MS, PhD); chemical engineering (MS, PhD); electrical and computer engineering (MS, PhD); engineering and applied sciences (MS, PhD); materials science (MS, PhD); mechanical engineering (MS, PhD). *Application deadline:* For fall admission, 2/1 (priority date). *Application fee:* $25. *Dean,* Kevin Parker, 716-275-4151.

Institute of Optics Students: 74 full-time (14 women), 4 part-time (1 woman); includes 5 minority (1 African American, 2 Asian Americans or Pacific Islanders, 2 Hispanic Americans), 27 international. 208 applicants, 16% accepted, 14 enrolled. *Faculty:* 14. Expenses: Contact institution. *Financial support:* Fellowships, research assistantships, teaching assistantships, tuition waivers (full and partial) available. Financial award application deadline: 2/1. In 2001, 9 master's, 7 doctorates awarded. Offers optics (MS, PhD). *Application deadline:* For fall admission, 2/1 (priority date). *Application fee:* $25. *Application Contact:* Joan Christian, Graduate Program Secretary, 585-275-7764. *Director,* Wayne Knox, 585-273-5520.

Eastman School of Music Students: 243 full-time (147 women), 20 part-time (9 women); includes 20 minority (2 African Americans, 15 Asian Americans or Pacific Islanders, 3 Hispanic Americans), 100 international. 780 applicants, 29% accepted, 103 enrolled. *Faculty:* 80. Expenses: Contact institution. *Financial support:* Fellowships, teaching assistantships, tuition waivers (full and partial) available. Financial award application deadline: 2/1. In 2001, 86 master's, 23 doctorates awarded. *Degree program information:* Part-time programs available. Offers composition (MA, MM, DMA, PhD); conducting (MM, DMA); education (MA, PhD); jazz studies/contemporary media (MM); music education (MM, DMA); musicology (MA, PhD); pedagogy of music theory (MA); performance and literature (MM, DMA); piano accompanying and chamber music (MM, DMA); theory (MA, PhD). *Application deadline:* For fall admission, 2/1. *Application fee:* $50. *Application Contact:* Charles Krusenstjerna, Director of Admissions, 585-274-1060. *Director,* James Undercofler, 585-274-1010.

Margaret Warner Graduate School of Education and Human Development Students: 74 full-time (51 women), 235 part-time (166 women); includes 42 minority (28 African Americans, 5 Asian Americans or Pacific Islanders, 9 Hispanic Americans), 4 international. 217 applicants, 86% accepted, 95 enrolled. *Faculty:* 20. Expenses: Contact institution. *Financial support:* Fellowships, teaching assistantships, tuition waivers (full and partial) available. Financial award application deadline: 2/1. In 2001, 53 master's, 14 doctorates awarded. *Degree program information:* Part-time and evening/weekend programs available. Offers education and human development (MAT, MS, Ed D, PhD). *Application deadline:* For fall admission, 2/1. Applications are processed on a rolling basis. *Application fee:* $25. *Application Contact:* Jennifer Steward, Director, of Admissions, 716-275-3969. *Dean,* Raffaella Borasi, 585-275-8300.

School of Medicine and Dentistry Students: 776 full-time (375 women), 93 part-time (58 women); includes 205 minority (48 African Americans, 119 Asian Americans or Pacific Islanders, 36 Hispanic Americans, 2 Native Americans), 151 international. 4,772 applicants, 10% accepted, 223 enrolled. *Faculty:* 578. Expenses: Contact institution. *Financial support:* Fellowships, research assistantships, teaching assistantships, Federal Work-Study, tuition waivers (full and partial), and training grant fellowships available. Support available to part-time students. In 2001, 102 first professional degrees, 41 master's, 40 doctorates awarded. *Degree program information:* Part-time programs available. Offers medicine (MD); medicine and dentistry (MD, MA, MPH, MS, PhD, Certificate). Electronic applications accepted. *Dean,* Dr. David Guzick, 716-275-7181.

Graduate Programs in Medicine and Dentistry Students: 374 full-time (162 women), 93 part-time (58 women); includes 65 minority (14 African Americans, 35 Asian Americans or Pacific Islanders, 16 Hispanic Americans), 149 international. 467 applicants, 35% accepted, 123 enrolled. *Faculty:* 158. Expenses: Contact institution. *Financial support:* Fellowships, research assistantships, teaching assistantships, scholarships/grants and tuition waivers (full and partial) available. Financial award application deadline: 2/1. In 2001, 41 master's, 40 doctorates awarded. *Degree program information:* Part-time programs available. Offers biochemistry (MS, PhD); biophysics (MS, PhD); genetics, genomics and development (MS, PhD); health services research and policy (PhD); marriage and family therapy (MS); medical statistics (MS); medicine and dentistry (MA, MPH, MS, PhD, Certificate); microbiology (MS, PhD); neurobiology and anatomy (MS, PhD); neuroscience (MS, PhD); oral biology (MS); pathology (MS, PhD); pharmacology (MS, PhD); physiology (MS, PhD); public health (MPH); statistics (MA, PhD); toxicology (MS, PhD). *Application deadline:* For fall admission, 2/1 (priority date). *Application fee:* $25. Electronic applications accepted. *Application Contact:* Maureen Goodman, Head, 585-275-2933. *Senior Associate Dean,* Paul La Celle, 585-275-4522.

School of Nursing Students: 40 full-time (38 women), 123 part-time (110 women); includes 8 minority (4 African Americans, 2 Asian Americans or Pacific Islanders, 2 Hispanic Americans), 7 international. 75 applicants, 83% accepted, 48 enrolled. *Faculty:* 22 full-time (20 women), 8 part-time/adjunct (7 women). Expenses: Contact institution. *Financial support:* In 2001–02, 23 students received support, including 8 fellowships with full and partial tuition reimbursements available (averaging $7,900 per year), 8 research assistantships with full and partial tuition reimbursements available (averaging $3,000 per year), 2 teaching assistantships with full and partial tuition reimbursements available (averaging $1,500 per year); scholarships/grants, traineeships, tuition waivers (partial), and unspecified assistantships also available. Support available to part-time students. Financial award application deadline: 6/30. In 2001, 49 master's, 4 doctorates, 15 other advanced degrees awarded. Offers nursing (MS, PhD, Certificate). *Application deadline:* For fall admission, 2/15 (priority date); for spring admission, 9/15 (priority date). *Application fee:* $25. *Application Contact:* Elaine Andolina, Director of Admissions, 585-275-2375, Fax: 585-756-8299, E-mail: elaine_andolina@urmc.rochester.edu. *Dean,* Dr. Patricia Chiverton, 585-275-5451, Fax: 585-273-1268, E-mail: patricia_chiverton@urmc.rochester.edu.

William E. Simon Graduate School of Business Administration Students: 584 full-time (158 women), 209 part-time (68 women); includes 74 minority (19 African Americans, 36 Asian Americans or Pacific Islanders, 17 Hispanic Americans, 2 Native Americans), 310 international. 1,935 applicants, 30% accepted, 334 enrolled. *Faculty:* 48. Expenses: Contact institution. *Financial support:* Fellowships, research assistantships, teaching assistantships, tuition waivers (full and partial) available. In 2001, 323 master's, 3 doctorates awarded. *Degree program information:* Part-time and evening/weekend programs available. Offers business administration (MBA, MS, PhD). *Application deadline:* Applications are processed on a rolling basis. *Application fee:* $75. *Dean,* Charles Plosser, 585-275-3316.

Announcement: The University of Rochester offers more than 40 programs that lead to the Doctor of Philosophy degree. Doctor of Medicine, Doctor of Education, and Doctor of Musical Arts degrees are also offered. The MA and MS are offered in several fields, along with MBA, MPH, and MM degrees. Graduate admission is decentralized, allowing faculty members in each college/department to administer their own programs. Requests for program information and admission materials should be directed to the appropriate academic department. World Wide Web: http://www.rochester.edu

UNIVERSITY OF ST. AUGUSTINE FOR HEALTH SCIENCES, St. Augustine, FL 32086

General Information Proprietary, coed, graduate-only institution. *Enrollment by degree level:* 315 master's, 104 doctoral. *Graduate faculty:* 20 full-time (11 women), 31 part-time/adjunct (7 women). *Tuition:* Full-time $16,000; part-time $285 per semester hour. *Required fees:* $85. Tuition and fees vary according to course load and program. *Graduate housing:* On-campus housing not available. *Student services:* Campus employment opportunities, free psychological counseling, international student services, low-cost health insurance, teacher training. *Collection:* 2,200 titles. *Research affiliation:* Flagler Physical Therapy (clinical practice).

Computer facilities: 14 computers available on campus for general student use. A campuswide network can be accessed. Internet access is available. *Web address:* http://www.usa.edu/.

General Application Contact: Julie T. Cook, Director of Enrollment Services, 904-826-0084 Ext. 207, Fax: 904-826-0085, E-mail: jcook@usa.edu.

GRADUATE UNITS

Graduate Programs Students: 288 full-time (167 women), 131 part-time (50 women); includes 55 minority (21 African Americans, 16 Asian Americans or Pacific Islanders, 11 Hispanic Americans, 7 Native Americans), 8 international. 400 applicants, 75% accepted. *Faculty:* 20 full-time (11 women), 31 part-time/adjunct (7 women). Expenses: Contact institution. *Financial support:* In 2001–02, 5 students received support; teaching assistantships, career-related internships or fieldwork, institutionally sponsored loans, scholarships/grants, and tuition waivers (partial) available. Support available to part-time students. In 2001, 187 master's, 37 doctorates awarded. *Degree program information:* Part-time programs available. Postbaccalaureate distance learning degree programs offered (minimal on-campus study). Offers occupational therapy (MOT, OTD); physical therapy (DPT). *Application deadline:* For fall admission, 1/15 (priority date); for spring admission, 6/15 (priority date). *Application fee:* $50. *Application Contact:* Julie T. Cook, Director of Enrollment Services, 904-826-0084 Ext. 207, Fax: 904-826-0085, E-mail: jcook@usa.edu.

Division of Advanced Studies 20 applicants, 100% accepted. *Faculty:* 22 part-time/adjunct (5 women). Expenses: Contact institution. *Financial support:* In 2001–02, 1 teach-

University of St. Augustine for Health Sciences (continued)

ing assistantship was awarded; career-related internships or fieldwork and tuition waivers (partial) also available. Support available to part-time students. In 2001, 8 master's, 3 doctorates awarded. *Degree program information:* Part-time programs available. Postbaccalaureate distance learning degree programs offered (minimal on-campus study). Offers advanced studies (MH Sc, DH Sc). *Application deadline:* For fall admission, 10/1 (priority date). *Application Contact:* Julie T. Cook, Director of Enrollment Services, 904-826-0084 Ext. 207, Fax: 904-826-0085, E-mail: jcook@usa.edu. *Director,* Dr. Richard Jensen, 904-826-0084 Ext. 262, Fax: 904-826-0085, E-mail: rhjensen@usa.edu.

Division of Entry-Level Physical Therapy Average age 26. 300 applicants, 67% accepted. *Faculty:* 20 full-time (11 women), 7 part-time/adjunct (5 women). Expenses: Contact institution. Offers entry-level physical therapy (DPT). *Application deadline:* For fall admission, 1/15 (priority date); for spring admission, 6/15 (priority date). *Application fee:* $50. *Application Contact:* Julie T. Cook, Director of Enrollment Services, 904-826-0084 Ext. 207, Fax: 904-826-0085, E-mail: jcook@usa.edu. *Director,* Dr. Gary Gorniak, 904-826-0084 Ext. 219, Fax: 904-826-0085, E-mail: ggorniak@usa.edu.

See in-depth description on page 1243.

UNIVERSITY OF ST. FRANCIS, Joliet, IL 60435-6169

General Information Independent-religious, coed, comprehensive institution. *Enrollment:* 160 full-time matriculated graduate/professional students (120 women), 1,040 part-time matriculated graduate/professional students (848 women). *Enrollment by degree level:* 1,200 master's. *Graduate faculty:* 13 full-time (7 women), 70 part-time/adjunct (32 women). *Tuition:* Part-time $340 per credit hour. *Graduate housing:* Room and/or apartments available on a first-come, first-served basis to single students; on-campus housing not available to married students. Typical cost: $5,580 (including board). Room and board charges vary according to board plan and housing facility selected. Housing application deadline: 6/30. *Student services:* Campus employment opportunities, campus safety program, career counseling, disabled student services, exercise/wellness program, free psychological counseling, low-cost health insurance, teacher training, writing training. *Library facilities:* University of St. Francis Library. *Online resources:* library catalog, web page, access to other libraries' catalogs. *Collection:* 184,000 titles, 710 serial subscriptions, 2,800 audiovisual materials.

Computer facilities: 147 computers available on campus for general student use. A campuswide network can be accessed from student residence rooms. Internet access and online class registration are available. *Web address:* http://www.stfrancis.edu/.

General Application Contact: Sheryl Paul, Executive Director, 800-735-7500, Fax: 815-740-5032, E-mail: spaul@stfrancis.edu.

GRADUATE UNITS

College of Health Arts, Graduate and Professional Studies Students: 105 full-time (74 women), 939 part-time (765 women); includes 111 minority (67 African Americans, 23 Asian Americans or Pacific Islanders, 20 Hispanic Americans, 1 Native American) Average age 39. 394 applicants, 73% accepted, 214 enrolled. *Faculty:* 7 full-time (2 women), 57 part-time/adjunct (21 women). Expenses: Contact institution. *Financial support:* In 2001–02, 75 students received support. Tuition waivers (partial) available. Support available to part-time students. Financial award applicants required to submit FAFSA. In 2001, 211 degrees awarded. *Degree program information:* Part-time and evening/weekend programs available. Offers health arts, graduate and professional studies (M Ed, MBA, MS, MSM). *Application deadline:* For fall admission, 8/15 (priority date); for spring admission, 12/15 (priority date). Applications are processed on a rolling basis. *Application fee:* $25. Electronic applications accepted. *Application Contact:* Sheryl Paul, Executive Director, 800-735-7500, Fax: 815-740-5032, E-mail: spaul@stfrancis.edu. *Dean,* Dr. Lyle Hicks, 815-740-3600, Fax: 815-740-3537, E-mail: lhicks@stfrancis.edu.

UNIVERSITY OF SAINT FRANCIS, Fort Wayne, IN 46808-3994

General Information Independent-religious, coed, comprehensive institution. *Enrollment:* 33 full-time matriculated graduate/professional students (23 women), 153 part-time matriculated graduate/professional students (105 women). *Enrollment by degree level:* 186 master's. *Graduate faculty:* 20 full-time (13 women), 5 part-time/adjunct (4 women). *Tuition:* Part-time $430 per hour. *Required fees:* $10 per hour. *Graduate housing:* Room and/or apartments available on a first-come, first-served basis to single students; on-campus housing not available to married students. *Student services:* Campus employment opportunities, career counseling, disabled student services, free psychological counseling, international student services, low-cost health insurance. *Library facilities:* University Library plus 1 other. *Online resources:* library catalog, web page, access to other libraries' catalogs. *Collection:* 85,544 titles, 580 serial subscriptions.

Computer facilities: 135 computers available on campus for general student use. Internet access is available. *Web address:* http://www.sf.edu/.

General Application Contact: David McMahan, Director of Admissions, 260-434-3264, Fax: 260-434-7590, E-mail: dmcmahan@sf.edu.

GRADUATE UNITS

Graduate School Students: 33 full-time (23 women), 153 part-time (105 women); includes 9 minority (7 African Americans, 2 Asian Americans or Pacific Islanders), 2 international. Average age 34. 129 applicants, 84% accepted. *Faculty:* 20 full-time (13 women), 5 part-time/adjunct (4 women). Expenses: Contact institution. *Financial support:* In 2001–02, 55 students received support. Career-related internships or fieldwork, Federal Work-Study, scholarships/grants, and unspecified assistantships available. Support available to part-time students. Financial award applicants required to submit FAFSA. In 2001, 45 degrees awarded. *Degree program information:* Part-time and evening/weekend programs available. Offers business administration (MBA, MS); fine art (MA); general psychology (MS); mental health counseling (MS); nursing (MSN); physician assistant studies (MS); school counseling (MS Ed); special education (MS Ed). *Application deadline:* For fall admission, 7/1 (priority date); for spring admission, 11/1 (priority date). Applications are processed on a rolling basis. *Application fee:* $20. *Application Contact:* David McMahan, Director of Admissions, 260-434-3264, Fax: 260-434-7590, E-mail: dmcmahan@sf.edu. *Chair,* Dr. Marcia Sauter, 260-434-7464, Fax: 260-434-7404, E-mail: msauter@sf.edu.

UNIVERSITY OF SAINT MARY OF THE LAKE–MUNDELEIN SEMINARY, Mundelein, IL 60060

General Information Independent-religious, men only, graduate-only institution. *Graduate faculty:* 36 full-time (3 women), 19 part-time/adjunct (4 women). *Tuition:* Full-time $13,152; part-time $300 per credit hour. *Graduate housing:* Room and/or apartments guaranteed to single students; on-campus housing not available to married students. Typical cost: $1,873 (including board). Housing application deadline: 8/1. *Student services:* Campus employment opportunities, campus safety program, free psychological counseling, international student services, low-cost health insurance, multicultural affairs office. *Library facilities:* Feehan Memorial Library. *Collection:* 180,000 titles, 400 serial subscriptions.

Computer facilities: 20 computers available on campus for general student use. A campuswide network can be accessed from student residence rooms. Internet access is available. *Web address:* http://www.vocations.org/.

General Application Contact: Rev. John F. Canary, Rector-President, 847-566-6401, Fax: 847-566-7330.

GRADUATE UNITS

School of Theology Students: 245 full-time (2 women), 9 part-time (2 women); includes 21 minority (5 African Americans, 8 Asian Americans or Pacific Islanders, 8 Hispanic Americans), 80 international. Average age 32. 82 applicants, 95% accepted. *Faculty:* 36 full-time (3 women), 19 part-time/adjunct (4 women). Expenses: Contact institution. *Financial support:* Career-related internships or fieldwork available. In 2001, 36 M Divs, 5 doctorates, 3 other advanced degrees awarded. *Degree program information:* Part-time programs available. Offers theology (M Div, STB, D Min, Certificate, STL). *Application deadline:* Applications are processed on a rolling basis. *Application fee:* $0. Electronic applications accepted. *Application Contact:* Rev. John F. Canary, Rector-President, 847-566-6401, Fax: 847-566-7330. *Academic Dean,* Rev. John G. Lodge, 847-566-6401.

UNIVERSITY OF ST. MICHAEL'S COLLEGE, Toronto, ON M5S 1J4, Canada

General Information Independent-religious, coed, graduate-only institution. *Enrollment by degree level:* 71 first professional, 18 master's, 47 doctoral, 20 other advanced degrees. *Graduate faculty:* 12 full-time (3 women), 16 part-time/adjunct (8 women). *Graduate tuition:* Tuition charges are reported in Canadian dollars. *Tuition:* Full-time $4,912 Canadian dollars; part-time $460 Canadian dollars per course. Tuition and fees vary according to program and student level. *Graduate housing:* Room and/or apartments available on a first-come, first-served basis to single students; on-campus housing not available to married students. Typical cost: $7,300 Canadian dollars (including board). Housing application deadline: 8/15. *Student services:* Campus employment opportunities, campus safety program, career counseling, disabled student services, international student services, low-cost health insurance. *Library facilities:* John Kelly Library plus 1 other. *Online resources:* library catalog, web page. *Collection:* 350,000 titles, 461 serial subscriptions, 190 audiovisual materials.

Computer facilities: 100 computers available on campus for general student use. A campuswide network can be accessed from student residence rooms and from off campus. Internet access and online class registration are available. *Web address:* http://www.utoronto.ca/stmikes/theology/.

General Application Contact: Wilma Stoyanoff, Registrar, 416-926-7140, Fax: 416-926-7294, E-mail: w.stoyanoff@utoronto.ca.

GRADUATE UNITS

Faculty of Theology Students: 84 full-time (35 women), 72 part-time (42 women); includes 9 minority (2 African Americans, 5 Asian Americans or Pacific Islanders, 2 Hispanic Americans), 28 international. Average age 38. 54 applicants, 56% accepted, 27 enrolled. *Faculty:* 12 full-time (3 women), 16 part-time/adjunct (8 women). Expenses: Contact institution. *Financial support:* In 2001–02, 54 students received support, including 2 research assistantships (averaging $2,500 per year), 5 teaching assistantships (averaging $4,200 per year); scholarships/grants, tuition waivers (partial), and bursaries also available. Financial award application deadline: 3/31. In 2001, 19 first professional degrees, 6 master's, 13 doctorates awarded. *Degree program information:* Part-time programs available. Postbaccalaureate distance learning degree programs offered (minimal on-campus study). Offers theology (M Div, MA, MRE, MTS, D Min, PhD, Th D); theology and Jewish studies (MA). *Application deadline:* For fall admission, 6/15 (priority date); for spring admission, 10/15. Applications are processed on a rolling basis. *Application fee:* $25. Electronic applications accepted. *Application Contact:* Wilma Stoyanoff, Registrar, 416-926-7140, Fax: 416-926-7294, E-mail: w.stoyanoff@utoronto.ca. *Dean,* Dr. Anne Anderson, CSJ, 416-926-7265, Fax: 416-926-7294, E-mail: anne.anderson@utoronto.ca.

UNIVERSITY OF ST. THOMAS, St. Paul, MN 55105-1096

General Information Independent-religious, coed, university. *Enrollment:* 687 full-time matriculated graduate/professional students (354 women), 4,597 part-time matriculated graduate/professional students (2,274 women). *Enrollment by degree level:* 65 first professional, 4,718 master's, 198 doctoral, 303 other advanced degrees. *Graduate faculty:* 192 full-time (79 women), 349 part-time/adjunct (113 women). *Tuition:* Part-time $401 per credit. Tuition and fees vary according to degree level and program. *Graduate housing:* On-campus housing not available. *Student services:* Campus employment opportunities, campus safety program, career counseling, child daycare facilities, disabled student services, exercise/wellness program, free psychological counseling, international student services, low-cost health insurance, multicultural affairs office. *Library facilities:* O'Shaughnessy-Frey Library plus 2 others. *Online resources:* library catalog, web page, access to other libraries' catalogs. *Collection:* 312,092 titles, 2,528 serial subscriptions, 6,158 audiovisual materials.

Computer facilities: 843 computers available on campus for general student use. A campuswide network can be accessed from student residence rooms and from off campus. Internet access and online class registration are available. *Web address:* http://www.stthomas.edu/.

General Application Contact: Dr. Angeline Barretta-Herman, Associate Vice President for Academic Affairs, 651-962-6033, Fax: 651-962-6702, E-mail: a9barrettahe@stthomas.edu.

GRADUATE UNITS

Graduate Studies Students: 687 full-time (354 women), 4,597 part-time (2,274 women); includes 475 minority (169 African Americans, 220 Asian Americans or Pacific Islanders, 59 Hispanic Americans, 27 Native Americans), 495 international. Average age 33. 1,791 applicants, 82% accepted. *Faculty:* 192 full-time (79 women), 349 part-time/adjunct (113 women). Expenses: Contact institution. *Financial support:* In 2001–02, 1,328 students received support, including 5 fellowships (averaging $4,800 per year), 18 research assistantships (averaging $944 per year); teaching assistantships, career-related internships or fieldwork, institutionally sponsored loans, and scholarships/grants also available. Support available to part-time students. Financial award application deadline: 4/1; financial award applicants required to submit FAFSA. In 2001, 12 first professional degrees, 1,326 master's, 29 doctorates, 181 other advanced degrees awarded. *Degree program information:* Part-time and evening/weekend programs available. Postbaccalaureate distance learning degree programs offered (no on-campus study). Offers social work (MSW). Electronic applications accepted. *Application Contact:* Dr. Angeline Barretta-Herman, Associate Vice President for Academic Affairs, 651-962-6033, Fax: 651-962-6702, E-mail: a9barrettahe@stthomas.edu. *Interim Vice President for Academic Affairs,* Dr. Susan L. Alexander, 651-962-6033, Fax: 651-962-6702, E-mail: slalexander@stthomas.edu.

College of Arts and Sciences Students: 10 full-time (5 women), 119 part-time (86 women); includes 2 minority (1 African American, 1 Asian American or Pacific Islander), 3 international. Average age 33. 37 applicants, 89% accepted. *Faculty:* 35 full-time (18 women), 16 part-time/adjunct (14 women). Expenses: Contact institution. *Financial support:* In 2001–02, 47 students received support, including 5 fellowships (averaging $4,800 per year); research assistantships, teaching assistantships, career-related internships or fieldwork, institutionally sponsored loans, and scholarships/grants also available. Support available to part-time students. Financial award application deadline: 4/1; financial award applicants required to submit FAFSA. In 2001, 21 degrees awarded. *Degree program information:* Part-time and evening/weekend programs available. Offers art history (MA); arts and sciences (MA); Catholic studies (MA); English (MA); music education (MA). *Dean of the College of Arts and Sciences,* Dr. Thomas B. Connery, 651-962-6000, Fax: 651-962-6930, E-mail: tbconnery@stthomas.edu.

College of Business Students: 245 full-time (104 women), 2,344 part-time (1,071 women); includes 171 minority (54 African Americans, 72 Asian Americans or Pacific Islanders, 33 Hispanic Americans, 12 Native Americans), 150 international. Average age 32. 852 applicants, 76% accepted. *Faculty:* 78 full-time (22 women), 154 part-time/adjunct (38 women). Expenses: Contact institution. *Financial support:* In 2001–02, 403 students received support; fellowships, research assistantships, career-related internships or fieldwork, institutionally sponsored loans, and scholarships/grants available. Support available to part-time students. Financial award application deadline: 4/1; financial award applicants required to submit FAFSA. In 2001, 642 master's, 23 other advanced degrees awarded. *Degree program information:* Part-time and evening/weekend programs available. Postbaccalaureate distance learning degree programs offered. Offers accounting (MBA, Certificate); business (MBA, MBC, MIM, MS, Certificate); business administration (MBA, Certificate); business communication (MBC); business writing (Certificate); electronic commerce (MBA); environmental management (MBA); finance (MBA); financial services management (MBA); franchise management (MBA, Certificate); government contracts (MBA, Certificate); health care management (MBA, Certificate); human resource management (MBA, Certificate); human resource management—development (Certificate); human resource management—organizational development (Certificate); human resource management—training (Certificate); human resource management–compensation (Certificate); human resource management–employee benefits (Certificate); human resource management–generalist (Certificate); human resource management–law (Certificate); information management (MBA); insurance and risk management (MBA); internal communication (Certificate); international finance (MIM, Certificate); international human resource management (Certificate); international human resources (MIM, Certificate); international managerial communication (MIM, Certificate); international marketing (MIM, Certificate); management (MBA); management communication (Certificate); manufacturing systems (MBA, MIM, Certificate); marketing (MBA); marketing communication (Certificate); medical group management (MBA); nonprofit management (MBA, Certificate); public relations (Certificate); real estate (MBA); real estate appraisal (MS, Certificate); self-designed (MIM); software systems (MIM, Certificate); sports and entertainment management (MBA); survey of professional communication (Certificate); venture management (MBA, Certificate). *Application deadline:* For fall admission, 4/1 (priority date); for spring admission, 12/1 (priority date). Applications are processed on a rolling basis. *Application Contact:* Martha Ballard, Director of Faculty and Student Services, 651-962-4226, Fax: 651-962-4260, E-mail: mbballard@stthomas.edu. *Interim Dean,* Dr. Jeanne Buckeye, 651-962-4206, Fax: 651-962-4260.

Graduate School of Applied Science and Engineering Students: 136 full-time (49 women), 984 part-time (277 women); includes 194 minority (62 African Americans, 123 Asian Americans or Pacific Islanders, 7 Hispanic Americans, 2 Native Americans), 332 international. Average age 32. 331 applicants, 98% accepted. *Faculty:* 12 full-time (2 women), 78 part-time/adjunct (7 women). Expenses: Contact institution. *Financial support:* In 2001–02, 236 students received support; fellowships, research assistantships, institutionally sponsored loans and scholarships/grants available. Support available to part-time students. Financial award application deadline: 4/1; financial award applicants required to submit FAFSA. In 2001, 248 master's, 29 other advanced degrees awarded. *Degree program information:* Part-time and evening/weekend programs available. Offers applied science and engineering (MMSE, MS, MSDD, MSS, Certificate); engineering and technology management (Certificate); manufacturing systems (MS); manufacturing systems engineering (MMSE); software engineering (MS, MSDD, MSS, Certificate); technology management (MS). *Application deadline:* For fall admission, 8/1 (priority date); for spring admission, 1/1 (priority date). Applications are processed on a rolling basis. *Application fee:* $30. Electronic applications accepted. *Application Contact:* Dr. Angeline Barretta-Herman, Associate Vice President for Academic Affairs, 651-962-6033, Fax: 651-962-6702, E-mail: a9barrettahe@stthomas.edu.

Graduate School of Professional Psychology Students: 42 full-time (34 women), 124 part-time (98 women); includes 19 minority (8 African Americans, 6 Asian Americans or Pacific Islanders, 4 Hispanic Americans, 1 Native American) Average age 34. 41 applicants, 76% accepted, 29 enrolled. *Faculty:* 8 full-time (4 women), 15 part-time/adjunct (8 women). Expenses: Contact institution. *Financial support:* In 2001–02, 91 students received support; fellowships, research assistantships, institutionally sponsored loans and scholarships/grants available. Support available to part-time students. Financial award application deadline: 4/1. In 2001, 34 master's, 8 doctorates, 6 other advanced degrees awarded. *Degree program information:* Part-time and evening/weekend programs available. Offers counseling psychology (MA, Psy D); family psychology (Certificate). *Application deadline:* For fall admission, 10/1; for winter admission, 2/1; for spring admission, 4/1. *Application fee:* $50. *Application Contact:* Dr. Mary M. Brant, Assistant Professor, 651-962-4641, Fax: 651-962-4651, E-mail: mmbrant@stthomas.edu. *Dean,* Dr. Burton Nolan, 651-962-4650, Fax: 651-962-4651, E-mail: bnolan@stthomas.edu.

Saint Paul Seminary School of Divinity Students: 69 full-time (3 women), 48 part-time (34 women); includes 7 minority (2 African Americans, 3 Asian Americans or Pacific Islanders, 2 Hispanic Americans), 1 international. Average age 36. 40 applicants, 100% accepted. *Faculty:* 14 full-time (4 women), 2 part-time/adjunct (0 women). Expenses: Contact institution. *Financial support:* In 2001–02, 67 students received support; fellowships, research assistantships, institutionally sponsored loans and scholarships/grants available. Support available to part-time students. Financial award application deadline: 4/1; financial award applicants required to submit FAFSA. In 2001, 12 first professional degrees, 7 master's, 3 doctorates awarded. *Degree program information:* Part-time and evening/weekend programs available. Offers divinity (M Div, MA, D Min); ministry (D Min); pastoral studies (MA); religious education (MA); theology (MA). *Application deadline:* For fall admission, 6/1 (priority date). Applications are processed on a rolling basis. *Application fee:* $30. *Application Contact:* Rev. Ronald Bowers, Vice Rector and Admission Chair, 651-962-5068, Fax: 651-962-5790, E-mail: rjbowers@stthomas.edu. *Rector,* Bp. Frederick Campbell, 651-962-5052, Fax: 651-962-5790, E-mail: fcampbell@stthomas.edu.

School of Education Students: 58 full-time (46 women), 937 part-time (660 women); includes 61 minority (31 African Americans, 12 Asian Americans or Pacific Islanders, 10 Hispanic Americans, 8 Native Americans), 9 international. Average age 35. 315 applicants, 78% accepted. *Faculty:* 33 full-time (20 women), 70 part-time/adjunct (37 women). Expenses: Contact institution. *Financial support:* In 2001–02, 333 students received support; fellowships, research assistantships, career-related internships or fieldwork, institutionally sponsored loans, and scholarships/grants available. Support available to part-time students. Financial award application deadline: 4/1; financial award applicants required to submit FAFSA. In 2001, 302 master's, 63 doctorates, 81 other advanced degrees awarded. *Degree program information:* Part-time and evening/weekend programs available. Offers curriculum and instruction (MA, Ed D, Ed S); education (MA, Ed D, Certificate, Ed S); educational leadership and administration (MA, Ed D, Certificate, Ed S); organization learning and development (MA, Ed D, Certificate); reading and language technology (Certificate); special education (MA, Certificate); teacher education (MA). *Application deadline:* For fall admission, 6/1 (priority date); for spring admission, 11/1 (priority date). Applications are processed on a rolling basis. *Application fee:* $50. *Application Contact:* Myrna Engebretson, Admissions Counselor, 651-962-5430, Fax: 651-962-5169, E-mail: mlengebretso@stthomas.edu. *Dean,* Dr. Miriam Williams, 651-962-4435, Fax: 651-962-6930, E-mail: mqwilliams@stthomas.edu.

See in-depth description on page 1245.

UNIVERSITY OF ST. THOMAS, Houston, TX 77006-4696

General Information Independent-religious, coed, comprehensive institution. *Enrollment:* 271 full-time matriculated graduate/professional students (121 women), 707 part-time matriculated graduate/professional students (431 women). *Enrollment by degree level:* 60 first professional, 912 master's, 6 doctoral. *Graduate faculty:* 48 full-time, 37 part-time/adjunct. *Tuition:* Full-time $8,550; part-time $475 per credit. *Required fees:* $11 per term. *Graduate housing:* Room and/or apartments available on a first-come, first-served basis to single students; on-campus housing not available to married students. Typical cost: $3,020 per year ($5,920 including board). Room and board charges vary according to board plan and housing facility selected. Housing application deadline: 7/1. *Student services:* Campus employment opportunities, campus safety program, career counseling, free psychological counseling, international student services. *Library facilities:* Doherty Library plus 1 other. *Online resources:* library catalog, web page, access to other libraries' catalogs. *Collection:* 226,593 titles, 3,400 serial subscriptions, 1,148 audiovisual materials.

Computer facilities: 143 computers available on campus for general student use. A campuswide network can be accessed from student residence rooms and from off campus. Internet access is available. *Web address:* http://www.stthom.edu/.

General Application Contact: Gerald E. Warren, Assistant Director of Admissions, 713-525-3500, Fax: 713-525-3558, E-mail: admissions@stthom.edu.

GRADUATE UNITS

Cameron School of Business Students: 174 full-time (89 women), 317 part-time (143 women); includes 151 minority (50 African Americans, 32 Asian Americans or Pacific Islanders, 69 Hispanic Americans), 130 international. Average age 30. 204 applicants, 91% accepted, 142 enrolled. *Faculty:* 22 full-time, 10 part-time/adjunct. Expenses: Contact institution. *Financial support:* In 2001–02, 76 students received support, including 6 fellowships (averaging $1,829 per year); Federal Work-Study, scholarships/grants, and unspecified assistantships also available. Support available to part-time students. Financial award application deadline: 3/1; financial award applicants required to submit FAFSA. In 2001, 136 degrees awarded. *Degree program information:* Part-time and evening/weekend programs available. Offers business (MBA, MIB, MSA, MSIS). *Application deadline:* For fall admission, 6/30; for spring admission, 10/31. Applications are processed on a rolling basis. *Application fee:* $35. *Application Contact:* Yolanda Salinas, Graduate Services Assistant, 713-525-2115, Fax: 713-525-2110, E-mail: salinas@stthom.edu. *Dean,* Dr. Yhi-Min Ho, 713-525-2100, Fax: 713-525-2110, E-mail: yhiminho@stthom.edu.

Center for Thomistic Studies Students: 4 full-time (0 women), 17 part-time (5 women); includes 4 minority (2 Asian Americans or Pacific Islanders, 2 Hispanic Americans), 3 international. Average age 33. 6 applicants, 100% accepted, 5 enrolled. *Faculty:* 11 full-time (1 woman). Expenses: Contact institution. *Financial support:* In 2001–02, 9 students received support, including 8 fellowships (averaging $9,872 per year); Federal Work-Study and scholarships/grants also available. Support available to part-time students. Financial award application deadline: 3/1; financial award applicants required to submit FAFSA. In 2001, 2 master's, 2 doctorates awarded. *Degree program information:* Part-time programs available. Offers philosophy (MA, PhD). *Application deadline:* For fall admission, 3/15 (priority date). Applications are processed on a rolling basis. *Application fee:* $0. *Director,* Dr. Daniel McInerny, 713-525-3591, Fax: 713-942-3464, E-mail: mac@stthom.edu.

Program in Liberal Arts Students: 27 full-time (16 women), 100 part-time (77 women); includes 36 minority (14 African Americans, 4 Asian Americans or Pacific Islanders, 16 Hispanic Americans, 2 Native Americans), 9 international. Average age 39. 51 applicants, 100% accepted, 40 enrolled. Expenses: Contact institution. *Financial support:* In 2001–02, 33 students received support, including 3 fellowships (averaging $1,917 per year); institutionally sponsored loans and scholarships/grants also available. Support available to part-time students. Financial award application deadline: 3/1; financial award applicants required to submit FAFSA. In 2001, 27 degrees awarded. *Degree program information:* Part-time and evening/weekend programs available. Offers liberal arts (MLA). *Application deadline:* Applications are processed on a rolling basis. *Application fee:* $35. *Director,* Dr. Janice Gordon-Kelter, 713-525-6951, Fax: 713-525-6924, E-mail: jgk@stthom.edu.

School of Education Students: 10 full-time (all women), 203 part-time (174 women); includes 57 minority (24 African Americans, 3 Asian Americans or Pacific Islanders, 29 Hispanic Americans, 1 Native American), 3 international. Average age 35. 64 applicants, 100% accepted, 31 enrolled. *Faculty:* 10 full-time, 12 part-time/adjunct. Expenses: Contact institution. *Financial support:* In 2001–02, 30 students received support, including 9 fellowships (averaging $1,422 per year); Federal Work-Study and scholarships/grants also available. Support available to part-time students. Financial award application deadline: 3/1; financial award applicants required to submit FAFSA. In 2001, 32 degrees awarded. *Degree program information:* Part-time and evening/weekend programs available. Offers education (M Ed). *Application deadline:* Applications are processed on a rolling basis. *Application fee:* $35. *Application Contact:* Paula C. Hollis, Secretary, 713-525-3541, Fax: 713-525-3871, E-mail: hollisp@stthom.edu. *Dean,* Dr. Ruth M. Strudler, 713-525-3546, Fax: 713-525-3871, E-mail: strudler@stthom.edu.

School of Theology Students: 56 full-time (6 women), 70 part-time (32 women); includes 40 minority (5 African Americans, 21 Asian Americans or Pacific Islanders, 14 Hispanic Americans), 15 international. Average age 39. 47 applicants, 100% accepted, 39 enrolled. *Faculty:* 5 full-time, 15 part-time/adjunct. Expenses: Contact institution. *Financial support:* In 2001–02, 8 students received support, including 5 fellowships (averaging $1,055 per year); Federal Work-Study and scholarships/grants also available. Support available to part-time students. Financial award application deadline: 3/1; financial award applicants required to submit FAFSA. In 2001, 10 first professional degrees, 22 master's awarded. *Degree program information:* Part-time programs available. Offers theology (M Div, MAPS, MAT). *Application deadline:* For fall admission, 8/15 (priority date); for spring admission, 12/1. Applications are processed on a rolling basis. *Application fee:* $35. *Application Contact:* Marianne Strzelecki, Director of Admissions, 713-686-4345 Ext. 288, Fax: 713-683-8673, E-mail: strezlm@stthomas.edu. *Dean,* Rev. Louis T. Brusatti, CM, 713-686-4345 Ext. 287, Fax: 713-683-8673, E-mail: brusatti@stthom.edu.

UNIVERSITY OF SAN DIEGO, San Diego, CA 92110-2492

General Information Independent-religious, coed, university. CGS member. *Enrollment:* 1,175 full-time matriculated graduate/professional students (630 women), 863 part-time matriculated graduate/professional students (473 women). *Enrollment by degree level:* 975 first professional, 879 master's, 184 doctoral. *Graduate faculty:* 159 full-time (64 women), 135 part-time/adjunct (65 women). *Graduate housing:* On-campus housing not available. *Student services:* Campus employment opportunities, career counseling, child daycare facilities, disabled student services, free psychological counseling, international student services, low-cost health insurance, multicultural affairs office, teacher training, writing training. *Library facilities:* Helen K. and James S. Copley Library plus 1 other. *Online resources:* library catalog, access to other libraries' catalogs. *Collection:* 500,000 titles, 2,600 serial subscriptions, 14,000 audiovisual materials. *Research affiliation:* Old Globe Theater (dramatic arts), Hubbs Marine Research Center (marine science, ocean studies).

Computer facilities: 260 computers available on campus for general student use. A campuswide network can be accessed from student residence rooms and from off campus. Internet access and online class registration are available. *Web address:* http://www.sandiego.edu/.

General Application Contact: Mary Jane Tiernan, Director of Graduate Admissions, 619-260-4524, Fax: 619-260-4158, E-mail: grads@sandiego.edu.

GRADUATE UNITS

College of Arts and Sciences Students: 44 full-time (27 women), 84 part-time (45 women); includes 24 minority (2 African Americans, 10 Asian Americans or Pacific Islanders, 12 Hispanic Americans), 3 international. Average age 31. 312 applicants, 27% accepted. *Faculty:* 42 full-time (23 women), 39 part-time/adjunct (14 women). Expenses: Contact institution. *Financial support:* Fellowships with partial tuition reimbursements, teaching assistantships with partial tuition reimbursements, career-related internships or fieldwork, Federal Work-Study, institutionally sponsored loans, scholarships/grants, tuition waivers (partial), and unspecified assistantships available. Support available to part-time students. Financial award application deadline: 5/1; financial award applicants required to submit FAFSA. In 2001, 35 degrees awarded. *Degree program information:* Part-time and evening/weekend programs available. Offers arts and sciences (MA, MFA, MS); dramatic arts (MFA); history (MA); international relations (MA); marine science (MS); pastoral care and counseling (MA); practical theology (MA). *Application deadline:* Applications are processed on a rolling basis. *Application fee:* $45. Electronic applications accepted. *Application Contact:* Mary Jane Tiernan, Director of Graduate Admissions, 619-260-4524, Fax: 619-260-4158, E-mail: grads@sandiego.edu. *Dean,* Dr. Patrick Drinan, 619-260-4545, Fax: 619-260-4162, E-mail: pdrinan@sandiego.edu.

Hahn School of Nursing and Health Sciences Students: 41 full-time (40 women), 85 part-time (83 women); includes 24 minority (4 African Americans, 6 Asian Americans or Pacific Islanders, 11 Hispanic Americans, 3 Native Americans), 1 international. Average age 41. 78 applicants, 90% accepted. *Faculty:* 9 full-time (all women), 16 part-time/adjunct (14 women). Expenses: Contact institution. *Financial support:* Fellowships, institutionally sponsored loans, scholarships/grants, and traineeships available. Support available to part-time students. Financial award application deadline: 5/1; financial award applicants required to submit FAFSA. In 2001, 32 master's, 3 doctorates awarded. *Degree program information:* Part-time and evening/weekend programs available. Offers adult nurse practitioner (MSN, Post Master's Certificate); case management for vulnerable populations (MSN); family nurse practitioner (MSN, Post Master's Certificate); health care systems (MSN); nursing science (PhD); pediatric nurse practitioner (MSN, Post Master's Certificate). *Application deadline:* For fall admission, 5/1 (priority date); for spring admission, 11/1 (priority date). Applications are processed on a rolling basis. *Application fee:* $45. Electronic applications accepted. *Application Contact:* Mary Jane Tiernan, Director of Graduate Admissions, 619-260-4524, Fax: 619-260-4158, E-mail: grads@sandiego.edu. *Dean,* Dr. Janet Rodgers, 619-260-4550, Fax: 619-260-6814, E-mail: rodgers@sandiego.edu.

School of Business Administration Students: 143 full-time (57 women), 158 part-time (62 women); includes 60 minority (3 African Americans, 29 Asian Americans or Pacific Islanders, 26 Hispanic Americans, 2 Native Americans), 38 international. Average age 31. 381 applicants, 54% accepted. *Faculty:* 35 full-time (5 women), 4 part-time/adjunct (2 women). Expenses: Contact institution. *Financial support:* In 2001–02, 84 fellowships (averaging $1,600 per year) were awarded; career-related internships or fieldwork, Federal Work-Study, institutionally

University of San Diego (continued)

sponsored loans, scholarships/grants, and unspecified assistantships also available. Support available to part-time students. Financial award application deadline: 5/1; financial award applicants required to submit FAFSA. In 2001, 160 degrees awarded. *Degree program information:* Part-time and evening/weekend programs available. Offers business administration (IMBA, MBA); electronic commerce (MSEC); executive leadership (MSEL); global leadership (MSGL). *Application deadline:* For fall admission, 5/1 (priority date); for spring admission, 11/15 (priority date). Applications are processed on a rolling basis. *Application fee:* $45. Electronic applications accepted. *Application Contact:* Dr. C. David Light, Graduate Program Director, 619-260-4871, Fax: 619-260-4891, E-mail: dlight@sandiego.edu. *Dean,* Dr. Curtis Cook, 619-260-4886, Fax: 619-260-4891, E-mail: sbadean@sandiego.edu.

School of Education Students: 172 full-time (132 women), 225 part-time (149 women); includes 111 minority (19 African Americans, 26 Asian Americans or Pacific Islanders, 58 Hispanic Americans, 8 Native Americans), 18 international. Average age 33. 358 applicants, 75% accepted. *Faculty:* 20 full-time (9 women), 39 part-time/adjunct (30 women). Expenses: Contact institution. *Financial support:* In 2001–02, 353 students received support, including 69 fellowships with tuition reimbursements available; career-related internships or fieldwork, Federal Work-Study, institutionally sponsored loans, unspecified assistantships, and stipends also available. Support available to part-time students. Financial award application deadline: 5/1; financial award applicants required to submit FAFSA. In 2001, 113 master's, 8 doctorates awarded. *Degree program information:* Part-time and evening/weekend programs available. Postbaccalaureate distance learning degree programs offered. Offers counseling (MA); education (M Ed, MA, MAT, Ed D); educational leadership (M Ed); leadership studies (MA, Ed D); learning and teaching (M Ed, MAT, Ed D); marital and family therapy (MA). *Application fee:* $45. *Application Contact:* Mary Jane Tiernan, Director of Graduate Admissions, 619-260-4524, Fax: 619-260-4158, E-mail: grads@sandiego.edu. *Dean,* Dr. Paula A. Cordeiro, 619-260-4540, Fax: 619-260-6835, E-mail: cordeiro@sandiego.edu.

School of Law Students: 776 full-time (375 women), 314 part-time (136 women); includes 258 minority (28 African Americans, 126 Asian Americans or Pacific Islanders, 90 Hispanic Americans, 14 Native Americans), 35 international. Average age 28. 3,082 applicants, 41% accepted. *Faculty:* 53 full-time (18 women), 37 part-time/adjunct (5 women). Expenses: Contact institution. *Financial support:* In 2001–02, 920 students received support, including 60 research assistantships (averaging $4,000 per year); career-related internships or fieldwork, Federal Work-Study, institutionally sponsored loans, and scholarships/grants also available. Support available to part-time students. Financial award application deadline: 3/1; financial award applicants required to submit FAFSA. In 2001, 302 first professional degrees, 92 master's awarded. *Degree program information:* Part-time and evening/weekend programs available. Offers business and corporate law (LL M); comparative law (LL M); general studies (LL M); international law (LL M); law (JD); taxation (LL M, Diploma). *Application deadline:* For fall admission, 2/1 (priority date). Applications are processed on a rolling basis. *Application fee:* $50. Electronic applications accepted. *Application Contact:* Carl J. Eging, Director of Admissions and Financial Aid, 619-260-4528, Fax: 619-260-2218, E-mail: eging@sandiego.edu. *Dean,* Daniel B. Rodriguez, 619-260-4527, Fax: 619-260-2218, E-mail: danr@sandiego.edu.

See in-depth description on page 1247.

UNIVERSITY OF SAN FRANCISCO, San Francisco, CA 94117-1080

General Information Independent-religious, coed, university. *Enrollment:* 2,477 full-time matriculated graduate/professional students (1,501 women), 724 part-time matriculated graduate/professional students (444 women). *Enrollment by degree level:* 646 first professional, 2,243 master's, 312 doctoral. *Graduate faculty:* 148 full-time (46 women), 311 part-time/adjunct (121 women). *Tuition:* Full-time $14,400; part-time $800 per unit. Tuition and fees vary according to degree level, campus/location and program. *Graduate housing:* Room and/or apartments available on a first-come, first-served basis to single students; on-campus housing not available to married students. Typical cost: $5,450 per year ($8,710 including board). Room and board charges vary according to board plan, campus/location and housing facility selected. *Student services:* Campus employment opportunities, career counseling, disabled student services, free psychological counseling, international student services, low-cost health insurance, multicultural affairs office, teacher training. *Library facilities:* Gleeson Library plus 2 others. *Online resources:* library catalog, web page, access to other libraries' catalogs. *Collection:* 755,000 titles, 2,706 serial subscriptions, 1,730 audiovisual materials. *Research affiliation:* NASA–Ames Research Center.

Computer facilities: 250 computers available on campus for general student use. A campuswide network can be accessed from student residence rooms and from off campus. Internet access and online class registration are available. *Web address:* http://www.usfca.edu/.

General Application Contact: 415-422-6563, Fax: 415-422-2217.

GRADUATE UNITS

College of Arts and Sciences Students: 401 full-time (197 women), 66 part-time (41 women); includes 85 minority (17 African Americans, 41 Asian Americans or Pacific Islanders, 21 Hispanic Americans, 6 Native Americans), 116 international. Average age 33. 526 applicants, 81% accepted, 236 enrolled. *Faculty:* 51 full-time (9 women), 60 part-time/adjunct (19 women). Expenses: Contact institution. *Financial support:* In 2001–02, 303 students received support; fellowships, research assistantships, teaching assistantships, career-related internships or fieldwork, Federal Work-Study, institutionally sponsored loans, and tuition waivers (partial) available. Support available to part-time students. Financial award application deadline: 3/2; financial award applicants required to submit FAFSA. In 2001, 145 degrees awarded. *Degree program information:* Part-time and evening/weekend programs available. Offers arts and sciences (MA, MFA, MS); Asia Pacific studies (MA); biology (MS); chemistry (MS); computer science (MS); economics (MA); environmental management (MS); sports and fitness management (MA); theology (MA); writing (MA, MFA). *Application deadline:* Applications are processed on a rolling basis. *Application fee:* $55 ($65 for international students). *Dean,* Dr. Stanley Nel, 415-422-6373.

College of Professional Studies Students: 622 full-time (413 women); includes 216 minority (76 African Americans, 92 Asian Americans or Pacific Islanders, 43 Hispanic Americans, 5 Native Americans), 15 international. Average age 37. 267 applicants, 81% accepted, 185 enrolled. *Faculty:* 11 full-time (2 women), 111 part-time/adjunct (41 women). Expenses: Contact institution. *Financial support:* In 2001–02, 247 students received support. Available to part-time students. Application deadline: 3/2; In 2001, 296 degrees awarded. *Degree program information:* Part-time and evening/weekend programs available. Offers health services administration (MPA); human resources and organization development (MHROD); information systems (MS); nonprofit administration (MNA); professional studies (MHROD, MNA, MPA, MS); public administration (MPA). *Application fee:* $55 ($65 for international students). *Application Contact:* 415-422-6000. *Dean,* Dr. Larry Brewster, 415-422-6254.

Graduate School of Management Students: 347 full-time (145 women), 174 part-time (72 women); includes 96 minority (9 African Americans, 69 Asian Americans or Pacific Islanders, 15 Hispanic Americans, 3 Native Americans), 184 international. Average age 30. 555 applicants, 89% accepted, 188 enrolled. *Faculty:* 44 full-time (6 women), 37 part-time/adjunct (7 women). Expenses: Contact institution. *Financial support:* In 2001–02, 162 students received support; fellowships, research assistantships, teaching assistantships, career-related internships or fieldwork, Federal Work-Study, and institutionally sponsored loans available. Support available to part-time students. Financial award application deadline: 3/2; financial award applicants required to submit FAFSA. In 2001, 232 degrees awarded. *Degree program information:* Part-time and evening/weekend programs available. Offers finance and banking (MBA); international business (MBA); management (MBA); marketing (MBA); professional business administration (MBA); telecommunications management and policy (MBA). *Application deadline:* For fall admission, 7/1 (priority date); for spring admission, 11/30. Applications are processed on a rolling basis. *Application Contact:* Cathy Fusco, Director, MBA Program, 415-422-6314, Fax: 415-422-2502, E-mail: mbausf@usfca.edu. *Dean,* Dr. Gary Williams, 415-422-6771, Fax: 415-422-2502.

School of Education Students: 489 full-time (367 women), 361 part-time (258 women); includes 240 minority (74 African Americans, 65 Asian Americans or Pacific Islanders, 91 Hispanic Americans, 10 Native Americans), 35 international. Average age 37. 692 applicants, 96% accepted, 379 enrolled. *Faculty:* 34 full-time (22 women), 97 part-time/adjunct (50 women). Expenses: Contact institution. *Financial support:* In 2001–02, 552 students received support; fellowships, research assistantships, teaching assistantships available. Financial award application deadline: 3/2; financial award applicants required to submit FAFSA. In 2001, 190 master's, 67 doctorates awarded. *Degree program information:* Part-time and evening/weekend programs available. Offers Catholic school leadership (MA, Ed D); Catholic school teaching (MA); counseling (MA); counseling psychology (Psy D); education (MA, Ed D, Psy D); educational technology (MA); international and multicultural education (MA, Ed D); learning and instruction (MA, Ed D); multicultural literature for children and young adults (MA); organization and leadership (MA, Ed D); private school administration (Ed D); teaching English as a second language (MA). *Application fee:* $55 ($65 for international students). *Dean,* Dr. Paul Warren, 415-422-6525.

School of Law Students: 533 full-time (310 women), 113 part-time (64 women); includes 201 minority (31 African Americans, 117 Asian Americans or Pacific Islanders, 50 Hispanic Americans, 3 Native Americans), 32 international. Average age 28. 1,997 applicants, 47% accepted, 250 enrolled. *Faculty:* 28 full-time (9 women), 34 part-time/adjunct (9 women). Expenses: Contact institution. *Financial support:* In 2001–02, 565 students received support. Career-related internships or fieldwork, Federal Work-Study, and institutionally sponsored loans available. Support available to part-time students. Financial award application deadline: 3/2; financial award applicants required to submit FAFSA. In 2001, 190 degrees awarded. *Degree program information:* Part-time and evening/weekend programs available. Offers law (JD). *Application deadline:* For fall admission, 4/1. Applications are processed on a rolling basis. *Application fee:* $50. *Application Contact:* Saralynn T. Ferrara, Director of Admissions, 415-422-6586. *Dean,* Jeffrey Brand, 415-422-6304.

School of Nursing Students: 63 full-time (60 women), 9 part-time (all women); includes 34 minority (4 African Americans, 25 Asian Americans or Pacific Islanders, 5 Hispanic Americans) Average age 30. 68 applicants, 82% accepted, 12 enrolled. *Faculty:* 7 full-time (all women), 6 part-time/adjunct (4 women). Expenses: Contact institution. *Financial support:* In 2001–02, 46 students received support. Institutionally sponsored loans available. Financial award application deadline: 3/2. In 2001, 16 degrees awarded. *Degree program information:* Part-time programs available. Offers advanced practice nursing-nurse practitioner and clinical nurse specialist (MSN); nursing administration (MSN). *Application deadline:* Applications are processed on a rolling basis. *Application fee:* $40. *Dean,* Dr. John Lantz, 415-422-6681, Fax: 415-422-6877, E-mail: lantzj@usfca.edu.

See in-depth description on page 1249.

UNIVERSITY OF SASKATCHEWAN, Saskatoon, SK S7N 5A2, Canada

General Information Province-supported, coed, university. *Enrollment:* 1,326 full-time matriculated graduate/professional students, 441 part-time matriculated graduate/professional students. *Graduate faculty:* 999 full-time, 236 part-time/adjunct. *Graduate tuition:* Tuition and fees charges are reported in Canadian dollars. *Tuition:* Part-time $161 Canadian dollars per credit. *Required fees:* $479 Canadian dollars. *Graduate housing:* Rooms and/or apartments available on a first-come, first-served basis to single and married students. *Student services:* Campus employment opportunities, campus safety program, career counseling, child daycare facilities, disabled student services, free psychological counseling, international student services, low-cost health insurance, teacher training, writing training. *Library facilities:* University of Saskatchewan Main Library plus 7 others. *Online resources:* library catalog, web page, access to other libraries' catalogs. *Collection:* 1.7 million titles, 14,170 serial subscriptions. *Research affiliation:* Canada Agriculture, Saskatchewan Research Council, University Hospital, Innovation Place.

Computer facilities: 900 computers available on campus for general student use. A campuswide network can be accessed from off campus. Internet access is available. *Web address:* http://www.usask.ca/.

General Application Contact: Tammy Morrison, Information Contact, 306-966-5751, Fax: 306-966-5756, E-mail: morrisont@admin.usask.ca.

GRADUATE UNITS

College of Dentistry Students: 116 full-time (44 women). Average age 25. 211 applicants, 12% accepted. *Faculty:* 22 full-time (5 women), 65 part-time/adjunct (11 women). Expenses: Contact institution. *Financial support:* In 2001–02, 15 students received support. Career-related internships or fieldwork and scholarships/grants available. Financial award application deadline: 1/15. In 2001, 22 degrees awarded. Offers dentistry (DMD). *Application deadline:* For fall admission, 1/15. *Application fee:* $50. *Application Contact:* V. J. Millar, Director of Academic and Student Affairs, 306-966-5119, Fax: 306-966-5126, E-mail: valerie.millar@usask.ca. *Dean,* C. G. Baker, 306-966-5122, Fax: 306-966-5126, E-mail: charles.baker@usask.ca.

College of Graduate Studies and Research Students: 1,326 full-time, 441 part-time. *Faculty:* 999 full-time, 236 part-time/adjunct. Expenses: Contact institution. *Financial support:* In 2001–02, 600 students received support; fellowships, research assistantships, teaching assistantships, career-related internships or fieldwork available. Financial award application deadline: 1/31. In 2001, 435 master's, 63 doctorates awarded. *Degree program information:* Part-time programs available. Offers toxicology (M Sc, PhD, Diploma). *Application deadline:* For fall admission, 7/1 (priority date). Applications are processed on a rolling basis. *Application fee:* $50. *Application Contact:* Tammy Morrison, Information Contact, 306-966-5751, Fax: 306-966-5756, E-mail: morrisont@admin.usask.ca. *Dean,* Dr. Tom Wishart, 306-966-5759, E-mail: gradstudies@usask.ca.

College of Agriculture Students: 172. *Faculty:* 101. Expenses: Contact institution. *Financial support:* Fellowships, research assistantships, teaching assistantships, career-related internships or fieldwork available. Financial award application deadline: 1/31. *Degree program information:* Part-time programs available. Offers agricultural economics (M Sc, MA, PhD); agriculture (M Ag, M Sc, MA, PhD); animal and poultry science (M Sc, PhD); applied microbiology and food science (M Sc, PhD); plant sciences (M Sc, PhD); soil science (M Sc, PhD). *Application deadline:* For fall admission, 7/1 (priority date). Applications are processed on a rolling basis. *Application fee:* $50. *Dean,* J. E.M. Barber, 306-966-4050, Fax: 306-966-8894.

College of Arts and Sciences Expenses: Contact institution. *Financial support:* Fellowships, research assistantships, teaching assistantships available. Financial award application deadline: 1/31. *Degree program information:* Part-time programs available. Offers archaeology and anthropology (MA, PhD); art and art history (MFA); arts and sciences (M Math, M Mus, M Sc, MA, MFA, PhD, Diploma); biology (M Sc, PhD, Diploma); chemistry (M Sc, PhD); computer science (M Sc, PhD); drama (MA); economics (MA); English (MA, PhD); geography (M Sc, MA, PhD); geological sciences (M Sc, PhD, Diploma); history (MA, PhD); languages and linguistics (MA); mathematics and statistics (M Math, MA, PhD); music (MA); native studies (MA, PhD); philosophy (MA); physics (M Sc, PhD); political studies (MA, PhD); psychology (MA, PhD); sociology (MA, PhD); women's and gender studies (MA, PhD). *Application deadline:* For fall admission, 7/1 (priority date). Applications are processed on a rolling basis. *Application fee:* $50. *Dean,* Dr. Kenneth Coates, 306-966-4232, Fax: 306-966-8839.

College of Commerce Students: 105. *Faculty:* 60. Expenses: Contact institution. *Financial support:* Fellowships, research assistantships, teaching assistantships available. Financial award application deadline: 1/31. *Degree program information:* Part-time programs available. Offers accounting (M Sc, MP Acc); commerce (M Sc, MBA, MP Acc, PhD, Diploma); finance and management science (M Sc); industrial relations and organizational behavior (M Sc); management and marketing (M Sc). *Application deadline:* For fall admission, 7/1 (priority date). Applications are processed on a rolling basis. *Application fee:* $50. *Dean,* Dr. V. L. Pearson, 306-966-4786, Fax: 306-966-5408.

College of Education Students: 316. *Faculty:* 51. Expenses: Contact institution. *Financial support:* Fellowships, research assistantships, teaching assistantships available. Financial award application deadline: 1/31. *Degree program information:* Part-time programs available. Offers curriculum studies (M Ed, PhD, Diploma); education (M Ed, MC Ed, PhD, Diploma); educational administration (M Ed, PhD, Diploma); educational foundations (M Ed, MC Ed, PhD, Diploma); educational psychology (M Ed, PhD, Diploma). *Application deadline:* For fall admission, 7/1 (priority date). Applications are processed on a rolling basis. *Application fee:* $50. *Dean,* Dr. K. Jacknicke, 306-966-7647, Fax: 306-966-7624.

College of Engineering Students: 286. *Faculty:* 69. Expenses: Contact institution. *Financial support:* Fellowships, research assistantships, teaching assistantships available. Financial award application deadline: 1/31. Offers agricultural and bioresource engineering (M Eng, M Sc, PhD); biomedical engineering (M Eng, M Sc, PhD); chemical engineering (M Eng, M Sc, PhD); civil engineering (M Eng, M Sc, PhD); electrical engineering (M Eng, M Sc, PhD); engineering (M Eng, M Sc, PhD, Diploma); environmental engineering (M Eng, M Sc, PhD, Diploma); mechanical engineering (M Eng, M Sc, PhD, Diploma). *Application deadline:* For fall admission, 7/1 (priority date). Applications are processed on a rolling basis. *Application fee:* $50. *Acting Dean,* Dr. R. Billinton, 306-966-5273, Fax: 306-966-5205.

College of Kinesiology Students: 30. *Faculty:* 41. Expenses: Contact institution. *Financial support:* Fellowships, research assistantships, teaching assistantships available. Financial award application deadline: 1/31. Offers kinesiology (M Sc, PhD, Diploma). *Application deadline:* For fall admission, 7/1 (priority date). Applications are processed on a rolling basis. *Application fee:* $50. *Application Contact:* Dr. E. Sprigings, Graduate Chair, 306-966-6481, Fax: 306-966-6502, E-mail: sprigings@sask.usask.ca. *Dean,* Dr. M. S. Tremblay, 306-966-6465, Fax: 306-966-6502.

College of Nursing Students: 34. *Faculty:* 19. Expenses: Contact institution. *Financial support:* Fellowships, research assistantships, teaching assistantships available. Financial award application deadline: 1/31. *Degree program information:* Part-time programs available. Offers nursing (MN). *Application deadline:* For fall admission, 7/1 (priority date). Applications are processed on a rolling basis. *Application fee:* $50. *Application Contact:* G. Laing, Graduate Chair, 306-966-6229, Fax: 306-966-6703. *Dean,* B. Horsburgh, 306-966-6223, Fax: 306-966-6703, E-mail: beth.horsburgh@usask.ca.

College of Pharmacy and Nutrition Students: 32. *Faculty:* 23. Expenses: Contact institution. *Financial support:* Fellowships, research assistantships, teaching assistantships available. Financial award application deadline: 1/31. Offers pharmacy and nutrition (M Sc, PhD). *Application deadline:* For fall admission, 7/1 (priority date). Applications are processed on a rolling basis. *Application fee:* $50. *Application Contact:* Dr. F. Remillard, Graduate Chair, 306-966-6345, Fax: 306-966-6377. *Dean,* Dr. D. Gorecki, 306-966-6328, Fax: 306-966-6377, E-mail: dennis.gorecki@usask.ca.

College of Law Students: 343. Average age 26. 23 applicants, 17% accepted. *Faculty:* 38. Expenses: Contact institution. *Financial support:* In 2001–02, 4 students received support, including 2 fellowships. Financial award application deadline: 1/31. In 2001, 90 LL Bs, 3 master's awarded. Offers law (LL B, LL M). *Application deadline:* For spring admission, 2/1 (priority date). Applications are processed on a rolling basis. *Application fee:* $50. *Application Contact:* Dana L. Kingsbury, Administrative Officer and Executive Assistant to the Dean, 306-966-5872, Fax: 306-966-5900, E-mail: dana.kingsbury@usask.ca. *Dean,* R. E. Bilson, 306-966-5910, E-mail: beth.bilson@usask.ca.

College of Medicine Students: 331 full-time, 16 part-time. *Faculty:* 140. Expenses: Contact institution. *Financial support:* In 2001–02, 80 students received support, including 3 fellowships; research assistantships, teaching assistantships, scholarships/grants also available. Financial award application deadline: 1/31. In 2001, 55 first professional degrees, 16 master's, 9 doctorates awarded. Offers anatomy and cell biology (M Sc, PhD); biochemistry (M Sc, PhD, Diploma); community health and epidemiology (M Sc, PhD); medicine (MD, M Sc, PhD, Diploma); microbiology (M Sc, PhD); obstetrics and gynecology (M Sc, PhD); pathology (M Sc, PhD); pharmacology (M Sc, PhD); physiology (M Sc, PhD); psychiatry (M Sc, PhD); surgery (M Sc, PhD). *Application deadline:* For fall admission, 7/1 (priority date). Applications are processed on a rolling basis. *Dean,* Dr. W. Albritton, 306-966-6135, Fax: 306-966-6164.

Western College of Veterinary Medicine *Faculty:* 72 full-time, 30 part-time/adjunct. Expenses: Contact institution. *Financial support:* Fellowships, teaching assistantships available. Financial award application deadline: 1/31. Offers herd medicine and theriogenology (M Sc, M Vet Sc, PhD, Diploma); large animal clinical sciences (M Sc, M Vet Sc, PhD, Diploma); small animal clinical sciences (M Sc, M Vet Sc, PhD); toxicology (M Sc, PhD, Diploma); veterinary anatomy (M Sc); veterinary anesthesiology, radiology and surgery (M Vet Sc); veterinary biomedical sciences (M Sc, M Vet Sc, PhD); veterinary internal medicine (M Vet Sc); veterinary medicine (DVM, M Sc, PhD); veterinary microbiology (M Sc, M Vet Sc, PhD); veterinary pathology (M Sc, M Vet Sc, PhD); veterinary physiological sciences (M Sc, PhD). *Application deadline:* For fall admission, 7/1 (priority date). *Application fee:* $50. *Dean,* Dr. A. Livingston, 306-966-7447, Fax: 306-966-8747.

Announcement: The University of Saskatchewan offers high-quality graduate education at the master's (MA, MFA, M Math, M PAcc, MN, M Ag, M Sc, M Ed, MC Ed, M Eng, LL M, MBA, and M Vet Sc) and PhD levels in most disciplines. Actual programs of study and areas of research depend on special interests of faculty members and the facilities available. Strong programs are available in basic sciences, applied sciences, the health sciences, veterinary medicine, the humanities, native studies, and the social sciences. Interdisciplinary offerings are available. Innovation Place, an internationally known research park, houses 95 tenants in the agricultural environmental sciences and resources sector. Inquiries are invited.

THE UNIVERSITY OF SCRANTON, Scranton, PA 18510

General Information Independent-religious, coed, comprehensive institution. CGS member. *Enrollment:* 237 full-time matriculated graduate/professional students (164 women), 365 part-time matriculated graduate/professional students (229 women). *Enrollment by degree level:* 602 master's. *Graduate faculty:* 151 full-time (55 women), 24 part-time/adjunct (12 women). *Tuition:* Part-time $539 per credit. *Required fees:* $25 per term. *Graduate housing:* Room and/or apartments available to single students; on-campus housing not available to married students. *Student services:* Campus employment opportunities, career counseling, free psychological counseling, international student services, multicultural affairs office. *Library facilities:* Harry and Jeanette Weinberg Memorial Library plus 1 other. *Online resources:* library catalog, web page, access to other libraries' catalogs. *Collection:* 433,900 titles, 7,553 serial subscriptions, 12,460 audiovisual materials. *Research affiliation:* Everhart Museum (art and general science), Lackawanna River Corridor Association (environment), Allied Services (rehabilitation), Pennsylvania State University, Community Medical Center (health services), Wyoming Valley Health Care System (nursing).

Computer facilities: 777 computers available on campus for general student use. A campuswide network can be accessed from student residence rooms and from off campus. Internet access and online class registration are available. *Web address:* http://www.scranton.edu/.

General Application Contact: James L. Goonan, Director of Admissions, 570-941-6304, Fax: 570-941-5995, E-mail: goonanj1@scranton.edu.

GRADUATE UNITS

Graduate School Students: 237 full-time (164 women), 365 part-time (229 women); includes 23 minority (6 African Americans, 12 Asian Americans or Pacific Islanders, 4 Hispanic Americans, 1 Native American), 73 international. Average age 30. 390 applicants, 91% accepted. *Faculty:* 151 full-time (55 women), 24 part-time/adjunct (12 women). Expenses: Contact institution. *Financial support:* In 2001–02, 73 students received support, including 73 teaching assistantships with full tuition reimbursements available (averaging $6,900 per year); career-related internships or fieldwork, Federal Work-Study, and teaching fellowships also available. Support available to part-time students. Financial award application deadline: 3/1. In 2001, 252 degrees awarded. *Degree program information:* Part-time and evening/weekend programs available. Offers accounting (MBA); adult health nursing (MS); biochemistry (MA, MS); chemistry (MA, MS); clinical chemistry (MA, MS); community counseling (MS); early childhood education (MS); educational administration (MS); elementary education (MS); elementary school administration (MS); English (MA); enterprise management technology (MBA); family nurse practitioner (MS); finance (MBA); general business administration (MBA); health administration (MHA); history (MA); human resources (MS); human resources administration (MS); human resources development (MS); international business (MBA); management information systems (MBA); marketing (MBA); nurse anesthesia (MS); occupational therapy (MS); operations management (MBA); organizational leadership (MS); physical therapy (MPT); professional counseling (CAGS); reading education (MS); rehabilitation counseling (MS); school counseling (MS); secondary education (MS); secondary school administration (MS); software engineering (MS); theology (MA). *Application fee:* $50. *Application Contact:* James L. Goonan, Director of Admissions, 570-941-6304, Fax: 570-941-5995, E-mail: goonanj1@scranton.edu. *Acting Dean,* Dr. Rose Sebastianelli, 570-941-7600, Fax: 570-941-5995, E-mail: sebastianellir1@scranton.edu.

See in-depth description on page 1251.

UNIVERSITY OF SIOUX FALLS, Sioux Falls, SD 57105-1699

General Information Independent-religious, coed, comprehensive institution. *Graduate housing:* Rooms and/or apartments available to single and married students.

GRADUATE UNITS

Program in Business Administration *Degree program information:* Part-time and evening/weekend programs available. Offers business administration (MBA).

Program in Education *Degree program information:* Part-time and evening/weekend programs available. Offers leadership (M Ed); reading (M Ed); technology (M Ed). Summer admission only.

UNIVERSITY OF SOUTH ALABAMA, Mobile, AL 36688-0002

General Information State-supported, coed, university. CGS member. *Enrollment:* 1,619 full-time matriculated graduate/professional students (1,027 women), 931 part-time matriculated graduate/professional students (672 women). *Enrollment by degree level:* 251 first professional, 2,071 master's, 150 doctoral, 78 other advanced degrees. *Graduate faculty:* 455 full-time (108 women), 27 part-time/adjunct (9 women). Tuition, state resident: full-time $3,048. Tuition, nonresident: full-time $6,096. *Required fees:* $320. *Graduate housing:* Rooms and/or apartments available to single and married students. Typical cost: $3,746 (including board) for single students. Housing application deadline: 6/1. *Student services:* Campus employment opportunities, campus safety program, career counseling, disabled student services, free psychological counseling, international student services, low-cost health insurance, multicultural affairs office, writing training. *Library facilities:* University Library plus 1 other. *Online resources:* library catalog, access to other libraries' catalogs. *Collection:* 578,615 titles, 3,981 serial subscriptions, 13,349 audiovisual materials. *Research affiliation:* Dauphin Island Marine Laboratory, Alabama Universities/Tennessee Valley Authority Research Consortia (chemical engineering), Naval Aerospace Medical Research Laboratory, Marine Environmental Sciences Consortium.

Computer facilities: 325 computers available on campus for general student use. A campuswide network can be accessed from student residence rooms and from off campus. Internet access is available. *Web address:* http://www.southalabama.edu/.

General Application Contact: Dr. James L. Wolfe, Associate Vice President for Research and Dean of the Graduate School, 334-460-6310.

GRADUATE UNITS

College of Medicine Students: 284 full-time (135 women), 3 part-time (1 woman); includes 51 minority (32 African Americans, 15 Asian Americans or Pacific Islanders, 2 Hispanic Americans, 2 Native Americans), 10 international. *Faculty:* 217 full-time (45 women), 22 part-time/adjunct (5 women). Expenses: Contact institution. *Financial support:* In 2001–02, 6 research assistantships were awarded; fellowships, institutionally sponsored loans also available. In 2001, 65 first professional degrees, 3 doctorates awarded. Offers biochemistry and molecular biology (PhD); cellular biology and neuroscience (PhD); medicine (MD, PhD); microbiology and immunology (PhD); pharmacology (PhD); physiology (PhD). *Application fee:* $25. *Dean,* Dr. Robert A. Kreisberg, 334-460-7189.

Graduate School Students: 1,335 full-time (892 women), 928 part-time (671 women); includes 358 minority (295 African Americans, 30 Asian Americans or Pacific Islanders, 16 Hispanic Americans, 17 Native Americans), 282 international. Average age 32. 1,182 applicants, 69% accepted. *Faculty:* 281 full-time (68 women), 5 part-time/adjunct (4 women). Expenses: Contact institution. *Financial support:* In 2001–02, 19 fellowships, 78 research assistantships, 25 teaching assistantships were awarded. Career-related internships or fieldwork, institutionally sponsored loans, and traineeships also available. Support available to part-time students. Financial award application deadline: 4/1. In 2001, 489 master's, 5 doctorates, 22 other advanced degrees awarded. *Degree program information:* Part-time and evening/weekend programs available. *Application deadline:* For fall admission, 9/1 (priority date). Applications are processed on a rolling basis. *Application fee:* $25. *Associate Vice President for Research and Dean,* Dr. James L. Wolfe, 334-460-6310.

College of Allied Health Professions Students: 157 full-time (128 women), 18 part-time (15 women); includes 17 minority (9 African Americans, 6 Asian Americans or Pacific Islanders, 2 Native Americans), 2 international. 77 applicants, 31% accepted. *Faculty:* 8 full-time (2 women). Expenses: Contact institution. *Financial support:* In 2001–02, 7 fellowships, 1 research assistantship were awarded. Career-related internships or fieldwork also available. Support available to part-time students. Financial award application deadline: 4/1. In 2001, 84 degrees awarded. Offers allied health professions (MHS, MPT, MS, PhD); communication sciences and disorders (PhD); physical therapy (MPT); physician assistant studies (MHS); speech and hearing sciences (MS). *Application deadline:* For fall admission, 9/1 (priority date). Applications are processed on a rolling basis. *Application fee:* $25. *Application Contact:* Dr. Stephen Hood, Director of Graduate Studies, 334-380-2600. *Dean,* Dr. Daniel Sellers, 334-380-2785.

College of Arts and Sciences Students: 133 full-time (78 women), 90 part-time (52 women); includes 21 minority (17 African Americans, 1 Asian American or Pacific Islander, 1 Hispanic American, 2 Native Americans), 18 international. 179 applicants, 69% accepted. *Faculty:* 118 full-time (27 women), 3 part-time/adjunct (2 women). Expenses: Contact institution. *Financial support:* In 2001–02, 12 fellowships, 43 research assistantships, 13 teaching assistantships were awarded. Career-related internships or fieldwork also available. Support available to part-time students. Financial award application deadline: 4/1. In 2001, 50 master's, 1 doctorate awarded. *Degree program information:* Part-time and evening/weekend programs available. Offers arts and sciences (MA, MPA, MS, PhD, Certificate); biological sciences (MS); communication arts (MA); English (MA); gerontology (Certificate); history (MA); marine sciences (MS, PhD); mathematics (MS); psychology (MS); public administration (MPA); sociology (MA). *Application deadline:* For fall admission, 9/1 (priority date). Applications are processed on a rolling basis. *Application fee:* $25. *Application Contact:* Dr. Stephen Thomas, Associate Dean, 334-460-6280. *Dean,* Dr. John Friedl, 334-460-6280.

College of Education Students: 455 full-time (363 women), 577 part-time (466 women); includes 240 minority (217 African Americans, 6 Asian Americans or Pacific Islanders, 10 Hispanic Americans, 7 Native Americans), 20 international. 301 applicants, 85% accepted. *Faculty:* 49 full-time (17 women). Expenses: Contact institution. *Financial support:* In 2001–02, 23 research assistantships, 10 teaching assistantships were awarded. Career-related internships or fieldwork also available. Support available to part-time students. Financial award application deadline: 4/1. In 2001, 164 master's, 4 doctorates, 22 other advanced degrees awarded. *Degree program information:* Part-time programs available. Offers art/music education (M Ed); business education (M Ed); counseling (M Ed, MS, Ed S); early childhood education (M Ed, Ed S); education (M Ed, MS, PhD, Ed S); education of the emotionally disturbed (M Ed); education of the gifted (M Ed); educational administration (M Ed, Ed S); educational media (M Ed, MS); elementary education (M Ed, Ed S); exercise technology (MS); health education (M Ed); instructional design (MS); instructional design and development (PhD); learning disability (M Ed); leisure services (MS); mentally retarded (M Ed); multihandicapped education (M Ed); natural science education (M Ed); physical education (M Ed, Ed S); reading (M Ed); science education (M Ed); secondary education (M Ed, Ed S); special education (M Ed, Ed S); therapeutic

University of South Alabama (continued)

recreation (MS). *Application deadline:* For fall admission, 9/1 (priority date). Applications are processed on a rolling basis. *Application fee:* $25. *Dean,* George E. Uhlig, 334-460-6205.

College of Engineering Students: 102 full-time (13 women), 34 part-time (4 women); includes 4 minority (2 African Americans, 2 Asian Americans or Pacific Islanders), 120 international. 215 applicants, 66% accepted. *Faculty:* 22 full-time (0 women). Expenses: Contact institution. *Financial support:* In 2001–02, 4 research assistantships were awarded; career-related internships or fieldwork and institutionally sponsored loans also available. Support available to part-time students. Financial award application deadline: 4/1. In 2001, 18 degrees awarded. *Degree program information:* Part-time programs available. Offers chemical engineering (MS Ch E); computer and electrical engineering (MSEE); engineering (MS Ch E, MSEE, MSME); mechanical engineering (MSME). *Application deadline:* For fall admission, 9/1 (priority date). Applications are processed on a rolling basis. *Application fee:* $25. *Application Contact:* Dr. Russell M. Hayes, Director of Graduate Studies, 334-460-6117. *Interim Associate Dean,* Dr. B. Keith Harrison, 334-460-6140.

College of Nursing Students: 289 full-time (245 women), 126 part-time (105 women); includes 58 minority (43 African Americans, 8 Asian Americans or Pacific Islanders, 4 Hispanic Americans, 3 Native Americans), 2 international. 275 applicants, 92% accepted. *Faculty:* 9 full-time (all women), 1 (woman) part-time/adjunct. Expenses: Contact institution. *Financial support:* Research assistantships, traineeships available. Support available to part-time students. Financial award application deadline: 4/1. In 2001, 91 degrees awarded. *Degree program information:* Part-time and evening/weekend programs available. Postbaccalaureate distance learning degree programs offered (minimal on-campus study). Offers adult health nursing (MSN); community mental health nursing (MSN); maternal child nursing (MSN). *Application deadline:* For fall admission, 8/1 (priority date). Applications are processed on a rolling basis. *Application fee:* $25. *Application Contact:* Information Contact, 334-434-3413, Fax: 334-434-3425. *Dean,* Dr. Debra C. Davis, 334-434-3414.

Division of Computer and Information Sciences Students: 102 full-time (17 women), 27 part-time (4 women); includes 7 minority (3 African Americans, 3 Asian Americans or Pacific Islanders, 1 Native American), 88 international. 153 applicants, 60% accepted. *Faculty:* 10 full-time (1 woman). Expenses: Contact institution. *Financial support:* In 2001–02, 4 research assistantships were awarded; career-related internships or fieldwork and institutionally sponsored loans also available. Support available to part-time students. Financial award application deadline: 4/1. In 2001, 25 degrees awarded. *Degree program information:* Part-time and evening/weekend programs available. Offers computer science (MS); information science (MS). *Application deadline:* For fall admission, 9/1 (priority date). Applications are processed on a rolling basis. *Application fee:* $25. *Dean,* Dr. David Feinstein, 334-460-6390.

Mitchell College of Business Students: 97 full-time (48 women), 56 part-time (25 women); includes 11 minority (4 African Americans, 4 Asian Americans or Pacific Islanders, 1 Hispanic American, 2 Native Americans), 32 international. 105 applicants, 54% accepted. *Faculty:* 17 full-time (6 women). Expenses: Contact institution. *Financial support:* In 2001–02, 7 research assistantships were awarded Support available to part-time students. Financial award application deadline: 4/1. In 2001, 57 degrees awarded. *Degree program information:* Part-time and evening/weekend programs available. Offers accounting (M Acct); business (M Acct, MBA); general management (MBA). *Application deadline:* For fall admission, 9/1 (priority date). Applications are processed on a rolling basis. *Application fee:* $25. *Dean,* Dr. Carl Moore, 334-460-6419.

See in-depth description on page 1253.

UNIVERSITY OF SOUTH CAROLINA, Columbia, SC 29208

General Information State-supported, coed, university. CGS member. *Enrollment:* 3,519 full-time matriculated graduate/professional students (1,993 women), 3,778 part-time matriculated graduate/professional students (2,639 women). *Graduate faculty:* 1,387 full-time (406 women), 324 part-time/adjunct (139 women). Tuition, state resident: full-time $4,434. Tuition, nonresident: full-time $9,854. Tuition and fees vary according to program. *Graduate housing:* Rooms and/or apartments available to single and married students. *Student services:* Campus employment opportunities, career counseling, child daycare facilities, disabled student services, exercise/wellness program, free psychological counseling, international student services, low-cost health insurance, multicultural affairs office. *Library facilities:* Thomas Cooper Library plus 7 others. *Online resources:* library catalog, web page, access to other libraries' catalogs. *Collection:* 3.2 million titles, 20,468 serial subscriptions, 44,089 audiovisual materials. *Research affiliation:* E. I. du Pont de Nemours and Company (engineering, chemical engineering), Westinghouse/Savannah River Corporation (environmental restoration, hazardous waste remediation), Motorola Corporation–Energy Production Division (electrochemical engineering), Glaxo-Wellcome, Inc. (pharmaceuticals), NCR Corporation (electrical and computer engineering).

Computer facilities: 11,000 computers available on campus for general student use. A campuswide network can be accessed from student residence rooms and from off campus. Internet access and online class registration are available. *Web address:* http://www.sc.edu/.

General Application Contact: Dale Moore, Director of Graduate Admissions, 803-777-4243, Fax: 803-777-2972, E-mail: dm@gwm.sc.edu.

GRADUATE UNITS

College of Pharmacy Students: 276 full-time (196 women), 5 part-time (1 woman); includes 39 minority (32 African Americans, 5 Asian Americans or Pacific Islanders, 1 Hispanic American, 1 Native American), 11 international. Average age 29. 150 applicants, 48% accepted. *Faculty:* 33 full-time (7 women), 4 part-time/adjunct (0 women). Expenses: Contact institution. *Financial support:* In 2001–02, 3 fellowships with partial tuition reimbursements (averaging $16,000 per year), 5 research assistantships with partial tuition reimbursements (averaging $14,000 per year), 7 teaching assistantships with partial tuition reimbursements (averaging $14,000 per year) were awarded. Career-related internships or fieldwork, Federal Work-Study, institutionally sponsored loans, and scholarships/grants also available. In 2001, 65 first professional degrees, 6 doctorates awarded. *Degree program information:* Part-time programs available. Offers pharmaceutical sciences (MS, PhD); pharmacy (Pharm D, MS, PhD). *Application deadline:* For fall admission, 1/15. *Application fee:* $35. Electronic applications accepted. *Application Contact:* Dr. Joseph W. Kosh, Graduate Director, 803-777-2705, Fax: 803-777-8356, E-mail: wise@cop.sc.edu. *Dean,* Dr. Farid Sadik, 803-777-4151, Fax: 803-777-2775, E-mail: sadik@cop.sc.edu.

The Graduate School Students: 3,371 full-time (1,934 women), 2,900 part-time (1,914 women); includes 928 minority (738 African Americans, 88 Asian Americans or Pacific Islanders, 85 Hispanic Americans, 17 Native Americans), 890 international. Average age 32. 5,979 applicants, 48% accepted, 2072 enrolled. *Faculty:* 1,006 full-time (279 women), 17 part-time/adjunct (6 women). Expenses: Contact institution. *Financial support:* Fellowships, research assistantships, teaching assistantships, career-related internships or fieldwork, Federal Work-Study, institutionally sponsored loans, scholarships/grants, traineeships, tuition waivers (full and partial), unspecified assistantships, and graders, tutors available. Support available to part-time students. In 2001, 1,827 master's, 228 doctorates, 92 other advanced degrees awarded. *Degree program information:* Part-time and evening/weekend programs available. Postbaccalaureate distance learning degree programs offered. Offers gerontology (Certificate). *Application deadline:* For fall admission, 7/1; for spring admission, 11/15. Applications are processed on a rolling basis. *Application fee:* $40. Electronic applications accepted. *Application Contact:* Dale Moore, Director of Graduate Admissions, 803-777-4243, Fax: 803-777-2972, E-mail: dm@gwm.sc.edu. *Dean,* Dr. Gordon B. Smith, 803-777-4811, Fax: 803-777-2972.

College of Criminal Justice *Degree program information:* Part-time and evening/weekend programs available. Postbaccalaureate distance learning degree programs offered. Offers criminal justice (MCJ). Electronic applications accepted.

College of Education Students: 461 full-time (342 women), 647 part-time (469 women); includes 207 minority (184 African Americans, 8 Asian Americans or Pacific Islanders, 12 Hispanic Americans, 3 Native Americans), 17 international. Average age 34. 529 applicants, 49% accepted, 194 enrolled. *Faculty:* 77 full-time (37 women), 43 part-time/adjunct (24 women). Expenses: Contact institution. *Financial support:* In 2001–02, 4 fellowships, 72 research assistantships with partial tuition reimbursements (averaging $5,200 per year), 8 teaching assistantships with partial tuition reimbursements (averaging $6,500 per year) were awarded. Career-related internships or fieldwork, Federal Work-Study, institutionally sponsored loans, tuition waivers (partial), and unspecified assistantships also available. Support available to part-time students. In 2001, 290 master's, 46 doctorates, 38 other advanced degrees awarded. *Degree program information:* Part-time and evening/weekend programs available. Postbaccalaureate distance learning degree programs offered (minimal on-campus study). Offers art education (IMA, MAT); business education (IMA, MAT); community and occupational education (M Ed); counseling education (PhD, Ed S); curriculum and instruction (Ed D); early childhood education (M Ed, MAT, PhD); education (IMA, M Ed, MA, MAT, MS, MT, Ed D, PhD, Certificate, Ed S); educational administration (M Ed, MA, PhD, Ed S); educational psychology, research (M Ed, PhD); educational technology (M Ed); elementary education (M Ed, MAT, PhD); English (MAT); foreign language (MAT); foundations in education (PhD); health education (MAT); health education administration (Ed D); higher education and student affairs (M Ed); higher education leadership (Certificate); language and literacy (M Ed, PhD); mathematics (MAT); physical education (IMA, MAT, MS, PhD); science (IMA, MAT); secondary education (IMA, M Ed, MA, MAT, MT, PhD); social studies (IMA, MAT); special education (M Ed, MAT, PhD); teaching (Ed S); theatre and speech (IMA, MAT). *Application deadline:* For fall admission, 7/15; for winter admission, 11/15. *Application fee:* $40. Electronic applications accepted. *Application Contact:* 803-777-6732, Fax: 803-777-3068, E-mail: teach@gwm.sc.edu. *Dean,* Dr. Les Sternberg, 803-777-3828, Fax: 803-777-3035, E-mail: lstern@gwm.sc.edu.

College of Engineering and Information Technology Students: 324 full-time (76 women), 146 part-time (21 women); includes 334 minority (16 African Americans, 309 Asian Americans or Pacific Islanders, 9 Hispanic Americans) Average age 30. 827 applicants, 49% accepted. *Faculty:* 86 full-time (7 women). Expenses: Contact institution. *Financial support:* In 2001–02, 5 fellowships (averaging $9,600 per year), 177 research assistantships with partial tuition reimbursements (averaging $15,000 per year), 42 teaching assistantships with partial tuition reimbursements (averaging $14,400 per year) were awarded. Career-related internships or fieldwork, institutionally sponsored loans, and scholarships/grants also available. In 2001, 163 master's, 22 doctorates awarded. *Degree program information:* Part-time and evening/weekend programs available. Postbaccalaureate distance learning degree programs offered (minimal on-campus study). Offers chemical engineering (ME, MS, PhD); civil engineering (ME, MS, PhD); computer science and engineering (ME, MS, PhD); electrical engineering (ME, MS, PhD); engineering and information technology (ME, MS, PhD); mechanical engineering (ME, MS, PhD); software engineering (MS). *Application deadline:* For fall admission, 3/1 (priority date); for spring admission, 11/1. Applications are processed on a rolling basis. *Application fee:* $40, Electronic applications accepted. *Application Contact:* Mike Perkins, Student Services Manager, 803-777-4177, Fax: 803-777-0027, E-mail: perkins@engr.sc.edu. *Dean,* Dr. Ralph E. White, 803-777-3270, Fax: 803-777-9597, E-mail: white@engr.sc.edu.

College of Hospitality, Retail, and Sport Management *Degree program information:* Part-time programs available. Postbaccalaureate distance learning degree programs offered (minimal on-campus study). Offers hospitality (MHRTA); hospitality, retail, and sport management (MHRTA). Electronic applications accepted.

College of Journalism and Mass Communications Students: 52 full-time (39 women), 34 part-time (15 women). Average age 29. 72 applicants, 63% accepted, 31 enrolled. *Faculty:* 26 full-time (9 women), 1 part-time/adjunct (0 women). Expenses: Contact institution. *Financial support:* In 2001–02, 20 students received support, including 1 fellowship (averaging $16,000 per year), 3 research assistantships (averaging $10,000 per year), 4 teaching assistantships (averaging $10,000 per year); career-related internships or fieldwork, Federal Work-Study, and unspecified assistantships also available. Financial award application deadline: 2/15. In 2001, 19 master's, 1 doctorate awarded. *Degree program information:* Part-time programs available. Offers journalism and mass communications (MA, MMC, PhD). *Application deadline:* For fall admission, 7/1 (priority date); for spring admission, 11/15. Applications are processed on a rolling basis. *Application fee:* $40. Electronic applications accepted. *Application Contact:* Sandra M. Hughes, Director, Graduate Student and Research Services, 803-777-5166, Fax: 803-777-1267, E-mail: sandra.hughes@usc.jour.sc.edu. *Interim Dean,* Dr. Henry T. Price, 803-777-4105, Fax: 803-777-4103, E-mail: henry.price@usc.jour.sc.edu.

College of Liberal Arts *Degree program information:* Part-time and evening/weekend programs available. Offers anthropology (MA); archives (MA); art education (IMA, MA, MAT); art history (MA); art studio (MA); clinical/community psychology (PhD); creative writing (MFA); English (MA, PhD); English education (MAT); experimental psychology (MA, PhD); foreign languages (MAT); geography (MA, MS, PhD); geography education (IMA); German (MA); historic preservation (MA); history (MA, PhD); history education (IMA, MAT); international studies (MA, PhD); liberal arts (IMA, MA, MAT, MFA, MMA, MPA, MS, PhD, Certificate); linguistics (MA, PhD); media arts (MMA); museum (MA); museum management (Certificate); philosophy (MA, PhD); political science (MA, PhD); public administration (MPA); public history (MA, Certificate); religious studies (MA); school psychology (PhD); sociology (MA, PhD); Spanish (IMA, MA, MAT); studio art (MFA); teaching English as a foreign language (Certificate); theater (IMA, MA, MAT, MFA); women's studies (Certificate). Electronic applications accepted.

College of Library and Information Science Students: 85 full-time (70 women), 361 part-time (318 women); includes 27 minority (22 African Americans, 2 Asian Americans or Pacific Islanders, 3 Hispanic Americans), 5 international. Average age 37. 147 applicants, 76% accepted. *Faculty:* 14 full-time (8 women), 7 part-time/adjunct (4 women). Expenses: Contact institution. *Financial support:* In 2001–02, 9 fellowships with partial tuition reimbursements (averaging $9,500 per year), 30 research assistantships with partial tuition reimbursements were awarded. Career-related internships or fieldwork, scholarships/grants, and unspecified assistantships also available. Support available to part-time students. Financial award application deadline: 4/1; financial award applicants required to submit FAFSA. In 2001, 170 master's, 19 other advanced degrees awarded. *Degree program information:* Part-time programs available. Postbaccalaureate distance learning degree programs offered (no on-campus study). Offers library and information science (MLIS, Certificate, Specialist). *Application deadline:* For fall admission, 4/1 (priority date); for spring admission, 10/1 (priority date). Applications are processed on a rolling basis. *Application fee:* $40. Electronic applications accepted. *Application Contact:* Sharon Allen, Admissions Contact, 803-777-3887, Fax: 803-777-0457, E-mail: sharona@gwm.sc.edu. *Dean,* Dr. Fred W. Roper, 803-777-3858, Fax: 803-777-7938.

College of Nursing Students: 43 full-time (42 women), 85 part-time (83 women); includes 16 minority (10 African Americans, 1 Asian American or Pacific Islander, 4 Hispanic Americans, 1 Native American), 1 international. Average age 43. 31 applicants, 90% accepted, 22 enrolled. *Faculty:* 16 full-time (15 women), 1 (woman) part-time/adjunct. Expenses: Contact institution. *Financial support:* In 2001–02, 38 students received support, including 10 research assistantships (averaging $2,233 per year), 2 teaching assistantships (averaging $800 per year); scholarships/grants, traineeships, and unspecified assistantships also available. Financial award application deadline: 4/1; financial award applicants required to submit FAFSA. In 2001, 40 master's, 4 doctorates, 1 other advanced degree awarded. *Degree program information:* Part-time programs available. Offers advanced practice nursing in clinical and psychiatric mental health (Certificate); advanced practice nursing in primary care and women's health (Certificate); clinical nursing (MSN); community mental health and psychiatric health nursing (MSN); health nursing (MSN); nursing (ND); nursing administration (MSN); nursing science (PhD). *Application deadline:* For fall admission, 7/1; for winter admission, 5/1; for spring admission, 11/15. Applications are processed on a rolling basis. *Application fee:* $35. Electronic applications accepted. *Application Contact:* Cheryl Nelson-Jackson, Student Services Coordinator, 803-777-3754, Fax: 803-777-0616, E-mail: cheryl.nelsonjackson@sc.edu. *Dean,* Dr. Mary Ann Parsons, 803-777-3119, Fax: 803-777-2072, E-mail: maryann.parsons@sc.edu.

College of Science and Mathematics *Degree program information:* Part-time and evening/weekend programs available. Offers applied statistics (CAS); biology (MS, PhD); biology education (IMA, MAT); chemistry and biochemistry (IMA, MAT, MS, PhD); ecology, evolution and organismal biology (MS, PhD); environmental geoscience (PMS); geological sciences (MS, PhD); marine science (MS, PhD); mathematics (MA, MS, PhD); mathematics education (M Math, MAT); molecular, cellular, and developmental biology (MS, PhD); physics and astronomy (IMA, MAT, MS, PhD); science and mathematics (IMA, M Math, MA, MAT, MIS, MS, PMS, PhD, CAS); statistics (MIS, MS, PhD). Electronic applications accepted.

College of Social Work Students: 320 full-time, 132 part-time; includes 177 minority (131 African Americans, 39 Asian Americans or Pacific Islanders, 5 Hispanic Americans, 2 Native Americans) Average age 34. 550 applicants, 38% accepted. *Faculty:* 27 full-time (16 women), 26 part-time/adjunct (17 women). Expenses: Contact institution. *Financial support:* In 2001–02, 174 students received support, including 2 fellowships with partial tuition reimbursements available, 117 research assistantships with partial tuition reimbursements available; teaching assistantships, career-related internships or fieldwork, Federal Work-Study, and institutionally sponsored loans also available. Financial award application deadline: 5/1. In 2001, 245 master's, 4 doctorates awarded. Offers social work (MSW, PhD). *Application deadline:* For fall admission, 3/1. *Application fee:* $35. Electronic applications accepted. *Application Contact:* Dr. John T. Gandy, Associate Dean, 803-777-5190, Fax: 803-777-3498. *Dean,* Dr. Frank B. Raymond, 803-777-4886, Fax: 803-777-3498.

The Darla Moore School of Business Students: 681 full-time (276 women), 230 part-time (51 women); includes 70 minority (20 African Americans, 34 Asian Americans or Pacific Islanders, 14 Hispanic Americans, 2 Native Americans), 202 international. Average age 29. 1,334 applicants, 54% accepted, 420 enrolled. *Faculty:* 96 full-time (16 women). Expenses: Contact institution. *Financial support:* In 2001–02, 317 students received support, including 46 fellowships with partial tuition reimbursements available (averaging $2,694 per year), 133 research assistantships with partial tuition reimbursements available (averaging $1,986 per year), 27 teaching assistantships with partial tuition reimbursements available (averaging $9,782 per year); career-related internships or fieldwork, Federal Work-Study, and institutionally sponsored loans also available. Financial award application deadline: 2/1. In 2001, 393 master's, 10 doctorates awarded. *Degree program information:* Part-time and evening/weekend programs available. Postbaccalaureate distance learning degree programs offered (minimal on-campus study). Offers business administration (MBA, MS, PhD); business measurement and assurance (M Acc); economics (MA, PhD); human resources (MHR); international business (MIBS); international business administration (IMBA); taxation (M Acc). *Application deadline:* For fall admission, 2/1 (priority date). Applications are processed on a rolling basis. *Application fee:* $35. Electronic applications accepted. *Application Contact:* Reena Lichtenfeld, Director of Admissions, 803-777-6749, Fax: 803-777-0414, E-mail: rlichten@moore.sc.edu. *Dean,* Joel A. Smith, 803-777-3178, Fax: 803-777-9123, E-mail: smithj@moore.sc.edu.

Norman J. Arnold School of Public Health Students: 265 full-time (187 women), 256 part-time (203 women); includes 88 minority (73 African Americans, 10 Asian Americans or Pacific Islanders, 4 Hispanic Americans, 1 Native American), 63 international. Average age 27. 537 applicants, 47% accepted, 108 enrolled. *Faculty:* 67 full-time (31 women), 3 part-time/adjunct (2 women). Expenses: Contact institution. *Financial support:* Fellowships with partial tuition reimbursements, research assistantships with partial tuition reimbursements, teaching assistantships with partial tuition reimbursements, career-related internships or fieldwork, scholarships/grants, traineeships, and unspecified assistantships available. Support available to part-time students. In 2001, 185 master's, 30 doctorates, 16 other advanced degrees awarded. *Degree program information:* Part-time programs available. Postbaccalaureate distance learning degree programs offered. Offers alcohol and drug studies (Certificate); biostatistics (MPH, MSPH, Dr PH, PhD); communication sciences and disorders (MCD, MS, MSP, PhD); environmental quality (MPH, MSPH, PhD); epidemiology (MPH, MSPH, Dr PH, PhD); exercise science (MS, DPT, PhD); general public health (MPH); hazardous materials management (MPH, MSPH, PhD); health administration (MHA, MPH, Dr PH, PhD); health education administration (Ed D); health promotion and education (MAT, MPH, MS, MSPH, Dr PH, PhD); industrial hygiene (MPH, MSPH, PhD); public health (MAT, MCD, MHA, MPH, MS, MSP, MSPH, DPT, Dr PH, Ed D, PhD, Certificate); school health education (Certificate). *Application deadline:* Applications are processed on a rolling basis. *Application fee:* $35. Electronic applications accepted. *Application Contact:* Angela Everett, Director, Office of Student and Alumni Services, 803-777-5031, Fax: 803-777-4783. *Dean,* Dr. Harris Pastides, 803-777-5032, Fax: 803-777-4783, E-mail: hpastides@gwm.sc.edu.

School of Music Offers composition (MM, DMA); conducting (MM, DMA); jazz studies (MM); music education (MM Ed, PhD); music history (MM); music performance (Certificate); music theory (MM); opera theater (MM); performance (MM, DMA); piano pedagogy (MM, DMA). Electronic applications accepted.

School of the Environment *Degree program information:* Part-time programs available. Postbaccalaureate distance learning degree programs offered (no on-campus study). Offers earth and environmental resources management (MEERM); environment (MEERM). Electronic applications accepted.

School of Law Students: 706 full-time (304 women); includes 57 minority (49 African Americans, 5 Asian Americans or Pacific Islanders, 3 Hispanic Americans), 6 international. Average age 24. 1,295 applicants, 35% accepted. *Faculty:* 45 full-time (2 women), 24 part-time/adjunct (1 woman). Expenses: Contact institution. *Financial support:* In 2001–02, 15 fellowships with partial tuition reimbursements were awarded; career-related internships or fieldwork, Federal Work-Study, scholarships/grants, tuition waivers (partial), and unspecified assistantships also available. Financial award application deadline: 4/15; financial award applicants required to submit FAFSA. In 2001, 215 degrees awarded. Offers law (JD). *Application deadline:* For fall admission, 2/15. Applications are processed on a rolling basis. *Application fee:* $40. *Application Contact:* John S. Benfield, Assistant Dean of Admissions, 803-777-6606, Fax: 803-777-7751, E-mail: johnb@law.law.sc.edu. *Dean,* John E. Montgomery, 803-777-6617, Fax: 803-777-5827, E-mail: johnm@law.law.sc.edu.

School of Medicine Students: 395 full-time (180 women), 35 part-time (22 women); includes 72 minority (35 African Americans, 36 Asian Americans or Pacific Islanders, 1 Hispanic American), 10 international. Average age 26. 1,287 applicants, 15% accepted. *Faculty:* 258 full-time (76 women), 50 part-time/adjunct (24 women). Expenses: Contact institution. *Financial support:* In 2001–02, 318 students received support, including 38 research assistantships with partial tuition reimbursements available (averaging $15,000 per year); fellowships, teaching assistantships, career-related internships or fieldwork, Federal Work-Study, institutionally sponsored loans, and unspecified assistantships also available. Financial award application deadline: 4/1; financial award applicants required to submit FAFSA. In 2001, 71 first professional degrees, 38 master's, 8 doctorates awarded. Offers biomedical science (MBS, MNA, PhD); genetic counseling (MS); medicine (MD, MBS, MNA, MRC, MS, PhD, Certificate); nurse anesthesia (MNA); psychiatric rehabilitation (Certificate); rehabilitation counseling (MRC). *Application deadline:* For fall admission, 12/1. Applications are processed on a rolling basis. *Application fee:* $45. Electronic applications accepted. *Application Contact:* Dr. Richard A. Hoppmann, Associate Dean for Medical Education and Academic Affairs, 803-733-1531, Fax: 803-733-3328, E-mail: hoppmann@med.sc.edu. *Dean,* Dr. Larry R. Faulkner, 803-733-3200.

See in-depth description on page 1255.

UNIVERSITY OF SOUTH CAROLINA AIKEN, Aiken, SC 29801-6309

General Information State-supported, coed, comprehensive institution. *Enrollment:* 9 full-time matriculated graduate/professional students (7 women), 134 part-time matriculated graduate/professional students (116 women). *Enrollment by degree level:* 143 master's. *Graduate faculty:* 8 full-time (3 women), 3 part-time/adjunct (2 women). Tuition, state resident: part-time $220 per semester hour. Tuition, nonresident: part-time $466 per semester hour. *Graduate housing:* Room and/or apartments available on a first-come, first-served basis to single students; on-campus housing not available to married students. *Student services:* Campus employment opportunities, campus safety program, career counseling, child daycare facilities, disabled student services, exercise/wellness program, free psychological counseling, multicultural affairs office. *Library facilities:* Gregg-Graniteville Library. *Online resources:* library catalog, web page, access to other libraries' catalogs. *Collection:* 138,077 titles, 853 serial subscriptions.

Computer facilities: 350 computers available on campus for general student use. A campuswide network can be accessed. *Web address:* http://www.usca.edu/.

General Application Contact: Karen Morris, Graduate Studies Coordinator, 803-641-3489, E-mail: karenm@usca.edu.

GRADUATE UNITS

Program in Applied Clinical Psychology Students: 9 full-time (7 women), 7 part-time (all women). Expenses: Contact institution. Offers applied clinical psychology (MS). *Application deadline:* Applications are processed on a rolling basis. *Application fee:* $35. Electronic applications accepted. *Application Contact:* Karen Morris, Graduate Studies Coordinator, 803-641-3489, E-mail: karenm@usca.edu. *Chair,* Dr. Edward Callen, 803-641-3446, Fax: 803-641-3726, E-mail: edc@usca.edu.

UNIVERSITY OF SOUTH CAROLINA SPARTANBURG, Spartanburg, SC 29303-4999

General Information State-supported, coed, comprehensive institution. *Graduate faculty:* 13 full-time (8 women). Tuition, state resident: full-time $4,652; part-time $196 per credit. Tuition, nonresident: full-time $11,100; part-time $505 per credit. *Required fees:* $4 per credit. *Graduate housing:* On-campus housing not available. *Student services:* Campus employment opportunities, campus safety program, child daycare facilities, disabled student services, low-cost health insurance, multicultural affairs office. *Library facilities:* University of South Carolina Spartanburg Library. *Online resources:* library catalog, web page, access to other libraries' catalogs. *Collection:* 156,558 titles, 3,151 serial subscriptions, 11,119 audiovisual materials.

Computer facilities: 254 computers available on campus for general student use. A campuswide network can be accessed from student residence rooms and from off campus. Internet access and online class registration are available. *Web address:* http://www.uscs.edu/.

General Application Contact: Dr. Anne Shelley, Director of Graduate Programs, 864-503-5551, Fax: 864-503-5574, E-mail: ashelley@uscs.edu.

GRADUATE UNITS

Graduate Programs *Faculty:* 13 full-time (8 women). Expenses: Contact institution. *Financial support:* College work study, Federal Family Education Loan Programs available. Financial award application deadline: 7/15; financial award applicants required to submit FAFSA. *Degree program information:* Part-time and evening/weekend programs available. Offers early childhood education (M Ed); elementary education (M Ed). *Application deadline:* Applications are processed on a rolling basis. *Application fee:* $25. *Director of Graduate Programs,* Dr. Anne Shelley, 864-503-5551, Fax: 864-503-5574, E-mail: ashelley@gw.uscs.edu.

THE UNIVERSITY OF SOUTH DAKOTA, Vermillion, SD 57069-2390

General Information State-supported, coed, university. *Enrollment:* 3,405 matriculated graduate/professional students. *Graduate faculty:* 422 full-time, 41 part-time/adjunct. Tuition, state resident: full-time $1,700; part-time $95 per credit hour. Tuition, nonresident: full-time $5,027; part-time $279 per credit hour. *Required fees:* $1,062; $59 per credit hour. *Graduate housing:* Rooms and/or apartments available to single students and available on a first-come, first-served basis to married students. Typical cost: $1,000 per year ($1,800 including board) for single students; $2,300 per year ($3,100 including board) for married students. Room and board charges vary according to board plan. *Student services:* Campus employment opportunities, career counseling, child daycare facilities, disabled student services, free psychological counseling, international student services, low-cost health insurance, multicultural affairs office. *Library facilities:* I. D. Weeks Library plus 2 others. *Online resources:* library catalog, access to other libraries' catalogs. *Collection:* 1.5 million titles, 2,862 serial subscriptions, 3,766 audiovisual materials.

Computer facilities: 1,800 computers available on campus for general student use. A campuswide network can be accessed from student residence rooms and from off campus. Internet access is available. *Web address:* http://www.usd.edu/.

General Application Contact: Stephanie M. Bucklin, Administrative Assistant, 605-677-6287, Fax: 605-677-5202, E-mail: sbuckli@usd.edu.

GRADUATE UNITS

Graduate School Students: 2,855. 1,570 applicants, 37% accepted. *Faculty:* 202 full-time (39 women), 47 part-time/adjunct (6 women). Expenses: Contact institution. *Financial support:* Research assistantships, teaching assistantships, career-related internships or fieldwork, Federal Work-Study, scholarships/grants, and clinical assistantships available. Support available to part-time students. In 2001, 367 master's, 52 doctorates, 22 other advanced degrees awarded. *Degree program information:* Part-time programs available. Offers administrative studies (MS); interdisciplinary studies (MA). *Application fee:* $35. *Dean, Graduate School,* Dr. Royce C. Engstrom, 605-677-6287, Fax: 605-677-5202.

College of Arts and Sciences Students: 260. *Faculty:* 82 full-time (13 women), 19 part-time/adjunct (2 women). Expenses: Contact institution. *Financial support:* Research assistantships, teaching assistantships, career-related internships or fieldwork, Federal Work-Study, scholarships/grants, and clinical assistantships available. Support available to part-time students. Financial award applicants required to submit FAFSA. In 2001, 104 master's, 16 doctorates awarded. *Degree program information:* Part-time programs available. Postbaccalaureate distance learning degree programs offered. Offers arts and sciences (MA, MNS, MPA, MS, PhD); audiology (MA); biology (MA, MNS, MS, PhD); chemistry (MA, MNS); clinical psychology (MA, PhD); computer science (MA); English (MA, PhD); history (MA); human factors (MA, PhD); mathematics (MA, MNS); political science (MA); public administration (MPA); sociology (MA); speech communication (MA); speech-language pathology (MA). *Application deadline:* Applications are processed on a rolling basis. *Application fee:* $35. *Application Contact:* Robert Fuller, Graduate Recruiter, 605-677-5435, E-mail: rfuller@usd.edu. *Acting Dean,* Dr. Susan Wolfe.

College of Fine Arts Students: 52. 57 applicants, 53% accepted. *Faculty:* 23 full-time (3 women), 5 part-time/adjunct (0 women). Expenses: Contact institution. *Financial support:* Research assistantships, teaching assistantships available. In 2001, 23 degrees awarded. Offers art (MFA); fine arts (MA, MFA, MM); mass communications (MA); music (MM); theatre (MA, MFA). *Application deadline:* Applications are processed on a rolling basis. *Application fee:* $35. *Acting Chair,* John A. Day, 605-677-5636.

School of Business Students: 266. 98 applicants, 72% accepted. *Faculty:* 10 full-time (0 women), 4 part-time/adjunct (1 woman). Expenses: Contact institution. *Financial support:* Research assistantships, teaching assistantships, Federal Work-Study available. Support available to part-time students. Financial award applicants required to submit FAFSA. In 2001, 56 degrees awarded. Offers accounting (MP Acc); business (MBA, MP Acc); business administration (MBA). *Application deadline:* Applications are processed on a rolling basis. *Application fee:* $35. *Application Contact:* Dr. Diane Duin, Director of Graduate Studies, 605-677-5232. *Dean,* Dr. Diane Hoadley, 605-677-5455.

School of Education Students: 485. 166 applicants, 61% accepted. *Faculty:* 35 full-time (12 women), 8 part-time/adjunct (2 women). Expenses: Contact institution. *Financial support:* Research assistantships, teaching assistantships, career-related internships or fieldwork and Federal Work-Study available. Support available to part-time students. Financial award applicants required to submit FAFSA. In 2001, 102 master's, 55 doctorates, 22 other advanced degrees awarded. *Degree program information:* Part-time programs available. Offers counseling and psychology in education (MA, Ed D, Ed S); curriculum and instruction (Ed D, Ed S); education (MA, MS, Ed D, PhD, Ed S); educational administration (MA, Ed D, Ed S); elementary education (MA); health, physical education and recreation (MA); secondary education (MA); special education (MA); technology for education and training (MS, Ed S). *Application deadline:* Applications are processed on a rolling basis. *Application fee:* $35. *Acting Dean,* Dr. Jeri Engelking, 605-677-5437.

The University of South Dakota (continued)

School of Law Students: 181 full-time, 3 part-time; includes 16 minority (3 African Americans, 1 Asian American or Pacific Islander, 2 Hispanic Americans, 10 Native Americans), 1 international. Average age 27. 300 applicants, 61% accepted, 81 enrolled. *Faculty:* 15 full-time (3 women), 2 part-time/adjunct (0 women). Expenses: Contact institution. *Financial support:* In 2001–02, 86 students received support, including 24 research assistantships with partial tuition reimbursements available (averaging $4,070 per year); career-related internships or fieldwork, Federal Work-Study, scholarships/grants, and unspecified assistantships also available. Financial award application deadline: 4/1; financial award applicants required to submit FAFSA. In 2001, 54 degrees awarded. *Degree program information:* Part-time programs available. Offers law (JD). *Application deadline:* For fall admission, 3/1 (priority date). Applications are processed on a rolling basis. *Application fee:* $35. Electronic applications accepted. *Application Contact:* Jean Henriques, Admissions Officer/Registrar, 605-677-5443, Fax: 605-677-5417, E-mail: lawreq@usd.edu. *Dean,* Barry R. Vickrey, 605-677-5443.

School of Medicine Students: 366 (221 women); includes 24 minority (15 Asian Americans or Pacific Islanders, 1 Hispanic American, 8 Native Americans) Average age 26. *Faculty:* 153 full-time, 258 part-time/adjunct. Expenses: Contact institution. *Financial support:* In 2001–02, 197 students received support; fellowships, research assistantships, teaching assistantships, career-related internships or fieldwork, institutionally sponsored loans, scholarships/grants, traineeships, tuition waivers (partial), and unspecified assistantships available. Financial award application deadline: 5/1; financial award applicants required to submit FAFSA. In 2001, 50 first professional degrees, 52 master's, 4 doctorates awarded. *Degree program information:* Part-time programs available. Offers cardiovascular research (MA, PhD); cellular and molecular biology (MA, PhD); medicine (MD, MA, MS, PhD); molecular microbiology and immunology (MA, PhD); neuroscience (MA, PhD); occupational therapy (MS); physical therapy (MS); physiology and pharmacology (MA, PhD). *Application fee:* $35. *Application Contact:* Dr. Paul C. Bunger, Dean, Medical Student Affairs, 605-677-5233, Fax: 605-677-5109, E-mail: pbunger@usd.edu. *Dean,* Dr. Robert Talley, 605-357-1300.

See in-depth description on page 1257.

UNIVERSITY OF SOUTHERN CALIFORNIA, Los Angeles, CA 90089

General Information Independent, coed, university. CGS member. *Enrollment:* 10,550 full-time matriculated graduate/professional students (5,032 women), 3,243 part-time matriculated graduate/professional students (1,215 women). *Enrollment by degree level:* 2,586 first professional, 6,803 master's, 3,660 doctoral, 744 other advanced degrees. *Graduate faculty:* 1,351 full-time (389 women), 752 part-time/adjunct (245 women). *Tuition:* Full-time $25,060; part-time $844 per unit. *Required fees:* $473. *Graduate housing:* Rooms and/or apartments available on a first-come, first-served basis to single and married students. Typical cost: $5,916 per year ($8,614 including board) for single students; $5,916 per year ($8,614 including board) for married students. *Student services:* Campus employment opportunities, campus safety program, career counseling, child daycare facilities, disabled student services, exercise/wellness program, free psychological counseling, international student services, low-cost health insurance, multicultural affairs office, teacher training, writing training. *Library facilities:* Doheny Memorial Library plus 22 others. *Online resources:* library catalog, web page. *Collection:* 3.5 million titles, 28,661 serial subscriptions, 3.2 million audiovisual materials. *Research affiliation:* Norris Cancer Hospital (medicine), Doheny Eye Institute (medicine), John Tracy Clinic (education), Children's Hospital Los Angeles (medicine), Rancho Los Amigos Medical Center (medicine).

Computer facilities: 2,300 computers available on campus for general student use. A campuswide network can be accessed from student residence rooms and from off campus. Internet access, on-line degree progress, grades, financial aid summary are available. *Web address:* http://www.usc.edu/.

General Application Contact: Laurel Baker Tew, Director of Enrollment Services, 213-740-0070, Fax: 213-740-8826, E-mail: tew@usc.edu.

GRADUATE UNITS

Graduate School *Degree program information:* Part-time programs available.

Annenberg School for Communication Students: 318 full-time (229 women), 20 part-time (12 women). Average age 30. 655 applicants, 48% accepted, 138 enrolled. *Faculty:* 52 full-time (15 women), 90 part-time/adjunct (25 women). Expenses: Contact institution. *Financial support:* In 2001–02, 15 fellowships with full tuition reimbursements (averaging $19,500 per year), 24 research assistantships with full tuition reimbursements (averaging $13,500 per year), 83 teaching assistantships with full tuition reimbursements (averaging $13,500 per year) were awarded. Career-related internships or fieldwork, Federal Work-Study, institutionally sponsored loans, scholarships/grants, health care benefits, tuition waivers (partial), and unspecified assistantships also available. Support available to part-time students. Financial award application deadline: 12/15; financial award applicants required to submit FAFSA. In 2001, 131 master's, 10 doctorates awarded. Offers broadcast journalism (MA); communication (MA, PhD); communication management (MA); Global Communication (MA); global communication (MA); international journalism (MA); print journalism (MA); strategic public relations (MA). *Application deadline:* For fall admission, 5/1 (priority date); for spring admission, 11/1. Applications are processed on a rolling basis. *Application fee:* $65 ($75 for international students). *Application Contact:* Anne Marie Elona Campian, Director of Student Services, 213-740-0903, Fax: 213-740-8036, E-mail: campian@usc.edu. *Dean,* Dr. Geoffrey Cowan, 213-740-6180, Fax: 213-740-3772, E-mail: gcowan@usc.edu.

College of Letters, Arts and Sciences *Degree program information:* Part-time programs available. Offers anthropology (PhD); applied demography (MS); applied mathematics (MA, MS, PhD); art history (MA, PhD, Certificate); chemical physics (PhD); chemistry (MA, MS, PhD); classics (MA, PhD); clinical psychology (PhD); comparative literature (MA, PhD); computational linguistics (MS); earth sciences (MS, PhD); East Asian languages and cultures (MA, PhD); East Asian studies (MA); economic development programming (MA); economics (MA, PhD); English (MA, PhD); environmental studies (MA, MS); French (MA, PhD); geography (MA, MS, PhD); history (MA, PhD); international relations (MA, PhD); kinesiology (MA, MS, PhD); letters, arts and sciences (MA, MPW, MS, PhD, Certificate); linguistics (MA, PhD); marine environmental biology (MS, PhD); marriage and family therapy (PhD); mathematics (MA, PhD); molecular and computational biology (MS, PhD); neuroscience (PhD); philosophy (MA, PhD); physics (MA, MS, PhD); political economy (MA); political economy and public policy (PhD); political science (MA, PhD); professional writing (MPW); psychology (MA, PhD); Slavic languages and literatures (MA, PhD); social anthropology (PhD); social ethics (MA, PhD); sociology (MA, MS, PhD); statistics (MS); visual anthropology (MA).

Leonard Davis School of Gerontology Students: 59 full-time (46 women), 25 part-time (18 women); includes 21 minority (3 African Americans, 16 Asian Americans or Pacific Islanders, 2 Hispanic Americans), 9 international. Average age 29. 70 applicants, 70% accepted, 32 enrolled. *Faculty:* 15 full-time (5 women), 29 part-time/adjunct (10 women). Expenses: Contact institution. *Financial support:* In 2001–02, fellowships with partial tuition reimbursements (averaging $18,000 per year), research assistantships with full tuition reimbursements (averaging $3,111 per year), teaching assistantships with full tuition reimbursements (averaging $3,111 per year) were awarded. Career-related internships or fieldwork, Federal Work-Study, institutionally sponsored loans, and scholarships/grants also available. Financial award application deadline: 2/15; financial award applicants required to submit FAFSA. In 2001, 14 master's, 2 doctorates awarded. *Degree program information:* Part-time programs available. Postbaccalaureate distance learning degree programs offered. Offers gerontology (MS, PhD, Certificate). *Application deadline:* For fall admission, 2/1 (priority date); for spring admission, 10/1 (priority date). Applications are processed on a rolling basis. *Application fee:* $65 ($75 for international students). *Application Contact:* Steve Arbuckle, Public Communications Manager, 213-821-5452, Fax: 213-740-0792, E-mail: arbuckle@usc.edu. *Dean,* Dr. Elizabeth Zelinski, 213-740-4918, E-mail: zelinski@usc.edu.

Marshall School of Business Offers accounting (M Acc); business (M Acc, MBA, MBT, MS, PhD); business administration (MBA, MS, PhD); business taxation (MBT); finance and business economics (MBA); information and operations management (MS); international business (MBA).

School of Architecture Offers architecture (M Arch); building science (MBS); landscape architecture (ML Arch).

School of Cinema-Television Offers cinema-television (MA, MFA, PhD); critical studies (MA, PhD); film and video production (MFA); film, video, and computer animation (MFA); interactive media (MFA); producing (MFA); screen and television writing (MFA).

School of Education Offers administration and policy (PhD); college student personnel services (MS); communication handicapped (MS); counseling psychology (MS, PhD); curriculum and instruction (Ed D, PhD); curriculum and teaching (MS); education (MS, Ed D, PhD, MFCC); educational leadership (MS); educational psychology (MS, PhD); instructional technology (MS); international and intercultural education (MS); language, literacy, and learning (PhD); learning handicapped (MS); marriage, family and child counseling (MFCC); pupil personnel services (K–12) (MS); teaching English as a second language (MS).

School of Engineering *Degree program information:* Part-time programs available. Offers aerospace and mechanical engineering (MS, PhD, Engr); applied mechanics (MS); biomedical engineering (MS, PhD); biomedical imaging and telemedicine (MS); chemical engineering (MS, PhD, Engr); civil engineering (MS, PhD, Engr); computer aided engineering (ME, Certificate); computer engineering (MS, PhD); computer networks (MS); computer science (MS, PhD); construction engineering (MS); construction management (MCM); earthquake engineering (MS); electrical engineering (MS, PhD, Engr); engineering (MCM, ME, MS, PhD, Certificate, Engr); engineering management (MS); environmental engineering (MS, PhD); industrial and systems engineering (MS, PhD, Engr); manufacturing engineering (MS); materials engineering (MS); materials science (MS, PhD, Engr); multimedia and creative technologies (MS); ocean engineering (MS); operations research (MS); petroleum engineering (MS, PhD, Engr); robotics and automation (MS); software engineering (MS); soil mechanics and foundations (MS); structural engineering (MS); structural mechanics (MS); systems architecture and engineering (MS); transportation engineering (MS); VLSI design (MS); water resources (MS).

School of Fine Arts Offers fine arts (MFA, MPAS); public art studies (MPAS).

School of Health Affairs Offers biokinesiology (MS, PhD); health affairs (MA, MS, DPT, PhD, Certificate); nursing (MS, Certificate); occupational science (PhD); occupational therapy (MA); physical therapy (MS, DPT).

School of Policy, Planning and Development Offers health administration (MHA); planning (M Pl); planning and development studies (MPDS, DPDS); policy, planning and development (M Pl, MHA, MPA, MPDS, MPP, MRED, DPA, DPDS, PhD, Certificate); public administration (MPA, DPA, PhD, Certificate); public policy (MPP); real estate development (MRED); urban and regional planning (PhD).

School of Social Work Offers social work (MSW, PhD).

School of Theatre *Degree program information:* Part-time programs available. Offers design (MFA); playwriting (MFA).

Thorton School of Music Offers choral and church music (MM, DMA); conducting (MM); early music performance (MA); historical musicology (PhD); history and literature (MA); jazz (MM); music (MA, MM, MM Ed, DMA, PhD); music education (MM, MM Ed, DMA); performance (MM, DMA); theory and composition (MA, MM, DMA, PhD).

Keck School of Medicine Students: 1,035 full-time (501 women), 21 part-time (16 women); includes 439 minority (38 African Americans, 309 Asian Americans or Pacific Islanders, 87 Hispanic Americans, 5 Native Americans), 174 international. Average age 27. 5,658 applicants. *Faculty:* 1,178 full-time (364 women), 54 part-time/adjunct (23 women). Expenses: Contact institution. *Financial support:* In 2001–02, 798 students received support, including 18 fellowships with full tuition reimbursements available, 138 research assistantships with full tuition reimbursements available (averaging $19,430 per year), 20 teaching assistantships with full tuition reimbursements available (averaging $19,430 per year); career-related internships or fieldwork, Federal Work-Study, institutionally sponsored loans, scholarships/grants, traineeships, and tuition waivers (full and partial) also available. Support available to part-time students. In 2001, 160 first professional degrees, 50 master's, 25 doctorates awarded. Offers medicine (MD, MPH, MS, PhD). Electronic applications accepted. *Application Contact:* Oralia Gonzales, Administrative Services Manager, 323-442-1607, Fax: 323-442-1610, E-mail: oraliago@hsc.usc.edu. *Dean,* Dr. Stephen J. Ryan, 323-442-6444.

Graduate Programs in Medicine Students: 376 full-time (212 women), 21 part-time (16 women); includes 116 minority (10 African Americans, 84 Asian Americans or Pacific Islanders, 22 Hispanic Americans), 162 international. Average age 28. 691 applicants. *Faculty:* 219 full-time (68 women), 13 part-time/adjunct (4 women). Expenses: Contact institution. *Financial support:* In 2001–02, 248 students received support, including 18 fellowships with full tuition reimbursements available, 138 research assistantships with full tuition reimbursements available (averaging $19,430 per year), 20 teaching assistantships with full tuition reimbursements available (averaging $19,430 per year); career-related internships or fieldwork, Federal Work-Study, institutionally sponsored loans, scholarships/grants, traineeships, and tuition waivers (full and partial) also available. Support available to part-time students. In 2001, 50 master's, 25 doctorates awarded. Offers anatomy and cell biology (MS, PhD); applied biostatistics/epidemiology (MS); biochemistry and molecular biology (MS, PhD); biometry/epidemiology (MPH); biostatistics (MS, PhD); cell and neurobiology (MS, PhD); epidemiology (PhD); experimental and molecular pathology (MS); health behavior research (MPH, PhD); health promotion (MPH); medicine (MPH, MS, PhD); molecular epidemiology (MS, PhD); molecular microbiology and immunology (MS, PhD); pathobiology (PhD); physiology and biophysics (MS, PhD); preventive nutrition (MPH); public health (MPH). *Application fee:* $55. Electronic applications accepted. *Application Contact:* Oralia Gonzales, Administrative Services Manager, 323-442-1607, Fax: 323-442-1610, E-mail: oraliago@hsc.usc.edu. *Interim Associate Dean for Scientific Affairs,* Dr. John T. Nicoloff, 323-442-1607, Fax: 323-442-1610, E-mail: jnicolof@hsc.usc.edu.

Law School Offers law (JD).

School of Dentistry Offers craniofacial biology (MS, PhD); dentistry (DDS, MS, PhD, Certificate).

School of Pharmacy Offers molecular pharmacology and toxicology (MS, PhD); pharmaceutical economics and policy (MS, PhD); pharmaceutical sciences (MS, PhD); pharmacy (Pharm D, MS, PhD); regulatory sciences (MS).

See in-depth description on page 1259.

UNIVERSITY OF SOUTHERN COLORADO, Pueblo, CO 81001-4901

General Information State-supported, coed, comprehensive institution. *Enrollment:* 66 full-time matriculated graduate/professional students (25 women), 41 part-time matriculated graduate/professional students (24 women). *Enrollment by degree level:* 107 master's. *Graduate faculty:* 24 full-time (7 women), 4 part-time/adjunct (1 woman). Tuition, state resident: full-time $1,746; part-time $97 per credit. Tuition, nonresident: full-time $8,298; part-time $461 per credit. *Required fees:* $445; $97 per credit. $582 per semester. Tuition and fees vary according to course load. *Graduate housing:* Room and/or apartments available on a first-come, first-served basis to single students; on-campus housing not available to married students. Typical cost: $2,484 per year ($5,164 including board). Room and board charges vary according to board plan. Housing application deadline: 8/1. *Student services:* Campus employment opportunities, campus safety program, career counseling, child daycare facilities, disabled student services, exercise/wellness program, free psychological counseling, grant writing training, international student services, low-cost health insurance, writing training. *Library facilities:* University of Southern Colorado Library. *Online resources:* library catalog, web page, access to other libraries' catalogs. *Collection:* 270,761 titles, 1,327 serial subscriptions, 16,862 audiovisual materials.

Computer facilities: 521 computers available on campus for general student use. A campuswide network can be accessed from student residence rooms and from off campus. Internet access is available. *Web address:* http://www.uscolo.edu/.

General Application Contact: Pamela L. Anastassiou, Director, Admissions and Records, 719-549-2461, Fax: 719-549-2419, E-mail: anastass@uscolo.edu.

GRADUATE UNITS

College of Education, Engineering and Professional Studies Students: 16 full-time (4 women), 18 part-time (3 women); includes 5 minority (1 African American, 3 Hispanic Americans, 1 Native American), 20 international. Average age 29. 30 applicants, 87% accepted. *Faculty:* 5 full-time (1 woman), 1 part-time/adjunct (0 women). Expenses: Contact institution. *Financial support:* In 2001–02, 1 fellowship (averaging $17,000 per year), 1 research assistantship with partial tuition reimbursement (averaging $13,000 per year), 2 teaching assistantships with partial tuition reimbursements (averaging $8,300 per year) were awarded. Career-related internships or fieldwork, Federal Work-Study, institutionally sponsored loans, and scholarships/grants also available. Financial award application deadline: 3/1; financial award applicants required to submit FAFSA. In 2001, 23 degrees awarded. *Degree program information:* Part-time and evening/weekend programs available. Offers education, engineering and professional studies (MS); industrial and systems engineering (MS). *Application deadline:* For fall admission, 7/19 (priority date); for spring admission, 11/30 (priority date). *Application fee:* $35. *Application Contact:* Dr. Huseyin Sarper, Graduate Coordinator, 719-549-2889, Fax: 719-549-2519, E-mail: sarper@uscolo.edu. *Dean,* Dr. Hector R. Carrasco, 719-549-2696, Fax: 719-549-2519, E-mail: carrasco@uscolo.edu.

College of Science and Mathematics *Degree program information:* Part-time programs available. Offers science and mathematics (MS).

Hasan School of Business Students: 26 full-time (12 women), 23 part-time (15 women); includes 12 minority (all Hispanic Americans), 7 international. Average age 36. 41 applicants, 85% accepted, 24 enrolled. *Faculty:* 9 full-time (2 women), 1 (woman) part-time/adjunct. Expenses: Contact institution. *Financial support:* In 2001–02, 10 research assistantships with partial tuition reimbursements (averaging $3,172 per year) were awarded; scholarships/grants and unspecified assistantships also available. Financial award applicants required to submit FAFSA. In 2001, 37 degrees awarded. *Degree program information:* Part-time and evening/weekend programs available. Offers business (MBA). *Application deadline:* For fall admission, 8/18 (priority date); for spring admission, 1/12 (priority date). Applications are processed on a rolling basis. *Application fee:* $35. *Application Contact:* Pamela L. Anastassiou, Director, Admissions and Records, 719-549-2461, Fax: 719-549-2419, E-mail: anastass@uscolo.edu. *Dean,* Dr. Rex D. Fuller, 719-549-2142, Fax: 719-549-2909, E-mail: rfuller@uscolo.edu.

Program in Applied Natural Science Students: 19 full-time (12 women), 5 part-time (4 women); includes 2 minority (1 African American, 1 Hispanic American), 2 international. Average age 28. 8 applicants, 75% accepted, 6 enrolled. *Faculty:* 10 full-time (4 women). Expenses: Contact institution. *Financial support:* In 2001–02, 7 students received support, including 1 fellowship (averaging $1,000 per year), 5 teaching assistantships (averaging $8,500 per year); research assistantships, career-related internships or fieldwork, scholarships/grants, and unspecified assistantships also available. Financial award application deadline: 3/1; financial award applicants required to submit FAFSA. In 2001, 7 degrees awarded. *Degree program information:* Part-time and evening/weekend programs available. Offers applied natural science (MS). *Application deadline:* For fall admission, 4/30 (priority date). Applications are processed on a rolling basis. *Application fee:* $35. *Professor of Biology and Dean,* Dr. Helen M. Caprioglio, 719-549-2815, Fax: 719-549-2732, E-mail: hcaprio@uscolo.edu.

UNIVERSITY OF SOUTHERN INDIANA, Evansville, IN 47712-3590

General Information State-supported, coed, comprehensive institution. CGS member. *Enrollment:* 97 full-time matriculated graduate/professional students (79 women), 393 part-time matriculated graduate/professional students (264 women). *Enrollment by degree level:* 490 master's. *Graduate faculty:* 59 full-time (20 women), 16 part-time/adjunct (3 women). Tuition, state resident: full-time $1,361; part-time $151 per hour. Tuition, nonresident: full-time $2,732; part-time $304 per hour. *Required fees:* $60; $23 per semester. Tuition and fees vary according to course load. *Graduate housing:* Rooms and/or apartments available on a first-come, first-served basis to single and married students. Typical cost: $2,520 per year ($5,512 including board) for single students; $2,520 per year ($5,512 including board) for married students. Room and board charges vary according to board plan and housing facility selected. Housing application deadline: 3/1. *Student services:* Campus employment opportunities, campus safety program, career counseling, child daycare facilities, disabled student services, exercise/wellness program, free psychological counseling, international student services, low-cost health insurance, multicultural affairs office. *Library facilities:* David L. Rice Library plus 1 other. *Online resources:* library catalog, web page, access to other libraries' catalogs. *Collection:* 248,546 titles, 3,302 serial subscriptions, 7,563 audiovisual materials.

Computer facilities: 750 computers available on campus for general student use. A campuswide network can be accessed from student residence rooms and from off campus. Internet access and online class registration are available. *Web address:* http://www.usi.edu/.

General Application Contact: Dr. Peggy F. Harrel, Director, Graduate Studies, 812-465-7015, Fax: 812-464-1956, E-mail: pharrel@usi.edu.

GRADUATE UNITS

Graduate Studies Students: 97 full-time (79 women), 393 part-time (264 women); includes 24 minority (13 African Americans, 6 Asian Americans or Pacific Islanders, 4 Hispanic Americans, 1 Native American), 13 international. Average age 33. 475 applicants, 86% accepted, 273 enrolled. *Faculty:* 59 full-time (20 women), 16 part-time/adjunct (3 women). Expenses: Contact institution. *Financial support:* In 2001–02, 162 students received support. Federal Work-Study, institutionally sponsored loans, scholarships/grants, tuition waivers (full and partial), and unspecified assistantships available. Financial award application deadline: 3/1; financial award applicants required to submit FAFSA. In 2001, 130 degrees awarded. *Degree program information:* Part-time and evening/weekend programs available. *Application deadline:* Applications are processed on a rolling basis. *Application fee:* $25. *Director,* Dr. Peggy F. Harrel, 812-465-7015, Fax: 812-464-1956, E-mail: pharrel@usi.edu.

School of Business Students: 14 full-time (7 women), 99 part-time (41 women); includes 3 minority (2 African Americans, 1 Asian American or Pacific Islander), 5 international. Average age 29. 82 applicants, 61% accepted, 44 enrolled. *Faculty:* 26 full-time (3 women). Expenses: Contact institution. *Financial support:* In 2001–02, 19 students received support. Federal Work-Study, institutionally sponsored loans, scholarships/grants, tuition waivers (full and partial), and unspecified assistantships available. Financial award application deadline: 3/1; financial award applicants required to submit FAFSA. In 2001, 30 degrees awarded. *Degree program information:* Part-time and evening/weekend programs available. Offers accounting and business law (MSA); business (MBA, MSA); business administration (MBA). *Application deadline:* For fall admission, 8/15. Applications are processed on a rolling basis. *Application fee:* $25. *Application Contact:* Director, MBA Program, 812-464-1803. *Dean,* Dr. Philip C. Fisher, 812-465-1681, E-mail: pfisher@usi.edu.

School of Education and Human Services Students: 66 full-time (59 women), 124 part-time (100 women); includes 13 minority (9 African Americans, 2 Asian Americans or Pacific Islanders, 2 Hispanic Americans), 4 international. Average age 31. 132 applicants, 70% accepted, 82 enrolled. *Faculty:* 18 full-time (9 women), 2 part-time/adjunct (0 women). Expenses: Contact institution. *Financial support:* In 2001–02, 80 students received support. Federal Work-Study, institutionally sponsored loans, scholarships/grants, tuition waivers (full and partial), and unspecified assistantships available. Financial award application deadline: 3/1; financial award applicants required to submit FAFSA. In 2001, 77 degrees awarded. *Degree program information:* Part-time and evening/weekend programs available. Offers education and human services (MS, MSW); elementary education (MS); secondary education (MS); social work (MSW). *Application deadline:* Applications are processed on a rolling basis. *Application fee:* $25. *Application Contact:* Dr. Charles Price, Director, 812-464-1939, E-mail: cprice@usi.edu. *Dean,* Dr. Thomas Pickering, 812-464-1811, E-mail: tpickeri@usi.edu.

School of Liberal Arts Students: 3 full-time (2 women), 29 part-time (21 women). Average age 38. 13 applicants, 77% accepted, 9 enrolled. *Faculty:* 20 part-time/adjunct (5 women). Expenses: Contact institution. *Financial support:* In 2001–02, 10 students received support. Federal Work-Study, institutionally sponsored loans, scholarships/grants, tuition waivers (full and partial), and unspecified assistantships available. Financial award application deadline: 3/1; financial award applicants required to submit FAFSA. In 2001, 6 degrees awarded. *Degree program information:* Part-time and evening/weekend programs available. Offers liberal arts (MA); liberal studies (MA). *Application deadline:* For fall admission, 8/15 (priority date). Applications are processed on a rolling basis. *Application fee:* $25. *Application Contact:* Dr. Thomas M. Rivers, Director, 812-464-1753, E-mail: trivers@usi.edu. *Dean,* Dr. Iain L. Crawford, 812-464-1855, E-mail: crawford@usi.edu.

School of Nursing and Health Professions Students: 14 full-time (11 women), 109 part-time (96 women); includes 7 minority (2 African Americans, 3 Asian Americans or Pacific Islanders, 1 Hispanic American, 1 Native American), 3 international. Average age 37. 117 applicants, 73% accepted, 84 enrolled. *Faculty:* 13 full-time (12 women), 1 part-time/adjunct (0 women). Expenses: Contact institution. *Financial support:* In 2001–02, 42 students received support. Federal Work-Study, institutionally sponsored loans, scholarships/grants, tuition waivers (full and partial), and unspecified assistantships available. Financial award application deadline: 3/1; financial award applicants required to submit FAFSA. In 2001, 17 degrees awarded. Offers health administration (MHA); nursing (MSN); nursing and health professions (MHA, MSN, MSOT); occupational therapy (MSOT). *Application deadline:* Applications are processed on a rolling basis. *Application fee:* $25. *Dean,* Dr. Nadine Coudret, 812-465-1151, E-mail: ncoudret@usi.edu.

School of Science and Engineering Technology Average age 35. 9 applicants, 56% accepted, 3 enrolled. *Faculty:* 5 full-time (0 women). Expenses: Contact institution. *Financial support:* In 2001–02, 2 students received support. Federal Work-Study, institutionally sponsored loans, scholarships/grants, tuition waivers (full and partial), and unspecified assistantships available. Financial award application deadline: 3/1; financial award applicants required to submit FAFSA. *Degree program information:* Part-time and evening/weekend programs available. Offers industrial management (MS); science and engineering (MS). *Application deadline:* Applications are processed on a rolling basis. *Application fee:* $25. *Dean,* Dr. Jerome Cain, 812-464-1977, E-mail: jcain@usi.edu.

UNIVERSITY OF SOUTHERN MAINE, Portland, ME 04104-9300

General Information State-supported, coed, comprehensive institution. *Enrollment:* 938 full-time matriculated graduate/professional students (605 women), 1,156 part-time matriculated graduate/professional students (806 women). *Enrollment by degree level:* 251 first professional, 1,830 master's, 13 doctoral. *Graduate faculty:* 140. Tuition, state resident: part-time $200 per credit. Tuition, nonresident: part-time $560 per credit. *Graduate housing:* Room and/or apartments available to single students; on-campus housing not available to married students. *Student services:* Campus employment opportunities, career counseling, child daycare facilities, disabled student services, exercise/wellness program, free psychological counseling, international student services, low-cost health insurance, multicultural affairs office, teacher training. *Library facilities:* University of Southern Maine Library plus 4 others. *Online resources:* library catalog, web page, access to other libraries' catalogs. *Collection:* 620,000 titles, 7,600 serial subscriptions, 2,500 audiovisual materials. *Research affiliation:* Maine Medical Center, Foundation for Blood Research.

Computer facilities: 440 computers available on campus for general student use. A campuswide network can be accessed from student residence rooms and from off campus. Internet access and online class registration are available. *Web address:* http://www.usm.maine.edu/.

General Application Contact: Mary Sloan, Director of Graduate Admissions, 207-780-4236, Fax: 207-780-4969, E-mail: msloan@usm.maine.edu.

GRADUATE UNITS

College of Arts and Science Students: 16 full-time, 37 part-time; includes 1 minority (Asian American or Pacific Islander) 20 applicants, 80% accepted. *Faculty:* 8 full-time (1 woman), 5 part-time/adjunct (2 women). Expenses: Contact institution. *Financial support:* In 2001–02, 3 research assistantships were awarded; career-related internships or fieldwork and Federal Work-Study also available. Support available to part-time students. In 2001, 6 degrees awarded. *Degree program information:* Part-time and evening/weekend programs available. Offers American and New England studies (MA); arts and science (MA). *Application deadline:* For fall admission, 3/15 (priority date); for spring admission, 10/1. *Application fee:* $25. *Application Contact:* Mary Sloan, Director of Graduate Admissions, 207-780-4236, Fax: 207-780-4969, E-mail: msloan@usm.maine.edu. *Dean,* Dr. F. C. McGrath, 207-780-4221.

College of Education and Human Development *Degree program information:* Part-time and evening/weekend programs available. Postbaccalaureate distance learning degree programs offered. Offers adult education (MS, CAS); counselor education (MS, CAS); education and human development (MS, MS Ed, CAS, Certificate); educational leadership (MS Ed, CAS, Certificate); English as a second language (MS Ed, CAS); extended teacher education (MS Ed, Certificate); industrial/technology education (MS Ed); literacy education (MS Ed, CAS); school psychology (MS); special education (MS).

College of Nursing and Health Professions Students: 50 full-time (44 women), 39 part-time (37 women); includes 1 minority (Native American) Average age 43. 73 applicants, 81% accepted, 34 enrolled. *Faculty:* 23 full-time (22 women), 6 part-time/adjunct (all women). Expenses: Contact institution. *Financial support:* In 2001–02, 9 research assistantships with tuition reimbursements (averaging $1,060 per year), 2 teaching assistantships with tuition reimbursements (averaging $1,060 per year) were awarded. Career-related internships or fieldwork, Federal Work-Study, scholarships/grants, traineeships, tuition waivers (full and partial), and unspecified assistantships also available. Support available to part-time students. Financial award application deadline: 2/15; financial award applicants required to submit FAFSA. In 2001, 32 degrees awarded. *Degree program information:* Part-time programs available. Postbaccalaureate distance learning degree programs offered (minimal on-campus study). Offers adult health nursing (PMC); clinical nurse specialist adult health care management (MS); clinical nurse specialist psychiatric-mental health nursing (MS); family nursing (PMC); nurse practitioner adult health nursing (MS); nurse practitioner family nursing (MS); nurse practitioner psychiatric/mental health nursing (MS); psychiatric-mental health nursing (PMC). *Application deadline:* For fall admission, 3/1. *Application fee:* $50. *Application Contact:* Mary Sloan, Director of Graduate Admissions, 207-780-4236, Fax: 207-780-4969, E-mail: msloan@usm.maine.edu. *Dean,* Dr. Jane Marie Kirschling, 207-780-4404, Fax: 207-780-4997, E-mail: jane.kirschling@usm.maine.edu.

Edmund S. Muskie School of Public Service Students: 31 full-time (17 women), 105 part-time (61 women); includes 3 minority (2 African Americans, 1 Asian American or Pacific Islander), 6 international. Average age 28. 50 applicants, 80% accepted. *Faculty:* 6 full-time (2 women), 13 part-time/adjunct (4 women). Expenses: Contact institution. *Financial support:* In 2001–02, 5 fellowships with partial tuition reimbursements (averaging $5,000 per year), 15 research assistantships with partial tuition reimbursements (averaging $5,000 per year) were awarded. Teaching assistantships with partial tuition reimbursements, career-related internships or fieldwork, Federal Work-Study, scholarships/grants, traineeships, tuition waivers (full), and unspecified assistantships also available. Support available to part-time students. Financial award application deadline: 4/1; financial award applicants required to submit CSS PROFILE. In 2001, 27 degrees awarded. *Degree program information:* Part-time and evening/weekend programs available. Postbaccalaureate distance learning degree programs offered (minimal on-campus study). Offers community planning and development (MCPD, Certificate); health policy and management (MS, Certificate); public policy and management (MPPM, PhD); public service (MCPD, MPPM, MS, PhD, Certificate). *Application deadline:* For fall admission, 3/1 (priority date); for winter admission, 12/1 (priority date). Applications are processed on a rolling basis. *Application fee:* $50. Electronic applications accepted. *Application Contact:* Carlene R. Goldman, Director of Student Affairs, 207-780-4864, Fax: 207-780-4417, E-mail: cgold@usm.maine.edu. *Dean,* Karl R. Braithwaite, 207-780-4563, Fax: 207-780-4417, E-mail: kbraithw@usm.maine.edu.

Program in Occupational Therapy Students: 33 full-time (27 women), 3 part-time (all women); includes 1 minority (Asian American or Pacific Islander) Average age 33. 17 applicants,

University of Southern Maine (continued)

71% accepted. *Faculty:* 3 full-time (all women), 5 part-time/adjunct (all women). Expenses: Contact institution. *Financial support:* In 2001–02, 1 research assistantship (averaging $1,200 per year), 2 teaching assistantships (averaging $1,200 per year) were awarded. Fellowships with partial tuition reimbursements, scholarships/grants and tuition waivers (partial) also available. Financial award application deadline: 3/1; financial award applicants required to submit FAFSA. In 2001, 22 degrees awarded. *Degree program information:* Part-time programs available. Offers occupational therapy (MOT). *Application deadline:* Applications are processed on a rolling basis. *Application fee:* $50. *Application Contact:* Ben Turner, Administrative Assistant, 207-753-6523, Fax: 207-753-6555, E-mail: turnerb@usm.maine.edu. *Director,* Roxie M. Black, 207-753-6515, Fax: 207-753-6555, E-mail: rblack@usm.maine.edu.

School of Applied Science, Engineering, and Technology *Degree program information:* Part-time and evening/weekend programs available. Offers applied immunology and molecular biology (MS); applied science, engineering, and technology (MS); computer science (MS); manufacturing systems (MS).

School of Business Students: 30 full-time (14 women), 111 part-time (43 women); includes 1 minority (Hispanic American), 1 international. Average age 31. 51 applicants, 82% accepted, 37 enrolled. *Faculty:* 18 full-time (6 women), 2 part-time/adjunct (1 woman). Expenses: Contact institution. *Financial support:* In 2001–02, 3 research assistantships (averaging $7,200 per year), 3 teaching assistantships (averaging $7,200 per year) were awarded. Career-related internships or fieldwork, Federal Work-Study, scholarships/grants, tuition waivers (full and partial), and unspecified assistantships also available. Support available to part-time students. Financial award application deadline: 2/15; financial award applicants required to submit FAFSA. In 2001, 28 degrees awarded. *Degree program information:* Part-time and evening/weekend programs available. Offers accounting (MSA); business administration (MBA). *Application deadline:* For fall admission, 8/1 (priority date); for spring admission, 12/1 (priority date). Applications are processed on a rolling basis. *Application fee:* $50. *Application Contact:* Dr. John B. Jensen, Co-Director, MBA Program, 207-780-4184, Fax: 207-780-4662, E-mail: mba@usm.maine.edu. *Dean,* Dr. John W. Bay, 207-780-4020, Fax: 207-780-4662, E-mail: johnbay@usm.maine.edu.

University of Maine School of Law Students: 221 full-time (117 women), 9 part-time (4 women); includes 11 minority (4 African Americans, 1 Asian American or Pacific Islander, 3 Hispanic Americans, 3 Native Americans), 1 international. Average age 29. 529 applicants, 54% accepted, 95 enrolled. *Faculty:* 18 full-time (6 women), 6 part-time/adjunct (3 women). Expenses: Contact institution. *Financial support:* In 2001–02, 198 students received support. Career-related internships or fieldwork, Federal Work-Study, scholarships/grants, and tuition waivers (full and partial) available. Support available to part-time students. Financial award application deadline: 2/1; financial award applicants required to submit FAFSA. In 2001, 89 degrees awarded. Offers law (JD). *Application deadline:* For fall admission, 2/15. Applications are processed on a rolling basis. *Application fee:* $50. *Application Contact:* Rebecca Warsinsky, Admissions Coordinator, 207-780-4341, Fax: 207-780-4239, E-mail: rebeccaw@usm.maine.edu. *Dean,* Colleen A. Khoury, 207-780-4344, Fax: 207-780-4239, E-mail: ckhoury@usm.maine.edu.

UNIVERSITY OF SOUTHERN MISSISSIPPI, Hattiesburg, MS 39406

General Information State-supported, coed, university. CGS member. *Enrollment:* 1,230 full-time matriculated graduate/professional students (724 women), 1,159 part-time matriculated graduate/professional students (768 women). *Enrollment by degree level:* 1,484 master's, 608 doctoral, 297 other advanced degrees. *Graduate faculty:* 624 full-time (239 women), 133 part-time/adjunct (62 women). Tuition, state resident: full-time $3,416; part-time $190 per credit hour. Tuition, nonresident: full-time $7,932; part-time $441 per credit hour. *Graduate housing:* Rooms and/or apartments available on a first-come, first-served basis to single students and available to married students. Typical cost: $2,760 per year for single students; $2,566 per year for married students. *Student services:* Campus employment opportunities, career counseling, disabled student services, free psychological counseling, international student services. *Library facilities:* Cook Memorial Library plus 4 others. *Online resources:* library catalog, web page. *Collection:* 217,634 titles, 21,134 audiovisual materials.

Computer facilities: 600 computers available on campus for general student use. Internet access is available. *Web address:* http://www.usm.edu/.

General Application Contact: Dr. Susan Siltanen, Director of Graduate Admissions, 601-266-5137, Fax: 601-266-5138.

GRADUATE UNITS

Graduate School Students: 1,230 full-time (724 women), 1,159 part-time (768 women); includes 330 minority (271 African Americans, 17 Asian Americans or Pacific Islanders, 34 Hispanic Americans, 8 Native Americans), 171 international. Average age 31. 2,010 applicants, 80% accepted. *Faculty:* 624 full-time (239 women), 133 part-time/adjunct (62 women). Expenses: Contact institution. *Financial support:* Fellowships with full and partial tuition reimbursements, research assistantships with full and partial tuition reimbursements, teaching assistantships with full and partial tuition reimbursements, career-related internships or fieldwork, Federal Work-Study, institutionally sponsored loans, scholarships/grants, traineeships, tuition waivers (full and partial), and unspecified assistantships available. Support available to part-time students. Financial award application deadline: 3/15. In 2001, 818 master's, 112 doctorates awarded. *Degree program information:* Part-time and evening/weekend programs available. *Application deadline:* Applications are processed on a rolling basis. *Application fee:* $0 ($25 for international students). *Application Contact:* Dr. Susan Siltanen, Director of Graduate Admissions, 601-266-5137, Fax: 601-266-5138. *Interim Dean,* Dr. Donald Cotten, 601-266-4369.

College of Business Administration Students: 67 full-time (32 women), 95 part-time (38 women); includes 10 minority (8 African Americans, 1 Asian American or Pacific Islander, 1 Hispanic American), 13 international. Average age 28. 126 applicants, 79% accepted. *Faculty:* 69. Expenses: Contact institution. *Financial support:* In 2001–02, 36 research assistantships with full tuition reimbursements (averaging $3,200 per year) were awarded; Federal Work-Study and institutionally sponsored loans also available. Support available to part-time students. Financial award application deadline: 3/15. In 2001, 69 degrees awarded. *Degree program information:* Part-time and evening/weekend programs available. Offers business administration (MBA); professional accountancy (MPA); systems management (MSSM). *Application deadline:* For fall admission, 7/15 (priority date); for spring admission, 11/15 (priority date). Applications are processed on a rolling basis. *Application fee:* $0 ($25 for international students). Electronic applications accepted. *Application Contact:* Sue Fayard, Manager of Graduate Business Programs, 601-266-4653, Fax: 601-266-4639, E-mail: sue.fayard@usm.edu. *Dean,* Dr. William Gunther, 601-266-4659, Fax: 601-266-5814.

College of Education and Psychology Students: 248 full-time (171 women), 388 part-time (264 women); includes 124 minority (107 African Americans, 4 Asian Americans or Pacific Islanders, 11 Hispanic Americans, 2 Native Americans), 15 international. Average age 35. 546 applicants, 40% accepted. *Faculty:* 89. Expenses: Contact institution. *Financial support:* Research assistantships with full tuition reimbursements, teaching assistantships with full and partial tuition reimbursements, career-related internships or fieldwork, Federal Work-Study, institutionally sponsored loans, and tuition waivers (partial) available. Financial award application deadline: 3/15. In 2001, 293 master's, 52 doctorates awarded. *Degree program information:* Part-time programs available. Offers adult education (M Ed, Ed D, PhD, Ed S); alternative secondary teacher education (MAT); business technology education (MS); early childhood education (M Ed, Ed S); education and psychology (M Ed, MA, MAT, MATL, MS, Ed D, PhD, Ed S); education of the gifted (M Ed, Ed D, PhD, Ed S); educational administration (M Ed, Ed D, PhD, Ed S); elementary education (M Ed, Ed D, PhD, Ed S); instructional technology (MS); psychology (M Ed, MA, MS, PhD, Ed S); reading (M Ed, MS, Ed S); secondary education (M Ed, MS, Ed D, PhD, Ed S); special education (M Ed, Ed D, PhD, Ed S); technical occupational education (MS). *Application deadline:* Applications are processed on a rolling basis. *Application fee:* $0 ($25 for international students). Electronic applications accepted. *Dean,* Dr. Carl R. Martray, 601-266-4568.

College of Health and Human Sciences Students: 219 full-time (150 women), 128 part-time (94 women); includes 81 minority (67 African Americans, 6 Asian Americans or Pacific Islanders, 5 Hispanic Americans, 3 Native Americans), 13 international. Average age 30. 310 applicants, 67% accepted. *Faculty:* 76. Expenses: Contact institution. *Financial support:* Fellowships with full and partial tuition reimbursements, research assistantships with full and partial tuition reimbursements, teaching assistantships with full and partial tuition reimbursements, career-related internships or fieldwork, Federal Work-Study, institutionally sponsored loans, scholarships/grants, and tuition waivers (partial) available. Financial award application deadline: 3/15. In 2001, 126 master's, 9 doctorates awarded. *Degree program information:* Part-time and evening/weekend programs available. Offers early intervention (MS); family and consumer studies (MS); health and human sciences (MPH, MS, MSW, Ed D, PhD); health education (MPH); health policy/administration (MPH); human nutrition (MS); human performance (MS, Ed D, PhD); institution management (MS); marriage and family therapy (MS); nutrition and food systems (PhD); occupational/environmental health (MPH); public health nutrition (MPH); recreation (MS); social work (MSW); sport administration (MS). *Application deadline:* Applications are processed on a rolling basis. *Application fee:* $0 ($25 for international students). Electronic applications accepted. *Dean,* Dr. Jane Boudreaux, 601-266-5253.

College of International and Continuing Education Students: 28 full-time (15 women), 20 part-time (9 women); includes 4 minority (3 African Americans, 1 Hispanic American), 2 international. Average age 32. 26 applicants, 85% accepted. *Faculty:* 10 full-time (1 woman), 1 part-time/adjunct (0 women). Expenses: Contact institution. *Financial support:* Fellowships, research assistantships, teaching assistantships available. Financial award application deadline: 3/15. In 2001, 10 degrees awarded. Offers economic development (MS); geography (MS); international and continuing education (MS, PhD); international development (PhD). *Application deadline:* For spring admission, 1/3. Applications are processed on a rolling basis. *Application fee:* $0 ($25 for international students). Electronic applications accepted. *Dean,* Dr. Tim W. Hudson, 601-266-4344, E-mail: tim.hudson@usm.edu.

College of Liberal Arts Students: 270 full-time (162 women), 344 part-time (253 women); includes 66 minority (51 African Americans, 3 Asian Americans or Pacific Islanders, 11 Hispanic Americans, 1 Native American), 42 international. Average age 34. 556 applicants, 58% accepted. *Faculty:* 196. Expenses: Contact institution. *Financial support:* Fellowships with full tuition reimbursements, research assistantships with full and partial tuition reimbursements, teaching assistantships with full and partial tuition reimbursements, career-related internships or fieldwork, Federal Work-Study, institutionally sponsored loans, scholarships/grants, tuition waivers (full and partial), and unspecified assistantships available. Financial award application deadline: 3/15. In 2001, 179 master's, 18 doctorates awarded. *Degree program information:* Part-time and evening/weekend programs available. Postbaccalaureate distance learning degree programs offered. Offers administration of justice (PhD); anthropology (MA); communication (MA, MS, PhD); corrections (MA, MS); English (MA, PhD); foreign languages and literatures (MATL); history (MA, MS, PhD); juvenile justice (MA, MS); law enforcement (MA, MS); liberal arts (MA, MATL, MLIS, MS, PhD, SLS); library and information science (MLIS, SLS); philosophy (MA); political science (MA, MS); public relations (MS); speech and hearing sciences (MA, MS, PhD). *Application deadline:* Applications are processed on a rolling basis. *Application fee:* $0 ($25 for international students). Electronic applications accepted. *Dean,* Dr. Glenn T. Harper, 601-266-4315.

College of Marine Sciences Students: 37 full-time (11 women), 15 part-time (7 women); includes 5 minority (3 African Americans, 2 Hispanic Americans), 9 international. Average age 32. 58 applicants, 31% accepted. *Faculty:* 23. Expenses: Contact institution. *Financial support:* Research assistantships with full tuition reimbursements, teaching assistantships with full tuition reimbursements, institutionally sponsored loans available. Financial award application deadline: 3/15. In 2001, 21 master's, 5 doctorates awarded. *Degree program information:* Part-time programs available. Offers hydrography (MS); marine science (MS, PhD); marine sciences (MS, PhD). *Application deadline:* Applications are processed on a rolling basis. *Application fee:* $0 ($25 for international students). Electronic applications accepted. *Dean,* Dr. D. Jay, 228-872-4211.

College of Nursing Students: 65 full-time (59 women), 70 part-time (64 women); includes 15 minority (12 African Americans, 1 Asian American or Pacific Islander, 2 Native Americans) Average age 39. 39 applicants, 46% accepted. *Faculty:* 38 full-time (all women). Expenses: Contact institution. *Financial support:* Research assistantships with full tuition reimbursements, Federal Work-Study and traineeships available. Financial award application deadline: 3/15. In 2001, 30 degrees awarded. *Degree program information:* Part-time and evening/weekend programs available. Offers adult health nursing (MSN); community health nursing (MSN); ethics (PhD); family nurse practitioner (MSN); leadership (PhD); nursing service administration (MSN); policy analysis (PhD); psychiatric nursing (MSN). *Application deadline:* For fall admission, 8/9 (priority date); for spring admission, 11/1 (priority date). Applications are processed on a rolling basis. *Application fee:* $0 ($25 for international students). Electronic applications accepted. *Dean,* Dr. Deolinda Mignor, 601-266-5445, Fax: 601-266-5927.

College of Science and Technology Students: 227 full-time (94 women), 73 part-time (26 women); includes 18 minority (14 African Americans, 2 Asian Americans or Pacific Islanders, 2 Hispanic Americans), 63 international. Average age 30. 529 applicants, 36% accepted. *Faculty:* 159. Expenses: Contact institution. *Financial support:* Fellowships, research assistantships with full tuition reimbursements, teaching assistantships with full tuition reimbursements, career-related internships or fieldwork, Federal Work-Study, institutionally sponsored loans, and tuition waivers (full) available. Support available to part-time students. Financial award application deadline: 3/15. In 2001, 61 master's, 20 doctorates awarded. *Degree program information:* Part-time and evening/weekend programs available. Offers analytical chemistry (MS, PhD); biochemistry (MS, PhD); computer science (MS); engineering technology (MS); environmental biology (MS, PhD); geology (MS); inorganic chemistry (MS, PhD); marine biology (MS, PhD); mathematics (MS); medical technology (MS); microbiology (MS, PhD); molecular biology (MS, PhD); organic chemistry (MS, PhD); physical chemistry (MS, PhD); physics and astronomy (MS); polymer science (MS, PhD); science and mathematics education (M Ed, MS, Ed D, PhD); science and technology (M Ed, MS, Ed D, PhD); scientific computing (PhD). *Application deadline:* Applications are processed on a rolling basis. *Application fee:* $0 ($25 for international students). *Dean,* Dr. Robert Lochhead, 601-266-4883, Fax: 601-266-5829.

College of the Arts Students: 68 full-time (29 women), 27 part-time (13 women); includes 7 minority (6 African Americans, 1 Hispanic American), 14 international. Average age 32. 49 applicants, 67% accepted. *Faculty:* 76. Expenses: Contact institution. *Financial support:* Teaching assistantships with full tuition reimbursements, career-related internships or fieldwork, Federal Work-Study, institutionally sponsored loans, and tuition waivers (partial) available. Support available to part-time students. Financial award application deadline: 3/15. In 2001, 29 master's, 8 doctorates awarded. *Degree program information:* Part-time programs available. Offers art education (MAE); arts (MAE, MFA, MM, MME, DMA, DME, PhD); church music (MM); conducting (MM); history and literature (MM); music education (MME, DME, PhD); performance (MM); performance and pedagogy (DMA); theatre and dance (MFA); theory and composition (MM); woodwind performance (MM). *Application deadline:* For fall admission, 8/9 (priority date). Applications are processed on a rolling basis. *Application fee:* $0 ($25 for international students). *Dean,* Dr. Mary Ann Stringer, 601-266-4984.

UNIVERSITY OF SOUTH FLORIDA, Tampa, FL 33620-9951

General Information State-supported, coed, university. CGS member. *Enrollment:* 2,990 full-time matriculated graduate/professional students (1,727 women), 3,329 part-time matriculated graduate/professional students (2,096 women). *Enrollment by degree level:* 400 first professional, 5,458 master's, 1,408 doctoral. *Graduate faculty:* 1,557 full-time (573 women), 140 part-time/adjunct (39 women). Tuition, state resident: part-time $166 per credit hour. Tuition, nonresident: part-time $573 per credit hour. *Required fees:* $17 per term. *Graduate housing:* Room and/or apartments available on a first-come, first-served basis to single students; on-campus housing not available to married students. Housing application deadline: 7/1. *Student services:* Campus employment opportunities, campus safety program, career counseling, child daycare facilities, disabled student services, exercise/wellness program, free psychological counseling, international student services, low-cost health insurance, multicultural affairs office. *Library facilities:* Tampa Campus Library plus 2 others. *Online resources:* library catalog, web page, access to other libraries' catalogs. *Collection:* 1.9 million titles, 9,607 serial subscriptions, 148,986 audiovisual materials. *Research affiliation:* H. L. Moffitt Cancer Center, Shriners Hospitals, Tampa General Hospital, Harris Corporation (electronics), All Children's Hospital, Veterans Administration Medical Center.

Computer facilities: 500 computers available on campus for general student use. A campuswide network can be accessed from student residence rooms and from off campus. Internet access and online class registration are available. *Web address:* http://www.usf.edu/.

General Application Contact: Dr. Dale E. Johnson, Dean, Graduate School, 813-974-2846, Fax: 813-974-5762, E-mail: dej@grad.usf.edu.

GRADUATE UNITS

College of Graduate Studies Students: 2,990 full-time (1,727 women), 3,329 part-time (2,096 women); includes 1,029 minority (376 African Americans, 204 Asian Americans or Pacific Islanders, 427 Hispanic Americans, 22 Native Americans), 675 international. Average age 34. 4,701 applicants, 50% accepted. *Faculty:* 1,415. Expenses: Contact institution. *Financial support:* Fellowships with full and partial tuition reimbursements, research assistantships with full and partial tuition reimbursements, teaching assistantships with full and partial tuition reimbursements, career-related internships or fieldwork, Federal Work-Study, institutionally sponsored loans, scholarships/grants, tuition waivers (full and partial), and unspecified assistantships available. Support available to part-time students. Financial award applicants required to submit FAFSA. In 2001, 1,819 master's, 155 doctorates awarded. *Degree program information:* Part-time and evening/weekend programs available. Postbaccalaureate distance learning degree programs offered. Offers applied behavior analysis (MA); cancer biology (PhD). *Application fee:* $20. Electronic applications accepted. *Application Contact:* Pat Pekovsky, Director of Graduate Admissions, 813-974-7918, Fax: 813-974-7343, E-mail: ppekovsky@grad.usf.edu. *Dean,* Dr. Dale E. Johnson, 813-974-2846, Fax: 813-974-5762, E-mail: dej@grad.usf.edu.

College of Arts and Sciences Students: 1,049 full-time (694 women), 994 part-time (693 women); includes 306 minority (105 African Americans, 44 Asian Americans or Pacific Islanders, 152 Hispanic Americans, 5 Native Americans), 125 international. Average age 34. 1,782 applicants, 45% accepted, 508 enrolled. *Faculty:* 518 full-time (201 women), 9 part-time/adjunct (5 women). Expenses: Contact institution. *Financial support:* In 2001–02, 73 fellowships with full and partial tuition reimbursements, 222 research assistantships with full and partial tuition reimbursements, 364 teaching assistantships with full and partial tuition reimbursements were awarded. Career-related internships or fieldwork, Federal Work-Study, institutionally sponsored loans, scholarships/grants, tuition waivers (full and partial), and unspecified assistantships also available. Support available to part-time students. Financial award applicants required to submit FAFSA. In 2001, 144 master's, 14 doctorates awarded. *Degree program information:* Part-time and evening/weekend programs available. Postbaccalaureate distance learning degree programs offered (minimal on-campus study). Offers American studies (MA); analytical chemistry (MS, PhD); applied anthropology (MA, PhD); applied linguistics (MA); applied mathematics (PhD); arts and sciences (MA, MLA, MPA, MS, MSW, Au D, PhD); audiology (Au D); aural rehabilitation (MS); biochemistry (MS, PhD); biology (PhD); botany (MS); cellular and molecular biology (PhD); clinical psychology (PhD); communication (MA, PhD); communication sciences and disorders (PhD); criminology (MA, PhD); ecology (PhD); engineering science/physics (PhD); English (MA, PhD); environmental policy and management (MS); experimental psychology (PhD); French (MA); geography (MA); geology (MA, PhD); gerontology (MA); history (MA); hydrogeology (MA); industrial/organizational psychology (PhD); inorganic chemistry (MS, PhD); liberal arts (MLA); library and information sciences (MA); linguistics (MA); marine biology (MS, PhD); mass communications (MA); mathematics (MA, PhD); microbiology (MS); organic chemistry (MS, PhD); philosophy (MA, PhD); physical chemistry (MS, PhD); physics (MA); physiology (PhD); political science (MA); polymer chemistry (PhD); public administration (MPA); rehabilitation and mental health counseling (MA); religious studies (MA); school library media (MA); social work (MSW); sociology (MA); Spanish (MA); speech language pathology (MS); teaching English as a second language (MA); women's studies (MA); zoology (MS). *Application fee:* $20. Electronic applications accepted. *Application Contact:* Wanda MacLean, Administrative Assistant, 813-974-6922, Fax: 813-974-4075, E-mail: maclean@chuma1.cas.usf.edu. *Interim Dean,* Dr. Renu Khator, 813-874-2503, Fax: 813-974-5911.

College of Business Administration Students: 377 full-time (141 women), 510 part-time (208 women); includes 160 minority (31 African Americans, 51 Asian Americans or Pacific Islanders, 76 Hispanic Americans, 2 Native Americans), 80 international. Average age 31. 822 applicants, 49% accepted, 261 enrolled. *Faculty:* 140 full-time (32 women). Expenses: Contact institution. *Financial support:* Fellowships, research assistantships, teaching assistantships, Federal Work-Study, institutionally sponsored loans, and unspecified assistantships available. Support available to part-time students. Financial award applicants required to submit FAFSA. In 2001, 108 master's, 1 doctorate awarded. *Degree program information:* Part-time and evening/weekend programs available. Offers accounting (M Acc); business (PhD); business administration (Exec MBA, M Acc, MA, MBA, MS, PhD); business administration for physicians (Exec MBA); economics (MA); information systems and decision science (MS); management (MS). *Application fee:* $20. *Application Contact:* Wendy Baker, Assistant Director of Graduate Programs, 813-974-3335, Fax: 813-974-4518, E-mail: mba@coba.usf.edu. *Dean,* Robert L. Anderson, 813-974-4281, Fax: 813-974-3030, E-mail: randers@coba.usf.edu.

College of Education Students: 533 full-time (410 women), 1,023 part-time (783 women); includes 250 minority (129 African Americans, 22 Asian Americans or Pacific Islanders, 90 Hispanic Americans, 9 Native Americans), 30 international. Average age 36. 863 applicants, 57% accepted, 391 enrolled. *Faculty:* 166 full-time (97 women). Expenses: Contact institution. *Financial support:* In 2001–02, 151 teaching assistantships with full tuition reimbursements were awarded; fellowships with full tuition reimbursements, research assistantships with full tuition reimbursements, career-related internships or fieldwork, Federal Work-Study, institutionally sponsored loans, and scholarships/grants also available. Support available to part-time students. Financial award applicants required to submit FAFSA. In 2001, 100 master's, 14 doctorates, 20 other advanced degrees awarded. *Degree program information:* Part-time and evening/weekend programs available. Offers adult education (MA, Ed D, PhD, Ed S); business technology education (MA); college student affairs (M Ed); counselor education (MA); distributive and marketing education (MA); early childhood education (M Ed, MAT, PhD); education (M Ed, MA, MAT, Ed D, PhD, Ed S); education of the emotionally disturbed (MA); education of the mentally handicapped (MA); educational leadership (M Ed, Ed D, Ed S); educational measurement and research (M Ed, PhD, Ed S); elementary education (MA, Ed D, PhD, Ed S); English education (M Ed, MA, PhD); foreign language education (M Ed, MA); gifted education (MA); higher education (PhD, Ed S); industrial technical education (MA); instructional technology (M Ed, PhD); interdisciplinary education (PhD, Ed S); junior college teaching (MA); learning disabilities (MA); mathematics education (M Ed, MA, PhD, Ed S); middle school education (M Ed); music education (MA, PhD); physical education (MA); reading education (M Ed, MA, PhD, Ed S); school psychology (PhD, Ed S); science education (M Ed, MA, PhD, Ed S); secondary education (PhD); social science education (M Ed, MA); special education (Ed D, PhD, Ed S); theater education (MA); varying exceptionalities (MA); vocational education (MA, Ed D, PhD, Ed S). *Application deadline:* For fall admission, 6/1; for spring admission, 10/15. *Application fee:* $20. Electronic applications accepted. *Application Contact:* Diane Briscoe, 813-974-3406, Fax: 813-974-3391, E-mail: briscoe@tempest.coedu.usf.edu. *Dean,* Constantine Heins, 813-974-3400, Fax: 813-974-3826.

College of Engineering Students: 432 full-time (108 women), 268 part-time (43 women); includes 93 minority (17 African Americans, 39 Asian Americans or Pacific Islanders, 35 Hispanic Americans, 2 Native Americans), 373 international. 1,620 applicants, 43% accepted, 210 enrolled. *Faculty:* 87 full-time (7 women), 1 part-time/adjunct (0 women). Expenses: Contact institution. *Financial support:* Fellowships with full tuition reimbursements, research assistantships with full and partial tuition reimbursements, teaching assistantships with full tuition reimbursements, career-related internships or fieldwork, Federal Work-Study, institutionally sponsored loans, tuition waivers (partial), and unspecified assistantships available. Support available to part-time students. Financial award applicants required to submit FAFSA. In 2001, 55 master's, 4 doctorates awarded. *Degree program information:* Part-time and evening/weekend programs available. Offers biomedical engineering (MSBE); chemical engineering (M Ch E, ME, MS, MS Ch E, PhD); civil engineering (MCE, MSCE, PhD); computer engineering (M Cp E, MS Cp E); computer science (MCS, MSCS); computer science and engineering (PhD); electrical engineering (ME, MSEE, PhD); engineering (ME, MSE); engineering management (ME, MIE, MSIE); engineering science (PhD); industrial engineering (ME, MIE, MSIE, PhD); mechanical engineering (ME, MME, MSME, PhD). *Application deadline:* For fall admission, 6/1; for spring admission, 10/15. Applications are processed on a rolling basis. *Application fee:* $20. Electronic applications accepted. *Associate Dean,* Louis A. Martin-Vega, 813-974-3780, Fax: 813-974-5094, E-mail: csmith@eng.usf.edu.

College of Marine Science Students: 60 full-time (34 women), 47 part-time (22 women); includes 11 minority (3 African Americans, 1 Asian American or Pacific Islander, 7 Hispanic Americans), 9 international. Average age 30. 109 applicants, 27% accepted, 19 enrolled. *Faculty:* 27 full-time (5 women). Expenses: Contact institution. *Financial support:* Fellowships with partial tuition reimbursements, research assistantships with partial tuition reimbursements, teaching assistantships with partial tuition reimbursements available. In 2001, 1 master's, 1 doctorate awarded. *Degree program information:* Part-time and evening/weekend programs available. Offers marine science (MS, PhD). *Application deadline:* For fall admission, 6/1; for spring admission, 11/1. Applications are processed on a rolling basis. *Application fee:* $20. *Application Contact:* Dr. Edward VanVleet, Coordinator, 727-553-1165, Fax: 727-553-1189, E-mail: advisor@marine.usf.edu. *Dean,* Dr. Peter R. Betzer, 727-553-1130, Fax: 727-553-1189, E-mail: pbetzer@marine.usf.edu.

College of Nursing Students: 99 full-time (88 women), 152 part-time (137 women); includes 35 minority (20 African Americans, 7 Asian Americans or Pacific Islanders, 7 Hispanic Americans, 1 Native American) 101 applicants, 60% accepted, 49 enrolled. *Faculty:* 34 full-time (33 women), 2 part-time/adjunct (both women). Expenses: Contact institution. *Financial support:* Fellowships with full tuition reimbursements, research assistantships with partial tuition reimbursements, teaching assistantships with partial tuition reimbursements, Federal Work-Study and institutionally sponsored loans available. Support available to part-time students. Financial award application deadline: 6/30; financial award applicants required to submit FAFSA. In 2001, 26 master's, 3 doctorates awarded. *Degree program information:* Part-time programs available. Offers nursing (MS, PhD). *Application deadline:* For fall admission, 6/1 (priority date); for spring admission, 10/15 (priority date). Applications are processed on a rolling basis. *Application fee:* $20. *Application Contact:* Dr. Mary Evans, Coordinator of Student Affairs, 813-974-9305, Fax: 813-974-5418, E-mail: mevans@hsc.usf.edu. *Dean,* Patricia A. Burns, 813-974-2191, Fax: 813-974-5418, E-mail: pburns@com1.med.usf.edu.

College of Public Health Students: 200 full-time (131 women), 243 part-time (156 women); includes 118 minority (58 African Americans, 26 Asian Americans or Pacific Islanders, 32 Hispanic Americans, 2 Native Americans), 21 international. Average age 34. 395 applicants, 36% accepted, 84 enrolled. *Faculty:* 16 full-time (8 women), 2 part-time/adjunct (both women). Expenses: Contact institution. *Financial support:* Fellowships with full tuition reimbursements, research assistantships with full and partial tuition reimbursements, career-related internships or fieldwork, Federal Work-Study, institutionally sponsored loans, and unspecified assistantships available. Support available to part-time students. Financial award applicants required to submit FAFSA. In 2001, 61 master's, 2 doctorates awarded. *Degree program information:* Part-time and evening/weekend programs available. Postbaccalaureate distance learning degree programs offered (minimal on-campus study). Offers community and family health (MPH, MSPH, PhD); environmental and occupational health (MPH, MSPH, PhD); epidemiology and biostatistics (MPH, MSPH, PhD); health policy and management (MHA, MPH, MSPH, PhD); public health (MHA, MPH, MSPH, PhD); public health practice (MPH). *Application deadline:* For fall admission, 6/1; for spring admission, 10/15. Applications are processed on a rolling basis. *Application fee:* $20. *Application Contact:* Magdalene Argiry, Director of Student Services, 813-974-6665, Fax: 813-974-4718, E-mail: margiry@com1.med.usf.edu. *Dean,* Dr. Charles S. Mahan, 813-974-3623, Fax: 813-974-4718, E-mail: cmahan@com1.med.usf.edu.

College of Visual and Performing Arts Students: 50 full-time (27 women), 44 part-time (21 women); includes 15 minority (5 African Americans, 10 Hispanic Americans), 6 international. Average age 32. 105 applicants, 50% accepted, 37 enrolled. *Faculty:* 79 full-time (29 women), 3 part-time/adjunct (1 woman). Expenses: Contact institution. *Financial support:* Fellowships with full tuition reimbursements, research assistantships, teaching assistantships with full tuition reimbursements, career-related internships or fieldwork, Federal Work-Study, institutionally sponsored loans, tuition waivers (partial), and unspecified assistantships available. Support available to part-time students. Financial award applicants required to submit FAFSA. *Degree program information:* Part-time and evening/weekend programs available. Offers art (MFA); art education (MA); art history (MA); choral conducting (MM); composition (MM); instrumental conducting (wind instruments) (MM); jazz studies (MM); performance (MM); theory (MM); visual and performing arts (MA, MFA, MM). *Application fee:* $20. *Application Contact:* Janet L. S. Moore, Associate Dean and Graduate Director, 813-974-0402, Fax: 813-974-2091, E-mail: jmoore@arts.usf.edu. *Dean,* Ron Jones, 813-974-2301.

School of Architecture and Community Design Students: 41 full-time (12 women), 21 part-time (10 women); includes 11 minority (1 African American, 4 Asian Americans or Pacific Islanders, 6 Hispanic Americans), 5 international. Average age 32. 60 applicants, 57% accepted, 14 enrolled. *Faculty:* 8 full-time (0 women), 1 (woman) part-time/adjunct. Expenses: Contact institution. *Financial support:* In 2001–02, 1 fellowship with partial tuition reimbursement, 2 teaching assistantships with partial tuition reimbursements were awarded. Research assistantships, Federal Work-Study, institutionally sponsored loans, scholarships/grants, and unspecified assistantships also available. Support available to part-time students. Financial award applicants required to submit FAFSA. In 2001, 16 degrees awarded. Offers architecture and community design (M Arch). *Application deadline:* For fall admission, 3/1 (priority date); for spring admission, 8/1 (priority date). Applications are processed on a rolling basis. *Application fee:* $20. Electronic applications accepted. *Application Contact:* Carol Trent, Admissions/Registrar Office, 813-974-4031, Fax: 813-974-2557, E-mail: trent@arch.usf.edu. *Director,* Stephen Schreiber, 813-974-6017, Fax: 813-974-2557, E-mail: schreiber@arch.usf.edu.

College of Medicine Students: 128 full-time (64 women), 4 part-time (all women); includes 23 minority (5 African Americans, 9 Asian Americans or Pacific Islanders, 8 Hispanic Americans, 1 Native American), 24 international. Average age 29. 1,666 applicants, 10% accepted, 144 enrolled. *Faculty:* 380 full-time (116 women), 101 part-time/adjunct (23 women). Expenses: Contact institution. *Financial support:* Fellowships, research assistantships, teaching assistantships, Federal Work-Study, institutionally sponsored loans, and unspecified assistantships available. Support available to part-time students. Financial award applicants required to submit FAFSA. In 2001, 2 master's, 2 doctorates awarded. *Degree program information:* Part-time programs available. Offers medicine (MD, MS, PhD); physical therapy (MS). *Application fee:* $20. Electronic applications accepted. *Application Contact:* Dr. Joseph J. Krzanowski, Associate Dean for Research and Graduate Affairs, 813-974-4181, Fax: 813-974-4317, E-mail: jkrzanow@com1.med.usf.edu. *Dean,* Dr. Robert M. Daugherty, 813-974-2196, Fax: 813-974-3886.

Graduate Programs in Medical Sciences Expenses: Contact institution. *Financial support:* Fellowships, research assistantships, institutionally sponsored loans available. Support available to part-time students. Financial award applicants required to submit FAFSA. Offers anatomy (PhD); biochemistry and molecular biology (PhD); medical microbiology and immunology (PhD); medical sciences (PhD); pathology (PhD); physiology and biophysics (PhD). *Application fee:* $20. *Associate Dean for Research and Graduate Affairs,* Dr. Joseph J. Krzanowski, 813-974-4181, Fax: 813-974-4317, E-mail: jkrzanow@com1.med.usf.edu.

H. Lee Moffitt Cancer Center and Research Institute Offers oncology (PhD). Electronic applications accepted.

See in-depth description on page 1261.

THE UNIVERSITY OF TAMPA, Tampa, FL 33606-1490

General Information Independent, coed, comprehensive institution. *Enrollment:* 138 full-time matriculated graduate/professional students (70 women), 358 part-time matriculated graduate/professional students (205 women). *Enrollment by degree level:* 496 master's. *Graduate faculty:* 41 full-time (13 women). *Tuition:* Full-time $6,048; part-time $336 per credit. *Required fees:* $35 per semester. *Graduate housing:* Room and/or apartments available on a first-come, first-served basis to single students; on-campus housing not available to married students. Typical cost: $5,890 (including board). Room and board charges vary according to board plan and housing facility selected. *Student services:* Campus employment opportunities, campus safety program, career counseling, exercise/wellness program, free psychological counseling, international student services, writing training. *Library facilities:* Merl Kelce Library. *Online resources:* library catalog, web page. *Collection:* 250,850 titles, 854 serial subscriptions, 3,733 audiovisual materials. *Research affiliation:* Tech Village (technology-based incubator), Human Resources Institute (human resources research).

Computer facilities: 250 computers available on campus for general student use. A campuswide network can be accessed from student residence rooms and from off campus. Internet access is available. *Web address:* http://www.ut.edu/.

General Application Contact: Barbara P. Strickler, Vice President for Enrollment, 888-646-2738, Fax: 813-258-7398, E-mail: admissions@ut.edu.

GRADUATE UNITS

John H. Sykes College of Business Students: 116 full-time (50 women), 270 part-time (116 women); includes 56 minority (16 African Americans, 10 Asian Americans or Pacific Islanders, 29 Hispanic Americans, 1 Native American), 96 international. Average age 30. 191 applicants, 77% accepted, 98 enrolled. *Faculty:* 41 full-time (13 women). Expenses: Contact institution. *Financial support:* Research assistantships with tuition reimbursements, career-related internships or fieldwork and unspecified assistantships available. Support available to part-time students. Financial award applicants required to submit FAFSA. In 2001, 97 degrees awarded. *Degree program information:* Part-time and evening/weekend programs available. Offers accounting (MBA); entrepreneurship (MBA); information systems management (MBA); international business (MBA); management (MBA); management of technology (MSTIM). *Application deadline:* For fall admission, 8/15 (priority date). Applications are processed on a rolling basis. *Application fee:* $35. *Application Contact:* Dr. Mary B. Prescott, Director of Graduate Programs, 813-253-6211, Fax: 813-259-5403, E-mail: mprescott@ut.edu. *Dean and Co-Chief Academic Officer*, Dr. Joseph E. McCann, 813-253-6211, Fax: 813-258-7408, E-mail: jmccan@ut.edu.

Nursing Program Students: 109 (100 women); includes 13 minority (4 African Americans, 1 Asian American or Pacific Islander, 4 Hispanic Americans, 4 Native Americans) Average age 35. *Faculty:* 4 full-time (all women). Expenses: Contact institution. *Financial support:* Research assistantships with tuition reimbursements, career-related internships or fieldwork and unspecified assistantships available. Support available to part-time students. Financial award applicants required to submit FAFSA. In 2001, 30 degrees awarded. *Degree program information:* Part-time and evening/weekend programs available. Postbaccalaureate distance learning degree programs offered (minimal on-campus study). Offers adult nurse practitioner (MSN); family nurse practitioner (MSN); nursing administration (MSN); nursing education (MSN). *Application deadline:* For fall admission, 8/20 (priority date). Applications are processed on a rolling basis. Electronic applications accepted. *Application Contact:* Barbara P. Strickler, Vice President for Enrollment, 888-646-2738, Fax: 813-258-7398, E-mail: admissions@ut.edu. *Director*, Dr. Nancy Ross, 813-253-6223, Fax: 813-258-7214, E-mail: nross@alpha.utampa.edu.

THE UNIVERSITY OF TENNESSEE, Knoxville, TN 37996

General Information State-supported, coed, university. CGS member. *Enrollment:* 3,805 full-time matriculated graduate/professional students (2,189 women), 2,104 part-time matriculated graduate/professional students (1,213 women). *Enrollment by degree level:* 728 first professional, 3,308 master's, 1,418 doctoral, 42 other advanced degrees. *Graduate faculty:* 1,247 full-time (367 women), 29 part-time/adjunct (14 women). Tuition, state resident: full-time $4,280; part-time $233 per hour. Tuition, nonresident: full-time $12,066; part-time $666 per hour. Tuition and fees vary according to program. *Graduate housing:* Rooms and/or apartments guaranteed to single and married students. Typical cost: $2,250 per year ($4,402 including board) for single students; $4,020 per year for married students. Housing application deadline: 2/1. *Student services:* Campus employment opportunities, campus safety program, career counseling, child daycare facilities, disabled student services, free psychological counseling, international student services, low-cost health insurance, multicultural affairs office, teacher training, writing training. *Library facilities:* John C. Hodges Library plus 6 others. *Online resources:* library catalog, web page, access to other libraries' catalogs. *Collection:* 24.4 million titles, 17,628 serial subscriptions, 175,541 audiovisual materials. *Research affiliation:* Oak Ridge National Laboratory–Biology Division (engineering, science), Lockheed Martin Corporation (engineering), Exxon Corporation (materials science), Atlantic Richfield Company (chemistry), Control Data Corporation (engineering), University of Tennessee (science, engineering).

Computer facilities: 1,000 computers available on campus for general student use. A campuswide network can be accessed from student residence rooms and from off campus. Internet access and online class registration are available. *Web address:* http://www.tennessee.edu/.

General Application Contact: Diana Lopez, Director of Graduate Admissions and Records, 865-974-3251, Fax: 865-974-6541, E-mail: gsinfo@utk.edu.

GRADUATE UNITS

College of Law Students: 467 full-time (222 women); includes 69 minority (53 African Americans, 7 Asian Americans or Pacific Islanders, 7 Hispanic Americans, 2 Native Americans) Average age 25. 1,069 applicants, 36% accepted, 156 enrolled. *Faculty:* 29 full-time (11 women), 28 part-time/adjunct (10 women). Expenses: Contact institution. *Financial support:* In 2001–02, 361 students received support, including 124 fellowships (averaging $5,630 per year), 7 research assistantships with full tuition reimbursements available (averaging $10,668 per year); career-related internships or fieldwork, Federal Work-Study, and institutionally sponsored loans also available. Support available to part-time students. Financial award application deadline: 3/1; financial award applicants required to submit FAFSA. In 2001, 144 degrees awarded. Offers law (JD). *Application deadline:* For fall admission, 2/15 (priority date). *Application fee:* $15. Electronic applications accepted. *Application Contact:* Janet S. Hatcher, Admissions and Financial Aid Adviser, 865-974-4131, Fax: 865-974-1572, E-mail: hatcher@libra.law.utk.edu. *Director of Admissions and Career Services*, Dr. Karen R. Britton, 865-974-4131, Fax: 865-974-1572, E-mail: lawadmit@libra.law.utk.edu.

Graduate School Students: 3,805 full-time (2,189 women), 2,104 part-time (1,213 women); includes 547 minority (342 African Americans, 74 Asian Americans or Pacific Islanders, 61 Hispanic Americans, 70 Native Americans), 678 international. *Faculty:* 1,247 full-time (367 women), 29 part-time/adjunct (14 women). Expenses: Contact institution. *Financial support:* In 2001–02, 967 research assistantships with full tuition reimbursements, 912 teaching assistantships with full tuition reimbursements were awarded. Fellowships with full tuition reimbursements, career-related internships or fieldwork, Federal Work-Study, institutionally sponsored loans, and unspecified assistantships also available. Financial award application deadline: 2/1; financial award applicants required to submit FAFSA. In 2001, 202 first professional degrees, 1,687 master's, 239 doctorates awarded. *Degree program information:* Part-time and evening/weekend programs available. Postbaccalaureate distance learning degree programs offered (minimal on-campus study). Offers aviation systems (MS); comparative and experimental medicine (MS, PhD). *Application deadline:* Applications are processed on a rolling basis. Electronic applications accepted. *Application Contact:* Diana Lopez, Director of Graduate Admissions and Records, 865-974-3251, Fax: 865-974-6541, E-mail: gsinfo@utk.edu. *Interim Dean of Graduate Studies*, Dr. Anne Mayhew, 865-974-3251, Fax: 865-974-6541, E-mail: mayhew@utk.edu.

College of Agricultural Sciences and Natural Resources Students: 187 (90 women); includes 16 minority (9 African Americans, 3 Asian Americans or Pacific Islanders, 2 Hispanic Americans, 2 Native Americans) 186 applicants, 50% accepted. *Faculty:* 115 full-time (12 women). Expenses: Contact institution. *Financial support:* In 2001–02, 2 fellowships with full tuition reimbursements, 124 research assistantships with full tuition reimbursements, 23 teaching assistantships with full tuition reimbursements were awarded. Career-related internships or fieldwork, Federal Work-Study, institutionally sponsored loans, and unspecified assistantships also available. Financial award application deadline: 2/1; financial award applicants required to submit FAFSA. In 2001, 62 master's, 6 doctorates awarded. *Degree program information:* Part-time programs available. Postbaccalaureate distance learning degree programs offered (minimal on-campus study). Offers agribusiness (MS); agricultural economics (MS); agricultural education (MS); agricultural extension education (MS); agricultural sciences and natural resources (MS, PhD); animal anatomy (PhD); biosystems engineering (MS, PhD); biosystems engineering technology (MS); breeding (MS, PhD); entomology (MS); floriculture (MS); food science and technology (MS, PhD); forestry (MS); landscape design (MS); management (MS, PhD); nutrition (MS, PhD); physiology (MS, PhD); plant pathology (MS); public horticulture (MS); rural sociology (MS); turfgrass (MS); wildlife and fisheries science (MS); woody ornamentals (MS). *Application deadline:* For fall admission, 2/1 (priority date). Applications are processed on a rolling basis. *Application fee:* $35. Electronic applications accepted. *Dean*, Dr. C. A. Speer, 865-974-7303.

College of Architecture and Design Students: 32 full-time (12 women), 3 part-time (1 woman); includes 1 minority (Hispanic American) 28 applicants, 36% accepted. *Faculty:* 23 full-time (2 women), 2 part-time/adjunct (1 woman). Expenses: Contact institution. *Financial support:* Fellowships, teaching assistantships, career-related internships or fieldwork, Federal Work-Study, institutionally sponsored loans, and unspecified assistantships available. Financial award application deadline: 2/1; financial award applicants required to submit FAFSA. In 2001, 12 degrees awarded. Offers architecture and design (M Arch). *Application deadline:* For fall admission, 2/1 (priority date). Applications are processed on a rolling basis. *Application fee:* $35. Electronic applications accepted. *Application Contact:* Jon Coddington, Graduate Representative, E-mail: jcodding@utk.edu. *Dean*, Marleen Davis, 865-974-5265, Fax: 865-974-0656.

College of Arts and Sciences Students: 924 full-time (478 women), 461 part-time (206 women); includes 84 minority (48 African Americans, 20 Asian Americans or Pacific Islanders, 12 Hispanic Americans, 4 Native Americans), 221 international. 1,554 applicants, 47% accepted. *Faculty:* 518 full-time (98 women), 39 part-time/adjunct (10 women). Expenses: Contact institution. *Financial support:* In 2001–02, 133 fellowships, 232 research assistantships, 575 teaching assistantships were awarded. Career-related internships or fieldwork, Federal Work-Study, institutionally sponsored loans, and unspecified assistantships also available. Financial award application deadline: 2/1; financial award applicants required to submit FAFSA. In 2001, 274 master's, 113 doctorates awarded. *Degree program information:* Part-time and evening/weekend programs available. Offers accompanying (MM); American history (PhD); analytical chemistry (MS, PhD); applied linguistics (PhD); applied mathematics (MS); archaeology (MA, PhD); arts and sciences (M Math, MA, MFA, MM, MPA, MS, MSP, PhD); audiology (MA, PhD); behavior (MS, PhD); biochemistry and cellular and molecular biology (MS, PhD); biological anthropology (MA, PhD); botany (MS, PhD); ceramics (MFA); chemical physics (PhD); choral conducting (MM); clinical psychology (PhD); composition (MM); computer science (MS, PhD); costume design (MFA); criminology (MA, PhD); cultural anthropology (MA, PhD); drawing (MFA); ecology (MS, PhD); energy, environment, and resource policy (MA, PhD); English (MA, PhD); environmental chemistry (MS, PhD); environmental planning (MSP); European history (PhD); evolutionary biology (MS, PhD); experimental psychology (MA, PhD); French (MA, PhD); genome science and technology (MS, PhD); geography (MS, PhD); geology (MS, PhD); German (MA, PhD); graphic design (MFA); hearing science (PhD); history (MA); inorganic chemistry (MS, PhD); instrumental conducting (MM); inter-area studies (MFA); Italian (PhD); jazz (MM); land-use planning (MSP); lighting design (MFA); mathematical ecology (PhD); mathematics (M Math, MS, PhD); media arts (MFA); medical ethics (MA, PhD); microbiology (MS, PhD); modern foreign languages (PhD); music education (MM); music theory (MM); musicology (MM); organic chemistry (MS, PhD); painting (MFA); performance (MFA, MM); philosophy (MA, PhD); physical chemistry (MS, PhD); physics (MS, PhD); piano pedagogy and literature (MM); plant physiology and genetics (MS, PhD); political economy (MA, PhD); political science (MA, PhD); polymer chemistry (MS, PhD); Portuguese (PhD); printmaking (MFA); psychology (MA); public administration (MPA); real estate development planning (MSP); religious studies (MA); Russian (PhD); scene design (MFA); sculpture (MFA); Spanish (MA, PhD); speech and hearing science (PhD); speech and language pathology (PhD); speech and language science (PhD); speech pathology (MA); theatre technology (MFA); theoretical chemistry (PhD); transportation planning (MSP); watercolor (MFA); zooarchaeology (MA, PhD). *Application deadline:* For fall admission, 2/1. *Application fee:* $35. Electronic applications accepted. *Dean*, Dr. Lorayne Lester, 865-974-5331.

College of Business Administration Students: 476 full-time (172 women), 41 part-time (19 women); includes 39 minority (15 African Americans, 17 Asian Americans or Pacific Islanders, 5 Hispanic Americans, 2 Native Americans), 108 international. 913 applicants, 43% accepted. *Faculty:* 101 full-time (17 women), 1 part-time/adjunct (0 women). Expenses: Contact institution. *Financial support:* In 2001–02, 9 fellowships, 6 research assistantships, 91 teaching assistantships were awarded. Career-related internships or fieldwork, Federal Work-Study, institutionally sponsored loans, unspecified assistantships, and merit-based fellowships also available. Financial award application deadline: 2/1; financial award applicants required to submit FAFSA. In 2001, 261 master's, 23 doctorates awarded. *Degree program information:* Part-time programs available. Postbaccalaureate distance learning degree programs offered (minimal on-campus study). Offers accounting (M Acc, PhD); business administration (M Acc, MA, MBA, MS, PhD); economics (MA, PhD); finance (MBA, PhD); industrial statistics (MS); industrial/organizational psychology (PhD); logistics and transportation (MBA, PhD); management (PhD); management science (MS, PhD); marketing (MBA, PhD); operations management (MBA); professional business administration (MBA); statistics (MS, PhD); systems (M Acc); taxation (M Acc). *Application deadline:* For fall admission, 2/1. Applications are processed on a rolling basis. *Application fee:* $35. Electronic applications accepted. *Application Contact:* Dr. Sarah Gardial, Assistant Dean, 865-974-5033, Fax: 865-974-3826, E-mail: sgardial@utk.edu. *Dean*, Dr. Jan Williams, 865-974-5061.

College of Communications Students: 62 full-time (41 women), 38 part-time (23 women); includes 11 minority (10 African Americans, 1 Hispanic American), 15 international. 153 applicants, 39% accepted. *Faculty:* 25 full-time (8 women). Expenses: Contact institution. *Financial support:* In 2001–02, 1 fellowship, 1 research assistantship, 19 teaching assistantships were awarded. Career-related internships or fieldwork, Federal Work-Study, institutionally sponsored loans, and unspecified assistantships also available. Financial award application deadline: 2/1; financial award applicants required to submit FAFSA. In 2001, 29 master's, 7 doctorates awarded. *Degree program information:* Part-time and evening/weekend programs available. Postbaccalaureate distance learning degree programs offered (no on-campus study). Offers advertising (MS, PhD); broadcasting (MS, PhD); communications (MS, PhD); information sciences (PhD); journalism (MS, PhD); public relations (MS, PhD); speech communication (MS, PhD). *Application deadline:* For fall admission, 2/1 (priority date). Applications are processed on a rolling basis. *Application fee:* $35. Electronic applications accepted. *Application Contact:* Dr. Edward Caudill, Head, 865-974-6651, Fax: 865-974-3896, E-mail: ccaudill@utk.edu. *Dean*, Dr. Dwight Teeter, 865-974-3031, Fax: 865-974-3896.

College of Education Students: 680 full-time (480 women), 377 part-time (243 women); includes 87 minority (69 African Americans, 12 Asian Americans or Pacific Islanders, 2 Hispanic Americans, 4 Native Americans), 49 international. 701 applicants, 52% accepted. *Faculty:* 91 full-time (30 women), 3 part-time/adjunct (1 woman). Expenses: Contact institution. *Financial support:* In 2001–02, 6 fellowships, 3 research assistantships, 46 teaching assistantships were awarded. Career-related internships or fieldwork, Federal Work-Study, institutionally sponsored loans, and unspecified assistantships also available. Financial award application deadline: 2/1; financial award applicants required to submit FAFSA. In 2001, 467 master's, 57 doctorates, 30 other advanced degrees awarded. *Degree program information:* Part-time and evening/weekend programs available. Postbaccalaureate distance learning degree programs offered (no on-campus study). Offers adult education (MS); art education (MS); college student personnel (MS); counseling education (PhD);

counseling psychology (PhD); cultural studies in education (PhD); curriculum (MS, Ed S); curriculum education research and evaluation (PhD); curriculum, educational research and evaluation (Ed D); early childhood education (PhD); early childhood special education (MS); education (MS, Ed D, PhD, Ed S); education of deaf and hard of hearing (MS); education psychology (PhD); educational administration and policy studies (Ed D, PhD); educational administration and supervision (MS, Ed S); educational psychology (Ed D); elementary education (MS, Ed S); elementary teaching (MS); English education (MS, Ed S); exercise science (MS, PhD); foreign language/ESL education (MS, Ed S); individual and collaborative learning (MS); industrial technology (PhD); instructional technology (MS, Ed D, Ed S); literacy, language education and ESL education (PhD); literacy, language education, and ESL education (Ed D); mathematics education (MS, Ed S); mental health counseling (MS); modified and comprehensive special education (MS); reading education (MS, Ed S); rehabilitation counseling (MS); school counseling (MS, Ed S); school psychology (PhD, Ed S); science education (MS, Ed S); secondary teaching (MS); social foundations (MS); social science education (MS, Ed S); socio-cultural foundations of sports and education (PhD); special education (Ed S); sport management (MS); sport studies (MS); teacher education (Ed D, PhD). *Application deadline:* For fall admission, 2/1 (priority date). Applications are processed on a rolling basis. *Application fee:* $35. Electronic applications accepted. *Application Contact:* Dr. Tom George, Associate Dean, 865-974-0907, Fax: 865-974-8718, E-mail: tgeorge1@utk.edu. *Dean*, Dr. Glennon Rowell, 865-974-2201, E-mail: growell@utk.edu.

College of Engineering Students: 297 full-time (66 women), 252 part-time (48 women); includes 31 minority (18 African Americans, 9 Asian Americans or Pacific Islanders, 3 Hispanic Americans, 1 Native American), 175 international. 771 applicants, 53% accepted. *Faculty:* 134 full-time (5 women), 11 part-time/adjunct (1 woman). Expenses: Contact institution. *Financial support:* In 2001–02, 11 fellowships, 130 research assistantships, 46 teaching assistantships were awarded. Career-related internships or fieldwork, Federal Work-Study, institutionally sponsored loans, and unspecified assistantships also available. Financial award application deadline: 2/1; financial award applicants required to submit FAFSA. In 2001, 155 master's, 36 doctorates awarded. *Degree program information:* Part-time and evening/weekend programs available. Postbaccalaureate distance learning degree programs offered. Offers aerospace engineering (MS, PhD); applied artificial intelligence (MS); biomedical engineering (MS, PhD); chemical engineering (MS, PhD); civil engineering (MS, PhD); composite materials (MS, PhD); computational mechanics (MS, PhD); electrical engineering (MS, PhD); engineering (MS, PhD); engineering management (MS); engineering science (MS, PhD); environmental engineering (MS); fluid mechanics (MS, PhD); industrial engineering (PhD); manufacturing systems engineering (MS); materials science and engineering (MS, PhD); mechanical engineering (MS, PhD); nuclear engineering (MS, PhD); optical engineering (MS, PhD); polymer engineering (MS, PhD); product development and manufacturing (MS); solid mechanics (MS, PhD); traditional industrial engineering (MS). *Application deadline:* For fall admission, 2/1 (priority date). Applications are processed on a rolling basis. *Application fee:* $35. Electronic applications accepted. *Interim Dean*, Dr. Fred Tompkins, 865-974-5321.

College of Human Ecology Students: 200 full-time (150 women), 185 part-time (134 women); includes 32 minority (23 African Americans, 8 Asian Americans or Pacific Islanders, 1 Hispanic American), 43 international. 233 applicants, 51% accepted. *Faculty:* 70 full-time (30 women), 2 part-time/adjunct (0 women). Expenses: Contact institution. *Financial support:* In 2001–02, 2 fellowships, 14 research assistantships, 66 teaching assistantships were awarded. Career-related internships or fieldwork, Federal Work-Study, institutionally sponsored loans, and unspecified assistantships also available. Financial award application deadline: 2/1; financial award applicants required to submit FAFSA. In 2001, 109 master's, 22 doctorates awarded. *Degree program information:* Part-time and evening/weekend programs available. Offers child and family studies (MS, PhD); community health (PhD); community health education (MPH); early childhood education (MS); gerontology (MPH); health planning/administration (MPH); health promotion and health education (MS); hospitality management (MS); human ecology (MPH, MS, PhD); human resource development (PhD); nutrition (MS); nutrition science (PhD); public health (MPH); recreation administration (MS); recreation, tourism, and hospitality management (MS); retail and consumer sciences (MS); retailing and consumer sciences (PhD); safety (MS); teacher licensure (MS); textile science (MS, PhD); textiles, retailing and consumer sciences (MS); therapeutic recreation (MS); tourism (MS); training and development (MS). *Application deadline:* For fall admission, 2/1 (priority date). Applications are processed on a rolling basis. *Application fee:* $35. Electronic applications accepted. *Dean*, Dr. James D. Moran, 865-974-5223, Fax: 865-974-2617, E-mail: jmoran@utk.edu.

College of Nursing Students: 87 full-time (80 women), 26 part-time (25 women); includes 7 minority (4 African Americans, 3 Asian Americans or Pacific Islanders), 1 international. 67 applicants, 37% accepted. *Faculty:* 27 full-time (all women). Expenses: Contact institution. *Financial support:* In 2001–02, 3 fellowships, 1 research assistantship were awarded. Teaching assistantships, Federal Work-Study, institutionally sponsored loans, and unspecified assistantships also available. Financial award application deadline: 2/1; financial award applicants required to submit FAFSA. In 2001, 42 master's, 4 doctorates awarded. *Degree program information:* Part-time programs available. Offers nursing (MSN, PhD). *Application deadline:* For fall admission, 2/1 (priority date). Applications are processed on a rolling basis. *Application fee:* $35. Electronic applications accepted. *Application Contact:* Dr. Martha Alligood, Graduate Representative, 865-974-7606, E-mail: stuservices@cn.gw.utk.edu. *Dean*, Dr. Joan L. Creasia, 865-974-4151, Fax: 865-974-3569, E-mail: jcreasia@utk.edu.

College of Social Work Students: 305 full-time (263 women), 110 part-time (94 women); includes 72 minority (61 African Americans, 4 Asian Americans or Pacific Islanders, 5 Hispanic Americans, 2 Native Americans), 6 international. 356 applicants, 50% accepted. *Faculty:* 33 full-time (19 women). Expenses: Contact institution. *Financial support:* In 2001–02, 8 fellowships, 9 research assistantships were awarded. Teaching assistantships, career-related internships or fieldwork, Federal Work-Study, institutionally sponsored loans, and unspecified assistantships also available. Financial award application deadline: 2/1; financial award applicants required to submit FAFSA. In 2001, 220 master's, 1 doctorate awarded. *Degree program information:* Part-time programs available. Offers clinical social work practice (MSSW); social welfare management and community practice (MSSW); social work (PhD). *Application deadline:* For fall admission, 2/1 (priority date). Applications are processed on a rolling basis. *Application fee:* $35. Electronic applications accepted. *Dean*, Dr. Karen Sowers, 865-974-3175, Fax: 865-974-4803, E-mail: kmsowers@utk.edu.

College of Veterinary Medicine Students: 257 full-time (182 women); includes 11 minority (3 African Americans, 2 Asian Americans or Pacific Islanders, 3 Hispanic Americans, 3 Native Americans), 4 international. 246 applicants, 30% accepted. *Faculty:* 83 full-time (19 women). Expenses: Contact institution. *Financial support:* In 2001–02, 1 fellowship, 10 research assistantships, 5 teaching assistantships were awarded. Career-related internships or fieldwork, institutionally sponsored loans, and unspecified assistantships also available. Financial award application deadline: 2/1; financial award applicants required to submit FAFSA. In 2001, 62 degrees awarded. Offers veterinary medicine (DVM). *Application deadline:* For fall admission, 11/1. *Application fee:* $25. *Application Contact:* Dr. James Brace, Associate Dean, E-mail: jbrace@utk.edu. *Dean*, Dr. Michael J. Blackwell, 865-974-7263, Fax: 865-974-4773.

School of Information Sciences Students: 47 full-time (38 women), 137 part-time (105 women); includes 7 minority (4 African Americans, 3 Asian Americans or Pacific Islanders), 6 international. 128 applicants, 69% accepted. *Faculty:* 11 full-time (6 women), 1 part-time/adjunct (0 women). Expenses: Contact institution. *Financial support:* In 2001–02, 1 fellowship, 16 teaching assistantships were awarded. Research assistantships, Federal Work-Study, institutionally sponsored loans, and unspecified assistantships also available. Financial award application deadline: 2/1; financial award applicants required to submit FAFSA. In 2001, 86 degrees awarded. *Degree program information:* Part-time programs available. Postbaccalaureate distance learning degree programs offered (no on-campus study). Offers information sciences (MS). *Application deadline:* For fall admission, 2/1 (priority date). Applications are processed on a rolling basis. *Application fee:* $35. Electronic applications accepted. *Application Contact:* Dr. Kristie Atwood, Graduate Representative, E-mail: katwood@utk.edu. *Head*, Dr. Elizabeth Aversa, 865-974-2148, Fax: 865-974-4967, E-mail: aversa@utk.edu.

See in-depth description on page 1263.

THE UNIVERSITY OF TENNESSEE AT CHATTANOOGA, Chattanooga, TN 37403-2598

General Information State-supported, coed, comprehensive institution. CGS member. *Enrollment:* 436 full-time matriculated graduate/professional students (272 women), 825 part-time matriculated graduate/professional students (478 women). *Enrollment by degree level:* 1,208 master's, 53 other advanced degrees. *Graduate faculty:* 129 full-time (49 women), 27 part-time/adjunct (15 women). Tuition, state resident: full-time $3,752; part-time $228 per hour. Tuition, nonresident: full-time $10,282; part-time $565 per hour. *Graduate housing:* Room and/or apartments available on a first-come, first-served basis to single students; on-campus housing not available to married students. Typical cost: $2,600 per year. Room charges vary according to housing facility selected. Housing application deadline: 8/1. *Student services:* Campus employment opportunities, campus safety program, career counseling, child daycare facilities, disabled student services, exercise/wellness program, free psychological counseling, international student services, teacher training, writing training. *Library facilities:* Lupton Library. *Online resources:* library catalog, web page, access to other libraries' catalogs. *Collection:* 479,007 titles, 2,768 serial subscriptions, 15,448 audiovisual materials. *Research affiliation:* Gulf Coast Research Laboratory, Tennessee Valley Authority, Highland Biological Field Station (NC).

Computer facilities: 300 computers available on campus for general student use. A campuswide network can be accessed from student residence rooms and from off campus. Internet access and online class registration are available. *Web address:* http://www.utc.edu/.

General Application Contact: Dr. Deborah E. Arfken, Dean of Graduate Studies, 865-425-1740, Fax: 865-425-5223, E-mail: deborah-arfken@utc.edu.

GRADUATE UNITS

Graduate Division Students: 436 full-time (272 women), 825 part-time (478 women); includes 150 minority (101 African Americans, 26 Asian Americans or Pacific Islanders, 19 Hispanic Americans, 4 Native Americans), 49 international. Average age 31. 660 applicants, 84% accepted, 312 enrolled. *Faculty:* 129 full-time (49 women), 27 part-time/adjunct (15 women). Expenses: Contact institution. *Financial support:* Fellowships, research assistantships, career-related internships or fieldwork, Federal Work-Study, institutionally sponsored loans, scholarships/grants, and unspecified assistantships available. Support available to part-time students. Financial award application deadline: 4/1; financial award applicants required to submit FAFSA. In 2001, 449 master's, 9 other advanced degrees awarded. *Degree program information:* Part-time and evening/weekend programs available. *Application deadline:* For fall admission, 8/1 (priority date); for spring admission, 12/1 (priority date). Applications are processed on a rolling basis. *Application fee:* $25. *Dean of Graduate Studies*, Dr. Deborah E. Arfken, 865-425-1740, Fax: 865-425-5223, E-mail: deborah-arfken@utc.edu.

College of Arts and Sciences Students: 83 full-time (46 women), 106 part-time (58 women); includes 22 minority (19 African Americans, 2 Asian Americans or Pacific Islanders, 1 Hispanic American), 1 international. Average age 29. 148 applicants, 87% accepted, 70 enrolled. *Faculty:* 38 full-time (14 women), 5 part-time/adjunct (3 women). Expenses: Contact institution. *Financial support:* Fellowships, research assistantships, Federal Work-Study and institutionally sponsored loans available. Financial award application deadline: 4/1; financial award applicants required to submit FAFSA. In 2001, 78 degrees awarded. *Degree program information:* Part-time and evening/weekend programs available. Offers arts and sciences (MA, MM, MPA, MS); English (MA); environmental sciences (MS); industrial/organizational psychology (MS); music (MM); public administration (MPA); research psychology (MS); school psychology (MS). *Application deadline:* For fall admission, 8/1 (priority date); for spring admission, 12/1 (priority date). Applications are processed on a rolling basis. *Application fee:* $25. *Application Contact:* Dr. Deborah E. Arfken, Dean of Graduate Studies, 865-425-1740, Fax: 865-425-5223, E-mail: deborah-arfken@utc.edu. *Dean*, Dr. Herbert Burhenn, 423-425-4635, Fax: 423-425-4279, E-mail: herbert-burhenn@utc.edu.

College of Business Administration Students: 74 full-time (41 women), 271 part-time (116 women); includes 50 minority (25 African Americans, 15 Asian Americans or Pacific Islanders, 10 Hispanic Americans), 14 international. Average age 28. 162 applicants, 85% accepted, 94 enrolled. *Faculty:* 23 full-time (5 women), 6 part-time/adjunct (2 women). Expenses: Contact institution. *Financial support:* Fellowships, research assistantships, Federal Work-Study and institutionally sponsored loans available. Support available to part-time students. Financial award application deadline: 4/1; financial award applicants required to submit FAFSA. In 2001, 175 degrees awarded. *Degree program information:* Part-time and evening/weekend programs available. Offers accountancy (M Acc); business administration (MBA); economics (MBA); finance (MBA); marketing (MBA); operations/production (MBA); organizational management (MBA). *Application deadline:* For fall admission, 8/1 (priority date); for spring admission, 12/1 (priority date). Applications are processed on a rolling basis. *Application fee:* $25. *Application Contact:* Dr. Deborah E. Arfken, Dean of Graduate Studies, 865-425-1740, Fax: 865-425-5223, E-mail: deborah-arfken@utc.edu. *Dean*, Dr. Richard P. Casavant, 423-425-4313, Fax: 423-425-5255, E-mail: richard-casavant@utc.edu.

College of Education and Applied Professional Studies Students: 161 full-time (108 women), 294 part-time (234 women); includes 51 minority (39 African Americans, 3 Asian Americans or Pacific Islanders, 5 Hispanic Americans, 4 Native Americans), 5 international. Average age 33. 183 applicants, 95% accepted, 98 enrolled. *Faculty:* 32 full-time (16 women), 9 part-time/adjunct (5 women). Expenses: Contact institution. *Financial support:* Fellowships, research assistantships, Federal Work-Study and institutionally sponsored loans available. Support available to part-time students. Financial award application deadline: 4/1; financial award applicants required to submit FAFSA. In 2001, 137 degrees awarded. *Degree program information:* Part-time and evening/weekend programs available. Offers athletic training (MS); curriculum and instruction (M Ed); early childhood education (M Ed); education and applied professional studies (M Ed, MS, Ed S); educational specialist (Ed S); elementary administration (M Ed); guidance and counseling (M Ed); reading (M Ed); secondary administration (M Ed); secondary education (M Ed); special education (M Ed). *Application deadline:* For fall admission, 8/1 (priority date); for spring admission, 12/1 (priority date). Applications are processed on a rolling basis. *Application fee:* $25. *Application Contact:* Dr. Deborah E. Arfken, Dean of Graduate Studies, 865-425-1740, Fax: 865-425-5223, E-mail: deborah-arfken@utc.edu. *Dean*, Dr. Mary Tanner, 423-425-4249, Fax: 423-425-4044, E-mail: mary-tanner@utc.edu.

College of Engineering and Computer Sciences Students: 18 full-time (5 women), 71 part-time (13 women); includes 8 minority (6 African Americans, 2 Asian Americans or Pacific Islanders), 28 international. Average age 33. 88 applicants, 48% accepted, 18 enrolled. *Faculty:* 16 full-time (3 women), 1 part-time/adjunct (0 women). Expenses: Contact institution. *Financial support:* Fellowships, research assistantships, Federal Work-Study and institutionally sponsored loans available. Support available to part-time students. Financial award application deadline: 4/1; financial award applicants required to submit FAFSA. In 2001, 10 degrees awarded. *Degree program information:* Part-time and evening/weekend programs available. Offers computer science (MS); engineering (MS); engineering management (MS). *Application deadline:* For fall admission, 8/1 (priority date); for spring admission, 12/1 (priority date). Applications are processed on a rolling basis. *Application fee:* $25. *Application Contact:* Dr. Deborah E. Arfken, Dean of Graduate Studies, 865-425-1740, Fax: 865-425-5223, E-mail: deborah-arfken@utc.edu. *Acting Dean*, Dr. Phil M. Kazemersky, 423-425-4121, Fax: 423-425-5229, E-mail: phil-kazemersky@utc.edu.

College of Health and Human Services Students: 100 full-time (72 women), 83 part-time (58 women); includes 19 minority (12 African Americans, 4 Asian Americans or Pacific Islanders, 3 Hispanic Americans), 1 international. Average age 30. 79 applicants, 92% accepted, 32 enrolled. *Faculty:* 19 full-time (11 women), 6 part-time/adjunct (5 women). Expenses: Contact institution. *Financial support:* Fellowships, research assistantships, Federal Work-Study and institutionally sponsored loans available. Support available to part-time students. Financial award application deadline: 4/1; financial award applicants

The University of Tennessee at Chattanooga (continued)

required to submit FAFSA. In 2001, 58 degrees awarded. *Degree program information:* Part-time and evening/weekend programs available. Offers administration (MSN); adult health (MSN); criminal justice (MSCJ); education (MSN); family nurse practitioner (MSN); health and human services (MSCJ, MSN, MSPT); nurse anesthesia (MSN); physical therapy (MSPT). *Application deadline:* For fall admission, 8/1 (priority date); for spring admission, 12/1 (priority date). Applications are processed on a rolling basis. *Application fee:* $25. *Application Contact:* Dr. Deborah E. Arfken, Assistant Provost for Graduate Studies, 423-425-4667, Fax: 423-425-4478, E-mail: darfken@utcvm.utc.edu. *Dean,* Dr. Galan Janeksela, 423-425-4133, Fax: 423-425-4132, E-mail: galan-janeksela@utc.edu.

Announcement: UTC offers one education specialist program, 19 master's programs, and 8 certificate programs in accounting, athletic training, business, computer science, criminal justice, education, engineering, engineering management, English, environmental science, music, nursing, physical therapy, psychology, and public administration. Sixty concentrations are available: school leadership, community counseling, executive MBA, industrial/organizational psychology, nurse anesthesia, family nurse practitioner studies, research psychology, school counseling, school psychology, special education, and teacher licensure. Emphasis on small classes/seminars. Graduate assistantships in every program. Fellowships for Tennessee minority students. Excellent computer facilities. Scenic campus within walking distance of Chattanooga's business/tourist district. Easy driving to mountains, lakes, historic parks, major Southern cities. Students can send e-mail to gstudies@cecasun.edu or visit the Web site at http://www.utc.edu/gradstudies.

THE UNIVERSITY OF TENNESSEE AT MARTIN, Martin, TN 38238-1000

General Information State-supported, coed, comprehensive institution. CGS member. *Enrollment:* 360 matriculated graduate/professional students (232 women). *Enrollment by degree level:* 360 master's. *Graduate faculty:* 133. *Tuition, area resident:* Full-time $3,796; part-time $213 per hour. Tuition, nonresident: full-time $10,326; part-time $576 per hour. *Graduate housing:* Rooms and/or apartments guaranteed to single students and available to married students. Housing application deadline: 3/1. *Student services:* Campus employment opportunities, campus safety program, career counseling, child daycare facilities, free psychological counseling, international student services, low-cost health insurance. *Library facilities:* Paul Meek Library plus 1 other. *Online resources:* library catalog, web page, access to other libraries' catalogs. *Collection:* 436,366 titles, 2,654 serial subscriptions, 10,858 audiovisual materials. *Research affiliation:* University of Tennessee Research Corporation (science and technology), National Writing Project (humanities), U.S. Department of Commerce (distance learning), Department of Education (academic extensions).

Computer facilities: 185 computers available on campus for general student use. A campuswide network can be accessed from student residence rooms and from off campus. *Web address:* http://www.utm.edu/.

General Application Contact: Linda L. Arant, Administrative Secretary, 731-587-7012, Fax: 731-587-7499, E-mail: larant@utm.edu.

GRADUATE UNITS

Graduate Studies Students: 360 (232 women). 184 applicants, 97% accepted, 120 enrolled. *Faculty:* 133. Expenses: Contact institution. *Financial support:* In 2001–02, 68 students received support, including 3 research assistantships with full tuition reimbursements available (averaging $5,048 per year), 5 teaching assistantships with full tuition reimbursements available (averaging $6,314 per year); fellowships with full tuition reimbursements available, career-related internships or fieldwork, scholarships/grants, tuition waivers (partial), and unspecified assistantships also available. Support available to part-time students. Financial award application deadline: 3/1. In 2001, 128 degrees awarded. *Degree program information:* Part-time programs available. Postbaccalaureate distance learning degree programs offered (no on-campus study). *Application deadline:* Applications are processed on a rolling basis. *Application fee:* $25 ($50 for international students). *Application Contact:* Linda L. Arant, Administrative Secretary, 731-587-7012, Fax: 731-587-7499, E-mail: larant@utm.edu. *Interim Assistant Vice Chancellor and Dean of Graduate Studies,* Dr. Victoria S. Seng, 731-587-7012, Fax: 731-587-7499, E-mail: vseng@utm.edu.

College of Agriculture and Applied Sciences Students: 31 (19 women). 31 applicants, 100% accepted, 21 enrolled. *Faculty:* 18. Expenses: Contact institution. *Financial support:* In 2001–02, 3 students received support; fellowships, research assistantships with full tuition reimbursements available, teaching assistantships, scholarships/grants, tuition waivers (partial), and unspecified assistantships available. Support available to part-time students. Financial award application deadline: 3/1. In 2001, 11 degrees awarded. *Degree program information:* Part-time programs available. Offers agricultural operations management (MSAOM); agriculture and applied sciences (MSAOM, MSFCS); child development and family relations (MSFCS); food science and nutrition (MSFCS). *Application deadline:* For fall admission, 7/1 (priority date). Applications are processed on a rolling basis. *Application fee:* $25 ($50 for international students). *Dean,* Dr. James Byford, 731-587-7250, E-mail: jbyford@utm.edu.

College of Business and Public Affairs Students: 163 (86 women). 78 applicants, 96% accepted, 50 enrolled. *Faculty:* 31. Expenses: Contact institution. *Financial support:* In 2001–02, 28 students received support, including 2 research assistantships with full tuition reimbursements available (averaging $4,128 per year), 3 teaching assistantships with full tuition reimbursements available (averaging $5,740 per year); fellowships, career-related internships or fieldwork, tuition waivers (partial), and unspecified assistantships also available. Support available to part-time students. Financial award application deadline: 3/1. In 2001, 91 degrees awarded. *Degree program information:* Part-time programs available. Postbaccalaureate distance learning degree programs offered (no on-campus study). Offers accounting (M Ac); business administration (MBA); business and public affairs (M Ac, MBA). *Application deadline:* Applications are processed on a rolling basis. *Application fee:* $25 ($50 for international students). *Application Contact:* Dr. Richard Griffin, Coordinator, 731-587-7308, Fax: 731-587-7241, E-mail: bagrad@utm.edu. *Dean,* Dr. Ernst Moser, 731-587-7227, Fax: 731-587-7241, E-mail: emoser@utm.edu.

College of Education and Behavioral Sciences Students: 166 (127 women). 75 applicants, 96% accepted, 49 enrolled. *Faculty:* 35. Expenses: Contact institution. *Financial support:* In 2001–02, 37 students received support, including 3 teaching assistantships with full tuition reimbursements available (averaging $5,740 per year); fellowships, research assistantships with full tuition reimbursements available, career-related internships or fieldwork, scholarships/grants, tuition waivers (partial), and unspecified assistantships also available. Support available to part-time students. Financial award application deadline: 3/1. In 2001, 23 degrees awarded. *Degree program information:* Part-time programs available. Postbaccalaureate distance learning degree programs offered (minimal on-campus study). Offers community mental health (MS Ed); education (MS Ed); educational administration and supervision (MS Ed); school counseling (MS Ed); teaching (MS Ed). *Application deadline:* Applications are processed on a rolling basis. *Application fee:* $25 ($50 for international students). *Application Contact:* Dr. Bonnie Daniel, Interim Coordinator, 731-587-7129, Fax: 731-587-7975, E-mail: bdaniel@utm.edu. *Dean,* Dr. B. C. DeSpain, 731-587-7127, Fax: 731-587-7975, E-mail: despain@utm.edu.

THE UNIVERSITY OF TENNESSEE HEALTH SCIENCE CENTER, Memphis, TN 38163-0002

General Information State-supported, coed, upper-level institution. CGS member. *Graduate faculty:* 745 full-time, 169 part-time/adjunct. *Graduate housing:* Room and/or apartments available to single students; on-campus housing not available to married students. Housing application deadline: 2/28. *Student services:* Campus employment opportunities, campus safety program, career counseling, child daycare facilities, disabled student services, free psychological counseling, low-cost health insurance. *Library facilities:* Health Science Library plus 2 others. *Collection:* 165,200 titles, 1,784 serial subscriptions. *Research affiliation:* Saint Jude's Children's Research Hospital, Veterans Administration Medical Center, LePasses Rehabilitation Center, LeBonheur Children's Medical Center.

Computer facilities: 100 computers available on campus for general student use. A campuswide network can be accessed from student residence rooms and from off campus. Internet access is available. *Web address:* http://www.utmem.edu/.

General Application Contact: Ida Mosby, Director of Admissions, 901-448-5560, Fax: 901-448-7772, E-mail: imosby@utmem.edu.

GRADUATE UNITS

College of Allied Health Sciences Students: 140 full-time (99 women); includes 24 minority (16 African Americans, 6 Asian Americans or Pacific Islanders, 1 Hispanic American, 1 Native American) Average age 24. 78 applicants, 50% accepted. *Faculty:* 7 full-time (5 women), 12 part-time/adjunct (8 women). Expenses: Contact institution. *Financial support:* Institutionally sponsored loans available. Support available to part-time students. Financial award application deadline: 2/15. In 2001, 4 degrees awarded. *Degree program information:* Part-time programs available. Offers allied health sciences (MPT, MSPT). *Application deadline:* For fall admission, 1/15 (priority date); for winter admission, 9/1 (priority date); for spring admission, 3/1 (priority date). *Application fee:* $50. Electronic applications accepted. *Application Contact:* Ida Mosby, Director of Admissions, 901-448-5560, Fax: 901-448-7772, E-mail: lmosby@utmem.edu. *Dean,* Dr. Susan P. Mansfield, 901-528-5581, Fax: 901-528-7545.

College of Dentistry Students: 312 full-time (85 women); includes 52 minority (28 African Americans, 19 Asian Americans or Pacific Islanders, 4 Hispanic Americans, 1 Native American) 254 applicants, 32% accepted. *Faculty:* 68 full-time (6 women), 56 part-time/adjunct (12 women). Expenses: Contact institution. *Financial support:* In 2001–02, 278 students received support. Federal Work-Study and minority scholarships available. Support available to part-time students. Financial award application deadline: 2/15. In 2001, 72 first professional degrees, 4 master's awarded. Offers dentistry (DDS, MS). *Application deadline:* For fall admission, 12/31. Applications are processed on a rolling basis. *Application fee:* $50. Electronic applications accepted. *Application Contact:* Ida Mosby, Director of Admissions, 901-448-5560, Fax: 901-448-7772, E-mail: lmosby@utmem.edu. *Dean,* Dr. William F. Slagle, 901-528-6200, Fax: 901-528-7104.

College of Graduate Health Sciences Students: 264 full-time (108 women); includes 116 minority (18 African Americans, 95 Asian Americans or Pacific Islanders, 3 Hispanic Americans) Average age 25. 606 applicants, 11% accepted. *Faculty:* 180 full-time (38 women), 6 part-time/adjunct (3 women). Expenses: Contact institution. *Financial support:* In 2001–02, 2 fellowships, 85 research assistantships, 40 teaching assistantships were awarded. Career-related internships or fieldwork, Federal Work-Study, institutionally sponsored loans, and tuition waivers (full and partial) also available. Support available to part-time students. Financial award application deadline: 2/25; financial award applicants required to submit FAFSA. In 2001, 45 degrees awarded. *Degree program information:* Part-time programs available. Offers anatomy and neurobiology (PhD); bacterial pathogenesis (PhD); biochemistry (PhD); health sciences (MS, PhD); immunology (PhD); microbiology (PhD); molecular and cell biology (PhD); molecular biology (PhD); nursing (PhD); pathology (MS, PhD); pharmaceutical sciences (MS, PhD); pharmacology (MS, PhD); physiology and biophysics (MS, PhD); signal transduction (PhD); structural biology (PhD); virology (PhD). *Application deadline:* For fall admission, 5/15 (priority date). *Application fee:* $0. Electronic applications accepted. *Application Contact:* Ida Mosby, Director of Admissions, 901-448-5560, Fax: 901-448-7772, E-mail: lmosby@utmem.edu. *Dean,* Dr. Richard Peppler, 901-448-5538.

School of Biomedical Engineering Students: 37 full-time (14 women); includes 19 minority (3 African Americans, 16 Asian Americans or Pacific Islanders) Average age 25. 112 applicants, 12% accepted. *Faculty:* 7 full-time (0 women). Expenses: Contact institution. *Financial support:* Research assistantships, teaching assistantships, career-related internships or fieldwork, Federal Work-Study, institutionally sponsored loans, and tuition waivers (full) available. Support available to part-time students. Financial award application deadline: 2/25. In 2001, 10 degrees awarded. *Degree program information:* Part-time programs available. Offers biomedical engineering (MS, PhD). *Application deadline:* For fall admission, 5/15. *Application fee:* $0. Electronic applications accepted. *Application Contact:* Ida Mosby, Director of Admissions, 901-448-5560, Fax: 901-448-7772, E-mail: lmosby@utmem.edu. *Chairman,* Dr. Frank A. DiBianca, 901-448-7099, Fax: 901-448-7387, E-mail: fdibianca@utmem.edu.

College of Medicine Students: 679 full-time (272 women); includes 173 minority (97 African Americans, 68 Asian Americans or Pacific Islanders, 5 Hispanic Americans, 3 Native Americans) Average age 24. 1,639 applicants, 10% accepted. *Faculty:* 517 full-time (104 women), 86 part-time/adjunct (18 women). Expenses: Contact institution. *Financial support:* In 2001–02, 522 students received support. Career-related internships or fieldwork, Federal Work-Study, and institutionally sponsored loans available. Support available to part-time students. Financial award application deadline: 2/15. In 2001, 162 degrees awarded. Offers medicine (MD). *Application deadline:* For fall admission, 11/15. Applications are processed on a rolling basis. *Application fee:* $50. Electronic applications accepted. *Application Contact:* Ida Mosby, Director of Admissions, 901-448-5560, Fax: 901-448-7772, E-mail: lmosby@utmem.edu. *Dean,* Dr. Hank Herrod, 901-528-5529, Fax: 901-528-7683, E-mail: hherrod@utmem.edu.

College of Nursing Students: 136 full-time (100 women); includes 21 minority (16 African Americans, 1 Asian American or Pacific Islander, 2 Hispanic Americans, 2 Native Americans) Average age 29. *Faculty:* 20 full-time (19 women), 2 part-time/adjunct (both women). Expenses: Contact institution. *Financial support:* Fellowships, teaching assistantships, Federal Work-Study and traineeships available. Support available to part-time students. Financial award application deadline: 2/15. In 2001, 19 master's, 3 doctorates awarded. *Degree program information:* Part-time programs available. Offers nursing (MSN, PhD). *Application deadline:* For fall admission, 3/15; for winter admission, 9/1. *Application fee:* $50. Electronic applications accepted. *Application Contact:* Ida Mosby, Director of Admissions, 901-448-5560, Fax: 901-448-7772, E-mail: lmosby@utmem.edu. *Dean,* Dr. Donna Hathaway, 901-528-6128, Fax: 901-577-4121, E-mail: dhathaway@utmem.edu.

College of Pharmacy Students: 396 full-time (267 women); includes 62 African Americans, 18 Asian Americans or Pacific Islanders, 1 Hispanic American Average age 23. 289 applicants, 36% accepted. *Faculty:* 43 full-time (7 women), 37 part-time/adjunct (17 women). Expenses: Contact institution. *Financial support:* In 2001–02, 221 students received support; fellowships, research assistantships, teaching assistantships, career-related internships or fieldwork, Federal Work-Study, institutionally sponsored loans, and tuition waivers (full) available. Support available to part-time students. Financial award application deadline: 2/15. In 2001, 99 degrees awarded. Offers pharmacy (Pharm D, MS, PhD). *Application deadline:* For fall admission, 2/1. *Application fee:* $50. *Application Contact:* Ida Mosby, Director of Admissions, 901-448-5560, Fax: 901-448-7772, E-mail: lmosby@utmem.edu. *Dean,* Dr. Dick R. Gourley, 901-528-6036, Fax: 901-528-7053, E-mail: rgourley@utmem.edu.

THE UNIVERSITY OF TENNESSEE–OAK RIDGE NATIONAL LABORATORY GRADUATE SCHOOL OF GENOME SCIENCE AND TECHNOLOGY, Oak Ridge, TN 37830-8026

General Information State-supported, coed, graduate-only institution. *Enrollment by degree level:* 5 master's, 17 doctoral. *Graduate faculty:* 1 full-time (0 women), 69 part-time/adjunct (15 women). Tuition, state resident: part-time $208 per hour. Tuition, nonresident: part-time $627 per hour. *Required fees:* $22 per hour. Tuition and fees vary according to program. *Graduate housing:* Rooms and/or apartments available on a first-come, first-served basis to single and married students. *Student services:* Campus safety program, career counseling, disabled student services, free psychological counseling, international student services, low-cost health insurance, multicultural affairs office, teacher training. *Library facilities:* Life Sciences Division Library. *Research affiliation:* Oak Ridge National Laboratory.

Computer facilities: A campuswide network can be accessed from student residence rooms and from off campus. Internet access and online class registration are available. *Web address:* http://bio.lsd.ornl.gov/gst/index.html.

General Application Contact: Kay Gardner, Program/Resource Specialist, 865-574-1227, Fax: 865-576-4149, E-mail: gardnerrk@ornl.gov.

GRADUATE UNITS

Graduate Program Students: 22 full-time (11 women). Average age 32. 75 applicants, 13% accepted, 10 enrolled. *Faculty:* 1 full-time (0 women), 70 part-time/adjunct (16 women). Expenses: Contact institution. *Financial support:* In 2001–02, 14 students received support, including 10 research assistantships with full tuition reimbursements available (averaging $18,000 per year); fellowships, institutionally sponsored loans and tuition waivers (full) also available. Financial award application deadline: 3/31. In 2001, 1 master's, 2 doctorates awarded. Offers genome science and technology (MS, PhD). *Application deadline:* For fall admission, 1/15 (priority date). Applications are processed on a rolling basis. *Application fee:* $35. Electronic applications accepted. *Application Contact:* Kay Gardner, Program/Resource Specialist, 865-574-1227, Fax: 865-576-4149, E-mail: gardnerrk@ornl.gov. *Director*, Dr. Jeffrey M. Becker, 865-574-1227, Fax: 865-576-4149, E-mail: jbecker@utk.edu.

THE UNIVERSITY OF TENNESSEE SPACE INSTITUTE, Tullahoma, TN 37388-9700

General Information State-supported, coed, primarily men, graduate-only institution. *Graduate faculty:* 41 full-time (1 woman), 8 part-time/adjunct (0 women). Tuition, state resident: full-time $4,730; part-time $208 per semester hour. Tuition, nonresident: full-time $15,028; part-time $627 per semester hour. *Required fees:* $10 per semester hour. One-time fee: $35. *Graduate housing:* Room and/or apartments available on a first-come, first-served basis to single students; on-campus housing not available to married students. *Student services:* Campus employment opportunities, career counseling, free psychological counseling, international student services, low-cost health insurance. *Library facilities:* UTSI Library. *Collection:* 23,927 titles, 175 serial subscriptions, 80 audiovisual materials. *Research affiliation:* U.S. Air Force–Arnold Engineering Development Center, Technical University (Aachen, Germany).

Computer facilities: 25 computers available on campus for general student use. A campuswide network can be accessed from student residence rooms and from off campus. Internet access is available. *Web address:* http://www.utsi.edu/.

General Application Contact: Dr. Alfonso Pujol, Assistant Vice President and Dean for Student Affairs, 931-393-7432, Fax: 931-393-7346, E-mail: apujol@utsi.edu.

GRADUATE UNITS

Graduate Programs Students: 53 full-time (11 women), 129 part-time (18 women); includes 6 minority (2 African Americans, 3 Asian Americans or Pacific Islanders, 1 Hispanic American), 29 international. 72 applicants, 69% accepted, 35 enrolled. *Faculty:* 41 full-time (1 woman), 8 part-time/adjunct (0 women). Expenses: Contact institution. *Financial support:* In 2001–02, 5 fellowships with full and partial tuition reimbursements, 53 research assistantships with full tuition reimbursements were awarded. Career-related internships or fieldwork, Federal Work-Study, and tuition waivers (full and partial) also available. Financial award applicants required to submit FAFSA. In 2001, 56 master's, 8 doctorates awarded. *Degree program information:* Part-time programs available. Postbaccalaureate distance learning degree programs offered. Offers aerospace engineering (MS, PhD); applied mathematics (MS); aviation systems (MS); chemical engineering (MS); electrical engineering (MS, PhD); engineering and applied science (MS, PhD); engineering management (MS); engineering sciences (MS, PhD); mechanical engineering (MS, PhD); mechanics (MS, PhD); metallurgical engineering (MS, PhD); physics (MS, PhD). *Application deadline:* Applications are processed on a rolling basis. *Application fee:* $35. Electronic applications accepted. *Application Contact:* Dr. Alfonso Pujol, Assistant Vice President and Dean for Student Affairs, 931-393-7432, Fax: 931-393-7346, E-mail: apujol@utsi.edu. *Chief Operating Officer*, Dr. John Caruthers, 931-394-7213, Fax: 931-394-7211, E-mail: jcaruthe@utsi.edu.

THE UNIVERSITY OF TEXAS AT ARLINGTON, Arlington, TX 76019

General Information State-supported, coed, university. CGS member. *Enrollment:* 2,173 full-time matriculated graduate/professional students (892 women), 2,678 part-time matriculated graduate/professional students (1,529 women). *Enrollment by degree level:* 4,259 master's, 592 doctoral. *Graduate faculty:* 411 full-time (98 women), 42 part-time/adjunct (10 women). *Tuition, area resident:* Full-time $2,268. Tuition, nonresident: full-time $6,264. *Required fees:* $839. Tuition and fees vary according to course load. *Graduate housing:* Rooms and/or apartments available on a first-come, first-served basis to single and married students. Typical cost: $2,163 per year ($4,124 including board) for single students. *Student services:* Campus employment opportunities, campus safety program, career counseling, child daycare facilities, disabled student services, exercise/wellness program, free psychological counseling, international student services, multicultural affairs office, teacher training, writing training. *Library facilities:* Central Library plus 2 others. *Online resources:* library catalog, web page, access to other libraries' catalogs. *Collection:* 694,357 titles, 4,738 serial subscriptions, 3,097 audiovisual materials.

Computer facilities: 700 computers available on campus for general student use. A campuswide network can be accessed from student residence rooms and from off campus. Online class registration is available. *Web address:* http://www.uta.edu/.

General Application Contact: Dr. Phil Cohen, Dean of Graduate Studies, 817-272-3186, Fax: 817-272-2625, E-mail: graduate.school@uta.edu.

GRADUATE UNITS

Graduate School Students: 2,173 full-time (892 women), 2,678 part-time (1,529 women). Average age 35. Expenses: Contact institution. *Financial support:* Fellowships, research assistantships, teaching assistantships, career-related internships or fieldwork, Federal Work-Study, institutionally sponsored loans, scholarships/grants, traineeships, and tuition waivers (partial) available. Financial award application deadline: 6/1; financial award applicants required to submit FAFSA. In 2001, 12 degrees awarded. *Degree program information:* Part-time and evening/weekend programs available. Postbaccalaureate distance learning degree programs offered (no on-campus study). Offers environmental science and engineering (MS, PhD); health care administration (MS); interdisciplinary studies (MA, MS); logistics (MS); management of technology (MS). *Application deadline:* For fall admission, 6/16. Applications are processed on a rolling basis. *Application fee:* $25 ($50 for international students). *Dean of Graduate Studies*, Dr. Phil Cohen, 817-272-3186, Fax: 817-272-2625, E-mail: graduate.school@uta.edu.

College of Business Administration Students: 370 full-time (172 women), 597 part-time (227 women); includes 158 minority (46 African Americans, 62 Asian Americans or Pacific Islanders, 46 Hispanic Americans, 4 Native Americans), 267 international. Average age 31. 597 applicants, 78% accepted, 280 enrolled. *Faculty:* 54 full-time (9 women), 5 part-time/adjunct (1 woman). Expenses: Contact institution. *Financial support:* In 2001–02, 100 students received support, including 5 fellowships (averaging $1,000 per year), 14 research assistantships (averaging $6,432 per year), 80 teaching assistantships (averaging $10,000 per year); career-related internships or fieldwork, Federal Work-Study, institutionally sponsored loans, and scholarships/grants also available. Financial award application deadline: 6/1; financial award applicants required to submit FAFSA. In 2001, 284 master's, 9 doctorates awarded. *Degree program information:* Part-time and evening/weekend programs available. Postbaccalaureate distance learning degree programs offered (no on-campus study). Offers accounting (MBA, MP Acc, MS, PhD); business administration (PhD); business statistics (PhD); economics (MA, PhD); finance (MBA, PhD); information systems (MBA, MS, PhD); management (MBA, PhD); management sciences (MBA); marketing (MBA, PhD); marketing research (MS); personal and human resources management (MBA); real estate (MBA, MS); taxation (MS, PhD). *Application deadline:* For fall admission, 6/15; for spring admission, 10/15. Applications are processed on a rolling basis. *Application fee:* $25 ($50 for international students). *Application Contact:* Alisa Johnson, Director, 817-272-3004, Fax: 817-272-5799, E-mail: question@uta.edu. *Dean*, Dr. Daniel Himarios, 817-272-3061, Fax: 817-272-2073, E-mail: himarios@uta.edu.

College of Engineering Students: 971 full-time (183 women), 426 part-time (76 women); includes 126 minority (12 African Americans, 95 Asian Americans or Pacific Islanders, 17 Hispanic Americans, 2 Native Americans), 1,077 international. Average age 27. 2,269 applicants, 80% accepted, 442 enrolled. *Faculty:* 89 full-time (5 women), 12 part-time/adjunct (1 woman). Expenses: Contact institution. *Financial support:* Fellowships, research assistantships, teaching assistantships, career-related internships or fieldwork, Federal Work-Study, institutionally sponsored loans, scholarships/grants, and tuition waivers (partial) available. Financial award application deadline: 6/1; financial award applicants required to submit FAFSA. In 2001, 251 master's, 20 doctorates awarded. *Degree program information:* Part-time programs available. Offers aerospace engineering (M Engr, MS, PhD); biomedical engineering (MS, PhD); civil and environmental engineering (M Engr, MS, PhD); computer science and engineering (M Engr, M Sw En, MCS, MS, PhD); electrical engineering (M Engr, MS, PhD); engineering (M Engr, M Sw En, MCS, MS, PhD); industrial and manufacturing systems engineering (M Engr, MS, PhD); materials science and engineering (M Engr, MS, PhD); mechanical engineering (M Engr, MS, PhD). *Application deadline:* For fall admission, 6/16. Applications are processed on a rolling basis. *Application fee:* $25 ($50 for international students). *Application Contact:* Dr. Theresa A. Maldonado, Associate Dean for Research and Graduate Studies, 817-272-5725, Fax: 817-272-2548, E-mail: maldonado@uta.edu. *Dean*, Dr. Bill D. Carroll, 817-272-5725, Fax: 817-272-5110, E-mail: carroll@uta.edu.

College of Liberal Arts Students: 83 full-time (47 women), 273 part-time (167 women); includes 51 minority (12 African Americans, 9 Asian Americans or Pacific Islanders, 28 Hispanic Americans, 2 Native Americans), 22 international. Average age 36. 144 applicants, 94% accepted, 91 enrolled. *Faculty:* 95 full-time (29 women), 13 part-time/adjunct (4 women). Expenses: Contact institution. *Financial support:* Fellowships, research assistantships, teaching assistantships, career-related internships or fieldwork, Federal Work-Study, institutionally sponsored loans, and tuition waivers (partial) available. Financial award application deadline: 6/1; financial award applicants required to submit FAFSA. In 2001, 57 master's, 32 doctorates awarded. Offers anthropology (MA); criminology and criminal justice (MA); English (MA); French (MA); German (MA); history (MA, PhD); humanities (MA); liberal arts (MA, MM, PhD); linguistics (MA, PhD); literature (PhD); political science (MA); rhetoric (PhD); sociology (MA); Spanish (MA). *Application deadline:* For fall admission, 6/16. Applications are processed on a rolling basis. *Application fee:* $25 ($50 for international students). *Dean*, Dr. Richard Cole, 817-272-3071, Fax: 817-272-3255, E-mail: cole@uta.edu.

College of Science Students: 162 full-time (80 women), 95 part-time (53 women); includes 53 minority (20 African Americans, 18 Asian Americans or Pacific Islanders, 14 Hispanic Americans, 1 Native American), 65 international. Average age 32. 141 applicants, 83% accepted, 61 enrolled. *Faculty:* 83 full-time (6 women), 7 part-time/adjunct (2 women). Expenses: Contact institution. *Financial support:* In 2001–02, 27 fellowships (averaging $1,000 per year), 61 research assistantships (averaging $14,000 per year), 102 teaching assistantships (averaging $15,500 per year) were awarded. Career-related internships or fieldwork, Federal Work-Study, institutionally sponsored loans, and tuition waivers (partial) also available. Financial award application deadline: 6/1; financial award applicants required to submit FAFSA. In 2001, 33 master's, 12 doctorates awarded. *Degree program information:* Part-time and evening/weekend programs available. Offers applied chemistry (PhD); biology (MS); chemistry (MS); experimental psychology (PhD); geology (MS); interdisciplinary science (MA); mathematical sciences (PhD); mathematics (MS); physics (MS); physics and applied physics (PhD); psychology (MS); quantitative biology (PhD); science (MA, MS, PhD). *Application deadline:* For fall admission, 6/16. Applications are processed on a rolling basis. *Application fee:* $25 ($50 for international students). *Application Contact:* Dr. Robert McMahon, Associate Dean, 817-272-3492, Fax: 817-272-3511, E-mail: r.mcmahon@uta.edu. *Dean*, Dr. Neal J. Smatresk, 817-272-3491, Fax: 817-272-3511, E-mail: smatresk@uta.edu.

School of Architecture Students: 92 full-time (37 women), 28 part-time (13 women); includes 18 minority (1 African American, 7 Asian Americans or Pacific Islanders, 10 Hispanic Americans), 14 international. Average age 30. 61 applicants, 82% accepted, 26 enrolled. *Faculty:* 16 full-time (0 women). Expenses: Contact institution. *Financial support:* In 2001–02, 5 fellowships with partial tuition reimbursements (averaging $1,000 per year), 2 research assistantships with partial tuition reimbursements (averaging $4,820 per year), 8 teaching assistantships with partial tuition reimbursements (averaging $4,820 per year) were awarded. Career-related internships or fieldwork and tuition waivers (partial) also available. Financial award application deadline: 6/1; financial award applicants required to submit FAFSA. In 2001, 26 degrees awarded. *Degree program information:* Part-time and evening/weekend programs available. Offers architecture (M Arch, MLA); landscape architecture (MLA). *Application deadline:* For fall admission, 6/16. Applications are processed on a rolling basis. *Application fee:* $25 ($50 for international students). Electronic applications accepted. *Application Contact:* Craig Kuhner, Graduate Adviser and Assistant Dean, 817-272-2801, Fax: 817-272-5098, E-mail: kuhner@uta.edu. *Interim Dean*, Martha LaGess, 817-272-2801, Fax: 817-272-5098, E-mail: lagess@uta.edu.

School of Education Students: 91 full-time (59 women), 580 part-time (470 women); includes 214 minority (145 African Americans, 7 Asian Americans or Pacific Islanders, 60 Hispanic Americans, 2 Native Americans), 3 international. Average age 38. 532 applicants, 98% accepted, 324 enrolled. *Faculty:* 19 full-time (14 women). Expenses: Contact institution. *Financial support:* In 2001–02, 5 fellowships were awarded Financial award application deadline: 6/1; financial award applicants required to submit FAFSA. In 2001, 145 degrees awarded. *Degree program information:* Part-time and evening/weekend programs available. Postbaccalaureate distance learning degree programs offered. Offers curriculum and instruction (M Ed); educational administration (M Ed); teaching (M Ed T). *Application deadline:* For fall admission, 6/16. Applications are processed on a rolling basis. *Application fee:* $25 ($50 for international students). *Application Contact:* Dr. Ted Chase, Graduate Advisor, 817-272-2591, Fax: 817-272-7624, E-mail: chaset@uta.edu. *Dean*, Dr. Jeanne M. Gerlach, 817-272-2591, Fax: 817-272-2530, E-mail: gerlach@uta.edu.

School of Nursing Students: 26 full-time (23 women), 219 part-time (196 women); includes 33 minority (12 African Americans, 9 Asian Americans or Pacific Islanders, 7 Hispanic Americans, 5 Native Americans), 2 international. Average age 39. 76 applicants, 100% accepted, 53 enrolled. *Faculty:* 16 full-time (all women), 1 (woman) part-time/adjunct. Expenses: Contact institution. *Financial support:* In 2001–02, 24 fellowships with partial tuition reimbursements (averaging $3,000 per year), 6 research assistantships (averaging $7,992 per year), 7 teaching assistantships (averaging $10,080 per year) were awarded. Career-related internships or fieldwork and traineeships also available. Financial award application deadline: 6/1; financial award applicants required to submit FAFSA. In 2001, 56 degrees awarded. *Degree program information:* Part-time and evening/weekend programs available. Offers administration/supervision of nursing (MSN); nurse practitioner (MSN); teaching of nursing (MSN). *Application deadline:* For fall admission, 6/16. Applications are processed on a rolling basis. *Application fee:* $25 ($50 for international students). *Application Contact:* Dr. Susan Grove, Graduate Adviser, 817-272-2776, Fax: 817-272-5006, E-mail: grove@uta.edu. *Dean*, Dr. Elizabeth C. Poster, 817-272-2776, Fax: 817-272-5006, E-mail: poster@uta.edu.

School of Social Work Students: 298 full-time (250 women), 247 part-time (209 women); includes 140 minority (73 African Americans, 14 Asian Americans or Pacific Islanders, 50 Hispanic Americans, 3 Native Americans), 6 international. Average age 34. 227 applicants, 98% accepted, 173 enrolled. *Faculty:* 25 full-time (13 women), 1 part-time/adjunct (0 women). Expenses: Contact institution. *Financial support:* In 2001–02, 355 students received support, including 14 fellowships (averaging $1,000 per year), 10 teaching assistantships (averaging $8,000 per year); research assistantships, career-related internships or fieldwork, Federal Work-Study, institutionally sponsored loans, scholarships/grants, and unspecified assistantships also available. Financial award application deadline: 6/1; financial award applicants required to submit FAFSA. In 2001, 201 master's, 8 doctorates awarded. *Degree program information:* Part-time and evening/weekend programs available. Postbaccalaureate distance learning degree programs offered (minimal on-campus study). Offers social work (MSSW, PhD). *Application deadline:* For fall admission, 3/15. *Application fee:* $25 ($50 for international students). *Application Contact:* Dr. Donald K. Granvold, Graduate Adviser, 817-272-3613, Fax: 817-272-5229, E-mail: granvold@uta.edu. *Dean*, Dr. Santos H. Hernandez, 817-272-3181, Fax: 817-272-5229, E-mail: herns@uta.edu.

School of Urban and Public Affairs Students: 54 full-time (25 women), 121 part-time (70 women). Average age 35. 67 applicants, 96% accepted, 48 enrolled. *Faculty:* 14 full-time (6 women), 2 part-time/adjunct (0 women). Expenses: Contact institution. *Financial support:* In 2001–02, 10 fellowships (averaging $1,500 per year), 5 research assistantships (averag-

The University of Texas at Arlington (continued)

ing $4,000 per year) were awarded. Teaching assistantships, career-related internships or fieldwork and Federal Work-Study also available. Financial award application deadline: 6/1; financial award applicants required to submit FAFSA. In 2001, 21 master's, 6 doctorates awarded. *Degree program information:* Part-time and evening/weekend programs available. Offers city and regional planning (MCRP); public administration (MPA); urban and public administration (PhD); urban and public affairs (MA, MCRP, MPA, PhD). *Application deadline:* For fall admission, 6/16. *Application fee:* $25 ($50 for international students). *Dean,* Dr. Richard Cole, 817-272-3071, Fax: 817-272-3255, E-mail: cole@uta.edu.

See in-depth description on page 1265.

THE UNIVERSITY OF TEXAS AT AUSTIN, Austin, TX 78712-1111

General Information State-supported, coed, university. CGS member. *Enrollment:* 12,007 matriculated graduate/professional students (5,653 women). *Enrollment by degree level:* 1,667 first professional, 5,806 master's, 4,534 doctoral. *Graduate faculty:* 2,653. Tuition, state resident: full-time $3,159. Tuition, nonresident: full-time $6,957. Tuition and fees vary according to program. *Graduate housing:* Rooms and/or apartments available to single and married students. *Student services:* Campus employment opportunities, campus safety program, career counseling, child daycare facilities, disabled student services, exercise/wellness program, free psychological counseling, grant writing training, international student services, low-cost health insurance, teacher training, writing training. *Library facilities:* Perry-Castañeda Library plus 18 others. *Online resources:* library catalog, web page, access to other libraries' catalogs. *Collection:* 4.3 million titles, 50,165 serial subscriptions, 573,254 audiovisual materials.

Computer facilities: 4,000 computers available on campus for general student use. A campuswide network can be accessed from student residence rooms and from off campus. Internet access, e-mail are available. *Web address:* http://www.utexas.edu/.

General Application Contact: Pat Ellison, Director, Graduate and International Admissions Center, 512-475-7398, Fax: 512-475-7395, E-mail: p.ellison@mail.utexas.edu.

GRADUATE UNITS

College of Pharmacy Offers pharmacy (Pharm D, MS Phr, PhD). Electronic applications accepted.

Graduate School Students: 10,576. *Faculty:* 1,774. Expenses: Contact institution. *Financial support:* Fellowships with full and partial tuition reimbursements, research assistantships with full and partial tuition reimbursements, teaching assistantships with full and partial tuition reimbursements, career-related internships or fieldwork, Federal Work-Study, institutionally sponsored loans, scholarships/grants, traineeships, tuition waivers (partial), and staff assistantships, teaching associateships available. Support available to part-time students. Financial award applicants required to submit CSS PROFILE or FAFSA. *Degree program information:* Part-time and evening/weekend programs available. Offers computational and applied mathematics (MA, PhD); Russian, East European and Eurasian studies (MA); science and technology commercialization (MS); writing (MFA). Electronic applications accepted. *Application Contact:* Pat Ellison, Director, Graduate and International Admissions Center, 521-475-7398, Fax: 512-475-7395, E-mail: p.ellison@mail.utexas.edu. *Vice President and Dean,* Dr. Teresa A. Sullivan, 512-471-4511, Fax: 512-471-7620, E-mail: tsullivan@mail.utexas.edu.

College of Communication *Degree program information:* Part-time programs available. Offers advertising (MA, PhD); communication (MA, MFA, PhD); communication sciences and disorders (MA, PhD); communication studies (MA, PhD); film/video production (MFA); journalism (MA, PhD); radio-television-film (MA, PhD). Electronic applications accepted.

College of Education *Degree program information:* Part-time programs available. Offers academic educational psychology (M Ed, MA); counseling education (M Ed); counseling psychology (PhD); curriculum and instruction (M Ed, MA, Ed D, PhD); education (M Ed, MA, MHRDL, Ed D, PhD); educational administration (M Ed, Ed D, PhD); foreign language education (MA, PhD); health education (M Ed, MA, Ed D, PhD); human development and education (PhD); kinesiology (M Ed, MA, Ed D, PhD); learning cognition and instruction (PhD); mathematics education (M Ed, MA, PhD); quantitative methods (PhD); school psychology (PhD); science education (M Ed, MA, PhD); special education (M Ed, MA, Ed D, PhD). Electronic applications accepted.

College of Engineering Students: 1,475 full-time (277 women), 411 part-time (71 women); includes 170 minority (26 African Americans, 92 Asian Americans or Pacific Islanders, 48 Hispanic Americans, 4 Native Americans), 1,070 international. Average age 28. 4,000 applicants, 27% accepted, 371 enrolled. *Faculty:* 227 full-time (21 women), 72 part-time/adjunct (6 women). Expenses: Contact institution. *Financial support:* In 2001–02, 293 fellowships with partial tuition reimbursements (averaging $3,160 per year), 756 research assistantships with full tuition reimbursements (averaging $14,000 per year), 305 teaching assistantships with partial tuition reimbursements (averaging $13,000 per year) were awarded. Career-related internships or fieldwork, Federal Work-Study, institutionally sponsored loans, scholarships/grants, tuition waivers (partial), and academic assistantships, tutorships also available. Support available to part-time students. Financial award applicants required to submit FAFSA. In 2001, 416 master's, 132 doctorates awarded. *Degree program information:* Part-time and evening/weekend programs available. Offers aerospace engineering (MSE, PhD); architectural engineering (MSE); biomedical engineering (MSE, PhD); chemical engineering (MSE, PhD); civil engineering (MSE, PhD); electrical and computer engineering (MSE, PhD); energy and mineral resources (MA, MS); engineering (MA, MS, MSE, PhD); engineering mechanics (MSE, PhD); environmental and water resources engineering (MSE); manufacturing systems engineering (MSE); materials science and engineering (MSE, PhD); mechanical engineering (MSE, PhD); operations research and industrial engineering (MSE, PhD); petroleum and geosystems engineering (MSE, PhD). *Application fee:* $50 ($75 for international students). Electronic applications accepted. *Dean,* Dr. Ben G. Streetman, 512-471-1166, Fax: 512-475-7072, E-mail: bstreet@mail.utexas.edu.

College of Fine Arts Students: 624 (368 women); includes 5 African Americans, 28 Hispanic Americans 637 applicants, 35% accepted. Expenses: Contact institution. *Financial support:* Fellowships with partial tuition reimbursements, research assistantships, teaching assistantships, career-related internships or fieldwork, institutionally sponsored loans, scholarships/grants, health care benefits, tuition waivers (partial), unspecified assistantships, and assistant instructorships available. Support available to part-time students. In 2001, 92 master's, 45 doctorates awarded. *Degree program information:* Part-time programs available. Offers art education (MA); art history (MA, PhD); design (MFA); fine arts (M Music, MA, MFA, DMA, PhD); music (M Music, DMA, PhD); studio art (MFA); theatre (MA, MFA, PhD). *Application fee:* $50 ($75 for international students). Electronic applications accepted. *Dean,* Robert Freeman, 512-471-1655, Fax: 512-471-5784.

College of Liberal Arts Students: 1,985 (986 women). 3,275 applicants, 27% accepted. Expenses: Contact institution. *Financial support:* Fellowships with full and partial tuition reimbursements, research assistantships with partial tuition reimbursements, teaching assistantships with partial tuition reimbursements, career-related internships or fieldwork, Federal Work-Study, institutionally sponsored loans, scholarships/grants, traineeships, tuition waivers (partial), and assistant instructorships available. Financial award applicants required to submit CSS PROFILE or FAFSA. In 2001, 275 master's, 127 doctorates awarded. *Degree program information:* Part-time programs available. Offers American studies (MA, PhD); Arabic studies (MA, PhD); archaeology (MA, PhD); Asian cultures and languages (MA, PhD); Asian studies (MA, PhD); classics (MA, PhD); comparative literature (MA, PhD); economics (MA, MS Econ, PhD); English (MA, PhD); folklore and public culture (MA, PhD); French (MA, PhD); geography (MA, PhD); Germanic studies (MA, PhD); government (MA, PhD); Hebrew studies (MA, PhD); Hispanic literature (MA, PhD); history (MA, PhD); Ibero-Romance philology and linguistics (MA, PhD); Latin American studies (MA, PhD); liberal arts (MA, MS Econ, PhD); linguistic anthropology (MA, PhD); linguistics (MA, PhD); Luso-Brazilian literature (MA, PhD); Middle Eastern studies (MA); Persian studies (MA, PhD); philosophy (MA, PhD); physical anthropology (MA, PhD); psychology (PhD); Romance linguistics (MA, PhD); Slavic languages and literatures (MA, PhD); social anthropology (MA, PhD); sociology (MA, PhD). *Application fee:* $50 ($75 for international students). Electronic applications accepted. *Dean,* Richard Lariviere, 512-471-4141.

College of Natural Sciences Students: 1,336 (413 women); includes 95 minority (7 African Americans, 52 Asian Americans or Pacific Islanders, 33 Hispanic Americans, 3 Native Americans) 504 international. 2,539 applicants, 32% accepted, 370 enrolled. Expenses: Contact institution. *Financial support:* Fellowships with partial tuition reimbursements, research assistantships with partial tuition reimbursements, teaching assistantships with partial tuition reimbursements, career-related internships or fieldwork, Federal Work-Study, institutionally sponsored loans, and scholarships/grants available. In 2001, 149 master's, 156 doctorates awarded. *Degree program information:* Part-time programs available. Offers analytical chemistry (MA, PhD); astronomy (MA, PhD); biochemistry (MA, PhD); biological sciences (MA, PhD); cell and molecular biology (PhD); cellular and molecular biology (PhD); child development and family relations (MA, PhD); computer sciences (MA, MSCS, PhD); ecology, evolution and behavior (MA, PhD); genetics and developmental biology (PhD); geological sciences (MA, MS, PhD); inorganic chemistry (MA, PhD); marine science (MA, PhD); mathematics (MA, PhD); microbiology (MA, PhD); microbiology and immunology (PhD); natural sciences (MA, MS, MS Stat, MSCS, PhD); nutrition (MA); nutritional sciences (MA, PhD); organic chemistry (MA, PhD); physical chemistry (MA, PhD); physics (MA, MS, PhD); plant biology (MA, PhD); statistics (MS Stat). *Application fee:* $50. Electronic applications accepted. *Dean,* Mary Ann Rankin, 512-4713255.

Graduate School of Library and Information Science Students: 305 (243 women); includes 41 minority (2 African Americans, 5 Asian Americans or Pacific Islanders, 33 Hispanic Americans, 1 Native American) 35 international. Average age 27. 164 applicants, 74% accepted. *Faculty:* 20 full-time, 9 part-time/adjunct. Expenses: Contact institution. *Financial support:* Fellowships, research assistantships, teaching assistantships, career-related internships or fieldwork, Federal Work-Study, and tuition waivers (partial) available. Support available to part-time students. Financial award application deadline: 2/1. In 2001, 137 master's, 3 doctorates awarded. *Degree program information:* Part-time programs available. Offers library and information science (MLIS, PhD). *Application deadline:* For fall admission, 2/1 (priority date); for winter admission, 5/1; for spring admission, 10/1. Applications are processed on a rolling basis. *Application fee:* $50 ($75 for international students). Electronic applications accepted. *Application Contact:* Dr. Philip Doty, Graduate Adviser, 512-471-3746, Fax: 512-471-3971, E-mail: pdoty@gslis.utexas.edu. *Dean,* Andrew I. Dillon, 512-471-3828, Fax: 512-471-3971.

The Institute for Neuroscience Students: 24 full-time (12 women). 81 applicants, 22% accepted, 12 enrolled. *Faculty:* 60 full-time. Expenses: Contact institution. *Financial support:* In 2001–02, 15 students received support, including 2 fellowships with tuition reimbursements available (averaging $15,000 per year), 6 research assistantships with tuition reimbursements available, 5 teaching assistantships with tuition reimbursements available (averaging $12,500 per year) Financial award application deadline: 2/1. In 2001, 2 degrees awarded. Offers neuroscience (MA, PhD). *Application deadline:* For fall admission, 1/15 (priority date). *Application fee:* $50 ($75 for international students). Electronic applications accepted. *Application Contact:* Dr. Rueben Gonzales, Graduate Adviser, 512-471-3640, Fax: 512-471-0390, E-mail: ins_uta@psy.utexas.edu. *Director,* Dr. Creed W. Abell, 512-471-3640, Fax: 512-471-2181, E-mail: dirins@uts.cc.utexas.edu.

Lyndon B. Johnson School of Public Affairs Students: 236 full-time (129 women), 38 part-time (24 women); includes 52 minority (11 African Americans, 14 Asian Americans or Pacific Islanders, 26 Hispanic Americans, 1 Native American), 32 international. Average age 26. 365 applicants, 64% accepted. *Faculty:* 26 full-time (6 women), 15 part-time/adjunct (2 women). Expenses: Contact institution. *Financial support:* In 2001–02, 221 students received support, including 187 fellowships with full and partial tuition reimbursements available (averaging $4,100 per year), 50 research assistantships with partial tuition reimbursements available (averaging $3,500 per year), 13 teaching assistantships with partial tuition reimbursements available (averaging $5,200 per year); career-related internships or fieldwork, institutionally sponsored loans, scholarships/grants, and tuition waivers (partial) also available. Financial award application deadline: 2/1. In 2001, 91 master's, 4 doctorates awarded. *Degree program information:* Part-time programs available. Offers public affairs (MP Aff); public policy (PhD). *Application deadline:* For fall admission, 1/15; for spring admission, 10/1 (priority date). Applications are processed on a rolling basis. *Application fee:* $50 ($75 for international students). Electronic applications accepted. *Application Contact:* Dr. Pat Wong, Graduate Adviser, 512-471-2956, Fax: 512-471-1835, E-mail: patwong@mail.utexas.edu. *Dean,* Dr. Edwin Dorn, 512-471-3200, Fax: 512-471-4697, E-mail: eddorn@mail.utexas.edu.

McCombs School of Business Students: 1,417 (582 women). 3,376 applicants, 29% accepted, 537 enrolled. *Faculty:* 159 full-time (39 women), 56 part-time/adjunct (14 women). Expenses: Contact institution. *Financial support:* Fellowships with full and partial tuition reimbursements, research assistantships with full and partial tuition reimbursements, teaching assistantships with partial tuition reimbursements, career-related internships or fieldwork, Federal Work-Study, institutionally sponsored loans, scholarships/grants, and tuition waivers (partial) available. Financial award applicants required to submit FAFSA. In 2001, 686 master's, 16 doctorates awarded. Offers accounting (MPA, PhD); business (MBA); business administration (MBA, MHRDL, MPA, PhD); finance (PhD); human resource development leadership (MHRDL); management (PhD); management sciences and information systems (PhD); marketing administration (PhD). Electronic applications accepted. *Dean,* Robert G. May, 512-471-5921.

School of Architecture Students: 209 full-time (92 women), 16 part-time (12 women); includes 20 minority (1 African American, 7 Asian Americans or Pacific Islanders, 12 Hispanic Americans), 27 international. 442 applicants, 39% accepted. Expenses: Contact institution. *Financial support:* In 2001–02, 6 fellowships with partial tuition reimbursements (averaging $10,000 per year), 6 research assistantships with partial tuition reimbursements (averaging $9,000 per year), 25 teaching assistantships with partial tuition reimbursements (averaging $9,000 per year) were awarded. Career-related internships or fieldwork, institutionally sponsored loans, scholarships/grants, and tuition waivers (partial) also available. Financial award application deadline: 2/1. In 2001, 85 degrees awarded. Offers architecture (M Arch, MS Arch St, MSCRP, PhD); community and regional planning (MSCRP, PhD). *Application deadline:* For fall admission, 2/1; for spring admission, 10/1. *Application fee:* $50 ($75 for international students). Electronic applications accepted. *Application Contact:* Lawrence Speck, Graduate Adviser, 512-471-0134, E-mail: lwspeck@mail.utexas.edu. *Dean,* Frederick Steiner, 512-471-1922.

School of Nursing Students: 131 full-time (119 women), 49 part-time (47 women); includes 37 minority (11 African Americans, 7 Asian Americans or Pacific Islanders, 18 Hispanic Americans, 1 Native American), 14 international. Average age 38. 102 applicants, 87% accepted. *Faculty:* 27 full-time (25 women), 14 part-time/adjunct (13 women). Expenses: Contact institution. *Financial support:* In 2001–02, 4 fellowships, 5 research assistantships, 18 teaching assistantships were awarded. Scholarships/grants and traineeships also available. Financial award application deadline: 2/1. In 2001, 45 master's, 13 doctorates awarded. *Degree program information:* Part-time programs available. Offers nursing (MSN, PhD). *Application deadline:* For fall admission, 2/1. *Application fee:* $50 ($75 for international students). Electronic applications accepted. *Application Contact:* Margaret Hill, Graduate Coordinator, 512-471-7927, Fax: 512-232-4777, E-mail: nugrad@uts.cc.utexas.edu. *Dean,* Dr. Dolores Sands, 512-471-4100, Fax: 512-471-4910, E-mail: dsands@mail.utexas.edu.

School of Social Work Students: 205 full-time, 70 part-time. Average age 28. 190 applicants, 92 enrolled. *Faculty:* 36 full-time (25 women), 15 part-time/adjunct (11 women). Expenses: Contact institution. *Financial support:* Fellowships, career-related internships or fieldwork, Federal Work-Study, institutionally sponsored loans, scholarships/grants, and unspecified assistantships available. Financial award application deadline: 2/1; financial award applicants required to submit FAFSA. In 2001, 126 master's, 4 doctorates awarded. *Degree program information:* Part-time programs available. Offers social work (MSSW, PhD). *Application deadline:* For fall admission, 2/1 (priority date); for spring admission, 10/1. Applications are processed on a rolling basis. *Application fee:* $50 ($75 for international students). *Application Contact:* David Springer, Graduate Advisor, 512-471-9819, E-mail: sswinfo@utxums.cc.utexas.edu. *Dean,* Dr. Barbara White, 512-471-1937.

School of Law Students: 1,443 full-time (698 women); includes 258 minority (37 African Americans, 78 Asian Americans or Pacific Islanders, 137 Hispanic Americans, 6 Native

Americans), 34 international. Average age 26. 4,451 applicants, 24% accepted, 484 enrolled. *Faculty:* 73 full-time (23 women), 103 part-time/adjunct (45 women). Expenses: Contact institution. *Financial support:* In 2001–02, 1,300 students received support, including 100 research assistantships (averaging $1,800 per year), 31 teaching assistantships (averaging $3,500 per year); career-related internships or fieldwork, scholarships/grants, and tuition waivers (full) also available. Financial award application deadline: 3/31; financial award applicants required to submit FAFSA. In 2001, 455 first professional degrees, 25 master's awarded. Offers law (JD, LL M). *Application deadline:* For fall admission, 2/1. *Application fee:* $65. Electronic applications accepted. *Dean,* William C. Powers, 512-232-1120, Fax: 512-471-6987, E-mail: wpowers@mail.law.utexas.edu.

Announcement: The University of Texas at Austin is one of the nation's premier research institutions, offering graduate education in more than 90 separate and joint-degree programs. In-depth information about the University, Graduate School, faculty, graduate degree programs, admissions (including an electronic Web application), and financial aid is available via the World Wide Web. Prospective students are strongly urged to access the Graduate School's Web site at http://www.utexas.edu/ogs.

THE UNIVERSITY OF TEXAS AT BROWNSVILLE, Brownsville, TX 78520-4991

General Information State-supported, coed, upper-level institution. CGS member. *Graduate housing:* On-campus housing not available.

GRADUATE UNITS

Graduate Studies and Sponsored Programs *Degree program information:* Part-time and evening/weekend programs available. Postbaccalaureate distance learning degree programs offered (minimal on-campus study).

College of Liberal Arts *Degree program information:* Part-time and evening/weekend programs available. Offers behavioral sciences (MAIS); English (MA); government (MAIS); history (MAIS); interdisciplinary studies (MAIS); liberal arts (MA, MAIS); Spanish (MA).

College of Science, Mathematics and Technology *Degree program information:* Part-time and evening/weekend programs available. Offers biological sciences (MSIS).

School of Business *Degree program information:* Part-time and evening/weekend programs available. Postbaccalaureate distance learning degree programs offered (minimal on-campus study). Offers business (MBA).

School of Education *Degree program information:* Part-time and evening/weekend programs available. Postbaccalaureate distance learning degree programs offered (minimal on-campus study). Offers counseling and guidance (M Ed); curriculum and instruction (M Ed); early childhood education (M Ed); educational administration (M Ed); educational technology (M Ed); elementary education/bilingual endorsement option (M Ed); English as a second language (M Ed); reading specialist (M Ed); special education/educational diagnostician (M Ed); supervision (M Ed).

School of Health Sciences Offers health sciences (MSPHN).

THE UNIVERSITY OF TEXAS AT DALLAS, Richardson, TX 75083-0688

General Information State-supported, coed, university. CGS member. *Enrollment:* 1,816 full-time matriculated graduate/professional students (760 women), 1,630 part-time matriculated graduate/professional students (700 women). *Enrollment by degree level:* 2,914 master's, 527 doctoral. *Graduate faculty:* 293 full-time (57 women), 46 part-time/adjunct (16 women). Tuition, state resident: full-time $1,440; part-time $84 per credit. Tuition, nonresident: full-time $5,310; part-time $295 per credit. *Required fees:* $1,835; $87 per credit. $138 per term. *Graduate housing:* Rooms and/or apartments available on a first-come, first-served basis to single and married students. Typical cost: $5,914 (including board) for single students; $5,914 (including board) for married students. *Student services:* Campus employment opportunities, campus safety program, career counseling, child daycare facilities, disabled student services, exercise/wellness program, free psychological counseling, grant writing training, international student services, low-cost health insurance, multicultural affairs office, teacher training, writing training. *Library facilities:* Eugene McDermott Library plus 2 others. *Online resources:* library catalog, web page, access to other libraries' catalogs. *Collection:* 447,496 titles, 3,831 serial subscriptions, 2,011 audiovisual materials.

Computer facilities: 428 computers available on campus for general student use. A campuswide network can be accessed from student residence rooms and from off campus. Internet access and online class registration are available. *Web address:* http://www.utdallas.edu/.

General Application Contact: Austin Cunningham, Dean for Graduate Studies, 972-883-2234.

GRADUATE UNITS

Erik Jonsson School of Engineering and Computer Science Students: 786 full-time (214 women), 381 part-time (104 women); includes 153 minority (9 African Americans, 134 Asian Americans or Pacific Islanders, 9 Hispanic Americans, 1 Native American), 889 international. Average age 27. 2,614 applicants, 40% accepted. *Faculty:* 59 full-time (5 women), 8 part-time/adjunct (3 women). Expenses: Contact institution. *Financial support:* In 2001–02, 4 fellowships with full tuition reimbursements (averaging $3,000 per year), 101 research assistantships with full tuition reimbursements (averaging $5,234 per year), 105 teaching assistantships with full tuition reimbursements (averaging $5,130 per year) were awarded. Career-related internships or fieldwork, Federal Work-Study, institutionally sponsored loans, and scholarships/grants also available. Support available to part-time students. Financial award application deadline: 4/30; financial award applicants required to submit FAFSA. In 2001, 313 master's, 14 doctorates awarded. *Degree program information:* Part-time and evening/weekend programs available. Offers computer science (MS, PhD); electrical engineering (MSEE, PhD); engineering and computer science (MS, MSEE, MSTE, PhD); microelectronics (MSEE); telecommunications (MSEE, MSTE). *Application deadline:* For fall admission, 7/15; for spring admission, 11/15. Applications are processed on a rolling basis. *Application fee:* $25 ($75 for international students). Electronic applications accepted. *Application Contact:* Sheila R. Fleming, Student Development Specialist for Engineering and Computer Science, 972-883-4155, Fax: 972-883-2813, E-mail: fleming@utdallas.edu. *Dean,* Dr. William P. Osborne, 972-883-2974, Fax: 972-883-2813, E-mail: wosborne@utdallas.edu.

School of Arts and Humanities Students: 85 full-time (48 women), 127 part-time (94 women); includes 22 minority (3 African Americans, 6 Asian Americans or Pacific Islanders, 9 Hispanic Americans, 4 Native Americans), 12 international. Average age 38. 94 applicants, 68% accepted. *Faculty:* 35 full-time (14 women), 7 part-time/adjunct (3 women). Expenses: Contact institution. *Financial support:* In 2001–02, 56 teaching assistantships with tuition reimbursements (averaging $4,934 per year) were awarded; fellowships, research assistantships, Federal Work-Study, institutionally sponsored loans, and scholarships/grants also available. Support available to part-time students. Financial award application deadline: 4/30; financial award applicants required to submit FAFSA. In 2001, 20 master's, 9 doctorates awarded. *Degree program information:* Part-time and evening/weekend programs available. Offers humanities (MA, MAT, PhD). *Application deadline:* For fall admission, 7/15; for spring admission, 11/15. Applications are processed on a rolling basis. *Application fee:* $25 ($75 for international students). Electronic applications accepted. *Application Contact:* Sherry Clarkson, Administrative Assistant, 972-883-2756, Fax: 972-883-2989, E-mail: ah-grad-info@utdallas.edu. *Dean,* Dr. Dennis M. Kratz, 972-883-2984, Fax: 972-883-2989, E-mail: dkratz@utdallas.edu.

School of General Studies Students: 5 full-time (all women), 25 part-time (18 women); includes 12 minority (5 African Americans, 2 Asian Americans or Pacific Islanders, 4 Hispanic Americans, 1 Native American), 2 international. Average age 36. 20 applicants, 70% accepted. *Faculty:* 4 full-time (3 women), 1 (woman) part-time/adjunct. Expenses: Contact institution. *Financial support:* In 2001–02, 1 teaching assistantship with tuition reimbursement (averaging $2,361 per year) was awarded; fellowships, research assistantships, career-related internships or fieldwork, Federal Work-Study, institutionally sponsored loans, and scholarships/grants also available. Support available to part-time students. Financial award application deadline: 4/30; financial award applicants required to submit FAFSA. In 2001, 13 degrees awarded. *Degree program information:* Part-time and evening/weekend programs available. Offers interdisciplinary studies (MA). *Application deadline:* For fall admission, 7/15; for spring admission, 11/15. Applications are processed on a rolling basis. *Application fee:* $25 ($75 for international students). Electronic applications accepted. *Application Contact:* Sandy Bowen, Administrative Assistant, 972-883-2350, Fax: 972-883-2440, E-mail: gs-grad-info@utdallas.edu. *Dean,* Dr. George Fair, 972-883-2323, Fax: 972-883-2440, E-mail: gwfair@utdallas.edu.

School of Human Development Students: 208 full-time (189 women), 53 part-time (42 women); includes 49 minority (11 African Americans, 21 Asian Americans or Pacific Islanders, 17 Hispanic Americans), 27 international. Average age 28. 284 applicants, 31% accepted. *Faculty:* 30 full-time (15 women), 10 part-time/adjunct (6 women). Expenses: Contact institution. *Financial support:* In 2001–02, 20 research assistantships with tuition reimbursements (averaging $5,283 per year), 55 teaching assistantships with tuition reimbursements (averaging $3,780 per year) were awarded. Fellowships, career-related internships or fieldwork, Federal Work-Study, institutionally sponsored loans, and scholarships/grants also available. Support available to part-time students. Financial award application deadline: 4/30; financial award applicants required to submit FAFSA. In 2001, 98 master's, 6 doctorates awarded. *Degree program information:* Part-time and evening/weekend programs available. Offers applied cognition and neuroscience (MS); audiology (Au D); communications disorders (MS); human development (MS, Au D, PhD); human development and communication sciences (PhD); human development and early childhood disorders (MS). *Application deadline:* For fall admission, 7/15; for spring admission, 11/15. Applications are processed on a rolling basis. *Application fee:* $25 ($75 for international students). Electronic applications accepted. *Application Contact:* Dr. Robert D. Stillman, Head, 972-883-3106, Fax: 972-883-3022, E-mail: stillman@utdallas.edu. *Dean,* Dr. Bert Moore, 972-883-2357, Fax: 972-883-2491, E-mail: bmoore@utdallas.edu.

School of Management Students: 493 full-time (208 women), 857 part-time (369 women); includes 267 minority (40 African Americans, 178 Asian Americans or Pacific Islanders, 45 Hispanic Americans, 4 Native Americans), 450 international. Average age 31. 967 applicants, 40% accepted. *Faculty:* 57 full-time (5 women), 9 part-time/adjunct (2 women). Expenses: Contact institution. *Financial support:* In 2001–02, 3 research assistantships with tuition reimbursements (averaging $6,875 per year), 120 teaching assistantships with tuition reimbursements (averaging $5,034 per year) were awarded. Fellowships, career-related internships or fieldwork, Federal Work-Study, institutionally sponsored loans, and scholarships/grants also available. Support available to part-time students. Financial award application deadline: 4/30; financial award applicants required to submit FAFSA. In 2001, 604 master's, 3 doctorates awarded. *Degree program information:* Part-time and evening/weekend programs available. Postbaccalaureate distance learning degree programs offered. Offers accounting (MS); business administration (EMBA, MBA); international management studies (MA, PhD); management (EMBA, MA, MBA, MS, PhD); management and administrative sciences (MS); management science (PhD). *Application deadline:* For fall admission, 7/15; for spring admission, 11/15. Applications are processed on a rolling basis. *Application fee:* $25 ($72 for international students). Electronic applications accepted. *Application Contact:* David B. Ritchey, Director of Advising, 972-883-2701, Fax: 972-883-6425, E-mail: davidr@utdallas.edu. *Dean,* Dr. Hasan Pirkul, 972-883-2705, Fax: 972-883-2799, E-mail: hpirkul@utdallas.edu.

School of Natural Sciences and Mathematics Students: 178 full-time (33 women), 83 part-time (64 women); includes 37 minority (7 African Americans, 17 Asian Americans or Pacific Islanders, 12 Hispanic Americans, 1 Native American), 111 international. Average age 31. 394 applicants, 52% accepted. *Faculty:* 74 full-time (7 women), 9 part-time/adjunct (0 women). Expenses: Contact institution. *Financial support:* In 2001–02, 2 fellowships, 64 research assistantships with tuition reimbursements (averaging $5,670 per year), 79 teaching assistantships with tuition reimbursements (averaging $2,615 per year) were awarded. Career-related internships or fieldwork, Federal Work-Study, institutionally sponsored loans, scholarships/grants, and unspecified assistantships also available. Support available to part-time students. Financial award application deadline: 4/30. In 2001, 49 master's, 25 doctorates awarded. *Degree program information:* Part-time and evening/weekend programs available. Offers applied mathematics (MS, PhD); biology (MS, PhD); chemistry (MS); engineering mathematics (MS); geosciences (MS, PhD); industrial chemistry (D Chem); mathematical science (MS, PhD); mathematics education (MAT); molecular and cell biology (MS, PhD); natural sciences and mathematics (MAT, MS, D Chem, PhD); physics (MS, PhD); science education (MAT); statistics (MS, PhD). *Application deadline:* For fall admission, 7/15; for spring admission, 11/15. Applications are processed on a rolling basis. *Application fee:* $25 ($75 for international students). Electronic applications accepted. *Dean,* Dr. Richard Caldwell, 972-883-2516, Fax: 972-883-6371, E-mail: caldwell@utdallas.edu.

School of Social Sciences Students: 61 full-time (32 women), 104 part-time (40 women); includes 43 minority (24 African Americans, 11 Asian Americans or Pacific Islanders, 7 Hispanic Americans, 1 Native American), 28 international. Average age 36. 119 applicants, 65% accepted. *Faculty:* 34 full-time (8 women), 2 part-time/adjunct (1 woman). Expenses: Contact institution. *Financial support:* In 2001–02, 3 fellowships, 11 research assistantships with tuition reimbursements (averaging $4,946 per year), 28 teaching assistantships with tuition reimbursements (averaging $5,017 per year) were awarded. Career-related internships or fieldwork, Federal Work-Study, institutionally sponsored loans, and scholarships/grants also available. Support available to part-time students. Financial award application deadline: 4/30; financial award applicants required to submit FAFSA. In 2001, 38 master's, 9 doctorates awarded. *Degree program information:* Part-time and evening/weekend programs available. Offers applied economics (MS); applied sociology (MA, MS); geographic information sciences (MS); political economy (PhD); public affairs (MPA); social sciences (MA, MPA, MS, PhD). *Application deadline:* For fall admission, 7/15; for spring admission, 11/15. Applications are processed on a rolling basis. *Application fee:* $25 ($75 for international students). Electronic applications accepted. *Application Contact:* Dr. Ewel Elliot, Director of Graduate Studies, 972-883-2066, Fax: 972-883-2735, E-mail: eelliott@utdallas.edu. *Dean,* Dr. James Murdoch, 972-883-2280, Fax: 972-883-2735, E-mail: murdoch@utdallas.edu.

THE UNIVERSITY OF TEXAS AT EL PASO, El Paso, TX 79968-0001

General Information State-supported, coed, university. CGS member. *Enrollment:* 916 full-time matriculated graduate/professional students, 1,662 part-time matriculated graduate/professional students. *Enrollment by degree level:* 2,091 master's, 212 doctoral, 275 other advanced degrees. *Graduate faculty:* 673 full-time, 250 part-time/adjunct. Tuition, state resident: full-time $2,450. Tuition, nonresident: full-time $6,000. *Graduate housing:* Room and/or apartments available on a first-come, first-served basis to single students; on-campus housing not available to married students. Housing application deadline: 5/1. *Student services:* Campus employment opportunities, career counseling, child daycare facilities, disabled student services, exercise/wellness program, free psychological counseling, grant writing training, international student services, low-cost health insurance, teacher training, writing training. *Library facilities:* University Library. *Collection:* 961,247 titles, 3,005 serial subscriptions.

Computer facilities: A campuswide network can be accessed from student residence rooms and from off campus. *Web address:* http://www.utep.edu/.

General Application Contact: Dr. Charles H. Ambler, Dean of the Graduate School, 915-747-5491 Ext. 7886, Fax: 915-747-5788, E-mail: cambler@utep.edu.

GRADUATE UNITS

Graduate School Students: 916 full-time, 1,662 part-time; includes 1,466 minority (61 African Americans, 48 Asian Americans or Pacific Islanders, 1,349 Hispanic Americans, 8 Native Americans), 244 international. Average age 36. *Faculty:* 673 full-time, 250 part-time/adjunct. Expenses: Contact institution. *Financial support:* In 2001–02, 365 students received support; fellowships with partial tuition reimbursements available, research assistantships with partial tuition reimbursements available, teaching assistantships with partial tuition reimbursements available, career-related internships or fieldwork, Federal Work-Study, institutionally sponsored loans, and tuition waivers (full and partial) available. Support available to part-time students. Financial award application deadline: 3/15; financial award applicants required to submit FAFSA. In 2001, 438 master's, 28 doctorates awarded. *Degree program information:* Part-time and evening/weekend programs available. Postbaccalaureate distance learning degree

The University of Texas at El Paso (continued)

programs offered. Offers art (MA); border history (MA); clinical psychology (MA); communication (MA); creative writing in English (MFA); creative writing in Spanish (MFA); English and American literature (MA); environmental science and engineering (PhD); experimental psychology (MA); history (MA, PhD); liberal arts (MA, MAIS, MAT, MFA, MM, MPA, PhD); linguistics (MA); materials science and engineering (PhD); music education (MM); music performance (MM); political science (MA, MPA); professional writing and rhetoric (MA); psychology (PhD); sociology (MA); Spanish (MA); teaching English (MAT); theatre arts (MA). *Application deadline:* For fall admission, 7/1 (priority date); for spring admission, 11/1 (priority date). Applications are processed on a rolling basis. *Application fee:* $15 ($65 for international students). Electronic applications accepted. *Application Contact:* Information Contact, 915-747-5491, Fax: 915-747-5788, E-mail: gradschool@utep.edu. *Dean of the Graduate School,* Dr. Charles H. Ambler, 915-747-5491 Ext. 7886, Fax: 915-747-5788, E-mail: cambler@utep.edu.

College of Business Administration Students: 304 (124 women); includes 183 minority (7 African Americans, 14 Asian Americans or Pacific Islanders, 162 Hispanic Americans) 49 international. Average age 30. 74 applicants, 95% accepted. Expenses: Contact institution. *Financial support:* In 2001–02, research assistantships with partial tuition reimbursements (averaging $18,750 per year), teaching assistantships with partial tuition reimbursements (averaging $15,000 per year) were awarded. Fellowships with partial tuition reimbursements, career-related internships or fieldwork, Federal Work-Study, institutionally sponsored loans, scholarships/grants, and tuition waivers (partial) also available. Support available to part-time students. Financial award application deadline: 3/15; financial award applicants required to submit FAFSA. In 2001, 48 degrees awarded. *Degree program information:* Part-time and evening/weekend programs available. Postbaccalaureate distance learning degree programs offered. Offers accounting (MACY); business administration (MACY, MBA, MS); economics and finance (MS). *Application deadline:* For spring admission, 11/1 (priority date). Applications are processed on a rolling basis. *Application fee:* $15 ($65 for international students). Electronic applications accepted. *Application Contact:* Dr. Charles H. Ambler, Dean of the Graduate School, 915-747-5491 Ext. 7886, Fax: 915-747-5788, E-mail: cambler@utep.edu. *Dean,* Dr. Charles Crespy, 915-747-5241, Fax: 915-747-5147.

College of Education Students: 560 (446 women); includes 432 minority (15 African Americans, 5 Asian Americans or Pacific Islanders, 410 Hispanic Americans, 2 Native Americans) 5 international. Average age 34. 72 applicants, 94% accepted. Expenses: Contact institution. *Financial support:* In 2001–02, research assistantships with partial tuition reimbursements (averaging $16,642 per year), teaching assistantships with partial tuition reimbursements (averaging $13,314 per year) were awarded. Fellowships, career-related internships or fieldwork, Federal Work-Study, institutionally sponsored loans, scholarships/grants, tuition waivers (partial), and unspecified assistantships also available. Financial award application deadline: 3/15; financial award applicants required to submit FAFSA. In 2001, 124 degrees awarded. *Degree program information:* Part-time and evening/weekend programs available. Offers education (M Ed, MA, Ed D); educational leadership and foundations (M Ed, MA, Ed D); educational psychology and special services (M Ed, MA); teacher education (M Ed, MA). *Application deadline:* For spring admission, 11/1 (priority date). Applications are processed on a rolling basis. *Application fee:* $15 ($65 for international students). Electronic applications accepted. *Application Contact:* Dr. Charles H. Ambler, Dean of the Graduate School, 915-747-5491 Ext. 7886, Fax: 915-747-5788, E-mail: cambler@miners.utep.edu. *Dean,* Dr. Arturo Pacheco, 915-747-5572, Fax: 915-747-5755, E-mail: apacheco@miners.utep.edu.

College of Engineering Students: 382 (87 women); includes 115 minority (3 African Americans, 5 Asian Americans or Pacific Islanders, 107 Hispanic Americans) 102 international. Average age 28. Expenses: Contact institution. *Financial support:* In 2001–02, research assistantships with partial tuition reimbursements (averaging $21,125 per year), teaching assistantships with partial tuition reimbursements (averaging $16,900 per year) were awarded. Fellowships with partial tuition reimbursements, career-related internships or fieldwork, Federal Work-Study, institutionally sponsored loans, scholarships/grants, and tuition waivers (partial) also available. Financial award application deadline: 3/15; financial award applicants required to submit FAFSA. In 2001, 78 degrees awarded. *Degree program information:* Part-time and evening/weekend programs available. Offers civil engineering (MS); computer engineering (MS, PhD); computer science (PhD); electrical engineering (MS, PhD); engineering (MEENE, MIT, MS, MSENE, PhD); environmental engineering (MEENE, MSENE); industrial engineering (MS); manufacturing engineering (MS); mechanical engineering (MS); metallurgical engineering (MS). *Application deadline:* For fall admission, 7/1 (priority date); for spring admission, 11/1 (priority date). Applications are processed on a rolling basis. *Application fee:* $15 ($65 for international students). Electronic applications accepted. *Application Contact:* Dr. Charles H. Ambler, Dean of the Graduate School, 915-747-5491 Ext. 7886, Fax: 915-747-5788, E-mail: cambler@miners.utep.edu. *Dean,* Dr. Andrew H. Swift, 915-747-5460.

College of Health Sciences Students: 207 (152 women); includes 117 minority (3 African Americans, 4 Asian Americans or Pacific Islanders, 107 Hispanic Americans, 3 Native Americans) 1 international. Average age 34. 47 applicants, 98% accepted. Expenses: Contact institution. *Financial support:* In 2001–02, research assistantships with partial tuition reimbursements (averaging $18,825 per year), teaching assistantships with partial tuition reimbursements (averaging $18,000 per year) were awarded. Career-related internships or fieldwork, Federal Work-Study, institutionally sponsored loans, scholarships/grants, and tuition waivers (partial) also available. Support available to part-time students. Financial award application deadline: 3/15; financial award applicants required to submit FAFSA. In 2001, 68 degrees awarded. *Degree program information:* Part-time and evening/weekend programs available. Postbaccalaureate distance learning degree programs offered. Offers adult health (MSN); allied health (MPT, MS); community health (MSN); community health/family nurse practitioner (MSN); health and physical education (MS); health sciences (MPT, MS, MSN); kinesiology and sports studies (MS); nurse midwifery (MSN); nursing administration (MSN); parent-child nursing (MSN); physical therapy (MPT); psychiatric/mental health nursing (MSN); speech language pathology (MS); women's health care/nurse practitioner (MSN). *Application deadline:* For spring admission, 11/1 (priority date). Applications are processed on a rolling basis. *Application fee:* $15 ($65 for international students). Electronic applications accepted. *Application Contact:* Dr. Charles H. Ambler, Dean of the Graduate School, 915-747-5491 Ext. 7886, Fax: 915-747-5788, E-mail: cambler@utep.edu. *Dean,* Dr. John Conway, 915-747-7280, Fax: 915-747-7207, E-mail: jconway@utep.edu.

College of Science Students: 151 (61 women); includes 60 minority (2 African Americans, 1 Asian American or Pacific Islander, 57 Hispanic Americans) 31 international. Average age 34. Expenses: Contact institution. *Financial support:* In 2001–02, research assistantships with partial tuition reimbursements (averaging $21,812 per year), teaching assistantships with partial tuition reimbursements (averaging $17,450 per year) were awarded. Fellowships with partial tuition reimbursements, career-related internships or fieldwork, Federal Work-Study, institutionally sponsored loans, scholarships/grants, and tuition waivers (partial) also available. Support available to part-time students. Financial award application deadline: 3/15; financial award applicants required to submit FAFSA. In 2001, 28 degrees awarded. *Degree program information:* Part-time and evening/weekend programs available. Offers bioinformatics (MS); Biological Science (PhD); biological Science (MS); chemistry (MS); Environmental Science and Engineering (PhD); geological sciences (MS, PhD); geophysics (MS); interdisciplinary studies (MSIS); mathematical sciences (MAT, MS); physics (MS); science (MAT, MS, MSIS, PhD); statistics (MS). *Application deadline:* For fall admission, 7/1; for spring admission, 11/1. Applications are processed on a rolling basis. *Application fee:* $15 ($65 for international students). Electronic applications accepted. *Application Contact:* Dr. Charles H. Ambler, Dean of the Graduate School, 915-747-5491 Ext. 7886, Fax: 915-747-5788, E-mail: cambler@utep.edu. *Dean,* Dr. Thomas E. Brady, 915-747-5536, Fax: 915-747-6807, E-mail: tbrady@miners.utep.edu.

See in-depth description on page 1267.

THE UNIVERSITY OF TEXAS AT SAN ANTONIO, San Antonio, TX 78249-0617

General Information State-supported, coed, university. CGS member. *Enrollment:* 702 full-time matriculated graduate/professional students (323 women), 1,586 part-time matriculated graduate/professional students (1,002 women). *Enrollment by degree level:* 2,200 master's, 88 doctoral. *Graduate faculty:* 238 full-time (67 women), 70 part-time/adjunct (21 women). Tuition, state resident: full-time $2,268; part-time $126 per credit hour. Tuition, nonresident: full-time $6,066; part-time $337 per credit hour. *Required fees:* $781. Tuition and fees vary according to course load. *Graduate housing:* Rooms and/or apartments available on a first-come, first-served basis to single and married students. Typical cost: $8,151 (including board) for single students; $8,151 (including board) for married students. *Student services:* Campus employment opportunities, career counseling, disabled student services, exercise/wellness program, free psychological counseling, international student services, low-cost health insurance, multicultural affairs office. *Library facilities:* John Peace Library plus 1 other. *Online resources:* library catalog, web page. *Collection:* 521,009 titles, 2,665 serial subscriptions, 24,752 audiovisual materials. *Research affiliation:* Southwest Research Center (engineering).

Computer facilities: 800 computers available on campus for general student use. A campuswide network can be accessed from student residence rooms and from off campus. Internet access and online class registration are available. *Web address:* http://www.utsa.edu/.

General Application Contact: George E. Norton, Associate Vice President, 210-458-4530, Fax: 210-458-7716.

GRADUATE UNITS

College of Business Students: 229 full-time (79 women), 325 part-time (136 women); includes 144 minority (12 African Americans, 15 Asian Americans or Pacific Islanders, 114 Hispanic Americans, 3 Native Americans), 71 international. Average age 32. 417 applicants, 72% accepted, 231 enrolled. *Faculty:* 37 full-time (7 women), 16 part-time/adjunct (1 woman). Expenses: Contact institution. *Financial support:* Career-related internships or fieldwork and Federal Work-Study available. Support available to part-time students. Financial award application deadline: 3/31. In 2001, 161 degrees awarded. *Degree program information:* Part-time and evening/weekend programs available. Offers accounting (MP Acct, MS); business (MA, MBA, MP Acct, MS, MSIT, MSMOT, MT); business economics (MBA); economics (MA); finance (MBA, MS); information systems (MSIT); management (MSMOT); management science and statistics (MBA); public management (MP Acct); taxation (MT). *Application deadline:* For fall admission, 7/1. Applications are processed on a rolling basis. *Application fee:* $25. *Application Contact:* George E. Norton, Associate Vice President, 210-458-4530, Fax: 210-458-7716. *Dean,* Dr. Bruce O. Bublitz, 210-458-4313.

College of Education and Human Development Students: 160 full-time (119 women), 770 part-time (621 women); includes 479 minority (48 African Americans, 19 Asian Americans or Pacific Islanders, 407 Hispanic Americans, 5 Native Americans), 18 international. Average age 34. 539 applicants, 91% accepted, 123 enrolled. *Faculty:* 42 full-time (22 women), 29 part-time/adjunct (15 women). Expenses: Contact institution. *Financial support:* Research assistantships, career-related internships or fieldwork and Federal Work-Study available. In 2001, 242 degrees awarded. Offers bicultural studies (MA); bicultural-bilingual studies (MA); counseling (MA); culture and languages (PhD); curriculum and instruction (MA); early childhood and elementary education (MA); education and human development (MA, Ed D, PhD); education-adult and higher education (MA); educational leadership and policy studies (MA, Ed D); educational psychology/special education (MA); reading and literacy (MA); teaching English as a second language (MA). *Application deadline:* For fall admission, 7/1. Applications are processed on a rolling basis. *Application fee:* $25. *Dean,* Dr. Blandina Cardenas, 210-458-4370, Fax: 210-458-4487.

College of Engineering Students: 53 full-time (11 women), 70 part-time (11 women); includes 29 minority (2 African Americans, 6 Asian Americans or Pacific Islanders, 21 Hispanic Americans), 49 international. Average age 29. 98 applicants, 91% accepted, 49 enrolled. *Faculty:* 21 full-time (1 woman), 4 part-time/adjunct (0 women). Expenses: Contact institution. *Financial support:* Research assistantships, teaching assistantships, career-related internships or fieldwork, institutionally sponsored loans, and scholarships/grants available. Financial award application deadline: 3/31. In 2001, 22 degrees awarded. *Degree program information:* Part-time and evening/weekend programs available. Offers civil engineering (MSCE); electrical engineering (MSEE); engineering (MSCE, MSEE, MSME); mechanical engineering (MSME). *Application deadline:* For fall admission, 7/1; for spring admission, 12/1. Applications are processed on a rolling basis. *Application fee:* $25. *Dean,* Dr. Zorica Pantic-Tanner, 210-458-5526.

College of Liberal and Fine Arts Students: 81 full-time (37 women), 213 part-time (138 women); includes 101 minority (3 African Americans, 2 Asian Americans or Pacific Islanders, 92 Hispanic Americans, 4 Native Americans), 9 international. Average age 33. 164 applicants, 81% accepted, 105 enrolled. *Faculty:* 75 full-time (29 women), 5 part-time/adjunct (1 woman). Expenses: Contact institution. *Financial support:* Fellowships, research assistantships, teaching assistantships, career-related internships or fieldwork, Federal Work-Study, institutionally sponsored loans, and tuition waivers (partial) available. Support available to part-time students. In 2001, 65 degrees awarded. *Degree program information:* Part-time and evening/weekend programs available. Offers anthropology (MA); architecture (M Arch); art and art history (MA, MFA); English (MA); history (MA); liberal and fine arts (M Arch, MA, MFA, MM, MS); music (MM); political science (MA); psychology (MS); sociology (MS); Spanish (MA). *Application deadline:* For fall admission, 7/1; for spring admission, 12/1. Applications are processed on a rolling basis. *Application fee:* $25. *Dean,* Dr. Alan E. Craven, 210-458-4350, Fax: 210-458-4347.

College of Public Policy Students: 8 full-time (4 women), 77 part-time (36 women); includes 40 minority (2 African Americans, 2 Asian Americans or Pacific Islanders, 36 Hispanic Americans) Average age 33. 47 applicants, 70% accepted, 27 enrolled. *Faculty:* 9 full-time (2 women), 1 part-time/adjunct (0 women). Expenses: Contact institution. *Financial support:* Research assistantships, career-related internships or fieldwork and Federal Work-Study available. In 2001, 14 degrees awarded. Offers justice policy (MS); public administration (MPA); public policy (MPA, MS). *Application deadline:* For fall admission, 7/1. Applications are processed on a rolling basis. *Application fee:* $25. *Vice Provost Downtown,* Dr. Jesse T. Zapata, 210-458-2700, Fax: 210-458-2424.

College of Sciences Students: 171 full-time (73 women), 131 part-time (60 women); includes 89 minority (3 African Americans, 9 Asian Americans or Pacific Islanders, 73 Hispanic Americans, 4 Native Americans), 84 international. Average age 31. 267 applicants, 79% accepted, 139 enrolled. *Faculty:* 54 full-time (6 women), 15 part-time/adjunct (4 women). Expenses: Contact institution. *Financial support:* Fellowships, research assistantships, teaching assistantships, career-related internships or fieldwork, Federal Work-Study, and institutionally sponsored loans available. Support available to part-time students. In 2001, 66 master's, 4 doctorates awarded. *Degree program information:* Part-time and evening/weekend programs available. Offers biology (MS, PhD); biology and biotechnology (MS); biotechnology (MS); chemistry (MS); computer science (MS, PhD); environmental sciences (MS); geology (MS); mathematics (MS); neurobiology (PhD); sciences (MS, PhD). *Application deadline:* For fall admission, 7/1. Applications are processed on a rolling basis. *Application fee:* $25. *Dean,* Dr. William H. Scouten, 210-458-4450.

THE UNIVERSITY OF TEXAS AT TYLER, Tyler, TX 75799-0001

General Information State-supported, coed, comprehensive institution. *Enrollment:* 142 full-time matriculated graduate/professional students (93 women), 447 part-time matriculated graduate/professional students (313 women). *Enrollment by degree level:* 589 master's. *Graduate faculty:* 136 full-time (53 women), 19 part-time/adjunct (10 women). Tuition, state resident: part-time $44 per credit hour. Tuition, nonresident: part-time $262 per credit hour. *Required fees:* $58 per credit hour. $76 per semester. *Graduate housing:* On-campus housing not available. *Student services:* Campus employment opportunities, career counseling, disabled student services, exercise/wellness program, free psychological counseling, writing training. *Library facilities:* Robert Muntz Library. *Online resources:* library catalog, web page. *Collection:* 216,365 titles, 1,534 serial subscriptions, 10,772 audiovisual materials.

Computer facilities: 300 computers available on campus for general student use. A campuswide network can be accessed from student residence rooms and from off campus. Internet access is available. *Web address:* http://www.uttyler.edu/.

General Application Contact: Carol A. Hodge, Office of Graduate Studies, 903-566-5642, Fax: 903-566-7068, E-mail: chodge@mail.uttly.edu.

GRADUATE UNITS

Graduate Studies Students: 142 full-time (93 women), 447 part-time (313 women); includes 94 minority (55 African Americans, 14 Asian Americans or Pacific Islanders, 18 Hispanic Americans, 7 Native Americans), 12 international. *Faculty:* 136 full-time (53 women), 19 part-time/adjunct (10 women). Expenses: Contact institution. *Financial support:* Fellowships, research assistantships, teaching assistantships, career-related internships or fieldwork, Federal Work-Study, institutionally sponsored loans, and scholarships/grants available. Support available to part-time students. Financial award applicants required to submit FAFSA. In 2001, 139 degrees awarded. *Degree program information:* Part-time and evening/weekend programs available. Postbaccalaureate distance learning degree programs offered (minimal on-campus study). Offers allied health/interdisciplinary studies (MSIS); clinical exercise physiology (MS); computer information systems (MAT); computer science (MS); engineering (M Engr); engineering and computer science (M Engr, MAIS, MAT, MS, MSIS); health and kinesiology (M Ed); interdisciplinary studies (MAIS, MSIS); kinesiology (MS); kinesiology/interdisciplinary studies (MSIS); nurse practitioner (MSN); nursing and health sciences (M Ed, MS, MSIS, MSN). *Application deadline:* For fall admission, 5/31; for spring admission, 10/31. Applications are processed on a rolling basis. *Application fee:* $0 ($50 for international students). Electronic applications accepted. *Application Contact:* Carol A. Hodge, Office of Graduate Studies, 903-566-5642, Fax: 903-566-7068, E-mail: chodge@mail.uttly.edu. *Graduate Coordinator,* 903-566-7402.

College of Arts and Sciences Students: 35 full-time (20 women), 114 part-time (78 women); includes 28 minority (22 African Americans, 4 Hispanic Americans, 2 Native Americans), 2 international. Average age 36. 23 applicants, 100% accepted. *Faculty:* 60 full-time (14 women), 10 part-time/adjunct (4 women). Expenses: Contact institution. *Financial support:* Teaching assistantships, Federal Work-Study available. Support available to part-time students. Financial award application deadline: 7/1; financial award applicants required to submit FAFSA. In 2001, 23 degrees awarded. *Degree program information:* Part-time and evening/weekend programs available. Postbaccalaureate distance learning degree programs offered. Offers art (MA, MAIS, MAT, MFA); arts and sciences (MA, MAIS, MAT, MFA, MPA, MS, MSIS); biology (MAT, MS); communication (MAT); criminal justice (MAIS, MS); economics (MAIS); English (MA, MAT); history (MA, MAT); interdisciplinary studies (MA, MAIS, MS, MSIS); mathematics (MAIS, MAT, MS); music (MAIS, MAT); political science (MA, MAIS, MAT); public administration (MPA); sociology (MAIS, MAT, MS). *Application deadline:* Applications are processed on a rolling basis. *Application fee:* $0. Electronic applications accepted. *Application Contact:* Carol A. Hodge, Office of Graduate Studies, 903-566-5642, Fax: 903-566-7068, E-mail: chodge@mail.uttly.edu. *Dean,* Dr. Donna Dickerson, 903-566-7397, Fax: 903-566-7377, E-mail: ddickers@mail.uttyl.edu.

College of Business and Technology Students: 177 (86 women); includes 33 minority (12 African Americans, 5 Asian Americans or Pacific Islanders, 15 Hispanic Americans, 1 Native American) 4 international. Average age 30. 87 applicants, 68% accepted. *Faculty:* 17 full-time (6 women), 3 part-time/adjunct (1 woman). Expenses: Contact institution. *Financial support:* Research assistantships, career-related internships or fieldwork available. Financial award application deadline: 7/1. In 2001, 24 degrees awarded. *Degree program information:* Part-time and evening/weekend programs available. Postbaccalaureate distance learning degree programs offered (no on-campus study). Offers business administration (MBA); general management (MBA); health care track (MBA); technology (MS). *Application fee:* $0 ($50 for international students). *Application Contact:* Dr. Mary Fischer, CBA Coordinator of Graduate Studies, 903-566-7433, Fax: 903-566-7372, E-mail: mfischer@mail.uttyl.edu. *Dean,* Dr. Jim Tarter, 903-566-7360.

College of Education and Psychology Students: 35 full-time (30 women), 203 part-time (162 women); includes 27 minority (15 African Americans, 2 Asian Americans or Pacific Islanders, 7 Hispanic Americans, 3 Native Americans), 3 international. Average age 35. *Faculty:* 36 full-time (20 women), 5 part-time/adjunct (4 women). Expenses: Contact institution. *Financial support:* Teaching assistantships, career-related internships or fieldwork, Federal Work-Study, institutionally sponsored loans, and scholarships/grants available. Support available to part-time students. Financial award application deadline: 4/1; financial award applicants required to submit FAFSA. In 2001, 73 degrees awarded. *Degree program information:* Part-time and evening/weekend programs available. Offers art (MAT); biology (MAT); clinical psychology (MS); computer information systems (MAT); counseling psychology (MA); curriculum and instruction (M Ed); early childhood education (M Ed, MA); education and psychology (M Ed, MA, MAT, MS, MSIS, Certificate); educational administration (M Ed); English (MAT); history (MAT); interdisciplinary studies (MS, MSIS); journalism (MAT); mathematics (MAT); music (MAT); political science (MAT); reading (M Ed, MA, Certificate); school counseling (MA); school principal (Certificate); school superintendent (Certificate); secondary teaching (MAT); sociology (MAT); special education (M Ed, MA, Certificate); speech communication (MAT); theatre (MAT). *Application fee:* $0 ($50 for international students). *Application Contact:* Jim Hutto, Dean of Enrollment Management, 903-566-8204, Fax: 903-566-7068. *Dean,* Dr. J. Milford Clark, 903-566-7050, Fax: 903-566-7036, E-mail: mclark@mail.uttyl.edu.

College of Sciences and Mathematics Students: 16 full-time (6 women), 21 part-time (9 women); includes 7 minority (4 African Americans, 3 Asian Americans or Pacific Islanders), 8 international. Average age 31. 20 applicants, 100% accepted. *Faculty:* 19 full-time (1 woman). Expenses: Contact institution. *Financial support:* In 2001–02, 3 research assistantships (averaging $6,000 per year), 4 teaching assistantships (averaging $6,000 per year) were awarded. Financial award application deadline: 7/1; financial award applicants required to submit FAFSA. In 2001, 8 degrees awarded. *Degree program information:* Part-time programs available. Offers sciences and mathematics (MA, MS). *Application deadline:* Applications are processed on a rolling basis. *Application fee:* $0. *Application Contact:* Carol A. Hodge, Office of Graduate Studies, 903-566-5642, Fax: 903-566-7068, E-mail: chodge@mail.uttly.edu. *Dean,* Dr. L. Lynn Sherrod, 903-566-7400, Fax: 903-566-7189, E-mail: lsherrod@mail.uttyl.edu.

THE UNIVERSITY OF TEXAS HEALTH SCIENCE CENTER AT HOUSTON, Houston, TX 77225-0036

General Information State-supported, coed, upper-level institution. CGS member. *Enrollment:* 3,025 matriculated graduate/professional students. *Graduate faculty:* 782 full-time (288 women), 238 part-time/adjunct (113 women). Tuition, state resident: full-time $2,736; part-time $76 per credit hour. Tuition, nonresident: full-time $10,584; part-time $294 per credit hour. *Required fees:* $642. *Graduate housing:* Rooms and/or apartments available on a first-come, first-served basis to single and married students. *Student services:* Campus safety program, career counseling, child daycare facilities, free psychological counseling, international student services, low-cost health insurance. *Library facilities:* Houston Academy of Medicine-Texas Medical Center Library plus 3 others. *Online resources:* library catalog, web page, access to other libraries' catalogs. *Collection:* 270,649 titles, 2,778 serial subscriptions.

Computer facilities: A campuswide network can be accessed from off campus. Internet access and online class registration are available. *Web address:* http://www.uth.tmc.edu/.

General Application Contact: Lois B. Monroe, Registrar, 713-500-3334, Fax: 713-500-3356, E-mail: uthschro@admin4.hsc.uth.tmc.edu.

GRADUATE UNITS

Dental Branch Students: 255 full-time (120 women); includes 106 minority (10 African Americans, 76 Asian Americans or Pacific Islanders, 19 Hispanic Americans, 1 Native American) Average age 26. 684 applicants, 10% accepted, 65 enrolled. Expenses: Contact institution. *Financial support:* In 2001–02, 15 students received support. Institutionally sponsored loans and scholarships/grants available. Financial award applicants required to submit FAFSA. In 2001, 56 degrees awarded. Offers dentistry (DDS). *Application deadline:* For fall admission, 11/1. Applications are processed on a rolling basis. *Application fee:* $80. Electronic applications accepted. *Application Contact:* Dr. H. Philip Pierpont, Associate Dean for Student Affairs, 713-500-4151, Fax: 713-500-4425, E-mail: studentaffairs@mail.db.uth.tmc.edu. *Dean,* Dr. Ronald Johnson, 713-500-4151, Fax: 713-500-4425.

Graduate School of Biomedical Sciences Students: 444 full-time (227 women); includes 92 minority (13 African Americans, 46 Asian Americans or Pacific Islanders, 31 Hispanic Americans, 2 Native Americans), 124 international. Average age 27. 452 applicants, 42% accepted, 118 enrolled. *Faculty:* 476 full-time (113 women). Expenses: Contact institution. *Financial support:* In 2001–02, 15 fellowships, 357 research assistantships, 10 teaching assistantships were awarded. Institutionally sponsored loans and scholarships/grants also available. Financial award application deadline: 1/15. In 2001, 24 master's, 51 doctorates awarded. Offers biochemistry and molecular biology (MS, PhD); biomedical sciences (MS, PhD); cancer biology (MS, PhD); cell and regulatory biology (MS, PhD); environmental and molecular carcinogenesis (MS, PhD); genes and development (MS, PhD); genetic counseling (MS); human and molecular genetics (MS, PhD); immunology (MS, PhD); medical physics (MS, PhD); microbiology and molecular genetics (MS, PhD); molecular pathology (MS, PhD); neuroscience (MS, PhD); oral biomaterials (MS); pharmacology (MS, PhD); physiology (MS, PhD); reproductive biology (MS, PhD); toxicology (MS, PhD); virology and gene therapy (MS, PhD). *Application deadline:* For fall admission, 1/15 (priority date); for spring admission, 11/1. Applications are processed on a rolling basis. *Application fee:* $10. Electronic applications accepted. *Application Contact:* Dr. Victoria P. Knutson, Assistant Dean of Admissions, 713-500-9860, Fax: 713-500-9877, E-mail: victoria.p.knutson@uth.tmc.edu. *Dean,* Dr. George M. Stancel, 713-500-9880, Fax: 713-500-9877, E-mail: george.m.stancel@uth.tmc.edu.

Studies in Biomathematics and Biostatistics Students: 1 full-time (0 women); minority (Asian American or Pacific Islander) Average age 27. 3 applicants, 67% accepted. *Faculty:* 17 full-time (5 women). Expenses: Contact institution. *Financial support:* Fellowships, research assistantships, institutionally sponsored loans available. Financial award application deadline: 1/15. Offers biomathematics (MS, PhD). *Application deadline:* For fall admission, 1/15 (priority date); for spring admission, 11/1. Applications are processed on a rolling basis. *Application fee:* $10. Electronic applications accepted. *Application Contact:* Dr. Victoria P. Knutson, Assistant Dean of Admissions, 713-500-9860, Fax: 713-500-9877, E-mail: victoria.p.knutson@uth.tmc.edu. *Coordinator,* Dr. Dennis Johnston, 713-792-2617, Fax: 713-792-4262, E-mail: djohnsto@notes.mdacc.tmc.edu.

Medical School Students: 830 full-time (351 women); includes 234 minority (26 African Americans, 104 Asian Americans or Pacific Islanders, 99 Hispanic Americans, 5 Native Americans) Average age 22. 2,602 applicants, 10% accepted, 204 enrolled. *Faculty:* 583 full-time (209 women), 108 part-time/adjunct (46 women). Expenses: Contact institution. *Financial support:* In 2001–02, 730 students received support. Scholarships/grants and health care benefits available. Financial award application deadline: 3/1; financial award applicants required to submit FAFSA. In 2001, 186 degrees awarded. Offers medicine (MD). *Application deadline:* For fall admission, 11/1. *Application fee:* $55 ($100 for international students). Electronic applications accepted. *Application Contact:* Dr. Albert E. Gunn, Associate Dean for Admissions, 713-500-5118, Fax: 713-500-0604, E-mail: albert.e.gunn@uth.tmc.edu. *Dean,* Dr. L. Maximilian Buja, 713-500-5010.

School of Nursing Students: 469 full-time (338 women), 137 part-time (122 women); includes 197 minority (71 African Americans, 62 Asian Americans or Pacific Islanders, 61 Hispanic Americans, 3 Native Americans), 4 international. Average age 33. *Faculty:* 53 full-time (47 women), 41 part-time/adjunct (36 women). Expenses: Contact institution. *Financial support:* In 2001–02, 101 students received support; research assistantships with tuition reimbursements available, teaching assistantships with tuition reimbursements available, institutionally sponsored loans, scholarships/grants, traineeships, and tuition waivers (full) available. Support available to part-time students. *Degree program information:* Part-time programs available. Offers nursing (MSN, DSN). *Application deadline:* For fall admission, 5/1 (priority date). Applications are processed on a rolling basis. *Application fee:* $10. Electronic applications accepted. *Application Contact:* Laurie G. Rutherford, Student Affairs, 713-500-2101, E-mail: laurie.g.rutherford@uth.tmc.edu. *Dean,* Dr. Patricia Starck, 713-500-2100, Fax: 713-500-2107.

School of Public Health Students: 273 full-time (183 women), 617 part-time (436 women); includes 339 minority (77 African Americans, 115 Asian Americans or Pacific Islanders, 143 Hispanic Americans, 4 Native Americans), 108 international. Average age 35. 787 applicants, 44% accepted, 171 enrolled. *Faculty:* 124 full-time (61 women), 9 part-time/adjunct (5 women). Expenses: Contact institution. *Financial support:* In 2001–02, 156 students received support. Traineeships and stipends available. Support available to part-time students. Financial award applicants required to submit FAFSA. In 2001, 115 master's, 32 doctorates awarded. *Degree program information:* Part-time programs available. Postbaccalaureate distance learning degree programs offered (no on-campus study). Offers public health (MPH, MS, Dr PH, PhD). *Application deadline:* For fall admission, 3/1; for spring admission, 9/1. Applications are processed on a rolling basis. *Application fee:* $10. Electronic applications accepted. *Application Contact:* Stephanie M. Tamborello, Office of Student Affairs, 713-500-9030, Fax: 713-500-9068, E-mail: stamborello@sph.uth.tmc.edu. *Dean,* Dr. R. Palmer Beasley, 713-500-9050, Fax: 713-500-9068.

THE UNIVERSITY OF TEXAS HEALTH SCIENCE CENTER AT SAN ANTONIO, San Antonio, TX 78229-3900

General Information State-supported, coed, upper-level institution. CGS member. *Enrollment by degree level:* 1,183 first professional, 147 master's, 235 doctoral, 42 other advanced degrees. *Graduate faculty:* 243 full-time (93 women), 44 part-time/adjunct (11 women). Tuition, state resident: full-time $378; part-time $42 per credit. Tuition, nonresident: full-time $2,358; part-time $262 per credit. *Required fees:* $310 per semester. Tuition and fees vary according to course load. *Graduate housing:* On-campus housing not available. *Student services:* Campus safety program, free psychological counseling, international student services, low-cost health insurance. *Library facilities:* Dolph Briso Library. *Collection:* 192,576 titles, 2,501 serial subscriptions. *Research affiliation:* Veterans Administration Hospital, Southwest Foundation for Research and Education, Southwest Research Institute, University Hospital.

Computer facilities: 1,000 computers available on campus for general student use. A campuswide network can be accessed from off campus. Internet access is available. *Web address:* http://www.uthscsa.edu/.

General Application Contact: James B. Peak, Senior Director of Student Services and Registrar, 210-567-2621, Fax: 210-567-2685, E-mail: peak@uthscsa.edu.

GRADUATE UNITS

Dental School Students: 353; includes 112 minority (6 African Americans, 43 Asian Americans or Pacific Islanders, 60 Hispanic Americans, 3 Native Americans) Average age 24. 594 applicants, 9% accepted. *Faculty:* 117 full-time, 84 part-time/adjunct. Expenses: Contact institution. *Financial support:* In 2001–02, 311 students received support; teaching assistantships, institutionally sponsored loans available. Financial award application deadline: 3/1; financial award applicants required to submit FAFSA. In 2001, 81 first professional degrees, 15 master's, 17 other advanced degrees awarded. Offers dentistry (DDS, MS, Certificate). *Application deadline:* For fall admission, 11/1. *Application fee:* $75. Electronic applications accepted. *Application Contact:* Lisa Serna, Office of Admissions and Student Services, 210-567-2674, E-mail: serna@uthscsa.edu. *Associate Dean for Student Affairs,* Dr. D. Denee Thomas, 210-567-3752, Fax: 210-567-4776, E-mail: thomasd@uthscsa.edu.

Graduate School of Biomedical Sciences Students: 238 full-time (124 women), 150 part-time (117 women); includes 93 minority (16 African Americans, 16 Asian Americans or Pacific Islanders, 60 Hispanic Americans, 1 Native American), 74 international. Average age 31. 465 applicants, 36% accepted, 117 enrolled. *Faculty:* 243 full-time (93 women), 44 part-time/adjunct (11 women). Expenses: Contact institution. *Financial support:* Fellowships, research assistantships, teaching assistantships, career-related internships or fieldwork, Federal Work-Study, institutionally sponsored loans, and tuition waivers (full) available. Support available to part-time students. Financial award applicants required to submit FAFSA. In 2001, 74 master's, 38 doctorates awarded. *Degree program information:* Part-time and evening/weekend

The University of Texas Health Science Center at San Antonio (continued)
programs available. Offers biochemistry (MS, PhD); biomedical sciences (Pharm D, MS, MSN, PhD, Certificate); cellular and structural biology (PhD); microbiology (MS, PhD); molecular medicine (MS, PhD); pharmacology (PhD); physiology (MS, PhD); radiological sciences (MS, PhD). *Application deadline:* For fall admission, 4/1; for spring admission, 9/1. Applications are processed on a rolling basis. *Application Contact:* Dr. Terry M. Mikiten, Associate Dean, 210-567-3711, Fax: 210-567-3719, E-mail: mikiten@uthscsa.edu. *Interim Dean*, Dr. Merle S. Olson, 210-567-3709, Fax: 210-567-3719, E-mail: olsonm@uthscsa.edu.

School of Nursing Students: 35 full-time (28 women), 116 part-time (101 women); includes 40 minority (13 African Americans, 3 Asian Americans or Pacific Islanders, 23 Hispanic Americans, 1 Native American) Average age 41. 66 applicants, 89% accepted, 55 enrolled. *Faculty:* 32 full-time (31 women). Expenses: Contact institution. *Financial support:* Research assistantships, teaching assistantships, institutionally sponsored loans available. Financial award application deadline: 4/1. In 2001, 63 master's, 3 doctorates awarded. *Degree program information:* Part-time and evening/weekend programs available. Offers nursing (MSN, PhD). *Application deadline:* For fall admission, 4/1; for spring admission, 10/1. *Application fee:* $15. *Application Contact:* Dr. Beverly Robinson, Associate Dean, 210-567-5815, Fax: 210-567-3813, E-mail: robinsonb@uthscsa.edu. *Dean*, Dr. Janet Allan, 210-567-5800.

Medical School Offers medicine (MD).

School of Allied Health Sciences Expenses: Contact institution. Offers allied health sciences).

THE UNIVERSITY OF TEXAS MEDICAL BRANCH, Galveston, TX 77555

General Information State-supported, coed, upper-level institution. CGS member. *Enrollment:* 1,244 full-time matriculated graduate/professional students (651 women), 121 part-time matriculated graduate/professional students (90 women). *Enrollment by degree level:* 823 first professional, 328 master's, 214 doctoral. *Graduate faculty:* 256 full-time (63 women), 15 part-time/adjunct (4 women). Tuition, state resident: full-time $1,134; part-time $42 per credit hour. Tuition, nonresident: full-time $6,831; part-time $253 per credit hour. *Required fees:* $473; $8 per credit hour. $71 per term. Tuition and fees vary according to course load. *Graduate housing:* Room and/or apartments available on a first-come, first-served basis to single students; on-campus housing not available to married students. Housing application deadline: 6/1. *Student services:* Campus employment opportunities, campus safety program, career counseling, child daycare facilities, disabled student services, exercise/wellness program, free psychological counseling, international student services, low-cost health insurance, multicultural affairs office. *Library facilities:* Moody Medical Library. *Online resources:* library catalog, web page, access to other libraries' catalogs. *Collection:* 247,096 titles, 1,986 serial subscriptions. *Research affiliation:* Shriners Hospitals (burns and wound healing).

Computer facilities: 160 computers available on campus for general student use. A campuswide network can be accessed from student residence rooms and from off campus. Internet access is available. *Web address:* http://www.utmb.edu/.

General Application Contact: Vicki Brewer, Registrar, 409-772-1215, Fax: 409-772-4466, E-mail: student.admissions@utmb.edu.

GRADUATE UNITS

Graduate School of Biomedical Sciences Students: 231 full-time (124 women), 72 part-time (42 women); includes 59 minority (10 African Americans, 22 Asian Americans or Pacific Islanders, 22 Hispanic Americans, 5 Native Americans), 72 international. Average age 33. 386 applicants, 31% accepted, 77 enrolled. *Faculty:* 307 full-time (79 women). Expenses: Contact institution. *Financial support:* In 2001–02, 71 students received support, including fellowships (averaging $18,000 per year), research assistantships (averaging $18,000 per year), teaching assistantships (averaging $18,000 per year); career-related internships or fieldwork, Federal Work-Study, institutionally sponsored loans, traineeships, and unspecified assistantships also available. Support available to part-time students. Financial award applicants required to submit FAFSA. In 2001, 19 master's, 32 doctorates awarded. *Degree program information:* Part-time programs available. Offers biochemistry (MS, PhD); biomedical sciences (MA, MMS, MS, PhD); cell biology (MS, PhD); cellular physiology and molecular biophysics (MS, PhD); emerging and tropical infectious diseases (PhD); experimental pathology (PhD); genetics (MS, PhD); medical humanities (MA, PhD); medical science (MMS); microbiology and immunology (MS, PhD); molecular biology (PhD); neuroscience (PhD); nursing (PhD); pharmacology (MS, PhD); preventive medicine and community health (MS, PhD); structural biology (PhD); toxicology (PhD). *Application deadline:* Applications are processed on a rolling basis. *Application fee:* $25 ($50 for international students). Electronic applications accepted. *Application Contact:* Robert C. Bennett, Associate Dean for Administration and Student Affairs, 409-772-2665, Fax: 409-747-0772, E-mail: rbennett@utmb.edu. *Dean*, Dr. Cary W. Cooper, 409-772-2665, Fax: 409-747-0772, E-mail: ccooper@utmb.edu.

Nursing Doctoral Students: 51 full-time (49 women), 66 part-time (58 women); includes 17 minority (7 African Americans, 1 Asian American or Pacific Islander, 9 Hispanic Americans), 3 international. Average age 24. 82 applicants, 33% accepted. *Faculty:* 29 full-time (all women), 5 part-time/adjunct (4 women). Expenses: Contact institution. *Financial support:* Research assistantships, teaching assistantships, Federal Work-Study, institutionally sponsored loans, and traineeships available. Support available to part-time students. In 2001, 31 degrees awarded. *Degree program information:* Part-time programs available. Postbaccalaureate distance learning degree programs offered (minimal on-campus study). Offers nursing (MSN). *Application deadline:* For fall admission, 2/1; for spring admission, 8/1. Applications are processed on a rolling basis. *Application fee:* $25. Electronic applications accepted. *Application Contact:* Richard Lewis, Registrar, 409-772-1215, Fax: 409-772-5056, E-mail: rlewis@utmb.edu. *Director*, Dr. Jeanette C. Hartshorn, 409-772-7311, Fax: 409-747-1519, E-mail: jhartsho@utmb.edu.

School of Allied Health Sciences Offers allied health sciences (MPT); physical therapy (MPT). Electronic applications accepted.

School of Medicine Students: 823 full-time (379 women); includes 400 minority (77 African Americans, 154 Asian Americans or Pacific Islanders, 166 Hispanic Americans, 3 Native Americans), 2 international. Average age 26. 2,529 applicants, 10% accepted, 208 enrolled. Expenses: Contact institution. *Financial support:* In 2001–02, 667 students received support. Federal Work-Study, institutionally sponsored loans, scholarships/grants, and tuition waivers (full and partial) available. Financial award applicants required to submit FAFSA. In 2001, 183 degrees awarded. Offers medicine (MD). *Application deadline:* For fall admission, 11/1. *Application fee:* $55 ($100 for international students). *Application Contact:* Dr. Lauree Thomas, Associate Dean for Admissions and Student Affairs, 409-772-1442, Fax: 409-772-5148, E-mail: lauthoma@utmb.edu. *Dean*, Dr. Stanley M. Lemon, 409-772-2671, Fax: 409-772-9598, E-mail: smlemon@utmb.edu.

THE UNIVERSITY OF TEXAS OF THE PERMIAN BASIN, Odessa, TX 79762-0001

General Information State-supported, coed, comprehensive institution. *Enrollment:* 629 matriculated graduate/professional students. *Enrollment by degree level:* 629 master's. *Graduate faculty:* 59 full-time (19 women). Tuition, state resident: full-time $1,746. Tuition, nonresident: full-time $5,292. *Required fees:* $523. Tuition and fees vary according to course load. *Graduate housing:* Rooms and/or apartments available on a first-come, first-served basis to single and married students. Typical cost: $1,900 per year for single students. Housing application deadline: 6/14. *Student services:* Career counseling, free psychological counseling, low-cost health insurance, multicultural affairs office, teacher training, writing training. *Collection:* 267,531 titles, 723 serial subscriptions.

Computer facilities: 130 computers available on campus for general student use. A campuswide network can be accessed from student residence rooms and from off campus. Internet access is available. *Web address:* http://www.utpb.edu/.

General Application Contact: Dr. J. Tillapaugh, Director of Graduate Studies, 915-552-2530, Fax: 915-552-2109, E-mail: tillapaugh_j@utpb.edu.

GRADUATE UNITS

Graduate School *Degree program information:* Part-time and evening/weekend programs available.

College of Arts and Sciences *Degree program information:* Part-time and evening/weekend programs available. Offers applied behavioral analysis (MA); arts and sciences (MA, MS); biology (MS); clinical psychology (MA); criminal justice administration (MS); English (MA); geology (MS); history (MA); physical education (MA); psychology (MA).

School of Business *Degree program information:* Part-time and evening/weekend programs available. Offers accountancy (MPA); business (MBA, MPA); management (MBA).

School of Education Offers counseling (MA); early childhood education (MA); education (MA); educational administration (MA); elementary education (MA); reading (MA); secondary education (MA); special education (MA); supervision (MA).

THE UNIVERSITY OF TEXAS–PAN AMERICAN, Edinburg, TX 78539-2999

General Information State-supported, coed, comprehensive institution. CGS member. *Enrollment:* 391 full-time matriculated graduate/professional students (235 women), 1,260 part-time matriculated graduate/professional students (825 women). *Graduate faculty:* 137 full-time (40 women), 34 part-time/adjunct (9 women). Tuition, state resident: part-time $212 per semester hour. Tuition, nonresident: part-time $367 per semester hour. *Graduate housing:* Room and/or apartments available on a first-come, first-served basis to single students; on-campus housing not available to married students. Typical cost: $1,540 per year ($2,622 including board). Room and board charges vary according to board plan and housing facility selected. *Student services:* Campus safety program, career counseling, disabled student services, free psychological counseling, international student services, low-cost health insurance. *Library facilities:* Learning Resource Library. *Collection:* 418,750 titles, 2,669 serial subscriptions, 24,412 audiovisual materials. *Research affiliation:* Management Planning Research Association, Inc. (curriculum and professional development).

Computer facilities: 500 computers available on campus for general student use. A campuswide network can be accessed from off campus. Internet access and online class registration are available. *Web address:* http://www.panam.edu/.

General Application Contact: Dr. Michael Faubion, Interim Chair, 956-381-3561, E-mail: mfc838@panam.edu.

GRADUATE UNITS

College of Arts and Humanities Students: 296. *Faculty:* 57 full-time (16 women). Expenses: Contact institution. *Financial support:* In 2001–02, 25 teaching assistantships were awarded; Federal Work-Study, institutionally sponsored loans, and tuition waivers (partial) also available. Support available to part-time students. In 2001, 32 degrees awarded. *Degree program information:* Part-time and evening/weekend programs available. Offers arts and humanities (MA, MAIS, MFA, MSIS, MMus); English (MA, MAIS); English as a second language (MA); history (MA, MAIS); interdisciplinary studies (MAIS, MSIS); music (MMus); Spanish (MA); speech communication (MA); studio art (MFA); theatre (MA). *Application fee:* $0. *Application Contact:* Dr. Michael Faubion, Interim Chair, 956-381-3561, E-mail: mfc838@panam.edu. *Dean*, Dr. Rodolfo Rocha, 956-381-2175, Fax: 956-381-2177, E-mail: rochar@panam.edu.

College of Business Administration *Degree program information:* Part-time and evening/weekend programs available. Offers business administration (MBA, MS, PhD); computer information systems (MS, PhD).

College of Education *Degree program information:* Part-time and evening/weekend programs available. Offers administration (M Ed); counseling and guidance (M Ed); early childhood education (M Ed); education (M Ed, MA, D Phil, Ed D); educational diagnostics (M Ed); educational psychology (D Phil); elementary bilingual education (M Ed); elementary education (M Ed); gifted and talented education (M Ed); kinesiology (M Ed); reading (M Ed); school psychology (MA); secondary education (M Ed); special education (M Ed); supervision (M Ed).

College of Health Sciences and Human Services Students: 76 full-time (63 women), 79 part-time (63 women); includes 128 minority (1 African American, 5 Asian Americans or Pacific Islanders, 122 Hispanic Americans) Average age 30. 131 applicants, 66% accepted. *Faculty:* 21 full-time (11 women), 3 part-time/adjunct (1 woman). Expenses: Contact institution. *Financial support:* In 2001–02, 46 students received support, including 12 fellowships with full tuition reimbursements available (averaging $7,200 per year), 3 research assistantships (averaging $2,000 per year), 8 teaching assistantships (averaging $3,500 per year); career-related internships or fieldwork, Federal Work-Study, institutionally sponsored loans, and scholarships/grants also available. Support available to part-time students. Financial award applicants required to submit FAFSA. In 2001, 48 degrees awarded. *Degree program information:* Part-time and evening/weekend programs available. Offers adult health nursing (MSN); communication sciences and disorders (MA); family nurse practitioner (MSN); health sciences and human services (MA, MS, MSN, MSSW); pediatric nurse practitioner (MSN); rehabilitation counseling (MS); social work (MSSW). *Interim Dean*, Dr. William J. McIntyre, 956-381-2292, Fax: 956-384-5054, E-mail: mcintyrew@panam.edu.

College of Science and Engineering *Degree program information:* Part-time and evening/weekend programs available. Offers biology (MS); computer science (MS); mathematics (MS); science and engineering (MS).

College of Social and Behavioral Sciences *Degree program information:* Part-time and evening/weekend programs available. Postbaccalaureate distance learning degree programs offered (minimal on-campus study). Offers criminal justice (MS); psychology (MA); public administration (MPA); social and behavioral sciences (MA, MPA, MS); sociology (MS).

THE UNIVERSITY OF TEXAS SOUTHWESTERN MEDICAL CENTER AT DALLAS, Dallas, TX 75390

General Information State-supported, coed, upper-level institution. *Enrollment:* 450 full-time matriculated graduate/professional students (212 women). *Graduate faculty:* 271 full-time (43 women), 65 part-time/adjunct (15 women). Tuition, state resident: full-time $990. Tuition, nonresident: full-time $6,062. *Required fees:* $843. *Graduate housing:* Rooms and/or apartments available on a first-come, first-served basis to single and married students. Housing application deadline: 5/1. *Student services:* Campus employment opportunities, campus safety program, disabled student services, exercise/wellness program, free psychological counseling, grant writing training, international student services, low-cost health insurance, writing training. *Library facilities:* University of Texas Southwestern Library. *Online resources:* library catalog, web page, access to other libraries' catalogs. *Collection:* 257,782 titles, 2,865 serial subscriptions.

Computer facilities: 150 computers available on campus for general student use. A campuswide network can be accessed from off campus. Internet access is available. *Web address:* http://www.utsouthwestern.edu/.

General Application Contact: Dr. Nancy E. Street, Assistant Dean, 214-648-6708, Fax: 214-648-2102, E-mail: nancy.street@utsouthwestern.edu.

GRADUATE UNITS

Southwestern Graduate School of Biomedical Sciences Students: 450 full-time (212 women); includes 72 minority (6 African Americans, 39 Asian Americans or Pacific Islanders, 25 Hispanic Americans, 2 Native Americans), 106 international. *Faculty:* 271 full-time (43 women), 65 part-time/adjunct (15 women). Expenses: Contact institution. *Financial support:* Fellowships, research assistantships, teaching assistantships, career-related internships or fieldwork, Federal Work-Study, institutionally sponsored loans, scholarships/grants, traineeships, and tuition waivers (full and partial) available. Financial award application deadline: 3/15; financial award applicants required to submit FAFSA. In 2001, 29 master's, 55 doctorates awarded. Offers biological chemistry (PhD); biomedical communications (MA); biomedical engineering (MS, PhD); biomedical sciences (MA, MPAS, MPT, MS, PhD); cell regulation (PhD); clinical psychology (PhD); genetics and development (PhD); immunology (PhD); integrative biology (PhD); medical science (PhD); molecular biophysics (PhD); molecular microbiology (PhD); neuroscience (PhD); physical therapy (MPT); physician assistant studies

(MPAS); radiological sciences (MS, PhD); rehabilitation counseling psychology (MS). *Application fee:* $0. Electronic applications accepted. *Application Contact:* 214-648-3606, Fax: 214-648-3289, E-mail: reggs@mednet.swmed.edu. *Acting Dean,* Dr. Philip S. Perlman, 214-648-2174, Fax: 214-648-2102, E-mail: perlman@utsw.swmed.edu.

Southwestern Medical School Students: 813 full-time (324 women); includes 356 minority (44 African Americans, 229 Asian Americans or Pacific Islanders, 82 Hispanic Americans, 1 Native American), 6 international. Average age 25. 2,518 applicants, 13% accepted, 204 enrolled. *Faculty:* 1,164 full-time, 192 part-time/adjunct. Expenses: Contact institution. *Financial support:* In 2001–02, 700 students received support. Federal Work-Study and institutionally sponsored loans available. Financial award application deadline: 3/15; financial award applicants required to submit FAFSA. In 2001, 203 degrees awarded. Offers medicine (MD). *Application deadline:* For fall admission, 10/15. *Application fee:* $45. Electronic applications accepted. *Application Contact:* Dr. Scott Wright, Administrative Director of Admission Committee, 214-648-2670, Fax: 214-648-3289, E-mail: admissions@utsouthwestern.edu. *Dean,* Dr. Robert Alpern, 214-648-2509.

THE UNIVERSITY OF THE ARTS, Philadelphia, PA 19102-4944

General Information Independent, coed, comprehensive institution. *Enrollment:* 97 full-time matriculated graduate/professional students (75 women), 59 part-time matriculated graduate/professional students (41 women). *Enrollment by degree level:* 156 master's. *Graduate faculty:* 33 full-time (13 women), 36 part-time/adjunct (19 women). *Tuition:* Part-time $938 per credit. Full-time tuition and fees vary according to campus/location. *Graduate housing:* On-campus housing not available. *Student services:* Campus employment opportunities, campus safety program, career counseling, disabled student services, free psychological counseling, international student services. *Library facilities:* Albert M. Greenfield Library plus 2 others. *Online resources:* library catalog, web page. *Collection:* 118,496 titles, 534 serial subscriptions, 307,149 audiovisual materials. *Research affiliation:* The Franklin Institute (general science education), Philadelphia Museum of Art (arts and culture), School District of Philadelphia (education).

Computer facilities: 365 computers available on campus for general student use. A campuswide network can be accessed. Internet access is available. *Web address:* http://www.uarts.edu/.

General Application Contact: Barbara Elliott, Director of Admissions, 215-717-6049, Fax: 215-717-6045, E-mail: admissions@uarts.edu.

GRADUATE UNITS

College of Art and Design Students: 82 full-time (68 women), 58 part-time (40 women); includes 20 minority (10 African Americans, 4 Asian Americans or Pacific Islanders, 6 Hispanic Americans), 11 international. Average age 33. 124 applicants, 75% accepted, 59 enrolled. *Faculty:* 20 full-time (13 women), 25 part-time/adjunct (16 women). Expenses: Contact institution. *Financial support:* In 2001–02, 79 students received support, including 79 fellowships (averaging $5,590 per year); career-related internships or fieldwork, scholarships/grants, and unspecified assistantships also available. Support available to part-time students. Financial award application deadline: 3/15; financial award applicants required to submit FAFSA. In 2001, 33 degrees awarded. *Degree program information:* Part-time programs available. Offers art and design (MA, MAT, MFA, MID); art education (MA); book arts/printmaking (MFA); ceramics (MFA); industrial design (MID); museum education (MA); museum exhibition planning and design (MFA); painting (MFA); sculpture (MFA); visual arts (MAT). *Application deadline:* For fall admission, 3/1 (priority date); for spring admission, 11/15 (priority date). Applications are processed on a rolling basis. *Application fee:* $40 ($75 for international students). *Application Contact:* Barbara Elliott, Director of Admissions, 215-717-6049, Fax: 215-717-6045, E-mail: admissions@uarts.edu. *Dean,* Stephen Tarantal, 215-717-6120, Fax: 215-717-6389.

College of Performing Arts Students: 15 full-time (7 women), 1 (woman) part-time; includes 4 minority (2 African Americans, 1 Asian American or Pacific Islander, 1 Hispanic American) Average age 26. 18 applicants, 78% accepted, 11 enrolled. *Faculty:* 6 full-time (1 woman), 18 part-time/adjunct (1 woman). Expenses: Contact institution. *Financial support:* In 2001–02, 20 fellowships (averaging $5,590 per year) were awarded; career-related internships or fieldwork and unspecified assistantships also available. Support available to part-time students. Financial award application deadline: 3/15; financial award applicants required to submit FAFSA. In 2001, 22 degrees awarded. *Degree program information:* Part-time programs available. Offers performing arts (MAT, MM). *Application deadline:* For fall admission, 3/1 (priority date); for spring admission, 11/15 (priority date). Applications are processed on a rolling basis. *Application fee:* $40 ($75 for international students). *Application Contact:* Barbara Elliott, Director of Admissions, 215-717-6049, Fax: 215-717-6045, E-mail: admissions@uarts.edu. *Interim Dean,* Dewitt Jack, 215-717-6125, E-mail: jdewitt@uarts.edu.

School of Music Students: 15 full-time (7 women), 1 (woman) part-time; includes 4 minority (2 African Americans, 1 Asian American or Pacific Islander, 1 Hispanic American) Average age 26. 18 applicants, 78% accepted, 11 enrolled. *Faculty:* 6 full-time (1 woman), 18 part-time/adjunct (1 woman). Expenses: Contact institution. *Financial support:* In 2001–02, 20 fellowships (averaging $5,590 per year) were awarded; career-related internships or fieldwork and unspecified assistantships also available. Support available to part-time students. Financial award application deadline: 3/15; financial award applicants required to submit FAFSA. In 2001, 22 degrees awarded. *Degree program information:* Part-time programs available. Offers jazz studies (MM); music education (MAT). *Application deadline:* For fall admission, 3/1 (priority date); for spring admission, 11/15 (priority date). Applications are processed on a rolling basis. *Application fee:* $75 for international students. Electronic applications accepted. *Application Contact:* Barbara Elliott, Director of Admissions, 215-717-6049, Fax: 215-717-6045, E-mail: admissions@uarts.edu. *Director,* Marc Dicciani, 215-717-6342, Fax: 215-545-8056, E-mail: mdicciani@uarts.edu.

UNIVERSITY OF THE DISTRICT OF COLUMBIA, Washington, DC 20008-1175

General Information District-supported, coed, comprehensive institution. CGS member. *Enrollment:* 77 full-time matriculated graduate/professional students (54 women), 239 part-time matriculated graduate/professional students (163 women). *Enrollment by degree level:* 316 master's. *Graduate faculty:* 30. Tuition, district resident: full-time $3,564; part-time $198 per credit hour. Tuition, nonresident: full-time $5,922; part-time $329 per credit hour. *Required fees:* $270; $135 per term. *Graduate housing:* On-campus housing not available. *Student services:* Campus employment opportunities, campus safety program, career counseling, child daycare facilities, disabled student services, free psychological counseling, international student services, low-cost health insurance, multicultural affairs office. *Library facilities:* Learning Resources Division Library plus 1 other. *Online resources:* library catalog, web page, access to other libraries' catalogs. *Collection:* 544,412 titles, 591 serial subscriptions, 19,548 audiovisual materials.

Computer facilities: 50 computers available on campus for general student use. A campuswide network can be accessed. *Web address:* http://www.udc.edu/.

General Application Contact: LaVerne Hill Flannigan, Processor, Graduate Applications, 202-274-5008.

GRADUATE UNITS

College of Arts and Sciences Students: 41 full-time (31 women), 93 part-time (70 women); includes 112 minority (99 African Americans, 2 Asian Americans or Pacific Islanders, 11 Hispanic Americans), 2 international. Average age 35. 178 applicants. Expenses: Contact institution. *Financial support:* Fellowships, research assistantships, teaching assistantships, career-related internships or fieldwork and Federal Work-Study available. In 2001, 31 degrees awarded. *Degree program information:* Part-time and evening/weekend programs available. Offers arts and sciences (MA, MS, MST); early childhood education (MA); special education (MA). *Application deadline:* For fall admission, 6/15 (priority date); for spring admission, 11/1. Applications are processed on a rolling basis. *Application fee:* $20. *Application Contact:* LaVerne Hill Flannigan, Director of Admission, 202-274-6069. *Acting Dean,* Dr. Bertha Minus, 202-274-5194.

Division of Arts and Education Students: 41 full-time (31 women), 93 part-time (70 women); includes 112 minority (99 African Americans, 2 Asian Americans or Pacific Islanders, 11 Hispanic Americans), 2 international. Average age 35. 74 applicants. Expenses: Contact institution. *Financial support:* Fellowships, research assistantships available. *Degree program information:* Part-time and evening/weekend programs available. Offers arts and education (MA, MS); English (MA); special education (MA); speech and language pathology (MS). *Application deadline:* For fall admission, 6/15 (priority date); for spring admission, 11/15. Applications are processed on a rolling basis. *Application fee:* $20. *Application Contact:* LaVerne Hill Flannigan, Director of Admission, 202-274-6069.

Division of Science and Mathematics Average age 35. 33 applicants, 30% accepted, 4 enrolled. Expenses: Contact institution. In 2001, 1 degree awarded. *Degree program information:* Part-time and evening/weekend programs available. Offers mathematics (MST); science and mathematics (MA, MST). *Application deadline:* For fall admission, 6/15 (priority date); for spring admission, 11/1. Applications are processed on a rolling basis. *Application fee:* $20. *Application Contact:* LaVerne Hill Flannigan, Director of Admission, 202-274-6069. *Head,* Dr. Freddie Dixon, 202-274-7401.

Division of Urban Affairs, Social, and Behavioral Sciences Students: 10 full-time (5 women), 40 part-time (27 women); includes 48 minority (44 African Americans, 4 Hispanic Americans), 1 international. Average age 35. Expenses: Contact institution. In 2001, 11 degrees awarded. Offers clinical psychology (MS); counseling (MS); urban affairs, social, and behavioral sciences (MS). *Application deadline:* For fall admission, 6/15 (priority date); for spring admission, 11/1 (priority date). Applications are processed on a rolling basis. *Application fee:* $20. *Head,* Dr. Sheila Harmon-Martin, 202-474-7407.

David A. Clarke School of Law Students: 133 full-time (86 women); includes 94 minority (76 African Americans, 4 Asian Americans or Pacific Islanders, 14 Hispanic Americans) Average age 30. 427 applicants, 22% accepted, 41 enrolled. *Faculty:* 16 full-time (9 women), 17 part-time/adjunct (5 women). Expenses: Contact institution. *Financial support:* In 2001–02, fellowships (averaging $2,000 per year); career-related internships or fieldwork, Federal Work-Study, scholarships/grants, and tuition waivers (full and partial) also available. Financial award application deadline: 5/1; financial award applicants required to submit FAFSA. In 2001, 38 degrees awarded. Offers law (JD). *Application deadline:* For fall admission, 3/15. Applications are processed on a rolling basis. *Application fee:* $35. Electronic applications accepted. *Application Contact:* Vivian W. Canty, Director of Admission, 202-274-7336, Fax: 202-274-5583, E-mail: vcanty@law.udc.edu. *Dean,* Katherine S. Broderick, 202-274-7400, Fax: 202-274-5583, E-mail: kbroderi@law.udc.edu.

School of Business and Public Administration Students: 24 full-time (15 women), 41 part-time (21 women); includes 52 minority (47 African Americans, 2 Asian Americans or Pacific Islanders, 3 Hispanic Americans), 6 international. Average age 29. 71 applicants, 55% accepted. Expenses: Contact institution. *Financial support:* Career-related internships or fieldwork and Federal Work-Study available. In 2001, 14 degrees awarded. *Degree program information:* Part-time and evening/weekend programs available. Offers business administration (MBA); business and public administration (MBA, MPA); public administration (MPA). *Application deadline:* For fall admission, 6/15 (priority date); for spring admission, 11/1. Applications are processed on a rolling basis. *Application fee:* $20. *Application Contact:* LaVerne Hill Flannigan, Director of Admission, 202-274-6069. *Dean,* Dr. Herbert Quigley, 202-282-7000.

UNIVERSITY OF THE INCARNATE WORD, San Antonio, TX 78209-6397

General Information Independent-religious, coed, comprehensive institution. *Enrollment:* 187 full-time matriculated graduate/professional students (90 women), 577 part-time matriculated graduate/professional students (386 women). *Enrollment by degree level:* 639 master's, 125 doctoral. *Graduate faculty:* 59 full-time (28 women), 28 part-time/adjunct (12 women). *Tuition:* Full-time $8,010; part-time $445 per hour. *Required fees:* $270; $25 per hour. One-time fee: $30. *Graduate housing:* Room and/or apartments available to single students; on-campus housing not available to married students. Typical cost: $2,960 per year ($12,570 including board). *Student services:* Campus employment opportunities, career counseling, exercise/wellness program, free psychological counseling, international student services, low-cost health insurance. *Library facilities:* J.E. and L.E. Mabee Library plus 1 other. *Online resources:* library catalog, web page. *Collection:* 235,000 titles, 3,436 serial subscriptions, 36,441 audiovisual materials.

Computer facilities: 200 computers available on campus for general student use. A campuswide network can be accessed from student residence rooms and from off campus. Internet access and online class registration are available. *Web address:* http://www.uiw.edu/.

General Application Contact: Andrea Cyterski, Director of Admissions, 210-829-6005, Fax: 210-829-3921, E-mail: cyterski@universe.uiwtx.edu.

GRADUATE UNITS

School of Graduate Studies and Research Students: 187 full-time (90 women), 577 part-time (386 women); includes 295 minority (45 African Americans, 13 Asian Americans or Pacific Islanders, 236 Hispanic Americans, 1 Native American), 128 international. Average age 35. 435 applicants, 74% accepted. *Faculty:* 59 full-time (28 women), 28 part-time/adjunct (12 women). Expenses: Contact institution. *Financial support:* Fellowships, research assistantships, teaching assistantships, career-related internships or fieldwork, Federal Work-Study, institutionally sponsored loans, traineeships, and tuition waivers (partial) available. Support available to part-time students. In 2001, 169 master's, 4 doctorates awarded. *Degree program information:* Part-time and evening/weekend programs available. Offers graduate studies (M Ed, MA, MAA, MAMT, MBA, MS, MSN, PhD); multidisciplinary studies (MA). *Application deadline:* For spring admission, 12/31. Applications are processed on a rolling basis. *Application fee:* $20. *Application Contact:* Andrea Cyterski, Director of Admissions, 210-829-6005, Fax: 210-829-3921, E-mail: cyterski@universe.uiwtx.edu. *Dean,* Gilberto M. Hinojosa, 210-829-3157, Fax: 210-829-3559, E-mail: hinojosa@universe.uiwtx.edu.

College of Education Students: 69 full-time (29 women), 183 part-time (135 women); includes 90 minority (15 African Americans, 7 Asian Americans or Pacific Islanders, 68 Hispanic Americans), 52 international. Average age 35. 164 applicants, 59% accepted. *Faculty:* 20 full-time (10 women), 9 part-time/adjunct (6 women). Expenses: Contact institution. In 2001, 38 master's, 2 doctorates awarded. *Degree program information:* Evening/weekend programs available. Offers adult education (M Ed, MA); early childhood education (M Ed, MA); education (M Ed, MA); education of the hearing impaired (M Ed); educational diagnostics (M Ed, MA); elementary education (M Ed, MA); instructional technology (MA); international education (M Ed, MA); international education/entrepreneurship (PhD); mathematics education (PhD); mathematics teaching (MS); organizational development (MAA); organizational leadership (PhD); organizational learning (M Ed, MA); physical education (M Ed, MA); reading (M Ed, MA); reading specialist (M Ed, MA); secondary teaching (M Ed, MA); special education (M Ed, MA); teaching (M Ed, MA). *Application deadline:* For fall admission, 8/15 (priority date); for spring admission, 12/31. Applications are processed on a rolling basis. *Application fee:* $20. *Application Contact:* Andrea Cyterski, Director of Admissions, 210-829-6005, Fax: 210-829-3921, E-mail: cyterski@universe.uiwtx.edu. *Dean,* Dr. Patricia Watkins, 210-829-2762, Fax: 210-829-2765, E-mail: watkins@universe.uiwtx.edu.

College of Humanities, Arts, and Social Sciences Students: 11 full-time (7 women), 57 part-time (42 women); includes 24 minority (1 African American, 23 Hispanic Americans), 3 international. Average age 36. 32 applicants, 75% accepted. *Faculty:* 8 full-time (5 women), 2 part-time/adjunct (1 woman). Expenses: Contact institution. *Financial support:* Federal Work-Study, institutionally sponsored loans, and tuition waivers (partial) available. In 2001, 17 degrees awarded. *Degree program information:* Part-time and evening/weekend programs available. Offers communication arts (MA); English (MA); humanities, arts, and social sciences (MA); religious studies (MA). *Application deadline:* For spring admission, 12/31. Applications are processed on a rolling basis. *Application fee:* $20. *Application Contact:* Andrea Cyterski, Director of Admissions, 210-829-6005, Fax: 210-829-3921, E-mail: cyterski@universe.uiwtx.edu. *Dean,* Dr. Donna Aronson, 210-829-6022, Fax: 210-829-3880, E-mail: aronson@universe.uiwtx.edu.

University of the Incarnate Word (continued)

School of Business and Applied Arts and Sciences Students: 54 full-time (26 women), 240 part-time (138 women); includes 132 minority (18 African Americans, 1 Asian American or Pacific Islander, 111 Hispanic Americans, 2 Native Americans), 35 international. Average age 33. 173 applicants, 84% accepted. *Faculty:* 14 full-time (2 women), 12 part-time/adjunct (1 woman). Expenses: Contact institution. *Financial support:* Career-related internships or fieldwork, Federal Work-Study, institutionally sponsored loans, and tuition waivers (partial) available. Support available to part-time students. In 2001, 83 master's, 2 doctorates awarded. *Degree program information:* Part-time and evening/weekend programs available. Offers business administration (MBA); business and applied arts and sciences (MAA, MBA, PhD); general management (MAA); international administration (MAA); organization development (MAA); organizational leadership (PhD); sports management (MAA). *Application deadline:* For fall admission, 8/15 (priority date); for spring admission, 12/31. Applications are processed on a rolling basis. *Application fee:* $20. *Application Contact:* Andrea Cyterski, Director of Admissions, 210-829-6005, Fax: 210-829-3921, E-mail: cyterski@universe.uiwtx.edu. *Dean,* Dr. Robert Ryan, 210-829-3924, Fax: 210-829-3169, E-mail: ryan@universe.uiwtx.edu.

School of Mathematics, Sciences and Engineering Students: 8 full-time (3 women), 40 part-time (26 women); includes 23 minority (3 African Americans, 1 Asian American or Pacific Islander, 19 Hispanic Americans), 4 international. Average age 34. 18 applicants, 83% accepted. Expenses: Contact institution. *Financial support:* Research assistantships, teaching assistantships available. In 2001, 18 degrees awarded. *Degree program information:* Part-time and evening/weekend programs available. Offers biology (MA, MS); mathematics (MAMT, MS, PhD); mathematics, sciences and engineering (MA, MAMT, MS, PhD). *Application deadline:* For fall admission, 8/15 (priority date); for spring admission, 12/31. Applications are processed on a rolling basis. *Application fee:* $20. *Application Contact:* Andrea Cyterski, Director of Admissions, 210-829-6005, Fax: 210-829-3921, E-mail: cyterski@universe.uiwtx.edu. *Dean,* Dr. David Elizandro, 210-829-2717, Fax: 210-829-3153, E-mail: elizandro@universe.uiwtx.edu.

School of Nursing and Health Professions Students: 13 full-time (all women), 38 part-time (34 women); includes 20 minority (6 African Americans, 3 Asian Americans or Pacific Islanders, 11 Hispanic Americans), 2 international. Average age 37. 38 applicants, 82% accepted. *Faculty:* 8 full-time (5 women), 2 part-time/adjunct (1 woman). Expenses: Contact institution. *Financial support:* Research assistantships, teaching assistantships, career-related internships or fieldwork, Federal Work-Study, and traineeships available. Support available to part-time students. In 2001, 7 degrees awarded. *Degree program information:* Part-time and evening/weekend programs available. Offers nursing (MSN); nursing and health professions (MS, MSN); nutrition (MS). *Application deadline:* For fall admission, 8/15 (priority date); for spring admission, 12/31. Applications are processed on a rolling basis. *Application fee:* $20. *Application Contact:* Andrea Cyterski, Director of Admissions, 210-829-6005, Fax: 210-829-3921, E-mail: cyterski@universe.uiwtx.edu. *Dean,* Dr. Kathleen Light, 210-829-3982, Fax: 210-829-3174.

See in-depth description on page 1269.

UNIVERSITY OF THE PACIFIC, Stockton, CA 95211-0197

General Information Independent, coed, university. CGS member. *Enrollment:* 1,916 full-time matriculated graduate/professional students (1,047 women), 596 part-time matriculated graduate/professional students (337 women). *Graduate faculty:* 378 full-time, 230 part-time/adjunct. *Tuition:* Full-time $21,150; part-time $661 per unit. *Required fees:* $375. *Graduate housing:* Rooms and/or apartments available on a first-come, first-served basis to single and married students. Housing application deadline: 7/1. *Student services:* Campus employment opportunities, campus safety program, career counseling, child daycare facilities, disabled student services, free psychological counseling, international student services, low-cost health insurance, multicultural affairs office, teacher training. *Library facilities:* Holt Memorial Library plus 1 other. *Online resources:* library catalog, web page, access to other libraries' catalogs. *Collection:* 689,733 titles, 3,747 serial subscriptions, 8,377 audiovisual materials. *Research affiliation:* Lawrence Hall of Science.

Computer facilities: 274 computers available on campus for general student use. A campuswide network can be accessed from student residence rooms and from off campus. Internet access and online class registration are available. *Web address:* http://www.uop.edu/.

General Application Contact: Dr. Robert Brodnick, Research and Graduate Studies, 209-946-2261, Fax: 209-946-2858, E-mail: gradschool@uop.edu.

GRADUATE UNITS

Graduate School Students: 796 full-time (533 women), 210 part-time (132 women); includes 522 minority (17 African Americans, 448 Asian Americans or Pacific Islanders, 50 Hispanic Americans, 7 Native Americans), 37 international. 384 applicants, 60% accepted. Expenses: Contact institution. *Financial support:* Fellowships with full and partial tuition reimbursements, research assistantships, teaching assistantships with full and partial tuition reimbursements, Federal Work-Study, institutionally sponsored loans, and unspecified assistantships available. Support available to part-time students. Financial award application deadline: 3/1. In 2001, 16 master's, 6 doctorates awarded. *Degree program information:* Part-time programs available. Offers biochemistry (MS, PhD); biological sciences (MS); chemistry (MS, PhD); communication (MA); intercultural relations (MA); international studies (MA); music therapy (MA); psychology (MA); sport sciences (MA). *Application deadline:* For fall admission, 3/1 (priority date); for spring admission, 10/1 (priority date). Applications are processed on a rolling basis. *Application fee:* $50. *Application Contact:* Information Contact, 209-946-2261, Fax: 209-946-2858, E-mail: gradschool@uop.edu. *Dean,* Dr. Denis J. Meerdink, 209-946-2261, Fax: 209-946-2858, E-mail: gradschool@uop.edu.

Conservatory of Music Students: 6 full-time (3 women), 4 part-time (all women); includes 1 minority (Asian American or Pacific Islander), 2 international. Average age 30. 9 applicants, 33% accepted, 1 enrolled. *Faculty:* 2 part-time/adjunct (both women). Expenses: Contact institution. *Financial support:* Teaching assistantships, institutionally sponsored loans available. Support available to part-time students. Financial award application deadline:3/1. In 2001, 1 degree awarded. Offers music (MA, MM); music education (MM). *Application deadline:* For fall admission, 3/1 (priority date); for spring admission, 10/1 (priority date). Applications are processed on a rolling basis. *Application fee:* $50. *Application Contact:* Dr. David Wolfe, Information Contact, 209-946-3194, E-mail: dwolfe@uop.edu. *Dean,* Dr. Steven Anderson, 209-946-2417.

Eberhardt School of Business Students: 30 full-time (14 women), 28 part-time (9 women); includes 9 minority (5 Asian Americans or Pacific Islanders, 4 Hispanic Americans), 4 international. Average age 30. 54 applicants, 67% accepted, 22 enrolled. Expenses: Contact institution. *Financial support:* Fellowships, research assistantships, Federal Work-Study and institutionally sponsored loans available. Support available to part-time students. Financial award application deadline: 3/1; financial award applicants required to submit FAFSA. In 2001, 37 degrees awarded. *Degree program information:* Part-time programs available. Offers business (MBA). *Application deadline:* For fall admission, 7/31 (priority date); for spring admission, 11/30. Applications are processed on a rolling basis. *Application fee:* $50. *Application Contact:* Dr. John Pfaff, MBA Director, 209-946-2874, Fax: 209-946-2586, E-mail: jpfaff@uop.edu. *Dean,* Dr. Mark Plovnick, 209-946-2466, Fax: 209-946-2586, E-mail: mplovnick@uop.edu.

School of Education Students: 66 full-time (52 women), 123 part-time (82 women); includes 52 minority (11 African Americans, 24 Asian Americans or Pacific Islanders, 15 Hispanic Americans, 2 Native Americans), 9 international. 102 applicants, 80% accepted. *Faculty:* 15 full-time (8 women). Expenses: Contact institution. *Financial support:* In 2001–02, 13 teaching assistantships were awarded; institutionally sponsored loans also available. Support available to part-time students. Financial award application deadline: 3/1. Offers curriculum and instruction (M Ed, MA, Ed D); education (M Ed); educational administration (MA, Ed D); educational counseling and psychology (MA); educational psychology (MA, Ed D); educational research (MA); school psychology (Ed D, PhD, Ed S); special education (MA). *Application deadline:* For fall admission, 3/1 (priority date); for spring admission, 10/15. Applications are processed on a rolling basis. *Application fee:* $50. *Dean,* Dr. Jack Nagle, 209-946-2683, E-mail: jnagle@uop.edu.

McGeorge School of Law Students: 609 full-time (316 women), 313 part-time (158 women); includes 168 minority (34 African Americans, 93 Asian Americans or Pacific Islanders, 27 Hispanic Americans, 14 Native Americans) Average age 24. 1,592 applicants, 73% accepted, 386 enrolled. *Faculty:* 39 full-time (12 women), 31 part-time/adjunct (7 women). Expenses: Contact institution. *Financial support:* In 2001–02, 528 students received support, including 9 fellowships, 20 research assistantships (averaging $6,485 per year); career-related internships or fieldwork, Federal Work-Study, institutionally sponsored loans, and scholarships/grants also available. Support available to part-time students. Financial award applicants required to submit FAFSA. In 2001, 261 first professional degrees, 19 master's awarded. *Degree program information:* Part-time and evening/weekend programs available. Offers government and public policy (LL M); international waters resources law (LL M, JSD); law (JD); transnational business practice (LL M). *Application deadline:* For fall admission, 5/1 (priority date). Applications are processed on a rolling basis. *Application fee:* $40. Electronic applications accepted. *Application Contact:* 916-739-7105, Fax: 916-739-7134, E-mail: admissionsmcgeorge@uop.edu. *Dean,* Elizabeth Rindscopf Parker, 916-739-7151, E-mail: elizabeth@uop.edu.

School of Dentistry Students: 452 full-time (172 women); includes 182 minority (4 African Americans, 161 Asian Americans or Pacific Islanders, 13 Hispanic Americans, 4 Native Americans) Average age 30. 2,174 applicants, 13% accepted. *Faculty:* 60 full-time (7 women), 271 part-time/adjunct (87 women). Expenses: Contact institution. *Financial support:* In 2001–02, 374 students received support. Institutionally sponsored loans, scholarships/grants, and stipends available. Support available to part-time students. Financial award application deadline: 3/2; financial award applicants required to submit FAFSA. In 2001, 142 DDSs, 6 master's awarded. Offers dentistry (DDS, MSD); international dental studies (DDS); orthodontics (MSD). *Application fee:* $75. *Application Contact:* Dr. Craig Yarborough, Associate Dean for Institutional Advancement and Student Services, 415-929-6491. *Dean,* Dr. Arthur A. Dugoni, 415-929-6424.

School of Pharmacy Students: 726 full-time (480 women), 27 part-time (14 women); includes 467 minority (5 African Americans, 431 Asian Americans or Pacific Islanders, 28 Hispanic Americans, 3 Native Americans), 27 international. Average age 25. 300 applicants, 43% accepted. Expenses: Contact institution. *Financial support:* In 2001–02, 15 teaching assistantships were awarded; career-related internships or fieldwork, Federal Work-Study, institutionally sponsored loans, and tuition waivers (full and partial) also available. Support available to part-time students. Offers Pharmaceutical Sciences (MS, PhD); pharmaceutics and medicinal chemistry (MS, PhD); pharmacy (Pharm D, MS, PhD); pharmacy practice (MS, PhD); physical therapy (MS); physiology/pharmacology (MS, PhD); speech-language pathology (MS). *Application fee:* $50. *Application Contact:* Cyndi Porter, Outreach Officer, 209-946-3957, Fax: 209-946-2410, E-mail: cporter@uop.edu. *Dean,* Dr. Philip Oppenheimer, 209-946-2561, Fax: 209-946-2410.

UNIVERSITY OF THE SACRED HEART, San Juan, PR 00914-0383

General Information Independent-religious, coed, comprehensive institution. *Enrollment:* 64 full-time matriculated graduate/professional students (56 women), 439 part-time matriculated graduate/professional students (312 women). *Enrollment by degree level:* 482 master's, 21 other advanced degrees. *Graduate faculty:* 20 full-time (14 women), 27 part-time/adjunct (11 women). *Tuition:* Full-time $2,880; part-time $160 per credit. *Required fees:* $200 per term. *Graduate housing:* Room and/or apartments available on a first-come, first-served basis to single students; on-campus housing not available to married students. Typical cost: $1,950 per year. Housing application deadline: 5/31. *Student services:* Career counseling, free psychological counseling. *Library facilities:* Maria Teresa Guevara Library plus 1 other. *Online resources:* library catalog, web page, access to other libraries' catalogs. *Collection:* 1,525 serial subscriptions, 67,048 audiovisual materials.

Computer facilities: 300 computers available on campus for general student use. A campuswide network can be accessed from off campus. *Web address:* http://www.sagrado.edu/.

General Application Contact: 787-728-1515 Ext. 2314, Fax: 787-268-8843, E-mail: acarrasquillo@sagrado.edu.

GRADUATE UNITS

Graduate Programs Students: 64 full-time (56 women), 439 part-time (312 women); all minorities (all Hispanic Americans) 156 applicants, 78% accepted, 96 enrolled. *Faculty:* 20 full-time (14 women), 27 part-time/adjunct (11 women). Expenses: Contact institution. *Financial support:* In 2001–02, 85 students received support, including 4 fellowships; tuition waivers (partial) also available. Financial award application deadline: 6/30. In 2001, 48 master's, 35 other advanced degrees awarded. *Degree program information:* Part-time and evening/weekend programs available. Offers advertising (MA); contemporary culture and means (MA); human resource management (MBA); instruction systems and education technology (M Ed); journalism and mass communication (MA); management information systems (MBA); marketing (MBA); medical technology (Certificate); natural science (Certificate); occupational health (MS); public relations (MA); taxation (MBA). *Application deadline:* For fall admission, 5/15. *Application fee:* $25. *Application Contact:* Dr. Lydia Espinet, Dean, Academic and Student Affairs, 787-728-1515 Ext. 1262, Fax: 787-268-8843, E-mail: lespinet@sagrado.edu. *Dean, Academic and Student Affairs,* Dr. Lydia Espinet, 787-728-1515 Ext. 1262, Fax: 787-268-8843, E-mail: lespinet@sagrado.edu.

UNIVERSITY OF THE SCIENCES IN PHILADELPHIA, Philadelphia, PA 19104-4495

General Information Independent, coed, university. *Enrollment:* 50 full-time matriculated graduate/professional students (32 women), 26 part-time matriculated graduate/professional students (18 women). *Enrollment by degree level:* 47 master's, 29 doctoral. *Graduate faculty:* 30 full-time (7 women), 17 part-time/adjunct (7 women). *Tuition:* Full-time $17,122; part-time $713 per credit. *Required fees:* $26 per credit. *Graduate housing:* On-campus housing not available. *Student services:* Campus employment opportunities, campus safety program, career counseling, free psychological counseling, international student services, low-cost health insurance, writing training. *Library facilities:* Joseph W. England Library. *Online resources:* library catalog, web page, access to other libraries' catalogs. *Collection:* 76,000 titles, 809 serial subscriptions.

Computer facilities: 105 computers available on campus for general student use. A campuswide network can be accessed from student residence rooms and from off campus. Internet access is available. *Web address:* http://www.usip.edu/.

General Application Contact: Dr. Rodney J. Wigent, Dean, College of Graduate Studies, 215-596-8937, Fax: 215-895-1185, E-mail: graduate@usip.edu.

GRADUATE UNITS

College of Graduate Studies Average age 32. 101 applicants, 40% accepted. *Faculty:* 27 full-time (4 women), 19 part-time/adjunct (11 women). Expenses: Contact institution. *Financial support:* In 2001–02, teaching assistantships with full and partial tuition reimbursements (averaging $13,000 per year); fellowships with full tuition reimbursements, research assistantships with full tuition reimbursements, institutionally sponsored loans, scholarships/grants, traineeships, and tuition waivers (full and partial) also available. Support available to part-time students. Financial award application deadline: 5/1. In 2001, 5 master's, 6 doctorates awarded. *Degree program information:* Part-time and evening/weekend programs available. Offers biochemistry (PhD); biomedical writing (MS); cell biology and biotechnology (MS); chemistry (MS, PhD); health policy (MS, PhD); health psychology (MS); pharmaceutical business (EMBA); pharmaceutics (MS, PhD); pharmacognosy (MS, PhD); pharmacology (MS, PhD); pharmacy administration (MS); toxicology (MS, PhD). *Application deadline:* For fall admission, 5/1; for spring admission, 10/1. Applications are processed on a rolling basis. *Application fee:* $45. Electronic applications accepted. *Dean,* Dr. Rodney J. Wigent, 215-596-8937, Fax: 215-895-1185, E-mail: graduate@usip.edu.

Philadelphia College of Pharmacy Offers pharmacy (Pharm D); pharmacy practice (Pharm D).

UNIVERSITY OF THE SOUTH, Sewanee, TN 37383-1000

General Information Independent-religious, coed, comprehensive institution. *Graduate housing:* Rooms and/or apartments available on a first-come, first-served basis to single and married students. Housing application deadline: 4/15.

GRADUATE UNITS

School of Theology *Degree program information:* Part-time programs available. Offers theology (M Div, MA, STM, D Min). MA open to foreign students.

UNIVERSITY OF THE VIRGIN ISLANDS, Charlotte Amalie, VI 00802-9990

General Information Territory-supported, coed, comprehensive institution. *Enrollment:* 19 full-time matriculated graduate/professional students (all women), 132 part-time matriculated graduate/professional students (104 women). *Enrollment by degree level:* 151 master's. *Graduate faculty:* 13 full-time (6 women), 2 part-time/adjunct (1 woman). *Tuition, area resident:* Part-time $228 per credit. Tuition, nonresident: part-time $456 per credit. *Graduate housing:* On-campus housing not available. *Student services:* Career counseling. *Library facilities:* Ralph M. Paiewonsky Library. *Online resources:* library catalog, web page. *Collection:* 106,361 titles, 940 serial subscriptions.

Computer facilities: 100 computers available on campus for general student use. A campuswide network can be accessed from off campus. *Web address:* http://www.uvi.edu/.

General Application Contact: Carolyn Cook, Director of Admissions and New Student Services, 340-693-1224, Fax: 340-693-1155, E-mail: ccook@uvi.edu.

GRADUATE UNITS

Graduate Programs Students: 19 full-time (all women), 132 part-time (104 women); includes 112 minority (107 African Americans, 1 Asian American or Pacific Islander, 4 Hispanic Americans), 26 international. Average age 36. 70 applicants, 81% accepted, 31 enrolled. *Faculty:* 13 full-time (6 women), 2 part-time/adjunct (1 woman). Expenses: Contact institution. *Financial support:* In 2001–02, 2 students received support. Career-related internships or fieldwork and scholarships/grants available. Financial award application deadline: 4/15. In 2001, 52 degrees awarded. *Degree program information:* Part-time and evening/weekend programs available. Offers public administration (MPA). *Application deadline:* For fall admission, 4/30; for spring admission, 10/30. Applications are processed on a rolling basis. *Application fee:* $20. *Application Contact:* Carolyn Cook, Director of Admissions and New Student Services, 340-693-1224, Fax: 340-693-1155, E-mail: ccook@uvi.edu. *Senior Vice President and Provost,* Dr. Laverne Ragster, 340-693-1200, E-mail: lragster@uvi.edu.

Division of Business Administration Students: 3 full-time (all women), 26 part-time (19 women); includes 24 minority (23 African Americans, 1 Asian American or Pacific Islander), 1 international. Average age 33. 13 applicants, 92% accepted, 6 enrolled. *Faculty:* 4 full-time (0 women), 1 part-time/adjunct (0 women). Expenses: Contact institution. *Financial support:* Application deadline: 4/15. In 2001, 26 degrees awarded. *Degree program information:* Part-time and evening/weekend programs available. Offers business administration (MBA). *Application deadline:* For fall admission, 4/30; for spring admission, 10/30. *Application fee:* $20. *Application Contact:* Carolyn Cook, Director of Admissions and New Student Services, 340-693-1224, Fax: 340-693-1155, E-mail: ccook@uvi.edu. *Chairperson,* Dr. Greg Braxton-Brown, 340-693-1301, Fax: 340-693-1311, E-mail: gbraxto@uvi.edu.

Division of Education Students: 16 full-time (all women), 98 part-time (80 women); includes 80 minority (76 African Americans, 4 Hispanic Americans), 25 international. Average age 36. 56 applicants, 79% accepted, 24 enrolled. *Faculty:* 8 full-time (6 women), 1 (woman) part-time/adjunct. Expenses: Contact institution. *Financial support:* In 2001–02, 2 students received support. Scholarships/grants available. Financial award application deadline: 4/15. In 2001, 23 degrees awarded. *Degree program information:* Part-time and evening/weekend programs available. Offers education (MAE). *Application deadline:* For fall admission, 4/30; for spring admission, 11/30. *Application fee:* $20. *Application Contact:* Carolyn Cook, Director of Admissions and New Student Services, 340-693-1224, Fax: 340-693-1155, E-mail: ccook@uvi.edu. *Chairperson,* Dr. Linda V. Thomas, 340-693-1328, Fax: 340-693-1385, E-mail: lthomas2@uvi.edu.

UNIVERSITY OF TOLEDO, Toledo, OH 43606-3398

General Information State-supported, coed, university. CGS member. *Enrollment:* 1,434 full-time matriculated graduate/professional students (681 women), 2,011 part-time matriculated graduate/professional students (1,274 women). *Graduate faculty:* 408. Tuition, state resident: full-time $7,278; part-time $303 per hour. Tuition, nonresident: full-time $15,731; part-time $699 per hour. *Required fees:* $43 per hour. *Graduate housing:* On-campus housing not available. *Student services:* Campus employment opportunities, campus safety program, career counseling, child daycare facilities, disabled student services, exercise/wellness program, free psychological counseling, grant writing training, international student services, low-cost health insurance, multicultural affairs office, teacher training, writing training. *Library facilities:* Carlson Library plus 3 others. *Online resources:* library catalog, web page, access to other libraries' catalogs. *Collection:* 1.3 million titles, 4,527 serial subscriptions, 7,224 audiovisual materials. *Research affiliation:* NASA–Glen Research Center at Lewis Field (aerospace engineering), Merck and Company (pharmaceutical research), Midwest Astronomical Data Reduction and Analysis Facility (astronomy), Edison Industrial Systems Center (systems integration, quality control, mathematical modeling), Ohio Aerospace Institute (aerospace research), National Renewable Energy Laboratory (thin films, photovoltaics).

Computer facilities: 1,700 computers available on campus for general student use. A campuswide network can be accessed from student residence rooms and from off campus. Internet access and online class registration, online transcripts, student account and grade information are available. *Web address:* http://www.utoledo.edu/.

General Application Contact: Dr. Richard A. Hudson, Interim Vice Provost for Graduate Education and Dean of the Graduate School, 419-530-1979, Fax: 419-530-7946.

GRADUATE UNITS

College of Law Students: 326 full-time (156 women), 124 part-time (50 women); includes 28 minority (19 African Americans, 4 Asian Americans or Pacific Islanders, 4 Hispanic Americans, 1 Native American) Average age 27. 983 applicants, 51% accepted, 167 enrolled. *Faculty:* 32 full-time (12 women), 16 part-time/adjunct (4 women). Expenses: Contact institution. *Financial support:* In 2001–02, 424 students received support, including 16 research assistantships (averaging $900 per year), 26 teaching assistantships (averaging $750 per year); career-related internships or fieldwork, Federal Work-Study, and scholarships/grants also available. Support available to part-time students. Financial award application deadline: 7/7; financial award applicants required to submit FAFSA. In 2001, 139 degrees awarded. *Degree program information:* Part-time and evening/weekend programs available. Offers law (JD). *Application deadline:* For fall admission, 6/1 (priority date). Applications are processed on a rolling basis. *Application fee:* $30. Electronic applications accepted. *Application Contact:* Carol E. Frendt, Assistant Dean of Law Admissions, 419-530-4131, Fax: 419-530-4345, E-mail: law.admissions@utoledo.edu. *Dean,* Phillip J. Closius, 419-530-2379, Fax: 419-530-4526.

Graduate School Students: 1,434 full-time (681 women), 2,011 part-time (1,274 women); includes 315 minority (224 African Americans, 47 Asian Americans or Pacific Islanders, 34 Hispanic Americans, 10 Native Americans), 789 international. Average age 33. 3,326 applicants, 47% accepted. *Faculty:* 408. Expenses: Contact institution. *Financial support:* In 2001–02, 4 fellowships, 292 research assistantships, 438 teaching assistantships were awarded. Career-related internships or fieldwork, Federal Work-Study, institutionally sponsored loans, tuition waivers (full), and administrative assistantships, tuition scholarships also available. Support available to part-time students. Financial award applicants required to submit FAFSA. In 2001, 739 master's, 76 doctorates, 19 other advanced degrees awarded. *Degree program information:* Part-time and evening/weekend programs available. Postbaccalaureate distance learning degree programs offered. *Application deadline:* Applications are processed on a rolling basis. *Application fee:* $30. Electronic applications accepted. *Application Contact:* Graduate School Office, 419-530-4723, Fax: 419-530-4724, E-mail: gradsch@utnet.utoledo.edu. *Interim Vice Provost for Graduate Education and Dean of the Graduate School,* Dr. Richard A. Hudson, 419-530-1979, Fax: 419-530-7946.

College of Arts and Sciences Students: 331 full-time (157 women), 124 part-time (92 women); includes 43 minority (32 African Americans, 7 Asian Americans or Pacific Islanders, 2 Hispanic Americans, 2 Native Americans), 145 international. Average age 32. 523 applicants, 60% accepted. *Faculty:* 180. Expenses: Contact institution. *Financial support:* In 2001–02, 71 research assistantships, 242 teaching assistantships were awarded. Fellowships, career-related internships or fieldwork, Federal Work-Study, institutionally sponsored loans, tuition waivers (full), and administrative assistantships, tuition scholarships also available. Support available to part-time students. In 2001, 128 master's, 25 doctorates awarded. *Degree program information:* Part-time and evening/weekend programs available. Offers analytical chemistry (MES, MS, PhD); anthropology (MAE); applied mathematics (MS); arts and sciences (MA, MAE, MES, MLS, MM, MPA, MS, PhD); biological chemistry (MES, MS, PhD); biology (MES, MS, PhD); clinical psychology (PhD); earth, ecological and environmental sciences (MS); economics (MA, MAE); English as a second language (MAE); English language and literature (MA, MAE); experimental psychology (MA, PhD); French (MA, MAE); geography (MA); German (MA, MAE); history (MA, MAE, PhD); inorganic chemistry (MES, MS, PhD); liberal studies (MLS); mathematics (MA, MES, PhD); music education (MM); organic chemistry (MES, MS, PhD); performance (MM); philosophy (MA); physical chemistry (MES, MS, PhD); physics (MES, MS, PhD); planning (MA); political science (MA); public administration (MPA); sociology (MA, MAE); Spanish (MA, MAE); statistics (MS). *Application fee:* $30. Electronic applications accepted. *Chair,* Dr. David Stern, 419-530-6185.

College of Business Administration Students: 277 full-time (90 women), 244 part-time (80 women); includes 23 African Americans, 4 Asian Americans or Pacific Islanders, 8 Hispanic Americans, 168 international. Average age 30. 382 applicants, 80% accepted, 165 enrolled. *Faculty:* 42. Expenses: Contact institution. *Financial support:* In 2001–02, 68 research assistantships, 12 teaching assistantships were awarded. Fellowships, career-related internships or fieldwork, Federal Work-Study, institutionally sponsored loans, tuition waivers (full), and administrative assistantships, tuition scholarships also available. Support available to part-time students. Financial award application deadline: 4/1; financial award applicants required to submit FAFSA. In 2001, 186 master's, 2 doctorates awarded. *Degree program information:* Part-time and evening/weekend programs available. Offers accounting (MBA, MSA); business administration (MBA, MS, MSA, PhD); decision sciences (MBA); finance and business economics (MBA); information systems (MBA); international business entrepreneurship and strategy (MBA); management (MBA); manufacturing management (MS, PhD); marketing (MBA); operations management (MBA). *Application deadline:* For fall admission, 8/1 (priority date). Applications are processed on a rolling basis. *Application fee:* $30. Electronic applications accepted. *Interim Dean,* Dr. Sonny S. Ariss, 419-530-4060, Fax: 419-530-7260, E-mail: mba@uoft01.utoledo.edu.

College of Education and Allied Professions Students: 155 full-time (114 women), 496 part-time (390 women); includes 84 minority (66 African Americans, 7 Asian Americans or Pacific Islanders, 8 Hispanic Americans, 3 Native Americans), 14 international. Average age 36. 512 applicants, 88% accepted. *Faculty:* 97 full-time (36 women). Expenses: Contact institution. *Financial support:* In 2001–02, 22 research assistantships, 12 teaching assistantships were awarded. Fellowships, career-related internships or fieldwork, Federal Work-Study, institutionally sponsored loans, tuition waivers (full), and administrative assistantships, tuition scholarships also available. Support available to part-time students. Financial award application deadline: 4/1; financial award applicants required to submit FAFSA. In 2001, 195 master's, 34 doctorates, 1 other advanced degree awarded. *Degree program information:* Part-time and evening/weekend programs available. Offers business education (ME, DE, PhD, Ed S); curriculum and instruction (ME, DE, PhD, Ed S); early childhood education (DE, PhD, Ed S); early childhood, physical and special education (ME); education (ME, MES, DE, PhD, Ed S); education theory and social foundations (ME); educational administration and supervision (ME, Ed S); educational education and supervision (DE); educational media (DE, PhD, Ed S); educational psychology (ME, DE, PhD); educational research and measurement (DE, PhD); educational sociology (DE, PhD); elementary education (DE, PhD, Ed S); foundation of education (ME, DE, PhD); foundations of education (DE, PhD); higher education (ME, PhD); history of education (DE, PhD); philosophy of education (DE, PhD); secondary education (ME, DE, PhD, Ed S); special education (ME, DE, PhD, Ed S); vocational education (ME, Ed S). *Application deadline:* Applications are processed on a rolling basis. *Application fee:* $30. Electronic applications accepted. *Head,* Dr. Linda B. Murphy, 419-530-2026, Fax: 419-530-7719.

College of Engineering Students: 253 full-time (47 women), 265 part-time (35 women); includes 6 minority (5 African Americans, 1 Asian American or Pacific Islander), 424 international. Average age 26. 1,944 applicants, 27% accepted. *Faculty:* 79 full-time (9 women). Expenses: Contact institution. *Financial support:* In 2001–02, 508 students received support, including 2 fellowships with full tuition reimbursements available, 119 research assistantships with full tuition reimbursements available, 144 teaching assistantships with full tuition reimbursements available; Federal Work-Study, scholarships/grants, tuition waivers (full), and unspecified assistantships also available. Support available to part-time students. Financial award application deadline: 4/1. In 2001, 199 master's, 14 doctorates awarded. *Degree program information:* Part-time and evening/weekend programs available. Postbaccalaureate distance learning degree programs offered (minimal on-campus study). Offers bioengineering (MS, PhD); chemical engineering (MS); civil engineering (MS); computer science (MS); ecology (PhD); electrical engineering (MS); engineering (PhD); engineering sciences (PhD); general engineering (MS); industrial engineering (MS); mechanical engineering (MS). *Application deadline:* For fall admission, 5/31 (priority date). Applications are processed on a rolling basis. *Application fee:* $30. Electronic applications accepted. *Application Contact:* Dr. Martin A. Abraham, Associate Dean, Research and Graduate Studies, 419-530-7391, Fax: 419-530-7392, E-mail: martin.abraham@utoledo.edu. *Interim Dean,* Dr. Nagi Naganathan, 419-530-8000, Fax: 419-530-8006, E-mail: nagi.naganathan@utoledo.edu.

College of Health and Human Services Students: 31 full-time (21 women), 71 part-time (51 women). 68 applicants, 78% accepted, 38 enrolled. Expenses: Contact institution. *Financial support:* In 2001–02, 4 research assistantships, 22 teaching assistantships were awarded. In 2001, 40 master's, 14 doctorates awarded. Offers counseling and mental health services (ME, PhD); health education (DE, PhD); kinesiology (MS); physical education (DE, PhD); public health and rehabilitative services (MES, MPH); recreation and leisure studies (ME); school psychology (ME, Ed S); speech language pathology (ME). *Application fee:* $30. *Dean,* Dr. Jerome M. Sulivan, 419-530-4180.

College of Pharmacy Offers administrative pharmacy (MSPS); industrial pharmacy (MSPS); medicinal and biological chemistry (MS, PhD); pharmaceutical science (MSPS); pharmacology (MSPS); pharmacy (Pharm D, MS, MSPS, PhD). Electronic applications accepted.

See in-depth description on page 1271.

UNIVERSITY OF TORONTO, Toronto, ON M5S 1A1, Canada

General Information Province-supported, coed, university. CGS member. *Graduate housing:* Rooms and/or apartments available on a first-come, first-served basis to single students and available to married students. *Research affiliation:* Center for Addiction and Mental Health, Hospital for Sick Children, Pontifical Institute of Medieval Studies, Royal Ontario Museum, Canadian Institute for Theoretical Astrophysics, Fields Institute for Research in Mathematical Sciences.

GRADUATE UNITS

Faculty of Dentistry Offers dental anesthesia (M Sc); dental public health (M Sc); dentistry (DDS, M Sc, PhD, Diploma); endodontics (M Sc); oral and maxillofacial surgery and anesthesia (M Sc); oral pathology (M Sc); oral radiology (M Sc); orthodontics (M Sc); pediatric dentistry (M Sc); periodontology (M Sc); prosthodontics (M Sc).

Faculty of Law *Degree program information:* Part-time programs available. Offers law (LL B, LL M, MSL, SJD).

Faculty of Medicine Offers medicine (MD).

University of Toronto (continued)

School of Graduate Studies *Degree program information:* Part-time and evening/weekend programs available.

Humanities Division *Degree program information:* Part-time programs available. Offers ancient and medieval philosophy (PhD); ancient studies (MA, PhD); classical studies (MA, PhD); comparative literature (MA, PhD); drama (MA, PhD); East Asian studies (MA, PhD); English (MA, PhD); French language and literature (MA, PhD); Germanic languages and literatures (MA, PhD); history (MA, PhD); history and philosophy of science and technology (MA, PhD); history of art (MA, PhD); humanities (LL M, M Ed, M Sc, MA, MA(T), MH Sc, MM St, MSW, Mus Doc, Mus M, Ed D, PhD, SJD); Italian studies (MA, PhD); linguistics (MA, PhD); medieval studies (MA, PhD); museum studies (MM St); music (MA, Mus Doc, PhD); Near and Middle Eastern civilizations (MA, PhD); performance (Mus M); philosophy (MA, PhD); religious studies (MA, PhD); Slavic languages and literatures (MA, PhD); South Asian studies (MA, PhD); Spanish and Portuguese (MA, PhD); women's studies (LL M, M Ed, M Sc, MA, MH Sc, MSW, Ed D, PhD, SJD).

Life Sciences Division *Degree program information:* Part-time programs available. Offers aging and the life course (M Sc, MA, MH Sc, MIS, MN, MSW, PhD); alcohol, tobacco, and other psychoactive substances (M Sc, MA, MI St, MSW, PhD); anatomy and cell biology (M Sc, PhD); biochemistry (M Sc, PhD); bioethics (LL M, M Sc, MA, MH Sc, PhD, SJD); biomedical communications (M Sc BMC); biomolecular structure (PhD); botany (M Sc, PhD); cardiovascular sciences (M Sc, PhD); community health (M Sc, MH Sc, PhD); developmental biology (PhD); environmental studies (M Sc, M Sc F, MA); forestry (M Sc F, MFC, PhD); genetic counseling (M Sc); immunology (M Sc, PhD); laboratory medicine and pathobiology (M Sc, MH Sc, PhD); life sciences (LL M, M Sc, M Sc BMC, M Sc F, MA, MA Sc, MFC, MH Sc, MI St, MIS, MN, MSW, PhD, SJD); medical biophysics (M Sc, PhD); medical science (M Sc, PhD); molecular and medical genetics (M Sc, PhD); neuroscience (M Sc, PhD); nursing science (M Sc, MN, PhD); nutritional sciences (M Sc, PhD); pharmaceutical sciences (M Sc, PhD); pharmacology (M Sc, PhD); physiology (M Sc, PhD); psychology (MA, PhD); rehabilitation science (M Sc); speech-language pathology (M Sc, MH Sc, PhD); toxicology (M Sc, M Sc F, MA, MA Sc, PhD); zoology (M Sc, PhD).

Physical Sciences Division *Degree program information:* Part-time programs available. Offers aerospace science and engineering (M Eng, MA Sc, PhD); applied science and engineering (M Eng, M Eng Tel, M Sc, MA Sc, MH Sc, PhD); astronomy (M Sc, PhD); biomedical engineering (M Eng, M Sc, MA Sc, PhD); chemical engineering and applied chemistry (M Eng, MA Sc, PhD); chemistry (M Sc, PhD); civil engineering (M Eng, MA Sc, PhD); clinical biomedical engineering (MH Sc); computer science (M Sc, PhD); electrical and computer engineering (M Eng, M Eng Tel, MA Sc, PhD); environmental engineering (M Eng, MA Sc, PhD); geology (M Sc, MA Sc, PhD); integrated manufacturing (M Eng); mathematics (M Sc, MMF, PhD); mechanical and industrial engineering (M Eng, MA Sc, PhD); metallurgy and materials science (M Eng, MA Sc, PhD); physical sciences (M Eng, M Eng Tel, M Sc, MA Sc, MH Sc, MMF, PhD); physics (M Sc, PhD); software engineering (M Eng, M Sc); statistics (M Sc, PhD); welding engineering (M Eng, MA Sc).

Social Sciences Division *Degree program information:* Part-time and evening/weekend programs available. Offers anthropology (M Sc, MA, PhD); architecture, landscape and design (M Arch, MLA, MUD); criminology (MA, PhD); economics (MA, PhD); education (M Ed, MA, MA(T), Ed D, PhD); ethnic and pluralism studies (M Sc, MA, MN, MSW, PhD); geography (M Sc, MA, PhD); industrial relations (MIR, PhD); information studies (MI St, PhD); international relations (MA); management (EMBA, MBA, MMPA, PhD); management and economics (PhD); planning (M Sc Pl); political science (MA, PhD); Russian and East European studies (MA); social sciences (EMBA, M Arch, M Ed, M Sc, M Sc Pl, MA, MA(T), MBA, MI St, MIR, MIS, MLA, MLS, MMPA, MN, MSW, MUD, Ed D, PhD); social work (MSW, PhD); sociology (MA, PhD).

UNIVERSITY OF TRINITY COLLEGE, Toronto, ON M5S 1H8, Canada

General Information Independent-religious, coed, graduate-only institution. *Enrollment by degree level:* 56 first professional, 9 master's, 12 doctoral, 29 other advanced degrees. *Graduate faculty:* 4 full-time (1 woman), 10 part-time/adjunct (2 women). *Graduate tuition:* Tuition and fees charges are reported in Canadian dollars. *Tuition:* Part-time $410 Canadian dollars per credit. One-time fee: $353 Canadian dollars part-time. *Graduate housing:* Room and/or apartments available on a first-come, first-served basis to single students; on-campus housing not available to married students. Typical cost: $7,610 Canadian dollars (including board). Housing application deadline: 7/15. *Student services:* Campus employment opportunities, campus safety program, career counseling, child daycare facilities, free psychological counseling, international student services, low-cost health insurance. *Library facilities:* The John W. Graham Library. *Online resources:* library catalog, web page, access to other libraries' catalogs. *Collection:* 150,000 titles, 360 serial subscriptions, 1,474 audiovisual materials.

Computer facilities: 41 computers available on campus for general student use. A campuswide network can be accessed from student residence rooms and from off campus. Internet access and online class registration are available. *Web address:* http://www.trinity.utoronto.ca/.

General Application Contact: Rachel Richards, Administrative Assistant to the Dean, Faculty of Divinity, 416-978-2133, Fax: 416-978-4949, E-mail: divinity@trinity.utoronta.ca.

GRADUATE UNITS

Faculty of Divinity *Degree program information:* Part-time and evening/weekend programs available. Offers ministry (Diploma); ministry for church musicians (Diploma); theology (M Div, MTS, Th M, D Min, Th D, Diploma, L Th). Member of the Toronto School of Theology.

UNIVERSITY OF TULSA, Tulsa, OK 74104-3189

General Information Independent-religious, coed, university. CGS member. *Enrollment:* 851 full-time matriculated graduate/professional students (368 women), 499 part-time matriculated graduate/professional students (196 women). *Enrollment by degree level:* 645 master's, 126 doctoral, 579 other advanced degrees. *Graduate faculty:* 231 full-time (55 women), 4 part-time/adjunct (0 women). *Tuition:* Full-time $9,540; part-time $530 per credit hour. *Required fees:* $80. One-time fee: $230 full-time. *Graduate housing:* Rooms and/or apartments available on a first-come, first-served basis to single and married students. Typical cost: $2,700 per year ($5,400 including board) for single students; $3,000 per year ($5,800 including board) for married students. *Student services:* Campus employment opportunities, campus safety program, career counseling, child daycare facilities, disabled student services, exercise/wellness program, free psychological counseling, international student services, low-cost health insurance, multicultural affairs office, teacher training, writing training. *Library facilities:* McFarlin Library plus 1 other. *Online resources:* library catalog, web page, access to other libraries' catalogs. *Collection:* 900,000 titles, 9,100 serial subscriptions, 13,300 audiovisual materials.

Computer facilities: 718 computers available on campus for general student use. A campuswide network can be accessed from student residence rooms and from off campus. Internet access is available. *Web address:* http://www.utulsa.edu/.

General Application Contact: Dr. Janet A. Haggerty, Dean of Research and Graduate Studies, 918-631-2336, Fax: 918-631-2073, E-mail: grad@utulsa.edu.

GRADUATE UNITS

College of Law Students: 469 full-time (192 women), 108 part-time (61 women); includes 84 minority (34 African Americans, 4 Asian Americans or Pacific Islanders, 46 Native Americans), 6 international. Average age 27. 876 applicants, 62% accepted. *Faculty:* 40 full-time (16 women), 27 part-time/adjunct (8 women). Expenses: Contact institution. *Financial support:* In 2001–02, fellowships (averaging $25,000 per year); Federal Work-Study and scholarships/grants also available. Support available to part-time students. Financial award applicants required to submit FAFSA. In 2001, 163 degrees awarded. *Degree program information:* Part-time programs available. Offers American Indian and indigenous law (LL M); comparative and international law (LL M); law (JD). *Application deadline:* Applications are processed on a rolling basis. *Application fee:* $30. Electronic applications accepted. *Application Contact:* George A. Justice, Assistant Dean of Admissions and Financial Aid, 918-631-2709, Fax: 918-631-3630, E-mail: george-justice@utulsa.edu. *Dean,* Martin H. Belsky, 918-631-2400, Fax: 918-631-3126, E-mail: martin-belsky@utulsa.edu.

Graduate School Students: 396 full-time (175 women), 375 part-time (133 women); includes 67 minority (15 African Americans, 13 Asian Americans or Pacific Islanders, 14 Hispanic Americans, 25 Native Americans), 254 international. Average age 30. 831 applicants, 82% accepted, 363 enrolled. *Faculty:* 203 full-time (44 women), 4 part-time/adjunct (0 women). Expenses: Contact institution. *Financial support:* In 2001–02, 131 students received support; fellowships with full and partial tuition reimbursements available, research assistantships with full and partial tuition reimbursements available, teaching assistantships with full and partial tuition reimbursements available, career-related internships or fieldwork, Federal Work-Study, institutionally sponsored loans, scholarships/grants, tuition waivers (partial), and unspecified assistantships available. Support available to part-time students. Financial award application deadline: 2/1; financial award applicants required to submit FAFSA. In 2001, 186 master's, 20 doctorates awarded. *Degree program information:* Part-time and evening/weekend programs available. *Application deadline:* Applications are processed on a rolling basis. *Application fee:* $30. Electronic applications accepted. *Dean of Research and Graduate Studies,* Dr. Janet A. Haggerty, 918-631-2336, Fax: 918-631-2073, E-mail: grad@utulsa.edu.

College of Arts and Sciences Students: 164 full-time (107 women), 71 part-time (51 women); includes 21 minority (3 African Americans, 5 Asian Americans or Pacific Islanders, 5 Hispanic Americans, 8 Native Americans), 19 international. Average age 31. 260 applicants, 77% accepted, 135 enrolled. *Faculty:* 99 full-time (29 women). Expenses: Contact institution. *Financial support:* Fellowships with tuition reimbursements, research assistantships with tuition reimbursements, teaching assistantships with tuition reimbursements, career-related internships or fieldwork, Federal Work-Study, scholarships/grants, tuition waivers (partial), and unspecified assistantships available. Support available to part-time students. Financial award application deadline: 2/1; financial award applicants required to submit FAFSA. In 2001, 92 master's, 9 doctorates awarded. *Degree program information:* Part-time and evening/weekend programs available. Offers anthropology (MA); art (MA, MFA); arts and sciences (MA, MFA, MS, MSMSE, MTA, PhD); clinical psychology (MA, PhD); education (MA); English language and literature (MA, PhD); history (MA); industrial/organizational psychology (MA, PhD); math/science education (MSMSE); speech-language pathology (MS); teaching arts (MTA). *Application deadline:* Applications are processed on a rolling basis. *Application fee:* $30. Electronic applications accepted. *Dean,* Dr. Thomas A. Horne, 918-631-2222, Fax: 918-631-3721, E-mail: thomas-horne@utulsa.edu.

College of Business Administration Students: 55 full-time (26 women), 199 part-time (64 women); includes 37 minority (11 African Americans, 3 Asian Americans or Pacific Islanders, 7 Hispanic Americans, 16 Native Americans), 23 international. Average age 30. 194 applicants, 97% accepted, 124 enrolled. *Faculty:* 32 full-time (9 women), 1 part-time/adjunct (0 women). Expenses: Contact institution. *Financial support:* Fellowships with full and partial tuition reimbursements, research assistantships with full and partial tuition reimbursements, teaching assistantships with full and partial tuition reimbursements, career-related internships or fieldwork, Federal Work-Study, institutionally sponsored loans, scholarships/grants, tuition waivers (partial), and unspecified assistantships available. Support available to part-time students. Financial award application deadline: 2/1; financial award applicants required to submit FAFSA. In 2001, 72 degrees awarded. *Degree program information:* Part-time and evening/weekend programs available. Postbaccalaureate distance learning degree programs offered (minimal on-campus study). Offers business administration (M Tax, MBA, METM, MS); chemical engineering (METM); computer science (METM); corporate finance (MS); electrical engineering (METM); geological science (METM); international finance (MS); investment and portfolio management (MS); mathematics (METM); mechanical engineering (METM); petroleum engineering (METM); risk management/financial engineering (MS); taxation (M Tax). *Application deadline:* Applications are processed on a rolling basis. *Application fee:* $30. Electronic applications accepted. *Application Contact:* Dr. W. Gale Sullenburger, Dean, 918-631-2213, E-mail: gale-sullenberger@utulsa.edu. *Dean,* Dr. W. Gale Sullenburger, 918-631-2213, E-mail: gale-sullenberger@utulsa.edu.

College of Engineering and Natural Sciences Students: 189 full-time (44 women), 93 part-time (16 women); includes 9 minority (1 African American, 5 Asian Americans or Pacific Islanders, 2 Hispanic Americans, 1 Native American), 212 international. Average age 28. 377 applicants, 79% accepted, 154 enrolled. *Faculty:* 72 full-time (6 women), 3 part-time/adjunct (0 women). Expenses: Contact institution. *Financial support:* Fellowships with full and partial tuition reimbursements, research assistantships with full and partial tuition reimbursements, teaching assistantships with full and partial tuition reimbursements, career-related internships or fieldwork, Federal Work-Study, scholarships/grants, tuition waivers (partial), and unspecified assistantships available. Support available to part-time students. Financial award application deadline: 2/1; financial award applicants required to submit FAFSA. In 2001, 43 master's, 13 doctorates awarded. *Degree program information:* Part-time programs available. Offers biological sciences (MS, PhD); chemical engineering (ME, MSE, PhD); chemistry (MS); computer science (MS, PhD); electrical engineering (ME, MSE); engineering and natural sciences (ME, METM, MS, MSE, PhD); geosciences (MS, PhD); mathematical sciences (MS); mechanical engineering (ME, MSE, PhD); petroleum engineering (ME, MSE, PhD). *Application deadline:* Applications are processed on a rolling basis. *Application fee:* $30. Electronic applications accepted. *Application Contact:* Information Contact, E-mail: grad@utulsa.edu. *Dean,* Dr. Steve J. Bellovich, 918-631-2288, E-mail: steven-bellovich@utulsa.edu.

See in-depth description on page 1273.

UNIVERSITY OF UTAH, Salt Lake City, UT 84112-1107

General Information State-supported, coed, university. CGS member. *Enrollment:* 3,981 full-time matriculated graduate/professional students (1,801 women), 1,443 part-time matriculated graduate/professional students (719 women). *Enrollment by degree level:* 889 first professional, 2,943 master's, 1,592 doctoral. *Graduate faculty:* 1,096 full-time (284 women), 157 part-time/adjunct (29 women). Tuition, state resident: part-time $320 per semester hour. Tuition, nonresident: part-time $1,135 per semester hour. *Required fees:* $143 per semester hour. Tuition and fees vary according to course load, degree level and program. *Graduate housing:* Rooms and/or apartments available on a first-come, first-served basis to single and married students. Typical cost: $2,193 per year ($4,646 including board) for single students; $9,400 per year ($11,853 including board) for married students. Room and board charges vary according to board plan and housing facility selected. *Student services:* Campus employment opportunities, campus safety program, career counseling, child daycare facilities, disabled student services, international student services, low-cost health insurance. *Library facilities:* Marriott Library plus 2 others. *Online resources:* library catalog, web page, access to other libraries' catalogs. *Collection:* 3.3 million titles, 21,853 serial subscriptions, 56,427 audiovisual materials.

Computer facilities: 5,000 computers available on campus for general student use. A campuswide network can be accessed from student residence rooms and from off campus. Internet access and online class registration, on-line classes are available. *Web address:* http://www.utah.edu/.

General Application Contact: Office of Admissions, 801-581-7281, Fax: 801-585-3034, E-mail: admissionweb_grad@saff.utah.edu.

GRADUATE UNITS

College of Pharmacy *Degree program information:* Part-time programs available. Offers medicinal chemistry (MS, PhD); pharmaceutics and pharmaceutical chemistry (MS, PhD); pharmacology and toxicology (MS, PhD); pharmacy (Pharm D, MS, PhD); pharmacy practice (MS).

Graduate School Students: 3,981 full-time (1,801 women), 1,443 part-time (719 women); includes 416 minority (36 African Americans, 178 Asian Americans or Pacific Islanders, 160 Hispanic Americans, 42 Native Americans), 848 international. Average age 32. 6,787 applicants, 41% accepted, 1672 enrolled. *Faculty:* 1,076 full-time (272 women), 300 part-time/adjunct (85 women). Expenses: Contact institution. *Financial support:* Fellowships with full and partial tuition reimbursements, research assistantships with full and partial tuition reimbursements, teaching assistantships with full and partial tuition reimbursements, career-related internships or fieldwork, Federal Work-Study, institutionally sponsored loans, scholarships/grants, and traineeships available. Support available to part-time students. Financial award application deadline: 3/1; financial award applicants required to submit FAFSA. In 2001, 995 master's, 220 doctorates awarded. *Degree program information:* Part-time and evening/weekend programs available. Offers statistics (M Stat). *Application deadline:* For fall admission, 5/1; for winter admission, 4/15; for spring admission, 11/1. *Application fee:* $40 ($60 for international students). Electronic applications accepted. *Application Contact:* Associate Vice President of Graduate Programs and Dean, 801-581-6925, Fax: 801-585-6749, E-mail: dchapman@park.admin.utah.edu. *Dean,* Dr. David S. Chapman, 801-581-6925, Fax: 801-585-6749, E-mail: dchapman@park.admin.utah.edu.

College of Education Students: 255 full-time (179 women), 293 part-time (199 women); includes 67 minority (11 African Americans, 19 Asian Americans or Pacific Islanders, 32 Hispanic Americans, 5 Native Americans), 4 international. Average age 37. 225 applicants, 44% accepted. *Faculty:* 44 full-time (20 women), 9 part-time/adjunct (7 women). Expenses: Contact institution. *Financial support:* In 2001–02, 31 fellowships with full tuition reimbursements, 5 research assistantships with full tuition reimbursements, 26 teaching assistantships with full and partial tuition reimbursements were awarded. Career-related internships or fieldwork, Federal Work-Study, institutionally sponsored loans, scholarships/grants, tuition waivers (full and partial), and unspecified assistantships also available. Support available to part-time students. Financial award applicants required to submit FAFSA. In 2001, 162 master's, 20 doctorates awarded. *Degree program information:* Part-time and evening/weekend programs available. Offers education (M Ed, M Stat, MA, MS, Ed D, PhD); education culture and society (M Ed, MA, MS, PhD); educational leadership and policy (M Ed, Ed D, PhD); educational psychology (M Ed, M Stat, MA, MS, PhD); special education (M Ed, MS, PhD); teaching and learning (M Ed, MA, MS, PhD). *Application fee:* $40 ($60 for international students). *Dean,* David J. Sperry, 801-581-8221, Fax: 801-581-5223, E-mail: david.sperry@ed.utah.edu.

College of Engineering Students: 381 full-time (66 women), 192 part-time (33 women); includes 178 minority (4 African Americans, 159 Asian Americans or Pacific Islanders, 11 Hispanic Americans, 4 Native Americans), 99 international. Average age 29. 903 applicants, 45% accepted. *Faculty:* 90 full-time (12 women), 15 part-time/adjunct (2 women). Expenses: Contact institution. *Financial support:* Fellowships, research assistantships, teaching assistantships, career-related internships or fieldwork, Federal Work-Study, institutionally sponsored loans, and traineeships available. Support available to part-time students. Financial award applicants required to submit FAFSA. In 2001, 68 master's, 29 doctorates awarded. *Degree program information:* Part-time programs available. Offers bioengineering (ME, MS, PhD); chemical and fuels engineering (M Phil, ME, MS, PhD); chemical engineering (M Phil, ME, MS, PhD); civil engineering (ME, MS, PhD); computing (M Phil, MS, PhD); electrical engineering (M Phil, ME, MS, PhD, EE); engineering (M Phil, ME, MS, PhD, EE); environmental engineering (ME, MS, PhD); materials science and engineering (ME, MS, PhD); mechanical engineering (ME, MS, PhD); nuclear engineering (ME, MS, PhD). *Application fee:* $40 ($60 for international students). *Application Contact:* Carolee Stout, Advisor, 801-581-6911, Fax: 801-581-8692, E-mail: cstout@coe.utah.edu. *Dean,* Gerald B. Stringfellow, 801-581-6911, Fax: 801-581-8692, E-mail: stringfellow@coe.utah.edu.

College of Fine Arts Students: 79 full-time (51 women), 40 part-time (21 women); includes 13 minority (10 Asian Americans or Pacific Islanders, 2 Hispanic Americans, 1 Native American), 6 international. Average age 34. 146 applicants, 42% accepted. *Faculty:* 65 full-time (25 women), 54 part-time/adjunct (20 women). Expenses: Contact institution. *Financial support:* Fellowships with full tuition reimbursements, research assistantships, teaching assistantships with full and partial tuition reimbursements, career-related internships or fieldwork, Federal Work-Study, institutionally sponsored loans, and scholarships/grants available. Financial award applicants required to submit FAFSA. In 2001, 44 master's, 3 doctorates awarded. *Degree program information:* Part-time programs available. Offers art history (MA); ballet (MA, MFA); ceramics (MFA); drawing (MFA); film studies (MFA); fine arts (M Mus, MA, MFA, PhD); graphic design (MFA); illustration (MFA); modern dance (MA, MFA); music (M Mus, MA, PhD); painting (MFA); photography/digital imaging (MFA); printmaking (MFA); sculpture/intermedia (MFA); theatre (MFA, PhD). *Application fee:* $40 ($60 for international students). *Application Contact:* Steve Roens, Associate Dean, 801-581-8420, E-mail: steve.roens@music.utah.edu. *Dean,* Phyllis A. Haskell, 801-581-6764, Fax: 801-581-3066, E-mail: phyllis.haskell@finearts.utah.edu.

College of Health Students: 295 full-time (204 women), 55 part-time (29 women); includes 21 minority (1 African American, 10 Asian Americans or Pacific Islanders, 9 Hispanic Americans, 1 Native American), 7 international. Average age 30. 396 applicants, 58% accepted. *Faculty:* 43 full-time (19 women), 9 part-time/adjunct (7 women). Expenses: Contact institution. *Financial support:* Fellowships, research assistantships, teaching assistantships, career-related internships or fieldwork, Federal Work-Study, and institutionally sponsored loans available. Financial award applicants required to submit FAFSA. In 2001, 88 master's, 11 doctorates awarded. *Degree program information:* Part-time programs available. Offers audiology (MA, MS); exercise and sport science (MS, Ed D, PhD); foods and nutrition (MS); health (M Phil, MA, MOT, MPT, MS, Ed D, PhD); health promotion and education (M Phil, MS, Ed D, PhD); occupational therapy (MOT); parks, recreation, and tourism (M Phil, MS, Ed D, PhD); physical therapy (MPT); speech-language pathology (MA, MS); speech-language pathology and audiology (PhD). *Application fee:* $40 ($60 for international students). *Dean,* John Dunn, 801-581-8537, Fax: 801-581-5580, E-mail: john.dunn@health.utah.edu.

College of Humanities Students: 213 full-time (128 women), 144 part-time (87 women); includes 31 minority (6 African Americans, 9 Asian Americans or Pacific Islanders, 15 Hispanic Americans, 1 Native American), 23 international. Average age 34. 413 applicants, 40% accepted. *Faculty:* 130 full-time (46 women), 30 part-time/adjunct (10 women). Expenses: Contact institution. *Financial support:* Fellowships, research assistantships, teaching assistantships, career-related internships or fieldwork, Federal Work-Study, and institutionally sponsored loans available. Financial award applicants required to submit FAFSA. In 2001, 55 master's, 22 doctorates awarded. *Degree program information:* Part-time programs available. Offers communication (M Phil, MA, MS, PhD); comparative literature (MA, PhD); creative writing (MFA); English (MA, PhD); French (MA, MAT); German (MA, MAT, PhD); history (MA, MS, PhD); humanities (M Phil, MA, MAT, MFA, MS, PhD); language pedagogy (MAT); linguistics (MA); Middle East studies (MA, PhD); philosophy (MA, MS, PhD); Spanish (MA, MAT, PhD). *Application fee:* $40 ($60 for international students). *Application Contact:* Maureen Mathison, Associate Dean, 801-581-6214, Fax: 801-585-5190, E-mail: maureen.mathison@m.cc.utah.edu. *Dean,* Robert D. Newman, 801-581-6214, Fax: 801-585-5190, E-mail: robert.newman@hum.utah.edu.

College of Mines and Earth Sciences Students: 99 full-time (25 women), 46 part-time (14 women); includes 40 minority (1 African American, 33 Asian Americans or Pacific Islanders, 6 Hispanic Americans), 18 international. Average age 30. 127 applicants, 53% accepted. *Faculty:* 37 full-time (5 women), 2 part-time/adjunct (0 women). Expenses: Contact institution. *Financial support:* Fellowships, research assistantships, teaching assistantships, career-related internships or fieldwork and institutionally sponsored loans available. Support available to part-time students. Financial award application deadline: 2/15. In 2001, 16 master's, 11 doctorates awarded. *Degree program information:* Part-time programs available. Offers geological engineering (ME, MS, PhD); geology (MS, PhD); geophysics (MS, PhD); metallurgical engineering (ME, MS, PhD); meteorology (MS, PhD); mines and earth sciences (ME, MS, PhD); mining engineering (ME, MS, PhD). *Application deadline:* For fall admission, 7/1. *Application fee:* $40 ($60 for international students). *Application Contact:* Sharon Christenson, Information Contact, 801-581-8767, Fax: 801-581-5560, E-mail: sharon@mines.utah.edu. *Dean,* Dr. Francis H. Brown, 801-581-8767, Fax: 801-581-5560, E-mail: brown@do01so.mines.utah.edu.

College of Nursing Students: 94 full-time (75 women), 102 part-time (90 women); includes 13 minority (7 Asian Americans or Pacific Islanders, 3 Hispanic Americans, 3 Native Americans), 5 international. Average age 37. 117 applicants, 79% accepted. *Faculty:* 24 full-time (17 women), 2 part-time/adjunct (1 woman). Expenses: Contact institution. *Financial support:* Fellowships, research assistantships, teaching assistantships, scholarships/grants available. In 2001, 71 master's, 4 doctorates awarded. *Degree program information:* Part-time programs available. Offers gerontology (MS, Certificate); nursing (MS, PhD, Certificate). *Application fee:* $40 ($60 for international students). *Application Contact:* Joyce Rathbun, Graduate Adviser, 801-581-8798, Fax: 801-581-4642, E-mail: jrathbun@nursac.nurs.utah.edu. *Dean,* Maureen Keefe, 801-581-8262, Fax: 801-581-4642, E-mail: maureen.keefe@nurs.utah.edu.

College of Science Students: 330 full-time (109 women), 93 part-time (28 women); includes 124 minority (4 African Americans, 112 Asian Americans or Pacific Islanders, 7 Hispanic Americans, 1 Native American), 30 international. Average age 31. 443 applicants, 55% accepted. *Faculty:* 129 full-time (11 women), 13 part-time/adjunct (2 women). Expenses: Contact institution. *Financial support:* Fellowships with full tuition reimbursements, research assistantships with full and partial tuition reimbursements, teaching assistantships with full and partial tuition reimbursements, career-related internships or fieldwork, scholarships/grants, and traineeships available. In 2001, 25 master's, 47 doctorates awarded. *Degree program information:* Part-time programs available. Offers biology (M Phil); chemical physics (PhD); chemistry (M Phil, MA, MS, PhD); ecology and evolutionary biology (MS, PhD); genetics (MS, PhD); mathematics (M Phil, M Stat, MA, MS, PhD); molecular biology (PhD); physics (MA, MS, PhD); science (M Phil, M Stat, MA, MS, PhD); science for secondary school teachers (MS); science teacher education (MS). *Application fee:* $40 ($60 for international students). *Application Contact:* Information Contact, 801-581-6958, E-mail: office@science.utah.edu. *Dean,* Peter J. Stang, 801-581-6958, Fax: 801-585-3169, E-mail: stang@chemistry.utah.edu.

College of Social and Behavioral Science Students: 165 full-time (84 women), 222 part-time (102 women); includes 39 minority (3 African Americans, 29 Asian Americans or Pacific Islanders, 6 Hispanic Americans, 1 Native American), 34 international. Average age 34. 475 applicants, 46% accepted. *Faculty:* 113 full-time (35 women), 29 part-time/adjunct (7 women). Expenses: Contact institution. *Financial support:* Fellowships, research assistantships, teaching assistantships, career-related internships or fieldwork, Federal Work-Study, and institutionally sponsored loans available. Support available to part-time students. In 2001, 78 master's, 14 doctorates awarded. *Degree program information:* Part-time programs available. Offers anthropology (MA, MS, PhD); economics (M Phil, M Stat, MA, MS, PhD); family and consumer studies (MS); geography (MA, MS, PhD); political science (MA, MS, PhD); psychology (M Stat, MA, MS, PhD); public administration (MPA, Certificate); social and behavioral science (M Phil, M Stat, MA, MPA, MS, PhD, Certificate); sociology (M Stat, PhD). *Application deadline:* For fall admission, 7/1. *Application fee:* $40 ($60 for international students). *Application Contact:* Stephen E. Reynolds, Associate Dean, 801-581-8620, E-mail: stephen.reynolds@csbs.utah.edu. *Director,* J. Steven Ott, 801-581-6781, Fax: 801-581-6957, E-mail: jsott@cppa.utah.edu.

David Eccles School of Business Students: 484 full-time (146 women), 61 part-time (20 women); includes 50 minority (3 African Americans, 30 Asian Americans or Pacific Islanders, 14 Hispanic Americans, 3 Native Americans), 39 international. Average age 31. 626 applicants, 55% accepted. *Faculty:* 51 full-time (17 women), 4 part-time/adjunct (0 women). Expenses: Contact institution. *Financial support:* In 2001–02, 30 teaching assistantships were awarded; fellowships, career-related internships or fieldwork and Federal Work-Study also available. In 2001, 178 master's, 6 doctorates awarded. *Degree program information:* Part-time and evening/weekend programs available. Offers accounting (M Pr A, PhD); business (M Pr A, MBA, MS, PhD); business administration (MBA, PhD); finance (MS, PhD). *Application deadline:* For fall admission, 2/15. *Application fee:* $40 ($60 for international students). *Application Contact:* Information Contact, 801-581-7785, Fax: 801-581-3666, E-mail: information@business.utah.edu. *Dean,* Jack Brittain, 801-581-7785, Fax: 801-581-3666, E-mail: dean@business.utah.edu.

Graduate School of Architecture Students: 68 full-time (21 women), 14 part-time (6 women); includes 8 minority (5 Asian Americans or Pacific Islanders, 3 Hispanic Americans), 7 international. Average age 28. 64 applicants, 45% accepted. *Faculty:* 12 full-time (1 woman), 4 part-time/adjunct (3 women). Expenses: Contact institution. *Financial support:* In 2001–02, 34 students received support, including 6 research assistantships with full tuition reimbursements available (averaging $8,250 per year), 26 teaching assistantships with partial tuition reimbursements available (averaging $8,250 per year); fellowships with full tuition reimbursements available, career-related internships or fieldwork, Federal Work-Study, and scholarships/grants also available. Financial award application deadline: 3/20. In 2001, 31 degrees awarded. *Degree program information:* Part-time programs available. Offers architecture (M Arch, MS). *Application deadline:* For fall admission, 3/1. *Application fee:* $40 ($60 for international students). *Application Contact:* Nicole Muhler, Admissions Adviser, 801-581-8254, Fax: 801-581-8217, E-mail: muhler@arch.utah.edu. *Dean,* William C. Miller, 801-581-8254, Fax: 801-581-8217, E-mail: william.c.miller@arch.utah.edu.

Graduate School of Social Work Students: 327 full-time (222 women), 25 part-time (16 women); includes 50 minority (7 African Americans, 14 Asian Americans or Pacific Islanders, 18 Hispanic Americans, 11 Native Americans), 2 international. Average age 35. 402 applicants, 58% accepted. *Faculty:* 17 full-time (11 women), 11 part-time/adjunct (5 women). Expenses: Contact institution. *Financial support:* Fellowships with full and partial tuition reimbursements, research assistantships with full and partial tuition reimbursements, teaching assistantships with full and partial tuition reimbursements, Federal Work-Study and institutionally sponsored loans available. Support available to part-time students. Financial award application deadline: 2/15; financial award applicants required to submit FAFSA. In 2001, 144 master's, 4 doctorates awarded. *Degree program information:* Part-time programs available. Offers social work (MSW, PhD). *Application deadline:* For fall admission, 12/1. *Application fee:* $50. *Application Contact:* Jeanette R. Drews, Associate Dean, 801-581-8828, Fax: 801-587-7956, E-mail: jdrews@socwk.utah.edu. *Dean,* Jannah H. Mather, 801-581-6194, Fax: 801-587-7956, E-mail: jmather@socwk.utah.edu.

School of Medicine Offers medicine (MD, M Phil, M Stat, MPH, MS, MSPH, PhD). Electronic applications accepted.

Graduate Programs in Medicine *Degree program information:* Part-time programs available. Offers biochemistry (MS, PhD); biostatistics (M Stat); experimental pathology (PhD); human genetics (MS, PhD); medical informatics (MS, PhD); medical laboratory science (MS); medicine (M Phil, M Stat, MPH, MS, MSPH, PhD); neurology and anatomy (M Phil, MS, PhD); neuroscience (PhD); oncological sciences (MS, PhD); physiology (PhD); public health (MPH, MSPH). Electronic applications accepted.

S.J. Quinney College of Law Students: 388 full-time (160 women); includes 46 minority (3 African Americans, 17 Asian Americans or Pacific Islanders, 19 Hispanic Americans, 7 Native Americans), 2 international. Average age 28. 908 applicants, 38% accepted, 138 enrolled. *Faculty:* 27 full-time (8 women), 21 part-time/adjunct (6 women). Expenses: Contact institution. *Financial support:* In 2001–02, 147 students received support, including 56 fellowships with full and partial tuition reimbursements available (averaging $8,354 per year), 2 research assistantships with partial tuition reimbursements available (averaging $3,500 per year); career-related internships or fieldwork, Federal Work-Study, institutionally sponsored loans, and scholarships/grants also available. Financial award application deadline: 3/15; financial award applicants required to submit FAFSA. In 2001, 128 degrees awarded. Offers law (JD, LL M). *Application deadline:* For fall admission, 2/1. Applications are processed on a rolling basis. *Application fee:* $50. *Application Contact:* Reyes Aguilar, Associate Dean for Admission and Financial Aid, 801-581-7479, Fax: 801-581-6897, E-mail: aguilarr@law.utah.edu. *Dean,* Scott Matheson, 801-581-6833, Fax: 801-581-6897.

UNIVERSITY OF VERMONT, Burlington, VT 05405

General Information State-supported, coed, university. CGS member. *Enrollment:* 1,497 matriculated graduate/professional students. *Enrollment by degree level:* 384 first professional, 805 master's, 308 doctoral. *Graduate faculty:* 702 full-time, 604 part-time/adjunct. Tuition, state resident: part-time $335 per credit. Tuition, nonresident: part-time $838 per credit. *Graduate housing:* Rooms and/or apartments available to single and married students. *Student services:* Career counseling, free psychological counseling, low-cost health insurance. *Library facilities:* Bailey-Howe Library plus 3 others. *Online resources:* library catalog, web page. *Collection:* 2.4 million titles, 20,216 serial subscriptions, 36,531 audiovisual materials. *Research affiliation:* W. Alton Jones Cell Science Center, Miner Institute (animal sciences).

Computer facilities: 685 computers available on campus for general student use. A campuswide network can be accessed from student residence rooms and from off campus. Internet access, e-mail, Web pages, on-line course support are available. *Web address:* http://www.uvm.edu/.

University of Vermont (continued)

General Application Contact: Ralph M. Swenson, Director of Admissions and Administration, 802-656-3160, Fax: 802-656-0519, E-mail: graduate.admissions@uvm.edu.

GRADUATE UNITS

College of Medicine Offers anatomy and neurobiology (PhD); biochemistry (MS, PhD); medicine (MD, MS, PhD); microbiology and molecular genetics (MS, PhD); molecular physiology and biophysics (MS, PhD); pathology (MS); pharmacology (MS, PhD).

Graduate College *Degree program information:* Part-time programs available. Offers cell and molecular biology (MS, PhD).

College of Agriculture and Life Sciences *Degree program information:* Part-time programs available. Offers agricultural biochemistry (MS, PhD); agriculture and life sciences (M Ext Ed, MAT, MS, MST, PhD); animal sciences (MS, PhD); biology (MST); botany (MAT, MS, PhD); community development and applied economics (M Ext Ed, MS); family and consumer sciences (MAT); field naturalist (MS); nutritional sciences (MS); plant and soil science (MS, PhD).

College of Arts and Sciences *Degree program information:* Part-time programs available. Offers arts and sciences (MA, MAT, MPA, MS, MST, PhD); biology (MS, PhD); biology education (MAT, MST); chemistry (MS, MST, PhD); chemistry education (MAT); clinical psychology (PhD); communication sciences (MS); engineering physics (MS); English (MA); English education (MAT); French (MA); French education (MAT); geography (MA, MAT); geology (MS); geology education (MAT, MST); German (MA); German education (MAT); Greek (MA); Greek and Latin (MAT); historic preservation (MS); history (MA); history education (MAT); Latin (MA); physical sciences (MST); physics (MAT, MS); political science (MA); psychology (PhD); public administration (MPA).

College of Education and Social Services *Degree program information:* Part-time programs available. Offers counseling (MS); curriculum and instruction (M Ed); education and social services (M Ed, MS, MSW, Ed D); educational leadership (M Ed); educational leadership and policy studies (Ed D); educational studies (M Ed); higher education and student affairs administration (M Ed); interdisciplinary studies (M Ed); reading and language arts (M Ed); social work (MSW); special education (M Ed).

College of Engineering and Mathematics *Degree program information:* Part-time programs available. Offers biomedical engineering (MS); biostatistics (MS); civil engineering (MS, PhD); computer science (MS); electrical engineering (MS, PhD); engineering and mathematics (MAT, MS, MST, PhD); materials science (MS, PhD); mathematics (MAT, MS, MST, PhD); mathematics education (MAT, MST); mechanical engineering (MS, PhD); statistics (MS).

School of Allied Health Sciences *Degree program information:* Part-time programs available. Offers allied health sciences (MPT, MS); biomedical technologies (MS); physical therapy (MPT).

School of Business Administration *Degree program information:* Part-time programs available. Offers business administration (MBA).

School of Natural Resources *Degree program information:* Part-time programs available. Offers forestry (MS); natural resources (MS, PhD); natural resources planning (MS, PhD); water resources (MS); wildlife and fisheries biology (MS).

School of Nursing Offers nursing (MS).

See in-depth description on page 1275.

UNIVERSITY OF VICTORIA, Victoria, BC V8W 2Y2, Canada

General Information Province-supported, coed, university. *Graduate housing:* Rooms and/or apartments available to single and married students. Housing application deadline: 2/1. *Research affiliation:* Dominion Astrophysical Observatory, Bamfield Marine Research Station (marine biology), Tri-University Meson Facility, Canada/France/Hawaii Telescope Observatory, Forest Research Centre (groundwater), Institute of Ocean Sciences (geography, oceanography).

GRADUATE UNITS

Faculty of Graduate Studies *Degree program information:* Part-time and evening/weekend programs available. Postbaccalaureate distance learning degree programs offered. Electronic applications accepted.

Faculty of Business *Degree program information:* Part-time programs available. Offers business (MBA).

Faculty of Education *Degree program information:* Part-time programs available. Postbaccalaureate distance learning degree programs offered (minimal on-campus study). Offers art education (M Ed); coaching studies (M Ed); counseling (M Ed, MA); curriculum and instruction (MA); curriculum studies (M Ed, MA); education (M Ed, M Sc, MA, PhD); educational administration (M Ed, MA); educational psychology (M Ed, MA, PhD); English language arts (M Ed, MA); language arts (PhD); leisure service administration (MA); mathematics education (M Ed); music education (M Ed, MA); science education (M Ed); social studies education (M Ed); sports and exercise science (M Sc, MA).

Faculty of Engineering *Degree program information:* Part-time and evening/weekend programs available. Offers computer science (M Sc, MA, PhD); electrical engineering (M Eng, MA Sc, PhD); engineering (M Eng, M Sc, MA, MA Sc, PhD); mechanical engineering (M Eng, MA Sc, PhD).

Faculty of Fine Arts Offers composition (M Mus, PhD); drawing (MFA); fine arts (M Mus, MA, MFA, PhD); history in art (MA, PhD); musicology (MA, PhD); painting (MFA); performance (M Mus); photography (MFA); printmaking (MFA); sculpture (MFA).

Faculty of Human and Social Development *Degree program information:* Part-time and evening/weekend programs available. Offers dispute resolution (MA); financial analysis (MPA); general policy analysis (MPA); human and social development (MA, MN, MSW); indigenous governance (MA); management science (MPA); personnel and industrial relations (MPA); planning and evaluation (MPA); policy fields (MPA); political and legal analysis (MPA). Electronic applications accepted.

Faculty of Humanities *Degree program information:* Part-time programs available. Offers American history (MA); applied linguistics (MA, PhD); British history (MA, PhD); Canadian history (MA, PhD); English (MA, PhD); European history (MA, PhD); French language and literature (MA); Germanic studies (MA); Greek and Roman studies (MA); humanities (MA, PhD); theoretical linguistics (MA, PhD). Electronic applications accepted.

Faculty of Science *Degree program information:* Part-time programs available. Offers applied mathematics (M Sc, MA, PhD); astronomy and astrophysics (M Sc, PhD); biochemistry (M Sc, PhD); cellular and developmental biology (M Sc, PhD); chemistry (M Sc, PhD); condensed matter physics (M Sc, PhD); forest biology (M Sc, PhD); geochemistry (M Sc, PhD); geophysics (M Sc, PhD); marine biology (M Sc, PhD); marine geology and geophysics (M Sc, PhD); medical physics (PhD); microbiology (M Sc, PhD); nuclear and particle studies (M Sc, PhD); ocean acoustics (M Sc, PhD); oceanography (M Sc, PhD); paleobiology (M Sc, PhD); paleoceanography (M Sc, PhD); plant and animal morphology (M Sc, PhD); pure mathematics (M Sc, MA, PhD); science (M Sc, MA, PhD); sedimentology (M Sc, PhD); statistics (M Sc, MA); stratigraphy (M Sc, PhD); systematic biology (M Sc, PhD); terrestrial and freshwater ecology (M Sc, PhD); theoretical physics (M Sc, PhD). Electronic applications accepted.

Faculty of Social Sciences *Degree program information:* Part-time programs available. Offers anthropology (MA); developmental psychology (M Sc, MA, PhD); economics (MA); experimental psychology (M Sc, MA, PhD); geography (M Sc, MA, PhD); human neuropsychology (M Sc, MA, PhD); political science (MA); social psychology (M Sc, MA, PhD); social sciences (M Sc, MA, PhD); sociology (MA, PhD).

Faculty of Law Students: 394 full-time (227 women), 17 part-time (14 women). Average age 28. 1,045 applicants, 13% accepted. *Faculty:* 28 full-time (11 women), 28 part-time/adjunct (7 women). Expenses: Contact institution. *Financial support:* In 2001–02, 211 students received support. Career-related internships or fieldwork, institutionally sponsored loans, scholarships/grants, health care benefits, unspecified assistantships, and course prizes, merit-based awards available. Support available to part-time students. Financial award application deadline: 9/15. In 2001, 94 degrees awarded. *Degree program information:* Part-time programs available. Offers law (LL B). *Application deadline:* For fall admission, 2/1. Applications are processed on a rolling basis. *Application fee:* $50. Electronic applications accepted. *Application Contact:* Neela Paige, Admissions Assistant, 250-721-8151, Fax: 250-721-6390, E-mail: lawadmss@uvic.ca. *Dean,* Andrew J. Petter, 250-721-8147, Fax: 250-472-7299, E-mail: apetter@uvic.ca.

UNIVERSITY OF VIRGINIA, Charlottesville, VA 22903

General Information State-supported, coed, university. CGS member. *Enrollment:* 5,250 full-time matriculated graduate/professional students (2,449 women), 443 part-time matriculated graduate/professional students (248 women). *Enrollment by degree level:* 1,603 first professional, 1,995 master's, 2,087 doctoral, 8 other advanced degrees. *Graduate faculty:* 1,979 full-time (538 women), 209 part-time/adjunct (95 women). Tuition, state resident: full-time $3,988. Tuition, nonresident: full-time $17,078. *Required fees:* $1,190. *Graduate housing:* Rooms and/or apartments available on a first-come, first-served basis to single and married students. Typical cost: $2,260 per year ($4,970 including board) for single students. Housing application deadline: 6/1. *Student services:* Campus employment opportunities, campus safety program, career counseling, child daycare facilities, disabled student services, exercise/wellness program, free psychological counseling, grant writing training, international student services, low-cost health insurance, multicultural affairs office, teacher training, writing training. *Library facilities:* Alderman Library plus 14 others. *Online resources:* library catalog, web page, access to other libraries' catalogs. *Collection:* 3.3 million titles, 51,237 serial subscriptions, 282,798 audiovisual materials. *Research affiliation:* National Radio Astronomy Observatory, Federal Executive Institute, The Judge Advocate General's School, U.S. Army.

Computer facilities: 1,859 computers available on campus for general student use. A campuswide network can be accessed from student residence rooms and from off campus. Internet access and online class registration are available. *Web address:* http://www.virginia.edu/.

General Application Contact: Dean of Appropriate School, 434-924-0311.

GRADUATE UNITS

College and Graduate School of Arts and Sciences Students: 1,611 full-time (777 women), 68 part-time (30 women); includes 123 minority (50 African Americans, 45 Asian Americans or Pacific Islanders, 25 Hispanic Americans, 3 Native Americans), 286 international. Average age 28. 3,283 applicants, 37% accepted, 401 enrolled. *Faculty:* 601 full-time (156 women), 104 part-time/adjunct (46 women). Expenses: Contact institution. *Financial support:* Fellowships with partial tuition reimbursements, research assistantships, teaching assistantships with tuition reimbursements, career-related internships or fieldwork, Federal Work-Study, institutionally sponsored loans, traineeships, tuition waivers (full and partial), and unspecified assistantships available. Financial award applicants required to submit FAFSA. In 2001, 194 master's, 139 doctorates awarded. *Degree program information:* Part-time programs available. Offers anthropology (MA, PhD); art history (MA, PhD); arts and sciences (MA, MAT, MFA, MS, PhD); Asian and Middle Eastern languages and cultures (MA); astronomy (MA, PhD); biochemistry (PhD); bioethics (MA); biological and physical sciences (MS); biology (MA, MS, PhD); biology education (MAT); biophysics (PhD); biotechnology (PhD); cell and molecular biology (PhD); cell biology (PhD); cell biology/anatomy (PhD); chemistry (MA, MS, PhD); chemistry education (MAT); classical art and archaeology (MA, PhD); classics (MA, MAT, PhD); clinical investigation (MS); clinical psychology (PhD); creative writing (MFA); drama (MFA); economics (MA, PhD); English (MA, MAT, PhD); environmental sciences (MA, MS, PhD); epidemiology (MS); foreign affairs (MA, PhD); French (MA, MAT, PhD); Germanic languages and literatures (MA, MAT, PhD); government (MA, MAT, PhD); health care informatics (MS); health care resource management (MS); health services research and outcomes evaluation (MS); history (MA, MAT, PhD); immunology (PhD); infectious disease (MS, PhD); Italian (MA); linguistics (MA); mathematics (MA, MS, PhD); microbiology (PhD); molecular genetics (PhD); molecular physiology and biological physics (PhD); music (MA, MAT); neuroscience (PhD); pharmacology (PhD); philosophy (MA, PhD); physics (MA, MAT, MS, PhD); physiology (PhD); psychology (MA, PhD); religious studies (MA, PhD); Slavic languages and literatures (MA, PhD); sociology (MA, PhD); Spanish (MA, MAT, PhD); statistics (MS, PhD); surgery (MS); teaching Spanish (MAT). *Application deadline:* Applications are processed on a rolling basis. *Application fee:* $40. Electronic applications accepted. *Associate Dean for Graduate Programs,* Duane J. Osheim, 434-924-7184, Fax: 434-924-3084, E-mail: grad-as@virginia.edu.

Curry School of Education Students: 614 full-time (465 women), 187 part-time (119 women); includes 93 minority (65 African Americans, 18 Asian Americans or Pacific Islanders, 9 Hispanic Americans, 1 Native American), 27 international. Average age 31. 1,213 applicants, 43% accepted, 181 enrolled. *Faculty:* 106 full-time (49 women), 6 part-time/adjunct (4 women). Expenses: Contact institution. *Financial support:* Fellowships, Federal Work-Study available. Financial award applicants required to submit FAFSA. In 2001, 372 master's, 65 doctorates, 17 other advanced degrees awarded. Offers administration and supervision (M Ed, Ed D, Ed S); communication disorders (M Ed); counselor education (M Ed, Ed D, Ed S); curriculum and instruction (M Ed, Ed D, Ed S); education (M Ed, MT, Ed D, PhD, Ed S); educational policy studies (M Ed, Ed D); educational psychology (M Ed, Ed D, Ed S); health and physical education (M Ed, Ed D); higher education (Ed D, Ed S); special education (M Ed, Ed D, Ed S).. *Application deadline:* For fall admission, 3/1; for spring admission, 11/15. Applications are processed on a rolling basis. *Application fee:* $40. Electronic applications accepted. *Application Contact:* Linda Berry, Student Enrollment Coordinator, 434-924-0738, E-mail: lrb8e@virginia.edu. *Dean,* David W. Breneman, 434-924-3332, Fax: 434-924-0888.

Darden Graduate School of Business Administration Students: 511 full-time (151 women), 1 (woman) part-time; includes 82 minority (29 African Americans, 31 Asian Americans or Pacific Islanders, 20 Hispanic Americans, 2 Native Americans), 147 international. Average age 28. 2,825 applicants, 14% accepted, 248 enrolled. *Faculty:* 63 full-time (14 women), 4 part-time/adjunct (2 women). Expenses: Contact institution. *Financial support:* Fellowships, career-related internships or fieldwork available. In 2001, 237 master's, 2 doctorates awarded. Offers business administration (MBA, DBA, PhD). *Application deadline:* For fall admission, 3/15. Applications are processed on a rolling basis. *Application fee:* $100. Electronic applications accepted. *Application Contact:* Dawna Clarke, Director of Admissions, 434-924-4809, E-mail: darden@virginia.edu. *Dean,* Robert S. Harris, 434-924-4823.

McIntire School of Commerce Students: 46 full-time (17 women), 112 part-time (60 women); includes 21 minority (9 African Americans, 10 Asian Americans or Pacific Islanders, 2 Hispanic Americans), 20 international. Average age 26. 4 applicants, 0% accepted. *Faculty:* 61 full-time (18 women), 5 part-time/adjunct (2 women). Expenses: Contact institution. *Financial support:* Fellowships, research assistantships, teaching assistantships, career-related internships or fieldwork and Federal Work-Study available. Financial award application deadline: 3/31; financial award applicants required to submit FAFSA. In 2001, 63 degrees awarded. Offers accounting (MS); management information systems (MS). *Application deadline:* For fall admission, 3/1. Applications are processed on a rolling basis. *Application fee:* $60. Electronic applications accepted. *Application Contact:* Robert S. Kemp, Associate Dean for Graduate Programs, 434-924-3482, Fax: 434-924-7074, E-mail: mcintiregrad@virginia.edu. *Dean,* Carl P. Zeithaml, 434-924-3110.

School of Architecture Students: 163 full-time (102 women), 4 part-time (1 woman); includes 15 minority (8 African Americans, 5 Asian Americans or Pacific Islanders, 2 Hispanic Americans), 7 international. Average age 27. 644 applicants, 30% accepted, 72 enrolled. *Faculty:* 41 full-time (11 women), 22 part-time/adjunct (6 women). Expenses: Contact institution. *Financial support:* Fellowships, career-related internships or fieldwork, Federal Work-Study, and institutionally sponsored loans available. Financial award applicants required to submit FAFSA. In 2001, 90 master's, 4 doctorates awarded. Offers architectural history (M Arch H, PhD); architecture (M Arch, M Arch H, M Land Arch, MP, PhD); landscape architecture (M Land Arch); urban and environmental planning (MP). *Application fee:* $40. *Application Contact:* Tracey Critzer, Admissions Officer, 434-924-6442, E-mail: arch-admissions@virginia.edu. *Dean,* Karen Van Lengen, 434-924-7019.

School of Engineering and Applied Science Students: 560 full-time (129 women), 36 part-time (6 women); includes 41 minority (9 African Americans, 27 Asian Americans or Pacific Islanders, 5 Hispanic Americans), 274 international. Average age 27. 1,569 applicants, 24% accepted, 173 enrolled. *Faculty:* 165 full-time (23 women), 17 part-time/adjunct (3 women). Expenses: Contact institution. *Financial support:* Fellowships with full tuition reimbursements, research assistantships with full tuition reimbursements, teaching assistantships with full tuition reimbursements, career-related internships or fieldwork available. Financial award application deadline: 2/1; financial award applicants required to submit FAFSA. In 2001, 127 master's, 39 doctorates awarded. *Degree program information:* Part-time programs available. Postbaccalaureate distance learning degree programs offered (no on-campus study). Offers applied mechanics (MAM, MS); biomedical engineering (ME, MS, PhD); chemical engineering (ME, MS, PhD); computer science (MCS, MS, PhD); electrical and computer engineering (ME, MS, PhD); engineering and applied science (MAM, MCS, ME, MEP, MMSE, MS, PhD); engineering physics (MEP, MS, PhD); environmental engineering (ME, MS, PhD); materials science (MMSE, MS, PhD); mechanical and aerospace engineering (ME, MS, PhD); nuclear engineering (ME, MS, PhD); structural mechanics (ME, MS, PhD); systems engineering (ME, MS, PhD); transportation engineering and management (ME, MS, PhD); water resources (ME, MS, PhD). *Application deadline:* For fall admission, 8/1; for spring admission, 12/1. Applications are processed on a rolling basis. *Application fee:* $40. Electronic applications accepted. *Application Contact:* Bill Thurneck, 424-924-3155. *Dean,* Richard W. Miksad, 434-924-3593.

School of Law Students: 1,112 full-time (487 women), 1 (woman) part-time; includes 157 minority (65 African Americans, 62 Asian Americans or Pacific Islanders, 23 Hispanic Americans, 7 Native Americans), 56 international. Average age 25. 4,093 applicants, 27% accepted, 411 enrolled. *Faculty:* 94 full-time (26 women), 2 part-time/adjunct (1 woman). Expenses: Contact institution. *Financial support:* Fellowships, Federal Work-Study available. Financial award application deadline: 2/15; financial award applicants required to submit FAFSA. In 2001, 352 first professional degrees, 66 master's, 2 doctorates awarded. Offers law (JD, LL M, SJD). *Application deadline:* For fall admission, 1/15. *Application fee:* $65. *Application Contact:* Albert R. Turnbull, Associate Dean, 434-924-4676, Fax: 434-982-2128, E-mail: art@virginia.edu. *Dean,* John C. Jeffries, 434-924-7343.

School of Medicine Students: 540 full-time (236 women); includes 148 minority (32 African Americans, 107 Asian Americans or Pacific Islanders, 7 Hispanic Americans, 2 Native Americans), 1 international. Average age 25. *Faculty:* 804 full-time (202 women), 45 part-time/adjunct (27 women). Expenses: Contact institution. *Financial support:* Institutionally sponsored loans and scholarships/grants available. Financial award application deadline: 3/1; financial award applicants required to submit FAFSA. In 2001, 129 degrees awarded. Offers medicine (MD). *Application deadline:* For fall admission, 11/1. Applications are processed on a rolling basis. *Application fee:* $60. *Application Contact:* Beth A. Bailey, Director, Admissions Office, 434-924-5571, Fax: 434-982-2586, E-mail: bab7g@virginia.edu. *Dean,* Dr. Robert M. Carey, 434-924-5571.

School of Nursing Students: 93 full-time (85 women), 34 part-time (30 women); includes 11 minority (10 African Americans, 1 Asian American or Pacific Islander), 4 international. Average age 36. 66 applicants, 68% accepted, 29 enrolled. *Faculty:* 44 full-time (39 women), 4 part-time/adjunct (all women). Expenses: Contact institution. *Financial support:* Fellowships, research assistantships, teaching assistantships, Federal Work-Study and scholarships/grants available. Financial award application deadline: 4/1; financial award applicants required to submit FAFSA. In 2001, 35 master's, 6 doctorates awarded. Offers nursing (MSN, PhD). *Application deadline:* For fall admission, 2/1; for spring admission, 12/1. Applications are processed on a rolling basis. *Application fee:* $40. *Application Contact:* Clay Hysell, Assistant Dean for Graduate Student Services, 434-924-2743, E-mail: nur-osa@virginia.edu. *Dean,* B. Jeanette Lancaster, 434-924-0141.

UNIVERSITY OF WASHINGTON, Seattle, WA 98195

General Information State-supported, coed, university. CGS member. *Enrollment:* 8,809 full-time matriculated graduate/professional students (4,513 women), 1,774 part-time matriculated graduate/professional students (1,284 women). Tuition, state resident: full-time $5,539. Tuition, nonresident: full-time $14,376. *Required fees:* $390. Tuition and fees vary according to course load and program. *Graduate housing:* Rooms and/or apartments available on a first-come, first-served basis to single and married students. Typical cost: $4,194 per year ($5,415 including board) for single students; $6,174 per year for married students. Room and board charges vary according to board plan and housing facility selected. Housing application deadline: 5/1. *Student services:* Campus employment opportunities, campus safety program, career counseling, child daycare facilities, disabled student services, international student services, low-cost health insurance, multicultural affairs office, teacher training. *Library facilities:* Suzzallo/Allen Library plus 21 others. *Online resources:* web page. *Collection:* 5.8 million titles, 50,245 serial subscriptions, 1.4 million audiovisual materials. *Research affiliation:* Fred Hutchinson Cancer Research Center, Children's Hospital and Regional Medical Center (pediatric research).

Computer facilities: 285 computers available on campus for general student use. A campuswide network can be accessed from student residence rooms and from off campus. *Web address:* http://www.washington.edu/.

General Application Contact: Information Contact, 206-543-2100, Fax: 206-543-8798, E-mail: uwgrad@u.washington.edu.

GRADUATE UNITS

Graduate School Students: 7,069 full-time (3,605 women), 2,300 part-time (1,317 women); includes 1,242 minority (171 African Americans, 774 Asian Americans or Pacific Islanders, 226 Hispanic Americans, 71 Native Americans), 1,666 international. Average age 31. ###### applicants, 36% accepted, 2878 enrolled. *Faculty:* 3,134. Expenses: Contact institution. *Financial support:* Fellowships with full tuition reimbursements, research assistantships with full and partial tuition reimbursements, teaching assistantships with full and partial tuition reimbursements, career-related internships or fieldwork, Federal Work-Study, institutionally sponsored loans, scholarships/grants, traineeships, tuition waivers (full and partial), and unspecified assistantships available. Support available to part-time students. Financial award application deadline: 2/28; financial award applicants required to submit FAFSA. In 2001, 2,558 master's, 479 doctorates awarded. *Degree program information:* Part-time and evening/weekend programs available. Postbaccalaureate distance learning degree programs offered (minimal on-campus study). Offers biology for teachers (MS); education (M Ed, Professional Certificate); global trade, transportation, and logistics (Certificate); Graduate School (EMCIS, EMHA, LL M, LL M T, M Arch, M Ed, M Mus, MA, MAE, MAIS, MAT, MBA, MC, MFA, MFR, MHA, MI St, MIT, MLA, MLIS, MM, MMA, MME, MN, MOT, MP Acc, MPA, MPH, MPT, MRM, MS, MS Ch E, MSA, MSAA, MSCE, MSCM, MSD, MSE, MSEE, MSIE, MSIM, MSME, MSW, MUP, DMA, Ed D, PhD, Certificate, Professional Certificate); K-8 education (Certificate); museology (MA); Near and Middle Eastern studies (PhD); preservation planning and design (Certificate); principalship (Certificate); quantitative ecology and resource management (MS, PhD); school administration (Certificate); urban design (Certificate). *Application fee:* $52. Electronic applications accepted. *Application Contact:* 206-543-5929, Fax: 206-543-8798, E-mail: uwgrad@u.washington.edu. *Dean and Vice Provost,* Marsha L. Landolt, 206-543-5900, Fax: 206-685-3234.

Business School Students: 1,262 full-time (84 women), 134 part-time (31 women). Average age 28. 933 applicants, 39% accepted. *Faculty:* 95 full-time (14 women), 20 part-time/adjunct (7 women). Expenses: Contact institution. *Financial support:* In 2001–02, 117 students received support; fellowships, research assistantships, teaching assistantships, career-related internships or fieldwork, Federal Work-Study, scholarships/grants, and unspecified assistantships available. Financial award applicants required to submit FAFSA. In 2001, 174 master's, 11 doctorates awarded. *Degree program information:* Part-time and evening/weekend programs available. Offers business (MBA, MP Acc, PhD). *Application deadline:* For fall admission, 3/1 (priority date). Applications are processed on a rolling basis. *Application fee:* $50. Electronic applications accepted. *Application Contact:* Janna Trefren, Assistant Director, 206-543-4661, Fax: 206-616-7351, E-mail: mba@u.washington.edu. *Dean,* Yash Gupta, 206-543-4750.

College of Architecture and Urban Planning *Degree program information:* Part-time and evening/weekend programs available. Offers architecture (M Arch); architecture and urban planning (M Arch, MLA, MS, MSCM, MUP, PhD, Certificate); computer design (Certificate); construction management (MS, MSCM); historic preservation (Certificate); landscape architecture (MLA); lighting (Certificate); urban design (Certificate); urban design and planning (PhD); urban planning (MUP). Electronic applications accepted.

College of Arts and Sciences Students: 2,295 full-time (1,110 women), 340 part-time (156 women). *Faculty:* 1,202. Expenses: Contact institution. *Financial support:* In 2001–02, 507 fellowships with full tuition reimbursements (averaging $12,550 per year), 843 research assistantships with full tuition reimbursements (averaging $12,870 per year), 1,337 teaching assistantships with full and partial tuition reimbursements (averaging $12,348 per year) were awarded. Career-related internships or fieldwork, Federal Work-Study, institutionally sponsored loans, scholarships/grants, traineeships, tuition waivers (full and partial), unspecified assistantships, and readerships, lectureships also available. Support available to part-time students. Financial award application deadline: 2/28; financial award applicants required to submit FAFSA. In 2001, 406 master's, 230 doctorates awarded. *Degree program information:* Part-time and evening/weekend programs available. Offers acting (MFA); anthropology (MA, PhD); applied mathematics (MS, PhD); art (MFA); art and design (MFA); art history (MA, PhD); arts and sciences (M Mus, MA, MAIS, MAT, MC, MFA, MM, MS, DMA, PhD); astronomy (MS, PhD); atmospheric sciences (MS, PhD); botany (MS, PhD); Central Asian studies (MAIS); chemistry (MS, PhD); China studies (MAIS); Chinese language and literature (MA, PhD); classics (MA, PhD); classics and philosophy (PhD); communication (MA, MC, PhD); comparative literature (MA, PhD); comparative religion (MAIS); costume design (MFA); dance (MFA); directing (MFA); East European studies (MAIS); economics (MA, PhD); English (MA, MAT, MFA, PhD); English as a second language (MAT); French (MA, PhD); French and Italian studies (MA, PhD); genetics (PhD); geography (MA, PhD); geology (MS, PhD); geophysics (MS, PhD); German language and literature (MA); German literature and culture (PhD); Hispanic literacy and cultural studies (MA); history (PhD); international studies (MAIS); Italian (MA); Japan studies (MAIS); Japanese language and literature (MA, PhD); Korea studies (MAIS); lighting design (MFA); linguistics (MA, PhD); mathematics (MA, MS, PhD); Middle Eastern studies (MAIS); music (M Mus, MA, MM, DMA, PhD); music education (MA, PhD); Near Eastern languages and civilization (MA); philosophy (MA, PhD); physics (MS, PhD); political science (MA, PhD); psychology (PhD); Romance languages and literature (PhD); Romance linguistics (MA, PhD); Russian literature (MA, PhD); Russian studies (MAIS); Russian, East European and Central Asian studies (MAIS); Scandinavian studies (MA, PhD); scene design (MFA); Slavic linguistics (MA, PhD); sociology (MA, PhD); South Asian language and literature (MA, PhD); South Asian studies (MAIS); Spanish and Portuguese (MA); speech and hearing sciences (MS, PhD); statistics (MS, PhD); theory and criticism (PhD); women studies (MA, PhD); zoology (PhD). *Application deadline:* Applications are processed on a rolling basis. *Application fee:* $50. Electronic applications accepted. *Dean,* David C. Hodge, 206-543-5340.

College of Education *Degree program information:* Part-time and evening/weekend programs available. Offers curriculum and instruction (M Ed, Ed D, PhD); early childhood education (M Ed, Ed D, PhD); educational leadership and policy studies (M Ed, Ed D, PhD); educational psychology (M Ed, PhD); elementary special education (M Ed, Ed D, PhD); emotional and behavioral disabilities (M Ed); general special education (M Ed, Ed D, PhD); human development and cognition (M Ed, PhD); measurement and research (M Ed, PhD); school counseling (M Ed, PhD); school psychology (M Ed, PhD); severe disabilities (M Ed, Ed D, PhD); special education (M Ed, Ed D, PhD); teacher education (MIT). Electronic applications accepted.

College of Engineering Students: 967 full-time (254 women), 343 part-time (90 women); includes 163 minority (16 African Americans, 115 Asian Americans or Pacific Islanders, 24 Hispanic Americans, 8 Native Americans), 478 international. Average age 29. 2,066 applicants, 36% accepted, 311 enrolled. *Faculty:* 179 full-time (25 women), 11 part-time/adjunct (1 woman). Expenses: Contact institution. *Financial support:* In 2001–02, 105 fellowships with full tuition reimbursements (averaging $14,389 per year), 518 research assistantships with full tuition reimbursements (averaging $13,759 per year), 218 teaching assistantships with full tuition reimbursements (averaging $13,281 per year) were awarded. Career-related internships or fieldwork, Federal Work-Study, institutionally sponsored loans, scholarships/grants, traineeships, health care benefits, tuition waivers (full), unspecified assistantships, and stipend supplements also available. Support available to part-time students. Financial award application deadline: 2/28; financial award applicants required to submit FAFSA. In 2001, 327 master's, 81 doctorates awarded. *Degree program information:* Part-time and evening/weekend programs available. Postbaccalaureate distance learning degree programs offered (minimal on-campus study). Offers aeronautics and astronautics (MAE, MSAA, PhD); bioengineering (MME, MS, PhD); chemical engineering (MS Ch E, PhD); computer science (MS, PhD); electrical engineering (MSEE, PhD); engineering (EMCIS, MAE, MME, MS, MS Ch E, MSAA, MSCE, MSE, MSEE, MSIE, MSME, PhD); environmental engineering (MS, MSCE, MSE, PhD); hydraulic engineering (MSCE, MSE, PhD); industrial engineering (MSIE, PhD); inter-engineering specialization in materials science and engineering (MS); materials science and engineering (MS, PhD); materials science and engineering nanotechnology (PhD); mechanical engineering (MSE, MSME, PhD); structural and geotechnical engineering and mechanics (MS, MSCE, MSE, PhD); technical communication (MS); transportation and construction engineering (MS, MSCE, MSE, PhD). *Application deadline:* For fall admission, 7/1; for winter admission, 11/1; for spring admission, 2/1. *Application fee:* $50. Electronic applications accepted. *Application Contact:* Frank Ashby, Director, Student and Community Relations, 206-543-1770, Fax: 206-616-8554, E-mail: engradv@engr.washington.edu. *Dean,* Dr. Denice D. Denton, 206-543-0340, Fax: 206-685-0666, E-mail: denton@engr.washington.edu.

College of Forest Resources Students: 160 full-time (77 women), 186 part-time (158 women); includes 16 minority (1 African American, 10 Asian Americans or Pacific Islanders, 4 Hispanic Americans, 1 Native American) Average age 31. 172 applicants, 52% accepted, 47 enrolled. *Faculty:* 57 full-time (12 women), 16 part-time/adjunct (2 women). Expenses: Contact institution. *Financial support:* In 2001–02, 140 students received support, including 15 fellowships with full tuition reimbursements available (averaging $14,000 per year), 98 research assistantships with full tuition reimbursements available (averaging $14,000 per year), 27 teaching assistantships with full tuition reimbursements available (averaging $14,000 per year); career-related internships or fieldwork, Federal Work-Study, institutionally sponsored loans, scholarships/grants, traineeships, health care benefits, tuition waivers (full), and unspecified assistantships also available. Financial award application deadline: 1/15. In 2001, 38 master's, 12 doctorates awarded. Offers forest economics (MS, PhD); forest ecosystem analysis (MS, PhD); forest engineering/forest hydrology (MS, PhD); forest products marketing (MS, PhD); forest soils (MS, PhD); paper science and engineering (MS, PhD); quantitative resource management (MS, PhD); silviculture (MFR); silviculture and forest protection (MS, PhD); social sciences (MS, PhD); urban horticulture (MFR, MS, PhD); wildlife science (MS, PhD). *Application deadline:* For fall admission, 1/15 (priority date); for winter admission, 9/1; for spring admission, 11/1. Applications are processed on a rolling basis. *Application fee:* $50. Electronic applications accepted. *Application Contact:* Michelle Trudeau, Student Services Manager, 206-616-1533, Fax: 206-685-0790, E-mail: michtru@u.washington.edu. *Dean,* Dr. B. Bruce Bare, 206-685-0952, Fax: 206-685-0790, E-mail: bare@u.washington.edu.

College of Ocean and Fishery Sciences Offers aquatic and fishery sciences (MS, PhD); biological oceanography (MS, PhD); chemical oceanography (MS, PhD); marine affairs (MMA); marine geology and geophysics (MS, PhD); ocean and fishery sciences (MMA, MS, PhD); physical oceanography (MS, PhD). Electronic applications accepted.

Daniel J. Evans School of Public Affairs Students: 211 full-time (137 women), 65 part-time (39 women); includes 42 minority (7 African Americans, 25 Asian Americans or Pacific Islanders, 5 Hispanic Americans, 5 Native Americans), 16 international. Average age 30. 293 applicants, 76% accepted, 113 enrolled. *Faculty:* 28 full-time (8 women), 31 part-time/adjunct (13 women). Expenses: Contact institution. *Financial support:* In 2001–02, 60 students received support, including 20 fellowships with full tuition reimbursements available (averaging $5,000 per year), 32 research assistantships with full tuition reimbursements available (averaging $11,340 per year), 5 teaching assistantships with full tuition reimbursements available (averaging $11,340 per year); career-related internships or fieldwork, Federal Work-Study, institutionally sponsored loans, and tuition waivers (full and partial) also available. Support available to part-time students. Financial award application deadline: 2/28; financial award applicants required to submit FAFSA. In 2001, 82 degrees awarded. *Degree program information:* Part-time and evening/weekend programs available. Offers public affairs (MPA). *Application deadline:* For fall admission, 2/1. *Application fee:* $45. Electronic applications accepted. *Application Contact:* Linda Rylander Bale,

University of Washington (continued)

Director of Admissions, 206-543-4900, Fax: 206-543-1096, E-mail: evansuw@u.washington.edu. *Acting Dean,* Dr. Paul T Hill, 206-616-1648, Fax: 206-543-1096, E-mail: bicycle@u.washington.edu.

The Information School Students: 173 full-time (130 women), 130 part-time (96 women); includes 41 minority (6 African Americans, 26 Asian Americans or Pacific Islanders, 8 Hispanic Americans, 1 Native American), 8 international. Average age 33. 308 applicants, 63% accepted, 142 enrolled. *Faculty:* 10 full-time (5 women), 10 part-time/adjunct (6 women). Expenses: Contact institution. *Financial support:* In 2001–02, 71 students received support, including 28 fellowships with tuition reimbursements available (averaging $11,340 per year), 8 research assistantships with tuition reimbursements available (averaging $11,340 per year), 4 teaching assistantships with tuition reimbursements available (averaging $11,340 per year); career-related internships or fieldwork, Federal Work-Study, institutionally sponsored loans, scholarships/grants, health care benefits, tuition waivers (full and partial), and unspecified assistantships also available. Financial award application deadline: 2/28; financial award applicants required to submit FAFSA. In 2001, 86 degrees awarded. *Degree program information:* Part-time and evening/weekend programs available. Postbaccalaureate distance learning degree programs offered. Offers information management (MSIM); information science (PhD); library and information science (MLIS). *Application deadline:* For fall admission, 1/15. *Application fee:* $50. *Application Contact:* Student Services, 206-543-1794, Fax: 206-616-3152, E-mail: studentservices@ischool.washington.edu. *Dean,* Michael B. Eisenberg, 206-685-9937, Fax: 206-616-3152, E-mail: mbe@u.washington.edu.

School of Nursing *Degree program information:* Part-time programs available. Offers nursing (MN, MS, PhD).

School of Public Health and Community Medicine Students: 442 full-time (290 women), 86 part-time (56 women); includes 96 minority (11 African Americans, 62 Asian Americans or Pacific Islanders, 20 Hispanic Americans, 3 Native Americans), 85 international. Average age 30. 690 applicants, 47% accepted. Expenses: Contact institution. *Financial support:* Fellowships with tuition reimbursements, research assistantships with full and partial tuition reimbursements, teaching assistantships with full and partial tuition reimbursements, career-related internships or fieldwork, Federal Work-Study, institutionally sponsored loans, scholarships/grants, traineeships, health care benefits, tuition waivers (full and partial), and unspecified assistantships available. Support available to part-time students. In 2001, 118 master's, 29 doctorates awarded. *Degree program information:* Part-time and evening/weekend programs available. Postbaccalaureate distance learning degree programs offered (minimal on-campus study). Offers biostatistics (MPH, MS, PhD); environmental and occupational hygiene (PhD); epidemiology (MPH, MS, PhD); general environmental health (MPH); genetic epidemiology (MS); health services (MS, PhD); health services administration and planning (EMHA, MHA); industrial hygiene and safety (MS); international health (MPH); maternal/child health (MPH); nutritional sciences (MPH, MS, PhD); occupational medicine (MPH); pathobiology (MS, PhD); public health (MPH); public health and community medicine (EMHA, MHA, MI St, MPH, MS, PhD); public health genetics (MPH, MS, PhD); technology (MS); toxicology (MS, PhD). *Application deadline:* Applications are processed on a rolling basis. *Application fee:* $50. Electronic applications accepted. *Application Contact:* Dylan E Wilbanks, Assistant to the Associate Deans, 206-543-1144, Fax: 206-543-3813, E-mail: wilbanks@u.washington.edu. *Dean,* Dr. Patricia W. Wahl, 206-543-1144, Fax: 206-543-3813, E-mail: sphcm@u.washington.edu.

School of Social Work *Degree program information:* Evening/weekend programs available. Postbaccalaureate distance learning degree programs offered (minimal on-campus study). Offers social work (MSW, PhD).

School of Social Work, Tacoma Campus Average age 35. 72 applicants, 49% accepted, 29 enrolled. *Faculty:* 6 full-time (4 women), 2 part-time/adjunct (both women). Expenses: Contact institution. *Financial support:* In 2001–02, 30 students received support. Institutionally sponsored loans and scholarships/grants available. Support available to part-time students. Financial award application deadline: 2/28; financial award applicants required to submit FAFSA. In 2001, 28 degrees awarded. *Degree program information:* Part-time and evening/weekend programs available. Offers social work (MSW). *Application deadline:* For fall admission, 3/1 (priority date). *Application fee:* $50. Electronic applications accepted. *Application Contact:* Terri M. Simonsen, Adviser and Administrator, 253-692-5822, Fax: 253-692-5825. *Director,* Dr. Marcie M. Lazzari, 253-692-5828, Fax: 253-692-5825, E-mail: mlazzari@u.washington.edu.

School of Dentistry Offers dentistry (DDS, MS, MSD, PhD).

School of Law Students: 595 full-time (292 women), 59 part-time (24 women); includes 95 minority (5 African Americans, 56 Asian Americans or Pacific Islanders, 21 Hispanic Americans, 13 Native Americans), 93 international. Average age 26. 1,954 applicants, 24% accepted. *Faculty:* 38 full-time (18 women), 22 part-time/adjunct (8 women). Expenses: Contact institution. *Financial support:* In 2001–02, 326 students received support, including 8 fellowships (averaging $1,562 per year), 10 research assistantships (averaging $4,640 per year); career-related internships or fieldwork, Federal Work-Study, institutionally sponsored loans, scholarships/grants, and tuition waivers (partial) also available. Financial award application deadline: 2/28; financial award applicants required to submit FAFSA. In 2001, 163 first professional degrees, 83 master's awarded. Offers Asian law (LL M, PhD); intellectual property and technology (LL M); law (JD, LL M T); law of sustainable international development (LL M); taxation (LL M). *Application deadline:* For fall admission, 1/15. *Application fee:* $50. *Application Contact:* Sandra Madrid, Assistant Dean, 206-543-0199, Fax: 206-543-5671, E-mail: smadrid@u.washington.edu. *Dean,* W. H Knight, 206-685-3846, Fax: 206-543-5305, E-mail: whknight@u.washington.edu.

School of Medicine Students: 1,308 full-time (614 women), 21 part-time (15 women); includes 339 minority (22 African Americans, 178 Asian Americans or Pacific Islanders, 107 Hispanic Americans, 32 Native Americans), 48 international. Average age 28. *Faculty:* 1,583 full-time (458 women), 173 part-time/adjunct (109 women). Expenses: Contact institution. *Financial support:* Fellowships with full tuition reimbursements, research assistantships with full tuition reimbursements, teaching assistantships with full tuition reimbursements, career-related internships or fieldwork, Federal Work-Study, institutionally sponsored loans, traineeships, and tuition waivers (full and partial) available. Support available to part-time students. Financial award applicants required to submit FAFSA. In 2001, 151 first professional degrees, 15 master's, 48 doctorates awarded. *Degree program information:* Part-time programs available. Offers medicine (MD, MOT, MPT, MS, MSE, PhD). Electronic applications accepted. *Application Contact:* Patricia T. Fero, Admissions Officer, 206-543-7212, E-mail: askuwsom@u.washington.edu. *Vice President for Medical Affairs and Dean,* Dr. Paul G. Ramsey, 206-543-7718, Fax: 206-685-8767, E-mail: bmahoney@u.washington.edu.

Graduate Programs in Medicine Students: 509 full-time (221 women), 20 part-time (15 women). 3,031 applicants, 8% accepted. *Faculty:* 676 full-time (107 women), 146 part-time/adjunct (24 women). Expenses: Contact institution. *Financial support:* Fellowships with full tuition reimbursements, research assistantships with full tuition reimbursements, teaching assistantships with full tuition reimbursements, career-related internships or fieldwork, Federal Work-Study, institutionally sponsored loans, scholarships/grants, traineeships, tuition waivers (full and partial), and stipends available. Support available to part-time students. Financial award applicants required to submit FAFSA. In 2001, 15 master's, 48 doctorates awarded. *Degree program information:* Part-time programs available. Offers biochemistry (PhD); biological structure (PhD); biomedical and health informatics (MS); entry-level physical therapy (MPT); genome sciences (PhD); immunology (PhD); laboratory medicine (MS); medicine (MOT, MPT, MS, MSE, PhD); microbiology (PhD); molecular and cellular biology (PhD); molecular basis of disease (PhD); neurobiology and behavior (PhD); occupational therapy (MOT, MS); pathology (MS, PhD); pediatric physical therapy (MS); pharmacology (MS, PhD); physical therapy (MPT, MS); physiology and biophysics (PhD); rehabilitation medicine (MS); veterinary science (MS). *Application fee:* $35. Electronic applications accepted. *Application Contact:* Patricia T. Fero, Admissions Officer, 206-543-7212, E-mail: askuwsom@u.washington.edu.

School of Pharmacy *Degree program information:* Part-time and evening/weekend programs available. Postbaccalaureate distance learning degree programs offered. Offers medicinal chemistry (PhD); pharmaceutics (MS, PhD); pharmacy (Pharm D, MS, PhD).

UNIVERSITY OF WATERLOO, Waterloo, ON N2L 3G1, Canada

General Information Province-supported, coed, university. *Enrollment:* 1,814 full-time matriculated graduate/professional students (666 women), 415 part-time matriculated graduate/professional students (136 women). *Graduate faculty:* 810 full-time (165 women), 666 part-time/adjunct (122 women). *Graduate tuition:* Tuition and fees charges are reported in Canadian dollars. Tuition, province resident: part-time $1,648 Canadian dollars per term. Tuition, Canadian resident: part-time $4,162 Canadian dollars per term. *Required fees:* $148 Canadian dollars per term. *Graduate housing:* Rooms and/or apartments available on a first-come, first-served basis to single and married students. Typical cost: $4,746 Canadian dollars per year for single students. *Student services:* Campus employment opportunities, campus safety program, career counseling, child daycare facilities, disabled student services, exercise/wellness program, free psychological counseling, international student services, low-cost health insurance, teacher training. *Library facilities:* Dana Porter Library plus 7 others. *Online resources:* library catalog, web page, access to other libraries' catalogs. *Collection:* 2.9 million titles, 13,228 serial subscriptions. *Research affiliation:* Waterloo Maple Inc. (symbolic computation research), Bell Canada (bell university labs), ABB- Borrem Inc. (spectroscopy), Boeing North America (groundwater/contaminants), Com Dev International (telecommunications), Nortel (telecommunications).

Computer facilities: 6,000 computers available on campus for general student use. A campuswide network can be accessed from student residence rooms and from off campus. Internet access, e-mail are available. *Web address:* http://www.uwaterloo.ca/.

General Application Contact: Amy Aldous, Recruitment Manager, 519-888-4567 Ext. 5946, Fax: 519-746-3051, E-mail: aaldous@uwaterloo.ca.

GRADUATE UNITS

Graduate Studies Students: 1,814 full-time (666 women), 415 part-time (136 women). *Faculty:* 810 full-time (165 women), 666 part-time/adjunct (122 women). Expenses: Contact institution. *Financial support:* Fellowships with partial tuition reimbursements, research assistantships with partial tuition reimbursements, teaching assistantships with partial tuition reimbursements, career-related internships or fieldwork, Federal Work-Study, institutionally sponsored loans, scholarships/grants, and tuition waivers (partial) available. Support available to part-time students. In 2001, 561 master's, 117 doctorates awarded. *Degree program information:* Part-time and evening/weekend programs available. Postbaccalaureate distance learning degree programs offered (no on-campus study). *Application deadline:* Applications are processed on a rolling basis. *Application fee:* $75 Canadian dollars. *Application Contact:* Jeanette Nugent, Admissions and Recruitment Coordinator, 519-888-4567 Ext. 3933, Fax: 519-746-3051, E-mail: jnugent@uwaterloo.ca. *Dean,* Dr. Jacob G. Sivak, 519-888-4567 Ext. 3439, Fax: 519-746-3051, E-mail: jsivak@uwaterloo.ca.

Faculty of Applied Health Sciences Students: 72 full-time (44 women), 30 part-time (19 women). 140 applicants, 35% accepted. *Faculty:* 65 full-time (20 women), 38 part-time/adjunct (7 women). Expenses: Contact institution. *Financial support:* Fellowships, research assistantships, teaching assistantships, career-related internships or fieldwork, Federal Work-Study, institutionally sponsored loans, scholarships/grants, and tuition waivers (partial) available. In 2001, 27 master's, 11 doctorates awarded. *Degree program information:* Part-time programs available. Offers applied health sciences (M Sc, MA, PhD); health studies and gerontology (M Sc, PhD); kinesiology (M Sc, PhD); recreation and leisure studies (MA, PhD). *Application deadline:* For fall admission, 2/1. *Application fee:* $75 Canadian dollars. Electronic applications accepted. *Application Contact:* C. M. Kendrick, Graduate Studies Coordinator, 519-888-4567 Ext. 6149, Fax: 519-746-6776, E-mail: cmkendri@healthy.uwaterloo.ca. *Associate Dean,* Dr. S. Shaw, 519-888-4567 Ext. 3098, Fax: 519-746-6776, E-mail: sshaw@uwaterloo.ca.

Faculty of Arts Students: 325 full-time (184 women), 61 part-time (32 women). *Faculty:* 187 full-time (49 women), 104 part-time/adjunct (37 women). Expenses: Contact institution. *Financial support:* Fellowships, research assistantships, teaching assistantships, career-related internships or fieldwork and scholarships/grants available. In 2001, 201 master's, 20 doctorates awarded. *Degree program information:* Part-time and evening/weekend programs available. Offers accounting (M Acc, PhD); accounting-finance (M Acc); arts (M Acc, M Tax, MA, MA Sc, MFA, PhD); economics (MA); English (MA, PhD); French (MA); German (MA, PhD); history (MA, PhD); language and professional writing (MA); philosophy (MA, PhD); political science (MA); psychology (MA, MA Sc, PhD); public history (MA); Russian (MA); sociology (MA, PhD); studio art (MFA); taxation (M Tax). *Application deadline:* Applications are processed on a rolling basis. *Application fee:* $75 Canadian dollars. *Application Contact:* Dr. H. A. MacDougall, Associate Dean of the Arts, Graduate Studies and Research, 519-888-4567 Ext. 3133, Fax: 519-725-1749, E-mail: hmacdoug@watarts.uwaterloo.ca. *Dean,* Dr. R. Kerton, 519-888-4567 Ext. 2217, Fax: 519-746-4147, E-mail: dean@arts.uwaterloo.ca.

Faculty of Engineering Students: 597 full-time (123 women), 198 part-time (39 women). *Faculty:* 182 full-time (17 women), 140 part-time/adjunct (9 women). Expenses: Contact institution. *Financial support:* Fellowships, research assistantships, teaching assistantships, career-related internships or fieldwork, Federal Work-Study, and institutionally sponsored loans available. In 2001, 154 master's, 41 doctorates awarded. *Degree program information:* Part-time and evening/weekend programs available. Postbaccalaureate distance learning degree programs offered (no on-campus study). Offers applied operations research (M Eng, MA Sc, PhD); chemical engineering (M Eng, MA Sc, PhD); civil engineering (M Eng, MA Sc, PhD); electrical and computer engineering (M Eng, MA Sc, PhD); electrical and computer engineering (software engineering) (MA Sc); engineering (M Eng, MA Sc, PhD); information systems (M Eng, MA Sc, PhD); management of technology (M Eng, MA Sc, PhD); mechanical engineering (M Eng, MA Sc, PhD); mechanical engineering-design and manufacturing (MA Sc); systems design engineering (M Eng, MA Sc, PhD). *Application deadline:* Applications are processed on a rolling basis. *Application fee:* $75 Canadian dollars. *Application Contact:* Dr. A. Penlidis, Associate Dean of Graduate Studies, 519-888-4567 Ext. 3376, Fax: 519-746-1457, E-mail: penlidis@engmail.uwaterloo.ca. *Dean,* Dr. S. Chaudhuri, 519-888-4567 Ext. 3347, Fax: 519-746-1457, E-mail: s.chaudhuri@ece.uwaterloo.ca.

Faculty of Environmental Studies Students: 182 full-time (94 women), 48 part-time (19 women). 212 applicants, 48% accepted, 86 enrolled. *Faculty:* 58 full-time (12 women), 50 part-time/adjunct (10 women). Expenses: Contact institution. *Financial support:* In 2001–02, 18 research assistantships, 126 teaching assistantships were awarded. Career-related internships or fieldwork, institutionally sponsored loans, and scholarships/grants also available. Support available to part-time students. In 2001, 47 master's, 6 doctorates awarded. *Degree program information:* Part-time programs available. Offers architecture (M Arch); environment and resource studies (MES); environmental studies (M Arch, MA, MAES, MES, PhD); geography (MA, MES, PhD); local economic development (MAES); planning (MA, MES, PhD). *Application deadline:* For fall admission, 2/1 (priority date). *Application fee:* $75 Canadian dollars. *Application Contact:* Birgit G. Moscinski, Faculty Graduate Assistant, 519-888-6574 Ext. 6574, Fax: 519-746-2031, E-mail: bmoscins@fes.uwaterloo.ca. *Dean,* Dr. Geoffrey McBoyle, 519-888-4567 Ext. 2884, Fax: 519-746-2031, E-mail: gmcboyle@fes.uwaterloo.ca.

Faculty of Mathematics Students: 330 full-time (90 women), 35 part-time (7 women). 676 applicants, 32% accepted. *Faculty:* 169 full-time (26 women), 105 part-time/adjunct (11 women). Expenses: Contact institution. *Financial support:* Research assistantships, teaching assistantships, career-related internships or fieldwork and scholarships/grants available. In 2001, 64 master's, 13 doctorates awarded. *Degree program information:* Part-time programs available. Offers actuarial science (M Math); applied mathematics (M Math, PhD); combinatorics and optimization (M Math, PhD); computer science (M Math, PhD); computer science (software engineering) (M Math); computer science (statistics-computing) (M Math); mathematics (M Math, PhD); pure mathematics (M Math, PhD); statistics (M Math, PhD); statistics-biostatistics (M Math); statistics-computing (M Math); statistics-finance (M Math). *Application fee:* $75 Canadian dollars. *Application Contact:* Dr. G. Labahn, Associate Dean of Graduate Studies, 519-888-4567 Ext. 3294, E-mail: mathgrad@math.uwaterloo.ca. *Dean,* Dr. J. A. George, 519-888-4567 Ext. 3474, Fax: 519-746-0274, E-mail: jageorge@sparse1.uwaterloo.ca.

Faculty of Science Students: 307 full-time (131 women), 43 part-time (19 women). *Faculty:* 151 full-time (35 women), 202 part-time/adjunct (24 women). Expenses: Contact institution. *Financial support:* Fellowships, research assistantships, teaching assistantships, career-related internships or fieldwork and institutionally sponsored loans available. In 2001, 66 master's, 27 doctorates awarded. *Degree program information:* Part-time programs available. Offers biology (M Sc, PhD); chemistry (M Sc, PhD); earth sciences (M Sc, PhD); optometry (OD); physics (M Sc, PhD); science (OD, M Sc, PhD); vision science (M Sc, PhD). *Application deadline:* Applications are processed on a rolling basis. *Application Contact:* A. Kolic, Administrative Assistant, 519-888-4567 Ext. 3525, Fax: 519-746-2543, E-mail: akolic@scimail.uwaterloo.ca. *Associate Dean*, Dr. J. J. Heikkila, 519-888-4567 Ext. 3076, Fax: 519-746-2543, E-mail: haikkila@sciborg.uwaterloo.ca.

THE UNIVERSITY OF WEST ALABAMA, Livingston, AL 35470

General Information State-supported, coed, comprehensive institution. *Enrollment:* 176 full-time matriculated graduate/professional students (139 women), 173 part-time matriculated graduate/professional students (127 women). *Enrollment by degree level:* 349 master's. *Graduate faculty:* 24 full-time (6 women), 7 part-time/adjunct (2 women). Tuition, state resident: part-time $133 per semester hour. Tuition, nonresident: part-time $266 per semester hour. *Required fees:* $25 per term. Tuition and fees vary according to course load. *Graduate housing:* Rooms and/or apartments available on a first-come, first-served basis to single students and available to married students. Typical cost: $760 per year for single students; $1,255 per year for married students. *Student services:* Campus employment opportunities, career counseling, disabled student services, free psychological counseling, international student services. *Library facilities:* Julia Tutwiler Library. *Online resources:* library catalog, web page, access to other libraries' catalogs. *Collection:* 141,755 titles, 5,000 serial subscriptions, 6,900 audiovisual materials.

Computer facilities: 250 computers available on campus for general student use. A campuswide network can be accessed from student residence rooms and from off campus. Internet access is available. *Web address:* http://www.uwa.edu/.

General Application Contact: Dr. Joe B. Wilkins, Dean of Graduate Studies, 205-652-3647 Ext. 421, Fax: 205-652-3551, E-mail: livjbw@uwa.edu.

GRADUATE UNITS

School of Graduate Studies Students: 176 full-time (139 women), 173 part-time (127 women); includes 184 minority (182 African Americans, 2 Hispanic Americans), 1 international. *Faculty:* 24 full-time (6 women), 7 part-time/adjunct (2 women). Expenses: Contact institution. *Financial support:* In 2001–02, 25 students received support. Career-related internships or fieldwork, Federal Work-Study, scholarships/grants, and unspecified assistantships available. Support available to part-time students. Financial award applicants required to submit CSS PROFILE. In 2001, 120 degrees awarded. *Degree program information:* Part-time and evening/weekend programs available. *Application deadline:* For fall admission, 9/10 (priority date); for spring admission, 3/24. Applications are processed on a rolling basis. *Application fee:* $20 ($50 for international students). *Dean*, Dr. Joe B. Wilkins, 205-652-3647 Ext. 421, Fax: 205-652-3551, E-mail: jbw@uwa.edu.

College of Education Students: 176 full-time (139 women), 173 part-time (127 women); includes 184 minority (182 African Americans, 2 Hispanic Americans) *Faculty:* 13 full-time (4 women), 4 part-time/adjunct (2 women). Expenses: Contact institution. *Financial support:* In 2001–02, 13 students received support. Career-related internships or fieldwork, Federal Work-Study, scholarships/grants, and unspecified assistantships available. Support available to part-time students. Financial award applicants required to submit FAFSA. In 2001, 120 degrees awarded. *Degree program information:* Part-time and evening/weekend programs available. Offers continuing education (MSCE); early childhood education (M Ed); education (M Ed, MAT, MSCE); elementary education (M Ed); guidance and counseling (M Ed, MSCE); library media (M Ed); physical education (M Ed, MAT); school administration (M Ed); secondary education (M Ed, MAT); special education (M Ed). *Application deadline:* For fall admission, 9/10 (priority date); for spring admission, 3/24. Applications are processed on a rolling basis. *Application fee:* $20 ($50 for international students). *Dean*, Dr. Ann Jones, 205-652-3421, Fax: 205-652-3706.

College of Liberal Arts Students: 12 full-time (8 women), 31 part-time (17 women); includes 20 minority (all African Americans) *Faculty:* 8 full-time (1 woman), 1 part-time/adjunct (0 women). Expenses: Contact institution. *Financial support:* Career-related internships or fieldwork, Federal Work-Study, scholarships/grants, and unspecified assistantships available. Support available to part-time students. In 2001, 8 degrees awarded. Offers history (MAT); language arts (MAT); liberal arts (MAT); social science (MAT). *Application fee:* $20 ($50 for international students). *Chairperson*, Dr. Roy Underwood, 800-621-8044 Ext. 3457.

College of Natural Sciences and Mathematics Students: 11 full-time (8 women), 20 part-time (14 women); includes 19 minority (18 African Americans, 1 Hispanic American) *Faculty:* 4 full-time (0 women), 1 part-time/adjunct (0 women). Expenses: Contact institution. *Financial support:* Career-related internships or fieldwork, Federal Work-Study, scholarships/grants, and unspecified assistantships available. Support available to part-time students. In 2001, 9 degrees awarded. Offers biological sciences (MAT); mathematics (MAT); natural sciences and mathematics (MAT). *Application fee:* $20 ($50 for international students). *Dean*, Dr. Judy Massey, 800-621-3412.

THE UNIVERSITY OF WESTERN ONTARIO, London, ON N6A 5B8, Canada

General Information Province-supported, coed, university. *Graduate housing:* Rooms and/or apartments available to single and married students.

GRADUATE UNITS

Faculty of Graduate Studies *Degree program information:* Part-time and evening/weekend programs available. Postbaccalaureate distance learning degree programs offered. Electronic applications accepted.

Arts Division *Degree program information:* Part-time programs available. Offers arts (M Mus, MA, PhD); Canadian literature (MA); classical studies (MA); comparative literature (MA); English (PhD); English literature (MA); French (MA, PhD); music (M Mus, MA, PhD); philosophy (MA, PhD); Spanish (MA).

Biosciences Division *Degree program information:* Part-time programs available. Postbaccalaureate distance learning degree programs offered. Offers anatomy and cell biology (M Sc, PhD); audiology (M Cl Sc, M Sc); biochemistry (M Sc, PhD); biosciences (M Cl Sc, M Sc, MA, PhD); epidemiology and biostatistics (M Sc, PhD); family medicine (M Cl Sc); kinesiology (M Sc, MA, PhD); medical biophysics (M Sc, PhD); microbiology and immunology (M Sc, PhD); neuroscience (M Sc, PhD); occupational therapy (M Sc); pathology (M Sc, PhD); pharmacology and toxicology (M Sc, PhD); physical therapy (M Sc); physiology (M Sc, PhD); plant and environmental sciences (M Sc); plant sciences (M Sc, PhD); plant sciences and environmental sciences (PhD); plant sciences and molecular biology (M Sc, PhD); psychology (MA, PhD); speech-language pathology (M Cl Sc, M Sc); zoology (M Sc, PhD).

Center for the Study of Theory and Criticism Students: 23. 31 applicants, 29% accepted. *Faculty:* 21. Expenses: Contact institution. *Financial support:* In 2001–02, 18 teaching assistantships with full tuition reimbursements (averaging $8,264 Canadian dollars per year) were awarded; research assistantships with tuition reimbursements, scholarships/grants also available. Financial award application deadline: 4/1. In 2001, 8 degrees awarded. Offers theory and criticism (MA, PhD). *Application deadline:* For fall admission, 2/15. *Application fee:* $30 Canadian dollars. *Director*, Prof. Thomas Carmichael, 519-661-3442, E-mail: theory@uwo.ca.

Physical Sciences Division *Degree program information:* Part-time programs available. Offers applied mathematics (M Sc, PhD); astronomy (M Sc, PhD); chemistry (M Sc, PhD); computer science (M Sc, PhD); engineering science (M Eng, ME Sc, PhD); geology (M Sc, PhD); geology and environmental science (M Sc, PhD); geophysics (M Sc, PhD); geophysics and environmental science (M Sc, PhD); mathematics (MA, PhD); physical sciences (M Eng, M Sc, MA, ME Sc, PhD); physics (M Sc, PhD); statistical and actuarial sciences (M Sc, PhD); theoretical physics (PhD). Electronic applications accepted.

Social Sciences Division *Degree program information:* Part-time and evening/weekend programs available. Offers anthropology (MA); counseling (M Ed); curriculum studies (M Ed); economics (MA, PhD); education (M Ed); educational policy studies (M Ed); educational psychology/special education (M Ed); geography (M Sc, MA, PhD); history (MA, PhD); journalism (MA); library and information science (MLIS, PhD); nursing (M Sc N); political science (MA, MPA, PhD); social sciences (M Ed, M Sc, M Sc N, MA, MBA, MLIS, MPA, PhD, Diploma); sociology (MA, PhD).

Faculty of Law Offers law (LL B, Diploma).

Faculty of Medicine and Dentistry Average age 24. Expenses: Contact institution. *Financial support:* Fellowships, teaching assistantships, career-related internships or fieldwork, Federal Work-Study, and institutionally sponsored loans available. In 2001, 150 degrees awarded. Offers medicine (MD); medicine and dentistry (DDS, MD, M Cl D, M Cl Sc, M Sc, MA, PhD). *Dean*, Dr. Carol P. Herbert, 519-661-3459.

School of Dentistry Students: 161. *Faculty:* 115. Expenses: Contact institution. *Financial support:* Fellowships, career-related internships or fieldwork, Federal Work-Study, and institutionally sponsored loans available. In 2001, 40 first professional degrees, 5 master's awarded. Offers dentistry (DDS, M Cl D); orthodontics (M Cl D). *Application Contact:* Dr. A. H. Mamandras, Chair, 519-661-2111 Ext. 86114, Fax: 519-661-2075, E-mail: antonios.mamandras@fmd.uwo.ca.

Richard Ivey School of Business Students: 630 full-time (200 women). Average age 29. *Faculty:* 81 full-time (13 women). Expenses: Contact institution. *Financial support:* In 2001–02, 20 fellowships (averaging $5,000 Canadian dollars per year) were awarded; career-related internships or fieldwork, Federal Work-Study, institutionally sponsored loans, and scholarships/grants also available. Financial award application deadline: 4/1. In 2001, 200 master's, 50 doctorates awarded. Offers business (EMBA, MBA, PhD). *Application deadline:* For fall admission, 4/1. Applications are processed on a rolling basis. *Application fee:* $100 Canadian dollars. Electronic applications accepted. *Application Contact:* Joanne Shoveller, Director, MBA Program Office, 519-661-3212, Fax: 519-661-3431, E-mail: jshovell@ivey.uwo.ca. *Dean*, L. G. Tapp, 519-661-3279, Fax: 519-661-3485.

UNIVERSITY OF WEST FLORIDA, Pensacola, FL 32514-5750

General Information State-supported, coed, comprehensive institution. CGS member. *Enrollment:* 357 full-time matriculated graduate/professional students (228 women), 957 part-time matriculated graduate/professional students (615 women). *Enrollment by degree level:* 1,011 master's, 244 doctoral, 59 other advanced degrees. *Graduate faculty:* 157 full-time (54 women), 35 part-time/adjunct (16 women). Tuition, state resident: full-time $3,995; part-time $166 per credit hour. Tuition, nonresident: full-time $13,766; part-time $574 per credit hour. Tuition and fees vary according to campus/location. *Graduate housing:* Rooms and/or apartments available to single students and available on a first-come, first-served basis to married students. Typical cost: $5,440 (including board) for single students. Room and board charges vary according to housing facility selected. *Student services:* Campus employment opportunities, campus safety program, career counseling, child daycare facilities, disabled student services, free psychological counseling, international student services, low-cost health insurance. *Library facilities:* Pace Library. *Online resources:* library catalog, web page, access to other libraries' catalogs. *Collection:* 392,581 titles, 3,210 serial subscriptions, 10,182 audiovisual materials. *Research affiliation:* Autometric, Inc. (computer information systems).

Computer facilities: A campuswide network can be accessed from student residence rooms and from off campus. Internet access and online class registration are available. *Web address:* http://uwf.edu/.

General Application Contact: Susie Neeley, Director of Admissions, 850-474-2230, Fax: 850-474-2082, E-mail: admissions@uwf.edu.

GRADUATE UNITS

College of Arts and Sciences: Arts Students: 119 full-time (78 women), 110 part-time (71 women); includes 29 minority (10 African Americans, 5 Asian Americans or Pacific Islanders, 11 Hispanic Americans, 3 Native Americans), 4 international. Average age 31. 204 applicants, 58% accepted, 56 enrolled. *Faculty:* 48 full-time (19 women), 6 part-time/adjunct (3 women). Expenses: Contact institution. *Financial support:* Fellowships with partial tuition reimbursements, research assistantships with partial tuition reimbursements, teaching assistantships with partial tuition reimbursements, career-related internships or fieldwork, Federal Work-Study, institutionally sponsored loans, and tuition waivers (full and partial) available. Support available to part-time students. In 2001, 55 degrees awarded. *Degree program information:* Part-time and evening/weekend programs available. Offers applied politics (MA); arts and sciences: arts (MA, MAT); communication arts (MA); English (MA); history (MA); humanities (MA); political science (MA); psychology (MA). *Application deadline:* Applications are processed on a rolling basis. *Application fee:* $20. *Dean*, Dr. Martha D. Saunders, 850-474-2688, E-mail: msaunder@uwf.edu.

College of Arts and Sciences: Sciences Students: 31 full-time (12 women), 82 part-time (38 women); includes 19 minority (5 African Americans, 6 Asian Americans or Pacific Islanders, 6 Hispanic Americans, 2 Native Americans), 7 international. Average age 33. 89 applicants, 43% accepted, 19 enrolled. *Faculty:* 26 full-time (3 women), 2 part-time/adjunct (1 woman). Expenses: Contact institution. *Financial support:* Fellowships, research assistantships with partial tuition reimbursements, teaching assistantships with partial tuition reimbursements, career-related internships or fieldwork, Federal Work-Study, institutionally sponsored loans, and tuition waivers (full and partial) available. Support available to part-time students. In 2001, 52 degrees awarded. *Degree program information:* Part-time and evening/weekend programs available. Offers arts and sciences: sciences (MA, MAT, MS, MST); biology (MS); biology education (MST); coastal zone studies (MS); computer science (MS); general biology (MS, MST); mathematics (MA); mathematics education (MAT); statistics (MA); systems and control engineering (MS). *Application deadline:* For fall admission, 6/30. Applications are processed on a rolling basis. *Application fee:* $20. *Associate Dean*, Dr. Katheryn K. Fouché, 850-474-3160, E-mail: kfouche@uwf.edu.

College of Business Students: 49 full-time (22 women), 181 part-time (98 women); includes 40 minority (14 African Americans, 15 Asian Americans or Pacific Islanders, 10 Hispanic Americans, 1 Native American), 14 international. Average age 32. 126 applicants, 67% accepted, 49 enrolled. *Faculty:* 20 full-time (5 women), 5 part-time/adjunct (1 woman). Expenses: Contact institution. *Financial support:* In 2001–02, 16 fellowships (averaging $500 per year), 22 research assistantships with partial tuition reimbursements (averaging $5,400 per year) were awarded. Career-related internships or fieldwork, Federal Work-Study, and scholarships/grants also available. Support available to part-time students. Financial award application deadline: 4/1; financial award applicants required to submit FAFSA. In 2001, 73 degrees awarded. *Degree program information:* Part-time and evening/weekend programs available. Offers accounting (MA); business (MA, MBA); business administration (MBA). *Application deadline:* For fall admission, 6/30; for spring admission, 11/1. Applications are processed on a rolling basis. *Application fee:* $20. *Dean*, Dr. F. Edward Ranelli, 850-474-2348.

College of Professional Studies Students: 158 full-time (116 women), 584 part-time (408 women); includes 159 minority (102 African Americans, 25 Asian Americans or Pacific Islanders, 24 Hispanic Americans, 8 Native Americans), 19 international. Average age 39. 322 applicants, 66% accepted, 141 enrolled. *Faculty:* 62 full-time (27 women), 22 part-time/adjunct (11 women). Expenses: Contact institution. *Financial support:* In 2001–02, 4 fellowships (averaging $350 per year), 6 teaching assistantships (averaging $10,000 per year) were awarded. Research assistantships with tuition reimbursements, career-related internships or fieldwork, Federal Work-Study, institutionally sponsored loans, and tuition waivers (full and partial) also available. Support available to part-time students. In 2001, 206 master's, 16 doctorates, 61 other advanced degrees awarded. *Degree program information:* Part-time and evening/weekend programs available. Offers alternative education (M Ed); clinical teaching (MA); curriculum and instruction (M Ed); curriculum and instruction/alternative education (M Ed); education (M Ed, MA, MPA, MS, Ed D, Ed S); elementary education (M Ed); guidance and counseling (M Ed); habilitative science (MA); middle and secondary level education (M Ed); primary education (M Ed); reading (M Ed); special education-clinical teaching (MA); vocational education (M Ed). *Application deadline:* For fall admission, 6/30; for spring admis-

University of West Florida (continued)

sion, 11/1. Applications are processed on a rolling basis. *Application fee:* $20. *Dean,* Dr. Janet Pilcher, 850-474-2769, Fax: 850-474-3205.

Division of Administrative Studies Students: 9 full-time (6 women), 41 part-time (25 women); includes 12 minority (7 African Americans, 3 Asian Americans or Pacific Islanders, 2 Hispanic Americans) Average age 36. 24 applicants, 58% accepted, 11 enrolled. Expenses: Contact institution. *Financial support:* Fellowships, research assistantships, career-related internships or fieldwork, Federal Work-Study, institutionally sponsored loans, and tuition waivers (full and partial) available. Support available to part-time students. Financial award application deadline: 4/15. In 2001, 18 degrees awarded. *Degree program information:* Part-time and evening/weekend programs available. Offers public administration (MPA). *Application deadline:* For fall admission, 6/30; for spring admission, 11/1. Applications are processed on a rolling basis. *Application fee:* $20. *Chairperson,* Dr. Kato B. Keeton, 850-474-2184, E-mail: kkeeton@uwf.edu.

Division of Diversity Studies and Applied Research Students: 51 full-time (34 women), 389 part-time (265 women); includes 87 minority (55 African Americans, 15 Asian Americans or Pacific Islanders, 11 Hispanic Americans, 6 Native Americans), 15 international. Average age 39. 142 applicants, 62% accepted, 68 enrolled. Expenses: Contact institution. *Financial support:* Fellowships, career-related internships or fieldwork available. In 2001, 88 master's, 16 doctorates, 61 other advanced degrees awarded. *Degree program information:* Part-time and evening/weekend programs available. Offers curriculum and instruction (Ed D, Ed S); educational leadership (M Ed, Ed S). *Application deadline:* For fall admission, 6/30; for spring admission, 11/1. Applications are processed on a rolling basis. *Application fee:* $20. *Chairperson,* Dr. Godfrey Franklin, 850-474-2251.

Division of Health, Leisure, and Exercise Science Students: 30 full-time (20 women), 31 part-time (23 women); includes 15 minority (9 African Americans, 2 Asian Americans or Pacific Islanders, 4 Hispanic Americans), 2 international. Average age 31. 32 applicants, 94% accepted, 19 enrolled. Expenses: Contact institution. *Financial support:* Teaching assistantships available. In 2001, 28 degrees awarded. *Degree program information:* Part-time and evening/weekend programs available. Offers health and community education (MS); health, leisure, and sports (MS); physical education (MS). *Application deadline:* For fall admission, 6/30; for spring admission, 11/1. Applications are processed on a rolling basis. *Application fee:* $20. *Chairperson,* Dr. C. B. Williamson, 850-474-2594.

UNIVERSITY OF WEST LOS ANGELES, Inglewood, CA 90301-2902

General Information Independent, coed, upper-level institution. *Enrollment:* 22 full-time matriculated graduate/professional students (11 women), 136 part-time matriculated graduate/professional students (64 women). *Enrollment by degree level:* 158 first professional. *Graduate faculty:* 6 full-time (1 woman), 30 part-time/adjunct (6 women). *Tuition:* Full-time $13,365; part-time $495 per unit. *Required fees:* $140 per term. *Graduate housing:* On-campus housing not available. *Student services:* Career counseling, disabled student services, low-cost health insurance. *Library facilities:* Kelton Library. *Collection:* 33,000 titles, 250 serial subscriptions.

Computer facilities: 20 computers available on campus for general student use. Internet access is available. *Web address:* http://www.uwla.edu/.

General Application Contact: Lynda Freeman, Director of Admissions, 310-342-5200 Ext. 254, Fax: 310-342-5295, E-mail: lfreeman@uwla.edu.

GRADUATE UNITS

School of Law Students: 22 full-time (11 women), 136 part-time (64 women); includes 67 minority (33 African Americans, 21 Asian Americans or Pacific Islanders, 12 Hispanic Americans, 1 Native American) Average age 35. 67 applicants, 54% accepted, 26 enrolled. *Faculty:* 6 full-time (1 woman), 30 part-time/adjunct (6 women). Expenses: Contact institution. *Financial support:* Teaching assistantships, career-related internships or fieldwork, Federal Work-Study, and scholarships/grants available. Support available to part-time students. Financial award application deadline: 10/15; financial award applicants required to submit FAFSA. In 2001, 50 degrees awarded. *Degree program information:* Part-time and evening/weekend programs available. Offers law (JD). *Application deadline:* Applications are processed on a rolling basis. *Application fee:* $55. Electronic applications accepted. *Application Contact:* Lynda Freeman, Admissions Counselor, 310-642-5200 Ext. 254, Fax: 310-342-5292, E-mail: lfreeman@uwla.edu. *Acting Dean,* Anne E Arvin, 310-342-5200 Ext. 270, Fax: 310-342-5295, E-mail: aarvin@uwla.edu.

UNIVERSITY OF WINDSOR, Windsor, ON N9B 3P4, Canada

General Information Province-supported, coed, university. *Graduate housing:* Rooms and/or apartments available on a first-come, first-served basis to single and married students. Housing application deadline: 6/7. *Research affiliation:* Daimler/Chrysler Automotive Research and Development Centre.

GRADUATE UNITS

Faculty of Graduate Studies and Research *Degree program information:* Part-time and evening/weekend programs available.

Faculty of Arts and Social Sciences *Degree program information:* Part-time programs available. Offers arts and social sciences (MA, MFA, PhD); clinical psychology (PhD); English and creative writing (MA); English literature (MA); history (MA); philosophy (MA); political science (MA); psychology (MA, PhD); sociology (MA); sociology-social justice (PhD); visual arts (MFA).

Faculty of Education *Degree program information:* Part-time and evening/weekend programs available. Offers education (M Ed, PhD).

Faculty of Engineering *Degree program information:* Part-time programs available. Offers civil and environmental engineering (MA Sc, PhD); electrical engineering (MA Sc, PhD); engineering (MA Sc, PhD); engineering materials (MA Sc, PhD); industrial engineering (MA Sc); manufacturing systems engineering (PhD); mechanical engineering (MA Sc, PhD).

Faculty of Human Kinetics *Degree program information:* Part-time programs available. Offers human kinetics (MHK).

Faculty of Science *Degree program information:* Part-time programs available. Offers biochemistry (M Sc, PhD); biological sciences (M Sc, PhD); chemistry (M Sc, PhD); computer science (M Sc); earth sciences (M Sc); economics (MA); mathematics (M Sc, PhD); nursing (M Sc); physics (M Sc, PhD); science (M Sc, MA, MA Sc, PhD); statistics (M Sc, PhD).

Odette School of Business *Degree program information:* Evening/weekend programs available. Offers business administration (MBA).

THE UNIVERSITY OF WINNIPEG, Winnipeg, MB R3B 2E9, Canada

General Information Province-supported, coed, comprehensive institution. *Graduate housing:* On-campus housing not available.

GRADUATE UNITS

Faculty of Theology *Degree program information:* Part-time programs available. Offers marriage and family therapy (MMFT, Certificate); sacred theology (STM); theology (M Div).

Graduate Studies *Degree program information:* Part-time and evening/weekend programs available. Offers history (MA); public administration (MPA); religious studies (MA).

UNIVERSITY OF WISCONSIN–EAU CLAIRE, Eau Claire, WI 54702-4004

General Information State-supported, coed, comprehensive institution. CGS member. *Enrollment:* 112 full-time matriculated graduate/professional students (86 women), 212 part-time matriculated graduate/professional students (157 women). *Enrollment by degree level:* 324 master's. *Graduate faculty:* 359 full-time (120 women), 26 part-time/adjunct (14 women). Tuition, state resident: full-time $4,481; part-time $249 per credit. Tuition, nonresident: full-time $14,305; part-time $795 per credit. *Graduate housing:* Room and/or apartments available to single students; on-campus housing not available to married students. Typical cost: $2,150 per year ($3,560 including board). Housing application deadline: 4/1. *Student services:* Campus employment opportunities, campus safety program, career counseling, child daycare facilities, disabled student services, exercise/wellness program, free psychological counseling, grant writing training, international student services, low-cost health insurance, multicultural affairs office, teacher training, writing training. *Library facilities:* William D. McIntyre Library plus 1 other. *Online resources:* library catalog, web page, access to other libraries' catalogs. *Collection:* 703,340 titles, 3,376 serial subscriptions, 12,052 audiovisual materials. *Research affiliation:* Materials Research Society (physics), Oncology Nursing Society (nursing), Camille and Henry Dreyfus Foundation (chemistry).

Computer facilities: 925 computers available on campus for general student use. A campuswide network can be accessed from student residence rooms and from off campus. Internet access and online class registration are available. *Web address:* http://www.uwec.edu/.

General Application Contact: Robert Lopez, Director of Admissions, 715-836-5415, Fax: 715-836-2409, E-mail: admissions@uwec.edu.

GRADUATE UNITS

College of Arts and Sciences Students: 33 full-time (26 women), 21 part-time (10 women); includes 3 minority (1 Asian American or Pacific Islander, 1 Hispanic American, 1 Native American), 1 international. Average age 28. 61 applicants, 64% accepted, 33 enrolled. *Faculty:* 254 full-time (69 women), 21 part-time/adjunct (12 women). Expenses: Contact institution. *Financial support:* In 2001–02, 23 students received support, including 5 fellowships, 15 teaching assistantships (averaging $5,500 per year); career-related internships or fieldwork and Federal Work-Study also available. Financial award application deadline: 4/15; financial award applicants required to submit FAFSA. In 2001, 20 degrees awarded. Offers arts and sciences (MA, MS, MSE, Ed S); biology (MS); English (MA); history (MA); school psychology (MSE, Ed S). *Application deadline:* Applications are processed on a rolling basis. *Application fee:* $45. *Dean,* Dr. Ted Wendt, 715-836-2542, Fax: 715-836-3292, E-mail: wendtta@uwec.edu.

College of Business Students: 7 full-time (5 women), 38 part-time (19 women); includes 1 minority (Asian American or Pacific Islander), 4 international. Average age 28. 29 applicants, 83% accepted, 10 enrolled. *Faculty:* 35 full-time (6 women), 2 part-time/adjunct (0 women). Expenses: Contact institution. *Financial support:* In 2001–02, 16 students received support, including 3 fellowships, 3 teaching assistantships (averaging $3,800 per year); Federal Work-Study also available. Support available to part-time students. Financial award applicants required to submit FAFSA. In 2001, 21 degrees awarded. *Degree program information:* Part-time programs available. Offers business (MBA); business administration (MBA). *Application deadline:* For fall admission, 7/1; for spring admission, 12/1. Applications are processed on a rolling basis. *Application fee:* $45. *Dean,* Dr. V. Thomas Dock, 715-836-5509, Fax: 715-836-5263, E-mail: dockv@uwec.edu.

College of Professional Studies Students: 72 full-time (55 women), 153 part-time (128 women); includes 11 minority (2 African Americans, 4 Asian Americans or Pacific Islanders, 1 Hispanic American, 4 Native Americans), 6 international. Average age 33. 163 applicants, 90% accepted, 59 enrolled. *Faculty:* 70 full-time (45 women), 3 part-time/adjunct (2 women). Expenses: Contact institution. *Financial support:* In 2001–02, 102 students received support, including 7 fellowships, 21 teaching assistantships (averaging $5,200 per year); career-related internships or fieldwork and Federal Work-Study also available. Support available to part-time students. Financial award application deadline: 3/1; financial award applicants required to submit FAFSA. In 2001, 112 degrees awarded. *Degree program information:* Part-time programs available. Offers professional studies (MAT, MEPD, MS, MSE, MSN, MST). *Application deadline:* Applications are processed on a rolling basis. *Application fee:* $45. *Dean,* Dr. Mark Clark, 715-836-2722, Fax: 715-836-4892, E-mail: clarkw@uwec.edu.

School of Education Students: 23 full-time (14 women), 97 part-time (79 women); includes 4 minority (1 Hispanic American, 3 Native Americans), 3 international. Average age 35. 53 applicants, 87% accepted, 22 enrolled. *Faculty:* 23 full-time (15 women), 2 part-time/adjunct (1 woman). Expenses: Contact institution. *Financial support:* In 2001–02, 30 students received support, including 6 teaching assistantships (averaging $5,800 per year); career-related internships or fieldwork and Federal Work-Study also available. Financial award application deadline: 3/1; financial award applicants required to submit FAFSA. In 2001, 60 degrees awarded. Offers biology (MAT, MST); education (MAT, MEPD, MSE, MST); education and professional development (MEPD); elementary education (MST); English (MAT, MST); history (MAT, MST); mathematics (MAT, MST); reading (MST); special education (MSE). *Application deadline:* For fall admission, 7/1; for spring admission, 12/1. Applications are processed on a rolling basis. *Application fee:* $45. *Interim Associate Dean,* Dr. Carol Klun, 715-836-3671, Fax: 715-836-3245, E-mail: kluncl@uwec.edu.

School of Human Sciences and Services Students: 37 full-time (30 women), 6 part-time (3 women); includes 3 minority (1 African American, 2 Asian Americans or Pacific Islanders), 3 international. Average age 26. 75 applicants, 91% accepted, 19 enrolled. *Faculty:* 25 full-time (8 women), 1 (woman) part-time/adjunct. Expenses: Contact institution. *Financial support:* In 2001–02, 34 students received support, including 9 teaching assistantships; career-related internships or fieldwork and Federal Work-Study also available. Financial award application deadline: 3/1; financial award applicants required to submit FAFSA. In 2001, 20 degrees awarded. Offers communicative disorders (MS); environmental and public health (MS); human sciences and services (MS). *Application deadline:* For fall admission, 3/1. Applications are processed on a rolling basis. *Application fee:* $45. *Dean,* Dr. Patricia Christopherson, 715-836-5038, Fax: 715-836-4892, E-mail: kluncl@uwec.edu.

School of Nursing Students: 12 full-time (11 women), 50 part-time (46 women); includes 4 minority (1 African American, 2 Asian Americans or Pacific Islanders, 1 Native American) Average age 36. 35 applicants, 94% accepted, 18 enrolled. *Faculty:* 22 full-time (all women). Expenses: Contact institution. *Financial support:* In 2001–02, 38 students received support, including 3 teaching assistantships (averaging $3,400 per year); Federal Work-Study also available. Support available to part-time students. Financial award application deadline: 3/1; financial award applicants required to submit FAFSA. In 2001, 32 degrees awarded. *Degree program information:* Part-time programs available. Offers nursing (MSN). *Application deadline:* For fall admission, 2/1 (priority date); for spring admission, 12/1. Applications are processed on a rolling basis. *Application fee:* $45. *Interim Associate Dean,* Dr. Rita Kisting Sparks, 715-836-5287, Fax: 715-836-5925, E-mail: sparksrk@uwec.edu.

See in-depth description on page 1277.

UNIVERSITY OF WISCONSIN–GREEN BAY, Green Bay, WI 54311-7001

General Information State-supported, coed, comprehensive institution. *Enrollment:* 32 full-time matriculated graduate/professional students (17 women), 92 part-time matriculated graduate/professional students (61 women). *Enrollment by degree level:* 124 master's. *Graduate faculty:* 29 full-time (10 women), 7 part-time/adjunct (4 women). Tuition, state resident: full-time $4,020; part-time $223 per credit. Tuition, nonresident: full-time $13,844; part-time $769 per credit. *Required fees:* $872. Part-time tuition and fees vary according to course load and reciprocity agreements. *Graduate housing:* Room and/or apartments available on a first-come, first-served basis to single students; on-campus housing not available to married students. Typical cost: $2,100 per year ($4,000 including board). Room and board charges vary according to housing facility selected. Housing application deadline: 5/1. *Student services:* Campus employment opportunities, campus safety program, career counseling, disabled student services, free psychological counseling, international student services, low-cost health insurance, multicultural affairs office. *Library facilities:* Cofrin Library. *Online resources:* library catalog, web page, access to other libraries' catalogs. *Collection:* 259,941 titles, 8,012 serial subscriptions, 45,396 audiovisual materials. *Research affiliation:* Abbott Laboratories (anaerobic digestion systems), Research Corporation (examination of the function structure, gene of Fetuin), Kimberly Clark (sludge recovery), Robert E. Lee & Associates (endangered species survey for Brown County landfill site selection), R. W. Beck (Brown County waste-to-energy study).

Computer facilities: 550 computers available on campus for general student use. A campuswide network can be accessed from student residence rooms and from off campus. Internet access and online class registration, on-line degree progress are available. *Web address:* http://www.uwgb.edu/.

General Application Contact: Ronald D. Stieglitz, Associate Dean of Graduate Studies, 920-465-2123, Fax: 920-465-2718, E-mail: stieglir@uwgb.edu.

GRADUATE UNITS

Graduate Studies Students: 32 full-time (17 women), 92 part-time (61 women); includes 12 minority (1 African American, 3 Asian Americans or Pacific Islanders, 8 Native Americans), 6 international. Average age 33. *Faculty:* 29 full-time (10 women), 7 part-time/adjunct (4 women). Expenses: Contact institution. *Financial support:* In 2001–02, 4 research assistantships, 9 teaching assistantships were awarded. Career-related internships or fieldwork, Federal Work-Study, and institutionally sponsored loans also available. Financial award application deadline: 7/15; financial award applicants required to submit FAFSA. In 2001, 27 degrees awarded. *Degree program information:* Part-time and evening/weekend programs available. Offers applied leadership for teaching and learning (MS Ed); environmental science and policy (MS); management (MS). *Application deadline:* For fall admission, 8/1; for spring admission, 11/1. Applications are processed on a rolling basis. *Application fee:* $45. *Associate Dean*, Ronald D. Stieglitz, 920-465-2123, Fax: 920-465-2718, E-mail: stieglir@uwgb.edu.

UNIVERSITY OF WISCONSIN–LA CROSSE, La Crosse, WI 54601-3742

General Information State-supported, coed, comprehensive institution. CGS member. *Graduate housing:* Room and/or apartments available to single students; on-campus housing not available to married students. Housing application deadline: 5/1.

GRADUATE UNITS

Graduate Studies *Degree program information:* Part-time and evening/weekend programs available.

College of Business Administration *Degree program information:* Part-time and evening/weekend programs available. Offers business administration (MBA).

College of Health, Physical Education and Recreation *Degree program information:* Part-time and evening/weekend programs available. Offers adult fitness/cardiac rehabilitation (MS); community health (MS); community health education (MPH); general pedagogy (MS); general sports administration (MS); health, physical education and recreation (MPH, MS); human performance (MS); recreation (MS); school health (MS); special adaptive physical education (MS).

College of Liberal Studies Offers liberal studies (MS Ed, CAGS); school psychology (MS Ed, CAGS).

College of Science and Allied Health *Degree program information:* Part-time programs available. Offers biology (MS); clinical microbiology (MS); nurse anesthetist (MS); physical therapy (MSPT); science and allied health (MS, MSPT).

School of Education *Degree program information:* Part-time programs available. Offers college student development and administration (MS Ed); education (MEPD, MS Ed); elementary education (MEPD); emotional disturbance (MS Ed); K–12 (MEPD); learning disabilities (MS Ed); professional development (MEPD); reading (MS Ed); secondary education (MEPD).

See in-depth description on page 1279.

UNIVERSITY OF WISCONSIN–MADISON, Madison, WI 53706-1380

General Information State-supported, coed, university. CGS member. *Enrollment:* 9,139 full-time matriculated graduate/professional students (4,420 women), 1,917 part-time matriculated graduate/professional students (977 women). *Enrollment by degree level:* 2,357 first professional, 3,747 master's, 4,952 doctoral. *Graduate faculty:* 3,171 full-time (891 women), 831 part-time/adjunct (408 women). Tuition, state resident: full-time $7,361; part-time $399 per credit. Tuition, nonresident: full-time $20,499; part-time $1,282 per credit. *Required fees:* $34 per credit. Full-time tuition and fees vary according to course load, program, reciprocity agreements and student level. *Graduate housing:* Rooms and/or apartments available on a first-come, first-served basis to single and married students. Typical cost: $3,855 per year ($4,855 including board) for single students. Room and board charges vary according to board plan and housing facility selected. *Student services:* Campus employment opportunities, campus safety program, career counseling, child daycare facilities, disabled student services, exercise/wellness program, free psychological counseling, international student services, low-cost health insurance, multicultural affairs office, teacher training, writing training. *Library facilities:* Memorial Library plus 40 others. *Online resources:* library catalog, web page, access to other libraries' catalogs. *Collection:* 6.1 million titles, 66,000 serial subscriptions. *Research affiliation:* U.S. Department of Agriculture–Dairy Forage Research Center, Institute on Tropical Studies, University Research Association, U.S. Department of Agriculture–Forest Products Laboratory.

Computer facilities: 2,800 computers available on campus for general student use. A campuswide network can be accessed from student residence rooms and from off campus. Internet access is available. *Web address:* http://www.wisc.edu/.

General Application Contact: Graduate Admissions, 608-262-2433, Fax: 608-262-5134, E-mail: gradadmiss@mail.bascom.wisc.edu.

GRADUATE UNITS

Graduate School Students: 6,973 full-time (3,196 women), 1,771 part-time (878 women); includes 701 minority (194 African Americans, 248 Asian Americans or Pacific Islanders, 217 Hispanic Americans, 42 Native Americans), 2,350 international. Average age 30. ###### applicants, 35% accepted, 1968 enrolled. *Faculty:* 3,171 full-time (891 women), 831 part-time/adjunct (408 women). Expenses: Contact institution. *Financial support:* In 2001–02, 5,511 students received support, including 718 fellowships with full and partial tuition reimbursements available (averaging $10,925 per year), 2,302 research assistantships with full and partial tuition reimbursements available (averaging $13,763 per year), 1,713 teaching assistantships with full and partial tuition reimbursements available (averaging $9,590 per year); career-related internships or fieldwork, Federal Work-Study, institutionally sponsored loans, scholarships/grants, traineeships, health care benefits, tuition waivers (full and partial), and unspecified assistantships also available. Support available to part-time students. Financial award applicants required to submit FAFSA. In 2001, 1,828 master's, 660 doctorates awarded. *Degree program information:* Part-time and evening/weekend programs available. Postbaccalaureate distance learning degree programs offered (minimal on-campus study). Offers biophysics (PhD); cellular and molecular biology (PhD); developmental biology (PhD); endocrinology-reproductive physiology (MS, PhD); engineering (PDD); neuroscience (MS, PhD); professional practice (ME); technical Japanese (ME). *Application deadline:* Applications are processed on a rolling basis. *Application fee:* $45. Electronic applications accepted. *Application Contact:* Graduate Admissions, 608-262-2433, Fax: 608-262-5134, E-mail: gradadmiss@mail.bascom.wisc.edu. *Dean*, Dr. Martin Cadwallader, 608-262-1044.

College of Agricultural and Life Sciences Students: 847 full-time (423 women), 82 part-time (38 women); includes 61 minority (9 African Americans, 25 Asian Americans or Pacific Islanders, 24 Hispanic Americans, 3 Native Americans) Average age 30. 1,414 applicants, 21% accepted, 184 enrolled. *Faculty:* 265 full-time (44 women). Expenses: Contact institution. *Financial support:* In 2001–02, 36 fellowships, 290 research assistantships, 5 teaching assistantships were awarded. Career-related internships or fieldwork, Federal Work-Study, institutionally sponsored loans, traineeships, tuition waivers (full and partial), and project assistantships also available. Support available to part-time students. Financial award applicants required to submit FAFSA. In 2001, 86 master's, 93 doctorates awarded. *Degree program information:* Part-time programs available. Offers agricultural and applied economics (MA, MS, PhD); agricultural and life sciences (MA, MS, PhD); agricultural journalism (MS); agronomy (MS, PhD); animal sciences (MS, PhD); bacteriology (MS); biochemistry (MS, PhD); biological systems engineering (MS, PhD); biometry (MS); dairy science (MS, PhD); development (PhD); entomology (MS, PhD); family and consumer journalism (MS); food science (MS, PhD); forest science (MS, PhD); forestry (PhD); genetics (PhD); horticulture (MS, PhD); landscape architecture (MA, MS); mass communication (PhD); medical genetics (MS); molecular and environmental toxicology (MS, PhD); natural resources (MA, MS, PhD); nutritional sciences (MS, PhD); plant breeding and plant genetics (MS, PhD); plant pathology (MS, PhD); recreation resources management (MS); soil science (MS, PhD); wildlife ecology (MS, PhD). *Application fee:* $45. Electronic applications accepted. *Dean*, Elton D. Aberle, 608-262-4930, Fax: 608-262-4556, E-mail: elton.aberle@ccmail.adp.wisc.edu.

College of Engineering Students: 1,024 full-time (188 women), 127 part-time (15 women); includes 74 minority (16 African Americans, 29 Asian Americans or Pacific Islanders, 17 Hispanic Americans, 12 Native Americans), 526 international. 2,145 applicants, 33% accepted. *Faculty:* 176 full-time (14 women), 16 part-time/adjunct (3 women). Expenses: Contact institution. *Financial support:* Fellowships with full and partial tuition reimbursements, research assistantships with full tuition reimbursements, teaching assistantships with full tuition reimbursements, career-related internships or fieldwork, Federal Work-Study, institutionally sponsored loans, scholarships/grants, and unspecified assistantships available. Support available to part-time students. In 2001, 232 master's, 107 doctorates awarded. *Degree program information:* Part-time programs available. Postbaccalaureate distance learning degree programs offered (minimal on-campus study). Offers biomedical engineering (MS, PhD); chemical engineering (MS, PhD); civil and environmental engineering (MS, PhD); electrical engineering (MS, PhD); engineering (ME, MS, PhD, PDD); engineering mechanics (MS, PhD); environmental chemistry and technology (MS, PhD); geological engineering (MS, PhD); industrial engineering (MS, PhD); limnology and marine science (MS, PhD); manufacturing systems engineering (MS); materials science (MS, PhD); mechanical engineering (MS, PhD); metallurgical engineering (MS, PhD); nuclear engineering and engineering physics (MS, PhD); polymers (ME). *Application deadline:* Applications are processed on a rolling basis. *Application fee:* $45. Electronic applications accepted. *Application Contact:* Graduate Admissions, 608-262-2433, Fax: 608-262-5134, E-mail: gradadmiss@mail.bascom.wisc.edu. *Dean*, Paul S. Peercy, 608-262-3482, Fax: 608-262-6400, E-mail: peercy@engr.wisc.edu.

College of Letters and Science Students: 3,129 full-time (1,479 women), 689 part-time (321 women); includes 287 minority (73 African Americans, 107 Asian Americans or Pacific Islanders, 94 Hispanic Americans, 13 Native Americans), 817 international. Average age 30. 60 applicants, 85% accepted, 21 enrolled. *Faculty:* 917 full-time (254 women), 48 part-time/adjunct (8 women). Expenses: Contact institution. *Financial support:* In 2001–02, 207 fellowships (averaging $13,445 per year), 625 research assistantships with full tuition reimbursements (averaging $8,988 per year), 1,228 teaching assistantships with full tuition reimbursements (averaging $23,000 per year) were awarded. Career-related internships or fieldwork, Federal Work-Study, institutionally sponsored loans, traineeships, tuition waivers (full and partial), and project assistantships also available. Support available to part-time students. Financial award applicants required to submit FAFSA. In 2001, 758 master's, 324 doctorates awarded. *Degree program information:* Part-time and evening/weekend programs available. Postbaccalaureate distance learning degree programs offered (minimal on-campus study). Offers African languages and literature (MA, PhD); Afro-American studies (MA); anthropology (MA, MS, PhD); applied English linguistics (MA); art history (MA, PhD); astronomy (PhD); atmospheric and oceanic sciences (MS, PhD); biological psychology (PhD); botany (MS, PhD); cartography and geographic information systems (MS); chemistry (MS, PhD); Chinese (MA, PhD); choral (MM, DMA); classics (MA, PhD); clinical psychology (PhD); cognitive and perceptual sciences (PhD); communication arts (MA, PhD); communicative disorders (MS, PhD); comparative literature (MA, PhD); composition (MM, DMA); composition studies (PhD); computer sciences (MS, PhD); curriculum and instruction (PhD); developmental psychology (PhD); economics (PhD); English language and linguistics (PhD); ethnomusicology (MM, PhD); family and consumer journalism (PhD); French (MA, PhD); French studies (MFS, Certificate); geographic information systems (Certificate); geography (MS, PhD); geology (MS, PhD); geophysics (MS, PhD); German (MA, PhD); Greek (MA); Hebrew and Semitic studies (MA, PhD); history (MA, PhD); history of science (MA, PhD); industrial relations (MA, MS, PhD); instrumental (MM, DMA); international public affairs (MPIA); Italian (MA, PhD); Japanese (MA, PhD); journalism and mass communication (MA); languages and cultures of Asia (MA, PhD); Latin (MA); Latin American, Caribbean and Iberian studies (MA); letters and science (MA, MFA, MFS, MM, MPA, MPIA, MS, MSSW, DMA, PhD, Certificate); library and information studies (MA, PhD, Certificate); linguistics (MA, PhD); literature (MA, PhD); mass communication (PhD); mathematics (MA, PhD); music (MA, MM, DMA, PhD); music education (MM); musicology (MA, MM, PhD); performance (MM, DMA); philosophy (MA, PhD); physics (MA, MS, PhD); political science (MA, PhD); Portuguese (MA, PhD); psychology (PhD); public affairs (MPA); rural sociology (MS); Scandinavian studies (MA, PhD); Slavic languages and literature (MA, PhD); social and personality psychology (PhD); social welfare (PhD); social work (MSSW); sociology (MS, PhD); Southeast Asian studies (MA); Spanish (MA, PhD); statistics (MS, PhD); theatre and drama (MA, MFA, PhD); theory (MA, MM, PhD); urban and regional planning (MS, PhD); zoology (MA, MS, PhD). *Application fee:* $45. Electronic applications accepted. *Application Contact:* Debbie Klimek, Graduate School Department of Academic Services, 608-262-2433, Fax: 608-265-6742, E-mail: zgregan@bascom.wisc.edu. *Dean, College of Letters and Science*, Phillip R. Certain, 608-263-2303, Fax: 608-265-3564, E-mail: pcertain@ls.admin.wisc.edu.

Institute for Environmental Studies Students: 129 full-time (63 women), 37 part-time (20 women). 232 applicants, 45% accepted. *Faculty:* 10 full-time, 130 part-time/adjunct. Expenses: Contact institution. *Financial support:* In 2001–02, 106 students received support, including 8 fellowships with full tuition reimbursements available (averaging $13,187 per year), 29 research assistantships with full tuition reimbursements available (averaging $15,343 per year), 25 teaching assistantships with full tuition reimbursements available (averaging $9,181 per year); career-related internships or fieldwork, Federal Work-Study, scholarships/grants, traineeships, unspecified assistantships, and project assistantships also available. Financial award application deadline: 1/2. In 2001, 38 master's, 5 doctorates awarded. *Degree program information:* Part-time programs available. Offers conservation biology and sustainable development (MS); environmental monitoring (MS, PhD); environmental studies (MS, PhD); land resources (MS, PhD); water resources management (MS). *Application deadline:* For fall admission, 2/1; for spring admission, 10/15. *Application fee:* $45. Electronic applications accepted. *Application Contact:* James E. Miller, Program Assistant, 608-262-9206, Fax: 608-262-2273, E-mail: jemiller@facstaff.wisc.edu. *Director*, Thomas M. Yuill, 608-265-5296, Fax: 608-262-0014.

School of Business Students: 502 full-time (177 women), 121 part-time (44 women); includes 62 minority (27 African Americans, 17 Asian Americans or Pacific Islanders, 16 Hispanic Americans, 2 Native Americans), 184 international. Average age 29. 1,465 applicants, 31% accepted, 296 enrolled. *Faculty:* 76 full-time (11 women). Expenses: Contact institution. *Financial support:* In 2001–02, 335 students received support, including 117 fellowships with partial tuition reimbursements available (averaging $5,747 per year), 169 research assistantships with full tuition reimbursements available (averaging $5,638 per year), 98 teaching assistantships with full tuition reimbursements available (averaging $9,118 per year); career-related internships or fieldwork, Federal Work-Study, institutionally sponsored loans, scholarships/grants, and unspecified assistantships also available. Support available to part-time students. Financial award application deadline: 2/15. In 2001, 250 master's, 18 doctorates awarded. *Degree program information:* Part-time and evening/weekend programs available. Offers accounting (M Acc, MBA, MS, PhD); actuarial science (MS, PhD); agribusiness (MBA); arts administration (MA); business (M Acc, MA, MBA, MS, PhD); business administration (MBA); entrepreneurship (MBA); finance, investment, and banking (MBA, MS); general management (MBA); information systems analysis and design (MBA, MS); international business (MBA, MS); management and human resources (MBA, MS); manufacturing and technology management (MBA, MS); marketing (MBA); marketing research (MBA, MS); operations and information management (MBA, MS); real estate and urban land economics (MBA, MS); real estate appraisal and investment analysis (MS); risk management and insurance (MBA, MS, PhD); supply chain management (MBA, MS). *Application deadline:* For fall admission, 4/15. Applications are processed on a rolling basis. *Application fee:* $45. Electronic applications accepted. *Application Contact:* Cory Lathbury, Admissions, 608-262-4000, Fax: 608-265-4195, E-mail: uwmadmba@bus.wisc.edu. *Dean*, Dr. Michael M. Knetter, 608-262-1758.

University of Wisconsin–Madison (continued)

School of Education Expenses: Contact institution. *Financial support:* Fellowships, research assistantships, teaching assistantships, traineeships and project assistantships available. Offers art (MA, MFA); art education (MA); chemistry education (MS); commercial arts education (MA); continuing and vocational education (MS, PhD); counseling (MS); counseling psychology (PhD); curriculum and instruction (MS, PhD); education (MA, MFA, MS, PhD); education and mathematics (MA); educational administration (MS, PhD); educational policy studies (MA, PhD); educational psychology (MS, PhD); English education (MA); French education (MA); geography education (MS); German education (MA); kinesiology (MS, PhD); Latin education (MA); music education (MS); physics education (MS); rehabilitation psychology (MA, MS, PhD); science education (MS); Spanish education (MA); special education (MA, MS, PhD); therapeutic science (MS). *Application fee:* $38. *Dean*, W. Charles Read, 608-262-1763.

School of Human Ecology Students: 70 full-time (59 women), 30 part-time (22 women). Average age 36. 88 applicants, 28% accepted, 23 enrolled. *Faculty:* 39 full-time (28 women), 1 (woman) part-time/adjunct. Expenses: Contact institution. *Financial support:* In 2001–02, 1 fellowship with full tuition reimbursement, 4 research assistantships with full tuition reimbursements, 24 teaching assistantships with full tuition reimbursements were awarded. Scholarships/grants, health care benefits, and unspecified assistantships also available. In 2001, 17 master's, 12 doctorates awarded. Offers consumer behavior and family economics (MS, PhD); continuing and vocational education (MS, PhD); design studies (MS); design studies (PhD); family and consumer journalism (MS, PhD); human development and family studies (MS, PhD). *Application deadline:* For fall admission, 2/15 (priority date). Applications are processed on a rolling basis. *Application fee:* $45. Electronic applications accepted. *Application Contact:* Anthony Johnson, Assistant Dean, 608-262-2608, Fax: 608-265-3616, E-mail: sketheri@facstaff.wisc.edu. *Dean*, Robin A. Douthitt, 608-262-4847.

Law School Students: 796 full-time (369 women); includes 172 minority (47 African Americans, 64 Asian Americans or Pacific Islanders, 41 Hispanic Americans, 20 Native Americans), 13 international. Average age 26. 1,950 applicants, 36% accepted. *Faculty:* 50 full-time. Expenses: Contact institution. *Financial support:* Fellowships, research assistantships, teaching assistantships, career-related internships or fieldwork, Federal Work-Study, institutionally sponsored loans, and unspecified assistantships available. Support available to part-time students. Financial award application deadline: 3/1; financial award applicants required to submit FAFSA. In 2001, 255 first professional degrees, 7 master's, 8 doctorates awarded. *Degree program information:* Part-time programs available. Offers law (JD, LL M, MLI, SJD); legal institutions (MLI). *Application deadline:* For winter admission, 2/1. Applications are processed on a rolling basis. *Application fee:* $45. *Application Contact:* 608-262-5914. *Dean*, Kenneth B. Davis, 608-262-0618, Fax: 608-262-5485.

Medical School Expenses: Contact institution. *Financial support:* Fellowships with full tuition reimbursements, research assistantships with full tuition reimbursements, teaching assistantships with full tuition reimbursements, scholarships/grants, traineeships, and tuition waivers (full) available. *Degree program information:* Part-time programs available. Postbaccalaureate distance learning degree programs offered (minimal on-campus study). Offers medicine (MD, MS, PhD). Electronic applications accepted. *Dean*, Dr. Philip M. Farrell, 608-263-4910, Fax: 608-265-3286, E-mail: pmfarrel@facstaff.wisc.edu.

Graduate Programs in Medicine Expenses: Contact institution. *Financial support:* Fellowships with full tuition reimbursements, research assistantships with full tuition reimbursements, teaching assistantships with full tuition reimbursements, scholarships/grants, traineeships, and tuition waivers (full) available. *Degree program information:* Part-time programs available. Postbaccalaureate distance learning degree programs offered (minimal on-campus study). Offers biomolecular chemistry (MS, PhD); cancer biology (PhD); genetics and medical genetics (MS, PhD); health physics (MS); medical physics (MS, PhD); microbiology (PhD); molecular and cellular pharmacology (PhD); neurophysiology (PhD); pathology and laboratory medicine (PhD); physiology (PhD); population health (MS, PhD). *Application fee:* $45. Electronic applications accepted. *Associate Dean of Research and Graduate Studies*, Dr. Paul M. DeLuca, 608-265-0524, Fax: 608-265-0522, E-mail: pmdeluca@facstaff.wisc.edu.

School of Nursing *Degree program information:* Part-time programs available. Offers nursing (MS, PhD). Electronic applications accepted.

School of Pharmacy Offers pharmaceutical sciences (MS, PhD); pharmacy (Pharm D, MS, PhD); social and administrative sciences in pharmacy (MS, PhD).

School of Veterinary Medicine Offers anatomy (MS, PhD); biochemistry (MS, PhD); cellular and molecular biology (MS, PhD); comparative biosciences (MS, PhD); environmental toxicology (MS, PhD); neurosciences (MS, PhD); pharmacology (MS, PhD); physiology (MS, PhD); veterinary medicine (DVM, MS, PhD).

UNIVERSITY OF WISCONSIN–MILWAUKEE, Milwaukee, WI 53201-0413

General Information State-supported, coed, university. CGS member. *Enrollment:* 1,489 full-time matriculated graduate/professional students (881 women), 1,986 part-time matriculated graduate/professional students (1,178 women). *Enrollment by degree level:* 2,779 master's, 696 doctoral. *Graduate faculty:* 722 full-time (262 women). Tuition, state resident: full-time $6,180; part-time $535 per credit. Tuition, nonresident: full-time $19,482; part-time $1,366 per credit. Tuition and fees vary according to course load, program and reciprocity agreements. *Graduate housing:* Room and/or apartments available on a first-come, first-served basis to single students; on-campus housing not available to married students. Typical cost: $4,108 (including board) ; $4,108 (including board) for married students. Room and board charges vary according to board plan and housing facility selected. *Student services:* Campus employment opportunities, campus safety program, career counseling, child daycare facilities, disabled student services, free psychological counseling, international student services, low-cost health insurance, multicultural affairs office. *Library facilities:* Golda Meir Library. *Online resources:* library catalog, web page, access to other libraries' catalogs. *Collection:* 1.3 million titles, 9,986 serial subscriptions, 31,501 audiovisual materials. *Research affiliation:* Johnson Controls (environment), Wisconsin Electric Power Company (recycling), Electric Power Research Institute (composites), John Deere (surfaces), Astra Arcus USA (medicinal chemistry), Anteon Corporation (optics).

Computer facilities: 310 computers available on campus for general student use. A campuswide network can be accessed from off campus. *Web address:* http://www.uwm.edu/.

General Application Contact: General Information Contact, 412-229-4982, Fax: 414-229-6967, E-mail: gradschool@uwm.edu.

GRADUATE UNITS

Graduate School Students: 1,489 full-time (881 women), 1,986 part-time (1,178 women); includes 412 minority (217 African Americans, 96 Asian Americans or Pacific Islanders, 80 Hispanic Americans, 19 Native Americans), 427 international. Average age 32. 2,840 applicants, 59% accepted. *Faculty:* 722 full-time (262 women). Expenses: Contact institution. *Financial support:* In 2001–02, 101 fellowships with partial tuition reimbursements (averaging $15,000 per year), 61 research assistantships with partial tuition reimbursements (averaging $17,200 per year), 510 teaching assistantships with full tuition reimbursements (averaging $18,100 per year) were awarded. Career-related internships or fieldwork, Federal Work-Study, tuition waivers (partial), and unspecified assistantships also available. Support available to part-time students. Financial award application deadline: 4/15; financial award applicants required to submit FAFSA. In 2001, 1,063 master's, 99 doctorates awarded. *Degree program information:* Part-time and evening/weekend programs available. *Application deadline:* For fall admission, 1/1 (priority date); for spring admission, 9/1. Applications are processed on a rolling basis. *Application fee:* $45 ($75 for international students). *Application Contact:* General Information Contact, 414-229-4982, Fax: 414-229-6967, E-mail: gradschool@uwm.edu. *Dean of the Graduate School and Associate Provost for Research*, Dr. Wiliam R. Rayburn, 414-229-5483, Fax: 414-229-2348, E-mail: rayburn@uwm.edu.

College of Engineering and Applied Science Students: 83 full-time (15 women), 160 part-time (33 women); includes 27 minority (8 African Americans, 17 Asian Americans or Pacific Islanders, 1 Hispanic American, 1 Native American), 124 international. 320 applicants, 52% accepted. *Faculty:* 59 full-time (3 women). Expenses: Contact institution. *Financial support:* In 2001–02, 8 fellowships, 22 research assistantships, 54 teaching assistantships were awarded. Career-related internships or fieldwork, Federal Work-Study, and unspecified assistantships also available. Support available to part-time students. Financial award application deadline: 4/15. In 2001, 43 master's, 11 doctorates awarded. *Degree program information:* Part-time programs available. Offers computer science (MS, PhD); engineering (MS, PhD); engineering and applied science (MS, PhD). *Application deadline:* For fall admission, 1/1 (priority date); for spring admission, 9/1. Applications are processed on a rolling basis. *Application fee:* $45 ($75 for international students). *Dean*, Dr. William Gregory, 414-229-4126, E-mail: wgregory@uwm.edu.

College of Health Sciences Students: 68 full-time (60 women), 36 part-time (30 women); includes 9 minority (4 African Americans, 3 Asian Americans or Pacific Islanders, 2 Hispanic Americans), 7 international. Average age 27. 82 applicants, 61% accepted. *Faculty:* 34 full-time (21 women). Expenses: Contact institution. *Financial support:* In 2001–02, 3 fellowships, 12 teaching assistantships were awarded. Research assistantships, career-related internships or fieldwork, Federal Work-Study, and unspecified assistantships also available. Support available to part-time students. Financial award application deadline: 4/15. In 2001, 40 degrees awarded. *Degree program information:* Part-time programs available. Offers clinical laboratory science (MS); communication sciences and disorders (MS); health sciences (MS); human kinetics (MS); occupational therapy (MS). *Application deadline:* For fall admission, 1/1 (priority date); for spring admission, 9/1. Applications are processed on a rolling basis. *Application fee:* $45 ($75 for international students). *Dean*, Randall Lambrecht, 414-229-4712, E-mail: rsl@uwm.edu.

College of Letters and Sciences Students: 466 full-time (245 women), 496 part-time (304 women); includes 88 minority (41 African Americans, 25 Asian Americans or Pacific Islanders, 19 Hispanic Americans, 3 Native Americans), 172 international. Average age 32. 809 applicants, 60% accepted. *Faculty:* 343 full-time (105 women). Expenses: Contact institution. *Financial support:* In 2001–02, 45 fellowships, 39 research assistantships, 358 teaching assistantships were awarded. Career-related internships or fieldwork, Federal Work-Study, and unspecified assistantships also available. Support available to part-time students. Financial award application deadline: 4/15. In 2001, 157 master's, 50 doctorates awarded. *Degree program information:* Part-time programs available. Offers anthropology (MS, PhD); art history (MA); art museum studies (Certificate); biological sciences (MS, PhD); chemistry (MS, PhD); classics and Hebrew studies (MAFLL); clinical psychology (MS, PhD); communication (MA); comparative literature (MAFLL); economics (MA, PhD); English (MA, PhD); French and Italian (MAFLL); geography (MA, MS); geological sciences (MS, PhD); German (MAFLL); history (MA); human resources and labor relations (MHRLR); journalism and mass communication (MA); letters and sciences (MA, MAFLL, MHRLR, MILR, MPA, MS, PhD, Certificate); mathematics (MS, PhD); philosophy (MA); physics (MS, PhD); political science (MA, PhD); psychology (MS, PhD); public administration (MPA); Slavic studies (MAFLL); sociology (MA); Spanish (MAFLL); urban studies (MS, PhD). *Application deadline:* For fall admission, 1/1 (priority date); for spring admission, 9/1. Applications are processed on a rolling basis. *Application fee:* $45 ($76 for international students). *Interim Dean*, Richard Meadows, 414-229-5895, E-mail: meadows@uwm.edu.

Peck School of the Arts Students: 60 full-time (40 women), 34 part-time (19 women); includes 11 minority (5 African Americans, 2 Asian Americans or Pacific Islanders, 3 Hispanic Americans, 1 Native American), 5 international. Average age 32. 113 applicants, 39% accepted. *Faculty:* 66 full-time (29 women). Expenses: Contact institution. *Financial support:* In 2001–02, 12 fellowships, 18 teaching assistantships were awarded. Research assistantships, career-related internships or fieldwork, Federal Work-Study, and unspecified assistantships also available. Support available to part-time students. Financial award application deadline: 4/15. In 2001, 36 degrees awarded. *Degree program information:* Part-time programs available. Offers art (MA, MFA); art education (MA, MFA, MS); arts (MA, MFA, MM, MS); dance (MFA); film (MFA); music (MM); theatre (MFA). *Application deadline:* For fall admission, 1/1 (priority date); for spring admission, 9/1. Applications are processed on a rolling basis. *Application fee:* $45 ($75 for international students). *Dean*, William Robert Bucker, 414-229-4762, E-mail: rbucker@uwm.edu.

School of Architecture and Urban Planning Students: 138 full-time (45 women), 34 part-time (15 women); includes 14 minority (2 African Americans, 2 Asian Americans or Pacific Islanders, 9 Hispanic Americans, 1 Native American), 30 international. Average age 28. 184 applicants, 72% accepted. *Faculty:* 29 full-time (6 women). Expenses: Contact institution. *Financial support:* In 2001–02, 4 fellowships, 23 teaching assistantships were awarded. Research assistantships, career-related internships or fieldwork, Federal Work-Study, and unspecified assistantships also available. Support available to part-time students. Financial award application deadline: 4/15. In 2001, 54 master's, 2 doctorates awarded. *Degree program information:* Part-time programs available. Offers architecture (M Arch, PhD); architecture and urban planning (M Arch, MUP, PhD); urban planning (MUP). *Application deadline:* For fall admission, 1/1 (priority date); for spring admission, 9/1. Applications are processed on a rolling basis. *Application fee:* $45 ($75 for international students). *Dean*, Robert Greenstreet, 414-229-4016, E-mail: bobg@uwm.edu.

School of Business Administration Students: 205 full-time (74 women), 492 part-time (200 women); includes 57 minority (17 African Americans, 33 Asian Americans or Pacific Islanders, 4 Hispanic Americans, 3 Native Americans), 71 international. Average age 32. 482 applicants, 55% accepted. *Faculty:* 61 full-time (17 women). Expenses: Contact institution. *Financial support:* In 2001–02, 3 fellowships, 29 teaching assistantships were awarded. Research assistantships, career-related internships or fieldwork, Federal Work-Study, and unspecified assistantships also available. Support available to part-time students. Financial award application deadline: 4/15. In 2001, 229 master's, 4 doctorates awarded. *Degree program information:* Part-time and evening/weekend programs available. Offers business administration (MBA, MS, PhD). *Application deadline:* For fall admission, 1/1 (priority date); for spring admission, 9/1. Applications are processed on a rolling basis. *Application fee:* $45 ($75 for international students). *Application Contact:* Velagapudi K. Prasad, Associate Dean, 414-229-4235. *Representative*, Sarah Sandin, 414-229-5403, Fax: 414-229-2372, E-mail: ssandin@uwm.edu.

School of Education Students: 231 full-time (193 women), 426 part-time (317 women); includes 147 minority (97 African Americans, 11 Asian Americans or Pacific Islanders, 32 Hispanic Americans, 7 Native Americans), 8 international. Average age 35. 387 applicants, 57% accepted. *Faculty:* 66 full-time (36 women). Expenses: Contact institution. *Financial support:* In 2001–02, 17 fellowships, 6 teaching assistantships were awarded. Research assistantships, career-related internships or fieldwork, Federal Work-Study, and unspecified assistantships also available. Support available to part-time students. Financial award application deadline: 4/15. In 2001, 238 master's, 26 doctorates awarded. *Degree program information:* Part-time programs available. Offers administrative leadership and supervision in education (MS); cultural foundations of education (MS); curriculum planning and instruction improvement (MS); early childhood education (MS); education (MS, PhD); educational psychology (MS); elementary education (MS); exceptional education (MS); junior high/middle school education (MS); reading education (MS); secondary education (MS); teaching in an urban setting (MS); urban education (PhD). *Application deadline:* For fall admission, 1/1 (priority date); for spring admission, 9/1. Applications are processed on a rolling basis. *Application fee:* $45 ($75 for international students). *Dean*, Alfonzo Thurman, 414-229-4181, E-mail: athurman@uwm.edu.

School of Information Studies Students: 52 full-time (39 women), 99 part-time (81 women); includes 7 minority (3 African Americans, 1 Asian American or Pacific Islander, 2 Hispanic Americans, 1 Native American), 6 international. Average age 36. 151 applicants, 70% accepted. *Faculty:* 10 full-time (5 women). Expenses: Contact institution. *Financial support:* In 2001–02, 2 fellowships, 6 teaching assistantships were awarded. Research assistantships, career-related internships or fieldwork, Federal Work-Study, and unspecified assistantships also available. Support available to part-time students. Financial award application deadline: 4/15. In 2001, 85 degrees awarded. *Degree program information:* Part-time programs available. Offers information studies (MLIS, CAS). *Application deadline:* For fall admission, 1/1 (priority date); for spring admission, 9/1. Applications are processed on a rolling basis. *Application fee:* $45 ($75 for international students). *Representative*, Dietmar Wolfram, 414-229-4707, Fax: 414-229-4848, E-mail: dwolfram@uwm.edu.

School of Multidisciplinary Studies Students: 2 full-time (0 women). Expenses: Contact institution. *Financial support:* Fellowships, research assistantships, teaching assistantships, career-related internships or fieldwork and unspecified assistantships available. Support available to part-time students. Financial award application deadline: 4/15. Offers multidisciplinary studies (PhD). *Application deadline:* For fall admission, 1/1 (priority date); for spring admission, 9/1. Applications are processed on a rolling basis. *Application fee:* $45 ($75 for international students). *Application Contact:* Wendy Fall, Director of Student Services, 414-229-6569, Fax: 414-229-6967, E-mail: wendyf@uwm.edu.

School of Nursing Students: 38 full-time (37 women), 58 part-time (53 women); includes 5 minority (4 African Americans, 1 Asian American or Pacific Islander), 3 international. Average age 39. 25 applicants, 56% accepted. *Faculty:* 29 full-time (all women). Expenses: Contact institution. *Financial support:* In 2001–02, 2 fellowships, 1 teaching assistantship were awarded. Research assistantships, career-related internships or fieldwork, Federal Work-Study, and unspecified assistantships also available. Support available to part-time students. Financial award application deadline: 4/15. In 2001, 30 master's, 6 doctorates awarded. *Degree program information:* Part-time programs available. Offers nursing (MS, PhD). *Application deadline:* For fall admission, 1/1 (priority date); for spring admission, 9/1. Applications are processed on a rolling basis. *Application fee:* $45 ($75 for international students). *Application Contact:* Ellen K. Murphy, Representative, 414-229-5468. *Representative,* Sue Dean-Baar, 414-229-5468, Fax: 414-229-6474, E-mail: deanbaar@uwm.edu.

School of Social Welfare Students: 148 full-time (133 women), 151 part-time (126 women); includes 47 minority (36 African Americans, 1 Asian American or Pacific Islander, 8 Hispanic Americans, 2 Native Americans), 1 international. Average age 31. 292 applicants, 65% accepted. *Faculty:* 24 full-time (10 women). Expenses: Contact institution. *Financial support:* In 2001–02, 5 fellowships, 3 teaching assistantships were awarded. Research assistantships, career-related internships or fieldwork, Federal Work-Study, and unspecified assistantships also available. Support available to part-time students. Financial award application deadline: 4/15. In 2001, 151 degrees awarded. *Degree program information:* Part-time programs available. Offers criminal justice (MS); social welfare (MS, MSW); social work (MSW). *Application deadline:* For fall admission, 1/1 (priority date); for spring admission, 9/1. Applications are processed on a rolling basis. *Application fee:* $45 ($75 for international students). *Dean,* James A. Blackburn, 414-229-4400, E-mail: cushman@uwm.edu.

UNIVERSITY OF WISCONSIN–OSHKOSH, Oshkosh, WI 54901

General Information State-supported, coed, comprehensive institution. *Enrollment:* 147 full-time matriculated graduate/professional students (113 women), 1,068 part-time matriculated graduate/professional students (654 women). *Enrollment by degree level:* 1,215 master's. *Graduate faculty:* 247 full-time (83 women), 18 part-time/adjunct (7 women). Tuition, state resident: full-time $2,236; part-time $250 per credit. Tuition, nonresident: full-time $7,148; part-time $795 per credit. Tuition and fees vary according to program. *Graduate housing:* Room and/or apartments available on a first-come, first-served basis to single students; on-campus housing not available to married students. Typical cost: $2,776 per year ($4,598 including board). Housing application deadline: 4/15. *Student services:* Campus employment opportunities, campus safety program, career counseling, child daycare facilities, disabled student services, free psychological counseling, international student services, low-cost health insurance, multicultural affairs office. *Library facilities:* Forrest R. Polk Library. *Online resources:* library catalog, web page, access to other libraries' catalogs. *Collection:* 446,774 titles, 5,219 serial subscriptions, 9,102 audiovisual materials.

Computer facilities: 475 computers available on campus for general student use. A campuswide network can be accessed from student residence rooms and from off campus. Internet access and online class registration are available. *Web address:* http://www.uwosh.edu/.

General Application Contact: Greg Wypiszynski, Director, Graduate Admissions and Records, 920-424-1223, Fax: 920-424-0247, E-mail: wypiszyn@uwosh.edu.

GRADUATE UNITS

Graduate School Students: 147 full-time (113 women), 1,068 part-time (654 women); includes 49 minority (9 African Americans, 27 Asian Americans or Pacific Islanders, 9 Hispanic Americans, 4 Native Americans), 19 international. Average age 32. 362 applicants, 83% accepted. *Faculty:* 247 full-time (83 women), 18 part-time/adjunct (7 women). Expenses: Contact institution. *Financial support:* Fellowships, career-related internships or fieldwork, Federal Work-Study, institutionally sponsored loans, scholarships/grants, traineeships, tuition waivers (partial), and unspecified assistantships available. Financial award application deadline: 3/15; financial award applicants required to submit FAFSA. In 2001, 329 degrees awarded. *Degree program information:* Part-time and evening/weekend programs available. *Application deadline:* Applications are processed on a rolling basis. *Application fee:* $45. Electronic applications accepted. *Application Contact:* Greg Wypiszynski, Director, Graduate Admissions and Records, 920-424-1223, Fax: 920-424-0247, E-mail: wypiszyn@uwosh.edu. *Assistant Vice Chancellor,* Dr. Nancy Kaufman, 920-424-1223, E-mail: kaufman@uwosh.edu.

College of Business Administration Students: 457; includes 15 minority (1 African American, 12 Asian Americans or Pacific Islanders, 2 Hispanic Americans), 13 international. Average age 32. 107 applicants, 82% accepted. *Faculty:* 37 full-time (5 women), 1 part-time/adjunct (0 women). Expenses: Contact institution. *Financial support:* Institutionally sponsored loans, scholarships/grants, tuition waivers (partial), and unspecified assistantships available. Financial award application deadline: 3/15; financial award applicants required to submit FAFSA. In 2001, 99 degrees awarded. *Degree program information:* Part-time programs available. Offers business administration (MBA, MS); information systems (MS). *Application deadline:* For fall admission, 7/1 (priority date); for spring admission, 12/1 (priority date). Applications are processed on a rolling basis. *Application fee:* $45. Electronic applications accepted. *Application Contact:* Lynn Grancorbitz, Assistant Program Coordinator, 800-633-1430, Fax: 920-424-7413, E-mail: mba@uwosh.edu. *Dean,* Dr. E. Alan Hartman, 920-424-1424, E-mail: hartman@uwosh.edu.

College of Education and Human Services Students: 580; includes 24 minority (6 African Americans, 10 Asian Americans or Pacific Islanders, 5 Hispanic Americans, 3 Native Americans), 2 international. Average age 31. *Faculty:* 44 full-time (21 women), 4 part-time/adjunct (2 women). Expenses: Contact institution. *Financial support:* Career-related internships or fieldwork, institutionally sponsored loans, and scholarships/grants available. Financial award application deadline: 3/15; financial award applicants required to submit FAFSA. In 2001, 152 degrees awarded. *Degree program information:* Part-time and evening/weekend programs available. Offers counseling (MSE); cross-categorical (MSE); curriculum and instruction (MSE); early childhood: exceptional education needs (MSE); education and human services (MS, MSE); educational leadership (MS); non-licensure (MSE); reading education (MSE). *Application deadline:* Applications are processed on a rolling basis. *Application fee:* $45. Electronic applications accepted. *Application Contact:* 920-424-1223, Fax: 920-424-0247, E-mail: gradschool@uwosh.edu. *Dean,* Dr. Carmen I. Coballes-Vega, 920-424-3322, E-mail: coballes@uwosh.edu.

College of Letters and Science Students: 118; includes 9 minority (2 African Americans, 4 Asian Americans or Pacific Islanders, 2 Hispanic Americans, 1 Native American), 4 international. Average age 33. *Faculty:* 153 full-time (45 women), 9 part-time/adjunct (2 women). Expenses: Contact institution. *Financial support:* Career-related internships or fieldwork, Federal Work-Study, institutionally sponsored loans, scholarships/grants, and unspecified assistantships available. Financial award application deadline: 3/15; financial award applicants required to submit FAFSA. In 2001, 63 degrees awarded. *Degree program information:* Part-time and evening/weekend programs available. Offers biology (MS); English (MA); experimental psychology (MS); general agency (MPA); health care (MPA); industrial/organizational psychology (MS); letters and science (MA, MPA, MS); mathematics education (MS); physics (MS); speech and hearing science (MS). *Application deadline:* Applications are processed on a rolling basis. *Application fee:* $45. Electronic applications accepted. *Application Contact:* 920-424-1223, Fax: 920-424-0247, E-mail: gradschool@uwosh.edu. *Dean,* Dr. Michael Zimmerman, 920-424-1210, E-mail: mz@uwosh.edu.

College of Nursing Students: 59; includes 1 minority (Asian American or Pacific Islander) Average age 29. *Faculty:* 14 full-time (all women), 3 part-time/adjunct (2 women). Expenses: Contact institution. *Financial support:* Institutionally sponsored loans, scholarships/grants, traineeships, and unspecified assistantships available. Financial award application deadline: 3/15; financial award applicants required to submit FAFSA. In 2001, 12 degrees awarded. *Degree program information:* Part-time programs available. Offers family nurse practitioner (MSN); primary health care (MSN). *Application deadline:* For fall admission, 12/15. *Application fee:* $45. Electronic applications accepted. *Application Contact:* Dr. Rosemary Smith, Program Coordinator, 920-424-2106, E-mail: congrad@uwosh.edu. *Dean,* Dr. Merritt Knox, 920-424-3089, E-mail: knox@uwosh.edu.

UNIVERSITY OF WISCONSIN–PARKSIDE, Kenosha, WI 53141-2000

General Information State-supported, coed, comprehensive institution. *Enrollment:* 14 full-time matriculated graduate/professional students (8 women), 88 part-time matriculated graduate/professional students (41 women). *Enrollment by degree level:* 102 master's. *Graduate faculty:* 34 full-time (9 women). *Tuition, area resident:* Full-time $4,542; part-time $264 per credit. Tuition, nonresident: full-time $14,366; part-time $810 per credit. *Required fees:* $236; $27 per credit. Tuition and fees vary according to program. *Graduate housing:* Room and/or apartments available on a first-come, first-served basis to single students; on-campus housing not available to married students. Typical cost: $3,150 per year ($4,050 including board). *Student services:* Campus employment opportunities, campus safety program, career counseling, child daycare facilities, disabled student services, exercise/wellness program, free psychological counseling, international student services, low-cost health insurance, multicultural affairs office. *Library facilities:* Library-Learning Center. *Online resources:* library catalog, web page, access to other libraries' catalogs. *Collection:* 265,110 titles, 4,096 serial subscriptions, 18,007 audiovisual materials.

Computer facilities: 180 computers available on campus for general student use. A campuswide network can be accessed from student residence rooms and from off campus. *Web address:* http://www.uwp.edu/.

General Application Contact: Matthew Jensen, Director of Admissions, 262-595-2355, Fax: 264-595-2630, E-mail: matthew.jensen@uwp.edu.

GRADUATE UNITS

College of Arts and Sciences Students: 14 full-time (8 women); includes 1 minority (Asian American or Pacific Islander) Average age 25. 4 applicants, 100% accepted, 2 enrolled. *Faculty:* 11 full-time (3 women). Expenses: Contact institution. *Financial support:* In 2001–02, 7 students received support, including 6 research assistantships; career-related internships or fieldwork, Federal Work-Study, and unspecified assistantships also available. In 2001, 3 degrees awarded. Offers applied molecular biology (MAMB); arts and sciences (MAMB). *Application deadline:* For fall admission, 7/1 (priority date). Applications are processed on a rolling basis. *Application fee:* $45. *Application Contact:* Dr. M. Scott Thomson, Chair, 262-595-2547, Fax: 262-595-2056, E-mail: melvin.thomson@uwp.edu. *Dean,* Dr. Donald Cress, 262-595-2188, Fax: 262-595-2056, E-mail: donald.cress@uwp.edu.

School of Business and Technology Average age 27. 32 applicants, 84% accepted. *Faculty:* 24 full-time (7 women). Expenses: Contact institution. *Financial support:* Available to part-time students. Application deadline: 7/1. In 2001, 20 degrees awarded. *Degree program information:* Part-time and evening/weekend programs available. Offers business administration (MBA); business and technology (MBA, MSCIS); computer and information systems (MSCIS). *Application deadline:* For fall admission, 8/1; for spring admission, 12/15. Applications are processed on a rolling basis. *Application fee:* $45. Electronic applications accepted. *Application Contact:* Bradley Piazza, Assistant Dean, 262-595-2046, Fax: 262-595-2680, E-mail: bradley.piazza@uwp.edu. *Dean,* Dr. Marwan Wafa, 262-595-2266, Fax: 262-595-2680, E-mail: marwan.wafa@uwp.edu.

UNIVERSITY OF WISCONSIN–PLATTEVILLE, Platteville, WI 53818-3099

General Information State-supported, coed, comprehensive institution. *Enrollment:* 33 full-time matriculated graduate/professional students (23 women), 84 part-time matriculated graduate/professional students (58 women). *Enrollment by degree level:* 117 master's. *Graduate faculty:* 5 full-time (2 women), 90 part-time/adjunct (16 women). Tuition, state resident: full-time $4,564; part-time $224 per credit. Tuition, nonresident: full-time $14,388; part-time $769 per credit. Part-time tuition and fees vary according to course load. *Graduate housing:* Room and/or apartments available on a first-come, first-served basis to single students; on-campus housing not available to married students. Typical cost: $1,915 per year. Room charges vary according to board plan. Housing application deadline: 7/1. *Student services:* Campus employment opportunities, career counseling, child daycare facilities, disabled student services, free psychological counseling, international student services, low-cost health insurance, multicultural affairs office, teacher training. *Library facilities:* Karrmann Library. *Online resources:* library catalog, web page, access to other libraries' catalogs. *Collection:* 257,566 titles, 1,499 serial subscriptions.

Computer facilities: 250 computers available on campus for general student use. A campuswide network can be accessed from student residence rooms and from off campus. Internet access is available. *Web address:* http://www.uwplatt.edu/.

General Application Contact: Laurie Schuler, Admissions and Enrollment Management, 608-342-1125, Fax: 608-342-1122, E-mail: admit@uwplatt.edu.

GRADUATE UNITS

School of Graduate Studies Students: 33 full-time (23 women), 84 part-time (58 women); includes 9 minority (3 African Americans, 6 Asian Americans or Pacific Islanders), 5 international. 80 applicants, 64% accepted. *Faculty:* 5 full-time (2 women), 90 part-time/adjunct (16 women). Expenses: Contact institution. *Financial support:* Research assistantships with partial tuition reimbursements, career-related internships or fieldwork, Federal Work-Study, institutionally sponsored loans, scholarships/grants, and unspecified assistantships available. Support available to part-time students. In 2001, 38 degrees awarded. *Degree program information:* Part-time and evening/weekend programs available. Postbaccalaureate distance learning degree programs offered (no on-campus study). *Application deadline:* For fall admission, 7/1 (priority date); for spring admission, 11/1. Applications are processed on a rolling basis. *Application fee:* $45. Electronic applications accepted. *Application Contact:* Laurie Schuler, Admissions and Enrollment Management, 608-342-1125, Fax: 608-342-1122, E-mail: admit@uwplatt.edu. *Interim Dean,* Dr. David P. Van Buren, 608-342-1262, Fax: 608-342-1270, E-mail: vanburen@uwplatt.edu.

College of Business, Industry, Life Science, and Agriculture Students: 4 full-time (0 women), 10 part-time (2 women). 10 applicants, 60% accepted. *Faculty:* 39 part-time/adjunct (6 women). Expenses: Contact institution. *Financial support:* Research assistantships with partial tuition reimbursements, career-related internships or fieldwork, Federal Work-Study, institutionally sponsored loans, scholarships/grants, and unspecified assistantships available. Support available to part-time students. In 2001, 5 degrees awarded. *Degree program information:* Part-time programs available. Offers business, industry, life science, and agriculture (MS); industrial technology management (MS). *Application deadline:* For fall admission, 7/1 (priority date); for spring admission, 11/1. Applications are processed on a rolling basis. *Application fee:* $45. Electronic applications accepted. *Application Contact:* Laurie Schuler, Admissions and Enrollment Management, 608-342-1125, Fax: 608-342-1122, E-mail: admit@uwplatt.edu. *Dean,* Dr. Duane Ford, 608-342-1547, Fax: 608-342-1254, E-mail: fordd@uwplatt.edu.

College of Liberal Arts and Education Students: 39 full-time (32 women), 69 part-time (54 women); includes 3 minority (2 African Americans, 1 Asian American or Pacific Islander), 1 international. 65 applicants, 65% accepted. *Faculty:* 4 full-time (1 woman), 54 part-time/adjunct (14 women). Expenses: Contact institution. *Financial support:* Research assistantships with partial tuition reimbursements, career-related internships or fieldwork, Federal Work-Study, institutionally sponsored loans, scholarships/grants, and unspecified assistantships available. Support available to part-time students. In 2001, 20 degrees awarded. *Degree program information:* Part-time programs available. Offers adult education (MSE); counselor education (MSE); elementary education (MSE); liberal arts and education (MSE); middle school education (MSE); secondary education (MSE); vocational and technical

University of Wisconsin–Platteville (continued)

education (MSE). *Application deadline:* For fall admission, 7/1 (priority date); for spring admission, 11/1. Applications are processed on a rolling basis. *Application fee:* $45. Electronic applications accepted. *Application Contact:* Laurie Schuler, Admissions and Enrollment Management, 608-342-1125, Fax: 608-342-1122, E-mail: admit@uwplatt.edu. *Director*, Dr. Sally Standiford, 608-342-1131, Fax: 608-342-1409, E-mail: standifs@uwplatt.edu.

Distance Learning Center *Degree program information:* Part-time and evening/weekend programs available. Postbaccalaureate distance learning degree programs offered (no on-campus study). Offers criminal justice (MS); engineering (ME); project management (MS). Electronic applications accepted.

UNIVERSITY OF WISCONSIN–RIVER FALLS, River Falls, WI 54022-5001

General Information State-supported, coed, comprehensive institution. CGS member. *Enrollment:* 397 full-time matriculated graduate/professional students (285 women). *Enrollment by degree level:* 397 master's. *Graduate faculty:* 150 full-time (54 women), 6 part-time/adjunct (4 women). Tuition, state resident: full-time $2,257; part-time $278 per credit. Tuition, nonresident: full-time $7,169; part-time $824 per credit. Tuition and fees vary according to reciprocity agreements. *Graduate housing:* Room and/or apartments available on a first-come, first-served basis to single students; on-campus housing not available to married students. *Student services:* Campus employment opportunities, career counseling, child daycare facilities, free psychological counseling, international student services, multicultural affairs office, teacher training. *Library facilities:* Chalmer Davee Library. *Online resources:* library catalog, web page, access to other libraries' catalogs. *Collection:* 448,088 titles, 1,660 serial subscriptions, 7,500 audiovisual materials.

Computer facilities: 387 computers available on campus for general student use. A campuswide network can be accessed from student residence rooms and from off campus. Internet access and online class registration are available. *Web address:* http://www.uwrf.edu/.

General Application Contact: Julia M. Persico, Program Assistant III, 715-425-3843, Fax: 715-425-3185, E-mail: julia.m.persico@uwrf.edu.

GRADUATE UNITS

Outreach and Graduate Studies Students: 397 full-time (285 women). *Faculty:* 150 full-time (54 women), 6 part-time/adjunct (4 women). Expenses: Contact institution. *Financial support:* In 2001–02, 5 research assistantships (averaging $4,800 per year) were awarded; career-related internships or fieldwork, Federal Work-Study, and institutionally sponsored loans also available. Support available to part-time students. Financial award application deadline: 3/1; financial award applicants required to submit FAFSA. In 2001, 108 degrees awarded. *Degree program information:* Part-time programs available. Offers management (MM). *Application deadline:* Applications are processed on a rolling basis. *Application fee:* $45. Electronic applications accepted. *Application Contact:* Julia M. Persico, Program Assistant III, 715-425-3843, Fax: 715-425-3185, E-mail: julia.m.persico@uwrf.edu. *Dean*, Dr. Leon M. Zaborowski, 715-425-3350, Fax: 715-425-3185, E-mail: leon.zaborowski@uwrf.edu.

College of Agriculture, Food, and Environmental Sciences Students: 3 full-time (1 woman), 10 part-time (6 women). *Faculty:* 3 full-time (0 women). Expenses: Contact institution. *Financial support:* Research assistantships, Federal Work-Study available. Financial award application deadline: 3/1; financial award applicants required to submit FAFSA. In 2001, 4 degrees awarded. *Degree program information:* Part-time programs available. Offers agricultural education (MS); agriculture, food, and environmental sciences (MS). *Application deadline:* For fall admission, 3/1 (priority date). *Application fee:* $45. Electronic applications accepted. *Application Contact:* Julia M. Persico, Program Assistant III, 715-425-3843, Fax: 715-425-3185, E-mail: julia.m.persico@uwrf.edu. *Dean*, Dr. William A. Anderson, 715-425-3841, Fax: 715-425-3785.

College of Arts and Science Students: 76 full-time (42 women). *Faculty:* 81. Expenses: Contact institution. *Financial support:* Research assistantships, Federal Work-Study available. Financial award application deadline: 3/1. In 2001, 26 degrees awarded. *Degree program information:* Part-time programs available. Offers arts and science (MSE); language, literature, and communication education (MSE); mathematics education (MSE); science education (MSE); social science education (MSE). *Application deadline:* For fall admission, 3/1 (priority date). Applications are processed on a rolling basis. *Application fee:* $45. Electronic applications accepted. *Application Contact:* Julia M. Persico, Program Assistant III, 715-425-3843, Fax: 715-425-3185, E-mail: julia.m.persico@uwrf.edu. *Dean*, Dr. Gorden O. Hedahl, 715-425-3366, E-mail: gorden.o.hedahl@uwrf.edu.

College of Education and Professional Studies Students: 236 (195 women). Expenses: Contact institution. *Financial support:* Research assistantships, career-related internships or fieldwork and Federal Work-Study available. Financial award application deadline: 3/1; financial award applicants required to submit FAFSA. In 2001, 77 degrees awarded. *Degree program information:* Part-time programs available. Offers communicative disorders (MS); counseling (MSE); education (MS, MSE, Ed S); elementary education (MSE); reading (MSE); school psychology (MSE, Ed S); secondary education-communicative disorders (MSE). *Application fee:* $45. *Application Contact:* Julia M. Persico, Program Assistant III, 715-425-3843, Fax: 715-425-3185, E-mail: julia.m.persico@uwrf.edu. *Interim Dean*, Dr. Connie Foster, 715-425-3774, Fax: 715-425-0622, E-mail: connie.d.foster@uwrf.edu.

UNIVERSITY OF WISCONSIN–STEVENS POINT, Stevens Point, WI 54481-3897

General Information State-supported, coed, comprehensive institution. *Enrollment:* 160 full-time matriculated graduate/professional students (116 women), 172 part-time matriculated graduate/professional students (122 women). *Enrollment by degree level:* 332 master's. *Graduate faculty:* 264 full-time (74 women), 19 part-time/adjunct (4 women). Tuition, state resident: full-time $4,020; part-time $223 per credit. Tuition, nonresident: full-time $13,844; part-time $769 per credit. *Required fees:* $487; $54 per credit. *Graduate housing:* Room and/or apartments available on a first-come, first-served basis to single students; on-campus housing not available to married students. *Student services:* Campus employment opportunities, campus safety program, career counseling, child daycare facilities, disabled student services, exercise/wellness program, free psychological counseling, grant writing training, international student services, low-cost health insurance, multicultural affairs office, teacher training, writing training. *Library facilities:* Learning Resources Center. *Online resources:* library catalog, web page, access to other libraries' catalogs. *Collection:* 362,788 titles, 1,816 serial subscriptions.

Computer facilities: 700 computers available on campus for general student use. A campuswide network can be accessed from student residence rooms and from off campus. Internet access is available. *Web address:* http://www.uwsp.edu/.

General Application Contact: David Eckholm, Director of Admissions, 715-346-2441, E-mail: admiss@uwsp.edu.

GRADUATE UNITS

College of Fine Arts and Communication Students: 10 full-time (4 women), 24 part-time (17 women), 1 international. *Faculty:* 26 full-time (9 women), 1 part-time/adjunct (0 women). Expenses: Contact institution. *Financial support:* Teaching assistantships, career-related internships or fieldwork, Federal Work-Study, institutionally sponsored loans, and unspecified assistantships available. Support available to part-time students. Financial award application deadline: 5/1; financial award applicants required to submit FAFSA. In 2001, 6 degrees awarded. *Degree program information:* Part-time programs available. Offers fine arts and communication (MA, MM Ed); interpersonal communication (MA); mass communication (MA); music (MM Ed); organizational communication (MA); public relations (MA). *Application deadline:* For fall admission, 5/1 (priority date). Applications are processed on a rolling basis. *Application fee:* $45. *Dean*, Gerard McKenna, 715-346-4920, Fax: 715-346-2718.

College of Letters and Science Students: 4 full-time (3 women), 15 part-time (9 women), 1 international. *Faculty:* 170 full-time (40 women), 6 part-time/adjunct (1 woman). Expenses: Contact institution. *Financial support:* Research assistantships, teaching assistantships, Federal Work-Study and unspecified assistantships available. Support available to part-time students. Financial award application deadline: 5/1; financial award applicants required to submit FAFSA. In 2001, 3 degrees awarded. Offers biology (MST); business and economics (MBA); English (MST); history (MST); letters and science (MBA, MST). *Application deadline:* For fall admission, 5/1 (priority date). Applications are processed on a rolling basis. *Application fee:* $45. *Dean*, Justus Paul, 715-346-4224.

College of Natural Resources Students: 38 full-time (17 women), 24 part-time (12 women); includes 1 minority (African American), 1 international. *Faculty:* 30 full-time (3 women), 11 part-time/adjunct (3 women). Expenses: Contact institution. *Financial support:* Research assistantships, teaching assistantships, career-related internships or fieldwork, Federal Work-Study, and unspecified assistantships available. Support available to part-time students. Financial award application deadline: 5/1; financial award applicants required to submit FAFSA. In 2001, 27 degrees awarded. *Degree program information:* Part-time programs available. Offers natural resources (MS). *Application deadline:* For fall admission, 3/15 (priority date); for spring admission, 11/15. Applications are processed on a rolling basis. *Application fee:* $45. *Associate Dean*, Dr. Christina Thomas, 715-346-2853, Fax: 715-346-3624.

College of Professional Studies Students: 108 full-time (92 women), 109 part-time (84 women); includes 5 minority (2 Asian Americans or Pacific Islanders, 3 Hispanic Americans) *Faculty:* 38 full-time (22 women), 1 part-time/adjunct (0 women). Expenses: Contact institution. *Financial support:* Research assistantships, teaching assistantships, career-related internships or fieldwork, Federal Work-Study, and unspecified assistantships available. Support available to part-time students. Financial award application deadline: 5/1; financial award applicants required to submit FAFSA. In 2001, 166 degrees awarded. *Degree program information:* Part-time programs available. Offers professional studies (MS, MSE). *Application deadline:* For fall admission, 5/1 (priority date). Applications are processed on a rolling basis. *Application fee:* $45. *Dean*, Joan North, 715-346-3169.

School of Communicative Disorders Students: 59 full-time (58 women), 1 (woman) part-time. *Faculty:* 5 full-time (2 women). Expenses: Contact institution. *Financial support:* Research assistantships, teaching assistantships, Federal Work-Study and unspecified assistantships available. Financial award application deadline: 5/1; financial award applicants required to submit FAFSA. In 2001, 27 degrees awarded. Offers communicative disorders (MS). *Application deadline:* For fall admission, 2/15; for spring admission, 10/15. Applications are processed on a rolling basis. *Application fee:* $45. *Head*, Dr. Dennis Nash, 715-346-3920, Fax: 715-346-3751.

School of Education Students: 49 full-time (34 women), 88 part-time (64 women); includes 4 minority (2 Asian Americans or Pacific Islanders, 2 Hispanic Americans) *Faculty:* 15 full-time (11 women). Expenses: Contact institution. *Financial support:* Research assistantships, teaching assistantships, Federal Work-Study and unspecified assistantships available. Support available to part-time students. Financial award application deadline: 5/1; financial award applicants required to submit FAFSA. In 2001, 117 degrees awarded. Offers education—general/reading (MSE); educational administration (MSE); elementary education (MSE); guidance and counseling (MSE). *Application deadline:* For fall admission, 5/1 (priority date). Applications are processed on a rolling basis. *Application fee:* $45. *Head*, Dr. Leslie McClaine-Ruelle, 715-346-4430, Fax: 715-346-4846.

School of Health Promotion and Human Development *Faculty:* 11 full-time (6 women). Expenses: Contact institution. *Financial support:* Research assistantships, teaching assistantships, career-related internships or fieldwork, Federal Work-Study, and unspecified assistantships available. Support available to part-time students. Financial award application deadline: 5/1; financial award applicants required to submit FAFSA. In 2001, 16 degrees awarded. *Degree program information:* Part-time programs available. Offers human and community resources (MS); nutritional sciences (MS). *Application deadline:* For fall admission, 5/1 (priority date). Applications are processed on a rolling basis. *Application fee:* $45. *Associate Dean*, John Munson, 715-346-2830, Fax: 715-346-3751.

UNIVERSITY OF WISCONSIN–STOUT, Menomonie, WI 54751

General Information State-supported, coed, comprehensive institution. *Enrollment:* 288 full-time matriculated graduate/professional students (182 women), 247 part-time matriculated graduate/professional students (158 women). *Enrollment by degree level:* 510 master's, 25 other advanced degrees. *Graduate faculty:* 213 full-time (77 women). Tuition, state resident: full-time $4,915. Tuition, nonresident: full-time $12,553. *Graduate housing:* Room and/or apartments available to single students; on-campus housing not available to married students. Typical cost: $3,258 per year ($4,912 including board). *Student services:* Campus employment opportunities, career counseling, child daycare facilities, disabled student services, exercise/wellness program, free psychological counseling, international student services, low-cost health insurance, multicultural affairs office, teacher training. *Library facilities:* Library Learning Center. *Online resources:* library catalog, web page, access to other libraries' catalogs. *Collection:* 219,270 titles, 6,205 serial subscriptions, 16,047 audiovisual materials. *Research affiliation:* ElectroMed, Inc. (assistive technology assessment), Wisconsin Procurement Institute.

Computer facilities: 590 computers available on campus for general student use. A campuswide network can be accessed from student residence rooms and from off campus. Internet access and online class registration are available. *Web address:* http://www.uwstout.edu/.

General Application Contact: Anne E. Johnson, Graduate Student Evaluator, 715-232-1322, Fax: 715-232-2413, E-mail: johnsona@uwstout.edu.

GRADUATE UNITS

Graduate School Students: 288 full-time (182 women), 247 part-time (158 women); includes 47 minority (16 African Americans, 15 Asian Americans or Pacific Islanders, 9 Hispanic Americans, 7 Native Americans), 44 international. 321 applicants, 67% accepted, 192 enrolled. *Faculty:* 213 full-time (77 women). Expenses: Contact institution. *Financial support:* In 2001–02, 69 research assistantships were awarded; teaching assistantships, Federal Work-Study, scholarships/grants, and tuition waivers (full and partial) also available. Support available to part-time students. Financial award application deadline: 4/1; financial award applicants required to submit FAFSA. In 2001, 174 master's, 9 other advanced degrees awarded. *Degree program information:* Part-time programs available. Postbaccalaureate distance learning degree programs offered. *Application fee:* $45. *Application Contact:* Anne E. Johnson, Graduate Student Evaluator, 715-232-1322, Fax: 715-232-2413, E-mail: johnsona@uwstout.edu. *Associate Vice Chancellor*, Julie Furst-Bowe, 715-232-2421, E-mail: furst_bowe5@uwstout.edu.

College of Human Development Students: 208 full-time (154 women), 159 part-time (108 women); includes 23 minority (11 African Americans, 7 Asian Americans or Pacific Islanders, 2 Hispanic Americans, 3 Native Americans), 29 international. 231 applicants, 69% accepted, 143 enrolled. Expenses: Contact institution. *Financial support:* In 2001–02, 50 research assistantships were awarded; teaching assistantships, Federal Work-Study, scholarships/grants, and tuition waivers (full and partial) also available. Support available to part-time students. Financial award application deadline: 4/1; financial award applicants required to submit FAFSA. In 2001, 112 master's, 5 other advanced degrees awarded. *Degree program information:* Part-time programs available. Offers applied psychology (MS); counseling and psychological services (MS); education (MS); food and nutritional sciences (MS); guidance and counseling (MS); home economics (MS); hospitality and tourism (MS); human development (MS, MS Ed, Ed S); marriage and family therapy (MS); mental health counseling (MS); school psychology (MS Ed, Ed S); vocational rehabilitation (MS). *Application fee:* $45. *Application Contact:* Anne E. Johnson, Graduate Student Evaluator, 715-232-1322, Fax: 715-232-2413, E-mail: johnsona@uwstout.edu. *Dean*, Dr. John Wesolek, 715-232-2688, E-mail: wesolekj@uwstout.edu.

College of Technology, Engineering, and Management Students: 58 full-time (16 women), 122 part-time (58 women); includes 14 minority (2 African Americans, 4 Asian Americans or Pacific Islanders, 7 Hispanic Americans, 1 Native American), 11 international. 90 applicants, 90% accepted, 75 enrolled. Expenses: Contact institution. *Financial support:* In 2001–02,

18 research assistantships were awarded; teaching assistantships, Federal Work-Study and tuition waivers (full and partial) also available. Support available to part-time students. Financial award application deadline: 4/1; financial award applicants required to submit FAFSA. In 2001, 62 master's, 4 other advanced degrees awarded. *Degree program information:* Part-time programs available. Offers industrial and vocational education (Ed S); industrial/technology education (MS); management technology (MS); risk control (MS); technology, engineering, and management (MS, Ed S); training and development (MS); vocational education (MS). *Application deadline:* Applications are processed on a rolling basis. *Application fee:* $45. *Application Contact:* Anne E. Johnson, Graduate Student Evaluator, 715-232-1322, Fax: 715-232-2413, E-mail: johnsona@uwstout.edu. *Dean,* Dr. Bob Meyer, 715-232-1325, Fax: 715-232-1274.

UNIVERSITY OF WISCONSIN–SUPERIOR, Superior, WI 54880-4500

General Information State-supported, coed, comprehensive institution. CGS member. *Enrollment:* 84 full-time matriculated graduate/professional students (61 women), 324 part-time matriculated graduate/professional students (205 women). *Enrollment by degree level:* 408 master's. *Graduate faculty:* 33 full-time (12 women), 11 part-time/adjunct (8 women). Tuition, state resident: part-time $2,238 per semester. Tuition, nonresident: part-time $7,150 per semester. *Graduate housing:* Rooms and/or apartments available to single and married students. Typical cost: $2,084 per year ($3,812 including board) for single students; $3,500 per year for married students. Housing application deadline: 7/1. *Student services:* Campus employment opportunities, campus safety program, career counseling, child daycare facilities, disabled student services, exercise/wellness program, free psychological counseling, international student services, low-cost health insurance, multicultural affairs office, teacher training, writing training. *Library facilities:* Jim Dan Hill Library. *Online resources:* library catalog, web page, access to other libraries' catalogs. *Research affiliation:* Great Lakes Indian Fish and Wildlife Commission, Wisconsin Department of Natural Resources (biology), Environmental Protection Agency (biology), The Mexican National Institute for Ecology (biology), The Mexican Marine National Park Service (biology), Coastal Zone Management Institute and Authority of Belize (biology), Fisheries Department, Government of Belize (biology).

Computer facilities: 125 computers available on campus for general student use. A campuswide network can be accessed from student residence rooms and from off campus. Internet access and online class registration are available. *Web address:* http://www.uwsuper.edu/.

General Application Contact: Evelyn Hagfeldt, Program Assistant/Status Examiner, 715-394-8295, Fax: 715-394-8040, E-mail: ehagfeld@uwsuper.edu.

GRADUATE UNITS

Graduate Division Students: 84 full-time (61 women), 324 part-time (205 women); includes 17 minority (1 African American, 6 Asian Americans or Pacific Islanders, 10 Native Americans), 6 international. Average age 37. 93 applicants, 94% accepted. *Faculty:* 33 full-time (12 women), 11 part-time/adjunct (8 women). Expenses: Contact institution. *Financial support:* In 2001–02, 15 research assistantships with partial tuition reimbursements (averaging $8,500 per year) were awarded; fellowships with partial tuition reimbursements, career-related internships or fieldwork, Federal Work-Study, institutionally sponsored loans, scholarships/grants, traineeships, tuition waivers (partial), unspecified assistantships, and disadvantaged fellowships also available. Support available to part-time students. Financial award application deadline: 4/15; financial award applicants required to submit FAFSA. In 2001, 108 master's, 3 other advanced degrees awarded. *Degree program information:* Part-time and evening/weekend programs available. Postbaccalaureate distance learning degree programs offered (minimal on-campus study). Offers art education (MA); art history (MA); art therapy (MA); community counseling (MSE); educational administration (MSE, Ed S); elementary school counseling (MSE); emotional/behavior disabilities (MSE); human relations (MSE); instruction (MSE); learning disabilities (MSE); mass communication (MA); secondary school counseling (MSE); special education (MSE); speech communication (MA); studio arts (MA); teaching reading (MSE); theater (MA). *Application deadline:* For fall admission, 4/1 (priority date); for spring admission, 10/15 (priority date). Applications are processed on a rolling basis. *Application fee:* $45. *Application Contact:* Evelyn Hagfeldt, Program Assistant/Status Examiner, 715-394-8295, Fax: 715-394-8040, E-mail: ehagfeld@uwsuper.edu. *Dean of Facilities,* Dr. Rosemary Keefe, 715-394-8296, Fax: 715-394-8040, E-mail: rkeefe@uwsuper.edu.

UNIVERSITY OF WISCONSIN–WHITEWATER, Whitewater, WI 53190-1790

General Information State-supported, coed, comprehensive institution. CGS member. *Enrollment:* 89 full-time matriculated graduate/professional students (49 women), 932 part-time matriculated graduate/professional students (572 women). *Enrollment by degree level:* 1,120 master's. *Graduate faculty:* 332. Tuition, state resident: full-time $4,511; part-time $251 per credit. Tuition, nonresident: full-time $14,335; part-time $797 per credit. One-time fee: $45. Tuition and fees vary according to course load and program. *Graduate housing:* Room and/or apartments available on a first-come, first-served basis to single students; on-campus housing not available to married students. Typical cost: $2,200 per year ($3,580 including board). Housing application deadline: 9/1. *Student services:* Campus employment opportunities, campus safety program, career counseling, child daycare facilities, disabled student services, exercise/wellness program, free psychological counseling, grant writing training, international student services, low-cost health insurance, multicultural affairs office. *Library facilities:* Andersen Library. *Online resources:* library catalog, web page, access to other libraries' catalogs. *Collection:* 436,521 titles, 2,206 serial subscriptions, 18,617 audiovisual materials. *Research affiliation:* WEBCO (lightning radiative transfer).

Computer facilities: 700 computers available on campus for general student use. A campuswide network can be accessed from student residence rooms and from off campus. *Web address:* http://www.uww.edu/.

General Application Contact: Sally A. Lange, School of Graduate Studies, 262-472-1006, Fax: 262-472-5027, E-mail: gradschl@uww.edu.

GRADUATE UNITS

School of Graduate Studies Students: 89 full-time (49 women), 932 part-time (572 women); includes 77 minority (35 African Americans, 23 Asian Americans or Pacific Islanders, 13 Hispanic Americans, 6 Native Americans) Average age 26. 308 applicants, 91% accepted, 193 enrolled. *Faculty:* 332. Expenses: Contact institution. *Financial support:* In 2001–02, 50 students received support, including 38 research assistantships (averaging $8,889 per year); career-related internships or fieldwork, Federal Work-Study, unspecified assistantships, and out of state fee waiver also available. Support available to part-time students. Financial award application deadline: 3/15; financial award applicants required to submit FAFSA. In 2001, 262 degrees awarded. *Degree program information:* Part-time and evening/weekend programs available. Postbaccalaureate distance learning degree programs offered (no on-campus study). *Application deadline:* For fall admission, 7/15; for spring admission, 12/1. Applications are processed on a rolling basis. *Application fee:* $45. Electronic applications accepted. *Application Contact:* Sally A. Lange, School of Graduate Studies, 262-472-1006, Fax: 262-472-5027, E-mail: gradschl@uww.edu. *Dean,* Dr. Richard Lee, 262-472-5200, Fax: 262-472-5210, E-mail: gradschl@uww.edu.

College of Arts and Communications Average age 26. 7 applicants, 100% accepted, 4 enrolled. *Faculty:* 35. Expenses: Contact institution. *Financial support:* In 2001–02, 1 research assistantship (averaging $8,889 per year) was awarded; Federal Work-Study, unspecified assistantships, and out of state fee waiver also available. Support available to part-time students. Financial award application deadline: 3/15; financial award applicants required to submit FAFSA. In 2001, 10 degrees awarded. *Degree program information:* Part-time and evening/weekend programs available. Offers arts and communications (MS); corporate/public communication (MS); mass communication (MS). *Application deadline:* For fall admission, 7/15; for spring admission, 12/1. Applications are processed on a rolling basis. *Application fee:* $45. Electronic applications accepted. *Application Contact:* Sally A. Lange, School of Graduate Studies, 262-472-1006, Fax: 262-472-5027, E-mail: gradschl@uww.edu. *Dean,* Dr. John Heyer, 262-472-1221, Fax: 262-472-1436, E-mail: heyerj@uww.edu.

College of Business and Economics Students: 45 full-time (15 women), 477 part-time (221 women); includes 49 minority (19 African Americans, 20 Asian Americans or Pacific Islanders, 6 Hispanic Americans, 4 Native Americans) Average age 29. 175 applicants, 97% accepted, 118 enrolled. *Faculty:* 57. Expenses: Contact institution. *Financial support:* In 2001–02, 18 research assistantships (averaging $8,889 per year) were awarded; career-related internships or fieldwork, Federal Work-Study, unspecified assistantships, and out of state fee waiver also available. Support available to part-time students. Financial award application deadline: 3/15; financial award applicants required to submit FAFSA. In 2001, 110 degrees awarded. *Degree program information:* Part-time and evening/weekend programs available. Offers accounting (MBA); business and economics (MBA, MPA, MS, MS Ed); business education (MS); decision support systems (MBA); finance (MBA); healthcare (MBA); human resource management (MBA); international business (MBA); management (MBA); management computer systems (MS); marketing (MBA); operations and supply chain management (MBA); post-secondary (MS); school business management (MS Ed); secondary (MS); technology and training (MBA). *Application deadline:* For fall admission, 7/15; for spring admission, 12/1. Applications are processed on a rolling basis. *Application fee:* $45. Electronic applications accepted. *Application Contact:* Dr. Donald Zahn, Associate Dean, 262-472-1945, Fax: 262-472-4863, E-mail: zahnd@uww.edu. *Acting Dean,* Dr. Christine Clements, 262-472-1343, Fax: 262-472-4863, E-mail: clementc@uww.edu.

College of Education Students: 24 full-time (18 women), 412 part-time (324 women); includes 19 minority (12 African Americans, 3 Asian Americans or Pacific Islanders, 3 Hispanic Americans, 1 Native American) Average age 29. 91 applicants, 91% accepted, 56 enrolled. Expenses: Contact institution. *Financial support:* In 2001–02, 13 research assistantships (averaging $8,889 per year) were awarded; career-related internships or fieldwork, Federal Work-Study, unspecified assistantships, and out of state fee waiver also available. Support available to part-time students. Financial award application deadline: 3/15; financial award applicants required to submit FAFSA. In 2001, 123 degrees awarded. *Degree program information:* Part-time and evening/weekend programs available. Offers communicative disorders (MS); community counseling (MS); curriculum and instruction (MS); education (MS, MS Ed); educational administration (MS Ed); higher education (MS); safety (MS); school counseling (MS); special education (MS Ed). *Application deadline:* Applications are processed on a rolling basis. *Application fee:* $45. Electronic applications accepted. *Application Contact:* Sally A. Lange, School of Graduate Studies, 262-472-1006, Fax: 262-472-5027, E-mail: gradschl@uww.edu. *Dean,* Dr. Jeffrey Barnett, 262-472-1101, Fax: 262-472-5716, E-mail: barnettj@uww.edu.

College of Letters and Sciences Students: 20 full-time (16 women), 28 part-time (19 women); includes 6 minority (3 African Americans, 2 Hispanic Americans, 1 Native American) Average age 28. 35 applicants, 63% accepted, 20 enrolled. Expenses: Contact institution. *Financial support:* In 2001–02, 6 research assistantships with partial tuition reimbursements (averaging $8,889 per year) were awarded; Federal Work-Study, unspecified assistantships, and out of state fee waiver also available. Support available to part-time students. Financial award application deadline: 3/15; financial award applicants required to submit FAFSA. In 2001, 14 degrees awarded. *Degree program information:* Part-time and evening/weekend programs available. Offers letters and sciences (MPA, MS Ed, Ed S); public administration (MPA); school psychology (MS Ed). *Application deadline:* Applications are processed on a rolling basis. *Application fee:* $45. Electronic applications accepted. *Application Contact:* Sally A. Lange, School of Graduate Studies, 262-472-1006, Fax: 262-472-5027, E-mail: gradschl@uww.edu. *Dean,* Dr. Howard Ross, 262-472-1711, Fax: 262-472-5238, E-mail: rossh@uww.edu.

UNIVERSITY OF WYOMING, Laramie, WY 82071

General Information State-supported, coed, university. CGS member. *Enrollment:* 1,088 full-time matriculated graduate/professional students (527 women), 693 part-time matriculated graduate/professional students (406 women). *Graduate faculty:* 555 full-time (127 women), 60 part-time/adjunct (19 women). Tuition, state resident: full-time $2,895; part-time $161 per credit hour. Tuition, nonresident: full-time $8,367; part-time $465 per credit hour. *Required fees:* $491; $10 per credit hour. $2 per credit hour. Tuition and fees vary according to course load and program. *Graduate housing:* Rooms and/or apartments available on a first-come, first-served basis to single and married students. Typical cost: $2,877 per year ($5,059 including board) for single students; $4,500 per year for married students. Room and board charges vary according to board plan, campus/location and housing facility selected. Housing application deadline: 5/25. *Student services:* Campus employment opportunities, campus safety program, career counseling, child daycare facilities, disabled student services, free psychological counseling, international student services, low-cost health insurance, multicultural affairs office. *Library facilities:* Coe Library plus 7 others. *Online resources:* library catalog, web page, access to other libraries' catalogs. *Collection:* 19,720 titles, 14,737 serial subscriptions, 3,701 audiovisual materials. *Research affiliation:* National Park Service Research Center, Institute for Energy Research.

Computer facilities: 1,270 computers available on campus for general student use. A campuswide network can be accessed from student residence rooms and from off campus. Internet access and online class registration are available. *Web address:* http://www.uwyo.edu/.

General Application Contact: Julie Houchin, Credentials Analyst/Advising Assistant, 307-766-2287, Fax: 307-766-2374, E-mail: juliea@uwyo.edu.

GRADUATE UNITS

College of Law Students: 228 full-time (103 women). Average age 27. 435 applicants, 57% accepted, 90 enrolled. *Faculty:* 14 full-time (8 women), 5 part-time/adjunct (2 women). Expenses: Contact institution. *Financial support:* In 2001–02, 118 fellowships (averaging $1,665 per year), 7 teaching assistantships with full and partial tuition reimbursements were awarded. Research assistantships, career-related internships or fieldwork, Federal Work-Study, institutionally sponsored loans, and scholarships/grants also available. Financial award application deadline: 3/1; financial award applicants required to submit FAFSA. In 2001, 76 degrees awarded. Offers law (JD). *Application deadline:* For fall admission, 3/15. Applications are processed on a rolling basis. *Application fee:* $35. *Application Contact:* Robyn F. Kniffen, Director of Admission-College of Law, 307-766-6416, E-mail: lawadmis@wyo.edu. *Dean,* Jerry Parkinson, 307-766-6416, E-mail: jparkins@wyo.edu.

Graduate School Students: 860 full-time (424 women), 693 part-time (406 women); includes 58 minority (4 African Americans, 9 Asian Americans or Pacific Islanders, 28 Hispanic Americans, 17 Native Americans), 194 international. Average age 30. 867 applicants, 73% accepted. *Faculty:* 541 full-time (119 women), 55 part-time/adjunct (17 women). Expenses: Contact institution. *Financial support:* In 2001–02, research assistantships with full tuition reimbursements (averaging $8,667 per year), teaching assistantships with full tuition reimbursements (averaging $8,667 per year) were awarded. Fellowships, career-related internships or fieldwork, Federal Work-Study, institutionally sponsored loans, scholarships/grants, traineeships, tuition waivers (full and partial), and unspecified assistantships also available. Support available to part-time students. Financial award applicants required to submit FAFSA. In 2001, 407 master's, 63 doctorates, 5 other advanced degrees awarded. *Degree program information:* Part-time and evening/weekend programs available. Postbaccalaureate distance learning degree programs offered. *Application fee:* $40. Electronic applications accepted. *Application Contact:* Julie Houchin, Credentials Analyst/Advising Assistant, 307-766-2287, Fax: 307-766-2374, E-mail: juliea@uwyo.edu. *Dean,* Dr. Stephen E. Williams, 307-766-2287, Fax: 307-766-2374, E-mail: sewms@uwyo.edu.

College of Agriculture Students: 86 full-time (43 women), 50 part-time (26 women); includes 3 minority (1 African American, 1 Hispanic American, 1 Native American), 21 international. Average age 28. 72 applicants, 58% accepted. *Faculty:* 86 full-time (11 women). Expenses: Contact institution. *Financial support:* In 2001–02, 3 fellowships, 15 research assistantships, 32 teaching assistantships were awarded. Career-related internships or fieldwork, Federal Work-Study, institutionally sponsored loans, and tuition waivers (partial) also available. Financial award application deadline: 3/1. In 2001, 39 master's, 8 doctorates awarded. *Degree program information:* Part-time programs available. Offers agricultural

University of Wyoming (continued)

and applied economics (MS); agriculture (MS, PhD); agronomy (MS, PhD); animal sciences (MS, PhD); entomology (MS, PhD); family and consumer sciences (MS); food science and human nutrition (MS); molecular biology (MS, PhD); pathobiology (MS); rangeland ecology and watershed management (MS, PhD); reproductive biology (MS, PhD). *Application deadline:* Applications are processed on a rolling basis. *Application fee:* $40. Electronic applications accepted. *Dean,* Dr. Frank D. Galey, 307-766-4133, E-mail: fgaley@uwyo.edu.

College of Arts and Sciences Students: 347 full-time (169 women), 208 part-time (99 women); includes 25 minority (6 Asian Americans or Pacific Islanders, 17 Hispanic Americans, 2 Native Americans), 51 international. Average age 32. 252 applicants, 85% accepted. *Faculty:* 232 full-time (51 women), 43 part-time/adjunct (12 women). Expenses: Contact institution. *Financial support:* Fellowships, research assistantships, teaching assistantships, career-related internships or fieldwork, Federal Work-Study, institutionally sponsored loans, traineeships, and tuition waivers (full and partial) available. Financial award application deadline: 3/1. In 2001, 125 master's, 21 doctorates awarded. *Degree program information:* Part-time programs available. Offers American studies (MA); anthropology (MA, PhD); arts and sciences (MA, MAT, MFA, MM, MP, MPA, MS, MST, PhD); botany (MS, PhD); botany/water resources (MS); chemistry (MS, PhD); communication (MA); community and regional planning and natural resources (MP); English (MA); French (MA); geography (MA, MP, MST); geography/water resources (MA); geology (MS, PhD); geophysics (MS, PhD); German (MA); history (MA, MAT); history and literature (MA); international studies (MA); mathematics (MA, MAT, MS, MST, PhD); mathematics/computer science (PhD); music education (MA); natural science (MS, MST); performance (MM); philosophy (MA); political science (MA); psychology (MA, MS, PhD); public administration (MPA); rural planning and natural resources (MP); sociology (MA); Spanish (MA); statistics (MS, PhD); theory and composition (MA); zoology and physiology (MS, PhD). *Application deadline:* Applications are processed on a rolling basis. *Application fee:* $40. Electronic applications accepted. *Application Contact:* Dr. Janet Constantinides, Associate Dean, 307-766-4106, Fax: 307-766-2697, E-mail: asdean@uwyo.edu. *Dean,* Oliver Walter, 307-766-4106, Fax: 307-766-2697, E-mail: asdean@uwyo.edu.

College of Business Students: 130 full-time (53 women), 41 part-time (25 women); includes 6 minority (2 Asian Americans or Pacific Islanders, 2 Hispanic Americans, 2 Native Americans), 33 international. 119 applicants, 88% accepted. *Faculty:* 70 full-time (13 women), 1 (woman) part-time/adjunct. Expenses: Contact institution. *Financial support:* In 2001–02, 31 research assistantships, 10 teaching assistantships were awarded. Fellowships, career-related internships or fieldwork, Federal Work-Study, institutionally sponsored loans, and tuition waivers (partial) also available. Financial award application deadline: 3/1; financial award applicants required to submit FAFSA. In 2001, 51 master's, 5 doctorates awarded. *Degree program information:* Part-time and evening/weekend programs available. Postbaccalaureate distance learning degree programs offered (minimal on-campus study). Offers accounting (MS); business (MBA, MS, PhD); business administration (MBA); e-business (MS); economics (MS, PhD); finance (MS). *Application deadline:* Applications are processed on a rolling basis. *Application fee:* $40. *Dean,* Dr. Kenyon Griffin, 307-766-4194.

College of Education Students: 65 full-time (48 women), 249 part-time (163 women); includes 13 minority (3 African Americans, 1 Asian American or Pacific Islander, 4 Hispanic Americans, 5 Native Americans), 6 international. Average age 30. 86 applicants, 81% accepted. *Faculty:* 51 full-time (18 women). Expenses: Contact institution. *Financial support:* In 2001–02, 26 teaching assistantships with full tuition reimbursements (averaging $8,990 per year) were awarded; fellowships, research assistantships, career-related internships or fieldwork, Federal Work-Study, and scholarships/grants also available. Financial award application deadline: 3/1. In 2001, 70 master's, 27 doctorates, 5 other advanced degrees awarded. Postbaccalaureate distance learning degree programs offered. Offers adult and postsecondary education (MA, Ed D, PhD); counselor education (MA, PhD); curriculum and instruction (MA, Ed D, PhD); education (Ed S); educational leadership (MA, Ed D, Ed S); instructional technology (MS, Ed D, PhD); special education (MA, Ed S). *Application deadline:* Applications are processed on a rolling basis. *Application fee:* $40. Electronic applications accepted. *Application Contact:* William Berube, Associate Dean, 307-766-3145, Fax: 307-766-6668, E-mail: berube@uwyo.edu. *Dean,* Dr. Patricia McClurg, 307-766-3145, Fax: 307-766-6668, E-mail: patmc@uwyo.edu.

College of Engineering Students: 122 full-time (26 women), 44 part-time (9 women); includes 2 minority (both Hispanic Americans), 80 international. Average age 27. 180 applicants, 49% accepted. *Faculty:* 60 full-time (2 women), 5 part-time/adjunct (1 woman). Expenses: Contact institution. *Financial support:* Fellowships, research assistantships, teaching assistantships, career-related internships or fieldwork, Federal Work-Study, and institutionally sponsored loans available. Support available to part-time students. In 2001, 61 master's, 2 doctorates awarded. *Degree program information:* Part-time programs available. Offers atmospheric science (MS, PhD); chemical engineering (MS, PhD); civil engineering (MS, PhD); computer science (MS, Pro MS, PhD); electrical engineering (MS, PhD); engineering (MS, Pro MS, PhD); environmental engineering (MS); mechanical engineering (MS, PhD); petroleum engineering (MS, PhD). *Application deadline:* Applications are processed on a rolling basis. *Application fee:* $40. Electronic applications accepted. *Dean,* Dr. Ovid A. Plumb, 307-766-4257, Fax: 307-766-4444, E-mail: gplumb@uwyo.edu.

College of Health Sciences Students: 110 full-time (85 women), 101 part-time (84 women); includes 9 minority (2 Hispanic Americans, 7 Native Americans), 3 international. 158 applicants, 74% accepted. *Faculty:* 42 full-time (24 women), 6 part-time/adjunct (3 women). Expenses: Contact institution. *Financial support:* Fellowships, research assistantships, teaching assistantships, career-related internships or fieldwork, Federal Work-Study, institutionally sponsored loans, scholarships/grants, traineeships, tuition waivers (full), and unspecified assistantships available. Support available to part-time students. Financial award application deadline: 3/1. In 2001, 61 degrees awarded. *Degree program information:* Part-time programs available. Postbaccalaureate distance learning degree programs offered (minimal on-campus study). Offers audiology (MS); health sciences (MS, MSW); kinesiology and health (MS); nursing (MS); social work (MSW); speech-language pathology (MS). *Application fee:* $40. Electronic applications accepted. *Dean,* Dr. Robert O. Kelly, 307-766-6556, Fax: 307-766-6608, E-mail: rokelley@uwyo.edu.

See in-depth description on page 1281.

UPPER IOWA UNIVERSITY, Fayette, IA 52142-1857

General Information Independent, coed, comprehensive institution. *Graduate housing:* Rooms and/or apartments available to single and married students.

GRADUATE UNITS

Online MBA Program *Degree program information:* Part-time and evening/weekend programs available. Postbaccalaureate distance learning degree programs offered (no on-campus study). Offers accounting (MA); human resource management (MA); organizational development (MA); quality management (MA). Also available at Des Moines, Iowa campus; Madison, Wisconsin campus; and Waterloo, Iowa campus.

URBANA UNIVERSITY, Urbana, OH 43078-2091

General Information Independent-religious, coed, comprehensive institution. *Enrollment:* 74 part-time matriculated graduate/professional students (59 women). *Enrollment by degree level:* 74 master's. *Graduate faculty:* 1 full-time (0 women), 7 part-time/adjunct (2 women). *Tuition:* Part-time $270 per semester hour. *Required fees:* $65 per semester. *Graduate housing:* On-campus housing not available. *Student services:* Career counseling, teacher training. *Library facilities:* Swedenborg Memorial Library. *Online resources:* library catalog, web page, access to other libraries' catalogs. *Collection:* 61,600 titles, 800 serial subscriptions, 22,036 audiovisual materials.

Computer facilities: 69 computers available on campus for general student use. Internet access is available. *Web address:* http://www.urbana.edu/.

General Application Contact: Dr. John A. Forsthoefel, Director of Graduate Education Programs, 937-484-1394, Fax: 937-484-1365, E-mail: j.forsthoefel@voyager.net.

GRADUATE UNITS

Division of Education and Allied Professions Average age 27. 13 applicants, 92% accepted. *Faculty:* 1 full-time (0 women), 7 part-time/adjunct (2 women). Expenses: Contact institution. *Financial support:* Institutionally sponsored loans, tuition waivers (partial), unspecified assistantships, and register for 3 courses in any semester and pay for only two available. Support available to part-time students. Financial award application deadline: 6/1. In 2001, 11 degrees awarded. *Degree program information:* Part-time and evening/weekend programs available. Offers classroom education (M Ed). *Application deadline:* For fall admission, 8/16 (priority date); for winter admission, 1/3 (priority date); for spring admission, 6/1 (priority date). Applications are processed on a rolling basis. *Application fee:* $25. *Director of Graduate Education Programs,* Dr. John A. Forsthoefel, 937-484-1394, Fax: 937-484-1365, E-mail: j.forsthoefel@voyager.net.

URSULINE COLLEGE, Pepper Pike, OH 44124-4398

General Information Independent-religious, coed, primarily women, comprehensive institution. *Enrollment:* 44 full-time matriculated graduate/professional students (36 women), 182 part-time matriculated graduate/professional students (156 women). *Enrollment by degree level:* 226 master's. *Graduate faculty:* 8 full-time (6 women), 22 part-time/adjunct (14 women). *Tuition:* Full-time $9,612; part-time $534 per credit hour. *Graduate housing:* Room and/or apartments available on a first-come, first-served basis to single students; on-campus housing not available to married students. Typical cost: $5,000 (including board). Room and board charges vary according to board plan. Housing application deadline: 8/20. *Student services:* Career counseling, disabled student services, free psychological counseling, international student services, multicultural affairs office, teacher training. *Library facilities:* Ralph M. Besse Library. *Online resources:* library catalog, web page. *Collection:* 92,525 titles, 3,654 serial subscriptions, 7,495 audiovisual materials.

Computer facilities: 66 computers available on campus for general student use. A campuswide network can be accessed from student residence rooms. Internet access is available. *Web address:* http://www.ursuline.edu/.

General Application Contact: Dr. Catherine Hackney, Dean of Graduate Studies, 440-646-8119, Fax: 440-684-6088, E-mail: gradsch@ursuline.edu.

GRADUATE UNITS

Graduate Studies Students: 44 full-time (36 women), 182 part-time (156 women); includes 30 minority (29 African Americans, 1 Asian American or Pacific Islander) Average age 39. 235 applicants, 50% accepted, 82 enrolled. *Faculty:* 8 full-time (6 women), 22 part-time/adjunct (14 women). Expenses: Contact institution. *Financial support:* Career-related internships or fieldwork and Federal Work-Study available. Support available to part-time students. Financial award application deadline: 3/1; financial award applicants required to submit FAFSA. In 2001, 80 degrees awarded. *Degree program information:* Part-time programs available. Offers art therapy (MA); education (MA); liberal studies (MALS); ministry (MA); non-public educational administration (MA); nursing (MSN). *Application deadline:* For fall admission, 8/1 (priority date). Applications are processed on a rolling basis. *Application fee:* $25. Electronic applications accepted. *Application Contact:* Jo Mann, Secretary, 440-646-8119, Fax: 440-684-6088, E-mail: gradsch@ursuline.edu. *Dean of Graduate Studies,* Dr. Catherine Hackney, 440-646-8119, Fax: 440-684-6088, E-mail: gradsch@ursuline.edu.

UTAH STATE UNIVERSITY, Logan, UT 84322

General Information State-supported, coed, university. CGS member. *Enrollment:* 1,037 full-time matriculated graduate/professional students (395 women), 1,295 part-time matriculated graduate/professional students (564 women). Tuition, state resident: full-time $1,693. Tuition, nonresident: full-time $4,233. *Required fees:* $501. Tuition and fees vary according to program. *Graduate housing:* Rooms and/or apartments available on a first-come, first-served basis to single and married students. Typical cost: $1,860 per year ($3,050 including board) for single students; $3,600 per year for married students. Room and board charges vary according to board plan, campus/location and housing facility selected. *Student services:* Campus employment opportunities, campus safety program, career counseling, child daycare facilities, disabled student services, exercise/wellness program, free psychological counseling, international student services, low-cost health insurance, multicultural affairs office, teacher training, writing training. *Library facilities:* Merrill Library plus 4 others. *Online resources:* library catalog, web page, access to other libraries' catalogs. *Collection:* 1 million titles, 14,449 serial subscriptions, 27,594 audiovisual materials. *Research affiliation:* GenCorp Aerojet (aerospace engineering), John Deere (agricultural science research), Dairy Management, Inc. (dairy science research), Sensor Systems Group (aerospace engineering), Nicholas Research (computer engineering), Primary Flow Signal Inc. (water research).

Computer facilities: 850 computers available on campus for general student use. A campuswide network can be accessed from student residence rooms and from off campus. Internet access and online class registration are available. *Web address:* http://www.usu.edu/.

General Application Contact: Diana Thimmes, Admissions Officer, School of Graduate Studies, 435-797-1190, Fax: 435-797-1192, E-mail: gradsch@cc.usu.edu.

GRADUATE UNITS

School of Graduate Studies Students: 1,037 full-time (395 women), 1,295 part-time (564 women); includes 84 minority (8 African Americans, 32 Asian Americans or Pacific Islanders, 28 Hispanic Americans, 16 Native Americans), 502 international. 2,524 applicants, 51% accepted. Expenses: Contact institution. *Financial support:* Fellowships with partial tuition reimbursements, research assistantships with partial tuition reimbursements, teaching assistantships with partial tuition reimbursements, career-related internships or fieldwork, Federal Work-Study, institutionally sponsored loans, scholarships/grants, tuition waivers (full and partial), unspecified assistantships, and production assistantships, stipends available. Support available to part-time students. In 2001, 769 master's, 66 doctorates, 2 other advanced degrees awarded. *Degree program information:* Part-time and evening/weekend programs available. Postbaccalaureate distance learning degree programs offered (minimal on-campus study). *Application deadline:* For fall admission, 6/15; for spring admission, 10/15. Applications are processed on a rolling basis. *Application fee:* $40. *Application Contact:* Diana Thimmes, Admissions Officer, 435-797-1190, E-mail: grdschool@grad.usu.edu. *Dean,* Dr. Thomas Kent, 435-797-1189, Fax: 435-797-1192.

College of Agriculture Students: 39 full-time (9 women), 19 part-time (10 women), 11 international. Average age 30. 44 applicants, 39% accepted. Expenses: Contact institution. *Financial support:* Fellowships, research assistantships, teaching assistantships, career-related internships or fieldwork, Federal Work-Study, institutionally sponsored loans, scholarships/grants, and tuition waivers (full and partial) available. Support available to part-time students. In 2001, 23 master's, 1 doctorate awarded. *Degree program information:* Part-time programs available. Postbaccalaureate distance learning degree programs offered (minimal on-campus study). Offers agricultural systems technology (MS); agriculture (MS, PhD); animal science (MS, PhD); biometeorology (MS, PhD); bioveterinary science (MS, PhD); dairy science (MS); ecology (MS, PhD); plant science (MS, PhD); soil science (MS, PhD); toxicology (MS, PhD). *Application deadline:* For fall admission, 6/15; for spring admission, 10/15. Applications are processed on a rolling basis. *Application fee:* $40. *Interim Dean,* 435-797-2215.

College of Business Students: 196 full-time (67 women), 310 part-time (84 women); includes 17 minority (12 Asian Americans or Pacific Islanders, 4 Hispanic Americans, 1 Native American), 92 international. Average age 30. 406 applicants, 60% accepted. *Faculty:* 81 full-time (5 women), 5 part-time/adjunct (0 women). Expenses: Contact institution. *Financial support:* Fellowships with partial tuition reimbursements, research assistantships with partial tuition reimbursements, teaching assistantships with partial tuition reimbursements, career-related internships or fieldwork, Federal Work-Study, institutionally sponsored loans, tuition waivers (full and partial), and unspecified assistantships available. In 2001, 231 master's, 4 doctorates awarded. *Degree program information:* Part-time and evening/weekend programs available. Postbaccalaureate distance learning degree programs offered (no on-campus study). Offers accountancy (M Acc); applied economics (MS); business (M Acc, MA, MBA, MS, MSS, Ed D, PhD); business administration (MBA); business education (MS); business information systems (MS); business information systems and education

(Ed D); economics (MA, MS, PhD); education (PhD); human resource management (MSS). *Application deadline:* For fall admission, 6/15; for spring admission, 10/15. Applications are processed on a rolling basis. *Application fee:* $40. *Dean*, David B. Stephens, 435-797-2272.

College of Education Students: 223 full-time (124 women), 470 part-time (280 women); includes 33 minority (4 African Americans, 12 Asian Americans or Pacific Islanders, 8 Hispanic Americans, 9 Native Americans), 25 international. 532 applicants, 61% accepted. Expenses: Contact institution. *Financial support:* Fellowships with partial tuition reimbursements, research assistantships with partial tuition reimbursements, teaching assistantships with partial tuition reimbursements, career-related internships or fieldwork, Federal Work-Study, institutionally sponsored loans, tuition waivers (full and partial), unspecified assistantships, and stipends available. Support available to part-time students. In 2001, 241 master's, 22 doctorates, 2 other advanced degrees awarded. *Degree program information:* Part-time and evening/weekend programs available. Postbaccalaureate distance learning degree programs offered (no on-campus study). Offers audiology (Ed S); business information systems (Ed D, PhD); clinical/counseling/school psychology (PhD); communication disorders and deaf education (M Ed); communicative disorders and deaf education (MA, MS); curriculum and instruction (Ed D, PhD); education (M Ed, MA, MRC, MS, Ed D, PhD, Ed S); elementary education (M Ed, MA, MS); health, physical education and recreation (M Ed, MS); instructional technology (M Ed, MS, PhD, Ed S); rehabilitation counselor education (MRC); research and evaluation (Ed D, PhD); research and evaluation methodology (PhD); school counseling (MS); school psychology (MS); secondary education (M Ed, MA, MS); special education (M Ed, MS, Ed D, PhD, Ed S). *Application deadline:* For fall admission, 6/15; for spring admission, 10/15. Applications are processed on a rolling basis. *Application fee:* $40. *Application Contact:* Louann Parkinson, Administrative Assistant to the Dean, 435-797-1470, Fax: 435-797-3939, E-mail: luannp@coe.usu.edu. *Dean*, Gerry Giordano, 435-797-1437, Fax: 435-797-3939.

College of Engineering Students: 174 full-time (25 women), 103 part-time (12 women); includes 7 minority (1 African American, 2 Asian Americans or Pacific Islanders, 2 Hispanic Americans, 2 Native Americans), 162 international. Average age 28. 662 applicants, 44% accepted. Expenses: Contact institution. *Financial support:* Fellowships with partial tuition reimbursements, research assistantships with partial tuition reimbursements, teaching assistantships with partial tuition reimbursements, career-related internships or fieldwork, Federal Work-Study, institutionally sponsored loans, and tuition waivers (partial) available. Support available to part-time students. In 2001, 77 master's, 7 doctorates awarded. *Degree program information:* Part-time and evening/weekend programs available. Offers aerospace engineering (MS, PhD); biological and agricultural engineering (MS, PhD); civil and environmental engineering (ME, MS, PhD, CE); electrical engineering (ME, MS, PhD, EE); engineering (ME, MS, PhD, CE, EE); industrial technology (MS); irrigation engineering (MS, PhD); mechanical engineering (ME, MS, PhD). *Application deadline:* For fall admission, 6/15; for spring admission, 10/15. Applications are processed on a rolling basis. *Application fee:* $40. *Dean*, A. Bruce Bishop, 435-797-2775.

College of Family Life Students: 56 full-time (31 women), 47 part-time (32 women); includes 3 minority (1 African American, 2 Hispanic Americans), 21 international. Average age 32. 117 applicants, 48% accepted. *Faculty:* 21 full-time (13 women). Expenses: Contact institution. *Financial support:* Fellowships with tuition reimbursements, research assistantships with tuition reimbursements, teaching assistantships with tuition reimbursements, career-related internships or fieldwork, Federal Work-Study, institutionally sponsored loans, scholarships/grants, and tuition waivers (full and partial) available. Support available to part-time students. In 2001, 29 master's, 4 doctorates awarded. *Degree program information:* Part-time and evening/weekend programs available. Postbaccalaureate distance learning degree programs offered. Offers dietetic administration (MDA); family and human development (MFHD, MS); family life (MDA, MFHD, MFMS, MS, PhD); food microbiology and safety (MFMS); human environments (MS); marriage and family therapy (MS); molecular biology (MS, PhD); nutrition and food sciences (MS, PhD). *Application deadline:* For fall admission, 6/15; for spring admission, 10/15. Applications are processed on a rolling basis. *Application fee:* $40. *Interim Dean*, Von T. Mendenhall, 435-797-1538, Fax: 435-797-3485, E-mail: vonm@cc.usu.edu.

College of Humanities, Arts and Social Sciences Students: 101 full-time (55 women), 145 part-time (79 women); includes 12 minority (1 African American, 2 Asian Americans or Pacific Islanders, 6 Hispanic Americans, 3 Native Americans), 23 international. Average age 29. 190 applicants, 63% accepted. *Faculty:* 112 full-time (26 women), 7 part-time/adjunct (1 woman). Expenses: Contact institution. *Financial support:* Fellowships with partial tuition reimbursements, research assistantships with partial tuition reimbursements, teaching assistantships with partial tuition reimbursements, career-related internships or fieldwork, Federal Work-Study, institutionally sponsored loans, scholarships/grants, tuition waivers (partial), and production assistantships available. In 2001, 81 master's, 2 doctorates awarded. *Degree program information:* Part-time and evening/weekend programs available. Postbaccalaureate distance learning degree programs offered (minimal on-campus study). Offers advanced technical practice (MFA); American studies (MA, MS); art (MA, MFA); bioregional planning (MS); design (MFA); English (MA, MS); folklore (MA, MS); history (MA, MS, MSS); humanities, arts and social sciences (MA, MFA, MLA, MS, MSLT, MSS, PhD); journalism and communication (MA, MS); landscape architecture (MLA); political science (MA, MS); second language teaching (MSLT); sociology (MA, MS, MSS, PhD); theatre arts (MA, MFA). *Application deadline:* For fall admission, 6/15; for spring admission, 10/15. *Application fee:* $40. *Dean*, Elizabeth Grobsmith, 435-7971195.

College of Natural Resources Students: 59 full-time (20 women), 71 part-time (27 women); includes 3 minority (2 Hispanic Americans, 1 Native American), 13 international. Average age 27. 96 applicants, 40% accepted. *Faculty:* 46 full-time (2 women), 2 part-time/adjunct (1 woman). Expenses: Contact institution. *Financial support:* Fellowships with partial tuition reimbursements, research assistantships with partial tuition reimbursements, teaching assistantships with partial tuition reimbursements, career-related internships or fieldwork, Federal Work-Study, institutionally sponsored loans, and tuition waivers (full and partial) available. Support available to part-time students. In 2001, 30 master's, 7 doctorates awarded. *Degree program information:* Part-time programs available. Offers ecology (MS, PhD); fisheries biology (MS, PhD); forestry (MS, PhD); geography (MA, MS); natural resources (MA, MNR, MS, PhD); range science (MS, PhD); recreation resources management (MS, PhD); science program (MS, PhD); wildlife biology (MS, PhD). *Application deadline:* For fall admission, 6/15; for spring admission, 10/15. Applications are processed on a rolling basis. *Application fee:* $40. *Dean*, Dr. F. E. Busby, 435-797-2445.

College of Science Students: 189 full-time (64 women), 130 part-time (40 women); includes 9 minority (1 African American, 4 Asian Americans or Pacific Islanders, 4 Hispanic Americans), 155 international. 477 applicants, 41% accepted. *Faculty:* 121 full-time (16 women), 6 part-time/adjunct (1 woman). Expenses: Contact institution. *Financial support:* Fellowships with partial tuition reimbursements, research assistantships with partial tuition reimbursements, teaching assistantships with partial tuition reimbursements, career-related internships or fieldwork, Federal Work-Study, institutionally sponsored loans, scholarships/grants, and tuition waivers (partial) available. Support available to part-time students. In 2001, 57 master's, 19 doctorates awarded. *Degree program information:* Part-time and evening/weekend programs available. Offers applied statistics (MS); biochemistry (MS, PhD); biology (MS, PhD); chemistry (MS, PhD); computer science (MCS, MS, PhD); ecology (MS, PhD); geology (MS); mathematical sciences (PhD); mathematics (M Math, MS); physics (MS, PhD); science (M Math, MCS, MS, PhD). *Application deadline:* For fall admission, 6/15; for spring admission, 10/15. Applications are processed on a rolling basis. *Application fee:* $40. *Interim Dean*, Don Fresinger, 435-797-2478.

UTICA COLLEGE, Utica, NY 13502-4892

General Information Independent, coed, comprehensive institution.

GRADUATE UNITS

Department of Physical Therapy

Program in Economic Crime Management Postbaccalaureate distance learning degree programs offered (minimal on-campus study). Offers economic crime management (MS).

VALDOSTA STATE UNIVERSITY, Valdosta, GA 31698

General Information State-supported, coed, university. CGS member. *Enrollment:* 421 full-time matriculated graduate/professional students (311 women), 756 part-time matriculated graduate/professional students (631 women). *Enrollment by degree level:* 1,113 master's, 64 doctoral. *Graduate faculty:* 217 full-time (78 women). Tuition, state resident: full-time $1,746; part-time $97 per hour. Tuition, nonresident: full-time $6,966; part-time $387 per hour. *Required fees:* $594; $297 per semester. *Graduate housing:* Rooms and/or apartments available on a first-come, first-served basis to single and married students. Typical cost: $2,914 per year for single students; $2,914 per year for married students. Housing application deadline: 7/1. *Student services:* Campus employment opportunities, campus safety program, career counseling, child daycare facilities, disabled student services, exercise/wellness program, free psychological counseling, grant writing training, international student services, low-cost health insurance, multicultural affairs office, teacher training, writing training. *Library facilities:* Odom Library. *Online resources:* library catalog, access to other libraries' catalogs. *Collection:* 288,035 titles, 3,262 serial subscriptions, 62,677 audiovisual materials. *Research affiliation:* Georgia Marine Institute, Skidaway Institute of Oceanography.

Computer facilities: 2,400 computers available on campus for general student use. A campuswide network can be accessed from student residence rooms and from off campus. Internet access and online class registration are available. *Web address:* http://www.valdosta.edu/.

General Application Contact: Dr. Ernestine H. Clark, Dean, 229-333-5694, Fax: 229-245-3853, E-mail: eclark@valdosta.edu.

GRADUATE UNITS

Graduate School Students: 421 full-time (311 women), 756 part-time (631 women); includes 162 minority (138 African Americans, 9 Asian Americans or Pacific Islanders, 12 Hispanic Americans, 3 Native Americans) Average age 34. 544 applicants, 88% accepted. *Faculty:* 217 full-time (78 women). Expenses: Contact institution. *Financial support:* In 2001–02, 703 students received support, including 43 research assistantships with full tuition reimbursements available (averaging $2,452 per year), 4 teaching assistantships with full tuition reimbursements available (averaging $2,800 per year); career-related internships or fieldwork, institutionally sponsored loans, scholarships/grants, traineeships, tuition waivers (partial), and unspecified assistantships also available. Support available to part-time students. Financial award application deadline: 7/1; financial award applicants required to submit FAFSA. In 2001, 346 master's, 1 doctorate, 38 other advanced degrees awarded. *Degree program information:* Part-time and evening/weekend programs available. Postbaccalaureate distance learning degree programs offered. Offers library and information science (MLIS). *Application deadline:* For fall admission, 7/1; for spring admission, 11/1. Applications are processed on a rolling basis. *Application fee:* $20. Electronic applications accepted. *Application Contact:* Judy Tomberlin, Coordinator of Graduate Admissions, 229-333-5694, Fax: 229-245-3853, E-mail: jtomberli@valdosta.edu. *Dean*, Dr. Ernestine H. Clark, 229-333-5694, Fax: 229-245-3853, E-mail: eclark@valdosta.edu.

College of Arts and Sciences Students: 107 full-time (88 women), 120 part-time (97 women); includes 31 minority (25 African Americans, 1 Asian American or Pacific Islander, 5 Hispanic Americans) Average age 29. 147 applicants, 93% accepted. *Faculty:* 58 full-time (19 women). Expenses: Contact institution. *Financial support:* In 2001–02, 14 research assistantships with full tuition reimbursements (averaging $2,452 per year), 2 teaching assistantships with full tuition reimbursements (averaging $2,800 per year) were awarded. Career-related internships or fieldwork, institutionally sponsored loans, scholarships/grants, and unspecified assistantships also available. Support available to part-time students. Financial award application deadline: 7/1; financial award applicants required to submit FAFSA. In 2001, 101 degrees awarded. *Degree program information:* Part-time and evening/weekend programs available. Postbaccalaureate distance learning degree programs offered. Offers arts and sciences (MA, MPA, MS); city management (MPA); criminal justice (MS); English (MA); history (MA); marriage and family therapy (MS); public human resources (MPA); public sector (MPA); sociology (MS). *Application deadline:* For fall admission, 7/1 (priority date); for spring admission, 11/1. Applications are processed on a rolling basis. *Application fee:* $20. Electronic applications accepted. *Acting Dean*, Dr. Ron Barnette, 229-333-5699.

College of Business Administration Students: 5 full-time (3 women), 44 part-time (36 women); includes 6 minority (all African Americans) Average age 27. 27 applicants, 78% accepted. *Faculty:* 16 full-time (3 women). Expenses: Contact institution. *Financial support:* In 2001–02, 5 research assistantships with full tuition reimbursements (averaging $2,452 per year) were awarded; institutionally sponsored loans, scholarships/grants, and unspecified assistantships also available. Support available to part-time students. Financial award application deadline: 7/1; financial award applicants required to submit FAFSA. In 2001, 16 degrees awarded. *Degree program information:* Part-time programs available. Offers business administration (MBA). *Application deadline:* For fall admission, 7/1; for spring admission, 11/15. Applications are processed on a rolling basis. *Application fee:* $20. Electronic applications accepted. *Application Contact:* Dr. John Oliver, Program Coordinator and Head of Department of Management, 229-333-2233, Fax: 229-245-6498, E-mail: joliver@valdosta.edu. *Dean*, Dr. Kenneth L. Stanley, 229-333-5991, Fax: 229-245-6498, E-mail: kstanley@valdosta.edu.

College of Education Students: 253 full-time (174 women), 535 part-time (456 women); includes 103 minority (88 African Americans, 6 Asian Americans or Pacific Islanders, 6 Hispanic Americans, 3 Native Americans) Average age 28. 296 applicants, 80% accepted. *Faculty:* 75 full-time (31 women). Expenses: Contact institution. *Financial support:* In 2001–02, 13 research assistantships with full tuition reimbursements (averaging $2,452 per year) were awarded; institutionally sponsored loans, scholarships/grants, and unspecified assistantships also available. Support available to part-time students. Financial award application deadline: 7/1; financial award applicants required to submit FAFSA. In 2001, 171 master's, 1 doctorate, 38 other advanced degrees awarded. *Degree program information:* Part-time and evening/weekend programs available. Offers adult and vocational education (Ed D); business education (M Ed, Ed S); clinical/counseling psychology (MS); communication disorders (M Ed); early childhood education (M Ed, Ed S); education (M Ed, MAE, MME, MS, Ed D, Ed S); educational leadership (M Ed, Ed D, Ed S); industrial/organizational psychology (MS); kinesiology and physical education (M Ed); middle grades education (M Ed, Ed S); reading (M Ed, Ed S); school counseling (M Ed, Ed S); school psychology (M Ed, Ed S); secondary education (M Ed, Ed S); special education (M Ed, Ed S); vocational education (M Ed). *Application deadline:* For fall admission, 7/1; for spring admission, 11/1. Applications are processed on a rolling basis. *Application fee:* $20. Electronic applications accepted. *Acting Dean*, Dr. Thomas Reed, 229-333-5925, Fax: 229-333-7167, E-mail: treed@valdosta.edu.

College of Fine Arts Students: 5 full-time (4 women), 8 part-time (5 women); includes 5 minority (all African Americans) Average age 26. 2 applicants, 100% accepted. *Faculty:* 18 full-time (6 women). Expenses: Contact institution. *Financial support:* In 2001–02, 5 research assistantships with full tuition reimbursements (averaging $2,452 per year), 1 teaching assistantship with full tuition reimbursement (averaging $2,452 per year) were awarded. Institutionally sponsored loans, scholarships/grants, and unspecified assistantships also available. Support available to part-time students. Financial award application deadline: 7/1; financial award applicants required to submit FAFSA. In 2001, 4 degrees awarded. *Degree program information:* Part-time programs available. Offers fine arts (MME); music education (MME). *Application deadline:* For fall admission, 7/1. Applications are processed on a rolling basis. *Application fee:* $20. Electronic applications accepted. *Head*, Dr. Lanny D. Milbrandt, 229-333-5832, Fax: 229-245-3799, E-mail: lmilbran@valdosta.edu.

College of Nursing Students: 12 full-time (7 women), 13 part-time (12 women); includes 4 minority (3 African Americans, 1 Asian American or Pacific Islander) Average age 32. 15 applicants, 100% accepted. *Faculty:* 7 full-time (6 women). Expenses: Contact institution. *Financial support:* In 2001–02, 2 research assistantships with full tuition reimbursements (averaging $2,452 per year) were awarded; institutionally sponsored loans, scholarships/grants, and unspecified assistantships also available. Support available to part-time students. Financial award application deadline: 7/1; financial award applicants required to submit FAFSA. In 2001, 16 degrees awarded. *Degree program information:* Part-time programs available. Offers administration (MSN); community health nursing (MSN). *Application deadline:* For

Valdosta State University (continued)

fall admission, 7/1; for spring admission, 11/15. Applications are processed on a rolling basis. *Application fee:* $20. Electronic applications accepted. *Dean,* Dr. Maryann Reichenbach, 229-333-5959, E-mail: mreichenb@valdosta.edu.

Division of Social Work Students: 38 full-time (34 women), 26 part-time (19 women); includes 10 minority (all African Americans) Average age 28. 39 applicants, 77% accepted. *Faculty:* 4 full-time (2 women). Expenses: Contact institution. *Financial support:* In 2001–02, 2 research assistantships with full tuition reimbursements (averaging $2,452 per year) were awarded; career-related internships or fieldwork, institutionally sponsored loans, scholarships/grants, and unspecified assistantships also available. Financial award application deadline: 7/1; financial award applicants required to submit FAFSA. In 2001, 38 degrees awarded. Offers social work (MSW). *Application deadline:* For fall admission, 3/15. Applications are processed on a rolling basis. *Application fee:* $20. *Director,* Dr. Peggy Cleveland, 229-249-4864, Fax: 229-245-4341, E-mail: phclevel@valdosta.edu.

VALPARAISO UNIVERSITY, Valparaiso, IN 46383-6493

General Information Independent-religious, coed, comprehensive institution. *Enrollment:* 474 full-time matriculated graduate/professional students (237 women), 167 part-time matriculated graduate/professional students (105 women). *Enrollment by degree level:* 461 first professional, 180 master's, 2 other advanced degrees. *Tuition:* Full-time $5,400; part-time $300 per credit. *Graduate housing:* Room and/or apartments available on a first-come, first-served basis to single students; on-campus housing not available to married students. Typical cost: $3,100 per year ($3,530 including board). Room and board charges vary according to board plan. *Student services:* Campus employment opportunities, campus safety program, career counseling, disabled student services, free psychological counseling, international student services, low-cost health insurance, multicultural affairs office, writing training. *Library facilities:* Moellering Library plus 1 other. *Online resources:* library catalog, web page. *Collection:* 714,657 titles, 16,158 serial subscriptions, 84,570 audiovisual materials.

Computer facilities: 580 computers available on campus for general student use. A campuswide network can be accessed from student residence rooms and from off campus. Internet access is available. *Web address:* http://www.valpo.edu/.

General Application Contact: Dr. David L. Rowland, Dean, Graduate Studies and Continuing Education, 219-464-5313, Fax: 219-464-5381, E-mail: david.rowland@valpo.edu.

GRADUATE UNITS

Graduate Division Students: 54 full-time (40 women), 121 part-time (90 women); includes 11 minority (5 African Americans, 3 Asian Americans or Pacific Islanders, 3 Hispanic Americans), 5 international. Average age 36. 198 applicants, 87% accepted, 120 enrolled. Expenses: Contact institution. *Financial support:* Career-related internships or fieldwork, Federal Work-Study, institutionally sponsored loans, and unspecified assistantships available. Financial award applicants required to submit FAFSA. In 2001, 44 degrees awarded. *Degree program information:* Part-time and evening/weekend programs available. Offers applied behavioral science (MA); business administration (MBA); clinical mental health counseling (MA); counseling (MA); English (MALS); ethics, value and society (MALS); history (MALS); human behavior and society (MALS); initial licensure (M Ed); music (MM); school psychology (MA); special education (M Ed, MS Sp Ed); teaching and learning (M Ed); theology (MALS); theology and ministry (MALS); U.S.culture (MALS). *Application deadline:* Applications are processed on a rolling basis. *Application fee:* $30. *Dean, Graduate Studies and Continuing Education,* Dr. David L. Rowland, 219-464-5313, Fax: 219-464-5381, E-mail: david.rowland@valpo.edu.

College of Nursing Students: 8 full-time (all women), 31 part-time (30 women); includes 3 minority (1 African American, 1 Asian American or Pacific Islander, 1 Hispanic American) Average age 41. Expenses: Contact institution. *Financial support:* Career-related internships or fieldwork, Federal Work-Study, and institutionally sponsored loans available. Financial award applicants required to submit FAFSA. In 2001, 13 degrees awarded. *Degree program information:* Part-time and evening/weekend programs available. Offers nursing (MSN). *Application deadline:* Applications are processed on a rolling basis. *Application fee:* $30. *Dean,* Dr. Janet Brown, 219-464-5289, Fax: 219-464-5425, E-mail: janet.brown@valpo.edu.

School of Law *Degree program information:* Part-time programs available. Offers law (JD, LL M). Electronic applications accepted.

VANCOUVER SCHOOL OF THEOLOGY, Vancouver, BC V6T 1L4, Canada

General Information Independent-religious, coed, graduate-only institution. *Graduate housing:* Rooms and/or apartments guaranteed to single students and available to married students. Housing application deadline: 4/7.

GRADUATE UNITS

Graduate and Professional Programs Offers theology (M Div, MPS, MTS, Th M, D Min, Dip CS).

VANDERBILT UNIVERSITY, Nashville, TN 37240-1001

General Information Independent, coed, university. CGS member. *Enrollment:* 2,843 full-time matriculated graduate/professional students (1,457 women), 138 part-time matriculated graduate/professional students (80 women). *Graduate faculty:* 1,315 full-time (374 women). *Tuition:* Full-time $28,350. *Graduate housing:* Rooms and/or apartments available to single and married students. Housing application deadline: 5/1. *Student services:* Campus employment opportunities, campus safety program, career counseling, child daycare facilities, disabled student services, exercise/wellness program, free psychological counseling, international student services, low-cost health insurance, multicultural affairs office, teacher training, writing training. *Library facilities:* Jean and Alexander Heard Library plus 7 others. *Collection:* 1.7 million titles, 21,608 serial subscriptions, 43,182 audiovisual materials.

Computer facilities: 400 computers available on campus for general student use. A campuswide network can be accessed from student residence rooms and from off campus. Productivity and educational software available. *Web address:* http://www.vanderbilt.edu/.

General Application Contact: Information Contact, 615-343-2727, Fax: 615-343-9936.

GRADUATE UNITS

Divinity School *Degree program information:* Part-time programs available. Offers divinity (M Div, MTS).

Graduate School Students: 1,548 full-time (713 women), 118 part-time (71 women); includes 93 minority (54 African Americans, 19 Asian Americans or Pacific Islanders, 17 Hispanic Americans, 3 Native Americans), 511 international. Average age 30. 2,524 applicants, 40% accepted. *Faculty:* 710. Expenses: Contact institution. *Financial support:* Fellowships with full and partial tuition reimbursements, research assistantships with full tuition reimbursements, teaching assistantships with full tuition reimbursements, career-related internships or fieldwork, Federal Work-Study, institutionally sponsored loans, scholarships/grants, traineeships, and tuition waivers (full and partial) available. Support available to part-time students. In 2001, 241 master's, 173 doctorates awarded. *Degree program information:* Part-time programs available. Offers anthropology (MA, PhD); astronomy (MS); biochemistry (MS, PhD); biological sciences (MS, PhD); biomedical informatics (MS, PhD); biomedical sciences (PhD); cancer biology (MS, PhD); cell and developmental biology (MS, PhD); cellular and molecular pathology (PhD); chemistry (MA, MAT, MS, PhD); classical studies (MA, MAT, PhD); comparative literature (MA, PhD); economics (MA, MAT, PhD); educational leadership (MS, PhD); English (MA, MAT, PhD); fine arts (MA, MAT); French (MA, MAT, PhD); geology (MS); German (MA, MAT, PhD); hearing and speech sciences (MS, PhD); history (MA, MAT, PhD); Latin American studies (MA); liberal arts and science (MLAS); mathematics (MA, MAT, MS, PhD); medical physics (MS); microbiology and immunology (MS, PhD); molecular physiology and biophysics (PhD); neuroscience (PhD); nursing science (PhD); pharmacology (PhD); philosophy (MA, PhD); physics (MA, MAT, MS, PhD); policy development and program evaluation (MS, PhD); political science (MA, MAT, PhD); Portuguese (MA); psychology (MA, PhD); psychology and human development (MS, PhD); religion (MA, PhD); sociology (MA, PhD); Spanish (MA, MAT, PhD); Spanish and Portuguese (PhD); special education (MS, PhD); teaching and learning (MS, PhD). *Application deadline:* For fall admission, 1/15. *Application fee:* $40. Electronic applications accepted. *Application Contact:* Andrew J. Ozier, Admissions Coordinator, 615-343-2727, Fax: 615-343-9936, E-mail: mr.ozier@vanderbilt.edu. *Acting Dean,* William P. Smith, 615-343-2727, Fax: 615-343-9936, E-mail: william.p.smith@vanderbilt.edu.

Law School Students: 574 (274 women); includes 104 minority (58 African Americans, 33 Asian Americans or Pacific Islanders, 13 Hispanic Americans) 28 international. Average age 25. *Faculty:* 40 full-time (10 women), 34 part-time/adjunct (7 women). Expenses: Contact institution. *Financial support:* Career-related internships or fieldwork, Federal Work-Study, and institutionally sponsored loans available. Financial award application deadline: 2/28; financial award applicants required to submit CSS PROFILE or FAFSA. In 2001, 187 degrees awarded. Offers law (JD, LL M). *Application deadline:* For fall admission, 3/1 (priority date). Applications are processed on a rolling basis. *Application fee:* $50. Electronic applications accepted. *Application Contact:* Sonya G. Smith, Assistant Dean of Admissions, 615-322-6452. *Dean,* Kent D. Syverud, 615-322-2615.

Owen Graduate School of Management Students: 550 full-time (149 women); includes 49 minority (18 African Americans, 23 Asian Americans or Pacific Islanders, 8 Hispanic Americans), 106 international. Average age 28. 1,198 applicants, 45% accepted, 297 enrolled. *Faculty:* 46 full-time (7 women), 24 part-time/adjunct (4 women). Expenses: Contact institution. *Financial support:* In 2001–02, 35 students received support, including 35 fellowships with full and partial tuition reimbursements available (averaging $9,500 per year); career-related internships or fieldwork, Federal Work-Study, institutionally sponsored loans, scholarships/grants, and tuition waivers (full and partial) also available. Financial award application deadline: 5/1; financial award applicants required to submit FAFSA. In 2001, 294 master's, 2 doctorates awarded. *Degree program information:* Evening/weekend programs available. Offers business administration (MBA); executive business administration (MBA); finance (PhD); management (MBA, PhD); marketing (PhD); operations management (PhD); organization studies (PhD). *Application deadline:* For fall admission, 11/15 (priority date); for winter admission, 3/15 (priority date); for spring admission, 5/15. Applications are processed on a rolling basis. *Application fee:* $50. Electronic applications accepted. *Application Contact:* Todd D. Reale, Director of MBA Program and Admissions, 615-322-6469, Fax: 615-343-1175, E-mail: admissions@owen.vanderbilt.edu. *Dean,* William G. Christie, 615-322-2316, Fax: 615-343-7110, E-mail: bill.christie@owen.vanderbilt.edu.

Peabody College Students: 238 full-time (179 women), 86 part-time (61 women); includes 41 minority (37 African Americans, 3 Asian Americans or Pacific Islanders, 1 Native American), 20 international. Average age 32. 404 applicants, 70% accepted, 144 enrolled. *Faculty:* 91 full-time (43 women), 38 part-time/adjunct (25 women). Expenses: Contact institution. *Financial support:* In 2001–02, 170 students received support, including 85 fellowships with full and partial tuition reimbursements available, 116 research assistantships with full and partial tuition reimbursements available, 110 teaching assistantships with full and partial tuition reimbursements available; Federal Work-Study, institutionally sponsored loans, scholarships/grants, traineeships, tuition waivers (partial), and unspecified assistantships also available. Financial award application deadline: 5/1; financial award applicants required to submit FAFSA. In 2001, 117 master's, 24 doctorates awarded. *Degree program information:* Part-time programs available. Offers curriculum and instructional leadership (M Ed, Ed D); early childhood education (M Ed, Ed D); education (M Ed, Ed D); elementary education (M Ed, Ed D); English education (M Ed, Ed D); general administrative leadership (Ed D); higher education (M Ed, Ed D); human development counseling (M Ed); human resource development (M Ed); human, organizational and community development (M Ed); language and literacy education (Ed D); mathematics education (M Ed, Ed D); organizational leadership (M Ed); reading education (M Ed); school administration (M Ed, Ed D); science education (M Ed, Ed D); secondary education (M Ed); special education (M Ed); technology and education (M Ed). *Application deadline:* For fall admission, 1/15 (priority date); for spring admission, 11/1 (priority date). Applications are processed on a rolling basis. *Application fee:* $40. Electronic applications accepted. *Application Contact:* Betty S. Lee, Registrar, 615-322-8400, Fax: 615-322-8401, E-mail: peabody.admissions@vanderbilt.edu. *Dean,* Dr. Camilla P. Benbow, 615-322-8407, Fax: 615-322-8501, E-mail: camilla.benbow@vanderbilt.edu.

School of Engineering Students: 340 full-time (88 women), 25 part-time (4 women); includes 55 minority (20 African Americans, 31 Asian Americans or Pacific Islanders, 4 Hispanic Americans), 157 international. Average age 26. 642 applicants, 31% accepted, 114 enrolled. *Faculty:* 135 full-time (10 women), 12 part-time/adjunct (2 women). Expenses: Contact institution. *Financial support:* In 2001–02, 202 students received support, including 42 fellowships with full and partial tuition reimbursements available (averaging $10,299 per year), 161 research assistantships with full and partial tuition reimbursements available (averaging $17,268 per year), 114 teaching assistantships with full tuition reimbursements available (averaging $14,068 per year); career-related internships or fieldwork, Federal Work-Study, institutionally sponsored loans, scholarships/grants, traineeships, and tuition waivers (full and partial) also available. Support available to part-time students. Financial award application deadline: 1/15; financial award applicants required to submit CSS PROFILE or FAFSA. In 2001, 76 master's, 25 doctorates awarded. *Degree program information:* Part-time programs available. Offers biomedical engineering (M Eng, MS, PhD); chemical engineering (M Eng, MS, PhD); civil engineering (M Eng, MS, PhD); computer science (M Eng, MS, PhD); electrical engineering (M Eng, MS, PhD); engineering (M Eng, MS, PhD); environmental engineering (M Eng, MS, PhD); management of technology (M Eng, MS, PhD); materials science (M Eng, MS, PhD); mechanical engineering (M Eng, MS, PhD). MS and PhD offered through the Graduate School. *Application deadline:* For fall admission, 1/15; for spring admission, 11/1. *Application fee:* $40. Electronic applications accepted. *Application Contact:* Dr. Arthur K. Overholser, Associate Dean, 615-343-3773, Fax: 615-343-8006, E-mail: knowles.a.overholser@vanderbilt.edu. *Dean,* Dr. Kenneth F. Galloway, 615-322-0720, Fax: 615-343-8006, E-mail: kenneth.f.galloway@vanderbilt.edu.

School of Medicine Offers clinical investigation (MS); medicine (MD, MPH, MS, PhD); public health (MPH).

School of Nursing *Degree program information:* Part-time and evening/weekend programs available. Postbaccalaureate distance learning degree programs offered (minimal on-campus study). Offers adult acute care nurse practitioner (MSN); adult/correctional health nurse practitioner (MSN); family nurse practitioner (MSN); gerontology nurse practitioner (MSN); health systems management (MSN); neonatal nurse practitioner (MSN); nurse midwifery (MSN); nursing science (PhD); occupational health/adult health nurse practitioner (MSN); pediatric nurse practitioner (MSN); psychiatric-mental health nurse practitioner (MSN); women's health nurse practitioner (MSN). Electronic applications accepted.

VANDERCOOK COLLEGE OF MUSIC, Chicago, IL 60616-3731

General Information Independent, coed, comprehensive institution. *Enrollment:* 134 full-time matriculated graduate/professional students (62 women), 52 part-time matriculated graduate/professional students (29 women). *Enrollment by degree level:* 186 master's. *Graduate faculty:* 9 full-time (4 women), 60 part-time/adjunct (14 women). *Tuition:* Full-time $3,430; part-time $290 per credit. *Required fees:* $325; $150 per term. Tuition and fees vary according to course level and program. *Graduate housing:* Rooms and/or apartments available on a first-come, first-served basis to single and married students. Typical cost: $1,118 (including board) for single students; $1,118 (including board) for married students. Housing application deadline: 6/1. *Student services:* Career counseling. *Library facilities:* Harry Ruppel Memorial Library. *Online resources:* library catalog, web page, access to other libraries' catalogs. *Collection:* 5,521 titles, 93 serial subscriptions.

Computer facilities: 20 computers available on campus for general student use. A campuswide network can be accessed from student residence rooms and from off campus. Internet access is available. *Web address:* http://www.vandercook.edu/.

General Application Contact: George Pierard, Director of Graduate Admissions, 312-225-6288 Ext. 237, Fax: 312-225-5211, E-mail: gpierard@vandercook.edu.

GRADUATE UNITS

Program in Music Education *Degree program information:* Part-time programs available. Offers music education (MM Ed). Offered during summer only.

VANGUARD UNIVERSITY OF SOUTHERN CALIFORNIA, Costa Mesa, CA 92626-6597

General Information Independent-religious, coed, comprehensive institution. *Enrollment:* 116 full-time matriculated graduate/professional students (86 women), 133 part-time matriculated graduate/professional students (61 women). *Enrollment by degree level:* 249 master's. *Graduate faculty:* 8 full-time (2 women), 14 part-time/adjunct (7 women). *Tuition:* Part-time $386 per unit. Tuition and fees vary according to course load and program. *Graduate housing:* Rooms and/or apartments available on a first-come, first-served basis to single and married students. Typical cost: $3,150 per year ($4,966 including board) for single students; $5,000 per year ($6,800 including board) for married students. Room and board charges vary according to board plan, campus/location and housing facility selected. Housing application deadline: 5/15. *Student services:* Campus employment opportunities, career counseling, free psychological counseling, international student services, low-cost health insurance, teacher training. *Library facilities:* O. Cope Budge Library. *Online resources:* library catalog, web page. *Collection:* 212,676 titles, 1,066 serial subscriptions, 2,241 audiovisual materials.

Computer facilities: 140 computers available on campus for general student use. A campuswide network can be accessed from student residence rooms and from off campus. Internet access is available. *Web address:* http://www.vanguard.edu/.

General Application Contact: Alison Bray, Assistant Director of Graduate Admissions, 714-556-3610 Ext. 5499, Fax: 714-957-9317, E-mail: abray@vanguard.edu.

GRADUATE UNITS

Program in Clinical Psychology Students: 49 full-time (38 women), 17 part-time (11 women); includes 21 minority (4 African Americans, 3 Asian Americans or Pacific Islanders, 13 Hispanic Americans, 1 Native American), 1 international. Average age 29. 40 applicants, 95% accepted, 30 enrolled. *Faculty:* 2 full-time (1 woman), 2 part-time/adjunct (1 woman). Expenses: Contact institution. *Financial support:* In 2001–02, 63 students received support, including 22 research assistantships (averaging $3,000 per year), 22 teaching assistantships (averaging $3,000 per year); scholarships/grants and tuition waivers (full) also available. Financial award application deadline: 4/15; financial award applicants required to submit FAFSA. In 2001, 10 degrees awarded. *Degree program information:* Part-time and evening/weekend programs available. Offers clinical psychology (MS). *Application deadline:* For fall admission, 4/1 (priority date). *Application fee:* $30. *Application Contact:* Tim Sorrick, Program Coordinator, 714-556-3610 Ext. 350, Fax: 714-662-5226, E-mail: gradpsychinfo@vanguard.edu. *Director,* Dr. Martin Harris, 714-556-3610 Ext. 409, Fax: 714-662-5226, E-mail: mharris@vanguard.edu.

Program in Education Students: 51 full-time (41 women), 46 part-time (32 women); includes 16 minority (6 Asian Americans or Pacific Islanders, 9 Hispanic Americans, 1 Native American) Average age 25. 77 applicants, 64% accepted. *Faculty:* 5 full-time (3 women), 13 part-time/adjunct (8 women). Expenses: Contact institution. *Financial support:* In 2001–02, 82 students received support, including 3 fellowships (averaging $20,000 per year), 2 research assistantships (averaging $1,000 per year); teaching assistantships, scholarships/grants and tuition waivers (partial) also available. Support available to part-time students. Financial award application deadline: 3/1; financial award applicants required to submit FAFSA. In 2001, 14 degrees awarded. *Degree program information:* Evening/weekend programs available. Offers education (MA). *Application deadline:* For fall admission, 4/9 (priority date); for spring admission, 10/15 (priority date). Applications are processed on a rolling basis. *Application fee:* $30. *Application Contact:* Michelle Romo, Graduate Education Coordinator, 714-556-3610 Ext. 310, Fax: 714-966-5495, E-mail: mromo@vanguard.edu. *Director,* Dr. Jeff Hittenberger, 714-556-3610 Ext. 442, Fax: 714-966-5495, E-mail: jhittenberger@vanguard.edu.

Programs in Religion Students: 16 full-time (7 women), 70 part-time (18 women); includes 29 minority (4 African Americans, 4 Asian Americans or Pacific Islanders, 21 Hispanic Americans), 1 international. Average age 34. 43 applicants, 91% accepted, 33 enrolled. *Faculty:* 3 full-time (0 women), 9 part-time/adjunct (2 women). Expenses: Contact institution. *Financial support:* In 2001–02, 83 students received support, including 10 research assistantships (averaging $1,680 per year); teaching assistantships, career-related internships or fieldwork, scholarships/grants, and tuition waivers (partial) also available. Support available to part-time students. Financial award application deadline: 3/1. In 2001, 6 degrees awarded. *Degree program information:* Part-time and evening/weekend programs available. Offers religion (MA); theological studies (MTS). *Application deadline:* For fall admission, 4/1 (priority date); for spring admission, 10/1. Applications are processed on a rolling basis. *Application fee:* $30. *Application Contact:* Phyllis Derksen, Graduate Coordinator, 714-556-3610 Ext. 248, Fax: 714-957-9317, E-mail: pderksen@vanguard.edu. *Director,* Dr. Frank Macchia, 714-556-3610 Ext. 238, Fax: 714-957-9317, E-mail: fmacchia@vanguard.edu.

VASSAR COLLEGE, Poughkeepsie, NY 12604

General Information Independent, coed, comprehensive institution. *Tuition:* Full-time $27,550; part-time $3,250 per course. *Graduate housing:* On-campus housing not available. *Student services:* Campus employment opportunities, campus safety program, career counseling, child daycare facilities, disabled student services, exercise/wellness program, free psychological counseling, low-cost health insurance, multicultural affairs office. *Library facilities:* Vassar College Libraries. *Online resources:* library catalog, web page, access to other libraries' catalogs. *Collection:* 803,021 titles, 5,887 serial subscriptions, 16,635 audiovisual materials. *Research affiliation:* Alfred P. Sloan Foundation (humanities, social sciences), Ford Program.

Computer facilities: 300 computers available on campus for general student use. A campuswide network can be accessed from student residence rooms and from off campus. Internet access and online class registration, Ethernet are available. *Web address:* http://www.vassar.edu/.

General Application Contact: Alexander M. Thompson, Dean of Studies, 914-437-5257, E-mail: thompson@vassar.edu.

GRADUATE UNITS

Graduate Programs Expenses: Contact institution. *Financial support:* Career-related internships or fieldwork available. *Degree program information:* Part-time programs available. Offers biology (MA, MS); chemistry (MA, MS). Applicants accepted only if enrolled in undergraduate programs at Vassar College. *Application fee:* $60. *Dean of Studies,* Alexander M. Thompson, 914-437-5257, E-mail: thompson@vassar.edu.

VERMONT COLLEGE, Montpelier, VT 05602

General Information Independent, coed, comprehensive institution. *Graduate faculty:* 16 full-time (10 women), 55 part-time/adjunct (32 women). *Web address:* http://www.tui.edu/vermontcollege/.

VERMONT LAW SCHOOL, South Royalton, VT 05068-0096

General Information Independent, coed, graduate-only institution. *Enrollment by degree level:* 479 first professional, 31 master's. *Graduate faculty:* 40 full-time (16 women), 37 part-time/adjunct (9 women). *Tuition:* Full-time $22,164; part-time $792 per credit. One-time fee: $75 full-time. Tuition and fees vary according to degree level. *Graduate housing:* Rooms and/or apartments available on a first-come, first-served basis to single and married students. Housing application deadline: 8/1. *Student services:* Campus employment opportunities, campus safety program, career counseling, child daycare facilities, exercise/wellness program, free psychological counseling, low-cost health insurance, multicultural affairs office, writing training. *Library facilities:* Cornell Library. *Online resources:* library catalog, access to other libraries' catalogs. *Collection:* 230,204 titles, 2,667 serial subscriptions, 3,905 audiovisual materials.

Computer facilities: 50 computers available on campus for general student use. A campuswide network can be accessed from off campus. Internet access is available. *Web address:* http://www.vermontlaw.edu/.

General Application Contact: Kathy Hartman, Assistant Dean for Admissions and Financial Aid, 802-763-8303 Ext. 2239, Fax: 802-763-7071, E-mail: admiss@vermontlaw.edu.

GRADUATE UNITS

Law School Students: 510 full-time (237 women); includes 59 minority (23 African Americans, 14 Asian Americans or Pacific Islanders, 19 Hispanic Americans, 3 Native Americans), 8 international. Average age 27. 781 applicants, 66% accepted, 185 enrolled. *Faculty:* 40 full-time (16 women), 37 part-time/adjunct (9 women). Expenses: Contact institution. *Financial support:* In 2001–02, 493 students received support, including 2 fellowships with full tuition reimbursements available (averaging $5,000 per year); career-related internships or fieldwork, Federal Work-Study, institutionally sponsored loans, scholarships/grants, and tuition waivers (partial) also available. Support available to part-time students. Financial award application deadline: 2/15; financial award applicants required to submit FAFSA. In 2001, 174 first professional degrees, 84 master's awarded. *Degree program information:* Part-time programs available. Offers law (JD, LL M, MSEL). *Application deadline:* For fall admission, 3/15 (priority date). Applications are processed on a rolling basis. *Application fee:* $50. Electronic applications accepted. *Application Contact:* Kathy Hartman, Assistant Dean for Admissions and Financial Aid, 802-763-8303 Ext. 2239, Fax: 802-763-7071, E-mail: admiss@vermontlaw.edu. *Dean,* L. Kinvin Wroth, 802-763-8303 Ext. 2237, Fax: 802-763-2663, E-mail: seider@vermontlaw.edu.

Environmental Law Center Students: 31 full-time; includes 3 minority (2 Asian Americans or Pacific Islanders, 1 Native American) Average age 28. 82 applicants, 78% accepted. *Faculty:* 10 full-time (3 women), 8 part-time/adjunct (4 women). Expenses: Contact institution. *Financial support:* In 2001–02, 25 students received support, including 2 fellowships with full tuition reimbursements available (averaging $5,000 per year); career-related internships or fieldwork, Federal Work-Study, institutionally sponsored loans, scholarships/grants, and tuition waivers (partial) also available. Support available to part-time students. Financial award application deadline: 2/15; financial award applicants required to submit FAFSA. *Degree program information:* Part-time programs available. Offers environmental law (LL M, MSEL). *Application deadline:* For fall admission, 3/15 (priority date). Applications are processed on a rolling basis. *Application fee:* $50. *Application Contact:* Anne Mansfield, Assistant Director, 802-763-8303 Ext. 2338, Fax: 802-763-2940, E-mail: elcinfo@vermontlaw.edu. *Director,* Karin Sheldon, 802-763-8303 Ext. 2201, Fax: 802-763-2490, E-mail: elcinfo@vermontlaw.edu.

VICTORIA UNIVERSITY, Toronto, ON M5S 1K7, Canada

General Information Independent-religious, coed, graduate-only institution. *Enrollment by degree level:* 133 first professional, 4 master's, 45 doctoral, 25 other advanced degrees. *Graduate faculty:* 12 full-time (4 women), 10 part-time/adjunct (4 women). *International tuition:* $10,000 full-time. Tuition, province resident: full-time $4,968. *Required fees:* $940. Tuition and fees vary according to course load. *Graduate housing:* Rooms and/or apartments guaranteed to single students and available on a first-come, first-served basis to married students. Typical cost: $6,965 (including board) for single students; $8,000 per year for married students. Housing application deadline: 7/1. *Student services:* Campus employment opportunities, campus safety program, career counseling, free psychological counseling, international student services, teacher training, writing training. *Library facilities:* Emmanuel Library plus 2 others. *Online resources:* library catalog, web page, access to other libraries' catalogs. *Collection:* 9 million titles, 36,636 serial subscriptions.

Computer facilities: 14 computers available on campus for general student use. A campuswide network can be accessed from student residence rooms and from off campus. Internet access and online class registration are available. *Web address:* http://vicu.utoronto.ca/.

General Application Contact: Gerald T. Sheppard, Director for Advanced Degree Studies, Fax: 416-585-4516, E-mail: g.sheppard@utoronto.ca.

GRADUATE UNITS

Emmanuel College *Degree program information:* Part-time programs available. Offers theology (M Div, MA, MPS, MRE, MTS, Th M, D Min, PhD, Th D).

VILLA JULIE COLLEGE, Stevenson, MD 21153

General Information Independent, coed, comprehensive institution. *Enrollment:* 78 part-time matriculated graduate/professional students (33 women). *Enrollment by degree level:* 78 master's. *Graduate faculty:* 8 full-time (1 woman), 5 part-time/adjunct (0 women). *Tuition:* Part-time $385 per credit. *Required fees:* $100 per semester. One-time fee: $25 part-time. Part-time tuition and fees vary according to degree level. *Graduate housing:* On-campus housing not available. *Student services:* Career counseling, international student services. *Library facilities:* Villa Julie College Library. *Online resources:* library catalog, web page, access to other libraries' catalogs. *Collection:* 124,417 titles, 720 serial subscriptions, 2,288 audiovisual materials.

Computer facilities: 230 computers available on campus for general student use. A campuswide network can be accessed from student residence rooms and from off campus. Internet access is available. *Web address:* http://www.vjc.edu/.

General Application Contact: Judith B. Snyder, Admissions and Enrollment Services, 410-653-6400, Fax: 410-653-6405, E-mail: jsnyder@atec.vjc.edu.

GRADUATE UNITS

School of Graduate and Professional Studies Average age 35. *Faculty:* 6 full-time (1 woman), 6 part-time/adjunct (1 woman). Expenses: Contact institution. In 2001, 18 degrees awarded. *Degree program information:* Part-time and evening/weekend programs available. Offers Advanced Information Technologies (MS); Business and Technology Management (MS); E-Commerce (MS). *Application deadline:* For fall admission, 8/1; for spring admission, 12/31. Applications are processed on a rolling basis. *Application fee:* $25. *Application Contact:* Judith B. Snyder, Admissions and Enrollment Services, 410-653-6400, Fax: 410-653-6405, E-mail: jsnyder@atec.vjc.edu. *Dean,* Dr. Jean Blosser, 410-653-6400, Fax: 410-653-6405, E-mail: masters@vjc.edu.

VILLANOVA UNIVERSITY, Villanova, PA 19085-1699

General Information Independent-religious, coed, comprehensive institution. CGS member. *Enrollment:* 1,182 full-time matriculated graduate/professional students (568 women), 1,565 part-time matriculated graduate/professional students (701 women). *Enrollment by degree level:* 836 first professional, 1,876 master's, 35 doctoral. *Tuition:* Part-time $340 per credit. One-time fee: $115 full-time. Tuition and fees vary according to program. *Graduate housing:* On-campus housing not available. *Student services:* Career counseling, free psychological counseling, international student services, low-cost health insurance, multicultural affairs office. *Library facilities:* Falvey Library plus 2 others. *Online resources:* library catalog, web page, access to other libraries' catalogs. *Collection:* 1 million titles, 5,338 serial subscriptions, 8,000 audiovisual materials.

Computer facilities: 800 computers available on campus for general student use. A campuswide network can be accessed from student residence rooms and from off campus. Internet access and online class registration are available. *Web address:* http://www.villanova.edu/.

General Application Contact: Dr. Gerald Long, Dean, Graduate School of Liberal Arts and Sciences, 610-519-7090, Fax: 610-519-7096.

GRADUATE UNITS

College of Commerce and Finance Students: 97 full-time (39 women), 715 part-time (308 women); includes 46 minority (14 African Americans, 26 Asian Americans or Pacific Islanders, 6 Hispanic Americans), 6 international. Average age 32. 365 applicants, 84% accepted. *Faculty:* 69 full-time (17 women), 44 part-time/adjunct (11 women). Expenses: Contact institution. *Financial support:* In 2001–02, 22 research assistantships with tuition reimbursements (averaging $9,870 per year) were awarded Support available to part-time students. Financial award application deadline: 3/15. In 2001, 230 degrees awarded. *Degree program information:* Part-time and evening/weekend programs available. Postbaccalaureate distance learning degree programs offered. Offers accounting and professional consultancy (M Ac); business administration (MBA); commerce and finance (EMBA, LL M in Tax, M Ac, MBA, MT); executive business administration (EMBA). *Application deadline:* Applications are processed on a rolling basis. *Application fee:* $40. Electronic applications accepted. *Application Contact:*

Villanova University (continued)

Dr. Mohammad Najdawi, Director, Graduate Studies in Business, 610-519-4336, Fax: 610-519-6273, E-mail: m.najdawi@villanova.edu. *Dean*, Dr. Thomas F. Monahan, 610-519-4330, Fax: 610-519-7864.

College of Engineering Students: 80 full-time (19 women), 158 part-time (29 women); includes 24 minority (4 African Americans, 16 Asian Americans or Pacific Islanders, 4 Hispanic Americans), 51 international. Average age 26. 201 applicants, 60% accepted, 56 enrolled. *Faculty:* 51 full-time (4 women), 17 part-time/adjunct (0 women). Expenses: Contact institution. *Financial support:* In 2001–02, 58 students received support, including 10 research assistantships with full tuition reimbursements available (averaging $10,265 per year), 31 teaching assistantships with full tuition reimbursements available (averaging $10,265 per year); Federal Work-Study, scholarships/grants, and tuition waivers (full and partial) also available. Support available to part-time students. In 2001, 65 degrees awarded. *Degree program information:* Part-time and evening/weekend programs available. Offers chemical engineering (M Ch E); civil engineering (MCE); composite engineering (Certificate); computer engineering (MSCE); electrical engineering (MSEE); engineering (M Ch E, MCE, MME, MSCE, MSEE, MSTE, MSWREE, Certificate); machinery dynamics (Certificate); manufacturing (Certificate); mechanical engineering (MME); thermofluid systems (Certificate); transportation engineering (MSTE); water resources and environmental engineering (MSWREE). *Application deadline:* For fall admission, 8/1 (priority date); for spring admission, 12/1. Applications are processed on a rolling basis. *Application fee:* $40. Electronic applications accepted. *Dean*, Barry C. Johnson, 610-519-4940, Fax: 610-519-4941, E-mail: barry.johnson@villanova.edu.

College of Nursing Students: 44 full-time (34 women), 104 part-time (99 women); includes 13 minority (5 African Americans, 7 Asian Americans or Pacific Islanders, 1 Hispanic American) Average age 35. 48 applicants, 63% accepted, 30 enrolled. *Faculty:* 15 full-time (all women). Expenses: Contact institution. *Financial support:* In 2001–02, 38 students received support, including 4 teaching assistantships with full tuition reimbursements available (averaging $10,265 per year); institutionally sponsored loans, scholarships/grants, and traineeships also available. Financial award application deadline: 3/1. In 2001, 41 degrees awarded. *Degree program information:* Part-time programs available. Offers adult nurse practitioner (MSN, Post Master's Certificate); clinical case management (MSN, Post Master's Certificate); geriatric nurse practitioner (MSN, Post Master's Certificate); health care administration (MSN); nurse anesthetist (MSN, Post Master's Certificate); nursing education (MSN, Post Master's Certificate); pediatric nurse practitioner (MSN, Post Master's Certificate). *Application deadline:* For fall admission, 7/1 (priority date); for spring admission, 12/1 (priority date). Applications are processed on a rolling basis. *Application fee:* $25. *Graduate Director*, Dr. Claire Manfredi, 610-519-4907, Fax: 610-519-7650, E-mail: claire.manfredi@villanova.edu.

Graduate School of Liberal Arts and Sciences Students: 271 full-time (161 women), 586 part-time (315 women); includes 46 minority (19 African Americans, 9 Asian Americans or Pacific Islanders, 18 Hispanic Americans), 170 international. Average age 30. 674 applicants, 50% accepted. Expenses: Contact institution. *Financial support:* Fellowships, research assistantships, teaching assistantships, career-related internships or fieldwork, Federal Work-Study, and scholarships/grants available. Support available to part-time students. Financial award applicants required to submit FAFSA. In 2001, 273 master's, 2 doctorates awarded. *Degree program information:* Part-time and evening/weekend programs available. Offers applied statistics (MS); biology (MA, MS); chemistry (MS); classical studies (MA); community counseling (MS); computing sciences (MS); counseling and human relations (MS); criminal justice administration (MS); educational leadership (MA); elementary school counseling (MS); elementary teacher education (MA); English (MA); history (MA); human resource development (MS); Latin (MA); liberal arts and sciences (MA, MPA, MS, PhD); liberal studies (MA); mathematical sciences (MA); philosophy (MA, PhD); political science (MA, MPA); psychology (MS); public administration (MPA); secondary administration (MS); secondary school counseling (MS); secondary teacher education (MA); Spanish (MA); theatre (MA); theology (MA). *Application deadline:* For fall admission, 8/1 (priority date); for spring admission, 12/1. *Application fee:* $40. *Dean*, Dr. Gerald Long, 610-519-7090, Fax: 610-519-7096.

School of Law 1,789 applicants, 47% accepted, 257 enrolled. Expenses: Contact institution. *Financial support:* In 2001–02, 208 students received support, including 107 research assistantships; career-related internships or fieldwork, Federal Work-Study, institutionally sponsored loans, and scholarships/grants also available. Support available to part-time students. Financial award application deadline: 3/15; financial award applicants required to submit FAFSA. In 2001, 233 first professional degrees, 39 master's awarded. Offers law (JD, LL M in Tax, MT); taxation (LL M in Tax, MT). *Application deadline:* For fall admission, 3/1. Applications are processed on a rolling basis. *Application fee:* $75. Electronic applications accepted. *Application Contact:* David P. Pallozzi, Assistant Dean of Admissions, 610-519-7010, Fax: 610-519-6291, E-mail: admissions@law.villanova.edu. *Dean*, Mark A. Sargent, 610-519-7007, Fax: 610-519-6472.

See in-depth description on page 1283.

VIRGINIA COMMONWEALTH UNIVERSITY, Richmond, VA 23284-9005

General Information State-supported, coed, university. CGS member. *Enrollment:* 3,840 full-time matriculated graduate/professional students (2,337 women), 2,119 part-time matriculated graduate/professional students (1,367 women). *Enrollment by degree level:* 1,461 first professional, 3,473 master's, 756 doctoral, 222 other advanced degrees. Tuition, state resident: full-time $4,276; part-time $238 per credit. Tuition, nonresident: full-time $12,672; part-time $704 per credit. *Required fees:* $1,167; $43 per credit. *Graduate housing:* Room and/or apartments available on a first-come, first-served basis to single students; on-campus housing not available to married students. *Student services:* Campus employment opportunities, campus safety program, career counseling, disabled student services, exercise/wellness program, free psychological counseling, grant writing training, international student services, low-cost health insurance, multicultural affairs office, teacher training, writing training. *Library facilities:* James Branch Cabell and Tompkins-McCaw Library. *Online resources:* library catalog, web page, access to other libraries' catalogs. *Collection:* 1.2 million titles, 18,315 serial subscriptions, 39,090 audiovisual materials. *Research affiliation:* Center for Innovative Technology (biotechnology), Virginia Biotechnology Research Park, Theatre Virginia (equity theatre).

Computer facilities: 900 computers available on campus for general student use. A campuswide network can be accessed from student residence rooms and from off campus. *Web address:* http://www.vcu.edu/.

General Application Contact: Dr. Sherry T. Sandkam, Associate Dean, 804-828-6916, Fax: 804-828-6949, E-mail: ssandkam@grd1.grd.vcu.edu.

GRADUATE UNITS

Medical College of Virginia-Professional Programs Students: 1,402 full-time, 47 part-time; includes 463 minority (101 African Americans, 334 Asian Americans or Pacific Islanders, 24 Hispanic Americans, 4 Native Americans) Expenses: Contact institution. *Financial support:* Fellowships, research assistantships, teaching assistantships, career-related internships or fieldwork, Federal Work-Study, institutionally sponsored loans, and tuition waivers (full and partial) available. In 2001, 358 degrees awarded. *Degree program information:* Part-time programs available. Offers medicine (DDS, MD, Pharm D, MPH, MS, PhD, CBHS). *Application deadline:* Applications are processed on a rolling basis. *Vice President for Health Sciences and Dean, School of Medicine*, Dr. Hermes A. Kontos, 804-828-9771, Fax: 804-828-8002, E-mail: hakontos@vcu.edu.

School of Dentistry Students: 315 full-time, 5 part-time; includes 84 minority (18 African Americans, 57 Asian Americans or Pacific Islanders, 9 Hispanic Americans) 698 applicants, 14% accepted, 86 enrolled. Expenses: Contact institution. *Financial support:* Fellowships available. In 2001, 86 degrees awarded. Offers dentistry (DDS). *Application deadline:* For fall admission, 1/1. *Application fee:* $70. Electronic applications accepted. *Application Contact:* Dr. Marshall P. Brownstein, Assistant Dean of Student Affairs and Admissions, 804-828-9196, Fax: 804-828-5288, E-mail: mbrownstein@den1.den.vcu.edu. *Dean*, Dr. Ronald J. Hunt, 804-828-9183, Fax: 804-828-6072, E-mail: lmhunt@den..den.vcu.edu.

School of Medicine Students: 689 full-time; includes 229 minority (47 African Americans, 171 Asian Americans or Pacific Islanders, 9 Hispanic Americans, 2 Native Americans) 3,628 applicants, 11% accepted, 181 enrolled. Expenses: Contact institution. *Financial support:* Fellowships, research assistantships, teaching assistantships, career-related internships or fieldwork, Federal Work-Study, institutionally sponsored loans, and tuition waivers (full and partial) available. In 2001, 172 degrees awarded. Offers medicine (MD, MPH, MS, PhD, CBHS). *Application deadline:* For fall admission, 11/15. Applications are processed on a rolling basis. *Application fee:* $80. Electronic applications accepted. *Application Contact:* Dr. Cynthia M. Heldberg, Associate Dean, Admissions, 804-828-9629, Fax: 804-828-1246, E-mail: heldberg@som1.vcu.edu. *Vice President for Health Sciences and Dean, School of Medicine*, Dr. Hermes A. Kontos, 804-828-9771, Fax: 804-828-8002, E-mail: hakontos@vcu.edu.

School of Pharmacy Students: 384 full-time, 21 part-time; includes 150 minority (46 African Americans, 96 Asian Americans or Pacific Islanders, 7 Hispanic Americans, 1 Native American) 265 applicants, 45% accepted. Expenses: Contact institution. *Financial support:* Fellowships, research assistantships, teaching assistantships, institutionally sponsored loans available. Financial award application deadline: 3/1. In 2001, 97 degrees awarded. *Degree program information:* Part-time programs available. Offers pharmacy (Pharm D, MS, PhD). *Application deadline:* Applications are processed on a rolling basis. *Application fee:* $105. *Application Contact:* Betty B. Dobbie, Assistant to Dean, Admissions, 804-828-3001, Fax: 804-828-7436, E-mail: bbdobbie@vcu.edu. *Dean*, Dr. Victor A. Yanchick, 804-828-3006, Fax: 804-827-0002, E-mail: vayanchi@vcu.edu.

School of Graduate Studies Students: 2,448 full-time, 2,097 part-time. 4,699 applicants, 59% accepted. *Faculty:* 937. Expenses: Contact institution. *Financial support:* Fellowships, research assistantships, teaching assistantships, career-related internships or fieldwork, Federal Work-Study, institutionally sponsored loans, scholarships/grants, and tuition waivers (full and partial) available. Support available to part-time students. Financial award applicants required to submit FAFSA. In 2001, 1,129 master's, 104 doctorates awarded. *Degree program information:* Part-time and evening/weekend programs available. Offers interdisciplinary studies (MIS). *Application fee:* $30. *Application Contact:* Dr. Sherry T. Sandkam, Associate Dean, 804-828-6916, Fax: 804-828-6949, E-mail: ssandkam@vcu.edu. *Interim Dean, Graduate Studies*, Dr. Albert T. Sneden, 804-828-1674, Fax: 804-828-6949, E-mail: atsneden@vcu.edu.

Center for Environmental Studies Average age 33. 4 applicants, 50% accepted. Expenses: Contact institution. Offers environmental communication (MIS); environmental health (MIS); environmental policy (MIS); environmental sciences (MIS). *Application fee:* $30. *Application Contact:* Andrew Lacatell, Assistant Director, 804-828-7202, Fax: 804-828-0503, E-mail: adlacate@vcu.edu. *Director*, Dr. Gregory C. Garman, 804-828-7202, Fax: 804-828-0503, E-mail: gcgarman@vcu.edu.

Center for Public Policy Students: 20 full-time, 80 part-time; includes 33 minority (29 African Americans, 4 Asian Americans or Pacific Islanders) 38 applicants, 76% accepted. Expenses: Contact institution. *Financial support:* Fellowships, career-related internships or fieldwork and Federal Work-Study available. Support available to part-time students. Financial award applicants required to submit FAFSA. In 2001, 6 degrees awarded. Offers public policy and administration (PhD). *Application deadline:* For fall admission, 3/15. *Application fee:* $30. *Application Contact:* Dr. Melvin I. Urofsky, Graduate Program Director, 804-828-8033, Fax: 804-828-6838, E-mail: murofsky@vcu.edu. *Director*, Dr. Robert D. Holsworth, 804-828-8033, Fax: 804-828-6838, E-mail: rholswor@vcu.edu.

College of Humanities and Sciences Students: 406 full-time, 292 part-time; includes 139 minority (84 African Americans, 47 Asian Americans or Pacific Islanders, 6 Hispanic Americans, 2 Native Americans) 1,040 applicants, 35% accepted. Expenses: Contact institution. *Financial support:* Fellowships, research assistantships, teaching assistantships, career-related internships or fieldwork, Federal Work-Study, institutionally sponsored loans, scholarships/grants, and tuition waivers (full and partial) available. Support available to part-time students. In 2001, 192 master's, 24 doctorates, 20 other advanced degrees awarded. *Degree program information:* Part-time and evening/weekend programs available. Offers account management (MS); account planning (MS); applied mathematics (MS); applied physics (MS); applied social research (CASR); art direction (MS); biology (MS); chemistry (MS, PhD); clinical psychology (PhD); copywriting (MS); counseling psychology (PhD); creative writing (MFA); criminal justice (MS, CCJA); forensic science (MS); general psychology (PhD); history (MA); humanities and sciences (MA, MFA, MPA, MS, MURP, PhD, CASR, CCJA, CPM, CURP, Certificate); literature (MA); mass communications (MS); mathematics (MS); operations research (MS); physics (MS); political science and public administration (MPA); public management (CPM); sociology (MS); statistics (MS, Certificate); urban planning (MURP); urban revitalization (CURP); writing and rhetoric (MA). *Application fee:* $30. *Application Contact:* Dr. Albert T. Sneden, Interim Dean, Graduate Studies, 804-828-1674, Fax: 804-828-6949, E-mail: atsneden@vcu.edu. *Dean*, Dr. Stephen D. Gottfredson, 804-828-1674, Fax: 804-828-2171, E-mail: sdgottfr@vcu.edu.

School of Allied Health Professions Students: 452 full-time, 190 part-time; includes 152 minority (92 African Americans, 45 Asian Americans or Pacific Islanders, 12 Hispanic Americans, 3 Native Americans) 504 applicants, 65% accepted. Expenses: Contact institution. *Financial support:* Fellowships, research assistantships, teaching assistantships, career-related internships or fieldwork and tuition waivers (full and partial) available. In 2001, 179 master's, 3 doctorates, 13 other advanced degrees awarded. *Degree program information:* Part-time programs available. Offers advanced physical therapy (MS); aging studies (CAS); allied health professions (MHA, MS, MSHA, MSNA, MSOT, PhD, CAS, CPC); anatomy and physical therapy (PhD); clinical laboratory sciences (MS); entry-level physical therapy (MS); executive health administration (MSHA); gerontology (MS); health administration (MHA); health services organization and research (PhD); nurse anesthesia (MSNA); occupational therapy (MS, MSOT); patient counseling (MS, CPC); physiology and physical therapy (PhD); rehabilitation counseling (MS, CPC). *Application fee:* $30. *Application Contact:* Monica L. White, Director of Student Services, 804-828-7247, Fax: 804-828-8656, E-mail: mlwhite@hso.vcu.edu. *Interim Dean*, Dr. Cecil B. Drain, 804-828-7247, Fax: 804-828-8656, E-mail: cdrain@gems.vcu.edu.

School of Business Students: 157 full-time, 384 part-time; includes 133 minority (57 African Americans, 69 Asian Americans or Pacific Islanders, 6 Hispanic Americans, 1 Native American) 363 applicants, 63% accepted. Expenses: Contact institution. *Financial support:* Fellowships, research assistantships, teaching assistantships, Federal Work-Study, institutionally sponsored loans, and tuition waivers (full and partial) available. Support available to part-time students. Financial award application deadline: 3/15. In 2001, 164 master's, 1 doctorate awarded. *Degree program information:* Part-time and evening/weekend programs available. Offers accountancy (MS, PhD); accounting (M Acc, PhD); business administration (MBA, PhD); business administration and management (MBA, PhD); decision sciences (MS); economics (MA, MS); finance, insurance, and real estate (MS); human resources management and industrial relations (MS); information systems (MS, PhD); marketing and business law (MS); real estate and urban land development (MS, Certificate); tax (MS); taxation (M Tax). *Application deadline:* Applications are processed on a rolling basis. *Application fee:* $30. *Application Contact:* Tracy Green, Graduate Program Director, 804-828-1741, Fax: 804-828-7174, E-mail: tsgreen@vcu.edu. *Dean*, Dr. Michael L. Sesnowitz, 804-828-0072, Fax: 804-828-1600, E-mail: msesnowi@vcu.edu.

School of Education Students: 271 full-time, 842 part-time; includes 180 minority (151 African Americans, 16 Asian Americans or Pacific Islanders, 10 Hispanic Americans, 3 Native Americans) 303 applicants, 82% accepted. *Faculty:* 60. Expenses: Contact institution. *Financial support:* Fellowships, research assistantships, teaching assistantships, career-related internships or fieldwork, Federal Work-Study, institutionally sponsored loans, and tuition waivers (full and partial) available. Support available to part-time students. Financial award application deadline: 3/1. In 2001, 296 master's, 13 doctorates, 12 other advanced degrees awarded. *Degree program information:* Part-time programs available. Offers administration and supervision (M Ed); adult education and human resource development (M Ed); counselor education (M Ed); curriculum and instruction (M Ed); early childhood (M Ed); early education (MT); education (M Ed, MS, MT, PhD, Certificate); emotionally disturbed (M Ed, MT); learning disabilities (M Ed); mentally retarded (M Ed, MT); middle education (MT); physical education (MS); reading (M Ed); recreation, parks and tourism (MS); secondary education (MT, Certificate); severely/profoundly handicapped (M Ed); special education (MT). *Application fee:* $30. *Application Contact:* Dr. Michael D. Davis, Director, Graduate Studies, 804-828-6530, Fax: 804-827-0676, E-mail: mddavis@vcu.edu. *Interim Dean*, Dr. Richard J. Rezba, 804-828-3382, Fax: 804-828-1323.

School of Engineering Students: 17 full-time, 5 part-time; includes 7 minority (1 African American, 6 Asian Americans or Pacific Islanders) 45 applicants, 67% accepted. Expenses: Contact institution. In 2001, 1 degree awarded. Offers biomedical engineering (MS, PhD); computer science (MS); engineering (MS, PhD). *Application deadline:* For fall admission, 2/15; for spring admission, 11/15. *Application fee:* $30. *Application Contact:* Dr. Gerald E. Miller, Associate Dean for Graduate Affairs, 804-828-7263, Fax: 804-828-4454, E-mail: gemiller@vcu.edu. *Dean*, Dr. Robert J. Mattauch, 804-828-0190, Fax: 804-828-9866, E-mail: rjmatta@vcu.edu.

School of Medicine Graduate Programs Students: 348 (181 women); includes 110 minority (29 African Americans, 68 Asian Americans or Pacific Islanders, 9 Hispanic Americans, 4 Native Americans) 918 applicants, 59% accepted. Expenses: Contact institution. *Financial support:* Fellowships, research assistantships, teaching assistantships, career-related internships or fieldwork, Federal Work-Study, institutionally sponsored loans, and tuition waivers (full) available. In 2001, 53 master's, 36 doctorates, 23 other advanced degrees awarded. *Degree program information:* Part-time programs available. Offers anatomy (MS, PhD, CBHS); anatomy and physical therapy (PhD); biochemistry (PhD); biochemistry and molecular biophysics (MS, CBHS); biostatistics (MS, PhD); genetic counseling (MS); human genetics (PhD, CBHS); medicine (MPH, MS, PhD, CBHS); microbiology (PhD); microbiology and immunology (MS, CBHS); molecular biology and genetics (PhD); neurosciences (PhD); pathology (MS, PhD); pharmacology (PhD, CBHS); pharmacology and toxicology (MS); physiology (MS, PhD, CBHS); preventive medicine (MPH). *Application fee:* $30. *Application Contact:* Dr. Jan F. Chlebowski, Associate Dean for Graduate Education, 804-828-1023, Fax: 804-828-1473, E-mail: jfchlebo@vcu.edu. *Vice President for Health Sciences and Dean, School of Medicine*, Dr. Hermes A. Kontos, 804-828-9771, Fax: 804-828-8002, E-mail: hakontos@vcu.edu.

School of Nursing Students: 114 full-time, 106 part-time; includes 37 minority (15 African Americans, 17 Asian Americans or Pacific Islanders, 4 Hispanic Americans, 1 Native American) 117 applicants, 84% accepted. Expenses: Contact institution. *Financial support:* Fellowships, research assistantships, teaching assistantships, career-related internships or fieldwork and institutionally sponsored loans available. In 2001, 56 master's, 5 doctorates, 5 other advanced degrees awarded. *Degree program information:* Part-time and evening/weekend programs available. Offers adult health nursing (MS); child health nursing (MS); family health nursing (MS); health system (PhD); immuno competence (PhD); nurse practitioner (Certificate); nursing administration (MS); psychiatric-mental health nursing (MS); risk and resilience (PhD); women's health nursing (MS). *Application deadline:* For fall admission, 2/1 (priority date). *Application fee:* $30. *Application Contact:* Susan Lipp, Admissions Counselor, 804-828-5171, Fax: 804-828-7743, E-mail: slipp@vcu.edu. *Dean*, Dr. Nancy F. Langston, 804-828-5174, Fax: 804-828-7743, E-mail: nflangst@vcu.edu.

School of Pharmacy Graduate Programs Students: 36 full-time, 13 part-time; includes 28 minority (3 African Americans, 24 Asian Americans or Pacific Islanders, 1 Native American) 331 applicants, 51% accepted. Expenses: Contact institution. *Financial support:* Fellowships, research assistantships, teaching assistantships, institutionally sponsored loans available. In 2001, 3 master's, 8 doctorates awarded. Offers pharmacy (Pharm D, MS, PhD). *Application deadline:* For fall admission, 6/1. *Application fee:* $30. *Application Contact:* Dr. Howard T. Karnes, Associate Dean, 804-828-3819, Fax: 804-828-7436, E-mail: htkarnes@vcu.edu. *Dean*, Dr. Victor A. Yanchick, 804-828-3006, Fax: 804-827-0002, E-mail: vayanchi@vcu.edu.

School of Social Work Students: 294 full-time, 255 part-time; includes 114 minority (90 African Americans, 14 Asian Americans or Pacific Islanders, 10 Hispanic Americans) 483 applicants, 80% accepted. Expenses: Contact institution. *Financial support:* Fellowships, research assistantships, teaching assistantships, career-related internships or fieldwork, Federal Work-Study, institutionally sponsored loans, and tuition waivers (full and partial) available. Support available to part-time students. In 2001, 204 master's, 2 doctorates awarded. Offers social work (MSW, PhD). *Application fee:* $30. *Application Contact:* Joseph M. Mason, Associate Dean, 804-828-0703, Fax: 804-828-0716, E-mail: jamasonl@vcu.edu. *Dean*, Dr. Frank R. Baskind, 804-828-1030, Fax: 804-828-0716, E-mail: fbaskind@saturn.vcu.edu.

School of the Arts Students: 154 full-time, 141 part-time; includes 49 minority (18 African Americans, 22 Asian Americans or Pacific Islanders, 8 Hispanic Americans, 1 Native American) 316 applicants, 45% accepted. Expenses: Contact institution. *Financial support:* Fellowships, teaching assistantships, career-related internships or fieldwork, Federal Work-Study, institutionally sponsored loans, and tuition waivers (full and partial) available. Support available to part-time students. In 2001, 50 master's, 4 doctorates awarded. *Degree program information:* Part-time programs available. Offers acting (MFA); art education (MAE); art history (MA, PhD); arts (MA, MAE, MFA, MM, PhD); ceramics (MFA); composition (MM); costume design (MFA); directing (MFA); education (MM); fibers (MFA); furniture design (MFA); glassworking (MFA); interior environment (MFA); jewelry/metalworking (MFA); painting (MFA); pedagogy (MFA); performance (MM); photography—film (MFA); printmaking (MFA); scene design/technical theater (MFA); sculpture (MFA); visual communication (MFA). *Application fee:* $30. *Application Contact:* Michael Drought, Graduate Program Director, 804-828-2787, Fax: 804-828-6469, E-mail: mhdrough@vcu.edu. *Dean*, Dr. Richard E. Toscan, 804-828-2787, Fax: 804-828-6469.

See in-depth description on page 1285.

VIRGINIA POLYTECHNIC INSTITUTE AND STATE UNIVERSITY, Blacksburg, VA 24061

General Information State-supported, coed, university. CGS member. *Enrollment:* 3,875 full-time matriculated graduate/professional students (1,466 women), 2,272 part-time matriculated graduate/professional students (1,207 women). *Enrollment by degree level:* 4,488 master's, 1,659 doctoral. *Graduate faculty:* 1,514 full-time. Tuition, state resident: part-time $241 per hour. Tuition, nonresident: part-time $406 per hour. Tuition and fees vary according to program. *Graduate housing:* Room and/or apartments available on a first-come, first-served basis to single students; on-campus housing not available to married students. Housing application deadline: 5/16. *Student services:* Campus employment opportunities, career counseling, free psychological counseling, international student services. *Library facilities:* Newman Library plus 4 others. *Online resources:* library catalog, web page. *Collection:* 2 million titles, 18,281 serial subscriptions, 17,510 audiovisual materials. *Research affiliation:* NASA–Langley Research Center, National Computational Science Alliance, Thomas Jefferson National Accelerator Facility, Japanese National Laboratory for High Energy Physics, Oak Ridge National Laboratories.

Computer facilities: A campuswide network can be accessed from student residence rooms and from off campus. Internet access and online class registration are available. *Web address:* http://www.vt.edu/.

General Application Contact: Graduate School Receptionist, 540-231-9563.

GRADUATE UNITS

Graduate School Students: 3,875 full-time (1,466 women), 2,272 part-time (1,207 women); includes 339 minority (185 African Americans, 82 Asian Americans or Pacific Islanders, 64 Hispanic Americans, 8 Native Americans), 1,404 international. 8,174 applicants, 32% accepted. *Faculty:* 1,514 full-time. Expenses: Contact institution. *Financial support:* In 2001–02, 350 fellowships with full tuition reimbursements, 920 research assistantships with full tuition reimbursements (averaging $13,000 per year), 1,280 teaching assistantships with full tuition reimbursements (averaging $12,100 per year) were awarded. Career-related internships or fieldwork, Federal Work-Study, institutionally sponsored loans, tuition waivers (full and partial), and unspecified assistantships also available. Support available to part-time students. In 2001, 1,413 master's, 334 doctorates, 46 other advanced degrees awarded. *Degree program information:* Part-time and evening/weekend programs available. *Application deadline:* For fall admission, 12/15 (priority date). Applications are processed on a rolling basis. *Application fee:* $45. Electronic applications accepted. *Acting Dean*, Dr. Joseph Merola, 540-231-7581, Fax: 540-231-3714, E-mail: jmerola@vt.edu.

College of Agriculture and Life Sciences Students: 193 full-time (84 women), 54 part-time (27 women); includes 20 minority (9 African Americans, 3 Asian Americans or Pacific Islanders, 8 Hispanic Americans), 59 international. 295 applicants, 37% accepted, 70 enrolled. Expenses: Contact institution. *Financial support:* In 2001–02, fellowships with full tuition reimbursements (averaging $17,000 per year), research assistantships with full tuition reimbursements (averaging $15,000 per year), teaching assistantships with full tuition reimbursements (averaging $15,000 per year) were awarded. Career-related internships or fieldwork, Federal Work-Study, institutionally sponsored loans, tuition waivers (full and partial), and unspecified assistantships also available. Support available to part-time students. Financial award application deadline: 4/1. In 2001, 55 master's, 21 doctorates awarded. *Degree program information:* Part-time and evening/weekend programs available. Offers agribusiness (MS); agricultural economics (MS); agriculture and life sciences (MS, PhD); animal science (MS, PhD); animal science, dairy (PhD); applied economics (MS); biochemistry (MS, PhD); cell and molecular biology (PhD); crop and soil environmental sciences (MS, PhD); dairy science (MS); developmental and international economics (PhD); econometrics (PhD); entomology (MS, PhD); food science and technology (MS, PhD); genetics (PhD); horticulture (MS, PhD); macro and micro economics (PhD); markets and industrial organizations (PhD); plant pathology (MS, PhD); plant physiology (MS, PhD); poultry science (MS, PhD); public and regional/urban economics (PhD); resource and environmental economics (PhD); weed science (MS, PhD). *Application deadline:* For fall admission, 12/1 (priority date). Applications are processed on a rolling basis. *Application fee:* $45. Electronic applications accepted. *Dean*, Dr. L. A. Swiger, 540-231-4152, Fax: 540-231-4163.

College of Architecture and Urban Studies *Degree program information:* Part-time and evening/weekend programs available. Postbaccalaureate distance learning degree programs offered (minimal on-campus study). Offers architecture (M Arch, MS); architecture and urban studies (M Arch, MLA, MPA, MPIA, MS, MURP, PhD, CAGS); environmental design and planning (PhD); landscape architecture (MLA); public administration and policy (MPA, PhD, CAGS); public and international affairs (MPIA); urban and regional planning (MURP). Electronic applications accepted.

College of Arts and Sciences Students: 858 full-time (331 women), 422 part-time (251 women); includes 117 minority (45 African Americans, 46 Asian Americans or Pacific Islanders, 21 Hispanic Americans, 5 Native Americans), 367 international. 2,263 applicants, 38% accepted, 549 enrolled. *Faculty:* 400 full-time (90 women), 10 part-time/adjunct (0 women). Expenses: Contact institution. *Financial support:* In 2001–02, 115 research assistantships, 500 teaching assistantships were awarded. Fellowships, career-related internships or fieldwork, Federal Work-Study, institutionally sponsored loans, tuition waivers (full and partial), and unspecified assistantships also available. Support available to part-time students. In 2001, 247 master's, 47 doctorates awarded. *Degree program information:* Part-time programs available. Offers applied mathematics (MS, PhD); applied physics (MS, PhD); arts administration (MFA); arts and sciences (MA, MFA, MIS, MS, PhD); bio-behavioral sciences (PhD); botany (MS, PhD); chemistry (MS, PhD); clinical psychology (PhD); computer science (MS, PhD); costume design (MFA); developmental psychology (PhD); ecology and evolutionary biology (MS, PhD); economics (MA, PhD); English (MA); genetics and developmental biology (MS, PhD); geography (MS); geological sciences (MS, PhD); geophysics (MS, PhD); history (MA); industrial/organizational psychology (PhD); information systems (MIS); lighting design (MFA); mathematical physics (MS, PhD); microbiology (MS, PhD); philosophy (MA); physics (MS, PhD); political science (MA); property management (MFA); psychology (MS); pure mathematics (MS, PhD); scenic design (MFA); science and technology studies (MS, PhD); sociology (MS, PhD); stage management (MFA); statistics (MS, PhD); technical theatre (MFA); zoology (MS, PhD). *Application fee:* $45. *Dean*, Dr. Lay Nam Chang, 540-231-5422, Fax: 540-231-3380, E-mail: laynam@vt.edu.

College of Engineering Students: 1,179 full-time (203 women), 452 part-time (85 women); includes 140 minority (44 African Americans, 63 Asian Americans or Pacific Islanders, 32 Hispanic Americans, 1 Native American), 699 international. 3,196 applicants, 36% accepted. *Faculty:* 263 full-time (19 women). Expenses: Contact institution. *Financial support:* In 2001–02, 106 fellowships, 639 research assistantships, 249 teaching assistantships were awarded. Career-related internships or fieldwork, Federal Work-Study, institutionally sponsored loans, tuition waivers (full and partial), and unspecified assistantships also available. Support available to part-time students. Financial award application deadline: 1/15. In 2001, 389 master's, 103 doctorates awarded. *Degree program information:* Part-time and evening/weekend programs available. Offers aerospace engineering (M Eng, MS, PhD); bio-process engineering (M Eng, MS, PhD); chemical engineering (MS, PhD); civil engineering (M Eng, MS, PhD); computer engineering (MS, PhD); electrical engineering (MS, PhD); engineering (M Eng, MEA, MS, PhD); engineering administration (MEA); engineering mechanics (M Eng, MS, PhD); environmental engineering (MS); environmental sciences and engineering (MS); food engineering (M Eng, MS, PhD); industrial engineering (M Eng, MS, PhD); land and water engineering (M Eng, MS, PhD); materials science and engineering (M Eng, MS, PhD); mechanical engineering (M Eng, MS, PhD); mining and minerals engineering (M Eng, MS, PhD); nonpoint source pollution control (M Eng, MS, PhD); ocean engineering (MS); operations research (M Eng, MS, PhD); systems engineering (M Eng, MS); watershed engineering (M Eng, MS, PhD); wood engineering (M Eng, MS, PhD). *Application deadline:* For fall admission, 12/1 (priority date). Applications are processed on a rolling basis. *Application fee:* $45. Electronic applications accepted. *Interim Dean*, Dr. Malcolm J. McPherson, 540-231-6641.

College of Human Resources and Education Students: 1,633; includes 258 minority (198 African Americans, 33 Asian Americans or Pacific Islanders, 23 Hispanic Americans, 4 Native Americans), 93 international. 642 applicants, 59% accepted. *Faculty:* 171 full-time (93 women). Expenses: Contact institution. *Financial support:* Fellowships, research assistantships, teaching assistantships, career-related internships or fieldwork, Federal Work-Study, tuition waivers (full and partial), and unspecified assistantships available. Financial award application deadline: 3/1. In 2001, 318 master's, 82 doctorates, 20 other advanced degrees awarded. *Degree program information:* Part-time and evening/weekend programs available. Offers administration and supervision of special education (Ed D, PhD, Ed S); adult and continuing education (MA Ed, MS Ed, Ed D, PhD, CAGS); adult development and aging (MS, PhD); adult learning and human resource development (MS, PhD); apparel business and economics (MS, PhD); apparel product design and analysis (MS, PhD); apparel quality analysis (MS, PhD); child development (MS, PhD); clinical exercise physiology (MS, PhD); community and international nutrition (MS, PhD); consumer studies (MS, PhD); curriculum and instruction (MA Ed, Ed D, PhD, Ed S); educational counseling (MA Ed, Ed D, PhD, Ed S); educational leadership (MA Ed, Ed D, PhD, CAGS); educational research and evaluation (PhD); family financial management (MS, PhD); family studies (MS, PhD); foods (MS, PhD); health and physical education (MS Ed); hospitality and tourism management (MS, PhD); household equipment (MS, PhD); housing (MS, PhD); human resources and education (MA Ed, MS, MS Ed, Ed D, PhD, CAGS, Ed S); interior design (MS, PhD); marriage and family therapy (MS, PhD); muscle physiology and biochemistry (MS, PhD); nutrition (MS, PhD); nutrition in sports and chronic disease (MS, PhD); resource management (MS, PhD); vocational-technical education (MS Ed, Ed D, PhD). *Application deadline:* For fall admission, 12/1 (priority date). Applications are processed on a rolling basis. *Application fee:* $45. Electronic applications accepted. *Application Contact:* Associate Dean, 540-231-5380. *Dean*, Dr. J. M. Johnson, 540-231-6779, Fax: 540-231-7157.

College of Natural Resources Students: 107 full-time (36 women), 15 part-time (4 women); includes 2 minority (1 African American, 1 Hispanic American), 21 international. Average age 30. 122 applicants, 40% accepted, 32 enrolled. *Faculty:* 61. Expenses: Contact institution. *Financial support:* In 2001–02, 110 students received support, including fellowships with tuition reimbursements available (averaging $24,000 per year), research assistantships with tuition reimbursements available (averaging $19,200 per year), teaching assistantships with tuition reimbursements available (averaging $19,200 per year); career-related internships or fieldwork, Federal Work-Study, institutionally sponsored loans, scholarships/grants, health care benefits, tuition waivers (full and partial), and unspecified assistantships also available. Financial award application deadline: 4/1. In 2001, 23 master's,

Virginia Polytechnic Institute and State University (continued)

9 doctorates awarded. Postbaccalaureate distance learning degree programs offered (no on-campus study). Offers fisheries and wildlife sciences (MS, PhD); forest biology (MF, MS, PhD); forest biometry (MF, MS, PhD); forest management/economics (MF, MS, PhD); forest products marketing (MF, MS, PhD); industrial forestry operations (MF, MS, PhD); natural resources (MF, MS, PhD); outdoor recreation (MF, MS, PhD); wood science and engineering (MF, MS, PhD). *Application deadline:* For fall admission, 12/1 (priority date). Applications are processed on a rolling basis. *Application fee:* $25. Electronic applications accepted. *Application Contact:* Arlice K. Banks, 540-231-7051, Fax: 540-231-7664, E-mail: arbanks@vt.edu. *Dean,* Gregory N. Brown, 540-231-5481, Fax: 540-231-7664, E-mail: browngn@vt.edu.

Pamplin College of Business Students: 209 full-time (83 women), 246 part-time (88 women); includes 48 minority (20 African Americans, 18 Asian Americans or Pacific Islanders, 9 Hispanic Americans, 1 Native American), 92 international. 446 applicants, 55% accepted. *Faculty:* 116. Expenses: Contact institution. *Financial support:* In 2001–02, 209 students received support, including 11 fellowships with full and partial tuition reimbursements available (averaging $4,000 per year), 2 research assistantships with full tuition reimbursements available, 47 teaching assistantships with full tuition reimbursements available; career-related internships or fieldwork, institutionally sponsored loans, tuition waivers (full and partial), and unspecified assistantships also available. Financial award application deadline: 3/1. In 2001, 137 master's, 5 doctorates awarded. *Degree program information:* Part-time and evening/weekend programs available. Postbaccalaureate distance learning degree programs offered (no on-campus study). Offers accounting and information systems (M Acct, PhD); business (M Acct, MBA, MS, PhD); business administration (PhD); business administration/finance (MS, PhD); business administration/management (PhD); business administration/marketing (MS, PhD); business information technology (MS, PhD). *Application deadline:* For fall admission, 2/1 (priority date). Applications are processed on a rolling basis. *Application fee:* $45. Electronic applications accepted. *Application Contact:* Susan V. Vest, Enrollment Services Coordinator, 540-231-6152, Fax: 540-231-4487, E-mail: mba_info@vt.edu. *Dean,* Dr. Richard E. Sorensen, 540-231-6601, Fax: 540-231-4487.

Virginia-Maryland Regional College of Veterinary Medicine Students: 431 full-time (334 women), 15 part-time (6 women); includes 29 minority (18 African Americans, 6 Asian Americans or Pacific Islanders, 5 Hispanic Americans), 29 international. 826 applicants, 13% accepted. *Faculty:* 93 full-time (18 women), 2 part-time/adjunct (both women). Expenses: Contact institution. *Financial support:* In 2001–02, 263 students received support; fellowships, research assistantships, unspecified assistantships available. In 2001, 90 first professional degrees, 17 master's, 5 doctorates awarded. *Degree program information:* Part-time and evening/weekend programs available. Offers veterinary medical sciences (MS, PhD); veterinary medicine (DVM, MS, PhD). *Dean,* Dr. Peter Eyre, 540-231-7666, E-mail: cvmpxe@vt.edu.

VIRGINIA STATE UNIVERSITY, Petersburg, VA 23806-0001

General Information State-supported, coed, comprehensive institution. *Enrollment:* 50 full-time matriculated graduate/professional students (35 women), 735 part-time matriculated graduate/professional students (549 women). *Graduate faculty:* 41 full-time (11 women), 5 part-time/adjunct (0 women). *Tuition, area resident:* Full-time $2,446; part-time $113 per credit hour. Tuition, state resident: full-time $8,814; part-time $420 per credit hour. *Required fees:* $1,724; $31 per credit hour. *Graduate housing:* Room and/or apartments available to single students; on-campus housing not available to married students. Housing application deadline: 5/1. *Student services:* International student services, low-cost health insurance. *Library facilities:* Johnston Memorial Library. *Online resources:* library catalog, web page, access to other libraries' catalogs. *Collection:* 282,353 titles, 1,150 serial subscriptions. *Research affiliation:* Swiss Institute Nuclear Research Laboratory (physics), NASA–Langley Research Center (physics), Brookhaven National Laboratory (physics), Los Alamos National Laboratory–Continuous Electron Beam Accelerator Facility (physics).

Computer facilities: 491 computers available on campus for general student use. A campuswide network can be accessed. Internet access is available. *Web address:* http://www.vsu.edu/.

General Application Contact: Dr. Wayne F. Virag, Dean, Graduate Studies, Research, and Outreach, 804-524-5985, Fax: 804-524-5104, E-mail: wvirag@vsu.edu.

GRADUATE UNITS

School of Graduate Studies, Research, and Outreach Students: 50 full-time (35 women), 735 part-time (549 women). *Faculty:* 41 full-time (11 women), 5 part-time/adjunct (0 women). Expenses: Contact institution. *Financial support:* In 2001–02, 23 students received support; fellowships, career-related internships or fieldwork and Federal Work-Study available. Financial award application deadline: 5/1. In 2001, 110 degrees awarded. *Degree program information:* Part-time and evening/weekend programs available. Offers biology (MS); engineering, science and technology (M Ed, MS); interdisciplinary studies (MIS); mathematics (MS); mathematics education (M Ed); physics (MS); psychology (MS). *Application deadline:* For fall admission, 8/15. Applications are processed on a rolling basis. *Application fee:* $25. *Dean, Graduate Studies, Research, and Outreach,* Dr. Wayne F. Virag, 804-524-5985, Fax: 804-524-5104, E-mail: wvirag@vsu.edu.

School of Business *Faculty:* 4 full-time (0 women). Expenses: Contact institution. *Financial support:* Fellowships, Federal Work-Study available. Financial award application deadline: 5/1. In 2001, 2 degrees awarded. *Degree program information:* Part-time programs available. Offers business (MA); economics and finance (MA). *Application deadline:* For fall admission, 8/15. Applications are processed on a rolling basis. *Application fee:* $25. *Application Contact:* Dr. Wayne F. Virag, Dean, Graduate Studies, Research, and Outreach, 804-524-5985, Fax: 804-524-5104, E-mail: wvirag@vsu.edu. *Dean,* Dr. Sadie Gregory, 804-524-5166, Fax: 804-524-5104, E-mail: sgregory@vsu.edu.

School of Liberal Arts and Education *Faculty:* 24 full-time (7 women), 5 part-time/adjunct (0 women). Expenses: Contact institution. *Financial support:* Fellowships, Federal Work-Study available. Financial award application deadline: 5/1. In 2001, 93 degrees awarded. *Degree program information:* Part-time and evening/weekend programs available. Offers education (M Ed, MS); educational administration and supervision (M Ed, MS); English (MA); guidance (M Ed, MS); history (MA); liberal arts and education (M Ed, MA, MS, CAGS); vocational technical education (M Ed, MS, CAGS). *Application deadline:* For fall admission, 8/15. Applications are processed on a rolling basis. *Application fee:* $25. *Application Contact:* Dr. Wayne F. Virag, Dean, Graduate Studies, Research, and Outreach, 804-524-5985, Fax: 804-524-5104, E-mail: wvirag@vsu.edu. *Dean,* Dr. Leon Bey, 804-524-5930, E-mail: lbeg@vsu.edu.

VIRGINIA UNION UNIVERSITY, Richmond, VA 23220-1170

General Information Independent-religious, coed, comprehensive institution. *Graduate housing:* Room and/or apartments available on a first-come, first-served basis to single students; on-campus housing not available to married students.

GRADUATE UNITS

School of Theology *Degree program information:* Part-time and evening/weekend programs available. Offers theology (M Div, D Min).

VITERBO UNIVERSITY, La Crosse, WI 54601-4797

General Information Independent-religious, coed, comprehensive institution. *Graduate housing:* Rooms and/or apartments available to single and married students. Housing application deadline: 4/2.

GRADUATE UNITS

Graduate Program in Education *Degree program information:* Part-time and evening/weekend programs available. Offers education (MA). Courses held on weekends and during summer.

Graduate Program in Nursing Students: 30 full-time (all women), 5 part-time (all women). Average age 33. 8 applicants, 100% accepted. *Faculty:* 3 full-time (all women), 4 part-time/adjunct (all women). Expenses: Contact institution. *Financial support:* In 2001–02, 12 students received support. Institutionally sponsored loans, scholarships/grants, and traineeships available. Financial award application deadline: 6/1; financial award applicants required to submit FAFSA. In 2001, 16 degrees awarded. *Degree program information:* Part-time programs available. Offers nursing (MSN). *Application deadline:* For spring admission, 3/1 (priority date). Applications are processed on a rolling basis. *Application fee:* $25. *Application Contact:* School of Nursing Office, 608-796-3671. *Director,* Dr. Bonnie Nesbitt, 608-796-3688, Fax: 608-796-3668, E-mail: bjnesbitt@viterbo.edu.

WAGNER COLLEGE, Staten Island, NY 10301-4495

General Information Independent, coed, comprehensive institution. *Enrollment:* 139 full-time matriculated graduate/professional students (79 women), 214 part-time matriculated graduate/professional students (141 women). *Graduate faculty:* 27 full-time (13 women), 28 part-time/adjunct (15 women). *Tuition:* Full-time $13,320; part-time $740 per credit. *Graduate housing:* Room and/or apartments available to single students; on-campus housing not available to married students. Housing application deadline: 8/1. *Student services:* Campus employment opportunities, campus safety program, career counseling, child daycare facilities, disabled student services, exercise/wellness program, free psychological counseling, international student services, writing training. *Library facilities:* August Horrmann Library. *Online resources:* web page. *Collection:* 310,000 titles, 1,000 serial subscriptions. *Research affiliation:* Staten Island University Hospital.

Computer facilities: 150 computers available on campus for general student use. A campuswide network can be accessed from student residence rooms and from off campus. Internet access is available. *Web address:* http://www.wagner.edu/.

GRADUATE UNITS

Division of Graduate Studies *Degree program information:* Part-time and evening/weekend programs available. Offers elementary education (MS Ed); family nurse practitioner (Certificate); finance (MBA); international business (MBA); management (Exec MBA, MBA); marketing (MBA); microbiology (MS); nursing (MS); secondary education (MS Ed); special education (MS Ed); teaching English to speakers of other languages (MS Ed).

WAKE FOREST UNIVERSITY, Winston-Salem, NC 27109

General Information Independent-religious, coed, university. CGS member. *Graduate housing:* On-campus housing not available.

GRADUATE UNITS

Babcock Graduate School of Management Students: 232 full-time (52 women), 428 part-time (106 women); includes 83 minority (50 African Americans, 22 Asian Americans or Pacific Islanders, 10 Hispanic Americans, 1 Native American), 81 international. Average age 27. 734 applicants, 63% accepted, 272 enrolled. *Faculty:* 42 full-time (5 women), 15 part-time/adjunct (6 women). Expenses: Contact institution. *Financial support:* In 2001–02, 357 students received support. Career-related internships or fieldwork, institutionally sponsored loans, scholarships/grants, tuition waivers (full and partial), and unspecified assistantships available. Support available to part-time students. Financial award applicants required to submit FAFSA. In 2001, 283 degrees awarded. *Degree program information:* Part-time and evening/weekend programs available. Offers business administration (MBA); management (MBA). *Application deadline:* Applications are processed on a rolling basis. *Application fee:* $50. Electronic applications accepted. *Application Contact:* Mary Goss, Assistant Dean, 336-758-5422, Fax: 336-758-5830, E-mail: mary.goss@mba.wfu.edu. *Dean,* R. Charles Moyer, 336-758-5418, Fax: 336-758-5830, E-mail: charlie.moyer@mba.wfu.edu.

Graduate School *Degree program information:* Part-time programs available. Offers accountancy (MSA); analytical chemistry (MS, PhD); biology (MS, PhD); computer science (MS); English (MA); guidance and counseling (MA Ed); health and exercise science (MS); history (MA); inorganic chemistry (MS, PhD); liberal studies (MALS); mathematics (MA); organic chemistry (MS, PhD); pastoral counseling (MA); physical chemistry (MS, PhD); physics (MS, PhD); psychology (MA); religion (MA); secondary education (MA Ed); speech communication (MA). Electronic applications accepted.

School of Law Students: 473 full-time (225 women), 22 part-time (10 women); includes 57 minority (45 African Americans, 8 Asian Americans or Pacific Islanders, 3 Hispanic Americans, 1 Native American), 3 international. Average age 25. 1,734 applicants, 36% accepted. *Faculty:* 39 full-time, 28 part-time/adjunct. Expenses: Contact institution. *Financial support:* Career-related internships or fieldwork, Federal Work-Study, institutionally sponsored loans, and scholarships/grants available. Financial award application deadline: 4/30; financial award applicants required to submit FAFSA. In 2001, 153 degrees awarded. Offers law (JD, LL M). LL M for foreign law graduates in American law. *Application deadline:* For fall admission, 3/15. Applications are processed on a rolling basis. *Application fee:* $60. *Application Contact:* Melanie E. Nutt, Director of Admissions and Financial Aid, 336-758-5437, Fax: 336-758-4632, E-mail: admissions@law.wfu.edu. *Dean,* Robert K. Walsh, 336-758-5435, Fax: 336-758-4632.

School of Medicine Offers medicine (MD, MS, PhD). Electronic applications accepted.

Graduate Programs in Medicine Students: 194 full-time (105 women), 5 part-time (4 women); includes 25 minority (14 African Americans, 9 Asian Americans or Pacific Islanders, 1 Hispanic American, 1 Native American), 26 international. Average age 28. 282 applicants, 30% accepted, 47 enrolled. *Faculty:* 218 full-time (51 women). Expenses: Contact institution. *Financial support:* In 2001–02, 74 fellowships with tuition reimbursements, 113 research assistantships with tuition reimbursements were awarded. Teaching assistantships, scholarships/grants, traineeships, tuition waivers (full and partial), and unspecified assistantships also available. Financial award application deadline: 2/15; financial award applicants required to submit FAFSA. In 2001, 2 master's, 15 doctorates awarded. Offers bio-organic and macromolecular structure (PhD); biochemistry (PhD); cancer biology (PhD); clinical epidemiology and health services research (MS); comparative medicine (MS); medical engineering (PhD); medical genetics (MS); medicine (MS, PhD); microbiology and immunology (PhD); molecular and cellular pathobiology (MS, PhD); molecular genetics (PhD); molecular medicine (PhD); neurobiology and anatomy (PhD); neuroscience (PhD); pharmacology (PhD); physiology (PhD). *Application deadline:* For fall admission, 2/1. Applications are processed on a rolling basis. *Application fee:* $25. Electronic applications accepted. *Application Contact:* E-mail: bggrad@wfumbc.edu. *Dean of the Graduate School,* Dr. Gordon A. Melson, 336-716-4303, Fax: 336-716-0185, E-mail: melson@wfu.edu.

See in-depth description on page 1287.

WALDEN UNIVERSITY, Minneapolis, MN 55401

General Information Proprietary, coed, graduate-only institution. CGS member. *Enrollment by degree level:* 698 master's, 1,384 doctoral. *Graduate faculty:* 252 part-time/adjunct (105 women). *Tuition:* Full-time $8,900. Tuition and fees vary according to degree level and program. *Graduate housing:* On-campus housing not available. *Student services:* International student services. *Library facilities:* Indiana University Bloomington. *Online resources:* library catalog, web page, access to other libraries' catalogs. *Collection:* 6 million titles.

Computer facilities: Internet access and online class registration are available. *Web address:* http://www.waldenu.edu/.

General Application Contact: Rita Sawyer, Director of Student Enrollment, 800-444-6795, Fax: 941-498-7821, E-mail: request@waldenu.edu.

GRADUATE UNITS

Graduate Programs Students: 1,666 full-time (1,157 women), 415 part-time (284 women); includes 586 minority (465 African Americans, 34 Asian Americans or Pacific Islanders, 73 Hispanic Americans, 14 Native Americans), 55 international. Average age 45. 205 applicants, 64% accepted. *Faculty:* 252 part-time/adjunct (105 women). Expenses: Contact institution. *Financial support:* In 2001–02, 1,260 students received support, including 10 fellowships with partial tuition reimbursements available (averaging $1,500 per year); tuition waivers (partial) also available. Support available to part-time students. Financial award applicants required to submit FAFSA. In 2001, 49 master's, 98 doctorates awarded. *Degree program information:*

Part-time and evening/weekend programs available. Postbaccalaureate distance learning degree programs offered (minimal on-campus study). Offers applied management and decision sciences (PhD); education (PhD); educational change and technology innovation (MS); health services (PhD); human services (PhD); professional psychology (MS, PhD); public health (MS). *Application deadline:* For fall admission, 7/1; for winter admission, 10/1; for spring admission, 1/1. Applications are processed on a rolling basis. *Application fee:* $50. Electronic applications accepted. *Application Contact:* Rita Sawyer, Director of Student Enrollment, 800-444-6795, Fax: 941-498-7821, E-mail: request@waldenu.edu. *President*, Dr. Paula Peinovich, 612-338-7224, Fax: 612-338-5092, E-mail: ppeinovi@waldenu.edu.

See in-depth description on page 1289.

WALLA WALLA COLLEGE, College Place, WA 99324-1198

General Information Independent-religious, coed, comprehensive institution. *Enrollment:* 216 full-time matriculated graduate/professional students (172 women), 30 part-time matriculated graduate/professional students (21 women). *Enrollment by degree level:* 246 master's. *Graduate faculty:* 34 full-time (19 women), 14 part-time/adjunct (5 women). *Tuition:* Full-time $15,561; part-time $399 per credit. *Graduate housing:* Rooms and/or apartments available on a first-come, first-served basis to single and married students. Typical cost: $7,500 per year ($9,975 including board) for single students; $7,500 per year ($9,975 including board) for married students. *Student services:* Campus employment opportunities, career counseling, disabled student services, free psychological counseling, international student services, low-cost health insurance, multicultural affairs office. *Library facilities:* Peterson Memorial Library plus 3 others. *Online resources:* library catalog, web page, access to other libraries' catalogs. *Collection:* 128,747 titles, 1,317 serial subscriptions, 3,483 audiovisual materials.

Computer facilities: 108 computers available on campus for general student use. A campuswide network can be accessed from student residence rooms and from off campus. Internet access and online class registration are available. *Web address:* http://www.wwc.edu/.

General Application Contact: Dr. Joe G. Galusha, Dean of Graduate Studies, 509-527-2421, Fax: 509-527-2253, E-mail: galujo@wwc.edu.

GRADUATE UNITS

Graduate School Students: 216 full-time (172 women), 30 part-time (21 women); includes 38 minority (5 African Americans, 3 Asian Americans or Pacific Islanders, 11 Hispanic Americans, 19 Native Americans), 3 international. Average age 30. 193 applicants, 98% accepted. *Faculty:* 34 full-time (19 women), 14 part-time/adjunct (5 women). Expenses: Contact institution. *Financial support:* In 2001–02, 209 students received support, including 2 research assistantships, 4 teaching assistantships; career-related internships or fieldwork, Federal Work-Study, scholarships/grants, tuition waivers (partial), and unspecified assistantships also available. Support available to part-time students. Financial award application deadline: 4/1; financial award applicants required to submit FAFSA. In 2001, 120 degrees awarded. *Degree program information:* Part-time and evening/weekend programs available. Offers biological science (MS). *Application deadline:* Applications are processed on a rolling basis. *Application fee:* $50. Electronic applications accepted. *Application Contact:* Donna J. Fisher, Administrative Assistant to Graduate Dean, 509-527-2421, Fax: 509-527-2237, E-mail: fishdo@wwc.edu. *Dean*, Dr. Joe G. Galusha, 509-527-2421, Fax: 509-527-2253, E-mail: galujo@wwc.edu.

School of Education and Psychology Students: 6 full-time (5 women), 17 part-time (10 women); includes 3 minority (2 African Americans, 1 Hispanic American) Average age 34. 16 applicants, 100% accepted. *Faculty:* 9 full-time (3 women), 3 part-time/adjunct (0 women). Expenses: Contact institution. *Financial support:* In 2001–02, 11 students received support, including 2 research assistantships with tuition reimbursements available (averaging $3,000 per year), 1 teaching assistantship with partial tuition reimbursement available (averaging $3,000 per year); Federal Work-Study, tuition waivers (partial), and unspecified assistantships also available. Support available to part-time students. Financial award application deadline: 4/1; financial award applicants required to submit FAFSA. In 2001, 13 degrees awarded. *Degree program information:* Part-time programs available. Offers counseling psychology (MA); curriculum and instruction (M Ed, MA); educational leadership (M Ed, MA, MAT); literacy instruction (M Ed, MA, MAT); school counseling (M Ed, MA); special education (M Ed, MA, MAT); students at risk (M Ed, MA); teaching (MAT). *Application deadline:* For fall admission, 4/1 (priority date). Applications are processed on a rolling basis. *Application fee:* $50. Electronic applications accepted. *Application Contact:* Dr. Joe G. Galusha, Dean of Graduate Studies, 509-527-2421, Fax: 509-527-2253, E-mail: galujo@wwc.edu. *Dean*, Dr. Steve Pawluk, 509-527-2212, Fax: 509-527-2248, E-mail: pawlst@wwc.edu.

School of Social Work Students: 203 full-time (161 women), 12 part-time (11 women); includes 37 minority (5 African Americans, 3 Asian Americans or Pacific Islanders, 10 Hispanic Americans, 19 Native Americans) Average age 34. 177 applicants, 98% accepted. *Faculty:* 19 full-time (15 women), 10 part-time/adjunct (5 women). Expenses: Contact institution. *Financial support:* In 2001–02, 195 students received support. Career-related internships or fieldwork, Federal Work-Study, and scholarships/grants available. Support available to part-time students. Financial award application deadline: 4/1; financial award applicants required to submit FAFSA. In 2001, 93 degrees awarded. *Degree program information:* Part-time programs available. Offers social work (MSW). *Application deadline:* For fall admission, 7/15 (priority date). Applications are processed on a rolling basis. *Application fee:* $50. Electronic applications accepted. *Application Contact:* Dr. Joe G. Galusha, Dean of Graduate Studies, 509-527-2421, Fax: 509-527-2253, E-mail: galujo@wwc.edu. *Dean*, Dr. Wilma Hepker, 509-527-2273, Fax: 509-527-2253, E-mail: hepkwi@wwc.edu.

WALSH COLLEGE OF ACCOUNTANCY AND BUSINESS ADMINISTRATION, Troy, MI 48007-7006

General Information Independent, coed, upper-level institution. *Enrollment:* 103 full-time matriculated graduate/professional students (61 women), 1,965 part-time matriculated graduate/professional students (1,003 women). *Enrollment by degree level:* 2,068 master's. *Graduate faculty:* 14 full-time (5 women), 113 part-time/adjunct (26 women). *Tuition:* Part-time $318 per credit hour. *Required fees:* $110 per term. *Graduate housing:* On-campus housing not available. *Student services:* Campus employment opportunities, career counseling, disabled student services. *Library facilities:* Vollbrecht Library. *Online resources:* library catalog, web page, access to other libraries' catalogs. *Collection:* 33,100 titles, 450 serial subscriptions, 70 audiovisual materials.

Computer facilities: 298 computers available on campus for general student use. A campuswide network can be accessed from off campus. Internet access is available. *Web address:* http://www.walshcollege.edu/.

General Application Contact: Karen Mahaffy, Director of Admissions and Academic Advising, 248-823-1610, Fax: 248-689-0938, E-mail: kmahaffy@walshcollegegr.edu.

GRADUATE UNITS

Graduate Programs Students: 103 full-time (61 women), 1,965 part-time (1,003 women); includes 317 minority (203 African Americans, 74 Asian Americans or Pacific Islanders, 32 Hispanic Americans, 8 Native Americans), 62 international. Average age 34. 787 applicants, 87% accepted. *Faculty:* 14 full-time (5 women), 113 part-time/adjunct (26 women). Expenses: Contact institution. *Financial support:* In 2001–02, 732 students received support. Scholarships/grants available. Support available to part-time students. Financial award application deadline: 6/30; financial award applicants required to submit FAFSA. In 2001, 568 degrees awarded. *Degree program information:* Part-time and evening/weekend programs available. Offers accountancy (MSPA); business administration (MBA); business information technology (MSBIT); economics (MAE); finance (MSF); management (MSM); taxation (MST). *Application deadline:* For fall admission, 8/24 (priority date); for winter admission, 1/1 (priority date); for spring admission, 4/1 (priority date). Applications are processed on a rolling basis. *Application fee:* $25. Electronic applications accepted. *Application Contact:* Karen Mahaffy, Director of Admissions and Academic Advising, 248-823-1610, Fax: 248-689-0938, E-mail: kmahaffy@walshcollegegr.edu. *Vice President/Academic Dean*, Dr. Michael Wood, 248-689-8282, Fax: 248-689-0920, E-mail: mwood@walshcollege.edu.

WALSH UNIVERSITY, North Canton, OH 44720-3396

General Information Independent-religious, coed, comprehensive institution. *Graduate housing:* Rooms and/or apartments available on a first-come, first-served basis to single and married students. Housing application deadline: 7/15.

GRADUATE UNITS

Graduate Programs *Degree program information:* Part-time and evening/weekend programs available. Offers counseling and human development (MA); education (MA); management (MA); physical therapy (M Sc).

WARNER PACIFIC COLLEGE, Portland, OR 97215-4099

General Information Independent-religious, coed, comprehensive institution. *Enrollment:* 12 full-time matriculated graduate/professional students (2 women). *Enrollment by degree level:* 12 master's. *Graduate faculty:* 5 part-time/adjunct (0 women). *Tuition:* Full-time $2,880; part-time $320 per credit. *Graduate housing:* Rooms and/or apartments available to single and married students. Housing application deadline: 7/1. *Student services:* Campus employment opportunities, campus safety program, career counseling, child daycare facilities, exercise/wellness program, free psychological counseling, international student services, low-cost health insurance, multicultural affairs office, teacher training, writing training. *Library facilities:* Otto F. Linn Library. *Online resources:* library catalog, access to other libraries' catalogs. *Collection:* 54,000 titles, 400 serial subscriptions.

Computer facilities: 15 computers available on campus for general student use. A campuswide network can be accessed from student residence rooms and from off campus. Internet access is available. *Web address:* http://www.warnerpacific.edu/.

General Application Contact: Linda Azorr, Office of Extended Studies, 503-517-1327, Fax: 503-517-1353, E-mail: lazorr@warnerpacific.edu.

GRADUATE UNITS

Graduate Program Students: 12 full-time (2 women). *Faculty:* 5 part-time/adjunct (0 women). Expenses: Contact institution. *Financial support:* Career-related internships or fieldwork and Federal Work-Study available. Financial award application deadline: 7/1; financial award applicants required to submit FAFSA. In 2001, 2 degrees awarded. *Degree program information:* Part-time and evening/weekend programs available. Offers biblical studies (M Rel); Christian ministry (M Rel). Courses only offered at night and on weekends. *Application deadline:* Applications are processed on a rolling basis. *Application fee:* $25. *Application Contact:* Linda Azorr, Office of Extended Studies, 503-517-1327, Fax: 503-517-1353, E-mail: lazorr@warnerpacific.edu. *Director*, Dr. L. Bryan Williams, 503-517-1045, Fax: 503-755-8853, E-mail: bwilliams@warnerpacific.edu.

WARNER SOUTHERN COLLEGE, Lake Wales, FL 33859

General Information Independent-religious, coed, comprehensive institution.

GRADUATE UNITS

Department of Business Administration

WARREN WILSON COLLEGE, Asheville, NC 28815-9000

General Information Independent-religious, coed, comprehensive institution. *Enrollment:* 70 full-time matriculated graduate/professional students (49 women). *Enrollment by degree level:* 70 master's. *Graduate faculty:* 20 full-time (8 women). *Tuition:* Full-time $9,250. *Required fees:* $950. *Graduate housing:* Room and/or apartments guaranteed to single students; on-campus housing not available to married students. *Library facilities:* Pew Learning Center and Ellison Library. *Online resources:* library catalog, web page, access to other libraries' catalogs. *Collection:* 99,000 titles, 4,060 serial subscriptions, 1,731 audiovisual materials.

Computer facilities: 68 computers available on campus for general student use. A campuswide network can be accessed from student residence rooms and from off campus. Internet access, word processing, software are available. *Web address:* http://www.warren-wilson.edu/.

General Application Contact: Peter Turchi, Director, 828-771-3715, Fax: 828-771-7005.

GRADUATE UNITS

MFA Program for Writers Students: 70 full-time (49 women); includes 6 minority (3 African Americans, 3 Asian Americans or Pacific Islanders) Average age 35. 144 applicants, 11% accepted. *Faculty:* 20 full-time (8 women). Expenses: Contact institution. *Financial support:* In 2001–02, 43 students received support, including 1 fellowship; scholarships/grants also available. Financial award application deadline: 3/15; financial award applicants required to submit FAFSA. In 2001, 28 degrees awarded. Postbaccalaureate distance learning degree programs offered (minimal on-campus study). Offers creative writing (MFA). *Application deadline:* For fall admission, 3/15; for spring admission, 9/15. *Application fee:* $60. *Application Contact:* Amy Grimm, Program Assistant, 828-771-3715, Fax: 828-771-7005, E-mail: agrimm@warren.wilson.edu. *Director*, Peter Turchi, 828-771-3715, Fax: 828-771-7005.

WARTBURG THEOLOGICAL SEMINARY, Dubuque, IA 52004-5004

General Information Independent-religious, coed, graduate-only institution. *Enrollment by degree level:* 130 first professional, 42 master's. *Graduate faculty:* 19 full-time (5 women), 7 part-time/adjunct (2 women). *Tuition:* Full-time $6,300; part-time $220 per hour. *Required fees:* $300. One-time fee: $225 part-time. *Graduate housing:* Rooms and/or apartments available on a first-come, first-served basis to single and married students. Typical cost: $2,400 per year ($5,000 including board) for single students; $4,600 per year for married students. Room and board charges vary according to board plan and housing facility selected. Housing application deadline: 4/30. *Student services:* Campus employment opportunities, international student services, writing training. *Library facilities:* Reu Memorial Library. *Online resources:* library catalog, access to other libraries' catalogs. *Collection:* 85,601 titles, 248 serial subscriptions, 369 audiovisual materials. *Research affiliation:* Menighetsfakultet (Oslo, Norway), Augustana Theologische Hochschule (Neuendettelsau, Germany).

Computer facilities: 9 computers available on campus for general student use. A campuswide network can be accessed from student residence rooms and from off campus. Internet access is available. *Web address:* http://www.wartburgseminary.edu/.

General Application Contact: Rev. M. DeWayne Teig, Director of Admissions and Candidacy, 319-589-0204, Fax: 319-589-0333, E-mail: admissions@wartburgseminary.edu.

GRADUATE UNITS

Graduate and Professional Programs Students: 157 full-time (84 women), 15 part-time (10 women); includes 1 minority (African American), 10 international. Average age 33. 80 applicants, 85% accepted. *Faculty:* 19 full-time (5 women), 7 part-time/adjunct (2 women). Expenses: Contact institution. *Financial support:* In 2001–02, 119 students received support, including 18 research assistantships with partial tuition reimbursements available; career-related internships or fieldwork, Federal Work-Study, institutionally sponsored loans, and scholarships/grants also available. Financial award application deadline: 3/15; financial award applicants required to submit FAFSA. In 2001, 37 first professional degrees, 10 master's awarded. *Degree program information:* Part-time programs available. Offers theology (M Div, MA, MATDE, STM). *Application deadline:* For fall admission, 5/15 (priority date); for spring admission, 12/15. Applications are processed on a rolling basis. *Application fee:* $25. Electronic applications accepted. *Application Contact:* Rev. M. DeWayne Teig, Director of Admissions and Candidacy, 319-589-0204, Fax: 319-589-0333, E-mail: admissions@wartburgseminary.edu. *Dean*, Rev. Craig L. Nessan, 319-589-0207, Fax: 319-589-0333.

WASHBURN UNIVERSITY OF TOPEKA, Topeka, KS 66621

General Information City-supported, coed, comprehensive institution. *Enrollment:* 582 full-time matriculated graduate/professional students (298 women), 599 part-time matriculated graduate/professional students (369 women). *Enrollment by degree level:* 392 first profes-

Washburn University of Topeka (continued)

sional, 789 master's. *Graduate faculty:* 87 full-time (34 women), 34 part-time/adjunct (9 women). Tuition, state resident: part-time $150 per credit hour. Tuition, nonresident: part-time $307 per credit hour. *Required fees:* $14 per semester. *Graduate housing:* Room and/or apartments available on a first-come, first-served basis to single students; on-campus housing not available to married students. Typical cost: $6,525 (including board). *Student services:* Campus employment opportunities, campus safety program, career counseling, disabled student services, exercise/wellness program, free psychological counseling, international student services, low-cost health insurance, multicultural affairs office, teacher training, writing training. *Library facilities:* Mabee Library plus 2 others. *Online resources:* library catalog, web page, access to other libraries' catalogs. *Collection:* 1.5 million titles, 14,000 serial subscriptions.

Computer facilities: 200 computers available on campus for general student use. A campuswide network can be accessed from off campus. Internet access and online class registration are available. *Web address:* http://www.washburn.edu/.

General Application Contact: Nancy Tate, Interim Dean, 785-231-1010 Ext. 1633, E-mail: zztate@washburn.edu.

GRADUATE UNITS

College of Arts and Sciences Students: 16 full-time (15 women), 20 part-time (15 women); includes 8 minority (5 African Americans, 1 Asian American or Pacific Islander, 2 Hispanic Americans), 1 international. Average age 65. *Faculty:* 12 full-time, 3 part-time/adjunct. Expenses: Contact institution. *Financial support:* Research assistantships, teaching assistantships, career-related internships or fieldwork, Federal Work-Study, institutionally sponsored loans, and scholarships/grants available. Support available to part-time students. In 2001, 31 degrees awarded. *Degree program information:* Part-time and evening/weekend programs available. Offers arts and sciences (M Ed, MA, MLS); clinical psychology (MA); curriculum and instruction (M Ed); educational administration (M Ed); liberal studies (MLS); reading (M Ed); special education (M Ed). *Interim Dean,* Nancy Tate, 785-231-1010 Ext. 1633, E-mail: zztate@washburn.edu.

School of Applied Studies

School of Business Students: 21 full-time (9 women), 116 part-time (53 women); includes 10 minority (2 African Americans, 2 Asian Americans or Pacific Islanders, 3 Hispanic Americans, 3 Native Americans), 12 international. Average age 30. 53 applicants, 83% accepted, 41 enrolled. *Faculty:* 19 full-time (6 women), 4 part-time/adjunct (2 women). Expenses: Contact institution. *Financial support:* In 2001–02, 30 students received support. Available to part-time students. Application deadline: 3/1; In 2001, 48 degrees awarded. *Degree program information:* Part-time and evening/weekend programs available. Offers business (MBA). *Application deadline:* For fall admission, 7/1 (priority date); for spring admission, 11/15 (priority date). Applications are processed on a rolling basis. *Application fee:* $20 ($60 for international students). *Application Contact:* Kirk T. Haskins, Director of Student Affairs, 785-231-1010 Ext. 1307, Fax: 785-231-1063, E-mail: mba@washburn.edu. *Interim Dean,* Dr. Russell E. Smith, 785-231-1010 Ext. 1308, Fax: 785-231-1063, E-mail: zzsmir@washburn.edu.

School of Law Students: 393 full-time (167 women); includes 49 minority (18 African Americans, 11 Asian Americans or Pacific Islanders, 16 Hispanic Americans, 4 Native Americans), 4 international. Average age 28. 509 applicants, 71% accepted, 141 enrolled. *Faculty:* 29 full-time (9 women), 36 part-time/adjunct (7 women). Expenses: Contact institution. *Financial support:* In 2001–02, 365 students received support, including 15 research assistantships (averaging $2,570 per year), 27 teaching assistantships (averaging $2,570 per year); career-related internships or fieldwork, Federal Work-Study, and scholarships/grants also available. Support available to part-time students. Financial award application deadline: 4/1; financial award applicants required to submit CSS PROFILE or FAFSA. In 2001, 146 degrees awarded. Offers law (JD). *Application deadline:* For fall admission, 3/15 (priority date); for spring admission, 9/15 (priority date). Applications are processed on a rolling basis. *Application fee:* $30. Electronic applications accepted. *Application Contact:* James L. Nelson, Director of Admissions, 785-231-1185, Fax: 785-232-8087, E-mail: jnelson@washburn.edu. *Dean,* Dennis R. Honabach, 785-231-1010 Ext. 1662, Fax: 785-232-8087, E-mail: dhona@washburn.edu.

WASHINGTON AND LEE UNIVERSITY, Lexington, VA 24450-0303

General Information Independent, coed, comprehensive institution. *Enrollment:* 357 full-time matriculated graduate/professional students (155 women). *Enrollment by degree level:* 357 first professional. *Graduate faculty:* 33 full-time (10 women), 4 part-time/adjunct (0 women). *Tuition:* Full-time $20,020. *Required fees:* $221. *Graduate housing:* Room and/or apartments available to single students; on-campus housing not available to married students. Housing application deadline: 4/15. *Student services:* Campus employment opportunities, campus safety program, career counseling, disabled student services, exercise/wellness program, free psychological counseling, international student services, low-cost health insurance, multicultural affairs office, writing training. *Library facilities:* James G. Leyburn Library plus 4 others. *Online resources:* library catalog, web page, access to other libraries' catalogs. *Collection:* 603,758 titles, 2,856 serial subscriptions, 8,190 audiovisual materials.

Computer facilities: 224 computers available on campus for general student use. A campuswide network can be accessed from student residence rooms and from off campus. Internet access and online class registration, e-mail are available. *Web address:* http://www.wlu.edu/.

General Application Contact: Sidney Evans, Director of Admissions, 540-463-8503, Fax: 540-463-8488, E-mail: evans@wlu.edu.

GRADUATE UNITS

School of Law Students: 357 full-time (155 women). Average age 26. 1,637 applicants, 31% accepted. *Faculty:* 33 full-time (10 women), 4 part-time/adjunct (0 women). Expenses: Contact institution. *Financial support:* In 2001–02, 274 students received support; fellowships, career-related internships or fieldwork, Federal Work-Study, institutionally sponsored loans, and scholarships/grants available. Financial award application deadline: 2/15; financial award applicants required to submit FAFSA. In 2001, 120 degrees awarded. Offers law (JD). *Application deadline:* For fall admission, 2/1 (priority date). Applications are processed on a rolling basis. *Application fee:* $50. Electronic applications accepted. *Application Contact:* Sidney Evans, Director of Admissions, 540-463-8503, Fax: 540-463-8488, E-mail: evans@wlu.edu. *Head,* David F. Partlett.

WASHINGTON COLLEGE, Chestertown, MD 21620-1197

General Information Independent, coed, comprehensive institution. *Enrollment:* 3 full-time matriculated graduate/professional students (all women), 52 part-time matriculated graduate/professional students (29 women). *Enrollment by degree level:* 55 master's. *Graduate faculty:* 28 full-time (10 women), 7 part-time/adjunct (1 woman). *Tuition:* Full-time $4,380; part-time $730 per course. *Required fees:* $240; $40 per course. Tuition and fees vary according to course load. *Graduate housing:* On-campus housing not available. *Student services:* Campus employment opportunities, career counseling, low-cost health insurance. *Library facilities:* Clifton M. Miller Library. *Online resources:* library catalog, web page, access to other libraries' catalogs. *Collection:* 231,576 titles, 4,635 serial subscriptions, 5,561 audiovisual materials.

Computer facilities: 100 computers available on campus for general student use. A campuswide network can be accessed from student residence rooms and from off campus. Internet access, e-mail are available. *Web address:* http://www.washcoll.edu/.

General Application Contact: Todd A. Lineburger, Assistant to the Provost, 410-810-7131, Fax: 410-778-7850, E-mail: todd.lineburger@washcoll.edu.

GRADUATE UNITS

Graduate Programs Students: 3 full-time (all women), 52 part-time (29 women). *Faculty:* 28 full-time (10 women), 7 part-time/adjunct (1 woman). Expenses: Contact institution. In 2001, 9 degrees awarded. *Degree program information:* Part-time and evening/weekend programs available. Offers English (MA); history (MA); psychology (MA). *Application deadline:* Applications are processed on a rolling basis. *Application fee:* $40. *Application Contact:* Todd A. Lineburger, Assistant to the Provost, 410-810-7131, Fax: 410-778-7850, E-mail: todd.lineburger@washcoll.edu. *Provost and Dean of the College,* Dr. Joachim J. Scholz, 410-778-2800 Ext. 7730, Fax: 410-778-7275.

WASHINGTON STATE UNIVERSITY, Pullman, WA 99164

General Information State-supported, coed, university. CGS member. *Enrollment:* 1,740 full-time matriculated graduate/professional students (836 women), 1,165 part-time matriculated graduate/professional students (586 women). *Enrollment by degree level:* 1,812 master's, 939 doctoral, 184 other advanced degrees. *Graduate faculty:* 721 full-time (160 women), 49 part-time/adjunct (13 women). Tuition, state resident: full-time $6,088; part-time $304 per semester. Tuition, nonresident: full-time $14,918; part-time $746 per semester. Tuition and fees vary according to program. *Graduate housing:* Rooms and/or apartments available to single and married students. Typical cost: $4,000 per year ($8,000 including board) for single students; $4,500 per year for married students. Room and board charges vary according to housing facility selected. Housing application deadline: 3/1. *Student services:* Campus employment opportunities, campus safety program, career counseling, child daycare facilities, disabled student services, exercise/wellness program, free psychological counseling, grant writing training, international student services, low-cost health insurance, multicultural affairs office, teacher training, writing training. *Library facilities:* Holland Library plus 5 others. *Online resources:* library catalog, web page, access to other libraries' catalogs. *Collection:* 2 million titles, 28,026 serial subscriptions, 316,707 audiovisual materials. *Research affiliation:* Battelle Pacific Northwest Laboratories (biochemistry, engineering).

Computer facilities: 10,000 computers available on campus for general student use. A campuswide network can be accessed from student residence rooms and from off campus. Internet access and online class registration are available. *Web address:* http://www.wsu.edu/.

General Application Contact: Dr. Steven R. Burkett, Associate Dean, Graduate School, 509-335-6424, Fax: 509-335-1949, E-mail: sburkett@wsu.edu.

GRADUATE UNITS

College of Veterinary Medicine Expenses: Contact institution. *Financial support:* Fellowships, research assistantships with partial tuition reimbursements, teaching assistantships with partial tuition reimbursements, career-related internships or fieldwork, Federal Work-Study, institutionally sponsored loans, scholarships/grants, traineeships, and tuition waivers (partial) available. Support available to part-time students. Financial award application deadline: 3/1; financial award applicants required to submit FAFSA. In 2001, 63 first professional degrees, 5 master's, 6 doctorates awarded. *Degree program information:* Part-time programs available. Offers neuroscience (MS, PhD); veterinary clinical sciences (MS, PhD); veterinary comparative anatomy, pharmacology, and physiology (MS, PhD); veterinary medicine (DVM, MS, PhD); veterinary microbiology and pathology (MS, PhD); veterinary science (MS, PhD). *Application deadline:* Applications are processed on a rolling basis. Electronic applications accepted. *Application Contact:* Nancy L. Malcolm, Principal Assistant, 509-335-3064, Fax: 509-335-0160, E-mail: nmalcolm@vetmed.wsu.edu. *Dean,* Dr. Warwick M. Bayly, 509-335-9515, Fax: 509-335-0160, E-mail: wmb@vetmed.wsu.edu.

Graduate School Students: 1,740 full-time (836 women), 1,165 part-time (586 women); includes 282 minority (54 African Americans, 82 Asian Americans or Pacific Islanders, 103 Hispanic Americans, 43 Native Americans), 570 international. *Faculty:* 721 full-time (160 women), 49 part-time/adjunct (13 women). Expenses: Contact institution. *Financial support:* In 2001–02, 100 fellowships with tuition reimbursements (averaging $3,000 per year), 451 research assistantships with tuition reimbursements (averaging $11,500 per year), 702 teaching assistantships with tuition reimbursements (averaging $11,500 per year) were awarded. Career-related internships or fieldwork, Federal Work-Study, institutionally sponsored loans, scholarships/grants, traineeships, tuition waivers (partial), unspecified assistantships, and staff assistantships, teaching associateships also available. Support available to part-time students. Financial award applicants required to submit FAFSA. In 2001, 732 master's, 149 doctorates awarded. *Degree program information:* Part-time programs available. Campuses also located at Spokane, Tri-Cities, and Vancouver. *Application deadline:* Applications are processed on a rolling basis. *Application fee:* $35. Electronic applications accepted. *Application Contact:* Dr. Steven R Burkett, Associate Dean, 509-335-6424, Fax: 509-335-1949, E-mail: sburkett@wsu.edu. *Interim Dean,* Dr. Howard Grimes, 509-3356424, Fax: 509-3351949.

College of Agriculture and Home Economics Students: 224 full-time (120 women), 28 part-time (14 women); includes 17 minority (2 African Americans, 9 Asian Americans or Pacific Islanders, 4 Hispanic Americans, 2 Native Americans), 95 international. Expenses: Contact institution. *Financial support:* In 2001–02, 10 fellowships, 125 research assistantships with full and partial tuition reimbursements (averaging $11,500 per year), 48 teaching assistantships with full and partial tuition reimbursements (averaging $11,500 per year) were awarded. Career-related internships or fieldwork, Federal Work-Study, institutionally sponsored loans, tuition waivers (partial), unspecified assistantships, and staff assistantships, teaching associateships also available. Financial award application deadline: 4/1; financial award applicants required to submit FAFSA. In 2001, 68 master's, 22 doctorates awarded. *Degree program information:* Part-time programs available. Offers agribusiness (MA); agricultural economics (MA, PhD); agriculture and home economics (MA, MLA, MS, PhD); animal sciences (MS, PhD); apparel, merchandising and textiles (MA); crop sciences (MS, PhD); entomology (MS, PhD); food science (MS, PhD); horticulture (MS, PhD); human development (MA); human nutrition (MS); interior design (MA); landscape architecture (MLA); natural resources sciences (MS, PhD); nutrition (PhD); plant pathology (MS, PhD); plant physiology (MS, PhD); soil sciences (MS, PhD). *Application deadline:* Applications are processed on a rolling basis. *Application fee:* $35. Electronic applications accepted. *Application Contact:* Broderick Gant, Assistant to the Associate Dean and Director of Recruitment, 509-335-4562, Fax: 509-335-1065, E-mail: bgant@wsu.edu. *Dean,* Dr. James Zuiches, 509-335-4561.

College of Business and Economics Students: 143 full-time (49 women), 28 part-time (8 women); includes 12 minority (7 African Americans, 4 Asian Americans or Pacific Islanders, 1 Native American), 74 international. *Faculty:* 69. Expenses: Contact institution. *Financial support:* In 2001–02, 9 research assistantships with full and partial tuition reimbursements, 82 teaching assistantships with full and partial tuition reimbursements were awarded. Career-related internships or fieldwork, Federal Work-Study, institutionally sponsored loans, tuition waivers (partial), and teaching associateships also available. Financial award application deadline: 4/1; financial award applicants required to submit FAFSA. In 2001, 108 master's, 6 doctorates awarded. Offers accounting and business law (M Acc); accounting information systems and business law (M Acc); business administration (MBA, PhD); business and economics (M Acc, MA, MBA, MTM, PhD, Certificate); economics (MA, PhD); international business economics (Certificate); technology management (MTM). *Application deadline:* For fall admission, 3/1 (priority date). Applications are processed on a rolling basis. *Application fee:* $35. *Application Contact:* Dr. Val Miskin, Director, 509-335-7617, Fax: 509-335-4735, E-mail: mba@wsu.edu. *Interim,* Dr. Glenn Johnson, 509-335-3596, Fax: 509-335-4275, E-mail: arndtm@wsu.edu.

College of Education Students: 125 full-time (77 women), 72 part-time (42 women); includes 55 minority (17 African Americans, 14 Asian Americans or Pacific Islanders, 15 Hispanic Americans, 9 Native Americans), 14 international. *Faculty:* 47. Expenses: Contact institution. *Financial support:* In 2001–02, 44 research assistantships with full and partial tuition reimbursements, 28 teaching assistantships with full and partial tuition reimbursements were awarded. Career-related internships or fieldwork, Federal Work-Study, institutionally sponsored loans, tuition waivers (partial), and staff assistantships, teaching associateships also available. Financial award application deadline: 4/1; financial award applicants required to submit FAFSA. In 2001, 163 master's, 22 doctorates awarded. Offers counseling psychology (MA, PhD); curriculum and instruction (Ed D, PhD); diverse languages (M Ed, MA); education (M Ed, MA, MAT, MIT, MS, Ed D, PhD); educational leadership (M Ed, MA, Ed D, PhD); elementary education (M Ed, MA, MIT); kinesiology (M Ed, MS); literacy (M Ed, MA); literacy education (PhD); math education (PhD); recreation and leisure studies (M Ed, MS); secondary education (M Ed, MA). *Application fee:* $35. *Dean,* Dr. Judy Mitchell, 509-335-4853.

College of Engineering and Architecture Students: 241 full-time (56 women), 31 part-time (10 women); includes 11 minority (1 African American, 7 Asian Americans or Pacific Islanders, 3 Hispanic Americans), 154 international. *Faculty:* 107. Expenses: Contact institution. *Financial support:* In 2001–02, 80 research assistantships with full and partial tuition reimbursements, 90 teaching assistantships with full and partial tuition reimbursements were awarded. Fellowships, career-related internships or fieldwork, Federal Work-Study, institutionally sponsored loans, tuition waivers (partial), and teaching associateships also available. Financial award applicants required to submit FAFSA. In 2001, 114 master's, 17 doctorates awarded. Offers architecture (MS); chemical engineering (MS, PhD); civil engineering (MS, PhD); computer science (MS, PhD); electrical engineering (MS, PhD); engineering and architecture (MS, PhD); environmental engineering (MS); materials science (MS, PhD); mechanical engineering (MS, PhD). *Application deadline:* For fall admission, 3/1 (priority date). Applications are processed on a rolling basis. *Application fee:* $35. *Dean,* Dr. Anjan Bose, 509-335-5593.

College of Liberal Arts Students: 374 full-time (212 women), 77 part-time (46 women); includes 69 minority (17 African Americans, 10 Asian Americans or Pacific Islanders, 31 Hispanic Americans, 11 Native Americans), 53 international. *Faculty:* 210. Expenses: Contact institution. *Financial support:* In 2001–02, 42 research assistantships with full and partial tuition reimbursements, 278 teaching assistantships with full and partial tuition reimbursements were awarded. Fellowships with tuition reimbursements, career-related internships or fieldwork, Federal Work-Study, institutionally sponsored loans, scholarships/grants, tuition waivers (partial), and unspecified assistantships also available. Support available to part-time students. Financial award applicants required to submit FAFSA. In 2001, 155 master's, 32 doctorates awarded. Offers American studies (MA, PhD); anthropology (MA, PhD); ceramics (MFA); clinical psychology (PhD); communications (MA); composition (MA); criminal justice (MA); drawing (MFA); electronic imaging (MFA); English (MA, PhD); history (MA, PhD); liberal arts (MA, MFA, MPA, MS, PhD); music (MA); painting (MFA); photography (MFA); political science (MA, PhD); print making (MFA); psychology (MS, PhD); public affairs (MPA); sculpture (MFA); sociology (MA, PhD); Spanish (MA); speech and hearing sciences (MA); teaching of English (MA). *Application fee:* $35. Electronic applications accepted. *Dean,* Dr. Barbara Couture, 509-335-4581.

College of Pharmacy Students: 318 full-time (195 women), 13 part-time (10 women); includes 92 minority (7 African Americans, 79 Asian Americans or Pacific Islanders, 5 Hispanic Americans, 1 Native American), 10 international. *Faculty:* 36. Expenses: Contact institution. *Financial support:* In 2001–02, 3 fellowships, 6 research assistantships with full and partial tuition reimbursements, 6 teaching assistantships with full and partial tuition reimbursements were awarded. Federal Work-Study, institutionally sponsored loans, tuition waivers (partial), and staff assistantships, teaching associateships also available. Financial award application deadline: 4/1; financial award applicants required to submit FAFSA. In 2001, 6 master's, 5 doctorates awarded. Offers health policy and administration (MHPA); pharmaceutical science (Pharm D); pharmacology and toxicology (MS, PhD); pharmacy (Pharm D, MHPA, MS, PhD). *Application deadline:* For fall admission, 3/1. Applications are processed on a rolling basis. *Application fee:* $35. *Director,* Dr. Dennis Clifton, 509-335-7738, E-mail: clifton@wsu.edu.

College of Sciences Students: 289 full-time (107 women), 24 part-time (10 women); includes 20 minority (4 African Americans, 11 Asian Americans or Pacific Islanders, 4 Hispanic Americans, 1 Native American), 79 international. *Faculty:* 209. Expenses: Contact institution. *Financial support:* In 2001–02, 8 fellowships, 110 research assistantships, 187 teaching assistantships were awarded. Career-related internships or fieldwork, Federal Work-Study, institutionally sponsored loans, traineeships, tuition waivers (partial), and teaching associateships also available. Financial award applicants required to submit FAFSA. In 2001, 65 master's, 25 doctorates awarded. Offers analytical chemistry (MS, PhD); biochemistry and biophysics (MS, PhD); biological systems (MS, PhD); biology (MS); botany (MS, PhD); chemical physics (PhD); environmental science (MS, PhD); genetics and cell biology (MS, PhD); geology (MS, PhD); inorganic chemistry (MS, PhD); material science (MS, PhD); materials science (PhD); materials science and engineering (MS); mathematics (MS, DA, PhD); microbiology (MS, PhD); organic chemistry (MS, PhD); physical chemistry (MS, PhD); physics (MS, PhD); regional planning (MRP); sciences (MRP, MS, DA, PhD); zoology (MS, PhD). *Application deadline:* Applications are processed on a rolling basis. *Application fee:* $35. *Dean,* Dr. Leon Radziemski, 509-335-5548.

Intercollegiate College of Nursing Students: 24 full-time (16 women), 40 part-time (37 women); includes 2 minority (1 Hispanic American, 1 Native American) Average age 39. 58 applicants, 71% accepted. *Faculty:* 27 full-time (24 women). Expenses: Contact institution. *Financial support:* In 2001–02, 2 research assistantships, 6 teaching assistantships with full and partial tuition reimbursements were awarded. Federal Work-Study, institutionally sponsored loans, scholarships/grants, traineeships, and tuition waivers (partial) also available. Support available to part-time students. Financial award application deadline: 4/1; financial award applicants required to submit FAFSA. In 2001, 38 degrees awarded. *Degree program information:* Part-time programs available. Offers nursing (M Nurs). *Application deadline:* For fall admission, 3/15 (priority date); for spring admission, 11/15. Applications are processed on a rolling basis. *Application fee:* $35. Electronic applications accepted. *Application Contact:* Margaret Ruby, Administrative Assistant, 509-324-7334, Fax: 509-324-7336, E-mail: mruby@wsu.edu. *Dean,* Dr. Dorothy Detlor, 509-324-7333.

WASHINGTON STATE UNIVERSITY SPOKANE, Spokane, WA 99201-3899

General Information State-supported, coed, graduate-only institution.

GRADUATE UNITS

Graduate Programs Offers aging (Certificate); computer science (MS); criminal justice (MA); electrical engineering (MS); engineering management (MEM); health policy and administration (MHPA); human nutrition (MS); speech and hearing sciences (MA); teaching (MT); technology management (MTM).

Interdisciplinary Design Institute Offers architecture (MS); interior design (MA); landscape architecture (MS).

Program in Pharmacy Offers pharmacy (Pharm D).

See in-depth description on page 1291.

WASHINGTON STATE UNIVERSITY TRI-CITIES, Richland, WA 99352-1671

General Information State-supported, coed, graduate-only institution.

WASHINGTON STATE UNIVERSITY VANCOUVER, Vancouver, WA 98686

General Information State-supported, coed, graduate-only institution.

WASHINGTON THEOLOGICAL UNION, Washington, DC 20012

General Information Independent-religious, coed, graduate-only institution. *Graduate housing:* Room and/or apartments available on a first-come, first-served basis to single students; on-campus housing not available to married students.

GRADUATE UNITS

Graduate and Professional Programs *Degree program information:* Part-time programs available. Offers theology (M Div, MA, MAPS).

WASHINGTON UNIVERSITY IN ST. LOUIS, St. Louis, MO 63130-4899

General Information Independent, coed, university. CGS member. *Enrollment:* 4,234 full-time matriculated graduate/professional students (2,051 women), 932 part-time matriculated graduate/professional students (362 women). *Enrollment by degree level:* 1,080 first professional, 2,488 master's, 1,568 doctoral, 30 other advanced degrees. *Graduate faculty:* 2,095 full-time (577 women), 533 part-time/adjunct (208 women). *Tuition:* Full-time $26,900. *Graduate housing:* Rooms and/or apartments available on a first-come, first-served basis to single and married students. *Student services:* Campus employment opportunities, campus safety program, career counseling, free psychological counseling, grant writing training, international student services, low-cost health insurance, teacher training. *Library facilities:* John M. Olin Library plus 13 others. *Online resources:* library catalog, web page, access to other libraries' catalogs. *Collection:* 1.5 million titles, 21,017 serial subscriptions, 42,799 audiovisual materials.

Computer facilities: 2,500 computers available on campus for general student use. A campuswide network can be accessed from student residence rooms and from off campus. Internet access and online class registration, e-mail are available. *Web address:* http://www.wustl.edu/.

General Application Contact: 314-935-6880, Fax: 314-935-4887, E-mail: graduateschool@artsci.wustl.edu.

GRADUATE UNITS

George Warren Brown School of Social Work Students: 388 full-time (328 women), 52 part-time (40 women); includes 98 minority (56 African Americans, 18 Asian Americans or Pacific Islanders, 8 Hispanic Americans, 16 Native Americans), 92 international. Average age 29. 539 applicants, 87% accepted. *Faculty:* 28 full-time (14 women), 52 part-time/adjunct (32 women). Expenses: Contact institution. *Financial support:* In 2001–02, 334 students received support, including 166 fellowships with partial tuition reimbursements available (averaging $4,930 per year), 73 research assistantships with full tuition reimbursements available (averaging $3,000 per year), 49 teaching assistantships with full tuition reimbursements available (averaging $1,000 per year); career-related internships or fieldwork, Federal Work-Study, institutionally sponsored loans, and tuition waivers (partial) also available. Support available to part-time students. In 2001, 190 master's, 6 doctorates awarded. *Degree program information:* Part-time and evening/weekend programs available. Offers social work (MSW, PhD). *Application deadline:* Applications are processed on a rolling basis. *Application fee:* $35. Electronic applications accepted. *Application Contact:* Brian W. Legate, Director of Admissions, 314-935-6676, Fax: 314-935-4859, E-mail: msw@gwbmail.wustl.edu. *Dean and George Warren Brown Distinguished Professor of Social Work,* Dr. Shanti K. Khinduka, 314-935-6693, Fax: 314-935-8511, E-mail: khinduka@gwbmail.wustl.edu.

Graduate School of Arts and Sciences Students: 1,351 full-time (663 women), 24 part-time (15 women); includes 130 minority (30 African Americans, 73 Asian Americans or Pacific Islanders, 21 Hispanic Americans, 6 Native Americans), 323 international. 2,677 applicants, 27% accepted. Expenses: Contact institution. *Financial support:* In 2001–02, 824 students received support, including 213 fellowships with tuition reimbursements available (averaging $12,000 per year), 28 research assistantships with tuition reimbursements available (averaging $12,500 per year), 443 teaching assistantships with tuition reimbursements available (averaging $11,475 per year); career-related internships or fieldwork, Federal Work-Study, institutionally sponsored loans, scholarships/grants, traineeships, tuition waivers (full and partial), and unspecified assistantships also available. Support available to part-time students. In 2001, 213 master's, 140 doctorates awarded. *Degree program information:* Part-time and evening/weekend programs available. Offers American history (MA, PhD); anthropology (MA, PhD); art history (MA, PhD); arts and sciences (MA, MA Ed, MAT, MFAW, MM, MS, PhD); Asian history (MA, PhD); Asian language (MA); Asian studies (MA); audiology (MS); British history (MA, PhD); chemistry (MA, PhD); Chinese (MA, PhD); Chinese and comparative literature (PhD); classical archaeology (MA, PhD); classics (MA, MAT); clinical psychology (PhD); comparative literature (MA, PhD); deaf education (MS); earth and planetary sciences (MA); East Asian studies (MA); economics (MA, PhD); educational research (PhD); elementary education (MA Ed); English and American literature (MA, PhD); environmental science (MA); European history (MA, PhD); European studies (MA); French (MA, PhD); general experimental psychology (MA, PhD); geochemistry (PhD); geology (MA, PhD); geophysics (PhD); Germanic languages and literature (MA, PhD); history (PhD); Islamic and Near Eastern studies (MA); Japanese (MA, PhD); Japanese and comparative literature (PhD); Jewish studies (MA); Latin American history (MA, PhD); mathematics (MA, PhD); mathematics education (MAT); Middle Eastern history (MA, PhD); movement science (PhD); music (MA, MM, PhD); performing arts (MA); philosophy (MA, PhD); philosophy/neuroscience/psychology (PhD); physics (MA, PhD); planetary sciences (PhD); political economy and public policy (MA); political science (MA, PhD); Romance languages (MA, PhD); secondary education (MA Ed, MAT); social psychology (MA, PhD); social work (PhD); Spanish (MA, PhD); speech and hearing sciences (MA, PhD); statistics (MA, PhD); writing (MFAW). *Application deadline:* For fall admission, 1/15. Applications are processed on a rolling basis. *Application fee:* $35. Electronic applications accepted. *Application Contact:* Assistant to the Dean, 314-935-6880, Fax: 314-935-4887. *Dean,* Robert E. Thach, 314-935-6843, Fax: 314-935-4887, E-mail: annaliesa_hanebrink@aismail.wustl.

Division of Biology and Biomedical Sciences Students: 491 full-time (214 women); includes 72 minority (4 African Americans, 57 Asian Americans or Pacific Islanders, 10 Hispanic Americans, 1 Native American), 91 international. 856 applicants, 27% accepted. *Faculty:* 283 full-time (29 women). Expenses: Contact institution. *Financial support:* Fellowships, research assistantships, tuition waivers (full) available. Financial award application deadline: 1/1. In 2001, 57 doctorates awarded. Offers bio-organic chemistry (PhD); biochemistry (PhD); computational biology (PhD); developmental biology (PhD); ecology (PhD); environmental biology (PhD); evolutionary and population biology (PhD); evolutionary biology (PhD); genetics (PhD); immunology (PhD); molecular biophysics (PhD); molecular cell biology (PhD); molecular genetics (PhD); molecular microbiology and microbial pathogenesis (PhD); neurosciences (PhD); plant biology (PhD). *Application deadline:* For fall admission, 1/1 (priority date). Applications are processed on a rolling basis. *Application fee:* $0. Electronic applications accepted. *Application Contact:* Rosemary Garagnani, Director of Admissions, 800-852-9074, E-mail: admissions@dbbs.wustl.edu.

Henry Edwin Sever Graduate School of Engineering and Applied Science Students: 299 full-time (57 women), 278 part-time (61 women); includes 61 minority (14 African Americans, 44 Asian Americans or Pacific Islanders, 3 Hispanic Americans), 175 international. 1,193 applicants, 31% accepted, 191 enrolled. *Faculty:* 81 full-time (6 women), 156 part-time/adjunct. Expenses: Contact institution. *Financial support:* In 2001–02, 147 students received support, including 12 fellowships with full tuition reimbursements available, 131 research assistantships with full tuition reimbursements available, 4 teaching assistantships; career-related internships or fieldwork, Federal Work-Study, institutionally sponsored loans, scholarships/grants, health care benefits, and unspecified assistantships also available. Financial award applicants required to submit FAFSA. In 2001, 172 master's, 30 doctorates awarded. *Degree program information:* Part-time and evening/weekend programs available. Offers biomedical engineering (MS, D Sc); chemical engineering (MS, D Sc); civil engineering (MSCE); computer science (MS, D Sc); construction engineering (MCE); construction management (MCM); control engineering (MCE); electrical engineering (MSEE, D Sc); engineering and applied science (MCE, MCE, MCM, MEM, MIM, MS, MSCE, MSE, MSEE, MSEE, MTM, D Sc); environmental engineering (MS, D Sc); materials science and engineering (MS); materials science engineering (D Sc); mechanical engineering (MS, D Sc); structural engineering (MSE, D Sc); systems science and mathematics (MS, D Sc); systems science and mathematics and economics (D Sc); transportation and urban systems engineering (D Sc). *Application deadline:* For fall admission, 2/1. *Application fee:* $20. Electronic applications accepted. *Application Contact:* Elaine Halley, Director, Graduate Recruiting, 314-935-4849, E-mail: elainehalley@seas.wustl.edu. *Dean,* Christopher I. Byrnes, 314-935-6166.

John M. Olin School of Business Students: 313 full-time (69 women), 354 part-time (81 women); includes 104 minority (27 African Americans, 59 Asian Americans or Pacific Islanders, 15 Hispanic Americans, 3 Native Americans), 129 international. Average age 28. 1,322 applicants, 32% accepted. *Faculty:* 72 full-time (16 women), 16 part-time/adjunct (3 women).

Washington University in St. Louis (continued)

Expenses: Contact institution. *Financial support:* In 2001–02, 194 students received support; fellowships, research assistantships, career-related internships or fieldwork, Federal Work-Study, scholarships/grants, tuition waivers (full and partial), and unspecified assistantships available. Support available to part-time students. Financial award application deadline: 3/31. In 2001, 308 master's, 6 doctorates awarded. *Degree program information:* Part-time and evening/weekend programs available. Offers business (PhD); business administration (MBA); health services management (EMBA); manufacturing management (EMBA). *Application deadline:* For fall admission, 12/4 (priority date); for winter admission, 1/21 (priority date); for spring admission, 3/11 (priority date). *Application fee:* $80. Electronic applications accepted. *Application Contact:* Brad Pearson, Director of MBA Admissions, 314-935-7301, Fax: 314-935-6309, E-mail: mba@olin.wustl.edu. *Dean,* Stuart I. Greenbaum, 314-935-6344, Fax: 314-935-4074, E-mail: greenbaum@olin.wustl.edu.

School of Architecture Offers architecture (M Arch, MAUD); urban design (MAUD).

School of Art Students: 22 full-time (11 women); includes 1 minority (Hispanic American), 2 international. Average age 29. 69 applicants, 52% accepted, 11 enrolled. *Faculty:* 15 full-time (5 women), 6 part-time/adjunct (2 women). Expenses: Contact institution. *Financial support:* In 2001–02, 22 students received support, including 4 fellowships with partial tuition reimbursements available, 11 research assistantships with partial tuition reimbursements available, 11 teaching assistantships with partial tuition reimbursements available; career-related internships or fieldwork, Federal Work-Study, institutionally sponsored loans, scholarships/grants, and tuition waivers (partial) also available. Financial award application deadline: 2/1; financial award applicants required to submit FAFSA. In 2001, 13 degrees awarded. Offers ceramics (MFA); painting (MFA); photography (MFA); printmaking/drawing (MFA); sculpture (MFA). *Application deadline:* For fall admission, 1/15. *Application fee:* $30. *Application Contact:* Denise Ward-Brown, Director of Graduate Studies, 314-935-5884, Fax: 314-935-6462, E-mail: ddwardbr@art.wustl.edu. *Dean,* Jeff Pike, 314-935-6525, Fax: 314-935-4862, E-mail: jpike@art.wustl.edu.

School of Law Offers law (JD, LL M, MJS, JSD). Electronic applications accepted.

School of Medicine Students: 910 full-time (583 women), 49 part-time (36 women). Average age 23. Expenses: Contact institution. *Financial support:* Fellowships, research assistantships, career-related internships or fieldwork, Federal Work-Study, and institutionally sponsored loans available. Support available to part-time students. Financial award applicants required to submit FAFSA. In 2001, 125 first professional degrees, 209 master's awarded. Offers health administration (MHA); medicine (MD, MA, MHA, MHS, MSOT, DPT, OTD, PhD, PPDPT); movement science (PhD); occupational therapy (MSOT); physical therapy (MHS, DPT, PhD, PPDPT). *Application Contact:* Dr. W. Edwin Dodson, Associate Dean, 314-362-6848, Fax: 314-362-4658, E-mail: wumscoa@msnotes.wustl.edu. *Dean,* Dr. William A. Peck, 314-362-6827.

See in-depth description on page 1293.

WAYLAND BAPTIST UNIVERSITY, Plainview, TX 79072-6998

General Information Independent-religious, coed, comprehensive institution. *Enrollment:* 7 full-time matriculated graduate/professional students (2 women), 35 part-time matriculated graduate/professional students (25 women). *Enrollment by degree level:* 42 master's. *Graduate faculty:* 17 full-time (5 women), 4 part-time/adjunct (2 women). *Tuition:* Full-time $4,770; part-time $265 per credit hour. *Required fees:* $40 per semester. Tuition and fees vary according to course load. *Graduate housing:* Rooms and/or apartments available on a first-come, first-served basis to single and married students. Typical cost: $1,216 per year ($3,121 including board) for single students. *Student services:* Campus employment opportunities, career counseling, free psychological counseling, teacher training. *Library facilities:* J.E. and L.E. Mabee Learning Resource Center. *Online resources:* library catalog, web page, access to other libraries' catalogs. *Collection:* 111,824 titles, 360 serial subscriptions, 13,239 audiovisual materials.

Computer facilities: 297 computers available on campus for general student use. A campuswide network can be accessed from student residence rooms and from off campus. Internet access is available. *Web address:* http://www.wbu.edu/.

General Application Contact: Dr. Glenn Saul, Vice President of Academic Services, 806-291-3420, Fax: 806-291-1950, E-mail: saulg@mail.wbu.edu.

GRADUATE UNITS

Graduate Programs Students: 7 full-time (2 women), 35 part-time (25 women); includes 6 minority (3 African Americans, 3 Hispanic Americans) Average age 35. 5 applicants, 100% accepted. *Faculty:* 17 full-time (5 women), 4 part-time/adjunct (2 women). Expenses: Contact institution. *Financial support:* In 2001–02, 41 students received support. Federal Work-Study, institutionally sponsored loans, and scholarships/grants available. Support available to part-time students. Financial award application deadline: 5/1; financial award applicants required to submit FAFSA. In 2001, 10 degrees awarded. *Degree program information:* Part-time and evening/weekend programs available. Offers business administration/management (MA, MBA); education (M Ed); religion (MA); science (MS). *Application deadline:* Applications are processed on a rolling basis. *Application fee:* $35. *Vice President of Academic Services,* Dr. Glenn Saul, 806-291-3420, Fax: 806-291-1950, E-mail: saulg@mail.wbu.edu.

WAYNESBURG COLLEGE, Waynesburg, PA 15370-1222

General Information Independent-religious, coed, comprehensive institution. *Graduate housing:* Room and/or apartments available on a first-come, first-served basis to single students; on-campus housing not available to married students. Housing application deadline: 8/1.

GRADUATE UNITS

Graduate and Professional Studies *Degree program information:* Part-time and evening/weekend programs available. Offers business administration (MBA). Electronic applications accepted.

WAYNE STATE COLLEGE, Wayne, NE 68787

General Information State-supported, coed, comprehensive institution. CGS member. *Enrollment:* 28 full-time matriculated graduate/professional students (17 women), 285 part-time matriculated graduate/professional students (164 women). *Enrollment by degree level:* 306 master's, 7 other advanced degrees. *Graduate faculty:* 89 part-time/adjunct (33 women). *Graduate housing:* Room and/or apartments available to single students; on-campus housing not available to married students. Housing application deadline: 8/1. *Student services:* Campus safety program, career counseling, disabled student services, free psychological counseling, international student services, low-cost health insurance. *Library facilities:* U. S. Conn Library plus 1 other. *Online resources:* library catalog, web page, access to other libraries' catalogs. *Collection:* 149,821 titles, 2,520 serial subscriptions, 5,437 audiovisual materials. *Research affiliation:* Nebraska Business Development Center.

Computer facilities: 200 computers available on campus for general student use. A campuswide network can be accessed. *Web address:* http://www.wsc.edu/.

General Application Contact: Dr. Robert McCue, Dean of Graduate Studies, 402-375-7232.

GRADUATE UNITS

Graduate School Students: 28 full-time (17 women), 285 part-time (164 women); includes 11 minority (7 African Americans, 3 Hispanic Americans, 1 Native American), 4 international. Average age 34. *Faculty:* 89 part-time/adjunct (33 women). Expenses: Contact institution. *Financial support:* In 2001–02, 32 teaching assistantships with full tuition reimbursements (averaging $4,000 per year) were awarded; career-related internships or fieldwork also available. Financial award application deadline: 5/1; financial award applicants required to submit FAFSA. In 2001, 167 master's, 5 other advanced degrees awarded. Postbaccalaureate distance learning degree programs offered (no on-campus study). *Application deadline:* Applications are processed on a rolling basis. *Application fee:* $10. *Dean of the Graduate Studies,* Dr. Robert McCue, 402-375-7232.

Division of Business Students: 7 full-time (2 women), 61 part-time (32 women); includes 1 minority (African American), 2 international. Average age 34. *Faculty:* 11 part-time/adjunct (3 women). Expenses: Contact institution. *Financial support:* In 2001–02, 2 teaching assistantships with full tuition reimbursements (averaging $4,000 per year) were awarded; career-related internships or fieldwork also available. Financial award application deadline: 5/1; financial award applicants required to submit FAFSA. In 2001, 11 degrees awarded. Offers business (MBA). *Application deadline:* Applications are processed on a rolling basis. *Application fee:* $10. *Head,* Dr. Vaughn Benson, 402-375-7245.

Division of Education Students: 7 full-time (5 women), 183 part-time (111 women); includes 4 minority (1 African American, 2 Hispanic Americans, 1 Native American), 2 international. Average age 35. *Faculty:* 16 part-time/adjunct (9 women). Expenses: Contact institution. *Financial support:* In 2001–02, 2 teaching assistantships with full tuition reimbursements (averaging $4,000 per year) were awarded; career-related internships or fieldwork also available. Financial award application deadline: 5/1; financial award applicants required to submit FAFSA. In 2001, 137 master's, 5 other advanced degrees awarded. Offers alternative education (MSE); art education (MSE); business education (MSE); communication arts education (MSE); consumer science education (MSE); counselor education (MSE); curriculum and instruction (MSE); education (MSE, Ed S); education technology (MSE); educational administration (Ed S); elementary administration (MSE); elementary education (MSE); English as a second language (MSE); health and physical education/health (MSE); health and physical education/pedagogy (MSE); industrial technology education (MSE); mathematics education (MSE); music education (MSE); science education (MSE); secondary administration (MSE); social science education (MSE); special education (MSE). *Application deadline:* Applications are processed on a rolling basis. *Application fee:* $10. *Head,* Dr. Paul Theobald, 402-375-7389.

Division of Fine Arts Students: 1 (woman) full-time. Average age 23. *Faculty:* 3 part-time/adjunct (1 woman). Expenses: Contact institution. *Financial support:* In 2001–02, teaching assistantships (averaging $4,000 per year) Financial award application deadline: 5/1; financial award applicants required to submit FAFSA. Offers art education (MSE). *Application deadline:* Applications are processed on a rolling basis. *Application fee:* $10. *Head,* Dr. Pearl Hansen, 402-375-7359.

Division of Humanities Students: 4 full-time (3 women), 9 part-time (all women); includes 2 minority (both African Americans) Average age 33. *Faculty:* 23 part-time/adjunct (10 women). Expenses: Contact institution. *Financial support:* In 2001–02, 4 teaching assistantships with full tuition reimbursements (averaging $4,000 per year) were awarded; career-related internships or fieldwork also available. Financial award application deadline: 5/1; financial award applicants required to submit FAFSA. In 2001, 2 degrees awarded. Offers communication arts (MSE); English education (MSE). *Application deadline:* Applications are processed on a rolling basis. *Application fee:* $10. *Head,* Dr. Ed Battistella, 402-375-7394.

Division of Mathematics and Science Average age 39. *Faculty:* 12 part-time/adjunct (3 women). Expenses: Contact institution. *Financial support:* Teaching assistantships with full tuition reimbursements available. Financial award application deadline: 5/1; financial award applicants required to submit FAFSA. In 2001, 2 degrees awarded. Offers mathematics education (MSE); science education (MSE). *Application deadline:* Applications are processed on a rolling basis. *Application fee:* $10. *Head,* Dr. J. S. Johar, 402-375-7329.

Division of Physical Education Students: 8 full-time (6 women), 16 part-time (3 women); includes 3 minority (all African Americans) Average age 25. *Faculty:* 3 part-time/adjunct (0 women). Expenses: Contact institution. *Financial support:* In 2001–02, 6 teaching assistantships with full tuition reimbursements (averaging $4,000 per year) were awarded; career-related internships or fieldwork also available. Financial award application deadline: 5/1; financial award applicants required to submit FAFSA. In 2001, 10 degrees awarded. Offers coaching (MSE); exercise science (MSE); health education (MSE); sport administration/management (MSE). *Application deadline:* Applications are processed on a rolling basis. *Application fee:* $10. *Head,* Dr. Stephen Glass, 402-375-7301.

Division of Social Sciences Students: 1 full-time (0 women), 9 part-time (6 women); includes 1 minority (Hispanic American) Average age 34. *Faculty:* 16 part-time/adjunct (5 women). Expenses: Contact institution. *Financial support:* In 2001–02, 2 teaching assistantships with full tuition reimbursements (averaging $4,000 per year) were awarded; career-related internships or fieldwork also available. Financial award application deadline: 5/1; financial award applicants required to submit FAFSA. In 2001, 5 degrees awarded. Offers history (MSE); social science (MSE). *Application deadline:* Applications are processed on a rolling basis. *Application fee:* $10. *Head,* Dr. Jean Karlen, 402-375-7292.

WAYNE STATE UNIVERSITY, Detroit, MI 48202

General Information State-supported, coed, university. CGS member. *Enrollment:* 5,284 full-time matriculated graduate/professional students (2,624 women), 7,267 part-time matriculated graduate/professional students (4,099 women). *Enrollment by degree level:* 2,754 first professional, 7,385 master's, 1,366 doctoral, 1,046 other advanced degrees. *Graduate faculty:* 927. Tuition, state resident: full-time $3,764. Tuition and fees vary according to degree level and program. *Graduate housing:* Rooms and/or apartments available on a first-come, first-served basis to single students and available to married students. *Student services:* Campus employment opportunities, career counseling, child daycare facilities, free psychological counseling, international student services, low-cost health insurance. *Library facilities:* David Adamany Undergraduate Library plus 6 others. *Online resources:* library catalog, web page, access to other libraries' catalogs. *Collection:* 3.1 million titles, 18,236 serial subscriptions, 38,110 audiovisual materials. *Research affiliation:* Michigan Cancer Foundation, Michigan Educational Research Information Triad, Ford Motor Company (engineering), Kresge Eye Institute, Detroit Medical Center, Michigan Public Health Institute.

Computer facilities: 1,000 computers available on campus for general student use. A campuswide network can be accessed from student residence rooms and from off campus. Internet access and online class registration are available. *Web address:* http://www.wayne.edu/.

General Application Contact: Michael Wood, Associate Director, 313-577-3596, Fax: 313-577-3536, E-mail: admissions@wayne.edu.

GRADUATE UNITS

Graduate School Students: 3,245 full-time (1,740 women), 7,037 part-time (3,989 women); includes 2,072 minority (1,551 African Americans, 345 Asian Americans or Pacific Islanders, 140 Hispanic Americans, 36 Native Americans), 1,854 international. Average age 27. 8,760 applicants, 46% accepted, 2232 enrolled. *Faculty:* 680. Expenses: Contact institution. *Financial support:* In 2001–02, 89 fellowships, 377 research assistantships, 612 teaching assistantships were awarded. Career-related internships or fieldwork, Federal Work-Study, institutionally sponsored loans, scholarships/grants, and tuition waivers (full and partial) also available. Support available to part-time students. In 2001, 236 first professional degrees, 2,464 master's, 192 doctorates, 149 other advanced degrees awarded. *Degree program information:* Part-time and evening/weekend programs available. Offers alcohol and drug abuse studies (Certificate); archives administration (Certificate); developmental disabilities (Certificate); gerontology (Certificate); infant mental health (Certificate); interdisciplinary studies (PhD); library and information science (MLIS, Spec); molecular and cellular toxicology (MS, PhD). *Application fee:* $20 ($30 for international students). *Application Contact:* Michael Wood, Interim Director, 313-577-3577, Fax: 313-577-7536, E-mail: admissions@wayne.edu. *Interim Dean,* Dr. Hilary Ratner, 313-577-2170, Fax: 313-577-2903, E-mail: hilary.ratner@wayne.edu.

College of Education Students: 670 full-time (461 women), 2,065 part-time (1,489 women); includes 822 minority (723 African Americans, 39 Asian Americans or Pacific Islanders, 53 Hispanic Americans, 7 Native Americans), 53 international. 1,144 applicants, 69% accepted, 484 enrolled. *Faculty:* 60 full-time. Expenses: Contact institution. *Financial support:* In 2001–02, 3 fellowships, 2 research assistantships, 5 teaching assistantships were awarded. Career-related internships or fieldwork, Federal Work-Study, and institutionally sponsored loans also available. Support available to part-time students. In 2001, 591 master's, 50 doctorates, 88 other advanced degrees awarded. *Degree program information:* Evening/weekend programs available. Offers art education (M Ed); bilingual/bicultural education (M Ed); career and technical education (M Ed); counseling (M Ed, MA, Ed D, PhD, Ed S); curriculum and instruction (Ed D, PhD, Ed S); early childhood education (M Ed); education

(M Ed, MA, MAT, Ed D, PhD, Ed S); educational evaluation and research (M Ed, Ed D, PhD); educational leadership (M Ed); educational leadership and policy studies (Ed D, PhD); educational psychology (M Ed, Ed D); elementary education (M Ed, MAT); English education-secondary (M Ed); general administration and supervision (Ed D, PhD, Ed S); health education (M Ed); higher education (Ed D, PhD); instructional technology (M Ed, Ed D, PhD, Ed S); mathematics education (M Ed); physical education (M Ed); PK-12 education (MAT); reading (M Ed, Ed S); reading education (Ed D); recreation and park services (MA); rehabilitation counseling and community inclusion (MA); school and community psychology (Ed S); science education (M Ed); secondary education (MAT); social studies (M Ed); special education (M Ed, Ed D, PhD, Ed S); sports administration (MA). *Application deadline:* For fall admission, 7/1. *Application fee:* $20 ($30 for international students). *Application Contact:* Janice Green, Assistant Dean, 313-577-1605, E-mail: jwgreen@coe.wayne.edu. *Interim Dean,* Dr. Paula Wood, 313-577-4675, Fax: 313-577-3606, E-mail: pwood@wayne.edu.

College of Engineering Students: 586 full-time (98 women), 969 part-time (166 women); includes 142 minority (46 African Americans, 89 Asian Americans or Pacific Islanders, 7 Hispanic Americans), 1,028 international. 3,185 applicants, 42% accepted, 490 enrolled. *Faculty:* 85 full-time. Expenses: Contact institution. *Financial support:* In 2001–02, 7 fellowships, 83 research assistantships, 46 teaching assistantships were awarded. Career-related internships or fieldwork, Federal Work-Study, institutionally sponsored loans, scholarships/grants, and tuition waivers (full and partial) also available. Support available to part-time students. In 2001, 516 master's, 32 doctorates, 14 other advanced degrees awarded. *Degree program information:* Part-time programs available. Offers biomedical engineering (MS, PhD); chemical engineering (MS, PhD); civil and environmental engineering (MS, PhD); computer engineering (MS, PhD); electrical engineering (MS, PhD); electronics and computer control systems (MS); engineering (MS, PhD, Certificate); engineering management (MS); engineering technology (MS); environmental auditing (Certificate); hazardous materials management on public lands (Certificate); hazardous waste (MS, Certificate); hazardous waste control (Certificate); hazardous waste management (MS); industrial engineering (MS, PhD); manufacturing engineering (MS); materials science and engineering (MS, PhD, Certificate); mechanical engineering (MS, PhD); operations research (MS); polymer engineering (Certificate). *Application deadline:* For fall admission, 7/1 (priority date); for spring admission, 3/15. Applications are processed on a rolling basis. *Application fee:* $20 ($30 for international students). *Application Contact:* Steven Salley, Associate Dean, 313-577-3861, E-mail: ssalley@wayne.edu. *Interim Dean,* Dr. Ralph Kummler, 313-577-3780, Fax: 313-577-5300, E-mail: rkummler@che.eng.wayne.edu.

College of Fine, Performing and Communication Arts Students: 66 full-time (44 women), 231 part-time (149 women); includes 59 minority (46 African Americans, 5 Asian Americans or Pacific Islanders, 5 Hispanic Americans, 3 Native Americans), 25 international. 262 applicants, 42% accepted, 89 enrolled. *Faculty:* 55 full-time. Expenses: Contact institution. *Financial support:* In 2001–02, 5 fellowships, 51 research assistantships, 16 teaching assistantships were awarded. Career-related internships or fieldwork, Federal Work-Study, and institutionally sponsored loans also available. Support available to part-time students. In 2001, 61 master's, 13 doctorates, 1 other advanced degree awarded. Offers art (MA, MFA); art history (MA); choral conducting (MM); communication studies (MA, PhD); composition (MM); design and merchandising (MA); fine, performing and communication arts (MA, MFA, MM, MS, PhD, Certificate); music (MA); music education (MM); orchestral studies (Certificate); performance (MM); public relations and organizational communication (MA); radio-TV-film (MA, PhD); speech communication (MA, PhD); theatre (MA, MFA, PhD); theory (MM). *Application deadline:* For fall admission, 4/1. *Application fee:* $20 ($30 for international students). Electronic applications accepted. *Application Contact:* John Vander Weg, Associate Dean, 313-577-5747. *Dean,* Linda Moore, 313-577-5342, Fax: 313-577-5355, E-mail: linda.moore@wayne.edu.

College of Liberal Arts Students: 194 full-time (112 women), 453 part-time (270 women); includes 134 minority (110 African Americans, 7 Asian Americans or Pacific Islanders, 13 Hispanic Americans, 4 Native Americans), 82 international. 383 applicants, 59% accepted, 163 enrolled. *Faculty:* 153 full-time. Expenses: Contact institution. *Financial support:* In 2001–02, 37 fellowships, 5 research assistantships, 110 teaching assistantships were awarded. Career-related internships or fieldwork, Federal Work-Study, institutionally sponsored loans, scholarships/grants, and tuition waivers (full and partial) also available. Support available to part-time students. In 2001, 67 master's, 19 doctorates awarded. *Degree program information:* Evening/weekend programs available. Offers anthropology (MA, PhD); archival administration (Certificate); classics (MA); comparative literature (MA); criminal justice (MPA); economics (MA, PhD); English (MA, PhD); French (MA); German (MA); history (MA, PhD); Italian (MA); language learning (MA); liberal arts (MA, MPA, MS, PhD, Certificate); linguistics (MA); modern languages (PhD); Near Eastern studies (MA); philosophy (MA, PhD); political science (MA, PhD); public administration (MPA); sociology (MA, PhD); Spanish (MA). *Application fee:* $20 ($30 for international students). *Application Contact:* Janet Hankin, Associate Dean, 313-577-2517, E-mail: janet.hankin@wayne.edu. *Dean,* Lawrence Scaff, 313-577-2514, Fax: 313-577-8971, E-mail: l.scaff@wayne.edu.

College of Lifelong Learning Students: 37. 18 applicants, 56% accepted, 10 enrolled. *Faculty:* 10 full-time. Expenses: Contact institution. *Financial support:* Research assistantships available. In 2001, 6 degrees awarded. Offers interdisciplinary studies (MIS); lifelong learning (MIS). Electronic applications accepted. *Application Contact:* Dr. Stuart Henry, Associate Dean, 313-577-4627, E-mail: stuart.henry@wayne.edu. *Interim Dean,* Dr. Paula Wood, 313-577-4675, Fax: 313-577-5466, E-mail: pwood@wayne.edu.

College of Nursing Students: 50 full-time (47 women), 157 part-time (145 women); includes 30 minority (23 African Americans, 6 Asian Americans or Pacific Islanders, 1 Native American), 17 international. Average age 39. 108 applicants, 74% accepted, 63 enrolled. *Faculty:* 17 full-time. Expenses: Contact institution. *Financial support:* In 2001–02, 47 students received support, including 4 fellowships, 1 research assistantship, 1 teaching assistantship; Federal Work-Study, institutionally sponsored loans, scholarships/grants, and traineeships also available. Support available to part-time students. Financial award application deadline: 7/1; financial award applicants required to submit FAFSA. In 2001, 52 master's, 5 doctorates, 7 other advanced degrees awarded. *Degree program information:* Part-time programs available. Offers adult acute care nursing (MSN); adult primary care nursing (MSN); advanced practice nursing with women, neonates and children (MSN); child/adolescent psychiatric nursing (MSN); community health nursing (MSN); nursing (MSN, PhD, Certificate); nursing education (Certificate); psychiatric mental health nurse practitioner (MSN); transcultural nursing (Certificate). *Application deadline:* Applications are processed on a rolling basis. *Application fee:* $20 ($30 for international students). *Application Contact:* Mary Nies, Assistant Dean, 313-577-5137, E-mail: ag6457@wayne.edu. *Dean,* Dr. Barbara Redman, 313-577-4070, Fax: 313-577-4571, E-mail: b.redman@wayne.edu.

College of Science Students: 327 full-time (160 women), 464 part-time (232 women); includes 194 minority (170 African Americans, 9 Asian Americans or Pacific Islanders, 12 Hispanic Americans, 3 Native Americans), 29 international. 1,504 applicants, 29% accepted, 236 enrolled. *Faculty:* 173 full-time. Expenses: Contact institution. *Financial support:* In 2001–02, 23 fellowships, 93 research assistantships, 236 teaching assistantships were awarded. Career-related internships or fieldwork, Federal Work-Study, institutionally sponsored loans, and tuition waivers (full) also available. Support available to part-time students. In 2001, 137 master's, 63 doctorates, 7 other advanced degrees awarded. Offers applied mathematics (MA, PhD); audiology (MS); biological sciences (MA, MS, PhD); chemistry (MA, MS, PhD); clinical psychology (PhD); cognitive psychology (PhD); computer science (MA, MS, PhD); developmental psychology (PhD); electronics and computer control systems (MS); geology (MS); human development (MA); industrial/organizational psychology (PhD); mathematics (MA, PhD); molecular biotechnology (MS); nutrition and food science (MA, MS, PhD, Certificate); physics (MA, MS, PhD); psychology (MA, PhD); science (MA, MS, PhD, Certificate); scientific computing (Certificate); social psychology (PhD); speech language pathology (PhD); speech-language pathology (MA); statistics (MA, PhD). *Application fee:* $20 ($30 for international students). *Application Contact:* Alice Young, Associate Dean, 313-577-2515, E-mail: alice.young@wayne.edu. *Dean,* Robert Thomas, 313-577-2515, Fax: 313-577-9693, E-mail: robert_thomas@wayne.edu.

College of Urban, Labor and Metropolitan Affairs Students: 17 full-time (13 women), 111 part-time (72 women); includes 36 minority (34 African Americans, 2 Asian Americans or Pacific Islanders), 10 international. 75 applicants, 49% accepted, 24 enrolled. *Faculty:* 15 full-time. Expenses: Contact institution. *Financial support:* In 2001–02, 3 teaching assistantships were awarded; career-related internships or fieldwork and institutionally sponsored loans also available. Support available to part-time students. In 2001, 35 master's, 1 other advanced degree awarded. *Degree program information:* Part-time and evening/weekend programs available. Offers dispute resolution (MADR, Certificate); economic development (Certificate); geography (MA); industrial relations (MAIR); urban planning (MUP); urban, labor and metropolitan affairs (MA, MADR, MAIR, MUP, Certificate). *Application deadline:* For fall admission, 7/1. *Application fee:* $20 ($30 for international students). Electronic applications accepted. *Application Contact:* Robin Boyle, Associate Dean, 313-577-8711, Fax: 313-577-8800, E-mail: r.boyle@wayne.edu. *Interim Dean,* Alma Young, 313-577-5071, Fax: 313-577-8800.

Eugene Applebaum College of Pharmacy and Health Sciences Students: 183 full-time (137 women), 73 part-time (52 women); includes 43 minority (20 African Americans, 21 Asian Americans or Pacific Islanders, 1 Hispanic American, 1 Native American), 24 international. 343 applicants, 35% accepted, 92 enrolled. *Faculty:* 44 full-time. Expenses: Contact institution. *Financial support:* In 2001–02, 12 research assistantships were awarded; fellowships, teaching assistantships, career-related internships or fieldwork and scholarships/grants also available. Support available to part-time students. In 2001, 13 first professional degrees, 82 master's, 3 doctorates awarded. *Degree program information:* Part-time and evening/weekend programs available. Offers allied health professions (MS, MSPT, Certificate); clinical laboratory sciences (MS, Certificate); health systems pharmacy management (MS); industrial toxicology (Certificate); nurse anesthesia (MS); occupational health sciences (MS); occupational therapy (MS); ocupational safety (Certificate); pharmaceutical sciences (MS, PhD); pharmacy (Pharm D); pharmacy and allied health professions (Pharm D, MS, MSPT, PhD, Certificate); physical therapy (MSPT); physician assistant studies (MS). *Application fee:* $20 ($30 for international students). *Application Contact:* Steve Siconolfi, Associate Dean, 313-577-5875, E-mail: sfs@wizard.pharm.wayne.edu. *Dean,* Eberhard F. Mammen, 313-577-1278, Fax: 313-577-5589, E-mail: ah4559@wayne.edu.

Law School Students: 551 full-time (271 women), 351 part-time (148 women); includes 146 minority (90 African Americans, 34 Asian Americans or Pacific Islanders, 16 Hispanic Americans, 6 Native Americans), 20 international. 96 applicants, 58% accepted, 37 enrolled. *Faculty:* 33 full-time. Expenses: Contact institution. *Financial support:* In 2001–02, 460 students received support. Federal Work-Study available. Support available to part-time students. Financial award application deadline: 4/30; financial award applicants required to submit FAFSA. In 2001, 223 first professional degrees, 26 master's awarded. *Degree program information:* Part-time and evening/weekend programs available. Offers law (JD, LL M). *Application deadline:* For fall admission, 4/15. *Application fee:* $20 ($30 for international students). Electronic applications accepted. *Application Contact:* Linda Fowler Sims, Assistant Dean for Recruitment and Admissions, 313-577-3937, Fax: 313-577-9049, E-mail: ab2594@wayne.edu. *Dean,* Joan Mahoney, 313-577-3933, Fax: 313-577-2620.

School of Business Administration Students: 231 full-time (104 women), 1,193 part-time (462 women); includes 267 minority (156 African Americans, 89 Asian Americans or Pacific Islanders, 15 Hispanic Americans, 7 Native Americans), 169 international. 792 applicants, 47% accepted, 267 enrolled. *Faculty:* 34 full-time. Expenses: Contact institution. *Financial support:* In 2001–02, 8 research assistantships were awarded; career-related internships or fieldwork, Federal Work-Study, and scholarships/grants also available. Support available to part-time students. Financial award applicants required to submit FAFSA. In 2001, 476 degrees awarded. *Degree program information:* Part-time and evening/weekend programs available. Offers business administration (MBA); taxation (MS). *Application deadline:* For fall admission, 8/1; for spring admission, 4/1. *Application fee:* $20 ($30 for international students). Electronic applications accepted. *Application Contact:* Barbara Price, Associate Dean, 313-577-6275, E-mail: bprice@wayne.edu. *Dean,* Dr. Harvey Kahalas, 313-577-4500, Fax: 313-577-4557.

School of Social Work Students: 213 full-time (186 women), 332 part-time (296 women); includes 194 minority (170 African Americans, 9 Asian Americans or Pacific Islanders, 12 Hispanic Americans, 3 Native Americans), 29 international. Average age 34. 284 applicants, 68% accepted, 127 enrolled. *Faculty:* 13 full-time. Expenses: Contact institution. *Financial support:* Career-related internships or fieldwork, institutionally sponsored loans, scholarships/grants, and tuition waivers (partial) available. Support available to part-time students. Financial award application deadline: 5/1; financial award applicants required to submit FAFSA. In 2001, 293 master's, 8 other advanced degrees awarded. *Degree program information:* Part-time and evening/weekend programs available. Offers social work (MSW); social work practice with families and couples (Certificate). *Application deadline:* For fall admission, 3/31; for spring admission, 2/28. *Application fee:* $20 ($30 for international students). Electronic applications accepted. *Application Contact:* Janet Clerk-Joiner, Director I, 313-577-4402. *Dean,* Phyllis Vroom, 313-577-4409, Fax: 313-577-8770.

School of Medicine Students: 2,039 full-time (884 women), 230 part-time (110 women); includes 718 minority (276 African Americans, 409 Asian Americans or Pacific Islanders, 27 Hispanic Americans, 6 Native Americans), 418 international. *Faculty:* 247 full-time. Expenses: Contact institution. *Financial support:* In 2001–02, 10 fellowships, 137 research assistantships were awarded. Teaching assistantships, career-related internships or fieldwork, Federal Work-Study, institutionally sponsored loans, scholarships/grants, and tuition waivers (full and partial) also available. Support available to part-time students. In 2001, 183 first professional degrees, 45 master's, 38 doctorates awarded. *Degree program information:* Part-time and evening/weekend programs available. Offers medicine (MD, MS, PhD, Certificate). *Application fee:* $20. Electronic applications accepted. *Application Contact:* Dr. Kenneth C. Palmer, Assistant Dean, 313-577-5151, E-mail: kpalmer@med.wayne.edu. *Dean,* Dr. John D. Crissman, 313-577-1460, Fax: 313-577-8777, E-mail: jcrissm@med.wayne.edu.

Graduate Programs in Medicine Students: 273. Expenses: Contact institution. *Financial support:* Fellowships, research assistantships, teaching assistantships, career-related internships or fieldwork, Federal Work-Study, institutionally sponsored loans, scholarships/grants, and tuition waivers (full and partial) available. Support available to part-time students. *Degree program information:* Part-time and evening/weekend programs available. Offers anatomy and cell biology (MS, PhD); basic medical science (MS); biochemistry (MS, PhD); cancer biology (PhD); cellular and clinical neurobiology (PhD); community health (MS); community health services (Certificate); immunology and microbiology (MS, PhD); medical physics (PhD); medical research (MS); medicine (MS, PhD, Certificate); molecular biology and genetics (MS, PhD); pathology (PhD); pharmacology (MS, PhD); physical medicine and rehabilitation (MS); physiology (MS, PhD); radiological physics (MS). *Application fee:* $20 ($30 for international students). *Assistant Dean,* Dr. Kenneth C. Palmer, 313-577-5151, E-mail: kpalmer@med.wayne.edu.

WEBBER INTERNATIONAL UNIVERSITY, Babson Park, FL 33827-0096

General Information Independent, coed, comprehensive institution. *Enrollment:* 31 full-time matriculated graduate/professional students (16 women), 8 part-time matriculated graduate/professional students (4 women). *Enrollment by degree level:* 39 master's. *Graduate faculty:* 8 full-time (1 woman). *Tuition:* Part-time $300 per credit hour. *Student services:* Campus safety program, career counseling, disabled student services, exercise/wellness program, international student services. *Library facilities:* Grace and Roger Babson Library plus 1 other. *Collection:* 35,000 titles, 168 serial subscriptions, 11,073 audiovisual materials.

Computer facilities: 50 computers available on campus for general student use. Internet access, e-mail are available. *Web address:* http://www.webber.edu/.

General Application Contact: Jeanne Sobierajski, MBA Marketing Director, 863-638-2927, Fax: 863-638-2823, E-mail: webbercollegemba@hotmail.com.

Webber International University (continued)

GRADUATE UNITS

Graduate School Students: 31 full-time (16 women), 8 part-time (4 women). Average age 27. 45 applicants, 71% accepted. *Faculty:* 8 full-time (1 woman). Expenses: Contact institution. *Financial support:* In 2001–02, 8 students received support; fellowships with partial tuition reimbursements available available. Support available to part-time students. Financial award application deadline: 8/15; financial award applicants required to submit FAFSA. In 2001, 13 degrees awarded. *Degree program information:* Part-time and evening/weekend programs available. Offers business administration (MBA). *Application deadline:* For fall admission, 5/15 (priority date). Applications are processed on a rolling basis. *Application fee:* $50 ($75 for international students). *Application Contact:* Jeanne Sobierajski, MBA Marketing Director, 863-638-2927, Fax: 863-638-2823, E-mail: webbercollegemba@hotmail.com. *Dean,* Dr. Nikos Orphanoudakis, 863-638-2925, Fax: 863-638-2823.

WEBER STATE UNIVERSITY, Ogden, UT 84408-1001

General Information State-supported, coed, comprehensive institution. *Enrollment:* 69 full-time matriculated graduate/professional students (20 women), 185 part-time matriculated graduate/professional students (115 women). *Enrollment by degree level:* 254 master's. *Graduate faculty:* 32 full-time (11 women), 10 part-time/adjunct (5 women). Tuition, state resident: part-time $220 per credit hour. Tuition, nonresident: part-time $633 per credit hour. Tuition and fees vary according to course level and program. *Graduate housing:* Room and/or apartments available on a first-come, first-served basis to single students; on-campus housing not available to married students. Typical cost: $1,645 per year ($4,645 including board). *Student services:* Campus employment opportunities, campus safety program, career counseling, child daycare facilities, disabled student services, exercise/wellness program, free psychological counseling, grant writing training, international student services, low-cost health insurance, multicultural affairs office, teacher training, writing training. *Library facilities:* Stewart Library plus 1 other. *Online resources:* library catalog, web page, access to other libraries' catalogs. *Collection:* 648,743 titles, 2,278 serial subscriptions, 15,383 audiovisual materials. *Research affiliation:* One Stop Satellite Solutions (aerospace technology), American Honda Corporation (automobile manufacturing), Petroleum and Research Foundation (chemical research), Applied Biosciences Corporation (biosciences).

Computer facilities: 558 computers available on campus for general student use. A campuswide network can be accessed from student residence rooms and from off campus. Internet access and online class registration, Online Grades are available. *Web address:* http://weber.edu/.

General Application Contact: Christopher C. Rivera, Director of Admissions, 801-626-6046, Fax: 801-626-6747, E-mail: crivera@weber.edu.

GRADUATE UNITS

College of Education Students: 6 full-time (2 women), 101 part-time (75 women); includes 7 minority (1 Asian American or Pacific Islander, 6 Hispanic Americans), 2 international. Average age 39. 53 applicants, 96% accepted. *Faculty:* 17 full-time (7 women), 9 part-time/adjunct (5 women). Expenses: Contact institution. *Financial support:* In 2001–02, 24 students received support. Institutionally sponsored loans, scholarships/grants, tuition waivers (full and partial), and unspecified assistantships available. Support available to part-time students. Financial award application deadline: 2/1. In 2001, 40 degrees awarded. *Degree program information:* Part-time and evening/weekend programs available. Offers curriculum and instruction (M Ed); education (M Ed). *Application deadline:* For fall admission, 5/1 (priority date); for spring admission, 11/1 (priority date). Applications are processed on a rolling basis. *Application fee:* $55 ($70 for international students). *Application Contact:* Dr. Judith Mitchell, Director, 801-626-6626, Fax: 801-626-7427, E-mail: jmitchell@weber.edu. *Dean,* Dr. David M. Greene, 801-626-6273, Fax: 801-626-7427, E-mail: dgreene@weber.edu.

John B. Goddard School of Business and Economics Students: 62 full-time (18 women), 59 part-time (27 women); includes 8 minority (2 African Americans, 4 Asian Americans or Pacific Islanders, 2 Hispanic Americans), 5 international. Average age 31. 105 applicants, 70% accepted. *Faculty:* 13 full-time (4 women), 1 part-time/adjunct (0 women). Expenses: Contact institution. *Financial support:* In 2001–02, 13 students received support; research assistantships, teaching assistantships, Federal Work-Study, institutionally sponsored loans, scholarships/grants, and tuition waivers (full and partial) available. Financial award application deadline: 3/1. In 2001, 36 degrees awarded. *Degree program information:* Part-time and evening/weekend programs available. Postbaccalaureate distance learning degree programs offered. Offers accountancy (MP Acc); business administration (MBA); business and economics (MBA, MP Acc). *Application deadline:* Applications are processed on a rolling basis. *Application fee:* $30 ($45 for international students). Electronic applications accepted. *Dean,* Dr. Michael Vaughan, 801-626-6063, Fax: 801-626-7423, E-mail: mvaughan@weber.edu.

WEBSTER UNIVERSITY, St. Louis, MO 63119-3194

General Information Independent, coed, comprehensive institution. *Enrollment:* 3,889 full-time matriculated graduate/professional students (2,111 women), 9,016 part-time matriculated graduate/professional students (4,854 women). *Enrollment by degree level:* 12,689 master's, 44 doctoral, 172 other advanced degrees. *Graduate faculty:* 80 full-time (37 women), 1,339 part-time/adjunct (331 women). *Tuition:* Full-time $7,164; part-time $398 per credit hour. *Graduate housing:* Rooms and/or apartments available on a first-come, first-served basis to single students and available to married students. Typical cost: $6,400 (including board) for single students. Room and board charges vary according to board plan and housing facility selected. Housing application deadline: 7/1. *Student services:* Campus employment opportunities, campus safety program, career counseling, disabled student services, exercise/wellness program, free psychological counseling, international student services, multicultural affairs office, writing training. *Library facilities:* Eden-Webster Library. *Online resources:* library catalog, web page, access to other libraries' catalogs. *Collection:* 250,000 titles, 1,400 serial subscriptions, 8,700 audiovisual materials. *Research affiliation:* Repertory Theatre of St. Louis, Opera Theatre of St. Louis, World Affairs Council (international business education), Literacy Investment for Tomorrow, OASIS.

Computer facilities: 185 computers available on campus for general student use. A campuswide network can be accessed. Internet access and online class registration are available. *Web address:* http://www.webster.edu/.

General Application Contact: Denise Harrell, Associate Director of Graduate and Evening Student, 314-968-6983, Fax: 314-968-7116, E-mail: gadmit@webster.edu.

GRADUATE UNITS

College of Arts and Sciences Students: 712 full-time (578 women), 696 part-time (541 women); includes 680 minority (578 African Americans, 10 Asian Americans or Pacific Islanders, 88 Hispanic Americans, 4 Native Americans), 56 international. Average age 35. 439 applicants, 92% accepted, 401 enrolled. *Faculty:* 17 full-time (9 women), 182 part-time/adjunct (73 women). Expenses: Contact institution. *Financial support:* Career-related internships or fieldwork and Federal Work-Study available. Support available to part-time students. Financial award application deadline: 4/1; financial award applicants required to submit FAFSA. In 2001, 414 master's, 27 other advanced degrees awarded. *Degree program information:* Part-time and evening/weekend programs available. Postbaccalaureate distance learning degree programs offered. Offers arts and sciences (MA, MS, MSN, Certificate); counseling (MA); family systems nursing (MSN); gerontology (MA); international relations (MA); legal studies (MA); nurse anesthesia (MS); paralegal studies (Certificate). *Application deadline:* Applications are processed on a rolling basis. *Application fee:* $25 ($50 for international students). *Application Contact:* Denise Harrell, Associate Director of Graduate and Evening Student Admissions, 314-968-6983, Fax: 314-968-7116, E-mail: gadmit@webster.edu. *Acting Dean,* Dr. Janice I. Hooper, 314-968-7160, Fax: 314-968-7471, E-mail: hooperji@webster.edu.

Leigh Gerdine College of Fine Arts Students: 15 full-time (9 women), 35 part-time (21 women); includes 4 minority (all African Americans), 3 international. Average age 34. 21 applicants, 86% accepted, 15 enrolled. *Faculty:* 16 full-time (5 women), 20 part-time/adjunct (9 women). Expenses: Contact institution. *Financial support:* Fellowships, teaching assistantships, career-related internships or fieldwork and Federal Work-Study available. Support available to part-time students. Financial award application deadline: 4/1; financial award applicants required to submit FAFSA. In 2001, 2 degrees awarded. *Degree program information:* Part-time and evening/weekend programs available. Offers art (MA, MFA); arts management and leadership (MFA); church music (MM); composition (MM); conducting (MM); fine arts (MA, MFA, MM); jazz studies (MM); music education (MM); performance (MM); piano (MM). *Application deadline:* Applications are processed on a rolling basis. *Application fee:* $25 ($50 for international students). *Application Contact:* Denise Harrell, Associate Director of Graduate and Evening Student Admissions, 314-968-6983, Fax: 314-968-7116, E-mail: gadmit@webster.edu. *Dean,* Peter Sargent, 314-968-7006, Fax: 314-963-6048, E-mail: sargenpe@webster.edu.

School of Business and Technology Students: 3,045 full-time (1,429 women), 7,284 part-time (3,412 women); includes 3,881 minority (2,894 African Americans, 329 Asian Americans or Pacific Islanders, 583 Hispanic Americans, 75 Native Americans), 824 international. Average age 35. 3,149 applicants, 96% accepted, 2891 enrolled. *Faculty:* 21 full-time (4 women), 1,053 part-time/adjunct (198 women). Expenses: Contact institution. *Financial support:* Career-related internships or fieldwork and Federal Work-Study available. Support available to part-time students. Financial award application deadline: 4/1; financial award applicants required to submit FAFSA. In 2001, 3,222 master's, 4 doctorates, 2 other advanced degrees awarded. *Degree program information:* Part-time and evening/weekend programs available. Postbaccalaureate distance learning degree programs offered. Offers business (MA, MBA); business and technology (MA, MBA, MS, DM, Certificate); computer distributed systems (Certificate); computer resources and information management (MA, MBA); computer science (MS); computer science/distributed systems (MS); environmental management (MS); finance (MA, MBA); health care management (MA); health services management (MA, MBA); human resources development (MA, MBA); human resources management (MA); international business (MA, MBA); management (MA, MBA, DM); marketing (MA, MBA); procurement and acquisitions management (MA, MBA); public administration (MA); real estate management (MA, MBA); security management (MA, MBA); space systems management (MA, MBA, MS); telecommunications management (MA, MBA). *Application deadline:* Applications are processed on a rolling basis. *Application fee:* $25 ($50 for international students). *Application Contact:* Denise Harrell, Associate Director of Graduate and Evening Student Admissions, 314-968-6983, Fax: 314-968-7116, E-mail: gadmit@webster.edu. *Dean,* Dr. Benjamin Ola Akande, 314-968-5951, Fax: 314-968-7077.

School of Communications Students: 24 full-time (16 women), 100 part-time (76 women); includes 36 minority (32 African Americans, 2 Asian Americans or Pacific Islanders, 2 Hispanic Americans), 12 international. Average age 31. 147 applicants, 95% accepted, 119 enrolled. *Faculty:* 6 full-time (4 women), 13 part-time/adjunct (6 women). Expenses: Contact institution. *Financial support:* Career-related internships or fieldwork and Federal Work-Study available. Support available to part-time students. Financial award application deadline: 4/1; financial award applicants required to submit FAFSA. In 2001, 30 degrees awarded. *Degree program information:* Part-time and evening/weekend programs available. Offers media communication (MA). *Application deadline:* Applications are processed on a rolling basis. *Application fee:* $25 ($50 for international students). *Application Contact:* Denise Harrell, Associate Director of Graduate and Evening Student Admissions, 314-968-6983, Fax: 314-968-7116, E-mail: gadmit@webster.edu. *Dean,* Debra Carpenter, 314-968-7154, Fax: 314-963-6106, E-mail: carpenda@webster.edu.

School of Education Students: 95 full-time (80 women), 911 part-time (813 women); includes 117 minority (96 African Americans, 5 Asian Americans or Pacific Islanders, 14 Hispanic Americans, 2 Native Americans), 5 international. Average age 34. 209 applicants, 89% accepted, 159 enrolled. *Faculty:* 20 full-time (15 women), 71 part-time/adjunct (45 women). Expenses: Contact institution. *Financial support:* Career-related internships or fieldwork and Federal Work-Study available. Support available to part-time students. Financial award application deadline: 4/1; financial award applicants required to submit FAFSA. In 2001, 313 degrees awarded. *Degree program information:* Part-time programs available. Postbaccalaureate distance learning degree programs offered. Offers communications (MAT); early childhood education (MAT); education (MAT, Ed S); Education Leadership (Ed S); education technology (MAT); mathematics education (MAT); multidisciplinary studies (MAT); science education (MAT); social science education (MAT); special education (MAT). *Application deadline:* Applications are processed on a rolling basis. *Application fee:* $25 ($50 for international students). *Application Contact:* Denise Harrell, Associate Director of Graduate and Evening Student Admissions, 314-968-6983, Fax: 314-968-7116, E-mail: gadmit@webster.edu. *Dean,* Dr. Judith Walker DeFelix, 314-968-7423, Fax: 314-968-7118, E-mail: jwafelix@webster.edu.

WESLEYAN COLLEGE, Macon, GA 31210-4462

General Information Independent-religious, women only, comprehensive institution. *Enrollment:* 21 part-time matriculated graduate/professional students (20 women). *Enrollment by degree level:* 21 master's. *Graduate faculty:* 11 full-time (5 women), 3 part-time/adjunct (all women). *Tuition:* Full-time $1,200; part-time $200 per credit hour. Tuition and fees vary according to course load. *Graduate housing:* Room and/or apartments available on a first-come, first-served basis to single students; on-campus housing not available to married students. Typical cost: $7,250 (including board). Room and board charges vary according to housing facility selected. Housing application deadline: 5/1. *Student services:* Campus safety program, exercise/wellness program, free psychological counseling, teacher training. *Library facilities:* Lucy Lester Willet Memorial Library. *Online resources:* library catalog, web page, access to other libraries' catalogs. *Collection:* 140,923 titles, 650 serial subscriptions, 6,553 audiovisual materials.

Computer facilities: 35 computers available on campus for general student use. A campuswide network can be accessed from student residence rooms and from off campus. Internet access and online class registration are available. *Web address:* http://www.wesleyancollege.edu/.

General Application Contact: Dr. Juanita E. Carson, Director, Graduate Programs in Education, 478-757-5279, Fax: 478-757-5148, E-mail: jcarson@wesleyancollege.edu.

GRADUATE UNITS

Department of Education *Faculty:* 11 full-time (5 women), 3 part-time/adjunct (all women). Expenses: Contact institution. *Financial support:* Federal Work-Study and scholarships/grants available. Financial award application deadline: 4/1; financial award applicants required to submit FAFSA. In 2001, 4 degrees awarded. *Degree program information:* Part-time programs available. Offers early childhood education (MA); middle-level mathematics and middle-level science education (MA). *Application deadline:* For fall admission, 9/1 (priority date); for spring admission, 12/1 (priority date). Applications are processed on a rolling basis. *Application fee:* $30. *Director, Graduate Programs in Education,* Dr. Juanita E. Carson, 478-757-5279, Fax: 478-757-5148, E-mail: jcarson@wesleyancollege.edu.

WESLEYAN UNIVERSITY, Middletown, CT 06459-0260

General Information Independent, coed, university. CGS member. *Enrollment:* 188 full-time matriculated graduate/professional students (90 women), 267 part-time matriculated graduate/professional students (194 women). *Graduate faculty:* 97 full-time (20 women), 120 part-time/adjunct (48 women). *Tuition:* Full-time $19,716. *Required fees:* $671. Full-time tuition and fees vary according to program. *Graduate housing:* Rooms and/or apartments available to single and married students. Typical cost: $5,172 per year for single students; $7,200 per year for married students. Room charges vary according to housing facility selected. Housing application deadline: 7/19. *Student services:* Campus employment opportunities, campus safety program, career counseling, child daycare facilities, exercise/wellness program, free psychological counseling, international student services, low-cost health insurance, multicultural affairs office, writing training. *Library facilities:* Olin Memorial Library plus 3 others. *Online resources:* library catalog, web page, access to other libraries' catalogs. *Collection:* 1.2 million titles, 2,719 serial subscriptions, 42,137 audiovisual materials. *Research affiliation:* Cold Springs Marine Laboratory, Woods Hole Oceanographic Institution.

Computer facilities: 250 computers available on campus for general student use. A campuswide network can be accessed from student residence rooms and from off campus. Internet access and online class registration, electronic portfolio are available. *Web address:* http://www.wesleyan.edu/.

General Application Contact: Marina J. Melendez, Director of Graduate Student Services, 860-685-2390, Fax: 860-685-2439, E-mail: mmelendez@wesleyan.edu.

GRADUATE UNITS

Graduate Liberal Studies Program Students: 6 full-time (2 women), 267 part-time (194 women); includes 9 minority (all African Americans), 6 international. Average age 41. 273 applicants, 100% accepted. *Faculty:* 40 part-time/adjunct (12 women). Expenses: Contact institution. *Financial support:* In 2001–02, 64 students received support. Scholarships/grants available. Support available to part-time students. In 2001, 120 master's, 5 other advanced degrees awarded. *Degree program information:* Part-time and evening/weekend programs available. Offers liberal studies (MALS, CAS). *Application deadline:* For fall admission, 9/11; for spring admission, 1/24. Applications are processed on a rolling basis. *Application fee:* $50. *Application Contact:* Dolores Chowaniec, Students Records Specialist, 860-685-2900, Fax: 860-685-2901, E-mail: glsinquire@wesleyan.edu. *Associate Dean and Director,* Dr. Lori Hunter-Union, 860-685-2900, Fax: 860-685-2901, E-mail: lhunterunion@wesleyan.edu.

Graduate Programs Students: 182 full-time (88 women); includes 12 minority (6 African Americans, 4 Asian Americans or Pacific Islanders, 2 Hispanic Americans), 94 international. Average age 28. 565 applicants. *Faculty:* 97 full-time (20 women), 11 part-time/adjunct (2 women). Expenses: Contact institution. *Financial support:* Fellowships with tuition reimbursements, research assistantships with tuition reimbursements, teaching assistantships with tuition reimbursements, institutionally sponsored loans and tuition waivers (full and partial) available. Financial award applicants required to submit FAFSA. In 2001, 22 master's, 18 doctorates awarded. Offers astronomy (MA); biochemistry (MA, PhD); cell biology (PhD); chemical physics (MA, PhD); comparative physiology (PhD); developmental biology (PhD); earth sciences (MA); ethnomusicology (PhD); genetics (PhD); inorganic chemistry (MA, PhD); mathematics (MA, PhD); molecular biology (PhD); music (MA); neurophysiology (PhD); organic chemistry (MA, PhD); physical chemistry (MA, PhD); physics (MA, PhD); population biology (PhD); psychology (MA); theoretical chemistry (MA, PhD). Electronic applications accepted. *Application Contact:* Marina J. Melendez, Director of Graduate Student Services, 860-685-2579, Fax: 860-685-2579, E-mail: mmelendez@wesleyan.edu. *Vice President for Academic Affairs, Provost and Professor of History,* Dr. Judith C. Brown, 860-685-2010, E-mail: jbrown@wesleyan.edu.

WESLEY BIBLICAL SEMINARY, Jackson, MS 39206

General Information Independent-religious, coed, graduate-only institution. *Graduate housing:* Rooms and/or apartments available to single and married students.

GRADUATE UNITS

Graduate Programs *Degree program information:* Part-time programs available. Offers theology (M Div, MA, MACE).

WESLEY COLLEGE, Dover, DE 19901-3875

General Information Independent-religious, coed, comprehensive institution. *Enrollment:* 10 full-time matriculated graduate/professional students (8 women), 76 part-time matriculated graduate/professional students (50 women). *Enrollment by degree level:* 86 master's. *Graduate faculty:* 2 full-time (1 woman), 8 part-time/adjunct (4 women). *Tuition:* Full-time $4,500; part-time $1,500 per year. *Required fees:* $15 per semester. One-time fee: $35. *Graduate housing:* On-campus housing not available. *Student services:* Campus employment opportunities, campus safety program, career counseling, disabled student services, international student services, teacher training. *Library facilities:* Robert H. Parker Library. *Online resources:* library catalog, web page. *Collection:* 72,000 titles, 400 serial subscriptions, 1,814 audiovisual materials.

Computer facilities: 115 computers available on campus for general student use. A campuswide network can be accessed from student residence rooms. Internet access is available. *Web address:* http://www.wesley.edu/.

General Application Contact: Arthur Jacobs, Director of Admissions, 302-736-2517, Fax: 302-736-2301, E-mail: jacobsar@mail.wesley.edu.

GRADUATE UNITS

Graduate Business Program Average age 30. 1 applicant, 100% accepted. *Faculty:* 3 full-time (1 woman). Expenses: Contact institution. *Financial support:* Teaching assistantships with tuition reimbursements, unspecified assistantships available. In 2001, 4 degrees awarded. *Degree program information:* Part-time and evening/weekend programs available. Offers business administration (MBA). *Application deadline:* Applications are processed on a rolling basis. *Application fee:* $20. *Application Contact:* Arthur Jacobs, Director of Admissions, 302-736-2517, Fax: 302-736-2301, E-mail: jacobsar@mail.wesley.edu. *Director,* Dr. Robert Edelson, 302-736-2517, Fax: 302-736-2301, E-mail: edelsoro@mail.wesley.edu.

Graduate Education Program Students: 18 full-time (8 women), 17 part-time (10 women); includes 2 minority (both African Americans) Average age 30. 16 applicants, 63% accepted. *Faculty:* 4 full-time (2 women), 1 (woman) part-time/adjunct. Expenses: Contact institution. *Financial support:* In 2001–02, 7 students received support, including 7 teaching assistantships with full tuition reimbursements available (averaging $9,000 per year) In 2001, 11 degrees awarded. *Degree program information:* Part-time and evening/weekend programs available. Offers education and physical education (M Ed, MA Ed, MAT). *Application deadline:* Applications are processed on a rolling basis. *Application fee:* $20. *Application Contact:* Marie Cusick, Administrative Assistant, Office of Graduate and Evening Studies, 302-736-2352, Fax: 302-736-2301, E-mail: cusickca@mail.wesley.edu. *Director,* Dr. J. Thomas Sturgis, 302-736-2476, Fax: 302-736-2301, E-mail: sturgith@mail.wesley.edu.

Graduate Environmental Sciences Program Average age 30. 4 applicants, 100% accepted. *Faculty:* 1 full-time (0 women). Expenses: Contact institution. *Financial support:* Teaching assistantships with tuition reimbursements, unspecified assistantships available. In 2001, 4 degrees awarded. *Degree program information:* Part-time and evening/weekend programs available. Offers environmental sciences (MS). *Application deadline:* Applications are processed on a rolling basis. *Application fee:* $20. *Application Contact:* Arthur Jacobs, Director of Admissions, 302-736-2428, Fax: 302-736-2301, E-mail: jacobsar@mail.wesley.edu. *Director,* Dr. Bruce Allison, 302-736-2349, Fax: 302-736-2301, E-mail: allisobr@mail.wesley.edu.

Graduate Nursing Program Students: 23 full-time (22 women), 21 part-time (20 women). Average age 34. 12 applicants, 67% accepted. *Faculty:* 4 full-time (3 women), 2 part-time/adjunct (both women). Expenses: Contact institution. *Financial support:* In 2001–02, 12 students received support, including 4 teaching assistantships with tuition reimbursements available; career-related internships or fieldwork, institutionally sponsored loans, traineeships, and unspecified assistantships also available. Support available to part-time students. Financial award applicants required to submit FAFSA. In 2001, 13 degrees awarded. *Degree program information:* Part-time and evening/weekend programs available. Offers nursing (MSN). *Application deadline:* Applications are processed on a rolling basis. *Application fee:* $20. Electronic applications accepted. *Director,* Dr. Lucille C. Gambardella, 302-736-2512, Fax: 302-736-2548, E-mail: gambarlu@mail.wesley.edu.

WESLEY THEOLOGICAL SEMINARY, Washington, DC 20016-5690

General Information Independent-religious, coed, graduate-only institution. *Graduate housing:* Rooms and/or apartments available to single and married students. Housing application deadline: 7/1.

GRADUATE UNITS

Graduate and Professional Programs *Degree program information:* Part-time programs available. Offers theology (M Div, MA, MRE, MTS, D Min).

WEST CHESTER UNIVERSITY OF PENNSYLVANIA, West Chester, PA 19383

General Information State-supported, coed, comprehensive institution. CGS member. *Enrollment:* 391 full-time matriculated graduate/professional students (308 women), 1,251 part-time matriculated graduate/professional students (861 women). *Enrollment by degree level:* 1,411 master's, 231 other advanced degrees. *Graduate faculty:* 226. Tuition, state resident: full-time $4,600; part-time $256 per credit. Tuition, nonresident: full-time $7,554; part-time $420 per credit. *Required fees:* $44 per credit. *Graduate housing:* Room and/or apartments available on a first-come, first-served basis to single students; on-campus housing not available to married students. *Student services:* Campus employment opportunities, campus safety program, career counseling, child daycare facilities, disabled student services, exercise/wellness program, free psychological counseling, grant writing training, international student services, low-cost health insurance, multicultural affairs office. *Library facilities:* Francis Harvey Green Library plus 1 other. *Online resources:* library catalog, web page, access to other libraries' catalogs. *Collection:* 524,976 titles, 2,800 serial subscriptions. *Research affiliation:* Texas Instruments (mathematics), University Corporation for Atmospheric Research (geology and astronomy).

Computer facilities: 1,000 computers available on campus for general student use. A campuswide network can be accessed from student residence rooms and from off campus. Internet access and online class registration are available. *Web address:* http://www.wcupa.edu/.

General Application Contact: Dr. Gopal Sankaran, Interim Dean, 610-436-2943, Fax: 610-436-2763, E-mail: gradstudy@wcupa.edu.

GRADUATE UNITS

Graduate Studies Students: 391 full-time (308 women), 1,251 part-time (861 women); includes 113 minority (67 African Americans, 33 Asian Americans or Pacific Islanders, 11 Hispanic Americans, 2 Native Americans), 47 international. Average age 32. 1,029 applicants, 74% accepted. *Faculty:* 226. Expenses: Contact institution. *Financial support:* In 2001–02, 64 research assistantships with full tuition reimbursements (averaging $5,000 per year) were awarded; career-related internships or fieldwork, Federal Work-Study, tuition waivers (full and partial), and unspecified assistantships also available. Support available to part-time students. Financial award application deadline: 2/15. In 2001, 458 degrees awarded. *Degree program information:* Part-time and evening/weekend programs available. Postbaccalaureate distance learning degree programs offered (minimal on-campus study). *Application deadline:* For fall admission, 4/15 (priority date); for spring admission, 10/15. Applications are processed on a rolling basis. *Application fee:* $25. *Application Contact:* 610-436-2943, Fax: 610-436-2763, E-mail: gradstudy@wcupa.edu. *Interim Dean,* Dr. Gopal Sankaran, 610-436-2943, Fax: 610-436-2763, E-mail: gradstudy@wcupa.edu.

College of Arts and Sciences Students: 119 full-time (83 women), 211 part-time (131 women); includes 23 minority (10 African Americans, 11 Asian Americans or Pacific Islanders, 2 Hispanic Americans), 29 international. Average age 32. 331 applicants. *Faculty:* 87. Expenses: Contact institution. *Financial support:* In 2001–02, 37 research assistantships with full tuition reimbursements (averaging $5,000 per year) were awarded; unspecified assistantships also available. Support available to part-time students. Financial award application deadline: 2/15; financial award applicants required to submit FAFSA. In 2001, 107 degrees awarded. *Degree program information:* Part-time and evening/weekend programs available. Offers arts and sciences (M Ed, MA, MS, MSA, Certificate); biology (MS); chemistry (M Ed, MS); clinical chemistry (MS); clinical psychology (MA); communication studies (MA); computer science (MS, Certificate); English (MA); French (M Ed, MA); general psychology (MA); German (M Ed); gerontology (Certificate); history (M Ed, MA); industrial organizational psychology (MA); Latin (M Ed); long term care (MSA); mathematics (MA); philosophy (MA); physical science (MA); Spanish (M Ed, MA); teaching English as a second language (MA). *Application deadline:* For fall admission, 4/15 (priority date); for spring admission, 10/15. Applications are processed on a rolling basis. *Application fee:* $25. *Dean,* Dr. Jennie Skerl, 610-436-3521, E-mail: jskerl@wcupa.edu.

School of Business and Public Affairs Students: 44 full-time (29 women), 254 part-time (102 women); includes 30 minority (17 African Americans, 10 Asian Americans or Pacific Islanders, 3 Hispanic Americans), 13 international. Average age 34. 161 applicants. *Faculty:* 39. Expenses: Contact institution. *Financial support:* In 2001–02, 7 research assistantships with full tuition reimbursements (averaging $5,000 per year) were awarded; career-related internships or fieldwork and unspecified assistantships also available. Support available to part-time students. Financial award application deadline: 2/15; financial award applicants required to submit FAFSA. In 2001, 128 degrees awarded. *Degree program information:* Part-time and evening/weekend programs available. Offers business and public affairs (MA, MBA, MS, MSA, MSW); criminal justice (MS); economics/finance (MBA); executive business administration (MBA); general business (MBA); geography (MA); health services (MSA); human research management (MSA); individualized (MSA); leadership for women (MSA); long-term care (MSA); management (MBA); public administration (MSA); regional planning (MSA); social work (MSW); sport and athletic administration (MSA); sport and athletic training (MSA); technology and electronic commerce (MBA); training and development (MSA). *Application deadline:* For fall admission, 4/15 (priority date); for spring admission, 10/15. Applications are processed on a rolling basis. *Application fee:* $25. *Dean,* Dr. Christopher Fiorentino, 610-436-2930.

School of Education Students: 152 full-time (131 women), 577 part-time (488 women); includes 43 minority (31 African Americans, 5 Asian Americans or Pacific Islanders, 6 Hispanic Americans, 1 Native American), 2 international. Average age 31. 319 applicants. *Faculty:* 44. Expenses: Contact institution. *Financial support:* In 2001–02, 8 research assistantships with full tuition reimbursements (averaging $5,000 per year) were awarded; unspecified assistantships also available. Support available to part-time students. Financial award application deadline: 2/15; financial award applicants required to submit FAFSA. In 2001, 127 degrees awarded. *Degree program information:* Part-time and evening/weekend programs available. Offers counseling and educational psychology (M Ed, MS); early childhood and special education (M Ed); educational research (MS); elementary education (M Ed); elementary school counseling (M Ed); higher education counseling (MS); literacy (M Ed); professional and secondary education (M Ed, MS); reading (M Ed); secondary education (M Ed); secondary school counseling (M Ed); special education (M Ed); teaching and learning with technology (Certificate). *Application deadline:* For fall admission, 4/15 (priority date); for spring admission, 10/15. Applications are processed on a rolling basis. *Application fee:* $25. *Dean,* Dr. Tony Johnson, 610-436-2428.

School of Health Sciences Students: 73 full-time (65 women), 158 part-time (111 women); includes 15 minority (9 African Americans, 5 Asian Americans or Pacific Islanders, 1 Native American), 3 international. Average age 31. 179 applicants, 91% accepted. *Faculty:* 27. Expenses: Contact institution. *Financial support:* In 2001–02, 8 research assistantships with full tuition reimbursements (averaging $5,000 per year) were awarded; unspecified assistantships also available. Support available to part-time students. Financial award application deadline: 2/15; financial award applicants required to submit FAFSA. In 2001, 80 degrees awarded. *Degree program information:* Part-time and evening/weekend programs available. Postbaccalaureate distance learning degree programs offered (minimal on-campus study). Offers communicative disorders (MA); driver education (Certificate); environmental health (MS); exercise and sport physiology (MS); gerontology (MS); health sciences (M Ed, MA, MS, MSA, MSN, Certificate); health services (MSA); nursing (MSN); nursing education (MSN); physical education (MS); public health (MS); safety (Certificate); school health (M Ed); sport and athletic administration (MSA). *Application deadline:* For fall admission, 4/15 (priority date); for spring admission, 10/15. Applications are processed on a rolling basis. *Application fee:* $25. *Dean,* Dr. Donald E. Barr, 610-436-2825.

School of Music Students: 3 full-time (0 women), 51 part-time (29 women); includes 2 minority (both Asian Americans or Pacific Islanders) Average age 31. 35 applicants. *Faculty:* 31. Expenses: Contact institution. *Financial support:* In 2001–02, 5 research assistantships with full tuition reimbursements (averaging $5,000 per year) were awarded; career-related internships or fieldwork and unspecified assistantships also available. Support available to part-time students. Financial award application deadline: 2/15; financial award applicants required to submit FAFSA. In 2001, 16 degrees awarded. *Degree program information:*

West Chester University of Pennsylvania (continued)

Part-time and evening/weekend programs available. Offers accompanying (MM); composition (MM); music (MA, MM); music education (MM); music history (MA); music theory (MM); performance (MM); piano pedagogy (MM). *Application deadline:* For fall admission, 4/15 (priority date); for spring admission, 10/15. Applications are processed on a rolling basis. *Application fee:* $25. *Application Contact:* Dr. J. Bryan Burton, Graduate Coordinator, 610-436-2222, E-mail: jburton@wcupa.edu. *Dean,* Dr. Timothy Blair, 610-436-2739.

See in-depth description on page 1295.

WESTERN CAROLINA UNIVERSITY, Cullowhee, NC 28723

General Information State-supported, coed, comprehensive institution. CGS member. *Enrollment:* 385 full-time matriculated graduate/professional students (238 women), 709 part-time matriculated graduate/professional students (474 women). *Enrollment by degree level:* 857 master's, 43 doctoral, 194 other advanced degrees. *Graduate faculty:* 334 full-time (119 women). Tuition, state resident: full-time $1,072. Tuition, nonresident: full-time $8,704. *Required fees:* $1,171. *Graduate housing:* Rooms and/or apartments available to single students and guaranteed to married students. Typical cost: $1,919 per year ($3,563 including board) for single students; $3,628 per year ($5,272 including board) for married students. Housing application deadline: 6/1. *Student services:* Campus employment opportunities, career counseling, child daycare facilities, exercise/wellness program, free psychological counseling, international student services, low-cost health insurance. *Library facilities:* Hunter Library. *Online resources:* library catalog, web page, access to other libraries' catalogs. *Collection:* 527,866 titles, 2,926 serial subscriptions, 22,598 audiovisual materials. *Research affiliation:* North Carolina Center for the Advancement of Teaching.

Computer facilities: 351 computers available on campus for general student use. A campuswide network can be accessed from student residence rooms and from off campus. Internet access and online class registration, e-mail are available. *Web address:* http://www.wcu.edu/.

General Application Contact: Josie Bewsey, Assistant to the Dean, 828-227-7398, Fax: 828-227-7480, E-mail: jbewsey@email.wcu.edu.

GRADUATE UNITS

Graduate School Students: 385 full-time (238 women), 709 part-time (474 women); includes 50 minority (26 African Americans, 4 Asian Americans or Pacific Islanders, 6 Hispanic Americans, 14 Native Americans), 56 international. Average age 33. 740 applicants, 80% accepted, 312 enrolled. *Faculty:* 334 full-time (119 women). Expenses: Contact institution. *Financial support:* In 2001–02, 231 students received support, including 4 fellowships (averaging $6,000 per year), 91 research assistantships with full and partial tuition reimbursements available (averaging $3,581 per year), 136 teaching assistantships with full and partial tuition reimbursements available (averaging $5,048 per year); Federal Work-Study, institutionally sponsored loans, and scholarships/grants also available. Financial award application deadline: 3/15. In 2001, 322 master's, 6 doctorates, 5 other advanced degrees awarded. *Degree program information:* Part-time and evening/weekend programs available. *Application deadline:* Applications are processed on a rolling basis. *Application fee:* $35. *Application Contact:* Josie Bewsey, Assistant to the Dean, 828-227-7398, Fax: 828-227-7480, E-mail: jbewsey@email.wcu.edu. *Dean,* Dr. Abdul M. Turay, 828-227-7398, Fax: 828-227-7480, E-mail: aturay@email.wcu.edu.

College of Applied Science Students: 137; includes 2 minority (1 Hispanic American, 1 Native American), 1 international. 134 applicants, 80% accepted, 65 enrolled. *Faculty:* 47 full-time (29 women). Expenses: Contact institution. *Financial support:* In 2001–02, 18 students received support, including 1 fellowship (averaging $6,000 per year), 15 research assistantships with full and partial tuition reimbursements available (averaging $2,669 per year), 2 teaching assistantships with full and partial tuition reimbursements available (averaging $5,004 per year); Federal Work-Study, institutionally sponsored loans, and scholarships/grants also available. Financial award application deadline: 3/15; financial award applicants required to submit FAFSA. In 2001, 47 degrees awarded. *Degree program information:* Part-time and evening/weekend programs available. Offers applied science (MAT, MHS, MPT, MS, MSN); family and consumer sciences (MAT); health sciences (MHS); industrial and engineering technology (MS); nursing (MSN); physical therapy (MPT). *Application deadline:* Applications are processed on a rolling basis. *Application fee:* $35. *Application Contact:* Josie Bewsey, Assistant to the Dean, 828-227-7398, Fax: 828-227-7480, E-mail: jbewsey@email.wcu.edu. *Dean,* Dr. Dennis Depew, 828-227-7272, Fax: 828-227-7446.

College of Arts and Sciences Students: 89 full-time (46 women), 88 part-time (47 women); includes 15 minority (8 African Americans, 2 Asian Americans or Pacific Islanders, 1 Hispanic American, 4 Native Americans), 11 international. 105 applicants, 72% accepted, 50 enrolled. *Faculty:* 150 full-time (34 women). Expenses: Contact institution. *Financial support:* In 2001–02, 81 students received support, including 20 research assistantships with full and partial tuition reimbursements available (averaging $4,765 per year), 61 teaching assistantships with full and partial tuition reimbursements available (averaging $5,301 per year); fellowships, Federal Work-Study, institutionally sponsored loans, and scholarships/grants also available. Financial award application deadline: 3/15; financial award applicants required to submit FAFSA. In 2001, 66 degrees awarded. *Degree program information:* Part-time and evening/weekend programs available. Offers American history (MA); art education (MAT); arts and sciences (MA, MA Ed, MAT, MPA, MS); comprehensive education (MA Ed); comprehensive education—art (MA Ed); comprehensive education-biology (MA Ed); comprehensive education-chemistry (MA Ed); comprehensive education-English (MA Ed); comprehensive education-mathematics (MA Ed); music (MA); public affairs (MPA); social sciences (MAT); studio art (MA). *Application deadline:* For fall admission, 5/1 (priority date); for spring admission, 10/1 (priority date). Applications are processed on a rolling basis. *Application fee:* $35. *Application Contact:* Josie Bewsey, Assistant to the Dean, 828-227-7398, Fax: 828-227-7480, E-mail: jbewsey@email.wcu.edu. *Dean,* Dr. Robert Vartabedian, 828-227-7646, Fax: 828-227-7647, E-mail: vartabdn@email.wcu.edu.

College of Business Students: 64 full-time (27 women), 99 part-time (44 women); includes 7 minority (3 African Americans, 2 Asian Americans or Pacific Islanders, 2 Native Americans), 28 international. 135 applicants, 80% accepted, 51 enrolled. *Faculty:* 47 full-time (14 women). Expenses: Contact institution. *Financial support:* In 2001–02, 40 students received support, including 5 research assistantships with full and partial tuition reimbursements available (averaging $3,851 per year), 35 teaching assistantships with full and partial tuition reimbursements available (averaging $5,316 per year); fellowships, Federal Work-Study, institutionally sponsored loans, and scholarships/grants also available. Financial award application deadline: 3/15; financial award applicants required to submit FAFSA. In 2001, 50 degrees awarded. *Degree program information:* Part-time and evening/weekend programs available. Offers accountancy (M Ac); accounting (MPA); business administration (MBA); project management (MPM). *Application deadline:* For fall admission, 5/1 (priority date); for spring admission, 10/1 (priority date). Applications are processed on a rolling basis. *Application fee:* $35. *Application Contact:* Josie Bewsey, Assistant to the Dean, 828-227-7398, Fax: 828-227-7480, E-mail: jbewsey@email.wcu.edu. *Dean,* Dr. Ronald E. Shiffler, 828-227-7401, Fax: 828-227-7414, E-mail: rshiffler@email.wcu.edu.

College of Education and Allied Professions Students: 190 full-time (142 women), 287 part-time (222 women); includes 23 minority (13 African Americans, 1 Asian American or Pacific Islander, 4 Hispanic Americans, 5 Native Americans), 11 international. 337 applicants, 69% accepted, 158 enrolled. *Faculty:* 90 full-time (42 women). Expenses: Contact institution. *Financial support:* In 2001–02, 104 students received support, including 3 fellowships (averaging $6,000 per year), 63 research assistantships with full and partial tuition reimbursements available (averaging $3,601 per year), 38 teaching assistantships with full and partial tuition reimbursements available (averaging $4,397 per year); Federal Work-Study, institutionally sponsored loans, and scholarships/grants also available. Financial award application deadline: 3/15; financial award applicants required to submit FAFSA. In 2001, 169 master's, 6 doctorates, 5 other advanced degrees awarded. *Degree program information:* Part-time and evening/weekend programs available. Offers art education (MAT); behavioral disorders (MA Ed); biology (MAT); chemistry (MAT); clinical psychology (MA); communication disorders (MS); community college education (MA Ed); community counseling (MS); comprehensive education (MA Ed); comprehensive education-elementary education (MA Ed); comprehensive education-special education (MA Ed, MS); counseling (MA Ed, MS); education and allied professions (MA, MA Ed, MAT, MS, MSA, Ed D, Ed S); educational administration (MA Ed); educational leadership (Ed D, Ed S); educational supervision (MA Ed); elementary education (MA Ed); English (MAT); family and consumer sciences (MAT); general special education (MA Ed); human resource development (MS); learning disabilities (MA Ed); mathematics (MAT); mental retardation (MA Ed); middle grades education (MA Ed); physical education (MA Ed, MAT); reading (MAT); reading education (MAT); school administration (MSA); school counseling (MA Ed); school psychology (MA); secondary education (MAT); social sciences (MAT). *Application deadline:* Applications are processed on a rolling basis. *Application fee:* $35. *Application Contact:* Josie Bewsey, Assistant to the Dean, 828-227-7398, Fax: 828-227-7480, E-mail: jbewsey@email.wcu.edu. *Dean,* Dr. A. Michael Dougherty, 828-227-7311, Fax: 828-227-7388, E-mail: dougherty@email.wcu.edu.

See in-depth description on page 1297.

WESTERN CONNECTICUT STATE UNIVERSITY, Danbury, CT 06810-6885

General Information State-supported, coed, comprehensive institution. *Enrollment:* 28 full-time matriculated graduate/professional students (19 women), 574 part-time matriculated graduate/professional students (389 women). *Enrollment by degree level:* 602 master's. *Graduate faculty:* 64 full-time (25 women), 9 part-time/adjunct (3 women). Tuition, state resident: full-time $2,772; part-time $215 per credit hour. Tuition, nonresident: full-time $7,726. *Required fees:* $30 per term. *Graduate housing:* Rooms and/or apartments available on a first-come, first-served basis to single and married students. Typical cost: $4,182 per year for single students. Room charges vary according to board plan and housing facility selected. Housing application deadline: 6/13. *Student services:* Campus employment opportunities, career counseling, child daycare facilities, disabled student services, free psychological counseling, international student services, low-cost health insurance, multicultural affairs office. *Library facilities:* Ruth Haas Library plus 1 other. *Online resources:* library catalog, web page, access to other libraries' catalogs. *Collection:* 261,328 titles, 2,538 serial subscriptions, 10,846 audiovisual materials. *Research affiliation:* National Undergraduate Research Center.

Computer facilities: 400 computers available on campus for general student use. A campuswide network can be accessed from student residence rooms and from off campus. Internet access is available. *Web address:* http://www.wcsu.edu/.

General Application Contact: Chris Shankle, Associate Director of Graduate Admissions, 203-837-8244, Fax: 203-837-8338, E-mail: shanklec@wcsu.edu.

GRADUATE UNITS

Division of Graduate Studies Students: 28 full-time (19 women), 574 part-time (389 women); includes 21 minority (7 African Americans, 4 Asian Americans or Pacific Islanders, 8 Hispanic Americans, 2 Native Americans), 1 international. Average age 35. *Faculty:* 64 full-time (25 women), 9 part-time/adjunct (3 women). Expenses: Contact institution. *Financial support:* Fellowships, teaching assistantships, career-related internships or fieldwork available. Support available to part-time students. Financial award application deadline: 5/1; financial award applicants required to submit FAFSA. In 2001, 205 degrees awarded. *Degree program information:* Part-time and evening/weekend programs available. *Application deadline:* For fall admission, 8/1 (priority date). Applications are processed on a rolling basis. *Application fee:* $40. *Application Contact:* Chris Shankle, Associate Director of Graduate Admissions, 203-837-8244, Fax: 203-837-8338, E-mail: shanklec@wcsu.edu. *Enrollment Management Officer,* William Hawkins, 203-837-8241.

Ancell School of Business and Public Administration Students: 5 full-time (3 women), 122 part-time (53 women); includes 4 minority (2 Asian Americans or Pacific Islanders, 2 Hispanic Americans) Average age 35. *Faculty:* 16 full-time (4 women), 1 part-time/adjunct (0 women). Expenses: Contact institution. *Financial support:* In 2001–02, 4 fellowships were awarded; career-related internships or fieldwork also available. Support available to part-time students. Financial award application deadline: 5/1; financial award applicants required to submit FAFSA. In 2001, 57 degrees awarded. *Degree program information:* Part-time and evening/weekend programs available. Offers accounting (MBA); business administration (MBA); business and public administration (MBA, MHA, MS); health administration (MHA); justice administration (MS). *Application deadline:* For fall admission, 8/1 (priority date). Applications are processed on a rolling basis. *Application fee:* $40. *Application Contact:* Chris Shankle, Associate Director of Graduate Admissions, 203-837-8244, Fax: 203-837-8338, E-mail: shanklec@wcsu.edu. *Dean,* Dr. Allen Morton, 203-837-8521.

School of Arts and Sciences Students: 16 full-time (12 women), 127 part-time (71 women); includes 6 minority (2 African Americans, 1 Asian American or Pacific Islander, 3 Hispanic Americans), 1 international. Average age 38. *Faculty:* 25 full-time (8 women), 1 part-time/adjunct (0 women). Expenses: Contact institution. *Financial support:* Fellowships, teaching assistantships, career-related internships or fieldwork available. Support available to part-time students. Financial award application deadline: 5/1; financial award applicants required to submit FAFSA. In 2001, 17 degrees awarded. *Degree program information:* Part-time and evening/weekend programs available. Offers arts and sciences (MA, MFA); biological and environmental sciences (MA); earth and planetary sciences (MA); English (MA); history (MA); illustration (MFA); mathematics and computer science (MA); painting (MFA); theoretical mathematics (MA). *Application deadline:* For fall admission, 8/1 (priority date). Applications are processed on a rolling basis. *Application fee:* $40. *Application Contact:* Chris Shankle, Associate Director of Graduate Admissions, 203-837-8244, Fax: 203-837-8338, E-mail: shanklec@wcsu.edu. *Dean,* Dr. Carol Hawkes, 203-837-9400.

School of Professional Studies Students: 7 full-time (4 women), 325 part-time (265 women); includes 11 minority (5 African Americans, 1 Asian American or Pacific Islander, 3 Hispanic Americans, 2 Native Americans) Average age 33. *Faculty:* 23 full-time (13 women), 7 part-time/adjunct (3 women). Expenses: Contact institution. *Financial support:* Fellowships, career-related internships or fieldwork available. Support available to part-time students. Financial award application deadline: 5/1. In 2001, 131 degrees awarded. *Degree program information:* Part-time and evening/weekend programs available. Offers adult nurse practitioner (MSN); clinical nurse specialist (MSN); community counseling (MS); counselor education (MS); curriculum (MS); English education (MS); instructional technology (MS); mathematics education (MS); music education (MS); professional studies (MS, MSN); reading (MS); school counseling (MS); special education (MS). *Application deadline:* For fall admission, 8/1 (priority date). Applications are processed on a rolling basis. *Application fee:* $40. *Application Contact:* Chris Shankle, Associate Director of Graduate Admissions, 203-837-8244, Fax: 203-837-8338, E-mail: shanklec@wcsu.edu. *Dean,* Dr. Lynne Clark, 203-837-9500.

WESTERN GOVERNORS UNIVERSITY, Salt Lake City, UT 84117

General Information Independent, coed, comprehensive institution. *Enrollment:* 315 full-time matriculated graduate/professional students (177 women), 28 part-time matriculated graduate/professional students. *Enrollment by degree level:* 142 master's, 173 other advanced degrees. *Graduate faculty:* 4 full-time (3 women). *Tuition:* Full-time $3,600. *Student services:* Career counseling. *Library facilities:* WGU Central Library (online). *Online resources:* web page.

Computer facilities: Internet access and online class registration are available. *Web address:* http://www.wgu.edu/.

General Application Contact: Wendy Gregory, Enrollment Manager, 801-274-3280 Ext. 315, Fax: 801-274-3280 Ext. 315, E-mail: wgregory@wgu.edu.

WESTERN ILLINOIS UNIVERSITY, Macomb, IL 61455-1390

General Information State-supported, coed, comprehensive institution. CGS member. *Enrollment:* 684 full-time matriculated graduate/professional students (374 women), 1,054 part-time matriculated graduate/professional students (700 women). *Enrollment by degree level:* 1,682 master's, 56 other advanced degrees. *Graduate faculty:* 392 full-time (118 women), 16 part-time/adjunct (3 women). Tuition, state resident: part-time $108 per credit hour. Tuition, nonresident: part-time $216 per credit hour. *Required fees:* $33 per credit hour.

Graduate housing: Rooms and/or apartments available on a first-come, first-served basis to single and married students. Typical cost: $2,888 per year for single students. *Student services:* Campus employment opportunities, campus safety program, career counseling, disabled student services, exercise/wellness program, free psychological counseling, international student services, low-cost health insurance, multicultural affairs office, writing training. *Library facilities:* Western Illinois University Library plus 4 others. *Online resources:* library catalog, web page. *Collection:* 998,041 titles, 3,200 serial subscriptions, 3,445 audiovisual materials. *Research affiliation:* Pharmacia and Upjohn (psychology), Ameritech (education), Gloekner Foundation (agriculture), Chicago Zoological Society (biology), Petroleum Research Foundation (geology), Illinois Pork Producers Association (agriculture).

Computer facilities: 700 computers available on campus for general student use. A campuswide network can be accessed from off campus. Course registration available. *Web address:* http://www.wiu.edu/.

General Application Contact: Dr. Barbara Baily, Director of Graduate Studies, 309-298-1806, Fax: 309-298-2345, E-mail: grad-office@wiu.edu.

GRADUATE UNITS

School of Graduate Studies Students: 684 full-time (374 women), 1,054 part-time (700 women); includes 100 minority (53 African Americans, 12 Asian Americans or Pacific Islanders, 30 Hispanic Americans, 5 Native Americans), 190 international. Average age 31. 902 applicants, 57% accepted. *Faculty:* 392 full-time (118 women), 16 part-time/adjunct (3 women). Expenses: Contact institution. *Financial support:* In 2001–02, 457 students received support, including 436 research assistantships with full tuition reimbursements available (averaging $5,720 per year), 21 teaching assistantships with full tuition reimbursements available (averaging $7,140 per year) Financial award applicants required to submit FAFSA. In 2001, 633 master's, 40 other advanced degrees awarded. *Degree program information:* Part-time programs available. Postbaccalaureate distance learning degree programs offered (no on-campus study). *Application deadline:* Applications are processed on a rolling basis. *Application fee:* $0 ($25 for international students). Electronic applications accepted. *Director of Graduate Studies,* Dr. Barbara Baily, 309-298-1806, Fax: 309-298-2345, E-mail: grad-office@wiu.edu.

College of Arts and Sciences Students: 172 full-time (92 women), 97 part-time (66 women); includes 13 minority (12 African Americans, 1 Asian American or Pacific Islander), 31 international. Average age 30. 192 applicants, 68% accepted. *Faculty:* 152 full-time (40 women), 4 part-time/adjunct (0 women). Expenses: Contact institution. *Financial support:* In 2001–02, 140 students received support, including 132 research assistantships with full tuition reimbursements available (averaging $5,720 per year), 8 teaching assistantships with full tuition reimbursements available (averaging $7,140 per year) Financial award applicants required to submit FAFSA. In 2001, 72 master's, 10 other advanced degrees awarded. *Degree program information:* Part-time programs available. Offers arts and sciences (MA, MS, Certificate, SSP); biological sciences (MS); chemistry (MS); clinical/community mental health (MS); community development (Certificate); general psychology (MS); geography (MA); history (MA); literature and language (MA); mathematics (MS); physics (MS); political science (MA); psychology (MS, SSP); school psychology (SSP); sociology (MA); writing (MA); zoo and aquarium studies (Certificate). *Application deadline:* Applications are processed on a rolling basis. *Application fee:* $0 ($25 for international students). Electronic applications accepted. *Application Contact:* Dr. Barbara Baily, Director of Graduate Studies, 309-298-1806, Fax: 309-298-2345, E-mail: grad-office@wiu.edu. *Dean,* Dr. Phyllis Rippey, 309-298-1828.

College of Business and Technology Students: 158 full-time (55 women), 100 part-time (38 women); includes 10 minority (5 African Americans, 3 Asian Americans or Pacific Islanders, 1 Hispanic American, 1 Native American), 103 international. Average age 30. 240 applicants, 43% accepted. *Faculty:* 73 full-time (12 women). Expenses: Contact institution. *Financial support:* In 2001–02, 87 students received support, including 79 research assistantships with full tuition reimbursements available (averaging $5,720 per year), 8 teaching assistantships (averaging $7,140 per year) Financial award applicants required to submit FAFSA. In 2001, 112 degrees awarded. *Degree program information:* Part-time programs available. Offers accountancy (M Acct); business administration (MBA); business and technology (M Acct, MA, MBA, MS); computer science (MS); economics (MA); engineering technology (MS). *Application deadline:* Applications are processed on a rolling basis. *Application fee:* $0 ($25 for international students). Electronic applications accepted. *Application Contact:* Dr. Barbara Baily, Director of Graduate Studies, 309-298-1806, Fax: 309-298-2345, E-mail: grad-office@wiu.edu. *Dean,* Dr. David Beveridge, 309-298-2442.

College of Education and Human Services Students: 263 full-time (167 women), 849 part-time (591 women); includes 69 minority (33 African Americans, 7 Asian Americans or Pacific Islanders, 25 Hispanic Americans, 4 Native Americans), 51 international. Average age 34. 348 applicants, 65% accepted. *Faculty:* 120 full-time (49 women), 12 part-time/adjunct (3 women). Expenses: Contact institution. *Financial support:* In 2001–02, 160 students received support, including 160 research assistantships with full tuition reimbursements available (averaging $5,720 per year) Financial award applicants required to submit FAFSA. In 2001, 403 master's, 30 other advanced degrees awarded. *Degree program information:* Part-time and evening/weekend programs available. Postbaccalaureate distance learning degree programs offered (no on-campus study). Offers college student personnel (MS); counseling (MS Ed); counselor education (MS Ed, Certificate); distance learning (Certificate); early childhood education (Certificate); education administration and supervision (MS Ed, Ed S); education and human services (MA, MAT, MS, MS Ed, Certificate, Ed S); educational and interdisciplinary studies (MS Ed); elementary education (MS Ed, Certificate); graphics application (Certificate); health education (MS); instructional technology and telecommunications (MS); language literacy (Certificate); law enforcement and justice administration (MA); marriage and family counseling (Certificate); mathematics (Certificate); multimedia (Certificate); physical education (MS); Police Executive Certification (Certificate); reading (MS Ed, Certificate); recreation, park, and tourism administration (MS); science (Certificate); secondary education (MAT); social studies (Certificate); special education (MS Ed); sport management (MS); technology integration in education (Certificate); training development (Certificate). *Application deadline:* Applications are processed on a rolling basis. *Application fee:* $0 ($25 for international students). Electronic applications accepted. *Application Contact:* Dr. Barbara Baily, Director of Graduate Studies, 309-298-1806, Fax: 309-298-2345, E-mail: grad-office@wiu.edu. *Interim Dean,* Dr. Bonnie Smith, 309-298-1690.

College of Fine Arts and Communication Students: 91 full-time (60 women), 8 part-time (5 women); includes 8 minority (3 African Americans, 1 Asian American or Pacific Islander, 4 Hispanic Americans), 5 international. Average age 28. 122 applicants, 48% accepted. *Faculty:* 47 full-time (17 women). Expenses: Contact institution. *Financial support:* In 2001–02, 70 students received support, including 65 research assistantships with full tuition reimbursements available (averaging $5,720 per year), 5 teaching assistantships with full tuition reimbursements available (averaging $7,140 per year) Financial award applicants required to submit FAFSA. In 2001, 46 degrees awarded. *Degree program information:* Part-time programs available. Offers communication (MA); communication sciences and disorders (MS); fine arts and communication (MA, MFA, MS); music (MA); theatre (MFA). *Application deadline:* Applications are processed on a rolling basis. *Application fee:* $0 ($25 for international students). Electronic applications accepted. *Application Contact:* Dr. Barbara Baily, Director of Graduate Studies, 309-298-1806, Fax: 309-298-2345, E-mail: grad-office@wiu.edu. *Dean,* Dr. James M. Butterworth, 309-298-1552.

WESTERN INTERNATIONAL UNIVERSITY, Phoenix, AZ 85021-2718

General Information Proprietary, coed, comprehensive institution. *Enrollment:* 749 full-time matriculated graduate/professional students (359 women). *Enrollment by degree level:* 749 master's. *Graduate faculty:* 133 part-time/adjunct (30 women). Tuition, state resident: full-time $5,130. Tuition, nonresident: full-time $5,580. *Graduate housing:* On-campus housing not available. *Student services:* Disabled student services, international student services, writing training. *Library facilities:* Learning Resource Center. *Online resources:* web page. *Collection:* 7,500 titles, 125 serial subscriptions.

Computer facilities: 30 computers available on campus for general student use. A campuswide network can be accessed. Internet access is available. *Web address:* http://www.wintu.edu/.

General Application Contact: Karen Janitell, Director of Enrollment, 602-943-2311 Ext. 1063, Fax: 602-371-8637, E-mail: karen_janitell@apollogrp.edu.

GRADUATE UNITS

Graduate Programs in Business Students: 749 full-time (359 women). Average age 35. *Faculty:* 133 part-time/adjunct (30 women). Expenses: Contact institution. *Financial support:* In 2001–02, 103 students received support. Career-related internships or fieldwork, Federal Work-Study, and scholarships/grants available. Financial award applicants required to submit FAFSA. In 2001, 93 degrees awarded. *Degree program information:* Evening/weekend programs available. Offers business (MBA, MPA, MS); finance (MBA); information technology (MBA, MS); international business (MBA); management (MBA); marketing (MBA); public administration (MPA). *Application deadline:* Applications are processed on a rolling basis. *Application fee:* $85 ($100 for international students). *Application Contact:* Karen Janitell, Director of Enrollment, 602-943-2311 Ext. 1063, Fax: 602-371-8637, E-mail: karen_janitell@apollogrp.edu. *Director of Academic Affairs and Curriculum,* Kay Look, 602-943-2311 Ext. 1026, Fax: 602-943-3204, E-mail: kay.look@apollogrp.edu.

WESTERN KENTUCKY UNIVERSITY, Bowling Green, KY 42101-3576

General Information State-supported, coed, comprehensive institution. CGS member. *Enrollment:* 620 full-time matriculated graduate/professional students (333 women), 1,167 part-time matriculated graduate/professional students (841 women). *Enrollment by degree level:* 1,723 master's, 23 doctoral, 41 other advanced degrees. *Graduate faculty:* 355 full-time (121 women), 36 part-time/adjunct (14 women). *Tuition, area resident:* Part-time $167 per credit. Tuition, state resident: full-time $2,490. Tuition, nonresident: full-time $6,660; part-time $399 per credit. *Required fees:* $554. Part-time tuition and fees vary according to campus/location and reciprocity agreements. *Graduate housing:* Room and/or apartments guaranteed to single students; on-campus housing not available to married students. Typical cost: $1,890 per year ($3,990 including board). Housing application deadline: 4/1. *Student services:* Campus employment opportunities, career counseling, child daycare facilities, disabled student services, exercise/wellness program, free psychological counseling, international student services, low-cost health insurance. *Library facilities:* Helm-Cravens Library plus 3 others. *Online resources:* library catalog, web page, access to other libraries' catalogs. *Collection:* 967,067 titles, 10,156 serial subscriptions, 90,955 audiovisual materials. *Research affiliation:* Bowling Green Field Station for Animal Studies (U.S. Fish and Wildlife Service), Roybal Center (gerontology).

Computer facilities: 100 computers available on campus for general student use. A campuswide network can be accessed from student residence rooms and from off campus. Internet access and online class registration, on-line grade reports are available. *Web address:* http://www.wku.edu/.

General Application Contact: Dr. Elmer Gray, Dean, Graduate Studies, 270-745-2446, Fax: 270-745-5442, E-mail: graduate.studies@wku.edu.

GRADUATE UNITS

Graduate Studies Students: 620 full-time (333 women), 1,167 part-time (841 women); includes 133 minority (63 African Americans, 57 Asian Americans or Pacific Islanders, 9 Hispanic Americans, 4 Native Americans), 211 international. Average age 31. 1,561 applicants, 65% accepted. *Faculty:* 355 full-time (121 women), 36 part-time/adjunct (14 women). Expenses: Contact institution. *Financial support:* In 2001–02, 350 students received support, including 75 research assistantships with partial tuition reimbursements available (averaging $5,600 per year), 60 teaching assistantships with partial tuition reimbursements available (averaging $5,600 per year); career-related internships or fieldwork, Federal Work-Study, institutionally sponsored loans, tuition waivers (partial), and service awards also available. Support available to part-time students. Financial award application deadline: 4/1; financial award applicants required to submit FAFSA. In 2001, 508 master's, 6 other advanced degrees awarded. *Degree program information:* Part-time and evening/weekend programs available. Postbaccalaureate distance learning degree programs offered (minimal on-campus study). Offers administration (MA); environmental health (MS); gerontology (MS); healthcare administration (MHA); nursing (MSN); public health (MPH); public health education (MA Ed, MPH). *Application deadline:* For fall admission, 7/1 (priority date); for spring admission, 11/1 (priority date). Applications are processed on a rolling basis. *Application fee:* $30. *Application Contact:* Carolyn Darnell, Admissions Specialist, 270-745-2446, Fax: 270-745-6950, E-mail: graduate.studies@wku.edu. *Dean,* Dr. Elmer Gray, 270-745-2446, Fax: 270-745-6950, E-mail: graduate.studies@wku.edu.

College of Education and Behavioral Sciences 633 applicants, 86% accepted. *Faculty:* 89 full-time (36 women), 28 part-time/adjunct (11 women). Expenses: Contact institution. *Financial support:* Research assistantships with partial tuition reimbursements, teaching assistantships with partial tuition reimbursements, career-related internships or fieldwork, Federal Work-Study, institutionally sponsored loans, tuition waivers (partial), unspecified assistantships, and service awards available. Support available to part-time students. Financial award application deadline: 4/1; financial award applicants required to submit FAFSA. In 2001, 336 master's, 6 other advanced degrees awarded. *Degree program information:* Part-time and evening/weekend programs available. Postbaccalaureate distance learning degree programs offered (no on-campus study). Offers business education (MA Ed); communication disorders (MS); counseling and student affairs (Ed S); early childhood education (MA Ed); education (Ed S); education and behavioral sciences (MA, MA Ed, MS, Ed S); educational administration (MA Ed, Ed S); elementary education (MA Ed, Ed S); exceptional child education (MA Ed); guidance and counseling (MA Ed); library media education (MS); middle grades education (MA Ed); physical education (MA Ed, MS); psychology (MA); reading (MA Ed); recreation (MS); school administration (Ed S); school business administration (MA Ed); school psychology (Ed S); secondary education (MA Ed, Ed S). *Application deadline:* For fall admission, 7/1 (priority date); for spring admission, 11/1 (priority date). Applications are processed on a rolling basis. *Application fee:* $30. *Dean,* Dr. Karen Adams, 270-745-4664, Fax: 270-745-6474, E-mail: karen.adams@wku.edu.

Gordon Ford College of Business 112 applicants, 53% accepted. *Faculty:* 44 full-time (9 women), 1 part-time/adjunct (0 women). Expenses: Contact institution. *Financial support:* Research assistantships with partial tuition reimbursements, Federal Work-Study, institutionally sponsored loans, and service awards available. Support available to part-time students. Financial award application deadline: 4/1; financial award applicants required to submit FAFSA. In 2001, 37 degrees awarded. *Degree program information:* Part-time and evening/weekend programs available. Offers business administration (MBA). *Application deadline:* For fall admission, 7/1 (priority date); for spring admission, 11/1 (priority date). Applications are processed on a rolling basis. *Application fee:* $30. *Dean,* Dr. Robert Jefferson, 270-745-5866, Fax: 270-745-3893.

Ogden College of Science, and Engineering 308 applicants, 37% accepted. *Faculty:* 91 full-time (15 women), 2 part-time/adjunct (0 women). Expenses: Contact institution. *Financial support:* Research assistantships with partial tuition reimbursements, teaching assistantships with partial tuition reimbursements, career-related internships or fieldwork, Federal Work-Study, institutionally sponsored loans, traineeships, tuition waivers (partial), unspecified assistantships, and service awards available. Support available to part-time students. Financial award application deadline: 4/1; financial award applicants required to submit FAFSA. In 2001, 40 degrees awarded. *Degree program information:* Part-time and evening/weekend programs available. Offers agriculture (MA Ed, MS); biology (MA Ed, MS); chemistry (MA Ed, MS); computer science (MS); geography and geology (MS); mathematics (MA Ed, MS); science, technology, and health (MA Ed, MS). *Application deadline:* For fall admission, 7/1 (priority date); for spring admission, 11/1. Applications are processed on a rolling basis. *Application fee:* $30. *Dean,* Dr. Blaine Ferrell, 270-745-4448, Fax: 270-745-6471, E-mail: blaine.ferrell@wku.edu.

Potter College of Arts, Humanities and Social Sciences 112 applicants, 77% accepted. *Faculty:* 104 full-time (44 women), 3 part-time/adjunct (2 women). Expenses: Contact institution. *Financial support:* Research assistantships with partial tuition reimbursements,

Western Kentucky University (continued)

teaching assistantships with partial tuition reimbursements, career-related internships or fieldwork, Federal Work-Study, institutionally sponsored loans, tuition waivers (partial), unspecified assistantships, and service awards available. Support available to part-time students. Financial award application deadline: 4/1; financial award applicants required to submit FAFSA. In 2001, 62 degrees awarded. *Degree program information:* Part-time and evening/weekend programs available. Postbaccalaureate distance learning degree programs offered. Offers art education (MA Ed); arts and humanities (MA, MA Ed, MS); communication (MA); communication education (MA Ed); English (MA Ed); folk studies (MA); French (MA Ed); German (MA Ed); government (MA Ed); historic preservation (MA); history (MA, MA Ed); humanities (MA); literature (MA); music (MA Ed); sociology (MA, MA Ed); Spanish (MA Ed); teaching English as a second language (MA); writing (MA). *Application deadline:* For fall admission, 7/1 (priority date); for spring admission, 11/1. Applications are processed on a rolling basis. *Application fee:* $30. *Dean,* Dr. David Lee, 270-745-2344, Fax: 270-745-5734, E-mail: david.lee@wku.edu.

Announcement: The MS program in geoscience emphasizes hydrology, meteorology, climatology, environmental management, and geographic information systems. Specializations in city and regional planning and in international development are also offered. Students are strongly encouraged to write a master's thesis, although a nonthesis option is available.

See in-depth description on page 1299.

WESTERN MICHIGAN UNIVERSITY, Kalamazoo, MI 49008-5202

General Information State-supported, coed, university. CGS member. *Enrollment:* 2,989 full-time matriculated graduate/professional students (1,656 women), 2,786 part-time matriculated graduate/professional students (1,763 women). *Enrollment by degree level:* 3,709 master's, 542 doctoral, 1,524 other advanced degrees. *Graduate faculty:* 785 full-time (269 women), 14 part-time/adjunct. Tuition, state resident: part-time $186 per credit hour. Tuition, nonresident: part-time $442 per credit hour. *Required fees:* $602. One-time fee: $132 part-time. Tuition and fees vary according to course load. *Graduate housing:* Rooms and/or apartments available on a first-come, first-served basis to single and married students. Typical cost: $5,517 (including board) for single students. Room and board charges vary according to housing facility selected. Housing application deadline: 7/1. *Student services:* Campus employment opportunities, campus safety program, career counseling, child daycare facilities, disabled student services, exercise/wellness program, free psychological counseling, international student services, low-cost health insurance. *Library facilities:* Waldo Library plus 4 others. *Online resources:* library catalog, web page, access to other libraries' catalogs. *Collection:* 937,095 titles, 7,262 serial subscriptions, 125,347 audiovisual materials. *Research affiliation:* Argonne National Laboratory (particle physics), Central States Universities, Inc., Ames Research Center (manufacturing education), Copper Development Association, Inc. (plastics extrusion), Pharmacia and Upjohn Company (electron microscopy), Flowserve Corporation (mechanical pumps and seals).

Computer facilities: 2,000 computers available on campus for general student use. A campuswide network can be accessed from student residence rooms and from off campus. *Web address:* http://www.wmich.edu/.

General Application Contact: Admissions and Orientation, 616-387-2000, Fax: 616-387-2355.

GRADUATE UNITS

Graduate College Students: 2,989 full-time (1,656 women), 2,786 part-time (1,763 women); includes 521 minority (353 African Americans, 73 Asian Americans or Pacific Islanders, 76 Hispanic Americans, 19 Native Americans), 995 international. Average age 25. 3,914 applicants, 68% accepted, 1011 enrolled. *Faculty:* 785 full-time (269 women), 14 part-time/adjunct. Expenses: Contact institution. *Financial support:* In 2001–02, 18 fellowships with full tuition reimbursements (averaging $4,195 per year), 131 research assistantships with partial tuition reimbursements (averaging $983 per year), 575 teaching assistantships with partial tuition reimbursements (averaging $4,802 per year) were awarded. Career-related internships or fieldwork, Federal Work-Study, institutionally sponsored loans, and unspecified assistantships also available. Support available to part-time students. Financial award application deadline: 2/15; financial award applicants required to submit FAFSA. In 2001, 1,311 master's, 56 doctorates, 6 other advanced degrees awarded. *Degree program information:* Part-time and evening/weekend programs available. *Application deadline:* Applications are processed on a rolling basis. *Application fee:* $25. *Application Contact:* Admissions and Orientation, 616-387-2000, Fax: 616-387-2355. *Dean,* Dr. Donald E. Thompson, 616-387-3570.

College of Arts and Sciences Students: 757 full-time (416 women), 505 part-time (278 women); includes 142 minority (98 African Americans, 15 Asian Americans or Pacific Islanders, 24 Hispanic Americans, 5 Native Americans), 226 international. 953 applicants, 60% accepted, 260 enrolled. *Faculty:* 350 full-time (242 women), 1 part-time/adjunct. Expenses: Contact institution. *Financial support:* In 2001–02, 7 fellowships with full tuition reimbursements (averaging $4,195 per year), 71 research assistantships with partial tuition reimbursements (averaging $9,839 per year), 374 teaching assistantships with partial tuition reimbursements (averaging $4,802 per year) were awarded. Career-related internships or fieldwork, Federal Work-Study, and institutionally sponsored loans also available. Financial award application deadline: 2/15; financial award applicants required to submit FAFSA. In 2001, 360 master's, 28 doctorates, 6 other advanced degrees awarded. *Degree program information:* Part-time programs available. Offers anthropology (MA); applied behavior analysis (MA, PhD); applied economics (PhD); applied mathematics (MS); arts and sciences (MA, MDA, MFA, MPA, MS, DPA, PhD, Ed S); biological sciences (MS, PhD); biostatistics (MS); chemistry (MA, PhD); clinical psychology (MA, PhD); comparative religion (MA, PhD); computational mathematics (MS); creative writing (MFA); development administration (MDA); earth science (MS); economics (MA); English (MA, PhD); experimental analysis of behavior (PhD); experimental psychology (MA); geography (MA); geology (MS, PhD); graph theory and computer science (PhD); history (MA, PhD); industrial/organizational psychology (MA); mathematics (MA, PhD); mathematics education (MA, PhD); medieval studies (MA); molecular biotechnology (MS); organizational communication (MA); philosophy (MA); physics (MA, PhD); political science (MA, PhD); professional writing (MA); public affairs and administration (MPA, DPA); school psychology (PhD, Ed S); science studies (MA, PhD); sociology (MA, PhD); Spanish (MA); statistics (MS, PhD). *Application deadline:* For fall admission, 2/15 (priority date). Applications are processed on a rolling basis. *Application fee:* $25. *Application Contact:* Admissions and Orientation, 616-387-2000, Fax: 616-387-2355. *Dean,* Dr. Elise B. Jorgens, 616-387-4358.

College of Education Students: 575 full-time (419 women), 888 part-time (672 women); includes 136 minority (100 African Americans, 13 Asian Americans or Pacific Islanders, 16 Hispanic Americans, 7 Native Americans), 45 international. 644 applicants, 86% accepted, 207 enrolled. *Faculty:* 108 full-time (60 women), 7 part-time/adjunct. Expenses: Contact institution. *Financial support:* In 2001–02, 2 fellowships with full tuition reimbursements (averaging $4,195 per year), 6 research assistantships with partial tuition reimbursements (averaging $9,839 per year), 76 teaching assistantships with partial tuition reimbursements (averaging $4,802 per year) were awarded. Career-related internships or fieldwork and Federal Work-Study also available. Financial award application deadline: 2/15; financial award applicants required to submit FAFSA. In 2001, 469 master's, 26 doctorates awarded. *Degree program information:* Part-time programs available. Offers administration (MA); athletic training (MA); career and technical education (MA); coaching and sports studies (MA); counseling psychology (PhD); counselor education (MA, Ed D, PhD); counselor education and counseling psychology (MA, PhD); counselor psychology (MA); early childhood education (MA); education (MA, Ed D, PhD, Ed S); education and professional development (MA); educational leadership (MA, Ed D, PhD, Ed S); educational studies (MA, Ed D); educational technology (MA); elementary education (MA); evaluation, measurement, and research (MA, PhD); exercise science (MA); family and consumer sciences (MA); human resources development (MA); marriage and family therapy (MA); middle school education (MA); motor development (MA); physical education (MA); reading (MA); socio-cultural foundations and educational thought (MA); special education for handicapped children (MA). *Application deadline:* Applications are processed on a rolling basis. *Application fee:* $25. *Application Contact:* Admissions and Orientation, 616-387-2000, Fax: 616-387-2355. *Dean,* Dr. David A. England, 616-387-2960.

College of Engineering and Applied Sciences Students: 489 full-time (78 women), 123 part-time (20 women); includes 25 minority (8 African Americans, 13 Asian Americans or Pacific Islanders, 4 Hispanic Americans), 468 international. 1,511 applicants, 61% accepted, 223 enrolled. *Faculty:* 85 full-time (9 women), 1 part-time/adjunct. Expenses: Contact institution. *Financial support:* In 2001–02, 4 fellowships (averaging $4,056 per year), 17 research assistantships (averaging $9,839 per year), 64 teaching assistantships (averaging $4,802 per year) were awarded. Career-related internships or fieldwork and Federal Work-Study also available. Financial award application deadline: 2/15; financial award applicants required to submit FAFSA. In 2001, 103 master's, 2 doctorates awarded. *Degree program information:* Part-time programs available. Offers computer engineering (MSE, PhD); computer science (MS, PhD); construction management (MS); electrical engineering (MSE, PhD); engineering and applied sciences (MS, MSE, PhD); engineering management (MS); industrial engineering (MSE); manufacturing engineering (MS); materials science and engineering (MS); mechanical engineering (MSE, PhD); operations research (MS); paper and printing science and engineering (MS, PhD). *Application deadline:* For fall admission, 2/15 (priority date). Applications are processed on a rolling basis. *Application fee:* $25. *Application Contact:* Admissions and Orientation, 616-387-2000, Fax: 616-387-2355. *Dean,* Dr. Daniel M. Litynski, 616-387-4017.

College of Fine Arts Students: 63 full-time (31 women), 21 part-time (15 women); includes 4 minority (3 African Americans, 1 Asian American or Pacific Islander), 16 international. 95 applicants, 75% accepted, 28 enrolled. *Faculty:* 82 full-time (28 women). Expenses: Contact institution. *Financial support:* In 2001–02, 1 fellowship (averaging $4,056 per year), 53 teaching assistantships (averaging $4,802 per year) were awarded. Research assistantships, Federal Work-Study also available. Financial award application deadline: 2/15; financial award applicants required to submit FAFSA. In 2001, 29 degrees awarded. *Degree program information:* Part-time programs available. Offers fine arts (MA, MFA, MM); graphic design (MFA); music (MA, MM); performing arts administration (MFA); textile design (MA, MFA). *Application deadline:* For fall admission, 2/15 (priority date). Applications are processed on a rolling basis. *Application fee:* $25. *Application Contact:* Admissions and Orientation, 616-387-2000, Fax: 616-387-2355. *Dean,* Dr. Margaret Merrion, 616-387-5810.

College of Health and Human Services Students: 434 full-time (359 women), 65 part-time (51 women); includes 58 minority (41 African Americans, 7 Asian Americans or Pacific Islanders, 10 Hispanic Americans), 10 international. 448 applicants, 73% accepted, 150 enrolled. *Faculty:* 76 full-time (45 women), 4 part-time/adjunct. Expenses: Contact institution. *Financial support:* In 2001–02, 2 fellowships (averaging $4,056 per year), 8 research assistantships (averaging $9,839 per year), 14 teaching assistantships (averaging $4,802 per year) were awarded. Federal Work-Study also available. Financial award application deadline: 2/15; financial award applicants required to submit FAFSA. In 2001, 197 degrees awarded. *Degree program information:* Part-time programs available. Offers audiology (MA); blind rehabilitation (MA); health and human services (MA, MS, MSW); occupational therapy (MS); physician assistant (MS); social work (MSW); speech pathology (MA). *Application fee:* $25. *Application Contact:* Admissions and Orientation, 616-387-2000, Fax: 616-387-2355. *Dean,* Dr. Janet Pisaneschi, 616-387-2638.

Haworth College of Business Students: 374 full-time (145 women), 238 part-time (74 women); includes 32 minority (11 African Americans, 15 Asian Americans or Pacific Islanders, 5 Hispanic Americans, 1 Native American), 190 international. 263 applicants, 88% accepted, 144 enrolled. *Faculty:* 73 full-time (13 women). Expenses: Contact institution. *Financial support:* In 2001–02, fellowships (averaging $4,056 per year), 8 research assistantships (averaging $9,839 per year), 14 teaching assistantships (averaging $4,802 per year) were awarded. Career-related internships or fieldwork and Federal Work-Study also available. Financial award application deadline: 2/15; financial award applicants required to submit FAFSA. In 2001, 153 degrees awarded. *Degree program information:* Part-time programs available. Offers accountancy (MSA); business (MBA, MSA); business administration (MBA). *Application deadline:* For fall admission, 2/15 (priority date). Applications are processed on a rolling basis. *Application fee:* $25. *Application Contact:* Admissions and Orientation, 616-387-2000, Fax: 616-387-2355. *Dean,* Dr. James Schmotter, 616-387-5050.

See in-depth description on page 1301.

WESTERN NEW ENGLAND COLLEGE, Springfield, MA 01119-2654

General Information Independent, coed, comprehensive institution. *Enrollment:* 1,462 matriculated graduate/professional students. *Enrollment by degree level:* 492 first professional, 970 master's. *Graduate faculty:* 61 full-time (16 women), 80 part-time/adjunct (23 women). *Tuition:* Part-time $429 per credit. *Required fees:* $9 per credit. $20 per semester. *Graduate housing:* On-campus housing not available. *Student services:* Campus safety program, career counseling, disabled student services, exercise/wellness program, free psychological counseling, low-cost health insurance, writing training. *Library facilities:* D'Amour Library plus 1 other. *Online resources:* library catalog, web page. *Collection:* 118,364 titles, 2,260 serial subscriptions, 2,989 audiovisual materials.

Computer facilities: 250 computers available on campus for general student use. A campuswide network can be accessed from student residence rooms and from off campus. Internet access is available. *Web address:* http://www.wnec.edu/.

General Application Contact: Dr. Janet Castleman, Director of Continuing Education, 413-782-1750, Fax: 413-782-1779, E-mail: jcastlem@wnec.edu.

GRADUATE UNITS

School of Business Average age 29. 162 applicants, 48% accepted. *Faculty:* 18 full-time (4 women), 17 part-time/adjunct (0 women). Expenses: Contact institution. *Financial support:* Available to part-time students. Application deadline: 4/1; In 2001, 541 degrees awarded. *Degree program information:* Part-time and evening/weekend programs available. Offers accounting (MBA, MSA); business administration (accelerated) (MBA); business administration (general) (MBA); criminal justice administration (MSCJA); finance (MBA); health care management (MBA); human resources (MBA); international business (MBA); management information systems (MBA); marketing (MBA); procurement and contracting (MBA). *Application deadline:* Applications are processed on a rolling basis. *Application fee:* $30. *Application Contact:* Dr. Janet Castleman, Director of Continuing Education, 413-782-1750, Fax: 413-782-1779, E-mail: jcastlem@wnec.edu. *Dean,* Dr. Stanley Kowalski, 413-782-1224.

School of Engineering Average age 29. 11 applicants, 27% accepted. *Faculty:* 17 full-time (0 women), 2 part-time/adjunct (0 women). Expenses: Contact institution. *Financial support:* Teaching assistantships available. Support available to part-time students. Financial award application deadline: 4/1; financial award applicants required to submit FAFSA. In 2001, 12 degrees awarded. *Degree program information:* Part-time and evening/weekend programs available. Offers computer and engineering information systems (MSEE); computer engineering (MSEE); engineering (MSEE, MSEM, MSME); mechanical engineering (MSME); production management (MSEM). *Application deadline:* Applications are processed on a rolling basis. *Application fee:* $30. *Application Contact:* Dr. Janet Castleman, Director of Continuing Education, 413-782-1750, Fax: 413-782-1779, E-mail: jcastlem@wnec.edu. *Dean,* Dr. Carl E. Rathmann, 413-782-1273 Ext. 1285, E-mail: crathman@wnec.edu.

School of Law Students: 260 full-time (139 women), 232 part-time (120 women); includes 65 minority (31 African Americans, 11 Asian Americans or Pacific Islanders, 20 Hispanic Americans, 3 Native Americans), 4 international. Average age 30. 915 applicants, 59% accepted, 154 enrolled. *Faculty:* 19 full-time (6 women), 37 part-time/adjunct (15 women). Expenses: Contact institution. *Financial support:* Career-related internships or fieldwork, Federal Work-Study, institutionally sponsored loans, and scholarships/grants available. Support available to part-time students. Financial award application deadline: 4/1; financial award applicants required to submit FAFSA. In 2001, 153 degrees awarded. *Degree program information:* Part-time and evening/weekend programs available. Offers law (JD). *Application deadline:* For fall admission, 3/15 (priority date). Applications are processed on a rolling basis. *Application fee:* $35. *Application Contact:* Sherri Berendt, Director of Admissions, 413-782-1281,

E-mail: sberendt@law.wnec.edu. *Dean*, Dr. Arthur R. Gaudio, 413-782-2201, E-mail: agaudio@wnec.edu.

WESTERN NEW MEXICO UNIVERSITY, Silver City, NM 88062-0680

General Information State-supported, coed, comprehensive institution. *Enrollment:* 85 full-time matriculated graduate/professional students (52 women), 478 part-time matriculated graduate/professional students (339 women). *Enrollment by degree level:* 403 master's. *Graduate faculty:* 40 full-time (20 women), 11 part-time/adjunct (4 women). Tuition, state resident: full-time $1,314; part-time $73 per credit. Tuition, nonresident: full-time $5,104. *Required fees:* $230 per semester. *Graduate housing:* Rooms and/or apartments available on a first-come, first-served basis to single and married students. Typical cost: $2,806 per year ($4,926 including board) for single students; $3,140 per year for married students. Housing application deadline: 6/30. *Student services:* Campus employment opportunities, campus safety program, career counseling, child daycare facilities, disabled student services, exercise/wellness program, free psychological counseling, low-cost health insurance, multicultural affairs office. *Library facilities:* Miller Library plus 2 others. *Online resources:* library catalog, web page, access to other libraries' catalogs. *Collection:* 245,146 titles, 236 serial subscriptions.

Computer facilities: 85 computers available on campus for general student use. Internet access is available. *Web address:* http://www.wnmu.edu/.

General Application Contact: Betsy Miller, Assistant Director of Admissions, 505-538-6106, Fax: 505-538-6127, E-mail: millerb@iron.wnmu.edu.

GRADUATE UNITS

Graduate Division Students: 74 full-time (50 women), 398 part-time (278 women); includes 165 minority (4 African Americans, 5 Asian Americans or Pacific Islanders, 100 Hispanic Americans, 56 Native Americans), 2 international. *Faculty:* 42 full-time (24 women), 7 part-time/adjunct (2 women). Expenses: Contact institution. *Financial support:* In 2001–02, 3 fellowships (averaging $6,000 per year), 15 research assistantships (averaging $4,500 per year) were awarded. Career-related internships or fieldwork, Federal Work-Study, tuition waivers (partial), and unspecified assistantships also available. Support available to part-time students. Financial award application deadline: 4/1; financial award applicants required to submit FAFSA. In 2001, 96 degrees awarded. *Degree program information:* Part-time and evening/weekend programs available. Offers business (MBA); interdisciplinary programs (MA). *Application deadline:* Applications are processed on a rolling basis. *Application fee:* $0. Electronic applications accepted. *Application Contact:* Betsy Miller, Assistant Director of Admissions, 505-538-6106, Fax: 505-538-6127, E-mail: millerb@iron.wnmu.edu. *Dean*, Dr. Faye N. Vowell, 505-538-6317, Fax: 505-538-6182.

School of Education Students: 59 full-time (41 women), 350 part-time (255 women); includes 153 minority (4 African Americans, 5 Asian Americans or Pacific Islanders, 96 Hispanic Americans, 48 Native Americans) *Faculty:* 11 full-time (5 women), 7 part-time/adjunct (5 women). Expenses: Contact institution. *Financial support:* In 2001–02, 2 fellowships were awarded; tuition waivers (partial) also available. Financial award application deadline: 4/1; financial award applicants required to submit FAFSA. In 2001, 84 degrees awarded. Offers counselor education (MA); elementary education (MAT); reading (MAT); school administration (MA); secondary education (MAT); special education (MAT). *Application deadline:* Applications are processed on a rolling basis. *Application fee:* $0. Electronic applications accepted. *Application Contact:* Betsy Miller, Assistant Director of Admissions, 505-538-6106, Fax: 505-538-6127, E-mail: millerb@iron.wnmu.edu. *Dean*, Dr. Jerry Harmon, 505-538-6414, Fax: 505-538-6417, E-mail: harmonj@silver.unmu.edu.

WESTERN OREGON UNIVERSITY, Monmouth, OR 97361-1394

General Information State-supported, coed, comprehensive institution. *Enrollment:* 127 full-time matriculated graduate/professional students (72 women), 206 part-time matriculated graduate/professional students (150 women). *Enrollment by degree level:* 333 master's. *Graduate faculty:* 191 full-time (87 women), 25 part-time/adjunct (13 women). *Graduate housing:* Rooms and/or apartments available on a first-come, first-served basis to single and married students. *Student services:* Campus employment opportunities, campus safety program, career counseling, child daycare facilities, disabled student services, exercise/wellness program, free psychological counseling, international student services, low-cost health insurance, multicultural affairs office, teacher training, writing training. *Library facilities:* Wayne Lynn Hamersly Library. *Online resources:* library catalog, web page, access to other libraries' catalogs. *Collection:* 257,194 titles, 1,700 serial subscriptions, 2,562 audiovisual materials.

Computer facilities: 277 computers available on campus for general student use. A campuswide network can be accessed from student residence rooms and from off campus. Internet access is available. *Web address:* http://www.wou.edu/.

General Application Contact: Alison Marshall, Director of Admissions, 503-838-8211, Fax: 503-838-8067, E-mail: marshaa@wou.edu.

GRADUATE UNITS

Graduate Programs Students: 127 full-time (72 women), 206 part-time (150 women). Average age 36. 187 applicants, 72% accepted. *Faculty:* 191 full-time (87 women), 25 part-time/adjunct (13 women). Expenses: Contact institution. *Financial support:* In 2001–02, 155 students received support, including 6 research assistantships with full tuition reimbursements available (averaging $1,233 per year), 20 teaching assistantships with full tuition reimbursements available (averaging $851 per year); career-related internships or fieldwork, Federal Work-Study, and tuition waivers (full and partial) also available. Support available to part-time students. Financial award application deadline: 3/1; financial award applicants required to submit FAFSA. In 2001, 167 degrees awarded. *Degree program information:* Part-time and evening/weekend programs available. Postbaccalaureate distance learning degree programs offered (minimal on-campus study). *Application deadline:* Applications are processed on a rolling basis. *Application fee:* $50. *Application Contact:* Alison Marshall, Director of Admissions, 503-838-8211, Fax: 503-838-8067, E-mail: marshaa@wou.edu. *Director of Graduate Studies*, Dr. Joseph W. Sendelbaugh, 503-838-8730, Fax: 503-838-8228, E-mail: sendelj@wou.edu.

College of Education Students: 120 full-time (69 women), 202 part-time (149 women). Average age 36. *Faculty:* 95 full-time (57 women), 11 part-time/adjunct (7 women). Expenses: Contact institution. *Financial support:* In 2001–02, 6 research assistantships with full and partial tuition reimbursements (averaging $1,233 per year), 18 teaching assistantships with full and partial tuition reimbursements (averaging $870 per year) were awarded. Career-related internships or fieldwork, Federal Work-Study, and tuition waivers (full and partial) also available. Support available to part-time students. Financial award application deadline: 3/1; financial award applicants required to submit FAFSA. In 2001, 173 degrees awarded. *Degree program information:* Part-time and evening/weekend programs available. Postbaccalaureate distance learning degree programs offered (minimal on-campus study). Offers bilingual education (MS Ed); deaf education (MS Ed); early childhood education (MS Ed); education (MAT, MS Ed); health (MS Ed); humanities (MAT, MS Ed); information technology (MS Ed); initial licensure (MAT); learning disabilities (MS Ed); mathematics (MAT, MS Ed); multihandicapped education (MS Ed); rehabilitation counseling (MS Ed); science (MAT, MS Ed); social science (MAT, MS Ed); teacher education (MAT, MS Ed). *Application deadline:* Applications are processed on a rolling basis. *Application fee:* $50. *Application Contact:* Alison Marshall, Director of Admissions, 503-838-8211, Fax: 503-838-8067, E-mail: marshaa@wou.edu. *Dean*, Dr. Meredith Brodsky, 503-838-8825, Fax: 503-838-8228, E-mail: brodskm@wou.edu.

College of Liberal Arts and Sciences Students: 7 full-time (3 women), 4 part-time (1 woman); includes 1 minority (Native American) Average age 35. *Faculty:* 96 full-time (30 women), 14 part-time/adjunct (6 women). Expenses: Contact institution. *Financial support:* In 2001–02, 2 teaching assistantships with full tuition reimbursements (averaging $676 per year) were awarded; research assistantships with full tuition reimbursements, career-related internships or fieldwork, Federal Work-Study, and tuition waivers (full and partial) also available. Support available to part-time students. Financial award application deadline: 3/1; financial award applicants required to submit FAFSA. In 2001, 3 degrees awarded. *Degree program information:* Part-time and evening/weekend programs available. Offers correctional administration (MA, MS); liberal arts and sciences (MA, MS). *Application deadline:* Applications are processed on a rolling basis. *Application fee:* $50. *Application Contact:* Alison Marshall, Director of Admissions, 503-838-8211, Fax: 503-838-8067, E-mail: marshaa@wou.edu. *Dean*, Dr. James Chadney, 503-838-8226, Fax: 503-838-8034, E-mail: chadney@wou.edu.

WESTERN SEMINARY, Portland, OR 97215-3367

General Information Independent-religious, coed, graduate-only institution. *Enrollment by degree level:* 161 first professional, 325 master's, 102 doctoral, 17 other advanced degrees. *Graduate faculty:* 29 full-time (4 women), 35 part-time/adjunct (9 women). *Tuition:* Part-time $275 per credit hour. Tuition and fees vary according to degree level. *Graduate housing:* On-campus housing not available. *Student services:* Campus employment opportunities, campus safety program, career counseling, international student services, low-cost health insurance, writing training. *Library facilities:* Cline-Tunnell Library. *Online resources:* library catalog, access to other libraries' catalogs. *Collection:* 47,278 titles, 729 serial subscriptions, 11,348 audiovisual materials.

Computer facilities: 8 computers available on campus for general student use. A campuswide network can be accessed from off campus. Internet access is available. *Web address:* http://www.westernseminary.edu/.

General Application Contact: Dr. Robert W. Wiggins, Registrar/Dean of Student Development, 503-517-1820, Fax: 503-517-1801, E-mail: rwiggins@westernseminary.edu.

GRADUATE UNITS

Graduate Programs Students: 194 full-time (88 women), 549 part-time (177 women); includes 128 minority (20 African Americans, 93 Asian Americans or Pacific Islanders, 14 Hispanic Americans, 1 Native American), 28 international. Average age 32. 375 applicants, 92% accepted. *Faculty:* 29 full-time (4 women), 35 part-time/adjunct (9 women). Expenses: Contact institution. *Financial support:* Fellowships, career-related internships or fieldwork, institutionally sponsored loans, and scholarships/grants available. Support available to part-time students. Financial award applicants required to submit FAFSA. In 2001, 32 first professional degrees, 68 master's, 16 doctorates awarded. *Degree program information:* Part-time and evening/weekend programs available. Offers biblical studies (Certificate); church education (MA, D Min); counseling (MA); hospital chaplaincy (Certificate); intercultural ministry (M Div, MA, D Miss, Certificate); marriage and family counseling (MA, MFT); pastoral counseling (M Div); theology (MA, Th M); women's ministries (MA, Certificate). *Application deadline:* For fall admission, 8/1 (priority date); for winter admission, 12/1 (priority date); for spring admission, 3/1 (priority date). Applications are processed on a rolling basis. *Application fee:* $40. *Application Contact:* Dr. Robert W. Wiggins, Registrar/Dean of Student Development, 503-517-1820, Fax: 503-517-1801, E-mail: rwiggins@westernseminary.edu. *Academic Dean*, Dr. Randal R. Roberts, 503-517-1860, Fax: 503-517-1859, E-mail: rroberts@westernseminary.edu.

WESTERN STATES CHIROPRACTIC COLLEGE, Portland, OR 97230-3099

General Information Independent, coed, upper-level institution. *Enrollment:* 331 full-time matriculated graduate/professional students (102 women). *Enrollment by degree level:* 331 first professional. *Graduate faculty:* 36 full-time (12 women), 32 part-time/adjunct (14 women). *Tuition:* Full-time $15,897. *Required fees:* $720. *Graduate housing:* On-campus housing not available. *Student services:* Campus employment opportunities, exercise/wellness program, free psychological counseling, international student services, low-cost health insurance. *Library facilities:* W. A. Buden Library plus 1 other. *Online resources:* library catalog, access to other libraries' catalogs. *Collection:* 14,700 titles, 365 serial subscriptions. *Research affiliation:* Oregon Center for Complimentary and Alternative Medicine in Craniofacial Disorders (complimentary and alternative medicine), Oregon Center for Complimentary and Alternative Medicine (complimentary and alternative medicine), Consortial Center for Chiropractic Research (Palmer Chiropractic College, Davenport, IA) (chiropractic).

Computer facilities: 15 computers available on campus for general student use. *Web address:* http://www.wschiro.edu/.

General Application Contact: Dr. Lee Smith, Director of Admissions, 800-641-5641, Fax: 503-251-5723, E-mail: lsmith@wschiro.edu.

GRADUATE UNITS

Professional Program Students: 331 full-time (102 women); includes 24 minority (2 African Americans, 15 Asian Americans or Pacific Islanders, 5 Hispanic Americans, 2 Native Americans), 85 international. Average age 26. 145 applicants, 53% accepted. *Faculty:* 36 full-time (12 women), 32 part-time/adjunct (14 women). Expenses: Contact institution. *Financial support:* In 2001–02, 298 students received support. Career-related internships or fieldwork and scholarships/grants available. Support available to part-time students. Financial award applicants required to submit FAFSA. In 2001, 125 degrees awarded. Offers chiropractic (DC). *Application deadline:* Applications are processed on a rolling basis. *Application fee:* $50. *Director of Admissions*, Dr. Lee Smith, 800-641-5641, Fax: 503-251-5723, E-mail: lsmith@wschiro.edu.

WESTERN STATE UNIVERSITY COLLEGE OF LAW, Fullerton, CA 92831-3000

General Information Proprietary, coed, graduate-only institution. *Enrollment by degree level:* 460 first professional. *Graduate faculty:* 21 full-time (9 women), 34 part-time/adjunct (12 women). *Tuition:* Full-time $22,168; part-time $7,460 per term. *Required fees:* $70 per term. *Graduate housing:* On-campus housing not available. *Student services:* Campus employment opportunities, campus safety program, career counseling, disabled student services, free psychological counseling, low-cost health insurance, writing training. *Library facilities:* Law Library. *Online resources:* library catalog, web page. *Collection:* 93,416 titles, 3,070 serial subscriptions.

Computer facilities: 51 computers available on campus for general student use. A campuswide network can be accessed from off campus. Internet access, Lexis, Westlaw, Dialog, Nexis, Cali, Authority are available. *Web address:* http://www.wsulaw.edu/.

General Application Contact: Paul D. Bauer, Assistant Dean of Admission, 714-738-1000 Ext. 2600, Fax: 714-441-1748, E-mail: adm@wsulaw.edu.

GRADUATE UNITS

Professional Program Students: 225 full-time (123 women), 235 part-time (103 women); includes 195 minority (28 African Americans, 83 Asian Americans or Pacific Islanders, 81 Hispanic Americans, 3 Native Americans) Average age 31. 1,010 applicants, 53% accepted, 157 enrolled. *Faculty:* 21 full-time (9 women), 34 part-time/adjunct (12 women). Expenses: Contact institution. *Financial support:* Federal Work-Study and scholarships/grants available. Support available to part-time students. Financial award application deadline: 9/21; financial award applicants required to submit FAFSA. In 2001, 116 degrees awarded. *Degree program information:* Part-time and evening/weekend programs available. Offers law (JD). *Application deadline:* For fall admission, 4/1 (priority date); for spring admission, 10/1 (priority date). Applications are processed on a rolling basis. *Application fee:* $50. Electronic applications accepted. *Application Contact:* Paul D. Bauer, Assistant Dean of Admission, 714-738-1000 Ext. 2600, Fax: 714-441-1748, E-mail: adm@wsulaw.edu. *Dean*, Dr. James F. Hogg, 714-738-1000 Ext. 2900, Fax: 714-526-1062, E-mail: jamesh@wsulaw.edu.

WESTERN THEOLOGICAL SEMINARY, Holland, MI 49423-3622

General Information Independent-religious, coed, graduate-only institution. *Enrollment by degree level:* 116 first professional, 28 master's, 20 doctoral. *Graduate faculty:* 14 full-time (3 women), 4 part-time/adjunct (0 women). *Tuition:* Full-time $6,832; part-time $214 per credit. *Required fees:* $85. One-time fee: $30. *Graduate housing:* Rooms and/or apartments available on a first-come, first-served basis to single and married students. *Student services:* Campus employment opportunities, disabled student services. *Library facilities:* Beardslee Library plus 1 other. *Online resources:* web page. *Collection:* 109,662 titles, 442 serial subscriptions.

Western Theological Seminary (continued)

Computer facilities: 12 computers available on campus for general student use. A campuswide network can be accessed from off campus. Internet access is available. *Web address:* http://www.westernsem.org/.

General Application Contact: Rev. Mark Poppen, Director of Admissions, 616-392-8555, Fax: 616-392-7717, E-mail: mark@westernsem.org.

GRADUATE UNITS

Graduate and Professional Programs Students: 131 full-time (41 women), 33 part-time (15 women); includes 1 minority (African American), 9 international. Average age 29. 92 applicants, 67% accepted, 50 enrolled. *Faculty:* 14 full-time (3 women), 4 part-time/adjunct (0 women). Expenses: Contact institution. *Financial support:* In 2001–02, 50 fellowships were awarded; career-related internships or fieldwork, institutionally sponsored loans, and scholarships/grants also available. Support available to part-time students. Financial award applicants required to submit FAFSA. In 2001, 24 first professional degrees, 10 master's, 3 doctorates awarded. *Degree program information:* Part-time programs available. Offers theology (M Div, M Th, MRE, D Min). *Application deadline:* For fall admission, 7/1 (priority date). Applications are processed on a rolling basis. *Application fee:* $30. *Application Contact:* Rev. Mark Poppen, Director of Admissions, 616-392-8555, Fax: 616-392-7717, E-mail: mark@westernsem.org. *President*, Dr. Dennis Voskuil, 616-392-8555, Fax: 616-392-7717, E-mail: dennis@westernsem.org.

WESTERN UNIVERSITY OF HEALTH SCIENCES, Pomona, CA 91766-1854

General Information Independent, coed, graduate-only institution. *Enrollment by degree level:* 1,099 first professional, 336 master's. *Graduate faculty:* 85 full-time (36 women), 7 part-time/adjunct (3 women). *Graduate housing:* On-campus housing not available. *Student services:* Campus safety program, career counseling, disabled student services, exercise/wellness program, free psychological counseling, low-cost health insurance, teacher training. *Collection:* 18,000 titles, 350 serial subscriptions. *Web address:* http://www.westernu.edu/.

General Application Contact: Susan M. Hanson, Director of Admissions, 909-469-5329, E-mail: shanson@westernu.edu.

GRADUATE UNITS

College of Allied Health Professions Offers allied health professions (MPT, MS); health professions education (MS); physical therapy (MPT); physician assistant studies (MS).

College of Grad Nursing *Degree program information:* Part-time and evening/weekend programs available. Postbaccalaureate distance learning degree programs offered. Offers family nurse practitioner (MSN).

College of Osteopathic Medicine of the Pacific Offers osteopathic medicine (DO).

College of Pharmacy Offers pharmacy (Pharm D).

WESTERN WASHINGTON UNIVERSITY, Bellingham, WA 98225-5996

General Information State-supported, coed, comprehensive institution. CGS member. *Graduate housing:* Rooms and/or apartments available on a first-come, first-served basis to single and married students. Housing application deadline: 5/1. *Research affiliation:* National Council for Air and Stream Improvement (water research/effluent toxicity), Amoco (international oil and chemical products company).

GRADUATE UNITS

Graduate School *Degree program information:* Part-time programs available.

College of Arts and Sciences *Degree program information:* Part-time programs available. Offers anthropology (MA); arts and sciences (M Ed, MA, MS); biology (MS); chemistry (MS); communication sciences and disorders (MA); computer science (MS); English (MA); general psychology (MS); geology (MS); history (MA); human movement and performance (MS); mathematics (MS); mental health counseling (MS); physical education (M Ed); political science (MA); psychology (MS); school counseling (M Ed); science education (M Ed); sociology (MA); technology (M Ed).

College of Business and Economics *Degree program information:* Part-time and evening/weekend programs available. Offers business and economics (MBA).

College of Fine and Performing Arts *Degree program information:* Part-time programs available. Offers art (M Ed); fine and performing arts (M Ed, M Mus, MA); music (M Mus); theatre (MA).

Huxley College of Environmental Studies *Degree program information:* Part-time programs available. Offers environmental science (MS); environmental studies (MS); geography (MS).

Woodring College of Education *Degree program information:* Part-time programs available. Postbaccalaureate distance learning degree programs offered (minimal on-campus study). Offers adult education (M Ed); education (M Ed, MA, MIT); educational administration (M Ed); elementary education (M Ed); exceptional children (M Ed); rehabilitation counseling (MA); secondary education (M Ed, MIT); student personnel administration (M Ed).

WESTFIELD STATE COLLEGE, Westfield, MA 01086

General Information State-supported, coed, comprehensive institution. *Enrollment:* 31 full-time matriculated graduate/professional students (25 women), 298 part-time matriculated graduate/professional students (202 women). *Enrollment by degree level:* 279 master's, 20 other advanced degrees. *Graduate faculty:* 21 full-time (9 women), 29 part-time/adjunct (10 women). Tuition, state resident: part-time $155 per credit. Tuition, nonresident: part-time $165 per credit. *Graduate housing:* On-campus housing not available. *Student services:* Career counseling, exercise/wellness program, free psychological counseling, low-cost health insurance, multicultural affairs office. *Library facilities:* Ely Library. *Online resources:* library catalog, web page, access to other libraries' catalogs. *Collection:* 124,363 titles, 819 serial subscriptions, 2,379 audiovisual materials.

Computer facilities: 230 computers available on campus for general student use. A campuswide network can be accessed from student residence rooms and from off campus. Internet access is available. *Web address:* http://www.wsc.ma.edu/.

General Application Contact: Russ Leary, Admissions Clerk, 413-572-8022, Fax: 413-572-5227, E-mail: rleary@wisdom.wsc.mass.edu.

GRADUATE UNITS

Division of Graduate Studies and Continuing Education Students: 24 full-time (16 women), 270 part-time (190 women); includes 15 minority (9 African Americans, 6 Hispanic Americans) Average age 32. *Faculty:* 21 full-time (9 women), 29 part-time/adjunct (10 women). Expenses: Contact institution. *Financial support:* In 2001–02, 11 research assistantships with full and partial tuition reimbursements (averaging $1,600 per year) were awarded; teaching assistantships, career-related internships or fieldwork, Federal Work-Study, and tuition waivers (full and partial) also available. Support available to part-time students. Financial award application deadline: 4/1; financial award applicants required to submit CSS PROFILE. In 2001, 94 master's, 3 other advanced degrees awarded. *Degree program information:* Part-time and evening/weekend programs available. Offers counseling/clinical psychology (MA); criminal justice (MS); early childhood education (M Ed); elementary education (M Ed); English (MA); history (M Ed); intensive special needs education (M Ed); mental health counseling/psychology (MA); middle school education (M Ed); occupational education (M Ed); physical education (M Ed); reading (M Ed); school administration (M Ed, CAGS); secondary education (M Ed); special education (M Ed); special needs education (M Ed); technology for educators (M Ed). *Application deadline:* Applications are processed on a rolling basis. *Application fee:* $30. *Application Contact:* Russ Leary, Admissions Clerk, 413-572-8022, Fax: 413-572-5227, E-mail: rleary@wisdom.wsc.mass.edu. *Dean*, Dr. Catherine Lilly, 413-572-8030, Fax: 413-572-5227, E-mail: clilly@wisdom.wsc.mass.edu.

WESTMINSTER COLLEGE, New Wilmington, PA 16172-0001

General Information Independent-religious, coed, comprehensive institution. *Enrollment:* 4 full-time matriculated graduate/professional students (2 women), 147 part-time matriculated graduate/professional students (94 women). *Enrollment by degree level:* 151 master's. *Graduate faculty:* 5 full-time (3 women), 8 part-time/adjunct (3 women). *Graduate housing:* On-campus housing not available. *Student services:* Career counseling, multicultural affairs office. *Library facilities:* McGill Memorial Library plus 1 other. *Online resources:* library catalog, web page. *Collection:* 230,000 titles, 827 serial subscriptions.

Computer facilities: 158 computers available on campus for general student use. A campuswide network can be accessed from student residence rooms and from off campus. Internet access is available. *Web address:* http://www.westminster.edu/.

General Application Contact: Dr. Darwin W. Huey, Graduate Director, 724-946-7186, Fax: 724-946-7171, E-mail: hueydw@westminster.edu.

GRADUATE UNITS

Programs in Education Students: 4 full-time (2 women), 147 part-time (94 women); includes 3 minority (all African Americans) *Faculty:* 5 full-time (3 women), 8 part-time/adjunct (3 women). Expenses: Contact institution. *Financial support:* Career-related internships or fieldwork and scholarships/grants available. In 2001, 77 degrees awarded. *Degree program information:* Part-time and evening/weekend programs available. Offers administration (M Ed, Certificate); elementary education (M Ed); general education (M Ed); guidance and counseling (M Ed, Certificate); reading (M Ed, Certificate); supervision and curriculum (M Ed, Certificate). *Application deadline:* For fall admission, 8/15 (priority date); for spring admission, 1/8 (priority date). Applications are processed on a rolling basis. *Application fee:* $20. *Graduate Director*, 724-946-7186, Fax: 724-946-7171, E-mail: hueydw@westminster.edu.

WESTMINSTER COLLEGE, Salt Lake City, UT 84105-3697

General Information Independent, coed, comprehensive institution. *Enrollment:* 133 full-time matriculated graduate/professional students (63 women), 362 part-time matriculated graduate/professional students (141 women). *Enrollment by degree level:* 495 master's. *Graduate faculty:* 48 full-time, 27 part-time/adjunct. *Tuition:* Full-time $10,656; part-time $592 per credit. *Required fees:* $210. *Graduate housing:* On-campus housing not available. *Student services:* Campus employment opportunities, campus safety program, career counseling, disabled student services, free psychological counseling, low-cost health insurance, teacher training. *Library facilities:* Giovale Library plus 1 other. *Online resources:* library catalog, web page. *Collection:* 102,632 titles, 1,807 serial subscriptions, 3,930 audiovisual materials.

Computer facilities: 238 computers available on campus for general student use. A campuswide network can be accessed from student residence rooms. Internet access and online class registration are available. *Web address:* http://www.westminstercollege.edu/.

General Application Contact: Philip J. Alletto, Vice President for Student Development and Enrollment Management, 801-832-2200, Fax: 801-484-3252, E-mail: admispub@westminstercollege.edu.

GRADUATE UNITS

The Bill and Vieve Gore School of Business Students: 86 full-time, 246 part-time; includes 20 minority (11 Asian Americans or Pacific Islanders, 9 Hispanic Americans), 5 international. Average age 34. 151 applicants, 62% accepted, 79 enrolled. *Faculty:* 31 full-time, 16 part-time/adjunct. Expenses: Contact institution. *Financial support:* In 2001–02, 140 students received support. Scholarships/grants and tuition remissions available. Support available to part-time students. Financial award applicants required to submit FAFSA. In 2001, 124 master's, 51 other advanced degrees awarded. *Degree program information:* Part-time and evening/weekend programs available. Postbaccalaureate distance learning degree programs offered (minimal on-campus study). Offers business (MBA, Certificate); business administration (MBA, Certificate). *Application deadline:* For fall admission, 8/1 (priority date). Applications are processed on a rolling basis. *Application fee:* $30. Electronic applications accepted. *Application Contact:* Philip J. Alletto, Vice President for Student Development and Enrollment Management, 801-832-2200, Fax: 801-484-3252, E-mail: admispub@westminstercollege.edu. *Dean*, Dr. James Seidelman, 801-832-2600, Fax: 801-484-3767, E-mail: c-seidel@westminstercollege.edu.

St. Mark's-Westminster School of Nursing and Health Sciences Students: 26 full-time, 1 part-time; includes 1 minority (Asian American or Pacific Islander) Average age 40. 25 applicants, 64% accepted, 15 enrolled. *Faculty:* 7 full-time. Expenses: Contact institution. *Financial support:* In 2001–02, 23 students received support. Scholarships/grants and tuition remissions available. Support available to part-time students. Financial award applicants required to submit FAFSA. In 2001, 15 degrees awarded. *Degree program information:* Part-time and evening/weekend programs available. Postbaccalaureate distance learning degree programs offered (minimal on-campus study). Offers nursing (MSN); nursing and health sciences (MSN). *Application deadline:* For fall admission, 3/1 (priority date). Applications are processed on a rolling basis. *Application fee:* $30. Electronic applications accepted. *Application Contact:* Philip J. Alletto, Vice President for Student Development and Enrollment Management, 801-832-2200, Fax: 801-484-3252, E-mail: admispub@westminstercollege.edu. *Dean*, Dr. Kathleen A. Emrich, 801-832-2168, Fax: 801-467-8601, E-mail: kemrich@westminstercollege.edu.

School of Arts and Sciences Students: 10 full-time, 64 part-time; includes 2 minority (both Native Americans) Average age 36. 36 applicants, 78% accepted, 24 enrolled. *Faculty:* 3 full-time, 4 part-time/adjunct. Expenses: Contact institution. *Financial support:* In 2001–02, 38 students received support. Scholarships/grants and tuition remissions available. Support available to part-time students. Financial award applicants required to submit FAFSA. In 2001, 17 degrees awarded. *Degree program information:* Part-time and evening/weekend programs available. Offers arts and sciences (MPC); professional communication (MPC). *Application deadline:* For fall admission, 8/1 (priority date). Applications are processed on a rolling basis. *Application fee:* $30. Electronic applications accepted. *Application Contact:* Philip J. Alletto, Vice President for Student Development and Enrollment Management, 801-832-2200, Fax: 801-484-3252, E-mail: admispub@westminstercollege.edu. *Dean*, Dr. Mary Jane Chase, 801-832-2300, Fax: 801-466-6916, E-mail: m-chase@westminstercollege.edu.

School of Education Students: 9 full-time, 26 part-time; includes 2 minority (1 Hispanic American, 1 Native American) Average age 38. 9 applicants, 78% accepted, 6 enrolled. *Faculty:* 7 full-time, 7 part-time/adjunct. Expenses: Contact institution. *Financial support:* Scholarships/grants and tuition remissions available. Support available to part-time students. Financial award applicants required to submit FAFSA. In 2001, 18 degrees awarded. *Degree program information:* Part-time and evening/weekend programs available. Offers education (M Ed). *Application deadline:* For fall admission, 8/1 (priority date). Applications are processed on a rolling basis. *Application fee:* $30. Electronic applications accepted. *Application Contact:* Philip J. Alletto, Vice President for Student Development and Enrollment Management, 801-832-2200, Fax: 801-484-3252, E-mail: admispub@westminstercollege.edu. *Dean*, Dr. Janet Dynak, 801-832-2470, Fax: 801-487-9507, E-mail: j-dynak@wcslc.edu.

WESTMINSTER THEOLOGICAL SEMINARY, Philadelphia, PA 19118

General Information Independent-religious, coed, primarily men, graduate-only institution. *Enrollment by degree level:* 226 first professional, 125 master's, 173 doctoral, 162 other advanced degrees. *Graduate faculty:* 20 full-time (0 women), 32 part-time/adjunct (5 women). *Tuition:* Full-time $8,280; part-time $345 per hour. *Required fees:* $20 per semester. Full-time tuition and fees vary according to course level, course load, degree level, campus/location, program and student's religious affiliation. *Graduate housing:* Room and/or apartments available on a first-come, first-served basis to single students; on-campus housing not available to married students. *Student services:* Campus employment opportunities, campus safety program, international student services, low-cost health insurance, multicultural affairs office, writing training. *Library facilities:* Montgomery Library. *Online resources:* library catalog. *Collection:* 119,956 titles, 810 serial subscriptions, 18 audiovisual materials.

Computer facilities: 16 computers available on campus for general student use. A campuswide network can be accessed. Internet access is available. *Web address:* http://www.wts.edu/.

General Application Contact: Dan Cason, Director of Admissions, 215-887-5511, Fax: 215-887-5404, E-mail: admissions@wts.edu.

GRADUATE UNITS

Graduate and Professional Programs Students: 305 full-time (37 women), 381 part-time (88 women); includes 215 minority (35 African Americans, 165 Asian Americans or Pacific Islanders, 10 Hispanic Americans, 5 Native Americans), 80 international. Average age 35. 440 applicants, 81% accepted. *Faculty:* 21 full-time (0 women), 37 part-time/adjunct (5 women). Expenses: Contact institution. *Financial support:* In 2001–02, 310 students received support. Scholarships/grants and tuition waivers (partial) available. Financial award application deadline: 5/30; financial award applicants required to submit FAFSA. In 2001, 31 first professional degrees, 27 master's, 19 doctorates, 1 other advanced degree awarded. *Degree program information:* Part-time and evening/weekend programs available. Offers apologetics (Th M); Biblical counseling (Certificate); biblical studies (MAR); Christian studies (Certificate); church history (Th M); counseling (M Div, MAR); general studies (M Div, MAR); hermeneutics and Bible interpretations (PhD); historical and theological studies (PhD); New Testament (Th M); Old Testament (Th M); pastoral counseling (D Min); pastoral ministry (M Div, D Min); systematic theology (Th M); theological studies (MAR); urban missions (M Div, MA, MAR, D Min). *Application deadline:* For fall admission, 3/1 (priority date); for spring admission, 9/30 (priority date). Applications are processed on a rolling basis. *Application fee:* $25. *Application Contact:* Dan Cason, Director of Admissions, 215-887-5511, Fax: 215-887-5404, E-mail: admissions@wts.edu. *Executive Vice President*, J. Stafford Carson, 215-887-5511, Fax: 215-887-5404, E-mail: scarson@wts.edu.

WESTMINSTER THEOLOGICAL SEMINARY IN CALIFORNIA, Escondido, CA 92027-4128

General Information Independent-religious, coed, primarily men, graduate-only institution. *Graduate faculty:* 11 full-time (0 women), 18 part-time/adjunct (2 women). *Tuition:* Part-time $265 per unit. One-time fee: $25 part-time. *Graduate housing:* Rooms and/or apartments available on a first-come, first-served basis to single students and available to married students. Housing application deadline: 1/1. *Student services:* Campus employment opportunities, career counseling, international student services. *Online resources:* library catalog, web page, access to other libraries' catalogs. *Collection:* 39,500 titles, 240 serial subscriptions.

Computer facilities: 8 computers available on campus for general student use. Internet access and online class registration are available.

General Application Contact: Elisa Hickernell, Admissions Coordinator, 760-480-8474, Fax: 760-480-0252, E-mail: admissions@wtscal.edu.

GRADUATE UNITS

Programs in Theology *Degree program information:* Part-time programs available. Offers biblical studies (MA); historical theology (MA); theological studies (M Div, MA).

WESTON JESUIT SCHOOL OF THEOLOGY, Cambridge, MA 02138-3495

General Information Independent-religious, coed, graduate-only institution. *Enrollment by degree level:* 75 first professional, 44 master's, 12 doctoral, 50 other advanced degrees. *Graduate faculty:* 21 full-time (5 women), 13 part-time/adjunct (4 women). *Tuition:* Part-time $490 per credit. *Required fees:* $300; $100 per semester. *Graduate housing:* Rooms and/or apartments available on a first-come, first-served basis to single and married students. Typical cost: $395 per year for single students; $575 per year for married students. Housing application deadline: 3/15. *Student services:* Campus employment opportunities, career counseling, disabled student services, international student services, low-cost health insurance, writing training. *Library facilities:* Weston/EDS Library. *Online resources:* library catalog, web page, access to other libraries' catalogs. *Collection:* 226,166 titles, 1,177 serial subscriptions, 518 audiovisual materials.

Computer facilities: 1 computer available on campus for general student use. Internet access is available. *Web address:* http://www.wjst.edu/.

General Application Contact: Karen Ann McLennan, Director of Admissions and Financial Aid, 617-492-1960, Fax: 617-492-5833, E-mail: kmclennan@wjst.edu.

GRADUATE UNITS

Graduate and Professional Programs Students: 138 full-time (34 women), 47 part-time (30 women); includes 12 minority (6 Asian Americans or Pacific Islanders, 6 Hispanic Americans), 26 international. Average age 31. 112 applicants, 84% accepted. *Faculty:* 21 full-time (5 women), 13 part-time/adjunct (4 women). Expenses: Contact institution. *Financial support:* In 2001–02, 67 students received support; fellowships with partial tuition reimbursements available, career-related internships or fieldwork, scholarships/grants, and tuition waivers (full and partial) available. Support available to part-time students. Financial award application deadline: 3/15; financial award applicants required to submit FAFSA. In 2001, 15 first professional degrees, 23 master's, 4 doctorates, 18 other advanced degrees awarded. *Degree program information:* Part-time programs available. Offers divinity (M Div); sacred theology (STD, STL); spiritual direction (MA); theological studies (MTS); theology (Th M, PhD). *Application deadline:* For fall admission, 3/15 (priority date); for spring admission, 11/1 (priority date). Applications are processed on a rolling basis. *Application fee:* $50. *Application Contact:* Karen Ann McLennan, Director of Admissions and Financial Aid, 617-492-1960, Fax: 617-492-5833, E-mail: kmclennan@wjst.edu. *Dean*, Fr. John R. Sachs, SJ, 617-492-1960, Fax: 617-492-5833, E-mail: jrsachs@wjst.edu.

WEST TEXAS A&M UNIVERSITY, Canyon, TX 79016-0001

General Information State-supported, coed, comprehensive institution. *Enrollment:* 222 full-time matriculated graduate/professional students (118 women), 673 part-time matriculated graduate/professional students (418 women). *Enrollment by degree level:* 895 master's. *Graduate faculty:* 114 full-time (33 women), 81 part-time/adjunct (27 women). Tuition, state resident: part-time $120 per hour. Tuition, nonresident: part-time $253 per hour. *Graduate housing:* Rooms and/or apartments available on a first-come, first-served basis to single students and available to married students. *Student services:* Campus employment opportunities, career counseling, child daycare facilities, disabled student services, exercise/wellness program, free psychological counseling, international student services, low-cost health insurance, multicultural affairs office, writing training. *Library facilities:* Cornette Library. *Online resources:* library catalog, web page, access to other libraries' catalogs. *Collection:* 301,412 titles, 5,905 serial subscriptions, 1,464 audiovisual materials. *Research affiliation:* Pantex (chemistry), Agricultural Research (agricultural), Owens Cornings (sports exercise), Agriculture Experiment Station (agriculture), Engineering Experiment Station (math/science).

Computer facilities: 800 computers available on campus for general student use. A campuswide network can be accessed from student residence rooms and from off campus. Internet access and online class registration are available. *Web address:* http://www.wtamu.edu/.

General Application Contact: Dr. James R. Hallmark, Dean of the Graduate School, 806-651-2730, Fax: 806-651-2733, E-mail: jhallmark@mail.wtamu.edu.

GRADUATE UNITS

College of Agriculture, Nursing, and Natural Sciences Students: 54 full-time (25 women), 113 part-time (66 women); includes 17 minority (3 African Americans, 1 Asian American or Pacific Islander, 11 Hispanic Americans, 2 Native Americans), 18 international. Average age 34. 141 applicants, 85% accepted, 141 enrolled. *Faculty:* 15 full-time (1 woman), 20 part-time/adjunct (2 women). Expenses: Contact institution. *Financial support:* In 2001–02, 4 research assistantships with tuition reimbursements (averaging $6,500 per year), 37 teaching assistantships with partial tuition reimbursements (averaging $6,750 per year) were awarded. Career-related internships or fieldwork, Federal Work-Study, institutionally sponsored loans, scholarships/grants, traineeships, and tuition waivers (partial) also available. Support available to part-time students. Financial award applicants required to submit FAFSA. In 2001, 56 degrees awarded. *Degree program information:* Part-time and evening/weekend programs available. Offers agricultural business and economics (MS); agriculture (MS); agriculture, nursing, and natural sciences (MS, MSN); animal science (MS); biology (MS); chemistry (MS); engineering technology (MS); environmental science (MS); mathematics (MS); nursing (MSN); plant science (MS). *Application deadline:* Applications are processed on a rolling basis. *Application fee:* $25 ($75 for international students). Electronic applications accepted. *Application Contact:* Gail A. Hall, Secretary, 806-651-2752, Fax: 806-651-2733, E-mail: graduateschool@mail.wtamu.edu. *Dean*, Dr. James Clark, 806-651-2585, Fax: 806-651-2609, E-mail: jclark@mail.wtamu.edu.

College of Education and Social Sciences Students: 56 full-time (39 women), 314 part-time (213 women); includes 39 minority (8 African Americans, 3 Asian Americans or Pacific Islanders, 24 Hispanic Americans, 4 Native Americans), 2 international. Average age 30. 348 applicants, 79% accepted, 348 enrolled. *Faculty:* 26 full-time (8 women), 14 part-time/adjunct (7 women). Expenses: Contact institution. *Financial support:* In 2001–02, research assistantships with partial tuition reimbursements (averaging $6,500 per year), 13 teaching assistantships with partial tuition reimbursements (averaging $6,750 per year) were awarded. Career-related internships or fieldwork, Federal Work-Study, institutionally sponsored loans, and tuition waivers (partial) also available. Support available to part-time students. Financial award applicants required to submit CSS PROFILE or FAFSA. In 2001, 125 degrees awarded. *Degree program information:* Part-time and evening/weekend programs available. Postbaccalaureate distance learning degree programs offered (minimal on-campus study). Offers administration (M Ed); counseling education (M Ed); criminal justice (MA); curriculum and instruction (M Ed); education and social sciences (M Ed, MA, MS); educational diagnostician (M Ed); educational technology (M Ed); elementary education (M Ed); history (MA); political science (MA); professional counseling (MA); psychology (MA); reading (M Ed); secondary education (M Ed, MA); sports and exercise science (MS). *Application deadline:* Applications are processed on a rolling basis. *Application fee:* $25 ($75 for international students). Electronic applications accepted. *Dean*, Dr. Ted Guffy, 806-651-2600, Fax: 806-651-2601, E-mail: tguffy@mailwtamu.edu.

College of Fine Arts and Humanities Students: 33 full-time (21 women), 64 part-time (46 women); includes 11 minority (3 African Americans, 6 Hispanic Americans, 2 Native Americans), 7 international. Average age 34. 102 applicants, 97 enrolled. *Faculty:* 32 full-time (13 women), 17 part-time/adjunct (6 women). Expenses: Contact institution. *Financial support:* In 2001–02, research assistantships (averaging $6,500 per year), 25 teaching assistantships with partial tuition reimbursements (averaging $6,700 per year) were awarded. Fellowships, career-related internships or fieldwork, Federal Work-Study, institutionally sponsored loans, and tuition waivers (partial) also available. Support available to part-time students. Financial award applicants required to submit CSS PROFILE or FAFSA. In 2001, 52 degrees awarded. *Degree program information:* Part-time and evening/weekend programs available. Offers art (MA); communication (MA); communication disorders (MS); English (MA); fine arts and humanities (MA, MFA, MM, MS); music (MA); performance (MM); studio art (MFA). *Application deadline:* Applications are processed on a rolling basis. *Application fee:* $25 ($75 for international students). Electronic applications accepted. *Dean*, Dr. Sue Park, 806-651-2777, Fax: 806-651-2779, E-mail: spark@mail.wtamu.edu.

Program in Interdisciplinary Studies Students: 7 full-time (5 women), 25 part-time (15 women); includes 8 minority (2 Asian Americans or Pacific Islanders, 6 Hispanic Americans), 1 international. Average age 34. 17 applicants, 17 enrolled. Expenses: Contact institution. *Financial support:* Federal Work-Study and institutionally sponsored loans available. Support available to part-time students. Financial award applicants required to submit CSS PROFILE or FAFSA. In 2001, 17 degrees awarded. *Degree program information:* Part-time and evening/weekend programs available. Postbaccalaureate distance learning degree programs offered (minimal on-campus study). Offers interdisciplinary studies (MA, MS). *Application deadline:* Applications are processed on a rolling basis. *Application fee:* $25 ($75 for international students). Electronic applications accepted. *Dean of the Graduate School*, Dr. James R. Hallmark, 806-651-2730, Fax: 806-651-2733, E-mail: jhallmark@mail.wtamu.edu.

T. Boone Pickens College of Business Students: 64 full-time (26 women), 123 part-time (52 women); includes 17 minority (4 African Americans, 2 Asian Americans or Pacific Islanders, 11 Hispanic Americans), 44 international. Average age 34. 163 applicants, 163 enrolled. *Faculty:* 18 full-time (6 women), 8 part-time/adjunct (4 women). Expenses: Contact institution. *Financial support:* In 2001–02, research assistantships (averaging $6,500 per year), 3 teaching assistantships with partial tuition reimbursements (averaging $6,700 per year) were awarded. Career-related internships or fieldwork, Federal Work-Study, institutionally sponsored loans, and tuition waivers (partial) also available. Support available to part-time students. Financial award applicants required to submit CSS PROFILE or FAFSA. In 2001, 70 degrees awarded. *Degree program information:* Part-time and evening/weekend programs available. Postbaccalaureate distance learning degree programs offered (minimal on-campus study). Offers accounting (MP Acc); business (MBA, MP Acc, MS); business administration (MBA); finance and economics (MS). *Application deadline:* Applications are processed on a rolling basis. *Application fee:* $25 ($75 for international students). Electronic applications accepted. *Dean*, Dr. John Cooley, 806-651-2530, Fax: 806-651-2927, E-mail: jcooley@mail.wtamu.edu.

See in-depth description on page 1303.

WEST VIRGINIA SCHOOL OF OSTEOPATHIC MEDICINE, Lewisburg, WV 24901-1196

General Information State-supported, coed, graduate-only institution. *Enrollment by degree level:* 294 first professional. *Graduate faculty:* 36 full-time (10 women), 96 part-time/adjunct (13 women). Tuition, state resident: full-time $13,594. Tuition, nonresident: full-time $33,644. *Graduate housing:* On-campus housing not available. *Student services:* Campus employment opportunities, career counseling, exercise/wellness program, free psychological counseling, multicultural affairs office. *Library facilities:* WVSOM Library. *Online resources:* library catalog, web page. *Collection:* 19,662 titles, 476 serial subscriptions, 2,599 audiovisual materials.

Computer facilities: 22 computers available on campus for general student use. A campuswide network can be accessed from off campus. Internet access is available. *Web address:* http://www.wvsom.edu.

General Application Contact: John N. Gorby, Director of Admissions, 304-645-6270 Ext. 373, Fax: 304-645-4859, E-mail: jgorby@wvsom.edu.

GRADUATE UNITS

Professional Program Students: 294 full-time (139 women); includes 13 minority (1 African American, 9 Asian Americans or Pacific Islanders, 1 Hispanic American, 2 Native Americans) Average age 28. 1,408 applicants, 11% accepted, 80 enrolled. *Faculty:* 36 full-time (10 women), 96 part-time/adjunct (13 women). Expenses: Contact institution. *Financial support:* In 2001–02, 280 students received support, including 6 teaching assistantships with partial tuition reimbursements available (averaging $10,656 per year); Federal Work-Study, scholarships/grants, tuition waivers (full), and unspecified assistantships also available. Financial award application deadline: 4/1; financial award applicants required to submit FAFSA. In 2001, 67 degrees awarded. Offers osteopathic medicine (DO). *Application deadline:* For fall admission, 2/15. Applications are processed on a rolling basis. *Application fee:* $125. Electronic applications accepted. *Application Contact:* John N. Gorby, Director of Admissions, 304-645-6270 Ext. 373, Fax: 304-645-4859, E-mail: jgorby@wvsom.edu. *President*, Dr. Olen E. Jones, 304-645-6270 Ext. 200, Fax: 304-645-4859.

WEST VIRGINIA UNIVERSITY, Morgantown, WV 26506

General Information State-supported, coed, university. CGS member. *Enrollment:* 3,778 full-time matriculated graduate/professional students (1,866 women), 2,875 part-time matriculated graduate/professional students (1,963 women). *Enrollment by degree level:* 1,241 first professional, 4,404 master's, 1,008 doctoral. *Graduate faculty:* 1,242 full-time (374 women), 406 part-time/adjunct (227 women). Tuition, state resident: full-time $2,791. Tuition, nonresident: full-time $8,659. *Required fees:* $1,002. Tuition and fees vary according to program. *Graduate housing:* Rooms and/or apartments available on a first-come, first-served basis to single students and available to married students. *Student services:* Campus employ-

West Virginia University (continued)

ment opportunities, campus safety program, career counseling, disabled student services, exercise/wellness program, free psychological counseling, international student services, low-cost health insurance, teacher training, writing training. *Library facilities:* Wise Library plus 9 others. *Online resources:* library catalog, web page, access to other libraries' catalogs. *Collection:* 1.4 million titles, 7,905 serial subscriptions, 42,040 audiovisual materials. *Research affiliation:* Polymer Alliance Zone (polymer recycling research), NASA IV and V Center (GOCO addressing software verification/validation), Institute for Software Research (software engineering), International Telemedicine Collaboration (telemedicine, telehealth and tele-education), West Virginia National Guard Drug Detection, Homeland Security, National Energy Technology Laboratory (fossil energy and environmental research).

Computer facilities: 1,600 computers available on campus for general student use. A campuswide network can be accessed from student residence rooms and from off campus. Internet access is available. *Web address:* http://www.wvu.edu/.

General Application Contact: Information Contact, 800-344-WVU1, Fax: 304-293-3080, E-mail: wvuinfo@wvu.edu.

GRADUATE UNITS

College of Business and Economics Students: 134 full-time (64 women), 166 part-time (61 women); includes 18 minority (8 African Americans, 7 Asian Americans or Pacific Islanders, 3 Hispanic Americans), 53 international. Average age 30. 524 applicants, 55% accepted. *Faculty:* 60 full-time (10 women), 6 part-time/adjunct (5 women). Expenses: Contact institution. *Financial support:* In 2001–02, 33 research assistantships, 18 teaching assistantships were awarded. Fellowships, career-related internships or fieldwork, Federal Work-Study, institutionally sponsored loans, tuition waivers (full and partial), and graduate administrative assistantships also available. Financial award application deadline: 2/1; financial award applicants required to submit FAFSA. In 2001, 151 master's, 5 doctorates awarded. *Degree program information:* Part-time and evening/weekend programs available. Offers accounting (MPA); business administration (MBA); business analysis (MA); business and economics (MA, MBA, MPA, MS, PhD); econometrics (PhD); industrial economics (PhD); industrial relations (MS); international economics (PhD); labor economics (PhD); mathematical economics (MA, PhD); monetary economics (PhD); public finance (PhD); public policy (MA); regional and urban economics (PhD); statistics and economics (MA). *Application fee:* $45. *Dean,* Dr. Jay Coats, 304-293-4092, Fax: 304-293-5652, E-mail: jay.coats@mail.wvu.edu.

College of Creative Arts Students: 75 full-time (37 women), 27 part-time (18 women); includes 5 minority (4 African Americans, 1 Asian American or Pacific Islander), 23 international. Average age 31. 111 applicants, 22% accepted. *Faculty:* 64 full-time (23 women), 11 part-time/adjunct (6 women). Expenses: Contact institution. *Financial support:* In 2001–02, 6 research assistantships, 46 teaching assistantships were awarded. Career-related internships or fieldwork, Federal Work-Study, institutionally sponsored loans, tuition waivers (full and partial), and graduate administrative assistantships also available. Financial award applicants required to submit FAFSA. In 2001, 29 master's, 5 doctorates awarded. *Degree program information:* Part-time programs available. Offers acting (MFA); art education (MA); art history (MA); ceramics (MFA); creative arts (MA, MFA, MM, DMA, PhD); graphic design (MFA); music composition (MM, DMA, PhD); music education (MM, DMA, PhD); music history (MM); music performance (MM, DMA, PhD); music theory (MM); painting (MFA); printmaking (MFA); sculpture (MFA); studio art (MA); theatre design/technology (MFA). *Application deadline:* For fall admission, 3/1 (priority date); for spring admission, 11/1. Applications are processed on a rolling basis. *Application fee:* $45. *Application Contact:* Dr. William J. Winson, Associate Dean, 304-293-4841 Ext. 3121, Fax: 304-293-2533, E-mail: william.winsor@mail.wvu.edu. *Dean,* Dr. Bernie Schultz, 304-293-4841, Fax: 304-293-3550, E-mail: bernie.schultz@mail.wvu.edu.

College of Engineering and Mineral Resources Students: 480 full-time (88 women), 172 part-time (50 women); includes 17 minority (3 African Americans, 12 Asian Americans or Pacific Islanders, 2 Hispanic Americans), 367 international. Average age 27. 814 applicants, 66% accepted. *Faculty:* 112 full-time (9 women), 13 part-time/adjunct (2 women). Expenses: Contact institution. *Financial support:* In 2001–02, 242 research assistantships, 84 teaching assistantships were awarded. Fellowships, career-related internships or fieldwork, Federal Work-Study, institutionally sponsored loans, tuition waivers (full and partial), and graduate administrative assistantships also available. Financial award application deadline: 2/1; financial award applicants required to submit FAFSA. In 2001, 213 master's, 21 doctorates awarded. *Degree program information:* Part-time programs available. Offers aerospace engineering (MSAE, MSE, PhD); chemical engineering (MS Ch E, PhD); civil engineering (MSCE, MSE, PhD); computer engineering (PhD); computer science (MS, PhD); electrical engineering (MSE, MSEE, PhD); engineering (MSE); engineering and mineral resources (MS, MS Ch E, MS Min E, MSAE, MSCE, MSE, MSEE, MSEM, MSIE, MSME, MSPNGE, MSSE, PhD); industrial engineering (MSE, MSIE, PhD); mechanical engineering (MSE, MSME, PhD); mining engineering (MS Min E, PhD); occupational hygiene and occupational safety (MS); petroleum and natural gas engineering (MSPNGE, PhD); safety and environmental management (MS); safety management (MS); software engineering (MSSE). *Application fee:* $45. *Application Contact:* Dr. Afzel Noore, Associate Dean, Academic Affairs, 304-293-4821 Ext. 2210, Fax: 304-293-2037, E-mail: afzel.noore@mail.wvu.edu. *Dean,* Dr. Eugene Cilento, 304-293-2111 Ext. 2413, Fax: 304-293-4139, E-mail: eugene.cilento@mail.wvu.edu.

College of Human Resources and Education Students: 489 full-time (368 women), 856 part-time (664 women); includes 54 minority (31 African Americans, 7 Asian Americans or Pacific Islanders, 9 Hispanic Americans, 7 Native Americans), 32 international. Average age 33. 614 applicants, 56% accepted. *Faculty:* 70 full-time (29 women), 19 part-time/adjunct (12 women). Expenses: Contact institution. *Financial support:* In 2001–02, 124 students received support, including 44 research assistantships, 80 teaching assistantships; fellowships, career-related internships or fieldwork, Federal Work-Study, institutionally sponsored loans, tuition waivers (full and partial), and graduate administrative assistantships also available. Financial award applicants required to submit FAFSA. In 2001, 364 master's, 34 doctorates awarded. *Degree program information:* Part-time and evening/weekend programs available. Offers behavioral disorders K-12 (MA); counseling (MA); counseling psychology (PhD); curriculum and instruction (Ed D); early intervention (preschool) (MA); educational leadership (MA, Ed D); educational psychology (MA, Ed D); elementary education (MA); gifted education 5-12 (MA); gifted education K-8 (MA); higher education administration (MA); higher education curriculum and teaching (MA); human resources and education (MA, MS, Ed D, PhD); information and communication systems (MA); instructional design and technology (MA); mentally impaired (MA); professional development (MA); public school administration (MA); reading (MA); rehabilitation counseling (MS); secondary education (MA); severe/profound handicaps (MA); special education (MA, Ed D); specific learning disabilities K-12 (MA); speech pathology and audiology (MS); technology and society (MA); technology education (MA, Ed D). *Application fee:* $45. *Interim Dean,* Dr. Anne Nardi, 304-293-5703 Ext. 1811, Fax: 304-293-7565, E-mail: anne.nardi@mail.wvu.edu.

College of Law Students: 420 full-time (177 women), 19 part-time (10 women); includes 30 minority (19 African Americans, 6 Asian Americans or Pacific Islanders, 4 Hispanic Americans, 1 Native American), 5 international. Average age 26. 511 applicants, 50% accepted. *Faculty:* 24 full-time (8 women), 18 part-time/adjunct (4 women). Expenses: Contact institution. *Financial support:* In 2001–02, 355 students received support, including 3 research assistantships, 9 teaching assistantships; fellowships, career-related internships or fieldwork, Federal Work-Study, institutionally sponsored loans, tuition waivers (full), and graduate administrative assistantships, graduate resident assistantships also available. Support available to part-time students. Financial award application deadline: 3/1. In 2001, 133 degrees awarded. *Degree program information:* Part-time programs available. Offers law (JD). *Application deadline:* For fall admission, 3/1. Applications are processed on a rolling basis. *Application fee:* $45. *Application Contact:* Janet Long Armistead, Assistant Dean for Admissions and Student Affairs, 304-293-7320, Fax: 304-293-6891, E-mail: janet.armistead@mail.wvu.edu. *Dean,* John W. Fisher, 304-293-3199, Fax: 304-293-6891, E-mail: john.fisher@mail.wvu.edu.

Davis College of Agriculture, Forestry and Consumer Sciences Students: 168 full-time (77 women), 43 part-time (25 women); includes 4 minority (1 African American, 2 Asian Americans or Pacific Islanders, 1 Hispanic American), 51 international. Average age 29. *Faculty:* 86 full-time (18 women), 11 part-time/adjunct (7 women). Expenses: Contact institution. *Financial support:* In 2001–02, 96 research assistantships, 29 teaching assistantships were awarded. Career-related internships or fieldwork, Federal Work-Study, institutionally sponsored loans, and tuition waivers (full and partial) also available. Financial award application deadline: 2/1; financial award applicants required to submit FAFSA. In 2001, 56 master's, 16 doctorates awarded. *Degree program information:* Part-time programs available. Offers agricultural and resource economics (MS); agricultural biochemistry (PhD); agricultural education (MS); agricultural extension education (MS); agriculture, forestry and consumer sciences (M Agr, MS, MSF, MSFCS, PhD); agronomy (MS); animal and food sciences (PhD); animal and veterinary sciences (MS); animal breeding (MS, PhD); animal nutrition (PhD); animal physiology (PhD); animal sciences (MS); biochemical and molecular genetics (MS, PhD); breeding (MS); cytogenetics (MS, PhD); descriptive embryology (MS, PhD); developmental genetics (MS); entomology (MS); environmental microbiology (MS); experimental morphogenesis (MS); family and consumer sciences (MSFCS); food sciences (MS); forest resource science (PhD); forestry (MSF); horticulture (MS); human genetics (MS, PhD); immunogenetics (MS, PhD); life cycles of animals and plants (MS, PhD); molecular aspects of development (MS, PhD); mutagenesis (PhD); mutagenetics (MS); natural resource economics (PhD); nutrition (MS); oncology (MS, PhD); physiology (MS); plant and soil sciences (PhD); plant genetics (MS, PhD); plant pathology (MS); population and quantitative genetics (PhD); population and quantitative genetics (MS); production (MS); production management (PhD); recreation, parks and tourism resources (MS); regeneration (MS, PhD); reproductive physiology (MS, PhD); teaching vocational-agriculture (MS); teratology (MS, PhD); toxicology (MS, PhD); wildlife and fisheries resources (MS). *Application fee:* $45. *Application Contact:* Dr. Dennis K. Smith, Associate Dean, 304-293-2691 Ext. 4521, Fax: 304-293-3740, E-mail: denny.smith@mail.wvu.edu. *Dean,* Dr. Cameron R. Hackney, 304-293-2395 Ext. 4530, Fax: 304-293-3740, E-mail: cameron.hackney@mail.wvu.edu.

Eberly College of Arts and Sciences Students: 641 full-time (348 women), 406 part-time (276 women); includes 47 minority (21 African Americans, 13 Asian Americans or Pacific Islanders, 6 Hispanic Americans, 7 Native Americans), 225 international. Average age 31. *Faculty:* 273 full-time (72 women), 94 part-time/adjunct (55 women). Expenses: Contact institution. *Financial support:* In 2001–02, 98 research assistantships, 335 teaching assistantships were awarded. Fellowships, career-related internships or fieldwork, Federal Work-Study, institutionally sponsored loans, tuition waivers (full and partial), and graduate administrative assistantships also available. Financial award application deadline: 2/1; financial award applicants required to submit FAFSA. In 2001, 370 master's, 34 doctorates awarded. *Degree program information:* Part-time and evening/weekend programs available. Post-baccalaureate distance learning degree programs offered. Offers African history (MA, PhD); African-American history (MA, PhD); American history (MA, PhD); American public policy and politics (MA); analytical chemistry (MS, PhD); animal behavior (MS); Appalachian/regional history (MA, PhD); applied mathematics (MS, PhD); applied physics (MS, PhD); applied social research (MA); arts and sciences (MA, MALS, MFA, MLS, MPA, MS, MSW, PhD); astrophysics (MS, PhD); behavior analysis (PhD); cellular and molecular biology (MS, PhD); chemical physics (MS, PhD); clinical psychology (MA, PhD); communication in instruction (MA); communication theory and research (MA); comparative literature (MA); condensed matter physics (MS, PhD); corporate and organizational communication (MA); creative writing (MFA); development psychology (PhD); discrete mathematics (PhD); East Asian history (MA, PhD); elementary particle physics (MS, PhD); energy and environmental resources (MA); environmental plant biology (MS, PhD); European history (MA, PhD); French (MA); geographic information systems (PhD); geography (MA, PhD); geography-regional development (PhD); geology (MS, PhD); geomorphology (MS, PhD); geophysics (MS, PhD); German (MA); GIS/cartographic analysis (MA); history of science and technology (MA, PhD); hydrogeology (MS); hydrology (PhD); inorganic chemistry (MS, PhD); interdisciplinary mathematics (MS); international and comparative public policy and U.S. politics (MA); Latin American history (MA); legal studies (MLS); liberal studies (MALS); linguistics (MA); literary/cultural studies (MA, PhD); materials physics (MS, PhD); mathematics for secondary education (MS); organic chemistry (MS, PhD); paleontology (MS, PhD); petrology (MS, PhD); physical chemistry (MS, PhD); plant systematics (MS); plasma physics (MS, PhD); political science (PhD); population genetics (MS); public policy analysis (PhD); pure mathematics (MS); regional development and urban planning (MA); solid state physics (MS, PhD); Spanish (MA); statistical physics (MS, PhD); statistics (MS); stratigraphy (MS, PhD); structure (MS, PhD); teaching English to speakers of other languages (MA); theoretical chemistry (MS, PhD); theoretical physics (MS, PhD); writing (MA). *Application fee:* $45. *Application Contact:* Dr. Fred L. King, Associate Dean for Graduate Studies, 304-293-4611 Ext. 5205, Fax: 304-293-6858, E-mail: fred.king@mail.wvu.edu. *Dean,* Dr. M. Duane Nellis, 304-293-4611 Ext. 5204, Fax: 304-293-6858, E-mail: duane.nellis@mail.wvu.edu.

School of Applied Social Science Students: 157 full-time (109 women), 136 part-time (101 women). Average age 31. *Faculty:* 19 full-time (9 women), 10 part-time/adjunct (9 women). Expenses: Contact institution. *Financial support:* In 2001–02, 21 research assistantships, 25 teaching assistantships were awarded. In 2001, 151 degrees awarded. Offers aging and health care (MSW); applied social science (MPA, MSW); children and families (MSW); mental health (MSW); public administration (MPA). *Assistant Dean,* Dr. David G. Williams, 304-293-2614 Ext. 3154, Fax: 304-293-8814, E-mail: david.williams@mail.wvu.edu.

Perley Isaac Reed School of Journalism Students: 30 full-time (18 women), 6 part-time (4 women); includes 2 minority (both African Americans), 4 international. Average age 25. 32 applicants, 53% accepted. *Faculty:* 11 full-time (6 women), 11 part-time/adjunct (5 women). Expenses: Contact institution. *Financial support:* In 2001–02, 2 research assistantships, 12 teaching assistantships were awarded. Career-related internships or fieldwork, Federal Work-Study, institutionally sponsored loans, tuition waivers (full and partial), and graduate administrative assistantships also available. Financial award application deadline: 2/1; financial award applicants required to submit FAFSA. In 2001, 11 degrees awarded. *Degree program information:* Part-time programs available. Offers journalism (MSJ). *Application deadline:* For fall admission, 7/15 (priority date); for spring admission, 11/15. Applications are processed on a rolling basis. *Application fee:* $45. *Application Contact:* Dr. R. Ivan Pinnell, Director of Graduate Studies, 304-293-3505 Ext. 5404, Fax: 304-293-3072. *Dean,* Dr. Christine Martin, 304-293-3505 Ext. 5413, Fax: 304-293-3072, E-mail: chris.martin@mail.wvu.edu.

School of Dentistry Students: 169 full-time (65 women), 1 (woman) part-time; includes 15 minority (1 African American, 13 Asian Americans or Pacific Islanders, 1 Hispanic American), 4 international. Average age 25. 1,257 applicants, 4% accepted. *Faculty:* 49 full-time (12 women), 7 part-time/adjunct (3 women). Expenses: Contact institution. *Financial support:* In 2001–02, 4 research assistantships, 1 teaching assistantship were awarded. Federal Work-Study and institutionally sponsored loans also available. Financial award application deadline: 3/1; financial award applicants required to submit FAFSA. In 2001, 37 first professional degrees, 8 master's awarded. *Degree program information:* Part-time programs available. Offers basic science (MS); dentistry (DDS, MS); education/administration (MS); endodontics (MS); office management (MS); orthodontics (MS); prosthodontics (MS); special patients (MS). *Application deadline:* Applications are processed on a rolling basis. *Application Contact:* Dr. Louise M. Veselicky, Graduate School Admissions Officer, 304-293-7307, Fax: 304-293-7440, E-mail: lveselicky@hsc.wvu.edu. *Dean,* Dr. James J. Koelbl, 304-293-2521, Fax: 304-293-2859, E-mail: jkoelbl@hsc.wvu.edu.

School of Medicine Students: 549 full-time (248 women), 74 part-time (53 women); includes 89 minority (13 African Americans, 71 Asian Americans or Pacific Islanders, 4 Hispanic Americans, 1 Native American), 29 international. Average age 27. *Faculty:* 456 full-time (147 women), 80 part-time/adjunct (34 women). Expenses: Contact institution. *Financial support:* In 2001–02, 52 research assistantships, 47 teaching assistantships were awarded. Fellowships, career-related internships or fieldwork, Federal Work-Study, institutionally sponsored loans, tuition waivers (full and partial), and graduate administrative assistantships also available. Financial award applicants required to submit FAFSA. In 2001, 81 first professional degrees, 151 master's, 8 doctorates awarded. *Degree program information:* Part-time and evening/weekend programs available. Offers exercise physiology (MS, PhD); medicine (MD, MOT, MPH, MPT, MS, PhD); occupational therapy (MOT); physical therapy (MPT). *Application fee:* $45. *Application Contact:* Dr. Stephen E. Alway, Director, Graduate Programs, 304-293-0772, Fax: 304-293-7105, E-mail: salway@hsc.wvu.edu. *Dean,* Dr. Robert M. D'Alessandri, 304-293-4511, Fax: 304-293-4973, E-mail: rdalessandri@hsc.wvu.edu.

Graduate Programs in Health Sciences Students: 110 full-time (55 women), 65 part-time (49 women); includes 12 minority (5 African Americans, 5 Asian Americans or Pacific Islanders, 1 Hispanic American, 1 Native American), 26 international. Average age 29. Expenses: Contact institution. *Financial support:* In 2001–02, 34 research assistantships, 39 teaching assistantships were awarded. Fellowships, career-related internships or fieldwork, Federal Work-Study, institutionally sponsored loans, tuition waivers (full and partial), and graduate administrative assistantships also available. Financial award applicants required to submit FAFSA. In 2001, 94 master's, 8 doctorates awarded. *Degree program information:* Part-time and evening/weekend programs available. Postbaccalaureate distance learning degree programs offered (minimal on-campus study). Offers autonomic pharmacology (MS, PhD); biomedical pharmacology (MS, PhD); cardiovascular physiology (MS, PhD); cell physiology (MS, PhD); chemotherapy (MS, PhD); clinical chemistry (MS); community health promotion (MS); community health/preventative medicine (MPH); developmental anatomy (MS); developmental biology (MS); endocrine pharmacology (MS, PhD); endocrine physiology (MS, PhD); energy transduction (MS); enzymes and serum proteins (PhD); enzymology (MS); ernal physiology (PhD); gene expression (MS, PhD); genetics (MS, PhD); gross anatomy (MS, PhD); health sciences (MPH, MS, PhD); hematology (MS); hormonal regulation/metabolism (MS, PhD); immunohematology (MS); immunology (MS, PhD); membrane biogenesis (MS, PhD); microbiology (MS); microscopic anatomy (MS, PhD); molecular and deevlo9pmental anatomy (PhD); molecular virology (MS); muscle physiology (MS, PhD); mycology (PhD); neural physiology (MS, PhD); neuroanatomy (MS, PhD); neuropharmacology (MS, PhD); nucleic acids (MS, PhD); nutritional oncology (PhD); parasitology (MS, PhD); pathogenic bacteriology (MS, PhD); physiology (MS, PhD); protein chemistry (MS); renal physiology (MS); respiratory physiology (MS); secretory mechanisms (PhD); toxicology (MS, PhD); virology (MS, PhD). *Application fee:* $45. *Application Contact:* Claire Noel, Graduate Adviser, 304-293-7116, Fax: 304-293-7038, E-mail: cnoel@hsc.wvu.edu. *Interim Associate Dean/Graduate Coordinator*, Dr. Charles R. Craig, 304-293-7206, Fax: 304-293-7038, E-mail: ccraig@hsc.wvu.edu.

School of Nursing Students: 38 full-time (35 women), 28 part-time (23 women); includes 1 minority (African American) Average age 36. 43 applicants, 93% accepted. *Faculty:* 37 full-time (36 women), 5 part-time/adjunct (all women). Expenses: Contact institution. *Financial support:* In 2001–02, 18 students received support, including 4 research assistantships; career-related internships or fieldwork, Federal Work-Study, institutionally sponsored loans, tuition waivers (full and partial), and graduate administrative assistantships also available. Financial award application deadline: 2/1; financial award applicants required to submit FAFSA. In 2001, 37 degrees awarded. *Degree program information:* Part-time programs available. Postbaccalaureate distance learning degree programs offered (minimal on-campus study). Offers nurse practitioner (Certificate); nursing (MSN, DSN). *Application deadline:* For fall admission, 6/1; for spring admission, 10/1. *Application fee:* $45. *Application Contact:* Dr. Mary Jane Smith, Associate Dean for Graduate Programs, 304-293-4298, Fax: 304-293-5483, E-mail: mjsmith@hsc.wvu.edu. *Dean*, Dr. E. Jane Martin, 304-293-4831, Fax: 304-293-6826, E-mail: ejmartin@hsc.wvu.edu.

School of Pharmacy Students: 275 full-time (158 women), 27 part-time (19 women); includes 7 minority (4 African Americans, 1 Asian American or Pacific Islander, 1 Hispanic American, 1 Native American), 20 international. Average age 24. 100 applicants, 20% accepted. *Faculty:* 29 full-time (12 women), 1 part-time/adjunct (0 women). Expenses: Contact institution. *Financial support:* In 2001–02, 17 research assistantships, 8 teaching assistantships were awarded. Career-related internships or fieldwork, Federal Work-Study, institutionally sponsored loans, and tuition waivers (full and partial) also available. Financial award application deadline: 2/1; financial award applicants required to submit FAFSA. In 2001, 20 first professional degrees, 1 master's, 2 doctorates awarded. Offers administrative pharmacy (PhD); behavioral pharmacy (MS, PhD); biopharmaceutics/pharmacokinetics (PhD); biopharmaceutics/pharmacokinetics (MS); clinical pharmacy (Pharm D); industrial pharmacy (MS); medicinal chemistry (MS, PhD); pharmaceutical chemistry (MS, PhD); pharmaceutics (MS, PhD); pharmacology and toxicology (MS); pharmacy (MS); pharmacy administration (MS). *Application deadline:* For fall admission, 3/1 (priority date). *Application fee:* $45. *Application Contact:* Dr. Patrick S. Callery, Assistant Dean for Graduate Programs, 304-293-1482, Fax: 304-293-2576, E-mail: pcallery@hsc.wvu.edu. *Dean*, Dr. George R. Spratto, 304-293-5101, Fax: 304-293-5483, E-mail: gspratto@hsc.wvu.edu.

School of Physical Education Students: 78 full-time (26 women), 26 part-time (12 women); includes 9 minority (8 African Americans, 1 Hispanic American), 8 international. Average age 26. 140 applicants, 71% accepted. *Faculty:* 21 full-time (6 women), 14 part-time/adjunct (0 women). Expenses: Contact institution. *Financial support:* In 2001–02, 4 research assistantships, 58 teaching assistantships were awarded. Career-related internships or fieldwork, Federal Work-Study, institutionally sponsored loans, tuition waivers (full and partial), and graduate administrative assistantships also available. Support available to part-time students. Financial award application deadline: 2/1; financial award applicants required to submit FAFSA. In 2001, 49 master's, 4 doctorates awarded. Offers athletic coaching (MS); athletic training (MS); exercise physiology (Ed D); physical education/teacher education (MS, Ed D); sport management (MS); sport psychology (MS, Ed D). *Application deadline:* For fall admission, 3/1 (priority date). *Application fee:* $45. *Application Contact:* Carol Straight, Student Records Assistant, 304-293-3295 Ext. 5265, Fax: 304-293-4641, E-mail: cstraight@mail.wvu.edu.

WEST VIRGINIA UNIVERSITY INSTITUTE OF TECHNOLOGY, Montgomery, WV 25136

General Information State-supported, coed, comprehensive institution. *Enrollment:* 20 full-time matriculated graduate/professional students (5 women), 1 part-time matriculated graduate/professional student. *Enrollment by degree level:* 21 master's. *Graduate faculty:* 10 full-time (1 woman). Tuition, state resident: full-time $3,248; part-time $180 per credit. Tuition, nonresident: full-time $7,852; part-time $436 per credit. *Graduate housing:* Room and/or apartments available to single students; on-campus housing not available to married students. Typical cost: $4,682 (including board). *Student services:* Campus employment opportunities, campus safety program, career counseling, free psychological counseling, international student services, low-cost health insurance. *Library facilities:* Vining Library plus 1 other. *Online resources:* library catalog, web page, access to other libraries' catalogs. *Collection:* 166,292 titles, 605 serial subscriptions.

Computer facilities: 625 computers available on campus for general student use. A campuswide network can be accessed from student residence rooms and from off campus. Internet access is available. *Web address:* http://www.wvutech.edu/.

General Application Contact: Dr. M. Sathyamoorthy, Dean, 304-442-3161, Fax: 304-442-1006.

GRADUATE UNITS

College of Engineering Students: 20 full-time (5 women), 1 part-time, 20 international. Average age 24. 35 applicants, 77% accepted. *Faculty:* 10 full-time (1 woman). Expenses: Contact institution. *Financial support:* In 2001–02, 21 teaching assistantships with full tuition reimbursements (averaging $4,000 per year) were awarded; career-related internships or fieldwork, Federal Work-Study, and institutionally sponsored loans also available. Financial award application deadline: 3/15. In 2001, 2 degrees awarded. *Degree program information:* Part-time programs available. Offers control systems engineering (MS); engineering (MS). *Application deadline:* For fall admission, 3/15 (priority date). Applications are processed on a rolling basis. *Application fee:* $10. *Application Contact:* Robert P. Scholl, Registrar, 304-442-3167, Fax: 304-442-3097, E-mail: rscholl@wvutech.edu. *Dean*, Dr. M. Sathyamoorthy, 304-442-3161, Fax: 304-442-1006.

WEST VIRGINIA WESLEYAN COLLEGE, Buckhannon, WV 26201

General Information Independent-religious, coed, comprehensive institution. *Graduate housing:* Room and/or apartments available to single students; on-campus housing not available to married students.

GRADUATE UNITS

Department of Business & Economics *Degree program information:* Part-time and evening/weekend programs available. Offers business (MBA).

WHEATON COLLEGE, Wheaton, IL 60187-5593

General Information Independent-religious, coed, comprehensive institution. *Enrollment:* 260 full-time matriculated graduate/professional students (133 women), 196 part-time matriculated graduate/professional students (99 women). *Enrollment by degree level:* 354 master's, 69 doctoral. *Graduate faculty:* 41 full-time (10 women), 6 part-time/adjunct (1 woman). *Tuition:* Part-time $410 per hour. *Graduate housing:* Rooms and/or apartments available on a first-come, first-served basis to single and married students. Typical cost: $3,670 per year ($6,050 including board) for single students; $9,600 per year for married students. Housing application deadline: 4/1. *Student services:* Campus employment opportunities, campus safety program, career counseling, exercise/wellness program, free psychological counseling, grant writing training, international student services, low-cost health insurance, multicultural affairs office, writing training. *Library facilities:* Buswell Memorial Library plus 1 other. *Online resources:* library catalog, web page, access to other libraries' catalogs. *Collection:* 342,746 titles, 3,264 serial subscriptions, 32,761 audiovisual materials.

Computer facilities: 150 computers available on campus for general student use. A campuswide network can be accessed from student residence rooms and from off campus. Internet access is available. *Web address:* http://www.wheaton.edu/.

General Application Contact: Julie A. Huebner, Director of Graduate Admissions, 630-752-5195, Fax: 630-752-5935, E-mail: gradadm@wheaton.edu.

GRADUATE UNITS

Graduate School Students: 260 full-time (133 women), 196 part-time (99 women); includes 30 minority (12 African Americans, 13 Asian Americans or Pacific Islanders, 4 Hispanic Americans, 1 Native American), 8 international. Average age 30. 446 applicants, 71% accepted, 231 enrolled. *Faculty:* 41 full-time (10 women), 6 part-time/adjunct (1 woman). Expenses: Contact institution. *Financial support:* In 2001–02, 235 students received support, including 10 teaching assistantships; career-related internships or fieldwork, Federal Work-Study, scholarships/grants, and unspecified assistantships also available. Financial award application deadline: 3/1; financial award applicants required to submit FAFSA. In 2001, 200 master's, 11 doctorates awarded. *Degree program information:* Part-time programs available. Offers advanced biblical studies (Certificate); biblical and theological studies (MA); biblical archaeology (MA); biblical exegesis (MA); biblical studies (MA, Certificate); Christian history and theology (MA); clinical psychology (MA, Psy D); educational ministries (MA); evangelism (MA); evangelism and spiritual formation (MA); intercultural studies/teaching English as a second language (MA); interdisciplinary studies (MA); missions/intercultural studies (MA); religion in American life (MA); secondary level (MAT); teaching English as a second language (Certificate). *Application deadline:* For fall admission, 3/1 (priority date); for spring admission, 11/1. Applications are processed on a rolling basis. *Application fee:* $30. *Application Contact:* Julie A. Huebner, Director of Graduate Admissions, 630-752-5195, Fax: 630-752-5935, E-mail: gradadm@wheaton.edu.

See in-depth description on page 1305.

WHEELING JESUIT UNIVERSITY, Wheeling, WV 26003-6295

General Information Independent-religious, coed, comprehensive institution. CGS member. *Enrollment:* 83 full-time matriculated graduate/professional students (43 women), 134 part-time matriculated graduate/professional students (92 women). *Enrollment by degree level:* 217 master's. *Graduate faculty:* 22 full-time (10 women), 13 part-time/adjunct (1 woman). *Tuition:* Full-time $7,740; part-time $430 per credit hour. *Required fees:* $145; $60 per semester. One-time fee: $25. Full-time tuition and fees vary according to program. *Graduate housing:* Rooms and/or apartments available on a first-come, first-served basis to single and married students. Typical cost: $3,330 per year ($6,390 including board) for single students; $6,100 per year ($12,100 including board) for married students. Room and board charges vary according to housing facility selected. *Student services:* Campus employment opportunities, campus safety program, career counseling, disabled student services, exercise/wellness program, free psychological counseling, international student services, low-cost health insurance, multicultural affairs office. *Library facilities:* Bishop Hodges Learning Center plus 1 other. *Online resources:* library catalog, access to other libraries' catalogs. *Collection:* 153,094 titles, 487 serial subscriptions, 5,308 audiovisual materials.

Computer facilities: 75 computers available on campus for general student use. A campuswide network can be accessed from student residence rooms and from off campus. Internet access is available. *Web address:* http://www.wju.edu/.

General Application Contact: Tricia Lollini, Graduate Admissions Counselor, 304-243-2250, Fax: 304-243-4441, E-mail: tlollini@wju.edu.

GRADUATE UNITS

Department of Business Students: 25 full-time (10 women), 77 part-time (45 women); includes 4 minority (1 African American, 2 Asian Americans or Pacific Islanders, 1 Hispanic American), 7 international. Average age 31. 43 applicants, 91% accepted, 29 enrolled. *Faculty:* 6 full-time (0 women), 6 part-time/adjunct (0 women). Expenses: Contact institution. *Financial support:* In 2001–02, 21 students received support. Unspecified assistantships available. Financial award application deadline: 5/1; financial award applicants required to submit FAFSA. In 2001, 33 degrees awarded. *Degree program information:* Part-time and evening/weekend programs available. Offers accounting (MS); business administration (MBA). *Application deadline:* For fall admission, 8/1 (priority date); for spring admission, 12/15 (priority date). Applications are processed on a rolling basis. *Application fee:* $25. Electronic applications accepted. *Application Contact:* Tricia Lollini, Graduate Admissions Counselor, 304-243-2250, Fax: 304-243-4441, E-mail: tlollini@wju.edu. *Director*, Gilbert E. Dwyer, 304-243-2087, Fax: 304-243-8703, E-mail: gildwyer@wju.edu.

Department of Nursing Students: 5 full-time (4 women), 35 part-time (33 women). Average age 38. 24 applicants, 96% accepted, 10 enrolled. *Faculty:* 6 full-time (all women), 1 (woman) part-time/adjunct. Expenses: Contact institution. *Financial support:* In 2001–02, 10 students received support. Scholarships/grants and unspecified assistantships available. Financial award application deadline: 5/1; financial award applicants required to submit FAFSA. In 2001, 9 degrees awarded. *Degree program information:* Part-time and evening/weekend programs available. Postbaccalaureate distance learning degree programs offered (minimal on-campus study). Offers nursing (MSN). *Application deadline:* For fall admission, 8/1 (priority date); for spring admission, 12/15 (priority date). Applications are processed on a rolling basis. *Application fee:* $25. Electronic applications accepted. *Application Contact:* Tricia Lollini, Graduate Admissions Counselor, 304-243-2250, Fax: 304-243-4441, E-mail: tlollini@wju.edu. *Chair*, Dr. Rose M. Kutlenias, 304-243-2227, Fax: 304-243-4441, E-mail: rosekut@wju.edu.

Department of Physical Therapy Students: 43 full-time (22 women); includes 1 minority (African American) Average age 25. 21 applicants, 100% accepted, 10 enrolled. *Faculty:* 6 full-time (4 women), 5 part-time/adjunct (0 women). Expenses: Contact institution. *Financial support:* Application deadline: 5/1; In 2001, 33 degrees awarded. Offers physical therapy (MSPT). *Application deadline:* For fall admission, 3/1 (priority date); for spring admission, 7/1 (priority date). Applications are processed on a rolling basis. *Application fee:* $25. Electronic applications accepted. *Director*, Dr. Letha B. Zook, 304-243-2432, Fax: 304-243-2042, E-mail: lezook@wju.edu.

Department of Theology Students: 9 full-time (6 women), 12 part-time (5 women). Average age 37. 9 applicants, 89% accepted, 5 enrolled. *Faculty:* 3 full-time (0 women). Expenses: Contact institution. *Financial support:* In 2001–02, 17 students received support. Scholarships/grants and unspecified assistantships available. Financial award application deadline: 5/1; financial award applicants required to submit FAFSA. In 2001, 3 degrees awarded. *Degree program information:* Part-time and evening/weekend programs available. Offers applied theology (MA). *Application deadline:* For fall admission, 7/1 (priority date); for spring admission, 12/15 (priority date). Applications are processed on a rolling basis. *Application fee:* $25. Electronic applications accepted. *Application Contact:* Tricia Lollini, Graduate Admissions Counselor, 304-243-2250, Fax: 304-243-4441, E-mail: tlollini@wju.edu. *Director*, Dr. Kristopher Willumsen, 304-243-2240, Fax: 304-243-4441, E-mail: kristw@wju.edu.

Teacher Preparation Program Average age 31. 12 applicants, 100% accepted, 9 enrolled. *Faculty:* 1 full-time (0 women), 1 part-time/adjunct (0 women). Expenses: Contact institution.

Wheeling Jesuit University (continued)

Financial support: In 2001–02, 9 students received support. Scholarships/grants available. Financial award application deadline: 5/1; financial award applicants required to submit FAFSA. *Degree program information:* Part-time and evening/weekend programs available. Post-baccalaureate distance learning degree programs offered (minimal on-campus study). Offers teacher preparation (MASMED). *Application deadline:* Applications are processed on a rolling basis. *Application fee:* $25. Electronic applications accepted. *Application Contact:* Carol A. Carroll, Graduate Secretary, 304-243-2344, Fax: 304-243-4441, E-mail: ccarroll@wju.edu. *Director*, Dr. H. Lawrence Jones, 304-243-2344, Fax: 304-243-4441, E-mail: hljones@wju.edu.

WHEELOCK COLLEGE, Boston, MA 02215

General Information Independent, coed, primarily women, comprehensive institution. *Enrollment:* 211 full-time matriculated graduate/professional students (181 women), 263 part-time matriculated graduate/professional students (257 women). *Enrollment by degree level:* 474 master's. *Graduate faculty:* 36 full-time (30 women), 32 part-time/adjunct (27 women). *Tuition:* Full-time $21,600; part-time $600 per credit. *Graduate housing:* Room and/or apartments available on a first-come, first-served basis to single students; on-campus housing not available to married students. Typical cost: $8,450 per year. Housing application deadline: 5/1. *Student services:* Campus employment opportunities, campus safety program, career counseling, disabled student services, exercise/wellness program, low-cost health insurance, teacher training, writing training. *Library facilities:* Wheelock College Library. *Online resources:* library catalog, web page, access to other libraries' catalogs. *Collection:* 96,500 titles, 546 serial subscriptions.

Computer facilities: 120 computers available on campus for general student use. A campuswide network can be accessed from student residence rooms and from off campus. Internet access is available. *Web address:* http://www.wheelock.edu/.

General Application Contact: Deborah A. Sheehan, Director of Graduate Admissions and Student Financial Planning, 617-879-2178, Fax: 617-232-7127, E-mail: dsheehan@wheelock.edu.

GRADUATE UNITS

Graduate School Students: 211 full-time (181 women), 263 part-time (257 women); includes 68 minority (49 African Americans, 7 Asian Americans or Pacific Islanders, 11 Hispanic Americans, 1 Native American), 40 international. Average age 28. 182 applicants, 93% accepted, 116 enrolled. *Faculty:* 36 full-time (30 women), 32 part-time/adjunct (27 women). Expenses: Contact institution. *Financial support:* In 2001–02, 10 teaching assistantships with tuition reimbursements (averaging $3,500 per year) were awarded; career-related internships or fieldwork, Federal Work-Study, institutionally sponsored loans, scholarships/grants, and unspecified assistantships also available. Support available to part-time students. Financial award application deadline: 4/1; financial award applicants required to submit FAFSA. In 2001, 306 degrees awarded. *Degree program information:* Part-time and evening/weekend programs available. Postbaccalaureate distance learning degree programs offered (minimal on-campus study). Offers child development and early childhood education (MS); child life and family centered care (MS); development and intervention (MS); early childhood education (MS); education (MS, MSW, CAGS); elementary education (MS); family studies (CAGS); family support and parent education (MS); family, culture, and society (MS); language, literacy, and reading (MS); leadership and policy in early care and education (MS, CAGS); school leadership (MS); social work and education (MSW); teacher as a leader (MS); teaching students with special needs (MS). *Application deadline:* For fall admission, 7/1 (priority date); for spring admission, 11/1 (priority date). Applications are processed on a rolling basis. *Application fee:* $35 ($40 for international students). *Application Contact:* Deborah A. Sheehan, Director of Graduate Admissions and Student Financial Planning, 617-879-2178, Fax: 617-232-7127, E-mail: dsheehan@wheelock.edu. *Dean*, 617-879-2196, Fax: 617-232-7127.

WHITTIER COLLEGE, Whittier, CA 90608-0634

General Information Independent, coed, comprehensive institution. *Enrollment:* 417 full-time matriculated graduate/professional students (235 women), 348 part-time matriculated graduate/professional students (215 women). *Enrollment by degree level:* 765 first professional, 99 master's. *Graduate faculty:* 34 full-time (16 women), 42 part-time/adjunct (16 women). *Tuition:* Part-time $385 per unit. *Required fees:* $385 per unit. *Graduate housing:* On-campus housing not available. *Student services:* Campus employment opportunities, campus safety program, career counseling, child daycare facilities, free psychological counseling, low-cost health insurance, multicultural affairs office, teacher training. *Library facilities:* Bonnie Bell Wardman Library plus 1 other. *Online resources:* library catalog, web page, access to other libraries' catalogs. *Collection:* 225,337 titles, 1,357 serial subscriptions.

Computer facilities: 150 computers available on campus for general student use. A campuswide network can be accessed from student residence rooms and from off campus. *Web address:* http://www.whittier.edu/.

General Application Contact: David J. Muller, Vice President for Academic Affairs and Dean of Faculty, 562-907-4200 Ext. 4204, Fax: 562-907-4940, E-mail: dmuller@whittier.edu.

GRADUATE UNITS

Graduate Programs Average age 26. 102 applicants, 97% accepted, 99 enrolled. *Faculty:* 4 full-time (2 women), 9 part-time/adjunct (4 women). Expenses: Contact institution. *Financial support:* In 2001–02, 14 fellowships were awarded; research assistantships, career-related internships or fieldwork and tuition waivers (full) also available. In 2001, 29 degrees awarded. *Degree program information:* Part-time and evening/weekend programs available. Offers educational administration (MA Ed); elementary education (MA Ed); secondary education (MA Ed). *Application deadline:* Applications are processed on a rolling basis. *Application fee:* $60. *Application Contact:* Catherine George, Credential Analyst, 562-907-4200 Ext. 4443, Fax: 562-464-4596, E-mail: cgeorge@whittier.com. *Vice President for Academic Affairs and Dean of Faculty*, David J. Muller, 562-907-4200 Ext. 4204, Fax: 562-907-4940, E-mail: dmuller@whittier.edu.

Whittier Law School Students: 373 full-time (217 women), 280 part-time (152 women); includes 272 minority (45 African Americans, 127 Asian Americans or Pacific Islanders, 96 Hispanic Americans, 4 Native Americans), 5 international. Average age 30. 1,225 applicants, 63% accepted, 209 enrolled. *Faculty:* 28 full-time (11 women), 36 part-time/adjunct (18 women). Expenses: Contact institution. *Financial support:* In 2001–02, 555 students received support, including 27 fellowships with full and partial tuition reimbursements available (averaging $3,800 per year), 8 research assistantships, 25 teaching assistantships; career-related internships or fieldwork, Federal Work-Study, institutionally sponsored loans, and scholarships/grants also available. Support available to part-time students. Financial award application deadline: 4/15; financial award applicants required to submit FAFSA. In 2001, 165 degrees awarded. *Degree program information:* Part-time and evening/weekend programs available. Offers foreign legal studies (LL M); law (JD). *Application deadline:* For fall admission, 3/15 (priority date); for spring admission, 11/1. Applications are processed on a rolling basis. *Application fee:* $50. *Application Contact:* Patricia Abracia, Director of Admissions, 714-444-4141 Ext. 123, Fax: 714-444-0250, E-mail: info@law.whittier.edu. *Dean*, Neil H. Cogan, 714-444-4141 Ext. 111, Fax: 714-444-0855.

WHITWORTH COLLEGE, Spokane, WA 99251-0001

General Information Independent-religious, coed, comprehensive institution. *Enrollment:* 64 full-time matriculated graduate/professional students (39 women), 147 part-time matriculated graduate/professional students (107 women). *Enrollment by degree level:* 211 master's. *Graduate faculty:* 16 full-time, 55 part-time/adjunct. *Tuition:* Full-time $11,790; part-time $300 per credit. Tuition and fees vary according to class time, course load and program. *Graduate housing:* Room and/or apartments available on a first-come, first-served basis to single students; on-campus housing not available to married students. Typical cost: $3,250 per year ($5,680 including board). Room and board charges vary according to board plan and housing facility selected. Housing application deadline: 5/1. *Student services:* Campus employment opportunities, career counseling, disabled student services, exercise/wellness program, free psychological counseling, international student services, low-cost health insurance, multicultural affairs office, teacher training, writing training. *Library facilities:* Harriet Cheney Cowles Library. *Online resources:* library catalog, web page. *Collection:* 17,982 titles, 773 serial subscriptions.

Computer facilities: 150 computers available on campus for general student use. A campuswide network can be accessed from student residence rooms and from off campus. *Web address:* http://www.whitworth.edu/.

General Application Contact: Fred Pfursich, Office of Admissions, 509-777-1000 Ext. 3212, E-mail: fpfursich@whitworth.edu.

GRADUATE UNITS

School of Education *Degree program information:* Part-time and evening/weekend programs available. Offers education (M Ed, MA, MAT, MIT).

Graduate Studies in Education *Degree program information:* Part-time and evening/weekend programs available. Offers education administration (M Ed); English as a second language (MAT); gifted and talented (MAT); guidance and counseling (M Ed); physical education and sport administration (MA); reading (MAT); school counselors (M Ed); social agency/church setting (M Ed); special education (MAT); teaching (MIT).

School of Global Commerce and Management Students: 30 full-time (13 women), 8 part-time (2 women); includes 12 minority (1 African American, 10 Asian Americans or Pacific Islanders, 1 Hispanic American), 16 international. Average age 29. 23 applicants, 57% accepted, 13 enrolled. *Faculty:* 3 full-time (0 women), 17 part-time/adjunct (11 women). Expenses: Contact institution. *Financial support:* In 2001–02, 20 students received support; fellowships with tuition reimbursements available, career-related internships or fieldwork, Federal Work-Study, institutionally sponsored loans, and scholarships/grants available. Support available to part-time students. Financial award application deadline: 3/1. In 2001, 16 degrees awarded. *Degree program information:* Part-time and evening/weekend programs available. Offers international management (MIM). *Application deadline:* For fall admission, 4/1 (priority date); for spring admission, 11/1 (priority date). Applications are processed on a rolling basis. *Application fee:* $35. Electronic applications accepted. *Application Contact:* Dr. Jake Semeijn, Assistant Director, Program Coordination, Marketing and Recruitment, 509-777-3742, Fax: 509-777-3723, E-mail: kkirschner@whitworth.edu. *Dean*, Dr. Kyle B. Usrey, 509-777-1000, Fax: 509-777-3723, E-mail: kusrey@whitworth.edu.

WICHITA STATE UNIVERSITY, Wichita, KS 67260

General Information State-supported, coed, university. CGS member. *Enrollment:* 1,134 full-time matriculated graduate/professional students (481 women), 2,184 part-time matriculated graduate/professional students (1,285 women). *Graduate faculty:* 457 full-time (161 women), 21 part-time/adjunct (13 women). Tuition, state resident: full-time $1,888; part-time $105 per credit. Tuition, nonresident: full-time $6,129; part-time $341 per credit. *Required fees:* $345; $19 per credit. $17 per semester. Tuition and fees vary according to course load and program. *Graduate housing:* Rooms and/or apartments available on a first-come, first-served basis to single and married students. Typical cost: $4,120 (including board) for single students; $4,800 (including board) for married students. Room and board charges vary according to board plan and housing facility selected. *Student services:* Campus employment opportunities, campus safety program, career counseling, child daycare facilities, disabled student services, exercise/wellness program, free psychological counseling, international student services, low-cost health insurance, multicultural affairs office, teacher training. *Library facilities:* Ablah Library plus 2 others. *Online resources:* library catalog, web page, access to other libraries' catalogs. *Collection:* 1.1 million titles, 12,055 serial subscriptions, 2,572 audiovisual materials. *Research affiliation:* Boeing Aircraft Company (aeronautical engineering), Raytheon Aircraft Company (aeronautical engineering), Cessna Aircraft Company (aeronautical engineering), Bombardier (aeronautical engineering).

Computer facilities: 1,500 computers available on campus for general student use. A campuswide network can be accessed from student residence rooms and from off campus. Internet access is available. *Web address:* http://www.wichita.edu/.

General Application Contact: Dr. Susan K. Kovar, Dean of the Graduate School, 316-978-3095, Fax: 316-978-3253, E-mail: susan.kovar@wichita.edu.

GRADUATE UNITS

Graduate School Students: 1,134 full-time (481 women), 2,184 part-time (1,285 women); includes 300 minority (94 African Americans, 122 Asian Americans or Pacific Islanders, 63 Hispanic Americans, 21 Native Americans), 764 international. Average age 34. 2,426 applicants, 59% accepted, 740 enrolled. *Faculty:* 457 full-time (161 women), 21 part-time/adjunct (13 women). Expenses: Contact institution. *Financial support:* In 2001–02, 9 fellowships (averaging $2,648 per year), 247 research assistantships (averaging $5,288 per year), 274 teaching assistantships with partial tuition reimbursements (averaging $5,856 per year) were awarded. Career-related internships or fieldwork, Federal Work-Study, institutionally sponsored loans, scholarships/grants, traineeships, tuition waivers (full and partial), and unspecified assistantships also available. Support available to part-time students. Financial award application deadline: 4/1; financial award applicants required to submit FAFSA. In 2001, 771 master's, 34 doctorates awarded. *Degree program information:* Part-time and evening/weekend programs available. *Application deadline:* Applications are processed on a rolling basis. *Application fee:* $25 ($40 for international students). Electronic applications accepted. *Application Contact:* Margaret E. Wood, Assistant to the Dean, 316-978-3095, Fax: 316-978-3253, E-mail: margaret.wood@wichita.edu. *Dean of the Graduate School*, Dr. Susan K. Kovar, 316-978-3095, Fax: 316-978-3253, E-mail: susan.kovar@wichita.edu.

College of Education Students: 154 full-time (110 women), 924 part-time (686 women); includes 63 minority (25 African Americans, 10 Asian Americans or Pacific Islanders, 19 Hispanic Americans, 9 Native Americans), 14 international. Average age 37. 295 applicants, 66% accepted, 161 enrolled. *Faculty:* 55 full-time (36 women), 1 (woman) part-time/adjunct. Expenses: Contact institution. *Financial support:* In 2001–02, 17 research assistantships (averaging $4,565 per year), 3 teaching assistantships with full tuition reimbursements (averaging $5,926 per year) were awarded. Fellowships, career-related internships or fieldwork, Federal Work-Study, institutionally sponsored loans, scholarships/grants, traineeships, and unspecified assistantships also available. Support available to part-time students. Financial award application deadline: 4/1; financial award applicants required to submit FAFSA. In 2001, 238 master's, 7 doctorates awarded. *Degree program information:* Part-time and evening/weekend programs available. Offers communications sciences (MA, PhD); counseling (M Ed); curriculum and instruction (M Ed); education (M Ed, MA, Ed D, PhD, Ed S); education administration (M Ed, Ed D); educational psychology (M Ed); physical education (M Ed); school psychology (Ed S); special education (M Ed); sports administration (M Ed). *Application deadline:* For spring admission, 1/1. Applications are processed on a rolling basis. *Application fee:* $25 ($40 for international students). Electronic applications accepted. *Dean*, Dr. Jon Engelhardt, 316-978-3301, Fax: 316-978-3302, E-mail: jon.engelhardt@wichita.edu.

College of Engineering Students: 347 full-time (26 women), 330 part-time (43 women); includes 70 minority (5 African Americans, 57 Asian Americans or Pacific Islanders, 7 Hispanic Americans, 1 Native American), 461 international. Average age 27. 893 applicants, 59% accepted, 182 enrolled. *Faculty:* 40 full-time (1 woman), 2 part-time/adjunct (0 women). Expenses: Contact institution. *Financial support:* In 2001–02, 110 research assistantships (averaging $4,832 per year), 34 teaching assistantships with full tuition reimbursements (averaging $4,298 per year) were awarded. Fellowships, career-related internships or fieldwork, Federal Work-Study, institutionally sponsored loans, scholarships/grants, traineeships, and unspecified assistantships also available. Support available to part-time students. Financial award application deadline: 4/1; financial award applicants required to submit FAFSA. In 2001, 98 master's, 15 doctorates awarded. *Degree program information:* Part-time and evening/weekend programs available. Offers aerospace engineering (MS, PhD); electrical engineering (MS, PhD); engineering (MEM, MS, PhD); industrial and manufacturing engineering (MEM, MS, PhD); mechanical engineering (MS, PhD). *Application deadline:* For fall admission, 7/1 (priority date); for spring admission, 1/1. Applications are processed on a rolling basis. *Application fee:* $25 ($40 for international students). Electronic applications accepted. *Dean*, Dr. Dennis Siginer, 316-978-3400, Fax: 316-978-3853, E-mail: dennis.siginer@wichita.edu.

College of Fine Arts Students: 65 full-time (35 women), 67 part-time (53 women); includes 8 minority (2 African Americans, 2 Asian Americans or Pacific Islanders, 3 Hispanic

Americans, 1 Native American), 11 international. Average age 36. 55 applicants, 65% accepted, 30 enrolled. *Faculty:* 50 full-time (20 women), 6 part-time/adjunct (4 women). Expenses: Contact institution. *Financial support:* In 2001–02, 32 teaching assistantships with full tuition reimbursements (averaging $5,261 per year) were awarded; research assistantships, career-related internships or fieldwork, Federal Work-Study, institutionally sponsored loans, and unspecified assistantships also available. Support available to part-time students. Financial award application deadline: 4/1; financial award applicants required to submit FAFSA. In 2001, 35 degrees awarded. *Degree program information:* Part-time programs available. Offers art education (MA); fine arts (MA, MFA, MM, MME); music (MM); music education (MME); studio arts (MFA). *Application deadline:* For fall admission, 7/1 (priority date); for spring admission, 1/1. Applications are processed on a rolling basis. *Application fee:* $25 ($40 for international students). Electronic applications accepted. *Dean,* Dr. Walter Myers, 316-978-3389, Fax: 316-978-3951, E-mail: walter.myers@wichita.edu.

College of Health Professions Students: 140 full-time (97 women), 131 part-time (115 women); includes 21 minority (6 African Americans, 9 Asian Americans or Pacific Islanders, 5 Hispanic Americans, 1 Native American), 35 international. Average age 33. 228 applicants, 59% accepted, 90 enrolled. *Faculty:* 28 full-time (20 women), 4 part-time/adjunct (3 women). Expenses: Contact institution. *Financial support:* In 2001–02, 7 research assistantships (averaging $4,726 per year), 16 teaching assistantships with full tuition reimbursements (averaging $3,836 per year) were awarded. Career-related internships or fieldwork, Federal Work-Study, institutionally sponsored loans, tuition waivers (full and partial), and unspecified assistantships also available. Support available to part-time students. Financial award application deadline: 4/1; financial award applicants required to submit FAFSA. In 2001, 69 degrees awarded. *Degree program information:* Part-time programs available. Offers clinical specialization (MSN); health professions (MPH, MPT, MSN); health sciences (MPH, MPT); nursing administration (MSN); physical therapy (MPT); public health (MPH); teaching of nursing (MSN). *Application deadline:* Applications are processed on a rolling basis. *Application fee:* $25 ($40 for international students). Electronic applications accepted. *Dean,* Dr. Peter A. Cohen, 316-978-3600, Fax: 316-978-3025, E-mail: cohen@chp.twsu.edu.

Fairmount College of Liberal Arts and Sciences Students: 330 full-time (174 women), 476 part-time (275 women); includes 86 minority (42 African Americans, 27 Asian Americans or Pacific Islanders, 14 Hispanic Americans, 3 Native Americans), 165 international. Average age 34. 723 applicants, 55% accepted, 172 enrolled. *Faculty:* 188 full-time (50 women), 20 part-time/adjunct (12 women). Expenses: Contact institution. *Financial support:* In 2001–02, 9 fellowships (averaging $2,648 per year), 58 research assistantships (averaging $4,862 per year), 183 teaching assistantships with full tuition reimbursements (averaging $6,504 per year) were awarded. Career-related internships or fieldwork, Federal Work-Study, institutionally sponsored loans, and unspecified assistantships also available. Support available to part-time students. Financial award application deadline: 4/1; financial award applicants required to submit FAFSA. In 2001, 180 master's, 12 doctorates awarded. *Degree program information:* Part-time and evening/weekend programs available. Offers anthropology (MA); applied mathematics (PhD); biological sciences (MS); chemistry (MS, PhD); communication (MA); community/clinical psychology (PhD); computer science (MS); creative writing (MA, MFA); criminal justice (MA); English (MA, MFA); environmental science (MS); geology (MS); gerontology (MA); history (MA); human factors (PhD); liberal arts and sciences (MA, MFA, MPA, MS, MSW, PhD); liberal studies (MA); mathematics (MS); physics (MS); political science (MA); psychology (MA); public administration (MPA); social work (MSW); sociology (MA); Spanish (MA); statistics (MS). *Application deadline:* For spring admission, 1/1. Applications are processed on a rolling basis. *Application fee:* $25 ($40 for international students). Electronic applications accepted. *Acting Dean,* Dr. William Bischoff, 316-978-3100, Fax: 316-978-3234, E-mail: bill.bischoff@wichita.edu.

W. Frank Barton School of Business Students: 98 full-time (39 women), 256 part-time (113 women); includes 33 minority (6 African Americans, 15 Asian Americans or Pacific Islanders, 8 Hispanic Americans, 4 Native Americans), 75 international. Average age 30. 232 applicants, 61% accepted, 105 enrolled. *Faculty:* 40 full-time (7 women), 2 part-time/adjunct (1 woman). Expenses: Contact institution. *Financial support:* In 2001–02, 8 research assistantships (averaging $5,562 per year), 1 teaching assistantship with full tuition reimbursement (averaging $5,000 per year) were awarded. Federal Work-Study, institutionally sponsored loans, and unspecified assistantships also available. Support available to part-time students. Financial award application deadline: 4/1; financial award applicants required to submit FAFSA. In 2001, 112 degrees awarded. *Degree program information:* Part-time and evening/weekend programs available. Offers accountancy (MPA); business (EMBA, MBA, MS); business economics (MA); economic analysis (MA); economics (MA); professional accountancy (MPA). *Application deadline:* For fall admission, 7/1 (priority date); for spring admission, 1/1. Applications are processed on a rolling basis. *Application fee:* $25 ($40 for international students). Electronic applications accepted. *Dean,* Dr. John Beehler, 316-978-3200, Fax: 316-978-3845, E-mail: j.beehler@wichita.edu.

See in-depth description on page 1307.

WIDENER UNIVERSITY, Chester, PA 19013-5792

General Information Independent, coed, comprehensive institution. CGS member. *Enrollment:* 1,471 full-time matriculated graduate/professional students (816 women), 1,691 part-time matriculated graduate/professional students (943 women). *Graduate faculty:* 204 full-time, 314 part-time/adjunct. *Tuition:* Part-time $500 per credit. *Required fees:* $25 per semester. *Graduate housing:* Rooms and/or apartments available on a first-come, first-served basis to single students and available to married students. Housing application deadline: 5/30. *Student services:* Campus employment opportunities, career counseling, child daycare facilities, exercise/wellness program, free psychological counseling, international student services. *Library facilities:* Wolfgram Memorial Library. *Online resources:* library catalog, web page, access to other libraries' catalogs. *Collection:* 161,632 titles, 2,286 serial subscriptions, 12,663 audiovisual materials. *Research affiliation:* Advanced Technology Center (engineering), Riverfront Development Corporation (engineering, management), Small Business Administration.

Computer facilities: 310 computers available on campus for general student use. A campuswide network can be accessed from student residence rooms and from off campus. Internet access is available. *Web address:* http://www.widener.edu/.

General Application Contact: Dr. Stephen C. Wilhite, Associate Provost for Graduate Studies, 610-499-4351, Fax: 610-499-4277, E-mail: stephen.c.wilhite@widener.edu.

GRADUATE UNITS

College of Arts and Sciences *Degree program information:* Part-time and evening/weekend programs available. Offers arts and sciences (MA, MPA); criminal justice (MA); liberal studies (MA); public administration (MPA).

School of Business Administration *Degree program information:* Part-time and evening/weekend programs available. Offers accounting information systems (MS); business administration (MBA, MHA, MHR, MS); health and medical services administration (MBA, MHA); human resource management (MHR, MS); taxation (MS). Electronic applications accepted.

School of Engineering *Degree program information:* Part-time and evening/weekend programs available. Offers chemical engineering (ME); civil engineering (ME); computer and software engineering (ME); electrical/telecommunication engineering (ME); engineering (ME); engineering management (ME); mechanical engineering (ME).

School of Human Service Professions *Degree program information:* Part-time and evening/weekend programs available. Offers human service professions (M Ed, MS, MSW, Ed D, Psy D).

Center for Education *Degree program information:* Part-time and evening/weekend programs available. Offers adult education (M Ed); counseling in higher education (M Ed); counselor education (M Ed); early childhood education (M Ed); educational foundations (M Ed); educational leadership (M Ed); educational psychology (M Ed); elementary education (M Ed); English and language arts (M Ed); health education (M Ed); higher education leadership (Ed D); home and school visitor (M Ed); human sexuality (M Ed); mathematics education (M Ed); middle school education (M Ed); principalship (M Ed); reading and language arts (Ed D); reading education (M Ed); school administration (Ed D); science education (M Ed); social studies education (M Ed); special education (M Ed); technology education (M Ed). Electronic applications accepted.

Center for Social Work Education *Degree program information:* Part-time programs available. Offers social work education (MSW). Electronic applications accepted.

Institute for Graduate Clinical Psychology Offers clinical psychology (Psy D); clinical psychology and health and medical services administration). Electronic applications accepted.

Institute for Physical Therapy Education Offers physical therapy education (MS).

School of Law at Wilmington Students: 638 full-time (313 women), 474 part-time (221 women); includes 108 minority (67 African Americans, 23 Asian Americans or Pacific Islanders, 17 Hispanic Americans, 1 Native American), 4 international. Average age 26. 305 applicants. *Faculty:* 54 full-time (22 women), 38 part-time/adjunct (8 women). Expenses: Contact institution. *Financial support:* Career-related internships or fieldwork, Federal Work-Study, institutionally sponsored loans, and scholarships/grants available. Support available to part-time students. Financial award application deadline: 2/15; financial award applicants required to submit FAFSA. In 2001, 13 master's, 331 doctorates awarded. *Degree program information:* Part-time programs available. Offers corporate law and finance (LL M); health law (LL M, MJ, D Law); juridical science (SJD); law (JD). *Application deadline:* For fall admission, 5/15; for spring admission, 12/1. Applications are processed on a rolling basis. *Application fee:* $60. *Application Contact:* Barbara L. Ayars, Assistant Dean of Admissions, 302-477-2210, Fax: 302-477-2224, E-mail: barbara.l.ayars@law.widener.edu. *Dean,* Douglas E. Ray, 302-477-2100, Fax: 302-477-2282, E-mail: douglas.e.ray@widener.edu.

School of Nursing *Degree program information:* Part-time and evening/weekend programs available. Offers nursing (MSN, DN Sc, PMC). Electronic applications accepted.

Widener University School of Law Students: 235 full-time (109 women), 156 part-time (68 women); includes 39 minority (11 African Americans, 15 Asian Americans or Pacific Islanders, 13 Hispanic Americans) Average age 26. 607 applicants, 58% accepted. *Faculty:* 21 full-time (8 women), 16 part-time/adjunct (7 women). Expenses: Contact institution. *Financial support:* Fellowships, research assistantships, career-related internships or fieldwork, Federal Work-Study, institutionally sponsored loans, and scholarships/grants available. Support available to part-time students. Financial award application deadline: 2/15; financial award applicants required to submit FAFSA. In 2001, 118 degrees awarded. *Degree program information:* Part-time programs available. Offers law (JD). *Application deadline:* For fall admission, 5/15. Applications are processed on a rolling basis. *Application fee:* $60. Electronic applications accepted. *Application Contact:* Barbara L. Ayars, Assistant Dean of Admissions, 302-477-2210, Fax: 302-477-2224, E-mail: barbara.l.ayars@law.widener.edu. *Dean,* Douglas E. Ray, 302-477-2100, Fax: 302-477-2282, E-mail: douglas.e.ray@widener.edu.

Announcement: Widener University has all the ingredients to make graduate studies a success. Students can choose from a wide variety of practically focused programs, most of which carry the highest possible accreditation. Small classes taught by experienced, dedicated faculty members provide the ideal environment to work in teams, learn from each other's experiences, and build professional networks. Flexible scheduling and convenient evening and Saturday classes are available. Extensive support is also available through Widener's state-of-the-art library and computing facilities and excellent Career Advising and Planning Services Office.

See in-depth description on page 1309.

WILFRID LAURIER UNIVERSITY, Waterloo, ON N2L 3C5, Canada

General Information Province-supported, coed, comprehensive institution. *Graduate housing:* Rooms and/or apartments available on a first-come, first-served basis to single students and available to married students. Housing application deadline: 4/1.

GRADUATE UNITS

Faculty of Graduate Studies

Faculty of Arts Offers arts (MA, MES, PhD); English (MA, PhD); geography and environmental studies (MA, MES, PhD); history (MA, PhD); philosophy (PhD); political science (MA); religion and culture (MA).

Faculty of Science Offers community psychology (MA); general/experimental psychology (MA); science (MA).

Faculty of Social Work *Degree program information:* Part-time programs available. Offers social work (MSW, PhD).

School of Business and Economics *Degree program information:* Part-time and evening/weekend programs available. Offers business administration (MBA); economics (MA).

Waterloo Lutheran Seminary Students: 34 full-time (16 women), 45 part-time (26 women); includes 9 minority (8 Asian Americans or Pacific Islanders, 1 Hispanic American), 2 international. Average age 33. 22 applicants, 95% accepted, 20 enrolled. *Faculty:* 9 full-time (1 woman), 7 part-time/adjunct (3 women). Expenses: Contact institution. *Financial support:* In 2001–02, 36 students received support. Career-related internships or fieldwork, institutionally sponsored loans, and scholarships/grants available. In 2001, 5 first professional degrees, 28 master's awarded. *Degree program information:* Part-time programs available. Offers Christian ethics (M Th); divinity (M Div); homiletics (M Th); ministry (D Min); pastoral counseling (M Th); theological studies (MTS). *Application fee:* $25. *Principal and Dean,* Dr. Richard Crossman, 519-884-1970 Ext. 3512, E-mail: rcrossma@wlu.ca.

WILKES UNIVERSITY, Wilkes-Barre, PA 18766-0002

General Information Independent, coed, comprehensive institution. *Enrollment:* 286 full-time matriculated graduate/professional students (174 women), 1,640 part-time matriculated graduate/professional students (1,150 women). *Enrollment by degree level:* 252 first professional, 1,674 master's. *Graduate faculty:* 106 full-time, 85 part-time/adjunct. *Tuition:* Full-time $14,304; part-time $596 per credit hour. *Required fees:* $312; $13 per credit hour. Tuition and fees vary according to program. *Graduate housing:* On-campus housing not available. *Student services:* Career counseling, free psychological counseling, international student services, low-cost health insurance, multicultural affairs office. *Library facilities:* Eugene S. Farley Library. *Online resources:* library catalog, access to other libraries' catalogs. *Collection:* 175,249 titles, 4,831 serial subscriptions, 10,973 audiovisual materials.

Computer facilities: 700 computers available on campus for general student use. A campuswide network can be accessed from student residence rooms and from off campus. Internet access and online class registration are available. *Web address:* http://www.wilkes.edu/.

General Application Contact: Dr. Bonnie Bedford, Dean of Graduate Studies, 570-408-4600, Fax: 570-408-7860, E-mail: bedford@wilkes.edu.

GRADUATE UNITS

College of Arts, Sciences, and Professional Studies Students: 39 full-time (21 women), 1,635 part-time (1,146 women); includes 17 minority (5 African Americans, 1 Asian American or Pacific Islander, 11 Hispanic Americans), 5 international. Average age 35. Expenses: Contact institution. *Financial support:* Career-related internships or fieldwork, Federal Work-Study, tuition waivers (full and partial), and unspecified assistantships available. Financial award application deadline: 2/28; financial award applicants required to submit FAFSA. In 2001, 530 degrees awarded. *Degree program information:* Part-time and evening/weekend programs available. Offers accounting (MBA); arts, sciences, and professional studies (MBA, MS, MS Ed, MSEE, MSN); educational computing (MS Ed); educational development and strategies (MS Ed); educational leadership (MS Ed); electrical engineering (MSEE); elementary education (MS Ed); finance (MBA); health care (MBA); human resource management (MBA); international business (MBA); marketing (MBA); mathematics (MS, MS Ed); nursing (MSN); physics (MS Ed); secondary education (MS Ed). *Application deadline:* Applications are processed on a rolling basis. *Application fee:* $30. *Dean of Graduate Studies,* Dr. Bonnie Bedford, 570-408-4600, Fax: 570-408-7860, E-mail: bedford@wilkes.edu.

Wilkes University (continued)

Nesbitt School of Pharmacy Students: 247 full-time (153 women), 5 part-time (4 women); includes 23 minority (4 African Americans, 16 Asian Americans or Pacific Islanders, 2 Hispanic Americans, 1 Native American), 2 international. Average age 23. Expenses: Contact institution. In 2001, 60 degrees awarded. Offers pharmacy (Pharm D). *Application deadline:* Applications are processed on a rolling basis. *Dean,* Dr. Bernard Graham, 570-408-4280, Fax: 570-408-7828, E-mail: grahamb@wilkes.edu.

WILLAMETTE UNIVERSITY, Salem, OR 97301-3931

General Information Independent-religious, coed, comprehensive institution. *Enrollment:* 632 full-time matriculated graduate/professional students (306 women), 31 part-time matriculated graduate/professional students (12 women). *Enrollment by degree level:* 416 first professional, 247 master's. *Graduate faculty:* 32 full-time (7 women), 66 part-time/adjunct (13 women). *Tuition:* Full-time $18,050; part-time $602 per credit. *Required fees:* $50. Tuition and fees vary according to course load, degree level and program. *Graduate housing:* Room and/or apartments available on a first-come, first-served basis to single students; on-campus housing not available to married students. Typical cost: $5,400 per year ($6,150 including board). Room and board charges vary according to board plan and housing facility selected. Housing application deadline: 6/1. *Student services:* Campus employment opportunities, campus safety program, career counseling, free psychological counseling, international student services, low-cost health insurance. *Library facilities:* Mark O. Hatfield Library plus 1 other. *Online resources:* library catalog, web page, access to other libraries' catalogs. *Collection:* 279,574 titles, 1,569 serial subscriptions, 8,456 audiovisual materials.

Computer facilities: 200 computers available on campus for general student use. A campuswide network can be accessed from student residence rooms and from off campus. *Web address:* http://www.willamette.edu/.

General Application Contact: Dr. Robin C. Brown, Vice President for Enrollment, 503-370-6303, Fax: 503-375-5363, E-mail: rbrown@williamette.edu.

GRADUATE UNITS

College of Law Students: 418 full-time (189 women), 4 part-time (2 women); includes 44 minority (9 African Americans, 28 Asian Americans or Pacific Islanders, 4 Hispanic Americans, 3 Native Americans), 5 international. Average age 26. 742 applicants, 57% accepted. *Faculty:* 26 full-time (8 women), 9 part-time/adjunct (2 women). Expenses: Contact institution. *Financial support:* In 2001–02, 246 students received support; research assistantships, career-related internships or fieldwork, Federal Work-Study, scholarships/grants, and tuition waivers (full and partial) available. Financial award application deadline: 3/1; financial award applicants required to submit FAFSA. In 2001, 130 degrees awarded. *Degree program information:* Part-time programs available. Offers law (JD). *Application deadline:* For fall admission, 4/1 (priority date). Applications are processed on a rolling basis. *Application fee:* $50. Electronic applications accepted. *Application Contact:* Lawrence Seno, Assistant Dean for Admissions and Communications, 503-370-6282, Fax: 503-370-6375, E-mail: law-admission@willamette.edu. *Dean,* Symeon C. Symeonides, 503-370-6402, Fax: 503-370-6828, E-mail: symeon@willamette.edu.

George H. Atkinson Graduate School of Management Students: 152 full-time (56 women), 16 part-time (6 women); includes 12 minority (1 African American, 6 Asian Americans or Pacific Islanders, 4 Hispanic Americans, 1 Native American), 53 international. Average age 26. 174 applicants, 83% accepted, 83 enrolled. *Faculty:* 14 full-time (3 women), 14 part-time/adjunct (2 women). Expenses: Contact institution. *Financial support:* In 2001–02, 110 students received support, including 11 research assistantships (averaging $1,200 per year); career-related internships or fieldwork, Federal Work-Study, and scholarships/grants also available. Support available to part-time students. Financial award application deadline: 7/1; financial award applicants required to submit FAFSA. In 2001, 71 degrees awarded. *Degree program information:* Part-time programs available. Offers business (MBA); government (MBA); not-for-profit management (MBA). *Application deadline:* For fall admission, 3/31 (priority date). Applications are processed on a rolling basis. *Application fee:* $50. Electronic applications accepted. *Application Contact:* Judy O'Neill, Assistant Dean and Director of Admissions, 503-370-6167, Fax: 503-370-3011, E-mail: joneill@willamette.edu. *Dean,* Bryan Johnston, 503-370-6440, Fax: 503-370-3011, E-mail: johnstob@willamette.edu.

School of Education Students: 92 full-time (74 women); includes 5 minority (1 African American, 4 Asian Americans or Pacific Islanders) Average age 26. 153 applicants, 76% accepted, 92 enrolled. *Faculty:* 10 full-time (9 women), 130 part-time/adjunct. Expenses: Contact institution. *Financial support:* In 2001–02, 75 students received support, including fellowships (averaging $3,000 per year); career-related internships or fieldwork, institutionally sponsored loans, scholarships/grants, and tuition waivers (partial) also available. Financial award application deadline: 2/1; financial award applicants required to submit FAFSA. In 2001, 78 degrees awarded. Offers teaching (MAT). *Application deadline:* For fall admission, 2/1 (priority date). Applications are processed on a rolling basis. *Application fee:* $35. *Application Contact:* Dr. Robin C. Brown, Vice President for Enrollment, 503-370-6303, Fax: 503-375-5363, E-mail: rbrown@williamette.edu. *Director,* Dr. Richard L. Biffle, 503-370-6294, Fax: 503-375-5478, E-mail: rbiffle@willamette.edu.

WILLIAM CAREY COLLEGE, Hattiesburg, MS 39401-5499

General Information Independent-religious, coed, comprehensive institution. *Enrollment:* 276 full-time matriculated graduate/professional students (193 women), 462 part-time matriculated graduate/professional students (390 women). *Enrollment by degree level:* 738 master's. *Graduate faculty:* 33 full-time (16 women), 20 part-time/adjunct (15 women). *Tuition:* Part-time $220 per semester hour. *Required fees:* $80 per semester hour. Tuition and fees vary according to program. *Graduate housing:* Rooms and/or apartments available on a first-come, first-served basis to single and married students. Typical cost: $3,549 (including board) for single students. *Student services:* Career counseling, free psychological counseling. *Library facilities:* I. E. Rouse Library. *Collection:* 109,746 titles, 587 serial subscriptions.

Computer facilities: 30 computers available on campus for general student use. Internet access is available. *Web address:* http://www.wmcarey.edu/.

General Application Contact: Dr. Tommy King, Dean of Graduate Admissions, 601-318-6774, Fax: 601-318-6454, E-mail: tommy.king@wmcarey.edu.

GRADUATE UNITS

Graduate School Students: 276 full-time (193 women), 462 part-time (390 women); includes 181 minority (169 African Americans, 2 Asian Americans or Pacific Islanders, 8 Hispanic Americans, 2 Native Americans), 3 international. *Faculty:* 33 full-time (16 women), 20 part-time/adjunct (15 women). Expenses: Contact institution. *Financial support:* Federal Work-Study and scholarships/grants available. Support available to part-time students. Financial award applicants required to submit FAFSA. In 2001, 314 degrees awarded. *Degree program information:* Part-time programs available. Offers business (MBA); counseling psychology (MS); industrial and organizational psychology (MS). *Application deadline:* Applications are processed on a rolling basis. *Application fee:* $25. *Application Contact:* Dr. Tommy King, Dean of Graduate Admissions, 601-318-6774, Fax: 601-318-6454, E-mail: tommy.king@wmcarey.edu. *Vice President of Academic Affairs,* Dr. Lloyd L. Ezell, 601-318-6101, Fax: 601-318-6413, E-mail: lloyd.ezell@wmcarey.edu.

School of Education Students: 88 full-time (73 women), 386 part-time (341 women); includes 95 African Americans, 4 Hispanic Americans, 1 Native American, 1 international. *Faculty:* 20 full-time (11 women), 15 part-time/adjunct (12 women). Expenses: Contact institution. *Financial support:* Federal Work-Study and scholarships/grants available. Support available to part-time students. In 2001, 205 degrees awarded. *Degree program information:* Part-time programs available. Offers art education (M Ed); art of teaching (M Ed); educational leadership (M Ed); elementary education (M Ed); English education (M Ed); gifted education (M Ed); secondary education (M Ed); special education (M Ed). *Application fee:* $25. *Application Contact:* Dr. Tommy King, Dean of Graduate Admissions, 601-318-6774, Fax: 601-318-6454, E-mail: tommy.king@wmcarey.edu. *Dean,* Dr. Bonnie Holder, 601-318-6139, Fax: 601-318-6185, E-mail: bonnie.holder@wmcarey.edu.

WILLIAM MITCHELL COLLEGE OF LAW, St. Paul, MN 55105-3076

General Information Independent, coed, graduate-only institution. *Enrollment by degree level:* 1,015 first professional. *Graduate faculty:* 36 full-time (14 women), 161 part-time/adjunct (67 women). *Tuition:* Full-time $20,140; part-time $14,600 per year. *Required fees:* $30; $30 per year. *Graduate housing:* Rooms and/or apartments available to single and married students. Typical cost: $7,845 (including board) for single students; $7,845 (including board) for married students. *Student services:* Campus employment opportunities, campus safety program, career counseling, disabled student services, free psychological counseling, international student services, multicultural affairs office, writing training. *Library facilities:* Warren E. Burger Library. *Online resources:* library catalog, web page, access to other libraries' catalogs. *Collection:* 173,742 titles, 4,215 serial subscriptions, 627 audiovisual materials.

Computer facilities: 355 computers available on campus for general student use. A campuswide network can be accessed from off campus. Internet access is available. *Web address:* http://www.wmitchell.edu/.

General Application Contact: James H. Brooks, Dean of Students, 651-290-6362, Fax: 651-290-7535, E-mail: admissions@wmitchell.edu.

GRADUATE UNITS

Professional Program Students: 537 full-time (302 women), 478 part-time (247 women); includes 105 minority (40 African Americans, 42 Asian Americans or Pacific Islanders, 17 Hispanic Americans, 6 Native Americans), 13 international. Average age 29. 1,022 applicants, 66% accepted. *Faculty:* 36 full-time (14 women), 161 part-time/adjunct (67 women). Expenses: Contact institution. *Financial support:* In 2001–02, 849 students received support, including 55 research assistantships (averaging $2,000 per year); Federal Work-Study, scholarships/grants, and tuition waivers (full and partial) also available. Support available to part-time students. Financial award application deadline: 3/15; financial award applicants required to submit FAFSA. In 2001, 250 degrees awarded. *Degree program information:* Part-time and evening/weekend programs available. Offers law (JD). *Application deadline:* For fall admission, 6/28. Applications are processed on a rolling basis. *Application fee:* $45. *Application Contact:* James H. Brooks, Dean of Students, 651-290-6362, Fax: 651-290-7535, E-mail: admissions@wmitchell.edu. *President and Dean,* Harry J. Haynsworth, 651-290-6310, Fax: 651-290-6426.

WILLIAM PATERSON UNIVERSITY OF NEW JERSEY, Wayne, NJ 07470-8420

General Information State-supported, coed, comprehensive institution. CGS member. *Enrollment:* 155 full-time matriculated graduate/professional students (101 women), 679 part-time matriculated graduate/professional students (551 women). *Enrollment by degree level:* 834 master's. Tuition, state resident: part-time $322 per credit. Tuition, nonresident: part-time $468 per credit. *Graduate housing:* Room and/or apartments available on a first-come, first-served basis to single students; on-campus housing not available to married students. *Student services:* Campus employment opportunities, campus safety program, career counseling, child daycare facilities, disabled student services, exercise/wellness program, free psychological counseling, international student services, low-cost health insurance, multicultural affairs office, teacher training, writing training. *Library facilities:* Sarah Byrd Askew Library. *Online resources:* library catalog, web page, access to other libraries' catalogs. *Collection:* 291,852 titles, 1,950 serial subscriptions, 13,997 audiovisual materials.

Computer facilities: 150 computers available on campus for general student use. A campuswide network can be accessed from student residence rooms. *Web address:* http://www.wpunj.edu/.

General Application Contact: Danielle Liautaud Watkins, Graduate Admissions Counselor, 973-720-3579, Fax: 973-720-2035, E-mail: liautaudd@wpunj.edu.

GRADUATE UNITS

College of Business Students: 26 full-time (7 women), 56 part-time (26 women); includes 19 minority (9 African Americans, 7 Asian Americans or Pacific Islanders, 3 Hispanic Americans) 61 applicants, 31% accepted, 14 enrolled. Expenses: Contact institution. *Financial support:* Research assistantships with full tuition reimbursements, unspecified assistantships available. Support available to part-time students. Financial award application deadline: 4/1; financial award applicants required to submit FAFSA. In 2001, 16 degrees awarded. *Degree program information:* Part-time and evening/weekend programs available. Offers business (MBA). *Application deadline:* Applications are processed on a rolling basis. *Application fee:* $35. Electronic applications accepted. *Application Contact:* Danielle Liautaud, Graduate Admissions Counselor, 973-720-3579, Fax: 973-720-2035, E-mail: liautaudd@wpunj.edu. *Dean,* Jess Bononico, Fax: 973-720-2809.

College of Education Students: 29 full-time (18 women), 397 part-time (349 women); includes 23 minority (14 African Americans, 2 Asian Americans or Pacific Islanders, 7 Hispanic Americans) 218 applicants, 52% accepted. Expenses: Contact institution. *Financial support:* Research assistantships with full tuition reimbursements, career-related internships or fieldwork, Federal Work-Study, and unspecified assistantships available. Support available to part-time students. Financial award application deadline: 4/1; financial award applicants required to submit FAFSA. In 2001, 105 degrees awarded. Offers counseling (M Ed); counseling services (M Ed); education (M Ed, MAT); educational leadership (M Ed); elementary education (M Ed, MAT); reading (M Ed); special education (M Ed). *Application deadline:* Applications are processed on a rolling basis. *Application fee:* $35. Electronic applications accepted. *Application Contact:* Danielle Liautaud, Graduate Admissions Counselor, 973-720-3579, Fax: 973-720-2035, E-mail: liautaudd@wpunj.edu. *Dean,* Leslie Agard-Jones, 973-720-2413, Fax: 973-720-2955.

College of Science and Health Students: 44 full-time (39 women), 104 part-time (99 women); includes 27 minority (3 African Americans, 12 Asian Americans or Pacific Islanders, 10 Hispanic Americans, 2 Native Americans) 180 applicants, 35% accepted. Expenses: Contact institution. *Financial support:* In 2001–02, 36 students received support; research assistantships with full tuition reimbursements available, career-related internships or fieldwork and unspecified assistantships available. Support available to part-time students. Financial award application deadline: 4/1; financial award applicants required to submit FAFSA. In 2001, 53 degrees awarded. *Degree program information:* Part-time and evening/weekend programs available. Offers biotechnology (MS); general biology (MA); limnology and terrestrial ecology (MA); molecular biology (MA); nursing (MSN); physiology (MA); science and health (MA, MS, MSN); speech pathology (MS). *Application deadline:* Applications are processed on a rolling basis. *Application fee:* $35. Electronic applications accepted. *Application Contact:* Danielle Liautaud, Graduate Admissions Counselor, 973-720-3579, Fax: 973-720-2035, E-mail: liautaudd@wpunj.edu. *Dean,* Dr. Eswar Phadia, 973-720-2194.

College of the Arts and Communication Students: 24 full-time (11 women), 35 part-time (24 women); includes 9 minority (4 African Americans, 3 Asian Americans or Pacific Islanders, 1 Hispanic American, 1 Native American) 120 applicants, 43% accepted, 26 enrolled. Expenses: Contact institution. *Financial support:* In 2001–02, 3 students received support; research assistantships with full tuition reimbursements available, career-related internships or fieldwork, Federal Work-Study, and unspecified assistantships available. Support available to part-time students. Financial award application deadline: 4/1; financial award applicants required to submit FAFSA. In 2001, 17 degrees awarded. *Degree program information:* Part-time and evening/weekend programs available. Offers arts and communication (MA, MFA, MM); media studies (MA); music (MM); visual arts (MA). *Application deadline:* Applications are processed on a rolling basis. *Application fee:* $35. Electronic applications accepted. *Application Contact:* Danielle Liautaud, Graduate Admissions Counselor, 973-720-3579, Fax: 973-720-2035, E-mail: liautaudd@wpunj.edu. *Dean,* Ofelia Garcia, 973-720-2231.

College of the Humanities and Social Sciences Students: 32 full-time (26 women), 87 part-time (53 women); includes 14 minority (2 African Americans, 2 Asian Americans or Pacific Islanders, 10 Hispanic Americans) 118 applicants, 55% accepted, 48 enrolled. Expenses: Contact institution. *Financial support:* In 2001–02, 13 students received support; research assistantships with full tuition reimbursements available, teaching assistantships with full tuition reimbursements available, unspecified assistantships available. Support available to part-time students. Financial award application deadline: 4/1; financial award applicants required to submit FAFSA. In 2001, 26 degrees awarded. *Degree program information:* Part-time and evening/weekend programs available. Offers applied clinical psychology (MA); English (MA); history (MA); humanities and social sciences (MA); sociology (MA). *Application deadline:* Applications are processed on a rolling basis. *Application fee:* $35. Electronic applications accepted. *Application Contact:* Danielle Liautaud, Graduate Admissions Counselor, 973-720-3579, Fax: 973-720-2035, E-mail: liautaudd@wpunj.edu. *Dean,* Dr. Isabel Tirado, 973-720-2413, Fax: 973-720-2955.

See in-depth description on page 1311.

WILLIAMS COLLEGE, Williamstown, MA 01267

General Information Independent, coed, comprehensive institution. *Graduate housing:* Room and/or apartments available to single students; on-campus housing not available to married students. *Research affiliation:* Clark Art Institute.

GRADUATE UNITS

Program in the History of Art *Degree program information:* Part-time programs available. Offers history of art (MA). Offered jointly with Sterling and Francine Clark Art Institute.

WILLIAM WOODS UNIVERSITY, Fulton, MO 65251-1098

General Information Independent-religious, coed, comprehensive institution. *Enrollment:* 665 full-time matriculated graduate/professional students (420 women), 5 part-time matriculated graduate/professional students (1 woman). *Enrollment by degree level:* 670 master's. *Graduate faculty:* 15 full-time (5 women), 220 part-time/adjunct (74 women). *Tuition:* Part-time $240 per credit hour. Tuition and fees vary according to program. *Graduate housing:* On-campus housing not available. *Student services:* Campus safety program, career counseling, exercise/wellness program, international student services. *Library facilities:* Dulany Library. *Online resources:* library catalog, web page, access to other libraries' catalogs. *Collection:* 93,917 titles, 26,773 audiovisual materials.

Computer facilities: 105 computers available on campus for general student use. A campuswide network can be accessed from student residence rooms. Internet access is available. *Web address:* http://www.williamwoods.edu/.

General Application Contact: Barbara Danuser, Recruitment Representative, 800-995-3199, Fax: 573-592-1164, E-mail: cgas@williamwoods.edu.

GRADUATE UNITS

Graduate and Adult Studies Students: 665 full-time (420 women), 5 part-time (1 woman); includes 77 minority (17 African Americans, 52 Asian Americans or Pacific Islanders, 5 Hispanic Americans, 3 Native Americans) Average age 34. 381 applicants, 96% accepted. *Faculty:* 15 full-time (5 women), 220 part-time/adjunct (74 women). Expenses: Contact institution. *Financial support:* Institutionally sponsored loans available. Financial award applicants required to submit FAFSA. In 2001, 310 degrees awarded. *Degree program information:* Evening/weekend programs available. Offers accounting (MBA); administration (M Ed); curriculum and instruction (M Ed); health management (MBA). *Application deadline:* Applications are processed on a rolling basis. *Application fee:* $25. Electronic applications accepted. *Application Contact:* Barbara Danuser, Recruitment Representative, 800-995-3199, Fax: 573-592-1164, E-mail: cgas@williamwoods.edu. *Associate Provost,* Dr. Betty R. Tutt, 573-592-4354, Fax: 573-592-1164, E-mail: btutt@williamwoods.edu.

WILMINGTON COLLEGE, New Castle, DE 19720-6491

General Information Independent, coed, comprehensive institution. *Enrollment:* 446 full-time matriculated graduate/professional students (307 women), 1,667 part-time matriculated graduate/professional students (1,192 women). *Enrollment by degree level:* 1,961 master's, 152 doctoral. *Graduate faculty:* 28 full-time, 158 part-time/adjunct. *Tuition:* Full-time $4,788; part-time $266 per credit. *Required fees:* $50; $25 per semester. Tuition and fees vary according to course level, course load, degree level, campus/location and program. *Graduate housing:* On-campus housing not available. *Student services:* Career counseling, disabled student services, international student services, teacher training. *Library facilities:* Robert C. and Dorothy M. Peoples Library plus 1 other. *Online resources:* library catalog, web page. *Collection:* 111,000 titles, 500 serial subscriptions, 6,795 audiovisual materials.

Computer facilities: 100 computers available on campus for general student use. Internet access is available. *Web address:* http://www.wilmcoll.edu/.

General Application Contact: Michael Lee, Director of Admissions and Financial Aid, 302-328-9407 Ext. 102, Fax: 302-328-5164, E-mail: inquire@wilmcoll.edu.

GRADUATE UNITS

Division of Behavioral Science Students: 9 full-time (6 women), 79 part-time (64 women); includes 21 minority (19 African Americans, 2 Hispanic Americans) *Faculty:* 6 full-time (2 women), 35 part-time/adjunct (15 women). Expenses: Contact institution. *Financial support:* Applicants required to submit FAFSA. In 2001, 25 degrees awarded. *Degree program information:* Part-time and evening/weekend programs available. Offers community counseling (MS); criminal justice studies (MS); student affairs and college counseling (MS). *Application deadline:* For fall admission, 4/15. *Application fee:* $25. *Application Contact:* Michael Lee, Director of Admissions and Financial Aid, 302-328-9407 Ext. 102, Fax: 302-328-5164, E-mail: inquire@wilmcoll.edu. *Chair,* James Wilson, 302-328-9401 Ext. 154, Fax: 302-328-5164, E-mail: jwils@wilmcoll.edu.

Division of Business Students: 179 full-time (105 women), 415 part-time (237 women); includes 111 minority (92 African Americans, 7 Asian Americans or Pacific Islanders, 9 Hispanic Americans, 3 Native Americans) *Faculty:* 7 full-time (2 women), 75 part-time/adjunct (25 women). Expenses: Contact institution. *Financial support:* Applicants required to submit FAFSA. In 2001, 234 degrees awarded. *Degree program information:* Part-time and evening/weekend programs available. Offers business administration (MBA); health care administration (MBA, MS); human resource management (MS); management (MS); public administration (MS); transport and logistics (MS). *Application deadline:* Applications are processed on a rolling basis. *Application fee:* $25. *Application Contact:* Michael Lee, Director of Admissions and Financial Aid, 302-328-9407 Ext. 102, Fax: 302-328-5164, E-mail: inquire@wilmcoll.edu. *Chair,* Dr. Raj Parikh, 302-328-9401 Ext. 284, Fax: 302-328-7021, E-mail: rpari@wilmcoll.edu.

Division of Education Students: 315 full-time (188 women), 851 part-time (622 women); includes 94 minority (84 African Americans, 1 Asian American or Pacific Islander, 9 Hispanic Americans) *Faculty:* 11 full-time (6 women), 210 part-time/adjunct (85 women). Expenses: Contact institution. *Financial support:* Applicants required to submit FAFSA. In 2001, 338 master's, 29 doctorates awarded. *Degree program information:* Part-time and evening/weekend programs available. Offers applied education technology (M Ed); elementary and secondary school counseling (M Ed); elementary special education (M Ed); elementary studies (M Ed); innovation and leadership (Ed D); reading (M Ed); school leadership (M Ed). *Application deadline:* For fall admission, 4/30. Applications are processed on a rolling basis. *Application fee:* $25. *Application Contact:* Michael Lee, Director of Admissions and Financial Aid, 302-328-9407 Ext. 102, Fax: 302-328-5164, E-mail: inquire@wilmcoll.edu. *Chair,* Dr. Barbara Raetsch, 302-328-9401 Ext. 163, Fax: 302-328-7081, E-mail: braet@wilmcoll.edu.

Division of Nursing Students: 82 full-time (72 women), 49 part-time (45 women); includes 21 minority (18 African Americans, 2 Hispanic Americans, 1 Native American), 1 international. *Faculty:* 8 full-time (all women), 15 part-time/adjunct (12 women). Expenses: Contact institution. *Financial support:* In 2001–02, 28 fellowships with tuition reimbursements (averaging $2,200 per year) were awarded; traineeships also available. Financial award applicants required to submit FAFSA. In 2001, 41 degrees awarded. *Degree program information:* Part-time programs available. Offers adult nurse practitioner (MSN); family nurse practitioner (MSN); gerontology (MSN); leadership (MSN); nursing (MSN). *Application deadline:* For fall admission, 3/31 (priority date). Applications are processed on a rolling basis. *Application fee:* $25. *Application Contact:* Michael Lee, Director of Admissions and Financial Aid, 302-328-9407 Ext. 102, Fax: 302-328-5164, E-mail: inquire@wilmcoll.edu. *Chair,* Mary Letitia Gallagher, 302-328-9401 Ext. 161, Fax: 302-328-7081, E-mail: tgall@wilmcoll.edu.

WINEBRENNER THEOLOGICAL SEMINARY, Findlay, OH 45839-0478

General Information Independent-religious, coed, graduate-only institution. *Enrollment by degree level:* 41 first professional, 19 master's, 11 doctoral. *Graduate faculty:* 9 full-time (1 woman), 5 part-time/adjunct (0 women). *Tuition:* Full-time $7,089; part-time $330 per credit. *Required fees:* $12 per trimester. *Graduate housing:* Rooms and/or apartments available on a first-come, first-served basis to single and married students. Typical cost: $5,100 per year for single students; $5,100 per year for married students. Housing application deadline: 7/1. *Student services:* Campus employment opportunities, career counseling, free psychological counseling, international student services. *Library facilities:* Winebrenner Seminary Library. *Online resources:* library catalog, access to other libraries' catalogs. *Collection:* 44,488 titles, 145 serial subscriptions, 728 audiovisual materials.

Computer facilities: 2 computers available on campus for general student use. A campuswide network can be accessed from off campus. Internet access is available. *Web address:* http://www.winebrenner.edu/.

General Application Contact: Jennifer J. Cobb, Admissions Counselor, 419-422-4824 Ext. 158, Fax: 419-422-3999, E-mail: admissions@winebrenner.edu.

GRADUATE UNITS

Professional Studies Students: 43 full-time (9 women), 28 part-time (13 women); includes 7 minority (6 African Americans, 1 Native American) Average age 42. 16 applicants, 100% accepted, 14 enrolled. *Faculty:* 9 full-time (1 woman), 5 part-time/adjunct (0 women). Expenses: Contact institution. *Financial support:* In 2001–02, 44 students received support. Career-related internships or fieldwork, institutionally sponsored loans, scholarships/grants, and tuition waivers (partial) available. Support available to part-time students. Financial award application deadline: 7/1; financial award applicants required to submit FAFSA. In 2001, 6 first professional degrees, 4 master's awarded. *Degree program information:* Part-time and evening/weekend programs available. Offers family ministry (MA); pastoral studies (Certificate, Diploma); theological study (MA); theological/ministerial studies (D Min); theology/ministerial studies (M Div). *Application deadline:* For fall admission, 8/15 (priority date); for winter admission, 12/15 (priority date); for spring admission, 4/15 (priority date). Applications are processed on a rolling basis. *Application fee:* $25. *Application Contact:* Jennifer J. Cobb, Admissions Counselor, 419-422-4824 Ext. 158, Fax: 419-422-3999, E-mail: admissions@winebrenner.edu. *Academic Dean,* Dr. Gene C. Crutsinger, 419-422-4824 Ext. 162, Fax: 419-422-3999, E-mail: wts@winebrenner.edu.

WINGATE UNIVERSITY, Wingate, NC 28174-0159

General Information Independent-religious, coed, comprehensive institution. *Enrollment:* 104 part-time matriculated graduate/professional students (58 women). *Enrollment by degree level:* 104 master's. *Graduate faculty:* 9 full-time (2 women), 2 part-time/adjunct (0 women). *Tuition:* Full-time $12,900; part-time $430 per semester hour. *Required fees:* $155 per semester. *Graduate housing:* Rooms and/or apartments available on a first-come, first-served basis to single and married students. Typical cost: $2,730 per year for single students. Housing application deadline: 8/15. *Student services:* Campus employment opportunities, career counseling, teacher training. *Library facilities:* Ethel K. Smith Library plus 2 others. *Online resources:* library catalog, web page. *Collection:* 110,000 titles, 600 serial subscriptions, 8,011 audiovisual materials.

Computer facilities: 75 computers available on campus for general student use. A campuswide network can be accessed from student residence rooms and from off campus. Internet access is available. *Web address:* http://www.wingate.edu/.

General Application Contact: Dr. Robert A. Shaw, Vice President for Academic Affairs, 704-233-8123, Fax: 704-233-8125, E-mail: rshaw@wingate.edu.

GRADUATE UNITS

Program in Education Average age 33. 13 applicants, 100% accepted, 11 enrolled. *Faculty:* 2 full-time (1 woman), 1 part-time/adjunct (0 women). Expenses: Contact institution. *Financial support:* In 2001–02, 5 students received support. Available to part-time students. Applicants required to submit FAFSA. In 2001, 9 degrees awarded. *Degree program information:* Part-time and evening/weekend programs available. Offers elementary education (MA Ed, MAT). *Application deadline:* For fall admission, 8/15 (priority date). Applications are processed on a rolling basis. *Application fee:* $0. *Application Contact:* Phyllis Starnes, Secretary, Thayer School of Education, 704-233-8075, Fax: 704-233-8273, E-mail: phylstar@wingate.edu. *Dean, Thayer School of Education,* Dr. Sarah Harrison-Burns, 704-233-8078, Fax: 704-233-8273, E-mail: shburns@wingate.edu.

School of Business and Economics Average age 29. 38 applicants, 79% accepted. *Faculty:* 7 full-time (1 woman), 1 part-time/adjunct (0 women). Expenses: Contact institution. *Financial support:* In 2001–02, 7 students received support. Federal Work-Study available. Support available to part-time students. Financial award application deadline: 8/1; financial award applicants required to submit FAFSA. In 2001, 26 degrees awarded. *Degree program information:* Part-time programs available. Offers business (MBA). *Application deadline:* For fall admission, 8/15 (priority date); for spring admission, 12/15 (priority date). Applications are processed on a rolling basis. *Application fee:* $25 ($50 for international students). Electronic applications accepted. *Application Contact:* Kathryn Rowell, MBA Coordinator, 704-233-8148, Fax: 704-233-8146, E-mail: karowell@wingate.edu. *Dean,* Dr. E. Hampton Pitts, 704-233-8148, Fax: 704-233-8146.

WINONA STATE UNIVERSITY, Winona, MN 55987-5838

General Information State-supported, coed, comprehensive institution. *Enrollment:* 114 full-time matriculated graduate/professional students (95 women), 350 part-time matriculated graduate/professional students (284 women). *Graduate faculty:* 66 full-time (36 women). Tuition, state resident: part-time $158 per semester hour. Tuition, nonresident: part-time $247 per semester hour. *Required fees:* $22 per credit. *Graduate housing:* Room and/or apartments available to single students; on-campus housing not available to married students. Housing application deadline: 3/2. *Student services:* Campus employment opportunities, campus safety program, career counseling, child daycare facilities, free psychological counseling, international student services, low-cost health insurance. *Library facilities:* Maxwell Library. *Online resources:* library catalog, web page, access to other libraries' catalogs. *Collection:* 243,500 titles, 1,950 serial subscriptions.

Computer facilities: 1,400 computers available on campus for general student use. A campuswide network can be accessed from student residence rooms and from off campus. Internet access is available. *Web address:* http://www.winona.edu/.

General Application Contact: Dr. Pauline Christensen, Director of Graduate Studies, 507-457-5088, E-mail: pchristensen@vax2.winona.msus.edu.

GRADUATE UNITS

Graduate Studies Students: 114 full-time (95 women), 350 part-time (284 women). 104 applicants, 84% accepted, 59 enrolled. *Faculty:* 90 full-time (46 women). Expenses: Contact institution. *Financial support:* Fellowships, research assistantships, career-related internships or fieldwork, Federal Work-Study, traineeships, and unspecified assistantships available. Support available to part-time students. In 2001, 125 degrees awarded. *Degree program information:* Part-time and evening/weekend programs available. *Application deadline:* Applications are processed on a rolling basis. *Application fee:* $20. Electronic applications accepted. *Director,* Dr. Pauline Christensen, 507-457-5088, E-mail: pchristensen@vax2.winona.msus.edu.

College of Education Students: 102 full-time (84 women), 263 part-time (206 women); includes 1 minority (Native American) 19 applicants, 100% accepted, 18 enrolled. *Faculty:* 27 full-time (13 women). Expenses: Contact institution. *Financial support:* Fellowships, career-related internships or fieldwork, Federal Work-Study, and unspecified assistantships available. Support available to part-time students. In 2001, 36 degrees awarded. *Degree program information:* Part-time and evening/weekend programs available. Offers counselor education (MS); education (MS); elementary school administration (MS); general school administration (MS); learning disabilities (MS); mild to moderate mentally handicapped (MS); secondary school administration (MS); special education (MS). *Application deadline:*

Winona State University (continued)

For fall admission, 8/8 (priority date); for spring admission, 2/17. Applications are processed on a rolling basis. *Application fee:* $20. *Dean,* Dr. Carol Anderson, 507-457-5570.

College of Liberal Arts Students: 1 full-time (0 women), 10 part-time (4 women). 3 applicants, 100% accepted, 5 enrolled. *Faculty:* 15 full-time (5 women). Expenses: Contact institution. *Financial support:* Career-related internships or fieldwork, Federal Work-Study, and unspecified assistantships available. Support available to part-time students. In 2001, 5 degrees awarded. *Degree program information:* Part-time programs available. Offers English (MA, MS); liberal arts (MA, MS). *Application deadline:* For fall admission, 7/26 (priority date); for spring admission, 12/8. Applications are processed on a rolling basis. *Application fee:* $20. *Dean,* Dr. Peter Henderson, 507-457-5017, E-mail: phenderson@vax2.winona.msus.edu.

College of Nursing Students: 11 full-time (all women), 78 part-time (74 women); includes 3 minority (1 African American, 2 Asian Americans or Pacific Islanders) 37 applicants, 78% accepted, 8 enrolled. *Faculty:* 20 full-time (16 women). Expenses: Contact institution. *Financial support:* In 2001–02, 3 research assistantships were awarded; traineeships also available. In 2001, 20 degrees awarded. Offers nursing (MS). *Application deadline:* For fall admission, 2/1. *Application fee:* $20. *Graduate Director,* Dr. Timothy Gaspar, 507-457-5122, E-mail: tgaspar@winona.msus.edu.

WINSTON-SALEM STATE UNIVERSITY, Winston-Salem, NC 27110-0003

General Information State-supported, coed, comprehensive institution.

GRADUATE UNITS

Area of Elementary Education

Department of Physical Therapy

WINTHROP UNIVERSITY, Rock Hill, SC 29733

General Information State-supported, coed, comprehensive institution. *Enrollment:* 257 full-time matriculated graduate/professional students (154 women), 165 part-time matriculated graduate/professional students (34 women). *Enrollment by degree level:* 691 master's, 8 other advanced degrees. *Graduate faculty:* 162 full-time (52 women). Tuition, state resident: full-time $4,546; part-time $189 per credit hour. Tuition, nonresident: full-time $8,326; part-time $356 per credit hour. *Required fees:* $40; $20 per semester. *Graduate housing:* Rooms and/or apartments available to single and married students. Housing application deadline:3/1. *Student services:* Campus employment opportunities, campus safety program, career counseling, disabled student services, exercise/wellness program, free psychological counseling, international student services, low-cost health insurance, multicultural affairs office. *Library facilities:* Dacus Library. *Online resources:* library catalog, web page, access to other libraries' catalogs. *Collection:* 638,454 titles, 2,706 serial subscriptions, 1,826 audiovisual materials.

Computer facilities: 250 computers available on campus for general student use. A campuswide network can be accessed from student residence rooms and from off campus. Internet access is available. *Web address:* http://www.winthrop.edu/.

General Application Contact: Sharon B. Johnson, Director of Graduate Studies, 800-411-7041, Fax: 803-323-2292, E-mail: johnsons@winthrop.edu.

GRADUATE UNITS

College of Arts and Sciences Students: 52 full-time (38 women), 69 part-time (50 women); includes 14 minority (11 African Americans, 1 Asian American or Pacific Islander, 2 Hispanic Americans), 5 international. Average age 32. *Faculty:* 71 full-time (24 women). Expenses: Contact institution. *Financial support:* Career-related internships or fieldwork, Federal Work-Study, scholarships/grants, and unspecified assistantships available. Support available to part-time students. Financial award application deadline: 2/1; financial award applicants required to submit FAFSA. In 2001, 41 master's, 9 other advanced degrees awarded. *Degree program information:* Part-time programs available. Offers arts and sciences (M Math, MA, MLA, MS, SSP); biology (MS); English (MA); history (MA); human nutrition (MS); liberal arts (MLA); mathematics (M Math); psychology (MS, SSP); Spanish (MA). *Application deadline:* Applications are processed on a rolling basis. *Application fee:* $35 ($50 for international students). Electronic applications accepted. *Application Contact:* Sharon B. Johnson, Director of Graduate Studies, 800-411-7041, Fax: 803-323-2292, E-mail: johnsons@winthrop.edu. *Dean,* Dr. Thomas F. Moove, 803-323-2368, E-mail: moovet@winthrop.edu.

College of Business Administration Students: 102 full-time (38 women), 114 part-time (59 women); includes 39 minority (30 African Americans, 6 Asian Americans or Pacific Islanders, 3 Hispanic Americans), 21 international. Average age 31. *Faculty:* 29 full-time (9 women). Expenses: Contact institution. *Financial support:* Federal Work-Study, scholarships/grants, and unspecified assistantships available. Support available to part-time students. Financial award application deadline: 2/1; financial award applicants required to submit FAFSA. In 2001, 72 degrees awarded. *Degree program information:* Part-time and evening/weekend programs available. Postbaccalaureate distance learning degree programs offered (no on-campus study). Offers business administration (MBA). *Application deadline:* For fall admission, 7/15 (priority date); for spring admission, 12/1. Applications are processed on a rolling basis. *Application fee:* $35 ($50 for international students). Electronic applications accepted. *Application Contact:* Sharon B. Johnson, Director of Graduate Studies, 800-411-7041, Fax: 803-323-2292, E-mail: johnsons@winthrop.edu. *Dean,* Dr. Roger Weikle, 803-323-2186, Fax: 803-323-3960, E-mail: weikler@winthrop.edu.

College of Education Students: 93 full-time (75 women), 242 part-time (195 women); includes 101 minority (97 African Americans, 2 Asian Americans or Pacific Islanders, 1 Hispanic American, 1 Native American), 2 international. Average age 32. *Faculty:* 29 full-time (13 women). Expenses: Contact institution. *Financial support:* Career-related internships or fieldwork, Federal Work-Study, scholarships/grants, and unspecified assistantships available. Support available to part-time students. Financial award application deadline: 2/1; financial award applicants required to submit FAFSA. In 2001, 90 degrees awarded. *Degree program information:* Part-time programs available. Offers agency counseling (M Ed); education (M Ed, MAT, MS); educational leadership (M Ed); elementary education (M Ed); middle level education (M Ed); physical education (MS); reading education (M Ed); school counseling (M Ed); secondary education (M Ed, MAT); special education (M Ed). *Application deadline:* For fall admission, 7/15 (priority date); for spring admission, 12/1. Applications are processed on a rolling basis. *Application fee:* $35 ($50 for international students). Electronic applications accepted. *Application Contact:* Sharon B. Johnson, Director of Graduate Studies, 800-411-7041, Fax: 803-323-2292, E-mail: johnsons@winthrop.edu. *Dean,* Dr. Patricia Graham, 803-323-2151, Fax: 803-323-4369, E-mail: grahamp@winthrop.edu.

College of Visual and Performing Arts Students: 10 full-time (3 women), 9 part-time (2 women); includes 2 minority (1 African American, 1 Hispanic American), 3 international. Average age 30. *Faculty:* 33 full-time (6 women). Expenses: Contact institution. *Financial support:* Federal Work-Study, scholarships/grants, and unspecified assistantships available. Support available to part-time students. Financial award application deadline: 2/1; financial award applicants required to submit FAFSA. In 2001, 5 degrees awarded. *Degree program information:* Part-time programs available. Offers art (MFA); art education (MA); conducting (MM); music education (MME); performance (MM); visual and performing arts (MA, MFA, MM, MME). *Application deadline:* Applications are processed on a rolling basis. *Application fee:* $35 ($50 for international students). Electronic applications accepted. *Application Contact:* Sharon B. Johnson, Director of Graduate Studies, 800-411-7041, Fax: 803-323-2292, E-mail: johnsons@winthrop.edu. *Dean,* Dr. Andrew Svedlow, 803-323-2323, Fax: 803-323-2333, E-mail: svedlowa@winthrop.edu.

WISCONSIN SCHOOL OF PROFESSIONAL PSYCHOLOGY, Milwaukee, WI 53225-4960

General Information Independent, coed, graduate-only institution. *Enrollment by degree level:* 10 master's, 38 doctoral. *Graduate faculty:* 3 full-time (all women), 32 part-time/adjunct (13 women). *Tuition:* Part-time $550 per credit hour. *Graduate housing:* On-campus housing not available. *Student services:* Career counseling, free psychological counseling. *Library facilities:* Curriculum Support Library. *Collection:* 4,000 titles, 7 serial subscriptions.

Computer facilities: 4 computers available on campus for general student use. Internet access is available. *Web address:* http://www.execpc.com/~wspp/.

General Application Contact: Dr. Howard J. Haven, Dean, 414-464-9777, Fax: 414-358-5590, E-mail: karen-wspp@msh.com.

GRADUATE UNITS

Program in Clinical Psychology Students: 14 full-time (all women), 31 part-time (27 women); includes 6 minority (3 African Americans, 1 Asian American or Pacific Islander, 2 Hispanic Americans), 1 international. Average age 38. 40 applicants, 23% accepted. *Faculty:* 3 full-time (all women), 32 part-time/adjunct (13 women). Expenses: Contact institution. *Financial support:* In 2001–02, 6 students received support. Clinical service assistantships, library aid assistantships available. Support available to part-time students. In 2001, 6 master's, 8 doctorates awarded. *Degree program information:* Part-time and evening/weekend programs available. Offers clinical psychology (MA, Psy D). *Application deadline:* For fall admission, 4/15 (priority date); for spring admission, 10/15 (priority date). Applications are processed on a rolling basis. *Application fee:* $100. *Application Contact:* Karen A. Kilman, Assistant to the President, 414-464-9777, Fax: 414-358-5590, E-mail: karen-wspp@msn.com.

WOODBURY UNIVERSITY, Burbank, CA 91504-1099

General Information Independent, coed, comprehensive institution. *Graduate housing:* Room and/or apartments available to single students; on-campus housing not available to married students. Housing application deadline: 5/1.

GRADUATE UNITS

Business Administration Program *Degree program information:* Part-time and evening/weekend programs available. Offers business administration (MBA).

WORCESTER POLYTECHNIC INSTITUTE, Worcester, MA 01609-2280

General Information Independent, coed, university. CGS member. *Enrollment:* 470 full-time matriculated graduate/professional students (132 women), 361 part-time matriculated graduate/professional students (92 women). *Enrollment by degree level:* 674 master's, 133 doctoral, 24 other advanced degrees. *Graduate faculty:* 195 full-time (30 women), 35 part-time/adjunct (5 women). *Tuition:* Part-time $796 per credit. *Required fees:* $20; $752 per credit. One-time fee: $30 full-time. *Graduate housing:* On-campus housing not available. *Student services:* Campus employment opportunities, campus safety program, career counseling, disabled student services, exercise/wellness program, free psychological counseling, grant writing training, international student services, low-cost health insurance, multicultural affairs office, teacher training, writing training. *Library facilities:* Gordon Library. *Online resources:* library catalog, web page, access to other libraries' catalogs. *Collection:* 170,000 titles, 1,400 serial subscriptions. *Research affiliation:* Tufts University (veterinary medicine), University of Massachusetts Medical Center at Worcester, Alden Research Laboratory (hydraulics), Massachusetts Biotechnology Research Institute, Central Massachusetts Manufacturing Partnership, Manufacturing Assistance Center.

Computer facilities: 1,000 computers available on campus for general student use. A campuswide network can be accessed from student residence rooms and from off campus. Internet access and online class registration are available. *Web address:* http://www.wpi.edu/.

General Application Contact: Louise Campbell, Administrative Assistant, 508-831-5301, Fax: 508-831-5717, E-mail: gao@wpi.edu.

GRADUATE UNITS

Graduate Studies Students: 470 full-time (132 women), 361 part-time (92 women); includes 55 minority (8 African Americans, 37 Asian Americans or Pacific Islanders, 10 Hispanic Americans), 396 international. 1,569 applicants, 54% accepted, 279 enrolled. *Faculty:* 195 full-time (30 women), 35 part-time/adjunct (5 women). Expenses: Contact institution. *Financial support:* In 2001–02, 286 students received support, including 35 fellowships with full tuition reimbursements available (averaging $12,809 per year), 86 research assistantships with full and partial tuition reimbursements available (averaging $17,256 per year), 125 teaching assistantships with full and partial tuition reimbursements available (averaging $12,942 per year); career-related internships or fieldwork, institutionally sponsored loans, scholarships/grants, and tuition waivers (partial) also available. Financial award application deadline: 2/15; financial award applicants required to submit FAFSA. In 2001, 245 master's, 17 doctorates awarded. *Degree program information:* Part-time and evening/weekend programs available. Postbaccalaureate distance learning degree programs offered (minimal on-campus study). Offers applied mathematics (MS); applied statistics (MS); biochemistry (MS, PhD); biology (MS); biomedical engineering (M Eng, MS, PhD, Certificate); biomedical sciences (PhD); biotechnology (MS, PhD); chemical engineering (MS, PhD); chemistry (MS, PhD); civil and environmental engineering (M Eng, MS, PhD, Advanced Certificate, Certificate); clinical engineering (M Eng); computer science (MS, PhD, Advanced Certificate, Certificate); electrical and computer engineering (MS, PhD, Advanced Certificate, Certificate); engineering (M Eng, MBA, MME, MS, PhD, Advanced Certificate, Certificate); financial mathematics (MS); fire protection engineering (MS, PhD, Advanced Certificate, Certificate); industrial mathematics (MS); management (MBA, Certificate); manufacturing engineering (MS, PhD, Certificate); marketing and technological innovation (MS); materials science and engineering (MS, PhD, Certificate); mathematical science (PhD, Certificate); mathematics (MME); mechanical engineering (M Eng, MS, PhD, Advanced Certificate); operations and information technology (MS); physics (MS, PhD); power systems engineering (MS, PhD). *Application deadline:* For fall admission, 2/1 (priority date); for spring admission, 10/15 (priority date). Applications are processed on a rolling basis. *Application fee:* $60. Electronic applications accepted. *Application Contact:* Louise Campbell, Administrative Assistant, 508-831-5248, Fax: 508-831-5717, E-mail: gao@wpi.edu. *Director,* Jeanne M. Gosselin, 508-831-5301, Fax: 508-831-5717, E-mail: grad_admiss@wpi.edu.

See in-depth description on page 1313.

WORCESTER STATE COLLEGE, Worcester, MA 01602-2597

General Information State-supported, coed, comprehensive institution. *Enrollment:* 78 full-time matriculated graduate/professional students (67 women), 775 part-time matriculated graduate/professional students (545 women). *Enrollment by degree level:* 853 master's. *Graduate faculty:* 71 full-time (43 women), 24 part-time/adjunct (13 women). *Tuition:* Part-time $120 per credit hour. *Graduate housing:* On-campus housing not available. *Student services:* Campus safety program, career counseling, disabled student services, free psychological counseling, international student services, low-cost health insurance, multicultural affairs office, teacher training, writing training. *Library facilities:* Learning Resources Center. *Online resources:* library catalog, web page, access to other libraries' catalogs. *Collection:* 1,137 serial subscriptions, 11,963 audiovisual materials.

Computer facilities: 250 computers available on campus for general student use. A campuswide network can be accessed from student residence rooms. Internet access is available. *Web address:* http://www.worcester.edu/.

General Application Contact: Nicole Brown, Graduate Admissions Counselor, 508-929-8787, Fax: 508-929-8100, E-mail: nbrown@worcester.edu.

GRADUATE UNITS

Graduate Studies Students: 78 full-time (67 women), 775 part-time (545 women); includes 51 minority (18 African Americans, 9 Asian Americans or Pacific Islanders, 19 Hispanic Americans, 5 Native Americans), 6 international. Average age 37. 278 applicants, 61% accepted, 122 enrolled. *Faculty:* 71 full-time (43 women), 25 part-time/adjunct (14 women). Expenses: Contact institution. *Financial support:* In 2001–02, 54 students received support, including 10 research assistantships with full tuition reimbursements available (averaging $5,000 per year); career-related internships or fieldwork, Federal Work-Study, institutionally sponsored loans, scholarships/grants, and unspecified assistantships also available. Support available to part-time students. Financial award application deadline: 3/1; financial award applicants required to submit FAFSA. In 2001, 154 degrees awarded. *Degree program* *information:* Part-time and evening/weekend programs available. Offers biotechnology (MS); community health nursing (MS); early childhood education (M Ed); elementary education (M Ed); English (M Ed); health care administration (MS); health education (M Ed); history (M Ed); leadership and administration (M Ed); middle school education (M Ed, Certificate); non-profit management (MS); occupational therapy (MOT); reading (M Ed, Certificate); secondary education (M Ed, Certificate); speech-language pathology (MS); teacher education (M Ed). *Application fee:* $10 ($40 for international students). *Application Contact:* Andrea Wetmore, Graduate Admissions Counselor, 508-929-8120, Fax: 508-929-8100, E-mail: awetmore@worcester.edu. *Acting Dean of Graduate Studies and Continuing Education,* Dr. William H. White, 508-929-8125, Fax: 508-929-8100, E-mail: wwhite@worcester.edu.

WRIGHT INSTITUTE, Berkeley, CA 94704-1796

General Information Independent, coed, graduate-only institution. *Graduate housing:* On-campus housing not available.

GRADUATE UNITS

Graduate School of Psychology Offers psychology (Psy D).

WRIGHT STATE UNIVERSITY, Dayton, OH 45435

General Information State-supported, coed, university. CGS member. *Enrollment:* 1,556 full-time matriculated graduate/professional students (811 women), 1,946 part-time matriculated graduate/professional students (1,252 women). *Enrollment by degree level:* 343 first professional, 2,306 master's, 239 doctoral, 9 other advanced degrees. *Graduate faculty:* 749 full-time (232 women), 354 part-time/adjunct (195 women). Tuition, state resident: full-time $7,161; part-time $225 per quarter hour. Tuition, nonresident: full-time $12,324; part-time $385 per quarter hour. Tuition and fees vary according to course load, degree level and program. *Graduate housing:* Rooms and/or apartments available on a first-come, first-served basis to single students and available to married students. Typical cost: $3,798 per year ($5,193 including board) for single students; $5,970 per year for married students. *Student services:* Campus employment opportunities, campus safety program, career counseling, child daycare facilities, disabled student services, exercise/wellness program, free psychological counseling, grant writing training, international student services, low-cost health insurance, multicultural affairs office, teacher training, writing training. *Library facilities:* Paul Laurence Dunbar Library plus 2 others. *Online resources:* library catalog, web page. *Collection:* 695,805 titles, 5,312 serial subscriptions. *Research affiliation:* Wright-Patterson Air Force Base (research and development, systems and logistics), Wright-Patterson Air Force Base Medical Center, Veterans Administration Medical Center, Scott-Kettering Magnetic Resonance Research Laboratory (medical science), Edison Biotechnology Center, Edison Materials Technology Center (processing).

Computer facilities: 450 computers available on campus for general student use. A campuswide network can be accessed from student residence rooms and from off campus. *Web address:* http://www.wright.edu/.

General Application Contact: Gerald C. Malicki, Assistant Dean and Director of Graduate Admissions and Records, 937-775-2976, Fax: 937-775-2453, E-mail: jerry.malicki@wright.edu.

GRADUATE UNITS

School of Graduate Studies Students: 1,006 full-time (486 women), 1,322 part-time (854 women); includes 168 minority (113 African Americans, 32 Asian Americans or Pacific Islanders, 18 Hispanic Americans, 5 Native Americans), 365 international. Average age 31. 1,503 applicants, 75% accepted. *Faculty:* 735 full-time (226 women), 348 part-time/adjunct (155 women). Expenses: Contact institution. *Financial support:* In 2001–02, 300 fellowships with full tuition reimbursements, 170 research assistantships with full tuition reimbursements, 141 teaching assistantships with full tuition reimbursements were awarded. Career-related internships or fieldwork, Federal Work-Study, institutionally sponsored loans, tuition waivers (full and partial), and unspecified assistantships also available. Support available to part-time students. Financial award applicants required to submit FAFSA. In 2001, 981 master's, 9 doctorates, 1 other advanced degree awarded. *Degree program information:* Part-time and evening/weekend programs available. Offers interdisciplinary studies (MA, MS). *Application deadline:* Applications are processed on a rolling basis. *Application fee:* $25. Electronic applications accepted. *Application Contact:* Gerald C. Malicki, Assistant Dean and Director of Graduate Admissions and Records, 937-775-2976, Fax: 937-775-2453, E-mail: jerry.malicki@wright.edu. *Dean and Associate Provost for Research,* Dr. Joseph F. Thomas, 937-775-3336, Fax: 937-775-2357, E-mail: jay.thomas@wright.edu.

College of Education and Human Services Students: 180 full-time (140 women), 627 part-time (509 women); includes 41 minority (36 African Americans, 2 Asian Americans or Pacific Islanders, 2 Hispanic Americans, 1 Native American), 2 international. Average age 34. 301 applicants, 95% accepted. Expenses: Contact institution. *Financial support:* In 2001–02, 40 fellowships with full tuition reimbursements were awarded; research assistantships, teaching assistantships, career-related internships or fieldwork, Federal Work-Study, institutionally sponsored loans, tuition waivers (full and partial), and unspecified assistantships also available. Support available to part-time students. Financial award applicants required to submit FAFSA. In 2001, 394 master's, 1 other advanced degree awarded. *Degree program information:* Part-time and evening/weekend programs available. Offers advanced curriculum and instruction (Ed S); advanced educational leadership (Ed S); business education (M Ed, MA); business, technology, and vocational education (M Ed, MA); chemical dependency (MRC); classroom teacher education (M Ed, MA); computer/technology education (M Ed, MA); counseling (M Ed, MA, MS); early childhood education (M Ed, MA); education and human services (M Ed, MA, MRC, MS, Ed S); educational administrative specialist: teacher leader (M Ed, MA); educational administrative specialist: vocational education administration (M Ed, MA); educational leadership (M Ed, MA); gifted educational needs (M Ed, MA); health, physical education, and recreation (M Ed, MA); higher education-adult education (Ed S); intervention specialist (M Ed, MA); library/media (M Ed, MA); mild to moderate educational needs (M Ed, MA); moderate to intensive educational needs (M Ed, MA); pupil personnel services (M Ed, MA); rehabilitation counseling (MRC); severe disabilities (MRC); student affairs in higher education-administration (M Ed, MA); superintendent (Ed S); vocational education (M Ed, MA). *Application fee:* $25. *Application Contact:* Gerald C. Malicki, Assistant Dean and Director of Graduate Admissions and Records, 937-775-2976, Fax: 937-775-2453, E-mail: jerry.malicki@wright.edu. *Dean,* Dr. Gregory R. Bernhardt, 937-775-2822, Fax: 937-775-4855, E-mail: gregory.bernhardt@wright.edu.

College of Engineering and Computer Science Students: 310 full-time (66 women), 120 part-time (22 women); includes 28 minority (10 African Americans, 14 Asian Americans or Pacific Islanders, 4 Hispanic Americans), 248 international. Average age 29. 958 applicants, 75% accepted. Expenses: Contact institution. *Financial support:* In 2001–02, 65 fellowships with full tuition reimbursements, 81 research assistantships with full tuition reimbursements, 31 teaching assistantships with full tuition reimbursements were awarded. Federal Work-Study, institutionally sponsored loans, tuition waivers (full and partial), and unspecified assistantships also available. Support available to part-time students. Financial award applicants required to submit FAFSA. In 2001, 169 master's, 4 doctorates awarded. *Degree program information:* Part-time and evening/weekend programs available. Offers biomedical and human factors engineering (MSE); biomedical engineering (MSE); computer engineering (MSCE); computer science (MS); computer science and engineering (PhD); electrical engineering (MSE); engineering (PhD); engineering and computer science (MS, MSCE, MSE, PhD); human factors engineering (MSE); materials science and engineering (MSE); mechanical and materials engineering (MSE); mechanical engineering (MSE). *Application fee:* $25. *Dean and Director, Engineering Ph.D. Program,* Dr. James E. Brandeberry, 937-775-5001, Fax: 937-775-5009, E-mail: james.brandeberry@wright.edu.

College of Liberal Arts Students: 98 full-time (66 women), 80 part-time (49 women); includes 20 minority (17 African Americans, 2 Hispanic Americans, 1 Native American), 5 international. Average age 33. 113 applicants, 95% accepted. Expenses: Contact institution. *Financial support:* In 2001–02, 34 fellowships with full tuition reimbursements, 12 research assistantships with full tuition reimbursements, 30 teaching assistantships with full tuition reimbursements were awarded. Federal Work-Study, institutionally sponsored loans, and unspecified assistantships also available. Support available to part-time students. Financial award applicants required to submit FAFSA. In 2001, 73 degrees awarded. *Degree program information:* Part-time programs available. Offers composition and rhetoric (MA); criminal justice and social problems (MA); English (MA); history (MA); humanities (M Hum); international and comparative politics (MA); liberal arts (M Hum, M Mus, MA, MPA); literature (MA); music education (M Mus); teaching English to speakers of other languages (MA); urban administration (MPA). *Application fee:* $25. *Dean,* Dr. Mary Ellen Mazey, 937-775-2225, Fax: 937-775-2707, E-mail: mary.mazey@wright.edu.

College of Nursing and Health Students: 46 full-time (45 women), 124 part-time (117 women); includes 16 minority (13 African Americans, 1 Asian American or Pacific Islander, 2 Hispanic Americans) Average age 39. 45 applicants, 100% accepted. Expenses: Contact institution. *Financial support:* In 2001–02, 15 fellowships with full tuition reimbursements were awarded; research assistantships, teaching assistantships, Federal Work-Study, institutionally sponsored loans, and unspecified assistantships also available. Support available to part-time students. Financial award application deadline: 6/1; financial award applicants required to submit FAFSA. In 2001, 64 degrees awarded. *Degree program information:* Part-time and evening/weekend programs available. Offers acute care nurse practitioner (MS); administration of nursing and health care systems (MS); adult health (MS); child and adolescent health (MS); community health (MS); family nurse practitioner (MS); nurse practitioner (MS); nursing and health (MS); school nurse (MS). *Application deadline:* For fall admission, 4/15 (priority date). *Application fee:* $25. *Application Contact:* Theresa A. Haghnazarian, Director of Student and Alumni Affairs, 937-775-2592, Fax: 937-775-4571, E-mail: theresa.haghnazarian@wright.edu. *Dean,* Dr. Patricia A. Martin, 937-775-3131, Fax: 937-775-4571, E-mail: patricia.martin@wright.edu.

College of Science and Mathematics Students: 231 full-time (110 women), 69 part-time (32 women); includes 26 minority (14 African Americans, 7 Asian Americans or Pacific Islanders, 3 Hispanic Americans, 2 Native Americans), 37 international. Average age 29. 337 applicants, 50% accepted. Expenses: Contact institution. *Financial support:* In 2001–02, 84 fellowships with full tuition reimbursements, 73 research assistantships with full tuition reimbursements, 77 teaching assistantships with full tuition reimbursements were awarded. Career-related internships or fieldwork, Federal Work-Study, institutionally sponsored loans, tuition waivers (full and partial), and unspecified assistantships also available. Support available to part-time students. Financial award applicants required to submit FAFSA. In 2001, 106 master's, 9 doctorates awarded. *Degree program information:* Part-time and evening/weekend programs available. Offers anatomy (MS); applied mathematics (MS); applied statistics (MS); biochemistry and molecular biology (MS); biological sciences (MS); biomedical sciences (PhD); chemistry (MS); earth science education (MST); environmental geochemistry (MS); environmental geology (MS); environmental sciences (MS); geological sciences (MS); geophysics (MS); human factors and industrial/organizational psychology (MS, PhD); hydrogeology (MS); mathematics (MS); medical physics (MS); microbiology and immunology (MS); petroleum geology (MS); physics (MS); physics education (MST); physiology and biophysics (MS); science and mathematics (MS, MST, PhD). *Application fee:* $25. *Dean,* Dr. Michele Wheatly, 937-775-2611, Fax: 937-775-3068, E-mail: michele.wheatly@wright.edu.

Raj Soin College of Business Students: 137 full-time (59 women), 297 part-time (125 women); includes 35 minority (21 African Americans, 8 Asian Americans or Pacific Islanders, 5 Hispanic Americans, 1 Native American), 71 international. Average age 30. 230 applicants, 89% accepted. Expenses: Contact institution. *Financial support:* In 2001–02, 32 fellowships with full tuition reimbursements, 1 research assistantship with full tuition reimbursement, 3 teaching assistantships with full tuition reimbursements were awarded. Career-related internships or fieldwork, Federal Work-Study, institutionally sponsored loans, and unspecified assistantships also available. Support available to part-time students. Financial award applicants required to submit FAFSA. In 2001, 168 degrees awarded. *Degree program information:* Part-time and evening/weekend programs available. Offers accountancy (M Acc); business (M Acc, MBA, MS); business economics (MBA); e-commerce (MBA); finance (MBA); international business (MBA); logistics management (MBA); management (MBA); management information systems (MBA); marketing (MBA); operations management (MBA); project management (MBA); social and applied economics (MS). *Application fee:* $25. *Application Contact:* Mike Evans, Graduate Director, 937-775-2437, Fax: 937-775-3545, E-mail: michael.evans@wright.edu. *Dean,* Dr. Berkwood Farmer, 937-775-3242, Fax: 937-775-3545.

School of Medicine Students: 344 full-time (184 women), 8 part-time (2 women); includes 64 minority (50 African Americans, 9 Asian Americans or Pacific Islanders, 5 Hispanic Americans), 2 international. Average age 24. *Faculty:* 135 full-time (34 women), 17 part-time/adjunct (1 woman). Expenses: Contact institution. *Financial support:* In 2001–02, 3 research assistantships with full tuition reimbursements were awarded; fellowships, teaching assistantships, unspecified assistantships also available. Financial award applicants required to submit FAFSA. In 2001, 76 first professional degrees, 7 master's awarded. Offers aerospace medicine (MS); medicine (MD, MS, PhD); pharmacology and toxicology (MS). *Application Contact:* Dr. Paul G. Carlson, Associate Dean for Student Affairs and Admissions, 937-775-2934, Fax: 937-775-3672, E-mail: paul.carlson@wright.edu. *Dean,* Dr. Howard Part, 937-775-3010, Fax: 937-775-3672, E-mail: howard.part@wright.edu.

School of Professional Psychology Students: 105 full-time (72 women), 2 part-time (1 woman); includes 30 minority (20 African Americans, 3 Asian Americans or Pacific Islanders, 7 Hispanic Americans), 9 international. Average age 29. *Faculty:* 21 full-time (5 women), 2 part-time/adjunct (1 woman). Expenses: Contact institution. *Financial support:* In 2001–02, 30 fellowships with full tuition reimbursements were awarded; teaching assistantships, career-related internships or fieldwork, Federal Work-Study, institutionally sponsored loans, and unspecified assistantships also available. Financial award application deadline: 4/15; financial award applicants required to submit FAFSA. In 2001, 20 degrees awarded. Offers clinical psychology (Psy D). *Application deadline:* For fall admission, 12/15. *Application fee:* $30. *Application Contact:* Leona L. Gray, Director, Student Services/Admissions, 937-775-3492, Fax: 937-775-3493, E-mail: leona.gray@wright.edu. *Dean,* Dr. John R. Rusisill, 937-775-3490, Fax: 937-775-3434, E-mail: john.rudisill@wright.edu.

WYCLIFFE COLLEGE, Toronto, ON M5S 1H7, Canada

General Information Independent-religious, coed, graduate-only institution. *Enrollment by degree level:* 55 first professional, 76 master's, 40 doctoral, 7 other advanced degrees. *Graduate faculty:* 10 full-time (1 woman), 8 part-time/adjunct (2 women). *Graduate tuition:* Tuition and fees charges are reported in Canadian dollars. *Tuition:* Part-time $423 Canadian dollars per course. *Required fees:* $7 Canadian dollars per course. $66 Canadian dollars per semester. *Graduate housing:* Rooms and/or apartments guaranteed to single students and available on a first-come, first-served basis to married students. Typical cost: $6,250 Canadian dollars (including board) for single students; $8,000 Canadian dollars per year for married students. Housing application deadline: 5/1. *Student services:* Campus employment opportunities, career counseling, free psychological counseling, international student services, low-cost health insurance. *Library facilities:* Graham Library plus 50 others. *Online resources:* library catalog, web page, access to other libraries' catalogs. *Collection:* 30,000 titles, 120 serial subscriptions, 237 audiovisual materials.

Computer facilities: 4 computers available on campus for general student use. A campuswide network can be accessed from off campus. Internet access and online class registration are available. *Web address:* http://www.chass.utoronto.ca/wycliffe/.

General Application Contact: Marie Soderlund, Registrar, 416-946-3530, Fax: 416-946-3545, E-mail: wycliffe.registrar@utoronto.ca.

GRADUATE UNITS

Division of Advanced Degree Studies Students: 39 full-time (8 women), 13 part-time (3 women); includes 9 minority (1 African American, 8 Asian Americans or Pacific Islanders), 6 international. Average age 35. 29 applicants, 114% accepted. *Faculty:* 6 full-time (1 woman), 1 (woman) part-time/adjunct. Expenses: Contact institution. *Financial support:* In 2001–02, 3 fellowships (averaging $20,000 per year), 2 research assistantships (averaging $5,500 per year), 10 teaching assistantships (averaging $5,500 per year) were awarded. Scholarships/grants and bursaries also available. Support available to part-time students. Financial award application deadline: 5/1. In 2001, 2 master's, 5 doctorates awarded. *Degree program*

Wycliffe College (continued)

information: Part-time programs available. Offers theology (MA, Th M, D Min, PhD, Th D). *Application deadline:* For fall admission, 1/15 (priority date). *Application fee:* $100. *Application Contact:* Paula Thomas, Recruitment, Admissions Officer, 416-946-3525, Fax: 416-946-3545, E-mail: pj.thomas@utoronto.ca. *Director*, Dr. Terence Donaldson, 416-946-3537, Fax: 416-946-3545, E-mail: terry.donaldson@utoronto.ca.

Division of Basic Degree Studies Students: 54 full-time (20 women), 73 part-time (41 women); includes 22 minority (6 African Americans, 14 Asian Americans or Pacific Islanders, 1 Hispanic American, 1 Native American), 2 international. Average age 37. 48 applicants, 79% accepted. *Faculty:* 10 full-time (1 woman), 8 part-time/adjunct (2 women). Expenses: Contact institution. *Financial support:* In 2001–02, 52 students received support. Career-related internships or fieldwork, scholarships/grants, and bursaries available. Support available to part-time students. Financial award application deadline: 5/1. In 2001, 11 first professional degrees, 7 master's awarded. *Degree program information:* Part-time programs available. Offers Christian Studies (Diploma). *Application deadline:* For fall admission, 5/1; for winter admission, 11/1. *Application fee:* $0. *Application Contact:* Paula Thomas, Recruitment, Admissions Officer, 416-946-3525, Fax: 416-946-3545, E-mail: pj.thomas@utoronto.ca. *Director*, Dr. Marion Taylor, 416-946-3542, Fax: 416-946-3545, E-mail: m.taylor@utoronto.ca.

XAVIER UNIVERSITY, Cincinnati, OH 45207

General Information Independent-religious, coed, comprehensive institution. *Enrollment:* 579 full-time matriculated graduate/professional students (331 women), 1,467 part-time matriculated graduate/professional students (738 women). *Enrollment by degree level:* 1,961 master's, 85 doctoral. *Graduate faculty:* 112 full-time (45 women), 96 part-time/adjunct (47 women). *Tuition:* Part-time $450 per hour. *Graduate housing:* Rooms and/or apartments available to single and married students. Typical cost: $1,860 per year ($3,360 including board) for single students; $1,955 per year ($3,545 including board) for married students. Room and board charges vary according to board plan and housing facility selected. *Student services:* Campus employment opportunities, campus safety program, career counseling, disabled student services, exercise/wellness program, free psychological counseling, international student services, low-cost health insurance, multicultural affairs office, teacher training, writing training. *Library facilities:* McDonald Library plus 1 other. *Online resources:* library catalog, web page, access to other libraries' catalogs. *Collection:* 200,044 titles, 1,586 serial subscriptions, 4,292 audiovisual materials.

Computer facilities: 200 computers available on campus for general student use. A campuswide network can be accessed from student residence rooms and from off campus. Internet access is available. *Web address:* http://www.xu.edu/.

General Application Contact: John Cooper, Director of Graduate Services, 513-745-3357, Fax: 513-745-1048, E-mail: xugrad@xu.edu.

GRADUATE UNITS

College of Arts and Sciences Students: 6 full-time (2 women), 76 part-time (54 women); includes 8 minority (5 African Americans, 2 Hispanic Americans, 1 Native American) Average age 36. 44 applicants, 66% accepted. *Faculty:* 25 full-time (11 women). Expenses: Contact institution. *Financial support:* In 2001–02, 55 students received support, including 16 teaching assistantships with full tuition reimbursements available (averaging $1,500 per year); career-related internships or fieldwork, scholarships/grants, tuition waivers (partial), and unspecified assistantships also available. Support available to part-time students. In 2001, 9 degrees awarded. *Degree program information:* Part-time and evening/weekend programs available. Offers arts and sciences (MA); English (MA); humanities (MA); theology (MA). *Application deadline:* For fall admission, 8/15 (priority date). Applications are processed on a rolling basis. *Application fee:* $35. Electronic applications accepted. *Application Contact:* John Cooper, Director of Graduate Services, 513-745-3357, Fax: 513-745-1048, E-mail: xugrad@xu.edu. *Dean*, Dr. Janice B. Walker, 513-745-3101, Fax: 513-754-1099, E-mail: walker@xu.edu.

College of Social Sciences Students: 384 full-time (273 women), 607 part-time (440 women); includes 111 minority (86 African Americans, 12 Asian Americans or Pacific Islanders, 11 Hispanic Americans, 2 Native Americans), 6 international. Average age 32. 625 applicants, 61% accepted. *Faculty:* 52 full-time (27 women), 73 part-time/adjunct (40 women). Expenses: Contact institution. *Financial support:* In 2001–02, 659 students received support, including 24 research assistantships (averaging $1,500 per year), 48 teaching assistantships (averaging $1,500 per year); career-related internships or fieldwork, scholarships/grants, traineeships, and residency stipends also available. Support available to part-time students. In 2001, 418 degrees awarded. *Degree program information:* Part-time and evening/weekend programs available. Offers agency and community counseling (M Ed); clinical psychology (Psy D); community counseling (M Ed, MA); criminal justice (MS); educational administration (M Ed); elementary education (M Ed); forensic nursing (MSN); health services administration (MHSA); healthcare law (MSN); human resource development (M Ed); Montessori (M Ed); multicultural literature for children (M Ed); nursing administration (MSN); psychology (MA); reading specialist (M Ed); school counseling (M Ed); school nursing (MSN); secondary education (M Ed); social sciences (M Ed, MA, MHSA, MS, MSN, Psy D, Certificate); special education (M Ed); sport administration (M Ed). *Application fee:* $35. *Application Contact:* John Cooper, Director of Graduate Services, 513-745-3357, Fax: 513-745-1048, E-mail: xugrad@xu.edu. *Dean*, Dr. Neil Heighberger, 513-745-3119, Fax: 513-745-1058, E-mail: heighber@xu.edu.

Williams College of Business Students: 189 full-time (56 women), 784 part-time (244 women); includes 85 minority (34 African Americans, 34 Asian Americans or Pacific Islanders, 13 Hispanic Americans, 4 Native Americans), 57 international. Average age 30. 471 applicants, 63% accepted, 227 enrolled. *Faculty:* 51 full-time (19 women), 23 part-time/adjunct (7 women). Expenses: Contact institution. *Financial support:* In 2001–02, 120 students received support, including 29 research assistantships with full and partial tuition reimbursements available (averaging $1,800 per year); career-related internships or fieldwork and scholarships/grants also available. Support available to part-time students. Financial award application deadline: 4/1. In 2001, 357 degrees awarded. *Degree program information:* Part-time and evening/weekend programs available. Offers accounting (MBA); business (Exec MBA, MBA); business administration (Exec MBA, MBA); e-commerce (MBA); entrepreneurship (MBA); finance (MBA); human resources (MBA); international business (MBA); management information systems (MBA); marketing (MBA). *Application deadline:* For fall admission, 8/1 (priority date); for winter admission, 12/1 (priority date); for spring admission, 4/1 (priority date). Applications are processed on a rolling basis. *Application fee:* $35. Electronic applications accepted. *Application Contact:* Jennifer Bush, Director of Enrollment Services, 513-745-3525, Fax: 513-745-2929, E-mail: xumba@xu.edu. *Dean*, Dr. Michael Webb, 513-745-3528, Fax: 513-745-2929, E-mail: webbm@xu.edu.

XAVIER UNIVERSITY OF LOUISIANA, New Orleans, LA 70125-1098

General Information Independent-religious, coed, comprehensive institution. CGS member. *Enrollment:* 746 full-time matriculated graduate/professional students (536 women), 116 part-time matriculated graduate/professional students (96 women). *Enrollment by degree level:* 470 first professional, 392 master's. *Graduate faculty:* 39 full-time (13 women), 76 part-time/adjunct (32 women). *Tuition:* Part-time $200 per hour. *Required fees:* $200 per semester. Tuition and fees vary according to program. *Graduate housing:* On-campus housing not available. *Student services:* Career counseling, child daycare facilities, disabled student services, exercise/wellness program, free psychological counseling, low-cost health insurance, teacher training. *Library facilities:* Xavier Library plus 1 other. *Collection:* 108,583 titles, 2,339 serial subscriptions, 4,984 audiovisual materials.

Computer facilities: 250 computers available on campus for general student use. A campuswide network can be accessed from student residence rooms and from off campus. *Web address:* http://www.xula.edu/.

General Application Contact: Marlene C. Robinson, Director of Graduate Admissions, 504-483-7487, Fax: 504-485-7921, E-mail: mrobinso@xula.edu.

GRADUATE UNITS

College of Pharmacy Students: 460 full-time (327 women), 10 part-time (6 women); includes 349 minority (283 African Americans, 60 Asian Americans or Pacific Islanders, 5 Hispanic Americans, 1 Native American), 34 international. Average age 33. 298 applicants, 49% accepted. *Faculty:* 34 full-time (11 women), 4 part-time/adjunct (0 women). Expenses: Contact institution. *Financial support:* Career-related internships or fieldwork, Federal Work-Study, institutionally sponsored loans, and scholarships/grants available. Support available to part-time students. Financial award application deadline: 4/1; financial award applicants required to submit FAFSA. In 2001, 115 degrees awarded. Offers pharmacy (Pharm D). *Application deadline:* For fall admission, 12/15. *Application fee:* $25. *Application Contact:* Cathy Jones, Admissions Counselor, 504-483-7427, Fax: 504-485-7930, E-mail: cjjones@xula.edu. *Dean*, Dr. Wayne T. Harris, 504-483-7421, Fax: 504-485-7930, E-mail: wharris@xula.edu/.

Graduate School Students: 286 full-time (209 women), 106 part-time (90 women); includes 335 minority (330 African Americans, 2 Asian Americans or Pacific Islanders, 3 Hispanic Americans) Average age 31. 60 applicants, 97% accepted, 58 enrolled. *Faculty:* 5 full-time (2 women), 72 part-time/adjunct (32 women). Expenses: Contact institution. *Financial support:* Career-related internships or fieldwork, scholarships/grants, and tuition waivers (partial) available. Support available to part-time students. In 2001, 102 degrees awarded. *Degree program information:* Part-time and evening/weekend programs available. Offers administration and supervision (MA); curriculum and instruction (MA); guidance and counseling (MA); nurse anesthesiology (MS). *Application deadline:* For fall admission, 7/1; for spring admission, 12/1. Applications are processed on a rolling basis. *Application fee:* $30. *Application Contact:* Marlene C. Robinson, Director of Graduate Admissions, 504-483-7487, Fax: 504-485-7921, E-mail: mrobinso@xula.edu. *Dean*, Dr. Alvin J. Richard, 504-483-7487, Fax: 504-485-7921, E-mail: arichard@xula.edu.

Institute for Black Catholic Studies Students: 36 full-time (18 women); includes 30 minority (28 African Americans, 1 Asian American or Pacific Islander, 1 Hispanic American) *Faculty:* 10 part-time/adjunct (5 women). Expenses: Contact institution. *Financial support:* Career-related internships or fieldwork and scholarships/grants available. In 2001, 1 degree awarded. *Degree program information:* Part-time programs available. Offers pastoral theology (Th M). *Application deadline:* For fall admission, 7/1; for spring admission, 12/1. Applications are processed on a rolling basis. *Application fee:* $65. *Application Contact:* Marlene C. Robinson, Director of Graduate Admissions, 504-483-7487, Fax: 504-485-7921, E-mail: mrobinso@xula.edu. *Director*, Sr. Eva Regina Martin, 504-483-7691, Fax: 504-485-7921.

YALE UNIVERSITY, New Haven, CT 06520

General Information Independent, coed, university. CGS member. *Enrollment:* 5,420 full-time matriculated graduate/professional students, 184 part-time matriculated graduate/professional students. *Graduate faculty:* 3,330. *Graduate housing:* Rooms and/or apartments available on a first-come, first-served basis to single and married students. Housing application deadline: 6/1. *Student services:* Campus employment opportunities, campus safety program, career counseling, disabled student services, free psychological counseling, international student services, low-cost health insurance. *Library facilities:* Sterling Memorial Library plus 20 others. *Online resources:* library catalog, web page, access to other libraries' catalogs. *Collection:* 10.8 million titles, 57,377 serial subscriptions. *Research affiliation:* Howard Hughes Medical Institute, J. B. Pierce Foundation (environmental physiology), Haskins Laboratories (speech, hearing, reading).

Computer facilities: 350 computers available on campus for general student use. A campuswide network can be accessed from student residence rooms and from off campus. *Web address:* http://www.yale.edu/.

General Application Contact: Admissions Information, 203-432-2772, E-mail: graduate.admissions@yale.edu.

GRADUATE UNITS

Divinity School Students: 388 (179 women); includes 40 minority (24 African Americans, 10 Asian Americans or Pacific Islanders, 5 Hispanic Americans, 1 Native American) 47 international. Average age 30. 469 applicants, 65% accepted, 142 enrolled. *Faculty:* 36 full-time (10 women), 15 part-time/adjunct (5 women). Expenses: Contact institution. *Financial support:* In 2001–02, 304 students received support, including 304 fellowships (averaging $8,000 per year); career-related internships or fieldwork, Federal Work-Study, institutionally sponsored loans, and scholarships/grants also available. Support available to part-time students. Financial award application deadline: 3/1; financial award applicants required to submit FAFSA. In 2001, 65 first professional degrees, 60 master's awarded. *Degree program information:* Part-time programs available. Offers divinity (M Div, MAR, STM). *Application deadline:* For fall admission, 2/1 (priority date); for spring admission, 10/15. *Application fee:* $75. *Application Contact:* Anna T. Ramirez, Associate Dean of Admissions and Financial Aid, 203-432-9802, Fax: 203-432-7475, E-mail: anna.ramirez@yale.edu. *Dean*, Dr. Harold W. Attridge, 203-432-5306, Fax: 203-432-9712, E-mail: harold.attridge@yale.edu.

Graduate School of Arts and Sciences *Degree program information:* Part-time programs available. Offers African studies (MA); African-American studies (MA, PhD); American studies (MA, PhD); anthropology (MA, PhD); applied mathematics (M Phil, MS, PhD); applied mechanics and mechanical engineering (M Phil, MS, PhD); applied physics (MS, PhD); archaeological studies (MA); arts and sciences (M Phil, MA, MS, PhD); astronomy (MS, PhD); biophysical chemistry (PhD); cell biology (PhD); cellular and molecular physiology (PhD); chemical engineering (MS, PhD); classics (PhD); comparative literature (PhD); computer science (PhD); developmental biology (PhD); East Asian languages and literatures (PhD); East Asian studies (MA); ecology and evolutionary biology (PhD); economics (PhD); electrical engineering (MS, PhD); English language and literature (MA, PhD); environmental sciences (PhD); experimental pathology (PhD); forestry (PhD); French (MA, PhD); genetics (PhD); geochemistry (PhD); geophysics (PhD); Germanic language and literature (MA, PhD); history (MA, PhD); history of art (PhD); history of medicine and the life sciences (MS, PhD); immunobiology (PhD); inorganic chemistry (PhD); international and development economics (MA); international relations (MA); Italian language and literature (PhD); linguistics (PhD); mathematics (MS, PhD); mechanical engineering (M Phil, MS, PhD); medieval studies (MA, PhD); meteorology (PhD); mineralogy and crystallography (PhD); molecular biology (PhD); molecular biophysics and biochemistry (MS, PhD); music (MA, PhD); Near Eastern languages and civilizations (MA, PhD); neurobiology (PhD); neuroscience (PhD); oceanography (PhD); organic chemistry (PhD); paleoecology (PhD); paleontology and stratigraphy (PhD); petrology (PhD); pharmacology (PhD); philosophy (PhD); physical chemistry (PhD); physics (PhD); plant sciences (PhD); political science (PhD); psychology (MS, PhD); religious studies (PhD); Renaissance studies (PhD); Russian and East European studies (MA); Slavic languages and literatures (MA, PhD); sociology (PhD); Spanish and Portuguese (MA, PhD); statistics (MS, PhD); structural geology (PhD).

School of Architecture Students: 172 full-time (61 women); includes 27 minority (3 African Americans, 16 Asian Americans or Pacific Islanders, 8 Hispanic Americans), 42 international. 504 applicants, 36% accepted, 77 enrolled. *Faculty:* 4 full-time (1 woman), 37 part-time/adjunct (11 women). Expenses: Contact institution. *Financial support:* In 2001–02, 126 students received support; fellowships, teaching assistantships, Federal Work-Study and institutionally sponsored loans available. Financial award application deadline: 2/1. In 2001, 57 degrees awarded. Offers architecture (M Arch, M Env Des). *Application deadline:* For fall admission, 1/3. *Application fee:* $70. *Application Contact:* 203-432-2291, Fax: 203-432-7175. *Dean*, Robert A. M. Stern, 203-432-2279, Fax: 203-432-7175.

School of Art Students: 119 full-time (67 women); includes 24 minority (5 African Americans, 14 Asian Americans or Pacific Islanders, 4 Hispanic Americans, 1 Native American), 19 international. Average age 27. 863 applicants, 8% accepted, 58 enrolled. *Faculty:* 13 full-time (4 women), 81 part-time/adjunct (33 women). Expenses: Contact institution. *Financial support:* In 2001–02, 90 students received support, including 55 teaching assistantships (averaging $1,500 per year); Federal Work-Study and scholarships/grants also available. Financial award application deadline: 3/1; financial award applicants required to submit FAFSA. In 2001, 55 degrees awarded. Offers graphic design (MFA); painting/printmaking (MFA); photography (MFA); sculpture (MFA). *Application deadline:* For fall admission, 1/15. *Application fee:* $75. *Application Contact:* Patricia Ann DeChiara, Director of Academic Affairs,

203-432-2600, E-mail: artschool.info@yale.edu. *Dean,* Richard Benson, 203-432-2606, E-mail: barbara.shanley@yale.edu.

School of Drama Students: 179 full-time (101 women); includes 29 minority (11 African Americans, 9 Asian Americans or Pacific Islanders, 7 Hispanic Americans, 2 Native Americans), 20 international. Average age 29. 1,082 applicants, 7% accepted, 65 enrolled. *Faculty:* 71 part-time/adjunct (27 women). Expenses: Contact institution. *Financial support:* In 2001–02, 179 students received support. Career-related internships or fieldwork, Federal Work-Study, and scholarships/grants available. Financial award application deadline: 2/15; financial award applicants required to submit FAFSA. In 2001, 66 master's, 2 doctorates awarded. Offers drama (MFA, DFA, Certificate). *Application deadline:* For fall admission, 1/15. *Application fee:* $60. *Application Contact:* Registrar's Office, 203-432-1507, Fax: 203-432-9668. *Dean/Artistic Director,* James Bundy, 203-432-1505.

School of Forestry and Environmental Studies *Degree program information:* Part-time programs available. Offers forestry and environmental studies (MES, MF, MFS, DFES, PhD).

School of Medicine Students: 497 full-time (234 women); includes 229 minority (46 African Americans, 139 Asian Americans or Pacific Islanders, 39 Hispanic Americans, 5 Native Americans), 24 international. Average age 24. 2,469 applicants, 8% accepted. *Faculty:* 1,349 full-time (405 women), 1,850 part-time/adjunct (555 women). Expenses: Contact institution. *Financial support:* In 2001–02, 387 students received support. Institutionally sponsored loans and scholarships/grants available. Financial award application deadline: 4/1; financial award applicants required to submit FAFSA. In 2001, 108 degrees awarded. *Degree program information:* Part-time programs available. Offers medicine (MD, MMS, MPH, MS, PhD); physician associate (MMS). *Application deadline:* For fall admission, 11/1. *Application fee:* $65. Electronic applications accepted. *Application Contact:* Richard A. Silverman, Director of Admissions, 203-785-2643, Fax: 203-785-3234, E-mail: medical.admissions@yale.edu. *Dean,* Dr. David A. Kessler, 203-785-4672, Fax: 203-785-7437.

Combined Program in Biological and Biomedical Sciences (BBS) Students: 66 full-time. 799 applicants, 25% accepted, 66 enrolled. *Faculty:* 250 full-time. Expenses: Contact institution. *Financial support:* In 2001–02, 66 students received support, including fellowships with full tuition reimbursements available (averaging $21,000 per year), research assistantships with full tuition reimbursements available (averaging $21,000 per year), teaching assistantships with full tuition reimbursements available (averaging $21,000 per year) Offers bioinformatics and computational biology (PhD); biological and biomedical sciences (PhD); cell biology and molecular physiology (PhD); genetics, development, and molecular biology (PhD); immunology (PhD); microbiology (PhD); molecular biophysics and biochemistry (PhD); molecular cell biology, genetics, and development (PhD); neuroscience (PhD); pharmacological sciences and molecular medicine (PhD); physiology and integrative medical biology (PhD). *Application deadline:* For fall admission, 1/2. *Application fee:* $80. Electronic applications accepted. *Application Contact:* Dr. John Alvaro, Administrative Director, 203-785-3735, Fax: 203-785-3734, E-mail: bbs@yale.edu. *Director,* Dr. Lynn Cooley, 203-785-5067, E-mail: bbs@yale.edu.

School of Public Health Students: 283 full-time, 10 part-time; includes 78 minority (12 African Americans, 56 Asian Americans or Pacific Islanders, 10 Hispanic Americans), 41 international. Average age 27. 390 applicants, 74% accepted, 122 enrolled. *Faculty:* 55 full-time (24 women), 39 part-time/adjunct (9 women). Expenses: Contact institution. *Financial support:* In 2001–02, 21 fellowships with full tuition reimbursements (averaging $12,560 per year), 4 research assistantships with full tuition reimbursements (averaging $24,910 per year) were awarded. Teaching assistantships with full tuition reimbursements, career-related internships or fieldwork, Federal Work-Study, institutionally sponsored loans, scholarships/grants, and tuition waivers (full and partial) also available. Support available to part-time students. Financial award application deadline: 4/1; financial award applicants required to submit FAFSA. In 2001, 104 master's, 12 doctorates awarded. *Degree program information:* Part-time programs available. Offers biostatistics (MPH, MS, PhD); chronic disease epidemiology (MPH, PhD); environmental health (MPH, PhD); epidemiology of microbial diseases (MPH, PhD); global health (MPH); health policy and administration (MPH, PhD); parasitology (PhD). MS and PhD offered through the Graduate School. *Application deadline:* Applications are processed on a rolling basis. *Application fee:* $60. *Application Contact:* Jacqui Comshaw, Director of Admissions, 203-785-2844, Fax: 203-785-4845, E-mail: eph.admissions@yale.edu. *Dean and Chairman,* Dr. Michael H. Merson, 203-785-2867, Fax: 203-785-6103, E-mail: michael.merson@yale.edu.

School of Music Students: 208 full-time (104 women); includes 31 minority (2 African Americans, 21 Asian Americans or Pacific Islanders, 8 Hispanic Americans), 74 international. Average age 23. 540 applicants, 22% accepted, 76 enrolled. *Faculty:* 21 full-time (5 women), 32 part-time/adjunct (5 women). Expenses: Contact institution. *Financial support:* In 2001–02, 179 students received support, including 179 fellowships (averaging $13,900 per year); Federal Work-Study and institutionally sponsored loans also available. Financial award application deadline: 2/28; financial award applicants required to submit FAFSA. In 2001, 81 master's, 7 doctorates, 5 other advanced degrees awarded. Offers music (MM, MMA, DMA, AD, Certificate). *Application deadline:* For fall admission, 1/16 (priority date). Applications are processed on a rolling basis. *Application fee:* $100. Electronic applications accepted. *Application Contact:* Suzanne M. Stringer, Registrar and Financial Aid Administrator, 203-432-4151, Fax: 203-432-7448, E-mail: suzanne.stringer@yale.edu. *Dean,* Robert Blocker, 203-432-4160, Fax: 203-432-7542.

School of Nursing Students: 206 full-time (188 women), 41 part-time (34 women); includes 27 minority (4 African Americans, 12 Asian Americans or Pacific Islanders, 11 Hispanic Americans), 5 international. Average age 30. 288 applicants, 46% accepted, 97 enrolled. *Faculty:* 55 full-time (50 women), 39 part-time/adjunct (36 women). Expenses: Contact institution. *Financial support:* In 2001–02, 188 students received support, including 63 fellowships (averaging $2,004 per year), 11 research assistantships with tuition reimbursements available (averaging $29,895 per year); Federal Work-Study, institutionally sponsored loans, scholarships/grants, and traineeships also available. Support available to part-time students. Financial award applicants required to submit FAFSA. In 2001, 76 master's, 4 doctorates, 5 other advanced degrees awarded. *Degree program information:* Part-time programs available. Offers nursing (MSN, DN Sc, Post Master's Certificate). *Application deadline:* For fall admission, 11/15 (priority date); for spring admission, 1/15 (priority date). Applications are processed on a rolling basis. *Application fee:* $50. *Application Contact:* Sharon E. Sanderson, Director, Student Recruitment and Placement, 203-737-2258, Fax: 203-737-5409, E-mail: sharon.sanderson@yale.edu. *Dean,* Catherine L. Gilliss, 203-785-2393, Fax: 203-785-6455, E-mail: catherine.gilliss@yale.edu.

Yale Law School Students: 632 full-time. Average age 25. 3,042 applicants, 10% accepted. *Faculty:* 67 full-time, 24 part-time/adjunct. Expenses: Contact institution. *Financial support:* Fellowships available. Financial award application deadline: 3/15; financial award applicants required to submit FAFSA. In 2001, 198 first professional degrees, 27 master's, 4 doctorates awarded. Offers law (JD, LL M, MSL, JSD). *Application deadline:* For fall admission, 2/15. Applications are processed on a rolling basis. *Application fee:* $55. Electronic applications accepted. *Application Contact:* Jean Webb, Director of Admissions, 203-432-4995, E-mail: admissions.law@yale.edu. *Dean,* Anthony T. Kronman, 203-432-1660.

Yale School of Management Students: 463 full-time (127 women); includes 76 minority (9 African Americans, 60 Asian Americans or Pacific Islanders, 7 Hispanic Americans), 189 international. Average age 28. 2,101 applicants, 20% accepted, 238 enrolled. *Faculty:* 52 full-time (8 women), 40 part-time/adjunct (4 women). Expenses: Contact institution. *Financial support:* In 2001–02, 286 students received support; fellowships, research assistantships, teaching assistantships, career-related internships or fieldwork, institutionally sponsored loans, and scholarships/grants available. Financial award application deadline: 2/15; financial award applicants required to submit FAFSA. In 2001, 224 master's, 2 doctorates awarded. Offers accounting (PhD); business administration (MBA); financial economics (PhD); management (MBA, PhD); marketing (PhD). *Application deadline:* For fall admission, 11/15 (priority date); for winter admission, 1/15 (priority date); for spring admission, 3/15 (priority date). *Application fee:* $180. Electronic applications accepted. *Application Contact:* James R. Stevens, Director of Admissions, 203-432-5932, Fax: 203-432-7004, E-mail: mba.admissions@yale.edu. *Dean,* Jeffrey E. Garten, 203-432-6035, Fax: 203-432-5092, E-mail: jeffrey.garten@yale.edu.

YESHIVA BETH MOSHE, Scranton, PA 18505-2124

General Information Independent-religious, men only, comprehensive institution.

YESHIVA DERECH CHAIM, Brooklyn, NY 11218

General Information Independent-religious, men only, comprehensive institution.

YESHIVA KARLIN STOLIN RABBINICAL INSTITUTE, Brooklyn, NY 11204

General Information Independent-religious, men only, comprehensive institution. *Graduate housing:* On-campus housing not available.

YESHIVA OF NITRA RABBINICAL COLLEGE, Mount Kisco, NY 10549

General Information Independent-religious, men only, comprehensive institution.

YESHIVA SHAAR HATORAH TALMUDIC RESEARCH INSTITUTE, Kew Gardens, NY 11418-1469

General Information Independent-religious, men only, comprehensive institution.

YESHIVATH VIZNITZ, Monsey, NY 10952

General Information Independent-religious, men only, comprehensive institution.

YESHIVATH ZICHRON MOSHE, South Fallsburg, NY 12779

General Information Independent-religious, men only, comprehensive institution.

GRADUATE UNITS

Graduate Programs *Degree program information:* Part-time programs available.

YESHIVA TORAS CHAIM TALMUDICAL SEMINARY, Denver, CO 80204-1415

General Information Independent-religious, men only, comprehensive institution.

YESHIVA UNIVERSITY, New York, NY 10033-3201

General Information Independent, coed, university. CGS member. *Graduate housing:* On-campus housing not available.

GRADUATE UNITS

Albert Einstein College of Medicine Offers medicine (MD, PhD).

Sue Golding Graduate Division of Medical Sciences Offers anatomy (PhD); biochemistry (PhD); cell and developmental biology (PhD); cell biology (PhD); developmental and molecular biology (PhD); medical sciences (PhD); microbiology and immunology (PhD); molecular genetics (PhD); molecular pharmacology (PhD); neuroscience (PhD); pathology (PhD); physiology and biophysics (PhD).

Azrieli Graduate School of Jewish Education and Administration *Degree program information:* Part-time and evening/weekend programs available. Offers Jewish education and administration (MS, Ed D, Specialist).

Benjamin N. Cardozo School of Law Offers general law (LL M); intellectual property law (LL M); law (JD). Electronic applications accepted.

Bernard Revel Graduate School of Jewish Studies Students: 34 full-time (11 women), 79 part-time (35 women). Average age 27. *Faculty:* 9 full-time (0 women), 6 part-time/adjunct (1 woman). Expenses: Contact institution. *Financial support:* In 2001–02, 45 fellowships with full and partial tuition reimbursements (averaging $4,840 per year) were awarded; institutionally sponsored loans, scholarships/grants, and tuition waivers (full and partial) also available. Support available to part-time students. Financial award application deadline: 3/1. In 2001, 6 master's awarded. *Degree program information:* Part-time programs available. Offers Jewish studies (MA, PhD). *Application deadline:* Applications are processed on a rolling basis. *Application fee:* $25. *Application Contact:* Sheniagia Alise Warren, Executive Secretary, 212-960-5254, Fax: 212-960-5245, E-mail: swarren@ymail.yu.edu. *Dean,* Dr. Arthur Hyman, 212-960-5253, Fax: 212-960-5245, E-mail: ahyman@ymail.yu.edu.

Ferkauf Graduate School of Psychology Students: 296 full-time (201 women), 64 part-time (44 women); includes 59 minority (16 African Americans, 14 Asian Americans or Pacific Islanders, 29 Hispanic Americans), 38 international. Average age 28. 570 applicants, 13% accepted. *Faculty:* 28 full-time (13 women), 73 part-time/adjunct (40 women). Expenses: Contact institution. *Financial support:* In 2001–02, 43 fellowships (averaging $5,000 per year), 26 research assistantships (averaging $2,000 per year), 79 teaching assistantships (averaging $2,000 per year) were awarded. Career-related internships or fieldwork, Federal Work-Study, institutionally sponsored loans, and scholarships/grants also available. Support available to part-time students. Financial award application deadline: 4/15. In 2001, 13 master's, 83 doctorates awarded. *Degree program information:* Part-time programs available. Offers clinical psychology (Psy D); developmental psychology (PhD); general psychology (MA); health psychology (PhD); psychology (MA, PhD, Psy D); school/clinical-child psychology (Psy D). *Application fee:* $50. *Application Contact:* Elaine Schwartz, Assistant Director of Admissions, 718-430-3820, Fax: 718-430-3960, E-mail: eschart@ymail.yu.edu. *Dean,* Dr. Lawrence J. Siegel, 718-430-3941, Fax: 718-430-3960.

Wurzweiler School of Social Work Students: 179 full-time (134 women), 264 part-time (208 women); includes 137 minority (88 African Americans, 6 Asian Americans or Pacific Islanders, 42 Hispanic Americans, 1 Native American), 25 international. Average age 34. 505 applicants, 50% accepted, 199 enrolled. *Faculty:* 23 full-time (12 women), 32 part-time/adjunct (19 women). Expenses: Contact institution. *Financial support:* In 2001–02, 352 students received support. Career-related internships or fieldwork, institutionally sponsored loans, and scholarships/grants available. Financial award application deadline: 5/15; financial award applicants required to submit FAFSA. In 2001, 156 master's, 5 doctorates awarded. *Degree program information:* Part-time and evening/weekend programs available. Offers social work (MSW, PhD). *Application deadline:* For fall admission, 5/1 (priority date); for spring admission, 10/31. Applications are processed on a rolling basis. *Application fee:* $35. *Application Contact:* Michele Sarracco, Director of Admissions, 212-960-0811, Fax: 212-960-0822. *Dean,* Dr. Sheldon R. Gelman, 212-960-0820.

YORK COLLEGE OF PENNSYLVANIA, York, PA 17405-7199

General Information Independent, coed, comprehensive institution. *Enrollment:* 22 full-time matriculated graduate/professional students (9 women), 152 part-time matriculated graduate/professional students (67 women). *Enrollment by degree level:* 174 master's. *Graduate*

York College of Pennsylvania (continued)

faculty: 17 full-time (3 women), 1 part-time/adjunct (0 women). *Tuition:* Part-time $330 per credit. *Required fees:* $96 per term. *Graduate housing:* On-campus housing not available. *Student services:* Campus safety program, career counseling, child daycare facilities, free psychological counseling, international student services, low-cost health insurance. *Library facilities:* Schmidt Library plus 1 other. *Online resources:* library catalog, web page, access to other libraries' catalogs. *Collection:* 300,000 titles, 1,400 serial subscriptions, 11,000 audiovisual materials.

Computer facilities: 250 computers available on campus for general student use. A campuswide network can be accessed from student residence rooms and from off campus. Internet access and online class registration are available. *Web address:* http://www.ycp.edu/.

General Application Contact: John F. Barbor, MBA Coordinator, 717-815-1491, Fax: 717-849-1653, E-mail: jbarbor@ycp.edu.

GRADUATE UNITS

Department of Business Administration Students: 22 full-time (9 women), 152 part-time (67 women). Average age 33. 77 applicants, 86% accepted. *Faculty:* 17 full-time (3 women), 1 part-time/adjunct (0 women). Expenses: Contact institution. *Financial support:* Available to part-time students. Application deadline: 4/15; In 2001, 51 degrees awarded. *Degree program information:* Part-time and evening/weekend programs available. Offers accounting/finance (MBA); general business (MBA); health care management (MBA); human resource management (MBA); information systems (MBA); management (MBA); marketing (MBA). *Application deadline:* For fall admission, 7/15 (priority date); for spring admission, 12/15. Applications are processed on a rolling basis. *Application fee:* $30. *MBA Coordinator,* John F. Barbor, 717-815-1491, Fax: 717-849-1653, E-mail: jbarbor@ycp.edu.

YORK UNIVERSITY, Toronto, ON M3J 1P3, Canada

General Information Province-supported, coed, university. *Enrollment:* 2,707 full-time matriculated graduate/professional students, 1,637 part-time matriculated graduate/professional students. *Graduate faculty:* 1,454 full-time (569 women), 165 part-time/adjunct (56 women). *Graduate tuition:* Tuition and fees charges are reported in Canadian dollars. *International tuition:* $7,637 Canadian dollars full-time. *Tuition, area resident:* Full-time $3,340 Canadian dollars; part-time $782 Canadian dollars per term. Tuition, Canadian resident: part-time $1,909 Canadian dollars per term. *Required fees:* $464 Canadian dollars. One-time fee: $106 Canadian dollars part-time. *Graduate housing:* Rooms and/or apartments available on a first-come, first-served basis to single and married students. *Student services:* Campus employment opportunities, campus safety program, career counseling, child daycare facilities, disabled student services, exercise/wellness program, free psychological counseling, grant writing training, international student services, low-cost health insurance, multicultural affairs office, teacher training, writing training. *Library facilities:* Scott Library plus 4 others. *Online resources:* library catalog, web page, access to other libraries' catalogs. *Collection:* 2.2 million titles, 13,651 serial subscriptions. *Research affiliation:* Imperial Oil LMT, National Palace Museum (Taiwan), Unicorn Children's Foundation (developmental and learning disorders), Smithsonian Institution (astronomy, physics, space), Beijing Municipality (management training), German Academic Exchange (German studies).

Computer facilities: 1,200 computers available on campus for general student use. A campuswide network can be accessed from student residence rooms and from off campus. Internet access and online class registration are available. *Web address:* http://www.yorku.ca/.

General Application Contact: J. Campanelli, Student Affairs Officer, 416-736-5126, Fax: 416-736-5592, E-mail: josecamp@yorku.ca.

GRADUATE UNITS

Faculty of Graduate Studies Students: 2,707 full-time (1,441 women), 1,637 part-time (868 women), 426 international. 4,005 applicants, 35% accepted, 884 enrolled. *Faculty:* 1,454 full-time (569 women), 165 part-time/adjunct (56 women). Expenses: Contact institution. *Financial support:* In 2001–02, 165 fellowships, 880 research assistantships, 1,147 teaching assistantships were awarded. Career-related internships or fieldwork, institutionally sponsored loans, tuition waivers (partial), and fee bursaries also available. In 2001, 532 master's, 89 doctorates awarded. *Degree program information:* Part-time and evening/weekend programs available. Offers communication and culture (MA, PhD); French studies (MA); interdisciplinary studies (MA); social work (MSW); translation (MA); women's studies (MA, PhD). *Application fee:* $60. Electronic applications accepted. *Application Contact:* J. Campanelli, Student Affairs Officer, 416-736-5126, Fax: 416-736-5592, E-mail: josecamp@yorku.ca. *Dean,* John W. Lennox, 416-76-5329.

Faculty of Arts Students: 1,018 full-time (571 women), 176 part-time (99 women), 178 international. 1,786 applicants, 34% accepted, 344 enrolled. *Faculty:* 663 full-time (239 women), 63 part-time/adjunct (19 women). Expenses: Contact institution. *Financial support:* Fellowships, research assistantships, teaching assistantships, tuition waivers (partial) and fee bursaries available. In 2001, 193 master's, 63 doctorates awarded. *Degree program information:* Part-time programs available. Offers arts (M Sc, MA, PhD); economics (MA, PhD); English (MA, PhD); geography (M Sc, MA, PhD); history (MA, PhD); kinesiology and health science (M Sc, MA, PhD); mathematics and statistics (MA, PhD); philosophy (MA, PhD); political science (MA, PhD); psychology (MA, PhD); social and political thought (MA, PhD); social anthropology (MA, PhD); sociology (MA, PhD). *Application fee:* $60. Electronic applications accepted. *Application Contact:* J. Campanelli, Student Affairs Officer, 416-736-5126, Fax: 416-736-5592, E-mail: josecamp@yorku.ca. *Dean,* Robert Drummond, 416-736-5260.

Faculty of Education Students: 51 full-time (45 women), 224 part-time (184 women), 7 international. 180 applicants, 52% accepted, 79 enrolled. *Faculty:* 62 full-time (37 women), 6 part-time/adjunct (5 women). Expenses: Contact institution. *Financial support:* In 2001–02, 12 fellowships (averaging $9,930 per year), 22 research assistantships (averaging $6,486 per year), 25 teaching assistantships (averaging $10,218 per year) were awarded. Fee bursaries also available. In 2001, 36 master's, 2 doctorates awarded. *Degree program information:* Part-time programs available. Offers education (M Ed, PhD). *Application deadline:* For fall admission, 2/1. *Application fee:* $60. Electronic applications accepted. *Director,* Celia Haig-Brown, 416-736-5018.

Faculty of Environmental Studies Students: 324 full-time (197 women), 52 part-time (35 women), 34 international. 358 applicants, 61% accepted, 141 enrolled. *Faculty:* 39 full-time (16 women). Expenses: Contact institution. *Financial support:* In 2001–02, 23 fellowships (averaging $7,750 per year), 106 research assistantships (averaging $8,035 per year), 55 teaching assistantships (averaging $10,093 per year) were awarded. Tuition waivers (partial) and fee bursaries also available. In 2001, 92 master's, 5 doctorates awarded. *Degree program information:* Part-time programs available. Offers environmental studies (MES, PhD). *Application deadline:* For fall admission, 3/1. *Application fee:* $60. Electronic applications accepted. *Director,* Barbara Rahder, 416-736-5252.

Faculty of Fine Arts Students: 136 full-time (80 women), 35 part-time (25 women), 15 international. 329 applicants, 30% accepted, 69 enrolled. *Faculty:* 110 full-time (53 women), 44 part-time/adjunct (24 women). Expenses: Contact institution. *Financial support:* Fellowships, research assistantships, teaching assistantships, tuition waivers (partial) and fee bursaries available. In 2001, 50 master's, 3 doctorates awarded. *Degree program information:* Part-time programs available. Offers art history (MA); composition (MA); dance (MA); film and video (MA, MFA); fine arts (MA, MFA, PhD); musicology and ethnomusicology (MA, PhD); theatre (MFA); visual arts (MFA). *Application fee:* $60. Electronic applications accepted. *Dean,* Phillip Silver, 416-736-5136.

Faculty of Pure and Applied Science Students: 216 full-time (88 women), 68 part-time (24 women), 46 international. 628 applicants, 19% accepted, 78 enrolled. *Faculty:* 199 full-time (22 women), 41 part-time/adjunct (4 women). Expenses: Contact institution. *Financial support:* Fellowships, research assistantships, teaching assistantships, career-related internships or fieldwork, tuition waivers (partial), and fee bursaries available. In 2001, 40 master's, 12 doctorates awarded. *Degree program information:* Part-time and evening/weekend programs available. Offers biology (M Sc, PhD); chemistry (M Sc, PhD); computer science (M Sc, PhD); earth and space science (M Sc, PhD); physics and astronomy (M Sc, PhD); pure and applied science (M Sc, MA, PhD). *Application fee:* $60. *Dean,* G. Wu, 416-736-5051.

Osgoode Hall Law School Students: 52 full-time (27 women), 40 part-time (20 women), 13 international. 124 applicants, 25% accepted, 20 enrolled. *Faculty:* 53 full-time (21 women), 4 part-time/adjunct (1 woman). Expenses: Contact institution. *Financial support:* In 2001–02, 29 fellowships (averaging $4,939 per year), 24 research assistantships (averaging $7,734 per year), 16 teaching assistantships (averaging $10,688 per year) were awarded. Fee bursaries also available. In 2001, 9 degrees awarded. *Degree program information:* Part-time and evening/weekend programs available. *Application deadline:* For fall admission, 1/31. *Application fee:* $60. Electronic applications accepted. *Director,* Craig Scott, 416-736-5046.

Schulich School of Business Students: 714 full-time (288 women), 592 part-time (244 women). Average age 30. 1,401 applicants, 50% accepted, 423 enrolled. *Faculty:* 84 full-time (20 women), 36 part-time/adjunct (16 women). Expenses: Contact institution. *Financial support:* In 2001–02, 832 students received support, including fellowships (averaging $5,000 per year), research assistantships (averaging $3,000 per year), teaching assistantships (averaging $7,000 per year); career-related internships or fieldwork, institutionally sponsored loans, scholarships/grants, traineeships, unspecified assistantships, and fee bursaries also available. Support available to part-time students. Financial award application deadline: 4/1. In 2001, 577 master's, 5 doctorates awarded. *Degree program information:* Part-time and evening/weekend programs available. Offers business (EMBA, IMBA, MBA, MPA, PhD). *Application deadline:* For fall admission, 3/1; for winter admission, 8/15. Applications are processed on a rolling basis. *Application fee:* $125. Electronic applications accepted. *Application Contact:* Carol Pattenden, Assistant Director, Admissions, 416-736-5060, Fax: 416-650-8174, E-mail: admissions@schulich.yorku.ca. *Dean,* Dr. D. J. Horváth, 416-736-5070, Fax: 416-736-5763, E-mail: dhorvath@schulich.yorku.ca.

YO SAN UNIVERSITY OF TRADITIONAL CHINESE MEDICINE, Los Angeles, CA 90066

General Information Private, coed, graduate-only institution. *Enrollment by degree level:* 167 master's. *Graduate faculty:* 3 full-time (2 women), 25 part-time/adjunct (9 women). *Tuition:* Full-time $7,425. *Required fees:* $105. *Graduate housing:* On-campus housing not available. *Student services:* Campus employment opportunities, international student services. *Library facilities:* Yo San University Library. *Collection:* 1,900 titles, 11 serial subscriptions, 156 audiovisual materials.

Computer facilities: 2 computers available on campus for general student use. Internet access is available. *Web address:* http://www.yosan.edu/.

General Application Contact: Matthew Titus, Director of Admissions, 310-577-3000 Ext. 24, Fax: 310-577-3033, E-mail: admissions@yosan.edu.

GRADUATE UNITS

Program in Acupuncture and Traditional Chinese Medicine Students: 167 (114 women); includes 48 minority (8 African Americans, 24 Asian Americans or Pacific Islanders, 13 Hispanic Americans, 3 Native Americans) 3 international. Average age 32. 35 applicants, 89% accepted. *Faculty:* 3 full-time (2 women), 25 part-time/adjunct (9 women). Expenses: Contact institution. *Financial support:* In 2001–02, 112 students received support. Federal Work-Study available. Support available to part-time students. Financial award applicants required to submit FAFSA. In 2001, 28 degrees awarded. *Degree program information:* Part-time programs available. Offers acupuncture and traditional Chinese medicine (MATCM). *Application deadline:* For fall admission, 8/4; for winter admission, 12/3; for spring admission, 3/31. Applications are processed on a rolling basis. *Application fee:* $50 ($100 for international students). *Application Contact:* Matthew Titus, Director of Admissions, 310-577-3000 Ext. 24, Fax: 310-577-3033, E-mail: admissions@yosan.edu. *Academic Dean,* Keiko Cronin, 310-577-3000 Ext. 24, Fax: 310-577-3033.

YOUNGSTOWN STATE UNIVERSITY, Youngstown, OH 44555-0001

General Information State-supported, coed, comprehensive institution. CGS member. *Graduate housing:* Room and/or apartments available on a first-come, first-served basis to single students; on-campus housing not available to married students. Housing application deadline: 9/1. *Research affiliation:* St. Elizabeth Hospital Medical Center (biomedical research), Ohio Supercomputer Center (computational chemistry), Edison Materials Technology Center, Cleveland Advanced Manufacturing Program (applied engineering).

GRADUATE UNITS

Graduate School *Degree program information:* Part-time and evening/weekend programs available.

College of Arts and Sciences *Degree program information:* Part-time programs available. Offers arts and sciences (MA, MS, Certificate); biological sciences (MS); chemistry (MS); economics (MA); English (MA); environmental studies (MS); history (MA); industrial/institutional management (Certificate); mathematics (MS); risk management (Certificate).

College of Education *Degree program information:* Part-time and evening/weekend programs available. Offers counseling (MS Ed); early and middle childhood education (MS Ed); education (MS Ed, Ed D); educational administration (MS Ed); educational leadership (Ed D); gifted and talented education (MS Ed); secondary education (MS Ed); special education (MS Ed); teaching—elementary education (MS Ed); teaching—secondary reading (MS Ed).

College of Fine and Performing Arts *Degree program information:* Part-time and evening/weekend programs available. Offers fine and performing arts (MM); music education (MM); music history and literature (MM); music theory and composition (MM); performance (MM).

College of Health and Human Services *Degree program information:* Part-time and evening/weekend programs available. Offers criminal justice (MS); health and human services (MHHS); nursing (MSN); physical therapy (MPT).

Warren P. Williamson Jr. College of Business Administration *Degree program information:* Part-time and evening/weekend programs available. Offers accounting (MBA); business administration (EMBA, MBA); executive business administration (EMBA); finance (MBA); management (MBA); marketing (MBA).

William Rayen College of Engineering *Degree program information:* Part-time and evening/weekend programs available. Offers civil, chemical, and environmental engineering (MSE); electrical engineering (MSE); engineering (MSE); mechanical and industrial engineering (MSE).

Essays: In-Depth Descriptions of Institutions Offering Graduate and Professional Work

The In-Depth Descriptions in this section present an overview of accredited graduate and professional schools in the United States and U.S. territories and institutions in Canada, Mexico, Europe, and Africa that are accredited by U.S. accrediting bodies. Critical information sought by all prospective graduate students—regardless of their intended field of study—has been supplied by the schools themselves.

In addition to listing the degree programs available, each entry gives valuable information on research facilities, financial aid opportunities, tuition rates, living and housing costs, students, the faculty, location, the university, and application criteria—in short, facts that all prospective graduate students need to know about an institution when selecting a graduate program.

After using the In-Depth Descriptions and the other sections of this volume to identify those universities that are appropriate to your needs, refer to the other five volumes for specific program information. Graduate and professional schools and colleges within the institutions represented in Book 1 are considered in detail in Books 2–6, which cover the humanities, arts, and social sciences; the biological sciences; the physical sciences, mathematics, agricultural sciences, the environment, and natural resources; engineering and applied sciences; and business, education, health, information studies, law, and social work, respectively.

ACADEMY OF ART COLLEGE

Programs of Study

The Academy of Art College offers Master of Fine Arts (M.F.A.) degrees in advertising (art direction, account planning, copyrighting, television commercials), computer arts (2D and 3D modeling, animation, new media, publishing, special effects, Web design, video games), fashion (design, textiles, fashion illustration, knitwear, merchandising), fine art (painting, sculpture, printmaking, jewelry, ceramics, bronze casting, neon, jewelry making, lithography, metal arts), graphic design (branding, corporate identity, packaging, print), illustration (2D animation, cartooning, children's books, editorial, feature film animation), industrial design (car design, product design, toy design, furniture design), interior architecture and design (commercial and residential design, architecture, furniture design), motion pictures and television (art direction, screenwriting, special effects, acting, producing, directing, editing, cinematography, advertising film), and photography (architecture, advertising, digital documentary, editorial, fashion, fine art, photojournalism, portraiture, landscape). The Academy of Art College graduate candidate engages in a unique interdisciplinary approach to M.F.A. degree preparation. Comprising studio work and academic investigation, the M.F.A. program extends for a period of 2½ years. Attainment of the M.F.A. degree requires the graduate candidate to successfully complete 27 units of studio courses, 18 units of directed study, 12 units of academic study, and 6 units of electives, for a total of 63 units.

Research Facilities

At the Academy, the graduate candidate is met with a dedicated and sophisticated approach to studying art and design. State-of-the-art facilities and equipment are paired with instruction by an accomplished faculty. Graduate student needs are accommodated by offering evening, weekday, and weekend classes. All graduate candidates have access to specialized computer labs to develop advanced software expertise related to their area of discipline.

The Academy's eight-story Digital Arts Center offers students access to an incredible array of technology. The center has more than 700 computer workstations, including 100 Silicon Graphics workstations, 300 Adobe premiere workstations, and 200 autoCAD workstations. Students also have the use of fourteen Avid digital editing suites, seven multitrack sound editing studios, one dedicated blue screen studio, and various other video equipment.

The Academy Library houses more than 28,000 books and magazines, as well as 375 CD-ROM titles, 100,000 slides, and 1,200 videos. Computers with Internet access are available to students as well as an online catalog, color scanners, and color and black-and-white copiers. Workshops and electronic study guides are also available.

The Academy Resource Center offers all students free learning support services that include study hall, tutoring, mentoring, midpoint review and study skills workshops, a writing lab, a state-of-the-art multimedia language lab, an English for Art Program, and a Conversation Partner Program.

Financial Aid

The Academy offers need-based financial aid packages consisting of grants, loans, and work-study to eligible students. Low-interest loans are available to all eligible students. As financial aid programs, procedures, and eligibility requirements change frequently, applicants should contact the Financial Aid office for current requirements at 79 New Montgomery Street, 3rd Floor, San Francisco, California 94105, or by telephone at the toll-free number listed below.

Cost of Study

Tuition for 2000 was $550 per credit unit for graduate study. There is a nonrefundable $120 registration fee, $100 of which is applicable toward tuition. Lab fees run from $25 to $400 per semester, depending on the class. Tuition and fees are subject to change at any time. The Academy operates an artists' supply store with substantial discounts for registered students. The Academy has most of the expensive technical equipment available for students to borrow or available for use in a lab context. It is estimated that the total cost of attending the Academy for one year for a student taking 30 units is $17,725, including tuition, fees, and supplies.

Living and Housing Costs

The Academy operates eight campus housing facilities within the city. Several housing options are offered, and costs vary from $6600 to $10,000 per academic year (fall and spring semesters). For further information, students may contact the Academy Housing Office directly at 415-263-7727 or by e-mail at housing@academyart.edu.

Student Group

The M.F.A. program accommodates more than 700 students. Of those, 55 percent are women, and 40 percent are international. Approximately 35 percent of the students receive financial aid.

Student Outcomes

The M.F.A. placement rate for 1999 was 89 percent. Companies that hired M.F.A. graduates in 2000 include Hal Riney, McCann Erickson, Wolfe Doyle, and USAGreetings for advertising; JINX, Manex, PeopleSoft, iPrint, KRON, Egreetings, and DNA Productions for computer arts; Nieman Marcus, Gap, Silver Wear NY, and Nicole Miller for fashion; Landor Associates, Primo Angeli, Impact Design, and Maddocks & Co. for graphic design; ILM, Disney, LucasArts, Marvel Comics, and Totally Games for illustration; Northstar, Ford/Lincoln Mercury, and Ruszel Woodworks for industrial design; Gensler, Hendler Design, and Holey & Associates for interior architecture and design; and Fox News, WB Channel 20, and Pixar Animation Studios for motion pictures and television.

Location

The city of San Francisco is one of the great cultural centers of the world, a melting pot of diversity, ethnicity, and creativity that has spawned major museums and galleries, world-class opera and theaters, dance companies, film production and recording studios, technological innovation, performing artists ranging from classical to popular music, and numerous other cultural opportunities. The city offers myriad locations for field trips and studio visits. World-renowned artists display their creations in the Academy's large Bush Street gallery. The Academy of Art College is an urban institution that both draws upon and contributes to the cultural wealth of the community in which it resides.

The College

In 1929, Academy of Art College founder Richard S. Stephens, who was the advertising creative director of *Sunset* magazine, acted on his belief that "aspiring artists and designers, given proper instruction, hard work, and dedication, can learn the skills needed to become successful professionals." When Richard A. Stephens succeeded his father as president in 1951, he added a Foundations Department to ensure that all students comprehended the basic principles of traditional art and design. In 1966 the Academy officially became a college, with approval from the California Department of Education to issue a Bachelor of Fine Arts degree. In another decade, the Master of Fine Arts degree was offered. Five more buildings were purchased, and by 1992, there were more than 2,500 Academy students. In that year, the leadership of the Academy was turned over to the third generation in the family, Elisa Stephens, granddaughter of the school's founder. Today, the Academy of Art College is the largest private art and design school in the nation and has an enrollment of more than 6,000 students from nearly every country in the world. One third of the student body is made up of international students. The school maintains a fleet of buses to connect the different points of the campus, all of which are in the city limits of San Francisco, one of the world's most vibrant and beautiful cities. The faculty, which is 90 percent part-time and made up of working art and design professionals, is recruited from all across the nation, drawn to the creative and intellectual center that is the Bay Area.

Applying

Admission to the M.F.A. program requires official transcripts indicating at least the completion of a bachelor's degree, the submission of a portfolio of work (portfolio requirements vary by discipline), a statement of intent outlining graduate study goals, a resume, and two letters of recommendation. Admission to the program is permitted at the beginning of each semester. Students should contact the Graduate Admissions Office for further details.

Correspondence and Information

Academy of Art College Graduate Admissions
P.O. Box 192290
San Francisco, California 94119
Telephone: 415-274-2222
800-544-ARTS (toll-free)
Fax: 415-263-4124
E-mail: info@academyart.edu
World Wide Web: http://www.academyart.edu

DEPARTMENT DIRECTORS

Advertising: Brian McCarthy, B.A., St. John's.
Computer Arts – Animation: Dan Brick, M.S., MIT.
Computer Arts – New Media: Gordon Silveria, B.F.A., Academy of Art College.
Fashion: Simon Ungless, M.A., St. Martin's School of Art (U.K.).
Fine Art Painting and Illustration: William Maughan, B.F.A., Art Center College of Design.
Fine Art Sculpture and Printmaking: Charlene Modena, M.A., San Francisco State.
Graphic Design: Jana Anderson, B.A., UCLA.
Industrial Design Studios: David Cole, B.A., Lanchester Polytechnic (U.K.).
Interior Architecture and Design: David Anttila, M.S., Pratt.
Motion Pictures and Television: Jack Isgro, B.A., St. John Fisher; David Pfeil, Art Center College of Design.
Photography: Jim Wood, B.A., Art Center College of Design.

The city of San Francisco is a dynamic setting for campus life at the Academy.

ALFRED UNIVERSITY

Graduate School

Programs of Study

Alfred University offers graduate programs leading to the Doctor of Psychology and Master of Arts degrees in school psychology; the Master of Business Administration; the Master of Science in Education degree in twelve program areas, all leading to New York State teacher or school counselor certification; the Master of Professional Studies degree in community services administration; the Master of Fine Arts degree in ceramic art, electronic integrated arts, glass art, and sculpture; the Master of Science degree in biomedical materials engineering science, ceramic science, glass science, materials science and engineering, and mechanical, electrical, or ceramic engineering; and the Doctor of Philosophy degree in ceramics and glass science.

The Doctor of Philosophy degree in school psychology is a 115-credit-hour program that leads to state and national certification as well as New York State license eligibility. The Master of Arts in School Psychology is a three-year, 77-credit-hour program that leads to permanent certification in New York State as well as national certification. Both programs are accredited by the National Association of School Psychologists (NASP) and the American Psychological Association (APA). The Master of Business Administration requires a maximum of 55 credit hours but may be completed in a one-year, 30-credit-hour program if the student has an undergraduate degree in business. The Master of Science in Education degree is offered in the following areas: elementary education, literacy teacher studies, secondary education (art, biology, business, chemistry, earth science, English, mathematics, physics, and social studies), and counseling. Elementary education, literacy teacher, and secondary education are 30-credit-hour programs requiring one year of full-time study, leading to New York State teacher certification. The Counseling Program is a two-year, 60-credit-hour program, and upon successful completion of the first 36 credit hours and a comprehensive examination, the candidate is eligible to receive the master's degree and has satisfied the academic requirements for a provisional certificate in school counseling. An additional 24 credits satisfy the academic requirements for New York State permanent certification in school counseling. The Master of Professional Studies in community services administration is a 30-credit-hour program, with an additional 3-credit-hour internship required for students without an employment background in an agency. Successful completion of the program requires an oral comprehensive examination. The Doctor of Philosophy degree in ceramics or glass science requires 90 credits. The Master of Fine Arts degree requires two years residence.

Research Facilities

Extensive laboratory and studio facilities support the engineering and art programs. Alfred University's two libraries, Herrick Memorial Library and Scholes Library of Ceramics, hold more than 320,000 volumes, 1,500 periodical titles in print and 5,000 in electronic format, and 120,000 other documents. The libraries share an online catalog and provide access to hundreds of electronic databases in both general and specialized fields. Access to the Internet and library catalogs worldwide is provided. General purpose and specialized computing labs located throughout the campus provide access to diverse operating systems such as Windows, Macintosh, Unix, and Linux. These labs are open an average of 77 hours per week during the semester. Research centers on campus include the Lea R. Powell Institute for Children and Families, Center for Rural School Psychology, the NSF Industry/University Center for Biosurfaces, the Whiteware Research Center, NYS Center for Advanced Ceramic Technology, the Center for Family Business, and the Institute for Electronic Arts.

Financial Aid

Assistantships are available to qualified full-time graduate students. Generally, assistantships provide a one-half tuition grant but may range up to full tuition. Full tuition grants are available under the Opportunity Fellowship Program. Students in the Master of Fine Arts program receive a full tuition grant and a $4750 stipend for the academic year. Students in the publicly endowed engineering program receive a full tuition grant and a $17,000 stipend for the academic year.

Cost of Study

Tuition for the 2002–03 academic year is $24,720 (endowed sector), and it was $13,892 for the New York State College of Ceramics in 2001–02.

Living and Housing Costs

A limited number of residence hall accommodations are available for single students on campus. Room and board cost $8392 for the 2002–03 academic year. Students should contact the Office of Residence Life for further information about both on- and off-campus housing.

Student Group

The University has approximately 2,000 undergraduate and 340 graduate students, drawn from thirty-eight states and fifteen countries. About 180 graduate students study part-time and are generally working professionals seeking advanced degrees in their fields.

Location

Alfred University is located in Alfred, New York, a college town 70 miles south of Rochester, 90 miles southeast of Buffalo, and 60 miles west of Corning. Nestled among the pine-sheltered foothills of the Allegheny Mountains, this popular recreation area is close to ski slopes and the water sports and fishing of the Finger Lakes region. New York City is 6 hours away via the Southern Tier Expressway/I-86.

The University

Alfred University, founded in 1836, is the second-oldest coeducational school in the United States and represents an unusual blend of private and public financing. The University is composed of the privately endowed College of Business, the College of Liberal Arts and Sciences, the College of Engineering and Professional Studies, and the New York State College of Ceramics (the School of Ceramic Engineering and Sciences and the School of Art and Design).

Applying

To be eligible for admission, an applicant must hold a four-year baccalaureate degree from an accredited college or university, and the undergraduate record must clearly indicate ability to perform credibly at the graduate level. Applicants must submit a brief personal statement of objectives and reasons for applying to the Graduate School, including professional goals, interests, and a specific plan for studies at Alfred. In addition, applicants should have two letters of recommendation (three for School Psychology Program applicants) and official transcripts of all completed academic work sent directly to the Graduate School Office. Official scores on the GRE General Test are required of applicants to the School Psychology Program. Official scores on the GMAT are required of applicants to the M.B.A. program. Interviews are required for the School Psychology and Counseling Programs. A portfolio is required for applicants to the M.F.A. program. Official TOEFL scores are required of international students whose native language is not English. An application fee of $50 is charged, but is waived if the application is made online.

Correspondence and Information

Office of Graduate Admissions
Alfred University
Saxon Drive
Alfred, New York 14802-1232
Telephone: 607-871-2141
800-541-9229 (toll-free)
E-mail: gradinquiry@alfred.edu
World Wide Web: http://www.alfred.edu/gradschool

THE FACULTY

David Szczerbacki, Provost and Vice President for Academic and Statutory Affairs; Ph.D., Buffalo.

PROGRAM DIRECTORS AND DEPARTMENTAL RESEARCH

Art

M.F.A. in Ceramic Art: Andrea Gill, Associate Professor of Ceramic Art; M.F.A., Alfred.
M.F.A. in Glass Art: Stephen Edwards, Professor of Glass; M.F.A., Illinois State.
M.F.A. in Sculpture: Stephen Edwards, Professor of Glass; M.F.A., Illinois State.
M.F.A. in Electronic Integrated Arts: Joseph Scheer, Associate Professor of Printmaking; M.A., M.F.A., New Mexico.

Business Administration

Lori Hollenbeck, Director, M.B.A. Program; M.B.A., Alfred.

Community Services Administration

Robert A. Heineman, Professor of Political Science; Ph.D., American. Research: paradigms for political analysis, program implementation, judicial policy.

Education

Counseling: James F. Curl, Professor of Education; Ph.D., Pittsburgh. Research: group therapy and practice, college student personnel.
Elementary Education and Literacy Teacher: Katherine D. Wiesendanger, Professor of Education; Ed.D., Mississippi State. Research: remedial reading methodology, characteristics of effective reading programs, psychology of reading.

Engineering and Sciences

Biomedical Materials Engineering Science: Alan H. Goldstein, Professor of Biology; Ph.D., Arizona. Research: biomedical materials engineering, characterization of molecular and cell biology events at the surface of biomaterials, protein and metabolic engineering for biomaterials applications, molecular dynamic simulations of protein binding to materials.
Ceramic Engineering: Ronald S. Gordon, Professor and Dean, Materials Science and Engineering; Sc.D., MIT. Research: ceramic materials processing and characterization, synthesis of ceramic powders, grain growth and microstructure development, thermodynamics, solid-state electrochemistry, high-temperature mechanical properties of polycrystalline ceramics and ion-conducting solid electrolytes.
Ceramic Science: Ronald S. Gordon, Professor and Dean, Materials Science and Engineering; Sc.D., MIT. Research: ceramic materials processing and characterization, synthesis of ceramic powders, grain growth and microstructure development, thermodynamics, solid-state electrochemistry, high-temperature mechanical properties of polycrystalline ceramics and ion-conducting solid electrolytes.
Electrical Engineering: James T. Lancaster, Professor of Electrical Engineering; Ph.D., Virginia Tech. Research: computer usage in power systems, deposition of thin films, decision and control, superconductors.
Glass Science: Ronald S. Gordon, Professor and Dean, Materials Science and Engineering; Sc.D., MIT. Research: ceramic materials processing and characterization, synthesis of ceramic powders, grain growth and microstructure development, thermodynamics, solid-state electrochemistry, high-temperature mechanical properties of polycrystalline ceramics and ion-conducting solid electrolytes.
Materials Science and Engineering: Ronald S. Gordon, Professor and Dean, Materials Science and Engineering; Sc.D., MIT. Research: ceramic materials processing and characterization, synthesis of ceramic powders, grain growth and microstructure development, thermodynamics, solid-state electrochemistry, high-temperature mechanical properties of polycrystalline ceramics and ion-conducting solid electrolytes.
Mechanical Engineering: William F. Hahn, Associate Professor of Mechanical Engineering; M.S.M.E., Ph.D., Illinois. Research: kinematics, machine design, manufacturing machinery and equipment, finite element methods for product design.

School Psychology

John D. Cerio, Professor of School Psychology; Ph.D., Boston College. Research: counseling psychology, family therapy, play therapy, personality assessment.

ALLIANT INTERNATIONAL UNIVERSITY

Graduate Programs

Programs of Study

Alliant International University (AIU) offers graduate programs in psychology, business, organizational studies, education, arts and sciences, and social and policy studies. Flexible scheduling allows students to take classes either full- or part-time in the evenings and on weekends. Prospective students should note that not all programs are offered at all locations. Alliant International offers graduate studies through its six colleges.

The California School of Organizational Studies (CSOS) offers master's programs in change leadership (M.A.), industrial/organizational psychology (M.A. and M.S.), organizational behavior (M.A.O.B. and M.S.O.B.), and organizational psychology (M.A.O.P.). CSOS offers doctoral programs in consulting psychology (Ph.D.), industrial/organizational psychology (Ph.D. and Psy.D.), organizational consulting (Psy.D.); organizational development (Psy.D.), and organizational psychology (Ph.D.). There is also a dual doctorate program in industrial/organizational psychology and clinical psychology (Ph.D.) and a joint master's in organizational behavior/clinical or forensic doctoral program (Psy.D. or Ph.D.).

The California School of Professional Psychology (CSPP) offers master's programs in clinical psychopharmacology (M.S.); counseling psychology (M.A.); marital and family therapy (M.A.); marriage, family and child counseling: family behavioral health program designed for American Indian students (M.A.); and psychophysiology and biofeedback (M.S.). CSPP offers doctoral programs in clinical psychology (Ph.D. and Psy.D.); health psychology (Ph.D.); marital and family therapy (Psy.D.); and a joint master's in organizational behavior/clinical doctorate (Psy.D. or Ph.D.).

The College of Arts and Sciences (CAS) offers a multicultural emphasis in its master's program in international relations (M.A.). Perennially ranked in the top three nationally in its percentage of international students, the college stresses understanding and appreciation of cultural diversity, societal interdependence, and global perspectives. Its culturally diverse faculty, working in uniquely rich, multicultural classrooms, is committed to preparing students for leadership.

The Graduate School of Education (GSOE) offers master's degrees, including the M.A. in education with the following concentrations: educational administration, teaching, teaching English to speakers of other languages (TESOL), and technology and learning. Master's in school psychology, including the Pupil Personnel Services Credential, CTC approval pending (M.A.) doctoral studies lead to Ed.D. degrees in educational leadership, TESOL, and technology and learning. There are also some specialized degrees including a doctorate/master's in cross-cultural studies (M.A. in education and Ed.D.); doctorate in school psychology, including the Pupil Personnel Services Credential, CTC approval pending (Psy.D.); and doctorate, advanced standing in school psychology (Psy.D.).

The School of Social and Policy Studies (SSPS) focuses on the effects of social systems, communities, and culture on human behavior. The program in culture and human behavior (Psy.D.) uses an interdisciplinary model, combining psychology, sociology, and anthropology to educate individuals to become leaders in applying cultural psychology principles in program evaluation, diversity training, and consulting. The forensic psychology program (Ph.D. and Psy.D.) offers interdisciplinary study of law and psychology, criminal/civil justice, and mental health.

The United States International College of Business (USICB) offers the unique dynamics of a truly international faculty, student body, alumni, and curriculum. USICB provides its students with a wide range of knowledge, skills, and problem-solving abilities to successfully manage businesses in a changing international environment. Master's programs lead to the degree of M.B.A., M.I.B.A., or M.S. Doctoral programs lead to the Doctor of Business Administration (D.B.A.) degree with concentrations in strategic management and international business specializing in finance or marketing.

Research Facilities

Alliant International offers excellent research facilities throughout the system. The libraries of AIU maintain a diverse available collection of more than 160,000 books, 1,150 current print journal subscriptions, twelve electronic database subscriptions, approximately 995 psychological test titles, 1,700 audiotapes, and more than 1,200 videotapes. Each campus library is a resource for a variety of research topics and works in cooperation with several other four-year institutions in the immediate area. Each academic school or college has research clusters, labs, and/or other research resources to support original and applied research that supports original scholarly and applied research.

Financial Aid

Financial aid is available to graduate students in the form of long-term, low-interest loans (Federal Perkins Loans, Federal Stafford Student Loans and Federal Unsubsidized Stafford Loans, and Federal Supplemental Loans for Students) and part-time employment (Federal Work-Study). Research assistantships are also available. Financial aid usually carries from one campus location to another, except for Federal Work-Study. For complete information, students should contact the Financial Aid Office on the San Diego campus.

Cost of Study

Tuition usually ranges from $350 to $725 per unit, depending on the program. Graduate students usually take three 4-unit courses per quarter. On the Kenya campus, the cost in 2001–02 was 5766 Kenya shillings (approximately $73) per unit, and on the Mexico campus, the cost was 1841 pesos (approximately $190) per unit.

Living and Housing Costs

Room and board on the San Diego campus cost $8265 for the academic year for a private room and $6365 for double occupancy. On the Kenya campus, room and board cost about 36,190 Kenyan shillings (approximately $725) per quarter, double occupancy. On-campus housing is not available at the Mexico campus.

Student Group

The Student Body Government Association is the elected governing student body. Through the council, students provide input to the administration, govern extracurricular activities and participate in other areas of student life.

Student Outcomes

Alliant International alumni have successful careers internationally and domestically with financial institutions, government agencies, multinational corporations, export companies, not-for-profit groups, educational institutions, professional psychology, practice, and entrepreneurial enterprises. Their employers include Sachy & Sachy; Solaronics; Synex International; Central Ohio Psychiatric Hospital; public school districts; state, local, and federal government; and the California Psychological Association.

Location

Alliant International University has ten locations—Fresno; Irvine; Los Angeles; Sacramento; two in San Diego; two in the San Francisco Bay Area, including administrative headquarters; Mexico City, Mexico; and Nairobi, Kenya.

The University

Alliant International University was founded in 2001 through the combination of United States International University (USIU) and Alliant University/California School of Professional Psychology. AIU offers a chance to learn from a globally oriented faculty and to study with fellow students from more than fifty-eight countries. The University's mission is to educate citizens of the world, ensuring the acquisition of knowledge and competencies that are essential to live, lead, and solve problems in a global society.

Applying

First-year and transfer applicants may be admitted year-round. Later applications are processed as quickly as possible on a space-available basis. The completed application form, application fees, and supporting documents should be on file in the Office of Admissions at least thirty days prior to the term for which the applicant desires admission. These items should be sent to the Office of Admissions.

Correspondence and Information

Office of Admissions
Alliant International University
10455 Pomerado Road
San Diego, California 92131

Telephone: 858-635-4772
Fax: 858-635-4739
E-mail: admissions@alliant.edu
World Wide Web: http://www.alliant.edu

SCHOOL HEADS

Judith E. N. Albino, University President; Ph.D, Texas.
Nancy Birdwell, Vice President for Development; B.A., Texas Tech.
Soroya Moore Coley, Vice President for Academic Affairs; Ph.D, Bryn Mawr.
Joseph M. Marron, Vice President for Student Services and Enrollment Management; Ed.D., Vanderbilt.
Patricia Mullen, Vice President of Enrollment and Student Services; B.A., Williams.
Ramona Kunard, Systemwide Dean, College of Arts and Sciences and Interim Systemwide Dean, School of Social and Policy Studies; Ph.D., Minnesota.
Rodney Lohman, Systemwide Dean, California School of Organizational Studies; Ph.D., Michigan State.
Adele S. Rabin, Systemwide Dean, California School of Professional Psychology; Ph.D., Houston.
Mink Stavenga, Systemwide Dean, College of Business and Management; D.B.A., US International.
Karen Schuster Webb, Systemwide Dean, Graduate School of Education; Ph.D., Indiana.

Alliant International University is a twenty-first century global university combining the strengths of the programs, faculty members, and students of the California School of Professional Psychology and United States International University.

Educating citizens of the world.

Students in front of the Walter Library on the San Diego campus.

AMERICAN UNIVERSITY

College of Arts and Sciences

Programs of Study

Graduate programs leading to the master's and/or the Ph.D. degrees are offered in anthropology, chemistry, economics, education, history, mathematics education, psychology, sociology, and statistics. The master's degree only is offered in art history, arts management, biology, computer science, dance, development finance and banking, educational leadership, environmental science, ethics and peace, financial economics for public policy, French studies, health fitness management, information systems, literature, mathematics, philosophy, public anthropology, sociology–international training and education, Spanish: Latin American studies, special education–learning disabilities, statistics for policy analysis, teaching English to speakers of other languages (TESOL), and toxicology. A Master of Arts in Teaching degree and Master of Fine Arts degrees in creative writing and in painting, sculpture, or printmaking are also available. In addition, the College offers graduate certificates in applied economics, applied statistics, arts management, dance, dance and health fitness management, environmental assessment, information systems, secondary teaching, teaching English to speakers of other languages (TESOL), toxicology, and translation. Many graduate degrees can be completed on either a full- or part-time basis.

Research Facilities

The Bender Library and Learning Resources Center house more than 743,000 volumes and 3,100 periodical titles as well as extensive microform collections and a nonprint media center. In addition, more than fourteen indexes in compact disc format are searchable through library microcomputers. Graduate students have unlimited borrowing privileges at six other college and university libraries in the Washington Research Library Consortium, all accessible through the library's online system, ALADIN. ALADIN contains upwards of 80 databases and may also be used to hold or renew library books, perform quick searches for Internet resources, or tap into Lexis-Nexis/Academic Universe and electronic reference subscriptions from any computer with Web access. Dozens of other research collections, including the Library of Congress, are readily available locally. The Media Center provides equipment and materials for research and instructional purposes. Microcomputer resources are extensive and can be used 24 hours a day at various campus locations, including specialized terminal locations such as the Social Science Research Lab. Statistical software packages such as SYSTAT, SPSS, and SAS are available. Research laboratories and workshops are located in the Departments of Psychology, Biology, and Chemistry, which also have close working relationships with other laboratries, such as the National Institutes of Health. A language resource center, studio and performing art facilities, the Kreeger Music Library, and the University's National Center for Health Fitness offer additional resources for student work.

Each spring, the College of Arts and Sciences sponsors a daylong Student Research Conference, featuring symposia, performances, and paper presentations by students from a wide variety of disciplines.

Financial Aid

Fellowships, scholarships, and graduate assistantships are available to full-time students. Special opportunity grants for members of minority groups (African American, Hispanic American, Asian or Pacific Islander American, American Indian, or Alaskan Native American) parallel the regular honor awards and take the form of assistantships and scholarships. Research and teaching fellowships provide stipends plus tuition. Graduate assistantships provide up to 18 credit hours of tuition remission per year.

Cost of Study

For the 2001–02 academic year, tuition was $793 per credit hour. AU anticipates a 4 percent increase in tuition in 2002–03.

Living and Housing Costs

Although many graduate students live off campus, the University provides graduate dormitory rooms and apartments. The Off-Campus Housing Office maintains a referral file of rooms and apartments. Housing costs in Washington, D.C., are comparable to those in other major metropolitan areas.

Student Group

Students come from all over the United States and from more than 150 other countries. In 2000–01, 17 percent of the University's graduate student body were members of minority groups, and about 16 percent of the graduate students were international students. The number of degree-seeking women is 1,917 and men, 1,275. The total number of part-time to full-time degree-seeking students is 1,748 to 1,444. There are 174 nondegree graduate students who are women and 111 who are men. The total number of part-time to full-time nondegree graduate students is 256 to 29.

Student Outcomes

American University's emphasis on experiential education outside the classroom provides a stepping-stone to a future career. Graduates of the College of Arts and Sciences' programs have pursued doctoral studies, entered academic and policy-oriented careers, become professional artists and performers, and found employment in private industry in the United States and around the world.

Location

The national capital area offers students access to an outstanding variety of educational, cultural, and governmental resources that enrich the graduate degree programs through practical applications of theoretical studies. Opportunities for research, internships, cooperative education placements, and full- or part-time jobs exist in every discipline, from the arts and humanities to the social and natural sciences. Local shuttle bus and rail transportation from the campus provides easy access to sites such as the John F. Kennedy Center for the Performing Arts, the World Bank, the Smithsonian Institution, the National Gallery of Art, the National Zoo, the President's Council on Physical Fitness and Sports, the Department of the Treasury, NASA/Goddard Space Flight Center, the Lab School of Washington, the Consumer Product Safety Commission, the National Endowment for the Arts, the Holocaust Museum, the Department of Health and Human Services, embassies, and private corporations.

The University

American University was founded as a Methodist institution, chartered by Congress in 1893, and intended originally for graduate study only. The University is located on an 84-acre site in a residential area of northwest Washington. As a member of the Consortium of Universities of the Washington Metropolitan Area, American University can offer its degree candidates the option of taking courses at other consortium universities for residence credit.

Applying

The College of Arts and Sciences uses a rolling application process. However, for international applicants, it is highly recommended that completed applications for the fall semester are submitted by June 1 for accurate processing. Applications for awards must be received by February 1. Online or downloadable application forms may be obtained on the Web at http://www.american.edu/cas/admissions. The cost to apply is $50 for the online application submitted electronically or $80 for the paper-based application submitted by mail, including those that are downloaded. Admission consideration is open to all qualified candidates without regard to race, color, national origin, religion, sex, or handicap.

Correspondence and Information

College of Arts and Sciences
American University
McKinley 100
4400 Massachusetts Avenue, NW
Washington, D.C. 20016-8012
Telephone: 202-885-2453
E-mail: CASGRAD@american.edu
World Wide Web: http://www.american.edu/cas/admissions

DEPARTMENTAL CHAIRPERSONS AND GRADUATE ADMISSIONS CONTACTS

Anthropology (M.A., Ph.D.): (telephone: 202-885-1830; e-mail: anthro@american.edu)
William Leap, Chairperson and Admissions Contact; Ph.D., SMU.
Art (M.A., M.F.A.): (telephone: 202-885-1670; e-mail: art@american.edu)
Ron Haynie, Chairperson and M.F.A. Admissions Contact; M.F.A., American. (M.F.A. ITALY Program Contact: Sonia@american.edu)
Norma Broude, M.A. Admissions Contact; Ph.D., Columbia.
Biology (M.A., M.S.): (telephone: 202-885-2176; e-mail: biology@american.edu)
Catherine Schaeff, Chairperson; Ph.D., Queen's at Kingston.
Victoria Connaughton, M.S. Admissions Contact; Ph.D., Delaware.
Chemistry (M.S., Ph.D.): (telephone: 202-885-1750; e-mail: chem@american.edu)
Albert Cheh, M.S. and Ph.D. Admissions Contact; Ph.D., Berkeley.
Computer Science and Information Systems (M.S.): (telephone: 202-885-1470; e-mail: csis@american.edu)
Richard Gibson, Chairperson and M.S. Admissions Contact; Ph.D., Maryland, College Park.
Economics (M.A., Ph.D.): (telephone: 202-885-3770; e-mail: econ2@american.edu)
Larry Sawers, Chairperson; Ph.D., Michigan.
Mieke Meurs, Ph.D. Admissions Contact; Ph.D., Massachusetts Amherst.
Colin Bradford, M.A. Admissions Contact; Ph.D., Columbia.
Education (M.A., M.A.T., Ph.D.): (telephone: 202-885-3720; e-mail: educate@american.edu)
Lynn Fox, Dean; Ph.D., Johns Hopkins.
Sarah Irvine, M.A. in Educational Technology Admissions Contact; Ph.D., Arizona State.
Fred Jacobs, Ph.D. Admissions Contact; Ph.D., Pennsylvania.
Sophia Kountz, M.A.Ed. Leadership, M.A.T., Certification in Secondary Education, and M.A. Specialized Studies Admissions Contact; M.A., American.
Sally Smith, M.A. in Special Education Admissions Contact; M.A., NYU.
Environmental Science (M.S.): (telephone: 202-885-2178; e-mail: dculver@american.edu)
David Culver, M.S. Admissions Contact; Ph.D., Yale.
Kiho Kim, M.S. Admissions Contact; Ph.D., SUNY at Buffalo.
Health and Fitness (M.S.): (telephone: 202-885-6275; e-mail: healthfitness@american.edu)
Robert Karch, Chairperson and Admissions Contact; Ed.D., American.
History (M.A., Ph.D.): (telephone: 202-885-2401; e-mail: history@american.edu)
Valerie French, Chairperson and M.A. and Ph.D. Admissions Contact; Ph.D., UCLA.
Language and Foreign Studies (M.A.): (telephone: 202-885-2381; e-mail: lfs@american.edu)
Olga Rojer, Chairperson; Ph.D., Maryland, College Park.
Consuelo Hernández, M.A. in Spanish: Latin American Studies Admissions Contact; Ph.D., NYU.
Danielle Rodamar, M.A. in French Studies Admissions Contact; Ph.D., Michigan.
Brock Brady, M.A. in TESOL Admissions Contact; M.A., Portland State. (e-mail: tesol@american.edu)
Literature (M.A., M.F.A.): (telephone: 202-885-2971; e-mail: lit@american.edu)
Jonathan Loesberg, Chairperson; Ph.D., Cornell.
Roberta Rubenstein, M.A. Admissions Contact; Ph.D., University of London.
Kermit Moyer, M.F.A. Admissions Contact; Ph.D., Northwestern.
Mathematics and Statistics (M.A., M.S., Ph.D.): (telephone: 202-885-3120; e-mail: mathstat@american.edu)
Mary Gray, Chairperson and M.A. in Mathematics Admissions Contact; Ph.D., Kansas.
Virginia Stallings, Ph.D. in Math Education Admissions Contact; Ph.D., Southern Mississippi.
Robert Jernigan, M.S. and Ph.D. in Statistics Admissions Contact; Ph.D., South Florida.
Performing Arts (M.A.): (telephone: 202-885-3439/3413; e-mail: dpa@american.edu)
Robert Goler, General Department Contact and M.A. in Arts Management Admissions Contact; M.A., Case Western Reserve.
Philosophy and Religion (M.A.): (telephone: 202-885-2925; e-mail: philrel@american.edu)
Amy Oliver, Chairperson; Ph.D., Massachusetts.
Lucinda Peach, M.A. Admissions Contact; Ph.D., Indiana.
Psychology (M.A., Ph.D.): (telephone: 202-885-1710; e-mail: psychology@american.edu)
Tony Riley, Chairperson; Ph.D., Washington (Seattle).
Michele Carter, M.A. in Psychology Admissions Contact; Ph.D., Vanderbilt.
Carol Weissbrad, Ph.D. (Clinical) Psychology Admissions Contact; Ph.D., Northwestern.
Bryan D. Fantie, Ph.D. (Behavioral Neuroscience) Psychology Admissions Contact, Ph.D., Dalhousie.
Sociology (M.A., Ph.D.): (telephone: 202-885-2475; e-mail: socio@american.edu)
Bette Dickerson, Chairperson; Ph.D., Washington State.
Samih Farsoun, M.A. and Ph.D. Admissions Contact; Ph.D., Connecticut.
Wendy Bokhorst-Heng, International Training and Education Program Admissions Contact; Ph.D., Toronto. (telephone: 202-885-3723; e-mail: itep@american.edu)

ANGELO STATE UNIVERSITY

Graduate School

Programs of Study

Angelo State University offers programs in twenty-two areas of study leading to Master of Arts, Master of Business Administration, Master of Education, Master of Public Administration, Master of Physical Therapy, Master of Science, and Master of Science in Nursing degrees as well as an integrated B.B.A./M.B.A. degree.

Major areas of study include accounting, animal science, biology, business administration, communications, counseling psychology (with Texas state licensure as a Licensed Professional Counselor or a psychological associate), curriculum and instruction, educational diagnostics, educational guidance and counseling, English (traditional research thesis and creative writing thesis options), general psychology, history, industrial/organizational psychology, interdisciplinary studies, international studies, kinesiology, nursing, physical therapy, public administration, reading specialization, and school administration. All programs in education meet the academic requirements for the Texas State Professional Certificate in their area.

Research Facilities

The Porter Henderson Library has comprehensive electronic resources, including an online catalog and a campuswide fiber-optic computer network with Internet connectivity. The total library holdings surpass 1 million items in a variety of formats. Resources include a partial depository for federal documents, a depository for Texas state documents, and the West Texas Collection, which contains numerous primary sources in the forms of diaries, journals, and memoirs of early settlers and pioneers from Texas.

The 6,000-acre Management, Instruction, and Research Center is a multipurpose agricultural production and wildlife management area. This multimillion-dollar complex includes four instructional and research laboratories for animal science, animal anatomy and physiology, animal reproduction, animal nutrition, wildlife management, wool and mohair technology, and plant and range sciences.

The graduate programs are supported by seven state-of-the-art microcomputer labs, more than 100 software packages, and a 20:1 student-computer ratio. Additional special facilities include the Small Business Development Center, International Trade Office, Language Learning Center, and school-based clinics.

Financial Aid

Carr Academic Scholarships, ranging from $1000 to $3000 for the academic year, have summer extensions available plus full tuition and fees and are awarded on a competitive basis to full-time graduate students. Part-time graduate students are eligible for Part-time Carr Scholarships, which cover tuition and fees. Carr Research Scholarships in the amount of $3000 plus itemized expenses up to $500 are available to support research projects.

Teaching assistantships paying $9381 per academic year are available in some departments. Students must have completed 18 hours of graduate work in the field in which they teach and meet other criteria. Graduate assistantships pay a maximum of $5204 per academic year and are available in most departments. Summer assistantships, residence hall assistantships, and student loans are also available.

Cost of Study

For the 2000–01 regular fall and spring semesters, tuition for students taking 9 semester credit hours per year was $1672 for Texas residents and $5542 for nonresidents. Additional expenses include the cost of books and supplies, parking fees, and special course fees. Tuition and fees are subject to change without notice.

Living and Housing Costs

Limited dormitory housing is available. Information about on-campus housing may be obtained from the Residence Life Office (915-942-2035).

Student Group

Graduate student enrollment is approximately 400, and the total student population is 6,200. The graduate group is composed of 66 percent women, with approximately two thirds of all students attending part-time.

Location

Angelo State University is located in San Angelo, Texas (population 93,000). San Angelo, county seat of Tom Green County, is located in the heart of west Texas at the juncture of the Middle and North Concho Rivers. The city is a trading and shopping center for persons in the ranching, farming, and oil industries and is an important medical and retirement center. Three lakes, a symphony orchestra, theaters, art galleries, museums, good shopping districts, proximity to the Texas hill country, and its famous friendly attitude make San Angelo an attractive place to live and study.

The University and The School

Angelo State University, established in 1965, is a regional comprehensive institution of higher learning offering programs in the liberal and fine arts, sciences, teacher education, education for the health professions, and business administration. The purpose of the Graduate School is to provide advanced specialized training that will strengthen the academic and professional competence of the students. The graduate programs are designed to develop students' capacities for independent study, train students in the techniques of research, and acquaint them with research in their fields of study. Angelo State University is part of the Texas State University System.

Applying

All persons seeking admission to the Graduate School must complete and file an application and residency form, which is available in the back of the bulletin, on the Web, or in the office of the Graduate School. An official copy of all transcripts of credits from all colleges and universities attended must be received directly from the institution(s). M.B.A. applicants must submit GMAT scores; applicants to all other programs must submit GRE scores (nursing students may substitute MAT scores). A $25 application fee is required of domestic students and $50 of international students. Students may apply for fall, spring, or summer admission, with the exception of Master of Physical Therapy (M.P.T.) applicants. Applications for the M.P.T. program are accepted in the fall preceding the summer when classes begin.

Correspondence and Information

The Graduate School
Angelo State University
Box 11025, ASU Station
San Angelo, Texas 76909

Telephone: 915-942-2169
Fax: 915-942-2194
E-mail: graduate.school@angelo.edu
World Wide Web: http://www.angelo.edu/dept/grad_school

DEPARTMENT HEADS AND GRADUATE PROGRAM ADVISORS

Accounting, Economics, Finance: Dr. Norman Sunderman, Department Head and Program Advisor (telephone: 915-942-2046).
Animal Science: Dr. Gil Engdahl, Department Head; Dr. Cody Scott, Program Advisor (telephone: 915-942-2027).
Biology: Dr. J. Kelly McCoy, Department Head; Dr. Bonnie Amos, Program Advisor (telephone: 915-942-2189).
Business Administration: Tom Badgett, Department Head; Dr. Karen Torres, Program Advisor (telephone: 915-942-2383).
Communications: Dr. Jack Eli, Department Head; Dr. June H. Smith, Program Advisor (telephone: 915-942-2032).
Education: Dr. John J. Miazga, Department Head (telephone: 915-942-2052, Ext. 255).
- Curriculum and Instruction, Elementary Education: Dr. Judith Hakes, Program Advisor (telephone: 915-942-2052, Ext. 257).
- Curriculum and Instruction, Instructional Technology: Dr. Nancy Hadley, Program Advisor (telephone: 915-942-2052, Ext. 252).
- Curriculum and Instruction, Secondary Education: Dr. Nancy Hadley, Program Advisor (telephone: 915-942-2052, Ext. 252).
- Curriculum and Instruction, Special Education: Dr. Mack McCoulskey, Program Advisor (telephone: 915-942-2052, Ext. 269).
- Curriculum and Instruction, Reading: Dr. Cheryl Hines, Program Advisor (telephone: 915-942-2052, Ext. 254).
- Guidance and Counseling: Dr. David Tarver, Program Advisor (telephone: 915-942-2052, Ext. 262).
- Reading Specialist: Dr. Cheryl Hines, Program Advisor (telephone: 915-942-2052, Ext. 254).
- School Administration: Dr. Robert Lowe and Dr. Fritz Leifeste, Program Advisors (telephone: 915-942-2052, Ext. 253 or 266).
- Superintendent Certificate: Dr. Robert Lowe, Program Advisor (telephone: 915-942-2052, Ext. 253).

English: Dr. James Moore, Department Head; Dr. Terence A. Dalrymple, Program Advisor (telephone: 915-942-2273).
Government: Dr. Ed C. Olson, Department Head (telephone: 915-942-2262).
- International Studies: Dr. Roberto Garza, Program Advisor.
- Public Administration: Dr. Jack Barbour, Program Advisor.

History: Dr. Charles Endress, Department Head; Dr. James Ward, Program Director (telephone: 915-942-2324).
Interdisciplinary Studies: Dr. Carol Diminnie, Program Advisor (telephone: 915-942-2169).
Kinesiology: Dr. Melanie Croy, Department Head; Dr. Earl Yarbrough, Program Director (telephone: 915-942-2173).
Nursing: Dr. Edward Russell, Department Head; Dr. Leslie Mayrand, Program Advisor (telephone: 915-942-2060).
Physical Therapy: Dr. Kathleen Cegles, Department Head; Mark Pape, Program Advisor (telephone: 915-942-2545)
Psychology: Dr. William Davidson, Department Head.
- Counseling Psychology: Dr. Sangeeta Singg, Program Advisor (telephone: 915-942-2068, Ext. 251).
- General Psychology: Dr. James Forbes, Program Advisor (telephone: 915-942-2068, Ext. 249).
- Industrial/Organizational Psychology: Dr. Kraig Schell, Program Advisor (telephone: 915-942-2766, Ext. 224).

ANTIOCH NEW ENGLAND GRADUATE SCHOOL

Graduate Programs

Programs of Study

Master's degree programs are offered in applied psychology, education, environmental studies/resource management and administration, and management, and doctoral degrees are offered in clinical psychology and environmental studies. Programs are designed for the motivated adult learner. Integrating internships and practica with academic studies, programs provide a scholarly, practice-oriented education. Classes meet one to two days per week. The master's programs range from 40 to 60 credits and may take fifteen months to 2½ years to complete. The doctoral program in clinical psychology can be completed in five years, and the Ph.D. in environmental studies in four years.

The Department of Applied Psychology offers the M.A. in counseling psychology, in counseling psychology with a substance abuse/addictions counseling concentration, in marriage and family therapy, and in dance/movement therapy with a counseling psychology minor and the M.Ed. in dance/movement therapy and in substance abuse counseling. The Department of Clinical Psychology offers a Psy.D. in clinical psychology. The Department of Education offers the M.Ed. in elementary and early childhood education, with concentrations in Integrated Learning, Waldorf, and science and environmental education, as well as an Experienced Educators Program offering an M.Ed. in Foundations of Education, with concentrations in professional development and Education by Design™. The Department of Environmental Studies offers an M.S. in environmental studies and in resource management and administration and a Ph.D. in environmental studies. The Department of Organization and Management offers an M.Ed. weekend program in administration and supervision, a Master of Human Services Administration, and a Master of Science in management. A Master of Arts in Interdisciplinary Studies is also offered.

Research Facilities

Antioch New England Institute, the Graduate School's sustainable communities research and application center, works with local communities, states, national governments, and other public and nonprofit organizations to develop sustainable, citizen-based solutions. It conducts community leadership research and training, community profiles, research on regional sustainability indicators, endangered species research, natural resource inventories, and community-based environmental education programs. The institute houses three centers, the Howes Center for Community Engagement, the Center for Environmental Education, and the Craiglow Center for Applied Research and Policy. The Department of Clinical Psychology houses the Center for Research on Psychological Practice and the Antioch Psychological Services Center. The focused library collection includes books, journals, conference proceedings, audio and video materials, curriculum materials, dissertations and theses, and government documents. Services include computerized access to bibliographic databases, interlibrary loan networks, Internet access, audiovisual equipment, and online library services. Students have access to 38,000 cataloged books and documents and 1,600 journal titles as well as the 300,000-volume collection at Antioch College in Yellow Springs, Ohio.

Financial Aid

Antioch New England participates in Federal Stafford Loan, Federal Perkins Loan, and Federal Work-Study programs. There are on-campus work-study positions available. Many interning students are paid for their work through the work-study program. Fellowships awarded include the Howard M. and Sondra D. Bender Fellowship (Dance/Movement Therapy Program), the Waldorf Teacher Training Fellowship, the Reader's Digest Fellowship, and the Racial/Ethnic Fellowship. In 1999–2000, Antioch New England awarded $224,000 in Federal Perkins Loans, $545,000 in Federal Work-Study awards, and more than $8.5 million in Federal Stafford and alternative loans. An interest-free payment plan is available.

Cost of Study

Students pay an established semester charge, which varies by program, for each semester registered. In 2002–03, tuition for master's degree programs ranges from $2750 to $5050 for the summer semester and $2850 to $6350 for the fall and spring semesters. Doctoral programs cost $3600 to $4100 for the summer semester and $4650 to $9500 for the fall and spring semesters. Tuition and fee rates are subject to change each academic year, effective with the summer term. Students should contact the Office of Admissions for more information.

Living and Housing Costs

Antioch New England Graduate School does not provide housing. Privately owned apartments and houses are available in the area. For students who relocate to the Keene region, living expenses are budgeted at $1100 per month.

Student Group

The 1,200 graduate students enrolled have an average of three to six years of professional experience and are seeking further accreditation in their fields, professional development, or a career change. The average age is 38, and 66 percent are women. Approximately 80 percent commute from the six New England states; another 7 percent come from New York State and the remainder from other states, Australia, Canada, Germany, India, Israel, Italy, Korea, and Switzerland.

Location

Antioch New England is centrally located in Keene, New Hampshire, in the picturesque Mount Monadnock region of southern New Hampshire. A small city with well-developed business, social, and educational resources, Keene is well connected to many parts of New England, and students can commute from considerable distances. Albany, New York, and Boston, Massachusetts, are 2 hours by car. Management programs are also offered in Portsmouth, New Hampshire. Experienced Educator cluster sites are located throughout New England.

The Graduate School

Antioch New England is a private, independent graduate school that offers graduate programs and training directed at enhancing the quality of life, the environment, work and learning settings, and human relationships. The integration of internships and practica with academic studies is a fundamental aspect of all programs. Little value is placed on competitiveness, except in the pursuit of academic excellence. Qualitative scales and narrative assessment are used to evaluate student learning. Most students continue employment while pursuing their degrees. There are three semesters. Entry points for master's programs vary depending upon department and program.

Applying

Applications for all master's programs are reviewed on a rolling basis. Applicants are encouraged to use a self-managed application procedure. A personal interview is required. Completed applications for the doctoral program in clinical psychology must be received by January 10, 2003, for entry in September of that year, and, for the doctoral program in environmental studies, they must be received by February 1, 2003, for June entry. All prospective students are encouraged to attend a departmental information session and visit classes before applying.

Correspondence and Information

Office of Admissions
Antioch New England Graduate School
40 Avon Street
Keene, New Hampshire 03431-3552

Telephone: 603-357-6265
603-357-7254 (TTY/TDD)
Fax: 603-357-0718
E-mail: admissions@antiochne.edu
World Wide Web: http://www.antiochne.edu

THE FACULTY

Listed below are department chairpersons and program directors.

Department of Applied Psychology: Julia Halevy, Dott. Ped., Chairperson.
M.A. Program in Counseling Psychology and Counseling Psychology with a Concentration in Substance Abuse/Addictions Counseling: Diane Kurinsky, Ed.D., Director.
M.A. Program in Marriage and Family Therapy: David Watts, Ed.D., Director.
M.A. in Dance/Movement Therapy with a Minor in Counseling Psychology: Susan Loman, M.A., ADTR, Director.

Department of Clinical Psychology: Roger L. Peterson, Ph.D., Chairperson.

Department of Education: Peter R. Eppig, M.Ed., Chairperson
M.Ed. Teacher Certification Programs: David Sobel, M.Ed.
M.Ed. Experienced Educators Program: Tom Julius, Ed.D., Director.
M.Ed. Waldorf Program: Torin Finser, Ph.D., Director.
M.Ed. Education by Design™: Marcea Gustafson, M.S., Director.

Department of Environmental Studies: Mitchell Thomashow, Ed.D., Chairperson.
M.S. Program in Resource Management and Administration: Joy N. Ackerman, M.S., and Michael H. Simpson, M.A., M.S., Co-directors.
M.S. Program in Conservation Biology: Jon Atwood, Ph.D., Director.
M.S. Program in Environmental Education: Cynthia B. Thomashow, M.S.T., M.Ed., Director.
M.S. Teacher Certification Programs: Jimmy Karlan, Ed.D., Academic Director.
Doctoral Studies: Mitchell Thomashow, Ed.D., Academic Director.

Department of Organization and Management: Steven P. Guerriero, Ph.D., Chairperson.

Antioch New England challenges its community to improve the quality of life locally and globally through research, community action, professional service, and stewardship of the natural world.

Antioch New England provides a transformative education by linking the worlds of scholarship and activism and by fostering the process of lifelong learning.

Antioch New England is a place where many people reflect a high level of personal and professional self-reflection and awareness.

ANTIOCH UNIVERSITY McGREGOR

ANTIOCH UNIVERSITY MCGREGOR

Graduate School

Programs of Study

Antioch University McGregor offers graduate programs in management, management for community college professionals, conflict resolution, educational leadership, and teacher licensure and a Master of Arts in the student's field of choice through the Individualized Liberal and Professional Studies (ILPS) Program.

The Master of Arts in Management Program attracts students who want to enhance their lives and career options by developing managerial skills. The program prepares graduates for careers in a global community by developing their capacity to adapt to societal change. This is an intensive two-year M.A. program offered on Saturdays and is intended for full-time students. Students come into this program at various phases of their careers in corporate, industrial, government, and not-for-profit organizations.

The Master of Arts in Management for Community College Professionals Program provides a unique educational experience for current and aspiring community college managers and administrators. The curriculum includes the traditional management disciplines while focusing on issues relevant to community college professionals. This is a limited-residency two-year program. Courses are offered through a combination of face-to-face meetings during residencies and online study.

The Master of Arts in Conflict Resolution Program is an internationally recognized program with a reputation for graduating students who are highly skilled and knowledgeable theorist-practitioners. This is an eight-quarter, half-time program. Students attend two 14-day residencies, participate in online courses, and complete a practicum. Students may bring up to 9 quarter credit hours of prior learning.

The Teacher Licensure Program provides course work and preparation required for an Ohio license in order to teach in public schools. Graduates must be able to connect with diverse classrooms, be creative and competent, and be compassionate teachers in the twenty-first century. Age groups and concentrations are mild to moderate intervention specialist (grades PK–12), early childhood education (grades PK–3), middle childhood education (grades 4–9), and adolescent and young adult (grades 7–12).

The Ohio Principal Licensure Program prepares principals who are up to meeting the challenges of school administration with effective and innovative leadership skills. This program is characterized by a practical and realistic orientation to school administration. There is a strong emphasis on curricular and instructional leadership issues.

The Master of Education (M.Ed.) in Educational Leadership Program prepares educational administrators and teachers who are capable of dynamic leadership and innovative change in today's fast-paced school climate. Antioch University McGregor provides its students with a classroom-based, experiential approach to leadership that emphasizes understanding the reasons behind actions. This approach, combined with practical organizational and management skills, makes this a program that fully equips grade PK–12 educators to manage diverse educational environments that foster lifelong learning.

A Master of Arts through the ILPS Program allows students to collaborate with an Antioch faculty adviser who is an expert in a field of study to design courses and a Master of Arts degree. This M.A. allows students to meet their own personal, educational, and professional needs while maintaining high academic standards. This is a limited-residency program that can be taken either as a distance learning program or as a program local to the student, depending on the student's preferences and academic resources.

Research Facilities

Students have access to the Olive Kettering Library, located in Yellow Springs, Ohio. The library houses a collection of more than 325,000 volumes, including extensive files of bound periodicals, many of which date back to the nineteenth century. In addition, it offers information in microform (more than 46,000 pieces) and carries subscriptions to more than 900 periodicals. The Kettering Library is a member of OhioLink, a consortium of the libraries of seventy-eight Ohio colleges and universities.

Financial Aid

Antioch participates in the Federal Stafford Student Loan, the Federal Perkins Loan, and Federal Work-Study programs. Other payment options are available. Approximately 50 percent of students receive financial aid.

Cost of Study

Each program of study differs in cost depending on the number of credits needed to graduate. Antioch is a moderately priced private higher education institution. Average tuition costs to complete a graduate degree program range from $14,000 to $22,000.

Living and Housing Costs

The University does not offer on-campus housing. Students either commute or are enrolled in limited-residency programs.

Student Group

Most students are working professionals. Student activities focus on events organized within the academic programs.

Location

Antioch University McGregor is located in Yellow Springs, Ohio.

The University

Founded in 1852, Antioch University has had a proud history of progressive education for more than 150 years. Under the guidance of Horace Mann, the father of public education, Antioch was the first college to offer equal opportunities to women and one of the first colleges to admit African-American students. Antioch continued to break ground by including community participation and service as an integral part of the higher education curriculum. In 1996, Antioch received the prestigious John D. and Catherine T. MacArthur Foundation Award for creative genius in recognition of its history of innovative education. Today, Antioch University has six campuses across the United States: Antioch College and Antioch University McGregor in Yellow Springs, Ohio; Antioch University Seattle in Washington; Antioch New England Graduate School in New Hampshire; and Antioch Southern California in Los Angeles and Santa Barbara.

Applying

Applications are accepted throughout the year. Financial aid applications should be submitted six weeks before the quarter begins to ensure timely receipt of aid, loans, and grants. Applicants must take part in a personal interview with the Admissions Committee. GRE or GMAT scores are not required for admission. Applications may be submitted online at the Web site listed below.

Correspondence and Information

Office of Student and Alumni Services
Antioch University McGregor
800 Livermore Street
Yellow Springs, Ohio 45387

Telephone: 937-769-1818
Fax: 937-769-1805
E-mail: sas@mcgregor.edu
World Wide Web: http://www.mcgregor.edu

FACULTY

Students should visit http://www.mcgregor.edu for a complete list of faculty member research interests and a listing of associated faculty members by program.

Getinet Belay, Associate Professor of Intercultural Relations and Co-Chair of Intercultural Relations Department; Ph.D., Berlin. Interaction and identity, communication and culture, cultural globalization, cyberculture/cybercommunity, cultural studies.
Steven J. Brzezinski, Academic Dean and Faculty; Ph.D., Illinois. Teaching interests, marketing.
Robert Dizney, Associate Professor of Education; M.Ed., Miami (Ohio). Appalachian culture, gender bias, foreign languages, queer theory, writing and reading instruction, reading styles, learning styles, cooperative learning.
Helen Epps, Associate Faculty; M.Ed., Ashland. Teacher education and licensure.
Barbara Gellman-Danley, President and Faculty; Ph.D., Oklahoma. Educational technology.
Jane Gordon, Associate Professor of Psychology; Ph.D., SUNY at Albany. Personality formation, attitude formation, racism and discrimination.
Beverly Guterman, Professor of Education and Director of Teacher Education; Ed.D., Indiana. Comprehensive school reform, democratic curricula and public education, interaction of student and school cultures, program evaluation and assessment.
Katherine Hale, Professor and Chair of Conflict Resolution; Ph.D., Oklahoma. Conflict studies curriculum design, collaborative decision-making processes, communication and conflict, comparative models of mediation.
Linda Johnston, Assistant Professor of Conflict Resolution; Ph.D., George Mason. Health-related conflicts, racial and ethnic conflicts, narrative analysis, worldview theory.
James Malarkey, Professor of Humanities; Ph.D., Texas at Austin. World classics and contemporary life, Middle East, North Africa.
Beloo Mehra, Assistant Professor of Education; Ph.D., Illinois at Urbana-Champaign. Cultural models of schooling, immigrant and multicultural education, qualitative and practitioner research in education.
Marge Mott, Professor of Education; Ph.D., Dayton. Education, art.
Diane Nelson, Associate Professor of Teacher Education; Ph.D., Miami (Ohio). Integration of multicultural literature into classroom instruction, partners in learning, community-based collaborative leadership techniques.
Virginia Paget, Professor of Educational Administration and Director of ILPS Program; Ph.D., Washington (St. Louis). Organizational change, school reform and the public, deliberative democracy.
Michael Robinson, Associate Professor of Management and Director of Graduate Management; M.A., Antioch McGregor. Leadership development, organizational change, small-group process, team building.
Jon Saari, Associate Professor of English; Ph.D., Bowling Green State. Twentieth-century and contemporary novels, contemporary autobiography and memoir, contemporary American culture, film studies.
Zak Sharif, Associate Professor and Chair of Ohio Principal Licensure; Ph.D., Miami (Ohio). Cultural studies.
Sherry Sutton, Faculty, Teacher Education; M.Ed., Wright State. Multicultural education, urban education, school reform.
Linda Tibbetts, Associate Faculty; M.B.A., Wright State. Human resources management.
Iris Weisman, Associate Professor of Higher Education and Chair of ILPS Program; Ed.D., North Carolina State. Higher education administration, community college leadership, educational program planning.
Linda Ziegahn, Associate Professor of Adult Education and Co-Chair of Intercultural Relations Department; Ph.D., Michigan State. Transformative learning, cultural issues, online communication, social networks, adult education.

ANTIOCH UNIVERSITY SEATTLE

Graduate Programs

Programs of Study

Antioch University Seattle offers graduate degree programs in art therapy, education, environment and community, management, organizational psychology, psychology, and whole systems design. Post-master's certificates in art therapy and foster care and adoption therapy are also offered.

The graduate programs in education provide a collaborative and challenging academic environment that continues Antioch's long tradition of progressive education. The graduate programs in education emphasize current research and its implications for student learning, the integration of theory and practice, multidimensional learning, and leadership for educational change. Antioch values and builds on the skills, knowledge, and talents that students bring to their graduate work.

The M.A. in education is for experienced educators. This program offers two options: the campus-based program (full- or part-time) for K–12 and adult educators and the site-based program (full-time) that is designed primarily for K–12 teachers.

The Graduate Teacher Certification Program is a full-time postbaccalaureate program for adults interested in becoming certified elementary, middle, or high school teachers. Students may earn a Washington State Teaching Certificate in four quarters or certification plus a master's in education in six quarters. Students come to the program with backgrounds in fields such as art, business, social service, homemaking, law, and engineering.

The M.A. in psychology programs offer clinical and individualized options. Clinical options include mental health counseling and couple and family therapy and can be extended to include art therapy. Graduates are able to meet the educational requirements for Washington State licensure as a mental health counselor or a couple and family therapist. The individualized option includes a self-directed, self-designed program for those who wish to pursue individualized and interdisciplinary studies in psychology (e.g., applying psychology as teachers, consultants, mediators, personal coaches, or trainers) or for those who wish to interweave psychology with another discipline for social action, interventions, ecopsychology, and community development. Postgraduate certificates are also offered in art therapy and foster care and adoption.

The M.A. in organizational psychology prepares students to transform and revitalize organizations and communities. Students gain an understanding of self, the ability to nurture relationships, and a practical understanding of organizations, systems, and intervention. Graduates work as project managers; practitioners; trainers; human resource managers; line managers in corporations, government and nonprofit groups, and start ups; and are self-employed professionals.

The M.S. in management program is designed to prepare working adults to be leaders of progressive change in their organizations. Students enter in September and go through the two-year degree program as part of a cohort and learning community. Classes are scheduled each month in a three-day weekend format from September to June. In the first year the program integrates collaborative leadership skills with an academic introduction to economics, finance strategy, marketing, ethics, and organizational behavior. In the second year, students participate in the design of their studies and focus on critical management issues that they face in their work environments. Teamwork, collaborative learning, and personal mastery are major emphases throughout the program.

The M.A. in environment and community program is for practitioners and educators who want to be leaders and problem solvers in fostering environmental stewardship and accountability. Students represent many professions and vocations and arrive from all over the United States and other countries. The program accommodates those students with a Pacific Northwest focus and those with a national/international focus. Students enter as part of a cohort in fall or spring quarter and complete six 9-day intensive sessions over a two-year period. They conduct much of the course work in their own region, focusing on issues related to that region.

The M.A. in whole systems design program brings together science, the humanities, and design to prepare students to go beyond the narrow problem definitions and thinking of the status quo. Students learn to understand a situation in terms of its context, interrelationships, and dynamics and to imagine and create new possibilities for taking action in the world. Students are prepared to bring wisdom, clarity, skill, and creativity to their work for practical engagement and positive change in their organizations, communities, cultures, and personal lives. The whole systems design program offers two options. The individualized option allows students to set their own degree focus, combining their individual interests with program requirements. Students in this option combine course work (usually meeting once per week) and individualized study and is available only in Seattle. The organization systems renewal option (OSR) is designed for people facilitating organizational change, whether managers, internal or external consultants, or individuals in leadership roles. OSR is a two-year cohort-based learning community that meets for extended weekends and two weeklong sessions and is available in Seattle and Chicago.

Research Facilities

In addition to Antioch's library and computer labs, Antioch students have complete access to the University of Washington's extensive main research library and its eighteen branch libraries.

Financial Aid

Antioch participates in the Federal Stafford Loan, the Federal Perkins Loan, Federal Work-Study Programs, Pell Grants, and Supplemental Educational Opportunity Grants. Other state aid and payment options are available. Approximately 71 percent of students receive financial aid.

Cost of Study

Each degree program differs in cost depending on the number of credits needed to graduate. Antioch is a moderately priced private, nonprofit higher education institution. Average tuition costs to complete a graduate degree program range from $18,200 to $29,000.

Living Costs

The University does not offer on-campus housing. Most students commute and work full- or part-time. A typical graduate student's monthly budget for housing, food, and personal expenses is $1300.

Student Group

Most students are working professionals. Student activities focus on events organized within the academic programs.

Location

Antioch University Seattle is located in downtown Seattle, Washington.

The University

Founded in 1852, Antioch University has had a proud history of progressive education for more than 140 years. Under the guidance of Horace Mann, the father of public education, Antioch was the first college to offer equal opportunities to women and one of the first colleges to admit African-American students. The commitment continues today, as community participation and service is an integral part of the higher education curriculum. In 1996, Antioch received the prestigious John D. and Catherine T. MacArthur Foundation Award for creative genius in recognition of its history of innovative education. Today, Antioch University has six campuses across the United States: Antioch College and the McGregor School of Graduate Studies in Yellow Springs, Ohio; Antioch University Seattle in Washington; Antioch New England Graduate School in New Hampshire; and Antioch Southern California in Los Angeles and Santa Barbara.

Applying

Applications are accepted throughout the year. Late applications may be considered if space is available in the program. Visiting and international students are welcome. Applicants must take part in a personal interview before acceptance to a program. GRE or GMAT scores are not required for admission. Financial aid applications should be submitted six to ten weeks before the quarter starts to ensure timely receipt of aid, loans, and grants.

Correspondence and Information

To request a school catalog or for more information:

Admissions
Antioch University Seattle
2326 Sixth Avenue
Seattle, Washington 98121
Telephone: 206-268-4202
Fax: 206-441-3307
E-mail: admissions@antiochsea.edu
World Wide Web: http://www.antiochsea.edu

PROGRAM DIRECTORS/CHAIRS

Graduate Education Programs: Tina Dawson, Ed.D., Virginia Tech.
Graduate Psychology Programs: Liang Tien, Psy.D., Denver.
Graduate Management Program: Mark Hower, M.S., Antioch.
Graduate Environment and Community Programs: Jonathan Scherch, Ph.D., Tennessee.
Graduate Whole Systems Design Program: Betsy Geist, Ph.D., Union (Ohio).
Graduate Organizational Psychology Program: Barbara Spraker, M.R.E., Drew; M.B.A., City (Seattle).

Challenging classes are designed to complement the schedules of working adults.

The educational goals of the student directs the learning process.

Antioch University Seattle offers the only Master of Arts degree in environment and community in the world.

ARCADIA UNIVERSITY

Graduate and Professional Studies

Programs of Study

The Master of Arts (M.A.) degree is offered in English, humanities, and counseling. English offers an integrated approach to the study of various kinds of written communication. Humanities provides an interdisciplinary study of one of the following areas: literature and language; fine arts, theater, and music; or history, philosophy, and religion, from the perspective of related disciplines. Depending on the track selected, the counseling degree prepares psychologists for work in community, industry, or health settings or in elementary and/or secondary school counseling.

The Master of Arts in Education (M.A.Ed.) program offers areas of concentration in such disciplines as art education, biology, chemistry, computer education, environmental education, health education, history, mathematics, music, philosophy, psychology, religion, and written communication. The environmental education program is a certification program that is offered in cooperation with the nearby Schuylkill Center for Environmental Education.

The Master of Education (M.Ed.) program includes areas of concentration in art education, biology, chemistry, computer education, early childhood education, educational leadership, elementary education, language arts, library science, mathematics education, reading, secondary education, special education, supervision, and written communication. Pennsylvania certification is available in all of the above areas except computer education and language arts. Certification is also available in pupil personnel services.

The Master of Science in Genetic Counseling (M.S.G.C.) is earned through a two-year, full-time program that includes academic and clinical experience. The program prepares counselors to deal with the new medical technologies related to human genetics and reproduction and to communicate effectively with clients.

The Master of Science in Public Health (M.S.P.H.) is an entry-level degree into the field of public health. It trains graduates to work effectively as public-health professionals in a wide array of health-related organizations.

The Master of Science in Health Education (M.S.H.Ed.) is designed for students interested in directing health programs in community and institutional settings.

The Doctorate in Physical Therapy (D.P.T.) is earned through a full-time, entry-level program that provides the academic study and clinical experience required by the American Physical Therapy Association for work as a professional physical therapist. The program consists of three academic years of formal course work integrated with clinical internships. The program is accredited by the APTA.

The Transitional Doctorate of Physical Therapy (D.P.T.) is a transitional pathway for practicing clinicians intending to make their final education congruent with students graduating from entry-level D.P.T. programs.

The Master of Arts in International Peace and Conflict Resolution (M.A.I.P.C.R.) prepares students for career positions in nongovernmental organizations (NGOs) and intergovernmental organizations (IGOs).

The Master of Science in Physician Assistant Studies (M.S.P.A.S.) is earned through a two-year educational program divided into didactic course work, clinical instruction, and clinical rotations.

The Certificate of Advanced Study (C.A.S.) program is a post-master's program that allows specialization and research in an area of education but does not lead to a doctoral degree.

Research Facilities

The Landman Library has 139,203 volumes, more than 57,000 units of microfilm, and 798 print periodical subscriptions. Students have access to several online bibliographical databases, and materials are made available through interlibrary loan and through membership in a cooperative group of academic libraries. For students of science, psychology, and physical therapy, there are excellent laboratory facilities in Marion Angell Boyer Hall. Internet services for students include the World Wide Web, Telnet, file transfer protocol (ftp), and e-mail. Software applications available include Microsoft Office, statistical and graphing packages, image-editing programs, and a variety of other software for class use. Programming languages available include C++, the Microsoft Visual Studio languages, SAS, Delphi/Pascal, Prolog, MS Assembler, and others. Working environments and operating systems include Windows NT/2000 and browsers. Student laboratories are located in Boyer Hall, which houses three PC labs and one Macintosh lab; in the library; and in the Educational Enhancement Center in Taylor Hall. The CD-ROM network for research, located in the library, has been replaced by online database subscriptions. In addition, some academic departments (such as Fine Arts, Biology, and Psychology) maintain computer equipment for their specific disciplines. Brubaker Hall also houses three PC-equipped teaching classrooms.

Financial Aid

A limited number of graduate assistantships and scholarships are available for qualified students.

Cost of Study

Tuition for 2001–02 was $420 per credit. Tuition for the physical therapy, genetic counseling, physician assistant studies, and international peace and conflict resolution programs ranges from $17,000 to $23,000 per academic year.

Living and Housing Costs

A limited number of residence life assistantships are available for qualified students. Rooms and/or apartments are available to single students.

Student Group

Graduate enrollment at Arcadia University consists of approximately 1,200 students. The majority of students study part-time, except for those in the genetic counseling, international peace and conflict resolution, and physician assistant studies programs, which require a two-year, full-time commitment. The Doctorate in Physical Therapy requires a three-year, full-time commitment.

Location

The University is located in a suburb of Philadelphia, 14 miles from the center of the city. Theaters, museums, and the Philadelphia Orchestra are half an hour away by train or car. On campus, there are always a variety of lectures, concerts, and plays.

The University

Arcadia University, founded in 1853, is a comprehensive university committed to providing an education that integrates liberal learning with career preparation. The University operates one of the largest, campus-based centers in this country for study abroad and supports a wide array of cultural, intellectual, and recreational activities.

Applying

Admission to graduate programs is based on an overall evaluation of credentials, including the applicant's undergraduate record, which should show approximately a B average or better in the major field. Applicants to programs other than genetic counseling, international peace and conflict resolution, physical therapy, and physician assistant studies should apply at least six weeks before the semester in which they plan to enroll. A $50 application fee must accompany the application. Applicants to the genetic counseling, physical therapy, and physician assistant studies programs must apply by January 15. The deadline to apply to the international peace and conflict resolution program is April 1. Applicants who do not fulfill admission requirements or who have undergraduate deficiencies may be admitted conditionally. Applications and supporting documents should be sent to the appropriate office listed below.

Correspondence and Information

For certification programs and programs in counseling, education, English, health education, and humanities:

Office of Graduate and Professional Studies
Arcadia University
450 South Easton Road
Glenside, Pennsylvania 19038-3295
Telephone: 215-572-2925
800-767-0031 (toll-free)
Fax: 215-572-2126
E-mail: grad@arcadia.edu

For full-time programs in genetic counseling, physical therapy, physician assistant studies, public health, and international peace and conflict resolution:

Office of Enrollment Management
Arcadia University
450 South Easton Road
Glenside, Pennsylvania 19038-3295
Telephone: 215-572-2910
877-272-2342 (toll-free)
Fax: 215-572-4049
E-mail: admiss@arcadia.edu

FACULTY HEADS AND PROGRAM COORDINATORS

Michael L. Berger, Vice President for Academic Affairs and Provost; Ed.D., Columbia.
Mark P. Curchak, Dean of Graduate and Professional Studies; Ph.D., Berkeley.
Maureen Guim, Assistant Dean of Graduate Studies; M.Ed., Arcadia.

Chairpersons

Biology: John Hoffman, Associate Professor; Ph.D., Michigan.
Chemistry: Chester M. Mikulski, Associate Professor; Ph.D., Drexel.
Education: Steve Gulkus, Associate Professor; Ph.D., West Virginia.
English: Jo Ann Weiner, Associate Professor; Ph.D., Florida.
Fine Arts: Robert Mauro, Associate Professor; M.F.A., Pratt.
Foreign Languages: Carol Klein, Assistant Professor; Ph.D., Illinois.
International Peace and Conflict Resolution: Warren Haffar, Assistant Professor; Ph.D., Pennsylvania.
Mathematics: Edward F. Wolff, Associate Professor; Ph.D., Massachusetts.
Music: William V. Frabizio, Associate Professor; D.Mus.A., Temple.
Philosophy/Religion: Finabarr W. O'Connor, Professor; Ph.D., Pennsylvania.
Physical Therapy: Rebecca Craik, Associate Professor; Ph.D., Temple.
Physician Assistant Studies: Michael Dryer, Professor; M.P.H., New York Medical College.
Psychology: Barbara Nodine, Professor; Ph.D., Massachusetts.
Public Health (M.S.): Andrea Crivelli-Kovach, Assistant Professor; Ph.D., Temple.

Coordinators

Certificate of Advanced Study (C.A.S.): Steven P. Gulkus, Associate Professor; Ph.D., West Virginia.
Computer Education (M.A.Ed., M.Ed.): Steven P. Gulkus, Associate Professor; Ph.D., West Virginia.
Counseling (M.A.): Samuel M. Cameron, Professor: Ph.D., Pennsylvania.
Early Childhood Education (M.Ed.): Christina Ager, Assistant Professor; Ph.D., Lehigh.
Educational Leadership (M.Ed.): Steven S. Goldberg, Professor; J.D., Brooklyn Law; Ph.D., Pennsylvania.
English (M.A., M.A.Ed.): Richard Wertime, Professor; Ph.D., Pennsylvania.
Environmental Education (M.A.Ed.): Deborah Pomeroy, Assistant Professor; Ed.D., Harvard.
Genetic Counseling (M.S.G.C.): Deborah Eunpu, Program Director; M.S., C.G.C., Sarah Lawrence.
Health Education (M.S., M.A.Ed.): Andrea Crivelli-Kovach, Assistant Professor; Ph.D., Temple.
Humanities (M.A.): Richard Wertime, Professor; Ph.D., Pennsylvania.
International Peace and Conflict Resolution (M.A.): Warren Haffar, Director; Ph.D., Pennsylvania.
Language Arts (M.Ed.): Bette Goldstone, Assistant Professor; Ed.D., Temple.
Public Health (M.S.): Andrea Crivelli-Kovach, Assistant Professor; Ph.D., Temple.
Reading (M.Ed.): Steven P.Gulkus, Associate Professor; Ph.D., West Virginia.
Science Education (M.A.Ed., M.Ed.): Deborah Pomeroy, Assistant Professor; Ed.D., Harvard.
Supervision (M.Ed.): Steven S. Goldberg, Professor; J.D., Brooklyn Law; Ph.D., Pennsylvania.

ARGOSY UNIVERSITY–SARASOTA

Graduate Programs

Programs of Study

The School of Psychology offers the Doctor of Education (Ed.D.) degree in counseling, organizational leadership, and pastoral community counseling. These three Ed.D. programs consist of 60 credit hours beyond the master's degree, including 42–45 credit hours of course work and 15–18 credit hours of dissertation. Each degree program is designed to meet the special requirements of working professionals motivated to develop their knowledge and skills in their chosen or desired careers. These programs offer students the opportunity to prepare for working in various settings with the skills and credentials necessary to pursue leadership, supervisory, training, and teaching positions in the professions. Each program intentionally integrates the engagement of knowledge, the development of skills, reflective practice, and research in a manner that offers students an opportunity to prepare to address their professional activities effectively and in an ethically responsible manner. The School also offers the Educational Specialist (Ed.S.) degree in school counseling in a 30-credit-hour program that is designed for experienced school teachers who have master's degrees and desire to meet the specialization requirements for certification in guidance counseling (K–12) in the state of Florida. The Master of Arts (M.A.) degree programs in guidance counseling and mental health counseling are 60-credit-hour programs that are offered to give human service providers the extensive knowledge and range of skills necessary to function effectively in their professions. Courses and curricula for the M.A. programs are designed to parallel prevailing licensure and certification requirements in counseling as closely as possible. Because of variations among states, each student should check with regional authorities to confirm such requirements.

The School of Business offers the Doctor of Business Administration (D.B.A.) in the following areas: accounting, information systems, international business, management, and marketing. The D.B.A. is a practice-oriented program of study and is structured to permit students to earn an advanced degree with minimal interruption to their careers. A maximum of seven years is permitted to complete the 60-credit-hour program, which includes 45 credit hours of course work and 15 credit hours of dissertation. The 36-credit-hour Master of Business Administration (M.B.A.) degree program is a regional in-residence program for students commuting to Sarasota, Tampa, and Clearwater to attend evening and/or Saturday classes. Students have a maximum of three years to complete the master's program. Several business certificate programs are offered for people who would like to supplement their degrees within specialty areas.

The School of Education offers the Doctor of Education (Ed.D.) degree in educational leadership and curriculum and instruction (K–12 and higher education). Both of these programs consist of 60 credit hours beyond the master's degree, including 45 credit hours of course work and 15 credit hours of dissertation. The Educational Specialist (Ed.S.) degree requires 30 credit hours beyond the master's degree and is available in educational leadership and curriculum and instruction for those who work in K–12 school systems. The Master of Education (M.Ed.) requires 39 hours of course work and is offered as a regional in-residence program for students in or near Sarasota, Tampa, or Clearwater. The degree is available in either curriculum and instruction or educational leadership.

Research Facilities

The library houses a specialized collection of books, journals, dissertations, CD-ROMs, computers, and online databases to support the studies and research of students and faculty members in the fields of business, education, counseling, and psychology. These resources are supplemented through interlibrary loan agreements. When working off campus, students have access to library support and resources via Embanet, the University's electronic communication intranet.

Financial Aid

Financial aid is available for those who qualify. Argosy University participates in federal student loan programs and the Federal Work Study Program. Some students may qualify for veteran's assistance. While the University provides assistance in the administrative function of the program, the financial aid loan is a binding agreement between the student and the lender. Approximately 30 percent of students are receiving financial aid assistance.

Cost of Study

Full-time tuition and fees vary by program. Students who wish to obtain current tuition and fee information should contact the campus admissions office or visit the University's Web site (listed below).

Living and Housing Costs

Students typically reside at local hotels and motels when they attend one-week in-resident intersessions. The University maintains a list of motels and hotels that have agreed to offer discounted rates to Argosy University–Sarasota students. Although many students secure car rentals, the University offers a limited shuttle service between certain motels and the campus during intersession periods.

Student Group

There are 2,231 students, 56 percent of whom are women, enrolled at Argosy University–Sarasota. The enrollment by college is as follows: School of Education, 995; School of Business, 497; and School of Psychology, 653; and students-at-large, 86. The following percentages reflect the degree level of student enrollment: bachelor's, 3.8 percent; master's, 15.9 percent; educational specialist, .9 percent; doctorate, 75.4 percent; and student-at-large, 4 percent.

Location

Sarasota, Florida, is a culturally rich seaside community located on the southwest coast of Florida, approximately 50 miles south of Tampa. The University occupies modern facilities on 17th Street at Honore Avenue in northeast Sarasota. The Tampa campus offers courses for regional students at its branch sites in Tampa and Largo, Florida.

The University

Formerly the University of Sarasota, Argosy University–Sarasota was established in 1969 to serve the educational needs of adult working professionals. The University is an independent, coeducational institution of higher learning accredited by the Higher Learning Commission and a member of the North Central Association of Colleges and Schools (telephone: 312-263-0456; http://www.ncahigherlearningcommission.org) to award bachelor's, master's, educational specialist, and doctoral degrees. The programs of study are generally offered in a flexible format to accommodate the schedules of working professionals who wish to pursue an advanced degree with minimal interruption to their careers. Students can meet their in-residence course requirements by attending intensive one-week sessions that are typically scheduled to coincide with traditional fall, winter, spring, and summer breaks. Approximately half of a program's course work can be completed off campus as distance tutorials with assigned faculty members.

Applying

The University has a rolling admissions process whereby the admissions committee meets on a monthly basis to review all completed application packets that have been received since the last meeting. A $50 application fee is required.

Correspondence and Information

Admissions Office
Argosy University–Sarasota
5250 17th Street
Sarasota, Florida 34235
Telephone: 941-379-0404
Fax: 941-279-5964
World Wide Web: http://www.argosyu.edu

FACULTY HEADS AND RESEARCH AREAS

One of the most outstanding aspects of Argosy University–Sarasota is the dedication of the faculty members and their ability to cultivate a supportive learning environment. Faculty members believe that their primary roles are those of mentor, teacher, and co-learner.

School of Business

Pete Simmons, Dean; Ph.D. (industrial/organizational psychology), South Florida.

Faculty areas of research specialization include marketing, business policy, information systems, ethics, law, accounting, international trade, and organizational management.

School of Education

Nancy Hoover, Dean; Ed.D. (educational administration), Louisville.

School of Psychology

Douglas G. Riedmiller, Dean; Psy.D. (clinical psychology), Florida Institute of Technology.

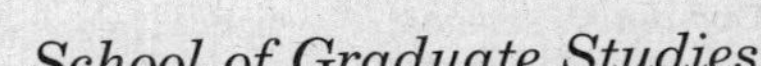

ARMSTRONG ATLANTIC STATE UNIVERSITY

A Unit of the University System of Georgia

School of Graduate Studies

Programs of Study

Armstrong Atlantic State University (AASU) offers master's-level degrees in the following areas: adult education, computer science, criminal justice, early childhood education, middle grades education, secondary education (broadfield science education, broadfield social science education, business education, English education, mathematics education), special education (behavior disorders, learning disabilities, speech/language pathology), health services administration, history, nursing, nursing/health services administration (dual degree), physical therapy, public health, and sports medicine. Graduate certificates in health services administration and gerontology are offered, and post-master's nursing certificates are offered in adult-health clinical nurse specialist studies, adult nurse practitioner studies, and nursing administration.

A minimum of half of the hours required for the degree must be earned in residence. AASU courses taken off campus as part of an approved external degree program are considered to have been completed in residence.

Research Facilities

The library collections consist of approximately 800,000 items, including 185,000 book volumes, 600,000 microforms, and 9,000 individual audiovisual titles, including compact discs, records, laser discs, slides, and video recordings. In addition, the library subscribes to 1,043 journals and newspapers. A special collection, the Florence Powell Minis Collection, contains publications of the University, published works by Savannah authors, and published material about Savannah and the surrounding area. The collection also includes first editions by Conrad Aiken, Flannery O'Connor, and other Savannah authors. Through participation in state, regional, and national resource-sharing agreements with other libraries, Lane Library is able to borrow and obtain for its clientele materials that are not available at Armstrong Atlantic. Interlibrary loan materials arrive by UPS, fax, and electronic delivery services. Off-campus library services for Armstrong Atlantic programs are supported by local libraries. Off-campus students may access library resources at home by accessing the online catalog, ORCA. Interlibrary loans may also be requested through ORCA. In addition, more than 100 databases are available on GALILEO, a system of databases shared among the thirty-four University System of Georgia libraries. GALILEO may be accessed by registered Armstrong Atlantic students from home via password. Laptop computers are available to graduate students. Computer labs are located at various sites on campus. A technology help desk facility is also available.

Financial Aid

Employment programs, grants, loans, out-of-state tuition waivers, scholarships, fellowship programs, and graduate assistantships are available. For more information, students should visit the Web site below. Students may also request information via e-mail at the address below.

Cost of Study

For the 2001–02 two-semester academic year, tuition and fees for full-time study (12 or more semester hours) were $2702 for Georgia residents and $9662 for nonresidents.

Living and Housing Costs

For the academic year 2001–02, single student housing in the residence hall on campus could be obtained for $2753 per semester, which included a food service fee of $965 per semester. Many graduate students elect to live in apartments that are close to campus or in historic downtown Savannah.

Student Group

The total enrollment of 5,747 students in fall 2001 included 5,061 undergraduates and 686 graduate students. Of the 686 graduate students, 36.6 percent were enrolled full-time (9 or more semester hours) and 63.4 percent were enrolled part-time (8 or fewer semester hours). Approximately 87 percent were Georgia residents, and the remainder were either out-of-state residents or international students. The average age of graduate students was 35 years.

The Graduate Student Coordinating Council provides representation for graduate students on campus. Many academic areas also offer graduate student associations.

Location

Armstrong Atlantic students find much to enjoy about living in the city of Savannah, the major urban area (population 280,000) of coastal Georgia. Atlanta, Georgia, is a 4½-hour drive away, and Jacksonville, Florida, and Columbia, South Carolina, are each 2 hours away from AASU.

AASU is located on a 250-acre campus in a residential area of the city, which promotes a feeling of freedom and security on campus. Savannah, Georgia's founding city, has all the historic and cultural variety of a metropolitan city, with the added advantage of the ocean at its back door. A temperate climate encourages year-round outdoor activities and recreation.

The University

Armstrong Atlantic was founded in 1935 as Armstrong Junior College to enhance educational opportunities in the community. Armstrong Atlantic State University now offers seventy-five academic programs and majors in the College of Arts and Sciences, the College of Health Professions, the College of Education, and the School of Graduate Studies. AASU is a part of the University System of Georgia, which includes thirty-four state-operated institutions of higher education.

A total of 250 faculty members teach at the University; 160 hold graduate faculty membership.

Applying

An application can be obtained by contacting the School of Graduate Studies or through the World Wide Web at the address below. The following additional graduate study information may be viewed on line: the graduate catalog, financial aid guidelines, student services, assistantship guidelines, thesis guidelines, and faculty research interests.

Correspondence and Information

School of Graduate Studies
11935 Abercorn Street
Armstrong Atlantic State University
Savannah, Georgia 31419
Telephone: 912-927-5377
Fax: 912-921-5586
E-mail: graduate@mail.armstrong.edu
World Wide Web: http://www.armstrong.edu

GRADUATE COORDINATORS

Computer Science: Raymond Greenlaw, Graduate Coordinator, Department of Computer Science (telephone: 912-927-5600; fax: 912-921-2083; e-mail: greenlaw@drake.armstrong.edu). The M.S.C.S. degree provides students with the opportunity to study a broad range of computer science subjects in-depth.

Criminal Justice: Kathy Bennett, Graduate Coordinator, Department of Criminal Justice, Social and Political Science (telephone: 912-927-5296; fax: 912-921-5876; E-mail: bennetka@mail.armstrong.edu). The criminal justice program is one of only three such programs in Georgia. The program is housed within University Hall, which is the same building that the Law Enforcement Training Center (Regional Police Academy) is housed, and in proximity to the Regional Office of the Georgia Bureau of Investigation and State Crime Lab. Upon completion of the M.S.C.J. degree, students are eligible for careers in criminal justice agency administration, planning, policy development and analysis, and management.

Education: Jo Ann Coleman, Graduate Coordinator, College of Education (telephone: 912-921-5689; fax: 912-921-5587; E-mail: graduate@mail.armstrong.edu). A master's degree in education is the minimal entry degree for administrative positions and college teaching. Critical fields are middle grades education, science education, mathematics education, and special education.

Health Services Administration: Joey Crosby, Graduate Coordinator, Department of Health Science (telephone: 912-921-7316; fax: 912-921-7350; E-mail: crosbyjo@mail.armstrong.edu). As one of only three designated regional health profession education centers in the University System of Georgia, AASU offers the M.H.S.A. program. Students wishing to design, implement, and manage health delivery systems learn the fundamentals of strategic planning, marketing, administration, and finance and the intricacies of the skills necessary to assist those who strive to maintain the health of others.

History: Christopher Hendricks, Graduate Coordinator, Department of History (telephone: 912-927-5283; fax: 912-921-5581; E-mail: hendrich@mail.armstrong.edu). Savannah provides an excellent laboratory for the student of history. Students may concentrate their graduate studies in one of the following three areas: American history, European history, or public history. Aside from a nationally recognized preservation program that supports the preservation of historical records as well as historical buildings, Savannah contains the city and county legal and political records, the Georgia Historical Society and its archives, several noteworthy museums, and a cosmopolitan population that is interested in recording and learning about its various ethnic and religious cultures.

Nursing: Camille Stern, Graduate Coordinator, Department of Nursing (telephone: 912-927-5311; fax: 921-920-6579; E-mail: youngsue@mail.armstrong.edu). The graduate program in nursing offers registered professional nurses the opportunity to pursue a master's degree in nursing in one of four tracks: adult clinical nurse specialist studies, adult nurse practitioner studies, advanced practice nursing, and nursing administration. Post-master's nursing certificates are available in adult clinical nurse specialist studies, adult nurse practitioner studies, and nursing administration. The RN options track is available for nurses with a diploma or associate degree in nursing to enter and progress through the baccalaureate and the master's degrees.

Nursing/Health Services Administration (Dual Degree): Camille Stern, Graduate Coordinator, Department of Nursing (telephone: 912-927-5311; fax: 921-920-6579; E-mail: youngsue@mail.armstrong.edu). The graduate programs in nursing and health services administration offer registered professional nurses the opportunity to pursue a dual master's degree with a specialty focus in nursing and health services administration.

Physical Therapy: David Lake, Graduate Coordinator, Department of Physical Therapy (telephone: 912-921-2327; E-mail: lakedavi@mail.armstrong.edu). The physical therapy program is a full-time program involving seven semesters of study. It involves twenty-nine weeks of full-time clinical practice and an additional five weeks of part-time clinical experiences. This program uses a modified problem-based learning (PBL) approach. The program maintains an active learning environment that promotes independent thinking. This program offers the option of entering as a graduate student or to enter the program without a baccalaureate degree and become a graduate student after completing the first two semesters of the program. The Department of Physical Therapy received the 1999 Regents' Teaching Excellence Award for Departments in the University of Georgia.

Public Health: Jacquie Fraser, Graduate Coordinator, Department of Health Science (telephone: 912-921-5480; fax: 912-921-7350; E-mail: streatsa@mail.armstrong.edu). The M.P.H. degree provides the student with a mastery of the appropriate theory, content/knowledge, and application of skills in areas of public health specific to the student's interest, as well as the ability to plan, implement, and evaluate programs that influence behavioral change conducive to the positive health of the community.

Sports Medicine: Kristinn Heinrichs, Graduate Coordinator (telephone: 912-921-7346; fax: 912-921-7350; E-mail: heinrikr@mail.armstrong.edu). The program of study prepares the graduate student to advance in his or her chosen field and/or to extend his or her practice to sports medicine.

ASSUMPTION COLLEGE

Graduate School

Programs of Study

Assumption College offers four graduate programs that lead to a master's degree. These are the Business Administration (M.B.A.), Counseling Psychology, Rehabilitation Counseling, and Special Education Programs. In addition, the Counseling Psychology and Rehabilitation Counseling Programs offer a Certificate of Advanced Graduate Studies and the Business Administration Program offers a Certificate of Professional Study in Business for advanced study in business.

Research Facilities

The College's Emmanuel d'Alzon Library's steadily growing holdings currently consist of more than 190,000 volumes, and the library subscribes to more than 1,100 journals. Electronic resources include more than 500 e-journals and over 80 databases. Assumption participates in local, regional, and national library networks.

The Media Center houses a professional TV studio widely used for sign-language practice, practice-teaching, debating, foreign language study, and interviewing techniques.

Assumption provides a sophisticated computer network for student use. The computer labs and classrooms contain both IBM-compatible Pentium machines and Apple Power PC and Macintosh G3 and G4 systems. The multimedia production lab is equipped with Mac G3 and G4 computers, with multiple scanners and CD writers, and two Media 100 systems for video editing.

The student computing facilities include more than 160 microcomputers. Students have complete access to e-mail and World Wide Web resources. A number of statistical packages and programming languages are also available.

Financial Aid

Fellowships and traineeships are offered on a competitive basis by the Counseling Psychology and Rehabilitation Counseling Programs, respectively. There are some campus aid opportunities available to graduate students as resident directors and assistants and in career services. Federal Stafford Loans are available for eligible students.

Cost of Study

The 2002–03 tuition for all graduate students is $352 per credit, with most courses being 3 credits. There is a $20 registration fee required per semester.

Living and Housing Costs

Assumption College does not provide graduate student housing. The Office of Residential Life assists students in finding housing in the vicinity. Graduate students who are resident directors or assistants are provided housing. Dining facilities are available.

Student Group

The total enrollment at Assumption College is about 2,400 students, of whom approximately 330 are graduate students.

Location

Assumption College occupies a suburban campus in Worcester, approximately 3 miles from the center of the city. Worcester is located approximately 50 minutes west of Boston. Cultural attractions in Worcester include the Worcester Art Museum, the Higgins Armory Museum, and the American Antiquarian Society. In addition, Worcester has several theater companies. The large college and university population in the area, as well as the Worcester Centrum, attracts an array of theatrical, musical, and artistic groups each year. Worcester is both an industrial center and a university community, home to nine of the fourteen institutions of higher learning that constitute the Worcester Consortium of Higher Education.

The College

Assumption College, a coeducational Catholic liberal arts college, was founded in 1904. Located on 175 acres of land, the entire campus was relocated and rebuilt after a 1953 tornado completely devastated the original site. The mission of the College at the graduate level is to provide programs designed primarily to prepare students for careers.

Applying

An application form, official transcripts of undergraduate and graduate records, and letters of recommendation (two for the M.B.A. and Rehabilitation Counseling Programs and three for the Counseling Psychology and Special Education Programs), preferably from professors of the proposed major study area or from employment supervisors, should be sent to the Director of Graduate Enrollment Management and Services. Applicants to the psychology program must have completed six courses in psychology at the undergraduate level, with a minimum cumulative grade point average of 3.0. Students should contact individual departments for GPA admission requirements. The GMAT is required for M.B.A. candidates. (Some waivers may apply.) Applications are reviewed on a rolling admissions basis. Specific deadlines apply for fellowships, financial aid, and registration. International applicants who native language is not English must provide TOEFL scores and certified translations of transcripts in addition to the above requirements. An evaluation of an international transcript may be required to determine if the degree obtained is equivalent to an American bachelor's degree. Applications are encouraged from qualified persons of all cultural, racial, religious, and ethnic groups.

Correspondence and Information

Director of Graduate Enrollment Management and Services
Assumption College
500 Salisbury Street
Worcester, Massachusetts 01609
Telephone: 508-767-7387
Fax: 508-767-7030
World Wide Web: http://www.assumption.edu

THE GRADUATE FACULTY

Adrian O. Dumas, M.B.A., Director of Graduate Enrollment Management and Services.
Daniel G. Provost, Assistant Director of Graduate Services.

Business Administration: Joseph T. Foley, Director of the M.B.A. Program; M.S., M.B.A., Northeastern. Frank A. Marino, Graduate Advisor; M.B.A., Northeastern; M.S.T., Bentley. Egidio A. Diodati, M.B.A., Suffolk. Colleen A. Fahy, Ph.D., SUNY at Binghamton. Jennifer M. Gregorski, M.B.A., Boston College. Carol P. Harvey, Ed.D., Massachusetts Amherst. Jeffery G. Hunter, D.B.A., Golden Gate. Demetrius Kantarelis, Ph.D., Clark. Gerald D. McCarthy, Ph.D., Pennsylvania. Jeanne M. McNett, Ph.D., Massachusetts Amherst. Saeed Mohaghegh, M.B.A., Clark. Melvin E. Murphy, M.B.A., Akron.

Counseling Psychology: Leonard A. Doerfler, Director of the Counseling Psychology Program; Ph.D., Missouri–Columbia. Paula Fitzpatrick, Ph.D., Connecticut. Maria D. Kalpidou, Ph.D., LSU. Amy C. Lyubchik, Ph.D., Rochester. Edmund F. O'Reilly, Ph.D., SUNY at Albany. Peter F. Toscano Jr., Ph.D., SUNY at Stony Brook.

Rehabilitation Counseling: David E. St. John, Acting Director of the Institute for Social and Rehabilitation Services; Ed.D., Clark. A. Lee Pearson, Director of Graduate Studies/ISRS; M.Ed., Boston College; C.A.G.S., Northeastern. Nancy Adams, M.S., Portland. Thomas P. McCarthy, Sc.D., Boston University. John R. Pelletier, Sc.D., Boston University. Philip Quinn, Sc.D., Boston University. Susan R. Sabelli, M.A., C.A.G.S., Assumption. Susan Scully, Ph.D., Michigan. David L. Siddle, Ph.D., Boston College. Charles K. Stuart, Ed.D., Northern Colorado.

Special Education: Mary E. Kielbasa, Chair of the Department of Education; Ed.D., Boston University. Claudia Aitken, Ed.D., Nova Southeastern. Veronica Gold, Ed.D., Clark. Mary Anne Mariani, Ph.D., Boston College. Christine Miller, M.S., Vermont. Joseph Vandergrift, Ph.D., Duquesne. Nanho VanderHart, Ph.D., Iowa.

Fuller Hall houses classrooms and faculty offices.

The Campus Center.

AUBURN UNIVERSITY

Graduate School

Programs of Study

The Graduate School offers programs leading to the Doctor of Philosophy in aerospace engineering, agronomy and soils, animal and dairy sciences, biological sciences, biomedical sciences, botany and microbiology, chemical engineering, chemistry, civil engineering, computer science and software engineering, counseling psychology, counselor education, curriculum and teaching, discrete and statistical sciences, economics, electrical and computer engineering, English, entomology, fisheries and allied aquacultures, forestry, health and human performance, history, horticulture, human development and family studies, industrial and systems engineering, management, materials engineering, mathematics, mechanical engineering, nutrition and food science, pharmaceutical sciences, physics, plant pathology, poultry science, psychology, public administration, rehabilitation and special education, wildlife science, and zoology. The Doctor of Education is also offered with major areas of specialization including counseling and counseling psychology; educational foundations, leadership, and technology; health and human performance; and vocational and adult education. The Specialist in Education degree may be earned in all departments of the College of Education. The M.S. and M.A. are available in many areas, along with nonthesis master's degrees in a number of fields. Minors also are available in biochemistry, ecology, economic development, environmental studies, molecular biology, sports management, and urban forestry. The Graduate Outreach Program offers graduate-level courses to off-campus students in engineering, business administration, accountancy, rehabilitation, and special education, and hotel and restaurant management. Auburn University has identified seven areas as peaks of excellence in graduate education: cell and molecular biosciences, detection and food safety, fisheries and allied aquacultures, forest sustainability, information technology, poultry products' safety and quality, and transportation. Students in these areas receive special consideration and support.

Research Facilities

The University, which has a graduate faculty of more than 1,100, provides various specialized facilities for graduate research. Among these are the Space Power Institute, the Alabama Microelectronics Science and Technology Center, the Advanced Manufacturing Technology Center, the Agricultural Experiment Station, the Engineering Experiment Station, the Scott-Ritchey Small Animal Research Facility, the Center for the Arts and Humanities, the Center for Aging Studies, the National Center for Asphalt Technology, the Truman Pierce Institute for the Advancement of Teacher Education, the Institute for Biological Detection Systems, the Pulp and Paper Research and Education Center, the Dauphin Island Sea and Gulf Coast Research Laboratories, and the International Center for Aquaculture. Auburn is a member of the Oak Ridge Associated Universities Research Participation Program and has access to the facilities of the National Laboratory at Oak Ridge, the Savannah River Laboratory, the laboratories of the Puerto Rico Nuclear Center, and the University of Tennessee Atomic Energy Commission Agricultural Research Laboratory.

The main library has more than 2 million bound books and more than 2 million other books and materials in microformat. Subscriptions are maintained for 20,800 serials, including 12,800 journals. High-speed computer searches may be made in approximately 750 fields. The catalog is Web-based, including data bases, full-text materials, electronic document delivery, and digitized collections. The library is a U.S. depository, receiving government publications and documents; a map reference library with a collection of more than 124,700 maps; and a depository for U.S. patents. University Archives has more than 900 manuscript collections, 150,000 photographs, 7,060 oral history tapes and audio cassettes, and 4,400 motion picture reels.

Auburn University has complete Internet access through the Alabama Research and Education Network and is a member of the Internet II/UCAID consortium. This includes supercomputing capabilities and a fiber optic Ethernet network linking all buildings and offices on campus. Auburn is ranked among the top twenty-five most-wired universities in the United States.

Financial Aid

Auburn University funds approximately 1,400 graduate assistantships annually. Many additional assistantships are provided through grants and contracts from external sources. Graduate teaching and research fellowships, which cover tuition and fees, are available for graduate assistants.

Cost of Study

Full-time (10 to 15 hours) tuition and fees for 2001–02 were $1525 per semester for Alabama residents and $4575 per semester for out-of-state residents. Nonresident fees do not apply to out-of-state students receiving a one-fourth-time or greater appointment as a graduate teaching assistant, research assistant, or assistant.

Living and Housing Costs

On-campus and off-campus housing is available to graduate students. The University maintains dormitories for men and women as well as apartments for married students. Room and board on campus per semester are $4600. Off-campus housing includes a wide selection of apartments, private dormitories, and mobile-home facilities, averaging $2000 per semester. The director of housing provides information. The estimated student cost for one calendar year, including fees and room and board, is $15,350 for in-state and $24,500 for out-of-state students.

Student Group

The total enrollment is almost 22,000, of whom 3,000 are graduate students. The student population comprises more than 11,000 men and more than 10,000 women. Represented are every state, the District of Columbia, Puerto Rico, the Virgin Islands, and more than eighty countries. Graduate School enrollment includes more than 1,200 women, more than 200 students from minority groups, and 800 international students. More than half of the graduate students are employed by the University as teaching or research assistants.

Location

The main campus of 1,871 acres occupies the entire southwest quadrant of the city of Auburn. The city's population is about 38,000, including resident students, in an area of 23 square miles. Auburn is 50 miles northeast of Montgomery, 110 miles southeast of Birmingham, and 115 miles southwest of Atlanta. Interstate 85 provides convenient access to Montgomery and Atlanta. The area has brief, mild winters and abundant sunshine.

The University

Auburn is a state-assisted, comprehensive, Doctoral/Research university—extensive (Carnegie classification), with a storied past dating from 1856. It has a long tradition of academic excellence and graduate education, awarding its first undergraduate degree in 1860 and its first graduate degree in 1870. Since then it has awarded more than 30,000 graduate degrees, including 4,000 doctorates. The largest university in Alabama, Auburn has twelve colleges and schools in addition to the Graduate School—Agriculture, Architecture, Business, Education, Engineering, Forestry and Wildlife Sciences, Human Sciences, Liberal Arts, Nursing, Pharmacy, Sciences and Mathematics, and Veterinary Medicine. More than ninety buildings occupy a campus of Southern charm graced with stately trees and abundant flowers. Auburn is accredited by the Southern Association of Colleges and Schools.

Applying

Minimum requirements include a baccalaureate degree from an accredited four-year college or university and satisfactory scores on the General Test of the GRE or, in business, the Graduate Management Admission Test (GMAT). Some departments also require satisfactory scores on a GRE Subject Test. All application materials should be received six weeks before planned enrollment.

Correspondence and Information

Dr. Stephen L. McFarland
Acting Associate Vice Provost for Academic Affairs
and Dean of the Graduate School
Hargis Hall
Auburn University, Alabama 36849-5122

Telephone: 334-844-4700
Fax: 334-844-4348
E-mail: gradadm@auburn.edu
World Wide Web: http://www.grad.auburn.edu

AREAS OF INSTRUCTION

The names of the programs and the degrees offered are listed along with the telephone number to call for information. The area code for all telephone numbers is 334. E-mail addresses are available through the Graduate School Web site (http://www.grad.auburn.edu).

Accountancy (M.Ac.): 844-5340.
Aerospace Engineering (M.A.E., M.S., Ph.D.): 844-4874.
Agricultural Economics (M.Ag., M.S., Ph.D.): 844-4800.
Agronomy and Soils (M.Ag., M.S., Ph.D.): 844-4100.
Anatomy, Physiology, and Pharmacology (M.S., Ph.D.): 844-4427.
Animal and Dairy Sciences (M.Ag., M.S., Ph.D.): 844-4160.
Biochemistry and Cell/Molecular Biology (minor): 844-4043.
Biological Sciences (M.S., Ph.D.): 844-4830.
Biomedical Sciences (M.S., Ph.D.): 844-6697.
Botany and Microbiology (M.S., Ph.D.): 844-4830.
Building Science (M.B.C.): 844-4518.
Business (M.S., M.B.A.): 844-4060.
Chemical Engineering (M.Ch.E., M.S., Ph.D.): 844-4827.
Chemistry (M.S., Ph.D.): 844-4043.
Civil Engineering (M.C.E., M.S., Ph.D.): 844-4320.
Communication (M.A.): 844-2727.
Communication Disorders (M.C.D., M.S.): 844-9600.
Community Planning (M.C.P.): 844-4516.
Computer Science and Software Engineering (M.S.W.E., M.S., Ph.D.): 844-4330.
Consumer Affairs (M.S.): 844-4084.
Counseling and Counseling Psychology (M.Ed., M.S., Ed.D., Ed.S., Ph.D.): 844-5160.
Curriculum and Teaching (M.Ed., M.S., Ed.S., Ph.D.): 844-4434.
Discrete and Statistical Sciences (M.A.M., M.P.S., M.S., Ph.D.): 844-5111.
Ecology (minor): 844-5053.
Economic Development (minor): 844-5370.
Economics (M.S., Ph.D.): 844-4910.
Educational Foundations, Leadership, and Technology (M.Ed., M.S., Ed.S., Ed.D., Ph.D.): 844-4460.
Electrical and Computer Engineering (M.E.E., M.S., Ph.D.): 844-1800.
English (M.A., Ph.D.): 844-4620.
Entomology (M.Ag., M.S., Ph.D.): 844-2553.
Environmental Studies (minor): 844-4850.
Graduate Outreach (off-campus programs in engineering, accountancy, business administration, rehabilitation and special education, and hotel and restaurant management): 844-5300.
Finance (M.S.): 844-5344.
Fisheries and Allied Aquacultures (M.Aq., M.S., Ph.D.): 844-4786.
Forestry (M.F., M.S., Ph.D.): 844-1007.
French (M.A., M.F.S.): 844-4345.
Geology (M.S.): 844-4282.
Health and Human Performance (M.Ed., M.S., Ed.S., Ed.D., Ph.D.): 844-4483.
History (M.A., Ph.D.): 844-4360.
Horticulture (M.Ag., M.S., Ph.D.): 844-4862.
Human Development and Family Studies (M.S., Ph.D.): 844-4151.
Industrial Design (M.I.D.): 844-2364.
Industrial and Systems Engineering (M.I.E., M.S., Ph.D.): 844-4340.
Integrated Textile and Apparel Science (Interdepartmental M.S., Ph.D.): 844-4123.
Large Animal Surgery and Medicine (M.S., Ph.D.): 844-6697.
Management (M.M.I.S., M.S., Ph.D.): 844-4071.
Marketing and Transportation (M.S.): 844-4035.
Materials Engineering (M.Mtl.E., M.S., Ph.D.): 844-4820.
Mathematics (M.A.M., M.S., Ph.D.): 844-4290.
Mechanical Engineering (M.M.E., M.S., Ph.D.): 844-4820.
Nutrition and Food Science (M.S., Ph.D.): 844-4261.
Pathobiology (M.S., Ph.D.): 844-4539.
Pharmacal Sciences (M.S.): 844-4037.
Pharmaceutical Sciences (Interdepartmental Ph.D.): 844-4037.
Pharmacy Care Systems (M.S.): 844-5152.
Physics (M.S., Ph.D.): 844-4264.
Plant Molecular Biology (minor): 844-5003.
Plant Pathology (M.Ag., M.S., Ph.D.): 844-5003.
Poultry Science (M.Ag., M.S., Ph.D.): 844-4133.
Psychology (M.S., Ph.D.): 844-4412.
Public Administration (M.P.A., Ph.D.): 844-5370.
Radiology (M.S., Ph.D.): 844-5045.
Rehabilitation and Special Education (M.Ed., M.S., Ed.S., Ph.D.): 844-5943.
Small Animal Surgery and Medicine (M.S., Ph.D.): 844-6003.
Sociology (M.A., M.S.): 844-5049.
Spanish (M.A., M.H.S.): 844-4345.
Sports Management (minor): 844-4483.
Statistics (M.P.S., M.S.): 844-5111.
Technical and Professional Communication (M.T.P.C.): 844-4620
Textile Science (M.S.): 844-4123.
Urban Forestry (minor): 844-4862.
Vocational and Adult Education (M.Ed., M.S., Ed.S., Ed.D.): 844-4460.
Wildlife Science (M.S., Ph.D.): 844-1007.
Zoology (M.S., M.Z.S., Ph.D.): 844-4830.

AUDREY COHEN COLLEGE

AUDREY COHEN COLLEGE

Master of Public Administration

Program of Study

The Master of Public Administration degree program at Audrey Cohen College is a graduate degree especially designed for working administrators or for individuals seeking to develop administrative acumen while working in a variety of nonprofit, profit, and public service arenas. The goal of this one-year master's degree program is to use management to create a systemic enhancement in the quality of services that the organization provides. Graduate students accomplish this by using their place of employment as a setting for on-site research and its evaluation to take place. This is followed by an articulation of a plan of action based on the interpretation of those results and the implementation of a pilot program addressing the needs of the organization, which leads to long-range planning and proposal writing. These are the three purposes of administration. The College's unique purpose-centered system of education is copyrighted and patented.

The student population is composed of all levels of working administrators across all sectors of administration and from a wide array of colleges and universities, including other graduate institutions. All course work is integrated each semester through the Constructive Action, a document that fuses theory with practice and demonstrates mastery of the three purposes. This unique methodology provides a dynamic counterpart to the traditional case study method and guides the graduate student/working administrator with concrete ways to assess real problems and issues. Through the Constructive Action, the classroom and the workplace become one, and upon its completion, a fully integrated, holistic administrative treatise is presented. This document evidences the analysis of a work challenge, the articulation of a mode of action as an immediate response to that analysis, the initiation of a service innovation that comes about through analysis, and an assessment and proposal for the future based on the results. All classes are conducted as seminars and teach toward the Constructive Action. In this manner, all learning is integrated toward the purpose of the semester. Students explore the dimensions of learning, action, and assessment appropriate for professional development as administrators. These classes typically include Values and Ethics, Self and Others, Systems, Skills, and a Purpose Seminar that directs the Constructive Action. Studies in the first semester focus on the purpose of "Identifying Service Needs" and typically include Values and Ethics for Administrative Decision Making, Human Development in the Social Context, Evaluating Service Delivery System, and Principles and Techniques of Evaluation Research. Constructive Actions are as varied as the organizations that sponsor the student administrators and have included the first HIV education guidelines for women, new emergency room triage systems mandated in New York State, establishing an AIDS pavilion at a major metropolitan medical center, and fine-tuning constituent services in a prominent congressman's office.

Research Facilities

The College has a highly specialized social service and management collection developed with the needs of service organizations, their managers, and service providers in mind. This technologically sophisticated library is cataloged by the Library of Congress system. The collection is augmented through cooperative library networks, which allow graduate students to use the vast resources of the excellent libraries, both public and private, in the New York area. It is a member of the Metropolitan Reference and Research Library Agency (METRO) and the Conference Board, and it has inter-library agreements with several universities in the area. The library has full Internet access and currently subscribes to a number of online services, such as Dialog, Pro Quest Direct, and First Search. An extensive array of CD-ROM databases complements the collection. In addition, an extensive collection of support software is available for student use through the Graduate Learning Center.

Financial Aid

The Presidential Scholarship Program and the Mayor's Graduate Scholarship Program (both funded by the College and awarded on merit alone) amount to a maximum of $1200 per semester. In addition, the graduate program features the Kenneth B. Facey Memorial Award, a prestigious scholarship awarded to a student in the third term whose academic performance merits special acknowledgment. Students are eligible to participate in a wide range of federal loan programs as well as to utilize deferred payment plans or use credit cards (MasterCard, Visa, and Discover) for payment. Students are encouraged to explore the wide range of private foundation support for scholarship assistance, and many receive tuition assistance from their employers.

Cost of Study

Tuition for 2002–03 is $5700 per semester (three semesters are featured annually). Books and supplies are an additional $300 to $350 per semester. College resources at the current time make it possible to ensure the current tuition through program completion (provided the student stays enrolled).

Living and Housing Costs

Audrey Cohen College does not maintain dormitories or provide off-campus housing assistance. Students are primarily from the metropolitan New York area and commute from their homes.

Student Group

There are a total of 180 matriculated students in the graduate program, 42 men and 138 women. More than 80 percent receive financial aid. Students range in age from 24 to 60. Urban and suburban profit and nonprofit service organizations and public and government agencies continue to employ the greatest concentration of administrative placements and include local borough/city/county government, state and national government agencies, international organizations, all levels of public and private educational institutions, gerontological institutes and other health-care providers, housing organizations, institutes of human development, corporate training and development, substance abuse facilities, foster care, advocacy, victims' services, and legal service organizations.

Student Outcomes

Recent graduates have secured positions as administrative directors, executive directors/CEOs, assistant commissioners, case managers, associate/assistant directors, budget programmers, chairpersons, coordinators, rehabilitation specialists, program directors, and other administrative appointments appropriate to wide range of service organizations.

Location

New York City is home to the world's largest number of government agencies and nonprofit organizations. The city's position as a center of international commerce, education, and culture is excellent for the study of contemporary management issues. The College's downtown Manhattan location is convenient to all public transportation and is minutes from the leading organizations where student administrators are employed.

The College

The dynamic graduate degree complements the two undergraduate schools of the College, where students from all programs engage in a curriculum that is both professionally challenging and academically rewarding. The atmosphere is collegial and professional. More than 50 percent plan on continuing their graduate study, and 30 percent have already moved on to law schools and schools of social work, education, divinity, counseling, and graduate business at both second master's and doctoral levels. New organizations have emerged directly from the graduate constructive actions completed in this one-year master's program.

Applying

Applications may be submitted for classes starting in September, January, and May. Application deadlines are one month prior to the start date of the new semester. A completed application includes an application for graduate study, a signed letter of agreement, a field supervisor's information form, two letters of recommendation, and a data sheet. Upon receipt of all the required materials, applicants are contacted for the admission interview. After the interview, applicants are requested to write two 300-word essays on an assigned topic. A $45 application fee is required.

Correspondence and Information

Mr. Steven K. Lenhart
Director of Graduate Admission
Audrey Cohen College
75 Varick Street
New York, New York 10013
Telephone: 212-343-1234 Ext. 5001, 2700, or 2704
800-33-THINK (toll-free)
World Wide Web: http://www.audreycohen.edu

THE FACULTY AND THEIR AREAS OF SPECIALIZATION

Bert Bernier, Ph.D., Birmingham (England). Islamic studies.
Bruce R. Buglione, Ed.D., Columbia Teachers College. Urban policy.
Peter Campanelli, Psy.D., Rutgers. Clinical psychology, community psychology, organizational behavior, public policy.
Steven Cresap, Ph.D., Cornell. Modern European intellectual history, values clarification, ethics.
Humphrey Crookendale, Dean; J.D., Howard. Law and social policy, impact on state and local municipalities.
Theodor Damian, Ph.D., Fordham. Moral philosophy.
Silvio Dobry, Ph.D., Fordham. Human resources, criminal justice, social justice.
Sebastian Douglas, M.S.W., Fordham.
Richard Grallo, Ph.D., NYU; K.M.O.S.J. Educational psychology, statistics, research methodologies.
Charles Gray, D.S.W., Yeshiva. Social policy, public administration, systems analysis, social welfare.
Louise Hedge, M.S.A., Audrey Cohen College. Applied research in mental health.
Gregory Jose, Ph.D., NYU. Public policy analysis, administrative theory and practice.
Ishola Kukumo, Ph.D., Columbia. Political science.
Lola Langley, Ph.D., Walden. Gerontology, social policy.
Rosalia Lapena, Ph.D., Centro Escolar (Philippines). Economics, business management, national and international security.
Michael Maurer, Ph.D., D.M.N., Chicago Theological Seminary. Religion and personality, pastoral counseling.
Louis H. Tietje, Ph.D., Union Theological Seminary (New York). Applied ethics, social and political philosophy, ethics and social policy.

AZUSA PACIFIC UNIVERSITY

Graduate Programs

Programs of Study

Azusa Pacific University (APU) offers graduate programs in the College of Liberal Arts and Sciences, the School of Business and Management, the School of Education and Behavioral Studies, the School of Music, the School of Nursing, and the Haggard Graduate School of Theology.

The Master of Business Administration program leads to or enhances a career in business. The Master of Human and Organizational Development is designed for the experienced professional in a position of leadership within a particular organizational context. The M.S. in applied computer science and technology fills the need for specialists in microcomputer science and technology at the professional level. The Master of Education program has concentrations in physical education and educational technology. The M.A. in education has concentrations in administration, special education, pupil personnel services, teaching, curriculum and instruction, and language and literacy development. The M.A. degree in clinical psychology offers an emphasis in marital and family therapy. The Psy.D. in clinical psychology retains a commitment to providing a comprehensive education in psychological science as the foundation for any training in psychology that emphasizes the service orientation of a clinical degree. The curriculum fulfills the academic requirement for California licensing. The Master of Music program in performance is designed to enhance musical performance as it relates to ministry. The Master of Music Education is for educators who desire additional preparation in the teaching field and challenges them to excel in the field. The M.S. in Nursing degree program prepares students in advanced theory and practice in a specialized clinical area of nursing. This program offers emphases in administration, education, adult nursing, parent-child, family nurse practitioner, and parish nursing as well as numerous post-master's credentials. Students are prepared to assume a functional role as clinical specialist, educator, or administrator of nursing services. The combination of theory, research, and professional development prepares graduates for doctoral study. The Master of Education in college student affairs is designed for those interested in working with students in the college environment. The program, which is based in the social sciences and founded upon the Christian view of humanity, enables the student affairs professional to appraise the nature, characteristics, and needs of college students; analyze and implement student development programs in relation to student needs and institutional objectives; and integrate student development theory in a practical hands-on setting. The M.A. in social science with an emphasis on leadership studies is designed for experienced professionals who hold positions of leadership. The nature of the degree is interdisciplinary, intercultural, international, and organizational. The intent of the M.A. is to provide an action research emphasis for informed decision making and organizational development. The M.A. degree with an emphasis in Teaching English to Speakers of Other Languages (TESOL) and the certificate in TESOL combine theory and practice for the student and are offered within the basic parameters of Christian service and ministry. The M.A. in pastoral studies program is directed toward persons seeking preparation in specialized fields of ministry, such as educational ministries, church development, and urban intercultural ministries. The Master of Divinity program prepares students for professional ministry in the church. The core curriculum provides students with solid training in biblical, theological, and ministerial studies. The M.A. in religion program prepares those who plan to teach Bible or theology in Christian schools or colleges and serves as a foundation for doctoral studies. The Master of Arts in nonprofit leadership and theology equips nonprofit leaders and managers to effect change. The M.A. in Christian education is for persons seeking preparation in the specialized field of educational ministries with available emphasis in youth ministry. The Doctor of Education in educational leadership prepares students for school and district-level administration. The Doctor of Ministry builds on the Master of Divinity degree and provides additional professional opportunities for those in this field. The Master of Physical Therapy program is pledged to excellence in total patient care and research and dedicated to the optimization of human health and the efficiency of human function. The physical therapy program is accredited by the Commission on Accreditation in Physical Therapy Education of the American Physical Therapy Association.

Research Facilities

The APU libraries include the William V. Marshburn Memorial Library, the Hugh and Hazel Darling Library, the Stamps Theological Reference Room, and six center libraries located at the Los Angeles, Temecula Valley/Menifee, Orange, San Bernardino, San Diego, and Ventura regional centers. A unified catalog identifies more than 175,000 volumes, media items, and periodical titles. More than 630,000 microforms include the New York Times and Educational Resources Information Center collections. The University network provides access to more than 100 electronic information databases. These electronic systems include indexing and abstracting databases, more than 8,000 full-text journals searchable by the Serials Solutions database, an additional 2,000 electronic books through NetLibrary and the Library of American Civilization.

The Information and Media Technology (IMT) Computer Center, located on the East Campus, is equipped with 40 PC workstations, 25 Macintosh workstations, and 3 HP Laser Jet printers operating on a Linux-based local area network. Software available includes Microsoft Office Professional, SPSS, word processing, spreadsheets, medical programs, and databases, as well as a variety of specialty programs.

Financial Aid

Three types of financial aid are available to students attending Azusa Pacific University, including scholarships and grants, educational loans, and student employment (on and off campus). Scholarships and grants do not have to be repaid and may be used to pay for educational expenses. Educational loans may be applied for and require repayment. The federal government provides low-interest loans to students. Private lenders provide educational loans to students who are either credit worthy or credit ready. APU provides numerous job opportunities for students needing additional resources to pay for their education.

Cost of Study

Graduate tuition for most programs is $395 per unit.

Living and Housing Costs

There is no on-campus housing available for students. Average monthly rents off campus are $700 to $800.

Location

Azusa Pacific University lies 26 miles northeast of Los Angeles, nestled in the San Gabriel Valley. The surrounding mountains provide a rugged, wilderness-like backdrop to the campus. The 52-acre East Campus is situated on the foothills on the corner of Alosta and Citrus avenues, the West Campus (within ¼ mile) rests on 21 acres, and the Graduate Center and most of the graduate program facilities reside in the Administration West location.

The University

Azusa Pacific is a comprehensive Christian, evangelical university. Total enrollment exceeds 6,800, of whom more than 3,100 are graduate students. A community of disciples and scholars, APU seeks to advance the work of God in the world through academic excellence in liberal arts and professional programs of higher education that encourage students to develop a Christian perspective of truth and life. APU offers more than forty areas of undergraduate study, twenty master's degree programs, and three doctorates.

Applying

Students should apply online at the Internet address listed below.

Correspondence and Information

Graduate Center
Azusa Pacific University
901 East Alosta Avenue
P.O. Box 7000
Azusa, California 91702-7000
Telephone: 626-815-4570
Fax: 626-815-4571
E-mail: graduatecenter@apu.edu
World Wide Web: http://www.apu.edu

International applicants:
Office of International Student Services
Azusa Pacific University
901 East Alosta Avenue
P.O. Box 7000
Azusa, California 91702-7000, USA
Telephone: 626-812-3055
Fax: 626-812-3801
E-mail: iss@apu.edu

DEANS

Haggard Graduate School of Theology: Dr. Lane Scott. (Interim)
School of Business and Management: Dr. Ilene Bezjian.
School of Education and Behavioral Studies: Dr. Alice V. Watkins.
School of Music: Dr. Duane Funderburk.
School of Nursing: Dr. Rose Lieglar.
College of Liberal Arts and Sciences: Dr. David Weeks.

Wilden Hall of Business and Management.

BARD

BARD COLLEGE

Graduate Programs

Programs of Study

In addition to its undergraduate curriculum, Bard College has the following four graduate programs: the Milton Avery Graduate School of the Arts (MFA), founded in 1981; the Bard Center for Environmental Policy (BCEP), created in 1999; the Center for Curatorial Studies and Art in Contemporary Culture (CCS), founded in 1990; and the Bard Graduate Center for Studies in the Decorative Arts (BGC), founded in 1993. The arts, environmental policy, and curatorial studies programs are conducted on the Bard campus. The decorative arts program takes place at the Bard Graduate Center's facilities in New York City. Each graduate program has an interdisciplinary focus and utilizes the expertise of the Bard College faculty members and of renowned artists, scholars, and specialists to create a dynamic, rigorous learning environment.

The Milton Avery Graduate School of the Arts confers the Master of Fine Arts (M.F.A.) degree. The Bard Center for Environmental Policy offers several options. Most students elect the two-year program that leads to the Master of Science in Environmental Policy (M.S.E.P.). Active professionals in environment-related fields who meet certain requirements may qualify for the master's degree after a one-year course of study. A Professional Certificate in Environmental Policy is awarded after completion of the August workshops and the first-year curriculum. Options also include a dual master's program (M.Sc. and M.A.) with the BGC and the Master's International Program with the Peace Corps. The two-year program of the Bard Graduate Center for Studies in the Decorative Arts confers the M.A. degree or the Ph.D. degree, which is awarded in the history of the decorative arts, design, and culture. The two-year program of the Center for Curatorial Studies leads to an M.A. degree as well.

For more information on the Bard Cetner for Environmental Policy, students should consult *Peterson's Guide to Graduate Programs in the Physical Sciences, Mathematics, Agricultural Sciences, the Environment & Natural Resources.*

For more information on the Bard Graduate Center for Studies in the Decorative Arts, students should consult *Peterson's Guide to Graduate Programs in the Humanities, Arts, and Social Sciences.*

Research Facilities

All graduate students have free access to the Henderson Computer Center and full borrowing privileges at the Bard College library complex, which holds an extensive collection of books, journals, videos, slides, videodiscs, and microforms and has access to special facilities ideal for students in the individual programs. The Bard Graduate Center in New York City has a specialized library of 20,000 volumes on the decorative arts and related disciplines. Students on the Bard campus have remote access from the College library to information on BGC's holdings. The Center for Curatorial Studies' Marieluise Hessel Collection consists of more than 1,000 paintings, sculptures, photographs, works on paper, artists' books, videos, and video installations from the mid-1960s to present day. CCS's library has 10,000 books and exhibition catalogs as well as an archive of 750 artist and subject files.

The Bard College Ecology Field Station is located on the shores of the Hudson River and houses a laboratory, computer facilities, a library, and an herbarium. Hudsonia Ltd., an independent, nonprofit environmental research institute, and The Hudson River National Estuarine Research Reserve of the New York State Department of Environmental Conservation are based at the field station and have research programs for which they maintain boats, equipment, and a library available to Bard students.

Financial Aid

Financial aid is available to students through scholarships, fellowships, grants, and loans.

Cost of Study

In 2001–02, the tuition was $11,309 per year for CCS, $6659 for MFA, and $742 per credit for BGC (M.A. degree). BCEP tuition for the two-year M.S.E.P. degree was $16,900 for the first year and $10,760 for the second year. The BCEP one-year M.S.E.P. and Professional Certificate in Environmental Policy programs were $17,010. Additional fees are minimal.

Living and Housing Costs

There is no campus housing for graduate students, although a variety of affordable houses and apartments can be rented in proximity to the Bard College campus.

Student Group

Each year, the programs have an entering class of approximately 12 students for CCS, 28 for MFA, 18 for BCEP, and 25 for BGC.

Location

Bard College is located in Annandale-on-Hudson, New York, 2 hours north of New York City on 600 acres of fields and forested land on the east shore of the Hudson River. Much of the campus is part of a historic district, encompassing nineteenth-century mansions and award-winning contemporary facilities. The campus is adjacent to 1,400 acres of nature preserve and a national estuarine sanctuary.

The College

Founded in 1860, Bard College attracts students from across the country to its undergraduate and graduate programs. Through small classes and personalized attention, students are encouraged to pursue intensive study in their areas of special interest, with a view to achieving a broad cultural outlook and intellectual understanding. The graduate programs provide specialized training with particular attention to career preparation. Throughout its history, Bard has been known for its innovative educational initiatives, including the graduate programs, and its public role in the cultural and educational life of the nation.

Applying

Application forms and information for CCS, BCEP, MFA, and BGC graduate programs and financial aid can be obtained from the addresses provided below or on the World Wide Web (http://www.bard.edu).

Correspondence and Information

Graduate Admissions
Bard Center for Environmental Policy
Bard College
Annandale-on-Hudson, New York 12504-5000
Telephone: 845-758-7073
Fax: 845-758-7636
E-mail: cep@bard.edu
World Wide Web: http://www.bard.edu/cep

Graduate Admissions
Center for Curatorial Studies
Bard College
Annandale-on-Hudson, New York 12505-5000
Telephone: 845-758-7598
Fax: 845-758-2442
E-mail: ccs@bard.edu
World Wide Web: http://www.bard.edu

Admissions Office
Bard Graduate Center for Studies
in the Decorative Arts
18 West 86th Street
New York, New York 10024
Telephone: 212-501-3000
Fax: 212-501-3079
E-mail: admissions@bgc.bard.edu
World Wide Web: http://www.bard.edu

Milton Avery Graduate School of the Arts
Bard College
Annandale-on-Hudson, New York 12504-5000
Telephone: 845-758-7481
Fax: 845-758-7507
E-mail: hsimmons@bard.edu
World Wide Web: http://www.bard.edu

THE FACULTY

The Center for Curatorial Studies

Marcia Acita, M.F.A., North Carolina at Chapel Hill. Assistant Director of the Museum Center for Curatorial Studies.
Konstantin Akinsha, Ph.D., All Union Research Institute of Art History (Moscow). Faculty, Center for Curatorial Studies.
Norton Batkin, Ph.D., Harvard. Art history and philosophy. Director of the Graduate Program, Center of Curatorial Studies.
Luca Bonetti, independent conservator, New York City.
Michael Brenson, Ph.D., Johns Hopkins. Art critic, New York City.
Jennifer Burns, Ph.D., CUNY Graduate Center. Faculty, Center for Curatorial Studies.
Susan Cahan, Ph.D. candidate, CUNY Graduate Center. Curator and Director of Arts Programs, Peter Norton Family Foundation.
Lynne Cooke, Ph.D., London. Curator, Dia Center for the Arts.
Amanda Cruz, B.A., NYU. Director, Center for Curatorial Studies and Art in Contemporary Culture.
Aruna D'Souza, Ph.D., NYU. Faculty, Center for Curatorial Studies and Art in Contemporary Culture.
Elizabeth Frank, Ph.D., Berkeley. Joseph E. Harry Professor of Modern Languages and Literature, Bard College.
Andrea Fraser, Artist. Whitney Museum of American Art Independent Study Program.
Thelma Golden, B.A., Smith. Associate Curator, Whitney Museum of American Art.
Vivian Heller, Ph.D., Yale. Writing tutor, Center for Curatorial Studies and Art in Contemporary Culture.
Maria Hlavajova, M.A., Comenius (Slovakia). Independent curator, Amsterdam, Netherlands and Bratislava, Slovakia.
Mary Jane Jacob, M.A., Michigan. Independent curator, Chicago.
Merlin James, M.A., Royal College of Art, London. Artist and critic.
Diane Lewis, B. Arch., Cooper Union. Associate Professor, Irwin S. Chanin School of Architecture, Cooper Union.
Stephen Melville, Ph.D., Chicago. Associate Professor, Department of Art History and Adjunct Associate Professor, Department of English, Ohio State University.
Ivo Mesquita, M.A., São Paulo. Independent curator, São Paulo, Brazil.
Helen Molesworth, Ph.D., Cornell. Curator of contemporary art, Baltimore Museum of Art.
Piotr Piotrowski, Ph.D., Adam Mickiewicz (Poland). Professor of Art History, Adam Mickiewicz University, Poland.
Mari Carmen Ramirez, Ph.D., Chicago. Curator of Latin American Art, Archer M. Huntington Art Gallery, University of Texas at Austin.
Robert Storr, M.F.A., Art Institute of Chicago. Curator, Department of Painting and Sculpture, Museum of Modern Art.
John Vinci, B.Arch., IIT. Architect, Chicago.

The Bard Center for Environmental Policy (* Affiliated Faculty)

Ana Arana, M.S., Columbia.
Daniel Berthold-Bond, Ph.D., Yale.
Lee Breckenridge,* J.D., Harvard.
Hillary Brown,* M.Arch., Yale.
James Chace, A.B., Harvard.
Kris Feder, Ph.D., Temple.
Stuart E. G. Findlay,* Ph.D., Georgia.
Joanne Fox-Przeworski, Ph.D., Washington (St. Louis). Director, Bard Center for Environmental Policy. Former Director for North America of the United Nations Environment Programme.
Michael Glantz, Ph.D., Pennsylvania.
Ann Goodman,* Ph.D., Chicago.
Francesca T. Grifo,* Ph.D., Cornell.
Robert Henshaw,* Ph.D., Iowa.
Felicia Keesing, Ph.D., Berkeley.
Erik Kiviat, Ph.D., Union (Ohio).
Lori Knowles,* LL.M., Wisconsin–Madison.
William T. Maple, Ph.D., Kent State.
Ruben A. Mnatsakanian, Ph.D., Moscow State University (Russia).
Paul Szasz,* LL.B., Cornell.
Michael Tibbetts, Ph.D., Wesleyan.
Kathleen Weathers,* Ph.D., Rutgers.

The Milton Avery Graduate School of Arts

Peggy Ahwesh. Filmmaker.
David Behrman. Composer/electronic artist.
Bob Bielecki. Technical adviser.
Nayland Blake. Sculptor.
Michael Brenson. Art critic/historian, curator.
Nancy Bowen. Sculptor.
Lydia Davis. Writer.
Cecilia Dougherty. Filmmaker.
Mark Alice Durant. Photographer.
Barbara Ess. Photography.
Heinz Inso Fenkl. Writer.
Stephen Frailey. Photography.
Kenji Fujita. Sculptor.
Arthur Gibbons. Director. Sculptor.
Regina Granne. Painter.
Charles Hagen. Photographer.
Arturo Herrera. Painter.
Peter Hutton. Filmmaker.
Suzanne Joelson. Painter.
Ann Lauterbach. Poet.
Judy Linn. Photographer.
Nicholas Maw. Composer.
Josip Novakovich. Fiction writer and essayist.
Yvonne Rainer. Film/video.
Leslie Scalapino. Writer.
Carolee Schneemann. Film/performance.
Nancy Shaver. Sculptor.
Amy Sillman. Painter.
Matthew Stadler. Writer.
Richard Teitelbaum. Composer.
Robin Tewes. Painter.
Lynne Tillman. Writer.
Oliver Wasow. Photographer.
Stephen Westfall. Painter.

The Bard Graduate Center for Studies in the Decorative Arts

Kenneth Ames, Ph.D., Pennsylvania. American nineteenth-century decorative arts and material culture.
Beth Holman, Ph.D., NYU. Renaissance art, material culture and decorative arts.
Patricia Kirkham, Ph.D., London. Eighteenth- and nineteenth-century English furniture, twentieth-century design/cultural studies, cinema studies.
François Louis, Ph.D., Zurich. Art history of Tang and Song China, Chinese goldsmithing.
Michele Majer, M.A., NYU. Costume studies.
Andrew Morrall, Ph.D., Courtauld Institute. Fourteenth- to eighteenth-century European arts.
Amy Ogata, Ph.D., Princeton. Nineteenth- and twentieth-century design history.
Derek E. Ostergard, B.A., American. Nineteenth- and twentieth-century decorative arts.
Sarah B. Sherrill, B.A., Smith. European, American, and Oriental carpets.
Elizabeth Simpson, Ph.D., Pennsylvania. Arts of the ancient world.
Susan Weber Soros, Director; Ph.D., Royal College of Art. Furniture studies.
Nina Stritzler-Levine, M.A., Cooper-Hewitt Museum/Parsons. Twentieth-century decorative arts.
Stephanie Walker, Ph.D., NYU. European sculpture and decorative arts.

For a list of recent BGC adjunct faculty members, students should consult *Peterson's Guide to Graduate Programs in the Humanities, Arts, and Social Sciences.*

BARRY UNIVERSITY

Graduate Programs

Programs of Study

Barry University offers more than fifty quality degree programs that prepare students for a successful career change and advancement. Classes are offered on evenings or Saturdays for many of the programs, thereby meeting the needs of the working professional. The faculty is well attuned to the learning styles of adult students. The experience at Barry is academically rewarding and challenging, with interaction with professionals who bring real-world experience to the classroom.

The School of Arts and Sciences offers the M.A. in communication, pastoral ministry for Hispanics, and theology; the M.S. in clinical psychology, communication, organizational communication, and school psychology; and the M.F.A. and M.A. in photography. The M.A. in pastoral theology is offered in Venice, Florida. The Doctor of Ministry (D.M.) is offered at the Miami Shores campus. The School of Natural and Health Sciences offers the M.S. in anesthesiology, biology, biomedical sciences, health services administration, and occupational therapy. The School of Business offers the Master of Business Administration (M.B.A.). Concentrations are available in finance, international business, management, health services administration, marketing, management information systems, and accounting. The School of Business also offers the M.S. in e-commerce. The School of Education offers programs in counseling (M.S., and Ed.S.) with specializations in guidance and counseling; marital, couple and family counseling/therapy; mental health counseling; rehabilitation counseling; and a dual specialization in marital, couple and family counseling/therapy and mental health counseling. The Ph.D. in counseling is also offered. The M.S. is offered in educational computing and technology, educational leadership, elementary education, and exceptional student education; guidance and counseling; and Montessori education, pre-K–primary education, and reading. The M.S. is also offered in higher education administration, human resource development and administration, and human resource development and administration with a specialization in not-for-profit/religious organizations. The Ed.S. is available in educational computing and technology, educational leadership, exceptional student education, guidance and counseling, Montessori education, and pre-K–primary education. The Ph.D. program in leadership and education has specializations in educational technology, exceptional student education, higher education administration, human resource development, and leadership. The School of Law offers the Juris Doctor (J.D.) degree. The School of Nursing offers the M.S.N. in nurse practitioner studies, nursing administration, and nursing education; a dual program that leads to the M.S.N./M.B.A; and the Ph.D. in nursing. There are also bridge options for qualified RNs with bachelor's degrees in fields other than nursing to earn an M.S.N. and an accelerated option for qualified RNs to move seamlessly to the M.S.N. The School of Graduate Medical Sciences offers the Master of Science in anatomy (M.S.) and a Physician Assistant Program leading to the Master of Clinical Medical Science (M.C.M.Sc.). Programs leading to the Doctor of Podiatric Medicine and Surgery (D.P.M.) and the D.P.M./M.B.A. dual degree are also available. The School of Social Work offers programs that lead to the M.S.W. and the Ph.D. in social work. The Advanced Standing M.S.W. Program is available to students with a recent B.S.W. from a school whose program is accredited by the Council on Social Work Education. The School of Human Performance and Leisure Sciences offers the Master of Science in Sport Management (M.S.S.M.) and an M.S.S.M./M.B.A. dual program. The M.S. in movement science is also available, with specializations in athletic training, biomechanics, exercise science, and sport and exercise psychology. The School of Adult and Continuing Education offers the M.S. in information technology and the M.A. in liberal studies.

None of the graduate programs requires a foreign language for admission or graduation.

Research Facilities

Campus facilities include the Monsignor William Barry Library, photography and digital imaging labs, a human performance lab, an athletics training room, a biomechanics lab, a complete television production studio, an academic computing center, multimedia business classrooms, art studios, a performing arts center, a nursing lab, the Classroom of Tomorrow, and several other well-equipped science labs.

Financial Aid

Financial aid is available. Professional scholarships are available for full-time social workers, educators, nurses, or members of a religious community. Some schools offer scholarships and other forms of financial assistance. Barry University also participates in the Federal Family Loan Program and applicable state Florida financial aid programs. Students should contact the specific school for details. Additional information is available from the Associate Director of Financial Aid (telephone: 305-899-3673; e-mail: finaid@mail.barry.edu).

Cost of Study

Tuition for 2001–02 was $520 per credit hour for most programs, except those in the Schools of Podiatric Medicine, Education (Ph.D. program), Social Work (Ph.D. program), and Nursing (Ph.D. program).

Living and Housing Costs

On-campus housing is not available for graduate students. Assistance is provided in locating off-campus housing.

Student Group

The total University enrollment for 2001–02 was 8,691, with 2,784 students registered in the graduate and professional programs. The majority of the graduate students are studying part-time in evening and weekend classes.

Location

The University's 122-acre campus is located in the village of Miami Shores, 7 miles north of downtown Miami and 14 miles south of Fort Lauderdale. This ideal location provides students with access to one of the nation's most dynamic multicultural environments and all of its business, cultural, and recreational opportunities.

The University

Barry University is an international, Catholic, coeducational institution with a history of distinguished graduate programs. Founded in 1940, the University has grown steadily in size and diversity, while maintaining a low student-faculty ratio, thus providing for the individual needs of its academic community.

Applying

Applicants are expected to have earned a 3.0 cumulative GPA or above in undergraduate work. They are usually required to submit scores on standardized tests (such as the GRE, MAT, MCAT, or GMAT); the specific test requirement depends on the program. Some programs have additional requirements. International applicants whose native language is not English are required to submit a TOEFL score of at least 550 (paper-based) or 213 (computer-based). The minimum acceptable score is higher for the Physician Assistant program. Students are admitted for any term, except in the School of Podiatric Medicine and most programs in the School of Natural and Health Sciences. The student's application and credentials (transcripts, recommendations, and test scores) should be sent to the address below and should be received at least thirty days prior to the beginning of the term for which admission is desired.

Correspondence and Information

Office of Admission
Barry University
11300 Northeast Second Avenue
Miami Shores, Florida 33161-6695
Telephone: 305-899-3100
800-695-2279 (toll-free)
Fax: 305-899-2971
E-mail: admissions@mail.barry.edu
World Wide Web: http://www.barry.edu/gradprograms

FACULTY HEADS

School of Natural and Health Sciences
Sr. John Karen Frei, O.P., Ph.D., Miami (Florida); Associate Vice President and Dean.
Anesthesiology: Dolores Maxey-Gibbs, M.S., Barry; Program Director, CRNA.
Biology: Ralph Laudan, Ph.D., Rutgers; Associate Dean and Program Director.
Biomedical Sciences: Ralph Laudan, Ph.D., Rutgers; Associate Dean and Program Director.
Health Services Administration: Len Sperry, M.D./Ph.D., Northwestern; Program Director.
Occupational Therapy: Douglas Mitchell, M.S., Wayne State; Program Director.
School of Arts and Sciences
Laura S. Armesto, Ph.D., Miami (Florida); Associate Vice President for Undergraduate Studies and Dean.
Clinical Psychology: Linda Peterson, Ph.D., Miami (Florida); Associate Dean and Chairperson.
Communication: Laura S. Armesto, Ph.D., Miami (Florida); Acting Chair.
Pastoral Ministry for Hispanics: Rev. Mario B. Vizcaino, Ph.D., Gregorian (Rome); Director, Southeast Pastoral Institute.
Photography: Dan Ewing, Ph.D., Michigan; Chairperson.
School Psychology: Agnes Shine, Ph.D., Ball State; Program Advisor.
Theology: Mark Wedig, O.P., Ph.D., Catholic University; Program Chair.
School of Business
Jack Scarborough, Ph.D., Maryland; Dean.
School of Education
Sr. Evelyn Piche, O.P.; Ph.D., Michigan State; Dean.
Dr. John Dezek, Ed.D., Western Michigan; Associate Dean, Graduate Studies.
Counseling (Ph.D.)—campus: Maureen Duffy, Ph.D., Nova Southeastern; Program Director.
Counseling (Ph.D.)—Orlando: Kathleen Douglas, Ph.D., Florida; Program Coordinator.
Educational Computing and Technology (M.S., Ed.S.)—campus: Donna Lenaghan, Ed.D., Virginia Tech.; Program Director.
Educational Leadership (M.S., Ed.S.)—campus: Candace Lacey, Ph.D., Barry; Program Director.
Educational Leadership (Ph.D., Ed.D.)—campus: John Enger, Ph.D., Iowa; Program Coordinator.
Educational Leadership (M.S., Ed.S., Ed.D.)—Orlando: Joseph Flora, Ed.D., Arkansas; Program Coordinator.
Elementary Education (M.S.)—campus: Catheryn Weitman, Ph.D., Texas A&M; Program Director.
Exceptional Student Education (M.S., Ed.S.)—campus: Judy Harris-Looby, Ph.D., Miami (Florida); Program Director.
Exceptional Student Education (Ph.D.)—campus: Clara Wolman, Ph.D., Minnesota; Program Coordinator.
Guidance and Counseling (M.S., Ed.S.)—campus: John Marszalek, Ph.D., Mississippi State; Program Coordinator.
Guidance and Counseling (M.S., Ed.S.)—Orlando: Kathleen Douglas, Ph.D., Florida; Program Coordinator.
Human Resource Development and Administration (M.S., Ed.S.)—campus: Toni Powell, Ph.D., Florida State; Program Director.
Human Resource Development and Administration (M.S., Ed.S.)—Ft. Myers: Madeleine Doran, Ed.D., South Florida; Program Coordinator.
Human Resource Development and Administration (M.S., Ed.S.)—Orlando: Rosalyn Vaughn, Ph.D., Southern Illinois; Program Coordinator.
Human Resource Development and Administration (M.S., Ed.S.)—Treasure Coast: Christine King, Ph.D., Oklahoma; Program Coordinator.
Human Resource Development (Ph.D.)—campus: Betty Hubschman, Ed.D., Florida International; Program Coordinator.
Human Resource Development (Ph.D.)—Orlando: Susan Fisher, M.B.A., Rollins; Program Coordinator.
Leadership and Education (Ph.D.)—campus: John Dezek, Ed.D., Western Michigan; Program Director.
Marital, Couple, and Family Counseling/Therapy (M.S., Ed.S.)—campus: Maureen Duffy, Ph.D., Nova Southeastern; Program Director.
Marital, Couple, and Family Counseling/Therapy (M.S., Ed.S.)—Orlando: Kathleen Douglas, Ph.D., Florida; Program Coordinator.
Mental Health Counseling (M.S., Ed.S.)—campus: Maureen Duffy, Ph.D., Nova Southeastern; Program Director.
Mental Health Counseling (M.S., Ed.S.)—Orlando: Kathleen Douglas, Ph.D., Florida; Program Coordinator.
Montessori: Elementary and Pre-K–Primary (M.S., Ed.S.)—campus: Ijya Tulloss, Ed.D., Nova Southeastern; Program Director.
Pre-K–Primary (M.S., Ed.S.)—campus: Dianna Radeloff, Ph.D., Michigan; Program Director.
Reading (M.S., Ed.S.)—campus: Ann Murphy, Ed.D., Miami (Florida); Program Director.
Rehabilitation Counseling (M.S., Ed.S.)—campus: Maureen Duffy, Ph.D., Nova Southeastern; Program Director.
School of Human Performance and Leisure Sciences
G. Jean Cerra, Ph.D., Missouri; Dean.
Gayle Workman, Ph.D., Ohio State; Associate Dean and Department Chair.
Movement Science—Athletic Training: Carl Cramer, Ed.D., Kansas State; Program Director.
Movement Science—Biomechanics: Monique Butcher, Ph.D., Texas Women's; Program Coordinator.
Movement Science—Exercise Science: Connie Mier, Ph.D., Texas; Program Coordinator.
Movement Science—Sport and Exercise Psychology: Gualberto Cremades, Ph.D., Houston; Program Coordinator.
Sport Management: Leta Hicks, Ph.D., Oklahoma State; Coordinator of Graduate Programs.
School of Law
Stanley M. Talcott, J.D., Nebraska; Dean.
Frank L. Schiavo, J.D., Villanova; Associate Dean.
School of Nursing
Pegge L. Bell, Ph.D., Virginia; Dean.
Janyce Dyer, DNSc., Catholic University; Associate Dean of Graduate Programs.
Kathleen Papes, Ed.D., Florida Atlantic; Associate Dean for Administrative Affairs.
Linda Perkel, Ph.D., Barry; Associate Dean for Undergraduate Programs.
Nursing Administration: Claudette Spalding, M.S.N., Barry; Program Advisor.
Nursing Education: Carrol Gold, Ph.D., Northwestern; Program Advisor.
Nurse Practitioner Studies: Claudia Hauri, Ed.D., Florida; Program Advisor.
Ph.D. Program: Janyce Dyer, Catholic University; Dean of Graduate Programs.
School of Graduate Medical Sciences
Chet Evans, D.P.M., California College of Podiatric Medicine; Dean.
Physician Assistant Program
Doreen Parkhurst, M.D., Boston University; Program Director.
School of Social Work
Stephen M. Holloway, Ph.D., Columbia; Dean.
William E. Buffum, Ph.D., Case Western Reserve; Associate Dean.
Ph.D. Program: Elane Nuehring, Ph.D., Florida State; Director.

Outside Andreas School of Business.

Students looking at X-ray.

BAYLOR UNIVERSITY

The Graduate School

Programs of Study

Approximately 1,300 students pursue doctoral degrees in sixteen programs, master's degrees in approximately sixty-five programs of study, and an educational specialist degree at the main campus in Waco. The U.S. Academy of Health Sciences offers master's degrees in health-care administration and in physical therapy (entry-level) at Ft. Sam Houston, Texas, and the Doctor of Science in Physical Therapy (D.Sc.P.T.) at Ft. Sam Houston and West Point, New York (for federal personnel and specially targeted nonfederal applicants). The School of Nursing in Dallas offers master's degrees in advanced neonatal nursing, family nurse practitioner studies, and nursing administration and management. Joint degrees are available in association with the Law School and Truett Theological Seminary.

Many graduate programs at Baylor consistently receive high national rankings, including entrepreneurship, music, religion, speech pathology, physical therapy, and nursing. The Psy.D. (Doctor of Psychology) clinical psychology program at Baylor is the oldest and longest accredited university Psy.D. program in the nation and has a national reputation for producing outstanding practicing clinical psychologists.

Research Facilities

The University Libraries house collections totaling more than 2.2 million volumes (including government documents), more than 8,300 serials, and numerous online search databases. Collections include the Armstrong Browning Library, Baylor Collections of Political Materials, Dawson Institute of Church-State Studies, Caston Law Library, Moody Memorial Library, Jones Library (for sciences and engineering), School of Education Learning Resource Center, School of Nursing Learning Resource Center, and the Texas Collection.

Research facilities include the Centers for American and Jewish Studies; Analytical Spectroscopy; Applied Geographic and Spatial Research; Astrophysics, Space Physics and Engineering Research; Community Research and Development; Family and Community Ministries; Ministry Effectiveness; Renewable Aviation Fuels Development; Wastewater Certification Center; and the Keck Seismological Observatory.

Strecker Museum and the Biology Department herbarium house research collections of vertebrates and plants from the Southwest and Mexico. Field study in Central America is supported through Chapala Ecology Station and Environmental Studies' field programs. Baylor operates a PBS television station and a National Public Radio station.

An active Graduate Student Association promotes professional development via a travel awards program.

Financial Aid

Students in most graduate programs receive some sort of financial support from the University, usually in the form of graduate assistantships and/or tuition remission. Information about this source of support can be obtained directly from the individual graduate programs. Paid health insurance is available to doctoral students who are instructors of record. Other sources of financial aid include Federal Stafford Student Loans, a low-interest loan made by a bank or credit union; Texas Tuition Equalization Grants, a program provided by the state legislature for residents of Texas; the Federal Work-Study Program, which provides part-time campus jobs for students with financial need; and private alternative loan programs.

Cost of Study

For academic year 2002–03, the tuition rate for domestic and international students is $654 per semester hour. Fees applicable to most students include the general student fee ($47 per credit hour; maximum $625 per semester), technology fee ($107 per semester), and vehicle registration fee ($175 annually). Most other fees are program specific. Books, supplies, and room and board expenses are additional.

Living and Housing Costs

Most graduate students live in off-campus apartments and houses. Private apartments range from $200 to $1350 per month. Limited on-campus housing for graduate and married students is available. The cost of a dormitory room is $1264 per person, per semester. The cost of board in the University dining halls is $1494 per semester.

Student Group

The total enrollment at Baylor University is approximately 14,000 students, of whom more than 1,300 are graduate students. The student body is diverse, representing numerous ethnic groups, religious affiliations, and countries of origin, although most graduate students come from Texas and the surrounding states. Slightly more than half the graduate student population is female. Most graduate students are full-time students.

Student Outcomes

Graduates of Baylor's graduate programs tend to be successful in their professional pursuits. Many go on for further graduate study in programs at other universities. Many pursue study in professional programs in medicine, dentistry, and an array of allied health professions. Many others take positions in business, industry, and government.

Location

The Baylor University campus is located along the Brazos River in Waco, a central Texas city of 200,000. Local attractions include recreational facilities at Lake Waco, the Cameron Park Zoo, historic homes, museums, and theaters featuring local and national productions. Waco can be reached by air, rail, bus, and interstate highway. Waco is a 2-hour drive from Austin and Dallas/Ft. Worth.

The University

Chartered in 1845 by the Republic of Texas and affiliated with the Baptist General Convention of Texas, Baylor University is the oldest institution of higher learning in Texas and the world's largest Baptist university. The mission of Baylor University is to educate men and women for worldwide leadership and service by integrating academic excellence and Christian commitment within a caring community.

Applying

Admission requires formal application. Applicants must hold a bachelor's degree from an accredited institution in the United States or proof of equivalent training at a foreign institution of higher learning. A completed application packet consists of the application form, application fee ($25 to $50 depending on the program), official transcripts from all institutions where course work has been taken, official results of exams (GRE General, Subject; GMAT; other program-required standardized measures), three letters of recommendation, and supplemental items required by certain programs.

Correspondence and Information

Applications, the Graduate Catalog, and other information are available on the Graduate School Web site or from the Graduate Admissions Office.

The Graduate School
Baylor University
P.O. Box 97264
Waco, Texas 76798-7264

Telephone: 800-BAYLORU (menu option 2) (toll-free)
E-mail: graduate_school@baylor.edu
World Wide Web: http://www.baylor.edu/Graduate_School/

ADMINISTRATIVE FACULTY

THE GRADUATE SCHOOL
J. Larry Lyon, Dean; Ph.D., Texas.
Kenneth T. Wilkins, Associate Dean; Ph.D., Florida.

THE COLLEGE OF ARTS AND SCIENCES
Wallace L. Daniel, Dean; Ph.D., North Carolina.
American Studies: Donald Greco, Ph.D., Illinois at Urbana-Champaign.
Biology: Keith Hartberg, Ph.D., Notre Dame.
Chemistry: Marianna Busch, Ph.D., Florida State.
Communication Disorders: Kathy Whipple, Ph.D., Memphis State.
Communication Sciences and Studies: Michael F. Korpi, Ph.D., Iowa.
English: Maurice Hunt, Ph.D., Berkeley.
Environmental Studies: Susan Bratton, Ph.D., Texas at Dallas.
Geology: Thomas Goforth, Ph.D., Southern Methodist.
History: James SoRelle, Ph.D., Kent State.
Journalism: Doug Ferdon, Ph.D., North Texas.
Mathematics: Edwin Oxford, Ph.D., New Mexico State.
Modern Foreign Languages: Manuel Ortuño, Ph.D., Michigan.
Museum Studies: Calvin Smith, M.S., Eastern New Mexico.
Neuroscience: Jim Patton, Ph.D., Baylor.
Philosophy: Robert Baird, Ph.D., Emory.
Physics: Darden Powers, Ph.D., Caltech.
Political Science: James Curry, Ph.D., Kansas.
Psychology: Jim Patton, Ph.D., Baylor.
Religion: William Brackney, Ph.D., Temple.
Sociology: Harold Osborne, Ph.D., LSU.
Theater Arts: Stan Denman, Ph.D., Pittsburgh.

THE HANKAMER SCHOOL OF BUSINESS
Terry Maness, Dean; Ph.D., Indiana.
Linda Livingstone, Associate Dean for Graduate Business Programs; Ph.D., Oklahoma State.
Accounting: Charles Davis, Ph.D., North Carolina.
Economics: Steve Green, Ph.D., Brown.

THE SCHOOL OF EDUCATION
Robert Yinger, Dean; Ph.D., Michigan State.
Curriculum and Instruction: Betty Conaway, Ph.D., LSU.
Educational Administration: Albert Smith, Ph.D., Michigan.
Educational Psychology: Terrill Saxon, Ph.D., Kansas.
Health, Human Performance, and Recreation: Deborah Johnston, Ed.D., Arkansas.

THE SCHOOL OF ENGINEERING AND COMPUTER SCIENCE
Benjamin Kelley, Dean; Ph.D., Kentucky.
Computer Science: Don Gaitros, Ph.D., Missouri–Rolla.

THE SCHOOL OF MUSIC
William May, Dean; Ph.D., Kansas.
Harry Elzinga, Director of Graduate Programs; Ph.D., Indiana.

THE SCHOOL OF NURSING
Phyllis Karns, Dean; Ph.D., Wyoming.
Pauline Johnson, Director of Graduate Programs; Ph.D., Texas Woman's.

THE SCHOOL OF SOCIAL WORK
Preston Dyer, Chairperson; Ph.D., Texas Woman's.
Center for Family and Community Minstries: Diana Garland, Ph.D., Louisville.

INSTITUTE OF BIOMEDICAL STUDIES
Darden Powers, Director; Ph.D., Caltech.

J. M. DAWSON INSTITUTE OF CHURCH-STATE STUDIES
Derek Davis, Director; Ph.D., Texas at Dallas.

INSTITUTE OF STATISTICS
Tom Bratcher, Director; Ph.D., SMU.

ACADEMY OF HEALTH SCIENCES, UNITED STATES ARMY
Health Care Administration: Comdr. Daniel Dominguez, Ph.D., Iowa.
Physical Therapy (entry-level): Lt. Colonel Timothy Flynn, Ph.D., Penn State.
Physical Therapy (D.Sc.P.T.): Josef Moore, Ph.D., Virginia (West Point). Matt Garber, D.Sc.P.T., Baylor (Ft. Sam Houston).

Program of Study

The Master of Business Administration (M.B.A.) covers the tools and methods required to run a business. The program requires 36 credit hours of course work. The schedule of course offerings permits an individual working full time to complete all the requirements for the M.B.A. degree in 18 months (2 classes per term).

Students who do not have an undergraduate degree in business generally take the Foundation (12 credits) and the Core (24 credits) to complete the degree. M.B.A. concentrations are offered in the following: accounting, finance, international management, and management information systems. This program is offered in class and online.

The Master of Science in Computer Information Systems program has strong elements of both business and computer/telecommunication subjects. Students with business or computer undergraduate preparation typically finish the program with 36 credits of graduate work. For the students without a computer background, there are 9 additional prerequisites credits. This program is offered in class and online.

The Master of Science in Health Care Administration program provides clinical health-care providers with an opportunity to pursue in depth the various areas of planning, organizing, leading, and controlling as they provide administrative guidance to others within their health-related organization. This program is offered online.

The Master of Arts in Management program develops a working knowledge of the application of quantitative techniques, marketing analysis, human resource management, financial analysis, influencing behavior in organizations, and sensitivity to the legal environment in which operations occur. This program is offered in class and online.

The Master of Arts in Leadership program encourages individual thought, synthesis of group contribution, and assimilation of practical and theoretical teachings. Its mission is to combine leadership philosophy derived from great leaders and their writings, with concepts and theoretical models of organizational leadership. This program is offered in class and online.

The Master of Science in Human Services program has two options for students: a 36-hour program that emphasizes youth services and a 48-hour program that emphasizes the clinical aspects of human services. The youth services option is designed for students whose main goal is a general master's degree with an emphasis on preparation for direct and administrative service roles rather than therapy or counseling roles.

The clinical options enables students to gain a stronger foundation in clinical assessment and treatment topics. It also provides students the benefits of a recommended supervised experience of 450 contact hours in preparation for application for the Nebraska Department of Health and Human Services Provisional Licensed Mental Health Practitioner or Certified Provisional Alcohol/Drug Abuse Counselor. Students are also prepared for any further graduate education. This program is offered only in class.

Research Facilities

The Bellevue University state-of-the-art library provides compete access to extensive research material from anywhere in the world on-site and online. In addition, Assisted and unassisted services are available on-site and online. Both provide complete bibliographic searches on a research topic and copies of articles cited in bibliographic search. Services available include the following: The Encyclopedia Americana, which contains all the informative full-text articles found in print or in CD-ROM versions, including thousands of hypertext links to Web sites featuring additional pertinent data; Health Source Plus, an online database covering general health magazines and professional health-care journals; LexisNexis Academic Universe, a service that combines searchable access to more than 2.8 billion documents from thousands of sources covering news and financial, medical, and legal information. The vast majority of the titles on LexisNexis Academic Universe are available in full text, with a limited number available in abstract form. The service covers newspapers, magazines, wire services, federal and state court opinions, federal and state statutes, federal regulations, and SEC filings such as 10-K's, 10-Q's, and their exhibits. News information is updated daily and wire services several times daily; ProQuest Direct, one of the world's largest collections of information that includes articles summaries from more than 4,000 publications, with many in full-text/full-image format; FirstSearch, containing more than 60 databases, some full-text, spanning numerous subjects that are updated regularly; and netLibrary, the most comprehensive collection of online books and resource materials available. Using netLibrary, students access a wide range of scholarly and reference materials entirely online.

Financial Aid

Financial aid assistance is available from the federal and state government, the institution, and private sources. Financial aid includes scholarships, work-study programs, and student loans. Scholarships do not have to be repaid. Federal Work-Study allows a student to work and earn money. Student loans must be repaid. In general, all U.S. citizens and eligible noncitizens enrolled in an approved degree program may apply for financial aid. For additional information, students may telephone 402-293-3762.

Cost of Study

For 2002–03, individual courses per credit hour in class are $275, and $295 online. The sixteen-month Cohort program is $10,125, and $10,845 online.

Living and Housing Costs

Student housing is available for graduate students. Students may contact 402-293-2088 for more information.

Student Group

The total University enrollment for fall 2001 was 3,925 with 720 students registered in graduate programs. The majority of graduate students study part-time in evening and online classes.

The University

Bellevue University is one of Nebraska's largest fully accredited independent colleges. Programs serve the needs of more than 4,000 students annually and cater to working adult students as well as traditional undergraduate students. Benefits include accelerated degree-completion programs; online programs, an online library, and cooperative credit transfer agreements. Associate degrees are accepted in full, and credit is given for corporate and military training.

Applying

To apply, students must transmit the application online or by mail, pay fees, and submit transcripts for evaluation. Admissions counselors work with students to complete the official admissions process. An educational degree plan is completed for each student defining requirements needed to achieve each student's degree goal.

Correspondence and Information

Information Center
Bellevue University
Telephone: 402-293-3769
800-756-7920 (toll-free)
E-mail: kld@bellevue.edu
World Wide Web: http://www.bellevue.edu

FACULTY

The Bellevue University full-time and adjunct faculty consists of 95 men and 53 women, teaching students from freshman to graduate level. The student-faculty ratio is 20:1. For most classes and programs, Bellevue University employs adjunct faculty members who are professionals in their respective fields. Faculty members are screened to ensure each is current on issues and technology.

BENEDICTINE UNIVERSITY

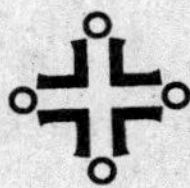

Graduate Programs

Programs of Study

Benedictine University offers ten graduate degrees, including the Master of Business Administration (M.B.A.) in two formats: the Evening MBA Program (with concentrations in accounting, entrepreneurship, financial management, health administration, human resource management, integrated marketing communications, international business, management consulting, and organizational leadership) and the Accelerated MBA Program; a Master of Science (M.S.) in clinical psychology; a Master of Arts in education (M.A.Ed.) with concentrations in elementary education, secondary education, and special education; a Master of Education (M.Ed.) with concentrations in special education/collaborative teaching, curriculum and instruction/collaborative teaching, curriculum and instruction/general, training and development, and leadership and administration; a Master of Science in exercise and physiology and fitness management; a Master of Arts (M.A.) in liberal studies; a Master of Science in management information systems with concentrations in business administration, financial reporting systems, health administration, integrated marketing communication, and management and organizational behavior; a Master of Science in management and organizational behavior with concentrations in management and organizational behavior, human service administration, human resources management, health administration, organization development, management in a professional technical environment, and international management; and a Masters of Public Health (M.P.H.) with concentrations in community administration of health care, health education, long-term care and management.

The University also offers a Ph.D. in organization development and certificates in managed-care business administration, change management consulting, e-commerce, health administration, international management, human resource management, long-term care, management consulting, management in a professional technical environment, organization development, practice management, service management, and training and development.

Research Facilities

The University Library is the central depository on campus for all media research materials. The collection contains more than 165,000 cataloged items, approximately 30,000 federal government documents, and a variety of audiovisual educational items. The library receives nearly 1,000 periodical and newspaper titles regularly. The Dialog computer research service makes available online more than 200 scholarly and commercial databases. Through participation in the OCLC network, the library offers interlibrary loan access to all libraries in the United States and Canada. The library also receives direct delivery of books through its membership in ILLINET.

Financial Aid

The only form of financial aid generally available to graduate students at Benedictine University is a Federal Stafford Student Loan. Graduate students may borrow up to $18,500 a year (a minimum of $10,000 must be in unsubsidized Stafford Loans). These low-interest loans may be used for tuition, fees, books, living expenses and other college-related costs. Loan applicants are required to submit the Free Application for Federal Student Aid (FAFSA). Federal regulations require demonstration of financial need to quality for the Federal Stafford Student Loan program.

Cost of Study

The 2001–02 tuition was $510 per semester credit hour and $370 per quarter credit hour, except for the Accelerated MBA.

Living and Housing Costs

On-campus apartments are available. Accommodations in surrounding communities range from moderate to expensive.

Student Group

Today, Benedictine University enrolls approximately 2,000 undergraduate and 1,000 graduate students across all programs. The programs attract students of diverse academic, social, and cultural backgrounds and ages.

Location

Benedictine University is located near the village of Lisle, about 1 mile west of Route 53. It is about 25 miles from downtown Chicago and a 5-minute drive from the Route 53 exit of the East-West Tollway (Interstate 88). From the east and west, it is easily accessible from Ogden Avenue (Route 34). The North-South Tollway's Maple Avenue exit is 2 miles east of the campus. Students take advantage of the many cultural and recreational facilities located in Chicago and the surrounding area.

The University

Benedictine University is an independent, coeducational University founded in 1887 by the Benedictine monks of St. Procopius Abbey. The University, which has an operating budget exceeding $14 million, has demonstrated financial stability. Benedictine University is a comprehensive, multifaceted university oriented by Christian values and affiliated with the Benedictine Order of the Catholic Church.

Applying

Requirements for admission include a bachelor's degree with a grade point average of at least 2.75 (on a 4.0 scale). For testing details, student-at-large options, and further information, students may contact the Office of Graduate Admissions.

Correspondence and Information

Office of Graduate Admissions
Benedictine University
5700 College Road
Lisle, Illinois 60532

Telephone: 630-829-6200
Fax: 630-829-6584
E-mail: gradadm@ben.edu
World Wide Web: http://www.ben.edu

THE FACULTY AND THEIR RESEARCH

Bruce S. Buchowicz, Professor of Business Administration; Ph.D., Northwestern, 1988. Dr. Buchowicz's consulting and research interests include management of innovation and technology, entrepreneurship, top management teams, corporate governance, and executive succession and compensation.

John A. Cicero, Dean of the College of Business, Technology, and Professional Programs and Professor of Computer Science; Ph.D., IIT, 1984. Dr. Cicero's interests include object-oriented development programming languages, software engineering, numerical analysis, modeling/simulation, computer ethics, and computer literacy.

Jane Crabtree, Associate Professor of Business and Management; Ph.D., Temple, 1996. Dr. Crabtree is doing research on career management practices and international management. She has taught classes in Asia and has a background in human resources, strategic management, computer information systems, and international business.

David A. Dibblee, Associate Professor of Business and Director of the Executive MBA Program for Senior Healthcare Administrators; Ed.D. candidate, Northern Illinois; CPA. Dr. Dibblee's research interests include changing the higher education accounting curriculum, adult education methods and practices, and the application of accounting to service.

John Kevin Doyle, Associate Professor; Ph.D., Syracuse, 1976.

Sandra Gill, Associate Professor of Business; Ph.D., Fielding Institute, 1998.

Alan Gorr, Associate Professor; Ph.D., Iowa, 1971; M.P.H., Illinois at Chicago, 1976. His professional experiences include five short-term consultancies with the World Health Organization in Africa and Southeast Asia. He is coeditor of the *Handbook of Health Professions Education*.

Barbara T. Grabowski, Professor and Director of the Management Information Systems Program; Ph.D., Northwestern, 1985. Dr. Grabowski is doing research on technology curriculum issues and the effect of strategic management of information technology on corporate performance.

Peter Healey, Professor and Director of Exercise Physiology and Fitness Management Programs; Ph.D., University of Health Sciences (Chicago), 1981. Dr. Healey has published research in the areas of weight training and aerobic performance/activity.

Jim F. Iaccino, Professor in Experimental Psychology; Ph.D., DePaul, 1982. Dr. Iaccino has published texts as well as journal articles on left brain–right brain differences, bizarre imagery, and Jungian analysis of film genres.

Eileen M. Kolich, Professor of Education; Ph.D., Penn State, 1985. Dr. Kolich specializes in reading theory and assessment, curriculum development, and clinical supervision.

James D. Ludema, Associate Professor of Organization Development; Ph.D., Case Western Reserve, 1996. Dr. Ludema has lived and worked in Asia, Africa, and Latin America and has served as consultant to a variety of organizations in the profit, nonprofit, and government sectors. His research interests include the human and organization dimensions of global change, business and sustainable development, the power of hope in building communities and organizations, organizational storytelling, and large-group methodologies for helping diverse stakeholder groups find common ground.

Ralph D. Meeker, Professor of Physics and Computer Science and Associate Academic Dean; Ph.D., Iowa State, 1970. Dr. Meeker has had research and development experience at AT&T Bell Laboratories and Argonne National Laboratory, and has been a consultant to other organizations. He has developed a multiprocessor packet switching system and a real-time operating system.

Susan M. Mikula, Professor of History; Ph.D., Syracuse, 1974. Dr. Mikula's area of expertise is East European history in the nineteenth and twentieth centuries, especially in questions of nationalism, political structures, and ethnic relations. Her research area focuses more specifically on the relations of Czechs and Slovaks and on the politics of ethnicity in that region.

Dianne R. Moran, Assistant Professor of Psychology and Counseling Psychology; Ph.D., Notre Dame, 1988. Dr. Moran's areas of interest include human development through the life span; behavior disorders of childhood, particularly autism; and applied behavior analysis.

Dan Nohl, Associate Professor; Ph.D., IIT, 1990.

Margaret O'Leary, Associate Professor of Business Administration; M.D., George Washington, 1980; M.B.A., Benedictine University, 1999. Dr. O'Leary's consulting, research, and writing interests focus on health-care performance measurement and improvement.

Charlotte P. Ross, Associate Professor of Education; Ph.D., Wisconsin–Madison, 1989. Dr. Ross specializes in behavioral disorders, behavior management, and family systems theory.

Alexey Shukin, Professor and Director of Counseling Psychology; Ph.D., Chicago, 1964. Dr. Shukin's primary areas of interest include client-therapist interaction, empathic skills training, therapist as a problem in psychotherapy, language of emotions and attitudes, and nonverbal behavior and phenomenology of emotional meanings.

Peter F. Sorensen Jr., Professor and Director of Management and Organizational Behavior and Organization Development; Ph.D., IIT, 1971. Dr. Sorensen has experience in a wide range of management development activities and in organizational assessment at such organizations as the Chicago Metropolitan YMCA, the Continental National American Group, the Illinois State Correction System, and Johnson & Johnson.

Jon Colby Swanson, Professor of Public Health; Ph.D., Illinois, 1972. Dr. Swanson's teaching interests include drug abuse and alcohol education, stress management, psychopharmacology, health education methods, and research methods. His research interests include attention-deficit disorder, psychopharmacology, and biological and chemical bases of behavior.

Ram Tenkasi, Associate Professor of Organization Development; Ph.D., Case Western Reserve, 1994. Dr. Tenkasi's research focuses on the areas of organizational knowledge and learning, technical and social innovations, and organizational transitions and change. He has obtained funding from several agencies, including the National Science Foundation.

Jim Zoda, Associate Professor; Ph.D., Northern Illinois, 1979.

BENNINGTON COLLEGE

Graduate Programs

Programs of Study

Bennington College's graduate programs are built on the belief that making new work is at the heart of the educational process.

The combined Bachelor of Arts/Master of Arts in Teaching Program may be entered at the graduate or undergraduate level. For those who begin the program with a B.A., the M.A.T. is generally a full-time, two-year program; its three main elements are immersion in a discipline or craft, a full year of classroom teaching, and a weekly education seminar. (Bennington is authorized to recommend licensure in early childhood, elementary, and secondary education.)

The low-residency Master of Fine Arts (M.F.A.) in writing and literature is a two-year program that involves ten-day residencies on campus during January and June of each year. Between residencies, students correspond directly with a nationally renowned core faculty of writers. Students are expected to devote at least 25 hours each week to their writing and reading and to create a portfolio of fiction, nonfiction, or poetry.

In the low-residency Master of Arts in Teaching a Second Language (M.A.T.S.L.), students study French or Spanish during three intensive weeks over two summers and a final week in the third summer. During the year, they carry out projects of their own design with close guidance and support from faculty members. The program is designed for new and veteran teachers who want to improve their language ability, while sharpening their teaching skills and help define the future of foreign language teaching.

The Master of Fine Arts in visual and performing arts offers candidates who have already reached a level of mature artistic expression in dance, drama, music, or the visual arts a chance to deepen and refine their specific artistic medium. Dance and theater students, especially, are expected to have experience in the field. The studio-based M.F.A. requires a two-year, four-semester, on-campus commitment.

The Master of Arts in Liberal Studies Program is designed to provide a context for students with a capacity for self-direction to explore relationships across the traditional boundaries of disciplines. Students create an individual program of courses; a minimum of 64 credits is required to fulfill the degree, which may be pursued on a full- or part-time basis.

The postbaccalaureate program is intended for students who have completed a bachelor's degree and have decided to pursue a career in medicine or the allied health sciences but who have not yet taken all the required science courses necessary for admission to medical school. This full-time, full-year or two-term program (depending on previous course work) is distinguished by its small class sizes and the ability of students to work with faculty members in current research.

Research Facilities

The 120,000-square-foot Visual and Performing Arts Center (VAPA) contains three black box theaters with state-of-the-art technical support, the Usdan Art Gallery, and studios for music, dance, video, painting, architecture, ceramics, sculpture, printmaking, and photography. Bennington also houses one of the largest sprung wood floors in the world, especially designed for dance performance. Most facilities in VAPA are available for student use 24 hours a day. The Dickinson Science Building includes fully equipped science labs, a computer center with audio/video digitizing and processing capabilities, and the language lab. Bennington's Center for Audio Technologies consolidates all campus music/audio technology; facilities include an electronic music studio, a computer instructional studio, a digital audio studio, and a lab equipped for the production of graphics, computer art, and multimedia projects. Architecture and design programs are enhanced by computer-aided design (CAD). Also available to graduate students is the Early Childhood Center, a licensed preschool and kindergarten that allows childhood development and education students to observe and work directly with children.

Financial Aid

For master's and first-year postbaccalaureate students who are U.S. citizens, aid is available through the Federal Stafford Student Loan Program.

Cost of Study

In 2001–02, tuition for the M.F.A. in visual and performing arts, M.A.T., and M.A.L.S. programs was $15,400 per year. The M.F.A. in writing and literature cost $11,150 per year and the postbaccalaureate program cost $16,800 per year plus $3700 for the summer term, if required. Tuition for the M.A.T.S.L. with summer room and board was $8960.

Living and Housing Costs

Master's and postbaccalaureate students live off campus. Students may participate in the College's board plan, which cost $2100 in 2001–02.

Student Group

Bennington's graduate programs are highly selective and are best suited for students who have a strong sense of what they want from graduate work and know how to assume responsibility for the design of their education. In the process of their education, all Bennington students must confront the question of what a real education is. The College currently enrolls more than 100 graduate students in its residential and low-residency programs.

Location

Bennington's 550-acre campus is nestled among the Green Mountains of southwestern Vermont—less than 1 hour from Albany and 3½ hours from both New York City and Boston. The region surrounding the College is renowned for its outdoor activities, including hiking, downhill and cross-country skiing, and canoeing.

The College

Bennington College, a liberal arts college founded in 1932, began as and remains an invitation to learn. Bennington is committed to the belief that teachers should do what they teach and bring to the classroom an engagement with their discipline learned through active practice in the world. Because both students and teachers are actively engaged in the work at hand, the relationship between them is richly collaborative; students participate in faculty work as much as the reverse.

Applying

Applications for the M.F.A. in visual and performing arts are due by February 1; students are notified by April 1. Financial aid applications are due March 1. For the M.A.L.S., applications are due by March 1; students are notified by May 1. Financial aid applications are due March 1. M.A.T. applications are due by March 1; students are notified by May 1. Financial aid applications are due March 1. The preferred application deadline for the M.A.T.S.L. is April 1; late applications continue to be accepted if there is room in the program. Students are notified on a rolling basis and financial aid applications are due April 1. For the M.F.A. in writing and literature, the application deadline for June entrance is March 15; notification is in mid-April and financial aid applications are due April 1. For January entrance, applications are due by September 15; students are notified by mid-October and financial aid applications are due by October 1. Normally, a bachelor's degree is required to enter the M.F.A. in writing and literature program, but this can be waived if the original work submitted for consideration warrants an exception. Students should submit applications to the Writing Programs Office (address below). For the Postbaccalaureate Program, applications (including financial aid applications) are due by February 15. Students are notified as soon as a decision is made. Notification of all financial aid awards is made on a rolling basis. Faculty members reserve the right to request an interview of all candidates.

Correspondence and Information

Coordinator of Graduate Admissions
Office of Admissions & the First Year
Bennington College
Bennington, Vermont 05201
Telephone: 802-440-4312
800-833-6845 (toll-free)
Fax: 802-440-4320
E-mail: admissions@bennington.edu
World Wide Web: http://www.bennington.edu

For M.F.A. in writing and literature, contact:
Writing Seminars Office
Bennington College
Bennington, Vermont 05201
Telephone: 802-440-4452
Fax: 802-442-4453
E-mail: writing@bennington.edu

THE FACULTY AND THEIR RESEARCH

David Anderegg, Ph.D., Clark, 1985. Psychology.
Steven Bach, Ph.D., USC. Film, literature.
Rina Banerjee, M.F.A., Yale, 1995. Drawing.
Barry Bartlett, M.F.A., Alfred, College of Ceramics, 1977. Ceramics.
Douglas Bauer, Ph.D., SUNY at Albany, 1984. Literature.
April Bernard, A.B., Harvard, 1978. Literature.
Thomas Bogdan. Studied voice with Adele Addison, acting at Bloomfield College, and dance with Guy Alessandro. Voice.
Kitty Brazleton, D.M.A., Columbia, 1994. Music composition.
Joel Chadabe, M.M., Yale, 1962. Electronic music.
Ronald Cohen, Ph.D., Michigan, 1966. Psychology.
Dan Coleman, Ph.D., Cornell, 1998. Teacher education.
Terry Creach, B.S., Oregon, 1972. Dance.
Mary DeBey, Ph.D., SUNY at Albany, 1994. Teacher education.
Norman Derby, Ph.D., MIT, 1976. Physics, astronomy.
Carol Diehl, M.F.A., School of Visual Arts. Painting.
Ida Faiella, M.A., SUNY at Stony Brook. Voice.
Mansour Farhang, Ph.D., Claremont, 1970. History.
Thomas Farrell, B.M., SUNY College at Potsdam, 1980. Design for dance and drama, media studies.
Marianne Finckel, B.A., Bennington, 1944. Piano.
Peggy Florin, M.F.A., Bennington, 1989. Dance instruction.
Janet Foley, Ph.D., Maine, 1996. Chemistry.
Michael Giannitti, M.F.A., Yale, 1987. Lighting design.
Juan Gomez, Ph.D., Kansas, 1999. Mathematics/science.
Ricky Ian Gordon, B.A., Carnegie Mellon, 1977. Music composition.
Milford Graves. Attended CUNY, City College; New York Community College; and Eastern School for Physicians Aides, Occidental Institute of Chinese Studies. Music.
Lucy Grealy, M.F.A., Iowa Writers Workshop, 1988. Literature.
Maxine Henryson, M.F.A., Illinois, 1986. Photography.
Edward Hoagland, A.B., Harvard, 1955. Literature.
Wayne Hoffmann-Ogier, M.A., Maine, 1972. Expository writing.
Daniel Hofstadter, B.A., Columbia, 1966. Literature.
Jon Isherwood, M.F.A., Syracuse, 1987. Sculpture.
Kirk Jackson, M.F.A., Yale, 1998. Drama.
Dina Janis, School of Visual Arts and private coaching, 1985–2000. Drama.
Jonathan Kline, M.F.A., RIT, 1984. Photography.
Roberta Levitow, M.F.A., Stanford. Drama.
Nino Mendolia, M.F.A., Yale. Digital art.
Daniel Michaelson, M.F.A., Columbia, 1970. Costume design, mediation.
Michael L. Mishkind, Ph.D., SUNY at Stony Brook, 1981. Biology.
Catherine Mosley, M.F.A., Columbia, 1970. Printmaking.
Randall Neal, M.F.A., Bennington, 1981. Electronic music.
Ann Pibal, M.F.A., Iowa, 1995. Painting.
Miroslava Prazak, Ph.D., Yale, 1992. Anthropology.
Ruben Puentedura, Ph.D., Harvard, 1990. Chemistry, media and computer studies.
Jean Randich, M.F.A., Yale, 1994. Drama.
Irving Rappaport, Ph.D., Caltech, 1953. Biology, immunology.
Sue Rees, M.F.A., Syracuse, 1986. Sculpture, drawing, performance design.
Bill Reichblum, M.F.A., Columbia, 1985. Drama.
Dana Reitz, M.F.A., Bennington, 1994. Dance.
Lloyd Richards, M.F.A., Yale. Drama.
Stephen Sandy, Ph.D., Harvard, 1963. Literature.
Gladden Schrock, M.F.A., Yale, 1964. Drama.
Susan Sgorbati, M.F.A., Bennington, 1986. Dance, mediation.
Michael Shamberg. Film, video.
Allen Shawn, M.A., Columbia, 1976. Music, composition.
Donald Sherefkin, B.A., Cooper Union, 1978. Architecture.
Elizabeth Sherman, Ph.D., Vermont, 1977. Biology.
Stephen Siegel, M.S., Juilliard. Music, composition.
David Slavitt, M.A., Columbia, 1957. Literature.
Dean Snyder, M.F.A., Art Institute of Chicago, 1978. Sculpture.
Andrew Spence, M.F.A., California, Santa Barbara, 1971. Painting.
Sally Sugarman, M.S./C.A.S., SUNY at Albany, 1990. Childhood and media studies.
Carol Symes, Ph.D., Harvard, 1998. History.
Perry Tymeson, B.F.A., Nova Scotia College of Art and Design, 1973. Printmaking.
Glen Van Brummelen, Ph.D., Simon Fraser, 1993. Mathematics.
Paul Voice, Ph.D., Witwatersrand (South Africa), 1997. Philosophy.
Bruce Weber, Ph.D., California, San Diego, 1968. Chemistry.
Bruce Williamson, M.A., Hunter, 1989. Music.
Kerry Woods, Ph.D., Cornell, 1980. Biology, ecology.
Janis Young, M.F.A., Arizona, 1987. Drama.

Regional Center for Languages and Cultures

Isabelle Kaplan, Director; C.A.P.E.S., Dijon (France), 1962. Professional development workshops, foreign language pedagogy, special teaching projects.
Clorinda Davila-Keller, Ph.D., California, Davis, 2000. Spanish.
Virginie Delfosse-Reese, Ph.D., Iowa, 1990. French, technology and language learning/teaching, historical perspectives in literature.
Peter Jones, M.A., Columbia, 1991. English as a second language.
Nicholas Lasoff, Director, Language Media Lab; M.A., Middlebury, 1990. German, technology.
Carol Meyer, M.A.T., School for International Training, 1995. Spanish, development of curriculum and activities for elementary foreign language education.
Montserrat Mochon, M.A., Granada (Spain), 1986. Spanish.
Noëlle Rouxel-Cubberly, M.A., Tours (France), 1998. French, humanities and modern languages.
Tina Sebastiani, M.A., Universita per Stranieri, Sienna (Italy), 2001. Italian.
Shunzhu Wang, Ph.D., Purdue, 2001. Chinese, Chinese literature and literary theory.
Ikuko Yoshida, M.A., St. Michael's (Toronto), 1997. Japanese.

M.F.A. in Writing and Literature Core Faculty

Douglas Bauer, Ph.D., SUNY at Albany. Fiction.
April Bernard, A.B., Harvard. Poetry.
Sven Birkerts, B.A., Michigan. Nonfiction.
Susan Cheever, B.A., Brown. Nonfiction.
Martha Cooley, B.A., Trinity. Fiction.
Elizabeth Cox, B.A., North Carolina. Fiction.
Thomas Sayers Ellis, M.F.A., Brown. Poetry.
Maria Flook, M.F.A., Iowa. Fiction.
Lynn Freed, Ph.D., Columbia. Fiction.
Amy Gerstler, M.F.A., Bennington. Poetry.
Lucy Grealy, M.F.A., Iowa. Nonfiction.
Amy Hempel, B.A., California State, San Jose. Fiction.
Jane Hirschfield, B.A., Princeton. Poetry.
David Lehman, Ph.D., Columbia. Poetry.
Phillip Lopate, Ph.D., Union (Ohio). Nonfiction.
Alice Mattison, Ph.D., Harvard. Fiction.
Jill McCorkle, M.A., Hollins. Fiction.
Askold Melnyczuk, M.A., Boston University. Fiction.
Rick Moody, M.F.A., Columbia. Fiction.
Ed Ochester, M.A., Harvard. Poetry.
George Packer, B.A., Yale. Nonfiction.
Liam Rector, Director; M.P.A., Harvard. Poetry.
Bob Shacochis, M.F.A., Iowa. Nonfiction.
Jason Shinder, M.A., California, Davis. Poetry.

BOSTON COLLEGE

Graduate School of Arts and Sciences

Programs of Study

The Graduate School of Arts and Sciences at Boston College offers programs that lead to the degrees of Ph.D., M.A., and M.S. in the humanities, social sciences, and natural sciences. A list of departments and faculty contacts is presented on the reverse of this page. Prospective applicants may contact the Graduate Arts and Sciences Admission Office or their departments of interest for application materials and program requirements.

Research Facilities

Research is an important part of the intellectual life at Boston College. Faculty members, graduate students, and undergraduates collaborate in a range of research strategies across the disciplines and professional schools, including laboratory studies, survey research, archival and textual research, theory development, and field and basic research. In addition to the work of individual faculty units, Boston College supports the collaborative work of faculty members and students across the university through the following centers and institutes: the Boisi Center for Religion and American Public Life; the Center for Child, Family, and Community Partnerships (CCFCP); the Center for Christian-Jewish Learning; the Center for Corporate Citizenship (CCC); the Center for East Europe, Russia, and Asia; the Center for Ignatian Spirituality; the Center for International Higher Education; the Center for Retirement Research; the Center for the Study of Testing, Evaluation, and Educational Policy (CSTEEP); the Center for Work and Family (CWF); the Institute of Medieval Philosophy and Theology; the Institute for Scientific Research; the Institute for the Study and Promotion of Race and Culture (ISPRC); the Irish Institute; the Jesuit Institute; the Lonergan Center; the Management Center; the Matrix: Resources for the Study of Women's Religious Communities; the Mathematics Institute; the Social Welfare Research Institute (SWRI); the Watershed Institute; and the Weston Observatory. Boston College provides its students with state-of-the-art facilities for learning, including a full range of computer services, online access to databases, and a library system with more than 1.9 million books, periodicals, and government documents and 3.4 million microform units. The library's membership in the Boston Library Consortium provides access to ten major research libraries in the Boston area, and an interlibrary loan system provides further resources.

Financial Aid

Assistantships, fellowships, and tuition scholarships are available to promising students and include the Boston College Graduate Fellowships for American Minority Students and the Presidential Fellowships. The amounts of these awards and the number of years for which they may be renewable vary among Graduate School departments. The university's Student Financial Services Office administers and awards need-based federal financial aid programs, including loans and work-study.

Cost of Study

Tuition was $736 per credit in 2001–02 (most courses are 3 credits). Full-time students without health insurance through another source were required to purchase health insurance through the university at a cost of $580 per year. Full-time students were also charged a $15 registration fee and a $25 activity fee each semester.

Living and Housing Costs

Most graduate students live off campus in nearby apartments. The university's Housing Office maintains lists of available housing and lists of students looking for roommates. Local realtors are also helpful. For information, students should contact Off-Campus Housing, Rubenstein Hall, or call 617-552-3075.

Student Group

The Graduate School of Arts and Sciences enrolls approximately 1,100 students representing a wide variety of national and cultural backgrounds. Students participate in the Graduate Student Association, the Graduate International Student Association, and the Graduate AHANA Association, which are involved in both academic and social activities.

Location

The university's main campus is located 6 miles from downtown Boston, with direct access to the city via trolley. Metropolitan Boston offers a fine setting for graduate study. Boston College graduate students can cross-register for courses at Brandeis, Tufts, and Boston Universities. The numerous local colleges make the city a mecca for students seeking academic, social, and cultural enrichment. The Boston College campus offers many programs and facilities for cultural, athletic, and other extracurricular pursuits.

The College

Founded in 1863, Boston College is one of the oldest Jesuit universities in the United States. The total graduate student enrollment of approximately 4,500 students is distributed among seven schools: the Graduate Schools of Arts and Sciences, Education, Management, Nursing, and Social Work; the Law School; and the College of Advancing Studies.

Applying

Prospective applicants are encouraged to contact the Graduate Arts and Sciences Admission Office to obtain application information. The application deadline is February 1 (deadline for psychology and theology departments is January 2).

Correspondence and Information

Graduate Arts and Sciences Admission Office
221 McGuinn Hall
Boston College
Chestnut Hill, Massachusetts 02467

Telephone: 617-552-3265
Fax: 617-552-3700
E-mail: gsasinfo@bc.edu
World Wide Web: http://www.bc.edu/gsas

GRADUATE ARTS AND SCIENCES DIVISIONS, PROGRAMS, AND PROGRAM DIRECTORS

Students who wish to contact a Program Director via e-mail may do so by using the following format: firstname.lastname@bc.edu.

HUMANITIES

Biblical Studies (M.A.): Dr. Lisa Cahill, 617-552-4602.
English (Ph.D.): Dr. Amy Boesky, 617-552-3701.
English (M.A., M.A.T., C.A.G.S.): Dr. Elizabeth Wallace, 617-552-3701.
French (Ph.D., M.A., M.A.T.): Dr. Dwayne Carpenter, 617-552-3820.
Greek (M.A.): Dr. Charles Ahern, 617-552-3661.
Hispanic Studies (Ph.D., M.A., M.A.T.): Dr. Dwayne Carpenter, 617-552-3820.
History (Ph.D., M.A., M.A.T.): Dr. Robin Fleming, 617-552-3871.
Irish Studies/English (M.A.): Dr. Philip O'Leary, 617-552-3938.
Italian (M.A.): Dr. Dwayne Carpenter, 617-552-3820.
Latin (M.A., M.A.T.): Dr. Charles Ahern, 617-552-3661.
Linguistics (M.A.): Dr. Maxim Shrayer, 617-552-3910.
Medieval Studies/History (M.A.): Dr. Robin Fleming 617-552-3871.
Medieval Studies/Romance Languages (Ph.D.): Dr. Dwayne Carpenter, 617-552-3820.
Pastoral Ministry (M.A.): Dr. Harold Horell, 617-552-8440.
Philosophy (Ph.D., M.A.): Dr. Arthur Madigan, 617-552-3847.
Religion and Education (Ph.D.): Dr. Harold Horell, 617-552-8440.
Romance Literatures (Ph.D.): Dr. Dwayne Carpenter, 617-552-3820.
Russian (M.A.): Dr. Maxim Shrayer, 617-552-3910.
Slavic Studies (M.A.): Dr. Maxim Shrayer, 617-552-3910.
Theological Ethics (Ph.D.): Dr. Lisa Cahill, 617-552-4602.
Theology (Ph.D., M.A.): Dr. Lisa Cahill, 617-552-4602.

SOCIAL SCIENCES

Economics (Ph.D., M.A.): Dr. Frank Gollop, 617-552-3683.
Political Science (Ph.D., M.A.): Dr. Susan Shell, 617-552-4160.
Psychology (Ph.D.): Dr. Ellen Winner, 617-552-4100.
Sociology (Ph.D., Ph.D./M.B.A., M.A., M.A./M.B.A.): Dr. Eve Spangler, 617-552-2133.

NATURAL SCIENCES

Biology (Ph.D., M.S., M.S.T.): Dr. Daniel Kirschner 617-552-3540.
Chemistry (Ph.D., M.S., M.S.T.): Dr. Paul Davidovits, 617-552-3605.
Geology (M.S., M.S.T.): Dr. John Ebel, 617-552-3641.
Geophysics (M.S.): Dr. John Ebel, 617-552-3641.
Mathematics (M.A., M.S.T.): Dr. Daniel Chambers, 617-552-3750.
Physics (Ph.D., M.S., M.S.T.): Dr. Rein Uritam, 617-552-3576.

BOSTON UNIVERSITY

Graduate School of Arts and Sciences

Programs of Study

The Graduate School of Arts and Sciences at Boston University offers forty-two M.A. programs and thirty-two Ph.D. programs in the humanities, social sciences, and natural sciences. There is, in addition, one division within the Graduate School that provides formal linkage to other professional graduate opportunities at Boston University: the Division of Religious and Theological Studies.

Freestanding M.A. programs within the Graduate School are offered through some research centers and institutes.

Additional academic options may be pursued through cross-registration in any of the University's other schools and colleges, including the University Professors' Program. Through an area consortium arrangement, students may also register for courses at many other graduate schools in the Boston area.

Research Facilities

The Boston University library system holds more than 4.5 million volumes in books and microform. Central service is provided by the Mugar Memorial Library. Among the units contained within this central facility are a music library, an African Studies library, and a department of Special Collections, containing rare books and manuscripts. Numerous departmental libraries are located throughout the campus. An interlibrary loan system further extends the available resources, and a consortium arrangement enables graduate students to use the facilities of many Boston area academic and research libraries.

The University provides laboratories for research and training in disciplines ranging from the physical sciences to the dramatic arts. The recently constructed Metcalf Center for Science and Engineering, for example, houses state-of-the-art facilities for science and engineering students. The University's Academic Computing Center, the Center for Computational Science, and individual departments provide computing resources, from parallel supercomputers to personal workstations, interconnected on a campuswide broadband network.

Financial Aid

Highly qualified graduate students are eligible for Presidential Fellowships and Dean's Fellowships, which include full tuition scholarships and a stipend of $15,000 for the 2002–03 academic year. Teaching fellowships provide stipends that range from $13,500 to $14,500 for 2002–03, plus a tuition scholarship. The Martin Luther King Jr. Fellowships are available to African-American students beginning graduate studies in any department. A wide variety of grants and awards (e.g., graduate scholarships and research assistantships) are made annually by individual departments and centers. In addition, graduate students at Boston University are eligible to participate in a variety of federally funded programs.

Cost of Study

For 2002–03, full-time tuition is $27,042 for the academic year. Part-time tuition is $845 per credit hour. The registration fee is $40 per semester, and the George Sherman Union fee is $79 per semester. Graduate students enrolled for continuing study pay $1690 per semester. The estimated cost of books and supplies is $931 per year.

Living and Housing Costs

A limited number of rooms and apartments in University residences are available for graduate students. Information may be obtained from the Housing Office, 985 Commonwealth Avenue. The Office of Rental Property, 19 Deerfield Street, will supply information about off-campus housing.

Costs of living in Boston are comparable to those in any large metropolitan city. Average housing costs range from $850 to $1200 per month.

Student Group

The Graduate School has 1,649 students, of whom approximately 51 percent are women and 32 percent come from abroad.

Location

The character of Boston results from a rich blend of its historical heritage, active cultural life, and contemporary growth in business, technology, and medicine. Some sixty colleges and universities are located in Greater Boston. Within Boston's compact central area are a host of galleries, the Public Garden, an active theater district, and the Freedom Trail, along which are located some of the most important landmarks in U.S. history. The Museum of Fine Arts, open without charge to Boston University students, has notable Oriental, Egyptian, American portrait, and French Impressionist collections. The Boston Symphony Orchestra, the Opera Company of Boston, and many fine chamber and jazz groups offer annual seasons; the Boston Pops season includes free outdoor summer concerts. Boston is the home of the Red Sox, the New England Patriots, the Celtics, and the Bruins.

The University

Boston University is an independent, coeducational, nonsectarian university. Founded by the Methodist Episcopal Church for the improvement of theological training, it has since its incorporation in 1869 been fully open to women and to all minorities. Its more than 22,463 full-time students and more than 3,500 faculty members contribute to its ranking as one of the world's largest independent universities. The main campus, on the south bank of the Charles River just west of downtown Boston, houses the Graduate School of Arts and Sciences, the College of Arts and Sciences, the School of Law, the School of Management, Metropolitan College, the College of Communication, Sargent College of Allied Health Professions, the School of Social Work, the School of Theology, and the University Professors' Program. On the medical campus are the School of Medicine, the School of Public Health, the Goldman School of Dental Medicine, and University Hospital.

Applying

Applications for admission with financial aid consideration for the fall semester must be received by January 15 for most programs; students should refer to the *Graduate School Bulletin* for exceptions. Some departments accept students in the spring semester, for which applications must be received by October 15 for financial aid consideration. Applications must include official transcripts from all colleges and universities attended, letters of recommendation from at least 2 faculty members in the proposed field of graduate study, and official results of the Graduate Record Examinations (General and Subject Tests) and/or the Miller Analogies Test, as required by the department to which the student is applying. Students from abroad must also submit the International Student Data Form and official English translations of all academic records. Students whose native language is not English must submit results of the Test of English as a Foreign Language. A nonrefundable application fee of $60 is required of all applicants. This fee cannot be waived.

Although financial aid competitions within individual programs begin in early January, students who wish to be considered for special Graduate School fellowships are urged to submit their application with all supporting documents by December 1.

Correspondence and Information

Graduate School of Arts and Sciences
Boston University
705 Commonwealth Avenue
Boston, Massachusetts 02215

Telephone: 617-353-2696
World Wide Web: http://www.bu.edu/bulletins/GRS

FACULTY HEADS

Departments, Divisions, and Programs
African American Studies Program: Ronald K. Richardson, Associate Professor; Ph.D., SUNY at Binghamton.
American and New England Studies Program: Bruce Schulman, Associate Professor; Ph.D., Stanford.
Anthropology Department: Thomas Barfield, Professor; Ph.D., Harvard.
Applied Linguistics Program: Mary Catherine O'Connor, Assistant Professor; Ph.D., Berkeley.
Archaeology Department: Julie Hansen, Professor; Ph.D., Minnesota.
Art History Department: Jonathan Ribner, Associate Professor; Ph.D., NYU.
Astronomy Department: W. Jeffrey Hughes, Professor; Ph.D., Imperial College (London).
Biology Department: Geoffrey Cooper, Professor; Ph.D., Miami (Florida).
Biostatistics Program: Ralph B. D'Agostino, Professor; Ph.D., Harvard.
Cellular Biophysics Program: M. Carter Cornwall, Professor; Ph.D., Utah.
Chemistry Department: Thomas Tullius, Professor; Ph.D., Stanford.
Classical Studies Department: Jeffrey Henderson, Professor; Ph.D., Harvard.
Cognitive and Neural Systems Program: Stephen Grossberg, Professor; Ph.D., Rockefeller.
Computer Science Department: Azer Bestavros, Associate Professor; Ph.D., Harvard.
Creative Writing: Leslie Epstein, Professor; D.F.A., Yale.
Earth Sciences Department: Richard Murray, Associate Professor; Ph.D., Berkeley.
Economics Department: Larry Kotlikoff, Professor; Ph.D., Harvard.
English Department: Bonnie Costello, Professor; Ph.D., Cornell.
Geography Department: Curtis Woodcock, Professor; Ph.D., California, Santa Barbara.
History Department: Charles Dellheim, Professor; Ph.D., Yale.
International Relations Department: Eric Goldstein, Professor; Ph.D., Cambridge.
Boston University Marine Program: Jelle Atema, Professor; Ph.D., Michigan.
Mathematics and Statistics Department: Steven Rosenberg, Professor; Ph.D., Berkeley.
Modern Foreign Languages and Literatures Department: Dorothy Kelly, Professor; Ph.D., Yale.
Music Department: John Daverio, Professor; Ph.D., Boston University.
Neuroscience Department: Howard Eichenbaum, Professor; Ph.D., Michigan.
Philosophy Department: Charles Griswold, Professor; Ph.D., Penn State.
Physics Department: Lawrence Sulak, Professor; Ph.D., Princeton.
Political Science Department: David Mayers, Professor; Ph.D., Chicago.
Preservation Studies: Richard Candee, Professor; Ph.D., Pennsylvania.
Program in Molecular Biology, Cell Biology, and Biochemistry: Gary R. Jacobson, Professor and Director; Ph.D., Stanford.
Psychology Department: Henry Marcucella, Professor; Ph.D., Boston University.
Division of Religious and Theological Studies: John Clayton, Professor; Ph.D., Cambridge.
Sociology Department: Peter Yeager, Associate Professor; Ph.D., Wisconsin.
Sociology/Social Work (Interdisciplinary): Judith Gonyea, Associate Professor; Ph.D., Washington (Seattle).
Women's Studies: Mary White, Professor and Director; Ph.D., Harvard.

Centers and Institutes
Center for Adaptive Systems: Stephen Grossberg, Professor; Ph.D., Rockefeller.
African Studies Center: James C. McCann, Professor; Ph.D., Michigan State.
Center for Anxiety and Related Disorders: David Barlow, Professor; Ph.D., Vermont.
Center for Archaeological Studies: James Wiseman, Professor; Ph.D., Chicago.
Institute for Astrophysical Research: Dan Clemens, Associate Professor; Ph.D., Massachusetts Amherst.
Institute for Classical Traditions: Meyer Reinhold, Professor; Ph.D., Columbia; Wolfgang Haase, Professor; Ph.D., Tübingen (Germany).
Center for Computational Science: Claudio Rebbi, Professor; Ph.D., Turin.
Institute for the Study of Conflict, Ideology, and Policy: Uri Ra'anan, Professor; Ph.D., Oxford.
International Center for East Asian Archaeology and Cultural History: Robert Murowchick, Research Associate Professor; Ph.D., Harvard.
Center for Ecology and Conservation Biology: Thomas Kunz, Profesor; Ph.D., Kansas.
Institute for Economic Development: Dilip Mookherjee, Professor; Ph.D., London School of Economics.
Editorial Institute: Christopher Ricks, Professor; D.Litt. (hon.), Oxford; Geoffrey Hill, Professor; D.Litt (hon.), Oxford.
Center for Einstein Studies: John J. Stachel, Professor; Ph.D., Stevens.
Center for Energy and Environmental Studies: Cutler Cleveland, Associate Professor; Ph.D., Illinois.
International History Institute: Cathol Nolan, Associate Professor; Ph.D., Toronto.
Center for International Relations: Andrew J. Bacevich, Associate Professor; Ph.D., Princeton.
Center for Judaic Studies: Steven Katz, Professor; Ph.D., Harvard.
Institute for Medieval History: Thomas Glick, Professor; Ph.D., Harvard.
Center for Milennial Studies: Richard Landes, Associate Professor; Ph.D., Princeton.
Center for the Philosophy and History of Science: Alfred Tauber, Professor; M.D., Tufts.
Institute for Philosophy and Religion: Leroy Rouner, Professor; Ph.D., Columbia.
Center for Polymer Studies: H. Eugene Stanley, Professor; Ph.D., Harvard.
Institute on Race and Social Division: Glenn Loury, Professor; Ph.D., MIT.
Center for Remote Sensing: Farouk El-Baz, Research Professor; Ph.D., Missouri–Rolla.
Science and Mathematics Education Center: Kenneth Brecher, Professor; Ph.D., MIT.
Center for Space Physics: Supriya Chakrabarti, Professor; Ph.D., Berkeley.
Center for Transportation Studies: T. R. Lakshmanan, Professor; Ph.D., Ohio State.

Boston University along the Charles River.

Marsh Chapel.

The campus along Commonwealth Avenue.

BOWLING GREEN STATE UNIVERSITY

Graduate College

Programs of Study

Bowling Green State University (BGSU) offers Doctor of Philosophy (Ph.D.) programs in American culture studies (communication, English (rhetoric), history, popular culture, and sociology), biological sciences, communication disorders, English (rhetoric), higher education administration, history, interdisciplinary studies, interpersonal communication, mass communication, mathematics, philosophy (applied), photochemical sciences, psychology (clinical, developmental, experimental, industrial, and quantitative), sociology, and theater. A Doctor of Education (Ed.D.) degree is also offered in leadership studies. Other graduate and specialist programs include technology management (consortium degree), education specialist (administration and supervision, mathematics supervision, reading, and school psychology), and specialist in applied biology (immunohematology). Certificates are offered in ethnic studies, gerontology, and women's studies.

BGSU offers the Master of Accountancy (M.Acc.) degree. The Master of Arts (M.A.) degree is offered in American culture studies, art, college student personnel, communication studies, economics, English (rhetoric and writing, literature, literature/creative writing), French, German, guidance and counseling, history, interdisciplinary studies, mathematics, philosophy, political science (dual degree with German only), popular culture, psychology, scientific and technical communication, sociology, Spanish, teaching English as a second language, and theater. The Master of Arts in Teaching (M.A.T.) degree is offered in American culture studies, biological sciences, chemistry, French, geology, German, history, mathematics, physics, Spanish, and theater. The Master of Arts/Science is offered in interdisciplinary studies. The Master of Business Administration (M.B.A.) degree is offered in finance, management information systems, marketing, and supply chain management. The Master of Education (M.Ed.) degree is offered in business education; career and technology education; classroom technology; curriculum and teaching; educational administration and supervision; guidance and counseling; human movement, sport, and leisure studies (developmental kinesiology, recreation and leisure, sport administration); interdisciplinary studies; reading; school psychology; and special education. BGSU also offers the Master of Family and Consumer Sciences (M.F.C.S.) degree. The Master of Fine Arts (M.F.A.) degree is offered in fine art, and creative writing. The Master of Industrial Technology (M.I.T.) is offered in construction management and technology and manufacturing technology. BGSU also offers the Master of Music (M.M.), Master of Organization Development (M.O.D.), Master of Public Administration (M.P.A.), Master of Public Health (M.P.H.), and the Master of Rehabilitation Counseling (M.R.C.) degrees. The Master of Science (M.S.) degree is offered in applied statistics, biological sciences, chemistry, communication disorders, computer science, criminal justice geology, and physics.

Ph.D. requirements include a minimum of 90 semester hours of graduate work beyond the baccalaureate and two semesters of residence. A minimum of 30 semester hours of graduate work beyond the baccalaureate is required for the master's degree; the choice of Plan I (thesis option) or Plan II (comprehensive examination option) is available in most programs. The Graduate College at BGSU is committed to helping students identify personal and professional goals. Through a comprehensive set of facilities and programs, opportunities are provided to pursue high-quality graduate education in an environment conducive to advanced study and research.

Research Facilities

The University libraries have approximately 2 million volumes and approximately 1.6 million microforms, including subscriptions to 6,000 periodicals and 600,000 government documents. In addition to providing a range of regular and specialized research facilities, the University supports a number of research centers and institutes. These include the Center for Archival Collections, the Center for Governmental Research and Public Service, the Center for Photochemical Sciences, the Center for the Study of Popular Culture, the National Drosophila Species Resource Center, the Center for Microscopy and Microanalysis, the Institute for Great Lakes Research, the Institute for Psychological Research and Application, the Management Center, the Philosophy Documentation Center, the Population and Society Research Center, the Reading Center, the Social Philosophy and Policy Center, and the Statistical Consulting Center.

Financial Aid

Departmental assistantships in 2001–02 provided tuition scholarships and stipend payments totaling as much as $34,476 for master's assistantships and $38,517 for doctoral assistantships. About 80 percent of the University's full-time graduate students are awarded assistantship or fellowship support. Student employment and loans are available as sources of graduate student support.

Cost of Study

Tuition in 2001–02 was $350 per credit hour for Ohio residents and $648 per credit hour for nonresidents. Full-time students were assessed a combined fee of $544 per semester for general and registration fees.

Living and Housing Costs

On-campus housing is not available for graduate students. Numerous apartments and other housing are available near the campus. For more information, those interested should contact Off-Campus Housing at 419-372-2458 or go online at http://www.bgsu.edu/offices/sa/campus/housing/rentalservices.html.

Student Group

The University maintains an enrollment of about 17,000 undergraduates and approximately 2,900 graduate students on the main campus. Students represent all fifty states and fifty countries. The opportunities to meet people and exchange ideas at Bowling Green are greatly enhanced by the residential nature of the campus.

Location

Bowling Green is a northwestern Ohio community, located 23 miles south of Toledo and within a 100-mile radius of Ann Arbor, Detroit, Cleveland, and Columbus. The community offers numerous recreational and cultural programs that supplement the activities offered by the University.

The University

Bowling Green, a state-assisted university, was founded in 1910. The University has a 1,250-acre campus.

Graduate programs are offered in six academic colleges—Arts and Sciences, Business Administration, Education and Human Development, Health and Human Services, Musical Arts, and Technology—within the Graduate College. Each year, the University invites visiting scholars, guest artists, and celebrities to lecture, perform, and meet informally with students to exchange ideas and information.

Applying

Applicants must have graduated with a baccalaureate degree from a regionally accredited college or university. Assistantships are awarded for the academic year beginning in the fall semester. Applicants for financial aid are encouraged to complete the admission process by January 15. The application for admission to the Graduate College should be submitted with a $30 nonrefundable application fee. Students should apply six months in advance for admission to a Ph.D. program; for a master's program, three months in advance. International students should allow more time for the application process. Two official transcripts from all colleges attended are required. GRE General Test or GMAT scores must be submitted. TOEFL scores must be submitted by all applicants whose first language is not English. Three letters of recommendation must be forwarded to the department to which admission is requested.

Correspondence and Information

Office of Graduate Admissions
120 McFall Center
Bowling Green State University
Bowling Green, Ohio 43403-0180

Telephone: 419-372-2791
E-mail: prospct@bgnet.bgsu.edu
World Wide Web: http://www.bgsu.edu/colleges/gradcol/

FACULTY HEADS

Graduate College (All telephone numbers are preceded by the area code 419.)
Heinz Bulmahn, Ph.D., Vice Provost for Research and Dean of the Graduate College, 372-7714.
Terry Lawrence, Ph.D., Assistant Dean for Graduate Admissions, 372-7710.

Academic Deans
Don Nieman, Ph.D., Dean, College of Arts and Sciences, 372-2340.
William Balzer, Ph.D., Dean, Continuing Education, Summer, and International Programs, 372-8183.
Lorraine Haricombe, J.D., Interim Dean of Libraries and Learning Resources, 372-2856.
Richard Kennell, Ph.D., Dean, College of Musical Arts 372-2188.
Ernest Savage, Ph.D., Interim Dean, College of Technology, 372-2438.
Josué Cruz, Ph.D., Interim Dean, College of Education and Human Development, 372-7403.
James A. Sullivan, Ph.D., Dean, College of Business Administration, 372-8795.
Linda Petrocino, Ph.D., Dean, College of Health and Human Services, 372-8243.

Degree Program Graduate Coordinators
Additional information may be obtained by contacting the following faculty members or by writing in care of the department.
Accountancy: Alan Lord, Ph.D., 372-8045 (alord@cba.bgsu.edu).
American Culture Studies: Don McQuarie, Ph.D. (Director), 372-0586 (dmcquar@bgnet.bgsu.edu).
Applied Statistics: Nancy Boudreau, Ph.D., 372-8396 (nboudre@bgnet.bgsu.edu).
Art: Charles Kanwischer, M.F.A., 372-9395 (ckanwis@bgnet.bgsu.edu).
Biological Sciences: Stan Smith, Ph.D., 372-8259 (stanlee@bgnet.bgsu.edu).
Business Administration: Carmen Castro-Rivera, Ph.D., 372-2488 (ccastro@cba.bgsu.edu).
Business Education: Linda Good, Ph.D., 372-2085 (lgood@bgnet.bgsu.edu).
Chemistry: Thomas Kinstle, Ph.D., 372-2658 (tkinstl@bgnet.bgsu.edu).
Classroom Technology: Gregg Brownell, Ph.D., 372-7392 (gbrowne@bgnet.bgsu.edu).
College Student Personnel: Michael Coomes, Ph.D., 372-7157 (mcoomes@bgnet.bgsu.edu).
Communication Disorders: Larry Small, Ph.D., 372-7182 (lsmall@bgnet.bgsu.edu).
Communication Studies: Bettina Heinz, Ph.D., 372-9486 (bheinz@bgnet.bgsu.edu).
Computer Science: Laura Leventhal, Ph.D., 372-2765 (leventha@cs.bgsu.edu).
Creative Writing: Larissa Szporluk, Ph.D. (Director), 372-8370 (slariss@bgnet.bgsu.edu).
Criminal Justice: Michael Buerger, Ph.D., 372-8905 (mbuerge@bgnet.bgsu.edu).
Curriculum and Teaching: Leigh Chiarelott, Ph.D., 372-7352 (lchiare@bgnet.bgsu.edu).
Economics: Peter VanderHart, Ph.D., 372-8070 (pvander@cba.bgsu.edu).
Education Administration and Supervision: Michael Dannells, Ph.D. (Chair), 372-7305 (michaed@bgnet.bgsu.edu).
Education Foundations and Inquiry: Daniel Fasco Jr., Ph.D. (Chair), 372-9184 (dfasko@bgnet.bgsu.edu).
English: Sue Carter, Ph.D., 372-6864 (scarter@bgnet.bgsu.edu).
Ethnic Studies: Theresa Mah, Ph.D., 372-7118 (tmah@bgnet.bgsu.edu).
Family and Consumer Sciences: Rebecca Pobocik, Ph.D., 372-7849 (pobocik@bgnet.bgsu.edu).
Geology: Sheila Roberts, Ph.D., 372-0354 (sjrober@bgnet.bgsu.edu).
German, Russian, and East Asian Languages: Christina Guenther, Ph.D., 372-7589 (cguenth@bgnet.bgsu.edu).
Guidance and Counseling: Sherlon Brown, Ph.D., 372-7311 (sbrown@bgnet.bgsu.edu).
Higher Education Administration: Judy Alston, Ph.D. (Chair), 372-7313 (jalston@bgnet.bgsu.edu).
History: Scott Martin, Ph.D., 372-8767 (smartin@bgnet.bgsu.edu).
Human Movement, Sport, and Leisure Studies: Julie Lengfelder, D.A., 372-2878 (jlengfe@bgnet.bgsu.edu).
Leadership Studies: Patrick Pauken, Ph.D. (Chair), 372-2550 (paukenp@bgnet.bgsu.edu).
Mathematics and Statistics: Steve Seubert, Ph.D., 372-2179 (sseuber@bgnet.bgsu.edu).
Musical Arts: Penny Kruse, Ph.D., 372-2757 (krusep@bgnet.bgsu.edu).
Organizational Development: Joyce Steffan, Ph.D., 372-8823 (steffan@cba.bgsu.edu).
Philosophy: Sara Worley, Ph.D., 372-2899 (sworley@bgnet.bgsu.edu).
Photochemical Sciences: Michael Ogawa, Ph.D., 372-2809 (mogawa@bgnet.bgsu.edu).
Physics and Astronomy: Lewis Fulcher, 372-2635 (fulcher@bgnet.bgsu.edu).
Popular Culture: Carl Holmberg, Ph.D., 372-8172 (cholmbe@bgnet.bgsu.edu).
Psychology: Eric Dubow, Ph.D., 372-2556 (edubow@bgnet.bgsu.edu).
Public Administration: Mark Simon, Ph.D. (Chair), 372-7386 (msimon@bgnet.bgsu.edu).
Public Health: Hailu Kassa, Ph.D., 372-9615 (hkassa@bgnet.bgsu.edu).
Reading: Michael French, Ph.D., 372-7356 (mfrench@bgnet.bgsu.edu).
Rehabilitation Counseling: Jay Stewart, Ph.D., 372-7301 (jstewar@bgnet.bgsu.edu).
Romance Languages/French: Katherine Roberts, Ph.D., 372-9440 (krobert@bgnet.bgsu.edu).
Romance Languages/Spanish: Nathan Richardson, Ph.D., 372-8043 (nrichar@bgnet.bgsu.edu).
School Psychology: Audrey Ellenwood, Ph.D., 372-9848 (aellenw@bgnet.bgsu.edu).
Sociology: Steve Cernkovich, Ph.D., 372-2743 (scernko@bgnet.bgsu.edu).
Special Education: Lessie Cochran, Ph.D., 372-7298 (llcochr@bgnet.bgsu.edu).
Technical Writing: Bill Coggin, Ph.D. (Director), 372-7552 (bcoggin@bgnet.bgsu.edu).
Technology: Donna Trautman, Ph.D., 372-7575 (dktraut@bgnet.bgsu.edu).
Theater: Jonathan Chambers, Ph.D., 372-9618 (jonathc@bgnet.bgsu.edu).
Women's Studies: Opportune Zongo, Ph.D., 372-7396 (ozongo@bgnet.bgsu.edu).

"Electric Falcon," the electric automobile developed by the College of Technology.

Professor Roger Ptak with students and a telescope in the Physics and Astronomy Observatory.

Theater production of "The Good Times are Killing Me."

BRADLEY
UNIVERSITY

BRADLEY UNIVERSITY

Graduate School

Programs of Study

Bradley University's Graduate School has programs leading to master's degrees in thirty-one disciplines within the Foster College of Business Administration, the Slane College of Communications and Fine Arts, and the Colleges of Education and Health Sciences, Engineering and Technology, and Liberal Arts and Sciences. The Foster College of Business Administration offers the M.B.A. with a general management focus as well as concentrations in managerial accounting, finance, information technology, management, marketing, and health care administration; a Master of Science degree in accounting; and an Executive M.B.A. program focusing on leadership. The Slane College of Communications and Fine Arts offers the M.A. and M.F.A. in art with areas of concentration in painting, sculpture, printmaking, ceramics, and photography. The College of Education and Health Sciences offers the M.A. in curriculum and instruction, educational administration, human development counseling, human service administration, and learning disabilities. The College also offers an M.S. in nursing with concentrations in administration and nurse-administered anesthesia and a Master of Physical Therapy (M.P.T.). The College of Engineering and Technology provides programs leading to the M.S.C.E., M.S.E.E., M.S.I.E., M.S.Mf.E., and M.S.M.E. All offer research and theses opportunities. The College of Liberal Arts and Sciences offers an M.S. in biology; an M.S. in chemistry for part-time students; an M.S. in computer information systems; an M.S. in computer science in the areas of numerical methods, systems programming, and information storage and retrieval; and an M.A. in English, with emphases in literature and writing. Support courses are offered in geological sciences, history, mathematics, philosophy, political science, and sociology. In addition, the Graduate School offers a Master of Liberal Studies (M.L.S.) degree program. The Graduate School seeks to increase access to its programs by offering many of its courses during the late afternoons and evenings to accommodate working students.

Research Facilities

The Graduate School and the Office for Research and Sponsored Programs at the University provide the focus for faculty and student research activities. Special centers of activity, such as those within the Center for Business and Economic Research and the Materials Testing and Research Lab, bring the University's human resources to bear on the problems of industry, business, and the community. Other special centers are the Illinois Manufacturing Extension Center and the Center for Energy Assessment. Bradley's Cullom-Davis Library, which has more than 1.3 million items, is research oriented. Students and faculty members have bibliographic access to holdings throughout the country through OCLC, a computerized bibliographic network that allows access to 6,000 libraries in the U.S. and other countries. The library holds major microform collections, including the Educational Resources Information Center (ERIC) documents, Library of American Civilization, and Library of English Literature. University computing facilities include high-end Sun engineering workstations, high-end Macintosh work stations, and campuswide computer labs as well as networked residence halls and selected apartments. Also on campus is the Caterpillar Global Communications Center with its innovative telecommunications center.

Financial Aid

The Graduate School offers teaching, research, and administrative assistantships to qualified full-time and part-time students. Awards are made on a competitive basis. Full-time students with full-time assistantships can earn up to 18 hours of tuition per year and an average stipend of $5000 per year. Part-time students with part-time assistantships earn a proportionately smaller amount. The Graduate School offers academic excellence, minority, and need-based scholarships to both full-time and part-time students; scholarship awards may cover up to one half of the cost of tuition. Caterpillar Masters Fellowships are awarded annually on a competitive basis to outstanding students who have graduated from an accredited university, demonstrated superior academic achievement, and are committed to research or creative production. The fellowships provide an annual stipend between $8000 and $12,000, in addition to a full-tuition waiver. UPS Fellowships and Scholarships, for qualified students who are members of minority groups, award full-tuition support and stipends for fellowship recipients. The University participates in the USX loan program, which offers favorable interest rates for students in business, computer science, and engineering. Information regarding other loans is available through the financial aid office at Bradley.

Cost of Study

For 2001–02, full-time tuition (12–16 credit hours) was $7615 per semester. Credit-hour tuition was as follows: 1–7 hours, $415 per semester hour; 7½–11½ hours, $515 per semester hour. Tuition for the Master of Liberal Studies program was $220 per semester hour.

Living and Housing Costs

Living expenses vary, but students should anticipate a cost of at least $800 per month for room, board, and miscellaneous expenses.

Student Group

The Graduate School enrolls approximately 850 students, from a wide variety of academic and occupational backgrounds. Roughly half of the graduate students are women; about one third are international students.

Student Outcomes

Bradley University's graduate students experience great success in finding employment in their fields. The Smith Career Center assists students in defining career goals, creating a job-search plan, obtaining career-related work experience, and making contact with prospective employers. Caterpillar, Inc., and other major companies employ many graduates in the fields of engineering, business, and computer science. Bradley's nurse administration, nurse-administered anesthesia, and physical therapy programs have provided excellent employees for the area hospitals.

Location

Bradley University is located in the heart of Illinois, in Peoria, a metropolitan area of 350,000, midway between Chicago and St. Louis. Peoria is large enough to provide a wide range of recreational, cultural, and professional activities and yet small enough to maintain a strong community spirit.

The University

Bradley University was founded in 1897 as a nonsectarian institution of higher education. Its purpose was and is to provide its students with a means of living independent, industrious, and useful lives. The University is characterized by strong professional programs based on an extensive liberal arts and sciences background.

Applying

Students must have completed their baccalaureate education prior to their intended enrollment date and have their application materials submitted to the Graduate School at least six weeks before the date they intend to register. Applications for graduate assistantships and scholarships must be received by March 1 for fall and October 1 for spring entry. Required examinations are the GRE General Test for biology and electrical engineering, the GMAT for the M.B.A. and accounting programs, and the MAT or GRE for education and nursing. Art applicants must meet portfolio requirements. International applicants must submit TOEFL scores and show financial resources sufficient to cover tuition and living costs. An application fee and two letters of reference are required of all applicants.

Correspondence and Information

Graduate School, Bradley University
118 Bradley Hall
Peoria, Illinois 61625

Telephone: 309-677-2375
Fax: 309-677-3343
E-mail: bugrad@bradley.edu
World Wide Web: http://www.bradley.edu/grad

GRADUATE PROGRAM ADVISERS

Foster College of Business
Business: Edward L. Sattler; Ph.D., Illinois; John Gillett, Ph.D., North Texas State; Jack Russell (EMBA).
Slane College of Communication and Fine Arts
Art: Kenneth H. Hoffman; M.F.A., San Francisco Art Institute.
College of Education and Health Sciences
Leadership in Educational Administration: Stan Huff, Ed.D., Texas A&M.
Leadership in Human Service Administration: Jenny Tripses, Ph.D., Illinois State.
Human Development Counseling: Jenny Tripses, Ph.D., Illinois State.
Curriculum and Instruction: Barbara S. Penelton; Ed.D., Indiana.
Nursing Administration: Francesca A. Armmer; Ph.D., Indiana State.
Nursing Administered Anesthesia: Francesca A. Armmer; Ph.D., Indiana State.
Physical Therapy: Mary Jo Mays; Ph.D., Nebraska.
College of Engineering and Technology
Civil Engineering: Robert W. Fuessle; Ph.D., Illinois.
Electrical Engineering: Prasad Shastry; Ph.D., Indiana Institute of Technology.
Industrial Engineering: Fariborz "Fred" Tayyari; Ph.D., Texas Tech.
Manufacturing Engineering: Saeed Saboury; Ph.D., Imperial.
Mechanical Engineering: Desh Paul Mehta; Ph.D., Iowa State.
College of Liberal Arts and Sciences
Biology: Janet L. Gehring; Ph.D., Illinois.
Chemistry: Kristy McQuade, Ph.D., Wisconsin.
Computer Information Systems: Jiang-bo Liu; Ph.D., Washington (St. Louis).
Computer Science: Jiang-bo Liu; Ph.D., Washington (St. Louis).
English: Robert Prescott, Ph.D., Illinois.
Liberal Studies: Max A. Taylor; Ph.D., MIT.

Graduate engineering students working on a class project in the engineering lab.

Peters Recital Hall is located in the Dingeldine Music Center, the site for more than eighty solo and ensemble recitals, plus concerts by University bands, choirs, and guest artists.

Bradley Hall is one of forty-one buildings located on the University's 75-acre campus.

BRANDEIS UNIVERSITY

Graduate School of Arts and Sciences

Programs of Study

Doctoral study is the foundation of the Graduate School of Arts and Sciences (GSAS). Required teaching and research components are an integral part of the educational development of all doctoral students. Ph.D. degrees are offered in American and comparative history, anthropology, biochemistry, chemistry, computer science, English and American literature, mathematics, molecular and cell biology, musicology and music composition, Near East and Judaic studies, neuroscience, physics, politics, psychology, sociology, structural biology, and biophysics. In addition, terminal master's degrees are offered in most of the Ph.D. programs; master's and postbaccalaurete programs are offered in classics, genetic counseling, Jewish communal service, Jewish studies, premedical studies, studio art, teaching of Hebrew, and theater arts. Joint master's degrees are offered in women's studies with anthropology, English, Near Eastern and Judaic studies, or sociology.

Research Facilities

Research facilities include the Volen National Center for Complex Systems, the Gordon Public Policy Center, the Lown School of Near Eastern and Judaic Studies, the Rosenstiel Basic Medical Sciences Research Center, the Tauber Institute for the Study of European Jewry, and the Goodman Institute for the Study of Zionism.

The University's four libraries house nearly 1 million volumes, 838,000 microtexts, 345,000 government documents, 31,000 audio recordings, and 6,500 journals. Students have access to VAX systems and Macintosh and DOS computers at three microcomputer clusters. The Spingold Theater Center and the Slosberg Music Center provide state-of-the-art performance spaces, as well as other areas for every facet of the performing arts. The Rose Art Museum is the focal point for the University's collection of contemporary art, which is without parallel in the greater Boston area.

Financial Aid

All doctoral candidates are offered a 100 percent tuition scholarship and fellowship, renewable for at least four years. Advanced doctoral candiates may apply for a number of other awards, including the Dissertation Year Fellowship, a University Prize Instructorship, and the Sachar Awards for research and study abroad. A limited number of need-based and merit-based awards for up to 50 percent of tuition are available to master's candidates.

Cost of Study

Tuition for the 2002–03 academic year is $27,345, or $13,672 per semester. Tuition for the postbaccalaureate studio art and artist's diploma programs is $13,672, or $6836 per semester. Tuition for postbaccalaureate premedical studies and part-time residence is $3418 per course, per term.

Living and Housing Costs

Most students live either in Waltham or Cambridge/Somerville. Both areas have large student populations; many local services are easily accessible to students without a car at Brandeis. On-campus housing is extremely limited, and preference is usually given to first-year international students from outside North America.

The coordinators of Graduate Student Services actively assist graduate students with their housing search. A large-scale house hunting weekend is held every July. In addition, Graduate Student Services monitors an e-mail list of available rental units and those seeking apartments and maintains a Web page that includes links to local housing Web sites and classified advertisements. The cost of living is comparable to that of most large metropolitan areas.

Student Group

The Graduate School of Arts and Sciences student profile is a diverse one, with students from all parts of the United States and various countries around the world. More than 1,000 students are enrolled in the Graduate School, of whom 28 percent are international, 47 percent are women, and 90 percent are full-time students. The average age of the GSAS student is 30 years.

Student Outcomes

After completing their programs, graduates regularly go on to positions in academics and in industry. Recent graduates have obtained tenure-track positions at Yale, Rutgers, Colgate, Boston College, University of California (Berkeley), and Virginia Commonwealth University. Postdoctoral positions have been held at Harvard Medical School, Yale Medical School, University of Pennsylvania Medical School, Massachusetts Institute of Technology, Boston College, the Joslin Clinic, and Beth Israel Hospital. Placements in the private sector include those at IBM, Chase Manhattan Bank, and Dupont-Merck.

Location

The Greater Boston area is rich in culture, education, and opportunities. Brandeis University, located just 10 miles west of Boston, consists of more than 90 buildings on 235 acres of rolling land and is in proximity to museums, theaters, and other attractions of the city, as well as to ocean beaches, canoeing on the Charles River, historic towns, and countryside for hiking or cross-county skiing. Brandeis is easily accessible by major routes and by public transportation.

The University

Brandeis University is a private, coeducational, and nonsectarian institution of high education and research. Founded in 1948, Brandeis brings to American higher education a unique cultural perspective reflecting Jewish traditions of scholarship and community service and the commitment to social justice personified by Louis Dembitz Brandeis, the distinguished Supreme Court Justice for whom the University is named. While Brandeis maintains a special relationship with the Jewish community, it is not affiliated with any religious organizations; it offers no theological instruction and it welcomes students and faculty members of all backgrounds and beliefs.

Applying

The Graduate School generally accepts students for the fall semester, and electronic application is encouraged. The deadline for applications to the Ph.D. programs is January 15; deadlines to the master's and postbaccalaureate programs vary by department. Applications submitted electronically require a $50 application fee. Applications submitted via mail require a $60 fee. Admission to the graduate programs is based on each applicant's prior scholastic achievement, statement of purpose, letters of recommendation, and for most programs, results of the GRE. Applications for the programs in theater or studio arts will be evaluated on the basis of the applicant's writing sample and portfolio or audition, as appropriate. Nonnative speakers of English must submit official results of the TOEFL, with a minimum score of 600 on the paper-based test or a minimum score of 250 on the computer-based test.

Correspondence and Information

Brandeis University
Graduate School of Arts and Sciences
P.O. Box 9110 MS 031
Waltham, Massachusetts 02454-9110

Telephone: 781-736-3410
Fax: 781-736-3412
E-mail: gradschool@brandeis.edu
World Wide Web: http://www.brandeis.edu/gsas

THE FACULTY AND THEIR RESEARCH

American History: Office: 781-736-2270; Ph.D., M.A.: delorenzo@brandeis.edu.
Anthropology: Office: 781-736-2210; Ph.D., M.A.: hunt@brandeis.edu; joint M.A. with Women's Studies: slamb@brandeis.edu.
Biochemistry: Office: 781-736-2300; Ph.D.: lolsen@brandeis.edu.
Biophysics and Structural Biology: Office: 736-3100; Ph.D.: biophysics@brandeis.edu.
Chemistry: Office: 781-736-2500; Ph.D.: chemadm@brandeis.edu.
Classics: Office: 781-736-2180; M.A.: johnston@brandeis.edu.
Comparative History: Office: 781-736-2270; Ph.D., M.A.: delorenzo@brandeis.edu.
Computer Science: Office: 781-736-2701; Ph.D., M.A.: maf@cs.brandeis.edu.
English and American Literature: Office: 781-736-2130; Ph.D., joint M.A. with Women's Studies: chaucer@brandeis.edu.
Genetic Counseling: Professor Judith Tsipis: 781-736-3165, Professor Kathryn Kim: 781-736-3108; M.S.: gc@bio.brandeis.edu.
Jewish Communal Service: Office: 781-736-2990; M.A., M.A./M.B.A., joint M.A. with NEJS: hornstein@brandeis.edu.
Mathematics: Office: 781-736-3051; Ph.D.: maths@brandeis.edu.
Molecular and Cell Biology: Biology Office: 781-736-3100; M.S., Ph.D.: sen@brandeis.edu.
Music: Office: 781-736-3311; Composition and Theory Ph.D., M.F.A., M.A.; Musicology Ph.D., M.F.A., M.A.: redgate@brandeis.edu.
Near Eastern and Judaic Studies: Office: 781-736-2957; Ph.D., M.A., Diploma, Certificate, joint M.A. with Jewish Communal Service: judaica@brandeis.edu.; joint Ph.D., M.A. with Sociology: fishman@brandeis.edu; joint M.A. with Women's Studies: brooten@brandeis.edu.
Neuroscience: Biology Office: 781-736-3145; Ph.D., M.S.: marder@brandeis.edu.
Physics: Office: 781-736-2800; Ph.D.: physics1@brandeis.edu.
Politics: Office: 781-736-2750; Ph.D., M.A.: colocouris@brandeis.edu.
Premedical Studies: Office: 781-736-3465; Certificate: jlewis@brandeis.edu.
Studio Art: Office: 781-736-2656; Certificate: wardwell@brandeis.edu.
Psychology: Office: 781-736-3301; Ph.D.: lachman@brandeis.edu; M.A.: tcross@brandeis.edu.
Sociology: Office: 781-736-2631; Ph.D., M.A.: khansen@brandeis.edu; joint M.A with Women's Studies: reinharz@brandeis.edu.
Theater Arts: Office: 781-736-3340; M.F.A., Acting, Design, Playwriting: artaud@brandeis.edu.

BROOKLYN COLLEGE OF THE CITY UNIVERSITY OF NEW YORK

Division of Graduate Studies

Programs of Study

The Brooklyn College Division of Graduate Studies offers more than sixty full-time or part-time programs leading to the Master of Arts, Master of Fine Arts, Master of Music, Master of Professional Studies, Master of Public Health, Master of Science, and Master of Science in Education degrees and to a number of professional certificates in education. In addition, there are more than six doctoral programs of the City University of New York that can be pursued on the Brooklyn College campus: biology, chemistry, computer and information science, earth and environmental sciences, physics, and psychology. These programs are part of the thirty-one doctoral programs offered through the Graduate Center of the City University of New York on its constituent college campuses. The following Master of Arts programs are offered in the liberal arts and sciences: art history, biology, chemistry, community health (community health education, thanatology), computer and information science (graphics/multimedia), economics, economics-accounting, English, French, geology, history, Judaic studies, liberal studies, mathematics, music (musicology, performance practice), physics, political science (urban policy and administration), psychology (experimental, industrial/organizational), sociology, Spanish, speech (public communication), and theater (history and criticism). Programs leading to the Master of Fine Arts degree include art (digital art, drawing and painting, photography, sculpture), creative writing (fiction, playwriting, poetry), television production, and theater (acting, design and technical production, directing, dramaturgy, performing arts management). Programs leading to the Master of Music degree include composition and performance. The program leading to the Master of Public Health degree in community includes community health, health-care management, and health-care policy and administration. Programs leading to the Master of Science degree include audiology, exercise science and rehabilitation, information systems, nutrition, physical education (psychosocial aspects of physical activity, sports management), speech-language pathology, and television and radio. The teacher-education program offers Master of Arts programs in art and music (all grades), and in biology, chemistry, English, French, mathematics, physics, social studies, and Spanish (adolescent education, grades 7–12). The Master of Science in Education is offered with specializations in childhood education (bilingual teaching, liberal arts, mathematics, science and environmental education, grades 1–6); early childhood education (birth–grade 2); health education (all grades); literacy education; middle childhood specialist studies: mathematics (grades 1–5); physical education (all grades); and teaching students with speech and language disabilities. Advanced certificate programs are offered in school administration and supervision, guidance and counseling, music education, and school psychology.

Research Facilities

The new, state-of-the-art library collection houses a collection of more than 1.3 million volumes, and additional special libraries are available on campus for art, music, classics, economics, and speech communication arts and sciences. A number of research centers are available on campus, many of which publish their own scholarly research. These include the Africana Research Center, the Archaeological Research Center, the Center for Italian-American Studies, the Wolfe Institute for the Humanities, the Center for Nuclear Theory, the Applied Sciences Institute, the Institute for Studies in American Music, the Center for Latino Studies, the Children's Studies Center, and the Center for the Study of World Television. Other special facilities include solid-state and solar-energy laboratories, nuclear physics laboratories, an astronomical observatory, an Infant Study Center, an Early Childhood Center, a greenhouse, an electronic music studio and a Center for Computer Music, a Speech and Hearing Center (and affiliated Center for Assistive Technology), and a Computer Center linked to City University's installation, one of the largest academic computer centers in the country.

Financial Aid

Federal and state aid programs that are available to eligible students include the Federal Perkins Loan, College Work-Study, and Federal Stafford Student Loan programs; Veterans Administration Education Benefits; and New York State Tuition Assistance Program. Fellowships, lectureships, and research assistantships are available through College funds, research grants, and outside agencies. Students may also apply for Fulbright scholarships and other international fellowships. Students can apply through their major department. Financial aid availability and eligibility requirements are subject to change by state and federal legislative action.

Cost of Study

In 2001–02, tuition for New York State residents was $185 per credit, with a maximum tuition each term of $2175. Tuition for nonresidents and international students was $320 per credit, with a maximum tuition each term of $3800. The consolidated fee was $80.10 per semester and $45.85 for summer term. Tuition and fees are subject to change without notice.

Living and Housing Costs

For the 2001–02 academic year, dependent students budgeted a minimum of about $700 for books and supplies, $700 for local transportation, $4500 for meals and personal expenses, and $3800 for at-home expenses. Independent students budgeted the same amounts for books, supplies, and transportation, as well as about $8000 for food and living expenses for the nine-month academic year.

Student Group

Approximately 5,000 students from all over the world attend the Division of Graduate Studies—72 percent are women and 83 percent attend part-time. The average age of students is 29. Many students are employed in the public schools and are studying for advanced degrees and certificates.

Location

The many different cultures of Brooklyn contribute to the wide ethnic diversity of the College. The borough offers such resources as the Brooklyn Botanical Garden, Brooklyn Museum of Art, Brooklyn Academy of Music, New York Aquarium, Prospect Park, and the Brooklyn Public Library at Grand Army Plaza, one of the largest public libraries in New York. All major IND and IRT trains, including the number 2 and number 5 trains to Flatbush Avenue and the D train to Avenue H, are easily accessible from the College. On-campus parking for students is available on a limited basis.

The College

In 1930, Brooklyn College was established as the first four-year, coeducational liberal arts urban college in New York. The Division of Graduate Studies was established in 1935, and in 1961 the College became part of the City University of New York. Approximately 11,000 undergraduate and 6,000 graduate students are enrolled in more than 125 degree and certificate programs. Brooklyn College by and accredited by the Middle States Association of Colleges and Schools; its programs are registered by the New York State Department of Education and accredited by the Association of American Universities, American Association of University Women, the Educational Standards Board of the American Speech-Language-Hearing Association, the Council on Education in Public Health, and the Northeastern Association of Graduate Schools.

Applying

Applicants must have a baccalaureate degree from an accredited institution and have completed an approved program with a minimum average of B in the major and B– overall. Some programs require the GRE. Applications and supporting credentials, including official transcripts, must be received by March 1 for the summer and fall terms, November 1 for the spring term, and March 1 for selected teacher-education programs. Late applicants may also submit their applications on a rolling basis; acceptance is determined solely by the department. Students may request an application from the Office of Admissions or apply online at the Web site listed below.

Correspondence and Information

Office of Admissions
1602 James Hall
Brooklyn College of the City University of New York
Brooklyn, New York 11210-2889

Telephone: 718-951-5914
World Wide Web: http://www.brooklyn.cuny.edu

THE FACULTY

Christoph M. Kimmich, President; D.Phil., Oxford.
Roberta S. Matthews, Provost; Ph.D., SUNY at Stony Brook.
Richard Pizer, Dean of Graduate Studies and Research; Ph.D., Brandeis.
Deborah A. Shanley, Dean of the School of Education; Ed.D., Columbia.
Anselma Rodriguez, Coordinator of Graduate Studies; M.S., Fordham; M.A., CUNY, Brooklyn.

DEPARTMENT AND PROGRAM HEADS

Art. Michael Mallory, Chairperson and Counselor for the Graduate M.A. Program in Art History; Ph.D., Columbia.
Rick Brazill, Graduate Deputy; M.F.A., Yale.
Biology. Ray Gavin, Chairperson and Graduate Deputy; Ph.D., Iowa.
Chemistry. Dominick A. Labianca, Professor and Chairperson; Ph.D., Michigan.
Darryl Howery, Graduate Deputy; Ph.D., North Carolina.
Computer and Information Science. Aaron M. Tenenbaum, Chairperson; Ph.D., NYU.
Graduate Deputies: Keith Harrow, Ph.D., NYU, and Gerald Weiss, Ph.D., NYU.
Conservatory of Music. Nancy Hager, Director; Ph.D., CUNY Graduate Center.
Paul Shelden, Graduate Deputy; D.M.A., Maryland.
Economics. Antony Arcadi, Chairperson; M.A., CUNY, Brooklyn.
Gary Testa, Graduate Deputy; M.B.A., St. John's.
Education. Deborah A. Shanley, Dean; Ed.D., Columbia.
Peter Taubman, Graduate Deputy; Ed.D., Columbia.
Early Childhood Education; Lorraine M. Harner, Ph.D., Columbia.
Elementary Education; Tibbi Duboys, Interim Program Head; Ph.D., Fordham.
Secondary Education; Peter Taubman, Ed.D., Columbia.
Educational Administration and Supervision (Advanced Certificate). Stephan Brumberg, M.A.T., Ed.D., Harvard.
Education of the Speech and Hearing Handicapped. Ronald L. Feldman (Speech Department), Program Head; Ph.D., NYU.
Guidance and Counseling (Advanced Certificate, M.S. in Education). Hollyce Giles, Program Head; Ph.D., Columbia.
Literacy. Margaret Waters, Program Head; Ph.D., Fordham.
Mathematics. David Fuys, Program Head, Elementary Education; Ed.D., Columbia.
School Psychology (for School Psychologist, Advanced Certificate, M.S. in Education). Laura H. Barbanel, Program Head; Ed.D., Columbia.
English. Herbert Perluck, Chairperson; Ph.D., Brown.
Nancy Black, Graduate Deputy; Ph.D., Columbia.
M.F.A. in Creative Writing. Maurice Kramer, Graduate Deputy; Ph.D., Harvard.
Louis Asekoff, Program Director, Poetry; M.A., Brandeis.
Jonathan Baumbach, Program Director, Fiction; Ph.D., Stanford.
Jack Gelber, Program Director, Playwriting; B.S., Illinois.
General Science. George Moriber, Interdepartmental Coordinator; Ph.D., NYU.
Geology. Nehru E. Cherukupalli, Chairperson; Ph.D., Columbia.
David Seidemann, Graduate Deputy; Ph.D., Yale.
Health and Nutrition Sciences. Erika Friedmann, Chairperson; Ph.D., Pennsylvania.
Kathleen Axen, Graduate Deputy; Ph.D., Columbia.
History. Philip Gallagher, Chairperson and Graduate Deputy; Ph.D., Notre Dame.
Judaic Studies. Sara Reguer, Chairperson; Ph.D., Columbia.
Herbert Druks, Graduate Deputy; Ph.D., NYU.
Master of Liberal Arts and Science. George Brinton, Graduate Deputy; Ph.D., Washington (Seattle).
Mathematics. George Shapiro, Chairperson; Ph.D., Harvard.
William Miller, Graduate Deputy; M.A., CUNY, Brooklyn.
Teacher Education Program, Secondary Education in Mathematics.
Modern Languages and Literatures. Carolyn Richmond, Professor and Chairperson; Ph.D., Wisconsin.
William Sherzer, Graduate Deputy; Ph.D., Princeton.
Physical Education. Charles Tobey, Chairperson; Ed.D., Columbia.
Donald Michielli, Graduate Deputy; Ph.D., Ohio State.
Physics. Peter Lesser, Chairperson; Ph.D., Rochester.
Ming Kung Liou, Graduate Deputy; Ph.D., Manitoba.
Political Science. Vincent Fucillo, Chairperson; Ph.D., NYU.
Mark Ungar, Graduate Deputy; Ph.D., NYU.
Psychology. R. Glen Hass, Chairperson; Ph.D., Duke.
Benzion Chanowitz, Graduate Deputy; Ph.D., CUNY Graduate Center.
Social Studies (Teacher Education Program, Secondary Education in Social Studies). Vincent J. Fuccillo, Interdepartmental Coordinator; Ph.D., NYU.
Sociology. Jerome Krase, Chairperson; Ph.D., NYU.
Marvin Koeningsberg, Graduate Deputy; Ph.D., NYU.
Speech. Timothy Gura, Chairperson; Ph.D., Northwestern.
Gail Gurland, Graduate Deputy; Ph.D., CUNY Graduate Center.
Speech and Hearing Clinic. Oliver Bloodstein, Director; Ph.D., Iowa.
Teacher Education Program, Teaching Speech. Timothy Gura, Chairperson; Ph.D., Northwestern.
Television/Radio. Hal Himmelstein, Chairperson; Ph.D., Ohio.
George Dessart, Graduate Deputy; B.S., Trinity College.
Theater. Benito Ortolani, Chairperson; Ph.D., Vienna.

DISTINGUISHED PROFESSORS

Lennart Anderson (Art), M.F.A., Cranbrook Academy of Art.
Jack Flam (Art), Ph.D., NYU.
Gerald Friedman (Geology), Ph.D., Columbia.
Rohit Parikh (Computer and Information Science), Ph.D., Harvard.
Fred H. Pollak (Physics), Ph.D., Chicago.
Theodore Raphan (Computer and Information Science), Ph.D., CUNY Graduate Center.
Martin Schreibman (Biology), Ph.D., NYU.
Anthony Sclafani (Psychology), Ph.D., Chicago.
Carl M. Shakin (Physics), Ph.D., Harvard.
Hans Trefousse (History), Ph.D., Columbia.

CALIFORNIA POLYTECHNIC STATE UNIVERSITY, SAN LUIS OBISPO

Graduate Programs

Programs of Study

Programs leading to the Master of Science (M.S.) degree are offered in agriculture, architecture, biological sciences, engineering, forestry sciences, mathematics, kinesiology, industrial and technical studies, and psychology. Master of Arts (M.A.) programs are offered in education and English. The Master of City and Regional Planning (M.C.R.P.) degree and the Master of Business Administration (M.B.A.) degree are also offered. M.S. engineering programs include aerospace engineering, civil and environmental engineering, computer science, electrical engineering, industrial engineering, and mechanical engineering as well as specializations in bioengineering, biochemical engineering, biomedical engineering, integrated technology management, materials engineering, and water engineering. The M.S. program in agriculture offers specializations in agribusiness, agricultural education, agricultural engineering, animal science, crop science, dairy products technology, environmental horticulture science, food science and nutrition, general agriculture, irrigation, and soil science. An agribusiness specialization is available in the M.B.A. program. The M.A. program in education offers specializations in counseling and guidance, curriculum and instruction, educational administration, literacy and reading, and special education.

Joint master's programs are offered, including the Engineering Management Program (M.B.A./M.S.), the Transportation Planning Program (M.C.R.P./M.S.), and the M.B.A./B.Arch. Program as well as other joint M.B.A./M.S. or M.A. programs.

Emphasis in the professional programs is on applied research and preparation for employment, but many graduates of California Polytechnic State University's (Cal Poly) master's programs continue on to doctoral studies. The average duration of a Cal Poly master's program is two years. Many programs require completion of a traditional thesis; others offer the alternative of a comprehensive examination or a research project. Many opportunities exist for involvement in challenging advanced research projects, both on and off campus.

Research Facilities

Graduate students have access to specialized instrumentation and research opportunities through a number of research centers and institutes. These include Applied Research and Development Facilities and Activities (Engineering), the Collaborative Agent Design Research Center, the Dairy Products Technology Center, the Environmental Biotechnology Institute, the Irrigation Training and Research Center, and the Urban Forest Ecosystems Institute. The College of Engineering's Advanced Technology Laboratories, completed in 1999, provide specialized laboratories and state-of-the-art equipment for faculty and student research. Further information can be found on the World Wide Web at http://www.calpoly.edu/~rgp/research. The library collection of 2,554,332 items includes books, periodicals, journals, art prints, microforms, government documents, maps, audiovisual materials, and various special collections. It is a selective depository for U.S. and California state documents and for U.S. nuclear power plant documents. Access is provided to a wide range of electronic indexes, full-text databases, and an online catalog of the collection. Campuswide computing systems include an IBM 9672–R24 CMOS mainframe computer, HP and other UNIX servers, Sun Enterprise Java Development labs, and advanced workstations. A multimedia development center is available in the library for student use.

Financial Aid

Sources of assistance include federal student loans, grants, scholarships, and work-study opportunities. The University offers a limited number of fellowships. Qualified students may find support through the Veterans Administration, Social Security Administration, State Rehabilitation Program, or Bureau of Indian Affairs. Many programs attempt to support all graduate students through research or teaching assistantships.

Cost of Study

Registration fees (including the health plan and other campus fees) for California residents in 2001–02 were $752.50 per quarter. Out-of-state and international students paid tuition of $164 per credit in addition to registration fees.

Living and Housing Costs

A limited number of double-occupancy residence hall rooms in a predominately undergraduate community are available at a cost of $6707 per academic year for room and board. Off-campus monthly housing rates for houses or apartments range from $900 to $2000 (two bedrooms) and $1200 to $2400 (three bedrooms). Rent for a private room in a house or apartment ranges from $300 to $600 per month. These rates apply to housing within a 20-mile radius of the University. The estimated cost for off-campus housing and food is $6000 per academic year. Personal expenses and transportation costs average around $2500 per academic year. More housing information is available on the World Wide Web (http://www.housing.calpoly.edu).

Student Group

Graduate student enrollment for fall 2001 was 1,013 out of a total of 18,066 students. About 36 percent are pursuing teaching credentials; the remainder are enrolled in master's programs. The master's programs with the largest number of students are education, business administration, agriculture, computer science, English, psychology, biology, and engineering. In fall 2001, 56 percent of graduate students were women; 22 percent were members of minority groups. The average course load for graduate students in fall 2001 was 10.5 units.

Student Outcomes

Graduates of Cal Poly's master's programs in engineering, architecture, business, and agriculture find ready employment in the private sector. Graduates of the M.S. in psychology program are prepared for Marriage, Family, and Child Counseling (MFCC) licensing. A significant number of graduates continue on to doctoral programs; many pursue teaching careers at the community college level. Graduates of the M.A. program in education advance their careers in elementary and secondary school teaching, counseling, and administration.

Location

San Luis Obispo is a pleasant, progressive city of approximately 48,000, situated 12 miles from the Pacific Ocean—midway between San Francisco and Los Angeles—in a region of growing renown for its viticulture. An exceptionally beautiful natural environment and temperate climate provide year-round recreational opportunities. Numerous concerts, theater offerings, and other cultural activities are available throughout the year. Annual events include the SLO Criterium and the Mozart Festival.

The University

Founded in 1901 as the California Polytechnic School, Cal Poly has evolved into a leading undergraduate polytechnic university. Consistently recognized by *U.S. News & World Report* as one of the top comprehensive universities in the West, it is particularly noted for its programs in engineering, architecture, and agriculture. A "learn by doing" philosophy permeates the curriculum and defines a unique educational experience. Graduates of Cal Poly are highly sought after by industry for the depth and breadth of their knowledge and their ability to apply it to real-world situations.

Applying

Application completion deadlines for master's programs are April 1 for summer quarter, July 1 for fall quarter, November 1 for winter quarter, and March 1 for spring quarter. Because graduate program coordinators may select earlier file completion dates, applicants should check with the department of interest for appropriate filing periods. Graduate coordinators should also be contacted for individual program requirements, such as letters of reference, interviews, and GRE or GMAT testing. Applications for Cal Poly scholarships and the Free Application for Federal Student Aid (FAFSA) are due by March 2. Applications can be requested via the World Wide Web (http://www.calpoly.edu/~finaid to request a Cal Poly scholarship application; http://www.fafsa.ed.gov to apply for federal aid with the FAFSA).

Correspondence and Information

Students should address all inquiries on graduate programs to the specific program coordinator indicated on the reverse of this page. All applications should be completed online and are available at http://www.csumentor.edu.

Admissions Office
California Polytechnic State University, San Luis Obispo
San Luis Obispo, California 93407

Telephone: 805-756-2311
Fax: 805-756-5400
World Wide Web: http://www.calpoly.edu/

DEANS AND GRADUATE PROGRAM COORDINATORS

Graduate Programs: Susan Opava, Dean of Research and Graduate Programs; Ph.D., Michigan. (E-mail: sopava@calpoly.edu)

College of Agriculture: David J. Wehner, Acting Dean; Ph.D., Penn State. (E-mail: dwehner@calpoly.edu)
Mark D. Shelton, Associate Dean/Graduate Coordinator; Ph.D., Utah State. (E-mail: mshelton@calpoly.edu)

Agribusiness Specialization: James Ahern, Coordinator, Ph.D., Utah. (E-mail: jahern@calpoly.edu)
Dairy Products Technology Specialization: Rafael Jimenez-Flores, Coordinator; Ph.D., California, Davis. (E-mail: rjimenez@calpoly.edu)

College of Architecture: Martin Harms, Dean; Ph.D., Pennsylvania. (E-mail: mharms@calpoly.edu)

Architecture: Jens Pohl, Coordinator; Ph.D., Sydney (Australia). (E-mail: jpohl@calpoly.edu)
City and Regional Planning: Linda Day, Coordinator; Ph.D., Syracuse. (E-mail: lday@calpoly.edu); Michael Boswell, Coordinator; Ph.D., Florida State. (E-mail: mboswell@calpoly.edu)
M.C.R.P./M.S. Engineering/Transportation Planning Specialization: Linda Day, Coordinator; Ph.D., Syracuse. (E-mail: lday@calpoly.edu)

College of Business: William Pendergast, Dean; Ph.D., Columbia. (E-mail: wpenderg@calpoly.edu)

General M.B.A.: Earl Keller, Coordinator; Ph.D., Washington (Seattle). (E-mail: eckeller@calpoly.edu)
Agribusiness Specialization: James Ahern, Coordinator; Ph.D., Maryland. (E-mail: jahern@calpoly.edu)
M.B.A./M.S. Engineering Management Program: Donald White, Coordinator; Ph.D., Case Western Reserve. (E-mail: dwhite@calpoly.edu)
M.B.A./B.Arch.: Allan Cooper, Coordinator; M.Arch., Cornell. (E-mail: acooper@calpoly.edu)
Industrial and Technical Studies: Anthony Randazzo, Coordinator; Ph.D., Washington State. (E-mail: arandazz@calpoly.edu)

College of Engineering: Peter Lee, Dean; Ph.D., Tulane. (E-mail: plee@calpoly.edu)

Aerospace Engineering: Daniel Biezad, Coordinator; Ph.D., Purdue. (E-mail: dbiezad@calpoly.edu)
Civil and Environmental Engineering: Eric Kasper, Coordinator; Ph.D., Berkeley. (E-mail: ekasper@calpoly.edu)
Computer Science: Gene Fisher, Coordinator; Ph.D., California, Irvine. (E-mail: gfisher@calpoly.edu)
Electrical Engineering: Fred DePiero, Coordinator; Ph.D., Tennessee. (E-mail: fdepiero@calpoly.edu)
Industrial Engineering Specialization: Tali Freed, Coordinator; Ph.D., Berkeley. (E-mail: tfreed@calpoly.edu)
Mechanical Engineering: Saeed Niku, Coordinator; Ph.D., California, Davis. (E-mail: sniku@calpoly.edu)
Biochemical Engineering Specialization: Nirupam Pal, Coordinator; Ph.D., NJIT. (E-mail: npal@calpoly.edu)
Bioengineering Specialization: Daniel Walsh, Coordinator; Ph.D., RPI. (E-mail: dwalsh@calpoly.edu)
Integrated Technology Management Specialization: Donald White, Coordinator; Ph.D., Case Western Reserve. (E-mail: dwhite@calpoly.edu)
Materials Engineering Specialization: Robert Heidersbach, Coordinator; Ph.D., Florida. (E-mail: rheiders@calpoly.edu)
Water Engineering Specialization: Charles Burt, Coordinator; Ph.D., Utah State. (E-mail: cburt@calpoly.edu)

College of Liberal Arts: Harry Hellenbrand, Dean; Ph.D., Stanford. (E-mail: hhellenb@calpoly.edu)

English: John Battenburg, Coordinator; Ph.D., Purdue. (E-mail: jbattenb@calpoly.edu)
Psychology: Michael Selby, Coordinator; Ph.D., Memphis State. (E-mail: mselby@calpoly.edu)

College of Science and Math: Philip Bailey, Dean; Ph.D., Purdue. (E-mail: pbailey@calpoly.edu)

Biological Sciences: Dennis Frey, Coordinator; Ph.D., Oklahoma State. (E-mail: dfrey@calpoly.edu)
Mathematics: Myron Hood, Coordinator; Ph.D., Washington (St. Louis). (E-mail: mhood@calpoly.edu)
Kinesiology: Steven C. Davis, Coordinator; Ph.D., Penn State. (E-mail: sdavis@calpoly.edu)

University Center for Teacher Education: Bonnie Konopak, Dean; Ph.D., California, Santa Barbara. (E-mail: bkonopak@calpoly.edu)

Counseling and Guidance: David Duran, Coordinator; Ph.D., Stanford. (E-mail: dduran@calpoly.edu)
Curriculum and Instruction: Susan McBride, Coordinator; Ph.D., Akron. (E-mail: smcbride@calpoly.edu)
Educational Administration: Rita King, Coordinator; Ph.D., San Diego. (E-mail: rking@calpoly.edu)
Literacy and Reading: Roberta Herter, Coordinator; Ph.D., Michigan. (E-mail: rherter@calpoly.edu)
Special Education: Dennis Nulman, Coordinator; Ph.D., USC. (E-mail: dnulman@calpoly.edu)

CALIFORNIA STATE UNIVERSITY, DOMINGUEZ HILLS

Graduate Studies

Programs of Study

Programs leading to the Master of Arts (M.A.) degree are offered in behavioral science (with options in negotiation and conflict management and gerontology), education (with options in technology-based education, counseling, educational administration, multicultural education, physical education administration, teaching/curriculum, and an individualized program), English, humanities, humanities external degree, special education, psychology (clinical), and sociology. A Master of Arts in teaching mathematics is also offered. Master of Science (M.S.) programs are offered in biology, clinical science (with options in cytotechnology and medical technology), health science (with options in physician's assistant and professional studies), marriage and family therapy, nursing, and quality assurance. A Master of Business Administration (M.B.A.) and a Master of Public Administration (M.P.A.) are also offered. The master's degree program in interdisciplinary studies is offered as either a Master of Arts or a Master of Science, depending on the program course work.

Programs of study are primarily focused on research, preparation for employment, and providing a solid foundation for doctoral studies. The average duration of a Dominguez Hills master's program is two years. Some programs require completion of a thesis, while others offer the alternative comprehensive exam or project. Opportunities exist for involvement in challenging research projects, both on and off campus.

Research Facilities

Graduate students have access to various research opportunities through a number of research facilities and laboratories. Such facilities include the Center for Urban Research and Learning, the Southern California Ocean Studies Consortium, the Desert Studies Consortium, a 20-acre nature preserve, a tissue culture laboratory, and a vivarium. Use of laboratories and facilities are also provided through Cedars-Sinai and UCLA Medical Centers, Specialty Laboratories, and Quest Diagnostic Laboratories.

California State University, Dominguez Hills (CSUDH), has gained national recognition for student collaboration in externally funded faculty research.

Financial Aid

Sources of financial assistance include federal student loans, grants, and work-study opportunities. The University offers a limited number of fellowships and scholarships. Students should visit the Office of Financial Aid Web site at http://www.csudh.edu/fin_aid for more information. The Office of Graduate Studies offers support to students involved in mentored research through fellowships, a forgivable loan program, and a predoctoral program. Support is available to enable students to present their work at professional meetings. Students should visit the Graduate Studies Web site at http://somc.csudh.edu/graduatestudies/ for further information.

Cost of Study

Registration fees (including health services and other fees) for California residents in 2000–01 averaged $1500 per semester. Nonresidents paid tuition of $246 per semester unit in addition to registration fees.

Living and Housing Costs

University housing consists of 134 double- and triple-occupancy, fully furnished apartment units located at the east end of the campus. The average on-campus housing cost (including meals) for the academic year is $5698. Off-campus monthly rental costs range from $500 to $900 for a studio or one-bedroom apartment. Total off-campus living and housing costs average approximately $7614 per academic year.

Student Group

Graduate student enrollment averages about 5,100 out of 12,800 students; 50 percent are enrolled in master's programs and 50 percent are pursuing teaching credentials and other objectives. The highest enrolled master's programs are education, business administration, behavioral sciences, and the distance learning humanities program. The majority of students are part-time evening students with an average course load of 6 units. Campus diversity is strong, with a 74 percent minority population.

Location

California State University, Dominguez Hills, is a diverse, comprehensive public university located in the suburban city of Carson and primarily serving the greater Los Angeles metropolitan area. Carson sits just a few miles from the beaches, the Long Beach Aquarium, L.A. County Museum of Art, the Getty Center, and Disneyland. CSUDH is known to have the safest campus in the CSU system.

The University

CSUDH is located on the historic Rancho San Pedro, the oldest Spanish land grant in the Los Angeles area. The land was in the Dominguez family from 1784 until its public acquisition to establish a university in 1960. CSUDH has a multicultural community committed to excellence and educating a student population of unprecedented diversity for leadership roles. University programs enable students to develop intellectually, personally, and professionally as they apply knowledge and hands-on expertise to real-world situations.

Applying

Applications are first accepted on November 1 for the following fall semester and September 1 for the following spring. Applicants should check with the individual department for application filing deadlines and for specific program requirements, such as supplemental applications, letters of recommendation, interviews, and test requirements. Applications for scholarships may be accessed through the Financial Aid Office on the Web at http://www.csudh.edu/fin_aid. The Free Application for Federal Student Aid (FAFSA) may be accessed on the Internet at http://www.fafsa.ed.gov.

Correspondence and Information

Students should address all inquiries to the Office of Graduate Studies via e-mail at graduate@research.csudh.edu or by phone at 310-243-3693. Completed applications should be sent to the Admissions Office. Online applications are available at http://www.csumentor.edu/AdmissionApp.

Admissions Office
California State University, Dominguez Hills
1000 East Victoria Street
Carson, California 90747
Telephone: 310-243-3300
World Wide Web: http://www.csudh.edu
http://somc.csudh.edu/graduatestudies (Graduate Studies)

FACULTY AND THEIR RESEARCH

Charmayne Bohman, Professor of Education; Ph.D., Claremont. Female identity, object relations theory-based counseling, educational reform, adolescent psychology.
Robert Christie, Professor of Sociology; Ph.D., Missouri. Urban anthropology, urban and regional planning, population and migration.
James Cooper, Professor of Education; Ph.D., Iowa. Reading assessment reform, graduate retention, at-risk assessment.
Miguel Dominguez, Professor of Foreign Languages and Humanities; Ph.D., UCLA. Bilingual education, at-risk students.
Larry Ferrario, Professor of English; Ph.D., USC. Rhetoric and composition; effective teacher education.
Lois Feuer, Professor of English and Humanities; Ph.D., California, Irvine. Shakespeare.
Farah Fisher, Professor of Education; Ph.D., USC. Distance education, educational technology, assessment.
Ken Ganeezer, Professor of Physics; Ph.D., UCLA. Nutrinos, biomedical research on bone density.
Diane Henschel, Professor of Psychology; Ph.D., Berkeley. Child abuse, child development.
Louise Ivers, Professor of Art and Humanities; Ph.D., New Mexico. Latin American architecture, central California studies.
Pamela Krochalk, Professor of Health Science; Dr.P.H., UCLA. Aging, alternative health care, community disease prevention.
Cecile Lindsay, Professor of Foreign Languages; Ph.D., California, Irvine. Twentieth-century French literature, critical theory, feminist theory.
Leonardo Martinez, Professor of Chemistry; Ph.D., California, San Diego. Science education, physical chemistry, biophysics.
Brendan McNulty, Professor of Earth Sciences; Ph.D., California, Santa Cruz. Plate tectonics, geochemistry, natural disasters.
Jerry Moore, Professor of Anthropology; Ph.D., California, Santa Barbara. Archaeology of pre-Columbian Peru and Baja California.
Maria Hurtado Ortiz, Professor of Psychology; Ph.D., California, Riverside. Child care, cross-cultural psychology.
Laura Robles, Professor of Biology; Ph.D., California, Santa Barbara. Biomedical research, cell signaling in the retina of the octopus.
Silvia Santos, Professor of Psychology; Ph.D., California, Riverside. Violence in special populations.
Dale Scherba, Professor of Education; Ph.D., Stanford. Counselor education, gender, self-esteem, cognitive psychology.
Michael Shafer, Professor of English; Ph.D., California, San Diego. Romantic literature, feminist literature.
Lyle Smith, Professor of English; Ph.D., Harvard. Writing assessment, myth and archetypes.
Frank Stricker, Professor of History and Humanities; Ph.D., Princeton. U.S. history, poverty, policy, and postwar government economics.
Lee Talley, Professor of English; Ph.D., Princeton. Victorian novel, women writers, interdisciplinary studies.
Sara Waller, Professor of Philosophy; Ph.D., Loyola Chicago. Dolphin behavior, conceptual flexibility.
Andrea White, Professor of English; Ph.D., USC. Ethnic literature, journals, world literature.

CAMBRIDGE COLLEGE

Graduate Programs for Working Adults

Programs of Study

The College offers two graduate degrees: a Master of Education (M.Ed.) in the fields of education, counseling psychology, or integrated studies; and a Master of Management. Each program includes a two-credit professional/management seminar for two to four terms and an independent learning or research project. The College also offers postgraduate certificates of advanced graduate study (CAGS) in educational leadership and counseling psychology. Depending on the number of credits, a program may be completed in three to six terms (one to two years).

In education, concentrations in education or integrated studies (32 credits) prepare teachers, other educators, and administrators. Certification in Elementary Education (37 credits), geared for adults who have worked extensively with children, prepares students for Massachusetts certification in elementary education. The National Institute for Teaching Excellence (NITE) is an intensive summer program primarily for educators who live outside Massachusetts and teach in urban settings. Students in this program who have 12 credits of previous graduate work can earn the M.Ed. degree (32 credits total) by completing course work during the summer and following up in the fall with a faculty-directed teaching practicum and thesis project. The 37-credit Certification in School Administration Program is for education professionals interested in certification as school administrators. Three programs prepare educators for certification as Teachers of Students with Special Needs: Provisional Certification With Advanced Standing (39 credits), Standard Certification (37 credits), or Dual Certification in Elementary Education and Special Education (43 credits). The Certification as Library Media Specialist Program (38 credits) prepares library media specialists to plan, implement, and administer a library media program. There is also a 32-credit program in teaching with Internet technologies and a 32-credit program for school nurse education. The individualized M.Ed. in integrated studies is a 32-credit distance learning program for motivated, independent learners with a clear academic focus and professional goals who live outside Massachusetts. Each student creates a concentration with a theme that links an interest in education, counseling psychology, or management (or some combination of these) with supporting studies in the arts and sciences.

The counseling psychology area includes a 36-credit degree with a practicum and a 36-credit program in psychological studies for students who do not intend to provide direct counseling services. Other programs provide professional training for counselors, leading to licensure or certification. These programs include mental health counseling (62 credits), marriage and family therapy (62 credits), school guidance counseling (39 credits), school adjustment counseling (62 credits), and counseling practice (50 credits). A 13-credit certificate program is available in elder care. The requirements for CADAC certification can be included in some of these programs.

The Master of Management degree program (35 credits) provides a core curriculum in management and specialized certificates in negotiation and conflict resolution, diversity, organization development, entrepreneurship and small business management, business, nonprofit and public organization management, and health-care management. These certificates are also available on a noncredit basis for professional development.

Access, the accelerated graduate studies program, provides introductory and intermediate-level graduate study for qualified applicants to the master's degree programs who have college-level academic skills, a career goal, and some college credits. An earned undergraduate degree is required of all graduate programs that prepare students for certification by the Massachusetts Department of Education.

The CAGS program provides opportunities for practicing professionals who hold master's degrees. They address changes in the field; secure certification, recertification, or licensure; qualify recipients for promotions or increases in salary; and help participants gain skills for new and challenging professional responsibilities. CAGS programs are available in counseling psychology: marriage and family therapy, mental health counseling, and school guidance counseling; and in educational leadership: educational specialist in curriculum and instruction, school administration, and special education.

Research Facilities

M.Ed. students have access to the Gutman Library of the Harvard Graduate School of Education. Management students have borrowing privileges at the Sawyer Library at Suffolk University. The College has online periodicals databases, including general and business periodicals. The College's Center for Learning and Assessment Services has a variety of assessment and instructional resources. At the computer lab, students have access to PCs and software.

Financial Aid

The primary source of funding for most Cambridge College students is the Federal Stafford Student Loan program. Eligible students may borrow up to $18,500 per academic year. A limited number of College scholarships are awarded based upon need. Information about other loans and funding sources is available from the Financial Aid Office.

Cost of Study

Graduate tuition rates for 2001–02 were $350 per credit, and CAGS courses were $375 per credit. Students are also assessed a one-time degree processing fee of $110. The cost of books and other materials varies by course.

Living and Housing Costs

Most of the College's programs are intended for adults who live and work within commuting distance of the College's sites; therefore, no housing is provided. For the summer National Institute for Teaching Excellence (NITE) program, the College arranges room and board for each participant, at an approximate cost of $2450 to $5000 (summer 2001).

Student Group

By design, the College attracts a student body diverse in ethnicity, race, economic status, age, and educational experience. Of its 2,900 adult learners, all have had at least five years' working experience, approximately 65 percent are women, and 40 percent are people of color. The average age of the student body is 39. Students seek graduate degrees to acquire necessary credentials and skills for professional advancement or to make the transition to another career.

Location

The College has two locations, the main campus in Cambridge and the western Massachusetts location in Springfield. Depending on demand, some courses are also scheduled at suburban locations in the greater Boston area.

The College

Cambridge College is an independent institution of higher education, fully accredited by the New England Association of Schools and Colleges. It was founded to serve adult professionals through a student-centered curriculum that includes knowledge and skill development relevant to their work and lives and equips them to become lifelong learners. The student-faculty ratio is approximately 17:1. The academic year consists of two 15-week fall and spring terms and an 8-week summer term. Classes are scheduled around the needs of the working adult and meet primarily during the evening, with some weekend courses. The College also offers a baccalaureate program designed for working adults.

Applying

New classes are admitted in September, January, and June. The minimum requirements for admission to the graduate program are at least three years of work experience after high school, an undergraduate degree from an accredited college or university or willingness to demonstrate the ability to succeed in graduate study through the completion of the Access program, and acceptance by the admissions committee. Depending upon their program, students may transfer in 9 to 12 credits of graduate work completed at other accredited institutions. Students must complete the application materials, including a personal statement, and take the College's writing assessment. International students must complete the TOEFL with a minimum score of 550 on the paper-based TOEFL or 213 on the computer-based TOEFL. No other standardized tests are required, as the College uses its own assessment techniques to evaluate candidacy. Applicants are assigned an individual admissions representative who guides them through the application process.

Correspondence and Information

Office of Enrollment Services
Cambridge College
1000 Massachusetts Avenue
Cambridge, Massachusetts 02138
Telephone: 617-868-1000
800-877-4723 (toll-free)
Fax: 617-349-3561
World Wide Web: http://www.cambridge.edu

Cambridge College
570 Cottage Street
Springfield, Massachusetts 01104
Telephone: 413-747-0204
800-829-GRAD (toll-free)
Fax: 413-747-0613

THE FACULTY

Chief Academic Officer and Dean of the College: Joseph Reed, Ph.D.
Director of the Springfield campus: Joseph Miglio, M.Ed., Boston University.

Access Program

Coordinator: Pedro Schuck, Ed.D., Boston University.
Coordinator, Springfield campus: Abigail Dolinger, M.Ed., Cambridge College.

Department of Counseling Psychology

Director: Robert Prague, M.Ed., Boston College.
Coordinator, Springfield campus: Deborah Merriman, M.Ed., Cambridge College.
Elder Care Program Coordinator: Claire Fialkov, Ph.D., Boston University.
Marriage and Family Therapy Program Coordinators: Claire Fialkov, Ph.D., Boston University; Jacqueline Gagliardi, C.A.G.S., Bridgewater State.
Mental Health Counseling, School Guidance and Adjustment Counseling Programs Coordinator: John Carew, Ph.D., Boston College.

Many faculty are practicing professionals in various areas of counseling psychology, and the department maintains an extensive network of partnerships with community organizations. Students may utilize this resource to obtain the internships needed for certification and licensure and to conduct research for their independent research projects.

CAGS in Counseling Psychology

Director: Margaret Sablove, Ed.D.

Department of Education

National Institute for Teaching Excellence Program Director: Ezat Parnia, Ph.D., Claremont.
School Administration Program Coordinator: Kathleen Buckley, Ed.D., Boston College.
Special Education Program Coordinator: Anthony DeMatteo, Ed.D., Boston University.
Library Media Specialist Program Coordinator: Joseph Angelo, Ed.D., Boston University.
Elementary Teacher Certification Program Coordinator: Farideh Oboodiat, Ph.D., Texas.
Individual M.Ed. in Integrated Studies Program Coordinator: Linda Ostrander, Ph.D., Union (Ohio); D.M.A. Boston University.

Many faculty are practicing professionals in various areas of education, and the department maintains an extensive network of partnerships with area schools. Students may utilize this resources to obtain the practica, internships, and clinical experiences required for certification and to conduct research for their independent learning projects.

CAGS in Educational Leadership

Director: Kathleen Buckley, D.Ed.

Department of Management

Director: Mary Ann Joseph, Ph.D., Northwestern.
Coordinator, Springfield campus: Richard Turner, Ph.D., Nova.

The department maintains an extensive network of partnerships with area businesses and organizations. Students may utilize this resource to conduct research for their independent learning projects.

CARDEAN UNIVERSITY

Master of Business Administration Degree Program

Programs of Study

Cardean University's Master of Business Administration (M.B.A.) program builds general management skills and requires students to achieve a wide breadth of competencies. There are fifteen 3-credit-hour courses required to complete the program. Students can choose to complete their degree in a flexible time frame ranging from two to four years.

There are six core requirement courses (18 credits), which consist of Corporate Finance, Financial Accounting, Leading and Managing Organizations (1 and 2), Principles of Marketing, and Effective Communication.

There are two distribution requirements (6 credits), consisting of Strategy and Economics and Analysis and Control. To fulfill the Strategy and Economics distribution requirement, students may select one of two courses: Principles of Competitive Strategy or Managerial Economics. To fulfill the Analysis and Control distribution requirement, students may select one of three courses: Operations, Managerial Accounting, or Decision Models.

Seven elective courses (21 credits) are selected from seventeen different subject areas. Prospective students should visit the University Web site listed below for a complete course catalog.

Research Facilities

Cardean University maintains an online library consisting of references and resources to assist students in course research and to broaden their business knowledge. As Cardean University is a completely online university, there are no specialized laboratories or equipment available to students.

Financial Aid

Cardean's advising staff is available to help understand the range of options available to students to finance their M.B.A. studies. Options available include employer reimbursement, veterans' benefits, loans from financial institutions, scholarships, and fellowships.

Prospective students should contact Cardean's admissions department at the e-mail address listed below if they have questions about financial issues.

Cost of Study

The M.B.A. tuition is $30,000 ($2000 per course) plus the cost of course materials (approximately $2000 total). These costs do not include Internet access fees.

Living and Housing Costs

Since Cardean University offers all of its courses over the Internet, living and housing costs are not applicable.

Student Group

More than 200 students have been admitted to the Cardean M.B.A. program. Approximately 50 students reside outside of the U.S. Nearly all of the students are part-time.

Cardean students are generally looking to advance their careers through business education, but they do not have the time or the lifestyle to accommodate full-time, site-based studies.

Student Outcomes

Cardean courses provide a problem-based learning experience that emulates real-world business projects. This model ensures that Cardean knowledge is highly relevant in the workplace. Cardean students have commented on the value of this approach, and the fact that learning is immediately applicable to their jobs.

Location

The offices of Cardean University are located in Deerfield, Illinois, about 25 miles northwest of Chicago. Cardean University is completely online and is located at the Web site listed below.

The University

Cardean University, founded in 1999, is an online learning community for working professionals. Its mission is to provide superior online business education for individuals around the world. Through the power of the Internet, Cardean provides a wide range of professional education courses, including an online M.B.A. degree. Cardean University's cognitive and learning scientists, pedagogical experts, and instructional designers work directly with faculty members from a consortium of top business universities, such as Carnegie Mellon University, Columbia Business School, the London School of Economics and Political Science, Stanford University, and the University of Chicago.

Applying

To apply for admission into Cardean's M.B.A. program, please complete the following requirements: application form available at the Web site listed below, an official transcript from an undergraduate institutions showing successful completion of a bachelor's degree or equivalent, a $75 nonrefundable application fee, an interview with an academic adviser, and for international students whose native language is not English, evidence of proficiency in English (a bachelor's degree or equivalent from an institution where courses are taught in English or a TOEFL score of at least 550). Neither the Graduate Management Admissions Test (GMAT) nor the Graduate Records Examination (GRE) is required.

Correspondence and Information

Student Advising
Cardean University
500 Lake Cook Road
Suite 150
Deerfield, Illinois 60015
Telephone: 847-444-8289
866-948-1289 (toll-free)
E-mail: admissions@cardean.edu
World Wide Web: http://www.cardean.edu

THE FACULTY AND THEIR RESEARCH

Cardean faculty members are unique in that they are rigorously trained to instruct in the online environment. One third of the faculty members hold doctorate degrees, one third hold master's degrees, and the remaining third hold other advanced degrees.

Consortium faculty members from our consortium schools (Columbia Business School, Stanford University, the University of Chicago Graduate School of Business, Carnegie Mellon, and the London School of Economics and Political Science) sponsor Cardean courses by contributing to the course content and approach. The consortium faculty members collaborate with Cardean faculty members to design and develop the courses, deliverables, learning resources, and other supporting materials that allow Cardean students to master the course learning outcomes and create the overall Cardean experience.

Research at Cardean focuses on new pedagogical and delivery methods for delivering superior learning solutions over the Internet.

More information about Cardean faculty members can be found at http://www.cardean.edu.

CASE WESTERN RESERVE UNIVERSITY

Graduate Studies Programs

Programs of Study

Graduate programs leading to master's and/or Ph.D. degrees are offered in the following fields: humanities and social sciences—American studies, anthropology, art education, art history, communication sciences, comparative literature, English, French, history, music education, music history, music performance, political science, psychology, sociology, and theater/contemporary dance; sciences—astronomy, biology, chemistry, computer science, geological sciences, mathematics, physics, and statistics; engineering—aerospace, biomedical, chemical, civil, computer, electrical, macromolecular, materials science, mechanical, and systems; biomedical sciences—anatomy, anesthesiology, biochemistry, bioethics, biophysics, biostatistics, cell biology, environmental health sciences, epidemiology, exercise physiology, genetic counseling, genetics, microbiology, molecular biology, molecular virology, neurosciences, nursing, nutrition, pathology, pharmacology, physiology, public health nutrition, and systems physiology; and professional programs—accountancy, health systems management, information systems, labor and human resource policy, management, management policy, marketing, operations research, organizational behavior, public health, and social welfare.

Research Facilities

The University has extensive modern laboratory and computing facilities for experimental research. The central library of the University, with more than 1,125 fiber-optic ports, contains more than 1.9 million volumes. These facilities are supplemented by the resources of neighboring cultural and educational institutions, including the Cleveland Public Library, which has approximately 3 million volumes.

Financial Aid

Financial assistance to graduate students is available on a competitive basis through fellowships, scholarships, traineeships, graduate assistantships, and special appointments in research. Some awards provide dependency allowances. Loans on deferred-repayment plans are also offered. Jobs for spouses (except those on F-1 visas) are available in the Cleveland area.

Students applying for these awards generally should have completed application forms on file by March 1.

Cost of Study

Tuition is charged at the rate of $938 per semester hour in 2002–03. To be considered full-time, a student must register for a minimum of 9 semester hours each semester. The medical insurance fee for all students is estimated at $700 per academic year.

Living and Housing Costs

Limited campus residences for unmarried graduate students are available. The cost of room and board averages $8610 for the academic year 2002–03. Most graduate students live in affordable apartments in the vicinity of the University.

Married graduate students may contact the University's Off-Campus Housing Office in Yost Hall or telephone 216-368-3780 for information and assistance.

Overall annual expenses are estimated to total $26,194 for 2002–03.

Student Group

The total University enrollment in the fall of 2002 was 9,530. Of this number, 2,128 were enrolled in the Graduate School, 3,793 in the professional schools, and 3,609 in the undergraduate units.

Student Outcomes

Available information on recent master's graduates shows that 33 percent continued graduate or professional studies at Case Western Reserve and elsewhere, while 58 percent joined major industrial and business corporations and various government agencies. Recent doctoral graduates gained postdoctoral (18 percent) or academic (28 percent) positions nationwide; obtained employment in business, industry, and government (47 percent); and established private consultant services (1 percent). Most international graduates assumed leadership roles in comparable settings on returning to their countries.

Location

In addition to the rich musical, artistic, and recreational opportunities available to students in University Circle, Metropolitan Cleveland provides a wide range of national sports events, entertainment, and theater.

The University is located about 4 miles east of downtown Cleveland adjacent to Cleveland Heights, one of the city's large residential suburbs.

The University

Case Western Reserve University was established in 1967 with the joining of Western Reserve University (founded in 1826) and Case Institute of Technology (founded in 1880), which had occupied adjoining campuses since 1883. It is located in Cleveland's famed University Circle—one of the largest cultural and educational centers in the nation. In the 500-acre Circle are located more than forty educational, scientific, medical, cultural, social service, and religious institutions, including the world-famed Cleveland Orchestra and Cleveland Museum of Art. Many of these institutions are affiliated with the University in joint educational programs at the graduate level.

Applying

In most programs, students may be admitted to graduate study at the beginning of any regular semester—fall, spring, or summer. Unless specified otherwise in program materials, applications must be received at least thirty days prior to the beginning of the semester for which the student is applying. Most fellowships, traineeships, and assistantships are, however, awarded for the academic year beginning in late August, and applicants for these awards should observe the March 1 deadline.

Correspondence and Information

For general information:
School of Graduate Studies
Case Western Reserve University
Cleveland, Ohio 44106-7027
Telephone: 216-368-4390
Fax: 216-368-4250

For application forms and program materials:
Department Assistant
Department of (specify)
Case Western Reserve University
Cleveland, Ohio 44106
World Wide Web: http://www.cwru.edu/provost/gradstudies/

THE FACULTY

Dean of Graduate Studies: Lenore A. Kola, Ph.D., Boston.

DEANS AND DEPARTMENT HEADS

Arts and Sciences: Dean Samuel M. Savin, Ph.D., Caltech.
Anthropology: Melvyn C. Goldstein, Ph.D., Washington (Seattle). (http://www.cwru.edu/artsci/anth/anth.html)
Art History and Education: Ellen G. Landau, Ph.D., Delaware. (http://www.cwru.edu/artsci/arth/arth/html)
Astronomy: R. Earle Luck, Ph.D., Texas. (http://burro.astr.cwru.edu/dept/)
Biology: Norman B. Rushforth, Ph.D., Cornell. (http://www.cwru.edu/artsci/biol/biol.htm)
Chemistry: Lawrence M. Sayre, Ph.D., California. (http://www.cwru.edu/artsci/chem/)
Communication Sciences: Claire Penn, Ph.D. (http://cwru.edu/artsci/cosi/cosi.htm)
English: Gary Stonum, Ph.D., Johns Hopkins. (http://cwru.edu/artsci/engl/engl.html)
Geological Sciences: Philip O. Banks, Ph.D., CalTech. (http://www.cwru.edu/artsci/geol/files/geol.html)
History: Carroll Pursell, Ph.D., Berkeley. (http://www.cwru.edu/artsci/hsty/)
Mathematics: James C. Alexander, Ph.D., Johns Hopkins. (http://www.cwru.edu/artsci/math/)
Modern Languages and Literatures: Margaretmary Daley, Ph.D., Yale. (http://www.cwru.edu/artsci/modlang/)
Music History and Education: Quentin Quereau, Ph.D., Yale. (http://music.cwru.edu/)
Physics: Lawrence M. Krauss, Ph.D., MIT. (http://phys.cwru.edu/)
Political Science: Vincent E. McHale, Ph.D., Penn State. (http://www.cwru.edu/artsci/posc/)
Psychology: Robert L. Greene, Ph.D., Yale. (http://www.cwru.edu/artsci/pscl/)
Sociology: Eva Kahana, Ph.D., Chicago. (http://socwww.cwru.edu)
Statistics: Wojbor A. Woyczynski, Ph.D., Wroclaw. (http://sun.cwru.edu)
Theater Arts: Ron Wilson, B.G.S., Kansas. (http://www.cwru.edu/artsci/thtr/)

Engineering: Dean Robert F. Savinell, Ph.D., Pittsburgh.
Biomedical Engineering: Patrick E. Crago, Ph.D., Case Western Reserve. (http://bme.cwru.edu)
Chemical Engineering: Chung-Chiun Liu, Ph.D., Iowa State. (http://www.cwru.edu/cse/eche/)
Civil Engineering: Robert Mullen, Ph.D., Northwestern. (http://ecivwww.cwru.edu/civil)
Electrical Engineering and Computer Science: B. Ross Barmish, Ph.D., Cornell. (http://www.eecs.cwru.edu)
Macromolecular Science: Alexander M. Jamieson, Ph.Phil., Oxford. (http://www.sci.cwru.edu/cse/emac/)
Materials Science and Engineering: Gary M. Michal, Ph.D., Stanford. (http://vulcan2.cwru.edu)
Mechanical and Aerospace Engineering: Joseph M. Prahl, Ph.D., Harvard. (http://www.mae1.cwru.edu/mae/)

Medicine—Basic Sciences: Dean Nathan A. Berger, M.D., Hahnemann.
Anatomy: Joseph LaManna, Ph.D., Duke. (http://www.cwru.edu/med/anatomy/)
Anesthesiology: Howard Nearman, M.D., Case Western Reserve. (http://www.anesth.com/)
Biochemistry: Michael Weiss, M.D., Ph.D., Harvard. (http://www.cwru.edu/med/biochemistry/home.html)
Biomedical Ethics: Stuart Youngner, M.D., Case Western Reserve. (http://www.cwru.edu/med/bioethics/bioethics.html)
Environmental Health Sciences: G. David McCoy, Ph.D., Connecticut. (http://mediswww.meds.cwru.edu/dept/evhs/evhs/htm)
Epidemiology and Biostatistics: Alfred A. Rimm, Ph.D., Rutgers. (http://epbiwww.cwru.edu/)
Genetics: Terry Hassold, Ph.D., Michigan State. (http://genetics.cwru.edu)
Molecular Biology and Microbiology: Lloyd Culp, Ph.D., MIT. (http://www.cwru.edu/med/microbio/mbio.htm)
Neurosciences: Lynn T. Landmesser, Ph.D., UCLA. (http://neurowww.cwru.edu)
Nutrition: Henri Brunengraber, Ph.D., M.D., Libre (Brussels). (http://www.cwru.edu/med/nutrition/home.html)
Pathology: Gearge Perry, Ph.D., California. (http://www.cwru.edu/med/pathology)
Pharmacology: John H. Nilson, Ph.D., New Mexico. (http://pharmacology.cwru.edu/)
Physiology and Biophysics: Antonio Scarpa, Ph.D., M.D., Padua (Italy). (http://physiology.cwru.edu/)

Applied Social Sciences: Dean Darlyne Bailey, Ph.D., Case Western Reserve. (http://www.msass.cwru.edu)

Dentistry: Dean Jerold S. Goldberg, D.D.S., Case Western Reserve. (http://www.cwru.edu/dental/casewebsite/)

Management: Dean Mohsen Anvari, Ph.D., Case Western Reserve. (http://weatherhead.cwru.edu/)
Management Ph.D. Program: Bo Carlsson, Ph.D., Stanford. (http://weatherhead.cwru.edu/degree/phd_mgmt/)
Operations Research: Matthew J. Sobel, Ph.D., Stanford. (http://weatherhead.cwru.edu/degree/phd_opre/)
Organizational Behavior: Richard E. Boyatzis, Ph.D., Harvard. (http://weatherhead.cwru.edu/degree/phd_orbh/)
Organizational Development and Analysis: Richard Boyatzis, Ph.D., Harvard. (http://weatherhead.cwru.edu/msoda/default.shtml)

Master of Public Health: Scott Frank, M.D., Michigan. (http://epbiwww.cwru.edu/pages/program_frames.html)

Nursing: Dean May L. Wykle, Ph.D., Case Western stReserve. (http://fpb.cwru.edu/)

THE CATHOLIC UNIVERSITY OF AMERICA

Graduate Studies

Programs of Study

In the School of Arts and Sciences, the University offers programs of study that lead to the Doctor of Philosophy degree in anthropology, biology, comparative literature, education, English language and literature, French, German, Greek and Latin, history (Latin American, medieval Europe, modern Europe, religion and society in the late medieval and early modern world, and United States), Italian, physics, politics (American government, political theory, and world politics), psychology, rhetoric, Romance languages and literatures, Semitic and Egyptian languages and literatures, sociology, and Spanish. Master's degrees are also granted in these programs as well as in accounting, chemical education, classics, congressional studies, drama, economics, financial management, human resources management, international affairs, international political economics, and Irish studies.

In the School of Religious Studies, there are doctoral programs in biblical studies, church history, religion and religious education, and theology. Master's programs are available in these areas as well as in history of religions and liturgical studies. Canonical programs in canon law (J.C.L. and J.C.D.) are offered as well as pontifical degrees in biblical studies (S.S.L. and S.S.D.) and ecclesiastical degrees in theology (S.T.D. and S.T.L.).

Programs of study that lead to master's and Ph.D. degrees are also offered in the Schools of Engineering, Music, Nursing, and Philosophy and in the National Catholic School of Social Service. The Schools of Architecture, Law, and Library and Information Science also offer the appropriate professional degrees.

In addition to interdisciplinary programs in early Christian studies and medieval and Byzantine studies, numerous opportunities for study in joint programs are available.

Research Facilities

The Catholic University of America libraries house approximately 1.5 million volumes in the John K. Mullen of Denver Memorial Library, six campus libraries, and the White Law Library. Special strengths in the collection include religious studies; language studies; philosophy; canon law; early Christian, medieval, and Renaissance history; nursing; music; Celtic languages and literatures; and Semitic languages. Manuscript collections include 3.5 million items that relate to Catholic Church history, immigration, American labor history, social welfare movements, and early photography. Other research facilities that are available to students include 10,000 volumes of fifteenth- to eighteenth-century rare books in the Clementine Library, more than 55,000 volumes on the history and culture of Portuguese-speaking peoples in the Oliveira Lima Library, the Institute for Christian Oriental Research, the Gregorian chant microfilm collection, and the Latin American Center for Graduate Studies in Music collection. The University is connected to the Internet via SURAnet, and there are more than 1,000 microcomputers and terminals on campus. The University is a member of the Oak Ridge Associated Universities and the Folger Institute of Renaissance and Eighteenth-Century Studies. The Washington Research Library Consortium provides access to millions of volumes that are owned by the six member libraries through a combined online catalog, direct borrowing, and a delivery service. Resources include ALADIN (the catalog of books, journals, periodical articles, and document citations), document delivery services, Internet access, and direct-dial access to numerous scholarly indexes and services. In addition, students have access to the collections of the Library of Congress, the Dumbarton Oaks Center for Byzantine Studies, the Folger Shakespeare Library, and the National Library of Medicine.

Financial Aid

Fellowships, scholarships, and teaching and research assistantships are awarded on the basis of academic excellence and promise. Need-based aid, such as student loans and work-study assistance, is also available.

Cost of Study

Tuition in 2002–03 is $21,050 per academic year for full-time graduate and other postbaccalaureate students ($21,230 for engineering and architecture students and $27,180 for law students). Tuition for part-time students is $810 per credit hour ($990 for law).

Living and Housing Costs

Meal plans in University dining halls range in price from $1620 to $4138 per academic year; costs are subject to change at the beginning of each academic year. On-campus housing ranges in price from approximately $5460 for a double room to $7612 for a single room per academic year. Off-campus housing information can be found at http://housing.cua.edu/och.

Student Group

The University's total enrollment is 5,510, including approximately 2,923 graduate and professional students.

Location

Students have ready access to the exceptional academic and recreational opportunities of the area. Washington, D.C., is a major cultural center as well as the seat of the federal government and the location of national educational, labor, political, and trade associations. The Smithsonian Institution, the National Gallery of Art, the Phillips Collection, and the Kennedy Center for the Performing Arts are among the many museums, galleries, and centers in the area.

The University is located on a spacious, 144-acre campus in a residential area of northeast Washington that is easily accessible from all parts of the metropolitan area. There is a Metrorail station at the campus.

The University

The Catholic University of America was founded in 1887 as the national institution of learning of the Catholic Church in the United States. Beginning as a center for graduate study, it soon evolved into a comprehensive university with undergraduate and professional programs as well. The University gives primacy to scholarship and scientific research and to the training of future scholars through its graduate programs. It is committed to the advancement of learning and particularly to the development of knowledge in the light of Christian revelation.

Applying

Decisions concerning admission to graduate study are made by the academic deans of the schools. Applications and supporting documents should be submitted to the Office of Graduate Admissions by the deadline specified by the respective department or school. A priority application deadline of February 1 is used for most programs. There is an application fee of $55. Applications for need-based financial aid should be submitted to the Office of Financial Aid.

Admission is open to qualified men and women of any age, color, disability, race, religion, or national or ethnic origin.

Correspondence and Information

For information about specific programs, prospective students should visit the graduate Web site (http://graduate.cua.edu). An inquiry form and application materials are available online. Questions regarding the application process should be directed to:

Office of Graduate Admissions
110 McMahon Hall
The Catholic University of America
Washington, D.C. 20064

Telephone: 202-319-5057

DEANS AND CHAIRS OF GRADUATE STUDIES

Many of the deans, department chairs, and program directors can be reached via e-mail. Please visit the CUA Web site at http://www.cua.edu and locate the appropriate program pages for contact information.

John J. Convey, Provost.
Peter Cimbolic, Vice Provost and Dean of Graduate Studies.

Arts and Sciences. Lawrence Poos, Dean.
Anthropology: Jon Anderson.
Biology: Venigalla Rao.
Business and Economics: Kevin S. Forbes.
Chemistry: Gregory Brewer.
Comparative Literature: Stephen K. Wright.
Drama: Thomas Donahue.
Early Christian Studies: Philip Rousseau.
Education: Shauvan Wall.
English Language and Literature: Stephen Wright.
Greek and Latin: Linda Safran.
History: Lawrence R. Poos.
Irish Studies: Christina Mahony.
Medieval and Byzantine Studies: Thérèse-Anne Druart.
Modern Languages and Literatures: Mario Rojas.
Physics: Charles J. Montrose.
Politics: Stephen Schneck.
Psychology: Marc M. Sebrechts.
Semitic and Egyptian Languages and Literatures: Michael P. O'Connor.
Sociology: Chefu Lee.

Engineering. Charles Nguyen, Dean.
Biomedical Engineering: Mark Mirotznik.
Civil Engineering: Timothy W. Kao.
Electrical Engineering: Nadar Namazi.
Engineering Management: Donald Purcell.
Mechanical Engineering: T. Steven Brown.

Philosophy. Kurt Pritzl, O.P., Dean.

Religious Studies. Stephen Happel, Dean.
Biblical Studies: Francis T. Gignac, S.J.
Canon Law: John Beal.
Church History: Nelson H. Minnich.
Liturgical Studies: David Power.
Religion and Religious Education: Margaret Mary Kelleher, O.S.U.
Theology: James Wiseman.

Deans of Other Graduate and Professional Schools
School of Architecture and Planning: Gregory K. Hunt.
Columbus School of Law: Douglas W. Kmiec.
School of Library and Information Science: Peter Liebscher.
The Benjamin T. Rome School of Music: Murry Sidlin.
School of Nursing: Ann Marie Brooks.
National Catholic School of Social Service: James R. Zabora.

CENTRAL CONNECTICUT STATE UNIVERSITY

School of Graduate Studies

Programs of Study

Using the faculties of the University's four academic schools (Arts and Sciences, Business, Education and Professional Studies, and Technology), the Graduate School offers degree programs in forty-one fields of study. Master of Arts (M.A.) programs are provided in biological sciences, English, history, information design, mathematics, modern languages, psychology, and public history. Master of Science (M.S.) degrees are available in most education specializations, such as art, business, counselor, early childhood, elementary, music, physical, secondary, special, and technology education; educational leadership; educational technology; foundations; reading; and teaching English to speakers of other languages (TESOL). M.S. degrees are also available in biological sciences (including nurse anesthesia), communication, criminal justice, data mining, engineering technology, geography, international studies, marriage and family therapy, mathematics, natural sciences, Spanish, technology management, and an interdisciplinary program of computer information technology. Many of these programs have specializations that students may elect as a specific concentration of study.

Also available are the Master of Business Administration (M.B.A.) in international business, which prepares graduates for leadership positions in the multinational business environment, and the new Ed.D. program in educational leadership—the first doctoral program at Central Connecticut State University (CCSU)—which serves educational leaders in Connecticut through an innovative program of study integrating course work and field studies grounded in authentic inquiry. Faculty members and doctoral candidates work together to improve educational opportunities for the children and young people of Connecticut.

In addition, CCSU has Sixth-Year Certificate programs in educational leadership and reading as well as programs for teacher and professional certification. Prospective educators/teachers can complete requirements for certification in elementary, middle-level, and secondary education; in special areas, such as art, music, physical, and technology education; and in TESOL. Through these programs, students also prepare for careers as school counselors, media specialists, intermediate administrators/supervisors, and reading consultants. There are also special certificate programs in prehealth and cell and molecular biology as well as planned programs of study beyond the master's for teachers and school personnel and students interested in other areas and disciplines.

Research Facilities

The Elihu Burritt Library provides access to more than 2 million books (via CONSULS), a wide array of electronic databases and online resources, and special collections, ranging from the unparalleled collection of Polish American materials to the Equity Archive. Information Services coordinates computer facilities and provides networked microcomputers as well as remote terminals that link students to a mainframe computer on the campus and to computing resources throughout the Connecticut State University. Central Connecticut is also part of the international network of computers (Internet). State-of-the-art hardware and software for computer-integrated manufacturing (CIM) and computer-assisted design and drafting (CADD) are available in the laboratories of the School of Technology.

Financial Aid

Graduate assistantships are available for qualified full-time and part-time students who wish to work with faculty members in teaching, research, or laboratory supervision. Graduate assistants receive a stipend (up to $9600 for a full-time assignment during 2000–01) and a waiver of some costs related to University attendance. Information about the Federal Stafford Student Loan programs and other forms of financial assistance for graduate students is available from the Financial Aid Office (860-832-2200). On-campus employment and off-campus work opportunities are available in the Hartford–New Britain metropolitan area.

Cost of Study

Tuition and fees are established and modified by the Board of Trustees. Currently, the cost for full-time study charged to Connecticut residents is $2437 per semester in tuition and fees. Out-of-state students pay tuition and fees of $5411. Students accepted for admission pay a nonrefundable graduate enrollment fee of $150, which is deducted from a later tuition bill. Tuition for part-time study is currently $190 per credit hour for courses numbered 100–499 and $220 per credit hour for graduate courses numbered 500–699. A part-time registration fee of $52 is also charged. Students registering for online courses have different course fees.

Living and Housing Costs

Current estimated expenses for two semesters of study, including living expenses as well as tuition and fees, are approximately $15,000 for Connecticut residents and $21,000 for nonresident and international students. A typical two-bedroom apartment in the New Britain area rents for $600 a month. Dormitory space is available only for a limited number of international graduate students. A campus meal plan is available.

Student Group

The total University enrollment is about 12,000, with approximately 7,000 attending full-time and 5,000 attending part-time. Approximately 2,400 graduate students enroll each semester, including 400 who attend full-time. International students constitute nearly 10 percent of the full-time enrollment.

Student Outcomes

Graduates of CCSU earn positions in major corporations, government, education, and the professions. Others pursue doctoral studies to prepare for eventual careers in colleges or universities as instructional or research faculty members.

Location

A suburban 140-acre campus, the University is conveniently located 15 minutes by car from Connecticut's capital city of Hartford and 2 hours from New York and Boston. Cultural and recreational opportunities abound. Central Connecticut is within driving distance of upper New England ski resorts, an hour from the Connecticut shore, and 2 hours from Rhode Island's beaches.

The University

Central Connecticut State University, a university in the Connecticut State University system, was founded in 1849 as the state's first public institution of higher learning. Recognized for nearly 150 years for its superior teacher training and education programs, Central has expanded its traditions to include offerings that prepare graduates for careers in business, industry, the sciences, the arts, and government. Advanced-degree programs have been offered since 1954. The quality of a CCSU education was honored by the Association of American Colleges and Universities when it selected the University as one of only sixteen "leaderships institutions" in the nation. And CCSU has been acclaimed by a noted college guide book as one of the "great colleges for the real world."

Applying

Prospective students must submit an application form, a $40 fee, and official transcripts from all colleges and universities attended. Applications are accepted throughout the year but should be received by August 1 for fall semester admission and December 1 for spring semester admission. International students and assistantship applicants should apply by May 1 and October 1, respectively. A bachelor's degree from a regionally accredited institution of higher education and an undergraduate average of at least 2.7 are required. As described in the graduate catalog, some departments have established earlier application deadlines or have additional requirements, including the GMAT (for M.B.A. in international business applicants) and the GRE (for Ed.D. in education leadership applicants). International students must demonstrate competence in English through the TOEFL.

Correspondence and Information

Kevin Oliva
Associate Director of Recruitment and Admissions
Graduate Studies Programs
Central Connecticut State University
New Britain, Connecticut 06050-4010

Telephone: 860-832-2350
Fax: 860-832-2362
E-mail: abraham@ccsu.edu
World Wide Web: http://www.ccsu.edu/grad

FACULTY AND DEPARTMENT HEADS

Deans

Graduate Studies: Dr. Paulette Lemma, Associate Vice President for Academic Affairs and Dean.
School of Arts and Sciences: Dr. Susan Pease, Interim Dean.
School of Business: Dr. Daniel J. Miller, Dean.
School of Education and Professional Studies: Dr. Ellen Whitford, Dean.
School of Technology: Dr. Zdzislaw Kremens, Dean.

Department Heads

The following chairpersons of departments offering graduate programs may be contacted for information about departmental offerings and admissions criteria. (The telephone area code for all numbers is 860.)

Art: Professor Sherinatu Fafunwa-Ndibe (832-2620).
Biological Sciences: Dr. Ruth Rollin (832-2645).
Chemistry: Dr. Timothy Shine (832-2675).
Communication: Dr. Sarafin Mendez-Mendez (832-2690).
Counseling and Family Therapy: Dr. James Malley (832-2145).
Criminology and Criminal Justice: Dr. Stephen Cox (832-3141).
Educational Leadership: Dr. Anthony Rigazio-DiGilio (832-2130).
Engineering Technology: Dr. John Bean (832-1825)
English: Dr. Loftus Jestin (832-2740).
Geography: Dr. Brian Sommers (832-2785).
History: Dr. Heather Munro Prescott (832-2800).
Manufacturing and Construction Management: Dr. Paul Resetarits (832-1830).
Mathematical Sciences: Dr. Timothy Craine (832-2835).
Modern Language: Dr. Louis Auld (832-2875).
Music: Dr. Pamela Perry (832-2900).
Physical Education and Health Fitness Studies: Dr. David Harackiewicz (832-2155).
Physics and Earth Science: Dr. Ali Antar (832-2930).
Psychology: Dr. Frank Donis (832-3100).
Reading and Language Arts: Dr. Helen Abadiano (832-2175).
Special Education: Dr. Ernest Pancsofar (832-2400).
Teacher Education: Dr. Nancy Hoffman (832-2145).
Technology, Vocational-Technical Education: Dr. Peter Rodrigues (832-1850).

Program Coordinators

The following persons may be contacted for information about interdisciplinary programs.

Ed.D./Educational Leadership: Dr. Richard Arends (832-2152).
M.B.A./International Business: Dr. Jean Lefebvre (832-3210).
M.S./Business Education: Dr. George Claffey (832-3210).
M.S./Data Mining: Dr. Daniel Larose (832-2322).
M.S./International Studies: Dr. Ronald Fernandez (832-3755).
M.S./Science and Science Education: Dr. Sandra Burns (832-2934).
M.S./TESOL: Dr. Andrea Osborne (832-2748).

CENTRAL MICHIGAN UNIVERSITY

College of Graduate Studies

Programs of Study

Doctoral degrees are available in applied experimental psychology, audiology, clinical psychology, educational leadership, history, industrial/organizational psychology, mathematics, and school psychology. Specialist's degrees are available in general educational administration and school psychology. Master's degrees are available in administration; art; biology; broadcast and cinematic arts; business administration; business education; chemistry; clinical psychology; community leadership; computer science; counseling; early childhood education; economics; educational administration; educational technology; elementary education; English composition and communication; English creative writing, English language and literature; exercise science; fine arts; general/experimental psychology; geographic information systems; health promotion and program management; history; human development and family studies; humanities; industrial education; industrial and organizational psychology; industrial management and technology; information systems; international administration; library, media, and technology; mathematics; middle-level education; music; nutrition and dietetics; physical education; physical therapy; physician assistant studies; physics; political science; public administration; recreation, park, and leisure services administration; school principalship; secondary education; social and criminal justice; sociology; Spanish; special education; speech-language pathology; speech communication and dramatic arts; sports administration; and teaching English to speakers of other languages (TESOL). Certificate programs are available in business computing, general administration, health services administration, hospitality and tourism administration, human resources administration, information resource management, international administration, leadership, public administration, and software engineering administration.

Research Facilities

State-of-the-art Charles V. Park Library holds nearly a million printed volumes and provides both on- and off-campus users access to CMU's printed and digital library holdings as well as information resources worldwide. The library features seating for more than 2,600 patrons as well as an array of group-study facilities, a high-technology multimedia auditorium, a café, and an extended-hours study area. The Clarke Historical Library, widely recognized for its valuable collections relating to the history of Michigan, the Old Northwest, and the Great Lakes area, is also housed here. The University has an IBM 9672 Enterprise server; IBM, IBM-compatible, and Macintosh microcomputers; and laser printers—all available for student use. The equipment is housed in laboratories and departmental clusters throughout campus. A computer laboratory with terminals and microcomputers is open and staffed 24 hours a day. The Research Collection of the Center for Cultural and Natural History includes more than 130,000 biological specimens, artifacts, and historical items. Departments have discipline-specific special facilities to support the research activities of their students and faculty members. For example, an astronomical observatory supports the work of the physics department. The computer science department has a mainframe VAX 8530, as well as a computer vision laboratory. The Industrial and Educational Technology Building has a robotics laboratory. Science departments enjoy state-of-the-art facilities in the Dow Science Complex. On-campus clinics are operated by the speech and hearing, psychology, and counseling programs. CMU also owns a 252-acre woodland, 22 miles north of Mt. Pleasant; 43 acres of historic Beaver Island in northern Lake Michigan; and Cathedral Woods near campus. All are used as natural laboratories for instruction and research.

Financial Aid

The University offers Graduate Research Fellowships for master's- and specialist's-level students, Doctoral Research Fellowships for doctoral students, and King-Chávez-Parks Fellowships for master's- and doctoral-level students from minority groups. All programs provide a stipend and a 30-credit tuition scholarship. Teaching and research assistantships, which provide a stipend and a 20-credit tuition scholarship, are also available. Domestic students can apply for loans, Federal Work-Study, and Michigan Work-Study programs. The University facilitates internship and co-op opportunities off-campus.

Cost of Study

Tuition for 2001–02 ranged from $162.60 to $175.80 per semester hour for Michigan residents and from $323 to $348.80 per semester hour for nonresidents. Recipients of CMU fellowships and assistantships as well as graduate students who have at least one parent who is a CMU alumnus are considered Michigan residents for tuition purposes.

Living and Housing Costs

The University provides furnished apartments for single and married graduate students. Rent covers the cost of utilities, local telephone, and cable television. In 2001–02, the cost of single student housing ranged from $316 to $481 per month. For those who prefer to live off campus, everything from single-family houses to major apartment complexes are available. Information regarding University housing and meal plans is available from the Housing and Dining Services Office in Bovee Center.

Student Group

The University's enrollment is 27,797 students. This includes more than 2,000 graduate students in on-campus programs and 6,000 in off-campus programs.

Location

The 480-acre campus of Central Michigan University is located in Mt. Pleasant, a growing city of about 25,000. The community blends vintage homes and a downtown area with modern office buildings, shopping centers, and government facilities. One can easily reach lakes, woods, and ski slopes to the north. Detroit, Ann Arbor, Saginaw, Grand Rapids, and Lansing are 50 to 150 miles away.

The University

The University was founded in 1892. Its academic departments are organized into six colleges. There are many cultural and recreational opportunities on campus. The Office for Institutional Diversity sponsors multicultural programs and activities designed to foster an appreciation for human diversity throughout the University. The Office for International Education offers programs and services to students from seventy-two countries. Visual arts are exhibited in the University gallery. Vocal and instrumental ensembles perform frequently. Students perform in and produce plays at the University theater. Professional productions in theater, music, and dance are presented. The departments sponsor discipline-related lectures, and the University sponsors a speaker's series. In sports, CMU competes at the NCAA Division I level (seven men's sports and nine women's sports) and is a member of the Mid-American Conference. The state-of-the-art Student Activity Center provides outstanding opportunities for recreation and fitness activities.

Applying

Applications are available from the College of Graduate Studies. Students should apply at least six weeks prior to the start of the semester in which they wish to enroll. International students should apply at least six months prior to the desired time of enrollment. Intermediate and advanced courses in academic English are available to international students who achieve a minimum TOEFL score of 500 (213 on the computer-based version). Since certain programs have earlier application deadlines and certain others require submission of GRE or GMAT scores, prospective students should contact the relevant academic department to learn about requirements and deadlines.

Correspondence and Information

Department of (specify)
Central Michigan University
Mt. Pleasant, Michigan 48859

College of Graduate Studies
Central Michigan University
Mt. Pleasant, Michigan 48859
Telephone: 989-774-GRAD
Fax: 989-774-1857
E-mail: grad@cmich.edu
World Wide Web: http://www.grad.cmich.edu

FACULTY HEADS

James H. Hageman, Ph.D., Dean.
Gail P. Scukanec, Ph.D., Associate Dean.

Administration: D. Terry Rawls, Ed.D., Director of Master of Science in Administration.
Art: Nedra Frodge, M.F.A., Chairperson.
Biology: John Scheide, Ph.D., Chairperson.
Broadcast and Cinematic Arts: Peter Orlik, Ph.D., Chairperson.
Business Administration: Daniel E. Vetter, Ph.D., Director, M.B.A. Program.
Business Information Systems: Monica Holmes, Ph.D., Chairperson.
Chemistry: Karl Lindfors, Ph.D., Chairperson.
Communication Disorders: Renny Tatchell, Ph.D., Chairperson.
Computer Science: Gongzhu Hu, Ph.D., Chairperson.
Counseling/Special Education: Richard Fox, Ph.D., Chairperson.
Economics: Michael Shields, Ph.D., Chairperson.
Educational Administration and Community Leadership: Rena Richtig, Ph.D., Chairperson.
English: Stephen Holder, Ph.D., Chairperson.
Foreign Languages, Literatures, and Cultures: James Jones, Ph.D., Chairperson.
Geography: Robert Aron, Ph.D., Chairperson.
History: John Robertson, Ph.D., Chairperson.
Human Environmental Studies: Usha Chowdhary, Ph.D., Chairperson.
Humanities: Ronald Primeau, Ph.D., Director of Humanities.
Industrial Engineering and Technology: Daniel Chen, Ph.D., Chairperson.
Mathematics: Sidney Graham, Ph.D., Chairperson.
Music: Randi L'Hommedieu, Ph.D., Chairperson.
Physical Education and Sport: James Hornak, Ed.D., Chairperson.
Physics: Stanley Hirschi, Ph.D., Chairperson.
Political Science: Lawrence Sych, Ph.D., Chairperson.
Psychology: Timothy Hartshorne, Ph.D., Chairperson.
Recreation, Park, and Leisure Services Administration: Roger Coles, Ed.S., Chairperson.
School of Health Sciences: Jeffrey Betts, Ph.D., Chairperson.
School of Rehabilitation and Medical Sciences: Herm Triezenberg, Ph.D., Chairperson.
Sociology, Anthropology, and Social Work: Rodney Kirk, Ph.D., Chairperson.
Speech Communication and Dramatic Arts: Denny Bettisworth, Ph.D., Chairperson.
Teacher Education and Professional Development: William Merrill, Ph.D., Chairperson.

Dr. Patricia Kelly reviews X-rays with a group of physician assistant studies students.

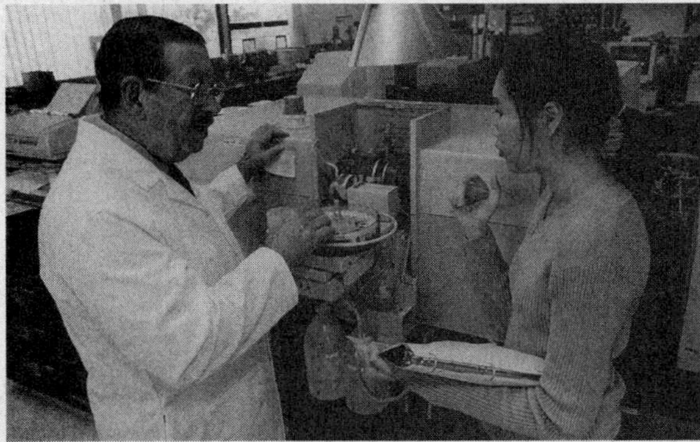

Dr. Bob Howell works with chemistry graduate student Khaekhai Chaiwong of Thailand.

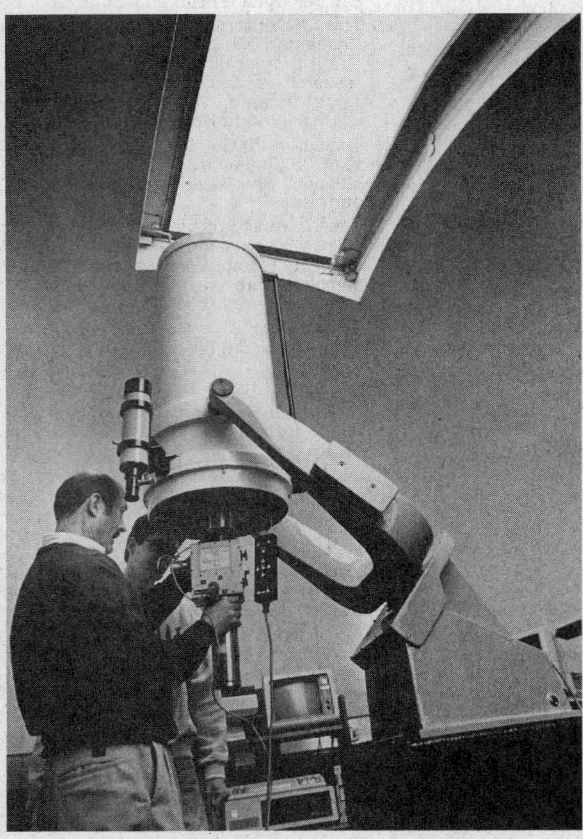

A computer-controlled 16-inch telescope is an example of the modern equipment that supports learning and research activities.

CENTRAL MISSOURI STATE UNIVERSITY

Graduate Studies

Programs of Study

Central Missouri State University offers programs leading to the Master of Arts, Master in Business Administration, Master of Science, Master of Science in Education, Education Specialist, and cooperative doctoral degrees. Areas of study include accountancy, agricultural technology, aviation safety, biology, business administration, business and office education, criminal justice administration, communication disorders, curriculum and instruction, economics, educational technology, English, history, human environmental sciences, industrial hygiene, industrial management, industrial technology, information technology, library information technology, library science and information services, mass communication, mathematics (applied mathematics), music, occupational safety management (fire science, industrial safety, loss control, public safety, security, and transportation safety), physical education: exercise and sport science, psychology, reading, rural nursing, school administration, school counseling, social gerontology, social studies, sociology, special education, speech communication, student personnel administration, teaching English as a second language, technology and occupational education (technology education and occupational education), and theater. The University also offers Education Specialist degrees in administration (elementary school principalship, secondary school principalship, superintendency, and higher education), curriculum and instruction, and human services (criminal justice administration, guidance and counseling, industrial arts and technology, learning resources, occupational safety management, special education, and public services). The two cooperative doctoral programs include the Ph.D. in technology management, with Indiana State University as the degree-granting institution, and the Ed.D. in education leadership, with the University of Missouri–Columbia as the degree-granting institution.

Research Facilities

The Office of Sponsored Programs in The Graduate School provide research support for students and faculty members.

The new $30.5-million James C. Kirkpatrick Library houses more than 2.4 million items in print and nonprint formats, CD-ROM databases, a historical children's literature collection, an online public access catalog, and a variety of information networks.

Information Services provides academic computing support using an ATM-based high-speed network with more than 2,000 attached workstations. The network is connected to a Windows NT network domain supported by a cluster of network servers for application, Web, data, and mail services. The networked environment provides Internet connectivity and is connected to an IBM 2003-115 mainframe, providing research support through products such as SAS. Information Services also provides HELP Desk and basic consulting services.

Financial Aid

Graduate assistantships, providing a competitive stipend and waiver of graduate academic fees, are available to qualified students under the terms of a nine-month contract. Scholarships include the Graduate Student Regents Scholarship, the Irvin L. and Edna A. Peters Memorial Graduate Student Scholarship, the Warren C. Lovinger Graduate Student Scholarship, and Presidential Fellowships. The University participates in a full range of federal financial aid programs, including grants, loans, and student employment.

Cost of Study

Graduate tuition for 2001–02 was $175 per credit hour for Missouri residents and $348 for nonresident students. Extended Campus rates are variable.

Living and Housing Costs

In 2001–02, double rooms cost $1395 per semester and single rooms cost $1930 per semester. The one-bedroom apartment rent ranges from $422 to $496 per month, and rent for two-bedroom apartments ranges from $465 to $518 per month. A limited number of economy suites are available for $450 per month (one-, two-, or three-person occupancy). The University has beautiful accommodations for students with families. Graduate students can build their own meal plans or select from three other meal plan packages with costs ranging up to $810 per semester.

Student Group

Total enrollment at Central Missouri State University exceeds 11,000 students, nearly 2,000 of whom are doing postgraduate work. The student-faculty ratio is 17:1. International students and ethnic minority students are encouraged to apply. Students attend the University from all fifty states and approximately sixty countries. Enrolled graduate students automatically become members of the Graduate Student Association.

Location

Central Missouri State University is located 50 miles southeast of Kansas City, in Warrensburg, Missouri. It is easily accessible by highway, bus, and passenger rail service.

The University

Founded in 1871, Central is a public university with a statewide mission in professional technology that has been fully integrated into a comprehensive liberal arts curriculum. Four colleges offer degree programs encompassing more than 150 areas of study at the undergraduate and graduate levels. Providing top-quality education at affordable cost is one of the institution's top priorities, as is its commitment to rigorous academic standards and thorough career preparation. The campus includes instructional buildings, residence halls, full-service dining, superb athletic facilities, and a spacious University Union. Other facilities on the 1,240-acre campus include a 300-acre recreational and biological research area with fishing lakes, a heated outdoor pool, and an 18-hole golf course; the Max B. Swisher Skyhaven Airport; 100,000-watt public television and radio stations; and the University Farm.

Applying

A nonrefundable fee of $25 is required for U.S. students applying for admission to a graduate studies program. International students pay a $50 fee.

Correspondence and Information

The Graduate School
Central Missouri State University
Ward Edwards 1800
Warrensburg, Missouri 64093

Telephone: 660-543-4328 (admissions information)
660-543-4621 (enrollment information)
800-729-2678 (toll-free)
E-mail: gradinfo@cmsu1.cmsu.edu
World Wide Web: http://www.cmsu.edu/graduate

Central Missouri State University

Master's Degree Programs and Coordinators

Accountancy: John A. Elfrink, Ph.D. (660-543-4245)
Agricultural Technology: Frederick D. Worman, Ph.D. (660-543-4191)
Aviation Safety: John Horine, Ed.D. (660-543-4457)
Biology: Stephen Mohler, M.A. (660-543-8684)
Business Administration: Kim Andrews, Ph.D. (660-543-8597)
Business/Office Education: Rebecca Limback, Ed.D. (660-543-4248)
Communication: Barbara Baker, Ph.D. (660-543-4469)
Communication Disorders: Carl Harlan, Ph.D. (660-543-4606)
Criminal Justice: Joseph B. Vaughn, Ph.D. (660-543-4188)
Curriculum and Instruction: Wayne Williams, Ed.D. (660-543-8701)
Economics: John A. Elfrink, Ph.D. (660-543-4245)
Educational Technology: C. Diana Smith, Ed.D. (660-543-8636)
English: Joseph Lewandowski, Ph.D. (660-543-8696)
History: Mary Ellen Rowe, Ph.D. (660-543-8713)
Industrial Hygiene: Dianna Bryant, M.S. (660-543-4971)
Industrial Management: John Sutton, Ph.D. (660-543-4439)
Industrial Technology: John Sutton, Ph.D. (660-543-4439)
Information Technology: Sam S. Ramanujan, Ph.D. (660-543-8565)
Library Science and Information Services: Linda Lillard, M.L.S. (660-543-8633)
Mathematics: Shing So, Ph.D. (660-543-8839)
Music: J. Franklin Fenley, Ed.D. (660-543-4530)
Occupational Safety Management: Omer Frank, Ph.D. (660-543-4412)
Physical Education, Exercise, and Sport Science: Curtis Reams, Ed.D. (660-543-8875)
Psychology: Jonathan Smith, Ph.D. (660-543-4185)
Reading, K–12: Carol Mihalevich, Ph.D. (660-543-8731)
Rural Family Nursing: M. Elaine Frank-Ragan, Ph.D. (660-543-4775)
School Administration: Janice C. Reynolds, Ed.D. (660-543-4341)
School Counseling: Patricia Ferris, Ph.D. (660-543-4185)
Social Gerontology: Shawn Kelly, Ph.D. (660-543-4903)
Social Studies: Yvonne Johnson, Ph.D. (660-543-8680)
Sociology: Yuh Lin Hu, Ph.D. (660-543-8790)
Special Education: B. Louise Keisker, Ph.D. (660-543-8768)
Student Personnel Administration: David Sundberg, Ph.D. (660-543-8628)
Teaching English as a Second Language: Dennis Muchisky, Ph.D. (660-543-8711)
Technology and Occupational Education: Michael Wright, Ed.D. (660-543-4452)
Theatre: Richard Herman, Ph.D. (660-543-8793)

Education Specialist Degree Programs and Coordinators

Administration (Elementary School Principalship, Secondary School Principalship, Superintendency): Janice C. Reynolds, Ed.D. (660-543-4341)
Higher Education: David Sundberg, Ph.D. (660-543-8628)
Curriculum and Instruction: Wayne Williams, Ed.D. (660-543-4235)
Human Services (Industrial Arts and Technology): Michael Wright, Ed.D. (660-543-8891)
Learning Resources: Linda Lillard, M.L.S. (660-543-8633)
Guidance and Counseling: Patricia Ferris, Ph.D. (660-543-4185)
Special Education: B. Louise Keisker, Ph.D. (660-543-8768)
Public Services: Alice Greife, Ph.D. (660-543-4411)

Cooperative Doctoral Degree Programs and Coordinators

Ph.D. in Technology (Indiana State University): John Sutton, Ph.D. (660-543-4439)
Ed.D. in Educational Leadership (University of Missouri–Columbia): Jim Machell, Ph.D. (660-543-4341)

CENTRAL WASHINGTON UNIVERSITY

Graduate Studies and Research

Programs of Study

Central Washington University (CWU) offers programs that lead to the following degrees: Master of Arts, Master of Arts for Teachers, Master of Education, Master of Fine Arts, Master of Music, Master of Professional Accountancy, and Master of Science. Master of Arts programs include art (M.A. and M.F.A.), English (literature, TESL), history, and theater production (summers only). Master of Science degree programs are available in biological sciences; chemistry; counseling psychology; engineering technology; experimental psychology; family and consumer sciences; geology; organization development (weekends only); physical education, health, and leisure studies; and resource management. There is a Master of Professional Accountancy in accounting program. A Master of Arts for Teachers of mathematics is available, in the summer only. Master of Education programs include administration, business and marketing education, master teacher, reading specialist, school counseling, school psychology, special education, and supervision and curriculum.

A minimum of 45 quarter credits is needed for the master's degree, though some programs require more credits. As the capstone project, programs may require a thesis, a project, or a comprehensive examination in lieu of the thesis. A final oral examination is standard for most programs.

CWU encourages collaborative research among graduate students and faculty members. It is committed to ensuring that graduate students gain as much hands-on experience as possible in their programs. A measure of CWU's success is that one of its graduate students recently won the prestigious Western Association of Graduate Schools' Distinguished Thesis Award and others have won awards for art. Music students have performed with nationally recognized orchestras and at the Metropolitan Opera. Graduate students regularly give conference presentations, exhibitions, and performances. They typically conduct research as part of federally sponsored grants in such areas as biological sciences, geographic information systems, geology, and resource management.

Research Facilities

In addition to its library, CWU's massive science facility and the completely renovated education building augment CWU's instructional and research facilities. The Psychology Research facility houses the Chimpanzee and Human Communications Institute. The Geographic Information Systems Laboratory, Applied Social Data Center, and Community Psychology Services Clinic provide students with exceptional research opportunities. Computing services include access to the Internet, an online public catalog, and online bibliographic retrieval services. A state archives facility makes CWU the largest repository of state documents in central Washington.

Financial Aid

Graduate assistantships are available in each of CWU's departments offering graduate degrees. Approximately 40 percent of all full-time enrolled graduate students received appointments in 2001–02. About two thirds of the graduate assistants teach; the remainder serve as research assistants and a few perform service functions. The stipend package for the 2001–02 academic year was $11,923. Other financial support can be obtained through the Office of Financial Aid from federal and state sources for students demonstrating financial need. There are also employment opportunities on and off campus. Furthermore, graduate students may apply for travel and research funds on a competitive basis through the Office of Graduate Studies and Research.

Cost of Study

Graduate tuition for 2001–02 was $1616 per quarter for full-time (10–18 quarter credit hours) Washington State residents and $4924 per quarter for nonresidents. For resident part-time students tuition was $161.60 per credit hour and $492.40 per credit hour for nonresidents. There was a $45 per quarter health service fee, a $35 per quarter athletic fee, and a $25 per quarter technology fee. The cost of tuition for summer school was $135 per credit hour for both in-state and out-of-state graduate students.

Living and Housing Costs

University Housing Services offers a variety of apartments starting at $365 per month for a studio and running up to $525 for a three-bedroom apartment. Rents off-campus range between $275 and $600 per month depending upon size and extras. The University also makes available rooms in residence halls for graduate students. Assistance with locating off-campus housing is available as well. Dining Services offers reasonably priced, quarterly contracts in its four dining halls. Meals vary at each location, and there are several meal plan options from which to choose.

Student Group

As of the fall quarter 2001, there were 772 graduate students at CWU enrolled in twenty-seven programs across nineteen departments; they make up 9 percent of the University's 8,421 students. Graduate classes are small and there are regular opportunities to work closely with professors and fellow students. The largest graduate programs are in education, psychology, and resource management. Other departments average between 12 and 30 enrolled graduate students.

Location

CWU's main campus is in Ellensburg, a safe and friendly community that prides itself on quality living. Students experience a small-town atmosphere, with diverse cultural and social fare. CWU's proximity to Seattle, the Cascade Mountains, Puget Sound, Yakima, the Yakima River Valley, and the Columbia River recreational areas makes its location extremely attractive for year-round recreation as well as for those interested in a wide range of research opportunities. Ellensburg, population 15,400, enjoys four distinct seasons and abundant sunshine.

The University

CWU, one of six state-assisted universities, was founded in 1890 as the Washington State Normal School. It began offering graduate programs in the fall of 1947 and became a comprehensive university in 1977. Fully accredited, CWU offers instruction not only in Ellensburg, but also in Lynnwood, Moses Lake, SeaTac, Steilacoom, Tacoma, Wenatchee, and Yakima. The campus, an appealing mixture of traditional and modern architecture, consists of eighty-three buildings, stretching across 380 acres of shaded lawns that are criss-crossed by two canals and framed by evergreens, landscaped malls, and walks. Points of interest include an award winning Japanese garden, an arts complex housing the Sarah Spurgeon Gallery, musical performance halls, a theater, and Nicholson Athletic Pavilion.

Applying

Application materials may be obtained from the address below. The application fee is $35. Applicants should have earned at least a 3.0 GPA over the last 60 semester hours (90 quarter hours) of graded course work. Some programs require scores on the General Test of the GRE. Students whose native language is not English must score at least 550 (paper-based) or 213 (computer-based) on the TOEFL. Students should contact the relevant department as they may need to supply other materials when submitting the application. Priority consideration will be given to applications received by April 1 for fall quarter admissions. Assistantship applications should be submitted by February 15 for the following academic year. Financial aid applications should be made directly to the Office of Financial Aid by March 1.

Correspondence and Information

Graduate Studies and Research
Central Washington University
400 East 8th Avenue
Ellensburg, Washington 98926-7510

Telephone: 509-963-3103
Fax: 509-963-1799
E-mail: masters@cwu.edu
World Wide Web: http://www.cwu.edu/~masters

GRADUATE AFFAIRS

The area code is 509 for all telephone and fax numbers.

Graduate Studies and Research
Telephone: 963-3103; fax: 963-1799; e-mail: masters@cwu.edu.
Richard Mack, Interim Associate Vice President; Ph.D., Colorado State.
Raymond Z. Riznyk, Director of University Research; Ph.D., Oregon State.

Graduate Programs and Contacts

Accounting (M.P.A.): Professional accountancy. Ronald Tidd, Graduate Coordinator; Ph.D., Minnesota. (telephone: 963-3340; fax: 963-2466; e-mail: mpa@cwu.edu)

Administrative Management and Business Education (M.Ed.): Business education, marketing education. V. Wayne Klemin, Department Chair and Graduate Coordinator; Ed.D., Utah State. (telephone: 963-2611; fax: 963-1721; e-mail: kleminw@cwu.edu)

Art (M.A., M.F.A.): Ceramics, drawing, jewelry and metal-smithing, mixed media, painting, photography, sculpture, wood design. Michael Chinn, Department Chair and Graduate Coordinator; M.F.A., California State, Long Beach. (telephone: 963-2665; fax: 963-1918; e-mail: chinnm@cwu.edu)

Biological Sciences (M.S.): Botany, stream ecology and fisheries, microbiology-parasitology, terrestrial ecology. Lixing Sun, Graduate Coordinator; Ph.D., SUNY Health Science Center at Syracuse. (telephone: 963-2731; fax: 963-2730; e-mail: lixing@cwu.edu)

Chemistry (M.S.): Analytical, biological, inorganic, medicinal, organic, physical. Anthony Diaz, Graduate Coordinator; Ph.D., Oregon State. (telephone: 963-2811; fax: 963-1050; e-mail: diaza@cwu.edu)

Curriculum and Supervision (M.Ed.): Master teacher, elementary teaching, middle school teaching, secondary school teaching. Osman Alawiye, Department Chair and Graduate Coordinator; Ph.D., New Mexico State. (telephone: 963-3412; fax: 963-1452; e-mail: alawiyeo@cwu.edu)

English (M.A.): Literature, TESL/TEFL. Gerald Stacy, Graduate Coordinator; Ph.D., Bowling Green. (telephone: 963-1546; fax: 963-1561; e-mail: stacyg@cwu.edu)

Family and Consumer Sciences (M.S.): Family studies, nutrition studies, family and consumer sciences education. Jan Bowers, Department Chair and Graduate Coordinator; Ph.D., Kansas State. (telephone: 963-2766; fax: 963-2787; e-mail: bowersj@cwu.edu)

Geology (M.S.): Tectonics, neotectonics, geomorphology, climate change. Jeffrey Lee, Graduate Coordinator; Ph.D., Stanford. (telephone: 963-2702; fax: 963-2821; e-mail: jeff@geology.cwu.edu)

History (M.A.): Colonial America, Western America, American women's history, modern Europe, Russia, modern Japan, Latin America, East Africa. Daniel Herman, Graduate Coordinator; Ph.D., Berkeley. (telephone: 963-1655; fax: 963-1654; e-mail: hermand@cwu.edu)

Industrial and Engineering Technology (M.S.): Engineering technology. Walter Kaminski, Department Chair and Graduate Coordinator; Ph.D., Florida. (telephone: 963-1756; fax: 963-1795; e-mail: kaminski@cwu.edu)

Mathematics (M.A.T.): Teaching mathematics (summer only). Mark Oursland, Graduate Coordinator; Ed.D., Montana State. (telephone: 963-2103; fax: 963-3226; e-mail: lewiss@cwu.edu)

Music (M.M.): Theory, composition, conducting, performance, pedagogy, music education. Peter Gries, Department Chair and Graduate Coordinator; D.M., Oregon. (telephone: 963-1216; fax: 963-1239; e-mail: griesp@cwu.edu)

Organization Development (M.S.): Organization development (weekends only). Anthony Stahelski, Graduate Coordinator; Ph.D., UCLA. (telephone: 963-2501; fax: 963-2307; e-mail: stahelsa@cwu.edu)

Physical Education, Health Education, and Leisure Services (M.S.): Exercise science, health education, health promotion, leisure services, physical education teaching/coaching sports and athletic administration. Leo D'Aquisto, Graduate Coordinator; Ed.D., Northern Colorado. (telephone: 963-1911; fax: 963-1848; e-mail: acquisto@cwu.edu)

Psychology (M.S., M.Ed.): Counseling psychology, experimental psychology, organizational psychology (M.S.), school counseling, school psychology (M.Ed.). Philip Tolin, Department Chair and Graduate Coordinator; Ph.D., Iowa. (telephone: 963-2381; fax: 963-2307; e-mail: tolin@cwu.edu)

Resource Management (M.S.): Stream flow, water quality and riparian management, natural resources policy, wildlife and fisheries economics, resource systems, cultural resource management, geographic information systems, linkages between cultural and natural resource management. Steven Hackenberger, Program Co-Director; Ph.D., Washington State (telephone: 963-3201; fax: 963-2315; e-mail: hackenbe@cwu.edu); Anthony Gabriel, Program Co-Director; Ph.D., Guelph. (telephone: 963-1188; fax: 963-1047; e-mail: gabriela@cwu.edu)

Teacher Education (M.Ed.): Administration, reading specialist, special education, supervision and curriculum. David Shorr, Department Chair and Graduate Coordinator; Ed.D., Washington (Seattle). (telephone: 963-1461; fax: 963-1162; e-mail: henryv@cwu.edu)

Theatre Arts (M.A.): Theater production (summer only). George Bellah, Department Co-Chair and Graduate Coordinator; M.F.A., North Carolina at Greensboro. (telephone: 963-1766; fax: 963-1767; e-mail: bellahg@cwu.edu)

CHAPMAN UNIVERSITY

Graduate Studies

Programs of Study

Chapman offers the Juris Doctor (law) and the M.A. in criminal justice, education, educational psychology, English, film studies, organizational leadership, psychology, school counseling, special education, teaching (elementary), and teaching (secondary). It offers the M.S. in food science and nutrition and human resources. Also offered are a Master of Business Administration, a Master of Fine Arts in creative writing, a Master of Fine Arts in film and television production, and a Doctor of Physical Therapy. Public school credential programs include multiple subjects/CLAD and BCLAD, single subjects, pupil personnel school counseling (PPSC), pupil personnel school psychology (PPSP), special education dual specialist credentials, special education specialist, and administrative services credentials. Many of the degree programs offer specializations. Credential programs can be combined with one of the degree programs in education.

Required units vary with each degree; however, each program comprises courses that best prepare students to continue a career or enter a new profession. Program requirements include advancement to degree candidacy after the completion of 12 units and a comprehensive examination, taken at the end of or during the final semester of course work. Some programs offer a thesis project option in place of the comprehensive examination. One or two internship courses that provide practical experience in the student's field are required for most programs. Course work from other accredited institutions may be transferred; a maximum of 12 credits may be applied to a program. At least 24 credits must be taken in residence.

Research projects are essential to many degree programs and are undertaken in research courses or through cooperative education. Because class sizes are kept small, students can readily communicate with faculty members about research projects and general academic work.

Research Facilities

Research facilities include the nationally recognized Chapman University Center for Economic Research, a state-of-the-art human performance laboratory and research vivarium, food science and nutrition food-tasting and research laboratories, and a community clinic for psychological counseling and research. The computer lab has DEC MicroVAX and NCR Tower facilities, and there are also IBM PC and Apple Macintosh laboratories. Library holdings include nearly 200,000 volumes: books, 1,914 journals, films, recordings, videocassettes, CDs, computer software, and other media software. Chapman has the largest collection of Albert Schweitzer memorabilia in the western United States; a permanent exhibit is on display in the Argyros Forum.

Financial Aid

Many financial aid opportunities are available for qualified students, including Chapman University Scholarships and loans, which are based on need and academic achievement; graduate assistantships; residence life positions; employment; California State Graduate Fellowships; Federal Stafford Student Loans; Benefits for Veterans and Dependents; and an employer-paid tuition plan. Students interested in any of these opportunities should contact the Financial Aid Office (714-997-6741).

Cost of Study

Tuition for 2001–02 varied by program. Part-time and full-time students, as well as California and non-California residents, were charged the same tuition rate. Tuition for a full-time student (9 credits per semester) was approximately $3960 to $5850 per academic year, depending on the student's program. Books and personal expenses add to annual costs.

Living and Housing Costs

Chapman offers limited housing for graduate students. Off-campus housing is available. For additional information, students should telephone the Residence Life Office (714-997-6604).

Student Group

Graduate study programs enroll more than 1,200 students each year on the Orange campus. Courses are scheduled so that both full- and part-time students can attend. Many students have been working in their field and bring practical experience to the classroom; they come from many states and countries, and about 50 percent of them are women. Students who choose to enroll at Chapman want a small-campus atmosphere, personalized attention, a superior faculty, and the education that will enable them to succeed in a highly competitive professional world. Opportunities for graduates are plentiful due to the concentration of business and industry in Orange County and throughout southern California. People for whom graduates may eventually work sit on many College advisory boards.

Location

Chapman is located in Orange, a pleasant community of 95,000. Approximately 30 miles northeast is Los Angeles, but minutes away are citrus groves, farmlands and pastures, and ocean beaches. The Anaheim Arena, Anaheim Convention Center, Disneyland, Disney's California Adventure, Knotts Berry Farm, and Edison International Field are also nearby.

The University

Chapman is an independent, private institution and has provided liberal and professional education of distinction since it was founded in 1861 by the Christian Church (Disciples of Christ). It has continued to meet the needs of its students with fine academic programs and individualized attention. Undergraduate and graduate degree programs are offered on the main campus and at thirty-one Academic Centers throughout the United States. The graduate curricula are designed to offer advanced study in specific disciplines to broaden and deepen a student's knowledge. Faculty members include distinguished academicians and noted professional practitioners. Chapman is accredited by and is a member of the Western Association of Schools and Colleges. It is also a member of the Independent Colleges of Southern California, the College Entrance Examination Board, the Western College Association, the Association of Independent California Colleges and Universities, the American Council on Education, the American Association of Colleges for Teacher Education, the Division of Higher Education of the Christian Church (Disciples of Christ), and the American Assembly of Collegiate Schools of Business. It is also accredited by the Institute of Food Technologists. Its teacher training and credential programs are approved by the California State Department of Education. The physical therapy program is approved by the Commission on Accreditation in the Physical Therapy Education of the American Physical Therapy Association and by the Physical Therapy Examining Committee of the Board of Medical Quality Assurance of the State of California. The M.B.A. program is fully accredited by AACSB–The International Association for Management Education. The School of Law is provisionally approved by the American Bar Association.

Applying

Students are admitted in the fall, spring, and summer. Applicants should submit $40 and a completed Application for Graduate Studies; transcripts of all postsecondary work, showing the completion of a bachelor's degree; scores on the GMAT, GRE (General or Subject test), MAT, MSAT, or SSAT (and TOEFL for international students); two letters of recommendation; and a statement of intent. Departments, however, should be consulted for specific program requirements.

Correspondence and Information

Office of Graduate Admission
Argyros Forum, Room 304
Chapman University
Orange, California 92866

Telephone: 714-997-6786
Fax: 714-997-6713
E-mail: shoover@chapman.edu
World Wide Web: http://www.chapman.edu

PROGRAM DIRECTORS

Business Administration: Thomas Turk, Associate Professor, School of Business and Economics; Ph.D., California, Irvine.

School Counseling: Michael Hass, Assistant Professor and Coordinator of Counselor Education Programs; Ph.D., California, Irvine.

Creative Writing: Matthew Schneider, Associate Professor of English and Program Director of Graduate Programs; Ph.D., UCLA.

Criminal Justice: Becky Ballestero, Director of Criminal Justice Program; M.S., California State, Long Beach.

Education: Barbara Tye, Professor of Education; Ed.D., Texas Tech.

Educational Psychology: Michael Hass, Assistant Professor and Coordinator of Educational Psychology Programs; Ph.D., California, Irvine.

English: Matthew Schneider, Associate Professor of English and Program Director of Graduate Programs; Ph.D., UCLA.

Film and Television Production and Film Studies: Robert Bassett, Professor of Communications and Dean, School of Film and Television; M.A., Chicago; M.A., Claremont.

Food Science and Nutrition: Fred Caporaso, Professor of Food Science; Chair, Department of Food Science and Nutrition; and Program Director; Ph.D., Penn State.

Human Resources: Amy Hurley, Chair, Department of Human Resources and Career Counseling; Ph.D., NYU.

Law: Joanne K. Punu, Associate Dean for Admission and Financial Aid; M.B.A., Hawaii.

Organizational Leadership: J. Marcus Maier, Associate Professor and Director of the M.A. in Organizational Leadership Program; Ph.D., Cornell.

Physical Therapy: Donald L. Gabard, Chair, Division of Physical Therapy; Ph.D., USC.

Psychology: John Flowers, Chair, Division of Psychology, and Program Director of Psychology; Ph.D., USC.

Special Education: Don Cardinal, Associate Professor of Education; Ph.D., Claremont.

Argyros Forum.

CHESTNUT HILL COLLEGE

Graduate Programs

Programs of Study

The Graduate Division of Chestnut Hill College offers master's degree and certificate programs in counseling psychology, education, applied technology, holistic spirituality/spiritual direction or health care, and administration of human services. The division also offers a Psy.D. in clinical psychology, state certification programs, and a variety of post-master's programs. The M.A. and M.S. programs in counseling psychology and human services include specializations in child and adolescent therapy, marriage and family therapy, trauma studies, and addictions counseling, or students may opt for a generalist curriculum. These programs prepare students for licensure in Pennsylvania and other states. Post-master's certificates are available in all areas of specialization. The Doctor of Clinical Psychology program is open to the applicant who has a master's degree in counseling or a closely related field. For the strong applicant with a bachelor's degree in psychology, the combined M.S./Psy.D. program is available. All programs offered by the Department of Professional Psychology are practitioner based, and classes are taught by faculty members who are actively working in the field. Master's-level courses are also offered on the DeSales University campus in Center Valley, Pennsylvania. The Education Department offers the M.Ed. in elementary education, early childhood education, and educational leadership (with principal certification). Students may also opt for state certification programs: elementary education, elementary education with certification in special education, early childhood education, and various secondary education areas. Reading specialist and principal certification programs are available for qualified applicants. A Montessori specialization certification (AMS) is also offered. The majority of courses in the Educational Leadership program are offered in the distance/on-site format. The Applied Technology program offers the M.S. in applied technology in two distinct strands—educational and transformational applications. Educational Applications is designed for the teacher eager to develop the technical skills and conceptual framework necessary for the appropriate use of technology in the learning environment. Reading and Technology focuses on the reading/language arts curriculum that culminates in state certification in reading. Education and Technology helps teachers develop new leadership skills and expertise in the use of technology in the achievement of curricular goals and applications of constructivist principles to today's changing classroom milieu. Transformational Applications is designed for people involved in technology who are challenged by impending cultural changes brought about by that technology. The goal of its specializations (instructional design and leadership and technology) is the preparation of professionals to assume leadership roles in the transformation of their work environments. Additional post-master's certificates, as well as postbaccalaureate professional certificates, are available in most areas of specialization. The majority of course work for these programs is offered through a distance/on-site format. The M.A. programs in holistic spirituality include holistic spirituality/spiritual direction, holistic spirituality/health care, and several certificate programs: spiritual direction, health care, specialized study in spirituality, and applied spirituality (post-master's). Each of the programs combines academic rigor with experiential learning in ways that promote the integration of theory and praxis. As an integral component of the regular academic-year offerings, the holistic spirituality program presents an annual summer Festival of Spirituality featuring nationally known theologians in public lectures, extended conversations, and intensive course formats. Each summer's festival is designed to advance the relationships between spirituality and the Bible, justice issues, and/or ecological concerns. The M.S. program in administration of human services combines courses in management, public policy, and social issues to prepare students for supervisory and leadership positions in health and human-service organizations. With an emphasis on social change and diversity, this degree provides a comprehensive knowledge base about organizations, their philosophy and structure, and the specialized services that are provided. This program is offered in an accelerated format.

Research Facilities

Chestnut Hill College provides access to state-of-the-art hardware and software in five computer labs and a new building offering computer access from every workstation. The Logue Library offers an electronic research center, an online catalog, and 140,000 volumes on three floors of open stacks. Among the electronic resources are ERIC, PsychINFO, LexisNexis, ProQuestReligion, JSTOR, EBSCOhost Elite, and Wilson OmniFile Mega, MLA. Specialized psychology demonstration rooms are available for live observation and taping of clinical sessions. Studio TV labs are used by the applied technology program; video editing and specialized multimedia development labs are used by other graduate programs.

Financial Aid

Chestnut Hill College offers a limited number of graduate assistantships for students at the master's level. The majority of students finance their education through student loans and work reimbursement arrangements. The Financial Aid Office is available to assist students with the loan application process. Some graduate programs (education and holistic spirituality) offer a discounted tuition to teachers and those in church-affiliated ministry.

Cost of Study

Tuition for 2002–03 is $425 per credit for the administration of human services, counseling psychology, and holistic spirituality programs; $400 per credit for the applied technology program; $380 per credit for the education program; and $615 per credit for the doctoral program in clinical psychology.

Living and Housing Costs

A variety of urban and suburban housing options are available within an easy commute to the campus. Limited on-campus housing is abailable for some Graduate Division summer sessions.

Student Group

With classes primarily in the evening and on weekends, the Graduate Division at Chestnut Hill College caters to the needs of the working professional. Ordinarily, degree programs must be completed within six years of matriculation. Within that time frame, students can choose their own pace for most programs; some opt to study full-time, while others take one or two courses per semester. Small classes and a welcoming atmosphere make Chestnut Hill College an excellent choice for traditional students as well as working professionals and those who wish to change careers.

Location

Chestnut Hill College is located in the northwestern corner of Philadelphia, easily accessible to all of the Philadelphia neighborhoods, outlying areas, and adjoining states. It is also near numerous cultural, athletic, and recreational activities in the region. The campus has a suburban feel, while remaining accessible through public transportation and major routes.

The College

Chestnut Hill College is a Catholic College founded by the Sisters of St. Joseph in 1924 as a college for women. In 2003, the undergraduate College becomes coeducational. The Accelerated and Graduate Divisions have been coeducational since their inception. The Graduate Division provides a quality education that takes into equal account the academic, professional, and personal needs of both women and men. The programs in the Graduate Division prepare adult students for professions in applied technology, counseling psychology, education, holistic spirituality/spiritual direction or health care, and administration of human services. A doctoral degree in clinical psychology (Psy.D.) is also offered. The aim of these graduate programs is to graduate professionals who are skilled, ethical, knowledgeable, and confident practitioners in their respective fields.

Applying

Applications for all programs are considered on a rolling admissions basis. Master's degree students may begin in any semester: fall, spring, or summer. Psy.D. and M.S./Psy.D. classes begin in the fall. All applicants are evaluated on the basis of the entire application packet, which includes the application, transcripts of all previous college study, three letters of recommendation, MAT or GRE General Test scores, and a Statement of Professional Goals. Special admission requirements apply to Psy.D. and M.S./Psy.D. programs. Interviews with department chairs are required; interviews with the Director of Graduate Admissions are available.

Correspondence and Information

For master's program information and application:

Director of Graduate Admissions
Chestnut Hill College
9601 Germantown Avenue
Philadelphia, Pennsylvania 19118-2693
Telephone: 215-248-7020
215-248-7170 (graduate office)
Fax: 215-248-7161
E-mail: graddiv@chc.edu
World Wide Web: http://www.chc.edu

For Psy.D. and M.S./Psy.D. program information and application:

Mary Steinmetz
Director of Psy.D. Admissions
Chestnut Hill College
9601 Germantown Avenue
Philadelphia, Pennsylvania 19118-2693
Telephone: 215-248-7077
215-248-7170 (graduate office)
Fax: 215-248-7155
E-mail: profpsyc@chc.edu
World Wide Web: http://www.chc.edu

THE FACULTY

Note: Research interests of the Psy.D. faculty members are available on the Web at http://www.chc.edu/graduate/psydfac.htm. Information on the entire faculty can be found at http://www.chc.edu/faculty/.

Scott W. Browning, Associate Professor of Psychology; M.Ed., Boston University; Ph.D., California School of Professional Psychology–Berkeley.
David Borsos, Assistant Professor of Psychology; M.Ed., Antioch; Ph.D., Temple.
Dominic Cotugno, Assistant Professor and Chair, Division of Education; Ed.D., Temple.
Mary Kay Flannery, S.S.J., Assistant Professor of Religious Studies; D.Min., Catholic Theological Union at Chicago.
Elaine R. Green, Associate Professor of Sociology and Coordinator, Administration of Human Services Program; Ed.D., Temple.
Nancy Havens, Assistant Professor of Education; Ed.D., Temple.
Molly Hindman, Assistant Professor of Psychology; Psy.D., Hahnemann.
Jessica Kahn, Associate Professor of Computer Technology; M.Ed., Temple; Ph.D., Pennsylvania.
Honor Keirans, S.S.J., Associate Professor of Education; Ed.D., Temple.
Thomas E. Klee, Associate Professor of Psychology; Ph.D., Temple.
Judith Marsh, Assistant Professor of Psychology and Chair, Department of Professional Psychology; Ph.D., Pittsburgh.
Louise A. Mayock, S.N.D., Assistant Professor of Computer Technology; M.T.S., Catholic University; Ed.D., Pennsylvania.
Georgia McWhinney, Associate Professor of Education; M.A.T., Harvard; Ph.D., Pennsylvania.
Joseph A. Micucci, Associate Professor of Psychology; Ph.D., Minnesota.
Catherine Nerney, S.S.J., Associate Professor of Religious Studies and Chair, Religious Studies Department/Holistic Spirituality Program; Ph.D., Catholic University.
Carol Pate, Assistant Professor of Education; Ed.D., Indiana.
Roseann Quinn, S.S.J., Assistant Professor of Religious Studies and Acting Dean of the Graduate Division; M.Ed., Boston College; D.Min., Catholic Theological Union at Chicago.
Cheryll Rothery, Assistant Professor of Psychology and Director of Clinical Training, Department of Professional Psychology; Psy.D., Rutgers.
Margaret H. Vogelson, Professor of Education; M.Ed., Ph.D., Temple.

CHRISTOPHER NEWPORT UNIVERSITY

Graduate Studies

Programs of Study

Christopher Newport University offers masters' programs in teaching, applied physics and computer science, industrial/organizational psychology, environmental science, and public safety leadership.

The Master of Arts in Teaching (M.A.T.) is a practitioner-oriented program that requires 33 to 36 credit hours to complete. M.A.T. students select a concentration from the content areas of language arts, mathematics, science, or history.

The Master of Science (M.S.) in applied physics and computer science, a 30- to 36-credit-hour program, emphasizes experimentation, instrumentation, and computer analysis. The department has a strong record of research in solid state (lasers and superconductors), nuclear physics, artificial intelligence, instrumentation and advanced computer systems, and pattern recognition.

The Master of Science in applied psychology offers a concentration in industrial/organizational psychology with a strong foundation in psychological theory and research and emphasizes the knowledge, skills, and abilities to apply psychology in organizational settings. The 33- to 36-credit-hour program includes a thesis or practicum option. Graduates are prepared for employment in business, industry, and government settings.

The Master of Science in environmental science is a 36-credit-hour program that provides a solid background in ecological and environmental conservation theory. Students develop the skills required for employment with environmental assessment/monitoring businesses and state governmental agencies in the growing field of environmental monitoring and conservation.

The Master of Public Safety Leadership degree is unique in its orientation to the challenge of promoting and ensuring the future safety of the public. Graduates of the 36-credit-hour program are prepared for positions in public safety and city/county management.

Research Facilities

The M.S. in applied physics is supported by major teaching-research labs: the Photonics and Laser Lab, the Solid State Sensors Lab, the Advanced Chip Design Lab, the Information Systems Lab, and a computer lab. Participation in funded research at the Thomas Jefferson National Accelerator Facility and the NASA Langley Research Center may be available. Christopher Newport University is one of four universities involved in a new state-of-the-art research consortium, the Applied Research Center. The M.S. in applied psychology is supported with a group process/human relations laboratory and a computer laboratory. The M.S. in environmental science is housed in a newly remodeled building that contains fourteen modern and well-equipped laboratories and twenty-three support areas. Included are three walk-in controlled environment chambers and a new greenhouse. The department has large ecological study sites in forested areas and rural areas and at a lake.

Financial Aid

Financial aid consists of scholarships, grants, graduate assistantships, loans, and employment opportunities. The priority filing date for applying for financial aid for the following academic year is March 1. Later dates are established on an annual basis for the student loan programs. To be eligible for programs, students must be admitted as degree-seeking graduate students and be enrolled at least on a half-time basis (some programs may require full-time), in good academic standing, making satisfactory academic progress, and U.S. citizens or permanent residents. Students interested in receiving financial aid are strongly encouraged to view the CNU Web site at http://www.cnu.edu/admin/finaid/.

Cost of Study

For the 2001–02 academic year the academic tuition was $150 per credit hour for in-state students and $392 per credit hour for out-of-state students. In addition, students pay a $20 registration fee, a $100 parking fee, and a $25 graduation fee. Graduate book costs are estimated at $400 per semester.

Living and Housing Costs

The 2002–03 annual rate for room and board is $5750 (single occupancy is $300 more per semester). New student apartments have ten-month leases at $5495 for the 2002–03 academic year. Off-campus apartments in the neighborhood of CNU currently rent for an average of $5980 per year for one bedroom.

Student Outcomes

Graduates of the programs have selected positions at area research laboratories such as NASA and Thomas Jefferson National Accelerator Facility and at companies such Northrop Grumman, Dallas Semiconductor, and Logicon; with the federal government, including U.S. Department of Justice; with state law enforcement agencies, city governments, and national and regional consulting firms; and in elementary, middle, and high schools.

Location

The University is located in suburban Newport News, Virginia, midway between Williamsburg and Virginia Beach. Newport News is located on the lower Virginia Peninsula in the Hampton Roads area. The area supports a variety of businesses, manufacturing concerns, health-care providers, government installations, research facilities, schools, colleges, and cultural and recreational facilities.

The University

Christopher Newport University is the youngest comprehensive university in Virginia and has been described by *U.S. News & World Report* as "young, hot, and growing." The academic areas of the University are organized into the College of Liberal Arts and Sciences and the School of Business. The graduate programs are administered by the Associate Dean of Liberal Arts and Sciences and the Associate Director of Graduate Admissions and Records. Instruction and research are carried out by the graduate faculty members.

Applying

Students should have baccalaureate degrees from regionally accredited colleges or universities with a minimum grade point average of 3.0 on a 4.0 scale. For all programs except the M.A.T., students must provide scores from the GRE taken within the last five years. The M.A.T. program requires scores from the PRAXIS I (reading, writing, and mathematics) or from the specialty area test of the PRAXIS series. Letters of recommendation and essays may also be required.

Application deadlines for degree-seeking students are July 1 for fall semester, November 15 for spring semester, and April 15 for summer sessions. After these deadlines, applicants may apply to enter as nondegree students, or, if a program determines that the student meets degree-seeking qualifications and the program has available space, the student may be admitted as degree-seeking. Graduate application forms and admission standards can be found at the Web site listed below.

Correspondence and Information

For information about graduate programs:

Ms. Lyn Sawyer, M.Ed.
Associate Director of Graduate Admissions and Records

Telephone: 757-594-7544
E-mail: gradstdy@cnu.edu.
World Wide Web: http://www.cnu.edu/gradstudies/

Applications should be mailed to:

Office of Admissions
Ms. Susan Chittenden
Christopher Newport University
1 University Place
Newport News, Virginia 23606

THE FACULTY AND THEIR RESEARCH

MASTER OF SCIENCE IN ENVIRONMENTAL SCIENCE

Harold Cones, Professor of Biology and Department Chair; Ph.D., Bowling Green State. Urban ecosystem dynamics, ecotourism, marine biology, history of technology. Selected as a Virginia Outstanding Professor by the State Council of Higher Education for Virginia.

Tarek Abdel-Fattah, Assistant Professor of Chemistry; Ph.D., Northeastern. Environmental remediation technology, catalysis and manotechnology for aerospace applications.

Rob Atkinson, Assistant Professor of Biology; Ph.D., Virginia Tech. Restoration of damaged ecosystems.

Russ Benedict, Assistant Professor of Biology; Ph.D., Nebraska–Lincoln. Ecology and distribution of bats, ecology and evolution of shrews, general biology of mammals.

Ken Chang, Professor of Chemistry; Ph.D., Notre Dame. Spectroscopy, radiation.

Jim Reed, Professor of Biology; Ph.D., Tulane. Lke ecosystem studies, bottlenose dolphin utilization of Chesapeake Bay tributaries.

Barbara Savitzky, Associate Professor of Biology; Ph.D., Tennessee. Ecology of reptiles and amphibians, vertebrate biology, animal behavior.

Gary Whiting, Associate Professor of Biology and Department Graduate Coordinator; Ph.D., South Carolina. GIS, wetlands ecology, biogeochemistry.

MASTER OF SCIENCE IN APPLIED PHYSICS AND COMPUTER SCIENCE

Joshua Anyiwo, Associate Professor; Ph.D., Colorado State. Computational physics, fluid dynamics.

A. Martin Buoncristinani, Professor and Chair; Ph.D., Notre Dame. Electrooptical properties of materials.

Randall Caton, Professor; Ph.D., CUNY. Superconductivity, science education.

David Doughty, Professor; Ph.D., Pennsylvania. High-energy physics, high-speed triggering and data acquisition.

David Game, Associate Professor; Ph.D., Old Dominion. Applied network theory; fiber-optic communications.

John Hardie, Assistant Professor; Ph.D., Pittsburgh. Nuclear physics, scientific computing, physics education.

David Hibler, Associate Professor; Ph.D., Texas at Austin. Artificial intelligence, neural nets, genetic algorithms.

Robert Hodson, Associate Professor; Ph.D., Florida State. Computer architecture, real-time systems.

Peter Knipp, Associate Professor; Ph.D., Chicago. Solid-state physics.

Lynn Lambert, Associate Professor; Ph.D., Delaware. Artificial intelligence, natural language processing, linguistics.

Nikita Pougachev, Associate Professor; Ph.D., Russian Academy of Sciences. Atmospheric physics.

Rauf Selim, Associate Professor; Ph.D., Temple. Superconductivity, computer interfaces.

Antonio Siochi, Associate Professor; Ph.D., Virginia Tech. Interactive software systems.

Ming Zhang, Ph.D., ECNU. Neural systems, artificial intelligence, pattern recognition, image processing.

PSYCHOLOGY

Thomas D. Berry, Associate Professor; Ph.D., Virginia Tech. Organizational and interpersonal feedback, health and safety, system leadership, evaluation and change.

Kelly Cartwright, Assistant Professor; Ph.D., Arkansas. Cognitive development, language, literacy, gender issues.

Dianne Catanzaro, Associate Professor; Ph.D., Old Dominion. Attitudes toward affirmative action, service encounter and service quality, gay/lesbian issues.

Dorothy Doolittle, Professor, Associate Dean College of Liberal Arts and Sciences, and Director of Graduate Studies; Ph.D., Tennessee. Personality and job performance, sexual harassment, organizational justice.

Jeffrey Gibbons, Assistant Professor; Ph.D., Kansas State. Theoretical and applied memory research pertaining to enhanced word recognition, relation of story telling to mood and the fading affect bias, memory for rumors (News Headlines), gender stereotypes and character identification in news stories, existential moments.

Timothy R. Marshall, Associate Professor of Psychology and Chairman; Ph.D., Virginia Tech. Developmental psychology, social and emotional development.

GOVERNMENT AND PUBLIC POLICY

Peter M. Carlson, Associate Professor; D.P.A., USC; Former Assistant Director/Regional Director for the Federal Bureau of Prisons. Prison administration, organizational change, organizational culture.

Robert E. Colvin, Assistant Professor; Ph.D., Virginia Commonwealth; Former commissioner with Virginia Alcoholic Beverage Control Department, former Executive Director of the Virginia Legislature's State Crime Commission, former Manager of the Virginia's Office of Consumer Affairs, lobbyist, and organizational development consultant. Values leadership, gender and leadership, organizational leadership.

Gary S. Green, Associate Professor; Ph.D., Pennsylvania. White collar crime, juvenile justice, deterrence, criminal justice administration.

Harry Greenlee, Associate Professor and Director of Legal Studies; J.D., Ohio State. Mediation and employment law.

Tammy Hall, Assistant Professor. Ph.D., Virginia Tech. Ethics, leadership, executive education, public management. Professor Hall has worked in private sector in human resources and the nonprofit sector in community services and development.

Quentin Kidd, Assistant Professor; Ph.D., Texas Tech; Director of the Joseph Center for the Study of Local, State and Regional Politics. Civic engagement and southern politics.

Buck G. Miller, Professor; Ph.D., NYU. Leadership, change leadership perception and organizational leadership.

MASTER OF ARTS IN TEACHING

Biology

Harold Cones, Professor; Ph.D., Bowling Green State.
Russ Benedict, Assistant Professor; Ph.D., Nebraska of Lincoln.
Rob Atkinson, Associate Professor; Ph.D., Virginia Tech.
Jim Reed, Professor; Ph.D., Tulane.
Gary Whiting, Associate Professor; Ph.D., South Carolina.
Barbara Savitsky, Associate Professor; Ph.D., Tennessee at Knoxville.

Education

Sandra Bryan, Professor; Ed.D. Auburn.
Jane Bailey, Associate Professor; Ed.D., William and Mary.
Adriana Dorrington, Assistant Professor; Ed.D., Toronto.
Marsh Sprague, Associate Professor of Education and Program Coordinator; Ed.D., Miami (Florida).

English

Roberta Rosenburg, Professor; Ph.D., North Carolina at Chapel Hill.
Kara Keeling, Associate Professor; Ph.D., Indiana.
Scott Pollard, Associate Professor; Ph.D., California, Irvine.
Jean Filetti, Assistant Professor; Ph.D., Toledo.
Terry Lee, Associate Professor; Ph.D., Syracuse.
Roark Mulligan, Associate Professor; Ph.D., Oregon.
Jay Paul, Professor; Ph.D., Michigan State.
Rebecca Wheeler, Assistant Professor; Ph.D., Chicago.

History

Shumet Sihagne, Associate Professor; Ph.D., Illinois.
Tim Morgan, Associate Professor; Ph.D., William and Mary.
Theodora Bostick, Professor; Ph.D., Illinois.
Mario Mazzerella, Professor; Ph.D., American.

Mathematics

Bobbye Bartels, Associate Professor; Ph.D., Illinois.
Stavrula Kostakii-Gailey, Professor; Ed.D., North Carolina at Greensboro.
Martin Bartelt, Professor; Ph.D., Wisconsin.
Brian Bradie, Associate Professor; Ph.D., Clarkson.
Parviz Khalili, Professor; Ph.D., Michigan.
Hongwei Chen, Associate Professor; Ph.D., North Carolina.

THE CITY COLLEGE OF THE CITY UNIVERSITY OF NEW YORK

Graduate Programs

Programs of Study

The City College of New York (CCNY) is similar to a small university offering a rich program of graduate study through the College of Liberal Arts and Science and the Schools of Architecture, Education, and Engineering. The College of Liberal Arts and Science offers the Master of Arts (M.A.) in anthropology (applied urban), art history, biochemistry, biology, chemistry, economics, English (creative writing and English literature), history, international relations, mathematics (pure mathematics, probability, statistics, and operations research), museum studies, music, physics, psychology, sociology, and Spanish and the Master of Fine Arts (M.F.A.) in art. The School of Architecture, Urban Design and Landscape Architecture offers the Master of Architecture and Urban Planning (M.U.P.) in urban design. The Department of Media and Communication Arts offers professional studies leading to the M.F.A. in media arts production. The School of Education offers both the Master of Science in Education (M.S.Ed.) degree in administration and supervision, bilingual education K–12 (Chinese, Haitian-Creole, and Spanish), developmental and remedial reading, early childhood education, elementary education (curriculum and teaching), special education, special education–bilingual, and TESOL-bilingual. In addition, the Master of Arts in Education (M.A.Ed.) degree is offered in art education, English education, science education, mathematics education, and social studies. A bilingual component may be added to each of these programs. The School of Engineering offers both the Master of Engineering (M.E.) and the Master of Science (M.S.) in biomedical, chemical, civil, electrical, and mechanical engineering and computer science. Advanced certificate programs are offered in administration and supervision and developmental and remedial reading. Interdepartmental programs are offered in air pollution control, engineering mechanics, and environmental engineering.

Research Facilities

The Morris Raphael Cohen Library in the North Academic Center houses more than 1 million volumes and is the largest in the CUNY system. Besides its general collection, it contains facilities for architecture, engineering, music, and science. Many library processes are computerized for rapid and efficient access to information. The University-wide Integrated Library System (CUNY Plus) provides online access to most holdings at both City College and all the libraries in the CUNY system. The Marshak Science Building houses more than 200 teaching and research laboratories, a planetarium, a weather station, an electron microscope, laser research facilities, a science and engineering library, and a physical education complex. The School of Engineering houses the Benjamin Levich Institute for Physiochemical Hydrodynamics, the Center for Biomedical Engineering, the Clean Fuels Institute, the Center for Water Resources and Environmental Research, the Institute for Municipal Waste Research, the Earthquake Research Center, and the Institute for Ultrafast Spectroscopy and Lasers. The School of Engineering also provides a wide range of networked computer facilities for both teaching and research.

Financial Aid

Graduate study at CCNY is supported by a combination of student fees, state funds, private and foundation contributions, and federal research grants. The Office of Financial Aid administers federal and state grants, loans, and work-study programs. The College offers a number of nonteaching assistantships and part-time teaching lectureships plus a number of tuition fee waivers. These programs are administered by the Financial Aid Office. For more information, students should contact the Financial Aid Office at 212-650-5819 or Ext. 6656.

Cost of Study

Tuition for state residents is $185 per credit ($2175 full-time per semester). For nonresidents and international students, tuition is $320 per credit ($3800 full-time per semester).

Living and Housing Costs

The College does not provide on-campus housing. Apartments and studios can be found independently throughout the five boroughs of New York City. Estimated living expenses for one year are $8500.

Student Group

The student body reflects a wide range of ethnic and cultural diversity. Students come from more than 100 different countries and speak more than 90 languages. Most are from Africa, Asia, the Caribbean, Latin America, and Europe. The students lend an international flavor to the campus and reflect the ethnic diversity of New York City. This has led City College to develop extensive international linkages. There are student and faculty exchanges with universities in Africa, Asia, Israel, and the Dominican Republic. The total student enrollment is approximately 10,500; of these, 2,416 are graduate students.

Location

The campus occupies 35 acres in upper Manhattan along Convent Avenue in an area known as St. Nicholas Heights in Harlem. It is an urban campus within easy commuting distance of midtown Manhattan.

The College

The City College of New York is the oldest institution in the City University of New York system. Founded in 1847 as the Free Academy, it was first housed at 23rd Street and Lexington Avenue. The name was changed in 1866 to the College of the City of New York; now it is called "City" or "CCNY." Although it originally granted only the bachelor's degree, CCNY began fifty-six years ago to expand its program offering to advanced levels. Since 1961, it has offered a wide range of master's programs, and through the City University of New York offers doctoral study on campus in the sciences, all branches of engineering, computer science, and psychology. CCNY is known for its commitment to academic excellence combined with access to higher education. Immigrants and their children have historically used the College as a vehicle for upward mobility.

Applying

Graduate study is open to well-qualified students who possess a bachelor's degree from an accredited U.S. institution or the equivalent from an international institution, and have an adequate background in the field of study they wish to pursue. Students are evaluated based on their previous academic record, generally with a minimum B average (3.0) required; letters of recommendation from scholars with whom they have studied; and writing samples, portfolios, and auditions (required by some programs only). International students whose native language is not English and who do not have a resident alien card must take the TOEFL (Test of English as a Foreign Language).

Correspondence and Information

Office of Graduate Admissions
Administration Building
The City College of the City University of New York
138th Street and Convent Avenue
New York, New York 10031
Telephone: 212-650-6977
Fax: 212-650-6417
E-mail: admissions@ccny.cuny.edu
World Wide Web: http://www.ccny.cuny.edu/

THE FACULTY

City College's faculty represents a broad range of disciplines, and many of its members have earned the nation's highest forms of recognition—Guggenheim and Fulbright awards—as well as grants amounting to millions of dollars in support of their research and scholarship. The faculty is internationally known for its research activities.

CITY UNIVERSITY

Graduate Division

Programs of Study

City University offers graduate education in six degree areas: Master of Business Administration, Master of Public Administration, Master of Arts, Master of Education, Master in Teaching, and Master of Science. Graduate certificate programs are also available in the areas of business and public administration management and finance, technology, and education. In keeping with City University's mission to make education accessible and convenient, graduate classes may be taken during the day, in the evening, or on weekends. Because classroom attendance is not always possible, City University also offers the majority of its graduate programs through distance learning.

City University's M.B.A. and M.P.A. programs are created with input from industry leaders and incorporate such concepts as technology, marketing, finance, ethics, and global economies. Students may choose from several emphasis areas: financial management, general management, information systems, managerial leadership, human resource management, marketing, individualized study, personal financial planning, or project management. M.P.A. students may choose from the one of six emphasis areas including general management, human resource management, managerial leadership, information systems, individualized study, or project management. Students may also choose to pursue a combined M.B.A/M.P.A. program. M.B.A. and M.P.A. programs require 45–60 credit hours of course work. City University offers a 45-credit-hour M.A. program in the disciplines of business and social services. The M.A. in management focuses on developing leadership capacities and "people management" for achieving organizational goals. The M.A. program in counseling psychology prepares students to counsel individuals and families in a variety of capacities. This program involves classroom and field-based experience and requires 70 credit hours of course work. The Master of Education program enables professionals to continue teaching while enhancing their skills and education. M.Ed. students may choose specialties in curriculum and instruction, educational leadership and principal certification, educational technology, guidance and counseling, and reading and literacy. Weekend classes are team-taught by practitioners offering experiential learning that can be applied directly to the classroom. Many courses in this program are also available by distance learning. The program requires 49–59 credit hours of course work, depending on the student's chosen speciality. The Master in Teaching with Teacher Certification is a unique, 64-credit program that provides for career transition into the field of education for those who already hold a bachelor's degree but lack teacher certification. The program combines classroom teaching and course work and is complete in twelve months of full-time attendance. There is also a special two-year format available for paraeducators. The program prepares students to be teachers in Washington State and is not available through distance learning. The Master of Science program offers majors in three areas: project management, computer systems, and organization and management. The project management program emphasizes systems, processes, and application of critical skills that pertain to the stages and concerns of project management as needed by industry and government. The computer systems program presents students with an in-depth study of the areas of importance to the professional working in informational technology today. Computer systems majors are available in four emphasis areas: C++ programming, Web development, individualized study, or Web programming languages. The organization and management program focuses on developing leadership capacities and "people management" for achieving organizational goals. Master in Science programs require 45 credit hours of course work.

With the exception of the Master of Arts degree, graduate programs generally do not require a thesis. M.Ed. candidates may elect to complete a thesis, project, or internship. M.B.A., M.P.A., and M.S. candidates complete a capstone course and project, with research embedded throughout the course of study.

Research Facilities

City University's library offers an abundance of information resources in paper, microfiche, and electronic formats. Its holdings include 33,000 titles in the general print collection and more than 500,000 titles on microfiche. The library subscribes to 1,600 periodical titles in paper format as well as indexing to several thousand titles online, many of which include full text. Most resources are indexed on the University's Web site. Reference and interlibrary loan services are offered to all students through the library's toll-free telephone number and e-mail. To serve certain education programs, the library maintains branches in Everett, Tacoma, and Vancouver, Washington. In addition, City University has formed cooperative agreements with appropriate libraries to extend library privileges to students in selected cities.

Financial Aid

Whenever possible, City University strives to help its students meet the financial challenges associated with a high-quality education. Several financial assistance programs are available, including student loans, scholarships, federal grants, and Federal Work-Study. More information on these programs and their application deadlines is available through the Student Financial Services Office.

Cost of Study

Graduate tuition for the 2001–02 academic year was $324 per credit, or $972 for a 3-credit course. The tuition rate is the same for both in-class and distance learning study. Other fees may apply, depending on the specific course of study. Tuition rates for the 2002–03 academic year are expected to increase by approximately 6 percent.

Living and Housing Costs

City University does not provide student housing, and the cost of living varies at each location. In the Seattle area, rental expenses for a one-bedroom apartment are approximately $850 per month.

Student Group

The graduate student body is diverse, ranging from students who have just completed baccalaureate work, to those holding advanced degrees, to mature adults returning to school after twenty or more years in the work force (or at home). The average age of the graduate students is 36. Most students are employed full-time and bring a wealth of experience to the classroom. More than 5,000 graduate students are enrolled at all locations. Of these, 52 percent are women and 32 percent are international students.

Location

City University's mission is to make education available to all who desire it. This is accomplished by maintaining a decentralized campus and by establishing locations where there is a demonstrated interest in quality higher education. City University operates from locations throughout the Pacific Northwest, Europe and Asia. Students all over the United States, as well as overseas may complete a degree through the distance learning format.

The University

City University is the largest private institution of higher learning in the Northwest, with more than 35,000 graduates. The University upholds its philosophy that everyone should have access to high-quality higher education by offering programs that are credible and convenient, thus allowing people to enhance their lives through education without interrupting other personal and professional commitments. A not-for-profit institution, City University has been a respected member of the Northwest's academic community since 1973 and is accredited by the Commission on Colleges of the Northwest Association of Schools and Colleges and AACSB International–The Association to Advance Collegiate Schools of Business.

Applying

City University is a professional institution for a professional student body. Because of this, the University has an open door admissions policy. Students may begin a degree program in any quarter, and there is no deadline for applications. The Office of Admissions and Student Services and the Office of International Student Services can provide more information on additional admissions requirements.

Correspondence and Information

Graduate Admissions
City University
11900 NE First Street
Bellevue, Washington 98005
Telephone: 425-637-1010; 425-450-4660 (TTY/TDD)
800-426-5596 (toll-free)
Fax: 425-709-5361
E-mail: info@cityu.edu
World Wide Web: http://www.cityu.edu

THE FACULTY

The combination of academic strength and practical expertise is a characteristic of City University's faculty and ensures the relevancy, currency, and credibility of instruction. Leaders from the business community and law, government, human services, civic, and research organizations are members of the City University faculty. All have strong academic preparation, and most are active professionals in their particular fields.

The University's senior administration and faculty have a University-wide role in quality assurance, academic policies and standards, curricular development, and instructional quality. They oversee the University's hundreds of adjunct faculty members.

Art Rogers, Executive Vice President, Academic Affairs; M.A., Chapman, 1992.
Stephen Guild, Director, Faculty Development; Ph.D., Massachusetts Amherst, 1972.
Verla Peterson, Dean, Library Services; M.A., M.L.S., Wisconsin, 1989.
Scott Mason, Interim Dean, European Programs; M.A., George Mason, 1991.

Gordon Albright School of Education
Margaret Davis, Dean; Ed.D., Seattle, 1980.
John Armenia, Director, M.Ed., Educatonal Leadership and Principal Certification; Ph.D., Washington State, 1978.
Dee Bayne, Senior Faculty, M.Ed., General Programs/Curriculum and Instruction, Reading and Literacy; M.A., Pacific Lutheran, 1972.
Margaret Chow, Director, Master in Teaching; Ed.D., Seattle, 1979.
Paul Drotz, Senior Faculty, Master in Teaching; Ed.D., Idaho, 1973.
Gary Eubanks, Senior Faculty, Master in Teaching; M.Ed., Central Washington, 1974.
Anne Foley, Senior Faculty, M.Ed., Educational Leadership and Principal Certification; Ph.D., Washington (Seattle), 1984.
Dan Hanson, Director, M.Ed., General Programs/Educational Technology; M.A., Lesley, 1994.
Richard Hayden, Senior Faculty, M.Ed., Guidance and Counseling; M.A., California Polytechnic, 1978.
Allen Nakano, Senior Faculty, Master in Teaching; M.Ed., Seattle, 1986.
Fara Nizamani, Senior Faculty, Master in Teaching; M.A., Barry, 1990.
Leann Nolan, Senior Faculty, Master in Teaching; M.Ed., Central Washington, 1969.
Michael Peters, Certification, Endorsement, Placement Specialist; M.Ed., City (Seattle), 1995.
Naomi Petersen, Senior Faculty, Master in Teaching; M.A., Chapman, 1986.
Verl Quast, Director, M.Ed., Guidance and Counseling; M.A., Pacific Lutheran, 1970.
Molly Ross, Senior Faculty, Master in Teaching; M.Ed., City (Seattle), 1995.
Craig Schieber, Senior Faculty, M.Ed., General Programs/Core; Ed.D., Seattle Pacific, 1999.
Barbara Scott-Johnson, Senior Faculty, Master in Teaching; M.Ed., Oregon State, 1973.
Tad Shipman, Senior Faculty, Master in Teaching; M.Ed., Puget Sound, 1979.
Ginny Tresvant, Senior Faculty, Master in Teaching; Ed.D., Seattle, 1979.

School of Business and Management
Carl Adams, Associate Dean; M.B.A., Golden Gate, 1978.
Joseph Flaherty, Director, ESL Language Assistance; M.A.T., Washington (Seattle), 1992.
Teresita Ireneo, Academic Coordinator, Canada; Ph.D., Angeles (Philippines), 1992.
Kathy Disney-Kantner, Director, Project Management; M.B.A., City (Seattle), 1998.
Thomas Cary, Program Director, General Education; J.D., California, Hastings Law, 1993.
Jodey Lingg, Senior Faculty, Economics; M.S., Idaho, 1990.
Carol Leffall, Program Director, Management; M.B.A., City (Seattle), 1995.
Kay Chomic, Senior Faculty, Marketing; M.B.A., Golden Gate, 1991.
Arah Martin, Senior Faculty, Management; M.A., Antioch Seattle, 1989.
Susan Mundy, Senior Faculty, Accounting; M.B.A., St. Martin's, 1998.
Marvin Will, Senior Faculty, Finance; Ph.D., Cambridge, 1975.
Sean Neely, Senior Faculty, Computer Systems; M.I.L.S., Washington (Seattle), 1987.
Belle Lee, Senior Faculty, Computer Systems; M.B.A., National Cheng Chi, 1995.
Ed Razon, Senior Faculty, Computer Systems; M.S., De La Salle (Philippines), 1996.

School of Human Services and Applied Behavioral Science
Elizabeth Fountain, Program Director, Counseling Psychology; M.A., Seattle, 1989.
Arden Henley, Program Director, Counseling Psychology; M.A., Duquesne, 1972.
Karen Langer, Clinic Director; M.Ed., Arizona, 1983.
Karen Lilly, Senior Faculty, Counseling Psychology; M.A., Pepperdine, 1988.
Theresa Wildt, Senior Faculty, Counseling Psychology; M.S., Oregon, 1980.

City University's Administrative Center in Renton, Washington.

CLARION UNIVERSITY OF PENNSYLVANIA

Division of Graduate Studies

Programs of Study

Clarion University awards the degrees of Master of Arts, Master of Business Administration, Master of Education, Master of Science, and Master of Science in Library Science. The Master of Arts is offered in English; the Master of Education in elementary education, mathematics, reading, and science education; and the Master of Science in biology, communication education and mass media technology, communication sciences and disorders, nursing, and special education. The M.S. in nursing is a joint program offered by Clarion, Edinboro, and Slippery Rock University of Pennsylvania. In addition, the Division offers a reading specialist certification program, an elementary education certification program for undergraduate majors in secondary education, a Certificate of Advanced Study in Library Science, school library media certification, and an Instructional Technology Specialist Certificate.

Clarion University is accredited by the Middle States Association of Colleges and Schools. The graduate program in business administration is accredited by AACSB International–The Association to Advance Collegiate Schools of Business. The graduate program in communication sciences and disorders is accredited by the Council on Academic Accreditation of the American Speech-Language-Hearing Association. The graduate program in library science is accredited by the American Library Association. The graduate program in nursing is accredited by the National League for Nursing Accrediting Commission. Clarion University of Pennsylvania is a member of the American Association of State Colleges and Universities and the American Association of Colleges for Teacher Education.

Research Facilities

Facilities supporting graduate programs at Clarion University include modern science laboratories supplied with excellent instrumentation, well-equipped clinical support areas for special education and communication sciences and disorders, a modern business administration building, technologically equipped classrooms for library science, radio and television studios and experimental audiovisual facilities in communication, and a fully equipped word processing lab.

The University libraries grow continuously to meet the instructional, informational, and research needs of the students, faculty members, and others in the academic community. Library resources on the main campus and on the Venango campus include 390,000 printed volumes and 1.88 million nonprint items. The libraries subscribe to more than 4,000 periodicals, including more than 3,000 journals that are available in electronic form over the Internet. In addition, reference sources, government documents, and other information sources can be accessed through the libraries' homepage (http://www.clarion.edu/library). A catalog shared among the fourteen University libraries in the Pennsylvania State System of Higher Education allows students to access the total holdings of that system.

The George R. Lewis Center for Computing Services is the site of Clarion University's central computing system, which utilizes a Digital Equipment Corporation VMS cluster consisting of two model 6460 CPUs plus two Alpha 4100s and two Alpha 2100s. Telephone registration is handled by a Touchnet communication system. Computing Services supports twelve general student access labs located in various buildings across the Clarion and Venango Campuses.

All students have access to the Internet and e-mail and are provided with the capability to create personal Web pages. Academic services for instruction and research include the following computer languages and packages: COBOL, FORTRAN, BASIC, Pascal, TSP, SAS, ADA, C, C++, SPSS, and business simulations.

Financial Aid

Graduate assistantships are awarded on a competitive basis for the nine-month academic year and are renewable. In 2002–03, compensation for a graduate assistant is either $2000 for 10 hours per week and a waiver of one half tuition or $4000 for 20 hours per week and a waiver of full tuition. Interested students should apply to the appropriate academic office or to the Division of Graduate Studies. Additional information regarding financial aid is available through the Office of Financial Aid.

Cost of Study

In 2001–02, graduate tuition and fees for Pennsylvania residents were $2850 per semester for full-time study (9 to 15 hours) or $317 per hour part-time. Out-of-state students paid $4327 for full-time study or $481 per hour part-time. Tuition and fees are subject to change without notice. The cost of books is estimated at $400 per semester.

Living and Housing Costs

University-owned housing is available to graduate students for $1822 per semester. Housing throughout the town of Clarion, though at a premium, is available at costs ranging from $500 to $700 per month. The Office of Residence Life has information regarding private housing. In 2002–03, food service can be obtained in the University Dining Hall for $737 per semester.

Student Group

The total enrollment at Clarion University is more than 6,000 students, of whom more than 470 are graduate students. The graduate enrollment represents many states and several other countries.

Location

Clarion is located high on the Allegheny Plateau overlooking the Clarion River. The rural setting is one of Pennsylvania's most scenic resort areas. The rolling, wooded countryside, interspersed with small farms, offers some of the best outdoor recreational opportunities to be found anywhere in northwestern Pennsylvania, with the Clarion River and its tributaries providing an ideal setting for boating, swimming, and other aquatic sports.

The University

Founded in 1867 as Carrier Seminary, the institution has evolved to a state normal school, to Clarion State Teachers College, to Clarion State College, and finally to Clarion University of Pennsylvania of the State System of Higher Education. Clarion's 99-acre main campus has thirty-eight buildings. It is within the Borough of Clarion, some 2 miles north of Interstate 80 at Exits 9 and 10, and is approximately 2 hours' driving time from the urban centers of Pittsburgh, Erie, and Youngstown. Clarion's 64-acre Venango Campus, located in Oil City, has four buildings, including the modern Suhr Library. The McKeever Environmental Education Center is located in Mercer County.

Applying

Admission materials may be obtained from the Division of Graduate Studies. The application for admission should be received at least thirty days prior to the semester for which the student seeks entrance. Assistantships are generally awarded in the spring for the following fall semester. Application for an assistantship should be made before March 1.

Correspondence and Information

Division of Graduate Studies
Clarion University of Pennsylvania
Clarion, Pennsylvania 16214

Telephone: 814-393-2337
Fax: 814-393-2722
World Wide Web: http://www.clarion.edu/graduatestudies

DEPARTMENT AND PROGRAM HEADS

Brenda Sanders Dédé, Assistant Vice President for Academic Affairs; Ed.D., Texas Southern.

Biology: Andrew Turner, Ph.D., Michigan State.
Business: Robert Balough, Ph.D., Northern Illinois.
Communication Education and Mass Media Technology: Joanne Washington, Ph.D., Indiana Bloomington.
Communication Sciences and Disorders: Janis Jarecki-Liu, Ph.D., Kent State.
Elementary Education: Vickie Harry, Ph.D., Penn State.
English: Herb Luthin, Ph.D., Berkeley.
Library Science: Bernard Vavrek, Ph.D., Pittsburgh.
Mathematics: Benjamin Freed, Ph.D., Kent State.
Nursing: Joyce White, Dr.P.H., Pittsburgh.
Reading: Vickie Harry, Ph.D., Penn State.
Science Education: Bruce Smith, Ph.D., Penn State.
Special Education: Sally M. Sentner, D.Ed., Penn State.

CLARK UNIVERSITY

Graduate School

Programs of Study

The Graduate School of Clark University offers the following degrees: Doctor of Philosophy, Master of Arts, Master of Arts in Education, Master of Arts in Liberal Arts, Master of Business Administration, Master of Public Administration, Master of Science in Finance, and Master of Science in Professional Communications.

The Doctor of Philosophy is conferred in biology, the biomedical sciences (in cooperation with the Worcester Foundation for Biomedical Research and Worcester Polytechnic Institute), chemistry, economics, geography, history, physics, psychology, and women's studies. Postdoctoral training is conducted in geography, psychology, and the sciences. An interdisciplinary Ph.D. program, on an individually designed basis, is also available.

The Master of Arts is awarded in biology, chemistry, education, English, environmental science and policy, history, international development, liberal arts, physics, and psychology. The Master of Business Administration and the Master of Science in Finance are offered in the Graduate School of Management. The Graduate School also offers accelerated B.A./M.A. programs in biology, chemistry, communications, education, environmental affairs, finance, history, international development, management, and physics.

An academic year of study in residence, which is eight courses, is a minimum requirement for a master's degree. One year of full-time study in residence, not less than eight courses beyond the master's, is required for the doctorate. Study in residence is broadly defined as graduate work done at Clark University under the immediate personal supervision of at least one member of the University faculty.

Cooperative work in some departments can be arranged with other colleges in the area as well as with the Worcester Foundation for Biomedical Research and the University of Massachusetts Medical School.

Research Facilities

The Arthur B. Sackler Science Center emphasizes the interdisciplinary nature of the sciences at Clark and provides teaching amphitheaters and seminar rooms, research laboratories, computer facilities, and a science library. The psychology department is also equipped with laboratory and computer facilities. The Graduate School of Geography has a modern cartography laboratory and the Guy H. Burnham Map and Aerial Photography Library.

The Robert Hutchings Goddard Library provides fine quarters for large collections in all graduate fields. Most graduate departments provide study space for graduate students and maintain equipment necessary for study and research.

Financial Aid

Graduate fellowships and scholarships are provided by the University for well-qualified graduate students. Financial aid is also available through grants from special funds, sponsored research grants, and a University graduate loan fund. Several departments participate in national fellowship programs.

Cost of Study

Tuition for the academic year 2002–03 is $25,600. Special fees include health insurance, a diploma fee of $150 for the doctorate and $100 for the master's degree, and a fee of $200 per semester for students who have completed all formal University and departmental residence requirements.

Living and Housing Costs

Living accommodations for both married and single graduate students are available a short distance from the campus at various costs. The University has a limited number of on-campus rooms available for single graduate students.

Student Group

During 2001–02, there were 436 full-time and 381 part-time graduate students in residence, of whom 376 were men and 441 were women. Approximately two thirds of the graduate students receive financial assistance in the form of remission of tuition and/or stipends in amounts that vary depending upon the field of study.

Location

Worcester, a city of diversified industry, is a rapidly emerging educational and cultural center. It has ten schools of higher learning with more than 10,000 students, as well as a modern medical school. Major cultural attractions include the Worcester Art Museum, Higgins Armory Museum, Worcester Historical Society, Worcester Public Library, and American Antiquarian Society. Worcester's Civic Center, the Centrum, offers a wide variety of popular performing artists and athletic events. The Worcester Music Festival presents an annual series of concerts. Theatrical productions, symphonic concerts, light operas, folk festivals, and lecture series are offered regularly. Boston and Cambridge are less than an hour's drive away.

The University

Clark University was founded as a graduate institution in 1887 and awarded its first doctorate in 1891. Undergraduate liberal arts education was established in 1902. The University has twenty-seven major buildings situated on a 35-acre campus. The Robert Hutchings Goddard Library was opened in 1969 and is nationally known for its design as well as its holdings. It was named in honor of the father of the Space Age, who was a Clark alumnus and professor of physics at Clark from 1914 until 1942.

Applying

Applicants from American and other institutions should contact the department in which they expect to do their major work. Application deadlines for admission and financial aid vary by department. Students should contact the department or program of interest for the date. An application fee of $40 is charged. Further information can be obtained from the University's Web site at the address below.

Correspondence and Information

Chair, Department of (specify)
Clark University
Worcester, Massachusetts 01610
World Wide Web: http://www.clarku.edu

THE FACULTY

The chairpersons of departments and the directors of interdepartmental programs offering graduate work at Clark are listed below.

Biology: Dr. Thomas Leonard.
Chemistry: Dr. Mark Turnbull.
Community Development: Dr. William F. Fisher.
Economics: Dr. Wayne B. Gray.
Education: Dr. Thomas Del Prete.
English: Dr. SunHee Gertz.
Environmental Science and Policy: Dr. William F. Fisher.
Geography: Dr. Susan Hanson.
History: Dr. Janette Greenwood.
International Development: Dr. William F. Fisher.
Liberal Arts: Dr. Thomas Massey.
Management: Dr. Edward J. Ottensmeyer.
Physics: Dr. S. Leslie Blatt.
Psychology: Dr. Jaan Valsiner.
Public Administration: Dr. Max Hess.
Women's Studies: Dr. Cynthia L. Enloe.

CLEVELAND STATE UNIVERSITY

College of Graduate Studies and Research

Programs of Study

Cleveland State University (CSU) offers master's degrees in accountancy and financial information systems, applied communication theory and methodology, biology, business administration (graduate certificates in health care administration; health care total quality management and continuous quality improvement; urban real estate development and finance; and data-driven marketing planning available), chemical engineering, chemistry, civil engineering, engineering mechanics, computer and information science, economics, education (counselor education; curriculum and instruction; educational administration; postsecondary education and supervision; and a graduate certificate in adult learning and development), electrical and computer engineering, English, environmental engineering, environmental science, environmental studies, health sciences, physical therapy, occupational therapy, (graduate certificates in ergonomics/human factors; and culture, communication, and health care available), history (art history specialization available), industrial and manufacturing engineering, labor relations and human resources, mathematics, mechanical engineering, music, philosophy (graduate certificate in advanced bioethics available), physics, psychology (clinical counseling and experimental psychology, post-master's in school psychology, graduate certificate in gerontology, and professional diversity training available), public administration, public health, social work, sociology, Spanish, speech pathology, urban planning, and urban studies (graduate certificates in urban geographic information systems, nonprofit management, urban economic development, and urban real estate development and finance available). Three post-master's programs grant degrees in educational administration, counseling and pupil personnel administration, and school psychology beyond the master's level. Doctoral programs in biology, business administration, clinical/analytical chemistry, engineering (specialization in applied biomedical engineering available), urban education, and urban studies and public affairs also are offered. Most master's degree programs have a 32-semester-hour minimum requirement and can be completed in one year of full-time study. Part-time graduate students constitute a large component of graduate enrollment. Graduate courses generally are offered in the late afternoon and evening for the benefit of the part-time student.

Research Facilities

The Science Research Center provides graduate students in biology and chemistry with modern laboratories and up-to-date research equipment. In addition, the Cleveland Clinic Foundation Research Institute is a partner in the research offerings in the clinical chemistry, engineering, and biology doctoral degree programs. The Cleveland MetroHealth Center is a partner in the master's degree programs in chemistry and speech pathology. The NASA-Glenn Research Center annually sponsors more than $5 million in research at the University. The Advanced Manufacturing Center provides an opportunity for collaborative research sponsored by the College of Engineering and private industry. The University Library supports Cleveland State's instructional and research programs through resources and services made available to students both in-house and over the Internet. The library contains more than 900,000 volumes of print resources, 7,200 serial subscriptions (both online and in print), more than 100 online research databases, 670,000 microforms, and substantial holdings of sound recordings, curriculum materials, art slides, films, videotapes, and multimedia products. The library provides more than 100 public computers connected to the Internet for access to online resources. Information on library holdings is available online through SCHOLAR at http://www. scholar.csuohio.edu/.

Financial Aid

Graduate teaching, research, and administrative assistantships are available in most departments that offer graduate degrees. A full-time graduate assistant may be awarded a stipend ($3480 minimum per term for master's level, and $3900 minimum per term for doctoral level in 2001–02) in addition to tuition support. Graduate assistants are required to provide 10, 15, or 20 hours of service per week in the department's research and/or teaching program. Graduate tuition grants also are available to qualified students. Funds permitting, Doctoral Dissertation Research Expense Awards and Travel Awards to present research at professional meetings and conferences are available on a competitive basis to qualified doctoral students. There also are funds awarded to graduate students on the basis of need through the Financial Aid Office.

Cost of Study

Graduate courses cost $263 per semester credit hour for Ohio residents and $520 for nonresidents in 2001–02. Tuition for a full-time load (13–16 semester credit hours) was $3419 per term for Ohio residents and $6763 for nonresidents.

Living and Housing Costs

Dormitory accommodations are available for full-time students; however, there are no housing facilities for married students. Convenient off-campus apartments in downtown Cleveland or in the nearby suburbs are available at varying costs. The campus is easily accessible by public transportation.

Student Group

Approximately 16,000 students attend CSU, of whom approximately 5,000 are enrolled in graduate work.

Location

Cleveland State University, an urban university, enjoys a close relationship with its community. Cooperative work-study programs and student internships with community institutions are available. Because the campus is located to downtown Cleveland and near university Circle, students can easily take advantage of the city's outstanding cultural offerings. The famed Cleveland Orchestra, the Playhouse Square Foundation theaters, the Cleveland Playhouse, and Karamu House present full seasons of concerts, drama, and dance. Students also have access to the Cleveland Museum of Art, the Museum of Natural History, the Cleveland Historical Society, the Cleveland Health Museum, Cleveland Public Library, the Great Lakes Science Center, and the S.S. Mather Maritime Museum.

The University

Cleveland State University was created in 1964 by an act of the Ohio General Assembly. University facilities include the Main Classroom Building; the twenty-story Rhodes Tower, which houses faculty offices, the library, University Center; the Business College and Law Library complex, the Convocation Center, the Cole Center, the Health Science and Physical Education complex, the Intramural Sports Center, an outdoor soccer field and tennis courts, the Theater Arts Building, the Law College, the Music and Communication Building, and the Urban Affairs complex.

The University consists of six academic colleges: The College of Arts and Sciences, the James J. Nance College of Business Administration, the College of Education, the Fenn College of Engineering, the Maxine Goodman Levin College of Urban Affairs, and the Cleveland-Marshall College of Law. Thirty-seven master's degrees, six doctoral degrees, and five additional advanced degrees and 12 graduate certificate programs are offered. Special programs include continuing education, women's studies, cooperative education, student development, and black studies. The graduate faculty has more than 500 members.

Applying

Graduate applicants are required to have a 2.75 cumulative grade point average or better (on a 4.0 scale) and may be asked to submit the results of the Graduate Record Examination, Graduate Management Admissions Test, Miller Analogies Test, or English language proficiency tests, as appropriate. At the time of application, students must submit a $30 nonrefundable application fee payable in U.S. currency. Applicants must submit transcripts from all colleges previously attended and two recommendation letters as appropriate. Applications, including transcripts, and all supporting materials must be received in the Office of Graduate Admissions by July 26 for fall term, December 16 for spring term, and April 17 for summer term, with the following exceptions: the deadline for the D.B.A. program is January 15 for fall admission only; for the professional psychology program, January 15 for fall admission only; for the speech pathology program, March 1 for summer or fall admission only; for the Ph.D. in Urban Education program, March 15; for social work, March 15, for the accelerated M.B.A. program, June 1, and for the Executive M.B.A. program, July 1.

Correspondence and Information

Office of Graduate Admissions
Campus Box G
Cleveland State University
1983 East 24th Street
Cleveland, Ohio 44115-2440
World Wide Web: http://www.csuohio.edu/gradcollege

GRADUATE FACULTY DEANS AND DEPARTMENT CHAIRPERSONS

Vice Provost for Research and Dean of Graduate Studies: Mark A. Tumeo, Ph.D.
Associate Dean of Graduate Studies and Director of Graduate Admissions: William C. Bailey, Ph.D.
Director of Graduate Programs: Dianne Rahm, Ph.D.

Arts and Sciences: Earl Anderson, Ph.D., Dean (Interim).
Art: George Mauersberger, M.F.A., Chairperson.
Biological, Geological, and Environmental Sciences: Michael Gates, Ph.D., Chairperson.
Chemistry: Stan Duraj, Ph.D., Chairperson.
Communications: Susan Kogler-Hill, Ph.D., Chairperson.
Economics: Jon D. Harford, Ph.D., Chairperson.
English: John Gerlach, Ph.D., Chairperson (Interim).
Health Sciences: Bette Bonder, Ph.D., Chairperson (Interim).
History: Donald Ramos, Ph.D., Chairperson.
Mathematics: Sherwood D. Silliman, Ph.D., Chairperson.
Modern Languages: Anita Stoll, Ph.D., Chairperson.
Music: Eric Ziolek, Ph.D., Chairperson.
Nursing: Noreen Frisch, Ph.D., Chairperson.
Philosophy: Jane McIntyre, Ph.D., Chairperson.
Physics: Myron Kaufman, Ph.D., Chairperson.
Political Science: Donald E. Schulz, Ph.D., Chairperson.
Psychology: Mark H. Ashcraft, Ph.D., Chairperson.
Social Work: Maggie Jackson, Ph.D., Chairperson.
Sociology: Peter Meiksins, Ph.D., Chairperson.
Speech Pathology: Benjamin Wallace, Ph.D., Chairperson.

Business Administration: Rosemary Ramsey, Ph.D. (Interim).
Accelerated M.B.A.: Patricia Hite, Director.
Doctor of Business Administration Director: Augustine Lado, Ph.D.
Executive M.B.A.: Patricia Hite, Director.
M.B.A. Director: Benoy Joseph, Ph.D.
Master of Public Health (M.P.H.): Brenda Stevenson Marshall, Ph.D.
Accounting and Business Law: Lawrence A. Kreiser, Ph.D., Chairperson.
Computer and Information Science: Donald G. Golden, Ph.D. Chairperson.
Finance: Lawrence A. Kreiser, Ph.D., Chairperson.
Health-Care Administration: Brenda Stevenson-Marshall, Ph.D., Chairperson.
Management & Labor Relations: Ronald Coccari, Ph.D., Chairperson. (Interim).
Marketing: Marian Webb, Ph.D., Chairperson.
Operations Management & Business Statistics: Ronald Coccari, Ph.D., Chairperson. (Interim).

Education: James McLoughlin, Ph.D., Dean.
Ph.D. Program Director: Carl F. Rak, Ph.D.
Counseling, Administration, Supervision, and Adult Learning: Elliott R. Ingersoll, Ph.D., Chairperson.
Curriculum and Foundations: Francine Peterman, Ph.D., Chairperson.
Health, Physical Education, Recreation, and Dance: Vincent J. Melograno Jr., Ed.D.
Specialized Instructional Programs: Clifford T. Bennett, Ph.D., Chairperson.

Engineering: John Hemann, Ph.D., Dean (Interim).
Doctoral Program Director: Joan M. Bellovich, Ph.D.
Chemical Engineering: Orhan Talu, Ph.D., Chairperson.
Civil and Environmental Engineering: Paul Bosela, Ph.D., Chairperson.
Electrical and Computer Engineering: Eugenio Villaseca, Ph.D., Chairperson.
Engineering Technology: Donald J. Anthan, MSEE, Chairperson. (Acting).
Industrial and Manufacturing Engineering: Joseph Svestka, Ph.D., Chairperson.
Mechanical Engineering: Mounir B. Ibrahim, Ph.D., Chairperson.

Law: Steven Steinglass, J.D., Dean.

Urban Affairs: Mark S. Rosentraub, Ph.D., Dean.

COLLEGE OF CHARLESTON, THE GRADUATE SCHOOL

Graduate Studies

Programs of Study

The College of Charleston offers sixteen master's-level programs with the following five degrees: Master of Arts (M.A.), Master of Arts in Teaching (M.A.T.), Master of Education (M.Ed.), Master of Public Administration (M.P.A.), and Master of Science (M.S.). These degrees are offered in the general program areas of accountancy, bilingual legal interpreting, computer and information sciences, education, English, environmental studies, history, marine biology, mathematics, and public administration. In addition, the College offers four certificate programs, two in English for speakers of other languages (ESOL) one in bilingual legal interpreting, and one in applied mathematics.

The School of Business and Economics offers the M.S. in accountancy. The School of Education offers the M.A.T. and M.Ed. in early childhood education, elementary education, and special education. The School of Humanities and Social Sciences offers the M.A. in bilingual legal interpreting, computer and information sciences, English, and history and the M.P.A. The School of Sciences and Mathematics offers the M.S. in marine biology and mathematics and jointly offers two interdisciplinary degrees: the M.Ed. in science and mathematics (for teachers) with the School of Education and the M.S. in environmental studies with the School of Humanities and Social Sciences.

Research Facilities

General research at the College of Charleston is supported by the main library on campus, which houses books, periodicals, government documents, microtexts, and special collections in all subject areas that support the curriculum. In addition, the Marine Resources Library at Fort Johnson houses extensive holdings of the College of Charleston, the South Carolina Department of Natural Resources, and NOAA's Fisheries Science Center. Also, through an agreement with other local institutions, students have access to the collections of four other local schools. There are several computing centers on campus that serve students seven days a week. These centers offer a wide range of services, including technical assistance, general Internet connectivity, e-mail, and text and graphics scanning.

Marine biology students study, attend classes, and conduct research at the Grice Marine Laboratory at Fort Johnson on the Charleston harbor. In addition to the facilities of the Grice Laboratory, students have the opportunity to utilize the other facilities at Fort Johnson, such as those supported by NOAA and the South Carolina Department of Natural Resources. The College is a member of Oak Ridge Associated Universities (ORAU), a consortium of colleges and universities that help students and faculty members gain access to federal research facilities throughout the country.

Financial Aid

The College uses the Free Application for Federal Student Aid (FAFSA) to award all federal- and state-sponsored financial aid programs offered through the School. Graduate students are eligible for direct federal loans through the Office of Financial Assistance and Veterans Affairs. The College's graduate programs also offer assistantships and other fellowships and awards. Information on these is usually specific to each program.

Cost of Study

Students should contact the Graduate School Office for 2002–03 tuition and fee information.

Living and Housing Costs

Other than dormitory space available at Grice Marine Laboratory, graduate students must make arrangements for their own accommodations in Charleston. The Residence Life Office offers an accommodations guide, and there are rental properties close to the downtown campus. Depending upon the number of students sharing a living space and the type of housing, costs range upward from $400 per month, exclusive of utilities.

Student Group

In fall 2002, there were more than 1,700 graduate students and 10,000 undergraduate students at the College of Charleston. The student population represents all fifty states and American possessions and sixty-five other countries.

Location

The College is located in beautiful, historic downtown Charleston, a community founded on the Atlantic coast more than 300 years ago. While steeped in the history and traditions of the Lowcountry, the Charleston tri-county area is a major urban center of South Carolina. The cultural life of the city includes symphony, dance, and museums. Charleston hosts the Spoleto Festival, U.S.A.; the MOJA Arts Festival; the Southeastern Wildlife Exposition; the famous Cooper River Bridge Run; and a new state-of-the-art aquarium. Popular entertainers perform regularly throughout the area, and the College's School of the Arts offers more than 150 performances, lectures, and exhibits during the year. The region's subtropical climate makes outdoor activities enjoyable throughout the year. There are beaches, resorts, parks, and wildlife refuges within easy driving distance of the city. Hiking, sailing, kayaking, and golfing are a few of the available activities, along with exploring old plantations and other historic sites.

The College

Since its inception in 1770, the College of Charleston has been committed to offering a strong liberal arts education. The College is currently developing proposals for new programs in arts management, computer science, historic preservation, and middle school education.

Applying

Individuals interested in applying should thoroughly acquaint themselves with the application deadlines for the program in which they are interested. These deadlines are found in the *Graduate Catalog,* which can be seen on the College's Web page, listed below, or by e-mailing the Graduate School Office to request a printed packet. The application fee is $35 for all programs except bilingual legal interpreting, which has a $50 application fee.

Correspondence and Information

Graduate School Office
College of Charleston
Suite 310, Randolph Hall
Charleston, South Carolina 29424

Telephone: 843-953-5614
Fax: 843-953-1434
E-mail: gradsch@cofc.edu
World Wide Web: http://www.cofc.edu/gradschool

AREAS OF RESEARCH

Accountancy: The faculty research interests in the M.S. in accountancy program include accounting, business law, economics, finance, marketing, not-for-profit, systems, and taxation. Courses are offered in financial reporting and theory, information systems, tax research, auditing, organization behavior, managerial accounting, and policy.

Bilingual Legal Interpreting: The faculty of the bilingual legal interpreting program is interested in legal interpretation and translation, language and culture, law and legal systems, Spanish, and Spanish education. A comprehensive, sequenced, and integrated series of courses is designed to provide students with the competencies, techniques, and research skills required of a professional legal interpreter.

Computer and Information Sciences: Research interests among the faculty from both campuses are current and diverse. They include database, distributed computing, computational geometry, real-time 3-D perspective visualization, global optimization, human-computer interaction, networks, parallel algorithms, programming languages, software engineering, design theory, and artificial intelligence. The faculty has ties to various private industry and government organizations within the Charleston area.

Early Childhood, Elementary, and Special Education: The faculty members in the programs in education focus their research on areas such as behavior disorders, early childhood education, elementary education, special education (behavior disorders, learning disabilities, and mental disabilities), and technology in education. Professors prepare M.A.T. degree candidates with no previous background in education to become certified teachers and help students who have completed all requirements for certification to seek the M.Ed. degree. The programs in early childhood and elementary education focus on the education of children from preschool to grade 8. The fundamental and specialized curricula in elementary education are designed to develop the competencies needed to teach the major academic areas of the elementary curriculum. The special education programs provide three areas of study within special education, emotional disabilities, learning disabilities, and mental disabilities. There is ample fieldwork built into the special education program to allow students to have experience working with exceptional children.

Science and Mathematics for Teachers: The faculty for this program is interdisciplinary and highly diverse, with research interests that include astronomy, biological sciences, chemistry (physical and analytical), curriculum development, education policy studies, education technology, elementary education, geology and mineralogy, marine biology, mathematics and mathematical modeling, mathematics education, middle and secondary science education, physics, and special education. The faculty helps certified teachers build science and mathematics concepts in K through 12 classrooms.

English: The faculty research interests include African-American literature; American and British literature, including modern, eighteenth-, and nineteenth-century literature; creative writing; English language; European fiction; poetry; Southern literature; and women's literature. Professors offer graduate-level instruction in British literature, American literature, and composition and rhetoric.

Environmental Studies: Faculty research interests include astronomy, biological sciences, biostatistics, chemistry (physical and analytical), climatology, coastal plain stratigraphy, environmental politics, geology, groundwater modeling, hydrogeology, mineralogy, marine biology, molecular ecology, physics, population biology, policymaking, problem definition and political power, and public administration. The interdisciplinary Master of Science in environmental studies program offers two major tracks: policy and science. The program's aim is to ensure that students are exposed to the complex, multidisciplinary arenas within which environmental issues are analyzed, understood, debated, and addressed.

History: Faculty research interests in history include American, Native American, Latin American, modern Europe, modern Germany, military, intellectual, U.S. South, Far East, Russia, nineteenth-century, China, social, and cultural. The program offers students historical studies with concentrations in United States, European, Asian, African, and Latin American history.

Marine Biology: Research areas include biological oceanography, marine environmental sciences, fisheries, aquaculture, marine ornithology, marine biomedical sciences, marine biotechnology, resource management, benthic ecology, evolutionary biology, and marine biodiversity. The program provides the knowledge and skills that allow students to either continue their education toward further graduate study or to pursue professional employment in the marine sciences field. Because of the broad scope of faculty interests and facilities, an extremely wide variety of research and training opportunities are available on the relatively unspoiled and biologically rich South Carolina coast.

Mathematics: The faculty members have research interests in areas such as statistics, time series, number theory, numerical linear algebra and optimization, functional analysis, dynamical systems, nonlinear elasticity, topology, probability, math logic, logic/set theory, statistical quality control, and complex/real analysis. Professors help prepare students for professional opportunities in business, industry, and government that require training in the mathematical sciences at the graduate level. The program provides a good background for those who might eventually pursue a doctoral-level degree and provides an option for secondary school teachers to enhance their math skills. Students can enhance their skills in areas such as applied mathematics, algebra and discrete mathematics, computational mathematics, analysis, and probability and statistics.

Public Administration: Areas of faculty research interest include organizational theory, state and local administration, public management, environmental politics, statistical methodology, intergovernmental relations, public policy process, budgetary process, administrative theory, administrative law, personnel, financial administration, and computer applications. The M.P.A. program concentrates on public administration and public policy, with a goal of preparing graduates for careers as professional public administrators. The program trains students to assume increasingly complex responsibilities at the local, state, and federal level and places a strong emphasis on developing skills for effective public management while remaining sensitive to the ethical roles and responsibilities of public administrators.

COLLEGE OF MOUNT ST. JOSEPH

Graduate Studies

Programs of Study

The College of Mount St. Joseph offers three graduate degrees: a Master of Arts in education and a Master of Arts in religious studies with a concentration in spiritual and pastoral care, and a Master of Science (M.S.) in organizational leadership.

The master's degree program in education is designed to meet the needs of college graduates who are experienced or prospective teachers. An intensive course of study integrates theory, experience, and field work in diverse educational settings. The Master of Arts in education degree is earned through successful completion of a minimum of 34 to 37 semester hours of graduate credit and a comprehensive examination. Areas of concentration include art, inclusive early childhood education, professional development, professional foundations, reading, and special education. Courses are offered in late afternoons, evenings, summer, and occasionally on weekends.

The master's degree program in religious studies with a concentration in spiritual and pastoral care is designed to enhance and integrate the interpersonal, systems, and theological skills of health-care professionals, educators, and ministers who serve in diverse populations and social contexts. Small classes, academic advising, and personal attention provide an environment conducive to learning, the development of pastoral competence, and a true sense of community. Core courses are offered on weekends, so adult students can continue working while completing degree requirements (36 credit hours) in two years. A final project, designed to blend theory with practice and academic studies with work experience, includes the research, design, implementation, and evaluation of a pastoral ministry area based on the learning accomplished in the program. This final project is linked as closely as possible to the student's present or projected ministry and is completed under the supervision of program faculty members.

The Master of Science degree in organizational leadership takes a multidisciplinary approach and emphasizes values, spirituality, and ethics. It is designed for individuals who have, or aspire to, leadership roles within their current organization. This program focuses on effective leadership skills to utilize in any type of organization. Areas of study include leadership, people and organizations, organizational decision making, and technology. The M.S. requires 39 credit hours and can be completed in less than two years. All courses are offered on Saturdays.

Research Facilities

The Mount's Archbishop Alter Library owns more than 90,000 items and provides patrons with access to materials held in other libraries as well. Two services, document delivery and interlibrary loan, facilitate the prompt acquisition of materials available anywhere in the country.

With FOCUS, the library's online public access catalog, patrons may search for materials available at the College library and other area libraries. OHIOLINK, a statewide network of public universities and private colleges, provides quick access to library books. Library patrons have full access to the World Wide Web and the Internet.

Financial Aid

Financial aid is available to all students enrolled at the Mount, with priority given to those who demonstrate financial need. Any student requesting financial aid must complete a financial aid application. In addition, the Sisters of Charity award three $1000 scholarships each year to female graduate students in education or religious studies. To qualify, applicants must take at least 12 credit hours during the academic year.

A special grant is available to any student enrolled in the religious studies graduate program who is a paid or volunteer minister serving in a congregation, hospital, health-care facility, social service agency, diocese, or educational institution. This College of Mount St. Joseph Ministry Tuition Grant reduces tuition during the summer semester to $175 per credit hour and tuition in all other semesters to $225 per credit hour. Verification of employment/volunteer service and submission of an FAFSA form are required.

A tuition voucher is available to students who enroll in the graduate education program. The voucher reduces tuition on the first class in the graduate education program to $100 per credit hour.

Cost of Study

Tuition is $382 per credit hour for education and religious studies and $425 per credit hour for organizational leadership studies.

Living and Housing Costs

There are numerous apartments for rent in the immediate area, and the cost of living is very reasonable.

Student Group

Total enrollment at the Mount exceeds 2,300. There are currently 160 graduate students—32 men and 128 women. Sixty-three percent of graduate students are part-time, 37 percent are full-time, and 36 percent receive financial aid. Graduate students generally come from Ohio, Kentucky, and Indiana.

Location

The Mount's campus is located in suburban Cincinnati, just 7 miles west of downtown. Students can enjoy all the arts, entertainment, sports, fine restaurants, and shopping of a major metropolitan city.

The College

The College of Mount St. Joseph is a Catholic college that provides its students with an interdisciplinary liberal arts and professional education emphasizing values, integrity, and social responsibility. Small class sizes encourage individualized learning, and the Mount offers its students opportunities for career experience, leadership development, and service learning as well as a wide range of student activities. In addition to the graduate programs, the Mount offers forty-three bachelor's programs, ten associate programs, and a Master of Physical Therapy program (which requires undergraduate entrance).

The Mount is fully accredited by the North Central Association of Colleges and Schools and is consistently ranked among the top Midwest regional universities for quality, value, and a high graduation rate by *U.S. News & World Report* in its guide to America's Best Colleges. In addition, the Mount is one of a select group of 100 colleges and universities nationwide to be recognized in *The Templeton Guide* for building the character of its students. *Rugg's Recommendation on the Colleges* ranked the Mount as one of the nation's finest choices for "selective" programs in art, business, education, and nursing.

Applying

Students interested in applying should contact the appropriate department directly to obtain application forms and other departmental materials.

Correspondence and Information

Office of Admission
College of Mount St. Joseph
5701 Delhi Road
Cincinnati, Ohio 45233

Telephone: 513-244-4805
800-654-9314 (toll-free)
World Wide Web: http://www.msj.edu

THE FACULTY

Religious Studies Department (John Trokan, D.Min., Associate Professor and Chair; Telephone: 513-244-4496; Fax: 513-244-4788; E-mail: john_trokan@mail.msj.edu)

Sister Mary Bookser, S.C., Adjunct; Ph.D, Union (Ohio).
Florence Caffrey Bourg, Assistant Professor; Ph.D., Boston College.
Kay Clifton, Professor; Ph.D., Iowa.
Alan deCourcy, Assistant Professor; D.Min., United Theological Seminary (Ohio).
Sister Marge Kloos, S.C., Assistant Professor; D.Min., United Theological Seminary (Ohio).
Deirdre LaNoue, Associate Professor; Ph.D., Baylor.
John Trokan, Associate Professor and Chair; D.Min., St. Mary of the Lake Seminary.

Education Department (Clarissa Rosas, Ph.D., Associate Professor and Chair; Telephone: 513-244-4812; Fax: 513-244-4867; E-mail: clarissa_rosas@mail.msj.edu)

Sharon Kesterson Bollen, Professor; Ed.D., Cincinnati.
Jerry Boyle, Adjunct; Ed.D., Cincinnati.
Lowell Flint, Associate Professor; Ed.D., Duke.
Michele C. Gerent, Assistant Professor; Ph.D., Florida.
James Green, Assistant Professor; Ph.D., Ohio State.
Mary Ann Haubner, Professor; Ph.D., Purdue.
Judith Z. Hotz, Instructor; Ed.D., Cincinnati.
Liz Hunter, Adjunct; Ph.D., Miami (Ohio).
Pam Korte, Adjunct; M.A., Louisville.
Craig Lloyd, Adjunct; M.F.A., Cincinnati.
Daniel Mader, Professor; M.A., Cincinnati.
Vesta Mickel, Associate Professor; Ed.D., Cincinnati.
Teresa Orloff, Assistant Professor; Ed.D., Cincinnati.
Barbara Reid, Associate Professor; Ph.D., Illinois.
Clarissa Rosas, Associate Professor and Chair, Ph.D., New Mexico.
Richard Sparks, Associate Professor; Ed.D., Cincinnati.
Sandra L. Starkey, Associate Professor; Ph.D., Claremont.
Sister Francis Marie Thrailkill, O.S.U, Associate Professor; Ed.D, Nova.
Loyola Walter, Assistant Professor; M.F.A., Cincinnati.

Organizational Leadership Department (Lonnie Supnick, Ph.D., Director; Telephone: 513-244-4330; Fax: 513-244-4654; E-mail: lonnie_supnick@mail.msj.edu)

John Ballard, Associate Professor; Ph.D., Purdue.
Yaping Gao, Adjunct Instructor; Ph.D., Purdue.
Michele Geiger, Assistant Professor; Ph.D., Purdue.
Kim Hunter, Assistant Professor; M.B.A., Toledo.
John Miriam Jones, S.C., Adjunct Instructor; Ph.D., Notre Dame.
Scott Sportsman, Associate Professor; Ph.D., Illinois.
Ron White, Professor; Ph.D., Kentucky.

COLLEGE OF MOUNT SAINT VINCENT

Graduate Studies

Programs of Study

The College of Mount Saint Vincent offers three graduate degree programs: a Master of Science (M.S.) in allied health studies, nursing, and urban/multicultural education.

The M.S. in allied health studies program offers six concentrations: addictions, child and family health, community health education, counseling, health-care management, and health-care systems and policy. This unique major is rooted in health psychology. It allows students with baccalaureate degrees in diverse disciplines to pursue a career-oriented program that enables them to work in health-related settings, including positions in hospitals, clinics, private practices, health maintenance organizations, and pain clinics.

The M.S. in nursing program offers four programs of study: clinical nurse specialist, nursing administration, and adult and family nurse practitioner studies. These programs prepare nurses for the complex decision making process necessary in today's health-care environment by incorporating three graduate business courses into the curriculum.

The M.S. in education focuses on urban/multicultural education and is a values-centered program reflecting the belief that learning and culture are inseparable, as are relationships among learner, teacher, environment, and purpose for learning.

Research Facilities

The library contains more than 170,000 volumes, 616 current periodical subscriptions, 9,585 microfilms, and 6,000 audiovisual units (recordings, films, and cassettes). Other facilities include the Audiovisual Center, the Special Collections room, and the Curriculum Center. The library has access via computer to bibliographic information in libraries across the country.

Financial Aid

Full-time or part-time students may be eligible for New York's Tuition Assistance Program (TAP), which is an income-based program available to families who have resided in New York State at least one calendar year. The College also recommends Stafford Student Loans. A number of lab assistantships are also available to qualified nursing students on an annual basis.

Cost of Study

Graduate tuition for the 2002–03 academic year is $520 per credit for students in education and allied health studies and $550 per credit for nursing students. There is a graduate nursing clinical fee (NURS-600) of $130 and technology fees of $50 for full-time students and $25 for part-time students.

Living and Housing Costs

Room and board for the 2002–03 academic year are $7500. The cost of books, supplies, and personal items is approximately $1500. Married students are required to live off campus.

Student Group

The graduate programs enroll a total of 350 students, of which 25 are full-time and 325 are part-time.

Location

The campus, in the Riverdale area of the Bronx in New York City, features 70 acres of rolling lawns, wooded fields, stone walls, and several buildings designated as New York City landmarks. The campus is 11 miles from mid-Manhattan and easily accessible by subway or bus, offering students an array of cultural and recreational opportunities.

The College

College of Mount Saint Vincent, a coeducational liberal arts college, is a private, independent institution in a public trust. Founded by the Sisters of Charity of New York in 1847 as an academy, it became a four-year college in 1910 and coeducational in 1974. The Graduate School's mission is to provide students the opportunity for academic excellence and professional leadership.

Applying

Applicants for graduate study must hold a bachelor's degree from an accredited school, have earned an undergraduate GPA of at least 3.0 and/or have completed 6 graduate credits as a nonmatriculated student at the College with a grade of at least 3.0 in each course. Each candidate must also pass a Writing Sample Exam and submit a $50 application fee, two references, and an official undergraduate transcript.

Correspondence and Information

Admissions Office
College of Mount Saint Vincent
6301 Riverdale Avenue
Riverdale, New York 10471-1093
Telephone: 718-405-3267
800-605-CMSV (toll-free)
Fax: 718-549-7945
E-mail: admissns@cmsv.edu
World Wide Web: http://www.cmsv.edu

THE FACULTY AND THEIR RESEARCH

Susan Apoid, Associate Professor and Chair of Graduate Nursing; Ph.D., Adelphi.
Eileen M. Brady, Associate Professor of Psychology; Ph.D., Fordham.
Barbara Jaffin Cohen, Professor and Director of Nursing Program; Ed.D., Columbia.
Carol DeFelice, Associate Professor of Nursing; Ed.D., Columbia.
Rita Scher Dytell, Professor of Allied Health Studies; Ph.D., CUNY Graduate Center.
Sr. Margaret Egan, S.C., Professor and Chairperson of Teacher Education; Ed.D., Yeshiva.
Beverly C. Fineman, Associate Professor of Nursing; Ed.D., Columbia.
Mary Fuller, Associate Professor and Associate Chairperson of Psychology; Ph.D., Fordham.
Eva Humbach, Visiting Instructor of Nursing; M.S. Pace.
Muriel Kneeshaw, Associate Professor of Nursing; Ed.D., Columbia.
Deborah Kramer, Associate Professor of Nursing; Ed.D., Columbia.
Edward H. Meyer, Professor and Chairperson of Economics and Business; M.B.A., J.D., NYU.
Arlene Moliterno, Associate Professor of Teacher Education; Ph.D., Fordham.
Rosemarie Pace, Associate Professor of Teacher Education; Ed.D., St. John's (New York); A.P.D., Fordham.
Dale Patrias, Associate Professor of Sociology; Ph.D., NYU.
Ron Scapp, Associate Professor of Teacher Education and Director of Graduate Education Program, Ph.D., SUNY at Stony Brook.
Kathleen J. Schmalz, Assistant Professor of Health Education; Ed.D., Columbia.
Barbara Shimmel, Professor and Chairperson of Health Education; Ed.D., Columbia.
Justine Taddeo, Associate Professor of Nursing; Ed.D., Columbia.
Bridget Weeks, Assistant Professor of Nursing; M.S.N., CUNY, Lehman.
Lizzette Zayas, Assistant Professor of Business and Teacher Education; J.D., Rutgers.

THE COLLEGE OF NEW JERSEY

Graduate Programs

Programs of Study

The College of New Jersey offers the following advanced degrees: Master of Arts (M.A.) in audiology, counselor education, English, and speech pathology; Master of Arts in Teaching (M.A.T.) in elementary education, secondary education, and special education; Master of Education (M.Ed.) in educational leadership, elementary education, health education, learning disabilities teacher/consultant, physical education, reading, secondary education, special education, and teaching English as a second language; Master of Science (M.S.) in educational technology; Master of Science in Nursing (M.S.N.) in adult nurse practitioner and family nurse practitioner; and Educational Specialist (Ed.S.) in marriage and family therapy.

Graduate certificate programs are offered in alcohol and chemical dependency counseling; bilingual education; family nurse practitioner; learning disabilities teacher/consultant studies; reading specialist; reading teacher; school licensure, preschool–grade 3; school nurse; secondary education; substance awareness coordinator; supervisor; teacher certification for international schools; teacher of the handicapped; and teaching English as a second language.

Graduate courses are given in the evenings for the convenience of the majority of graduate students, who are pursuing degrees while being employed full-time.

Research Facilities

The Roscoe L. West Library houses more than 560,000 volumes and 200,000 microforms and subscribes to more than 1,400 periodicals. The library subscribes to more than 75 electronic indexes, including full-text resources. The Endeavor/Voyager library online catalog and an interlibrary loan program further extend the library's research resources. The library is an active participant in a number of library networks, including the New Jersey Virtual Academic Library Environment (VALE).

The School of Education houses a speech, language, and hearing center. The College has met the challenge of the computer field's phenomenal growth with installations of computer facilities in each of its seven schools.

Financial Aid

The College of New Jersey offers financial aid to qualified matriculated students through a combination of loans, grants, and/or employment. To be considered for all financial aid programs, students must submit the Free Application for Federal Student Aid (FAFSA) to the College Financial Assistance Office. Full and partial graduate assistantships are available to qualified full-time students on a competitive basis.

Cost of Study

Because it is state supported, TCNJ can offer graduate programs of the highest quality at two thirds to one half the cost of private colleges and universities in the area. Tuition and fees for all graduate courses in 2001–02 were $396.19 per semester hour of credit for New Jersey residents and $534.64 per semester hour of credit for out-of-state residents. (Tuition and fees are subject to change by action of the New Jersey State Legislature.)

Living and Housing Costs

As nearly all of TCNJ's graduate students attend classes part-time in the evenings, the College does not offer on-campus housing for graduate students. Graduate students who seek housing in the area can get assistance from the Office of Residence Life.

Student Group

The College of New Jersey had an enrollment of approximately 5,900 undergraduate students and 1,150 graduate students in 2001–02.

Student Outcomes

The College of New Jersey's excellent reputation has afforded graduates outstanding opportunities when entering their professional fields. Many TCNJ graduates receive job placements through various on-campus recruitment programs sponsored by the Office of Career Services.

Location

The College of New Jersey is located on 289 acres in suburban Ewing, New Jersey, 7 miles from the state capital in Trenton. Woodlands and two lakes surround the academic and residential buildings. More than thirty major buildings make up the physical plant, most of which are built in the classic Georgian colonial architecture. The campus is 30 miles from Philadelphia and 60 miles from New York's theaters, museums, and other attractions. The nearby towns of Princeton and New Hope offer additional cultural activities.

The College

Founded in 1855, the College has grown from its early years as a teachers' college to a multipurpose institution comprising seven schools: Art, Media, and Music; Business; Culture and Society; Education; Engineering; Nursing; and Science. Graduate study is available in Culture and Society, Education, and Nursing.

TCNJ introduced its first advanced degree program, a Master of Science in elementary education, in 1947. Over the years, the number of graduate programs has steadily increased. At present there are more than thirty specialized graduate degree and certificate programs.

TCNJ's academic programs are accredited by the Middle States Association of Colleges and Schools, the National Council for Accreditation of Teacher Education (NCATE), and by appropriate professional associations.

Applying

Students of proven ability with undergraduate degrees in appropriate fields are eligible to apply for graduate study. Applications and transcripts of all previous college or university work should be forwarded to the Office of Graduate Studies, along with the $50 nonrefundable application fee. Acceptable scores on the appropriate national standardized tests are required. Application deadlines for matriculation are April 15 for the summer session and fall semester and October 15 for the spring semester. The fall semester deadline for audiology and speech pathology is March 1. These programs do not admit students for the spring semester. The special admission deadlines are August 1 for the fall semester and December 1 for the spring semester.

Correspondence and Information

Suzanne H. Pasch, Dean
Frank Cooper, Director
Office of Graduate Studies
The College of New Jersey
P.O. Box 7718
Ewing, New Jersey 08628
Telephone: 609-771-2300
Fax: 609-637-5105
E-mail: graduate@tcnj.edu
World Wide Web: http://www.TCNJ.edu/~graduate

DEANS AND PROGRAM COORDINATORS

SCHOOL OF CULTURE AND SOCIETY
Deborah Compte, Interim Dean; Ph.D., Princeton.

Graduate Program Coordinators
English: Michael Robertson, Associate Professor; Ph.D., Princeton.

SCHOOL OF EDUCATION
Lawrence Marcus, Interim Dean; M.A., Columbia.

Graduate Program Coordinators
Audiology: Lynn Z. Smith, Assistant Professor; Ph.D., CUNY Graduate Center.
Counselor Education: Roland Worthington, Professor; Ph.D., Utah. Mary Lou Ramsey, Professor; Ed.D., Fairleigh Dickinson. Charlene Alderfer, Associate Professor; Ed.D., Massachusetts at Amherst.
Educational Leadership: Richard Farber, Professor and Department Chair; Ed.D., Temple. Donald Leake, Associate Professor; Ph.D., Ohio State.
Educational Technology: Amy G. Dell, Professor; Ph.D., Rochester.
Elementary Education: Stuart Carroll, Assistant Professor; Ph.D., Syracuse. Brenda Leake, Associate Professor; Ph.D., Ohio State.
Health and Physical Education: Aristomen Chilakos, Professor; Ph.D., Temple.
International and Overseas Administration and Supervision: Yiqiang Wu, Assistant Professor; Ph.D., Texas A&M.
Reading: Jean Wong, Assistant Professor; Ph.D., UCLA.
School Licensure, Preschool–Grade 3: Blythe Hinitz, Professor; Ed.D., Temple.
Secondary Education: Richard Farber, Professor and Department Chair; Ed.D., Temple. Ruth Palmer, Associate Professor; Ph.D., Howard.
Special Education: Amy G. Dell, Professor; Ph.D., Rochester.
Speech Pathology: Debra M. Garrett, Assistant Professor; Ph.D., Howard.
TESOL/Bilingual Education: Yiqiang Wu, Assistant Professor; Ph.D., Texas A&M.

SCHOOL OF NURSING
Susan Bakewell-Sachs, Dean; Ph.D., Pennsylvania; CRNP.

Graduate Program Coordinator
Claire Lindberg, Associate Professor; Ph.D., Rutgers. Priscilla O'Connor, Associate Professor; Ph.D., Temple.

MAJOR RESEARCH PROJECTS

Grant Awards
Adaptive technology center; Dr. Amy Dell, School of Education.
Advanced education nursing traineeship program; Dr. Claire Lindberg, School of Nursing.
Infant functional status and discharge management; Dr. Susan Bakewell-Sachs, School of Nursing.
New Jersey teacher preparation quality and capacity initiative; Mr. Lawrence Marcus, School of Education.
Preparing special and elementary educators to use inquiry and design-based learning; Dr. Amy Dell, School of Education.
Provisional teacher program; Dr. Anthony Evangelisto, School of Education.

Support of Scholarly Activity Awards (SOSA)
Conversation analysis of native/nonnative speakers; Dr. Jean Wong, School of Education.
Facilitating transition from school to employment for individuals with challenging behavior; Dr. Shridevi Rao, School of Education.
HIV symptom distress project; Dr. Claire Lindberg, School of Nursing.
Identifying the skills of successful deaf readers; Dr. Christopher McAuliffe, School of Education.
Issues of literacy and teaching elementary students of color; Dr. Deborah Thompson, School of Education.
The reception of Dante and Chaucer within the work of their literary successors; Dr. Glenn Steinberg, School of Culture and Society.
When boys become parents: understanding and helping teen fathers; Dr. Mark Kiselica, School of Education.
Writing the republic; Dr. David Blake, School of Culture and Society.

The College of New Jersey's tree-lined campus, which provides spectacular fall foliage, offers a beautiful residential setting for students all year long.

The clock tower above Green Hall, the main administration building on campus, is a well-known symbol of TCNJ tradition.

Many students spend time studying or just relaxing by one of the two lakes that form part of the northern border of the College's suburban 255-acre campus.

THE COLLEGE OF NEW ROCHELLE

Graduate School

Programs of Study

The Graduate School of The College of New Rochelle offers the M.S.Ed. in the fields of childhood education, creative teaching and learning, dual certification: special education/childhood education, dual certification: special education/early childhood education, early childhood education, literacy education, multilingual/multicultural education, school administration and supervision, special education, and speech-language pathology. It offers the M.S. in the fields of art therapy, career development, communication studies, community/school psychology, gerontology, guidance and counseling, and studio art. An M.A. degree in art education is offered. The College of New Rochelle certificates are offered in the professional areas of art museum education, bilingual education, communication studies, creative teaching and learning, staff development, staff development-special education, thanatology, gerontology, and career development. A professional diploma in school district administration and supervision is offered.

The coeducational Graduate School is sensitive to the working and parenting responsibilities of the large portion of its student body who study part-time and therefore provides convenient access to graduate education. Courses are offered on the main campus in New Rochelle. The Graduate School permits courses tailored to the needs of area professionals to run through Teacher Center sites throughout the metropolitan New York area, Nassau, Suffolk, Westchester, Orange, and Sullivan counties. In some instances, these sites run selected graduate programs.

Flexible scheduling meets the needs of working professionals who are part-time students, with courses offered on weekday evenings at 4 and 6:30 p.m. and on weekends. Fall semester is followed by winter intersession; spring semester is followed by two summer sessions plus an August Institute.

Research Facilities

In addition to the libraries and museums of New York City, on-campus Gill Library houses one of the largest collections of print and nonprint resources in Westchester County. The library, which is newly renovated to meet the needs of the twenty-first century, subscribes to more than 1,400 periodicals and numerous online subscription databases. It is open seven days a week and until 11 p.m. five nights a week. Gill Library uses the Web-based INNOPAC system to provide an online catalog to the library's holdings as well as Internet access and selected CD-ROM databases. As a member of WALDO, Gill Library also participates in WebPALS, a computerized catalog that provides online information about the holdings of Westchester-area academic, public, and special libraries. Collections of note include the ERIC Collection of educational documents, the Kutscher Collection of works in thanatology, and the Zierer Collection of materials in art therapy.

The Mooney Center provides technological support for all academic programs. Its facilities include a TV studio, photo labs, and model classroom. The Center's desktop publishing, computer graphics, and Macintosh classrooms are available for work in graphic arts and communication studies. The computer laboratories are designed for individual student use and are open seven days a week and until 11 p.m. five nights a week.

The Castle Gallery, located in historic Leland Castle, opened its doors more than a decade ago. It enjoys an excellent reputation for the quality and diversity of its exhibitions and for its innovative programs that enhance campus activities and contribute to the academic experience. In addition, the Mooney Center Exhibit Hall features faculty and student art exhibits. These spaces function as a cultural resource for the entire community.

The Graduate Division of Education, through its Education Center, provides diagnostic and remedial services to students, children, and adults in the larger community.

Financial Aid

College-funded financial aid is available in the form of assistantships and partial scholarships, which are awarded on the basis of merit and need. Assistantships provide both a stipend and tuition for full-time students, and require 15 hours of service per week. New York State and federal grant and loan programs provide additional sources of assistance. Application deadlines are specified in the *Financial Aid Information Packet.*

Cost of Study

Tuition is $415 per credit hour in 2002–03. Fees and tuition are specified in the *Graduate School Catalog.*

Living and Housing Costs

The third floor of Angela Hall offers single-room suites for graduate men and women. The lounge area has kitchen accommodations. Residential housing rates include board.

Off-campus housing is available for graduate students in the nearby residential community. A listing of available apartments is on file in the Office of Student Life at 914-654-5365.

The College's food service in the Student Campus Center offers a full range of dining options for commuter and resident students.

Student Group

The Graduate School, founded in 1969, continues its commitment to educate men and women for leadership in the service professions and the corporate world. Small in size (1,000-student enrollment) with ongoing academic advisement, students pursue a course of study to achieve their career goals. Graduate students, the majority from the surrounding tristate area, earn degrees and certificates in programs that accommodate students on a full- or part-time basis.

Location

The College's location combines the advantages of a tranquil suburban campus thirty minutes from New York City with its vast repository of cultural riches. The College's 20-acre campus in Westchester County is located in a pleasant residential neighborhood of New Rochelle, within a few blocks of open green parks and the public beaches of Long Island Sound. The College is easily reached by major highways from Queens, New York City, New Jersey, Connecticut, and upstate New York. The New Rochelle Metro North train station (a 30-minute ride from New York City) and buses from points in Westchester and the Bronx stop within a few blocks of the College.

The College

The College, founded in 1904, offers its various academic programs through four schools: Arts and Sciences, Graduate School, Nursing, and New Resources (undergraduate liberal arts for adults only).

Applying

Admission is on a rolling basis. Applications and all supporting materials for admission must be submitted one month prior to the start of a session. A personal interview with the Division Head and an on-site writing sample are required before a student is accepted into a program; both are scheduled upon receipt of the application packet.

Correspondence and Information

Nancy Brown, Ed.D.
Graduate Dean
The College of New Rochelle
29 Castle Place
New Rochelle, New York 10805-2339
Telephone: 914-654-5334
Fax: 914-654-5593
World Wide Web: http://www.cnr.edu

THE FACULTY

The expertise of the Graduate School's full-time professors is complemented by its cadre of adjunct professors who specialize in the fields in which they teach.

DIVISION HEADS

Division of Art and Communication Studies: Dr. Basilio Monteiro, Chapel G12, Telephone: 914-654-5279. E-mail: bmonteiro@cnr.edu
Programs:
- Art Education
- Art Therapy
- Communication Studies (Public Relations, Corporate and Organizational Communication, Advertising)
- Studio Art

Certificate Programs:
- Art Museum Education
- Communication Studies

Division of Education: Dr. John Koster, Chidwick 103, Telephone: 914-654-5322. E-mail: jkoster@cnr.edu. Assistant Division Head: Louise Challop, Chidwick 103, Telephone: 914-654-5330. E-mail: lchallop@cnr.edu
Programs:
- Childhood Education
- Creative Teaching and Learning
- Dual Certification: Special Education/Childhood Education
- Dual Certification: Special Education/Early Childhood Education
- Early Childhood Education
- Literacy Education
- Multilingual/Multicultural Education
- School Administration and Supervision
- Special Education
- Speech-Language Pathology

Professional Diploma:
- Administration and Supervision

Certificate Programs:
- Bilingual Education
- Creative Teaching and Learning
- Staff Development
- Staff Development–Special Education

Division of Human Services: Chidwick 204, Telephone: 914-654-5561
Programs:
- Career Development
- Community/School Psychology
- Gerontology
- Guidance and Counseling

Certificate Programs:
- Gerontology
- Thanatology
- Career Development

COLLEGE OF ST. CATHERINE

Graduate Programs

Programs of Study

The College of St. Catherine offers eight master's degree programs. The M.A. is available in education, nursing, occupational therapy, organizational leadership, and theology. Master of Library and Information Science (M.L.I.S.), Master of Physical Therapy (M.P.T.), and Master of Social Work (M.S.W.) programs also are offered. Graduate programs focus on advanced knowledge in both theoretical and applied aspects of these fields. All are committed to excellence and to integrating liberal arts with professional disciplines. Central themes in all programs are ethics and leadership; a holistic view of the individual, including the spiritual dimension; social justice; critical analysis; and interactive, integrative learning.

St. Catherine's graduate programs are coeducational. Many courses are offered in the late afternoon and evening or on weekends. Most programs can be completed in two to three years of full-time study; part-time study is available for most programs. The M.P.T. is a three-year, full-time, day-scheduled program with a strong clinical education component. M.A. in nursing (MANU) graduates are eligible to write the nurse practitioner examination in selected specialties; full-time students receive preference. The M.S.W., offered jointly with the University of St. Thomas in St. Paul, Minnesota, prepares students for clinical practice in social work. The M.L.I.S., offered cooperatively with Dominican University in River Forest, Illinois, is accredited by the American Library Association. The M.A. in organizational leadership (MAOL) is a management program that focuses on ethics and leadership. The M.A. in education (MAED) offers options for both licensed teachers and individuals who wish to become licensed. The M.A. in theology (MATH) provides academic training in Christian thought with emphasis on spirituality. The M.A. in occupational therapy (MAOT) offers both an entry-level and postprofessional option.

Research Facilities

The College participates in Cooperating Libraries in Consortium (CLIC) comprising library facilities from 52 libraries on the Minnesota State University's online catalog system. CLIC puts more than 1 million volumes and a subscription list of 5,000 periodicals at students' disposal. A complete catalog of the CLIC collection plus daily delivery of books makes CLIC a fully operative part of campus library resources. The computer center, located in the library, provides access to numerous online research services and provides computing work stations for student use in the center and at numerous locations around campus.

Financial Aid

Graduate students may apply for financial assistance from a variety of sources: state and federal loan programs, grants, assistantships, scholarships, and work-study programs. Most funding is available to students enrolled for at least a half-time course of study. Nurse traineeships are awarded to MANU students based upon available federal funds. Assistantships are awarded in the MAOL, MATH, and M.S.W. programs; students should consult program directors for details. Students applying for financial aid must complete a Free Application for Federal Student Aid (FAFSA). All application materials for financial aid should be submitted by April 1 for the following year of study. Information is available from the Office of Financial Aid at 651-690-6540.

Cost of Study

Tuition for the M.L.I.S., MANU, MAOT, M.P.T., and MAOL programs is $495 per credit. Tuition for the MATH program is $400 per credit. Tuition for the M.S.W. program is $443 per credit. Tuition for the MAED program is $375 per credit.

Living and Housing Costs

Campus housing is available to all students enrolled for 6 or more credits per term. Residence hall fees range from $1391 to $1809 per semester; apartments from $909 to $2910 (one- and two-bedroom units available). Board fees are $1070 per semester. Numerous off-campus rental units can be found in the multicollege community that surrounds the campus.

Student Group

Graduate students at the College of St. Catherine represent a diverse range of ages and life experiences.

Location

Set in an attractive, well-kept neighborhood in St. Paul, Minnesota, the College of St. Catherine is part of a close-knit community of colleges and universities that includes the University of Minnesota Twin Cities campuses. A nationally known and varied arts community thrives, offering cultural and entertainment activities. Metro and statewide park systems provide year-round fitness and recreational opportunities. Convenient transit and freeway systems provide access to attractions throughout the metro area.

The College

The College of St. Catherine is the largest and most comprehensive Catholic college for women in the nation. Founded in 1905 by the Sisters of St. Joseph of Carondelet, the College is recognized for academic excellence and forward-looking innovation to meet students' intellectual, spiritual, and professional needs. The College enrolls more than 4,400 students on campuses in St. Paul and Minneapolis. The St. Paul campus offers Bachelor of Arts and Bachelor of Science degrees to women and graduate degrees to women and men. The coeducational Minneapolis campus offers associate degrees and certificates in health-care and human-services fields. St. Catherine's is accredited by the North Central Association of Colleges and Secondary Schools, the Commission on Accreditation in Physical Therapy Education, Accreditation Council for Occupational Therapy, American Occupational Therapy Association, the Council on Social Work Education, the Minnesota Board of Nursing, the National Council for the Accreditation of Teacher Education, and the National League for Nursing Accrediting Commission.

Applying

Each program has an established application process. Interested students should contact the Office of Graduate Admission for program brochures and application materials. All applicants must submit an application with a nonrefundable fee, transcripts from each postsecondary school attended demonstrating a cumulative grade point average of 3.0 (on a 4.0 scale), and letters of recommendation. Some programs require one of the standardized tests (GRE or MAT). Some have specific work experience requirements, and some require interviews.

Correspondence and Information

Office of Graduate Admission, #4024
The College of St. Catherine
2004 Randolph Avenue
St. Paul, Minnesota 55105-1794

Telephone: 651-690-6933
800-945-4599 Ext. 6933 (toll-free)
E-mail: graduate_studies@stkate.edu

THE FACULTY AND THEIR RESEARCH

The College of St. Catherine graduate faculty members are active both as scholars and respected professionals and carry a common commitment to excellence in teaching. They maintain a dedication to continuing their own professional development in order to ensure command of their field and ongoing relevance in times of rapid cultural change and expansion of knowledge. Although faculty members are encouraged to engage in research and do so, their first commitment is to teaching. A low student-faculty ratio provides an exciting learning environment that encourages individual exploration.

Master of Arts in Education
Beverly Schuler, Director; Ed.D., Nova Southeastern.

Master of Library and Information Science
Mary Wagner, Director; M.L.S., Washington (Seattle).

Master of Arts in Nursing
Ruth Brink, Director; Ph.D. candidate, Minnesota.

Master of Arts in Occupational Therapy
Julie Bass Haugen, Director; Ph.D., Minnesota.

Master of Arts in Organizational Leadership
Julie Belle White-Newman, Director; Ph.D., Minnesota.

Master of Physical Therapy
Debra O. Sellheim, Director; M.A., North Dakota.

Master of Social Work
Barbara W. Shank, Director; Ph.D., Minnesota.

Master of Arts in Theology
Shawn Madigan, Director; Ph.D., Catholic University.

The College of St. Catherine recently upgraded and expanded its collection of PCs and has developed a laptop computer leasing program.

The College is located in one of St. Paul's most charming residential areas, only 10 minutes from downtown Minneapolis and St. Paul.

Our Lady of Victory Chapel, which is listed on the National Register of Historic Places, stands at the focal point of the campus.

THE COLLEGE OF SAINT ROSE

Programs of Study

The College of Saint Rose offers graduate programs leading to the degrees of Master of Arts, Master of Science, Master of Science in Education, and Master of Business Administration. Graduate programs are specially designed to meet the needs of part-time students, although most programs also serve students who attend full-time. Graduate courses are scheduled in the late afternoon and evening to accommodate the large number of students whose days are filled with other activities. Part-time students usually finish in 2 or 3 years, full-time students in 1½ years.

Fields of study include accounting, art education, business administration, communication disorders, computer information systems, counseling, early childhood education, educational administration and supervision, educational psychology, elementary education, English, history and political science, music, music education, public communications, reading, school psychology, secondary education, special education, and teacher education. The College of Saint Rose also offers a joint J.D./M.B.A. degree with Albany Law School and a full-time, daytime M.B.A. program, in addition to the evening business program. The College also offers graduate certificates in educational computing, applied technology, nonprofit management, and educational administration and supervision.

The objectives of Saint Rose graduate study are to encourage intellectual curiosity, foster creative thought, and promote careful research and professional competence. To these ends, programs are designed to provide essential core materials and to allow options for electives. The programs in elementary education, teacher education, and special education also lead, with appropriate planning and advisement, to professional teaching certification. In addition to a master's degree, certification only is available for secondary education, educational administration and supervision, and counseling students.

Small classes, opportunities for independent study, and, in many programs, internships or various practicum or fieldwork experiences facilitate the learning process. Through the College's membership in the Hudson-Mohawk Association of Colleges and Universities, full-time students may cross-register for graduate courses at other institutions in the Capital Region.

The College operates on an academic year of two 15-week semesters, fall and spring, and two 6-week summer semesters. The accounting and M.B.A. programs offer three 11-week sessions.

Research Facilities

The Neil Hellman Library houses 203,299 volumes, 825 periodical subscriptions, 282,304 titles on microform, and a collection of rare books. Students requiring additional information can borrow books and articles through the College's membership in a nationwide interlibrary loan cooperative. Graduate students have access to computer labs featuring IBM and Macintosh computers with Internet access. The Music Building provides state-of-the-art facilities for music majors at Saint Rose, including the Saints and Sinners Sound Studio, a sixteen-track professional recording studio, and the Henry and Alice Cooper Finks Music Library. In addition, the Pauline K. Winkler Speech-Language-Hearing Center is the College's on-campus clinic, where Saint Rose students work with clients under faculty supervision. Cabrini Hall houses the Career Center, the Writing Center, and the Learning Center. The College's 27,000-square-foot Science Center features the modern equipment that students may encounter in the workplace. The Picotte Hall Art Center houses the Saint Rose Art Gallery, as well as classrooms, studio space, graphic design computer labs, darkrooms, and one of the largest screen printing studios in New York State. All art education graduate students are allocated their own studio space in which to create a body of work for exhibition in the Graduate Art Show.

Financial Aid

Saint Rose serves graduate students through a variety of federal, state, and institutional programs, which include loans, grants, and employment opportunities. Graduate assistantships and merit, multicultural, international, and second-chance scholarships are available to matriculated students. Matriculating graduate students may apply for campus-based assistance (college assistantships and Federal Perkins Loan) by completing the Free Application for Federal Student Aid (FAFSA). The College deadline for the receipt of these documents is March 1 for the fall semester and November 15 for the spring semester.

Cost of Study

The cost of graduate tuition in 2002–03 is $402 per credit hour. A $15 registration fee is payable at each registration.

Living and Housing Costs

There is an abundance of private housing accommodations close to the Saint Rose campus. Graduate students can choose from a variety of one- and two-bedroom apartments located in the Pine Hills neighborhood, many of which can be found near bus routes. Typical monthly rents range from $350 to $550.

Student Group

Saint Rose has a total enrollment of 4,411 students, of whom 1,555 are graduate students. Approximately 80 percent of the graduate students attend part-time. Students come from colleges and universities throughout the United States and other countries, with the largest number from New York and neighboring states. In addition to students who are pursuing a degree, Saint Rose welcomes individuals who are taking courses toward teaching certification and students who seek personal or professional enrichment.

Location

Albany offers extensive cultural and recreational opportunities. In addition to the many extracurricular activities offered by Saint Rose and several other colleges in the area, students may enjoy the Albany Symphony Orchestra and various theater groups, museums, galleries, and historic sites. The College's location in the capital of New York State provides a special opportunity for students to seek involvement with a large variety of government agencies. New York City, Boston, and Montreal are all less than a 4-hour drive from Saint Rose.

The College

The College of Saint Rose, founded in 1920, is a private, coeducational liberal arts and sciences college with a strong tradition of academic excellence and service to the community. Located in Albany's Pine Hills residential neighborhood, the College enjoys all the advantages of a major metropolitan area. Its 25-acre campus, comprised of a combination of modern buildings and traditional Victorian homes, creates an informal environment that is conducive to personal, as well as professional, growth and enrichment. Saint Rose supports educational innovation and faculty-student interaction. Faculty members and students often are engaged in joint research projects. The College is fully accredited by the Middle States Association of Colleges and Schools, the Board of Regents of the University of the State of New York, the National Association of Schools of Art and Design, the Educational Standards Board of the American Speech-Language-Hearing Association, the Association of Collegiate Business Schools and Programs, and the National Association of Schools of Music.

Applying

Applicants must file an application form, official transcripts of all postsecondary work, a statement of purpose, two letters of recommendation for graduate study, and any other forms of evidence to support their credentials by the application deadline before the beginning of the semester in which they wish to begin study. The application deadline for the fall semester is July 15; for the spring semester, it is November 15. Candidates applying to the Communication Disorders Program must submit their applications by March 15 for fall admission and by October 1 for spring admission. Some applicants for the M.B.A. or the M.S. in accounting program are required to submit Graduate Management Admission Test scores. The nonrefundable application fee is $30. A complete catalog and application is available at the Web address listed below.

Correspondence and Information

Dean of Graduate, Adult and Continuing Education Admissions
The College of Saint Rose
432 Western Avenue
Albany, New York 12203-1490
Telephone: 518-454-5143
800-637-8556 Ext. 3 (toll-free)
Fax: 518-458-5479
E-mail: ace@mail.strose.edu
World Wide Web: http://www.strose.edu

DEANS OF SCHOOLS, PROGRAM CHAIRS, AND DESCRIPTIONS

SCHOOL OF ARTS AND HUMANITIES
Maria de la Camara, Dean; Ph.D., Case Western Reserve.

Art Education (Master of Science)
Karene Faul, Chair; M.F.A., Notre Dame.
Provides permanent certification for those who are provisionally certified in art education as well as those who have a background in fine arts, but no teaching experience. Curriculum emphasizes studio work.
Public Communications (Master of Arts)
Gary McLouth, Chair; Ph.D., SUNY at Albany.
Offers concentrations in journalism and public relations for communications professionals who want to build on skills that they use in the workplace.
English (Master of Arts)
Catherine Cavanaugh, Chair; Ph.D., SUNY at Binghamton.
With concentrations in literature and writing, this program can be tailored to meet students' personal and professional needs. Fulfills the academic requirement for permanent certification for those who are provisionally certified to teach English at the secondary level.
History/Political Science (Master of Arts)
Keith Haynes, Chair; Ph.D., Northern Illinois.
Focuses on the historical, political, and international dimensions of the American experience. Fulfills the academic requirement for permanent certification for those who are provisionally certified to teach social studies at the secondary level.
Music (Master of Arts)
Paul Evoskevich, Chair; M.M., Rochester (Eastman).
Provides an in-depth study of the aesthetics, theory, and styles of music literature through performance, score analysis, and research. Students may tailor their degree program by choosing one of four concentrations.
Music Education (Master of Science)
Paul Evoskevich, Chair; M.M., Rochester (Eastman).
Prepares students to teach music in grades K–12 by providing a specialized, in-depth study of learning and teaching music. Meets the needs of current teachers pursuing permanent certification, as well as those who have undergraduate degrees in music but no teaching experience.

SCHOOL OF BUSINESS
Severin C. Carlson, Dean; D.B.A., Indiana.

Accounting (Master of Science)
Thomas Amyot, Chair; M.S., Saint Rose.
Qualifies students in New York State to take the CPA exam, provided they have 60 credits of liberal arts courses and 45 credits of undergraduate business courses. Also geared toward students who already work in accounting but want to advance in their field and those who want to enter the field of accounting for the first time.
Business/Economics (Master of Business Administration)
Susan Raynis, Chair; Ph.D., Colorado State.
Provides students with the skills and knowledge to become effective managers in today's rapidly changing and competitive business environment. Offers an accelerated part-time option for working professionals and a one-year, full-time intensive option with an internship component.

SCHOOL OF EDUCATION
Crystal J. Gips, Dean; Ed.D., Boston University.

Communication Disorders (Master of Science in Education)
John Pickering Jr., Chair; Ph.D., Ohio.
Accredited by the American Speech-Language-Hearing Association and approved by New York State to license speech-language pathologists and to certify teachers of the speech and hearing handicapped.
Counseling (Master of Science in Education)
Jelane Kennedy, Chair; Ed.D., William and Mary.
Offers concentrations in school counseling, community counseling, and college student personnel.
Early Childhood Education (Master of Science in Education)
Designed for those who want to work with children in nursery schools, early childhood centers, Head Start programs, or elementary schools.
Educational Administration (Master of Science in Education)
Designed for educators who wish to become certified as administrators, principals, or superintendents at the school and/or school district levels.
Educational Psychology (Master of Science in Education)
Richard Brody, Chair; Ph.D., SUNY at Albany.
Designed for those with no prior experience in education and for those who have a background in education and want to expand their skills and expertise. Also fulfills the academic requirement for permanent certification for those who are provisionally certified in elementary, secondary, or special education.
Elementary Education (Master of Science in Education)
Designed for students who want to teach at the elementary school level and who are not yet provisionally certified.
Reading (Master of Science in Education)
Margaret McLane, Chair; Ph.D., SUNY at Albany.
Designed for teachers who have provisional teaching certification in elementary education, secondary education, or special education and want additional certification in reading.
School Psychology (Master of Science in Education)
Prepares students for careers as certified school psychologists.
Secondary Education (Master of Science in Education)
Designed for anyone who wants to teach at the middle or high school level. Fulfills all the education course work requirements for provisional certification to teach biology, chemistry, English, mathematics, social studies, or Spanish in grades 7–12.
Special Education (Master of Science in Education)
Margaret McLane, Chair; Ph.D., SUNY at Albany.
Prepares teachers to address the variety of needs among students with disabilities and is designed for those with and without provisional certification in special education.
Teacher Education (Master of Science in Education)
Designed to provide a master's degree leading to permanent teaching certification in grades K–12, under New York State requirements.

SCHOOL OF MATHEMATICS AND SCIENCES
Chris Arney, Dean; Ph.D., Rensselaer.

Computer Information Systems (Master of Science)
Neal Mazur, Chair; Ph.D., Arizona State.
A part-time, evening program designed for students with some experience in computer technology and programming who wish to advance their skills and knowledge in areas such as software design and programming, computer architecture, and database theory.

COLLEGE OF STATEN ISLAND OF THE CITY UNIVERSITY OF NEW YORK

Graduate Degree Programs

Programs of Study

The College of Staten Island offers Master of Arts (M.A.) degrees in cinema studies, English, history, and liberal studies. Master of Science (M.S.) degrees are offered in adult health nursing, biology, computer science, environmental science, mental retardation and developmental disabilities, and neuroscience. A combined Bachelor of Science (B.S) and Master of Science degree in physical therapy is offered. Master of Science in Education (M.S.Ed.) degrees are offered in childhood (elementary) education, adolescence (secondary) education (biology, English, mathematics, or social studies), and special education. The College offers an advanced certificate in educational leadership (elementary or secondary). Master's degree programs and the advanced certificate program generally require a minimum of 30 credits. Degree candidates are expected to meet the specific requirements of the graduate program to which they are accepted. The College of Staten Island also participates with the City University of New York (CUNY) Graduate School and University Center and Brooklyn College in a doctoral program in polymer chemistry and with the Graduate School and University Center in a doctoral program in computer science. In cooperation with the Center for Developmental Neuroscience and Developmental Disabilities, the College participates in CUNY doctoral subprograms in neuroscience (biology), learning processes (psychology), polymer chemistry, and computer science.

Research Facilities

The academic buildings house approximately 200 modern laboratories and classrooms. Academic and research programs are served by a computer network that allows students and faculty members full access to specialized software, the World Wide Web, online library resources, and e-mail. All major computer languages and software packages are supported. The College houses an IBM 4381 computer, and students can access the University's IBM 3090/400 system. The library holds up to 300,000 volumes, computer facilities for database searching, periodical subscriptions, and media services. The College library is a member of the City University of New York integrated library system. Students and faculty members have free access to ERIC as well as various databases on CD-ROM or via the Internet. The College's devotion to research is evident in its maintenance of the Center for Development Neuroscience and Developmental Disabilities and the Center for Environmental Science. In addition, the Center for the Arts, complete with a 900-seat auditorium, a 450-seat fully equipped theater, a recital hall, an experimental theater, an art gallery, a conference center, a lecture hall, and studios, provides facilities for teaching and public assembly.

Financial Aid

The Office of Student Financial Assistance administers federal and state grant, loan, and work-study programs to assist students with financial need to attend the College of Staten Island. Students should contact the Office of Student Financial Assistance early in the admissions process to discuss eligibility requirements and responsibilities. The College offers a limited number of tuition waivers for matriculated graduate students who demonstrate need. In some departments, graduate assistant positions are available for full-time graduate students, and information about these positions may be obtained from the individual program departments.

Cost of Study

In 2001–02, tuition for New York State residents was $185 per credit, plus $65 for each additional contact hour, or $2175 per semester for 12 or more credits. Tuition for nonresidents was $320 per credit, plus $85 for each additional contact hour, or $3800 per semester for 12 or more credits.

Living and Housing Costs

For the 2000–01 academic year, dependent students budgeted a minimum of $500 for books and supplies, $675 for local transportation, $1860 for meals and personal expenses, and $1500 for expenses at home. Independent students budgeted the same amounts for books, supplies, and transportation, plus $7780 for food and living expenses for a nine-month academic year.

Student Group

More than 1,400 graduate students enrolled at the College of Staten Island in the 2001 fall semester. The graduate population reflects a wide range of ethnicity, social and economic backgrounds, educational and professional experiences, and aspirations.

Location

The College of Staten Island is located in New York City in the Borough of Staten Island. Completed in 1994, the 204-acre campus of the College of Staten Island is the largest one for a college in New York City. Set in a parklike landscape, the campus is centrally located on Staten Island and is accessible by automobile and public transportation.

The College

The College of Staten Island, a senior college of the City University of New York, was founded in 1976 through the union of two existing colleges—Richmond College and Staten Island Community College. Richmond College, an upper-division college that offered undergraduate and graduate degrees to students who had successfully completed the first two years of college at the Staten Island Community College (founded in 1955) or elsewhere, was founded in 1965. The College of Staten Island is the only public senior college of higher learning on Staten Island. The College offers fully accredited undergraduate and graduate programs.

Applying

Requirements for admission and application deadlines vary by program and department. Students should contact the Office of Recruitment and Admissions for additional information or to arrange an admissions interview or campus tour.

Correspondence and Information

Mary Beth Reilly, Director of Recruitment and Admissions
Office of Recruitment and Admissions
North Administration Building (2A), Room 404
College of Staten Island
2800 Victory Boulevard
Staten Island, New York 10314
Telephone: 718-982-2010
Fax: 718-982-2500
E-mail: recruitment@postbox.csi.cuny.edu
World Wide Web: http://www.csi.cuny.edu

GRADUATE PROGRAM FACULTY HEADS

Adult Health Nursing: Margaret Lunney, Ph.D., Professor, Department of Nursing.
Biology: Jacqueline LeBlanc, Ph.D., Professor, Department of Biology.
Cinema Studies: David Gerstner, Ph.D., Assistant Professor, Department of Performing and Creative Arts.
Computer Science: Miriam Tausner, Ph.D., Associate Professor, Department of Computer Science.
Educational Leadership: David Seeley, J.D., Ed.D., Professor; Susan Sullivan, Ed.D., Assistant Professor; Department of Education.
Elementary Education: Jed Luchow, Ed.D., Associate Professor, Department of Education.
English: Richard Currie, Ph.D., Associate Professor, Department of English Speech and World Literature.
Environmental Science: Alfred Levine, Ph.D., Professor, Department of Engineering Science and Physics; Center for Environmental Science.
History: Steven Stearns, Ph.D., Associate Professor, Department of History.
Liberal Studies: David Traboulay, Ph.D., Professor, Department of History.
Secondary Education: Eileen Donoghue, Ed.D., Associate Professor, Department of Education.
Special Education: Effie Simmonds, Ed.D., Professor, Department of Education.

COLLEGE OF WILLIAM AND MARY

Graduate Studies

Programs of Study

The Faculty of Arts and Sciences offers M.A., M.S., and Ph.D. programs in a number of disciplines and the Master of Public Policy. The Psy.D. in clinical psychology is offered in collaboration with neighboring institutions through the Virginia Consortium Program in Clinical Psychology, which awards the degree. Joint-degree programs leading to M.B.A./M.P.P., M.S. in marine science/M.P.P., M.S. in computational operations research/M.P.P., J.D./M.A. in American studies, and J.D. with law/M.P.P. are also offered. The School of Business Administration offers a full-time M.B.A., an evening M.B.A., an Executive M.B.A., and a Master of Accounting (M.A.C.). Joint-degree programs in law (M.B.A./J.D.) and public policy (M.B.A./M.P.P.) are also offered. The School of Education offers an M.A.Ed. in elementary school teaching (with an emphasis in reading, language, and literacy), secondary school teaching, and gifted education; an M.Ed. in counseling, educational leadership (with emphases in general K–12 administration and higher education administration), school psychology, and special education; an Ed.S. in school psychology; and an Ed.D. and Ph.D. in counselor education and educational policy planning and leadership (with emphases in general K–12 administration, gifted education administration, higher education, and special education administration). *U.S. News & World Report* ranks William and Mary among the top fifty in a national survey of 191 doctoral degree–granting schools of education. The College was also ranked sixth in the country in the quality of its teaching. The Marshall-Wythe School of Law offers the J.D. and LL.M. degrees as well as three joint degrees: J.D./M.A. in American studies, J.D./M.B.A., and J.D./M.P.P. The School of Marine Science offers M.S. and Ph.D. programs in marine science with specializations in biological, chemical, geological, and physical oceanography; marine resource management; marine fisheries science; and toxicology and pathology.

Research Facilities

The libraries of the College are the central Earl Gregg Swem Library; the chemistry, physics, geology, biology, and music libraries; the Marshall-Wythe Law Library; the School of Marine Science Library; the Professional Resource Center in the School of Business Administration; and the Learning Resource Center/Curriculum Library in the School of Education. Specialized laboratories, equipment, publication organizations, collections, and other facilities are available in a variety of departments and institutes, including the Applied Research Center, which houses the Jefferson Lab library; the Omohundro Institute of Early American History and Culture; the Virginia Institute of Marine Science; the Center for Archaeological Research; the Archaeological Conservation Center; the Institute for the Bill of Rights; Millington Life Sciences Hall; Muscarelle Museum; the Center for Public Policy Research; and the William Small Physical Laboratory. Research opportunities are extended in conjunction with neighboring organizations that include the Colonial Williamsburg Foundation, the Thomas Jefferson National Accelerator Facility, the Eastern State Hospital, the National Center for State Courts, and the Langley Research Center of the National Aeronautics and Space Administration. Graduate students and faculty members are working at national laboratories and accelerator installations throughout the world.

Financial Aid

Fellowships, scholarships, institutional and grant-funded assistantships, internships, apprenticeships, work-study arrangements, and loans are available. Duties are limited so that assistants can progress toward their degrees at the normal pace. Most of the funds are assigned through the departments and schools. While there is often some flexibility, early application is recommended.

Cost of Study

For the 2001–02 academic year, tuition and fees for two semesters of full-time study, by school, are as follows: Graduate Arts and Sciences, School of Marine Science, and Graduate School of Education, $5740 for Virginia residents and $17,276 for nonresidents; Virginia Consortium Program in Clinical Psychology, $2175 for residents and nonresidents; School of Law, $10,400 for Virginia residents and $19,750 for nonresidents; full-time M.B.A. program, $9322 for Virginia residents and $19,670 for nonresidents; and M.A.C. program, $7690 for residents and $17,374 for nonresidents.

Living and Housing Costs

For academic year 2001–02, the estimated cost of living for a single student totaled $11,995 plus tuition. Conveniently located College housing for graduate and professional students is available for $1749 per semester. Many graduate and professional students elect to live off campus.

Student Group

The total enrollment of 7,489 in fall 2001 included 5,604 undergraduates and 1,331 graduate and professional students (159 of these were unclassified). Most are full-time students who live on or in the vicinity of the campus. In each faculty, there is an active graduate student association.

Location

Williamsburg is on a Chesapeake Bay peninsula between the York and James rivers, on Interstate 64, 50 miles from Richmond, 45 miles from Norfolk, and 150 miles from Washington, D.C. It is the center of a historic and popular tourist area that includes Colonial Williamsburg, Yorktown, Jamestown, a major water-sports region, and an exceptional concentration of cultural activities. Williamsburg has direct limousine service to the Newport News, Norfolk, and Richmond airports, and bus and railway service is also available.

The College

Although it retains the historic name under which it was chartered in 1693, the College of William and Mary has in fact been a small research university for a long time. In 1779, it established the first chair of law in the United States. The College is now organized as a Faculty of Arts and Sciences and Schools of Business Administration, Education, Law, and Marine Science. The 1,200-acre main campus in Williamsburg encompasses most of the activities of the university and includes buildings ranging in age from those built around the time of the granting of the royal charter to recent construction. The School of Marine Science campus is located at Gloucester Point.

Applying

There are substantial variations in deadlines and procedures among the departments and schools, and applicants should request information from those in their areas of interest as soon as possible. Most programs are designed for students who wish to begin their studies in the fall semester. It is recommended that applications be completed as early as January 5, particularly by those who seek financial aid.

Correspondence and Information

For more information about the College's programs, students can access the World Wide Web at http://www.wm.edu/.

Dean of Research and Graduate Studies
Faculty of Arts and Sciences
College of William and Mary
P.O. Box 8795
Williamsburg, Virginia 23187
Telephone: 757-221-2467
Fax: 757-221-4874
Web: http://www.wm.edu/graduate

M.B.A. Admissions
School of Business Administration
College of William and Mary
P.O. Box 8795
Williamsburg, Virginia 23187
Telephone: 757-221-2900
Fax: 757-221-2958
E-mail: admissions@business.wm.edu
Web: http://business.wm.edu/mba

Dean of Graduate Studies
School of Marine Science
College of William and Mary
P.O. Box 1346
Gloucester Point, Virginia 23062
Telephone: 804-684-7106

Dean of Admissions
Marshall-Wythe School of Law
College of William and Mary
P.O. Box 8795
Williamsburg, Virginia 23187
Telephone: 757-221-3785

Associate Dean of Academic Programs
School of Education
College of William and Mary
P.O. Box 8795
Williamsburg, Virginia 23187
Telephone: 757-221-2317

Virginia Consortium Program in Clinical Psychology
Administrative Office
Pembroke 2, Suite 301
287 Independence Boulevard
Virginia Beach, Virginia 23462
Telephone: 757-518-2550
Web: http://www.vcpcp.odu.edu/vcpcp

DEPARTMENT CONTACTS AND RESEARCH AREAS

FACULTY OF ARTS AND SCIENCES

American Studies (M.A., Ph.D., J.D./M.A. with law): Dr. Richard Lowry, Graduate Studies Director (rslowr@wm.edu). Program encourages students to use interdisciplinary approaches to explore the diverse past and present cultures of the peoples of the United States. The program has special strengths in African-American studies, cultural studies, popular and material cultures, cultural and intellectual history, American literature, and the history of the book.

Anthropology (M.A., Ph.D.): Dr. Norman F. Barka, Graduate Director (nfbark@wm.edu). The M.A. is designed as a terminal degree to prepare students in historical archaeology and related professions. The Ph.D. program prepares students for long-term research and teaching in anthropology with specializations in historical archaeology and historical anthropology. Faculty specialities emphasize comparative colonialism, the African diaspora, Native America, the archaeology of Colonial America and the Caribbean, and CRM. Practical training in field, laboratory, and museum conservation methods is available in various courses, including summer field schools. Students have access to unparalleled historical, archaeological, and museum resources, as well as opportunities to participate in a wide variety of ongoing projects in the Williamsburg area, Dutch West Indies, and Bermuda.

Applied Science (M.S., Ph.D.): Dr. Eric Bradley, Chair (elbrad@as.wm.edu). Offers an interdisciplinary program in the physical sciences, which is cooperatively offered by the core faculty of applied science and participating faculty from biology, chemistry, computer science, mathematics, and physics, as well as NASA-Langley, Jefferson Lab, and VIMS. Research specializations of core and affiliated faculty members include applied mathematics and modeling, thin films, computational materials, interface and surface science, processing materials with light and plasmas, nondestructive evaluation, medical imaging, solid-state NMR, and composite and polymer materials science.

Biology (M.A.): Dr. Stanton Hoegerman, Graduate Director (sfhoeg@wm.edu). Program is designed for students who desire additional training before pursuing an advanced program or entering the job market. Graduates go on to doctoral programs, including medicine and law as well as traditional Ph.D. programs in biology, or find employment in environmental analysis or pharmaceuticals/biotechnology.

Chemistry (M.S. and joint M.S./Ph.D. program with Applied Science): Dr. Chris Abelt, Graduate Director (cjabel@wm.edu). Program offers a thesis-based degree in areas of biochemistry and organic, inorganic, physical, and polymer and analytical chemistry. The program is designed for students who desire additional academic experience before pursuing an industrial career, a professional degree, or a Ph.D. degree.

Computer Science (M.S., Ph.D.): Dr. Gianfranco Ciardo, Graduate Director (ciardo@cs.wm.edu). Research areas include computer systems and architecture, parallel and distributed processing, performance modeling, logical verification and model checking, databases, high-performance computing, numerical linear algebra and optimization, parallel mesh generation, algorithms, and artificial intelligence. Interdisciplinary research opportunities can be found nearby at NASA-Langley, Jefferson Lab, and the Applied Science department. (http://www.cs.wm.edu)

History (M.A., Ph.D.): Dr. Cindy Hahamovitch, Graduate Director (gradap@wm.edu). Ph.D. students specialize in American history; M.A.-level students may also specialize in selected areas of English or European history. In cooperation with the Institute of Early American History and Culture, Colonial Williamsburg, and Swem Library, the department offers students practical work experience through apprenticeships in archives and manuscripts, scholarly publishing, humanities computing, historical archaeology, and teaching.

Physics (M.A., M.S., Ph.D.): Dr. Marc Sher, Graduate Admissions (sher@physics.wm.edu). Research specialties include accelerator physics; atomic, molecular, and optical physics; nuclear and particle physics; plasma theory and nonlinear dynamics; condensed matter physics; and computational physics. Collaborative research efforts and the proximity of NASA-Langley and Jefferson Lab bring graduate students into contact with the international community.

Psychology (M.A.): Dr. Lee Kirkpatrick, M.A. Graduate Director (lakirk@wm.edu). M.A. program includes core courses in all major subfields, a yearlong statistics sequence, a professional development seminar, and opportunities to conduct research with faculty members whose publications are on a par with faculties in the top quarter of Ph.D.-granting institutions.

Psychology (Psy.D.): Dr. Neill Watson, Chair and Director of Clinical Training (npwats@wm.edu). The Psy.D. degree is offered by the Virginia Consortium Program in Clinical Psychology (the College of William and Mary, Eastern Virginia Medical School, Norfolk State University, and Old Dominion University) and provides education and training for the practice of clinical psychology. (http://www.vcpcp.odu.edu/vcpcp)

Public Policy (M.P.P., J.D./M.P.P. with law, M.B.A./M.P.P. with business, M.S./M.P.P. with marine science): Professor Elaine McBeth, Admissions Director (mcbeth@wm.edu). Two-year interdisciplinary program prepares students for careers in public service through training in economics and quantitative analysis, with instruction in political, legal, and organizational environments in which policy is made and implemented.

SCHOOL OF BUSINESS ADMINISTRATION

M.B.A., M.B.A./J.D., M.B.A./M.P.P.: Kathy Pattison, Director of M.B.A. Admissions (admissions@business.wm.edu). William and Mary provides a broad management education in a personalized environment that offers open access to faculty members and one-on-one interaction with some of today's most intriguing corporate leaders. Students achieve a thorough grounding in management theory and practice through the uniquely integrated curriculum, which addresses the complexities of multidisciplinary business issues. Elective courses and study-abroad opportunities provide concentrated study in specialized fields, while internships and field studies consulting projects provide hands-on experience in identifying, researching, and proposing solutions for real business problems.

M.A.C.: Ellen Lemieux, Assistant Director, Master of Accounting Program (account@business.wm.edu). A full-time, one-year residential program at Williamsburg, Virginia, the M.A.C. program has been built upon the nationally recognized excellence in William and Mary's accounting and M.B.A. programs. Offering a unique curriculum that blends both required accounting core courses and M.B.A. electives taught by highly respected faculty members, the M.A.C. program provides an extremely practical and valuable learning experience.

SCHOOL OF EDUCATION

M.Ed., M.A.Ed., Ed.D., Ed.S., Ph.D.: Thomas Ward, Associate Dean of Academic Programs (tjward@wm.edu). Programs prepare teachers for elementary, middle, and secondary education; prepare specialists in counseling, gifted education, and school psychology; and prepare students for educational policy, planning, and leadership roles for K–12 and higher education. Programs are organized into three divisions: curriculum and instruction; educational policy, planning, and leadership; and school psychology and counseling education.

MARSHALL-WYTHE SCHOOL OF LAW

J.D., LL.M., J.D./M.A. in American Studies, J.D./M.B.A., J.D./M.P.P.: Faye F. Shealy, Associate Dean of Admission (lawadm@wm.edu). The School is home to the Institute of Bill of Rights Law, which sponsors programs on emerging constitutional issues, and the Legal Skills Program, a nationally recognized model for teaching professional skills and ethics. The Supreme Court Preview, held each fall, includes nationally known journalists and academic commentators. The faculty includes nationally and internationally recognized experts in a wide range of subjects. Students, faculty members, administrators, and staff members maintain an exceptionally collegial learning and scholarly community.

SCHOOL OF MARINE SCIENCE

M.S., Ph.D.: Michael Newman, Dean of Graduate Studies (newman@vims.edu). School is located at the Virginia Institute of Marine Science and emphasizes the study of estuaries and coastal oceanography. Organized into five departments (biology, environmental science, fisheries, physical science, and coastal and ocean policy), the School also contributes to the College-wide environmental science and policy curriculum. Research focuses on the Chesapeake Bay area as well as national and international research projects. Considerable attention is also paid to advisory services and outreach in response to both public and private needs and interests.

COLORADO SCHOOL OF MINES

Graduate School

Programs of Study

The Colorado School of Mines (CSM) offers graduate education and research in areas related to the environment, energy, minerals, and materials. Advanced degrees are offered in chemical engineering and petroleum refining, chemistry, engineering and technology management, engineering systems, environmental science and engineering, geochemistry, geology and geological engineering, geophysics and geophysical engineering, materials science, mathematical and computer sciences, metallurgical and materials engineering, mineral economics, mining and earth systems engineering, petroleum engineering, and physics. Interdisciplinary programs are arranged to suit the student's particular career goals.

The Master of Science and Master of Engineering degrees require a minimum of 24 semester hours of acceptable course work and 12 hours of research credit plus a thesis or an engineering report. Nonthesis degree programs generally requiring 36 semester hours are available in chemical engineering and petroleum refining, engineering and technology management, engineering systems, environmental science and engineering, materials science, mathematical and computer science, mineral economics, mining engineering, and petroleum engineering. The School accepts a maximum of 9 semester hours of transfer credit for thesis degree programs and 15 semester hours for nonthesis degrees.

Course work requirements for the Ph.D. degree are established by the major department. The minimum credit hour requirement for the Ph.D. degree is 72 hours beyond the bachelor's degree, of which the Ph.D. thesis shall be no less than 24 hours. Each doctoral candidate is required to take a minimum of 12 semester hours of graduate credit in a minor field.

Postbaccalaureate professional degree programs emphasizing graduate-level work require a minimum of 30 hours of course work. These programs are designed for individuals who have been employed professionally and have the desire to enhance their education or for those who wish to change careers. Professional degree programs are offered in engineering geology, exploration geosciences, geological engineering, geophysical engineering, geophysics, and hydrogeology.

Graduate certificate programs are offered in international political economy through the Liberal Arts and International Studies Division. Each program requires two 15-hour certificates. Students specialize in one of six areas: resources, Latin America, Asia-Pacific, Middle East, Sub-Saharan Africa, or Eurasia.

Research Facilities

CSM maintains twenty-five research centers and institutes dedicated to various aspects of research in the fields of environment, minerals, energy, and materials. Major areas include exploration, mineral and petroleum production, environmental sciences and engineering, fuels science and engineering, materials science and engineering, automated and expert systems, and bioengineering (including bioenergy, biomaterials, and intelligent biomedical devices). Central Colorado is the home of numerous companies and high-tech industries working in these fields, and the nearby Rocky Mountains provide an excellent laboratory for educational fieldwork in the earth science disciplines. Located within a short distance of the CSM campus are valuable research facilities, including those of the U.S. Geological Survey, the National Park Service, the National Renewable Energy Laboratory, the U.S. Bureau of Reclamation, and the National Institute of Standards and Technology. CSM's proximity to the University of Colorado and Colorado State University provides opportunities for collaborative research and study in a wide variety of fields.

Financial Aid

Financial aid in the form of graduate research and teaching assistantships, as well as industrial, state, and federal fellowships, is available to full-time graduate students on a competitive basis. Financial assistance is provided to approximately 72 percent of all full-time graduate students.

Cost of Study

Tuition for the 2001–02 academic year was $2470 per semester for state residents and $8035 per semester for nonresidents. Student fees were $340 per semester, and health insurance cost approximately $400 per semester. A one-time graduation fee of $244 is also charged for the master's degree and $275 is charged for the Ph.D.

Living and Housing Costs

Single-student apartments are available in 1- to 3-bedroom units, with rents ranging from $550 to $990 per month. Family housing is available in 1- and 2-bedroom units at rents ranging from $550 to $635 per month. There is also a wide variety of private housing in the Golden and West Denver areas.

Student Group

The graduate enrollment of approximately 700 is composed of full- and part-time students. The latter are mainly practicing professionals working in the Denver area. Approximately 37 percent are international students, representing sixty-seven different nations. Thirty percent of the graduate students are women.

Location

The School is located in Golden, a community of 15,000 people in the eastern foothills of the Rocky Mountains, about 15 minutes west of Denver. Colorado's world-famous ski resorts are a short drive from campus, and the Rocky Mountains offer a variety of year-round outdoor activities. Hiking, backpacking, camping, fishing, hunting, bicycling, rock climbing, rafting, kayaking, and white-water canoeing are popular activities in Colorado. Golden's mild and dry climate has more than 300 sunny days a year.

The School

CSM offers engineering and applied science programs with a special focus on resource production and utilization. Founded in 1874 to support a growing mining industry in the Colorado territory, the school became the Colorado School of Mines when Colorado became a state in 1876. As the School grew, its mission widened from a focus on nonfuel minerals to encompass a broad range of engineering and science disciplines dealing with energy, minerals, materials, and the environment.

Applying

Interested individuals wishing to apply for graduate studies at the Colorado School of Mines should provide a duplicate set of transcripts from previous colleges, GRE scores, and three letters of recommendation. Applications can be accessed on line at the Web address listed below.

Correspondence and Information

Application forms are also available from:

Office of Graduate Studies
Colorado School of Mines
Golden, Colorado 80401

Telephone: 303-273-3247
800-446-9488 (toll-free)
Fax: 303-273-3244
E-mail: grad-school@mines.edu
World Wide Web: http://www.mines.edu/Admiss/grad

PROGRAMS, FACULTY HEADS, AND AREAS OF SPECIALIZATION

Chemical Engineering: Dr. James F. Ely, Head (303-273-3885). Surface and interfacial engineering, membranes, fuels science, theoretical and computational thermodynamics, thermophysical properties, polymers, new materials, mathematical modeling, dermal transport, gas hydrates, kinetic modeling, fuel cells; Colorado Institute for Fuels and Energy Research, Center for Hydrate Research, Colorado Institute for Macromolecular Science and Engineering.

Chemistry and Geochemistry: Dr. Paul Jagodzinski, Head (303-273-3622). Environmental chemistry, exploration geochemistry, biogeochemistry, organic geochemistry, fossil fuel chemistry, alternative clean fuels, catalysis and surface chemistry, polymer chemistry, surface analysis, computational materials chemistry, separation science.

Economics and Business: Dr. Roderick G. Eggert, Director (303-273-3981). Applied microeconomics; natural resource economics; quantitative business methods; energy and mineral markets; international trade and economic development; environmental policy and compliance; business and investment decision making, including operations research/operations management; decision making under uncertainty; discounted cashflow analysis; financial risk management; corporate finance. International joint-degree program in petroleum economics and management with Institut Français du Pétrole; joint-degree program with University of Denver School of Law; new master's degree in engineering and technology management.

Engineering: Dr. Joan P. Gosink, Director (303-273-3650). Analytical design, automated systems, biomedical systems, combustion, computer modeling of engineering systems, energy conversion, geotechnical and structural engineering, granular mechanics, intelligent automated systems, mechanics and materials, neural network applications, offshore mechanics, process simulation. Center for Advanced Control of Energy and Power Systems; Center for Automation, Robotics and Distributed Intelligence; Center for Combustion and Environmental Research; Center for Intelligent Biomedical Devices and Musculoskeletal Systems, Geomechanics Research Center, Particle Science and Technology Group. Web site: http://egweb.mines.edu

Environmental Science and Engineering: Dr. Robert Siegrist, Director (303-273-3473). Water and wastewater treatment, environmental biotechnology, environmental chemistry and radiochemistry, site characterization and remediation, environmental systems modeling.

Geology and Geological Engineering: Dr. Murray W. Hitzman, Head (303-384-2127). Predictive sediment modeling, aquifer-contaminant flow modeling, waste management, water-rock interactions, petroleum geology, mineral deposits, economic geology, geotechnical engineering, environmental geology, groundwater engineering, petrology, structural geology.

Geophysics and Geophysical Engineering: Dr. Terence K. Young, Head (303-273-3454). Applied geophysics, including seismic exploration, seismic data processing, gravity and geomagnetic fields, electrical and electromagnetic mapping and sounding, ground-penetrating radar, petrophysics, borehole geophysics, well logging, satellite remote sensing, groundwater exploration and exploitation, geohazard mitigation, mathematical geophysics, environmental and geotechnical geophysics. Center for Wave Phenomena; Reservior Characterization Project; Center for Petrophysics, Gravity and Magnetics Research Consortium; Geophysics Field Camp; Near-Surface Seismology Group; Rock Physics Laboratory; Physical Acoustics Laboratory. Web site: http://www.geophysics.mines.edu

Liberal Arts and International Studies: Dr. Arthur B. Sacks, Director (303-273-3590). International political economy of area studies, international political economy of resources and the environment, theories of globalization, case studies of global corporations, international political risk assessment and mitigation, theories of international political economy, comparative development theories of regions, political economy of ethnicity, theories and empirical case studies of comparative regimes, global political geography, comparative political cultures.

Materials Science: Dr. John J. Moore, Program Director (303-273-3660). Bonding theory, ceramics, coatings, composites, surface engineering, thin-films and advanced coatings, electronic materials, joining science, materials chemistry, mechanics of materials, metal and alloy systems, phase transformations, photovoltaic materials, polymeric materials, biomaterials, nuclear materials, solid-state physics, solid-state thermodynamics, structural and structured defects, surfaces/interfaces, transport and kinetics; Center for Welding and Joining Research, Colorado Center for Advanced Ceramics, Colorado Center for Simulation of Materials and Engineering, Advanced Coatings and Surface Engineering Laboratory, Center for Solar and Electronic Materials, Advanced Steel Processing and Products Research Center.

Mathematical and Computer Sciences: Dr. Graeme Fairweather, Head (303-273-3860). Applied mathematics: direct and inverse scattering, inverse problems, mathematical finance, micro-local analysis, numerical analysis, scientific computing, symbolic computing, wave propagation. Computer science: algorithms, computer networking, databases, graphics, mobile computing, visualization. Statistics: biostatistics, epidemiological methods, statistical seismic data processing, statistical regularization of inverse problems. Center for Wave Phenomena; Center for Automation, Robotics and Distributed Intelligence.

Metallurgical and Materials Engineering: Dr. John J. Moore, Head (303-273-3770). Physical and mechanical metallurgy, physicochemical processing (extractive metallurgy and waste processing, materials synthesis and processing, materials process modeling and control), ceramic engineering, metals, intermetallics, ceramics, glasses, thin films, coatings, surface engineering, photovoltaics, electronic materials processing, corrosion, forming, castings, welding, electroceramics, composites and smart materials of these components; Advanced Steel Processing and Products Research Center, Center for Welding and Joining Research, Colorado Center for Advanced Ceramics, W. J. Kroll Institute for Extractive Metallurgy, Colorado Center for Simulation of Materials and Engineering, Center for Solar and Electronic Materials, Advanced Coatings and Surface Engineering Laboratory.

Mining Engineering: Dr. Tibor G. Rozgonyi, Head (303-273-3700). Mine evaluation and planning, geostatistics, underground excavations, rock mechanics, mechanical fragmentation, mine productivity analysis, intelligent decision support systems, mechanical excavation systems, bulk material handling, mineral processing; Earth Mechanics Institute, Edgar Experimental Mine, Western Mining Resource Center.

Petroleum Engineering: Dr. Craig W. Van Kirk, Head (303-273-3740). Reservoir management; field development; computer simulation; geostatistics; interdisciplinary integration of petroleum engineering, geology, and geophysics; petroleum economics; enhanced oil and gas production; subsidence; drilling in space and laser drilling; well completion design; sand control; dynamic rock mechanics; petrophysics; geochemistry; hydrocarbon hydrates; multiphase flow in pipelines; fluid flow in porous media; and environmental issues.

Physics: Dr. James A. McNeil, Head (303-273-3844). Condensed-matter physics and materials science: photovoltaics; surface physics; nanophysics; scanning probe microscopy; high-pressure physics; granular materials; X-ray, electron, Mössbauer, and Raman spectroscopies; theoretical condensed-matter physics; X-ray scattering. Nuclear physics: experimental low-energy nuclear physics, theoretical nuclear physics, high-temperature fusion plasma diagnostics, nuclear astrophysics, environmental nuclear physics. Applied optics: ultra-short pulses, optical properties of interfaces and surfaces, laser physics and quantum optics. Center for Solar and Electronic Materials, Center for Commercial Applications of Combustion in Space.

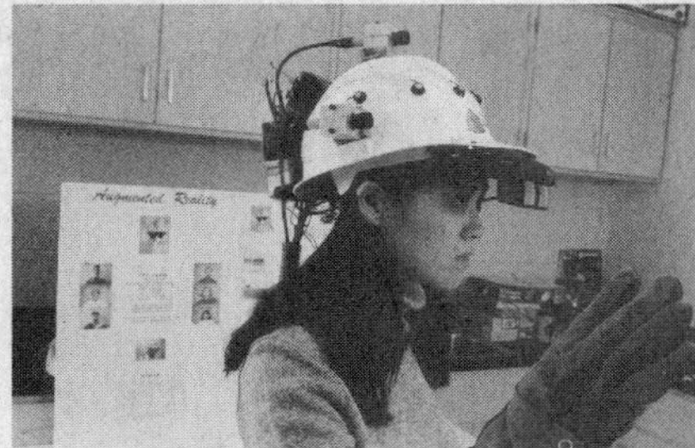

An engineering student uses an augmented reality system.

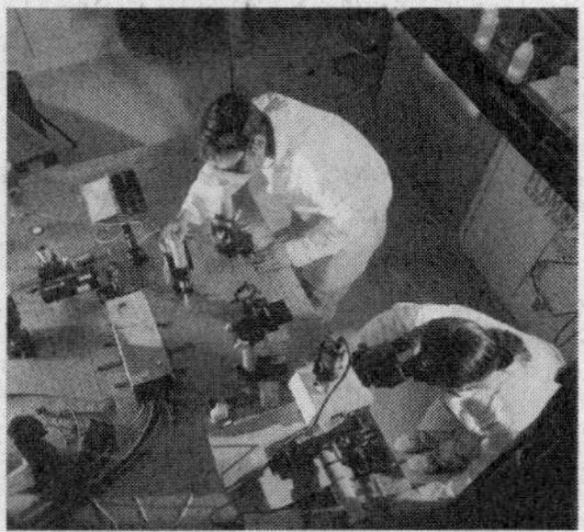

Chemical engineering students engage in materials synthesis by optical tweezing.

COLUMBIA COLLEGE CHICAGO

Graduate School

Programs of Study

The Graduate School of Columbia College Chicago offers programs of study leading to a master's degree in ten fields. Following a non-traditional approach, the M.F.A. program in architectural studies focuses on specific areas such as architectural imaging, furniture construction, and building material specialist studies, encouraging full immersion in each. The program in arts, entertainment, and media management (AEMM) applies the techniques of successful business management to the special needs of the arts through four concentrations: media management, the music business, and visual or performing arts management. The ATDA-approved program in dance/movement therapy integrates theoretical, clinical, and experiential approaches to dance and movement in the field of psychotherapy, preparing graduates for careers as clinicians, researchers, and educators. The program in film and video offers the M.F.A. degree and emphasizes development in both narrative and documentary forms. The writing and directing curriculum is production oriented and prepares students for independent or industry careers. The M.A. program in interdisciplinary arts encourages professional artists and educators in the five arts to collaborate to develop original art and performances, integrated arts programs, opportunities in arts administration, and the book and paper arts. The M.F.A. program in interdisciplinary book and paper arts encourages students to develop a personal focus and to stretch the art form into installation, set design, and performance. The M.F.A. in interdisciplinary arts and media uses emerging technology with personal vision and voice in conjunction with the artists art form. The M.F.A. program in interior architecture permits focus in such areas as facility design and management, hospitality, furniture design, and decorative arts. The M.A. in journalism program offers specialized training in public affairs reporting at the local, state, and national levels. Educational Studies offers a Master of Arts in Teaching (M.A.T.) degree program that prepares candidates for state of Illinois initial teacher certification in one of three areas: special certificate in art (K–12), elementary education (K–9), and elementary education (K–9) with the necessary course work for permanent bilingual approval. Supporting a broad range of contemporary photographic practice, the M.F.A. and M.A. programs in photography combine aesthetic and expressive development with advanced technical training, preparing students to become both successful professional photographers and fine artists. The program in writing offers three concentrations that use the celebrated Story Workshop approach: in the M.F.A. program in creative writing, students are guided through self-discovery and critique to meet the demands of professional writing, producing book-length fiction, nonfiction, and dramatic works; in the M.A. program in the teaching of writing, students learn to write professionally and also to teach. The department also offers a combined M.F.A./M.A. program of study.

Research Facilities

In addition to its general collection, the Columbia College Library houses the George S. Lurie Memorial Collection of books and resource materials on art, photography, and film, as well as a center containing the Black Music Resource Collection. The Columbia College Script Collection has one of the country's largest collections of motion-picture and television scripts. The library is linked by computer and direct delivery to more than forty academic libraries in Illinois, and it also offers a nationwide network for interlibrary loans and computerized bibliographic database search services.

Financial Aid

Each year, the Graduate School offers a limited number of Follett Fellowships and Graduate Opportunity Awards to students applying for fall admission. The awards are renewable, provided that the student continues to meet program standards for satisfactory academic progress. The Office of Financial Aid administers federal and state loan programs. Tuition may be paid in installments.

Cost of Study

For the 2002–03 academic year, graduate tuition is $463 per credit hour. A number of graduate courses, particularly in advanced technical areas, require additional class fees; typically, these range from $15 to $100 per course. There is also a registration fee of $50 per term and a student activity fee of $40 per term ($20 for part-time students). Entering students are charged a library deposit of $30, which is refunded upon withdrawal or graduation. There is a graduation fee of $100. Full-time students pay a U-pass fee of $70.

Living and Housing Costs

Columbia is an urban college serving commuter students, and limited on-campus housing is available. The city's public transportation network enables students to live in any part of Chicago or the suburbs and still reach the College quickly and easily. Costs of living are as varied as those in any large metropolitan area.

Student Group

In the 2001–02 academic year, the College had 513 graduate students; about 35 percent were full-time students. The average age was 32; 36 percent were members of minority groups, and 67 percent were women. The College's total enrollment in 2001–02 was 9,500 students.

Location

Chicago has numerous cultural, educational, and recreational resources. Near the College are the Chicago Public Library, the Field Museum, the Art Institute, Orchestra Hall, Adler Planetarium, Auditorium Theater, the Chicago City Ballet, Shedd Aquarium, music conservatories, and several other colleges.

The College

Columbia College Chicago is a modern, urban institution. Its fifteen-story main building is on South Michigan Avenue, overlooking Grant Park and Lake Michigan. Columbia is an independent liberal arts college that prepares creative people for careers in film; photography; theater, music, and dance; graphic and fine arts; writing; television and radio; journalism; marketing communication; and management.

Applying

To be considered for fall admission, U.S. applicants must complete their files by January 3 for film and video, by March 15 for early admission decisions in creative writing, by March 15 for interdisciplinary arts programs and for dance/movement therapy, and by August 1 for all other programs. Fall or spring applicants for Follett Fellowships or Graduate Opportunity Awards must complete their files by March 15. For selected spring term admission, the deadline to complete the file is November 15.

International students must submit a supplemental application form, essay, and official TOEFL score by November 15 for spring programs and by March 15 for all interdisciplinary arts programs, dance/movement therapy, and early admission for creative writing and by June 15 for all other programs except film and video, which has a January 3 deadline.

Correspondence and Information

Graduate School
Columbia College Chicago
600 South Michigan Avenue
Chicago, Illinois 60605-1996
Telephone: 312-344-7260
E-mail: gradsch@popmail.colum.edu
World Wide Web: http://www.colum.edu/graduate

THE FACULTY

Architectural Studies & Interior Design
Joclyn Oats, M.Arch., Coordinator of the Master's Program. Yvonne Gajewski, M.S. Ted Garnett, M. Arch. Jean Guarino, M.A. Kevin Henry, M.F.A. Melinda Palmore, M.Arch. Tim Whitman, M.A.

Arts, Entertainment, and Media Management
J. Dennis Rich, Ph.D., Chairperson. Clark Greene, B.A. Phyllis Johnson, M.Mgmt. Dawn Larsen, J.D. Angelo Luciano, M.S. Joseph Roberts, Ph.D. Dolores Smith, M.A. Irwin Steinberg, M.A. Charles Suber, B.A. Paulette Whitfield, M.B.A. James Kimo Williams, M.A. Carol Yamamoto, M.B.A.

Creative Writing/Teaching of Writing
Randall Albers, Ph.D., Chairperson. Andrew Allegretti, M.A. Don DeGrazia, M.F.A. Ann Hemenway, M.F.A. Gary Johnson, M.A. Eric May, B.A. Patricia Ann McNair, M.F.A. John Schultz. Betty Shiflett, B.A. Shawn Shiflett, M.A.

Dance/Movement Therapy
Susan Imus, M.A., Chairperson; ADTR, LCPC. Andrea Brown, M.Ed.; ADTR, LCPC, NCC, LSW. Lisa Goldman, M.A.; ADTR, LCPC. Dawna Gutzman, M.D. Lenore Hervey, Ph.D.; ADTR, NOC, REAT. Stacey Hurst, M.A.; ADTR., LCPC. Kris Larsen, M.A.; ADTR, LCPC. Pam Margueles, LCSW, ADTR. Margaret Mason, M.A.; ADTR, LCPC. Mollie Ryan, M.A.; ADTR, LCPC. Ellen Stone-Belic, M.A., A.M.; CSW.

Educational Studies
Ava Belisle-Chatterjee, Ph.D., Chairperson. Abour Cherif, Ph.D. Clara Fitzpatrick, M.A. Mary Pat Garr, M.A. Philip Kluhoff, Ph.D.

Film and Video
Doreen Bartoni, M.A. Cari Callis, M.A. Judd Chesler, Ph.D. Dan Dinello, M.F.A. Ron Falzone, M.F.A. Tom Fraternigo, M.F.A. Chappelle Freeman, M.F.A. Paula Froehle, M.F.A. Karla Rae Fuller, Ph.D. Ted Harden, M.F.A. Paul Hettel, B.S., B.A. Chris Peppy, B.A. Russell Porter. Mehmaz Saeed-Vafa, M.F.A. Bruce Sheridan, B.A. Donald Smith, M.F.A. Josef Steiff, M.F.A. Christopher Swider, B.A. Wenhwa Tsao, M.F.A.

Graduate Laban Certificate in Movement Analysis
Carol-Lynne Moore, Ph.D.; CMA. Calvin Jarrell, M.F.A., M.A.; CMA. Cate Deicher, M.A.; CMA.

Interdisciplinary Arts
Suzanne Cohan-Lange, M.A., Chairperson. Jeff Abell, M.M. Sherry Antoninini, M.F.A. Ron Boyd, B.A. Melissa J. Craig, M.F.A. Joan Dickinson, M.A. William Drendel, Director of Book and Paper Arts. Jenny Magnus, B.A. Jeanine Mellinger, M.F.A. Audrey Niffenegger, M.F.A. Andrea Peterson, M.F.A. Michael Piazza, M.F.A. Nana Shineflug, M.A.

Journalism
Norma Green, Ph.D., Director. Thom Clark, B.A. Hank DeZutter, M.S.J. Maria Donato, M.A. Lorraine Forte, M.S.J. Peter Gorner, B.S. Carolyn Hulse, M.A. Curtis Lawrence, M.S.J. Barry Rice, M.S.J. Len Strazewski, M.A., M.S. Lillian Williams, M.S.J.

Photography
Bob Thall, M.F.A, Chairperson. Paul D'Amato, M.F.A. Barbara Kasten, M.F.A., Graduate Coordinator. Dawoud Bey, M.F.A. Elizabeth Ernst, M.S. William G. Frederking, M.F.A. Peter LeGrand, M.A. Judy Natal, M.F.A Corey Postiglione, M.F.A. Sabrina Raaf, M.F.A. Accra Shepp, M.F.A. Thomas Shirley, M.F.A. Lynn Sloan, M.S. Peter Hunt Thompson, M.A.

COLUMBIA UNIVERSITY

Graduate School of Arts and Sciences

Programs of Study

The Graduate School of Arts and Sciences at Columbia University offers programs of study leading to the degree of Doctor of Philosophy in anatomy and cell biology; anthropology; applied physics; architecture; art history and archaeology; astronomy; biochemistry and molecular biophysics; biological sciences; biostatistics; business; cellular, molecular, and biophysical studies; chemical engineering and applied chemistry; chemical physics; chemistry; civil engineering and engineering mechanics; classical studies; classics; communications; computer science; Earth and environmental sciences; East Asian languages and cultures; ecology, evolution, and environmantal biology; economics; education; electrical engineering; English and comparative literature; environmental health sciences; epidemiology; French and Romance philology; genetics and development; Germanic languages; history; industrial engineering and operations research; Italian; mathematics; mechanical engineering; medical informatics; metallurgical and mineral engineering; microbiology; Middle East and Asian languages and cultures; mining; music; neurobiology and behavior; nutrition; pathology; pharmacology; philosophy; physics; physiology and cellular biophysics; political science; psychology; religion; Slavic languages; social work; sociology; sociomedical sciences; Spanish and Portuguese; statistics; theater; and urban planning. The Graduate School also offers M.A. programs in African-American studies; art history and archaeology; anthropology; biotechnology, classical studies; classics; conservation biology; dental sciences; East Asian languages and cultures; East Asian regional studies; English and comparative literature; French and romance philology; French cultural studies; Germanic languages; Italian; Japanese pedagogy (summer only); mathematics; mathematics of finance; Middle East and Asian languages and cultures; modern art; museum anthropology; music; philosophical foundations of physics; philosophy; political science; quantitative methods in the social sciences; religion; Russian, Eurasian, and European regional studies; Slavic cultures; Slavic languages; sociology; Spanish and Portuguese; and statistics and two dual M.A./M.S. degree programs in earth and environmental sciences journalism and religion and journalism with the School of Journalism. The information telephone number for obtaining separate applications for the liberal studies M.A. program in American, East Asian, human rights, Islamic, Jewish, medieval, modern European, and South Asian studies is 212-854-4932.

Research Facilities

Columbia University's research facilities are too numerous to be listed, but in every area of study the University's excellent facilities are supplemented by the rich resources of the city of New York.

Financial Aid

A comprehensive program of financial aid, including teaching and research fellowships, is available. Applicants who file financial aid forms by the deadline are automatically considered for any Columbia-administered awards for which they may be eligible. Applicants are urged to compete for all national, regional, and foundation fellowships in addition to those available at Columbia.

Cost of Study

Tuition and fees for 2001–02 were $28,900, based on a flat tuition payment of $13,764 per semester, plus fees for a full-time course load for which the student earns 2 residence units. Six units are required for the Ph.D., although up to 2 units of advanced standing may be given for previous graduate work leading to an M.A. or other appropriate professional degree. With the exception of traveling fellows, students are expected to remain registered until they have completed all the requirements for the degree.

Living and Housing Costs

Most graduate students live in off-campus housing, although the University is increasing its facilities for both single and married students. All graduate students awarded fellowships are guaranteed housing.

Student Group

Of the approximately 23,000 students at Columbia University, 3,400 are students in the various departments and subcommittees of the Graduate School of Arts and Sciences. The vast majority of these 3,400 students are engaged in full-time completion of the requirements for the Ph.D.

Location

The incomparable city of New York is indisputably the greatest college town on earth. Cultural appetites can be sated at any of the innumerable theaters, museums, concert halls, opera houses, movie plexes, bookstores, and street fairs within a walk or subway hop from the Columbia campus. Retreat from concrete can be found at large verdant parks or at the beaches and mountains just a short drive away from the metropolitan area.

The School

The Graduate School of Arts and Sciences is historically divided into the humanities, social sciences, and natural sciences. In addition to these three disciplinary areas, there are a number of doctoral program subcommittees. A student is admitted to one of the departments or a subcommittee, and his or her course of study is directed by the regulations established by that department or subcommittee.

Applying

In order to be guaranteed consideration for admission and financial aid for the autumn term, all students must submit the completed application form, required transcripts, and all supporting materials by January 3. To be considered for admission only, international students and overseas applicants must file applications by March 30 for consideration (without fellowship) on a space-available basis. All other students must apply before April 1. Only in exceptional circumstances can applications submitted after these dates be considered. Students should contact the specific department or program of interest for detailed information.

Students who do not hold degrees from colleges or universities in which English is the classroom language or for whom English is not the native language are required to submit scores on the TOEFL, administered in other countries by the Educational Testing Service.

General descriptions of all programs and procedures are to be found on the Graduate School of Arts and Sciences Web page: http://www.columbia.edu/cu/gsas. Students can download the application or apply online through this site. Students who cannot access the Web and need a hard copy of the application booklet can request one from the address below.

Correspondence and Information

Office of Student Affairs
Graduate School of Arts and Sciences
107 Low Memorial Library
Mail Code: 4304
Columbia University
535 West 116th Street
New York, New York 10027
Telephone: 212-854-4737
Fax: 212-854-2863
E-mail: gsas-admit@columbia.edu
World Wide Web: http://www.columbia.edu

FACULTY HEADS

Department Chairs
Anatomy and Cell Biology: Michael D. Gershon, 630 West 168th Street.
Anthropology: Nicholas Dirks, 452 Schermerhorn.
Applied Physics and Applied Math: Michael E. Mauel, 206 Seeley W. Mudd.
Art History and Archaeology: Joseph Connors, 826 Schermerhorn.
Astronomy: Jacqueline van Gorkom, 1328 Pupin.
Biochemistry and Molecular Biophysics: David Hirsh, 630 West 168th Street.
Biological Sciences: Carol Privas, 600 Fairchild.
Chemistry: Gerard Parkin, 344 Havemeyer.
Civil Engineering and Engineering Mechanics: Rimas Vaicaitis, 610 Seeley W. Mudd.
Classics: Gareth Williams, 617 Hamilton.
Computer Science: Kathleen R. McKeown, 450 Computer Science.
Earth and Environmental Engineering, Materials Science and Engineering: Peter Schlosser, 918 Mudd.
Earth and Environmental Sciences: Dennis Hayes, Lamont-Doherty Geological Observatory.
East Asian Languages and Cultures: Harno Shirane, 407 Kent.
Ecology, Evolution, and Environmental Biology: Marina Cords, 1004 Schermerhorn Extension.
Economics: Don Davis, 1022 International Affairs.
Electrical Engineering: Charles Zukowski, 1312 Seeley W. Mudd.
English and Comparative Literature: Jonathan Arac, 602 Philosophy.
French and Romance Philology: Pierre Force, 517 Philosophy.
Genetics and Development: Franklin Costantini, 701 West 168th Street.
Germanic Languages: Dorothea von Muecke, 319 Hamilton.
History: Alan Brinkley, 611 Fayerweather.
Industrial Engineering and Operations Research: Donald Goldfarb, AC, 322 Seeley W. Mudd.
Italian: Teodolinda Barolini, 502 Hamilton.
Mathematics: Robert Friedman, 509 Mathematics.
Mechanical Engineering: W. Michael Lai, 220 Seeley W. Mudd.
Microbiology: Saul Silverstein, 701 West 168th Street.
Middle East and Asian Languages and Cultures: Hamid Dabashi, 602 Kent.
Music: Elaine Sisman, 703 Dodge.
Pathology: Michael Shelanski, 630 West 168th Street.
Pharmacology: Robert S. Kass, 630 West 168th Street.
Philosophy: Haim Gaifman, 708 Philosophy.
Physics: Steven Kahn, 704 Pupin.
Physiology and Cellular Biophysics: Samuel C. Silverstein, 630 West 168th Street.
Political Science: Bob Shapiro, 714 International Affairs.
Psychology: Don Hood, 406 Schermerhorn.
Religion: Ryuichi Abe, 617 Kent.
Slavic Languages: Irina Reyfman, 708 Hamilton.
Sociology: Peter Bearman, 413 Fayerweather.
Spanish and Portuguese: Patricia Grieve, Casa Hispánica, 305.
Statistics: Shaw-Hwa Lo, 618 Mathematics.

Chairs of Doctoral Program Subcommittees
Architecture: Kenneth Frampton, 400 Avery.
Biostatistics: Bruce Levin, 600 West 168th Street.
Business: John Donaldson, 804 Uris.
Integrated Program in Cellular, Molecular, and Biophysical Studies at the College of Physicians and Surgeons: Ronald Liem, 630 West 168th Street.
Chemical Physics: Phil Pechukas, 959 Chandler.
Classical Studies: W. V. Harris, 613 Fayerweather.
Communications: Andrea Tucher, 201 Journalism.
Education: Robert O. McClintock, 218 Main.
Environmental Health Sciences: Joseph H. Graziano, 600 West 168th St.
Epidemiology: Ezra Susser, 600 West 168th Street.
Medical Informatics: Edward Shortliffe, 161 Fort Wash Avenue, 13th Floor.
Neurobiology and Behavior: John Koester, 722 W. 168th Street.
Nutrition: Richard Deckelbaum, 701 West 168th Street.
Social Work: Brenda McGowan, 708 McVickar, 622 West 113th Street.
Sociomedical Sciences: Peter Messeri, 600 West 168th Street.
Theatre: James Shapiro and Arnold Aronson, 602 Philosophy.
Urban Planning: Elliott D. Sclar, 413 Avery.

Chairs of Master's Programs (Interdisciplinary)
African-American Studies: Steven Gregory, 758 Schermerhorn Extension.
Biotechnology: Carol Lin, 600 Fairchild.
Conservation Biology: Don Melnick, 1004 Schermerhorn Extension.
Dental Sciences: Letty Moss-Salentijn, 630 West 168th Street.
Earth and Environmental Sciences Journalism: Kim Kastens, Lamont-Doherty Geological Observatory.
East Asia (Regional Studies): Madeleine Zelin, 914 International Affairs.
French Cultural Studies in Paris, France: Beatrice Terrien, 109 Low.
Human Rights: Louis Henkin, 8E3 Law.
Japanese Pedagogy: Paul Anderer, 407 Kent.
Liberal Studies: Steven Laymon, 108 Low.
Mathematics, with specialization in Mathematics of Finance: Ioannis Karatzas, 511 Mathematics.
Modern Art: Rosalind Krauss, 826 Schermerhorn.
Museum Anthropology: Terry D'Altroy, 452 Schermerhorn.
Philosophical Foundations of Physics: David Albert, 708 Philosophy; Allan Blaer, 704 Pupin.
Quantitative Methods in the Social Sciences: Andrew Gelman, 618 Mathematics.
Philosophy; Patricia Grieve, 305 Casa Hispánica.
Russia, Eurasia, and Eastern Europe (Regional Studies): Cathy Nepomayaschy, 1214 International Affairs.
Slavic Cultures: Frank J. Miller, 708 Hamilton.
Statistics: Shaw-Hwa Lo, 618 Mathematics.

CONCORDIA UNIVERSITY

School of Graduate Studies

Programs of Study

Concordia University offers programs leading to doctoral and master's degrees, graduate diplomas, and graduate certificates. Ph.D.'s are awarded in administration, art education, art history, biology, building studies, chemistry, civil engineering, communication, computer science, economics, educational technology, electrical and computer engineering, history, mathematics, mechanical engineering, psychology, and religion. There are also interdisciplinary programs that lead to the Ph.D. in humanities and the Ph.D. in a special, individualized program. The minimum residence requirement is two years of full-time study or the equivalent in part-time study. All Ph.D. programs are a minimum of 90 credits. Students entering without having completed a master's degree normally require more time. It is rare to complete a Ph.D. in less than three years. All Ph.D. programs require a thesis.

Master's degrees (M.A., M.A.Sc., M.Sc., M.Eng., M.Comp.Sc., M.Ap.Comp.Sc., M.B.A., M.T.M., or M.F.A.) are available in applied linguistics, art education, art history, biology, business administration (executive option, international aviation option), chemistry, child study, computer science, creative arts therapies, economics, educational studies, educational technology, engineering (aerospace, building, civil, electrical and computer, and mechanical), English, film studies, history, human systems intervention, investment management, Judaic studies, mathematics, media studies, philosophy, psychology, public policy and public administration (with an option in geography), religion, social and cultural anthropology, sociology, studio arts, teaching of mathematics, theological studies, and traductologie. Most master's programs require 45 credits and have a one year's minimum residence. Programs in business administration, studio arts, and educational technology require more than 45 credits and take proportionately longer. Many master's programs have a nonthesis option.

Diplomas are offered in accountancy, administration, adult education, advanced music performance, communication studies, community economic development, computer science, economic policy, environmental impact assessment, instructional technology, investment management, journalism, traduction, and sports administration. Diploma programs are 30 or more credits, normally take one year of full-time study, and do not require a thesis.

Graduate certificates are offered in anglais/français en langue et techniques de localisation, building studies, community organizational development, cultural affairs event management, digital technologies in design art practice, e-business, environmental engineering, management accounting, management of health-care organizations, mechanical engineering, software systems for mechanical and aerospace engineering, urban development studies, and users interface design for software systems. Graduate certificates are normally 15 credits, can be completed in one year, and do not require a thesis.

One credit is deemed the equivalent of 45 hours of work by the student, which includes lectures, laboratory sessions, seminars, research, and preparation of assignments. The minimum full-time credit load for an individual graduate student is 24 credits over twelve months.

Research Facilities

The Universities libraries have a rapidly expanding collection of reference and research materials and an extensive collection of government documents and newspapers on microfilm, microfiche, and microcard. The expanded Vanier Library houses unusual special collections. The main library has been designated a full depository library for Canadian federal government documents. Various cooperative arrangements exist with other research libraries in the Montreal area. Modern buildings house the well-equipped engineering and science laboratories, used for both teaching and research. A CDC CYBER 170/835 dual-processor computer is available for use by graduate students.

Financial Aid

Scholarships and fellowships are available on a competitive basis; Concordia fellowships are currently valued at $2900 per term (master's level) and $3600 per term (doctoral level). All dollar amounts are in Canadian funds. Certain fellowships have a higher value. Work at the University in the form of part-time lecturer contracts, teaching assistantships, and research assistantships is limited. Information about the possibility of this kind of work is available from the graduate program in which the applicant hopes to enroll. The Graduate Awards Directory, obtainable on diskette at nominal cost from the School of Graduate Studies, gives details about many awards tenable at Concordia and elsewhere. International students are strongly advised to apply for awards available to them from their own country or through agencies in their own country.

Cost of Study

For 2002–03, tuition for Québec residents is $1251.24 per year (second- and third-cycle programs) and for non-Québec residents, $3009.39 per year (second-cycle programs) and $1251.24 per year (third-cycle programs); tuition for international students is $6876.24 per year; tuition for international students in second-cycle programs in the John Molson School of Business is $9000 per year. Students pay a number of miscellaneous fees, which are assessed at the time of registration. International students must also pay approximately $480 for health insurance.

Living and Housing Costs

The expenses for a single student for an eight-month stay total approximately $13,000 (lodging, $5000; books and supplies, $1000; groceries, $4200; clothing, $800; transportation, $600; and miscellaneous, $1400).

Student Group

There are approximately 3,700 graduate students enrolled in the University. A significant number are bilingual and/or come from multicultural backgrounds.

Location

Montreal is the second-largest city in Canada, with a population of nearly 3 million. Roughly three quarters of the population is French speaking. Montreal has all the attractions one would expect of a large cosmopolitan area: many theatres and museums, a rich musical life, numerous places of historic interest, and beautiful parks, including the famous Mount Royal Park. The climate is variable, with temperatures ranging from 30°C in summer to -20°C in winter.

The University

Concordia University is one of four universities in the Montreal area. It was formed in 1974, when Sir George Williams University and Loyola College of Montreal merged the green spaces of the Loyola Campus and the urban downtown campus of Sir George Williams to complement each other. There are nearly 27,000 students enrolled in graduate and undergraduate programs. An interuniversity agreement makes it possible for graduate students to elect a certain number of their courses from any one of Montreal's four universities regardless of where they are enrolled.

Applying

Applications can be obtained from the School of Graduate Studies. There is a $50 application fee. Along with the application form, applicants must provide three academic assessments and arrange for official transcripts of university-level work to be sent directly by the registrar of the institution attended. Application deadlines vary for each program. While most students begin their degrees in the fall term, some programs accept students in the summer or the winter term. The deadline for financial aid applications is February 1.

Correspondence and Information

School of Graduate Studies, Concordia University
1455 de Maisonneuve Boulevard, West
Montreal, Québec H3G 1M8
Canada

Telephone: 514-848-3800
Fax: 514-842-2812
E-mail: gradadm@alcor.concordia.ca
World Wide Web: http://graduatestudies.concordia/ca

FACULTY RESEARCH AREAS

Accountancy: financial and management accountancy, behavioural accountancy, accountancy education, auditing, management control in nonprofit organizations.
Administration: decision sciences and management information systems; finance; management; marketing; community services, public and parapublic; health and health-care delivery; arts, cultural affairs, and event management; sport administration.
Adult Education: staff development, literacy, learning in the workplace, professional development, self-directed learning, human relations training.
Aerospace: aeronautics and propulsion, avionics and control, structures and materials, space engineering.
Applied Linguistics: teaching English as a second/foreign language, second language learning, evaluation of language programs, teacher education for second/foreign language learning.
Art Education: development of symbolization and aesthetic response in children; the early development of artists; history of art education; museum education; adult education; multicultural and aboriginal issues; women in art and art education; built environment education; response to art; postmodernism; digital technologies and art education, ethnography; life-history; oral history; action research; descriptive research; feminist research; video and photographic documentation; community-based video; studio-based inquiry, studio theory, and practice.
Art History: Amerindian and Inuit art and architecture; North American architecture, craft, painting, photography, and sculpture, as well as other media, from the seventeenth to the twenty-first centuries; European art and theory from the Middle Ages to the present; art criticism; cultural studies; feminist and gender studies; industrial archaeology and museum studies.
Biology: animal biology, cell biology/biochemistry, ecology and behaviour, microbiology/molecular biology, plant biochemistry and biotechnology.
Building Engineering: computer-aided design, performance of building envelope and materials, building environment (HVAC, acoustics, illumination, air quality), building and energy, wind effects on buildings, building structures and construction management.
Business Administration: professional M.B.A., Executive M.B.A., International Aviation M.B.A.
Chemistry and Biochemistry: analytical and bioanalytical chemistry, biochemistry and biophysical chemistry, bioinorganic and physical inorganic chemistry, physical organic chemistry, computational chemistry, materials and solid-state chemistry.
Child Study: children's social behaviour in day care settings, children and technology, historical perspectives on child care, early childhood curriculum, popular culture of youth and children, health and well-being, gender issues, teaching and teacher education, family and children, international issues in early childhood education, learning and cognition and educational psychology.
Civil Engineering: structural engineering, bridge engineering, structural mechanics, earthquake engineering, water resources, fluids engineering, geotechnical engineering, transportation.
Communication: nature and conception of audiences, cultural studies, rhetorical strategies in communication, future studies, film production and policy, television aesthetics, feminism and cultural theory, development communication, political communication and the interface of technology and culture.
Computer Science: computer systems and VLSI architecture; database and information systems; parallel and distributed computing; mathematics of computation; pattern recognition, artificial intelligence, image processing; programming languages and methodology; software engineering; theoretical computer science.
Creative Arts Therapies: art psychotherapy, rehabilitation through art and drama, sandplay therapy, guided imagery in music, development and creative art therapy assessments, narrative therapy, storytelling as therapeutic process, art and psychoanalysis (postmodern theory French School of Thought).
Economics: econometrics, microeconomics, macroeconomics, international trade and finance, labour economics, economic development and planning, financial and monetary economics, economic dynamics, regional economics, environmental and natural resources economics, public economics and industrial organization.
Educational Studies: cooperative learning and classroom processes; social aspects of microtechnology; gender and education; education of immigrants and minorities; sociology of education and issues of differences; political education; education, work, and leisure; social history of education and history of educational ideas; women and development; curricular deliberation; experiential education; professional development; literacy and education; education in developing countries.
Educational Technology: Computer-based learning, computer-supported collaborative learning, distance learning, classroom processes, human performance technology applications, program evaluation, educational evaluation and new technologies, corporate applications of educational technology, systemic modeling of educational systems, learning styles and strategies, multimedia research and development.
Electrical and Computer Engineering: systems, control, and robotics; circuits and systems; communications; computer communications and protocols; signal processing; high-performance architecture; software engineering; VLSI systems; microelectronics; microwaves and optoelectronics; antennas and electromagnetic compatibility; power electronics and adjustable speed drives.
English: English literature from the Middle Ages to the present; European, Canadian, American, and postcolonial literature; genres; creative writing; composition; women's literature.
Etudes Françaises: writing, translation, court interpretation.
Film Studies: Canadian film, experimental film, gay and lesbian film making, experimental documentary and ethnography, Third World cinemas and auteur studies, film acting, film and philosophy, Japanese cinema, Indian cinema, documentary film, feminist theory, film theory and American cinema.
Finance: international financing consortia, efficiency of capital markets, financing of small and medium-sized businesses, corporate finance, capital markets, business economics.
Geography: policy-oriented studies, with an emphasis on urban, environmental, and social issues, including watershed management, port development and planning, urban design, immigration, sustainable forestry, indigenous resource management, and metropolitan government.
History: Canadian, European, and American history and Non-Western history (India, China, the Caribbean, Africa). Genres include genocide, antisemitism, and human rights; race and slavery in the Western hemisphere; colonialism; women's and gender history; urban history; pacifism; cultural history; intellectual history; religious history; and historiography.
Humanities: interdisciplinary doctoral studies in the humanities, social sciences, and fine arts.
Human Systems Intervention: applications of group development and small-group leadership, organizational development and change interventions, cross-cultural perspectives of management and leadership, coaching and mentoring relationships, community intervention and interventions with community workers.
Journalism: ethics, Québec media, broadcast public affairs.
Mathematics: number theory-computational algebra, mathematical physics–differential geometry, dynamical systems, statistics-actuarial mathematics, mathematics education.
Mechanical Engineering: computational fluid dynamics, industrial control systems and robotics, composites, mechanical systems and manufacturing, microfabrication and micromechatronics, thermofluid and propulsion, biomedical and human factor engineering, vehicle systems engineering, industrial engineering.
Music: advanced music performance.
Philosophy: history of philosophy, logic and philosophy of logic, ethics, political philosophy and value theory, epistemology, metaphysics, philosophy of science and social sciences, contemporary philosophy.
Political Science: public policy and public administration, geography, Canadian and Québec politics, interest groups and community politics, environmental and consumer law, elements of public law.
Psychology: appetitive motivation and drug dependence; behaviour disorders; health psychology; human development and developmental processes; perception, cognition, and neuropsychology; sexual and sex-related behaviour.
Religion: comparative religious ethics; ancient, medieval, and modern Judaism; women and religion; Christianity; Islam; Hinduism; Buddhism; sociology and philosophy of religion; new religious movements.
Social and Cultural Anthropology: gender from a cross-cultural perspective, economic anthropology, legal anthropology, anthropological linguistics, development, urban anthropology, community, ethnic studies, ethnographic writing, visual anthropology, information technologies, popular culture, youth culture, race, the politics of identity, globalization and transnationalism.
Sociology: faculty interests range from the sociology of business to religion, ethnic relations, and popular culture.
Specialized Individualized Programs: innovative studies that cross more than one recognized field.
Studio Arts: film production, open media, painting, photography, print media, sculpture, ceramics and fibres.
Theological Studies: Biblical periods, patristic age, fundamental and applied ethics, spirituality and contemporary theology.

DARTMOUTH COLLEGE

DARTMOUTH COLLEGE

Graduate School

Programs of Study

Dartmouth awards the A.M. degree in comparative literature and electroacoustic music and the M.S. degree in computer science, earth sciences, evaluative clinical sciences, and physics. The Ph.D. degree is awarded in biochemistry, biology, chemistry, computer science, earth sciences, engineering sciences, evaluative clinical sciences, genetics, mathematics, microbiology/immunology, pharmacology/toxicology, physics/astronomy, physiology, and psychological and brain sciences. A special program leading to the degree of Master of Arts in Liberal Studies (M.A.L.S.) is also offered. An interactive, cross-disciplinary program, the Molecular and Cellular Biology (MCB) program, is offered in the life sciences. It is comprised of faculty members from the College of Arts and Sciences, the Dartmouth Medical School, and the Thayer School of Engineering.

Graduate degrees are also offered by the professional Schools of Medicine (M.D.), Engineering (M.E., M.S., Ph.D.), and Business Administration (M.B.A.).

Dartmouth's graduate programs are small and selective and are designed to provide more flexibility than the traditional Ph.D. program usually allows. Breadth within the discipline, significant teaching experience, and a broadly conceived research-thesis project are the basic elements in each of the graduate programs. Research achievement is naturally the most fundamental aspect of the Ph.D. program, and the limited enrollment in each program ensures the student a close apprentice/colleague relationship with his or her research supervisor. Most students are expected to teach during part of their graduate career, and considerable emphasis is placed on carefully supervised teaching experience of increasing responsibility.

Research Facilities

Several significant research and teaching facilities at Dartmouth have been designed to encourage contact and intellectual exchange among scholars in related disciplines. The Sherman Fairchild Physical Sciences Center and the Burke Chemistry Laboratory building house programs in geology, chemistry, and physics and provide a common library, service shops, and computing facilities. Similarly, the Gilman Biomedical Center provides related facilities and space for the programs in biology, biochemistry, pharmacology, and physiology, and the Murdough Center serves as a connecting link for cooperative programs between engineering and business administration. Moore Hall, which houses the department of psychological and brain sciences, provides modern facilities for training in psychology and cognitive neuroscience, including the first MRI in the country dedicated to basic research.

All residence halls, classrooms, laboratories, and offices are networked at Dartmouth. Innovative ways are used to integrate personal computers into the curriculum, administration, and operation as well as the daily life of all members of the Dartmouth community. More than 12,000 network ports, a campuswide wireless network, and a variety of utilities make access to central computers and the Internet easy. The Computing Services group also maintains several clusters of personal computers and workstations throughout the campus for faculty and student use. Berry Library, at the geographic and intellectual hub of the campus, houses the central machine room with a wide variety of computers for academic and administrative needs and general-purpose use. The center is open 24 hours a day, seven days a week and is a centrally located hub of information technology activity.

Financial Aid

Most students in the Ph.D. programs receive financial assistance through a program of scholarships, fellowships, and loans. These are made possible by Dartmouth funds and by federal and private fellowships and traineeships. Dartmouth is an authorized lender under the Federal Stafford Student Loan Program. In 2001–02, fellowships for first-year students carried stipends of $1370 per month plus a scholarship covering full tuition. Insofar as is consistent with the duration of individual awards, each student's program of course work, teaching, and research is designed to promote most effectively his or her academic progress without reference to the source of financial support.

Cost of Study

Tuition for the academic year 2002–03 is $27,600. Full tuition scholarships are generally awarded to all admitted students.

Living and Housing Costs

The College assists graduate students in arranging for appropriate housing, either in College facilities or in private accommodations in the Hanover area. College-owned apartments are available at various rents for graduate students.

Student Group

Dartmouth is coeducational. The undergraduate student body numbers approximately 4,000. The graduate and professional school enrollment is about 1,375; approximately 500 of these students are enrolled in the graduate programs of arts and sciences.

Location

Dartmouth College is located in Hanover, New Hampshire, a town of about 6,000 on the border of New Hampshire and Vermont. Hanover is less than 3 hours' driving distance from Boston and Albany and about 4 hours from Montreal. The Hanover area provides excellent opportunities for hiking, canoeing, climbing, and skiing and is near many of northern New England's lake and skiing resorts.

The College

The Hopkins Center for the Performing Arts serves as the cultural focus of the College. The center sponsors an active film society, two full concert series, and a very active drama program. In addition, all students and faculty members have access to workshops for sculpture, painting, and various craft forms as well as to membership in various choral and instrumental music groups. Dartmouth also makes available to its graduate students the extensive facilities of the Dartmouth Outing Club and the Dartmouth College Athletic Council.

Applying

Each program has its own application form, which can be obtained by contacting the individual department. In general, an application requires a completed application, a college transcript, three letters of recommendation, and scores from the General Test of the Graduate Record Examinations. All application materials should be sent directly to the department in which the prospective student wishes to specialize. Particular details, as well as the application packet, can be obtained from each graduate program. Dartmouth College is committed to its policy of nondiscrimination. A statement of this policy and the mechanism for redress of grievances can be found in the College's *Affirmative Action Plan 1982–92* (revised June 1985). For a copy, interested students should call 603-646-3197.

Correspondence and Information

Department of (specify intended major)
Dartmouth College
Hanover, New Hampshire 03755-3526
Telephone: 603-646-2106
World Wide Web: http://www.dartmouth.edu/~gradstdy/

DEANS AND DEPARTMENTAL CHAIRS

Carol L. Folt, Dean of Graduate Studies.
Gary L. Hutchins, Assistant Dean of Graduate Studies.

Biochemistry
Professor Ta Yuan Chang, Dartmouth Medical School, 7200 Vail Building, Room 405 (telephone: 603-650-1622).

Biological Sciences
Professor Mark McPeek, 6044 Gilman Hall, Room 406 (telephone: 603-646-2389).

Chemistry
Professor Dean E. Wilcox, 214 Burke Hall (telephone: 603-646-2874).

Comparative Literature
Professor John Kopper, B-2 Parker (telephone: 603-646-3281).

Computer Science
Professor David Nicol, 6211 Sudikoff Laboratory, Room 224 (telephone: 603-646-3385).

Earth Sciences
Professor Leslie J. Sonder, 6105 Fairchild Hall, 224 Fairchild (telephone: 603-646-2372).

Evaluative Clinical Sciences
Professor Gerald O'Connor, Dartmouth Medical School, 564W Borwell (telephone: 603-650-1680).

Genetics
Professor Jay Dunlap, Dartmouth Medical School, 7400 Remsen Hall, Room 701 (telephone: 603-650-1494).

Master of Arts in Liberal Studies
Professor Don Pease, 6092 Wentworth Hall, Room 116 (telephone: 603-646-3592).

Mathematics
Professor Dana Williams, 6188 Bradley Hall, 201 Choate Hse. (telephone: 603-646-2990).

Microbiology and Immunology
Professor Michael W. Fanger, Dartmouth Medical School, 7556 Borwell, Room 603W (telephone: 603-650-7505).

Molecular and Cellular Biology
Professor Ronald Taylor, 7550 Vail Building, Room 106 (telephone: 603-650-1632)

Music
Professor Larry Polansky, 6187 Hopkins Center, Room 49 (telephone: 603-646-2139).

Pharmacology and Toxicology
Professor Ethan Dmitrovsky, Dartmouth Medical School, 7650 Remsen Hall, Room 523 (telephone: 603-650-1667).

Physics and Astronomy
Professor Mary Hudson, 6127 Wilder Laboratory, Room 101 (telephone: 603-646-2976).

Physiology
Professor Donald Bartlett, Dartmouth Medical School, 7700 Remsen Hall, Room 618 (telephone: 603-646-7723).

Psychological and Brain Sciences
Professor Howard Hughes, 105 Moore Hall (telephone: 603-646-3181).

Thayer School of Engineering
Professor William Lotko, 8000 Cummings Hall, Room 217B (telephone: 603-646-3485).

The Sherman Fairchild Physical Sciences Center.

Research lab in Sherman Fairchild Physical Sciences Center.

The Burke Chemistry Laboratory building.

DEPAUL UNIVERSITY

College of Liberal Arts and Sciences Graduate Studies

Programs of Study

The College offers graduate programs leading to the degree of Doctor of Philosophy in philosophy and psychology (clinical, industrial/organizational, and experimental). The master's degree is offered in biological sciences, chemistry, communication, economics, English, health law and policy, history, interdisciplinary studies, international public service management, international studies, liberal studies, mathematical sciences, mathematics education, nursing, philosophy, physics, general psychology, public services, sociology, and writing. Certificate programs in communication, nursing, psychology, public services, and writing are available for midcareerists in those disciplines and other professionals.

Research Facilities

The University libraries contain more than 689,000 volumes, more than 8,900 periodical subscriptions, and an extensive microcard and microfilm collection. Special collections include Dickens, Horace, sports, an extensive collection of Napoleonic materials, and various rare books and incunabula. The library computer system allows access to 800 other Illinois libraries.

Various computer facilities, resources, and support services are available. More than 400 workstations are available for student use in laboratories and classrooms throughout all campuses. Dial-in access is available around the clock on the main systems. Students receive free e-mail addresses and low-cost Internet access.

Financial Aid

DePaul University provides a number of teaching and research assistantships to degree-seeking, full-time graduate students. Annual awards are typically $6000 to $12,000 stipends and include tuition waivers. Applications should be made directly to the chairperson of the appropriate department. Nominations for these assistantships are generally made during the spring quarter of the previous academic year.

The Financial Aid Office assists interested students in applying to the Federal Perkins Loan and Federal Stafford Student Loan programs.

Cost of Study

In 2001–02, graduate tuition for liberal arts and sciences programs was $362 per quarter hour. Full-time graduate study consists of at least 8 quarter hours per quarter. Fees vary according to the course of study.

Living and Housing Costs

The Student Life Office has listings of apartments and residential hotels near the Lincoln Park campus. Rents vary greatly in the Chicago area.

Student Group

DePaul University is the largest Catholic university in the U.S., with an enrollment of more than 19,000. Graduate enrollment in liberal arts and sciences is 1,100, half of whom are full-time students. The LA&S graduate student population is diverse; approximately 25 percent are members of minority groups, 50 percent are women, and 26 percent are over the age of 30. Many of these students are working full-time, often in the business and financial communities clustered around the Loop. Ninety-eight percent of all students are from the greater Chicago area, and 85 percent of the alumni still reside there.

Student Outcomes

Graduates of the College find a diversity of positions. Most find employment in the Chicago area, many continue in professional and other advanced degree programs, and some accept postdoctoral and faculty appointments. For example, recent graduates teach at Loyola of Chicago, Seattle, and Santa Clara; conduct research at Harvard; write for Abbott Laboratories; work for the Civic Federation of Chicago; study law at Michigan; and pursue the Ph.D. at Northwestern, Chicago, and Wisconsin.

Location

DePaul is located in a culturally and academically rich urban environment. The Loop campus is minutes away from the Art Institute; Orchestra Hall; museums of art, natural history, and science; and the LaSalle Street business district. Eighty percent of DePaul's students work to help finance their education and find that the downtown location provides many employment opportunities. At the Lincoln Park campus, revitalization of the community has paralleled the expansion of University facilities. The area's potpourri of stores, theaters, musical groups, and events reflects the broad spectrum of interests of the people who live and work in the area.

The University serves the needs of the Chicago community in many ways, such as providing the public with the facilities of the Mental Health Clinic, its Learning Disabilities Center, and the DePaul Legal Clinic.

The University

DePaul University is one of the largest Catholic universities in the world. Founded in 1898 by the Vincentian Fathers, the University strives to be urban in style while maintaining the heritage of St. Vincent de Paul: the perfection of the person through professional involvement with others at every level.

Many graduate programs schedule classes in the evening and on weekends. DePaul's two urban campuses are easily reached by public transportation; the Loop campus is at the south end of Chicago's downtown area, and the 25-acre Lincoln Park campus is located on the city's north side. There are suburban satellite campuses as well: O'Hare, Naperville, South/Oak Forest, and Lake Forest.

Numerous student organizations offer extensive opportunities for participation in both community and University activities. There are music performance groups, theater groups, student publications, sports, and honor and service societies. Athletic facilities include two gymnasiums, a swimming pool, racquetball courts, and extensive physical education equipment.

Applying

Application materials for the College of Liberal Arts and Sciences may be received by sending a request to the address given below. Addresses for other graduate programs and professional programs are given on the reverse of this page. The College of Liberal Arts and Sciences has no general admission test; however, some departments require the General Test of the Graduate Record Examinations. Students should consult the *Graduate Bulletin* for details. The application fee is $25 ($40 for psychology programs). Most departments allow students to begin their course work in any academic quarter; however, communication, international studies, psychology, and philosophy department programs begin in the autumn quarter. The application deadlines are as follows: January 15 for clinical psychology, January 31 for industrial/organizational psychology, February 15 for philosophy, and February 28 for general experimental psychology. Interested applicants should contact the Graduate Information Office for communication and international studies deadlines. Students desiring loans are encouraged to apply before May 1 to receive maximum consideration.

Correspondence and Information

Graduate Information Office
DePaul University
1 East Jackson Boulevard
Chicago, Illinois 60604

Telephone: 312-362-8300
Fax: 312-362-5749
E-mail: admitdpu@wppost.depaul.edu
World Wide Web: http://www.depaul.edu

PROGRAM DIRECTORS

Liberal Arts and Sciences Programs

Dean: Michael L. Mezey, Ph.D.
Associate Dean: Charles S. Suchar, Ph.D.

Biological Sciences: John V. Dean, Ph.D.
Chemistry: Wendy Wolbach, Ph.D.
Communication: Bruno Teboul, Ph.D.
Economics: Michael Miller, Ph.D.
English: Eric Selinger, Ph.D.
History: Warren Schultz, Ph.D.
Interdisciplinary Studies: Fassil Demissie, Ph.D.
International Studies: Michael McIntyre, Ph.D.
Liberal Studies: David Gitomer, Ph.D.
Mathematical Sciences: Effat Moussa, Ph.D.
Mathematics Education: Jeffrey Bergen, Ph.D.
Nursing: Susan Poslusny, Ph.D., RN.
Philosophy: Will McNeill, Ph.D.
Physics: Ross Hyman, Ph.D.
Clinical Psychology: LaVome Robinson, Ph.D.
Experimental Psychology: Ching-Fan Sheu, Ph.D.
General Psychology–Lincoln Park: George Michel, Ph.D.
General Psychology–Naperville: Joseph Ferrari, Ph.D.
Industrial/Organizational Psychology: Alice Stuhlmacher, Ph.D.
Public Services: J. Patrick Murphy, C.M., Ph.D.
Sociology: Kenneth Fidel, Ph.D.
Writing: Craig Sirles, Ph.D.

Other Graduate and Professional Programs

College of Law: Teree E. Foster, J.D., Dean; 9th Floor, 25 East Jackson Boulevard, Chicago, Illinois 60604 (Telephone: 312-362-8701).
Graduate School of Business: Arthur Kraft, Ph.D., Dean; Karen M. Stark, M.B.A., Assistant Dean and Director; 12th Floor, Lewis Center, 25 East Jackson Boulevard, Chicago, Illinois 60604 (Telephone: 312-362-8810).
School of Computer Science, Telecommunications and Information Systems: Helmut Epp, Ph.D., Dean; Administration Center 401, 243 South Wabash Avenue, Chicago, Illinois 60604 (Telephone: 312-362-8381).
School of Education: Sandra Jackson, Ph.D., Acting Dean; Schmitt Academic Center, 2320 North Kenmore, Chicago, Illinois 60614 (Telephone: 773-325-8106).
School of Music: Donald E. Casey, Ed.D., Dean; Room 205, Fine Arts, 804 West Belden, Chicago, Illinois 60614 (Telephone: 773-325-7260).
School for New Learning: Susanne Dumbleton, Ph.D., Dean; Administration Center 700, 243 South Wabash Avenue, Chicago, Illinois 60604 (Telephone: 312-362-8001).
Theatre School: John Culbert, M.F.A., Acting Dean; 2135 North Kenmore, Chicago, Illinois 60614 (Telephone: 773-325-7917).

DOMINICAN COLLEGE OF BLAUVELT

Graduate Programs

Programs of Study

Dominican College offers graduate programs in nursing (family nurse practitioner), occupational therapy (OT), physical therapy, and special education. These programs are offered in formats that take into consideration the professional and personal commitments of working adults. The nursing program is offered in an evening format, with each class meeting once a week. The occupational therapy, physical therapy, and special education programs are offered on weekends; classes are offered approximately every third weekend.

The M.S. in nursing, family nurse practitioner program, is designed to prepare an advanced practice nurse–family nurse practitioner. The curriculum for the master's degree program integrates current trends in nurse practitioner research, practice, and education. Emphasis is placed on integration of practice and theory across diverse settings where primary care is delivered within the context of family-centered care. Students engage in classroom instruction and experiential teaching–learning opportunities that prepare them in assessment, role development, and in-depth clinical practice. Students are encouraged to take electives that strengthen teaching, clinical practice, and/or research interests.

The College offers an entry-level B.S./M.S. degree in occupational therapy for new college students, transfers, COTAs, and students holding other degrees. The program prepares its graduates for entry-level practice and provides graduates with the skills necessary to respond to societal trends and changes in human services. Its problem-solving approach develops the student's clinical reasoning and critical-thinking skills. A postprofessional master's degree in OT leadership has been registered by the NYSED and is offered as needed.

The M.S. in physical therapy program, a full-time weekend program, employs a curricular design that addresses the theoretical framework integrated with the clinical decision-making processes and critical-inquiry skills. The program promotes distinguished physical therapy education in a challenging and supportive environment. Graduates of the program are entry-level therapists who are able to meet the ever-changing health-care environment and to provide services that address the needs of the whole client. Details of the program and accreditation status are available from the Office of Admissions.

The College offers two M.S. in education programs. One of the programs has an emphasis on teaching students with multiple needs, preparing certified special education teachers to work with a learner who has a special educational and/or health-related needs, and who may be medically fragile as well. The second program focuses on certifying teachers of the blind and visually impaired.

Research Facilities

All the graduate programs require research by way of projects or papers. Dominican College has an Institutional Review Board that adheres to federal policy on all research activities involving human subjects. The College supports research activities by providing online databases that can be accessed in the library, computer laboratories, and the residence hall as well as from off-campus locations. These online databases include First Search, SearchBank, Proquest Direct, and Dialog@Carl.

Financial Aid

The Financial Aid Office assists graduate students with obtaining various kinds of low-interest loans. Some students may be eligible for federal/state aid.

Cost of Study

For the academic year 2001–02, the tuition for the master's-level courses was $472 per credit.

Living and Housing Costs

Since most of the graduate programs meet in a weekend format and the participants are active professionals, the students choose to commute from their homes.

Student Group

The College has a total student body of approximately 1,700 graduate and undergraduate students.

Student Outcomes

The programs are intended to prepare professionals in their respective fields. They provide significant enhancement of skills of those students who are already working in the field and allow for professional and career enhancement.

Location

The College is located in Rockland County, New York. The beautiful Hudson Valley campus is located 17 miles north of New York City. The College is easily reached by car or public transportation and from the major airports of New York and New Jersey.

The College

Dominican College of Blauvelt, founded by the sisters of St. Dominic of Blauvelt, New York, is located in Rockland County. Dominican College, chartered by the University of the State of New York and accredited by the Middle States Association of Colleges and Schools, is an independent coeducational four-year college. The College does not discriminate on the basis of sex, race, color, religion, disability, or national or ethnic origin.

Applying

Applicants for master's degree programs must have a bachelor's degree from an accredited college or university. They should submit a completed application along with the application fee, three letters of recommendation, and transcripts from all institutions the candidate has attended. Each program has specific additional admissions requirements.

Correspondence and Information

Joyce Elbe
Director of Admissions
Dominican College of Blauvelt
470 Western Highway
Orangeburg, New York 10962
Telephone: 866-4DC-INFO (toll-free)
Fax: 845-365-3150
E-mail: admissions@dc.edu
World Wide Web: http://www.dc.edu

THE FACULTY

Sandra Countee, Associate Professor and Program Director, Occupational Therapy Program; Ph.D., NYU.
Valerie G. Olson, Assistant Professor of Health Sciences and Program Administrator, Physical Therapy Program; Ph.D., Seton Hall.
Rona Shaw, Professor of Special Education; Ed.D., Columbia Teachers College.
Lynne Weissman, Assistant Professor and Director, Nurse Practitioner Program; M.S., Columbia; PNP.

The fully equipped 25,000-square-foot Hennessy Center is available to all students and features a 1,000-seat gymnasium, physical fitness center, suspended track, locker rooms, athletic department offices, and a multipurpose room for student gatherings.

In September 2000, the second floor of Granito Dining Center was opened, giving students access to a newly developed student health complex, a video conferencing center and satellite downlink facility, and a new bookstore.

Commencement 2001.

DRAKE UNIVERSITY

Graduate Programs

Programs of Study

Drake University offers top-quality programs leading to master's, specialist, and doctoral degrees. The College of Business and Public Administration offers the Master of Business Administration (M.B.A.), the Master of Public Administration (M.P.A.), and the Master of Accounting (M.Acc.). The M.B.A. program, accredited by AACSB International–The Association to Advance Collegiate Schools of Business, and the M.P.A. may be combined with a degree in law or pharmacy. Although the joint programs require full-time enrollment, students seeking graduate programs within the College of Business and Public Administration only may enroll on either a full-time or part-time basis, since most courses are offered as evening classes. Many degree programs and numerous endorsements are available through the School of Education. Degrees include the Master of Arts in Teaching (M.A.T.) and Master of Science in Teaching (M.S.T.), which are designed to help individuals who want to teach at the secondary or elementary levels become certified teachers while earning a master's degree. Additional degrees include the Master of Science (M.S.) in rehabilitation administration; rehabilitation counseling; rehabilitation placement; and adult learning, performance, and development. Also offered are the Master of Science in Education (M.S.E.) in counseling (elementary and secondary); community agency counseling; educational leadership (elementary and secondary); early childhood education; effective teaching, learning, and leadership; and special education. The Educational Specialist (Ed.S.) and Doctor of Education (Ed.D.) are offered in education leadership. The College of Pharmacy and Health Sciences offers the Doctor of Pharmacy (Pharm.D.) degree and joint programs. Drake Law School, one of the twenty-five oldest law schools in the country, offers the J.D. and joint programs. Through joint degree programs, students may obtain a degree in law combined with advanced degrees in business, public administration, political science, social work, or agricultural economics.

Research Facilities

State-of-the-art physical facilities are available in many disciplines. The recently constructed Pharmacy and Science Hall provides students with technologically advanced research resources. Cowles Library, the main university library, holds more than 500,000 volumes and an extensive collection of database searching facilities. Computer labs are available in both the Cowles and Law Library as well as a 24-hour lab in the Dial Computer Center. Opperman Hall and Law Library, built in 1993, has won several architectural and design awards and has received international recognition. The Law Library includes two computer labs, WESTLAW and LEXIS legal research training centers, access to the Internet, and CD-ROM-based research.

Financial Aid

The Office of Student Financial Planning offers financial information and services to graduate students. Graduate assistantships are available in a limited number of fields and are administered and awarded through application to specific departments. Student loans (for U.S. citizens only) and part-time employment, both on and off campus, are also available. The Office of Student Financial Planning also has information about other scholarship possibilities. Drake's Law School Office of Admission has additional information about scholarship opportunities within the Law School. Students working for companies that offer tuition assistance may enroll in the Employer Tuition Support Payment Plan. This plan provides the option of a delayed payment based on the anticipated tuition reimbursement provided by the student's employer.

Cost of Study

Many students enroll in a maximum of 9 credit hours each term and are therefore charged tuition on a per-credit-hour basis. The general tuition rate for part-time graduate students ranges from $290 to $360 per credit hour. In most programs, students enrolling in 10 or more hours are charged the full-time tuition cost of $18,800 for each academic year.

Living and Housing Costs

The cost of living in the Des Moines area is low compared to many metropolitan areas, particularly in housing expenses. Numerous apartment options are available within the Drake neighborhood and are within walking distance of the campus. On-campus adult student housing is quite limited, with one residence hall offering both one- and two-bedroom apartments. Off-campus rent varies but generally ranges from $400 to $650 per month.

Student Group

Approximately 1,600 students are enrolled in Drake's graduate, law, and pharmacy programs. Of those, approximately 500 are full-time law and pharmacy students. Graduate programs other than law and pharmacy offer the majority of courses either in the evening or on weekends, which allows many adults who are working full-time to pursue their degree while continuing to work. Students find that attendance with other professionals in the area brings an added dimension to their experience, as does attending class with 260 international students representing almost sixty countries. Faculty members are available to assist and advise students and to supervise their research. Classes are small enough to allow for maximum interaction.

Student Outcomes

Drake alumni live in all fifty states and many other countries and hold positions as corporate CEOs, teachers, journalists, and state supreme court justices. Drake graduates are leaders in their fields, including education, business, journalism, pharmacy, and law. Upon graduation, students are prepared for not only their first employment opportunity, but also for advancement beyond their first position. Those already working are prepared to advance within their companies or seek other opportunities. Drake is known for educating students for the variety of careers they may have throughout their lifetimes and for teaching students to be flexible and manage and create positive change. The graduating class of 2000–01 had an overall placement rate of 98.8 percent.

Location

Drake University's scenic campus is located in a residential neighborhood in Des Moines, a medium-sized city of 400,000 people. As Iowa's capital and largest city, Des Moines is a metropolitan center for business (especially insurance), government, publishing, broadcasting, advertising, and the arts. The quality of life is enriched by the people of Iowa, who are noted for their friendliness, honesty, strong work ethic, and educational values. The Des Moines International Airport, which is served by major airlines, is just 15 minutes by car from the safe campus, and the University's 120-acre community is within 10 minutes of downtown Des Moines. Des Moines was named by Kiplinger's *Personal Finance* as one of the country's fifteen "super cities" where "people are moving and opportunity is knocking." Because of its central U.S. location, the climate in Iowa has a cycle of four distinct seasons.

The University

Founded in 1881, Drake University is a highly ranked private, independent university that is nationally recognized for teaching excellence and academic reputation within a student-centered learning environment. The University is accredited by the North Central Association of Colleges and Schools, and professional programs are accredited by their corresponding professional associations. Drake's faculty members are very accessible for advising and mentoring, and the overall student-faculty ratio is 13:1. More than 94 percent of the faculty members hold the highest degree in their field.

Applying

Applications may be obtained from the Office of Graduate Admission at the address below or online at https://www.applyweb.com/apply/drakeg. A graduate information request form is available at http://www.drake.edu/admissions/inquiry/graduate.html. Most programs offer rolling admission; however, applications to the doctoral programs and certain other programs do have specific deadlines. Some programs also offer admission for the fall term only; most consider students for fall, spring, and summer admission. Students must submit the application for admission, application fee, official transcripts from each college or university previously attended, and appropriate entrance examination score reports as well as any additional information specified by the department to which the student is applying.

Correspondence and Information

Ann J. Martin, Graduate Coordinator
Office of Graduate Admission
Drake University
2507 University Avenue
Des Moines, Iowa 50311
Telephone: 515-271-3871 or 800-443-7253 Ext. 3871 (toll-free in the U.S.)
Fax: 515-271-2831
E-mail: gradadmission@drake.edu
ann.martin@drake.edu
World Wide Web: http://www.drake.edu

FACULTY HEADS

David Maxwell, President; Ph.D., Brown.
Ronald J. Troyer, Provost; Ph.D., Western Michigan.

Web Sites by School or College

College of Business and Public Administration: http://www.drake.edu/cbpa/grad/index.html
College of Pharmacy and Health Sciences: http://pharmacy.drake.edu
Law School: http://www.law.drake.edu
School of Education: http://www.educ.drake.edu

DREW UNIVERSITY

The Caspersen School of Graduate Studies

Programs of Study

The Caspersen School of Graduate Studies offers students an opportunity to pursue graduate studies in a setting that emphasizes small class size, individual attention from faculty mentors, and the ability to explore a wide range of scholarly interests through intensive independent work and tutorials. The program in English literature (M.A., Ph.D.) offers courses in most areas of British and American literature, with particular emphasis on the modern period. The interdisciplinary modern history and literature program (M.A., Ph.D.), which covers the period from the early eighteenth century to the late twentieth century, provides students the ability to concentrate in either American or European intellectual and cultural history. The women's studies program (M.A., Ph.D. concentration) allows students to specialize in historical/literary or religious/theological perspectives. The book history program (M.A.) offers study in the history of written communication. Drew also offers five programs in the field of religion and theology. Biblical studies and early Christianity (M.A., Ph.D.) encompasses two subfields: the New Testament and the religion of ancient Israel. The religion and society program (M.A., Ph.D.) offers students the ability to concentrate in anthropology, sociology, psychology, or ethics. The theological and religious studies program (M.A., Ph.D.) encompasses theological, historical, and philosophical approaches to the study of religion. The liturgical studies program (M.A., Ph.D.) offers ecumenical study in the history and theology of Christian liturgy. The interdisciplinary Wesleyan and Methodist studies program (M.A., Ph.D.) encompasses Methodist origins, history, and thought.

Drew offers two additional degree programs. The interdisciplinary arts and letters program (M.Litt., D.Litt.) emphasizes broad competence in the liberal arts, while the innovative medical humanities program (C.M.H., M.M.H., D.M.H.), conducted jointly by Drew and Raritan Bay Medical Center, addresses topics such as biomedical ethics, medical narrative, and the history of medicine. Full- or part-time study is available.

The M.A. is designed to be completed in a minimum of one academic year and includes course work, demonstrated reading knowledge of one foreign language, and a thesis. The Ph.D. program includes two years of course work, demonstrated reading knowledge of two foreign languages, comprehensive examinations, and a dissertation. Requirements differ for the arts and letters and medical humanities programs. Students should contact Graduate Admissions for specific information.

Research Facilities

The Rose Memorial Library houses 462,498 volumes plus a large collection of manuscripts, journals, and other primary source material. It also has an unusually large collection of periodicals with special strengths in the basic areas of graduate study offered at Drew. The library is a depository for the publications of the federal government and the state of New Jersey. It also collects the official documents of the United Nations. The Center for Holocaust Studies is located on campus, and the United Methodist Archive and History Center, adjacent to the library, houses one of the most extensive collections of American religious history and Methodistica in the world.

Financial Aid

Financial aid may take the form of scholarships, loans, employment, or any combination of these. Both need and achievement are taken into account in determining the amount of assistance to be made available. Merit-based awards range from 40 percent of tuition to 100 percent of tuition plus stipend. Applicants must file financial aid forms.

Cost of Study

Tuition for full-time M.A. and Ph.D. study in 2002–03 is $24,408 per year. Tuition is prorated for part-time study, but a minimum of three courses must be taken for credit each year. Arts and letters and medical humanities tuition is $716 per credit, with reduced rates for senior citizens and full-time educators on a space-available basis.

Living and Housing Costs

Drew offers a variety of housing options in dormitories or apartments for both single and married students. For 2002–03, the cost is approximately $4000 to $10,000 for the academic year, depending on size requirements. Meal plans can be provided for a modest additional charge. Commuter rooms are also available.

Student Group

The total University enrollment is 2,418 students; of this number, 541 are in the Graduate School. Of the total number of graduate students, 55 percent are women, 17 percent are international students, and 15 percent are self-identified members of minority groups.

Student Outcomes

Drew seeks to actively place its graduates. Most Drew graduates from the doctoral program go on to teach in colleges and universities. Others choose to enter related fields; Drew graduates work for publishing houses, government and nonprofit agencies, church organizations, and similar employers.

Location

Drew is located on a beautiful, 186-acre campus in Madison, New Jersey (population 18,000), 25 miles west of Manhattan. Commuter rail and bus lines provide easy access to New York City and all its educational, cultural, and entertainment opportunities.

The University

One of the major characteristics of the Graduate School is the emphasis on interdisciplinary studies. Its size allows for graduate education on a personal level with many small seminars, one-to-one tutorials, and classes that encourage discussion and lively interaction. Faculty members excel in teaching as well as in scholarship and research.

Applying

Evaluation of an applicant's qualifications for admission is based upon previous course work and grade point average, three letters of recommendation from professors, a personal statement, and an academic writing sample. GRE General Test scores are required of U.S. and Canadian citizens. International students who are not native English speakers are required to submit recent TOEFL and TWE scores. To present a competitive application, students should have a grade point average of 3.5 (on a 4.0 scale) or better. M.A. and Ph.D. candidates are admitted for the fall semester only. Arts and letters and medical humanities candidates may be admitted for the fall, spring, or summer semester and have different application requirements. The deadline for receipt of financial aid forms for M.A. and Ph.D. candidates is February 15. Applicants to all other programs should contact Graduate Admissions for information on financial aid deadlines.

Prospective students are encouraged to attend the Graduate Open House held each fall.

Correspondence and Information

Director of Graduate Admissions
Drew University
Madison, New Jersey 07940

Telephone: 973-408-3110
Fax: 973-408-3242
E-mail: gradm@drew.edu
World Wide Web: http://www.drew.edu/grad

THE FACULTY

S. Wesley Ariarajah, Professor of Ecumenical Theology; Ph.D., London.
Fran Bernstein, Assistant Professor of History; Ph.D., Columbia.
Karen McCarthy Brown, Professor of Anthropology and Sociology of Religion; Ph.D., Temple.
Virginia Burrus, Associate Professor of Early Church History; Ph.D., Graduate Theological Union.
Janet Burstein, Professor of English; Ph.D., Drew.
William Campbell, Affiliate Professor of Parasitology, RISE; Ph.D., Wisconsin.
Ashley Carter, Affiliate Professor of Physics and Mathematics, RISE; Ph.D., Brown.
Michael Christensen, Affiliate Assistant Professor of Spirituality; Ph.D., Drew.
Gabriel M. Coless, Affiliate Professor of Church History; S.Th.D., Pontificio Instituto Liturgico (Rome).
Robert Corrington, Associate Professor of Philosophic Theology; Ph.D., Drew.
Charles Courtney, Professor of Philosophy of Religion; Ph.D., Northwestern.
David A. Cowell, Professor of Political Science; Ph.D., Georgetown.
Paolo Cucchi, Professor of French and Italian and Dean; Ph.D., Princeton.
J. Christopher Cunningham, Assistant Professor of English; Ph.D., UCLA.
Donald Dayton, Affiliate Professor of Historical Theology; Ph.D., Chicago.
Carlos de la Torre, Assistant Professor of Sociology; Ph.D., New School.
Lala Kalyan Dey, Associate Professor of New Testament; Th.D., Harvard.
Delight W. Dodyk, Affiliate Professor of History; Ph.D., Rutgers.
Darrell J. Doughty, Professor of New Testament; D.Theol., Göttingen (Germany).
Lillie Edwards, Associate Professor of History and African-American Studies; Ph.D., Chicago.
Heather M. Elkins, Associate Professor of Worship and Liturgical Studies; Ph.D., Drew.
William Elkins, Affiliate Assistant Professor of Hermeneutics; Ph.D., Drew.
Victoria Erickson, Associate Professor of Sociology of Religion; Ph.D., CUNY Graduate Center.
Mark Freeman, Assistant Professor of Psychology; Ph.D., Temple.
Brett Gary, Assistant Professor of History; Ph.D., Pennsylvania.
David M. Graybeal, Professor of Church and Society; Ph.D., Yale.
James Paul Hala, Professor of English; Ph.D., Michigan.
Sara Henry-Corrington, Associate Professor of Art; Ph.D., Berkeley.
Herbert B. Huffmon, Professor of Old Testament; Ph.D., Michigan.
Ada-Maria Isasi-Diaz, Associate Professor of Theology and Ethics; Ph.D., Union Theological Seminary (New York).
Sandra Jamieson, Associate Professor of English; Ph.D., SUNY at Binghamton.
Donald G. Jones, Professor of Religion; Ph.D., Drew.
Laurel Kearns, Associate Professor of Sociology of Religion; Ph.D., Emory.
Catherine Keller, Professor of Constructive Theology; Ph.D., Claremont.
David Kohn, Professor of History of Science; Ph.D., Massachusetts.
Wendy Kolmar, Professor of English; Ph.D., Indiana.
Edwina Lawler, Associate Professor of German and Russian; Ph.D., Drew.
Perry Leavell Jr., Professor of History; Ph.D., Tulane.
Robin Leaver, Affiliate Professor of Liturgical Studies; Th.D., Groningen (Netherlands).
H. Leedom Lefferts Jr., Professor of Anthropology; Ph.D., Colorado.
John Lenz, Associate Professor of Classics; Ph.D., Columbia.
Neal Levi, Assistant Professor of English; Ph.D. Columbia.
Otto Maduro, Associate Professor of Latin American Christianity; Ph.D., Louvain.
Thomas Magnell, Professor of Philosophy; D.Phil., Oxford.
Jason Merrill, Assistant Professor of Russian History and Literature; Ph.D., Kansas.
William Messmer, Associate Professor of Political Science; Ph.D., Ohio State.
Paul Meyendorff, Adjunct Professor of Eastern Orthodox Studies: Ph.D., Notre Dame.
Jo Ann Middleton, Director of Medical Humanities; Ph.D., Drew.
James Mills, Professor of Psychology; Ph.D., Columbia.
Stephen Moore, Professor of New Testament Studies; Ph.D., Trinity College (Ireland).
A. Johan Noordsij, Affiliate Professor of Psychiatry; M.D., Leiden (Netherlands).
Frank Occhiogrosso, Professor of English; Ph.D., Johns Hopkins.
Thomas C. Oden, Henry Anson Buttz Professor of Theology; Ph.D., Yale.
James O'Kane, Professor of Sociology; Ph.D., NYU.
Nadine Ollman, Professor of English; Ph.D., Pennsylvania.
James H. Pain, Henry and Annie M. Pfeiffer Professor of Religion and Dean; D.Phil., Oxford.
Dale Patterson, Affiliate Assistant Professor of American Religious Studies; Ph.D., Drew.
Philip Peek, Professor of Anthropology; Ph.D., Indiana.
Virginia Phelan, Director of Arts and Letters; Ph.D., Rutgers.
Arthur Pressley, Associate Professor of Pastoral Care; Ph.D., Northwestern.
Jonathan W. Reader, Associate Professor of Sociology; Ph.D., Cornell.
Robert Ready, Professor of English; Ph.D., Columbia.
Richard S. Rhone, Professor of Political Science; Ph.D., Penn State.
Charles L. Rice, Professor of Homiletics; Ph.D., Duke.
William B. Rogers, Affiliate Professor of History and Associate Dean; Ph.D., Drew.
Joseph Romance, Assistant Professor of Political Science; Ph.D., Rutgers.
Jonathan Rose, Assistant Professor of History; Ph.D., Pennsylvania.
Kenneth E. Rowe, Professor of Church History; Ph.D., Drew.
Peggy Samuels, Assistant Professor of English; Ph.D., CUNY Graduate Center.
Suzanne Selinger, Assistant Professor of Bibliography and Research; Ph.D., Yale.
Douglas W. Simon, Professor of Political Science; Ph.D., Oregon.
Merrill M. Skaggs, Professor of English; Ph.D., Duke.
Geraldine Smith-Wright, Professor of English; Ph.D., Rutgers.
William D. Stroker, Professor of Religion; Ph.D., Yale.
Shirley Sugerman, Affiliate Associate Professor of Religion; Ph.D., Drew.
Jesse T. Todd Jr., Assistant Professor of American Religious Studies; Ph.D., Columbia.
Carol Ueland, Associate Professor of Russian; Ph.D., Columbia.
Linda Van Blerkom, Associate Professor of Anthropology; Ph.D., Colorado.
Joan M. Weimer, Professor of English; Ph.D., Rutgers.
Charles J. Wetzel, Professor of History; Ph.D., Wisconsin.
Traci West, Associate Professor of Ethics and African-American Studies; Ph.D., Union Theological Seminary (New York).
Lynne Westfield, Assistant Professor of Christian Education; Ph.D., Union.
James F. White, Thompson Visiting Professor of Liturgics; Ph.D., Duke.
Anne Bagnall Yardley, Associate Professor of Music; Ph.D., Columbia.
Charles Yrigoyen Jr., Affiliate Professor of Church History; Ph.D., Temple.

DREXEL UNIVERSITY

Graduate Studies

Programs of Study

Drexel University offers graduate programs leading to the Doctor of Philosophy, Master of Science, and Master of Business Administration degrees. Many programs include options for part-time studies; nondegree students are also welcome to pursue graduate course work in most programs.

Programs leading to the Doctor of Philosophy degree are offered in the College of Arts and Sciences (bioscience and biotechnology, chemistry, education, mathematics, clinical psychology, nutrition and food sciences, physics, and atmospheric science), College of Business and Administration (business administration), College of Engineering (chemical, civil, electrical and computer, materials, mechanical engineering), and the College of Information Science and Technology. In addition, the Ph.D. may be earned through two multidisciplinary schools. The School of Biomedical Engineering, Science and Health Systems offers the Ph.D. in biomedical engineering and biomedical science. The School of Environmental Science, Engineering and Policy offers the Ph.D. in environmental engineering and environmental science.

Programs leading to the Master of Science degree are offered in the College of Arts and Sciences (bioscience and biotechnology, chemistry, mathematics, computer science, education, human nutrition/food science and nutrition, physics and atmospheric science, publication management, science of instruction, and technical and science communication), College of Business and Administration (M.B.A. and M.S. degrees in accounting, decision sciences, finance, marketing, and taxation), Nesbitt College of Design Arts (arts administration, fashion design, and interior design), College of Engineering (M.E. and M.S. degrees in biochemical, chemical, civil, electrical and computer, materials, mechanical, and telecommunications engineering and in engineering geology and engineering management), College of Information Science and Technology (library and information science, and information systems), School of Biomedical Engineering, Science, and Health Systems (biomedical engineering and biomedical science), School of Environmental Science, Engineering, and Policy (environmental engineering and environmental science), and through the multidisciplinary program in software engineering.

The Master of Business Administration degree program can include specialization in one of fourteen areas of business study. A general M.B.A. can be earned through a series of special courses offered only on Saturdays. All required course work for the M.B.A. degree may be completed in the evenings.

Research Facilities

Drexel University is a major research institution, with basic and applied research complementing the studies listed above. A modern and expanding physical plant hosts research that is supported by a formal research grant program. Detailed descriptions of the research programs and the facilities that serve them may be found in specific program brochures and individual departments. Drexel's library also offers extensive resources.

Financial Aid

Financial aid is available for full-time students. This aid includes teaching and research assistantships, fellowships, work-study grants, student loans, and on-campus employment. Assistantships carry tuition remission benefits as well as monthly stipends.

Cost of Study

In 2002–03, students are billed at the rate of $515 to $667 per credit hour, depending upon their program of study. In addition, there is a general University fee of $142 per term for full-time students and $82 per term for part-time students.

Living and Housing Costs

Ample off-campus housing is available in the neighborhoods bordering campus. For the nine-month academic year, transportation and living expenses for a single student are estimated at $13,500.

Student Group

The University has a total enrollment of approximately 13,500 students, of whom 2,550 are graduate students (650 full-time and 1,900 part-time).

Location

Drexel University is located in the University City section of Philadelphia. The educational atmosphere is enhanced by Philadelphia's ample cultural, historical, corporate, and technological resources. The campus is within a 5-minute walk of Amtrak's 30th Street Station, which is adjacent to the Schuylkill Expressway (I-76). Drexel is also served by local bus, streetcar, and subway lines.

The University

The University was founded in 1891 by Anthony J. Drexel, a Philadelphia financier and philanthropist, as Drexel Institute of Art, Science, and Industry. It later became Drexel Institute of Technology and finally, in 1970, Drexel University. Drexel operates under a four-term calendar, with graduate and undergraduate studies offered year-round.

Applying

Application forms are available from the Office of Graduate Admissions. Some programs require admission tests (GRE, GMAT), and a few require interviews. At least two recommendations are required. International students must provide a TOEFL score that is less than two years old. Students typically enter in the fall term. However, for many programs, applicants may apply with the intention of enrolling in any of Drexel's four terms (these begin in January, March, June, and September). Application deadlines vary accordingly. The student is advised to confer with the Office of Graduate Admissions or the departmental adviser (see reverse).

Drexel has a rolling admission review program. Those wishing consideration for assistantships, however, are encouraged to apply for the fall term and submit their credentials by January 1, as support decisions by departments are made soon thereafter. All applications require a nonrefundable $50 fee.

Correspondence and Information

Office of Graduate Admissions
Drexel University
3141 Chestnut Street
Philadelphia, Pennsylvania 19104

Telephone: 215-895-6700
E-mail: admissions@drexel.edu
World Wide Web: http://www.drexel.edu

FACULTY HEADS

PROGRAMS OF STUDY, DEPARTMENTAL GRADUATE ADVISERS, AND SELECTED AREAS OF STUDY/RESEARCH

(All phone numbers are in area code 215.)

College of Arts and Sciences
Bioscience and Biotechnology (M.S., Ph.D.): Biochemistry, molecular biology, biotechnology, microbiology, ecology, physiological ecology. Dr. A. Philip Handel, 895-2428.
Chemistry (M.S., Ph.D.): Analytical chemistry, inorganic and bioinorganic chemistry, organic chemistry, physical chemistry, materials polymer chemistry, environmental chemistry, atmospheric chemistry. Dr. Peter Wade, 895-2652.
Clinical Psychology (M.S., Ph.D., Advanced Professional Certificate): Gerontology, personality assessment, medical psychology. Dr. David Cibon, 895-2402.
Mathematics and Computer Science (M.S., Ph.D.; Ph.D. available only in mathematics): Symbolic mathematic computation, functional analysis, parallel and distributed systems, software engineering, special functions and asymptotic analysis, biostatistics and biomathematics, combinatorics and differential equations. Dr. Robert Boyer, 895-1854.
Nutrition and Food Science (M.S., Ph.D.): Human nutrition, food science and nutrition. Dr. A. Philip Handel, 895-2428.
Physics and Atmospheric Science (M.S., Ph.D.): Nuclear and particle physics, atomic and molecular physics, condensed matter physics, biological physics, environmental and educational physics, atmospheric science, astrophysics. Dr. Frank Ferrone, 895-2778.
School of Education (M.S., Ph.D.): Certification in elementary education and in secondary education (emphases in biology, chemistry, earth and space science, general science, mathematics, physics). Larry Keiser, 895-6770.
Technical and Science Communication and Publication Management (M.S.). Dr. Alexander Friedlander, 895-1819.

College of Business and Administration
Business Administration (M.B.A., M.B.A. Online, Advanced Professional Certificate): Accounting control, banking management, business economics, financial management, organizational and human resource management, international business, investment management, management science, management information systems, management of production and operating systems, marketing management, quality science, statistical analysis, taxation. Dr. Thomas Wieckowski, 895-1791.
Accounting (including Taxation) (M.S). Dr. Anthony Curatola, 895-1453.
Finance (M.S.). Dr. Michael Gombola, 895-1743.
Ph.D. Dr. Jeffrey Greenhaus, 895-2139. Accounting, decision sciences, economics, finance, marketing, organizational science, strategic management.

College of Engineering
Chemical Engineering and Biochemical Engineering (M.S., Ph.D.): Process dynamics and control, environmental engineering, process design, semiconductor processing, biochemical engineering, heat and mass transfer, simulation and process modeling. Dr. Masoud Soroush, 895-1710.
Civil Engineering (M.S., Ph.D.): Environmental engineering, geosynthetic engineering, water and wastewater treatment, highway engineering, coastal engineering, hydrology, structural models and engineering, engineering geology, hazardous waste containment, construction materials. Dr. Jonathan Cheng, 895-2996.
Electrical and Computer Engineering (M.S., Ph.D.): Electrophysics, microwave-lightwave engineering, ultrasonics and ultrasound, signal processing, communications, controls, circuits, electromagnetic fields, image processing, computer vision, power systems, artificial intelligence, optics, superconductivity. Dr. Bahram Nabet, 895-6761.
Engineering Geology (M.S.): Environmental geology, geophysics, groundwater hydrology, hydrogeology, surface hydrology. Dr. Edward Doheny, 895-2344.
Engineering Management Program (M.S.): Financial management, technical marketing, construction management, quality and manufacturing management, utility and energy management. Dr. Stephen Smith, 895-2354.
Materials Engineering (M.S., Ph.D.): Ceramics, polymer processing, biomaterials, powder and physical metallurgy, fibrous materials, composites. Dr. Wei-Heng Shih, 895-6636.
Mechanical Engineering (M.S., Ph.D.): Structural dynamics, biomechanics, dynamic systems and controls, CAD/CAM, thermal sciences, nuclear engineering, fluid mechanics, combustion and fuels chemistry, manufacturing, robotics, thermodynamics, aerodynamics, robotics. Dr. Sorin Siegler, 895-2316.

College of Information Science and Technology
Library and Information Science (M.S., M.S.I.S., Ph.D., Advanced Professional Certificate). M.S.: library and information science. Master of Science in Information Systems: analysis/design of software-intensive systems. Ph.D.: information systems design/evaluation; management; scholarly communication. Ms. Anne Tanner, 895-2485.

Multidisciplinary Program
Software Engineering (M.S.). Three tracks are available.
Computer science. Dr. Spiros Mancoridis, 895-6824.
Engineering. Dr. Mohana Shankar, 895-6632.
Information science. Dr. Greg Hislop, 895-2179.

Nesbitt College of Design Arts
Arts Administration (M.S.). Professor Cecelia Fitzgibbon, 895-4913.
Architecture (M.S.). Assistant Department Head: Walter Moleski, 895-6090.
Fashion and Visual Studies (M.S.). Professor Kathy Martin, 895-4941.
Interiors and Graphic Studies (M.S.). Professor Rena Cumby, 895-4943.

School of Biomedical Engineering, Science and Health Systems (M.S., Ph.D.): Biomaterials/biotechnology, biomechanics, biomedical signal processing, biosensors, bioelectrodes and biotelemetry, biophysics, biostatistics, cardiovascular dynamics and instrumentation, computer applications to health care, medical imaging and image processing, medical ultrasound, neural networks and systems, sensory systems, clinical engineering, rehabilitation engineering. Dr. William Freedman, 895-2249. Biomedical science, Dr. Donald McEachron, 895-1382.

School of Environmental Science, Engineering and Policy (M.S., Ph.D.): Air pollution, applied ecology, environmental assessment, environmental chemistry, environmental health/industrial hygiene, environmental microbiology, hazardous waste, solid waste, water/wastewater treatment, water resources. Dr. Claire Welty, 895-2281.

DUKE UNIVERSITY

Graduate School

Programs of Study

Duke University offers programs of study leading to the degree of Doctor of Philosophy in art history, biochemistry, biological anthropology and anatomy, biology, biomedical engineering, business administration, cell biology, chemistry, civil and environmental engineering, classical studies, computer science, cultural anthropology, earth and ocean sciences (geology), ecology, economics, electrical and computer engineering, English, environment, genetics, German studies, history, immunology, literature, mathematics, mechanical engineering and materials science, microbiology, molecular cancer biology, music, neurobiology, pathology, pharmacology, philosophy, physics, political science, psychology, religion, Romance studies, sociology, and statistics and decision sciences. Master's degree work is also available in many of these study areas.

In addition, the following programs of study offer master's degree study only: East Asian studies, international development policy, public policy studies, Slavic languages and literatures, teaching, and the interdisciplinary programs in the humanities and in liberal studies.

Although the following programs do not offer individual degrees, they do provide areas of study and course work that enhance the degree programs listed above: aging and human development, area studies (African and African-American studies, Bioinformatics and Genome Technology, Canadian studies, Latin American studies, and Slavic, Eurasian, and East European studies), biological chemistry, cell and molecular biology, cellular and biosurface engineering, computational science and engineering, demography, developmental biology, developmental psychology, health policy, hydrology, medieval and Renaissance studies, molecular biophysics, nonlinear and complex systems, political economy, toxicology, tropical conservation, and women's studies.

Research Facilities

Among the facilities for research and study are the University libraries, which contain 4.5 million volumes, including many noteworthy holdings and special collections of international reputation. Extensive computing facilities and services are available to all students, including free accounts on the main computer system and access to the global Internet. The Duke Medical Center and Hospital, a part of the University located on campus, ranks among the outstanding health-care centers of the world. The University encompasses a complex of modern laboratory facilities including the Phytotron, an integrated series of plant-growth rooms providing forty-six separately controlled environments; the morphometrics laboratory; the primate center; the vivarium; the Duke Marine Laboratory at Beaufort, North Carolina; the hyperbaric/hypobaric unit located in the F. G. Hall Laboratory for Environmental Research; the Triangle Universities Nuclear Laboratory (TUNL); the Duke Free Electron Laser Laboratory; the Paul M. Gross Chemical Laboratory; and numerous other scientific and medical laboratories located in departments across the campus. The 7,700-acre Duke Forest serves as an outdoor laboratory for study in forestry and allied fields.

Financial Aid

Awards for financial assistance to graduate students are based on academic merit. These awards include the James B. Duke Fellowships, which provide an annual stipend supplement of $4000 to any other award the student secures; the University Scholars Program Fellowships, which provide full tuition and fees plus a stipend; departmentally administered fellowship stipends (ranging in value from $14,000 to $20,250) and tuition scholarships (for full or partial tuition); assistantships for teaching and research; and traineeships. Special awards, including Duke Endowment Fellowships, are available for minority students. Financial aid for students who demonstrate need is available in the form of loans and through the Federal Work-Study Program.

Cost of Study

Tuition is charged on a per-semester basis for Ph.D. students and on a per-unit basis for master's and nondegree students. For the academic year 2002–03, tuition and fees for Ph.D. study are estimated to be $24,600. The per-unit tuition charge for master's degree students is estimated to be $820, with 12 units per semester defined as a full-time program of study. There is a registration fee of $1500 each semester.

Living and Housing Costs

University housing for the academic year 2002–03 averages about $5600 for a single student, and meals average about $4200. Plentiful off-campus housing is available at various rates.

Student Group

Of a total University enrollment of 13,060 in 2001–02, there were 2,287 students registered in the Graduate School. Graduate students come from most of the fifty states and from more than seventy countries.

Location

Duke is located in Durham, a city of more than 200,000 in a metropolitan area of approximately 1 million people midway between the Atlantic Ocean and the Appalachian Mountains. Outdoor recreation is possible all year, and the cultural life of the community is well developed in all of the arts. The University is situated on wooded hills that constitute part of the 7,700-acre Duke Forest. Nearby are the University of North Carolina at Chapel Hill (8 miles south) and North Carolina State University in Raleigh, the state capital (25 miles east). These two institutions, along with Duke, constitute the points of the well-known Research Triangle Park of North Carolina, the site of the laboratories and research facilities of many government agencies and major pharmaceutical, medical, chemical, and computer corporations.

The University and The School

Duke is a private university that dates as a corporate entity from 1924. However, its roots go back more than 150 years to the Union Institute, founded in 1838. The Graduate School has a faculty of more than 1,000 members, teaching approximately 900 courses and seminars; a reciprocal agreement with the University of North Carolina at Chapel Hill, North Carolina Central University in Durham, and North Carolina State University at Raleigh enables Duke students to enroll in courses at those nearby institutions. In addition to the programs in the Graduate School proper, other graduate programs at Duke are offered in the schools of business, divinity, environment, law, medicine, and nursing.

Applying

Electronic application forms are available at the Graduate School's World Wide Web address (listed below). Applications are reviewed competitively, with careful consideration given to every aspect of the application—academic records, letters of recommendation, Graduate Record Examinations scores, and the candidate's own statements. All departments require the GRE General Test; some require a Subject Test as well. Students whose native language is not English must also submit test scores from the Test of English as a Foreign Language (TOEFL); a minimum TOEFL score of 550 (paper-based test) or 213 (computer-based test) is required. For an applicant to be guaranteed consideration for fall admission and financial aid, the completed application forms and all supporting materials must be submitted together and postmarked no later than December 31.

Correspondence and Information

Graduate School Admissions Office
127 Allen Building
Box 90065
Duke University
Durham, North Carolina 27708-0065

Telephone: 919-684-3913
E-mail: grad-admissions@duke.edu (Include name of department/program in the subject line.)
World Wide Web: http://www.gradschool.duke.edu

FACULTY HEADS

Lewis M. Siegel, Ph.D., Dean of the Graduate School and Vice Provost.
A. Leigh DeNeef, Ph.D., Professor of English and Associate Dean.

Directors of Graduate Studies

Art History: Annabel Wharton, Ph.D. (telephone: 919-684-2495).
Biochemistry: Terrence Oas, Ph.D. (telephone: 919-684-4363).
Biological Anthropology and Anatomy: Carel Van Schaik, Ph.D. (telephone: 919-660-7390).
Biology: William Morris, Ph.D. (telephone: 919-684-5257).
Biomedical Engineering: Monty Reichert, Ph.D. (telephone: 919-660-5151).
Business Administration: James R. Bettman, Ph.D. (telephone: 919-660-7851).
Cell Biology: Blanche Capel, Ph.D. (telephone: 919-684-6390).
Chemistry: Richard MacPhail, Ph.D. (telephone: 919-660-1536).
Civil and Environmental Engineering: Tomasz Hueckel, Ph.D. (telephone: 919-660-5205).
Classical Studies: Diskin Clay, Ph.D. (telephone: 919-684-8873).
Computer Science: Robert Wagner, Ph.D. (telephone: 919-660-6536).
Cultural Anthropology: Charles Piot, Ph.D. (telephone: 919-681-3264).
Earth and Ocean Sciences (Geology): Lincoln Pratson, Ph.D. (telephone: 919-681-8077).
East Asian Studies: Nan Lin, Ph.D. (telephone: 919-660-5610).
Ecology: James Clark, Ph.D. (telephone: 919-660-7402).
Economics: Kent Kimbraugh, Ph.D. (telephone: 919-660-1846).
Electrical and Computer Engineering: Peter Marinos, Ph.D. (telephone: 919-660-5257).
English: Sarah Beckwith, Ph.D. (telephone: 919-684-5275).
Environment: Kenneth Knoerr, Ph.D. (telephone: 919-613-8030).
Genetics: Robin Wharton, Ph.D. (telephone: 919-681-4365).
German Studies: James Rolleston, Ph.D. (telephone: 919-681-3098).
History: Ronald Witt, Ph.D. (telephone: 919-684-8201).
Humanities: A. Leigh DeNeef, Ph.D. (telephone: 919-681-3252).
Immunology: Garnett Kelsoe, Ph.D. (telephone: 919-613-7936).
International Development Policy: Francis Lethem, Ph.D. (telephone: 919-613-7332).
Liberal Studies: Donna Zapf, Ph.D. (telephone: 919-684-3222).
Literature: Kenneth Surin, Ph.D. (telephone: 919-684-4364).
Mathematics: Les Saper, Ph.D. (telephone: 919-660-2843).
Mechanical Engineering and Materials Science: Laurens Howle, Ph.D. (telephone: 919-660-5331).
Microbiology: David J. Pickup, Ph.D. (telephone: 919-684-2480).
Molecular Cancer Biology: Ann Marie Pendergast, Ph.D. (telephone: 919-681-8086).
Music: Scott Lindroth , Ph.D. (telephone: 919-660-3307).
Neurobiology: Dona Chikaraishi, Ph.D. (telephone: 919-681-4269).
Pathology: Soman Abraham, Ph.D. (telephone: 919-684-3630).
Pharmacology: Donald McDonnell, Ph.D. (telephone: 919-684-6035).
Philosophy: Ted Schmaltz, Ph.D. (telephone: 919-660-3059).
Physics: Henry Weller, Ph.D. (telephone: 919-660-2633).
Political Science: Rom Coles, Ph.D. (telephone: 919-660-4310).
Psychology: Reiko Mazuka, Ph.D. (telephone: 919-660-5702), and Carol Eckerman, Ph.D. (telephone: 919-660-5705).
Public Policy Studies: Frederick Mayer, Ph.D. (telephone: 919-613-7338).
Religion: Eric Meyers, Ph.D. (telephone: 919-660-3517).
Romance Studies: Margaret Greer, Ph.D. (telephone: 919-660-3102).
Slavic Languages and Literatures: Jehanne Gheith, Ph.D. (telephone: 919-660-3147).
Sociology: Nan Lin, Ph.D. (telephone: 919-660-5610).
Statistics and Decision Sciences: Jim Berger , Ph.D. (telephone: 919-684-4531).
Teaching: Rosemary Thorne (telephone: 919-684-4353).

Directors of Interdisciplinary Programs

African and African-American Studies: Thavolia Glymph, Ph.D. (919-668-1625).
Asian-Pacific Studies Institute: Nan Lin, Ph.D. (telephone: 919-684-2604).
Canadian Studies Program: John Thompson, Ph.D. (telephone: 919-684-2343).
Center for Bioinformatics and Computational Biology (certificate program): Jeffery Vance, Ph.D. (telephone: 919-681-5696).
Center for Cellular and Biosurface Engineering: Monty Reichert, Ph.D. (telephone: 919-660-5151).
Center for Demographic Studies: Kenneth Manton, Ph.D. (telephone: 919-684-6126).
Center for Documentary Studies: Charles Thompson (telephone: 919-660-3657).
Center for Health Policy, Law, and Management: Christopher Conover, Ph.D. (telephone: 919-684-8026).
Center for Hydrologic Science: Miguel Medina, Ph.D. (telephone: 919-660-5195).
Center for Latin American and Caribbean Studies: Orin Starn, Ph.D. (telephone: 919-684-3221).
Center for Mathematics and Computation in Life Sciences and Medicine: Michael Reed, Ph.D. (telephone: 919-660-2808).
Center for Nonlinear and Complex Systems: Robert Behringer, Ph.D. (telephone: 919-660-2550).
Center for Slavic, Eurasian, and East European Studies: Edna Andrews, Ph.D. (telephone: 919-660-3142).
Center for the Study of Aging and Human Development: Harvey Jay Cohen, M.D./Ph.D. (telephone: 919-660-7502).
Center for Tropical Conservation: John W. Terborgh, Ph.D. (telephone: 919-490-9081).
Medical Historian Training Program: Peter English, M.D./Ph.D. (telephone: 919-684-8206).
Medical Scientist Training Program: Salvatore Pizzo, M.D./Ph.D. (telephone: 919-684-2412).
Program for the Study of Democracy, Institutions, and Political Economy: John Aldrich, Ph.D. (telephone: 919-660-4346).
Program in Computational Science and Engineering: William Allard, Ph.D. (telephone: 919-660-2861).
Program in Medieval and Renaissance Studies: A. Leigh DeNeef, Ph.D. (telephone: 919-681-3252).
University Program in Biological Chemistry: Eric J. Toone, Ph.D. (telephone: 919-681-3484).
University Program in Cell and Molecular Biology: Danny Lew, Ph.D. (telephone: 919-613-8627).
University Program in Genetics: Marcy Speer, Ph.D. (telephone: 919-684-2702).
University Program in Molecular Biophysics: John York, Ph.D. (telephone: 919-681-6414).
University Program in Toxicology: Ted Slotkin, Ph.D. (telephone: 919-681-8015).
Wetland Center: Curtis Richardson, Ph.D. (telephone: 919-613-8009).
Women's Studies: Robyn Wiegman, Ph.D. (telephone: 919-684-5683).

DUQUESNE UNIVERSITY

McAnulty Graduate School of Liberal Arts

Programs of Study

The McAnulty Graduate School of Liberal Arts offers a broad, diversified program of advanced study in a variety of academic disciplines. The graduate program gives qualified students the opportunity to broaden their knowledge in a chosen area of study, to acquire proficiency and experience in the traditional academic pursuits of scholarship and research, to contribute to the advancement of human knowledge as teachers and scholars in a personalized academic setting, to increase their professional competence, and to enhance their knowledge of current issues. Areas of study include traditional humanistic disciplines and newly designed interdisciplinary programs in liberal studies.

The Graduate School offers advanced degree programs in six disciplines at the doctoral level and in sixteen disciplines at the master's level. The Doctor of Philosophy is offered in English, health-care ethics, philosophy, psychology, rhetoric, and theology. The Master of Arts is offered in archival, museum, and editing studies; church administration and canon law; computational mathematics; conflict resolution; corporate communications; English; health-care ethics; history; liberal studies; multimedia technology; pastoral ministry; philosophy; psychology; rhetoric and philosophy of communication; social and public policy; and theology.

While no residence requirements are in effect for any master's program, all work toward this degree must be completed within six years. Doctoral candidates are expected to spend at least one year in full-time residence, during which they register for no less than 9 credits for two semesters. Doctoral students are also required to maintain continuous semester registration during their course of study at the University and to complete all degree requirements within seven years of their qualifying examinations.

Research Facilities

The University's five-story Gumberg Library houses more than 400,000 volumes, more than 3,400 periodicals and journals, and a large collection of microprint and audiovisual materials. A modern research facility, the library also has graduate study carrels, typing rooms, and group study and reading areas. Special collections housed in the library include the African Collection, a regional resource for the study of African cultures and societies; the Rabbi Herman Hailperin Collection, a historical collection on Judeo-Christian scholarship during the Middle Ages; and the Center for World Literature in Phenomenology, an extensive collection of writings in phenomenological psychology and philosophy. The library facilities of Duquesne University, the University of Pittsburgh, Carnegie Mellon University, and the Carnegie Library of Pittsburgh combine to form one of the largest regional library resource centers in the United States.

Financial Aid

The various departments of the Graduate School award a limited number of graduate assistantships, both teaching and research, and tuition scholarships. Assigned on a competitive basis to students with outstanding academic records, these awards are made for an initial one-year period, with reappointments extended on the basis of proven competence and good academic standing. Assistantships normally provide a stipend along with waivers of both tuition and the University fee.

Cost of Study

Graduate tuition for 2000–01 was set at $588 per credit.

Living and Housing Costs

Students should contact the Graduate School for living and housing information.

Student Group

Duquesne University has a total enrollment of more than 10,000 students in its nine schools. With more than 700 students and 100 faculty members in its Graduate School of Liberal Arts, the University offers the graduate student a highly personalized learning and advisement environment.

Location

One of the few private Catholic downtown universities in the United States, Duquesne University, from its position adjacent to Pittsburgh's main business section, offers ready access to the many cultural, social, and entertainment attractions of the city. Within walking distance of the campus are Heinz Hall for the Performing Arts (home of the symphony, opera, ballet, theater, and other musical and cultural institutions), the Civic Arena (center for indoor sporting events and various exhibitions and conventions), Three Rivers Stadium (for outdoor sporting events), and South Side (an entertainment and nightlife center). The libraries, museums, art galleries, and music hall of the Carnegie Institute in the Oakland area are easily accessible by public transportation, whose routes pass immediately adjacent to the campus, or by private automobile. As one of the ten largest metropolitan areas in the United States, Pittsburgh also offers many professional career opportunities for its residents.

The University

Founded in 1878 by the Fathers and Brothers of the Congregation of the Holy Ghost, Duquesne University provides the opportunity for a superior private education for students from many backgrounds without regard to sex, race, creed, color, national or ethnic origins, non-performance-related handicap, or veteran status. Duquesne's beautiful, 40-acre, self-contained campus on the bluff overlooking downtown Pittsburgh is the safest in Pennsylvania and one of the safest in the nation.

Applying

Applications for admission to graduate study with financial aid should be submitted no later than May 1 for the academic year beginning in the following September. Applications for admission without financial aid may be made up to one month prior to the beginning of the term in which the student desires to begin graduate work. All applications require official transcripts of previous undergraduate and graduate work and three letters of recommendation. The Graduate School's bulletin and application forms are available by writing or calling the office of the Graduate School.

Correspondence and Information

Linda L. Rendulic, Assistant to the Dean
McAnulty Graduate School of Liberal Arts
Duquesne University
Pittsburgh, Pennsylvania 15282
Telephone: 412-396-6400
Fax: 412-396-5265
World Wide Web: http://www.duq.edu/liberalarts/frontpage/graduate.html

THE FACULTY

The University faculty consists of more than 300 full-time professors. The Graduate School faculty consists of more than 100 experienced teachers and scholars, of whom 90 percent or more have attained the highest degrees conferred in their academic disciplines.

Constance D. Ramirez, Professor and Dean of the McAnulty Graduate School of Liberal Arts.
G. Evan Stoddard, Associate Dean of the Graduate School.

Ronald Arnett, Professor and Chair, Department of Communication and Rhetorical Studies.
James Hanigan, C.S.Sp., Professor and Chair, Department of Theology.
Douglas Harper, Chair, Department of Sociology.
Jean Hunter, Professor; Chair, Department of History; and Director, Liberal Studies Program.
Michael Irwin, Associate Professor and Director, Social and Public Policy.
David Kelly, Professor and Director, Health Care Ethics.
Charles Rubin, Chair, Department of Political Science.
John Shepherd, Associate Professor and Director, Multimedia.
Russell Walsh, Professor and Chair, Department of Psychology.
Wallace Watson, Professor and Interim Chair, Department of English.
William Wurzer, Professor and Chair, Department of Philosophy.

Graduate classes at Duquesne are small, and students are ensured personal attention.

The Gumberg Library has nearly half a million volumes and provides comfortable study areas.

D'YOUVILLE COLLEGE

Graduate Studies

Programs of Study

Degree programs leading to the Master of Science are offered in clinical nurse specialist studies in community health nursing, health services administration, international business, nurse practitioner studies (master's degree and post-master's certificate), nursing (with choice of clinical focus), occupational therapy, physical therapy, and elementary, secondary, special education, and TESOL. Graduate teacher certification programs are available in elementary, secondary, and special education. Advanced certificate programs in addictions in the community, advanced orthopedic physical therapy, clinical research associate studies, health services administration, long-term-care administration, manual physical therapy, and nursing and health-related professions education are also available. Five-year B.S./M.S. degrees are offered in dietetics, international business, nursing, and occupational therapy.

Research Facilities

D'Youville's Library Resources Center contains 95,995 volumes, including microtext and software, and subscribes to 730 periodicals and newspapers. The Health Science Building houses laboratories, activity and daily living labs for the health professions, and additional laboratories for physics, chemistry, quantitative analysis, and computer science.

Financial Aid

In order to apply for federal aid, the Free Application for Federal Student Aid (FAFSA) must be completed. Graduate students must be matriculated for 6 or more credits in a degree program. Sources of federal aid include Federal Perkins Loans, the Federal Work-Study Program, Veterans' Benefits, Federal Stafford Student Loans, and Graduate Nursing Loans. The New York State Tuition Assistance Program (TAP) is available to full-time (at least 12 credit hours), matriculated graduate students who are residents of New York State. D'Youville College offers three forms of scholarships for graduate students matriculated in a master's degree program, including the Program Merit Scholarship, the Disadvantaged Student Scholarship, and the Retention Award. Nurse traineeship assistance is available to students enrolled for a minimum of 9 credit hours per semester in the Graduate Nursing Program. Canadian students (citizens and landed immigrants) are offered a 20 percent tuition reduction and may also apply for the Ontario Student Assistance Program (OSAP). Private education loans are also available to both U.S. and Canadian citizens.

Cost of Study

Graduate tuition for 2002–03 is $460 per credit hour. A general fee of between $30 and $60 is required and is based on credit hours taken. A Student Association fee of $2 per credit hour is applied toward concerts, yearbooks, activities, and guest lectures. A technology fee of $75 is required of all full-time students ($50 for part-time students).

Living and Housing Costs

Marguerite Hall, the residence facility, houses male and female students on separate floors, with the exception of the designated coed floors. For 2002–03, room and board cost $3280 per semester. Overnight accommodations are available at a rate of $22 per night (space permitting).

Student Group

Graduate degree programs are enhanced by a 13:1 student-faculty ratio. There is an enrollment of 1,103 full-time and 422 part-time graduate students. Seventy-seven percent of the student population are women, 3 percent are from minority groups, and 62 percent are international students.

Location

D'Youville's location is ideally set in a residential community of Buffalo, New York. D'Youville College is minutes from the Peace Bridge to Canada and is approximately 90 minutes from Toronto and 25 minutes from Niagara Falls, making it a gateway to recreation areas in western New York and Ontario.

The College

D'Youville College is a private, coeducational liberal arts and professional college located in residential Buffalo, New York, approximately 1 mile from the Peace Bridge. The Grey Nuns founded D'Youville College in 1908. With a student population of just over 2,400, D'Youville offers its students the diversity and resources of a much larger college and the attention and accessibility that is usually attributed to a small college. The College's 7-acre campus offers students comprehensive facilities, modern computer labs, state-of-the-art medical labs, and modern classrooms.

Applying

Applications are reviewed on a rolling admissions basis once a candidate's file is complete. All candidates must have earned a baccalaureate degree from an accredited college or university. A baccalaureate degree in nursing from an approved or accredited college or university and RN licensure are required for admission to the graduate nursing programs. Licensure as a registered nurse in New York State and a minimum of one year of experience as a registered nurse are required of all candidates applying to the nurse practitioner studies programs. Admission to graduate programs is based on an overall evaluation of credentials, including the applicant's undergraduate record, which should show approximately a B average or better in the major field. Applicants who do not fulfill admission requirements may be admitted provisionally. Applicants whose native language is not English must submit a minimum TOEFL score of 550. The College does not require Graduate Record Examinations (GRE) or Miller Analogies Test (MAT) scores.

Correspondence and Information

Linda E. Fisher
Director of Graduate Admissions
D'Youville College
One D'Youville Square
320 Porter Avenue
Buffalo, New York 14201-9985
Telephone: 716-881-7676
800-777-3921 (toll-free)
Fax: 716-881-7779
E-mail: fisherl@dyc.edu
World Wide Web: http://www.dyc.edu

THE FACULTY

Education

Ronald Banks, Assistant Professor; Ph.D. candidate, SUNY at Buffalo.
Jamie DeWaters, Professor; Ph.D., SUNY at Buffalo.
Robert Di Sibio, Professor and Director of Teacher Certification; Ed.D., Indiana of Pennsylvania.
Sheila G. Dunn, Associate Professor and Department Chair; Ed.D., SUNY at Buffalo.
Robert J. Gamble, Associate Professor; Ph.D., SUNY at Buffalo.
Mark Garrison, Assistant Professor; Ph.D. candidate, SUNY at Buffalo.
Nancy M. Kaczmarek, GNSH, Associate Professor and Assistant Department Chair; Ph.D., SUNY at Buffalo.
James Lalley, Assistant Professor; Ph.D., SUNY at Buffalo.
Hilary Lochte, Assistant Professor; Ph.D. candidate, Wyoming.
Cathleen March, Assistant Professor; Ph.D., SUNY at Buffalo.
Robert Miller, Assistant Professor; Ph.D., SUNY at Buffalo.
Amable Paulino, Assistant Professor; Ph.D., Wisconsin–Madison.
Thomas Schiera, Assistant Professor; Ph.D., SUNY at Buffalo.
Sheila Taylor-King, Assistant Professor; Ph.D. candidate, Wyoming.
Thomas Traverse, Assistant Professor; M.A., SUNY at Buffalo.
Scott Waltz, Assistant Professor; Ph.D., SUNY at Buffalo.
Stephen E. Williams, Assistant Professor; Ed.D., Clark.

Health Services Administration

Ardyce Lightner, Professor and Chair; Ed.D. (business education), Northern Colorado; J.D., Dayton. Health management.
Elizabeth Miranda, Assistant Professor; J.D., SUNY at Buffalo.
James Notaro, Assistant Professor; Ph.D., North Carolina at Chapel Hill.
Judith H. Schiffert, Assistant Professor ; Ed.D., SUNY at Buffalo.

International Business

Joseph Fennell, Associate Professor; M.B.A., Columbia.
Bonnie Fox-Garrity, Assistant Professor; M.A., North Carolina at Chapel Hill.
Kushnood Haq, Assistant Professor; Ph.D. (international trade), SUNY at Buffalo.

Nursing

Joan Cookfair, Professor; Ed.D., SUNY at Buffalo. Community health nursing, HIV/AIDS, teaching strategies, transcultural nursing, strategies to facilitate critical thinking.
Carol A. Gutt, Associate Professor; Ed.D., SUNY at Buffalo. Wellness, child health, curriculum, women's health, women's issues, stress management, leadership roles.
Paul Hageman, Associate Professor; Ph.D., NYU. Nursing science/theory explication, integration/metaphysics and science, holistic health, caring science.
Dorothy Hoehne, Associate Professor; Ph.D., SUNY at Buffalo. Pediatrics, hospice with adults and children, instruction, experimental/qualitative research, spouse and child abuse, wellness, rehabilitation, curriculum.
Janet T. Ihlenfeld, Professor; Ph.D., SUNY at Buffalo. Parent-child nursing, patient teaching, stress, social support, quantitative research models, child abuse, statistics.
Verna Kieffer, Assistant Professor and Department Chair; D.N.S., SUNY at Buffalo. Adult health, critical care, qualitative research, quality of life issues, professional practice issues.
Edith Malizia, Assistant Professor and Assistant to the Chair; Ed.D., SUNY at Buffalo. Adult health, professional issues, professional socialization, leadership and management.

Occupational Therapy

Merlene Gingher, Associate Professor and Department Chair; Ed.D., SUNY at Buffalo. Gerontic occupational therapy, range of motion in the elderly.
Elizabeth Stanton, Assistant Professor; Ph.D., SUNY at Buffalo, Mental health issues, hospice care, culture and health.

Physical Therapy

James Karnes, Associate Professor; Ph.D., SUNY at Buffalo. Neuroanatomy/enruophysiology, gross anatomy, functional morphology.
Penelope Klein, Associate Professor; Ed.D., Syracuse. Tai chi, health-care systems and cost analysis.
Lynn Rivers, Assistant Professor and Department Chair; Ph.D. candidate, SUNY at Buffalo.
John Rousselle, Associate Professor; Ed.D., SUNY at Buffalo. Exercise physiology, psychophysiology, wellness, health education.

EAST CAROLINA UNIVERSITY

Graduate School

Programs of Study

East Carolina University offers a wide range of graduate programs. There are seventy-one master's degree programs and twelve doctoral degrees in the College of Arts and Sciences and eleven professional schools. Post-master's programs leading to the Certificate of Advanced study (C.A.S.) and Educational Specialist (Ed.S.) are also offered. (A listing is available on overleaf.)

The minimum requirement for all master's, C.A.S., and Ed.S. programs is successful completion of 30 semester hours and a comprehensive examination. A thesis and demonstrated proficiency in research skills are required in most M.A. and M.S. programs. Ph.D. programs in the biomedical sciences require completion of a minimum of 58 semester hours, candidacy examinations, and a dissertation. The Ed.D. program requires 60 semester hours, including an internship and a dissertation, and full-time residency for one year. Most master's, C.A.S., and Ed.S. programs can be completed in one calendar year of full-time study; part-time students can take up to six calendar years to complete their programs. Ph.D. students must complete all requirements no later than the end of the twelfth semester, including summers, following initial enrollment.

Research Facilities

Joyner Library houses approximately 1,014,510 bound volumes, 1.7 million pieces of microfilm, more than 5,900 periodical subscriptions, 865,858 government documents, and nearly 900 manuscript collections. It subscribes to Dialog Information Retrieval Service, with access to 200 databases. The map collection contains 97,450 maps and charts. The Music Library, a branch of Joyner, houses some 58,000 items, including books, periodicals, scores, and video and sound recordings. The Health Sciences Library is located at the Brody Medical Sciences Building and houses about 180,000 bound volumes, 30,800 units of microfilm, and 1,542 periodical and serial publications.

The Computing and Information Systems Center serves as an instructional laboratory facility in direct support of computer-related course work. The Academic Computing unit maintains various instructional and research software packages and provides technical assistance to faculty and graduate research users. A remote link to the Research Triangle Park provides access to a wide variety of instructional software and supercomputing capabilities. The campus has received national recognition for its computer networking infrastructure.

East Carolina University has renewed and strengthened its commitment to research, scholarship, and creative activity for both faculty and students. Extramural support for University activities has gone from $9.6 million to more than $40 million in the last nine years. The faculty have particular strengths in biomedical sciences, coastal studies, the fine arts, maritime history, and exercise physiology. The University continues to develop educational programs in response to regional needs in human service and health professions; endeavors draw on such cross-disciplinary research efforts as the Center on Aging and the Institute for Coastal and Marine Resources.

Financial Aid

A limited number of graduate assistantships and fellowships, ranging in value from $800 to $17,000, are available. These are awarded through the departments and schools. A limited number of waivers are available for nonresident students that allow these students to pay the resident tuition rate. Inquiries about assistantships, fellowships, and fee waivers should be addressed to academic units. Information on loans, work-study programs, and other work opportunities is available from the Financial Aid Office.

Cost of Study

In spring 2002, tuition and fees for a North Carolina resident for full-time graduate study were $1318 per semester; for a nonresident, the total was $5682. Tuition and fees are subject to change.

Living and Housing Costs

Housing and board are available on campus for unmarried students at a cost of approximately $1430 per semester for room and $1170 per semester for board. All charges are subject to change. There are no University residences for married students, but rental accommodations are available in Greenville.

Student Group

The University faculty of 1,274 provided instruction for 18,174 students in the fall of 2001, including 2,614 graduate students and 291 students in the School of Medicine. In addition, 1,044 graduate students were enrolled in distance education courses offered through the Division of Continuing Education. There are more than 67,500 living alumni who reside in all fifty states and some thirty other countries. Out-of-state students make up 14 percent of the student body.

Location

The main campus is adjacent to the downtown area of Greenville, a city of more than 60,000 people. Greenville, the hub of the eastern North Carolina coastal plain and a business, medical, and university center, is located 80 miles east of Raleigh and is accessible by highway and nearby airports. It is within easy driving distance of coastal resorts and the Outer Banks. The campus of the School of Medicine is adjacent to Pitt County Memorial Hospital, a 734-bed facility that serves as the teaching hospital for the School of Medicine.

The University

East Carolina University, North Carolina's third-largest institution of higher learning, was founded in 1907 as a state-supported teacher training school and became a liberal arts college in 1941. Developing and growing rapidly, ECU became a state university in 1967 and a constituent campus of the University of North Carolina System in 1972. The University serves as a focal point in eastern North Carolina for higher education in many fields, including its professional schools of Allied Health Sciences, Art, Business, Computer Science and Communication, Education, Health and Human Performance, Human Environmental Sciences, Industry and Technology, Medicine, Music, Nursing, and Social Work. The Health Sciences Division includes the Schools of Medicine, Nursing, and Allied Health Sciences. The Academic Division includes the College of Arts and Sciences, with seventeen departments; nine professional schools; the Graduate School; Undergraduate Studies; the Division of Continuing Education and Summer School; the Institute for Coastal and Marine Resources; the BB&T Center for Leadership Development; and the Office of Cooperative Education.

Applying

Applications must be received by June 1 for fall enrollment and by October 15 for enrollment in the spring. Some academic units have earlier deadlines. Master's degree candidates planning to enroll in the fall who want to be considered for out-of-state tuition waivers must submit applications by February 1. All applications must include a completed application form, official transcripts of all prior academic work, letters of recommendation, appropriate standardized test scores, and a nonrefundable application fee of $45.

Correspondence and Information

Graduate School
East Carolina University
131 Ragsdale Hall
Greenville, North Carolina 27858-4353

Telephone: 252-328-6012
Fax: 252-328-6071
E-mail: gradschool@mail.ecu.edu
World Wide Web: http://www.ecu.edu

GRADUATE DEGREE PROGRAMS AND PROGRAM DIRECTORS

Dr. Paul D. Tschetter, Senior Associate Dean of the Graduate School. (252-328-6012)
Dr. Max C. Poole, Associate Dean of the Graduate School.

College of Arts and Sciences
Anthropology (M.A.): Linda Wolfe, Ph.D. (252-328-6766)
Biology (M.S.): Gerhard Kalmus, Ph.D. (252-328-6306)
Chemistry (M.S.): Art Rodriguez, Ph.D. (252-328-6228)
Economics (M.S.): John Bishop, Ph.D. (252-328-6756)
English (M.A., M.A.Ed.): James Holte, Ph.D. (252-328-4291)
Geography (including Planning) (M.A.): Scott Lecce, Ph.D. (252-328-1047)
Geology (M.S.): Terri Woods, Ph.D. (252-328-6379)
History (including Maritime History) (M.A., M.A.Ed.): Carl Swanson, Ph.D. (252-328-6485)
Mathematics (M.A., M.A.Ed.): John Daughtry, Ph.D. (252-328-1904)
Molecular Biology and Biotechnology (M.S.): Gerhard Kalmus, Ph.D. (252-328-6306)
Physics (M.S., Ph.D.): Larry Toburen, Ph.D. (252-328-1861)
Psychology, Clinical (M.A.): Thomas Durham, Ph.D. (252-328-6118)
Psychology, General (M.A.): John Cope, Ph.D. (252-328-6497)
Psychology, School (M.A.): Michael Brown, Ph.D. (252-328-4170)
Public Administration (M.P.A.): Carmine Scavo, D.P.A. (252-328-6130)
Sociology (M.A.): Robert Edwards, Ph.D. (252-328-6883)

School of Allied Health Sciences
Communication Sciences and Disorders (M.S., Ph.D.): Mike Rastatter, Ph.D. (252-328-4467)
Occupational Therapy (M.S.): Anne Dickerson, Ph.D. (252-328-4439)
Physical Therapy (M.P.T.): Gregg Givens, Ph.D. (252-328-4450)
Rehabilitation Studies (including Substance Abuse and Vocational Evaluation) (M.S.): Paul Alston, Ph.D. (252-328-4452)

School of Art
Art (M.A., M.F.A., M.A.Ed.): Jackie Leebrick, M.F.A. (252-328-6140)

School of Business
Accounting (M.S.A.): Rick Niswander, Ph.D. (252-328-6970)
Business Administration (M.B.A.): Rick Niswander, Ph.D. (252-328-6970)

School of Computer Science and Communication
Computer Science (M.S.): Ronnie Smith, Ph.D. (252-328-1906)

School of Education
Adult Education (M.A.Ed.): Vivian Mott, Ed.D. (252-328-6856)
Business and Vocational Education (M.S.): Lilla Holsey, Ed.D. (252-328-6762)
Counselor Education (M.A.Ed.): John Schmidt, Ed.D. (252-328-6856)
Educational Administration and Supervision (Ed.S.): Lynn Bradshaw, Ed.D. (252-328-6444)
Educational Leadership (Ed.D.): Kermit Buckner, Ed.D. (252-328-1119)
Elementary Education (M.A.Ed.): Patricia Anderson, Ed.D. (252-328-6833)
Instructional Technology Education (M.A.Ed., M.S.): Constance Mellon, Ph.D. (252-328-4338)
Master of Arts in Teaching (M.A.T.): Patricia Anderson, Ed.D. (252-328-6833)
Library Science (M.L.S., CAS): Constance Mellon, Ph.D. (252-328-4338)
Middle Grades Education (M.A.Ed.): Ann Bullock, Ed.D. (252-328-1126)
Reading Education (M.A.Ed.): Katherine Misulis, Ph.D. (252-328-6830)
School Administration (M.S.A.): Dan Wait, Ed.D. (252-328-1096)
Science Education (M.A., M.A.Ed.): Scott Watson, Ph.D. (252-328-6219)
Special Education (Learning Disabilities and Mental Retardation) (M.A.Ed.): Melissa Engleman, Ph.D. (252-328-6400)

School of Health and Human Performance
Exercise and Sport Science (M.A., M.A.Ed.): James Decker, Ph.D. (252-328-0001)
Health Education (M.A., M.A.Ed.): Michael Felts, Ph.D. (252-328-4636)
Recreation and Leisure Services Administration (M.S.): Hans Vogelsong, Ph.D. (252-328-0020)

School of Human Environmental Sciences
Child Development and Family Relations (M.S.): Mel Markowski, Ph.D. (252-328-6908)
Marriage and Family Therapy (M.S.): David A. Dosser, Ph.D. (252-328-4850)
Nutrition and Dietetics (M.S.): Margie Gallagher, Ph.D. (252-328-4222)

School of Industry and Technology
Environmental Health (M.S.E.H.): Dan Sprau, Ph.D. (252-328-4249)
Industrial Technology (M.S.): Charles Coddington, Ph.D. (252-328-2482)
Occupational Safety (M.S.): Mark Friend, Ph.D. (252-328-2114)

School of Medicine
Anatomy and Cell Biology (Ph.D.): Ronald Dudek, Ph.D. (252-816-2849)
Biochemistry (Ph.D.): George Kasparek, Ph.D. (252-816-2681)
Microbiology and Immunology: Henry Stone, Ph.D. (252-816-2702)
Pharmacology (Ph.D.): Saeed Dar, Ph.D. (252-816-2885)
Physiology (Ph.D.): Mike Van Scott, Ph.D. (252-816-3654)

School of Music
Music (M.M.): Rodney Schmidt, D.M.A. (252-328-6282)

School of Nursing
Nursing (M.S.N.): Judy Bernhardt, Ph.D. (252-328-4302)

School of Social Work
Criminal Justice (M.S.): Mary Jackson, Ph.D. (252-328-1448)
Social Work (M.S.W.): Brent Angell, Ed.D. (252-328-4204)

Interdisciplinary and Multidisciplinary Programs
Bioenergetics (Ph.D.): James Decker, Ph.D. (252-328-0001)
Biological Sciences (Ph.D.): Donald Hoffman, Ph.D. (252-816-2807)
Coastal Resources Management (Ph.D.): Lauriston King, Ph.D. (252-328-2484)
International Studies (M.A.I.S.): Lester Zeager, Ph.D. (252-328-6408)

EASTERN ILLINOIS UNIVERSITY

Graduate Studies

Programs of Study

Eastern Illinois University offers programs of study leading to the specialist degree in educational administration and school psychology. Students may also pursue the Master of Business Administration. The following programs of study lead to the Master of Arts degree: art, clinical psychology, economics, English, gerontology, history (with a historical administration option), music, mathematics (with a mathematics education option), political science, and speech communication. The following programs of study lead to the Master of Science degree: biological sciences, chemistry, college student affairs, communication disorders and sciences, counseling, family and consumer sciences (with an option in dietetics), and technology. The University offers the Master of Science in natural sciences with concentrations in biological sciences, chemistry, physics, and earth science. Programs of study leading to the Master of Science in education include educational administration, elementary education, physical education, and special education. Through the School of Technology, the University also offers three certificate programs in computer technology, quality systems, and work performance improvement. Students may also pursue postbaccalaureate teacher certification or nondegree professional development courses.

Research Facilities

Following a $22.5-million renovation and expansion completed in 2002, Booth Library's patrons are enjoying many new enhancements, including study tables wired for data and power; new group-study rooms; improved accessibility throughout the building, including an atrium staircase and three elevators; and browsable media collections. The library collection consists of more than 926,000 cataloged volumes, approximately 1.3 million microtexts, as well as maps, music scores, and pamphlets selected to support the University's educational mission. The government documents collection includes United States and Illinois State publications. Booth Library is also home to the Coles Ballenger Teachers' Center housing K–12 curriculum materials, an extensive juvenile collection, and a variety of nonprint materials related to teachers and teaching. Leisure-time reading interests are served through materials from the general book, serial, and newspaper collections, as well as the latest bestsellers, films, and popular materials.

Booth Library's public catalog is available through ILLINET Online, the statewide network of forty-five academic libraries. The reference collection consists of 55,000 volumes. Library Technology Services provides students with computer labs, media equipment, and nonprint materials such as sound recordings and videotapes. Study carrels equipped for independent viewing and listening are provided, as well as group listening/viewing rooms.

Eastern provides several computer labs for student use. Individual departments also provide research facilities for graduate students. There is a strong history at Eastern of graduate students working with faculty members on a variety of sponsored research projects. The Graduate School provides a series of competitive grant programs to promote and support graduate research. Programs include Graduate School Research/Creative Activity Awards, Williams Travel Awards, and Master's Thesis Awards.

Financial Aid

Graduate assistantships are available in the areas of teaching and research for qualified graduate students. The Housing Department offers residential assistantships. Service assistantships are offered in a limited number of nonacademic offices. Completed assistantship applications should be submitted to the appropriate department by February 15 each year. Individual departments may establish other deadlines. The assistantships include a tuition waiver and a monthly stipend for the contract period. Program and service fees are not waived as part of the tuition waiver scholarship. As an additional benefit, a summer tuition waiver is offered to graduate assistants. Students interested in assistantships should contact individual departments for specific details. In addition to graduate assistantships, students may qualify for the Federal Work-Study Program, student employment, federal loans, and various private scholarships. International students may qualify for a limited number of International Student Scholarships.

Cost of Study

Tuition for 2002–03 graduate study at Eastern Illinois University ranges from $110.35 per credit hour for resident tuition to $330.95 for nonresident tuition. Fees are $693 for full-time residents and nonresidents who enroll for 12 or more semester hours and $52.50 per semester hour for part-time residents and nonresidents. The fees cover textbook rental, health and accident insurance, and programs and services.

Living and Housing Costs

Housing for families and single graduate students is available at a cost of $1643 per semester for a 1½-room apartment, $1730 per semester for a two-room apartment, and $1532 per semester for a super-efficiency apartment. These apartments are designed to provide inexpensive living facilities for graduate students.

Student Group

Total enrollment at Eastern Illinois University in fall 2001 was 10,531. This number includes 1,416 graduate students. Graduate students are represented by the Graduate Student Advisory Council, an organization made up of student representatives from each program. A variety of activities are available for students at Eastern, including the use of the Student Recreation Center, which offers a fitness center, racquetball courts, basketball courts, volleyball courts, an indoor track, and a swimming pool. Numerous outdoor courts, playing fields, and a jogging trail are also available.

Location

Eastern Illinois University is located in Charleston, Illinois, the county seat of Coles County, in east-central Illinois. The city has a population of approximately 20,000. Two State Highways, 16 and 130, go through Charleston and provide access to Interstates 57 and 70. Amtrak service is available in Mattoon, which is approximately 10 miles from Charleston. The larger communities of Champaign-Urbana, Decatur, and Terre Haute are within 1 hour's driving distance.

The University

The University was established as Eastern Illinois State Normal School in 1895 by the Illinois General Assembly. In response to growth and change, the institution became Eastern Illinois State Teachers College in 1921, Eastern Illinois State College in 1947, and Eastern Illinois University in 1957. The campus is located on 320 acres and consists of seventy-two buildings, including twelve residence halls and seventeen apartment buildings. The University also owns wooded tracts near Charleston, which are used for nature study and life science research.

Applying

Domestic applicants submit an application, a $30 application fee, and transcripts verifying completion of a baccalaureate degree from an accredited institution approved by Eastern Illinois University. Additional requirements such as test scores (GRE, GMAT, MAT) and departmental applications may be required by some degree programs. Admission and assistantship applications are available on the Web at http://www.eiu.edu/~graduate/ or http://www.eiu.edu for electronic application.

International applicants must submit an international application, a $30 application fee, an approved financial affidavit form, an official raised-seal transcript, and required admission test scores (GRE, GMAT, MAT, and TOEFL); TOEFL scores of at least 550 are required. International application materials are available on the Web at http://www.eiu.edu/interntl/~index.html.

Correspondence and Information

The Graduate School
Eastern Illinois University
600 Lincoln Avenue
Charleston, Illinois 61920

Telephone: 217-581-2220
Fax: 217-581-6020
World Wide Web: http://www.eiu.edu/~graduate/

THE FACULTY AND THEIR RESEARCH

DEANS
Robert M. Augustine, Ph.D., Dean of the Graduate School, Research, and International Programs.
James K. Johnson, M.F.A., Dean of the College of Arts and Humanities.
Mary Anne Hanner, Ph.D., Dean of the College of Sciences.
Elizabeth Hitch, Ph.D., Dean of the College of Education and Professional Studies.
Martha Brown, Ph.D., Interim Dean of the Lumpkin College of Business and Applied Sciences.

GRADUATE PROGRAMS AND FACULTY COORDINATORS
The area code for all phone numbers is 217.

College of Arts and Humanities
Master of Arts in Art: Mr. David Griffin (Telephone: 581-2059; E-mail: cfdg1@eiu.edu)
Master of Arts in English: Dr. Susan Bazargan (Telephone: 581-3765; E-mail: cfsxb@eiu.edu)
Master of Arts in History: Dr. Mark Voss-Hubbard (Telephone: 581-3124; E-mail: cfmv@eiu.edu)
Master of Arts in History, Historical Administration Option: Dr. Nora Pat Small (Telephone: 581-6380; E-mail: cfnps@eiu.edu)
Master of Arts in Music: Dr. Peter Hesterman (Telephone: 581-3677; E-mail: cfpdh@eiu.edu)
Master of Arts in Speech Communication: Dr. Shane Miller (Telephone: 581-6306; E-mail: cfsam@eiu.edu)

College of Education and Professional Studies
Specialist in Education in Educational Administration: Dr. Charles Rohn (Telephone: 581-6667; E-mail:cfcar@eiu.edu)
Master of Science in Education in Educational Administration: Dr. Charles Rohn (Telephone: 581-6667; E-mail: cfcar@eiu.edu)
Master of Science in Education in Elementary Education: Dr. Merribeth D. Bruning (Telephone: 581-5728; E-mail:csclf@eiu.edu)
Master of Science in Counseling: Dr. Richard Roberts (Telephone: 581-2400; E-mail: cfrlr@eiu.edu)
Master of Science in College Student Affairs: Dr. Richard Roberts (Telephone: 581-2400; E-mail: cfrlr@eiu.edu)
Master of Science in Physical Education: Dr. Scott Crawford (Telephone: 581-6363; E-mail: cfscc@eiu.edu)
Master of Science in Education in Special Education: Dr. Christy Hooser (Telephone: 581-5315; E-mail: cfcmh1@eiu.edu)

Lumpkin College of Business And Applied Sciences
Master of Business Administration: Dr. Cheryl Noll (Telephone: 581-6933; E-mail: cfcln@eiu.edu)
Postbaccalaureate Certificate in Accounting
Master of Science in Family and Consumer Sciences: Dr. Frances Murphy (Telephone: 581-6997; E-mail: cfflm@eiu.edu)
Master of Science in Family and Consumer Sciences, Dietetics Option: Dr. Frances Murphy (Telephone: 581-6997; E-mail: cfflm@eiu.edu)
Master of Arts in Gerontology: Dr. Jeanne Snyder (Telephone: 581-7843; E-mail: cfjrs3@eiu.edu)
Master of Science in Technology: Dr. Peter Ping Liu (Telephone: 581-6267; E-mail: pingliu@www.eiu.edu)
- Certificate in Work Performance Improvement
- Certificate in Quality Systems
- Certificate in Computer Technology

College of Sciences
Specialist in School Psychology: Dr. J. Michael Havey (Telephone: 581-3523; E-mail: cfjmh@eiu.edu)
Master of Science in Biological Sciences: Dr. Charles Costa (Telephone: 581-2520; E-mail: cfcjc@eiu.edu)
Master of Science in Natural Sciences
- Concentration in Biological Sciences: Dr. James McGaughey (Telephone: 581-2928; E-mail: cfjam@eiu.edu)
- Concentration in Chemistry: Dr. Ellen Keiter (Telephone: 581-2521; E-mail: cfeak@eiu.edu)
- Concentration in Physics: Dr. Keith Andrew (Telephone: 581-3220; E-mail: cfkxa@eiu.edu)
- Concentration in Earth Science: Dr. Alan Baharlou (Telephone: 581-2626; E-mail: cfab@eiu.edu)

Master of Science in Chemistry: Dr. Carol Deakyne (Telephone: 581-6379; E-mail: cfcad@eiu.edu)
Master of Science in Communication Disorders and Sciences: Mr. Frank Goldacker (Telephone: 581-2712; E-mail: cffeg@eiu.edu)
Master of Arts in Economics: Dr. Eric Hake (Telephone: 581-6333; E-mail: cferh2@eiu.edu)
Master of Arts in Mathematics: Dr. Jonell Comerford (Telephone: 581-5902; E-mail: cfjac@eiu.edu)
Master of Arts in Mathematics, Education Option: Dr. Max Gerling; (Telephone: 581-6281: E-mail: cfmog@eiu.edu)
Master of Arts in Political Science: Dr. Andrew McNitt (Telephone: 581-6219; E-mail: cfadm01@eiu.edu)
Master of Arts in Clinical Psychology: Dr. William Kirk (Telephone: 581-6415; E-mail: cfwgk@eiu.edu)

EASTERN WASHINGTON UNIVERSITY

Graduate Programs

Programs of Study

Eastern Washington University offers the Master of Arts degree in college instruction, English (teaching English as a second language, English in public schools, literature, rhetoric, composition, and technical communication), history, interdisciplinary studies, and music (composition, general music, music education, performance). The Master of Education degree is offered in adult education, curriculum and instruction, early childhood education, educational leadership, elementary teaching, foundations of education, French, instructional media and technology, literacy specialist studies, school library media administration, science education, social science education, supervising (clinic) teaching, and computer- and technology-supported education. The Master of Fine Arts degree is awarded in creative writing. Eastern also offers the Doctor of Physical Therapy (D.P.T.), Master of Public Administration, Master of Business Administration, Master of Social Work, and a master's in urban and regional planning. Master of Science degrees are awarded in biology; college instruction; communication disorders; communications; computer science; applied psychology (community college teaching, counseling, developmental psychology, mental health counseling, school counseling school psychology); interdisciplinary studies; mathematics; physical education; and psychology (clinical, experimental, school psychology). Quarter credits required for graduation range from 45 to 109, depending on the master's program. The D.P.T. program requires 161 credits. All programs require at least a 3.0 cumulative grade point average, with no more than two courses below 2.5. All programs require a final comprehensive examination. Most programs require a thesis or research paper, and some also require written exams to be taken in the final quarter before graduation.

Research Facilities

Research opportunities are numerous on Eastern's Cheney campus and in Spokane. Programs offer modern facilities and actively encourage faculty-student research collaboration. Applied psychology offers video formats for instructional and practice purposes and a computer instructional lab for standard CAI exercises and integrated learning packages. Biology students have research opportunities in more than a dozen specialty fields. A recently remodeled and equipped campus facility houses the latest biological research equipment. Modern computing facilities with access to a wide array of hardware and software offer strong support to the computer science degree program. Other programs provide equally advantageous opportunities for research in their own facilities or shared facilities, such as Eastern's JFK Library and other research centers.

Financial Aid

Graduate assistantships are available in a majority of the departments offering master's degrees. In most cases, assistantships require teaching. The stipend for 2001–02 was $6870 for the academic year. Graduate assistants who work 20 hours per week may receive a waiver of all or a portion of their tuition in addition to the stipend. Assistantships are competitive. Applications should be submitted by February 15 for the following year. Financial aid in the form of tuition waivers or work-study awards is also available for students demonstrating financial need; application should be made directly to the University Financial Aid Office by February 1.

Cost of Study

In 2001–02, full-time resident tuition was $1586 per quarter, or $4758 per year. Nonresidents paid $4677 per quarter, or $14,031 per year. Part-time resident students (9 credits or less) paid $158 per credit ($316 minimum per quarter). Part-time nonresidents paid $467 per credit ($934 minimum per quarter).

Living and Housing Costs

Eastern offers a 21-and-over residence hall; rates are for single rooms and include the meal plan and vary by quarter. Yearly rates are $4677–$6443, depending on the meal plan. If reserved quarterly, rates are higher. Family housing is available in four University-administered apartment complexes. Monthly rates range from $207 to $538, depending on size and location. Off-campus apartments or rental homes are readily available in Cheney and Spokane. Incentive grants of $600 for a double or single room come with the standard meal plan. The deadline for signing up for these grants is May 1.

Student Group

Eastern has approximately 1,050 active graduate students, 60 percent of whom are women. Seventy-two percent of graduate students are enrolled full-time. Graduate programs in business administration, communications, computer science, creative writing, nursing, physical therapy, public administration, and urban and regional planning are offered in Spokane. The largest graduate programs are education (176 students), social work (264 students), physical therapy (91 students), and applied psychology (83 students). The average enrollment for all graduate programs is 54 students.

Student Outcomes

According to a recent survey of 1994–95 and 1998–99 graduates, more than 90 percent are employed and 6 percent are pursuing further graduate study. The graduates are employed as systems analysts, medical technicians, environmental biologists, city planners, physical therapists, school psychologists, mental health counselors, social workers, CPA firm managers, and community college or public school teachers.

Location

Cheney, home of Eastern's main campus, is a farming community and university town with a population of 8,800. Spokane, with facilities that house Eastern's health science and professional programs, is a metropolitan area with a population of 417,000 and is the gateway to a vast region offering hiking, camping, skiing, boating, and sightseeing.

The University

Eastern was established in 1882 as a small academy to educate teachers. Over the years, Eastern has evolved to meet the changing needs of students who want to be competitive in the worlds of business and technology. Today, the University maintains the largest graduate school of any comprehensive institution in Washington State. Eastern's tree-shaded 350-acre campus offers an ideal atmosphere for learning. Campus structures range from historic to modern.

Applying

Application forms and catalogs are available from the Graduate Studies Office and on the Web site (listed below). A $35 fee must accompany the application, along with two official transcripts from all colleges and universities attended. Applicants must submit score reports from the Graduate Record Examination (if required by the department) or from the Graduate Management Admission Test (for M.B.A. applicants). A minimum GPA of 3.0 in the last 60 semester or 90 graded quarter credits is required for admission.

Correspondence and Information

Complete information on Eastern's graduate programs may be obtained by contacting the Graduate Studies Office at the following address:

EWU Graduate Studies Office
Eastern Washington University
206 Showalter
Cheney, Washington 99004-2444

Telephone: 509-359-6297
Fax: 509-359-6044
E-mail: gradprograms@mail.ewu.edu
World Wide Web: http://www.ewu.edu/gradprog/

FACULTY HEADS

ADMINISTRATION

Ronald H. Dalla, Ph.D., Vice Provost and Dean of Graduate and Undergraduate Studies.
Larry Briggs, Ph.D., Associate Vice President for Graduate Studies.

Graduate Program Directors

Applied Psychology: Armin W. Arndt, Ph.D.; Valerie Appleton, Ph.D.
Biology: A. Ross Black, Ph.D.; Margaret A. O'Connell, Ph.D.; Dona Boggs, Ph.D.
Business Administration: M. David Gorton, M.B.A.
College Instruction: Elaine Ackerman.
Communication Disorders: Roberta Jackson, Ph.D.
Communications: Igor Klyukanov, Ph.D.
Computer Science: Linda Kieffer, Ph.D.; Timothy Rolfe, Ph.D. (M.S. Program).
Creative Writing: Gregory Spatz, M.F.A.
Education: Judy Leach, Ph.D.
English: Dana Elder, Ph.D.; Judy Logan, Ph.D.; Lynn Briggs, Ph.D.; LaVona Reeves, Ph.D.
History: Michael Conlin, Ph.D.
Mathematics: Yves Nievergelt, Ph.D.
Modern Languages (French): Alys S. Seifert, M.A.
Music: David Dolata, Ph.D.
Nursing: Anne Hirsch, Ph.D.
Physical Education: Alan Coelho, Ed.D.
Physical Therapy: Meryl R. Gersh, M.M.S; Donna Eldin, Ph.D.
Psychology: Gail Hicks, Ph.D.; Leonard Stern, Ph.D.; Peter Buerger, Ph.D.
Public Administration: Larry S. Luton, Ph.D.
Social Work: Lynne Morris, Ph.D..
Urban and Regional Planning: William J. Kelley, Ph.D.

JFK Library and the quad on Eastern's Cheney campus.

The master's program in computer science provides a balance between practical, up-to-date, applications-oriented content and a strong theoretical framework for continued learning.

Students in the Master of Social Work practicum utilize regional agency settings for integration of their course work knowledge.

EAST STROUDSBURG UNIVERSITY OF PENNSYLVANIA

Graduate Studies

Programs of Study

East Stroudsburg University of Pennsylvania offers graduate studies leading to the M.A., M.Ed., M.P.H., and M.S. degrees. In addition, graduate programs are available in twenty-four different areas of teacher certification. The Master of Arts degree is awarded with a major in history or political science. The Master of Education degree is awarded in biological sciences, elementary education, general sciences, health and physical education, history, instructional technology, political science, reading, secondary education, and special education. The Master of Public Health degree is awarded with a concentration in community health education. This program is accredited by the Council of Education for Public Health. The Master of Science degree is awarded with a major in biology, cardiac rehabilitation and exercise science, computer science, general science, health education, physical education, and speech-language pathology. The Certification Program includes, among others, the School Administration Program leading to the elementary and/or secondary principal certification and the cooperative program with Penn State University for the superintendent's letter of eligibility, the reading specialist certification, and the special education supervisor certificate. Students may complete programs of study that lead to a Pennsylvania Instructional I or Instructional II teaching certificate. ESU's educational programs are accredited by NCATE. Graduate programs provide internship opportunities, well-equipped laboratories, computer facilities, and comprehensive Web-based research databases.

Research Facilities

Kemp Library houses 341,891 monographs, 93,428 periodical volumes, and 1,278,265 pieces of microform material. The library is a depository for both U.S. government documents and Pennsylvania state publications, totaling 76,915 documents. The library uses an integrated online library system for both its automated catalog and for circulation. CD-ROM searching by microcomputer is available in addition to online searching. The Curriculum Materials Center provides teacher-trainees with a special collection of 7,600 items that includes a selection of textbooks currently used in schools throughout the country and a comprehensive collection of school courses of study. The University's computer center functions to support both administrative and academic computing. The center provides management, maintenance, and administration of all computing resources on campus used to support these two areas. A data network, connecting many buildings on the campus, is used to provide access to the administrative computer, the academic computers, and the library computers from any networked PC on campus. Seventy-five DEC workstations, seventy Macintoshes, and more than 350 PC-type microcomputers connect faculty members and students to resources throughout the world via the Internet. Stroud Hall contains classrooms, lecture halls, and computer and language laboratories. Beers Lecture Hall, which opened in 1998, seats 140 students and serves as a distance learning facility. The Fine and Performing Arts Center consists of two theaters, an art gallery, a concert hall, and classrooms. Other major classroom buildings include the Moore Biology building with laboratories for biological sciences, a large greenhouse, and a wildlife museum; recently renovated Gessner Science Hall with laboratories for physics and chemistry; DeNike Center for Human Services with laboratory areas for recreation and leisure services management, nursing, and health; LaRue Hall with laboratories for speech pathology and audiology; and Rosenkrans Hall with offices and the media, communication, and technology department. Koehler Fieldhouse contains the human performance laboratories used for exercise science, cardiac rehabilitation, and sports medicine teaching and research.

Financial Aid

Financial aid, including the Federal Stafford Student Loan program, is available to graduate students. More than 100 graduate assistantships are offered to students each semester. Graduate assistantships provide a stipend of $2500 to $5000 for a nine-month appointment and waiver of tuition (including out-of-state tuition). International students are eligible to apply for graduate assistantships.

Cost of Study

The basic tuition fee for the 2001–02 academic year for full-time Pennsylvania residents was $4600 per year. Out-of-state students paid $7554. The general fee was $806 per year. All costs are subject to change.

Living and Housing Costs

On-campus housing is available but not guaranteed to graduate students. The Office of Off-Campus Student Housing keeps listings of apartments and rooms, many within walking distance of the campus. Students living off campus may take meals in the University dining facility. International students are required to live and eat on campus during the first semester they are enrolled. The 2002–03 on-campus costs are $2768 per year for room and ranges from $946 to $1578 for board, depending on the meal plan chosen.

Student Group

East Stroudsburg University of Pennsylvania has a total enrollment of about 5,800 students. About 1,000 are graduate students. Pennsylvania residents account for about 83 percent of the student body; women comprise 70 percent of the graduate enrollment, and more than 25 percent attend full-time.

Location

East Stroudsburg University is nestled in the foothills of the Pocono Mountains in northeastern Pennsylvania. The combination of quiet woodlands, mountain streams, and refreshing clean air has made the Poconos famous as a resort area for more than 100 years. Students take advantage of the many scenic, historic, and recreational sites, including the Delaware Water Gap, Bushkill Falls, and the Pocono ski areas. The area offers fine restaurants and resorts, high-caliber entertainment, outstanding shopping, and year-round recreation, including hiking, skiing, and water sports. There is an excellent opportunity for weekend employment. The University, which is located in East Stroudsburg (Exit 51 off I-80), is within easy reach of major highway systems and commercial air services. The campus is approximately 75 miles west of New York City, 85 miles northeast of Philadelphia, 40 miles southeast of the Wilkes-Barre/Scranton area, and 40 miles northeast of the Allentown/Bethlehem/Easton area. Students and faculty members alike enjoy the opportunities and advantages of visits to the metropolitan areas.

The University

East Stroudsburg University is one of the fourteen institutions in the Pennsylvania State System of Higher Education. Founded in 1893 as a normal school to prepare teachers, the institution changed its name in 1927 to East Stroudsburg State Teachers College and again in 1960 to East Stroudsburg State College, reflecting the addition of a liberal arts and sciences curriculum. In 1983 it achieved university status. Today, the University awards the master's degree in twenty areas of specialization.

Applying

Application forms for admission are available from the graduate school office at the address below. Students should submit an application for admission, a nonrefundable $25 application fee, and an official transcript of all undergraduate work. If courses were taken at more than one institution, a transcript is required from each institution attended. Applications must be submitted between before July 31 for the fall semester and before and December 15 for the spring semester. Earlier submission for some programs is requested.

Correspondence and Information

James Fagin, Ph.D.
Dean, Graduate Studies and Research
East Stroudsburg University
East Stroudsburg, Pennsylvania 18301

Telephone: 570-422-3536
866-837-6130 (toll-free)
Fax: 570-422-3506
E-mail: grad@po-box.esu.edu
World Wide Web: http://www.esu.edu

GRADUATE PROGRAMS AND FACULTY CONTACTS

Biology
Dr. Jane Huffman, Program Graduate Coordinator (telephone: 570-422-3716). Master of Science: thesis, nonthesis, nonresearch options. Master of Education: thesis, nonthesis, nonresearch options. Faculty areas of research include management of environmental resources, marine science, wildlife diseases/parasitology, animal behavior and migrating bird biology, protozoology, developmental biology of ferns/plant ecology, and molecular biology.

Computer Science
Dr. Richard Prince, Program Graduate Coordinator (telephone: 570-422-3772). Master of Science: research emphasis (highlights software engineering). Special interests of research include artificial intelligence, discrete algorithms, robotics, and expert systems.

Elementary Education
Professor Margaret Stish, Graduate Program Coordinator (telephone: 570-422-3752). Master of Education: thesis, project, or extended programs options.

General Science
Dr. Sharmaine Cady, Program Graduate Coordinator (telephone: 570-422-3264). Master of Science: thesis or nonthesis options. Master of Education: thesis or nonthesis options. Graduate work in biology, chemistry, physics, geography, mathematics, and computer science. Programs provide for breadth and depth characteristics of a general science degree.

Health Sciences
Dr. Tisha Waring, Program Graduate Coordinator (telephone: 570-422-3565). Master of Science with major in health education: research and nonresearch options. Master of Public Health with concentration in community health education. Program accredited by the Council of Education for Public Health.

History
Professor Joe Jarvis, Department Chair/Graduate Program Coordinator (telephone: 570-422-3252). Master of Arts: thesis required. Master of Education: thesis and nonthesis options.

Instructional Technology
Dr. Elzar Camper, Jr., Graduate Coordinator. (telephone: 570-422-3646). Master of Education in Instructional Technology. Instructional Technology Certificate (K–12). Prospective students should contact the department coordinator for details.

Movement Studies and Exercise Science
Professor Shala Davis, Graduate Program Coordinator (telephone: 570-422-3106). Master of Education: major in health and physical education or concentration in sport management. Master of Science: major in physical education or cardiac rehabilitation and exercise science. Thesis, research project, and comprehensive examination options. Special application and admission required for CRES program.

Political Science
Professor Merlyn Clarke, Department Chair and Graduate Program Coordinator (telephone: 570-422-3286). Master of Arts: thesis required. Master of Education: thesis and nonthesis options.

Reading
Dr. Fred Fedorko, Graduate Program Coordinator (telephone: 570-422-3416). Master of Education: major in reading includes certification as a reading specialist. Certification as reading specialist also available without the M.Ed.

Secondary Education
Dr. Faith Waters, Graduate Program Coordinator (telephone: 570-422-3358). Master of Education: area of concentration required. Extended study option with comprehensive exam or research problem option available. Principal certification program for elementary and/or secondary. Cooperative doctoral program/superintendent's letter of eligibility with Temple University. Teacher intern program for college graduates to enter teaching profession in secondary school of Pennsylvania.

Special Education
Dr. Teri Burcroff, Graduate Program Coordinator (telephone: 570-422-3559). Master of Education: major in special education. Thirty-six-credit or thesis program option for holders of special education teaching certificate. Nonspecial education certified 36-credit or 31-credit research options available. Special education supervisor advanced certificate also available.

Speech Pathology and Audiology
Dr. Robert Ackerman, Graduate Program Coordinator (telephone: 570-422-3681). Master of Science: major in speech-language pathology. Forty-two credits and appropriate clinical practicum and comprehensive examination.

EAST TENNESSEE STATE UNIVERSITY

School of Graduate Studies

Programs of Study

East Tennessee State University (ETSU) was recognized by the *Kaplan/Newsweek College Catalog 2002* as a top university in the category of "schools that offer the best value for your tuition dollar." The ETSU School of Graduate Studies offers more than fifty majors within fourteen master's degree programs, five certificate programs, and three doctoral programs, and ETSU also offers the Doctor of Medicine (M.D.) degree. Pending approval, the Doctor of Audiology (Aud.D.) and the Master of Social Work (M.S.W.) programs will admit students in 2003. Certificate programs are offered in business, gerontology, nursing, health-care management, and archival studies. In addition to the Ed.D. in educational leadership and policy analysis, the new D.S.N., and the Ph.D. in biomedical sciences, the M.D. is offered through the James H. Quillen College of Medicine, recognized by prestigious national organizations for its programs in rural and primary-care medicine. Extramural support has increased from $6 million in 1991 to more than $31 million in 2000, including more than $3 million in funding from the NIH. A new $36-million basic sciences building, Stanton-Gerber Hall, opened in 2002.

Research Facilities

The $28-million Charles C. Sherrod Library has 192,000 square feet, can hold 800,000 volumes, and contains more than 1 million microforms, 2,124 periodical subscriptions, and more than 350,000 federal and state documents and maps. It seats 1,800, has multiple computer stations, and houses 420 individual study carrels, including a number of private rooms, all network accessible, for students working on theses or dissertations. Twenty-five laptop computers are available for in-library use, with 4-hour checkout. Four public microcomputer labs containing PCs and Macintoshes provide access to the campus e-mail server, the Internet, and the library online catalog system. More than 700 terminals and nine open computer labs are also provided. A large number of other departmental and dedicated labs, as well as multimedia classrooms, meet specialized needs of individual programs. The Archives of Appalachia and the law collection provide access to political, social, historical, and cultural records of the southern Appalachian Mountains.

Financial Aid

ETSU offers approximately 600 graduate assistantships, including Geier Awards for African Americans; stipends begin at $5000 for a nine-month contract, in addition to full remission of in-state and out-of-state tuition. Tuition scholarships also provide full remission of in-state and out-of-state tuition. In addition to departmental assignments, assistantships and tuition scholarships are available in nonacademic departments across the campus, such as University Housing, the Sherrod Library, and various administrative offices. Fellowships, work-study programs, and federal loans are available through the Office of Financial Aid. Information regarding all types of financial aid is available on the Web at http://www.etsu.edu/gradstud/finaid.htm.

Cost of Study

In 2001, graduate students paid $220 per semester hour, to a maximum of $1998 per semester. Nonresident graduate students paid an out-of-state fee of $490 per semester hour, to a maximum of $5234 per semester. Graduate assistants and tuition scholars received remission of the graduate tuition fee.

Living and Housing Costs

For single students, residence halls (double occupancy) were available at costs ranging from $825 to $970 per semester in 2001–02; a furnished efficiency for single graduate students was $260 per month. A 300-bed apartment complex offers 25 four-bedroom units and 100 two-bedroom apartments; all are fully furnished, with kitchens and washers and dryers, and have common living rooms, balconies or patios, and telephone jacks, television jacks, and data jacks in each bedroom and living room. A clubhouse and recreational facilities are available to all occupants. Rent is variable, depending upon occupancy and terms of lease.

Student Group

In fall 2001, approximately 12,000 students were enrolled. Graduate students accounted for about 2,000 of that total.

Location

The main campus of ETSU is located in Johnson City, 100 miles northeast of Knoxville and near the state lines of Virginia, Kentucky, West Virginia, North Carolina, and South Carolina. The Tri-Cities Metropolitan Statistical Area (MSA) is the eighty-fourth-largest in the country, with a population of more than 462,300. The Tri-Cities Tennessee/Virginia area is the nation's only region to be designated an "All America City." Situated just a few miles from Interstates 81 and 181, ETSU is easily accessible by automobile and is served by Tri-Cities Regional Airport. The campus has 366 tree-shaded acres and more than seventy buildings. Off-campus sites include ETSU at Bristol, ETSU at Greeneville, ETSU at Kingsport, and the Nave Center in Elizabethton. Recreational opportunities include boating, tennis, golf, skiing (snow and water), white-water rafting, fishing, jogging, biking, hiking, and more. This region provides tenancy to six area hospitals affiliated with the University, including the adjacent James H. Quillen Veterans Affairs Medical Center. ETSU's Division of Health Sciences (Medicine, Nursing, and Public and Allied Health) and the regional med-tech community comprise the only center for health sciences between Knoxville and Roanoke, Virginia.

The University

Founded in 1911, ETSU is one of six universities (forty-five postsecondary institutions) governed by the Tennessee Board of Regents, the nation's sixth-largest higher education system, providing programs to some 182,000 students. Accredited by the Commission on Colleges of the Southern Association of Colleges and Schools, ETSU has seven colleges—Arts and Sciences, Business, Education, Medicine, Applied Science and Technology, Nursing, and Public and Allied Health—and the Schools of Continuing Studies and Graduate Studies. ETSU offers more courses through interactive television than any other institution in Tennessee and a wide range of evening and online courses that appeal to students who work full-time. The University's growth includes a new 100,000-square-foot Center for Physical Activity recreational complex and the new Scott M. Niswonger Digital Media Center that houses ETSU's internationally acclaimed advanced visualization design graphics lab. In short, ETSU is large enough to offer many choices in programs and activities but small enough to avoid the intimidation and anonymity of a larger university.

Applying

Application for admission to graduate study is open to any person with a bachelor's degree from a regionally accredited institution. All domestic application materials should be filed with the School of Graduate Studies at least six weeks prior to the semester in which the applicant plans to enroll. International applications must be received twelve weeks prior to the expected date of enrollment. Application forms are available on the University's Web site (http://www.etsu.edu/gradstud/gradad.htm). Students can request a paper application by e-mail or by writing to the address below. The current application fee, which is subject to change, is $25 for U.S. residents and $35 for international students.

Correspondence and Information

School of Graduate Studies
Box 70720
East Tennessee State University
Johnson City, Tennessee 37614-1710
Telephone: 423-439-4221
E-mail: gradsch@etsu.edu
World Wide Web: http://www.etsu.edu/gradstud

PROGRAM CONTACTS

Listed below are the graduate school administration and the graduate coordinators of the various programs with the graduate degree(s) available in each area. Direct telephone contacts may be made by dialing area code 423 plus 439 and the number given for each program.

Wesley Brown, Dean, School of Graduate Studies (4221)
Roberta Herrin, Associate Dean, School of Graduate Studies (4221)
Linda Wyatt, Administrative Assistant (6146)
Sonja Jackson, Admissions Counselor/Recruiter (6149)

College of Applied Science and Technology
Caroll Hyder, Interim Dean
Computer and Information Sciences (M.S.): Martin Barrett (7409), Phil Pfeiffer (5355)
Clinical Nutrition (M.S.): Beth Lowe (7537)
Technology (M.S.): Hugh Broome (7817)

College of Arts and Sciences
Rebecca Pyles, Interim Dean
Art (M.A., M.F.A.): David Logan (5393)
Biology (M.S.): Celia McIntosh (5838)
Chemistry (M.S.): Hamid Kasmai (6917)
Communication, Professional (M.A.): Jack Mooney (4168)
Criminal Justice and Criminology (M.A.): Larry Miller (5964)
English (M.A.): Mark Holland (6681)
History (M.A.): Dale Schmitt (6698)
Mathematical Sciences (M.A.): Robert Gardner (6977)
Microbiology (M.S.): Eric Mustain (7672)
Music (M.Mu.Ed.): Benjamin Caton (4405)
Psychology (M.A.):
    Clinical: Jon Ellis (6658)
    General: Otto Zinser (6657)
Sociology and Anthropology (M.A.): Martha Copp (7056)

College of Business
Linda R. Garceau, Dean
Accountancy (M.Acc.): Martha Pointer (5314)
Business Administration Certificate: Ronald Green (5314)
Master of Business Administration (M.B.A.): Ronald Green (5314)
Public Management (M.P.M.): Lon Felker (6631)
City Management (M.C.M.): Lon Felker (6631)

College of Education
Martha Collins, Dean
Counseling (M.A.): Brent Morrow (4187)
Early Childhood Education (M.A., M.Ed.): Laurelle Phillips (7903)
Educational Leadership and Policy Analysis (M.Ed., Ed.S., Ed.D.): Terry Tollefson (7617), Russell Mays (7629), Russ West (7619)
Educational Media and Educational Technology (M.Ed.): Karilee Freeberg (7598)
Elementary and Secondary Education (M.Ed.):
    Elementary: Edward Dwyer (7593)
    Secondary: Karilee Freeberg (7598)
Elementary and Secondary Education (M.A.T.):
    Elementary: Rhona Cummings (7588)
    Secondary: Marjorie Anderson (7599)
Physical Education, Exercise and Sport Sciences (M.A., M.Ed.): Tom Coates (5261), Lynda Reeves (5358)
Reading Education (M.A., M.Ed.): Edward Dwyer (7593)
Reading and Storytelling (M.A., M.Ed.): Joseph Sobol (7863)
Special Education (M.Ed.): Martha Coutinho (7689)

College of Nursing
Joellen Edwards, Dean
Nursing (M.S.N., D.S.N.): Patricia Smith (4624)
Advanced Nurse Practitioner Certificate: Patricia Smith (4624)

College of Public and Allied Health
Wilsie Bishop, Dean
Communicative Disorders (M.S.)
    Audiology: Marc Fagelson (4583)
    Speech Pathology: Lynn Williams (7188)
Environmental Health (M.S.E.H.): Creg Bishop (4540)
Gerontology Certificate: Creg Bishop (4540)
Health Care Management Certificate: Patricia Smith (4624)
Physical Therapy (M.P.T.): Duane Williams (8786)
Public Health (M.P.H.): Richard Wissell (4427)

James H. Quillen College of Medicine
Ronald Franks, Dean of Medicine and Vice President for Health Affairs
Biomedical Sciences (M.S., Ph.D.)
    Assistant Dean: Mitchell Robinson (4658)
    Anatomy and Cell Biology: Paul Monaco (6717)
    Biochemistry: Sankhavaram Panini (8014)
    Microbiology: K. Jane Mayberry-Carson (6227)
    Pharmacology: Richard Kostrzewa (6321)
    Physiology: Tom Ecay (4739)

School of Continuing Studies
Norma McRae, Dean of Continuing Studies and Vice Provost for Public Service
Liberal Studies (M.A.L.S.): Marie Tedesco (4223)

EMERSON COLLEGE

Graduate Programs

Programs of Study

The School of Communication has three graduate departments: Communication, Journalism, and Communication Sciences and Disorders. These departments offer programs of study leading to the degrees of Master of Arts (M.A.) in global marketing communication and advertising, health communication, integrated marketing communication, management and organizational communication, print and multimedia journalism, and broadcast journalism and Master of Science (M.S.) with a concentration in speech-language pathology.

The School of the Arts has three graduate departments: Writing, Literature, and Publishing; Visual and Media Arts; and Performing Arts. These departments offer programs of study leading to the degrees of Master of Fine Arts (M.F.A.) in creative writing and Master of Arts in publishing and writing, audio production, television/video production, new media production, and theater education.

Emerson operates on a semester calendar. The number of credit hours to be completed varies according to the program. A minimum of 40 credits is required for the Master of Arts degree.

Research Facilities

The Emerson College Library houses more than 190,000 print and nonprint items that focus on the communication arts and sciences. Through membership in the Fenway Consortium, graduate students have access to more than 2 million volumes. Computer-assisted reference services provide bibliographic databases through DIALOG, BRS, and other online services. The On-line Computer Library Center is used for student research support. Visual and media arts facilities include two fully equipped production studios complete with professional-quality studio cameras, two film/video screening rooms, eight ¾-inch U-matic editing suites, one Avid digital nonlinear film composer editing system, Interformat and Paltex computer-assisted video production suites, twenty digital field production units, thirty Media 100 digital editing stations, and a state-of-the-art audio mix-to-pix suite. Emerson also maintains two student-operated radio stations (WECB-FM and the award-winning WERS-FM, 88.9) and an on-campus television channel (the Emerson Channel).

The Robbins Speech, Language, and Hearing Center; the Thayer-Lindsley Parent-Centered Pre-School Nursery for hearing-impaired children; the Early Childhood Communication Center; the Center for Acquired Communication Disorders; and the Children's Hospital Group Language Therapy Program provide facilities for clinical training and research for students studying communication sciences and disorders.

Financial Aid

Financial aid is available to graduate students in the form of need-based loans and awards based on academic merit. Merit awards consist of teaching, research, clinical, and administrative assistantships. The deadline for applicants interested in merit-based awards is February 1.

Cost of Study

Tuition for the 2002–03 academic year is $660 per credit. Other fees, including health insurance and health services fees, are approximately $700 per year.

Living and Housing Costs

Though Emerson does not offer on-campus housing to graduate students, the College's Office of Off-Campus Student Services assists graduate students in arranging for private accommodations in the Boston area. Costs of living in Boston are comparable to those in any large metropolitan city.

Student Group

There are approximately 3,400 students at Emerson, of whom about 900 are enrolled in graduate programs. The Graduate Student Association provides lectures, social activities, and grants to graduate students. Other graduate student activities include a comedy troupe, a video production company, and a literary journal.

Student Outcomes

Emerson's Career Services Office provides internship and job placement and lifetime career assistance, listing more than 1,500 positions in the United States and Europe. Internships are available in media, corporate, nonprofit, theatrical, medical, and political organizations. Recent employers and internship sites include ABC; AIDS Action; Arnold Communication; the *Atlantic Monthly;* Avid Technology; Boston Public Schools; Children's Hospital (Boston); the *Christian Science Monitor;* CNN; Dana-Farber Cancer Institute; Dreamworks SKG; Genzyme; Hill Holliday; Little, Brown & Company; Pfizer Pharmaceuticals; Spaulding Rehabilitation Hospital; Tom Snyder Productions; the Wang Center; and the World Health Organization.

Location

Located in the heart of Boston near Beacon Hill and the Boston Common, Emerson lies in the midst of one of the nation's largest media and publishing markets and corporate centers. Boston also provides nearly 100 communication disorders practicum sites through its outstanding speech and hearing centers.

Emerson is within walking distance of the Theater District, the Public Garden, Newbury Street shopping, the Charles River Esplanade, and the Freedom Trail. Fenway Park, Harvard Square, and the Museum of Fine Arts, open without charge to Emerson students, are also minutes from the campus. Graduate students in certain programs may spend a semester at Emerson's Los Angeles campus, working at internships by day and taking classes with Emerson professors and industry professionals in the late afternoon and evening. Furnished housing is adjacent to the Los Angeles Center and just minutes from Universal Studios, Warner Bros., and NBC.

The College

Emerson College is an independent, privately supported, coeducational, specialized college. Founded in Boston in 1880, it is the only four-year undergraduate and graduate college in the nation entirely devoted to the communication arts and sciences.

Applying

Admission to the graduate programs is based on a combination of factors, including academic performance, GRE/GMAT scores, letters of recommendation, personal and professional experience, writing samples, and potential contributions to the proposed major field of study. An application and fee of $55 ($75 for international students) must be submitted along with official transcripts from all undergraduate and graduate institutions attended and three letters of recommendation. International students must also submit results of the Test of English as a Foreign Language (TOEFL). The GRE General Test (or, in some cases, the GMAT) is required.

Emerson College encourages applications from graduating college seniors and from individuals who wish to reenter the job market, seek a career change, or strengthen their credentials. Part-time enrollment and evening classes are available in several of the program areas.

Correspondence and Information

Office of Graduate Admission
Emerson College
120 Boylston Street
Boston, Massachusetts 02116
Telephone: 617-824-8610
Fax: 617-824-8614
E-mail: gradapp@emerson.edu
World Wide Web: http://www.emerson.edu

FACULTY HEADS

Director of Graduate Studies: Donna Schroth, Ed.D.

School of Communication: Stuart J. Sigman, Ph.D., Dean.
- Department of Communication: Phillip Glenn, Ph.D., Chair.
- Department of Journalism: Gerald F. Lanson, M.A., Chair.
- Department of Communication Sciences and Disorders: Cynthia Bartlett, Ph.D., Acting Chair.

School of the Arts: Grafton J. Nunes, M.F.A., Dean.
- Department of Performing Arts: Maureen Shea, Ph.D., Chair.
- Department of Visual and Media Arts: Robert Sabal, M.F.A., Chair.
- Department of Writing, Literature, and Publishing: Robin Riley Fast, Ph.D., Acting Chair.

Emerson College is located in the historic Back Bay section of Boston, within minutes of the thriving business and theater districts.

Dean Stuart Sigman of the School of Communication, Management, and Policy chats with graduate students.

EMORY UNIVERSITY

Graduate School of Arts and Sciences

Programs of Study

The Graduate School of Arts and Sciences offers the Master of Arts in educational studies, film studies, Jewish studies, and music and sacred music; the Master of Science in biostatistics, mathematics, and mathematics and computer science; and the Master of Science in clinical research in epidemiology. Professional degrees awarded are Master of Education and Master of Arts in Teaching. A Diploma for Advanced Study in Teaching is also available.

The Doctor of Philosophy is offered in anthropology, art history, biological and biomedical sciences, biomedical engineering, biostatistics, business, chemistry, comparative literature, economics, educational studies, English, epidemiology, French, history, liberal arts, mathematics, nursing, philosophy, physics, political science, psychology, religion, sociology, Spanish, and women's studies.

Programs within the Graduate Division of Biological and Biomedical Sciences include biochemistry, cell and developmental biology, genetics and molecular biology, immunology and molecular pathogenesis, microbiology and molecular genetics, molecular and systems pharmacology, neuroscience, nutrition and health sciences, and population biology, ecology, and evolution. A six-year Medical Scientist Program leads to a combined M.D./Ph.D. The Graduate Institute of the Liberal Arts offers programs of interdisciplinary study. Area concentrations in interdisciplinary study are American and African-American studies and culture, history, and theory. Programs in the Psychology Department include clinical psychology, cognitive and developmental psychology, and neuroscience and animal behavior. Programs within the Graduate Division of Religion include ethics and society; Hebrew Bible; historical studies in theology and religion; New Testament; person, community, and religious practices; theological studies; West and South Asian religion; and the J.D./Ph.D. program. A joint Ph.D. program in biomedical engineering is offered with the Georgia Institute of Technology.

M.A. and M.S. degrees require a minimum of two semesters of residence; M.Ed. and M.A.T. degrees and the diploma require at least three semesters of residence; a minimum of four semesters of residence are required for the Ph.D.

Research Facilities

The library resources of Emory University are encompassed in six facilities: the Robert W. Woodruff Library for Advanced Studies, Asa Griggs Candler Library, James Samuel Guy Chemistry Library, Hugh F. MacMillian Law Library, Robert W. Woodruff Health Sciences Library, and Pitts Theology Library. Collections in the University number 2.7 million volumes, 2.4 million microforms, 50,000 reels of microfilm, 7,700 linear feet of manuscripts, more than 22,300 serial and periodical subscriptions, and a growing inventory of nonprint materials.

Additional facilities include the Information Technology Division, Yerkes Regional Primate Research Center, and the Michael C. Carlos Museum. The Carter Center of Emory University provides resources for the study of national and international policy issues.

Financial Aid

All Emory University graduate fellowships are based on academic merit. They include the George W. Woodruff Fellowship, which provides an annual stipend supplement to the departmental award, plus tuition, for five years; the Emory Minority Graduate Fellowship, which provides stipend and tuition for five years; and departmental awards, which include stipend and tuition scholarships. All applications are due by January 20. Some departments have earlier deadlines; prospective students should check with the department. Tuition assistance grants are awarded to some teachers admitted to master's programs in the Division of Educational Studies. Information regarding extra-University financial aid (loans, work study, or veterans' benefits) may be obtained from the Financial Aid Office.

Cost of Study

In 2002–03, tuition is $1074 per semester hour, or $12,885 for a full load (12 semester hours or more); the computing fee is $50 per semester; and the student activity and recreation fee is $126 per semester. Additional costs include a thesis-binding fee of $45, a thesis copyright fee of $45, a dissertation-binding fee of $85, and a dissertation copyright fee of $45.

Living and Housing Costs

A variety of on-campus and off-campus housing is available. On-campus housing includes a graduate and professional residential complex offering accommodations ranging from a high-rise tower for single students to attractive efficiencies and one- and two-bedroom garden apartments. All students must provide proof of medical insurance.

Student Group

Total University enrollment is more than 11,000. In the fall of 2001, total enrollment in degree programs in the Graduate School of Arts and Sciences was 1,408: 585 men and 823 women. Eighteen percent were international students, and 90 percent of the students received merit awards.

Location

Emory University's wooded campus is located in an attractive residential section of Atlanta. Easily accessible by bus and metro from Emory, downtown Atlanta provides an exciting, progressive atmosphere with many recreational and cultural activities, often with reduced rates for students. Increased attention is being paid to the city's past and its historical development and the revitalization of the downtown area. With a population of 3 million, Atlanta is relatively close to the Appalachian Mountains, the Atlantic coast, and the Gulf coast.

The University

Founded by the Methodist Church in 1836, Emory received its university charter in 1915 and moved from Oxford, Georgia, to the northeast Atlanta campus. The University comprises the Graduate School of Arts and Sciences, Emory College, Oxford College, and the medical, nursing, law, business administration, public health, allied health, and theology schools. The Graduate School of Arts and Sciences was organized as a division of the University in 1919. Extracurricular activities are plentiful.

Applying

Minimum requirements for admission include a baccalaureate degree from an accredited four-year college, an undergraduate academic average of C, an academic average of B for the last two undergraduate years, and satisfactory scores on the General Test of the GRE. Applicants are considered without regard to race, color, national origin, religion, sex, sexual orientation, age, handicap, or veteran status. Applications may be obtained by writing to the address below. Applications are due by January 20. Some departments have earlier deadlines; students should check with the department.

Correspondence and Information

Graduate School of Arts and Sciences
202 Administration Building
Emory University
Atlanta, Georgia 30322

Telephone: 404-727-6028
E-mail: inquiry@gsas.emory.edu
World Wide Web: http://www.emory.edu/GSOAS/

FACULTY HEADS AND THEIR RESEARCH

Anthropology: Carol M. Worthman, Chair; Ph.D., Harvard, 1978. Biological anthropology, human reproduction, human development, developmental epidemiology, biocultural and life history theory.
Art History: Clark Poling, Chair; Ph.D., Columbia, 1973. Early twentieth-century French and German art and theory, with an emphasis on surrealism.
Division of Biological/Biomedical Sciences: Bryan Noe, Director; Ph.D., Minnesota, Twin Cities, 1971. Structure and subcellular localization of peptide hormones, enzymology of precursor-to-hormone processing.
Biomedical Engineering: Don P. Giddens, Chair; Ph.D., Georgia Tech, 1967. Fluid mechanics applied to cardiovascular disease, Doppler velocimetry and ultrasound, hemodynamics.
Biostatistics: Michael H. Kutner, Chair; Ph.D., Texas A&M, 1971. Estimation and hypothesis testing for analysis of variance models with missing cells, model diagnostics, clinical trials methodology, statistical collaboration, and statistical education.
Business: Ajay Kohli, Chair; Ph.D., Pittsburgh, 1986. Marketing organizations, marketing management and strategy, sales force management, business/industrial marketing.
Chemistry: Jay Justice, Chair; Ph.D., North Carolina, 1974. Analytical, neurochemistry, and biophysical.
Clinical Research: John Boring, Chair; Ph.D., Florida, 1961. Infectious disease epidemiology, reproductive health.
Comparative Literature: Cathy Caruth, Chair; Ph.D., Yale, 1988. English and German romanticism, literary theory, psychoanalytic writing, trauma theory.
Economics: Jerry Thursby, Chair; Ph.D., North Carolina. Econometrics, international trade and licensing of university technologies.
Educational Studies: Eleanor Main, Chair; Ph.D., North Carolina at Chapel Hill. Urban education and educational policy, urban politics and policy, Southern politics.
English: William Gruber, Chair; Ph.D., Washington State, 1979. Drama, history of drama; comedy; missing persons: character and characterization on the modern stage; comic theaters: studies in performance and audience response.
Epidemiology: John Boring, Director, Epidemiology; Ph.D., Florida, 1961. Infectious disease epidemiology, reproductive health.
Film Studies: David A. Cook, Chair; Ph.D., Virginia, 1971. Soviet and post-Soviet cinema, Eastern European and Middle Eastern cinema; post–World War II American film, wide-screen technologies, major figures (Stanley Kubrick, Alfred Hitchcock, Orson Welles).
French: Carol Herron, Chair; Ph.D., Wisconsin–Madison, 1978. French and second language acquisition and classroom research.
Graduate Institute of the Liberal Arts: Christine Levenduski, Chair; Ph.D., Minnesota, 1989. American studies, early American literature.
History: James V. H. Melton, Chair; Ph.D., Chicago, 1982. Enlightenment Europe, early modern German and Habsburg history, historiography.
Jewish Studies: Deborah Lipstadt, Director; Ph.D., Brandeis, 1976. Modern Jewish studies, history of the Holocaust, women in Judaism.
Mathematics and Computer Science: Dwight Duffus, Chair; Ph.D., Calgary, 1978. Combinatorics, ordered sets.
Music: Steven Everett, Chair; Ph.D., Illinois, 1988.
Nursing: Annette C. Frauman, Chair; Ph.D., Texas, 1991. Social and adaptive development of children with chronic renal failure, particularly the adaptive behaviors associated with managing a complex care regimen.
Philosophy: David Carr, Chair; Ph.D., Yale, 1966. Recent continental European philosophy, Husserl, and the philosophy of history.
Physical, Materials, and Computational Sciences (PMACS): Dale Edmundson, Director of Graduate Studies; Ph.D., Arizona, 1970. Structure and function of oxidation-reduction enzymes.
Physics: Raymond DuVarney, Chair; Ph.D., Clark, 1968. Experimental solid-state physics: muon spin resonance.
Political Science: Thomas Walker, Chair; Ph.D., Kentucky, 1970. Constitutional law, judicial behavior.
Psychology: Darryl Neill, Chair; Ph.D., Chicago, 1972. Psychobiology.
Division of Religion: Laurie Patton, Chair; Ph.D., Chicago. History of Indian religions, particularly Vedic interpretation and the role of mythological narratives and magical practices in Indian commentarial texts; comparative mythology and literary theory in the study of religion.
Sociology: John Boli, Chair; Ph.D., Stanford, 1976. World culture and international organizations since 1850, transnational corporations in world-cultural context since 1970, structure and process in the world polity, citizenship and civil society.
Spanish: Hazel Gold, Chair; Ph.D., Pennsylvania, 1976. Nineteenth- and twentieth-century Spanish literature, narrative theory.
Women's Studies: Frances Smith-Foster, Chair; Ph.D., California, San Diego, 1976. African-American literature.

EMPORIA STATE UNIVERSITY

Graduate Studies

Programs of Study

Emporia State University (ESU) offers courses leading to the Master of Arts in English and history. The Master of Science is offered in art therapy, biology, business education, curriculum and instruction (effective practitioner studies, national board certification, curriculum leadership), early childhood, educational administration, health and physical education, instructional design and technology, master teacher studies (subject matter, reading specialist studies, teaching ESL), mathematics, mental health counseling, physical sciences (chemistry, earth science, physics, and physical sciences education options), psychology, rehabilitation counseling, school counseling, school psychology, special education, and student personnel in higher education. The Master of Arts in Teaching is offered in social sciences. The School also offers Master of Business Administration (general or accounting concentration), Master of Library Science, and Master of Music degree programs.

The Specialist in Education (Ed.S.) degree is offered in school psychology, and the Ph.D. is offered in library and information management.

The University conducts an academic year of two semesters plus a nine-week summer session in which graduate courses are offered in every field.

The University is accredited by the North Central Association of Colleges and Schools and is a member of the Council of Graduate Schools in the United States. Its programs are recognized by the American Chemical Society and the National Association of Schools of Music and accredited by the National Council for Accreditation of Teacher Education, the American Library Association, the American Art Therapy Association, the Council on Rehabilitative Education, the Kansas State Department of Education, and the Council for Accreditation of Counseling and Related Educational Programs (CACREP).

Research Facilities

Library Services in the William Allen White Library contains more than 733,000 volumes and more than 1 million items on microfilm. The library provides online and CD-ROM access to bibliographic and some full-text databases. Other resources are available via the Internet at public access microcomputers located in White Library. Materials not available at ESU can be requested from other libraries throughout the country by utilizing the interlibrary loan services. Other key sources or resource areas are the special collections department in White Library and the University Archives, located in Anderson Library on the west campus. The Departments of Biological Sciences and Physical Sciences have the Jones Biotechnology Laboratories and the Jones Environmental Chemistry Laboratories, with state-of-the-art equipment. The University operates four natural areas for biological research in tall grass prairie, upland and deciduous forest, and marshland. The Department of Psychology and Special Education has a state-of-the-art research laboratory for students and faculty members. The Department of Early Childhood/Elementary Teacher Education operates the only lab school on a university campus in Kansas. The lab school serves as a valuable research and training facility. The Department of Counselor Education and Rehabilitation Programs supports a state-of-the-art counseling clinic for training students and providing service to the community.

Financial Aid

Most departments offering graduate work, as well as numerous other units within the University, award graduate assistantships. During the academic year, the University employs at least 175 graduate assistants. To qualify for an assistantship, an applicant must have a minimum overall grade point average of 2.5 for four years or 2.75 for the last two years of undergraduate study, based on a 4.0 scale. Students may be eligible for fee reductions during each term in which they hold an assistantship appointment. Nonresident full-time graduate assistants are assessed fees at the same rate as residents of Kansas.

Cost of Study

In 2002–03, fees for a full graduate course load are estimated at $1356 per semester for state residents and $3468 per semester for nonresidents. For the summer session, resident fees are $123 per credit hour, and nonresident fees are $299 per credit hour. Fees are subject to change by action of the Board of Regents.

Living and Housing Costs

The Office of Residential Life offers graduate students a number of cost-effective living arrangements. On-campus apartments rent for $230 per month (utilities included). The apartment complex five blocks east of campus features one- and two-bedroom units that rent for $195 to $280 per month, depending on furnishings. Students can contact the office by telephone at 316-341-5264 or by e-mail (reslife@emporia.edu) for more information.

Student Group

The total on-campus enrollment is approximately 4,868, with about 500 full-time and 1,100 part-time graduate students. About 30 percent of the full-time graduate students receive financial assistance of some kind; 6 percent are international students. In 2000, 7 Ed.S. degrees, 325 master's degrees, and 1 Ph.D. degree were conferred.

Student Outcomes

Approximately 60 percent of the graduates find employment in their major fields of study within the state of Kansas, 29 percent of the graduates are employed in their major field of study outside the state of Kansas, 2 percent find employment outside their major field of study, 5 percent continue their education, and 4 percent are unemployed.

Location

Emporia, with a population of more than 26,000, is an educational, industrial, trade, and medical center serving 60,000 people in east-central Kansas. It is situated on the eastern edge of the famous Bluestem region of the Flint Hills and is surrounded by numerous lakes and recreational facilities. The city is located on the Kansas Turnpike, Interstate Highway 35. Three major metropolitan areas of the state—Topeka, Kansas City, and Wichita—are within 100 miles.

The University

The University, founded in 1863, has a long, diverse, and exciting history, which is reflected in its twenty-three different graduate programs in teaching, library science and information management, business, and liberal arts and sciences. Although all programs are of high quality, the University is particularly well known for its teacher education and library and information management programs. At ESU, small class sizes are the norm.

Applying

Applications for admission to the Graduate School should be made thirty days before the first day of an enrollment period. Some academic departments have earlier deadlines. For admission as a master's degree student, an applicant must have a minimum grade point average of 2.5 in the last 60 hours of undergraduate study. Applicants for the M.A. in English and the M.S. in special education must have at least a 2.75 grade point average or at least a 3.0 in the major. Applicants for the Specialist in Education degree must hold a master's degree from an accredited college or university with grades of B or better in three fourths of the credit hours taken for the degree. Applicants for the M.S. in psychology, school psychology, or art therapy must have a cumulative grade point average of at least 3.0 or at least 3.25 for the last 60 hours of an undergraduate program.

Correspondence and Information

Graduate Studies and Research
Campus Box 4003
Emporia State University
Emporia, Kansas 66801-5087

Telephone: 316-341-5403
800-950-GRAD (toll-free)
Fax: 316-341-5909
E-mail: gradinfo@emporia.edu
World Wide Web: http://www.emporia.edu/grad

FACULTY HEADS

The following list shows specializations, research, and/or exhibits of the faculty within each graduate program and the chair or graduate adviser of each department.

Biological Sciences (M.S.): Derek Zelmer, Ph.D., Director of Graduate Studies. Animal and plant ecology, animal behavior, cellular and molecular biology, ecology and physiology of grassland plants, endocrinology, entomology, environmental biochemistry and physiology, evolutionary biology, fisheries and wildlife management, ichthyology, immunology, invertebrate and vertebrate zoology, mammalogy, microbiology, ornithology, population and molecular genetics, plant and animal anatomy/physiology, plant and animal taxonomy/systematics, science education, soil science, virology.

Business and Business Education (M.B.A., M.S. in business education): Sajjad Hashmi, Ph.D., Dean. M.B.A. faculty research interests include accounting, computer information systems, finance, economics, international business, management, and marketing. The research interests of faculty members teaching in the Master of Science in business education program include business teacher education, and vocational education.

Counselor Education and Rehabilitation Programs (M.S.): David Kaplan, Ph.D., Chair. Mental health counseling, K–12 school counseling, rehabilitation counseling, student personnel services in higher education.

Early Childhood/Elementary Teacher Education (M.S.): Lawrence Lyman, Ph.D., Chair. Master teacher (reading specialist, teaching ESL, subject matter), early childhood education (early childhood curriculum and instruction, early childhood special education), postbaccalaureate teacher certification. Faculty specializations include authentic assessment, cooperative learnihg, curriculum integration, Reading Recovery, inclusion, and multicultural education. Distance learning is available for many courses in all programs.

English (M.A.): Mel Storm, Ph.D., Director of Graduate Studies. Programs offered include rhetoric, composition, creative writing, and English and American literatures. Courses for in-service teachers and for those who wish to pursue careers in community college teaching are also available. Dual master's degrees are offered with the School of Library and Information Management. Faculty specializations include medieval literature and language, Renaissance literature, eighteenth- and nineteenth-century British literature, nineteenth-century American literature, twentieth-century American literature, contemporary literature, world literature, women's studies, American studies, young adult fiction, English education, creative writing, folklore, popular culture, gender and ethnic studies, critical theory, rhetoric and composition, linguistics, and journalism.

Health, Physical Education and Recreation (M.S.): Mark Stanbrough, Ph.D., Chair. Administration, athletic training, coaching, exercise physiology, health education, pedagogy, philosophy of sports, psychology and sociology of sport. The M.S. in physical education may be fully completed via the World Wide Web.

History (M.A.): Gregory Schneider, Ph.D., Director of Graduate Studies. American history: archives and museums, oral history, Great Plains, history of Kansas, social and cultural history, nineteenth- and twentieth-century history, local and family history, Colonial history, Black history, Native American history, women's history, military history; European history: ancient and medieval, Eastern Europe, nineteenth- and twentieth-century Europe, Reformation, Renaissance, World Wars I and II; history of science.

Instructional Design and Technology (M.S.): Armand Seguin, Ed.D., Chair. Instructional design and technology. A number of courses are offered via the World Wide Web (http://idt.emporia.edu).

Library and Information Management (M.L.S., Ph.D.): Robert Grover, Ph.D., Dean. Analysis of information services and delivery systems, community analysis, economics of information, information brokering, information management, information transfer, library and information science education, management of library and information systems, organization and retrieval of information, psychology of information use, sociology of information, technology applications to information storage and retrieval. Dual master's degrees offered with the Departments of Music, History, Social Sciences, and English and the School of Business. School library media and information management certification is also available. Regional programs are offered in Colorado, North Dakota, Utah, and Oregon.

Mathematics (M.S.): Larry Scott, Ph.D., Chair. Applied mathematics, combinatorics, commutative algebra and field theory, computer science, functional analysis, mathematics education, numerical solutions of differential equations, optimization, probability and statistics, real and complex analysis, topology.

Music (M.M.): Marie C. Miller, Ph.D., Chair. Concentration in music education or performance. Areas of study and research include elementary and secondary music education; choral and instrumental conducting; vocal and instrumental methods and performance; jazz performance and instruction; applied studies in voice, keyboard, woodwinds, brass, strings, and percussion; music computer applications.

Physical Sciences (M.S.): DeWayne Backhus, Ph.D., Chair. Emphasis in chemistry, earth science, physical science teaching, or physics. All programs are designed to prepare students for additional degree work at the doctoral level, for industrial or government employment, or for teaching. Research opportunities are available in a number of areas within each discipline; NASA-funded research exists in each discipline emphasis.

Psychology and Special Education (M.S., Ed.S.): Kenneth A. Weaver, Ph.D., Chair. Clinical, general-experimental, and industrial/organizational psychology; special education: behavior disorders, mental retardation, learning disabilities, interrelated, teaching the gifted; art therapy; school psychology; special education administration. Faculty specializations: teaching psychology at the secondary level; psychometrics; inclusion; assessment; neuropsychology; cognition/retrieval process; child abuse; special education attrition; behavioral toxicology, smoking, and stress; clinical applications of art; developmental psychology; psychology of gender; cheating; statistics learning; performance appraisal; control theory; language abilities; autobiographical memory; narrative development; adolescent art therapy; human resources practices in organizations; mental retardation; and autism. A number of courses are delivered via ITV, Telenet, and the Internet.

School Leadership/Middle and Secondary Teacher Education (M.S.): Jerry Will, Ph.D., Chair. Degree and certification programs in elementary and secondary school leadership, district-level school leadership, curriculum and instruction (effective practitioner studies, national board certification, curriculum leadership), secondary education, and postbaccalaureate teacher certification. Varied courses are offered via ITV, the World Wide Web, Telenet, and ATM.

Social Sciences (M.A.T.): Gregory Schneider, Ph.D., Director of Graduate Studies. American history, geography, philosophy, political science, social studies education, world history.

Relaxing campus environment.

Interactive classes.

Technology in the classroom.

FAIRLEIGH DICKINSON UNIVERSITY

Graduate Studies

Programs of Study

Nearly fifty full- and part-time graduate programs are offered through FDU's four degree-granting colleges on its two northern New Jersey campuses. Graduate study is offered at the Maxwell Becton College of Arts and Sciences at the College at Florham; University College: Arts, Sciences, and Professional Studies and the New College of General and Continuing Studies on the Metropolitan Campus, which both offer a number of programs on the College at Florham campus; and the Samuel J. Silberman College of Business Administration, which offers programs on both campuses. The majority of FDU's graduate classes are scheduled during the evenings and on weekends for the convenience of the working professional. Not all programs are offered on both campuses.

Master of Science (M.S.) programs are offered in biology, chemistry (with a concentration in pharmaceutical chemistry), computer science, electrical engineering, electronic commerce, hospitality management studies, management information systems, mathematics, medical technology, nursing (adult nurse practitioner with a concentration in administration or education), physics, and systems sciences (with a concentration in environmental studies).

Master of Arts (M.A.) programs are offered in corporate and organizational communication, education for certified teachers, educational leadership (pending state approval), English and comparative literature, history, international studies, learning disabilities, multilingual education, political science, psychology (applied social and community, clinical counseling, general-experimental, general-theoretical, industrial, organizational behavior for managers, personnel, and school psychology), and science (with concentrations in cosmetic science, elementary science specialist, and science teaching specialist).

Master of Arts in Teaching (M.A.T.) programs are available in elementary education (with certification in grades K–8, including preschool), English as a second language, and subject area certification grades K–12 in biological sciences, chemistry, English language and literacy, mathematics, physical sciences, social studies, and world languages.

Master of Business Administration (M.B.A.) programs are offered in accounting for nonaccountants, entrepreneurial studies, finance, global management, health systems management, human resource management, international business, management, management for executives, management for information systems professionals, marketing, and pharmaceutical-chemical studies.

Students may earn a joint M.A./M.B.A. degree in corporate and organizational communications and management and industrial psychology and human resource management.

Professional degree programs are available in the Master of Administrative Sciences (M.A.S.), Master of Public Administration (M.P.A.) (with specializations in public management, nursing management, and health-care administration), and the Master of Science in Taxation (M.S.T.).

FDU offers a nationally recognized, five-year, full-time Ph.D. program in clinical psychology that is fully accredited by the American Psychological Association. The program adheres to the scientist/practitioner model, requiring a number of clinical and research practicums in addition to an extensive classroom curriculum. A doctoral dissertation and a one-year clinical internship are required of all students. Program faculty interests include work in adult, child, and family therapy; childhood anxiety disorders; gerontology; quantitative methods; personality assessment; addictive behaviors; adult attachment processes; and gender bias. A doctoral program in school psychology leading to the Psy.D. is also available for the practicing professional.

Research Facilities

FDU offers a wide range of library, computer, health-care skills, and scientific laboratory equipment on both campuses to support student and faculty member research in virtually all graduate disciplines. In addition, the University supports the dissemination of research activities through special departmental centers and research institutes.

Financial Aid

A limited number of research, honors research, teaching, and graduate administrative fellowships are available at FDU. Some programs, such as the Master of Arts in Teaching (M.A.T.) and the Master of Public Administration (M.P.A.), offer paid internships. Eligible students may borrow up to $10,000 in subsidized or unsubsidized loans under the Federal Stafford Student Loan program. In addition, FDU offers students a number of attractive flexible financing programs.

Cost of Study

Tuition for most graduate programs in 2002–03 is $681 per credit. An annual technology fee of $194 for part-time students or $420 for full-time students is also assessed. Annual graduate fees were $392 for full-time students and $160 for part-time students. Several programs, such as the executive M.B.A., M.B.A. in global management, and the M.A. in psychology (with a concentration in organizational behavior for managers) carry an inclusive full program fee.

Living and Housing Costs

FDU provides limited housing for graduate students. The University's Office of Student Life also can provide interested students with a listing of off-campus housing.

Student Group

There are a total of 3,035 graduate students enrolled at Fairleigh Dickenson University. The College of Business Administration has 867 students; Becton College enrolls 320 students; University College has 1,418 students; and New College has 422 students.

Location

FDU has two major campus locations in northern New Jersey. The Metropolitan Campus is located less than 10 miles from New York City among seventy-three buildings on a modern, 125-acre site in Teaneck. The College at Florham is situated in the heart of New Jersey's growing corporate center. The campus's Georgian-style buildings span 177 acres of wooded grounds on what was once a private estate.

The University

Founded in 1942, FDU is New Jersey's largest private university, with nearly 10,000 students. In addition to its two major northern New Jersey campuses, FDU also offers graduate studies to residents of central New Jersey through its Fort Monmouth extension center in Eatontown. During the summer term, overseas studies for graduate students are offered in many disciplines at FDU's historic campus in Wroxton, England. In accordance with the University's mission of service to diverse local, national, and international constituencies, in 1996 FDU also established an overseas location in Israel at the Bio Technical Institute in Tel Aviv.

Applying

Students can apply for graduate admission for the fall, spring, or summer semester. Requirements vary from program to program, but all require a baccalaureate degree from an accredited institution. To be considered for admission, an FDU application for graduate admission and official transcripts of previous college work must be filed. In some cases, letters of recommendation may be required. Depending on the college in which admission is sought, test scores on the Graduate Record Examinations, Graduate Management Admission Test, or Praxis must be submitted.

Correspondence and Information

Metropolitan Campus
Office of Graduate Admissions
Fairleigh Dickinson University
1000 River Road
Teaneck, New Jersey 07666
Telephone: 201-692-2551
Fax: 201-692-2560
World Wide Web: http://www.fdu.edu

College at Florham
Office of Graduate Admissions
Fairleigh Dickinson University
285 Madison Avenue
Madison, New Jersey 07940
Telephone: 973-443-8905
Fax: 973-443-8088
World Wide Web: http://www.fdu.edu

RESEARCH AREAS

College of Arts and Sciences, College at Florham

Barbara G. Salmore, Ph.D., Dean. Departments of Biological and Allied Health Sciences; Chemistry and Geological Sciences; English, Communications, and Philosophy; Visual and Performing Arts; Mathematics, Computer Science, and Physics; Modern Languages and Literature; Psychology; and Social Sciences and History.

The faculty of the Maxwell Becton College of Arts and Sciences offers master's degree programs that emphasize applied research in a variety of disciplinary and interdisciplinary areas. Becton faculty members also serve as the directors or editors of a journal of student research in psychology, two professional journals (*Literary Studies* and the *New Jersey Journal of Communication*), the Fairleigh Dickinson University Press, and the University's Corporate Communications Institute. The faculty's research specializations include:

Psychology: gambling, risk-taking behavior, and drive reduction theory; reduction of reinforcement frequency and increases in response-force requirements as aversive unconditioned stimuli; interpersonal power as an approach to conceptualizing psychopathology; bioenergetic techniques in treating psychopathology; neuropsychology of perception and cognitive processes; the effect of mass media on interpersonal awareness; organizational psychology, including managers' perceptions of problematic employee behavior and techniques for behavioral change; problems of the visibly handicapped.

Social Sciences and History: peaceful transitions to democracy, Japanese defense policy, campaign finance reform, campaign strategies and electoral behavior, race and gender in the antebellum South, the portrayal of sexual norms in women's magazines, anthropology of law, twentieth-century intellectual history, constitutional law and American politics, child soldiers, self-society relationships in the U.S. and the Middle East, concepts of culture in the U.S. in the Middle East, globalization and culture.

Arts and Humanities: digital image processing, animation, and video; literary studies, including Shakespeare and nineteenth- and twentieth-century American authors; history and theory of communications; corporate and organizational communication.

Natural Sciences, Computer Science, and Mathematics: pharmaceutical chemistry; interdiffusion of gold and titanium thin-film specimens; microbiology and virology; marine biology; implementation of programming languages, computational complexity, analysis, watermarking techniques, statistics, and actuarial science; quadratic and Hermitian forms.

College of Business Administration, Metropolitan Campus and College at Florham

Departments of Accounting, Economics, Finance and International Business, Management, Marketing, and Information Systems. Also includes the Office of Executive and Special Programs (which includes the Executive M.B.A., Health Systems Management, Global M.B.A., M.S. in accounting, M.S. in taxation, and Pharmaceutical/Chemical Studies), and the George Rothman Institute of Entrepreneurial Studies.

The faculty of the Silberman College of Business is committed to exemplary teaching and scholarship. Research activities are an integral part of accomplishing the mission of the college. Research work, which includes textbooks, journal articles, conference papers, and presentations before professional organizations keep the faculty current in its fields. The College also coordinates a number of applied research projects that are conducted for major corporations, manufacturing and industrial firms, and related organizations. The knowledge and experience gained through their research activities is adopted into lecture material and shared with students. Key research areas include entrepreneurship, both corporate and small ventures; enterprise resource planning; information systems management issues; integrated marketing communications; strategic pricing; human resource management and development; and Austrian economics, specifically Hayek.

New College of General and Continuing Studies, Metropolitan Campus and College at Florham

Kenneth T. Vehrkens, Dean. School of Hotel, Restaurant and Tourism Management.

Applied research in hospitality management, including an internship with the Greater Atlantic City Hotel-Motel. Association and numerous research opportunities with the properties in the New York/New Jersey area.

Public Administration Institute: Applied research on problems in state and local government, administrative justice, emergency planning and management, administrative science, health services management, performance evaluation, and comparative health systems.

University College: Arts, Sciences, and Professional Studies, Metropolitan Campus

Michael B. Sperling, Ph.D., Dean. School of Communication Arts, School of Computer Science and Information Systems; Peter Sammartino School of Education; School of Engineering and Engineering Technology; School of Natural Sciences; Henry P. Becton School of Nursing and Allied Health; School of History, Political, and International Studies; and School of Psychology. Other programs within the College include sociology, criminal justice, and physical education.

There has been a growing emphasis on original research and scholarship by the faculty members and graduate students of the University College. Seasonal affective disorder, eating problems, personality development and psychological testing are among the research projects of the clinical psychology doctoral program. American writers of the nineteenth and twentieth centuries are the focus of the English and comparative literature department, while the Sammartino School of Education conducts innovative research in learning disabilities and bilingual education. Science and engineering faculty members receive research funding for work in such diverse areas as high-temperature superconductivity, underwater digital imaging enhancement, digital image transmission, and ADA computer programming language. The campus's Wiener Library contains nearly 250,000 volumes and 1,600 periodicals and includes diverse special collections. The College also offers graduate students access to a wide range of computer resources and outstanding science research equipment in its biology, chemistry, and engineering laboratories. Examples of additional research projects within University College by area of specialization are:

Arts and Humanities: origins of civilization; the Middle East and its problems; Soviet studies; constitutional law and the Supreme Court; world regions and international relations; international law and organizations; study of American playwright Lanford Wilson; the star-spangled screen; American World War II films; popular culture in twentieth-century America; handling of time in William Faulkner; film history; media effects; advertising outcomes and effects; role of culture and language education at the school level; development of bicultural instructional materials for teaching; adult development as it concerns change agents, self-esteem; leadership related to learning by children with educational handicaps; use of ESL strategies in developing standard English among black English speakers. The School of Education is also involved in a variety of educational and research programs in cooperation with state and local agencies and school systems, as well as with the federal Department of Education.

Behavioral and Social Sciences: clinical psychology; personality assessment; psychological consequences of exposure to toxics; obesity; factors of sexual harassment; program evaluation; quantitative methods; jury selection.

Nursing and Allied Health: critical thinking; educational technology and pedagogy; obesity and stressful life events; parenting behaviors and perceived competence, perceived health status; ethnography of community health nursing.

Science and Engineering: aquatic ecology; prokaryotic and eukaryotic metabolism; protozoan genetics and ecology; industrial applications of bacterial enzymes; biofouling of reverse osmosis membranes; hormone function using monoclonal antibodies; multimedia applications in histology and parasitology; enzyme inhibitors; cell culture media (growth factors); natural product antimicrobial testing; development of text systems to access environmental toxicity; physical and colloid chemistry (membranes); geochemistry (carbonate chemistry of water); theoretical organic chemistry (computational methods); consumer-provided cooperation in the transit-planning process; high-resolution, far-infrared spectroscopy; infrared optics (optical properties of solids and powders); computer simulation (sociological theory in pattern evasions); computer methods in engineering and statistical applications; software reuse; management information systems; operation systems; organizational memory; optics (light wave technology); optical communications; parallel and fault-tolerant systems; electronic commerce; pattern recognition; computer engineering; wireless and digital communications; digital signal and image processing; computer networks.

In addition to its two campuses in northern New Jersey, FDU also owns and operates its own campus in Wroxton, England.

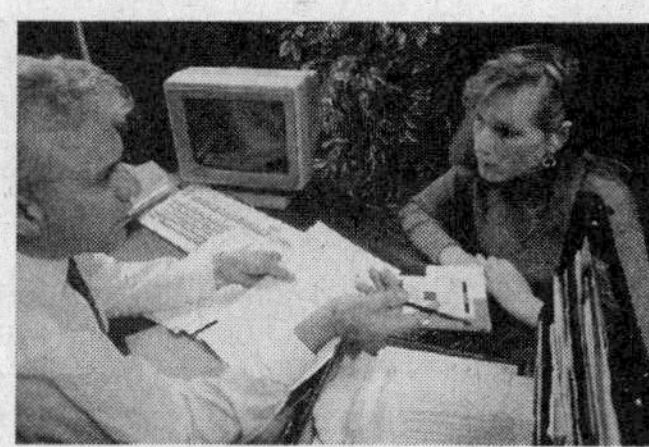

The University offers more than fifty career-oriented graduate programs.

FITCHBURG STATE COLLEGE

Graduate Education

Programs of Study

Fitchburg State College (FSC) offers Master of Arts/Master of Arts in Teaching (M.A./M.A.T.) degrees in biology, English, history, and mathematics and Master of Education degrees in arts education; early childhood, elementary, middle school, and secondary education; general studies in education; occupational education; science education; special education; and technology education. Master of Science (M.S.) degrees are offered in communications/media, computer science, counseling (psychological and school guidance), criminal justice, and nursing (forensic). The College also offers Master of Business Administration (M.B.A.) degrees. Certificates of Advanced Graduate Study (CAGS) are offered in educational leadership and management, interdisciplinary studies, and teacher leadership. The Fitchburg State College academic year consists of two 15-week semesters (fall and spring), two intensive five-week summer terms, and a five-week intensive winter term. Graduate courses in all degree fields and in other nondegree areas of study are offered in both the fall and spring sessions, and many courses are also offered during the two summer sessions as well as during the winter session.

Research Facilities

The College Library provides 98 hours of weekly service, online access to the library's catalog, and more than 100 databases via the library's home page. The local area network provides ready access to its heavily utilized subscription services. There are approximately 263,000 volumes and 1,467 current periodicals, supplemented by the 445,000-item Education Resources Information Center (ERIC). Additional services include interlibrary loans, reciprocal borrowing privileges, and specialized collections for criminal justice and nursing.

The College Computer Center serves the general administrative, educational, and research needs of the campus. The Tricord ES8000 mainframe serves the administrative computing needs of the College. An Alpha Server 2100 acts as the central locus for faculty and staff members and students, providing an enhanced environment for computer science applications, e-mail, and Internet access capabilities. A Proliant DHCP server hosts TCP/IP to the entire campus. Five accessible general-purpose labs and five living learning centers exist for general academic use. Falcon Net, FSC's major telecommunications upgrade, offers each classroom and residence hall high-speed T-1 network connectivity, making possible the full potential of distance learning and videoconferencing and a scalable infrastructure prepared for the growth of tomorrow.

Financial Aid

Graduate scholarships, in the form of tuition and fee waivers, are available in amounts ranging from $110 to $1790 per year. The application deadline is February 1 of each academic year. Students admitted to a graduate program may apply for graduate assistantships. Graduate assistants are paid $5500 for the academic year, are awarded a tuition waiver for 24 semester hours for the academic year, must carry a load of 6 semester hours per semester, and are required to work no more than 20 hours per week. Applications for graduate assistantships are due annually by May 15. Matriculated graduate students who enroll in a minimum of 5 semester hours per term may apply for the Federal Perkins Loan, the Federal Work Study Program, and Federal Direct Subsidized and Unsubsidized Loans.

Cost of Study

Graduate tuition for 2001–02 was $150 per credit. An additional comprehensive fee of $75 per student and a capital projects fee of $7 per credit were charged each semester.

Living and Housing Costs

On-campus housing options range from traditional halls to suites and apartments. Each room has a phone, cable, and data access. On-campus housing costs for 2001–02 averaged $2910 for the year for double occupancy. Singles are available on a space-available basis. Board plans are required for on-campus residents and range from $1800 to $2000 per year.

Student Group

In fall 2001, there were 2,283 matriculated part-time graduate students, including CAGS program students. Approximately 350 graduate degrees and CAGS are conferred annually.

Student Outcomes

Recent Fitchburg State College graduate program alumni are teachers at various levels in Massachusetts public school systems (including special and vocational education); psychological counselors in schools, colleges, hospitals, and public agencies; or management and management information systems specialists in both the public and private sectors. Eighty-nine percent of graduate program alumni are employed full-time, with 67 percent earning salaries in excess of $35,000. Almost 90 percent of graduates report they are satisfied with both their graduate major and their current employment.

Location

Fitchburg State College, the third-largest of Massachusetts state colleges, is located in the attractive Montachusett region of north central Massachusetts, an hour's drive from Boston and just minutes from some of New England's finest skiing, camping, hiking, and fishing spots.

The College

Fitchburg State College integrates an interdisciplinary, multicultural, liberal arts and sciences core program with selected strong professional and arts and sciences majors at both the undergraduate and graduate levels. A comprehensive public college, Fitchburg State College is committed to providing excellent yet accessible and affordable lifelong learning opportunities in undergraduate, graduate, and continuing education. A dynamic force in New England, the College shares leadership and resources with and draws expertise from the Montachusett region of Massachusetts. Valuing the diversity of the learning community, the College helps students become personally and professionally responsible citizens by promoting their intellectual, social, and ethical development.

Applying

The College employs a rolling admissions policy. Deadlines vary. MAT, GRE, or GMAT (M.B.A.) scores are required for degree programs. Students must have a degree from an accredited four-year institution with a GPA of 2.8 or better. For more information, students should visit FSC's Web site, listed below.

Correspondence and Information

Graduate Education
Fitchburg State College
160 Pearl Street
Fitchburg, Massachusetts 01420-2697
Telephone: 978-665-3208
Fax: 978-665-3658
E-mail: gce@fsc.edu
World Wide Web: http://www.fsc.edu

GRADUATE DEAN AND PROGRAM CHAIRS

Dorothy Boisvert, Interim Dean of Graduate Studies; Ed.D., Massachusetts Lowell (telephone: 978-665-3240; e-mail: dboisvert@fsc.edu).

GRADUATE PROGRAM CHAIRS

CAGS—Teacher Leadership

CAGS—Educational Leadership and Management
Daniel Nomishan, Chair; Ed.D., Indiana of Pennsylvania (978-665-3516; dnomishan@fsc.edu).

CAGS—Interdisciplinary Studies
Harry Semerjian, Chair; Ed.D., Massachusetts (978-665-3279; hsemerjian@fsc.edu).

M.A./M.A.T.—Biology
George Babich, Chair; Ph.D., New Hampshire (978-665-3245; gbabich@fsc.edu).

M.A./M.A.T.—Earth Science
Lawrence Guth, Chair; Ph.D., Rice (978-665-3082; lguth@fsc.edu).

M.A./M.A.T.—English
Marilyn McCaffrey, Chair; Ed.D., Boston University (978-665-3362; mmccaffrey@fsc.edu).

M.A./M.A.T.—History
Teresa Thomas, Chair; Ph.D., Clark (978-665-4587; tthomas@fsc.edu).

M.A.T.—Mathematics
Lucy Dechene, Chair; Ph.D., California, Riverside (978-665-3077; ldechene@fsc.edu).

Master of Business Administration (M.B.A.)
Joseph McAloon, Chair; M.S.P.A., Massachusetts (978-665-3125; jmcaloon@fsc.edu).

M.Ed.—Arts in Education
Harry Semerjian, Chair; Ed.D., Massachusetts (978-665-3279; hsemerjian@fsc.edu).

M.Ed.—Educational Leadership and Management
Daniel Nomishan, Chair; Ed.D., Indiana of Pennsylvania (978-665-3516; dnomishan@fsc.edu).

M.Ed.—Early Childhood/Elementary/Middle School Education
George Miller, Co-Chair; Ph.D., Michigan (978-665-3191; gmiller@fsc.edu).
Pamela Hill, Co-Chair; Ed.D., Boston University (978-665-3515; phill@fsc.edu).

M.Ed.—General Studies
George Miller, Co-Chair; Ph.D., Michigan (978-665-3191; gmiller@fsc.edu).
Pamela Hill, Co-Chair; Ed.D., Boston University (978-665-3515; phill@fsc.edu).

M.Ed.—Occupational Education
James Alicata, Chair; Ed.D., Massachusetts (978-665-3047; jalicata@fsc.edu).

M.Ed.—Science Education
George Babich, Chair; Ph.D., New Hampshire (978-665-3245; gbabich@fsc.edu).

M.Ed.—Secondary Education
Nancy Kelly, Chair; Ph.D., Massachusetts (978-665-3447; nkelly@fsc.edu).

M.Ed.—Special Education
Elaine Francis, Co-Chair; Ed.D., Massachusetts (978-665-3501; efrancis@fsc.edu).

M.Ed.—Technology Education
Stanley Bucholc, Chair; Ed.D., West Virginia (978-665-3256; sbucholc@fsc.edu).

M.S.—Communications/Media
Randy Howe, Chair; Ed.D., Boston University (978-665-3544; rhowe@fsc.edu).

M.S.—Computer Science
Nadimpalli Mahadev, Chair; Ph.D., Waterloo (978-665-3270; nmahadev@fsc.edu).

M.S.—Counseling
Mike Bloomfield, Chair (Mental Health Counseling and School Guidance Counseling); Ed.D., Massachusetts (978-665-3610; mbloomfield@fsc.edu).

M.S.—Nursing (Forensic)
Andrea Wallen, Chair; Ed.D., Massachusetts (978-665-3033; awallen@fsc.edu).

GRADUATE CERTIFICATE PROGRAM DIRECTORS

Certificate in Adolescent and Family Therapy
Mike Bloomfield, Chair; Ed.D., Massachusetts (978-665-3610; mbloomfield@fsc.edu).

Certificate in Child Protective Services
Cynthia Crosson-Tower, Director; Ed.D., Massachusetts (978-665-3348; ccrossen@fsc.edu).

Certificate in Communications/Media
Randy Howe, Director; Ed.D., Boston University (978-665-3544; rhowe@fsc.edu).

Certificate in Early Intervention
Anne Howard, Co-Chair; Ph.D., Brandeis (978-665-3309; anhoward@fsc.edu).

Fine Arts Directors Program Certificate
Harry Semerjian, Director; Ed.D., Massachusetts (978-665-3279; hsemerjian@fsc.edu).

Forensic Case Work Certificate
Mary King, Director; Ed.D., Massachusetts (978-665-4178; mking@fsc.edu).

Forensic Nursing Certificate
Andrea Wallen, Director; Ed.D., Massachusetts (978-665-3033; awallen@fsc.edu).

School to Career Certificate
Stanley Bucholc, Director; Ed.D., West Virginia (978-665-3256; sbucholc@fsc.edu).

Substance Abuse Services Certificate
G. Jefferson Breen, Director; Ed.D., Clark (978-665-3601; gjbreen@fsc.edu).

FLORIDA INSTITUTE OF TECHNOLOGY

Graduate School

Programs of Study

The Graduate School offers master's, education specialist's (Ed.S.), and doctoral degree programs. The School of Business offers the M.B.A. degree. The College of Engineering offers Ph.D. and M.S. degrees in aerospace engineering, applied mathematics, chemical engineering, civil engineering, computer engineering, computer science, electrical engineering, environmental science, mechanical engineering, ocean engineering, and oceanography. Master's programs are also offered in computer information systems, engineering management, environmental resources management, and software engineering. The College of Science and Liberal Arts offers master's and doctoral degrees in applied mathematics, biological sciences, chemistry, physics, science education, and space sciences. Master's degrees are offered in applied mathematics, computer education, environmental education, math education, operations research, and technical and professional communication. The Ed.S. degree in science education is also awarded. The School of Psychology offers the Psy.D. degree in clinical psychology, the M.S. in applied behavior analysis, and the M.S. and Ph.D. in industrial/organizational psychology. The School of Aeronautics offers a Master of Science degree in aeronautics with specializations in airport development and management and aviation safety and a Master of Science degree in aviation human factors.

Research Facilities

Laboratories on campus are equipped for research in the various programs of study. These are supplemented by the Life Science Research Complex, Applied Research Laboratories, Claude Pepper Institute for Aging and Therapeutic Research, Reproductive Biology Laboratory, Center for Energy Alternatives, and aquaculture and marine research facilities at Oceanside in Vero Beach. Additional facilities include a solar energy research laboratory and laboratories for optical and solid-state physics, environmental and water pollution analysis, electromagnetics, materials testing and research, electron microscopy, and cytogenetics, as well as in numerous other areas.

The Academic and Research Computing Services (ARCS) provides graduate students with a wide range of computing resources for course work and research. These resources include a Sun Enterprise 3000 and Harris Lab 5227 with several Sun SPARC and GSI Workstations. These machines are connected internally as part of the campus network and externally to the Internet. Many programs and departments have their own computing resources that are also connected to the campus network. Access to these computing resources is available in computer labs and academic units and through dial-up lines. Programming languages supported include C, Pascal, ADA, Fortran, and C++. A staff of professionals is available to assist users with consultation and documentation. In addition to these resources, ARCS maintains a large microcomputer center in the Library Pavilion.

Financial Aid

Graduate student assistantships for instruction and research are available to well-qualified master's and doctoral degree students. Assistantships carry stipends plus a tuition waiver. In some cases, a tuition waiver alone may be awarded for a limited amount of service. Assistantships for master's degree students are normally for an academic year; assistantships for doctoral students are renewable on a yearly basis.

Cost of Study

Tuition for graduate study is $690 per semester hour in 2002–03. A tuition deposit of $300 (deducted from the first semester's tuition charge) is required of all new students. Books are estimated to cost $550 per year.

Living and Housing Costs

Room and board on campus cost approximately $2500 per semester in 2002–03. On-campus housing (dormitories and apartments) is available for full-time single and married graduate students, but priority for dormitory rooms is given to undergraduate students. Many apartment complexes and rental houses are available near the campus.

Student Group

Graduate students constitute more than one fourth of the students attending Florida Tech's Melbourne campus. Enrolled graduate and undergraduate students represent forty-nine states and more than eighty countries.

Location

Melbourne is located on the central east coast of Florida. The area offers a delightful year-round subtropical climate and is 10 minutes from the ocean beaches. Kennedy Space Center and the massive NASA complex are just 45 minutes north of Melbourne. The city of Orlando, Walt Disney World, and EPCOT are 1 hour west of the Florida Tech main campus.

The Institute

Florida Institute of Technology is a distinctive, independent university, founded in 1958 by a group of scientists and engineers to fulfill a need for specialized, advanced educational opportunities on the Space Coast of Florida. Florida Tech is the only comprehensive, independent scientific and technological university in the southeast. Supported by both industry and the community, Florida Tech is the recipient of many research grants and contracts, a number of which provide financial support for graduate students.

Applying

Forms for applying to the Graduate School and for assistantships are sent on request. Applications for assistantships must be submitted by February 15. Department of Biology students must complete the application process by March 1. Doctor of Psychology and Applied Behavior Analysis applicants must complete the application process by January 15 and begin their program of study in the fall. Electronic application and related forms are available on the Florida Tech Web page (listed below) under "admissions."

Correspondence and Information

Graduate Admissions Office
Florida Institute of Technology
150 West University Boulevard
Melbourne, Florida 32901-6975
Telephone: 321-674-8027
800-944-4348 (toll-free)
Fax: 321-723-9468
E-mail: grad-admissions@fit.edu
World Wide Web: http://www.fit.edu

DEPARTMENT HEADS AND PROGRAM CHAIRS

The faculty members listed below will be pleased to answer inquiries concerning programs and degrees or to provide general university information.

VICE PRESIDENT OF RESEARCH AND GRADUATE PROGRAMS

R. L. Sullivan, Ph.D.

SCHOOL OF AERONAUTICS

N. T. Stevens, Ph.D., Dean.

Airport Development and Management (M.S.): N. Villaire, Ed.D., Program Chairman.
Aviation Safety (M.S.): N. Villaire, Ed.D., Program Chairman.
Aviation Human Factors (M.S.): N. Villaire, Ed.D., Program Chairman.

SCHOOL OF BUSINESS

A. T. Hollingsworth, Ph.D., Dean.
B. Pierce, Ph.D., Associate Dean.

Business Administration (M.B.A.).

SCHOOL OF PSYCHOLOGY

M. B. Kenkel, Psy.D., Dean.

Applied Behavior Analysis (M.S.): José Martinez-Diaz, Ph.D., Chair.
Clinical Psychology (Psy.D.): P. D. Faber, Ph.D., Director.
Industrial/Organizational Psychology (M.S.): R. Griffith, Ph.D., Chair.

COLLEGE OF ENGINEERING

J. R. Bailey, Ph.D., Dean.
E. H. Kalajian, Ph.D., Associate Dean.
F. M. Ham, Ph.D., Associate Dean.

Chemical Engineering (M.S., Ph.D.): P. A. Jennings, Ph.D., Chair.
Civil Engineering (M.S., Ph.D.): A. Pandit, Ph.D., Chair.
Computer Sciences (M.S., Ph.D.): W. Shoaff, Ph.D., Chair.
Electrical and Computer Engineering (M.S., Ph.D.): J. Wheeler, Ph.D., Department Head.
Engineering Management (M.S.): M. Shaikh, Ph.D., Program Director.
Marine and Environmental Systems (M.S., Ph.D.): G. Maul, Ph.D., Department Head.
Mechanical and Aerospace Engineering (M.S., Ph.D.): J. Engblom, Ph.D., Department Head.

COLLEGE OF SCIENCE AND LIBERAL ARTS

G. Nelson, Ph.D., Dean.
R. L. Alford, Ph.D., Associate Dean.
T. Oswalt, Ph.D., Associate Dean.

Applied Mathematics (M.S., Ph.D.): V. Lakshmikatham, Ph.D., Head.
Biological Sciences (M.S., Ph.D.): G. N. Wells, Ph.D., Head.
Chemistry (M.S., Ph.D.): M. W. Babich, Ph.D., Head.
Computer Education and Environmental Education (M.S.): R. H. Fronk, Ph.D., Head.
Operations Research (M.S., Ph.D.): M. Shaw, Ph.D., Head.
Physics and Space Sciences (M.S., Ph.D.): L. Baksay, Ph.D., Head.
Science Education and Mathematics Education (M.S., Ed.S., Ph.D.): R. H. Fronk, Ph.D., Head.
Technical and Professional Communication (M.S.): N. Matar, Ph.D., Head.

Evans Library.

Crawford Science Building.

FLORIDA INTERNATIONAL UNIVERSITY

University Graduate School

Programs of Study

Graduate programs are offered at Florida International University (FIU) in the following fields (asterisks denote fields in which only a master's degree is offered): *African New World studies, *architecture, *landscape architecture, biology, chemistry, *comparative sociology, *creative writing, economics, *English, *environmental studies, *forensic science, geology, history, international studies, *Latin American and Caribbean studies, *linguistics, *mathematical sciences, physics, political science, psychology, *religious studies, Spanish, statistics, *visual arts, computer science, *music, *music education, business administration, *finance, *international business, management information systems, *accounting, *taxation, *administration and supervision of vocational education, adult education, *art education, counselor education, curriculum and instruction, *early childhood education, educational leadership, *elementary education, *English education, *English for non-English speakers (TESOL), exceptional student education, *health education, *health occupations education, human resource development, *international development education, *math education, *modern language education, *parks and recreation management, *physical education, *reading education, *science education, *social studies education, *special education, *technical education, *technology education, school psychology, *urban education, *vocational home economics education, *vocational industrial education, educational administration and supervision, *biomedical engineering, civil engineering, *computer engineering, *construction management, electrical engineering, *engineering management, *environmental engineering, *environmental and urban systems, *industrial engineering, mechanical engineering, dietetics and nutrition, *nursing, *occupational therapy, *physical therapy, *public health, *hotel and food service management, *mass communication, *criminal justice, *health services administration, public administration, social welfare, *social work, and speech-language pathology.

Research Facilities

The libraries at University Park and the Biscayne Bay Campus house more than 1 million volumes along with numerous periodicals, maps, microfilms, institutional archives, curriculum materials, and government documents. Access to 9,300 periodicals and serials is available. Interlibrary loan services offer access to holdings at major libraries throughout the country, and the online catalog gives information about the collections of all the libraries in the State University System of Florida. Special research centers and institutes include the following: the Academy for the Art of Teaching, the High-Performance Database Research Center, the Hemispheric Center for Environmental Technology, the International Hurricane Center, the Latin American and Caribbean Center, and the Southeast Florida Center on Aging.

Financial Aid

Graduate students may qualify for assistantships and fellowships and other awards that are offered through FIU's schools, colleges, and departments. To apply, students should contact the departmental dean's office. A limited number of awards are available for students who demonstrate need through the Free Application for Federal Student Aid (FAFSA). The form is available at all U.S. colleges and universities.

Cost of Study

The average tuition and fees for full-time, in-state graduate students is $1600 per semester. For the 2001–02 academic year, credit-hour fees for graduate students were $161.98 per credit hour for Florida residents and $569.14 per credit hour for out-of-state students. Tuition and fees are subject to change.

Living and Housing Costs

Graduate student housing is available at University Park (telephone: 305-348-4190) and the Biscayne Bay Campus (telephone: 305-919-5587).

Student Group

The graduate student community includes 6,500 students from all fifty states and more than 110 nations.

Student Outcomes

Graduates of the University proceed to a wide variety of academic and professional careers in academic institutions, government agencies, nonprofit organizations, private industry, and entrepreneurial enterprises.

Location

Located in suburban west Miami-Dade County, the 342-acre University Park campus is notable for its distinctive architecture, lush tropical landscape, and impressive outdoor sculpture park. The Biscayne Bay Campus is situated on 200 acres on Biscayne Bay in North Miami, which encompasses a natural mangrove preserve. FIU also operates academic sites in Davie and Pembroke Pines.

The University

FIU is a public, multicampus research university and a member of the State University System of Florida. The University, designated by the Carnegie Foundation as a Doctoral/Research University–Extensive, offers more than 100 graduate and advanced academic and professional degrees.

Applying

Applicants who have earned a bachelor or master's degree or equivalent from a regionally accredited institution or a recognized institution of higher learning are welcome to apply. The Admissions Office must receive official transcripts, diplomas, and/or certificates directly from all previously attended institutions. Documents in a language other than English must be translated by an official translation agency. Applicants must submit GRE or GMAT scores. Students whose native language is not English must also submit TOEFL scores.

Correspondence and Information

Office of Admissions
Florida International University
Charles E. Perry Building, Room 140
University Park
Miami, Florida 33199-0001
Telephone: 305-348-2363
800-955-8771 (toll-free; TDD via FRS)
Fax: 305-348-3648
E-mail: admiss@fiu.edu
World Wide Web: http://www.fiu.edu

THE FACULTY AND THEIR PROGRAMS

COLLEGE OF ARTS AND SCIENCES

African–New World Studies: Jean Rahier.
Biology: Joel Trexler.
Chemistry: Kevin O'Shea.
Computer Science: Raimund Ege.
Creative Writing: Lester Standiford.
Economics: Devashish Mitra.
English: Joan Baker.
Environmental Studies: Mahader Bhat.
Forensic Science: Jose Almirall.
Geology: Dean Whitman.
History: Joseph Patrouch.
International Relations: Roderick Neumann.
Latin American and Caribbean Studies: Theodore Young.
Linguistics: Feryal Yavas.
Mathematics: Bao Qin Li.
Modern Languages: Reinaldo Sanchez.
Music: Orlando J. Garcia.
Physics: Xuewen Wang.
Political Science: Timothy Power.
Psychology: Jonathan Tubman.
Religious Studies: Lesley Northup.
Sociology: Chris Girard.
Statistics: Carlos Brain.
Visual Arts: William Maguire

COLLEGE OF BUSINESS ADMINISTRATION

Accounting: Dana Forgione.
Business Administration: Paul Miniard.
Finance: Shahid Hamid.
International Business: Lea Pacheco.
Management: Steven Beste, Ellie Browner, and Vincent Daniels.
Management Information Systems: Dinesh Batra.

COLLEGE OF EDUCATION

Adult Education and Human Resource Development: Jo Gallagher.
Art Education: David Chang.
Community Mental Health: Jethro Toomer.
Counselor Education: Adriana McEachern.
Curriculum and Instruction: Steve Fain and Charles Bleiker.
Early Childhood Education: Alicia Mendoza.
Educational Administration/Supervision: Peter Cistone.
Elementary Education: Lynne Miller and Lisbeth Dixon-Krauss.
English Education: Linda Spears-Bunton.
English for Non-English Speakers (TESOL): Aida Perez-Prado.
Exceptional Student Education: Patricia Barbetta.
Health Education/Exercise Physiology: Richard Lopez.
Higher Education/Community College Teaching: Janice R. Sandiford.
Home Economics Education: Sandra Poirier.
International Development Education: John Carpenter.
Mathematics Education: Edwin McClintock.
Modern Languages: Arnilda Bahia.
Parks and Recreation Management: Daniel Dustin and Alexis McKenney.
Physical Education: Charmaine DeFrancesco and Robert Wolff.
Reading Education: Joyce Fine.
School Psychology: Philip J. Lazarus.
Science Education: Luis A. Martinez Perez.
Social Studies Education: Mohammed Farouk.
Special Education: Howard Rosenberg.
Technical Education: Dominic Mohamed.
Urban Education: Delia Garcia and M. D. Thiranarayanan.

COLLEGE OF ENGINEERING

Biomedical Engineering: Richard Schoephoerster.
Civil Engineering: Irtishad Ahmad.
Construction Management: Syed M. Ahmed.
Electrical and Computer Engineering: Jean Andrian.
Engineering Management: Shih-Ming Lee.
Environmental Engineering: Wolfgang Rogge.
Industrial Engineering: Marc Resnick.
Mechanical Engineering: Norman Munroe.

COLLEGE OF HEALTH AND URBAN AFFAIRS

Criminal Justice: Valerie Patterson.
Dietetics and Nutrition: Michelle Ciccazzo.
Health Services Administration: Valerie Patterson.
Nursing: Marie-Luise Friedman.
Occupational Therapy: Susan Kaplan.
Physical Therapy: Leonard Elbaum.
Public Administration: Valerie Patterson and Allan Rosenbaum.
Public Health: Richard Patton.
Social Welfare: David Cohen.
Social Work: Nan Van De Bergh.
Speech Language Pathology: Lemietta McNeilly.

SCHOOL OF HOSPITALITY MANAGEMENT

Hotel and Food Service Management: Adele Smith.

SCHOOL OF JOURNALISM AND MASS COMMUNICATION

Advertising/Public Relations: Kathleen Donnelley.
Journalism/Broadcasting: Mario Diament.

SCHOOL OF ARCHITECTURE

Architecture: William McMinn.
Landscape Architecture: Marta Canaves.

FLORIDA STATE UNIVERSITY

Graduate Studies

Programs of Study

Florida State University (FSU), a Carnegie Research I university, offers doctoral programs in seventy areas and master's programs in ninety-nine areas. Advanced master's and specialist degrees are offered in twenty-eight programs. The University is composed of seventeen colleges and schools: Arts and Sciences; Business; Communication; Criminology; Education; Engineering; Human Sciences; Law; Information Studies; Medicine; Motion Pictures, Television, and Recording Arts; Music; Nursing; Social Sciences; Social Work; Theater; and Visual Arts and Dance. Students may pursue a number of interdisciplinary degrees, and several joint-degree programs are available.

FSU ranks among the top fifty universities in the country in the number of doctoral degrees awarded annually.

Research Facilities

Florida State University libraries contain approximately 2.1 million volumes, more than 18,000 serials, and more than 5 million other items. The libraries are committed to innovative use of new electronic technologies to enhance the research capabilities of students and faculty members. The University has more than eighty research centers, institutes, and special laboratories. Prominent among these are the National High Magnetic Field Laboratory, which is dedicated to research in supermagnetic fields and has application in the life sciences, transportation, and materials research. Among other research facilities are the Super FN Tandem Van de Graff Accelerator in Nuclear Research; the Institute for Molecular Biophysics; the Learning Systems Institute, which focuses on instructional systems design technology; the Institute for Science and Public Affairs, which focuses on assisting state and private agencies and the related units on aging, populations studies, family studies, and policy studies; the Marine Laboratory, which is located on the northern Gulf; the Geophysical Fluid Dynamics Institute; several centers devoted to atmospheric, oceanic, and climatic studies; the Center for Materials Research and Technology; and the Center for Music Research.

Financial Aid

Graduate students may compete for many forms of financial assistance for graduate study. There is an annual competition for nonduty University fellowships with stipends ranging from $15,000 to $20,000, plus tuition waivers with some departments supplementing this amount. All graduate programs offer teaching or research assistantships, with some programs funding most of their enrolled graduate students. Assistantship stipends vary from program to program, but in combination with tuition waivers they are competitive with other universities. Student loans are available through the Office of Financial Aid, 4474 UCT, Florida State University, Tallahassee, Florida 32306 (World Wide Web: http://www.ais.fsu.edu/finaid).

Cost of Study

Tuition and fees for an in-state resident for 2001–02 were $3738 for the academic year; this is based on 12 hours of graduate enrollment each term. The comparable amount for out-of-state graduate students was $12,828. Most students who receive a fellowship or an assistantship have both in-state and out-of-state tuition waived.

Living and Housing Costs

The University provides some housing for graduate students, but the majority of graduate students secure private housing, much of it within walking distance or free bus service of the University. There are many apartment complexes in Tallahassee and private dormitories near the University. For more information about housing, students can contact Housing, 108 CAW, Florida State University, Tallahassee, Florida 32306 (World Wide Web: http://www.housing.fsu.edu). Generally, the cost of living in Tallahassee is moderate.

Student Group

Florida State enrolled more than 34,000 students in 2001–02, including more than 6,300 graduate students, of whom 65 percent were full-time. The overall student body is 56 percent women, and members of minority groups constitute 23 percent of all students. All fifty states and a large number of other countries are represented in the student body.

Student Outcomes

FSU awards more than 1,400 master's degrees and approximately 285 doctoral degrees each year. Students find many rewarding opportunities ranging from faculty positions in colleges and universities to postdoctoral appointments in other leading universities. The University has a Career Center to assist graduate students, and departments actively assist graduates in their search for employment.

Location

FSU is located in Tallahassee, the capital of Florida and the home of two other educational institutions, Florida A&M University, a historically black university, and Tallahassee Community College. Tallahassee is situated about 40 miles from the Gulf of Mexico, with some of the world's most beautiful beaches within an easy drive. The climate permits year-round outdoor activity. Recreation and sports activities abound for both participants and observers. Cultural activities are very rich as well. The outstanding Schools of Music and Theater are the catalysts for several series of plays, musical performances, and operas, and the University operates both public television and radio stations. A new culture and science center is slated to open soon in downtown Tallahassee.

The University

FSU is a fully-accredited public university and functions as a component of the ten-member State University System of Florida. While the University provides an extensive and high-quality undergraduate program, it has a central mission in graduate education and research. Its mission statement recounts that "the University's primary role is to serve as a center for advanced graduate and professional studies while emphasizing research and providing excellence in undergraduate programs." It has a distinguished faculty that has regularly included Nobel laureates and members of prestigious national academic societies. Its expenditures in sponsored research exceed $130 million per year. For more information about Florida State University, students can access the World Wide Web page (http://www.fsu.edu).

Applying

Students may apply online (http://admissions.fsu.edu/gradonline.html) or fill out the general application for admission, which is available from Graduate Admissions; seek information about a program online (http://admissions.fsu.edu/forms/grad.html); and contact the academic department to which they are applying if they wish to be considered for financial assistance. While there are University-wide requirements for admission, the requirements for each program are set by the faculty members in that program and may be higher than University-wide requirements. The GRE General Test is required of all students (GMAT for business). Applications are carefully reviewed with due consideration to the academic record, test scores, letters of recommendation, and expressions of interest. A TOEFL score of 550 or better is required for applicants whose native language is not English. While admission deadlines vary by department, students should submit all materials by early January to be considered for all forms of financial assistance.

Correspondence and Information

For admissions:
Graduate Admissions
A2500 UCA
Florida State University
Tallahassee, Florida 32306-2400
Telephone: 850-644-3420
Fax: 850-644-0197
E-mail: gradstds@www.fsu.edu
World Wide Web:
http://www.fsu.edu/~gradstds

For specific programs:
(Department or Program)
Florida State University
Tallahassee, Florida 32306

For graduate studies:
Office of Graduate Studies
408 Westcott
Florida State University
Tallahassee, Florida 32306-1410
Telephone: 850-644-3500
Fax: 850-644-2969

DIRECTORS OF GRADUATE PROGRAMS

COLLEGE OF ARTS AND SCIENCES

American and Florida Studies (M.A.): Dr. John Fenstermaker (telephone: 850-644-0202; e-mail: jfenstermaker@english.fsu.edu). **Anthropology (M.S.):** Dr. Rochelle Marrinan (telephone: 850-644-8149; e-mail: rmarrina@garnet.fsu.edu). **Biological Science (Ph.D.):** Judy Bowers (telephone: 850-644-3023; e-mail: bowers@bio.fsu.edu). **Chemistry (Ph.D.):** Ginger Martin (telephone: 850-644-8434; e-mail: gmartin@chem.fsu.edu). **Classics (Ph.D.):** Dr. Christopher Pfaff (telephone: 850-644-0306; e-mail: cpfaff@mailer.fsu.edu). **Computer Science (Ph.D.):** David Gaitros (telephone: 850-644-4055; e-mail: gaitros@cs.fsu.edu). **English (Ph.D.):** Dr. David Johnson (telephone: 850-644-2753; e-mail: djohnson@english.fsu.edu). **Geology (Ph.D. and M.S.):** Dr. Roy Odom (telephone: 850-644-6706; e-mail: odom@magnet.fsu.edu). **Geophysical Fluid Dynamics (Ph.D.):** Dr. Albert Barcilon (telephone: 850-644-4596; e-mail: barcilon@gfdi.fsu.edu). **History (Ph.D.):** Dr. Peter Garretson (telephone: 850-644-9516; e-mail: pgarret@mailer.fsu.edu). **Humanities (Ph.D.):** Dr. Leon Golden (telephone: 850-644-0314; e-mail: lgolden@mailer.fsu.edu). **Mathematics (Ph.D.):** Dr. Sam Huckaba (telephone: 850-644-1479; e-mail: huckaba@math.fsu.edu). **Meteorology (Ph.D.):** Ms. Terri Johnson (telephone: 850-644-8582; e-mail: johnson@met.fsu.edu). **Modern Languages (Ph.D.):** Dr. Stacey Burch (telephone: 850-644-8397; e-mail: sburch@mailer.fsu.edu). **Molecular Biophysics (Ph.D.):** Dr. Laura Keller (telephone: 850-644-5780; e-mail: lkeller@bio.fsu.edu). **Neuroscience (Ph.D.):** Dr. Michael Meredith (telephone: 850-644-3427; e-mail: mmered@neuro.fsu.edu). **Oceanography (Ph.D.):** Dr. David Thistle (telephone: 850-644-6700; e-mail: lupiani@ocean.fsu.edu). **Philosophy (Ph.D.):** Dr. Peter Dalton (telephone: 850-644-0229; e-mail: pdalton@mailer.fsu.edu). **Physics (Ph.D.):** Dr. Kirby Kemper (telephone: 850-644-2338; e-mail: kirby@phy.fsu.edu). **Psychology (Ph.D.):** Dr. Ellen Berler (telephone: 850-644-2040; e-mail: berler@psy.fsu.edu). **Religion (Ph.D.):** Dr. Kathleen Erndl (telephone: 850-644-0205; e-mail: kerndl@mailer.fsu.edu). **Statistics (Ph.D.):** Dr. Pi-Erh Lin (telephone: 850-644-6697; e-mail: lin@stat.fsu.edu).

COLLEGE OF BUSINESS

Accounting (Ph.D.): Dr. Allen Bathke (telephone: 850-644-7888; e-mail: abathke@cob.fsu.edu). **Business Administration (M.B.A.):** Dr. Patrick Maroney (telephone: 850-644-4070; e-mail: pmarone@cob.fsu.edu). **Finance (Ph.D.):** Dr. William A. Christiansen (telephone: 850-644-8202; e-mail: wchrist@cob.fsu.edu). **Information and Management Sciences (Ph. D. and M.S.):** Dr. Joey George (telephone: 850-644-7449; e-mail: jgeorge@cob.fsu.edu). **Management (Ph.D.):** Dr. Bruce Lamont (telephone: 850-644-9846; e-mail: blamont@cob.fsu.edu). **Management Information Systems (M.S.):** Dr. David Paradics (telephone: 850-644-3888; e-mail: dparadic@cob.fsu.edu). **Marketing (Ph.D.):** Dr. Ron Goldsmith (telephone: 850-644-4401; e-mail: rgoldsm@garnet.acns.fsu.edu). **Risk Management and Insurance (Ph.D.):** Dr. Kevin Eastman (telephone: 850-644-8218; e-mail: keastma@cob.fsu.edu).

COLLEGE OF COMMUNICATION

Communications (Ph.D.): Dr. Steve McDowell (telephone: 850-644-2276; e-mail: smcdowel@mailer.fsu.edu). **Communication Disorders (Ph.D.):** Dr. Amy Wetherby (telephone: 850-644-8456; e-mail: awetherb@garnet.acns.fsu.edu).

SCHOOL OF CRIMINOLOGY (Ph.D.): Dr. Bruce Bullington (telephone: 850-644-7377; e-mail: bbulling@mailer.fsu.edu).

COLLEGE OF EDUCATION

Early Childhood Education (Ph.D.): Dr. Charles Wolfgang (telephone: 850-644-8484; e-mail: wolfgang@coe.fsu.edu). **Educational Foundations and Policy Studies (Ph.D.):** Dr. Carolyn Herrington (telephone: 850-644-7077; e-mail: cherrington@lsi.fsu.edu). **Educational Leadership (Ph.D. and M.S.):** Dr. Michael Biance (telephone: 850-644-3583; e-mail: biance@coe.fsu.edu). **Educational Research (Ph.D.):** Dr. John Keller (telephone: 850-644-8790; e-mail: jkeller@mailer.fsu.edu). **Elementary Education (Ph.D.):** Dr. Janice Flake (telephone: 850-644-8481; e-mail: jflake@mailer.fsu.edu). **English Education (Ph.D.):** Dr. Sissi Carroll (telephone: 850-644-2997; e-mail: pcarroll@garnet.acns.fsu.edu). **Health Education (M.S.):** Dr. Mary Sutherland (telephone: 850-644-2122; e-mail: sutherl@coe.fsu.edu). **Instructional Systems (Ph.D.):** Dr. John Keller (telephone: 850-644-4592; e-mail: keller@coe.fsu.edu). **Leisure Services and Studies (M.S.):** Dr. Jean Mundy (telephone: 850-644-3854). **Mathematics Education (Ph.D):** Dr. Elizabeth Jakubowski (telephone: 850-644-0365; e-mail: ejakubow@coe.fsu.edu). **Multilingual/Multicultural Education (Ph.D.):** Dr. Frank Brooks (telephone: 850-644-3240; e-mail: fbrooks@garnet.acns.fsu.edu). **Physical Education (Ph.D.):** Aubrey Kent (telephone: 850-644-7174; e-mail: kent@coe.fsu.edu). **Psychological Services Education (Ph.D.):** Dr. Stephen Rollin (telephone: 850-644-3854; e-mail: rollin@coe.fsu.edu). **Reading Education (Ph.D.):** Dr. Diana Scott-Simmons (telephone: 850-644-8472; e-mail: dscott@coe.fsu.edu). **Rehabilitation Services (Ph.D.):** Dr. Jane Burkhead (telephone: 850-644-3854; e-mail: burkhead@coe.fsu.edu). **Science Education (Ph.D.):** Dr. Alejandro Gallard (telephone: 850-644-7813; e-mail: agallard@garnet.acns.fsu.edu). **Social Science Education (Ph.D.):** Dr. Sande Milton (telephone: 850-644-8168; e-mail: milton@coe.fsu.edu). **Special Education (Ph.D.):** Dr. Mary Frances Hanline (telephone: 850-644-8417; e-mail: hanline@coe.fsu.edu).

COLLEGE OF ENGINEERING

Chemical Engineering (Ph.D.): Dr. Srinivas Palanki (telephone: 850-410-6149; e-mail: palanki@eng.fsu.edu). **Civil Engineering (Ph.D.):** Dr. Nur Yazdani (telephone: 850-410-6125; e-mail: yazdani@eng.fsu.edu). **Electrical Engineering (Ph.D.):** Dr. Frank Gross (telephone: 850-410-6410; e-mail: gross@eng.fsu.edu). **Industrial Engineering (Ph.D.):** Dr. Chun Zhang (telephone: 850-410-6355; e-mail: chzhang@eng.fsu.edu). **Mechanical Engineering (Ph.D.):** Dr. Farrukh Alvi (telephone: 850-410-6336; e-mail: alvi@eng.fsu.edu).

COLLEGE OF HUMAN SCIENCES

Family and Child Sciences (Ph.D.): Dr. Connor Walters (telephone: 850-644-3217; e-mail: cwaltersc@mailer.fsu.edu). **Marriage and the Family (Ph.D.):** Dr. Mary Hicks (telephone: 850-644-7741; e-mail: mhicks@mailer.fsu.edu). **Nutrition, Food, and Exercise Sciences (Ph.D.):** Dr. Doris Abood (telephone: 850-644-4796; e-mail: dabood@mailer.fsu.edu). **Textiles and Consumer Sciences (Ph.D.):** Dr. Jeanne Heitmeyer (telephone: 850-644-5578; e-mail: jheitmey@mailer.fsu.edu).

SCHOOL OF INFORMATION STUDIES (Ph.D./M.A./M.S.): Dr. Don Latham (telephone: 850-644-7272; e-mail: latham@lis.fsu.edu); **(M.S.):** Dr. Kathleen Burnett (telephone: 850-644-5772; e-mail: kburnett@lis-two.fsu.edu); **(Ph.D.):** Dr. Ron Blazek (telephone: 850-644-8112; e-mail: blazek@lis.fsu.edu).

COLLEGE OF LAW (J.D.): Mark Seidenfeld (telephone: 850-644-4759; e-mail: mseidenf@law.fsu.edu).

COLLEGE OF MEDICINE (M.D.): Dr. Helen Livingston (telephone: 850-644-8938; e-mail: hlivings@mailer.fsu.edu).

SCHOOL OF MOTION PICTURE, TELEVISION, AND RECORDING ARTS (M.F.A.): Dr. Reb Braddock (telephone: 850-644-2621; e-mail: rbraddock@filmschool.fsu.edu).

SCHOOL OF MUSIC (Ph.D. and M.M.): Dr. Seth Beckman (telephone: 850-644-5848; e-mail: seth.beckman@music.fsu.edu).

SCHOOL OF NURSING (Ph.D. and M.S.): Jeanne Flannery (telephone: 850-644-5626; e-mail: jflanner@mailer.fsu.edu).

COLLEGE OF SOCIAL SCIENCES

Asian Studies (M.A. or M.S.): Dr. Burt Atkins (telephone: 850-644-4418; e-mail: batkins@garnet.acns.fsu.edu). **Demography/Population Center (M.S.):** Dr. William Serow (telephone: 850-644-1762; e-mail: wserow@coss.fsu.edu). **Economics (M.A.):** Dr. Thomas Zuehlke (telephone: 850-644-7206; e-mail: tzuehlke@garnet.acns.fsu.edu). **Geography (Ph.D.):** Dr. Phillip Steinberg (telephone: 850-644-1706; e-mail: psteinbe@coss.fsu.edu). **International Affairs (M.A. or M.S.):** Dr. Burt Atkins (telephone: 850-644-4418; e-mail: batkins@garnet.acns.fsu.edu). **Political Science (Ph.D./M.A./M.S.):** Dr. Charles Barrilleaux (telephone: 850-644-7643; e-mail: cbarille@garnet.acns.fsu.edu). **Public Administration and Policy (Ph.D.):** Dr. Richard Feiock (telephone: 850-644-3525; e-mail: rfeiock@garnet.acns.fsu.edu); **(M.P.A.):** Dr. Fran Berry (telephone: 850-644-7603; e-mail: fberry@garnet.acns.fsu.edu). **Russian and East European Studies (M.A. or M.S.):** Dr. Ljubisa Adamovich (telephone: 850-644-7097; e-mail: plollis@mailer.fsu.edu). **Sociology (Ph.D.):** Dr. Harry Dahms (telephone: 850-644-2135; e-mail: hdahms@garnet.acns.fsu.edu). **Urban and Regional Planning (Ph.D.):** Dr. Greg Thompson (telephone: 850-644-8521; e-mail: gthompsn@garnet.acns.fsu.edu); **(M.S.P.):** Dr. Robert Deyle (telephone: 850-644-8512; e-mail: rdeyle@garnet.acns.fsu.edu).

SCHOOL OF SOCIAL WORK (Ph.D.): Dr. Wendy Crook (telephone: 850-644-9596; e-mail: wcrook@mailer.fsu.edu); **(M.S.W.):** Dr. Pam Graham (telephone: 850-644-1201; e-mail: pgraham@mailer.fsu.edu).

SCHOOL OF THEATRE (Ph.D. and M.F.A.): Dr. Carrie Sandahl (telephone: 850-644-4303; e-mail: csandahl@mailer.fsu.edu).

SCHOOL OF VISUAL ARTS AND DANCE

Art (M.F.A.): Professor Robert Fichter (telephone: 850-644-6474; e-mail: rficht@mailer.fsu.edu). **Art Education (Ph.D.):** Dr. Sally McRorie (telephone: 850-644-1915; e-mail: smcrorie@mailer.fsu.edu). **Art History (Ph.D.):** Dr. Robert Neuman (telephone: 850-644-2584; e-mail: rneuman@mailer.fsu.edu). **Arts Administration (M.A.):** Dr. Sally McRorie (telephone: 850-644-1915; e-mail: smcrorie@mailer.fsu.edu). **Dance (M.F.A.):** Professor Elizabeth Patenaude (telephone: 850-644-1023; e-mail: pphillip@mailer.fsu.edu). **Interior Design (M.F.A./M.A./M.S.):** Professor Tock Ohazama (telephone: 850-644-1436; e-mail: tohazama@mailer.fsu.edu).

FORDHAM UNIVERSITY

Graduate School of Arts and Sciences

Programs of Study

The Graduate School of Arts and Sciences is committed to the education of talented men and women in the liberal arts and sciences and offers programs of advanced study in a number of academic disciplines. Areas of study include both the traditional humanistic and scientific disciplines and interdisciplinary programs that may be oriented academically, toward the achievement of career goals, or for personal enrichment.

Master's and doctoral degrees are offered in biological sciences, classics, economics, English, history, philosophy, political science, psychology, sociology, and theology. Master's degrees are also offered in computer science and public communications. Interdisciplinary programs include master's degrees in international political economy and development and humanities and sciences, as well as a master's degree and a doctoral-level program in medieval studies.

Research Facilities

The combined libraries of the University contain more than 1.8 million bound volumes and more than 14,000 periodicals and serials. The main collection is in the William D. Walsh Family University Library, an open-stack library that seats 1,600 readers. The Law School library and the Gerald Quinn Library Lincoln Center may also be used by Fordham students. In addition to the University libraries, graduate students may use the New York Public Library system, and they also have access to the libraries of the City University of New York, Columbia University, New School University, and New York University through the New York City Doctoral Consortium. The library subscribes to several computerized online services and data search networks.

The Computing Center houses up-to-date equipment that is available for use by students, faculty members, and administrators at all times of the day and night. It also maintains an extensive array of software packages. Terminals located at various sites on all three campuses provide convenient access for users.

Separate laboratory facilities are maintained by a number of departments, including biology, communications, computer science, and psychology. The 114-acre Louis Calder Conservation and Ecology Study Center in Armonk, New York, includes a limnological laboratory, an entomology laboratory, a 10-acre lake for ichthyological studies, and forest and swamp habitats for year-round teaching and research in ecology and conservation. In addition, the University is affiliated with a number of outside agencies, including the New York Botanical Garden and the New York Zoological Society.

Financial Aid

The Graduate School awards a number of graduate assistantships and fellowships, both teaching and research, as well as some that require no service. All assistantships and fellowships include stipends, and recipients usually receive a separate tuition scholarship. They are assigned on a competitive basis to full-time students with outstanding academic records, and reappointments are extended on the basis of proven competence and good academic standing. Scholarships for members of underrepresented groups are also available.

Cost of Study

Tuition for the 2001–02 academic year was $625 per credit. Normally, a master's degree requires 30–36 credits and a doctoral degree 60–72 credits beyond the baccalaureate. Annual general fees are $300.

Living and Housing Costs

Rental costs for single students living in University apartments range from $5000 to $5200 a year. Shared rental units range from $400 to $600 per month in the immediate off-campus neighborhood. An up-to-date rental database is maintained by the Office of the Associate Dean.

Student Group

Of the approximately 14,000 students attending Fordham University, about 900 are enrolled in the various departments and programs of the Graduate School. Students come from all areas of the United States and many other countries. Many enroll either full-time or part-time in pursuit of a degree; some take individual courses for professional advancement or personal enrichment.

Location

New York City exposes students to the best the world has to offer in art, culture, and business and has the highly diversified atmosphere of a truly international city. Fordham encourages students to make the best possible use of the opportunities the city offers in class, at work, and during their leisure time. Professors draw upon the resources of the city to enrich their courses. Students experience the city in a variety of personal, individual ways. The University is located in a neighborhood that has been rated as one of the safest in the country.

The University

Fordham is a university in the Jesuit tradition. Founded in 1841, it is governed as an institution under a charter granted by the State of New York. The Graduate School of Arts and Sciences is one of ten colleges and schools at Fordham University. Founded in 1916, it carries on Fordham's oldest academic tradition, the education of talented men and women in the liberal arts and sciences, at the postgraduate level.

Applying

Application and recommendation forms are available from the Office of Graduate Admissions. All applicants must submit a completed application form, official transcripts, results of the Graduate Record Examinations, and three letters of recommendation. Some departments have additional requirements for which students should consult the current Graduate School of Arts and Sciences' *Bulletin.*

Applications are accepted throughout the year for most programs, but they must be received by January 16, 2002, to be guaranteed consideration for financial aid. Psychology applications must be received by January 8, 2002.

Students from abroad must have superior scholastic records and proficiency in written and spoken English. All international students are required to submit scores on the TOEFL.

Detailed descriptions of programs and procedures are to be found in the Graduate School of Arts and Sciences' *Bulletin.* Requests for additional information should be directed to the address given below.

Correspondence and Information

Office of Admissions
Graduate School of Arts and Sciences
216 Keating Hall
Fordham University
441 E. Fordham Road
Bronx, New York 10458

Telephone: 718-817-4416
Fax: 718-817-3566
E-mail: fuga@fordham.edu
World Wide Web: http://www.fordham.edu/gsas/

FACULTY HEADS

Nancy Busch, Interim Dean; Ph.D., Penn State.
William P. Baumgarth, Associate Dean; Ph.D., Harvard.
Craig W. Pilant, Assistant Dean; Ph.D., Fordham.

Department of Biological Sciences: Berish Y. Rubin, Chair; Ph.D., CUNY Graduate Center.
Department of Classical Languages and Literature: John R. Clark, Chair; Ph.D., Cornell.
Department of Communication and Media Studies: Paul Levenson, Director of Graduate Studies; Ph.D., NYU.
Department of Computer and Information Science: D. Frank Hsu, Chair; Ph.D., Michigan.
Department of Economics: Dominick Salvatore, Chair; Ph.D., CUNY Graduate Center.
Department of English Language and Literature: Christopher L. GoGwilt, Chair; Ph.D., Princeton.
Department of History: Richard F. Gyug, Chair; Ph.D., Toronto.
Humanities and Sciences Program: E. Doyle McCarthy, Director; Ph.D., Fordham.
International Political Economy and Development: Henry M. Schwalbenberg, Director; Ph.D., Columbia,
Medieval Studies Program: Maryanne Kowaleski, Director; Ph.D., Toronto.
Philosophical Resources Program: Joseph W. Koterski, S.J., Director; Ph.D., St. Louis.
Department of Philosophy: Dominic J. Balestra, Chair; Ph.D., St. Louis.
Department of Political Science: Richard S. Fleisher, Chair; Ph.D., Illinois.
Department of Psychology: Mary E. Procidano, Chair; Ph.D., Indiana.
Department of Sociology: Orlando Rodriguez, Chair; Ph.D., Columbia.
Department of Theology: Harry P. Nasuti, Chair; Ph.D., Yale.

RESEARCH

Biology. Two main areas of research are available: cell and molecular biology and ecology. Cell and molecular biology research programs include molecular and cellular analysis of immune response to cancer; immunomodulators and their molecular mechanisms of action; eukaryotic gene expression and RNA processing; genetic basis of aging; genetic toxicology; cytogenetic and molecular analysis of chromosomes; spermatogenesis and early development; cellular differentiation; regeneration in invertebrates; neuronal differentiation, structure, function, and analysis; role of growth factors. The ecology program spans behavioral, population, community, and ecosystem levels. Areas of emphasis include conservation biology, forest-microbial dynamics and function, ecology of phytoplankton and bacteria, insect-parasitoid interactions, medical entomology, paleoecology, plant-insect interactions, primate behavior and ecology, systematics and evolution of fishes, and vertebrate physiological ecology.

Classical Languages and Literature. Current research interests range widely over Greek poetry, historiography, religion, archaeology, and philosophy; Latin lyric, elegiac, and epic poetry and historiography; Roman topography; textual criticism; the intellectual life of late antiquity; medieval and Renaissance Latin; and Latin paleography.

Communication and Media Studies. Current research emphasizes the ethical, social, and humanistic dimensions of the public communications media. Other areas of interest include public radio, telecommunications, and international communications. The Donald McGannon Communication Research Center sponsors and facilitates research in these and other areas.

Computer and Information Science. Current research and concentrations are available in the following areas: information systems and applications, artificial intelligence, communications and networks, and computation and algorithms. Courses available include software system design, computer architecture, parallel computation, computer security and ethics, data communications and networks, graph theory and network design, internet computing and Java programming, data base systems, and artificial intelligence.

Economics. Research interests are broad, with perhaps slightly more emphasis given to areas of applied rather than theoretical economics. Topics include development economics, financial economics, international economics, monetary economics, and industrial organization

English Language and Literature. The research interests of the faculty members are represented in virtually every field of English and American literature, from Old English literature to twentieth-century British and American literature as well as literary criticism and critical theory. The English department has particular strength in eighteenth-century literature and culture.

History. Current research interests range over diverse areas of medieval history, including England, France, Germany, Italy, and Spain, and include concentrations on the medieval Church, particularly liturgy, monasticism and canon law, medieval society and economy, notably women and family, towns, and trade; cultural history; and legal history. In European history the concentrations are Tudor-Stuart England; early modern and modern Britain, Ireland, France, and Germany; Protestant and Catholic reformations; European intellectual history; gender history; and Imperial and Soviet Russia. In American history research areas include women in colonial and modern America, Thomas Jefferson and the Republican era, the Civil War, the American South, the New Deal, foreign relations, African-American history, urban studies, immigration, and Latin America.

International Political Economy and Development. Current research efforts focus primarily on the interaction of political and economic institutions in the functioning of the global economy and their respective roles in facilitating political modernization and economic development. Ongoing research projects include the politics of economic stabilization programs, trade policies and economic growth, foreign assistance and economic reform efforts, and the political foundations of poverty. Participating faculty members have traditionally specialized in the following areas: corporative and international politics, development studies (project management, finance and development, economic and political development, community and social development), emerging markets and country risk analysis, international business and finance, and international and development economics.

Medieval Studies. The Center for Medieval Studies offers an interdisciplinary M.A. and a doctoral certificate in medieval studies, giving students the opportunity to broaden their knowledge of the Middle Ages and to integrate in a coherent whole the various facets of medieval civilization. Disciplines participating in the program include art, classics, English, history, modern languages and literature (French, German, Italian, and Spanish), music, philosophy, political science, and theology.

Philosophy. The department seeks to maintain a wide diversity of research interests and competencies. While strong in the history of philosophy, it has special capabilities in continental philosophy, analytic philosophy, classical American philosophy, medieval philosophy, and philosophy of religion. With respect to both historical and contemporary perspectives, it has strengths in epistemology and metaphysics as well as moral and political philosophy.

Political Science. Faculty members teach courses leading to the M.A. in the history of political philosophy, from classical to contemporary. Areas in American politics include institutions, political behavior, public policy, and urban politics. The department also offers M.A. and minor fields in political economy and comparative/international politics.

Psychology. Research is being undertaken in both basic and applied clinical and developmental psychology and psychometrics. Current clinical research interests are behavior therapy, family therapy, health psychology, neuropsychology, child therapy, social supports, and treatment planning and evaluation. Developmental research employs a life-span orientation in research on developmental processes and in the application of developmental principles to the design, implementation, and evaluation of prevention and intervention programs and to the assessment of children and families. Psychometrics research focuses on the quantitative aspects of psychology, especially test constructing, personnel selection, program evaluation, and advanced statistical procedures.

Sociology. Research centers on three specialization areas. Demography research includes family planning program efforts and fertility behavior; career histories and contraceptive behavior; gender, ethnic, and racial inequalities in the labor force; U.S. metropolitan migration; and residential segregation. Ethnic/minority research includes household structure among Dominican and Colombian immigrants, comorbidity of mental illness and problem behavior among Hispanic adolescents, and migration and adaptation of Hispanic groups. Sociology of religion research includes fundamentalist Catholic organizations, religion and social movements, and the abortion controversy and Catholic social thought. Other faculty research includes the sociology of emotions and the society of knowledge. The department also offers M.A. specialization in justice and criminology studies.

Theology. Faculty research represents the three areas of specialization in the department. In the biblical section, faculty research includes exegetical, theological, narrative, and historical interpretations. The historical theology faculty does research in Greek and Latin patristics, medieval theology, nineteenth- and twentieth-century European and American religious thought, and U.S. religious history. The systematic theology faculty, focusing on contemporary Catholic theology, is engaged in research in fundamental theology, Karl Rahner, liberation and feminist theologies, Christian social ethics, and moral theology.

GEORGE FOX UNIVERSITY

Graduate School

Programs of Study The Master of Arts in Teaching (M.A.T.), offered in Newberg, is a full-time day program that begins in June and is completed in three semesters over eleven months. The part-time evening program in Portland begins in late August, is designed for those who want to continue employment, and takes five semesters to complete. A second part-time program, M.A.T. in Your Community is completed over four semesters. Classes at time of publication are offered in Portland and Salem. Additional locations are being considered.

The Master of Education (M.Ed.) is for educators seeking advanced training. In addition to the fall and spring semesters, courses are offered in the summer, both part-time and online.

The Doctor of Education (Ed.D.) program prepares educators to be leaders in their chosen specialties at the K–12 levels. Students have the opportunity to complete the program in about four years through summer on-campus course work, Internet-based offerings during the school year, and independent study.

The Administrative License Program is designed either as a stand-alone program or as part of the M.Ed. or Ed.D. programs. Curricula leading to the Initial Administrative License, Continuing Administrative/Initial Superintendent's License, and Continuing Superintendent's License are offered.

The Master of Business Administration (M.B.A.) program is part-time and consists of 40 semester hours over twenty-six months. The human dimension of management, communication, leadership, ethics, change, problem solving, decision making, and globalization are some of the themes explored in the curriculum. M.B.A. classes meet at the University's Portland Center.

The Master of Divinity (M.Div.) program prepares men and women for denominational ordination or recording. The student may concentrate studies in chaplaincy, pastoral studies, biblical studies, Christian ministries, spiritual formation, marriage and family counseling, or Christian history and thought. The degree requires completion of 96 semester hours. Classes are offered at George Fox Evangelical Seminary in Portland.

The Doctor of Ministry (D.Min.) in leadership and spiritual formation is the highest professional degree for those in parish or related ministries, and is designed to engage ministry professionals in the integration of their experience with new knowledge, research, and reflection. The degree consists of 36 semester hours. The M.Div. degree or its equivalent is required for admission. On-site classes are offered in four 2-week modules at the University's Portland Center.

The Master of Arts in Christian ministries is a professional degree that prepares the student for ordination or recording or for work as a lay minister. Studies may be concentrated in church leadership, adult ministries, urban ministries, spiritual formation, or family ministries. Completion of this degree requires 64 semester hours. Classes are offered at George Fox Evangelical Seminary in Portland.

The Master of Arts in Theological Studies (M.A.T.S.) program prepares the scholar for doctoral work beyond the seminary level. The program is designed for men and women who desire graduate study in the field of theological studies with an emphasis in either biblical studies or Christian history and thought. The degree consists of 64 semester hours. Classes are offered at George Fox Evangelical Seminary in Portland.

The Doctor of Clinical Psychology (Psy.D.) program is based on the practitioner-scholar model, which puts more emphasis on clinical skills than the more traditional, research-oriented scientist-practitioner model leading to the Ph.D. This full-time, APA-accredited, five-year program consists of four years of full-time study followed by a year of full-time internship. Classes are offered in Newberg.

The Master of Arts in counseling program is designed for men and women who desire graduate study and preparation for becoming a licensed professional counselor. Sixty-four semester hours are required for the degree, which can be completed at the student's own pace. This degree is offered in Portland and Salem.

Recognizing the special training and expertise required for working effectively with couples and families, the University offers the Master of Arts in marriage and family therapy degree. This program prepares those intending to become licensed marriage and family therapists. The degree consists of 79 semester hours and is offered in Portland.

The Master of Arts in organizational leadership program is designed to develop leaders for a broad range of organizations, including business, health care, education, the church, and the public sector. The 36-semester-hour program consists of fifteen courses, including a service learning project and an action research product and is offered in Boise.

Research Facilities The University maintains libraries at both its Newberg and Portland Center campuses. The Murdock Learning Center on the Newberg campus houses more than 140,000 volumes and receives more than 900 periodical titles. The Portland Center library houses 70,000 volumes and receives more than 300 periodicals. In addition to an online catalog, the library system is a member of OCLC, with direct access to a database of more than 38 million bibliographic records that represent holdings on thousands of member libraries in the region. The University is also a member of the Portland Area Library System (PORTALS) and Orbis, a consortium of academic libraries with a union catalog located at the University of Oregon. University students may also use the Portland State University library as well as numerous other state university and private libraries in Oregon and Washington.

Financial Aid The University participates in Federal Stafford Student Loans programs. Scholarships are available for selected programs.

Cost of Study Tuition varies by program. Applicants should contact the Office of Graduate Admission for specific program costs.

Living and Housing Costs A wide variety of housing is available in Newberg and throughout the Portland metropolitan area. On-campus housing is not available for graduate students. It is the student's responsibility to make all housing arrangements.

Student Group Overall enrollment at George Fox University is 2,730 students. Of those, 1,092 are enrolled in graduate programs (965 master's level and 127 doctoral level).

Location Newberg, Oregon (population 17,000) is home to the residential campus, a 75-acre tree-shaded area in a historic residential neighborhood, 23 miles from Portland. Hess Creek Canyon, a natural setting of trees, ferns, and wildflowers, runs through campus.

The Portland Center, near Interstate 5 and Highways 217 and 99W, is utilized by classes for the University's George Fox Evangelical Seminary; graduate business, counseling, and education; and undergraduate degree-completion programs.

The University George Fox is a Christ-centered university noted for its academic excellence. Founded in 1891 by Quaker pioneers, it has grown to a community of more than 2,700 students and faculty and staff members. From the beginning, its purpose has been to demonstrate the meaning of Jesus Christ by offering a caring educational community in which each individual can achieve the highest intellectual and personal growth and participate responsibly in the world's concerns.

Applying To be admitted to any of the graduate programs, an applicant must have a baccalaureate degree from an accredited college or university, with at least a 3.0 GPA over the last two years of course work. Certain application requirements differ among the graduate programs. Information may be obtained by contacting the Office of Graduate Admission. The application fee is a $40 (nonrefundable). Generally, a $200 matriculation deposit is required of all accepted applicants.

Correspondence and Information

Office of Graduate Admission
George Fox University
414 North Meridian Street #6149
Newberg, Oregon 97132
Telephone: 503-554-2260
800-631-0921 (toll-free)
E-mail: graduate.admission@georgefox.edu
World Wide Web: http://www.georgefox.edu

THE FACULTY AND THEIR RESEARCH

Wayne V. Adams, Director, Graduate School of Clinical Psychology; Ph.D., Syracuse. Postdoctoral work in pediatric psychology, coauthor of three nationally normed psychological tests of cognition.

Mark E. Ankeny, Assistant Professor of Education and Director, Doctor of Education Program; Ph.D., Oregon. History of education, ethics, principles of management and supervision.

Daniel Brunner, Associate Professor of Church History and Pastoral Studies; D.Phil., Oxford. Reformation and pietist church history, spiritual formation, pastoral studies and discipleship.

Robert E. Buckler, Professor of Psychology; M.D., Georgetown. Addiction psychology, forensic psychiatry, epidemiology of mental disorders.

Rodger K. Bufford, Professor of Psychology and Director of Integration, Graduate School of Clinical Psychology; Ph.D., Illinois. Psychology of religion, spiritual well-being, Christian counseling, techniques in psychotherapy; author of *The Human Reflex: Behavioral Psychology in Biblical Perspective and Counseling the Demonic;* coauthor of Templeton Foundation award papers on spiritual health and Christian counseling distinctives.

Roy L. Bunch, Director, Master of Arts in Teaching Night Program; Ed.D., Portland State. Designer of online instruction programs in language arts and social studies for middle school students, workshop leader on teaching writing with the Oregon Analytical Model of writing instruction.

Charles J. Conniry Jr., Assistant Professor Of Pastoral Ministry and Director, Doctor of Ministry Program; Ph.D., Fuller Theological Seminary. Systematic theology, pastoral ministry, modern and postmodern philosophy, American religious history.

Stephen Delamarter, Associate Professor of Old Testament and Hebrew; Ph.D., Claremont. Biblical history and archaeology, manuscript discoveries, hermeneutics, contemporary church music.

James D. Foster, Professor of Psychology and Dean, Graduate and Professional Studies; Ph.D., Ohio State. Developmental psychology with a focus on adulthood and aging, moral development; coauthor of *Christians in the Crossfire.*

Kathleen Kleiner Gathercoal, Professor of Psychology and Director of Research, Graduate School of Clinical Psychology; Ph.D., Case Western Reserve. Face perception and recognition, mental retardation, and infants' vision development; Quaker/Friends higher education, postmodernism, and culture shift.

Jules D. Glanzer, Dean, George Fox Evangelical Seminary; D.Min., Fuller Theological Seminary. Church planting, pastoral ministry, faith-based leadership development, natural church development.

W. Scott Headley, Associate Professor of Education and Chair, Department of Teacher Education; Ph.D., Ohio State.

Thomas F. Johnson, Professor of Biblical Theology; Ph.D., Duke. Christian theology, spiritual formation, biblical studies; author of *A Commentary of the Letters of John.*

Karin B. Jordan, Director, Counseling Program; Ph.D., University of Georgia. Author of *Foundations in Psychotherapy: Clinical Wisdom, Skill Development, and Practice* and *The Student and Supervisor Handbook.* Author of twenty-one professional journal articles and eight book chapters.

Randolph Michael, Associate Professor of Marriage and Family Therapy; D.Min., Midwestern Baptist Theological Seminary. International clinic services, effective interpersonal communication and team building, clinical supervision, organizational consulting and training.

Glenn T. Moran, Professor of Education and Director, Boise Center; Ed.D., Northern Colorado. Collaborative management, leadership.

MaryKate Morse, Associate Professor of Spiritual Formation and Pastoral Studies; Ph.D., Gonzaga. Biblical perspectives on gender issues, leadership and congregations, spiritual formation.

Mary Olson, Assistant Professor of Management; Ph.D., Idaho. Adult learning programs.

Asbjorn Osland, Assistant Professor of Business and Director, Master of Business Administration Program; Ph.D., Case Western Reserve. International business, total quality, case writing.

Donna Kalmbach Phillips, Associate Professor of Education and Director, Master of Arts in Teaching Day Program; Ed.D., Oregon State. Language arts/social studies methods, instruction of academically gifted students, integration of curriculum.

Gary L. Railsback, Associate Professor of Education and Director, Master of Education Program; Ph.D., UCLA. Moral and ethical issues in education, faith development of college students, technology for classroom teachers, higher education marketing.

R. Larry Shelton, Richard B. Parker Professor of Wesleyan Theology; Th.D., Fuller Theological Seminary. Church staff and program development, church history and theology, Christianity and culture, ethics of leadership and management.

Laura K. Simmons, Assistant Professor of Christian Ministries; Ph.D., Fuller Theological Seminary. The religious writings of Dorothy L. Sayers, practical theology, church music ministries.

Daniel Sweeney, Associate Professor of Counseling; Ph.D., North Texas. Children (play therapy) and parenting issues, projective psychotherapy techniques, psychology/theology integration.

Kent Yinger, Assistant Professor of Biblical Studies; Ph.D., Sheffield (England). New Testament studies, Pauline theology, New Testament Greek, missions.

GEORGE MASON UNIVERSITY

Graduate Programs

Programs of Study

George Mason University (GMU) graduate programs at the doctoral level are the Ph.D. in bioinformatics, biosciences, computational sciences and informatics, computer science, conflict analysis and resolution, cultural studies, earth systems science, economics, education, electrical and computer engineering, environmental science and public policy, history, information technology, nursing, psychology, and public policy; and a D.A. in community college education. The Juris Doctor (J.D.) and the Juris Master are offered at the School of Law, which holds classes on the Arlington Campus. The University also offers programs at the master's level, conferring the M.A. in art and visual technology, biosciences, communication, economics, English, English (linguistics), foreign languages (French and Spanish), history, international commerce and policy, music, nursing, psychology, sociology, telecommunications, and transportation policy, operations, and logistics; M.M. in music; the M.S. in applied and engineering physics, applied and engineering statistics, bioinformatics, biotechnology, biology, chemistry, civil and infrastructure engineering, computational sciences, computer engineering, computer science, conflict analysis and resolution, earth systems science, e-commerce, electrical engineering, enterprise engineering policy, environmental science and policy, exercise fitness and health promotion, geographic and cartographic sciences, health sciences, information systems, knowledge management, mathematics, nursing, operations research, software engineering, statistical sciences, systems engineering, technology management, and telecommunications; the M.S.W. in social work; the M.Ed. in counseling and development (school, community/agency, and higher education), curriculum and instruction (adult education, early childhood education, elementary education, secondary education, multilingual/multicultural education, English as a second language, foreign language and Latin, and advanced studies in teaching and learning), education leadership, instructional technology, and special education; the Master of Business Administration; the Master of Public Administration; and the Master of Fine Arts in art and visual technology, creative writing, and dance. A Master of Arts in Interdisciplinary Studies (M.A.I.S.) is offered, with tracks in individualized studies and liberal studies. The M.A.I.S. in individualized studies includes faculty-sponsored concentrations in political science, recreation resources management, and video-based production. The Master of Arts in New Professional Studies (M.N.P.S.) is also offered, with tracks in biosciences, biotechnology, forensic biosciences, organizational learning, peace operations, and teaching.

Research Facilities

Research at GMU is expanding rapidly in breadth and volume. External funding, which has increased by nearly 50 percent in the last two years, is distributed across most of the major academic units and offers a variety of opportunities for graduate research assistantships in most fields of study. At GMU, advanced computational capabilities are used in research in fields ranging from computational fluid dynamics, bioinformatics, and computer engineering to public policy and history. Facilities for research in the modern biosciences and genomics are expanding rapidly both at the Fairfax and Prince William campuses. The Shared Research Instrumentation Facility at Fairfax houses advanced analytical instrumentation shared across the physical and biological sciences. GMU students and faculty members are active participants in the experimental research programs of nearby federal agencies, including NIST, NRL, USGS, and NASA Goddard Space Flight Center. The GMU research libraries at Fairfax and Arlington are substantially augmented through the Washington Research Library Consortium and the Virtual Library of Virginia, which together give GMU students and faculty members user privileges at more than twenty major academic research libraries. The central computing facility houses Compaq Alpha Servers running the Digital UNIX operating system as well as an HP 9000C server running HP-UX and an IBM 9121-511 running OS/390. Public laboratories of Windows-based and Apple Macintosh microcomputers are located in major buildings. Special-purpose labs include the advanced Internet lab, the geographic information systems (GIS) and special analysis lab, departmental labs, and research labs housing special equipment (such as the Intel hypercube for parallel processing). State-of-the-art fiber and Gigabit Ethernet data networks enable individuals both on and off campus to access central computers, connect to the online catalog, and transfer data between mainframes and workstations.

Financial Aid

GMU annually awards a limited number of three-year fellowships for beginning high-potential doctoral students. These fellowships carry stipends of up to $12,000 and tuition waivers of up to 9 hours per regular semester. The University offers assistantships in research and instruction that are awarded without regard to financial need. A student holding an assistantship must have degree status and take a minimum of 6 graduate credit hours per semester. Stipends range from $7995 to $10,860 in 2002–03. A limited number of tuition waivers are available for graduate assistants. All fellowship awards, assistantships, and tuition waivers are offered by individual departments. Financial aid and scholarship information is available on the Web (http://apollo.gmu.edu/finaid). Applicants may request specific scholarship applications by contacting the Scholarship Coordinator, Office of Student Financial Aid, 4400 University Drive, MS 3B5, Fairfax, Virginia 22030 (telephone: 703-993-2353). U.S. citizens and permanent residents applying for student loans must complete the FAFSA.

Cost of Study

The tuition and fees for the 2002–03 academic year are $208.50 per credit hour for in-state students and $571.50 per credit hour for out-of-state students. Tuition and fees may vary for some graduate programs and are subject to change.

Living and Housing Costs

On-campus housing is provided to graduate students on a space-available basis. Prices for the 2002–03 academic year range from $3490 to $4500. Meal plans are available to both resident and commuter students. For more information, applicants should visit the Web (http://www.gmu.edu/student/living). Off-campus housing is available in the immediate Fairfax community at prevailing local rates.

Student Group

In fall 2001, GMU enrolled 24,897 students, of whom 8,332 were graduate and professional students. A majority of graduate students are currently employed in the Washington area and take advantage of courses given in the evening or on weekends. Employment opportunities for graduates are excellent.

Location

GMU is in the center of Fairfax County, in a suburban community of more than 1 million that is just 16 miles west of Washington, D.C. The Greater Washington area offers museums, historic sites, and entertainment as well as the outdoor excitement of the Chesapeake Bay and the Blue Ridge Mountains, all within a short drive of Fairfax. Fairfax County has one of the highest per-family incomes in the nation. Selected programs are offered at the Arlington and Prince William campuses.

The University

Established in 1957, George Mason's Fairfax campus is nestled in a heavily-wooded tract of 583 acres and includes a 10,000-seat sports arena and entertainment complex, a Center for the Arts with a 2,000-seat concert hall theater, and a two-pool Aquatic and Fitness Center complex. As the state university in Northern Virginia, GMU is a rapidly growing institution with state-of-the art facilities and programs that focus on interdisciplinary learning. George Mason continues to grow and is poised to lead the way in higher education and workforce training.

Applying

Applicants are encouraged to go to the Web for graduate application materials at http://www.admissions.gmu.edu. Requests for paper applications may be directed to the address or e-mail listed below. Applicants must submit an application form, two official copies of all transcripts, an application fee, a Virginia Domicile Classification form, examination scores from standardized tests, letters of recommendation, and all other forms required by specific departments. International students must also submit external evaluations of international transcripts, a minimum TOEFL score of 575 (paper-based) or 230 (computer-based), proof of financial support, and bank statements. Applicants are encouraged to apply early. Deadlines vary by department and are published in the application packet and on the Web. The deadlines for international students are one month prior to those published for domestic students.

Correspondence and Information

Graduate Admissions Information
George Mason University
4400 University Drive, MSN: 3A4
Fairfax, Virginia 22030-4444
Telephone: 703-993-2407
Fax: 703-993-2392
E-mail: gmugrad@admissions.gmu.edu
World Wide Web: http://www.gmu.edu

PROGRAM CONTACTS AND RESEARCH AREAS

Art and Visual Information Technology: Dr. Scott M. Martin (telephone: 703-993-4574; e-mail: avt@gmu.edu). Digital arts (M.A. program); digital arts, InterArts, painting, photography, printmaking, and sculpture (M.F.A. programs). **Biology:** Dr. George E. Andrykovitch (telephone: 703-993-1050; e-mail: biologygrad@gmu.edu). Evolutionary genetics, genomics, pathogenic microbiology, microbial ecology, population ecology, fungal physiology, vertebrate physiology, entomology, lichenology, paleobotany, field botany. **Biosciences:** Dr. Robert F. Smith (telephone: 703-993-1398; e-mail: biosciphd@gmu.edu). Neurosciences, functional genomics, systematics and evolutionary biology, astrobiology, bioethics. **Bioinformatics:** Dr. Glenda Wilson (telephone: 703-993-8487; e-mail: scs@gmu.edu). Analysis (M.S.), computational biology (Ph.D.), computational neuroscience (Ph.D.), customized tools (M.S.), microbial genomics and diversity (Ph.D.), modern biotechnology (M.S.), applied cell and molecular biology (Ph.D.). **Business/School of Management:** Dr. Andres Fortino (telephone 703-993-2140; e-mail masonmba@som.gmu.edu). M.B.A., executive M.B.A., technology management. **Chemistry:** Dr. Gerald L. Roberts (telephone 703-993-1456; e-mail chemgrad@gmu.edu). Biochemistry, environmental chemistry, synthetic materials, theoretical chemistry, fuels, analytical chemistry. **Civil, Environmental and Infrastructure Engineering:** Dr. Mark Houck (telephone: 703-993-1675; e-mail: civil@gmu.edu). Transportation, water resources, environmental engineering, inventive design. **Computational Sciences (School of):** Dr. Peter A. Becker (telephone 703-993-1990; e-mail: scs@gmu.edu). Astrophysics, material science, biology, chemistry, fluid dynamics, applied mathematics, physics, space sciences, statistics, and earth systems and global change. **Computer Science:** Dr. Henry J. Hamburger (telephone: 703-993-1530; e-mail: csinfo@cs.gmu.edu). Image analysis, parallel and distributed computation, graphics, vision and robotics, machine learning. **Conflict Analysis and Resolution:** Dr. Sara Cobb (telephone: 703-993-1300; e-mail: scobb@gmu.edu). Cultural, ethnic, organizational, and public sector conflict; multiparty, multinational, and social psychological dimensions of conflict. **Communication:** Dr. Cindy Lont (telephone: 703-993-1314; e-mail: commgrad@gmu.edu). Public relations, organizational, crisis and risk communication. **Community College Education (D.A.):** Dr. Gail Kettlewell (telephone: 703-993-2310; e-mail: dance@gmu.edu). Community college teaching, program combines courses in college teaching with a concentration in a knowledge area. **Creative Writing:** William B. Miller, M.F.A. (telephone: 703-993-1180; e-mail: writing@gmu.edu). Poetry, fiction, nonfiction. **Cultural Studies:** Dr. Roger N. Lancaster (telephone: 703-993-2851; e-mail: cultural@gmu.edu). Critical studies of race, ethnicity, and nation; film and media, science and technology, gender/sexuality, and political economy. **Dance:** Karen A. Studd, M.S., CMA (telephone 703-993-1114; e-mail: dance@gmu.edu). Modern dance, performance, choreography, teaching. **Earth Systems Science:** Dr. Menas Kafatos (telephone: 703-993-1990; e-mail: scs@gmu.edu). Global systems, atmosphere, biosphere, observation and quantitative analysis. **E-commerce:** Dr. Daniel Menasce (telephone: 703-993-1673; e-mail: ms-ecomm@ite.gmu.edu). Management, public policy, and information technology aspects, developing electronic commerce solutions. **Economics:** Dr. Richard E. Wagner (telephone: 703-993-1135; e-mail: econgrad@gmu.edu). Public choice, Austrian economics, law and economics. **Education (Graduate School of):** Dr. Mark Goor (telephone 703-993-4648; e-mail: gseinfo@gmu.edu). NCATE approved programs, National Board for Teaching Standards preparation, professional development schools, instructional technology partnerships with schools and businesses, individualized doctoral programs, emphasis on leadership in research and practice. **Electrical and Computer Engineering:** Dr. Andre Manitius (telephone: 703-993-1569; e-mail: ece@gmu.edu). Communications, computer engineering, control and robotics, electromagnetics, electronics, optoelectronics, signal processing. **English:** Dr. Roger Lathbury (telephone: 703-993-1185; e-mail: englgrad@gmu.edu). Literature, cultural studies, linguistics, professional writing and editing, the teaching of writing and literature. **Enterprise Engineering and Policy:** Dr. Ray Sommer (telephone: 703-993-8099; e-mail: sppapp@gmu.edu). Policy, regulatory, modern process management methods, process-oriented enterprise systems, enterprise design, implementation execution, process optimization. **Environmental Science and Policy:** Dr. Ronald Stewart (telephone 703-993-3187; e-mail: espp@gmu.edu). Aquatic and terrestrial ecology, human ecology, urban/suburban sustainability, conservation of biodiversity, environmental management, international environmental policy. **Foreign Languages:** Dr. Mark Goldin (telephone: 703-993-1231; e-mail: language@gmu.edu). Literature of Spain, Spanish America and the French-speaking world, Spanish and French linguistics, foreign language learning and teaching. **Geographic and Cartographic Sciences:** Dr. David Wong (telephone 703-993-1212; e-mail: ges@gmu.edu). GIS, remote sensing; population; water resources; political representation; spatial statistics. **History and Art History** (telephone: 703-993-1250; e-mail: historygrad@gmu.edu): Dr. Rosemarie Zagarri. U.S., European, and comparative world history (M.A. program). Dr. Suzanne Smith. U.S., European, and comparative world history (Ph.D. program), public history, constitutional studies, new media/information technology. **Information and Software Engineering:** Dr. Sushil Jajodia (telephone: 703-993-1640; e-mail: ise@gmu.edu). Databases, information security, information systems integration, e-commerce, software engineering. **Information Technology:** Dr. Stephen G. Nash (telephone: 703-993-1505; e-mail: itegrad@gmu.edu). See listings for Civil, Environmental and Infrastructure Engineering, Computer Science, Electrical and Computer Engineering, Information and Software Engineering, Statistics, Systems Engineering and Operations Research, and Telecommunications. **Interdisciplinary Studies:** Dr. John Radner (telephone: 703-993-8762; e-mail: mais@gmu.edu). Concentrations in political science, recreation resources management, video-based production, with option for individualized studies. **International Commerce and Policy:** Dr. Kris McCord. (telephone: 703-993-2268; e-mail: icp@gmu.edu). International trade/finance, international commerce/economics, international marketing/technology, and telecommunications/transportation. **Liberal Studies:** Dr. Young-chan Ro (telephone: 703-993-1292; e-mail: libstudies@gmu.edu). Multidisciplinary and multicultural approaches to human ideas and values, cultural studies, philosophy, religious studies, women's studies, social and political questions within cultural contexts. **Linguistics:** Dr. Steven H. Weinberger (telephone: 703-993-1180; e-mail: englgrad@gmu.edu). TESL, phonology, syntax, second language acquisition. **Mathematical Science:** Dr. David F. Walnut (telephone: 703-993-1460; e-mail: mathgrad@gmu.edu). Applied mathematics, dynamical systems, computational mathmatics, combinatorics, topology, logic. **Music:** Dr. Tom Owens (telephone: 703-993-1236; e-mail: music@gmu.edu). Performance, music education, composition, instrumental and choral conducting. **Nursing and Health Science:** Dr. James Vail (telephone: 703-993-1947; e-mail: nursinfo@gmu.edu). Health policy, health services research, health work force, rural health. **Organizational Learning:** Dr. Mark Addleson (telephone: 703-993-3804; e-mail: psol@gmu.edu). Learning organizations/knowledge management, methodology of social inquiry, Austrian economics. **Physics (Applied and Engineering):** Dr. Paul So (telephone: 703-993-1280; e-mail: physics@gmu.edu). Applied, computational, particle/nuclear, planetary, and solar physics; astrophysics/astronomy; complex systems; physics and astronomy education. **Psychology:** Dr. James E. Maddux (telephone: 703-993-1342; e-mail: psycgrad@gmu.edu). Applied developmental (M.A. and Ph.D.), clinical (Ph.D., APA accredited), human factors/applied cognition (M.A. and Ph.D.), school (M.A.), industrial/organizational (M.A. and Ph.D.), biopsychology (M.A. and Ph.D.). **Public Administration:** Dr. Lawrence C. Walters (telephone: 703-993-1411; e-mail: mpa@gmu.edu). Public management; policy studies; public and nonprofit finance; state and local government; environmental science and public policy; health policy and administration; administration of justice; information policy and administration; nonprofit, human resources, and international management. **Public Policy:** Dr. Kingsley E. Haynes (telephone: 703-993-8200; e-mail: spp@gmu.edu). Science and technology policy; regional development policy; society, values, and policy; governance and public management policy; organizational informatics. **Social Work:** Dr. Sunny Harris Rome (telephone: 703-993-2030; e-mail: socwork@gmu.edu). Social policy, advocacy, management, community organization, child welfare, gerontology, human rights, domestic violence, substance abuse. **Sociology:** Dr. Linda Kalof (telephone: 703-993-1441; e-mail: socgrad@gmu.edu). Race, ethnicity, and gender; sociological theory; applied sociology; criminology/delinquency; conflict resolution; culture. **Statistics (Applied and Engineering):** Dr. Paul So (telephone: 703-993-1280; e-mail: statistics@gmu.edu). Computational statistics, visualization, data mining. **Systems Engineering and Operations Research:** Dr. Karla Hoffman (telephone: 703-993-1670; e-mail: seor@gmu.edu). Decision processes, discrete event simulation, air transportation, network analysis, dynamic systems, optimization methods, queuing, inference analysis, telecommunications, military applications. **Telecommunications (M.A.):** Dr. Michael R. Kelley (telephone: 703-993-1314; e-mail: telecom@gmu.edu). Educational technology, information systems, systems modeling, international telecommunications, management organization and policy, network technologies and applications, production theory and practice, telecommunication systems, wireless communications. **Telecommunications (M.S.):** Dr. Jeremy Allnutt (telephone: 703-993-3810; e-mail: msintcom@gmu.edu). Communication networks, architecture, modeling, performance analysis, protocols, broadband communications, high-performance computer networks, wireless and mobile communications. **Transportation Policy, Operations and Logistics:** Dr. Jonathan L. Gifford (telephone: 703-993-2275; e-mail: tpol@gmu.edu). Highway and urban transportation policy, aviation policy, and advanced technology in transportation systems.

THE GEORGE WASHINGTON UNIVERSITY

Columbian College of Arts and Sciences

Programs of Study

Graduate programs leading to both the Ph.D. degree and the master's degree are offered in American studies, biochemistry, biological sciences, biostatistics, chemistry, economics, English, epidemiology, genetics, geoscience, history, hominid paleobiology, mathematics, physics, political science, public policy, and statistics.

The Ph.D. degree only is offered in American religious history, counseling, human sciences, immunology, molecular and cellular oncology, neuroscience, pharmacology, and psychology (including clinical, cognitive neuropsychology, and industrial/organizational/applied social). A Psy.D. degree is offered in clinical psychology.

Master's degrees are also offered in anthropology, art history, art therapy, computer fraud investigation, criminal justice, environmental and resource policy, fine arts (including ceramics, design, interior design, painting, photography, printmaking, sculpture, and visual communication), forensic sciences, geography, history of religion, legislative affairs, media and public affairs, museum studies, philosophy and social policy, political management, public policy, organizational sciences (human resources management and organizational management), religion (Hinduism and Islam), security management, sociology, speech-language pathology, telecommunication, theater (with concentrations in theater design and classical acting), and women's studies. Graduate certificate programs are offered in art therapy, computer fraud investigation, leadership coaching, museum studies, organizational management, security management, survey design and data analysis, and women's studies.

The University cooperates with the Smithsonian Institution and the Library of Congress in offering doctoral programs in American studies, with the Smithsonian and other area museums in offering the art history and museum studies programs, and with the Folger Institute of Renaissance and Eighteenth-Century Studies in programs in English. A cooperative agreement also exists with the Shakespeare Theatre's Academy of Classical Acting for the M.F.A. in classical acting and with the Thomas Jefferson National Accelerator Facility for the doctoral program in nuclear physics. In many of the doctoral programs, close but informal relations are maintained with various government and private organizations, in particular with the National Institutes of Health, National Institute of Standards and Technology, and Naval Research Laboratory. Through the Consortium of Universities of the Washington Metropolitan Area, graduate students may supplement their course work at ten other area universities.

The University operates on an academic year of two semesters and two 5-week summer sessions.

Research Facilities

The University library collections, totaling approximately 2 million volumes, 18,000 periodical subscriptions, and 1.2 million microforms, are housed in the Gelman Library and the libraries of the School of Medicine and Health Sciences and the George Washington University Law School. Students also have access to the Library of Congress, the libraries of the other members of the Consortium of Universities of the Washington Metropolitan Area, public libraries, many of the specialized government agency libraries, the National Archives, and numerous other special collections in the Washington area.

Research facilities at the Foggy Bottom and Virginia campuses include nuclear detection laboratories and an Institute for Materials Science. The services of the University Computer Center are available to students and faculty members.

Financial Aid

Many departments award graduate teaching assistantships and University fellowships in varying amounts. In addition, some departments offer research fellowships and grants. Information about loans can be obtained from the University's Office of Student Financial Assistance. Information concerning part-time employment and cooperative education can be obtained from the Career Center.

Cost of Study

For the 2001–02 academic year, on-campus tuition was $742.50 per credit hour. Other fees apply.

Living and Housing Costs

The Office of Campus Life provides information on off-campus housing and hosts apartment-hunting weekends during the summer. The cost of living in the Washington area is comparable to that in other major metropolitan centers.

Student Group

The total student body includes 14,000 full-time students and 8,000 part-time students. Enrollment in graduate programs in the arts and sciences is 1,800, with 850 in doctoral programs. Students come from throughout the country and the world, representing all fifty states and 130 countries.

Location

The George Washington University is located in Washington, D.C., in an area characterized by an attractive mixture of federal government buildings, office buildings, and residential housing. The White House, the Department of State, the Kennedy Center for the Performing Arts, the World Bank, the International Monetary Fund, and some of the most important museums and libraries in the world are within minutes of the University. This part of the city, known traditionally as Foggy Bottom, places students at the governmental, cultural, and historic center of Washington, D.C., and is an unusually pleasant and attractive setting for an urban university. With a subway station located on campus, the University is easily accessible from many parts of the city and Virginia and Maryland suburbs.

The University

The George Washington University, chartered by Congress in 1821, is private and nonsectarian. It holds regional accreditation from the Middle States Association of Colleges and Schools. The campus, located four blocks west of the White House, is a mixture of large new buildings, traditional town houses, and older classroom and dormitory buildings.

Applying

Applicants must demonstrate academic excellence, based on a baccalaureate degree from an accredited institution. Scores from the GRE General Test, letters of recommendation, transcripts from all schools attended, and a statement of purpose are required from most applicants. Applicants for any M.F.A. program need not submit GRE scores. International applicants are required to submit TOEFL scores. Some departments require other documentation, such as GRE Subject Test scores, writing samples, and/or portfolios.

Admission deadlines vary by program. For specific information, consult the Graduate Application packet or the Web site listed below. Admissions submitted after deadlines are considered on a space-available basis.

Correspondence and Information

Applications for graduate admission are available on line or for applicants to download from the Web page listed below. The University bulletin is also available on the Web (http://www.gwu.edu).

Graduate Admissions
Columbian College of Arts and Sciences
The George Washington University
Washington, D.C. 20052

Telephone: 202-994-6210
Fax: 202-994-6213
E-mail: csasgrad@gwu.edu
World Wide Web: http://www.gwu.edu/~ccas

FACULTY HEADS

Interim Dean: Jean Folkerts, Ph.D., Kansas.
Associate Dean for Graduate Studies: Michael Moses, Ph.D., Monash (Australia).

American Studies: Phyllis M. Palmer, Ph.D., Ohio State.
Anthropology: Alison S. Brooks, Ph.D., Harvard.
Art: David Bjelajac, Ph.D., North Carolina.
Art Therapy: Ann Milles, M.A., Concordia.
Biochemistry: Allan L. Goldstein, Ph.D., Rutgers.
Biological Sciences: Robert P. Donaldson, Ph.D., Michigan State.
Biomedical Sciences: Stephan Ladisch, M.D., Pennsylvania.
Biostatistics: John Lachin, Sc.D., Pittsburgh.
Chemistry: Michael King, Ph.D., Harvard.
Earth and Environmental Science: John Lewis, D.Phil., Oxford.
Economics: Harry S. Watson, Ph.D., Indiana.
English: Faye Moskowitz, M.A., George Washington.
Environmental and Resource Policy: Henry C. Merchant, Ph.D., Rutgers.
Epidemiology: Dante Verme, Ph.D., George Washington.
Forensic Sciences: David A. Rowley, Ph.D., Illinois.
Genetics: Diana Johnson, Ph.D., Chicago.
Geography: Dorn McGrath, M.C.P., Harvard.
History: Edward Berkowitz, Ph.D., Northwestern.
Hominid Paleobiology: Bernard Wood, Ph.D., London (England).
Human Sciences: Alf Hiltebeitel, Ph.D., Chicago.
Immunology: David W. Scott, Ph.D., Yale.
Legislative Affairs: Charles Cushman, Ph.D., North Carolina.
Mathematics: Daniel Ullman, Ph.D., Berkeley.
Media and Public Affairs: Jerol Manheim, Ph.D., Northwestern.
Molecular and Cellular Oncology: Steven R. Patierno, Ph.D., Texas at Houston.
Museum Studies: Ildiko DeAngelis, J.D., American.
Neuroscience: Vincent Chiappinelli, Ph.D., Connecticut.
Pharmacology: Vincent Chiappinelli, Ph.D., Connecticut.
Philosophy and Social Policy: Robert Paul Churchill, Ph.D., Johns Hopkins.
Physics: William Parke, Ph.D., George Washington.
Political Management: Chris Arterton, Ph.D., MIT.
Political Science: Jeffrey Henig, Ph.D., Northwestern.
Professional Psychology: James Miller, Ph.D., Yale.
Psychology: Rolf Peterson, Ph.D., Iowa.
Public Policy: Joseph J. Cordes, Ph.D., Wisconsin.
Religion: Paul Duff, Ph.D., Chicago.
Sociology: Gregory Squires, Ph.D., Michigan State.
Speech and Hearing: Geralyn Schulz, Ph.D., Maryland.
Statistics: Tapan Nayak, Ph.D., Pittsburgh.
Telecommunication: Christopher H. Sterling, Ph.D., Wisconsin–Madison.
Theatre and Dance: Leslie Jacobson, M.F.A., Boston University.
Women's Studies: Diane Bell, Ph.D., Australian National.

A view of the George Washington University's campus.

The Academic Center, which houses the Columbian College of Arts and Sciences; the art, music, history, and English as a foreign language departments; and the Computer Center.

THE GRADUATE SCHOOL AND UNIVERSITY CENTER OF THE CITY UNIVERSITY OF NEW YORK

Programs of Study

The Graduate School and University Center of the City University of New York, known as the Graduate Center, offers the Doctor of Philosophy, Doctor of Musical Arts, Master of Arts, and Doctor of Social Welfare degrees.

Doctoral programs are offered in anthropology, art history, biochemistry, biology, business, chemistry, classics, comparative literature, computer science, criminal justice, earth and environmental sciences, economics, educational psychology, engineering, English, French, Hispanic and Luso-Brazilian literatures, history, linguistics, mathematics, music, philosophy, physics, political science, psychology, social welfare, sociology, speech and hearing sciences, theater, and urban education.

Masters's programs at the Graduate Center are offered in classics (offered jointly with New York University), comparative literature, liberal studies, linguistics, philosophy, and political science. Other master's degree programs are given by the senior colleges of the University. Among the interdisciplinary courses of study available are research, cognitive science, cultural studies, health and society, language and literacy, Latin American and Caribbean studies, European Union studies, and public policy and urban studies. Certificate programs exist in American studies, film studies, medieval studies, Renaissance studies, and women's studies.

Research Facilities

Centers, institutes, and research groups at the Graduate Center are varied and provide extraordinary research opportunities. The Graduate School's Mina Rees Library collection consists of more than 272,000 volumes. There are about 600,000 microforms (microfiche and reels of microfilm), more than 222,000 art slides, numerous scores, and more than 2,000 sound recordings. The library system of the City University of New York includes the libraries of all the CUNY colleges, which house more than 6 million volumes and 31,000 currently received periodicals in a variety of languages. The central building of the New York Public Library, located just a few blocks from the Graduate Center, provides more than 6 million volumes of information for reference use.

Financial Aid

Financial assistance programs include fellowships, grants, assistantships, traineeships, loans, and Federal Work-Study Program assignments. Special awards are available to minority group students.

Cost of Study

For 2001–02, full-time tuition was $2175 per semester for first-level doctoral (up to 45 credits), master's, and nonmatriculated students (state residents) and $3800 per semester for out-of-state and international students. The cost for second-level doctoral students (from 45 credits to completion of required course work) was $1360 per semester for state residents and $3025 for nonresidents. The cost for third-level doctoral students (from completion of required course work to completion of degree) was $540 per semester for state residents and $1080 for nonresidents. In addition to tuition, a student activities fee of $29.60 per semester is charged. Tuition and charges are subject to change by action of the Board of Trustees of CUNY.

Living and Housing Costs

Housing information (both residence and off-campus) is available from the Office of Residence Life (telephone: 212-817-7480).

Student Group

In the fall of 2000, nearly 4,000 full-time students were enrolled at the Graduate Center. Minority groups constituted about 23 percent of the doctoral population. The majority of students are residents of New York State; about 28 percent represent students from other parts of the United States and international students.

Location

The Graduate Center is located on a new campus at 365 Fifth Avenue in Manhattan. Housed in a landmark building, the new campus has been designed to accommodate the particular needs of doctoral-level studies and research. Students are able to enjoy the extraordinary cultural diversity of the Center's cosmopolitan milieu. Most doctoral programs are located at the Graduate Center, but science and professional programs are offered at the CUNY senior colleges.

The School

The Graduate School and University Center of the City University of New York, established in 1961 to integrate graduate work on the doctoral level, represents a consortium of programs and institutions within the City University. The 1,600-member doctoral faculty consists primarily of scholars on the faculties of the senior colleges and the Graduate Center and also includes researchers from such specialized New York City institutions as the New York Botanical Garden, the Metropolitan Museum of Art, and the American Museum of Natural History. A thoroughly stimulating and congenial intellectual atmosphere prevails. The Graduate Center's new campus features a science center, enhanced library facilities, seminar rooms, an expanded dining commons, state-of-the-art computing facilities, and a cultural/conference complex including an auditorium, a recital hall, a black-box theater, a film screening room, and an art gallery.

Applying

Completed application forms, transcripts, test scores, and all other supporting material must be submitted to the Admissions Office by the following deadlines: January 1 for clinical psychology, neuropsychology, and all music (D.M.A. and Ph.D., except late D.M.A. performance); January 8 for anthropology (for those students seeking consideration for financial aid); January 15 for criminal justice (applicants must file a duplicate application and immediately make direct contact with the program), English (for those students seeking consideration for financial aid)(writing sample required), Hispanic and Luso-Brazilian literatures (for those students seeking consideration for financial aid), and linguistics; February 1 for biology, French (writing sample required: one paper for B.A. applicants; two papers or thesis for M.A. applicants), biopsychology, experimental cognition psychology, industrial and organizational psychology, social-personality psychology, and sociology; February 15 for school psychology area of educational psychology and urban education; March 1 for business, history (writing sample of no more than fifteen pages required), developmental psychology, environmental psychology, experimental psychology, learning processes psychology, music (late D.M.A. performance), social welfare (professional writing sample required), speech and hearing sciences, and theater; April 1 for anthropology (for those students not seeking financial aid) and English (for those students not seeking financial aid) (writing sample required); and April 15 for Hispanic and Luso-Brazilian literatures (for those students not seeking financial aid) and for all other programs. The deadline for spring admission is November 15. Spring enrollment is not permissible in anthropology, business, computer science, criminal justice, educational psychology, English, linguistics, music, psychology, social welfare, sociology, theater, or urban education.

Correspondence and Information

For information about a particular program:
Executive Officer
Program in (specify)
The Graduate Center
365 Fifth Avenue
New York, New York 10016
Telephone: 212-817-7000

For admission and registration information:
Admissions Office
The Graduate Center
365 Fifth Avenue
New York, New York 10016
Telephone: 212-817-7470
World Wide Web: http://www.gc.cuny.edu/

For other information:
Provost's Office
The Graduate Center
365 Fifth Avenue
New York, New York 10016
Telephone: 212-817-7200
World Wide Web: http://www.gc.cuny.edu/

FACULTY HEADS

Administration
Frances Degen Horowitz, President.
William P. Kelly, Provost and Senior Vice President.
Linda N. Edwards, Associate Provost and Dean for Academic Affairs.

Executive Officers
Anthropology: Professor Louise Lennihan, Graduate Center.
Art History: Professor Patricia Mainardi, Graduate Center.
Biochemistry: Professor Horst Schulz, Graduate Center.
Biology: Professor Richard L. Chappell, Graduate Center.
Business: Dean Gloria Thomas, Baruch College, 17 Lexington Avenue, New York, New York 10010.
Chemistry: Professor Gerald Koeppl, Graduate Center.
Classics (M.A. and Ph.D.): Professor Dee L. Clayman, Graduate Center.
Comparative Literature (M.A. and Ph.D.): Professor William Coleman, Graduate Center.
Computer Science (M.A. and Ph.D.): Professor Theodore Brown, Graduate Center.
Criminal Justice: Professor Mary S. Gibson, John Jay College, 899 10th Avenue, Suite 411, New York, New York 10019.
Earth and Environmental Sciences: Professor Jeffrey P. Osleeb, Graduate Center.
Economics: Professor Thom Thurston, Graduate Center.
Educational Psychology: Professor Alan L. Gross, Graduate Center.
Engineering: Mumtaz Kassir, City College School of Engineering, Convent Avenue and 138th Street, New York, New York 10031.
English: Professor Joan Richardson, Graduate Center.
French: Professor Francesca Canadé Sautman, Graduate Center.
Hispanic and Luso-Brazilian Literatures: Professor Lía Schwartz, Graduate Center.
History: Professor James Oakes, Graduate Center.
Liberal Studies (M.A.): Professor Rachel Brownstein, Graduate Center.
Linguistics: Professor Charles Cairns, Graduate Center.
Mathematics: Professor Alvany Rocha, Graduate Center.
Music: Professor David Olan, Graduate Center.
Musical Arts: Professor David Olan, Graduate Center; Professor Peter Basquin, Deputy Executive Officer.
Philosophy (M.A. and Ph.D.): Professor Michael Devitt, Graduate Center.
Physics: Professor Louis S. Celenza, Graduate Center.
Political Science (M.A. and Ph.D.): Professor W. Ofuatey-Kodjoe, Graduate Center.
Psychology: Professor Joseph Glick, Graduate Center.
Biopsychology: Professor Peter Moller, Hunter College, 695 Park Avenue (68th Street), New York, New York 10021.
Clinical Psychology: Professor Steven Tuber, Psychological Center, City College, North Academic Complex, Convent Avenue and 136th Street, New York, New York 10031.
Developmental Psychology: Professor Anna Stetsenko, Graduate Center.
Environmental Psychology: Professor David Chapin, Graduate Center.
Experimental Cognition: Professor John Antrobus, City College, North Academic Complex, Convent Avenue and 136th Street, New York, New York 10031.
Experimental Psychology: Cognition, Learning and Perception: Professor Arthur Reber, Brooklyn College, James Hall, Room 5315, Bedford Avenue and Avenue H, Brooklyn, New York 11210.
Industrial and Organizational Psychology: Professor Joel Lefkowitz, Baruch College, 17 Lexington Avenue, New York, New York 10010.
Learning Processes: Professor Bruce Brown, Queens College, Rasran Hall, Room 201, 65-30 Kissena Boulevard, Flushing, New York 11367.
Neuropsychology: Professor Jeffery M. Halperin, Queens College, 65-30 Kissena Boulevard, Flushing, New York 11367.
Social Personality: Professor William Cross, Graduate Center.
Social Welfare: Professor Michael Fabricant, Hunter College School of Social Work, Room 901, 129 East 79th Street, New York, New York 10029.
Sociology: Professor Philip Kasinitz, Graduate Center.
Speech and Hearing Sciences: Professor Robert Goldfarb, Graduate Center.
Theatre: Professor Pamela Sheingorn, Graduate Center.
Urban Education: Professor Jay Lemke, Graduate Center.

The Graduate Center's new campus is in a landmark building located at Fifth Avenue and 34th Street, redesigned for the needs of a twenty-first century doctoral studies institution.

The new CUNY Graduate Center Campus at 365 Fifth Avenue in New York City.

GRADUATE SCHOOL OF FIGURATIVE ART OF THE NEW YORK ACADEMY OF ART

Graduate Program

Programs of Study

The Graduate School of Figurative Art of the New York Academy of Art offers Master of Fine Arts (M.F.A.) degree programs in figurative art that emphasize anatomy, figure drawing, perspective, and traditional techniques of painting and sculpture. Students concentrate in figure painting, drawing, or sculpture and also pursue course work in écorché construction, anatomical drawing, figure structure, structural drawing of casts and objects, perspective, history of composition and design, history of painting or sculpture techniques, and the contemporary figure. During the final year of instruction, students work with the adviser of their choice to complete an artwork or series of artworks that are exhibited in the annual Diploma Works Exhibition at the New York Academy of Art.

Research Facilities

The Academy occupies a newly renovated, five-story building in lower Manhattan's Tribeca district. The cast iron landmark houses a collection of nineteenth-century plaster casts of classical, Renaissance, and later European sculpture; an anatomy classroom that includes skeletal specimens and plaster dissection casts; additional classrooms where students are instructed in drawing, painting, and sculpture; semi-private studios for students; and a library that emphasizes anatomical studies and figurative art.

Financial Aid

All applicants (including non-U.S. citizens) may apply for a scholarship. The Graduate School of Figurative Art awards scholarships to outstanding students in the full-time program, ranging from $1000 to $5000 annually. U.S. citizens or permanent residents may apply for federally guaranteed student loans of up to $27,000 per academic year.

Cost of Study

In 2002–03, for students enrolled in the two-year program, the full-time tuition is $16,750 per academic year. Tuition for students enrolled in the one-year, three-semester program is $25,000; international student tuition is $24,000. All students pay a materials/services fee of $325 per semester.

Living and Housing Costs

There is no university housing, but the School assists students in finding accommodations.

Student Group

Students come from throughout the United States and abroad. Approximately 18 percent of the total enrollment of 123 are international students.

Student Outcomes

Graduates have served on the faculties of schools such as Pratt Institute; School of Visual Arts; Parsons School of Design; New School University; the University of Pennsylvania; CUNY, Queens; Mercy College; St. John's (New York); the University of the Arts; Montserrat College of Art; the University of North Florida; New World School of the Arts; the Philbrook Art Museum School; the Hotchkiss School; and Han Nam University (Korea). Many have also held group and solo exhibitions throughout the U.S. and abroad.

Location

The Graduate School is located in the lower Manhattan landmark district of Tribeca. Tribeca is adjacent to SoHo, which is noted for its galleries, museums, and large population of artists.

The University

The Graduate School of Figurative Art offers the only graduate program in the nation devoted to the study of art based on the human figure. It is the School's goal to provide students with sufficient conceptual knowledge of anatomy, perspective, geometry, and the effects of light on form to render the human figure from the imagination as well as from life. The common theme running through the variety of courses offered in the School's highly integrated curriculum is the need to understand the complex nature of the human form and its relationship to the creation of vital contemporary art.

Applying

Required materials include the application for admission and statement of goals, a $75 nonrefundable application fee, official transcripts from undergraduate colleges, two letters of recommendation, a slide portfolio, a self-addressed stamped envelope for return of the portfolio, and TOEFL scores if the applicant is an international student whose native language is not English.

Entrance to the one- and two-year program is for the fall semester only. Conditionally admitted students begin in the summer semester. The deadline for submission of applications for both programs is April 15. The recommended deadline for students seeking merit scholarship consideration is March 15. Those seeking to apply after either deadline should contact the Office of Admissions.

Correspondence and Information

Office of Admissions and Financial Aid
Graduate School of Figurative Art
of the New York Academy of Art
111 Franklin Street
New York, New York 10013
Telephone: 212-966-0300
Fax: 212-966-3217
E-mail: info@nyaa.edu
World Wide Web: http://www.nyaa.edu

THE FACULTY AND THEIR AREAS OF INTEREST

Steven Assael, Adjunct Faculty (painting and drawing). He received his bachelor's degree from Pratt Institute and the School of Visual Arts, and is a recipient of the Elizabeth Breenshields Foundation Grant, Charles Roman Award, and the ED Foundation Grant. His work has been exhibited throughout the U.S. in solo exhibitions at Forum Gallery, the Tatistcheff Gallery, the More Gallery, and the Staempfli Gallery, and in group shows at the Arkansas Arts Center in Little Rock, Arkansas; the Flint Institute of Art in Flint, Michigan; the Kemper Museum in Kansas City, Missouri; the Yale University Museum in New Haven, Connecticut; the Queens Museum of Art in Flushing, New York; and the New York State Museum in Albany, New York. He had a ten-year retrospective at the Frye Museum in Seattle, Washington. He is currently represented by the Forum Gallery. Lindenhill Books has published a book on his drawings, and articles on his work have appeared in *ARTnews* and *Art in America*.

Lisa Bartolozzi, Adjunct Faculty (painting). She earned a B.F.A. from the University of Delaware and an M.F.A. from Washington University in St. Louis. She has taught at Indiana University's Herron School of Art, the Delaware Institute for Arts in Education, and the University of Delaware.

Harvey Citron, Full-Time Faculty (sculpture and drawing). He graduated from Pratt Institute and received a Diploma from the Accademia di Belli Arti in Rome. He has taught at the University of the Arts and has exhibited sculptures in New York City, Chicago, and Pennsylvania.

Beth Cohen, Adjunct Faculty (art history). She earned a B.A. in the history of art from Queens College and an M.A. and a Ph.D. from the Institute of Fine Arts at New York University. She has received numerous grants and awards, including four fellowships from the Metropolitan Museum of Art and three fellowships from the National Gallery of Art, where she recently served as a Visiting Senior Fellow.

Patrick David Connors, Adjunct Faculty (drawing). He studied at the Pennsylvania Academy of the Fine Arts and the University of Pennsylvania, where he received a B.F.A. His most recent solo exhibition was at the Gross-McCleaf Gallery in Philadelphia. He is the author of *Thomas Eakins and His Perspective*.

Peter Cox, Adjunct Faculty (painting and drawing). He earned a B.A. from the College of the Holy Cross and an M.A. from Catholic University. He has taught at the Fashion Institute of Technology, the National Academy of Design, and the Art Students League.

José Dejesús, Adjunct Faculty (sculpture and drawing). He earned a B.S. from the Inter American University of Puerto Rico and an M.F.A. from the Graduate School of Figurative Art. He has taught at Parsons School of Design and Altos de Chavon in the Dominican Republic. A recipient of the National Arts Club's Ruth Mellon Memorial Sculpture Award, his work has been exhibited in New York City and the Dominican Republic.

Jon deMartin, Adjunct Faculty (drawing and painting). He graduated from Pratt Institute and studied with Nelson Shanks and Daniel E. Greene. His paintings and drawings have been exhibited throughout the New York metropolitan area.

Vincent Desiderio, Adjunct Faculty (painting). He graduated from Haverford College and studied at the Accademia di Belli Arti in Florence and the Pennsylvania Academy of the Fine Arts. He has been the recipient of a Pollock-Krasner Foundation Grant, two National Endowment for the Arts grants, and the Everson Museum of Art Purchase Prize.

Martha Mayer Erlebacher, Adjunct Faculty (anatomy and drawing). She earned her bachelor's and master's degrees from Pratt Institute. She has received an Ingram Merrill Foundation Grant, a Mellon Venture Fund Grant, a National Endowment for the Arts Senior Fellowship, and a Pennsylvania Council on the Arts Fellowship in the visual arts.

Eric Fischl, Adjunct Faculty (painting). He received a B.F.A. from the California Institute of the Arts. For the past sixteen years, he has had at least two solo exhibitions a year in galleries and museums throughout the U.S. and Europe. He has been the subject of a retrospective at the Whitney Museum of American Art, and his works are in numerous private and public collections, including that of the Metropolitan Museum of Art.

Gerry Hoag, Adjunct Faculty (anatomy). He received a B.F.A. from Massachusetts College of Art and an M.F.A. from Boston University. He has taught at both of these institutions as well as at the Art Institute of Boston and Montserrat College. His sculptures have been exhibited at the Boston Center for the Arts, Massachusetts College of Art, and Boston University.

John Horn, Adjunct Faculty (sculpture and anatomy). He earned his bachelor's degree from the Philadelphia College of Art and his master's degree from Queens College. He has worked on several major historical conservation projects, such as the Arch of Constantine, and on restoration of cast collections at the Metropolitan Museum of Art, the Capitolini Museum, the Roman Forum, and the Kunstmuseum in Bonn.

John Jacobsmeyer, Adjunct Faculty (painting). He graduated from the University of New Hampshire and earned an M.F.A. in painting and printmaking from Yale University. He has taught at the University of New Hampshire, Brandeis University, the College of Charleston, and Savannah College of Art and Design.

Deane G. Keller, Adjunct Faculty (drawing). He earned a B.A. in art history from Yale University, a B.F.A. in sculpture and painting from the John Herron Art Institute at Indiana University, and an M.A. in education from Saint Joseph's College. His artwork is in the collections of the Brandywine River Museum, the Wadsworth Atheneum, and the Slater Memorial Museum.

Leonid Lerman, Adjunct Faculty (sculpture and drawing). He received an M.F.A. from the Moukhina College of Art and Design in St. Petersburg. A recipient of the James Wilburt Johnston Sculpture Award, his work has appeared in numerous exhibitions, including a solo exhibition at the Duke University Museum of Art, the Riskin-Sinow Gallery in San Francisco, and the McKee Gallery in New York City.

David Loeb, Adjunct Faculty (painting and art history). He earned a B.F.A. from Boston University and an M.F.A. from Indiana University. His awards include a Fulbright Travel Grant to France, a Ford Foundation Grant, a Pollock-Krasner Foundation Grant, a Yaddo Residency Fellowship, and a Berkshire Museum Purchase Award.

Louis Marinaro, Adjunct Faculty (anatomy). He received degrees from Yale University and the Philadelphia College of Art, where he studied with Walter Erlebacher. He teaches at the University of Michigan and has exhibited throughout the United States.

Randolph L. McIver, Adjunct Faculty (anatomy). He earned a B.A. in art education from the University of Texas at El Paso, a B.F.A. in painting from the Art Center College of Design in Pasadena, California, and an M.F.A. from the Graduate School of Figurative Art. He has taught at the Barrett Art Center in Poughkeepsie, New York, and the Guild Hall in East Hampton, New York.

Randolph Melick, Full-Time Faculty (drawing and anatomy). He earned a bachelor's degree from Princeton University and a master's degree from the Graduate School of Figurative Art. His work has been exhibited in San Francisco and New York City and is represented in many private collections.

George Nista, Adjunct Faculty (sculpture and art history). He earned a B.A. from the Catholic University of America and an M.F.A. in sculpture from Pratt Institute. He is an instructor at the Art Institute of Philadelphia and was previously an Associate Professor at Drexel University.

Leonard Petrillo, Adjunct Faculty (drawing and art history). He earned a bachelor's degree from the Swain School of Design and a master's degree from Brooklyn College. He has taught at Brooklyn College, the Fashion Institute of Technology, and the Brooklyn Museum Art School. He has had solo exhibitions at the First Street Gallery and the Cast Iron Gallery.

Phyllis Purves-Smith, Adjunct Faculty (anatomy and drawing). She earned a B.F.A. at Cooper Union and an M.F.A. at Temple University's Tyler School of Art. She is an Associate Professor at the University of the Arts.

Edward Schmidt, Full-Time Faculty (painting and drawing). He earned a bachelor's degree from Pratt Institute and a master's degree from Brooklyn College. He has received grants from the Greenshields Foundation, the Ingram Merrill Foundation, and the National Endowment for the Arts. He has exhibited throughout the United States and Europe and was the 1983 winner of the American Academy in Rome Fellowship in painting.

Wade Schuman, Adjunct Faculty (painting, drawing, and art history). He studied at the Pennsylvania Academy of Fine Arts and the Rhode Island School of Design. He has exhibited paintings and drawings in New York, Pennsylvania, Germany, and France. He has received a Visual Arts Fellowship Grant for painting from the Pennsylvania Council on the Arts. He recently had a solo exhibition at Forum Gallery in New York City.

Robert Taplin, Adjunct Faculty (sculpture). He is a graduate of Pomona College and a recipient of a National Endowment for the Arts Fellowship.

Elsa Johnson Tarantal, Adjunct Faculty (sculpture). She earned a B.F.A. at Cooper Union; an M.S. at the University of Baroda in Gujarat, India; and an M.F.A. at the University of Pennsylvania. She is currently an Associate Professor at the Philadelphia College of Art and Design of the University of the Arts.

Hong Nian Zhang, Adjunct Faculty (painting and drawing). He studied at the China Central Art Academy and the City University of New York. His most recent solo exhibitions have been at the Loretta Goodwin Gallery in Birmingham, Alabama, and the Imavision Gallery in Taipei, Taiwan.

Brenda Zlamany, Adjunct Faculty (painting). She earned a B.A. at Wesleyan University. Her awards include grants from the New York Foundation for the Arts and the Mid-Atlantic Arts Foundation of the National Foundation for the Arts.

GRAND VALLEY STATE UNIVERSITY

Graduate Studies

Programs of Study

Grand Valley State University offers twenty graduate major programs and enrolls approximately 3,500 graduate students each year. Graduate programs include Master of Business Administration, Master of Science in accounting, Master of Science in biology, Master of Science in communications, Master of Science in computer information systems (distributed computing, information systems management, object-oriented technology, and software engineering), Master of Science in criminal justice (labor relations, policy formulations and planning, public administration, and social work), Master of Education (early childhood education, educational leadership, educational technology, elementary education, gifted and talented, middle and high school, adult and higher education, college student affairs leadership, TESOL, reading, and special education), Master of Science in engineering (manufacturing engineering, mechanical engineering, manufacturing operations), Master of Health Science, Master of Science in nursing (clinical emphases: adult, child, elderly, family, mental health, and women; functional roles: administration, advanced practice, case management, education), Master of Science in occupational therapy, Master of Science in physical therapy, Master of Science in physician assistant studies, Master of Public Administration (criminal justice, health administration, nonprofit management and leadership, and public management), Master of Social Work, and Master of Taxation. Certificates are also available in business (e-commerce), computer science, education, engineering, nursing, and public administration.

Research Facilities

The Steelcase Graduate Library, located in the DeVos Center, has a robotic automatic retrieval system that houses 2,600 book bins in a 40-foot-high storage facility and contains approximately 250,000 books. This retrieval system is only found at two other libraries in the country. The library is also the home to the Grand Rapids Bar Association's law library. The Steelcase Graduate Library houses an extensive reference collection with an emphasis on law and business. The GVSU library system houses more than 700,000 volumes, 3,200 periodical subscriptions, and 21,096 reels of microfilm. Computer facilities are available throughout the campus and all labs run on MS Office Suite, SPSS, SAS, SAP, and departmental-specific applications for course instruction. In addition to having wireless access in the main plaza, there are multiple network connections throughout the DeVos Center. DeVos also has forty kiosk stations for access to e-mail, student records, and Library resources.

Financial Aid

Grand Valley State University offers graduate assistantships through various departments to help students finance their education. Many assistantships cover tuition and include a stipend for hours worked in conjunction with faculty members. Domestic students may also apply for federal student aid. Tuition reimbursement options are available through some local employers.

Cost of Study

Tuition for 2002–03 is $242 per credit hour for in-state students and $525 per credit hour for out-of-state and international students. There are no additional fees charged to students for tuition or academic programs. Students who qualify for a graduate assistantship are considered Michigan residents for tuition purposes.

Living and Housing Costs

Grand Valley State University offers housing for graduate students at the Pew Campus, in downtown Grand Rapids. Housing 180 students, Secchia Hall has one-, two-, three- and four-bedroom units and is located directly across the street from the academic facilities. The most recent costs range from $450 to $700 per month. Off-campus housing within walking distance of the campus is readily available in the Grand Rapids community.

Student Group

The graduate student population at Grand Valley State University ranges from full-time students directly out of an undergraduate program to part-time students with many years of professional experience. Approximately 65 percent of the students are female and a small percentage are international students who represent more than thirty countries.

Location

The Pew Campus, located in downtown Grand Rapids, comprises the majority of Grand Valley's graduate programs. Located on a 15-acre site just west of the Grand River, Grand Valley is in the heart of the city. Grand Rapids is the second largest city in Michigan, with a vibrant economy and a revitalized downtown that provides students numerous social and professional opportunities. As the University continues to grow, many regional sites offer graduate programs at locations such as Muskegon, Holland and Traverse City.

The University

Grand Valley State University was established in 1963 in Allendale, Michigan. Grand Valley enrolls approximately 20,400 students, approximately 3,500 of whom are graduate students. The Pew Campus in downtown Grand Rapids is the only full-service campus in the city and houses the majority of Grand Valley's graduate programs. The DeVos Center is a 250,000-square-foot facility that includes a state-of-the-art library, more than sixty classrooms and laboratories, faculty and staff offices, and more than 320 computers for student use. Currently under construction is a Health Professions Building, set for completion in the fall of 2003. The five-story, 215,000-square-foot facility will support advances in teaching and research technology for our health professions programs.

Correspondence and Information

Grand Valley State University
Graduate Admissions
401 W. Fulton
117B DeVos Center
Grand Rapids, Michigan 49504
Telephone: 616-771-6674
800-748-0246 (toll-free)
Fax: 616-486-6476
E-mail: go2gvsu@gvsu.edu
World Wide Web: http://www.gvsu.edu

GRADUATE PROGRAM DIRECTORS

Priscilla Kimboko, Ph.D., Dean of Graduate Studies and Grants Administration

Business: Dave Mielke, Ph.D.
Communications: Alex Nesterenko, Ph.D.
Computer Science and Information Systems: Paul Leidig, Ph.D.
Criminal Justice: Doug McKenzie, Ph.D., J.D.
Education: Ann Mulder, Ph.D.
Engineering: Paul Plotkowski, Ph.D.
Health Science: Debra Burg, Ph.D.
Nursing: Phyillis Gendler, Ph.D.
Occupational Therapy: Barb Hooper, M.S., OTR.
Physical Therapy: John Peck, Ph.D.
Physician Assistant Studies: Thomas Marks, M.D.
Public Administration: Dan Balfour, Ph.D.
Social Work: Rod Mulder, Ph.D.
Taxation: Rick Harris, J.D., LL.M., C.P.A.

GRATZ COLLEGE

Graduate Programs

Programs of Study

Gratz College offers of broad array of graduate programs in areas of Judaic study that lead to Master of Art degrees in Jewish Communal Studies (M.A.J.C.S.), Jewish Education (M.A.J.Ed.), Jewish Music (M.A.J.Mu.), Jewish Studies (M.A.J.S.), Jewish Liberal Studies (M.A.J.L.S.), and Education. Gratz also offers five programs that lead to Certificate status—Jewish education, Jewish music, Jewish communal studies, Judaica librarianship, and Israel studies.

Gratz participates in several joint programs with other Philadelphia-area institutions in which a student can matriculate at both institutions. A program in Jewish communal studies with the University of Pennsylvania leads to both a Master of Social Work from the University of Pennsylvania's School of Social Work and a Master of Arts or Certificate in Jewish Communal Studies from Gratz. The joint program in Jewish special needs education with La Salle University allows students to earn both the M.A.J.Ed. and credits toward Pennsylvania certification in special education. The joint program in Jewish education with the Reconstructionist Rabbinical College (RRC) allows RRC students to simultaneously earn the M.A.J.Ed. from Gratz, while a joint program in Jewish music with RRC allows its students to simultaneously earn the M.A.J.Mu. from Gratz. The joint program with Chestnut Hill College enables students to earn the M.A.J.Ed. and an M.A. in early childhood education and/or Pennsylvania certification in early childhood education.

Research Facilities

The Tuttleman Library is a specialized library devoted to Judaic and Hebraic studies. Its multilingual collection, primarily English, Hebrew, and Yiddish, consists of more than 100,000 items, including books, periodicals, microfilms, sheet music, recordings, videos, and CD-ROMs. The library's special collections include the Rare Book Room, which features Jewish books of early printing (sixteenth–eighteenth centuries), some limited editions, facsimiles of rare books and manuscripts, archival materials, and a Haggadah collection of more than 400 items. The Schreiber Jewish Music Library has one of the most extensive collections of its kind in the United States, including more than 20,000 books, scores, records, and tapes related to Jewish music and theater. The Gratz College Holocaust Oral History Archive was established to collect, preserve, and make available the taped testimonies of Holocaust survivors, of which 800 are on file.

Financial Aid

State, federal, and Gratz College–sponsored loans and grants are available to incoming students. Students should request a financial aid form by calling the Financial Aid Office. Work-study opportunities, a limited number of fellowships, and possible stipends for students currently teaching in supplementary schools are available. One third of tuition must be paid at registration. Deferred tuition payment plans on the balance are available.

Cost of Study

Full-time graduate tuition (12–18 credits per semester) is $4975 per semester. Senior citizens (over 65) receive a 25 percent discount. Part-time graduate students are billed at $466 per credit. Nonmatriculated graduate students are billed at $207 per credit. International students requiring visas must pay an annual $125 processing and service fee.

Living and Housing Costs

There is no College housing for graduate students. The Office of Admissions assists students in obtaining privately owned accommodations that are suited to their needs.

Student Group

Students from a wide range of personal and professional backgrounds from the United States, Israel, and other countries are drawn to Gratz, offering the kind of diversity of background, religious practice, and beliefs that contributes much to its learning environment. Approximately 450 students are enrolled in the graduate programs.

Student Outcomes

Alumni have gone on to occupy senior professional positions in the Jewish community of North America, Israel, and other countries in such fields as Jewish education, Jewish communal service, academia, the rabbinate, and cantorate. Others have achieved distinction in law, medicine, and business while occupying leadership positions in the Jewish community.

Location

Gratz is located on the Mandell Education Campus in Melrose Park, Pennsylvania, a Montgomery Country suburb that is 6 miles north of Philadelphia. The center of the 28-acre campus is the Ann Newman Building, which contains the Tuttleman Library, a student lounge, and a bookstore.

The University

Gratz College is the oldest independent, nondenominationally affiliated college of Jewish studies in the Western Hemisphere. Founded in 1895, it traces its origins back to a trust established in 1856 by banker, philanthropist, and community leader Hyman Gratz. Originally established as a Hebrew teacher's college, it has emerged as a general college of Jewish studies.

Applying

Applicants to graduate programs must have a bachelor's degree from an accredited college or university. Some degree programs have additional prerequisite requirements that can be fulfilled through undergraduate classroom work, by examination, or by evaluation. An applicant is required to submit a personal statement with a completed application and transcripts from any graduate or undergraduate general or Jewish institutions attended. At its discretion, the admissions committee may require satisfactory GRE or Miller Analogies Test scores for master's degree candidates. Two letters of recommendation are also required, and candidates for the master's programs should expect a preadmission interview. Gratz College accepts students on a rolling admissions basis. International students whose native language is not English are required to demonstrate proficiency in English through the TOEFL unless they have studied at an institution at which English was the sole medium of instruction.

Correspondence and Information

Office of Admissions
Gratz College
7605 Old York Road
Melrose Park, Pennsylvania 19027
Telephone: 215-635-7300 Ext. 140
800-475-4635 Ext. 140 (toll-free)
Fax: 215-635-7320
E-mail: admissions@gratz.edu
World Wide Web: http://www.gratzcollege.edu

THE FACULTY

Jonathan Rosenbaum, Professor of Religion and President; Ph.D., Harvard.

Uziel Adini, Professor of Hebrew Literature and Education; Ed.D., Dropsie.
Elizabeth Bloch-Smith, Visiting Assistant Professor of Bible; Ph.D., Chicago.
Michael A. Carasik, Visiting Assistant Professor of Bible; Ph.D., Brandeis.
Joseph Davis, Assistant Professor of Jewish Thought; Ph.D., Harvard.
Marsha Bryan Edelman, Associate Professor of Music; Ed.D., Columbia.
Allen Glicksman, Adjunct Associate Professor of Sociology; Ph.D., Pennsylvania.
Deana Glickstein, Instructor in Education; M.A., St. John's (New York).
David Green, Assistant Professor of Jewish Communal Service; D.Min., Hartford Seminary.
Daniel Harris, Visiting Professor of Literature; Ph.D., Yale.
Diane A. King, Associate Professor of Education; Ph.D., Dropsie.
Jerry M. Kutnick. Associate Professor of History and Jewish Thought; Ph.D., Brandeis.
Emilie Passow, Visiting Assistant Professor of Literature; Ph.D., Columbia.
Nili Rabinovitz, Instructor in Hebrew Language; M.A., Hahnemann.
Diana L. Ramsey, Instructor in Education; M.A., Kean.
Ruth Sandberg, Leonard and Ethel Landau Assistant Professor of Rabbinics; Ph.D., Pennsylvania.
Sharon Schanzer, Instructor in Education; Ph.D., Bryn Mawr.
Ilene S. Schneider, Assistant Professor of Education; Ed.D., Temple.
Ofira Seliktar, Adjunct Associate Professor of Israel Studies; Ph.D., Strathclyde (Scotland).
Hayim Sheynin, Adjunct Associate Professor of Jewish Literature; Ph.D., Pennsylvania.
Michael Steinlauf, Associate Professor of History; Ph.D., Brandeis.
Ira Stone; Adjunct Professor of Literature; M.H.L., Jewish Theological Seminary; Rabbi.
Kerima M. Swartz, Instructor in Education; M.S., Temple.
Saul P. Wachs, Rosaline B. Feinstein Professor of Education; Ph.D., Ohio State.

HAMPTON UNIVERSITY

Graduate College

Programs of Study

The programs of the Graduate College are designed to prepare students for professional competence in a specific field and for prospective graduate study. Graduate programs leading to the Master in Teaching degree are offered for early childhood, middle school, and secondary education. The Graduate College also offers the Master of Arts (M.A.) degree in biology, communicative sciences and disorders, counseling, elementary education, and special education. In addition, students may pursue the Master of Science (M.S.) degree in applied mathematics, biology, chemistry, computer science, medical science, nursing, and physics; the Master of Business Administration (M.B.A.); the Ph.D. in nursing and physics; and the Doctor of Physical Therapy (D.P.T.).

Programs are planned in consultation with the student's faculty adviser. Specific requirements vary with the department, but in most instances candidates for the Master of Arts degree must complete a minimum of 30–32 semester hours and have the option of writing a thesis, completing a special project, or taking a comprehensive examination.

Candidates for the Master of Science degree in applied mathematics, biology, chemistry, and physics are required to complete a minimum of 32 semester hours, including a thesis. Nursing majors, who must complete a minimum of 45 semester hours, have a choice of a thesis or a comprehensive examination. The Master of Business Administration degree requires between 36 and 60 semester hours, and the Ph.D. in physics requires a minimum of 72 semester hours.

Research Facilities

The William R. and Norma B. Harvey Library, which opened in 1992, is a major focal point of the academic environment of Hampton University. Besides housing an extensive collection of books and periodicals, it serves as a partial depository of U.S. government documents. The distinctive George Foster Peabody Collection, which consists of more than 25,000 items by and about African Americans, is housed in a specially designed room in the Harvey Library.

Other research facilities include computer resources with state-of-the-art mainframes, parallel processors and numerous microcomputers connected via a fiber-optic local area network. The University's science facilities include an observatory with a 16-inch telescope, the Marine Science Center for Coastal and Environmental Studies, the Science and Technology Building, and the Olin Engineering Building. Selected research centers include the Center for Non-linear Analysis, the Nuclear/High Energy Physics Research of Excellence, the Research Center for Optical Physics, and the National Center for Minority Special Educational Research. The Hampton University Museum has an outstanding collection of art, including pieces from sub-Saharan Africa, Asia, Oceania, and American Indians.

Financial Aid

Financial aid is available in the form of fellowships; traineeships; teaching, research, laboratory, and residence hall assistantships; loans; and part-time employment. Assistantship and fellowship stipends generally range from $3200 to $17,000 per academic year and may include varying levels of tuition support.

Cost of Study

In 2000–01, tuition was $9966 for two academic semesters for students taking 10–17 semester hours and $245 per semester hour for those taking 1–9 hours. Nonrefundable fees and book costs amount to approximately $1000 per year.

Living and Housing Costs

Most graduate students live off campus. The University Office of Off-Campus Housing provides assistance in locating housing. Limited on-campus accommodations are available in University-owned apartments. Off-campus housing expenses for single students are estimated at $4800 per year.

Student Group

In 2000–01, the total University enrollment was more than 5,743 students, 415 of whom were enrolled in the Graduate College. The student body is drawn from sixty-one states, territories, and countries. Approximately 50 percent of the graduate students are enrolled full-time. About 95 percent of the Graduate College alumni are employed in their chosen fields.

Location

Hampton University is located in Hampton, Virginia, 27 miles north of Norfolk and 80 miles southeast of Richmond. The University was built on Virginia's peninsula, where the James and York rivers join. The region is richly steeped in early American history: a Kecoughtan native community once stood near the University grounds, and the historic communities of Jamestown, Yorktown, and Williamsburg are all within a 45-minute drive. The city of Hampton is the oldest community in the United States to be continuously occupied by English-speaking people. Hampton is accessible by car, bus, or train as well as direct airline service via Newport News/Williamsburg and Norfolk.

The University

Chartered in the city of Hampton, Elizabeth City County, Virginia, Hampton University was founded by Gen. Samuel Chapman Armstrong in April 1868, in the first days of Reconstruction, in order to assist recently freed slaves in obtaining an "education for life." In line with its broadening educational program, the University inaugurated graduate courses in 1928 and awarded its first master's degree in 1932. The graduate offerings have continued to expand with the addition of a Ph.D. in physics program.

Applying

Applications for admission should be mailed directly to the Graduate College at the address provided below. Students may be admitted to the Graduate College at the beginning of the fall or spring semester or at the beginning of the summer session.

Correspondence and Information

Dean
Graduate College
Hampton University
Hampton, Virginia 23668
Telephone: 757-727-5454 or 5496
Fax: 757-727-5084
E-mail: hugrad@hamptonu.edu
World Wide Web: http://www.hamptonu.edu

THE FACULTY

Rodney D. Smith, Vice President for Planning and Dean of the Graduate College; Ed.D., Harvard, 1986.
Donna W. Dabney, Graduate College Counselor; M.S., Prairie View A&M, 1982.

Deans
Continuing Education: W. O. Lawton, Ed.D., George Washington, 1982.
School of Business: Sid Credle, Ph.D., Texas at Austin, 1989.
School of Engineering and Technology: Morris H. Morgan III, Ph.D., Rensselaer, 1978.
School of Liberal Arts and Education: Mamie E. Locke, Ph.D., Miami (Florida), 1981.
School of Nursing: Pamela V. Hammond, Ph.D., Old Dominion, 1992.
School of Science: Donald A. Whitney, Associate Dean; Ph.D., Virginia, 1977.

Program Heads and Coordinators
Applied Mathematics: Carolyn Morgan, Professor and Chair; Ph.D., Union (New York), 1982.
Applied Mathematics: Abolghassem Miamee, Professor and Director of Graduate Program; Ph.D., Michigan State, 1973.
Biology: Elaine Eatman, Professor; Ph.D., Howard, 1966.
Business Administration: Edward Pyatt, Professor; Ph.D., Temple, 1985.
Chemistry: Isai T. Urasa, Professor; Ph.D., Colorado State, 1977.
Communicative Sciences and Disorders: Robert M. Screen, Professor and Chair; Ph.D., Michigan State, 1968.
Communicative Sciences and Disorders: Pollie S. Murphy, Associate Professor; Ph.D., Memphis State, 1982.
Computer Science: Edward Hill Jr., Associate Professor; D.Sc., George Washington, 1977.
Counseling: Theresa Ford, Assistant Professor; Ph.D., William and Mary, 2000.
Elementary Education: Wanda S. Mitchell, Assistant Professor; Ed.D., William and Mary, 1995.
Master in Teaching: Martha Williams, Ph.D., Virginia Tech, 1979.
Medical Science: Harold J. Marioneaux Jr., Assistant Professor; Meharry Medical College, 1981.
Nursing (master's program): Shirley V. Gore, Associate Professor; Ph.D., North Carolina, 1996.
Nursing (doctoral program): Pamela V. Hammond, Professor; Ph.D., Old Dominion, 1992.
Physical Therapy: Marilys Randolph, Associate Professor; Ph.D., Howard, 1991; PT.
Physics: Donald Whitney, Associate Professor; Ph.D., Virginia, 1977.
Special Education: Martha Williams, Ph.D., Virginia Tech, 1979.

Academy Building, one of five national historic landmark buildings on campus.

The William R. and Norma B. Harvey Library, a state-of-the-art facility constructed in 1992.

A view of the campus waterfront along the Hampton River.

HARVARD UNIVERSITY

Graduate School of Arts and Sciences

Programs of Study

The Graduate School of Arts and Sciences offers master's and Ph.D. degrees under fifty-two departments, committees, and divisions within the Harvard Faculty of Arts and Sciences (FAS). It also offers a joint M.D./Ph.D. program in cooperation with the Harvard Medical School and a special program in Health Science and Technology with the Medical School and the Massachusetts Institute of Technology. A list of departments is presented on the following page. In many departments, the master's degree is awarded only in progress to the doctorate, and applications for the master's degree only are not accepted. Common to all programs are a residence requirement, a tuition requirement, and a requirement of continuous registration from admission until completion of the degree program. Candidates for a master's degree must complete a minimum of one year of full-time study in residence at full tuition (see below). The requirements for the Ph.D. vary considerably from subject to subject, but in all departments a minimum of two years of full-time study in residence at full tuition is required. Candidates for the Ph.D. are normally expected to demonstrate language proficiency, pass general or qualifying examinations, and write a thesis based on original research. Application forms and pamphlets describing the requirements and programs of particular departments may be obtained from the Office of Admissions and Financial Aid (see below).

Research Facilities

The University offers outstanding resources for study and research. The University library system has holdings of more than 11 million volumes and is composed of three main libraries—Widener Memorial, Lamont, and Hilles—and more than ninety other collections. These include special libraries in rare books and manuscripts, art, science, geology, Asian studies, government, music, and anthropology, and separate libraries in many departments and research institutes. Several computing facilities with DEC and IBM mainframes and microcomputers are available for research, computing, thesis work, and word processing. Special research facilities in the sciences include the Center for Astrophysics, which combines the Harvard Observatory and the Smithsonian Astrophysical Observatory; the Center for Earth and Planetary Sciences; the Harvard Forest; the University Herbaria; and laboratories in chemistry, biology, biochemistry, physics, applied sciences, anthropology, and medical sciences. Facilities and institutes in the social sciences and humanities include the Harvard-Yenching Institute, the Fairbank Center for East Asian Research, the Edwin O. Reischauer Institute for Japanese Studies, the Center for Middle Eastern Studies, the Center for Jewish Studies, the Center for the Study of World Religions, the Center for European Studies, the Ukrainian Research Institute, the Russian Research Center, the Committee on Latin American and Iberian Studies, the Committee on African Studies, the Harvard Institute for International Development, the Center for International Affairs, the Center for American Political Studies, the W. E. B. DuBois Institute for Afro-American Studies, the Center for Urban Studies, the Carpenter Center for the Visual Arts, and the Loeb Drama Center. The University museums are also available for research and study: these include the Fogg and Arthur M. Sackler art museums, the Peabody Museum of Archaeology and Ethnology, the Semitic Museum, the Museum of Comparative Zoology, the Botanical Museum, and the Mineralogical Museum. Research affiliations are maintained with a variety of other institutions, including the Woods Hole Oceanographic Institute, the Arnold Arboretum, Dumbarton Oaks Library, the Center for Hellenic Studies, and Villa i Tatti.

Financial Aid

Assistance is available through Harvard and outside fellowships, assistantships, federal work-study, and loans. Financial aid is based on need, as determined by the Office of Admissions and Financial Aid, and may be supplemented by merit awards when funds are available. Most admitted students are guaranteed full, need-based support for two years of study. In the third and following years, most students can support themselves through teaching and research. If necessary, loan funds are usually available to supplement these sources.

Cost of Study

All students must register for full-time study. For the academic year 2002–03, tuition and fees are $26,400 for those in the first two years of study. Reduced tuition of $8174 is charged to students in the third and fourth years. Those in later years pay a facilities fee of $3430 per year if they are in residence. A health insurance fee of $1020 per year is included in the cost for students in residence. Students on leave to conduct research and advanced students living outside the Cambridge area pay an active file fee of $300 per year.

Living and Housing Costs

Costs of most goods and services are somewhat higher in the Boston area than in many other metropolitan areas. For 2002–03, the average ten-month budget for a single student is about $16,100. Dormitory rooms rent for $3822 to $6132 per year; board is available at an additional cost in some cases. Rents for University-owned apartments range from $996 to $2434 per month.

Student Group

The Graduate School of Arts and Sciences has an enrollment of about 3,000. The student body is extremely diverse. About 24 percent of the students are international; 43 percent are women. Approximately 28 percent are in humanities programs, while some 35 percent are in natural sciences and 37 percent in social sciences. Asian Americans constitute more than 4 percent of the student body, while the underrepresented minority community is about 10 percent. The wide range of interests of the students is reflected in a variety of organizations and activities.

Location

Most facilities of the University are located in Cambridge, adjacent to Boston. The two cities and their environs offer wide cultural and recreational opportunities. The University itself has excellent athletic facilities and sponsors numerous arts and public affairs activities. Within the area are many opportunities for public service. Other resources include museums, music, drama, dance, and sports. Recreational areas on the Atlantic coast and in the mountains and forests of New England are easily accessible.

The University

Harvard University is a complex of the Faculty of Arts and Sciences and nine other professional and graduate faculties. The FAS comprises Harvard and Radcliffe Colleges and the Graduate School of Arts and Sciences. Founded in 1636, Harvard College is the oldest college in the United States. The Graduate School of Arts and Sciences (founded in 1872) is the largest graduate institution in the University.

Applying

Students are admitted to graduate study only at the beginning of the academic year; there are no admissions for the spring term. The application deadlines are: natural sciences, December 16; social sciences and humanities, January 2. The application fee is $80.

Correspondence and Information

Office of Admissions and Financial Aid
Graduate School of Arts and Sciences
Byerly Hall, 2nd Floor
Harvard University
8 Garden Street
Cambridge, Massachusetts 02138
Telephone: 617-495-5315
E-mail: admiss@fas.harvard.edu
World Wide Web: http://www.gsas.harvard.edu

OFFICERS AND PROGRAMS IN THE GRADUATE SCHOOL OF ARTS AND SCIENCES

Peter T. Ellison, Dean of the Graduate School of Arts and Sciences and Professor of Anthropology.
Margo N. Gill, Administrative Dean of the Graduate School of Arts and Sciences.

DEPARTMENTS AND COMMITTEES AND GRADUATE DEGREES AWARDED FOR 2001–02

Humanities
Department of Afro-American Studies (Ph.D.).
Department of Celtic Languages and Literatures (A.M., Ph.D.).
Department of Classics (Ph.D.).
Department of Comparative Literature (Ph.D.).
Department of East Asian Languages and Civilizations (Ph.D.).
Department of English and American Literature and Language (Ph.D.).
Department of Germanic Languages and Literatures (A.M., Ph.D.).
Committee on History and East Asian Languages (Ph.D.).
Department of History of Art and Architecture (Ph.D.).
Committee on Inner Asian and Altaic Studies (Ph.D.).
Department of Linguistics (Ph.D.).
Department of Music (A.M., Ph.D.).
Department of Near Eastern Languages and Civilizations (A.M., Ph.D.).
Department of Philosophy (A.M., Ph.D.).
Committee on Regional Studies—East Asia (A.M.).
Committee on the Study of Religion (Ph.D.).
Department of Romance Languages and Literatures (A.M., Ph.D.).
Department of Sanskrit and Indian Studies (A.M., Ph.D.).
Department of Slavic Languages and Literatures (Ph.D.).

Natural Sciences
Department of Astronomy (Ph.D.).
Committee on Biological Sciences in Dental Medicine (Ph.D.)
Committee on Biological Sciences in Public Health (Ph.D.)
Committee on Biophysics (Ph.D.).
Committee on Chemical Physics (Ph.D.).
Department of Chemistry and Chemical Biology (Ph.D.).
Department of Earth and Planetary Sciences (Ph.D.).
Division of Engineering and Applied Sciences (S.M., M.E., Ph.D.).
The Harvard Forest (M.F.S.).
Division of Health Science and Technology (M.D./Ph.D., Ph.D.).
Department of Mathematics (Ph.D.).
M.D./Ph.D. Program.
Division of Medical Sciences (Ph.D.).
Department of Molecular and Cellular Biology (Ph.D.).
Department of Organismic and Evolutionary Biology (Ph.D.).
Department of Physics (Ph.D.).
Department of Statistics (A.M., Ph.D.).

Social Sciences
Department of Anthropology (A.M., Ph.D.).
Committee on Architecture, Landscape Architecture and Urban Planning (Ph.D.).
Committee on Business Economics (Ph.D.).
Department of Economics (Ph.D.).
Department of Government (Ph.D.).
Committee on Health Policy (Ph.D.).
Department of History (Ph.D.).
Committee on the History of American Civilization (Ph.D.).
Department of History of Science (A.M., Ph.D.).
Committee on Information Technology and Management (Ph.D.)
Committee on Middle Eastern Studies (A.M., Ph.D.).
Committee on Organizational Behavior (Ph.D.).
Committee on Political Economy and Government (Ph.D.).
Department of Psychology (Ph.D.).
Committee on Public Policy (Ph.D.).
Committee on Regional Studies—Russia, Eastern Europe, and Central Asia (A.M.).
Committee on Social Policy (Ph.D.)
Department of Sociology (Ph.D.).

HAWAI'I PACIFIC UNIVERSITY

Graduate Studies

Programs of Study

Hawai'i Pacific University offers leading master's degree programs in business administration, communication, diplomacy and military studies, economics, global leadership, information systems, nursing, organizational change, and teaching English as a second language. The Master of Business Administration (M.B.A.) program offers concentrations in accounting, economics, finance, human resource management, international business, management, marketing, information systems, e-business, and travel industry management. The M.B.A. program requires 45 semester hours of graduate work. Prerequisite study in business subjects may be required.

The Master of Science in Information Systems (M.S.I.S.) is designed to create a generation of decision-makers expert in information technology, systems design, and problem solving with automated resources. Students lacking a background in the technical, scientific, and analytical realms are required to complete selected prerequisites to fully prepare for the program. Forty-two semester hours of graduate work are required to complete the program.

The Master of Arts in Human Resource Management (M.A./HRM) emphasizes the study and practices of human relations and managing personnel. These include human resource planning, recruitment and selection, compensation management and benefits, human resource development, labor-management relations, employment law, safety and health, and global perspective on human resources. Some undergraduate prerequisites may be required. The program requires completion of 42 semester hours of graduate work.

The Master of Arts in Global Leadership (M.A./GL) is designed to prepare students to become leaders in all types of organizations that include multinational, governmental, and not-for-profit organizations. Courses include Comparative Management Systems, Global Markets in Transition, International Business Management, and Systems Management. Some prerequisites may be required. Forty-two hours of graduate work are required to complete the program.

The Master of Arts in Organizational Change (M.A./OC) emphasizes the management, design, implementation, and application of organizational change. Courses include Organizational Development, Managing Organizational Culture, Design and Implementation of Organizational Change, and Applications of Organizational Change. Some prerequisite courses may be required. Forty-two hours of graduate work are required to complete the program.

The Master of Science in Nursing (M.S.N.) offers concentrations for those interested in becoming family nurse practitioners or community health clinical nurse specialists. Students who have an RN but lack a Bachelor of Science in Nursing may enter the RN to MSN Pathway. Forty-two semester hours are required to complete the M.S.N. with a family nurse practitioner concentration, and 48 semester hours are required to complete the M.S.N. with a clinical nurse specialist concentration.

The Master of Arts in Communication (M.A./COM) is designed to prepare students for careers in business communication, marketing, advertising, mass media, public relations, entertainment, broadcast or print journalism, sales, the Internet, writing, or education. Some prerequisite courses may be required. Forty-two hours of graduate work are required to complete the program.

The Master of Arts in Teaching English as a Second Language (M.A.T.E.S.L.) requires 37 semester hours of graduate work. Courses include English Phonology and the Teaching of Pronunciation, English Syntax and the Teaching of Grammar, and Methods of Teaching Oral/Aural English. Some prerequisite courses may be required.

The Master of Arts in Diplomacy and Military Studies (M.A./DMS) explores the complex relationships of politics, society, and the military. The M.A./DMS degree is useful for those who are professional military officers or work in government positions. Some prerequisites may be required. The M.A./DMS program requires 42 hours of graduate work.

Research Facilities

To support graduate studies, University libraries, with a collection exceeding 159,000 volumes, add an average of 2,500 volumes annually, 15 percent of which are on business topics. A significant number of business reference books, including national and international business directories, investment and financial services, accounting and tax information sources, and a collection of annual reports, are available. Periodical titles number more than 1,700, and 200,000 pieces of microfiche and 5,200 rolls of microfilm are maintained. Dial-up access to local area databases of public and state university library catalogs, legislative information, and business-oriented statistical data is available in the library. Other in-house, business-related and commercially vendored databases support specialized information needs. The University's accessible on-campus computer center houses more than 100 IBM-compatible microcomputers, with stand-alone support and networked configurations that support the graduate program's integrated computer applications approach.

Financial Aid

The University participates in all federal financial aid programs designated for graduate students. These programs provide aid in the form of subsidized (need-based) and unsubsidized (non-need-based) Federal Stafford Student Loans. Through these loans, funds may be available to cover a student's entire cost of education. To apply for aid, students must submit the Free Application for Federal Student Aid (FAFSA) after January 1. Mailing of student award letters usually begins in April. The University also offers several institutional scholarships and assitantships.

Cost of Study

For the 2002–03 academic year, tuition is $4920 per semester. Books and supplies cost approximately $1500 for the entire program.

Living and Housing Costs

The University has both on-campus residence halls and an apartment referral service. Cost of living for a single student for two semesters (nine months) is $18,215, including tuition, books, housing, food, health insurance, and miscellaneous expenses.

Student Group

University enrollment currently stands at more than 8,000, including more than 1,200 graduate students. All fifty states and more than eighty countries are represented.

Location

The University has two campuses, 8 miles apart, connected by a shuttle system. The downtown Honolulu campus is situated within the center of the business and financial capital of the Pacific. Hawai'i Loa campus is located in a suburban, residential setting on 135 acres of green countryside.

The University

Hawai'i Pacific University is the largest private postsecondary institution in the state of Hawai'i. The University is coeducational, with a faculty of more than 300, a student-faculty ratio of 20:1, and an average class size of 24. A wide range of counseling and other student support services are available. There are some fifty-five student organizations on campus, including the Graduate Student Organization.

Applying

Hawai'i Pacific University seeks students with academic promise, outstanding career potential, and high motivation. Applicants should complete and forward a Graduate Admissions Application, have official transcripts sent from all colleges or universities attended, and forward two letters of recommendation. International students should submit results of the TOEFL. Admissions decisions are made on a rolling basis, and applicants are notified between one and two weeks after all documents have been submitted. Applicants are encouraged to submit their applications online at the Web address listed below.

Correspondence and Information

Graduate Admissions
Hawai'i Pacific University
1164 Bishop Street, Suite 911
Honolulu, Hawai'i 96813

Telephone: 808-544-0279
866-GRAD-HPU (toll-free)
Fax: 808-544-0280
E-mail: graduate@hpu.edu
World Wide Web: http://www.hpu.edu/grad

THE FACULTY AND THEIR RESEARCH

Richard Chepkevich, M.S., USC. Information systems.
Larry Cross, Ph.D., Colorado. Economics.
Thomas Crowley, J.D., Hawai'i. Law.
Cheryl Ann Crozier, M.B.A., Hawai'i Pacific. Human resource management.
Patrick Doran, Ph.D., Georgia. Information systems.
Eric Drabkin, Ph.D., UCLA. Economics.
Peter Freeman, M.A., Florida. Communication arts.
Stanley Ghosh, Ph.D., Indiana. Strategic planning.
W. Gerald Glover, Ph.D., Florida. Quality assurance.
Randall Harakal, J.D., Widener. Law.
Bradford Harrison, M.B.A., Hawai'i Pacific. Business administration.
Gordon L. Jones, Ph.D., New Mexico. Computer applications, information systems.
Thomas Kam, M.B.A., Hawai'i. Business administration.
John Karbens, M.B.A., Ed.D., Hawai'i; CPA, CMA, CIA. Accounting, finance.
John Kros, Ph.D., Virginia. Systems engineering.
Lola Lackey, M.B.A., Seattle. Marketing, management.
David Lohmann, Ph.D., Arizona State. Marketing, management.
Ernesto Lucas, Ph.D., Hawai'i. Agricultural economics.
Ward Mardfin, Ph.D., Hawai'i. Economics.
Gunter Meissner, Ph.D., Kiel (Germany). Mathematics, derivatives.
Michael Miller, M.S., Hawai'i Pacific. Information systems.
Wallace (John) Nabers, LL.B., Duke. Law.
Ronald Paglinawan, M.S., USC. EDP auditing.
Roy Reeber, M.B.A., Pepperdine; M.S., USC. International business management, systems management.
Rodney Romig, Ph.D., Nebraska. Economics.
Lawrence Rowland, M.S., USC. Systems management.
Michael Seiler, D.B.A., Cleveland. Finance.
Derek Shigesato, J.D., Georgetown. Law.
Ronald Slepecki, M.S.I.S., Hawai'i Pacific. Information systems.
Mary Smith, M.S., Hawai'i Pacific. Information systems.
Paul Stipek, M.S., Naval Postgraduate School. Information systems.
Bradley Tamm, J.D., Western State Law. Law.
Shue-Jane Thompson, M.S., Hawai'i Pacific. Information systems.
Edwin Van Gorder, Ph.D., Stanford. Mathematics, management.
Phillip Viehl, M.B.A., Hawai'i Pacific. Finance.
James Waddington, M.B.A., Hawai'i; CPA. Accounting.
Richard Ward, Ed.D., USC. Human resource management, safety management.
Warren Wee, M.B.A., Hawai'i; Ph.D., Washington (Seattle); CPA. Accounting.
Arthur Whatley, Ph.D., Texas. Management, economics.
Leslie Wiletzky, M.A., SUNY College at Buffalo; M.P.A., Penn State. Human resource management.
Alfred Zimermann, M.B.I.S., Georgia State. Business information systems.
Larry Zimmerman, M.S., USC. Systems management.

Graduation day.

HEBREW COLLEGE

Graduate Studies

Programs of Study

Hebrew College offers two graduate degrees—a Master of Jewish Education (M.J.Ed.) and a Master of Arts in Jewish studies (M.A.) and several certificates.

The M.J.Ed., offered through the Shoolman Graduate School of Jewish Education, prepares students to pursue careers or upgrade professional credentials in the expanding field of Jewish education. Students may pursue specialty tracks in day school education, Jewish family education, early childhood Jewish education, special education in Jewish settings, school administration, youth leadership, or Jewish camp administration. The M.J.Ed. program balances formal, academic study with independent work and practical internship experience. Students are required to develop a foundation in Jewish education, general education, and Jewish studies; the 42-credit program is also individualized to support the needs and goals of each student. The Shoolman Graduate School of Jewish Education also offers certificates in Jewish family education, early childhood Jewish education, Jewish day school education, Jewish special education, and Jewish informal education, youth leadership, and camping.

The 39-credit M.A. provides a solid academic base in Jewish studies, which may be used as a foundation for rabbinic or cantorial school, or for an advanced degree in Jewish scholarship. Curricula emphasize text study and Hebrew literacy; from the study of texts in the original Hebrew, students master the subject matter and develop the skills needed to continue independent scholarship. Through a sequence of core-text courses that focus on primary sources of the biblical, rabbinic, medieval and modern periods, students gain a broad understanding of Jewish thought, history, culture, and civilization. Students specialize in an area of interest—a discipline, period, or subject—and demonstrate mastery through a major project in their final semester.

Certificate programs include a certificate in Jewish communal and clinical social work, which may be earned separately or in conjunction with a master's in social work from Simmons College. Through its Jewish Music Institute, the College also offers certificates in Jewish music and Jewish cantorial arts.

Students benefit from the College's cross-registration agreements with several nearby colleges and universities, including Boston University, Boston College, Brandeis University, Andover Newton Theological School, Simmons College, the University of Massachusetts Boston, and Northeastern University.

Typically, graduate students complete their course work within two years, although part-time students may take additional time to complete the programs.

Research Facilities

The Hebrew College Library contains more than 110,000 holdings, with special collections in modern Hebrew literature, Jewish medical ethics, Jewish education, Jewish genealogy, Holocaust studies, Hassidism, and Jewish children's literature. Through the Research Libraries Information Network, users can access a database of 53 million books, journals, maps, records, and cassettes drawn from the Judaica collections across the country, including that of the Jewish Theological Seminary in New York, Harvard University, Yale University, Princeton University, and Brandeis University.

Financial Aid

The College works with each student to develop a financial aid package. Awards are made on the basis of financial need. Preference is given to students who apply for financial aid by April 15. The College participates in all federal programs as well as in numerous scholarship programs offered by various Jewish communal organizations. The Hebrew College Stone-Teplow Families' Fund provides Jewish educators working at least 12 hours a week—including teachers, youth leaders, family educators, educational leaders, and camp professionals—with a 25 percent reduction in Hebrew College tuition on all courses taken for credit. Several Shoolman fellowships are available for students who show outstanding academic achievement and demonstrate significant promise in the field of Jewish education.

The Hebrew College Fellows Program encompasses several one-year, renewable fellowships for both full- and part-time study, awarded on a competitive basis to outstanding students enrolled in the College's Master of Jewish Education and Master of Arts in Jewish studies degree programs. The Dr. David M. Gordis Fellowship is granted to students who demonstrate exceptional potential for Jewish communal leadership. The Betty and Irving Brudnick Fellowship is awarded to an outstanding student in the field of Jewish studies. The Abraham and Sadie Shapiro Family Fellowships are given to students who are pursing a career in Jewish education and are committed to postgraduate service in the Boston Jewish community. The Edith and Eliot Shoolman Fellowship is awarded to students who are currently active in the field of Jewish education as teachers or administrators. The Betsy and Dr. Martin P. Solomon Graduate Fellowship is granted to outstanding graduate students in the field of Jewish education.

Cost of Study

Tuition for the 2002–03 academic year is $565 per credit hour.

Student Group

Although most students are drawn from the Jewish community, Hebrew College is nonsectarian and does not discriminate in admission or any matter in regard to age, gender, religion, handicap, race, color, national origin, or sexual orientation. Hebrew College students join the community of thousands of students enrolled at Boston-area colleges and universities.

Location

In December 2001, Hebrew College moved to a new, 7-acre campus in Newton Centre, a beautiful Boston suburb within easy reach of Boston's many outstanding colleges, universities, and cultural institutions. The state-of-the-art campus, designed by architect Moshe Safdie, includes new classrooms, lecture halls, administrative offices, parking facilities, a student center, cafeteria, and library. Later construction phases include an auditorium and more classrooms.

The College

Founded in 1921, Hebrew College maintains a historic commitment to Jewish learning and scholarship within a pluralistic, nonsectarian environment. Through intensive training in Jewish texts, history, literature, ethics, and Hebrew language, the College prepares students to become literate participants in the global Jewish community. Hebrew College offers graduate and undergraduate degrees and certificates in all aspects of formal and nonformal Jewish education as well as Jewish studies and Jewish music; the College also serves students of all ages through its Prozdor High School, Camp Yavneh, Ulpan, and Center for Adult Jewish Learning. In addition, the College created and directs Me'ah—One Hundred Hours of Adult Jewish Learning, a two-year program of adult study. Hebrew College is also the East Coast home of the California-based Wilstein Institute of Jewish Policy Studies, a policy research think-tank committed to the study of pivotal issues facing American Jews and the formulation of strategies to help ensure the continued growth and vitality of Jewish life.

Applying

The graduate programs of Hebrew College are open to qualified students holding a bachelor's degree from an accredited four-year college or university. Applicants are asked to provide two letters of recommendation, transcripts, and a personal statement. For the M.J.Ed., applicants are also required to provide GRE scores. All prospective students are encouraged to contact the College early in the process to arrange for an interview and campus visit.

Correspondence and Information

Ina Regosin, Dean of Students
Hebrew College
160 Herrick Road
Newton Centre, Massachusetts 02459

Telephone: 617-559-8610
800-866-4814 (toll-free)
Fax: 617-559-8601
E-mail: admissions@hebrewcollege.edu
World Wide Web: http://www.hebrewcollege.edu

THE FACULTY

Tzvi I. Abusch, Professor of Biblical Languages and Civilizations; Ph.D., Harvard.
Avi Bernstein-Nahar, Assistant Professor of Jewish Thought; Ph.D., Stanford.
Helen Cohen, Lecturer, Early Childhood Institute; M.S., Lesley.
Steven Copeland, Assistant Professor of Jewish Thought and Education; Ph.D., Harvard.
David M. Gordis, Professor of Rabbinics and President; Ph.D. and Rabbinic Ordination, Jewish Theological Seminary.
Sherry Israel, Visiting Associate Professor of Jewish Family Education; Ph.D., UCLA.
Joshua Jacobson, Visiting Professor of Jewish Music and Director, Zamir Chorale (Artists-in-Residence); D.M.A., Cincinnati.
Judith Kates, Professor of Jewish Women's Studies; Ph.D., Harvard.
Robert Kegan, Visiting Professor of Developmental Psychology; Ph.D., Harvard.
Shalva Klement, Instructor in Hebrew Language, Ulpan, and Prozdor; B.A., Hebrew.
Hila Kobliner, Visiting Instructor in Jewish Education; M.A., Harvard.
Michelle Kwitkin-Close, Visiting Lecturer in Hebrew; Ph.D. candidate, Harvard.
Lisa Lahey, Visiting Lecturer in Developmental Psychology; Ed.D., Harvard.
Barry Mesch, Stone/Teplow Families' Professor of Jewish Thought and Provost; Ph.D., Brandeis.
Jacob Meskin, Assistant Professor of Jewish Thought; Ph.D., Princeton.
Gabi Mezger, Instructor in Hebrew Language, Ulpan; Diploma, Music Teacher's Seminary (Israel), M.Ed., Boston College.
Shai Nathanson, Instructor in Hebrew Language and Director, Hebrew Language Programs and Ulpan; M.A., Lesley.
Hankus Netzky, Visiting Professor of Music; M.M., New England Conservatory.
Nehemia Polen, Professor of Jewish Thought; Ph.D., Boston University; Rabbinic Ordination, Ner Israel Rabbinical.
Gila Ramras-Rauch, Lewis H. and Selma Weinstein Professor of Jewish Literature; Ph.D., Bar Ilan (Israel).
Ina Regosin, Lecturer in Early Childhood Education, Dean of Students, and Director, Early Childhood Institute and Early Childhood Directors' Institute; M.S., Wheelock.
Susie Rodenstein, Visiting Lecturer in Jewish Education and Lecturer in Early Childhood Education; M.A., Harvard.
Sol Schimmel, Professor of Jewish Education and Psychology; Ph.D., Wayne State.
Judith Segal, Professor of Library Science and Director of the Library; D.L.S., Columbia.
Harvey Shapiro, Assistant Professor of Jewish Education and Dean, Shoolman Graduate School of Jewish Education; Ph.D. Hebrew Union–Jewish Institute of Religion (Los Angeles).
Scott Sokol, Adjunct Associate Professor of Jewish Music and Director, Jewish Music Institute; Ph.D., Johns Hopkins.
David Starr, Lecturer in Jewish History and Dean of Me'ah; Ph.D. candidate, Columbia; Rabbinic Ordination, Jewish Theological Seminary.
Naomi Steiner, Visiting Instructor in Hebrew; B.A./M.A. candidate, Hebrew University.
Joseph Stern, Assistant Professor of Jewish Law; Ph.D., Boston College; Rabbinic Ordination, Yeshiva.
Maurice Tuchman, Director Emeritus of Library Services; D.A. (library science), Simmons.
Arnold Wieder, Professor Emeritus of Rabbinic Literature; Ph.D., Brandeis; Rabbinic Ordination, Yeshiva.

HUNTER COLLEGE OF THE CITY UNIVERSITY OF NEW YORK

Programs of Study

Hunter College offers Master of Arts (M.A.) degrees in anthropology, art history, biochemistry, biological sciences, communications, economics, English literature, French, geography, history, Italian, mathematics, music, physics, psychology, Spanish, theater, and urban affairs. A Master of Public Health (M.P.H.) is offered in community health education and in public health nutrition. Master of Science (M.S.) degrees are offered in communication sciences, environmental and occupational health sciences, nursing (adult nurse practitioner, community health, gerontological, maternal/child, medical/surgical, pediatric nurse practitioner, psychiatric), social research, and speech and hearing handicapped. Master of Science in Education (M.S.Ed.) degrees are offered in elementary education–bilingual, childhood education, guidance and counseling, rehabilitation counseling, and special education (childhood, deaf, blind, severe/multiple). Master of Arts (M.A.) degrees in education are offered in biology (7–12), chemistry (7–12), physics (7–12), secondary education (English, French, Italian, Latin, mathematics, music (K–12), social studies, Spanish) and teaching English to speakers of other languages. Advanced certificates are offered in educational supervision and administration and pediatric nurse practitioner studies. Hunter also offers a Master of Fine Arts (M.F.A.) in art and creative writing, a Master of Physical Therapy (M.P.T.), a Master of Social Work (M.S.W.), and a Master in Urban Planning (M.U.P.). Master's degree programs generally require a minimum of 30 credit hours, the successful completion of a thesis or an equivalent substitute as determined by the department, and the demonstration of a reading knowledge of one foreign language or its equivalent as determined by the department. Hunter College is a major participant in the City University of New York doctoral programs. In many programs, the master's course of study is equal to the first year of university doctoral work.

Research Facilities

The collections of the Hunter College libraries are housed in the Jacqueline Grennan Wexler Library and the Art Slide Library (located at the main campus) as well as in the branch libraries at the Brookdale Campus and the School of Social Work. The libraries hold 750,000 volumes, 2,300 periodicals, and a nonprint collection that includes more than 1 million microforms and 250,000 art slides, as well as records, tapes, scores, music CDs, and videos. New computer, multimedia, and Internet labs were recently installed, and the first CD-ROM network was created. The CD-ROM network provides access to indexes, abstracts, and complete texts and multimedia resources. Access to the World Wide Web is available through Internet labs. In addition, many individual programs have their own specialized labs, research facilities, or clinics. Students should contact the academic department in which they are interested for further information.

Financial Aid

The Office of Financial Aid administers federal and state grant, loan, and work-study programs to assist students who need financial help to attend Hunter College. Students should contact the financial aid office for further information. In addition, traineeships, assistantships, fellowships, and grants are available from certain departments; students should contact the individual department for further information.

Cost of Study

In 2001–02, tuition for New York State residents was $185 per credit plus $65 for each additional contact hour or $2175 per semester for 12 or more credits. Tuition for nonresidents was $320 per credit plus $85 for each additional contact hour or $3800 per semester for 12 or more credits.

Living and Housing Costs

The Hunter College Residence Hall is currently undergoing extensive renovations. This will take the dormitories off line for the semesters occurring during the year 2001–02. More information can be obtained at http://www.hunter.cuny.edu/~reslife or by contacting the Hunter College Residence Hall at 212-481-4310.

Student Group

The 4,590 graduate students enrolled at Hunter College in fall 2001 represented a rich diversity of races, ages, and creeds. In the 2000–01 academic year, 950 master's degrees were awarded in a variety of fields.

Location

The College is anchored by its main campus at 68th Street and Lexington Avenue, a modern complex of four buildings interconnected by skywalks. The Division of the Schools of Health Professions, which includes the Hunter-Bellevue School of Nursing, one of the nation's largest nursing programs, and the School of Health Sciences, noted for its outstanding programs, is located at the Brookdale Campus on East 25th Street. The Hunter College School of Social Work, recently listed among the top twenty schools of its kind in the nation by *U.S. News & World Report,* is uptown, at East 79th Street. The Campus Schools at Park Avenue and East 94th Street—an elementary school and a high school for the gifted—are renowned (as is the College itself) for their tradition of academic excellence. On Manhattan's west side, Hunter's Studio Art Building provides students with an 8,000-square-foot gallery and their own individual studio space.

The College

Hunter College, the second-oldest college in the City University of New York System, is a coeducational, fully accredited college with a large and diverse faculty in the liberal arts and sciences and in several professional schools. In most of its programs, the College offers both undergraduate and graduate degrees. Hunter was established in 1870 as the Female Normal and High School in response to a very real need for more and better teachers in the city of New York. Because of the dramatic changes that have taken place in New York, Hunter has been able to grow from a small women's college for teachers to a coeducational, comprehensive group of liberal arts departments and professional schools. Publicly funded, Hunter became a part of the City University of New York when that system was created in 1961. Hunter celebrated its 125th anniversary in 1995. Today, with nearly 20,000 students, Hunter is the largest public college in New York City. The College continues to educate women—currently almost 71 percent of the total enrollment—and, since 1951, men.

Applying

Requirements for admission and application deadlines vary from program to program. Students should contact the appropriate office indicated below for details.

Correspondence and Information

For all programs except the School of Social Work:
Hunter College
Office of Admissions
695 Park Avenue
New York, New York 10021-5085
Telephone: 212-772-4490
Fax: 212-650-3336
E-mail: admissions@hunter.cuny.edu
World Wide Web: http://www.hunter.cuny.edu

For inquiries concerning the School of Social Work:
Hunter College School of Social Work
129 East 79 Street
New York, New York 10021
Telephone: 212-452-7005
E-mail: admissions.hcssw@hunter.cuny.edu
World Wide Web: http://www.hunter.cuny.edu/socwork

FACULTY ADVISERS

Arts and Sciences
Anthropology: Marc Edelman (telephone: 212-772-5659).
Art History: Emily Braun (telephone: 212-650-3756).
Art (studio): Joel Carreiro (telephone: 212-650-3398).
Biochemistry: Maria Tomasz (telephone: 212-772-5387).
Biological Sciences: Rivka Rudner (telephone: 212-772-5231).
Creative Writing: Elena Georgiou (telephone: 212-772-5164).
Economics: Cordelia Reimers (telephone: 212-772-5444).
English Literature: Sylvia Tomasch (telephone: 212-772-5079).
French: Julia Przybos (telephone: 212-772-5097).
Geography: Marianna Pavlovskaya (telephone: 212-772-5320).
History: Barbara Welter (telephone: 212-772-5480).
Integrated Media Arts: Jay Roman (telephone: 212-772-4470).
Italian: Maria Paynter (telephone: 212-772-5090).
Mathematics (Applied): Edward Binkowski (telephone: 212-772-4715).
Mathematics (Pure): Edward Binkowski (telephone: 212-772-4715).
Music: Poundie Burstein (telephone: 212-772-5152).
Physics: Steven Greenbaum (telephone: 212-772-4973).
Psychology: Martin Chodorow (telephone: 212-772-5618).
Social Research: Naomi Kroeger (telephone: 212-772-5581).
Spanish: Carlos Hortas (telephone: 212-772-5108).
Theater: Mira Felner (telephone: 212-772-5149).
Urban Affairs: Elaine Walsh (telephone: 212-772-5595).
Urban Planning: William Milczarski (telephone: 212-772-5601).

Health Professions
Communication Science: Dava Waltzman (telephone: 212-481-4467).
Speech and Hearing Handicapped: Carol Silverman (telephone: 212-481-4467).
Community Health Education: Philip Alcabes (telephone: 212-481-5111).
Environmental and Occupational Health Science: Jack Caravanos (telephone: 212-481-5111).
Public Health Nutrition: Arlene Spark (telephone: 212-481-7590).
Physical Therapy: Gary Krasilovsky (telephone: 212-481-4469).

Nursing
Adult Nurse Practitioner: Carole Birdsall (telephone: 212-481-7585).
Community Health Nursing: Kathleen Nokes (telephone: 212-481-7594).
Community Health Nursing/Education: Kathleen Nokes (telephone: 212-481-7594).
Gerontological Nursing: Steve Baumann (telephone: 212-481-4457).
Maternal/Child Nursing: Janet Natapoff (telephone: 212-481-5070)
Medical/Surgical Nursing: Joan Sayre (telephone: 212-481-4343).
Pediatric Nurse Practitioner: Janet Natapoff (telephone: 212-481-5070).
Psychiatric Nursing: Joan Sayre (telephone: 212-481-4343).

Education
Guidance and Counseling: Mary Kopala (telephone: 212-772-4714).
Rehabilitation Counseling: John O'Neill (telephone: 212-772-4720).
Childhood Special Education: Timothy Lackaye (telephone: 212-772-4777).
Special Education–Deaf: Kate GarnettSara Schley (telephone: 212-772-4701).
Special Education–Blind: Roseanne Silberman (telephone: 212-772-4740).
Special Education–Severe/Multiple: Roseanne Silberman (telephone: 212-772-4740).
Early Childhood Special Education: Shirley Cohen (telephone: 212-772-4708).
Supervision and Administration: Janet Patti (telephone: 212-772-4692).
Teaching English to Speakers of Other Languages (TESOL): Donald Byrd (telephone: 212-772-4691).
Childhood Education (grades 1–6): Arlene Smith (telephone: 212-772-4667).
Childhood Education (bilingual): Yvonne DeGaetano (telephone: 212-772-4683).
Early Childhood Education (birth–grade 2): Christina Taharally (telephone: 212-772-4679).
Literacy (birth–grade 6): Marianna Pavlovskaya (212-772-5320).
Biology (7–12): Rivka Rudner (telephone: 212-772-5231).
Chemistry (7–12): Pam Mills (telephone: 212-772-5331).
Earth Science: Marianna Pavlovskaya (telephone: 212-772-5320).
English: Sylvia Tomasch (telephone: 212-772-5079).
French: Julia Przybos (telephone: 212-772-5097).
Italian: Maria Paynter (telephone: 212-772-5090).
Latin: Ronni Ancona (telephone: 212-772-4962).
Math: Edward Binkowski (telephone: 212-772-4715).
Music (K–12): Poundie Burstein (telephone: 212-772-5152).
Physics (7–12): Rodney Varley (telephone: 212-772-5252).
Social Studies: Barbara Welter (telephone: 212-772-5480).
Spanish: Carlos Hortas (telephone: 212-772-5108).

ILLINOIS INSTITUTE OF TECHNOLOGY

Graduate College

Programs of Study

Illinois Institute of Technology (IIT) offers graduate degree and certificate programs in engineering and the sciences, architecture, design, technical communication, public administration, psychology, business, and law at five locations in Chicago and the surrounding suburbs. In addition, courses in many programs are offered via interactive television, at more than fifty public and corporate sites in the Chicago area; some courses and degree programs are offered via videoconferencing and/or online.

Doctoral programs include applied mathematics, architecture, biology, biomedical engineering, chemical engineering, chemistry, civil engineering, computer science, design, electrical engineering, environmental engineering, mathematics education, mechanical and aerospace engineering, metallurgical and materials engineering, molecular biochemistry and biophysics, physics, psychology, and science education.

The Master of Science degree is offered in applied mathematics, biology, chemical engineering, chemical engineering and computer science (dual-degree program), chemistry, civil engineering, computer science, computer science for teachers, computer engineering, design, electrical engineering, environmental engineering, food process engineering, food safety and technology, information architecture, manufacturing engineering, mathematics education, mechanical and aerospace engineering, metallurgical and materials engineering, molecular biochemistry and biophysics, personnel and human resources development, physics, psychology, rehabilitation counseling, science education, and technical communication and information design.

Professional master's (nonthesis) degrees are offered in analytical chemistry, architecture, chemical engineering, chemistry, construction engineering and management, design, electrical and computer engineering, electricity markets, environmental engineering, food process engineering, geoenvironmental engineering, geotechnical engineering, health physics, information technology and management, manufacturing engineering, manufacturing technology and operations, materials and chemical synthesis, mathematics education, mechanical and aerospace engineering, metallurgical and materials engineering, public administration, public works, science education, structural engineering, telecommunications and software engineering, and transportation engineering.

Certificate programs are offered in biological, chemical, and physical sciences (analytical method development; analytical spectroscopy; characterization of inorganic and organic materials; chromatography, synthesis, and characterization of organic materials; and synthesis and characterization of inorganic materials); chemical and environmental engineering (air resources bioengineering, food process engineering, food safety and technology, hazardous waste engineering, indoor air quality, particle processing, pharmaceutical processing, physiology for pharmaceutical applications, polymer synthesis and characterization/processing, process operations management, water and wastewater treatment); civil and architectural engineering (construction management, earthquake and wind engineering design, geoenvironmental engineering, infrastructure engineering and management, and transportation systems planning); computer science (educational technology, intelligent information systems, Internet, networking and telecommunications, and software engineering); electrical and computer engineering (advanced electronics, applied electromagnetics, communications systems, computer engineering, control systems, electricity markets, power engineering, signal processing, and wireless communications engineering); Institute of Psychology: rehabilitation psychology (psychiatric rehabilitation); and Lewis Department of Humanities: (ethics in the workplace: business, engineering and government, instructional design, and technical communications).

Research Facilities

All academic units at IIT have the laboratories and equipment essential for high-level graduate study. Faculty members and students also engage in research at IIT's renowned research centers. IIT's library system includes the Paul Galvin Library on the Main Campus, the Downtown Campus Information Center, the Chicago-Kent Law Library, the Stuart Graduate School of Business Library, and the Louis W. Biegler Library at the Rice Campus. IIT's Computing and Network Services maintains excellent computing laboratories featuring networked PCs and workstation clusters. Academic units, research centers, and faculty members have additional dedicated computer networks for their academic and research activities.

Financial Aid

Financial assistance in the form of fellowships, teaching assistantships, research assistantships, and scholarships are awarded to a limited number of candidates with outstanding credentials. These awards include varying stipends and full or partial tuition. Loans for eligible students may be arranged through the Financial Aid Office. Primary consideration for graduate financial aid is given to applications received before March 1 for fall, September 1 for spring, and April 1 for summer.

Cost of Study

In 2002–03, tuition is $610 per credit hour. International students are required to register for a minimum of 9 credits or the equivalent per semester. Some programs typically require a course load of 12 to 15 credit hours per semester.

Living and Housing Costs

Housing is available for graduate students in IIT residence halls; the 2002–03 cost of room and board ranges from $5842 to $7704. Unfurnished IIT apartments are available for graduate students at costs ranging from $579 to $1145 per month, including utilities. Early application for apartments is recommended. Several off-campus apartment complexes are located within walking distance of various IIT campuses.

Student Group

IIT's total enrollment in 2001–02 was approximately 6,050. Of this number, 1,060 were enrolled as full-time graduate students and 1,501 as part-time graduate students; 1,842 were undergraduates and the remainder were enrolled at the Chicago-Kent College of Law or the Stuart Graduate School Of Business.

Location

IIT's Main Campus is located 3 miles south of Chicago's Loop. The Main Campus, designed by Ludwig Mies van der Rohe and regarded internationally as a landmark of 20th century architecture, occupies fifty buildings on a 120-acre site, and includes research institutes, libraries, laboratories, residence halls, a sports center, and other facilities. The Downtown Campus is in the Loop near the city's financial trading, banking, and legal centers. The Institute of Design is in the North Loop. The Rice Campus is in suburban Wheaton, convenient to the Interstate 88 research and technology corridor west of the city. The Moffett Campus is in southwest suburban Summit-Argo.

The Institute

Illinois Institute of Technology was formed in 1940 by the merger of Armour Institute of Technology (founded 1890) and Lewis Institute (founded 1896). IIT is a member of the prestigious Association of Independent Technological Universities (AITU).

Applying

Students may be admitted to graduate studies at the beginning of fall or spring semesters. Applications and all supporting documents should be received in the Graduate Admissions Office not later than June 1 or November 1 for matriculation in the fall or spring semester, respectively. The application deadline for the summer session is May 1. Deadlines for architecture and psychology are earlier. Applications that include requests for consideration for financial aid should be submitted by the March 1 for fall and September 1 for spring deadlines. Deadlines may vary depending on the degree program. Detailed information and online application forms are available at http://www.grad.iit.edu.

Correspondence and Information

Graduate College
Illinois Institute of Technology
3300 South Federal Street, Room 301A
Chicago, Illinois 60616

Telephone: 312-567-3024
E-mail: inquiry.grad@iit.edu
World Wide Web: http://www.grad.iit.edu

GRADUATE DEGREE AND CERTIFICATE PROGRAMS

College of Architecture: M.Arch, Ph.D. Areas of specialization: tall buildings, long-span structures, mixed-use buildings, energy-conscious design, computer-aided design, urban planning and design.

Department of Applied Mathematics: M.S., Ph.D. Areas of specialization: applied analysis, computational mathematics, discrete applied mathematics, stochastic analysis.

Department of Biological, Chemical and Physical Sciences

Biology: M.S., M.A.S.*, Ph.D., graduate certificate programs. Areas of specialization: biochemistry, biotechnology, cell and molecular biology, microbiology.

Chemistry: M.S., M.A.S.*, Ph.D., graduate certificate programs. Areas of specialization: analytical chemistry, environmental chemistry, materials chemistry, organic chemistry, polymer chemistry, chemical and materials synthesis.

Molecular Biochemistry and Biophysics: M.S., Ph.D. Areas of specialization: biological chemistry, biological physics, cell and molecular biology, structural biology.

Physics: M.S., M.A.S.*, Ph.D. Areas of specialization: accelerator physics, computational physics, condensed-matter physics, health physics, high-energy physics, structural biophysics.

Department of Chemical and Environmental Engineering

Chemical Engineering: M.S., M.Ch.E, Ph.D., graduate certificate programs. Areas of specialization: bioengineering, electrochemical science and engineering, energy/environment/economics, environmental engineering, food process engineering, particle technology, pharmaceutical processing, polymer science/engineering, process design/control.

Environmental Engineering: M.S., M.A.S.*, Ph.D. Areas of specialization: air pollution engineering, chemical engineering, environmental chemistry, environmental resource management, hazardous-waste engineering, water/wastewater engineering.

Department of Civil and Architectural Engineering

Civil Engineering: M.S., M.A.S.*, Ph.D., graduate certificate programs. Areas of specialization: architectural engineering, construction management and engineering, geotechnical engineering, public works, structural engineering, transportation engineering.

Department of Computer Science

Computer Science: M.S., M.A.S.*, Master of Science for Teachers, Ph.D., graduate certificate programs. Areas of specialization: intelligent information systems, telecommunications and networking, software engineering.

Department of Electrical and Computer Engineering

Electrical and Computer Engineering: M.S., M.A.S.*, Ph.D., graduate certificate programs. Areas of specialization: computer architecture, computer networks, control systems, digital signal processing, medical imaging, microelectronics, microwave electronics, power electronics, power systems, VLSI design, wireless communications.

Lewis Department of the Humanities

Technical Communications and Information Design: M.S., graduate certificate programs. Areas of specialization: information architecture, technical communication and information design.

Department of Mechanical, Materials Mechanical and Aerospace Engineering

Mechanical and Aerospace Engineering: M.S., M.A.S., Ph.D., graduate certificate programs. Areas of specialization: design and manufacturing, dynamics and controls, fluid dynamics, solid mechanics, thermal sciences.

Manufacturing Engineering: M.S., M.A.S., graduate certificate programs. Area of specialization: manufacturing engineering.

Metallurgical and Materials Engineering: M.S., M.A.S., Ph.D., graduate certificate programs. Areas of specialization: advanced metals and materials, manufacturing process engineering, polymer and ceramic science/engineering.

Pritzker Institute of Medical Engineering: Ph.D. in biomedical engineering.

Department of Social Sciences

Public Administration: M.P.A. Area of specialization: public administration.

Institute of Psychology: M.S., M.A.S.*, Ph.D., graduate certificate programs. Areas of specialization: rehabilitation counseling, clinical psychology, personnel and human resource development, industrial/organizational psychology, psychiatric rehabilitation, rehabilitation psychology.

Institute of Design: M.S., M.A.S.*, Ph.D. Areas of specialization: photography, human-centered design, design planning.

Stuart School of Business: M.B.A., M.S. in finance, M.S. in environmental management, M.S. in marketing communications., M.S. in operations/technology management, Ph.D. in management science.

Chicago Kent College of Law: J.D., J.D./M.B.A., J.D./M.S. in financial markets and trading.

Center for Law and Financial Markets: M.S. in financial markets and trading, M.S. in financial markets and regulation.

For details on programs in business, applicants should call 312-906-6544 or visit http://www.stuart.iit.edu. For details on programs in law, applicants should call 312-906-5020 or visit http://www.kentlaw.edu.

IIT RESEARCH CENTERS

Selected Research Centers at IIT include:

The Center for Accelerator and Particle Physics provides a locus for interdisciplinary activities at IIT aimed at the continued development of research in elementary particle physics, at developing new particle-accelerator technologies, and at education and outreach both to the educational, business, philanthropic, and general public sectors and promotes involvement in research programs through a close working relationship with other universities in the region and with Fermilab. Daniel Kaplan, Director.

The Electric Power and Power Electronics Center (EPPEC) contributes to research and development in electric power and power electronics technologies. The center sponsors technical studies for industrial partners, visits by technical scientists on related subjects, scholarships for potential candidates, and degree programs and short courses on electric power and power electronics. Mohammad Shahidehpour, Director; Ali Emadi, Assistant Director.

The Center for Electrochemical Science and Engineering conducts basic and applied research primarily in fuel cells and batteries, while preparing students for a career in advanced energy technology. Robert J. Selman, Director; Eugene Smotkin, Assistant Director.

The Center for Excellence in Polymer Science and Engineering, established with a grant from Amoco Foundation, concentrates research and educational efforts on processing raw polymer materials into finished products, analyzing the properties of polymers, and manufacturing and recycling polymers. David Venerus, Director.

The Center for Synchrotron Radiation Research and Instrumentation promotes application of the tools and techniques of synchrotron radiation to science and engineering research, with a particular focus on developing experimental beam line facilities to serve the needs of various collaborative access teams at the Advanced Photon Source at Argonne National Laboratory. Tim Morrison, Director.

Energy+Power Center offers research and education programs that respond to the needs of the energy and power industries. The center's activities include the Energy/Environmental/Economics (E3) program. Henry R. Linden, Director.

The Fluid Dynamics Research Center conducts experiments and theoretical studies on fluid flow management and control, particularly in the area of boundary layer turbulence, applying the principles of computational fluid dynamics. The center is the site of the National Diagnostic Facility, the world's largest university wind tunnel, fully dedicated to basic research, and is supported by the Air Force Office of Scientific Research and the Office of Naval Research. David R. Williams, Director.

The Particle Technology and Crystallization Center (PTCC) is devoted to research in the areas of nucleation, crystallization, particle technology, and characterization, aimed at faster development of new pharmaceutical compounds, development of new solid forms, and reduced time to bring a new compound to market. The center is a collaboration of IIT, Purdue University, and Massachusetts Institute for Technology. Alan Myerson, Director of the Center for IIT.

The National Center for Food Safety and Technology at the IIT Moffett Campus is a consortium comprised of IIT, IITRI, the U.S. Food and Drug Administration, the University of Illinois and industrial sponsors, to advance the safety and quality of the food supply, through research and education programs and extensive pilot plant facilities in food biotechnology, food packaging and food process control. Charles E. Sizer, Director.

The Pritzker Institute of Medical Engineering explores the application of engineering instrumentation and concepts to the solution of health-care problems in such areas as implantable drug infusion devices, cardiac pacing, implantable microstimulators, and assistive devices. Vincent Turitto, Director.

The Thermal Processing Technology Center performs high-quality basic and applied research in thermal processing technology of interest to the primary metals and manufacturing industry. Multidisciplinary research teams provide innovative solutions to industrial materials processing problems. Dr. Philip Nash, Director.

---

*Professional Master's Degrees (nonthesis only): A generic name used here for a wide variety of professional master's degrees in several of the areas of specialization.

ILLINOIS STATE UNIVERSITY

Graduate School

Programs of Study

Illinois State University offers graduate programs in the Colleges of Applied Science and Technology, Arts and Sciences, Business, Education, Fine Arts, and Nursing.

The College of Applied Science and Technology offers the M.S. in agribusiness; applied computer science; environmental health and safety; health, physical education, and recreation; and industrial technology. Both the M.A. and M.S. degrees are offered by the Departments of Criminal Justice Sciences and Family and Consumer Sciences.

The College of Arts and Sciences offers the Ph.D. in biological sciences, English studies, mathematics education, and school psychology. Both the M.A. and the M.S. are available in communication, economics, English, historical archaeology, history, mathematics, political science, psychology, sociology, speech pathology/audiology, and writing. The M.S. degree is also offered in biological sciences, chemistry, and geohydrology, and the M.A. is also offered in foreign languages. The S.S.P. degree is awarded in school psychology.

The College of Business offers the M.B.A. The M.S. and B.S./M.P.A. are offered in accounting.

The College of Education offers the Ph.D. in educational administration and the Ed.D. in curriculum and instruction, educational administration, and special education. The M.S. is awarded in curriculum and instruction, educational administration, and special education. The M.S. in Education is offered in curriculum and instruction, educational administration, reading, and special education.

The College of Fine Arts offers the M.F.A., M.A, and M.S. in both art and theater. The Department of Music offers both the M.M. and the M.M.Ed. degrees. An M.S. in Arts Technology is also offered.

The College of Nursing offers an M.S.N. degree and a Post-Master's FNP certificate.

Research Facilities

The University library provides extensive access to state and national databases in addition to its own collection of more than 1.9 million volumes. The University maintains both an elementary and a secondary laboratory school in which graduate students may conduct educational research. Each department at Illinois State University provides students with both the laboratories and equipment needed for graduate study and access to the University's comprehensive computer services.

Financial Aid

Federal Perkins Loans, Federal Stafford Student Loans, and Federal Work-Study awards are offered to students with demonstrated financial need. State grants include Illinois Military Scholarships and various teacher shortage, minority, and administration scholarships. Both teaching and research assistantships, including tuition waivers, are arranged through individual departments. GI bill benefits, plus fellowship/traineeship programs and several privately financed scholarships, are available.

Cost of Study

In 2002–03, tuition and fees for full-time (12 hours) state resident students are $2003 per semester; out-of-state students pay $3663.

Living and Housing Costs

The University offers a variety of room options in residence halls and a number of meal plans from which to choose. The 2002–03 cost of room and board is $4548 per year for a multiple-occupancy room and the basic meal plan. Single and married graduate students (with or without dependents) may qualify for University-owned apartments. Enrollment in a degree program is required. Rental rates in 2001–02 ranged from $266 to $378 per month. Early application for apartments is recommended.

Student Group

Illinois State University's total enrollment is approximately 20,000; of this number, about 3,000 are enrolled as full- or part-time graduate students. Men and women are enrolled in approximately equal numbers, and minority groups are represented.

Location

Illinois State University is located in the twin cities of Bloomington-Normal (population 100,000) and is easily accessible by car, bus, train, or plane. Amtrak offers train service to and from Chicago, Milwaukee, St. Louis, and points along the way, and various bus lines provide service to all points in the state. Airlines provide daily passenger service to Chicago, Detroit, Minneapolis, St. Louis, Denver, and points west. The Bloomington-Normal area is reached by one of the best highway systems in the state; the twin cities serve as the hub for Interstates 74, 55, and 39 and U.S. 51, the major north-south route in Illinois.

The University

Abraham Lincoln drafted the documents establishing Illinois State Normal University, which was founded in 1857 as the first public institution of higher education in Illinois. The University first began offering graduate work in several departments in 1943. In the 1960s, after more than a century as a single-purpose teacher-education institution, Illinois State began to offer liberal arts as well as teacher-education programs, introduced doctoral-level curricula, and renamed the institution Illinois State University.

Applying

Any student who has completed work for a bachelor's degree from a regionally accredited institution may apply for admission to the Graduate School. Students at the master's level and Specialist in School Psychology (S.S.P.) level should file an application and arrange for Graduate Record Examinations General and Subject Test scores (if required by a department) and official transcripts to be sent at the time of application. The Graduate Management Admission Test is required for applicants to the College of Business. Applicants to the Master of Fine Arts and doctoral programs should file their materials at the time of application.

Correspondence and Information

Office of Admissions
Hovey Hall 201
Campus Box 2200
Illinois State University
Normal, Illinois 61790-2200

Telephone: 309-438-2181
800-366-2478 (toll-free)
309-438-2006 (TTY/TDD)
E-mail: gradadm@ilstu.edu
World Wide Web: http://www.ilstu.edu/admissions

FACULTY HEADS

Gary D. McGinnis, Vice President of Graduate Studies, Research, and International Education.
Sandra L. Little, Director of Graduate Studies.

Deans
College of Applied Science and Technology: J. Robert Rossman, Ph.D.
College of Arts and Sciences: John Freed, Ph.D.
College of Business: Dixie L. Mills, Ph.D.
College of Education: Dianne Ashby, Ph.D.
College of Fine Arts: Roosevelt Newson, Ph.D.
Mennonite College of Nursing: Nancy Ridenour, Ph.D.
University Libraries: Cheryl Elzy, C.A.S.

Graduate Program Directors
Accounting: Max Rexroad, Ph.D.
Agriculture: Kerry Tudor, Ph.D.
Applied Computer Science: Tibor Gyires, Ph.D.
Art: Ron Mottram, M.S.
Biological Sciences: Charles Thompson, Ph.D.
Chemistry: John Hansen, Ph.D.
Communication: Mark E. Comadena, Ph.D.
Criminal Justice Sciences: Beverly Smith, Ph.D.
Curriculum and Instruction: Dent Rhodes, Ph.D. (Doctoral Program); Vicky Morgan, Ph.D. (Master's Program).
Economics: Hassan Mohammadi, Ph.D.
Educational Administration and Foundations: Patricia Klass, Ph.D.
English: Ron Strickland, Ph.D.
Family and Consumer Sciences: Maria Canabal, Ph.D.
Foreign Languages: Alice Berry, Ph.D.
Geohydrology: James Carter, Ph.D.
Health, Physical Education, and Recreation: William Vogler, Ph.D.
Historical Archaeology: Charles Orser, Ph.D.
History: Lee Beier, Ph.D.
Industrial Technology: Dan Brown, Ph.D.
Mathematics: Norma Presmeg, Ph.D. (Doctoral Program); Mike Plantholt, Ph.D. (Master's Program).
M.B.A.: Lee Graf, D.B.A.
Music: Joe Neisler, M.M.
Nursing: Sara Campbell, D.N.S.; Denise Wilson, Ph.D.
Political Science: Lane Crothers, Ph.D.
Psychology: Mark Swerdlik, Ph.D. (S.S.P. and Doctoral Programs); Sam Catanzaro, Ph.D. (Master's Program).
Reading: Kathleen Crawford, Ph.D.
Sociology and Anthropology: Barbara Heyl, Ph.D.
Specialized Educational Development: Barbara Fulk, Ph.D. (Doctoral Program); Cindy Lawson, Ph.D. (Master's Program).
Speech Pathology and Audiology: Linda Bowman, M.S.
Theatre: Kim Pereira, Ph.D.

IMMACULATA COLLEGE

College of Graduate Studies

Programs of Study

Immaculata College offers programs of study leading to the Master of Arts in counseling psychology, cultural and linguistic diversity (bilingual studies and teaching English to speakers of other languages), educational leadership, music therapy, nutrition education (with an ADA Dietetic Internship), and organization leadership (with a concentration in organizational effectiveness). Also available are curricula leading to the Doctor of Education (Ed.D.) in educational leadership, the Doctor of Psychology (Psy.D.) in clinical psychology, and the Doctor of Psychology (Psy.D.) in school psychology. The Doctor of Psychology in clinical psychology is accredited by the American Psychological Association. Pennsylvania certification for school nurses, school superintendents, intermediate unit directors, elementary and secondary school teachers, school psychologists, elementary and secondary school guidance counselors, principals, special education, and supervisor for curriculum and instruction, special education, and speciality areas is also offered. Certificates are available in teaching English to speakers of other languages (TESOL), expressive arts, organizational effectiveness, and existential humanistic psychotherapy.

The total semester hours required in each master's program are as follows: 48 credits in counseling psychology (48 with elementary school counselor certification, 51 with secondary school counselor certification, 60 with school psychologist certification); 39 credits in cultural and linguistic diversity; 36 credits in educational leadership; 40 credits in music therapy; 45 credits in nutrition education; and 39 credits in organization leadership.

An unusual feature of the programs is the liberal arts focus in the required 9-credit core curriculum. The core, along with course work in the area of specific concentration, provides an integrative, holistic, and humanistic approach to graduate education. Through close, ongoing advisement as well as the curriculum and career counseling, each student's personal development is assisted and monitored while he or she acquires the strong theoretical and practical preparation necessary for responsible professional practice.

The College of Graduate Studies is sensitive to the needs of the adult learner. Classes are offered in the late afternoon, evenings, and weekends to accommodate both part-time and full-time students. Innovative accelerated courses covering special topics are offered in intensive time blocks for elective credit or seminar experience.

Research Facilities

Gabriele Library is a freestanding 52,000-square-foot library that offers the latest advances in Internet and electronic access. With subscriptions to ERIC, PsycInfo, Registry of Nursing Research, Academic Abstracts, CINAHL, FirstSearch, and LEXIS-NEXIS, the Gabriele Library serves the needs of students who are conducting research in the areas of education, psychology, business, science, humanities, health, and many other fields. With online journal services, such as Project Muse and Academic Press, there is full-text availability of a wide variety of quality research journals. These resources are in addition to the fully integrated online book catalog. The library offers an AV/computer room with stereo, VCR, laserdisc, and other audiovisual equipment as well as PCs and printers; a fully equipped media classroom; closed-circuit TV room; video-editing room; group study rooms; and a digitized microfilm/fiche reader/printer.

Financial Aid

Seventy percent of the students receive financial aid. Federal Stafford Student Loans (subsidized and unsubsidized) and Federal Perkins Loans are available to students enrolled at least half-time in any discipline. Merit scholarships are awarded annually in a competitive process.

Cost of Study

Estimated tuition for 2002–03 is $400 per credit for 500- and 600-level courses and $640 per credit for 700-level courses. The general College fee is $50 each semester. The practicum fee varies with the program. The graduation fee is approximately $100.

Living and Housing Costs

Most students commute to campus. The College is located in a rapidly growing suburban area offering many off-campus housing options, the cost of which varies widely.

Student Group

Total enrollment at Immaculata College is approximately 3,000. The graduate student body of 800 women and men comprises recent college graduates, professionals with several years of experience in their field, and those returning to study after a number of years.

Students Outcomes

Students leaving Immaculata College's graduate programs typically are quickly engaged in positions with the helping professions. Many students come to Immaculata College's graduate programs to study part-time, while continuing their full-time employment with an eye toward advancement as a result of their studies. Other graduates report that their degree at Immaculata College has allowed them to make a complete career change, and that they have generally found employment within a few months of graduation in fields that are closely allied to their studies. Employers frequently report their satisfaction with the quality and depth of preparation they find in the Immaculata graduates they hire.

Location

Immaculata's 390-acre campus overlooks the rapidly growing Chester Valley and is located in Frazer, Pennsylvania, on the Main Line, about 20 miles west of Philadelphia. Proximity to Philadelphia provides access to a great many cultural, academic, and recreational facilities. The College's close working relationships with the surrounding community offer excellent resources for internships, practicums, and professional experiences.

The College

Immaculata is a fully accredited Catholic liberal arts college. Founded in 1920 by the Sisters, Servants of the Immaculate Heart of Mary, the College began the Graduate Division in 1983.

The expansion of program offerings in the College of Graduate Studies is yet another example of Immaculata's continuing commitment to meeting the needs of a rapidly changing, highly complex, and diversified society. Immaculata's tradition of excellence and creative, responsive innovation is exemplified in its College of Graduate Studies.

Applying

The deadlines for those seeking admission to the Psy.D. programs in clinical or school psychology are November 1 for a January start, March 1 for a May start, or June 1 for a September start. Application deadlines for the Ed.D. program are November 1, March 1, and June 1. The application fee is $50. Applications to the master's and certification/certificate programs are welcomed throughout the year and should be accompanied by a $25 application fee. Applicants are to forward official transcripts of all completed undergraduate and graduate work, three recommendations from academic and professional sources, and a writing sample. Application materials, interview appointments, and campus visit information are available by writing, calling, or e-mailing the College of Graduate Studies, Immaculata College. Open houses are held three times per year.

Additional requirements may include acceptable scores on either the Miller Analogies Test or the Graduate Record Examinations. Music therapy applicants are required to take a music entrance exam. Educational leadership and administration program candidates must provide a copy of their teaching certificate, and school psychology doctoral students must provide a copy of their certification. Applicants should contact the graduate office for more specific program requirements and information.

Correspondence and Information

College of Graduate Studies
King Road, Campus Box 500
Immaculata College
Immaculata, Pennsylvania 19345-0500

Telephone: 610-647-4400 Ext. 3211 or 3212
Fax: 610-993-8550
E-mail: graduate@immaculata.edu

THE FACULTY

Faculty members are listed below according to department. Those who also teach in the core are indicated by an asterisk.

Sr. Ann M. Heath, Dean of the College of Graduate Studies; Ph.D., Bryn Mawr.

Core
Ann Reinsmith, D.Min., Eastern Baptist Theological Seminary.
Joseph P. Healy, Ph.L., Saint Paul.
Thomas E. Legere, Ph.D., Union (Ohio).
Sr. Jane Anne Molinaro, Ph.D., Ohio State.

Cultural and Linguistic Diversity
Margaret van Naerssen, Coordinator; Ph.D., USC.
Mufid James Hannush,, Ph.D., Duquesne.
Kalala Kabongo-Mianda, Ph.D., Pennsylvania.
Joanna Labov, Ph.D., Pennsylvania.
Suzanne Tapper, M.A., Rutgers.

Educational Leadership/Administration
Sr. Anne Marie Burton, Chair; Ed.D., Temple.
Percy Bland, Ed.D., Immaculata.
Karen Brofee, Ed.D., Temple.
Joseph J. Corabi, Ed.D., Widener.
Sr. Carol Anne Couchara, Ed.D., Lehigh.
Karen Florentine, Ed.D., Immaculata.
Thomas Kent, Ed.D., Pennsylvania.
Lee McFadden, Ed.D., Immaculata.
David Morgan, Ed.D., Pennsylvania.
Kathleen Nolan, Ph.D., Saint Louis.
Dianna Richardson, Ph.D., Virginia Tech.
Carolyn Trohoski, Ed.D., Pennsylvania.
John Wingerter, Ed.D., Temple.
Mary Ellen Wrabley, Ed.D., Temple.
*Charlotte R. Zales, Ed.D., Lehigh.

Music Therapy
Sr. Jean Anthony Gileno, Chair; Ph.D., Temple; MT-BC.
George Allen, Ph.D., Temple.
*JoEllyn Beck, Ph.D., Temple; MT-BC.
Paul Butler, B.Mus., Kutztown; M.F.P.
*William Carr, D.M.A., Catholic University.
Robert Cerulli, M.M., Trenton State.
Sr. Cecile Marie Phelan, D.M.A., Temple.
Joseph F. Reilly, M.A., Immaculata; MT-BC.

Nutrition Education
Laura B. Frank, Chair; Ph.D., Temple.
Sr. M. Carroll Isselmann, Ed.D., Rutgers; RD.
Susan W. Johnston, M.S., West Chester; RD.
Lorraine Matthews, M.S., Drexel; RD.
Diane Mattiford, M.B.A., St. Joseph's (Philadelphia); RD.
Vicki Schwartz, M.S., Drexel; RD, CNSD.

Organization Studies
Janice Marks Jacobs, Chair; Ph.D., Temple.
Janet F. Kane, Ed.D., Johns Hopkins.
Rod Napier, Ph.D., Chicago.
Judy Passerini, M.S., Penn State.
Julie Roberts, Ph.D., Temple.
Julie Ryan, Ph.D., Capella.
Ed Travis, Ed.D., Massachusetts.

Psychology
Jed A. Yalof, Chair; Psy.D., Illinois School of Professional Psychology; ABPP.
Pamela Abraham, Psy.D, Baylor.
*Sr. Kathleen Mary Burns, Ed.D., Virginia.
Maria Cuddy-Casey, Ph.D., Nova Southeastern.
Barbara W. Domingoes, Ph.D., Bryn Mawr.
Janet L. Etzi, Psy.D., Widener.
Sabrina Ford, Ph.D., Iowa.
Charles Gleich, Ph.D., Tennessee.
Paul Haughton, Psy.D., Hahnemann.
Joanne Hirko, Ph.D., Southern California University for Professional Studies.
Sr. Agnes Hughes, Ph.D., Fordham.
Todd Lewis, Ph.D., Drexel.
Marijo Lucas, Ph.D., Auburn.
Monica McHale-Small, Ph.D., Pennsylvania.
*Sr. Jeannine Marie O'Kane, Ph.D., Fordham.
*Ronald Pekala, Ph.D., Michigan State.
Angela Roman, M.A., Towson.
Bonnie Clement Socket, Ph.D., Temple.

RESEARCH

Cultural and Linguistic Diversity (M.A.): Second-language acquisition, sociolinguistics, phonology, Caribbean literature and culture, ESL, TESOL.

Counseling Psychology (M.A.), Clinical Psychology (Psy.D.), and **School Psychology (Psy.D.):** Supervision, ethics, psychology of teaching, gender, gerontology, sexuality, cultural diversity, women's issues, psychoanalytic psychotherapy, existentialism.

Educational Leadership/Administration (M.A., Ed.D.): Performance assessment, cooperative learning, school-based management, special education, whole language.

Music Therapy (M.A.): Biofeedback music laboratory research, experimental research in music therapy, sound beam, world music, improvisation.

Nutrition Education (M.A.): Obesity and weight control, nutrition counseling, mentoring of students in dietetics, multicultural nutrition, pediatric nutrition.

INDIANA STATE UNIVERSITY

School of Graduate Studies

Programs of Study

Indiana State University offers graduate programs in the College of Arts and Sciences and the Schools of Business, Education, Health and Human Performance, Nursing, and Technology.

The College of Arts and Sciences offers the Ph.D. in geography and life sciences and the Psy.D. in clinical psychology. The Department of Art offers the M.F.A. The Department of Music offers M.M. and M.M.E. degrees. The Department of Political Science offers the M.P.A. Both the M.A. and the M.S. are available in communication, criminology, English, foreign languages, history, life sciences, political science, psychology, science education, and sociology. The M.A. degree is also offered in art, earth sciences, geography, and humanities. The M.S. degree is also offered in chemistry, family and consumer sciences, geology, and social studies. The School of Business offers the M.B.A. The School of Education offers the Ph.D. in curriculum and instruction, educational administration, and guidance and psychological services with specializations in either counseling psychology or school psychology. The Ed.S. degree is offered in school psychology and school administration. The M.Ed. is offered in curriculum and instruction, early childhood education, elementary education, reading, school administration, school counselor, and school psychology. The M.A. and M.S. are awarded in communication disorders, counseling psychology, educational media, educational psychology, special education, and student affairs administration. The M.S. is offered in marriage and family therapy. The School of Health and Human Performance offers the M.A. and M.S. in athletic training, health, physical education, and recreation and sport management. The School of Nursing awards the M.S. in nursing and a combined M.S./M.B.A. in nursing/business administration. The School of Technology offers the M.A. and M.S. in technology education; the M.S. in electronics and computer technology, human resource development, and industrial technology; and the Ph.D. in technology management.

Research Facilities

Indiana State University Libraries house more than 1 million items and subscribe to more than 5,000 periodicals. These can be accessed through an online system that also connects with other college libraries in Terre Haute and Indiana. All students enrolled at ISU can receive a computer account, which gives them access to the University computer network. Several departments offer specialized research facilities. The Psychology Clinic serves as a training facility for clinical psychology doctoral students. The Porter School Psychology Center provides research opportunities for students in counseling and school psychology. The ISU Remote Sensing Laboratory specializes in earth resources analysis using computer-aided processing of satellite data. The Technology Services Center engages in cooperative research with industry using CAD/CAM and other related technologies. A Radiation Laboratory provides students experience with the latest technology. The Center for Research and Management Services utilizes students to provide research for local area and statewide businesses in fields of economic development and targeted industry studies.

Financial Aid

Graduate students may apply through the School of Graduate Studies for master's-level assistantships, both academic year and summer; doctoral-level fellowships, both academic year and summer; scholarships or tuition and fee waivers, exclusive of building and student services fees, for up to 21 hours per academic year; Paul A. Witty Fellowships for students specializing in the education of gifted and creative children; and the Gertrude and Theodore Debs Memorial Fellowship for students specializing in American labor and reform movements. Applications received prior to March 1 will be given preference. Graduate students interested in the Federal Perkins Loan (National Direct Student Loans), Federal Stafford Student Loan program, PLUS loans, or College Work-Study Program should contact the Office of Student Financial Aid.

Cost of Study

Tuition and fees for the 2000–01 academic year were $154 per semester hour for in-state students and $351 per semester hour for out-of-state students. The maximum load for fall and spring semesters is 12 semester hours. Summer Session I runs eight weeks with three-, five-, and eight-week class options. A maximum of 9 credit hours may be earned during Session I. Summer Session II runs five weeks, and a maximum of 6 credit hours may be earned.

Living and Housing Costs

The basic hall rate is $4603 for a residence hall room. Family apartments are available as furnished or unfurnished and have one- to three-bedroom options. Costs range from $349 to $550 per month, including utilities and campus phone. Low-cost housing is also available in the surrounding community.

Student Group

The Indiana State University graduate student population of more than 1,600 is characterized by diversity. Students come to Indiana State University from all fifty states and from sixty-two countries. International students comprise 13 percent of the graduate student population, while students from outside of Indiana comprise another 17 percent. Approximately 6 percent of the graduate student population are students of color. Fifty-four percent of the graduate students are women. The average graduate student age is 33.

Location

The campus is located adjacent to the central business district of Terre Haute, Indiana, which is an industrial and commercial city of approximately 61,000 located in west-central Indiana. Cultural activities include amateur and professional theatrical productions, symphonies, and art exhibits. Excellent county and state parks are within easy driving distance. The city is convenient to the four major metropolitan areas of Indianapolis, St. Louis, Chicago, and Cincinnati.

The University and The School

Indiana State University has a tradition of dedicated interest in high-quality graduate education. Indiana State University has grown during its 133-year history from Indiana State Normal School to Indiana State Teachers College and Indiana State College to full university status. The School offers a variety of graduate programs, with more than sixty courses of study leading to a master's or doctoral degree. Since there are only approximately 1,500 graduate students, this diversity of programs assures a close mentoring experience and significant research opportunities.

Applying

All application materials should be received by the School of Graduate Studies at least two months prior to the student's first registration. Applicants should check with the department for specific deadlines or additional information required by the department. All applicants must submit a $35 nonrefundable application fee and official transcript from each institution previously attended. International students must submit a TOEFL score of 550 or better. Students applying to the Ed.S., doctoral, and selected master's programs must submit scores on the General Test of the Graduate Record Examinations and five letters of recommendation. M.B.A. applicants must submit scores on the Graduate Management Admission Test. M.F.A. applicants must submit twenty works completed in the preceding eighteen months.

Correspondence and Information

Dr. K. K. Bentil, AIC
Dean
School of Graduate Studies
Indiana State University
Terre Haute, Indiana 47809

Telephone: 812-237-3087
Fax: 812-237-8060
E-mail: kbentil@indstate.edu
World Wide Web: http://www.indstate.edu/sogs

THE FACULTY

Deans
Diane Michelfelder, Ph.D.; Dean, College of Arts and Sciences.
David R. Hopkins, Ph.D.; Dean, School of Business.
C. Jack Maynard, Ph.D.; Dean, School of Education
K. K. Bentil, Ph.D.; Dean, School of Graduate Studies; AIC.
Barbara Passmore, Ph.D.; Dean, School of Health and Human Performance and Professor of Physical Education.
Bonnie Saucier, Ph.D.; Dean, School of Nursing and Professor of Nursing.
W. Tad Foster, Ph.D.; Dean, School of Technology and Professor of Construction Technology.

Department Chairpersons and Directors of Graduate Studies
Art: dele jegede, Ph.D., Acting Chairperson.
Athletic Training: Mitchell L. Cordova, Ph.D., Acting Chairperson and Assistant Professor.
Chemistry: Arthur Halpern, Ph.D., Chairperson and Professor.
Communication: Richard Vincent, Ph.D., Chairperson and Professor.
Communication Disorders and Special Education: Ravic Ringlaben, Ph.D., Chairperson.
Counseling: Michele Boyer, Ph.D., Chairperson and Professor.
Criminology: Jeffrey Schrink, Ph.D., Chairperson and Professor.
Curriculum, Instruction, and Media Technology: Susan Powers, Ed.D., Acting Chairperson.
Educational and School Psychology: Michael Bahr, Ph.D., Chairperson and Professor.
Educational Leadership, Administration, and Foundations: Joanne Burrows, Ph.D., Chairperson.
Electronics and Computer Technology: Ngoba Maloba, Ph.D., Chairperson and Associate Professor.
Elementary and Early Childhood Education: Elizabeth Jared, Ph.D., Chairperson and Associate Professor.
English: Ronald Baker, Ph.D., Chairperson and Professor.
Family and Consumer Sciences: Frederica Kramer, Ph.D., Chairperson and Professor.
Geography, Geology, and Anthropology: William Dando, Ph.D., Chairperson and Professor.
Health and Safety: Portia Plummer, H.S.D., Chairperson and Professor.
History: Robert Hunter, Ph.D., Chairperson and Professor.
Humanities: Donald Jennermann, Ph.D.; Chairperson and Professor.
Industrial and Mechanical Technology: Michael Hayden, Ph.D., Chairperson and Associate Professor.
Industrial Technology Education: Anthony Gilberti, Ph.D., Chairperson and Professor.
Languages, Literatures, and Linguistics: Ronald Dunbar, Ph.D., Chairperson and Professor.
Life Sciences: Charles Amlaner, Ph.D., Chairperson and Professor.
Manufacturing and Construction Technology: Gordon Minty, Ph.D., Chairperson and Professor.
Mathematics and Computer Science: Richard Easton, Ph.D., Chairperson and Professor.
Music: Todd Sullivan, Ph.D., Interim Chairperson.
Nursing: Kathleen D. Pickrell, Ph.D., Chairperson.
Physical Education: John Ozmun, Ph.D., Acting Chairperson and Associate Professor.
Physics: Arthur Halpern, Ph.D., Acting Chairperson.
Political Science: H. Michael Erisman, Ph.D., Chairperson and Professor.
Psychology: Douglas Herrmann, Ph.D., Chairperson and Professor.
Recreation and Sport Management: Steve Smidley, Ph.D., Acting Chairperson.
Science Education: Stan Shimer, Ph.D., Director.
Sociology: Morris Medley, Ph.D., Chairperson and Professor.
Technology Management: Bruce Dallman, Ph.D., Ph.D. Consortium Director.
Urban-Regional Studies: Robert Larson, Ph.D., Director and Associate Professor of Geography.

INDIANA UNIVERSITY OF PENNSYLVANIA

Graduate School and Research

Programs of Study

The Graduate School and Research at IUP offers programs of study leading to the Doctor of Education, Doctor of Psychology, and Doctor of Philosophy degrees in the areas of administration and leadership studies (educational administration track or human services track), clinical psychology, criminology, curriculum and instruction, English, and school psychology. Master of Arts, Master of Science, Master of Business Administration, Master of Education, and Master of Fine Arts degrees are available in adult/community education, applied mathematics, art, biology, business administration, business workforce/development, chemistry, community counseling, criminology, early childhood education, education, educational psychology, education of exceptional persons, elementary and middle school mathematics, elementary or secondary school counseling, English (English education, generalist English, literature, or teaching English to speakers of other languages), food and nutrition, geography, history, industrial and labor relations, literacy, mathematics, music, nursing, physics, professional growth, psychology, public affairs, safety sciences, sociology, speech-language pathology, sport science, and student affairs in higher education. The M.B.A. executive track and a few other programs are offered in the Pittsburgh and Johnstown areas. The Graduate School and Research also offers specialization or certification through a post-master's educational psychology program and a principal's certification program.

Basic requirements for the doctoral degrees include spending a minimum of two semesters (or summer session equivalents) in residence at IUP, passing qualifying examinations, and presenting and defending a dissertation. The thesis is optional in most master's degree programs.

The University operates on an academic year of two semesters, plus two summer sessions of five weeks each.

Research Facilities

The University library contains more than 793,000 book volumes, 3,300 periodical subscriptions, and 1.7 million units of microform materials and other documents and is a select federal depository. The computer center is housed in the same building as the Graduate School and Research and is available to members of the University community at all times. Specialized laboratories and research equipment are available for advanced master's, post-master's, and doctoral students. There are numerous research centers on campus.

Financial Aid

Graduate assistantships are available to qualified applicants in most degree programs. For 2001–02, assistantship awards ranged between $4740 and $5660 at the master's level and between $5930 and $6330 at the doctoral level, plus tuition waiver. Various loan opportunities are available. Funds exist to support student research and attendance at professional meetings to present papers.

Cost of Study

In 2001–02, full-time graduate tuition was $2300 for in-state students and $3777 for out-of-state students. Tuition for part-time study was $256 per semester credit for in-state students and $420 per credit for out-of-state students. Full-time students paid an activity fee of $66 per semester; part-time students paid $29.50. Each semester, an educational service and facilities fee of $230 ($25.60 per credit hour for part-time students) and a registration fee of $20 per semester were assessed. Costs are subject to change.

Living and Housing Costs

University residence halls and off-campus rooms and apartments are available. Costs vary depending upon room size, proximity, and whether or not meals are included in the arrangement.

Student Group

Approximately 1,675 students are enrolled in programs leading to the various graduate degrees. The total University enrollment is approximately 13,400, equally distributed between men and women. Students represent American minority groups, most states, and a number of countries.

Location

Indiana, Pennsylvania, a community of 28,000, is 59 miles northeast of Pittsburgh. A wide variety of cultural and recreational activities in urban, suburban, and rural settings are available in and near the town of Indiana and in Pittsburgh.

The University

Founded as a higher education institution in 1875 and designated a university in 1965, IUP is a Doctoral I institution with three campuses and more than 700 faculty members.

Applying

An admissions packet is available from the Graduate Office; requests should be sent to the Graduate School and Research. Brochures and other information describing individual programs are available directly from most department chairpersons, whose names appear on the reverse of this page.

Correspondence and Information

Graduate School and Research
Stright Hall
210 South Tenth Street
Indiana University of Pennsylvania
Indiana, Pennsylvania 15705-1081
Telephone: 724-357-2222
Fax: 724-357-4862
E-mail: graduate_admissions@grove.iup.edu
World Wide Web: http://www.iup.edu.graduate/

THE FACULTY

Listed below are IUP's graduate degree program areas. Each is followed by the name of the chairperson of the appropriate department and his or her campus address.

PROGRAM AREAS

Administration and Leadership Studies, Education Track: Dr. George Bieger, Davis 305.
Administration and Leadership Studies, Human Services Track: Dr. Harvey Holtz, McElhaney 102.
Adult/Community Education: Dr. Trenton Ferro, Stouffer 206.
Art: Dr. Vaughn Clay, Sprowls 115.
Biology: Dr. W. Barkley Butler, Weyandt 114.
Business Administration: Dr. Krish Krishnan, Eberly 402.
Business and Workforce Development: Dr. Wayne Moore, Eberly 224.
Chemistry: Dr. Ruiess Ramsey, Weyandt 143.
Clinical Psychology: Dr. Mary Lou Zanich, Uhler 101.
Counseling: Dr. Claire Dandeneau, Stouffer 206B.
Criminology: Dr. Dennis Giever, McElhaney G1.
Curriculum and Instruction: Dr. George Bieger, Davis 305.
Early Childhood Education: Dr. George Bieger, Davis 305.
Educational Psychology: Dr. Mary Ann Rafoth, Stouffer 246.
Education of Exceptional Persons: Dr. Richard Nowell, Davis 203.
English: Dr. Gail Berlin, Leonard 110.
Food and Nutrition: Dr. Joanne Steiner, Ackerman 10.
Geography: Dr. Robert Sechrist, Leonard 10.
History: Dr. Gary Bailey, Keith 205.
Industrial and Labor Relations: Dr. James Byers, Keith 3.
Literacy: Dr. George Bieger, Davis 305.
Master's in Education: Dr. George Bieger, Davis 305.
Mathematics: Dr. Gerald Buriok, Stright 233.
Music: Dr. Lorraine Wilson, Cogswell 101.
Nursing: Dr. Jodell Kuzneski, Johnson 210.
Physics: Mr. Richard Roberts, Weyandt 56A.
Public Affairs: Dr. David Chambers, Keith Annex 103W.
Safety Sciences: Dr. Lon Ferguson, Johnson 116.
School Psychology: Dr. Mary Ann Rafoth, Stouffer 246.
Sociology: Dr. Harvey Holtz, McElhaney 102.
Speech-Language Pathology: Dr. Richard Nowell, Davis 203.
Sport Science: Dr. James Mill, Zink 225.
Student Affairs in Higher Education: Dr. Ronald Lunardini, Stouffer 206.

IONA COLLEGE

School of Arts and Science and Hagan Business School Graduate Programs

Programs of Study

Iona College offers graduate programs leading to the degree of Master of Arts, Master of Science, Master of Science in Education, Master of Science in Teaching, and Master of Business Administration. Fields of study in the School of Arts & Science include communication arts (corporate communication or public relations), computer science, counseling (family and pastoral), criminal justice, education (elementary science, secondary subjects, multicultural education, school administration and supervision), educational technology, English, health services administration, history, journalism, psychology (experimental, applied, certification in school counseling or school psychology), Spanish, teaching (elementary or secondary subjects—designed for career changers), and telecommunications. Certificate programs are available in communication arts, counseling, educational technology, mass communications, health services administration, and telecommunications. From the Hagan School of Business, the M.B.A. degree is available with concentrations in financial management, management, marketing, human resource management, and information and decision technology management. Certificates are available in e-commerce and international business.

Graduate programs at Iona College are taught on the main campus in New Rochelle and at Iona's Rockland Graduate Center in Orangeburg, New York. These programs are specially designed to meet the needs of part-time students, although many programs serve a student who would like to attend full-time. Classes are conveniently scheduled in the late afternoon and early evening to accommodate students' workdays. Depending on the number of credits required of a graduate program, a dedicated part-time student can expect to complete his or her degree in as little as two years. Each program is designed with a core requirement and elective courses. Internships and practicum experiences are built into many programs so students may gain hands-on experience.

Research Facilities

The heart of Iona's research facilities is its two libraries, the Ryan Library and the Arrigoni Technology Center. Ryan houses nearly 1,400 periodicals and 250,000 volumes, and Arrigoni is home to research and computer laboratories. Iona belongs to three interlibrary programs that allow online access to millions of volumes. Iona College possesses more than 500 networked computers, and there are two fully networked computer labs located at Iona's branch campus in Rockland County. Computer lab assistants are available to help students with their questions, and one lab stays open 24 hours a day, seven days a week. All students have e-mail accounts and access to the Internet.

Financial Aid

Iona College serves graduate students through a variety of state, federal, and institutional programs, which include loans, grants, scholarships, and assistantships. Scholarships are available based on undergraduate GPA or GRE or GMAT scores. Assistantships are available to students who can work a maximum of 20 hours per week on campus. Tuition and an hourly stipend are provided to these students. To be eligible for state and federal loans, students must complete the FAFSA and the Iona College loan application.

Cost of Study

The cost of graduate tuition for the 2001–02 academic year was $525 per credit hour. A $45 registration fee is payable at the time of registration.

Living and Housing Costs

While on-campus housing is not available to graduate students, the Housing Office at Iona College maintains an extensive list of housing accommodations close to the campus. Rents may range from $400 per month for a room in a private house to $800 for a one-bedroom apartment.

Student Group

There are approximately 1,400 students enrolled in graduate programs at Iona College. The majority of these students are employed full-time and attend classes on a part-time basis in the evenings.

Student Outcomes

Companies that employ Iona graduates include American Express, Avon, Bristol-Meyers, Gannett Co., IBM, Sports Illustrated, Texaco Inc., and Xerox.

Location

Iona's main campus is located in New Rochelle in lower Westchester County. It offers all the benefits of a traditional college campus. Iona's Rockland Graduate Center is located in the city of Orangeburg, New York, on the west shore of the Hudson River. The Center provides people on the west side of the Hudson River with a convenient location to study. The proximity of both campuses to New York City allows students to take advantage of the many cultural and employment opportunities that are available in the city.

The College

Founded in 1940 by the Christian Brothers order of the Catholic Church, Iona is an independent coeducational institution with a total enrollment of 5,000 students. Iona is accredited by the Middle States Association of Colleges and Schools and is a member of many different organizations.

Applying

Applications for Iona's School of Arts & Science graduate programs are available by mail or can be completed on the Iona Web site. The completed application must be received with the application fee, official transcripts from all postsecondary schools, and three letters of recommendation. An interview is required for the communication arts, journalism, and counseling programs and is strongly recommended for all other programs. The graduate catalog contains information regarding GPA criteria and the GRE requirements for each program.

Candidates for the Hagan School of Business may enter the graduate program in the fall (September), winter (November), or spring (March) trimester or in the summer session. The completed application, with fee, must be accompanied by two letters of recommendation, official transcripts from all postsecondary schools, and GMAT scores. All documents must be received no later than two weeks prior to the start of the session for which the candidate is applying.

Correspondence and Information

Office of Graduate Admissions
School of Arts & Science
Iona College
715 North Avenue
New Rochelle, New York 10801
Telephone: 914-633-2502
800-231-IONA (toll-free)
Fax: 914-633-2277
WWW: http://www.iona.edu

Director of M.B.A. Admissions
Hagan School of Business
Iona College
715 North Avenue
New Rochelle, New York 10801
Telephone: 914-633-2288
Fax: 914-633-2012
WWW: http://www.iona.edu/hagan

Iona College–Rockland Graduate Center
One Dutch Hill Road
Orangeburg, New York 10962
Telephone: 845-359-2252
Fax: 845-359-2261
WWW: http://www.iona.edu

DEPARTMENT AND PROGRAM HEADS

Helen Bauer, Professor and Chair of English; Ph.D., CUNY.
Robert Burns, Assistant Professor and Chair of Pastoral Counseling; Ph.D., St. John's.
James Carpenter, Professor and Chair of Mathematics; Ed.D., Columbia.
Frank Fazio, Associate Professor and Chair of Biology; Ph.D., Fordham.
Paul Greene, Associate Professor and Chair of Psychology; Ph.D., LIU.
Jack Heil, Assistant Professor and Chair of Health Care Programs; Ph.D., Missouri.
Victoria Ketz, Assistant Professor and Chair of Foreign Language; M.Phil., Columbia.
Francis J. McGrath, Professor and Chair of Finance, Business Economics, and Legal Studies; Ph.D., Fordham.
Robert Mealia, Assistant Professor and Chair of Criminal Justice; M.P.A., CUNY, John Jay; M.A., Ph.D., SUNY at Albany.
Donald Moscato, Professor and Chair of Information and Decision Technology Management and Accounting; Ph.D., Columbia.
Lucy Murphy, Professor and Chair of Education; Ph.D., Vanderbilt.
Catherine Ricardo, Professor and Graduate Program Coordinator, Department of Computer and Information Sciences; Ph.D., Columbia.
Frederica Rudell, Associate Professor and Chair of Marketing; Ph.D., Columbia.
Dennis Schmidt, Assistant Professor and Chair of History and Political Science; Ph.D., New School.
Orly Shachar, Assistant Professor of Mass Communication; Ph.D., Boston University.
Ursula Wittig-Berman, Associate Professor and Chair of Management; Ph.D., CUNY, Baruch.

IOWA STATE UNIVERSITY

Graduate College

Programs of Study

Iowa State University provides outstanding facilities for graduate study and research in the Colleges of Agriculture, Business, Design, Education, Engineering, Family and Consumer Sciences, Liberal Arts and Sciences, and Veterinary Medicine. Faculty members from more than 100 graduate programs offer advanced study opportunities. Advanced degrees include the research-oriented Master of Arts, Master of Science, and Doctor of Philosophy degrees; in certain fields, the Master of Science without thesis and the Master of Arts without thesis; and the advanced technical or professional degrees of Master of Accounting, Master of Agriculture, Master of Architecture, Master of Business Administration, Master of Community and Regional Planning, Master of Education, Master of Engineering, Master of Family and Consumer Sciences, Master of Fine Arts, Master of Landscape Architecture, Master of Public Administration, and Master of School Mathematics.

Although there is flexibility in planning each student's graduate program, certain minimum requirements are set for advanced degrees by the graduate faculty as well as by individual programs. Minimum Graduate College requirements include maintaining a B average and generally completing the degree requirements within five years for a master's degree and seven years for the Ph.D. Graduate students are advised by almost 1,500 graduate faculty members, who have been selected because their research activity, professional involvement, and publications qualify them to guide the research of graduate students.

Research Facilities

Graduate assistants play an integral role in the research of numerous institutes, centers, and laboratories at Iowa State. Major research units associated with the University include the Ames Laboratory, the Plant Sciences Institute, the National Soil Tilth Laboratory, the National Animal Disease Center, the Institute for Physical Research and Technology, the Iowa Agriculture and Home Economics Experiment Station, Iowa State University's Biotechnology Program, the Leopold Center for Sustainable Agriculture, the Center for Agricultural and Rural Development, the Center for Transportation Research and Education, the Veterinary Medical Research Institute, the Institute for Social and Behavioral Research, the Ames Center for Animal Health, the Statistical Laboratory, the Center for Academic Information Technology, the Center for Designing Foods to Improve Nutrition, the Iowa Energy Center, and the Information Assurance Center.

The University library, with a collection exceeding 2 million volumes and an equally extensive number of nonprint holdings, is nationally recognized for its collections in the basic and applied fields of the biological and physical sciences. Its major strengths for research include holdings in agriculture, design arts, statistics, and veterinary medicine. An online catalog system provides computerized access to the collections from on and off campus.

Financial Aid

Graduate assistantships, fellowships, and special research grants have been established to encourage graduate study and promote research. Information on these awards is available from individual programs. The Graduate College also sponsors a program of additional first-year tuition scholarship awards to attract outstanding students. Recipients of these one- or two-year awards receive a scholarship for up to half of the resident tuition. Other types of financial aid include a deferred fee payment plan, Federal Direct Student Loans (low-interest, deferred repayment), and University Emergency Loans.

Cost of Study

In 2002–03, the graduate fees for a semester of full-time study total $2194 for state residents and $6457 for nonresidents. Fees for a partial schedule or for off-campus courses are determined on a per-hour basis. Students appointed to graduate assistantships are considered full-time students and are assessed the state resident fees. Most assistants also qualify for a scholarship credit of up to $1097.

Living and Housing Costs

The University provides housing for single and married graduate students. Proposed costs for 2002–03 range from $3970 per academic year for a double-occupancy residence hall room to as low as $462 per month for a University student apartment. Students may also secure off-campus rooms, apartments, or duplexes in Ames and the surrounding communities. The costs for off-campus housing ranges from $500 to more than $1000 per month, depending on the size and location of the housing.

Student Group

In 2001–02, 27,823 students, including 4,363 graduate students, enrolled at the University. Most graduate students attend full-time; 40 percent are women, and 34 percent are international students. More than 50 percent are awarded graduate assistantships.

Location

The University is situated on a 1,000-acre tract in Ames, Iowa (population, 50,000), 35 miles north of the state capital of Des Moines. Ames is at the crossroads of three interstate highways: running north and south, I-35, and running east and west, U.S. 30 and (30 miles to the south) I-80. The city offers a calendar of social, cultural, and athletic activities that surpasses that of many other metropolitan areas. Students, faculty, and Ames residents are a cosmopolitan group, representing more than 120 countries. The city maintains more than 700 acres of woods, streams, and open meadows as parks, and the general atmosphere of Ames is relaxed and friendly.

The University

Iowa State was chartered in 1858 and became the land-grant institution for the state of Iowa after the passage of the Morrill Act. Graduate study was offered almost as soon as classes began in 1868, and the first graduate degree was conferred in 1877. The University's motto, Science with Practice, suggests the importance placed on both the learning of theory and the discovery of applications in the many areas in which Iowa State excels.

Applying

The graduate admissions bulletin contains directions for applying, contacts, and admission requirements for each graduate program, and an application packet to be completed and returned to the Office of Admissions. This booklet may be requested from the Office of Admissions at the address given below. Normally the application, accompanied by a $30 application fee ($50 for international students) and an official transcript from each college attended, should be sent to the Office of Admissions by March 1 for summer or fall admission, and October 1 for spring admission. Since many programs have earlier deadlines, applicants should correspond with the appropriate program, which can also provide guidance about graduate assistantships, fellowships, and special research grants. Students may also apply to Iowa State online by accessing the Graduate College's Web site at the address listed below.

Correspondence and Information

For program information:

Graduate Program of (specify)
Iowa State University
Ames, Iowa 50011

For general application information:

Office of Admissions
Alumni Hall
Iowa State University
Ames, Iowa 50011-2010

Telephone: 800-262-3810 (toll-free)
E-mail: grad_admissions@iastate.edu
World Wide Web: http://www.grad-college.iastate.edu

FIELDS OF STUDY

To request more information on Iowa State's major areas of study, students are encouraged to contact the following programs directly. The telephone area code for each program is 515.

Accounting: M.A.A.A. (294-8118).
Aerospace Engineering: M.Eng., M.S., Ph.D. (294-2694).
Agricultural Economics: M.S., Ph.D. (294-2701).
Agricultural Education: M.S., Ph.D. (294-5904).
Agricultural Engineering: M.Eng., M.S., Ph.D. (294-4025).
Agricultural History and Rural Studies: Ph.D. (294-5620).
Agricultural Meteorology: M.S., Ph.D. (294-1361).
Agronomy: M.S. (294-1361).
Analytical Chemistry: M.S., Ph.D. (294-7810).
Animal Breeding and Genetics: M.S., Ph.D. (294-4524).
Animal Ecology: M.S., Ph.D. (294-6148).
Animal Nutrition: M.S., Ph.D. (294-4524).
Animal Physiology: M.S., Ph.D. (294-4524).
Animal Science: M.S., Ph.D. (294-4524).
Anthropology: M.A. (294-7139).
Applied Mathematics: M.S., Ph.D. (294-0393).
Applied Physics: M.S., Ph.D. (294-5441).
Architectural Studies: M.S. (294-2187).
Architecture: M.Arch., M.Arch./M.B.A., M.Arch./M.C.R.P. (294-2187).
Art and Design: M.A. (294-6724).
Astrophysics: M.S., Ph.D. (294-5441).
Biochemistry: M.S., Ph.D. (294-2231).
Bioinformatics and Computational Biology: M.S., Ph.D. (294-5122).
Biophysics: M.S., Ph.D. (294-2231).
Botany: M.S., Ph.D. (294-0367).
Businesss: M.S. (294-8118).
Business Administration: M.B.A., M.Arch./M.B.A., M.B.A./M.C.R.P., M.B.A./M.S. (Statistics) (294-8118).
Chemical Engineering: M.Eng., M.S., Ph.D. (294-7643).
Chemistry: M.S., Ph.D. (294-7810).
Civil Engineering: M.S., Ph.D. (294-2861).
Community and Regional Planning: M.C.R.P, M.Arch./M.C.R.P., M.B.A./M.C.R.P., M.L.A./M.C.R.P., M.P.A./M.C.R.P. (294-8958).
Computer Engineering: M.S., Ph.D. (294-2667).
Computer Science: M.S., Ph.D. (294-8361).
Condensed Matter Physics: M.S., Ph.D. (294-5441).
Crop Production and Physiology: M.S., Ph.D. (294-1361).
Earth Science: M.S., Ph.D. (294-4477).
Ecology and Evolutionary Biology: M.S., Ph.D. (294-7252).
Economics: M.S., Ph.D. (294-2701).
Education: M.Ed., M.Ed. Practitioner, M.S., Ph.D. (294-1241).
Electrical Engineering: M.S., Ph.D. (294-2667).
Engineering Mechanics: M.Eng., M.S., Ph.D. (294-2694).
English: M.A. (294-2477).
Entomology: M.S., Ph.D. (294-7400).
Exercise and Sport Science: M.Ed., M.S. (294-8650).
Family and Consumer Sciences: M.F.C.S. (294-5982).
Family and Consumer Sciences Education: M.Ed., M.S., Ph.D. (294-5307).
Fisheries Biology: M.S., Ph.D. (294-6148).
Food Science and Technology: M.S., Ph.D. (294-6442).
Food Service and Lodging Management: M.S., Ph.D. (294-7474).
Forestry: M.S., Ph.D. (294-1458).
Genetics: M.S., Ph.D. (294-7697).
Geology: M.S., Ph.D. (294-4477).
Graphic Design: M.F.A. (294-6724).
Health and Human Performance: Ph.D. (294-8650).
High Energy Physics: M.S., Ph.D. (294-5441).
History: M.A. (294-4672).
History of Technology and Science: M.A., Ph.D. (294-5956).
Horticulture: M.S., Ph.D. (294-2751).
Human Development and Family Studies: M.S., Ph.D. (294-6321).
Immunobiology: M.S., Ph.D. (294-7252).
Industrial Education and Technology: M.S., Ph.D. (294-2539).
Industrial Engineering: M.S., Ph.D. (294-0126).
Industrial Relations: M.S. (294-2701).
Information Assurance: M.S. (294-8307).
Information Systems: M.S. (294-8118).
Inorganic Chemistry: M.S., Ph.D. (294-7810).
Integrated Visual Arts: M.F.A. (294-6725).
Interdisciplinary Graduate Studies: M.A., M.S. (294-4531).
Interior Design: M.F.A. (294-6724).
Journalism and Mass Communication: M.S. (294-4342).
Landscape Architecture: M.L.A., M.L.A./M.C.R.P. (294-5676).
Materials Science and Engineering: M.S., Ph.D. (294-1214).
Mathematics: M.S., M.S.M., Ph.D. (294-0393).
Meat Science: M.S., Ph.D. (294-4524).
Mechanical Engineering: M.S., Ph.D. (294-9474).
Meteorology: M.S., Ph.D. (294-9874).
Microbiology: M.S., Ph.D. (294-1630).
Molecular, Cellular, and Development Biology: M.S., Ph.D. (294-7252).
Neuroscience: M.S., Ph.D. (294-7252).
Nuclear Physics: M.S., Ph.D. (294-5441).
Nutrition: M.S., Ph.D. (294-9304).
Operations Research: M.S. (294-0126).
Organic Chemistry: M.S., Ph.D. (294-7810).
Physical Chemistry: M.S., Ph.D. (294-7810).
Physics: M.S., Ph.D. (294-5441).
Physiology: M.S., Ph.D. (294-2440).
Plant Breeding: M.S., Ph.D. (294-1361).
Plant Pathology: M.S., Ph.D. (294-1741).
Plant Physiology: M.S., Ph.D. (294-0132).
Political Science: M.A. (294-3764).
Professional Agriculture: M.Ag. (294-0895).
Psychology: M.S., Ph.D. (294-1743).
Public Administration: M.P.A., M.P.A./M.C.R.P., C.P.M. (294-7256).
Rhetoric and Professional Communication: Ph.D. (294-2477).
Rural Sociology: M.S., Ph.D. (294-8312).
School Mathematics: M.S.M. (294-8169).
Sociology: M.S., Ph.D. (294-8312).
Soil Science: M.S., Ph.D. (294-1361).
Statistics: M.S.,M.B.A./M.S., Ph.D. (294-3440).
Sustainable Agriculture: M.S., Ph.D. (294-6061).
Systems Engineering: M.Eng. (294-8731).
Teaching English as a Second Language/Applied Linguistics: M.A., (294-2477)
Textiles and Clothing: M.S., Ph.D. (294-5284).
Toxicology: M.S., Ph.D. (294-7697).
Transportation: M.S. (294-8103).
Veterinary Anatomy: M.S., Ph.D. (294-2440).
Veterinary Clinical Sciences: M.S. (294-2061).
Veterinary Microbiology: M.S., Ph.D. (294-5776).
Veterinary Pathology: M.S., Ph.D. (294-3386).
Veterinary Preventive Medicine: M.S. (294-3837).
Water Resources: M.S., Ph.D. (294-8921).
Wildlife Biology: M.S., Ph.D. (294-6148).
Zoology: M.S., Ph.D. (294-3909).

ITHACA COLLEGE

Division of Graduate Studies

Programs of Study

Ithaca College has a proud tradition of master's-level instruction built on excellence in undergraduate professional programs. For more than half a century the Division of Graduate Studies has offered master's programs in music and physical education. Current graduate programs also include business administration, communications, music, music education, exercise and sport sciences, occupational therapy, physical therapy, speech-language pathology, and teaching students with speech and language disabilities.

While faculty members at the College are productive scholars and performers in their own right, they hold teaching as their highest priority. They involve graduate students in the conduct of their scholarly pursuits, providing a rich, student-centered learning environment. Faculty members are also active in their respective professions, which keep curricula current with professional developments and consistent with the high standards of external licensing and accrediting bodies.

Ithaca graduate programs integrate professional preparation with the enhancement of analytic and evaluative skills and provide opportunities for interpretation and constructive decision making. Students gain experience applying their newly developed professional abilities, independent thinking, and intellectual initiative within a supportive educational and professional environment. Graduates assume positions as active professionals committed to continued learning and advancement of their professions.

Research Facilities

The library is open 99 hours a week to provide a complete range of information services and resources in both electronic and print formats. Academic Computing and Client Services (ACCS) maintains an extensive collection of programming languages, data-analysis packages, and business programs to support the curriculum. ACCS supports microcomputer facilities with more than 400 microcomputers on the campus-wide network.

Financial Aid

A limited number of assistantships are available in each of the master's degree programs on a competitive basis. Assistantships supplement tuition and offer a small salary in exchange for on-campus responsibilities.

Cost of Study

The 2002–03 graduate tuition rate is $660 per credit hour.

Living and Housing Costs

The College maintains no housing facilities for graduate students. Off-campus housing is available at various rates. Several meal plans are available in the College dining halls. The following are 2001–02 prices: $872 for five meals per week, $1961 for ten meals per week, and $2156 for ten, fourteen, or twenty meals per week with bonus dollars.

Student Group

Approximately 250 students are enrolled in graduate programs.

Location

Ithaca, New York, is also the site of Cornell University. A majority of the city's 29,000 permanent residents are academically oriented, while a transient population of some 23,000 students, artists, scientists, and scholars enriches its unique academic atmosphere. Many visitors are drawn to Ithaca by the striking beauty of the scenery, the opportunities for outdoor life, and the cultural activity of a cosmopolitan community where there is extensive interest in the humanities, sciences, music, and drama. Students have frequent occasions to share in and contribute to these interests and opportunities.

The College

Constructed on a naturally terraced hillside, the unobstructed view of the surrounding countryside provides one of the finest vistas in the Finger Lakes region. The facilities were designed to take advantage of that view and to blend with the natural beauty of the terrain. Residence halls, dining halls, and academic buildings are located in spacious, closely knit units at the center of the site. Classrooms, laboratories, lecture halls, and specialized facilities have been designed to utilize modern teaching technology. The campus is surrounded by an abundance of recreational facilities, including an outdoor Olympic-size swimming pool, fitness trail, playing fields, and tennis courts. Recent construction includes additions to the Schools of Music and Health Sciences and Human Performance. A new fitness center has also recently been completed.

Applying

Applications for admission, with the necessary transcripts and recommendations, must be received by the Division of Graduate Studies no later than March 1 for fall and summer semesters and December 1 for spring. The exception to this is the speech-language pathology program, which has a deadline of February 1. The General Test of the Graduate Record Examinations is required by speech-language pathology and exercise and sport sciences.

Admission requirements include a bachelor's degree from an accredited college, a minimum 3.0 undergraduate GPA, and typically an undergraduate major or the equivalent in the proposed field. Application forms and catalogs may be obtained by writing to the address below.

Correspondence and Information

Dr. Garry L. Brodhead
Associate Provost and Dean of Graduate Studies
Division of Graduate Studies
Ithaca College
111 Towers Concourse
Ithaca, New York 14850-7142
Telephone: 607-274-3527
Fax: 607-274-1263
E-mail: gradstudies@ithaca.edu
World Wide Web: http://www.ithaca.edu

THE FACULTY

Business Administration

Joseph Cheng, Associate Professor; Ph.D., SUNY at Binghamton. Donald Eckrich, Professor; D.B.A., Kentucky. Eileen Kelly, Professor; Ph.D., Cincinnati. Patricia Libby, Associate Professor; Ph.D., Michigan. Donald Lifton, Associate Professor; Ph.D., Cornell. Gregor Macy, Associate Professor; Ph.D., Indiana. Michael McCall, Associate Professor and Chair; Ph.D., Arizona State. Hormoz Movassaghi, Associate Professor; Ph.D., Wisconsin. Abraham Mulugetta, Professor; Ph.D., Wisconsin. Margaret Nowicki, Assistant Professor; Ph.D., Colorado at Boulder. Gwen Seaquist, Associate Professor; J.D., Mississippi. Donald Simmons, Associate Professor; Ph.D., SUNY at Binghamton. Fahri Unsal, Professor; Ph.D., Cornell. M. Raquibuz Zaman, Professor; Ph.D., Cornell.

Communications

Marie Garland, Assistant Professor; Ph.D., Ohio State. Diane M. Gayeski, Associate Professor; Ph.D., Maryland. Rama Hart, Assistant Professor; Ph.D., Case Western Reserve. Sandra L. Herndon, Professor and Chair of Graduate Programs; Ph.D., Southern Illinois. Ari Kissiloff, Assistant Professor; M.S., Ithaca. Gordon Rowland, Associate Professor; Ph.D., Indiana. Steven A. Seidman, Associate Professor; Ph.D., Indiana.

Exercise and Sport Sciences

Mary DePalma, Professor; Ph.D., Cornell. Jeff Ives, Assistant Professor; Ph.D., Massachusetts. Betsy A. Keller, Associate Professor, Ph.D., Massachusetts. Victor H. Mancini, Professor; Ed.D., Boston University. Tom Pfaff, Assistant Professor; Ph.D., Syracuse. Kent Scriber, Professor; Ed.D., Syracuse. Gary A. Sforzo, Professor and Chair of Graduate Programs; Ph.D., Maryland. Greg Shelley, Assistant Professor; Ph.D., Utah. John Sigg, Associate Professor, Ph.D., Toledo. Tom Swensen, Assistant Professor, Ph.D., Tennessee. Janet Wiggleworth, Assistant Professor; Ph.D., Indiana. Deborah A. Wuest, Professor, Ed.D., Boston University.

Music

Mary Arlin, Professor (Theory); Ph.D., Indiana. Carole Bigler, Lecturer; B.M., Syracuse. Diane Birr, Assistant Professor (Piano); M.M., Indiana. Randie Blooding, Assistant Professor (Voice); D.M.A., Ohio State. Stephen Brown, Professor (Guitar and Jazz Studies); M.M., Ithaca. Verna Brummett, Assistant Professor (Music Education); Ed.D., Illinois. Frank Campos, Associate Professor (Trumpet and Music Education); M.M., North Texas State. Pablo Cohen, Adjunct Assistant Professor (Classical Guitar); M.M., Temple. Grant Cooper, Professor (Orchestra Conductor); M.M., Tulsa. Craig Cummings, Associate Professor (Music History); Ph.D., Indiana. Lawrence A. Doebler, Professor (Director of Chorale Music); M.M., Washington (St. Louis). D. Kim Dunnick, Professor (Trumpet); D.M., Indiana. Richard Faria, Assistant Professor (Clarinet); M.M., Michigan State. Mark Fonder, Associate Professor (Music Education); Ed.D., Illinois. Read Gainsford, Assistant Professor; B.M., Auckland. Janet Galvan, Professor (Music Education); Ed.D., North Carolina. Michael Galvan, Professor (Clarinet and Music Education); M.M., Illinois. Angus Godwin, Professor (Voice); M.A., Columbia. Lee Goodhew, Associate Professor (Bassoon); M.M., SMU. Patrick Hansen, Assistant Professor; M.M., Missouri. Allison Evans Henry, Adjunct Assistant Professor; D.M.A., Rochester (Eastman). Rebecca Jemian, Assistant Professor (Theory); Ph.D., Indiana. Timothy A. Johnson, Assistant Professor; Ph.D., SUNY at Buffalo. Keith A. Kaiser, Assistant Professor; M.M., Redlands. Deborah Martin, Assistant Professor (Piano); D.M., Indiana. Steven Mauk, Professor (Saxophone); D.M.A., Michigan. Carol McAmis, Professor (Voice); M.M., Kansas. Wendy Herbener Mehne, Associate Professor (Flute); D.M.A., Wisconsin. Phiroze Mehta, Professor (Piano); M.M., Massachusetts. Deborah Montgomery, Professor (Voice); M.M., Illinois. Debra Moree, Associate Professor (Viola and Violin); M.M., Indiana. Henry Neubert, Professor (Double Bass); M.M., Northwestern. Timothy A. Nord, Assistant Professor (Music Technology); Ph.D., Wisconsin. Arthur Ostrander, Dean (Theory); Ph.D., Indiana Bloomington. David Pacun, Assistant Professor (Theory); Ph.D., Chicago. David Parks, Professor (Voice); D.M.A., Arizona. Patrice Pastore, Associate Professor (Voice); M.M., New England Conservatory. William Pelto, Associate Professor (Theory); Ph.D., Texas. Elizabeth Peterson, Assistant Professor (Music Education); M.M., Northwestern. Stephen G. Peterson, Associate Professor; Ph.D., Northwestern. Mark Radice, Associate Professor (Music History); Ph.D., Rochester (Eastman). Beth A. Ray, Assistant Professor; D.M.A., Texas at Austin. Sanford Reuning, Adjunct Assistant Professor (Suzuki Strings); B.M., Illinois. Harold Reynolds, Associate Professor (Trombone); D.M.A., Rochester (Eastman). Peter Rothbart, Associate Professor (Electroacoustic); D.M.A., Cleveland Institute of Music. Kelly Samarzea, Assistant Professor; D.M., Indiana. Alex Shuhan, Assistant Professor (French Horn); B.M., Rochester (Eastman). Elizabeth P. Simkin, Associate Professor (Cello); M.M., Rochester (Eastman). Gordon Stout, Professor (Percussion) and Chair of Performance Studies; M.M., Rochester (Eastman). David Unland, Associate Professor (Baritone and Tuba); M.S., Illinois at Urbana-Champaign. John White, Assistant Professor; Ph.D., Indiana. Dana Wilson, Professor (Composition); Ph.D., Rochester (Eastman). Gregory Woodward, Professor (Music Composition) and Chair of Graduate Programs in Music; D.M.A., Cornell.

Speech-Language Pathology/Audiology

Luanne Andersson, Assistant Professor; Ph.D., Connecticut. Douglas E. Cross, Associate Professor; Ph.D., Tennessee. Barbara Ann Johnson, Professor; Ph.D., Florida. Richard J. Schissel, Associate Professor; Ph.D., Penn State. Kal M. Telage, Professor; Ph.D., Ohio. E. W. Testut, Associate Professor and Chair; Ph.D., Oklahoma.

JOHN F. KENNEDY UNIVERSITY

Programs of Study

John F. Kennedy University (JFKU) offers thirteen master's degrees, a Juris Doctor (J.D.) degree, and a Doctor of Psychology (Psy.D.) degree. The School of Liberal Arts offers M.A. degrees in museum studies and teaching. The School of Management offers graduate degrees in business administration and career development. The Graduate School of Professional Psychology offers M.A. degrees in counseling psychology, organizational psychology, and sport psychology and a Psy.D. The Graduate School for Holistic Studies offers M.A. degrees in consciousness studies, counseling psychology, holistic health education, transformative arts, and transpersonal psychology and an M.F.A. in studio arts. The School of Law offers the J.D.

Research Facilities

The University's central library is the Robert M. Fisher Library, located on the Orinda campus (main campus). There is also a branch library on the Campbell campus. In addition to the Fisher Library, the University's resources include the Law Library and the Career Development Center Library. The collections total more than 80,000 volumes and 1,260 periodical subscriptions. All holdings are available in the libraries' Web catalog. The libraries have particularly strong collections in education, business, religion, clinical and transpersonal psychology, holistic studies, liberal arts, law, management, and museum studies. The libraries offer Web access to six electronic indexes as well as in-house use of several CD-ROM databases and Web links to electronic resources and libraries.

The University has four computer labs: two at its Orinda campus, one at its Law School in Walnut Creek, and one at the Campbell campus. All labs have IBM PCs with Internet access.

The University operates three counseling centers and a career development center. The three counseling centers provide high-quality, affordable psychotherapy to the community and offer supervised training for advanced students in counseling psychology programs. The Career Development Center provides comprehensive career management services. The center offers low-cost counseling, workshops, and other services for career planning, advancement, and change. Its resource library has information on careers, labor market trends, and potential employers received daily from Bay Area employers.

Financial Aid

Many financial aid opportunities are available for qualified students, including the Federal Pell Grant; Federal Supplemental Educational Opportunity Grant; Cal Grants A, B and T; Federal Perkins Loan; Federal Subsidized Stafford Loan; Federal Unsubsidized Stafford Loan; Federal PLUS Loan; and John F. Kennedy Scholarships. Students interested in any of these opportunities should contact the Financial Aid Office at 925-258-2385.

Cost of Study

Tuition for the 2001–02 academic year was as follows: Orinda campus, $348 per unit; Campbell campus, $374 per unit; law, $523 per semester unit; and Psy.D., $446 per unit.

Living and Housing Costs

There is no housing office at JFKU; no on-campus housing facilities are provided.

Student Group

There are student associations at JFKU campuses in Walnut Creek (law), Orinda, and Campbell. Peer Advising Offices are located at the Orinda and Walnut Creek campuses.

Location

John F. Kennedy University is located in Orinda, California, approximately 25 minutes east of San Francisco. There are branch campuses throughout the Bay Area, including the School of Law in Walnut Creek and a satellite campus in Campbell, which offers courses from the Graduate School of Professional Psychology, the Graduate School for Holistic Studies, and the School of Liberal Arts. Counseling centers are located in Sunnyvale, Pleasant Hill, and Oakland. The Career Development Center is located in Orinda. The Arts and Consciousness Gallery is located in Berkeley.

The University

John F. Kennedy University is accredited by the Western Association of Schools and Colleges. The School of Law is accredited by the Committee of Bar Examiners of the State Bar of California.

Applying

All graduate degree programs except law require a bachelor's degree from a regionally accredited institution. Application deadlines vary by program. Applicants should submit a completed application form with a $50 fee, official transcripts of all postsecondary education, and a personal statement. An in-person or telephone interview is also required. Specific programs may have additional requirements. The LSAT is required for law school, and the TOEFL is required for international students.

Correspondence and Information

Admissions and Records Office
John F. Kennedy University
12 Altarinda Road
Orinda, California 94563-2603
Telephone: 925-258-2211
Fax: 925-258-2083
World Wide Web: http://www.jfku.edu

PROGRAM DIRECTORS

Graduate School for Holistic Studies
Ray Greenleaf, Associate Professor and Chair of Transpersonal Psychology; M.A., John F. Kennedy, 1981.
Michael Grady, Associate Professor and Chair of Arts and Consciousness; M.F.A., Pratt, 1990.
Vernice Solimar, Associate Professor and Chair of Integral Studies; Ph.D., California Institute of Integral Studies, 1986.
Greg Bogart, Assistant Professor and Program Director, Holistic Studies, Campbell Campus; Ph.D., Saybrook Institute, 1992.

School of Law
Michael J. Guarino, Dean; J.D., Southwestern, 1975.

School of Liberal Arts
Marjorie Schwarzer, Chair, Department of Museum Studies; M.B.A., Berkeley, 1983.
Susan Kwock, Associate Professor of Education and Chair, Department of Education; Ed.D., San Francisco, 1988.
Suzanne West, Chair, Department of Liberal Arts; M.A., John F. Kennedy, 1986.

School of Management
Sue Aiken, Associate Professor of Career Development and Chair, M.A. in Career Development Program; M.A., John F. Kennedy, 1982.
Larisa Genin, Associate Professor of Business and Chair, M.B.A. Program; Ph.D., Golden Gate, 2001.
Michael Lee, Associate Professor of Business and Chair, Undergraduate Business Program; M.B.A., Golden Gate, 1983.

Graduate School of Professional Psychology
Jorge Partida, Professor of Psychology and Director, Psy.D. Program; Psy.D., Illinois School of Professional Psychology, 1992.
Rhonda James, Professor of Psychology and Director, M.A. in Counseling Psychology Program; M.A., John F. Kennedy, 1984.
Maurice Monette, Professor of Psychology and Chair, M.A. in Organizational Psychology Program; Ed.D., Columbia University, 1977.
Gail Solt, Professor of Psychology and Chair, M.A. in Sport Psychology Program; M.A., John F. Kennedy, 1987.

Graduate School for Holistic Studies

Consciousness Studies (M.A.): This program embraces a holistic philosophy that integrates body, mind, and spirit and emphasizes the interconnectedness of all life. It examines the nature of self and reality and supports personal and social transformation. Areas of concentration include dream studies, myth and symbol, deep ecology, living systems and new sciences, East/West spirituality, and feminine views of self and soul.

Counseling Psychology (M.A.): Counseling psychology programs are offered with specializations in holistic studies, somatic psychology, and transpersonal psychology. All specializations provide sound, practical clinical training and emphasize diagnosis and assessment, marriage and family counseling, child therapy, individual development, and addiction studies, in addition to providing a holistic perspective on therapy. All meet the educational requirements for the California Marriage and Family Therapist (MFT) license.

Holistic Health Education (M.A.): The program emphasizes body-mind integration and a holistic approach to wellness. It prepares students to articulate a holistic health perspective and to contribute meaningfully to the multifaceted process of transformative health education.

Master of Fine Arts in Studio Arts (M.F.A.): This program enables students to develop a fully resolved, professional body of artwork that is based on authentic personal experience and spiritual investigation. Formal and critical vocabulary is enhanced through challenging critiques and studio work. Classes are offered at the JFKU Arts Annex in Berkeley.

Transformative Arts (M.A.): This program facilitates the student's search into the deepest dimensions of art, spirituality, personal growth, and cultural expression. It allows students to combine their work as artists with positive models that allow them to share their experience of creative process with the community. After completing a series of core courses aimed at deepening personal creative experience, students learn techniques to bring creative growth to others.

Transpersonal Psychology (M.A.): This program provides a thorough theoretical grounding in the field of transpersonal psychology, with a balance between cognitive and experiential learning.

School of Law

Juris Doctor (J.D.): The School of Law offers a four-year day and evening program leading to the degree of Juris Doctor and is accredited by the Committee of Bar Examiners of the State Bar of California. The program emphasizes both theoretical knowledge and an understanding of the law's practical application. Students have a diversity of life experiences that enrich classroom discussion. A high-quality legal education is offered with courses on every subject tested on the Bar Examination as well as a variety of electives.

School of Liberal Arts

Museum Studies (M.A.): Program offers specializations in administration, collections management, and public programming. The curriculum emphasizes innovative concepts and methodology for more socially responsible museums. Students apply classroom knowledge during internships in museums around the country.

Teaching (M.A.): Program provides the opportunity for practitioners to thoroughly research an area of interest and test their ideas in the classroom. It is composed of 50 units for the professional clear credential and an additional 18-unit sequence. Program emphasizes urban, multicultural teaching and community-based teaching with emphasis on hands-on and progressive teaching. Multiple-, single-subject, and CLAD credentials are offered.

School of Management

Business Administration (M.B.A): Program prepares students for upper-managerial and executive-level careers in today's global economy. Course work addresses a wide range of business topics, with an emphasis on analytical. Entrepreneurial and leadership compentencies. Specializations are offered in e-commerce, general management, and leadership.

Career Development (M.A.): Program prepares students to counsel and assist people who are making work-related decisions and transitions. The program's interdisciplinary approach combines a solid background in work and societal issues, labor market analysis, and job search strategies with vocational assessment and career counseling techniques. Some courses are available through the University's distance learning program.

Graduate School of Professional Psychology

Counseling Psychology (M.A.): This degree emphasizes marriage, family, and child counseling. The curriculum provides in-depth knowledge of systemic and individual approaches to treatment through a combination of experiential learning, theory, and fieldwork. Optional specializations are available in addiction studies, child and adolescent therapy, couple and family therapy, conflict resolution, cross-cultural counseling, expressive arts therapy, and sport psychology. This program meets the educational requirements for the California Marriage and Family Therapist (MFT) license.

Doctor of Psychology (Psy.D.): This program is designed for individuals seeking the highest level of training to become applied clinical psychologists. It prepares graduates for multiple roles that contemporary psychologists must fill to competently serve their communities. Practical applications and advanced clinical training are emphasized throughout the program. All aspects of the program include its core commitment to diversity.

Organizational Psychology (M.A.): Students learn to apply the basic principles and processes of psychology to businesses, community and government agencies, and educational institutions. The program emphasizes communication and interpersonal issues and how to improve relationships within organizations to facilitate growth and maximize benefits. The core curriculum includes work in organizational theory, problem-solving skills, cross-cultural awareness, group facilitation, and conflict resolution.

Sport Psychology (M.A.): This program trains students in the field of sport psychology and in the interpersonal and applied aspects of psychology. One of the few existing degree programs in the U.S. that integrates counseling psychology with sport psychology, its counseling curriculum focuses on basic counseling skills, group dynamics, and psychopathology. Sport psychology course work covers optimal performance, techniques of coaching, social issues, substance abuse, and sport-based issues pertaining to child, adolescent, and family counseling.

JOHNS HOPKINS UNIVERSITY

Zanvyl Krieger School of Arts and Sciences and Whiting School of Engineering

Programs of Study

Degree programs leading to the Ph.D. are offered in the Humanities Center and in the Departments of Anthropology, Biology, Biomedical Engineering, Biophysics, Chemical Engineering, Chemistry, Civil Engineering, Classics, Cognitive Science, Computer Engineering, Computer Science, Earth and Planetary Sciences, Economics, Electrical Engineering, English, Geography and Environmental Engineering, German, History, History of Art, History of Science/Medicine and Technology, Materials Science and Engineering, Mathematical Sciences, Mathematics, Mechanical Engineering, Near Eastern Studies, Philosophy, Physics and Astronomy, Political Science, Psychology, Romance Languages, and Sociology.

A degree program leading to the M.A. is offered in the Writing Seminars. Master's degree programs are also offered in the Departments of Biomedical Engineering, Chemical Engineering, Civil Engineering, Classics, Computer Science, Electrical and Computer Engineering, Geography and Environmental Engineering, German, History, History of Art, Institute for Policy Studies, Materials Science and Engineering, Mathematical Sciences, Mechanical Engineering, and Sociology.

Emphasis is placed on mastery of a field of study and on creative research. There are no formal school-wide requirements measured in numbers of courses or credits. Each program is planned in consultation with a department or committee after reviewing the individual's attainments and areas of interest.

Specific requirements for the Ph.D. include a minimum of two consecutive semesters of registration as a full-time, resident graduate student; certification by a department or program committee that all departmental or committee requirements have been fulfilled; a dissertation approved by at least 2 referees appointed by the department or committee; and a Graduate Board oral examination.

The continuing process of education and research in the University setting requires involvement beyond the formal preparation for a degree. Postdoctoral training, therefore, is an integral part of many departmental programs.

Research Facilities

Major research activities and laboratories are integral to the Hopkins experience. The Milton S. Eisenhower Library houses the University's major collections. The quality and quantity of its collections and services make it one of the country's foremost research libraries. Other important Hopkins libraries include the Welch Medical Library, the Peabody Institute Library, and the Library of the School of Advanced International Studies (SAIS). The Homewood campus is also home to the Space Telescope Science Institute, administered for NASA by the Association of Universities for Research in Astronomy, the research center for the Hubble Space Telescope. Collaboration between the Institute and Hopkins scientists makes the University a world center for astronomical research. The Zanvyl Krieger Mind/Brain Institute is an interdisciplinary research center devoted to the study of neural mechanisms of higher mental functions, with emphasis on perception. Through the study of neuroanatomy, neurophysiology, computational neuroscience, neurology, and psychology, critical questions regarding the brain and how it operates are addressed.

Financial Aid

Most graduate students receive either full or partial fellowships, which include a tuition waiver as well as a stipend or salary. Also, there are fellowship awards made directly to students by government agencies, private foundations, and business and industrial corporations. Other aid, in the form of long-term student loans and employment, is administered by the Office of Student Financial Services. Notification of awards is made no later than the first week of April, and recipients are expected to respond to the offer no later than April 15.

Cost of Study

The matriculation fee, a one-time charge payable at the time of entrance, is $500. Tuition is approximately $27,390 for 2002–03; however, most graduate students receive a full or partial tuition fellowship.

Living and Housing Costs

During 2002–03, room and board costs are about $8650 for single students for a nine-month period. However, room and board costs vary depending on proximity to campus and choice of living arrangements. Other costs are books and supplies (up to $3350 per year) and travel expenses. All students are required to have health insurance either through the University at a cost of approximately $1000 per year or through a private insurer.

Student Group

Approximately 375–450 men and women representing a wide range of interests and a variety of backgrounds are selected each year for graduate study by the various academic departments. Students come from all areas of the United States as well as from many other countries. Approximately 40 percent of the graduate students are women.

Location

The campus is in a residential neighborhood of both single-family homes and apartments, located 4 miles from downtown Baltimore. There are churches, restaurants, drugstores, grocery stores, and other shops nearby. The 140-acre tree-lined Homewood campus offers a wide variety of areas for gatherings and recreation. Generally, graduate students find that their social as well as their academic lives tend to center on their departments. The three most widely used buildings are the Milton S. Eisenhower Library, the Newton H. White Jr. Athletic Center, and the Hopkins Union, the University student center.

The University

Privately endowed, Johns Hopkins University was founded in 1876 as the first American educational institution committed to the university idea of giving its students and faculty the freedoms of choice and opportunity that are necessary for learning and creativity to flourish. It remains committed to this idea. Johns Hopkins is a small coeducational university. The Schools of Arts and Sciences and Engineering are located on the Homewood campus in north Baltimore. In order to preserve close intellectual association, the University community and the student-faculty ratio are intentionally small. Currently enrolled are approximately 3,900 undergraduate, 1,400 graduate, and 140 postdoctoral students. The faculty numbers about 365.

Applying

Requests for applications and literature should be made to the department of the University in which the student desires to do graduate work. The completed application form, transcripts, letters of recommendation, and other supporting materials that any particular department requires are to be sent directly to that department. All applicants are advised to submit recent scores from the General Test of the Graduate Record Examinations. Although in most cases applications for fellowships must be made no later than January 15, application deadlines vary among departments; therefore, students should contact the appropriate department for details.

Correspondence and Information

Office of Graduate Admissions
Johns Hopkins University
3400 North Charles Street
Baltimore, Maryland 21218

Telephone: 410-516-8174
E-mail: grad_adm@jhu.edu
World Wide Web: http://www.jhu.edu (home page)
http://www.jhu.edu/~admis/grad.html
(graduate admissions)

Academic Department (specify)
Johns Hopkins University
3400 North Charles Street
Baltimore, Maryland 21218

DEANS AND DEPARTMENTAL CHAIRS

The mailing address for Deans and Departmental Chairs is: Johns Hopkins University, 3400 North Charles Street, Baltimore, Maryland 21218. The area code for all numbers listed below is 410.

SCHOOL OF ARTS AND SCIENCES

Daniel H. Weiss, Dean.
Steven R. David, Associate Dean for Academic Affairs.
Gary K. Ostrander, Associate Dean for Research.

Department, Location, Chair, Telephone, and E-mail

Anthropology: 404B Macaulay Hall, Gyanendra Pandey, Chair; 516-7271 (dklautky@jhu.edu).
Biology: 144 Mudd, Victor G. Corces, 516-5502 (joan@jhu.edu).
Biophysics: 110 Jenkins, Eaton E. Lattman, 516-7245 (TCJenkin@jhunix.hcf.jhu.edu); Molecular Biophysics: D. Draper, 516-5197 (tcjenkins@jhu.edu).
Chemistry: 138 Remsen, Paul J. Dagdigian, 516-7429 (chem.grad.adm@jhu.edu).
Classics: 130 Gilman, H. Alan Shapiro, 516-7556 (gmiller@jhu.edu).
Cognitive Science: 237 Krieger, Luigi Burzio 516-5250 (inquire@cogsci.jhu.edu).
Earth and Planetary Sciences: 301 Olin, Peter Olson, 516-7034 (cspangler@jhu.edu).
Economics: 440 Mergenthaler, Louis J. Maccini, 516-7601 (econ@jhu.edu).
English: 146 Gilman, Frances Ferguson, 516-4311 (susieh@jhu.edu).
German: 245 Gilman, Rainer Nägele. 516-7508 (rita.braun@jhu.edu).
History: 312 Gilman, Gabrielle Spiegel, 516-7575 (leb1@jhu.edu).
History of Art: 268 Mergenthaler, Walter S. Melion, 516-7117 (arthist@jhu.edu).
History of Science/Medicine and Technology: 216A Ames, Sharon Kingsland, Vice Chair; 516-7501 (eford@jhu.edu).
Humanities Center: 113 Gilman, Michael Fried, 516-7619 (mphilip@jhu.edu).
Mathematics: 404 Krieger, Christopher Sogge, 516-7399 (grad@math.jhu.edu).
Near Eastern Studies: 128 Gilman, Betsy M. Bryan, 516-7499 (vwild@jhu.edu).
Philosophy: 347 Gilman, Michael WIlliams, 516-7524 (cc1@jhu.edu).
Physics and Astronomy: 366 Bloomberg, Paul D. Feldman, 516-7344 (admissions@pha.jhu.edu).
Policy Studies: 540 Wyman, Sandra J. Newman, Director; 516-4167 (maps@jhu.edu).
Political Science: 338 Mergenthaler, William E. Connolly, 516-7540 (political.science@jhu.edu).
Psychological and Brain Sciences: 222 Ames, Michela Gallagher, 516-6175 (krach@jhu.edu).
Romance Languages and Literatures: 330 Gilman, Stephen G. Nichols, 516-7226 (romance@jhu.edu).
Sociology: 533 Mergenthaler, Andrew J. Cherlin, 516-7627 (sociology@jhu.edu).
Writing Seminars: 135 Gilman, Jean McGarry, 516-6286 (regina@jhu.edu).

WHITING SCHOOL OF ENGINEERING

Ilene J. Busch-Vishniac, Dean
Andrew Douglas, Associate Dean for Academic Affairs.
Marc Donohue, Associate Dean for Research.

Department, Location, Chair, Telephone, and E-mail

Biomedical Engineering: 318 Clark Hall, Murray B. Sachs; Master's: 516-5282 (mmoody@bme.jhu.edu); Ph.D.: 955-3131 (emccann@bme.jhu.edu).
Chemical Engineering: 225 Maryland, Michael E. Paulaitis, 516-7170 (che@jhu.edu).
Civil Engineering: 207A Latrobe, Nicholas P. Jones, 516-8680 (civil@jhu.edu).
Computer Science: 224 NEB, Rao Kosaraju, 516-7451 (linda@cs.jhu.edu).
Electrical and Computer Engineering: 105 Barton, Gerard G. L. Meyer, 516-7031 (eceapps@jhu.edu).
Geography and Environmental Engineering: 313 Ames, Marc Parlange, 516-7092 (Dogee@jhu.edu).
Materials Science and Engineering: 102 Maryland, Peter C. Searson, 516-8145 (dmse.admissions@jhu.edu).
Mathematical Sciences: 104 Whitehead, Edward Scheinerman, 516-7198 (lutz@jhu.edu).
Mechanical Engineering: 200 Latrobe, K. T. Ramesh, 516-7154 (drace@jhu.edu).

JOHNSON & WALES UNIVERSITY

Alan Shawn Feinstein Graduate School

Programs of Study

The Alan Shawn Feinstein Graduate School at Johnson & Wales University offers an M.B.A. degree in hospitality administration and an M.B.A. degree in global business with concentration choices in accounting, financial management, international trade, marketing, and organizational leadership. The School also offers an M.A. degree in teacher education for students with a business or food service undergraduate degree. An Ed.D. in educational leadership completes the programs offered at the Feinstein Graduate School. Classes are presented in both a day and evening schedule, and students with the appropriate business background can complete some programs in twelve months. The focus of all graduate programs is to provide students with the educational experiences that will help them attain employment in their chosen careers or enhance opportunities for advancement in their current employment. Very simply, the University's graduate programs teach people what they need to know to succeed in every economy.

Research Facilities

The main library, located on the first two floors of University Hall, is the central site of the Johnson & Wales University Library Network. This network currently includes the libraries of the following campuses: Charleston, South Carolina; Norfolk, Virginia; North Miami, Florida; and Worcester, Massachusetts. The main Providence facility holds a collection of resource materials to serve the research needs of the University community, especially students in the School of Arts & Sciences, the College of Business, the Feinstein Graduate School, the Hospitality College, and the School of Technology. The College of Culinary Arts has its own library on the Harborside campus.

All graduate students have access to IBM computer labs, a multimedia center, and other specialized computer laboratories.

Financial Aid

The Feinstein Graduate School offers graduate assistantships as well as Federal Stafford Student Loans for those who qualify. International students, as well as domestic students, can apply for student employment on campus.

Cost of Study

Tuition for the 2002–03 academic year is $220 per quarter credit hour. (Three semester credits equal 4.5 quarter credits.) Total tuition is between $11,880 and $17,265. Payment options include term and monthly installment payment plans.

Living and Housing Costs

Graduate student housing is very limited, but an off-campus housing office maintains listings of apartments available locally. Students should anticipate costs of $7000 to $8500 per year for off-campus housing, food, and utilities.

Student Group

In 2001–02, there were approximately 675 students enrolled in graduate programs at Johnson & Wales University, the majority of whom are employed while pursuing their degree. Forty-six percent of the student population are international students from sixty-one countries.

Student Outcomes

The objective of the Feinstein Graduate School is to meet the diverse needs of the global market. Graduates of the School's programs have entered positions that include management, administration, marketing, technology, accounting, and teaching. Organizations from around the globe, such as Sony, Ritz-Carlton, Citibank, and the Leromme Jerusalem Hotel, have hired the School's graduates.

Location

Johnson & Wales University is situated in Providence, Rhode Island, amidst a thriving business and academic community. Besides having a permanent population of 150,000, Providence is also a part-time home to more than 17,000 students from Johnson & Wales University, Brown University, Providence College, Rhode Island College, and Rhode Island School of Design. The arts are plentiful, from the plays of the Trinity Square Repertory Company to the musicals, ballets, operas, and current pop and comedy stars to be found at the Providence Performing Arts Center and the Civic Center. Providence is a reasonable driving distance from Newport, Rhode Island's beaches, and Boston.

The University

Johnson & Wales University is a private, nonprofit, coeducational institution that offers students an opportunity to pursue practical career education in business, food service, hospitality, technology, and teacher education. Associate, bachelor's, and master's degree programs permit students to select the educational program most suited to their career interests and objectives.

Applying

Students are encouraged to apply early, as program enrollment is very limited. Applicants must submit a signed application, official transcripts documenting all undergraduate work, and two letters of recommendation. A statement of purpose is suggested. GMAT scores are recommended but not required. International applicants should also include documentation showing financial support and a TOEFL score, unless they wish to enter the ESL program or they have graduated from an American university. New students may apply for the terms starting in September, December, March, and June. Applicants wishing to enroll in the twelve-month program can start only in the September term.

Correspondence and Information

Alan Shawn Feinstein Graduate Admissions Office
Johnson & Wales University
8 Abbott Park Place
Providence, Rhode Island 02903
Telephone: 401-598-1015
800-342-5598 Ext. 1015 (toll-free outside Rhode Island)
Fax: 401-598-1286
E-mail: gradadm@jwu.edu
World Wide Web: http://www.jwu.edu

THE FACULTY

Administration
Dr. Joe Goldblatt, CSEP, Dean and Professor of the Alan Shawn Feinstein Graduate School.
Frank Pontarelli, Ed.D., Director, Center for Education and Ed.D. Program in Educational Leadership.

Faculty
Paul Colbert, Associate Professor; Ph.D., Boston College.
Kevin Fountain, Associate Professor; M.S.T., Bryant; J.D., Suffolk; CPA.
Gary Gray, Associate Professor; M.B.A., Babson.
Paul Hodges, Assistant Professor and Program Director of Teacher Education; M.A., Rhode Island.
Ralph Jasparro, Associate Professor; Ph.D., Clayton.
Stacey L. Kite, Assistant Professor; M.S., Johnson & Wales.
Patt Manheim, Professor; Ph.D., Cornell.
William Millett, Associate Professor; Ph.D., Iowa.
Charles Mojkowski, Associate Professor; Ed.D., Boston University.
Alexander Portnyagin, Associate Professor; Ph.D., Moscow State.
Thomas Rossi, Assistant Professor; M.S., Lesley.
Frank Satterthwaite Jr., Associate Professor and Director of Center for Global Enterprise Leadership; Ph.D., Yale.
Lisa Sisco, Associate Professor; Ph.D., New Hampshire.
Martin Sivula, Associate Professor and Director of Center for Research; Ph.D., Connecticut.
Jane Sjogren, Associate Professor; Ph.D., Stanford.
Esmond D. Smith, Associate Professor; Ph.D., Salve Regina.
Kenneth Walker, Associate Professor; Ed.D., Boston University.

Adjunct Faculty
John Ball, C.A.G.S., Connecticut.
Elgin Boyce, C.A.G.S., Connecticut.
Theodore Butzbach, M.Ed., Rhode Island College.
Gary D'Orsi, M.B.A., Johnson & Wales.
James Dutra, M.B.A., Providence; M.S.T., Bryant.
Edward P. Mara, Ed.D., Nova.
Raymond Massotti, C.A.G.S., Boston University.
Joseph McWilliams Jr., M.B.A., Salve Regina.
Nick O'Donohoe, Ph.D., Syracuse.
Frank A. Pontarelli, Ph.D., Connecticut.
Carlos Rodriguez, Ph.D., Arizona.
Henry Silva, M.B.A., Providence.
Lisa M. Stepanski, Ph.D., New Hampshire.
Everett Zurlinden, M.B.A., Johnson & Wales.

JONES INTERNATIONAL UNIVERSITY

Graduate Studies

Programs of Study

As the Internet's first fully online, accredited university, Jones International University (JIU) offers Master of Business Administration (M.B.A.), Master of Education (M.Ed.) in e-learning, and Master of Arts (M.A.) in business communication degree programs that provide a high-quality online education. JIU provides vast educational opportunities by delivering curricula designed specifically for the Internet by content experts from prestigious institutions such as Cornell University; Thunderbird, the American Graduate School of International Management; Carnegie Mellon University; and the London School of Economics. Jones International University students may choose from a selection of undergraduate, graduate, and certificate programs in a wide variety of fields.

JIU offers educational excellence at the student's convenience. Discussions, interactions, lectures, and assignments can all be reviewed online from the convenience and comfort of the student's own home. Even the library is fully online. With students from more than 100 countries, the collection of perspectives, cultures, and experience gives an outstanding education and global perspective.

Jones International University offers seven M.B.A. programs in global enterprise management, health-care management, entrepreneurship, information technology management, negotiation and conflict management, project management, and e-commerce. M.Ed. in e-learning programs include research and assessment, corporate training and knowledge management, global leadership and administration, library and resource management, technology and design, and generalist studies. Courses are offered in accelerated eight-week and traditional twelve-week programs. New classes start each month, and applications are accepted throughout the year.

Research Facilities

Access to information and a library of resources is an essential key to a good education. Through Jones' e-global library, students have 24-hour-a-day online access to the resources they need to find the information they want. The JIU library is composed of several elements, all geared to serve the needs of time-constrained adult learners. It includes more than 20 electronic databases; more than eighty research guides; an Internet-based resource collection of nearly 6,000 handpicked, content-rich Web sites; access to more than 325 federal government sites that are categorized by subject and contain more than 150,000 documents; and access to more than 775 government-agency sites. In addition, the Jones e-global library offers tutorials that help students navigate the Internet more efficiently and effectively; reference assistance from librarians is available by e-mail.

Financial Aid

Students who would like to apply for student loans may apply for P.L.A.T.O.–The Classic Student Loan®. JIU also offers Career Training Loans, a financial assistance program available through SLM Financial Corporation, a Sallie Mae company. This cost-effective program has fast approval processing, high acceptance rates, and secured and unsecured options. Both loan options are available to individuals who are U.S. citizens, U.S. nationals, or permanent U.S. residents.

Students may be qualified for financial assistance under the Montgomery GI Bill, the Dependents' Educational Assistance Program, the Veteran's Educational Assistance Program, and employer-based reimbursement programs.

Cost of Study

Course tuition for each 3-credit graduate class is $925. There is a one-time admission application fee of $75; however, students may enroll in classes without applying for admission to the degree program. A $40 technology fee is also assessed per course.

Living and Housing Costs

Since all of Jones International University's courses are offered entirely online, students do not encounter extra living or housing costs in addition to their current living expenses.

Student Group

The Jones International University student body consists of students from a wide range of cultures and backgrounds. JIU has students in more than 100 countries. They range from 25 to 70 years old. Most are employed and are looking to JIU to help them further their careers with a master's degree.

Location

All JIU courses take place entirely on the Internet. Travel to additional locations is never required. JIU's administrative offices are located in Englewood, Colorado.

The University

Since 1993, Jones International University has been at the forefront of the online education revolution, creating relevant, content-rich executive, undergraduate, and graduate-level programs for motivated adult learners. In recognition of the quality of its programs, JIU became the first fully online educational institution to be awarded regional accreditation by the Higher Learning Commission of the North Central Association of Colleges and Schools (NCA).

Applying

For admission to the graduate degree programs, students must submit documentation of an earned bachelor's degree, in the form of an official transcript from a college or university that is accredited regionally or by the Distance Education Training Council. A minimum GPA of 2.5 is required. Students must complete the JIU application package, including submission of a two- to three-page statement of professional accomplishments and goals, a current resume, three professional or academic letters of reference, and a $75 nonrefundable application fee. Master of Arts in business communications applicants must also prove proficiency in public speaking and business writing through various documented methods.

Students may apply online at the Web site listed below.

Correspondence and Information

For more information, students should contact:

Enrollment Center
Jones International University
9697 East Mineral Avenue
Englewood, Colorado 80112
Telephone: 303-784-8247
800-811-5663 (toll-free in the U.S.)
Fax: 303-784-8547
E-mail: info@international.edu
World Wide Web: http://www.jonesinternational.edu

THE FACULTY

Jones International University has a world-class faculty from leading universities around the world. The course content is designed specifically for the online learning environment by experts who are recognized among the foremost authorities in their fields. These content experts have led groundbreaking research in business, economics, education, communication, and information technology. Industrial giants, including IBM, General Motors, and AT&T, as well as governments around the world, have benefited from their expertise. JIU offers a faculty with a unique combination of scholarship and real-world experience.

KANSAS STATE UNIVERSITY

The Graduate School

Programs of Study

Kansas State University's (KSU) Graduate School offers advanced study in sixty-four master's degree programs and forty-three doctoral programs, with more than 3,000 graduate students enrolled. There is an increasing emphasis on innovative interdisciplinary programs.

Opportunities exist for research and scholarly activities in the areas of agriculture, architecture and design, biochemistry, business administration, education, engineering, food science, genetics, human ecology, humanities and fine arts, natural sciences, social sciences, and veterinary medicine. Examples of areas for graduate study and research include atomic physics, automated manufacturing, software engineering, space biology, infectious disease research, prairie ecology, rural sociology, wheat genetics, molecular biology, theater, cancer biology, materials science, industrial and organizational psychology, military history, high-energy physics, and milling science.

The Graduate School requires 30 semester hours beyond the bachelor's degree to obtain the master's degree, although some programs require more than 30 semester hours. Many programs require a substantial research project, although a nonthesis option is available in some programs, and in the professional programs, that option predominates.

Doctoral programs require 90 semester hours beyond the bachelor's degree to obtain a Ph.D. and 94 semester hours beyond to obtain an Ed.D. Both programs include original research and a dissertation. Admission to candidacy requires the successful completion of the preliminary examinations.

The Division of Continuing Education offers many courses and degree programs through distance education, using a variety of delivery methods, including the World Wide Web, videotapes, audiotapes, Telenet 2, and other technologies. KSU offers the following through distance learning: the Adult and Continuing Education Master's Program (Kansas City, Salina, or Wichita), an Agribusiness Master's Degree, the Educational Administration and Leadership Master's Program, Engineering Degree Programs, the Classroom Technology Specialty in Elementary/Secondary Education Program, and English as a Second Language Specialty in Elementary/Secondary Education Program.

Post-baccalaureate certificates provide a means to recognize mastery in a specialized area or to supplement a graduate degree. KSU currently offers certificate programs in the areas of air quality, business administration, classroom technology, community planning, complex fluid flow, family financial planning, international studies, occupational health psychology, technical writing and professional communication, and women's studies. Certificate programs in other areas are being developed.

Research Facilities

KSU ranks among the nation's top seventy public research universities, with a growing foundation of research infrastructure to support vigorous training in scholarly research. The campus contains numerous specialized centers of interdisciplinary focused research, and these provide graduate students with dynamic training in their disciplines. Students should consult the KSU Graduate School home page for a partial listing of these centers (see Web site below).

Financial Aid

Nearly half of KSU graduate students receive some type of financial assistance, including university graduate fellowships, teaching and research assistantships, or other forms of university employment and loans. Full tuition waivers are given to graduate teaching assistants who receive at least a four-tenths-time appointment, and tuition reductions are available for graduate research assistants.

The KSU Office of Student Financial Assistance administers the federal assistance programs, work-study programs, and loans for which graduate students are eligible.

Cost of Study

For 2001–02, tuition for Kansas residents ranged from $113.40 for 1 graduate credit hour per semester to $1814.40 for 16 credit hours. Nonresident tuition ranged from $357.75 for 1 graduate credit hour per semester to $5724 for 16 credit hours. Campus privilege fees, which range from $64.00 to $251, are also charged.

Overall annual expenses, including living expenses, for a full-time student who completes 27 hours and is paying nonresident tuition, are about $18,900.

Living and Housing Costs

KSU has 432 apartment units for graduate students. Married couples with children and single parents have priority. One-bedroom apartments on a semester basis range from $281 to $293 per month, and two-bedroom apartments range from $331 to $344 per month. On a yearly basis in Williams Place, one-bedroom apartments range from $362 to $411 per month, and two-bedroom apartments range from $431 to $496 per month.

Student Group

The KSU graduate student population of more than 3,000 is made up of an almost equal number of men and women. International students from more than 100 countries make up about one–fourth of the population. About two–thirds of all graduate students are nontraditional (age 25 or older or married).

Student Outcomes

KSU graduates are highly sought after. They often receive multiple job offers, and many find employment well before graduation. They are leaders in public and private sectors, at government agencies, and at all levels of business and the private sector.

A sample of employers includes the National Institutes of Health, Argonne and Sandia National Labs, Nintendo, Merck, Pfizer, Cargill, Kellogg's, Hershey Foods, Anheuser-Busch, Motorola, AT&T Bell Labs, Texas Instruments, Rockwell International, and Sprint.

Location

KSU's picturesque 668-acre campus features many buildings of native limestone. KSU is centrally located in Manhattan (population 40,000), about 125 miles west of Kansas City. Manhattan has a new municipal airport, excellent schools, a daily newspaper, and numerous recreational facilities and cultural offerings. International festivals, Cinco de Mayo, Juneteenth, and Native American observances are held annually.

The University

Founded in 1863 as the first land-grant college, KSU is an internationally recognized, comprehensive research university with excellent academic programs carried out in a lively intellectual and cultural atmosphere.

In 1996, the University received the National Science Foundation's Recognition Award for the Integration of Research and Education. KSU was one of only ten universities selected.

Since 1974, KSU has ranked in the top 1 percent of all U.S. universities in the number of its graduates selected as Rhodes scholars.

Applying

Students should request admission applications and supplementary program information directly from the department or program coordinator. The Graduate School forwards correspondence to the appropriate program.

U.S. citizens should have all application materials on file by February 1 to receive priority consideration for full admission and for consideration for fellowships or graduate assistantships for the following fall semester. International students should apply no later than six months prior to the term in which they wish to enroll.

Correspondence and Information

The Graduate School
103 Fairchild Hall
Kansas State University
Manhattan, Kansas 66506-1103

Telephone: 800-651-1816 (toll-free in the U.S.)
785-532-6191 (outside the U.S.)
Fax: 785-532-2983
E-mail: grad.admissions@gradresearch.grad.ksu.edu
World Wide Web: http://www.ksu.edu/grad

PROGRAMS AND COORDINATORS

Students should contact the program coordinators listed below for more information.

COLLEGE OF AGRICULTURE

Agribusiness (M.S.): Allen Featherstone.
Agricultural Economics (M.S., Ph.D.): Ted Schroeder.
Agronomy (M.S., Ph.D.): Richard Vanderlip.
Animal Sciences and Industry (M.S., Ph.D.): Ernest Minton.
Entomology (M.S., Ph.D.): Sonny Ramaswamy.
Grain Science and Industry (M.S., Ph.D.): Katherine Tilley.
Horticulture (M.S., Ph.D.): Channa Rajashekar.
Plant Pathology (M.S., Ph.D.): Fred Schwenk.

COLLEGE OF ARCHITECTURE AND DESIGN

Postprofessional Master's Program in Architecture: Vladimir Krstic.
Professional Master's Programs: Landscape Architecture (M.L.A.): Dan Donelin.
Regional and Community Planning (M.R.C.P.): Al Keithley.

COLLEGE OF ARTS AND SCIENCES

Sciences and Mathematics

Biology and Microbiology (M.S., Ph.D.): David Rintoul.
Chemistry (M.S., Ph.D.): Robert Hammaker.
Geology (M.S., cooperative Ph.D. with the University of Kansas) Jack Oviatt.
Mathematics (M.S., Ph.D.): David Surowski.
Physics (M.S., Ph.D.): Tim Bolton.
Statistics (M.S., Ph.D.): John Boyer.

Humanities and Fine Arts

English (M.A.): Greg Eiselein.
Fine Arts (M.F.A.): Louann Culley.
History (M.A., Ph.D.): Sue Zschoche.
Modern Languages (M.A.): Claire Dehon.
Music (M.M.): Al Cochran.
Speech Communication, Theater, and Dance (M.A.): Speech, Charles Griffin; Theater, Daniel Davy.

Social Sciences

Economics (M.A., Ph.D.): Yang-Ming Chang.
Geography (M.A.): David Kromm.
Kinesiology (M.S.): Mary McElroy.
Mass Communication (M.S.): Robert Meeds.
Political Science (M.A.): Scott Tollefson.
Psychology (M.S., Ph.D.): John Uhlarik.
Public Administration (M.P.A.): Krishna Tummala.
Sociology (M.A., Ph.D.): Richard Goe.

COLLEGE OF BUSINESS ADMINISTRATION

Accountancy (M.Acc.): Dave Vruwink.
Business Administration (M.B.A.): Dave Vruwink.

COLLEGE OF EDUCATION

Students should contact Linda P. Thurston for information related to the following programs.

Adult, Occupational, and Continuing Education (M.S., Ed.D., Ph.D.).
Curriculum and Instruction (Ed.D., Ph.D.).
Educational Administration (M.S., Ed.D.).
Educational Psychology (Ed.D.).
Elementary Education (M.S.).
Secondary Education (M.S.).
Special Education (M.S., Ed.D.).
Student Counseling and Personnel Services (M.S., Ed.D., Ph.D.).

COLLEGE OF ENGINEERING

Architectural Engineering (M.S.): Charles Burton.
Biological and Agricultural Engineering (M.S., Ph.D.): Naiqian Zhang.
Chemical Engineering (M.S., Ph.D.): James Edgar.
Civil Engineering (M.S., Ph.D.): Hani Melhem.
Computing and Information Sciences (M.S., Ph.D.): David Gustafson.
Electrical and Computer Engineering (M.S., Ph.D.): Anil Pahwa.
Engineering Management (M.E.M.): E. Stanley Lee.
Industrial Engineering (M.S., Ph.D): E. Stanley Lee.
Mechanical Engineering (M.S., Ph.D.): Kevin Lease.
Nuclear Engineering (M.S., Ph.D.): Kevin Lease.
Operations Research (M.S.): E. Stanley Lee.
Software Engineering:(M.S.E.): David Gustafson.

COLLEGE OF HUMAN ECOLOGY

Apparel, Textiles and Interior Design (M.S.): Elizabeth McCullough.
Family Studies and Human Services (M.S.): Ann Smit.
Food Service, Hospitality Management, and Dietetics Administration (M.S.): Virginia Moxley.
Human Ecology (Ph.D.): Elizabeth McCullough.
Human Nutrition (M.S., Ph.D.): Food Science, Edgar Chambers IV; Nutrition, Sung Koo.
Institutional Management (M.S.): Virginia Moxley.

COLLEGE OF VETERINARY MEDICINE

Anatomy and Physiology (M.S.): Mark Weiss.
Clinical Sciences (M.S.): James Roush.
Pathobiology (M.S., Ph.D.): George Stewart.
Physiology (Ph.D.): Mark Weiss.

GRADUATE CERTIFICATE PROGRAMS

Air Quality: Larry Erickson and Mo Hosni.
Business Administration: Lynn Waugh.
Classroom Technology: College of Education.
Community Planning: Al Keithley.
Complex Fluid Flows: Chris Sorensen and Mo Hosni.
Family Financial Planning: John Grable, Joyce Cantrell, Debra Wood.
International Service: Scott Tollefson.
Occupational Health Psychology: Clive Fullagar.
Technical Writing and Professional Communications: Thomas Deans.
Women's Studies: Jackie Spears.

INTERDISCIPLINARY PROGRAMS

Food Science (M.S., Ph.D.): Ike Jeon.
Genetics (M.S., Ph.D.): George Liang.

KEAN UNIVERSITY

Graduate School

Programs of Study

The Nathan Weiss College of Graduate Studies of Kean University offers a wide variety of master's degree programs that address the needs of industry, education, and social services. Master of Arts degrees are available in the following areas: behavioral sciences, counselor education, early childhood education, educational administration, educational media specialization, educational psychology, fine arts, instruction and curriculum, liberal studies, mathematics education, reading specialization, special education, and speech-language pathology.

In addition to the M.A. degree programs, the University offers Master of Science degrees in accounting, biotechnology, computing, statistics, and mathematics; exercise science; graphic communications technology management; management information systems; and occupational therapy; the Master of Science in Nursing; the Master of Social Work; and the Master of Public Administration. The Master of Science in Nursing/Master of Public Administration is a dual-degree program. Also offered are the Professional Diploma in School Psychology and in Marriage and Family Therapy, as well as the post-master's Learning Disability Teacher Consultant certificate.

Students with an undergraduate liberal arts major may enter the Classroom Instruction or Early Childhood M.A. programs, which are special programs that grant an initial teaching certificate in elementary or early childhood education after the first year.

Most classes are scheduled during the evening to accommodate students who work full-time. Classes meet once a week during the fall and spring semesters; during the summer, students may take classes during the day or evening.

Research Facilities

The Nancy Thompson Library is a comprehensive learning center with 271,000 volumes (including bound periodicals and 1,350 periodical subscriptions), 92,000 microfilms, and an extensive journal collection. Included are rare books and printed materials, the New Jersey Collection, and the papers of Congresswoman Florence P. Dwyer. Available materials are greatly expanded through an interlibrary loan system, and the University utilizes an online computerized retrieval system from several national databases that facilitates rapid bibliographic retrieval. In addition, the holdings of all institutions of the Consortium of East New Jersey are available to Kean University students through the Nancy Thompson Library. The Holocaust Resource Center contains a vast collection of encyclopedia and text on Holocaust survivors, all of which is indexed for use by scholars, historians, teachers, and students. This center is affiliated with the Video Archive for Holocaust Testimonies, Sterling Library, Yale University.

The Instructional Resource Center (IRC) provides a variety of nonprint materials, electronic and conventional audiovisual equipment, and comprehensive media services. The nonprint instructional materials collection, which includes films, filmstrips, slides, audiotapes, media kits, video cassettes, and video discs, has approximately 7,400 titles.

Laboratory facilities include the Teaching Performance Center, Reading Institute, Campus School, Institute of Child Study, and Comprehensive Evaluation Clinic (Clinic in Learning Disabilities and Clinic in Audiology Disabilities).

Research affiliates include the Cerebral Palsy Center, Camp Union, and Aid to Children with Learning Disabilities, as well as a statewide computer network that exceeds student needs in virtually all cases.

Financial Aid

The University offers approximately 150 graduate assistantships, which are limited to full-time matriculated students (taking a minimum of 9 graduate credits per semester). Students receive a weekly stipend plus a waiver of tuition and fees.

A limited number of scholarships are available to graduate students as are institution-sponsored loans.

Cost of Study

Full-time graduate tuition and fees were $6780.40 for 2000–01 for New Jersey residents and $9106.40 for out-of-state students. Part-time graduate tuition and fees were $283.10 per credit for 2000–01 for New Jersey residents and $347.10 per credit for out-of-state students.

Living and Housing Costs

Limited on-campus housing is available for graduate students; off-campus apartments are available in the nearby vicinity.

Student Group

The 12,000 full- and part-time graduate and undergraduate students form a heterogeneous student body representing diverse cultural backgrounds. The graduate student population of about 2,000 is primarily part-time, with approximately 17 percent attending on a full-time basis.

The graduate student community is diverse in terms of ethnic background and age. A number of graduate students return for purposes of making career changes or upgrading professional skills and competencies. Graduate students often work cooperatively in research seminars and study groups, exchanging ideas and questions and learning, to a considerable extent, from one another. Practical experience is provided through internships in many of the programs.

Student Outcomes

Of the master's degree recipients in a recent year, approximately 74 percent went into teaching and education-related fields, 11 percent into administrative and business professions, and 15 percent into other occupations.

Location

Kean University's location in Union, New Jersey, is accessible to all major highways and is minutes away from an international airport. New York City is approximately 10 miles away.

The University

Established in 1855 as Newark Normal School, Kean University celebrated its 140th year in 1995. It offers degrees in the humanities, education, sciences, government, technology, and business. The University observed the 50th year of its graduate programs in the academic year 1998–99.

The University has received national acclaim for its innovative assessment and retention programs. The University offers a wide variety of cultural and social events. The New Jersey Ballet, a resident dance company, offers several performances throughout the year.

A delightful contrast to the surrounding urban area, the campus is 122 acres of rolling lawns and wooded areas with a graceful, meandering stream. An additional 28 acres on Kean's east campus are used for both intercollegiate and intramural recreation and student-oriented activities.

Applying

A formal application; a $35 fee; scores on the GRE General Test, the GMAT, the Miller Analogies Test, or the PRAXIS exam; and official transcripts of all previous college work are required for admission in most programs. A personal interview and references may also be required.

Correspondence and Information

Office of Graduate Admissions
T-106
Kean University
Union, New Jersey 07083

Telephone: 908-527-2665
E-mail: grad-adm@kean.edu
World Wide Web: http://www.kean.edu

FACULTY COORDINATORS

Kean University has 353 full-time faculty members, of whom 275 hold doctorates and 36 hold terminal degrees in their respective disciplines and also have distinguished themselves in their fields through research and publications. Adjunct faculty members drawn from the professions, business, and industry bring with them practical knowledge of their fields as well as academic qualifications. Graduate students receive personal attention, support, and guidance from the faculty and from the Office of Graduate Studies. The faculty-student ratio, which averages 1:17, allows for small classes and enables instructors to work closely with their students.

Accounting (M.S.): Dr. Eric Carlsen.
Behavioral Sciences (M.A.)
  Option: Business and Industry Counseling. Dr. Rhoda Feigenbaum.
  Option: Human Behavior and Organization Psychology. Dr. Henry L. Kaplowitz.
  Option: Psychological Services. Dr. Kit Ng.
Biotechnology (M.S.): Dr. Kristie Reilly.
Computing, Statistics and Mathematics (M.S.): Dr. Francine Abeles.
Counselor Education (M.A.): Dr. Juneau Gary.
  Option: Alcohol and Drug Abuse Counseling.
  Option: Business and Industry Counseling.
  Option: Community/Agency Counseling
  *Option: School Counseling.
Early Childhood Education (M.A.): Dr. Michael Knight.
  Option: Advanced Curriculum and Teaching.
  Option: Administration in Early Childhood and Family Studies.
  Option: Education for Family Living.
*Educational Administration (M.A.): Dr. Leonard Elovitz.
  Option: Program for Principals and Supervisors.
  Option: Program for Supervisors.
  Option: Program for School Business Administrators.
*Educational Media Specialization (M.A.): Dr. Hilary Crew.
*Educational Psychology (M.A.): Dr. Dennis Finger.
Exercise Science (M.S.): Dr. Walter Andzel
Fine Arts Education (M.A.)
  Option: Studio Art. Professor Richard Buncamper.
  *Option: Certification. Dr. Michael Desiano.
  *Option: Fine Arts Supervision. Dr. Michael Desiano.
Graphic Communications Technology Management (M.S.): Dr. Cyril Nwako.
Instruction and Curriculum (M.A.)
  Option: Mastery in Teaching. Dr. Sharon Brendzel.
  Option: Mathematics/Science/Computer Education. Dr. Sharon Brendzel.
  *Option: Bilingual/Bicultural Education. Dr. Gilda Del Risco.
  *Option: Teaching English as a Second Language. Professor Dr. Betsy Rodriguez-Bachiller.
  *Option: Classroom Instruction. Dr. Sharon Brendzel.
  *Option: Earth Science. Dr. Charles Murphy.
Liberal Studies (M.A.): Dr. John Gruesser.
Management Information Systems (M.S.): Dr. Thomas Abraham and Professor Jack Ryder.
Mathematics Education (M.A.): Dr. Francine Abeles.
  Option: Teaching of Mathematics.
  *Option: Supervision of Mathematics Education.
  Option: Computer Applications.
Nursing (M.S.N.): Dr. Dula Pacquiao.
Nursing/Public Administration (M.S.N./M.P.A.): Dr. Dula Pacquiao and Dr. Susan Ault.
Occupational Therapy (M.S.): Dr. Karen Stern.
Public Administration (M.P.A.): Dr. Jon Erickson.
  Option: Environmental Management.
  Option: Health Care Administration. Dr. Susan Ault.
*Reading Specialization (M.A.): Dr. Joan Kastner.
  Option: Basic Skills Specialist.
  Option: Adult Literacy.
  Reading Specialist (certification only).
  Teaching of Reading (certification only).
Social Work (M.S.W.): Dr. Alan Lightfoot.
  Option: Advanced Standing.
Special Education (M.A.): Dr. Beverly Kling.
  Option: Emotionally Disturbed and Socially Maladjusted.
  Option: Mental Retardation.
  Option: Preschool Handicapped.
  Option: Learning Disabilities.
*Speech-Language Pathology (M.A.): Dr. Barbara Glazewski.

Professional Diplomas:
  Marriage and Family Therapy: Dr. Kit Ng.
  School Psychology: Dr. Dennis Finger.

*Post-Master's Programs:
  Learning Disabilities Teacher Consultant. Dr. Marie C. Segal.
  Licensed Professional Counseling. Dr. Juneau Gary.

**Leads to New Jersey certification.*

The Holocaust Resource Center.

Dr. Frank Esposito, Dean of Nathan Weiss College of Graduate Studies.

The Kean Building.

KUTZTOWN UNIVERSITY OF PENNSYLVANIA

College of Graduate Studies

Programs of Study

The College of Graduate Studies at Kutztown University offers a variety of programs leading to the M.Ed., M.A., M.L.S. (Master of Library Science), M.B.A. (Master of Business Administration), M.P.A. (Master of Public Administration), and M.S. degrees. Certification programs are also offered.

The Master of Education degree is offered in art education; elementary education; reading; instructional technology; elementary and secondary school counseling; student affairs in higher education; and secondary education with cognate areas in biology, curriculum and instruction, English, mathematics, and social studies.

The Master of Science degree is offered in computer and information science and telecommunications.

The Master of Arts degree is offered in counseling psychology and English.

It is possible to earn a graduate degree at Kutztown University while concurrently completing course work for teaching certification or extending a valid teaching certificate to include new fields. Pennsylvania maintains cooperative agreements with many states so that earning certification in Pennsylvania means that the candidate will be eligible for certification in some other states.

Research Facilities

The Rohrbach Library is the focal point of academic life at Kutztown University. The library houses collections of books, periodicals, pamphlets, newspapers, maps, microforms, nonprint media, and electronic resources. At present, the collection consists of more than 492,117 volumes, representative federal and state documents, 45,000 maps, approximately 10,000 periodicals and newspapers, 15,000 units of nonprint media, and more than 1 million units of various kinds of microforms. The library provides electronic access to several full-text databases and reference resources over the University's network. The map collection is one of the finest in the state and includes Braille maps, city plans, and topographic and raised relief maps. The library has a state-of-the-art facility with network access to the Web and the Internet and has installed Endeavor's Voyager integrated library system.

The Curriculum Materials Center provides a wide range of the newest teaching and learning resources for examination, evaluation, and curriculum revision.

The Audiovisual Center, located on the ground floor of the library, administers a comprehensive collection of audiovisual materials and equipment. In addition, the Audiovisual Center houses a microcomputer laboratory, microcomputer software collection, and a materials production area.

Rohrbach Library provides numerous services to faculty and students. These include the circulation of open-collection and reserve materials, online database searching, interlibrary loan services, document delivery services, motion enhancement services, and electronic reference services.

The Rohrbach Library staff is responsible for developing and organizing the library collections and for administering programs of library orientation and bibliographic instruction. Librarians meet frequently with classes from all areas of curriculum to discuss specialized research tools.

Financial Aid

Various types of financial aid, in the form of grants and loans, are available to eligible graduate students who are enrolled either full-time or half-time (at least 6 hours). Financial aid in the form of Stafford loans is available to eligible students. Students should direct inquiries for information to the Financial Aid Office. A number of graduate assistantships are available. A stipend, accompanied by a tuition waiver, is offered to qualified students. Graduate assistants must take at least 9 semester hours for a full academic load. No more than 12 hours of course work are permitted for any one semester. Under supervision for a maximum of 20 hours each week, graduate assistants assume responsibilities that are related to their professional interests.

Cost of Study

Basic tuition and fees for the 2001–02 academic year for full-time Pennsylvania resident students taking 9–15 credits were $2718 per semester. Resident students taking fewer than 9 credits were billed at $297 per credit. Out-of-state students were assessed $4195 for full-time study or $478 per credit for fewer than 9 credits. (Tuition and fees are subject to change.)

Living and Housing Costs

Housing for graduate students in University residence halls is offered only during the summer session and on a space-available basis. Students should direct inquiries for information to the Office of Housing and Residence Life. Privately owned apartments and houses are available near the campus.

Student Group

In 1999–2000, total enrollment was 7,190; 860 were graduate students. Most of the graduate students (87 percent) are studying part-time, and 73 percent are women.

Location

With access to both the Lehigh and Schuylkill River Valleys, Kutztown University is located in the heart of the Pennsylvania Dutch country of the Commonwealth of Pennsylvania. A short drive of 7 miles via Pennsylvania Route 737 provides easy access to Interstate Highway 78, connecting New York City and Harrisburg, Pennsylvania. Kutztown is equidistant (16 miles) from Reading and Allentown, Pennsylvania, along Route 222. Commercial bus transportation is available from Kutztown to Reading, Philadelphia, New York City, and Washington, D.C. The University is located 25 miles west of Lehigh Valley Airport and 18 miles east of Reading Airport.

The University

Established in 1866 as a school to prepare teachers, Kutztown was authorized to award the bachelor's degree in 1926. Teacher education, including elementary and secondary education and a variety of special fields, such as art education and library science, has always played an important part in the development of the institution. On January 8, 1960, the governor of the commonwealth approved legislation making Kutztown a center of learning that would offer the youth of Pennsylvania the best possible education in the arts and sciences as well as in teacher education. The year before, Kutztown State College had been authorized to grant master's degrees in art education and elementary education.

Under the new statement of mission, the College began to develop a richness and breadth that encompasses the liberal arts and sciences, the fine and performing arts, teacher education, and other professional programs at the undergraduate and graduate levels. In 1983, Kutztown State College became Kutztown University.

Applying

The Graduate Office coordinates the admissions process. All applications and instructions should be obtained from the Director of Graduate Studies of the College of Graduate Studies. The payment of a nonrefundable $35 fee must accompany the completed application. Brochures and other information describing graduate programs are available from the departments listed on the reverse of this page. Descriptions of programs and courses also are available in the graduate catalog.

Correspondence and Information

Dr. Charles Cullum, Dean
College of Graduate Studies
Kutztown University
Kutztown, Pennsylvania 19530
Telephone: 610-683-4200
World Wide Web: http://www.kutztown.edu/academics/graduate

GRADUATE PROGRAMS AND FACULTY

Art Education. John H. White, Program Coordinator (610-683-4520); Susan Allport-Schneider; Nicholas N. Bowen; James G. Chaney; Harry Krizan; Anna Kuo; James Malenda; Thomas F. Schantz; Barbara J. Schulman; George W. Sorrels Jr.; Marilyn Stewart; Peter W. Traugott.

Business Administration. Theodore A. Hartz, Program Coordinator (610-683-4576); Okan Akcay; Arifeen Daneshyar; Mark Dinger; Kenneth Ehrensal; Philip R. Evans; Thomas Grant; Keshav Gupta; John Hamrick; Eileen Hogan; James M. Hvidding; Jonathan Kramer; Donald Kreps; James Luizer; H. Albert Margolis; James Ogden; Norman C. Sigmond; Abdulwehab Sraiheen; David D. Wagaman; Ronald L. Werley; Girma Zelleke.

Computer and Information Science. William Bateman, Program Coordinator (610-683-4410); Robert J. Buff; Linda Day; Henry G. Gordon; Deepak Khanna; Vivian G. Mosca; Thomas L. Pirnot; Oskars Rieksts; Joseph C. Thomas; Francis J. Vasko.

Counselor Education/Counseling Psychology. Margaret A. Herrick, Program Coordinator (610-683-4204); Emmanuel Akillas; Deborah Barlieb; Jo Cohen-Hamilton; Kelly Kenney; Sandra McSwain; Anita M. Meehan; George K. Muugi; G. Dennis Rains; Thomas A. Seay; Ronald W. Stoffey; Robert M. Voytas; C. Bruce Warner.

Elementary Education. Elsa Geskus, Program Coordinator (610-683-4262), faculty evaluation, language arts; Jorie Borden, language arts, student teaching; Jeanie H. Burnett, reading, gifted education; Sandra A. Chambers, reading, language arts; Sally Knappenberger, social studies, discipline; Charles E. Marple, social studies, international education; Alicia Montoya, multicultural education, language arts; T. Kelley Neyhart, math education, urban education; Lisa Potylycki, language arts, mathematics; Mary Ellen Swoyer, language arts, children's literature.

English. Guiyou Huang, Program Coordinator (610-683-4353); Dennis Bonser; Edwin E. Christian; Mary Theresa Hall; Jerome M. Hand; Judith Kennedy; David C. Laubach; James I. McNelis III; James W. Nechas; Arnold E. Newman; August J. Nigro; Elaine Reed; Louis A. Schwartz; Raymond D. Tumbleson.

Instructional Technology. Lynn Milet, Program Coordinator (610-683-1598); Robert A. Gray; Charles F. Roth Jr.

Library Science. Kathryn Holland, Program Coordinator (610-683-4300); Daniel R. Cates.

Computer Information Science. William Bateman, Program Coordinator (610-683-4410); Paul Ache; Robert J. Buff; Deborah Frantz; Glenna Y. Gebhard; Henry G. Gordon; William E. Jones Jr.; Deepak Khanna; Anthony A. Matz; Vivian G. Mosca; Larry R. Mugridge; Thomas L. Pirnot; Oskars Rieksts; Charles E. Trafford; Francis J. Vasko.

Public Administration. Paula A. Duda, Program Coordinator (610-683-4449); Gary B. Brey; Jack Treadway; Cheryl H. Wilf.

Reading Specialist. Beth M. Herbine, Program Coordinator (610-683-4271); Jeanie H. Burnett; Sandra Chambers; Edward J. Earley; Linda J. Gibbs.

Secondary Education. Kathleen A. Dolgos, Program Coordinator (610-683-4259); Joseph Elias; Joseph E. McSparran; Theresa M. Stahler; Dale Titus.

Telecommunications. David Kintsfather, Program Coordinator (610-683-4492); Leonard J. Barish; Joseph R. Chuk; Helen E. Clinton; Darrell D. Dahlman; Daryl Fairchild; Andrew R. Skitko Jr.

LAMAR UNIVERSITY

Graduate School

Programs of Study

Doctoral degrees are offered in the following disciplines: deaf education (Ed.D.), chemical engineering, civil engineering, industrial engineering, mechanical engineering, and electrical engineering (D.E.).

Master's degrees are offered in audiology (M.S.), applied criminology (M.S.), biology (M.S.), business administration (M.B.A.), chemical engineering (M.E. and M.E.S.), chemistry (M.S.), civil engineering (M.E. and M.E.S.), community and counseling psychology (M.S.), computer science (M.S.), counseling and development (M.Ed.), deaf studies/habilitation (M.S.), educational administration (M.Ed.), electrical engineering (M.E. and M.E.S.), elementary education (M.Ed.), engineering management (M.E.M.), English (M.A.), environmental engineering (M.S.), environmental studies (M.S.), family and consumer science (M.S.), history (M.A.), industrial engineering (M.E. and M.E.S.), industrial and organizational psychology (M.S.), kinesiology (M.Ed.), mathematics (M.S.), mechanical engineering (M.E. and M.E.S.), music (M.Mu.), music education (M.Mu.Ed.), nursing administration (M.S.), public administration (M.P.A.), secondary education (M.Ed.), special education (M.Ed.), speech-language pathology (M.S.), supervision (M.Ed.), theater (M.S.), and visual arts (art history) (M.A).

Teaching certification is available in the areas of counseling, educational diagnostician, elementary education, mental retardation, midmanagement administrator (principal), reading specialist, school superintendent, secondary education, special education supervisor, supervisor, and visiting teacher. The Early Childhood Development Center is a tool that provides University students direct observation of young children who exhibit typical and atypical development, as well as the opportunity to investigate effective teaching strategies for promoting optimal development among young children.

Research Facilities

The eight-story Mary and John Gray Library building dominates the campus from its central location. The library occupies seven floors and possesses an online public-access catalog to more than 1 million volumes and 3,000 periodicals. In addition to a collection of books and periodicals, the library provides access to state and federal government documents and participates in the library networks that extend access to information resources. The library coordinates multimedia programs on campus and has a basic collection of equipment and materials for central distribution.

The Research Office is administered by the Associate Vice President for Research, who chairs the research council. This office promotes and funds internal research; oversees sponsored programs and technology transfer, as well as patent, copyright, and intellectual property policies; establishes liaisons between the University and state and national funding sources; and assures that proposed projects comply with institutional and governmental regulations. This office also provides assistance to faculty members in the development and submission of grant/project proposals by locating funding sources and providing editorial assistance in proposal preparation.

Financial Aid

Financial assistance in the form of loans, grants, scholarships, tuition fee waivers, and the Federal Work-Study Program is available for a number of qualified students. Details may be obtained upon request from the Director of Financial Aid, P.O. Box 10042, Beaumont, Texas 77710. Teaching and research assistantships are available in the various graduate departments. Additional information may be obtained either from the department chair or from the Dean of the College of Graduate Studies.

Cost of Study

The current tuition rate for a Texas resident is $86 per hour for the summer and $148 per hour for fall and spring. Non-Texas resident tuition is $281 per hour for all sessions.

Living and Housing Costs

A variety of living options are available and include modern furniture, semiprivate rooms, carpet, central heating and air conditioning, and various color schemes in the dormitories. Apartment accommodations in newly remodeled buildings are also available. Questions concerning housing and rates can be directed to the Residence Life Office, Lamar University, P.O. Box 10041, Beaumont, Texas 77710.

Student Group

The student body consists of 8,027 undergraduate students, 915 master's students, and 28 doctoral students. The majority of undergraduate enrollment is from Jefferson and Orange Counties, while the Graduate School population is largely international. The average age of the Graduate School student is 33.

Student Outcomes

At the spring 2001 commencement, there were eighteen master's degrees awarded for arts and sciences, seven for business, fourteen for education, thirty-five master's and two doctoral degrees in engineering, and seven master's in fine arts.

Location

The Lamar University campus is located in Beaumont, Texas. With a population of more than 114,000, Beaumont is a diversified city, home not only to the University but also businesses and industry stemming from a strong petrochemical and agriculture base. World-renowned companies are located in Beaumont to take advantage of the area's resources and its educational workforce.

The University

Lamar University originated on March 8, 1923, with the plans for "a junior college of the first class." On June 8, 1942, classes were held for the first time on the present campus. In 1962, the Graduate School was established, and the doctorate of engineering and the doctorate in education in deaf education were established in 1971 and in 1993, respectively. Lamar is proud to be part of the Texas State University System and eagerly anticipates the evolving needs of its students.

Applying

General admission information can be found on the Web site at the address listed below or in the graduate catalog. Graduate students must meet the general standards and may have to meet more stringent standards, depending upon the department. Domestic students must submit all materials at least thirty days before registration.

Correspondence and Information

Graduate Admissions
Lamar University
P.O. Box 10078
Beaumont, Texas 77710

Telephone: 409-880-8356
Fax: 409-880-8414
E-mail: intladm@hal.lamar.edu
World Wide Web: http://www.lamar.edu

FACULTY HEADS

College of Arts and Sciences
Brenda S. Nichols; D.N.Sc., Indiana.

College of Business
Charles Hawkins (Interim Dean); Ph.D., LSU.

College of Education and Human Development
Carl Westerfield; Ph.D., Toledo.

College of Engineering
Jack R. Hopper; Ph.D., LSU.

College of Fine Arts and Communication
Russ Schultz; Ph.D., North Texas State.

Graduate Studies and Research/Admissions
Jerry W. Bradley; Ph.D., Texas Christian.

LESLEY UNIVERSITY

Graduate School of Arts and Social Sciences

Programs of Study

The Graduate School of Arts and Social Sciences of Lesley University offers programs of study in counseling and psychology, creative arts in learning, environmental education, expressive therapies, independent study degree, intercultural relations, and interdisciplinary studies.

Lesley offers a Doctor of Philosophy degree in expressive therapies, a Master of Arts degree in counseling psychology with the option of a specialization in school counseling, and a Master of Arts degree in clinical mental health counseling with specializations in holistic counseling, expressive therapies counseling, and school and community counseling. A certificate only program in school counseling and a Certificate of Advanced Graduate Study are also offered. Dual-degree programs with the School of Undergraduate Studies are available.

A Master of Education degree in creative arts in learning is offered with specializations in multicultural education and an individually designed program. A Curriculum and Instruction Program with a specialization in creative arts in learning and a Certificate of Advanced Graduate Study are also offered. A joint program is offered with the School of Education that leads to provisional and standard teacher certification in early childhood (Pre-K–3), elementary (1–6), and middle school (5–9) education. A Master of Education degree program in art education is also offered.

The Lesley/Audubon collaborative programs offer a Master of Science degree in environmental education and a Master of Science degree in ecological teaching and learning.

A Master of Arts degree in expressive therapies is offered with specializations in art therapy, dance therapy, music therapy, mental health counseling, and an individually designed specialization. A Certificate in Expressive Therapy for mental health professionals and a Certificate of Advanced Graduate Study are also available.

A Master of Arts degree in intercultural relations is offered with specializations in intercultural training and consulting, managing culturally diverse human resources, international education exchange, international student advising, multicultural education, intercultural health and human services, development project administration, intercultural conflict resolution, and an individually designed specialization. A Certificate of Advanced Graduate Study is also available.

Lesley University offers a Master of Arts degree, a Master of Education degree, and a Certificate of Advanced Graduate Study in independent study. In this nontraditional program, students design their own programs of study, which are pursued through independent study.

The Interdisciplinary Studies Program offers a Master of Arts degree that allows students the opportunity to focus their degree through an individualized specialization. Students draw from graduate-level courses across the four schools of Lesley University. A graduate certificate program in integrative holistic health studies is also available.

An Institute for Mind-Body Studies provides advanced graduate training and research.

Research Facilities

The Ludcke Library maintains a working collection of books, periodicals, microfilm and microfiches, curriculum materials, nonprint materials, and software resources. The Library provides Internet resources and database access to general and subject-specific resources appropriate to the subject focuses of the University. The Kresge Center for Teaching Resources provides instructional resources for individual and group instruction, and the Microcomputer Center houses the Instructional Computing activities of the University, including a collection of educational software. Through the Fenway Consortium students can access thirteen other libraries in the Boston-Cambridge area.

Financial Aid

The Lesley University Financial Aid Office administers all federal financial aid programs. There are opportunities in college teaching, advising, and research activities, as well as field placements. A limited number of assistantships are awarded by semester or academic year. Most positions require about 10 to 15 hours of work per week.

Cost of Study

Tuition for on-campus graduate students is $490 per credit for 2001–02; tuition for off-campus graduate students is $315 per credit. Most courses are 3 credits. Graduate degree requirements vary from 33 to 60 credits, depending upon the student's program and past experience. Book and supply costs average $400 per year. The Independent Study Degree Program's cost is $15,300, all inclusive.

Living and Housing Costs

Housing is not available for graduate students on campus. Information on local housing and assistance in obtaining it are available upon request from the Residence Life Office of Student Affairs.

Student Group

The graduate on-campus and off-campus enrollment at Lesley University consists of approximately 5,000 students—men and women ranging in age from their mid 20s to their early 70s, in all stages of professional development. Students come from fifty states and thirty-two countries. Most have worked in the professional field of their choice and returned to graduate school to upgrade their training, learn new skills, or change careers.

Location

Lesley University occupies a campus near Harvard Square in Cambridge, an area that benefits from the many advantages of the cities of Boston and Cambridge. The University is connected to downtown Boston by public transportation. Within a 6-mile radius are numerous historical sites and cultural attractions, including theaters, museums, and concerts. Off-campus programs are available across the United States and Internationally.

The University

Lesley University, founded in 1909 as a women's teaching college, continues its commitment to educating undergraduate women while also offering graduate and Ph.D. programs for women and men in the fields of education, human services, management, and the arts. With today's student in mind, Lesley University has successfully pioneered a wide variety of flexible programs for adult learners that share a commitment to quality, innovation, and the integration of theory with practice.

Lesley offers degree programs through four schools: the School of Undergraduate Studies, which includes the primarily residential Women's College, the coeducational Adult Baccalaureate College, and the Threshold Program; the Graduate School of Arts and Social Sciences; the School of Education; and the School of Management. The University also supports several centers and hosts a variety of academic and professional conferences and institutes. Lesley programs operate throughout Massachusetts and in fourteen other states, as well as at affiliated international sites.

There are four semesters of courses at Lesley: a fourteen-week fall semester, a four-week January mini-semester, a fourteen-week spring semester, and a twelve-week summer session (with two-week to five-week course options). Day and evening courses on campus and intensive weekend classes off campus permit maximum flexibility in arranging schedules. Students need not be degree candidates to take courses at the Graduate School of Arts and Social Sciences.

Applying

Applications are reviewed and acted upon as they are completed. Applications from international students not residing in the United States should be completed by April 1 for the fall semester and October 1 for the spring semester. Requirements for admission to graduate degree programs are a bachelor's degree (for the M.A. and M.Ed. programs) or a master's degree (for the C.A.G.S.) from a regionally accredited college or university as well as a satisfactory grade average, official transcripts of undergraduate and graduate work, three letters of recommendation, a written personal statement, and a nonrefundable $50 application fee. Application materials should be requested from the Office of Admissions for Graduate and Adult Baccalaureate Programs.

Correspondence and Information

Office of Admissions
Graduate and Adult Baccalaureate Programs
Lesley University
29 Everett Street
Cambridge, Massachusetts 02138-2790
Telephone: 617-349-8300
800-999-1959 Ext. 8300 (toll-free)
Fax: 617-349-8313
World Wide Web: http://www.lesley.edu

THE ADMINISTRATION AND FACULTY

Martha B. McKenna, Associate Professor and Dean of the Graduate School of Arts and Social Sciences; Ed.D., Columbia.
Thomas L. Geraty, Assistant Professor and Associate Dean of the Graduate School of Arts and Social Sciences; Ph.D. (LICSW), Simmons.
Linda Harris, Assistant Dean of the Graduate School of Arts and Social Sciences; M.A.L.S., Wesleyan (Connecticut).

Division Directors

Julia Byers, Professor and Director of the Expressive Therapies Program; Ed.D., Toronto.
Sharlene Cochrane, Associate Professor and Director of the Interdisciplinary and Individualized Programs; Ph.D., Boston College.
Susan Cohen, Director of Program Evaluation and Research Group (PERG); M.Ed., Lesley.
Gene Diaz, Associate Professor and Director of the Creative Arts in Learning Program; Ph.D., New Orleans.
Lisa Hoshmand, Professor and Director of Counseling and Psychology Division; Ph.D., Hawaii.
Vivien Marcow-Speiser, Professor and Director of International and Collaborative Projects; Ph.D., Union (Ohio).

Faculty

Kate Austin, Assistant Professor of Creative Arts in Learning; Ph.D. candidate, Union (Ohio).
John Aram, Professor of Independent Studies; Ph.D., MIT.
Mariagnese Cattaneo, Professor of Expressive Therapies; Ph.D., Union (Ohio).
Claudia Christie, Associate Professor of Interdisciplinary and Individualized Studies; Ph.D., Columbia.
Sylvia Cowan, Associate Professor of Intercultural Relations; Ed.D., Boston University.
Paul Crowley, Professor of Counseling and Psychology; Ph.D., Catholic University.
Arlene Dallalfar, Assistant Professor of Intercultural Relations; Ph.D., UCLA.
Karen Estrella, Assistant Professor of Expressive Therapies; Ph.D. candidate, Fielding Institute.
Michele Forinash, Assistant Professor of Expressive Therapies; D.A., NYU.
Susan Gere, Associate Professor of Counseling and Psychology; Ph.D., Simmons.
Joi Gresham, Assistant Professor of Creative Arts in Learning; Ed.D. candidate, Massachusetts Amherst.
Jay Jones, Associate Professor of Intercultural Relations; Ph.D., Boston College.
Jared Kass, Professor of Counseling and Psychology; Ph.D., Union (Ohio).
Lynn Kass, Instructor of Independent Study Degree Program; M.A.T., Antioch (Ohio). .
Michael Kemeh, Assistant Professor of Creative Arts in Learning; Ph.D., Kansas State.
Dalia Llera, Associate Professor of Counseling and Psychology; Ed.D., Harvard.
Elijah Mirochnik, Assistant Professor of Creative Arts in Learning; Ph.D., Berkeley.
Marion Nesbit, Associate Professor of Interdisciplinary and Individualized Studies; Ph.D., Texas at Austin.
Louise Pascale, Instructor of Creative Arts in Learning; Ph.D. candidate, Lesley.
Vivian Poey, Assistant Professor of Creative Arts in Learning; M.F.A., Rhode Island School of Design.
Mary Clare Powell, Associate Professor of Creative Arts in Learning; Ed.D., Massachusetts Amherst.
Rick Reinkraut, Associate Professor of Counseling and Psychology; Ph.D., Connecticut; Ed.D, Harvard.
Eleanor Roffman, Professor of Counseling and Psychology; Ed.D., Boston University.
Peter Rowan, Associate Professor of Expressive Therapies; B.A., Boston University.
Priscilla Sanville, Associate Professor of Creative Arts in Learning; Ph.D., Union (Ohio).
Robert Shreefter, Assistant Professor of Creative Arts in Learning; M.F.A., North Carolina at Chapel Hill.
Susan Spaniol, Assistant Professor of Expressive Therapies; Ed.D., Boston University.

LIBERTY UNIVERSITY

Graduate Studies

Programs of Study

Liberty University offers programs leading to graduate degrees within the College of Arts and Sciences, the School of Education, the School of Religion (including Liberty Baptist Theological Seminary), the School of Business and Government, and the Distance Learning program.

The School of Education offers the Master of Education (M.Ed.) and the Doctor of Education (Ed.D.). Master's degree concentrations are offered in administration and supervision, secondary education, elementary education, reading, school counseling, early childhood education, gifted education, and special education. Campus programs are designed so that students can complete all requirements in three or more summers. The Ed.D. in educational leadership offers concentrations in administration, curriculum, and instruction. A cognate in any one of twelve areas and a research component complete the Ed.D. program. The M.Ed. and Ed.D. degrees are also available through the Distance Learning program.

The College of Arts and Sciences offers the Master of Arts in Counseling and the Master of Science in Nursing. The Liberty Baptist Theological Seminary offers programs leading to the Master of Divinity; the Master of Arts in Religious Studies; the Master of Religious Education, with concentrations in church growth, youth, leadership, counseling, praise and worship, and cross-cultural studies; the Master of Theology; and the Doctor of Ministry. The School of Business and Government offers the Master of Business Administration.

The Distance Learning program offers the following distance learning adult degree programs: Master of Arts in Counseling, Master of Arts in Religion, Master of Business Administration, Master of Divinity, Master of Education, Doctor of Education, and Doctor of Ministry. Courses are taken via VHS videocassette or online and are designed for those who are unable to take courses on campus. However, some residence is required for most graduate programs.

Students are actively involved with their faculty adviser from the beginning of their program. Most programs can be completed in two years of full-time study. The Ed.D, the M.Div., and the D.Min. are three-year programs. The M.A. in Counseling requires a practicum and an internship.

The University, including Liberty Baptist Theological Seminary, is accredited by the Southern Association of Colleges and Schools (SACS) and the Transnational Association of Christian Colleges and Schools and is approved by the State Council of Higher Education for Virginia.

Research Facilities

The A. Pierre Guillermin Library contains more than 300,000 volumes and subscribes to more than 8,000 periodicals, including many full-text versions of books and journals available via the Internet to residential and off-campus students. The library subscribes to several electronic database services via the Internet, including ATLA Religion Index, Cambridge Scientific Abstracts, CCH Internet Tax Research Network, Christian Periodical Index, Dow Jones Interactive, EBSCOhost, FirstSearch, GaleNet's Literature Resource Center, InfoTrac, LEXIS-NEXIS Academic Universe, netLibrary, ProQuest Direct, and OVID. Participation in the OCLC international library network and the Virtual Library of Virginia (VIVA) enables Liberty to share library services within and beyond the state of Virginia. The library maintains an Electronic Information Center with thirty-four Pentium workstations where students can search the Internet and access Microsoft Office software and an Electronic Classroom, which provides instruction in the latest electronic resources. Liberty University is located within 1 to 3 hours of several major research libraries in Virginia and North Carolina.

The Information Technology Resource Center, open between 7:30 a.m. and 2 a.m., Sunday to Thursday, and from 9 a.m. to 9 p.m. on Saturday, provides Liberty University students access to 230 computers, twenty-four of which are powerful Mac G4 machines used primarily for graphic design. A full range of software titles (more than 200) are available, including Photoshop, Quark, Illustrator, MS Office 2000 application suite, all Oracle titles and tools, system development tools, animal sound analysis tools, SPSS, chemical tools, and Mathematica. A special graduate lab is in the developmental stage. The Zinngrabe Biblical Research Lab provides advanced academic research to the School of Religion and the Liberty Baptist Theological Seminary. For more information, students can visit the center's Web site at http://www.liberty.edu/itrc.

Financial Aid

The preferred submission date for all financial aid materials is April 15. Students may request the Free Application for Federal Student Aid by calling the Financial Aid Office at 434-582-2270. The most readily available source of financial aid for graduate students is the Federal Stafford Student Loan Program. Students may contact either the Financial Aid Office or their local financial institution to obtain further information or to apply. Many students are financially assisted in the seminary by tuition scholarships. The student should be aware that institutional funds for scholarships and grants are limited.

Cost of Study

In 2002–03, tuition for resident graduate programs is $285 per credit hour for the Master of Arts in counseling, $245 per credit hour for the Master of Science in nursing, $235 per credit hour for the Doctor of Ministry, and $165 per credit hour for seminary degree programs. The Distance Learning Program tuition is $235 per credit hour. Videotapes, workbooks, and textbooks cost extra. Seminary tuition is $150 per credit hour. Books cost approximately $350 per semester.

Living and Housing Costs

Housing costs average from $350 to $500 per month. The Student Development Office maintains a listing of housing opportunities that is available upon request. Single students should budget approximately $7500 per year, and married students should budget approximately $12,000 per year. Information on newspapers, apartment guides, and local businesses is available upon request. Single students aged 30 and under who are enrolled full-time may live in the dormitories. In 2002–03, dormitory room and board cost $2550 per semester. Cost of living figures are approximate and vary according to the student's standard of living.

Student Group

Currently, 350 graduate students are enrolled on campus, and 500 graduate students are enrolled through the Distance Learning Program.

Location

Liberty University is located in the heart of Virginia in Lynchburg (population 70,000), with the scenic Blue Ridge Mountains as a backdrop. The city is more than 200 years old and is noted for its culture, beauty, and educational advantages. Nearby are such sites as Appomattox Court House; Natural Bridge; Thomas Jefferson's Monticello; Washington, D.C.; and other places of interest.

Lynchburg offers a wide variety of activities for recreation and entertainment through its excellent sports facilities and programs, cultural events, Fine Arts Center, beautiful parks and streams, and ample shopping plazas and malls. Lynchburg is accessible by air, train, and bus.

The University

Founded in 1971 by Dr. Jerry Falwell, Liberty University provides a Christian, coeducational, comprehensive education. The graduate faculty is composed of dedicated scholars who work closely with each student.

Applying

Students should submit all admissions materials to the Office of Graduate Admissions by August 1 for fall entry and by December 1 for spring entry. The Ed.D. and all Master of Arts and Master of Education programs require the GRE, and the D.Min. requires the Miller Analogies Test (MAT) (the GRE may be substituted). Applicants must submit two official copies of transcripts from completed baccalaureate programs and any previous graduate schools attended. Applicants to the Th.M. and D.Min. programs must submit transcripts proving completion of the M.Div. at an accredited institution. In addition, applicants must submit a completed health record that is sent with the letter of admission. One or more academic recommendations is required for all master's-level programs. The D.Min. requires three letters of reference from colleagues in the ministry. A $35 application fee is required.

Correspondence and Information

Office of Graduate Admissions
Liberty University
1971 University Boulevard
Lynchburg, Virginia 24502
Telephone: 800-543-5317 (toll-free)
World Wide Web: http://www.liberty.edu

THE FACULTY

Ronald Allen, Associate Professor of Counseling; Ed.D., Sarasota.
John Balmer, Assistant Professor of Missions and Director, Center for World Missions; Th.M., Dallas Theological Seminary.
David Barnett, Dean, Library Services; D.Min., Liberty.
W. David Beck, Professor of Philosophy and Associate Vice President, Academic Affairs; Ph.D., Boston University.
Bruce K. Bell, Professor of Business and Dean, School of Business and Government; Ph.D., Walden.
Ellen L. Black, Adjunct Professor of Education; Ed.D., Temple.
James A. Borland, Professor of Biblical Studies and Theology; Th.D., Grace Theological Seminary.
Wayne A. Brindle, Professor of Biblical Studies; Th.D., Dallas Theological Seminary.
Deanna Britt, Associate Professor of Nursing and Chair, Nursing; Ph.D., Virginia Tech.
Rebecca F. Carwile, Professor of Education and Associate Dean, Education; Ed.D., Alabama.
Don H. Clark, Associate Professor of Educational Ministries; Ph.D., Southwestern Baptist Theological Seminary.
John Cooley, Adjunct Professor of Education; J.D., Washington and Lee; Ph.D., Baptist Christian.
Carl J. Diemer, Professor of Church History and New Testament; Th.D., Southwestern Baptist Theological Seminary.
John W. Donaldson, Professor of Geography and Education; Ph.D., Michigan.
Pauline Donaldson, Professor of Education; Dean, College of General Studies; and Director, Interdisciplinary and General Studies; Ed.D., Virginia.
Linda Eure, Associate Professor of Counseling; Ph.D., Regent University (Virginia).
Paul R. Fink, Professor of Pastoral Ministries; Th.D., Dallas Theological Seminary.
James Freerksen, Director, D.Min. Program; Th.M., Central Theological Seminary; Ph.D., Grace Theological Seminary.
John George, Professor of Business and Associate Dean, Graduate Studies; Ph.D., Alabama.
John Gianopulos, Adjunct Professor of Religion; Ed.D., Loyola.
Ronald L. Giese Jr., Associate Professor of Biblical Studies; Coordinator, Seminary Distance Learning Program; and Associate Dean, Seminary; Ph.D., Wisconsin–Madison.
Cynthia Goodrich, Assistant Professor of Nursing; Ed.D., Sarasota.
Gary R. Habermas, Distinguished Professor of Apologetics and Philosophy and Chairman, Department of Philosophy; Ph.D., Michigan State.
Harvey Hartman, Associate Professor of Biblical Studies; Th.D., Grace Theological Seminary.
Ronald E. Hawkins, Professor of Counseling and Practical Theology and Dean, College of Arts and Sciences; D.Min., Westminster Theological Seminary (Philadelphia); Ed.D., Virginia Tech.
Craig Hinkson, Assistant Professor of Theology and Philosophy and Director, Graduate Studies; Ph.D., Chicago.
Clarence Holland, Associate Professor of Education; Ed.D., Oklahoma.
Jerald Hubbard, Adjunct Professor of Education; Ed.D., Nova.
Kathie Johnson, Associate Professor of Education and Chairman, Teacher Education; Ed.D., Virginia.
Luke Kauffman, Associate Professor of Pastoral Ministries; D.Min., Luther Rice.
C. Daniel Kim, Professor of Church History and Missions; Th.D., Dallas Theological Seminary.
Donnie Lawrence, Associate Professor of Education; Ph.D., Kansas.
David Lawson, Assistant Professor of Counseling; Psy.D., Biola.
Larry L. Lilley, Professor of Business and Chairman, Department of Business Management; D.B.A., Nova.
Danny Lovett, Professor of Evangelism and Dean, Liberty Baptist Theological Seminary; D.Min., Reformed Theological Seminary.
Robert Mastin, Associate Professor of Counseling; Ph.D., US International.
William Matheny, Professor of History and Missions and of Cross-Cultural Studies; Ph.D., Texas Christian.
Tim Mink, Associate Professor of Pastoral Care and Coordinator, EDP Seminary Program; Ph.D., North Texas.
Daniel R. Mitchell, Professor of Theological Studies and Associate Dean, Seminary; Th.D., Dallas Theological Seminary.
John Morrison, Associate Professor of Theological Studies; Ph.D., Virginia.
John J. Pantana, Professor of Education; Ed.D., Virginia.
Karen Parker, Professor of Education and Dean, School of Education; Ed.D., Miami (Florida).
Kenneth Reeves, Assistant Professor of Counseling; Ed.D., Northern Illinois.
Frank J. Schmitt, Professor of Educational Ministries and Director, Doctor of Ministry Program; M.B.A., Lynchburg; Ed.D., New Orleans Baptist Theological Seminary.
Charles Schneider, Adjunct Professor of Education; Ed.D., Nova.
William Scott, Associate Professor of Counseling; Ed.D., New Orleans Baptist Theological Seminary.
Hila J. Spear, Associate Professor of Nursing and Director, Graduate Studies in Nursing; Ph.D., Virginia.
Randal J. Spear, Adjunct Professor of Education; Ed.D., Virginia Tech.
Jean St. Clair, Assistant Professor of Nursing and Director, Generic Nursing; Ph.D., Virginia Commonwealth.
Patricia Thompson, Assistant Professor of Counseling and Psychology and Executive Director, Distance Learning Program; Ed.D., Sarasota.
Elmer Towns, Distinguished Professor of Systematic Theology and Dean, School of Religion; D.Min., Fuller Theological Seminary; D.D., Baptist Bible College of Pennsylvania.

LONG ISLAND UNIVERSITY, C.W. POST CAMPUS

Graduate Programs

Programs of Study

The College of Liberal Arts and Sciences offers M.A. degrees in English, history, interdisciplinary studies, political science, psychology, and Spanish; M.S. degrees in applied mathematics, biology, environmental studies, and interdisciplinary studies; and a Psy.D. degree in clinical psychology. The College of Liberal Arts and Sciences offers a number of accelerated five-year degree programs combining a broad-based liberal arts background at the bachelor's level with professional training at the master's level: B.S./M.S. (biology); B.A. (international studies)/M.B.A. (international business); B.A./M.A. (political science); and B.A. (political science)/M.P.A. (health-care administration). The College of Management offers the M.B.A. with concentrations in finance, international business, logistics and supply chain management, management, management information systems, and marketing; M.S. degrees are offered in accountancy, criminal justice, criminal justice (security administration concentration), and taxation; M.P.A. degrees are offered in health-care administration and public administration. Advanced certificates are also offered in business, gerontology, and nonprofit management. The College of Management also offers accelerated programs, including an M.P.A. (health-care administration)/J.D. and a J.D./M.B.A. in conjunction with Touro Law Center; B.S./M.S. (accountancy); B.A./M.S. (criminal justice); B.S./M.P.A. (health-care administration); and B.S./M.P.A. (public administration). The College of Information and Computer Science offers a Ph.D. in information studies; an M.S. in library and information science, information systems, management engineering, and computer science education; and an advanced certificate in archives and records management. The School of Education offers M.S.Ed. degrees for teachers of special education, school administration and supervision, and for reading teachers; M.A. degrees in teaching English to speakers of other languages (TESOL) and speech language pathology; M.S. degrees in early childhood and childhood education, school counseling, computers in education, and mental health counseling; and M.S. degrees in the following areas of secondary education: biology, art (K–12), music (K–12), Spanish, English, mathematics, earth science, and social studies. Advanced certificate programs are also offered for school district administrator studies and school business administration. C.W. Post also offers thirty-six dual bachelor's/master's degree programs in education and dual certification master's degree programs in childhood/literacy and childhood/special education. The School of Visual and Performing Arts offers M.A. degrees in art, clinical art therapy, interactive media arts, music, and theater; an M.F.A. degree is offered in fine arts and design. The School of Health Professions offers M.S. degrees in cardiovascular perfusion, clinical laboratory management, nutrition, advanced practice nursing, family nurse practitioner studies, and biomedical science (with specializations in hematology, immunology, medical chemistry, or medical microbiology). Accelerated B.S./M.S. degrees include nursing/family nurse practitioner studies and nursing/advanced practice nursing. Advanced certificates in advanced practice nursing and dietetic intership are also offered. Master's degree students have five years in which to complete their course of study. For the College of Liberal Arts and Sciences there is a requirement of 30 to 42 credits, depending on the degree chosen. Entrance and thesis requirements vary, depending on the program. In the arts, the M.A. programs require 33–36 credits and a thesis; the M.F.A. program requires 60 credits, including a thesis. For all art programs a portfolio review is required. The M.B.A. program requires 36–60 credits. M.S. programs in professional accountancy require a maximum of 60 credits. M.S. degrees in taxation require a maximum of 48 credits. The M.P.A. is a 48-credit program; the M.S. in criminal justice is a 36-credit program, including a thesis. Education degrees require 30–38 credits; a thesis is optional. All advanced certificates and counseling degrees require 60–62 credits. The M.S. in library and information science requires 36 credits and a thesis is optional. Through weekend college, students may earn graduate credits toward degrees in education, criminal justice, health administration, public administration, and medical biology.

Research Facilities

The B. Davis Schwartz Memorial Library is one of the largest research libraries in New York and houses 2.6 million books and periodicals as part of a University-wide system. This multilevel library is a digital powerhouse with high-speed Web connections and wireless communications, online subscriptions, and more than 100 database services. It also features the nationally respected Center for Business Research, Media Center, and Government Information Collection. C.W. Post is home to the Center for Aging, the Financial Markets Research Center, and the Electronic Educational Village. Science, art, and education facilities are fully equipped.

Financial Aid

Various assistantships are available through each department. Financial aid is also available through federal financial aid programs, including the Federal William T. Ford Direct Loan, Federal Perkins Loan, and Federal Work-Study Program. In addition, full-time students may be eligible for state grants. A graduate scholarship provides awards of up to $100 per credit depending on the major and grade point average. The awarding of this scholarship is not based on financial need and does not prevent the student from applying for other types of financial assistance. Continuing graduate students who are high achievers may be considered for a Graduate Incentive Award. Deadline dates apply. Scholarships/grants are given on a funds-available basis.

Cost of Study

Tuition for 2001–02 was $572 per credit plus college fees for all majors except Psy.D, speech-language pathology, M.B.A., and Ph.D. Additional expenses include books and laboratory, thesis, and graduation fees. Fees are subject to change.

Living and Housing Costs

C.W. Post provides housing for graduate students.

Student Group

There are more than 3,700 graduate students from over forty-five countries around the world. Students can enroll in either part-time or full-time study.

Location

C.W. Post is located on a beautiful 308-acre estate in the suburban Long Island community of Brookville. Major shopping centers in the immediate area include good restaurants, movie theaters, and department stores. The campus is only 40 minutes from New York City. Bus transportation is available from the Long Island Railroad station in Hicksville.

The University

C.W. Post Campus is one of six campuses of Long Island University, the eighth-largest independent university in the country. The many facilities available for student use include a modern concert theater, the Interfaith Center, the Klar Intercultural Student Center, stables, and recreational facilities such as a football stadium and a new mulitmillion dollar recreation center. The Hillwood Commons campus center houses an outstanding museum and film theater.

Applying

Students wishing to apply for admission to any program should request a graduate bulletin and an application from the Office of Graduate Admissions. Deadlines exist for certain graduate degree programs. Interested applicants should contact the Office of Admissions for further information. An online application is available at http://www.liu.edu/postapp.

Correspondence and Information

Office of Graduate Admissions
Long Island University, C.W. Post Campus
720 Northern Boulevard
Brookville, New York 11548-1300
Telephone: 516-299-2900
Fax: 516-299-2137
E-mail: enroll@cwpost.liu.edu
World Wide Web: http://www.liu.edu

FACULTY HEADS

C.W. POST CAMPUS DEANS

College of Liberal Arts and Sciences: Katherine C. Hill-Miller, Acting Dean; Ph.D., Columbia.
College of Management: Robert J. Sanator, Ph.D., Polytechnic.
School of Education: Robert Manheimer, Acting Dean; Ed.D., Columbia.
School of Health Professions: Theodora Grauer, Ph.D., Adelphi.
College of Information and Computer Science: Michael Koenig, Dean, Ph.D., Drexel.
School of Visual and Performing Arts: Lynn Croton, M.A., Columbia Teachers College.

DEPARTMENT CHAIRPERSONS

Art: Jerome Zimmerman, M.F.A., Rhode Island School of Design.
Biology: Michael Shodell, Ph.D., Berkeley.
Biomedical Science: R. R. Modesto, Ph.D., IIT.
Clinical Psychology: Robert Keisner, Director of Program; Ph.D., Massachusetts.
College of Management
- Accounting: Lawrence Kalbers, Director, School of Professional Accountancy; Ph.D., Penn State.
- Criminal Justice: Harvey Kushner, Ph.D., NYU.
- Finance: Vincent Massaro, Ph.D., Notre Dame.
- Health Care and Public Administration: Matthew Cordaro, Ph.D., Cooper Union
- Management: Anthony Akel, Ph.D., Northwestern.
- Marketing: P. M. Rao, Ph.D., NYU.

Media Arts: Barbara Fowles, Ph.D., Yeshiva.
Computer Science: Susan Fife-Dorchak, Ph.D., Nova.
Earth and Environmental Science: Margaret Boorstein, Ph.D., Columbia.
Education
- Administration and Leadership: Richard K. White, Ed.D., NYU.
- Counseling: A. Scott McGowan, Ph.D., Fordham.
- Curriculum and Instruction: Anthony DeFalco, Ed.D., Rutgers.
- Educational Technology: Michael Byrne, Ph.D., Michigan State; Bette Schneiderman, Ph.D., Hofstra.
- Health, Physical Education and Movement Science: Mary Trotto, Ph.D., West Virginia.
- Special Education and Literacy: Alvin Kravitz, Ed.D., Hofstra.
- Communication Science and Disorders: Dianne Slavin, Ph.D., NYU.

English: Edmund Miller, Ph.D., SUNY at Stony Brook.
Foreign Languages: Sheila Gunther, M.A., Pennsylvania.
History: Roger Goldstein, Ph.D., Columbia.
Mathematics: Neo Cleopa, Ph.D., Adelphi.
Music: Alexander Dashnaw, M.M., Northwestern.
Nursing: Minna Kapp, Ed.D., Columbia.
Nutrition: Frances Gizis, Ph.D., NYU.
Political Science/International Studies: Roger Goldstein, Ph.D., Columbia.
Psychology: Gerald Lachter, Ph.D., CUNY, Queens.
Theater and Film: Cara Gargano, Ph.D., CUNY Graduate Center.

LOUISIANA STATE UNIVERSITY IN SHREVEPORT

Graduate Studies

Programs of Study

The College of Business at Louisiana State University in Shreveport (LSUS) offers the M.B.A. A concentration in health-care management is available with the completion of 12 hours of elective course work in the area of health care. The College of Education offers the M.Ed., with concentrations in gifted education, supervision, counselor K–12, ancillary counselor K–12, reading specialist, administration, early childhood education, elementary education, secondary education, special education, exercise and wellness, and a discipline from liberal arts/sciences; the M.S. in counseling psychology; and the School Psychology Specialist (S.P.S.). The College of Liberal Arts offers the M.A. in liberal arts and the M.S. in human services administration. The College of Sciences offers the M.S. in systems technology.

Research Facilities

The Noel Memorial Library houses more than 250,000 items organized by the Library of Congress Classification. The library is a select depository for the United States Government Publications Office and for Louisiana state documents. It maintains two special collections, including archival records, historical manuscripts, and the James Smith Noel collection of more than 250,000 volumes in 128 broad subject areas. On the campus, there are eighteen computing labs, two institutes (the Red River Watershed Management Institute and the Sports Science Institute), and the International Lincoln Center for American Studies.

Financial Aid

Federal Stafford Student Loans are available to graduate students pursuing at least 6 hours per semester. The University offers a number of assistantships for both full-time and part-time graduate students. Students should contact the specific program's director for more details. For additional information about financial aid, students should contact the Director of Financial Aid at 318-797-5363.

Cost of Study

Tuition and fees total $185 per credit hour for Louisiana residents and $410 for nonresidents.

Living and Housing Costs

The University Court Apartments offers four-bedroom and efficiency apartments with either nine-month or twelve-month contracts. Each includes a one-time furniture payment per contract ranging from $261 to $516. Prices range from $1067 to $2214 per semester but are less in the summer. Each has a full-service kitchen.

Student Group

The total University enrollment was 4,113 for fall 2001, with 694 graduate students; 3,934 for spring 2002, with 681 graduate students; and 2,109 for summer 2002, with 519 graduate students. The majority of graduate students are part-time and take evening classes.

Location

The University is located on a 200-acre tract on Highway 1 in south Shreveport, north Louisiana's largest metropolitan area, with a population of 350,000, and the business center of the surrounding Ark-La-Tex, with a population of 1.5 million. Shreveport is located in the northwest corner of Louisiana, 200 miles east of Dallas, Texas, and 230 miles north of Baton Rouge, Louisiana.

The University

Louisiana State University in Shreveport is the only public comprehensive university in the largest metropolitan center in the region. Established in 1967, LSUS is an independent member of the LSU system and has a Carnegie classification of Master's University I. *The Gourman Report* has ranked LSUS as third among Louisiana universities in quality of academic programs, behind Tulane and LSU A&M (both with a Carnegie classification of Doctoral/Research University–Extensive). LSUS is accredited by the Southern Association of Colleges and Schools.

Applying

Applicants should have earned a minimum 2.5 cumulative GPA in undergraduate work. Most programs require submission of scores on standardized tests (GRE or GMAT). All programs have additional requirements. Students whose native language is not English must submit a TOEFL score of at least 550. Students are admitted to any term. The application and credentials (transcripts and test scores) should be received at the address below at least thirty days prior to the term for which admission is desired.

Correspondence and Information:

Office of Admission and Records
Louisiana State University in Shreveport
One University Place
Shreveport, Louisiana 71115
Telephone: 318-797-5061
Fax: 318-797-5286
E-mail: admissions@pilot.lsus.edu
World Wide Web: http://www.lsus.edu

THE FACULTY

College of Business Administration

Douglas Bible, Ph.D., Ohio State. Lisa Burke, Ph.D., Indiana. Chengho Hsieh, Ph.D., LSU. Karen James, D.B.A., Southern Illinois Carbondale. Lorraine Krajewski, Ph.D., Arizona State. Binshan Lin, Ph.D., LSU. John Masters, Ph.D., North Texas. Sanjay Menon, Ph.D., McGill. Frederick Parker, J.D., LSU. Raymond Taylor, Ph.D., Southern Illinois Carbondale. John Vassar, Ph.D., North Texas State. Tim Vines, Ph.D., Tennessee.

College of Education

Ronald Byrd, Ph.D., Florida State. Yong Dai, Ph.D., Brigham Young. Cay Evans, Ph.D., Georgia. Jean Hollenshead, Ph.D., Santo Tomas (Philippines). Yong Hwang, Ph.D., SUNY at Buffalo. Martha Mangin, Ph.D., South Carolina. Meredith Nelson, Ph.D., New Orleans. Rebecca Nolan, Ph.D., Texas A&M. Kyle Pierce, Ed.D., Auburn. Merikay Ringer, Ph.D., Southern Mississippi. Patricia Stanley, Ph.D., East Texas State. Timothy Winter, Ph.D., Tennessee at Knoxville.

College of Liberal Arts

David Anderson, Ph.D., Northwestern. Larry Anderson, Ph.D., Illinois at Chicago. LaMoyne Batten, M.F.A., Indiana. Stephen Brennan, Ph.D., Tulane. Megan Conway, Ph.D., Tulane. Norman Dolch, Ph.D., Missouri. Thomas DuBose, Ph.D., Texas. Milton Finley, Ph.D., Florida State. Terry Harris, Ph.D., Missouri. Lloyd Klein, Ph.D., CUNY Graduate Center. Merrell Knighten, Ph.D., LSU. James Lake, Ph.D., Delaware. Dorie LaRue, Ph.D., Southwestern Louisiana. Michael Leggiere, Ph.D., Florida State. Johnette McCrery, Ph.D., Maryland. Charles Moore, Ph.D., Syracuse. Bernadette Palombo, Ph.D., Claremont. William Pederson, Ph.D., Oregon. Marguerite Plummer, Ph.D., Texas at Dallas. Sura Rath, Ph.D., Texas A&M. Jeffrey Sadow, Ph.D., New Orleans. Mary Ann Shaw, Ph.D., Texas A&M. Helen Taylor, Ph.D., Connecticut. Lynn Walford, Ph.D., LSU.

College of Sciences

Stephanie Aamodt, Ph.D., Vanderbilt. Krishna Agarwal, Ph.D., SUNY at Stony Brook. Stephen Banks, Ph.D., Nottingham (England). Elizabeth Bida, Ph.D., Tennessee. Gary Boucher, Ph.D., Louisiana Tech. Beverly Burden, Ph.D., Wisconsin–Madison. Judith Covington, Ph.D., Southwestern Louisiana. Adrienne Critcher, Ph.D., Iowa. Julien Doucet, Ph.D., Tulane. David Foley, Ph.D., IIT. Mary Ann Foley, Ph.D., Texas A&M. James Goodrich, Ph.D., Texas at Austin. Dalton Gossett, Ph.D., Texas A&M. Wayne Gustavson, Ph.D., Oklahoma. Laurence Hardy, Ph.D., New Mexico. James Ingold, Ph.D., Miami (Ohio). Robert Kalinsky, Ph.D., Ohio State. Jeff Key, M.S.S.T., LSU in Shreveport. Vaughan Langman, Ph.D., Alaska. Myron Cran Lucas, Ph.D., Washington State. Steven Lynch, Ph.D., California, Davis. Richard Mabry, Ph.D., South Florida. John Sigle, Ph.D., Texas A&M. Cynthia Sisson, Ph.D., South Carolina. Paul Sisson, Ph.D., South Carolina. Carlos Spaht, Ph.D., LSU. Richard Thompson, Ph.D., Oklahoma State. William Vekovius, Ph.D., LSU. Robb Wilson, Ph.D., Michigan.

LOYOLA MARYMOUNT UNIVERSITY

Programs of Study

Loyola Marymount University offers more than forty master's degrees in programs aimed primarily at serving working professionals in the Southern California area. The College of Liberal Arts grants degrees in the fields of English, philosophy, pastoral studies, and theology. The Department of English offers a degree with an emphasis in creative writing, rhetoric/composition, or literature. The College of Business Administration offers an M.B.A. program that is open to applicants who hold a bachelor's degree in any field. The program is accredited by the American Assembly of Collegiate Schools of Business. The School of Film and Television offers an M.F.A. degree in the fields of film production, television production, and screenwriting. The Department of Marital and Family Therapy offers a master's degree program with an emphasis in clinical art therapy. The program is accredited by the American Art Therapy Association. The College of Science and Engineering grants Master of Science degrees in the areas of computer science, engineering and production management, and environmental science. The college also offers a Master of Science in Engineering degree in the fields of civil (environmental), electrical, and mechanical engineering. The School of Education grants Master of Arts degrees in bilingual education, counseling, educational psychology, elementary education, secondary education, special education, and TESL/multicultural education. The school also offers the Master of Education degree in administration, child and adolescent literacy, general education, and literacy and language arts. The fields of specialty in the Master of Arts in Teaching degree program are biology, communication arts, English, history, Latin, learning and teaching, mathematics, and social studies. Ten credential and four certificate programs are also offered at the School of Education.

Research Facilities

Graduate students have access to all computer labs on campus. Equipment includes Digital MicroVAX, IBM, Apple IIe, and Macintosh computer systems. Internet access is available. The recently remodeled Von der Ahe Library contains more than 363,000 volumes, 101,000 microforms, 2,900 current periodicals, and access, via an interlibrary system, to the major research facilities at UCLA's libraries.

Financial Aid

The University maintains an Office of Financial Aid to assist graduate students who require financial aid. LMU offers financial aid in the form of scholarships, grants, loans, teaching assistantships, research assistantships, and graduate assistantships.

Cost of Study

Tuition for the 2001–02 academic year for most programs is $575 per unit (most classes are 3 units). The M.B.A. and engineering and production management programs are $710 per unit. The clinical art therapy program in the Department of Marital and Family Therapy is $600 per unit, and programs in the School of Film and Television are $600 per unit.

Living and Housing Costs

Room and board in the surrounding residential area average $8000 for the academic year. Students should contact the Graduate Admissions Office for assistance in locating appropriate accommodations. Public transportation is available near the campus. Limited on-campus housing is available.

Student Group

Organizations such as the M.B.A. Student Association and the Student Advocates of Bilingual Education offer graduate students a forum for discussion and networking within specific fields of interest. LMU services include low-cost health insurance, free psychological counseling, career counseling and placement, emergency short-term loans, campus employment opportunities, campus safety programs, and counseling and support for international students. Recreational facilities are open to all students.

Location

Loyola Marymount is situated in an ideal location for living and learning. The campus is located in a peaceful residential neighborhood of Los Angeles. LMU sits high on a bluff overlooking the Pacific Ocean and Marina del Rey, with easy access to the San Diego (405), Marina (90), and Century (105) freeways. Its beautiful campus provides an exceptional setting for academic and campus life. The Los Angeles metropolitan area, with one of the most diverse populations in the country, also provides students with many stimulating cultural opportunities.

The University

Loyola Marymount, founded in 1911, is a Catholic, independent university in the educational tradition of the Society of Jesus (Jesuits) and the Religious of the Sacred Heart of Mary. The University is accredited by the Western Association of Schools and Colleges. The students and faculty and staff members bring a vast diversity of backgrounds and traditions to the campus. LMU offers small class size and personal interaction between students and faculty. The University emphasizes academic excellence for the total development of the student and for the building of a more just society.

Applying

Applicants must hold a bachelor's or higher degree from a regionally accredited institution. The GRE is required for most programs; the M.B.A. program requires the GMAT. Individual programs may have specific deadlines, prerequisites, or additional paperwork requirements. Applicants must submit a graduate application with a nonrefundable $35 fee, a statement of intent, and two official transcripts of all previous college-level work with the Graduate Admissions Office prior to the pertinent deadline. Students must submit financial aid applications to the Office of Financial Aid by June 1 to be considered for aid for the following fall. Students may apply online at http://www.embark.com.

Correspondence and Information

Graduate Admissions Office
University Hall, Suite 2500
Loyola Marymount University
One LMU Drive
Los Angeles, California 90045-2659

Telephone: 310-338-2721
888-946-5681 (toll-free)
Fax: 310-338-6086
E-mail: gradapps@lmumail.lmu.edu
World Wide Web: http://www.lmu.edu/graduate

PROGRAM DIRECTORS

Stephanie August, Director of Computer Science and Electrical Engineering Programs; Ph.D., UCLA, 1991. (310-338-5973)
Paul A. De Sena, Director of Educational Counseling Program; Ph.D., Penn State, 1963. (310-338-2863)
Victoria L. Graf, Coordinator of Special Education Program; Ph.D., California, Riverside, 1980. (310-338-2863)
Richard P. Hadley Jr., Director of Communication Arts Program; Ph.D., USC, 1989. (310-338-2779)
Paul Harris, Director of English Program; Ph.D., California, Irvine, 1991. (310-338-4452)
Rachelle Katz, Director of M.B.A. Program; Ph.D., Stanford, 1980. (310-338-2848)
Scott W. Kester, Coordinator of Educational Psychology Program; Ph.D., Oklahoma, 1969. (310-338-2863)
Albert Koppes, Dean of School of Education; Ph.D., USC, 1973. (310-338-2863)
Magaly Lavadenz, Coordinator of General and Bilingual Education Programs; Ph.D., USC, 1994. (310-338-2863)
Debra Linesch, Chair of the Marital and Family Therapy (Clinical Art Therapy) Department; Ph.D., Union (Ohio), 1992. (310-338-4562)
Edmundo Litton, Coordinator of Teaching Program; Ed.D., San Francisco. (310-338-2863)
Mary McCullough, Coordinator of Administration Program; Ph.D., USC, 1992. (310-338-2863)
Mel I. Mendelson, Director of Engineering and Production Management Program; Ph.D., Northwestern, 1973. (310-338-6020)
Mark Morelli, Director of Philosophy Program; Ph.D., Toronto, 1981. (310-338-7384)
Irene Oliver, Coordinator of Elementary Education Program; Ed.D., Pepperdine, 1997. (310-338-2863)
Bohdan Oppenheim, Director of Mechanical Engineering Program; Ph.D., Southampton (England), 1980. (310-338-2825)
Michael O'Sullivan, Director of Counseling Psychology Program; Ph.D., Saint Louis, 1983. (310-338-3015)
Candace A. Poindexter, Coordinator of Reading/Language Arts Program; Ph.D., UCLA, 1985. (310-338-2863)
Joe Reichenberger, Director of Civil Engineering and Environmental Science Programs; M.S.C.E., USC, 1967. (310-338-2830)
Jeffrey S. Siker, Director of Theological and Pastoral Studies; Ph.D., Princeton Theological Seminary, 1989. (310-338-4556)

Loyola Marymount University campus.

LOYOLA UNIVERSITY CHICAGO

Graduate School

Programs of Study

The Graduate School is dedicated to the training of talented women and men who strive for understanding and truth in a humane environment. Programs of advanced study with academic and applied orientations are offered in humanities, social science, and natural science disciplines, as well as in interdisciplinary science areas and dual-degree programs.

Master's and doctoral degrees are offered in administration and supervision, anatomy, biochemistry, chemistry, child development, clinical psychology, counseling, developmental psychology, educational and school psychology, educational leadership and policy studies, English, higher education, history, microbiology, molecular biology, neuroscience, nursing, perception, pharmacology, philosophy, physiology, political science, research methodology, social psychology, social work, sociology, and theology. Master's degrees are offered in biology, Chicago studies, community counseling, computer science, criminal justice, curriculum and instruction, human resources, industrial relations, mathematical sciences, organization development, pastoral counseling, Spanish, training and development, and women's studies. The M.Div. degree is offered through the Institute of Pastoral Studies. Interdisciplinary areas include doctoral programs in neuroscience and in molecular biology. Dual degrees are available in M.D./Ph.D., M.D./M.S., and J.D./M.A. programs.

Research Facilities

The combined libraries of the University contain more than 1 million volumes, with standing orders for more than 7,800 serials, 650,000 microforms, and 21,000 pieces of audiovisual material. The library subscribes to several computerized online services, data search networks, and interlibrary access and loan programs.

The Academic Computing Service, with centers on all campuses, houses up-to-date equipment and software for use by students and faculty. To ensure convenient access to all users, programming advisers are housed on all campuses; terminals and personal computers are located throughout the University.

Specialized laboratory facilities are maintained in the basic medical science, science, and social science departments.

Financial Aid

The Graduate School awards graduate fellowships and assistantships totaling more than $2 million annually. These awards are assigned on a competitive basis for a period of one year to students with outstanding records. Reappointments are made on the basis of good academic standing and proven competence. In most instances, the award includes a full tuition scholarship and a stipend; teaching and/or research services are required in some departments and for some awards.

Cost of Study

Tuition for the 2002–03 academic year is $548 per credit hour.

Living and Housing Costs

There is limited graduate housing available on campus. Housing costs in the Chicago area vary considerably. Information is available through the Graduate School.

Student Group

Of the approximately 14,000 students attending Loyola University of Chicago, more than 1,500 are enrolled in the various departments and programs of the Graduate School. Students come from all areas of the United States and many other countries.

Student Outcomes

More than 100,000 Loyola alumni are spread throughout every state of the nation and in at least 121 countries throughout the world. Among their ranks are hundreds of CEOs of major corporations and health-care institutions, dozens of state and national legislators, scores of circuit court and federal judges, and a number of presidents of nationally recognized universities.

Location

Chicago, the nation's third-largest city, is an international center for academics, art, business, culture, and sports. The University operates an academic medical center and four higher education campuses, three in the Chicago area and one in Rome, Italy.

The University

Founded in 1870, Loyola is a Jesuit, Catholic university dedicated to excellence in teaching, research, health care, and community service. Programs in the University's nine schools and colleges focus not only on intellectual growth but also on the social, cultural, and spiritual development of the students they serve.

Applying

Applications are available from the Graduate School. All applicants must submit a completed application form and official transcripts. Most departments and programs also require the results of the Graduate Record Examinations. Additional material is required by some departments. Students should consult the *Graduate School Bulletin* for details. Applicants may apply online at the Web address listed below.

Applications are accepted throughout the year by most departments. Students who wish to be considered for need-based financial aid and merit awards must have their completed applications on file by February 1. Because there are some exceptions to this deadline, students should consult the *Graduate School Bulletin* for details.

Students from abroad must have proficiency in written and spoken English. Students for whom English is not the native language are required to submit scores from the TOEFL. Students from other countries are tested for competence in the English language and may have to take ESL courses.

Detailed descriptions of programs and procedures are found in the *Graduate School Bulletin.* Requests for additional information and applications should be directed to the address given below.

Correspondence and Information

The Graduate School
Loyola University of Chicago
6525 North Sheridan Road
Chicago, Illinois 60626
Telephone: 773-508-3396
Fax: 773-508-2460
E-mail: grad-phd-ma-ms@luc.edu
World Wide Web: http://www.luc.edu/schools/grad

FACULTY HEADS

William A. Yost, Associate Vice President for Research and Dean of the Graduate School; Ph.D., Indiana.

Research activities vary among programs and departments. For details and descriptions in an area of interest, students should contact the chair of the department or director of the program.

Basic Medical Science
Biochemistry: Mary Manteuffel, Director, Ph.D., North Carolina at Chapel Hill. (708-216-3370)
Cell and Molecular Physiology: Donald M. Bers, Chair; Ph.D., UCLA. (708-216-6305)
Cell Biology, Neurobiology, and Anatomy: John Clancy Jr., Chair; Ph.D., Iowa. (708-216-3352)
Microbiology: Katherine Knight, Chair; Ph.D., Indiana. (708-216-3384)
Molecular Biology: Alan Wolfe, Director; Ph.D., Arizona. (708-216-5814)
Neuroscience: E. J. Neafsey, Director; Ph.D., UCLA. (708-216-3355)
Nursing: Sheila Haas, Dean; Ph.D., Illinois at Chicago. (312-508-3255)
Pharmacology: Israel Hanin, Chair; Ph.D., UCLA. (708-216-6595)

Education
Child Development: Barbara T. Bowman, President, Erikson Institute; M.A., Chicago. (312-280-7302)
Curriculum Instruction and Educational Psychology: David Prasse, Chair; Ph.D., Indiana State. (847-853-3318)
Leadership, Foundations, and Counseling Psychology: Terry Williams, Chair; Ph.D., Florida State. (847-853-3354)

Humanities
Classical Studies: John P. Murphy, S.J., Chair; Ph.D., Fordham. (773-508-3650)
English: Frank Fennell, Chair; Ph.D., Northwestern. (773-508-2240)
History: Anthony Cardoza, Chair; Ph.D., Princeton. (773-508-2220)
Modern Languages and Literature: Paolo Giordano, Chair; Ph.D., Indiana. (773-508-2856)
Philosophy: Paul Moser, Chair; Ph.D., Vanderbilt. (773-508-2733)
Theology: John McCarthy, Chair; Ph.D., Chicago. (773-508-2347)

Sciences
Biology: Jeffrey L. Doering, Chair; Ph.D., Chicago. (773-508-3627)
Chemistry: Kenneth Olsen, Chair; Ph.D., Duke. (773-508-3100)
Mathematical Sciences: Joseph H. Mayne, Chair; Ph.D., IIT. (773-508-3574)

Social Sciences
Criminal Justice: Arthur J. Lurigio, Chair; Ph.D., Loyola, Chicago. (312-915-7565)
Political Science: John Pelissero, Acting Chair; Ph.D., Oklahoma. (773-508-3047)
Psychology: Isiaah Crawford, Chair; Ph.D., DePaul. (773-508-3001)
Sociology: Peter Whalley, Chair; Ph.D., Columbia. (773-508-3453)

Specialized Programs
Center for Organization Development: Homer Johnson, Director; Ph.D., Illinois at Urbana-Champaign. (312-915-6609)
Industrial Relations: Homer Johnson, Director; Ph.D., Illinois at Urbana-Champaign. (312-915-6609)
Pastoral Studies: Mary Elsbernd, Acting Director; Ph.D., Louvain (Belgium). (773-508-2320)

Loyola's strong commitment to teaching and research encourages a collaborative relationship between graduate students and faculty members.

At Loyola, graduate faculty members take time to mentor and advise students.

Graduate students at Loyola University Medical Center study and do research in a nationally recognized clinical research and health-care facility.

LYNN UNIVERSITY

College of Graduate Studies

Programs of Study

Lynn's innovative graduate programs are state-of-the-art, reflecting the University's commitment to preparing its graduates to meet the challenges of the twenty-first century. The 36-credit Master of Business Administration (M.B.A.) has four specializations that take advantage of the University's Florida location, the rich experience of its faculty members, and the exchange with international students:

International management cultivates individual managerial expertise to meet complex, multinational corporate business interests of the twenty-first century.

Health-care administration offers challenges and opportunities as dynamic transitions and transformations occur in the health-care industry.

Hospitality administration has crossed traditional borders and is now increasingly international, with worldwide career possibilities.

Sports and recreation administration provides a view of the national and international sports scene and its business enterprises.

The Master of Science in Administration (M.S.) degree (36 credits) is available in the following specializations:

Criminal justice administration promotes a clear understanding of the global issues facing law enforcement, while integrating sound business principles and practices expected of modern police administrators.

Emergency Planning and Administration provides leadership in dealing with the demands of managing emergencies and disasters.

Biomechanical Trauma focuses on the complex nature of biomechanical trauma and its treatment.

Health-care administration (with or without a nursing home administrator licensure option) is a 42-credit degree focusing on the industry's intense scrutiny and profound challenges in defining and providing high-quality medical and/or long-term care.

The Master of Education (M.Ed.) in varying exceptionalities (36-credit research-oriented degree with certification in varying exceptionalities) or the M.Ed. in varying exceptionalities and an E.S.O.L. endorsement option (a 42-credit practitioner-oriented degree) are also offered.

The Ph.D. degree in educational leadership prepares graduates to create responsive academic and non-academic educational systems in our global society.

Research Facilities

The state-of-the-art Eugene and Christine Lynn Library contains more than 80,000 volumes and subscribes to 759 professional journals. The library belongs to a resource-sharing consortium, the Southeast Florida Library Information Network (SEFLIN), which provides members with timely access to information documents. Through this membership, Lynn University students have direct online access to 11.4 million bibliographic holdings of member libraries. Lynn students also have borrowing privileges in the academic member libraries.

The Lynn Library provides access to twenty CD-ROM databases on a local area network and online, including MEDLINE Professional, AGELINE, ABI INFORM (a business index), F&S (an international business index), and Lodging and Restaurant Index.

Graduate students can use one of the workstations in several locations across the campus, including the library and computer labs.

Financial Aid

Student loans are available along with a limited number of graduate assistantships. Special scholarships are available for educators and law enforcement professionals. International students may apply for graduate and research assistantships, but do not qualify for federal financial aid.

Cost of Study

The 2001–02 cost per credit hour was $440, with the exception of the M.S. in criminal justice administration, which was $315 per credit hour, and the M.Ed., which had a scholarship of $135 per credit hour for all public and private education employees that reduced the cost to $305 per credit hour. There is a $30 nonrefundable registration fee each term for all programs.

Living and Housing Costs

Graduate students live in apartments or houses within commuting distance of the campus. The typical cost of books and supplies for a full-time graduate student for three terms is $1000.

Student Group

Lynn University and its DeHoernle International Center welcome a diverse mix of students, representing more than seventy countries. The University has a historical tradition of emphasizing the development of a multicultural and international perspective. Faculty members and students share a commitment to develop the knowledge and skills necessary for global leadership dedicated to improving the quality of life of the planet and its inhabitants.

Alumni have pursued careers as administrators and leaders in long-term care, researchers and practitioners in education, business leaders, CEOs of multinational corporations, and innovators in their fields of specialization.

Location

Lynn University is located in Boca Raton, on the southeast coast of Florida, which serves as headquarters for many international corporations involved in trade and commerce. Located in a city of 96,000 people, midway between Palm Beach and Fort Lauderdale, Boca Raton residents have access to an array of tricounty cultural and recreational events year-round. Boca Raton is a tourist mecca with an ideal climate, whatever the season.

The University

Founded in 1962, Lynn University offers innovative graduate programs combining state-of-the-art knowledge and an individualized, student-centered approach to learning. Emphasis is placed on a combination of the practical and theoretical, and study-abroad opportunities or internships/practicums are available in most concentrations. Faculty members are mentors, educators, and role models who encourage individual talents and abilities of each student. Placed in the context of a global orientation, the result is a graduate who has a broadened world view and the professional knowledge and skills to be a critical thinker and an innovative leader. Lynn University is accredited by the Southern Association of Colleges and Schools to offer associate, bachelor's, master's, and doctoral degrees.

Applying

Applicants must complete an application of admission and provide the following materials: two letters of reference, a resume with a statement of professional goals, official transcripts from all schools and colleges attended, and scores from the GMAT for the M.B.A. or the MAT or GRE for all other concentrations and the M.Ed. and the Ph.D. In addition, international students must provide a bank statement or verification of finances, an English translation of the official transcripts, and TOEFL scores. There is a nonrefundable application fee of $50.

Correspondence and Information

Office of Graduate Admission
Lynn University
3601 North Military Trail
Boca Raton, Florida 33431-5598

Telephone: 561-237-7846
800-544-8035 (toll-free)
Fax: 561-237-7965
E-mail: admission@lynn.edu
World Wide Web: http://www.lynn.edu

THE FACULTY

Eldon Bernstein, Professor, School of Business; Ph.D., Connecticut, 1991. Marketing.
Bernard Brucker, Professor, Department of Biomechanical Trauma and Research; Ph.D., NYU, 1977. Learned voluntary control of systolic blood pressure.
Karen A. Casey-Acevedo, Associate Professor and Dean of Graduate Studies; Ph.D., SUNY at Albany, 1994. Impact of visitation on the disciplinary behavior of inmate mothers.
Richard Cohen, Associate Professor, School of Education; Ed.D., Kansas, 1978. Nontraditional teaching techniques for diverse student populations.
Frederick Dembowski, Professor, College of Education; Ed.D., Rochester, 1978.
Linsley DeVeau, Professor and Dean, School of Hotel, Restaurant and Recreation Administration; Ed.D., Bridgeport, 1994; M.B.A., New Haven, 1992; Certified Hospitality Account Executive, Certified Hotel Administrator, Certified Human Resource Executive. Safety management, labor relations.
James Downey, Associate Professor, School of Hotel, Restaurant and Recreation Administration; Ph.D., Purdue, 1977. Financial management in the hospitality industry.
Fariden Farazmand, Assistant Professor, College of Business; Ph.D., Syracuse, 1989; Economics. Agglomeration economics and optimal location of industries in the U.S.
Robert Green, Associate Professor, School of Business; D.B.A., Nova Southeastern, 1997.
Rita Nacken Gugel, Professor and Chairperson, Department of Gerontology and Health Services; Ph.D., NYU, 1979. Geriatrics and gerontology, long-term care administration, Alzheimer's disease.
William Leary, Professor, College of Education; Ed.D., Boston University, 1972; Ed.D., Harvard, 1973. The teaching of law as a form of moral education at Dorchester High School, planning and implementation of an eight-point program for the Boston public school system.
James Miller, Professor, School of Business; Ph.D., American, 1975; The human side of management.
Ralph Norcio, Associate Professor, School Of Business; Ph.D., Union (Ohio), 1994; M.B.A., Cornell, 1975; CPA. Entrepreneurship.
Virginia Salus, Director of Field Placement, School of Education; Ph.D., George Washington, 1991. Teaching methods, special education, effective teaching, nontraditional learning.
Cheryl Serrano, College of Education; Ph.D., Florida State, 1987. The effectiveness of cross-level peer involvement in the acquisition of English as a second language by Spanish-speaking migrant children.
Cindy Skaruppa, Professor of Education; Ph.D., 1993. School-based management.
Richard Thomas, Associate Professor, School of Hotel, Restaurant and Recreation Administration; Ph.D., Florida State, 1969. Effects of cerebral lateralization on motor skill enhancement, dynamic balance and its correlation to the performance of leisure time skills.
Carole Warshaw, Associate Professor, School of Education; Ed.D., St. John's, 1993. Special education, varying exceptionalities.
Richard A. Young, Professor, School of Hotel, Restaurant and Recreation Administration; Ph.D., Bowling Green State, 1975. Methods of teaching ethics in the sports and athletics arena.

A part of the campus of Lynn University, in Boca Raton, Florida.

MALONE COLLEGE

The Graduate School

Programs of Study

Malone College offers graduate programs leading to the Master of Arts in education; the Master of Arts in Christian ministries, with areas of study in family and youth ministries, leadership in the church, and pastoral counseling; and the Master of Business Administration.

The purpose of the graduate program in education is to provide advanced study in the areas of curriculum development, instructional technology, reading, intervention specialist (special education), curriculum and instruction/professional development (for administrative specialist license), school counseling, and community counseling to meet the professional needs of Ohio educators and community counselors. Teacher education programs range from 36 to 48 semester hours and meet Ohio standards for additional teaching endorsements or school counseling licensure. The programs can be completed in two to three years. The Community Counseling Core, approved by the State of Ohio Counselor and Social Worker Board to meet the educational requirements for professional counselor licensure in Ohio, provides preparation for those who wish to serve as professional counselors in agency or professional settings.

The purpose of the Master of Arts in Christian ministries program is to enhance students' understanding of God and the mission of Christianity through biblical, theological, and practical ministerial studies. Students are strongly encouraged to engage in some form of ministry while enrolled in the program. This degree requires 36 semester hours and can be completed in two years.

The Master of Business Administration degree program is designed to provide advanced study for individuals preparing to lead and manage organizations. This 37 to 49 semester-hour program is taken in a cohort format and can be completed in two years.

Research Facilities

The Everett L. Cattell Library information is available via the Internet with a new state of-the-art library system. The library has more than 153,000 book and periodical volumes, 1,300 current periodical subscriptions, and various microfiche and multimedia materials. More than 90 computer-based periodical indexes and reference databases are available to students. Through its membership in OPAL, Malone is a member of OhioLINK, a statewide central catalog and resource-sharing consortium for most of Ohio's universities and colleges. Through OCLC, students have access to over 44 million titles in more than 26,000 libraries. Malone College also has e-books available. Five computer labs are available for classes and general student use. The Education Lab is set up for educational media and desktop publishing. The Counselor Training Center, opened in 2002, is located in Founders Hall.

Financial Aid

The Federal Stafford Loan (subsidized or unsubsidized) is available to students who need financial assistance. One graduate assistantship with a full tuition grant and a stipend is available.

Cost of Study

Tuition for the 2001–02 academic year is as follows: the graduate program in education, $330 per semester hour; the graduate program in Christian ministries, $245 per semester hour; and the graduate program in business administration, $370 per semester hour.

M.B.A. prerequisite courses tuition is $225 per semester hour and Continuing Studies Workshops tuition is $125 per semester hour.

Living and Housing Costs

Most graduate students commute to Malone College. For further information, students should contact the Graduate School.

Student Group

Malone College has approximately 280 graduate students and a total enrollment of approximately 2,000 students. The majority of graduate students at Malone College are working professionals seeking advanced degrees in their fields.

Location

Malone College is located in Canton, Ohio, just one mile east of I-77 and the Professional Football Hall of Fame. Conveniently located via interstates, the College is one hour south of Cleveland, two hours west of Pittsburgh, and 2½ hours northeast of Columbus.

The College

Malone College has grown from the dreams and labors of an energetic Friends couple, Walter and Emma Malone. In 1957, Cleveland Bible College moved to Canton and was renamed Malone College to honor its founders. Malone College is a Christian liberal arts college, widely recognized today for producing exceptional graduates, not only for the marketplace, but for all aspects of life. Malone's commitment to this approach has led to a vibrant balance between faith and learning at the College.

Applying

Applicants should complete the application and return it to the Graduate School with a nonrefundable $20 fee (waived for Malone College Alumni). In addition, applicants should have two letters of recommendation (three for counseling programs) and official transcripts of all completed academic work sent directly to the Graduate School. Entry interviews are part of the application process. Applicants must meet the individual requirements of their chosen programs.

Correspondence and Information

The Graduate School
Malone College
515 25th Street NW
Canton, Ohio 44709-3897
Telephone: 330-471-8224
800-257-4723 (toll-free)
E-mail: gradschool@malone.edu
World Wide Web: http://www.malone.edu

THE FACULTY

Marietta Daulton, Associate Professor of Education and Dean of the Graduate School; Ed.D., Kentucky.

Education and Counseling Program

Alice E. Christie, Associate Professor of Education and Interim Director of Graduate Program in Education; Ph.D., Kent State.
Martha J. Cook, Professor of Education; Ed.D., Akron.
Andrea M. Farenga, Assistant Professor of Education: Ed.D., Illinois State.
Marshall L. Holmes, Assistant Professor of Education; Ed.D., Akron.
Patricia L. Long, Professor of Education: Ed.D., Akron.
Kenneth G. McCurdy, Assistant Professor of Counseling and Coordinator of Counseling Programs; M.S., Scranton.
Daniel R. Merz, Associate Professor of Counseling; Ph.D., Ohio.
David E. Snyder, Assistant Professor of Education; Ed.D., Nova Southeastern.

Christian Ministries Program

David N. Entwistle, Associate Professor of Psychology and Counselor Education; Psy.D., Biola.
Stephen K. Moroney, Associate Professor of Theology and Pastoral Counseling; Ph.D., Duke.
Larry D. Reinhart, Professor of Christian Education and Director of Graduate Program in Christian Ministries; Ph.D., Trinity Evangelical Divinity School.
Joel R. Soza, Assistant Professor of Biblical Studies; M.A., Ashland Theological Seminary.
Duane F. Watson, Professor of New Testament Studies; Ph.D., Duke.

M.B.A. Program

John P. Harris, Professor of Business Administration; Ph.D., Kent State.
Dennis D. Kincaid, Professor of Business Administration; Ph.D., Kent State.
Thomas A. Kratzer, Professor of Business Administration; Ph.D., Iowa.
Michael J. Ophardt, Assistant Professor of Business Ethics; Ph.D., Duquesne.
Roy C. Ramsaroop, Professor of Business Administration; Ph.D. Saint Louis.
Chrei L. Ramsburg, Professor of Business Administration; J.D., Akron.
Albert H. Smith, Associate Professor of Business Administration; M.B.A., Ohio State.
John C. Wilson, Assistant Professor of Business Administration; M.B.A., Notre Dame.

MANHATTAN COLLEGE

Graduate Division

Programs of Study

The Graduate Division offers seventeen major areas of study leading to master's degrees in education, engineering, and biotechnology.

The School of Education and Human Services offers master's degrees in three areas. The M.A. in counseling program is directed toward work in guidance and psychology, with the goal of preparing the candidate for the role of a school or sports counselor. The program for alcohol/substance abuse counselors consists of 36 credits. The Master of Science in Education (M.S.E.) program in special education is geared toward the professional preparation of teachers of exceptional individuals. Within this area there is a program with a concentration in adaptive physical education. These programs require 33 credits of graduate courses, a major research paper, and a practicum. The M.S.E. program in administration and supervision focuses on the preparation of school administrators and supervisors and requires completion of 33 credits of graduate courses, including an internship and a major research paper. Postdegree professional diplomas are available in each of these three programs and are granted on completion of 18 to 27 credits of course work.

The School of Engineering offers several programs of study leading to M.S. degrees in civil, chemical, computer, electrical, environmental, and mechanical engineering, as well as an M.E. (Environmental) degree. Part-time and full-time programs are available. The completion of 30 credits of graduate course work is required.

The biotechnology program draws upon faculty members from various disciplines of biology, chemistry, physics, and mathematics. Courses cover such areas as biochemistry, bioinformatics, combinatorial chemistry, genomics, high throughput screening, molecular biology, molecular modeling, recombinant DNA technology, and structural biology

Research Facilities

There are more than thirty scientific and engineering laboratories at Manhattan College. Most notable of these are the modern language lab, the multimedia center, the computer information systems lab, and a state-of-the-art Research and Learning Center, which houses laser and microcomputer design labs as well as special rooms for robotics, graphics, drafting, and senior projects. The psychology, biology, and sociology laboratories, located at the College of Mount Saint Vincent (about 10 minutes from campus), are available to students through a cooperative program. The Nuclear Engineering Lab includes a low-power critical reactor of the open pool type, a subcritical water-moderated reactor, and a subcritical graphite pile reactor. Manhattan College's libraries house 200,000 volumes and 1,500 periodical titles, plus several rare book collections.

Financial Aid

Financial aid is available through departmental fellowships, scholarships, and grants. The College offers limited loan opportunities to matriculated students, and some lab and research assistantships are available.

Cost of Study

Tuition per credit varies, depending on the program. Graduate education courses are $395 per credit; engineering courses are $520 per credit. There is a $50 registration fee per semester.

Living and Housing Costs

Studio and one-bedroom apartments near Manhattan College begin at $550 per month.

Student Group

Of the 429 students enrolled in Manhattan's Graduate Division, 185 are women and 244 are men, 363 are part-time students, and 66 study full-time, including 14 international students. A vast majority of the students have prior professional experience in their field.

Student Outcomes

Approximately 165 representatives, including many of Manhattan's well-placed alumni, from various professional fields come to the campus each year to interview and recruit students for career opportunities. Manhattan College has consistently exceeded national averages in the number of students placed in professional positions as well as in the number of recruiters coming to campus to interview students. Manhattan students who participated in cooperative education had a higher placement/graduate school attendance rate than the general population. For example, students from the class of 1998 in the School of Science who participated in cooperative education had a 100 percent placement/graduate school attendance rate.

Location

Just 12 miles north of midtown Manhattan and about a mile from Westchester County, the main campus of the College is situated on the heights above Van Cortlandt Park in the Riverdale section of the Bronx. Riverdale, an upper-middle-class community and the home of many New York business, political, and educational leaders, offers an ideal blend of the calm and quiet of a residential, suburban setting with easy access to the many advantages of New York City.

The College

Manhattan College was founded in 1853 and is a private independent liberal arts college under the sponsorship of the Brothers of the Christian Schools. Currently, 3,024 full-time and part-time undergraduate and graduate students are enrolled in more than thirty-six major fields of study. Of the 254 faculty members, 171 are full-time, 83 are part-time, and 90 percent hold doctoral degrees; the student-faculty ratio is 15:1. The College has been ranked first in New York State among private, primarily undergraduate colleges whose alumni have earned doctoral degrees in the arts, sciences, education, and engineering, as well as fifth nationally for engineering and science doctorates and fourteenth nationally for doctoral degrees in the arts, sciences, and education. The College ranked seventh among all liberal arts colleges whose graduates have become top corporate executives.

Applying

Application forms for admission on a matriculated or nonmatriculated basis are furnished by the Admission Center on request. Filing for admission should be completed before May 2 for engineering and biotechnology summer sessions, June 10 for the education summer session, August 10 for fall session applicants, and January 7 for spring session applicants. Students seeking admission into the full-time engineering programs must have completed their application by February 1 if they are applying for a fellowship or scholarship for the fall semester.

Correspondence and Information

William J. Bisset Jr.
Assistant Vice President for Enrollment Management
Manhattan College
Riverdale, New York 10471

Telephone: 800-MC-2-XCEL (toll-free)
Fax: 718-862-8019
E-mail: admit@manhattan.edu
World Wide Web: http://www.manhattan.edu

THE FACULTY AND THEIR RESEARCH

Manhattan College prides itself on being able to provide research opportunities for students, thus enhancing their educational experience. Below, the Graduate Division programs are listed with the dean and program contact person, along with the areas of faculty specialization.

SCHOOL OF ENGINEERING
Richard Heist, Ph.D., Purdue.
Chemical Engineering. Helen C. Hollein, Chairperson; Eng.Sc.D., NJIT.
Civil Engineering. Walter P. Saukin, Chairperson; Ph.D., CUNY, City College.
Electrical Engineering and Computer Engineering. Br. Henry Chaya, F.S.C., Chairperson; Ph.D., Princeton.
Environmental Engineering and Science. James A. Mueller, Chairperson; Ph.D., Wisconsin.
Mechanical Engineering. Daniel W. Haines, Chairperson; Eng.Sc.D., Columbia.
Faculty specializations: Structural analysis, hydrology, water and waste treatment, toxicology, analysis of natural water systems, air pollution control, biotechnology, advanced separation processes, hazardous waste incineration, fields analysis, microwaves, heat transfer, magnetic resonance imaging, enzyme analysis, mathematical modeling.

SCHOOL OF EDUCATION AND HUMAN SERVICES
William J. Merriman, Ph.D., NYU.
Counseling and Special Education. Elizabeth M. Kosky, Program Advisor; Ed.D., Miami (Florida).
School Administration and Supervision. Sr. Remigia Kushner, C.S.J., Program Advisor; Ph.D., Fordham.
Faculty specializations: Leadership theory and the role of the principal, at-risk students and adaptive curriculum, engineer-physiologist partnership in rehabilitative design, local cooperation between regular education and special education teachers, physiological development patterns in childhood, psychoneural influences on learning, site-based school management of inner-city parochial schools, sports counseling, adapting physical education for special needs population.

BIOTECHNOLOGY PROGRAM
Edward Brown, Dean; Ph.D., NYU.
Abhijit Mitra, Director; Ph.D., Columbia.

MANHATTANVILLE COLLEGE

School of Graduate and Professional Studies

Programs of Study

The School of Graduate and Professional Studies at Manhattanville College offers five programs of study at the master's level. The three Master of Science (M.S.) programs (leadership and strategic management, organizational management and human resource development, and management communications) are offered in convenient weekend class schedules. Executives presently employed in their field of expertise design the curriculum and teach the classes. Two Master of Arts (M.A.) programs are also offered (liberal studies and writing), with courses scheduled in either the daytime or the evening. All master's programs have been developed to be completed within two years.

The Master of Science in leadership and strategic management is a 39-credit program providing advanced training in strategic management and planning and fostering the development of effective leadership skills. The learning is current, streamlined, and designed to allow managers and executives to excel in a rapidly changing and increasingly global work environment. Degree requirements include twelve courses and a final integrative project.

The Master of Science in organizational management and human resource development is a 36-credit program that provides training in human resource administration and organizational management for professionals who are already employed in or looking to enter the human resource field. Emphasis is on a strong theoretical background as well as development of practical, administrative, and management skills for individuals in corporations, small businesses, government, education, and the not-for-profit sector. Degree requirements include ten courses and a 6-credit thesis.

The Master of Science in management communications, a 36-credit program, provides advanced training in developing a communications strategy that is integrated with an organization's marketing and financial objectives and executing this strategy using advanced media approaches and technology. Students learn the principles of effective communications in global settings and the communication issues involved in marketing brand management and public relations. Degree requirements include eleven courses and a final integrative project.

The Master of Arts in Liberal Studies (M.A.L.S.), a 30-credit program, has been aptly described as a "time for your mind." This unique master's degree program cuts across many disciplines—art, literature, music, psychology, religion, sociology, philosophy, history, and politics. The M.A.L.S. is designed for adult and part-time students in that it is self-paced and flexibly scheduled.

The Master of Arts in writing is a 32-credit program designed for writers, aspiring writers, and teachers of writing. The program enables students who have completed undergraduate degrees to develop their skills in writing while deepening their knowledge of the humanities. All required courses are scheduled in the evening, with the exception of the intensive Summer Writers' Week and Writers' Weekend. A final project of an original piece of writing is required.

Research Facilities

The Manhattanville College library is considered one of the leading college libraries in the Northeast. The library owns approximately 275,000 volumes and bound periodicals, 2,600 audiovisual materials, and an extensive microform collection. The library subscribes to nearly 1,000 print journals and has a broad and expanding range of electronic journals, databases, search services, abstracts, indexes, and other tools. An educational resource center has curriculum materials to assist new teachers.

Financial Aid

Federal Stafford Student Loans, as well as a deferred payment plan, are available for graduate students. For further information, prospective students can contact the Office of Financial Aid, Reid Hall, Purchase, New York, 10577 (telephone: 914-323-5357).

Cost of Study

Tuition was $450 per credit in 2001–02. There was a semester registration fee of $35; some courses may have fees.

Living and Housing Costs

Most School of Graduate and Professional Studies students live off campus and work in communities throughout Westchester and the surrounding counties. For campus housing information, students should call Residence Life at 914-323-5217.

Student Group

There are approximately 270 students in the School of Graduate and Professional Studies at Manhattanville College. The average age is 35.

Location

Manhattanville's 100-acre suburban campus is located in New York's Westchester County, just minutes from White Plains to the west and Greenwich, Connecticut, to the east. It is 25 miles from the heart of Manhattan. Many prominent corporate offices—Philip Morris, IBM, MasterCard, Pepsico, and Texaco—are headquartered nearby. Public transportation stops on the campus.

The College

Manhattanville, whose mission is to educate ethically and socially responsible leaders for the global community, is a coeducational, independent liberal arts college. Manhattanville attracts bright students who seek the challenge of a demanding curriculum at an independent liberal arts college. Currently, there are approximately 1,400 undergraduate students and 750 graduate students. The college was founded in New York City in 1841 and moved to its present location in Purchase, New York, in 1952.

Applying

Applications to the School of Graduate and Professional Studies are reviewed on a continuing basis. Applicants are encouraged to apply at least sixty days in advance of the semester for which matriculation is sought (fall, winter, spring, summer I, or summer II). Application requirements are the submission of a completed application form, an application fee, an interview, two recommendations, and official transcripts of all previous undergraduate and graduate college work. Under certain circumstances, limited study as a nonmatriculated student is permitted.

Correspondence and Information

Andrea Covell, Ph.D.
Assistant Dean
Graduate and Professional Studies
Manhattanville College
2900 Purchase Street
Purchase, New York 10277

Telephone: 914-694-3425
Fax: 914-694-3488
E-mail: dowdr@mville.edu
World Wide Web: http://www.mville.edu

THE FACULTY

School of Graduate and Professional Studies Administration

Ruth Dowd, R.S.C.J., Professor of Philosophy and Dean; Ph.D. Fordham.
Donald J. Richards, Assistant Professor of History and Associate Dean; Ph.D., Notre Dame; M.B.A., LIU.
Andrea J. Covell, Assistant Dean; Ph.D., USC.

Master of Arts in Writing

Patricia Gauch, Ph.D., Drew.
John Herman, Ph.D., Berkeley.
Catherine Lewis, M.S., M.A., Florida State.

ADJUNCT FACULTY

Master of Science Programs (Management Communication, Leadership and Strategic Management, Organizational Management and Human Resource Development)

Laurie J. Bilik, M.B.A., NYU. President, Global Human Resources, Inc.
Cynthia Brosnan, M.B.A., NYU. Management development consultant.
Harriet W. Cabell, Ed.D. Alabama, M.L.E., Harvard. Cabell & Associates.
Ed Cheney, M.A., Syracuse, M.A., Columbia. Vice President, Strategic Communication, Global Consumer Business, Citigroup (Citibank).
Michael Crystal, M.B.A., Ph.D., Connecticut. Advanced Management Program, Stanford. Managing Principal, Myriad Development Group.
Keith T. Darcy, M.B.A., Iona. Executive Vice President, IBJ Whitehall Bank & Trust.
Tanya M. Odom, Ed.M., Harvard. Affiliate, Towers Perrin.
David R. Pipsky, Ph.D., Hofstra. Manager in Organizational Effectiveness, Sony Electronics.
Thomas Schwartz, Ph.D., UCLA. President, Tri-State Nannies.
William Stopper, M.B.A., Connecticut. Partner, The Walker Group.
Dotti Templeton, M.S., Manhattanville. Employee Relations Consultant, Towers Perrin.
Morrison Webb, J.D., Harvard.

MARQUETTE UNIVERSITY

Graduate School

Programs of Study

The Marquette University Graduate School offers doctoral degree programs (Ph.D. or Ed.D.) in the following fields: biology; biomedical engineering; chemistry; civil engineering; clinical psychology; counseling and educational psychology; educational policy and leadership; electrical and computer engineering; English; history; materials science and engineering; mathematics, statistics, and computer science; mechanical engineering; philosophy; and religious studies.

Master's degrees are offered in all of the above programs as well as in accounting, advertising, broadcast and electronic communication, business administration, communication studies, computing, counseling, dentistry, dispute resolution, economics, engineering management, foreign languages and literature (Spanish), health care technologies management, human resources, international affairs, journalism, mass communication, materials science, medieval studies, nursing (including post-master's certificates), political science, public service (with programs in administration of justice, dispute resolution, gerontology, and health-care administration), speech-language pathology, and theology. Also available is an interdisciplinary Ph.D. program that combines two or more of the University's graduate departments, allowing the student to create a unique doctoral program. Specific nondegree certificate programs are available in civil engineering, communication, dentistry, dispute resolution, educational policy and leadership, electrical and computer engineering, gerontology, mechanical engineering, and nursing.

Professional degrees are offered in law (J.D.) and dentistry (D.D.S.). In addition, the University offers dual-degree programs that combine a professional (J.D. or D.D.S.) degree with a traditional graduate degree. The Department of Biomedical Engineering offers a joint program with the Medical College of Wisconsin that leads to a doctoral degree in functional imaging technology. Marquette University also offers five- or six-year bachelor's to master's degree programs in engineering, nursing, economics, physical therapy, physician assistant studies, political science, and speech pathology.

Research Facilities

Marquette's Memorial, Science, and Law Libraries contain more than 1.2 million volumes of books and bound journals, 6,000 e-journals and e-books, and 10,000 serial subscriptions. The library online catalog system, MARQCAT, provides access to book and periodical holdings, electronic indexes to journal literature, and directional information on library hours, staff, programs, and services. Memorial Library also includes the Department of Special Collections and the University Archives, which contains 6,000 cubic feet of archival and manuscript collections and more than 6,000 rare books.

Thematic research centers and institutes include the Center for Intelligent Systems, Controls, and Signal Processing; the Center for Mass Media Research; the Center for Family Business; the National Sports Law Institute, Wisconsin Geriatric Center; the Parenting Center; the Bradley Institute for Democracy and Public Values; the Hartman Family Literacy Center; the Center for Dispute Resolution Education; the Orthopedic and Rehabilitation Engineering Center; and the Center for Highway and Traffic Engineering.

Financial Aid

Fellowships, assistantships, scholarships, and a wide variety of grants and loans are available for qualified graduate students. Competition deadlines for non-need-based University-funded financial aid are February 15 for the fall semester, November 15 for the spring semester, and April 15 for summer sessions I and II. Teaching and research assistantships include full tuition and stipends that range from $10,520 to $15,650 per year in 2001–02. Numerous grants, including the Arthur J. Schmitt, Smith Family, and Rev. John P. Raynor, S.J. Fellowships, include stipends of up to $13,000 and varying amounts of tuition. Need-based scholarships, grants, loans, and work-study programs are available through the Office of Student Financial Aid.

Cost of Study

Graduate school tuition is $565 per credit hour with the following exceptions: business administration courses, $585; dental graduate courses, $755; graduate education courses, $420; and English as a Second Language courses, $470 per credit hour.

Living and Housing Costs

Limited on-campus graduate student housing is available in the form of efficiencies ($367 per month), studios ($292 to $432 per month), one-bedroom apartments ($440 to $728 per month), two-bedroom apartments ($896 to $1028 per month), two and a half-bedroom apartments ($1136 to $1168 per month), and three-bedroom apartments ($1226 to $1334 per month). A wide variety of off-campus apartments are available for rent.

Student Group

The 2,300 Marquette graduate students comprise a diverse group. Sixty-five percent are part-time students, 51 percent are women, and 15 percent are international students. Approximately one-third of the graduate students receive financial aid through the Graduate School Office in the form of assistantships, fellowships, and scholarships.

Location

Marquette University is located on an 80-acre urban campus that is adjacent to downtown Milwaukee. Approximately 75 percent of the campus is contained within a mall area that is closed to traffic. Milwaukee offers a multitude of cultural, social, and athletic opportunities, including art galleries, college and professional sports teams, symphony and professional ballet companies, and numerous thespian groups and community playhouses. The Milwaukee lakefront is a beautiful area that hosts various musical and ethnic fests almost continuously throughout the summer. The University's proximity to downtown offers access to many world-class businesses, including Harley Davidson, Northwestern Mutual Life, Allen Bradley Corporation, and others. Many of these businesses interview regularly at Marquette, offer internships and paid research opportunities, and serve as sites for professional and continuing-education classes.

The University

Marquette University is an independent, coeducational institution of higher learning that was founded in 1881 by members of the Society of Jesus, a Catholic religious order established in 1540 by St. Ignatius Loyola. Marquette is named after Father Jacques Marquette (1637–1675), a French Jesuit missionary and explorer in North America. The University offers graduate or first professional degrees in ten of its eleven colleges. While Marquette University continues to stress the liberal arts, it offers cutting-edge education and research in the sciences and engineering fields. The University remains committed to offering an education marked by intellectual excellence, the Judeo-Catholic tradition, and service to others.

Applying

Most departments accept applications and will admit applicants at any time if all required materials are received at least six weeks before the beginning of the term (at least four months for international students). Application forms are available from the Graduate School Office and must be submitted with a $40 nonrefundable application processing fee. The M.B.A. and business-related programs require GMAT, and most other programs require GRE or MAT scores. The Test of English as a Foreign Language (TOEFL) is required of all students whose native language is not English. Letters of recommendation and personal interviews may be required. Specific application requirements are available in the Graduate School Office, listed in the *Bulletin,* and found on the Internet at the address below.

Correspondence and Information

Office of the Graduate School
Marquette University
Holthusen Hall, 305
P.O. Box 1881
Milwaukee, Wisconsin 53201-1881

Telephone: 414-288-7137
Fax: 414-288-1902
E-mail: mugs@marquette.edu
World Wide Web: http://www.grad.marquette.edu (Graduate School)
http://info.orsp.mu.edu (Research and grants)

THE FACULTY

Department Chairs and Program Directors

Accounting: Dr. Don Giacomino, Chair.
Biology: Dr. Brian Unsworth, Chair.
Biomedical Engineering: Dr. Jack Winters, Chair.
Bioinformatics: Dr. Anne Clough, Director of Graduate Studies.
Business Administration: Dr. David Shrock, Dean.
Chemistry: Dr. Charles Wilkie, Chair.
Civil and Environmental Engineering: Dr. Thomas H. Wenzel, Chair.
Clinical Psychology: Dr. Robert Lueger, Chair.
Communication Studies: Dr. William Elliott, Dean.
Counseling and Educational Psychology: Dr. Tim Melchert, Chair.
Dentistry: Dr. William Lobb, Dean.
Dispute Resolution: Ms. Eva Soeka, Director.
Economics: Dr. Brian Brush, Chair.
Educational Policy and Leadership: Dr. William Pink, Chair.
Electrical and Computer Engineering: Dr. Ed Yaz, Chair.
Engineering Management: Dr. James Rice, Director of Graduate Studies.
English: Dr. Tim Machan, Chair.
Foreign Languages and Literature: Dr. Belén Castañeda, Chair.
History: Dr. Lance Grahn, Chair.
Human Resources: Dr. Tim Keaveny, Chair.
International Affairs: Dr. H. Richard Friman, Chair.
Mathematics, Statistics, and Computer Science: Dr. John Simms, Chair.
Mechanical and Industrial Engineering: Dr. Kyle Kim, Chair.
Medieval Studies: Dr. Ronald Zupko, Director.
Nursing: Dr. Madeline Wake, Dean.
Philosophy: Rev. John Jones, Chair.
Physical Therapy: Dr. Lawrence Pan, Chair.
Physician Assistant Studies: Mr. Tim Gengembre, Chair.
Political Science: Dr. H. Richard Friman, Chair.
Public Service: Dr. Thomas Jablonsky, Director.
Speech-Language Pathology: Dr. Edward Korabic, Chair.
Theology and Religious Studies: Dr. Philip Rossi, Chair.

Centers, Institutes, and Laboratories

Biomechanics Research Laboratory: Dr. Gerald Harris.
Center for Applied Economic Analysis: Dr. Steven Crane.
Center for Biomedical Engineering and Biomathematics: Dr. Gerald Harris.
Center for Dispute Resolution Education: Professor Eva Soeka.
Center for Energy Studies: Dr. Richard Gaggioli.
Center for Ethics Studies: Dr. Robert Ashmore.
Center for Family Business: Ms. Sandra Shirk.
Center for Highway and Traffic Engineering: Dr. Ronald Sonntag.
Center for Industrial Processes and Productivity: Dr. Otto Widera.
Center for Intelligent Systems: Dr. Ronald Brown.
Center for Mass Media Research: Dr. Robert Griffith.
Center for Sensor Technology: Dr. Fabian Josse.
Center for Supply Chain Management: Dr. DaeSoo Kim.
Center for Teaching Excellence: Dr. David Buckholdt.
Center for the Study of Entrepreneurship.
Center for Water Quality: Dr. Alphonse Zanoni.
Concrete Laboratory: Dr. Thomas H. Wenzel.
Deburring and Surface Finishing Laboratory: Dr. Robert Stango.
Hartman Literacy and Learning Center: Dr. Lauren Leslie.
High-Field NMR Spectroscopy Laboratory: Dr. Sheldon Cremer.
Human Function Laboratory: Dr. Guy Simoneau.
Industrial Ergonomics Laboratory: Dr. Richard Marklin.
Industrial Mathematics Group: Dr. George Corliss.
Institute for Family studies: Dr. Michael Phayer.
Institute for the Transformation of Learning: Dr. Howard Fuller.
Institute for Urban Environmental Risk Management: Dr. Vladimir Novotny.
Institute for Natural Family Planning: Dr. Richard J. Fehring.
Institute for Urban Life: Dr. Thomas Jablonsky.
Institute of the Catholic Media: Dr. William Thorn.
Les Aspin Center for Government: Rev. Timothy O'Brien.
National Sports Law Institute: Professor Matthew Mitten.
Orthopedic and Rehabilitation Engineering Center: Dr. Gerald Harris.
Parenting Center: Dr. Robert Fox.
Rapid Prototyping Center: Dr. Vikram Cariapa.
Surface Mount Technology Group: Dr. Nicholas J. Nigro.
Wisconsin Geriatric Education Center: Dr. Anthony Iacopino; Ms. Stacy Barnes.

MARSHALL UNIVERSITY

Graduate College

Programs of Study

The Graduate College at Marshall University offers programs of study leading to the degrees of Master of Arts, Master of Science, Master of Business Administration, Master of Arts in Teaching, Master of Arts in Journalism, Master of Science in Nursing, Master of Science in Engineering, Ed.D., and Doctor of Philosophy in biomedical sciences. Education Specialist degrees are also available in school psychology and education (adult and technical education, counseling, leadership studies, and in curriculum and instruction). A Psy.D. degree program will be initiated in fall 2002. (See the reverse side of this page for a detailed listing of graduate programs and the directors or department chairpersons involved in the programs.) These graduate programs provide students with outstanding opportunities for advanced professional preparation, basic research, and applied research.

There are three basic requirements for the master's degree: a minimum of 36 credit hours in graduate courses or 32 hours if a thesis option is chosen, including 6 hours for the thesis; a minimum grade point average of 3.0 (B) in all graduate courses applicable to the degree; and the comprehensive assessment, which can be written, oral, or both and which is taken when the student is nearing completion of all course work.

Since more than half of the graduate students at Marshall University attend on a part-time basis while working, a special effort is made to offer graduate courses in the late afternoon and evening. Full-time graduate students usually complete the master's degree requirements in one or two calendar years, part-time students in three or four years. The English as a Second Language Institute is available to international students.

Research Facilities

Marshall University Research Corporation is the contract and financial management agent for research/service contracts and grants of the University, with funding in excess of $20 million annually from such sources as the National Science Foundation, the National Institutes of Health, and the Economic Development Administration. Marshall maintains the University Computer Center, University Theater, Psychology Clinic, Speech Clinic, Writing Center, Learning Resources Center, language laboratory, chemistry and physics laboratories, mathematics laboratory, WMUL-FM, WPBY-TV, instructional television, extensive facilities in the Departments of Art and Music, and biomedical science facilities for DNA research. The John Deaver Drinko Library is a state-of-the-art electronic information center. The James Morrow Library houses one of the largest collections of antebellum Southern materials in the world. In addition, General Chuck Yeager has donated his memorabilia to Marshall.

Financial Aid

Graduate teaching and research assistantships are available in most departments offering the master's degree. Information can be obtained from the individual department chairpersons. Inquiries about work-study opportunities, loans, and other forms of financial assistance should be directed to the Financial Aid Office. A brochure is available from the Dean of the Graduate College's office.

Cost of Study

Full-time West Virginia residents paid a total enrollment fee of $1442 per regular semester in 2001–02. Full-time nonresidents paid $4079 per regular semester. (Fees are subject to change.) Part-time students enrolling for 8 hours or less paid fees on the basis of a graduated hourly scale. Metro fees, a reduced fee structure for out-of-state students from certain counties of Ohio, Virginia, Maryland, and Kentucky, were $2748 per semester. There are additional fees for students in the health professions and in the College of Business.

Living and Housing Costs

The Huntington and Charleston areas offer a great variety of living accommodations, ranging from $250 per month upward. Men's and women's residence halls are located on the main campus; room and board for a single student ranged from $2554 to $2992 (nineteen meals weekly) per semester in 2001–02. (Fees are subject to change.) Married student housing units are located on the University Heights campus, within easy driving distance of the main campus.

Student Group

The University's total enrollment is approximately 16,000, of whom about 15 percent are out-of-state students. Enrollment in the Graduate College is approximately 4,000.

Location

Huntington, with a population of approximately 50,000, in a tri-state metropolitan region with a population of 300,000, is situated on the banks of the Ohio River. There is a well-planned park system on the south side of the community. Several major industries are located in this area, including the CSX railway, Special Metals Company, and ACF Industries. There are two television stations, five radio stations, numerous theaters, an amusement park, boating facilities, and swimming pools. The community is noted for its friendliness.

The South Charleston campus is located just outside the state capital, a city of 55,000 people. It is the political center of West Virginia and offers excellent restaurants, museums, and cultural centers.

The University

Founded in 1837, Marshall University is assisted by the state of West Virginia and is one of two universities comprising the University of West Virginia System. The main campuses are located in Huntington and South Charleston. The Graduate College was authorized in 1948. The University provides a broad program of cultural programs through the Artists Series and the Departments of Art, Music, and English. The School of Medicine graduated its first class in 1981. The West Virginia Graduate College and Marshall University merged in 1997.

Marshall University is accredited by the North Central Association of Colleges and Schools, and appropriate programs are accredited by the National Council for Accreditation of Teacher Education. It is a member of the Council of Graduate Schools. The business administration program is accredited by AACSB International–The Association to Advance Collegiate Schools of Business.

Applying

Admission is based on official transcripts of college credit; GRE, MAT, or GMAT scores; the information provided on the application form; and whatever examinations and conditions the Graduate College may require. Applications are due at least two weeks prior to the beginning of the term of anticipated enrollment. Many departments have earlier application deadlines.

Correspondence and Information

Leonard J. Deutsch
Dean of the Graduate College
Marshall University
Huntington, West Virginia 25755-2100
Telephone: 304-696-6606
E-mail: deutschl@marshall.edu
World Wide Web: http://www.marshall.edu

FACULTY HEADS

College of Business

Business Administration (M.B.A.): Dr. Michael Newsome, Director. Accounting, finance, management, marketing, economics.
Health Care Administration (M.S.): Dr. Andrew Sikula, Associate Dean of Graduate Programs.
Industrial Relations (M.S.): Dr. Andrew Sikula, Associate Dean of Graduate Programs.

College of Education

Adult and Technical Education (M.A., M.S.): Dr. LeVene A. Olson, Chairperson. Adult, business, career, cooperative, marketing, and vocational-technical education.
Counseling (M.A.): Dr. Violet Eash and Dr. Michael Burton, Program Coordinators. Elementary, secondary school, higher education, and agency counseling.
Educational Administration (M.A., Ed.D.): Dr. Mike Cunningham, Program Coordinator. Elementary and secondary school principal studies, higher education, supervision, school superintendent studies.
Family and Consumer Science (M.A.): Dr. Mary Jo Graham, Program Coordinator. Foods and nutrition, home management, consumer economics, teacher education.
Health and Physical Education (M.S.): Dr. Robert Barnett, Chairperson. Professional health education, professional physical education, athletic training, adult physical fitness, cardiac rehabilitation.
School Psychology (Ed.S.): Dr. Steve O'Keefe, Program Director.
Teacher Education (M.A.): Dr. Carl Johnson, Division Head. Early childhood, elementary, middle childhood, secondary, reading, and special education in the areas of behavioral disorders, gifted, learning disabilities, mentally impaired, and physically handicapped.
Teaching (M.A.T.): Dr. Tony Williams, Division Head. Certification for undergraduate content specialization.

College of Fine Arts

Art (M.A.): Professor Jean Miller, Chairperson. Painting, drawing, sculpture, graphics, ceramics, weaving, art history, art education.
Music (M.A.): Dr. Marshall Onofrio, Chairperson. Instrumental music, vocal music, church music, performance, history, literature, theory, composition, music supervision, teacher education.

College of Liberal Arts

Communication Studies (M.A.): Dr. Bert Gross, Chairperson. Speech communication.
Criminal Justice (M.S.): Professor Peggy Brown, Chairperson. Corrections and law enforcement.
English (M.A.): Dr. David Hatfield, Chairperson. American and English literature and language.
Geography (M.A., M.S.): Professor Larry Jarrett, Chairperson. Cultural geography, conservation, cartography.
History (M.A.): Dr. Steve Riddel, Chairperson. American, European, and Asian history.
Humanities (M.A.): Dr. Joyce East, Director of Flexible Interdisciplinary Program.
Political Science (M.A.): Dr. Simon Perry, Chairperson. American national and state government, comparative government, international governments, public administration, theory.
Psychology (M.A.): Dr. Marty Amerikaner, Chairperson. General-theoretical psychology, clinical psychology, and school psychology.
Sociology and Anthropology (M.A.): Dr. Ken Ambrose, Chairperson. General sociology, community development, industrial relations, sociology of the Appalachian region, medical anthropology.

College of Science

Biological Sciences (M.A., M.S.): Dr. Laura Jenski, Chairperson. Environmental biology, plant and animal taxonomy, aquatic ecology, plant cell biology, evolutionary biology and systematics, plant and animal physiology, biological science education.
Chemistry (M.S.): Dr. Daniel Babb, Chairperson. Organic, physical, and analytical chemistry; interdisciplinary program in physical science.
Mathematics (M.A.): Dr. Judith Silver, Chairperson. Algebra, topology, analysis, interdisciplinary program in physical science, teacher education.
Physical Science and Physics (M.A., M.S.): Dr. Ron Martino, Advisor. Interdisciplinary program in physical science, teacher education.

College of Information Technology and Engineering

Engineering (M.S.): Dr. Betsy Dulin, Chairperson. Areas of emphasis available in chemical engineering, engineering management, environmental engineering.
Environmental Science (M.S.): Dr. Tony Szwilski, Chairperson. Breadth in dealing with environmental issues, analytical tools for addressing state and national issues.
Information Systems (M.S.): Dr. Tom Hankins, Coordinator. Information system information analysis, design, development, effective use.
Safety Technology (M.S.): Dr. Allan Stern, Program Coordinator. Ergonomics, industrial hygiene, occupational safety and health, safety management, mine safety.
Technology Management (M.S.): Dr. Bernard Gillespie, Coordinator. Technology planning, quality and productivity management. Areas of emphasis: information technology, environmental management, manufacturing systems, transportation systems and technologies.

School of Medicine

Biomedical Science (M.S., Ph.D.): Dr. Louis H. Aulick, Coordinator. Biochemistry, anatomy, physiology, pharmacology, microbiology.
Forensic Science (M.S.): Dr. Terry Fenger. DNA and other forensic evidence from a scientific and legal perspective.

College of Nursing and Health Professionals

Communication Disorders (M.A.): Professor Kathy Chezik, Chairperson. Speech pathology and audiology.
Nursing (M.S.N.): Dr. Lynne Welch, Dean. Family nurse practitioner studies.

School of Journalism and Mass Communication

Journalism (M.A.J.): Dr. Harold C. Shaver, Dean of the School. News-editorial writing, public relations, broadcast-TV journalism, advertising, teacher education.

MARYMOUNT UNIVERSITY

Graduate Program

Programs of Study

Marymount University (MU) offers programs of study leading to the Master of Arts degree in humanities, human performance systems, human resource management, interior design, legal administration, literature and language, organization development, and psychology (with a counseling, school counseling, or forensic psychology focus); the Master of Business Administration; the Master of Education degree in elementary education, secondary education, English as a second language, learning disabilities, and Catholic school leadership; the Master of Science degree in business technologies, computer science, health-care management, health promotion management, information management, organizational leadership and innovation, and physical therapy; and the Master of Science in Nursing degree, with concentrations in critical-care nursing, nursing and health administration, and family nurse practitioner studies.

Graduate programs are coeducational and are designed to meet the career needs of both full-time students and part-time, employed students who wish to enhance their careers and update their professional credentials. Most courses are offered in the late afternoon and during evening hours. There are a number of program options that allow working students to schedule their graduate programs around different employment schedules; these options include weekend offerings, seven-week semesters involving two evenings per week, and traditional fifteen-week semesters involving one evening per week.

Research Facilities

On-campus facilities include the Emerson G. Reinsch Library, which also houses the Learning Resource Center and Instructional Media Center. The Reinsch Library is a member of the Washington Research Library Consortium, providing access to materials and services from other university libraries in the Washington area. The Information Technology Support Center is located on the main campus and supports the learning process with the latest technologies. The Computer Center supports the learning process with the latest technologies. Marymount's computer labs are comprised of PCs and Macintosh computers. Students have access to these systems at all campus locations. Because of the University's location in the Washington, D.C., metropolitan area, resources such as the Smithsonian Institution, National Gallery of Art, and Kennedy Center for the Performing Arts as well as the embassies of other nations provide cultural resources and informational programs to enhance student learning. Students at Marymount can also enjoy the rich and varied resources of government libraries. Other resources available locally include trade associations and such agencies as the Federal Communications Commission, the Food and Drug Administration, the National Institutes of Health, and the Securities and Exchange Commission. Ongoing congressional hearings, easily accessible by Metro transit, provide yet another resource for understanding legislative and regulatory trends and processes affecting business and education.

Financial Aid

A number of service assistantships are awarded to graduate students assigned to an academic school or an administrative office. The Federal Stafford Student Loan Program is a federally supported, need-based program through which students may borrow up to $8500 per academic year. The state provides Virginia Tuition Assistance Grants for full-time graduate study for Virginia state residents. The grants, which can be for up to $3000 in 2002–03, are not based on need. To apply for financial aid, a student must file the Free Application for Federal Student Aid (FAFSA). Cooperative arrangements are maintained with business employers for the provision of tuition assistance.

Cost of Study

Graduate tuition is $530 per credit hour for the 2002–03 academic year. Physical therapy tuition, including fees, is $17,300 per year (the physical therapy master's degree program is full-time).

Living and Housing Costs

Most Marymount graduate students live and work in the area and commute to classes. On-campus housing is currently reserved for undergraduate students. Apartment, town-house, and single-family home rentals are all available close to campus.

Student Group

In 2001–02, approximately 1,500 students were enrolled in graduate degree programs. The majority of Marymount graduate students have full-time jobs and attend the University part-time, taking evening and weekend courses. However, the physical therapy program is full-time, and other programs, such as psychological services, have a number of full-time students.

Location

Marymount University is located in Arlington, Virginia, minutes from Washington, D.C. Free University shuttle buses connect Marymount's main campus, Ballston campus, and the subway. Marymount's School of Business Administration, located at the Ballston campus, is just off Route 66 and two blocks from the Ballston-MU Metro station in Arlington. The University is a member of the Consortium of Universities of the Washington Metropolitan Area, which includes American University, the Catholic University of America, Gallaudet University, George Mason University, the George Washington University, Georgetown University, and the University of Maryland, among others.

The University

Marymount is a comprehensive, coeducational Catholic university, governed by an independent Board of Trustees. Founded in 1950 by the Religious of the Sacred Heart of Mary, Marymount emphasizes excellence in teaching, attention to the individual, and values and ethics across the curriculum. Marymount offers thirty-seven undergraduate majors and twenty-six graduate degree programs. It is accredited by the Southern Association of Colleges and Schools and approved by the State Council for Higher Education in Virginia; several of its professional programs are accredited by individual professional accrediting agencies.

Applying

Students are admitted on a full- or part-time basis for the September and January semesters and for the summer sessions. All applicants must submit an application with a $35 fee, transcripts of postsecondary work, and two letters of recommendation. Most programs also require standardized tests and interviews. Students are asked to contact the Office of Graduate Admissions for details regarding these requirements.

Correspondence and Information

Chris Domes
Vice President of Enrollment Management
Marymount University
2807 North Glebe Road
Arlington, Virginia 22207-4299

Telephone: 703-284-5901
800-548-7638 (toll-free)
Fax: 703-527-3815
E-mail: grad.admissions@marymount.edu
World Wide Web: http://www.marymount.edu

PROGRAM CHAIRS AND FACULTY RESEARCH AREAS

SCHOOL OF ARTS AND SCIENCES

Dr. Rosemary Hubbard, Dean (703-284-1560; rosemary.hubbard@marymount.edu).

Communications and Graphic Design: Barry Erdeljon, Chair (703-284-1652; barry.erdeljon@marymount.edu).

Fine and Applied Arts: Dr. Janice McCoart, Chair (703-284-1569; janice.mccoart@marymount.edu). Areas of expertise include art history and fashion design.

History and Politics: Christopher Snyder, Chair (703-284-3857; christopher.snyder@marymount.edu). Areas of faculty expertise include ancient and medieval British isles, constitutional law, international relations, political theory, public history, and U.S. history.

Humanities: Dr. Boyd Hagy, Chair (703-284-1577; boyd.hagy@marymount.edu). Areas of faculty expertise include modern poetry and theater production.

Interior Design: Bridget May, Chair (703-284-1671; bridget.may@marymount.edu). Areas of faculty expertise include historic preservation, illumination and acoustical design, design process, modern architecture, historic architecture and furnishings, and technology for interior design.

Literature and Language: Dr. Lillian Bisson, Chair (703-284-1563; lillian.bisson@marymount.edu). Areas of expertise include medieval literature, linguistics, origins of the novel, and nineteenth-century British literature.

Mathematics and Computer Science: Dr. Elsa Schaefer, Chair (703-284-1566; elsa.schaefer@marymount.edu). Areas of faculty research include software engineering, error-correcting codes, combinatorial algorithms, programming languages, and artificial intelligence and computational linguistics.

Science: Dr. Todd Rimkus, Chair (703-284-1559; todd.rimkus@marymount.edu).

SCHOOL OF BUSINESS ADMINISTRATION

Dr. Robert Sigethy, Dean (703-284-5910; robert.sigethy@marymount.edu).

Accounting, Economics, and Finance: Dr. Catherine England, Chair (703-284-5976; catherine.england@marymount.edu).

Human Resources: Dr. Karen Medsker, Chair (703-284-5959; karen.medsker@marymount.edu).

Information Management/Management Sciences: Dr. Carolyn Jacobson; Chair (703-284-5931, carolyn.jacobson@marymount.edu).

Legal Administration/Health-Care Management: Dr. Cynthia Hathaway, Chair (703-284-5934; cynthia.hathaway@marymount.edu).

Management/Marketing: James Ryerson, Chair (703-284-5926; james.ryerson@marymount.edu).

SCHOOL OF EDUCATION AND HUMAN SERVICES

Dr. Wayne Lesko, Dean (703-284-2620; wayne.lesko@marymount.edu).

Education: Dr. Alice Young, Chair (703-284-1632; aliceyoung@marymount.edu). Areas of faculty expertise include collaborative relationships and partnerships between public schools and universities on teacher education programs, stress and student teaching, and portfolio assessment of preservice teachers.

Forensic Psychology: Mary Lindahl, Chair (703-526-6825; mary.lindahl@marymount.edu).

Psychology: Dr. Carolyn Oxenford, Chair (703-284-1634; carolyn.oxenford@marymount.edu). Areas of research include social and emotional development of gifted adolescents, effects of media on children, the role of fathers in child development, occupational stress management, trends in counseling, social psychology, and organizational behavior.

School Counseling: Dr. Michele Garofalo (703-284-3822; michele.garofalo@marymount.edu).

Sociology/Criminal Justice: Dr. Michael Bolton, Chair (703-284-3824; michael.bolton@marymount.edu).

SCHOOL OF HEALTH PROFESSIONS

Dr. Theresa Cappello, Chair (703-284-1580; tess.cappello@marymount.edu).

Health and Human Performance: Dr. Liane Summerfield, Chair (703-284-1627; liane.summerfield@marymount.edu). Areas of research include obesity and weight management, health behavior management, and HIV prevention.

Nursing: Graduate Nursing: Christine Galante, Chair (703-284-6836; cgala77767@aol.com). Areas of research include health policy, nursing and health-care management, theory, and research.

B.S.N. Department: Dr. Rajamma George, Chair (703-284-6881; rajamma.george@marymount.edu). Areas of research include maternal-newborn nursing and medical-surgical nursing.

A.A.S. Department: Dr. Sharron Guillett, Chair (703-284-6879; sharron.guillett@marymount.edu). Areas of research include quality of life and children with disabilities.

Physical Therapy: Diana Venskus, Chair (703-284-5985; diana.venskus@marymount.edu). Areas of research include neurological rehabilitation, prosthetic rehabilitation, regeneration of the nervous system, and pediatric occupational therapy.

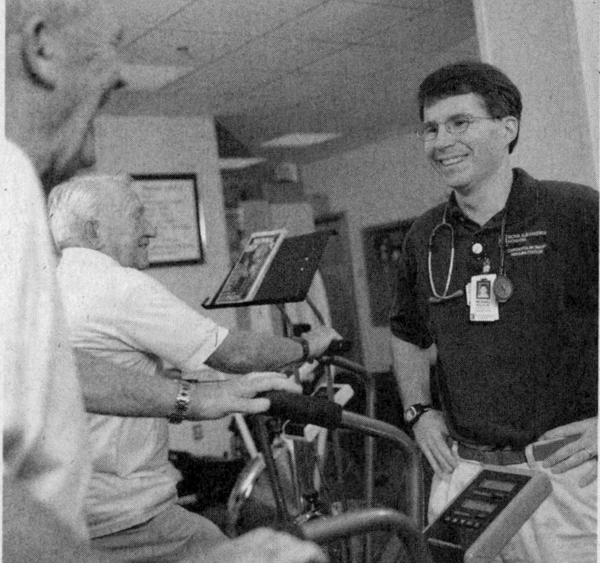

Mike Mulligan, M.S. in Health Promotion Management, works in the Cardiopulmonary Rehabilitation Center of area hospital.

At Marymount, classes are small and students receive individual attention.

MARYWOOD UNIVERSITY

Graduate School of Arts and Sciences

Programs of Study

The Graduate School of Arts and Sciences offers degree programs in eleven academic departments: Art, Business and Managerial Science, Communication Arts, Communication Sciences and Disorders, Counseling and Psychology, Education, Foods and Nutrition, Human Development, Music, Nursing and Public Administration, and Special Education. An interdisciplinary Ph.D. in human development is offered with specializations in educational administration, instructional leadership, social work, health promotion, and higher education administration. The M.A. degree is offered in art education, art therapy, church music, communication arts, counseling, music education, musicology, psychology (general/theoretical, clinical services), studio art, and teaching. The M.S. degree is available in management information systems, counseling (elementary and secondary school), school leadership, early childhood intervention, instructional technology, reading, foods and nutrition, special education, speech-language pathology, criminal justice, information sciences, and nursing administration. Additional degrees offered are the M.B.A., M.Ed. in instructional leadership, M.F.A., M.P.A., M.P.A./M.S.W. (a dual-degree program offered in cooperation with the Graduate School of Social Work), and an M.H.S.A.

A Psy.D. in clinical psychology has just been introduced; the first class began in fall 2001.

Certificates of Advanced Graduate Study can be earned in art, art therapy, counseling, psychology, and vocal pedagogy. Certification programs have been approved by the Pennsylvania Department of Education in thirty-three areas of specialization.

Research Facilities

Situated at the heart of Marywood's campus is the modern Learning Resources Center, consisting of the library and the media center. In addition to the more than 208,000 volumes and 1,100 periodical titles, the library collection includes more than 42,000 nonprint items. The library is open 88 hours a week, and a librarian is on duty to provide reference service during these hours. The library collection is accessible through an online database. In addition, CD-ROM databases are available to students and faculty members. The media center provides graphic, photographic, television, multi-image, and equipment services for the campus. The Instructional Media Laboratory is equipped and programmed as an auto-learning facility for media instruction. A fully equipped color television broadcasting studio is among the facilities that support the services offered to students. The University has integrated its library and academic computing services.

Financial Aid

Approximately 100 tuition scholarships are awarded each year by Marywood University to students in the Graduate School of Arts and Sciences. Assistantships and cultural diversity scholarships are available.

Students who are enrolled at least half-time (6 credits per semester) can borrow under the Federal Stafford Student Loan and/or Federal Supplemental Loans for Students programs. Application forms can be obtained from a local bank or credit union.

Cost of Study

Tuition for master's degree programs in the Graduate School of Arts and Sciences is $554 ($565 for the Master of Fine Arts program) per credit for 2002–03. Tuition for doctoral degree programs is $590 per credit. Tuition for classes taken at the Lehigh Valley Center is $570 per credit. General fees range from $180 to $650 per year. Deferred payment plans are offered.

Living and Housing Costs

On-campus housing is available for graduate students. Arrangements can be made for full-semester use of on-campus housing or for weekly use for a fixed amount of days by the semester. The Office of Student Affairs maintains a listing of private off-campus rooms and apartments. Meals can be obtained in the dining room of the Student Center at the University.

Student Group

The total enrollment at Marywood University in 2001–02 was about 3,000 students. Enrollment at the graduate level was approximately 1,200. Approximately 30 percent of the graduate student population is full-time. The majority of graduate students are from Pennsylvania, with about 15 percent coming from New York and New Jersey.

Student Outcomes

Eighty-nine percent of students who responded to an exit survey were employed full-time. Eighty-two percent of the respondents who gained full-time employment had obtained positions in their fields of study. Graduates were employed in a wide variety of fields that reflected the scope of available programs; examples include teachers, counselors, therapists, clinical supervisors, caseworkers, reading specialists, systems analysts, operations/purchase managers, chief information officers, and human resource managers.

Location

Marywood University is situated in a suburban area known as the Green Ridge section of Scranton. It is located a little more than 100 miles from New York to the east and from Philadelphia to the south. It is served by the Scranton–Wilkes-Barre International Airport and is easily accessible by a network of superhighways. The Pocono Mountains resort areas and several beautiful lakes can be reached within 45 minutes or less. Montage Mountain ski area is only 15 minutes away.

The Graduate School

Marywood University, founded by the Congregation of the Sisters, Servants of the Immaculate Heart of Mary of Scranton, Pennsylvania, opened in 1915. Today, in addition to the Undergraduate School, Marywood includes two graduate schools—the Graduate School of Arts and Sciences and the Graduate School of Social Work. Founded in 1922, the Graduate School of Arts and Sciences aims to assist students in acquiring the education and training essential to preparation for their chosen careers, career changes, and professional enrichment. Currently, the Graduate School of Arts and Sciences offers the widest variety of professional degree programs in northeastern Pennsylvania.

Applying

Application for programs other than the doctoral and master's programs in speech-language pathology should be made at least two months before the date of desired entry. Specific application deadlines for the 2003–04 academic year are as follows: for the Psy.D. program, January 15, 2003; for the Ph.D. program, February 1, 2003; and for the speech-language pathology program, February 15, 2003. Required documents include the completed application form with fee, official transcripts, and recommendations. Some departments have additional requirements. Most departments accept the GRE General Test or Miller Analogies Test scores as an entrance requirement. Students usually enter a program in the fall semester, but they may be admitted in the spring or summer sessions for most programs.

Correspondence and Information

Office of Graduate Admissions
Graduate School of Arts and Sciences
Marywood University
Scranton, Pennsylvania 18509
Telephone: 570-340-6002
E-mail: gsas_adm@ac.marywood.edu
World Wide Web: http://www.marywood.edu

THE FACULTY AND THEIR RESEARCH

Steven Alexander, Associate Professor of Art; M.F.A., Columbia, 1997. Abstract paintings, examining the metaphorical resonance of color, physicality and scale.
Francis J. Anzelmi, Coordinator of Criminal Justice Program; M.P.A., Marywood, 1979. Criminal reduction: a trilateral approach.
Dona Bauman, Assistant Professor of Special Education; Ph.D., Temple, 2000. Early childhood special education issues.
Sr. M. Benedicta Berendes, I.H.M., Professor of Music; Ph.D., Pittsburgh, 1973. Musicology, with special interest in medieval, Renaissance, and American music, liturgical music and liturgy.
Janet D. Bisset, Associate Professor of Communication Sciences and Disorders; Ph.D., Memphis, 1981; postdoctoral study in medical speech pathology at the Mayo Clinic. Cognitive responses of individuals with left- versus right-hemisphere brain damage.
Grace Bohr, Lecturer in Counseling and Psychology; M.F.T., Hahnemann, 1979. Family dynamics, development of constructive personal and family relationships.
Marianne E. Borja, Professor and Cochair of Nutrition and Dietetics; Ed.D., Temple, 1984. Community nutrition, food and the environment, food systems management, dietary methodology, health promotion.
John Charles Boylan, Professor of Counseling and Psychology; Ph.D., Pittsburgh, 1973. Practicum and supervision, medical aspects of sexual dysfunction.
Ed Brodsky, Lecturer in Art; M.F.A., Syracuse, 1985. Advertising design and communication.
Barbara J. Burkhouse, Professor of Education; Ed.D., Lehigh, 1973. Preservice teacher education, classroom computer applications.
Sr. Gail Cabral, I.H.M., Professor of Psychology; Ph.D., Catholic University, 1978. Myers-Briggs Type Indicator, psychology and religion.
Martin Raymond Michael Camarata, Assistant Professor of Business and Managerial Science; Ph.D., Virginia Commonwealth, 1997. Health care, service quality, relationship management, international business.
C. Estelle Campenni, Associate Professor of Psychology; Ph.D., Adelphi, 1987. State-dependent learning, gender and play.
Brooke Cannon, Associate Professor of Counseling and Psychology; Ph.D., SUNY at Binghamton, 1990. Neuropsychology, dementia, brain trauma.
John R. Connelly, Assistant Professor of Education; Ed.D., Syracuse, 1989. Investigation of schoolwide reform models.
Edward J. Crawley, Assistant Professor of Psychology and Counseling; Ph.D., SUNY at Binghamton, 1999. Auditory perception, spoken word recognition, music cognition.
Samir Dagher, Professor and Chair of Business; Ph.D., Ohio State, 1974. Acquisitions and mergers.
Lois K. Draina, Associate Professor of Education and Dean, Graduate School of Arts and Sciences; Ph.D., Virginia Commonwealth, 1985. Instructional leadership, educational administration, Catholic schools, school board development, teacher education.
U. Rex Dumdum, Associate Professor of Business and Managerial Science; Ph.D., SUNY at Binghamton, 1993. Problem formulation of ill-structured situations, comparative evaluation of information system methodologies.
Maureen Dunn-Touey, Clinical Coordinator, Dietetic Internship and Director, Distance Education Dietetic Internship Program; M.S., CUNY, Lehman, 1983. Medical nutrition therapy.
Robin Gallagher, Professor of Nursing; D.N.Sc., Widener, 1989. Women's health, pediatrics, community health.
Mary Alice Golden, Associate Professor and Chair of Nursing and Public Administration; Ph.D., Pennsylvania, 1989. Alzheimer's disease, communication, nursing research, aging and psychosocial issues in nursing, long-term care.
Mona R. Griffer, Associate Professor of Communication Sciences and Disorders; Ed.D., Nova Southeastern, 1997. High-risk infants and toddlers, family-centered early intervention clinical service delivery, pediatric language.
Robert A. Griffith, Professor of Art; M.F.A., Southern Illinois, 1976. Forged and fabricated metal sculpture.
Jay Hammeran, Assistant Professor of Communication Arts; M.P.W., University of Southern California, 1982. History of television, how film studies became involved in network television.
Lee Harrison, Professor and Cochair of Nutrition and Dietetics; Ph.D., NYU, 1984. Personality type (MBTI) and its effects on career choice, competence, and ability to predict success; nutrition support/critical care, food habits, health promotion, gerontological nutrition.
Sr. Cor Immaculatum Heffernan, I.H.M., Professor and Chair of Art; M.F.A., Syracuse, 1981. Cast bronze sculpture.
Peter T. Hoffer, Associate Professor of Art; M.F.A., Cranbrook Academy of Art, 1968. Possibilities of computer applications with traditional printmaking processes.
Ann M. Jablonski, R.S.C.J., Associate Professor of Education; Ph.D., Fordham, 1996. Novice-to-expert self-efficacy and cognitive processes, mentoring and internships in preservice teacher education, educational leadership, systems analysis and structural modeling.
Gale Jaeger, Associate Professor of Business and Managerial Science; Ed.D., Temple, 1998. Marketing, human resources.
Bradley Janey, Assistant Professor of Psychology and Counseling; Ph.D., Kansas State, 1999. Aggression and masculinity in boys, fathering, media violence.
Doug Lawrence, Assistant Professor of Communication Arts; Ph.D. candidate, Union (Ohio). The impact of student development through the use of all forms of mass communication, including oral interpretation, written delivery, and technology.
John Lemoncelli, Associate Professor of Counseling and Psychology; Ed.D., Temple, 1983. Adult survivors of abuse, clinical practice training, pastoral counseling.
Alan M. Levine, Professor of Nutrition and Dietetics; Ph.D., NYU, 1985. Sports nutrition, human performance, wellness/health promotion.
Marie Loftus, Professor of Mathematics and Director, Ph.D. Program in Human Development; Ed.D., Penn State, 1975. Health and life style habits of children; gender differences in mathematics.
George Marcinek, Assistant Professor of Business and Managerial Science; M.B.A., Scranton, 1981. Accounting.
Sarah Michelle Marvian, Assistant Professor of Counseling and Psychology; Ph.D., Temple, 1997. Family violence and attachment theory, clinical practice training and supervision and group psychotherapy.
Alice Elaine McDonnell, Professor and Assistant Chair of Nursing and Public Administration; Dr.P.H., Columbia, 1982. Gerontology, long-term care, role of hospices and other community resources in treatment of older cancer patients, Alzheimer's.
Paulette Merchel, Associate Professor of Communication Arts; Ph.D., Temple, 1994. Cognitive processing, children's theater, educational theater, television in education.
Michael Mirabito, Professor and Chair of Communication Arts; Ph.D., Bowling Green State, 1982. New communication technologies, computer applications in the communications field.
Nancy M. Nagy, Associate Professor of Education; Ph.D., Temple, 1994. Diagnostic reading, literacy and language development.
Edward J. O'Brien, Professor and Chair of Counseling and Psychology; Ph.D., Massachusetts at Amherst, 1980. Cognitive approaches to self-esteem change, stress and coping, outcomes assessment in mental health, multimedia training methods.
Samuel Olfano, Assistant Professor in Art; M.F.A., Cincinnati, 1995. Photography, both product and process, as a visual language expressive of linear thought and nonlinear being.
David J. Palmitter Jr., Associate Professor of Psychology and Counseling and Director of Psychological Services Center; Ph.D., George Washington, 1989. Child and adolescent disruptive behavioral disorders, psychological testing.
Pamela Parsons, Associate Professor in Art; M.F.A., Indiana, 1990. Exploration, from a feminine perspective, of visual imagery revealing the psychological underpinnings of modern daily living.
Linda Dugan Partridge, Assistant Professor of Art History; Ph.D., Delaware, 1992. Art of the United States, nineteenth-century art of natural history and John James Audubon.
Sue Perdew, Professor of Nursing; Ph.D., Pittsburgh, 1982. Forensics, pediatric AIDS, child abuse, community health.
Susan Perlis, Assistant Professor of Education; Ph.D., Temple, 2001. Multicultural education, learning theory, higher education.
Mathew Povse, Assistant Professor and Chair of Art; M.F.A., Cranbrook Academy of Art, 1973. Sculptural form, texture, and line in clay.
Sr. Miriam Joseph Reinhardt, I.H.M., Assistant Professor and Chair of Music; Ph.D., NYU, 1971. History of the Gregorian chant.
David Renjilian, Associate Professor of Psychology; Ph.D., Fairleigh Dickinson, 1990. Development of mental health training materials; stress, coping, and burnout in health-care professionals.
Anthony C. Russo, Associate Professor and Chair of Special Education; Ed.D., Maryland, 1976. Adult literacy, inclusion strategies.
Mary Salvaterra, C.S.J., Professor and Chair of Education; Ph.D., Syracuse, 1990. Catholic identity in higher education, educational leadership, teacher education, multiculturalism.
Gina Pazzaglia Sylvester, Assistant Professor of Nutrition and Dietetics; Ph.D., Penn State, 1999. Nutrition education, nutrition and the media, hunger issues.
Daniel Terfassa, Assistant Professor of Business and Managerial Science; D.P.S., Pace, 1998. Corporate finance, financial institutions, auditing.
Zoe Zehel, Assistant Professor in Communication Sciences and Disorders; Ph.D., Maryland, 1974. Adult speech and language disorders.

MEMORIAL UNIVERSITY OF NEWFOUNDLAND

School of Graduate Studies

Programs of Study

Memorial University offers thirty-four doctoral programs, sixty-five master's programs, and two graduate diplomas. Information is available in the University's *Prospectus* (available at http://www.mun.ca/sgs) or by writing to the address listed below.

Research Facilities

There are excellent facilities for research in earth resources and cold ocean engineering as well as social, educational, and economic development, including specialized on-campus archives, such as the Maritime History Archive and the Folklore and Language Archive. An additional major facility is a full-service cartographic production facility providing support for scholarly publication and research. Other research centres include the Ocean Sciences Centre in Logy Bay and the Health Sciences Centre. The Fisheries and Marine Institute of Memorial University houses North America's largest flume tank and a world-class marine simulator complex. The NRC Institute for Marine Dynamics houses a 200-meter towing tank. The academic buildings offer extensive computer systems, recording studios, and learning resource centres. The University's library system houses more than 1 million bound volumes as well as periodicals, microfiche and computerized materials, and audiovisual resources.

The University's central Department of Computing and Communications maintains a large state-of-the-art campus network connected to the Internet and to CA*bet, Canada's high-speed education and research network. The primary computer servers are UNIX-based. A full range of services for Windows, NT, Macintosh, and UNIX are available, including PC-based computing labs, general computing and network services, high-performance computing, a well-equipped digital media centre, consulting assistance, and a computer store.

Financial Aid

On the basis of academic merit, financial support is available for full-time students through a variety of sources. No special application is required, as all applicants to the School of Graduate Studies are considered for these awards if the student's interest in financial aid is indicated on the application. In addition to scholarships, teaching assistantships are available through individual departments. Non-Canadian citizens are restricted to on-campus employment.

Cost of Study

Canadian and permanent resident tuition fees for 2001–02 were Can$2574 for master's candidates per academic year (minimum of two years); a minimum one-year fee of Can$3543 was available for some master's programs. Doctoral candidates paid Can$3195 per academic year (minimum of three years). Students were also required to pay a graduate student organization fee of Can$20 per semester. International students were charged an additional 10 percent on tuition fees. International students are required to purchase annual health insurance (the rate varies from year to year) as a condition of registration in the fall semester. Students entering in the winter or spring semesters are charged on a prorated basis.

Living and Housing Costs

Fees for accommodations and meals vary, depending on the meal plan chosen and whether a single room or shared accommodations in a residence or in an apartment are chosen. The minimum annual cost of room and board is approximately Can$6700. Information on additional fees and charges can be obtained directly from the University at the time of application.

Student Group

There are more than 1,600 graduate students enrolled in the University, with 20 percent coming from multicultural backgrounds.

Location

Memorial University is situated in Canada's most easterly city, St. John's, Newfoundland, on the shores of the North Atlantic. The province is particularly well known for its natural beauty; its fresh, clean air; and the many small communities that dot its coasts. Boating, fishing, hiking, camping, hunting, and skiing are just some of the leisure-time activities that can be enjoyed short distances from the city. Newfoundland also has a rich tradition of folk culture and music that makes it distinct from any other place in North America. The city provides many recreational and cultural facilities and has a temperate climate varying from approximately 20°C in the summer to approximately 0°C in the winter.

The University

Memorial University is the only university in Newfoundland and Labrador and was established in remembrance of Newfoundlanders lost in active service during the First World War. Current enrollment is approximately 14,200 undergraduate and more than 1,600 graduate students.

Applying

Applications can be submitted online at the URL listed below, or by writing the School of Graduate Studies. A nonrefundable Can$40 fee is charged for processing applications. Requirements include three letters of recommendation, an official transcript, and confirmation of a degree; certain departments require standardized test scores. TOEFL scores are required for applicants whose primary language is not English. Application deadlines vary across disciplines.

Correspondence and Information

School of Graduate Studies
Memorial University of Newfoundland
St. John's, Newfoundland A1B 3X5
Canada
Telephone: 709-737-8200
Fax: 709-737-4702
E-mail: sgs@mun.ca
World Wide Web: http://www.mun.ca/sgs/

THE FACULTY

SCHOOL OF GRADUATE STUDIES

Gregory S. Kealey, Dean, School of Graduate Studies; Ph.D., FRSC, FRHistS.
C. R. Jablonski, Associate Dean, School of Graduate Studies; Ph.D.

Deans of Faculties
Arts: (Interim) J. Black, Ph.D.
Business Administration: R. W. P. Blake, Ph.D.
Education: B. J. Burnaby, Ph.D.
Engineering and Applied Science: R. Seshadri, Ph.D., P.Eng.
Medicine: M. I. Bowmer, M.D.
Science: C. R. Lucas, D.Phil.

Directors of Schools
Human Kinetics and Recreation: C. Higgs, Ph.D.
Nursing: C. A. Orchard, Ed.D.
Pharmacy: (Acting) L. Hensmam, Pharm.D.
Social Work: (Acting) J. Dempster, M.S.W.

Chairs of Interdisciplinary Programs
Aquaculture: J. Brown, Ph.D.
Biopsychology: J. Brown, Ph.D.; A. Storey, Ph.D.
Computational Science: W. Zuberek, Ph.D.
Employment Relations: To be appointed
Environmental Engineering and Applied Sciences: T. Husain, Ph.D.
Environmental Science: N. Gogan, Ph.D.
Humanities: R. Matthews, Ph.D.
Marine Studies: P. Fisher, Ph.D.
Women's Studies: D. Tye, Ph.D.

GRADUATE PROGRAMS

Arts/Humanities/Social Sciences
Anthropology (M.A., Ph.D.)
Classics (M.A.)
Economics (M.A.)
English Language and Literature (M.A., Ph.D.)
Folklore (M.A., Ph.D.)
French Studies (M.A.)
Geography (M.A., Ph.D.)
German Language and Literature (M.A., M.Phil.)
History (M.A., Ph.D.)
Humanities (M.Phil.)
Linguistics (M.A., Ph.D.)
Philosophy (M.A.)
Political Science (M.A.)
Religious Studies (M.A.)
Sociology (M.A., Ph.D.)
Women's Studies (M.W.S.)

Sciences
Aquaculture (M.Sc.)
Biochemistry (M.Sc., Ph.D.)
Biology (M.Sc., Ph.D.)
  Marine Biology (M.Sc., Ph.D.)
Biopyschology (M.Sc., Ph.D.)
Chemistry (M.Sc., Ph.D.)
  Instrumental Analysis (M.Sc.)
Computational Science (M.Sc., M.Sc. Cooperative)
Computer Science (M.Sc., Ph.D.)
Earth Sciences
  Geology (M.Sc., Ph.D.)
  Geophysics (M.Sc., Ph.D.)
Environmental Science (M.Env.Sci., M.Sc.)
Food Science (M.Sc., Ph.D.)
Geography (M.Sc., Ph.D.)
Mathematics (M.Sc., Ph.D.)
Physical Oceanography (M.Sc., Ph.D.)
Physics (M.Sc., Ph.D.)
Psychology
  Experimental Psychology (M.Sc., Ph.D.)
  Applied Social Psychology (M.A.S.P.)
Statistics (M.A.S., M.Sc., Ph.D.)

Professional Programs
Business Administration (M.B.A., E.M.B.A.)
Education
  Counselling Psychology (M.Ed.)
  Educational Leadership Studies (M.Ed.)
  Information Technology (M.Ed.)
  Postsecondary Studies (M.Ed.)
  Teaching and Learning Studies (M.Ed.)
Employment Relations (M.E.R.)
Engineering and Applied Science
  Civil Engineering (M.Eng., Ph.D.)
  Electrical and Computer Engineering (M.Eng., Ph.D.)
  Environmental Engineering and Applied Science (M.A.Sc.)
  Mechanical Engineering (M.Eng., Ph.D.)
  Ocean and Naval Architectural Engineering (M.Eng., Ph.D.)
Human Kinetics and Recreation
  Administration, Curriculum and Supervision (M.P.E.)
Marine Studies
  Fisheries Resource Management (M.M.S.)
Medicine
  Cancer (M.Sc., Ph.D.)
  Cardiovascular and Renal Sciences (M.Sc., Ph.D.)
  Clinical Epidemiology (graduate diploma)
  Community Health (graduate diploma, M.Sc., Ph.D.)
  Human Genetics (M.Sc., Ph.D.)
  Immunology (M.Sc., Ph.D.)
  Neurosciences (M.Sc., Ph.D.)
Music (M.Mus.)
Nursing (M.N.)
Social Work (M.S.W., Ph.D.)

MIAMI UNIVERSITY

Graduate School

Programs of Study

The Graduate School at Miami University offers programs leading to master's, specialist's, and doctoral degrees. Ph.D. programs are offered in botany, chemistry, educational leadership, English, geology, microbiology, political science, psychology, and zoology. The Doctor of Education (Ed.D.) degree is offered in the Department of Educational Leadership. There are more than fifty different master's degree programs and fields of concentration offered by thirty-six departments in five academic divisions and the Institute of Environmental Sciences. The degrees offered are Master of Accountancy, Master of Architecture, Master of Arts, Master of Arts in Teaching, Master of Business Administration, Master of Education, Master of Environmental Science, Master of Fine Arts, Master of Gerontological Studies, Master of Music, Master of Science, Master of Science in Statistics, Master of Systems Analysis, and Master of Technical and Scientific Communication. A post-master's degree program leads to the Specialist in Education (Ed.S.) degree in school psychology.

The doctorate requires a minimum of 60 semester hours beyond the master's degree, the passing of a comprehensive examination, and the writing and defense of a dissertation. Language and research requirements for the doctorate are determined by individual departments. Both practice-oriented and research-oriented master's degree programs are offered, generally requiring a minimum of 30 semester hours, although some programs require more. Practice-oriented programs generally require internships or practicum experience in appropriate professional positions.

Research Facilities

The University libraries on the central campus at Oxford contain more than 1.8 million cataloged volumes, a government-documents collection of 90,000 volumes, and more than 2.1 million microforms. At present, the libraries receive more than 10,000 current periodicals and newspapers. The Edgar W. King Library building has a seating capacity of 2,000. Its facilities include rooms for the visually handicapped and for small-group study, a microform reading area, a record library with listening rooms, a student lounge, and special collections. The Brill Science Library houses more than 200,000 cataloged volumes and 1,800 journals in the science disciplines; it has a seating capacity of 700. The Walter E. Havighurst Special Collections Library includes the Edgar W. King Collection of Early Juvenile Books, the Samuel F. Covington Collection of Ohio Valley History, rare books, and special research materials and manuscripts. In addition, collections are housed in branch libraries for art and architecture and for music on the Oxford campus, in the Rentschler Library on the Hamilton campus, and in the Gardner-Harvey Library on the Middletown campus. The McGuffey Museum, designated a National Historic Landmark, has one of the finest collections of McGuffey Readers in the United States.

Other research facilities include the Institute of Environmental Sciences, the Scripps Foundation for research in gerontology and demography, the Bachelor Wildlife Reserve, the Ecology Research Center, the Computer Centers, the Molecular Microspectroscopy Laboratory, child study and clinical psychology facilities, and a speech and hearing clinic. Major equipment (including electron microscopes, spectrophotometers, ultracentrifuges, nuclear magnetic resonators, and minicomputers), a greenhouse, and well-equipped laboratories support research in the science areas.

Financial Aid

Financial support includes graduate assistantships, associateships, and grants-in-aid (tuition waivers). Stipends for full awards for assistantships and scholarships ranged from $8498 to $13,184 for the academic year 2001–02, plus a waiver of in-state and out-of-state instructional fees. Award holders also receive a waiver of summer instructional fees and a scholarship of up to $1600 for study during summer sessions. Inquiries about assistantships or associateships should be addressed to the appropriate academic department or program.

Cost of Study

In 2001–02, the instructional fee was $2977 per semester for a full load (12 hours) for Ohio residents and an additional $3837 for nonresidents. The student fees were $560 per semester. Graduate award holders paid reduced student fees of $280 per semester.

Living and Housing Costs

On-campus apartments are available on a first-come, first-served basis. The cost in 2001–02 was $3051 per semester. Most graduate students live in apartments off campus in Oxford.

Student Group

Graduate students comprise approximately 10 percent of the 16,000 enrollment at Miami's Oxford campus. A limited number of graduate courses are also offered at Miami's regional campuses in Hamilton and Middletown. Approximately 53 percent of Miami's full-time graduate students are women, 9 percent are members of ethnic minorities, and 16 percent are international scholars.

Location

Miami University is located in a small-town setting in southwestern Ohio, approximately 35 miles from Cincinnati and 45 miles from Dayton. Oxford has a resident population of 17,500.

The University

Miami University is a state-assisted university. It was established in 1809 and is the second-oldest institution of higher education in Ohio. The University has been engaged in graduate education since 1826, and its first earned master's degree was awarded in 1830. In 1947, graduate study was coordinated into the Graduate School. Doctoral programs began in 1967, with the first doctoral degrees awarded in 1969.

Applying

Applications for admission must be received at least one month before classes begin. Applications for financial support for the academic year must be received by March 1 for the following fall semester.

Correspondence and Information

For U.S. students:
Graduate School
Bonham House
Miami University
Oxford, Ohio 45056
Telephone: 513-529-4125
Fax: 513-529-4127
E-mail: gradschool@muohio.edu

For international students:
Office of International Programs
Langstroth Cottage
Miami University
Oxford, Ohio 45056
Telephone: 513-529-5628
E-mail: instuapp@muohio.edu

FACULTY HEADS

The academic department chairpersons are listed below. Doctoral departments are indicated by an asterisk.

Robert C. Johnson, Associate Provost and Dean of the Graduate School; Ph.D., Illinois.
Cheryl B. Evans, Associate Dean of the Graduate School; Ph.D., Ohio State.

Accountancy: John Cumming, Ph.D., Illinois.
Architecture and Interior Design: Robert A. Benson, Ph.D., Michigan.
Art/Art Education: Jerry Morris, Ed.D., Penn State.
*Botany: David Francko, Ph.D., Michigan State.
*Chemistry and Biochemistry: Michael Novak, Ph.D., Cornell.
Communication: Mark McPhail, Ph.D., Massachusetts.
Comparative Religion: Peter Williams (Acting), Ph.D., Yale.
Decision Sciences: David Yen, Ph.D., Nebraska.
Economics: John D. Ferguson, Ph.D., Brown.
*Educational Leadership: Bernard Badiali, Ph.D., Penn State.
Educational Psychology: Alex Thomas, Ph.D., Toledo.
*English: Dianne Sadoff, Ph.D., Rochester.
Environmental Sciences: Gene E. Willeke, Ph.D., Stanford.
Family Studies and Social Work: Susan Cross Lipnickey (Acting), Ph.D., Ohio State; Ph.D., J.D., Northern Kentucky.
Finance: Saul W. Adelman, Ph.D., Georgia.
French and Italian: James Creech (Acting), Ph.D., Cornell.
Geography: James M. Rubenstein, Ph.D., Johns Hopkins.
*Geology: William Hart, Ph.D., Case Western Reserve.
Gerontological Studies: C. Barry Chabot (Interim), Ph.D., SUNY at Buffalo.
History: Charlotte Newman Goldy, Ph.D., SUNY at Binghamton.
Management: William Snavely, Ph.D., Nebraska.
Marketing: Thomas Speh, Ph.D., Michigan State.
Mathematics and Statistics: Mark A. Smith, Ph.D., Illinois.
M.B.A. Program: Judy Barille, M.B.A., Miami (Ohio).
*Microbiology: Anne Morris Hooke, Ph.D., Georgetown.
Music: Judith K. Delzell, Ph.D., Michigan.
Paper Science and Engineering: Martin D. Sikora, Ph.D., Institute of Paper Chemistry.
Philosophy: William McKenna, Ph.D., New School for Social Research.
Physical Education, Health, and Sport Studies: Robin S. Vealey (Interim), Ph.D., Illinois.
Physics: Michael Pechan (Acting), Ph.D., Iowa State.
*Political Science: Ryan Barilleaux. Ph.D., Texas.
*Psychology: Karen Maitland Schilling, Ph.D., Florida.
Spanish and Portuguese: Charles Ganelin, Ph.D., Chicago.
Systems Analysis: Douglas A. Troy (Acting), Ph.D., Waikato (New Zealand).
Teacher Education: James Shiveley (Acting), Ph.D., Ohio State.
Technical and Scientific Communications: Jean Ann Lutz, Ph.D., Rensselaer.
Theater: Paul K. Jackson Jr., Ph.D., Wisconsin–Madison.
*Zoology: Douglas B. Meikle, Ph.D., Bowling Green.

MICHIGAN STATE UNIVERSITY

Graduate School

Programs of Study

Thirteen colleges of Michigan State University are authorized to grant graduate degrees. Within these colleges, seventy-one departments offer approximately 200 programs of study in which the master's and/or doctoral degrees may be earned. Doctoral degree offerings are accounting; agricultural economics; agricultural education; agricultural engineering; agricultural technology and systems management; animal science; anthropology; applied mathematics; arts and letters interdisciplinary programs; biochemistry; botany and plant pathology; cell and molecular biology; chemical engineering; chemical physics; chemistry; civil engineering; communication; communication arts and sciences: mass media; computer science; counseling and school psychology; crop and soil science; curriculum teaching and educational policy; ecology; economics; educational psychology; electrical engineering; English; entomology; environmental engineering; evolutionary biology and behavior; family and child ecology; finance; fisheries and wildlife; food science; forestry; French language and literature; genetics; geography; geology; German; higher, adult, and lifelong education; history; horticulture; human environment: design and management; human nutrition; K–12 educational administration; kinesiology; large-animal clinical sciences; linguistics; management policy and strategy; marketing; materials science; mathematics; measurement and quantitative methods; mechanical engineering; mechanics; medical science training program; microbiology; music (composition, education, musicology, and theory); neuroscience; organizational behavior/personnel; park and recreation resources; pharmacology and toxicology; philosophy; physics; physiology; political science; production and operations management; psychology; rehabilitation counseling and school counseling; resource development; Russian; school psychology; social sciences interdisciplinary programs (options in criminal justice, industrial relations and human resources, social work, and urban and regional planning); sociology; Spanish language and literature; special education; statistics; theater; transportation/distribution; and zoology. Interdepartmental doctoral degree programs that link environmental toxicology, plant breeding and genetics, or urban studies with a traditional academic discipline are also available.

Research Facilities

With a rapidly growing collection of more than 4 million volumes, the University's libraries are well designed to serve educational and research programs. Fiber and broadband cable support a campuswide data and video network. Vector and parallel processing, geographic visualization, and database systems are available to all students and faculty members for both instruction and research. Shared facilities exist for electron microscopy, mass spectrometry, magnetic resonance, protein and nucleic acid sequencing, and materials fabrication.

A more complete listing of research facilities is found in the Graduate School catalog.

Financial Aid

More than 3,100 assistantships are available in the various departments of the Graduate School. In 2001–02, half-time assistantship stipends ranged from $1066 to $2134 per month. In addition to the stipend, substantial tuition waivers and health insurance are included for all assistants. During 2001–02, in addition to the above grants, more than 3,000 fellowships were held by graduate students. These included NSF fellowships, NIH and NIMH traineeships, Ford Foundation fellowships, and numerous other grants sponsored by industry, foundations, and government agencies. The University also offers graduate fellowships and out-of-state tuition awards. Many of the fellowships pay tuition and fees in addition to stipends.

MSU Distinguished Fellowships are awarded each year in a University-wide competition. The stipend is $20,000 per year plus tuition and fees.

MSU Student Aid Grants, Federal Perkins Loans, Supplemental Loans for Students (SLS), and Federal Stafford Student Loans are also available to graduate and professional students.

An Affirmative Action Graduate Assistantship Program provides funds to encourage the recruitment, enrollment, and support of underrepresented groups of men and women. Equal Opportunity Program fellowships are awarded on the basis of financial need and academic background.

Cost of Study

The University operates on the semester system. In 2001–02, the tuition for out-of-state graduate students was $494 per credit, and the tuition for in-state graduate students was $244 per credit.

Living and Housing Costs

Housing for 872 graduate students is provided in Owen Hall, the graduate residence center, where charges were $2156 per semester for a single-occupancy room, $1843 per semester for a double-occupancy room, and $2492 per semester for a designated single (single in a double-occupancy room) for 2001–02. These charges include $280 for a meal plan. Housing charges for each of the two 7-week summer sessions in 2001 were $905 for a single-occupancy room and $774 for a double-occupancy room. These charges included $118 for a meal plan.

The University also operates 2,284 one- and two-bedroom apartments for married students. These are furnished apartments that rent from $443 to $477 per month for one bedroom and from $491 to $528 per month for two bedrooms. This includes telephone and all other utilities.

Off-campus housing costs vary widely, depending on the quality of housing desired.

Student Group

The University has an enrollment of 44,227 students on the East Lansing campus; 4,530 of these are graduate students and 1,378 are graduate professional students.

Student Outcomes

During the last five years, on average, 91 percent of the doctoral degree recipients and 91.5 percent of the master's degree recipients have secured job placement. Graduates have chosen the following career paths over the last five years: 36 percent of the doctoral graduates and 6.5 percent of the master's graduates are with hospital or medical services; 36 percent of the doctoral graduates and 7 percent of the master's graduates are employed by colleges or universities; 3.5 percent of the doctoral graduates and 12 percent of the master's graduates are attending graduate school or postdoctoral assignments; 2 percent of the doctoral graduates and 14 percent of the master's graduates are employed in elementary or secondary schools; 9 percent of the doctoral graduates and 8 percent of the master's graduates are with governmental agencies; plus other exciting career directions too numerous to mention.

Location

East Lansing offers the advantages of a small university town, with entertainment, sports, and cultural events provided by an outstanding University program. Contiguous with Lansing, the capital of Michigan, and within 2 hours' driving time of Detroit, East Lansing also provides the advantages of city life.

The University

Founded in 1855, Michigan State University brought a new concept of higher education into being in the United States, combining education and research with public service. This approach set the pattern for the nation's land-grant institutions. The 5,315-acre campus, including the 2,100-acre main campus, is essentially an arboretum park, providing a dynamic environment and an excellent atmosphere for study and research.

Applying

Applications for admission and supporting documents should be received by the Office of Admissions and Scholarships in time to meet appropriate departmental deadlines. Since these vary, students should correspond with a specific department prior to the date of desired enrollment. If a student is also applying for a graduate assistantship, fellowship, or scholarship, application materials should be received several months earlier and at least by the deadline established for the award concerned.

Correspondence and Information

Department of (specify)
Michigan State University
East Lansing, Michigan 48824
World Wide Web: http://www.msu.edu/user/gradschl

Office of Admissions and Scholarships
Michigan State University
East Lansing, Michigan 48824
Telephone: 517-355-8332

FACULTY CHAIRS AND DIRECTORS

Graduate School
Robert Huggett, Ph.D., Vice President for Research and Graduate Studies.
Karen Klomparens, Ph.D., Dean of the Graduate School and Assistant Provost for Graduate Studies.

Department of Accounting: Dr. Susan Haka, Chairperson.
Department of Advertising: Dr. Kathy Petroni, Chairperson.
Department of Agricultural and Extension Education: Dr. Kirk Heinze, Acting Chairperson.
Department of Agricultural Economics: Dr. Larry Hamm, Chairperson.
Department of Agricultural Engineering: Dr. Ajit K. Srivastara, Chairperson.
Department of Animal Science: Dr. Maynard Hogberg.
Department of Anthropology: Dr. Lynne Goldstein, Chairperson.
Department of Art: Dr. James A. Hopfensperger, Chairperson.
Department of Audiology and Speech Science: Dr. Brad Rakerd, Chairperson.
Department of Biochemistry and Molecular Biology: Dr. William Smith, Chairperson.
Department of Botany and Plant Pathology: Dr. Ray Hammerschmidt, Interim Chairperson.
Department of Chemical Engineering and Materials Science: Dr. K. Jayaraman, Chairperson.
Department of Chemistry: Dr. Katharine Hunt, Chairperson.
Department of Civil and Environmental Engineering: Dr. R. Harichandran, Chairperson.
Department of Communication: Dr. Charles Atkin, Chairperson.
Department of Computer Science and Engineering: Dr. Wayne Dyksen, Chairperson.
Department of Counseling, Educational Psychology, and Special Education: Dr. Richard Prawat, Chairperson.
School of Criminal Justice: Dr. Edmund McGarrell, Director.
Department of Crop and Soil Sciences: Dr. Douglas Buhler, Chairperson.
Department of Economics: Dr. Roweena Pecchenino, Chairperson.
Department of Educational Administration: Dr. Philip Cusick, Chairperson.
Department of Electrical and Computer Engineering: Dr. Satish Udpa, Chairperson.
Department of English: Dr. Patrick O'Donnell, Chairperson.
Department of Entomology: Dr. Edward Gratius, Chairperson.
Department of Epidemiology: Dr. Nigel Paneth, Chairperson.
Department of Family and Child Ecology: Dr. Anne Soderman, Acting Chairperson.
Department of Finance: Dr. Geoffrey Booth, Chairperson.
Department of Fisheries and Wildlife: Dr. Thomas Coon, Acting Chairperson.
Department of Food Science and Human Nutrition: Dr. Mark Uebersax, Chairperson.
Department of Forestry: Dr. Daniel E. Keathley, Chairperson.
Department of Geography: Dr. Richard Groop, Chairperson.
Department of Geological Sciences: Dr. Michael Velbel, Chairperson.
Department of History: Dr. Lewis Siegelbaum, Chairperson.
Department of Horticulture: Dr. Ron Perry, Acting Chairperson.
School of Hospitality Business: Dr. Ronald F. Cichy, Director.
Department of Human Environment and Design: Dr. Dana Stewart, Chairperson.
School of Journalism: Dr. Stephen Lacy, Acting Director.
Department of Kinesiology: Dr. Deborah Feltz, Chairperson.
School of Labor and Industrial Relations: Dr. Theodore Curry, Director.
Department of Large Animal and Clinical Sciences: Dr. Frederik Derksen, Chairperson.
Department of Linguistics and Languages: Dr. David K. Prestel, Chairperson.
Department of Management: Dr. John Wagner III, Chairperson.
Department of Marketing and Supply Chain Management: Dr. Robert W. Nason, Chairperson.
Department of Mathematics: Dr. Peter Lappan, Chairperson.
Department of Mechanical Engineering: Dr. Ronald Rosenberg, Chairperson.
Department of Microbiology and Molecular Genetics: Dr. Jerry Dodgson, Chairperson.
School of Music: Dr. James Forger, Director.
College of Nursing: Dr. Marilyn Rothert, Dean.
Department of Osteopathic Manipulative Medicine: Dr. James Rechtien, Acting Chairperson.
School of Packaging: Dr. Bruce R. Harte, Director.
Department of Park, Recreation, and Tourism Resources: Dr. Joseph Fridgen, Chairperson.
Department of Pharmacology and Toxicology: Dr. Kenneth E. Moore, Chairperson.
Department of Philosophy: Dr. Stephen Esquith, Chairperson.
Department of Physical Medicine and Rehabilitation: Dr. Margaret Fankhauser, Acting Chairperson.
Department of Physics and Astronomy: Dr. Wolfgang Bauer, Chairperson.
Department of Physiology: Dr. William S. Spielman, Chairperson.
Department of Political Science: Dr. Richard Hula, Chairperson.
Department of Psychology: Dr. Neal Schmitt, Chairperson.
Department of Resource Development: Dr. Scott Witter, Acting Chairperson.
Department of Romance and Classical Languages: Dr. Diedre Dawson, Acting Chairperson.
Department of Small Animal Clinical Sciences: Dr. Curtis Probst, Chairperson.
School of Social Work: Dr. Gary Anderson, Director.
Department of Sociology: Dr. Thomas Conner, Chairperson.
Department of Statistics and Probability: Dr. Habib Salehi, Chairperson.
Department of Surgery: Dr. Richard E. Dean, Chairperson.
Department of Teacher Education: Dr. Stephen Koziol, Chairperson.
Department of Telecommunication: Dr. Mark Levy, Chairperson.
Department of Theatre: Dr. Frank Rutledge, Chairperson.
Department of Zoology: Dr. Richard Snider, Acting Chairperson.

MichiganTech

MICHIGAN TECHNOLOGICAL UNIVERSITY

Graduate School

Programs of Study

The University offers graduate instruction in many branches of engineering, science, and related technological and business fields. M.S. degree programs are available in applied science education, biological sciences, chemical engineering, chemistry, civil engineering, computer science, electrical engineering, engineering mechanics, environmental engineering, environmental engineering science, environmental policy, forestry, geological engineering, geology, geophysics, industrial archaeology, mathematics, mechanical engineering, metallurgical engineering, mineral economics, mining engineering, physics, and rhetoric and technical communication. The Ph.D. degree is offered in biological sciences, chemical engineering, chemistry, civil engineering, computer science, electrical engineering, forest molecular genetics and biotechnology, forest science, geological engineering, geology, mathematics, mechanical engineering–engineering mechanics, metallurgical engineering, mining engineering, physics, rhetoric and technical communication, and other nondepartmental engineering areas (computational science and environmental). The School of Forestry and Department of Civil and Environmental Engineering also offer an M.S. program in cooperation with the Peace Corps. The College of of Engineering recently initiated a Master of Engineering degree program.

Research Facilities

The J. Robert Van Pelt Library provides books, periodicals, microfiche/film, and access to electronic information to complement instructional and research needs. Access to library resources is through the automated system, Voyager. The library contains more than 780,000 volumes, including government documents, and receives more than 10,000 serials and periodicals. The collection is particularly strong in the physical and natural sciences, mathematics, and engineering. Individual departments maintain networked labs of PCs, Sun Workstations, or other specialized computational or visualization systems tailored to their research needs. In addition to departmental facilities, campuswide computer and network services are offered by Informational Technology (IT). The campus network is connected to the Internet, allowing virtually all faculty and graduate students easy access to all network and information services from the desktop.

All departments at Michigan Tech have the laboratories and equipment needed for graduate study, as well as access to many other facilities, such as those of the National Park Service Cooperative Studies Unit, the Forestry Sciences Laboratory (USDA, Forest Service), the Remote Sensing Institute, the Center for Advanced Manufacturing and Materials Processing, and the Keweenaw Research Center.

Financial Aid

Financial assistance includes fellowships and teaching and research assistantships. A number of doctoral dissertation fellowships are available. Stipends for teaching and research assistantships ranged from $8404 to $9758 for the 2001–02 academic year; in addition, tuition is paid by the University, and a health insurance subsidy is available. A Michigan minority fellowship program is available for doctoral students. Loans may be arranged through the Financial Aid Office.

Cost of Study

Tuition and fees for 2001–02 were $3009 per semester for residents of Michigan and $5831 per semester for nonresident graduate students. All students are responsible for a student activity fee of $131.30.

Living and Housing Costs

Michigan Tech residence halls have accommodations for 2,131 single students; application forms may be obtained from the Director of Residential Services. For married students, Michigan Tech has 352 one- and two-bedroom furnished apartments; applications for these may be obtained from the manager of Daniell Heights Apartments. Rooms, apartments, trailers, and houses are available in the community. Housing arrangements should be made as early as possible. Because the cost of housing is subject to change, representative costs are not stated.

Student Group

The University has an enrollment of approximately 6,300 students; nearly 700 are graduate students.

Student Outcomes

Graduates attain positions in academia, industry, and government agencies as faculty members, research engineer/scientists, and project engineers. In the past year, these positions have been obtained at such institutions as Caltech, Notre Dame, Purdue, Wayne State, the University of Central Florida, and the University of Missouri, and at such corporations as BASF, Ford, GE, GM, Kimberly Clark, and Tenneco. Master's program graduates have been accepted to doctoral programs at Illinois, Michigan State, Northern Arizona, Ohio State, Purdue, and SUNY at Stony Brook, among others.

Location

Michigan Tech's main campus stretches for about a mile along Portage Lake in Houghton, a city approximately 550 miles northwest of Detroit and 450 miles north of Chicago. Houghton is on the Keweenaw Peninsula, which extends into Lake Superior. Known for its rugged, unspoiled natural beauty, the area has been nicknamed "copper country" because of its rich history of copper mining. The main campus consists of about eighty buildings housing laboratories, classrooms, lecture halls, living accommodations, the library, the Memorial Union, the gymnasium, indoor tennis courts, and an ice arena. The University owns and operates an eighteen-hole golf course and a downhill ski run with a chair lift.

The University

Michigan Technological University is an independent unit in Michigan's state-supported system of higher education. Founded in 1885 as a mining college, it has since developed strengths in a variety of technological and business fields.

Applying

The application for admission and an official transcript of previous academic work at the undergraduate and graduate levels must be submitted to the Graduate School. A nonrefundable $30 application fee ($35 for international applications) must accompany the application. Applications should be submitted at least six weeks before the start of the applicant's desired quarter of entrance.

Correspondence and Information

Graduate School Office
Michigan Technological University
1400 Townsend Drive
Houghton, Michigan 49931-1295
Telephone: 906-487-2327
Fax: 906-487-2245
E-mail: gradadms@mtu.edu
World Wide Web: http://www.mtu.edu/

Chair, Department of (specify)
Michigan Technological University
1400 Townsend Drive
Houghton, Michigan 49931-1295

FACULTY HEADS

The administrative officers of the Graduate School and of the departments responsible for programs leading to graduate degrees are listed below:

Graduate School: J. Bruce Rafert, Ph.D., Dean.

Department of Biological Sciences: John H. Adler, Ph.D., Chair.
School of Business and Engineering Administration (Mineral Economics): Keith W. Lantz, Ph.D., Dean.
Department of Chemical Engineering: Michael E. Mullins, Ph.D., Interim Chair.
Department of Chemistry: Pushpalatha P. Murthy, Ph.D., Chair.
Department of Civil and Environmental Engineering: C. Robert Baillod, Ph.D., Chair.
Department of Computer Science: Linda Ott, Ph.D., Chair.
Department of Electrical and Computer Engineering: Timothy J. Schulz, D.Sc., Chair.
School of Forestry and Wood Products: Glenn D. Mroz, Ph.D., Dean.
Department of Geological Engineering and Sciences: Theodore J. Bornhorst, Ph.D., Chair.
Department of Humanities (Rhetoric and Technical Communication): Robert R. Johnson, Ph.D., Chair.
Department of Materials Science and Engineering: Calvin L. White, Ph.D., Chair.
Department of Mathematical Sciences: A. H. Baartmans, Ph.D., Chair.
Department of Mechanical Engineering–Engineering Mechanics: W. W. Predebon, Ph.D., Chair.
Department of Mining and Materials Processing Engineering: S. Komar K. Kawatra, Ph.D., Chair.
Department of Physics: Ravinda Pandey, Ph.D., Interim Chair.
Department of Social Science (Environmental Policy and Industrial Archaeology): Terry S. Reynolds, Ph.D., Chair.

Computational Science and Engineering Ph.D. Committee: Steven R. Seidel, Ph.D., Chair.
Environmental Engineering Ph.D. Committee: John C. Crittenden, Ph.D., Chair.

MTU's main campus features the famous inclined pine tree and is easily accessible from residence halls and apartments.

Michigan Tech students use the beautiful Keweenaw Peninsula as the ultimate outdoor laboratory.

MTU students have access to lasers and other high-technology equipment.

MILLERSVILLE UNIVERSITY OF PENNSYLVANIA

Graduate School

Programs of Study

Millersville University of Pennsylvania offers programs of study leading to the master's degree (M.A., M.B.A., M.Ed., M.S., and M.S.N.) in art, biology, business administration, early childhood, educational leadership, elementary education, English, foreign languages, history, mathematics, nursing, psychology, reading and language arts, school counseling, special education, sport management, and technology education. Students may also pursue graduate level supervisory and post-master's certification credentials.

The University calendar consists of two regular semesters, which begin in August and January, and modified summer sessions. The Foreign Language Department offers course work only through its innovative summer language institutes. Students may pursue graduate degrees on a full-time or part-time basis, but generally must complete their course of study within a five-year period.

Research Facilities

The Helen A. Ganser Library is the main research repository on campus, with approximately 1 million books, periodicals, and media resources. The library is a member of the Keystone Library and the Pennsylvania Academic Library Networks, which provide direct access to the collections of more than sixty academic libraries and to thousands of electronic abstracts, indexes, journals, and business services. It is also a depository for selected U.S. government publications and Pennsylvania state documents. State-of-the-art computer labs complement online computer labs across campus. A Marine Science Consortium, the Center for Regional Studies, the Center for Academic Excellence, the Center for Politics and Public Affairs, the Elizabeth Jenkins Early Childhood Learning Center, several multimedia art galleries, and more specialized research centers offer students a vast array of research opportunities.

Financial Aid

Graduate assistantships are awarded on a competitive basis to master's degree and graduate-level certification students. Remuneration for assistantships includes a first-year stipend of $4000 and a waiver of tuition fees to a maximum of 24 graduate credits in a calendar year. The stipend for second year studies is $4500. Assignments include most academic programs and many administrative offices. Student work-study positions are available, and the University administers a range of loan programs. Interested students should contact the Office of Graduate Studies. In order to receive full consideration, assistantship applications should be received no later than March 31.

Cost of Study

Tuition for the 2001–02 academic year was $256 per credit for in-state resident students and $420 per credit for out-of-state graduate students. Students also paid a general fee of $43.50 per credit. Tuition and fees are expected to increase slightly for the 2002–03 academic year.

Living and Housing Costs

Housing on campus for graduate students during the fall and spring semesters is limited. Summer accommodations are available by reservation. Affordable residential housing is available near the campus. For campus housing, students should contact the Resident Life Office at 717-872-3162. For assistance on off-campus housing, students should contact the Off-Campus Housing Office at 717-872-3707.

Student Group

The University's total enrollment for fall 2001 was 7,556, including 959 graduate students. The graduate enrollment includes students from numerous states and several countries. Many graduate students are engaged in or intend to pursue careers in teaching, while others have achieved success in varying professions. Students regularly go on to distinction in doctoral programs in the nation's finest universities. A Graduate Student Association represents the academic and social interests of the graduate student population.

Location

Millersville University is in Lancaster County, the heartland of central Pennsylvania and the rural Pennsylvania Dutch culture. Adjacent to the city of Lancaster, a thriving metropolitan area of diverse commercial and cultural institutions, the University is situated in a peaceful residential borough of tree-lined streets and gently rolling hills. The campus is a 1½-hour drive from Philadelphia and Baltimore, 2½ hours from Washington, D.C., and 3½ hours from New York City.

The University

Rated one of the finest regional universities in the country in several recent publications, Millersville University has a tradition of graduate education that dates back nearly half a century. Established in 1855 as the Commonwealth's first normal school, Millersville University is one of fourteen institutions in the State System of Higher Education. A multipurpose university situated on a 250-acre campus, Millersville blends the spirit of innovation with the strength of tradition in academic and professional programs that serve a diverse regional population. The campus itself reflects a combination of the old and the new, with beautiful Victorian buildings and state-of-the-art research labs and technology centers.

Applying

Applicants to degree programs must hold a baccalaureate degree from an accredited college or university. In addition to the application form, a $30 nonrefundable fee, official transcripts, and official GRE, MAT, or GMAT scores (depending on the program) are required. International students are required to submit a TOEFL score and financial information forms. Application deadlines are March 1 for summer and fall admission and October 1 for winter and spring admission. Students who do not meet regular admissions requirements may be granted probational admission status.

Correspondence and Information

Office of Graduate Studies
231 Lyle Hall
Millersville University of Pennsylvania
P.O. Box 1002
Millersville, Pennsylvania 17551-0302
Telephone: 717-872-3030
Fax: 717-871-2022
E-mail: gradstu@millersville.edu
World Wide Web: http://www.millersville.edu/~graduate

THE FACULTY AND THEIR RESEARCH

PROGRAM COORDINATORS

Art: Marianne S. Kerlavage, Ph.D., Wisconsin.
Biology: Daniel H. Yocom, Ph.D., SUNY at Stony Brook.
Business Administration: Howard Cox, Ph.D., Ohio State.
Early Childhood Education: Alice M. Meckley, Ph.D., Pennsylvania.
Elementary Education: Judith Wenrich, Ed.D., Lehigh.
English: Robert Carballo, Ph.D., Miami (Florida).
Educational Leadership: Nancy L. Smith, Ph.D., Georgia.
History: Saulius Suziedelis, Ph.D., Kansas.
Mathematics: Bernard L. Schroeder, Ph.D., Wisconsin.
Nursing: Barbara F. Haus, Ed.D., Lehigh.
Psychology and School Counseling: Claudia Haferkamp, Ph.D., Ball State.
Reading and Language Arts: Mary Ann C. Gray-Schlegel, Ed.D., North Carolina at Greensboro.
Special Education: Elba Rohena, Ed.D., Lehigh.
Sport Managment: Stanley Kabacinski, M.Ed., East Stroudsburg.
Technology Education: Joseph M. McCade, Ed.D., Virginia Tech.

Robotics and artificial intelligence research in the University's Intelligent Machines Laboratory.

Collaborative learning and research distinguish graduate programs in the School of Education.

Biemesderfer Center, formerly College Library, built 1893–5.

MILLS COLLEGE

Graduate Studies

Programs of Study

Graduate programs at Mills are offered to both men and women in the arts, sciences, and education, all programs for which the College has a reputation for excellence. Graduate degree programs include the Master of Arts or the Master of Fine Arts (M.F.A.) in creative writing, dance (choreography and performance) English, music (composition, performance and literature, electronic music and recording media), and studio art. In addition, the College offers the Master of Arts in the areas of child development/early childhood education, child life in hospitals, interdisciplinary computer science, and teaching. Special nondegree certificate graduate programs also attract students to Mills from many parts of the nation and the world. The highly competitive postbaccalaureate Pre-Medical Certificate Program is for college graduates who have decided to pursue a health professions career but lack the basic science courses. In computer science, a New Horizons Certificate Program is available to college graduates who find barriers in their path to graduate study or employment because of a lack of exposure to sophisticated computer concepts.

The Department of Education offers combined Master of Arts degree and teacher credential programs with specializations in early childhood, elementary, and secondary education and in the hospitalized child. A nationally recognized and successful model for preparation of math and science teachers recruits applicants in midcareer who wish to become teachers. Graduate students in the teacher preparation and child development programs benefit from fieldwork in the Mills College Children's School, a laboratory school that continues to maintain its reputation as a leader in the education of young children and the training of professionals in the field. In addition, Mills now offers a Master of Arts (M.A.) as well as a Doctor of Education (Ed.D.) degree and an Administrative Services Credential (ASC) in educational leadership. These programs prepare candidates for current challenges facing school administrators.

All graduate degree programs require at least two years of full-time study. Required courses of study range from ten courses (40 semester hours) to twelve courses (48 semester hours). Students must complete their degrees within five years after initial enrollment, except for the Master of Arts in Teaching, which allows a maximum of eight years for completion.

Research Facilities

The award-winning F. W. Olin Library has online facilities and vast rare book archives. Other facilities are the Mills College art collection and art gallery with more than 4,500 works; the Center for Contemporary Music with outstanding electronic music and recording facilities; computer facilities, which include VAX, NeXT, and Macintosh workstations and training; the Children's School; the Career Center; athletic facilities; spacious dance studios; and individual studios for graduate art students.

Financial Aid

Graduate teaching assistantships that give both a stipend and partial tuition remission are available in most departments, particularly to second-year students. These awards are limited and are usually not available to a student for more than one or two semesters. Alumnae tuition scholarships are also available to help cover partial tuition costs. Graduate students are often eligible for state and federal assistance programs, including the Federal Stafford Student Loan program.

Cost of Study

In 2001–02, tuition was $12,700 for the academic year. Other fees included a $500 studio fee for M.F.A. students, a $75 student teaching fee for credential students, and varying fees for music instruction and rental of practice rooms.

Living and Housing Costs

An on-campus graduate residence houses women and men in single rooms or suites. The cost for room and board was approximately $8350 for 2001–02.

Student Group

In 2001–02, the graduate student enrollment at Mills was 434. The undergraduate enrollment was more than 755. Approximately 26 percent of the graduate population were men, 20 percent were members of minority groups, and 1 percent were international students. Students come from many parts of the United States and many areas of the world. Mills encourages diversity in its student body and is working to increase diversity throughout the Mills academic community.

Location

Mills is located on a 135-acre wooded campus in Oakland, California, one of the most culturally diverse cities in the United States. The campus is minutes away from the East Bay Regional Redwood Parks, 20 minutes from downtown San Francisco, and 30 minutes from the beaches of the Pacific Ocean.

The College

Mills College, founded in 1852 as the first college in the West for women, continues its commitment to the education of women at the undergraduate level but has graduate programs open to both men and women. Mills remains a small, private, liberal arts college located in an urban center on a beautiful 135-acre campus noted for its tall eucalyptus and pines, rolling hills, and streams. Architecture on the campus includes Mills Hall, a Victorian-style campus center building that is listed on the National Register of Historic Places; gracious Spanish-style dormitories and classroom buildings, and contemporary building designs. Mills is accredited by the Western Association of Schools and Colleges.

Applying

Basic requirements for admission are an earned bachelor's degree or its equivalent from an accredited college or university and demonstrated intellectual potential or special performance in the field of study being sought. Application deadlines vary according to the program, with November 1 and February 1 being the standard deadlines for spring and fall admission, respectively.

Correspondence and Information

Office of Graduate Studies
Mills College
Oakland, California 94613
Telephone: 510-430-3309
Fax: 510-430-2159
E-mail: grad-studies@mills.edu
World Wide Web: http://www.mills.edu

GRADUATE DEPARTMENTS

Art: Hung Liu, M.F.A., California, San Diego.
Anna Murch, M.A., Royal College of Art (London).
Ron Nagle, B.A., San Francisco State.
Catherine Wagner, M.A., San Francisco State.
Gail Wright, M.F.A., San Francisco Art Institute.

Dance: Mary Cochran (Paul Taylor Dance Company).
Mary Ann Kinkead, M.A., Mills.
Kathleen McCormick, M.F.A., Mills.
Judith Rosenberg, M.M., Rochester (Eastman).
June Watanabe, B.A., UCLA.

Education: Lyda Beardsley, Ph.D., Berkeley.
Jane Bowyer, Ph.D., Berkeley.
David Donahue, Ph.D., Stanford.
Tomas Galguera, Ph.D., Stanford.
Joseph Kahne, Ph.D., Stanford.
Linda Kroll, Ph.D., Berkeley.
Vicki LaBoskey, Ph.D., Stanford.
Ginny Lee, Ph.D., Stanford.
Richard P. Mesa, Ph.D., Stanford.
Edna Mitchell, Ph.D., Missouri.
Linda Perez, Ph.D., Berkeley.
Anna Richert, Ph.D., Stanford.

English: Elmaz Abinader, Ph.D., Nebraska.
Chana Bloch, Ph.D., Berkeley.
Madeleine Kahn, Ph.D., Stanford.
Ajuan Mance, Ph.D., Michigan.
Edward Milowicki, Ph.D., Oregon.
Cornelia Nixon, Ph.D., Berkeley.
Stephen Ratcliffe, Ph.D., Berkeley.
Katherine Reiss, M.F.A., Michigan.
Ruth Saxton, Ph.D., Berkeley.
Cynthia Scheinberg, Ph.D., Rutgers.
Tom Strychacz, Ph.D., Princeton.
Elizabeth Willis, Ph.D., SUNY at Buffalo.

Interdisciplinary Computer Science: Steven Givant, Ph.D., Berkeley.
Matthew Merzbacher, Ph.D., UCLA.
Barbara Li Santi, Ph.D., California, Santa Barbara.
Ellen Spertus, Ph.D., MIT.
Zvezdelina Stankova-Frenkel, Ph.D., Harvard.
Susan Wang, Ph.D., Princeton.

Music: David Bernstein, Ph.D., Columbia.
John Bischoff, M.F.A., Mills.
Chris Brown, M.F.A., Mills.
Alvin Curran, M.A., Yale.
Michelle Fillion, Ph.D., Cornell.
Fred Frith, M.A., Cambridge.
Pauline Oliveros, B.A., San Francisco State.
Maggi Payne, M.Mus., Illinois.
Sandra Soderlund, D.M.A., Stanford.

Postbaccalaureate Pre-Medical Program: Sandra Banks, M.S., UCLA.
John Brabson, Ph.D., Illinois at Urbana-Champaign.
Steven Givant, Ph.D., Berkeley.
Richard Grow, Ph.D., California, Riverside.
David Keeports, Ph.D., Washington (Seattle).
Karen Swearingen, Ph.D., Berkeley.
Lisa Urey, Ph.D., MIT.
John Vollmer, Ph.D., USC.
Elizabeth Wade, Ph.D., Berkeley.
Cathy Wadeen, Ph.D., SUNY at Stony Brook.

MONMOUTH UNIVERSITY

Graduate School

Programs of Study

The Graduate School offers programs in several areas designed for students who wish to acquire advanced knowledge and skills in their chosen fields of study and to engage in research and other scholarly activities. The programs are administered through the School of Humanities and Social Sciences; the School of Nursing and Health Studies; the School of Business Administration; the School of Science, Technology and Engineering; and the School of Education. The School of Humanities and Social Sciences awards the Master of Arts (M.A.) in criminal justice, corporate and public communication, history, and psychological counseling, a Master of Arts in Liberal Arts (M.A.L.A.), and a Master of Social Work (M.S.W.). This school also offers a post-master's certificate in professional counseling; specialist certificates in public relations, media studies, and human resources communication; and a certificate in criminal justice administration. The School of Nursing and Health Studies offers a Master of Science in Nursing (M.S.N.) as well as a post-master's certificate in advanced practice nursing, a post-master's certificate in nursing education, a postbaccalaureate substance awareness coordinator certificate, a postbaccalaureate certificate in forensic nursing, and a postbaccalaureate school nurse certificate. The School of Science, Technology and Engineering awards Master of Science (M.S.) degrees in computer science and software engineering. Certificates are available in software development and software engineering. The School of Education offers two programs leading to master's degrees: the Master of Arts in Teaching (M.A.T.) and the Master of Science in Education (M.S.Ed.). The M.S.Ed. program offers concentrations in principal preparation, special education, reading specialist studies, and educational counseling. Certificate programs are offered in learning disabilities teacher-consultant, teacher of the handicapped, supervisor, and reading specialist. The School of Business Administration offers the Master of Business Administration (M.B.A.) program and the M.B.A. with a concentration in health-care management. Monmouth also offers an accelerated degree program, the Graduate Scholars Program, to enable students to achieve both a bachelor's and master's degree in five years of study.

Research Facilities

The Guggenheim Memorial Library is the informational center of the University and holds 220,000 volumes and 1,300 periodicals. The library maintains special collections pertaining to the state of New Jersey and prominent American scholar and social critic Lewis Mumford (1895–1990). The library is a selective depository for publications of the United States government. Interlibrary loan service is available through the On-Line College Library Center, allowing students access to the collections of more than 1,300 major resource libraries. The library also maintains several online CD-ROM search databases, which can be accessed by all of the University's major computer resources. The major components that support Monmouth's academic programs include UNIX, Windows NT, and Novell server systems that are connected by a sophisticated campus Ethernet network that spans twenty-three buildings and encompasses more than 1,000 workstations campuswide. Workstations that are specifically dedicated to student use are distributed among thirty instructional and open-use laboratories and include DEC Alpha servers, Silicon Graphics servers and workstations, SUN servers and workstations, Pentium servers and workstations, and Macintosh workstations. Laptop plug-in ports are available in convenient locations across the campus. A campus communications network (HawkNet) connects all Monmouth University computing resources to the Internet. All students receive a computer account that provides them with e-mail, World Wide Web browsing and authoring tools, and electronic access to the Guggenheim Library catalog.

Financial Aid

Financial aid is available through fellowships, assistantships, employment, and loans. Fellowships are awarded, upon application and approval, to qualified full-time students on the basis of outstanding undergraduate records and GRE scores. A limited number of assistantships and resident assistantships are available to continuing students, with preference given to those maintaining a high grade point average. To determine eligibility for all other forms of aid, applicants must file the FAFSA form, which is available from the Financial Aid Office. Monmouth University participates in the Federal Direct Student Loan Program, which makes both need- and non-need-based loans available to students who file the FAFSA.

Cost of Study

Tuition for study in 2001–02 for most programs was $523 per credit. Tuition was $523 per credit for the post-master's programs in education and $1588 per course for the software engineering program. A University fee is assessed each semester.

Living and Housing Costs

Housing on campus for graduate students may be obtained on a space-available basis. Due to Monmouth's proximity to the beach, there are ample off-campus housing opportunities that are conveniently located near the University. These accommodations are relatively inexpensive since the academic year is also the off-season for tourism. A file of off-campus residences for rent is maintained by the Office of Student Services.

Student Group

Monmouth University's total enrollment is 5,753 students, 1,475 of whom are enrolled in the Graduate School. The diverse student body includes many international students representing thirty-five different countries.

Location

Monmouth University is located less than 1 mile from the Atlantic Ocean on a 147-acre campus in the quiet, picturesque town of West Long Branch, New Jersey (population 7,800). The campus is only 1½ hours from both New York City and Philadelphia. Both can be easily accessed by train. Commuter bus service is also available. The surrounding area boasts numerous activities, restaurants, and cultural events. Its proximity to high-technology firms, financial institutions, and a thriving business-industrial sector provides current Monmouth students and graduates with limitless employment possibilities.

The University

Monmouth University is a private, moderate-sized coeducational teaching university committed to providing a learning environment that enables men and women to pursue their educational goals and realize their full potential for making significant contributions to their community and society. Small classes that allow for individual attention and student-faculty dialogue, together with careful academic advising and career counseling, are hallmarks of a Monmouth education. The Student Center houses the Office of Student Services, placement, computer laboratories, study lounges, a full-service cafeteria and campus pub, and student activities meeting rooms and offices. The University's NCAA Division I intercollegiate athletics program includes nine men's and ten women's teams.

Applying

An application for admission to the Graduate School includes a completed application form with application fee, official transcript of the undergraduate record, score reports from the appropriate entrance examination (e.g., GRE or GMAT), transcripts of any graduate work done elsewhere, and two letters of recommendation covering the candidate's personal and professional qualifications to pursue graduate work. International students must also provide evidence of English proficiency. The application deadlines are as follows: August 15 for the fall term, December 15 for the spring term, and May 15 for the summer sessions. Successful completion of the GMAT is required of those applying for the M.B.A. program. GRE test scores are required for those applying for programs in psychological counseling, nursing, criminal justice, and corporate and public communication. Students with work experience in communication may submit a portfolio in lieu of the GRE. An initial review of the complete application for admission is conducted by the Office of Adult and Graduate Admission and Enrollment. The file is then forwarded to the faculty director of the program for an admission decision. All correspondence should be conducted with the Office of Adult and Graduate Admission and Enrollment.

Correspondence and Information

Kevin L. Roane
Director of Graduate Admission
Monmouth University
West Long Branch, New Jersey 07764-1898
Telephone: 732-571-3452
800-320-7754 (toll-free)
Fax: 732-263-5123
E-mail: gradadm@monmouth.edu
World Wide Web: http://www.monmouth.edu

FACULTY HEADS AND PROGRAMS

Master of Arts in History (M.A.): Julius O. Adekunle, Program Director and Assistant Professor of History; Ph.D., Dalhousie.

The program accommodates students who wish to specialize in European or United States history. The program is designed not only for recent college graduates but also for secondary school teachers of history and social studies and professionals in government, the military, and business. Thesis and nonthesis options are available.

Master of Arts in Psychological Counseling (M.A.): Frances K. Trotman, Program Director and Associate Professor of Psychology; Ph.D., Columbia.

The program offers practical and theoretical courses in quantitative methods, intervention skills, and assessment methods. The program equips students with proficiencies in the traditional counseling field as well as in emerging areas. Upon completion of the program, students may pursue an advanced degree or enter the post-master's certification program.

Master of Arts in Liberal Arts (M.A.L.A.): Kenneth Campbell, Acting Program Director and Associate Professor of History; Ph.D., Delaware.

This program is an interdisciplinary approach to the graduate study of the humanities, the natural and applied sciences, and the social and behavioral sciences. Students are encouraged to cross disciplinary boundaries and to combine various areas into a degree program that satisfies personal curiosity and contributes to the achievement of professional objectives.

Master of Science in Software Engineering (M.S.): William Tepfenhart, Program Director and Associate Professor of Software Engineering; Ph.D., Texas at Dallas.

The software engineering program offers the first degree of its kind in New Jersey. Students learn to develop, validate, implement, and maintain high-quality software products. Specialization tracks are offered in embedded real-time systems, information management, organizational management, and telecommunications.

Master of Science in Computer Science (M.S.): A. A. Fredericks, Program Director and Professor of Computer Science; Ph.D., NYU.

The program includes concentrations in computer networks and intelligent information systems. The computer networks concentration includes study in analysis/modeling and simulation. The program is open to students with undergraduate degrees other than computer science (some preparatory work may be required).

Master of Science in Nursing (M.S.N.): Janet Mahoney, Program Director and Associate Professor of Nursing; Ph.D., NYU.

The nursing program is designed to prepare the professional nurse for advanced practice nursing. Concentrations are offered in adult or family nurse practitioner and nursing administration.

Master of Arts in Teaching (M.A.T.): David S. McCurry, Program Director and Assistant Professor of Curriculum and Instruction; Ed.D., Massachusetts.

The M.A.T. is offered for both certified teachers and those who wish to become certified teachers.

Master of Science in Education (M.S.Ed.): Lynn Andrews Romeo, Program Director and Associate Professor of Educational Leadership and Special Education; Ed.D., Rutgers.

M.S.Ed. programs include principal, educational counseling, special education, and reading specialist. Certification programs include learning disabilities-teacher consultant, classroom teacher of the handicapped, supervisor, and reading specialist.

Master of Business Administration (M.B.A.): Catherine Bianchi, Program Director of the M.B.A. Program; M.B.A., Monmouth (New Jersey).

The comprehensive M.B.A. program provides a balance of theory and practice. Students learn the business disciplines as well as specific organizational functions. Current issues and realistic applications of skill and knowledge are discussed with prominent business executives who serve as visiting lecturers and adjunct professors. The program requires between 30 and 48 credit hours of study, depending on the student's background.

Master of Business Administration (M.B.A.)—Concentration in Healthcare Management: Edward Christensen, Program Director and Assistant Professor of Management and Marketing; Ph.D., Rutgers.

The program prepares managers, health-care professionals, and business graduates for executive responsibilities in the health-care industry; nurses to move from patient care to administration; and doctors, dentists, and other health-care professionals for the business aspects of private practice or administration. The program requires between 33 and 54 credit hours of study, depending on the student's background.

Master of Arts in Criminal Justice (M.A.): Gregory J. Coram, Program Director and Associate Professor and Chair of Criminal Justice; Psy.D., Indiana State.

The program offers a broad perspective on the criminal justice system and its various institutions and processes. The curriculum provides a concentration in administration, which prepares criminal justice professionals or pre-career students for supervisory and administrative roles.

Master of Arts in Corporate and Public Communication (M.A.): Donald R. Swanson, Program Director and Associate Professor and Chair of Communication; Ed.D., Northern Colorado.

The program prepares students to become effective communication specialists in a number of fields, from interpersonal communication to mass media. Specialist certificates are available in human resources communication, public relations, and media studies.

Master of Social Work (M.S.W.): Mark E. Rodgers, Program Director, Associate Professor, and Chair of Social Work; D.S.W., Pennsylvania.

The program offers two concentrations—one in services to families and children and one in international and community development.

MONTCLAIR STATE UNIVERSITY

Graduate Programs

Programs of Study

Montclair State University is a major source of cultural, economic, and educational life in northern New Jersey. By foreseeing the ever-accelerating changes in the academic world, the University has recently pioneered the first doctoral program in pedagogy (Ed.D.) and added a new Master of Fine Arts (M.F.A.) in studio arts. Students have the opportunity to choose from more than 50 graduate programs, which include a variety of master's degrees, teaching certificates, and other certification programs.

The College of Education and Human Services offers the Master of Arts (M.A.) in administration and supervision; counseling, human services, and guidance; health education; human ecology; physical education; literacy; and educational media. The Master of Arts in Teaching (M.A.T.) degree is offered in many areas of instructional certification. The Master of Education (M.Ed.) is offered in the fields of critical thinking, education, and philosophy for children.

The College of Humanities and Social Sciences offers the M.A. degree in applied linguistics, applied sociology, communication sciences and disorders, educational psychology, English, French, legal studies, practical anthropology, psychology, social sciences, and Spanish.

The College of Sciences and Mathematics offers the Master of Science (M.S.) in biology, chemistry, computer science, geoscience, mathematics, and statistics. The College offers the M.A. degree in environmental studies.

The School of the Arts offers the M.F.A. degree in studio arts and the M.A. degree in fine arts, music, and speech and theater.

The School of Business offers the Master of Business Administration (M.B.A.) with concentrations in accounting, business economics, finance, international business, management information systems, and marketing. The M.A. degree is offered in business education and social sciences–economics.

Research Facilities

Montclair State's fully computerized on-campus microcomputer laboratories offer Internet access, individual e-mail accounts for students in good standing, and specialized software in numerous fields. A comprehensive multimedia environment provides for the most sophisticated technological classes and conferences.

The Harry A. Sprague Library houses a superior collection of 1.5 million items, with more than 2,600 periodical subscriptions, 32,000 government documents, 400,000 books, and 1 million media items, which include government and reference reports on microfilm, corporate annual reports, spoken-word and music recordings, and classical and award-winning productions on videotape. Electronic databases provide access to many resources. The library is a designated government documents depository. For further information, students should visit the library Web site (http://www.montclair.edu/library).

Financial Aid

In addition to the Federal Stafford Student Loan program, graduate students may apply for graduate assistantships or graduate scholarships. The graduate assistantships provide students with a $5000 master's-level stipend and a $10,000 doctoral-level stipend and cover University-wide tuition and fees. Students are required to work an average of 15 hours per week during a ten-month academic year. A small number of graduate scholarships are also available and cover University-wide tuition for one year. The deadlines for the assistantships and scholarships are March 1 and May 1, respectively. Prospective students should visit the University Web site or contact the Graduate School for additional information. Resident Hall assistantships are also available through the Office of Residence Life (telephone: 973-655-5188). For information on other assistance that may be available, prospective students should contact the Office of Student Financial Aid (telephone: 973-655-4461).

Cost of Study

For 2002–03, graduate tuition and fees begin at approximately $287 per credit for New Jersey residents and approximately $407 per credit for nonresidents and international students. Tuition and fees vary depending on the program and are subject to change.

Living and Housing Costs

Limited on- and off-campus housing is available. The estimated room and board cost for graduate students is $8300 per academic year. For more information, students should contact the Office of Residence Life (telephone: 973-655-5188).

Student Group

Of the total University enrollment of approximately 14,000 students, 3,500 are graduate students, with approximately 3 percent of the graduate population being international students. The majority of the graduate students are working professionals that enhance the programs by bringing a wealth of knowledge into the classrooms. Most graduate courses are offered in the evening hours to accommodate working students.

Location

The University is conveniently located on a beautiful 200-acre hilltop campus in Upper Montclair, New Jersey. This suburban town is surrounded by a rich diversity of cultural and recreational opportunities in northern New Jersey and in New York City, which is located 14 miles from campus.

The University

Since its establishment in 1908, Montclair State has been recognized for its high academic standards, outstanding faculty members, and vital academic programs. With more than 14,000 students and 450 full-time faculty members, Montclair State University is New Jersey's second-largest university, combining the breadth and scope of a large university with the small class size and individual attention of a small college. Montclair State began offering master's degrees in 1932, and a doctoral program was recently added. The University has been designated a Center of Excellence for the Fine and Performing Arts, and is the only institution in New Jersey to receive two Governor's Challenge for Excellence grants. The University is the home of the internationally renowned Institute for the Advancement of Philosophy for Children, the Center of Pedagogy, and the International Trade Center, all of which epitomize the University's belief in the scholarship of application—the practical application of knowledge.

Applying

Admission credentials are processed as soon as they are received. Most programs do not have specific deadlines and utilize rolling admissions. For those programs without a specific deadline, the Graduate School recommends that students submit their credentials as far in advance as possible from the semester they plan to begin their studies to ensure a timely review of their application. Some programs have fixed deadlines and students should refer to the admission packet for the most up-to-date information. The admission decision is based on a number of criteria, including the undergraduate grade point average, standardized test scores, letters of recommendation, and the statement of objectives. Some fine arts programs may also require a satisfactory portfolio review or successful completion of an audition.

Correspondence and Information

Graduate Admissions
The School of Graduate, Professional, and Continuing Education
Montclair State University
Upper Montclair, New Jersey 07043

Telephone: 973-655-5147
800-331-9207 (toll-free)
Fax: 973-655-7869
E-mail: graduate.school@montclair.edu
World Wide Web: http://www.montclair.edu/graduate

GRADUATE ADVISERS

Doctor of Education

Pedagogy: Dr. Cynthia Onore, Director of the Center of Pedagogy (973-655-4262 or 7691).

Master of Arts

Administration and Supervision: Dr. David Weischadle (973-655-5175 or 7335).
Applied Linguistics: Dr. Milton Seegmiller (973-655-7500).
Applied Sociology: Dr. Mary Holley (973-655-7229).
Business Education: Dr. Rosemary Macauley (973-655-7039 or 4269).
Communications Sciences and Disorders
  Speech Language Pathology: Dr. Gerard Caracciolo (973-655-4232).
Counseling, Human Services, and Guidance: Dr. Arlene King (973-655-5175 or 7184).
Curriculum and Teaching
  Early Childhood Special Education: Dr. Lucille Weistuch-Saffner (973-655-7360 or 4255).
  Learning Disabilities: Dr. Elaine Fine (973-655-7361).
Educational Psychology: Dr. Paul Locher (973-655-7381 or 5201).
English: Dr. Art Simon (973-655-7942 or 4249).
Environmental Studies
  Environmental Education: Dr. Nicholas Smith-Sebasto (973-655-7614 or 973-948-4603).
  Environmental Health: Dr. Harbans Singh (973-655-7383 or 4448).
  Environmental Management: Dr. Harbans Singh (973-655-7383 or 4448).
  Environmental Science: Dr. Harbans Singh (973-655-7383 or 4448).
Fine Arts: Dr. Dorothy Heard (973-655-4210 or 7295).
French: Dr. Kay Wilkins (973-655-5145).
Health Education: Dr. Reza Shahrokh (973-655-7115 or 4154).
Human Ecology: Dr. Shahla Wunderlich (973-655-4373 or 4171).
Legal Studies: Dr. Jack Baldwin-LeClair (973-655-7953 or 4152).
Music
  Music Education: Dr. Lisa DeLorenzo (973-655-7212).
  Music Performance: Dr. Ting Ho (973-655-7212).
  Music Therapy: Professor Karen Goodman (973-655-5268).
  Theory and Composition: Dr. Ting Ho (973-655-7212).
Physical Education: Dr. Michelle Fisher (973-655-7120 or 5253).
Practical Anthropology: Dr. Kenneth Brook (973-655-4119 or 7542).
Psychology: Dr. Kenneth Sumner (973-655-5203).
Reading: Dr. Diedre Glenn-Paul (973-655-7183).
Social Science
  Anthropology: Dr. Richard Franke (973-655-4133 or 4119).
  Economics: Dr. Harold Flint (973-655-7403 or 5255).
  History: Dr. Robert Cray (973-655-5261 or 5256).
Spanish: Dr. Vincent Bolletino (973-655-7510 or 4285)
Speech and Theatre
  Communication Arts: Dr. Michael Kent (973-655-7471 or 5130).
  Theatre: Dr. Suzanne Trauth (973-655-7000).

Master of Arts in Teaching

Initial Teacher Certification: Ms. Anne Baldinger (973-655-7976 or 4139).

Master of Business Administration: Dr. Eileen Kaplan (973-655-4306).

Master of Education: Dr. Catherine Becker (973-655-7201 or 5187).
Critical Thinking: Dr. Mark Weinstein (973-655-7041 or 5170).
Philosophy for Children: Dr. Megan Laverty (973-655-4351).

Master of Fine Arts: Professor John Czerkowicz (973-655-7294).

Master of Science

Biology: Dr. Dirk Vanderklein (973-655-5265 or 4397).
Biology Science Education: Professor Lynn English (973-655-5105 04 4397).
Chemistry: Dr. Mark Whitener (973-655-7166 or 5140)
Computer Science: Dr. James Benham (973-655-7249 or 4166).
Geoscience: Dr. Duke Ophori (973-655-7558 or 4448).
Mathematics: Dr. William Parzynski (973-655-7257 or 4263).
Statistics: Dr. William Parzynski (973-655-7257 or 4263).

Certificate Programs

American Dietetics Association (ADA): Dr. Carol Sokolik (973-655-4375).
Child Advocacy: Dr. Robert McCormick (973-655-4188).
CISCO: Dr. Dorothy Deremer (973-655-4166).
Collaborative Teaching for Inclusive Settings: Dr. Lucille Weistuch-Saffner (973-655-4255).
Exercise Science and Nutrition: Dr. Michele Fisher (973-655-7120).
Health Education: Dr. Reza Shahrokh (973-655-7115).
Molecular Biology: Dr. Quinn Vega (973-655-7178).
Music Therapy: Dr. Karen Goodman (973-655-5268 or 7212).
Object Oriented Computing: Dr. Dorothy Deremer (973-655-4166).
Paralegal Studies: Dr. Regina Judge (973-655-7390 or 4152).
Teaching English to Speakers of Other Languages: Dr. Longxing Wei (973-655-7501).
Translation and Interpretation in Spanish: Dr. Pamela Smorkaloff (973-655-4285).
Water Resource Management: Dr. Duke Ophori (973-655-7558 or 4448).

MOUNTAIN STATE UNIVERSITY

Graduate Studies

Programs of Study

Mountain State University, formerly the College of West Virginia, offers master's degree programs in criminal justice administration (M.C.J.A.), health science (M.H.S.), interdisciplinary studies (M.A. or M.S.), nursing (M.S.N.; concentrations in family nurse practitioner studies or administration/education), physician assistant studies (M.S.P.A.), and strategic leadership (M.S.S.L.). The University offers all its graduate programs at its Beckley, West Virginia, campus; the nursing program is also available in Martinsburg, West Virginia; and the strategic leadership program is offered at various sites throughout West Virginia. Many programs are also available to distance learners, with no residency requirement. Most programs feature a flexible structure that accommodates students who continue to work full- or part-time. Registration, advising, and other student services are available evenings as well as during the day and are also available to distance learners.

Research Facilities

Learning resources for graduate and undergraduate students include multimedia classrooms, computer laboratories, computer-assisted instruction, nursing and health assessment labs, and laboratories for the basic sciences. The Robert C. Byrd Learning Resource Center includes a student-centered library and media center. The collection comprises more than 90,000 titles, supplemented both by interlibrary loan and by extensive electronic resources, including ProQuest, CINAL (Cumulative Index to Nursing and Allied Health Literature), SIRS (Social Issues Resources Index), EBSCOhost, WESTLAW, Wilson Web, Newsbank, and Medline. The Learning Resource Center also features a media center and student computer facilities.

Financial Aid

Eligible graduate students may qualify for Federal Stafford Student Loans. Prospective students must submit the Free Application for Federal Student Aid (FAFSA) for determination of eligibility. Approximately 75 to 80 percent of graduate students receive some sort of financial assistance.

Cost of Study

Graduate tuition for 2001–02 ranged from $200 to $290 per credit hour, depending on the program. Payment plans are available. Additional fees are charged for graduation, thesis review, and thesis binding. Graduate students pay an average of $300 per semester for textbooks.

Living and Housing Costs

Many affordable housing opportunities are available in the neighborhoods surrounding the campus and in other nearby areas, which range from suburban to rural. Monthly rents average $300 to $600. Graduate students may also live in the residence hall on campus. Residence hall fees are $1191 per semester for double occupancy and $1785 per semester for a private room. Students living on campus are required to purchase one of the University's meal plans, which range from $365 a semester for a four-meal plan to $1290 a semester for a nineteen-meal plan.

Student Group

Mountain State University serves more than 3,000 students. Graduate enrollment and programming have grown steadily since the University's first graduate program was launched in 1998.

Location

The Mountain State University campus is located near downtown Beckley, West Virginia, a small city in the heart of the southern West Virginia mountains that serves as a regional center for business, health care, education, and tourism. Nearby recreational opportunities include whitewater rafting on the famed New and Gauley Rivers, skiing, hiking, climbing and rappelling, and other outdoor pursuits. Beckley is an hour's drive from the state capital of Charleston and just a few hours from Pittsburgh, Washington, and other eastern metropolitan areas.

The University

For nearly seventy years, Mountain State University has been a leader in overcoming barriers to higher education and in offering academic programs that combine a liberal arts foundation with career-oriented studies. The University features innovative programming, flexible learning arrangements, well-qualified and deeply committed faculty members, and outstanding student services, all in a relaxed atmosphere.

Graduate degree programs are offered through the University's School of Graduate Studies, some in conjunction with the School of Extended and Distance Learning.

Applying

While admission requirements vary from program to program, most programs require only a bachelor's degree from a regionally accredited institution. Nursing and physician assistant programs have more specific requirements.

A $25 application fee applies to the strategic leadership program; all other programs require a $50 reservation fee. In both cases, the fees are applied to the first semester's tuition.

Correspondence and Information

School of Graduate Studies
Mountain State University
P.O. Box 9003
Beckley West Virginia 25802-9003
Telephone: 304-253-7351
800-766-6067 (toll-free)
Fax: 304-253-0789
E-mail: gomsu@mountainstate.edu
World Wide Web: http://www.mountainstate.edu

THE GRADUATE FACULTY

Kay Blose, M.O.T.; OT/R.
M. Susan Bonifer, Ph.D.
Karen Bowling, M.S.N.; RN, RNP-C.
Lori Casto, Ph.D.
Sheila Dewhirst, Ph.D.
Patricia Gilliken, Ph.D.
Michelle Gompf, Ph.D.
M. Frances Hash, M.A.; CMA.
Patsy Haslam, Ed.D.; RN.
Brian Holloway, Ph.D.
Carter Kaplan, Ph.D.
Joan Klemballa, Ph.D.; RN, FNP-C.
Richard L'Heureux, Ph.D.
Everett Lilly, Ph.D.
Kenneth Miller, Ph.D.
Charles Milne, Ph.D.
Sixin Qian, Ph.D.
Jessica Sharp, Ph.D.; RN, FNP-C.
Krishna Shrestha, Ph.D.
Michael C. Stamper, Ph.D.
Dennis Stone, Ph.D.
Ruth Tunick, Ph.D.

MURRAY STATE UNIVERSITY

Graduate Studies

Programs of Study

Graduate degrees conferred by Murray State University are Master of Arts in clinical psychology; English; exercise and leisure studies; general psychology; geosciences; health, physical education, and recreation; history; mass communications; mathematics; organizational communication; and teaching English to speakers of other languages. Also offered are Master of Arts in Education in early elementary teaching, guidance and counseling, middle school teaching, reading and writing, school administration, secondary teaching, and special education; Master of Arts in Teaching in biology, chemistry, and mathematics; Master of Business Administration; Master of Music Education; Master of Public Administration; Master of Science in Nursing; Master of Science in agriculture, biology, chemistry, clinical psychology, mass communications, economics, general psychology, geosciences, human services, industrial education, interdisciplinary early childhood education, management of technology, mathematics, occupational safety and health, organizational communication, speech-language pathology, telecommunications systems management, and water science; and Specialist in Education in early elementary teaching, guidance and counseling (school guidance and counseling, community), middle school teaching, school administration, and secondary teaching.

Doctor of Education and Doctor of Philosophy in education areas are offered in cooperation with the University of Kentucky, the University of Memphis, and the University of Reading.

Research Facilities

Murray State University has two libraries. The Waterfield Library houses the circulating collection, reference sources, government documents, microforms, and periodicals. A centralized interlibrary loan service is maintained for the borrowing of research materials from other libraries. Online searching, including networked access to CD-ROM resources, access to full-text periodicals in remote electronic databases, and other literature, is also provided. Media and Curriculum Resources serves as a library and laboratory for students enrolled in the teacher education program. The Pogue Library contains a genealogy collection and other special library materials relating to the history and culture of western Kentucky and Tennessee. Legal Resources, located in the Pogue Library, consists of basic legal materials governing the United States and individual states. Together, the libraries subscribe to approximately 3,000 periodicals and serial titles annually.

Murray State University has several off-campus research facilities. These include three agricultural laboratory farms, the Hancock Biological Station, Murphy's Pond, the Breathitt Veterinary Center, and the Wickliffe Mounds Research Center.

Financial Aid

Graduate students may apply for grants, loans, part-time employment, and assistantships. Graduate teaching and research assistantships are available in most departments for highly qualified graduate students. The out-of-state portion of tuition is waived for those with an assistantship. Stipends for assistantships vary among departments. To qualify for a graduate assistantship, an entering graduate student must have an undergraduate GPA of at least 2.5 on a 4.0 scale from a regionally accredited institution. Exceptions may be made for one semester only in cases of assistantships in academic departments when an otherwise ineligible student has required expertise.

Cost of Study

In 2001–02, in-state tuition was $1439.50 per semester for full-time students ($168.50 per hour). Out-of-state tuition was $4003.50 per semester for full-time students ($449.50 per hour). The thesis binding fee is $6.50 per copy.

Living and Housing Costs

Murray State University offers graduate students on-campus housing in traditional residence halls ($1010 per semester, or $1615 for a private room) or one-bedroom apartments in College Courts ($405 per month). Murray has a variety of off-campus accommodations available in almost any price range. A recent newspaper listed apartments renting from $250 to $650 per month.

Student Group

Graduate enrollment for fall term 2001 was 1,873. Of this number, 634 were men and 1,239 were women. The part-time enrollment was 1,320, and full-time enrollment was 553. Twelve percent of the graduate students are international students. Sixty-five percent of all graduate students receive some form of financial aid.

Location

Murray State University is located in Murray (population 16,000) in western Kentucky. Murray is in a rural area located close to a national recreation area. Murray's fine arts organizations include the Playhouse in the Park, the Murray Civic Music Association, and the Murray Art Guild. The area also hosts several folk art and music festivals each year.

The University

Murray State University, founded in 1922, is a tax-supported institution composed of five colleges that offer a variety of graduate programs. Students come to the beautiful 232-acre campus from nearby, throughout the nation, and from around the world. Murray State has the best faculty-student ratio among state-supported universities in Kentucky. The main campus comprises seventy-one major buildings, and classes are also offered off-campus throughout the Jackson Purchase area.

Applying

Minimum University requirements for unconditional admission are an overall 2.75 grade point average (on a 4.0 scale) and a minimum score of 800 on the Graduate Record Examinations. Some degree programs have additional requirements for admission. A score of at least 500 on the TOEFL is required for international students. Some programs require a higher TOEFL score. While no application deadline is set by the University, applicants should submit all required materials at least two months before the enrollment date. The application fee is $20. Graduate assistantships are usually awarded in the spring preceding fall enrollment, but assistantships are occasionally awarded during the summer and fall.

Correspondence and Information

For more information about specific course requirements, all units of the University may be reached at the following address:

Graduate Office
Sparks Hall
Murray State University
P.O. Box 9
Murray, Kentucky 42071-0009
Telephone: 270-762-3741
800-272-4678 (toll-free)
World Wide Web: http://www.murraystate.edu

DEANS

College of Business and Public Affairs: Dr. Dannie Harrison (270-762-4181).
College of Education: Dr. Jack Rose (270-762-3817).
College of Health Sciences and Human Services: Dr. Betty Blodgett (270-762-3590).
College of Humanities and Fine Arts: Dr. Sandra Jordan (270-762-6936).
College of Science, Engineering and Technology: Dr. Neil Weber (270-762-3391).
School of Agriculture Director: Dr. Jim Rudolph (270-762-3328).

NATIONAL UNIVERSITY

Graduate Programs

Programs of Study

National University offers programs leading to the following degrees: Master of Business Administration; Global M.B.A.; Master of Fine Arts; Master of Education in cross-cultural teaching with a CLAD certificate; Master of Arts in Teaching; Master of Forensic Sciences; Master of Health Care Administration; Master of Public Administration; Master of Arts in counseling psychology, human behavior, human resource management, and management; and Master of Science in educational administration, educational counseling, educational technology, electronic commerce, instructional technology, school psychology, software engineering, special education, technology management, telecommunication systems management, and nursing.

Various areas of specialization are available in many degree programs. Most master's degree courses are conducted in one-month modules, allowing continuous enrollment throughout the calendar year and intensive study in one subject area at a time. Graduate programs and teaching credentials are offered primarily in the evening, but some degree programs are available during the day. Not all degree programs are offered at every location. Some programs and courses are available in an online format.

Research Facilities

National University's library has been developed with attention to the overall educational purpose of serving career-oriented adults. The University's library includes nearly 200,000 volumes, approximately 2,500 periodicals, approximately 2.5 million microforms, and 7,000 e-journal descriptions. Students have free access to the Library Resources Online System (LIBROS), which subscribes to 55 full-text online databases and more than 35,000 online book titles.

Financial Aid

Financial aid is available in the form of tuition scholarships. Rensselaer research and teaching assistantships and university, corporate, or national fellowships fund many of Rensselaer's full-time graduate students. Outstanding students may qualify for university-sponsored Rensselaer Graduate Fellowship Awards, which carry a minimum stipend of $16,000 and a full tuition and fees scholarship. All fellowship awards are calendar year awards for full-time graduate students. Summer support is also available in many departments. Low-interest, deferred repayment graduate loans are also available to U.S. citizens with demonstrated need.

Cost of Study

Tuition for 2002–03 is $332 per 1.5 quarter units. The cost of books and supplies varies for each course.

Living and Housing Costs

The cost of rooms for single students in residence halls or apartments ranges from $3866 to $6102 for the 2002–03 academic year. Family student housing, with a monthly rent of $620 to $755, is still available.

Student Group

More than 19,900 students are enrolled in the graduate programs annually. The average age of enrolled students is 34. Of these, 61 percent are women. Most students are employed full-time as middle- or upper-level management professionals or educators. Class discussions in graduate seminars are enhanced by the maturity, motivation, and varied backgrounds and work experiences of the students.

Location

National University offers graduate programs at locations in Fresno, Los Angeles, Orange County, San Bernardino, Redding, Sacramento, San Jose, and throughout San Diego County.

The University

Chartered in 1971, National University is a nonprofit, nonsectarian, independent institution accredited by the Western Association of Schools and Colleges. The University's academic goal is to provide educational opportunities in a meaningful format that prepares students for leadership roles while increasing their competence in specific academic areas. Students are encouraged to register for an entire degree program, taking courses in one-month modules of intensive study. Approximately 500 courses begin each month.

Applying

Applicants for master's programs must hold a bachelor's or higher degree from a regionally accredited college or university and have a minimum GPA of 2.5. Under certain conditions, admission on probation may be granted to applicants whose average is 2.0–2.49. All applicants must file a University application, pay a nonrefundable $60 application fee ($100 for international applicants), and have official transcripts sent to the records office from every college or university previously attended. The University sets no deadlines for receipt of applications for admission but operates under a continuous admission policy. Students may begin their studies any month of the year and pursue their program without delay, following the special one-course-per-month format.

Correspondence and Information

Admissions
National University
11255 North Torrey Pines Road
La Jolla, California 92037

Telephone: 619-563-7100 (San Diego)
760-945-6100 (Vista)
858-642-8000 (La Jolla)
714-429-5100 (Costa Mesa)
310-258-6600 (Los Angeles)
916-855-4100 (Sacramento)
909-806-3300 (San Bernardino)
408-236-1100 (San Jose)
559-256-4900 (Fresno)
209-475-1400 (Stockton)
661-864-2360 (Bakersfield)
530-226-4000 (Redding)
714-429-5300 (Orange)
619-830-6887 (Twenty Nine Palms)
800-NAT-UNIV (toll-free nationwide)
Fax: 858-642-8709
E-mail: advisor@nu.edu
World Wide Web: http://www.nu.edu

THE FACULTY

The National University faculty is composed of four tiers: full-time, associate, core adjunct, and adjunct faculty members. Full-time faculty members—whose primary responsibilities are teaching, scholarship, service, providing intellectual coordination with the part-time faculty members, professional development, student advising, and participation in the University's governance—are members of the University. Associate faculty members are skilled teachers who are able to make a half-time commitment (extended throughout the course of the year) to the University faculty. They are contracted to teach a designated number of courses per year; advise students on course, program, or career-related issues; participate in departmental, school, and University activities; and engage in scholarship relevant to their teaching. Core adjunct faculty members are skilled teachers whose principal professional commitments are elsewhere in their fields. They are contracted to teach a designated number of courses per year, advise students on course-related topics, and maintain currency in their professional and disciplinary fields. Adjunct faculty members are those assigned to teach one course at a time, advise students on course-related topics, and participate in faculty development activities without a need for deeper commitment to other aspects of University life.

All faculty members not only hold advanced degrees in their areas of expertise, but are respected professionals with many years of career experience. Learning is facilitated through lectures, outside reading, class discussions, case studies, and research projects relating to problems within the students' interests. The expansive knowledge of the students and the diversity of their backgrounds add richness to the group-learning experience.

National University's Academic and Administrative Center in La Jolla, California.

NEW COLLEGE OF CALIFORNIA

Graduate Programs

Programs of Study

The program in humanities and leadership (M.A.) represents a new area of study. It is aimed at helping leaders and potential leaders realize their full talents, often within the organizations where they currently work. Diverse leadership concepts and approaches portrayed in fiction, poetry, drama, and folktales are studied and assessed to determine their effectiveness and humanity. These readings are integrated with contemporary research on leadership, organizational behavior, and ethics. Program goals are accomplished via two Saturdays of seminars per month and independent study. A key emphasis area is in culture, environment, and sustainable community, offered at the College's Santa Rosa campus.

The program in Irish studies (M.A.) combines rigorous and creative academic study with practical experience in Ireland and the local Irish-American community. It explores Irish America and Irish politics, history, culture, and literature, examining the influences that have shaped the Irish at home and abroad. Students acquire the fundamentals of research methodology as applied to the investigation of sociological, psychological, historical, and literary aspects of Irish culture. Students study for two semesters at New College and then spend one to two semesters living and studying in Ireland or two semesters of independent study in the San Francisco Irish-American community. Classes and seminars take place two Saturdays a month and one to two evenings a week.

The New College Writers' Center, which also sponsors readings and a small-press bookstore on campus, comprises two unique master's programs in writing. The program in poetics (M.A./M.F.A.) unites critical study and the creative practice of poetry. Taught by well-known poets, the program builds from historical course work in English-language poetry, from the Renaissance to present day, into innovative writing seminars. Elective opportunities include translation, performance, printing, and magazine production. The M.F.A. in poetics and writing, together with substantial publication, makes its holders eligible to pursue teaching careers in four-year colleges. The M.A. in poetics may be approached with a view to pursuing doctoral study or to teaching English and/or writing in community colleges. The program community continually generates new magazines, chapbooks, and readings.

The program in writing and consciousness (M.A./M.F.A.) is designed to help the student create a writer's identity, stressing the importance of creative self-reliance. Students shape fiction or creative nonfiction while examining important prose texts from around the world. Notions of family, alienation, gender, and personal triumph and failure are addressed. The curriculum includes core reading courses, several levels of workshops, courses that concentrate on the master's thesis, and courses in literary theory. Program goals are accomplished via two Saturdays of seminars per month and independent study.

The program in psychology (M.A.) has one of the highest Marriage and Family Therapist (M.F.T.) license pass rates in the state, but it aims to go beyond the conventional M.F.T. program by joining concern about social justice with a sophisticated understanding of unconscious dynamics. The feminist psychology concentration is designed to help promote the mental health of women and their communities. It offers intensive training in psychodynamic theory and practice, family therapy, and feminist theory. The social-clinical concentration helps students develop the clinical skills, multicultural sensitivity, and political savvy needed for public therapy and private practice. Classes are held only two evenings per week, and the program can be completed in six trimesters.

The new Master of Arts in Teaching (M.A.T.) program focuses on critical environmental global literacy (CEGL). It is intended for credentialed teachers committed to providing their students with an understanding of the global interdependence of peoples and ecosystems. M.A.T.-CEGL students rigorously study global social, economic, and ecological realities while learning to create developmentally appropriate curricula and teaching strategies. Program goals are accomplished through a two-semester course of study and a thesis research project. Each project includes a one-week, small-team visit to a partner country in the developing world; a five-day workshop; and development of an international classroom-based student research project on a chosen aspect of local environmental concern.

Drawing on the grassroots women's spirituality and ecofeminist movements, the program in women's spirituality (M.A.) is an innovative course of study that reclaims women's history and prehistory, spiritual experience, and creative expression. The visual and symbolic languages of art and mythology are integrated with oral and written language to honor diverse expressions. The local feminist learning community offers mentoring. Each woman contributes her scholarship in a nonhierarchical structure, which allows for the reexamination of the nature of knowledge, exploration of new forms, and creation of new visions. Core courses and most specialized studies courses are held on weekends. Each student designs and undertakes a community practicum intended to enrich thesis research work and model a spiritually grounded approach to scholarship and social change.

M.A. programs, unless otherwise stated, require a minimum of 36 units and can be completed in three classroom semesters. M.F.A. programs require 54 units and can be completed in five classroom semesters. Other programs at New College include the oldest public-interest law school in the country, a multicultural/bilingual teacher credential program, and a science program.

Research Facilities

In addition to its resident collections, the College library offers access to other collections through a free online catalog and periodicals database search and interlibrary loans. Free Internet access is provided. Students may also employ the nearby University of California at Berkeley and San Francisco public libraries.

Financial Aid

New College graduate students may obtain federally administered financial aid (loans and work-study) according to their assessed need and eligibility. Lower-income students may apply for the California Graduate Fellowship. New College also offers partial tuition scholarships.

Cost of Study

Full-time tuition in all programs is approximately $4900 per semester.

Living and Housing Costs

New College of California has no residence facilities for graduate students. Housing costs in the surrounding community vary widely.

Student Group

New College graduate students come from diverse backgrounds but share interests in creative thinking and social justice. The total College population is approximately 900.

Location

The New College graduate programs are housed in three buildings on Valencia Street in San Francisco's historic Mission District. Coffeehouses, theaters, cultural centers, and bookstores abound.

The College

New College began in 1971. Its mission was the study of the humanities without rigid disciplinary separations and with an emphasis on teacher-student dialogue. Today the College mission also links personal development with social responsibility and emphasizes critical thinking, collaborative learning, and respect for diversity.

Applying

None of the programs has examination requirements. All programs require a bachelor's degree from an accredited college, official transcripts from all prior colleges or universities attended, and a $45 application fee. The priority deadline is March 1.

Correspondence and Information

Admissions Office
New College of California
741 Valencia Street
San Francisco, California 94110
Telephone: 415-437-3460
E-mail: admissions@newcollege.edu
World Wide Web: http://www.newcollege.edu

THE FACULTY AND THEIR RESEARCH

Irish Studies

Daniel Cassidy, Director; Ph.D., Columbia. His film *Uncensored Voices: War or Peace in Ireland* was featured at the San Francisco Film Arts Festival in 1995, and his earlier documentary on the North of Ireland, *Civil Rights and Civil Wrongs,* was nominated for an Emmy. His writings have appeared in the *New York Times Book Review, Atlantic,* the *San Francisco Chronicle,* and elsewhere.

Adrienne Murray, M.A., Trinity College (Dublin). She holds a "Fainne Or" for fluency in spoken Irish and has studied Irish poetry and prose, dialects, folklore, and syllabic poetry. Ms. Murray has taught Irish in Ireland, Russia, and the United States.

Ruth O'Hara, Ph.D., USC. She is a Research Psychologist at Stanford in the area of human development and an Assistant Professor at UCLA. Since 1984, she has taught on the influence of culture on human development, aging, and Irish/American cultural interaction. In 1993 she was awarded a Brookdale National Fellowship to study memory and aging.

Teaching (CEGL)

Sudia Paloma McCaleb, Director and Founder, New College Teacher Education Program; Ph.D. Author, *Building Communities of Learners: A Collaboration Among Teachers, Students, Family, and Community.* Research interests include parent-teacher collaboration and the use of art and music across the curriculum.

Psychology

Ali Chavoshian, Dean; Ph.D., Wright Institute. He is an experienced clinical supervisor who applies a psychoanalytic approach to his private practice, specializing in immigration issues, psychopathology, and object relations. Visiting Professor, Guilan University, Iran.

Hannnah Eckstein, Associate Dean; Ph.D. candidate, Wright Institute. She takes a psychoanalytic approach to cross-cultural issues, specializing in the psychology of women in transition. Research interests include the impacts of immigration and religious practices on women.

Jon Platania, Director, Community Counseling Center; Ph.D. He employs integrative analytic psychology as a licensed health and clinical psychologist and long-time mental health activist. Author, *Jung for Beginners, Psychology for Beginners, The Yoga of Recovery.*

Poetics

Tom Clark, M.A., Cambridge. Author, *White Thought, Like Real People, Junkets on a Sad Planet: Scenes from the Life of John Keats* (poetry), and of many other volumes of poetry, criticism, biography, and fiction. Scholarly interests include Charles Olson, Robert Creeley, Vietnam War literature, and the English Renaissance.

Adam Cornford, Chair; M.A., San Francisco State. Author, *Decision Forest, The Snarling Gift,* (in *Terminal Velocities*), *Animations* (poetry), and *O-Town* (prose memoir). Cofounded and coedited *Processed World* magazine, 1980–1992. Scholarly interests include William Blake, surrealism and negritude, and science fiction.

Gloria Frym, M.A., New Mexico. Author, *Distance No Object* and *How I Learned* (short stories) and *Homeless at Home* and *By Ear* (poetry). Scholarly interests include Emily Dickinson, the prose poem and the short story, and the fiction of Henry James.

David Meltzer. Author, *Writing Jazz, Reading Jazz,* and *Arrows: Selected Poems 1957–92,* among many other books of poetry, criticism, and nonfiction. Scholarly interests include Kaballah, American popular fiction, children's literature, and the poetics of prophecy.

Women's Spirituality

Rose Wognum Frances, Co-Director; M.F.A., Miami. Her mixed media works have been shown since 1970 in numerous museums and galleries, including the Smithsonian Institution. Research and teaching integrate the creative process, the language of myth and symbol, art history, and shamanism.

Anica Vesel Mander, Co-Director; Ph.D., Union (Ohio). Author, *Blood Ties: A Woman's History* and *From Butmir to Sarajevo: Re-searching Our Female Heritage and Healing Patriarchal Ravages* (in progress); coauthor, *Feminism as Therapy.* Research includes multiculturalism, gender, language, and identity. Recent fieldwork examines gender-related violence in Bosnia.

Judy Grahn. Internationally known poet, cultural theorist, and lesbian-feminist. Recipient, Lifetime Achievement Award in Lesbian Letters. Work centers on the desire for a reclamation of the values and aesthetics of the Sacred Feminine. Publications include *Blood, Bread, and Roses* and *Another Mother Tongue: Gay Words, Gay Worlds.*

Starhawk. Feminist, peace activist, and internationally acclaimed author. Books include *The Spiral Dance: A Rebirth of the Religion of the Great Goddess; Dreaming the Dark: Magic, Sex, and Politics*; and *Truth or Dare: Encounters with Power, Authority, and Mystery.*

Luisah Teish. Priestess of Oshun in the Yoruba tradition, actress, dancer, storyteller, feminist activist, choreographer, and teacher. Author, *Jambalaya: A Natural Woman's Book of Personal Charms* and *Practical Rituals and Carnival of the Spirit: Seasonal Celebrations and Rites of Passage.*

Writing and Consciousness

Juvenal Acosta, Ph.D. candidate, California, Davis. Author, *El Cazador de tatuajes (The Tattoo Hunter)* and *Tango de la cicatriz (Scar Tango). Light From a Nearby Window,* his anthology of 21 younger Mexican poets, won the Pen Oakland Award. Translator of Lawrence Ferlinghetti, Michael McClure, Jack Kerouac, and Louise Gluck.

Neeli Cherkovski. Author, *Animal, Elegy for Bob Kaufman,* and *Toltec Stone, Aztec Windows* (poetry); *Ferlinghetti: A Life, Bukowski: A Life,* and *Whitman's Wild Children* (criticism/biography). Currently working on *Walking the Mexican Mind* (essays) and completing a novel.

NEW MEXICO INSTITUTE OF MINING AND TECHNOLOGY

Graduate Studies

Programs of Study

New Mexico Institute of Mining and Technology offers graduate courses and research opportunities leading to the M.S. degree in biology, chemistry, computer science, engineering mechanics, environmental engineering, geochemistry, geology, geophysics, hydrology, mathematics, materials engineering, mineral engineering, petroleum engineering, and physics. A Master of Science in Teaching degree is offered for certified teachers of high school mathematics and science.

The Institute offers programs of study and research leading to the Ph.D. degree in chemistry, computer science, geochemistry, geology, geophysics, hydrology, materials engineering, petroleum engineering, and physics.

The Institute is strongly research oriented in fields of study dealing with natural physical resources, such as the atmosphere and water. Some research topics are crust-mantle geochemistry, volcanology (the Southwest and Antarctic), economic geology, stratigraphy and sedimentation, mineral exploration and recovery (including the biology and chemistry of leaching), fuel and energy research (production, use, and environmental considerations), nuclear and hazardous-waste hydrology, enhanced oil recovery, explosives (including the effect of high-energized and strain rates on materials), mine ventilation and fire control, seismological crustal studies, geotechnical and soil mechanics, environmental engineering, thunderstorm electrification and cloud physics, stellar and extragalactic processes, radio astronomy, and explosives and atmospheric chemistry.

Research Facilities

Graduate research opportunities are supported by a number of on-campus research groups, such as the New Mexico Bureau of Mines and Mineral Resources, the Petroleum Recovery Research Center, the Research and Development Office (including the Geophysical Research Center for geophysics, hydrology, and climatology and a Center for Explosives Technology Research), and the Sullivan Center of In-Situ Mining Research. Special facilities include the Langmuir Laboratory for Atmospheric Research (for studies of lightning, atmospheric physics, chemistry, and air quality), the Joint Observatory for Cometary Research, Waldo Experimental Mines, and the EMRTC Field Laboratory for explosives research. There are also materials characterization laboratories for structure/property correlation (TEM, SEM, EPMA, FIM, and mechanical testing). The Very Large Array Radio Telescope and the Very Large Baseline Array, both facilities of the National Radio Astronomy Observatory, are headquartered on the campus. Cooperative research opportunities are available with the Sandia National Laboratories and Kirtland Air Force Base in Albuquerque and with Los Alamos National Laboratories. Modern computer and library facilities and a wide range of modern analytical equipment are available, including a liquid scintillation spectrometer, a stable isotope mass spectrometer, automated XRF and XRD spectrometers, a microprobe, a neutron activation laboratory, a quadrupole mass spectrometer, FT-IR and GC/M spectrometers, GCs, HPLCs, seismological equipment, a thunderstorm-penetrating airplane, instrumented balloons and rockets, cloud physics radar, a supernova telescope, a fluid inclusion laboratory, and a quantitative mineralogy laboratory.

Financial Aid

In 2001, minimum stipends varied from $11,714 for nine months for beginning M.S. assistants to $30,000 for doctoral students who are on twelve-month appointments and have completed candidacy requirements.

Cost of Study

Tuition (based on a 12-credit-hour load) for 2001–02 was $2651.52 for residents and $8674.86 for nonresidents. Those on assistantship appointments qualify for resident tuition.

Living and Housing Costs

The cost of room and board for single students living in residence halls in 2001–02 was $2925 per semester. Housing for married students is available at prices starting at $435 per month for unfurnished one- or two-bedroom efficiency apartments. Housing in Socorro is also available.

Student Group

Tech has 1,338 students, of whom about 280 are graduate students. About 20 percent of the graduate students are women. International students from thirty-five countries constitute 10 percent of the student body.

Location

Socorro (population 9,000) is located in the Rio Grande Valley in a sparsely settled area of south-central New Mexico, 75 miles south of Albuquerque on Interstate 25. The campus is at an elevation of 1,400 meters. Nearby mountains reach 3,280 meters in elevation. The principal sources of income in New Mexico are scientific research, agriculture, minerals (including petroleum, copper, potash, and coal), lumbering, and tourism. New Mexico's cultural diversity provides an unusual political and social environment. Historic sites, ghost towns, and ancient Indian ruins are all within a short driving distance of the campus.

The Institute

New Mexico Tech, which started as the New Mexico School of Mines in 1889, has achieved international recognition in petroleum engineering, materials engineering, atmospheric physics, geosciences, mineral-resource engineering, and explosives technology. Its faculty is outstanding in such diverse areas as atmospheric physics, astrophysics, biomedical research, seismology, geochemistry, economic geology, mineral exploration, groundwater hydrology, bacterial leaching of ores, laser and ion surface modification, intermetallics, ceramic- and metal-matrix composites, solid oxide fuel cells, capacitor dielectrics and high-temperature superconductors, organic and environmental chemistry, and petroleum recovery.

Applying

Tech encourages interested people who have a bachelor's or master's degree from an accredited college and a record indicating potential for advanced study and research in science or engineering to apply for admission. Transcripts of previous college work, references from 3 professors and/or professionals, and GRE General Test and Subject Test scores are required. International students must also submit TOEFL scores.

Correspondence and Information

Dr. David B. Johnson
Dean of Graduate Studies
New Mexico Institute of Mining and Technology
801 Leroy Place
Socorro, New Mexico 87801
Telephone: 505-835-5513
800-428-TECH (8324) (toll-free)
E-mail: graduate@nmt.edu
World Wide Web: http://www.nmt.edu/~grad/

THE FACULTY AND THEIR RESEARCH

Biology. A. Smoake, Chairman: physiology, endocrinology. T. Kieft: environmental biology, microbiology. K. Kirk: biology of aging. R. Reiss: molecular biology and evolution. S. Rogelj: molecular biology, cell adhesion molecules.
Chemistry. T. Pietrass, Chair: inorganic chemistry, physical chemistry, nuclear magnetic resonance spectroscopy. D. Brandvold: biophysical chemistry, enzyme mechanisms, environmental chemistry, atmospheric chemistry. M. Heagy: organic chemistry, organic synthesis, physical organic chemistry. A. Komienko: organic chemistry, medicinal chemistry. S. Pandey: analytical chemistry, spectroscopy. C. Popp: atmospheric chemistry, environmental chemistry, geochemistry. L. Werbelow: theoretical chemistry, chemical physics, spectroscopy. O. Wingenter: atmospheric chemistry.
Computer Science. A. Sung, Chairman: computational intelligence and its applications, high-performance computing, multimedia, algorithms. C. Barefoot: combinatorics, algorithms, cryptography. W. Chang: multimedia and Internet technologies; data mining, analysis, and visualization; digital image and speech processing. K. Glass: complex systems modeling and analysis. J.-L. Lassez: bioinformatics, search engines. S. Mazumdar: database systems, massive storage systems, computational logic. H. Soliman: computer networks, neural networks.
Earth and Environmental Science. J. L. Wilson, Chairman: groundwater hydrology, numerical and analytic modeling, stochastic hydrology, colloid and bacterial transport. R. C. Aster: earthquake and volcanic seismology, seismic structure. R. S. Bowman: surface chemistry, groundwater contamination, solute transport. A. R. Campbell: metallic ore deposits, stable isotope geochemistry. K. C. Condie: trace-element and isotope geochemistry, Precambrian studies. L. B. Goodwin: spatial and temporal evolution of faults and shear zones, deformation mechanisms, fabric development, fluid flow in faults. B. Harrison: soil properties, recurrence intervals of earthquakes, soil salinization in arid environments, soil stability. J. Hendrickx: soil-water physics, vadose-zone hydrology, soil contamination. D. B. Johnson: biostratigraphy, Paleozoic depositional environments. P. R. Kyle: igneous geochemistry, Antarctic geology, volcanology. W. C. McIntosh: argon geochronology, Cenozoic volcanism in the Southwestern United States, Antarctic volcanism. B. McPherson: groundwater geology, basin-scale hydrogeologic modeling, coupled groundwater and heat-flow studies, saturated multiphase flow, fracture genesis. P. S. Mozley: environmental geology, sedimentary petrology, low-temperature geochemistry. D. I. Norman: metallic ore deposits, geochemistry of ore deposits, fluid inclusion studies. F. M. Phillips: groundwater chemistry, isotope hydrology, groundwater dating, Quaternary studies. J. W. Schlue: seismology, surface waves, crustal and upper mantle structure, rift studies, inverse methods. E. E. Small: hydroclimatology, regional climate change, geomorphology. H. J. Tobin: fault zone petrophysics and structure, subduction zone tectonics, reflection seismology.
Environmental Engineering. C. Richardson, Chairman: biological wastewater treatment, groundwater contamination, site remediation. M. Cal: air pollution control, gas-phase absorption, indoor air quality. B. Deng: environmental engineering, aquatic chemistry, groundwater remediation. F. Huang: hazardous waste management, biological and chemical waste treatment, environmental systems modeling, risk assessment.
Engineering Mechanics. H. Walling, Chairman: air-blast loading of structures, seismic response of structures, high-velocity impact of hardened structures, mitigation of effects of explosive detonations. P. Gerity: robotics, system integration, technology turnkey and licensing. W. C. Lyons: drilling mechanics, structural mechanics, structural vibrations. B. Melof: energetic materials, synthesis of explosives, explosives chemistry. A. R. Miller: finite-element analysis, explosive synthesis of materials, high-temperature systems. F. Norwood: shock waves, elastic waves, finite elements, computer applications. K. I. Oravecz: rock mechanics, instrumentation, high-precision displacement measurements. T. Sarkodie-Gyan: image analysis, robotics and automation, vibration and isolation systems, soft computing (genetic algorithms, neural computing, fuzzy systems), machine vision, pattern recognition, biomedical engineering, systems theory.
Mathematics. B. Borchers, Chairman: optimization, inverse problems. R. Aitbayev: numerical partial and differential equations, preconditioning of large sparse linear systems. D. Arterburn: functional analysis, real variables. I. Avramidi: mathematical physics. C. Barefoot: graph theory, applied mathematics. A. Hossain: theory and applications of statistics, regression diagnostics. G. Kerr: thermoelasticity, integral equations. M. Mojirsheibani: inference, nonparametric methods. S. Schaffer: applied mathematics, numerical analysis. W. Stone: differential equations, mathematical biology, industrial mathematics.
Materials Engineering. G. T. Bond, Chairman: electron microscopy, radiation damage, intermetallics, micromechanisms of deformation and fracture, hydrogen effects, CO_2 sequestration, biomimetic materials. T. D. Burleigh: corrosion mechanisms and mechanisms of corrosion protection. P. Fuierer: electronic ceramics, magnetic ceramics, sol-gel thin films. D. Hirschfeld: engineering ceramics and advanced composites, processing, protective coatings. O. T. Inal: plasma-assisted (HCD and DC) CVD; design/modification of reactive solder/braze alloys; radiation- , shock- and laser-exposure–induced defects; explosive ceramic and metal working; laser and plasma surface modification; enhancement of low-temperature ductility in ordered intermetallics; plasma spray deposition of oxide coatings. P. Lu: electron microscopy and high-resolution electron microscopy, electronic thin film, chemical vapor deposition. B. Majumdar: mechanisms and mechanics of deformation and fracture, thin films and interfaces, composites, advanced alloys. J. McCoy: polymer blends, phase transitions, interfaces.
Mineral Engineering. Navid Mojtabai, Chairman: rock blasting and fragmentation, ground vibration, geomechanics, mining applications. C. Aimone-Martin: rock blasting, ground vibration, soils mechanics, instrumentation, geostatistics. J. Barker: industrial minerals. W. X. Chavez Jr.: ore deposit genesis and natural resources utilization, mine waste assessment and remediation. I. Gundiler: hydrometallurgy, mineral processing. V. McLemore, economic geology. K. Oravescz, rock mechanics, surveying, instrumentation. I. Walder: geochemistry, mine waste assessment and remediation.
Petroleum and Chemical Engineering. T. Engler, Chairman, Petroleum Engineering: formation evaluation, petrophysics, unconventional gas recovery. D. Weinkauf, Chairman, Chemical Engineering: polymer engineering, plasma polymerization, membrane separations, microsensors. R. Bretz: transport phenomena, phase behavior, natural gas processing. J. Buckley: petrophysics and surface chemistry, reservoir wettability. H.-Y. Chen: well testing, reservoir mechanics. J. Dong: thin-film membrane reactors, solid oxide fuel cells. R. Grigg: gas flooding processes, phase behavior. H.-S. Jeon: polymer engineering, neutron scattering, polymer blends, anionic polymerization. R. Lee: natural gas storage, applied numerical methods, phase behavior. W. Lyons: drilling mechanics, air and gas drilling. J. Sampaio: directional drilling, offshore drilling. R. Seright: profile control, polymer, water, and chemical flooding. J. Taber: oil recovery processes, mechanisms. L. Teufel: rock mechanics; naturally fractured reservoir characterization; in situ stresses; reservoir simulation, including stress distribution; subsidence mechanisms.
Physics. Ken Minschwaner, Chairman: radiative transfer and climate, physics of the upper atmosphere. I Avramidi: mathematical physics, quantum field theory in curved space time, quantum gravity and gauge field theories. A. Blyth: atmospheric physics, physics of cloud particles. S. Colgate: astrophysics, plasma physics, atmospheric physics. K. Eack: production of energetic particles and gamma rays in thunderstorms. J. Eilek: plasma astrophysics, quasars, radio galaxies, pulsars. M. Goss: radio astronomy, interstellar medium. T. Hankins: radio astronomy of pulsars, instrumentation, signal processing. S. Huang: atmospheric radioactive and nonradioactive aerosol, sources and transport pathways, trace element analysis. D. Klinglesmith: astronomical instrumentation. P. Krehbiel: lightning and thunderstorm studies, radar meteorology. V. LeFebre: statistical physics, thermodynamics. E. Moore: cometary physics, astrophysics. D. Raymond: geophysical fluid dynamics, cloud physics. W. Rison: atmospheric electricity, radar meteorology, instrumentation. V. Romero: energetic materials, shock phenomena, high-energy physics. M. Rupen: gas and dust in galaxies, radio transients. G. Taylor: very long baseline radio astronomy, active galactic nuclei. S. Teare: adaptive optics, astronomical seeing, photometry and spectroscopy, telescope system. C. Watts: laboratory plasma physics, space and magnetosphere physics. J. Weatherall: high-energy astrophysics, plasma physics. D. Westpfahl: dynamics of spiral and dwarf galaxies. W. Winn: atmospheric physics, electrical discharges in gases, instrumentation. L. Young: star formation and the interstellar medium, dwarf and elliptical galaxies.

Macey Conference Center and Turtle Bay.

NEW SCHOOL UNIVERSITY

Graduate Faculty

Programs of Study

The Graduate Faculty, a division of New School University, awards the Master of Arts (M.A.), the Doctor of Philosophy (Ph.D.), and the Doctor of Social Science (D.S.Sc.) degrees in anthropology, economics, philosophy, political science, psychology (including clinical psychology), and sociology. Interdisciplinary M.A. programs are offered in historical studies and liberal studies. A consortium between the Graduate Faculty and five major New York City universities allows doctoral students to take approved courses at these other institutions.

Students have five years to complete all M.A. requirements and ten years to complete all Ph.D. requirements. Students in the doctoral program in clinical psychology have twelve years to complete all degree requirements.

The Graduate Faculty continues to embody the ideals that made the institution unique in 1933 when it was founded as the University in Exile—a haven for scholars and artists who were threatened by National Socialism. Building on the work of early faculty members such as economist Gerhard Colm, political scientist Hannah Arendt, psychologist Max Wertheimer, and sociologist Hans Speier, the Graduate Faculty is American in its progressive outlook and European in its scholarly traditions; it continues its long association with exiled intellectuals and dissenting public voices. Students are encouraged to work on contemporary issues such as democracy, human rights, and social policy reforms and, through innovative research and programs, to develop interdisciplinary perspectives and analyses within a critical framework.

Research Facilities

Research centers include the Center for Economic Policy Analysis; the Hannah Arendt Center; the European Union Center of New York; the International Center for Migration, Ethnicity, and Citizenship; the Committee on Western European Studies; the Janey Program in Latin America Studies; and the Transregional Center for Democratic Studies. These centers present students with research opportunities and provide extensive special programming.

New School University has three specialized libraries. The Fogelman Library, focusing on social sciences and philosophy, is in the Graduate Faculty building. The University is a member of several library consortia that provide students with a wealth of traditional and electronic resources and services as well as the broadest subject range. Students also have access to three computer centers that provide the necessary technology tools, multimedia, and computing programs to support the University community. The Academic Computer Center focuses on the needs of graduate students and is located at the Graduate Faculty.

Financial Aid

Financial assistance is available in the form of scholarships, fellowships, assistantships, federal loans, and work-study. The Office of Academic Affairs and Scholarships should be contacted early in the admissions process for eligibility requirements and responsibilities, and a financial aid application should be submitted with an admissions application. The fellowship and special scholarships deadline is January 15. Requests for other financial aid that are received after this deadline are considered on a rolling basis.

U.S. citizens and permanent residents applying for federal financial aid must file the Free Application for Federal Student Aid through the University Financial Aid Office by March 1.

Cost of Study

In 2002–03, estimated tuition and mandatory fees are $19,778 for 18 credits (two semesters).

Living and Housing Costs

For the 2002–03 academic year, living and housing costs are approximately $14,595 for a nine-month period. A single student should budget for $9900 in room and board, $900 for books and research, $585 for local transportation, $1800 for personal expenses, and $1410 for health insurance. International students must also budget for their travel to and from their home countries.

Student Group

Through January 2002, the Graduate Faculty has awarded 7,828 Master of Arts (M.A.), 150 Master of Social Science (M.S.Sc.), 1,717 Doctor of Philosophy (Ph.D.), and twenty-five Doctor of Science (D.S.Sc.) degrees. Current enrollment is composed of about 1,000 students from more than forty U.S. states and from more than seventy countries. The student population reflects a wide range of ethnic, social, and economic backgrounds and educational and professional experiences.

Location

New School University and the Graduate Faculty are located in the heart of Greenwich Village, one of New York's oldest and most eclectic neighborhoods. Historical and ersatz, the bohemian spirit abounds in its diversity of people, events, businesses, and arts. The University owns and utilizes buildings from 8th Street to 14th street, between 3rd and 6th Avenues.

The University and The Division

New School University pioneered the idea of lifelong university-level education for adults. It was created for teachers and students from different backgrounds who were willing to take risks for their intellectual and political beliefs. The Graduate Faculty is one of seven divisions that comprise the University's 7,000 undergraduate and graduate students.

The Graduate Faculty continues to draw strength from its European intellectual origins and has expanded to involve collaborations with scholars and public intellectuals in Latin America, Africa, and Asia.

Applying

Admission applicants must hold a bachelor's degree. The deadline for applications requesting fellowship and scholarship financial aid is January 15; all other admissions applications and requests for other financial aid are reviewed on a rolling basis. Applicants must meet the admission requirements of their intended department or committee. Only students with an M.A. degree may apply for admission to doctoral study. All other students must complete certain course requirements and pass a qualifying examination before being granted Ph.D. candidate status.

Correspondence and Information

Manny Lomax, Director of Admissions
Graduate Faculty Office of Admissions
New School University
65 Fifth Avenue
New York, New York 10003

Telephone: 212-229-5710
800-523-5411 (toll-free in the U.S.)

Fax: 212-989-7102
E-mail: gfadmit@newschool.edu
World Wide Web: http://www.newschool.edu/gf/guide

GRADUATE PROGRAM FACULTY

Anthropology: Deborah Poole, Associate Professor and Chair; Ph.D., Illinois, 1984.
Economics: Duncan Foley, Leo Model Professor and Chair; Ph.D., Yale, 1966.
Historical Studies: José Casanova, Professor of Sociology; Ph.D., New School, 1982.
Liberal Studies: James Miller, Professor and Chair; Ph.D., Brandeis, 1975.
Philosophy: Jay Bernstein, University Distinguished Professor of Philosophy; Ph.D., Edinburgh, 1975.
Political Science: David Plotke, Associate Professor and Chair; Ph.D., Berkeley, 1985.
Psychology: Michael Schober, Professor and Chair; Ph.D., Stanford, 1990.
Sociology: Terry Williams, Associate Professor of Sociology and Chair; Ph.D., CUNY Graduate Center, 1978.

NEW YORK INSTITUTE OF TECHNOLOGY

Graduate Division

Programs of Study

The Graduate Division offers sixteen programs in five academic centers.

The School of Management offers the M.B.A. and the M.S. in human resources management and labor relations. The M.B.A. has concentrations in accounting, e-commerce, finance, general management, international business, management of information systems, marketing, and personnel and industrial relations. The M.S. in human resources management and labor relations prepares students for careers in human resources management, personnel administration, compensation and benefits, training, and labor relations. In addition to the degree program, advanced-level certificates are offered in human resources administration and in labor relations.

The School of Arts, Sciences, and Communication offers the Master of Arts (M.A.) in communication arts. The M.A. degree in communication arts concentrates on mass communications, with specializations in media management and production, writing for the media, journalism, public relations and advertising, corporate communication, intercultural communication, design graphics, painting and studio art, and electronic cinematography.

The School of Education offers Master of Science degrees in counseling, instructional technology, and elementary education and a professional diploma in educational leadership and technology. The M.S. degree program in school counseling and the M.S. degree program in mental health counseling prepare professional counselors and development and human relations specialists who can practice effectively with individuals across the life span. The goal is to prepare effective professional counselors who can work with clients from diverse populations in a variety of human services and educational settings. The M.S. in instructional technology has two components. The industrial trainer component has its theory base in instructional systems design. The educational component provides infusion of technology into the curriculum. The M.S. in elementary education provides curriculum development skills through the study and practice of techniques that capitalize on the use of technology as well as more traditional methods. The School of Education also offers a certificate program in computers in education; registrants may apply the program's 18 credits toward the M.S. in instructional technology. The professional diploma program in educational leadership and technology prepares students to be thoughtful and effective school leaders who can articulate the integration of technology into K–12 curricula.

The School of Engineering and Technology offers the Master of Science degree in computer science, energy management, environmental technology, and electrical and computer engineering. The M.S. in computer science emphasizes the relationship between computers and their applications. It is an ideal program for students interested in systems programming, systems analysis, data communications, microprocessors, and computer graphics. The M.S. in environmental technology emphasizes the outstanding business opportunities available due to the increasing emphasis on the relationship between environmental concerns and governmental regulations. Specializations are offered in waste management, pollution prevention, and regulatory compliance. The M.S. in electrical and computer engineering emphasizes applied and design-oriented engineering skills and their underlying theoretical concepts. In addition to the traditional emphases on communications, microwaves, and electrooptics, there is a major component in engineering software design devised to advance professional practice. The M.S. in energy management provides professionals currently in business management or engineering with the most up-to-date knowledge in the field of energy management.

The School of Allied Health and Life Sciences offers the Master of Science in clinical nutrition, the Master of Professional Studies (M.P.S.) in human relations, the Master of Science in occupational therapy, and the Master of Science in physical therapy. The M.S. in clinical nutrition provides an in-depth study of the body of knowledge necessary to understand the relationships of food and nutrition to health and disease. The M.P.S. degree in human relations provides an interdisciplinary study of human behavior that prepares graduates for careers in industrial, clinical, and substance-abuse (alcoholism) counseling. Students completing the credentialed alcoholism counseling option meet all of the course work requirements needed to sit for the New York State credentialing examination and a portion of the experiential fieldwork requirements as well. The M.S. in physical therapy is accredited and satisfies all prerequisites for sitting for the licensure exam. The School of Allied Health Sciences also conducts the Approved Pre-Professional Practice Program (AP4) as a service to the community.

The School of Architecture and Design offers the Master of Architecture degree in urban and regional design. The postprofessional M.Arch. provides students with a thorough theoretical and historical understanding, through analysis and design, of the origin and function of cities and the geographic regions that embrace them.

Research Facilities

The Center for Labor and Industrial Relations conducts research into current problems in the workplace. Research projects in recent years have focused on training needs within the transit industry, regional labor market trends, and the needs of older workers. In addition, under the auspices of its six schools, including the New York College of Osteopathic Medicine, NYIT conducts ongoing research that has been integrated into its academic curricula. Opportunities for highly qualified graduate students to assist in this research are available each semester.

Financial Aid

Eligible students may apply for the New York Tuition Assistance Program (TAP) and federal grants available to graduate students. The Institute provides assistantships, work-study programs, and scholarships for public-sector employees and senior citizens as well as graduate students.

Cost of Study

Graduate tuition was $545 per credit in 2001–02.

Living and Housing Costs

For the 2001–02 academic year, the fees for the residence halls at Central Islip varied from $2040 to $2050 per semester. and the fees for the facility in Brooklyn varied from $3200 to $4800 per semester.

Meal plans for those living in the residence halls in Central Islip varied from $1500 to $1850 per semester. In addition, commuters were able to purchase weekly to monthly meal tickets, with costs ranging from $50 to $200.

Student Group

In order to accommodate students who work full-time, NYIT offers classes in the evenings and on weekends. Eighty-five percent of the students attend on a part-time basis.

Location

The Old Westbury Campus, located on the North Shore of Long Island, consists of wooded and landscaped acres. The Manhattan Campus is located at 61st Street and Broadway. The Central Islip Campus is a scenic tree-lined site on the south coast of Long Island.

The Institute

NYIT is an independent, fully accredited, nonsectarian institution with campuses in Manhattan and Long Island. Programs emphasize the development of innovative learning-teaching formats applicable to modern life-styles. NYIT is renowned for its research efforts and accomplishments in computer graphics; optics, lasers, and holography; robotics; ultrasonics; biomechanics; telecommunications; and high-definition television.

Applying

Applications are accepted on a continuous basis; the deadline for registration for each semester is the second class date. Requirements include a baccalaureate degree from an accredited college and a cumulative undergraduate GPA of 2.85 or better. M.B.A. students are required to submit GMAT scores. GRE scores may be required by other programs. Students must submit a completed application form, an official transcript of their undergraduate record, and any additional materials and information that may be required by the program as well as the $50 application fee. International students must demonstrate proficiency in English.

Correspondence and Information

Graduate Admissions Office
New York Institute of Technology
P. O. Box 8000
Old Westbury, New York 11568-8000

Telephone: 516-686-7519
800-345-NYIT (toll-free)
World Wide Web: http://www.nyit.edu

GRADUATE PROGRAM CONTACTS

For general information about NYIT's Graduate Division, students should contact the Dean of Graduate Studies or the Dean of Admissions and Financial Aid. For information about a specific program, students should call the number indicated.

Edward Guiliano, Ph.D., President (516-686-7630).
Dean of Admissions and Financial Aid (516-686-7519 or 800-345-NYIT, toll-free).

Master of Architecture: 516-686-7594
Master of Business Administration: 516-686-7972 or 212-261-1597.
Master of Science in Clinical Nutrition: 516-686-3803.
Master of Arts in Communication Arts: 516-686-7779.
Master of Science in Computer Science: 212-261-1640 or 516-686-7523.
Master of Science in Counseling (mental health and school): 516-686-7777.
Master of Science in Electrical and Computer Engineering: 516-686-7523.
Master of Science in Elementary Education: 516-686-7777.
Master of Science in Energy Management: 516-686-7578.
Master of Science in Environmental Technology: 516-686-7969.
Master of Professional Studies in Human Relations: 516-686-3882.
Master of Science in Human Resource Management and Labor Relations: 516-686-7722.
Master of Science in Instructional Technology: 516-686-7777.
Master of Science in Occupational Therapy: 516-686-3865.
Master of Science in Physical Therapy: 516-686-7696.

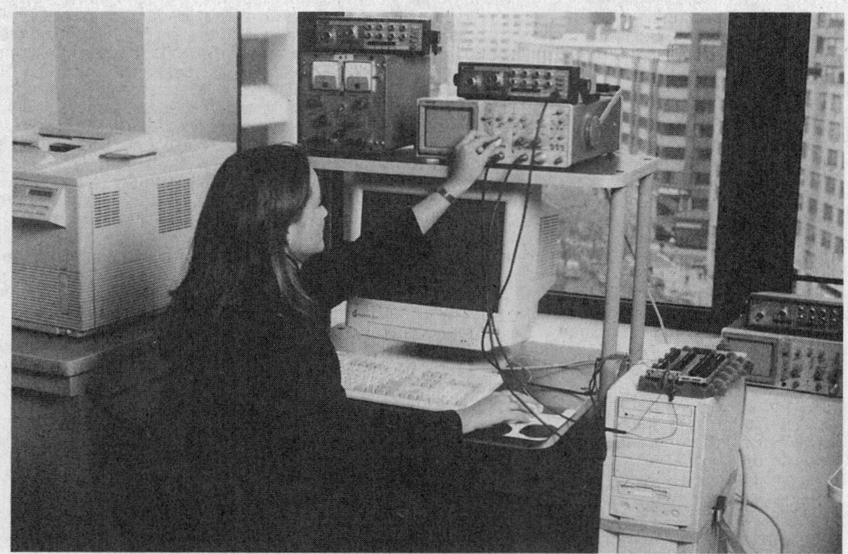

State-of-the-art electrical engineering lab at Manhattan campus.

Graduate students working together in a study group.

Computer graphics students work on a graduate project.

NEW YORK UNIVERSITY

Graduate School of Arts & Science

Programs of Study

The Graduate School of Arts & Science offers master's and doctoral degrees in forty-five departments and programs within the Faculty of Arts & Science, including a wide range of interdisciplinary programs. The Graduate School also offers dual degrees with the faculties of the School of Arts, the School of Business, the School of Public Service, the School of Law, the School of Medicine, and the School of Dentistry. The NYU Institutes for Advanced Study allow distinguished visiting faculty members from throughout the world to join specialists and graduate students at NYU in research activities. Graduate students may also study at La Pietra, NYU's Italian research center on the outskirts of Florence, as well as participate in other global exchange programs.

Departmental requirements for the Ph.D. degree vary among disciplines, but all candidates for the doctoral degree are expected to demonstrate language proficiency and complete a thesis that makes an original contribution to their field of study. Students must also pass departmental qualifying or comprehensive examinations.

Research Facilities

The Elmer Holmes Bobst Library and Study Center houses 2.7 million volumes while providing seating for 3,500 students. The library integrates into one enormous collection more than 2.2 million books, journals, microfilms, and other materials from various libraries of the University. It is one of the world's largest open-stack libraries. With the introduction of BOBCAT (for BOBst Library CATalog), the first online catalog in a New York City library, students may search the library's collections using computer terminals. Among the noteworthy resources of the Bobst Library are special collections in education, science, music, Near Eastern and Ibero-American languages and literatures, and Judaica and Hebraica; the Tamiment Institute Library on the history of the U.S. labor movement; the Fales Library of English and American Literature since 1750; the Robert Frost Library; and numerous rare books and manuscripts. The Avery Fisher Electronics and Media Center, also in Bobst, is a center for research in music and film, with extensive holdings of videos, scores, and recordings. The Courant Institute of Mathematical Sciences has a highly specialized research collection consisting of more than 60,000 volumes in mathematics, computer science, and physics. CDC CYBER, IBM 4341, DEC, and other nonspecialized computer systems are also available in the Courant Institute of Mathematical Sciences.

The NYU art collection and the Grey Art Gallery and Study Center emphasize interdisciplinary study for students, instructors, artists, and scholars, and their exhibits also serve the community at large.

Financial Aid

The financial aid program of the Graduate School of Arts & Science seeks to ensure that outstanding, academically qualified students have financial support while they work toward their degrees. The Graduate School offers an extensive program of support. Awards for fully-funded students include support for tuition, fees, NYU health insurance, and a stipend. The Henry Mitchell MacCracken Fellowship provides five years of full support for most entering doctoral students. This includes a one-time, $1000 Dean's Supplementary Fellowship grant for start-up research and educational expenses. New York University offers a full range of loan programs for students who require additional funding.

Cost of Study

In 2002–03, the estimated cost of tuition is $855 per credit, plus a registration fee of $48 per credit.

Living and Housing

University housing is available to full-time students.

Student Group

The total enrollment at New York University is more than 50,000, with approximately 1,100 Ph.D. students and 1,600 master's students enrolled in the Graduate School of Arts & Science. Students come to NYU from more than 200 undergraduate institutions, all fifty states, and from more than 100 other countries.

Location

New York University is an integral part of the metropolis of New York City—a global city that is also arguably the cultural, artistic, intellectual, and financial center of the nation. The University's chief center for study is at Washington Square in Greenwich Village, which has long been famous for its contributions to the fine arts, literature, and drama and for its personalized, independent style of living. New York University makes a significant contribution to the creative activity of the Greenwich Village area through the high concentration of its faculty members and students residing within a few blocks of the University.

The University

New York University is a private, metropolitan university. Founded in 1831, the University now comprises twelve schools, colleges, and divisions at four centers in Manhattan, seven international campuses, and a 500-acre site at Sterling Forest near Tuxedo, New York, where certain of the University's facilities—notably the Institute of Environmental Medicine—are located. Courses for the Graduate School of Arts & Science are offered primarily at Washington Square; however, courses are also held at the University's Medical Center, the David B. Kriser Dental Center, Sterling Forest, the Institute of Fine Arts, and in the cities of Prague, Florence, London, Paris, Cracow, and Salamanca. Special arrangements have also been made to enable students to use the facilities of such nearby institutions as the Metropolitan Museum of Art, the New York Botanical Garden, the Museum of Modern Art, the Osborn Laboratories for Marine Science, the New York Zoological Society, and the Strang Clinic for Preventive Medicine.

NYU is a member of the distinguished Association of American Universities. The University is accredited by the Middle States Association of Colleges and Schools. Graduate and professional accrediting agencies recognize its degrees in many categories.

Applying

Applications for admission are available from Graduate Enrollment Services at the Graduate School of Arts & Science. The completed application (with a $60 nonrefundable check or money order payable to New York University), three letters of academic reference, GRE scores, and official college transcripts in duplicate should be received by Graduate Enrollment Services before January 4 for fall admission with financial support. Prospective students should consult the Graduate School of Arts & Science *Bulletin* or Web site to identify departments that accept applications for the spring or summer term.

Correspondence and Information

Graduate School of Arts & Science
New York University
Cooper Station, P.O. Box 907
New York, New York 10276-0907

Telephone: 212-998-8050
E-mail: gsas.admissions@nyu.edu
World Wide Web: http://www.nyu.edu/gsas

FACULTY HEADS

Catharine R. Stimpson, Dean, Graduate School of Arts & Science; Ph.D., Columbia.
T. James Matthews, Vice Dean, Graduate School of Arts & Science; Ph.D., Brown.
J. David Slocum, Associate Dean, Academic and Student Life, Graduate School of Arts & Science; Ph.D., NYU.
Roberta S. Popik, Assistant Dean, Graduate Enrollment Services, Graduate School of Arts & Science; Ph.D., Northwestern.

Africana Studies: Michael Dash, Ph.D., West Indies.
American Studies: Andrew Ross, Ph.D., Kent, Canterbury (England).
Anthropology: Fred R. Myers, Ph.D., Bryn Mawr.
Basic Medical Sciences/Sackler Institute of Biomedical Sciences: Joel D. Oppenheim, Associate Dean; Ph.D., Loyola Chicago.
Biology: Philip Furmanski, Ph.D., Temple.
Biomaterials: John P. Legeros, Ph.D., Western Ontario.
Biomedical Sciences/Mount Sinai School of Medicine: Terry Ann Krulwich, Dean; Ph.D., Wisconsin.
Chemistry: Nicholas Geacintov, Ph.D., Syracuse.
Cinema Studies: Chris Straayer, Ph.D., Northwestern.
Classics: Michael Peachin, Ph.D., Columbia.
Comparative Literature: Richard Sieburth, Ph.D., Harvard.
Computer Science: Edmond Schonberg, Ph.D., Chicago.
Economics: Douglas Gale, Ph.D., Columbia.
English: John Guillory, Ph.D., Yale.
Environmental Health Sciences: Max Costa, Ph.D., Arizona.
Ergonomics and Biomechanics: Margareta Nordin, Med.Dr.Sci., Göteborg (Sweden).
European Studies: Martin Schain, Ph.D., Cornell.
Fine Arts: James R. McCredie, Ph.D., Harvard.
French: Thomas Bishop, Ph.D., Berkeley.
German: Avital Ronell, Ph.D., Princeton.
Hebrew and Judaic Studies: Lawrence Schiffman, Ph.D., Brandeis.
History: Robin D. G. Kelley, Ph.D., UCLA.
Humanities and Social Thought: Robin Nagle, Ph.D., Columbia.
Institute of French Studies: Edward Berenson, Ph.D., Rochester.
Italian: John Freccero, Ph.D., Johns Hopkins.
Journalism and Mass Communication: Jay Rosen, Ph.D., NYU.
Latin American and Caribbean Studies: Christopher Mitchell, Ph.D., Harvard.
Law and Society: Christine B. Harrington, Ph.D., Wisconsin.
Linguistics: Anna Szabolcsi, Ph.D., Hungarian Academy of Sciences.
Mathematics: Joel Spencer, Ph.D., Harvard.
Middle Eastern Studies: Michael Gilsenan, D.Phil., Oxford.
Museum Studies Program: Bruce Altshuler, Ph.D., Harvard.
Music: Gage Averill, Ph.D., Washington (Seattle).
Near Eastern Studies: Timothy Mitchell, Ph.D., Princeton.
Neural Science: Daniel Sanes, Ph.D., Princeton.
Performance Studies: Diana Taylor, Ph.D., Washington.
Philosophy: Paul Boghossian, Ph.D., Princeton.
Physics: Allen Mincer, Ph.D., Maryland.
Politics: Anna Harvey, Ph.D., Princeton.
Psychology: Marissa Carrasco, Ph.D., Princeton.
Religious Studies: Angela Zito, Ph.D., Chicago.
Russian and Slavic Studies: Charlotte Douglas, Ph.D., Texas at Austin.
Sociology: Kathleen Gerson, Ph.D., Berkeley.
Spanish and Portuguese: Kathleen Ross, Ph.D., Yale.

The view north along 5th Avenue seen from the center of New York University's Washington Square campus.

The entrance to the administrative offices of the Graduate School of Arts & Science, located at 6 Washington Square North.

NEW YORK UNIVERSITY

School of Continuing and Professional Studies

Programs of Study

The School of Continuing and Professional Studies at New York University (NYU) was founded more than sixty years ago as a separate school within the University and is the leading and largest institution of its kind in the nation, with annual enrollments of 60,000 in its many professional development and degree programs. It offers the following eleven master's degree programs, all connected with the high-opportunity core professions: the Master of Science in direct and interactive marketing, the Master of Science in hospitality industry studies, the Master of Science in management and systems, the Master of Science in publishing, the Master of Science in translation (online), the Master of Science in construction management, the Master of Science in digital imaging and design, the Master of Science in real estate, the Master of Science in tourism and travel management, the Executive Master of Science in hospitality industry studies (online), and the Executive Master of Science in tourism and travel management (online). Classes are taught by outstanding professionals as well as by experienced academicians. The curriculum for each program is planned under the guidance of boards of advisers.

Research Facilities

NYU's Elmer Holmes Bobst Library and Study Center, one of the largest open-stack research libraries in the world, houses more than 3.2 million volumes. Bobst is one of nine NYU libraries.

The Virtual College™ takes an innovative approach to developing and delivering graduate courses online. The online courses are the best available because they are both student-centered and feature high levels of interactivity with faculty members. The infrastructure of the online program helps students become organized. Every element is clearly mapped out: the syllabus, lectures, information about assignments, reading material, and the office hours of faculty members. At a glance, students know what courses they have registered for and what still needs to be completed to meet degree requirements.

The Jack Brause Library and Information Center is devoted exclusively to the subject matter of real estate and is the most comprehensive facility of its kind. It is a reliable source of information covering all aspects of the real-estate industry, including magazines, journals, market reports, statistical and economic data, books, maps, and specialized databases.

Financial Aid

To learn more about financial aid opportunities, program-administered scholarships, Veteran's benefits, and deferred payment tuition plans, students should visit the NYU financial aid Web site at http://www.nyu.edu/financial.aid. This Web site also provides directions for filing the Free Application for Federal Student Aid (FAFSA).

Cost of Study

Tuition for the 2002–03 academic year is $1000 per credit plus fees for part-time students. For full-time students (10–15 credits per semester), the cost of tuition is $10,000 plus fees per semester. Fees vary somewhat by program. The Board of Trustees of New York University reserves the right to alter these costs without notice.

Living and Housing Costs

Most graduate student housing is located within walking distance of the Washington Square campus and provides separate kitchen and bathroom facilities and laundry rooms. A free NYU shuttle bus links housing and academic facilities. An off-campus housing office is available to assist students.

Student Group

Most students are employed full-time and study on a part-time basis. The student population is representative of the global university, with individuals from Europe, Asia, Africa, and South America as well as the United States. Many students study online through offerings of The Virtual College™.

Location

NYU's Washington Square campus is located in historic Greenwich Village, within walking distance of Chinatown, Little Italy, and SoHo, one of New York City's major art centers. It is within minutes of Broadway and off-Broadway theaters as well as museums, restaurants, and major sightseeing locations.

Several graduate programs are located at 11 West 42nd Street, off Fifth Avenue in midtown Manhattan, close to shops, offices, theaters, and museums. NYU's Midtown Center is directly across the street from the New York Public Library.

The University and The School

New York University is one of the nation's largest private universities, offering students from around the country and throughout the world the advantages of outstanding educational experiences within the context of a great urban setting. The University is a member of the Association of American Universities and is accredited by the Middle States Association of Colleges and Schools. Its School of Continuing and Professional Studies has an international reputation for excellence in providing innovative education for working professionals. According to the Middle States Association's Commission of Higher Education, NYU's School of Continuing and Professional Studies is one of the largest and most responsive in the United States.

Application

Students may apply for fall or spring admission. Factors that are considered in evaluating applicants include the applicant's official transcripts of academic achievement in previous undergraduate and graduate course work, scores on the GRE or GMAT (TOEFL for international students), the nature and extent of previous work experience, letters of recommendation, and a statement of purpose.

Correspondence and Information

For more information and an application package, students should contact the School of Continuing and Professional Studies as listed below. Applicants must be sure to specify their area of interest.

Office of Admissions
Graduate Programs
School of Continuing and Professional Studies
New York University
145 Fourth Avenue, 2nd Floor
New York, New York 10003
Telephone: 212-998-7200 Ext. 416
Fax: 212-995-4675
E-mail: scps.gradadmissions@nyu.edu
World Wide Web: http://www.scps.nyu.edu/416

THE ADMINISTRATION

School of Continuing and Professional Studies Administration
David F. Finney, Dean, School of Continuing and Professional Studies; Ed.D.

Master of Science in Direct and Interactive Marketing
H. Griffin Walling, Associate Dean, Division of Professional and Industry Programs, School of Continuing and Professional Studies; Ed.D.
Renée Harris, Director, Marketing and Management Institute, School of Continuing and Professional Studies; M.S.

Master of Science in Hospitality Industry Studies
Lalia Rach, Associate Dean, Clinical Professor, and Director, Preston Robert Tisch Center for Hospitality, Tourism and Travel Administration; M.B.A., Ed.D.
Mark Warner, Clinical Associate Professor and Director of Graduate Programs, Preston Robert Tisch Center for Hospitality, Tourism and Travel Administration, School of Continuing and Professional Studies; M.A., D.P.A.

Master of Science in Management and Systems
H. Griffin Walling, Associate Dean, Division of Professional and Industry Programs, School of Continuing and Professional Studies; Ed.D.
Howard Deckelbaum, Director, Information Technologies Institute, School of Continuing and Professional Studies; M.S.

Master of Science in Publishing
H. Griffin Walling, Associate Dean, Division of Professional and Industry Programs, School of Continuing and Professional Studies; Ed.D.
Robert Baensch, Clinical Associate Professor and Director, Center for Publishing, School of Continuing and Professional Studies; B.A.

Master of Science in Real Estate
D. Kenneth Patton, Associate Dean, Clinical Professor and Silverstein Chair, Real Estate Institute, School of Continuing and Professional Studies; M.S.
Daniel Boffey, Director, Administration and Programs, Real Estate Institute, School of Continuing and Professional Studies; M.A.

Master of Science in Tourism and Travel Management
Lalia Rach, Associate Dean, Clinical Professor and Director, Preston Robert Tisch Center for Hospitality, Tourism and Travel Administration, School of Continuing and Professional Studies; M.B.A., Ed.D.
Mark Warner, Clinical Associate Professor and Director of Graduate Programs, Preston Robert Tisch Center for Hospitality, Tourism and Travel Administration, School of Continuing and Professional Studies; M.A., D.P.A.

NIAGARA UNIVERSITY

Graduate Studies

Programs of Study

Niagara University (NU) has three graduate divisions: Arts and Sciences, Business Administration, and Education.

The Division of Arts and Sciences offers a program leading to an M.S. in criminal justice. A full-time student can complete the program in one calendar year, while a part-time student can in two. This program provides students with the skills to anticipate, address, and correct problems faced by criminal justice professionals.

The Division of Business Administration offers programs leading to the M.B.A. degree with concentrations in general business, accounting, human resource management, strategic management, and international business. The program is practitioner focused and provides current or future business professionals with the skills necessary to become successful managers at both the middle and strategic levels of an organization. Economics, accounting, statistics, finance, team building, conflict resolution, and human behavior are featured in the curriculum.

The Division of Education offers programs leading to the M.A. and M.S. in education in foundations and teachings, special education, school counseling, administration and supervision, and school business administration. The College of Education also offers an M.S. degree and an advanced certificate in mental health counseling. The program strives to produce qualified professionals who can assume leadership roles in educational and other vocational settings.

Research Facilities

Niagara University's library has twice been named an "Electronic Doorway Library" by New York State. It contains more than 271,101 volumes and 4,700 periodicals, with the addition of 5,000 new volumes per year. Internet technology is also on the cutting edge. A science library is available in DePaul Hall, with access to Roswell Park Memorial Institute's Medical Scientific Library.

Financial Aid

Eligible students may apply for financial aid by filing the FAFSA. Federal loans such as Federal Perkins Loans and Federal Stafford Student Loans are available to eligible graduate students. Niagara University also offers financial aid through student employment programs that include graduate resident assistantships, graduate assistantships, and work study. There are a limited number of departmental tuition scholarships.

Cost of Study

Tuition per credit hour for the 2001–02 academic year was as follows: elementary and secondary education, $400; school and mental health counseling, administration, and supervision, $350; M.B.A., $490; and criminal justice, $400.

Living and Housing Costs

Housing for graduate students is offered based upon space availability. Graduate students are eligible to apply for resident status in May as soon as they are accepted into a graduate degree program.

Student Group

There are a total of 818 students (458 full-time and 360 part-time) enrolled in graduate programs.

Location

Niagara University is built on Monteagle Ridge, which overlooks the Niagara Gorge and the Niagara River. Conveniently located near Niagara Falls, the University is complemented by many historical, cultural, and natural attractions. Niagara offers a scenic suburban campus and is a short drive from Buffalo, New York, and Canada.

The University

Niagara University is a liberal arts university in the Vincentian tradition. Basic to the academic cocurricular and extracurricular programs at Niagara is the conviction that the students need to be prepared for productive roles in society and provided with the opportunity to fulfill their intellectual, physical, emotional, and spiritual potential. The NU experience introduces students to a comprehensive body of knowledge, encourages interest in intellectual matters and learning as a lifelong pursuit, provides the development of powers of discrimination and judgment, enriches their cultural lives, and fosters a commitment to ethical, intellectual, and social values.

Applying

Applications are submitted to the directors of each specific program of study or an online application may be submitted at http://www.niagara.edu/graduate. The application should be submitted with official transcripts, two letters of recommendation, GRE or GMAT scores, and a 500-word personal statement. Applications are accepted on a rolling basis. An interview is required.

Correspondence and Information

Mark E. Wojnowski, Assistant Dean for Graduate Recruitment
Graduate Studies
Ballo Hall
Niagara University
Niagara University, New York 14109
Telephone: 716-286-8700
800-462-2111 (toll-free)
Fax: 716-286-8710
E-mail: admissions@niagara.edu
World Wide Web: http://www.niagara.edu/graduate

THE FACULTY AND THEIR RESEARCH

College of Education

Debra A. Colley, Dean; Ph.D., SUNY at Buffalo. (e-mail: dcolley@niagara.edu; telephone: 716-286-8560)

Frank Calzi, Graduate Program Director, Administration and Supervision; Ph.D., SUNY at Buffalo. (e-mail: fcalzi@niagara.edu; telephone: 716-286-8553)

Robin W. Erwin Jr., Chair, Department of Education; Ph.D., SUNY at Buffalo. (e-mail: rewin@niagara.edu; telephone: 716-286-8551)

Salvatore J. Pappalardo, Professor and Graduate Program Director, School Counseling; Ed.D., SUNY at Albany. Organizational citizenship behaviors as they relate to the school and mental health counselor. (e-mail: sjp@niagara.edu; telephone: 716-286-8545)

College of Business Administration

John A. Helmuth, Dean; Ph.D., South Carolina.

Philip Scherer, M.B.A. Program Director; Ph.D., Missouri-Columbia. Ethics of using worker generated information to lay off employees. (e-mail: pscherer@niagra.edu; telephone: 716-286-8165)

College of Arts and Sciences

Nancy McGlen, Dean; Ph.D., Rochester. (e-mail: nmcglen@niagara.edu; telephone: 716-286-8059)

Timothy O. Ireland, Graduate Program Director, Criminal Justice; Ph.D., Albany. Long-term consequences of child victimization, causes of violence, consequences of child abuse and neglect, theories of crime and delinquency, violence in public housing. (e-mail: toi@niagara.edu; telephone: 716-286-8098)

NORFOLK STATE UNIVERSITY

Graduate Programs

Programs of Study

Norfolk State University offers sixteen programs through the Schools of Business, Education, Liberal Arts, Social Work, and Science and Technology. The following advanced degrees are offered: Master of Arts in applied sociology; Master of Arts in communications (mass communications, journalism, and interpersonal communication); Master of Arts in community/clinical psychology; Master of Arts in education of the gifted; Master of Science in materials science; Master of Music in music; Master of Arts in pre-elementary education; Master of Arts in severe disabilities; Master of Social Work and Doctor of Social Work; Master of Arts in urban affairs; Master of Arts and Master of Fine Arts in visual studies. Graduate programs at Norfolk State University are designed to provide opportunities for a quality education through the acquisition of knowledge, understanding, and skills. It is the philosophy of the University that all people, regardless of socioeconomic status, race, sex, age, disabling conditions, or national origin, are entitled to benefit from educational opportunities and advantages to the fullest extent of their capabilities. Graduate programs are organized and staffed to provide intellectual, professional, and social leadership skills that enable students to realize their fullest potential. Further, the programs strive to foster a sense of social responsibility as well as personal and professional worth so that graduates will be capable of providing leadership in and beyond the area of their special competence.

Research Facilities

The Lyman Beecher Brooks Library is a state-of-the-art facility that is fully automated. Students can search the library holdings online via the Virginia Tech Library System (VTLS). Approximately fifty search terminals are located throughout the building. The automated system facilitates the circulation of all library materials. The library also uses automated systems such as the Internet, Compuserve, Dialog, and others in order to assist users with research.

The Harrison B. Wilson Archives is the repository of the historical records of the University and its faculty, alumni, and students. In addition, the archives has the mission of collecting and preserving the historical records of African Americans in Virginia and making them available to researchers.

The Lois E. Woods Museum houses a collection of African art from fourteen countries representing forty groups and cultures. Included in the museum is a reference library that features more than 400 books on African art, folklore, and history.

The Virginia Beach Higher Education Center is operated cooperatively by Norfolk State University and Old Dominion University. It is geared primarily toward offering graduate-level courses. The Tri-Cities Higher Education Center is located in Portsmouth, Virginia, and offers yet another off-campus site where graduate instruction is available.

Financial Aid

The University offers numerous graduate fellowship awards each year to qualified students who have been admitted to full-time study for an advanced degree. Fellowship grants may be need-based or merit-based. A number of departmental and university stipends and tuition awards are available. The purpose of the financial aid program is to provide assistance to graduate students who, without such assistance, would not be able to earn an advanced degree. Applications and information regarding financial aid may be obtained from the Office of Student Financial Aid, Harrison B. Wilson Hall, Room 130; by calling 757-823-9381/8382; or from the Web site at http://www.nsu.edu. Inquiries regarding departmental grants may be made at the specific program office.

Cost of Study

Tuition for the 2001–02 academic year was $197 per semester hour for Virginia residents and $503 per semester hour for non-Virginia residents. Full-time study for graduate students, except in the School of Social Work, is 9 semester hours.

Living and Housing Costs

On-campus housing is provided for graduate students only in special circumstances. The Housing Office will assist in finding housing upon request.

Location

Norfolk State University is located in Norfolk, Virginia, and is proud to be one of the sixteen cities and counties that compose the area known as Hampton Roads. It serves as the home of the largest naval military installation in the world. Also, it is the home of numerous international businesses and governmental and military facilities such as the Joint Forces Staff College, the NASA Langley Research Center, and the Atlantic Headquarters of NATO. Located within 20 miles of the Atlantic Ocean and the Chesapeake Bay, Norfolk is a major tourist attraction. Places to visit include theme parks, an opera house, museums, theaters, beaches, and other historic sites. The city is easily accessible by air, train, bus, or car.

The University

Norfolk State University was founded in 1935. Brought to life in the midst of the Great Depression, it provided a setting in which the youth of the region could give expression to their hopes and aspirations. At its founding, it was named the Norfolk Unit of Virginia Union University. In 1942, Norfolk Polytechnic College became independent, and two years later an Act of the Virginia Legislature mandated that it become a part of Virginia State College. The University was able to pursue and expand its mission with even greater emphasis. In 1956, another Act of the Virginia Legislature enabled it to offer, for the first time, the baccalaureate degree. In 1969, the University became fully independent and was officially named Norfolk State College. In 1979, the College became Norfolk State University.

Enrollment at the University in spring 2001 totaled 6,668 students, 778 of whom were graduate students. The student body has an excellent ethnic and racial mix and draws from a broad geographical area.

Applying

Requirements for admission and application deadlines vary from program to program. Students should contact the appropriate offices of the Office of Graduate Studies for specific details.

Correspondence and Information

For all programs except the School of Social Work:
Office of Graduate Studies
Norfolk State University
700 Park Avenue
Norfolk, Virginia 23504
Telephone: 757-823-8015
World Wide Web:
http://www.nsu.edu

For inquiries concerning the School of Social Work:
Office of Admissions
Norfolk State University
School of Social Work
700 Park Avenue
Norfolk, Virginia 23504
Telephone: 757-823-8695

FACULTY

Applied Sociology
Dr. James Nolan (757-823-8436/8852)

Communications
Dr. Stanley Tickton (757-823-8594/2383)

Community/Clinical Psychology
Dr. Darlene Colson (757-823-8435)

Education of the Gifted
Dr. Gae Golembiewski (757-823-8736)

Master of Arts in Teaching
Dr. Sean Warner, Secondary Education (757-823-8111)
Dr. Mona Thornton, Early Childhood Education (757-823-8111)

Materials Science
Dr. Larry Mattix (757-823-2511)

Music
Dr. O'Neill Sanford (757-823-8544)

Pre-Elementary Education
Dr. Mona Thornton (757-823-2124)

Severe Disabilities
Dr. Helen Bessant-Byrd (757-823-8733)

Urban Affairs
Dr. Curtis Langley (757-396-6801)

Urban Education
Dr. Sean Warner (757-823-8178)

Visual Studies
Dr. Amelia Adams (757-823-8021)

Master of Social Work
Mrs. Margaret Kerekes (757-823-8696)

Doctor of Social Work
Dr. Rowena Wilson (757-823-8322)

The student body has a diverse ethnic and racial mix and draws from a broad geographical area.

Students receive individualized attention.

Recent graduates of Norfolk State University.

NORTH DAKOTA STATE UNIVERSITY

Graduate School

Programs of Study

North Dakota State University (NDSU) offers the Doctor of Philosophy, Master of Arts, Master of Business Administration, Master of Education, Master of Science, and Educational Specialist degrees.

The College of Agriculture offers the M.S. degree in agribusiness and applied economics, animal and range sciences, cereal and food science, plant sciences, entomology, food safety, horticulture, microbiology, plant pathology, and soil science and the Ph.D. degree in animal and range sciences, cereal science, entomology, food safety, molecular pathogenesis, plant pathology, plant sciences, and soil science.

In the College of Arts, Humanities and Social Sciences, the master's degree is offered in English, history, mass communication, social science (anthropology, sociology, political science), and speech communication and the Ph.D. is offered in communication and criminal justice.

The College of Business Administration offers the Master of Business Administration (M.B.A.) degree.

The College of Engineering and Architecture offers the M.S. in agricultural and biosystems engineering, civil engineering, electrical engineering, environmental engineering, industrial engineering and management, and mechanical engineering and the Ph.D. degree in engineering.

The College of Human Development and Education offers the master's degree in agricultural education, child development and family science, counseling and guidance, educational administration, family and consumer sciences education, health, nutrition and exercise science, and secondary education. A Ph.D. is offered in human development.

The College of Pharmacy offers both the M.S. and the Ph.D. in pharmaceutical sciences and the M.S. in nursing.

The College of Science and Mathematics awards M.S. and Ph.D. degrees in biochemistry, botany, chemistry, computer science, mathematics, physics, polymers and coatings sciences, psychology, statistics, and zoology.

The following programs are offered as interdisciplinary degrees: M.S. and Ph.D. in natural resources management and Ph.D. in cellular and molecular biology.

The educational specialist degree may be earned in educational administration.

Research Facilities

North Dakota State University possesses state-of-the-art facilities in magnetic resonance imaging, high-performance computing, electron microscopy, and computer chip assembly. Located adjacent to the campus, a new Research and Technology Park is expanding to house both academic research units and industrial partners, strengthening links between the University and technology-based companies. Research specializations in a wide variety of disciplines have resulted in establishment of the Center for Nanoscale Science and Engineering, NSF Coatings Cooperative Research Center, the Bio-imaging and Sensing Center, the Center for Protease Research, the Quentin Burdick Center for Cooperatives, the Center for Agricultural Policy and Trade Studies, the Great Plains Institute of Food Safety, the Upper Great Plains Transportation Institute, and the Institute for Regional Studies. As the state's land-grant institution, NDSU houses the North Dakota Agricultural Experiment Station and the Extension Service, with eight Research and Extension Centers across the state. An Internet2 institution, NDSU provides high-speed network access to classrooms and desktops, an Access Grid facility for global virtual conferencing, and high-speed connections to other universities and federal agencies for research and distance education. Library resources include more than 498,000 bound volumes, 40,000 maps, 4,400 current electronic and print subscriptions, and an extensive array of specialized full-text electronic databases, as well as an online catalog that interfaces with other regional, national, and international library catalogs.

Financial Aid

Graduate teaching and research assistantships are awarded to qualified students upon recommendations from individual departments and include tuition waivers for all graduate credits. Approximately half of the graduate students are awarded graduate assistantships. Student activity fees are not waived. Stipend amounts vary widely from department to department; the average is about $850 per month. The Graduate School has stipend enhancements for outstanding applicants. North Dakota's very successful National Science Foundation EPSCoR program is centered at NDSU and has just committed $300,000 per year in new monies for support of NDSU Ph.D. students and about $40,000 per year for master's degree student support. For more information, students should contact the Financial Aid Office (telephone: 701-231-7533).

Cost of Study

Tuition per credit, through 12 credits, is $145.08 for North Dakota residents; $178 for Minnesota residents; $206 for residents of Saskatchewan, Manitoba, South Dakota, and Montana; and $351.33 for other students. Student fees per credit, through 12 credits, were $21.58 in 2001–02.

Living and Housing Costs

Apartments for families, as well as single-occupancy units, are located on and near the University campus in University Village and Bison Court. For residence hall life, the combined room and meal plan costs approximately $3600 per academic year. Housing, utility, and food expenses for 2 people living on and off campus are estimated at $5520 and $6380, respectively.

Student Group

Current enrollment at NDSU is approximately 10,500 students on the central campus in Fargo. NDSU also serves several thousand additional people throughout the state in continuing education and extension programs. Graduate student enrollment is approximately 1,100 students, with about 60 percent attending full-time. International students comprise approximately 25 percent of the graduate student population, providing a wealth of diversity within both the academic and local communities.

Student Outcomes

North Dakota State University graduates more than 200 master's students and 35 Ph.D. students each year.

Location

With more than 170,000 people, Fargo-Moorhead is the largest metropolitan center between Minneapolis and Seattle and is nestled in the Red River Valley, rich in fertile farmlands. In Fargo-Moorhead, three universities and the technical colleges provide a wide variety of educational opportunities, while the community offers access to part-time jobs, internships, parks and other recreational facilities, entertainment, and cultural amenities.

The University

North Dakota State University, the state's first land-grant institution, was established in 1890. It is one of the two research institutions within North Dakota's university system of five 2-year schools, three 4-year schools, and three graduate institutions. NDSU is a comprehensive university that offers nationally recognized programs of study within a student-friendly community. Forty-one master's degree programs, twenty-five Ph.D. degree programs, and an educational specialist degree program in educational administration are offered. Seventy-five undergraduate majors are offered.

Applying

All application materials are due one month before registration for U.S. students; some departments have earlier deadlines. For international students, the completed application packet (application form, application fee, official transcripts, three letters of reference, and a personal statement) and required test scores should be received by the Graduate School by April 1 for fall semester and August 1 for spring semester.

Correspondence and Information

The Graduate School
North Dakota State University
P.O. Box 5790
Fargo, North Dakota 58105-5790

Telephone: 701-231-7033
Fax: 701-231-6524
E-mail: ndsu.grad.school@ndsu.nodak.edu
World Wide Web: http://www.ndsu.nodak.edu/gradschool
http://www.ndsu.nodak.edu

THE FACULTY

Listed below are North Dakota State University's deans, graduate degree programs, and corresponding phone numbers and e-mail addresses. (All phone numbers are in the 701 area code, with the exception of the nursing program.)

College of Agriculture: Patricia Jensen, J.D.
Agricultural and Biosystems Engineering: 231-7261. (E-mail: earl.stegman@ndsu.nodak.edu)
Agribusiness and Applied Economics: 231-7441. (E-mail: sshultz@ndsu.nodak.edu)
Animal and Range Sciences: 231-7641. (E-mail: dkirby@ndsu.nodak.edu)
Cereal Science: 231-7711. (E-mail: khalil.khan@ndsu.nodak.edu)
Entomology: 231-7582. (E-mail: gary.brewer@ndsu.nodak.edu)
Natural Resources Management: 231-8180. (E-mail: carolyn.grygiel@ndsu.nodak.edu)
Plant Pathology: 231-8362. (E-mail: ppth@ndsu.ext.nodak.edu)
Plant Sciences: 231-7971. (E-mail: albert.schneiter@ndsu.nodak.edu)
Soil Science: 231-8901. (E-mail: jimmie.richardson@ndsu.nodak.edu)
Veterinary and Microbiological Sciences: 231-7511. (E-mail: douglas.freeman@ndsu.nodak.edu)

College of Business Administration: Jay Leitch, Ph.D.
Business Administration: 231-8651. (E-mail: paul.brown@ndsu.nodak.edu)

College of Engineering and Architecture: Otto Helweg, Ph.D.
Civil Engineering: 231-7244. (E-mail: dinesh.katti@ndsu.nodak.edu)
Electrical Engineering: 231-7019. (E-mail: info@venus.ece.ndsu.nodak.edu)
Environmental Engineering: 231-7879. (E-mail: wei.lin@ndsu.nodak.edu)
Industrial Engineering: 231-7287. (E-mail: david.l.wells@ndsu.nodak.edu)
Mechanical Engineering: 231-8671. (E-mail: mary.stoa@ndsu.nodak.edu)

College of Human Development and Education: Virginia Clark Johnson, Ph.D.
Child Development and Family Science: 231-8268. (E-mail: james.deal@ndsu.nodak.edu)
Health, Physical Education and Recreation: 231-8681. (E-mail: brad.strand@ndsu.nodak.edu)
School of Education: 231-7127. (E-mail: jim.wigtil@ndsu.nodak.edu)
- Agricultural Education: 231-7439. (E-mail: anissa.wilhelm@ndsu.nodak.edu).
- Counseling Education: 231-7676. (E-mail: robert.nielson@ndsu.nodak.edu)
- Educational Leadership: 231-9732. (E-mail: vicki.ihry@ndsu.nodak.edu)
- Family and Consumer Sciences Education: 231-7101. (E-mail: anissa.wilhelm@ndsu.nodak.edu)

College of Arts, Humanities and Social Sciences: Thomas Riley, Ph.D.
Communication: 231-7705. (E-mail: ross.collins@ndsu.nodak.edu)
English: 231-7143. (E-mail: muriel.brown@ndsu.nodak.edu)
History: 231-8654. (E-mail: ndsu.history@ndsu.nodak.edu)
Political Science: 231-8567. (E-mail: robert.wood@ndsu.nodak.edu)
Sociology/Anthropology: 231-8657. (E-mail: gary.goreham@ndsu.nodak.edu)

College of Pharmacy: Charles Peterson, Ph.D.
Nursing: 218-236-4699. (E-mail: giedt@mnstate.edu)
Pharmaceutical Sciences: 231-7661. (E-mail: janelle.fortier@ndsu.nodak.edu)

College of Science and Mathematics: Alan White, Ph.D.
Biochemistry: 231-7678. (E-mail: derek.killilea@ndsu.nodak.edu)
Botany/Biology: 231-8679. (E-mail: william.bleier@ndsu.nodak.edu)
Cellular and Molecular Biology: 231-7405. (E-mail: mary.stewart@ndsu.nodak.edu)
Chemistry: 231-8694. (E-mail: greg.mccarthy@ndsu.nodak.edu)
Computer Science: 231-8562. (E-mail: carole.huber@ndsu.nodak.edu)
Mathematics: 231-8171. (E-mail: ndsu.math@ndsu.nodak.edu)
Physics: 231-8974. (E-mail: ndsu.physics@ndsu.nodak.edu)
Polymers and Coatings: 231-7633. (E-mail: ndsu.polycoat@ndsu.nodak.edu)
Psychology: 231-8622. (E-mail: ndsu.psych@ndsu.nodak.edu)
Statistics: 231-7532. (E-mail: ndsu.stats@ndsu.nodak.edu)
Zoology: 231-7087. (E-mail: william.bleier@ndsu.nodak.edu)

NORTHEASTERN UNIVERSITY

Graduate and Professional Schools

Programs of Study

The Graduate School of Arts and Sciences offers the Ph.D. in biology; chemistry; English; history; law, policy, and society (interdisciplinary); mathematics; physics; psychology; and sociology. The M.A. may be earned in economics, English, history, journalism, political science, public and international affairs, sociology, and writing. The M.S. is awarded in bioinformatics; biology; chemistry; law, policy, and society (interdisciplinary); mathematics; operations research (a joint program with the College of Engineering); and physics. The M.Ed. is awarded in curriculum and instruction (elementary and secondary). The M.Arch., M.P.A., and M.T.P.W. are also offered, as well as a certificate in information design. The M.A.T. is offered in biology, chemistry, economics, English, history, mathematics, physics, political science, and sociology. Teacher certification is offered in elementary, middle, secondary, and special education. The Graduate School of Bouvé College of Health Sciences offers the Ph.D. in biomedical science with specializations in pharmaceutics and drug-delivery systems, pharmacology, and toxicology, and an interdisciplinary program in biomedical science; the Ph.D. in school psychology and counseling psychology; the M.S. in applied behavioral analysis, applied educational psychology with options in school counseling and school psychology, audiology, clinical exercise physiology, college student development and counseling, general biomedical sciences, medical laboratory science, perfusion technology, pharmacology, physician assistant studies, and speech-language pathology, and in nursing with specializations in administration, community health, critical care, primary care, anesthesia, and psychiatric–mental health; M.S./M.B.A. and B.S.N./M.S. programs for A.D. and diploma-educated nurses; certification programs for master's-prepared nurses; the M.S. in counseling psychology; the M.S. in education with options in special needs and intensive special needs; and the C.A.G.S. in psychology, education, and the community. The Graduate School of Business Administration offers eight distinct programs: the Executive M.B.A., the High Technology M.B.A., the Cooperative Education M.B.A., the Part-Time M.B.A., the J.D./M.B.A., the M.D./M.B.A., the M.S./M.B.A. in nursing administration, and the M.S. in finance. The Graduate School of Professional Accounting offers a full-time, intensive fifteen-month program of study, including a three-month paid internship, leading to a joint M.S./M.B.A. The School also offers a part-time program leading to the M.S. in taxation. The Graduate School of Computer Science offers programs leading to the M.S. and Ph.D. The Graduate School of Criminal Justice offers an M.S. with options in administration and planning, criminology and research, security administration, or another field of concentration developed to suit individual needs. The Graduate School of Engineering offers programs in chemical engineering (Ph.D., M.S.), civil engineering (Ph.D., M.S.), computer engineering (Ph.D.), computer systems engineering (M.S.), electrical engineering (Ph.D., M.S.), engineering management (M.S.), industrial engineering (Ph.D., M.S.), information systems (M.S.), and mechanical engineering (Ph.D., M.S.). The School also offers the M.S. in operations research (a joint program with the Graduate School of Arts and Sciences). The School of Law offers a Co-operative Education Program leading to the J.D. Under the Co-op Program, students complete a traditional first year of academic studies, and for the remaining two years of study, students alternate every three months between working full-time as legal interns and attending classes. The School of Law also offers a J.D./M.S./M.B.A. with the Graduate School of Business Administration; a J.D./Ph.D. in law, policy, and society with the Graduate School of Arts and Sciences; and an M.P.H. with Tufts University. University College offers graduate-level certificate programs in bioinformatics essentials, human resources management, knowledge management, nonprofit management, and strategic Internet management.

Research Facilities

The University supports twenty-nine centers and institutes, including the Barnett Institute of Chemical and Biological Analysis, the Institute for Molecular Biotechnology, Nano Manufacturing Research Institute, Institute on Race and Justice, Domestic Violence Institute, Center for Interdisciplinary Research on Complex Systems, Brudnick Center on Violence and Conflict, Center for Advanced Microgravity Materials Processing, Center for the Study of Sport in Society, Center for Subsurface Sensing and AImagin Systems, Center for Technology Management, Center for Urban and Regional Policy, and the Marine Science Center. Special University facilities include the Electron Microscopy Center, Microfabrication Laboratory, and Molecular Modeling Center. A high-speed data network links users and facilities to the central campus to three satellite campuses, and to computing facilities around the world. Students have access to Compaq Alpha systems, public-access microcomputer labs (PC and Macintosh), a conferencing system, multimedia labs, and specialized computing equipment. Northeastern University is also an Internet2 site. University libraries contain approximately 936,500 volumes, 2,195,000 microforms, 163,400 government documents, 7,845 serial subscriptions, and 20,900 audio, video, and software titles.

Financial Aid

Northeastern awards need-based aid through the Federal Perkins Loan, Federal Work-Study, and Federal Stafford Student Loan programs and also offers minority fellowships and Martin Luther King Jr. Scholarships. The graduate schools offer assistance through teaching, research, and administrative assistantship awards that include tuition remission and a stipend typically ranging between $10,400 and $14,560 that requires 20 hours of work per week. Tuition assistantships that provide partial or full tuition remission and require 10 hours of work per week are also available.

Cost of Study

For 2001–02, tuition was $505 per credit in the Graduate Schools of Arts and Sciences, Bouvé College of Health Sciences, and Criminal Justice; $545 in the Graduate School of Computer Science; $535 in the Graduate School of Engineering; and $580 in the Graduate School of Business Administration and the M.S. in taxation and the M.S. in finance programs. Tuition for the School of Law was $26,820 annually; tuition was $25,920 per year in the Graduate School of Professional Accounting. Tuition for University College was $390 per credit.

Living and Housing Costs

For 2001–02, quarterly on-campus room rates for a single bedroom within an apartment ranged from $1765 to $2435. Single apartments ranged from $2455 to $2645. A shared bedroom in an apartment ranged from $1660 to $2165. On-campus housing for graduate students is limited and granted on a space-available basis. An off-campus referral service is available (telephone: 617-373-4872; e-mail: commuter@lynx.neu.edu). While there are several board options available, graduate students typically pay $1200 per quarter for ten meals per week.

Student Group

In fall 2001, 13,963 undergraduate and 4,217 graduate and professional students were enrolled at Northeastern University.

Location

Boston, Massachusetts, offers a rich cultural and intellectual history and is the premiere educational center of the country, with more than thirty-five colleges in the city region. Cultural offerings, which include several world-class museums, a bevy of art galleries, and the Boston Symphony, are diverse, and the city is home to people of every race, ethnicity, political persuasion, and religion. A public transportation system serves the greater Boston area, and there are subway and bus services convenient to the University.

The University

Building on its flagship cooperative education program, the century-old University links classroom learning with workplace experience and integrates professional preparation with study in the liberal arts and sciences. Northeastern has six undergraduate colleges, eight graduate and professional schools, two part-time undergraduate divisions and an extensive variety of research institutes and divisions. For more information, students should visit the Internet address listed below.

Applying

Correspondence should be addressed to the appropriate school. Application materials, official transcripts, and all required test scores, should be returned to the graduate school of intended study. Applications to most programs are processed on a rolling basis; however, many have an application deadline in early spring. Online applications are available for many schools.

Correspondence and Information

Graduate School of (specify)–PG
Northeastern University
360 Huntington Avenue
Boston, Massachusetts 02115
E-mail: See address for specific graduate school on reverse.
World Wide Web: http://www.northeastern.edu

FACULTY HEADS

David Hall, S.J.D., LL.M., Provost.
Ronald Hedlund, Ph.D., Vice Provost for Research and Graduate Education.

GRADUATE SCHOOL OF ARTS AND SCIENCES

Edward L. Jarroll, Ph.D., Interim Associate Dean for Faculty Affairs and Director of the Graduate School of Arts and Sciences, 124 Meserve Hall (617-373-3982). E-mail: gsas@neu.edu

Department Chairs

Biology: Susan Powers-Lee, Ph.D., Interim Chair, 414 Mugar Building (617-373-2260).
Chemistry: David A. Forsyth, Ph.D., 102 Hurtig Hall (617-373-2822).
Economics: Steven A. Morrison, Ph.D., 301 Lake Hall (617-373-2872).
Education: James W. Fraser, Ph.D., 50 Nightingale (617-373-4216).
English: Mary Loeffelholz, Ph.D., Acting Chair, 406 Holmes Hall (617-373-2512).
History: Laura Frader, Ph.D., 249 Meserve Hall (617-373-2660).
Journalism: Alan Schroeder, M.A., Acting Director, 102 Lake Hall (617-373-3236).
Law, Policy and Society: Leonard Buckle, Ph.D., and Suzann Thomas-Buckle, Ph.D., 305 Cushing Hall (617-373-5211, 617-373-4689).
Mathematics: Robert McOwen, Ph.D., 521 Lake Hall (617-373-2450).
Physics: Paul Champion, Ph.D., 110 Dana Hall (617-373-2902).
Political Science: Christopher Bosso, Ph.D., 305 Meserve Hall (617-373-2796).
Psychology: Stephen G. Harkins, Ph.D., 125 Nightingale Hall (617-373-3076).
Sociology and Anthropology: Luis Falcón, Ph.D., Acting Chair, 500 Holmes Hall (617-373-2686).

GRADUATE SCHOOL OF BOUVÉ COLLEGE OF HEALTH SCIENCES

Ena Vazquez-Nutall, Ed.D., Associate Dean and Graduate School Director, 203A Mugar Hall (617-373-2708). E-mail: w.purnell@nunet.neu.edu

School of Pharmacy

Daniel Robinson, Pharm.D., Dean, CLS, 205 Mugar Life Sciences Building (617-373-8917).

Department Chair

Biomedical Sciences: Vladimir Torchillin, Ph.D., 312 Mugar Hall (617-373-3206).

Program Directors

General Biomedical Science: Roger W. Giese, Ph.D., 110 Mugar Hall (617-373-3227).
Medical Laboratory Science: Mary Louise Turgeon, Ed.D., 206 Mugar Hall (617-373-4192).
Pharmacology: Ralph H. Loring, Ph.D., 211 Mugar Hall (617-373-3316).
Toxicology: Robert A. Schatz, Ph.D., 203A Mugar Hall (617-373-3369).
Ph.D. Programs: Robert A. Schatz, Ph.D., 203A Mugar Hall (617-373-3369).

School of Health Professions

Department Chairs

Cardiopulmonary and Excercise Sciences: William J. Gillespie, Ed.D., CPP, 117 Dockser Hall (617-373-5695).
Counseling and Applied Educational Psychology: Emmanuel J. Mason, Ph.D., 203 Lake Hall (617-373-3276).
Physicians Assistant Studies: Suzanne Greenberg, Sc.D., 202 Robinson Hall (617-373-3195).
Speech-Language Pathology and Audiology: Linda J. Ferrier, Ph.D., 133 Forsyth Hall (617-373-2892).

Program Directors

Applied Education
  School Counseling: M. Patricia Fetter, Ph.D., 209 Lake Hall (617-373-4486).
  School Psychology: Louis J. Kruger, Psy.D., 216 Lake Hall (617-373-5897).
Clinical Exercise Physiology: William J. Gillespie, Ed.D., CPP, 117 Dockser Hall (617-373-5695).
College Student Development: Vanessa D. Johnson-Durgans, Ed.D., 203 Lake Hall (617-373-2470).
Counseling Psychology: Mary B. Ballou, Ph.D., ABPP, 205 Lake Hall (617-373-5937).
Counseling Psychology, CAGS: Deborah F. Greenwald, Ph.D., 210A Lake Hall (617-373-2486).
Education Intensive Special Needs: Karin N. Lifter, Ph.D., 212B Lake Hall (617-373-5916).
Education Special Needs: Karin N. Lifter, Ph.D., 212B Lake Hall (617-373-5916).
Perfusion Technology: Eric B. Pepin, Ed.D., CPP, 100 Dockser (617-373-4183).
Rehabilitation Counseling: James F. Scorzelli, Ph.D., 207 Lake Hall (617-373-5919).
School and Counseling Psychology, Ph.D.: Karin N. Lifter, Ph.D., 212B Lake Hall (617-373-5916).
School Psychology, CAGS: Louis J. Kruger, Psy.D., 216 Lake Hall (617-373-5897).

School of Nursing

Margery Chisholm, Acting Dean, Ed.D., 102 Robinson Hall (617-373-3649).

Program Directors

B.S.N./M.S. and M.S./M.B.A.: Jane F. Aroian, Ed.D., RN, 207J Robinson Hall (617-373-3128).
Community Care: Abraham N. Ndiwane, Ed.D., 207F Robinson Hall (617-373-3124).
Critical Care/Neonatal: Elizabeth M. Howard, Ph.D., RN, ANP, 418A Robinson Hall (617-373-4590).
Nurse Anesthesia: Steve Alves, Ph.D. candidate, M.S., CRNA, 207D Robinson Hall (617-373-7962).
Nursing Administration: Jane F. Aroian, Ed.D., RN, 207J Robinson Hall (617-373-3128).
Primary Care: Michelle A. Beauchesne, D.N.Sc., PNP, 401A Robinson Hall (617-373-3621).
Psychiatric–Mental Health: Margaret Smith Hamilton, 106K Robinson Hall (617-373-3627).

GRADUATE SCHOOL OF BUSINESS ADMINISTRATION

Therese M. Hofmann, M.B.A., Associate Dean and Director of Graduate Programs, 400 Dodge Hall (617-373-5417).
Dennis Ramsier, M.B.A., Director of Co-op M.B.A. Program, 350 Dodge Hall (617-373-4264).

Department Coordinators

Accounting: Paul Janell, Ph.D., 404 Hayden Hall (617-373-4645).
Finance and Insurance: Paul Bolster, Ph.D., 413 Hayden Hall (617-373-5051).
General Management: Ravi Sarathy, Ph.D., 214 Hayden Hall (617-373-4806).
Human Resources: Frank Spital, Ph.D., 304 Hayden Hall (617-373-4722).
Management Science: Robert Parsons, M.A., M.B.A., 314 Hayden Hall (617-373-4749).
Marketing: Dan Dunn, D.B.A., 202 Hayden Hall (617-373-4563).

GRADUATE SCHOOL OF COMPUTER SCIENCE

Agnes H. Chan, Ph.D., Associate Dean and Director, 161 Cullinane Hall (617-373-2464). E-mail: csgradinfo@neu.edu

GRADUATE SCHOOL OF CRIMINAL JUSTICE

Jack McDevitt, Associate Dean for Research and Graduate Studies, 400 Churchill Hall (617-373-2813). E-mail: j.mcdevitt@neu.edu

GRADUATE SCHOOL OF ENGINEERING

Yaman Yener, Ph.D., Associate Dean for Research and Graduate Studies and Director of the Graduate School of Engineering, 130 Snell Engineering Center (617-373-2711). E-mail: grad-eng@coe.neu.edu

Department Chairs

Chemical Engineering: Ronald Willey, Ph.D., Acting Chair, 342 Snell Engineering Center (617-373-2989).
Civil and Environmental Engineering: Peter Furth, Ph.D., 400 Snell Engineering Center (617-373-2444).
Electrical and Computer Engineering: Fabrizio Lombardi, Ph.D., 409 Dana Hall (617-373-4159).
Information Systems: Ronald Perry, Ph.D., 140 Snell Engineering Center (617-373-4835).
Mechanical, Industrial, and Manufacturing Engineering: John Cipolla, Ph.D., 334 Snell Engineering Center (617-373-2740).

GRADUATE SCHOOL OF PROFESSIONAL ACCOUNTING

Cynthia Parker, M.S., M.B.A., Director, 412 Dodge Hall (617-373-4622).

SCHOOL OF LAW

Roger I. Abrams, J.D., Dean, 120 Knowles Hall (617-373-3307). E-mail: r.abrams@nunet.neu.edu
Diane L. Tsoulas, J.D., Associate Dean, 120 Knowles Hall (617-373-3307). E-mail: d.tsoulas@nunet.neu.edu
Mary O'Connell, J.D., Associate Dean of Academic Affairs, 80 Cargill Hall (617-373-3918). E-mail: m.oconnell@neu.edu

UNIVERSITY COLLEGE GRADUATE CERTIFICATE PROGRAM

Judith Stoessel, Ph.D., Interim Dean for Academic Programs, 295 Ryder Hall (617-373-2412). E-mail: ju.stoessel@nunet.neu.edu
Admissions: Julie Wollwerth, Graduate Coordinator (617-373-4299). E-mail: j.wollwerth@neu.edu

Northeastern UNIVERSITY

NORTHEASTERN UNIVERSITY

Graduate School of Arts and Sciences

Programs of Study

The Graduate School of Arts and Sciences offers the Doctor of Philosophy degree in biology, chemistry, English, history, mathematics, physics, psychology, public and international affairs, and sociology. An interdisciplinary program in law, policy, and society leads to the Doctor of Philosophy degree or to the Master of Science degree for students who have already earned a J.D. A combined M.S./J.D. program of study is also available. The Master of Arts or Master of Science degree is awarded in bioinformatics, biology, chemistry, economics, English, history, journalism, mathematics, physics, political science, sociology, and writing. Also offered are the degrees of Master of Architecture, Master of Education, Master of Public Administration, and Master of Technical and Professional Writing. The Master of Arts in Teaching degree is offered in biology, chemistry, economics, English, history, mathematics, physics, political science, and sociology. The Master of Science in Operations Research is offered in conjunction with the Graduate School of Engineering at Northeastern. A nondegree certificate program is available in information design. Teacher certification programs are offered in elementary, middle, and secondary education.

Research Facilities

The University supports twenty-nine centers and institutes, including the Barnett Institute of Chemical and Biological Analysis, the Institute for Molecular Biotechnology, the Nano Manufacturing Research Institute, the Institute on Race and Justice, the Domestic Violence Institute, Center for Interdisciplinary Research on Complex Systems, the Brudnick Center on Violence and Conflict, the Center for Advanced Microgravity Materials Processing, the Center for the Study of Sport in Society, the Center for Subsurface Sensing and Imaging Systems, the Center for Technology Management, the Center for Urban and Regional Policy, and the Marine Science Center. Special University facilities include the Electron Microscopy Center, the Microfabrication Laboratory, and the Molecular Modeling Center. A high-speed data network links users and facilities on the central campus to three satellite campuses and to computing facilities around the world. Students have access to Compaq Alpha systems, public-access computer labs (PC and Mac), a conferencing system, multimedia labs, and specialized computing equipment. Northeastern is also an Internet2 site.

University libraries contain approximately 936,500 volumes, 2,195,000 microforms, 163,400 government documents, 7,845 serial subscriptions, and 20,900 audio, video, and software titles. A central library contains technologically sophisticated services, including online catalog and circulation systems and a gateway to external networked information resources. Students have access to major research collections through the Boston Library Consortium.

Financial Aid

Northeastern University awards need-based financial aid to graduate students through the Federal Perkins Loan, Federal Work-Study, and Federal Stafford Student Loan programs. The University also offers a limited number of minority fellowships, Martin Luther King Jr. Scholarships, and Graduate Assistantships in Areas of National Need (GAANN). The graduate schools also provide financial assistance through teaching, research, and administrative assistantship awards that include tuition remission and a stipend typically ranging between $10,400 and $14,560 (departmentally specific). These assistantships require 20 hours of work per week. Also available are a number of tuition assistantships, which provide partial or full tuition remission and require 10 hours of work per week.

Cost of Study

Tuition for the 2001–02 academic year in the Graduate School of Arts and Sciences cost $505 per quarter hour of credit. Where applicable, special tuition charges are made for the thesis, the dissertation, teaching, practicums, or fieldwork. Other charges included the Student Center fee and health and accident insurance fee, which are required of all full-time students.

Living and Housing Costs

For 2001–02, quarterly on-campus room rates for a single bedroom within an apartment ranged from $1765 to $2435. Single apartments ranged from $2455 to $2645. A shared bedroom in an apartment ranged from $1660 to $2165 per quarter. On-campus housing for graduate students is limited and granted on a space-available basis. An off-campus referral service is available (telephone: 617-373-4872 or e-mail: commuter@lynx.neu.edu). While there are several board options available, graduate students typically pay $1200 per quarter for ten meals per week. A public transportation system serves the greater Boston area, and there are subway and bus services convenient to the University.

Student Group

In fall 2001, 13,757 undergraduate and 4,217 graduate students were enrolled at Northeastern University, representing a wide variety of academic, professional, geographic, and cultural backgrounds. The Graduate School of Arts and Sciences has 680 students, 73 percent of whom attend on a full-time basis. Because graduate classes are offered primarily in the evening, many students pursue programs on a part-time basis while maintaining full-time employment.

Location

Boston, Massachusetts, offers a rich cultural and intellectual history and is one of the premier educational centers of the country, with more than thirty-five colleges in the city region. Cultural offerings—including several world-class museums, art galleries, and the Boston Symphony—are diverse and the city is home to people of every race, ethnicity, and political and religious persuasion. Boston is steeped in New England tradition and offers world-class restaurants and a range of outdoor activities.

The University

Northeastern University, a private research institution located in Boston, Massachusetts, is a world leader in practice-oriented education. Building on its flagship cooperative education program, the century-old University links classroom learning with workplace experience and integrates professional preparation with study in the liberal arts and sciences. The University has six undergraduate colleges, eight graduate and professional schools, two part-time undergraduate divisions, and an extensive variety of research institutes and divisions. For more information, student should visit the Web site listed below.

Applying

Applications are due in many cases by March 15; however, deadlines vary by academic department and program, with some occurring as early as January 15. Applicants are urged to consult their department of interest for more information. The General and/or Subject Tests of the Graduate Record Examinations are required by most departments. Prospective students may obtain application materials on the University's Web site or by writing to the address below.

Correspondence and Information

Graduate School of Arts and Sciences
124 Meserve Hall-PG
Northeastern University
Boston, Massachusetts 02115

E-mail: gsas@neu.edu
World Wide Web: http://www.northeastern.edu

FACULTY HEADS, GRADUATE COORDINATORS, AND DEPARTMENTAL RESEARCH AREAS

Department e-mail and Web addresses are listed after the name of the department head.

Architecture. George Thrush, M.Arch., Harvard (gradarch@neu.edu; www.casdn.neu.edu/graduate).
Graduate Coordinator: George Thrush, M.Arch., 617-373-4637.
Urban architecture and design. M.Arch. applicants must have earned a bachlor's degree in architecture from Northeastern University.

Biology. Susan Powers-Lee, Ph.D., Berkeley (gradbio@neu.edu; www.dac.neu.edu/biology).
Graduate Coordinator: Donald P. Cheney, Ph.D., 617-373-2262.
Biochemistry, bioinformatics, botany, cell biology, developmental biology, ecology, immunology, marine biology, microbiology, molecular biology, neurobiology, physiology, vertebrate zoology.

Chemistry. David A. Forsyth, Ph.D., Berkeley (chemistry-grad-info@neu.edu; www.chem.neu.edu/gradprog.htm).
Graduate Coordinator: Patricia Ann Mabrouk, Ph.D., 617-373-2822.
Analytical biotechnology; analytical, inorganic, organic, and physical chemistry; bioorganic and medicinal chemistry; separation science; bioinorganic chemistry; electrochemical storage; energy conversion; inorganic reaction mechanisms; magnetic resonance; mass spectrometry; materials science; molecular modeling; natural products; organic reaction mechanisms; organic synthesis; solid-state chemistry; spectroscopy; theoretical chemistry.

Economics. Steven A. Morrison, Ph.D., Berkeley (gradecon@neu.edu; www.atsweb.neu.edu/economics).
Graduate Coordinator: Daryl A. Hellman, Ph.D., 617-373-7517.
Global economics, including trade, development, and privatization; policy analysis, including project evaluation, planning, regulation, and law; urban economics, including development, federalism, and environmental.

Education. James W. Fraser, Ph.D., Columbia (graded@neu.edu; www.casdn.neu.edu/~educate).
Graduate Coordinator: Joan Fitzgerald, Ph.D., 617-373-3644.
Master of Education in curriculum and instruction (elementary, secondary); Master of Arts in Teaching.

English. Mary Loeffelholz, Ph.D., Yale (gradenglish@neu.edu; www.casdn.neu.edu/~english).
Graduate Coordinator: Stuart Peterfreund, Ph.D., 617-373-3692.
British and American literature, literary theory, film and cultural studies, technical and professional writing, composition studies.

History. Laura Frader, Ph.D., Rochester (gradhistory@neu.edu; www.history.neu.edu).
Graduate Coordinator: Christina Gilmartin, Ph.D., 617-373-4449
World history; American, European, African, Asian, environmental, and public history in a global perspective.

Journalism. Alan Schroeder, M.P.A., Harvard (gradjourn@neu.edu; www.dac.neu.edu/journalism).
Graduate Coordinator: Laurel Leff, M.S.L., 617-373-3236.
Print and broadcast journalism, freedom of the press and democracy in Russia, journalism history, sports writing, media ethics, law of the press, Latin America, Holocaust studies, documentary film.

Law, Policy and Society. Suzann Thomas-Buckle, Ph.D., MIT; Leonard Buckle, Ph.D., MIT (lps@neu.edu; www.lps.neu.edu).
Graduate Coordinators: L. Buckle, Ph.D. and S. Thomas-Buckle, Ph.D., 617-373-4689.
Civil and human rights, corporate policy and public regulation, technology policy and society, criminal law and justice, economic development and trade law and policy, environmental regulation, health law and policy, organization and function of the judiciary, alternative dispute resolution, labor law and workplace organization.

Mathematics. Robert C. McOwen, Ph.D., Berkeley (mathdept@neu.edu; www.math.neu.edu/).
Graduate Coordinator: Alexandru Suciu, Ph.D., 617-373-4456.
Algebraic geometry, singularities, commutative algebra, representation theory, combinatorics, algebraic topology, differential topology, K-theory, differential geometry, partial differential equations, probability theory, statistics, harmonic analysis, mathematical physics.

Physics. Paul Champion, Ph.D., Illinois (gradphysics@neu.edu; www.physics.neu.edu).
Graduate Coordinator: Jorge V. José, Ph.D., 617-373-2927.
Astrophysics, biophysics, experimental high-energy and elementary particle physics, elementary particle and quantum field theory, supersymmetry, general relativity, experimental solid-state physics, low-temperature physics, medical physics, microwaves, mesoscopic physics, infrared and ultraviolet spectroscopy of condensed matter, laser-light scattering, neutron scattering, correlated electrons, low-dimensional quantum physics, high–magnetic field optical spectroscopy, metal-insulator transitions, Quantum Hall effect, high-temperature superconductivity, quantum chaos, solid-state theory, many-body theory, statistical mechanics, theoretical biophysics, theory of friction, quantum computing, nonlinear dynamics and pattern formation, electronic structure and spectroscopy of ordered and disordered materials, theoretical neurobiology and cell biology.

Political Science. Denis Sullivan, Ph.D., Michigan (gradpolisci@neu.edu; www.casdn.neu.edu/~polisci).
Graduate Coordinator: William Crotty, Ph.D., 617-373-4404.
Public policy and administration, political development and democratization, American politics and public policy, comparative politics, international relations, political behavior, state and urban politics, public management, political economy.

Psychology. Stephen G. Harkins, Ph.D., Missouri (psychology@neu.edu; www.psych.neu.edu).
Graduate Coordinator: Judith A. Hall, Ph.D., 617-373-3790.
Neuropsychology/psychobiology; sensation/perception; language/cognition; social/personality.

Sociology. Luis M. Falcón, Ph.D., Cornell (gradsoc@neu.edu; www.casdn.neu.edu/~socant/).
Graduate Coordinator: Maureen Kelleher, Ph.D., 617-373-2686.
Economic sociology, political economy, social policy and applied sociology, work professions and occupations, gender studies, violence and social conflict, Brudnick Center for the Study of Conflict and Violence, graduate certificate in women's studies.

NORTHERN ILLINOIS UNIVERSITY

Graduate School

Programs of Study

The University offers the Ph.D. in biological sciences, chemistry, economics, English, geology, history, mathematical sciences, physics, political science, and psychology. The Ed.D. is offered in adult continuing education, counseling, curriculum and instruction (curriculum leadership, elementary education, reading, and secondary education), educational administration, educational psychology, and instructional technology. Students may pursue the Educational Specialist degree in educational administration. There is a post-master's program leading to the Performer's Certificate in music. Also offered are the Master of Accounting Science, Master of Arts, Master of Business Administration, Master of Fine Arts, Master of Music, Master of Physical Therapy, Master of Public Administration, Master of Public Health (including health promotion and health services management), Master of Science, Master of Science in Education, and Master of Science in Taxation. These master's degrees are available in accountancy; adult continuing education; anthropology; applied family and child studies (marriage and family therapy); applied probability and statistics; art (art education, art history, and studio art); biological sciences (including human anatomical sciences and bioinformatics); business administration; chemistry; communication studies; communicative disorders (audiology, rehabilitation counseling, and speech-language pathology); computer science; counseling; curriculum and instruction (curriculum leadership, outdoor teacher education, and secondary education); early childhood education; economics; educational administration; educational research and evaluation; educational psychology; electrical engineering; elementary education; English; foreign languages (French and Spanish); foundations of education; geography; geology; history; industrial engineering; industrial management; instructional technology; management information systems; mathematical sciences (applied, computational, and pure mathematics and mathematics education); mechanical engineering; music; nursing; nutrition and dietetics; philosophy; physical education (adapted physical education and exercise physiology/fitness leadership); physical therapy; physics (applied physics, basic physics, and physics teaching); political science; psychology; public administration (comparative and developmental, fiscal, human services administration, public management and leadership, and urban management); public health; reading; school business management; sociology (including criminology); special education (behavior disorders; blind rehabilitation; early childhood special education; learning disabilities; multiply handicapped, deaf or blind; orientation and mobility; and visual impairments); sport management; taxation; and theater arts (acting and design and technology). Interdisciplinary concentrations and numerous certificates of graduate study are available.

Research Facilities

The libraries contain more than 1.7 million volumes, 18,000 current periodical titles, 2.9 million microform units, more than 228,000 maps, and more than 1.2 million government publications and are a member of the Center for Research Libraries and the Illinet Online (IO) System. A campuswide, fiber-optic, multi-gigabit data network (NIUnet) supports more than 8,000 PCs, workstations, and servers that provide access to electronic mail, the Internet, library services, and instructional and research resources for students, staff members, and faculty members. Student computer laboratories provide access to office productivity, electronic mail, Web browser, and instructional software as well as printers and scanners. Remote dial-in access to the Internet is provided by a 472-line modem pool supporting 56-kpbs and ISDN 128-kpbs connections. Specialized resources also exist in the Social Science Research Institute, Center for Biochemical and Biophysical Studies, Plant Molecular Biology Center, Center for Southeast Asian Studies, Northern Illinois Center for Accelerator and Detector Development, Center for Burma Studies, and the Center for Governmental Studies. Opportunities for research are available at the nearby Fermi National Accelerator Laboratory, Argonne National Laboratory, and the Field Museum of Natural History.

Financial Aid

Graduate assistantships for up to 20 hours per week of service pay a monthly stipend, which varies by department, and carry a tuition waiver scholarship. Graduate School fellowships, doctoral awards, and a number of other special fellowships and paid internships are offered on a competitive basis. Specific support is available to increase student diversity. A variety of loans are also available.

Cost of Study

Tuition for the 2002–03 academic year is $148 per semester hour for Illinois residents and $295 per semester hour for nonresidents (up to 12 semester hours). Fees for all on-campus graduate students are $47.40 per semester hour (up to 12 semester hours). Costs for off-campus courses vary.

Living and Housing Costs

Costs for room and board for the 2001–02 academic year varied from $2084 to $3785 per semester. Student Housing and Dining Services maintains a listing of off-campus housing vacancies at http://www.och.niu.edu.

Student Group

Total University enrollment in fall 2000 was 23,783, including 6,012 at the graduate level and 303 in the College of Law.

Location

DeKalb is located 65 miles west of Chicago's Loop and 45 miles southeast of Rockford. It has a population of about 35,000 and is the site of diverse manufacturing and agricultural operations. Courses are offered at numerous off-campus sites, including the University's facilities in Hoffman Estates, Naperville, and Rockford.

The University

The University offers postbaccalaureate programs in the Colleges of Business, Education, Engineering and Engineering Technology, Health and Human Sciences, Law, Liberal Arts and Sciences, and Visual and Performing Arts and is accredited by the Higher Learning Commission of the North Central Association of Colleges and Schools. Individual programs are accredited, as appropriate, by their respective accrediting bodies.

The University is a member of the National Association of State Universities and Land-Grant Colleges (NASULGC) and the Universities Research Association (URA) and is classified as a Doctoral/Research—Extensive institution by the Carnegie Foundation.

Applying

Application materials include an application form, official transcripts from each institution from which a postsecondary degree was earned and from each institution where graduate course work was undertaken, and letters of recommendation. Scores on the GRE General Test or on the GMAT or Miller Analogies Test may be required. Completed applications must be in the Graduate School by June 1 for fall admission, November 1 for spring, and April 1 for summer, with all supporting documents on file by August 1, January 1, and June 1, respectively. (Some programs have earlier deadlines). Students seeking financial aid must apply early. International students (except permanent residents and those currently residing in the United States) must submit applications and supporting documents by May 1 for fall admission and October 1 for spring. With some exceptions, applicants whose native language is not English must also submit recent official TOEFL scores and, to be considered for most teaching assistantships, recent official results of the TSE or of the SPEAK (administered at Northern Illinois University).

Correspondence and Information

Information on programs and financial aid may be obtained from the appropriate department chair or director of graduate studies (see reverse). Information on admission and application materials may be obtained from:

Graduate School, Adams Hall
Northern Illinois University
DeKalb, Illinois 60115-2864
Telephone: 815-753-0395
E-mail: gradsch@niu.edu
World Wide Web: http://www.niu.edu/grad

FACULTY CONTACT PERSONS

Listed below is the professor who is the chair or director of graduate studies for each department or area in which graduate studies may be pursued. Each may be contacted at the office indicated, Northern Illinois University, DeKalb, Illinois, 60115. Program information and the Graduate Catalog are also available via the Graduate School's World Wide Web site (http://www.niu.edu/grad).

Department of Accountancy: M.A.S. Program, John R. Simon; M.S.T. Program, James C. Young.
Adult Continuing Education: Contact the Department of Counseling, Adult and Health Education.
† **School of Allied Health Professions:** M.P.H. Program, William A. Oleckno; M.P.T. Program, M. J. Blaschak.
Department of Anthropology: Mark Mehrer.
School of Art: Adrian Tió.
* **Center for Biochemical and Biophysical Studies:** John L. A. Mitchell.
† **Department of Biological Sciences:** Carl N. von Ende.
Graduate Studies in Business: M.B.A. Program, Executive M.B.A. Program, Harold Wright.
Department of Chemistry and Biochemistry: Jon W. Carnahan.
Department of Communication: Jeffrey Chown.
Department of Communicative Disorders: Earl J. Seaver.
Department of Computer Science: Rodney Angotti.
† **Department of Counseling, Adult and Health Education:** Amy D. Rose.
Curricular Leadership: Contact the Department of Teaching and Learning.
Early Childhood Education: Contact the Department of Teaching and Learning.
Department of Economics: George Slotsve.
† **Department of Educational Psychology and Foundations:** Wilma R. Miranda.
Educational Research and Evaluation: Contact the Department of Educational Technology, Research and Assessment.
† **Department of Educational Technology, Research and Assessment:** Jeffrey B. Hecht.
Department of Electrical Engineering: Vincent McGinn.
Elementary Education: Contact the Department of Teaching and Learning.
† **Department of English:** David Gorman.
School of Family, Consumer, and Nutrition Sciences: Mary E. Pritchard.
Department of Finance: Richard J. Dowen.
† **Department of Foreign Languages and Literatures:** French, Susan Linden; Spanish, Mary Lee Cozad.
Foundations of Education: Contact the Department of Educational Psychology and Foundations.
Department of Geography: Fahui Wang.
† **Department of Geology and Environmental Geosciences:** James A. Walker.
† **Gerontology Program:** John F. Stolte.
* **Department of History:** Stephen Foster.
† **Department of Industrial Engineering:** Romualdas Kasuba.
Instructional Technology: Contact the Department of Educational Technology, Research and Assessment.
Department of Kinesiology and Physical Education: Lauriece L. Zittel.
Department of Leadership in Educational and Sport Organizations: Keith W. Lambrecht.
† **Department of Literacy Education:** Norman A. Stahl.
Department of Mathematical Sciences: Bernard J. Harris.
† **Department of Mechanical Engineering:** Shin-Min Song.
School of Music: C. T. Blickhan.
** **School of Nursing:** Marilyn Frank-Stromborg.
Department of Operations Management and Information Systems: Phyllis J. Zerull.
Department of Philosophy: James W. Dye.
Department of Physics: John C. Shaffer.
Department of Political Science: Dwight Y. King.
Department of Psychology: Charles E. Miller.
† **Division of Public Administration:** Vicki C. Clarke.
Reading: Contact the Department of Literacy Education.
Department of Sociology: Kay B. Forest.
* **Center for Southeast Asian Studies:** Susan D. Russell.
Special Education: Contact the Department of Teaching and Learning.
Division of Statistics: Sudhir Gupta.
† **Department of Teaching and Learning:** Antoinette Heinze.
† **Department of Technology:** Clifford R. Mirman.
School of Theatre and Dance: Alexander Gelman.
† **Women's Studies Program:** Amy Levin.

---

* *A graduate concentration is available in conjunction with a graduate degree in another academic field.*
† *A certificate of graduate study is available, with or without simultaneous pursuit of a graduate degree in another academic field; nearly forty certificates of graduate study are available.*
** *A post-master's certificate of graduate study is available.*

OAKLAND UNIVERSITY

Office of Graduate Study

Programs of Study

Oakland University (OU) offers seventy graduate degree and certificate programs at the master's, doctoral, and specialist levels. Doctoral degrees may be earned in applied mathematical sciences; biomedical science, with a specialization in health and environmental chemistry or medical physics; reading; physical therapy; and systems engineering. The Education Specialist degree is available in school administration. Master's degrees are offered in accounting; applied statistics; biology; business administration; executive M.B.A.; chemistry; computer science and engineering; counseling; curriculum, instruction and leadership; early childhood education; electrical and computer engineering; embedded systems; engineering management; English; exercise science; history; industrial applied mathematics; information systems engineering; information technology management; liberal studies; linguistics; mathematics; mechanical engineering; music; nursing; physical therapy; physics; public administration; reading and language arts; software engineering; special education; systems engineering; and training and development. In addition, graduate certificate programs are offered in administrator certification (education), business administration, clinical exercise science, complementary medicine and wellness, corporate and worksite wellness, exercise science, microcomputer applications, orthopedic manual physical therapy, pediatric rehabilitation, and statistical methods. Post-master's specializations are available in counseling and nurse practitioner studies. Oakland University also offers planned programs for teacher certification and endorsements. Graduate programs are linked closely to OU's research, scholarship, and public service activities. Students are assumed to be partners in the implementation of programs. In the process, they are educated in the methods of intellectual inquiry and critical analysis and trained in the skills needed for their chosen fields. Through this partnership, the goals and purposes of graduate education are fulfilled.

Research Facilities

Most University library materials and services are housed in Kresge Library. The library's automated catalog allows patrons to identify resources held not only in the Kresge Library but also in the collections of Wayne State University, the University of Detroit Mercy, Detroit Public Library, and numerous other libraries in the area. The Office of Computer and Information Services provides services to support the instructional, research, administrative, and public service activities of Oakland University. Departments have special discipline-specific facilities to support the research activities of their students and faculty members. These include the Public Affairs Research Laboratory, Meadow Brook Health Enhancement Institute, Cumulative Trauma Research Institute, Institute for Biochemistry and Biotechnology, Eye Research Institute, Center for Robotics and Advanced Automation, and Michigan Center for Automotive Research. Research dollars have increased every year for the past six years to the current level of $6.2 million.

Financial Aid

In order to assist eligible graduate students in financing their education, the University participates in the following programs: King/Chavez/Parks Fellowships, a limited number of which are available for qualified members of minority groups; the Federal Perkins Loan program; the Federal Work-Study Program; and the William Ford Federal Direct Loan Program. Graduate assistants are appointed by departments offering graduate degree programs. Stipends vary by discipline.

Cost of Study

The University operates on the semester system. For 2001–02, the tuition for in-state graduate students was $246 per credit, and the tuition for out-of-state graduate students was $508. Full-time graduate students normally carry 8 credits per semester.

Living and Housing Costs

The 2001–02 rate for room and board was $4978 for the academic year. Facilities with a selected number of single rooms are available to graduate students. For students with families, a limited number of two-bedroom town houses are available. The 2001–02 rent was $596 per month plus utilities.

Student Group

Total enrollment for fall 2001 was 15,875. Twenty-one percent of the total enrollment are graduate students. Within the graduate enrollment, 65 percent are women and 9.4 percent are members of ethnic minority groups. The diverse student body includes international students representing many different countries.

Location

Oakland University is located 25 miles north of Detroit in suburban Oakland county. OU is situated on 1,500 rolling acres near parks, recreational areas, and a large concentration of high-technology industries. Many Fortune 500 companies are located in proximity to campus, which facilitates student research and internship opportunities.

The University

Oakland University, founded in 1957, is a comprehensive state-supported institution of higher education. The University is organized into the College of Arts and Sciences and the Schools of Business Administration, Education and Human Services, Engineering and Computer Science, Health Sciences, and Nursing.

Applying

Application for admission and supporting documents must be submitted to the Office of Graduate Study in time to meet appropriate program deadlines for each semester. All application materials and deadline information may be obtained from the Office of Graduate Study. International applicants should submit both a University application and an international student application at least one year before the date they wish to enter the University.

Correspondence and Information

Office of Graduate Study
Oakland University
Rochester, Michigan 48309-4401

Telephone: 248-370-3167
Fax: 248-370-4114
E-mail: gradmail@oakland.edu
World Wide Web: http://www.oakland.edu/grad

FACULTY/PROGRAM COORDINATORS

Applied Mathematical Sciences (Ph.D.): Fiki Shillor, Ph.D. (telephone: 248-370-3426)
Biology (M.S., M.A.): Keith Berven, Ph.D. (telephone: 248-370-3550)
Business Administration (M.B.A., M.Acc., M.S. in information technology management, post-master's certificates in accounting, business economics, executive M.B.A., finance, human resources management, international business, management information services, marketing, and production/operations management): Darla Null (telephone: 248-370-3287)
Chemistry (Ph.D.): Kathleen Moore, Ph.D. (telephone: 248-370-2320)
Chemistry (M.S.): Paul Tomboulian, Ph.D. (telephone: 248-370-2320)
Counseling (Ph.D. in education): Luellen Ramey, Ph.D. (telephone: 248-370-4185)
Counseling (M.A., Post-master's specializations in advanced career counseling, child and adolescent counseling, mental health counseling, marriage and family counseling, and substance abuse counseling): Luellen Ramey, Ph.D. (telephone: 248-370-4185)
Curriculum, Instruction, and Leadership (M.Ed./Administrator Certificate): Jacqueline Lougheed, Ph.D. (telephone: 248-370-3070)
Early Childhood (Ph.D. in education): Sherri Oden, Ph.D. (telephone: 248-370-3077)
Early Childhood Education (M.Ed.): Andrew Gunsberg, Ph.D. (telephone: 248-370-3077)
Early Mathematics Education (graduate certificate): Andrew Gunsberg, Ph.D. (telephone: 248-370-3077)
Educational Leadership (Ph.D. in education): William Keane, Ph.D. (telephone: 248-370-3070)
Education Specialist (Ed.Spec.): Duane Moore, Ph.D. (telephone: 248-370-3070)
Engineering (Ph.D.): Bhushan Bhatt, Ph.D. (telephone: 248-370-2233)
Engineering (M.S. in systems, M.S. in electrical and computer science, M.S. in engineering management, M.S. in software engineering): Naim Kheir, Ph.D. (telephone: 248-370-2177)
Engineering (M.S. in computer science, M.S. in embedded systems, M.S. in information systems engineering, M.S. in software engineering): Ishwar Sethi, Ph.D. (telephone: 248-370-2200)
Engineering (M.S. in mechanical engineering): Gary Barber, Acting Chair; Ph.D. (telephone: 248-370-2210)
English (M.A.): Kathy Pfeiffer, Ph.D. (telephone: 248-370-2250)
Exercise Science (graduate certificates in clinical exercise science, corporate and worksite wellness, exercise science, and complementary medicine and wellness): Brian Goslin, Ph.D. (telephone: 248-370-4038)
History (M.A.): Carl Osthaus, Ph.D. (telephone: 248-370-3510)
Linguistics (M.A.): Michael Smith, Ph.D. (telephone: 248-370-2175)
Mathematics (M.S. in applied statistics, M.S. in industrial applied mathematics, M.A. in mathematics, graduate certificate in statistical methods, Ph.D. in applied mathematical science): Fiki Shillor, Ph.D. (telephone: 248-370-3439)
Music (M.M.): Jackie Wiggins, Ph.D. (telephone: 248-370-2036)
Nursing (M.S.N., Post-master's specialization in family nurse practitioner studies): C. Vincent, Ph.D., RN. (telephone: 248-370-4484)
Physical Therapy (D.P.T., D.Sc.P.T., M.S.): Beth Marcoux, Ph.D. (telephone: 248-370-4041)
Physical Therapy (Graduate certificate in orthopedic manual physical therapy): John Krauss, M.S.P.T.; OCS; FAAOMPT. (telephone: 248-370-4041)
Physical Therapy (Graduate certificate in pediatric rehabilitation): Chris Stiller Sermo, M.A.P.T. (telephone: 248-370-4041)
Physics (Ph.D.): Norman Tepley, Ph.D. (telephone: 248-370-3416)
Physics (M.S.): Gopalan Srinivasan, Ph.D. (telephone: 248-370-3416)
Public Administration (M.P.A.): Dale Nesbary, Ph.D. (telephone: 248-370-2352)
Reading (Ph.D.): Toni Walters, Ph.D. (telephone: 248-370-3065)
Reading (M.A.T.): Robert Schwartz, Ph.D. (telephone: 248-370-3065)
Reading (Graduate certificate in microcomputer applications): Anne Porter, Ph.D. (telephone: 248-370-3065)
Special Education (M.Ed. in special education, teacher endorsements in autistic impairment, emotional impairment, and learning disability): Carol Swift, Ph.D. (telephone: 248-370-3077)
Teacher Certification: Gretchen Parks. (telephone: 248-370-4182)
Training and Development (M.T.D.): James Quinn, Ph.D. (telephone: 248-370-4109)

OKLAHOMA STATE UNIVERSITY

Graduate College

Programs of Study

Oklahoma State University (OSU) is a major comprehensive research land-grant university that has engaged in creating and disseminating knowledge through research, instruction, and public service for more than 100 years. In fulfilling its mission, Oklahoma State University continually evolves and expands its role as a leader in meeting the changing needs of the state, national, and international communities.

OSU strives to provide an educational environment that fosters cultural diversity and rich intellectual exchange between faculty members and students. OSU offers ninety-one master's and seventy-one doctoral programs of study.

Research Facilities

OSU continues to expand its graduate research on the Stillwater campus. In addition, a market for research facilities and dollars at the new Tulsa, Oklahoma, campus is rapidly growing. During a seven-year period, beginning in 1991, OSU's expenditures for research and sponsored programs increased by 37 percent.

Financial Aid

Out-of-state tuition waivers are available for graduate students. Other financial aid opportunities include teaching and research assistantships, social justice waivers, and spousal tuition waivers. Full and partial in-state tuition waivers are also available. Financial aid is based upon the number of hours for which the student is enrolled. Some restrictions apply. Fellowships, including those through the Fulbright Foundation, National Science Foundation, and National Research Council, are also available.

Cost of Study

Tuition costs for Oklahoma residents for 2001–02, excluding health and semester fees, were $112.18 per credit hour. Nonresident costs were $317.63 per credit hour, excluding health and semester fees. The health fee was $54 for students.

Living and Housing Costs

Both Stillwater and OSU offer several housing alternatives that meet all types of graduate student needs. On-campus room and board expenses for nine months (two semesters) are approximately $6180. On-campus expenses for a student who attends for twelve months (fall, spring, and summer sessions) are approximately $8159. Off-campus expenses vary.

Student Group

The main campus at Oklahoma State University has approximately 21,000 students, of whom more than 4,500 are graduate students from forty-four states and ninety-one other countries. Another 660 graduate students are enrolled through the branch campus in Tulsa. In addition, the College of Veterinary Medicine and the College of Osteopathic Medicine enroll between 250 and 300 students each. Approximately 20 percent of graduate students are from other countries, and nearly 15 percent are members of minority groups.

Location

Oklahoma State University is located in Stillwater, a north-central Oklahoma community with a population of more than 42,000. Stillwater is approximately 60 miles from the Tulsa and Oklahoma City metropolitan areas and is readily accessible from other major population centers. The OSU campus is one of exceptional beauty, with modified Georgian-style architecture. The main campus encompasses 415 acres and has 200 permanent buildings.

The University

Oklahoma State University was founded on December 25, 1890, as Oklahoma Agricultural and Mechanical College, just twenty months after the Land Run of 1889. The first students assembled for class on December 14, 1891. As a land-grant university, OSU has a special commitment to serving all people and is dedicated to providing a multicultural environment for students and faculty and staff members. Oklahoma State University has enjoyed accreditation by the North Central Association of Colleges and Secondary Schools as a degree-granting institution since 1916. In the 1998 *Student Guide to America's 100 Best College Buys*, OSU was proclaimed America's Best College Buy for 1999.

Applying

Applications for admission should be sent to the Graduate College accompanied by a $25 nonrefundable processing fee ($50 nonrefundable fee for international applicants) and official transcripts from all institutions previously attended. Individual departments may require additional documentation. All documentation should be received by the Graduate College at least thirty days prior to the departmental deadline or the semester of expected enrollment. International students must submit all documentation at least five months prior to the semester of expected enrollment. As application deadlines vary from department to department, students should contact their programs of interest for more information. Students can apply online or download an application from the Graduate College Web site.

Correspondence and Information

Graduate College
Oklahoma State University
202 Whitehurst
Stillwater, Oklahoma 74078-1019
Telephone: 405-744-6368
Fax: 405-744-0355
E-mail: grad-i@okstate.edu
World Wide Web: http://gradcollege.okstate.edu

PROGRAMS OF STUDY

Agricultural Science and Natural Resources
Agricultural Economics: M.S., Ph.D.
Agricultural Education: M.S., Ph.D.
Agriculture: M.Ag.
Animal Breeding and Reproduction: Ph.D.
Animal Nutrition: Ph.D.
Animal Science: M.S.
Biochemistry and Molecular Biology: M.S., Ph.D.
Biosystems and Agricultural Engineering: M.En., M.S., Ph.D.
Clinical Psychology: Ph.D.
Crop Science: Ph.D.
Entomology: M.S., Ph.D.
Environmental Science: M.S., Ph.D.
Experimental Psychology: Ph.D.
Food Science: M.S., Ph.D.
Forest Resources: M.S.
Horticulture: M.S.
Plant Pathology: M.S., Ph.D.
Plant Science: Ph.D.
Plant and Soil Science: M.S.
Soil Science: Ph.D.

Arts and Sciences
Botany: M.S.
Chemistry: M.S., Ph.D.
Communication Sciences and Disorders: M.S.
Computer Science: M.S., Ph.D.
English: M.A., Ph.D.
Environmental Sciences: M.S., Ph.D.
Fire and Emergency Management: M.S.
Geography: M.S., Certification in GeoSystems
Geology: M.S.
History: M.A., Ph.D.
Mass Communications: M.S.
Mathematics: M.S., Ph.D.
Microbiology, Cell, and Molecular Biology: M.S., Ph.D.
Music Pedagogy and Performance: M.M.
Philosophy: M.A.
Physics: M.S., Ph.D.
Plant Science: Ph.D.
Political Science: M.A.
Psychology: M.S., Ph.D.
Sociology: M.S., Ph.D.
Statistics: M.S., Ph.D.
Technical Writing: M.A., Ph.D.
Theater: M.A.
Wildlife and Fisheries Ecology: M.S., Ph.D.
Zoology: M.S., Ph.D.

Business
Accounting: M.S., Ph.D.
Accounting Information Systems/Management Information Systems: M.S.
Business Administration: M.B.A., Ph.D.
Business Administration–Accounting: Ph.D.
Business Administration–Finance: Ph.D.
Business Administration–Management: Ph.D.
Business Administration–Marketing: Ph.D.
Economics: M.S., Ph.D.
Quantitative Financial Economics: M.S.
Telecommunications Management: M.S.

Education
Adult and Continuing Education: M.S., Ed.D.
Applied Behavioral Studies: M.S., Ed.D.
Applied Educational Studies: Ph.D.
Applied Exercise Science: M.S.
Aviation and Space Education: M.S., Ed.D.
College Interdisciplinary: Ed.D.
Community Counseling: M.S.
Counseling Psychology: Ph.D.
Counseling and Student Personnel: M.S.
Curriculum and Leadership Studies: M.S.
Curriculum and Social Foundations: Ph.D.
Educational Administration: Ed.S., Ed.D.
Educational Leadership Studies: M.S.
Educational Psychology: M.S., Ph.D.
Elem/Middle/Secondary Ed/K–12 Ed: M.S.
Elementary School Counseling: M.S.
Gifted and Talented: M.S.
Health and Human Performance: Ph.D.
Health Promotions: M.S.
Higher Education: M.S., Ed.D.
Human Resource Development: M.S., Ed.D.
Leisure: Ph.D.
Leisure Services Management: M.S.
Leisure Studies: M.S.
Occupational and Adult Education: M.S., Ed.D.
Occupational Education Studies: M.S., Ph.D.
Occupational/Vocational Education: Ed.D.
Physical Education: M.S.
Professional Education Studies: Ph.D.
Reading and Literacy: M.S.
Research and Evaluation: M.S., Ph.D.
School Administration: M.S.
School Psychology: M.S., Ed.S., Ph.D.
Secondary School Counseling: M.S.
Special Education: M.S., Ph.D.
Student Personnel Administration: Ph.D.
Student Personnel Service: M.S
Teaching, Learning, and Leadership: M.S..
Therapeutic Recreation: M.S.

Engineering, Architecture, and Technology
Architectural Engineering: M.Arch.Eng.
Architecture: M.Ar.
Biosystems and Agricultutal Engineering: M.En., M.S., Ph.D.
Chemical Engineering: M.En., M.S., Ph.D.
Civil Engineering: M.En., M.S., Ph.D.
Control Systems Engineering: M.S.
Electrical Engineering: M.En., M.S., Ph.D.
Engineering and Technology Management: M.S.
Environmental Engineering: M.En., M.S.
General Engineering: M.En.
Industrial Engineering and Management: M.S.
Manufacturing Systems Engineering: M.En.
Mechanical Engineering: M.En., M.S., Ph.D.

Human Environmental Sciences
Design, Housing, and Merchandising: M.S., Ph.D.
Family Financial Planning: M.S.
Family Relations and Child Development: M.S., Ph.D.
Hospitality Administration: M.S., Ph.D.
Human Environmental Sciences: M.S., Ph.D.
Nonprofit Services Administration: M.S.
Nutrition: M.S.
Nutritional Sciences: M.S., Ph.D.

Interdisciplinary
Gerontology: M.S.
Health Care Administration: M.S.
Photonics: M.S., Ph.D.

International Studies
International Studies: M.S.

Osteopathic Medicine
Biomedical Sciences: M.S., Ph.D.
Forensic Sciences: M.S., M.F.S.

Veterinary Physiological Sciences
Veterinary Biomedical Sciences: M.S., Ph.D.

OLD DOMINION UNIVERSITY

College of Arts and Letters Graduate Programs

Programs of Study

The College of Arts and Letters offers the Master of Arts (M.A.) in applied linguistics, applied sociology, English, history, humanities, international studies, and visual studies; the Master of Fine Arts (M.F.A.) in creative writing and visual studies; and the Doctor of Philosophy (Ph.D.) in international studies.

Research Facilities

Research centers and institutes include the Center for Regional and Global Study, the Social Science Research Center, and the Laboratory for Remote Sensing and Environmental Analysis. Research and creative work are also supported by the University's computer and multimedia laboratory and superior campus facilities. The University library provides a full complement of state-of-the-art services for all clientele. The library contains more than 2 million items, including monographs, government publications, periodicals and serials, microfilms, electronic resources, and maps that are currently accessible through the online public access catalog. Electronic services such as Internet access to indexes, abstracts, full-text journals, government publications, and statistics are among research services offered by the Reference and Research Services Department. Interlibrary loan services are available to faculty members and students from the Interlibrary Loan Office.

Financial Aid

Financial aid is available in the form of fellowships, research and teaching assistantships, and scholarships. The stipend generally ranged between $8000 and $11,000 for the 2000–01 academic year. In addition, full tuition scholarships are available in some programs. Low-interest, deferred-repayment graduate loans are also available to U.S. citizens who can demonstrate need.

Cost of Study

In-state tuition for 2001–02 was $202 per credit hour. Out-of-state tuition was $534 per credit hour. Other fees amounted to approximately $76 per semester.

Living and Housing Costs

The cost of a room for a single student in the residence halls ranged from $3340 to $5498 for the 2001–02 academic year. All residences are furnished, with local telephone service and utilities included. Other non-University housing options are available near the campus.

Student Group

The College of Arts and Letters conferred 92 graduate degrees during the 2000–01 academic year. Overall, Old Dominion University has approximately 19,000 students, one third of whom are graduate students, representing all fifty states and more than 100 countries.

Location

Old Dominion University is located in Norfolk, Virginia, one of seven major cities that make up Hampton Roads, an area with a population of 1.4 million. The campus is approximately 200 miles south of Washington, D.C.; within minutes of the world's largest naval base, the largest East Coast seaport, and the oceanfront; and only 30 minutes from the surf and sand of Virginia Beach. Since the early seventeenth century, the Hampton Roads area has been one of the world's major seaports, a hub of commerce and industry, and an area rich in military history.

The University

Founded in 1930 as the Norfolk division of the College of William and Mary, the University gained full independence as a state-supported college in 1962, taking on the name Old Dominion College. Its rapid expansion caused the governing board to change its name to Old Dominion University. Today, the institution is a powerhouse for higher education with its six colleges: the College of Arts and Letters, the College of Business and Public Administration, Darden College of Education, the College of Engineering and Technology, the College of Health Sciences, and the College of Sciences. Graduate students at Old Dominion currently choose from sixty-six master's degree programs, two certificates of advanced study, and twenty-two doctoral programs.

Applying

Applications and supporting credentials should be submitted well in advance of the preferred semester of entry to allow sufficient time for departmental review and processing. The application fee is $30. Prospective students should contact their respective departments of interest for requirements. Since the first departmental awards are made in February and March for the next full academic year, applicants requesting aid are encouraged to submit all required credentials by February 15 to ensure full consideration.

Correspondence and Information

For applications and admissions information:
Office of Admissions
108 Alfred B. Rollins Jr. Hall
Old Dominion University
Norfolk, Virginia 23529
Telephone: 757-683-4845
800-348-7926 (toll-free)
World Wide Web: http://www.odu.edu/~admissions

For program information:
Dean's Office, BAL 900
College of Arts and Letters
Old Dominion University
Norfolk, Virginia 23529-0076
Telephone: 757-683-3925
Fax: 757-683-5746
World Wide Web: http://www.odu.edu/al/do/

GRADUATE DEGREE PROGRAMS AND PROGRAM DIRECTORS

Applied Linguistics (M.A.): Janet M. Bing, Director. Telephone: 757-683-4030; fax: 757-683-3241; e-mail: linggpd@odu.edu.
The M.A. in applied linguistics has two emphases. The TESOL emphasis is for teachers of English as a second language either in the U.S. or abroad. The language variation emphasis is primarily for those who wish to pursue a Ph.D. in linguistics or cognitive science.

Applied Sociology (M.A.): Randy Gainey, Director. Telephone: 757-683-3791; fax: 757-683-5634; e-mail: socgpd@odu.edu.
The M.A. degree, offered jointly by Old Dominion University and Norfolk State University, serves as professional training for students who are seeking employment in federal, state, and local government agencies or in private-sector organizations. In addition, the M.A. program provides excellent academic training in the fundamentals of sociology for students who wish to pursue a Ph.D. in the social sciences. The program provides students with training in theory and methods as well as opportunities to participate in three areas of specialization: general sociology, criminal justice, and women's studies.

Creative Writing (M.F.A.): Michael Pearson, Director. Telephone: 757-683-4770; fax: 757-683-3241; e-mail: cwgpd@odu.edu.
The M.F.A. program is part of the English Department at Old Dominion University. In addition to taking workshops and craft courses with the M.F.A. faculty, students take courses with a dynamic faculty who have expertise in American, British, and world literature as well as literary theory, film studies, and rhetoric.

English (M.A.): Edward Jacobs, Director. Telephone: 757-683-3991; fax: 757-683-3241; e-mail: englgpd@odu.edu.
The M.A. program in English develops professional competency in literary analysis and interpretation and in writing. The program prepares students for further graduate study in English; for professional writing and editing; for teaching in secondary schools and colleges; for further study in such fields as anthropology, law, psychology, and philosophy; for careers in government and industry; and for professions involving analytical, literary, linguistic, or writing skills.

History (M.A.): Carolyn Lawes, Interim Director. Telephone: 757-683-3949; fax: 757-683-5644; e-mail: histgpd@odu.edu.
The Department of History offers courses of study leading to the M.A. degree with a major in history. Academic areas of interest include African-American, American, Asian, Civil War/Southern, classical, Colonial America, early modern world, intellectual and cultural, international relations/diplomatic, Latin American, medieval, military, modern European, Russian/Slavic, Virginia and local, and women's history.

Humanities (M.A.): Dana A. Heller, Director. Telephone: 757-683-3821; fax: 757-683-6191; e-mail: humgpd@odu.edu.
The multidisciplinary and interdisciplinary program allows students to pursue individualized programs of study through approved graduate courses from at least three of the following fields: art history, economics, English, foreign languages, history, music, philosophy, political science and geography, sociology and anthropology, communication and theater arts, and women's studies.

International Studies (M.A., Ph.D.): Kurt Taylor Gaubatz, Director. Telephone: 757-683-5700; fax: 757-683-5701; e-mail: isgpd@odu.edu.
The program provides a wide range of courses in history, international business, political science, international economics, political economy, sociology, and geography, as well as courses with a regional focus on Europe, China, Russia, the Middle East, and Latin America, leading to an M.A. or Ph.D. degree in international studies. Fields of concentration include international relations/American foreign policy, conflict and cooperation, political economy and development, and transnational issues.

Visual Studies (M.A., M.F.A.): Elliott C. Jones, Director. Telephone: 757-683-4047; fax: 757-683-5923; e-mail: artgpd@odu.edu.
The M.A./M.F.A. program in visual studies, offered jointly by Old Dominion University and Norfolk State University, offers concentrated individual programs utilizing the resources of both universities.

PACE UNIVERSITY

Graduate Programs

Programs of Study

Pace University offers a broad range of graduate degree and certificate programs through its six colleges and schools. All programs are fully described in the appropriate books of the *Peterson's* series. The Lubin School of Business offers M.S. degree programs with concentrations in accounting, accounting information systems, business economics, investment management, management science, operations planning and analysis, personal financial planning, and taxation. The M.B.A. degree is offered with concentrations in accounting, business economics, e-business, financial management, information systems, international business, management, marketing, operations planning and analysis, and taxation. The e.MBA@PACE program is a Web-based, online executive M.B.A. program that combines online learning with brief residencies. Also offered is the D.P.S. degree in business, as well as certificate programs. The Dyson College of Arts and Sciences offers M.S. degree programs in publishing, environmental science, forensic science, and counseling. The M.P.A. degree is offered with concentrations in management of government, health care, or nonprofit organizations. Certificate programs are offered in nonprofit management, health-care policy management, and long-term care management and practice. In conjunction with the School of Law and the Lubin School of Business, joint M.P.A./J.D. and M.P.A./M.B.A. degree programs are offered. In addition, four psychology programs are offered through Dyson: the Psy.D. in school-clinical child psychology, the M.S.Ed. in school psychology and bilingual school psychology, and the M.A. in psychology. The School of Computer Science and Information Systems offers M.S. degree programs in computer science, information systems, Internet technology for e-commerce, and telecommunications. Also offered is the D.P.S. in computing, as well as certificate programs in object-oriented programming, information systems, Internet technology, telecommunications, computer communications and networks, and computing for teachers. The School of Education offers graduate programs resulting in the M.S.T. and the M.S.Ed. with specializations in educational administration and supervision, educational technology, literacy, special education, and early childhood education. Advanced graduate certificate programs are available with concentrations in early childhood administration, middle/secondary school teaching, school business management, and educational administration. The Lienhard School of Nursing offers the M.S. in nursing, offering majors in family nurse practitioner, psychiatric nurse practitioner, women's health-care nurse practitioner, collaborative nursing informatics, and case management. The combined degree B.S.N./M.S. program allows graduates with baccalaureate degree in areas outside of nursing to complete both a second bachelor's and a master's degree in nursing. Advanced graduate certificate programs are available with concentrations in family nurse practitioner, psychiatric nurse practitioner, nursing informatics, and case management. The School of Law offers three-year (full-time) or four-year (part-time) J.D. degree programs. Certificate programs are available in the areas of health law, environmental law, and international law. Also offered is an advanced LL.M. degree in environmental law, an S.J.D. degree program, and combined J.D./M.B.A. and J.D./M.P.A. programs in conjunction with the Lubin School of Business and Dyson College of Arts and Science, respectively.

Research Facilities

The Pace University Library is a comprehensive teaching library and student-learning center. The library embodies the attributes of the "virtual library", combining the development of strong core collections with access and connectivity to global Internet resources in support of the University's broad and diversified curricula. Pace offers instructional services librarians, sophisticated computing technologies, a state-of-the-art electronic classroom, major information literacy initiatives, digital reference services, and multimedia applications. Pace's computer laboratories are linked to its high-speed data network and feature sophisticated hardware, utilizing the network and the Internet to facilitate learning. Pace has been recognized by *Yahoo! Internet Life* survey for the past two years as one of America's "Most Wired" Universities. Pace supports high-speed Internet/Internet2 access on every campus. There are almost 600 student accessible PCs with the latest hardware/software enhancements available. Pace provides e-mail, Web space, and file storage space for its student body. Many rooms are connected with real-time video for interactive distance classes.

Financial Aid

Pace University strives to provide opportunities to students of diverse backgrounds and circumstances. The University is committed to offering financial aid to students to the fullest extent of its resources. Pace's comprehensive student financial aid assistance program includes scholarship, graduate assistantships, student loans (federal and alternative plans), and tuition payment plans. Scholarships are awarded to students in recognition of superior academic achievement and are available for full- and part-time study. Highly qualified students may be eligible for assistantships awarded by departments, which paid stipends up to $5100 and tuition remission up to 24 credits during the 2001–02 academic year. Pace participates in all major federal and state financial aid programs such as Direct Loans, New York State Tuition Assistance Program (TAP), Perkins Loans, and Federal Work-Study. All students are encouraged to apply for these programs by filing the Free Application for Federal Student Aid (FAFSA). For further information, applicants should contact the Financial Aid Office.

Cost of Study

Graduate tuition varies by school. Tuition is charged per credit. For the 2001–02 academic year, tuition charges were: Dyson College of Arts and Sciences, $545 or $595 per credit depending on program; Lubin School of Business, $625; School of Computer Science and Information Systems, $625; School of Education, $545; Lienhard School of Nursing, $545. The School of Law charges $12,647 per semester for full-time study and $9498 per semester for part-time study.

Living and Housing Costs

Residence facilities are available in both New York City and Westchester. Double occupancy rooms cost $5070 for the 2001–02 academic year. University operated, off-campus housing is available in proximity of the New York City campus. A wide variety of rooms and apartments are also available for students in the New York City and Westchester County areas.

Student Group

Highly motivated, Pace students represent diversified personal, cultural, and educational backgrounds. Many students are employed and pursue graduate study for personal growth and career advancement opportunities and nearly 75 percent are enrolled part-time in evening classes. Current graduate and law school enrollment is nearly 4,600.

Location

Pace University is a multicampus institution with campuses in New York City and Westchester County. All locations are accessible by public transportation and within reach of cultural, business, and social resources and opportunities. The downtown Manhattan campus is near the financial district and City Hall. Pace's Midtown Center on Fifth Avenue is within a short distance of Times Square, the theater district, art museums, and Grand Central Station. The Pleasantville/Briarcliff campus in Westchester County is a suburban setting, surrounded by towns and villages offering various forms of recreation. The Graduate Center and the School of Law are located in White Plains among retail districts and corporate headquarters.

The University

Founded in 1906, Pace University is a private, nonsectarian, coeducational institution. Originally founded as a school of accounting, Pace Institute was designated Pace College in 1973. Through growth and various successes, it was renamed Pace University as approved by the New York State Board of Regents. Today, Pace offers comprehensive undergraduate, graduate, doctoral, and professional-level programs at several campus locations through six schools and colleges.

Applying

Admission to the graduate programs varies by school, program, and degree. Not all programs are available on all campuses. Applications may be submitted throughout the year, but should be submitted by August 1, December 1, and May 1 for the fall, spring, and summer semesters (one month earlier for international applications), respectively. Exceptions are the Psy.D. in school-clinical psychology and the M.S.Ed. in school psychology and bilingual school psychology (February 1, fall), the B.S.N./M.S. combined-degree program in nursing (March 1, summer), and the D.P.S. (July 1, fall; November 1, spring).

Correspondence and Information

Office of Graduate Admission
Pace University
1 Pace Plaza
New York, New York 10038
Telephone: 212-346-1531
Fax: 212-346-1585
E-mail: gradnyc@pace.edu
WWW: http://www.pace.edu

Office of Graduate Admission
Pace University
1 Martine Avenue
White Plains, New York 10606
Telephone: 914-422-4283
Fax: 914-422-4287
E-mail: gradwp@pace.edu
WWW: http://www.pace.edu

Office of Law School Admission
Pace University
78 North Broadway
White Plains, New York 10603
Telephone: 914-422-4210
Fax: 914-422-4010
E-mail: admissions@law.pace.edu
WWW: http://www.law.pace.edu

DEANS AND PROGRAM HEADS

Dyson College of Arts and Science

Gail Dinter-Gottleib, Dean; Ph.D., Weizmann (Israel).
Barbara Mowder, Director, Graduate Psychology Programs; Ph.D., Indiana.
Ross Robak, Coordinator, M.S. in Counseling Program; Ph.D., Hofstra.
Joseph Thomas, Interim Chair, Master of Public Administration Program.
Sherman Raskin, Chair, Department of English (New York City), and Director, M.S. in Publishing Program; M.A., Columbia.
Ellen Weiser, Director, M.S. in Environmental Science Program; Ph.D., CUNY.

Lubin School of Business

Arthur Centonze, Dean; Ph.D., NYU.
Peter Hoefer, Associate Dean and Director of Graduate Programs; Ph.D., CUNY Graduate Center.

School of Computer Science and Information Systems

Susan Merritt, Dean; Ph.D., NYU.

School of Education

Janet McDonald, Dean; Ph.D., SUNY at Albany.

Lienhard School of Nursing

Harriet Feldman, Dean; Ph.D., NYU.

School of Law

David S. Cohen, Dean; LL.B., Toronto.

PACIFIC LUTHERAN UNIVERSITY

Graduate Studies

Programs of Study

The University offers master's-level graduate degrees in four fields: business (M.B.A.), education (M.A.), nursing (M.S.N.), and social sciences (M.A.). Areas of specialization in education include classroom teaching, educational administration, initial certification, literacy education, and special education. The social sciences master's program offers a concentration in the area of marriage and family therapy. In nursing, concentrations include care and outcomes manager and nurse practitioner studies. The M.B.A. program offers a concentration in technology and innovative management.

Specific objectives for the University's graduate programs include increasing the breadth and depth of understanding of graduate students in their chosen disciplines, increasing students' knowledge of ongoing research in their fields of study, immersing students in research processes, developing students' abilities to do independent study and research, and preparing students to enter professional vocations or pursue advanced study leading to doctoral degrees.

The University offers a 4-1-4 calendar that consists of two 14-week semesters bridged by a 4-week January term. A minimum of 32 semester hours is required for each program. Individual programs may require more, depending upon prior preparation and specific degree requirements. Students must complete at least 24 of the required semester hours at PLU. Full-time students may complete most graduate programs in two years; however, some programs are designed to be completed in as little as fourteen months. Graduate students at PLU enjoy small classes and a high level of individual attention from the faculty.

Research Facilities

The Robert A. L. Mortvedt Library is the central multimedia learning resource center serving the entire University community. It contains more than 500,000 books and periodicals, microfilms, and audiovisual materials and receives more than 2,000 current magazines, journals, and newspapers. Computer access to other large libraries in the area combined with e-mail service allows students and faculty rapid access to many other sources for research. A large computer lab, located in the University Center, provides IBM PCs, Macintosh computers, and access to the University's DEC Alpha 3400 computer.

Financial Aid

Financial assistance for graduate students is available in the form of Federal Perkins and Federal Stafford Student Loans, graduate assistantships, and scholarships. In addition, students may be eligible for a PLUS loan to a maximum of $3000. A limited number of graduate assistantships are awarded to full-time students in amounts up to $5000 per year.

Cost of Study

Graduate tuition is charged at the rate of $578 per semester credit hour in 2002–03. Some programs have special rates.

Living and Housing Costs

The University has a selection of residence halls that provide comfortable living arrangements. Although these are primarily undergraduate residences, one hall is designed to accommodate graduate students, and any full-time student is welcome to apply for housing. Application may be made through the Residential Life Office. In the surrounding area there are numerous housing options available for off-campus living.

Student Group

The graduate student population for all programs totals approximately 250. Full-time students comprise about one half of the graduate population. Students come from throughout the United States and from several other countries.

Student Outcomes

More than 96 percent of recent M.B.A. graduates are employed and work in such diverse industries as manufacturing, aerospace, financial services, health care, accounting, and forest products. Graduates with the M.A. in education have accepted instructional and educational administrative positions across the state and region. Several graduates have been named Washington State Teacher of the Year. Graduates with the M.A. in social sciences (marriage and family therapy concentration) are employed, on average, one month after graduation as licensed/certified marriage and family therapists in mental health centers, social service organizations, group practices, and educational institutions. All students in the M.S.N. program who complete the care and outcomes management concentration have consistently been employed as managed-care coordinators and case managers. Graduates who complete the nurse practitioner studies concentration have been offered positions in ambulatory care settings.

Location

Pacific Lutheran University is located on a 126-acre campus immediately adjacent to the city of Tacoma (population 162,100). The campus is 40 miles south of Seattle and 20 miles south of Seattle-Tacoma International Airport. Located in the midst of the Puget Sound region, the campus is within a short drive of a wide variety of natural attractions including Mt. Rainier, the Olympic and Cascade mountain ranges, and numerous bodies of both salt and fresh water.

The University

Pacific Lutheran University is an independent, coeducational university affiliated with the Evangelical Lutheran Church in America. Total University enrollment is approximately 3,400. The faculty numbers approximately 260 and includes outstanding scholars with national and international reputations. The University academic structure consists of five professional schools (arts, business, education, nursing, and physical education) and a College of Arts and Sciences with three divisions (humanities, social sciences, and natural sciences). The University has superb academic and athletic facilities.

Applying

Further information and applications for graduate admission may be obtained from the Office of Admissions. All application evaluations are based on scholastic qualifications, letters of recommendation, a statement of goals, and preparation in the proposed field of study. Certain programs require scores on standardized examinations and personal interviews. Applications for admission to most programs are acted upon throughout the year. However, all application documents should be received six weeks prior to the semester in which enrollment is sought.

Correspondence and Information

Office of Admissions
Pacific Lutheran University
Tacoma, Washington 98447

Telephone: 253-535-7151
800-274-6758 (toll-free)
Fax: 253-535-5136
E-mail: admissions@plu.edu
World Wide Web: http://www.plu.edu

PROGRAM ADMINISTRATION

Loren J. Anderson, President.
James Pence, Provost and Dean of Graduate Studies.

Graduate Studies
James Pence, Provost and Dean of Graduate Studies.

Division of Social Sciences (M.A.)
Charles York, Chair of Marriage and Family Therapy.

School of Business (M.B.A.)
Catherine Pratt, Director of Graduate Programs.

School of Education (M.A.)
Doug Lamoreaux, Director of Graduate Programs.

School of Nursing (M.S.N.)
Emily Mize, Graduate Admissions Coordinator.

PENNSYLVANIA STATE UNIVERSITY HARRISBURG CAMPUS OF THE CAPITAL COLLEGE

Graduate Programs

Programs of Study

Pennsylvania State University Harrisburg Campus of the Capital College (Penn State Harrisburg) offers the Master of Arts (M.A.) in American studies, which explores American civilization through history, philosophy, folklore, and the arts; their relationships to economic, political, and social institutions; the M.A. in humanities, and interdisciplinary program; the Master of Business Administration (M.B.A.), a professionally oriented program for those seeking or holding management positions in business, engineering, scientific, technical, or health-care organizations; the Master of Education (M.Ed.), with a major in teaching and curriculum, designed for professional educators; the M.Ed., with a major in training and development, focusing on the special skills needed by training and development professionals in business, industry, health care, government, and human services; the M.Ed., with a major in health education, providing a broad background in health areas, the skills required to assess and deal with health educational needs, the theoretical basis for understanding health education research, and the knowledge to design, implement, and evaluate health education programs; the Master of Engineering (M.Eng.), with a major in engineering science, providing broad education in advanced aspects of engineering sciences and the opportunity for specialization; the M.Eng., with a major in environmental pollution control, offers an opportunity for engineers to specialize in various aspects of pollution control; the Master of Environmental Pollution Control (M.E.P.C.) or Master of Science (M.S.) in environmental pollution control focuses on aspects of air and water pollution control and solid-waste disposal; the Master of Arts in community psychology and social change, which emphasizes the use of psychology and sociology to meet social needs in the community; the Master of Public Administration (M.P.A.), for those in or seeking professional careers in government, health-care, human service, or public service organizations; the Ph.D. in public administration combining the traditions of the doctoral degree with flexible class schedules for part-time students and scholar/practitioners; the Doctor of Education (D.Ed.) in adult education, a program in which adult education is merged with such areas as counseling and the behavioral sciences, business and organizational development, science and engineering, public affairs, the humanities, and health education; the M.A. in applied clinical psychology, which prepares students to work as mental health professionals in a variety of settings and provides the academic training necessary for graduates to apply for master's-level licensing as mental-health professionals in the Commonwealth of Pennsylvania; the M.A. in applied behavior analysis, which is designed to teach graduate-level students to become proficient in the clinical practice of applied behavior analysis and to meet certification standards set by the Association for Behavior Analysis and the Behavior Analyst Certification Board (BACB); the M.S. in applied psychological research, which focuses on the development of research skills within the context of scientific training in psychology; the Master of Science in Information Systems (M.S.I.S.), offered within the School of Business for technically grounded, upper-level information resource managers with business organizations; the M.Eng. in electrical engineering, with concentrations in electronic communications systems, control systems, VLSI and computer engineering, and power systems; the Master of Health Administration (M.H.A.), for careers in a variety of health-care organizations; the Master of Science (M.S.) in computer science, for practical and theoretical applications; and the M.A. in community psychology and social change offering areas of study in children, youth, and family studies; environmental issues; and individual studies. Penn State Harrisburg and the Dickinson School of Law of the Pennsylvania State University offer cooperative, concurrent programs leading to J.D./M.B.A., J.D./M.P.A., J.D./E.P.C., and J.D./M.S.I.S. degrees, as well as a program with the Penn State College of Medicine at Hershey leading to the Ph.D. degree in pharmacology and an M.B.A.

Research Facilities

The new campus Library contains more than 263,000 volumes (growing by 6,000 a year) and subscribes to 1,567 periodicals. Microform holdings total 1 million units, including complete sets of ERIC, HRAF, Envirofiche, and Library of American Civilization. The resources of other libraries of the University are available through LIAS, an online integrated library system of the University Libraries. Students also have access to the resources of the Associated College Libraries of Central Pennsylvania, a consortium of area college libraries. The Computer Center provides support for instruction and research. Facilities include a nineteen-terminal microcomputer lab, a thirty-terminal microcomputer LAN, and a forty-terminal microcomputer LAN that accesses the library's online database search system and an IBM mainframe processing system located at University Park. Programming support is available through the center's staff. Penn State Harrisburg is also home to the Pennsylvania State Data Center.

Financial Aid

Internships, fellowships, graduate assistantships, graduate work-study awards, grants-in-aid programs, Guaranteed Student Loans, and a minority graduate student assistantship is available.

Cost of Study

In 2001–02, resident tuition was $3941 per semester for full-time study (12 or more credits) and $333 per credit for part-time study (1 to 11 credits). Pennsylvania nonresident full-time tuition was $7192 per semester, and part-time tuition was $600 per credit. Pennsylvania resident M.B.A. part-time tuition was $386 per credit. Pennsylvania nonresident M.B.A. part-time tuition was $733 per credit.

Living and Housing Costs

Ninety-two new apartment-style units accommodate a minimum of 356 occupants. Housing is close to classrooms, the new library, recreation activities, and food and support services. Each unit contains four bedrooms, two full bathrooms, a kitchen, living area, and washers and dryers.

Student Group

Most undergraduates come to the campus as juniors, and since the campus is a major graduate center, students are primarily mature individuals committed to continuing their education. The median age of graduate students is 31. There are approximately 1,500 graduate students, most of whom are employed full-time and attend classes on a part-time basis.

Location

The University is located 8 miles from Harrisburg, the state capital. The resources of local, state, and federal agencies; museums; archives; and the state library are nearby. Within 30 miles are the urban centers of York and Lancaster, small towns such as Hershey, and rural settings in pastoral Lancaster and Lebanon counties. Diverse business, cultural, industrial, agricultural, residential, and service opportunities abound. Three interstate highways converge in Harrisburg and provide access to Philadelphia, Baltimore, New York City, and Washington, D.C., which also are accessible via nearby rail and air service.

The University

Penn State Harrisburg has a small-college atmosphere, with a student body of about 3,500, yet it has the resources, academic standards, and assets of the state's comprehensive land-grant research university. Graduate programs are designed primarily for persons employed full-time in area businesses, schools, government agencies, and industries, and most courses are held in the evening. A variety of programs and services are offered through the Downtown and Eastgate Centers in Harrisburg.

Applying

Candidates must have a bachelor's degree from an accredited institution. Applicants generally are expected to have earned a GPA of at least 3.0 (4.0 scale). The GRE is required by some programs. The M.B.A. and M.S.I.S. programs require the GMAT. The M.P.A. program accepts the GRE General Test, GMAT, LSAT, or MAT. The Adult Education Program accepts the GRE or MAT. Candidates from countries in which English is not the primary language must earn at least 550 (paper-based test) or 213 (computer-based test) on the TOEFL. International transcripts must be evaluated by the Educational Credential Evaluators (ECE). ECE evaluations should accompany the application and transcripts.

Correspondence and Information

Enrollment Services
Pennsylvania State University Harrisburg Campus of the Capital College
777 West Harrisburg Pike
Middletown, Pennsylvania 17057
Telephone: 717-948-6250
800-222-2056 (toll-free)
E-mail: hbgadmit@psu.edu
World Wide Web: http://www.hbg.psu.edu

DEAN AND PROGRAM COORDINATORS

Howard G. Sachs, Professor (biology) and Associate Dean for Research and Graduate Studies; Ph.D., Clark, 1971.

Coordinators of Graduate Programs

Adult Education (D.Ed.): Edward W. Taylor, Associate Professor (adult education); Ph.D., Georgia, 1993.
Applied Psychology (M.A.): Michael A. Becker, Associate Professor (psychology); Ph.D., SUNY at Albany, 1984.
American Studies (M.A.): Simon J. Bronner, Distinguished Professor (American studies and folklore); Ph.D., Indiana, 1981.
Business Administration (M.B.A.): Robert K. Larson, Associate Professor (professional accountancy); Ph.D., Utah, 1993.
Community Psychology and Social Change (M.A.): Stephen R. Couch, Professor (sociology); Ph.D., SUNY, 1979.
Computer Science (M.S.): Thang Bui, Associate Professor (computer science); Ph.D., MIT, 1986.
Engineering Science (M.Eng.): Seroj Mackertich, Assistant Professor (engineering); Ph.D., Penn State, 1979.
Environmental Pollution Control (M.E.P.C.. M.Eng., M.S.): Samuel McClintock, Associate Professor (engineering); Ph.D., Virginia Tech, 1990.
Electrical Engineering (M.E.E.): Jerry F. Shoup, Associate Professor (engineering); Ph.D., Penn State, 1971.
Health Administration (M.H.A.); James T. Ziegenfuss, Professor (management and health-care systems); Ph.D., Pennsylvania, 1980.
Health Education (M.Ed.): Samuel W. Monismith, Assistant Professor (health education); D.Ed., Penn State, 1984.
Humanities (M.A.): Louise E. Hoffman, Associate Professor (humanities and history); Ph.D., Bryn Mawr, 1975.
Information Systems (M.S.I.S.): Gayle J. Yaverbaum, Professor (information systems); Ph.D., Temple, 1983.
Public Administration (M.P.A.): Jack Rabin, Professor (public administration and public policy); Ph.D., Georgia, 1972.
Public Administration (Ph.D.): Rupert F. Chisholm, Professor (management); Ph.D., Case Western Reserve, 1974.
Teaching and Curriculum (M.Ed.): Steven A. Melnick, Associate Professor (education); Ph.D., Connecticut, 1988.
Training and Development (M.Ed.): Barry O. Williams, Assistant Professor (instructional design); Ph.D., Penn State, 1995.

Vartan Plaza, with the college bookstore (left) and the Science and Technology Building (right).

The state-of-the-art library at Penn State Harrisburg.

THE PENNSYLVANIA STATE UNIVERSITY UNIVERSITY PARK CAMPUS

Graduate School

Programs of Study

Programs of graduate study are offered in the following fields (asterisks precede fields in which only a master's degree is offered; all other fields offer both master's and doctoral programs, except where noted): acoustics; adult education; aerospace engineering; agricultural, environmental, and regional economics; agricultural and extension education; agricultural and biological engineering; agronomy; *American studies; anatomy; animal science; anthropology; *applied behavior analysis; *applied clinical psychology; applied linguistics (Ph.D. only); *applied psychological research; *applied statistics; architectural engineering; *architecture; *art; art education; art history; astronomy and astrophysics; biobehavioral health; biochemistry and molecular biology; biochemistry, microbiology, and molecular biology; bioengineering; biology; *biotechnology; business administration; cell and molecular biology; chemical engineering; chemistry; civil engineering; communication disorders; *community psychology and social change; *community and economic development; comparative and international education; comparative literature; *composition/theory; computer science and engineering; *conducting; counseling psychology (Ph.D. only); counselor education; crime, law, and justice; curriculum and instruction; demography; earth sciences; ecology; economics; educational administration; educational psychology; educational theory and policy; electrical engineering; energy, environmental, and mineral economics; *engineering mechanics; *engineering science; engineering science and mechanics; English; entomology; environmental engineering; *environmental pollution control; food science; forest resources; French; fuel science; genetics; geoenvironmental engineering; geography; geosciences; German; *health administration; health education; *health evaluation sciences; health policy and administration; higher education; history; horticulture; hotel, restaurant, and institutional management; human development and family studies; *humanities; industrial engineering; *industrial health and safety; *industrial relations and human resources; *information science; information sciences and technology (Ph.D. only); *information systems; instructional systems; integrative biosciences; kinesiology; *laboratory animal medicine; *landscape architecture; leisure studies; *manufacturing engineering; *manufacturing systems engineering; mass communications (Ph.D. only); materials; materials science and engineering; mathematics; mechanical engineering; *media studies; meteorology; microbiology and immunology; *mineral engineering management; mineral processing; mining engineering; music and music education; *music theory; *music theory and history; neuroscience; nuclear engineering; nursing; nutrition; operations research; pathobiology; *performance; petroleum and natural gas engineering; pharmacology; philosophy; physics; physiology; *piano pedagogy and performance; plant pathology; plant physiology; political science; psychology; public administration; quality and manufacturing management; rural sociology; Russian and comparative literature; school psychology; sociology; software engineering; soil science; Spanish; special education; speech communication; statistics; systems engineering; *teaching and curriculum; *teaching English as a second language; *telecommunications studies; *theater; *training and development; *voice performance and pedagogy; wildlife and fisheries science; women's studies; workforce education and development; and *youth and family education. Level I Instructional, Supervisory, Educational Specialist, and Administrative certificates are offered.

Research Facilities

The University Libraries System has more than 4.3 million cataloged volumes, 39,000 current serials, and 4.7 million microforms. Automated services are provided through the Library Information Access System developed at Penn State. The Center for Academic Computing (CAC) is the principal provider of central academic computing services. The center operates computers capable of providing not only numerically intensive computing but also electronic access to higher education facilities and research centers worldwide. Penn State and Internet resources include electronic bulletin boards, news and conferencing systems, publications, library catalogs, research databases, discussion groups, and much more. Public laboratories with terminals and desktop computers provide facilities for those without their own equipment.

Financial Aid

Fellowships, traineeships, or assistantships are held by 66 percent of all University Park students. These awards involve remission of tuition and payment of stipends averaging $1430 per month. Awards are usually made by the student's department or on recommendation to another administrative unit. Student loans and work-study funds are available through the Office of Student Aid.

Cost of Study

In 2001–02, tuition for full-time study (except for medical students) was $3941 per semester for residents and $8071 per semester for nonresidents at all campuses except Penn State Great Valley, where tuition was $415 per credit for residents and $733 per credit for nonresidents.

Living and Housing Costs

Residence hall accommodations and University-owned apartments are available through the Assignment Office for Campus Residences (telephone: 814-865-7501).

Student Group

In fall 2001, 10,306 graduate students were enrolled. The University conferred 2,503 advanced degrees, including 541 doctorates, during the 2000–01 year.

Student Outcomes

Graduates of the University typically proceed to a wide variety of academic and nonacademic professional careers in colleges and universities, private industry, government, and nonprofit organizations.

Location

The main campus, University Park, is located in the center of the state in the borough of State College. Pittsburgh, Philadelphia, New York City, and Washington, D.C., are each within a few hours' travel by car and are readily accessible by bus or air. The beautiful mountain country surrounding the community offers seasonal recreation, including swimming, boating, hunting, fishing, hiking, camping, and skiing. Although Penn State is a major graduate and research institution, the community retains a collegiate atmosphere.

The Graduate School

Graduate study is offered in more than 150 major programs, and twenty-one types of advanced academic and professional degrees are conferred. The faculty of the Graduate School numbers about 2,600. In addition to the University Park campus, Penn State Great Valley near Philadelphia; Penn State Harrisburg, the Capital College; the College of Medicine at Hershey; and Penn State Erie, the Behrend College, offer graduate degree programs.

Applying

Admission is granted jointly by the Graduate School and the department to which the student is applying. Applicants interested in programs at Penn State Erie, the Behrend College; Penn State Great Valley; and Penn State Harrisburg, the Capital College, should apply directly to these campuses. Students should contact the Office of Certification and Educational Services, 181 Chambers Building, for information on Level I Instructional, Supervisory, Educational Specialist, or Administrative certificates. Students whose native language is not English or who have not received baccalaureate or master's degrees from an institution in which the language of instruction is English must submit TOEFL scores. Application materials and detailed information about specific graduate programs and GRE requirements are available from the individual graduate programs. Because the admission process is time consuming, applications should be submitted as early as possible.

Correspondence and Information

Graduate School
114 Kern Graduate Building
The Pennsylvania State University
University Park, Pennsylvania 16802

Telephone: 814-865-1795 (Graduate Enrollment Services)
E-mail: gadm@psu.edu
World Wide Web: http://www.gradsch.psu.edu

COLLEGES/CENTERS AND HEADS OF PROGRAMS

Unless otherwise indicated, the mailing address is the Pennsylvania State University, University Park, Pennsylvania 16802. (Penn State Harrisburg is in Middletown, Pennsylvania 17057; the Milton S. Hershey Medical Center, College of Medicine, is in Hershey, Pennsylvania 17033; Penn State Great Valley School of Graduate Professional Studies is in Malvern, Pennsylvania 19355; and Penn State Erie, the Behrend College, is in Erie, Pennsylvania 16563).

Agricultural Sciences
Agricultural and Biological Engineering: Roy Young, 250 Agricultural Engineering. Agricultural and Extension Education: Blannie Bowen, 323 Agricultural Administration. Agricultural, Environmental, and Regional Economics: David Blandford, 103 Armsby. Crop and Soil Sciences: A. Turgeon, 116 Agricultural Sciences and Industries. Dairy and Animal Science: Terry Etherton, 325 Henning. Entomology: Charles Pitt, 501 Agricultural Sciences and Industries. Food Science: John D. Floros, 111 Borland. Forest Resources: Larry Nielsen, 113 Ferguson. Horticulture: D. R. Decoteau, 102 Tyson. Pathobiology: Lorraine Sordillo, 115 Henning. Plant Pathology: Elwin Stewart, 212 Buckhout. Rural Sociology: David Blandford, 103 Armsby. Wildlife and Fisheries Science: Larry Nielson, 113 Ferguson. Youth and Family Education: Blannie Bowen, 323 Agricultural Administration.

Arts and Architecture
Architecture: James Wines, 206 Engineering C. Art History: Craig Zabel, 229 Arts. Composing: Richard Green, 233 Music. Composition/Theory: Richard Green, 233 Music. Conducting: Richard Green, 233 Music. Integrative Arts: William Kelly, 215 Wagner. Landscape Architecture: Brian Orland, 210 Engineering Unit D. Music and Music Education: Richard Green, 233 Music. Music Theory and History: Richard Green, 233 Music. Performance: Richard Green, 233 Music. Piano Pedagogy and Performance: Richard Green, 233 Music. Theater: Dan Carter, 103 Arts. Visual Arts: C. Garoian, 210 Patterson. Voice Performance and Pedagogy: Richard Green, 233 Music.

Business Administration
Business Administration: Judy Olian, 807 Business Administration.

Communications
Mass Communications: Richard Barton, 201 Carnegie. Media Studies: Richard Barton, 201 Carnegie. Telecommunications Studies: Richard Barton, 201 Carnegie.

Earth and Mineral Sciences
Energy, Environmental, and Mineral Economics: Adam Rose, 2217 EES. Energy and Geoenvironmental Engineering: Alan Scaroni, 118 Hosler. Geography: Roger Downs, 302 Walker. Geosciences: Rudy Slingerland, 503 Dieke. Materials Science and Engineering: Gary Messing, 121 Steidle. Meteorology: William Brune, 503 Walker.

Education
Adult Education: Fred Schied, 314 Keller; Robert Lesniak, Penn State Harrisburg. Counseling Psychology and Counselor Education: Robert Slaney, 327 Cedar. Curriculum and Instruction: Murray Nelson, 141 Chambers. Educational Administration: William Lowe Boyd, 300 Rackley. Educational Psychology: Robert Stevens, 227 Cedar. Educational Theory and Policy: David Baker, 300 Rackley. Higher Education: Dorothy Evensen, 400 Rackley. Instructional Systems: Alison Carr-Chellman 307 Keller. School Psychology: M. Watkins, 102 Cedar. Special Education: David McNaughton, 230 Cedar; Charles Hughes, Great Valley. Workforce Education and Development: Kenneth C. Gray, 301 Keller.

Engineering
Aerospace Engineering: Dennis McLaughlin, 229 Hammond. Agricultural and Biological Engineering: Roy Young, 250 Agricultural Engineering. Architectural Engineering: Richard Mistrick, 212 Engineering A. Chemical Engineering: J. L. Duda, 160 Fenske. Civil Engineering: Paul Jovanis, 212 Sackett. Computer Science and Engineering: R. Acharya, 218 Pond Lab. Electrical Engineering: W. Kenneth Jenkins, 121 Electrical Engineering East. Engineering Mechanics: R. P. McNitt, 212 EES. Engineering Science: R. P. McNitt, 212 EES; S. Mackertich, Penn State Harrisburg; David W. Russell, Great Valley. Environmental Engineering: Paul Jovanis, 212 Sackett. Industrial and Manufacturing Engineering: A. Ravindran, 310 Leonhard. Mechanical Engineering: Richard Benson, 137 Reber. Nuclear Engineering: J. Brenizer, 138 Reber.

Health and Human Development
Biobehavioral Health: Lynn Kozlowski, 315 Human Development East. Bioengineering: 205 Hallowell. Communication Disorders: Gordon Blood, 110 Moore. Health Policy and Administration: Diane Brannon, 104 Henderson. Hotel, Restaurant, and Institutional Management: William Andrew, 201H Mateer. Human Development and Family Studies: Leann Birch, 210 South Henderson. Kinesiology: M. Latash, 146 Recreation Building. Leisure Studies: Garry Chick, 201 Mateer. Nursing: S. Gueldner, 201 Human Development. Nutrition: M. Green, 126 South Henderson.

Hershey Medical Center
Biochemistry and Molecular Biology: Judith Bond. Cell and Molecular Biology: Robert Levenson. Health Evaluation Sciences: Mark Young. Laboratory Animal Medicine: C. M. Lang. Microbiology and Immunology: Richard Courtney. Neuroscience: Robert Milner. Pharmacology: Melvin L. Billingsley. Physiology: Leonard S. Jefferson.

Intercollege Graduate Degree Programs
Acoustics: Anthony Atchley, 217A Applied Science. Bioengineering: Herbert Lipowsky, 233 Hallowell. Demography: Gordon DeJong, 601 Oswald. Ecology: Christopher Uhl, 106 Mueller. Environmental Pollution Control: Herschel Elliot, 207 ASI; Samuel A. McClintock, Penn State Harrisburg; Lily Sehayek, Great Valley. Genetics: Douglas Cavener, 208 Mueller. Information Science: David Russell, Great Valley. Integrative Biosciences: Richard Frisque, University Park; J. Bond, Hershey. Materials: Barbara Shaw, 117 Hammond. Operations Research: Susan Xu, 335 Beam. Physiology: James Ultman, 106 Fenske. Plant Physiology: Teh-hui Kao, 318 Wartik. Quality and Manufacturing Management: M. Hottenstein, 344 Leonhard.

Liberal Arts
Anthropology: Dean Snow, 409 Carpenter. Comparative Literature: Caroline Eckhardt, 311 Burrowes. Crime, Law, and Justice: Barrett Lee, 201 Oswald Tower. Economics: Robert Marshall, 613 Kern. English: Don Bialostosky, 119 Burrowes. French: Thomas Hale, 325 South Burrowes. Germanic and Slavic Language and Literature: Gerhard Strasser, 311 Burrowes. History: A. G. Roeber, 108 Weaver. Industrial Relations and Human Resources: Mark Wardell, 101 Old Botany. Philosophy: John Stuhr, 240 Sparks. Political Science: Frank Baumgartner, 113 Burrowes. Psychology: Keith Crnic, 417 Moore. Russian and Comparative Literature: Caroline Eckhardt, 311 Burrowes. Sociology: Barrett Lee, 211 Oswald Tower. Spanish, Italian, and Portuguese: John Lipski, N354 Burrowes. Speech Communication: Michael Hecht, 234 Sparks. Teaching English as a Second Language: K. Johnson, 305 Sparks.

Penn State Erie, Behrend College
Business Administration: John Magenau; Manufacturing Systems Engineering: Robert Simoneau.

Penn State Great Valley School of Graduate Professional Studies
Business Administation: Ellen Foster-Curtis. Information Science: David Russell. Software Engineering: David Russell. Systems Engineering: David Russell.

Penn State Harrisburg
American Studies: Simon Bronner. Community Psychology and Social Change: Stephen Couch. Computer Science: Thang Bui. Electrical Engineering: J.F. Shoup. Engineering Science: S. Mackertich. Environmental Pollution Control: Samuel A. McClintock. Health Administration: James Ziegenfuss. Health Education: Samuel Monismith. Humanitites: Wm. J. Mahar. Information Systems: Gayle Yaverbaum. Public Administration: Steven Peterson. Teaching and Curriculum: Steven Melnick. Training and Development: Robert Lesniak.

School of Information Sciences and Technology
Information Sciences and Technology: David Hall, 2E Thomas.

Science
Astronomy and Astrophysics: Peter Mészáros, 525 Davey. Biochemistry, Microbiology, and Molecular Biology: Robert Schlegel, 108 Althouse. Biology: Douglas Cavener, 208 Mueller. Chemistry: Andrew Ewing, 152 Davey Lab. Mathematics: Svetlana Katok, 224 McAllister; Jack Stein, Great Valley. Physics: Jayanth Banavar, 104 Davey. Statistics: J. L. Rosenberger, 326 Thomas.

PEPPERDINE UNIVERSITY

Graduate School of Education and Psychology

Programs of Study

The Graduate School of Education and Psychology offers degree and credential programs designed to prepare teachers and educational administrators, psychologists and counselors, mental health administrators, consultants, change agents, and technology specialists.

Pepperdine offers a variety of graduate programs in education, leading to a Master of Science in Administration, a Master of Arts in Education, a Master of Arts in Educational Technology (85 percent on line, 15 percent face-to-face), and a Doctor of Education (Ed.D.). Several teaching credentials and Tier I and II administrative credentials are also offered.

The Ed.D. program has four unique concentrations: Educational Leadership, Administration, and Policy; Educational Technology; Organization Change; and Organizational Leadership. Each doctoral concentration has its own format designed for working professionals. The program in Organizational Leadership offers traditional classes at the Culver City and Orange County campuses on weeknights and weekends; the Educational Technology and the Educational Leadership, Administration, and Policy programs offer classes that are 60 percent face-to-face, 40 percent online; and the Organization Change program has a sequence-oriented, seminar-style curriculum held at various conference locations.

Psychology programs include a Master of Arts in Psychology, a Master of Arts in Clinical Psychology with an emphasis in marriage and family therapy, and a Doctor of Psychology (Psy.D.). Master's programs are designed for students to work at their own pace, with evening classes available for working professionals and a daytime program offered for full-time students. The Psy.D. program consists of three years of course work in addition to an internship. A dissertation is required.

Research Facilities

A computer network links each of the University's libraries, which collectively contain more than 800,000 books, bound journals, and microforms. Each facility has computer labs, and the West Los Angeles campus houses the Multimedia Center.

Financial Aid

Scholarships, grants, loans, assistantships, and payment plans are available to qualified students. Veterans should follow regular admission procedures and secure the certificate of eligibility from the Veterans Administration or the State of California. More than 70 percent of the students receive federal loans, and more than 35 percent receive Pepperdine-funded assistance.

Cost of Study

Charges for one trimester unit of instruction in 2002–03 varies from $645 to $820, depending upon the program.

Living and Housing Costs

While there is a limited amount of graduate housing available for clinical M.A. students at Malibu, the other campuses are in close proximity to apartment buildings and residential areas. Students can expect to budget approximately $15,000 annually for rent, utilities, food, transportation, and personal expenses.

Student Group

Total University enrollment is 7,700 and enrollment at the Graduate School of Education and Psychology is 1,500. Students range in age and experience, with many returning to the workforce or changing their careers, and others entering the programs upon completing their undergraduate degree.

Location

The headquarters for the Graduate School of Education and Psychology is Pepperdine University Plaza, located in Culver City, about 30 minutes west of downtown Los Angeles. The Malibu campus overlooks the Pacific Ocean from the Santa Monica Mountains. The San Fernando Valley Center is located in Encino, north of the Santa Monica Mountains. The Orange County center is just east of the John Wayne Airport in Irvine. The Ventura County Center is located in Westlake Village. Program offerings vary by location.

The University

Pepperdine, an independent, medium-sized Christian university, has two major campuses. Seaver College, the undergraduate residential college of letters, arts, and sciences; the School of Public Policy; and the School of Law are on an 830-acre campus overlooking the Pacific Ocean at Malibu. Headquarters for the Graduate School of Education and Psychology and the Graziadio School of Business and Management are in West Los Angeles.

Applying

Admission requirements vary by program. For more information, prospective students should contact the address given below.

Correspondence and Information

Office of Admissions
Graduate School of Education and Psychology
Pepperdine University
400 Corporate Pointe
Culver City, California 90230
Telephone: 800-347-4849 for education programs (toll-free)
800-888-4849 for psychology programs (toll-free)
World Wide Web: http://gsep.pepperdine.edu/

THE FACULTY

Education

Michael Botsford, Lecurer; Ed.D., USC.
Vance Caesar, Visiting Faculty; Ph.D., Walden.
Margot Condon, Assistant Director of Student Teaching; Ed.D., Pepperdine.
Kay Davis, Lecturer; Ed.D., Pepperdine.
Cynthia A. Dollins, Visiting Faculty; Ed.D., Pepperdine.
Christopher Ellsasser, Visiting Faculty; Ed.D., Columbia.
Mercedes Fisher, Associate Professor; Ph.D., Denver.
J. L. Fortson, Lecturer; Ed.D., San Francisco.
Cara L. Garcia, Professor; Ph.D., Arizona.
Nancy Harding, Assistant Professor; Ph.D., UCLA.
Diana Hiatt-Michael, Professor; Ed.D., UCLA.
Don Kobabe, Visiting Faculty; Ed.D., USC.
Cheryl Lampe, Visiting Faculty; Ed.D., Pepperdine.
Doug Leigh, Assistant Professor; Ph.D., Florida State.
Delores Lindsey, Visiting Faculty; Ph.D., Claremont.
Randall Lindsey, Distinguished Educator-in-Residence; Ph.D., Georgia State.
Farzin Madjidi, Associate Professor; Ed.D., Pepperdine.
Chester H. McCall Jr., Professor; Ph.D., George Washington.
John F. McManus, Professor; Ph.D., Connecticut.
Joan G. Mills-Buffehr, Professor; Ed.D., Pepperdine.
Robert Paull, Associate Professor; Ph.D., USC.
Linda G. Polin, Associate Professor; Ph.D., UCLA.
Linda Purrington, Visiting Faculty; Ed.D., Pepperdine.
Reyna G. Garcia Ramos, Assistant Professor; Ph.D., California, Santa Barbara.
Margaret Riel, Visiting Faculty; Ph.D., California, Irvine.
Marta E. Sanchez, Visiting Faculty; Ph.D., California, Santa Barbara.
June Schmieder, Associate Professor; Ph.D., Stanford.
Jack Scott, Distinguished Professor; Ph.D., Claremont.
Thomas E. Skewes-Cox, Visiting Faculty; Ph.D., UCLA.
Paul R. Sparks, Visiting Faculty; Ph.D., UCLA.
Ronald D. Stephens, Professor; Ed.D., USC.
Sue Talley, Visiting Faculty; Ed.D., Pepperdine.

Psychology

Joy Keiko Asamen, Professor; Ph.D., UCLA.
Louis John Cozolino, Professor; Ph.D., UCLA.
Robert A. deMayo, Associate Professor; Ph.D., UCLA.
Drew Erhardt, Associate Professor; Ph.D., UCLA.
David W. Foy, Professor; Ph.D., Southern Mississippi.
Pamela H. Harmell, Visiting Faculty; Ph.D., CSPP.
Shelly Prillerman Harrell, Associate Professor; Ph.D., UCLA.
Joanne Hedgespeth, Associate Professor; Ph.D., Biola.
James Hedstrom, Emeritus Professor; Ph.D., UCLA.
Clarence Hibbs, Professor; Ph.D., Iowa.
Susan Himelstein, Visiting Faculty; Ph.D., UCLA.
Robert Hohenstein, Visiting Faculty; Ph.D., American Commonwealth.
Barbara Ingram, Professor; Ph.D., USC.
David A. Levy, Professor; Ph.D., UCLA.
Dennis W. Lowe, Professor; Ph.D., Florida State.
Tomas Martinez, Professor; Ph.D., Michigan.
Cary L. Mitchell, Associate Professor; Ph.D., Kentucky.
Frances W. Neely, Professor; Ph.D., Kansas.
Lynn Rankin-Esquer, Assistant Professor; Ph.D., North Carolina.
Daryl Rowe, Professor; Ph.D., Ohio State.
Edward P. Shafranske, Professor; Ph.D., US International.
Stephane M. Woo, Associate Professor; Ph.D., UCLA.

The Malibu Campus.

Pepperdine University in West Los Angeles.

PRESCOTT COLLEGE

Graduate Programs

Programs of Study

Prescott College grants master's degrees in five broadly defined fields of study: counseling and psychology, education, environmental studies, humanities, and adventure education. Many students design interdisciplinary programs that combine two or more of these categories.

Approximately 200 students are enrolled in the limited-residency program; most programs are three or four terms in length (1½ to 2 years). Students must attend two 3-day weekend colloquia per term in Prescott, Arizona, unless they are enrolled in a site-based program. The majority of students continue to work full-time in their home communities while completing their course work through independent and community-based study.

Research Facilities

The Prescott College Library provides Master of Arts students with a full range of graduate-level services, including borrowing privileges, user instructions, and research assistance. Current holdings consist of approximately 24,000 books, 270 periodical subscriptions, and 1,300 audiocassettes and videocassettes. Online resources include licensed journal databases, reference materials, and electronic books. The library supplements its on-site collection with access to material from databases and libraries throughout the world. The library Web site is www.library.prescott.edu.

Financial Aid

The Financial Aid Office assists graduate students with obtaining many different kinds of low-interest loans. They also assist with scholarship searches.

Cost of Study

For the academic year 2002–03, tuition is $5220 per 18 to 24 quarter credits; tuition increases may occur in July of each year.

Living and Housing Costs

On-campus housing is not available for graduate students. The Student Services Office assists graduate students seeking off-campus housing if they choose to live in Prescott, Arizona.

Student Group

Approximately 200 students are enrolled in the distance learning graduate program.

Student Outcomes

Because many students are working professionals, the benefits derived from their participation in one of Prescott College's graduate programs include professional advancement and greater opportunities for lateral movement within their professions. Students also obtain the skills and education required for entrance into particular fields and positions, as well as the additional education and experience needed to prepare for doctoral education. Students also enroll because they are interested in continuing their education in order to enhance their own personal development.

Location

Prescott is located in central Arizona, about 2 hours from Phoenix, surrounded by national forest and high plains at an elevation of more than 5,200 feet. With four mild seasons and the beautiful surroundings, Prescott offers a diversity of outside activities, including rock climbing, hiking, mountain biking, and nearby canoeing, rafting, and snow skiing. The city has a population more than 35,000, including the 125-member Yavapai Apache Indian Tribe, and the county has a population of more than 150,000. Prescott is an interesting combination of old and new. There are more than 500 buildings in Prescott that are recorded on the National Register of Historic Places. Described by *Arizona Highways* magazine as "Everybody's Hometown," the community of Prescott is known for its fine quality of life, friendly atmosphere, and small-town charm. Because it has a growing spirit, the community strives to balance the needs of an environmentally conscious lifestyle with an expanding economy. Many of the College's students participate in municipal sports leagues. The town offers facilities for racquetball, tennis, swimming, and horseback riding. Many people are active in such fine arts endeavors as photography, music, weaving, and dance. Prescott is, in fact, home to a lively and growing artistic community. The Mountain Artists Guild and the Prescott Fine Arts Association make a substantial cultural impact. The Phoenix Symphony, visiting ballet and opera companies, and numerous art shows also provide regular programs.

The College

Prescott College was founded in 1966 based upon the idea that learning occurs in the world of experience as well as in the mind. Prescott College seeks to develop the whole person through a unified educational experience in which the acquisition of knowledge and skills is combined with the individual's search for identity and meaning. The College is accredited by the North Central Association of Colleges and Schools and grants bachelor's and master's degrees in several fields.

Applying

Applicants for the master's degree programs must have a bachelor's degree from an accredited college or university. They should submit a completed application along with the appropriate fee, two letters of recommendation, a résumé, a personal statement, a proposed study plan, and official transcripts from all colleges or universities attended. Fine arts, studio arts, and art therapy applicants are required to submit a minimum of twelve prints or slides or other portfolio or demonstration of work. Admission into all graduate programs is based on an overall assessment of each candidate, and no specific GPAs or thresholds are used.

Correspondence and Information

Admissions Office, Master of Arts Program
Prescott College
220 Grove Avenue
Prescott, Arizona 86301
Telephone: 800-628-6364 (toll-free)
Fax: 928-776-5242
E-mail: admissions@prescott.edu
World Wide Web: http://www.prescott.edu

THE FACULTY

The Master of Arts Program (MAP) is a community of students, advisers, and faculty with wide-ranging interests in a multitude of disciplines that both intersect and diverge significantly. The similarities and differences provide for rich interactions and dialogue within the community and with outside scholars and practitioners. The MAP faculty desires to engage with all who share its interests in the ongoing development and refinement of Prescott's educational process. With this in mind, faculty members in MAP have sought to identify their place in the community of learners, their uniqueness as a learning environment, and their commitment to having an impact on social, cultural, and environmental surroundings.

Steve Walters, Dean, Adult Degree Programs; Ed.D., Arizona State, 1985.

Joel Barnes, Prescott College RDP Faculty; M.S., Humboldt State, 1991.
Noël Caniglia, Education Core Faculty; M.S., Mankato State, 1979.
Jeanne Cashin, Counseling Psychology Core Faculty; Ph.D., Union Institute (Ohio).
Joan Clingan, MAP Program Coordinator and Humanities Core Faculty; M.A., Santa Monica, 1992.
Rick Medrick, Adventure Education Core Faculty; Ed.D., Northern Colorado, 1985.
Ericha Scott, Counseling Psychology Core Faculty; Ph.D., Union Institute (Ohio), 1999; M.Ed., Florida Atlantic, 1981; Post-Master's Graduate Art Therapy Certificate, Notre Dame (California), 1996.
Paul Sneed, Environmental Studies Core Faculty and Prescott College RDP Faculty; Ph.D., Hawaii, 1997.
Bill Walton, Director of the Prescott College Tucson Center and Humanities Core Faculty; M.A., Prescott, 1995.

QUEENS COLLEGE OF THE CITY UNIVERSITY OF NEW YORK

Graduate Programs in the Arts and Sciences

Programs of Study Queens College offers programs of study leading to the Master of Arts in applied linguistics, art history, biology, chemistry, computer science, English, French, geology, history, Italian, mathematics, music, physics, psychology, Spanish, speech pathology, and urban affairs. Master of Science degrees are offered in nutrition and exercise science and accounting. The interdisciplinary degrees of Master of Arts in Liberal Studies and Master of Arts in Social Sciences are also offered. The Master of Fine Arts degree is offered in studio art. Master of Science in Education programs are available in bilingual elementary education, counselor education, elementary school education, literacy education, school psychology, secondary school education (art; English; French; general science—biology, chemistry, earth science, and physics; home economics; Italian; mathematics; music; physical education; social studies; and Spanish), special education, and teaching English to speakers of other languages. Professional diplomas in applied behavior analysis, education, school psychology, and in administration and supervision at the elementary and secondary levels are also offered. For applicants who seek New York State provisional teacher certification but whose undergraduate programs did not include a background in education, the College offers postbaccalaureate advanced certificate programs in elementary education and secondary education (English, French, general science, Italian, mathematics, music, social studies, and Spanish). Bilingual certification programs are available in counselor education, school psychology, and special education. The Master of Library Science degree and a post-master's advanced certificate in librarianship are offered. Both programs are accredited by the American Library Association. Concentrations in various areas also exist in a number of departments. Applicants should contact the Office of Graduate Admissions for more information.

Queens College is a major participant in the doctoral programs of the City University of New York (CUNY). Persons interested in these programs should contact the CUNY Graduate Center, 365 Fifth Avenue, New York, New York 10016.

Research Facilities The extensive laboratory facilities of the College house up-to-date scientific instruments for research in biology, chemistry, computer science, geology, physics, psychology, and health and physical education. There is also a Low-Temperature Physics Laboratory. Computing equipment ranges from up-to-date, high-technology, personal computers to highly specialized minicomputers. There are diverse computer laboratories, including a well equipped social science research laboratory. The Graduate School of Library and Information Studies maintains a fully integrated computer-intensive facility.

Gertz Speech and Hearing Center provides a facility for research and clinical practice experience in communicative disorders. The College is home to an electronic music studio and to one of the best music libraries on the East Coast. It also shares facilities with the American Museum of Natural History, Brookhaven National Laboratory, the Lamont-Doherty Geological Observatory, and leading hospitals. The Benjamin S. Rosenthal Library holds 753,000 volumes, 3,860 print and electronic journal subscriptions, and an extensive collection of microform material. The library is a selective depository for many government publications. A reference area contains materials for research on a wide range of social science, humanities, education, and science topics. The library also houses significant collections of specialized materials. Access is provided via telephone page to electronic resources at http://www.qc.edu/library.

Financial Aid A limited number of graduate fellowships, some requiring teaching and/or research, may be available from individual departments through the Office of the Assistant to the Provost for Graduate Admissions. Other kinds of financial aid include New York State Tuition Assistance Program grants, Board of Trustees partial tuition waivers, Federal Perkins Loans, the Federal Direct Student Loan Program, and Federal Work-Study Program awards. Applicants should contact the Financial Aid Office for information. The Cooperative Education Program helps students gain both academic credit and work experience in paid positions.

Cost of Study In 2001–02, tuition per semester was $185 per credit (maximum $2175) for New York State residents and $320 per credit (maximum $3800) for nonresidents. Activities fees are additional.

Living and Housing Costs Queens College does not provide housing for its students. Students who desire housing find it available in the surrounding neighborhood.

Student Group Approximately 4,100 students are registered for master's and advanced certificate programs, and many CUNY doctoral students work under the direct supervision of Queens College faculty members. Students come from throughout the United States and from a number of countries. In 2000, 932 degrees and 97 certificates were awarded. The Graduate Student Association at Queens College, an elective body representing the interests of all graduate students, offers free help with income tax return preparation and legal counseling.

Location Queens College is located close to the attractions of Manhattan. Opera, concerts, theater, and gallery and museum exhibits are accessible by public transportation; students can get tickets to many attractions at reduced prices. There are also parks and ocean beaches located nearby in Queens and on Long Island.

The College Established in 1937, Queens College is a coeducational, publicly supported college with an emphasis on the liberal arts and sciences and education. Its attractive, tree-lined campus includes athletic fields, a gymnasium, a pool, tennis courts, and a performing arts center that schedules a lively calendar of events, with performances by internationally renowned artists. The College offers lectures, art exhibits, plays, concerts, dance recitals, and other cultural and educational programs to the community. An extensive construction program has recently added a music building, which includes a 500-seat recital hall with tracker organ; a science building that houses sophisticated laboratories and equipment; the Rosenthal Library, with shelf space for more than 1 million volumes and study carrels for 2,200 users; and a renovated art building. Queens College is registered by the New York State Department of Education and accredited by the Middle States Association of Colleges and Schools. The American Association of Colleges for Teacher Education includes the College in its list of member colleges.

Applying The admission decision is based on the baccalaureate record and evidence of the ability to pursue graduate work. The General Test and a Subject Test of the Graduate Record Examinations are required for admission to certain programs. For fall semester admission, applications should be filed by April 1; for spring semester admission, by November 1 (not all programs admit students in the spring). Applications for fine arts and school psychology must be filed by March 15 for fall admission and by October 15 for spring admission. Speech pathology applications must be filed by February 1 for fall admission (spring applications are not accepted). Financial aid applications should be filed as early as possible. This information is subject to change.

Correspondence and Information

For information about a particular program:

Chair (listed overleaf)
Department of (specify)
Queens College
Flushing, New York 11367

For admission and registration information:

Graduate Admissions Office
Queens College
Flushing, New York 11367
Telephone: 718-997-5200
Fax: 718-997-5193
E-mail: graduate_admissions@qc.edu

For other information:

Office of Graduate Studies
Queens College
Flushing, New York 11367
Telephone: 718-997-5190
Fax: 718-997-5193
E-mail: robert_engel@qc.edu

THE FACULTY

From its beginnings in 1937, Queens College has made every effort to build a faculty of dedicated teachers and scholars. The list of institutions that have conferred degrees on members of the faculty includes every major university in the United States and several major European universities. Faculty members have received numerous national and international awards and fellowships as well as many sponsored research and training grants through the College's Office of Research and Sponsored Programs.

Office of Graduate Studies and Research
Robert Engel, Ph.D., Assistant to Provost for Graduate Studies.
Mario Caruso, M.A., Director of Graduate Admissions.

The following is a list of the heads of departments that offer graduate programs at the College. An asterisk (*) indicates that there is no master's or advanced certificate program in this area, but faculty members participate in the Ph.D. program at the CUNY Graduate Center. A double asterisk indicates that the program is not currently accepting students.

Division of the Arts
Raymond Erickson, Ph.D., Dean of the Faculty for the Arts.
Art: James Saslow, Ph.D., Chair.
***Classical, Middle Eastern, and Asian Languages and Cultures:** Gopal Sukhu, Ph.D., Chair.
***Comparative Literature:** Clare L. Carroll, Ph.D., Chair.
Drama, Dance, and Theatre: Harry Feiner, Ph.D., Chair.
English: Nancy Comley, Ph.D., Chair.
***European Languages and Literatures:** Hermann Haller, Ph.D., Chair.
Hispanic Languages and Literatures: Emilio de Torre, Ph.D., Chair.
Linguistics and Communication Disorders: Helen S. Cairns, Ph.D., Chair.
Media Studies: Stuart Liebman, Ph.D., Chair.
Music: Rufus Hallmark, Ph.D., Chair and Director, Aaron Copland School of Music.

Division of Mathematics and the Natural Sciences
Robert Prezant, Ph.D., Dean of the Faculty for Mathematics and the Natural Sciences.
Biology: Harold Magazine, Ph.D., Chair.
Chemistry: Arthur D. Baker, Ph.D., Chair.
Computer Science: Ishim Phillips, Ph.D., Chair.
Earth and Environmental Sciences: Daniel Habib, Ph.D., Chair.
Family, Nutrition, and Exercise Sciences: Michael Toner, Ph.D., Chair.
Mathematics: Norman Weiss, Ph.D., Chair.
Physics: Steven Schwarz, Ph.D., Chair.
Psychology: Richard Bodnar, Ph.D., Chair.

Division of the Social Sciences
Donald Scott, Ph.D., Dean of the Faculty for the Social Sciences.
***Anthropology:** James Moore, Ph.D., Chair.
****Economics:** M. Anne Hill, Ph.D., Chair.
History: Frank Warren, Ph.D., Chair.
Library Science: Marianne Cooper, Ph.D., Chair and Director, Graduate School of Library and Information Studies.
Philosophy: Steven Hicks, Ph.D., Chair.
****Political Science:** Patricia Rachal, Ph.D., Chair.
Sociology: Milton Mankoff, Ph.D., Chair.
Urban Studies: Leonard Rodberg, Ph.D., Chair.

Division of Education
Philip M. Anderson, Ph.D., Acting Dean of the Faculty for Education.
Educational and Community Programs: David Goh, Ph.D., Chair.
Elementary and Early Childhood Education and Services: Helen Johnson, Ph.D., Chair.
Secondary Education and Youth Services: Eleanor Armour-Thomas, Ph.D., Chair.

Interdisciplinary Studies
Liberal Studies: Martin Pine, Ph.D., Graduate Adviser.
Social Sciences: Martin Hanlon, Ph.D., Graduate Adviser.

QUINNIPIAC
UNIVERSITY

QUINNIPIAC UNIVERSITY

Graduate Studies

Programs of Study

Quinnipiac University offers master's degrees in the areas of accounting, biomedical sciences, business administration, computer information systems, e-media, forensic nursing, health administration, journalism, molecular and cell biology, nurse practitioner studies, pathologists' assistant studies, physical therapy, physician assistant studies, and teaching as well as a Juris Doctor (J.D.) degree through the School of Law. Programs range in length from twelve months to three years. Both full- and part-time study are available in certain fields. Through its graduate programs, the University has recognized a substantial trend toward greater professionalism and the rapidly expanding body of knowledge in these fields. All graduate programs at the University share three foundations. Instruction is provided by a team of academicians who hold the highest available academic credentials and practicing professionals who hold advanced positions in their fields. Every graduate student is provided with the opportunity to obtain practical experience through residencies, internships, thesis research, special projects, clinical rotations, consulting practicums, or small laboratory classes. Study in all graduate programs is advanced and builds upon both undergraduate education and professional experience.

Research Facilities

All graduate and professional students have access to the materials in the Arnold Bernhard Library and the School of Law Library. Education students can utilize ERIC, PsychInfo, and the Wilson Full-Text Educational Service via the World Wide Web; assorted curriculum materials in all formats; a children/young adult literature collection; electronic and paper copies of periodicals; and a collection of current textbooks. Students in the School of Business can access ABI/Inform, LexisNexis, and Business Abstracts databases via the World Wide Web. Many business journals and business monographs are available. In the sciences, Science Direct, MEDLINE, and the Nursing Index are offered, among other Web-based resources. Librarians maintain a joint online catalog for the two libraries. Communications students utilize the Ed McMahon Mass Communications Center. The center provides students with hands-on experience in studios, radio and TV control rooms, video and audio editing suites, and the news technology center. Students in the programs offered through the School of Health Sciences utilize the facilities on campus in Echlin Health Sciences Center and the Clinical Skills Laboratory. Echlin Center houses classrooms designed for clinical practice in the health sciences, extensive computer and robotics equipment, and lecture halls and seminar rooms. The Clinical Skills Laboratory is a well-equipped simulation of a hospital setting. The Law Library contains more than 280,000 volumes and an extensive audiovisual collection. It is equipped with LEXIS and WESTLAW, computerized legal research systems, and IBM PCs for word processing and computer-assisted legal instruction programs.

Financial Aid

Graduate assistantships are available on a limited basis to both full- and part-time students. Some programs offer a combination of tuition waiver and/or stipend in return for assistance in areas such as faculty research, admissions, or other administrative departments. Some education students receive tuition waivers and stipends while they are participating in the Master of Arts in Teaching (M.A.T.) program. Pathologists' assistant and physician assistant students receive tuition waivers during the clinical portions of their programs. In addition, graduate students are eligible to apply for federal and commercial loan programs.

Cost of Study

Tuition for all graduate programs is computed per credit hour. In 2002–03, the tuition rate is $475 per credit hour. Students in some programs are charged by the semester. The tuition cost for the physician assistant studies program is approximately $42,000; for the pathologists' assistant studies program, approximately $34,000; for the M.A.T. program, approximately $18,000; and the tuition cost for the M.B.A. program is approximately $18,000. Part-time students pay a student fee of $25 per credit each semester. Full-time students are charged a student fee of $225 each semester. The University offers students a variety of payment plans, including deferred payment and installment programs, and cooperates fully with most employer reimbursement programs. Other expenses, such as books and supplies, vary by program. Information about financial aid and student budgets should be obtained directly from Quinnipiac's Financial Aid Office Graduate Division.

Living and Housing Costs

On-campus housing is available during the summer. The Office of Residential Life maintains a listing of nearby privately owned housing. Students can contact the Office of Residential Life at 203-582-8666 or visit the Web site listed below. Costs for off-campus housing range from $500 to $700 or more monthly. Housing is available in apartments and private homes.

Student Group

Quinnipiac University enrolls approximately 1,800 graduate students. Of these, approximately 900 are enrolled in Graduate Studies, with the remainder enrolled in the Law School. In Graduate Studies, 60 percent of the students are women and about 50 percent attend full-time. There is a small but growing number of international students and students of color on the Quinnipiac campus. Quinnipiac University has a firm commitment to increasing diversity on campus.

Location

Quinnipiac University is located on a beautiful campus in Hamden, Connecticut, a suburb of New Haven. Hamden is approximately 30 minutes from Hartford, 1½ hours from New York City, and 2 hours from Boston. Quinnipiac is located at the base of Sleeping Giant Park with more than 1,500 acres of wooded trails. New Haven is a vibrant city with much to offer, including theaters, art museums, shops, and restaurants. Hartford, the state capital, also offers historical and cultural attractions, concerts, and athletic events.

The University

The University comprises the Schools of Business, Communications, Health Sciences, and Law and the College of Liberal Arts. Quinnipiac University is a private, nondenominational institution of higher learning founded in 1929. Quinnipiac's mission is to provide a supportive and stimulating environment for the intellectual and personal growth of its students.

Applying

With the exception of the pathologists' assistant and physician assistant programs, application deadlines are rolling. Applications for the physician assistant program must be complete no later than December 1; for the pathologists' assistant program, applications must be complete by January 15. Interviews are required for the M.A.T., nursing, physician assistant, and pathologists' assistant programs. Files are reviewed upon receipt of all required materials. All application materials are submitted to the Graduate Admissions Office.

Correspondence and Information

For additional information or application materials, students should contact:

Graduate Admissions
Quinnipiac University
275 Mount Carmel Avenue
Hamden, Connecticut 06518

Telephone: 203-582-8672
800-462-1944 (toll-free)
Fax: 203-582-3443
E-mail: graduate@quinnipiac.edu
World Wide Web: http://www.quinnipiac.edu

PROGRAM DIRECTORS

School of Business

Accounting Program: Julia Brazelton, Director; Ph.D., South Carolina.

Computer Information Systems Program: Bruce White, Director; Ph.D., Nebraska.

Master of Business Administration: Mark Thompson, Director; Ph.D., Georgia State.
Areas of faculty research include the role of self-management and student entrepreneurship training, group decision support systems, expert systems, economic history, outsourcing of internal audit departments, international accounting, tax policy issues, consumer behavior, impact of tax policies on foreign direct investment, the African American in American business, psychological correlates of entrepreneurship, organizational development in public schools, opportunities for U.S. firms in Japan, strategy formulation, strategic management, small business, retail strategy, food marketing, and development of tax systems in former Communist countries of Eastern Europe.

Master of Health Administration: Ronald Rozett, Director; M.P.H., M.D., Harvard.
Areas of faculty research include group purchasing of health care, health-care regulation and legislation, health-care informatics, marketing, management of health-care professionals, quality management in health care, health services research, international health.

School of Communications

Program in E-media: Scott Barnett, Director; Ph.D., Columbia.

Program in Journalism: Arthur Hayes, Director; J.D., Quinnipiac.
Areas of faculty research include journalism, documentary, mass communication, film, media history, writing, media management, media research, law and ethics.

School of Health Sciences

Program in Forensic Nursing: Barbara Moynihan, Director; Ph.D., Connecticut.

Medical Laboratory Sciences and Molecular and Cell Biology: Kenneth Kaloustian, Director; Ph.D., New Hampshire. Charlotte Hammond, Director; Ph.D., Connecticut.
Areas of faculty research include biochemistry, clinical pathology, embryology, epidemiology, food and dairy bacteriology, forensic pathology, hematology, microbiology, molecular biology, molecular genetics, molecular pathology, parasitology, physiology and endocrinology.

Nurse Practitioner Program: Jeanne Levassuer, Director; Ph.D., Connecticut; APRN.
Areas of faculty research include transformational leadership, rehabilitation nursing, women's health.

Pathologists' Assistant Program: Kenneth Kaloustian, Director; Ph.D., New Hampshire.
Areas of faculty research include embryology, clinical pathology, biomedical photography and technology, epidemiology/public health, hematology, food and dairy bacteriology, radiology, physiology and endocrinology.

Physician Assistant Program: Cynthia Booth Lord, Director; M.H.S., Quinnipiac; PA-C.
Areas of faculty research include histology, family medicine, clinical pathology, radiology, biostatistics.

Physical Therapy: Russell Woodman, Director; D.P.T., Creighton; PT, FSOM, OCS.
Areas of faculty research include Parkinson's disease and biomechanics and the stroke patient.

College of Liberal Arts

Master of Arts in Teaching: Gloria Holmes, Director; Ph.D., SUNY at Stony Brook. Anne Dichele, Director; Ph.D., Connecticut.
Areas of faculty research include biology, fine arts, English, mathematics, history, political science, educational technology, special education, occupational therapy, curriculum and instruction, sociology.

RADFORD UNIVERSITY

College of Graduate and Extended Education

Programs of Study

Radford University offers the Educational Specialist (Ed.Spec.) degree in school psychology, the Master of Fine Arts (M.F.A.) degree in art, the Master of Business Administration (M.B.A.) degree, and the Master of Arts (M.A.) degree in communication sciences and disorders, criminal justice, English, music, music therapy, and psychology (clinical, counseling, experimental, and industrial/organizational). It offers the Master of Science (M.S.) degree in art education, communication sciences and disorders (language pathology), corporate and professional communication, counselor education, criminal justice, educational leadership, English, environmental and engineering geosciences, music education, music therapy, psychology (clinical, counseling, and industrial/organizational), reading, and special education (emotional/behavioral disorders and specific learning disabilities or mental retardation and severe disabilities); the Master of Science in Nursing (M.S.N.); and the Master of Social Work (M.S.W.).

Requirements for the M.A. and M.S. degrees range from 30 to 48 semester hours. Most departments offer both thesis and nonthesis options. The M.B.A. requires 36 semester hours; the M.S.N., 34 to 38 semester hours; the M.F.A., 60 semester hours; the M.S.W., 61 semester hours; and the Ed.Spec., 71 semester hours.

Research Facilities

The program in communication disorders maintains a Speech Science Laboratory for research. Graduate students in art have access to a foundry, a woodworking shop, and studios for sculpture, ceramics, crafts, drawing, painting, printmaking, graphic arts, fibers, jewelry, design, and art education. Facilities for music include a recording and score collection, a computer-equipped theory laboratory, the Center for Music Technology, and an electronic music laboratory. The psychology program has animal research facilities, human-subject testing rooms, social psychology research rooms, a physiology laboratory, the Center for Neuropsychology, and computer-support resources.

Financial Aid

Graduate assistantships valued up to $7440 per year in 2001–02 were available in the Academic Advising and Retention Program, art, business, communication sciences and disorders, corporate/professional communication, counselor education, criminal justice, education, English, music, nursing, psychology, and a variety of University offices. For more information, students should contact the Graduate College, Box 6928. Resident directorships, involving the supervision of undergraduates in the residence halls, are valued at $10,000. There are a few summer work fellowships, and student loan programs are also available. For more information, students should write to the Financial Aid Office at Box 6905.

Cost of Study

In 2001–02, tuition and fees were $2004 per semester for Virginia residents and $3877 per semester for nonresidents. Tuition per hour was $167 for Virginia residents and $323 for nonresidents. Costs are subject to change for 2002–03. The cost of books and supplies varies but averages $325 per semester.

Living and Housing Costs

A single student could expect living expenses of about $4000 per semester in 2001–02. A variety of housing is available in the community.

Student Group

Of the University's total student population of 8,800, approximately 1,200 are graduate students. Of these, about two thirds are women.

Location

The city of Radford is 45 miles southwest of Roanoke, Virginia, on Interstate Highway 81. It is located in the New River Valley between the Blue Ridge and Allegheny mountains. Radford has a population of 15,900, but the populations of nearby Christiansburg and Blacksburg combine with Radford's to total a substantially larger number. National forests, Claytor Lake, the Blue Ridge Parkway, and the Appalachian Trail provide a wide range of outdoor recreational opportunities.

The University

Radford is a medium-sized, coeducational, comprehensive university at which the student receives individual attention and never becomes submerged in great masses of other students. Since its first classes began in 1913, Radford has maintained a strong tradition of excellence in teaching and of attention to the needs of the individual student. Although the University has grown dramatically in recent years and has developed its programs to stay in the forefront of educational excellence, this emphasis on the student has been maintained.

Applying

For admission to the College of Graduate and Extended Education, all applicants should submit an application form, a Virginia domicile classification form, and at least two letters of recommendation. Transcripts of all previous college work should be supplied by the institutions at which the work was done. Test scores (GRE, MAT, GMAT) should be supplied by the testing agency. There is an application fee of $25.

Correspondence and Information

Graduate Studies Admissions
Box 6928
Radford University
Radford, Virginia 24142
Telephone: 540-831-5431
World Wide Web: http://www.radford.edu (Radford University)
http://www.radford.edu/gradcatalog/index.html (the Graduate College Catalog)
http://www.radford.edu/~gradcoll (online application)

THE GRADUATE FACULTY

Accounting and Finance. F. E. Amenkhienan, Chair; Ph.D., Mississippi. B. W. Chase, Ph.D., Virginia Commonwealth. D. V. Davidson, J.D., Indiana. S. E. Perumpral, Ph.D., Virginia Tech. C. C. Rose, Ph.D., Virginia Tech. J. B. Ross, Ph.D., Connecticut. L. K. Saubert, Ph.D., Wisconsin. R. W. Saubert, J.D., Drake. C. D. White, Ph.D., Ohio State.

Art. A. Jones, Chair; Ph.D., Case Western Reserve. S. Arbury, M.A., Rutgers. C. Brouwer, M.F.A., Western Michigan. T. Dodson, M.F.A., Edinboro. A. A. Feng, M.F.A., Radford. J. Knipe, M.F.A., Minnesota. J. Krebs, M.F.A., Kansas. P. L. Lawson, M.F.A., Georgia. E. Le Schock, M.Ed., Temple. D. Mercer, Ph.D., Georgia. H. Salam, D.F.A., Texas Tech. L. Sanders-Bustle, Ph.D., Virginia Tech. J. Spoon, M.A., Michigan State.

Communication Sciences and Disorders. R. Linville, Chair; Ph.D., Iowa. L. Adams, Ph.D., Tennessee. M. C. Calloway, M.A., Tennessee. D. Culbertson, Ph.D., Iowa. J. E. Nicely, Ph.D., Illinois. P. Rossi, M.S., Virginia Commonwealth. S. Singleton, M.A., Radford. M. Taylor, M.S., Radford. M. VanLue, Ph.D., Case Western Reserve. C. M. Waldron, Ph.D., Virginia Tech. B. Whisonant, M.S., Radford.

Corporate and Professional Communication. W. Kennan, Chair; Ph.D., Oklahoma. G. O. Brown, Ph.D., Maryland. T. J. Brunneau, Ph.D., Penn State. M. W. Cronin, Ph.D., Wayne State. D. Dobkins, Ph.D., Oklahoma. G. Grice, Ph.D., Texas at Austin. V. Hazelton, Ph.D., Oklahoma.

Counselor Education. D. Anderson, Chair; Ed.D., Virginia Tech. K. Eriksen, Ph.D., George Mason. A. Forrest, Ed.D., William and Mary. D. J. Gumaer, Ed.D., Florida. P. W. Harris, Ed.D., East Tennessee State. D. E. Hill, Ph.D., Alabama. K. Jordan, Ph.D., Virginia Tech. S. Lynch, Ph.D., Kansas State. L. Murray, Ph.D., Virginia Tech. W. R. Scott, Ph.D., Virginia Tech. P. Stanley, Ph.D., North Carolina. J. Strosnider, M.S., Appalachian State.

Criminal Justice. I. Van Patten, Chair; Ph.D., Virginia Tech. B. Abdul-Rauf, Ph.D., South Florida. M. Atwell, Ph.D., Saint Louis. T. W. Burke, Ph.D., CUNY, John Jay. J. Call, Ph.D., Georgia. M. Jordan, Ph.D., Missouri. W. M. Oliver, Ph.D., West Virginia. C. Tischler, Ph.D., Sam Houston State.

Educational Studies. D. H. Jackman, Chair; Ph.D., Minnesota. M. Aylesworth, Ed.D., Virginia. S. Bisset, M.S.Ed., Radford. E. C. Brandt, Ph.D., Connecticut. C. Butcher, Ph.D., South Florida. A. L. Corey, Ph.D., Syracuse. E. D. Dore, Ed.D., Northern Colorado. B. Foulks-Boyd, Ed.D., Pacific University. D. Gregory, M.S., George Peabody. P. M. Harris, Ph.D., North Carolina. H. R. Jahn, Ph.D., Michigan. J. James, M.S., Ed.D., Virginia Tech. R. W. Kolenbrander, Ph.D., Kansas State. D. Langrehr, Ph.D., Florida State. V. D. Linkous, Ed.D., Virginia Tech. R. J. Lockwood, Ed.D., Rutgers. S. J. Moore, Ed.D., Virginia Tech. J. K. Newhouse, Ph.D., Virginia Tech. S. S. Reyna, Ed.D., Virginia Tech. J. L. Sellers, Ed.D., Virginia Tech. P. Shoemaker, Ph.D., South Florida. R. C. Small Jr., Ph.D., Virginia.

English. R. F. Guruswamy, Chair; Ph.D., Kent State. M. P. Baker, Ph.D., Notre Dame. S. R. Christianson, Ph.D., Minnesota. L. Cubbison, Ph.D., Purdue. G. T. Edwards, Ph.D., Virginia. K. D. Gainer, Ph.D., Ohio State. K. Kelly, Ph.D., Florida State. R. P. Lanier Jr., Ph.D., Tennessee. C. Mathews, Ph.D., North Carolina. T. C. Poland, Ph.D., Georgia State. R. S. Riddle, Ph.D., Tennessee. D. C. Samson, Ph.D., North Carolina. J. Saperstein, Ph.D., New Hampshire. D. E. Secreast, Ph.D., Iowa. W. P. Self, Ed.D., Virginia Tech. H. Siebert, Ph.D., Iowa. R. Van Noy, Ph.D., Case Western Reserve. J. W. Wawrzycka, Ph.D., Southern Illinois. A. Weiss, Ph.D., Berkeley. P. T. Witkowsky, Ph.D., North Carolina.

Geology. S. Lenhart, Chair; Ph.D., Kentucky. W. P. Anderson, Ph.D., North Carolina State. E. H. Kastning, Ph.D., Texas. K. L. Knight, Ph.D., Iowa. P. Sethi, Ph.D., North Carolina. J. S. Tso, Ph.D., Virginia Tech. C. F. Watts, Ph.D., Purdue. R. C. Whisonant, Ph.D., Florida State.

Management and Marketing. A. L. Bures, Chair; Ph.D., Nebraska. H. M. Beheshti, Ph.D., Oklahoma State. B. K. Blaylock, Ph.D., Georgia State. F. B. Green, Ph.D., Virginia Tech. D. A. Henderson, Ph.D., Nebraska–Lincoln. J. D. Herrington, D.B.A., Mississippi State. J. M. Kopf, Ph.D., Arkansas. J. G. Lollar, Ph.D., Alabama. M. R. Mattson, Ph.D., Tennessee. H.-M. Tong, Ph.D., Nebraska. G. D. Wiggs, Ed.D., George Washington.

Music. E. C. Fellin, Chair; Ph.D., Wisconsin. J. E. Borling, M.M., Miami (Florida). M. D. Camphouse, M.M., Northwestern. D. Castonguay, M.A., Connecticut. C. W. Conger, M.M., Kentucky. D. C. Dabney, D.M.A., Michigan. R. K. Dean, M.M., Florida State. C. James, M.M., Indiana. N. Kats, M.F.A., Minnesota. B. P. Mahin, D.M.A., Johns Hopkins (Peabody). M. Meador, Ph.D., North Texas State. E. E. Mikenas, M.M., Manhattan. J. P. Scartelli, Ph.D., Miami (Florida). R. S. Trent, M.A., Trenton State. A. F. Wojtera, M.M., Northwestern. D. A. Zuschin, M.M., Yale.

Nursing. J. H. Boettcher, Chair; Ph.D., Texas at Austin. M. K. Bassett, M.S., Boston University. E. Birx, Ph.D., Texas at Austin. K. Carter, M.S.N., Virginia. K. S. Castleberry, Ph.D., Wisconsin–Madison. S. C. Cooper, M.S.N., Old Dominion. J. Cox, M.S., Radford. C. Gibbons, M.S., West Virginia. M. H. Gibson, M.S.N., Vanderbilt. K. V. Givens, Ed.D., Virginia Tech. J. McDaniel, Ph.D., Virginia Tech. M. Powell, D.N.S., Catholic University. S. Strauss, Ph.D., Washington. V. Weisz, M.S., Virginia Commonwealth.

Psychology. A. V. E. Harris, Chair; Ph.D., South Dakota. M. Aamodt, Ph.D., Arkansas. J. Aspelmeier, Ph.D., Kent State. J. E. Bucy, Ph.D., North Carolina. J. L. Chase, Ph.D., South Carolina. F. W. Clemens, Ed.D., Virginia. A. Elliott, Ph.D., Northern Illinois. C. H. Fischer, Ph.D., Tennessee. D. Friedman, Ph.D., South Carolina. D. M. Hall, Ph.D., North Carolina. R. Hiltonsmith, Ph.D., Vanderbilt (Peabody). P. A. Jackson, Ph.D., Kentucky. J. King, Ph.D., Virginia Tech. H. M. Lips, Ph.D., Northwestern. C. S. McKee, Ph.D., Nebraska. J. J. Montuori, Ph.D., Florida State. H. T. Mullis, Ph.D., Utah. T. W. Pierce, Ph.D., Maine. N. P. Reilly, Ph.D., Dartmouth. J. Willner, Ph.D., Dalhousie.

Social Work. M. Rigby, Chair; M.S.W., Case Western Reserve. A. Barnes, Ph.D., Washington (St. Louis). J. Burroughs, M.S.W., New Mexico Highlands. D. Cogswell, Ed.D., Virginia Tech. S. Culver, Ph.D., Chicago State. A. Dornberg, M.S.W., Illinois. R. Duncan-Datson, M.S.W., Florida International. D. Hodge, Ph.D., Chicago State. S. Kossak, Ph.D., South Carolina. L. Marais, M.S.W., Ed.D., Western Michigan. M. Risacher, M.S.W., Virginia Commonwealth. J. Smeltzer, M.S.W., Virginia Commonwealth.

Special Education. A. G. Anderson, Chair; Ed.D., Virginia Tech. A. Babkie, Ed.D., Florida Atlantic. D. Bays, Ph.D., Virginia Tech. J. B. Engelhard, Ed.D., Virginia Tech. C. H. Geller, Ph.D., Virginia Tech. R. E. Janney, Ph.D., Nebraska–Lincoln. N. Wheeler, Ed.D., Vanderbilt.

REGENT UNIVERSITY

Graduate Programs

Programs of Study

Regent University offers master's- and doctoral-level programs in business (M.B.A., Executive M.B.A., Professional M.B.A., M.A. in management, graduate certificate programs); communication and the arts (M.A. in communication [cinema-TV, theater, communication studies, script and screenwriting], M.A. in journalism, Master of Fine Arts [M.F.A.] in script and screenwriting, Ph.D. in communication); divinity (M.A. in biblical studies, M.A. in missiology, M.A. in practical theology, Master of Divinity [M.Div.], Doctor of Ministry [D.Min.]); education (Master of Education [M.Ed.], TESOL Certificate, Doctor of Education [Ed.D.], Certificate of Advanced Graduate Studies [C.A.G.S.] in education, Alternative Licensure Program); government (M.A. in public policy, M.A. in political management, Master of Public Administration [M.P.A.], Certificate of Advanced Graduate Studies [C.A.G.S.] in public policy); law (Juris Doctor [J.D.]); psychology and counseling (M.A. in counseling, M.A. in human services counseling, Certificate of Advanced Counseling Studies [C.A.C.S.], Doctor of Psychology [Psy.D.] in clinical psychology, Ph.D. in counselor education and supervision); and leadership studies (M.A. in organizational leadership, Certificate of Graduate Studies [C.G.S.] in leadership, Ph.D. in organizational leadership, Doctor of Strategic Leadership [D.S.L.], Certificate of Advanced Graduate Studies [C.A.G.S.] in leadership). Programs are offered on the Virginia Beach Campus, online (distance education) via the Worldwide Campus, and at the Graduate Center, Northern Virginia/D.C., and are fully accredited. Virtually all master's-level programs are available as joint degrees, which allows the student to earn two degrees in less time.

The following programs are offered at the Graduate Center, Northern Virginia/D.C., in Alexandria, Virginia: Professional M.B.A., M.A. in management, M.A. in biblical studies, M.A. in practical theology, M.Ed., TESOL Certificate, Alternative Licensure Program, M.A. in public policy, M.A. in political management, M.P.A., C.A.G.S. in public policy, M.A. in journalism, M.A. in counseling, and C.A.C.S. Some programs require online courses for the completion of the degree.

The following programs are offered online via the Worldwide Campus: Executive M.B.A., Professional M.B.A., M.A. in management, graduate certificate programs in business, M.A. in communication, M.A. in journalism, Ph.D. in communication, M.A. in biblical studies, M.A. in practical theology, M.Div., M.Ed., Ed.D., C.A.G.S. in education, TESOL Certificate, M.A. in public policy, M.A. in political management, M.P.A., C.A.G.S. in public policy, M.A. in organizational leadership, C.G.S. in leadership, Ph.D. in organizational leadership, D.S.L., C.A.G.S. in leadership, M.A. in human services counseling, and Ph.D. in counselor education and supervision. Some programs require on-campus courses and/or residencies.

Research Facilities

The University Library collections consist of more than 220,000 printed volumes, 700,000 microforms, and 13,000 audiovisual items, including films, CDs, laser discs, and audiocassettes and videocassettes. In addition, the library subscribes to more than 2,000 journals related to Regent's curriculum, has access to more than 6,000 full-text journal titles online, and has close to 200 electronic indexes and 75 full-text reference or journal databases via remote access. Databases available include WorldCat, ABI/Inform, NetLibrary, ATLA Religion Database, Academic Universe, Congressional Universe, Business & Company Resource Center, Dow Jones Interactive, ERIC Full Text, Education Full Text, ComIndex, ComAbstracts, Expanded Academic Index, Emerald Library, History Universe, JSTOR, Project Muse, PsycINFO, PsycArticles, Social Science Citation Index, International Index to the Performing Arts, Standard and Poors, and Digital Dissertations, to name a few.

Financial Aid

The University financial aid is institutionally and federally funded. More than 75 percent of the student body receives some form of financial assistance. In addition to need-based assistance grants, Regent offers scholarship awards based on academic merit, potential in the chosen area of study, professional experience, spiritual maturity, and clarity of goals. Applications for most awards are due by April 1; however, some deadlines vary. Regent participates in the Virginia state Tuition Assistance Grant Program. Graduate assistantships, campus jobs, Federal Stafford Student Loans, and alternative private education loans are also available.

Cost of Study

Tuition varies by program, as do additional fees. Tuition costs for the 2002–03 school year are as follows: Executive M.B.A., $740/credit hour; M.B.A., Professional M.B.A., M.A. in management, and graduate certificate programs in business, $535/credit hour; M.A. in communication, M.A. in journalism, M.F.A. in script and screenwriting, and Ph.D. in communication, $450/credit hour (subject to change for fall 2002); M.A. in missiology, M.A. in biblical studies, M.A. in practical theology, M.Div., and D.Min., $335/credit hour; M.Ed. and TESOL Certificate, $379/credit hour; Ed.D. and C.A.G.S. in education, $488/credit hour; M.A. in public policy, M.A. in political management, M.P.A., and C.A.G.S. in public policy, $450/credit hour; M.A. in organizational leadership and C.G.S. in leadership, $375/credit hour; Ph.D. in organizational leadership, D.S.L., and C.A.G.S. in leadership, $500/credit hour; J.D., $595/credit hour; M.A. in human services counseling and C.A.C.S., $400/credit hour; and Psy.D. in clinical psychology and Ph.D. in counselor education and supervision, $500/credit hour.

Living and Housing Costs

The Regent Village is less than 1 mile from the campus and consists of 112 two-bedroom, one-bath apartments; 56 two-bedroom, two-bath apartments; and 56 three-bedroom, two-bath apartments. Accommodations for a single person sharing an apartment cost between $300 and $335 per month; for a married couple, between $560 and $655 per month. Rent is subject to change.

Student Group

Regent University has an enrollment of more than 2,700 students. In a typical year, this population represents all fifty states, approximately sixty other countries, and more than 400 undergraduate institutions. Students range in age from 22 to 74, with the average age about 36.5. Approximately 50 percent are married.

Location

The main campus of stately Georgian-style buildings is located in Virginia Beach, Virginia. The University is privileged to share several hundred acres of pine-timbered land with the Christian Broadcasting Network. Within a 2-hour drive of Regent University are historic Yorktown, Jamestown, and Colonial Williamsburg. Richmond, the state capital, and Washington, D.C., are less than a 4-hour drive by car. The Graduate Center, Northern Virginia/D.C. campus, is located across from the King Street metro stop in Alexandria, Virginia. Regent University also offers programs online via its convenient, flexible Worldwide Campus.

The University

Regent University, incorporated in 1977, is accredited by the Commission on Colleges of the Southern Association of Colleges and Schools (1866 Southern Lane, Decatur, Georgia 30033-4097; telephone: 404-679-4501) to award bachelor's, master's, and doctoral degrees. The School of Law is fully accredited by the American Bar Association. The School of Divinity is accredited by the Association of Theological Schools (ATS). The Council for Accreditation of Counseling and Related Educational Programs (CACREP), a specialized accrediting body recognized by the Council for Higher Education Accreditation (CHEA), has conferred accreditation to the following program areas offered by the School of Psychology and Counseling of Regent University: community counseling and school counseling (M.A.).

Applying

An application packet may be requested from the mailing address below. Some applications are available online at http://www.regent.edu/admissions. Application requirements include submission of transcripts, graduate test scores (GRE, GMAT, LSAT, or MAT), a nonrefundable fee ranging from $30 to $100, a personal goals statement, and three recommendations (clergy, faculty, and general). Requirements vary slightly for law school applicants. Application deadlines vary by program.

Correspondence and Information

Central Enrollment Management
Regent University
1000 Regent University Drive
Virginia Beach, Virginia 23464
Telephone: 800-373-5504 (toll-free) (Central Admissions)
E-mail: admissions@regent.edu
World Wide Web: http://www.regent.edu

DEPARTMENT CONTACTS AND RESEARCH AREAS

Regent University offers the knowledge and information needed to succeed—tools that will foster one's role as a leader in today's society—through graduate degrees that are critical in today's culture. Regent programs integrate rigorous academics with biblical principles—an approach that prepares students to succeed personally and professionally.

GRADUATE SCHOOL OF BUSINESS
Dr. John Mulford, Dean. The Graduate School of Business offers the M.B.A.*, Professional M.B.A.*, Executive M.B.A., M.A. in management*, and graduate certificate programs*. The Graduate School of Business also offers the C12 Group M.B.A. for members of a C12 Group. *Concentrations include e-business, entrepreneurship, finance, human resource management, international business, marketing, nonprofit management, and organizational change and development.

COLLEGE OF COMMUNICATION AND THE ARTS
Dr. William Brown, Dean. The College's new Communication & Performing Arts Building is scheduled for completion in fall 2002. This state-of-the-art building features a 750-seat proscenium theater, a camera acting lab, a dance studio, a Foley sound stage, a television production studio, a back lot, film screening rooms, a 150-seat experimental theater, an aircraft cable grid, a 2,500-square-foot scenographic lab with paint floor and prop shop, two 1,200-square-foot rehearsal/performance movement classrooms, and much more.

School of Journalism
The M.A. in journalism offers areas of study in news journalism (print and broadcast), professional writing, and public relations. Students may study at the Virginia Beach Campus, at the Washington Graduate Journalism Center in Northern Virginia/D.C., or online via the Worldwide Campus. Research focus for the Ph.D. in communication may center on journalism.

School of Cinema-Television/Theatre Arts
Students in this school earn the M.A. in communication and may choose from a variety of concentrations. Cinema/television students may focus on directing, editing, producing, entertainment arts management, critical studies, or 3-D animation. Areas of study for theater arts majors include performance studies or design and technical theater. Students in script and screenwriting may focus on writing for theater or writing for cinema-television. The M.F.A. in script and screenwriting is also available. The Ph.D. in communication may include research in any of the above areas.

School of Communication Studies
The M.A. in communication may be pursued with an emphasis in communication studies or computer-mediated communication. The Ph.D. in communication may be pursued with an emphasis in communication studies. Research areas depend upon faculty area of expertise and student interest.

SCHOOL OF PSYCHOLOGY AND COUNSELING
Dr. Rosemarie Scotti Hughes, Dean. The school offers the M.A. in counseling and the C.A.G.S. in counseling, both with concentrations in community counseling and school counseling; the M.A. in human services counseling; the Psy.D. in clinical psychology; and the Ph.D. in educational psychology. The Council for Accreditation of Counseling and Related Educational Programs (CACREP), a specialized accrediting body recognized by the Council for Higher Education Accreditation (CHEA), has conferred accreditation to the following program areas offered by the School of Psychology and Counseling of Regent University: community counseling (M.A.) and school counseling (M.A.).

SCHOOL OF DIVINITY
Dr. Vinson Synan, Dean. The school offers the M.A. in biblical studies (biblical interpretation, Christian doctrine and history, English Bible, New Testament, and Old Testament); missiology (entrepreneurial tentmaking, interdisciplinary studies, ministry to Muslims, missions management, practical missiology, and TESOL); and practical theology (cell church leadership, church and ministry, interdisciplinary studies, and worship and renewal studies). The M.Div. offers areas of study in missiology (same concentrations as the M.A. in missiology) and practical theology (same concentrations as the M.A. in practical theology). The D.Min. offers areas of study in advanced cell leadership training, clinical pastoral education, and leadership and renewal and is also available in Korea. The School of Divinity is accredited by the Association of Theological Schools.

SCHOOL OF EDUCATION
Dr. Alan Arroyo, Dean. The school offers the M.Ed. with ten majors: Christian school program, cross-categorical special education, educational leadership, individualized degree plan, master teacher program, master teacher program/English as a second language, school-based security and community policing, TESOL, and TESOL/initial licensure with optional reading specialist endorsement. The Ed.D. offers seven cognates: K–12 school leadership, higher education administration, staff development/adult education, educational psychology, special education, distance education, and Christian education leadership. The C.A.G.S. in education, TESOL certificate, and an alternative licensure program are also available.

ROBERTSON SCHOOL OF GOVERNMENT
Dr. Kathaleen Reid-Martinez. The school offers the M.A. in public policy (strategic leadership, economic policy analysis, political philosophy, domestic policy analysis, and individualized); M.A. in political management (campaign management); M.P.A. (leadership studies); and the C.A.G.S. in public policy.

SCHOOL OF LAW
Jeffrey Brauch, Dean. The school offers the J.D. (full- or part-time with concentrations in Virginia law, general practice, dispute resolution, commercial, public law, academic, and constitutional law). The School of Law is accredited by the American Bar Association.

CENTER FOR LEADERSHIP STUDIES
Kathaleen Reid-Martinez, Executive Director. The center offers the M.A. in organizational leadership (organizational leadership, corporate communication leadership, educational leadership, church and ministry leadership, leadership in business, leadership in government, interdisciplinary studies, and computer-mediated communication); the C.G.S. in leadership; the Ph.D. in organizational leadership; the Doctor of Strategic Leadership; and the C.A.G.S. in leadership. All degree programs are offered online via the Worldwide Campus only. The Ph.D. and D.S.L. programs require a residency at the Virginia Beach campus for completion of the degree.

REGIS
UNIVERSITY
School for Professional Studies
GRADUATE PROGRAMS

REGIS UNIVERSITY

School for Professional Studies
Graduate Programs

Programs of Study

Regis University offers multiple graduate degree programs. Most programs provide the opportunity to focus studies within an area of emphasis, and many programs offer distance learning options. The Master of Business Administration (M.B.A.) degree represents 30 credit hours. Students may complete the general M.B.A. entirely online using Internet technologies. Emphasis areas in the Master of Science in Computer Information Technology (M.S.C.I.T.) include database technologies, e-commerce engineering, management of technology, networking technologies, and object-oriented technologies. The entire 36-credit-hour program may be completed online. The Master of Science in Management (M.S.M.) degree represents 36 credit hours and includes organizational leadership, project management, and computer information technology emphasis areas that can be completed online. The 36-credit-hour Master of Nonprofit Management (M.N.M.) is available in distance formats. The Master of Liberal Studies (M.L.S.) is offered through a mentored (guided independent) learning format. Emphasis areas are available in adult learning, training and development, language and communication, psychology (including Colorado Licensed Professional Counselor), and social sciences. The M.L.S. degree programs require 36 to 48 credit hours. The Master of Education (M.Ed.) is a 36-to-60-credit-hour program.

Research Facilities

Regis University Libraries are dedicated to providing a full range of library services and resources to Regis students and faculty members without regard to their geographic location. Dayton Memorial Library (DML) is the main library facility of Regis University, offering students a significant collection of print, multimedia, and online resources. DML includes 300 individual study stations, numerous group study rooms, individual faculty carrels, and shelving capacity for up to 350,000 volumes. RegisNet is available throughout the building, along with a multimedia production lab, and a state-of-the-art electronic classroom. Library computer workstations with access to online resources and word processing are located throughout the building.

Financial Aid

The primary sources of financial aid for graduate students are loans. Both subsidized need-based loans and unsubsidized loans for applicants without demonstrated need are available. The Regis University Office of Financial Aid is responsible for processing and administering the student loan program. Financial aid applications are accepted on a rolling basis for degree- or graduate certificate–seeking applicants. Students must be enrolled at least half time to utilize federal financial aid programs.

Cost of Study

For 2002–03, the per-credit-hour charges for classroom-based and and online (figures in parentheses) courses are $385 ($440) for the M.B.A. program, $335 ($360) for the M.S.C.I.T. program, $320 ($350) for the M.S.M. program, $295 ($310) for the M.N.M. program, $302 for the M.L.S. program, and $315 ($320) for the M.Ed. program. Additional expenses are a $75 application fee and an $80 graduation fee. The average per-course cost of books is $150.

Living and Housing Costs

University-sponsored housing is not available to graduate students. More then half of the students complete course work through distance education.

Student Group

Regis University Graduate Programs serves approximately 5,500 nontraditional working adult students. Classes are offered in the evening, online, or through guided independent study formats. The average age of incoming students is 36. Most students bring more than ten years of work experience to the program. The overall breakdown of men to women varies by program of study, but it is approximately even.

Student Outcomes

Regis graduate students represent midlevel to upper-level professionals who seek to enhance their skills in a rigorous interactive academic environment. Many pursue careers in business, computer information systems, counseling, or education. Graduates include systems engineers, database administrators, chief financial officers, marketing managers, human resources managers, trainers, licensed counselors, educators, and grant administrators.

Location

Regis University is located in Denver, Colorado. Students may complete course work at one of six campuses along the Front Range or through distance learning.

The School

To better meet the needs of adult students, Regis University created the School for Professional Studies in the mid-1970s. Last year, more than 12,000 students completed courses through the School. Courses are offered in the evenings and through Internet technologies (distance education) in eight-week accelerated formats. Regis has been nationally recognized as a leader in providing adults with innovative, professional, and personalized education programs.

Applying

Application materials may be obtained by sending a request to the address below or through the University's Web site. In addition to the application for admissions and a $75 application fee, the following materials are required for most programs of study: official transcripts from regionally accredited bachelor's degree–granting institutions, two letters of recommendation, a resume, and critical analysis essays. Individual programs may have additional requirements. Applicants who received an undergraduate degree from an institution outside the United States must meet additional requirements.

Correspondence and Information

Graduate Admissions Office
3333 Regis Boulevard L-16
Denver, Colorado 80221
Telephone: 303-458-4080
800-677-9270 (toll-free)
E-mail: masters@regis.edu
World Wide Web: http://www.regis.edu

THE FACULTY

Courses are taught by full-time and affiliate faculty members who are experts in their fields. Faculty members bring years of professional experience in their subject areas into the classroom and hold the academic credentials to teach at the graduate level.

RENSSELAER POLYTECHNIC INSTITUTE

Graduate Studies

Programs of Study

Rensselaer awards advanced degrees in the Schools of Architecture, Engineering, Humanities and Social Sciences, Management, and Science.

The School of Architecture offers the M.Arch. as a first professional degree for students with bachelor's degrees in any field; this program requires 3½ years of study. Applicants for the M.Arch. as a second professional degree, a one-year program, must have an undergraduate degree in architecture from an accredited program. An M.S. in building sciences, informatics, or architecture and an M.S. degree in lighting are also available.

The School of Engineering ranks among the top twenty-five engineering schools in the nation by the *U.S. News & World Report* survey and is ranked in the top ten by practicing engineers. The School offers Master of Engineering (M.Eng.), Master of Science (M.S.), Doctor of Engineering (D.Eng), and Doctor of Philosophy (Ph.D.) degrees. Programs include aeronautical engineering, biomedical engineering, chemical engineering, civil engineering, computer and systems engineering, decision sciences and engineering systems, electrical engineering, electric power, engineering physics, industrial and management engineering, manufacturing systems, materials engineering, mechanical engineering, nuclear engineering, operation research and statistics, and transportation. The M.Eng. program is a nonthesis degree intended for professional practice. A student with an accredited B.S. or its equivalent can typically complete this degree in one year.

The School of Science offers M.S. and Ph.D. programs in biology, chemistry, computer science, geology, mathematics, and physics. Master's degrees are available in applied mathematics, applied science, biochemistry and biophysics, and natural sciences.

The School of Management grants the degrees of M.B.A., M.S., and Ph.D., with a focus on the intersection of management and technology. An Executive M.B.A. is also offered.

The School of Humanities and Social Sciences offers the master's degree in communication and rhetoric; economics; ecological economics, values, and policy; electronic arts; philosophy; psychology; technical communication; and science and technology studies. A doctorate may be obtained in communication and rhetoric, ecological economics, and science and technology studies. Interdisciplinary programs are offered by most departments.

Research Facilities

Research is supported by such state-of-the-art facilities as the George M. Low Center for Industrial Innovation; the Rensselaer Libraries, whose electronic information systems provide access to collections, databases, and Internet resources from campus and remote terminals; the Rensselaer Computing System, which includes public UNIX workstations, a shared toolkit of applications for interactive learning and research and high-speed Internet connectivity; and a high-performance computing facility that includes an 18-node SP2 parallel computer with 68 CPUs. In addition, the academic departments have extensive research capabilities and equipment. There are also numerous centers and institutes, including Integrated Electronics and Electronic Manufacturing, Materials Research, Composite Materials and Structures, Lighting Research, Science and Technology Policy, Infrastructure and Transportation Studies, and the Geotechnical Centrifuge Research Center. Other research support units include the Fresh Water Institute and the Scientific Computation Center.

Financial Aid

Financial aid is available in the form of tuition scholarships. Rensselaer research and teaching assistantships and university, corporate, and national fellowships fund many of Rensselaer's full-time graduate students. Outstanding students may qualify for university-supported Rensselaer Graduate Fellowship Awards, which carry a minimum stipend of $16,000 and a full tuition and fees scholarship. All fellowship awards are calendar-year awards for full-time graduate students. Summer support is also available in many departments. Low-interest, deferred-repayment graduate loans are also available to U.S. citizens with demonstrated need.

Cost of Study

Full-time graduate tuition for the 2002–03 academic year is $26,400. Other additional costs (estimated living expenses, insurance, etc.) are projected to be around $11,940. Therefore, the cost of attendance for full-time graduate study is approximately $38,340. Part-time study and cohort programs are priced differently. Students should contact Rensselaer for specific cost information related to the program they wish to study.

Living and Housing Costs

The cost of rooms for single students in residence halls or apartments ranges from $3866 to $6102 for the 2002–03 academic year. Family student housing, with a monthly rent of $620 to $755, is also available.

Student Group

There are about 5,100 undergraduates and 1,880 graduate students representing all fifty states and more than eighty countries at Rensselaer.

Student Outcomes

Eighty-one percent of Rensselaer's 2001 graduate students were hired after graduation, earning starting salaries that averaged $67,019 for master's degree recipients.

Location

Troy, New York, is situated in the northeastern United States, 150 miles north of New York City. Rensselaer Polytechnic Institute is centrally located with easy driving access to Boston (3 hours); New York City (3 hours); Montreal (4 hours); Niagara Falls (5 hours); Baltimore, Maryland (6½ hours); and Washington, D.C. (7½ hours).

The University

Founded in 1824, and the oldest technological university in the English-speaking world, Rensselaer today is accredited by the Middle States Association of Colleges and Schools and is a private, nonsectarian, coeducational university. Rensselaer has five schools—Architecture, Engineering, Management, Science, and Humanities and Social Sciences—that offer a total of 104 graduate degrees in forty-two fields. A master's degree in information technology, offering many cross-disciplinary options, is also available.

Applying

Applications and all supporting credentials should be submitted well in advance of the preferred semester of entry to allow sufficient time for departmental review and processing. The application fee is $45. Since the first departmental awards are made in February for the next full academic year, applicants are encouraged to submit all required credentials by January 15 to ensure consideration.

Correspondence and Information

For written information about graduate work:

Department of (specify)
Graduate Admissions
Rensselaer Polytechnic Institute
Troy, New York 12180-3590
Telephone: 518-276-6216
World Wide Web: http://www.rpi.edu

For applications and admissions information:

Rensselaer Admissions
Rensselaer Polytechnic Institute
110 8th Street
Troy, New York 12180-3590
Telephone: 518-276-6216
Fax: 518-276-4072
E-mail: admissions@rpi.edu
World Wide Web: http://www.rpi.edu

AREAS OF RESEARCH

Aeronautical Engineering. Departmental projects generally are concerned with the design, operation, and handling of high-speed atmospheric and space vehicles. Interdisciplinary projects include the design and construction of advanced-composite aircraft structures, a miniature remotely piloted vehicle, transient heat transfer in spacecraft, aeroelasticity and structural analysis, helicopter technology (through the Center of Excellence in Rotorcraft Technology), computational and experimental fluid mechanics, and advanced propulsion.
Architecture. Programs are available in architecture (3½-year professional degree); lighting; informatics and architecture; building conservation; sonics in architecture; workplace design and computing; and advanced studies in architecture, emphasizing the theoretical, scientific, technical, and aesthetic potentials of tomorrow's workplace. (An asterisk denotes pending New York State approval.)
Bioinformatics. Design and applications of algorithms for sequence database searching, sequence alignment and sequence analysis, molecular modeling.
Biology. Molecular biology, biophysics, biochemistry, applied and environmental microbiology, plant biology, freshwater ecology, bioinformatics.
Biomedical Engineering. Biomaterials, biomechanics, biofluids, computational bioengineering, cellular and tissue bioengineering, computing and signal processing, systems physiology, biomedical imaging, and clinical medicine and anesthesiology, electrical impedance imaging.
Chemical Engineering. Interfacial phenomena; nonlinear diffusing; thermodynamics; combustion and high-temperature kinetics: generation of air pollutants; polymer engineering: biocatalysis and biochemical engineering; membrane and chromatographic separations; processing of semiconductors and other advanced materials; process control and design; and mesoscale/nanoscale engineering.
Chemistry. Biochemistry and biophysics, organic and bioorganic chemistry, natural products synthesis, medicinal chemistry, materials chemistry, polymer chemistry (synthesis and physical properties), analytical chemistry, inorganic chemistry, electrochemistry, coordination and organometallic chemistry, nuclear chemistry and radiochemistry, photochemistry (including laser techniques), physical chemistry, physical organic chemistry, solid-state chemistry and crystal growth, spectroscopy (laser, microwave, NMR, ESR, vibrational, fluorescence, and in situ environmental probes), and surface science.
Civil Engineering. Geotechnical, earthquake, structural, infrastructure, and transporting engineering; mechanics of composite materials and structures; and computational mechanics. Research activities emphasize advanced computer-based modeling techniques with direct ties to simulation and state-of-the-art field and laboratory testing.
Computer and Systems Engineering. Research and academic programs are available in intelligent network management, neural networks, wireless networks, software engineering, advanced image processing, parallel computation, digital signal processing, computer vision and pattern recognition, computational geometry, computer graphics and visualization, gigahertz microprocessor design, artificial intelligence and robotics, and distributed manufacturing systems.
Computer Science. Research and academic programs are available in computational science and engineering, computer vision, collaborative design, database systems, generic programming and software design, human computer interaction, medical imaging, networking, parallel and distributed computing, robotics, and theory and algorithms.
Decision Sciences and Engineering Systems. Programs are offered in industrial and management engineering, manufacturing systems engineering, operations research and statistics, and information systems. The program in industrial and management engineering combines the quantitative and behavioral sciences with the classical approach to industrial engineering as applicable in both manufacturing and service systems. The program in manufacturing systems engineering focuses on quality systems, information systems, management processes and technology, and systems modeling pertaining to manufacturing. The program in operations research and statistics offers advanced study in mathematical modeling optimization and statistical techniques applicable to a wide range of practical problems. Research at the doctoral level is conducted, with particular emphasis on information systems, manufacturing systems engineering, operations research and statistics, industrial engineering, and systems engineering.
Ecological Economics, Values and Policy. Program is focused on the theory and practice of sustainability: the economic, political, social, cultural, and ethical implications and interactions of science, technology, environment, and society.
Economics and Ecological Economics. The department offers an M.S. in economics and a Ph.D. in ecological economics. Areas of research include but are not limited to cost-benefit analysis, environmental valuation, natural resource economics, public sector economics, and regional economics. Ecological economics is concerned with the relationship between economic systems, society, and the environment.
Electrical Engineering. Research and academic programs are available in semiconductor device characterization, semiconductor power devices, multilevel interconnects, thermophotovoltaic devices, automation and robotics, multivariable and nonlinear control, agile manufacturing, communications and information processing, digital signal processing, advanced image processing, computer communication networks, gigahertz microprocessor design, multimedia systems, electronics manufacturing, and plasma diagnostics.
Electric Power Engineering. High-voltage transmission and compaction of equipment; large electrical apparatus design; experimental machine analysis; circuit interruption technology; electromagnetics; economic studies of systems; modeling of power systems and component devices; insulation systems; power electronics; adjustable speed drives; and advanced power systems relaying.
Electronic Arts. The program focuses on creative work in an intermedia context, including computer music, digital video art, computer imaging and animation, interactive technologies, and performance and installation, as well as historical and critical studies.
Environmental and Energy Engineering. The department offers degrees in environmental engineering, nuclear engineering, and engineering physics. Environmental engineering focuses on water quality including bioremediation and physicochemical techniques. Topics address disinfection by-product formation, pathogenic protozoan fate in reservoirs, sediment contaminant fate and transport, and mathematical modeling of these and other environmental processes. Research areas in nuclear engineering and engineering physics include fission and fusion reactor technology, nuclear data measurements, health physics, multiphase phenomena, and applied radiation.
Environmental Management and Policy. The department offers an M.S. (45 credits) from the Lally School of Management and Technology, whose graduates are leaders in business, government, environmental consulting, and non-profit organizations. Studies at Rensselaer integrate environmental strategies with core business and policy planning. The course work combines technical expertise in engineering and science with management trends and other business tools.
Environmental Science. Groundwater studies, limnology, and aqueous geochemistry.
Geology. Geochemistry, petrology, structural geology, tectonics, geophysics, seismology, surficial geology, hydrogeology, and planetary science.
Language, Literature, and Communication. The department offers an M.S. in technical communication and an M.S. and Ph.D. in communication and rhetoric. These programs emphasize the interdisciplinary nature of communication, combining the perspectives of technical writing, graphics, human-computer interaction (HCI), rhetorical theory, media studies, composition, speech communication, and literary study.
Management. The Lally School of Management and Technology offers an M.B.A., M.S., and Ph.D. in Management. The theory and practice of integrating management and technology, of turning innovations into commercial or competitive advantages, is interwoven throughout the programs.
Materials Science and Engineering. Metallic and ceramic materials processing; composite materials and structures; electronic materials; ceramics and glass; melting and solidification; welding and joining; surface and interfacial phenomena; nanostructured materials.
Mathematics. Applied mathematics and analysis, including methods of applied mathematics, differential equations, functional analysis, numerical analysis, applied geometry, mathematical programming, operations research, and applications of mathematics in the physical sciences, biological sciences, and engineering.
Mechanical Engineering and Mechanics. Applied mechanics, mechanics of materials, design, energy and thermal/fluid systems, computational and experimental heat transfer, computational and experimental fluid mechanics, manufacturing, structural analysis, advanced composite materials, aeroelasticity, tribology, dynamics and vibrations, computer-aided design, robotics, advanced manufacturing technology, and helicopter technology.
Philosophy. Cognitive science, philosophy of science and technology, artificial intelligence, social and political philosophy, phenomenology, aesthetics, oriental philosophy, metaphysics, and environmental philosophy.
Physics. Experimental and theoretical nuclear and particle physics, condensed-matter physics (surfaces and interfaces), astrophysics (interstellar matter and star formation), biophysics, theory of solids, optical physics, and educational research and development in physics.
Psychology. Personnel selection, performance appraisal, training, test development, leadership, motivation, group processes, decision making, organization theory, psychopharmacology, human factors and cognition, and the study of warning and behavioral compliance.
Science and Technology Studies. Social, historical, political, economic, and cultural dimensions of today's scientific and technological society with emphasis on the ethical and value dimensions.

RHODE ISLAND COLLEGE

Graduate Studies

Programs of Study

Rhode Island College offers graduate programs leading to the Master of Arts (M.A.), Master of Fine Arts (M.F.A.), Master of Arts in Teaching (M.A.T.), Master of Social Work (M.S.W.), Master of Education (M.Ed.), Master of Music Education, Master of Science (M.S.), and Master of Professional Accounting degrees and to the Certificate of Advanced Graduate Study (C.A.G.S.). The College also offers a joint Ph.D. program in education with the University of Rhode Island.

The M.A. is offered in agency counseling, agency counseling with concentration in alcohol/substance abuse, art, educational psychology, English, history, mathematics, media studies, and psychology. The M.F.A. is offered in theater. The areas of concentration for the M.A.T. program are art education, biology, elementary education, English, French, general science, history, mathematics, music, physical science, and Spanish. The M.Ed. is available in bilingual/bicultural education; counselor education; educational administration (elementary or secondary); elementary education; elementary education with a concentration in early childhood; health; individualized M.Ed.; reading; secondary education; special education with a concentration in behavior disorders, learning disabilities, preschool disabilities, secondary special needs, or severe and profound disabilities; teaching English as a second language; and technology education. The M.S. is available in industrial technology. The Master of Professional Accounting degree is available for accounting majors. The M.S.W. provides advanced concentrations in clinical practice and organizing policy and administration.

The C.A.G.S., a 30-semester-hour specialist's program beyond the master's degree, is offered in the following areas: counselor education, counselor education with concentration in mental health, educational administration, and school psychology.

Individualized graduate programs leading to the M.A., M.S., M.Ed., and C.A.G.S. degrees may be developed.

All master's degree programs require at least 30 semester hours of study. The agency counseling program requires 45 hours and the M.A.T. program, from 35 to 45 hours, depending on the concentration and the student's background. The M.Ed. programs require 36 hours. The M.S.W. program requires 61 hours.

Rhode Island College is accredited by the New England Association of Schools and Colleges. Degree programs are accredited by the National Association of Schools of Music, the National Association of State Directors of Teacher Education and Certification, and the National Council for Accreditation of Teacher Certification. Rhode Island College is a member of the Council on Social Work Education and the Council of Graduate Schools in the United States.

Research Facilities

The Adams Library houses more than 500,000 volumes and receives 2,200 periodical subscriptions. An additional campus library, the Curriculum Resources Center, contains books and media materials for educational studies. The Fogarty Life Science Building houses five environmental chambers, a liquid scintillation counter, a high-speed refrigerated centrifuge and a preparative ultracentrifuge, a modern animal room, an insectary, a chromatography room, and an interference microscope. For work in the physical sciences, the Clark Science Building has various spectrometers, including UV-visible–near IR, fluorescence, NMR, and atomic absorption; gas chromatographs; a polarographic analyzer; and a photochemical reactor. Computer facilities include an IBM 4341, DEC VAX-11/780s, IBM PC microcomputer laboratories, and local area network.

Financial Aid

Scholarships and graduate and teaching assistantships are available to full-time students. The stipend was $3500 to $4000 for 2001–02, plus remission of tuition and registration fees for one academic year and a summer session. Information on the departments or areas that offer assistantships is available in the fall; the application deadline is March 15. Traineeships are offered by the School of Social Work. Loan and work-study information may be obtained from the Financial Aid Office.

Cost of Study

Tuition for the 2001–02 academic year was $170 per semester hour for Rhode Island residents and $355 per semester hour for nonresidents. Additional fees were $159 per semester for full-time students and $93 per semester for part-time students. The School of Social Work has a separate fee schedule: $2425 per semester for full-time students who are Rhode Island residents and $3750 per semester for out-of-state full-time students (2001–02 figures). Part-time tuition in the School of Social Work was $170 per credit for Rhode Island residents and $355 per credit for out-of-state students.

Living and Housing Costs

On-campus housing for graduate students at Rhode Island College is very limited; the Housing Office should be contacted early for information. The cost of living in the Providence area is comparable to the national average.

Student Group

In the fall of 2000, the graduate programs had an enrollment of 285 full-time and 1,510 part-time students. Most students come from Rhode Island and nearby areas of southern New England.

Location

The location of Rhode Island College in Providence, the state capital, combines the advantages of city living with easy access to natural recreation areas. Providence is about an hour's drive from Boston and from Rhode Island's noted beaches in Newport and South County. Providence also has an active cultural and social life, which includes the nationally renowned Trinity Square Repertory Company, the Rhode Island School of Design's museum, and the Providence Civic Center, where many musical and sporting events are held.

The College

A state-supported coeducational institution, Rhode Island College is dedicated to educating students in the liberal arts and to providing curricula for professional and preprofessional studies. The total graduate and undergraduate enrollment is about 9,000. Graduate programs at the College were begun in the 1920s. The primary goal of the Graduate Division is to foster advanced study in the arts and sciences and to train professionals in the areas of public and social service. Rhode Island College has designed its graduate programs to meet the needs of many types of individuals. In most programs, students can study full- or part-time, days or evenings. Ample opportunities for graduate course work are also provided during the summer session.

Applying

Since admissions requirements vary according to program, applicants are urged to call or write for specific information. Scores on the General Test of the Graduate Record Examinations or Miller Analogies Test are required (departmental requirements may vary). Applications and all accompanying materials must be received by April 1 for the fall and by November 1 for the spring term. The M.S.W. program has a separate admissions procedure, and all applications and accompanying materials for this program must meet a February 1 deadline. All applicants to the College are charged a $25 application fee.

Correspondence and Information

Faculty of Arts and Sciences
Rhode Island College
Providence, Rhode Island 02908
Telephone: 401-456-8107

Feinstein School of Education and
Human Development
Rhode Island College
Providence, Rhode Island 02908
Telephone: 401-456-8110

School of Social Work
Rhode Island College
Providence, Rhode Island 02908
Telephone: 401-456-8042

Center for Management and Technology
Rhode Island College
Providence, Rhode Island 02908
Telephone: 401-456-8036

FACULTY HEADS

George D. Metrey, Interim Vice President for Academic Affairs; Ph.D., NYU.

Faculty of Arts and Sciences
Richard R. Weiner, Dean; Ph.D., Columbia.

Art: Stephen Fisher, M.F.A., Yale.
Biology: Kenneth Kinsey, Ed.D., Bowling Green State.
English: Joan Dagle, Ph.D., Brown.
French: Olga Juzyn, Ph.D., Brown.
History: Ronald Dufour, Ph.D., William and Mary.
Mathematics: Barry Schiller, A.M., California, Davis.
Music: P. William Hutchinson, Ph.D., Northwestern.
Physical Sciences: David Greene, Ph.D., Kentucky.
Psychology: Tom M. Randall, Ph.D., SUNY at Buffalo.
Spanish: Olga Juzyn, Ph.D., Brown.
Theatre: P. William Hutchinson, Ph.D., Northwestern.

School of Education and Human Development
John A. Bucci, Dean; Ed.D., Boston University.

Administration (Educational): Paul Tiskus, Ph.D., Indiana.
Counseling (Agency, Counselor Education): Murray H. Finley, Ph.D., Iowa.
Curriculum: Paul Tiskus, Ph.D., Indiana.
Educational Psychology: Murray Finley, Ph.D., Iowa.
Elementary Education: Patricia Cordeiro, Ed.D., Harvard.
Health Education: Ben Lombardo, Ed.D., Boston University.
Reading: Patricia Cordeiro, Ed.D., Harvard.
Secondary Education: Paul Tiskus, Ph.D., Indiana.
Special Education: John Gleason, Ed.D., Harvard.
Teaching English as a Second Language: Willis E. Poole, Ph.D., NYU.
Technology Education: James G. McCrystal, Ed.D., Maryland.

School of Social Work
George D. Metrey, Dean; Ph.D., NYU.

School of Management and Technology
James A. Schweikart, Dean; Ph.D., Indiana.

RIVIER COLLEGE

School of Graduate Studies

Programs of Study

The School of Graduate Studies at Rivier College offers programs leading to the following master's degrees: Master of Arts (M.A.) in clinical mental health counseling, writing, and literature; Master of Science (M.S.) in computer information systems, computer science, human resources management, nursing (family nursing, nursing education, and psychiatric mental health nursing); Master of Education (M.Ed.) in counselor education, curriculum and instruction, early childhood education, educational administration, learning disabilities and reading, elementary education, elementary education and general special education, elementary education and learning disabilities, educational studies, emotional/behavioral disabilities, learning disabilities, reading, and secondary education; Master of Business Administration (M.B.A.) with concentrations in accounting, marketing, quality management, and health care; Master of Arts in Teaching (M.A.T.) in English, mathematics, social studies, and Spanish; and Master of Arts/Master of Arts in Teaching (M.A./M.A.T.) in writing and literature. The Certificate of Advanced Graduate Study (C.A.G.S.) is offered in leadership and learning and nursing education.

Certificate programs are offered in computer information systems, computer science (client server applications and networking technologies), counseling, early childhood professional, family nursing, health-care administration, human resources management, management and organizational behavior, marketing, multicultural counseling or multicultural/bilingual counseling, nursing education (family nursing focus), parenting education, psychiatric/mental health nursing, quality management, and writing.

Research Facilities

The Regina Library and the Cho Education Resource Center are the resource libraries for students and faculty and staff members. Currently, the libraries hold more than 150,000 volumes, 400 journal titles, 80,000 microform units, and 29,000 audiovisual items to meet a diversified curriculum and the academic requirements of the Rivier College community. Electronic resources include online indexes and abstracts through EBSCO, Wilson Web, WESTLAW, document retrieval for more than 1,000 full-text journals, and other document delivery services. The Cho Education Resource Center provides specialized resources and services to students and faculty members in the education programs, including curriculum materials, children's literature, parenting resources, and educational software.

In addition, through Rivier College's participation in the New Hampshire College and University Council (NHCUC), students have access to twelve academic and research libraries with a collection of more than 3 million volumes.

The Academic Computer Center provides students with state-of-the-art hardware and software to facilitate research and learning. Graduate students have access to computers, including two networked classrooms. The Regina Library has an additional classroom with sixteen PCs and eight high-speed computers especially for bibliographic research. All computers are connected to the Rivier College network which provides direct access to the Internet and the World Wide Web.

Financial Aid

Many students are working professionals with full-time jobs who often receive financial aid from their employer through a tuition reimbursement program. A limited number of graduate assistantships are awarded as they become available. Students may also apply for one or more of the federal student aid programs, details of which may be obtained from the Financial Aid Office.

Cost of Study

Tuition for the graduate programs in 2002–03 is $374 per credit, except the tuition for the graduate nursing programs, which is $591 per credit.

Living and Housing Costs

A limited number of graduate housing units are provided on campus. The Office of Student Development provides listings and suggestions for students interested in off-campus housing. Meal plans are available to all students.

Student Group

Rivier College enrolls approximately 900 graduate students. Most are part-time students. Students may enter directly from an undergraduate program or may have several years of full-time work experience before entering an advanced degree program.

Location

Rivier College is located on a 64-acre campus 1 mile from downtown Nashua in a quiet, residential area. Easy access to Boston provides students with opportunities for intellectual, cultural, and social enrichment. Proximity to the seacoast and to the White Mountains of New Hampshire offers additional recreational advantages.

The College

Founded in 1933 by the Sisters of the Presentation of Mary, Rivier College is a coeducational institution offering approximately sixty undergraduate and graduate degree programs. Rivier offers a Catholic liberal education with a commitment to social justice, and is dedicated to the formation of intellect and character. The College is recognized for its broad-based curriculum, which emphasizes both the preparation of students for challenging and rewarding careers and the furthering of their personal growth.

Recognizing the value of all branches of knowledge, the College offers a traditional liberal arts curriculum with fields of specialization on the undergraduate level and advanced professional education on the graduate level.

Applying

A system of rolling admissions is employed for graduate study. Students may begin graduate programs in the fall semester (August) or the spring semester (January). Requirements for admissions to the graduate programs are a bachelor's degree (a master's degree for the C.A.G.S. programs) from a regionally accredited institution, a satisfactory grade average, official transcripts of undergraduate and graduate course work, three letters of recommendation, a written personal statement, and a nonrefundable $25 application fee. Certain programs require the submissions of scores from specified standardized entrance examinations. Scores on the TOEFL are required of all applicants whose native language is not English.

Correspondence and Information

Office of Graduate Admissions
School of Graduate Studies
Adrienne Hall
Rivier College
420 Main Street
Nashua, New Hampshire 03060
Telephone: 603-897-8229
E-mail: gadmissions@rivier.edu
World Wide Web: http://www.rivier.edu

THE GRADUATE FACULTY

Albert DeCiccio, Academic Dean of the College; Ph.D., Arizona State.

Business
Joseph Allard, Professor; Ed.D., Boston University.
Eric Drouart, Assistant Professor; M.S.B.A., Massachusetts Amherst.
Raymond Hubbard, Professor; Ed.D., Rutgers.
George Kaloudis, Professor; Ph.D., Kansas.
Maria Matarazzo, Associate Professor; D.B.A. (candidate), Nova Southeastern.

Computer Science/Mathematics
William Bonnice, Assistant Professor; Ph.D., George Washington.
Stephan Ehrlich, Professor; Ph.D., USC.
Bryan Higgs, Assistant Professor; Ph.D., Yale.
A. Darien Lauten, Assistant Professor and Department Chairperson; Ph.D., New Hampshire.
Teresa Magnus, Assistant Professor; Ph.D., Virginia.
Vladimir Riadov, Associate Professor; Ph.D., Moscow Institute of Technology.
Mihaela Sabin, Assistant Professor and Director of Computer Science Programs; Ph.D. (candidate), New Hampshire.

Education
Louise Auclair, Associate Professor; Ph.D., Boston College.
Mary Jane Benoit, Professor; Ph.D., Boston College.
Diane Connell, Associate Professor; Ed.D., Boston University.
Susan Gately, Associate Professor; Ph.D., Boston College.
Andrew Gersten, Assistant Professor; Ph.D., IIT.
Christy Hammer, Associate Professor; Ph.D., New Hampshire.
Patricia Howson, Associate Professor; Ph.D., Boston College.
Carol Langlier, Associate Professor; Ph.D., Northeastern.
Charles Mitsakos, Professor and Department Chairperson; Ed.D., Boston University.
Howard Muscott, Associate Professor; Ed.D., Columbia Teachers College.
Michael Tramonte, Associate Professor; Ed.D., Boston University.

History, Law, and Government
George Kaloudis, Professor; Ph.D., Kansas.
Martin Menke, Assistant Professor and Coordinator, M.A.T. in Social Studies; Ph.D., Boston College.

Modern Languages
Barry Jackson, Professor and Department Chairperson; Ph.D., Oregon.

English and Communication
Sharon Dean, Professor; Ph.D., New Hampshire.
Timothy Doherty, Assistant Professor; Ph.D., Massachusetts Amherst.
Marjorie Francoeur, Professor; M.A., Rivier.
Paul Lizotte, Professor; Ph.D., Penn State.
Larry Maness, Professor; M.F.A., Goddard.
Patricia Roberts, Professor and Director of M.A.T. Programs; Ed.D., Massachusetts Lowell.
Bradford Stull, Associate Professor and Department Chairperson; Ph.D., Illinois at Chicago.
Herman Tavani, Associate Professor and Chairperson, Philosophy; Ph.D., Temple.
Elizabethada Wright, Assistant Professor; Ph.D., Rensselaer.

Nursing
Karen Baranowski, Associate Professor and Chairperson, Baccalaureate and Graduate Nursing Programs; D.N.Sc., Yale.
Denise Baxter, Professor; Ed.D., Vanderbilt.
Doreen Cawley, Instructor of Nursing; N.D., Case Western Reserve.
Susan Murphy, Associate Professor; Ph.D., Boston College.
Christine O'Reilly, Assistant Professor; Ed.D., Massachusetts Lowell.
Ivor Pattison, Assistant Professor; Ph.D., Boston College.
Cathy St. Pierre, Associate Professor; Ph.D., Boston College.
Virginia Ryan, Professor; Ed.D., Boston College.
Grace Sullivan, Professor; D.N.Sc., Boston University.

ROBERT MORRIS UNIVERSITY

Programs of Study

Robert Morris University (RMU) offers the Master of Business Administration (M.B.A.) degree and the Master of Science (M.S.) degree in accounting, finance, sport management, marketing, business education, instructional leadership, communications and information systems, Internet information systems, information systems management, and taxation. The University also offers the Doctor of Science (D.Sc.) degree in information systems and communications.

Research Facilities

Facilities supporting the graduate programs at Robert Morris University include nine open-access computer laboratories, two physical libraries, and an electronic library offering an array of research databases. Twenty-eight classrooms have been equipped with advanced computer and presentation technology equipment to facilitate teaching and learning. The University is presently construction an Education Resource Center containing computers, software, and multimedia equipment dedicated to the needs of graduate and undergraduate education majors.

The University's two libraries house more than 130,000 volumes, 950 print periodicals, and a large collection of microprint, audiovisual, and government documents. The library has a state-of-the-art searchable catalog system, which was installed in 1999. The RMU Electronic Library offers continual off-campus access to 9 major research databases. The library is a member of numerous resource-sharing consortia that greatly extend the amount of materials available to support graduate education.

Financial Aid

Graduate loans are available for those who qualify. Students are encouraged to file the Free Application for Federal Student Aid (FAFSA). Robert Morris University participates in the William D. Ford Federal Direct Loan program and also offers various interest-free payment plans.

Cost of Study

Tuition for the 2001–02 academic year in the M.B.A. program and the M.S. programs in accounting, finance, sport management, marketing, Internet information systems, and communications and information systems, and information systems management was $410 per credit hour. Tuition for the M.S. programs in instructional leadership and business education was $374 per credit hour; the M.S. in taxation was $441 per credit hour; and the D.Sc. program had a flat fee of $17,000. The doctoral fee included tuition, fees, books and supplies, lodging during residency periods, and some meals.

Living and Housing Costs

Students find plenty of residential living opportunities around both campuses. The Moon Township campus presently has nine residence halls that house approximately 1,000 students. There are adequate residential housing options in Pittsburgh for students who take their course work in downtown Pittsburgh Center. The doctoral program fee includes the cost of the required residencies. These residencies take place at an off-campus location, and the costs are included in the fee, as indicated above.

Student Group

Of a student body of nearly 5,000 people, 1,000 are enrolled in professional graduate degree programs. The average age of graduate students is 32, with an age range of 22 to 70. Women comprise almost half of the student population. Students come from diverse professional and academic backgrounds.

Location

Robert Morris University has two locations. The main campus occupies 230 acres in suburban Moon Township, Pennsylvania, 17 miles northwest of downtown Pittsburgh and less than 15 minutes from Pittsburgh International Airport. RMU also has a campus in downtown Pittsburgh among the nation's sixth-largest concentration of Fortune 500 corporate headquarters. Students may also study certain programs at satellite locations in the South Hills and Cranberry areas of suburban Pittsburgh. Some graduate programs are offered exclusively at one location.

The University

Robert Morris University, founded in 1921, is a four-year, private, coeducational, independent institution. It has developed a national reputation for its strong business programs and offers more than thirty-five undergraduate degrees, thirteen master's programs, and the Doctor of Science in information systems and communications.

Applying

The graduate programs admit students on a rolling basis. However, students are encouraged to submit all required materials at least two months prior to the start of their desired term of entry. Applications can be filed through the University's Web site at the address below. Students should note that the M.S. in communications and information systems and the D.Sc. program require an interview as part of the final selection process.

Correspondence and Information

Office of Graduate Admission
Robert Morris University
881 Narrows Run Road
Moon Township, Pennsylvania 15108-1189
Telephone: 800-762-0097 (toll-free)
World Wide Web: http://www.rmu.edu

THE FACULTY

School of Communications and Information Systems

David Jamison, Dean; J.D., Michigan.
Frederick G. Kohun, Associate Dean; Ph.D., Carnegie Mellon.

Communications Faculty

Jay Carson, D.A., Carnegie Mellon.
Seth Finn, Ph.D., Stanford.
Arthur Grant, Ph.D., Wheaton (Illinois).
Ann D. Jabro, Ph.D., Penn State.
Barbara J. Levine, Ph.D., Wisconsin–Madison.
John D. O'Banion, Ph.D., Northern Illinois.
Linda Runyon, Ed.D., Houston.
James A. Seguin, Ph.D., Ohio State.

Computer and Information Systems Faculty

Valerie J. Harvey, Ph.D., Texas at Austin.
Linda Kavanaugh, Ph.D., Pittsburgh.
Frederick G. Kohun, Ph.D., Carnegie Mellon.
Joseph Laverty, Ph.D., Pittsburgh.
Walter Pilof, M.B.A., Xavier (Cincinnati).
Daniel M. Rota, Ph.D., Pittsburgh.
Robert J. Skovira, Ph.D., Pittsburgh.
John Turchek, M.Ed., Duquesne.
David F. Wood, Ph.D., Pittsburgh.
John Zeanchock, M.Ed., Indiana of Pennsylvania.

Education Faculty

Donna Cellante, Ed.D., Pittsburgh.
John E. Graham, Ed.D., Pittsburgh.
Jon Shank, Ed.D., Pittsburgh.

School of Business

Richard Stolz, Dean; Ph.D., Michigan State.
William T. Rupp, Associate Dean; Ph.D., Georgia.

Accounting and Taxation Faculty

Gerald J. Berenbaum, M.B.A., Massachusetts; CPA.
William G. Brucker, J.D., Duquesne.
Lois D. Bryan, M.B.A., Denver; CPA.
Charles Fazzi, Ph.D., Penn State.
Jerry W. Hanwell, J.D., Duquesne.

Finance and Economics Faculty

Robert G. Beaves, Ph.D., Iowa.
Mark J. Eschenfelder, Ph.D., Missouri.
Frank R. Flanegin, Ph.D., Central Florida.
Patrick J. Litzinger, Ph.D., Pittsburgh.

Management and Marketing Faculty

Joseph M. Correa, Ph.D., Washington (Seattle).
Nell T. Hartley, Ph.D., Vanderbilt.
Dean R. Manna, Ph.D., Pittsburgh.
Gayle J. Marco, Ph.D., Pittsburgh.
David A. Page, Ph.D., Harvard.
Charles Popovich, Ph.D., Pittsburgh.

Sport Management Faculty

Scott Branvold, Ed.D., Utah.
John Clark, Ph.D., Massachusetts.
David P. Synowka, Ph.D., Pittsburgh.

School of Engineering, Mathematics, and Science

Yildirm "Bill" Omurtag, Dean; Ph.D., Iowa State.
Winston Erevelles, Associate Dean; Ph.D., Missouri–Rolla.

Engineering Faculty

Stephen Aylor, Ph.D., Missouri–Rolla.
Winston Erevelles, Ph.D., Missouri–Rolla.
Derya Jacobs, Ph.D., Missouri–Rolla.
John Hayward, Ph.D., Penn State.

Mathematics and Science Faculty

Mark A. Ciancutti, Ph.D., Carnegie Mellon.
Renato Clavijo, Ph.D., Arkansas.
William Connor, Ph.D., Penn State.
Allen Lias, Ph.D., Pittsburgh.
Mark Maxwell, Ph.D., Oregon.
Daniel Short, Ph.D., Liverpool (England).

R·I·T

ROCHESTER INSTITUTE OF TECHNOLOGY

Graduate Studies

Programs of Study

The Rochester Institute of Technology (RIT) offers the following graduate programs of study: business, management, and communication: business administration (M.B.A., Executive M.B.A.), communication and media technologies (M.S.), human resource development (M.S.), finance (M.S.), hospitality-tourism management (M.S.), manufacturing management and leadership (M.S.), product development (M.S.), public policy (M.S.), senior-living management (Advanced Certificate), and service management (M.S.); computer science and information technology: computer science (M.S.), information technology (M.S.), interactive multimedia development (Advanced Certificate), and software development and management (M.S.); education: art education (M.S.T.), instructional technology (M.S.), school psychology (M.S.), school psychology and deafness (Advanced Certificate), and secondary education of students who are deaf and hard of hearing (M.S.); engineering and technology: applied statistics (M.S.), computer engineering (M.S.), computer-integrated manufacturing (M.S.), electrical engineering (M.S.), engineering management (M.E.), environmental health and safety management (M.S.), industrial engineering (M.E., M.S.); manufacturing engineering (M.E.), materials science and engineering (M.S.), mechanical engineering (M.E., M.S.), microelectronics manufacturing engineering (M.E., M.S.), packaging science (M.S.), statistical quality (Advanced Certificate), and systems engineering (M.E.); multidisciplinary studies: cross-disciplinary professional studies (M.S.), fine arts studio (M.F.A.), glass and glass sculpture (M.F.A.), graphic arts publishing (M.S.), graphic arts systems (M.S.), graphic design (M.F.A.), imaging arts/computer animation and film (M.F.A.), imaging arts/photography (M.F.A.), industrial design (M.F.A.), medical illustration (M.F.A.), metalcrafts and jewelry (M.F.A.), printing technology (M.S.), and woodworking and furniture design (M.F.A.); and science, mathematics, and imaging science: industrial and applied mathematics (M.S.), chemistry (M.S.), clinical chemistry (M.S.), color science (M.S.), and imaging science (M.S. and Ph.D.)

Research Facilities

State-of-the art technology in campus classrooms and laboratories reflects RIT's emphasis on career education. Six computer centers, a microchip-fabricating cleanroom, dedicated research laboratories, a student-operated restaurant, design studios, and more than 100 photography darkrooms provide students with the facilities they need to investigate and explore their academic fields. Wallace Library is the primary information source on campus, with full electronic access to research and data worldwide. It houses more than 750,000 items, including 350,000 books, 4,700 journals, 3,100 audio recordings, 6,700 film and video recordings, and 410,000 microforms. The online Infonet menu provides 24-hour access to a wide selection of resources, databases, the Internet, and the library's electronic catalog. Some of the nation's leading companies have supported research and teaching facilities that include the $22-million Center for Integrated Manufacturing Studies, the Sloan Printing Industry Center, and the Chester F. Carlson Center for Imaging Science. RIT's new Center for Excellence in Mathematics, Science and Technology showcases innovative teaching efforts using multimedia instructional technology. RIT offers opportunities to apply advanced technology to many areas of graduate study. Printing, design, and photography students merge these creative disciplines in the Electronic Still Photography Lab. Imaging science students analyze the latest in remote sensing capability from an on-campus remote-controlled observatory. Manufacturing management students evaluate production techniques in the manufacturing bays of the Center for Integrated Manufacturing Studies, and hospitality-tourism management students complete projects on their industry-standard SABRE computer system.

Financial Aid

Graduate scholarships and assistantships are available in most graduate departments. In addition, some departments offer externally funded stipends from corporate or government sources. Students should contact the appropriate department chairperson for additional information. Federal, state, and institutional aid are also available to those who qualify. Applicants seeking financial aid should submit the Free Application for Federal Student Aid (FAFSA) to the Office of Financial Aid by March 15 for consideration for entry for the following September.

Cost of Study

In 2001–02, the cost of full-time study (12–18 credit hours) was $7290 per quarter. The cost of part-time study (11 credit hours or fewer) was $613 per credit hour.

Living and Housing Costs

Housing Operations handles assignments for university-operated residence halls and more than 1,000 campus apartment units. Apartment rents begin at $665 per month for one-bedroom units for the academic year; reduced summer rates are available. In addition, there are several large local apartment complexes and individual living quarters within a short distance of the campus.

Student Group

The total enrollment at the Institute is 15,000. Enrollment in the graduate degree programs is 2,400.

Location

RIT's campus in suburban Rochester occupies 400 acres on a 1,300-acre site and is located close to the cultural and entertainment districts of Rochester. Gallery and museum exhibits, a philharmonic orchestra, and theaters are located in metropolitan Rochester.

The Institute

RIT is accredited by the Middle States Association of Colleges and Schools and the New York State Board of Regents. It is a privately endowed, nonsectarian institution of higher education. RIT has been a pioneer in professional and career development programs since its founding in 1829. Its principal task is preparing men and women with the knowledge, skills, and attitudes required for technological, managerial, and aesthetic competence. It strives to assist them to mature as perceptive, skilled, and incisive professionals. Each graduate program is built as a freestanding unit and is designed to fill a specific demand in a given field. The thrust of the graduate programs is toward state-of-the-art technology and business, the aesthetic areas of the fine arts, photography, printing, and career-oriented programs in communication, school psychology, and public policy.

Applying

Applicants should hold a bachelor's degree from a regionally accredited university and demonstrate, in the quality of undergraduate record, experience, and/or creative production, a genuine professional potential. Application deadlines vary by program, and applications must include all postsecondary official transcripts and degree certificates, a personal statement, two letters of recommendation, a $50 application fee, and a slide portfolio where applicable. In addition, some programs require GRE or GMAT scores, and a TOEFL score is required for students whose native language is not English.

Correspondence and Information

Office of Graduate Enrollment Services
Rochester Institute of Technology
Rochester, New York 14623-5604
E-mail: gradinfo@rit.edu
World Wide Web: http://www.rit.edu

GRADUATE PROGRAM CONTACTS

COLLEGE OF APPLIED SCIENCE AND TECHNOLOGY

Cross-Disciplinary Professional Studies
Richard Morales, Ph.D., Syracuse. (585-475-5230, cms@rit.edu)
Environmental, Health, and Safety Management
Joseph Rosenbeck, M.S., Central Missouri State. (585-475-6469)
Health Systems Administration
William Walence, Ph.D., Ohio. (585-475-7359, wwwcad@rit.edu)
Hospitality and Service Management
James Jacobs, Ph.D., SUNY at Buffalo. (585-475-6017, jwjism@rit.edu)
Human Resource Development
Dianne Mau, M.S., SUNY at Brockport. (585-475-5036, dcmhrd@rit.edu)
Instructional Technology
C. J. Wallington, Ph.D., USC. (585-475-2893, cjwici@rit.edu)
Packaging Science
Deanna Jacobs, M.S., RIT. (585-475-2278, dmjipk@rit.edu)

COLLEGE OF BUSINESS

Donald O. Wilson, Associate Dean, Ph.D., California, Irvine. (585-475-6798, dowbbu@rit.edu)

B. THOMAS GOLISANO COLLEGE OF COMPUTING AND INFORMATION SCIENCES

Computer Science
Roger S. Gaborski, Ph.D., Maryland, Baltimore. (585-475-7801, csgradcoord@cs.rit.edu)
Information Technology
Diane P. Bills, M.S., RIT. (585-475-6179, itgradcoord@it.rit.edu)

COLLEGE OF ENGINEERING

Center for Quality and Applied Statistics
Joseph Voelkel, Chair; Ph.D., Wisconsin–Madison. (585-475-2231, jgvcqa@rit.edu)
Computer Engineering
Andreas Savakis, Ph.D., North Carolina State. (585-475-2987, ce_chair@rit.edu)
Electrical Engineering
Soheil Dianat, Ph.D., George Washington. (585-475-2165, sadeee@rit.edu)
Industrial Engineering
Jacqueline Reynolds Mozrall, Ph.D., SUNY at Buffalo. (585-475-2598, jrmeie@rit.edu)
Mechanical Engineering
Edward C. Hensel, Ph.D., New Mexico State. (585-475-2162, echeme@rit.edu)
Microelectronics Engineering
Santosh Kurinec, Ph.D., Dehli (India). (585-475-6065, skkemc@rit.edu)

COLLEGE OF IMAGING ARTS AND SCIENCES

School of Art
Thomas Lightfoot, Ed.D., Columbia. (585-475-2657, trlfad@rit.edu)
School of Design
Nancy Ciolek, M.F.A., Indiana State. (585-475-2668, nacfad@rit.edu)
School for American Crafts
Richard Tanner, Certification of Mastery, Boston University. (585-475-5778, rdtffa@rit.edu)
School of Film and Animation
Malcolm Spaull, M.F.A., RIT. (585-475-7403, mgscdm@rit.edu)
School of Photographic Arts and Sciences
Willie Osterman, M.F.A., Oregon. (585-475-2725, wtopph@rit.edu)
School of Printing Management and Sciences
Len Leger, M.S., RIT. (585-475-6026, lwlppr@rit.edu)

COLLEGE OF LIBERAL ARTS

Communication and Media Technologies
Rudolph Pugliese, Ph.D., Temple. (585-475-5925, rrpgsl@rit.edu)
Public Policy
James Winebrake, Ph.D., Pennsylvania. (585-475-5291, jwjgpt@rit.edu)
School Psychology
Virginia Costenbader, Ph.D., Syracuse. (585-475-2765, vkcgsp@rit.edu)

NATIONAL TECHNICAL INSTITUTE FOR THE DEAF

Secondary Education of Students Who are Deaf or Hard of Hearing
Gerald Bateman, Ed.D., RIT. (585-475-6480 V/TTY, gcbnmp@rit.edu)

COLLEGE OF SCIENCE

Chemistry
Terence C. Morrill, Ph.D., Colorado. (585-475-2497, tcmsch@rit.edu)
Clinical Chemistry
James Aumer, M.S., Michigan Tech. (585-475-2526, jcascl@rit.edu)
Color Science
Roy S. Berns, Ph.D., Rensselaer. (585-475-2230, rsbpph@rit.edu)
Imaging Science
Harvey Rhody, Ph.D., Syracuse. (585-475-6215, herrc@rit.edu)
Materials Science and Engineering
K.S.V. Santhanam, Ph.D., Sri Venkateswara (India). (585-475-2920, ksssch@rit.edu)
Mathematics and Statistics
Richard Orr, M.S., SUNY at Buffalo. (585-475-2523, rjosma@rit.edu)

ROOSEVELT UNIVERSITY

Graduate Division

Programs of Study

The Graduate Division of Roosevelt University offers master's degrees in accounting, biotechnology and chemical science, business administration, computer science, creative writing, economics, education (educational leadership and organizational change, counseling and human services, early childhood, elementary education, reading, secondary education, and teacher leadership), English, history, hospitality and tourism management, human resource management, information systems, integrated marketing communications, interdisciplinary studies, international business, journalism, mathematical sciences, music (performance, theory, composition, jazz studies, musicology, orchestral studies, music education, and theater), political science, psychology, public administration, sociology (gerontology), Spanish, telecommunications, training and development, Web and distributed programming, and women's and gender studies. Doctor of Education degrees in educational leadership and organizational change as well as a Psy.D. in clinical psychology are available.

Research Facilities

The Murray-Green Library holds more than 225,000 volumes and a variety of research materials including periodicals and microforms. A full staff is on duty to assist student researchers at the downtown campus, and research services are also available at the Schaumburg Campus. Roosevelt University is a member of the Illinois Library Computer Services Organization (ILCSO), which operates a statewide online circulation system embracing 45 of the largest libraries in Illinois. It is also backed up by the OCLC international bibliographic network and subscribes to numerous online electronic database services.

Financial Aid

Loans, grants, and scholarships are available for qualified students in all departments of the graduate division. Assistantships that pay stipends and carry tuition waivers are offered in most departments. Graduate students may also apply for college work-study. Partial tuition grants are available to qualified part-time students. Many graduate students finance their education through loans or are reimbursed by their employers. Those interested in financial aid should see the Applying section below for deadlines.

Cost of Study

The 2001–02 tuition was $540 per graduate semester hour. Fees include a general student fee of $100 per term and, in some programs, laboratory and other small fees.

Living and Housing Costs

The University's Herman Crown Center provides reasonably priced housing for 350 men and women. The cost of living in Chicago is about the same as in most other major cities. Chicago offers many job opportunities, a myriad of inexpensive services and activities, and a wide choice of living quarters at a variety of rent levels.

Student Group

Approximately 550 full-time and 2,000 part-time graduate students attend classes at Roosevelt. Students of varied backgrounds and ages from many states and more than fifty other countries pursue graduate studies at the University. Most work part-time or full-time and find Roosevelt's scheduling flexibility well suited to their schedules.

Location

Roosevelt University's main campus is in two Michigan Avenue locations, the Auditorium Building and the Center for Professional Advancement, in the heart of Chicago's cultural center. Both are within easy commuting distance by car or public transportation. Students can take advantage of the many events and activities in the city. The Albert A. Robin Campus is located in northwest suburban Schaumburg, approximately 30 miles from downtown Chicago. The University bus schedules daily transport to and from each of the three campuses.

The University

From its founding as a private university in 1945, Roosevelt pioneered the education of adults and nontraditional students, creating a diverse learning environment for all students. Today, its educational programs are recognized nationwide, and students throughout Metropolitan Chicago and from around the world pursue degrees at its two campuses. Roosevelt's characteristics provide a number of graduate educational benefits: small classes that encourage an open exchange of ideas, outstanding faculty, excellent academic programs, scheduling flexibility to accommodate working students, and counseling and career planning services.

The Career Counseling and Placement Office assists students in finding part-time, full-time, and second-career positions. Its services remain available to Roosevelt graduates, who may take advantage of a full range of career counseling, planning, and placement opportunities.

Applying

Students should contact the Office of Graduate Admission indicating their field of interest. Priority deadlines for applications for admission are August 1 for the fall semester, December 1 for the spring semester, and April 15 for the summer terms. The application deadline for assistantships is February 15 for the following year and for partial scholarships the priority deadline is May 1. There is a $25 fee for domestic applications and $35 for international applications. International students must apply at least three months prior to the intended semester.

Correspondence and Information

Office of Graduate Admission
Roosevelt University
430 South Michigan Avenue
Chicago, Illinois 60605
Telephone: 312-341-3515
Fax: 312-341-4316
E-mail: applyru@roosevelt.edu
WWW: http://www.roosevelt.edu

Center for Professional Advancement
Roosevelt University
18 South Michigan Avenue
Chicago, Illinois 60603
Telephone: 312-281-3252
WWW: http://www.roosevelt.edu

Albert A. Robin Campus
Roosevelt University
1400 North Roosevelt Road
Schaumburg, Illinois 60173-4344
Telephone: 847-619-8600
Fax: 847-619-8636
E-mail: admitrc@roosevelt.edu
WWW: http://www.roosevelt.edu

GRADUATE PROGRAM DIRECTORS

Accounting: Michael Groner, Ph.D., Illinois at Urbana-Champaign.
Biotechnology and Chemical Science: Cornelius Watson, Ph.D., Wesleyan
Business Administration (Interdepartmental): Marilyn Nance, M.B.A., Roosevelt; CPA.
Computer Science and Telecommunications: Ray Wright, M.B.A., Loyola.
Counseling and Human Services: Bruce Dykeman, Ph.D., Wisconsin–Milwaukee.
Early Childhood Education: Shiela Coffin, M.S.Ed., Northern Illinois.
Economics: Steven Balkin, Ph.D., Wayne State.
Education/Teacher Leadership: Susan Belgrad, Ph.D., Illinois at Chicago.
Elementary Education: Alonza Everage, M.Ed., Chicago.
English: Lawrence Howe, Ph.D., Berkeley.
Gerontology: Daniel Krause, Ph.D., Illinois.
History: Leonard Stein, Ph.D., NYU.
Hospitality and Tourism Management: Gerald Bober, Ed.D., Northern Illinois.
Human Resource Management: Susan Burroughs, Ph.D., Tennessee.
Information Systems: Connie Wells, Ph.D., Minnesota.
Interdisciplinary Studies: Gary Wolfe, Ph.D., Chicago.
International Business: Alan Krabbenhoft, Ph.D., Wayne State.
Journalism: Linda Jones, M.S., Northwestern.
Marketing Communications: Linda Jones, M.S., Northwestern.
Mathematical Sciences: John Currano, Ph.D., Chicago.
Music: Linda Berna, Associate Dean; M.A., Roosevelt.
Political Science: Paul Green, Ph.D., Chicago.
Psychology: Edward Rossini, Ph.D., Loyola Chicago.
Public Administration: Paul Green, Ph.D., Chicago.
Secondary Education: Nona Burney, Ph.D., Cleveland State.
Sociology: Daniel Krause, Ph.D., Illinois.
Spanish: John Barry, Ph.D., Chicago.
Theater/Music Theater: Joel Fink, D.A., NYU; SEHNAP.
Training and Development: Kathleen Iverson, Ph.D., Loyola Chicago.
Women's and Gender Studies: Ann Brigham, Ph.D., Arizona.

The Murray-Green Library, located on the downtown campus.

The Robin Campus in Schaumburg is architecturally modern and decidedly horizontal, encompassing 225,000 square feet.

The downtown campus is located in the historic Auditorium Theatre building that overlooks Grant Park and Lake Michigan.

ROSEMONT COLLEGE

Graduate Studies

Programs of Study

Rosemont College offers programs leading to the Master of Arts in counseling psychology, English, English and publishing, and curriculum and instruction; the Master of Education in technology, mid-level education, and educational studies; the Master of Business Administration; and the Master of Science in management, criminal justice, and public safety.

Students may pursue graduate studies on a full-time or part-time basis. Summer sessions are offered for all programs. For more information on all programs, students should visit the College's Web site at http://www.rosemont.edu.

Research Facilities

The Rosemont College Library system spans several facilities and collections, including the Gertrude Kistler Memorial Library, the slide collection, and the Computer Center, which is located both in the library and in the Dorothy McKenna Brown Science Center. The College's library program strives to meet the study and research needs of the students and faculty members by combining traditional library strengths with state-of-the-art access to information and resource sharing.

Financial Aid

Subsidized and unsubsidized FFEL Stafford Student Loans are available to matriculated students enrolled at least half-time (6 credits per semester).

Cost of Study

Tuition for 2002–03 ranges from $1200 to $1500 per 3-credit course depending on the program. There are no registration fees.

Living and Housing Costs

On-campus housing is available for graduate students. The room cost per semester is $2200. Meal ticket options are also available.

Student Group

The Graduate School comprises primarily working professional men and women in their mid-twenties to their mid-fifties. Total enrollment for all graduate programs is approximately 400 students.

Student Outcomes

M.Ed. and curriculum students are employed in the education field as teachers, technology coordinators, curriculum developers, staff developers, supervisors, and administrators. English and publishing graduates work in publishing houses or in organizations that need professionals skilled in publishing. Graduates in counseling psychology provide direct client services or work in schools, mental health centers, hospitals, social service agencies, and day treatment centers. M.A. in English graduates teach at all levels; they also use their writing skills as entrepreneurs or for businesses that value employees with strong liberal arts backgrounds. Business degree students improve their critical thinking and communication abilities while developing more specific job-related skills.

Location

Rosemont College is located in Rosemont, Pennsylvania, one of several side-by-side college towns nestled among Philadelphia's historic Main Line suburbs. The College is easily accessible by car, train, or bus. Rosemont is ideally located no more than a day trip from New Jersey shore points, Longwood Gardens, the Pocono Mountains, New York City, Baltimore, and Washington, D.C.

The College

Rosemont College has a unique and progressive spirit of learning, engendered by an atmosphere of freedom and openness. Founded on the original Sinnott Estate, Rosemont received its charter as a college of liberal arts and was incorporated under the laws of the Commonwealth of Pennsylvania in 1922. In 1930, Rosemont was accredited by the Middle States Association of Colleges and Schools.

Applying

Applications for admission are required for all master's degrees and certificates. Applications are reviewed throughout the year. In some programs, application requirements include standardized test scores (MAT or GRE). The application fee is $50.

Correspondence and Information

Graduate Studies in Education
Rosemont College
1400 Montgomery Avenue
Rosemont, Pennsylvania 19010
Telephone: 610-526-2982
800-531-9431 (toll-free)
Fax: 610-526-2964
E-mail: gradstudies@rosemont.edu
World Wide Web: http://www.rosemont.edu

FACULTY HEADS AND PROGRAM DIRECTORS

Rosemont College's faculty members are dedicated academicians and practitioners with a genuine commitment to teaching at the graduate level. For more information on the entire faculty, students should visit the College's Web site at http://www.rosemont.edu.

Kenneth Bingham, Director of English and Publishing; M. A., Temple.
Debra G. Klinman, Dean of Graduate Studies and Codirector of Counseling Psychology; Ph.D., Temple.
Honour Moore, Dean of Continuing Studies; M.A., Villanova.
Kathleen Roney, Director of Mid-Level Education Program; Ed.D., Temple.
Edward Samulewicz, Codirector of Counseling Psychology; Ed.D., Lehigh.
Faye Senneca, Director of Curriculum and Instruction; Ed.D., Temple.
Robert J. Siegfried, Director of Technology in Education Program; Ph.D., Pittsburgh.
Erlis Glass Wickersham, Vice President for Academic Affairs; Ph.D., Bryn Mawr.

ROWAN UNIVERSITY

The Graduate School

Programs of Study

As a regional public university committed to teaching, Rowan combines liberal education with professional preparation and offers undergraduate through doctoral programs. The Rowan ambition is knowledge through study, responsibility through service, and character through challenge. At the graduate level, Rowan serves those interested not only in assuming positions of leadership within their respective professions but also in moving the profession forward in creative ways that enhance society. The University is accredited by the Middle States Association of Colleges and Schools, and its School of Education is accredited by the National Council for Accreditation of Teacher Education and the National Association of State Directors of Teacher Education and Credentials. Rowan music programs are accredited by the National Association of Schools of Music.

Rowan University offers graduate degree programs through six colleges. The College of Business Administration offers the Master of Business Administration (M.B.A.) and the Master Of Science (M.S.) in accounting. The College of Communication offers the Master of Arts (M.A.) in public relations and in writing. The College of Education offers M.A. degrees in administration, elementary education, environmental education, higher education, instructional technology, learning disabilities, reading, school and public librarianship, school psychology, special education, student personnel services, subject matter teaching (art, biological sciences, mathematics, music, and physical sciences), and supervision and curriculum and Master of Science in Teaching (M.S.T.) degrees in elementary education, secondary education, and special education as well as the Ed.D. in educational leadership. The College of Engineering grants M.S. degrees. The College of Liberal Arts and Sciences grants M.A. degrees in applied psychology and mathematics. The College of Fine and Performing Arts has two master's degree programs, one in music and one in theater. Rowan also offers certification programs, including associate educational media specialist, computers in education, elementary school language arts, elementary school math, ESL/bilingual education, learning disabilities, school business administration, school psychologist, supervisor, substance awareness, theater, and writing.

Research Facilities

The Campbell Library, a 118,000-square-foot facility opened in 1995, houses more than 350,000 books, documents, and multimedia materials. In addition, the library subscribes to almost 2,000 journals, many of which are available with full-text and images from a large number of online databases covering a wide range of subjects. The library also provides a number of specialized electronic databases in such fields as business, engineering, law, mathematics, and worldwide news coverage. Online databases are available on the campus network and can be accessed remotely by Rowan community members.

The library also houses extensive collections of microfilm and microfiche, as well as a special collection of New Jersey historical materials. The library is also a U.S. Government Depository Library.

The library building is equipped with seminar rooms for group study, lecture rooms, electronic reference areas, and a computer laboratory.

Financial Aid

Within the limits of the resources available, Rowan University provides financial assistance to all eligible graduate students on the basis of financial need. Students must enroll on at least a half-time basis to qualify. Rowan participates in two federal campus-based programs of assistance (Federal Direct Stafford Student Loan and College Work-Study programs). Residents of New Jersey may be eligible for a Garden State Scholarship. More information is available from the Financial Aid Office at 856-256-4250. Graduate and residence assistantships are offered to qualified full-time students (9 credits or more) and part-time students (6 credits). Graduate assistantships provide tuition waiver and a stipend in exchange for 10 to 20 hours of work provided to offices and programs on campus. Interested students should contact the Graduate School at 856-256-4051. Residence-life assistantships provide room, board, tuition waiver, and stipend.

Cost of Study

Full-time (9 credits or more) New Jersey residents paid $3967 per semester in spring 2002. Nonresidents paid $6091 for full-time study. Part-time New Jersey residents paid $333 per credit hour, and part-time nonresidents paid $510 per credit hour.

Living and Housing Costs

Housing is available in on- and off-campus apartments. In 2001–02, campus housing costs ranged from $1993 to $2330 per semester. Meal plans were available for approximately $1350 per semester.

Student Group

In spring 2002, 8,005 undergraduate students were enrolled at Rowan. Graduate enrollment included 1,370 students.

Location

Rowan University is located in Glassboro, New Jersey, a small town in a suburban area close to the cultural opportunities of Philadelphia (20 miles), New York City (120 miles), and Atlantic City (40 miles). Washington, D.C., is only 2½ hours by train from Philadelphia. Some of the best beaches on the East Coast are located within a 1–2 hours' drive. A wide range of sporting events, museums, theaters, restaurants, and libraries are readily accessible.

The University

Rowan University opened its doors with 236 students in 1923 as the Glassboro Normal School with a gift from the residents of Glassboro, New Jersey, of 25 acres. After seventy years as Glassboro State College, Henry and Betty Rowan gave the College a gift of $100 million in 1992, providing the means to transform the institution into a superior regional college. In 1994, an $8.6-million state-of-the-art recreational center opened on campus, and in 1995, a $16.8-million library opened. A $30-million engineering building has just been completed on campus. Construction began in 2001 on a new science building. In 1997, the college was granted university status in recognition of its increasing regional leadership role in the economic, educational, and cultural development of the southern New Jersey region.

Applying

Application forms for admission and for graduate assistantships may be obtained by calling or writing to the Graduate School. Online applications may be obtained from the Web site listed below. The admission decision is made after careful consideration of the student's transcripts, appropriate graduate admission test scores, letters of recommendation, and, in some cases, a personal interview.

Correspondence and Information

The Graduate School
Memorial Hall
Rowan University
Glassboro, New Jersey 08028

Telephone: 856-256-4050
Fax: 856-256-4436
World Wide Web: http://www.rowan.edu

DEANS AND PROGRAM COORDINATORS

College of Business Administration
Dr. Edward Schoen, Dean; J.D., Georgetown.
Graduate Program Coordinators:
Accounting: Dr. G. Romeo, 856-258-4384
Business: Dr. R. Parker, 856-256-4013.

College of Communication
Dr. George Tholtam, Dean; Ph.D., Bombay (India).
Graduate Program Coordinators:
Public Relations: Dr. D. Bagin, 856-256-4332.
Writing: Dr. D. Penrod, 856-256-4330.

College of Education
Graduate Program Coordinators:
Higher Education Administration: Dr. T. Monahan, 856-256-4748.
School Administration (Elementary): Dr. R. Capasso, 856-256-4702.
(Secondary): Dr. R. Capasso, 856-256-4702.
Elementary School Teaching: Dr. L. Molinari, 856-256-4500 Ext. 3803.
Environmental Education: G. Patterson, 856-256-4500 Ext. 3801.
Learning Disabilities: Dr. S. Bianco, 856-256-4500 Ext. 3796.
Master of Science in Teaching: Dr. C. Calliari, 856-256-4736.
Reading: Dr. C. Hasit, 856-256-4772.
School Business Administration: Dr. R. Capasso, 856-256-4702.
School Psychology: Dr. J. Klanderman, 856-256-4500 Ext. 3797.
Dr. R. Dihoff, 856-256-4500 Ext. 3776.
School and Public Librarianship: Dr. H. Willett, 856-256-4759.
Special Education: Dr. S. Urban, 856-256-4500 Ext. 3795.
Student Personnel Services: Dr. G. Ognibene, 856-256-4500 Ext. 3828.
Supervision (Health and Physical Education): Dr. T. Monahan, 856-256-4748.
Supervision and Curriculum Development: Dr. T. Monahan, 856-256-4748.
Subject Matter Teaching:
Art: Dr. J. Graziano, 856-256-4045.
Biological Sciences: Dr. R. Meagher, 856-256-4833.
Chemistry/Physics: Dr. R. Newland, 856-256-4856.
Music: Dr. L. Levinowitz, 856-256-4500 Ext. 3716.
Mathematics: Dr. M. Wright, 856-256-4500 Ext. 3873.
Educational Leadership Doctoral Program: Dr. R. Capasso, 856-256-4702.

College of Engineering
Dianne Dorlund, Dean; Ph.D., West Virginia.
Graduate Program Coordinator: Dr. T. R. Chandrupatla, 856-256-4632.

College of Fine and Performing Arts
Dr. Donald L. Gephardt, Dean; Ed.D., Washington (St. Louis).
Graduate Program Coordinators:
Music: V. Zuponcic, 856-256-4555
Theater: P. Graneto, 856-256-4392

College of Liberal Arts and Sciences
Dr. Jay Harper, Dean; Ph.D., SUNY at Stony Brook.
Graduate Program Coordinators:
Mathematics: Dr. M. Wright, 856-256-4500 Ext. 3873.
Applied Psychology: Dr. J. Cahill, 856-256-4500 Ext. 3520.

RUTGERS, THE STATE UNIVERSITY OF NEW JERSEY, CAMDEN

The Graduate School

Programs of Study

The Graduate School–Camden offers programs leading to M.A. and M.S. degrees in biology, chemistry, English, history, liberal studies, and mathematics; an M.P.T. in physical therapy; and an M.P.A. in public policy and administration. A comprehensive examination and demonstrated ability to write an expository or critical essay are required in each of these programs. A J.D. is offered by the Rutgers–Camden Law School and an M.B.A. by the Rutgers–Camden Business School. Other programs of graduate study on the Rutgers–Camden campus include an M.S. in Nursing offered by the College of Nursing in Newark, an M.S.W. offered by the School of Social Work in New Brunswick, and accelerated dual degrees for a J.D./M.P.A., a J.D./M.B.A., and a J.D./M.S.W. In all programs, there is ample opportunity for close contact with faculty members who are at the cutting edge of their disciplines, many of whom have not only national but also international reputations as scholars.

Research Facilities

The Paul Robeson Library contains more than 230,000 books, 100,000 government documents, and 210,000 pieces of microfilm and subscribes to more than 1,300 periodicals and other serials. It is a depository for publications of both the state and federal governments and, together with the Camden Law Library, receives a large percentage of the major publications issued by the United States Government Printing Office. Students also have access to more than 430,000 volumes and 1,300 serial publications located in the Law Library. These holdings in Camden are supplemented by approximately 2.8 million volumes contained within the Rutgers University libraries located in New Brunswick and Newark and available to Camden students through the Rutgers Request Service. IRIS, an online catalog, and more than 1,300 full-text journals and many bibliographic indexes are accessible on line from numerous locations on campus and from students' homes. In addition, because Rutgers belongs to the Research Libraries Group, students may obtain books from libraries outside Rutgers, including more than twenty of the largest libraries in the United States.

The Office of Computing Services operates central servers (Sun UNIX, Novell, and Macintosh) on a high-speed campus Ethernet backbone that links more than 170 public client workstations and consists of PCs, Sun Workstations, and Macintoshes. A full range of applications are maintained, including Web browsers, office suites, programming languages, and departmental-specific content. Rutgers is an active participant in the national Internet II Project. The Biology and Chemistry Departments have extensive facilities and equipment for research, such as Compaq Alpha and SGI computers for molecular design, a 300 MHz NMR machine, an electron microscope that magnifies 400,000 times, and the Pinelands Research Station, a major center for environmental studies. The Public Policy and Administration Department's Forum for Policy Research and Public Service engages in grant-funded projects and hosts a wide range of workshops and public forums.

Financial Aid

There are generous teaching fellowships for superior students in biology, chemistry, and English, which amounted to $13,700, remission of tuition, and other benefits in 2001–02. Graduate assistantships, scholarships, and research assistantships are available to M.P.A. students. Funding in the form of scholarships for students in other programs is limited. The Office of Financial Aid provides expert counseling to all students who wish to obtain low-interest loans, work-study opportunities, and other forms of financial assistance.

Cost of Study

In 2001–02, tuition for full-time students in the programs listed on the reverse of this page under the Graduate School, in social work, and in nursing and who are residents of New Jersey was $4266.75 per semester. Tuition for nonresident full-time students was $6008.75. Tuition for part-time students was $308 per credit hour for state residents and $454.50 per credit hour for nonresidents. The student fee was $422 for full-time students and $181 for part-time students. Tuition and fees for law and business students were slightly higher. Computer fees range from $20 to $100 depending on the number of student credit hours. Costs are subject to change.

Living and Housing Costs

There is ample housing for graduate students in modern, attractively furnished apartments (some for married students) that are owned and operated by the University. The housing fee for the 2001–02 academic year (September 1 through May 19) was $4392. The Camden Campus Center, located across the street, contains a food court that provides a deli, a salad bar, full-course meals, a grill, a dessert bar, a breakfast bar, a beverage area, and a pizza parlor. Classrooms, the library, a theater, and a gymnasium can all be reached by foot within 2 minutes.

Student Group

Rutgers University enrolls 50,000 students, more than 5,000 of whom study on the Camden campus. In addition to 750 law students, there are 650 students in the other graduate programs listed on the reverse of this page. Many students work during the day and take courses in the late afternoon or evening.

Location

The Rutgers–Camden campus is readily accessible from South Jersey suburbs, and it provides an ideal point of departure for further travels. It is located only a few hundred yards from the Benjamin Franklin Bridge, major highways, and the subway. Traveling by public transportation, one can reach the center of Philadelphia in only a few minutes, and the main railway station in Philadelphia and the University of Pennsylvania in half an hour.

The University

Rutgers, The State University of New Jersey, is one of the major state university systems in the nation, with a long and glorious history. The faculty members and students on the Camden campus take pride in being full-fledged members of the larger whole. Chartered in 1766 as Queen's College, the eighth institution of higher learning to be founded in what later became the United States, the University was renamed after Henry Rutgers in 1825, designated as the land-grant institution of New Jersey in 1864, and designated as The State University of New Jersey in 1945. The College of South Jersey at Camden was established as part of the University in 1950. The South Jersey Law School, established in 1926, became part of the University in the same year. The establishment of other graduate programs began in the 1970s. The Graduate School–Camden was established in 1981.

Applying

Application forms for all programs except law (see the reverse for information) may be obtained from the Camden Admissions Office. The application fee is $50. All of the programs except social work and liberal studies require candidates for degrees to submit scores on the GRE General Test (GMAT for business). Applicants may be admitted on a space-available basis as nonmatriculated students without taking the GRE. International students and students whose native language is not English must provide TOEFL scores. Students should consult with program directors concerning additional tests that may be required. Applications may be submitted well into the spring.

Correspondence and Information

Dr. Deborah E. Bowles
Director of Undergraduate and Graduate Admissions
Camden Admissions Office
Rutgers University
406 Penn Street
Camden, New Jersey 08102
Telephone: 856-225-6056
World Wide Web: http://www.camden.rutgers.edu/RUCAM/grad.html

DEANS, DIRECTORS, AND FACULTY OF THE GRADUATE SCHOOL

Deans

Margaret Marsh, Dean of the Graduate School; Ph.D. (History), Rutgers; 375 Armitage Hall, 856-225-6097.
Marie E. Cornelia, Associate Dean; Ph.D. (English), Fordham; 377 Armitage Hall, 856-225-6149.

Biology (M.S., M.B.T.). Joseph V. Martin, Director; Ph.D., USC; 217 Science Building, 856-225-6142.
Rocco Carsia, Ph.D., Rutgers. John Dighton, Ph.D., London. Robert C. Evans, Ph.D., Ohio State. Dennis J. Joslyn, Ph.D., Illinois. Hsin-yi Lee, Ph.D., Minnesota. Patrick J. McIlroy, Ph.D., Berkeley. Mark D. Morgan, Ph.D., California, Davis. Robert G. Nagele, Ph.D., Rutgers. William M. Saidel, Ph.D., MIT. Daniel Shain, Ph.D., Colorado State. Lisa Szeto, Ph.D., Columbia.
Faculty research: molecular and cellular biology, neurobiology, cell physiology, mycology, microbiology, ecology.

Chemistry (M.S.). Paul Maslen, Director, Ph.D., Cambridge. Georgia A. Arbuckle, Ph.D., Pennsylvania. Luke A. Burke, D.Sc., Louvain. Nancy Hopkins, Ph.D., Michigan. Sidney Katz, Ph.D., Pennsylvania. Alex Roche, Ph.D., Durham (England).
Faculty research: biochemistry, materials science, and inorganic, analytical, organic, physical, and theoretical chemistry.

English (M.A.; tracks in literature, the teaching of writing, Walt Whitman studies, and creative writing). Lisa Zeidner, Director; M.A., Johns Hopkins; 419 Armitage Hall, 856-225-6490.
Joseph Barbarese, Ph.D., Temple. Betsy Bowden, Ph.D., Berkeley. Marie E. Cornelia, Ph.D., Fordham. Richard Epstein, Ph.D., California, San Diego. Christopher Fitter, D.Phil., Oxford. M. A. Rafey Habib, D.Phil., Oxford. Tyler B. Hoffman, Ph.D., Virginia. Caroline Levine, Ph.D., London. William D. Lutz, Ph.D., Nevada, Reno. Timothy H. Martin, Ph.D., Pennsylvania. Donald L. Mull, Ph.D., Yale. Robert M. Ryan, Ph.D., Columbia. Geoffrey Sill, Ph.D., Penn State. Carol Singley, Ph.D., Brown. Lisa Zeidner, M.A., Johns Hopkins.
Faculty research: Creative writing; Chaucer, Shakespeare, Milton, and Defoe; religion and women in the Romantic and Victorian periods; Whitman, Wharton, and Joyce; critical theory, linguistics, and "doublespeak."

History (M.A.; tracks in American history, public history, and legal history). Philip Scranton, Director; Ph.D. Pennsylvania; 318 Armitage Hall, 856-225-6080.
Jeffrey M. Dorwart, Ph.D., Massachusetts. Nicole Eustace, Ph.D., Pennsylvania. Howard Gillette, Ph.D., Yale. Wayne Glasker, Ph.D., Pennsylvania. Janet Golden, Ph.D., Boston University. Xiao Bin Ji, Ph.D., Princeton. Andrew Lees, Ph.D., Harvard. Margaret Marsh, Ph.D., Rutgers. Jake Soll, Ph.D., Cambridge. Gerald Verbrugghe, Ph.D., Princeton. Allen L. Woll, Ph.D., Wisconsin.
Faculty research: economic and social history of Philadelphia and New Jersey political and constitutional history, history of cities, women and minorities, medicine and technology, military affairs, popular culture.

Liberal Studies (M.A.; interdisciplinary). Robert M. Ryan, Director; Ph.D., Columbia; 481 Armitage Hall, 856-225-6700.
Julianne Baird, Ph.D., Stanford (Music). Laurie Bernstein, Ph.D., Sonoma State (History). Stuart Charme, Ph.D., Chicago (Religion). Marie Cornelia, Ph.D., Fordham (English). Christine Cosentino-Dougherty, Ph.D., Columbia (German). Andrew Lees, Ph.D., Harvard (History). Robert Tarbell, Ph.D., Delaware (Art History). G. Alan Tarr, Ph.D., Chicago (Political Science). William Tucker, Ph.D., Princeton (Psychology). J. W. Whitlow, Ph.D., Yale (Psychology).
Faculty research: Romanticism, the Renaissance, early music, modern art, twentieth century German literature and history, constitutional law, social psychology.

Mathematics (M.S.; tracks in pure and applied mathematics, mathematical computer science, and teaching in the mathematical sciences). Gabor Toth, Director; Ph.D., Budapest; 310 Business and Science Building, 856-225-6538.
Leonard Bidwell, Ph.D., Pennsylvania. E. Roger Cowley, Ph.D., Cambridge. Joseph L. Gerver, Ph.D., Berkeley. Howard Jacobowitz, Ph.D., NYU. Martin L. Karel, Ph.D., Chicago. Debashis Kushary, Ph.D., Rutgers. Will Y. K. Lee, Ph.D., SUNY at Stony Brook. Haisheng Li, Ph.D., Rutgers. Mahesh G. Nerurkar, Ph.D., Minnesota. Yuchung J. Wang, Ph.D, Rutgers.
Faculty research: solid-state theory and computer simulations, automorphic forms, number theory, combinatorics, geometry, differential geometry, groups and ergodicity, partial differential equations, mathematical statistics and quality engineering, several complex variables.

Physical Therapy (M.P.T. accredited by CAPTE). Marie Koval Nardone, Director; M.S., Duke; 40 East Laurel Road, Suite 228, Stratford, New Jersey 08084, 856-566-6456; fax: 856-566-6458.
Patricia M. Adams Gillardon, M.P.T., UMDNJ-Rutgers. G. Edward Flickinger, M.B.A., West Chester. David M. Kietrys, M.S., Hahnemann. Dennise B. Krencicki, M.A., Columbia. Robert Marsico, M.P.T., UMDNJ-Rutgers. Joseph V. Martin, Ph.D., USC.
Faculty research: examination of influence of biomechanical constraints on motor control, management issues in physical therapy, cardiovascular function after paraplegia, teaching and learning, development of competence in physical therapy, situated cognition, posture and ergonomics, professional ethics.

Public Policy and Administration (M.P.A. accredited by NASPAA; tracks in public management, health-care management, and international development administration). James A. Dunn Jr., Director; Ph.D., Pennsylvania; 401 Cooper Street, 856-225-6359.
Jennifer M. Coston, Ph.D., USC. James Garnett, Ph.D., Syracuse. Sharon Gramby-Sobukwe, Ph.D., Temple. Richard Harris, Ph.D., Pennsylvania. Russell Harrison, Ph.D., North Carolina. Michael Lang, Ph.D., London. Sanjay Pandey, Ph.D., Syracuse.
Faculty research: housing, transportation, and health-care policy and management; survey research; ethics in government and the politics of regulation; executive communications, organizational behavior, and management information systems; nonprofit management; economic development of the Third World.

Other Graduate Programs on the Camden Campus

Business Administration (M.B.A. accredited by AACSB–The International Association for Management Education). Izzet Kenis, Director; Ph.D., NYU; Business and Science Building 221, 856-225-6711.

Law (J.D. accredited by ABA). Camille Andrews, Associate Dean of Enrollment; J.D., Rutgers; 406 Penn Street, Third Floor, Camden, New Jersey 08102, 856-225-6102.

Nursing (M.S. accredited by NLNAC). Marie O'Toole, Director; Ed.D., Rutgers; RN; 459 Armitage Hall, 856-225-6526.

Social Work (M.S.W. accredited by CSWE). Raymond Sanchez Mayers, Ph.D., Brandeis; 327 Cooper Street, 856-225-6346.

The Fine Arts Building contains the largest and best equipped theater in the southern part of New Jersey and the Stedman Art Gallery.

The Business and Science Building houses the School of Business and provides state-of-the-art facilities for computing that are used by students in many disciplines.

RUTGERS, THE STATE UNIVERSITY OF NEW JERSEY, NEWARK

Graduate School

Programs of Study

The Graduate School–Newark offers programs of study leading to a Doctor of Philosophy degree in biology*, chemistry, criminal justice, environmental science*, global affairs, management*, mathematical sciences*, integrative neuroscience, nursing, physics (applied)*, psychology, public administration, and urban systems. It offers programs leading to a master's degree in biology*, chemistry, computational biology*, English, environmental geology, environmental science*, global affairs, history*, jazz history and research, liberal studies, nursing, physics (applied)*, political science, public administration, and public health. The asterisks indicate joint/collaborative programs with NJIT and/or UMDNJ. Other graduate programs available on the Rutgers–Newark campus are master's programs in criminal justice, government accounting, management, professional accounting, and taxation and a J.D. degree through the School of Law. In general, doctoral students must satisfy the course requirements of their area of concentration, pass comprehensive examinations, present their research in an acceptable dissertation, and defend the dissertation in a public examination. Master's students pursue a course of study and must pass a comprehensive examination. While the master's thesis is an option in most programs, in some it is required. Specific requirements for both the doctoral and master's students are determined by the faculty of each program; additional information about these requirements should be obtained from the appropriate program director.

Opportunities for postdoctoral work are available in behavioral and neural sciences, biology, chemistry, and psychology. These programs also offer collaborative research opportunities for visiting scientists.

Research Facilities

Scientific laboratories feature scanning and transmission electron microscopes, a confocal microscope, an automated DNA sequencer, ultracentrifuges, a phosphorimager, scintillation and gamma counters, a solid-phase peptide synthesizer, AVIV circular dichroism spectrophotometer, a time-correlated single photon counting instrument, fluorescence spectrometer, UV-vis NIR spectrometer, 20 MeV electron accelerator, excimer-isotopic carbon dioxide and semiconductor lasers, Auger spectrometer, quadrupole mass spectrometer, Allegra 3-Tesla functional magnetic resonance imaging instrument, and much more.

Financial Aid

In 2002–03 University teaching assistantships provide a beginning annual salary of $16,302, remission of tuition, and other benefits. Fellowships and internships supported by federal, state, private, and University funds provide annual stipends of up to $14,000 and generally offer tuition remission. Program directors can provide information about support in their respective programs.

Cost of Study

In 2002–03, tuition for full-time students who are residents of New Jersey is $4106 per semester; for nonresident full-time students it is $6020. Tuition for part-time students is $338 per credit hour for New Jersey residents and $499.50 per credit hour for nonresidents. The student fee is $387 for full-time students and $119 for part-time students. The computer fee is $100 for full-time students and $20 to $47 for part-time students.

Living and Housing Costs

There is limited housing for graduate students in University-operated furnished apartments. The housing fee for the 2002–03 academic year (September 1 through May 15) is $5068; for the calendar year (September 1 through August 15), it is $6090.

Student Group

The University's total enrollment is 47,000 students, of whom 10,000 are in the seven schools and colleges on the Newark campus. The Graduate School–Newark enrolls about 1,250 students.

Location

The Rutgers–Newark campus is conveniently located in the center of a diverse and thriving educational, professional, and cultural community in the downtown area of New Jersey's largest city. Located just a few minutes from the Newark campus, the New Jersey Performing Arts Center is a major cultural venue for the greater New York and Newark metropolitan areas and has restored Newark's historic role as the center for arts and culture in New Jersey. Because of its central location, Rutgers–Newark is accessible to a number of major metropolitan areas. New York City can be reached within 20 minutes by train, Philadelphia within an hour by train, and Washington, D.C., within an hour by plane.

The University

Rutgers, The State University of New Jersey, was chartered in 1766 as Queen's College, the eighth institution of higher learning to be founded in the Colonies before the Revolutionary War. Queen's College opened its doors in New Brunswick in 1771 with one instructor and a handful of students. In 1825 the name of the college was changed to Rutgers to honor the former trustee and Revolutionary War veteran Col. Henry Rutgers. Rutgers College became the land-grant institution of New Jersey in 1864 and, almost 100 years later, after a period of phenomenal growth, was designated the State University of New Jersey in 1945. The University's Newark campus was created in 1946 when the University of Newark became part of Rutgers. The Graduate School–Newark was established in 1974. In addition to the Graduate School, Rutgers in Newark includes the College of Arts and Sciences, the College of Nursing, the Rutgers Business School, the School of Criminal Justice, the School of Law, and University College.

Applying

Applications are available upon request from the Office of Graduate and Professional Admission, or they may be downloaded from http://www.gradstudy.rutgers.edu. Applicants may also apply online. The application fee is $50. All programs, except the program in management, require that applicants submit scores on the General Test of the Graduate Record Examinations (GRE); the management program requires scores on the Graduate Management Admission Test (GMAT). Programs in biology, chemistry, and psychology require scores on a GRE Subject Test as well as on the GRE General Test. International students and students whose native language is not English must provide scores on the Test of English as a Foreign Language (TOEFL).

By law and by purpose, Rutgers, The State University of New Jersey, is dedicated to serve all people on an equal and nondiscriminatory basis.

Correspondence and Information

Office of Graduate & Professional Admission
Rutgers, The State University of New Jersey
249 University Avenue
Newark, New Jersey 07102
Telephone: 973-353-5205
World Wide Web: http://gradstudy.rutgers.edu

Program Director (specify)
Rutgers, The State University of New Jersey
Newark, New Jersey 07102
World Wide Web: http://rutgers-newark.rutgers.edu/gradnwk

PROGRAM DIRECTORS

Dr. Steven J. Diner, Acting Dean of the Graduate School and Provost; Dr. John W. Graham, Associate Dean (973-353-5834); Claire G. Bautista, Assistant Dean (973-353-5456); Adriana Afonso, Departmental Administrator (973-353-5197).

Biology (M.S., Ph.D.): Dr. Doina Ganea (973-353-1162). Research in neuroimmunology, cytoskeleton, signal transduction in animals and plants, computational neurobiology, molecular evolution, marine biology, environmental toxicology, and the parasitology of AIDS. Facilities are available for sophisticated techniques in molecular biology and biochemistry, microbial ecology, microscopic imaging, electron microscopy, woody plant physiology and development, and cell and tissue culture. Financial support is available to qualified candidates. (http://biology-newark.rutgers.edu/bio/)

Chemistry (M.S., Ph.D.): Dr. Phillip Huskey (973-353-5741). M.S. and Ph.D. degrees are offered on both a part-time and full-time basis in all major divisions of chemistry, including organic, inorganic, analytical, and physical chemistry and biochemistry. Financial support in the form of fellowships or assistantships is available to highly qualified applicants. (http://www.rutgers-newark.rutgers.edu/chemistry/)

Computational Biology (M.S.): Dr. Michael Recce, NJIT (973-596-3483); Dr. Doina Ganea, Program Coordinator, Rutgers–Newark (973-353-1162). Joint program offered by NJIT and Rutgers–Newark to address the need for personnel trained in both computer and biological sciences. Applicants with a background in either area gain expertise in the other, as well as take core courses that provide an understanding of computational biology. Areas of specialization are genomics, molecular modeling and drug discovery, computational neuroscience, biostatistics, and physiology.

Criminal Justice (M.A., Ph.D.): Dr. Bonita Veysey (973-353-1929). Research: criminal justice theory, policy, and planning; situational crime prevention; community supervision of offenders; sentencing theory; violence; youth gangs; substance abuse and aggression; juvenile justice; organized crime; law and criminal justice; prosecution and the courts; comparative systems; maritime crime; policing; globalization of crime; business and crime. (http://www.rutgers-newark.rutgers.edu/scj/)

English (M.A.): Dr. Sterling Bland (973-353-5279 Ext. 518). Research: medieval, Renaissance, and eighteenth-century literature; Romanticism; Victorian literature; nineteenth- and twentieth-century American and British literature; modernism; contemporary literature; Marxist, postcolonial, and feminist criticism; literature and technology; African-American literature. (http://english-newark.rutgers.edu/)

Environmental Geology (M.S.): Dr. Alexander Gates (973-353-5034). A collaborative program in environmental geology with the Departments of Geological Sciences of Rutgers–New Brunswick and Civil and Environmental Engineering of NJIT. Research: structural geology, radon, aqueous geochemistry, hydrogeology, stratigraphy, applied geophysics, mineralogy, and petrology. (http://geology2.rutgers.edu/grad.htm)

Environmental Science (M.S., Ph.D.): Dr. Alexander Gates 411 Boyden Hall, Rutgers–Newark (973-353-5034). Joint M.S. and Ph.D. program with NJIT. Chemical engineering, coastal processes, ecology, environmental chemistry, environmental engineering, geochemistry, geology, geophysics, and microbiology with emphasis on urban problems. (http://www.rutgers-newark.rutgers.edu/gradnwk/envsci/index.html)

Global Affairs (M.S., Ph.D.): Professor Alexander J. Motyl (973-353-5585). Offerings include an M.S. and a Ph.D. in global affairs. Programs are interdisciplinary, drawing on political science, history, economics, law, business, sociology, and anthropology to study the relationship between globalization and emerging forms of global governance. (http://newark.rutgers.edu/~cgcg/home.html)

History (M.A., M.A.T.): Dr. Jan Lewis (973-353-1469). Joint M.A. and M.A.T. degrees offered with NJIT. American social, cultural, political, intellectual, legal, and diplomatic history; African-American history and the history of women; history of technology, the environment, medicine, and public health; European and American political culture; European history and the histories of Asia, Africa, Latin America, and the Near and Middle East; world history and comparative economic development. (http://www.andromeda.rutgers.edu/~history/)

Jazz History and Research (M.A.): Dr. Lewis Porter (973-353-5600 Ext. 30). This unique program prepares students to do research, publishing, and teaching by relying on the renowned Institute of Jazz Studies, the largest jazz library in the world. The required twelve courses focus on historiography and research, including transcribing, musical analysis, archival research, and interviewing. Applicants should have a bachelor's degree in any field and basic competence in playing and reading music. (http://www.rutgers-newark.rutgers.edu/gradnwk/jazz/index.html)

Liberal Studies (M.A.L.S.): Dr. Josephine Grieder (973-353-1045). Conceptual and historical aspects of ethology; social theory; myth, drama, contemporary fiction, and film; bureaucracy; science and technology policy; poetry and criticism; history of philosophy; women's studies; ethics, philosophy of mind, and philosophy of religion; aesthetics; history of ideas from antiquity to the twenty-first century. (http://www.rutgers-newark.rutgers.edu/gradnwk/liberal/index.html)

Management (Ph.D.): Dr. Benjamin Melamed (732-445-3128). Research and doctoral training with majors possible in accounting, information systems, international business, finance, management science, marketing, and organization management. There are three majors in information systems: accounting information systems, computer information systems, and information technology. (http://accounting.rutgers.edu/raw/gsm/phd/)

Mathematical Sciences (Ph.D.): Dr. Ulrich Oertel (973-353-5156 Ext. 20). Joint program with NJIT. Research: low-dimensional topology, geometric group theory, Riemann surfaces, number theory, algebraic geometry, differential topology, representation theory, automorphic forms, harmonic analysis, Teichmuller theory. (http://www.andromeda.rutgers.edu/~nwkmath/grad/index.html)

M.D./Ph.D.: Dr. Barry Komisaruk (973-353-5853). Seven-year program leading to the M.D. from the New Jersey Medical School (NJMS)–University of Medicine and Dentistry of New Jersey (UMDNJ) and the Ph.D. from Rutgers–Newark. Students take two years of biomedical courses at NJMS, then conduct research at Rutgers–Newark for three years, and then return to NJMS for two years of clinical training. Students apply to both institutions simultaneously. Full tuition waiver plus annual salary support. Minority students encouraged to apply. (http://www.rutgers-newark.rutgers.edu/gradnwk/md_phd/index.html)

Integrative Neuroscience (Ph.D.): Dr. Ian Creese (Rutgers) (973-353-1080 Ext. 3200). Joint program with Rutgers–Newark and UMDNJ. The program offers specific research training in behavioral and cognitive neuroscience and molecular, cellular, clinical, and systems neuroscience. Research studies can emphasize either human, animal, or computational approaches. (http://llins.rutgers.edu)

Nursing (M.S., Ph.D.): Dr. Nancy Redeker (973-353-5326 Ext. 513). Research: care and health promotion of children, adolescents, and adults/aged; symptom management in HIV/AIDS, CHF, and renal failure; pain control alternatives and exercise in hypertension; QOL issues for women in menopause and with breast cancer and persons with multiple sclerosis and surgeries that change appearance; sleep patterns of hospitalized cardiac patients; patient-care outcomes in vulnerable populations; and high-tech home care. (http://nursing.rutgers.edu/academic-programs/phd.htm)

Physics (Applied; M.S., Ph.D.): Dr. Ken K. Chin, NJIT (973-596-3297) and Dr. Zhen Wu, Rutgers–Newark (973-353-1311). Joint program offered by the Physics Departments of Rutgers (Newark) and NJIT. Research: applied optics, ultrafast optical phenomena, solid-state physics–microelectronics, MBE (molecular beam epitaxy), materials science, free electron laser, surface science, biophysics, astrophysics, plasma physics, laser spectroscopy, quantum electronics.

Political Science (M.A.): Dr. Mary Segers (973-353-5591). International relations theory, public administration and bureaucracy, environmental politics and policy, policy formation and process evaluation, immigration policy, religion and politics, American human rights policy, generational ethnicity, ethics and international relations, gender and politics, international political economy. (http://nwk-web.rutgers.edu/gradnwk/polsci/index.html)

Psychology (Ph.D.): Dr. Maggie Shiffrar (973-353-1328; e-mail: gradprogram@psychology.rutgers.edu). Graduate training and research focusing on basic issues in cognitive and behavioral sciences, with concentrations in the areas of perception, attention, visual cognition, language, cognitive neuroscience, cognitive and perceptual development, social psychology, connectionist modeling, learning and memory, emotion, hormones and behavior, adaptive behavior, and computational neuroimaging. (http://www.psych.rutgers.edu/)

Public Administration (M.P.A., Ph.D.): Dr. Marc Holzer, Ph.D.; Dr. Alan Zalkind, M.P.A., Executive M.P.A. (973-353-5093). The goal of the program is to train and educate public sector leaders, researchers, and educators. Areas of concentration in the doctoral program include productive public management, policy analysis, urban systems, and comparative public management, policy analysis, urban systems, and comparative public management and global governance. The M.P.A. program concentrations include budgeting, education, health care, and nonprofit management. The program places special emphasis on training women and minorities. (http://www.rutgers-newark.rutgers.edu/pubadmin/)

Public Health (M.P.H.): Dr. Evan Stark (973-353-5052). Joint master's program offered by UMDNJ School of Public Health, NJIT, and Rutgers–Newark, in collaboration with the Public Health Research Institute. The program prepares students to work with communities to identify and assess health needs and problems, plan and implement solutions, monitor progress, and evaluate program outcomes. Specialty tracks are urban and environmental health, quantitative methods: biostatistics and epidemiology, and health policy and administration. All courses are offered in the late afternoon or evening. (http://www.rutgers-newark.rutgers.edu/gradnwk/mph/index.html)

Urban Systems (Ph.D.): Dr. Joseph M. Holtzman, UMDNJ (973-972-7133); Dr. Alan Sadovnik, Rutgers–Newark Urban Education Policy Coordinator (973-353-1216). Joint program offered by NJIT, UMDNJ, and Rutgers–Newark. The program is designed to prepare students to develop research-based knowledge in urban systems and to participate in the development, implementation, and evaluation of policy and services for urban populations.

Women's & Gender Studies (Graduate Concentration): Dr. Frances Bartkowski (973-353-5817). This four-course concentration can be taken through the programs in English, global affairs, history, liberal studies, political science, or public administration.

SACRED HEART UNIVERSITY

Graduate Studies

Programs of Study

Sacred Heart University offers master's degrees in nine fields of study: the Master of Arts in Health Systems Management; the Master of Arts in Religious Studies; the Master of Arts in Teaching, which may lead to Connecticut public school teacher certification in elementary or secondary education; the Master of Business Administration (M.B.A.), with concentrations in accounting, economics, finance, health-care administration, human resources, international business, management information systems, and marketing; the Master of Science in Chemistry; the Master of Science degree in Computer Science and Information Technology; the Master of Science in Nursing (M.S.N.), with a nursing administration or family nurse practitioner concentration; the Master of Science in Physical Therapy; and the Master of Science in Occupational Therapy.

A dual M.B.A./M.S.N. degree is also offered. The Master of Science in chemistry program may be completed through a twenty-one-month part-time format. Post-master's certificates are available in the educational administration and family nurse practitioner programs. Graduate certificates of study are available in computer and information technology, e-commerce, educational technology, financial management, health-care administration, human resource management, international business, management information systems, multimedia, and taxation. The Institute for Religious Education and Pastoral Studies at Sacred Heart University offers graduate courses in conjunction with the graduate education and graduate religious studies programs.

Each program is designed for students to maximize their potential through academic or internship experiences. Class sizes are generally small, allowing for frequent faculty and student contact. Many programs are available on a full-time or part-time basis. Courses are held locally throughout the calendar year in Fairfield, Stamford, Danbury, and Lisbon, Connecticut. The University currently offers the only academically accredited M.B.A. program in the Grand Duchy of Luxembourg.

Research Facilities

The Ryan-Matura Library holds more than 263,000 volumes and maintains 2,100 periodical subscriptions. Additional materials are available through interlibrary loan with colleges and universities located throughout the area. A number of state-of-the-art chemistry, physical therapy, occupational therapy, and computer science laboratories are available for student use. The University sponsors the Center for Christian-Jewish Understanding, an educational and research resource on current religious thought in Christianity and Judaism. A 4,500-square-foot physical therapy clinic is housed in the William H. Pitt Health and Recreation Center.

Financial Aid

A limited number of research and staff assistantships are available to graduate students. Off-campus internship opportunities that provide tuition waivers and/or stipends are available on a competitive basis through the Office of Career Development. Teaching internships, which provide full or partial tuition waivers toward the teacher certification or the Master of Arts in Teaching program, are available in area school districts. Financial aid in the form of GradEXCEL Loans, federal student loan programs, and deferred payment plans are available through the Office of Student Financial Assistance.

Cost of Study

Tuition for most graduate students is charged on a per-credit-hour basis. Rates for the 2001–02 academic year vary by program but range from $375 to $435 per credit. Tuition for the Master of Science in Physical Therapy program is approximately $16,125 for the 2001–02 academic year.

Living and Housing Costs

Most graduate students commute to campus. Rent for off-campus housing in neighboring communities ranges from $500 to $900 per month for a one-bedroom apartment. University housing is available for full-time graduate students on a space-available basis at an approximate cost of $3433 per semester.

Student Group

There are approximately 5,700 undergraduate and graduate students enrolled at Sacred Heart University. Graduate enrollment for the 2001–02 academic year exceeds 1,600 full- and part-time students. Nearly 60 percent are women, and 9 percent represent minority groups. The graduate student body represents seventeen states from New England to the Pacific Northwest, as well as thirteen countries.

Location

Established in 1639, Fairfield, Connecticut, is an attractive suburban community located 55 miles northeast of New York City. The community and surrounding area are considered one of the nation's more dynamic business and economic regions and are home to numerous Fortune 500 companies. The main campus is located on 56 acres near major thoroughfares and recreational areas.

The University

Sacred Heart University was founded in 1963 as a coeducational, independent, comprehensive institution in the Catholic intellectual tradition. Graduate programs are offered through the College of Arts and Sciences, College of Business, and College of Education and Health Professions. In recent years, the University has achieved phenomenal growth in enrollment, faculty, and facilities. It is the third-largest Catholic university in New England.

Applying

A bachelor's degree from a regionally accredited four-year college or university or its equivalent is required for admission. Other requirements vary for each program. All applicants must submit a completed application to the Office of Graduate Admissions. International applicants must have a minimum TOEFL score of 550 on the paper-based exam or 220 on the computer-based exam and are required to demonstrate the ability to finance their education for F-1 Visa eligibility.

Correspondence and Information

Sacred Heart University
Office of Graduate Admissions
5151 Park Avenue
Fairfield, Connecticut 06432-1000

Telephone: 203-365-7619
Fax: 203-365-4732
E-mail: gradstudies@sacredheart.edu
World Wide Web: http://www.sacredheart.edu/

THE FACULTY

College of Arts and Sciences

Claire Paolini, Dean; Ph.D., Tulane.
Chemistry: Babu George, Department Chair; Ph.D., New Mexico.
Computer Science and Information Technology: Domenick Pinto, Program Director; M.S., Polytechnic.
Religious Studies: Richard Grigg, Program Director; Ph.D., Iowa.

College of Business

Ben Boyer, Dean; Ph.D., UCLA.
Business: Mary Trefry, Director of Graduate Business Programs; Ph.D., Columbia.

College of Education and Health Professions

Patricia Walker, Dean; Ed.D., Loyola.
Education: Peter Gioiella, Chair and Program Director; Ph.D., NYU.
Nursing: Dori Sullivan, Program Director; Ph.D., Connecticut; RNC, CNA, CPHQ.
Occupational Therapy: Jody Bortone, Program Director; M.A., NYU; OTR/L.
Physical Therapy: Michael Emery, Program Director; Ed.D., Vermont.

SAGE GRADUATE SCHOOL

Programs of Study

Sage Graduate School, one of the Sage Colleges, offers an M.B.A. and a joint J.D./M.B.A. degree in association with Albany Law School. The community psychology program is the largest of its type in the U.S., offering an M.A. with tracks in general psychology, child care and children's services, community health education, and community counseling. A dietetic internship program, which leads to standing as a registered dietitian, is offered in conjunction with the American Dietetic Association. Programs in elementary education, guidance counseling, health education, literacy education, literacy/childhood special education, childhood special education, and a Master of Arts in Teaching (biology, English, mathematics, or social studies) lead to teacher certification in New York State; a post-master's certificate is offered in guidance and counseling. The Master of Science in Nursing (M.S.N.) is based on NLNAC-accredited programs in adult health or community health nursing, gerontological nurse practitioner studies, psychiatric–mental health nursing, or nurse practitioner studies. There is also a dual M.S.N. with an M.B.A. as well as a post-master's certificate in nursing. The M.S. in Public Administration offers concentrations in communications, public management, human services administration, and gerontology and the dietetic internship. The M.S. in health service administration offers tracks in management, gerontology, and the dietetic internship. The programs are flexible and carefully tailored to the needs of today's society and students who are preparing for professional leadership. Sage also offers degrees in chemical dependence administration, forensic psychology, and physical therapy. There are also certificate programs available.

Research Facilities

Two libraries house a collection of more than 350,000 volumes of books, periodicals, and audiotapes and videotapes and maintain more than 1,500 current periodical subscriptions. Students have access to other Capital District libraries as well as libraries nationwide.

Financial Aid

Student loans, graduate assistantships, scholarships, and state and federal assistance are available. For students in teacher certification programs, paid internships in the schools may be available.

Cost of Study

For 2002-03, the cost per credit hour is $415. The application fee is $40.

Living and Housing Costs

Residential options are available for women on the Troy campus. Total room and board charges are calculated on a monthly or yearly basis. Off-campus apartments ($500 to $600 per month) are available within walking distance of each campus.

Student Group

Currently, there are more than 1,000 matriculated women and men at Sage Graduate School. Many of the part-time students are already working in their fields of study. Most classes average between 10 and 25 students.

Student Outcomes

Through the Career Services and the Sage Graduate School Alumni Association, a network of linkages to professional positions in the Capital District are open to graduate students. Sage graduates are employed in the federal, state, and local governments; as directors of nursing homes; as nurse practitioners; as teachers in public and private schools; as managers in regional health-care facilities; and in the administration of for-profit and not-for-profit businesses and agencies.

Location

Sage Graduate School has two campuses, one in the historic district of downtown Troy and the other in the heart of New York's capital city, Albany. New York's Capital District (population 1.2 million) is easily accessible by air, bus, rail, and interstate highway transportation. The Capital District is only 3 hours from New York City, Boston, and Montreal.

The School

Founded in 1949, Sage Graduate School is one of the Sage Colleges, a federation of four educational institutions that includes Russell Sage College, Sage Junior College of Albany, and Sage Evening College. Sage Graduate School is a dynamic organization that serves adults who seek entrance into a variety of professions. The Sage Graduate School faculty members have professional backgrounds, real-world experience, and terminal degrees in the areas they represent.

Applying

The requirements for admission to Sage Graduate School are a baccalaureate degree from an accredited four-year college and a GPA of at least 2.75, two letters of recommendation, a current resume, and a one- to two-page typewritten career essay. Certain programs have higher admission requirements and require an interview prior to admission. Students not meeting these requirements may be eligible for provisional admission. Sage Graduate School accepts applications at any time during the year, but it should be noted that in order to apply for financial aid, students must apply for admission and be accepted. Financial aid applications can be processed within 30 days after a student has been accepted, provided they have completed the application process for financial aid. To apply to the occupational or physical therapy programs, students may call the Office of Admissions for special application procedures.

Correspondence and Information

Office of Admissions
Sage Graduate School
45 Ferry Street
Troy, New York 12180
Telephone: 518-244-6878
888-VERY-SAGE (toll-free)
Fax: 518-244-6880
E-mail: sgsadm@sage.edu
World Wide Web: http://www.sage.edu

THE FACULTY

Kim P. Baker, Assistant Professor of Education; Ph.D., SUNY at Albany.
Melodie Bell-Cavallino, Associate Professor of Nutrition Science; M.S., Sage Graduate.
Frederick A. Brandt, Associate Professor of Management; Ph.D., Arizona State.
James Brennan, Assistant Professor of Physical Therapy; M.S., Ohio State.
Joan E. Dacher, Assistant Professor of Nursing; Ph.D., SUNY at Albany.
Linda Davern, Assistant Professor of Education; Ph.D., Syracuse.
Leigh Davies, Assistant Professor of Creative Arts in Therapy; M.P.S., Pratt.
Martha M. Frank, Associate Professor of Occupational Therapy and Chair, Division of Health and Rehabilitation Sciences; M.S., Saint Rose.
Connell Frazer, Associate Professor of Education and Dean of Sage Graduate School; Ed.D., Northern Colorado.
Barbara E. Gioia, Assistant Professor of Education; Ph.D., SUNY at Albany.
Kathleen A. Gormley, Associate Professor of Education; Ed.D., SUNY at Albany.
Michael L. Hall, Associate Professor of Public Administration; Ph.D., Oklahoma.
Theresa Hartshorn-Hand, Instructor of Occupational Therapy; M.S. Sage Graduate.
Glenda Kelman, Associate Professor of Nursing; Ph.D., NYU.
Kathleen Kennedy, Assistant Professor of Nursing; M.S., Sage Graduate; RN.
David B. Kiner, Associate Professor of Marketing; M.B.A., Western New England.
Wendy Krupnick, Assistant Professor of Occupational Therapy; M.B.A., George Washington.
Peter McDermott, Associate Professor of Education; Ed.D., SUNY at Albany.
Francisco Melero, Associate Professor of Economics; Ph.D., Rensselaer.
William D. Niemi, Professor of Biology and Chair, Division of the Sciences; Ph.D., Vermont.
Patricia O'Connor, Professor of Psychology and Lorraine Walker Fellow in Psychology; Ph.D., NYU.
Mary Lou Peck, Associate Professor of Nursing; Ed.D., Columbia.
John J. Pelizza, Associate Professor of Health Education; Ph.D., New Mexico.
Arlene Pericak, Assistant Professor of Nursing; M.A., Lowell.
Linda Ceriale Peterson, Professor of Nursing; Ed.D., Massachusetts.
Barbara B. Pieper, Associate Professor of Nursing; Ph.D., Adelphi.
Joseph N. Prenoveau, Assistant Professor of Education; Ed.D., Columbia.
Jeffrey C. Rinehart, Professor of Public Administration; Ph.D., Penn State.
Bronna Romanoff, Assistant Professor of Psychology; Ph.D., SUNY at Albany.
Julia J. Rothenberg, Associate Professor of Education; Ph.D., SUNY at Albany.
Marjane Selleck, Associate Professor of Physical Therapy; M.S., Saint Rose.
Ellen Shapiro, Associate Professor of Physical Therapy; M.S., Long Island.
Marion Terenzio, Associate Professor of Music, Associate Professor of Psychology, and Chairperson, Faculty Council; Ph.D., Michigan State.
John Tribble, Associate Professor of Economics and Lawrence Family Foundation Professor in Economics and Business; Ph.D., Utah State.
Cynthia J. Ward, Associate Professor of Public Administration; Ph.D., Syracuse.
Susan Wheeler-Roy, Associate Professor of Psychology; Ed.D., SUNY at Albany.
Thomas L. Zane, Associate Professor of Education; Ph.D., West Virginia.

Frear House on the Sage Troy Campus.

Campus Center on the Albany Campus.

ST. JOHN'S UNIVERSITY

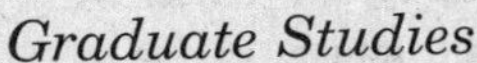

Programs of Study

St. John's University, through its six Graduate Divisions, offers a wide variety of graduate degrees, professional diplomas, and advanced certificates. St. John's College of Liberal Arts and Sciences offers the following areas of study and degrees: Chinese or East Asian studies (M.A.; Advanced Certificates in East Asian culture studies, Asian and African culture studies, and Chinese language), Latin American and Caribbean studies (Advanced Certificate), biology (M.S., Ph.D.), chemistry (M.S.), English (M.A., D.A.), government and politics (M.A., certificate programs in public administration and international law and diplomacy), government and politics/library science (M.A./M.L.S.), history (M.A.), modern world history (D.A.), library science (M.L.S., Advanced Certificate in Library and Information Studies), mathematics (M.A.), clinical psychology (Ph.D. in clinical general and clinical child), general experimental psychology (M.A.), school psychology (M.S., Psy.D.) and school psychology–bilingual track (M.S., Psy.D.), sociology (M.A.), Spanish (M.A.), speech-language pathology and audiology (M.A.), theology (M.A., Certificate in Catechetics and Religious Education, Certificate in Theology), and Ministerial Studies (M.Div.). The School of Education offers the following majors and degrees: adolescent education (biology 7–12, English 7–12, mathematics 7–12, social studies 7–12, Spanish 7–12 (M.S.)), childhood education (M.S.), childhood special education 1–6 (M.S.), early childhood education (M.S.), educational administration and supervision (M.S., P.D., Ed.D.), instructional leadership (P.D., Ed.D.), reading specialist studies (P.D.), teaching literacy B–6 (M.S., P.D.), teaching literacy 5–12 (M.S., P.D.), rehabilitation counseling (M.S., P.D.), school counselor (M.S., P.D.), school counselor with bilingual extension (M.S., P.D.), student development practice in higher education (M.S., P.D.), and teaching English to speakers of other languages (TESOL; M.S., P.D.). Certificate programs are available in special education (childhood) and (adolescent). Extension programs are offered in bilingual education. The Peter J. Tobin College of Business offers the M.B.A. in decision sciences, computer information systems for managers, executive management, finance, financial services, international finance, marketing, management, international business, accounting, risk and insurance management. The Peter J. Tobin College of Business also offers the M.S. in taxation, accounting and risk management, actuarial sciences, and forecasting and planning. Advanced Professional Certificate programs are also offered in each of these areas. The College of Pharmacy and Allied Health Professions offers the following degree programs: pharmaceutical sciences (M.S., Ph.D.), toxicology (M.S.), pharmaceutical science/library science (M.S./M.L.S.), pharmacy administration (M.S.), and pharmacy (Doctor of Pharmacy). The School of Law offers a Juris Doctor degree and a Master of Laws (LL.M.) in bankruptcy, as well as a combined M.A./J.D. in government and politics and law and an M.B.A./J.D. in a broad variety of business disciplines. The College of Professional Studies offers a degree in criminal justice leadership (M.P.S.). Qualified undergraduate students may earn a baccalaureate degree from St. John's College of Liberal Arts and Sciences or the College of Professional Studies and a J.D. degree from the School of Law in a six-year program.

Research Facilities

The main library of the University is in St. Augustine Hall, located on the Queens Campus. Together with the collections of the Loretto Memorial Library on the Staten Island Campus, the Law School Library, the Eastern Long Island Campus Library, the Rome Campus Library, and the Manhattan Campus Library, the total University library collections number 1.7 million volumes and include more than 6,000 periodic subscriptions. Collections include government documents and audiovisual materials. The libraries' Web site also includes subject pages that represent various disciplines and subjects related to the St. John's University curricula. Pentium workstations in each library provide access to these electronic formats as well as to the holdings of more than two dozen consortium libraries, electronic full-text databases, and information resources available on the Internet. The main library provides seating for more than 950 patrons, reference assistance during most library hours, interlibrary loan services that allow students to obtain materials from other libraries, and workshops on using electronic and other library resources. Well-equipped laboratories for research are also available.

Financial Aid

University Doctoral Fellowships, other doctoral fellowships, and assistantships are awarded annually to qualified graduate students. Scholarships based on academic achievement and financial need are also available. A complete listing may be found in the *Graduate Bulletin*. Information about graduate assistantships and application forms is available from the Office of Admission. Information about fellowships is available from the office of the Academic Dean of the particular graduate unit. Application for scholarships should be made to the Office of Financial Aid unless otherwise indicated. Full-time graduate students may also apply for awards through the Federal Perkins Loan and Federal Work-Study Programs; New York State residents may apply for aid through the New York State Tuition Assistance Program. Information concerning law school financial aid and scholarships is listed in the *Law School Bulletin*.

Cost of Study

Tuition for the 2002–03 academic year is $630 per credit. Courses taken toward programs in library and information sciences, school psychology, and speech pathology and audiology is $710 per credit; graduate programs in business administration (M.B.A.) are $655 per credit; courses taken toward the pharmacy program, the Psy.D. in school psychology, and the Ph.D. clinical psychology program are $790 per credit; and the master's in law program is $877 per credit. First-professional day law students pay $26,300, and night law students pay $19,730 per year.

Living and Housing Costs

The University offers on-campus housing facilities (room only) to graduate students at an annual cost of $6050.

Student Group

During the 2001–02 academic year, 4,138 graduate and first-professional students were enrolled.

Location

St. John's has three handsome, residential New York City campuses. The 100-acre Queens campus and the compact Staten Island campus are in quiet, suburban neighborhoods. The award winning, 10-story Manhattan "campus" is in Manhattan's financial center. There is also a 110-acre campus in Oakdale, Long Island.

The University

St. John's University is dedicated to the intellectual growth of its students and to the advancement of knowledge through research. It aims to help students attain a mastery of the preparation essential for success in a chosen career, the ability to think clearly and consistently, and a facility in written and oral communication.

Applying

Students applying must submit the application for admission, official transcripts of all college and university work, and GRE or GMAT or LSAT scores if required. These materials should be sent directly to Graduate Admission at the appropriate campus at least three months prior to the registration period. Specific program deadlines are as follows: Master of Science in speech-language pathology and audiology, March 1 for fall and October 1 for spring; Master of Science in school psychology, March 15; doctoral programs in clinical psychology and school psychology, February 1; doctoral programs in education, April 15; doctoral program in pharmacy, March 15; other doctoral programs as well as international students, June 1 for fall and November 1 for spring. Applicants should carefully review University and department admission requirements as described in the current *Graduate Bulletin* prior to applying. A nonrefundable application fee of $40 ($50 for law school applications) is required in the form of a personal check or money order.

Correspondence and Information

Queens and Manhattan Campus
St. John's University
8000 Utopia Parkway
Jamaica, New York 11439
Telephone: 718-990-2000 (in state)
888-9STJOHNS (toll-free)
Fax: 718-990-2096
E-mail: admissions@stjohns.edu
WWW: http://www.STJOHNS.edu

Staten Island Campus
St. John's University
300 Howard Avenue
Staten Island, New York 10301
Telephone: 718-390-4500
800-9STJOHNS (toll-free)
Fax: 718-390-4298

Rome Campus
St. John's University
Pontificio Oratorio di San Pietro
Via Santa Maria
Mediatrice 24
00165 Roma, Italia
Telephone: 011-39-06-636-937
Fax: 011-39-06-636-901
E-mail: info@stjohns.edu

DEANS AND CHAIRPERSONS

St. John's College of Liberal Arts and Sciences
Jeffrey W. Fagen, Ph.D., Dean.
Frank A. Biafora, Ph.D., Associate Dean.
Nicholas Healy, Ph.D., Associate Dean (Staten Island Campus).
Patrick P. McGuire, Ed.D., Assistant Dean.
Christine Rupp, M.A., Assistant Dean.
Asian Studies: John S. Lin, Ph.D., Director.
Biological Sciences: Jay Zimmerman, Ph.D., Chair.
Biological Sciences Ph.D. Program: Dipak Haldar, Ph.D., Director.
Chemistry: Neil D. Jespersen, Ph.D., Chair.
English: Stephen Sicari, Ph.D., Chair.
Government and Politics: Robert Pecorella, Ph.D., Chair.
History: Frank Ninkovitch, Ph.D., Chair.
Library and Information Sciences: Sherry Vellucci, D.L.S., Director.
Mathematics: Charles Traina, Ph.D., Chair.
Modern Foreign Languages: Gaetano Cipolla, Ph.D., Chair.
    Master's Program in Spanish: Marie-Lise Gazarian, Ph.D., Coordinator.
Modern World History: Frank J. Coppa, Ph.D., Director.
Psychology: Ray DiGiuseppe, Ph.D., Chair.
    Clinical Program: Jeffrey Nevid, Ph.D., Director.
    General Experimental: Leonard Brosgole, Ph.D., Coordinator.
    School Psychology: Sam Ortiz and Dawn Flanagan, Ph.D., Co-Directors.
Sociology and Anthropology: Dawn Esposito, Ph.D., Chair.
Speech Communication Sciences: Fredricka Bell-Berti, Ph.D., Chair.
    Speech Pathology–Audiology Program: Donna Geffner, Ph.D., Director.
Theology and Religious Studies: Rev. Jean-Pierre Ruiz, Ph.D., Chair.

The Peter J. Tobin College of Business
Peter J. Tobin, Dean.
Donna M. Narducci, Ed.D., Associate Dean and Director (Staten Island Campus).
Nejdet Delener, Ph.D., Associate Dean.
Susan McTiernan, M.S., Associate Dean.
William Swan, Ph.D., Associate Dean.
Susan McCall, M.B.A., Assistant Dean.
Susan Bradley, M.B.A., Assistant Dean (Staten Island Campus).
Nicole Bryan, M.B.A., Assistant Dean.
Niall Hegarty, M.B.A., Assistant Dean.
Kevin Shea, M.B.A., Assistant Dean (Staten Island Campus).
Accounting and Taxation: Adrian Fitzsimons, Ph.D., Chair.
Business Law: John Manna, J.D., Chair.
Computer Information Systems and Decision Sciences: Andrew Russakoff, Ph.D., Chair.
Economics and Finance: Thomas Liaw, Ph.D., Chair.
Management: John Angelidis, Ph.D., Chair.
Marketing: Sreedhar Kavil, Ph.D., Chair.
School of Risk Management, Insurance, and Actuarial Science: James Barrese, Ph.D., Chair.

School of Education and Human Services
Jerrold Ross, Ph.D., D.Hum.(Hon.), Dean.
Barbara J. Nelson, Ed.D., Associate Dean.
Sr. Ann McCarthy, CSJ, Ed.D., Assistant Dean.
Sr. Colleen T. Fogarty, O.P., Ph.D., Assistant Dean.
Steven S. Kuntz, Ph.D., Assistant Dean (Staten Island Campus).
Charisse Willis, P.D., Director, Undergraduate Advisement.
Kelly Ronayne, M.A., Assistant Dean.
Richard T. Scarpaci, Ph.D., Director, Field Experiences.
Lydia Haluski, B.A., Assistant to the Dean.
Maria Allegretti, B.S., Assistant to the Dean (Staten Island Campus).
Administration and Instructional Leadership: Gene Geisert, Ph.D., Chair.
Human Services and Counseling: Richard Sinatra, Ph.D., Chair.
Early Childhood, Childhood, and Adolescent Education: William Sanders, Ph.D., Chair.

College of Pharmacy and Allied Health Professions
Robert Mangione, Ed.D., Dean.
Joseph Brocavich, Pharm.D., Associate Dean.
John-Emery Konecsni, Ph.D., Assistant Dean.
Clinical Pharmacy Practice: Judith L. Beizer, Pharm.D., Chair.
Pharmaceutical Sciences: Louis Trombetta, Ph.D., Chair.
Pharmacy and Administrative Sciences: Somnath Pal, Ph.D., Chair.

College of Professional Studies
Kathleen Vouté MacDonald, Ed.D., Dean.
Criminal Justice and Legal Studies: Bernard Helldorfer, J.D., Chair.
Criminal Justice and Legal Studies: Thomas Ward, D.P.A., Director, Graduate Program.

School of Law
Joseph Bellacosa, J.D., Dean.
Robert Harrison, J.D., Assistant Dean and Director of Admission.

SAINT JOSEPH'S UNIVERSITY

Graduate School of Arts and Sciences

Programs of Study

Saint Joseph's University offers graduate study leading to the Master of Science in chemistry and chemistry education, computer science (concentration in information systems management), criminal justice (concentrations in administration, probation, parole and corrections, criminology), education (concentrations in business, chemistry, computer science, educational leadership, elementary and secondary certification, math, professional education, reading certification), gerontological services (concentrations in gerontological counseling, human services administration), health administration, health education (concentrations in employee assistance, nutrition marketing), nurse anesthesia, psychology, and training and organization development. The University also offers both a Master of Arts and a Master of Science in biology, as well as a postbaccalaureate certificate in purchase/acquisitions. Pennsylvania certification in the areas of curriculum supervision, principal, and superintendent at the elementary and secondary levels is also offered. Health administration is available on satellite campuses located at Albright College in Reading and at Ursinus College in Collegeville, both in Pennsylvania. Criminal justice is available at Albright. Post-master's certificates in health administration, employee assistance, nutrition marketing, training and development, and gerontological services are also offered. Saint Joseph's has also inaugurated a new doctoral program, an Ed.D. in educational leadership.

Research Facilities

The Francis A. Drexel Library, located near the center of campus, contains a collection of approximately 350,000 volumes, 750,000 holdings in microfilm and microfiche, and 1,850 current periodical subscriptions. It also serves as a selective depository for U.S. government documents. The library has an online public access catalog for searching its holdings, accessible from remote locations via the University's computer network. Patrons have access to the Internet and many subject-oriented databases through the campus network and the library's local area network. Reference librarians offer instruction in the use of the library's resources and can perform online searches of numerous external databases. Patrons also have direct borrowing access to more than 4.5 million volumes from members of the Tri-State College Library Cooperative as well as interlibrary loan access to more than 35 million volumes nationwide and in thirty-eight other countries and territories through the library's participation in the Online Computer Library Center.

More than 1,000 desktop computers are connected to the University's campuswide network from classrooms, offices, and three of the student residence halls, as well as from seven computer labs, four computer classrooms, and several e-mail labs available for use by students and faculty and staff members. The campus network provides access to e-mail and a large collection of application software packages, including word processing, spreadsheets, databases, statistical software, programming languages, and programmed learning modules used by faculty members in the presentation of course materials. Internet access is available through the World Wide Web, e-mail, telnet, ftp, Usenet, and Listserv software. The campuswide information system utilizes World Wide Web technology and is located at the address listed below.

Financial Aid

Graduate assistantships are available to qualified students. Scholarships are available to full-time teachers and administrators who are enrolled in a degree or certification program in education. The University work-study program is available to graduate students attending on at least a half-time basis, and these students may also apply for Federal Perkins and Federal Stafford Student loans and PHEA-HELP.

Cost of Study

Tuition for 2002–03 for graduate arts and sciences courses is $560 per credit; for graduate computer science courses, $600 per credit; and for graduate education and psychology courses, $600 per credit. Doctoral courses are $600 per credit.

Living and Housing Costs

On-campus housing is not available for graduate students, but accommodations are available in the area. Living costs in the greater Delaware Valley are reasonable compared with costs in other large urban centers.

Student Group

Total enrollment is approximately 7,000 students, 1,500 of whom are graduate students in Arts and Sciences. The majority of graduate students are attending part-time and are primarily professionals with several years of experience in their field.

Location

The 65-acre campus of Saint Joseph's University is conveniently situated on the western boundary of Philadelphia on wooded and landscaped grounds. It combines urban accessibility with the traditional charm of the area's well-known Main Line. The environment provides an aura of seclusion; yet the educational, cultural, and entertainment resources of metropolitan Philadelphia are easily accessible. Located near the Schuylkill Expressway (Route 76), the University is served by local bus and rail lines and is less than 20 minutes from Center City.

The University

As a Jesuit university founded in 1851, Saint Joseph's strives to be perceptibly Christian. Its focus as an institution is a commitment to high intellectual and ethical standards in the Jesuit tradition, to the education of leaders and agents of social change, to the development of intercultural and international awareness, and to the Ignatian heritage of service to others. Saint Joseph's has awarded graduate degrees since 1898 and in choosing the areas in which to offer graduate programs, has always sought those of direct benefit to professionals in the field.

Applying

Applications for admission are welcomed throughout the year and should be accompanied by a $30 application fee, a current resume, official transcripts of all undergraduate and graduate work completed, and three letters of recommendation from professional and/or academic sources. Specific requirements for the application process, including GPA and GREs, differ among the programs. A TOEFL score is required of all candidates from non-English-speaking countries. General application materials, interview appointments, and campus visit information are available by writing to or calling the Office of Graduate Programs.

Correspondence and Information

Graduate School of Arts and Sciences
Saint Joseph's University
5600 City Avenue
Philadelphia, Pennsylvania 19131-9977
Telephone: 610-660-1289
Fax: 610-660-3230
World Wide Web: http://www.sju.edu

GRADUATE PROGRAMS

Dr. Robert H. Palestini, Ed.D., Temple; Dean of Graduate and Continuing Studies.

- Biology
- Chemistry
- Computer Science
- Criminal Justice
- Education
- Gerontological Services
- Health Administration
- Health Education
- Nurse Anesthesia
- Psychology
- Public Safety and Environmental Protection
- Training and Organization Development

Barbelin Building, the original building on Saint Joseph's campus.

A faculty meeting at Haub Executive Center in McShain Hall.

Mandeville Hall.

SAINT LOUIS UNIVERSITY

Graduate Studies

Programs of Study

The Graduate School offers programs of advanced study in the following disciplinary units leading to the degrees indicated: aerospace engineering, M.S., M.S.(R); American studies, M.A., M.A.(R), Ph.D.; anatomy, M.S.(R), Ph.D.; biochemistry and molecular biology, Ph.D.; biology, M.S., M.S.(R), Ph.D.; business administration (international business/marketing), Ph.D.; chemistry, M.S., M.S.(R); communication, M.A., M.A.(R); communication sciences and disorders, M.A., M.A.(R); community health, M.P.H.; counseling and family therapy, M.A., Ph.D.; economics, M.A.; educational leadership, M.A., Ed.S., Ed.D., Ph.D.; educational studies, M.A., M.A.T., Ed.D., Ph.D.; endodontics, M.S.; English, M.A., M.A.(R), Ph.D.; French, M.A.; geology, M.S., M.S.(R); geophysics, M.S., M.S.(R), Ph.D.; health administration, M.H.A.; health-care ethics, Ph.D.; higher education, M.A., Ed.D., Ph.D.; historical theology, M.A., Ph.D.; history, M.A., M.A.(R), Ph.D.; mathematics, M.A., M.A.(R), Ph.D.; meteorology, M.Pr.Met., M.S.(R), Ph.D.; microbiology, Ph.D.; neurobiology, Ph.D.; nursing, M.S., M.S.(R), Ph.D.; nutrition and dietetics, M.S.; orthodontics, M.S.; pathology, Ph.D.; periodontics, M.S.; pharmacological and physiological science, Ph.D.; philosophy, M.A., M.A.(R), Ph.D.; psychology, M.S.(R), Ph.D.; public administration, M.A.P.A.; public health studies, Ph.D.; public policy analysis, Ph.D.; Spanish, M.A.; theology, M.A; urban affairs, M.A.U.A.; urban planning and real estate development, M.UPRED.

Certificates may be pursued parallel to degree study in rhetorical studies/writing pedagogy, Medieval studies, and Renaissance studies. Post-master's certificates are available in marriage and family therapy and in a variety of nursing specialities. Opportunities for combining degree programs that facilitate simultaneous training in one of the University's professional schools (e.g., law, medicine, business, or social services) are also available.

Research Facilities

The combined holdings of the University libraries total approximately 1.4 million volumes and some 14,300 continuations. Computer access is available to the libraries of the University of Missouri system. Special collections include 35 million pages of Vatican manuscripts and extensive theological holdings. The University is a member of the Center for Research Libraries (Chicago), and students also have access to the libraries of the University of Missouri and Washington University in St. Louis. Computer centers and research offices are staffed on both the Frost and Health Sciences Center campuses. The University's urban location has allowed the development of unique research opportunities with numerous public and private agencies and corporations.

Financial Aid

Financial assistance is available to qualified graduate students. Fellowships, traineeships, teaching, and research assistantships are awarded in most fields of study; full-tuition scholarships accompany stipends in many instances. Applications for appointments are available from Graduate School Admissions. Federal and state (Missouri) grants and loans and Federal Work-Study eligibility may be sought through the University's Office of Financial Aid; formal application and the need analysis are mandatory.

Cost of Study

The cost per Graduate School credit hour is $660 in 2002–03.

Living and Housing Costs

Limited on-campus housing exists for graduate and professional students. Numerous privately owned rooms and apartments are located within short distances from the University's campuses. Room and board costs for a single student and a married couple are currently estimated at $7300 and $11,200, respectively, for the nine-month academic year.

Student Group

Of the 11,300 students attending Saint Louis University's five campuses, approximately 1,900 are students in the Graduate School pursuing advanced degrees.

Location

The University's campuses are located in the midtown area between downtown and the west boundary of the city. Powell Hall, home of the St. Louis Symphony Orchestra, and shopping are within walking distance. Forest Park, the Missouri Botanical Garden, and professional sports facilities are easily accessible from the University. The city and Saint Louis University have a long-standing mutual commitment to each other's vitality and quality of life.

The University

Saint Louis University is a private Catholic institution of higher learning serving urban, regional, national, and international clienteles. The University was founded in 1818 and was chartered by the state in 1832 as the first institution of higher learning west of the Mississippi River. Its first M.A. and Ph.D. degrees were conferred in 1834 and 1880, respectively. More than 525 of the full-time faculty members hold graduate faculty appointments. The governance of the Graduate School is the responsibility of the Dean and the University Board of Graduate Studies. The University has been classified as a Research II university by the Carnegie Foundation for the Advancement of Teaching.

Applying

Application forms for admission and graduate assistantships can be obtained from the Graduate School Admissions office. The assistantship application should be filed by February 1 for fall consideration; the deadline for fall admission is July 1 for most programs. Forms for need-based assistance can be obtained from the Office of Scholarship and Financial Aid.

All international students whose native language is not English must submit official copies of TOEFL score reports. Most programs require GRE General Test scores of all applicants.

Correspondence and Information

Graduate School Admissions
Saint Louis University
3634 Lindell Boulevard
St. Louis, Missouri 63108
Telephone: 314-977-2240
E-mail: grequest@slu.edu
World Wide Web: http://www.slu.edu/colleges/gr

Office of Scholarship and Financial Aid
Saint Louis University
221 North Grand Boulevard
St. Louis, Missouri 63103
Telephone: 314-977-2350

FACULTY HEADS

Rev. Lawrence H. Biondi S.J., Ph.D., President.
Sandra H. Johnson, LL.M., J.D., Provost.

Officers of the Graduate School

Donald G. Brennan, Ph.D., Dean of the Graduate School/Associate Provost for Research.
Marcia D. Buresch, Ph.D., Associate Dean.
Robert J. Nikolai, Ph.D., Associate Dean.

Department and Program Chairpersons or Directors

Aerospace Engineering: Dr. Krishnaswamy Ravindra.
American Studies: Dr. Matthew Mancini.
Anatomy/Neurobiology: Dr. Paul Young.
Biochemistry: Dr. William Sly.
Biology: Dr. Richard Mayden.
Business Administration: Dr. Stephen Miller.
Chemistry: Dr. Vincent Spaziano.
Communication: Dr. John Pauly.
Communication Sciences and Disorders: Dr. Richard Maguire.
Community Health: Dr. Ross Brownson.
Counseling/Family Therapy: Dr. Nancy Morrison.
Economics: Dr. Muhammad Islam.
Education Leadership/Higher Education: Dr. William Rebore.
Education Studies: Dr. Ann Rule.
Endodontics: Dr. John Hatton.
English: Dr. Sara van den Berg.
Geoscience: Dr. Robert Hermann.
Health Administration: Dr. Claudia Campbell.
Health Care Ethics: Dr. Gerard Magill.
History: Dr. Thomas Madden
Mathematics: Dr. Michael May.
Meteorology: Dr. James Moore.
Microbiology: Dr. William Wold.
Modern/Classical Language: Rev. Anthony Daly.
Nursing (M.S.): Dr. Margie Edel.
Nursing (Ph.D.): Dr. Maryellen McSweeney.
Nutrition and Dietetics: Dr. Mildred Mattfeldt-Beman.
Orthodontics: Dr. Eustaquio Araujo.
Pathology: Dr. Richard Hoover.
Periodontics: Dr. Douglas Miley.
Pharmacological and Physiological Sciences: Dr. Thomas Westfall.
Philosophy: Rev. Theodore Vitali.
Psychology: Dr. Ronald Kellogg.
Public Health Studies: Dr. William True.
Public Policy Studies: Dr. Mary Domahidy.
Research Methodology: Dr. Terry Tomazic.
Theological Studies: Rev. John J. Mueller.

While most Department and Program Chairpersons and Directors also serve as the Admissions Director, the exceptions are listed below.

Aerospace Engineering: Dr. Marty Ferman.
Biochemistry: Dr. Margaret Weidman.
Biology: Dr. Gary Bulla.
Business Administration (M.B.A.): Mr. Casey Crane.
Business Administration (Ph.D.): Dr. Stephen Miller.
Communication: Dr. Robert Krizek.
Education Studies: Dr. Dorothy Miles.
French: Dr. Jean-Louis Pautrot.
Higher Education: Dr. Gerard Fowler.
History: Dr. T. Michael Ruddy.
Microbiology: Dr. H. Peter Zassenhaus.
Pathology: Dr. Jacki Kornbluth.
Pharmacological/Physiological Sciences: Dr. Barry Chapnick.
Psychology—Applied/Experimental: Dr. Donna LaVoie.
Psychology—Clinical: Dr. Michael Ross.
Public Administration: Dr. Mary Domahidy.
Spanish: Dr. Olga Arbelaez.
Theological Studies: Rev. Wayne Hellman.
Urban Affairs: Dr. Mary Domahidy.
Urban Planning and Real Estate Development: Dr. Mary Domahidy.
Aquinas Institute of Theology: Ron Knapp.
School of Law: Michael J. Kalnik.
School of Medicine: Dr. James Willmore.
School of Social Service: Dr. Jay Memmott.

The Gateway Arch on the Mississippi River frames the historic Old Courthouse and provides the background for a bronzed Olympic runner in Kiener Plaza in St. Louis, Missouri.

The Billikens basketball team is experiencing new success in Conference USA.

View of the John E. Connelly Plaza and mall, located on the Frost Campus.

SAINT PETER'S COLLEGE

Graduate Studies

Programs of Study

Saint Peter's College offers selected graduate degrees and certification programs. The Master of Business Administration is a 48-credit program and runs on a trimester calendar. Students can choose from five areas of concentration: finance, management information systems, marketing, international business, and management. The Master of Science in accountancy is a 30-credit program and also runs on a trimester calendar. Upon graduation, M.S. in accountancy students will have completed the 150 credit hours of education that became a requirement in the year 2000 in the state of New Jersey to sit for the Certified Public Accountant (CPA) examination. The 36-credit Master of Arts in education runs on a semester calendar and offers concentrations in administration and supervision, reading, and teaching. For students who earned their undergraduate degrees in an area other than education and want to be certified to teach nursery through eighth grade or ninth through twelfth grade, a 26-credit teacher certification program is offered. The Master of Science in Nursing degree program offers two concentrations: a 37-credit concentration in case management and a 39-credit concentration in primary-care adult nurse practitioner studies. For students who already possess a master's degree in nursing and want to earn a certificate as an adult nurse practitioner, a 25-credit post-master's certificate is offered.

Research Facilities

The libraries of Saint Peter's College provide extensive services and research facilities to the College community at both campuses. The Theresa and Edward O'Toole Library in Jersey City is fully automated, and the catalog is accessible via the campus network. The Jersey City and Englewood Cliffs libraries hold more than 300,000 volumes. Both libraries provide access to databases in business, nursing, and the humanities. The O'Toole Library also provides a computer lab for word processing and Internet access. The College's computer facilities offer an opportunity for students to have hands-on access to several state-of-the-art computer systems as well as a variety of microcomputers. The center has an open-door policy, which means that all students are granted access to the computer facilities. The College's computers are part of worldwide computer networks such as the Internet and Usenet. The networks allow students to communicate with other students and researchers. All students, upon registration, have free access to these networks.

Financial Aid

To make financing an education possible, Saint Peter's financial aid advisers help students explore the best means of affording their degree. Options include tuition deferment and installment plans, employer-sponsored tuition reimbursement plans, and student loans. Students should call a financial aid adviser at 201-915-9308 for more information.

Cost of Study

The cost of tuition for graduate study in 2002–03 is $615 per credit.

Living and Housing Costs

Housing on campus for graduate students can be obtained on a space-available basis.

Student Group

Saint Peter's College has a total enrollment of more than 3,300 undergraduate and graduate students. The diverse student body includes many international students representing seventy different countries.

Location

Saint Peter's College offers two campuses in convenient locations. The main campus has long been a landmark on Kennedy Boulevard in Jersey City, New Jersey. The College's atmosphere, architecture, and activity reflect a dynamic, vital, urban institution that offers important intellectual resources to the community. The New York City skyline, visible from Jersey City, is a constant reminder of the College's proximity to a major cultural and financial center. The branch campus at Englewood Cliffs in Bergen County, New Jersey, was established as a college for adults. The campus is perched on a bluff overlooking northern Manhattan and the Hudson River, located on the Palisades 1 mile north of the George Washington Bridge.

An off-site location at the Jersey City Waterfront affords graduate students the opportunity to take business courses at a convenient location close to their place of employment in downtown Jersey City. It is also conveniently located close to PATH and ferry transportation.

The College

Saint Peter's College, founded in 1872, is a Jesuit, Catholic, coeducational liberal arts college in an urban setting that seeks to develop the whole person in preparation for a lifetime of learning, leadership, and service in a diverse and global society. Committed to academic excellence and individual attention, Saint Peter's College provides education informed by values.

Applying

A complete graduate admissions application to one of Saint Peter's College graduate programs includes a $20 application fee, official undergraduate transcripts, official graduate transcripts, official score reports from the appropriate entrance examination (GRE, GMAT, or MAT), and three complete recommendation forms from professional or academic references. International applicants must submit all of the above plus an official, course-by-course foreign credential evaluation of undergraduate and graduate degrees as well as official TOEFL scores. An initial review of the complete application for admission is conducted by the Office of Graduate Admission. The file is then forwarded to a graduate program director for an admission decision. All correspondence should be conducted with the Office of Graduate Admission.

Correspondence and Information

Office of Graduate Admissions
Saint Peter's College
2641 Kennedy Boulevard
Jersey City, New Jersey 07306
Telephone: 201-915-9216
888-SPC-9933 (toll-free)
Fax: 201-432-6241
E-mail: gradadmit@spc.edu
World Wide Web: http://www.spc.edu

GRADUATE PROGRAMS

Master of Arts in Education (M.A.)

The Master of Arts in education program offers three areas of concentration: administration and supervision, reading, and teaching. Each concentration prepares teachers for certification by the state of New Jersey. The three concentrations have a set of foundation courses (9 credits), which are enhanced by specialized required courses and electives. The M.A. in education program is 36 credits and runs on a semester calendar.

For persons who earned their undergraduate degrees in an area other than education and want to be certified to teach nursery through eighth grade or ninth through twelfth grade, a 26-credit teacher certification program is offered. The program consists of six courses (18 credits) in addition to 8 credits in student teaching. The teacher certification program can be completed strictly in the evenings or strictly on the weekends. Students can also mix and match their class schedule by taking evening and weekend courses.

Master of Business Administration (M.B.A.)

The M.B.A. program at Saint Peter's has been designed to meet the changing requirements that are occurring in the business workplace. The M.B.A. program offers five concentrations: finance, management information systems, marketing, international business, and management. The M.B.A. is 48 credits, with a common core of 24 credits. The program runs on a trimester calendar, with courses offered in the evenings and on weekends. The M.B.A. program can be completed strictly in the evenings or strictly on the weekends. Students can also mix and match their class schedule by taking evening and weekend courses.

Master of Science in Accountancy (M.S.)

The 30-credit Master of Science in accountancy runs on a trimester calendar. This program keeps pace with changes in accounting practices and anticipates coming changes in the business environment. Furthermore, graduates of this program will have completed the 150 credit hours of education that will become a requirement in the year 2000 by the state of New Jersey to sit for the Certified Public Accountant (CPA) examination. The M.S. in accountancy can be completed strictly in the evenings or strictly on the weekends. Students can also mix and match their class schedule by taking evening and weekend courses.

Master of Science in Nursing (M.S.N.)

The Master of Science in Nursing program offers two areas of specialization: primary-care adult nurse practitioner studies and case management with a functional concentration in nursing administration. Both options consist of core courses that provide a foundation for graduate study and theoretical and clinical practica courses that prepare graduates for specialization in case management, nursing administration, or in primary care as adult nurse practitioners. The 37-credit M.S.N. in case management curriculum is offered on a trimester basis. The 39-credit M.S.N. adult nurse practitioner program is offered on a combined trimester/semester schedule.

For nurses who already possess a master's degree in nursing and want to earn a certificate as an adult nurse practitioner, a 25-credit, post-master's program is offered. Graduate study in nursing is offered exclusively at the Englewood Cliffs campus.

The College's campus is one of the first in New Jersey to offer students with remote-access-equipped laptops the ability to log onto the College system or the Internet anytime, anywhere on campus.

The Englewood Cliffs campus is specifically designed for adult learners and is conveniently located just 5 minutes from the George Washington Bridge.

ST. THOMAS UNIVERSITY

Graduate Programs

Programs of Study

St. Thomas University offers master's degree programs in business, counseling, management, and pastoral ministries. The University is fully accredited by the Southern Association of Colleges and Schools/Commission on Colleges. On-site and certificate programs are also offered in a number of specializations listed below.

In the Department of Arts and Sciences, programs in counseling include Master of Science degrees in guidance and counseling, mental health counseling, and marriage and family therapy. Prior teaching experience and certification at the elementary or secondary level are recommended for the guidance and counseling program. The University also offers a Ph.D. degree in practical theology and a Master of Arts in Pastoral Ministries, with specializations in campus young adult ministry, family ministry, pastoral counseling, peace education, religious education, and youth and deaf ministries. An interdisciplinary certificate program in loss and healing is also offered.

In the Department of Business Administration, the following master's degree programs are offered: Master of Accounting (M.Acc.), Master of International Business (M.I.B.), and Master of Business Administration (M.B.A.), with specializations in accounting, health management, international business, management, and sports administration.

In the Department of Management, the following master's degree programs are offered: Master of Science in Management (M.S.M.), with specializations in church business administration, general management, health management, human resource management, international business, justice administration, and public management, and Master of Science in sports administration.

In the Department of Education, the following master's degree programs are offered: Master of Science in Special Education, with a specialization in research, gifted education, and English for speakers of another language, and a Master of Science in educational administration. The department also offers an Educational Specialist degree and certificate in educational administration.

Individual programs vary from 30 to 45 graduate credit hours. Programs are structured to contain core courses, courses in the area of specialization, and electives. All students must maintain at least a B average in all course work, and, with the exception of those enrolled in the M.Acc. degree program, all students must pass a written comprehensive examination in order to graduate.

Research Facilities

The main library and law library contain more than 330,000 volumes and volume equivalences. In addition, the main library is a federal depository library. The libraries subscribe to almost 1,000 periodicals and microfilms. The library is a member of Southeast Florida Library Information Network (SEFLIN), which provides for the sharing of resources among south Florida libraries. Online computer searching systems and a media center are also available for student use. Moreover, two microcomputer centers are available to supplement the University data processing center. Media facilities include screening rooms, a language laboratory, an instructional television recording studio, a film and videotape collection room, and a radio station.

Financial Aid

Financial assistance is available to students in the form of graduate assistantships, community-based scholarships for full-time teachers and employees of the Archdiocese of Miami, and federal aid programs. Time-payment plans are also available. Outstanding students who are awarded graduate assistantships receive a tuition waiver for 9 credits per semester and a cash stipend. Qualified students in the pastoral ministries program receive 40 percent tuition scholarships. Tuition reimbursement for approved job-related graduate courses or programs may also be available.

Cost of Study

Tuition for students attending graduate programs during the 2002–03 academic year is $515 per credit.

Living and Housing Costs

On-campus room and board are available to graduate students through the Office of Student Life. Costs start at $6600 per year. Housing applications should be submitted by July 1. Family housing is not available on campus, but rental apartments abound in the surrounding area. Reasonably priced meals are available on campus.

Student Group

The total enrollment for the 2001–02 academic year was approximately 2,200 students. The graduate student population was approximately 600. St. Thomas University provides a learning environment that is intellectually challenging. Classes are small to foster maximum interaction between students and faculty members. Many students are working professionals who, along with the faculty members, help place theoretical approaches in the context of real-life practical experience. Evening courses are offered at convenient locations.

Location

Located between Fort Lauderdale and downtown Miami, the University is near numerous cultural and recreational facilities. The area's subtropical climate enables students to enjoy the nearby Atlantic Ocean beaches and many other natural attractions throughout the year. And numerous cities of Florida's Gold Coast are a short drive from campus. The city of Miami is a major international commercial and banking center.

The University

The University was originally founded in 1961 as Biscayne College by the order of Augustinian Friars. By 1984 the college had grown to such an extent that its status was changed to that of a university, and it was renamed St. Thomas University. The Law School was also founded in 1984 and received full accreditation from the American Bar Association in 1994. In addition, the Institute for Pastoral Ministries was established in 1981, the Institute for Human Rights in 1992, and the Center for Loss and Healing in 2000. St. Thomas is under the sponsorship of the Archdiocese of Miami.

Applying

Prospective students must have a bachelor's degree from an accredited college or university. The Graduate Admissions Committee considers applicants for admission on the basis of their academic record, personal and professional accomplishments, motivation, talents, recommendations, test results when required, and a personal statement. Applicants may be required to submit GRE, GMAT, or other test scores. International students must demonstrate adequate proficiency in English by submitting scores from the TOEFL. Detailed information about specific program requirements may be obtained by contacting the Office Of Graduate Admissions. Students may start any term throughout the year. However, early application is recommended.

Correspondence and Information

Office of Graduate Admissions
St. Thomas University
16400 Northwest 32nd Avenue
Miami, Florida 33054
Telephone: 305-628-6546
800-367-9006 (toll-free in Florida)
800-367-9010 (toll-free outside Florida)
Fax: 305-628-6591
E-mail: signup@stu.edu
World Wide Web: http://www.stu.edu

DEAN AND DEGREE PROGRAM COORDINATORS

SCHOOL OF GRADUATE STUDIES

Joseph Iannone, Dean; Ph.D., Notre Dame.

DEPARTMENT OF ARTS AND SCIENCES

Master of Science in Guidance and Counseling
Judy Bachay, Professor; Ph.D., Barry.

Master of Science in Marriage and Family Therapy
Barbara C. Buzzi, Associate Professor; Ph.D., Barry.

Master of Science in Mental Health Counseling
Lawrence C. Rubin, Associate Professor; Ph.D., Nova Southeastern.

Master of Arts in Pastoral Ministries
Mercedes Iannone, Professor and Director, Institute for Pastoral Ministries; D.Min., St. Mary's (Baltimore).

DEPARTMENT OF BUSINESS ADMINISTRATION

Master of Accounting
Craig Reese, Professor; Ph.D., Texas.

Master of Business Administration
Maria Delores Espino, Associate Professor; Ph.D., Florida State.

DEPARTMENT OF EDUCATION

Master of Science in Special Education and Educational Administration
Walter J. Cegelka, Associate Professor and Chair; Ed.D., Syracuse.

DEPARTMENT OF MANAGEMENT

Master of Science in Management
Nancy Borkowski, Professor; D.B.A., Nova Southeastern.

Master of Science in Sports Administration
Jan Bell, Professor and Chair; Ed.D., Temple.

SALVE REGINA UNIVERSITY

Graduate Programs

Programs of Study

Salve Regina University offers six master's degree programs and a Ph.D. degree program. Courses typically are scheduled one evening per week in order to accommodate students who work full-time. Most master's degree programs require attending courses on the main campus in Newport. Graduate courses are also offered at two satellite campuses in Lincoln and East Providence. For those interested in distance learning, four master's degree programs can be pursued through Graduate Extension Study (GES).

Approximately 450 students are enrolled in the six master's degree programs, which are comprised of administration of justice, business administration, health services administration, holistic counseling, humanities, international relations, and management. Approximately 60 students are enrolled in the Ph.D. Program in the Humanities, which is devoted to the interdisciplinary study of the impact of technology on the world and the future. Some graduate students work full-time and take courses part-time, taking one or two courses each semester and during the summer. Some, who are too far away to take a course at one of Salve Regina's campuses, enroll in the GES program, which allows them to take advantage of the distance learning option and earn a degree in business administration, human development, international relations, or management. Many on-campus students occasionally register for such courses when personal circumstances make it difficult to attend classes on campus.

Research Facilities

The McKillop Library, constructed in 1991, provides seating for more than 450 and has about 250,000 holdings. The library is connected to a fiber-optic network and to the University's telecommunications system. Twenty-four intelligent terminals provide access to the University host, the library host, and external databases. The bibliographic research room is equipped with a local area network, fifteen intelligent workstations, an instructor's workstation, and four printers. Online public access catalog and circulation systems are available to the University community, and many CD-ROM databases are available to library and off-campus users. The University has four academic computer labs in the library that serve students and the faculty. The workstations in each lab are linked to a local area network and are open seven days a week.

Financial Aid

The Financial Aid Office assists graduate students with obtaining many different kinds of low-interest loans. A few part-time internship opportunities are also available.

Cost of Study

For the academic year 2001–02, the cost for a typical 3-credit master's-level course was $900 ($300 per credit). The cost of a doctoral-level course was $1350 ($450 per credit).

Living and Housing Costs

On-campus housing is not available for graduate students. The Residence Office assists graduate students seeking off-campus housing, which is plentiful given that Newport is a worldwide tourist attraction.

Student Group

Approximately 450 full- and part-time students are enrolled in on-campus graduate courses, and 280 students are enrolled in distance learning classes, some of whom are also enrolled in on-campus courses.

Student Outcomes

Because many students are working professionals, the benefits derived from their participation in one of Salve Regina's graduate programs include professional advancement and greater opportunities for lateral movement within their professions. Younger students who enroll in the University with a recent bachelor's degree also benefit in two principal ways. They obtain the skills and education required for entrance into particular fields and positions as well as the additional education and experience they need to prepare themselves for doctoral education. Students also may enroll because they are interested in continuing their education in order to fuel their own personal development. This is particularly true of the students in the human development, humanities, and holistic counseling programs.

Location

Newport is a small resort city filled with architectural masterpieces, breathtaking natural beauty, and artistic delights. Tens of thousands of people visit Newport and its famous Bellevue Avenue mansions, seacoast, and shops each year. Salve Regina is located next to the Breakers, the most famous of all Newport mansions, and is adjacent to the Cliff Walk, a magnificent, winding pathway that rises high above the Atlantic Ocean. It is comprised of historically important mansions and attractive landscaping, and it is considered by many to be among the most beautiful campuses in the U.S. Newport is about 2 hours from Boston, about 3 hours from New York, and about 40 minutes from T. F. Green International Airport in Providence.

The University

Salve Regina College was chartered by the State of Rhode Island in 1934. A 1991 amendment to its charter, reflecting in part the significant development of its graduate programs, changed the name of the institution to Salve Regina University. The University was founded by the Sisters of Mercy and operates as an independent Catholic university dedicated to the liberal education of its students. The University is accredited by the New England Association of Schools and Colleges and offers baccalaureate and postbaccalaureate degrees in several fields.

Applying

Applicants for master's degree programs must have a bachelor's degree from an accredited college or university. They should submit a completed application along with the appropriate fee, a personal statement, two letters of recommendation, transcripts from all degree-granting institutions the applicant has attended, a transcript evaluation (if transcript is international), and official scores on either the MAT, GRE, GMAT, or LSAT. Students may also enroll in one or two courses without being formally admitted into the program. Formal admission into a program, however, requires submission of the above materials. There are additional requirements for applicants to the Ph.D. Program in the Humanities. Interested students should consult the graduate catalog or contact the Dean of Graduate Studies for these additional requirements. Admission into all graduate programs is based on an overall assessment of each candidate, and no specific cut-offs or thresholds are used.

Correspondence and Information

Graduate Admissions
Salve Regina University
100 Ochre Point Avenue
Newport, Rhode Island 02840

Telephone: 401-341-2338
800-637-0002 (toll-free)
Fax: 401-341-2973
E-mail: graduate_studies@salve.edu
World Wide Web: http://www.salve.edu

AREAS OF RESEARCH

Administration of Justice: Police theory, police ethics, computers and law, juvenile justice, comparative justice systems, the criminal justice process and management. Program Director: Dr. Thomas Svogun.

Business: Strategic planning and entrepreneurship, human resource management and business ethics, corporate stock repurchases, dividend policy, the impact of impending monetary union in Europe. Program Director: Dr. Myra Edelstein.

Health Services Administration: Quality of life for the elderly, biomedical ethics. Program Director: Dr. Joan Chapdelaine.

Holistic Counseling: Psychoneuroimmunology as a means to heal oneself, Gestalt theory and family therapy, human development, expressive arts in healing. Program Director: Dr. Peter Mullen.

Humanities: Meaning and effects of modern technology, mutual relations between art and technology, ethics and technology, human resources and technology, literature and technology, philosophy and technology, religion and technology, multidisciplinary insights on the humanities and technology. Program Director: Br. Theresa Madonna.

International Relations: World justice, harmony of international interests, international criminal justice, international political economy and development. Program Director: Dr. Daniel Trocki.

Many of the University's academic and administrative buildings look out on the Atlantic Ocean, guarded by Newport's world-famous Cliff Walk.

The McKillop Library, built in 1991, has approximately 250,000 holdings and provides seating for more than 450 people.

A student meets with a faculty member at the front entrance of McAuley Hall, home of the Salve Regina University Graduate Studies Office.

SARAH LAWRENCE COLLEGE

Graduate Programs

Programs of Study

Sarah Lawrence College has been a pioneer in several graduate fields, founding three outstanding programs in human genetics (genetic counseling), health advocacy, and women's history that have served as models nationwide. The College also offers master's degrees in areas where it has particular strength: creative writing, dance, theater, the art of teaching, and child development. The College believes in the importance of close and extensive collaboration with the faculty. Many of the graduate programs combine small seminar classes with individual student-faculty conferences. In all programs, opportunity for fieldwork is extensive and varied. Most graduate programs are for two years of full-time study and require 36 course credits. Part-time study may be arranged.

The Art of Teaching Program leads to a Master of Science degree leading to certification in early childhood (birth–grade2), childhood (grades 1–6), or early childhood education (birth–grade 6). Special features of the program include theoretical study of child development; empirical courses in curriculum planning with emphasis on mathematics, science, and language arts; and integration of theory and fieldwork from the first semester. Student teaching under master teachers is offered at the Sarah Lawrence Early Childhood Center and several Westchester County, New York City, and Connecticut school systems.

The Child Development Program leads to an M.A. and is for students who seek in-depth understanding of childhood functioning in the context of contemporary society. Study of theoretical perspectives and research in developmental psychology is integrated with fieldwork experience. The program is unique in its ongoing combination of theory and fieldwork. Graduates of the program are prepared for direct work with young children in a variety of settings, for teaching child development at an intermediate level, or for pursuing more advanced study in psychology and related fields.

The Dance Program leads to an M.F.A. and is based on the premise that dance is a distinctive art form, calling for the integration of body, mind, and spirit. Daily modern and ballet technique classes are required of all graduate students. Basic physical skills, strength, and control are required for the central focus of the program, the creative use of the dance medium. The student is exposed to vital aspects of the art as a performer, creator, and observer, with music as an integral part. The curriculum centers on choreography, dance improvisation, music improvisation, composition, and the teaching of dance. The dance program offers dancers the opportunity to grow under the guidance of an excellent faculty made up of dancers and dance scholars with professional experience in the New York area and abroad.

The Writing Program leads to an M.F.A. This program offers an uncommon opportunity for students to develop as poets or creative nonfiction or fiction writers under the close supervision of an internationally renowned faculty. At the center of the course of study are four successive seminars that students take during their two years in the program. In addition to the intensive student-faculty discussions in these seminars, students participate in individual conferences with faculty members every two weeks. This unique aspect of the Sarah Lawrence program provides further intensive scrutiny of students' writing and helps them create the substantial body of work needed to fulfill the program's requirements.

The Theatre Program leads to the M.F.A. and is based on the principle that learning comes through practical application, personal experience, and intensive workshops. Working with a faculty of New York City theater professionals, students explore playwriting, acting, directing, design, and technical work in small seminars, private tutorials, and collaborative projects.

Descriptions of the Health Advocacy Program, which leads to careers that promote patients' rights in an increasingly complex health-care system and is the only program of its kind in the country, and the Human Genetics (Genetic Counseling) Program, which pioneered the field of genetics services and continues to lead the way in the field of genetic counseling, can be found in Book 6 of Peterson's Annual Guides to Graduate Study.

The graduate program in women's history, the first in the nation to offer graduate study in the field, emphasizes the combination of scholarship and activism. A detailed description can be found in Book 2 of Peterson's Annual Guides to Graduate Study.

Research Facilities

The College's facilities include classrooms, laboratories, a computer center, and a state-of-the-art sports center; a modern library with 202,265 books and 880 periodicals, which is linked by computer to more than 6,000 other libraries; the Performing Arts Center, which consists of two theaters, a dance studio, and a concert hall; a music building, including a music library; a new Science Center; Early Childhood Center; Center for Graduate Studies; and Center for Continuing Education.

Financial Aid

All graduate grants and loans are awarded based on financial need as determined by information provided on the PROFILE and the FAFSA. Applicants with financial need are considered for Sarah Lawrence College gift aid, Federal Perkins Loans, and Federal Stafford Student Loans. Sarah Lawrence College is unable to offer federal financial aid to students who are not citizens or permanent residents of the United States. However, international students may apply for Sarah Lawrence gift aid by filling out the PROFILE. International students are also advised to investigate other financing opportunities offered by their governments or through private institutions.

Cost of Study

In 2002–03, tuition ranges from $700 to $796 per course credit, depending on the program.

Living and Housing Costs

Off-campus single rooms in local homes are available for $300 to $500 per month; sharing an apartment ranges from $500 to $700 per month. The minimum cost for an off-campus apartment in the area is $500 a month. Housing information is available from the Student Affairs Office and the Graduate Studies Office.

Student Group

Sarah Lawrence attracts students who seek a creative education and are eager to take responsibility for it. The College draws its 300 students from forty-nine states and thirty-one countries.

Location

The College is situated in the Bronxville/Yonkers community of Bronxville in southern Westchester County, just 15 miles north of midtown Manhattan in New York City. Highways and a commuter railroad make it possible to reach the city in about 30 minutes, enabling students to take advantage of its social, cultural, and intellectual riches and its internship possibilities.

The College

Founded in 1926, Sarah Lawrence is a small liberal arts college for men and women. It is a lively community of students, scholars, and artists, nationally renowned for its unique academic structure, which combines small classes with individual student-faculty conferences.

Applying

Applicants for graduate studies must have received a B.A. or an equivalent degree from an accredited college or university. They should request information on the program that interests them at the address or telephone number below. Applicants are asked to complete an application form and to furnish transcripts of all undergraduate work and two letters of recommendation, preferably from former teachers. Personal interviews may be arranged with the program directors and with the Director of Graduate Studies. The creative writing and the performing arts programs require demonstration of the candidate's ability. GRE scores are not required. Application deadlines vary according to program. The deadline for first consideration is February 1.

Correspondence and Information

Susan Guma
Director of Graduate Studies
Sarah Lawrence College
Bronxville, New York 10708-5999

Telephone: 914-395-2371
Fax: 914-395-2664
E-mail: grad@sarahlawrence.edu
World Wide Web: http://www.sarahlawrence.edu

THE FACULTY AND GRADUATE PROGRAM DIRECTORS

Art of Teaching

Sara Wilford, Director; M.S.Ed., M.Ed., Bank Street College of Education.
Mary Hebron, Associate Director; M.A., NYU.
Maggie Martinez DeLuca, M.S.Ed., Bank Street College of Education.
Jan Drucker, Ph.D., NYU.
Margery B. Franklin, Director; Ph.D., Clark.
Barbara Schecter, Ph.D., Columbia Teachers College.
Marsha Winoker, Ph.D., Yeshiva.

Child Development

Barbara Schecter, Director; Ph.D., Columbia Teachers College.
Carl Barenboim, Ph.D., Rochester.
Charlotte Doyle, Ph.D., Michigan.
Jan Drucker, Ph.D., NYU.
Marvin Frankel, Ph.D., Chicago.
Margery B. Franklin, Ph.D., Clark.
Elizabeth Johnston, D.Phil., Oxford.
Linwood Lewis, Ph.D., CUNY.
Sara Wilford, M.S.Ed., M.Ed., Bank Street College of Education.

Dance

Sara Rudner, Director; M.F.A., Bennington.
Penelope Dannenberg, M.F.A., UCLA.
Emmy Devine, B.A., Connecticut College.
Dan Hurlin, B.A., Sarah Lawrence.
John Jasqup.
Karen Levey, B.A., Adelphi.
Max Luna III.
Cassandra Phifer.
Joanne Robinson-Hill.
Sterling Swann, B.A., Vassar.
Rose Anne Thom, B.A., McGill.
Lance Westergard, B.F.A., Juilliard.
Jessica Wolf, B.A., NYU.
John Yannelli, M.F.A., Sarah Lawrence.

Health Advocacy

Marsha Hurst, Director; Ph.D., Columbia.
Bruce Berg, Ph.D., American.
Diane Borst, M.B.A., NYU.
Sayantani DasGupta, M.D./M.P.H., Johns Hopkins.
Frank De Sena, M.Phil., CUNY Graduate Center.
Rachel Grob, M.A., Sarah Lawrence.
Catherine M. Handy, Ph.D., NYU.
Alice Herb, LL.M., NYU.
Kristin Jones, Ph.D., CUNY Graduate Center
Margaret Keller, J.D., M.S., Columbia.
Terry Mizrahi, Ph.D., Virginia.
Jane Nusbaum, M.A., Sarah Lawrence.
Michael J. Smith, D.S.W., Columbia.
Laura Weil, M.A., Sarah Lawrence.

Human Genetics

Caroline Lieber, Director; M.S., Sarah Lawrence.
Bruce Haas, Associate Director; M.S., Sarah Lawrence.
Allen Bale, M.D., Massachusetts.
Dawn Cardeiro, M.S., Sarah Lawrence.
Suzanne Carter, M.S., Sarah Lawrence.
Elizabeth Cherniske, M.S., Sarah Lawrence.
Jessica Davis, M.D., Columbia.
Marvin Frankel, Ph.D., Chicago.
Elaine Gallin, Ph.D., CUNY
Elana Gizang-Ginsberg, Ph.D., Columbia.
Eva Bostein Griepp, M.D., NYU.
Susan Gross, M.D., Toronto.
Gayna Havens, M.S., Sarah Lawrence, M.A., New School for Social Research.
Susan Hodge, D.Sc., Washington (St. Louis).
Gordon Hutcheon, M.D., Tulane.
Suresh Jhanwar, M.D., Ph.D., Delhi.
Maureen Keating, M.S.A., Audrey Cohen College. (RNC, CNA)
Laura Long, M.s. Sarah Lawrence.
Robert Marion, M.D., Yeshiva (Einstein).
Diana Punales Morejon, M.S., Sarah Lawrence.
Sally Nolin, Ph.D., SUNY Health Science Center at Brooklyn.
Elsa Reich, M.S., Sarah Lawrence.
Gianine Rosenblum, Ph.D., Rutgers.
Susan Sklower-Brooks, M.D., CUNY, Mount Sinai.
Dorothy Warburton, Ph.D., McGill.

Theater

Shirley Kaplan, Director; A.A., Briarcliff; Academie de la Grande Chaumiere, Paris.
William D. McRee, Assistant Director; M.F.A., Sarah Lawrence.
Ernst Abuba.
Paul Austin, B.S., Emerson.
Edward Allen Baker, B.A., Rhode Island.
Lynn Brook, M.F.A., Art Institute of Chicago.
Kevin Confoy, B.A., Rutgers.
Michael Early, M.F.A., Yale.
June Ekman, B.A., Goddard; Illinois; ACAT certification, Alexander Technique.
Christine Farrell, M.F.A., Columbia.
Nancy Franklin, Member, Actors Studio and Ensemble Studio Theatre
Edward Gianfrancesco.
Dan Hurlin, B.A., Sarah Lawrence.
Rosette LaMont, Ph.D., Yale.
Doug MacHugh, M.F.A., Sarah Lawrence.
Greg MacPherson, B.A., Vermont.
John McCormack, B.A., Hamilton.
Cassandra Medley, Michigan.
Kym Moore, M.F.A., Massachusetts Amherst.
Carol Ann Pelletier, B.A., Brandeis.
Paul Rudd, B.A., Fairfield.
Arthur Sainer, M.A., Columbia.
Fanchon Miller Scheier, M.F.A., Sarah Lawrence.
James Shearwood, M.A., Smith.
Stuart Spencer.
Sterling Swan, B.A., Vassar.

Writing/Fiction

Mary La Chapelle, Director; M.F.A., Vermont.
Linsey Abrams, M.A., CUNY Graduate Center.
Melvin Jules Bukiet, M.F.A., Columbia.
Peter Cameron.
Carolyn Ferrell, M.A., CUNY, City College.
Myra Goldberg, M.A., CUNY Graduate Center.
Joshua Henkin, M.F.A., Michigan.
Kathleen Hill, Ph.D., Wisconsin.
William Melvin Kelley, Harvard.
Valerie Martin.
Mary Morris, Director; M.Phil., Columbia.
Brian Morton, B.A., Sarah Lawrence.
Lucy Rosenthal, M.S., Columbia; M.F.A., Yale.
Joan Silber, M.A., NYU.
Barbara Probst Solomon, B.S., Columbia.

Writing/Poetry

Thomas Lux, Director, Poetry Program; B.A., Emerson; University of Iowa Writers Workshop.
Billy Collins, M.A., California, Riverside.
Suzanne Gardinier, M.F.A., Columbia.
Marie Howe, M.F.A., Columbia.
Kate Knapp Johnson, M.F.A., Sarah Lawrence.
Joan Larkin, M.A., Arizona.
Tracie Morris.
Kevin Pilkington, M.A., Georgetown.
Vijay Seshadri, M.F.A., Columbia.

Writing/Creative Nonfiction

Mary Morris, M.Phil., Columbia.
Barbara Probst Solomon, B.S., Columbia.
Lawrence Weschler, B.A., California, Santa Cruz.

Women's History

Priscilla Murolo, Director; Ph.D., Yale. U.S. labor history.
Tara James, Associate Director.
Persis Charles, Ph.D., Tufts. Modern social and women's history, with particular emphasis on British and French history.
Eileen Ka-may Cheng, Ph.D., Yale. Nineteenth-century America, with a focus on intellectual and political history.
Lyde Cullen Sizer, Ph.D., Brown. Women's literary cultures, American popular culture, the American Civil War.
K. Komozi Woodard, Ph.D., Pennsylvania. African-American history and culture, with emphasis on the black freedom movement, American urban history, and ghetto formation.

Affiliate Faculty in Women's History

Julie Abraham, Lesbian and Gay Studies.
Bella Brodski, Literature.
Isabel De Sena, Spanish/Literature.
Eri Fujieda, Sociology.
Marsha Hurst, Health Advocacy.
Judith Kicinski, Literature.
Arnold Krupat, Literature.
Chikwenye Ogunyemi, Literature.
David Peritz, Political Science.
Mary Porter, Anthropology.
Marilyn Power, Economics.
Charlotte Price, Economics.
Sandra Robinson, Asian Studies.
Judith Rodenbeck, Art History.
Shahnaz Rouse, Sociology.
Barbara Schecter, Psychology.
David Valentine, Anthropology.
Pauline Watts, History.

The College is set on a 35-acre campus reminiscent of a rural English village.

SCHOOL FOR INTERNATIONAL TRAINING

Graduate Programs

Programs of Study

School for International Training (SIT) offers master's programs in Intercultural Service, Leadership and Management (M.A. in conflict transformation, M.A. in international education, M.A. in intercultural relations, M.A. in sustainable development, M.S. in organizational management, and M.A. in international and intercultural service) and in language teaching (M.A.T.).

The academic programs that lead to the Intercultural Service, Leadership and Management degrees develop the intercultural, managerial, and training skills necessary for careers in international and intercultural management. Alumni work in the fields of sustainable development, exchange management, global education, international student advising, cross-cultural training, and refugee relief. The program is based on the college's philosophy of learning through experience. It combines on-campus academic study with a minimum six-month professional-level internship and concludes with a capstone seminar. The organization that provides the internship can be located anywhere in the world and should be appropriate to the student's area of professional interest. Course work focuses on project management, development administration, training and organizational development, intercultural communication, and leadership and managerial skills. There is a special track for nongovernmental organization leaders and managers working in the global South, which begins with a postgraduate diploma program in Bangladesh.

With a focus on applied classroom practice, the academic program that leads to the M.A.T. degree is designed to prepare its graduates for a successful and effective career in language teaching. Concentrations offered are English to speakers of other languages (ESOL), French, and Spanish, and the program can be done as a one-academic-year program or in a two-summer format designed for working teachers. In the one-year program, students may choose either single or double language concentrations. The teaching internship, supervised by program faculty members during the winter quarter, is a period of rapid professional growth as the student is called upon to put theory into practice in the classroom and to make individual choices regarding teaching styles and approaches. The practical focus of the program serves to equip graduates to achieve a high professional standing in their field. Internship sites in the U.S. are located primarily in New England, and overseas sites used in recent years include Mexico, Morocco, and South Africa. Students in the academic-year format are eligible for public school certification after a second teaching internship during the fall following the course work. There is also an optional endorsement in bilingual-multicultural education (BME) available. The Summer M.A.T. Program consists of two 8-week sessions in consecutive summers, with the teaching practicum supervised by program faculty members during the intervening year. This format brings together experienced ESOL, French, and Spanish teachers from all over the world who can earn the M.A.T. degree without having to take time off from their jobs.

Research Facilities

To support the work of the faculty members and students, the college's Donald B. Watt Library includes a specialized collection consisting of some 32,000 volumes and 450 periodical titles and is supported by an interlibrary loan network. The library's reading and study areas are open 24 hours a day. The library also has various electronic and online databases available for research.

Financial Aid

The college participates in all federally sponsored financial aid programs, including the Federal Perkins Loan, Federal Work-Study, and Federal Stafford Student Loan programs. Institutional grants and scholarships are also offered. Financial aid is awarded based on need, with a few specific merit scholarships offered. Restricted scholarships are available for returned Peace Corps volunteers; staff from development management, refugee assistance, population control, and exchange organizations; and members of minority groups.

Cost of Study

Students are charged for their degree program, not annually. The total tuition and fees for graduate programs for the 2002–03 academic year are $26,084 for Intercultural Service, Leadership and Management degree candidates and $26,020 for M.A.T. degree candidates. Summer M.A.T. students pay half their tuition each summer.

Living and Housing Costs

The 2001–02 on-campus room and board costs for the Intercultural Service, Leadership and Management degree candidates ranged from $5986 to $7106. For M.A.T. degree candidates, the range was from $3682 to $5978. All costs depend on the type of accommodations and length of enrollment in the program.

Student Group

The student body of the college is diverse, with an annual enrollment of about 200 students who range in age from 20 to 45 or older. A typical group in residence may include students from twenty-five to thirty countries, many regions of the United States, and half a dozen basic language groups. The composition of the student body gives the campus a multicultural character that complements the academic programs. Many students have had extensive work experience, often in another culture, and are returning to school to acquire skills to help them advance professionally or change careers.

Location

The School for International Training is located in Brattleboro, a town in southeastern Vermont. By car, Brattleboro is about 2 hours from Boston and 4 hours from New York City and Montreal. Skiing, hiking, canoeing, and climbing can be enjoyed nearby. In addition, the area is a center for a thriving arts community that includes the Brattleboro Music Center, the Yellow Barn Music Festival, the Marlboro Summer Music Festival, numerous community theater and dance groups, visual artists, and fine craftsmen.

The School

Established in 1964, School for International Training is an accredited college specializing in developing individual and institutional capacities for responsible leadership in global and local contexts. It began in 1932 as The Experiment in International Living and remains one of the oldest international education service organizations in the world.

SIT came into its own in the 1960s shortly after The Experiment provided the original language and culture training for the U.S. Peace Corps. In fact, through a special arrangement, SIT graduate programs continue to offer students the opportunity to combine Peace Corps service with other degree requirements.

Accredited by the New England Association of Schools and Colleges, SIT is a global leader in language education, intercultural training, human resource development, policy advocacy, conflict mediation, and nongovernmental organization (NGO) partnership and management.

SIT also maintains two centers for on-campus research, training, and project management: the Center for Social Policy and Institutional Development and the Center for Teacher Education, Training and Research.

In addition to offering graduate degrees, SIT administers more than fifty study-abroad programs (for credit) in more than forty countries, available to undergraduate students enrolled in other colleges and universities.

Applying

Application forms for admission and financial aid are available through the Admissions Office. Applications are accepted throughout the year; admission decisions are made on a rolling basis throughout the year, upon completion of the student's file. Applications must be accompanied by a $45 nonrefundable application fee. Scores on the GRE are not required.

Correspondence and Information

Director of Admissions
School for International Training
Kipling Road
P.O. Box 676
Brattleboro, Vermont 05302-0676

Telephone: 802-257-7751
800-336-1616 (toll-free within the U.S.)
Fax: 802-258-3500
E-mail: admissions@sit.edu
World Wide Web: http://www.sit.edu

THE FACULTY

Master of Arts in Teaching

Marti Anderson, Ph.D. candidate.
Francis Bailey, Ed.D.
William Conley, M.A.T.
Andy Curtis, Ph.D.
Alvino Fantini, Ph.D.
Beatriz Fantini, M.A.T.
Donald Freeman, Ph.D., Dean, Department of Language Teacher Education.
Kathleen Graves, M.A.T.
Mike Jerald, M.A.T.
Diane Larsen-Freeman, Ph.D.
Paul Levasseur, Ed.D. candidate.
Bonnie Mennell, M.A.T.
Pat Moran, Ph.D.
Alex Silverman, M.A., Ph.D. candidate.
Elizabeth Tannenbaum, M.A.T.

Master of International and Intercultural Management

Kanthie Athukorala, Ed.D.
Sandra Basgall, Ph.D. candidate.
Karen Blanchard, Ph.D. candidate.
Charles Crowell, Ph.D. candidate.
Charlie Curry-Smithson, Ph.D. candidate.
Abdoul Diallo, Ph.D.
Linda Drake Gobbo, M.Ed., M.B.A.
Paula Green, Ed.D.
Claire Halverson, Ph.D.
Janaki Natarajan, Ph.D.
Richard Rodman, Ph.D.
Marla Solomon, Ed.D.
John Ungerleider, Ed.D.
Jeff Unsicker, Ph.D., Dean, Department of Global Issues and Intercultural Management.
Paul Ventura, M.S.
Ryland White, M.I.A.

On a hilltop in southern Vermont, SIT's 200-acre campus provides ample space for students to reflect on issues confronting the global community.

SCHOOL OF VISUAL ARTS

Graduate Programs

Programs of Study

In 1983, the School of Visual Arts (SVA), the largest independent undergraduate art college in the United States, introduced its first graduate offering, a Master of Fine Arts (M.F.A.) program in painting, drawing, and sculpture. Since that time, SVA has added five more graduate programs: a Master of Professional Studies (M.P.S.) in art therapy, a Master of Fine Arts in computer art, a Master of Fine Arts in design, a Master of Fine Arts in illustration as visual essay, and a Master of Fine Arts in photography and related media. In the fall of 2003, the college is scheduled to open its seventh graduate program: a Master of Arts in Teaching (M.A.T.). Each of these highly individual professional-degree programs shares certain important characteristics that reflect the School of Visual Arts' unique approach to the education of artists. The program in fine arts focuses on training students whose primary interest is the making of art. The program in illustration is predicated upon radical departure from the accepted methods of teaching and of making illustration. The college's program in computer art was the first in the country to base graduate training in computer art primarily upon aesthetic concerns of this field. SVA's program in design perceives the designer not merely as a form giver but as a content creator; design is seen as more than the reorganization of existing elements. The M.F.A. program in photography seeks to develop a new and personal vision in traditional areas of photography as well as investigating the impact of computer, film, and video technologies on the visual culture. The M.P.S. in art therapy curriculum examines a variety of approaches to the diagnosis and therapeutic treatment of challenged individuals while supporting the artistic development and creative endeavors of the artist-as-therapist. The M.A.T. in art education offers rigorous academic study coupled with requisite teaching experience that provide graduates with the essential knowledge and tools to teach art to children. The School of Visual Arts has long prided itself on the reputation and experience of its internationally renowned faculty members. It is the extraordinary caliber of the faculty member with whom the graduate student works that makes the realization of personal goals and the development of personal vision possible.

Research Facilities

SVA's location in New York City, extensive facilities, state-of-the-art equipment, faculty of professionals dedicated to excellence in the arts, and unique program philosophies offer graduate students the best opportunities for advanced study in the arts. SVA provides students the opportunity to exhibit their art in a number of campus galleries and in a professional gallery in SoHo. The Offices of Career Development and Alumni Affairs provide resources for networking and job opportunities. In addition to networked studio environments and private graduate painting and sculpture studios, the campus features buildings dedicated primarily to photography and sculpture. SVA has digital imaging and output centers and a commitment to maintaining technology that meets industry standards. Another invaluable resource to SVA students is the professional faculty members who work to prepare graduates to meet the challenges of the industry. The Visual Arts Library maintains distinctive multimedia collections; a growing collection of books, periodicals, picture files, slides, exhibition catalogs, film scripts, and videos; and other materials.

Financial Aid

The School of Visual Arts offers scholarships and other financial aid based upon need and merit. Approximately 75 percent of students receive some sort of aid. The School of Visual Arts uses federal, state, and institutional guidelines to determine student need. The Office of Financial Aid is able to provide more information on need-based assistance. Scholarships and assistantships are awarded through the admissions process for new students and by department chair and faculty members for continuing students.

Cost of Study

The tuition fee for the academic year 2002–03 for the art therapy, computer art, fine arts, illustration as visual essay, and photography departments is $19,320. Tuition for the design department is $21,790. Department lab fees range from $150 to $1100.

Living and Housing Costs

Housing costs range from $6800 to $9350 for the academic year 2002–03. The estimated cost for personal expenses for the academic year is $13,500.

Student Group

SVA has a full-time enrollment of 2,800 undergraduate and 300 graduate students. Thirty-six percent of the graduate students are international, and 57 percent are women.

Student Outcomes

The thoroughly professional orientation of the graduate programs is reflected in the internationally renowned faculty. Ultimately, it is the extraordinary caliber of the faculty with whom the graduate student works that makes the realization of personal goals and the development of personal vision possible. Students and graduates of SVA have had gallery exhibitions of their art work and had work published in many newspapers, magazines, and variety of print media. Graduates have also held internships with major multimedia, telecommunications, and production facilities in addition to winning numerous art awards nationally and abroad. SVA is a diverse environment in terms of subject matter as well as population.

Location

Because the College is well positioned in the heart of New York City, students have an opportunity to become acquainted with one of America's largest and most vibrant cities, the art and design capital of the world. Unlimited opportunities exist for constant involvement in the arts. Furthermore, the School of Visual Arts was conceived as a New York City institution from the beginning. The energy, the spirit, and the desire to be the best that characterize New York, embodied in SVA's renowned professional faculty, constantly challenge and inspire students. The unparalleled leadership and accomplishment of the city's arts and design communities demand excellence, and the School of Visual Arts prepares students to compete successfully in this environment.

The School

Founded in 1947, the School of Visual Arts has grown steadily and is today the largest undergraduate college of art in the country. SVA is located in midtown Manhattan in five buildings within walking distance of each other. The energetic atmosphere and the students' dedication to work most often impress visitors. Students come to SVA to gain access to the 800 faculty members who are working artists and who demonstrate a personal and professional commitment to excellence in the arts.

Applying

Applicants to the graduate degree program must have a bachelor's degree from a regionally accredited college or university or a diploma from a four-year professional art school. Applicants to the M.P.S. program in art therapy are required to have completed 12 credits in specific areas of psychology and 15 credits in studio art. Applicants to the M.A.T. program in art education are required either to have completed a minimum of 30 credits in studio art or demonstrate an equivalent level of skill in visual art, a minimum of 12 credits in art history, and proficiency in a language other than English. Applicants must complete and submit all application requirements no later than February 1, 2003.

Correspondence and Information

Rick Longo, Executive Director of Admissions
School of Visual Arts
209 East 23rd Street
New York, New York 10010
Telephone: 212-592-2100
800-436-4204 (toll-free)
Fax: 212-592-2288
E-mail: gradadmissions@adm.schoolofvisualarts.edu
World Wide Web: http://www.schoolofvisualarts.edu

THE FACULTY

Since the School of Visual Arts brings working professionals to its faculty, the 800 members comprise practicing artists, filmmakers, designers, and photographers. As a result of using working professionals to teach, the college has been able to attract some of the most prominent artists in New York.

M.A.T. Art Education

Rose Viggiano, Acting Chair

Michael Filan
Judith Kuspit
Gaetano LaRoche
Frank Migliorelli
Joyce Raimondo
Barbara Salander
Natalie J. Shifano
Virginia S. Stolarski
Ada Pujols Torres

M.P.S. Art Therapy

Deborah Farber, Chair

Vivien Abrams
Kimberly Bush
Jean Davis
Jennifer Drower
Emmanuel Hammer
Julia Kristeller
Judith Kuspit
Jennifer Mauro
Ellen McLean
Nefretete Rasheed

M.F.A. Computer Art

Bruce Wands, Chair

Victor Acevedo
Mark Bajuk
Michael Barron
Ed Bowes
Kathy Brew
Todd Brous
Kevin Brownie
Clay Budin
John Cabral
Robert Cavaleri
Kevin Centanni
Andy Deck
Joseph Dellinger
Tennessee Rice Dixon
Carl Edwards
Joseph Ferrari
Eric Furubotn
Bruce Gionet
Thyrza Nichols Goodeve
Edgar David Grana
Bonnie L. Hammer
Christine Heun
Perry Hoberman
G.H. Hovagimyan
Mary Lynn Kirby
Russet Lederman
Gary Leib
Jonathan Lipkin
Jarryd Lowder
Maria Manhattan
Sandra Jo McLean
Nikita Mikros
Joseph Nechvatal
Wells Packard
Christiane Paul
Gary Poster
Lynn Rawden
Steve Rittler
Gae Savannah
Mathew Schlanger
Richard Shupe
Ellen Zweig

M.F.A. Design

Steven Heller, Co-chair
Lita Talarico, Co-chair

Paola Antonelli
Marian Appellof
Eva Doman Bruck
John Carlin
Brian Collins
Stephen Doyle
Janet Froelich
Peter Girardi
Dorothy Globus
Keith Goddard
Steven Guarnaccia
Martin Kace
Maira Kalman
Julie Lasky
Warren Lehrer
Frank Martinez
Kevin O'Callaghan
Lynn Rawden
Howard Reeves
Stefan Sagmeister
Jeff Scher
Paula Scher
Bonnie Siegler
David Slatoff
Véronique Vienne
Eric Zimmerman

M.F.A. Fine Arts

David L. Shirey, Chair

Polly Apfelbaum
Perry Bard
Jake Berthot
Sam Cady
Petah Coyne
Monroe Denton
Sharon Fleischmann
Kenji Fujita
Johan Grimonprez
Lewis Holman
Will Insley
Thomas Lanigan-Schmidt
John Lees
Loren Madsen
Suzanne McClelland
Lucio Pozzi
David Row
Jerry Saltz
Joseph Santore
Gary Stephan
Sarah Sze
Ursula Von Rydingsvard
Jacqueline Winsor

M.F.A. Illustration As Visual Essay

Marshall Arisman, Chair

N. C. Couch
Gregory Crane
Carol Fabricatore
Mikro Ilic
Matthew B. Richmond
David Sandlin
Carl Nicholas Titolo
Mary Jo Vath
Michele Zackheim

M.F.A. Photography and Related Media

Charles Traub, Chair

Judith Barry
Robert Bowen
Ed Bowes
Sarah Charlesworth
Yolanda Cuomo
Gwen Darien
Nancy Davenport
Jeremy Dawson
Marvin Heiferman
Perry Hoberman
Carole Kismaric
Ken Kobland
Richard Leslie
Jonathan Lipkin
Paola Mieli
Mary Patierno
Philip Perkis
Christopher Phillips
Peter Rad
Shelley E. Rice
John Rilson
Collier Schorr
Shelly Silver
Shelly J. Smith
Stephen Sollins
Mark Stafford
Joel Sternfeld
Penelope Umbrico
Chris Verene
Simon Watson
Grahame Weinbren
Randy West
Bonnie Yochelson

SEATTLE UNIVERSITY

Graduate and Professional Programs

Programs of Study

Seattle University, serving more than 2,500 graduate and professional degree students, offers twenty-four degree and seventeen certificate programs at the graduate level. Designed to accommodate working professionals, Seattle University graduate programs offer evening and weekend classes as well as part-time study options.

The Albers School of Business and Economics offers the Master of Business Administration (M.B.A.), Master of International Business (M.I.B.), Master of Professional Accounting (M.P.Ac.), and Master of Science in Finance (M.S.F.) degrees, which are accredited by the AACSB International–The Association to Advance Collegiate Schools of Business. Several post-master's certificates are offered in the Albers School of Business and Economics. The College of Arts and Sciences offers the Master of Arts (M.A.) degree in psychology, the Master of Public Administration (M.P.A.), and the Executive Master in Not-for-Profit Leadership (M.N.P.L.). The School of Education offers graduate programs in educational leadership (Ed.D.), adult education and training (M.A. or M.Ed.), teaching English to speakers of other languages (M.A. or M.Ed.), counseling (M.A.), literacy for special needs (M.Ed.), special education (M.Ed.), school psychology (Ed.S.), curriculum and instruction (M.A. or M.Ed.), educational administration (M.A., M.Ed., or Ed.S.), and student development administration (M.A. or M.Ed.) as well as the Master in Teaching (M.I.T.) degree. Several post-master's certificates are also available. The School of Law, which is fully accredited by the American Bar Association, offers the Juris Doctor (J.D.) degree. A Master of Science in Nursing (M.S.N.) is offered by the School of Nursing in the areas of primary-care nurse practitioner studies and leadership in community nursing specialist studies. A new advanced practice immersion program is available for those without undergraduate degrees in nursing. A post-master's certificate in family primary-care nurse practitioner is also available. The School of Science and Engineering offered the first Master in Software Engineering (M.S.E.) degree in 1982 and continues to provide leadership in software engineering education through its M.S.E. program. The School of Theology and Ministry houses the Institute for Catholic Theological Studies and the Institute for Ecumenical Theological Studies and offers M.A. degrees in pastoral studies and transforming spirituality. In addition, the School offers the Master of Divinity (M.Div.) degree as well as post-master's certificates.

Research Facilities

The Lemieux Library houses a growing collection of 234,000 books, more than 1,300 online databases, 2,700 current periodical and serial subscriptions, 570,000 microforms, and a variety of media materials. The library currently offers fifteen CD-ROM databases and an online catalog that includes a gateway module connecting users to Internet resources. Library resources are strongest in subjects that correspond to graduate studies, including business, economics, education, psychology, software engineering, and religious studies. In addition to its collections, the library is a service center. The reference and information services staff assists students in ways that range from personal instruction in the use of the catalog to advising on both advanced and specialized research materials to the development of bibliographies.

Financial Aid

Seattle University offers scholarships, loans, and employment opportunities to eligible graduate students. A limited number of graduate assistantships are offered each year in student development administration. Students must be enrolled at least half-time (3 credits per quarter) to be eligible for financial assistance.

Cost of Study

Tuition for the 2002–03 academic year is assessed at the following rates: business, $544 per credit; education, $420 per credit; Master in Teaching, $420 per credit; Doctor of Education, $508 per credit; Institute of Public Service, $455 per credit; psychology, $455 per credit; nursing, $420 per credit; theology and ministry, $419 per credit; and software engineering, $544 per credit.

Living and Housing Costs

On-campus residence halls and apartments are available for graduate students. A single room costs $1924 per quarter, and a double room costs $1434 per quarter. Meal plans range from $494 to $1200 per quarter. Students living in Campion Tower or the Murphy Apartments are not required to participate in a meal plan, as cooking facilities are available on each residence floor. The University is centrally located on Seattle's First Hill, surrounded by a myriad of various off-campus housing opportunities. For more information about campus housing, students should contact the Residential Life Office (telephone: 206-296-6305).

Student Group

There are more than 5,900 students attending Seattle University, of whom 27 percent are graduate students and 17 percent are enrolled in the School of Law; 58 percent are women. Approximately 8 percent of students are international. Graduate programs are designed to serve and facilitate a diverse student population, with the majority of courses offered in the evenings and on weekends and a select number offered at satellite locations around the Puget Sound region.

Student Outcomes

Seattle University provides its graduates with advanced and in-depth knowledge in addition to practical experience gained through internships, student teaching, mentoring programs, or practicum experience. With this strong foundation, graduates enter careers as community leaders, politicians, administrators, educators, consultants, entrepreneurs, software developers, therapists, health-care providers, spiritual leaders, nonprofit executives, and lawyers, among many others. Seattle University's alumni include ambassadors, governors, scientists, ministers, judges, and prominent businesspeople.

Location

Seattle University is located in a port city of natural beauty. As the Pacific Northwest's largest city (and the twenty-fourth-largest metropolitan area in the United States), Seattle is a scenic and cultural center in a setting that includes breathtaking mountain views of the Cascades to the east and of the Olympics to the west. Skiing areas are within 60 minutes of campus. In addition to being situated along Puget Sound, Seattle also contains Lakes Union and Washington, both of which provide a wide variety of recreational opportunities. Seattle's residents love the outdoors, and areas for hiking, backpacking, and climbing are minutes from campus. Biking is also popular, and special trails for cycling and running are located throughout the city. Seattle's sights and sounds, rich ethnic diversity, celebrated restaurants, first-run entertainment, major-league athletics, theater, opera, and ballet enhance campus life. The city serves as an important extension of campus.

The University

Founded in 1891, Seattle University is one of twenty-eight Jesuit colleges and universities in the United States. Located in the heart of a metropolitan area, the University attracts more than 5,900 students, nearly 45 percent of whom are enrolled in graduate or professional programs. The average class size is 20, and the faculty-student ratio is 1:14.

Applying

For most graduate programs, applications are accepted each quarter. Program requirements, entry terms, and deadlines vary according to the individual program. International student deadlines are generally four to five months earlier than the general application deadline.

Correspondence and Information

Admissions Office
Graduate Programs
Seattle University
900 Broadway
Seattle, Washington 98122-4340
Telephone: 206-296-2000
800-426-7123 (toll-free outside Washington)
Fax: 206-296-5656
E-mail: grad-admissions@seattleu.edu
World Wide Web: http://www.seattleu.edu

DEANS

Albers School of Business and Economics: Joseph Phillips, Ph.D.
College of Arts and Sciences: Wallace Loh, Ph.D.
School of Education: Sue Schmitt, Ed.D.
School of Law: Rudolph Hasl, J.D., LL.M.
School of Nursing: Mary K. Walker, Ph.D.
School of Science and Engineering: George Simmons, Ph.D.
School of Theology and Ministry: Patrick Howell, SJ, D.Min.

Graduate classes are offered in the evenings and on the weekends to accommodate the schedules of working professionals.

The Pigott Building houses the Albers School of Business and Economics and has many state-of-the-art classrooms.

SETON HALL UNIVERSITY

Graduate Programs

Programs of Study

The College of Arts and Sciences offers the Master of Arts (M.A.) in Asian studies, corporate and public communication, English, Jewish-Christian studies, and museum professions; the Master of Science (M.S.) in biology, chemistry, and microbiology; the Master of Public Administration (M.P.A.); the Master of Healthcare Administration (M.H.A.), which is offered both on campus and online; the Master of Arts in Strategic Communication and Leadership (M.A.S.C.L.), which is offered on line; and the Ph.D. in chemistry. The College's Center for Public Service/Graduate Department of Public and Healthcare Administration offers certificate programs in health-care administration and nonprofit organization management. Nondegree courses are offered in physics, psychology, religious studies, and social work. The College of Education and Human Services offers the M.A. in counselor preparation, educational administration and supervision, elementary education, health professions education, human resources training and development, professional education, psychological studies, secondary education, and student personnel services (K–12) and the M.S. in marriage and family therapy. The Educational Specialist (Ed.S.) degree is offered in bilingual/bicultural education; cultural, humanistic, and professional studies; educational administration and supervision; instructional design and technology; marriage and family therapy; school and community psychology; and secondary education. An M.A. in Catholic leadership for experienced teachers is also offered. Doctoral degrees are offered in clinical psychology (Ph.D./Psy.D.), counseling psychology (Ph.D.), general administration (Ed.D.), higher education administration (Ed.D./Ph.D.), marriage and family therapy (Ph.D.), and school business administration (Ed.D.). The College also offers certification programs in bilingual/bicultural education, English as a second language, and advanced training in marriage and family therapy and elementary and secondary school guidance and counseling. The Stillman School of Business offers the M.B.A. in accounting, environmental affairs, finance, financial institutions, information systems, management, marketing, pharmaceutical operations, and sports management and the M.S. in accounting, international business, professional accounting, and taxation. Joint-degree offerings include the M.S. in international business/M.B.A., M.B.A./J.D., M.B.A./M.P.A., M.B.A./M.S. in nursing, and M.S. in international business/M.A. in diplomacy and international relations. The School of Diplomacy and International Relations offers the M.A. in diplomacy and international relations. The College of Nursing offers the M.S.N. in advanced practice nurse studies: nurse practitioner studies in acute care, adult, critical care, gerontological, pediatrics, school, and women's health care; nurse administrator; and nursing case management. An M.A. is offered in nursing education for nurses with an M.S. degree. Certification programs are offered in nursing management, nursing case management, primary health-care nurse practitioner, and school nurse. Immaculate Conception Seminary School of Theology offers M.A. degrees in pastoral ministry and theology and the Master of Divinity (M.Div.) degree. A concentration in church administration is also offered through the M.P.A. program administered by the University's Center for Public Service. Certificate programs are offered in bible teaching ministry, catechetical ministry, church administration, pastoral ministry, youth ministry, and administration of lay ministry formation. The School of Law offers the J.D., a joint M.B.A./J.D. program in cooperation with the Stillman Business School, and the M.S.J. and LL.M. in health law. The School of Graduate Medical Education offers an M.S.–Health Science degree with specialization in movement science–advanced clinical competence or educational strategies for practitioners, an entry-level M.S.–Physician Assistant in collaboration with the University of Medicine and Dentistry of New Jersey School of Health Related Professions, an M.S. in occupational therapy, and an M.S. in speech pathology. There is a doctoral degree in audiology (Sc.D.). Continuing medical education programs are available for health professionals.

Research Facilities

The Walsh Library, a state-of-the-art 155,000-square-foot building, houses 500,000 titles, 1,875 current periodicals, and an extensive collection of microform and other nonprint items, including videotapes, CD-ROM music, and other electronic media. Fahy Hall has twenty-eight classrooms, two TV studios, a Macintosh and IBM graphics lab, two classroom amphitheaters, and language and statistics labs. McNulty Hall has well-equipped science labs. The College of Nursing Building contains a multipurpose practice demonstration room with twelve hospital beds, an amphitheater, an independent study area, and a computer laboratory. Completed in 1997, Kozlowski Hall, a six-story facility with 126,000-square feet of academic space, features high-tech classrooms with computer and multimedia capabilities.

Financial Aid

Federal aid is available through fellowships, traineeships, and loans. The Office of Financial Aid, through the Educational Opportunity Office, offers EOF grants to those who document eligibility. Direct federal student loans are also available through the Office of Financial Aid to students enrolled at least half-time. Applications for graduate assistantships for full-time study are available from the schools that administer the graduate programs. Those seeking teaching assistantships in English, biology, and chemistry should contact those departments. The Office of Housing has information on resident assistantships, which pay for room, board, and partial tuition.

Cost of Study

In 2002, tuition was $870 per credit in the School of Law, $646 per credit in the School of Business, and $601 per credit in all other programs. A University fee is assessed each semester.

Living and Housing Costs

Seton Hall maintains a limited supply of housing accommodations for graduate students. The South Orange area provides a broad selection of living quarters within a convenient distance of the University.

Location

South Orange is located in a suburban setting about half an hour from Manhattan.

The University

Founded in 1856, Seton Hall is a private coeducational Catholic institution—the nation's oldest diocesan institution of higher education in the U.S. It is made up of nine colleges and schools, including University College. The total enrollment is about 10,000. The main campus comprises 58 acres in the village of South Orange. Seton Hall is accredited by the Middle States Association of Colleges and Schools and holds additional accreditations by the AACSB International–The Association to Advance Collegiate Schools of Business, the National League for Nursing Accrediting Commission, the American Bar Association, and the National Association of Schools of Public Affairs and Administration.

Applying

Applicants for admission to the College of Arts and Sciences must submit all credentials by July 1 for the fall semester, by November 1 for the spring semester, and by May 1 for the summer session. There is a rolling admission policy for corporate and public communication, public administration, health-care administration, M.A./M.P.A. with School of Diplomacy and International Relations, and online programs. The College of Education and Human Services has a rolling admissions policy for the M.A. in human resources training and development and the M.A. and Ed.S. in administration and supervision (K–12) and in New Jersey State Police Law Enforcement. Applicants for the College of Education and Human Services's other programs must submit all credentials by the following deadlines: Ph.D. programs in counseling and clinical psychology, January 15, fall semester; Ed.D. program in administration and supervision and the Ph.D. and Ed.D. programs in higher education administration, February 1 for the fall semester and October 1 for the spring semester; Ph.D. in marriage and family therapy, February 15, fall semester; and the Ed.D. in the Executive Ed.D. in Educational Administration (K–12) Program, December 1, spring semester. Applicants for the School of Theology must submit all credentials by August 1 for the fall semester and December 15 for the spring semester. The School of Theology has a rolling admissions policy for the summer session. Applicants for admission to the School of Law must submit all credentials by April 1 for fall entry. Applicants for the College of Nursing, the School of Business, the School of Graduate Medical Education, and the School of Diplomacy and International Relations should contact the respective advisement offices for application deadlines. Application requirements vary by program, but in general include a completed application form, three letters of reference, official transcripts from all undergraduate institutions attended, a statement of professional goals and/or resume, and official copies of appropriate test scores.

Correspondence and Information

Further information can be obtained by contacting the University via the Internet at http://www.shu.edu or at http://www.setonworldwide.net for online degree programs.

FACULTY HEADS

College of Arts and Sciences (telephone: 973-761-9022; World Wide Web: http://artsci.shu.edu)
Dean: James VanOosting, Ph.D., Northwestern.
Associate Dean: Joan Guetti, Ph.D., Rutgers.
Asian Studies: Gilbert Mattos, Chair; Ph.D., Washington (Seattle).
Biology: Sulie Chang, Chair; Ph.D., Ohio State.
Chemistry and Biochemistry: Richard D. Sheardy, Chair; Ph.D., Florida.
Communication: Donald N. Lombardi, Director; Ph.D., Fordham.
English: Martha Carpentier, Chair; Ph.D., Fordham.
Jewish-Christian Studies: Rabbi Asher Finkel, Chair; Ph.D., Tübingen (Germany).
Museum Professions: Barbara Cate, Director; M.A., Columbia.
Public and Healthcare Administration: Naomi Wish, Director; Ph.D., Rutgers.
Established as Seton Hall College in 1856, the College of Arts and Sciences is the oldest school of the University. The College offers graduate courses leading to the Master of Arts degree, with specializations in Asian studies (Chinese, Japanese, Asian area studies, and Asian bilingual/bicultural education), corporate and public communication, English, Jewish-Christian studies, and museum professions. The Master of Science degree is offered with specializations in biology, chemistry, and microbiology. The Center for Public Service/Graduate Department of Public and Healthcare Administration offers the Master of Public Administration and Master of Healthcare Administration degrees. The Doctor of Philosophy degree is offered in chemistry. The Master of Strategic Communication and Leadership and Master of Healthcare Administration are offered online through the Seton WorldWide (http://www.setonworldwide.net) Internet-based graduate degree program.

Stillman School of Business (telephone: 973-761-9220)
Dean: Karen Boroff, Ph.D., Columbia.
Associate Deans: Karen A. Passaro, M.B.A., J.D., Seton Hall; Joyce Strawser, Ph.D., Louisiana State.
Accounting and Taxation: James Greenspan, Chair; Ph.D., Texas A&M.
Center for Leadership Studies: Lisa McCauley Parles, J.D., Rutgers.
Center for Sports Management: Ann Mayo, Director; Ph.D., Ohio State.
Center for Tax Research: Brian Greenstein, Director; Ph.D., Houston.
Computing and Decision Sciences: David Rosenthal, Chair; Ph.D., Pennsylvania.
Economics: John Dall, Chair; Ph.D., Pennsylvania.
Finance and Legal Studies: Anthony Loviscek, Ph.D., West Virginia.
Management: Joan H. Coll, Ph.D., Fordham.
Marketing: Joseph Wisenblit, Chair; Ph.D., CUNY.
The Stillman School of Business is a professional school that educates students for responsible roles in the business community. Established in 1950, the School offers courses of graduate study leading to the Master of Business Administration and Master of Science in Taxation degrees. The graduate program has professional accreditation from the AACSB International–The Association to Advance Collegiate Schools of Business. Research and continuing education are essential components of the School of Business.

College of Education and Human Services (telephone: 973-761-9668)
Dean: Joseph DePierro, Ed.D., Rutgers.
Associate Deans: Rev. Kevin Hanbury, Ed.D., Seton Hall; Manina Dunn, Ed.D., Seton Hall.
Educational Administration and Supervision: Charles Mitchel, Chair; Ed.D., Fairleigh Dickinson.
Educational Studies: Roberta Devlin-Scherer, Chair; Ed.D., Temple.
Professional Psychology and Family Therapy: John Smith, Ed.D., Lehigh.
The College of Education and Human Services offers programs of graduate study leading to the Master of Arts in education, Doctor of Education, and Doctor of Philosophy degrees. These programs are designed for candidates who wish to prepare for careers in teaching, general professional development, educational leadership, and careers relating to the practice of counseling and psychology.

College of Nursing (telephone: 973-761-9306)
Dean: Phyllis Hansell, Ed.D., Columbia.
Associate Dean: Barbara Wright, Ph.D., NYU.
Recognizing the complexity of modern health-care delivery and the educational preparation needed to meet this challenge, Seton Hall University initiated a graduate nursing program in 1975. Fully accredited by the National League for Nursing Accrediting Commission, the Master of Science degree program now serves some 249 full- and part-time students.

School of Law (telephone: 973-642-8737)
Dean: Patrick Hobbs, LL.M., NYU; J.D., North Carolina at Chapel Hill.
Dean of Admissions and Financial Resource Management: William D. Perez.
The School of Law opened as a unit of Seton Hall University in 1951. It is the only law school in the state operated by a private university and, in addition to its three-year program, has a part-time evening division for employed students who cannot matriculate during the day. Total enrollment is more than 1,200, making it the largest law school in New Jersey and one of the largest in the nation. In addition to basic courses required in preparation for admission to the bar and professional practice in various states, the School offers advanced courses in contemporary legal trends in the health-care and technology industries and those engaged in private legal practice.

Immaculate Conception Seminary School of Theology (telephone: 973-761-9575; fax: 973-761-9577; e-mail: theology@shu.edu)
Rector/Dean: Rev. Monsignor Robert F. Coleman, J.C.D., Pontifical Gregorian (Rome).
Vice-Rector/Business Manager: Rev. Thomas P. Nydegger, M.Div., Immaculate Conception Seminary School of Theology.
Assistant Dean and Director of Lay Ministry: Dianne M. Traflet, S.T.D., Pontifical University of St. Thomas Aquinas (Rome); J.D., Seton Hall.
Associate Dean: Rev. Joseph Chapel, S.T.D., Academia Alphonsiana.
Immaculate Conception Seminary was founded in 1861 at South Orange, New Jersey, by James Roosevelt Bayley, the first bishop of Newark. Through its academic faculty, which constitutes the School of Theology, it offers graduate programs leading to a Master of Divinity, Master of Arts in Theology, and Master of Arts in Pastoral Ministry degrees.

School of Graduate Medical Education (telephone: 973-275-2800)
Dean: John Paterson, D.D.S., Pennsylvania.
Associate Deans: John Sensakovic, M.D., Ph.D., University of Medicine and Dentistry of New Jersey. Brian Shulman, Ph.D., Bowling Green State.
The School of Graduate Medical Education offers graduate programs directed toward the Master of Science in health sciences with specialization in movement science–advanced clinical competence, or educational strategies for practitioners, or the Master of Science–athletic training, occupational therapy, physician assistant, physical therapy, or speech-language pathology. Master's and doctoral degrees in audiology are also offered. The School, in collaboration with five participating medical institutions, offers residency programs for physicians and dentists in specialty areas such as anesthesia, family practice, internal medicine, neuroscience, obstetrics/gynecology, orthopedics, pediatrics, dentistry, oral and maxillofacial surgery, and podiatry. Continuing medical education programs are also offered by the School through conferences, seminars, courses, workshops, and mini-residency experiences for health-care providers.

School of Diplomacy and International Relations (telephone: 973-275-2515; fax: 973-275-2519; e-mail: diplomat@shu.edu; World Wide Web: http://diplomacy.shu.edu)
Dean: Clay Constantinou, LL.M., NYU.
Associate Deans: Marian Glenn, Ph.D., Tufts (academic affairs). Marilyn DiGiacobbe, B.A., Rutgers (external affairs).
The School of Diplomacy and International Relations was founded in 1997 in an alliance with the United Nations Association of the United States of America (UNA-USA). The School offers a 45-credit graduate program that leads to a Master of Arts (M.A.) in diplomacy and international relations. This program provides students with an understanding of international relations and the skills necessary to apply that knowledge. It is designed to train students to be effective managers and leaders in the United Nations system, other intergovernmental organizations, nongovernmental organizations (NGOs), international businesses, and governmental agencies involved in international affairs. The M.A. in diplomacy program provides a competency-based course of study that combines an interdisciplinary international studies curriculum taught from a global perspective with an international management and leadership curriculum. Students in the School undertake an extended internship program to develop important skills and regional specializations.

SETON HILL UNIVERSITY

Graduate Programs

Programs of Study

Certification is simultaneously available in some options of the Master of Arts in elementary education and the Master of Arts in special education for those students with no previous background in teaching. The curricula for both education degrees meet the standards established by the Pennsylvania Department of Education for certification.

The Master of Arts in art therapy, approved by the American Art Therapy Association, is designed to teach students the theory and skills necessary for the effective practice of visual and verbal therapy in a variety of therapeutic settings. A certificate program is also available to students who have already completed master's degrees in related fields.

The Master of Business Administration is designed to create a learning community committed to the study of management theory and contemporary business practice.

The Master of Arts in writing popular fiction is one of the only programs in the country that teaches writers to produce fiction that sells and that reaches a wide audience—mysteries, romance, children's literature, and science fiction.

The Master of Arts in counseling psychology is designed to expose students to the theory, practice, and research in psychology through a systems lens. Two specializations are available: couples and family therapy and art therapy.

The Master of Education in technologies enhanced learning offers advanced study for professionals in education, instruction, training, and development in a variety of settings. Professionals learn how to integrate technology into their teaching and training, whether in the classroom or in business. Specializations include instructional design and adult and special learning populations.

Research Facilities

Reeves Memorial Library serves as the University's information center. In the library, access to information is made easy through an automated catalog, CD-ROM databases, and online resources, such as EBSCOhost and LEXIS-NEXIS. In addition, students have access to thirteen Pentium labs, a Power Mac lab, a multimedia lab, and a Silicon Graphics lab. All students receive an Internet account for e-mail, navigating the Web, and conducting research.

Financial Aid

An institutional scholar's discount, loan opportunities, and work-study opportunities are currently available to make education at Seton Hill University more affordable. For those students who prefer to pay the University bill in monthly installments, Seton Hill offers a tuition payment plan.

Cost of Study

Tuition for the 2001–02 academic year was $400 per semester hour. A one-time application fee of $30 is also charged. Fees include a graduation fee of $100 and a project-binding fee of $40. Books and supplies range from approximately $50 to $100 per course.

Living and Housing Costs

Room and board costs for the 2001–02 academic year ranged from $2725 to $2830 per semester. Room and board costs for the 2001 summer semester were $150 per week. Nightly room charges were $10. Parking permits are $20 per year.

Student Group

Currently, there are 295 graduate students enrolled at the University—20 art therapy students, 54 in elementary education, 53 in special education, 36 in business administration, 62 in writing popular fiction, 44 in counseling psychology, and 26 in technologies enhanced learning. Forty-two of these students are full-time, while 253 students are enrolled on a part-time basis. Women comprise 211 of the total number of graduate students.

Location

Seton Hill University's 200-acre campus is located in Greensburg, Pennsylvania, which is easily accessible by car, train, or plane. Just 35 miles east of Pittsburgh, Greensburg enjoys all the advantages of a large city while maintaining a small-town atmosphere. The seat of Westmoreland County, Greensburg is home to the Westmoreland Museum of American Art, the Westmoreland Symphony Orchestra, Ohio Pyle recreation center, and Seven Springs ski resort.

The University and The Programs

Seton Hill is a Catholic, liberal arts university.

The degree programs in elementary education and art therapy began in 1995. The Master of Arts in special education program began in 1997. The master's degrees in management and writing popular fiction were first offered in 1998. The counseling psychology program began in 1999. The technologies enhanced learning program began in 2000.

Applying

All programs require a completed application and fee, official transcripts from all colleges and universities attended, and three recommendation forms. In addition, the master's programs in writing popular fiction, business administration, art therapy, technologies enhanced learning, and counseling psychology require a letter of intent. The writing popular fiction program requires a writing sample. The art therapy program requires a Miller Analogies Test score and an art portfolio of fifteen to twenty slides. Admission to the education programs requires a copy of any teaching certification held.

All non-native English speakers are required to take the TOEFL.

Correspondence and Information

Mary Kay Cooper
Director of Admissions and Adult Student Services
Seton Hill University
Seton Hill Drive
Greensburg, Pennsylvania 15601-1599
Telephone: 724-838-4221
800-826-6234 (toll-free)
Fax: 724-830-1294
E-mail: gadmit@setonhill.edu
World Wide Web: http://www.setonhill.edu

THE FACULTY

Elementary Education and Special Education

Alvaro Q. Barriga, Assistant Professor of Psychology; Ph.D., Ohio State.
Terrance E. DePasquale, Associate Professor of Education and Director of the Graduate Program in Elementary Education; Ed.D., Georgia.
Mary Ann Gawelek, Professor of Psychology; Ed.D., Boston University.
Daniel P. Gray, Assistant Professor of Education; Ed.D., Pittsburgh.
Frank Klapak, Associate Professor of Communication and Information Arts and Director of the Graduate Program in Technologies Enhanced Learning; Ph.D., Pittsburgh.
Sondra D. Lettrich, Associate Professor of Education and Director of the Graduate Program in Special Education; Ph.D., Pittsburgh.
Melanie Pampena, Instructor of Communication and Information Arts; M.S.Ed., Duquesne.

Art Therapy and Counseling Psychology

Alvaro Q. Barriga, Assistant Professor of Psychology; Ph.D., Ohio State.
Nina Denninger, Associate Professor and Director of the Graduate Program in Art Therapy; M.A., Goddard.
Terrance E. DePasquale, Associate Professor of Education and Director of the Graduate Program in Elementary Education; Ed.D., Georgia.
Mary Ann Gawelek, Professor of Psychology; Ed.D., Boston University.
Tracey Laszloffy, Associate Professor of Psychology; Ph.D., Syracuse.
Cynthia A. Magistro, Professor of Psychology; Ph.D., Duquesne.

Business Administration

Catherine Giunta, Assistant Professor of Management; M.A., Saint Francis (Pennsylvania).
Victoria Marie Gribschaw, S.C., Associate Professor of Management; Ph.D., Ohio State.
Paul Mahady, Assistant Professor of Management; M.B.A., Indiana of Pennsylvania.
Barbara Mistick, Associate Professor of Management and Director of the National Education Center for Women in Business (NECWB); M.B.A., Pittsburgh.
Mark Nolan, Assistant Professor of Management and Director of the Graduate Program in Management; M.B.A., New Mexico.

Writing Popular Fiction

Michael A. Arnzen, Assistant Professor of English; Ph.D., Oregon.
Lee Tobin McClain, Associate Professor of English and Director of the Graduate Program in Writing Popular Fiction; Ph.D., Colorado at Boulder.
Albert Wendland, Associate Professor of English; Ph.D., Pittsburgh.

Technologies Enhanced Learning

Terrance E. DePasquale, Associate Professor of Education and Director of the Graduate Program in Elementary Education; Ed.D., Georgia.
Mary Ann Gawelek, Professor of Psychology; Ed.D., Boston University.
Frank Klapak, Associate Professor of Communication and Information Arts and Director of the Graduate Program in Technologies Enhanced Learning; Ph.D., Pittsburgh.
Melanie Pampena, Instructor of Communication and Information Arts; M.S.Ed., Duquesne.

SHIPPENSBURG UNIVERSITY OF PENNSYLVANIA

School of Graduate Studies

Programs of Study

Shippensburg University of Pennsylvania offers programs of study leading to the master's degrees (M.A., M.B.A., M.Ed., M.P.A., and M.S.) in administration of justice, applied gerontology, applied history, biology, business administration, communication studies, computer science, counseling, curriculum and instruction, educational administration, geoenvironmental studies, information systems, public administration, psychology, reading, and special education. Students may also pursue postgraduate level supervisory and certification credentials.

Research Facilities

The Ezra Lehman Memorial Library houses more than 2 million items and provides access to electronic resources, including books and articles, that are accessible from students' personal computers 24 hours a day. Via the Keystone Library and Pennsylvania Academic Library networks students can access the collections of sixty academic libraries. The University maintains three general-purpose microcomputer laboratories (two are open 24 hours a day) and eighteen labs that have department or major specific software. The Center for Applied Research and Policy Analysis, the Center for Education and Human Services, the Center for Interdisciplinary Science, the Center for Juvenile Justice Training and Research, and the Center for Local and State Government offer students research opportunities in addition to department research projects.

Financial Aid

Graduate assistantships are awarded on a competitive basis without regard to financial need. They provide a tuition waiver as well as compensation on an hourly scale for work performed. Graduate assistants are required to work 250 hours during the semester and 150 hours during the summer. Applications should be filed by March 1. Residence director (RD) positions are available, with preference given to students enrolled in the counseling program. The RD position is a 12-month appointment, compensated with a salary, and free apartment and meal plan. RDs also receive a tuition waiver for 6 credits per semester and 3 credits per summer. The University is approved for training veterans and administers a range of loan programs. Funds are available to support student research and attendance at professional meetings to present papers.

Cost of Study

Tuition for 2001–02 was $256 per credit hour for in-state students and $420 per credit hour for out-of-state students. Students also pay an educational services fee of $22 per credit hour. A health services fee of $72 is charged to full-time students. The student union fee is $102 for full-time students and $51 for those attending part-time.

Living and Housing Costs

Off-campus housing is available to graduate students during the fall and spring semesters. For information, students should visit the Web site at http://www.ship.edu/~deanstu/OffCampus/. Housing is available on campus during the summer sessions. For housing information, contact the Dean of Students' office at 717-477-1164 or deanstu@ship.edu. Various meal plans are available, including Flex Accounts, which can be used like cash in any of the campus dining locations.

Student Group

The University enrolls approximately 1,000 graduate students and 6,000 undergraduate students. Most graduate students are part-time (78 percent) and female (63 percent). Graduate students represent various ethnicities, states, and countries. A Graduate Student Association Board represents the academic and social interests of graduate students. Student services include on-site day care, Women's Center, Multicultural Student Affairs, and Counseling Center.

Location

Shippensburg University is located in the Cumberland Valley of south central Pennsylvania, 40 miles southwest of Harrisburg. It is easily accessible from exits 24 northward and 29 south of Interstate 81 and the Blue Mountain and Carlisle interchanges of the Pennsylvania Turnpike.

The University

Founded in 1871, Shippensburg is consistently rated as one of the best universities in the Northeast. Shippensburg has offered graduate education since 1959 and is one of fourteen universities in Pennsylvania's State System of Higher Education.

Applying

Applicants must present a bachelor's degree from an accredited college or university and an official transcript. In addition, some academic departments may require an interview, additional test scores, goal statements, or letters of recommendation. The application fee is $30. Students may apply and check the status of their application online at http://www.ship.edu/admiss/grad.html.

Correspondence and Information

Office of Graduate Admissions
Shippensburg University
1871 Old Main Drive
Shippensburg, Pennsylvania 17257-2299
Telephone: 717-477-1213
800-822-8028
Fax: 717-477-4016
E-mail: admiss@ship.edu
World Wide Web: http://www.ship.edu/admiss/grad.html

THE FACULTY

Dean of Graduate Studies: James G. Coolsen, Ph.D., American.
Dean of Extended Studies: Kathleen M Howley, D.Ed., Penn State.
Dean of Graduate Admissions: Joseph G. Cretella, M.Ed., Kent State.

Administration of Justice: Robert M. Freeman, Ph.D., Maryland.
Applied Gerontology: Richard Wiscott, Ph.D., Akron.
Applied History: David F. Godshalk, Ph.D., Yale.
Biology: Michael McNichols, Ph.D., Virginia Tech.
Business Administration and Information Systems: Robert Rollins, D.Ed., Penn State.
Communication Studies: Edward J. Carlin, Ph.D., Bowling Green State.
Computer Science: Carole Wellington, Ph.D., North Carolina State.
Counseling: Thomas L. Hozman, Ph.D., Purdue.
Curriculum and Instruction, Reading, Special Education: Elizabeth Vaughn, Ph.D., South Florida.
Educational Leadership and Policy: Nancy Stankus, D.Ed., Penn State.
Geoenvironmental Studies: John Benhart, Ph.D., Syracuse.
Public Administration: Sara Grove, Ph.D., North Carolina.
Psychology: Ronald Mehiel, Ph.D., Washington (Seattle).

SLIPPERY ROCK UNIVERSITY OF PENNSYLVANIA

Graduate School

Programs of Study

Slippery Rock University offers the Master of Arts degree in community counseling, English, history, and student personnel; the Master of Science degree in accounting, exercise and wellness promotion, park and resource management, sport management, and sustainable systems (agroecology, built environment/energy management, permaculture, and sustainable resource management); the Master of Education degree in elementary education (elementary school mathematics/science and reading), elementary school counseling, secondary education (mathematics/science), secondary school counseling, and special education (master teacher, supervision, and mentally and physically handicapped); the Master of Science in Nursing degree (nurse practitioner studies); and the Doctor of Physical Therapy degree. The physical therapy program takes 116 semester hours and requires eight semesters (which includes two summers) for completion. A graduate certificate in gerontology is also available.

Except for the physical therapy program, two semesters comprise the academic year; summer sessions are arranged in one 3-week presession, two 5-week sessions, and one 7-week evening term. Up to 12 semester hours of graduate credit from an accredited institution may be transferred into most master's programs.

Research Facilities

More than 700,000 volumes, along with an extensive microfiche collection and major professional journals and newspapers, are housed in the Bailey Library. A large reference collection, including bibliographies, indexes, and abstracts, is available. A comprehensive materials center and an audiovisual center are also located in the library. One of the largest computer centers in western Pennsylvania is operated by the University. Slippery Rock University is part of a Marine Science Consortium with research facilities at Wallops Island in Virginia. In addition, the University operates a biology station at nearby Moraine State Park, is affiliated with the McKeever Environmental Learning Center near Sandy Lake, and owns 60 acres for environmental studies and research. Scanning and transmission electron microscopes, greenhouses, an Outdoor Recreational Instruction Laboratory, a planetarium, IBM and Apple computer laboratories, and modern equipment support research and instruction.

Financial Aid

For 2002–03, more than 125 graduate assistantships with tuition waived and stipends of $4000 were offered. Assistantships may be granted for up to two academic years, with full-time recipients working 20 hours a week and taking at least 9 graduate credits a semester. Application forms may be obtained from the unit supervisor/graduate program coordinator. Unconditional admission to the graduate studies program is a prerequisite for assistantship eligibility.

Loans are available to graduate students with definite need through the Federal Perkins Loan and the Pennsylvania Higher Education Assistance Agency programs. Special Education Graduate Fellowships for special education majors are available through the Bureau of Education for the Handicapped. Information on additional sources of financial aid can be obtained from the Financial Aid Office.

Cost of Study

In 2002–03, Pennsylvania residents who study full-time pay $2993 per semester; nonresidents pay $4621 per semester. The course fee per credit hour for part-time graduate students is $256 for residents and $420 for nonresidents. All fees are subject to change without notice.

Living and Housing Costs

On-campus housing for graduate students is available. In 2002–03, rooms and apartments within walking distance of the campus range in price from $180 to $430 per month, and board is available on campus starting at $955 per semester.

Student Group

Graduate enrollment for the fall semester of 2001 is more than 700. Approximately 1 graduate student in 3 is enrolled on a full-time basis.

Student Outcomes

Recent graduates of Slippery Rock University have found employment in many different fields. More than 90 percent of graduates have obtained employment in their field of study. This statistic includes 100 percent placement in the fields of physical therapy, special education, and counseling. These graduates are employed in a variety of different agencies, including hospitals, social service agencies, and counseling centers.

Location

Slippery Rock, a borough of about 3,000 people, adjoins the University. Small shops and restaurants are within two or three blocks of the center of the campus. Pittsburgh, one of the country's largest cities, is about 50 miles to the south, and Erie, located on Lake Erie, is 75 miles to the north. Youngstown, Ohio, is 30 miles to the west. The borough is served by commercial buses from these cities and is located within 10 miles of two major interstate highways, I-80 and I-79. Cultural and recreational activities abound in the area.

The University

In 1889, the citizens of Slippery Rock borough founded the University and gave it their town's picturesque name. The University is one of fourteen state-owned institutions of higher education in Pennsylvania. Its undergraduate academic divisions include the Colleges of Business, Information, and Social Sciences; Education; Health, Environment, and Science; and Humanities, Fine and Performing Arts. The current enrollment of the University is approximately 6,500 undergraduates and 700 graduate students.

Slippery Rock University is fully accredited by the Middle States Association of Colleges and Schools, and appropriate programs are accredited by the National Council for Accreditation of Teacher Education.

Applying

The basic requirement for admission to graduate study is graduation from an accredited university or college with a major in the area proposed for graduate study, a grade point average of at least 2.75 (on a 4.0 scale) on all work attempted, and acceptable scores on the General Test of the Graduate Record Examinations. A nonrefundable fee of $25 must accompany applications for admission to graduate study. An official transcript must be submitted from the college or university at which the baccalaureate degree was earned. Applications should be filed two months prior to the opening of the semester for which admission is sought. Applications for financial aid should be filed at the financial aid office at least six months before the student is to begin graduate study. Application to the physical therapy program requires a $35 nonrefundable application fee.

Correspondence and Information

Graduate Studies Office
Robert A. Lowry Center
Slippery Rock University
Slippery Rock, Pennsylvania 16057

Telephone: 724-738-2051
Fax: 724-738-2146
E-mail: graduate.studies@sru.edu
World Wide Web: http://www.sru.edu/depts/graduate/

GRADUATE PROGRAM COORDINATORS

The telephone numbers at the end of each entry below are equipped with voice mail.

Accounting: Susan Lubinski, J.D., Duquesne. (724-738-2013)
Allied Health: Michael Kennedy, Ph.D., Rensselaer. (724-738-2017)
Counseling and Educational Psychology: Donald Strano, Ed.D., Texas Tech. (724-738-2035)
Elementary Education/Early Childhood: John Burtch, Ph.D., Syracuse. (724-738-2042)
English: James Strickland, Ph.D., Indiana of Pennsylvania. (724-738-2043)
History: Larry Rotge, Ph.D., Ball State. (724-738-2053)
Nursing: Joyce White, Coordinator, M.S.N. program; Dr.P.H., Pittsburgh (724-738-2323); Mary Kavoosi, Chairperson, nursing department, Clarion University; Ph.D., Pittsburgh. (814-677-6107)
Parks and Recreational/Environmental Education: *Park and Resource Management, Environmental Education, Sustainable Systems:* Daniel Dziubek, Ed.D., Pittsburgh (724-738-2068).
Physical Education: Robin Ammon Jr., Ed.D., Northern Colorado. (724-738-2072)
Physical Therapy: Barbara Billek-Sawhney, Ed.D., Duquesne. (724-738-2080)
Secondary Education/Foundations of Education: Edwin Christmann, Ph.D., Old Dominion. (724-738-2041)
Special Education: Dennis Fair, Ph.D., Pittsburgh. (724-738-2085)

Sustainable energy sources are critical to the planet's future.

Teacher training programs are one of Slippery Rock's strengths.

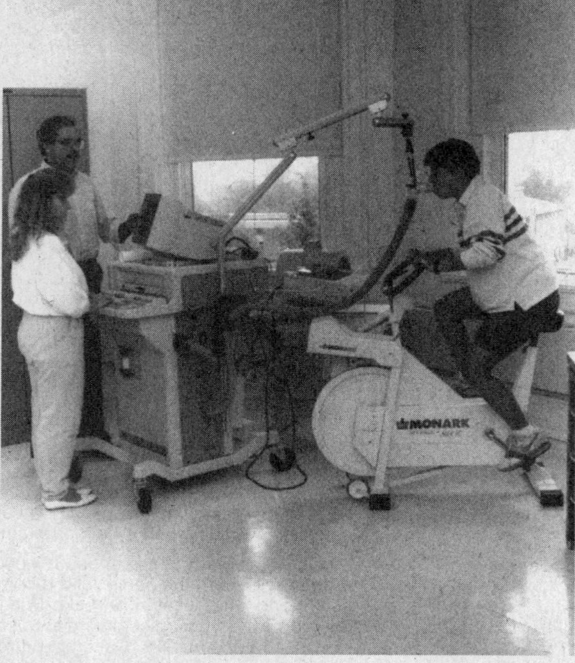

One of Slippery Rock's graduate degrees is the Doctor of Physical Therapy.

SOUTH DAKOTA SCHOOL OF MINES AND TECHNOLOGY

Graduate Division

Programs of Study

Master of Science degrees are offered in atmospheric sciences, chemical engineering, civil engineering, computer science, electrical engineering, geology/geological engineering, materials engineering and science, mechanical engineering, paleontology, and technology management. A master's degree requires a minimum of 30 semester hours, including research and a thesis, or 32 hours without a thesis. The maximum graduate load is 15 credit hours per semester. Up to 12 hours of graduate credit may be transferred from another institution. The normal period required for completion of the M.S. degree ranges from one to two years for most students. Research credits may be earned during the summer.

Programs leading to a Ph.D. degree are offered in atmospheric, environmental, and water resources (AEWR); in geology/geological engineering; and in materials engineering and science (MES). The Ph.D. program requires a minimum of 50 semester hours of course work and between 30 and 40 hours of research credits beyond the baccalaureate degree. (The AEWR program requires a total of 90 credits.) The Ph.D. programs also include qualifying and comprehensive examinations, language requirements, and a dissertation representing the culmination of between one and two academic years of full-time research. The residence requirement is two consecutive semesters.

Research Facilities

Facilities include a Computation Center with Sun and IBM RS-6000 computers and 140 clustered Pentium computers, most of which are on a local area network. Other facilities include the Engineering and Mining Experiment Station analytical laboratories; and the Museum of Geology, with its extensive mineral and paleontological collections. The library, with 217,500 volumes and more than 800 periodicals, is also a selective depository of U.S. government documents. The Institute of Atmospheric Sciences provides research and study opportunities in meteorology, atmospheric chemistry, cloud physics, remote sensing, hydrology, and biogeochemistry.

Research equipment includes X-ray diffractometers, a scanning electron microscope, a transmission electron microscope, an electron microanalyzer, FT infrared and Raman spectrometers, a simultaneous inductively coupled plasma (ICP) mass spectrometer, an API mass spectrometer, chromatographs, other analytical instruments, a variety of mechanical testing machines, lasers, and many other specialized items such as a T-28 instrumented research airplane.

Financial Aid

Teaching and research assistantships, and various fellowships are available. For the 2002–03 academic year, full-time teaching and research assistantships normally carry nine-month stipends that range from $8000 to $10,000. Supplementary summer assistantships may be offered with stipends of up to $2293 (M.S.) or $2454 (Ph.D.) per month. Full-year fellowships range up to $8240 for nine months. Information on other types of financial aid for U.S. students is available upon request from the Enrollment Management Services Office.

Cost of Study

Graduate tuition in 2002–03 is $98.65 per credit hour for state residents and $290.75 for nonresidents. Assistants on state contract pay one third the graduate resident rate if registered for 9 credit hours or more. In addition, students are assessed fees of approximately $95 per credit hour depending on the type of course. Other fees are added for a guarantee deposit, parking, late registration, and health insurance, as applicable.

Living and Housing Costs

Assistance in finding off-campus rooms and apartments is available from the Director of Housing. These rooms range in cost from $100 to $125 per week. Apartments rent for a minimum of $300 per month. On-campus board is payable by the meal or is available through plans ranging from $723 to $947 per semester. When available to graduate students, dormitory rooms cost $795 per semester for double occupancy or $1060 for a single room. Other costs are near national averages.

Student Group

Undergraduate enrollment (primarily science and engineering) is more than 2,400; there are normally 300 to 350 students registered in graduate programs. Of all students, approximately 35 percent are either nonresident or international; approximately 25 percent are women.

Location

Rapid City has a population of about 66,000. Described as the gateway to the Black Hills, it is located a short distance from the Mount Rushmore Memorial and the White River Badlands. Climatic conditions are favorable in winter and summer for a variety of recreational activities—skiing, biking, hunting, fishing, hiking, and camping—with easy access to mountain streams and lakes.

The School

In 1885, the territorial legislature established the Dakota School of Mines in Rapid City, where it served the frontier communities of the Black Hills as a mining college and a prospectors' analytical laboratory. Since 1900, however, the educational emphasis has shifted to include a broad spectrum of engineering and scientific disciplines. Research capabilities have steadily improved. Modern teaching and research laboratories characterize the science and engineering departments with particular emphasis in the atmospheric sciences, hydrology, both natural and man-made materials, automated manufacturing, and computer networks. Recent staff additions include those in atmospheric sciences, biology, chemistry, civil engineering, geology, physics, and metallurgical engineering. From fifty to sixty graduate degrees are awarded annually. The School is accredited by the North Central Association of Colleges and Schools. The chemistry programs are approved by the American Chemical Society.

Applying

Applications from U.S. residents should be received sixty days before the beginning of the semester of desired admittance. International students should apply 120 days prior to their expected date of matriculation. All individuals who have graduated from institutions with accredited engineering and science curricula are encouraged to apply. The Graduate Record Examinations are required of all applicants for admission to AEWR, atmospheric sciences, computer science, paleontology, geology/geological engineering, and MES; it is required of all applicants for admission to electrical and mechanical engineering who are (or will be) graduates of non-ABET-accredited schools. The GRE General Test is desirable but not required in other departments. A minimum score of 520 (paper-based test) or 190 (computer-based test) on the TOEFL is required (560/220 for admission without additional English tutoring) of applicants from non-English-speaking countries. GMAT or GRE scores are required for technology management.

Correspondence and Information

Dean of Graduate Education and Sponsored Programs
South Dakota School of Mines and Technology
501 East Saint Joseph Street
Rapid City, South Dakota 57701-3995

Telephone: 605-394-2493
E-mail: graduate.admissions@sdsmt.edu
World Wide Web: http://www.sdsmt.edu/admin/gesp/

PROGRAMS AND RESEARCH AREAS

Master of Science Program in Atmospheric Sciences
Program Director: P. R. Zimmerman, Ph.D., Colorado State. Telephone: 605-394-2291.
Research areas are listed below under Institute of Atmospheric Sciences.

Master of Science Program in Chemical Engineering
Program Director: M. S. McDowell, Ph.D., Iowa State. Telephone: 605-394-2421.
HPLC, NMR, FTIR, molecular modeling, biomass conversions, mining wastes characterization, hazardous waste incineration pollutants, environmental and forensic chemistries, combustion syntheses, natural products, synthetic plant growth regulators, organophosphorus chemistry, polymers and polymer/composites, kinetics and mechanisms of inorganic reactions, supermolecular assemblies, nanotechnology, supercritical fluids, process control.

Master of Science Program in Civil and Environmental Engineering
Program Director: Terje Preber, Ph.D., Wisconsin–Madison. Telephone: 605-394-2439.
Advanced materials, environmental engineering, geotechnical engineering, hazardous waste treatment and remediation, soil mechanics and hydraulics, structural engineering, water and wastewater treatment, water resources, and water quality engineering.

Master of Science Program in Computer Science
Program Director: Antonette Logar, Ph.D., Texas Tech. Telephone: 605-394-2471.
Artificial intelligence, fuzzy logic, neural networks, pattern recognition in satellite imagery, image processing, computer vision, computer graphics, database management systems, parallel and distributed systems, software engineering, mathematical foundations of computer science.

Master of Science Program in Electrical and Computer Engineering
Program Director: L. A. Simonson, Ph.D., South Dakota Mines and Tech. Telephone: 605-394-2451.
Circuit and systems theory, communication theory, control systems, digital systems, electric power, electrooptics, electromagnetics, instrumentation, material science, microcomputer/microprocessor applications, robotics, semiconductor processing.

Master of Science Program in Geology and Geological Engineering
Program Director: J. E. Fox, Ph.D., Wyoming. Telephone: 605-394-2461.
Bioremediation, Black Hills geology, economic geology, engineering geophysics, geochemistry, geographic information systems, geohydrology, gold deposits, groundwater, igneous and metamorphic petrology, mineralogy, ore-forming systems, pegmatite petrogenesis, remote sensing, sedimentology, stratigraphy, surficial processes, tectonics, vertebrate paleontology.

Master of Science Program in Materials Engineering and Science
Program Director: K. N. Han, Ph.D., Berkeley. Telephone: 605-394-2342.
Synthetic inorganic chemistry, polymer structure and properties, molecular modeling and dynamics, synthetic organic chemistry, supramolecular assembly, solid-phase microextraction technology, environmental chemistry, supercritical fluid extraction, metal ion activation of small molecules, electrochemistry, toxicity assessment, hydrometallurgy, interfacial phenomena, solution thermodynamics, metallurgic kinetics, transport phenomena, chlorination, polymer matrix composites, nanomechanics and micromechanics, phase transformation, strengthening mechanisms, fracture mechanics, X-ray diffraction, SEM/TEM microscopy, process control, artificial intelligence, NMR, FTIR, electronic and structural materials, electrical conductivity, photoconductivity, semiconductor materials, magnetic nanostructures, quantum wells, resonant tunneling devices.

Master of Science Program in Mechanical Engineering
Program Director: M. A. Langerman, Ph.D., Idaho. Telephone: 605-394-2401.
Computational transport phenomena, natural convection, enhanced cooling of microelectronics, advanced structural analysis, fatigue life of composite materials, stress analysis by moire method, computer-integrated manufacturing.

Master of Science Program in Paleontology
Program Director: Gale A. Bishop, Ph.D., Texas at Austin. Telephone: 605-394-2467
Mammalian paleontology emphasis, studies in paleoecology, micropaleontology, evolutionary processes, Oligocene/Miocene stratigraphy, continental faunas, museum methods.

Master of Science Program in Technology Management
Program Director: S. D. Kellogg, Ph.D., Texas at Austin. Telephone: 605-394-1271
Engineering economics, management science, quality management, systems engineering.

Doctor of Philosophy Program in Atmospheric, Environmental, and Water Resources
Program Directors: S. O. Farwell (at South Dakota School of Mines and Technology), Ph.D., Montana State. Telephone: 605-394-2493. V. R. Schaefer (South Dakota State University), Ph.D., Virginia Tech. Telephone: 605-688-6307.
A joint program with South Dakota State University at Brookings. Separate degrees awarded in atmospheric, environmental, and water resources with research areas in atmospheric, groundwater, and surface water science and engineering; atmospheric chemistry; resource conservation; hydrologic mapping and modeling; remote sensing/satellite imagery; physical meteorology; meteorological modeling; and agricultural and urban waste treatment.

Doctor of Philosophy Program in Geology and Geological Engineering
Program Director: J. E. Fox, Ph.D., Wyoming. Telephone: 605-394-2461
Research areas are listed above under the Master of Science Program.

Doctor of Philosophy Program in Materials Engineering and Science
Program Director: C. H. Jenkins, Ph.D., Oregon State. Telephone: 605-394-2406
Computational and continuum mechanics, composite materials, concrete technology, FT-IR spectroscopy, heterogeneous reaction kinetics, interfacial force microscopy, interfacial science, multiphase materials, polymer materials and processing, Raman spectroscopy, thermophysical and electronic properties.

RESEARCH UNITS AND RESEARCH AREAS

Institute of Atmospheric Sciences
Director: P. R. Zimmerman, Ph.D., Colorado State. Telephone: 605-394-2291.
Trace gas biogeochemistry, tropospheric chemistry, airborne measurements, atmospheric electricity, cloud physics, hailstorms, nucleation processes, mesoscale meteorology, numerical cloud modeling, radar meteorology, radiative transfer, land use and change, weather modification, climate change, hydrology.

South Dakota Space Grant Consortium
Director: S. O. Farwell, Ph.D., Montana State. Telephone: 605-394-2493. Deputy Director and Outreach Coordinator: Thomas Durkin, M.S., South Dakota Mines and Tech. Telephone: 605-394-1975.
Remote sensing and image processing techniques and applications; satellite and balloon platform measurement technology; tropospheric sampling and measurement methodology; biogeochemistry of S, N, and C compounds; climate change; statistics and experimental design; and K–12 educational activities in space and earth sciences.

Museum of Geology
Director: Gale A. Bishop, Ph.D., Texas at Austin. Telephone: 605-394-2467.
Biostratigraphy, evolution, mineralogy, museums, paleobiology, paleontology, taphonomy, sea turtle program.

SOUTHEASTERN UNIVERSITY

College of Graduate Studies

Programs of Study

Southeastern University offers master's degree programs in three principal areas: business management, computer science, and public administration. The Master of Business Administration has concentrations in accounting, business management, computer information systems, financial management, and marketing. The Master of Public Administration has concentrations in government management and health administration. The Master of Science concentration is in computer science.

The master's degree requires a minimum of 45 credit hours, which must be completed within seven years of the date of initial enrollment. All programs are offered on the weekend and weeknights to accommodate the working adult.

Research Facilities

The University's facilities include a modern, well-equipped library. The Washington campus library contains 45,000 volumes, 200 periodicals, and many audiovisual materials. The library maintains an Internet lab with seven workstations and a state-of-the-art computer network where students can use the latest reference materials on CD-ROM. A historical archival collection contains a wealth of materials on the growth of Southeastern University into the modern institution that it is today. Located in southwest Washington, D.C., the University is a short distance from major academic and research libraries, including the Library of Congress, and the Smithsonian Institution. The University is also a member of the Consortium of Universities of the Washington Metropolitan Area.

Financial Aid

Most financial aid awards are based on need, and eligible students are usually awarded a combination of loans in a financial aid package. Graduate students are also eligible for University-sponsored scholarships. Although the bulk of funds are committed to students entering in the fall term, financial aid applications should be submitted by April 15.

Cost of Study

In 2002, tuition for graduate students was $285 per credit hour. A $175 University fee is also charged at each registration. Books and supplies are estimated to cost $300 per term.

Living and Housing Costs

The University has no housing for students; however, the Office of Student Services maintains an active housing referral service, and it is easy to find housing in proximity of the University. Southeastern University has its own metro rail stop.

Student Group

More than 400 graduate students register in each quadmester. Graduate students come from the Washington, D.C., metropolitan area and from more than sixty nations. Most graduate students are employed full-time with federal and local government agencies, various branches of the armed services, and private industrial firms in the Washington area.

Location

Southeastern is within walking distance of the U.S. Capitol, various federal agencies, and L'Enfant Plaza. The Smithsonian Institution, the National Gallery of Art, the Arena Stage, and the Hirshhorn Museum are also nearby. Southeastern's location makes it convenient for many federal workers and others who live and work in Washington.

The University

Southeastern University's roots go back to 1879, when the Washington Young Men's Christian Association (YMCA) first sponsored formal programs of study, including courses in business training. Southeastern is chartered by the Congress of the United States, accredited by the Commission on Higher Education of the Middle States Association of Colleges and Schools, and is recognized by the Boards of Accountancy of the District of Columbia, Maryland, and Virginia. Southeastern provides, at a reasonable cost, a practical and useful education, which can be applied easily by students in their business, computer, and government degrees. The University strives to provide this type of education to students who historically have not been served by the traditional higher-education institutions in Washington, D.C.

Southeastern University operates on the quadmester system. Students are offered four full academic semesters each calendar year and receive 3 semester credits for each course. Advantages to the quadmester system are the flexible scheduling and the opportunity for students to take up to one third more courses during an academic year. The system is geared to meet the needs of today's working adult. Assistance is given to international students to meet immigration requirements. The four quadmesters—winter, spring, summer, and fall—begin respectively in early January, late March, early July, and late September. The quadmester system complements Southeastern's cooperative education program, and slightly expanded class sessions enable the faculty to use innovative teaching approaches.

Applying

Prospective students are encouraged to visit Southeastern University and are invited to meet with an admissions counselor to discuss the various programs and curricula. Application deadlines may be obtained by contacting the Graduate Admissions Office.

To be regularly admitted to a graduate degree program, a candidate must hold a bachelor's degree from a regionally accredited institution, or an equivalent degree from outside the United States. Applicants must submit two letters of recommendation and an essay. Applicants applying to the M.S. in computer science program must pass the general Graduate Record Examinations with a minimum score of 1200. All applications will be reviewed individually by the Southeastern University Admissions Committee.

Students who do not have undergraduate training in accounting, business management, economics, finance, mathematics, and statistics normally will be required to take introductory courses in those subjects.

Nondegree students may transfer to degree candidacy after completion of 6 graduate credit hours at Southeastern University with a cumulative average of 3.0 or better. Those with nondegree status, those who lack sufficient business-related or computer-related background, or students who demonstrate low proficiency in English may be considered for degree status after the successful completion of developmental or background course work.

A nonrefundable $45 application fee is required of all applicants. Official transcripts and other records should be sent directly to the Admissions Office. International students must also submit TOEFL scores and, for those seeking student visas, a statement of financial support. Applications are accepted for any of the four quadmesters.

Correspondence and Information

Graduate Admissions Office
Southeastern University
501 I Street, SW
Washington, D.C. 20024
Telephone: 202-265-5343 (COL-LEGE)
E-mail: admissions@admin.seu.edu
World Wide Web: http://www.seu.edu

THE FACULTY

Hossein Besharatian, D.Sc., George Washington. Operations research.
Manohar Bhide, Ph.D., Bombay (India). Theoretical physics.
Portia Bookhart, Ed.D., Virginia Tech. Curriculum and instruction.
Veronica Boutte, Ph.D., South Africa. Literature and philosophy.
Samuel Chang, Ph.D., George Mason. Computer science.
Fei (John) Chen, Ph.D., UCLA. Atmospheric sciences.
Patricia Ciuffreda, D.P.A. Nova Southeastern. Public administration.
Victor Dates, J.D., Georgetown.
Stephen Dike, Ph.D., West Virginia. Capital management.
Rudolph Douglas, Ph.D., Howard. Physical chemistry.
Abe Eftekhari, Ph.D., Texas at Arlington. Mathematical science.
Beverly Elson, Ph.D., Maryland. Art history.
William English, Ph.D., Purdue. Electrical engineering.
Gregory Fant, Ph.D., Nebraska–Lincoln. Public policy.
Hossein Firouzi, Ph.D., Southern Methodist. Electrical engineering.
Gregory Foster, D.P.A., George Washington. Public administration.
Gwendolyn Fox, Ph.D., Union (Ohio). Public policy.
Kassu Gebremarium, Ph.D., York. Political science.
Saiid Ganjalizadeh, Ph.D., George Mason. Information studies.
Lofti Geriesh, Ph.D., Kennedy Western.
Elaine Bourne Heath, Ph.D., Howard. Organizational communications.
Alfred Hernandez, J.D., California, Davis. Law.
Muhammad Islam, Ph.D., Northeastern. Economics.
Janet Jalloul, Ph.D., American. Educational administration.
Wilmer Johnson, Ph.D., Catholic University. Administration.
William Jones, Ph.D., Minnesota. American studies.
Jorge Lamas, Ph.D., George Washington. Economics.
Vivian Lusweti, Ph.D., Maryland. Comparative and international education.
Elsayed Mansour, D.Sc., George Mason. Information systems.
James McCarthy, LL.M., George Washington. Federal taxation.
John Milton, J.D., Rutgers. Law.
Vincent Okigbo, Ph.D. Howard. Communications.
Ephraim Okoro, Ph.D., Howard. Communications.
L. Parrish-White, LL.M. George Washington. Taxation.
Ann Pharr, Ph.D., Pittsburgh. Public administration.
Jianchun Qin, Ph.D., Illinois State. Environment science.
Hortense Roscoe, J.D., South Texas Law. Law.
Mohammed Safa, Ph.D., Ruhr (Germany). Economics.
Timothy Shaughnessy, Ph.D., Arizona State. Educational administration.
Michael Simms, Ph.D., Howard. Public adminstration.
Peter Smith, Ph.D., Penn State. Agricultural economics.
Philippa Smithey, Ph.D., American. Public administration.
Nagi Soliman, D.Sc., George Washington. Information systems.
Richard Sterling, Ph.D., Howard. Communications.
Judith Sutter, Ed.D., Maine. Counseling.
Thomas Tofighbaksh, J.D., Northern Virginia Law School. Law.
Richard Wilson, Ed.D., Texas Southern. Counseling.
Zhaohua Wu, Ph.D., Washington (Seattle). Atmospheric sciences.
Kwang-Su Yang, Ph.D., George Mason. Computational statistics.

SOUTHERN CONNECTICUT STATE UNIVERSITY

School of Graduate Studies

Programs of Study

Southern Connecticut State University (SCSU) offers graduate programs leading to the degrees of Master of Arts, Master of Science, Master of Science in Education, Master of Science in Nursing, Master of Library Science, Master of Public Health, Master of Social Work, Master of Marriage and Family Therapy, and Master of Business Administration. Graduate programs leading to the Sixth-Year Professional Diploma in special areas of education and library science are also offered.

The Master of Arts degree is awarded in English, history, psychology, Romance languages (French, Spanish, and Italian), and women's studies. The Master of Science degree is offered in biology; chemistry; communications disorders; computer science; instructional technology; recreation and leisure; research, measurement, and evaluation; sociology; and urban studies. The Master of Science in Education degree is awarded in art; bilingual/bicultural education; biology; chemistry; counseling; elementary education; English; environmental education; exercise science; foreign languages (French, Spanish, and Romance languages); history; mathematics; reading; school health education; school psychology; science education; and special education.

The Sixth-Year Professional Diploma is offered in counseling and school psychology, educational leadership, and education—classroom teacher specialist studies, educational foundations, library information studies, reading, special education, and science education.

Most graduate programs are offered in the evening for the convenience of part-time students. Students follow a planned program that includes completing course requirements and taking a comprehensive examination, preparing a thesis, or completing a special project, as appropriate.

Research Facilities

The Hilton C. Buley Library, Southern Connecticut State University's center of education and research, plays an indispensable part in the academic experience of every student. Buley Library provides more than 575,000 print and media volumes and access to more than 100 electronic databases. An online shared catalog expands available print and media resources to more than 2 million volumes. The library also provides 2,800 current periodical titles, 80,000 bound periodicals, and nearly 100,000 microform volumes.

Financial Aid

There are a limited number of teaching and research assistantships available. The chief source of aid is the Federal Stafford Loan. Application forms for this loan are available from commercial banks.

Cost of Study

Tuition for full-time study for the 2002–03 academic year is $5216 for state residents and $11,393 for out-of-state residents. Part-time study costs $265 per credit hour plus a $48 registration fee and an $8 per credit hour information technology fee each semester. Students in some programs are charged differential tuition.

Living and Housing Costs

On-campus housing is available for graduate students. Off-campus accommodations are also readily available close to the campus at a range of prices. Students may choose from a wide range of housing styles and options.

Student Group

Approximately 4,000 graduate students (including more than 700 full-time) are enrolled in graduate programs in five schools of the University. SCSU has consistently ranked as one of the top ten graduate schools in New England in terms of enrollment.

Location

New Haven, Connecticut's third-largest city, is home to three universities, three colleges, and several private schools. New Haven serves as the gateway to New England, where I-95 and I-91 intersect and provide access to New York and Boston.

The University

Southern Connecticut State University is one of four institutions of the Connecticut State University System, authorized by the state of Connecticut. It receives its principal financial support from legislative appropriations. It is the policy of Southern Connecticut State University to accept students without regard to race, color, creed, sex, age, national origin, or physical disability.

Applying

Application forms for the School of Graduate Studies are available in the Graduate Office, located in Room 118, Engleman Hall, or may be obtained by mail, telephone request, or on line. Students are advised to send the completed, signed application and official transcripts from every college and graduate school attended, along with a $40 application fee, to the Graduate Office. All other documents, such as requested letters of recommendation or any departmental forms, should be sent directly to the academic department to which application is being made. A personal interview with the appropriate department chairperson or a designated faculty member in the major area of study is a requirement for admission. Requests for appointments must be made to the department. The application and credentials should be submitted well in advance of the semester for which the student seeks admission.

Correspondence and Information

School of Graduate Studies
Southern Connecticut State University
501 Crescent Street, En 118
New Haven, Connecticut 06515-1355
Telephone: 203-392-5240
800-448-0661 (toll-free)
World Wide Web: http://www.southernct.edu/grad

FACULTY HEADS

Listed below is the chairperson or graduate coordinator of each department.

Art Education: Kathleen Connors, Coordinator.
Biology: Rebecca Lerud, Coordinator.
Business Administration: Omid Nodoushani, Coordinator.
Chemistry: Robert Snyder, Coordinator.
Communication Disorders: Marianne Kennedy, Chair.
Computer Science: Taraneh Seyed, Coordinator.
Counselor Education: Teri Olisky, Chair.
Education: Peter Barile, Chair.
Educational Foundations: Cynthia McDaniels, Coordinator.
Educational Leadership: Brian Perkins, Chair.
English: Vara Neverow, Chair.
Exercise Science: Robert Axtell, Coordinator.
Foreign Languages: Deane Hetric, Chair.
History: Polly Beals, Coordinator.
Library Science and Instructional Technology: Mary Brown, Chair.
Marriage and Family Therapy: J. Edward Lynch, Chair.
Mathematics: Martin Hartog, Coordinator.
Nursing: Olive Santavenere, Coordinator.
Psychology: James Mazur, Coordinator.
Public Health: Michael Perlin, Coordinator.
Reading: Irving Newman, Chair.
Recreation: James McGregor, Coordinator.
Research, Measurement, and Evaluation: William Diffley, Coordinator.
School Health: Doris Marino, Chair.
School Psychology: Michael Martin, Coordinator.
Science and Environmental Education: Susan Cusato, Chair.
Social Work: Todd Rofuth, Chair.
Sociology: Debra Emmelman, Coordinator.
Special Education: Stephen J. Feldman, Coordinator.
Urban Studies: Charles Small, Coordinator.
Women's Studies: Rosalyn Amenta and Vara Neverow, Co-Coordinators.

There are many opportunities for graduate students at SCSU to enroll in small classes and work closely with faculty.

The Hilton C. Buley Library.

SOUTHERN ILLINOIS UNIVERSITY CARBONDALE

Graduate School

Programs of Study

The Graduate School at Southern Illinois University Carbondale (SIUC) offers master's and doctoral programs (see reverse of page for listing). Students may design double-major master's programs and interdisciplinary doctoral programs with the approval of the Dean of the Graduate School. Master's degree programs vary from 30 to 60 semester hours, including thesis hours. Both thesis and nonthesis options are available in some programs. The doctoral degree is offered in twenty-six programs. Twenty programs offer direct entry and/or accelerated entry into doctoral programs. Although there is no Graduate School requirement that a certain number of semester hours be completed for the doctoral degree, some degree programs do have semester-hour requirements, and students must meet the residence requirements of the Graduate School. Six graduate certificate programs are also offered, including those in anatomy, art history, earth science, gerontology, plant ecology, and systematic biology (see page 4 of Graduate Catalog).

Research Facilities

In addition to containing approximately 2.5 million volumes, 3 million microforms, and 12,000 current periodicals, Morris Library also is at the forefront of providing electronic access to information. Multiple computer stations on each floor allow patrons to obtain information—often in full text—from local, state, national, and international sources; access is also available from across campus and remotely from home. The library is a member of Illinet Online, the statewide library automated catalog; the national Online Computer Library Center (OCLC), the world's largest bibliographic network; and the Association of Research Libraries (ARL), an exclusive consortium of 120 of the largest academic/research libraries in the country.

Campus computing and network infrastructure includes a campus fiber-optic gigabit "backbone"; an IBM mainframe computer (Multiprise 3000, H30); a cluster of specialized, Unix-based RISC servers, which offer access to e-mail, software downloading, computational resources, and statistical libraries; and a connection to the Internet through the Illinois Century Network. Infrastructure software includes a Web browser, an e-mail agent, and the full range of file-transfer, remote-login, and telecommunication software to enable state-of-the-art transactions with the campus network resources and the Internet. This software is available at no charge to students. SIUC is a member of Internet2.

The Office of Research Development and Administration helps faculty and staff members and students obtain external grants to support research. The office provides grant-related information and proposal development services, negotiates with funding agencies, processes grant awards, and oversees technology transfer. It also coordinates seed grant programs for research and administers research support facilities, such as the Nuclear Magnetic Resonance Facility and Integrated Microscopy and Graphics Expertise (IMAGE).

Financial Aid

Departments offer assistantships of $974 to $1300 per month for half-time duties in 2002. The Graduate School offers competitive eleven-month fellowships. Currently, these fellowships pay $1000 per month for master's students, $1100 per month for doctoral students, and dissertation research awards of $1204 per month. The Morris Doctoral Fellowship program offers $15,000 for each of five years of doctoral study to students of high scholastic standing. Fellowships for promising minority students are available through the Proactive Recruitment of Multicultural Professionals for Tomorrow (PROMPT) Program, the Graduate Dean's Fellowship (GDF), the Illinois Minority Graduate Incentive Program (IMGIP), and the Illinois Consortium for Educational Opportunity Program (ICEOP). Assistantships and fellowships carry tuition scholarships. Student employment, loans, and other tuition scholarships are also available. About 70 percent of all graduate students receive some form of SIUC financial aid.

Cost of Study

In-state tuition is $154 per semester credit hour (15 hours and up, $2310) in 2002–03. Out-of-state tuition is $308 per credit hour (15 hours and up, $4620). Fees vary from $277.13 (1 credit hour) to $599.40 (12 credit hours).

Living and Housing Costs

For married couples, students with families, and single graduate students, the University has 589 efficiency and one-, two-, and three-bedroom apartments that rent for $374 to $432 per month in 2002–03. Residence halls for single graduate students are also available, as well as accessible residence hall rooms and apartments for students with disabilities.

Student Group

Total University enrollment exceeds 21,000, including more than 4,000 graduate students. Men and women come from all fifty states and 113 other countries. About 53 percent of the graduate students are women, 23 percent are foreign nationals, and 13 percent are American minorities.

Location

SIUC is 350 miles south of Chicago and 100 miles southeast of St. Louis. Nestled in rolling hills bordered by the Ohio and Mississippi Rivers and enhanced by a mild climate, the area has state parks, national forests and wildlife refuges, and large lakes for outdoor recreation. Cultural offerings include theater, opera, concerts, art exhibits, and cinema. Educational facilities for the families of students are excellent.

The University

Southern Illinois University Carbondale is a comprehensive public university with a variety of general and professional education programs. The University offers associate, bachelor's, master's, and doctoral degrees; J.D. and M.D. degrees; and graduate certificate programs. The University is fully accredited by the North Central Association of Colleges and Schools. The Graduate School has an essential role in the development and coordination of graduate instruction and research programs. The Graduate Council has academic responsibility for determining graduate standards, recommending new graduate programs and research centers, and establishing policies to facilitate the research effort.

Applying

Students interested in admission to degree programs should contact the appropriate departments directly to obtain official Graduate School application forms and other departmental materials. Students interested in nondeclared (non-degree-program affiliated) status should contact the Graduate School directly at the telephone number listed below to obtain application materials. Students applying to degree programs should mail all application materials directly to the department. Regardless of where the official transcripts are eventually sent, such transcripts must be forwarded directly from the registrar of previously attended schools (other than SIUC). Applicants whose native language is not English must submit TOEFL scores. Standardized test scores, letters of reference, personal and professional data, and requests for financial assistance should be submitted to the department concerned. Students seeking a fellowship should submit all required documents before February 1; those applying for other sources of financial aid should submit materials as early in the spring as possible. Deadlines for financial aid awards are posted on the Graduate School Web site (listed below).

Correspondence and Information

Graduate School Admissions
Woody Hall B103
Southern Illinois University Carbondale
Carbondale, Illinois 62901-4716

Telephone: 618-536-7791
Fax: 618-453-4562
E-mail: gradschl@siu.edu
World Wide Web: http://www.siu.edu/gradschl

PROGRAM DIRECTORS

Accountancy (master's): Allan Karnes, Professor and Director.
Administration of Justice (master's): Thomas Castellano, Associate Professor and Director.
Agribusiness Economics (master's): Steven Kraft, Professor and Chair.
Animal Science (master's): Richard Roeder, Professor and Chair.
Anthropology (master's, Ph.D.): Jonathan Hill, Professor and Chair.
Applied Linguistics (master's): Glenn Gilbert, Professor and Chair.
Art (master's): Harris Deller, Professor and Director.
Behavior Analysis and Therapy (master's): Anthony Cuvo, Professor and Coordinator.
Biological Sciences (master's): Phillip Robertson, Professor and Director.
Business Administration (master's, Ph.D.): Richard Rivers, Professor and Acting Associate Dean of the College of Business and Administration.
Chemistry (master's, Ph.D.): Gerard V. Smith, Professor and Acting Chair.
Communication Disorders and Sciences (master's): Kenneth Simpson, Assistant Professor and Coordinator.
Computer Science (master's): William Wright, Professor and Chair.
Creative Writing (master's): Kevin Dettmar, Professor and Chair.
Economics (master's, Ph.D.): Richard Grabowski, Professor and Chair.
Education (Ph.D.): R. Keith Hillkirk, Professor and Dean of the College of Education.
- **Curriculum and Instruction** (master's, Ph.D.): William A. Henk, Professor and Chair.
- **Educational Administration** (master's, Ph.D.): Randy Dunn, Associate Professor and Chair.
- **Educational Psychology** (master's. Ph.D.): John Pohlmann, Professor and Chair.
- **Health Education** (master's, Ph.D.): David A. Birch, Professor and Chair.
- **Workforce Education and Development** (master's, Ph.D.): Fred Reneau, Professor and Chair.

Engineering:
- **Civil Engineering** (master's): Bruce De Vantier, Associate Professor and Interim Chair.
- **Electrical Engineering** (master's): Glafkos Galanos, Professor and Chair.
- **Mechanical Engineering** (master's): Suri Rajan, Professor and Acting Chair.
- **Mining Engineering** (master's): Satya Harpalani, Professor and Chair.

Engineering Science (Ph.D.): Hasan Sevim, Professor and Associate Dean of the College of Engineering.
English (master's, Ph.D.): Kevin Dettmar, Professor and Chair.
Environmental Resources and Policy (interdisciplinary Ph.D.):
- **Agribusiness Economics:** Steven Kraft, Professor and Chair.
- **Geography:** Christopher Lant, Professor and Chair.
- **Geology:** Michael Kruge, Professor and Chair.

Food and Nutrition (master's): Richard Roeder, Professor and Chair.
Foreign Languages and Literatures (French, Spanish) (master's): Frederick Betz, Professor and Chair.
Forestry (master's): John Phelps, Professor and Chair.
Geography (master's): Christopher Lant, Professor and Chair.
Geology (master's): Michael A. Kruge, Professor and Chair.
Higher Education (master's): Randy Dunn, Associate Professor and Chair.
History (master's, Ph.D.): Marjorie Morgan, Associate Professor and Chair.
Law (J.D.): Thomas F. Guernsey, Professor and Dean of the Law School.
Manufacturing Systems (master's): Gary Butson, Associate Professor and Chair.
Mass Communication and Media Arts (master's, Ph.D.): Thomas J. Johnson, Professor and Director.
Mathematics (master's, Ph.D.): Andrew Earnest, Professor and Chair.
Medicine (M.D.): Kevin Dorsey, Professor and Interim Dean of the School of Medicine.
Molecular Biology, Microbiology, and Biochemistry (M.S., Ph.D.): Peter Borgia, Professor and Director.
Molecular, Cellular, and Systemic Physiology (master's, Ph.D.): Richard Steger, Professor and Acting Chair.
Music (master's): Robert Weiss, Professor and Director.
Pharmacology (master's, Ph.D.): Carl Faingold, Professor and Chair.
Philosophy (master's, Ph.D.): Kenneth Stikkers, Professor and Chair.
Physical Education (master's): Peter Carroll, Assistant Professor and Acting Chair.
Physics (master's): Aldo Migone, Professor and Chair.
Plant Biology (master's, Ph.D.): Dale Vitt, Professor and Chair.
Plant and Soil Science (master's): John Russin, Professor and Chair.
Political Science (master's, Ph.D.): Uday Desai, Professor and Chair.
Psychology (master's, Ph.D.): Alan Vaux, Professor and Chair.
Public Administration (master's): Keith Snavely, Associate Professor and Director.
Recreation (master's): David A. Birch, Professor and Chair.
Rehabilitation (Rh.D.): James Bordieri, Professor and Interim Director of the Rehabilitation Institute.
Rehabilitation Administration and Services (master's): William Crimando, Professor and Coordinator.
Rehabilitation Counseling (master's): John Benshoff, Professor and Coordinator.
Social Work (master's): Sharon M. Keigher, Professor and Director of the School of Social Work.
Sociology (master's, Ph.D.): Robert Benford, Professor and Chair.
Special Education (master's): John Pohlmann, Professor and Chair.
Speech Communication (master's, Ph.D.): Nathan Stucky, Associate Professor and Chair.
Teaching English to Speakers of Other Languages (master's): Glenn Gilbert, Professor and Chair.
Theater (master's): Mark Varns, Associate Professor and Chair.
Workforce Education and Development (master's, Ph.D.): Fred Reneau, Professor and Chair.
Zoology (master's, Ph.D.): William Muhlach, Associate Professor and Chair.

Note: Students should see Mass Communication and Media Arts for cinema and photography, interactive multimedia, journalism, and telecommunications programs and Molecular, Cellular, and Systemic Physiology for physiology programs.

SOUTHERN ILLINOIS UNIVERSITY EDWARDSVILLE

Graduate Studies and Research

Programs of Study

Graduate Studies and Research awards the following degrees: Master of Arts in art therapy counseling, biological sciences, economics and finance, English, history, psychology, sociology, and speech communication; Master of Science in accountancy, biological sciences, chemistry, computer science, computing and information systems, economics and finance, environmental sciences, geographical studies, health care and nursing administration, mass communications, mathematics, medical-surgical nursing, nurse anesthesia, nurse educator, nurse practitioner studies, physics, psychiatric–mental health nursing, psychology, public health nursing, and speech language pathology; Master of Business Administration; Master of Fine Arts with studio areas in painting, sculpture, ceramics, textile art, drawing, printmaking, digital art, and metalsmithing or with a specialization in art education; Master of Marketing Research; Master of Music in music education or music performance; Master of Public Administration; Master of Science in Engineering in civil, electrical, or mechanical engineering; Master of Science in Education in educational administration, elementary education, instructional technology, kinesiology, secondary education with concentrations in eleven teaching areas, and special education; and the Master of Social Work. The Specialist degree is offered in educational administration and in school psychology. Cooperative doctoral study is offered in some degree programs through special arrangements with Southern Illinois University Carbondale. Postbaccalaureate and post-master's certificates are also offered in several fields.

Final examinations are required of all degree candidates. Projects that must be completed for master's programs include theses, research projects and papers, internships, practicums, exhibitions, or recitals.

Research Facilities

The University has laboratories for the technical sciences, education, human performance, anthropological studies, psychological studies, and urban studies, and it has practice facilities for fine arts, theater, and music. Lovejoy Library has more than 1 million bound volumes, 6,500 serials and periodicals, and 1.5 million microform units and maintains borrowing agreements with libraries locally and throughout the nation. Networked computers are available throughout the campus, including most offices, and numerous academic computing labs are available for use by graduate students. Problem-oriented programs have internship and practicum agreements with government, health, business, welfare, and educational agencies throughout the metropolitan St. Louis area.

Financial Aid

Teaching, research, and general assistantships are available, as are a number of special graduate awards, most of which carry stipends. Application for assistantships is made through department chairpersons. Application for some special awards is made through Graduate Studies and Research or Graduate Records. Student employment and various types of loans are available through the Office of Student Financial Aid. A first-semester residence scholarship for the fall semester is available for newly appointed, first-time graduate assistants.

Cost of Study

In 2002–03, tuition and fees for full-time graduate students are $2712 per academic year (fall and spring semesters) for Illinois residents and $5424 for the same time period for out-of-state students. Figures are based on 12 semester hours of enrollment each term and are subject to change. St. Louis–area residents taking 6 semester hours or fewer per term pay in-state tuition and fees.

Living and Housing Costs

In 2001–02, rent for on-campus apartments, managed by University Housing, range from $2746 for an academic year (fall through spring terms) for a single student sharing a furnished apartment with 3 other students to $889 a month for a three-bedroom furnished apartment for a family. (Rates are subject to change.) The Housing Office also has lists of available off-campus housing. Reasonably priced meals are served in the University cafeteria, and restaurant and meal plans are available through the University's dining services. Special housing arrangements can be made for graduate students.

Student Group

More than 12,400 students are enrolled, including 2,600 full- and part-time graduate students. Minority groups and other countries are well represented in the enrollment. Evening and weekend classes are offered to accommodate graduate students employed in area schools, businesses, and industries.

Location

The area surrounding the University is rich in cultural advantages. Three other major universities and a number of junior colleges share with Southern Illinois University Edwardsville (SIUE) a responsibility for offering advanced educational opportunities to many thousands of people. Live theater, art shows, museums, public parks, Cahokia Mounds, Missouri Botanical Gardens, and the Gateway Arch are some of the attractions of the general area. The St. Louis Symphony Orchestra offers both indoor and outdoor concerts. The area has a combination of farmland and urban concentrations. Thriving businesses and large industries offer opportunities for employment. Recreational opportunities for hikers, campers, and canoe enthusiasts exist in the wilderness preserves of the nearby Ozarks and southern Illinois. St. Louis, with its stadium, Edward Jones Dome, Savvis Center, Municipal Opera, and Lambert International Airport, is a 30-minute drive from the University.

The University

The University is situated on 2,660 acres of rolling hills. The main campus consists of large, modern buildings housing classrooms, laboratories, administrative offices, three undergraduate residence halls, an apartment complex, and a student center with cafeteria, restaurant, recreational facilities, bookstore, bowling alleys, and lounge areas. An athletics complex offers a wide range of recreational opportunities, including an indoor pool and student fitness center. Tennis courts, playing fields, and other recreational facilities are located on the periphery of the main campus. Low-cost bus service connects the campus with many nearby Illinois and Missouri centers and the University apartment complex. Ample parking space is provided for automobiles. An Art and Design Building opened in 1993, and an outstanding addition to campus music facilities opened in 1995. The School of Nursing has a new psychomotor skills lab, and the School of Engineering moved into a state-of-the-art building in fall 2000.

Applying

Students should file an application for admission with Graduate Admissions. Admission requirements vary for different programs. Requests for application forms, program information, and financial aid information should be sent to Graduate Admissions, Box 1047. Graduate applications and information are also available on the World Wide Web at http://www.register.siue.edu.

Correspondence and Information

Department Chairperson
Southern Illinois University Edwardsville
Edwardsville, Illinois 62026
World Wide Web: http://www.siue.edu/

FACULTY HEADS

THE GRADUATE SCHOOL

Dr. Stephen L. Hansen, Graduate Dean.
Dr. Gerald Pogatshnik, Associate Dean.

College of Arts and Sciences
Dr. M. Kent Neely, Dean.

Art and Design: Ivy Schroeder, Chair.
Art Therapy Counseling: Dr. Gussie Klorer, Program Director.
Biological Sciences: Dr. Richard Brugam, Chair.
Chemistry: Dr. James Eilers, Chair.
English Language and Literature: Dr. Charles Berger, Chair.
Environmental Sciences: Dr. Kevin Johnson, Program Director.
Geography: Dr. Wendy Shaw, Chair.
Historical Studies: Dr. Ellen Nore, Chair.
Mass Communications: Dr. Ralph Donald, Chair.
Mathematics: Dr. Ed Sewell, Chair.
Music: Dr. Ron Abraham, Chair.
Physics: Dr. Arthur Braundmeier, Chair.
Public Administration and Policy Analysis: Dr. T. R. Carr, Chair.
Social Work: Dr. Tom Regulus, Chair.
Sociology: Dr. Hugh Barlow, Chair.
Speech Communication: Dr. David Valley, Chair.

School of Business
Dr. Robert Carver, Dean.
Dr. Kathryn Martell, Associate Dean.

Accounting: Dr. Michael Costigan, Chair.
Business Administration: Dr. Kathryn Martell, Associate Dean.
Economics and Finance: Dr. Rik Hafer, Chair.
Management and Marketing: Dr. Donald E. Strickland, Chair.
Marketing Research: Dr. Donald E. Strickland, Chair; Dr. Jim Lynch, Graduate Program Director.

School of Education
Dr. Elliott Lessen, Dean.
Dr. Lela DeToye, Associate Dean; Dr. Don Baden, Associate Dean.

Curriculum and Instruction: Dr. Randy Smith, Chair.
Educational Leadership: Dr. Wayne Nelson, Chair.
Kinesiology and Health Education: Dr. John Baker, Chair.
Psychology: Dr. Bryce Sullivan, Chair.
Special Education and Communication Disorders: Dr. Thomas Shea, Chair.
Speech Language Pathology: Dr. Jean Harrison, Program Director.

School of Engineering
Dr. Paul Seaburg, Dean.

Civil Engineering: Dr. Nader Panahshahi, Chair.
Computing and Information Systems: Dr. Marilynn Livingston, Chair.
Electrical Engineering: Dr. Oktay Alkin, Chair.
Mechanical Engineering: Dr. Nader Saniei, Chair.

School of Nursing
Dr. Felissa L. Lashley, Dean.
Dr. Wendy Nehring, Acting Associate Dean.
Dr. Roslyn Sykes, Program Director.

SOUTHERN METHODIST UNIVERSITY

Graduate Studies

Programs of Study

Southern Methodist University offers a wide array of graduate degree programs. Dedman College of Humanities and Sciences offers the Master of Arts (M.A.) in anthropology (medical), applied economics, biology, economics, English, history, medieval studies, psychology (clinical-counseling), and religious studies; the Master of Science (M.S.) in applied geophysics, biology, chemistry, computational and applied mathematics, geology, geophysics, physics, and statistical science; the Master of Bilingual Education (M.B.E.); and the Doctor of Philosophy (Ph.D.) in anthropology, biology, computational and applied mathematics, economics, geology, geophysics, history, physics, psychology (general, clinical), religious studies, and statistical science.

The School of Engineering offers the Master of Science (M.S.) with majors in applied science, computer science, environmental systems management, facilities management, manufacturing systems management, operations research, software engineering, systems engineering, and telecommunications. In addition, the following are offered: the Master of Science in Civil Engineering with a specialization in structural engineering, Master of Science in Computer Engineering (M.S.C.E.), Master of Science in Electrical Engineering (M.S.E.E.), Master of Science in Engineering Management (M.S.E.M.), Master of Science in Environmental Engineering (M.S.En.E.), and the Master of Science in Mechanical Engineering (M.S.M.E.). The Doctor of Philosophy (Ph.D.) is offered in applied science, computer science, computer engineering, electrical engineering, mechanical engineering, and operations research; and the Doctor of Engineering (D.Engr.) in engineering management.

Meadows School of the Arts offers programs leading to the degrees of Master of Arts (M.A.) in art history and TV/radio; Master of Fine Arts (M.F.A.) in art, dance, and theater; Master of Music (M.M.) in choral conducting, music composition, music education, music history and literature, music performance, music theory, instrumental conducting, and piano performance and pedagogy; and Master of Music Therapy (M.M.T.).

The Edwin L. Cox School of Business offers the Master of Business Administration (M.B.A.) in general business and a Master of Science in accounting.

Through the School of Law, programs are available leading to the Juris Doctor (J.D.), Master of Laws (LL.M.) in comparative and international law and taxation, and Doctor of the Science of Law (S.J.D.).

Perkins School of Theology offers programs leading to the degrees of Master of Divinity (M.Div.), Doctor of Ministry (D.Min.), Master of Sacred Music (M.S.M.), Master of Religious Education (M.R.E.), and Master of Theological Studies (M.T.S.).

Dual degrees are available between economics and law (M.A., J.D.), business and law (J.D., M.B.A.), and business and arts administration (M.A., M.B.A.). An interdisciplinary program leading to the Master of Liberal Arts (M.L.A.) degree is available through the Division of Evening and Summer Studies.

Research Facilities

The University provides local computing facilities to handle most research projects. The campus is served by a distributed computing environment composed of equipment made by DEC, Sun, IBM, and Hewlett-Packard. These machines provide e-mail, World Wide Web access, and computing resources to the University community. Access to these machines is available via Telnet on the University network or through dialup connections. PPP access is available for persons who have a 14,400 kbs or a higher speed modem. Most academic research is run on one of the several DEC Alpha 2100s. The School of Engineering hosts a DEC Alpha 8200 with 2 GB of main memory and 9 GB of swap space for general campus computing of large jobs, which must be submitted on a batch basis. The school also provides engineering students with a large number of networked DEC, Sun, and PC workstations. The Institute for the Study of Earth and Man operates many Sun Workstations with related servers. SMU's libraries, with more than 7,000 periodicals and nearly 3 million volumes, provide extensive resources for research.

SMU provides many laboratories and other research facilities for students—the Solid State Technology Laboratory; the Fort Burgwin Research Center in Taos, New Mexico; the Dallas Seismological Observatory; the Geothermal Laboratory; the Engineering Material and Failure Analysis Laboratory; the Computational/Graphics Laboratory; the Robotics (CAM) Laboratory; and the Thermal Design Laboratory. A herbarium with an extensive plant collection is located at the Botanical Research Institute of Texas, Fort Worth.

Financial Aid

A number of tuition fellowships and partial and full teaching and research assistantships are available. Teaching and research assistantships can cover tuition and fees and paid stipends in the range of $4000 to $15,000 in 2002–03. Graduate students' spouses find that Dallas offers abundant opportunities for employment in a wide variety of fields.

Cost of Study

Tuition and fees vary by school. In 2002–03, Dedman College tuition is approximately $813 per semester credit hour and fees total $104 per semester credit hour.

Living and Housing Costs

For 2002–03, the cost of on-campus housing is approximately $2200 per person (double occupancy) each semester. Married student housing (one-bedroom apartment) is $4500 per academic year. Other on-campus room plans are available. Board, including sales tax, costs between $1300 and $1500 per semester.

Student Group

Of the approximately 10,000 students enrolled at SMU, more than 5,000 are graduate students in the humanities, sciences, social sciences, business, arts, engineering, theology, and law. Students come from all states and many other countries.

Student Outcomes

SMU graduates seeking employment locally have the advantage of looking in a city that has a diversified and healthy economy. Dallas is home to several corporate headquarters, including J. C. Penney and EDS. There are employment opportunities in the areas of business, banking, communications, high-tech, and manufacturing, with top companies like Nationsbank, Arthur Andersen, and Texas Instruments recruiting on campus. The Career Center, the M.B.A. Center, and the Law School Placement Service are some of the offices that assist students in the job placement process. Databases in these offices also include listings for research and teaching positions around the country.

Location

SMU is located 5 miles north of downtown Dallas on a 164-acre campus. Dallas is the eighth-largest city in the United States, and is the home of the nation's second leading fashion and apparel center, the third-largest concentration of high technology firms, and the fifth-largest financial center. Beyond the campus, the Dallas area provides an abundance of affordable housing, outstanding schools, shopping, public transportation, and cultural and entertainment opportunities.

The University

Established in 1911 by the United Methodist Church, SMU is a nonsectarian institution dedicated to academic excellence and freedom of inquiry. It has six undergraduate, graduate, and professional schools.

Applying

Students of proven ability with undergraduate preparation in appropriate fields are eligible to apply. For application materials and information, students should write to the admission office of the intended school of study. SMU does not discriminate on the basis of race, color, national or ethnic origin, sex, age, or disability.

Correspondence and Information

Admissions Office of (specify school)
Southern Methodist University
Dallas, Texas 75275
World Wide Web: http://www.smu.edu

For Dedman College:
Office of Research and Graduate Studies
P.O. Box 750240
Dallas, Texas 75275-0240
E-mail: smugrad@mail.smu.edu

FACULTY HEADS

Dean of Research and Graduate Studies: U. Narayan Bhat, Ph.D.

Meadows School of the Arts: Carole Brandt, Ph.D., Dean.
Art: James W. Sullivan, M.F.A.
Art History: Janis Bergman-Carton, Ph.D.
Arts Administration and Corporate Communications: Gregory Poggi, Ph.D.
Dance: Jeremy Blanton
Cinema-Television: Frank P. Tomasulo
Music: Robert Stroker, Ph.D.
Theatre: Kevin Paul Hofeditz, M.F.A.

Edwin L. Cox School of Business: Albert W. Niemi Jr., Ph.D., Dean.
Accounting/Law and Taxation: Joseph Magliolo III, Ph.D.
Business Policy/Organizational Behavior: Robin Pinkley, Ph.D.
Finance: Marc Reinganum, Ph.D.
Information Systems and Operations Management: Amit Basu, Ph.D.
Marketing: Daniel Howard, Ph.D.
Real Estate/Insurance/Business Law: William Brueggeman, Ph.D.

Dedman College: Jasper Neel, Ph.D., Dean.
Anthropology: Caroline Brettell, Ph.D.
Biology: Lawrence S. Ruben, Ph.D.
Chemistry: Edward R. Biehl, Ph.D.
Economics: Nathan Balke, Ph.D.
English: Dennis A. Foster, Ph.D.
Geological Sciences: Robert T. Gregory, Ph.D.
History: James K. Hopkins, Ph.D.
Mathematics: Douglas A. Reinelt, Ph.D.
Medieval Studies: Bonnie Wheeler, Ph.D., Director.
Physics: Fredrick Olness, Ph.D.
Psychology: Alan S. Brown, Ph.D.
Religious Studies: William S. Babcock, Ph.D.
Statistics: Richard F. Gunst, Ph.D.
Master of Liberal Arts: Robert A. Patterson, Ph.D., Dean.

School of Engineering: Stephen A. Szygenda, Ph.D., Dean.
Computer Science and Engineering: Hesham El-Rewini, Ph.D.
Electrical Engineering: Jerry D. Gibson, Ph.D.
Engineering Management, Information and Systems: Richard Barr, Ph.D.
Environmental and Civil Engineering: Edward Forest, Ph.D.
Mechanical Engineering: Yildirim Hurmuzlu, Ph.D.

School of Law: John B. Attanasio, LL.M., Dean.

Perkins School of Theology: Robin W. Lovin, Ph.D., Dean.

Dallas Hall Quadrangle, Southern Methodist University, Dallas, Texas.

SOUTHERN POLYTECHNIC STATE UNIVERSITY

Graduate Programs

Programs of Study

Southern Polytechnic State University (SPSU) offers the Master of Science degree, with majors in computer science, construction, engineering technology, management, quality assurance, software engineering, information technology, and technical and professional communication. The M.S. in computer science is designed to enhance career options for a broad mix of students, from those with an academic background in computer science and just beginning their careers to those who have worked for years as computer professionals and may have academic credentials in other fields. The M.S. in construction offers education in construction and project management to practicing construction professionals who are educated in related disciplines yet need or desire more knowledge in the construction process, to professionals who are educated in construction or construction management and wish to pursue the subject in greater depth, and to those who hold a baccalaureate degree and are actively pursuing a construction industry career but lack construction and project management education. The M.S. in engineering technology is offered to meet the needs of individuals who wish to pursue advanced studies in modern electrical, electronic, or computer technologies in order to fulfill their personal or career goals. The M.S. in management prepares managers to identify, acquire, and assimilate optimum technology requirements into products and operations, all of which are essential for a technology-intensive firm. The M.S. in quality assurance is offered in order to meet an established need in both manufacturing and service industries and focuses on total quality management and such analytical methods as statistics, process, analysis, and problem-solving techniques. The M.S. in technical and professional communication educates those who seek to begin their careers in the field of technical communication and provides a useful credential for current technical communicators who need advanced training to move ahead in their careers. The Master of Science in Software Engineering (M.S.S.E.) program meets the high demand for professional degrees in software engineering within the context of a nontraditional audience. It uses the life-cycle concept from traditional engineering, with an emphasis on specification, design, and implementation, but calls on the focused application of computer science concepts rather than those of traditional engineering. The Master of Science in Information Technology (M.S.I.T.) program focuses on the management of computer information technology incorporating both management and computer skills.

Research Facilities

SPSU maintains several computing facilities in the Academic Building and the Crawford Laboratory Building. These facilities provide computing resources for most computer-related courses at SPSU and contain an IBM RS6000 model 550 minicomputer, a DOS PC-based microcomputer lab, and a projects lab. Access to the academic computer is provided in a large user area that contains more than twenty text-based terminals, a number of graphics-based terminals and workstations, two 600-line-per-minute printers, and a laser printer. Via the RS6000, users can also connect to PeachNet, the regional network of the University System of Georgia, which provides full access to the Internet. The library collection consists of some 110,000 cataloged volumes, more than 1,500 periodical and serial titles, stand-alone CD-ROMs, various microforms, U.S. Geological Survey maps for the state of Georgia, and a circulating reserve collection of texts, tests, and tools. The automated library union catalog, On Line Library Information (OLLI), lists materials held by more than forty libraries throughout the state. Materials from these and other libraries nationwide may be obtained through the interlibrary loan service in the reference section. The Center for Quality Excellence (CQE) helps local and regional businesses become more effective competitors in the global marketplace. With the participation of the business community, the CQE assists organizations (private and public) with implementing total quality management concepts and methodologies as well as ISO 9000 and ISO 14000.

Financial Aid

Financial assistance includes loans, scholarships, part-time employment, and federal programs. Graduate students are eligible for Federal Perkins Loans, William D. Ford Direct Loans, and Stafford Direct Loans. Applicants for loans must submit the Free Application for Federal Student Aid (FAFSA). Teaching and research assistantships are available and are administered by each academic department. Availability and application procedures are available through the academic department of interest. Inquiries regarding financial assistance should be directed to the Office of Scholarships and Financial Aid.

Cost of Study

For the 2001–02 academic year, graduate tuition for Georgia residents was $2762. Out-of-state students paid $9722 per year. Books cost approximately $800.

Living and Housing Costs

Residence halls for single students are available on campus. In 2000–01, rental rates are approximately $2200 per year. The on-campus University Commons Apartments has annual rental rates of $4140 per student (two-bedroom unit) and $3540 per student (four-bedroom unit).

Student Group

The graduate programs at Southern Polytechnic State University are designed to enhance career options for a broad mix of students. In 2001–02, the University had an enrollment of approximately 3,600, including 600 graduate students.

Location

Southern Polytechnic is located in Marietta, one of the fastest-growing areas of Georgia, about 20 minutes from downtown Atlanta. The Cobb County Campus sits on 232 acres of wooded property, 90 acres of which are developed.

The University

Founded in 1948 as a school that offered two-year programs as part of Georgia Tech, Southern Polytechnic was named a senior college in 1970. It became independent of Georgia Tech in 1980 and began offering master's degrees in 1986. It was named Southern Polytechnic State University in 1996.

Applying

Admission to the graduate programs is based on the applicant's educational record, scores on the General Test of the Graduate Record Examinations or other specified test, and recommendations. Applicants must have a baccalaureate degree from an accredited school. Applications and supporting credentials should be received in the Office of Admissions by July 1 for fall semester, by November 1 for spring semester, and by April 1 for the summer term. Applications for financial aid are accepted at any time, but those received by March 15 for the following academic year are given priority.

Correspondence and Information

Office of Admissions
Southern Polytechnic State University
1100 South Marietta Parkway
Marietta, Georgia 30060-2896

Telephone: 770-528-7281
800-635-3204 (toll-free)
E-mail: admissions@spsu.edu
World Wide Web: http://www.spsu.edu

THE FACULTY

Listed below are the graduate coordinators for each of the graduate program areas.

Computer Science: Dr. Venu Dasigi, telephone: 770-528-7406, e-mail: compsci@spsu.edu.
Construction: Dr. Brian C. Moore, telephone: 770-528-3715, e-mail: bmoore@spsu.edu.
Engineering Technology: Dr. Omar Zia, telephone: 770-528-7308, e-mail: ozia@spsu.edu, Web site: http://ecet.spsu.edu.
Information Technology: Dr. Rebecca Rutherfoord, telephone: 770-528-7400, e-mail: brutherf@spsu.edu.
Management: Dr. Mohammed Obeidat, telephone: 770-528-7440, e-mail: mobeidat@spsu.edu.
Quality Assurance: Professor Lawrence Aft, telephone: 770-528-7243, e-mail: msqa@spsu.edu, Web site: http://www.msqa.edu.
Software Engineering: Dr. Venu Dasigi, telephone: 770-528-7406, email: compsci@spsu.edu.
Technical and Professional Communication: Dr. Mark Stevens, telephone: 770-528-7202, e-mail: mstevens@spsu.edu.

SOUTHWESTERN COLLEGE

Graduate Studies

Programs of Study

The purpose of the master's programs at Southwestern College is to prepare mental health professionals in counseling and art therapy. Graduate degrees at Southwestern College are based on the attainment of educational objectives in three areas: theoretical knowledge, applied skills, and character strength.

Both master's programs are two academic years in length. In year one, the emphasis is on students' exploration of their personal psychological transformation. This reflective emphasis provides insight into the nature of character development and the human condition. A foundation is laid for understanding the nature of change and its application in the helping professions. In year two, the emphasis is on students' professional identity and the development of clinical skills. Students acquire the competencies needed for facilitating change in others.

The master's program in counseling integrates effective modes of counseling, incorporating all levels of psychological functioning: imaginal, emotional, mental, and spiritual. This holistic approach fosters a creative sense of self and the potential for change.

The master's program in art therapy emphasizes the use of the visual arts as a therapeutic approach in clinical, educational, forensic, and rehabilitation settings. While visual art is the primary therapeutic modality, the creative process is supported by classroom instruction and experiences in the use of drama, movement, and music therapy.

Certificates in art therapy, grief counseling, school counseling, and action methods are also offered.

Research Facilities

The Quimby Memorial Library supports teaching and research in counseling, art therapy, applied psychology, and experiential education. The library contains approximately 14,000 books, journals, and audiovisual materials. Patrons have access to interlibrary loan and Pro Quest through the New Mexico State Library. The Quimby Memorial Library houses the second-largest metaphysical collection in the United States.

Financial Aid

Financial aid programs include Subsidized and Unsubsidized Federal Direct Student Loans, scholarships, and payment plans. A Free Application for Federal Student Aid (FAFSA) must be submitted at least three months before admission in order to have a loan guarantee in place at the time of registration. For the 2001–02 academic year, the maximum amount potentially awarded to a student in combined Subsidized and Unsubsidized Federal Direct Student Loans was $18,500. Students and their families should investigate local sources, such as service organizations, churches, Native American tribal affiliations, corporations, and foundations for scholarship and loan funds. A limited number of scholarships are available, including quarterly Southwestern College Scholarships.

Cost of Study

The current cost is $245 per quarter unit. The cost of study is dependent upon the number of units taken each quarter. Full-time study is $11,760 per year. Additional expenses for books and supplies are approximately $1000 per year. A graduation fee of $80 is required.

Living and Housing Costs

There is no housing available on campus. There are numerous apartment complexes nearby with rentals from the $550 to $800 price range, depending on size and number of bedrooms. There are several property managers available to help students find housing in the Santa Fe area. For more information, students should contact the Director of Admissions.

Student Group

Students choose Southwestern College because of the unique transformational nature of the programs offered. The age of students ranges from the early 20s to students in their 60s. Younger students tend to come directly from undergraduate programs and are preparing to enter their first profession. Older students have often had one or more careers and a wealth of life experience. The unifying characteristic of all students at the College is the commitment to self-knowledge and the desire to be of service to others.

Student Outcomes

Southwestern College graduates are uniquely qualified to take their place as transformational leaders in the world. Counseling graduates are well prepared to fulfill licensure requirements in mental health counseling. Graduates of the counseling and art therapy programs pursue successful careers in educational, mental health, and residential treatment settings and private practice. Graduates are able to apply for licensure in the state of New Mexico and other states. Art therapy graduates are eligible to apply for registration with the Art Therapy Credentials Board (ATCB).

Location

Southwestern College's campus is located in Santa Fe, the capital of New Mexico. At an altitude of 7,000 feet, Santa Fe offers stunning high-desert vistas and breathtaking sunsets. A mild four-season climate boasts 300 days of sunshine each year. This tricultural area offers outdoor recreation, museums, stage productions, the Santa Fe Opera, and Indian and Spanish markets.

The College

The roots of Southwestern College can be traced to 1945, when a group of forward-thinking individuals began a collection of metaphysical books to establish the Quimby Memorial Library. The collection included the manuscripts of Phineas Parkhurst Quimby, an American Transcendentalist. Quimby believed that the mind had great healing powers in regard to physical illness and that maintaining the mind/body connection could bring a person into balance. In 1976, Southwestern College, then called Quimby College, was dedicated. Today, the College continues to teach in a holistic, person-centered, and experiential way. The college is accredited by The Higher Learning Commission, and is a member of the North Central Association of Colleges and Schools (NCA). The art therapy program is approved by the American Art Therapy Association.

Applying

Southwestern College accepts students who have the motivation for self-discovery, a love of learning, and a quest for deeper meaning in their lives. Applicants are required to submit an application, a $50 application fee, a personal statement, a current resume, transcripts from each college previously attended, and three letters of recommendation. In addition, art therapy applicants must submit a portfolio of 12 to 15 slides of recent work. An admissions interview is required. Students may be admitted during the fall, winter, and spring quarters.

Correspondence and Information

Admissions
Southwestern College
P.O. Box 4788
Santa Fe, New Mexico 87502-4788
Telephone: 505-471-5756 Ext. 26
877-471-5756 Ext. 26 (toll-free)
E-mail: admissions@swc.edu
World Wide Web: http://www.swc.edu

FACULTY AND THEIR RESEARCH

Stephen Barrilleaux, Ph.D., Catholic University; Licensed Psychologist.
Gail Bell, M.A., New Mexico; LPCC, LPAT, LADAC. Addictions and art therapy.
Deborah Bergeron, M.A., New Mexico; ATR, LPAT, LPCC.
Rosvita Botkin, M.A., Lesley; Certified Expressive Therapist, ATR, LPAT, LPCC. Jungian art therapy.
Alan Brody, Ph.D. CUNY Graduate Center; LISW, CADC. Psychoanalytical psychotherapy and addictions.
Marylou Butler, Ph.D., Arizona State; Licensed Psychologist. Blending self and transpersonal psychology in psychotherapy.
Liz Cervio, M.S., St. Thomas; CADAC, LMFAT. Addictions.
Wendy Chapin, M.A., Southwestern (New Mexico). Performing arts.
Kate Cook, M.A., Antioch (Ohio); Certified Psychodrama Practitioner, LPCC, CPP, TEP. Psychodrama.
Larry Dettweiler, Ph.D., Minnesota; LPCC. Jungian and transpersonal approaches to developmental psychology.
Miles Diller, Ph.D., DePaul; Licensed Psychologist, Licensed School Psychologist, Certified Gestalt Therapist.
Helaine Foster, Ph.D., Pacifica Graduate; LPCC.
Cynthia Fulreader, M.A., Southwestern; LPC.
Geri Glover, Ph.D., North Texas; LPCC, NCC, Registered Play Therapist.
Molly Hunt, Psy.D., Denver; Licensed Clinical Psychologist.
Luanne Lee, M.A., Institute of Imaginal Studies; ATR-BC.
Louis R. Levin, Ph.D., Maryland; Licensed Psychologist. School psychology.
Lou Montgomery, M.F.A., Texas; M.A., Santa Monica. Expressive therapies.
Jay Navarro, Ph.D., California School of Professional Psychology–Fresno; LPCC. Native American medicine ways.
Katherine M. Ninos, M.A., Southwestern (New Mexico); LPC. Consciousness studies and transpersonal psychology.
Beth Prothro, Ph.D., Union (Ohio); LMHC, LMFT. Gestalt psychology.
Kate Rogers, M.S., St. Mary's (Minnesota).
Maria L. Santa-Maria, D.Min., San Francisco Theological Seminary; LPCC.
Janet Schreiber, Ph.D., Berkeley. Grief counseling and death education.
Kris Sly-Linton, M.A., New Mexico; ATR-BC, LPAT. Addictions and corrections.
George Tate, Th.D., Iliff School of Theology. Multicultural issues.
Christine Tiernan, M.A., Antioch (Ohio); ATR. Bereavement in art therapy.
Rober Waterman, Ed.D., New Mexico State; LPCC.
Susan Wilkinson, Ph.D., New Mexico; Licensed in Special Education, ATR-BC, LPAT. Program evaluation, assessment, and research in art therapy.

SOUTHWEST MISSOURI STATE UNIVERSITY

Graduate College

Programs of Study

Southwest Missouri State University (SMSU) offers forty-two graduate programs leading to the Master of Accountancy (M.Acc.), Master of Arts (M.A.), Master of Arts in Teaching (M.A.T.), Master of Business Administration (M.B.A.), Master of Health Administration (M.H.A.), Master of International Affairs and Administration (M.I.A.A.), Master of Music (M.M.), Master of Natural and Applied Science (M.N.A.S.), Master of Physical Therapy (M.P.T.), Master of Public Administration (M.P.A.), Master of Public Health (M.P.H.), Master of Science (M.S.), Master of Science in Education (M.S.Ed.), Master of Science in Nursing (M.S.N.), Master of Social Work (M.S.W.), Specialist in Education (Ed.S.), and Doctorate in Educational Leadership (Ed.D.), and Doctorate in Audiology (Au.D.) degrees. Programs of study are available in accounting, administrative studies, biology, business administration, cell and molecular biology, chemistry, communication, communication sciences and disorders, computer information systems, counseling, defense and strategic studies, educational administration, elementary education, English, health administration, health promotion and wellness management, history, instructional media technology, international affairs and administration, materials science, mathematics, music, natural and applied science, nurse anesthesia, nursing, physical therapy, physician assistant studies, plant science, psychology, public administration, public health, reading, religious studies, resource planning, secondary education, social work, special education, teaching, theater, and writing. All programs are accredited by the North Central Association of Colleges and Schools, and many programs are professionally accredited.

SMSU also offers accelerated master's programs and for-credit graduate certificate programs. Accelerated master's programs enable outstanding SMSU undergraduate students to begin graduate work while completing their undergraduate program. Accelerated master's programs are in the areas of accounting, business administration, cell and molecular biology, chemistry, materials science, mathematics, nursing, and public administration. The graduate certificate programs include conflict and dispute resolution, instructional technology specialist, post-master's nursing educator, post-master's nurse practitioner, sports management, project management, and sports management.

Research Facilities

The University libraries have comprehensive electronic resources, including an online catalog, CD-ROM databases, and Internet accessibility. SMSU is a member of the Center for Research Libraries and is a government document depository. Special facilities include a K–12 laboratory school and ten research centers, including the Center for Business and Economic Development, the Small Business Development Center, and the Center for Resource Planning and Management.

Financial Aid

Financial assistance is available through a variety of scholarships, graduate assistantships, grants, loans, and work-study programs. Most students who receive financial assistance do so through teaching or research graduate assistantships. Graduate assistantship stipends range from $6150 to $8200 for the nine-month academic year (2002–03) plus a full tuition scholarship (resident or nonresident) for up to 15 hours a semester. Students on academic-year assistantships also receive a 6-hour tuition scholarship for the summer term. Summer assistantships also are available. To be eligible for an assistantship, a student must be admitted to a graduate program and have a minimum GPA of 3.0 (cumulative or in the last 60 hours of course work) or a minimum GPA of 3.0 in 9 or more hours of graduate work.

Cost of Study

In 2002–03, graduate tuition is $148 per credit hour for in-state residents and $296 per credit hour for nonresidents. Internet courses in the administrative studies program are $165 per credit hour, courses in computer information systems are $395 per credit hour, and all other Internet courses are $215 per credit hour. Fees are subject to change at any time.

Living and Housing Costs

The average cost per year for room and board in residence halls is $4248. Exact rates depend on room style and meal plan. Furnished apartments are available for graduate, married, and nontraditional students for $353 to $470 per month. University and privately owned apartments are within a reasonable distance of the campus.

Student Group

Graduate student enrollment is 3,105, and the total student population is 18,252. Graduate student are from across the United States and from fifty-two countries.

Location

Southwest Missouri State University is located in Springfield, the third-largest population center in Missouri and a metropolitan service region of 250,000. Located in the heart of the Ozarks recreational area, the University is within easy driving distance of numerous recreational lakes, streams, and parks. The community of Springfield is supported by an industrial/manufacturing base and an expanding service industry in tourism, with people drawn by the natural beauty and recreation of the Ozarks and the musical attractions in nearby Branson. Springfield has an extensive health and medical economy serving southwest Missouri, northwest Arkansas, southeast Kansas, and northeast Oklahoma.

The University

Southwest Missouri State University was founded in 1905 and has evolved into a multipurpose institution that provides diverse instructional, research, and service programs. Today, it is a comprehensive university with the second-largest student enrollment in the state.

Applying

Southwest Missouri State University invites applications from students with strong records of undergraduate performance. A fee of $25 is required at the time of application, and the application is not complete until official transcripts of prior work are received. Accountancy, M.B.A., and CIS majors must submit official GMAT scores, and most other programs require GRE scores. The application deadline to avoid a late fee is three weeks prior to the beginning of the desired semester of entrance; however, students are strongly encouraged to submit required paperwork before this date to allow for appropriate processing time. Many programs admit students only once a year and have specific deadlines. Prospective students should refer to program admission requirements. The graduate catalog and admission application can be accessed at the World Wide Web site listed below.

Correspondence and Information

Frank Einhellig, Dean
Graduate College
Southwest Missouri State University
901 South National Avenue
Springfield, Missouri 65807
Telephone: 417-836-5335
417-836-4770 (MO Relay TDD)
866-SMS-GRAD (toll-free)
Fax: 417-836-6888
E-mail: graduatecollege@smsu.edu
World Wide Web: http://www.graduate.smsu.edu

FIELDS OF STUDY AND FACULTY ADVISERS

E-mail addresses of faculty members are in parentheses. All phone numbers are in area code 417.

Graduate College: Frank Einhellig, Dean (fae942f@smsu.edu); Charlene Berquist, Associate Dean (cab293f@smsu.edu); 836-5335.

Administrative Studies (M.S.): John Bourhis, Program Director (jsb806f@smsu.edu); 836-6390. This program is available on campus and as an Internet program. Options in applied communication, criminal justice, environmental management, and project management.

College of Arts and Letters: David O. Belcher, Dean (dob458f@smsu.edu); 836-5247.

Communication (M.A.): Carey Adams, Department Head (caa074f@smsu.edu); Randy Dillon, Program Coordinator; 836-5218.

English (M.A.): W. D. Blackmon, Department Head (wdb898f@smsu.edu); Jane Hoogestraat, Graduate Director (jah905f@smsu.edu); 836-5107. Tracks in literature, creative writing, and TESOL.

Music (M.M.): John Prescott, Department Head (jsp304f@smsu.edu); Robert Quebbeman, Graduate Advisor (rcq416f@smsu.edu); 836-5648. Program accredited by the National Association of Schools of Music. Options in conducting, theory and composition, pedagogy, performance, and education.

Theatre (M.A.): Robert Bradley, Department Head and Graduate Advisor. (rhb072f@smsu.edu); 836-5268. Program accredited by the NAST.

Writing (M.A.): Department of English; W. D. Blackmon, Department Head (wdb898f@smsu.edu); Jane Hoogestraat, Graduate Director (jah905f@smsu.edu); 836-5107. Tracks in rhetoric and composition and technical and professional writing.

College of Business Administration: Ronald Bottin, Dean (rrb639f@smsu.edu); 836-4408. Programs are accredited by AACSB International–The Association to Advance Collegiate Schools of Business.

Accounting (M.Acc.): Phillip Harsha, Director (pdh480f@smsu.edu); John Williams, Graduate Program Advisor (jrw783f@smsu.edu); 836-5414.

Business Administration (M.B.A.): D. Michael Fields, Associate Dean and Graduate Program Director (dmf603f@smsu.edu); 836-5646. Concentrations in economics, computer information systems, finance and general business, management, and marketing and quantitative analysis.

Computer Information Systems (M.S.): Jerry Chin, Department Head (jmc808f@smsu.edu); David Meinert, Graduate Advisor (dbm946f@smsu.edu); 836-4131. This program is available on the Internet.

Health Administration (M.H.A.): Department of Management; Barry Wisdom, Department Head (blw355f@smsu.edu); Robert Lunn, Graduate Director (rol561f@smsu.edu); 836-5415.

College of Education: David Hough, Dean (dah315f@smsu.edu); 836-5254. Programs accredited by NCATE and the Missouri State Department of Elementary and Secondary Education.

Counseling (M.S.): Charles Barké, Department Head (crb024f@smsu.edu); 836-5449. Options in secondary and elementary school counseling and community agency.

Educational Administration (Ed.S. and M.S.Ed.): William Agnew, Department Head (wja656f@smsu.edu); 836-5392. Options in elementary, secondary, special, and vocational education and superintendent studies.

Educational Leadership (Ed.D.): William Agnew, Department Head (wja656f@smsu.edu); Barbara Martin, Program Director (bnm919f@smsu.edu); 836-5392. Cooperative program with the University of Missouri–Columbia (UMC). The degree is conferred by UMC.

Elementary Education (M.S.Ed.): School of Teacher Education, Christopher Craig, Associate Dean and Director (cjc886f@smsu.edu); Cindy Wilson, Program Director (ckw081f@smsu.edu); 836-5796.

Instructional Media Technology (M.S.Ed.) and Graduate Certificate Program in Instructional Technology Specialist: School of Teacher Education, Christopher Craig, Associate Dean and Director (cjc886f@smsu.edu); Roger Tipling, Graduate Advisor (rmt853f@smsu.edu); 836-6769. Program is accredited by the AECT.

Reading (M.S.Ed.): School of Teacher Education, Christopher Craig, Associate Dean and Director (cjc886f@smsu.edu); Deanne Camp, Graduate Director (jdc628f@smsu.edu). Program is accredited by IRA.

Secondary Education (M.S.Ed.): For information, students should contact the area of emphasis department or Derek Mallett, Coordinator of Admissions and Recruitment (drm230t@smsu.edu); 417-836-5335 or 866-SMS-GRAD. Areas of emphasis include agriculture, art, biology, business, chemistry, earth science, English, geography, history, industrial education, mathematics, modern and classical languages, music, natural science, physical education, physics, political science, social science, speech and theater, and vocational family and consumer studies.

Special Education (M.S.Ed.): School of Teacher Education, Christopher Craig, Associate Dean and Director (cjc886f@smsu.edu); Linda Garrison-Kane, Graduate Advisor (lgh216f@smsu.edu)836-6769. Program is accredited by CEP.

Teaching (M.A.T.): School of Teacher Education, Christopher Craig, Associate Dean and Director (cjc886f@smsu.edu).

College of Health and Human Services: Cynthia Pemberton, Acting Dean (clp473f@smsu.edu); 836-4176.

Cell and Molecular Biology (M.S.): Department of Biomedical Sciences; Harold Falls, Department Head (hbf931f@smsu.edu); Al Gordon, Graduate Advisor (arg372f@smsu.edu); 836-5603.

Communication Sciences and Disorders (M.S.): Neil DeSarno, Department Head (njd579f@smsu.edu); 836-5368. Program options in audiology, education of the hearing impaired, and speech-language pathology. Programs are accredited by the American Speech-Language-Hearing Association and the Council of Education of the Deaf.

Health Promotion and Wellness Management (M.S.): Department of Health, Physical Education and Recreation, Alex Trombetta, Acting Department Head (adt964f@smsu.edu); Dalen Duitsman, Graduate Director (dmd271f@smsu.edu); 836-5370.

Nurse Anesthesia (M.S.): Department of Biomedical Sciences; Harold Falls, Department Head (hbf931f@smsu.edu); Al Gordon, Graduate Advisor (arg372f@smsu.edu); 836-5603. Program is accredited by Council on Accreditation of Nurse Anesthesia Education Programs.

Nursing (M.S.N.) and Graduate Certificate Programs for Nurse Educator and Nurse Practitioner: Kathryn Hope, Department Head and Program Director (klh895f@smsu.edu); 836-5310. Program is accredited by NLNAC. Options in family nurse practitioner and nurse educator.

Physical Therapy (M.P.T.): Mark Horacek, Department Head and Director (mjh421f@smsu.edu); 836-6179. Program is accredited by CAPTE.

Physician Assistant Studies (M.S.): Patricia Ragan, Department Head and Director (pdr692f@smsu.edu); 836-6151.

Psychology (M.S.): Fred Maxwell, Department Head (frm650f@smsu.edu); 836-5797. Industrial/organizational, clinical, and general psychology options.

Public Health (M.P.H.): Department of Health, Physical Education and Recreation; Alex Trombetta, Acting Department Head (adt964f@smsu.edu); Dalen Duitsman, Graduate Director (dmd271f@smsu.edu); 836-5370.

Social Work (M.S.W.): Anne B. Summers, Acting Director (abs901f@smsu.edu); Mary Ann Jennings, M.S.W. Program Director (maj398f@smsu.edu). Program is accredited by the Council on Social Work Education.

Sports Management Graduate Certificate Program: Department of Health, Physical Education and Recreation; Alex Trombetta, Acting Department Head (adt964f@smsu.edu); 836-5370.

College of Humanities and Public Affairs: Lorene H. Stone, Dean (lhs301f@smsu.edu).

Defense and Strategic Studies (M.S.): William Van Cleave, Department Head (vam979f@smsu.edu); 836-4137.

History (M.A.): Marc Cooper, Department Head (mac566f@smsu.edu); William Piston, Graduate Advisor (wgp936f@smsu.edu); 836-5511.

International Affairs and Administration (M.I.A.A.): Department of Political Science; Beat Kernen, Acting Department Head (brk265f@smsu.edu); Dennis Hickey, Graduate Advisor (dvh804f@smsu.edu)836-5630.

Public Administration (M.P.A.): Department of Political Science; Beat Kernen, Acting Department Head (brk265f@smsu.edu); Patrick Scott, Program Director (pgs074f@smsu.edu); 836-5630. Accredited by the National Association of Schools for Public Affairs and Administration.

Religious Studies (M.A.): James C. Moyer, Department Head (jcm625f@smsu.edu); Stan Burgess, Graduate Advisor (smb209f@smsu.edu); 836-5514.

College of Natural and Applied Sciences: Lawrence Banks, Dean (leb793f@mail.smsu.edu); 836-5249.

Biology (M.S.): Steven Jensen, Department Head (slj205f@smsu.edu); Tom Tomasi, Graduate Advisor (tet962f@smsu.edu); 836-5126.

Chemistry (M.S.): Tamara Jahnke, Department Head (tsj118f@smsu.edu); Vernon Thielmann, Graduate Advisor (vjt822f@smsu.edu); 836-5506.

Materials Science (M.S.): Department of Physics, Astronomy and Material Science; Ryan Giedd, Department Head (reg796f@smsu.edu); James Broerman, Graduate Advisor (jgb223f@smsu.edu); 836-5131.

Mathematics (M.S.): Yungchen Cheng, Department Head and Graduate Advisor (yuc471f@smsu.edu); 836-5112.

Natural and Applied Science (M.N.A.S.): Bill Cheek, Program Director (whc256f@smsu.edu); 836-6887. An interdisciplinary program in which students select concentrations in at least two of the following emphasis areas: agriculture, biology, chemistry, geography, geology and planning, mathematics, physics and astronomy, and technology.

Plant Science (M.S.): Department of Fruit Science; James Moore, Department Head (jfm594f@smsu.edu); Bill Cheek, Program Director (whc256f@smsu.edu); 836-6887.

Resource Planning (M.S.): Department of Geography, Geology, and Planning; James Skinner, Department Head (jls519f@smsu.edu); Bob Pavlowsky, Graduate Advisor (rtp138f@smsu.edu); 836-5800.

SPALDING UNIVERSITY

Graduate Programs

Programs of Study

Spalding University offers several levels of graduate study. Doctorates are offered in clinical psychology and education. The Doctor of Psychology (Psy.D.) in clinical psychology program is fully accredited by the American Psychological Association and includes tracks in general clinical psychology, health psychology, and child, adolescent, and family psychology. The programs emphasize the acquisition of the professional skills and competencies required for the practice of psychology and are built upon a foundation of psychological theory and research. The Doctor of Education (Ed.D.) in leadership education emphasizes values and ethics in leadership and serves people in traditional educational roles as well as in business, technical, health, and other areas. Applicants must have a master's degree in education or a related field. This cohort-based program is available in a traditional format with classes during the fall and spring semesters and a format appropriate to international students with on-campus classes during the summer and other formats throughout the year.

Master's degrees are offered in education, media librarianship, clinical psychology, nursing, occupational therapy, pastoral ministry, religious studies, social work, and creative writing. Within the School of Education, the following options are available: the M.A.T. (Master of Art in Teaching) with concentrations in initial teaching licensure in interdisciplinary early childhood education, library media specialist studies, learning behavior disorders, and elementary, middle, or high school education; the M.A. in education with cognate areas in school principalship, school guidance counseling, Montessori instruction, reading and writing, library media specialist studies, and other approved areas; and Rank I and Rank II programs. All programs are accredited by the National Council for Accreditation of Teacher Education (NCATE). The School of Professional Psychology offers an M.A. in clinical psychology, which qualifies the graduate to seek certification as a psychological associate in Kentucky, while the School of Social Work offers a Master of Social Work (M.S.W.) that is accredited by the Council on Social Work Education (CSWE). Following the University's long-standing tradition of innovative education within the field of nursing, four Master of Science in Nursing (M.S.N.) tracks are offered within the School of Nursing: leadership in nursing and health care, family nurse practitioner studies, adult nurse practitioner studies, and pediatric nurse practitioner studies. A post-master's nurse practitioner program is also offered. The Russell Institute of Religion and Ministry offers an M.A. in religious studies and in pastoral ministry. These prepare individuals for church work, teaching, or further academic study. The Auerbach School of Occupational Therapy offers an entry-level Master of Science (M.S.) in occupational therapy and is fully accredited by the Accreditation Council for Occupational Therapy Education (ACOTE) of the American Occupational Therapy Association (AOTA). The College of Arts and Sciences, Humanities Department, offers a Master of Fine Arts (M.F.A) in writing with concentrations in fiction, poetry, creative nonfiction, and writing for children. This brief-residency program consists of intensive ten-day sessions in October and May that are attended by all faculty members and students as they begin each semester, after which students and faculty members return home to correspond on an individual basis.

Research Facilities

The library provides print and nonprint materials, audiovisual equipment, services, and facilities to support the educational and research programs. There are more than 200,000 volumes in the collection, accessed via an automated catalog. These resources are augmented by external collections and services, particularly those of the Kentuckiana Metroversity, a consortium of seven colleges and universities in the metropolitan area that provides access to more than 3 million books and 20,000 journals. Access to further information is enhanced through online and CD-ROM databases and through Internet resources. Additional support is provided through document delivery services and SOLINET/OCLC. Study facilities include large loud-study rooms suitable for group work, while private study and research are supported by small rooms.

Financial Aid

The general types of financial assistance at Spalding University are graduate assistantships and scholarships, repayable aid (loans), work opportunities, and specific tuition remission programs in association with the School of Education/Jefferson County Public Schools, KHEAA, and Crusade for Children. Students should file the FAFSA and a Spalding aid application for loans and work opportunities. Assistantship and scholarship information is available from the graduate office.

Cost of Study

In 2001–02, the cost per credit hour was $400 for most master's programs, $470 for the doctoral program in education, $425 for the master's program in psychology, and $515 for the doctoral program in psychology. The tuition for the M.F.A. in writing was $4600 per semester.

Living and Housing Costs

Housing for single students, both undergraduate and graduate, is available at Morrison Hall on the University campus for $1150 per semester, single occupancy. Married students find ample housing in the surrounding area at varying rates. Daily and weekly dormitory rates are also available for graduate students.

Student Group

More than 600 graduate students with diverse backgrounds and various experiences are enrolled at Spalding. The majority are older students who work full-time and are attracted by the flexibility of the programs.

Location

The Spalding University campus is located between the business section of the city and Old Louisville, a neighborhood of elegant Victorian mansions that was the center of gracious living in the latter half of the nineteenth century. The University is a participant in an effort to preserve and restore the rich architectural heritage of the Louisville Central Area. The campus is adjacent to the Louisville Free Public Library and is within walking distance of performances of the Louisville Orchestra, Kentucky Opera Association, Louisville Ballet, Bach Society, Actors Theatre, and other cultural activities. The campus is also convenient to the schools, hospitals, and agencies used for preprofessional, clinical, and practicum experiences of the students.

The University

Spalding University has its roots in Nazareth College and Academy, established by the Sisters of Charity of Nazareth in 1814 in Bardstown, Kentucky. The name of the University is derived from and honors Catherine Spalding, the founder of the Sisters of Charity of Nazareth. Since the establishment of the Louisville campus in 1920, Spalding University has occupied the Tompkins-Buchanan-Rankin Mansion as the core of its now expanded campus. The University continues its tradition of service to the Louisville area by providing programs that include components of the liberal arts and sciences and professional education for men and women of all ages and from all sectors of society.

Historically, Spalding University has offered extensive programs for part-time students. Business and professional persons, in-service teachers, and others unable to attend college full-time have earned graduate degrees by attending evening and Saturday classes. Today, the University is maintaining its innovative stance at the cutting edge of educational service to the Louisville community and beyond.

Applying

Most graduate students may enter at the beginning of any term; however, students in psychology, the regular social work program, and the Ed.D. program are admitted only in the fall. Occupational therapy students are admitted in the spring. Advanced social work students begin in the summer. Prospective students should contact the Graduate Admissions Office to receive information and application materials.

Correspondence and Information

Cynthia Amback, Director of Graduate Admissions
Spalding University
851 South Fourth Street
Louisville, Kentucky 40203-2188

Telephone: 502-585-7105
800-896-8941 ext. 2105 (toll-free)
Fax: 502-992-2429
E-mail: gradadmissions@spalding.edu
World Wide Web: http://www.spalding.edu

THE FACULTY

Administration
Thomas R. Oates, University President; Ph.D., St. Louis.
Steven E. Hardin, Senior Vice President for Academic Affairs; Ph.D., Kansas.
Judith Plawecki, Associate Vice President for Academic Affairs and Dean of the Graduate School; Ph.D., Iowa.
Kathleen Nesbitt, Acting Dean of the College of Arts and Science; Ph.D., Michigan State.

Education
Gladys M. Busch, Professor; Ph.D., Indiana.
Karen Dunnagan, Assistant Professor; Ph.D., Ohio State.
Barbara Foster, Assistant Professor; Ed.D., Spalding.
Robert Hay, Associate Professor; Ed.D., Louisville.
William Lieshoff, Assistant Professor; Ph.D., Texas A&M.
Betty Lindsey, Associate Professor and Dean; Ed.D., Louisville.
Ann Riedling, Assistant Professor; Ed.D., Louisville.
Nikki Schweinbeck, Adjunct Assistant Professor; Ed.D., Spalding.
John G. Shaughnessy, CFX, Professor; Ed.D., Rutgers.
Mary Angela Shaughnessy, SCN, Professor; Ph.D., Boston College; J.D., Louisville.

Nursing
Veronica Abdur-Rahman, Associate Professor; Ph.D., Houston.
Cynthia Crabtree, Associate Professor and Dean; Ed.D., Spalding.
Pam King, Assistant Professor; M.S.N., Kentucky.
Ann Lyons, Associate Professor; D.N.S., Indiana.
Gracie Wishnia, Associate Professor; Ph.D., Louisville.

Occupational Therapy
Jeffrey Lederer, Assistant Professor; Ph.D., New Mexico.
Janis Renninger, Instructor; M.S., Indianapolis.
Laura S. Strickland, Assistant Professor; M.A., Houston.
L. Randy Strickland, Professor and Dean; Ed.D., North Carolina State.

Pastoral Ministry and Religious Studies
Adeline Fehribach, SCN, Assistant Professor; Ph.D., Vanderbilt.
Joseph Martos, Professor; Ph.D., DePaul.
Joseph T. Merkt, Assistant Professor; S.T.D., Catholic University.

Psychology
Catherine Aponte, Clinical Faculty; Psy.D., Spalding.
Thomas A. Bergandi, Professor; Ph.D., Ball State.
Sally Brenzel, Adjunct Associate Professor; Psy.D., Spalding.
James Cooksey, Associate Professor; Ph.D., Louisville.
John Embry, Adjunct Assistant Professor; Ph.D., Nebraska.
David Finke, Adjunct Assistant Professor; Ph.D., Michigan State.
Helene Finke, Adjunct Assistant Professor; Ph.D., Michigan State.
John A. James III, Associate Professor; Ph.D., Missouri.
Kenneth Linfield, Assistant Professor; Ph.D., Illinois.
Andrew Meyer, Adjunct Assistant Professor and Director of Health Psychology Emphasis; Ph.D., Missouri.
David L. Morgan, Associate Professor; Ph.D., Auburn.
Brenda Nash, Adjunct Assistant Professor; Ph.D., Kentucky.
T. Andrew Pearson, Adjunct Assistant Professor; Psy.D., Spalding.
Kevin Pernicano, Adjunct Assistant Professor; Ph.D., Notre Dame.
Patricia Pernicano, Clinical Faculty; Psy.D., Baylor.
Darlene Shelton, Assistant Professor and Director of Minority Student Recruitment and Retention; Ph.D., Southern Illinois.
Thomas G. Titus, Professor; Ph.D., Louisville.
April Vandeventer, Adjunct Assistant Professor; Psy.D., Spalding.
Marilyn Wagner, Adjunct Associate Professor; Ph.D., Memphis State.
Byron White, Adjunct Assistant Professor; Psy.D., Spalding.
Barbara Williams, Professor and Dean; Ph.D., Houston.
Diane Wohlfarth, Assistant Professor; Psy.D., Spalding.

Social Work
Desiree Brown-Daughtery, Instructor and Director of Field; M.S.S.W., Louisville.
Patricia Cummings, Assistant Professor; M.S.S.W., Louisville.
Helen Deines, Associate Professor and Interim Dean; Ed.D., Spalding.
Erlene Grise-Owens, Assistant Professor and Director; Ed.D., Spalding.
Jillian Johnson, Professor Emeritus; Ph.D., Washington State.
Kathy Lay, Assistant Professor; M.S.S.W., Louisville.
David Peterson, Assistant Professor; M.S.S.W., Louisville.
David Richart, Adjunct Associate Professor; Ph.D., Union (Ohio).
Wendy Turner, Assistant Professor; Ph.D., Ohio State.
Rita Valade, Assistant Professor; M.S.W., Catholic University.

University-Wide Studies
Paul Hoyt-O'Connor, Associate Professor of Philosophy; Ph.D., Boston College.
Larry Wayne Lewis, Associate Professor of Mathematics; Ph.D., Louisville.
Betty Shiffman, Associate Professor of English; Ph.D., Louisville.
Youn-Kyung Kim, Assistant Professor of English; Ph.D., Oklahoma State.

SPRINGFIELD COLLEGE

School of Graduate Studies

Programs of Study

Graduate study at Springfield College is designed to provide advanced professional preparation for qualified graduates of colleges and universities in the United States and abroad. Fourteen graduate programs, several with a number of subspecialty areas, are coordinated through the School of Graduate Studies. These programs are Art Therapy, Education (early childhood, elementary, secondary, school adjustment, special education), Healthcare Management, Health Sciences (applied exercise science, sports injury prevention and management), Health Studies (health promotion/wellness management, teacher certification program), Human Services, Movement Science (biomechanics, exercise physiology, clinical exercise physiology, science and research, interdisciplinary studies), Occupational Therapy, Physical Education (adapted physical education, advanced-level coaching, athletic administration, community physical education, sports management, sports psychology, sports studies, supervisor/director studies, teaching and administration), Physical Therapy, Psychology (athletic counseling, general counseling, industrial/organizational psychology, marriage and family therapy, mental health counseling, school guidance, student personnel in higher education), Recreation and Tourism (outdoor recreational management, recreational management, therapeutic recreational management), Rehabilitation Services (alcohol rehabilitation/substance abuse counseling, developmental disabilities, general counseling and casework, psychiatric rehabilitation/mental health counseling, special services, vocational evaluation/work adjustment), and Social Work. Graduate study is offered on three different levels, leading to the Master of Education, Master of Physical Education, Master of Science, Master of Social Work, Certificate of Advanced Study, Doctor of Physical Education, and combined M.S.W./J.D. degrees.

For the Master of Science in Human Services, course work is offered on weekends. The program lasts sixteen months, and students meet one weekend each month. A five-year human services experience (paid or volunteer) is required for admission. Master of Social Work candidates are able to attend classes on a part-time basis, every other weekend, or as full-time students two days a week.

Research Facilities

A well-equipped laboratory for physiology provides an area for student and faculty research. Experiments in the areas of kinesiology and exercise physiology are concerned with oxygen consumption and energy expenditure, strength, electrogoniometry, physical fitness, pulmonary function, and body density. Arrangements can also be made for work in cinematography and somatotyping. The Allied Health Center, the education curriculum laboratory, the College Counseling Center, a counseling laboratory with videotape facilities, a physical education tests and measurements laboratory, a biomechanics laboratory, the Computer Center, the College campgrounds, and the modern Babson Library offer campus opportunities for conducting research related to student interests and areas of study.

Financial Aid

Various types of financial assistance are available. Four All-College Tuition Scholarships are awarded each year. Teaching and research associateships are offered in art therapy, biology, chemistry, computer science, education, health studies, mathematics, multicultural affairs, occupational therapy, physical education, physical science, physics, psychology, recreation, rehabilitation services, and social sciences. These awards provide tuition waivers for a maximum of 24 semester hours per academic year, partial payment of health insurance, and a stipend. Graduate assistantships are also available in teaching, coaching, laboratory supervision, research, and administrative areas. A limited number of scholarships, ranging from $200 to the full cost of tuition, are provided for international students. The Financial Aid Office administers federal loan programs.

Cost of Study

For a typical full-time graduate student at Springfield College, tuition and fees for two semesters (nine months) amounted to $12,961 during the 2001–02 academic year. An ample schedule of courses is planned each summer, with the cost based mainly on the number of semester hours carried.

Living and Housing Costs

For 2001–02, the minimum meal plan cost $1480 per year. Both on- and off-campus housing are available. Entertainment costs and other personal expenses vary greatly from student to student. College-owned apartments cost approximately $5080 per academic year.

Student Group

During 2001–02, there were 1015 full-time graduate students enrolled in the various programs. An additional 405 part-time graduate students were also enrolled. Sixty-eight percent were women. Students were drawn from twenty-four states and twenty-one countries.

Student Outcomes

Graduates consistently declare themselves well prepared and qualified for employment in the professional fields of art; occupational and physical therapy; education; counseling psychology; sport, wellness, and recreation; and health and human services. The positions include teacher, coach, trainer, counselor, administrator, director, consultant, entrepreneur, and hands-on practitioner. Employers who have recently hired Springfield graduates include the YMCA, Old Sturbridge Village, Veterans Affairs Medical Centers, Baystate Health Systems, Goodwill Industries, Motorola, Harvard University, Rochester Americans, Converse, Advantage Health Corp., and Yale New Haven Hospital.

Location

The campus is located on Lake Massasoit, about 3 miles from the downtown area of Springfield, Massachusetts, offering the advantages of a small-town setting within a metropolitan area. The campus site covers 156 acres, including the 56-acre campground fronting on the lake.

The College is within a day's drive of major centers in the northeastern United States. Boston, the largest city in New England, is less than a 2-hour drive away, and New York City is only 3 hours away. The Green Mountains of Vermont and the White Mountains of New Hampshire are easily reached via modern highways going north. The entire area abounds in lakes, mountains, resorts, historic sites, museums, and other attractions.

The College

Springfield College is, and has been since its founding more than 100 years ago, concerned with the preparation of the total person—in spirit, in mind, and in body. Its professional curriculum has been specifically designed to prepare students for careers in what have come to be known as the "human-helping" professions. The College lists more than 30,000 alumni whose professional education at Springfield has enabled them to assume leadership positions in virtually all areas of community service, including recreation, physical education, counseling, psychological services, education, commerce and industry, community leadership and development, rehabilitation services, health promotion, and physical, art, occupational, and recreational therapy.

Applying

Applications for the Physical Therapy and Occupational Therapy Programs must be on file no later than December 1 and January 1, respectively. Applications are due by March 15 for the Master of Social Work degree. All other programs follow a rolling admissions process, in which files are reviewed as they become complete. The financial aid application deadline is March 1. Notification usually takes a minimum of six weeks from receipt of an application. Candidates lacking undergraduate prerequisites must make up their deficiencies without earning graduate credit for these. Standardized tests and interviews are not a regular part of the admission process for most master's and certificate students. However, the General Test of the GRE is required of health education, exercise science and sport studies, physical education, and physical therapy applicants. In some programs, personal interviews are a prerequisite to action on the application. Scores on the General Test of the GRE are also required of doctoral students.

Correspondence and Information

Donald J. Shaw Jr.
Director of Graduate Admissions
Box P.G.
Springfield College
Springfield, Massachusetts 01109
Telephone: 413-748-3225
Fax: 413-748-3694
World Wide Web: http://www.spfldcol.edu

THE FACULTY

There are nearly 100 faculty members teaching graduate-level courses. They hold degrees from colleges and universities in the United States and abroad, and approximately two thirds of them have doctorates. Many are authorities in their fields, and all members of the graduate faculty teach. In addition, many engage in research or writing projects as their teaching loads permit.

SCHOOL OF GRADUATE STUDIES

Dean: Betty L. Mann, Associate Professor of Physical Education; D.P.E., Springfield, 1984.
Director of Graduate Admissions: Donald J. Shaw Jr., M.Ed., Springfield, 1970.

Program Coordinators

Art Therapy: Leslie Abrahms, Assistant Professor of Art; Ph.D., Fordham, 1994.
Education: Sharon J. Washington, Associate Professor of Education; Ph.D., Ohio State, 1988.
Healthcare Management: John J. Doyle Jr., Professor of Economics; Ph.D., Clark, 1976.
Health Science: Charles J. Redmond, Associate Professor of Physical Education; M.S.P.T., Boston University, 1981.
Health Studies: John C. Smith, Assistant Professor of Health Education; Ph.D., Miami (Florida), 1983.
Human Services: Ann Marie Frisbe, Coordinator of Admissions, School of Human Services; B.A., St. Michael's, 1993.
Movement Science: Charles J. Redmond, Associate Professor of Physical Education; M.S.P.T., Boston University, 1981.
Occupational Therapy: Katherine Post, Assistant Professor of Occupational Therapy; M.S., Columbia, 1976.
Physical Education: Stephen Coulon, Associate Professor of Physical Education; Ph.D., Ohio State, 1987.
Physical Therapy: Linda Tsoumas, Associate Professor of Physical Therapy; M.S., Massachusetts, 1979.
Psychology: Barbara Mandell, Associate Professor of Psychology; Ed.D., Massachusetts, 1987.
Recreation and Tourism: Donald R. Snyder, Associate Professor of Recreation; Ph.D., Connecticut, 1987.
Rehabilitation Services: Thomas J. Ruscio, Professor of Rehabilitation; C.A.S., Springfield, 1966.
Social Work: Francine Vecchiolla, Dean, School of Social Work; Ph.D., Brandeis, 1987.

STATE UNIVERSITY OF NEW YORK AT ALBANY

Graduate Studies

Programs of Study

The Graduate Faculties offer programs of study in the College of Arts and Sciences, the School of Education; the School of Business, the School of Public Health, the Nelson A. Rockefeller College of Public Affairs and Policy, the School of Criminal Justice, the School of Information Science and Policy, and the School of Social Welfare.

Doctor of Philosophy programs are offered in anthropology, atmospheric science, biology, biomedical sciences, biometry and statistics, biopsychology, chemistry, clinical psychology, cognitive psychology, computer science, counseling psychology, criminal justice, curriculum and instruction, economics, educational administration, educational psychology, English, environmental health and toxicology, epidemiology, French, geology, history, industrial/organizational psychology, information science, mathematics, organizational studies, philosophy, physics, political science, public administration, reading, social/personality psychology, social welfare, sociology, and Spanish. A Doctor of Arts program is offered in humanistic studies. In addition, the Doctor of Psychology degree is offered in school psychology. A Doctor of Public Health degree is also offered. The Certificate of Advanced Study, involving a 60-credit curriculum, is awarded in counseling, court systems management, curriculum and instruction, information science, planning and policy analysis, public history, reading, Russian translation, and school psychology.

Master's degree programs are offered in accounting, Africana studies, anthropology, art (studio), atmospheric science, biodiversity and conservation, biology, biomedical sciences, biometry and statistics, business administration, chemistry, classics, communication, computer science, counseling, criminal justice, curriculum development and instructional technology, economics, educational administration, educational psychology and statistics, English, environmental health and toxicology, epidemiology, forensic molecular biology, French, general educational studies, geography, geology, health policy and management, history, information science, Latin American and Caribbean studies, liberal studies, library science, mathematics, philosophy, physics, political science, psychology, public administration, public affairs and policy, public health, reading, regional planning, rehabilitation counseling, Russian, social studies, social welfare, sociology, Spanish, special education, taxation, teaching English to speakers of other languages, teaching of academic subjects in secondary schools, theater, urban and regional planning, and women's studies.

Graduate certificates, comprising 15–18 credit hours of study, are offered in advanced public management, demography, geographic information systems and spatial analysis, Latin American and Caribbean studies, public sector management, regulatory economics, urban policy, and women and public policy.

Research Facilities

The State University of New York at Albany organizes research, special training facilities, and associated services through a variety of centers, clinics, institutes, laboratories, and other special units. Several of these are operated or sponsored jointly with other institutions and agencies. Two such research facilities are the internationally known Atmospheric Sciences Research Center and the Wadsworth Center for Laboratories and Research.

Financial Aid

University graduate fellowships and assistantships are available with stipends of $5000 to $18,000 for the academic year, plus consideration for tuition scholarship. Loans are available through the Federal Perkins and Federal Stafford Student loan programs. Financial aid is offered by the state of New York through the New York State Tuition Assistance Program and State University scholarships. There are several programs available for the support of graduate students from historically underrepresented segments of the population.

Cost of Study

Tuition was $5100 per academic year for full-time students who are residents of New York State; tuition was $8416 for nonresidents in 2000–01.

Living and Housing Costs

Residence hall facilities for unmarried students are available at $3488 per year for a double-occupancy room. On-campus apartments are available, ranging from $3924 to $4580 per person per year. Off-campus accommodations are readily available in the Albany area. Optional meal plans are available on campus from $1466 to $1752 per year.

Student Group

Of the 16,616 students at the State University of New York at Albany, 5,273 are graduate students; 2,159 of the latter study full-time. Students come from all parts of the United States and from forty other countries.

Location

Albany recently was designated an All-America City by the National Civic League and has abundant cultural and recreational opportunities. Located nearby are the Saratoga Performing Arts Center, summer home to the New York City Opera, New York City Ballet, and the Philadelphia Orchestra; Tanglewood, summer home to the Boston Symphony Orchestra; and Jacob's Pillow, which features prominent artists in ballet and other forms of the dancing arts. The area also lends itself naturally to winter and summer leisure activities. It is surrounded by the Berkshires and the Adirondack, Helderberg, Grafton, and Catskill mountains. Historic sites and vacation areas within driving distance include New York City, Boston, Cape Cod, Connecticut, Vermont, Montreal, Lake George, and Lake Champlain.

The University

The State University of New York at Albany is the oldest state-chartered public institution of higher education in New York. Established in 1844, and designated as a University Center of the State University of New York, Albany has a broad mission of undergraduate and graduate education, research, and public service. The main campus, designed by Edward Durell Stone, contains fourteen academic buildings within a common platform, all connected by a continuous roof and an enclosed below-level corridor. Although most classrooms and laboratories are on this campus, some are located at the downtown campus, and the School of Public Health Sciences is located in the State Health Laboratories in the Empire State Plaza and on the East Campus. In addition to classrooms and laboratories, there are the University libraries and the Performing Arts Center with several theaters, recital halls, rehearsal rooms, and instructional areas. Other special facilities include the Fine Arts Building, which houses one of the finest galleries in the Northeast, the Center for Environmental Science and Technology building, which houses the local branch of the National Weather Service, a computing center, and a linear accelerator for physics research.

Applying

The Office of Graduate Studies is a University-wide administrative unit generally responsible for the administration of graduate affairs and for the coordination of graduate programs offered by the several schools. Application forms may be obtained from the Office of Graduate Admissions and are available online at the Web site listed below.

Correspondence and Information

Office of Graduate Admissions, UAB-121
University at Albany
1400 Washington Avenue
Albany, New York 12222

Telephone: 518-442-3980
E-mail: graduate@uamail.albany.edu
World Wide Web: http://www.albany.edu

FACULTY HEADS

Karen R. Hitchcock, President.
Carlos Santiago, Provost and Vice President for Academic Affairs.
Christopher D'Elia, Vice President for Research.

College of Arts and Sciences: V. Mark Durand, Interim Dean.
Nelson A. Rockefeller College of Public Affairs and Policy: Frank Thompson, Dean.
School of Business: Richard Highfield, Dean.
School of Criminal Justice: James Acker, Interim Dean.
School of Education: Susan Philips, Interim Dean.
School of Information Science and Policy: Philip Eppard, Dean.
School of Public Health: Peter Levin, Dean.
School of Social Welfare: Katharine Briar-Lawson, Dean.

Views of the downtown and uptown campuses of the State University of New York at Albany.

STATE UNIVERSITY OF NEW YORK AT BINGHAMTON

Graduate School

Programs of Study

The Graduate School offers comprehensive advanced degree programs through the Harpur College of Arts and Sciences, the School of Management, the Decker School of Nursing, the School of Education and Human Development, and the Thomas J. Watson School of Engineering and Applied Science.

The Master of Arts (M.A.) and Doctor of Philosophy (Ph.D.) are offered in anthropology, art history, biological sciences, chemistry, comparative literature, economics, education, English, geological sciences, history, mathematical sciences, philosophy, political science, psychology, and sociology. The M.A. is also available in French, geography, Italian, philosophy, physics, public administration, Spanish, and theater. Master of Science (M.S.) degrees are offered in chemistry and physics. The Department of Music offers the Master of Music. A certificate program in translation studies is offered through the Center for Research in Translation.

The Thomas J. Watson School of Engineering and Applied Science offers M.S. degrees in computer science, electrical engineering, industrial engineering, mechanical engineering, and systems science. The Master of Engineering (M.Eng.) is offered, with specializations in computer, electrical, industrial, and mechanical engineering. The Ph.D. is offered in computer science, electrical engineering, mechanical engineering, systems science, and systems science with a specialization in manufacturing systems.

The School of Management offers the Ph.D. in management, the Master of Business Administration (M.B.A.), the M.S. in professional accounting, and the Executive M.B.A. (health-care and corporate). A combined-degree program leads to the M.B.A. in management/M.A. in history. The M.A. in social science is offered by the School of Education and Human Development. Within the field of education, the Master of Arts in Teaching, Master of Science in Teaching, Master of Science in Education, and Ed.D. in educational theory and practice are offered. A Certificate of Advanced Study in reading and language arts also is offered. The Decker School of Nursing offers the M.S., Ph.D., and certificate programs in community health primary care nurse practitioner, family nurse practitioner, and gerontological nurse practitioner studies.

Degree programs at the master's level normally require from one to two years of study. Doctoral degree programs usually require five years of study beyond the bachelor's degree.

Research Facilities

The University library system consists of the Glenn G. Bartle Library, with holdings in the social sciences and the humanities; a Science Library; and a Fine Arts Library. The total collection includes 3.8 million items, with much of its data accessible through an online catalog system. Resources are supplemented by memberships in academic library consortia, notably the Research Libraries Group, Inc. The University's main computers, an IBM ES 9000/500 and an IBM 9121-320, support instruction and research on campus as well as administrative data processing. Two DEC VAX 6440 computers and numerous microprocessors provide additional support for academic instruction.

Financial Aid

Many students hold traineeships, fellowships, or graduate, research, or teaching assistantships. Most awards include a full or partial tuition scholarship. Other sources include the New York State Tuition Assistance Program, Federal Stafford Student Loan, and Federal Work-Study programs and campus job opportunities.

Cost of Study

Full-time annual tuition in 2000–01 was $5100 for residents and $8416 for nonresidents. Additional charges per semester included an activity fee of $40 and a comprehensive fee of $336.50. These costs are subject to change without notice.

Living and Housing Costs

There is currently no on-campus housing available to graduate students as a result of an increased demand for housing in the undergraduate population. However, the greater majority of Binghamton's graduate students have always lived off campus. There is ample public transport (both by the county transit system and by the University's own bus system) serving the community surrounding the campus. The University offers assistance to students seeking off-campus accomodations through its Off Campus College at (http://www.binghamton.edu) for student services to off-campus living; or directly at (http://occ.binghamton.edu/new.htm) where available housing and prices are listed.

Student Group

In the fall of 2000, there were 1,335 men and 1,380 women enrolled in the Graduate School. Of these, 1,417 were full-time and 1,198 were part-time students. There were 100 doctoral degrees and 626 master's degrees awarded in May 2000.

Student Outcomes

Employment opportunities for master's and Ph.D. recipients of Binghamton include postdoctoral research at such institutions as Cornell, Duke, Indiana, and the Smithsonian Institution; faculty positions at such universities as Johns Hopkins, Penn State, and North Carolina; and career paths in government, health fields, industry, manufacturing, and commercial and private sector businesses throughout the country.

Location

The 606-acre suburban campus is located just west of Binghamton. The Finger Lakes and the Adirondack, Catskill, and Pocono mountains are nearby, providing opportunities for camping, hiking, skiing, sailing, or virtually any other outdoor activity. Binghamton is within an afternoon's drive of New York, Philadelphia, and other major urban centers.

The University and The School

Binghamton is one of four university centers in the State University of New York System. Campus facilities for music, drama, art, and cinema are exceptional and include the Floyd E. Anderson Center for the Performing Arts that contains a 1,200-seat theater with a retractable rear wall to provide outdoor seating for 2,500 more people. The University's Art Museum has a permanent collection representing all periods and also displays works from special loan exhibitions. The annual concert series of the Department of Music brings prominent soloists and chamber groups to campus. The Department of Theater stages more than twenty-five productions each year. An 8,500-square-foot greenhouse contains one of the finest botanical teaching collections in the Northeast. A number of major building and rehab projects are currently underway on campus.

Graduate programs were initiated in 1961 with the establishment of M.A. programs in English and mathematics. The first Ph.D. program was offered in 1965. The Graduate School prepares students for scholarly study, advanced research, teaching, and professional leadership. Its mission is service to the community, region, state, and nation through the advancement of knowledge and the development of human resources.

Applying

Holders of bachelor's degrees from any college or university of recognized standing are eligible to apply. Application materials are available from the Office of Graduate Admissions. Applicants for admission should submit scores from the GRE General Test and the appropriate Subject Test, if any. School of Management applicants should submit GMAT scores in lieu of GRE scores. International applicants must also submit TOEFL scores and provide proof of their ability to meet academic expenses. To ensure consideration for assistantship and fellowship awards, admission credentials should be received by February 15.

Correspondence and Information

Office of Graduate Admissions
Binghamton University
P.O. Box 6000
Binghamton, New York 13902-6000
Telephone: 607-777-2151

FACULTY HEADS

Graduate School
David G. Payne, Interim Dean of the Graduate School.
Allan L. Eller, Associate Dean of the Graduate School.

Harpur College of Arts and Sciences
Jean-Pierre Mileur, Dean.
Norah F. Henry, Associate Dean for Administration.
Donald Blake, Associate Dean for Academic Affairs.
Anthropology: Robert Herbert, Chairperson; G. Philip Rightmire, Director of Graduate Programs.
Art History: John Tagg, Chairperson; Oscar Vazquez, Director of Graduate Programs.
Biological Sciences: Rob Van Buslurle, Chairperson; Nancy Stamp, Director of Graduate Programs.
Chemistry: Alistair Lees, Chairperson; Eugene S. Stevens, Director of Graduate Programs; M. Stanley Whittingham, Director of Graduate Admissions.
Comparative Literature: Christopher Fynsk, Chairperson; Brett Levinson, Director of Graduate Studies.
Economics: Edward Kokkelenberg, Chairperson; Thomas Cowing, Director of Graduate Programs; Ron Britto, Director of Graduate Admissions.
English: David Bartine, Chairperson; Richard McLain, Director of Graduate Programs.
Geography: Shin-Yi Hsu, Chairperson; Burrell Montz, Director of Graduate Programs.
Geological Sciences: Robert DeMarco, Chairperson; David Jenkins, Director of Graduate Studies.
History: Don Quataert, Chairperson; Howard Brown, Director of Graduate Studies.
Mathematical Sciences: Erik Pedersen, Chairperson; Alex Feingold, Director of Graduate Programs; Fernando Guzman, Director of Graduate Admissions.
Music: Bruce Borton, Chairperson; Jonathan Biggers, Director of Graduate Programs.
Philosophy: Donald Weiss, Chairperson; Stephen Ross, Director of Graduate Studies (PIC); Max Pensley, Director of Graduate Studies (SPEL).
Physics: Srinivasa Venugopalan, Chairperson; Eric Cotts, Director of Graduate Programs.
Political Science: Michael McDonald, Chairperson; Chistopher Anderson, Director of Graduate Programs.
Psychology: Linda Spear, Chairperson; Albrecht Inhoff, Director of Graduate Programs.
Romance Languages: Salvador Fajardo, Chairperson; Rosemarie LaValva, Director of Graduate Programs.
Sociology: Dale Tomich, Chairperson; Kelvin Santiago-Valles, Director of Graduate Programs.
Theater: John Vestal, Chairperson; Allan Jackson, Director of Graduate Programs.

Thomas J. Watson School of Engineering and Applied Science
Charles R. Westgate, Dean.
Cynthia Sedgewick, Associate Dean for Academic Affairs and Administration.
John Fillo, Associate Dean for Research and External Affairs.
Computer Science: Kanad Ghose, Chairperson.
Electrical Engineering: Richard Plumb, Chairperson.
Industrial Engineering and Systems Science: Robert Emerson, Chairperson.
Mechanical Engineering: Ron Miles, Chairperson.

School of Education and Human Development
Ernest Rose, Dean.
Theodore W. Rector, Associate Dean.
Education: Thomas O'Brien, Director of Graduate Programs.
M.A. Social Science Program: Sue Crowley, Director of Graduate Programs.

School of Management
Glenn Pitman, Dean.
Richard Reeves-Ellington, Associate Dean.
Vincent Pasquale, Assistant Dean.
George Bobinski, Director of Executive Education.

Decker School of Nursing
Mary S. Collins, Dean.
Joyce Ferrario, Associate Dean.

SUNY BROCKPORT

STATE UNIVERSITY OF NEW YORK COLLEGE AT BROCKPORT

Graduate Studies

Programs of Study

SUNY College at Brockport is accredited by the Middle States Association of Colleges and Schools and the Board of Regents of the University of the State of New York. The College offers twenty-seven graduate programs, including an M.A. in communication, dance, English, history, liberal studies, mathematics, and psychology; an M.S. in biological sciences, computational science, family nurse practitioner studies, and recreation and leisure; an M.F.A. in dance and visual studies; an M.P.A. in public administration; an M.S.Ed. in counselor education, education in the graduate teacher certification areas listed below, educational administration, health education, physical education, and additional teacher certification areas as listed below; a Master of Science in Social Work (in collaboration with Nazareth College of Rochester); a C.A.S. (Certificate of Advanced Study) in counselor education, educational administration, and school business administration; and a post-master's program in family nurse practitioner studies.

Graduate teacher certification programs include bilingual education, biological and general science 7–12, chemistry and general science 7–12, childhood literacy birth–6, childhood special education, dance K–12, earth sciences and general science 7–12, elementary education preK–6, English 7–12, health education K–12, mathematics 7–12, physical education K–12, physics and general science 7–12, school administrator and supervisor, school business administrator, school district administrator, school counselor, and social studies 7–12.

Research Facilities

SUNY Brockport's Drake Memorial Library houses the largest collection among the SUNY four-year colleges, including 583,000 books and bound journals, 2 million microforms, 100,000 federal and state documents, subscriptions to 1,340 journals and magazines in print form, and online database subscriptions to 13,000 journal titles. The library's extended hours are particularly helpful for students whose classes meet in the evenings. Students can conduct online searches and download publications from remote sites. Students studying primarily at the downtown SUNY Brockport MetroCenter also use the SUNY Resource Library at the Bausch & Lomb Public Library, including PCs linked to the Internet and Drake Memorial Library. The campus's two-story computing center, with a Data Analysis Lab, is augmented by more than twenty satellite computing labs. The College's computing hardware includes 750 networked PC, Macintosh, and Sun stations that are available for students to utilize.

SUNY Brockport is home to seven centers, institutes, and unique academic endeavors that enrich the academic enterprise, including the Center for Applied Aquatic Science and Aquaculture, which coordinates programs in applied aquatic biology, aquaculture, and related sciences; Center for Philosophic Exchange, sponsoring programs of philosophic inquiry on academic and public issues; Child and Adolescent Stress Management Institute, offering preventive health programming to campus and public audiences; Congress on Research in Dance, providing opportunities for dance scholars, professionals, and graduate students to exchange ideas and methodologies through publication, conferences, and workshops; Monroe County Historian's Office, providing assistance with local history projects to county and village historians and the general public; Visual Studies Workshop, an affiliate of SUNY Brockport, offering courses and the M.F.A. program for Brockport graduate art students; and Writers Forum and Videotape Library, advancing the appreciation for and practice of the art of writing through sponsored public readings by writers of local, national, and international reputation.

Financial Aid

Of the 1,870 graduate students enrolled for fall 2001, 762 full- and part-time students received financial aid. Some graduate students hold teaching, graduate, and research assistantships. A number of competitive fellowship programs are available to graduate students, including opportunities for students who are members of underrepresented minority groups. Full or partial tuition scholarships accompany most assistantships and fellowships. Graduate Opportunity Tuition Scholarships are available to students who participated in undergraduate EOP, HEOP, or SEEK programs.

Cost of Study

Full-time tuition for 2002–03 is $5100 per academic year for New York State residents and $8416 per academic year for nonresidents. Part-time tuition is $213 per credit for residents and $351 per credit for nonresidents. All tuition rates are subject to adjustment by the Board of Trustees. College fees total $637 per academic year for full-time graduate students and $26.35 per credit for part-time students.

Living and Housing Costs

Housing for international graduate students is offered on a space-available basis. On-campus housing offers easy access to computing facilities, the library, recreational and dining facilities, and cultural events. All standard services are provided, including Internet and cable TV access and free laundry facilities. A double-occupancy room is $3930 per person per academic year. Meal plans currently range from $2080 to $2960 per academic year.

Student Group

SUNY Brockport's total enrollment for fall 2001 was 8,634 (3,544 men and 5,090 women), with a graduate student population of 1,870 (673 men and 1,197 women), of whom 295 (92 men and 203 women) were engaged in full-time study.

Location

SUNY Brockport's main campus is located in the village of Brockport, 16 miles west of Rochester, New York. Brockport combines the familiarity and friendliness of a small town with easy access to the opportunities of a metropolitan city. The College's 435-acre campus is only 10 miles from the southern shores of Lake Ontario, with its many parks and beaches; within short driving distance of New York State's renowned Finger Lakes; and within easy reach of area ski resorts. The College is 20 minutes by car from the Monroe County International Airport, 1 hour from Niagara Falls, and 3 hours from Toronto.

The College

Student success is at the heart of the College's mission statement, "Brockport . . . has the success of its students as its highest priority, emphasizing student learning and . . . committed to advancing teaching, scholarship, creative endeavors, and service . . ." The foundation for today's comprehensive institution was laid in 1841 with the opening of the Brockport Collegiate Institute. Over the years, the College expanded beyond its sole focus on teacher education to a comprehensive institution offering both baccalaureate and master's programs.

The campus includes sixty-six buildings, professional-quality athletic fields, and open and wooded land. Recent renovations include Hartwell Hall ($10 million), which houses several departments, including the Department of Dance, with theater and performance spaces; Lennon Hall Science Complex ($20 million); and the Seymour College Union, with expanded dining facilities, 24-hour computer lab, and enhanced student activity space.

Applying

Applications should be filed directly with the Office of Graduate Admissions. Deadlines for filing applications vary by department. Application forms and information describing the credentials required for admission to SUNY Brockport's graduate programs are available at the address below.

Correspondence and Information

The Office of Graduate Admissions
SUNY College at Brockport
350 New Campus Drive
Brockport, New York 14420

Telephone: 585-395-5465
585-395-2525
E-mail: gradadmit@brockport.edu
World Wide Web: http://www.brockport.edu/~graduate

GRADUATE PROGRAM ADMINISTRATORS AND DIRECTORS

The area code for all numbers is 585.

ADMINISTRATORS

Diane Elliott, Ed.D., Assistant Vice President for Graduate Studies and Research, 395-2525, delliott@brockport.edu
Julian Ortiz, Senior Graduate Admissions Advisor, 395-5456, jortiz@brockport.edu

DIRECTORS

School of Arts and Performance

Dean: Sharon Vasquez, M.F.A., 395-2350, svasquez@brockport.edu
Communication (M.A.): Bill Reed, Ph.D., 395-5290, breed@brockport.edu
Dance (M.A./M.F.A.): Susannah Newman, M.A., 395-5302, snewman@brockport.edu
Physical Education (M.S.Ed.): William Stier, Ed.D., 395-5331, bstier@brockport.edu
Visual Studies Workshop (M.F.A.): Christopher Burnett, M.F.A., 442-8676, cburnett@brockport.edu

School of Letters and Sciences

Dean: Michael A. Maggiotto, Ph.D., 395-2394, mmaggiot@brockport.edu
Biological Sciences (M.S.): Christopher Norment, Ph.D., 395-5748, cnorment@brockport.edu
Computational Sciences (M.S.): Osman Yasar, Ph.D., 395-2595, oyasar@brockport.edu
English (M.A.): David Hale, Ph.D., 395-5832, dhale@brockport.edu
History (M.A.): Jennifer Lloyd, Ph.D., 395-5680, jlloyd@brockport.edu
Liberal Studies (M.A.): Stuart Appelle, Ph.D., 395-2262, sappelle@brockport.edu
Mathematics (M.A.): Sanford Miller, Ph.D., 395-5178, smiller@brockport.edu
Psychology (M.A.): Janet Gillespie, Ph.D., 395-2433, jgillesp@brockport.edu

School of Professions

Dean: Joseph R. Mason, Ph.D., 395-2510, jmason@brockport.edu
Counselor Education (M.S.Ed./C.A.S.): Susan Seem, Ph.D., 395-5492, sseem@brockport.edu
Educational Administration (M.S.Ed./C.A.S.): Sandra Graczyk, Ed.D., 395-5802, slgrazak@aol.com
Education and Human Development (M.S.Ed.): Patricia Baker, Ph.D., 395-5552, pbaker@brockport.edu
Family Nurse Practitioner (M.S./post-master's): Linda Snell, Ph.D., 395-5323, lsnell@brockport.edu
Health Education (M.S.Ed.): Patti Follansbee, Ph.D., 395-5483, pfollans@brockport.edu
Public Administration (M.P.A.): James Fatula, Ph.D., 395-2375, jfatula@brockport.edu
Recreation and Leisure (M.S.): Joel Frater, Ed.D., 395-5338, jfrater@brockport.edu
Social Work* (M.S.W.): Estella Norwood Evans, Ph.D., CSW, ACSW, 327-7450, enevans@naz.edu
(*Greater Rochester Collaborative Master of Social Work with Nazareth College of Rochester)

STATE UNIVERSITY OF NEW YORK INSTITUTE OF TECHNOLOGY AT UTICA/ROME

School of Management, School of Information Systems and Engineering Technology, School of Arts and Sciences, and School of Nursing

Programs of Study

The School of Management offers three Master of Science programs in accountancy, in health services administration, and in business management, with concentrations available in health services management, human resources management, accounting and finance, and marketing. The accounting program, which is also available online and is registered in New York State to satisfy the 150-hour licensure requirement, prepares students for careers in public accounting, corporate accounting, not-for-profit accounting, and government accounting. Graduates are prepared to sit for professional accounting examinations that lead to credentials such as the CPA and CMA designations. The focus of course work in the business management program is on the use of quantitative and qualitative analysis in conjunction with financial, accounting, and economic principles to solve current and future business challenges. The health services and administration program, which is also available online, prepares students for management positions in the health-care industry. The School of Information Systems and Engineering Technology offers three graduate degrees. The Master of Science degree in computer and information science is designed to provide students with a strong theoretical and application-oriented education. Course offerings stress principles of problem-solving methodology that are required of computer professionals working in industry and education or those pursuing advanced degrees. The Master of Science in advanced technology program is an interdisciplinary program with an emphasis on practical applications. It is offered jointly by the electrical, industrial, and mechanical engineering technology departments and is designed for part-time students. A limited number of Internet-based online courses are available. The Master of Science in telecommunications is based on a solid core of telecommunications courses combined with computer science/information systems and business-related components to provide the breadth of knowledge to deal with design, management, and maintenance of complex telecommunication systems. The School of Arts and Sciences offers two Master of Science programs. The Master of Science in information design and technology (I.D.T.) meets the needs of professionals who use communication technologies to design and manage information. Students use a variety of computer-based tools to create original materials including Web pages, multimedia presentations, newsletters, and related desktop publishing documents in fields such as education, technical communication, public relations, marketing, instructional design and technology, government service, publications, and corporate communication. The Master of Science in applied sociology promotes the application of anthropological and sociological theory and research to design, implement, and evaluate organizationally based interventions. Students learn to integrate various methods of data collection and analysis to use in evaluating social programs. The School of Nursing offers three Master of Science programs, in nursing administration, in adult nurse practitioner, and in family nurse practitioner. The nursing administration program is specifically designed to prepare registered nurses to effectively manage the delivery of nursing services through the synthesis of theories of organization, leadership, and management with nursing theory, practice, and research. Graduates of the nurse practitioner programs are prepared to focus on health assessments, disease prevention, health promotion, and monitoring of chronic conditions to keep people healthy outside of hospitals and nursing homes. Graduates of the master's program are qualified to take the American Nurses Association's certification exam.

Research Facilities

Research facilities include a library containing 192,425 bound volumes, 65,396 microforms, and an extensive collection of professional journals, newspapers, and other national publications. The library serves as a depository for selected state and federal documents. The library participates in SUNYConnect, the state university virtual library, which offers many online resources. Graduate students also have access to interlibrary loans. Superb computing facilities include numerous laboratory environments consisting of more than 380 personal computers and workstations in a networked environment that extends to every classroom, office, and dormitory room. Internet access is provided through a fractional T-3 connection. The master's degree program in telecommunications is supported by three state-of-the-art voice, data, and network operations laboratories possessing more than $5 million in industry-donated equipment. The I.D.T. program is supported by a state-of-the-art networked computer lab and related technologies, including workstations designed for collaborative project work.

Financial Aid

Matriculated graduate students who are enrolled for at least 6 credit hours each semester and are in good academic standing are eligible to apply for aid from the following sources: Federal Work-Study Program, Federal Perkins Loan Program, and Federal Direct Student Loan Program. New York State residents who are enrolled for at least 12 hours are eligible to apply for aid from the Tuition Assistance Program. Graduate assistantships are awarded each academic year to selected students and generally include a state tuition waiver for work performed as a teaching assistant, research assistant, or administrative assistant. A limited number of Graduate Minority Fellowships, which include a state tuition waiver and stipend, are available to full-time students who are members of underrepresented groups.

Cost of Study

Estimated costs for full-time enrollment for the 2001–02 academic year included state resident tuition and fees of $5625 and out-of-state tuition and fees of $8941. Part-time tuition and fees for state residents were $234.35 per credit hour; for out-of-state students, $372.35 per credit hour.

Living and Housing Costs

The Institute provides town-house-style residence halls for 584 students at an estimated cost of $6240 for room and board. Residence halls are available on a first-come, first-served basis. Assistance in locating off-campus housing is provided. Students interested in living on campus will be considered for a residential scholarship.

Student Group

The Institute offers a small-college atmosphere, enrolling 2,537 undergraduate and graduate students. One hundred twenty-six graduate students are enrolled full-time and 365 part-time. The man-woman ratio is approximately 1:1. Eleven percent of the student population are from minority groups; 3.8 percent are international students. Students work closely with faculty members and receive individual attention. Close to 100 percent of students who have completed graduate programs at the Institute are working full-time in their professional field.

Location

The State University of New York (SUNY) Institute of Technology is situated in the geographic center of New York State. Utica is a cultural and recreational center for the Mohawk Valley Region. Museums, theaters, and restaurants are available nearby. The area is easily accessible by local and interstate bus services, Amtrak, and the Oneida County Airport.

The Institute

The State University of New York Institute of Technology was established in 1966 by the SUNY Board of Trustees to provide upper-division and graduate-level education in sciences and technologies. SUNY Institute of Technology continues to provide professionally oriented programs to meet the needs of undergraduate and graduate students and will begin offering select programs to freshmen in fall 2003. The campus is just north of the city of Utica; it includes three major academic, administrative, and student life buildings, two town house–style residential complexes, a facilities building, and a $14-million library scheduled for completion in fall 2002.

Applying

Applications to one of the graduate programs should be completed by June 1 for the fall semester and November 1 for spring. While the college does offer rolling admission in most programs, these application deadlines are required for international students. The Graduate Record Examinations (GRE) are required for the graduate programs in computer science, advanced technology, nursing administration, family nurse practitioner, and adult nurse practitioner. An undergraduate degree in nursing and RN licensure are also required for the nursing graduate programs. The Graduate Management Admission Test (GMAT) is required for the business management, health services administration, and accountancy programs. A minimum TOEFL score of 550, along with GRE or GMAT scores, is required for international students whose native language is not English (excluding international students who have earned an undergraduate degree in the United States). Personal interviews are encouraged but not required.

Correspondence and Information

Director of Admissions
SUNY Institute of Technology at Utica/Rome
P.O. Box 3050
Utica, New York 13504-3050
Telephone: 866-2SUNYIT (toll-free)
E-mail: admissions@sunyit.edu
World Wide Web: http://www.sunyit.edu

THE FACULTY AND THEIR RESEARCH

School of Arts and Sciences (Information Design and Technology, Applied Sociology)

David Hakken, Professor; Ph.D., American. Computerization and human needs, social policy.
Maarten Heyboer, Associate Professor; Ph.D. Virginia Tech. Computer-mediated communication and distance learning via the Internet.
Walter Johnston, Associate Professor; Ph.D., Cornell. Technical writing and editing.
Russell Kahn, Associate Professor; Ph.D., SUNY at Albany. Social implications of the Web, graphic design, Web design and computer software documentation.
Kenneth Mazlen, Associate Professor; Ph.D., SUNY at Albany. Social theory, white-collar crime, unemployment and crime.
Daniel J. Murphy, Associate Professor; Ph.D., Rensselaer. Technical communication, digital media and computer-mediated communication.
Alphonse Sallett, Associate Professor; Ph.D., Syracuse. Social theory, criminology and the sociology of drug use.
Steven Schneider, Associate Professor; Ph.D., MIT. Computer-mediated communication and computer-mediated instructional systems.
Linda Weber, Associate Professor; Ph.D., North Texas. Social practice, medical sociology, social psychology, health promotion, at-risk youth.
Lee Williams, Assistant Professor; Ph.D., Tennessee. Political sociology, social change, community, applied research methods, medical sociology, community forestry, social justice, rural development, participatory research and popular education.

School of Management (Accountancy, Business Management, and Health Services Administration)

Thomas Amlie, Assistant Professor; M.B.A., Ph.D., Maryland. Pension accounting, job cost accounting.
Lisa Calongne, Assistant Professor; Ph.D., Virginia Tech. Human resource management in small businesses, adult learning and needs assessment.
John E. Cook, Professor; Ph.D., Syracuse. Management, human resource management.
J. Allen Hall, Associate Professor; Ph.D., Iowa. Communications for business.
Richard J. Havranek, Associate Professor; Ph.D., Syracuse. Human resource management, computerization of personnel and other management information, strategy/policy.
Peter Karl, Associate Professor; J.D., Albany Law; M.B.A., Rensselaer; CPA. Tax, business law, real estate transactions, federal taxation.
William Langdon, Professor; Ph.D., Syracuse. Quantitative methods and finance.
Sarah Laditka, Associate Professor; Ph.D., Syracuse. Public administration, health and aging-related processes, health-care delivery systems, health-care data research.
Hoseoup Lee, Assistant Professor; Ph.D., Connecticut. Capital markets and accounting information systems.
James Morey, Associate Professor; M.B.A., George Washington; CPA. Hospital mergers/consolidations, nursing home establishment, expansion and acquisition, operational analysis.
Edward Petronio, Associate Professor; Ph.D., Syracuse. Business policy and organizational behavior.
Rafael F. Romero, Associate Professor; Ph.D., West Virginia. Emerging capital markets, international economics.
Gary Scherzer, Associate Professor; M.P.H., Tennessee. Public health, planning, marketing, health policy.
Thomas Tribunella, Associate Professor; Ph.D., RIT; CPA. Decision and accounting information systems.
Henry Vandenburgh, Assistant Professor; Ph.D., Texas at Austin. Health-care organizations.
Sanjay B. Varshney, Associate Professor and Dean and Chartered Financial Analyst with the New York Society of Security Analysts; Ph.D., LSU. Market microstructure trading analysis, corporate governance, security valuation and issuance.
Robert Yeh, Assistant Professor; Ph.D., Purdue. Quantitative marketing models, statistical applications and mathematical modeling in product designing and product improvement.
Linda Yu, Assistant Professor; Ph.D., Memphis. Fixed income securities pricing, term structure of interest rates, asset liquidity.

School of Information Systems and Engineering Technology (Advanced Technology, Computer Information Science, and Telecommunications)

Bruno Andriamanalimanana, Associate Professor; Ph.D., Lehigh. Combinatorics, coding theory and cryptography.
Orlando Baiocchi, Professor; Ph.D., University College (London). Electromagnetics, pulse propagation and nonlinear media.
Daniel Benicasa, Assistant Professor; Ph.D., Rensselaer. Digital signal processing, electrooptic systems, RF systems, communication intelligence systems.
Roger Cavallo, Professor; Ph.D., SUNY at Binghamton. Systems theory, systems methodology, conceptual modeling, probabilistic database theory.
Digendra Kumar Das, Associate Professor; Ph.D., Manchester (England). CAD/CAM/CIM, fluid/prognostics, turbomachinery and thermal sciences and MEMS.
Heather Dussault, Assistant Professor; Ph.D., Rensselaer. Nuclear engineering and science.
Patrick W. Fitzgibbons, Associate Professor of Telecommunications; Ph.D., SUNY at Buffalo. Network design, simulation, and management.
Larry Hash, Associate Professor of Telecommunications; Ph.D., North Carolina State. Wireless networks and services, LAN-WAN.
Atlas Hsie, Associate Professor; M.S. Michigan, M.S., Akron; CmfgE, CQE, CRE. Quality and reliability engineering, engineering economics, production management, CAM and robotics.
Naseem Ishaq, Associate Professor; Ph.D., London. Vision, VLSI and networking, computer-aided design.
Raymond G. Jesaitis, Professor; Ph.D., Cornell. Distributed systems, UNIX operating system, numerical methods.
Ernest J. Johnson, Lecturer; Ph.D. candidate, SUNY at Stony Brook. XSB logic programming, tabling systems, TST.
Daniel K. Jones, Assistant Professor; Ph.D., Pittsburgh; PE. Rehabilitation engineering and assistive technology, experimental fluid mechanics and FMS.
Yefim Kats, Assistant Professor; Ph.D., CUNY Graduate School. Automatic control systems, modeling, software development.
Kevin Lefebvre, Lecturer in Telecommunications; Ph.D., Connecticut. Information assurance, transport networks.
Michael J. Medley, Assistant Professor; Ph.D., Rennselaer. Lapped transform domain excision, adaptive nonlinear/linear filtering, RA -OFDM, wireless information assurance, integrated transmission and exploitation.
Rosemary Mullick, Associate Professor; Ph.D., Wayne State. Operating systems, artificial intelligence, computer networks, parallels between human cognition and artificial intelligence and human engineering.
Eugene J. Newman, Professor of Telecommunications; Ph.D., Wisconsin. International telecommunications policy and trade issues, project management.
Jorge Novillo, Professor; Ph.D., Lehigh. Combinatorics, complexity, artificial intelligence.
Michael Pittarelli, Professor; Ph.D., SUNY at Binghamton. Systems science, artificial intelligence, statistics, database theory.
Salahuddin Qazi, Associate Professor; Ph.D., Loughborough (England). Fiber optics, optical and wireless communications.
Mohamed Rezk, Associate Professor; D.Eng., Concordia. Circuit theory, computer-aided circuit design and digital filters.
Ronald Sarner, Distinguished Service Professor; Ph.D., SUNY at Binghamton. Data modeling, statistical inference in the social sciences, instructional computing.
Saumendra Sengupta, Professor; Ph.D., Waterloo. Systems modeling, computer networks and distributed systems, pattern recognition.
Scott Spetka, Associate Professor; Ph.D., UCLA. Distributed database systems and distributed query processing.
Anglo-Kamel Tadros, Associate Professor; Ph.D., Bradford (England). Mechanics of sheet metal forming, computer-aided engineering, finite element analysis.

School of Nursing (Nursing Administration, Family Nurse Practitioner, Adult Nurse Practitioner)

Esther G. Bankert, Associate Professor; Ph.D., SUNY at Albany. Critical thinking and instruction, ethical decision making models and moral development in the RN student.
Cathryn Barns, Assistant Professor; M.S., Syracuse. Adult health.
Mary Lou Wranesh Cook, Professor; Ph.D., SUNY at Albany. Helping relationship between home-care workers and family caregivers.
Louise Dean-Kelly, Associate Professor; D.N.S., SUNY at Buffalo. Definition of health and health-care practices through cross-cultural studies.
Deborah A. Hayes, Clinical Assistant Professor; M.S., SUNY at Binghamton. Family health.
Christeen Liang, Clinical Assistant Professor; M.S., SUNY at Binghamton. Women's health.
Jeannine D. Muldoon, Professor and Dean; Ph.D., Massachusetts Amherst. Health policy, technology in health care, privacy and security issues.
Maria Pappas-Rogich, Associate Professor; Dr.P.H., Pittsburgh. Gerontological health.
Victoria E. Rinehart, Associate Professor; Ed.D., Columbia Teachers College. Personality types and coping.
Kathleen F. Sellers, Assistant Professor; Ph.D., Adelphi. Nursing systems.
Pamela Slagle, Clinical Assistant Professor; M.S., SUNY at Stony Brook. Family health.
Carole E. Torok, Associate Professor; Ph.D., SUNY at Albany. RN students and wellness, writing across the curriculum.

STEVENS
Institute of Technology

STEVENS INSTITUTE OF TECHNOLOGY

Programs of Study

Stevens offers advanced programs in a broad range of engineering disciplines, the physical sciences, computer science, mathematics, management, and interdisciplinary programs as well as graduate certificate programs. The Department of Chemical, Biochemical, and Materials Engineering offers M.Eng., Ch.E., and Ph.D. degrees in chemical engineering, with concentrations in chemical engineering and polymer engineering; M.Eng. and Ph.D. degrees in materials engineering, with a concentration in microelectronics and photonics science and technology. The Department of Chemistry and Chemical Biology offers the M.S. degree in chemical biology, with a concentration in bioinformatics, and M.S. and Ph.D. degrees in chemistry, with concentrations in analytical chemistry, chemical biology, organic chemistry, physical chemistry, and polymer chemistry. The Department of Civil, Environmental, and Ocean Engineering offers M.Eng., C.E., and Ph.D. degrees in civil engineering, with concentrations in geotechnical/geoenvironmental engineering, structural engineering, and water resources engineering; M.Eng. and Ph.D. degrees in environmental engineering, with concentrations in environmental process, groundwater and soil pollution control, and inland and coastal environmental hydrodynamics; M.Eng. and Ph.D. degrees in ocean engineering, with concentrations in coastal engineering, hydrodynamics, naval architecture, and oceanography; the M.S. degree in construction management; and the M.S. degree in maritime systems, with concentrations in environmental engineering, structural engineering, management, and marine transportation. The Department of Computer Science offers M.S. and Ph.D. degrees in computer science, with concentrations in computer communication, database systems, programming languages and compilers, software design, and theoretical computer science, and the M.S. degree in quantitative software engineering. The Department of Electrical and Computer Engineering offers M.Eng., C.E., and Ph.D. degrees in computer engineering, with concentrations in computer systems, data communications and networks, digital systems design, image processing and multimedia, and software engineering; M.Eng., E.E., and Ph.D. degrees in electrical engineering, with concentrations in computer architecture and digital system design, signal processing for communications, telecommunications engineering, wireless communications, and microelectronics and photonics science and technology; and the M.Eng. degree in networked information systems, with concentrations in data communication networks, information networks, multimedia technologies, network systems technologies, networked information systems, business practices, and secure network systems. The Department of Mathematical Sciences offers the M.S. degree in applied mathematics, applied statistics, and stochastic systems analysis and optimization and the M.S. and Ph.D. degrees in mathematics. The Department of Mechanical Engineering offers M.Eng., M.E., and Ph.D. degrees in mechanical engineering, with concentrations in manufacturing systems, product design, and thermal engineering. The Department of Physics and Engineering Physics offers the M.Eng. degree in engineering physics (optics and solid state), with concentrations in microelectronics and photonics science and technology, and M.S. and Ph.D. degrees in physics. The Wesley J. Howe School of Technology Management offers the M.S. in information systems (MSIS), with concentrations in computer science, e-commerce, information management, project management, and telecommunications management; the M.S. degree in management, with concentrations in general management, global innovation management, information management, management planning, project management, and technology management; the M.S. degree in telecommunications management, with concentrations in business management and technical management; an Executive Master of Technology Management (EMTM) program; and Ph.D. degrees in information management and technology management.

Graduate certificate programs are also available in almost all programs and are usually four graduate courses that transfer directly to a master's degree at Stevens. Numerous off-campus corporate locations are also available.

Research Facilities

All departments have state-of-the-art research facilities. In addition, Stevens has developed research alliances, called "Centers," which strive to identify problems in U.S. competitiveness and develop solutions industry can implement. Major areas of research addressed by Centers include automated concurrent engineering, environmental and coastal engineering, highly filled materials technologies, the development of polymer processes, telecommunications, the effective management of manufacturing, and laser physics and quantum electronics technologies.

Stevens' Computer Center supports mainframe, minicomputer, and microcomputer systems. The library provides students with a wide range of information-gathering tools, such as an information retrieval system of bibliographical computer databases containing references to millions of documents.

Financial Aid

Assistantships, fellowships, scholarships, loan and deferred-payment plans, work-study, and employer tuition benefits are available to qualified students. In 2001–02, assistantships ranged from $13,000 to $15,000 for the stipend plus remission of tuition and fees; recipients devote 20 hours per week to teaching or research.

Cost of Study

Tuition for the 2002–03 academic year for courses offered in the School of Engineering (SOE) and the Arthur E. Imperatore School of Sciences and Arts (ISSA) is $750 per credit hour, which was equal to $2250 for a typical 3-credit-hour graduate course. (SOE and ISSA each require completion of ten courses for graduation.) Tuition for courses offered in the School of Technology Management (STM) is $625 per credit hour, which was equal to $1875 for a typical 3-credit-hour graduate course. (STM requires completion of 12 courses for graduation.)

Living and Housing Costs

Residence costs for 2001–02 ranged from $3030 to $5800 per academic year for an off-campus room to $5360 per academic year for on-campus married and graduate student apartments. Additional living expenses are approximately $4050 for thirty-eight weeks. Books and supplies cost about $500 per year.

Student Group

There is an exceptionally diverse group of about 2,570 graduate students at Stevens, nearly 80 percent of whom are enrolled part-time.

Location

Stevens is located on the west bank of the Hudson River in Hoboken, New Jersey, a community that has undergone a remarkable renaissance and become a popular residential and cultural center. The campus is 15 minutes from the center of New York City. World-famous year-round resort areas and beaches are less than 2 hours away.

The Institute

Founded in 1870, Stevens is a pioneer in technical education and a highly regarded independent center of study and research, accredited by MSACS, ABET, and CSAB. Total enrollment is approximately 4,170, and there are 130 full-time faculty members, more than 95 percent of whom hold the doctorate. A leader in integrating computers into engineering education, Stevens was the first university in the country to require freshmen to purchase personal computers. A campuswide computer network greatly expands the capabilities of the entire university community.

Applying

An application, transcripts, two recommendations, and a $50 application fee should be filed with the Dean of the Graduate School at least three to four weeks before the beginning of a semester for domestic applicants and three to four months before for international applicants. The fall semester begins in late August and the spring semester in mid-January. Additional information on financial aid may be obtained from the financial aid office. Registration should be completed at least a week before the term opening.

Correspondence and Information

Dr. Charles Suffel
Dean of the Graduate School
Stevens Institute of Technology
Castle Point on Hudson
Hoboken, New Jersey 07030
Telephone: 201-216-5234
World Wide Web: http://www.stevens-tech.edu

DEPARTMENT HEADS

ARTHUR E. IMPERATORE SCHOOL OF SCIENCES AND ARTS
Erich Kunhardt, Dean; Ph.D., Polytechnic of New York, 1976. Telephone: 201-216-5099.

Department of Chemistry and Chemical Biology
Frank T. Jones, Director; Ph.D., Dartmouth, 1981. Telephone: 201-216-5518.

Department of Computer Science
Stephen L. Bloom, Director; Ph.D., MIT, 1968. Telephone: 201-216-5439.

Department of Mathematical Sciences
Milos Dostal, Director; Ph.D., Czechoslovak Academy of Sciences, 1966. Telephone: 201-216-5448.

Department of Physics and Engineering Physics
Kurt H. Becker, Director; Ph.D., Saarbrücken, 1981. Telephone: 201-216-5671.

CHARLES V. SCHAEFER, JR. SCHOOL OF ENGINEERING
Bernard M. Gallois, Dean; Ph.D., Carnegie Mellon, 1980. Telephone: 201-216-5263.

Department of Chemical, Biochemical, and Materials Engineering
Woo Young Lee, Director; Ph.D., Georgia Tech, 1990. Telephone: 201-216-8307.

Department of Civil, Environmental, and Ocean Engineering
Richard I. Hires, Director; Ph.D., Johns Hopkins, 1968. Telephone: 201-216-5676.

Department of Electrical and Computer Engineering
Stuart Tewksbury, Director; Ph.D., Rochester, 1969. Telephone: 201-216-5623.

Department of Mechanical Engineering
Constantin Chassapis, Co-Director; Ph.D., CUNY Graduate Center, 1988. Telephone: 201-216-5564.

SCHOOL OF ENGINEERING–RESEARCH ALLIANCES/CENTERS

Center for Environmental Engineering
George P. Korfiatis, Director; Ph.D., Rutgers, 1984. Telephone: 201-216-5348.

Center for Product Lifecycle Management
George P. Korfiatis, Director; Ph.D., Rutgers, 1984. Telephone: 201-216-5348.

Davidson Laboratory
Michael S. Bruno, Director; Sc.D., MIT, 1986. Telephone: 201-216-5338.

Design and Manufacturing Institute (DMI)
Constantin Chassapis, Co-Director; Ph.D., CUNY Graduate Center, 1988. Telephone: 201-216-5564.
Souran P. Manoochehri, Co-Director; Ph.D., Wisconsin–Madison, 1986. Telephone: 201-216-5562.

Highly Filled Materials Institute
Dilhan M. Kalyon, Director; Ph.D., McGill, 1980. Telephone: 201-216-8225.

WESLEY J. HOWE SCHOOL OF TECHNOLOGY MANAGEMENT
Jerry MacArthur Hultin, Dean; J.D., Yale, 1972. Telephone: 201-216-8166.

General Management
C. Timothy Koeller, Director; Ph.D., Rutgers, 1979. Telephone: 201-216-5376.

Information Systems
Jerome N. Luftman, Director; Ph.D., Stevens, 1991. Telephone: 201-216-8255.

Project Management
Parviz Rad, Director; Ph.D., MIT, 1970. Telephone: 201-216-8126.

Executive Master of Technology Management (EMTM)
Donald N. Merino, Director; Ph.D., Stevens, 1975. Telephone: 201-216-8903.

Telecommunications Management
Audrey Curtis, Director; Ph.D., NYU, 1980. Telephone: 201-216-5524.

WESLEY J. HOWE SCHOOL OF TECHNOLOGY MANAGEMENT–RESEARCH ALLIANCES/CENTERS

Alliance for Technology Management (ATM)
Lawrence E. Gaswirt, Director; Ph.D., Princeton 1962. Telephone: 201-216-8941.

Center for Improved Engineering and Science Engineering (CIESE)
Edward A. Friedman, Director; Ph.D., Columbia, 1963. Telephone: 201-216-5188.

STONY BROOK UNIVERSITY, STATE UNIVERSITY OF NEW YORK

Graduate School

Programs of Study

Stony Brook is a leading research university offering graduate degree programs in the following fields of study: anatomical sciences/Ph.D.; anthropology (anthropological sciences)/M.A.; applied mathematics and statistics/M.S., Ph.D.; art (studio)/M.F.A.; art history and criticism/M.A., Ph.D.; biological science/M.A.; biomedical engineering/M.S., Ph.D.; biopsychology/Ph.D.; cellular and developmental biology/Ph.D.; chemistry/M.S., Ph.D.; clinical psychology/Ph.D.; coastal oceanography/Ph.D.; computer science/M.S., Ph.D.; dentistry/D.D.S.; dramaturgy/M.F.A.; earth and space sciences (geosciences)/M.S., Ph.D.; ecology and evolution/Ph.D.; economics/M.A., Ph.D.; electrical engineering/M.S., Ph.D.; English/M.A., Ph.D.; English (comparative literature)/M.A., Ph.D.; executive option M.B.A.; experimental psychology/Ph.D.; foreign language instruction (French, German, Italian, Russian, and TESOL)/D.A.; Germanic languages and literature/M.A.; genetics/Ph.D.; health-care policy and management/M.S.; Hispanic languages and literature/M.A., Ph.D.; history/M.A., Ph.D.; human resources management/M.P.S.; liberal studies/M.A.; linguistics/M.A., Ph.D.; management and policy/M.S.; marine environmental sciences/M.S.; materials science and engineering/M.S., Ph.D.; mathematics/M.A., Ph.D.; mechanical engineering/M.S., Ph.D.; medicine/M.D., M.D./Ph.D.; molecular biology and biochemistry/Ph.D.; molecular and cellular biology/Ph.D.; molecular and cellular pharmacology/Ph.D.; molecular microbiology/Ph.D.; music/M.A., Ph.D.; music performance/M.M., D.M.A.; neurobiology and behavior/Ph.D.; nursing (adult health, child health, family nurse, gerontological nurse, midwifery, neonatal, perinatal/women's health, psychiatric/mental health)/M.S.; oral biology and pathology/Ph.D.; philosophy/M.A., Ph.D.; physics/M.A., Ph.D.; physics (scientific instrumentation)/M.S.; physiology and biophysics/Ph.D.; physical therapy/M.S.; political science/M.A., Ph.D.; psychology/M.A.; public affairs/M.P.S.; Romance languages and literature (French, Italian)/M.A.; Slavic languages and literature/M.A.; social health psychology/Ph.D.; social work/M.S.W., M.S.W./J.D. (with the Touro College Law Center); social welfare/Ph.D.; sociology/M.A., Ph.D.; teaching grades 7–12 (biology, chemistry, earth science, English, French, German, Italian, physics, Russian, social studies)/M.A.T.; technological systems management/M.S., M.B.A.; technology management/M.S.; TESOL/M.A.; theater/M.A., Ph.D. (dramaturgy); and waste management/M.P.S. Stony Brook offers Advanced Graduate Certificates in biomedical engineering, coaching, community health, cultural studies, educational computing, environmental/occupational health and safety, health-care management, human resources management, information systems management, oceanic science, operations research, school administration and supervision, school district administration, software engineering, waste management, and women's studies. Postdoctoral certificates are available in endodontics, orthodontics, and periodontics.

Research Facilities

Research support is provided by the Frank Melville, Jr. Memorial Library; the Health Sciences Library; and six branch science libraries, holding more than 2 million volumes and 3 million publications in microformat. Sun, IBM, and DEC computers in the Division of Information Technology and in other academic departments are available for general research use. There are more than 800 publicly available state-of-the-art computers for student use. E-mail and Internet accounts are provided to all full-time students. Other research facilities include the Institute for Theoretical Physics, the Humanities Institute, and the Marine Science Research Center.

Financial Aid

Because Stony Brook is committed to attracting quality students, the Graduate School provides two competitive fellowships for U.S. citizens and permanent residents. Graduate Council fellowships are for outstanding doctoral candidates studying in any discipline, and the W. Burghardt Turner Fellowships target outstanding African-American, Hispanic American, and Native American students entering either a doctoral or master's degree program. For doctoral students, both fellowships provide an annual stipend of at least $15,600 for up to five years, as well as a full tuition scholarship. For master's students, the Turner Fellowship provides an annual stipend of $10,000 for up to two years, along with a full tuition scholarship. Health insurance subsidies are also provided within a scale depending on the size of the fellow's dependent family. Departments and degree programs award approximately 900 teaching and graduate assistantships and approximately 600 research assistantships on an annual basis. Full assistantships carry a stipend amount that usually ranges from $11,260 to $18,000, depending on the department.

Cost of Study

In 2001–02, full-time tuition was $2550 per semester for state residents and $4208 per semester for nonresidents. Part-time tuition was $213 per credit hour for residents and $351 per credit hour for nonresidents. Additional charges included an activity fee of $20.50 and a comprehensive fee of $287.50 per semester.

Living and Housing Costs

University apartments ranged in cost from approximately $208 per month to approximately $1180 per month, depending on the size of the unit. Off-campus housing options include furnished rooms to rent and houses and/or apartments to share that can be rented for $350 to $550 per month.

Student Group

Stony Brook's current enrollment is 20,855 students. Graduate students number 6,667 and come from all states in the nation, as well as from some seventy-five countries. International students, both graduate and undergraduate, represent about 9 percent of the total student body.

Location

Stony Brook's campus is approximately 50 miles east of Manhattan on the north shore of Long Island. The cultural offerings of New York City and Suffolk County's countryside and seashore are conveniently located nearby. Cold Spring Harbor Laboratories and Brookhaven National Laboratories are easily accessible from, and have close relationships with, the University.

The University

The University, established in 1957, achieved national stature within a generation. Founded at Oyster Bay, Long Island, the school moved to its present location in 1962. Stony Brook has grown to encompass more than 110 buildings on 1,100 acres. There are more than 1,568 faculty members, and the annual budget is more than $805 million. The Graduate Student Organization oversees the spending of the student activity fee for graduate student campus events. International students find the additional four-week Summer Institute in American Living very helpful. The Intensive English Center offers classes in English as a second language. The Career Development Office assists with career planning and has information on permanent full-time employment. Disabled Student Services has a Resource Center that offers placement testing, tutoring, vocational assessment, and psychological counseling. The Counseling Center provides individual, group, family, and marital counseling and psychotherapy. Day-care services are provided in four on-campus facilities. The Writing Center offers tutoring in all phases of writing.

Applying

Applicants are judged on the basis of distinguished undergraduate records (and graduate records, if applicable), thorough preparation for advanced study and research in the field of interest, candid appraisals from those familiar with the applicant's academic/professional work, potential for graduate study, and a clearly defined statement of purpose and scholarly interest germane to the program. A baccalaureate degree is required, with a minimum overall grade point average of 2.75 and an average grade of B in the major and related courses. Some programs require a higher GPA. Students should submit admission and financial aid applications by January 15 for the fall semester and by October 1 for the spring semester. Decisions are made on a rolling basis as space permits. The $50 application fee may be waived in some circumstances.

Correspondence and Information

For further information, students should contact the graduate program director listed on the following page (area code is 631) or phone or write:

Graduate School
State University of New York at Stony Brook
Stony Brook, New York 11794-4433

Telephone: 631-632-4723
Fax: 631-632-7243
E-mail: graduate.school@sunysb.edu
World Wide Web: http://www.grad.sunysb.edu/

THE FACULTY

According to the most recent independent, quantitative study, Stony Brook ranked among the top three public research universities in the nation on the basis of faculty productivity in research and scholarship. With the total research volume nearly doubling in the last decade and now exceeding $121 million annually, Stony Brook's researchers have propelled the University to the top position among all of New York's public institutions in Federally sponsored project funding. Adjusted for size, Stony Brook can claim more members of the most selective national bodies of scholars than any other public university in the Northeast. Stony Brook faculty members are part of the National Academy of Sciences, the National Academy of Engineering, and the American Academy of Arts and Sciences. Distinguished faculty members and some of their most outstanding accomplishments include C.N. Yang, Physics (emeritus), Nobel laureate; applied mathematician James Glimm, Dannie Heineman Prize for mathematics; mathematician James Milnor, Wolf Prize; neuroscientist Paul Adams, MacArthur Award; anatomist John Fleagle, MacArthur Award; George C. Williams, Ecology and Evolution (emeritus), Royal Swedish Academy of Sciences Crafoord Prize; anthropologist Patricia Wright, whose work was recently featured in the award-winning documentary, *Me and Isaac Newton,* MacArthur Award; mathematician Dennis Sullivan, King Faisal International Prize of Science; neuroscientist Gail Mandel, Howard Hughes Medical Institute Investigator.

BASIC HEALTH SCIENCES Craig Malbon, Vice Dean.
Anatomical Sciences: Cathy Forster, Director, 444-3114, catherine.forster@stonybrook.edu; Jack Stern, Chairperson.
Molecular and Cellular Pharmacology: Daniel Bogenhagen, Director, 444-3057, daniel.bogenhagen@stonybrook.edu; Francis Johnson, Chairperson.
Molecular Microbiology: James Konopka, Director, 632-8812, james.konopka@stonybrook.edu; Michael Hayman, Acting Chairperson.
Oral Biology and Pathology: Jerry Pollock, Director, 632-8923, jerry.pollock@stonybrook.edu; Israel Kleinberg, Chairperson.
Physiology and Biophysics: Suzanne Scarlata, Director, 444-2299, suzanne.scarlata@stonybrook.edu; Peter Brink, Chairperson.
Medical Scientist Training Program (M.D./Ph.D.): Paul Fisher, 444-3067, paul.fisher@stonybrook.edu.

DENTISTRY Barry Rifkin, Dean, 632-8950.
Erin E. Riley, D.M.D., Assistant Dean for Admissions and Student Affairs, 632-8871, erin.riley@stonybrook.edu.

HEALTH TECHNOLOGY AND MANAGEMENT Craig Lehmann, Dean.
Health Care Policy and Management and Community Health Education: Nanci Rice, Director, 444-3240, nanci.rice@stonybrook.edu; Alan Leiken, Chairperson.

MEDICINE Norman H. Edelman, Dean.
Grace Agnetti, Assistant Dean for Admissions, 444-2113, grace.agnetti@stonybrook.edu.

NURSING Lenora J. McClean, Dean.
Philip Tarantino, Director of Enrollment, 444-3282, philip.tarantino@stonybrook.edu.

SOCIAL WELFARE Frances Brisbane, Dean.
Ph.D. Program: Joel Blau, Director, 444-8361, joel.blau@stonybrook.edu.
M.S.W. Program: Linda Francis, Director, 444-3141, linda.francis@stonybrook.edu.

COLLEGE OF ARTS AND SCIENCES James Staros, Dean.
Anthropological Science (Ph.D.): Callum Ross, Director, 632-7606, callum.ross@stonybrook.edu.
Anthropology (M.A.): Diane Doran, Director, 632-7606, diane.doran@stonybrook.edu; Fred Grine, Chairperson.
Art: Barbara Frank, Director, 632-7270, barbara.frank@stonybrook.edu; James Rubin, Chairperson.
Biochemistry and Structural Biology: Steven O. Smith, Director, 632-1210, steven.o.smith@stonybrook.edu; William Lennarz, Chairperson.
Chemistry: Peter Tonge, Director, 632-7886, peter.tonge@stonybrook.edu; Iwao Ojima, Chairperson.
Comparative Literature: Ilona Rashkow, Director, 632-7456, ilona.rashkow@stonybrook.edu; Krin Gabbard, Chairperson.
Ecology and Evolution: Manuel Lerdau, Director, 632-8604, manuel.lerdau@stonybrook.edu; Walter Eanes, Chairperson.
Economics: Thomas Muench, Director, 632-7530, thomas.muench@stonybrook.edu; William Dawes, Chairperson.
English: Heidi Hutner, Director, 632-7373, heidi.hutner@stonybrook.edu; Peter Manning, Chairperson.
European Languages, Literatures, and Cultures: Nicholas Rzhevsky, Director, 632-7442, nicholas.rzhevsky@stonybrook.edu; Charles Franco, Chairperson.
Genetics: Peter Gergen, Director, 632-8812, john.peter.gergen@stonybrook.edu.
Geosciences: Martin Schoonen, Director, 632-8554, martin.schoonen@stonybrook.edu; Scott McLennan, Chairperson.
Hispanic Languages and Literature: Victoriano Roncero-Lopez, Director, 632-6935, victoriano.roncero-lopez@stonybrook.edu; Román de la Campa, Chairperson.
History: Chris Sellers, Director, 632-7490, christopher.sellers@stonybrook.edu; Ned Landsman, Chairperson.
Linguistics: Christina Bethin, Director, 632-7774, christina.bethin@stonybrook.edu; Daniel Finer, Chairperson.
Mathematics: Lowell E. Jones, Director, 632-8282, lowell.jones@stonybrook.edu; Detlef Gromoll, Chairperson.
Mathematics (Secondary Teaching Option): Bernard Maskit, Director, 632-8257, bernard.maskit@stonybrook.edu.
Molecular and Cellular Biology: Nancy Reich, Director, 632-8533, nancy.reich@stonybrook.edu; William Lennarz, Chairperson.
Music: David Lawton, Director, 632-7330, david.lawton@stonybrook.edu; Judith Lochhead, Chairperson.
Neurobiology and Behavior: Mary Kritzer, Director, 632-8630, mary.kritzer@stonybrook.edu; Lorne Mendell, Chairperson.
Philosophy: Jeff Edwards, Director, 632-7580, b.edwards@stonybrook.edu; Kelly Oliver, Chairperson.
Physics and Astronomy: Peter Stephens, Director, 632-8080, peter.stephens@stonybrook.edu; Paul Grannis, Chairperson.
Political Science: Jeffrey Segal, Director, 632-7667, jeffrey.segal@stonybrook.edu; Mark Schneider, Chairperson.
Psychology: Susan Brennan, Director, 632-7855, susan.brennan@stonybrook.edu; Nancy Squires, Chairperson.
Public Policy (M.A.): Paul Teske, 632-7667, paul.teske@stonybrook.edu.
Sociology: Ivan Chase, Director, 632-7730, ivan.chase@stonybrook.edu; Norman Goodman, Chairperson.
Theater Arts: Michael X. Zelenak, Director, 632-7280, michael.zelenak@stonybrook.edu.
Women's Studies: Mary Rawlinson, Director, 632-9176, mary.rawlinson@stonybrook.edu.

COLLEGE OF ENGINEERING AND APPLIED SCIENCE Yacov Shamash, Dean.
Applied Math and Statistics: Woo Jong Kim, Director, 632-8360, woo.kim@stonybrook.edu; James Glimm, Chairperson.
Biomedical Engineering: Partap Khalsa, Director, 444-2303, partap.khalsa@stonybrook.edu; Clinton Rubin, Chairperson.
Computer Science: Michael Kifer, Director, 632-8471, michael.kifer@stonybrook.edu; Arie Kaufman, Chairperson.
Computer Science (M.S.): Arthur Bernstein, Director, 632-8471, arthur.bernstein@stonybrook.edu.
Electrical and Computer Engineering: Yuan Yuan Yang, Director, 632-8400, yuanyuan.yang@stonybrook.edu; Serge Luryi, Chairperson.
Information Systems Management: T. Owen Carroll, Director, 632-7476, owen.carroll@stonybrook.edu.
Management and Policy (Harriman School): Jeff Casey, Director, 632-7296, jeff.casey@stonybrook.edu; Tom Sexton, Chairperson.
Materials Science: Sanjay Sampath, Director, 632-0812, sanjay.sampath@stonybrook.edu; Michael Dudley, Chairperson.
Mechanical Engineering: Lin-Shu Wang, Director, 632-8340, lin-shu.wang@stonybrook.edu; Fu-Pen Chiang, Chairperson.
Technology and Society: Sheldon Reaven, Director, 632-8765, sheldon.reaven@stonybrook.edu; Thomas Liao, Chairperson.

MARINE SCIENCE RESEARCH CENTER Marvin Geller, Dean.
Marine Sciences: Glenn Lopez, Director, 632-8681, glenn.lopez@stonybrook.edu.

SCHOOL OF PROFESSIONAL DEVELOPMENT Paul Edelson, Dean, 632-7050.
Graduate Degrees and Advanced Graduate Certificates for Evening, Part-Time, and Online Study: Sandra Romansky, Assistant Dean and Director, 632-7050, sandra.romansky@stonybrook.edu.

TEMPLE UNIVERSITY

of the Commonwealth System of Higher Education

Graduate School

Programs of Study

Doctor of Philosophy programs are offered in the following fields: African-American studies, anatomy and cell biology, anthropology, art history, biochemistry, biology, business administration, chemistry, communication sciences, computer and information sciences, counseling psychology, criminal justice, dance, economics, educational psychology, engineering, English, health studies, history, kinesiology, mass media and communication, mathematics, medicinal and pharmaceutical chemistry, microbiology and immunology, molecular biology and genetics, music education, pathology, pharmaceutics, pharmacology, philosophy, physical therapy, physics, physiology, political science, psychology, religion, school psychology, sociology, Spanish, statistics, and urban education.

The Doctor of Musical Arts is offered in music composition and music performance.

Doctor of Education degrees are awarded in educational administration, language education, and mathematics/science education.

Master's degree programs are offered in actuarial sciences; adult and organizational development; African-American studies; anthropology; applied communication; art education; art history; biochemistry; biology; broadcasting, telecommunications, and mass media; business administration; chemistry; civil and environmental engineering; computer and information sciences; counseling psychology; creative writing; criminal justice; curriculum, instruction, and technology in education; dance; early childhood education; economics; educational administration; educational psychology; electrical and computer engineering; elementary education; environmental health; geography; geology; health-care management/health-care financial management; health studies; history; inclusive school practices; journalism; kinesiology; liberal arts; linguistics; mathematics; mathematics and science education; mechanical engineering; medicinal and pharmaceutical chemistry; microbiology and immunology; music composition; music education; music history; music performance; music theory; music therapy; nursing; occupational therapy; oral biology; pharmaceutics; pharmacology; philosophy; physical therapy; physics; physiology; political science; public health; quality assurance and regulatory affairs; school health education; school psychology; social work; sociology; Spanish; speech, language, and hearing; sport and recreation administration; statistics; teaching a second and foreign language; therapeutic recreation; tourism and hospitality management; urban education; and urban studies. Also offered are an executive M.B.A. and an international M.B.A.

Master of Fine Arts degree programs are available in acting, crafts, dance, design/technical productions, directing, film and media arts, graphic arts and design, and painting, drawing, and sculpture.

Research Facilities

The University libraries contain more than 2 million volumes and provide reading space for 2,500 students. One mile north of the Academic Center is the Health Sciences Center at Broad and Ontario streets. Here are housed the Schools of Medicine, Dentistry, and Pharmacy; the College of Allied Health Professions; the Temple University Hospital; and the Medical Research Building, all of which offer excellent and varied facilities for research in many fields.

Financial Aid

Aid is available to qualified full-time students in the form of assistantships, traineeships, and fellowships funded by the University and various external agencies. All forms include a stipend plus tuition. Tuition scholarships are also available to qualified students. The specific type of aid offered to a particular student depends on the student's qualifications and program of study.

Cost of Study

Resident tuition for the 2001–02 academic year was $369 per credit hour for most graduate programs, $384 per credit hour for Allied Health, $381 per credit hour for the Tyler School of Art, $383 per credit hour for the Fox School of Business and Management, and $505 per credit hour for Pharmacy, including Quality Assurance and Regulatory Affairs. Nonresident tuition was $534 per credit hour for most graduate programs, $557 per credit hour for Allied Health, $557 per credit hour for the Tyler School of Art, $565 per credit hour for the Fox School of Business and Management, and $665 per credit hour for Pharmacy, including Quality Assurance and Regulatory Affairs.

Living and Housing Costs

On-campus housing is limited. Students should contact the Student Housing Office at 215-204-7223.

Student Group

Temple University, which has nearly 30,000 students, is one of the largest universities in the country. Since becoming a part of the Commonwealth System of Higher Education it has placed increased emphasis on upper-division and graduate work. A significant portion of the student body is from outside Philadelphia, although the institution primarily serves the greater metropolitan area of eastern Pennsylvania.

Location

Philadelphia is the fifth-largest city in the country and has a regional population of more than 7 million. It offers a variety of cultural attractions. The city has a world-renowned symphony orchestra, a ballet company, two professional opera companies, and a chamber music society. Besides attracting touring plays, Philadelphia enjoys a professional repertory theater and many amateur productions. All facilities for sports and recreation are easy to reach. The city is world famous for its historic shrines, parks, and eighteenth-century charm, which is carefully maintained in the oldest section. The climate is temperate; there is an average winter temperature of 33 degrees and an average summer temperature of 75 degrees.

The University

The development of Temple University has been in line with the ideal of "educational opportunity for the able and deserving student of limited means." With a rich heritage of populist tradition, Temple provides students with an opportunity for education of high quality without regard to race, creed, or station in life. Affiliation with the Commonwealth System of Higher Education undergirds Temple's character as a public institution.

Temple's academic programs are conducted on six campuses in central and north Philadelphia and its nearby suburbs. These locations, as well as numerous extension centers throughout eastern Pennsylvania, give Temple University the distinction of being a fast-growing institution with many superior facilities.

The main campus, located at Broad Street and Montgomery Avenue, is the site of the Colleges of Education, Engineering, Liberal Arts, and Science and Technology; the Esther Boyer College of Music and Department of Dance; the Schools of Communications and Theater, Law, Social Administration, and Tourism and Hospitality Management; and the Fox School of Business and Management.

Applying

Departmental deadlines for admissions and financial aid vary. Applicants should consult the Internet address listed below and the program in which they are interested. Notification regarding admission and financial aid is made once the application has been screened.

Correspondence and Information

Dr. Sheryl Burt Ruzek
Acting Dean of the Graduate School
501 Carnell Hall
Temple University
1803 North Broad Street
Philadelphia, Pennsylvania 19122-6095
Telephone: 215-204-1380
World Wide Web: http://www.temple.edu/grad

FACULTY HEADS

Graduate School: Sheryl Burt Ruzek, Acting Dean.
College of Allied Health Professions: Peter Doukas, Acting Dean.
Tyler School of Art: Rochelle Toner, Dean.
Fox School of Business and Management: M. Moshe Porat, Dean.
School of Communications and Theater: Concetta Stewart, Dean.
School of Dentistry: Martin F. Tansy, Dean.
College of Education: Joseph Ducette, Acting Dean.
College of Engineering: Keya Sadeghipour, Acting Dean.
School of Law: Robert Reinstein, Dean.
College of Liberal Arts: Morris Vogel, Acting Dean.
School of Medicine: Leon Malmud, Dean.
Esther Boyer College of Music and Department of Dance: Richard Broadhead, Acting Dean.
School of Pharmacy: Peter Doukas, Dean.
School of Podiatric Medicine: John A. Mattiacci, Dean.
College of Science and Technology: Chris Platsoucas, Dean.
School of Social Administration: Curtis Leonard, Dean.
School of Tourism and Hospitality Management: M. Moshe Porat, Dean.

A time for quiet study in Mitten Memorial Hall.

The view from Founder's Garden at Temple's main campus.

TEXAS A&M UNIVERSITY–COMMERCE

Graduate School

Programs of Study

The Graduate School at Texas A&M University–Commerce (A&M–Commerce) includes twenty-six academic departments and offers more than fifty major areas of study. Six departments offer doctoral degrees. Graduate degrees now offered by A&M–Commerce are the Master of Arts (M.A.), Master of Business Administration (M.B.A.), Master of Education (M.Ed.), Master of Fine Arts (M.F.A.), Master of Music (M.M.), Master of Science (M.S.), Master of Social Work (M.S.W.), Doctor of Education (Ed.D.), and Doctor of Philosophy (Ph.D.). The Graduate School is one of five academic divisions of the University, with the Colleges of Arts and Sciences, Business and Technology, Education and Human Services Division of Continuing Education, and Institutional Effectiveness.

Major areas of study at the master's level include agricultural sciences; agriculture education; art; biological sciences; broad-field sciences; business administration; chemistry; computer science; counseling; early childhood education; earth sciences; economics; educational administration; elementary education; English; health, kinesiology, and sports studies; higher education; history; industrial technology; interdisciplinary studies; learning technology and information systems; management; marketing; mathematics; music; physics; psychology; reading; secondary education; Spanish; special education; sociology; social work; theater; and training and development. Major areas of study leading to a doctoral degree include English; counseling; educational administration; educational psychology; and supervision, curriculum and instruction.

Research Facilities

The James G. Gee Library, named for A&M–Commerce's fifth president, is the academic center of the campus. The online catalog provides access to the library's collection of more than 1.8 million monographs, periodicals, microforms, and other processed materials (videotapes, sound recordings, and films). This total includes collections of juvenile and young adult literature, archival materials, curriculum guides, and maps. The University has been a selective depository for federal government publications since 1937 and for Texas state documents since 1963.

In support of graduate programs, the library provides Internet access to more than 50 databases, some containing the full text or full images of articles, plus access to several CD-ROM databases in the Gee Library and its Metroplex branch, or via the campuswide area network. Internet access to other library catalogs is also available. An interlibrary loan service delivers publications to Gee Library from libraries throughout Texas and the world. Viewing machines are available for microform items and reader-printers enable students to obtain hard copies of microform materials. The library's microform collections include ERIC (Educational Resources Information Center) documents. Photocopy machines are also available throughout the library. The library computer lab, located on the second floor, contains PCs and Macintosh computers; printers; and software for word processing, spreadsheet, presentation software, and access to the Internet. A&M–Commerce Gee Library is a member of the Phoenix Group of North Texas research libraries, TexShare, and AMIGOS Library Services, the OCLC regional support organization. TexShare membership gives students and faculty members access and borrowing privileges to most academic institutions statewide. The library has daily courier service to selected TexShare institutions, supporting rapid interlibrary loan service.

Among other research facilities at A&M–Commerce are the laboratories for arts and sciences and the University Farm.

Financial Aid

Graduate students who have full admission to a graduate degree program or a teacher certification program may be eligible for several forms of financial aid. These programs include the Texas Public Education Grant, on-campus employment, and several loan programs. For more information and application forms, applicants should contact the Office of Financial Aid, Texas A&M University, Commerce, Texas 75429 (telephone: 903-886-5910).

Cost of Study

Graduate tuition for 2001–02 for 9 semester credit hours was $1092.50 for Texas residents and $2991.50 for nonresidents; tuition for 12 semester hours was $1439 for Texas residents and $3971 for nonresidents. Out-of-state tuition is waived for full-time graduate and teaching assistants and for students living in bordering counties of Arkansas, Louisiana, and Oklahoma.

Living and Housing Costs

A variety of housing options is available. A&M–Commerce can accommodate more than 2,400 single students and 250 families in campus housing. The costs are reasonable and facilities are varied to meet a number of different lifestyles. The halls designed for family housing include 250 air-conditioned and centrally heated furnished apartments. Utilities, including basic telephone service, are furnished. For more information, students should call Housing Operations at 903-886-5797.

Student Group

More than 40 percent of the student enrollment at A&M–Commerce is made up of graduate students. The overall student population is approximately 75 percent Anglo-American, 15 percent African American, 5 percent Hispanic, 1 percent Asian American, 1 percent Native American, and 3 percent international. There are approximately 250 international students representing thirty-eight countries at the University.

Location

The 140-acre main campus of Texas A&M University-Commerce is located in Commerce, Texas (population 7,700), 65 miles northeast of Dallas, which is one of the world's leading metropolitan areas. Nearby are recreational areas such as Lakes Texoma, Tawakoni, and Cooper. Greenville, the seat of Hunt County, is 14 miles west of Commerce and has a population of more than 25,000. Graduate classes are also offered at the A&M–Commerce Metroplex Center, located in the Dallas suburb of Mesquite.

The University

A&M–Commerce has an enrollment of approximately 8,300 students who attend either the main campus in Commerce or one of the off-campus facilities at the Metroplex Center in Mesquite, Texas, the Universities Center in Dallas, or the Navarro Partnership in Corsicana, Texas. Distance education courses, including Internet courses, are other options for students. A&M–Commerce was founded in 1889 and joined the A&M system in 1996. The University has been granting master's degrees since 1936 and doctoral degrees since 1962.

Applying

Students should submit admission applications to the Graduate Office. Applications are also available online at the address listed below.

Correspondence and Information

Dr. Mathew Kanjirathinkal, Dean of Graduate Studies and Research
P.O. Box 3011
Commerce, Texas 75429
Telephone: 903-886-5163
Fax: 903-886-5165
E-mail: graduate_school@tamu-commerce.edu
World Wide Web: http://www.tamu-commerce.edu

DEPARTMENT HEADS AND THEIR RESEARCH

COLLEGE OF ARTS AND SCIENCES

Agricultural Sciences (903-886-5358)
Robert L. Williams, Assistant Professor; Ph.D., Texas Tech.

Art (903-886-5208)
Kay L. Coughenour, Professor; Ph.D., Kent State.

Biological and Earth Sciences (903-886-5378)
Don Royce Lee, Professor; Ph.D., Oregon State. Microbiology, food microbiology, *Salmonella.*

Chemistry and Physics (903-886-5488)
Ben M. Doughty, Professor and Head of Physics; Ph.D., Arkansas. Science education.

Communication and Theatre (903-886-5346)
John Hanners, Professor; Ph.D., Michigan State. Nineteenth-century American and British theatre history.

Computer Science and Information Systems (903-886-5409)
Sam Saffer, Professor; M.A.S., Ph.D., SMU.

History (903-886-5226)
Judy Ford, Assistant Professor; Ph.D., Fordham. Medieval history.

Literature and Languages (903-886-5260)
Gerald Duchovnay, Professor of English; Ph.D., Indiana.

Mathematics (903-886-5157)
Stuart Anderson, Professor; Ph.D., Oklahoma.

Music (903-886-5303)
Gene Lockhart, Associate Professor; M.M., Rochester (Eastman).

Social Work (903-886-5029)
Edward R. Skarnulis, Professor; M.S.W., Ph.D., Nebraska. Developmental disabilities, handicapped, mental retardation.

Sociology and Criminal Justice (903-886-5332)
R. A. Singh, Professor; Ph.D., Mississippi State.

COLLEGE OF BUSINESS AND TECHNOLOGY

Accounting (903-886-5659)
Wendell Edwards, Professor M.B.A., Texas A&M; Ph.D., North Texas; CPA.

Economics and Finance (903-886-5681)
Stephen Avard, Associate Professor; M.B.A., East Texas State; Ph.D., North Texas.

General Business and Systems Management (903-886-5692)
Donald E. English,, Professor; Ph.D., North Dakota.

Industrial and Engineering Technology (903-886-5474)
Jerry D. Parish, Professor; Ed.D., East Texas State.

Marketing and Management (903-886-5703)
Randall Y. Odom, Associate Professor; Ph.D., Mississippi.

COLLEGE OF EDUCATION

Counseling (903-886-5637)
Phyllis Erdman, Associate Professor; Ph.D., St. Mary's at San Antonio. Marriage and family therapy, clinical supervision training.

Educational Administration (903-886-5520)
David Thompson, Assistant Professor; Ph.D., Texas A&M.

Elementary Education (903-886-5537)
Wayne M. Linek, Associate Professor; Ph.D., Kent State. Teacher beliefs and student achievement, the impact of the professional development school model, pre-service and in-service teacher development as it relates to literacy teaching and teacher attrition.

Health and Physical Education(903-886-5308)
Fred Blohm, Professor; Ed.D., Arkansas.

Psychology and Special Education (903-886-5594)
Paul F. Zelhart, Professor; Ph.D., Alberta.

Secondary and Higher Education (903-886-5607)
William Ogden, Professor; Ph.D., Wisconsin.

TEXAS A&M UNIVERSITY–KINGSVILLE

College of Graduate Studies

Programs of Study

Through the College of Graduate Studies, fifty-seven master's degrees and three doctoral degrees are offered from five academic colleges.

The College of Agriculture and Human Sciences offers a joint Doctor of Philosophy (Ph.D.) in wildlife science with Texas A&M University in College Station; Master of Science (M.S.) degrees in agribusiness, agriculture education, animal science, plant and soil science, and range and wildlife management; and a Master of Science in Human Sciences (M.S.H.S.). The College of Arts and Sciences offers many degrees in a vast range of disciplines. Graduate degrees include the Master of Arts (M.A.) in English, history and politics, psychology, sociology, and Spanish; Master of Science (M.S.) in art, biology, chemistry, communication science and disorders, English, geology, gerontology, history and politics, mathematics, psychology, and sociology; and the Master of Music in music education. The College of Business Administration offers the Master of Business Administration (M.B.A.), M.S. with a major in business administration, and Master of Professional Accountancy (M.P.A.) in accounting. The College of Education offers Doctor of Education (Ed.D.) degrees in bilingual education and in educational leadership (the latter jointly with Texas A&M–Corpus Christi); Master of Education (M.Ed.) in adult education, early childhood, English as a second language, and special education; M.S. in reading specialization; and M.A. and M.S. degrees in bilingual education, counseling and guidance, educational administration, and kinesiology. The College of Engineering offers several interdisciplinary courses of study leading to M.S. and Master of Engineering (M.E.) degrees in chemical engineering, civil engineering, electrical engineering, environmental engineering, mechanical engineering, and natural gas engineering and M.S. degrees in computer science and in industrial engineering.

Research Facilities

Graduate study is supported by University and departmental attitudes and facilities. The James C. Jernigan Library contains more than 480,000 volumes and 700,000 microfiche documents, subscribes to 2,200 periodicals, and is a depository for selected U.S. government documents. Electronic information resources offer online and CD-ROM databases. Graduate students have interlibrary loan privileges providing access to nationwide library collections. Research is conducted through such centers, institutes, and laboratories as the Caesar Kleberg Wildlife Research Institute, the Citrus Center, the Monoclonal Antibody Facility, and the Geosciences Analytical Instrumentation Laboratory.

Financial Aid

Graduate students taking at least 9 hours of graduate courses are eligible for a variety of fellowships and research or teaching assistantships. Financial aid is available for up to 48 hours of graduate credits. The University participates in most federal and state grant, loan, and work-study programs. Non-Texas residents receiving approved fellowships or assistantships may be eligible to pay Texas resident tuition. University teaching and research assistantships provide annual stipends, while fellowships and internships supported by federal, state, and University funds provide stipends of $1000 to $14,000. International students are required to guarantee their support but are eligible, after enrollment, for in-state tuition rates if awarded competitive scholarships valued at a minimum of $1000. Inquiries about the availability of support should be addressed to the graduate coordinator of the various disciplines.

Cost of Study

Tuition and fees for 9 semester hours are $833 per semester for full-time graduate students who are Texas residents and $2759 per semester for non-Texas residents and international students.

Living and Housing Costs

The cost of living in south Texas is relatively low when compared to other areas of the country. Apartments and homes rent for $450 to $550 per month and up. Several apartment complexes and rental properties are within walking or short driving distance of the University. Dormitory rooms for unmarried students as well as family apartments are available at the University. Dorm residents may purchase optional meal plans. Student family apartments rent for less than $320 per month.

Student Group

The University enrollment is approximately 6,000; 1,091 are enrolled as graduate students. International students make up 13 percent of the graduate student enrollment. The overall student population, a multicultural mix of fifty-five countries and forth-three states, is 62 percent Hispanic, 28 percent Anglo-American, 4 percent African American, less than 1 percent Asian American and American Indian, and 4 percent international.

Location

Texas A&M University–Kingsville is located in semitropical south Texas. Kingsville is about 40 miles southwest of Corpus Christi, 153 miles southeast of San Antonio, and 120 miles north of Mexico. Kingsville (population 25,000) is in a semirural area that is easily accessible to urban areas. The King Ranch, one of the largest commercial ranches in the world, provides tours. Water sports and outdoor activities can be found nearby along the coastline. Corpus Christi offers many social and cultural activities, including museums, concerts, and plays, as well as shopping malls.

The University

Texas A&M University–Kingsville (formerly Texas A&I University) was established in 1925 as Texas State Teachers College and has since evolved into a comprehensive institution of higher education. The University became a part of the Texas A&M University System in 1989 and changed its named to Texas A&M University–Kingsville in 1993.

Applying

Candidates must submit admissions applications to the Admissions Office. Students must be admitted both to the College of Graduate Studies and to a specific program to take courses for graduate credit. The application fee is $35 for United States residents and $50 for international students. Students must have a GRE score of at least 1000 (verbal plus quantitative) and an undergraduate GPA of at least 3.0 on a 4.0 scale. International students are required to score a minimum of 500 on the Test of English as a Foreign Language (TOEFL), with engineering and business graduate programs requiring a TOEFL score of 550. Application deadlines for U.S. students are July 1 for fall, November 15 for spring, and April 15 for summer. Application deadlines for first-time international students are June 1 for fall, October 1 for spring, and April 1 for summer.

Correspondence and Information

Dr. Alberto M. Olivares, Dean
College of Graduate Studies
MSC 118–700 University Boulevard
Texas A&M University–Kingsville
Kingsville, Texas 78363-8202
Telephone: 361-593-2808
Fax: 361-593-3412
E-mail: koosrxx@tamuk.edu
World Wide Web: http://www.tamuk.edu/grad

COLLEGE DEANS AND GRADUATE COORDINATORS

Graduate School: Alberto M. Olivares, Dean; Ph.D., Texas A&M. (Telephone: 361-593-2808)

Agriculture and Human Science: Ronald Rosati, Dean; Ph.D., Iowa State. (Telephone: 361-593-3712)
Agricultural Programs (Master's): Gary McBryde, Associate Professor; Ph.D., Washington State.
Human Sciences: Anna P. McArthur, Associate Professor; Ph.D., Texas Tech.
Wildlife Science (Doctoral): Fred Bryant, Professor; Ph.D., Texas A&M.

Arts and Sciences: Mary R. Mattingly, Dean; Ph.D., Michigan State. (Telephone: 361-593-2761)
Art: Richard C. Scherpereel, Professor; Ed.D., Vanderbilt (Peabody).
Biology: James Pierce, Associate Professor; Ph.D., Texas at Austin.
Chemistry: Nicholas R. Beller, Associate Professor; Ph.D., New Mexico.
Communications and Theater Arts (Minor): Shari Schlehuser, Assistant Professor; Ph.D., Purdue.
Communication Science and Disorders (Master's): Shari Schlehuser, Assistant Professor; Ph.D., Purdue.
English: David Sabrio, Professor; Ph.D., South Carolina.
Geosciences: Michael A. Jordan, Associate Professor; Ph.D., Texas at Austin.
Gerontology: Trudy A. Anderson, Assistant Professor; Ph.D., Nebraska.
History: Leslie G. Hunter, Professor; Ph.D., Arizona.
Mathematics: Louis Thurston, Associate Professor; Ph.D., Carnegie-Mellon.
Music: Nancy King Sanders, Professor; D.M.A., Illinois at Urbana-Champaign.
Physics (Minor): Lionel D. Hewett, Professor; Ph.D., Missouri–Rolla.
Political Science: Jimmie D. Phaup, Professor; Ph.D., Arizona.
Psychology: Dorothy Pace, Professor; Ph.D., Oklahoma State.
Sociology: Joseph Domino, Professor; Ph.D., Georgia.
Spanish: Guillermo Valencia, Associate Professor; Ph.D., Florida.

Business Administration: Robert Diersing, Dean; Ph.D., Texas A&M. (Telephone: 361-593-3801)
Business Administration: Robert Diersing, Dean; Ph.D., Texas A&M.

Education: Freddie Litton, Dean; Ed.D., Northern Colorado. (Telephone: 361-593-2801)
Adult Education: Mark Walsh, Professor; Ph.D., Texas A&M.
Bilingual Education (Master's): Lento F. Maez, Associate Professor; Ph.D., California, Santa Barbara.
Bilingual Education (Doctoral): Gustavo Gonzalez, Professor; Ph.D., Texas at Austin.
Certification Programs: Glenna S. Cannon, Assistant Professor; Ph.D., Texas at Austin.
Counseling and Guidance: Fred T. Ponder, Associate Professor; Ph.D., North Texas.
Early Childhood: Deanna L. Nekovei, Assistant Professor; D.Ed., Massachusetts Amherst.
Educational Leadership (Doctoral): Robert Marshall, Associate Professor; Ed.D., Texas A&M.
Educational Administration (Master's): Ronald McKenzie, Professor; Ph.D., Texas at Austin.
Kinesiology: Albert Ruiz, Associate Professor; Ph.D., Texas A&M.
Reading Specialization: Shirley Ermis, Assistant Professor; Ed.D., Texas A&M–Kingsville.
Special Education: Grace A. Hopkins, Professor; Ph.D., Illinois.

Engineering: Phil V. Compton, Dean; Ph.D., Texas A&M. (Telephone: 361-593-2001)
Chemical Engineering: Robert W. Serth, Professor; Ph.D., SUNY at Buffalo.
Civil Engineering: Joseph Sai, Associate Professor; Ph.D., Texas A&M.
Computer Science: Chung S. Leung, Associate Professor; Ph.D., Florida Atlantic.
Electrical Engineering: T. Joe Boehm, Associate Professor; Ph.D., Oklahoma State.
Environmental Engineering: Andrew Ernest, Associate Professor; Ph.D., Texas A&M.
Industrial Engineering: Kambiz Farahmand, Associate Professor; Ph.D., Texas at Arlington.
Mechanical Engineering: Yousri Elkassabgi, Professor; Ph.D., Houston.
Natural Gas Engineering: Ali Pilehvari, Associate Professor; Ph.D., Tulsa.

TEXAS SOUTHERN UNIVERSITY

Graduate School

Programs of Study

The Graduate School at Texas Southern University (TSU) offers the Doctor of Philosophy, Doctor of Education, and several master's degrees in more than thirty academic programs. Doctoral degree offerings include the Doctor of Philosophy in environmental toxicology and the Doctor of Education. It is expected that the doctorate can be completed in a period of four to eight years.

Master's degrees are as follows: Master of Arts, Master of Business Administration, Master of City Planning, Master of Education, Master of Public Administration, and Master of Science.

Majors are available in the following fields: biology, chemistry, city planning, communication, counseling, curriculum and instruction, educational administration and supervision, English, environmental toxicology, general business, health and human performance, higher education, history, human services and consumer sciences, industrial technology, mathematics, music, psychology, public administration, secondary education, sociology, and transportation management and planning. Students may pursue research in all of the major disciplines offered at the graduate level. Research involves both basic and applied studies under the supervision of graduate faculty members. Students who complete graduate degrees are prepared to pursue careers in government, teaching, business, and industry and through private entrepreneurship. Because Houston is a major international city, opportunities exist for contacts with international entities through which careers may be developed.

Research Facilities

TSU occupies a modern campus valued at more than $225 million, which is located on 125 acres and consists of forty-four buildings. The Gray Hall building is a three-level facility of 50,790 gross square feet. It houses ten research laboratories totaling approximately 7,000 square feet and a modern small-animal care facility. Other research facilities include an environmental control chamber, a tissue culture laboratory, and biomedical research laboratories in Nabrit Science Building. Texas Southern's library is housed in a 135,000-square-foot recently renovated facility with more than 866,500 volumes. Opportunities are available for library loan privileges with other universities in the Houston area, including the city of Houston library system. Six special Research and Technology Transfer Centers provide opportunities for students and faculty members to obtain hands-on, practical experience in various aspects of environmental, social, and educational research. Other important units and committees of the University that exist and support research include the Grants and Contracts Office, the Faculty Organized Research Committee, and the Faculty Development and Sabbatical Leave Committee.

Financial Aid

Graduate students may apply for Guaranteed Student Loans, scholarships, and work-study through the Office of Financial Aid. Graduate assistantships are available in certain academic disciplines and may be secured through the head of the department in which the student is pursuing the degree. The University also has a scholarship program to which applications may be submitted through the Director of Financial Aid. The application deadline is April 30.

Cost of Study

The cost of study reflects tuition and fees as determined by resident/nonresident status and number of hours taken. Resident tuition and fees, except for the Thurgood Marshall School of Law, are approximately $1300 per semester (12 credit hours). Tuition and fees for a nonresident are approximately $3600. Besides regular fees, students should be aware that certain miscellaneous fees, such as laboratory fees, books and supplies, and parking decals, are extra. The University reserves the right to change tuition and other charges without notice as necessitated by University or legislative action. The exact cost for tuition and fees may be secured from the University registrar.

Living and Housing Costs

Students living in University housing can expect to pay an average rate of $2000 per semester for room and board. Married students and off-campus commuting students can expect to pay approximately $5000 to $8000 per year for housing. Yearly costs for out-of-state and international students are estimated to be $12,000 for single students, with an additional $3000 for a spouse and $1500 per child. Housing is available for graduate students in dormitories and in off-campus apartments.

Student Group

Texas Southern University's student population is approximately 8,000. This population, although predominantly African American and from Texas, includes a large corps of non-African Americans as well as international students from more than sixty countries. In the profile of the student body for fall 1998, the student population was 40.2 percent male and 59.8 percent female and 89 percent undergraduate and 11 percent graduate. Eighty percent were Texas residents, and 20 percent were out-of-state students or foreign nationals. In descending order, the students were 84.4 percent African Americans of non-Hispanic origin, 7.7 percent foreign nationals, 3.4 percent Hispanics, 3 percent whites of non-Hispanic origin, and 1.5 percent Asians, American Indians, or Alaskans.

Student Outcomes

Graduates of Texas Southern University influence the world through science, business, education, law, and the fine arts and include presidents of colleges or universities, presidents or CEOs of corporations, owners or entrepreneurs of businesses, elected officials, superintendents of school districts, engineers, pharmacists, lawyers, and judges.

Location

Texas Southern University is an urban comprehensive institution located in Houston, Texas, a metropolitan city of approximately 3 million. The institution has a long history of involvement in the international affairs of the city and serves as the host of a number of major national and international programs and conferences throughout the year.

The University and The School

The University occupies 125 acres in the southeastern section of Houston. The institution is a member of the National Collegiate Athletics Association, offers recreational and athletic facilities for many different types of sports and has a major cultural affairs series of programs and activities for students, faculty members, and the community.

The Graduate School was established as a unit of Texas Southern University when the institution was created by the Texas State Legislature in 1947. Since its establishment, the Graduate School has grown steadily and currently offers degree programs in thirty-two academic fields. Regular graduate faculty members have the doctorate degree and hold research and publication credits. Research and training are also supported by several centers of research and outreach, including the Economic Development Center, the Center for Excellence in Urban Education, the Center for Transportation Training and Research, the Mickey Leland Center on World Hunger and Peace, the Center on the Family, the Research Center for Minority Institutions, the Environmental Science Institute, the Center for Toxicological Studies, the Minority Biomedical Research Support Program (MBRS), the Environmental Research and Technology Transfer Center (ERT^2C), the Center on Aging for Horizons Intergenerational Wellness (CoA-HIW), and the Center for Cardiovascular Research.

Applying

Students seeking admission to the Graduate School of Texas Southern University should request application materials from the Graduate School Office. The minimum admission requirements for most graduate programs are an earned bachelor's degree from an accredited college or university and a minimum undergraduate GPA of 2.5 (or a 3.0 GPA on the last 60 semester hours of undergraduate course work); an acceptable GRE or GMAT score may be required for admission to certain degree programs. International students must have a score of at least 550 on the TOEFL. The completed application package should be submitted to the Dean of the Graduate School at Texas Southern University. Deadlines are July 15 for fall, November 15 for spring, and May 1 for summer.

Correspondence and Information

For information and to submit completed application packages, students should contact the address below:

Dean of the Graduate School
Texas Southern University
3100 Cleburne
Houston, Texas 77004

Telephone: 713-313-7233
Fax: 713-313-1876
E-mail: jones_jx@tsu.edu
World Wide Web: http://www.tsu.edu

THE FACULTY AND THEIR RESEARCH

Most graduate faculty members have had more than five years of college-level teaching experience and have published scholarly books and papers in leading journals. They are engaged in research projects supported by federal, state, or private grants.

This partial listing of faculty research provides an overview of the comprehensive nature of research in which faculty members are engaged at Texas Southern University. Prospective students should contact the head of the department to discuss specific research interests.

Some research in biology includes soil microorganisms, metabolites and their nematicidal properties, sickle cell anemia, neurophysiological aspects of L-tryptophan and quinolinic acid, ganglionic and renovascular adenosine receptors, phytoalexins in plants, and parasites of avian hosts. In the Department of Chemistry, research includes studies on lead using ruthenium, inorganic pollutants in mother's milk, volatile constituents of motor oil and their environmental impact, organic synthesis of sulphur, metal (pyrazoly) borate, and the HPLC uptake study of EDTA. Computer science faculty members and students study solar wind, superconducting compounds, and remote sensing. In the Department of English and Foreign Languages, studies are underway on the dialect style for African Americans. The Department of Fine Arts has research underway on the solo snare drum, while history, geography, and economics faculty members are engaged in the study of Africans in the exploration process, residential desegregation, Tanzanian history, African Americans in reconstruction, and the Harlem Renaissance. The faculty members in mathematics are engaged in the study of the minimum variance bound, Hamel basis for R∞, chaotic systems difference equations model, high-T_c trapped field magnets, oscillation, properties of higher order difference equations, and soluble quadratic congruencies. The Department of Psychology's research includes Holland's topology for African-American college students, abused males, and delinquent males. Sociology faculty members are studying Afrocentric contributions to knowledge, immunization rates of African Americans, Medicare beneficiaries in Texas, race and ethnic relationships, research methodologies, and the race complex phenomenon. The School of Education's faculty members are involved in such projects as field dependence/independence and performance, HISD's Apple Project, the acculturation of Latino children in U.S. society, preparing culturally responsive teachers for the twenty-first century, field-based teacher preparation programs, students who tutor students, learning climate in public schools, data-driven instruction, research to practice manifestations of fear of success, effective administrative competencies, minority retention, hazing as ritualistic violence, and school choice and vouchers. In the School of Business, research includes the study of perverse information incentives, output efficiency of minority-owned banks, methodological issues related to the measurement of consumer choice sets, strategic preferences, procedural and interactional justice, and power function for inverse Gaussian regression models. Several interdisciplinary research projects involve faculty members in the College of Pharmacy and Health Sciences. Research includes effects of a protease inhibitor dipyridamole on the disposition kinetics of antiviral nucleosides, epithelial transport of nucleosides, neurobehavioral toxicity of lead, neurotoxicity of toluene, functional alterations of insulin, diabetic vascular damage induced by allylamine, and diabetes/vascular smooth muscle cell studies. In the School of Technology, studies include high energy cells and batteries, renewable energy, and solar photovoltaic and solar heat pump studies. In the Department of Transporation, studies focus on transportation factors affecting port competitiveness, rural and small-town transportation, vanpooling for central-city commuters, megaports, demand management options, safety, and modal traffic.

Dean of the Graduate School
Joseph Jones, Ph.D.

Department Heads
Accounting: Ladelle Hyman, Ph.D.
Biology: Debabrata Ghosh, Ph.D.
Chemistry: John Sapp, Ph.D.
Communication: James Ward, Ph.D.
Curriculum and Instruction: Sumpter Brooks, Ed.D.
Educational Leadership and Counseling: Launey Roberts, Ed.D.
English: Betty Taylor-Thompson, Ph.D.
Fine Arts: Diane Jemison-Pollard, M.F.A.
General Business: K. V. Ramaswamy, Ph.D.
Health and Kinesiology: Thurman Robins, Ed.D.
History: Ethiopia Keleta, Ph.D.
Human Service and Consumer Science: Shirley Nealy, Ph.D.
Industrial Technology: Jessie Horner, Ed.D.
Mathematics: Della Bell, Ph.D.
Psychology: Leon Belcher, Ph.D.
Public Affairs: Theophilus Herrington, Ph.D.
Sociology: Betty Cox, Ed.D.
Transportation Management: Lei Yu, Ph.D.

TEXAS TECH UNIVERSITY

Graduate School

Programs of Study

Through its Graduate School, School of Law, School of Allied Health, School of Nursing, School of Pharmacy, and School of Medicine, Texas Tech offers a diverse range of graduate studies. The Graduate School offers degrees from eight academic colleges. The College of Agriculture offers the Doctor of Philosophy (Ph.D.), Master of Science (M.S.), Doctor of Education (Ed.D.), and Master of Agriculture (M.Ag.) in a variety of disciplines. In addition, the college offers the Master of Landscape Architecture (M.L.A.). The College of Architecture offers Master of Architecture (MAR), Master of Science (MSR), and Ph.D. degrees. The College of Arts and Sciences offers many degrees in a vast range of disciplines, including the Ph.D. in eighteen academic disciplines, Master of Arts (M.A.) in eighteen fields, and the Master of Science (M.S.) in twelve fields. Texas Tech's College of Business Administration offers Ph.D. in business administration, M.S. in business administration, Master of Science in Accounting (M.S.A.), and Master of Business Administation (M.B.A.) degree programs. Each degree offers concentrations in various areas. An M.B.A. is available as a joint degree with foreign languages, law, nursing, and medicine and also with architecture. The College of Education offers the Master of Education (M.Ed.) in twelve fields, the Doctor of Education (Ed.D.), and the Ph.D. The College of Engineering offers the Ph.D. in seven engineering fields, the M.S. in ten fields, the Master of Engineering (M.EN.), the Master of Environmental Engineering (M.EV.), and the Master of Environmental Technology Management (M.E.T.). The College of Human Sciences offers the M.S. as well as the Ph.D. in various fields. The College of Visual and Performing Arts offers Ph.D., M.A., Master of Fine Arts (M.F.A.), Master of Music (M.M.), and Master of Music Education (M.M.Ed.) degrees. In addition, the college offers the Doctor of Musical Arts (D.M.A.). Interdisciplinary degrees housed in the Graduate School include predesigned programs or self-designed programs that are coordinated to meet individual needs. Predesigned programs include applied linguistics, heritage management, museum science, public administration, sports health, and multidisciplinary science. Self-designed programs may be generated from any of the courses listed in the graduate catalog. Some of the more common minors or areas of interest include comparative literature, environmental evaluation, ethnic studies, fine arts management, land-use planning management and design, Latin American studies, legal studies, neural and behavioral science, risk-taking behavior, and women's studies. The School of Law offers the Doctor of Jurisprudence degree and joint-degree programs with the M.P.A., M.S. in agricultural economics, M.S. in accounting, and M.B.A. The School of Allied Health offers an M.S. in three disciplines: communication disorders (speech language pathology or audiology), occupational therapy, and physical therapy. The School of Nursing offers a Ph.D. in nursing, a Master of Science in Nursing, and a joint-degree program with the M.B.A. The School of Pharmacy offers the Doctor of Pharmacy (Pharm.D.). The School of Medicine offers the Doctor of Medicine, medical education in thirty residency programs, Ph.D. and M.S. degrees in six disciplines, and a joint M.B.A./M.D. degree.

Research Facilities

Graduate study is strongly supported by the University and its departments. The library houses over 4 million volumes and more than 27,000 serials. The high-performance computer center provides students up-to-date computing facilities. The Advanced Technology Learning Center gives students comprehensive access to the latest computer technology and software. Many departments feature their own library and computer facilities. Consistent dedication to quality and research has earned national and international respect for numerous departments. Every department has its own strengths, and each college possesses its special resources, centers for investigation, and research opportunities. A small sample of the numerous centers and institutes includes the Institute for Ergonomics Research, Institute for Banking and Financial Studies, Child Development Center, Center for Petroleum Mathematics, Southwest Center for German Studies, Institute for Disaster Research, International Center for Arid and Semi-Arid Land Studies, Center for the Study of Addiction, Center for Professional Development, and the Institute of Environmental and Human Health. In the new Carnegie classification, Texas Tech was rated as a Doctoral/Research University Extensive, the highest category for doctorate-granting institutions.

Financial Aid

Graduate students are eligible for an array of scholarships, fellowships, and research or teaching assistantships in many academic disciplines. Part-time employment is readily available both on and off campus. The University participates in most federal and state grant, loan, and work-study programs. Texas Tech University's Gelin Emergency Loan Fund is a special benefit for students in need. Non-Texas residents receiving approved scholarships, fellowships, or assistantships may be eligible to pay Texas resident tuition, which is among the lowest in the nation.

Cost of Study

Graduate School tuition for the 2002–03 academic year for Texas residents is $84 per semester credit hour, in addition to department tuition. Students employed at least half-time as teaching or research assistants pay the same tuition as Texas residents. The graduate nonresident tuition rate for residents of New Mexico, Oklahoma, Arkansas, and Louisiana who are legal residents of a county adjacent to Texas is $84 per semester credit hour, in addition to department tuition. Nonresident student tuition is $295 per semester credit hour, in addition to department tuition. Fees may vary but generally include the Texas Tech University identification fee, laboratory fee, informational technology fee, library fee, and general fees. Most fees are waived for half-time teaching and research assistants. Tuition and fees for law, nursing, pharmacy, allied health, and medicine vary and may be confirmed in the course catalog by contacting the school directly. Texas has no state income tax. Tuition and fees are subject to change.

Living and Housing Costs

Characteristics of Lubbock are low unemployment, low housing costs, and a low cost of living. On-campus living, meals included, in upperclass halls costs about $4800 per academic year. Abundant privately owned housing in the city meets most price and amenity demands.

Student Group

More than 50 percent of Texas Tech's 25,000 students have permanent homes more than 300 miles away, making Tech a residential campus. Students come from all parts of Texas, the nation, and more than 100 other countries. Tech's growing graduate and professional student population is about 4,300, most of whom are full-time students.

Location

With a population of 200,000, Lubbock enjoys all the services of a major city. The city has more than sixty parks, numerous cultural and civic events, and a modern and convenient international airport that hosts several major airlines. Lubbock is the principal trade, medical, and financial center in a rich agricultural and petroleum area. Situated on the high plains of west Texas, Lubbock is about an hour's flight from Dallas, Houston, Albuquerque, and Denver. Lubbock enjoys 265 annual days of sunshine, a warm and dry climate, and pleasant weather year-round.

The University

Founded in 1923, Texas Tech is a state-assisted major research university. Texas Tech's campus features expansive lawns and impressive landscaping with unique Spanish Renaissance architecture. The beautiful, spacious campus—one of the largest in the nation—is well equipped not only for research and study but also for cultural and recreational activities. A fulfilling after-study-hours life can be achieved by participating in the wide array of campus and community activities.

Applying

Application forms for admission can be provided upon request or accessed electronically through the Graduate School Web page (address listed below). Applications are accepted throughout the year for the fall, spring, and two summer terms. The Graduate School requires a $25 application fee for U.S. citizens and permanent residents and $50 for international applicants.

Correspondence and Information

Rosa H. Gallegos
Coordinator of Graduate School Recruitment
Texas Tech University
Graduate Admissions
P.O. Box 41030
Lubbock, Texas 79409-1030
Telephone: 806-742-2787
E-mail: rosa.gallegos@ttu.edu
World Wide Web: http://www.ttu.edu/gradschool

DEANS AND FACULTY HEADS

A current list of advisers can be found at http://www.ttu.edu/gradschool.

Graduate School: Ronald Anderson, Dean; Ph.D., Iowa State (telephone: 806-742-2781).
Interdisciplinary Studies: Allan Headley, Coordinator; Ph.D., Howard; Wendell Aycock, Coordinator; Ph.D., South Carolina.
Biotechnology and Genomics: David Knaff, Ph.D., Yale.
Museum Science and Heritage Management: Gary Edson, Ph.D., Tulane.
Public Administration: Phillip H. Marshall, Ph.D., Illinois.

Agricultural Sciences: John Abernathy, Dean; Ph.D., Illinois (telephone: 806-742-2810).
Agricultural and Applied Economics: Don Etheridge, Ph.D., North Carolina State.
Agricultural Education and Communication: Matt Baker, Ph.D., Ohio State.
Animal Science and Food Technology: Kevin Pond, Ph.D., Texas A&M.
Landscape Architecture: Alon Kvashny, Ed.D., West Virginia.
Plant and Soil Science: Dick Auld, Ph.D., Montana State.
Range and Wildlife and Fisheries Management: Ernest Fish, Ph.D., Arizona.

Architecture: John Borrelli, Interim Dean; Ph.D., Penn State (telephone: 806-742-3136).
Architecture: David A. Driskill, M.Arch., Catholic University.

Arts and Sciences: Jane L. Winer, Dean; Ph.D., Ohio State (telephone: 806-742-3833).
Art: Melody Weiler, M.F.A., Ohio.
Biological Sciences: Carleton Phillips, Ph.D., Kansas.
Chemistry and Biochemistry: Richard A. Bartsch, Ph.D., Brown.
Classical and Modern Languages and Literature: Peder G. Christiansen, Ph.D., Wisconsin.
Communication Studies: K. David Roach, Ed.D., Texas Tech.
Economics and Geography: Joseph E. King, Ph.D., Illinois.
English: Madonne Miner, Ph.D., SUNY at Buffalo.
Environmental Toxicology: Ronald J. Kendall, Ph.D., Virginia Tech.
Geosciences: Richard Peterson, Ph.D., Missouri.
Health, Exercise, and Sport Sciences: T. Gilmour Reeve, Ph.D., Texas A&M.
History: Bruce C. Daniels, Ph.D., Connecticut.
Mass Communications: Jerry Hudson, Ph.D., North Texas State.
Mathematics and Statistics: Lawrence Schovanec, Ph.D., Indiana.
Music: Gary Owens: Ph.D,.Wisconsin–Madison.
Philosophy: Frederick Suppe, Ph.D., Michigan.
Physics: Lynn Hatfield, Ph.D., Arkansas.
Political Science: Phillip Marshall, Ph.D., Illinois.
Psychology: Ruth Maki, Ph.D., Berkeley.
Sociology, Anthropology, and Social Work: Paul Johnson, Ph.D., Illinois.
Theater Arts: Norman Bert, Ph.D., Indiana.

Business Administration: Allen McInnes, Dean (telephone: 806-742-3188).
Accounting: Lane K. Anderson, Ph.D., Wisconsin–Madison.
Finance: Paul Goeble, Ph.D., Georgia.
Information and Quantitative Sciences (MIS): Surya Yadav, Ph.D., Georgia State.
Management: Kimberly Boal, Ph.D., Wisconsin–Madison.
Marketing: Robert Wilkes, Ph.D., Alabama.

Education: Greg Bowes, Dean; Ph.D., Northern Illinois (telephone: 806-742-1837).
Curriculum and Instruction: Billy Askins, Ed.D., North Texas.
Educational Psychology and Leadership: Gerald Parr, Ph.D., Colorado.

Engineering: William Marcy, Dean; Ph.D, Texas Tech (telephone: 806-742-3451).
Chemical Engineering: Gregory B. McKenna, Ph.D., Utah.
Civil Engineering: James McDonald, Ph.D., Purdue.
Computer Science: Daniel Cooke, Ph.D., Texas at Arlington.
Electrical Engineering: Jon Bredeson, Ph.D., Northwestern State.
Engineering Physics: James Gregory, Ph.D., Iowa State.
Engineering Technology: Ron Pigott, Ph.D., Pennsylvania.
Industrial Engineering: Milton L. Smith, Ph.D., Texas Tech.
Mechanical Engineering: Thomas D. Burton, Ph.D., Pennsylvania.
Petroleum Engineering: James F. Lea, Ph.D., SMU.
Software Engineering: Donald Bagert, Ph.D., Texas A&M.

Human Sciences: Linda Hoover, Interim Dean; Ph.D., Texas Woman's (telephone: 806-742-3031).
Education, Nutrition, and Restaurant-Hotel Management: Lynn Huffman, Ph.D., Texas A&M.
Human Development and Family Studies: Dean Busby, Ph.D., Brigham Young.
Merchandising, Environmental Design, and Consumer Economics: JoAnn Shroyer, Ph.D., Oklahoma State.

Visual and Performing Arts: Garry Owens, Dean; Ph.D., Wisconsin–Madison (telephone: 806-742-3825)
Art: John T. Morrow, M.S., Indiana.
Music and Theater: Garry Owens, Ph.D., Wisconsin–Madison.

Law: James Eissinger, Interim Dean; J.D., North Dakota (telephone: 806-742-3793).

Allied Health: Paul Brooke, Dean; Ph.D., Iowa; FACHE (telephone: 806-743-3223).
Communication Disorders: Rajinder Koul (Interim), Ph.D., Iowa.
Diagnostic and Primary Care: Hal S. Larsen, Ph.D., Nebraska.
Rehabilitation Services: H. H. Merrifield, Ph.D., Iowa.

Graduate School of Biomedical Sciences: Richard Homan, Dean; M.D., SUNY (telephone: 806-743-3000).
Cell Biology and Biochemistry: Harry M. Weitlauf, M.D., Washington (Seattle).
Microbiology and Immunology: Ronald Kennedy, Ph.D., Baylor College of Medicine.
Pharmacology: Reid Norman (Interim), Ph.D., Kansas.
Physiology: John Orem, Ph.D., New Mexico.

Nursing: Alexia Green, Dean; Ph.D., Texas Woman's; RN (telephone: 806-743-2737).

Medicine: Richard Homan, Dean; M.D., SUNY (telephone: 806-743-3000).

Pharmacy: Arthur A. Nelson Jr., Dean; R.Ph., Ph.D., Iowa (telephone: 806-356-4011).

TEXAS WOMAN'S UNIVERSITY

Graduate School

Programs of Study

Texas Woman's University (TWU) offers master's degrees through the Departments of Biology; Chemistry and Physics; English, Speech, and Foreign Languages; History and Government; Mathematics and Computer Science; Performing Arts (dance, drama, music); Psychology and Philosophy; Sociology and Social Work; Visual Arts; and Women's Studies; and the School of Management in the College of Arts and Sciences; through the Departments of Communication Sciences and Disorders; Healthcare Administration, Health Studies, Kinesiology, and Nutrition and Food Sciences in the College of Health Sciences; through the Departments of Family Sciences; Reading; Teacher Education; and the School of Library and Information Studies in the College of Professional Education; through the College of Nursing; and through the Schools of Occupational Therapy and Physical Therapy.

The University offers doctoral degrees in child development, counseling psychology, dance and related arts, early childhood education, family studies, family therapy, health studies, kinesiology, library science, molecular biology, nursing, nutrition, occupational therapy, physical therapy, reading education, rhetoric, school psychology, sociology, and special education.

In addition to the degree sequences offered by the University alone, TWU cooperates with sister institutions of the Federation of North Texas Area Universities to offer interinstitutional doctoral programs and graduate instruction in a number of disciplines.

Research Facilities

The University Library has holdings of 526,839 print volumes, 40,000 e-book volumes, 1,557,871 units in microform, 2,559 periodical and serial publications, more than 100 online databases offering access to thousands of full-text/full-image articles, and 85,067 audiovisual materials. The library's electronic resources are available through Internet access to students wherever they are located. Students have checking privileges at each member library of the statewide TexShare Program. The library is also connected via the Internet through Online Computer Library Center, Incorporated (OCLC), in Columbus, Ohio, with major academic and research libraries throughout the world for interlibrary borrowing and lending. The Women's Collection, with more than 45,000 print volumes and 3,500 linear feet of manuscript collections, is a national research collection on American women and women's issues. Specific facilities are available for nutrition, bone density, and other biomedical research. Facilities in the Institute for Clinical Services and Applied Nutrition, the Institute for Women's Health, the Speech and Hearing Clinic, the Stroke Center, and other program areas offfer opportunities for special study. Grants from individual donors, corporations, foundations, and federal and state governments support diverse research programs.

Financial Aid

The University provides a limited number of teaching and research assistantships for qualified graduate students as part of the educational and professional-preparation programs. Stipends vary according to the assignment and qualifications of applicants. Applications for assistantships may be obtained from the head of the academic unit in which the applicant intends to study. Student loans, campus employment, and a limited number of graduate scholarships are also available.

Cost of Study

In 2001–02, graduate tuition for Texas residents was $98 per semester hour. Graduate tuition for out-of-state students was $309 per semester hour. All students paid the following fees on a per semester credit hour basis: a minimum $3 per semester credit hour course fee (fee ranged from $3 to $200 per course), a student service fee of $15.91 ($143.19 maximum), a library use fee of $30, a transcript fee of $3, a medical service fee of $30, and a computer use fee of $6 ($15 minimum). Students also paid a publication fee of $10, a student identification card fee of $2, and a Student Center fee of $25. All rates are subject to change.

Living and Housing Costs

The University provides both single-room and apartment facilities for graduate students in its residence halls. In 2001–02, graduate students paid about $1100 per semester for a residence hall room (double occupancy). Family housing is available for married students with not more than one child and for single parents with a maximum of two children. Meal services are available in University dining halls. Costs for rooms and meals depend on individual needs and preferences. All rates are subject to change.

Student Group

Fall 2001 enrollment was approximately 8,000 students. Of these, 47 percent were enrolled in graduate programs. Qualified women and men are eligible for admission to all programs.

Location

With about 79,000 residents, Denton provides the benefits of a medium-sized city. The surrounding Dallas–Fort Worth metropolitan area (the nation's ninth-largest) offers rich cultural, entertainment, and recreational opportunities. TWU's Houston Center provides students with access to a metropolitan city with diverse opportunities, including clinical experiences that are available in the Texas Medical Center.

The University and The School

Established in 1901 by an act of the Texas legislature, Texas Woman's University is a public university offering baccalaureate, master's, and doctoral degree programs. It is a teaching and research institution, and its 270-acre main campus is located in Denton (35 miles north of Dallas–Fort Worth). Major centers for health science study are in Dallas, in the Parkland and Presbyterian Hospital complexes, and in Houston, in the heart of the Texas Medical Center. TWU is fully accredited by appropriate state, regional, and national agencies, including the Southern Association of Colleges and Schools. The Graduate School is a member of the Council of Graduate Schools in the United States, the Conference of Southern Graduate Schools, and the Academic Common Market of the Southern Regional Education Board.

Applying

Prospective students should file an application for admission to the Office of Student Records Processing no later than ninety days prior to registration.

Correspondence and Information

Additional information and application forms are available from:

Office of Student Records Processing
Box 425589
Texas Woman's University
Denton, Texas 76204-5589

Telephone: 940-898-3076
E-mail: gradschool@twu.edu
World Wide Web: http://www.twu.edu/o-grad/

DEPARTMENT AND PROGRAM HEADS

GRADUATE SCHOOL

Michael H. Droge, Dean of Graduate Studies and Research; Ph.D., UTMB Galveston.
Sondra Ferstl, Associate Dean for Research; Ph.D., Wisconsin.
Jennifer Martin, Associate Dean for Graduate Studies; Ph.D., Texas Woman's.

UNIVERSITY GENERAL DIVISIONS

Arts and Sciences: Richard Rodean, Interim Dean; Ph.D., Texas Tech.
Biology: Allen E. Waldo, Interim Chair; Ph.D., Washington State.
Chemistry and Physics: Carlton T. Wendel, Chair; Ph.D., Texas Tech.
English, Speech, and Foreign Languages: Hugh Burns, Chair; Ph.D., Texas at Austin.
History and Government: Jim R. Alexander, Chair; Ph.D., American.
Mathematics and Computer Science: Donald Edwards, Chair; Ph.D., Texas Christian.
Performing Arts: John Weinkein, Interim Chair; M.F.A., Drake.
Psychology and Philosophy: Daniel Miller, Chair; Ph.D., Ohio State.
School of Management: Paula Ann Hughes, Chair; Ph.D., North Texas.
Sociology and Social Work: Joyce E. Williams, Chair; Ph.D., Washington (St. Louis).
Visual Arts: John Weinkein, Chair; M.F.A., Drake.
Women's Studies: Claire Sahlin, Director; Ph.D., Harvard.

Professional Education: Keith Swigger, Dean; Ph.D., Iowa.
Family Sciences: Lora Ann Neill, Interim Chair; Ph.D., Texas Tech.
Reading: Cathy Zeek, Chair; Ph.D., TAMU-Commerce.
School of Library and Information Studies: Keith Swigger, Interim Director; Ph.D., Iowa.
Teacher Education: Donna Crenshaw, Chair; Ph.D., Texas Woman's.

INSTITUTE OF HEALTH SCIENCES

Health Sciences: Jean Pyfer, Dean; P.E.D., Indiana.
Communication Sciences and Disorders: Alfred H. White, Chair; Ph.D., Michigan State.
Healthcare Administration–Dallas: Robert Maurer, Director; Ph.D., Texas at Dallas.
Healthcare Administration–Houston: Kelley Moseley, Director; Dr.P.H., Texas at Austin.
Health Studies: Susan Ward, Chair; Ph.D., Virginia.
Kinesiology: Jerry Wilkerson, Chair; Ph.D., Indiana.
Nutrition and Food Sciences: Carolyn Bednar, Chair; Ph.D., Nebraska.

Nursing: Carolyn S. Gunning, Dean; Ph.D., Texas at Austin.

Occupational Therapy: Sally Schultz, Interim Dean; Ph.D., North Texas.

Physical Therapy: Carolyn K. Rozier, Dean; Ph.D., Oklahoma.

TWU welcomes men and women to its master's and doctoral programs.

THOMAS EDISON STATE COLLEGE

Graduate Studies

Programs of Study

Thomas Edison State College offers two master's degree programs that have broad appeal to adult students who desire to build professional expertise through completing quality, online degrees.

The Master of Science in Management (M.S.M.) degree serves employed adults with three to five years of professional experience in management. Designed in partnership with major corporations, the M.S.M. degree program integrates the theory and practice of management. Nearly 30 percent of students are from the nonprofit sector. Students may specialize in leadership, project management, management of substance abuse, or insurance programs. The M.S.M. leadership track requires two weekend residencies, one at the beginning of the program and one after the fifth semester. Students who participate in the residencies recommend them highly as a strong point for the program. The 36-semester-hour program is typically completed within twenty-two months.

The College's online Master of Arts in Professional Studies (M.A.P.S.) degree (36 semester hours) provides working professionals an opportunity to study the liberal arts from an applied perspective. Students work from the context of their ongoing professional work. Their study of professionalism, community, and change infuses their professional lives with a deeper understanding of the workplace and their responsibilities as professionals. Students acquire leadership tools as they gain a deeper appreciation of the value and relevance of the arts, sciences, and humanities to the practical concerns of the workplace. The M.A.P.S. program attracts a diverse student body working in positions such as museum curator, college business manager, computer networking specialist, nuclear engineer, and teacher.

Research Facilities

Thomas Edison State College students utilize the rich library research facilities of the New Jersey State Library, which is affiliated with Thomas Edison State College administers. Students have access to VALE, the Virtual Academic Libraries Environment, a system that provides access to a network of research libraries.

Financial Aid

Graduate students support their studies with employer tuition aid and loans. Unsubsidized loans are available to all accepted applicants. The Thomas Edison State College Office of Financial Aid is available to assist students.

Cost of Study

Tuition and fees are specified in the *Graduate Studies Prospectus and Application*. Books and materials are estimated at $200 to $300 per semester.

Living and Housing Costs

Thomas Edison State College graduate and undergraduate students complete course work through distance education. There are no College-based living and housing costs associated with an education through Thomas Edison State College.

Student Group

Students are working adults who maintain membership in their current professional associations. Graduates are invited to become active in the alumni association.

Location

Thomas Edison State College is located in the capital city of Trenton, New Jersey, but its reach is global. Students live and study in all fifty states and eighty other countries. The College's campus embraces the historic Kelsey Building at 101 West State Street and the adjacent Townhouse Complex, the Academic Center at 167 East Hanover Street, and the Kuser Mansion at 315 West State Street. Renovations were completed on five historic town houses in 1999, preserving of the nineteenth-century structures. This historical restoration project now houses the College's electronic classrooms, computer labs, educational conference and training rooms as well as the College's distance learning support, development, and delivery facilities, linking students and faculty members at dozens of colleges throughout the country and around the world.

The College

Founded in 1972, Thomas Edison State College provides adults with access to the best choices in higher education. One of New Jersey's twelve senior public institutions of higher education, the College offers two graduate degrees as well as twelve associate and baccalaureate degrees. Thomas Edison State College, a pioneer in the assessment of adult learning and use of educational technologies, enrolls more than 8,300 students. Undergraduate students earn degrees through assessment of their learning, transfer credit, independent study, and online courses. Graduate study is primarily online. The online courses require student interaction and collaboration, and intensive communications with faculty members is the norm. *Forbes* magazine identified the College as one of the top twenty colleges and universities in the nation in the use of technology to create learning opportunities for adults. The College is home to the John S. Watson Institute for Public Policy, which provides public policy analysis and other assistance to government, community groups, and the private sector. Thomas Edison State College is accredited by the Middle States Association of Colleges and Schools.

Applying

Applications are competitive. The programs are open to students with baccalaureate degrees in any field and three to five years of experience appropriate to the program. The application requires a statement of professional goals, an analysis of competencies for the Master of Science in Management or an essay for the Master of Arts in Professional Studies, undergraduate transcripts documenting the earned degree, and two letters of recommendation. Students are required to have computer access and be proficient in computer use. A minimum TOEFL score of 550 is required for applicants whose primary language in not English. The application fee of $75 is nonrefundable. Applications are accepted throughout the year, and students may apply online at the Web site listed below.

Correspondence and Information

Dr. Esther Taitsman
Associate Dean and Director of Graduate Studies
Office of Graduate Studies
Thomas Edison State College
101 West State Street
Trenton, New Jersey 08608-1176
Telephone: 609-984-1168
Fax: 609-633-8593
E-mail: info-msm@tesc.edu (M.S.M. program)
info-maps@tesc.edu (M.A.P.S. program)
World Wide Web: http://www.tesc.edu

ABOUT THE FACULTY

Thomas Edison State College consulting faculty members share with students their academic expertise (90 percent have earned the highest degree in their field), real-world work experience, and expertise in teaching online. Thomas Edison State College faculty members have earned their highest degrees from large public institutions such as Rutgers, Temple, and the Universities of California and Georgia as well as from private universities such as the University of Pennsylvania, the Fielding Institute, and Columbia University. Faculty members have experience working in or consulting with corporate and nonprofit organizations. M.S.M. faculty members have worked as senior managers in human resources, finance, operations research, communications, and public relations. M.A.P.S. faculty members have worked in communications and as academic faculty members and administrators, performing artists, and consultants, providing executive leadership programs. The faculty members at Thomas Edison have designed their courses specifically for the online environment. M.S.M. faculty members have been teaching online since 1996.

TIFFIN UNIVERSITY

School of Graduate Studies

Programs of Study

The Graduate School at Tiffin University offers graduate programs in two areas of study—business administration and criminal justice. The Master of Business Administration (M.B.A.) program is offered in a variety of ways, from an evening and weekend option to online Internet-based study. The program is fully and nationally accredited by the Association of Collegiate Business Schools and Programs (ACBSP). The program is also offered at various extension campuses located in Ohio. The Master of Criminal Justice (M.C.J.) program is a one-year Saturday-only program that is offered on the main campus in Tiffin, Ohio. The M.C.J. consists of two concentrations—justice administration and forensic psychology. The M.C.J. in justice administration is also offered online.

Research Facilities

The Tiffin University Library system holds approximately 60,000 volumes in books and microform. After its expansion in 1996, Pfeiffer Library is poised to provide increased services. The library has an outstanding collection of books and subscribes to more than 200 journals to support its academic programs. In addition to print resources, Pfeiffer Library provides its journal collection in microfiche format and has an expanding selection of CD-ROM databases, including periodical indexes. Special collections include the National Criminal Justice Reference Service Document collection and the University archives. Circulation is automated and requires the use of the bar code on the Tiffin University ID cards. Library services include reference assistance, photocopying, interlibrary loan, computerized bibliographic retrieval, and reserve items. The library is also part of the statewide network (OhioLINK) of university libraries. This allows faculty and staff members and students quick access to interlibrary loans, scholarly journals, and online databases.

Financial Aid

Federal programs determine the financial need from the information submitted by students on the Free Application for Federal Student Aid (FAFSA). The data provided in the FAFSA is analyzed and evaluated according to a formula approved by Congress and the Department of Education. A confidential report is then provided to Tiffin University, based upon which all applicants are given equitable consideration.

Cost of Study

For the 2001–02 academic year, the graduate tuition fee was $475 per credit hour. Tuition totaled approximately $15,200 for the M.B.A. program (32 credit hours) and $14,250 for the M.C.J. program (30 credit hours). The estimated cost of books was just under $400. There is a nonrefundable $50 processing fee for all M.B.A. and M.C.J. students.

Living and Housing Costs

A limited number of rooms and apartments within the University are available for graduate students. Information may be obtained from the Housing Office, in care of Residence Life. Residence Life also assists students interested in off-campus apartments. Being a rural community, the cost of living is reasonable, with housing costs ranging from $300 to $475 per month, plus utilities.

Student Group

The Graduate School has slightly more than 300 students, of whom approximately 40 percent are women and 20 percent are international.

Location

Tiffin, Ohio, is a quiet community located in a rural setting. Its location is in north central Ohio approximately 90 miles from Cleveland and Columbus, Ohio, and Detroit, Michigan. Tiffin is an historic community with numerous seasonal activities, ranging from festivals and county fairs to plays, comedy acts, and musical productions that can be seen at the historic Ritz Theater. Tiffin is proudly known as the "Education Community."

The University

Tiffin University was established in 1888 as a business university. During the last two decades, the University has grown and transformed to offer nationally accredited graduate and undergraduate degree programs in business administration, top-notch bachelor's and master's degrees in criminal justice, and distinctive liberal studies degrees. The campus at Tiffin is a blend of traditional historic buildings and modern complexes that create a vibrant and warm home for an educational community. Campus development during the last decade includes the construction of several new residence halls, a new student center, a new classroom building, and outdoor athletic facilities, as well as renovation of many of the University buildings. In addition to the growth at Tiffin, graduate and undergraduate programs of the University are offered at the Degree Centers at Lorain and Lima, Ohio, and at several sites in the Greater Cleveland area.

Applying

Applications for admission for the fall semester must be received by August 15. To be considered for financial assistance, applications should be submitted by mid-January. Applications must include official transcripts from all colleges and universities attended. Letters of recommendation are welcome, but not required. International students must also submit a financial statement and official English translations of all academic records. Students whose native language is not English must submit results of the Test of English as a Foreign Language (TOEFL).

Correspondence and Information

School of Graduate Studies
Tiffin University
155 Miami Street
Tiffin, Ohio 44883
Telephone: 800-968-6446 Ext. 3401 (toll-free)
Fax: 419-443-5002
World Wide Web: http://www.tiffin.edu
http://www.tiffin-global.org (online M.B.A.)

THE FACULTY

Business Faculty (M.B.A.)

John J. Millar, Professor and Dean, School of Business; Ph.D., Michigan State.
Raj V. Pathi, Professor and Vice President of Academic Affairs; Ph.D., Case Western Reserve.
Shawn P. Daly, Assistant Professor and Dean; Ph.D., Temple.
Lillian Drimmer, Assistant Professor; D.B.A., Cleveland State.
Debra S. Gatton, Assistant Professor; Ph.D., Kent State.
Nabarun Ghose, Associate Professor; D.B.A., Southern Illinois at Carbondale.
Barry Jacobs, Assistant Professor; Ph.D., Case Western Reserve.
Gabrial Jaskolka, Assistant Professor; Ph.D., SUNY at Buffalo.
Laura Ketter, Instructor; M.B.A., Tiffin.
Terry Sullivan, Instructor; J.D., Ohio Northern.
Martha J. Turner, Assistant Professor; Ph.D., Cornell.
Walter A. Verdon, Professor; Ph.D., Nebraska–Lincoln.
Walter A. Zielinski, Associate Professor; Ph.D., Union (Ohio).

Criminal Justice Faculty (M.C.J.)

Jack D. Collins, Associate Professor and Dean, School of Criminal Justice; Ed.D., Cincinnati.
Keith N. Haley, Professor and Dean, Off Campus Learning; M.S., Michigan State.
Elizabeth Athaide-Victor, Assistant Professor; Ph.D., Toledo.
John A. Bates, Professor; Ph.D., Massachusetts Amherst.
Steven D. Hurwitz, Associate Professor; Ph.D., Syracuse.
C. Joseph Saunders, Assistant Professor; Ph.D., Ohio.
Jeffrey J. Stockner, Professor; J.D., Ohio Northern.
James C. Todd, Professor; Ph.D., Akron.

TOWSON UNIVERSITY

Graduate School

Programs of Study

The Graduate School at Towson University (TU) prepares qualified students for career advancement, leadership positions, and further graduate study. The Graduate School offers three doctoral degree progams, thirty-three master's degree programs, and seventeen graduate certificate programs. The University schedules graduate-level classes for the convenience of part-time and full-time students.

The M.Ed. degree is offered in art education, early childhood education, elementary education, reading, secondary education, and special education. TU also offers the Master of Arts in Teaching (M.A.T.) for liberal arts graduates seeking to teach at the early childhood, elementary, or secondary school level.

The M.A. degree is offered in geography and environmental planning, humanities, liberal and professional studies, and psychology (with specializations in clinical psychology, counseling, experimental psychology, and school psychology). TU also offers the Certificate of Advanced Study in School Psychology and in Counseling Psychology.

The M.F.A. degree is offered in studio art and theater. The Master of Music (M.Mus.) degree is offered in music performance and composition, and a 15-hour Graduate Music Certificate is available.

The M.S. degree is offered in applied and industrial mathematics, applied gerontology, applied information technology, biology, communications management, computer science, environmental science, health science, human resource development, instructional technology, mathematics education, music education, nursing, occupational therapy, physician assistant studies, professional writing, social science, speech-language pathology, and women's studies.

Applied doctoral programs are offered in audiology (Au.D.), instructional technology (Ed.D.), and occupational science (Sc.D.).

Research Facilities

The Albert S. Cook Library is the hub of information resources for the University, with more than 700,000 book and nonbook items, more than 2,000 periodicals, a number of specialized collections, and online access to resources of other University System of Maryland libraries. Students use individual computer accounts to access information via the Internet and World Wide Web. Special institutes and research facilities on campus include the Regional Economic Studies Institute, the Geographic Information Systems Laboratory, the Speech-Language-Hearing Clinic, the Institute for Teaching and Research on Women, and the Center for Applied Information Technology.

Financial Aid

Graduate assistantships, low-interest loans, and a limited number of scholarships are available to help make graduate education affordable. Graduate assistantships provide free tuition and a stipend in exchange for full-time (20 hours per week) or part-time (10 hours per week) work, generally on campus. Ten-month and twelve-month positions are available. Federally sponsored loans are available to U.S. citizens with demonstrated need. Graduate Diversity Grants are designed to help African-American students who are Maryland residents, and the Charlotte W. Newcombe Foundation Scholarship for Women is designed for second-career women or women seeking career advancement.

Cost of Study

Tuition for 2001–02 was $211 per credit hour for Maryland residents and $435 per credit hour for nonresidents. Additional fees were $52 per credit hour.

Living and Housing Costs

Graduate students may live in residence halls or dorm-style apartments if space is available. Students living on campus can expect to pay about $2975 per semester for room and a dining plan. Another popular and convenient residence for both single and married graduate students is The Burkshire, a University-owned facility renting one- and two-bedroom apartments on twelve-month leases. Rental fees begin at $730 per month plus utilities.

Student Group

There are 3,021 graduate students currently enrolled at Towson, which has a total student body of 16,980. More than 75 percent of graduate students enroll part-time. The median age for graduate students is 31. About 6 percent are out-of-state residents, and 6 percent are international students. Members of minority groups comprise 19 percent of the total enrollment. The majority of students are attracted to applied graduate programs that can assist them in their professional careers.

Location

The University is situated on a 328-acre suburban campus located on the outskirts of Baltimore, Maryland. The city's many cultural resources include the Walters Art Museum, the Baltimore Museum of Art, Meyerhoff Symphony Hall, Center Stage, and the Lyric Theatre. In addition, the 100,000 students at twenty colleges and universities in the Baltimore metropolitan area have access to a wide array of lectures, fine arts programs, music, and library resources. The University also is less than an hour from Washington, D.C., and access is convenient by rail or car to Philadelphia and New York City.

The University

Towson University, founded in 1866 as Maryland's first teacher training institution, is a liberal arts–based, comprehensive metropolitan university, nationally recognized for its excellent programs in the arts and sciences, business, communication, fine arts, health sciences, and teacher education. The Graduate School offers doctoral degrees, master's degrees, and certificate programs to a student body composed mainly of working adults seeking professional and personal growth. Graduate students currently represent 18 percent of the student body.

Applying

The application fee is $40. Prospective students may apply online at the Web address listed below.

Correspondence and Information

For applications, admissions information, and information about specific graduate programs, students may contact:

The Graduate School
Towson University
8000 York Road
Towson, Maryland 21252
Telephone: 410-704-2501
Fax: 410-704-4675
E-mail: petgrad@towson.edu
World Wide Web: http://www.towson.edu/grad

GRADUATE PROGRAMS AND DIRECTORS

Applied and Industrial Math (M.S.): Geoff Goodson, Ph.D., Sussex (England).
Applied Gerontology (M.S.): Donna Wagner, Ph.D., Portland State.
Applied Information Technology (M.S., certificates): Ali Behforooz, Ph.D., Michigan State.
Art (M.F.A., M.Ed.): James Flood, Professor and Chair; M.A., Illinois.
Art Education (M.Ed.): Jane Bates, Ed.D., Arizona State.
Art, Studio (M.F.A.): Stuart Stein, M.F.A., Maryland Institute, College of Art.
Audiology (Au.D.): Diana Emanuel, Ph.D., Penn State.
Biology (M.S.): Larry Wimmers, Ph.D., Cornell; Scott Johnson, Ph.D., Calgary.
Chemistry Education (certificate): Frank Milio, M.S., Maryland.
Clinician-Administrator Transition (certificate): Patricia Alt, Ph.D., North Carolina.
Communications Management (M.S.): Mark McElreath, Ph.D., Wisconsin–Madison.
Computer Science (M.S.): Ramesh Karne, Ph.D., George Mason.
Early Childhood Education (M.Ed.): Edyth Wheeler, Ph.D., George Mason.
Elementary Education (M.Ed.): Linda Emerick, Ph.D., Connecticut.
Environmental Science (M.S., certificate): Jane Wolfson, Ph.D., Stony Brook, SUNY.
Geography and Environmental Planning (M.A.): Kent Barnes, Ph.D., Rutgers.
Health Science (M.S.): Susan Radius, Ph.D., Johns Hopkins.
Humanities (M.A.): George Hahn, Ph.D., Maryland.
Human Resource Development (M.S.): Larry Froman, Ph.D., Wayne State.
Instructional Technology (M.S., Ed.D.): David Wizer, Ph.D., Maryland.
Liberal and Professional Studies (M.A.): John Webster, Ed.D., Rutgers.
Management and Leadership Development (certificate): Filiz Tabak, Ph.D., Oklahoma State.
Mathematics Education (M.S.): Tadanobu Watanabe, Ph.D., Florida State.
Music (M.S., certificate): Michael Jothen, Ph.D., Ohio State.
Music Performance/Composition (M.Mus.): Luis Engelke, D.M.A., Arizona State.
Network Technologies (certificate): Ali Behforooz, Ph.D., Michigan State.
Nursing (M.S.): Joan Jordan, Ed.D., Morgan State.
Nursing Education (certificate): Joan Jordan, Ed.D., Morgan State.
Occupational Science (Sc.D.): Maggie Reitz, Ph.D., Maryland, College Park.
Occupational Therapy (M.S.): Sonia Lawson, M.Ed., Maryland.
Organizational Change (C.A.S.): Roxana DellaVeccia, Ph.D., Maryland.
Physician Assistant Studies (M.S.): Steven Collier, Ph.D., Georgia State.
Professional Writing (M.S.): Harvey Lillywhite, Ph.D., Utah.
Psychology, Clinical Psychology Track (M.A.): Barry Bass, Ph.D., Tennessee.
Psychology, Counseling Psychology Track (M.A., C.A.S.): Janet Anderson-Parente, Ph.D., Maryland.
Psychology, Experimental Psychology Track (M.A.): Michael Figler, Ph.D., Michigan State.
Psychology, School Psychology Track (M.A., C.A.S.): Susan Bartels, Ph.D., Virginia.
Reading (M.Ed.): Barbara Laster, Ed.D., Virginia Tech.
Reading Education (certificate): Barbara Laster, Ed.D., Virginia Tech.
Secondary Education (M.Ed.): Elizabeth Wilkins-Canter, Ph.D., Southern Illinois.
Social Science (M.S.): Nicole Dombrowski, Ph.D., NYU.
Software Engineering (certificate): Ali Behforooz, Ph.D., Michigan State.
Special Education (M.Ed.): Amy Pleet, Ed.D., George Washington.
Speech-Language Pathology (M.S.): Sharon Glennon, Ph.D., Penn State.
Strategic Public Relations and Integrated Communications (certificate): Mark McElreath, Ph.D., Wisconsin–Madison.
Teaching (M.A.T.): Debbie Piper, M.A., Maryland.
Theatre (M.F.A.): Juanita Rockwell, M.F.A., Connecticut; Ralph Blasting, Ph.D., Toronto.
Women's Studies (M.S.): Esther Wangari, Ph.D., New School.

TRINITY COLLEGE

School of Education
School of Professional Studies

Programs of Study

Trinity College offers coeducational graduate programs leading to the Master of Arts (M.A.), the Master of Arts in Teaching (M.A.T.), the Master of Education (M.Ed.), and the Master of Science in Administration (M.S.A.) degrees. These programs are designed to meet the needs of teachers, counselors, administrators, managers, entrepreneurs, and other professionals. Courses stress current issues, trends, the application of current research, and bridging the gap between theory and practice. Courses are conveniently scheduled for full- or part-time students who continue working while earning their graduate degrees. A variety of concentrations gives students the opportunity for intensive study in their degree program. The graduate degrees offered by the School of Education meet the certification requirements of the District of Columbia and are approved by NASDTEC.

Trinity's School of Education offers M.A.T. specializations in early childhood education (48 credits), elementary education (45 credits), secondary education (42 credits), and special education (48 credits). The M.Ed. in curriculum and instruction (36 credits) is offered with a focus on reading or on education for democracy, diversity, and social justice. Trinity also provides accelerated teacher certification to nondegree students.

In the areas of counseling and management, the School of Education offers the M.A. in community counseling (49 credits), school guidance and counseling (43 credits), and student development in higher education (45 credits). For students pursuing administrative or instructional leadership positions in educational settings, Trinity College offers an M.S.A. in educational administration (36 credits).

Trinity's School of Professional Studies offers the M.S.A. degree in organizational administration that prepares students for management or supervisory positions in government and not-for-profit settings.

Research Facilities

The Sister Helen Sheehan Library houses approximately 200,000 volumes, 600 periodicals, and numerous CD-ROM and online databases. As a member of the interlibrary loan and consortium libraries, Trinity provides students with access to all major academic libraries in the Washington, D.C., metropolitan area.

Financial Aid

The Financial Aid Office provides information about federal loan and work-study programs as well as the District of Columbia Matching Funds Programs.

Cost of Study

Tuition and fees for the 2000–01 academic year were $485 per credit hour for graduate courses. Students may contact the Admissions Office for current information about costs for other programs.

Living and Housing Costs

Graduate students may live on campus for the academic year.

Student Group

There are nearly 500 students in the graduate courses and programs at Trinity College. With most graduate courses offered in the evening and on Saturdays, the majority of students work and pursue their degrees part-time. Nine credits is the minimum load for full-time status, although most students enroll in six courses per semester.

Location

Trinity College's 26-acre wooded campus is located in a residential neighborhood in Washington, D.C., just 2 miles north of the U.S. Capitol. A free shuttle service runs between the campus and the Metro (commuter rail transportation for the greater Washington metropolitan area); campus parking is available. Trinity also provides a child-care center. All programs at Trinity are enlarged and enriched by the resources of the nation's capital.

The College and The School

Trinity College, founded in 1897 by the Sisters of Notre Dame, is one of the nation's first Catholic liberal arts colleges for women. The coeducational graduate programs were established in 1966 in response to the changing economic and educational needs of the District of Columbia and adjacent counties.

Applying

Candidates for admission must have completed a bachelor's degree from a regionally accredited institution with a minimum grade point average of 2.8. To apply, students should submit a completed application packet (the application, a two-page typed essay, two letters of recommendation, official transcripts from all colleges and universities attended, a current resume or CV, and a $35 nonrefundable application fee). An interview may be required. International applicants must also submit an official TOEFL score, a declaration/certification of finances, and an official transcript with translation and evaluation. Applications will not be reviewed until they are complete.

Applicants are encouraged to submit all materials at least two months in advance of the semester in which they wish to matriculate. Applicants may take up to 6 credits as nonmatriculating students, providing that they had a minimum undergraduate GPA of 2.8.

Correspondence and Information

Office of Admissions–Graduate Program
Trinity College
125 Michigan Avenue NE
Washington, D.C. 20017-1094
Telephone: 202-884-9400
800-492-6882 (toll-free)
Fax: 202-884-9229

THE FACULTY

School of Education

Gloria Grantham, Dean, School of Education; Ph.D., Pittsburgh.
Rosemarie Bosler, S.N.D., Associate Professor of Education; Ed.D., Catholic University.
Anne Coates-Conaway, Associate Professor of Counseling; Ph.D., Saint Louis.
Roberta Dorr, Assistant Professor of Education; Ph.D., Catholic University.
Shelly Gismondi, Assistant Professor of Education; Ph.D., Catholic University.
Cynthia Greer, Assistant Professor of Counseling; Ph.D., Florida State.
Robert F. Redmond, Associate Professor of Education; Ph.D., Maryland.
L. Lawrence Riccio, Professor of Education; Ed.D., George Washington.

School of Professional Studies

Sara Murray Thompson, Dean, School of Professional Studies; M.B.A., Colorado; Ph.D., Marquette.
Sharon Levin, Associate Professor of Business Administration; M.B.A., Loyola (Baltimore); CPA.
V. R. Nemani, Associate Professor of Business Administration; M.B.A., Iowa.
Beverly Whitest, Coordinator of Graduate Programs in Administration; Ph.D., Maryland, College Park.

TRUMAN STATE UNIVERSITY

Graduate Programs

Programs of Study

Truman State, Missouri's public liberal arts and sciences university, offers eight selective graduate programs leading to the Master of Accountancy, Master of Arts, Master of Arts in Education (including teacher certification), and Master of Science degrees. Areas of study include accountancy, biology, communication disorders, counseling, education, English, history, and music.

Most programs require a thesis or other capstone project. For example, the M.A.E. program offers a reflective case study option. Programs range from 30 to 48 semester hours.

Programs with special accreditation include: accountancy, accredited by the International Association for Management Education (AACSB); communication disorders, accredited by the American Speech-Language-Hearing Association (ASHA); counseling, accredited by the Council for Accreditation of Counseling and Related Educational Programs (CACREP); education, accredited by the National Council for Accreditation of Teacher Education (NCATE); and music, accredited by the National Association of Schools of Music (NASM).

Research Facilities

Truman's graduate programs offer a combination of theory and practical application. The University Library supports faculty and student research with a collection of 427,286 volumes, 1,509,988 microforms, and 3,700 serial subscriptions; interlibrary loan services; and access to bibliographic databases on line and on compact disc.

Academic computer facilities include seven computer classrooms with 219 stations, and 328 workstations in student labs, some available 24 hours a day. Internet access is available at no charge.

A $20.4 million renovation of the Ophelia Parrish Building became the new home to Truman's Fine Arts Division in 2000–01.

Truman's close association with the birthplace of osteopathic medicine, the Kirksville College of Osteopathic Medicine, offers students access to additional graduate-level faculty members and research opportunities. The science facilities will undergo a $24 million renovation and expnasion.

Financial Aid

Graduate teaching and research assistantships are available in many programs. Most assistantships include an $8000 stipend for a nine-month contract, as well as a waiver of in-state or out-of-state graduate tuition for up to 9 credit hours per academic semester. In addition, the University offers some divisional fellowships and private scholarships and participates in all major federal financial aid programs.

Cost of Study

Full-time graduate tuition for 2001–02 was $2036 per academic year for Missouri residents and $3706 for nonresident students. There is a student activity fee of $16 per academic semester.

Living and Housing Costs

In 2001–02, room and board in residence halls cost $4736 per person per year for a double room. Apartments rented for $1856 to $2216 per person per year. University family student housing was available for $3624 per year for a one-bedroom apartment and $4168 per year for a two-bedroom apartment. The apartments and the University family student housing include all utilities except electricity and telephone. Many privately owned apartment complexes close to the University are available to single students and families.

Student Group

Total enrollment at Truman State University is approximately 6,000, of whom about 200 are graduate students. International students and American students who are members of minority groups are encouraged to apply.

Location

Truman's campus comprises 140 acres, located in the heart of Kirksville, Missouri. Kirksville offers numerous social and cultural opportunities, including a variety of recreation areas, shops, restaurants, theaters, and churches. Recreation areas include Thousand Hills State Park and the 700-acre Forest Lake.

The University

Founded in 1867, Truman provides a world-class liberal arts and sciences education to a select number of high-ability students. The University offers forty-two undergraduate and nine graduate majors.

Truman is recognized nationally for offering top-quality education at an affordable cost to students. The University's achievements have been featured in such publications as *USA Today, Time, Money* magazine, *IBM Viewpoint,* the *Chronicle of Higher Education, U.S. News & World Report, Kiplinger's Personal Finance Magazine,* and *Changing Times.*

Applying

Truman State University invites applications from students with outstanding records of undergraduate performance. There is no application fee for American citizens. Application deadlines vary. Official transcripts from each college or university attended are required. In addition, scores on the appropriate entrance exam or exams must be submitted to the Graduate Office. Accountancy majors must submit the GMAT. The GRE General Test is required by all other programs. Prospective students are advised to take the required exam(s) prior to filing for admission.

Correspondence and Information

Graduate Office
203 McClain Hall
Truman State University
100 East Normal
Kirksville, Missouri 63501
Telephone: 660-785-4109
Fax: 660-785-7460
E-mail: gradinfo@truman.edu
World Wide Web: http://www2.truman.edu/gradinfo

PROGRAM DIRECTORS AND FACULTY RESEARCH AREAS

Accountancy: (AACSB accredited)
Program Director: Dr. Jeffrey Romine, Associate Professor of Accounting; CPA.
Areas of Faculty Research: EDP influences on internal auditing, accounting education, informational impacts on audit reports, managerial accounting, FASB's conceptual framework, accounting standards overload, applications of federal tax laws.

Biology
Program Director: Dr. Cynthia Cooper, Associate Professor of Biology.
Areas of Faculty Research: Ecology, systematics, and evolution (plant/insect/fungus interactions, plant reproductive ecology, ecological genetics, plant population biology, conservation biology, microbial ecology, fungal ecology, microbe-vertebrate interactions, plant taxonomy, biosystematics, aquatic ecology, rare plant ecology, evolution of Caribbean birds, ornithology, paleobotany, evolution of seed plants, evolution and ecology of marine invertebrates); cellular and molecular biology (maize genetics, nerve cell biology, carotenoid genetics, DNA repair, genetics of sperm development, microbial genetics, plant cell biology, membrane transport, steroid receptor biochemistry); physiology and anatomy (plant stress physiology, physiology of drug abuse, neurophysiology, parasitology/immunology, respiratory physiology); biology education (teaching technology and laboratory investigations).

Communication Disorders: (ASHE accredited)
Program Director: Dr. John Applegate, Professor of Communication Disorders.
Areas of Faculty Research: Speech and language characteristics of geriatric populations, microcomputer-assisted language intervention, orofacial anomolies, augmentative communication systems, child phonology, bilingual phonology.

Counseling: (CACREP accredited)
Program Director: Dr. Christopher Maglio, Associate Professor of Counseling.
Areas of Faculty Research: Adolescent behavior, behavior therapy, death anxiety, death education, grief counseling, marriage and family counseling, testing and assessment, self-concept, elementary guidance, curriculum development, and counselor supervision.

Education: (NCATE accredited)
Program Director: Dr. Sam Minner, Professor and Head of the Division of Education.
Areas of Teaching Specialty: Communication (speech, theater, journalism), English, elementary education, exercise science, foreign language (French, Spanish), history, mathematics, music, science, special education, visual arts.

English
Program Director: Dr. Bob Mielke, Professor of English.
Areas of Faculty Research: Composition and rhetorical theory, writing poetry and fiction, world literature, postcolonial literature, Old English language and literature, medieval drama, Chaucer and his contemporaries, Shakespeare and his contemporaries, British period literature from medieval through contemporary, Irish literature, Germanic literature, Joyce and his contemporaries, William Blake, Walt Whitman, William Faulkner, American period literature from early through contemporary, literary theory, film studies, cold war culture, cultural studies.

History
Program Director: Dr. Sally West, Assistant Professor of History.
Areas of Faculty Research: American history: diplomacy, intellectual, cultural, religious, Amish, gender, public, oral, Asian-American, colonial, revolutionary, Civil War, Jacksonian, U.S.-Latin American relations; European history: social, history of science and medicine, ancient Greece, early modern England, medieval and early modern England, medieval and early modern Europe and modern France, imperial Russia, disability studies; non-Western: modern China, Latin America, modern Japan and Africa, and modern France.

Music: (NASM accredited)
Program Director: Dr. Warren Gooch, Professor of Music.
Specialty Areas: Musicology, theory, composition, music education, conducting, orchestral instruments, piano, voice. Emphases: Research (thesis), performance (recital), composition (recital), conducting (recital).

TUFTS UNIVERSITY

Graduate School of Arts and Sciences

Programs of Study

The Graduate School of Arts and Sciences offers master's and doctoral programs in selected areas of the natural sciences, social sciences, and the humanities.

The Doctor of Philosophy degree is offered in biology, chemistry, child development, drama, English, history, mathematics, physics, and psychology. A highly selective interdisciplinary doctorate is available in other areas.

The Master of Arts degree may be earned in art history, art history and museum studies, child development, classical archaeology, classics, drama, economics, education, English, French, German, history, history and museum studies, mathematics, museum education, music, occupational therapy, philosophy, school psychology, and urban and environmental policy and planning. The Master of Science is offered in biology, chemistry, mathematics, occupational therapy, physics, and psychology. The Master of Arts in Teaching is available with concentrations in early childhood, elementary, and secondary education. The Master of Fine Arts degree is awarded in conjunction with the School of the Museum of Fine Arts, Boston. Tufts also offers the Master of Public Policy degree. A Certificate of Advanced Graduate Study may be earned in child development, education, and school psychology.

Full-time students can take one course per semester, for both a grade and credit, through cross-registration agreements with Boston College, Boston University, and Brandeis University.

Research Facilities

The University library system includes the Tisch Library, the Music Library, and the Edward Ginn Library of the Fletcher School. Through Tufts' membership in the Boston Library Consortium, graduate students also have library privileges at Boston College, Boston University, Brandeis University, Brown University, Massachusetts Institute of Technology, Northeastern University, University of Massachusetts, and Wellesley College. Drama students have access to the Harvard Theatre Collection.

Special research facilities for science and engineering students include the campus-based Science and Technology Center, which houses selected areas of research in physics and electrical and chemical engineering, as well as laboratory facilities in biology, chemistry, psychology, and electrical and civil engineering. Students are encouraged to pursue collaborative research at off-site facilities, which have included Fermilab, the Woods Hole Oceanographic Institute, and Brookhaven Laboratories. Many researchers carry out collaborative research with colleagues at nearby Boston universities.

Financial Aid

In 2001–02, the School awarded more than $4 million in tuition scholarships. Teaching and research assistantships are available, as are some fellowships. Tufts also awards need-based financial aid through the Federal Perkins Loan, Federal Work-Study, and Federal Stafford Student Loan programs.

Cost of Study

Tuition for 2002–03 is $28,264, which covers the full cost of one-year master's programs and one third the cost of doctoral programs. Tuition for two-year master's programs (occupational therapy, studio art, and urban and environmental policy) is $21,198 for the 2002–03 academic year. Tuition for the school psychology program is $24,731. Part-time tuition is $2826 per course. Other charges include student health insurance, a health service fee, and a student activity fee.

Living and Housing Costs

Living expenses are estimated at about $1000 a month. There is limited on-campus housing for graduate students. Rents for one-bedroom apartments in Medford and Somerville begin at approximately $800 per month. The cost of sharing an apartment averages about $550 per person. A public transportation system serves the greater Boston area and provides easy access to and from the campus.

Student Group

In 2001–02, 1,332 students were enrolled in the Graduate School of Arts and Sciences and the School of Engineering. Of these, 59 percent were women and 18 percent were international students.

Location

The main campus, which spans the Medford-Somerville city line, is 7 miles from downtown Boston, a city where the arts (music, drama, and dance), museums, and sporting events abound. Cape Cod beaches and the mountains and forests of Maine, New Hampshire, and Vermont can be easily reached.

The University

Chartered as a liberal arts college in 1852, today Tufts is a small, selective, private university offering opportunities for undergraduate, graduate, and professional education to more than 7,500 students. The Graduate School of Arts and Sciences, the Fletcher School of Law and Diplomacy, the School of Engineering, the Gerald J. and Dorothy R. Friedman School of Nutrition Science and Policy, the Sackler School of Graduate Biomedical Sciences, and the Schools of Dental Medicine, Medicine, and Veterinary Medicine offer graduate and/or professional education. The University is accredited by the New England Association of Schools and Colleges.

Applying

Deadlines for applications vary by program. Applicants are required to submit three letters of recommendation, official transcripts from all colleges and universities attended, and a personal statement. Most departments also require the results of the Graduate Record Examinations (GRE). Students whose native language is not English must submit official results of the Test of English as a Foreign Language (TOEFL). A minimum score of 550 (or 213 CBT) is required.

Correspondence and Information

Graduate and Professional Studies
Tufts University
Ballou Hall, First Floor
Medford, Massachusetts 02155

Telephone: 617-627-3395
Fax: 617-627-3016
World Wide Web: http://ase.tufts.edu/gradstudy

FIELDS OF STUDY AND FACULTY ADVISERS

Art and Art History: Cristelle Baskins (M.A. program); Andrew McClellan (Museum Studies); David Brown (M.F.A. program).
Biology: Barry Trimmer.
Chemistry: David Walt.
Child Development: Jayanthi Mistry.
Classics: Peter Reid (Classics); Jodi Magness (Classical Archaeology).
Drama: Laurence Senelick.
Economics: Yannis Ioannides; Jeffrey Zabel.
Education: Linda Beardsley (Teacher Education); Barbara Brizvela (Education Studies); Analúcia Schliemann (Museum Education); Caroline Wandle (School Psychology); Dorothy Pilla (Art Education).
English: Modhumita Roy.
French: Vincent Pollina.
German: Bernard Martin.
History: Steven Marrone.
Interdisciplinary Doctorate: Steven Marrone.
Mathematics: Montserrat Teixidor.
Music: Jane Bernstein (Musicology); David Locke (Ethnomusicology); John McDonald (Composition); Janet Schmalfeldt (Theory).
Occupational Therapy: Sharan Schwartzberg.
Philosophy: Mark Richard.
Physics: Roger Tobin.
Psychology: Robert Cook.
Urban and Environmental Policy and Planning: Francine Jacobs.

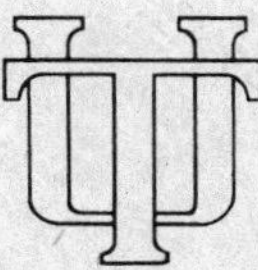

TULANE UNIVERSITY

Graduate School

Programs of Study

The Graduate School offers research-oriented programs leading to the degrees of Master of Arts, Master of Science, and Doctor of Philosophy and professionally oriented programs leading to the degrees of Master of Fine Arts and Master of Liberal Arts.

The Master of Arts degree is offered in the fields of anthropology, art history, chemistry, civic and cultural management, classical languages, economics, English, French, history, Italian, Latin American studies, mathematics, music, philosophy, political science, Portuguese, sociology, and Spanish.

The Master of Science degree is available in the fields of anatomy, anthropology, applied development, biochemistry, biology, biomedical engineering, biostatistics, chemical engineering, chemistry, civil engineering, computer science, electrical engineering, environmental statistics, epidemiology, geology, mathematics, mechanical engineering, microbiology and immunology, molecular and cellular biology, neuroscience, parasitology, pharmacology, physics, physiology, and psychology.

The Master of Fine Arts degree is available in the fields of art, music, and theater.

The Master of Liberal Arts program is offered by Tulane's University College in cooperation with the Graduate School. To enroll in the program, the student must first apply to University College for admission.

The Doctor of Philosophy degree is offered in the fields of anatomy, anthropology, biochemistry, biology, biomedical engineering, biostatistics, business administration, chemical engineering, chemistry, civil engineering, computer science, earth and ecosystem sciences, economics, electrical engineering, English, epidemiology, French, history, human genetics, international development, international health and development, Latin American studies, mathematics, mechanical engineering, microbiology and immunology, molecular and cellular biology, neuroscience, paleontology, parasitology, pharmacology, philosophy, physics, physiology, political science, psychology, social work, sociology, and Spanish. Special interdisciplinary programs also lead to the Ph.D. These are formal ad hoc interdepartmental programs, consisting of work taken in two or more departments, one of which has a doctoral program. To determine the feasibility of a program, an applicant should consult with the appropriate faculty member before making formal application.

Research Facilities

Howard-Tilton Memorial Library, the University's general library, features open stacks for all books, journals, microform texts, pamphlets, and reference materials, except rare books. Holdings of the various University libraries number more than 2 million in the general collection and an additional 15,000 periodical and serial subscriptions. The facilities of the University are well equipped for instruction and original research. In addition to the medical laboratories in the Medical Center complex, students have access to research facilities at the Tulane Riverside Research Laboratories, the Tulane Regional Primate Research Center, the Lindy Boggs Center for Energy and Biotechnology, and the U.S.-Japan Cooperative Biomedical Research Laboratories. Tulane's research and teaching centers include the Middle American Research Institute, the Roger Thayer Stone Center for Latin American Studies, the Murphy Institute of Political Economy, the Center for Archaeology, the Newcomb College Center for Research on Women, the Center for Bioenvironmental Research, the Southern Center of the National Institute for Global Environmental Change, and the Amistad Research Center.

Financial Aid

Financial assistance for graduate students is awarded primarily on the basis of academic merit and is available in the forms of part-time teaching or research assistantships, scholarships, fellowships, or combinations of these awards. The University offers financial assistance to qualified students through long-term loans, emergency loans, and a deferred-payment plan for tuition.

Cost of Study

Full-time tuition and fees for 2001–02 were $12,808 per semester. Tuition on a part-time basis was $1423 per credit hour plus fees.

Living and Housing Costs

A limited amount of housing is available for graduate students. Most graduate students live off campus, where costs vary greatly depending on the type of accommodation.

Student Group

Tulane enrolls 8,800 full-time and 1,900 part-time students each year. Of these, 925 are registered in the Graduate School. In recent years, graduate students have come to Tulane from approximately 300 colleges and universities in the United States as well as other countries.

Location

Tulane's eleven colleges and schools, with the exception of the medical divisions, are located on 100 acres in a residential area of New Orleans. New Orleans' mild climate, numerous parks, and proximity to the Gulf Coast provide opportunities for a wide variety of outdoor activities. The city's numerous art galleries and museums offer regularly scheduled exhibits throughout the year. New Orleans is famous for its French Quarter, Mardi Gras, Creole cuisine, and jazz.

The University

Tulane is a private nonsectarian university offering a wide range of undergraduate, graduate, and professional courses of study for men and women. The University's history dates from 1834, when a group of New Orleans doctors founded the Medical College of Louisiana, the first medical school in the Deep South and Southwest. In 1847, the newly chartered University of Louisiana in New Orleans added a Law Department and, three years later, a Collegiate Department, forerunner of the College of Arts and Sciences. Graduate work was first offered in 1883. In 1884 the University was organized under its present form of administration and renamed for Paul Tulane, a wealthy New Orleans merchant who endowed it generously.

Applying

For those requesting financial aid, the application deadline is February 1. The general deadlines for applying are July 1 for the fall semester, December 1 for the spring semester, and May 1 for the summer session. Students should write to the dean of the Graduate School for application forms. The Graduate School will not consider any student for admission until all of the following documents plus the $45 application fee have been received: a completed application form, three completed recommendation forms, official transcripts of all undergraduate and graduate work, and official results of the General and Subject tests of the GRE, taken within the last five years. International applicants for admission must present satisfactory evidence of competence in English by submitting an acceptable score on the TSE (Test of Spoken English), normally a minimum score of 220. If the TSE is not available in the applicant's area of the world, the TOEFL may be taken instead; 600 is the minimum TOEFL score acceptable for admission. Admission is based on academic accomplishments and promise, regardless of race, creed, or sex.

Correspondence and Information

Dean of the Graduate School
Tulane University
New Orleans, Louisiana 70118
Telephone: 504-865-5100
E-mail: graduate.school@tulane.edu
World Wide Web: http://www.tulane.edu/

THE FACULTY

Listed below are the departments in the Graduate School, with the chairperson of each.

Anatomy: Robert D. Yates, Ph.D.
Anthropology: Robert Hill, Ph.D.
Applied Development: William E. Bertrand, Ph.D.
Art: Arthur Okazaki, M.F.A.
Biochemistry: Jim Karam, Ph.D.
Biomedical Engineering: Richard Hart, Ph.D.
Biostatistics: Larry Webber, Ph.D.
Business Administration: John Trapani, Ph.D.
Cell and Molecular Biology: Ken Muneoka, Ph.D.
Chemical Engineering: Kyriakos Papadopoulos, Ph.D.
Chemistry: William L. Alworth, Ph.D.
Civic and Cultural Management: Janet Herrald, M.F.A.
Civil Engineering: Brian W. Baetz, Ph.D.
Classical Languages: Dennis Kehoe, Ph.D.
Computer Science: Parviz Rastgoufard, Ph.D.
Earth and Ecosystems Sciences: Thomas S. Bianchi, Ph.D.
Ecology, Evolution, and Organismal Biology: David Heins, Ph.D.
Economics: David Malueg, Ph.D.
Electrical Engineering: Parviz Rastgoufard, Ph.D.
English: Michael Kuczynski, Ph.D.
Environmental Statistics: Laura J. Steinberg, Ph.D.
Epidemiology: Roger Sherwin, Ph.D.
French and Italian: Hope Glidden, Ph.D.
Geology: George Flowers, Ph.D.
History: Richard Latner, Ph.D.
Human Genetics: Jess Thoene, Ph.D.
International Health and Development: Jane Bertrand, Ph.D.
Latin American Studies: Thomas Reese, Ph.D.
Mathematics: Michael Mislove, Ph.D.
Mechanical Engineering: Morteza Mehrabadi, Ph.D.
Microbiology and Immunology: John Clements, Ph.D.
Molecular and Cellular Biology: Barbara Beckman, Ph.D.
Music: Anthony Cummings, Ph.D.
Paleontology: George Flowers, Ph.D.
Parasitology: Donald J. Krogstad, M.D.
Pharmacology: Krishna Agrawal, Ph.D.
Philosophy: Ronna Burger, Ph.D.
Physics: John Perdew, Ph.D.
Physiology: Luis G. Navar, Ph.D.
Political Science: Thomas Langston.
Psychology: Jeffrey Lockman, Ph.D.
Social Work: Michael J. Zakour, Ph.D.
Sociology: Joel Devine, Ph.D.
Spanish and Portuguese: Nicasio Urbina, Ph.D.
Theatre: Barbara Hayley, M.F.A.

UNIVERSITÉ LAVAL

Faculty of Graduate Studies

Programs of Study

Ph.D.'s are awarded in administration and evaluation in education, administrative sciences, ancient civilization, animal sciences, anthropology, archeology, art history, biochemistry (biological science), biology, cellular and molecular biology (medicine), chemical engineering, chemistry, civil engineering, comunity health, computer science, didactics, earth sciences, economics, educational psychology, electrical engineering, English literature, epidemiology, ethnology of French-speaking people in North America, experimental medicine, food sciences and technology, forestry sciences, French and Québec literatures, geographical sciences, geomatics sciences, history, industrial relations, kinesiology, linguistics, literature and the screen and stage, mathematics, mechanical engineering, metallurgical engineering, microbiology (agriculture), microbiology (science), microbiology and immunology (medicine), mining engineering, music, neurobiology, nutrition, oceanography, orientation sciences, pharmacy, philosophy, physics, physiology-endocrinology, planning and regional development, plant biology, political science, psychology, religious sciences, social work, sociology, soil sciences, Spanish language and literature, teaching technology, theology, and wood sciences. An LL.D. degree in law is also offered. A D.Th.P. in Practical Theology is offered.

The Master of Arts degree (M.A.) is offered in administration and evaluation in education, ancient civilization, anthropology, archeology, art history, didactics, economics, educational psychology, English literature, ethnology of French-speaking people in North America, French and Québec literatures, French studies, history, human religion sciences, industrial relations, international relations, linguistics, literature and the screen and stage, mass communication, orientation sciences, philosophy, political science, politics analysis, psychology, sociology, Spanish language and literature, teaching technology, terminology and translation, theology, and visual arts.

The Master of Science degree (M.Sc.) is offered in aerospatial engineering, agricultural economics, agri-food engineering, agroforestry, animal sciences, architectural studies, biochemistry (sciences), biology, business studies, cellular and molecular biology (medicine), chemical engineering, chemistry, civil engineering, community health, computer science, dental sciences, earth sciences, electrical engineering, epidemiology, experimental medicine, food sciences and technology, forestry sciences, geomatics sciences, kinesiology, mathematics, mechanical engineering, metallurgical engineering, microbiology (agriculture), microbiology (science), microbiology and immunology (medicine), mining engineering, neurobiology, nursing, nutrition, pharmacy, pharmacy (hospital), physics, physiology-endocrinology, plant biology, soil sciences, speech therapy, statistics, and wood sciences. The University also offers master's degrees in architecture (M.Arch.), business administration (M.B.A.), geographical sciences (M.Sc.Geogr), law (LL.M.), music (M.Mus.), planning and regional development (M.ATDR.), psychology (M.Ps.), and social work (M.Serv.Soc.).

Diplomas are offered in accident prevention and occupational health and safety management, applied ethics, business administration, community pharmacy, consumer studies, educational practice, electronic business, industrial engineering, integrated rural development, international and transnational law, journalism (international), law of business, management accounting, museology, notarial law, nursing, organization management, public accountancy, public relations, software engineering, technological entrepreneurship, terminology and translation, urban infrastructure engineering, and women's studies.

Research Facilities

There is a wide range of research structures, such as centres, groups, and teams, either multidisciplinary or monodisciplinary. Faculty members and students have access to a variety of specialized laboratories and equipment. Laboratories are fully equipped with the latest computer facilities and databases. The University's libraries have more than 4 million documents, including up-to-date collections of reference and research materials, such as books, periodicals, journals, microfiches, CD-ROMs, audiovisual resources, and electronic data resources.

Financial Aid

Various forms of financial assistance from different sources are available to students, regardless of citizenship, who undertake graduate studies at Université Laval. Some of these programs include doctoral awards from the Fondation de l'Université Laval, the Fonds d'engagement des étudiants au doctorat (Can$2.0 million every year), merit scholarships at the master's level, assistantships, and research grants.

Cost of Study

Full-time tuition fees are Can$915.00 per session for Québec residents, French citizens, students enrolled in French-related programs, and students from countries who have signed an agreement with the Québec government. Other Canadian citizens and permanent residents must pay Can$2010.00 at the master's level and Can$915.00 at the Ph.D. level per session. For other students, session fees are Can$4515.00 at the master's level and Can$4080.00 at the Ph.D. level.

Living and Housing Costs

Though living expenses may vary from one person to another, an average of Can$11,000 should be budgeted to cover living and housing costs. International students must also buy health insurance, which costs about Can$525.

Student Group

In fall 2001, there were 6,954 graduate students enrolled at Laval (5,245 at the master's level and 1,709 at the Ph.D. level), of whom 3,675 were women. There were also 1,004 international students from sixty-seven countries.

Location

Université Laval is located in Québec City, the capital city of the province of Québec and one of the oldest cities in North America. In this historic city, designated by UNESCO as part of the World's Heritage, one can still feel the soul of the French period. Outside of the strong walls of its eighteenth-century fortification, Québec presents itself as a modern and dynamic city where one can find everything that makes life pleasant. Well known for its Winter Carnival, Québec offers a variety of cultural riches and activities year-round, such as numerous festivals, museums, movies, restaurants, theatres, and art galleries. Within 30 minutes of downtown, students can ski, skate, golf, swim, raft, or bike. Université Laval's campus, straddling Sainte-Foy and Sillery, is one of the most striking in the province of Québec. It covers 1.2 square kilometers and includes almost thirty buildings, all linked by 7.5 kilometers of underground walkways.

The University

As the first French-speaking university in North America, Laval traces its origins to 1663 when Monseigneur Francois de Montnorency Laval, the first Bishop of New France, founded Le Séminaire de Québec. In 1852, Queen Victoria granted Le Séminaire de Québec a Royal Charter, thus creating Université Laval. Until 1920, Université Laval was the only French university in Canada. Through the years, it contributed to the education of the French-speaking intellectual elite of Québec and Canada and graduated several Prime Ministers, artists, writers, musicians, and scientists . Considered a leading university since its foundation, Laval is today designated as a member of the Group of Ten - the ten top-ranked Canadian universities in terms of research. Its well-established reputation extends beyond Québec and Canada.

Applying

The admission deadline for the session that begins in September is February 1; for the January session, the deadlines are September 1 for students who live outside of Canada and November 1 for students who live in Canada; for the summer session, they are February 1 for students who live outside of Canada and April 1 for students who live in Canada. Late applications can be considered on a space-available basis. Candidates to graduate studies must be sponsored by three people, each of whom is required to send the University an evaluation of the candidate's general all-around research ability. Report forms are included in the admission pack. All documents submitted with an application must be official and translated in French or in English. The application fee is Can$30. The application can also be submitted through the Internet.

Correspondence and Information

For further information (in French) or to obtain the Admission Guide and an application form:

Bureau d'information et de promotion
2435 Pavillon Jean-Charles-Bonenfant
Université Laval
Québec, Québec G1K 7P4
Canada

Telephone: 418-656-2764
877-785-2825 (toll-free in Canada and the U.S.)
E-mail: info@vrd.ulaval.ca
World Wide Web: http://www.ulaval.ca

RESEARCH

At Université Laval, developing research is a strategic priority; therefore, research is an important part of the mission of every Faculty and Institute. At Laval, there are some 1,100 professors who receive more than Can$100 million in research grants yearly. This places Université Laval in the top Canadian universities in terms of research.

More than 130 groups, centres, laboratories, and institutes conduct high-level research at Université Laval. Of these 130 research bodies, thirty-three are accredited: the Inter-University Centre for Study in Letters, Arts, and Traditions (CELAT); the Nordic Studies Centre, (CEN); the Centre for Research on Interface Properties and Catalysis (CERPIQ); the Macromolecular Science and Engineering Research Centre (CERSIM); the Inter-University Centre for Algebraic Computation (CICMA); the Inter-University Centre for Québec Studies (CIEQ); the Centre for Optics, Photonics and Lasers (COPL); the Forest Biology Research Centre (CRBF); the Reproduction Biology Research Centre (CRBR); the Cancer Research Centre (CRC); the Centre for Research on the Literature of Québec (CRELIQ); the Centre for Research in Geomatics (CRG); the Horticulture Research Centre (CRH); the Infectiology Research Centre (CRI); the Inter-University Research Centre on Concrete (CRIB); the Neurobiology Research Centre (CRN); the Rheumatology and Immunology Research Centre (CRRI); the Interdisciplinary Group for Research on Finite Elements (GIREF); the Inter-University Group for Oceanographic Research in Québec (GIROQ); the Research Group in Oral Ecology (GREB); the Group for Research on Energy, Environment, and Natural Resource Economics (GREEN); the Group for Research on Psychosocial Maladjustment in Children (GRIP); the Québec Institute for Advanced International Studies (IQHEI); the Mont Mégantic Astronomical Observatory (OMM); the Dairy Sciences and Technology Research Centre (STELA); the Protein Function, Structure and Engineering Research Center (CREFSIP); the Inter-University Research Centre on Teacher Training and Teaching Profession (CRIFPE); the Network Organization Technology Research Centre (CENTOR); the Research Centre on Brain, Behaviour and Neuropsychiatry (CRCN); the Centre for Research in Economics of Agro-Food (CREA); the Research Centre on Applied Economy and Finance (CREFA); the Centre for Research on Energy Metabolism (CREME); the Oncology and Molecular Endocrinology Research Centre (CREMO); the Research Centre for Planning and Regional Development (CRAD); the Inter-University Research Centre on Education and Working Life (CRIEVAT); and the Research and Development Center for School Success (CRIRES).

More information about research at Université Laval is available on the World Wide Web (http://www.ulaval.ca/Al/rech_un.html).

UNIVERSITY AT BUFFALO, STATE UNIVERSITY OF NEW YORK

Graduate School

Programs of Study

The Graduate School offers 115 master's degree programs, eighty-eight doctoral degree programs, and four professional programs, as well as a number of certificate and dual-degree programs. Interdisciplinary research is available through more than forty centers and graduate groups. The graduate programs and departments fashion individual curricula to meet specific objectives. Each program establishes its own requirements for admission, its own assessment of satisfactory student progress, and its own mandates for satisfactory completion of the degree offered under a broad institutional mandate for excellence. Each department is responsible for admitting its own students. For the master's degree, one year of residence is required, as is one of the following: a comprehensive test, a thesis based on independent research, or an appropriate special project. For the doctoral degree, the residence requirement is one year; other requirements include an evaluation of the student's work in the doctoral program, an original dissertation, and an oral defense.

Research Facilities

The University at Buffalo (UB) has become a leader in developing and deploying an IT environment that empowers University members to accomplish their goals. Students and faculty members have multimedia e-mail; access to campus high-speed networks in laboratories, classrooms, and University residence halls and apartments; wireless access points on campus; Web access to extensive library resources; easy Web publishing; and extensive technical support and training. Through its digital initiative, the University libraries offer online access to major full-text information products covering journal literature, books, statistical data, worldwide newspapers, and hundreds of databases supporting research in the sciences, social sciences, humanities, and interdisciplinary studies. More than 2,200 personal computers and high-performance workstations are available to students in more than ninety public and departmental computing labs. Students also have access to computing on powerful clusters of UNIX time-sharing machines and to computational resources at one of the leading academic supercomputing sites in the U.S., the Center for Computational Research (CCR).

More than a dozen investigative centers and institutes are part of a research effort that exceeded $250 million in expenditures last year. The University enjoys an international reputation, attracting students from all over the world and maintaining scholarly exchanges with institutions in several nations. Some examples include the Center for Studies in American Culture; Center for Comparative and Global Studies Education; National Center for Geographic Information and Analysis; Center for Assistive Technology; Multidisciplinary Center for Earthquake Engineering Research; Environment and Society Institute; Institute for Research and Education on Women and Gender; New York State Center for Engineering Design and Industrial Innovation; Industry/University Center for Biosurfaces; Center for Excellence for Document Analysis and Recognition; Center for Research on Urban Social Work Practice; Center for Structural Biology; Center for Advanced Photonic and Electronic Materials; Center for Advanced Molecular Biology and Immunology; Comprehensive Oral Health Research Center; Center for Computational Research; Institute for Lasers, Photonics and Biophotonics; Research Institute on Addictions; and Center for Hearing and Deafness. New York State and private industry have recently committed $150 million for the Buffalo Center of Excellence in Bioinformatics. In addition to governmental and private foundation support for research, UB receives considerable industrial support through research collaborations and affiliations.

Financial Aid

Many students hold teaching, graduate, or research assistantships. A number of competitive fellowship programs are also available, including opportunities for students who are members of underrepresented minority groups. Full or partial tuition scholarships accompany most assistantships and fellowships. Graduate Opportunity Tuition Scholarships are available to students who participated in undergraduate EOP, HEOP, or SEEK programs. Students should contact the department chairperson for information and applications.

Cost of Study

Full-time tuition for 2001–02 was $2550 per semester for New York State residents and $4208 per semester for nonresidents. Part-time tuition was $213 per credit hour for residents and $351 per credit hour for nonresidents. Tuition in the professional schools is slightly higher. All tuition rates are subject to adjustment by the Board of Trustees.

Living and Housing Costs

A complex of two-bedroom town-house apartments opened in 1998, with twelve-month leases. Rents are approximately $770 per month plus utilities. These are available for married and unmarried graduate students. An apartment complex with studio and one- and two-bedroom apartments opened in fall 2000. Rents range from $511 to $547 per student, with all utilities except telephone service. In fall 2001 another new apartment complex opened with one- and two-bedroom apartments. Rents range from $505 to $572 per student, with all utilities except telephone service. Opening in fall 2002 is a new complex with two-bedroom town-house apartments for married and unmarried graduate students. Rents are $570 per student, with all utilities except telephone service.

Student Group

The total enrollment of 25,838 consists of 13,543 men and 12,295 women. Graduate students number 8,548. The student body includes representatives from more than 100 countries.

Location

Buffalo is a Great Lakes city on an international border with a metropolitan population of more than 1 million. It is a city of friendly neighborhoods with big city recreation for all tastes: professional sports (football, hockey, indoor soccer, lacrosse, and Triple-A baseball), the Buffalo Philharmonic Orchestra, a celebrated theater district, the renowned twentieth-century collection in the Albright-Knox Art Gallery, and a lively club scene. Buffalo enjoys four distinct seasons in a dramatic setting on Lake Erie and the Niagara River. Skiing, hiking, camping, sailing, boating, and Lake Erie beaches on both the U.S. and Canadian shores and the natural wonder of Niagara Falls are all nearby.

The University

The University at Buffalo is the largest and most comprehensive public research university in New York and New England. The University's two campuses make up the largest unit of the sixty-four-campus SUNY system. Its North Campus, the seat of most of its nonmedical sciences academic programs, occupies 2 square miles of fields and woods in suburban Amherst. It is one of the most modern university campuses in the nation. More than 5 million square feet of academic space, laboratories, libraries, residence halls, and recreation facilities have been built there since 1972. An expanded 30,000-seat football stadium, a $45-million Center for the Arts, the first building in a Natural Sciences complex, and an expanded Student Union have opened on the North Campus in the past five years. The University's South Campus, 3 miles away in the residential northeast corner of Buffalo, is now largely devoted to the health sciences. Buffalo's rapid transit system connects that campus with the city center and the waterfront.

Applying

Applications should be filed directly with the appropriate department. Deadlines for filing applications vary by department. Students should consult the appropriate director of graduate studies.

Correspondence and Information

Chair, Department of (specify)
University at Buffalo, State University of New York
Buffalo, New York 14260
Telephone: 716-645-2000
(request specific department)

The Graduate School
409 Capen Hall
University at Buffalo, State University of New York
Buffalo, New York 14260-1608
Fax: 716-645-6142
World Wide Web: http://www.buffalo.edu/grad/admissions

FACULTY HEADS

Deans and chairs are listed below. The area code is 716.

Dean of the Graduate School: Dr. Kerry S. Grant (645-6003).
Associate Provost and Executive Director of the Graduate School: Dr. Myron A. Thompson (645-6227).

ARCHITECTURE AND PLANNING
Dr. Levy, Interim Dean; Hayes Hall (829-3485). Architecture (M.Arch., M.Arch./M.B.A., M.Arch./M.U.P.): Dr. Kleinman. Urban and Regional Planning (M.U.P., M.Arch./M.U.P.): Dr. Sternberg.

ARTS AND SCIENCES
Dr. Stinger, Interim Dean; Clemens Hall (645-2711). Center for the Americas (M.A., Ph.D.): Dr. Mohawk. Anthropology (M.A., Ph.D., J.D./Ph.D.): Dr. Pollock. Art (M.F.A.): Dr. Henderson. Art History (M.A.): Dr. Carman. Biological Sciences (M.A., M.S., Ph.D.): Dr. Bisson. Chemistry (M.A., M.S., Ph.D.): Dr. Atwood. Classics (M.A., Ph.D.): Dr. Cole. Communicative Disorders and Sciences (M.A., Ph.D., Au.D.): Dr. Stathopoulous. Comparative Literature (M.A., Ph.D.): Dr. Irlam. Economics (M.A., Ph.D., Cert.): Dr. Ehrlich. English (M.A., Ph.D.): Dr. Conte. Geography (M.A., Ph.D., M.A./M.B.A.): Dr. Calkins. Geology (M.A., Ph.D.): Dr. Mitchell. History (M.A., Ph.D., J.D./Ph.D.): Dr. Ellis. Humanities (M.A.): Ms. Willbern. Linguistics (M.A., Ph.D.): Dr. Van Valin. Mathematics (M.A., Ph.D.): Dr. Schack. Modern Languages and Literature–French, German, and Spanish (M.A., Ph.D.): Dr. Feal. Music Composition, History and Theory (M.A., Ph.D.) and Music Performance (M.M.): Dr. Manes. Natural Science/Interdisciplinary (M.S.): Ms. Willbern. Philosophy (M.A., Ph.D., J.D./Ph.D.): Dr. Kearns. Physics (M.S., Ph.D.): Dr. Gonsalves. Political Science (M.A., Ph.D., J.D./Ph.D.): Dr Zagare. Psychology (M.A., Ph.D.): Dr. Meacham. Social Science/Interdisciplinary (M.S.): Ms. Willbern. Sociology (M.A., Ph.D., J.D./Ph.D.): Dr. Farrel.

DENTAL MEDICINE
Dr. Buchanan, Dean; Squire Hall (829-2836). Biomaterials (M.S.): Dr. Baier. Dentistry (D.D.S.): Dr. Joynt. Oral Biology (Ph.D.): Dr. Genco. Oral Sciences (M.S.): Dr. Mohl. Orthodontics (M.S., Cert.): Dr. Preston. Certificate Programs: Endodontics, Oral and Maxillofacial Surgery, Oral and Maxillofacial Pathology, Orthodontics, Pediatric Dentistry, Periodontics, and Prosthodontics.

EDUCATION
Dr. Greshman, Interim Dean; Baldy Hall (645-6481).
Counseling, School, and Educational Psychology: Dr. Janikowski: Counseling Psychology (Ph.D.), Counselor Education (Ph.D.), Educational Psychology (M.A., Ph.D.), General Education (Ed.M.), Rehabilitation Counseling (M.S.), School Counseling (Ed.M., Cert.), School Psychology (M.A.).
Learning and Instruction: Dr. Schroeder: Bilingual Education N–6 (Ed.M.), Elementary Education (Ed.M., Ed.D., Ph.D.), English Education (Ed.M., Ed.D., Ph.D.), Foreign and Second Language Education (Ed.M., Ed.D., Ph.D.), General Education (Ed.M.), Mathematics Education (Ed.M., Ph.D.), Music Education (M.A., Cert.), Reading Education (Ed.M., Ed.D., Ph.D.), School Administration and Supervision (Cert.), Science Education (Ed.M., Ed.D., Ph.D.), Social Studies Education (Ed.M.), Special Education (Ph.D.), Teaching English to Speakers of Other Languages (Ed.M.).
Educational Leadership and Policy: Dr. Jacobson: Educational Administration (Ed.M., Ed.D., Ph.D.), Educational Technology (Ed.M., Cert.), General Education (Ed.M.), Social Foundations (Ph.D.), Specialist in Educational Administration (Cert.).

ENGINEERING AND APPLIED SCIENCES
Dr. Karwan, Dean; Bonner Hall (645-2771). Chemical Engineering (M.E., M.S., Ph.D.): Dr. Lund. Civil, Structural, and Environmental Engineering (M.E., M.S., Ph.D.): Dr. Constantinou. Computer Science and Engineering (M.S., Ph.D.): Dr. Jayaraman. Electrical Engineering (M.E., M.S., Ph.D.): Dr. Malone. Industrial Engineering (M.E., M.S., Ph.D.): Dr. Batta. Mechanical and Aerospace Engineering (M.E., M.S., Ph.D.): Dr. Taulbee. Engineering Science (M.S.).

HEALTH RELATED PROFESSIONS
Dr. Trevisan, Interim Dean; Kimball Tower (829-3434). Biotechnical and Clinical Laboratory Science (M.S.): Dr. Kostyniak. Occupational Therapy (M.S.): Dr. Klick. Physical Therapy, Exercise, and Nutrition Sciences (M.S., D.P.T., Ph.D.): Dr. Cerny. Rehabilitation Science (Ph.D.): Dr. Fisher.

INFORMATICS
Dr. Penniman, Dean; Baldy Hall (645-6481). Communication (M.A., Ph.D.): Dr. Jacobson. Information and Communication (M.A.), Information and Library Science (M.L.S., Cert.), School Media Specialist (M.L.S.).

LAW
Dr. Olsen, Dean; O'Brian Hall (645-2052). Law (J.D., J.D./M.A., J.D./M.B.A., J.D./M.S.W., J.D./Ph.D.): Mr. Cox. Criminal Law (L.L.M.): Ms. Oreskovic.

MANAGEMENT
Dr. Newman, Interim Dean; Jacobs Management Center (645-3204). Accounting (M.S.), Business Administration (M.B.A.), Management (Ph.D.), Management Information Systems (M.S.), Manufacturing and Operations Management (M.S.).

MEDICINE AND BIOMEDICAL SCIENCES
Dr. Bernardino, Dean; Biomedical Education Building (829-3398). Anatomy and Cell Biology (M.A., Ph.D.): Dr. Mendel. Biochemistry (M.A., Ph.D.): Dr. Blumenthal. Biomedical Sciences (M.D./Ph.D.): Dr. Holm. Interdisciplinary Graduate Program in Biomedical Sciences (Ph.D.): Dr. Rabin. Medicine (M.D.): Dr. Klocke. Microbiology (M.A., Ph.D.): Dr. Hay. Molecular Cell Biology: Dr. Nicholson. Pathology (M.A., Ph.D.): Dr. Heffner. Pharmacology and Toxicology (M.A., M.S., Ph.D.): Dr. Rubin. Physiology and Biophysics (M.A., Ph.D.): Dr. Strauss. Social and Preventive Medicine (M.S., M.P.H., Ph.D.): Dr. Trevisan.

NURSING
Dr. Cranley, Dean; Kimball Tower (829-2533). Nursing (M.S., D.N.S., Cert.).

PHARMACY AND PHARMACEUTICAL SCIENCES
Dr. Anderson, Dean; Cooke Hall (645-2823). Pharmaceutics (M.S., Ph.D.): Dr. Jusko. Pharmacy (Pharm.D.).

ROSWELL PARK CANCER INSTITUTE
Dr. Michalek, Dean; Elm and Carlton Streets (845-2339). Biological Sciences (Cellular and Molecular Biology) (M.A., Ph.D.): Dr. Yates. Biophysics (Molecular and Cellular) (M.S., Ph.D.): Dr. Subjeck. Microbiology (Immunology) (Ph.D.): Dr. Soldano. Natural Sciences/Interdisciplinary (M.S.): Dr. Michalek. Pathology (Experimental) (M.A., Ph.D.): Dr. Asch. Pharmacology (Molecular Pharmacology and Cancer Therapeutics) (M.A., Ph.D.): Dr. Mihich.

SOCIAL WORK
Dr. Shulman, Dean; Baldy Hall (645-3381). Social Welfare (Ph.D.). Social Work (M.S.W., J.D./M.S.W.).

THE UNIVERSITY OF AKRON

Graduate School

Programs of Study

Master's degree programs are available in the following areas: accountancy, audiology, biology, business administration (accounting, electronic business, entrepreneurship, finance, global sales management, health services management, international business, international finance, management, management of technology, marketing, quality management, supply chain management), chemistry, communication, counseling psychology, economics (labor and industrial relations), education (administration, elementary, foundations, guidance and counseling, higher, physical, principal, secondary, special, technical), engineering (biomedical, chemical, civil, electrical, management specialization, mechanical, polymer), English (English composition), family and consumer sciences (child development, child life, clothing/textiles/interiors, family development, food sciences), geography (urban planning), geology (earth science, engineering, environmental, geophysics), history, management (human resources, information systems), mathematics (applied, computer science, engineering-applied), music (accompanying, composition, education, history and literature, performance, technology, theory), nursing, nutrition/dietetics, physics, political science (applied politics), polymer science, psychology (applied cognitive aging, industrial/organizational, industrial/gerontological), public administration, public health, social work, sociology, Spanish, speech-language pathology, statistics, taxation, theater arts (arts administration), and urban studies. Joint law/master's programs are available as well. Twenty-two graduate certificate programs are also offered.

Doctor of Philosophy programs are available in chemistry, counseling psychology, elementary education, engineering (applied mathematics, biomedical, environmental, materials, mechanics, polymer, systems, and transport processes), guidance and counseling, history, nursing, polymer science, psychology, secondary education, sociology, and urban studies and public affairs.

The Doctor of Education degree is offered in educational administration.

The University is fully accredited by the North Central Association of Colleges and Schools.

The minimum number of semester hours required for the master's degree is 30. In many departments the ability to perform independent study or research may be demonstrated by a program including a thesis, for which credit hours are given, or by a program culminating in one or more papers that have developed out of a seminar or similar activity.

The requirements for the doctoral degree are qualitative rather than quantitative; however, it usually takes at least three academic years of full-time graduate study beyond the baccalaureate to complete doctoral programs. The residence requirement is one academic year. The candidate must present a dissertation on a topic related to his or her major subject that embodies the results of original research and demonstrates high scholarship and must pass oral defense-of-thesis and dissertation examinations.

Applicants are advised to consult the *Graduate Bulletin* or to write to the chair of the relevant department for further details.

Research Facilities

Bierce Library has more than 1 million volumes and houses the Archives of History of American Psychology as well as an American History Research Center. Resources of the C. Blake McDowell Law Center Library are also available. The University offers access to computer databases through both Bierce Library and Information Services, which maintains an IBM 9672, an IBM 4381-R14, and a DECstation 5000. The $10.5-million science and engineering building provides ample facilities for the fields of engineering and biology. A Polymer Towers complex provides facilities for the College of Polymer Science and Polymer Engineering. A College of Business Administration building opened in 1991.

Financial Aid

Numerous fellowships and teaching and research assistantships, which ranged from $6000 to $14,400 in 2000–01, are available. These awards include waivers of tuition. Applicants must have a minimum 2.75 overall quality point average, with a 3.0 in the intended major field.

Cost of Study

Tuition was $200.10 per semester hour for Ohio residents and $364.40 per semester hour for out-of-state students for 2000–01. There was also a general service fee of $7.70 per semester hour to a maximum of $91.80 per semester. (Figures are subject to change.)

Living and Housing Costs

Limited on-campus housing is available for graduate students. Approximate costs per year for 2000–01 were $5350, including a meal plan, utilities, and local telephone charges. Information regarding on-campus graduate housing may be obtained from the Office of Residence Life and Housing, Bulger Hall, Room 109 (telephone: 330-972-7800).

Student Group

There are 22,878 students enrolled at the University of Akron. This figure includes 3,445 graduate students.

Location

Akron, with a rich heritage of industrial leadership in rubber and related products, has evolved into a center for high technology and service-oriented businesses. It provides northeastern Ohio with a stimulating blend of educational, cultural, recreational, commercial, research, and industrial resources.

The University

Founded in 1870 as Buchtel College by the Unitarians, the University of Akron became a municipal school in 1913 and a state university in 1967. A major building program is under way in accordance with a master plan. The campus is located near the central city and has a close relationship with all segments of the community.

Applying

For full admission, the applicant's transcript must show an overall quality point average from an accredited school of no less than 2.75 (2.0 is C; 3.0 is B) and the necessary background courses for the graduate program that he or she wishes to pursue. Provisional admission may be granted when the GPA is below 2.75. Applications should be filed with a nonrefundable $25 application fee ($50 application fee for international students) at least six weeks prior to the opening of the term for which admission is sought. The application deadline for fellowships, teaching assistantships, and research assistantships is March 1.

Correspondence and Information

Dean of the Graduate School
The University of Akron
Akron, Ohio 44325-2101
Telephone: 330-972-7663
E-mail: gradschool@uakron.edu

FACULTY HEADS

The Graduate School
Vice President for Research and Dean: George R. Newkome, Ph.D., Kent State.
Associate Dean: Lathardus Goggins, Ph.D., St. John's.

Listed below are the major departments or schools offering graduate degree programs, with the chair or director of each indicated.

Buchtel College of Arts and Sciences
Biology: Jerry N. Stinner, Ph.D., California, Riverside.
Chemistry: David S. Perry, Ph.D., Toronto.
Economics: Michael Nelson, Ph.D., Purdue.
English: Diana C. Reep, Ph.D., Wisconsin–Milwaukee.
Geography and Planning: Robert B. Kent, Ph.D., Syracuse.
Geology: John P. Szabo, Ph.D., Iowa.
History: Walter L. Hixson, Ph.D., Colorado.
Mathematics and Computer Science: Wolfgang Pelz, Ph.D., Virginia Tech.
Modern Languages: J. Christopher Eustis, Ph.D., Indiana Bloomington.
Physics: Robert R. Mallik, Ph.D., Leicester Polytechnic (England).
Political Science: David J. Louscher, Ph.D., Wisconsin.
Psychology: Linda M. Subich, Ph.D., Ohio State.
Public Administration and Urban Studies: Raymond W. Cox III, Ph.D., Virginia Tech.
Sociology: John F. Zipp, Ph.D., Duke.
Statistics: Chand Midha, Ph.D., Iowa State.

Business Administration
Director of Graduate Business Programs: James J. Divoky, D.B.A., Kent State.
Accountancy: Emeka O. Ofobike, Ph.D., Oregon.
Finance: David A. Redle, J.D., Akron.
Management: Jayprakash G. Patankar, Ph.D., Clemson.
Marketing: Dale M. Lewison, Ph.D., Oklahoma.

Education
Director for Graduate Studies (interim): James R. Rogers, Ph.D., Akron.
Counseling and Special Education: John J. Zarski, Ph.D., Ohio.
Curricular and Instructional Studies: Susan J. Olson, Ph.D., Penn State.
Educational Foundations and Leadership: Sharon D. Kruse, Ph.D., Minnesota.
Sports Science and Wellness Education: Philip J. Buckenmeyer, Ph.D., Maryland College Park.

Engineering
Biomedical Engineering: Mary C. Verstraete, Ph.D., Michigan State.
Chemical Engineering: Steven S. Chuang, Ph.D., Pittsburgh.
Civil Engineering: Wieslaw K. Binienda, Ph.D., Drexel. (interim)
Electrical Engineering: Jose Alexis De Abreu-Garcia, Ph.D., Queen's at Kingston. (interim)
Mechanical Engineering: Celal Batur, Ph.D., Leicester (England).

Fine and Applied Arts
Communication: Dudley B. Turner, Ph.D., Purdue.
Dance/Theatre and Arts Administration: Lucinda S. Lavelli, M.F.A., Case Western Reserve.
Family and Consumer Sciences: Virginia L. Gunn, Ph.D., Akron. (acting)
Music: William K. Guegold, Ph.D., Kent State.
Social Work: Virginia L. Fitch, Ph.D., Case Western Reserve.
Speech-Language Pathology and Audiology: James M. Lynn, Ph.D., Iowa.

Nursing
Dean: Cynthia F. Capers, Ph.D., Pennsylvania.
Coordinator, Master's Programs: Kathleen M. Ross-Alaolmolki, Ph.D., Case Western Reserve.

College of Polymer Science and Polymer Engineering
Polymer Engineering: Lloyd A. Goettler, Ph.D., Delaware.
Polymer Science: William J. Brittain, Ph.D., Caltech.

Bierce Library.

E. J. Thomas Performing Arts Hall.

THE UNIVERSITY OF ALABAMA AT BIRMINGHAM

Graduate School

Programs of Study

The University of Alabama at Birmingham (UAB) offers doctoral degrees in administration health services, applied mathematics, biochemistry, biology, biomedical engineering, biophysical sciences, biostatistics, cell biology, chemistry, computer and information sciences, early childhood education, educational leadership, environmental health engineering, environmental health sciences, epidemiology, health education/health promotion, materials engineering, materials science, medical genetics, medical sociology, microbiology, molecular and cellular pathology, neurobiology, nursing, nutrition science, pharmacology, physics, physiology and biophysics, psychology (medical, developmental, and behavioral neuroscience), public health, and vision science. Master's degrees are offered in accounting, anthropology, art history, biology, biomedical engineering, biostatistics, business administration, chemistry, civil engineering, clinical laboratory sciences, clinical nutrition, computer and information sciences, criminal justice, dentistry, education (all areas), electrical and computer engineering, English, environmental engineering, forensic science, health services administration, health informatics, history, materials engineering, mathematics, mechanical engineering, nurse anesthesia, nursing, occupational therapy, oral biology, physical therapy, physics, public administration, public health, sociology, and vision science. Interdisciplinary training programs that add to traditional doctoral programs are available in cell and molecular biology, cognitive science, forensic science, neuroscience, pharmaceutical design, and toxicology. Combined degree programs are available in many areas and include the M.D./Ph.D., O.D./Ph.D., D.D.S./Ph.D., Ph.D./M.P.H., Ph.D./M.B.A., and M.P.A./J.D.

Research Facilities

UAB is one of the leading research universities in the country, annually receiving more than $331 million in research and training grants. That amounts to more external funding than is granted to all other Alabama universities combined. UAB ranks twentieth in the nation in support from the National Institutes of Health and twenty-fifth for all federal research and development funding.

UAB's research enterprise is highly interdisciplinary. University-wide research centers house active basic and translational research programs in the areas of cancer, women's health, AIDS, arthritis, developmental and learning disabilities, aging, vision science, oral pathology, laser and photonics research, social medicine, metabolic bone disease, and obesity. Other schoolwide centers focus their research efforts on cystic fibrosis, cardiovascular research, cell matrix and adhesion, urban affairs, telecommunications, educational accountability, and biomaterials. Many centers house special research facilities, such as the transgenic animal/embryonic stem cell facility, the hybridoma core facility, the digital microscopy facility, and a 4.1 Tesla magnet for functional NMR imaging. Two major research libraries, the Mervyn H. Sterne Library and the Lister Hill Library of the Health Sciences, provide online access to the research literature in all areas of graduate study.

A major thrust of UAB research is moving technology into the marketplace. The OADI Technology Center is a business incubator facility that houses new advanced-technology companies in such areas as biotechnology, robotics, software development, and medical devices. The UAB Research Foundation serves as a conduit of information, discoveries, and inventions from researchers to business. In partnership with industry, it guides technology through laboratory observation, product development, and marketing. Other University-industry partnerships include student organizations such as the Industry Roundtable, which introduces students to career options outside academia by providing information and networking opportunities with business and industry.

Financial Aid

Each year, approximately 175 students are appointed as Graduate School fellows or assistants. Stipends range from approximately $10,000 to $17,500, plus full payment of tuition and fees. The individual graduate programs also offer similar awards. Some programs need teaching or laboratory assistants, some have federal and state research grants that are budgeted to include student assistants, and many need graders or lab tutors. UAB currently has approximately $10 million in training support from federal agencies. The Comprehensive Minority Faculty and Student Development Program offers four years of support to minority students enrolled in doctoral programs.

Cost of Study

Tuition in 2001–02 was $112 per semester hour for Alabama residents and $224 per semester hour for nonresident students.

Living and Housing Costs

UAB offers a number of reasonably priced apartments (efficiencies to two-bedroom units) for on-campus residence. The Housing Office also provides information on off-campus housing, including listings for short- and long-term lease facilities. Many reasonably priced apartments are located within easy walking distance of UAB.

Student Group

In 2001–02, there were more than 3,700 graduate students enrolled in UAB's thirty doctoral programs and forty-six master's programs. Many of these programs unite different disciplines and cross departmental and school lines, illustrating the strong interdisciplinary character of the University.

Location

Birmingham is located in the geographic heart of the Southeast, 2½ hours by interstate from Atlanta, 4 hours from Nashville, 6 hours from New Orleans, 5 hours from the Smoky Mountains, and 5 hours from the beaches of the Gulf of Mexico. Birmingham is a dynamic, progressive urban center of great natural beauty. Almost 1 million people live in the metropolitan area.

The University

The University of Alabama at Birmingham is a comprehensive research institution in Alabama's most populated city. With more than 100 major campus buildings occupying seventy city blocks on Birmingham's Southside, UAB has become a nationally and internationally respected center for educational, research, and service programs.

The University is composed of thirteen schools as well as hospitals and clinics that house internationally renowned patient-care programs. UAB includes the Schools of Arts and Humanities, Business, Dentistry, Education, Engineering, Health Related Professions, Medicine, Natural Sciences and Mathematics, Nursing, Optometry, Public Health, and Social and Behavioral Sciences and the Graduate School. Special assistance is given to adult learners through UAB Options. The Graduate School offers a comprehensive Professional Development Program to enhance students' communication skills, to provide training for teaching at the college level, and to prepare students to compete for grants and jobs.

Applying

UAB's admission process has two levels of review. The Graduate School sets general admission requirements, and each graduate program specifies its particular requirements. In general, the Graduate School welcomes applications from students who have earned a bachelor's degree from a regionally accredited academic institution, have good letters of evaluation, and have scored well on a recognized standardized test (usually the Graduate Record Examinations General Test). Each application is evaluated by the program faculty on the basis of all information available about the applicant.

Applications for admission are not processed until all credentials required by the Graduate School have been received. Prospective students can submit an application via the Internet from the Graduate School's Web page.

Correspondence and Information

The Graduate School
Room 511, Hill University Center
The University of Alabama at Birmingham
1400 University Boulevard
Birmingham, Alabama 35294-1150
E-mail: gradschool@uab.edu
World Wide Web: http://www.uab.edu/graduate

GRADUATE PROGRAM DIRECTORS

Accounting: Dr. Richard A. Turpen.
Administrative Health Services: Dr. Robert Hernandez and Dr. Gail McGhee.
Anthropology: Dr. Brian Hesse.
Applied Environmental Biotechnology: Dr. Joseph Gauthier.
Art History: Dr. Heather McPherson.
Biochemistry: Dr. Jamila Horabin.
Biology: Dr. Steven Watts.
Biomedical Engineering: Dr. Linda Lucas.
Biostatistics: Dr. Katharine Kirk.
Business–M.B.A.: Dr. Gail McGhee.
Cell Biology: Dr. James Collawn
Chemistry: Dr. Larry Krannich.
Civil Engineering/Environmental Health Engineering: Dr. Fouad H. Fouad.
Clinical Lab Sciences: Dr. Virginia Randolph.
Clinical Nutrition: Dr. Gayle Canfield.
Cell and Molecular Biology: Dr. David Bedwell.
Cognitive Science: Dr. Michael Sloane.
Computer and Information Sciences: Dr. Warren T. Jones.
Criminal Justice: Dr. John Sloan.
Curriculum–Instruction: Dr. Joe Burns.
Dentistry–Oral Biology: Dr. Firoz Rahemtulla.
Educational Leadership–Special Education: Dr. Boyd Rogan.
Education–Allied Health Sciences: Ms. Jean Keenon.
Electrical Engineering: Dr. Tom Jannett.
English: Dr. Kyle Grimes.
Environmental Health Science: Dr. Douglas Ruden.
Epidemiology: Dr. Ellen Funkhouser.
Forensic Science: Dr. Ray Liu.
Gerontology: Dr. Patricia Baker.
Health Administration: Dr. Steven O'Connor.
Health Education–Counseling: Dr. David Macrina.
Health Information Management: Dr. Helmuth Orthner.
History: Dr. Carolyn Conley.
Materials Engineering: Dr. Gregg Janowski.
Materials Science: Dr. Gregg Janowski.
Mathematics: Dr. Gilbert Weinstein.
M.D./Ph.D. Program: Dr. Jeff Kudlow.
Mechanical Engineering: Dr. B. J. Stephens.
Medical Genetics: Dr. Andrew Carroll.
Microbiology: Dr. Peter Burrows.
Neurobiology: Dr. Anne Theibert.
Neuroscience: Dr. Paul Gamlin.
Nurse Anesthesia: Mr. Joe Williams.
Nursing: Dr. Carol Dashiff.
Nutrition Sciences: Dr. Tim Nagy.
Occupational Therapy: Dr. Claudia Peyton.
Pathology: Dr. Joseph Messina.
Pharmaceutical Design: Dr. Ming Luo.
Pharmacology: Dr. Elias Meezan.
Physical Therapy: Dr. Sharon Shaw.
Physics: Dr. Yogesh Vohra.
Physiology: Dr. Lisa Schwiebert.
Psychology–Behavioral Neuroscience: Dr. Alan Randich.
Psychology–Developmental: Dr. Jan Wallender.
Psychology–Medical: Dr. Jesse Milby.
Public Administration: Dr. Akhlaque Haque.
Sociology/Medical Sociology: Dr. Jeffrey Clair.
Toxicology: Dr. Coral Lamartiniere.
Vision Science: Dr. Kent Keyser.

UNIVERSITY OF BRIDGEPORT

Graduate Studies

Programs of Study

The University offers programs leading to the Master of Science (M.S.), Master of Business Administration (M.B.A.), Executive Master of Business Administration (E.M.B.A.), Sixth Year Professional Diploma, Doctor of Education (Ed.D.) in educational leadership, and doctoral degrees in chiropractic (D.C.) and naturopathic medicine (N.D.).

The School of Business offers the M.B.A. and E.M.B.A. degrees with optional concentrations in accounting, computer applications, computer science, finance, global marketing, management, fashion merchandising, and human resources. The M.B.A. and E.M.B.A. are offered on a full-time, part-time, and accelerated-weekend basis at the Stamford campus and can be completed in twelve to eighteen months.

The School of Engineering and Design offers the M.S. in computer engineering, computer science, electrical engineering, mechanical engineering, and technology management. The M.S. in computer science is also offered on an accelerated basis and can be completed in less than eighteen months at the University's Stamford campus.

Programs in the School of Education and Human Resources lead to the M.S. in education, counseling, and human resources as well as to teacher certification from the state of Connecticut. The Education Internship program, which leads to the master's degree, gives students instruction and supervised work in schools tuition free. Specializations in counseling include community counseling, college student personnel services, and human resource development. The M.S. in human resource development is offered on a weekend basis of one weekend per month for 22 months at the University's Stamford Campus. The Sixth Year Professional Diploma is available in elementary and secondary education, counseling, and educational leadership. An Ed.D. degree is offered in educational leadership. A daytime Master of Education is available and can be completed in two years with courses scheduled just one day a week from 9–2.

The Nutrition Institute offers an M.S. degree in human nutrition. Students take courses one weekend per month for eighteen months. An online program is available via the Internet (e-mail: ubonline@bridgeport.edu). The College of Chiropractic offers the Doctor of Chiropractic degree, accredited by the Council on Chiropractic Education (CCE). It is the first university-based chiropractic college in the U.S. and the only one located in New England and the greater New York metropolitan area. The College of Naturopathic Medicine confers the Doctor of Naturopathic Medicine (N.D.) degree through a four-year residential professional program. The College is one of only four colleges in the U.S. to offer this degree within a traditionally based University and the only one located on the East Coast. The Acupuncture Institute's alternative health-care program is offered in the evenings or weekends and leads to an M.S. in acupuncture.

The University has an English Language Institute on campus offering intensive English language training for a variety of purposes, including preparation for those seeking admission to U.S. universities. The number of credit hours to be completed varies according to the program, as do requirements for theses, practicums, and internships.

Research Facilities

The University's Wahlstrom Library contains approximately 270,000 bound volumes, including bound journals and indexes and more than 1 million microforms. It subscribes to more than 1,200 periodicals and other serials in print and more than 6,000 full-text publications online. Access to about 7,400 electronic books is available. An extension library is maintained at the Stamford campus with extensive electronic access and a core collection of books and periodicals. The library also provides a free interlibrary loan service.

Financial Aid

Financial aid is available in the form of endowed scholarships, fellowships, Federal Stafford Student Loans, graduate assistantships, and internships. The University hires graduate students as residence hall directors and assistant hall directors. Additional information can be obtained from the Financial Aid Office (telephone: 203-576-4568). The University has a long-standing partnership with local corporations who provide employees with excellent educational opportunities that lead to degrees and career advancement. Graduate students seeking assistantships should contact their respective department directly.

Cost of Study

In 2002–03, full-time tuition is $408 per credit hour in the School of Education and Human Resources; $424 per credit hour in the School of Business; $437 per credit hour in the School of Engineering and Design; $7553 per semester in the College of Chiropractic; and $7553 per semester in the College of Chiropractic and College of Naturopathic Medicine. Students taking 12 credits or more are considered full-time.

Living and Housing Costs

Graduate students may reside either in the University's on-campus residence halls or in private (off-campus) apartments or rooms. The cost of off-campus living varies widely. Additional information related to on-campus residence may be obtained from the Office of Residential Life (telephone: 203-576-4395).

Student Group

There are approximately 1,800 graduate students enrolled at the University, representing many interests, professions, nationalities, and ages. Approximately 52 percent are women, 38 percent are international, and 20 percent are members of minority groups.

Location

The University of Bridgeport (UB), founded in 1927, is one of America's most internationally diverse campuses. It is situated on a quiet, urban campus on the shores of Long Island Sound, just 1 hour from New York City and less than 3 hours from Boston. UB's main campus in Bridgeport and its satellite campus in Stamford are at the heart of Fairfield County, Connecticut, which is home to the headquarters of many of the world's largest corporations.

The University

The University of Bridgeport offers a wide variety of graduate programs in computer science, computer engineering, counseling and human resources (human resource development, college student personnel, community counseling), education (from the master's to the Ed.D.), electrical engineering, human nutrition, mechanical engineering, and technology management as well as programs leading to the M.B.A., the Doctor of Naturopathic, and the Doctor of Chiropractic. Many of the programs are scheduled during the weekend and part-time to allow for maximum convenience for working adults. Weekend programs include the M.B.A. (twelve to eighteen months), human nutrition (eighteen months), human resource development (twenty-two months), and computer science (sixteen to eighteen months).

Accreditation for professional programs has been granted by a number of accrediting agencies, including the Engineering Accreditation Commission of the Accreditation Board for Engineering and Technology, Inc. (ABET); the National Association of Schools of Art and Design (NASAD); the Council on Dental Education of the American Dental Association; and the Commission on Accreditation of the Council on Chiropractic Education (CCE). The School of Business is internationally accredited by the Association of Collegiate Business Schools and Programs (ACBSP).

Applying

Students are encouraged to apply well in advance of the term they expect to enter but no later than thirty days before the beginning of the semester; students interested in the M.B.A. program should apply no later than sixty days prior to the beginning of the semester. Electronic applications are welcome. Students are generally admitted for the fall semester; however, transfer and advanced placement students are admitted for either the fall or spring semester.

Correspondence and Information

Office of Admissions
University of Bridgeport
126 Park Avenue
Bridgeport, Connecticut 06601
Telephone: 203-576-4552
800-EXCEL-UB (toll-free)
Fax: 203-576-4941
E-mail: admit@bridgeport.edu
World Wide Web: http://www.bridgeport.edu

FACULTY HEADS

School of Business

Dean: Paul Huo, Ph.D., Yale.
Director of M.B.A. and E.M.B.A. Studies: Diane Richardson, M.B.A., Bridgeport.

School of Engineering

Dean: Tarek Sobh, Ph.D., Pennsylvania.

Computer Science: Stephen Grodzinsky, Ph.D., Illinois.
Technology Management: Paul Bauer, Ph.D., Oklahoma State.
Mechanical Engineering: Tienko Ting, Acting Chair, Ph.D., Michigan.

School of Education and Human Resources

Dean: James Ritchie, Ed.D., Columbia Teachers College.

Counseling and Human Resources: Joseph Nechasek, Ph.D., SUNY at Buffalo.
Educational Leadership: John Mulcahy, Ph.D., Fordham.
Education Internship Program: Alfred G. Tufano, Ph.D., Wisconsin–Madison.

College of Chiropractic

Dean: Frank Zolli, D.C., New York Chiropractic.
Associate Dean: Anthony Onorato, D.C., National Chiropractic.

College of Naturopathic Medicine

Dean: Peter Martin, D.C., N.D., D.O. (G.B.), Palmer Chiropractic.

Acupuncture Institute

Director: Jennifer Brett, N.D., National College of Naturopathic Medicine.

Nutrition Institute

Director: Blonnie Thompson, Ph.D., Wake Forest.

UNIVERSITY OF CALIFORNIA, DAVIS

Graduate Studies

Program of Study

University of California (UC), Davis is an institution of outstanding academic excellence, offering every area of scholarship necessary for a complete, modern campus. Graduate students have an opportunity to work with and learn from accomplished faculty members recognized for their contributions to the research of their fields. Academic programs are consistently ranked among the best in the nation. UC Davis has more than eighty graduate programs offering the master's and doctoral degrees. Some programs are administered in the traditional departmental mechanism; however, many are offered by "graduate groups," self-governing organizations of faculty sponsoring graduate degree programs that are interdepartmental and usually interdisciplinary. More than half of the graduate majors at UC Davis are sponsored by graduate groups.

Research Facilities

The General Library at Davis includes five facilities: the Peter J. Shields Library, the Physical Sciences Library, the Loren D. Carlson Health Sciences Library, the UC Davis Medical Center Library in Sacramento, and the Agricultural Economics Library. An independent law library is located at the King Hall School of Law. The General Library contains more than 3.1 million volumes and receives 44,614 periodical and journal titles annually. The collections of the Physical Sciences Library consist of more than 333,777 volumes and 4,686 journal titles. The Carlson Health Sciences Library serves the Schools of Medicine and Veterinary Medicine with a collection of 280,318 volumes and approximately 3,200 periodical titles. It also houses a microcomputer facility for use of instructional software and multimedia by graduate students and faculty members in the health sciences. The MELVYL online catalog system contains the bibliographic records of the entire collections of the Physical Sciences, the Carlson Health Sciences, the UC Davis Medical Center, and the Law Libraries and most books and periodicals held in Shields Library and on the other eight campuses of the University of California. UC Davis has extensive research facilities in agricultural and biological sciences, arts and humanities, engineering, and the physical and social sciences (World Wide Web: http://gradstudies.ucdavis.edu/facility/facility.htm).

Financial Aid

Financial support is available in the form of teaching and research assistantships, financial aid, and fellowships/scholarships. Information and application materials for teaching assistantships are available from individual departments.

Financial aid, which is available to U.S. citizens, permanent residents, or immigrants only, is awarded on the basis of demonstrated financial need and is administered by the Financial Aid Office. Federal financial aid includes student loans, grants, and work-study. Students may apply for financial aid before being admitted. To be considered for any need-based award, students must file the FAFSA no later than March 2 prior to the fall quarter enrollment. This form is used to determine financial need only. Students can contact the Graduate Financial Aid Office for information.

Fellowships and graduate scholarships are awarded primarily on the basis of merit. Considered in evaluations are GRE scores, undergraduate and graduate GPAs, academic transcripts, a statement of purpose, letters of recommendation, and other documentation such as publications or awards. The minimum cumulative undergraduate GPA required for a stipend or in-state fee award is 3.5 (A=4.0). Applicants must be U.S. citizens, permanent U.S. residents, or immigrants. To be considered for a nonresident tuition award, applicants must be U.S. citizens or permanent U.S. residents who are not legal residents of California. New international students may be awarded nonresident tuition fellowships; the minimum GPA is 3.25. Applications for fellowships and graduate scholarships are due by January 15 for awards beginning in the fall quarter.

Cost of Study

For California residents, quarterly fees are $1611; for nonresidents, the cost is $5243 for fees plus tuition. Fees are subject to change without notice. All graduate students are required to purchase the Graduate Student Health Insurance Plan (GSHIP). The cost for the GSHIP, which is included in the above amounts, is $300 per quarter.

Living and Housing Costs

An average annual budget, including rent, food, fees, books and supplies, personal expenses, and transportation, is as follows: single resident, University housing, $15,684; single resident, non-University housing, $15,570; and student family, University housing, $13,611 (add $2011 for each dependent child). Non-California residents add tuition of $10,704.

Student Group

In 2000–01, the total enrollment was 26,104 students. Of these, 3,215 were graduate students. This number included 651 international students (eighty-five countries were represented). Forty-eight percent of graduate students were women and 90 percent received financial assistance. The ethnic diversity included 53 percent white, 11 percent Asian, 5 percent Latino, 2 percent African American, and 1 percent Native American; 9 percent did not report. Careers after graduation include university teaching and research and government and public- and private-sector employment.

Location

The UC Davis campus is adjacent to the city of Davis (population 60,000), 15 miles west of the state's capital, Sacramento, and 75 miles east of San Francisco and the Bay Area. The wineries of the Napa Valley are about an hour's drive to the northwest, Lake Tahoe and the ski slopes of the Sierra Nevada are 2 hours to the east, and the seacoast towns of Mendocino and Santa Cruz are about 150 miles to the north and south, respectively. There are many recreational resources in the outlying areas such as boating, swimming, sailing on the Delta or San Francisco Bay, skiing, and hiking, and the city of Davis has more than 90 miles of bikeways, more than two dozen tennis courts, three public swimming pools, a municipal golf course, and beautiful parks and greenbelts to add to the delights of small-town living.

The University

The University of California has nine campuses throughout the state—Berkeley, Davis, Irvine, Los Angeles, Riverside, San Diego, San Francisco, Santa Barbara, and Santa Cruz. A tenth campus is under construction at Merced. All are recognized nationally and internationally as among the largest and most distinguished centers of higher learning and research in the world. The faculty constitutes one of its most prized assets. University-wide, there are 24 Nobel Laureates and more than 300 members of the National Academy of Sciences, numbers that exceed any other college or university system. The campuses have an enrollment of more than 173,000 undergraduate, graduate, and professional students. Charged by the state with the three-fold mission of teaching, research, and public service, the University's preeminence results from its outstanding contributions to the expansion of knowledge, the education of six generations of Californians since the first graduating class in 1874, and the improvement of the health and well-being of people throughout the world.

UC Davis was established in 1906 as the agricultural teaching site for the University. In 1922 it began conferring the degree of Bachelor of Science in agriculture; some years later the College of Agriculture was established. In 1949 the School of Veterinary Medicine was opened, in 1951 a College of Letters and Science was founded, and in 1959 Davis became a general campus of the University. There are now three undergraduate colleges, a graduate division, and four professional schools. As a result, UC Davis has the most diversified teaching and research faculty in the nine-campus system. The campus is about 5,500 acres, including the experimental agriculture plots, a central quadrangle, and an arboretum on the banks of Putah Creek. Architecturally, the campus is a mix of old wooden buildings and new glass and concrete facilities.

Applying

All programs operate on the quarter system; admission is for the fall quarter only. The general application deadline is March 1 for international students and April 1 for domestic students. Many programs have earlier deadlines. The deadline for the application for financial support is January 15. Applications are available online at http://gradstudies.ucdavis.edu/b4apply.htm or from the address below. Information about a particular program is available from the program office.

Correspondence and Information

Office of Graduate Studies
250 Mrak Hall
University of California
One Shields Avenue
Davis, California 95616

Telephone: 530-752-0655
Fax: 530-752-6222
World Wide Web: http://gradstudies.ucdavis.edu/

CAMPUS ADMINISTRATION AND DEGREE PROGRAMS

Larry N. Vanderhoef, Chancellor of the Davis Campus.
Cristina González, Dean of Graduate Studies.

Agricultural and Resource Economics (M.S., Ph.D.)
Agricultural Education (Cred.)*
Agricultural and Environmental Chemistry (M.S., Ph.D.)
Animal Behavior (Ph.D.)
Anthropology (M.A., Ph.D.)
Applied Mathematics (M.S., Ph.D.)
Art (M.F.A.)
Atmospheric Science (M.S., Ph.D.)
Avian Science (M.S.)
Biochemistry and Molecular Biology (M.S., Ph.D.)
Biomedical Engineering (M.S., Ph.D.)
Biophysics (M.S., Ph.D.)
Biostatistics (M.S., Ph.D.)
Cell and Developmental Biology (M.S., Ph.D.)
Chemistry (M.S., Ph.D.)
Child Development (M.S.)
Community Development (M.S.)
Comparative Literature (M.A., Ph.D.)
Comparative Pathology (M.S., Ph.D.)
Computer Science (M.S., Ph.D.)
Cultural Studies (M.A., Ph.D.)
Dramatic Art (M.F.A., Ph.D.)
Ecology (M.S., Ph.D.)
Economics (M.A., Ph.D.)
Education (M.A., Ph.D., Cred., Ed.D.)
Engineering (M.Eng., D.Eng., M.S., Ph.D., Cert.)
- Applied Science
- Biological and Agricultural Engineering
- Chemical Engineering
- Civil and Environmental Engineering
- Electrical and Computer Engineering
- Material Science Engineering
- Mechanical and Aeronautical Engineering

English (M.A., Ph.D.)
- Creative Writing (M.A.)

Entomology (M.S., Ph.D.)
Epidemiology (M.S., Ph.D.)
Exercise Science (M.S.)
Food Science (M.S., Ph.D.)
Forensic Science (M.S.)
French (Ph.D.)
Genetics (M.S., Ph.D.)
Geography (M.A., Ph.D.)
Geology (M.S., Ph.D.)
German (M.A., Ph.D.)
History (Ph.D.)
History of Art (M.A.)
Horticulture and Agronomy (M.S.)
Human Development (Ph.D.)
Hydrologic Science (M.S., Ph.D.)
Immunology (M.S., Ph.D.)
International Agricultural Development (M.S.)
International Commercial Law (M.A.)
Linguistics (M.A.)
Mathematics (M.A., M.A.T., Ph.D.)
Medical Informatics (M.S.)
Microbiology (M.S., Ph.D.)
Music (M.A., Ph.D.)
Native American Studies (M.A., Ph.D.)
Neuroscience (Ph.D.)
Nutrition (M.S., Ph.D.)
Pharmacology and Toxicology (M.S., Ph.D.)
Philosophy (M.A., Ph.D.)
Physics (M.S., Ph.D.)
Physiology (M.S., Ph.D.)
Plant Biology (M.S., Ph.D.)
Plant Pathology (M.S., Ph.D.)
Plant Protection and Pest Management (M.S.)
Political Science (M.A./J.D., Ph.D.)
Population Biology (Ph.D.)
Psychology (Ph.D.)
Sociology (M.A., Ph.D.)
Soil Science (M.S., Ph.D.)
Spanish (M.A., Ph.D.)
Statistics (M.S., Ph.D.)
Textile Arts and Costume Design (M.F.A.)
Textiles (M.S.)
Transportation, Technology and Policy (M.S., Ph.D.)
Viticulture and Enology (M.S.)

**Denotes program currently closed. Students should contact the department for admission information.*

Reading area in the Peter J. Shields Library.

Eye on Mrak (the Last Laff), from the egghead series by Robert Arneson.

Group of graduate students at Commencement.

UNIVERSITY OF CENTRAL FLORIDA

Graduate Programs

Programs of Study

The University of Central Florida (UCF), the fastest-growing public university in Florida, offers more than eighty master's and doctoral programs. The Master of Arts degree is awarded in communication, communicative disorders, economics (applied), education, English, history, liberal studies, political science, psychology (clinical), sociology (applied), Spanish, theater, and TESOL. The Master of Science degree is offered in accounting, biology, chemistry (industrial), computer science, criminal justice, engineering (aerospace, civil, computer, environmental, electrical, industrial, and mechanical), health services administration, management, materials science and engineering, mathematical science, modeling and simulation, molecular biology and microbiology, nursing, optics, physical therapy, physics, psychology (clinical and industrial/organizational), statistical computing, and taxation. Also offered are the Master of Business Administration, Master of Education, Master of Public Administration, and Master of Social Work.

Ph.D. programs are offered in applied experimental and human factors psychology, biomolecular sciences, business administration, civil engineering, clinical psychology, computer engineering, computer science, education, electrical engineering, environmental engineering, industrial engineering, industrial and organizational psychology, materials science and engineering, mathematics, mechanical engineering, optics, physics, public affairs, and texts and technology. The Ed.D. and Ed.S. degrees are also offered in curriculum and instruction and in educational leadership. The Ed.S. degree is also offered in school psychology.

Research Facilities

UCF's research in optics and lasers, computer and simulation technologies, and microelectronics and materials is known around the world. UCF has a number of internationally recognized research centers and institutes: the Florida Solar Energy Center, the Center for Research and Education in Optics and Lasers, the Institute for Simulation and Training, the Advanced Materials Processing and Analysis Center, and the Center for Discovery of Drugs and Diagnostics. In 1997 UCF and the National Institute of Justice joined to establish the National Center for Forensic Science, the nation's first research center dedicated to combatting terrorism and bomb attacks.

Research facilities are also extensive in other areas. In the computer sciences, students and researchers have access to more than 1,000 microcomputers, a NeXT computer, an image processor, graphics terminals, and an entire lab devoted to computer-based graphics. Buttressing UCF's computer network is the parallel processing Intel supercomputer once used by the U.S. Navy. Access to other computer systems is available across Florida through the State University System (SUS) network.

The College of Engineering maintains modern research facilities for CAD/CAM, robotics, microelectronics, light wave research, laser and optics, mechanics, combustion, environmental engineering, and related research.

The chemistry department has access to laboratory instrumentation and scale-up and industrial control equipment. A fully equipped instrumental biofeedback research laboratory and psychological testing laboratory as well as physiological research laboratories and communicative disorders facilities are available for use in that field. Well-equipped laboratories are also available in the biological sciences, as are a greenhouse, an extensive herbarium, a vertebrate collection, and outstanding inland and coastal natural resources for fieldwork.

UCF is adjacent to the Central Florida Research Park, home of many research labs pursuing activities in simulation and training, lasers, optical filters, behavioral sciences, diagnostic test equipment, and oceanographic equipment.

For more information on the University's research facilities, students should visit the Web site at http://www.research.ucf.edu.

Financial Aid

Programs administered by the Student Financial Assistance Office include long-term loans and institutional emergency short-term loans. On-campus employment is also available. Information on in-state and out-of-state tuition waivers and teaching or research assistantships are available through the colleges. Approximately $2.5 million in University graduate fellowships is available.

Cost of Study

Tuition for 2001–02 was $162.24 per semester credit hour and thesis credit hour. Out-of-state fees were $569.40 per semester credit hour. Health fees paid by all students were $53 for fall and spring semesters and $39.75 for summer.

Living and Housing Costs

Many apartments are near UCF, some within walking distance for graduate students. No on-campus housing is available. Rent per month ranges from $400 for a one-bedroom apartment to $700 for a two-bedroom apartment.

Student Group

The 2001 fall enrollment was more than 35,000 students; the student body was almost equally divided between men and women. The University enrolled 4,840 graduate and 1,361 postbaccalaureate students. All age groups are represented, with most students between 21 and 40 years of age.

Location

UCF is located 15 miles from downtown Orlando, the home of many laser, electronic, and software firms. The Central Florida Research Park, one of the top ten in the United States and adjacent to the University, has numerous opportunities for part-time graduate student employment and internships.

The University

Established as a state university in 1963, the University admitted its first students in 1968.

Numerous disciplines at UCF are accredited by professional organizations. The University is accredited by the Southern Association of Colleges and Schools, the College of Business Administration by AACSB International–The Association to Advance Collegiate Schools of Business, and the College of Education by the Florida State Department of Education and the National Council for Accreditation of Teacher Education.

Applying

Prospective international students should apply to Graduate Studies at the address given below at least six months before the start of classes for the term in which they plan to enroll. Domestic applicants should contact Graduate Studies for the appropriate deadline. A $20 application fee, official transcripts, and GRE General Test scores (GMAT scores for business programs) are required of all applicants. TOEFL scores are required for international students. Additional documents and information may be required by individual degree programs.

Correspondence and Information

Office of Graduate Studies
University of Central Florida
P.O. Box 160112
Orlando, Florida 32816-0112

Telephone: 407-823-2766
E-mail: graduate@mail.ucf.edu
World Wide Web: http://www.graduate.ucf.edu

DEANS AND GRADUATE PROGRAM COORDINATORS

Patricia J. Bishop, Ph.D., Vice Provost and Dean for Graduate Studies; PE.
Ben B. Morgan Jr., Ph.D., Associate Dean.

Arts and Sciences: Kathryn Seidel, Dean; Robert Bledsoe, Ph.D., Florida.
Applied Sociology: David Gay, Ph.D., Duke.
Biological Science: John Weishampel, Ph.D., Virginia.
Communication: Burt Pryor, Ph.D., Michigan.
English: James Campbell, Ph.D., Notre Dame.
History: Rosalind Beiler, Ph.D., Pennsylvania.
Industrial Chemistry: Kevin Belfield, Ph.D., Syracuse.
Industrial Chemistry, Forensic Science: Jack Ballantyne, Ph.D., SUNY.
Liberal Studies: Elliot Vittes, Ph.D., Massachusetts.
Mathematics: Ram Mohapatra, Ph.D., Jabalpur (India).
Physics: Robert Peale, Ph.D., Cornell.
Political Science: Phillip Pollack, Ph.D., Minnesota.
Psychology, Applied Experimental/Human Factors: Eduardo Salas, Ph.D., Old Dominion.
Psychology, Clinical: Robert Kennerley, Ph.D., South Carolina.
Psychology, Clinical (Ph.D.): Mark Rapport, Ph.D.
Psychology, Industrial/Organizational: William Wooten, Ph.D., Memphis State.
Psychology, Industrial/Organizational (Ph.D.): Eugene Stone-Romero, Ph.D., California, Irvine.
Spanish: Alberto Villaneuva-Ghelfa, Ph.D., Florida International.
Statistical Computing: Jim Schott, Ph.D., Florida.
TESOL: Keith Folse, Ph.D., South Florida.
Texts and Technology: Paul Dombrowski, Ph.D., Rensselaer.
Theater: Julie Listengarten, Ph.D., Michigan.

Business Administration: Thomas Keon, Dean; Robert Ford, Ph.D., Arizona State.
Accounting: Linda Savage, Ph.D., Florida.
Applied Economics: KaSaundra Tomlin, Ph.D., Oregon.
Business Administration: Robert Ford, Ph.D., Arizona State.
Management: Foard Jones, Ph.D., Georgia.
Management Information Systems: Paul Cheney, Ph.D., Minnesota.
Taxation: Dale Bandy, Ph.D., Texas.

Education: Sandra Robinson, Dean; Michael Hynes, Ph.D., Kent State.

Engineering: Marty Wanielista, Dean; Issa Batarseh, Ph.D., Illinois at Chicago; PE.
Civil and Environmental: Roger Wayson, Ph.D., Vanderbilt.
Computer Science: Ronald Dutton, Ph.D., Washington State.
Electrical and Computer: Michael Georgiopoulos, Ph.D., Connecticut.
Industrial: Linda Malone, Ph.D., Virginia Tech.
Mechanical, Materials, and Aerospace: Alain Kassab, Ph.D., Florida.

Health and Public Affairs: Belinda McCarthy, Dean; Eileen Abel, Ph.D., Case Western.
Communicative Disorders: Linda Louko, Ph.D.
Criminal Justice: Kenneth Reynolds, Ph.D., New Orleans.
Health Sciences: Timothy Rotarius, Ph.D., Texas Tech.
Molecular Biology and Microbiology: Karl Chai, Ph.D., Medical University of South Carolina.
Nursing: Jean Kijek, Ph.D., NYU; RN.
Physical Therapy: Katherine Parry, Ph.D., Oklahoma.
Public Administration: Xiao Hu Wang, Ph.D., Florida International.
Public Affairs: Eileen Abel, Ph.D., Case Western.
Social Work: Paul Maiden, Ph.D., Maryland.

Optics: Erik W. Van Stryland, Director; David Hagan, Ph.D., Heriot-Watt (Edinburgh).

Interdisciplinary Programs:

Biomolecular Sciences: Diane Jacobs, Ph.D., Harvard.
Modeling and Simulation: Peter Kincaid, Ph.D., Ohio State.

UNIVERSITY OF CONNECTICUT

Graduate School

Programs of Study

The Graduate School of the University of Connecticut offers programs leading to the degrees of Master of Arts, Master of Science, Master of Business Administration, Master of Dental Science, Master of Engineering, Master of Fine Arts (offered in art and dramatic arts), Master of Music, Master of Public Administration, Master of Public Health, and Master of Social Work, as well as to the degrees of Doctor of Education (educational leadership), Doctor of Musical Arts, and Doctor of Philosophy.

Study leading to the degree of Master of Arts or Master of Science is offered in accounting; agricultural and resource economics; allied health; animal science; anthropology; biochemistry; biomedical engineering; biophysics; biotechnology; botany; cell biology; chemical engineering; chemistry; civil engineering; communication science; comparative literary and cultural studies; computer science and engineering; dramatic arts; ecology; economics; education; electrical engineering; English; entomology; environmental engineering; French; genetics; geography; geological sciences; German; history; human development and family studies; international studies; Italian; Judaic studies; linguistics; materials science; mathematics; mechanical engineering; medieval studies; metallurgy and materials engineering; microbiology; music; natural resources—land, water, and air; nursing; nutritional science; oceanography; pathobiology; pharmaceutical science; philosophy; physical therapy (offered only as a dual bachelor's/master's degree program); physics; physiology and neurobiology; plant science; political science; polymer science; psychology; sociology; Spanish; statistics; survey research; and zoology.

Study leading to the degree of Doctor of Philosophy is offered in adult learning; agricultural and resource economics; animal science; anthropology; biochemistry; biomedical engineering; biomedical science; biophysics; botany; business administration; cell biology; chemical engineering; chemistry; civil engineering; communication science; comparative literary and cultural studies; computer science and engineering; curriculum and instruction; ecology; economics; educational administration; educational psychology; educational studies; electrical engineering; English; entomology; environmental engineering; French; genetics; geography; geological sciences; German; history; human development and family studies; Italian; kinesiology; linguistics; materials science; mathematics; mechanical engineering; medieval studies; metallurgy and materials engineering; microbiology; music; natural resources–land, water, and air; nursing; nutritional science; oceanography; pathobiology; pharmaceutical science; philosophy; physics; physiology and neurobiology; plant science; political science; polymer science; psychology; social work; sociology; Spanish; special education; statistics; and zoology.

Research Facilities

The Homer Babbidge Library at Storrs seats 2,300 people in a wide variety of study facilities, including individually assigned research studies, group studies, and areas designed for the use of computers, videos, and microtext. The building contains more than 2 million volumes of the system's total of nearly 3 million volumes, as well as microtext, maps, manuscripts, archives, recordings, and other materials. The library's book and journal holdings as well as many periodical indexes are accessible through HOMER, the online information system. A wide array of electronic resources are available in the reference area of the Babbidge Library. The Thomas J. Dodd Research Center, dedicated in 1995, is a fully equipped research facility and a major archive for historic papers.

The University has several dozen centers and institutes that promote research in specialized areas of study.

Financial Aid

Available are graduate assistantships for teaching and research, tuition remission awards, Special Graduate Student Fellowships, named Graduate School fellowships, University predoctoral fellowships, doctoral dissertation fellowships, summer fellowships for doctoral and predoctoral students, and aid in a variety of forms for students in specific programs.

Cost of Study

Course-related fees in 2002–03 for full-time students total $3418 per semester for in-state students and $7964 per semester for out-of-state students. Fees for part-time study are prorated. Fees are subject to change without notice.

Living and Housing Costs

On-campus housing for graduate students is limited. In 2002–03, students living in the Graduate Residence are charged $1978 per semester or approximately $5700 for the calendar year. The board plan provides three meals a day, seven days per week, while classes are in session at a cost of $1532 per semester. Fees are subject to change without notice.

Student Group

Approximately 4,500 students are enrolled in graduate degree programs. About 1,500 are working toward doctoral degrees.

Location

Most graduate degree programs offered by the University are located at the Storrs campus, which is 25 miles northeast of Hartford. Storrs is a scenic, agricultural area. Degree programs in the biomedical sciences and the marine sciences are offered at the University of Connecticut Health Center in Farmington (near Hartford) and at the Marine Sciences Institute at Avery Point (on Long Island Sound), respectively.

The University

The University of Connecticut grew out of the Storrs Agricultural School, which was founded in 1881 as a direct result of the gift of land, money, and buildings presented to the Connecticut General Assembly by Charles and Augustus Storrs of Mansfield. Master's degree study was offered by 1920. The Graduate School was established officially in 1939, and the University conferred its first Ph.D.'s a decade later.

Applying

Applicants should consult the academic department or program of their choice concerning application deadlines. Many programs have early closing dates. Application to some programs may require scores on one or more graduate admission tests, an interview or audition, or demonstrated proof of adequate facility in English for international applicants (the TOEFL is generally required for international applicants whose native language is not English). The application packet contains a complete summary of these requirements.

Correspondence and Information

Graduate Admissions Office
Unit 1006
University of Connecticut
Storrs, Connecticut 06269-1006
Telephone: 860-486-3617
E-mail: gradschool@uconn.edu
World Wide Web: http://www.grad.uconn.edu/

FACULTY HEADS

Accounting: A. J. Rosman, Ph.D.
Adult and Vocational Education: E. F. Iwanicki, Ph.D.
Agricultural and Resource Economics: E. Pagoulatos, Ph.D.
Allied Health: J. W. Smey, Ed.D.
Animal Science: L. C. Faustman, Ph.D.
Anthropology: W. P. Handwerker, Ph.D.
Art: J. Thorpe, M.F.A.
Biochemistry: P. L. Yeagle, Ph.D.
Biomedical Engineering: J. D. Enderle, Ph.D.
Biomedical Science: B. E. Kream, Ph.D.
Biophysics: P. L. Yeagle, Ph.D.
Biotechnology: R. T. Vinopal, Ph.D.
Botany: G. J. Anderson, Ph.D.
Business Administration: T. G. Gutteridge, Ph.D.
Cell Biology: P. L. Yeagle, Ph.D.
Chemical Engineering: J. J. Helble, Ph.D.
Chemistry: S. Suib, Ph.D.
Civil Engineering: E. A. Smith, Ph.D.
Communication Science: H. R. Gilbert, Ph.D.
Comparative Literary and Cultural Studies: L. McNeece, Ph.D.
Computer Science: R. A. Ammar, Ph.D.
Curriculum and Instruction: M. A. Doyle, Ph.D.
Dental Science: R. L. MacNeil, D.D.S., M.Dent.Sc.
Dramatic Arts: G. M. English, M.F.A.
Ecology: G. J. Anderson, Ph.D.
Economics: K. Segerson, Ph.D.
Education: R. L. Schwab, Ph.D.
Educational Administration: E. F. Iwanicki, Ph.D.
Educational Psychology: S. M. Reis, Ph.D.
Educational Studies: M. A. Doyle, Ph.D.
Electrical Engineering: R. Magnusson, Ph.D.
Engineering: A. Faghri, Ph.D.
English: J. L. Abbott, Ph.D.
Entomology: G. J. Anderson, Ph.D.
Environmental Engineering: B. A. Holmén, Ph.D.
Family Studies: C. M. Super, Ph.D.
French: D. K. Herzberger, Ph.D.
Genetics: P. L. Yeagle, Ph.D.
Geography: D. M. Hanink, Ph.D.
Geological Sciences: T. B. Byrne, Ph.D.
German: D. K. Herzberger, Ph.D.
History: A. L. Waller, Ph.D.
International Studies: B. E. Bravo-Ureta, Ph.D.
Italian: D. K. Herzberger, Ph.D.
Judaic Studies: A. M. Dashefsky, Ph.D.
Kinesiology: C. M. Maresh, Ph.D.
Linguistics: D. C. Lillo-Martin, Ph.D.
Materials Science: H. L. Marcus, Ph.D.
Mathematics: C. I. Vinsonhaler, Ph.D.
Mechanical Engineering: T. Bergman, Ph.D.
Medieval Studies: T. J. Jambeck, Ph.D.
Metallurgy and Materials Engineering: J. E. Morral, Ph.D.
Microbiology: P. L. Yeagle, Ph.D.
Music: R. F. Miller, Ph.D.
Natural Resources: D. B. Schroeder, Ph.D.
Nursing: L. C. Dzurec, Ph.D.
Nutritional Science: C. J. Lammi-Keefe, Ph.D.
Oceanography: R. B. Whitlatch, Ph.D.
Pathobiology: H. J. Van Kruiningen, D.V.M., Ph.D., M.D.
Pharmaceutical Science: M. C. Gerald, Ph.D.
Philosophy: C. L. Elder, Ph.D.
Physical Therapy: S. Hasson, Ed.D.
Physics: W. C. Stwalley, Ph.D.
Physiology and Neurobiology: A. de Blas, Ph.D.
Plant Science: R. A. Ashley, Ph.D.
Political Science: J. T. Rourke, Ph.D.
Polymer Science: C. S. P. Sung, Ph.D.
Psychology: C. A. Lowe, Ph.D.
Public Administration: W. Simonsen, Ph.D.
Public Health: H. Hansen, Ph.D., M.D.
Social Work: K. Davidson, D.S.W.
Sociology: M. Wallace, Ph.D.
Spanish: D. K. Herzberger, Ph.D.
Special Education: S. M. Reis, Ph.D.
Statistics: D. Dey, Ph.D.
Zoology: G. J. Anderson, Ph.D.

M.B.A. students work on a project in the café in the newly constructed, state-of-the-art School of Business building.

Graduate study is offered in more than eighty fields of study. The Graduate School awards nearly 1,500 degrees each year.

A picnic was held on the plaza in front of the Homer Babbidge Library in late August 2001 to welcome new students to the campus.

UNIVERSITY OF DAYTON

Graduate School

Programs of Study

Programs leading to advanced degrees are offered through the College of Arts and Sciences and the Schools of Business, Education, Engineering, and Law.

Doctoral programs are available in biology; in theology; in aerospace, electrical, electrooptics, materials, and mechanical engineering; and in educational leadership. Both Ph.D. and D.E. degrees are offered in engineering.

The College of Arts and Sciences offers master's programs in applied mathematics, biology, chemistry, communication, computer science, English, history, management science, mathematics, pastoral ministries, philosophy, political science, psychology, public administration, and theological studies. Individual interdisciplinary studies are also available.

The School of Business Administration offers a Master of Business Administration with concentrations in finance, international business, management information systems, and manufacturing management. The J.D./M.B.A. joint degree is offered to students meeting the admission requirements of both the Law School and the School of Business Administration.

The School of Education offers a Master of Science in Education degree, with programs in elementary education, physical education, school administration, school counseling, school psychology, secondary education, and the preparation of educational research specialists and student service personnel in higher education. The School also offers an M.S.T. degree, the Educational Specialist in Educational Leadership degree, and a Ph.D. in educational leadership.

The School of Engineering offers the Master of Science in Aerospace Engineering, Chemical Engineering, Civil Engineering, Electrical Engineering, Electro-Optics, Engineering, Engineering Management, Engineering Mechanics, Materials Engineering, and Mechanical Engineering degrees.

The School of Law offers a Juris Doctor degree.

Research Facilities

All programs are supported by adequate library, laboratory, and off-campus practicum facilities. Arrangements for internships and field studies with local hospitals, government agencies, schools, treatment centers, and research and industrial groups are excellent. The University has an outstanding Research Institute, with a wide range of equipment and support facilities.

Financial Aid

All departments offering graduate work have graduate teaching or research assistantships available. In 2000–01, the full stipend ranged from $5500 upward, with remission of tuition and fees. Summer jobs and fellowships are often available.

Cost of Study

The cost of graduate courses varies. Tuition in 2001 for the School of Education was $262 per semester hour and $382 per doctoral semester hour. Tuition in 2001 for the College of Arts and Sciences and the School of Engineering was $453 per semester hour, $481 per semester hour for the M.B.A. program, and $494 per semester hour for doctoral programs.

Living and Housing Costs

Graduate students at the University of Dayton usually arrange for their own housing off campus, although the Housing Office will assist individuals who so desire.

Student Group

In fall 2001, the University enrolled 3,004 graduate students and 7,164 undergraduates, including full- and part-time students. During 2000, 674 master's and 28 doctoral degrees were conferred.

Location

Dayton is the center of a metropolitan area of 850,000 people located in southwestern Ohio. It is a center for the manufacture of precision products, and industry constitutes a major portion of the city's economy. At present, it has about 1,000 industrial plants. Dayton offers many cultural attractions, including the Dayton Art Institute, the Air Force Museum, the Museum of Natural History, the Dayton Civic Ballet, the Dayton Philharmonic Orchestra, and several dramatic groups. Numerous parks and similar facilities are available to the public for outdoor activities and recreation.

The University

Although the origins of the University date to 1850, it became known as the University of Dayton in 1920. A Catholic institution with a lay Board of Trustees, it strives to transmit the heritage of the past, to direct attention to the achievements of the present, and to alert students to the changes and challenges of the future. The University is a member of the Southwestern Ohio Council for Higher Education.

The University operates on a trimester system with a split third term. It is accredited by the North Central Association of Colleges and Schools. The programs in the School of Education are approved by the National Council for Accreditation of Teacher Education.

Applying

Completed applications should be on file not later than one month prior to a new term (August 1, December 1, or April 1). Applications must include the regular application form, with one official college transcript, three letters of recommendation, and, in several departments, results of the General Test and/or the Subject Tests of the Graduate Record Examinations. The Graduate Management Admission Test is required of all M.B.A. students. A $30 nonrefundable application fee is due upon application to the Graduate School.

Correspondence and Information

Vice President for Graduate Studies and Research
Dean, Graduate School
St. Mary's, Room 200
University of Dayton
300 College Park
Dayton, Ohio 45469-1620
E-mail: nancy.wilson@notes.udayton.edu
World Wide Web: www.udayton.edu/~gradsch/

FACULTY HEADS

Vice President for Graduate Studies and Research and Dean, Graduate School: Gordon A. Sargent, Ph.D.
Associate Vice President for Graduate Studies and Research, Graduate School: Katy E. Marre, Ph.D.
Assistant to the Vice President for Graduate Studies and Research and Dean of the Graduate School: Nancy A. Wilson
Dean of the College of Arts and Sciences: Paul J. Morman, Ph.D.
Dean of the School of Business Administration: Sam Gould, Ph.D.
Dean of the School of Education: Thomas J. Lasley, Ph.D.
Dean of the School of Engineering: Blake E. Cherrington, Ph.D.
Dean of the School of Law: Lisa A. Kloppenborg, Esq., J.D.

Chairs and Directors of Graduate Programs
Biology: John J. Rowe, Ph.D., Chair; Robert Kearns, Ph.D., Director.
Business Administration: Janis Glynn, Director.
Chemical Engineering: Tony E. Saliba, Ph.D., Chair.
Chemistry: Gary Morrow, Ph.D., Chair; Kevin Church, Ph.D., Director.
Civil and Environmental Engineering and Engineering Mechanics: Joseph E. Saliba, Ph.D., Chair.
Communication: Kathleen Watters, Ph.D., Chair; James Robinson, Ph.D., Director.
Computer Science: Jim Buckley, Ph.D., Chair; Ragrava Gowda, Ph.D., Director.
Counselor Education and Human Services: Thomas W. Rueth, Ph.D., Chair.
Educational Administration: Father Joseph Massucci, Ph.D., Chair.
Educational Leadership: James Biddle, Ph.D., Director.
Educational Specialist in Educational Leadership: Rev. Joseph Massucci, Ph.D.
Electrical and Computer Engineering: Partha Banerjee, Ph.D., Chair.
Electro Optics: Joe Haus, Ph.D., Director.
Engineering: Donald Moon, Ph.D.
Engineering Management and Systems: Edward Mykytka, Ph.D., Chair.
English: Brian Conniff, Ph.D., Chair; Faiza Shereen, Ph.D., Director.
Health and Sports Science: Lloyd Laubach, Ph.D., Chair.
History: Janet Bednarek, Ph.D., Chair.
Law: Francis J. Conte, J.D.
Management Science: Patrick J. Sweeney, Ph.D., Chair.
Materials Engineering: Tony Saliba, Ph.D., Chair; Daniel Eylon, Ph.D., Director.
Mathematics: Paul W. Eloe, Ph.D., Chair; Muhammed Islam, Ph.D., Director.
Mechanical and Aerospace Engineering: Kevin P. Hallinana, Ph.D., Chair.
Pastoral Ministries and Religious Studies: Terrence Tilley, Ph.D., Chair; Sandra Yocum Mize, Ph.D., Director.
Physics: J. Michael O'Hare, Ph.D., Chair.
Political Science: Christopher Duncan, Ph.D., Chair; Peter Nelson, Ph.D., Director.
Psychology: David Biers, Ph.D., Chair; Charles Kimble, Ph.D., Director.
Public Administration: Peter B. Nelson, Ph.D.
Teacher Education: Patricia Hart, Ph.D., Chair.
Theological Studies: Terrence Tilley, Ph.D.

UNIVERSITY OF DELAWARE

Graduate Studies

Programs of Study

The Doctor of Philosophy may be earned in animal science, art history, biological sciences, biomechanics and movement science, chemistry and biochemistry, climatology, computer and information sciences, criminology, economics, education, engineering (chemical, civil, electrical, materials science, and mechanical), English, entomology and applied ecology, environmental and energy policy, family studies, geology, history, linguistics, marine studies, mathematics, oceanography, operations research, physics, plant and soil sciences, political science, psychology, sociology, or urban affairs and public policy. The Master of Arts or Master of Science is offered in accounting, agricultural economics, animal science, art, art conservation, art history, biological sciences, chemistry and biochemistry, communication, computer and information sciences, criminology, early American culture, economics education and entrepreneurship, education, English, entomology and applied ecology, exercise science, food science, human nutrition, foreign languages and literatures, foreign languages and pedagogy, geography, geology, health promotion, history, individual and family studies, liberal studies, marine studies, mathematics, operations research, physics, plant and soil sciences, political science and international relations, psychology, public horticulture, sociology, statistics, and urban affairs and public policy. Also offered are the Doctor of Education; Master of Business Administration; Master of Education; Master of Chemical, Civil, Electrical, Materials Science, and Mechanical Engineering; Master of Environmental and Energy Policy; Master of Fine Arts; Master of Instruction; Master of Marine Policy; Master of Music; Master of Physical Therapy; Master of Public Administration; and Master of Science in Nursing.

Research Facilities

University libraries hold more than 2.4 million volumes, more than 2.9 million items on microtext, and more than 120,000 maps; subscribe to more than 19,000 periodicals and serials; and are a U.S. government and patent depository. They belong to the Association of Research Libraries and PALINET, through which they are connected on line to OCLC. They have online computer access to hundreds of databases available for customized searching. An online public access catalog, DELCAT, contains more than 1 million items. Students and faculty members use the University's high-speed campus network to access on-campus and off-campus computing and information resources and the Internet. University resources include Sun Microsystems SPARCcenter and SPARCserver systems, IBM RS/6000 systems, a Silicon Graphics power Challenge system, a Cray Research J-90 system, and other departmental systems. Microcomputers are available in departmental and general computing sites across campus. The campus network's connection to SURAnet allows full access to the Internet. Software available includes major programming languages, statistical and numerical packages, graphics programs, Internet tools, and text-processing programs. Excellent laboratory facilities are available in chemistry; agriculture; human resources; food science; nutritional science; psychology; education; physics; biological sciences; languages; chemical, civil, electrical, materials science, and mechanical engineering; and marine studies in Newark and Lewes. Cooperative programs are offered with the Henry Francis duPont Winterthur Museum in early American culture; the Hagley Museum and Library in American technological, business, and labor history; and the Longwood Gardens in public horticulture. Courses in museum curatorship and a program in art conservation augment these programs. The Mount Cuba Astronomical Observatory is associated with the Physics Department. The Bartol Research Institute is also located on the Newark campus. The University has many other centers and institutes.

Financial Aid

Fellowships and teaching assistantships that pay a stipend and tuition costs are available in all areas of graduate study. In 2002–03, stipends range from $9,000 to $18,000. Fellowships and traineeships are offered under a number of federal programs. Tuition-only scholarships are also available.

Cost of Study

In 2002–03, course fees for full-time students are $2535 per semester for Delaware residents and $7300 per semester for nonresidents. Fees for part-time students are $282 per credit for Delaware residents and $871 per credit for nonresidents. M.B.A. rates for Delaware residents are $356 per credit hour. The graduation fee is $35 for master's degrees and $95 for doctorates. Courses are offered during the main fall and spring semesters, plus winter and summer sessions.

Living and Housing Costs

Various living accommodations are available for both single and married students. Costs vary depending on the type of accommodation. Graduate students may purchase a board plan in the campus dining halls, ranging from five to twenty meals per week.

Student Group

In fall 2001, there were 2,060 full-time and 882 part-time graduate students among the 18,007 students on the Newark campus. Approximately 76 percent of the full-time students receive fellowships or assistantships. Fifty percent of the graduate students are women, and about 25 percent of the full-time students are international students. In 2001, 151 Ph.D.'s, ten Ed.D.'s, and 700 master's degrees were conferred.

Location

The University is located in Newark, Delaware, a pleasant college community of about 30,000 people, 14 miles southwest of Wilmington, halfway between Philadelphia and Baltimore. Newark enjoys the advantages of a small community while being an easy drive from Philadelphia, New York, Baltimore, and Washington. It is also close to the recreational areas on the Chesapeake Bay and the Atlantic Ocean. The College of Marine Studies also operates a Marine Studies Complex at Lewes.

The University

The University of Delaware, a land- and sea-grant institution, has a long and interesting history. An outgrowth of a small academy founded in 1743, it has been a degree-granting institution since 1834. Delaware College and the Women's College, an affiliate opened in 1914, were combined as coordinate colleges under the name of the University of Delaware in 1921. Separate classes for men and women were held until 1945, when the two institutions were merged into the present university structure. Graduate programs leading to a master's degree have been available since the turn of the century. Doctoral programs have been offered since the 1940s. In recent years, the University has greatly expanded its enrollment, physical plant, faculty, and the scope of its educational endeavors. University campuses consist of 2,346 acres with 449 buildings. Its artistically grouped buildings are mostly in the Georgian style.

Applying

The general application deadlines are July 1 for fall, December 1 for spring, and April 1 for summer sessions. Many programs have earlier deadlines. Applications may be sent through the Web or may be requested from either address given below. In addition to submitting the application and $50 application fee (international students must use a check drawn on a U.S. bank or International Postal Money Order to remit payment in U.S. currency), applicants must forward one official transcript of previous academic records, GRE General Test scores (or GMAT scores for business students), and three letters of recommendation. Applications for fellowships and assistantships are submitted with the application. The deadline for application for financial aid (loans) is March 1.

Correspondence and Information

Office of Graduate Studies
University of Delaware
Newark, Delaware 19716-1501

Telephone: 302-831-2129
Fax: 302-831-8745
WWW: http://www.udel.edu/admissions/appinfo.html (application and information)
http://www.udel.edu/GradAcademic/col-irf.html (admission inquiries)

Chair, Department (specify major)
University of Delaware
Newark, Delaware 19716

FACULTY HEADS

Accounting and Management Information Systems: K. St. Pierre, Ph.D.; CPA. Financial, managerial systems; auditing; taxation; international accounting.

Agricultural and Technology Education: J. Bacon, M.S. Teacher certification program in agricultural and natural resources education or technology education.

Agriculture and Resource Economics: T. W. Ilvento, Ph.D. Marketing, production economics, international agricultural trade, resource economics, rural development.

Animal and Food Sciences: J. K. Rosenberger, Ph.D. Nutrition, reproduction, animal or avian physiology, pathology, immunology, animal/food microbiology, molecular biology, biotechnology, food safety, packaging, process engineering.

Art: S. Alchon, Ph.D. Painting, sculpture, printmaking, ceramics, metals, photography.

Art Conservation: D. Norris, Ph.D. The conservation of art and cultural objects, especially furniture, textiles, paintings, prints, photographs, and decorative and archaeological objects. (In association with Winterthur Museum.)

Art History: A. Gibson, Ph.D. American, European (antiquity to present) art theory, decorative arts, history of photography.

Biological Sciences: D. Carson, Ph.D. Cellular, molecular, organismic, genetic, physiological, ecological, marine, developmental, microbiological, and neurobiological research.

Biomechanics and Movement Science: T. Buchanan, Ph.D. Interdisciplinary program in biomechanics, motor control, applied physiology, exercise physiology, and rehabilitation technology.

Business Administration: J. Sawyer, Ph.D. Finance, management, marketing, operations management, organizational behavior.

Chemical Engineering: M. Barteau, Ph.D. Biochemical and biomedical engineering, catalysis and surface science, chemical kinetics and reaction engineering, composite materials, electronic materials, polymer science and engineering, process control, rheology, thermodynamics, transport phenomena and separation processes.

Chemistry and Biochemistry: S. D. Brown, Ph.D. Analytical, inorganic, organic, and physical chemistry; biochemistry.

Civil Engineering: M. Chajes, Ph.D. Structural engineering and mechanics, water resources and environmental engineering, soil mechanics and foundations, ocean engineering, railroad engineering, transportation engineering, applied sciences.

Communication: J. A. Courtright, Ph.D. Interpersonal, small group, organizational, and mass communication; public relations.

Computer and Information Sciences: M. S. Carberry, Ph.D. Artificial intelligence, computational theory, networks and parallel computing, supercomputer compiler systems, symbolic computations.

Criminology: J. Best, Ph.D. Crime and delinquency, sociology of law, criminal justice systems, theory and methods.

Early American Culture: J. C. Curtis, Ph.D. Decorative arts and material culture in social and cultural contexts in the seventeenth, eighteenth, and nineteenth centuries. (In association with Winterthur Museum.)

Economics: S. Hoffman, Ph.D. Applied quantitative economics: labor economics, econometrics and information systems, international economics and development, finance, natural resources, urban and regional economics; economics for educators.

Education: C. Clark, Ph.D. Cognition and instruction; cognition, development, and instruction; college counseling; curriculum; educational policy; elementary/secondary education; ESL/bilingualism; exceptional children; exceptionality; leadership; measurement, statistics, and evaluation; school counseling; school psychology; student affairs practice in higher education.

Electrical and Computer Engineering: G. Arce, Ph.D. Communications and networks, control and optimization, computer engineering, image processing, solid-state electronics, electric/magnetic devices, optoelectronics, integrated optics, solar energy.

English: J. C. Beasley, Ph.D. English and American literature, literature and pedagogy.

Entomology and Applied Ecology: D. Tallamy, Ph.D. Plant-insect interactions, pest and wildlife management, insect ecology, genetics.

Environmental and Energy Policy: R. T. Sylves, Ph.D. Sustainable development, political economy of energy and environment, disasters and public policy, energy and environmental policy.

Exercise Science: S. Hall, Ph.D. Biomechanics, cardiac rehabilitation, exercise physiology, teacher education.

Foreign Languages and Literatures: R. A. Zipser, Ph.D. French, German, Spanish, comparative literature.

Geography: D. Leathers, Ph.D. Applied climatology, water and energy budget climatology, climatic modeling, synoptic climatology, urban environments, cultural-historical geography, social-economic geography.

Geology: J. Pizzuto, Ph.D. Geochemistry, geophysics, mineralogy, crystallography, sedimentation, paleoecology, petrology, stratigraphy, biostratigraphy, marine coastal geology, geochronology, geoarchaeology, micropaleontology, structure, planetology.

History: C. Haber, Ph.D. American history, European history, the history of science and technology, special programs in industrialization (Hagley), U.S. social and cultural history (American civilization), museum studies.

Hotel Restaurant and Institutional Management: F. DeMicco, Ph.D. Corporate hospitality information for managers, consultants, and hospitality systems.

Human Development and Family Studies: M. Ferrari, Ph.D. Child development, individual and family studies, gerontology, young exceptional children, family and community services.

Human Nutrition: J. L. Smith, Ph.D. Food and nutrient consumption patterns over the life cycle, health promotion education, determinants of food and nutrition practices.

Liberal Studies: G. May, Ph.D. History of ideas in the humanities (for adult learners), the connections between fields of knowledge.

Linguistics: W. Idsardi, Ph.D. Theoretical and applied linguistics, second-language acquisition, ESL, psycholinguistics, computational linguistics, text grammar, phonology, syntax, cognitive science.

Marine Studies: C. A. Thoroughgood, Ph.D. Marine biology and biochemistry, marine policy, oceanography, physical ocean science and engineering.

Materials Science and Engineering: J. F. Rabolt, Ph.D. Metal, polymer, and ceramic materials; composites; electronic, photovoltaic, and oxide superconducting materials; fracture; fatigue; surface phenomena; electron microscopy.

Mathematical Sciences: P. Broadbridge, Ph.D. Ordinary and partial differential equations, integral equations, function theory, optimization, numerical analysis, combinatorics, topology, probability, statistics.

Mechanical Engineering: T. Chou, Ph.D. Biomechanics, environment, composites and smart materials, chaos and controls, particle dynamics and turbulence, manufacturing and design, failure mechanics.

Music: R. Murray, Ph.D. Master's-level program with concentrations in performance and teaching.

Nursing: L. Plowfield, Ph.D. Geriatrics/gerontology; medical/surgical nursing (cardiopulmonary, oncology/immune deficiency); nursing of women and children; nursing administration; family nurse practitioner.

Operations Research: P. Krishnan, Ph.D. Mathematics; computer and information sciences; energy conversion; statistics; business administration; chemistry; marine studies; food and resource economics; process management; agricultural, civil, and electrical engineering; urban affairs; composite materials.

Physical Therapy: S. Binder-Macleod, Ph.D. Graduate entry-level program preparing physical therapy generalists for state licensure.

Physics: J. MacDonald, Ph.D. Astronomy, astrophysics, and space physics; condensed matter and materials physics; elementary particle theory; atomic, molecular, and optical physics; acoustics; biophysics; cosmic ray physics.

Plant and Soil Sciences: D. L. Sparks, Ph.D. Crop improvement: plant breeding/genetics, plant pathology, plant/cell tissue culture, plant physiology/anatomy; soil science: soil chemistry, soil fertility/plant nutrition, soil genesis, soil microbiology.

Political Science and International Relations: J. Pika, Ph.D. American/comparative government, global governance, international relations, political theory, public policy.

Psychology: B. Ackerman, Ph.D. Experimental and clinical psychology, with specialization in social psychology, cognition, perception, learning, biopsychology, neuroscience, development, emotions, personality, and human engineering. APA-approved.

Public Administration: E. Jacobson, Ph.D. Environment and energy management, financial management, international and development administration, nonprofit leadership, personnel administration and labor relations, urban management.

Public Horticulture: J. E. Swasey, Ph.D. Management and engineering of publicly oriented horticultural institutions.

Sociology: J. Best, Ph.D. Sociological theory, research methodology, deviance, urban sociology, sociology of sex and gender, organizations, disaster research.

Statistics: T. Ilvento, Ph.D. Theoretical foundations of statistics, statistical methods.

Theatre: S. Robbins, M.F.A. Professional theater training in acting, technical production, and stage management.

Urban Affairs and Public Policy: M. Wilder, Ph.D. Planning and governance, political economy, social policy analysis and evaluation, technology and society, urban policy, historic preservation, energy and environmental policy.

UNIVERSITY OF DENVER

Graduate Studies

Programs of Study

The University of Denver offers programs of study leading to master's, doctoral, and specialist degrees. The Doctor of Philosophy (Ph.D.) is available from many programs in the Arts and Humanities, Social Sciences, and the Natural Sciences, Mathematics, and Engineering; the College of Education; the Graduate School of International Studies; and the Graduate School of Social Work. A joint Ph.D. is available from the Department of Religious Studies and the Iliff School of Theology. The Doctor of Psychology (Psy.D.) is available from the Graduate School of Professional Psychology.

An Education Specialist (Ed.S.) degree is available from the College of Education. The Juris Doctor (J.D.) is available from the College of Law.

Master's degrees can be pursued in the Arts and Humanities, Social Sciences, and the Natural Sciences, Mathematics, and Engineering; Daniels College of Business; the College of Education; the Graduate School of International Studies; University College; the Graduate School of Professional Psychology; and the Graduate School of Social Work.

Various joint and interdisciplinary degrees, which combine study with two or more programs, are also available.

The College of Law, Daniels College of Business, the Graduate School of International Studies, the Graduate School of Social Work, the College of Education, the Department of Human Communications, and the Department of Psychology offer various dual degrees, which combine study in two programs and award two degrees.

In addition, the University of Denver offers students the opportunity to simultaneously enroll in any two graduate degree programs, thus creating flexible dual degrees. These programs must make academic and/or career preparation sense, and no more that 15 credits of each program can be counted toward the other program.

Research Facilities

The University of Denver libraries provide an extensive collection of volumes, periodical subscriptions, and microforms in all subjects covered by University courses and research. Penrose Library has been a U.S. government document depository since 1909. Penrose has numerous online search capabilities that include the Colorado Alliance of Research Libraries (CARL), LEXIS-NEXIS, Dialog, and other business and humanities indexes. In addition, Penrose has been selected by Higher Education Resource Services to provide scholarly information to the western United States. Students also have access to many other academic and public libraries. The University also possesses excellent media and computer facilities and state-of-the-art research laboratories on campus.

Financial Aid

Two kinds of financial aid are available for graduate students: need-based aid and merit-based aid. Students applying for either kind of aid must be accepted into an eligible graduate program at the University. Need-based financial aid consists of Direct Loans, Carl Perkins Loans, the Federal Work-Study Program, and Colorado Graduate Grants. Merit-based financial aid consists of Graduate Tuition Scholarships, Graduate Teaching and Research Assistantships, Colorado Graduate Fellowships, and Minority Student Fellowships. A student who seeks state and federal financial assistance to pursue graduate studies at the University must file the Free Applications for Federal Student Aid (FAFSA). For more information, students should contact the graduate school or department in which they wish to enroll.

Cost of Study

For the 2003–04 academic year, tuition is $630 per credit hour. Full-time tuition per quarter (12 to 18 hours) is $7560. There is an additional technology fee of $4 per credit hour with a maximum of $144 per academic year and an activity fee of $5 per quarter. In addition, there is an optional health services fee per quarter and a University insurance fee per six months (which is waived with proof of alternate insurance).

Living and Housing Costs

The yearly rate in 2002–03 for an on-campus one-bedroom apartment is $8022 ($6282 for a studio). The yearly rate for one person in an on-campus two-bedroom apartment is $5826. Off-campus apartments are available nearby and range from $650 to $725. A liberal estimate of total monthly living expenses (e.g., rent, board, books, and personal spending) is $1200.

Student Group

Approximately 5,525 graduate students attend the University and comprise more than one half of the University's total student enrollment of 9,444 students. Approximately 14 percent of the total student population consists of student members of ethnic minority groups.

Student Outcomes

Most graduate students at the University of Denver find employment within a year of graduation. Students who have received their doctoral degrees from the University have obtained teaching and research positions at universities throughout the U.S. and the world. Master's degree recipients have pursued work in various business sectors and with governments throughout the world. The University has a Career Center that actively works with students and alumni who are seeking employment.

Location

Mile-high Denver, with a population of about 1.8 million, is the financial, administrative, commercial, and sports center of the Rocky Mountain region. Denver offers many cultural and intellectual attractions, including numerous theater groups, an outstanding symphony orchestra, and fine museums. Denver has a mild climate, with an average of 300 sunny days a year. Excellent outdoor recreation of all kinds, especially skiing, may be enjoyed within an hour's drive of the University.

The University

In 1864, John Evans, second governor of the Colorado Territory, signed the charter establishing Colorado's first private university—the University of Denver. Founded in the spirit of westward expansion, the University is one of the few major private universities between Chicago and the West Coast. It maintains a strong tradition of pioneering philosophy and programming. Nationally recognized for graduate programming and the quality of the professional schools, the University prides itself on a 13:1 overall student-faculty ratio.

Applying

Each graduate program provides specific information about admission to that school and/or department. Application fees, deadlines, and requirements vary by school and department.

Correspondence and Information

For general information, students should contact:

Graduate Studies Admissions
University of Denver
2197 South University Boulevard, Room 216
Denver, Colorado 80208
Telephone: 303-871-2305
877-871-3119 (toll-free)
Fax: 303-871-4942
E-mail: grad-adm@du.edu
World Wide Web: http://www.du.edu/grad/gradadm.html

SCHOOLS, PROGRAMS, AND FACULTY

Listed below are the University of Denver's deans, graduate degree programs, and admissions phone numbers. All numbers are in area code 303.

ARTS AND HUMANITIES: Dean Gregg Kvistad, Ph.D., Berkeley.

Art and Art History: 871-2846 (e-mail: saah-gradinfo@du.edu).
English: 871-2266 (e-mail: engl-info@du.edu).
History: 871-2347 (e-mail: yford@du.edu).
Judaic Studies: 871-3012 (e-mail: judaic-studies@du.edu).
Languages and Literature: 871-2662 (e-mail: langs-lits@du.edu).
Music: 871-6973 (e-mail: marhuels@du.edu).
Philosophy: 871-2063 (e-mail: phil-grad-info@du.edu).
Religious Studies: 871-2740 (e-mail: rlgsol@denver.du.edu).

NATURAL SCIENCES, MATHEMATICS, AND ENGINEERING: Dean Jim Fogelman, Ph.D., Cornell.

Biological Sciences: 871-3661 (e-mail: rsanford@du.edu).
Chemistry and Biochemistry: 871-2435 (e-mail: chem-gradinfo@du.edu).
Computer Science: 871-2453 (e-mail: grad@cs.du.edu).
Engineering: 871-2102 (e-mail: engr08@denver.du.edu).
Geography: 871-2513 (e-mail: geog-info@du.edu).
Mathematics: 871-2911 (e-mail: info@math.du.edu).
Physics: 871-2238 (e-mail: phys-gradinfo@du.edu).

SOCIAL SCIENCES: Dean Gregg Kvistad, Ph.D., Berkeley.

Anthropology: 871-2406 (e-mail: anth02@denver.du.edu).
Economics: 871-2685 (e-mail: econ04@denver.du.edu).
Psychology: 871-3803 (e-mail: phoughta@du.edu).
School of Communication:
- **Digital Media Studies:** 871-2166 (e-mail: jrutenbe@du.edu).
- **Human Communication Studies:** 871-4313 (e-mail: joasmith@du.edu).
- **International and Intercultural Communication:** 871-2088 (e-mail: mcom07@denver.du.edu).
- **Mass Communication and Journalism Studies:** 871-2166 (e-mail: mcom06@denver.du.edu).
- **Public Relations and Advertising:** 871-2166 (e-mail: mcom06@denver.du.edu).

COLLEGE OF EDUCATION: Dean Virginia R. Maloney, Ph.D., George Washington. Contact: 871-2509 (e-mail: educ03@denver.du.edu).

COLLEGE OF LAW: Dean Mary Ricketson, J.D., Denver. Contact: 871-6103 (e-mail: admissions@mail.law.du.edu).

DANIELS COLLEGE OF BUSINESS: Dean James Griesemer, D.P.A., Colorado at Boulder. Contact: 871-3416; 800-622-4723 (toll-free) (e-mail: dcb@du.edu).

GRADUATE SCHOOL OF INTERNATIONAL STUDIES: Dean Tom Farer, J.D., Harvard. Contact: 871-2544; 877-474-7236 (toll-free) (e-mail: gsisadm@du.edu).

GRADUATE SCHOOL OF PROFESSIONAL PSYCHOLOGY: Dean Peter Buirski, Ph.D., Adelphi. Contact: 871-3873 (e-mail: ppsy02@denver.du.edu).

GRADUATE SCHOOL OF SOCIAL WORK: Dean Catherine Foster Alter, Ph.D., Maryland at Baltimore. Contact: 871-2841 (e-mail: gssw07@denver.du.edu).

UNIVERSITY COLLEGE: Academic Dean Kathy Gerhold, Ph.D., Northwestern. Contact: 871-3155 (e-mail: ucolinfo@du.edu).

UNIVERSITY OF DENVER

University College

Programs of Study

University College of the University of Denver offers six master's degrees and more than thirty certificate programs through evening, weekend, and distance delivery formats. Programs are offered in today's most relevant fields, including applied communication, alternative dispute resolution, American Indian studies, computer information systems, electronic commerce, environmental policy and management, geographic information systems, liberal studies, modern languages, network analysis and design, technology management, telecommunications, and women in computer science.

Research Facilities

Penrose Library houses more than 2.7 million volumes in total collection, including 5,102 journals and periodicals. A computer reference system connects the library with major libraries in the region and throughout the United States. The University of Denver also has more than thirty specialized research centers and institutions in a wide range of disciplines.

Financial Aid

Some financial aid programs are available to assist University College students who are unconditionally admitted to a master's degree program. Certificate candidates may also be eligible for financial aid upon verification of an earned baccalaureate degree by the admissions office. The University of Denver's Office of Student Financial Services handles all financial aid applications.

Cost of Study

University College offers more than one thousand courses per year, with costs ranging from $230 to $325 per credit hour and $108 to $190 per noncredit hour.

Living and Housing Costs

The majority of University College students commute, but graduate housing is available on the University of Denver campus. For more information, students can call 303-871-2246.

Student Group

The total number of graduate students for winter 1999 through fall 1999 was 1,589, with 868 degree students and 721 certificate students. Total enrollment for the same period was 10,342. The student population is 57 percent women. Students are generally working professionals with medium to high incomes and balance career, family, and community responsibilities. A growing number of students take classes for personal enrichment and are considered to be lifelong learners.

Location

The University of Denver campus is located in a residential neighborhood 20 minutes southeast of downtown Denver, Colorado. With a spectacular view of the Rocky Mountains, Denver bustles with economic, cultural, and recreational activity. The University now has invested in the campus more than $100 million in new buildings, classrooms, state-of-the-art labs, and sports facilities.

The University

The University of Denver was founded in 1864. In addition to traditional undergraduate programs, this fine institution offers innovative programs for adults. The non-traditional division was founded in 1983 on the premise that education for adults should be immediately applicable, career oriented, and guided by the industries served.

With more than forty national programming awards and many other distinctions from its peers, University College of the University of Denver is recognized as one of the very best providers of adult education in the nation, and programs are accredited by the North Central Association of Colleges and Schools.

Applying

University College has no entrance exam requirements, and no undergraduate degree is required for most certificate programs. However, to be accepted into a master's program, a bachelor's degree is required from a regionally accredited institution. An undergraduate GPA of 3.0 is required for both certificate and degree candidates. Those individuals with lower GPAs may qualify for conditional admission. Lifelong learners do not have to be a degree or certificate candidate.

Correspondence and Information

University College
University of Denver
2211 South Josephine Street
Denver, Colorado 80208
Telephone: 303-871-3354
Fax: 303-871-3303
E-mail: ucolinfo@du.edu
World Wide Web: http://www.universitycollege.du.edu

THE FACULTY

University College faculty members hold advanced degrees and are recognized professionals representing major corporations, businesses, and institutions in the Denver area.

THE ADMINISTRATION

University College Dean: Michele Bloom, M.A., Denver.
American Indian Studies: Tripp Baltz, M.L.S., Denver.
Applied Communication/Alternative Dispute Resolution: Susan Cook, Ph.D., Denver.
Computer Information Systems: Samuel A. Dosumu, Ph.D., Colorado.
Environmental Policy and Management: John A. Hill, Ph.D., UCLA.
Liberal Studies: Tripp Baltz, M.L.S., Denver.
Modern Languages: Kathryn Gerhold, Ph.D., Northwestern.
Technology Management: Richard Kettner-Polley, Ph.D., Harvard.
Telecommunications: Richard Kettner-Polley, Ph.D., Harvard.
Women in Computer Science: Samuel A. Dosumu, Ph.D., Colorado.

The University of Denver, founded in 1864, is the oldest institution of higher education in the Rocky Mountain Region and is the largest independent university in Colorado.

UNIVERSITY OF FLORIDA

Graduate School

Programs of Study

The University of Florida (UF) Graduate School offers the Ph.D. in eighty disciplines, in addition to the Doctor of Audiology, Doctor of Education, and Doctor of Plant Medicine degrees. There are master's programs in 111 disciplines, fourteen Engineer degree programs, and twelve Specialist in Education programs. In addition, a number of interdisciplinary concentrations are available at the doctoral level, and there are many successful joint-degree programs. Professional postbaccalaureate degrees are offered in dentistry, law, medicine, pharmacy, physician assistance, and veterinary medicine.

Research Facilities

Outstanding among UF's more than 100 interdisciplinary research and education centers, bureaus, and institutes are the Cancer Center, Engineering Research Center for Particle Science and Technology, the Brain Institute, the Archie Carr Center for Sea Turtle Research, the Florida Museum of Natural History, the Center for Environmental Systems Commercial Space Technology, the Center for Applied Optimization, the Database Systems Research and Development Center, and the National High Magnetic Field Laboratory partnership with Florida State University and Los Alamos.

UF's eight libraries contain more than 3.4 million cataloged volumes, approximately 25,000 serial titles, and 6.3 million microforms. Nationally significant research collections include the Latin American Collection, the Price Library of Judaica, the Map and Imagery Library, the Baldwin Library of Children's Literature, and the P. K. Yonge Library of Florida History, which is the state's preeminent Floridiana collection. The libraries also have particularly strong holdings in architectural preservation and eighteenth-century American architecture, late nineteenth- and early twentieth-century German state documents, rural sociology of Florida, and tropical and subtropical agriculture.

Financial Aid

UF offers 150 Alumni Graduate Fellowships to superior students entering Ph.D. and M.F.A. programs (http://www.aa.ufl.edu/fellows/). In addition, qualified graduate students are eligible for a number of other fellowships, assistantships, and awards (http://gradschool.rgp.ufl.edu/education/finaid.html). UF also has a substantial number of fellowships targeted specifically for students from underrepresented minority groups (http://rgp.ufl.edu/ogmp). Applications for these awards should be made to the appropriate department chair at the University of Florida on or before February 15 of each year.

Non-Florida tuition payments and in-state tuition payments are available to eligible graduate students who hold assistantships or certain fellowships. These payments cover most tuition charges.

Cost of Study

Tuition and fees for in-state residents in 2001–02 were $1964 per semester, based on 12 hours of graduate enrollment. The comparable amount for out-of-state graduate students was $6849. Near graduation, there are expenses for typing and duplicating a thesis (dissertation) and fees for library processing, microfilming, and publishing the dissertation abstract.

Living and Housing Costs

UF provides some variety in types of accommodations. The double room for two students is the most common. Air-conditioned dormitory rooms range from $1109 to $2290 per person per semester. Accommodations for single graduate or professional students in Diamond Apartment Village begin at $301 per person per month. At present, a one-bedroom unfurnished apartment off campus rents for about $475 per month.

Student Group

The 46,500 University of Florida students (fall 2001) come from more than 100 countries (4,700 international students), all fifty states, and every one of the sixty-seven counties in Florida. The ratio of men to women is 49:51. Seventy-three percent of UF students are undergraduates, 20 percent are graduate students, and 6 percent are in professional programs. There are 3,300 African-American students and 4,400 Hispanic-American students who attend UF.

Location

The Gainesville urban population is approximately 180,000. It is about an hour's drive from both the Atlantic and Gulf beaches. Although it is predominantly warm, in summer the temperature generally drops about 20 degrees at night, in winter there are short but stimulating cold spells, and the seasons change. Spring comes early, and the dogwoods and azaleas are spectacular.

The University

The University of Florida is a major public, land-grant, research university. The state's oldest, largest, and most comprehensive university, Florida is among the nation's most academically diverse universities. One of only seventeen land-grant universities in the Association of American Universities, Florida has a long history of established programs in international education, research, and service. UF is also noted for its outstanding intercollegiate sports program.

Applying

University requirements for graduate students are a minimum grade average of B for all upper-division undergraduate work, a minimum combined score of 1000 on the verbal and quantitative portions of the GRE General Test, and a baccalaureate degree from a regionally accredited college or university or the equivalent. Individual departments may have requirements higher than the University's. A TOEFL score of 550 or higher is required for applicants whose native language is not English. Deadlines are given in the University Calendar (http://gradschool.rgp.ufl.edu/gradcat/2001-2002/criticaldates.html).

Correspondence and Information

For general information:
Graduate Admissions Office
201 Criser Hall
University of Florida
P.O. Box 114000
Gainesville, Florida 32611-4000
Telephone: 352-392-1365 Ext. 7117

For program information:
Graduate Coordinator
(specify department or program)
College of (specify)
University of Florida
Gainesville, Florida 32611
World Wide Web: http://rgp.ufl.edu

COLLEGES AND PROGRAMS

College of Agricultural and Life Sciences (http://www.acprog.ifas.ufl.edu): Agricultural Educatión and Communication; Agricultural and Biological Engineering; Agronomy; Animal Sciences (Dairy and Poultry Sciences); Entomology and Nematology; Environmental Horticulture; Family, Youth, and Life Sciences; Fisheries and Aquatic Sciences; Food and Resource Economics; Food Science and Human Nutrition; Forest Resources and Conservation; Horticultural Sciences; Microbiology and Cell Science; Nutritional Sciences; Plant Medicine; Plant Molecular and Cellular Biology; Plant Pathology; Soil and Water Science; Wildlife Ecology and Conservation.

Warrington College of Business Administration (http://www.cba.ufl.edu): Accounting, Master of Business Administration (Arts Administration, Competitive Strategy, Decision and Information Sciences, Entrepreneurship, Finance, Global Management, Graham-Buffet Security Analysis, Health Administration, Human Resources Management, International Studies, Latin American Business, Management, Marketing, Private Enterprise and Public Policy, Real Estate, Sports Administration), Decision and Information Sciences, Economics, Finance, Insurance, International Business, Management, Marketing, Real Estate and Urban Analysis.

College of Dentistry (http://www.dental.ufl.edu): Dental Sciences: Endodontics, Orthodontics, Periodontics, Prosthodontics, Oral Biology.

College of Design, Construction, and Planning (http://www.arch.ufl.edu): Architecture, Building Construction, Interior Design, International Construction Management, Landscape Architecture, Urban and Regional Planning.

College of Education (http://www.coe.ufl.edu): Counselor Education, Curriculum and Instruction, Early Childhood Education, Educational Leadership, Educational Psychology, Elementary Education, English Education, Foreign Language Education, Foundations of Education, Higher Education Administration, Instruction and Curriculum, Marriage and Family Counseling, Mathematics Education, Mental Health Counseling, Reading Education, Research and Evaluation Methodology, School Counseling and Guidance, School Psychology, Science Education, Social Studies Education, Special Education, Student Personnel in Higher Education.

College of Engineering (http://www.eng.ufl.edu): Aerospace Engineering, Agricultural and Biological Engineering, Biomedical Engineering, Chemical Engineering, Civil Engineering, Coastal and Oceanographic Engineering, Computer and Information Sciences, Computer Engineering, Digital Arts and Sciences, Electrical and Computer Engineering, Engineering Mechanics, Engineering Science, Environmental Engineering Sciences, Industrial and Systems Engineering, Materials Science and Engineering, Mechanical Engineering, Nuclear Engineering Sciences.

College of Fine Arts (http://www.arts.ufl.edu): Art, Art Education, Art History, Digital Arts and Sciences, Museology, Music, Music Education, Theater and Dance.

College of Health and Human Performance (http://www.hhp.ufl.edu/): Exercise and Sport Sciences (Biomechanics, Exercise Physiology, Exercise and Sport Pedagogy, Motor Learning/Control, Special Physical Education/Exercise Therapy, Sport and Exercise Physiology, Sport Management); Health and Human Performance (Athletic Training/Sport Medicine, Biomechanics, Exercise Physiology, Health Behavior, Motor Learning/Control, Sport and Exercise Physiology, Therapeutic Recreation, Tourism and National Resource Recreation); Health Science Education; Public Health; Recreation, Parks, and Tourism.

College of Health Professions (http://www.hp.ufl.edu): Audiology, Clinical and Health Psychology, Health Administration, Health Services Research, Occupational Therapy, Physical Therapy, Public Health, Rehabilitation Counseling, Rehabilitation Science.

College of Journalism and Communications (http://www.jou.ufl.edu): Mass Communication: Advertising, International Communication, Journalism, Mass Communication Law, Public Relations, Telecommunication.

Levin College of Law (http://www.law.ufl.edu/): Comparative Law, Taxation.

College of Liberal Arts and Sciences (http://www.clas.ufl.edu): Anthropology, Astronomy, Audiology, Botany, Chemistry, Classical Studies, Communication Sciences and Disorders, Computer and Information Sciences, Counseling Psychology, English, French, Geography, Geology, German, History, Latin, Latin American Studies, Linguistics, Mathematics, Philosophy, Physics, Plant Molecular and Cellular Biology, Psychology, Religion, Romance Languages and Literatures, Sociology, Spanish, Statistics, Zoology.

College of Medicine (http://www.med.ufl.edu/): Biochemistry and Molecular Biology; Medical Sciences: Anatomy and Cell Biology; Biochemistry and Molecular Biology; Clinical Investigation; Genetics; Immunology and Microbiology; Molecular Cell Biology; Neuroscience; Pathology, Immunology, and Laboratory Medicine; Physiology and Pharmacology; Public Health.

College of Natural Resources and Environment (http://web.cnre.ufl.edu): Interdisciplinary Ecology.

College of Nursing (http://con.ufl.edu): Nursing Sciences: Adult Health, Family, Midwifery, Pediatric, Women's Health.

College of Pharmacy (http://www.cop.ufl.edu): Pharmaceutical Sciences: Medicinal Chemistry, Pharmacodynamics, Pharmacy, Pharmacy Health Care Administration.

College of Veterinary Medicine (http://www.vetmed.ufl.edu): Veterinary Medical Sciences: Forensic Toxicology, Large and Small Animal Clinical Sciences, Physiological Sciences, Infectious Diseases and Experimental Pathology.

Combined Bachelor's/Master's Programs (http://rgp.ufl.edu/gradcat): Accounting, Aerospace Engineering, Agricultural and Biological Engineering, Animal Sciences, Art (Digital Arts and Sciences), Biomedical Engineering, Computer Science, Computer Engineering, Decision and Information Sciences, Electrical and Computer Engineering, Engineering Science, Environmental Engineering Sciences, Exercise and Sport Sciences, Forest Resources and Conservation, Geography, Geological Sciences, Health Science Education, History, Interdiscplinary Ecology, Materials Science and Engineering, Mathematics, Nuclear and Radiological Engineering, Nursing, Physical Therapy, Plant Pathology, Political Science, Recreational Studies, Religion, Sociology, Statistics.

Innovative Program Options:
Distance Learning: Doctor of Audiology (http://web.csd.ufl.edu/aud.html), Master of Agriculture and Master of Agribusiness (http://disted.ifas.ufl.edu/master.htm), Master of Health Administration (http://www.hp.ufl.edu): Executive Program (Electronic), Master of Health Science (http://www.hp.ufl.edu/ot/), Master of International Construction Management (http://www.bcn.ufl.edu/c_menu/).
Engineering (http://www.eng.ufl.edu): Florida Engineering Education Delivery System (videotape).
Master of Business Administration (http://www.cba.ufl.edu): Internet M.B.A. (one- and two-year options), M.B.A. for Professions (twenty-seven month and one-year options), Executive M.B.A. option, Traditional M.B.A. (one- and two-year options).

Interdisciplinary Concentrations and Certificates (http://rgp.ufl.edu/gradcat): African Studies, Agroforestry, Animal Molecular and Cellular Biology, Biological Sciences, Chemical Physics, Ecological Engineering, Geographical Information Systems, Gerontology, Health Physics, Hydrologic Sciences, Imaging Science and Technology, International Development Policy and Administration, Manufacturing Systems Engineering, Medical Physics, Political Campaigning, Public Administration, Quantum Theory Project, Teaching English as a Second Language, Toxicology, Tropical Agriculture, Wetlands, Women's/Gender Studies.

Joint Programs (http://gradschool.rgp.ufl.edu/gradcat): With Law: J.D./M.A. (Anthropology, History, Latin American Studies, Public Affairs, Real Estate, or Sociology), J.D./M.Acc. (Accounting), J.D./M.A.M.C. (Mass Communication), J.D./M.A.U.R.P. (Urban and Regional Planning), J.D./M.B.A. (Business Administration), J.D./M.B.C. or M.S.B.C. (Building Construction), J.D./M.E. or M.S. (Electrical and Computer Engineering or Environmental Engineering Sciences), J.D./M.S. (Food and Resource Economics, Forest Resources and Conservation, Interdisciplinary Ecology, or Medical Sciences), J.D./M.S.E.S.S. or M.E.S.S. (Exercise and Sport Sciences), J.D./Ph.D. (Anthropology, Educational Leadership, Forest Resources and Conservation, History, Interdisciplinary Ecology, Mass Communications, Medical Sciences, or Psychology).
With Master of Business Administration: M.B.A./B.S.I.S.E. (Industrial and Systems Engineering), M.B.A./J.D. (Law), M.B.A./M.E.S.S. (Exercise and Sport Sciences), M.B.A./M.I.B. (Netherlands School of Business), M.B.A./M.I.M. (American Graduate School of International Management), M.B.A./M.S. or Ph.D. (Medical Sciences), M.B.A./Pharm.D. (Pharmacy). Other Combinations: M.S./M.Ed. (Medical Sciences/Educational Leadership), Ph.D./M.D. (Medical Sciences/Medicine), Ph.D./Pharm.D. (Pharmaceutical Sciences/Pharmacy).

UNIVERSITY OF GEORGIA

Graduate School

Programs of Study

The Doctor of Philosophy degree is offered in adult education, agricultural economics, agronomy, animal and dairy science, animal nutrition, anthropology, art, biochemistry and molecular biology, biological and agricultural engineering, business administration, cellular biology, chemistry, child and family development, communication sciences and disorders, comparative literature, computer science, counseling and student personnel services, counseling psychology, drama, early childhood education, ecology, economics, educational psychology, elementary education, English, entomology, exercise science, food science, foods and nutrition, forest resources, genetics, geography, geology, health promotion and behavior, higher education, history, horticulture, housing and consumer economics, instructional technology, language education, linguistics, marine sciences, mass communication, mathematics, mathematics education, medical microbiology, microbiology, middle school education, music, occupational studies, pharmacology (veterinary), pharmacy, philosophy, physical education and sport studies, physics, physiology (veterinary), plant biology, plant pathology, political science, poultry science, psychology, reading education, recreation and leisure studies, Romance languages, science education, social foundations of education, social science education, social work, sociology, special education, speech communication, statistics, textile sciences, toxicology, veterinary parasitology, and veterinary pathology.

Programs of study leading to the Master of Science degree are available in agricultural economics; agricultural engineering; agronomy; anatomy (veterinary); animal science; artificial intelligence; biochemistry and molecular biology; biological engineering; cellular biology; chemistry; child and family development; computer science; conservation ecology and sustainable development; dairy science; ecology; entomology; environmental economics; environmental health; food science; foods and nutrition; forest resources; genetics; geography; geology; horticulture; housing and consumer economics; marine sciences; medical microbiology; microbiology; pharmacology (veterinary); pharmacy; physics; physiology (veterinary); plant biology; plant pathology; poultry science; psychology; statistics; textiles, merchandising, and interiors; toxicology; veterinary parasitology; and veterinary pathology.

The degree of Master of Arts is offered in anthropology, art history, business administration, classical languages, comparative literature, economics, education, English, French, geography, German, Greek, history, journalism and mass communication, Latin, linguistics, mathematics, mathematics (nonthesis), music, nonprofit organizations, philosophy, political science, religion, Romance languages, sociology, Spanish, and speech communication.

Advanced professional degrees, including the Doctor of Education, Doctor of Musical Arts, Doctor of Public Administration, and Specialist in Education, are offered. Professional master's degrees are offered in accountancy, agricultural economics, agricultural extension, applied mathematical science, art education, avian medicine, business administration, crop and soil sciences, education, English, fine arts (art and drama), family and consumer sciences, food technology, forest resources, French, German, historic preservation, Internet technology, landscape architecture, law, marketing research, mass communication, music, music education, plant protection and pest management, public administration, Romance languages, social work, and Spanish.

The University operates on an academic year of two semesters, a presummer (May) session, and two summer sessions.

Research Facilities

The University libraries contain more than 3.4 million volumes and 5.6 million microforms. The science library, located in the Boyd Graduate Studies Research Center, has 710,000 volumes. The University is a member of Oak Ridge Associated Universities and the Organization for Tropical Studies. Among research programs in which graduate students participate are those conducted by the Complex Carbohydrate Research Center, the Institute of Ecology, the Institute for Behavioral Research, the Institute of Higher Education, the Center for Remote Sensing and Mapping Science, the Poultry Disease Research Center, and the Marine Sciences Program.

Financial Aid

Graduate students receive financial aid amounting to more than $34 million from various sources. In 2001–02, stipends started at $11,900 per year for master's students and $13,000 for doctoral students. Students who hold at least a one-third-time assistantship pay a matriculation fee of $25 and a modest activity fee. The Graduate School awards approximately 300 assistantships each year. Assistantships are available in most departments, and in some areas, postdoctoral fellowships are available. Spouses of graduate students may obtain work at the University, at several federal agencies located on campus, in the public schools, and in industry.

Cost of Study

Tuition in 2001–02 was $1971 per semester for residents and $6705 per semester for nonresident students who do not hold an assistantship.

Living and Housing Costs

Single student residence halls and family housing apartments are available on campus. In 2001–02, the rental rates for residence halls ranged from $1446 to $1906 per semester, and one- and two-bedroom unfurnished apartments rented for $340 to $580 per month. There are two meal plans: a five-day meal plan (Monday–Friday) and a seven-day meal plan.

Student Group

In 2001–02, the University had 32,317 students on campus, including 5,979 graduate students. In 2001, 1,721 graduate degrees were awarded. Of these, 384 were doctoral degrees.

Location

Athens, a town of approximately 101,000 people, is 65 miles east of Atlanta. The Great Smoky Mountains are 100 miles north of Athens, and the Atlantic coast is 200 miles to the southeast. Several large artificial lakes near Athens offer exceptional recreational opportunities. Athens has a number of large and small industries, giving it an excellent balance between industry and education.

The University

The University was chartered in 1785 and is the oldest chartered state university in the country. Classes began in 1801. It is one of the top institutions in the Southeast and is rapidly becoming one of the leading institutions in the country. A building program of more than $240 million is under way; part is under construction and part is in the planning stage. The University is both a land-grant and sea-grant institution.

Applying

Admission to the Graduate School is based on multiple criteria, including (but not limited to) the applicant's educational record, official scores on required entrance tests, and departmental recommendation. Applications and supporting credentials should be received in the Graduate Admissions Office by specific deadlines. The deadline for consideration for Graduate School assistantships is January 1 for the fall semester. Academic departments may have earlier deadlines for applicants and assistantship awards than those that follow: domestic student applications for the fall semester should be received by July 1; for the spring semester, by November 15; for the presummer session, by April 1; and for the summer semester (all other sessions), by May 1. International student applications for the fall semester should be received by April 15; for the spring semester, by October 15; and for the summer semester (all sessions), by February 15. An application processing fee of $30 is charged. Applicants are encouraged to apply online at the Web address listed below.

Correspondence and Information

For general information:
Office of Graduate Admissions
534 Boyd Graduate Studies Research Center
University of Georgia
Athens, Georgia 30602-7402
Telephone: 706-542-1787
E-mail: gradadm@uga.edu
World Wide Web: http://www.gradsch.uga.edu/

For program information:
Graduate Coordinator
(specify department or program)
College or School of (specify)
University of Georgia
Athens, Georgia 30602

COLLEGES AND PROGRAMS

College of Agricultural and Environmental Sciences (http://ugacescn.ces.uga.edu/caeshome/): agricultural economics, agricultural extension, agronomy, animal and dairy science, animal nutrition, biological and agricultural engineering, crop and soil sciences, entomology, environmental economics, environmental health, food science, horticulture, plant pathology, poultry science.

Franklin College of Arts and Sciences (http://ben.franklin.uga.edu/): anthropology, art, art history, artificial intelligence, biochemistry and molecular biology, cellular biology, chemistry, classics, comparative literature, computer science, conservation ecology and sustainable development, drama, English, French, genetics, geography, geology, German, Greek, history, Latin, linguistics, marine sciences, mathematics, mathematics nonthesis, microbiology, music, nonprofit organizations, philosophy, physics and astronomy, plant biology, political science, psychology, public administration, religion, Romance languages, sociology, Spanish, speech communication, statistics.

Terry College of Business (http://www.terry.uga.edu/): accounting, banking and finance, business administration, economics, legal studies, management, management science, management information systems, marketing research, real estate, risk management and insurance.

College of Education (http://www.coe.uga.edu/): adult education, agricultural education, art education, business education, college student affairs administration, communication sciences and disorders, counseling and student personnel services, counseling psychology, early childhood education, education of the gifted, educational leadership, educational psychology, elementary education, English education, exercise science, family and consumer sciences education, guidance and counseling, health promotion and behavior, higher education, human resource and organizational development, instructional technology, language education, marketing education, mathematics education, middle school education, music education, occupational studies, physical education and sports studies, reading education, recreation and leisure studies, school psychology, science education, social foundations of education, social science education, special education, teaching additional languages, technological studies.

College of Environment and Design (http://www.sed.uga.edu/): ecology, historic preservation, landscape architecture.

College of Family and Consumer Sciences (http://www.fcs.uga.edu/): child and family development; foods and nutrition; housing and consumer economics; textiles, merchandising, and interiors.

Warnell School of Forest Resources (http://www.uga.edu/wsfr/): forest resources.

Grady College of Journalism and Mass Communication (http://www.grady.uga.edu/): journalism, mass communication.

School of Law (http://www.lawsch.uga.edu/): law.

College of Pharmacy (http://www.rx.uga.edu/): clinical and administrative sciences, pharmaceutical and biomedical sciences.

School of Public and International Affairs (http://www.uga.edu/spia): international affairs, political science, public administration.

School of Social Work (http://www.ssw.uga.edu/): social work.

College of Veterinary Medicine (http://www.vet.uga.edu/): anatomy and radiology, avian medicine, large animal medicine, medical microbiology, pharmacology, physiology, small animal medicine, veterinary parasitology, veterinary pathology.

Interdisciplinary Concentrations and Certificates (http://graduate.gradsch.uga.edu/bulletin/): applied mathematical science, atmospheric sciences, computer systems engineering, conservation ecology and sustainable development, engineering physics, environmental ethics, geographic information science, gerontology, global policy studies, historic preservation, interdisciplinary qualitative studies, marriage and family therapy, nonprofit organizations, plant protection and pest management, women's studies.

UNIVERSITY OF HOUSTON–CLEAR LAKE

Graduate Study

Programs of Study

The University of Houston–Clear Lake (UHCL) confers five degrees in forty graduate majors: the Master of Arts (M.A.), the Master of Science (M.S.), the Master of Business Administration (M.B.A.), the Master of Healthcare Administration (M.H.A.), and the Master of Healthcare Administration/Master of Business Administration (M.H.A./M.B.A.). The following are the programs of study: accounting (M.S.), business administration (M.B.A.), environmental management (M.S.), finance (M.S.), health-care administration (M.H.A.), health-care administration/business administration (M.H.A./M.B.A.), human resource management (M.A.), management information systems (M.S.), and professional accounting (M.S.) in the School of Business and Public Administration; counseling (M.S.), curriculum and instruction (M.S.), early childhood education (M.S.), educational management (M.S.), instructional technology (M.S.), multicultural studies in education (M.S.), reading (M.S.), and school library and information science (M.S.) in the School of Education; biological sciences (M.S.), chemistry (M.S.), computer engineering (M.S.), computer science (M.S.), computer information systems (M.S.), environmental science (M.S.), mathematical sciences (M.S.), physical sciences (M.S.), software engineering (M.S.), and statistics (M.S.) in the School of Science and Computer Engineering; and behavioral sciences (M.A.), clinical psychology (M.A.), criminology (M.A.), cross-cultural studies (M.A.), family therapy (M.A.), fitness and human performance (M.A.), history (M.A.), humanities (M.A.), literature (M.A.), psychology (M.A.), school psychology (M.A.), sociology (M.A.), and studies of the future (M.S.) in the School of Human Sciences and Humanities.

Research Facilities

The Alfred R. Neumann Library contains more than 650,000 volumes in hard copy, microfilm, and electronic formats. The library receives 2,000 periodical subscriptions. It also offers 130 subscription databases containing electronically searchable abstracts and full-text articles from thousands of scholarly journals. UHCL students may also take advantage of the 2 million volumes of the University of Houston libraries. Texpress Courier Service offers delivery of books and articles from libraries all over Texas within a few days.

Financial Aid

Students may seek financial assistance in the form of loans, grants, scholarships, or part-time employment. Financial assistance is awarded based on demonstrated need as determined by federal and state regulations. Every effort is made to cover the difference between the cost of attending UHCL and the amount of support that a student and/or family can reasonably be expected to provide. Students applying to the Federal Stafford Student Loan Program must be enrolled for a minimum of 6 hours (known as three-quarter time). The University endeavors to ensure that all applications for financial assistance are evaluated in a consistent manner on the basis of a consistent interpretation of need. Students are required to submit the Free Application for Federal Student Aid (FAFSA); forms may be obtained from the institution where the applicant is currently enrolled or from the UHCL Office of Financial Aid. The deadline for filing the FAFSA is the April 1 preceding the academic year for which aid is being requested. Students who file after the deadline may be considered for aid if funds remain available. Although applications for financial assistance can be processed entirely by mail, the Office of Financial Aid welcomes the opportunity to confer with applicants personally. No action on initial requests for aid are taken until the applicant has been officially admitted.

Cost of Study

For 2002–03, Texas residents pay $120 for the first semester hour, $176 for the second semester hour, and $88 per hour after the second semester hour; nonresidents pay $253 per semester hour.

Living and Housing Costs

In 1995, UHCL opened its first on-campus apartment community. Efficiency and two- and four-bedroom units with computer hookups to campus in each bedroom, furniture option, pool/jacuzzi, clubhouse, and on-site resident staff are available for occupancy. Complete housing information packets are available by calling 281-286-5959.

Student Group

Adult students are the special focus of the University of Houston–Clear Lake. More than 75 percent of the students are employed full- or part-time. The average age is 32.

Student Outcomes

UHCL programs support the region's various technological, petrochemical, space, medical, education, computer, commercial, and international trade sectors. Advisory groups from many of these areas advise the schools in their program development to ensure relevancy and immediacy of the University's curriculum to the needs of the job market.

Location

The campus is located in Clear Lake, halfway between downtown Houston and the historic city of Galveston. It is adjacent to Armand Bayou Nature Preserve and the Lyndon B. Johnson Space Center (NASA). The serene wooded setting of the campus provides an ideal atmosphere for study and research, while the great resources of the dynamic Houston metropolitan area are easily accessible.

The University

The University of Houston–Clear Lake was established in 1971 as an upper-level undergraduate and graduate university to serve juniors, seniors, and graduate students. It is one of four campuses governed by the University of Houston System Board of Regents. It is composed of the Schools of Business and Public Administration, Education, Human Sciences and Humanities, and Science and Computer Engineering. UHCL is fully accredited by the Southern Association of Colleges and Schools. The University also has individual accredited programs. The School of Business and Public Administration maintains accreditation by the AACSB International–The Association to Advance Collegiate Schools of Business. The School of Education is accredited by the National Council for Accreditation of Teacher Education (NCATE), which covers all of the institution's initial teacher preparation and advanced educator preparation programs. The School of Education is also accredited by the Texas State Board for Educator Certification. The School of Human Sciences and Humanities holds accreditation by the Commission on Accreditation from Marriage and Family Therapy Education and the National Association of School Psychologists. In addition, the Humanities Program is a full member of the Association for Graduate Liberal Studies Program, and the Clinical Psychology Program is a member of the Council of Applied Masters Programs in Psychology. The university Counseling Services is accredited by the International Association of Counseling Services.

Applying

Any applicant who has earned a bachelor's degree from a regionally accredited college or university and who is eligible to return to the last institution attended may apply for graduate standing. Students must also provide scores on the standardized test specified by their academic division (GRE, GMAT, or MAT). Each program may have additional requirements for admission. To be accepted into a degree program, a student must meet all program admission requirements and obtain both the consent of the associate dean or program director and approval of a plan of study. Applications and supporting credentials should be submitted approximately ninety days before the start of the term in which the student wishes to enter. Students applying to the School of Business and Public Administration must submit applications and credentials by August 1 for fall entry, December 1 for spring entry, and May 1 for summer entry. International students must submit their applications and credentials to the University by March 1 for summer, June 1 for fall, and October 1 for spring.

Correspondence and Information

Office of Enrollment Services
University of Houston–Clear Lake
2700 Bay Area Boulevard
Houston, Texas 77058

Telephone: 281-283-2521
World Wide Web: http://www.uhcl.edu/admissions

THE FACULTY

Administration

President, William A. Staples, Ph.D.
Senior Vice President and Provost, Edward J. Hayes, Ph.D.
Associate Vice President for Academic Affairs, Andrea Bermudez, Ed.D.

School of Business and Public Administration

Dean, School of Business and Public Administration, William T. Cummings, Ph.D.
Associate Dean, School of Business and Public Administration, Joan Bruno, Ph.D.

School of Education

Dean, School of Education, Dennis W. Spuck, Ph.D.
Associate Dean, School of Education, James M. Sherrill, Ph.D.

School of Human Sciences and Humanities

Dean, School of Human Sciences and Humanities, Bruce Palmer, Ph.D.
Associate Dean, School of Human Sciences and Humanities, Howard Eisner, Ed.D.

School of Science and Computer Engineering

Dean, School of Science and Computer Engineering, Charles W. McKay, Ed.D.
Associate Dean, School of Science and Computer Engineering, Robert N. Ferebee, Ph.D.

Atrium II in the Bayou Building provides a focal point for study.

UNIVERSITY OF IDAHO

College of Graduate Studies

Programs of Study

As the land-grant institution and research center of the state of Idaho, the University of Idaho (UI) offers twenty-six doctoral programs, seven specialist degrees, and sixty-six master's degrees. Graduate students are able to pursue degrees full- or part-time.

All of the graduate programs are available on the main campus in Moscow. Graduate programs in education disciplines are available at UI's Coeur d'Alene and Boise centers, graduate programs in engineering and natural resources are available at UI's Boise center, and graduate programs in engineering disciplines and several physical science disciplines are available at the Idaho Falls center. In addition, engineering and psychology (human factors option) graduate programs are available through UI's Video Outreach Program on the Web and through compressed video.

The minimum requirements beyond a bachelor's degree for each graduate degree are as follows: for a doctoral degree, 78 semester credits of course work and a dissertation, successful completion of the departmental preliminary examination, and successful defense of the dissertation; for a specialist degree, 60 semester credits of course work and successful completion of the departmental comprehensive examination; and for a master's degree, between 30 and 60 semester credits (depending on the degree) and successful completion of a thesis, project, or comprehensive examination (depending on the degree).

Research Facilities

Research is a primary function of UI and is significant in each graduate department. UI currently participates in several Experimental Programs to Stimulate Competitive Research (EPSCoR) funded by the National Science Foundation, the Environmental Protection Agency, the National Institutes of Health, and the Department of Energy.

UI has three dozen additional research units, both within individual disciplines and encompassing several departments, including the the Center for Applied Thero-Dynamics Studies; the Center for Secure and Dependable Software; the National Institute for Advanced Transportation Technology; the Center for Hazardous Waste Remediation; the Forest, Wildlife and Range Experiment Station; the Glaciological and Arctic Sciences Institute; the Idaho Agricultural Experiment Station; the Idaho Cooperative Fish and Wildlife Research Unit; the Idaho Geological Survey; the Idaho Water Resources Research Institute; the Institute for Materials and Advanced Processes; the Environmental Research Institute; the Institute for Pacific Northwest Studies; the Laboratory of Anthropology; and the Microelectronics Research and Communications Institute.

The UI libraries contain approximately 2.5 million items, including more than 12,000 serial titles. The main library recently completed a major expansion and renovation.

Financial Aid

Many departments offer teaching assistantships or research assistantships, which include a waiver of nonresident tuition. Information on assistantships may be obtained directly from the appropriate department director of graduate studies. Financial aid is also available through the Federal Perkins Loan Program, the Federal Stafford Student Loan Program, and work-study grants. Information and applications can be provided by the Student Financial Aid Office.

Cost of Study

For 2001–02, full-time graduate fees were $1630 per semester for Idaho residents, with an additional fee of $3000 per semester for nonresidents. Resident students enrolled part-time paid $150 per credit; nonresidents paid an additional $95 per credit for part-time work. Full-time fees are charged for 8 credits or more. Fees are subject to change.

Living and Housing Costs

Graduate student housing is available through the University for $398 to $594 per month for apartments ranging in size from efficiencies to four-bedroom units. Residence hall room and board contracts are available for $3845 to $4973 for the academic year, depending on the meal plan chosen. Potential graduate students are advised to reserve housing early. Off-campus housing lists are available through the student government office (ASUI) in the Student Union Building.

Student Group

Total graduate enrollment at UI for fall 2001 was 2,230 students: 1,545 on the main campus in Moscow and 685 at UI's Coeur d'Alene, Boise, and Idaho Falls instructional centers and through the Outreach Programs. UI enrolls students from all fifty states and from seventy-eight other countries, providing cultural diversity as part of its educational mission.

Location

Moscow is located in the Idaho panhandle among the rolling hills of the Palouse. It is an agricultural and recreational area and is the cultural center of the region. Local music and theater productions have received international acclaim. Skiing and lake and river sports are within easy drives. Spokane is 88 miles north, and Seattle and Portland are each 6 hours west.

The University

The University of Idaho was created in 1889, a year before Idaho became a state. UI is a publicly supported, comprehensive land-grant institution with principal responsibility in Idaho for performing research and granting the Ph.D. degree. More than 750 faculty members participate in teaching and research. In addition to the accreditation of individual programs, the University is accredited by the Northwest Association of Schools and Colleges.

Applying

Information regarding program offerings, deadlines, and requirements and general University information as well as the online application for admission can be accessed on the University's Web site. Requests by mail should be forwarded to the Graduate Admissions Office with an indication of the department or program of interest. All application materials are to be forwarded to the Graduate Admissions Office. Official transcripts from every college and university attended should also be sent directly from the institution to the Graduate Admissions Office.

Correspondence and Information

For information on admission, students may contact:

Graduate Admissions Office
University of Idaho
P.O. Box 443019
Moscow, Idaho 83844-3019

Telephone: 208-885-4001
Fax: 208-885-6198
E-mail: gadms@uidaho.edu
World Wide Web: http://www.uidaho.edu

University of Idaho

FACULTY HEADS

Accountancy (M.Acct.): Marcia Niles (telephone: 885-7238; e-mail: niles@uidaho.edu)
Adult Education (Ed.S.Ad.Ed., M.S., M.Ed., doctoral; through College of Education): James Gregson (telephone: 885-2768; e-mail: jgregson@uidaho.edu)
Agricultural Economics (M.S.): James Nelson (telephone: 885-5217; e-mail: jnelson@uidaho.edu)
Agricultural Education (M.S.): Lou Riesenberg (telephone: 885-6358; e-mail: lriesenb@uidaho.edu)
Animal Physiology (Ph.D.): Mark McGuire (telephone: 885-7683; e-mail: mmcguire@uidaho.edu)
Animal Science (M.S.): Mark McGuire (telephone: 885-7683; e-mail: mmcguire@uidaho.edu)
Anthropology (M.A.): Donald Tyler (telephone: 885-6752; e-mail: dtyler@uidaho.edu)
Architecture (M.A., M.Arch.): Paul Windley (telephone: 885-6272; e-mail: pwindley@uidaho.edu)
Art (M.F.A., M.A.T.): Sally Machlis (telephone: 885-6976; e-mail: sallymac@uidaho.edu)
Biological and Agricultural Engineering (Ph.D., M.S., M.Engr.): James DeShazer (telephone: 885-6182; e-mail: jades@uidaho.edu)
Biological Sciences (M.Nat.Sc.): Pat McCarroll (telephone: 885-6329; e-mail: patm@uidaho.edu)
Botany (Ph.D., M.S.): Pat McCarroll (telephone: 885-6329; e-mail: patm@uidaho.edu)
Business Education (M.Ed.): James Gregson (telephone: 885-2768; e-mail: jgregson@uidaho.edu)
Chemical Engineering (Ph.D., M.S., M.Engr.): Jo Ann Rattey (telephone: 885-6793; e-mail: jrattey@uidaho.edu)
Chemistry (Ph.D., M.S., M.A.T.): Daniel Edwards (telephone: 885-6118; e-mail: edwards@uidaho.edu)
Civil Engineering (Ph.D., M.S., M.Engr.): Sunil Sharma (telephone: 885-6403; e-mail: ssharma@uidaho.edu)
Computer Engineering (M.S., M.Engr.): Susan Santos (telephone: 885-6554; e-mail: ssantos@ece.uidaho.edu)
Computer Science (Ph.D., M.S.): Rhonda Zenner (telephone: 885-6589; e-mail: rzenner@cs.uidaho.edu)
Counseling and Human Services (Ed.S.Couns.Hum.Serv., M.S., M.Ed., doctoral; through College of Education): James Gregson (telephone: 885-2768; e-mail: jgregson@uidaho.edu)
Creative Writing (M.F.A.): Bob Wrigley (telephone: 885-6823; e-mail: rwrigley@uidaho.edu)
Curriculum and Instruction (M.S., M.Ed., doctoral; through College of Education): George Canney (telephone: 885-7712; e-mail: gcanney@uidaho.edu)
Earth Science (M.A.T.): Bill McClelland (telephone: 885-4704; e-mail: wmcclell@uidaho.edu)
Economics (M.S.): S. M. Ghazanar (telephone: 885-7144; e-mail: ghazi@uidaho.edu)
Education (Ph.D., Ed.D., Ed.S.Ed.): Shirley Green (telephone: 885-7456; e-mail: shirleyg@uidaho.edu)
Educational Leadership (Ed.S.Ed.Ldrshp., M.S., M.Ed., doctoral; through College of Education): George Canney (telephone: 885-7712; e-mail: gcanney@uidaho.edu)
Educational Technology (M.Ed.): James Gregson (telephone: 885-2768; e-mail: jgregson@uidaho.edu)
Electrical Engineering (Ph.D., M.S., M.Engr.): Susan Santos (telephone: 885-6554; e-mail: ssantos@ece.uidaho.edu)
Engineering Management (M.Engr.): Sunil Sharma (telephone: 885-6403; e-mail: ssharma@uidaho.edu)
English (M.A., M.A.T.): Richard Fehrenbacher (telephone: 885-5563; e-mail: fehrenba@uidaho.edu)
English as a Second Language, Teaching (M.A.): Richard Fehrenbacher (telephone: 885-5563; e-mail: fehrenba@uidaho.edu)
Entomology (Ph.D., M.S.): Sonia Todd (telephone: 885-6930; e-mail: soniat@uidaho.edu)
Environmental Engineering (M.S., M.Engr.): Margrit von Braun (telephone: 885-6113; e-mail: vonbraun@uidaho.edu)
Environmental Science (M.S.): Margrit von Braun (telephone: 885-6113; e-mail: vonbraun@uidaho.edu)
Family and Consumer Sciences (M.S.): Linda Fox (telephone: 885-6546; e-mail: lfox@uidaho.edu)
Fishery Resources (M.S., doctoral; through College of Natural Resources): Karla Makus (telephone: 885-4006; e-mail: makus@uidaho.edu)
Food Science (M.S.): Denise Smith (telephone: 885-9234; e-mail: dsmith@uidaho.edu)
Forest Products (M.S., doctoral; through College of Natural Resources): Jan Pitkin (telephone: 885-9663; e-mail: jpitkin@uidaho.edu)
Forest Resources (M.S., doctoral; through College of Natural Resources): Brenda Haener (telephone: 885-7952; e-mail: bhaener@uidaho.edu)
Geography (Ph.D., M.S., M.A.T.): Dorota Wilk (telephone: 885-6216; e-mail: dwilk@uidaho.edu)
Geological Engineering (M.S., doctoral; through Materials Metallurgical Mining and Geological Engineering): Sam Froes (telephone: 885-7989; e-mail: froes@uidaho.edu)
Geology (Ph.D., M.S.): Bill McClelland (telephone: 885-4704; e-mail: wmcclell@uidaho.edu)
Geophysics (M.S.): Bill McClelland (telephone: 885-4704; e-mail: wmcclell@uidaho.edu)
History (Ph.D., M.A., M.A.T.): Richard Spence (telephone: 885-6551; e-mail: rspence@uidaho.edu)
Hydrology (M.S., doctoral; through Geological Sciences): Bill McClelland (telephone: 885-4704; e-mail: rspence@uidaho.edu)
Industrial Technology Education (M.S., M.Ed.): James Gregson (telephone: 885-2768; e-mail: jgregson@uidaho.edu)
Interdisciplinary Studies (M.A., M.S.): Roger Wallins (telephone: 885-6243; e-mail: rwallins@uidaho.edu)
Landscape Architecture (M.S.): Stephen Drown (telephone: 885-7448; e-mail: srdrown@uidaho.edu)
Manufacturing Engineering (M.S., M.Engr.): Ralph Budwig (telephone: 885-7454; e-mail: rbudwig@uidaho.edu)
Materials Science (M.S., doctoral; through Materials Metallurgical Mining and Geological Engineering): Sam Foes (telephone: 885-7989; e-mail: froes@uidaho.edu)
Mathematics (Ph.D., M.S., M.A.T.): Monte Boisen (telephone: 885-6742; e-mail: boisen@uidaho.edu)
Mechanical Engineering (Ph.D., M.S., M.Engr.): Ralph Budwig (telephone: 885-7454; e-mail: rbudwig@uidaho.edu)
Metallurgical Engineering (M.S., doctoral; through Materials Metallurgical Mining and Geological Engineering): Sam Froes (telephone: 885-7989; e-mail: froes@uidaho.edu)
Metallurgy (M.S.): Sam Froes (telephone: 885-7989; e-mail: froes@uidaho.edu)
Microbiology, Molecular Biology and Biochemistry (Ph.D., M.S.): Gregory Bohach (telephone: 885-6666; e-mail: gbohach@uidaho.edu)
Mining Engineering (M.S., doctoral; through Materials Metallurgical Mining and Geological Engineering): Sam Froes (telephone: 885-7989; e-mail: froes@uidaho.edu)
Mining Engineering-Metallurgy (Ph.D.): Sam Froes (telephone: 885-7989; e-mail: froes@uidaho.edu)
Music (M.A., M.Mus.): Mary DuPree (telephone: 885-7557; e-mail: mdupree@uidaho.edu)
Natural Resources (M.N.R.): Deena Winterton (telephone: 885-8981; e-mail: deenaw@uidaho.edu)
Physical Education (M.S., M.Ed., doctoral; through College of Education): Calvin Lathen (telephone: 885-7921; e-mail: call@uidaho.edu)
Physics (Ph.D., M.S., M.A.T.): Bernhard Stumpf (telephone: 885-7558; e-mail: bjstumpf@uidaho.edu)
Plant Science (Ph.D., M.S.): Sonia Todd (telephone: 885-6930; e-mail: soniat@uidaho.edu)
Political Science (Ph.D., M.A.): Donald Crowley (telephone: 885-7290; e-mail: crowley@uidaho.edu)
Professional Technology Education (Ed.S.Voc.Ed., M.S., M.Ed., doctoral; through College of Education): James Gregson (telephone: 885-2768; e-mail: jgregson@uidaho.edu)
Psychology (M.S.): Carol Berreth (telephone: 885-6324; e-mail: cberreth@uidaho.edu)
Public Administration (M.P.A.): Florence Heffron (telephone: 885-6120; e-mail: fheffron@uidaho.edu)
Rangeland Ecology and Management (M.S., doctoral; through College of Natural Resources): Kendall Johnson (telephone: 885-6537; e-mail: kjohnson@uidaho.edu)
Recreation (M.S.): Calvin Lathen (telephone: 885-7921; e-mail: call@uidaho.edu)
Resource Recreation and Tourism (M.S., doctoral; through College of Natural Resources): Lehigh McCarroll (telephone: 885-7911; e-mail: rrt@uidaho.edu)
School Psychology (Ed.S.Sch.Psych.): James Gregson (telephone: 885-2768; e-mail: jgregson@uidaho.edu)
Soil Science (Ph.D., M.S.): Sonia Todd (telephone: 885-6930; e-mail: soniat@uidaho.edu)
Special Education (Ed.S.Sp.Ed., M.S., M.Ed., doctoral; through College of Education): George Canney (telephone: 885-7712; e-mail: gcanney@uidaho.edu)
Statistics (M.S.): Barbara Olsen (telephone: 885-2929; e-mail: bolsen@uidaho.edu)
Systems Engineering (M.Engr.): Ralph Budwig (telephone: 885-7454; e-mail: rbudwig@uidaho.edu)
Theatre Arts (M.F.A.): David Lee-Painter (telephone: 885-6197; e-mail: davidlp@uidaho.edu)
Veterinary Science (M.S.): Mark McGuire (telephone: 885-7683; e-mail: mmcguire@uidaho.edu)
Wildlife Resources (M.S., doctoral; through College of Natural Resources): Karla Makus (telephone: 885-4006; e-mail: makus@uidaho.edu)
Zoology (Ph.D., M.S.): Pat McCarroll (telephone: 885-6329; e-mail: patm@uidaho.edu)

UNIVERSITY OF ILLINOIS AT SPRINGFIELD

Graduate Studies

Programs of Study

The University of Illinois at Springfield (UIS) offers master's degrees in eighteen academic programs within four distinct colleges. The College of Business and Management offers the M.A. in accountancy, the M.S. in management information systems, and the M.B.A. in business administration. The College of Education and Human Services offers the M.A. in educational leadership, human development counseling, and human services. The College of Liberal Arts and Sciences offers the M.A. in communication, English, history, and individual option and the M.S. in biology and computer science. The College of Public Affairs and Administration offers the M.A. in environmental studies, legal studies, political studies (two concentrations: practical politics and academic politics), and public affairs reporting and the M.P.A. in public administration, as well as a doctorate in public administration (D.P.A.). A full schedule of courses is offered in the evening and on weekends to accommodate working students. Instruction is also offered via the Internet and through other distance learning technologies.

Internship/practicum experiences are an integral component of several degree programs. A number of paid internship positions in state government and with campus units are also available.

Research Facilities

Brookens Library is a teaching facility that offers students immediate access to more than 520,000 volumes and 2,000 journal subscriptions. In addition, students are linked by computer to the collections of forty-four other academic libraries in the state. The library also houses a media services unit as well as an archives and special collections unit that offers students a chance to conduct research using primary sources. Opportunities for applied research are coordinated through UIS's public affairs centers, which share a common emphasis on coordinated, interdisciplinary approaches to problem solving, training, and communication.

Financial Aid

The Office of Financial Assistance administers institutional, local, state, and federal grant and loan programs. Every attempt is made to meet the needs of eligible students by "packaging" funds from available sources. A variety of graduate assistantships and internships, with stipends and tuition waivers, are available.

Cost of Study

The fall 2002 in-state tuition for graduate students is $123 per semester hour (1–16 hours). Tuition for nonresident graduate students is $369.60 per semester hour (1–16 hours). Additional fees are assessed. All rates are subject to change without notice.

Living and Housing Costs

Modern apartment-style on-campus housing is designed to meet the varying needs of individual students and student families. One-, two-, and four-bedroom furnished and unfurnished apartments and new four-bedroom townhouses were available at rates ranging from $684 to $2502 per semester in fall 2001. The Housing Office also maintains a listing of privately owned houses and apartments for rent in the Springfield area.

Student Group

In the 2001 fall semester, UIS enrolled more than 4,000 students, approximately 46 percent of whom were graduate students. While many of the full-time graduate students are in the traditional age group of 22 to 24, a sizable number are 30 and older. Nearly 66 percent of those enrolled are women. About 38 percent of UIS's students attend full-time. Approximately 12 percent are members of underrepresented groups, including American Indians, African Americans, Asian/Pacific Islanders, and Hispanics. In the fall of 2001 international students represented 4 percent of the total student population.

Student Outcomes

Many graduates of UIS have achieved leadership and management positions in state government, private industry, print and broadcast media, and not-for-profit associations.

Location

Springfield derives much of its character from its location in the state's rural heartland. Yet, with St. Louis less than 100 miles to the southwest and Chicago less than 200 miles to the northeast, Springfield offers its more than 100,000 residents easy access to these large urban centers. Major employers in the area are local, state, and federal government; health-care delivery systems; the banking industry; insurance companies; and other service industries.

The University

UIS emphasizes excellence in teaching, curricular flexibility, and public affairs instruction and research. Situated on 746 acres near Lake Springfield, the campus includes the Public Affairs Center with its 2,017-seat performing arts auditorium, a Health and Sciences Building, a television office, and a public radio station. All classes are taught by faculty members who also serve as student advisers and mentors. With a low student-faculty ratio, UIS is able to offer a small, private atmosphere at affordable state rates.

Applying

Admission to graduate studies is open to students who have earned a bachelor's degree from an accredited institution with a grade point average of 2.5 or better on a 4.0 scale. Students must also meet the requirements of the specific program in which they wish to enroll. Applicants to the D.P.A. program must also hold a master's degree (minimum GPA of 3.25). For maximum consideration, all applications and transcripts should arrive at least three months prior to the term in which the student wishes to begin course work. Requirements for each program are outlined in the UIS catalog, which is available upon request.

Correspondence and Information

Office of Admissions and Records
University of Illinois at Springfield
P.O. Box 19243
Springfield, Illinois 62794-9243
Telephone: 217-206-6626
800-252-8533 (toll-free)
Fax: 217-206-6620
World Wide Web: http://www.uis.edu

University of Illinois at Springfield

FACULTY HEADS

College of Business and Management
Dr. Paul McDevitt, Interim Dean.
Accountancy: Dr. John Nosari, Chair.
Business Administration: Dr. John Palmer, Director.
Management Information Systems: Dr. Rassule Hadidi, Chair.

College of Education and Human Services
Dr. Larry Stonecipher, Dean.
Educational Leadership: Dr. James Cherry, Convener.
Human Development Counseling: Dr. Larry Stonecipher, Convener.
Human Services: Dr. Rachell Anderson, Convener.

College of Liberal Arts and Sciences
Dr. William L. Bloemer, Dean.
Biology: Dr. Gary Butler, Convener.
Communication: Mary Bohlen, Convener.
Computer Science: Dr. Ted Mims, Convener
English: Dr. Marcellus Leonard, Convener.
History: Dr. Cecilia Cornell, Convener.
Individual Option: Dr. Jan Droegkamp, Convener.

College of Public Affairs and Administration
Dr. Glen Hahn Cope, Dean.
Environmental Studies: Dr. Malcolm Levin, Chair.
Legal Studies: Dr. Anne Draznin, Chair.
Political Studies: Dr. Calvin Mouw, Chair.
Public Administration: (M.P.A.) Dr. Anthony A. Sisneros, Director.
(D.P.A.) Dr. Beverly Bunch, Director.
Public Affairs Reporting: Charles N. Wheeler III, Director.
Public Health: Dr. Remi Imeokparia, Chair.

UofL

UNIVERSITY OF LOUISVILLE

Graduate School

Programs of Study

The Graduate School of the University of Louisville offers programs of study leading to the degree of Doctor of Philosophy in anatomical sciences and neurobiology, applied and industrial mathematics, art history, biochemistry and molecular biology, biostatistics–decision science, chemical engineering, chemistry, civil engineering, clinical psychology, computer science and engineering, English, environmental biology, epidemiology: clinical investigation sciences, experimental psychology, industrial engineering, microbiology and immunology, pharmacology and toxicology, physiology and biophysics, social work, and urban and public affairs. A Doctor of Audiology degree is also offered. The Doctor of Education degree is offered in three areas of concentration. Degree programs combining medicine or dentistry with a number of pure and applied science fields are also offered. Programs of study leading to the master's degree are available in more than sixty different areas, including interdisciplinary studies. The Master of Arts in Teaching degree is offered for prospective elementary, secondary, and junior college teachers.

Each student is expected to take those courses required for advancement of general knowledge in his or her discipline as well as courses in a field of specialization. Although guidelines for study have been established by each department, curricula may be tailored to meet the needs, abilities, and interests of the student. All appropriate courses offered by the University are open to the doctoral student, with permission of the instructor. The doctoral degree is awarded in recognition of creative scholarship and research, and therefore some degree of flexibility exists regarding curricular requirements. In general, a thesis or dissertation of significant value and quality, developed under the supervision of a faculty preceptor, is required. The doctoral student usually completes the program in about four to five years of full-time work, whereas the master's programs usually require two years of study.

Research Facilities

The University has a number of outstanding on-campus research facilities and, as a member of ORAU, provides access to the facilities and educational programs of Oak Ridge National Laboratory. The Kentucky Institute for the Environment and Sustainable Development provides an exciting venue for interdisciplinary research in environmental science, policy, and education. The Urban Studies Institute is in direct contact with the community through public service and research related to problems of urban life, community development, and city planning. New, state of-the-art research buildings have been constructed on the Health Sciences campus and house numerous centers and institutes, including Cellular Therapeutics, Genetics and Molecular Medicine, and Molecular Cardiology. The Kentucky Lions Eye Research Institute is a modern 75,000-square-foot facility equipped for molecular biological, biochemical, physicochemical, electrophysiological, morphometric, and transgenic studies of the eye and the visual system. The General Electric Factory Automation Laboratory provides a model factory environment and includes a rapid prototyping center, industrial robots, computer-aided engineering facilities, and space for research and development projects. The University Libraries, a member of the Association of Research Libraries, has holdings of more than 1.3 million volumes and microtexts and nearly 13,000 serials. Students also have access to the collections of six other area institutions.

Financial Aid

A number of awards are available. In general, teaching and research assistantships for 2002–03 vary from $10,000 to $15,000 in stipend and include full tuition remission and health insurance. Doctoral fellowships are available and carry a stipend of $18,000 plus full tuition remission and health insurance.

Cost of Study

In 2002–03, full-time tuition is $16,316 per year for nonresidents and $5924 per year for Kentucky residents. Student fees are prorated on a credit-hour basis; however, full-time is considered 9 credit hours each semester and 6 credit hours in the summer.

Living and Housing Costs

Housing is available for single and married students on the University of Louisville's main campus, 10 minutes from the Health Sciences Center. In 2002–03, a dormitory room for 2 students is approximately $2470 per year; a single room is $3720 per year. Partially furnished apartments for married students cost $498, $573, and $685 for an efficiency, one-bedroom, or two-bedroom apartment, respectively, including utilities.

Student Group

More than 4,300 graduate students are enrolled in various departments of the University. Approximately one fourth are working toward doctorates. Students come from all areas of the United States and a number of other countries.

Location

The greater Louisville area, situated on the Ohio River, includes more than three quarters of a million people. Resident opera, art, theater, choral, ballet, and orchestral societies provide Louisville with cultural resources beyond those typically available in cities of comparable size. The surrounding countryside is rich in natural resources; many local and state parks provide a variety of outdoor activities. Each May, the famed Kentucky Derby is held at Churchill Downs in Louisville.

The University

The University traces its history to 1798 with the founding of the Jefferson Seminary. It became the University of Louisville in 1846 and a part of the state university system in 1970. Among its major divisions are the College of Arts and Sciences, College of Business and Public Administration, Graduate School, Kent School of Social Work, Speed Scientific School (engineering), School of Law, School of Music, and College of Education and Human Development, which are located on the main campus about 2 miles from the downtown area. The School of Medicine, School of Dentistry, School of Nursing, and School of Public Health are located in the heart of a growing sixteen-square-block Health Sciences Center. The University of Louisville is a member of the Kentuckiana Metroversity, which aims at cooperative ventures among the six institutions of higher education in the area, and is a Doctoral/Research University–Extensive (among the top 3.8 percent in the nation) in the Carnegie rankings.

Applying

For application information and deadline dates, students should contact the department to which they wish to apply.

Correspondence and Information

Graduate School
University of Louisville
Louisville, Kentucky 40292
E-mail: graduate@louisville.edu
World Wide Web: http://www.graduate.louisville.edu

FACULTY HEADS

ADMINISTRATION

Ronald M. Atlas, Ph.D., Dean.
Richard W. Stremel Ph.D., Associate Dean.
Michael J. Cuyjet, Ed.D., Associate Dean.

PROGRAM AREAS AND AREAS OF ADVANCED TRAINING

All e-mail addresses are followed by @louisville.edu unless otherwise specified.

Accountancy: Julia Karcher, Ph.D., Director (e-mail: jnkarco1@gwise.louisville.edu).
Anatomical Sciences and Neurobiology: Fred Roisen, Ph.D., Chair (e-mail: fjrois01@gwise.louisville.edu).
Audiology: Ian M. Windmill, Ph.D., Director (e-mail: imwind01@gwise.louisville.edu).
Biochemistry and Molecular Biology: Robert Gray, Ph.D., Acting Chair (e-mail: rdgray01@gwise.louisville.edu).
Biology: Ronald Fell, Ph.D., Chair (e-mail: rfell). Advanced training: biosystematics, biotechnology, ecology, environmental biology, microbiology, molecular biology, physiology.
Biostatistics–Decision Science: W. Paul McKinney, M.D., Director (e-mail: wpmcki01).
Business Administration: Robert Taylor, Ph.D., Dean of the College of Business and Public Administration (e-mail: robert.l.taylor).
Chemical Engineering: Thomas L. Starr, Ph.D., Chair (e-mail: tlstar01@gwise.louisville.edu). Advanced training: advanced process control, advanced materials, catalysis, pollution prevention, polymer processing, chemical vapor deposition, chemical sensors, thin-film applications.
Chemistry: George Pack, Ph.D., Chair (e-mail: george.pack). Advanced training: analytical chemistry, inorganic chemistry, organic chemistry, physical chemistry, chemical physics.
Civil Engineering: Mark N. French, Ph.D., Director (e-mail: mnfren01). Advanced training: Civil and environmental engineering.
Classical and Modern Languages: Wendy Pfeffer, Ph.D., Chair (e-mail: pfeffer). Advanced training: French, Spanish.
Communicative Disorders: David R. Cunningham, Ph.D., Chair (e-mail: drcunn01@gwise.louisville.edu).
Computer Engineering and Computer Science: Adel S. Elmaghraby, Ph.D., Acting Chair (e-mail: aselma01@gwise.louisville.edu).
Computer Science and Engineering: Rammohan K. Ragade, Ph.D., Coordinator (e-mail: rkraga01@gwise.louisville.edu). Advanced training: computationally intensive applications, hardware engineering, software engineering.
Education: John F. Welsh, Ph.D., Acting Dean, College of Education and Human Development (e-mail: jfwels01); Linda Irwin-Devitis, Ed.D., Associate Dean (e-mail: ladevi01). Advanced training: Ed.D. in counseling and personnel services, educational administration, and educational supervision (includes a concentration in special education).
Electrical and Computer Engineering: Peter B. Aronhime, Ph.D., Director (e-mail: pbaron01).
English: Beth A. Boehm, Ph.D., Acting Chair and Director of Graduate Studies (e-mail: baboeh01@gwise.louisville.edu). Advanced training: computer-assisted instruction, critical theory, professional writing, rhetoric and composition, rhetoric of science, writing assessment, literature, literature with creative writing emphasis.
Epidemiology: Clinical Investigation Sciences: Carlton A. Hornung, Ph.D., M.P.H., Director (e-mail: cahorn01@gwise.louisville.edu)
Exercise Physiology: Bryant A. Stamford, Ph.D., Director (e-mail: bryant).
Expressive Therapies: Laura A. Cherry, Ph.D., Director (e-mail: lacher01).
Fine Arts: James T. Grubola, M.F.A., Chair (e-mail: grubola); Thomas Buser, Ph.D., Art History Program Director (e-mail: tabuse01@gwise.louisville.edu). Advanced training: architectural history, art history.
History: Thomas C. Mackey, Ph.D., Chair (e-mail: thomasmackey). Advanced training: ancient-medieval, modern European, U.S. history, U.S. history with oral-public history concentration.
Humanities: Elaine O. Wise, M.A., Chair (e-mail: elaine.wise).
Industrial Engineering: Suraj M. Alexander, Ph.D., Chair (e-mail: suraj.alexander). Advanced training: ergonomics and human factors, manufacturing engineering, production systems engineering, operations research and logistics.
Interdisciplinary Studies: Michael J. Cuyjet, Ed.D., Associate Dean, Graduate School (e-mail: cuyjet).
Justice Administration: Deborah G. Wilson, Ph.D., Chair (e-mail: dgwilson).
Mathematics: Kevin Clancey, Ph.D., Chair (e-mail: kfclan01). Advanced training: applied analysis, combinatorics and graph theory, financial and actuarial mathematics, functional equations.
Mechanical Engineering: Glen Prater Jr., Ph.D., Chair (e-mail: gprater).
Microbiology and Immunology: Robert D. Stout, Ph.D., Chair. (e-mail: bobstout). Advanced training: cellular and molecular immunology, genetics and pathogenesis, microbial physiology, molecular virology.
Music: Christopher P. Doane, Ph.D., Dean, School of Music (e-mail: cpdoan01); Jean M. Christensen, Ph.D., Chair, Music History (e-mail: jmchri01@gwise.louisville.edu). Advanced training: music history (Spanish medieval renaissance theory, early music performance, twentieth-century music history), music education, music performance, theory and composition; Robert Amchin, Ph.D., Chair (e-mail: robamchin@aol.com). Music education.
Nursing: Mary H. Mundt, Ph.D., Dean, School of Nursing (e-mail: mhmund01@gwise.louisville.edu). Advanced training: adult nurse practitioner, adult acute-care clinical specialist, neonatal nurse practitioner, psychiatric–mental health clinical specialist.
Oral Biology: John Firriolo, D.D.S., Director (e-mail: fjfirr01@gwise.louisville.edu).
Pharmacology and Toxicology: David Hein, Ph.D., Chair (e-mail: d.hein).
Physics: Joseph S. Chalmers, Ph.D., Chair (e-mail: chalmers).
Physiology and Biophysics: Irving G. Joshua, Ph.D., Chair (e-mail: igjosh01@gwise.louisville.edu). Advanced training: cardiopulmonary physiology, exercise physiology, hypertension, microcirculation, microvascular control mechanisms, smooth-muscle function.
Political Science: Charles E. Ziegler, Ph.D., Chair (e-mail: cezieg01@gwise.louisville.edu). Advanced training: American politics, urban politics, comparative politics and international relations, policy and administration.
Psychological and Brain Sciences: Dennis Molfese, Ph.D., Chair (e-mail: dmolfese). Advanced training: clinical psychology (anxiety disorders, behavioral medicine, forensics, mental health and aging), experimental psychology (cognition, perception and sensory physiology, social psychology, visual science).
Public Administration: Hank Savitch, Ph.D., Chair (e-mail: hvsavi01@gwise.louisville.edu). Advanced training: labor and public management, public policy and administration, urban development and environment.
Social Work: Terry Singer, Ph.D., Dean, Kent School of Social Work (e-mail: terry.singer); Ruth Huber, Ph.D., Director, Doctoral Program (e-mail: ruth.huber).
Sociology: Wayne M. Usui, Ph.D., Acting Chair (e-mail: wayne.usui).
Theater Arts: Russell J. Vandenbroucke, D.F.A., Chair (e-mail: rjvand01). Advanced training: acting, design/technical theater, directing.
Urban Planning: Thomas S. Lyons, Ph.D., Director (e-mail: tslyon01@gwise.louisville.edu). Advanced training: administration of planning organizations, land use and environmental planning, spatial analysis for planning.
Urban and Public Affairs: Steven Bourassa, Ph.D., Chair (e-mail: steven.bourassa). Advanced training: environmental policy and planning, urban planning and development, urban policy and administration.

UNIVERSITY OF MARYLAND, BALTIMORE

Graduate School

Programs of Study

The Graduate School at the University of Maryland, Baltimore (UMB) offers M.A., M.S., and Ph.D. degrees in the following areas: anatomy and neurobiology, applied and professional ethics, biochemistry, dental hygiene, epidemiology, gerontology (Ph.D. only) human genetics, marine-environmental-estuarine studies, medical and research technology, microbiology and immunology, molecular and cell biology, neuroscience and cognitive sciences, nursing, oral and craniofacial biological sciences (including cellular and molecular biology, infectious disease, and neuroscience), oral biology, oral pathology, pathology (forensic toxicology and medical pathology), pharmaceutical sciences, pharmacology and experimental therapeutics, pharmaceutical health services research, physical and rehabilitative science, physiology, preventive medicine, social work (Ph.D. only), and toxicology.

Several programs such as biochemistry, marine-environmental-estuarine studies, molecular and cell biology, neuroscience and cognitive sciences, and toxicology are offered jointly with the University of Maryland, Baltimore County (UMBC) in nearby Catonsville, Maryland, and the University of Maryland, College Park. There are also joint professional/graduate programs, including M.D./Ph.D., D.D.S./Ph.D., and D.D.S./M.S. programs.

Research Facilities

Grant and contract support to UMB totaled $225 million in fiscal year 2001. Major funding sources include the National Science Foundation (NSF), the National Institutes of Health (NIH), and the State of Maryland. In addition to benefiting from the resources of the six professional schools, UMB researchers work closely with investigators at the Medical Biotechnology Center, University of Maryland Medical System, the Veterans Affairs Medical Center, and other area universities. The Institute for Human Virology at UMB is world renowned for its research in related areas.

Financial Aid

Graduate research and teaching assistantships with stipends beginning at $18,000 as well as remission of tuition and health insurance are available to selected applicants. Graduate School fellowships and aid in the form of loans and work-study opportunities are also available.

Cost of Study

Tuition for graduate study was $281 per credit hour for Maryland residents and $503 per credit hour for nonresidents in 2001–02. Fees average approximately $200 per student per semester.

Living and Housing Costs

A limited number of on-campus rooms are available. Apartments and townhouses are available near campus in quiet, pleasant neighborhoods. The Housing and Student Union Office assists students in locating suitable housing.

Student Group

Of UMB's 6,000 students, nearly 1,300 are graduate students. Approximately 37 percent of the graduate population are enrolled in Ph.D. programs, 48 percent are master's degree candidates, and the remaining 15 percent are non-degree students.

Student Outcomes

Students who have completed their Ph.D. degrees from UMB within the past five years are currently pursuing postdoctoral research at major universities and government agencies such as the National Institutes of Health and the Food and Drug Administration; others are assistant professors at schools including the University of Chicago and the University of Cairo; also, many graduates are advancing drug development and delivery in the pharmaceutical industry and contributing to the research and policy activities of agencies as diverse as the Department of Defense, the Maryland Department of the Environment, and the Population Council of New York.

Location

Located in downtown Baltimore, UMB is just blocks from the city's famous Inner Harbor area. Oriole Park at Camden Yards, Ravens Stadium, the Galleria shopping area, the National Aquarium, and the Maryland Science Center are all within easy walking distance of the campus. UMB comprises much of the University Center area of Baltimore, a rapidly growing biotechnology and health science center. The campus also benefits from its proximity to the resources of Washington, D.C., as well as to the recreational areas of Western Maryland, Annapolis, and the Chesapeake Bay.

The University

The University of Maryland, Baltimore, is home to six professional schools (Law, Medicine, Dentistry, Pharmacy, Social Work, Nursing) in addition to the Graduate School. Chartered in 1807, UMB is Maryland's first public university. It is now one of America's fastest growing biomedical research centers. According to the National Science Foundation, the University is among America's top sixty universities in research and development spending. The Human Services/Health Sciences Library, the fifteenth largest of its kind in the United States, serves as the regional medical library for the National Library of Medicine. Moreover, *U.S. News & World Report* recently ranked UMB's School of Nursing, which offers its graduate programs through the Graduate School, sixth in the nation.

Applying

Degree-seeking candidates are required to submit a completed application form, a $50 application fee, three letters of recommendation, official transcripts from all prior institutions, and official GRE score reports. International students must submit official TOEFL score reports. Applicants should also consult application materials for program-specific requirements and deadline dates. The application is available at the World Wide Web address listed below.

Correspondence and Information

Interested individuals should write directly to the department chair or graduate program director of their area of interest for information on program opportunities and requirements and assistantships. For general information and applications, students should contact:

Keith T. Brooks, Director
Graduate Admissions and Enrollment Services
Graduate School
University of Maryland, Baltimore
621 West Lombard Street, Room 336
Baltimore, Maryland 21201
Telephone: 410-706-7131
410-706-7714 (TTY/TDD)
Fax: 410-706-3473
E-mail: gradinfo@umaryland.edu
World Wide Web: http://graduate.umaryland.edu

GRADUATE PROGRAMS

The following lists graduate degree programs, degrees offered, and the names of faculty members in charge of the administration of the graduate programs at UMB.

UMB GRADUATE SCHOOL

Dental School

Dental Hygiene: M.S.; Ms. Linda DeVore, Chair; Ms. M. Elaine Parker, Director.
Oral Biology: M.S.; Dr. Glenn Minah, Director.
Oral and Craniofacial Biological Sciences: M.S., Ph.D.; Dr. Ronald Dubner, Chair; Dr. Norman Capra, Director.
Cellular and Molecular Biology Track: Dr. Renty Franklin, Contact Person.
Infectious Disease Track: Dr. Robert Nauman, Contact Person.
Neuroscience Track: Dr. Norman Capra, Contact Person.
Oral Pathology: M.S.; Dr. John Sauk, Chair; Dr. Bernard Levy, Director.

School of Medicine

Anatomy and Neurobiology: Ph.D.; Dr. Michael T. Shipley, Chair; Dr. George Markelonis, Director.
Biochemistry: M.S., Ph.D.; Dr. Giuseppe Inesi, Chair; Dr. David Weber, Director.
Epidemiology and Preventive Medicine: M.S., Ph.D., M.S./M.D., M.D./Ph.D.; Dr. Paul Stolley, Chair; Dr. Patricia Langenberg, Director.
Gerontology: Ph.D.; Dr. Jay Magaziner, Director.
Human Genetics: M.S., Ph.D., M.D./Ph.D.; Dr. Miriam Blitzer, Director.
Medical and Research Technology: M.S.; Dr. Denise Harmening, Chair; Dr. Ivana Vucenik, Director.
Microbiology and Immunology: M.S., Ph.D.; Dr. Jan Cerny, Chair; Dr. Harry Mobley, Director.
Molecular and Cell Biology: Ph.D.; Dr. Peter Melera, Director.
Neuroscience and Cognitive Sciences: Ph.D.; Dr. Michael Shipley, Chair; Dr. Asaf Keller, Director.
Pathology: M.S., Ph.D., M.D./Ph.D.; Dr. Sanford Stass, Interim Chair; Dr. Anne Hamburger, Director.
Pharmacology and Experimental Therapeutics: M.S., Ph.D., M.D./Ph.D.; Dr. Edson Albuquerque, Chair; Dr. David Burt, Director.
Physical and Rehabilitative Science: Ph.D.; Dr. Jill Whitall, Director.
Physiology: M.S., Ph.D., M.D./Ph.D.; Dr. Mordecai Blaustein, Chair; Dr. Robert Koos, Director.

School of Nursing

Nursing: M.S., Ph.D.; Dr. Barbara Heller, Dean; Dr. Louise Jenkins, Director of Doctoral Program.

School of Pharmacy

Pharmaceutical Sciences: M.S., Ph.D.; Dr. Russell DiGate, Chair; Dr. James Polli, Director.
Pharmaceutical Health Services Research: M.S., Ph.D.; Dr. Gary Smith, Acting Chair; Dr. C. Daniel Mullins, Director.

School of Social Work

Social Work: Ph.D.; Dr. Jesse Harris, Dean; Dr. Julianne Oktay, Director.

Multicampus Programs

Applied and Professional Ethics: M.A.; Dr. Susan Dwyer (UMBC), Director.
Biochemistry: Ph.D.; Dr. David Weber, Joint Program Director.
Marine-Estuarine-Environmental Science: M.S., Ph.D.; Dr. Kennedy T. Paynter, Acting Executive Director (UMCP); Dr. Brian Bradley (UMBC) and Dr. Robert Nauman (UMB), Directors.
Toxicology: M.S., Ph.D.; Dr. Bruce Fowler, Director.

UNIVERSITY OF MARYLAND, BALTIMORE COUNTY

Graduate Studies

Programs of Study

The University of Maryland, Baltimore County (UMBC) Graduate School offers more than forty graduate degrees at the master's and doctoral levels and a number of postbaccalaureate certificates. Graduate degrees are offered in computer science and information systems, education, emergency health services, engineering, modern languages (French, German, Spanish), the liberal arts and humanities, the natural sciences and mathematics, public policy, social sciences, and the visual arts. A wide range of disciplinary, interdisciplinary, and professional programs prepare students for further graduate study, new careers, and career advancement.

More than 400 graduate faculty members, approximately 2,000 graduate students, and more than $80 million in external support for research and training provide a rich environment for graduate education. Graduates go on to careers in such fields as university teaching and research, business, industry, government, the arts, and education. Opportunities for interdisciplinary collaboration are encouraged through more than twenty UMBC research centers and institutes. Graduate students take advantage of the University's proximity to the vast array of Baltimore-Washington research sites. Research innovations are actively shared with industry and government partners through collaborative studies, joint training programs, shared facilities, and technology transfer.

The University of Maryland Graduate School, Baltimore, created in 1985, represents the combined graduate and research programs at UMBC and the University of Maryland, Baltimore (UMB). This combined graduate school provides UMBC students access to courses, practical experiences, and research opportunities—including the schools of law, medicine, pharmacy, dentistry, nursing, and social work—at the UMB campus.

Research Facilities

Exceptional research facilities are available to graduate students in all disciplines at UMBC. The University offers state-of-the-art computer facilities and well-equipped laboratories for research in the social, physical, and biological sciences. The University is home to six high-field NMR spectrometers, including an 800-MHz instrument as well as a high-resolution four-sector mass spectrometer; Fourier-transform ion cyclotron resonance mass spectrometer; and X-ray diffraction facility.

The Albin O. Kuhn Library has a collection of more than 750,000 books and bound journals, more than 4,000 current journals and subscriptions, and well over 1.5 million photographs, slides, maps, music scores, recordings, microforms, and government documents. In addition, graduate students have access to the other libraries of the University System of Maryland campuses as well as to the Peabody Library and the Enoch Pratt Free Library in Baltimore, the Library of Congress, and other outstanding libraries in the Baltimore-Washington area.

Financial Aid

Graduate assistantships (research, teaching, and administrative) are available to qualified, full-time, degree-seeking students and are awarded and administered through the departments. Doctoral assistantship levels are competitive with other major research universities. Financial aid for students who demonstrate need is available in the form of government loans, work-study opportunities, and grants-in-aid.

Cost of Study

Tuition for graduate courses for the 2001–02 academic year was $292 per credit hour for Maryland residents and $480 per credit hour for nonresidents. Nonrefundable fees were approximately $459 per semester (or $51 per credit hour) for a graduate student carrying a full 9-credit load.

Living and Housing Costs

Graduate students are able to find reasonably priced apartments in the Baltimore area with monthly rentals starting at about $500. Several apartment developments are located near campus. There is no graduate student housing on campus.

Student Group

UMBC has a current graduate school enrollment of approximately 1,500 students who come from thirty-eight states and thirty-nine countries. A wide variety of cultural events enrich campus life. There is an active Graduate Student Association and an Office of Graduate Student Life.

Location

UMBC is situated approximately 6 miles from downtown Baltimore on a 474-acre suburban site. A convenient shuttle bus links the campus to the surrounding residential neighborhoods, the downtown campus of UMB, the nearby Baltimore–Washington International Airport, and the Amtrak and commuter train stations. Students profit from the immense concentration of academic, cultural, and recreational facilities in the Baltimore-Washington urban centers.

The University

UMBC is a medium-sized research university. When founded in 1966, UMBC joined the state's oldest campus, the University of Maryland, Baltimore, in serving the public higher education and research needs of the Baltimore area. With more than 10,000 undergraduate, graduate, and postdoctoral students, UMBC is large enough to provide students with excellent training and research opportunities and small enough for close student-faculty interaction.

Applying

The application process involves submitting the completed application form, official college transcripts, and three letters of recommendation. Graduate Record Examinations (GRE) scores are required for most programs. International students are generally required to submit TOEFL scores. Details are available with the application materials. The application fee of $45 is neither waived nor deferred.

For information on programs or applications for assistantships, students may write to the appropriate Graduate Program Director. Program and course descriptions, class schedules, application forms, faculty research interests, and other campus information are available on the UMBC Web site (listed below). For applications and general admission information, students may contact the Office of Graduate Admissions at the address listed below.

Correspondence and Information

Office of Graduate Admissions
University of Maryland, Baltimore County
1000 Hilltop Circle
Baltimore, Maryland 21250
Telephone: 410-455-2537
Fax: 410-455-1130
E-mail: umbcgrad@umbc.edu
World Wide Web: http://www.umbc.edu

THE FACULTY

Dean, Graduate School: Dr. Scott A. Bass. Telephone: 410-455-2199.
Dean, College of Arts and Sciences: Dr. G. Rickey Welch. Telephone: 410-455-2385.
Dean, College of Engineering: Dr. Shlomo Carmi. Telephone: 410-455-3270.

GRADUATE PROGRAM DIRECTORS

COMPUTER SCIENCE AND INFORMATION SYSTEMS

Computer Science (M.S., Ph.D.): Dr. Charles Nicolas. Telephone: 410-455-1433; e-mail: sschne1@umbc.edu; Web site: http://www.cs.umbc.edu/

Information Systems (M.S., Ph.D.): Dr. Andrew Sears. Telephone: 410-455-3795; e-mail: ifsm-gradinfo@umbc.edu; Web site: http://www.ifsm.umbc.edu/

EDUCATION

Post-Baccalaureate Teacher Education (Early Childhood, Elementary, Secondary), Urban Teacher Education, Experienced Teacher Program, Training Systems, Distance Learning, ESOL/Bilingual (M.A., certificates): Dr. Susan Blunck. Telephone: 410-455-3388; e-mail: blackwel@umbc.edu; Web site: http://www.umbc.edu/education/

ENGINEERING

Chemical and Biochemical Engineering (M.S., Ph.D., certificate): Dr. Govind Rao. Telephone: 410-455-3400; e-mail: manderso@umbc.edu; Web site: http://www.umbc.edu/cbe/

Electrical Engineering (M.S., Ph.D.): Dr. Joel Morris. Telephone: 410-455-1433; e-mail: sschne1@umbc.edu; Web site: http://www.cs.umbc.edu/

Engineering Management (M.S.): Dr. Christian von Kerczek. Telephone: 410-455-3313; e-mail: kerczek@engr.umbc.edu; Web site: http://www.umbc.edu/GradProg/engm/html

Mechanical Engineering (M.S., Ph.D., certificates): Dr. Tim Topoleski. Telephone: 410-455-3330; e-mail: taylor@engr.umbc.edu; Web site: http://www.umbc.edu/engineering/me/

GERONTOLOGY

Gerontology (Ph.D.): Dr. Kevin Eckert. Telephone: 410-455-2960; e-mail: eckert@umbc.edu; Web site: http://www.gerontologyphd.umaryland.edu/

HEALTH

Emergency Health Services (M.S.): Dr. Rick Bissell. Telephone: 410-455-3776; e-mail: bissell@umbc.edu; Web site: http://ehs.umbc.edu/

LIBERAL ARTS AND THE HUMANITIES

Ethics (Applied and Professional) (M.A.): Dr. Susan Dwyer. Telephone: 410-455-2005; e-mail: dwyer@umbc.edu; Web site: http://www.umbc.edu/philosophy/mape/

Historical Studies (M.A.): Dr. Rebecca Boehling. Telephone: 410-455-2093; e-mail: boehling@umbc.edu; Web site: http://novell.umbc.edu/history/

Language, Literacy, and Culture (Ph.D.): Dr. JoAnn Crandall. Telephone: 410-455-2313/3061; e-mail: llc@umbc.edu; Web site: http://www.umbc.edu/llc/

MODERN LANGUAGES AND INTERCULTURAL COMMUNICATION

Intercultural Communication (M.A.): Dr. Ed Larkey. Telephone: 410-455-2109; e-mail: johnson@umbc.edu; Web site: http://www.umbc.edu/mml/mcc/

LIFE SCIENCES

Biochemistry (Ph.D.): Dr. Michael Summers. Telephone: 410-455-2491; e-mail: amahon1@gl.umbc.edu; Web site: http://research.umbc.edu/~smith/chem/chem.html

Biological Sciences (M.S., Ph.D.): Dr. Daphne Blumberg. Telephone: 877-UMBC-BIO; e-mail: biograd@umbc.edu; Web site: http://www.umbc.edu/biosci/

Chemistry (M.S., Ph.D.): Dr. William LaCourse. Telephone: 410-455-2491; e-mail: chemgrad@umbc.edu; Web site: http://research.umbc.edu/~smith/chem/chem.html

Marine, Estuarine and Environmental Science (M.S., Ph.D.): Dr. Thomas Cronin. Telephone: 877-UMBC-BIO; e-mail: biograd@umbc.edu; Web site: http://www.umbc.edu/biosci/

Molecular and Cell Biology (Ph.D.): Dr. Philip Farabaugh. Telephone: 877-UMBC-BIO; e-mail: biograd@umbc.edu; Web site: http://www.umbc.edu/biosci/

Molecular Biology (Applied) (M.S.): Dr. Nessly Craig. Telephone: 877-UMBC-BIO; e-mail: biograd@umbc.edu; Web site: http://www.umbc.edu/biosci/

Neuroscience and Cognitive Sciences (Ph.D.): Dr. Phyllis Robinson. Telephone: 877-UMBC-BIO; e-mail: biograd@umbc.edu; Web site: http://www.umbc.edu/biosci/

NATURAL SCIENCES AND MATHEMATICS

Mathematics (Applied) (M.S., Ph.D.): Dr. Rouben Rostamian. Telephone: 410-455-2412; e-mail: grad_info@math.umbc.edu; Web site: http://www.math.umbc.edu/

Physics (Applied) (M.S., Ph.D.): Dr. Michael Hayden. Telephone: 410-455-2513; e-mail: allison@umbc.edu; Web site: http://physics.umbc.edu/

Physics, Atmospheric (M.S., Ph.D.): Dr. Larrabee Strow. Telephone: 410-455-2513; e-mail: allison@umbc.edu; Web site: http://physics.umbc.edu/

Statistics (M.S., Ph.D.): Dr. Rouben Rostamian. Telephone: 410-455-2412; e-mail: grad_info@math.umbc.edu; Web site: http://www.math.umbc.edu/

PUBLIC POLICY

Economic Policy Analysis (M.A.): Dr. Wendy Takacs. Telephone: 410-455-2174; e-mail: econ-masters@umbc.edu; Web site: http://umbc.edu/economics/grad.html

Policy Sciences (M.P.S., Ph.D.): Dr. Marvin Mandell. Telephone: 410-455-3201; e-mail: gradposi@umbc.edu; Web site: http://www.umbc.edu/posi/

SOCIAL SCIENCES

Psychology, Applied Developmental (Ph.D.): Dr. Douglas Teti. Telephone: 410-455-2567; e-mail: cherelst@umbc.edu; Web site: http://www.umbc.edu/psyc/

Psychology, Human Services Psychology (M.A., Ph.D.): Dr. Christopher Murphy. Telephone: 410-455-2567; e-mail: cherelst@umbc.edu; Web site: http://www.umbc.edu/psyc/

Sociology (Applied) (M.A.): Dr. James Trela. Telephone: 410-455-3979; e-mail: marmstro@umbc.edu; Web site: http://www.umbc.edu/sociology/

VISUAL ARTS

Imaging and Digital Arts (M.F.A.): Professor Vin Grabill. Telephone: 410-455-2110; e-mail: grabill@umbc.edu; Web site: http://art.umbc.edu/

UNIVERSITY OF MARYLAND EASTERN SHORE

Graduate School

Programs of Study

The Graduate School offers the following degrees: Master of Science (M.S.), Master of Education (M.Ed.), Master of Physical Therapy (M.P.T.), Master of Arts in Teaching (M.A.T.), and Doctor of Philosophy (Ph.D.). The M.S. programs offered are applied computer science, agriculture and extension education, criminology and criminal justice, food and agricultural sciences, marine-estuarine-environmental sciences, rehabilitation counseling, and toxicology. The M.Ed. programs are in guidance and counseling, career and technology education, and special education. The M.A.T. program is for initial teacher certification in secondary schools. The M.P.T. program is in physical therapy. Ph.D. programs are offered in food science and technology, marine-estuarine-environmental sciences, and toxicology.

Effective in fall 2002, there will be a Ph.D. program in organizational leadership, and a Doctor of Physical Therapy (D.P.T.) program will replace the master's degree (M.P.T.) program.

For most master's programs, a minimum of 30 semester hours is required in acceptable course work and research credit toward a graduate degree. The M.S. programs in marine-estuarine-environmental sciences and toxicology require a thesis. The two agriculture master's programs, criminology and criminal justice, and rehabilitation counseling offer a thesis or nonthesis option. The M.P.T. program is a three-year program. Two doctoral programs (marine-estuarine-environmental sciences and toxicology) are interdisciplinary and intercampus (within the University System of Maryland). Applicants should consult the individual programs for specific requirements.

Research Facilities

Students have the opportunity to participate directly in ongoing research, development, and training projects. UMES is an 1890 land-grant and historically black institution, which conducts research and creative endeavors in the agricultural, environmental, and marine sciences; mathematics and computer applications; education and allied health; and other fields. Federal agency support includes the following: U.S. Departments of Agriculture, Commerce, Defense, Education, Energy, Health and Human Services, and the Interior; the National Science Foundation; the National Aeronautics and Space Administration; and the Agency for International Development.

There are a number of research and applications laboratories and facilities on campus and on the University's farm. Students also have access to other University System of Maryland, federal, and state facilities and field sites located throughout the state and region. Library and information resources may be accessed locally through the University System of Maryland Web site and the Internet.

Financial Aid

Limited financial assistance is available for qualified students, on the basis of merit and/or need, from institutional and sponsored funding. Examples of financial assistance are teaching, research and other types of assistantships, fellowships, traineeships, and federal work-study and loan programs.

Cost of Study

In 2001–02, tuition was $151 per semester credit hour for Maryland students and $272 per semester credit hour for out-of-state students. There was an application fee of $30.

Living and Housing Costs

Current monthly housing rates range from $200 for a room in a private or group home to $500 for an apartment in the local area. Limited University housing for single students is available on campus.

Student Group

UMES has a current graduate enrollment of about 300 students, both full- and part-time. About half the students are women, and 14 percent are international.

Student Outcomes

Students find employment in school systems as special, agriculture, and technology educators and guidance counselors as well as other certified high school teachers; in state agencies and private practice as guidance and rehabilitation counselors; in computer firms and educational settings as computer applications specialists; in private practice as physical therapists; and in federal, state, and local agencies and private businesses as marine, environmental, agricultural, and food scientists and criminology and criminal justice specialists.

Location

UMES is located in Princess Anne, a small town on the eastern shore of Maryland. The town dates back to 1733 and has many buildings and landmarks of historic interest. The area is quiet and ideally suited for a learning environment, yet it is only 2½ hours by car from the abundant cultural and recreational facilities of Washington, D.C., and Baltimore, Maryland. The state's famous seaside resort, Ocean City, is only 45 minutes from the campus. The campus is 13 miles south of the town of Salisbury, which provides shopping and recreational facilities.

The School

The University of Maryland Eastern Shore Graduate School has more than 80 graduate faculty members, who, through an elected Graduate Council, determine the policies, procedures, and degree requirements for the various graduate programs. Approved specialists from industry, government, and academia may also serve on student research committees as graduate faculty members.

The University of Maryland Eastern Shore Graduate School is a public research school that admits students without regard to sex, race, creed, or ethnic origin.

Applying

Completed application and other pertinent forms, official college/university transcripts, and three letters of evaluation are required. Some graduate programs have additional admission requirements. Admission deadlines vary by graduate program. International applicants need TOEFL scores or an equivalent and a certification of available finances for study. GRE General Test scores are or may be required in some cases for the programs in marine-estuarine-environmental sciences, physical therapy, food and agricultural sciences, special education, criminology and criminal justice, food science and technology, rehabilitation counseling, and applied computer science. Other programs may use the GRE as a criterion for admission. Education programs may require the PRAXIS examinations.

Correspondence and Information

Mr. C. Dennis Ignasias
Graduate Studies Office
University of Maryland Eastern Shore
Princess Anne, Maryland 21853-1299
Telephone: 410-651-6507, or 7966
Fax: 410-651-7571
E-mail: cdignasias@mail.umes.edu

THE FACULTY

Emmanuel Acquah, Associate Professor; Ph.D., Ohio State, 1976.
Ayodele J. Alade, Assistant Professor; Ph.D., Utah, 1981.
Arthur L. Allen, Associate Professor; Ph.D., Illinois, 1971.
Michael Almeida, Assistant Professor; Ph.D., SUNY at Buffalo, 1987.
Brenda Anderson, Assistant Professor; Ed.D., American, 1979.
Eugene L. Bass, Associate Professor; Ph.D., Massachusetts at Amherst, 1970.
Joseph Beatus, Assistant Professor; Ph.D., Maryland College Park, 1996.
Sarah B. Bing, Associate Professor; Ph.D., Georgia, 1976.
Raymond Blakely, Associate Professor; Ph.D., NYU, 1977.
Dixie Bounds, Associate Professor; Ph.D., Arizona, 1996.
Cheryl Bowers, Assistant Professor; Ph.D., Pennsylvania, 1997.
Eddie Boyd Jr., Assistant Professor; Ph.D., Oklahoma State, 1977.
Carolyn B. Brooks, Associate Professor; Ph.D., Oklahoma State, 1977.
Henry M. Brooks, Associate Director, Co-op Extension; Ph.D., Ohio State, 1975.
E. William Chapin, Assistant Professor; Ph.D., Princeton, 1969.
Leon L. Copeland, Associate Professor; Ed.D., Virginia Tech, 1977.
Clement L. Counts, Assistant Professor; Ph.D., Delaware, 1983.
Leon N. Coursey, Associate Professor; Ph.D., Ohio State, 1971.
Robert Dadson, Associate Professor; Ph.D., McGill, 1969.
June de Graft-Hanson, Research Associate; Ph.D., Maryland College Park, 1987.
Ejigou Demissie, Professor; Ph.D., Oklahoma State, 1982.
Stanley DeViney Jr., Associate Professor; Ph.D., Rutgers, 1983.
Joseph N. D. Dodoo, Assistant Professor; Ph.D., King's College (London), 1979.
Joseph J. Dudis, Assistant Professor; Ph.D., Johns Hopkins, 1970.
Dothel W. Edwards Jr. Assistant Professor; Rh.D., Southern Illinois at Carbondale, 1999.
Clayton W. Faubion, Assistant Professor; Ph.D., Arkansas, 1998.
Ann M. Flores, Assistant Professor; Ph.D., Ohio State, 2000.
Joan M. Fobbs, Associate Professor; Ph.D., Ohio State, 1988.
Kristian I. Garver, Research Assistant Professor; Ph.D., Clemson, 1999.
Tonya M. Gerald, Assistant Professor; Ph.D., Maryland at Baltimore, 1999.
Gian C. Gupta, Professor; Ph.D., Roorkee (India), 1966.
Youssef S. Hafez, Professor; Ph.D., California, Davis, 1975.
Thomas Handwerker, Associate Professor; Ph.D., Cornell, 1972.
Robert A. Harleston, Associate Professor; J.D., Georgetown, 1983.
Jeannine M. Harter-Dennis, Associate Professor; Ph.D., Illinois, 1977.
George Heath, Associate Professor; Ph.D., Minnesota, Twin Cities, 1985.
Thelma Hedgepeth, Associate Professor; Ph.D., Maryland Eastern Shore, 1989.
Nancy A. Horton, Assistant Professor; Ph.D., SUNY at Albany, 1995.
Steven Hughes, Associate Professor; Ph.D., Cornell, 1982.
C. Dennis Ignasias, Associate Professor; Ph.D., Michigan State, 1967; Ph.D., Wisconsin–Madison, 1973.
Roman Jesien, Assistant Professor; Ph.D., Maryland College Park, 1989.
Linda P. Johnson, Assistant Professor; Ph.D., Temple, 1995.
Jagmohan Joshi, Professor; Ph.D., Ohio State, 1972.
Gerald E. Kananen, Assistant Professor; Ph.D., Duquesne, 1968.
Frank C. Lin, Professor; Ph.D., Yale, 1965.
Gregory F. Martel, Assistant Professor; Ph.D., Maryland, College Park, 1998.
Dorothy M. Mattison, Associate Professor; Ph.D., George Washington, 1990.
Eric B. May, Associate Professor; Ph.D., Oregon State, 1982.
Theodore A. Mollett, Associate Professor; Ph.D., Purdue, 1980.
Mervalin Morant, Associate Professor; Ph.D., Purdue, 1988.
Thomas S. Mosely, Assistant Professor; Ph.D., Howard, 1997.
Brigid Noonan, Assistant Professor; Ph.D., Maryland, College Park, 1998.
Jonathan C. Odo, Assistant Professor; Ph.D., Florida State, 1997.
Joseph Okoh, Associate Professor; Ph.D., Howard, 1982.
Daniel Okunbor, Associate Professor; Ph.D., Illinois, 1993.
Ihekwoaba Onwudiwe, Assistant Professor; Ph.D., Florida State, 1993.
Emmanuel Onyeozili, Assistant Professor; Ph.D., Florida State, 1998.
Jack P. Pinion, Assistant Professor; Ph.D., George Washington, 1970.
Maryam Rahimi, Assistant Professor; Ph.D., Florida State, 1987.
Howard M. Rebach, Professor; Ph.D., Michigan State, 1968.
Joel H. Roache III, Associate Professor; Ph.D., Pennsylvania, 1967.
Douglas E. Ruby, Associate Professor; Ph.D., Michigan, 1976.
Anugrah Shaw, Professor; Ph.D., Texas Woman's, 1984.
George S. Shorter, Visiting Lecturer; Ph.D., Iowa State, 1981.
Gurbax Singh, Professor; Ph.D., Maryland College Park, 1971.
Jeurel Singleton, Lecturer; Ph.D., Ottawa, 1980.
David L. Spinner, Assistant Professor; Ph.D., Maryland at College Park, 1994.
Karen A. Verbeke, Associate Professor; Ph.D., Maryland College Park, 1982.
Yan Waguespack, Associate Professor; Ph.D., Tulane, 1990.
Shawn R. White, Assistant Professor; Ph.D., Clemson, 1997.
Niki C. Whitley, Assistant Professor; Ph.D., Mississippi State, 1998.
James W. Wiley, Assistant Professor; Ph.D., Miami, 1982.
Allen B. Williams, Assistant Professor; Ph.D., California, Santa Barbara, 1995.
Emin Yilmaz, Associate Professor; Ph.D., Michigan, 1970.
Ki Sun Yoon, Research Associate; Ph.D., Rhode Island, 1990.
Adil E. M. Yousif, Assistant Professor; Ph.D., Ohio, 1997.

UNIVERSITY OF MASSACHUSETTS AMHERST

Graduate School

Programs of Study

The Graduate School offers the Doctor of Philosophy degree in Afro-American studies, animal science, anthropology, astronomy, biochemistry, biology, chemical engineering, chemistry, civil engineering, communication, communication disorders, comparative literature, computer science, economics, electrical and computer engineering, English, entomology, exercise science, food science, forestry, geosciences, Germanic languages and literatures, Hispanic literatures and linguistics, history, industrial engineering and operations research, linguistics, management, mathematics, mechanical engineering, microbiology, molecular and cellular biology, music, neuroscience and behavior, nursing, organismic and evolutionary biology, philosophy, physics, plant and soil sciences, plant biology, political science, polymer science and engineering, psychology, public health, regional planning, resource economics, school psychology, sociology, sport studies, and wildlife and fisheries conservation. In several fields—all departments in the biological sciences, astronomy, chemistry, geology, and physics—degrees are awarded under the Five College Cooperative Ph.D. Program. The Doctor of Education degree is also offered.

Major fields in which courses leading to a master's degree are offered are accounting; Afro-American studies; animal science; anthropology; art; art history; astronomy; biochemistry; biology; chemical engineering; chemistry; Chinese; civil engineering; classics; communication; communication disorders; comparative literature; computer science; economics; education; electrical and computer engineering; engineering management; English; entomology; environmental engineering; exercise science; food science; forestry; French and Francophone studies; geography; geosciences; Germanic languages and literatures; Hispanic literatures and linguistics; history; hotel, restaurant, and travel administration; industrial engineering and operations research; Italian studies; Japanese; labor studies; landscape architecture; linguistics; management; manufacturing engineering; mathematics; mechanical engineering; microbiology; molecular and cellular biology; music; nursing; nutrition; organismic and evolutionary biology; philosophy; physics; plant and soil sciences; plant biology; political science; polymer science and engineering; psychology; public administration; public health; regional planning; resource economics; sociology; sport studies; theater; and wildlife and fisheries conservation. A Certificate of Advanced Graduate Study is awarded in the School of Education.

Research Facilities

Present library holdings include more than 5.4 million books, periodicals, serials, and government documents and more than 2.3 million items in microformat. In addition to discipline-oriented laboratories and equipment, special research facilities include the Donahue Institute for Government Services; the Labor Relations and Research Center; the Institute for Advanced Studies in the Humanities; the Marine Station at Gloucester, Massachusetts; the Polymer Research Institute; and the Environmental Institute. The Office of Information Technologies provides computing facilities for faculty members, staff members, and students; Internet connections through the campus network; World Wide Web support, LAN support, and desktop computing hardware and software support; multimedia development; and many training classes.

Financial Aid

Teaching assistantships, teaching associateships, research assistantships, and Graduate School and minority fellowships, carrying full tuition waivers, are available to qualified graduate students. NSF and NIH traineeships are also available. The Financial Aid Office assists students through the federal College Work-Study, Perkins Loan, and Stafford Student Loan programs.

Cost of Study

In fall 2002, graduate tuition is $2640 per year ($1320 per semester) for full-time Massachusetts residents and a maximum of $9940 per year ($4970 per semester) for nonresidents. A typical full course load is 9 credit hours. Part-time tuition is one twelfth of a full semester's tuition for each credit hour. Fees for health and other services averaged $5020 per year.

Living and Housing Costs

University residence room rent in 2002–03 is $3080 per year, with board charges of $2550 per year. The University owns and manages 345 unfurnished apartments for students with families, and an Off-Campus Housing Office maintains listings of privately owned living accommodations.

Student Group

Graduate students totaled 5,800 in fall 2001. They represented fifty states and consisted of 51 percent women and 14 percent minority students. More than half were supported by teaching assistantships, research assistantships, teaching associateships, and fellowships. Undergraduate enrollment was 18,268.

Location

Amherst is located in the Connecticut River Valley, approximately a 2-hour drive from Boston and 3 hours from New York. The area is semirural, with outdoor sports available during all seasons.

The University

The University of Massachusetts was founded in 1863 under the Morrill Land Grant Act. Its schools and colleges are the Graduate School; the Colleges of Arts and Sciences, Engineering, and Food and Natural Resources; and the Schools of Education, Management, Nursing, and Public Health and Health Sciences. Five Colleges, Inc., is a consortium composed of the University and Amherst, Hampshire, Mount Holyoke, and Smith Colleges. With their adviser's prior approval, students in any of the five colleges may enroll for courses at the others.

Applying

The application and application fee ($40 for U.S. citizens and permanent residents, $50 for international applicants) are due between December 1 and February 1 for September or summer session enrollment, depending on desired program of study, and by October 1 for January enrollment. The General Test of the Graduate Record Examinations (GRE) is required of nearly all applicants. Applicants to programs in management, sport studies, and hotel, restaurant, and travel administration are required to take the Graduate Management Admission Test (GMAT) instead of the GRE. The Test of English as a Foreign Language (TOEFL) is required of all applicants from non-English-speaking countries. Students are encouraged to apply online at http://www.umass.edu/gradschool/application/online/index.html.

Correspondence and Information

Graduate Admissions Office
Goodell Building
University of Massachusetts
Amherst, Massachusetts 01003
Telephone: 413-545-0721
Fax: 413-577-0010
World Wide Web: http://www.umass.edu/gradschool

FACULTY HEADS

John Lombardi, Chancellor.
John Dubach, Deputy Chancellor.
Charlena Seymour, Senior Vice Chancellor for Academic Affairs and Provost.
Frederick W. Byron, Vice Chancellor for Research.
James Walker, Graduate Dean.

College of Humanities and Fine Arts: Lee R. Edwards, Dean.
College of Natural Sciences and Mathematics: Leon Osterweil, Dean.
College of Social and Behavioral Sciences: Janet Rifkin, Dean.
School of Education: Andrew Effrat, Dean.
College of Engineering: Joseph I. Goldstein, Dean.
College of Food and Natural Resources: Cleve Willis, Dean.
School of Management: Thomas O'Brien, Dean.
School of Nursing: Eileen T. Breslin, Dean.
School of Public Health and Health Sciences: Stephen H. Gehlbach, Dean.

UNIVERSITY OF MASSACHUSETTS BOSTON

Graduate Studies

Programs of Study

The University of Massachusetts Boston offers master's and doctoral degree programs through the Graduate College of Education and the Colleges of Arts and Sciences, Management, Nursing, and Public and Community Service. The Master of Arts (M.A.) is awarded in American studies, applied linguistics (with three tracks: bilingual education, English as a second language, and foreign language pedagogy), critical and creative thinking, dispute resolution, English, history (with three tracks: history, historical archaeology, and history teaching), and sociology (applied). The B.A./M.A. accelerated program in applied sociology allows students to earn both a bachelor's degree in their field of interest and a master's degree in sociology in five years. The Master of Education (M.Ed.) is offered in counseling, educational administration, instructional design, school psychology, special education, and teacher education. The Master of Science (M.S.) is offered in biology, biotechnology and biomedical science, chemistry, computer science, environmental sciences, human services, nursing, physics (applied), and public affairs. The RN to M.S. Pathway Program offers registered nurses who hold NLNAC-approved diplomas or associate degrees the opportunity to concurrently pursue B.S. and M.S. nursing degrees. The Master of Business Administration (M.B.A.) is offered in business administration. A joint Master of Science/Master of Business Administration (M.S./M.B.A.) is offered through the M.S. in nursing program in collaboration with the M.B.A. program. The B.A./M.B.A. accelerated program allows students to earn both a bachelor's degree in liberal arts and the M.B.A. in five years. A Certificate of Advanced Graduate Study (C.A.G.S.) is offered in counseling, educational administration, and school psychology. The Doctor of Philosophy (Ph.D.) is offered in clinical psychology, computer science, environmental sciences, gerontology, nursing, and public policy. Environmental sciences has four tracks: environmental, coastal, and ocean sciences; environmental biology; green chemistry; and molecular, cellular, and organismal biology. The Doctor of Education (Ed.D.) is offered in higher education administration and urban school leadership. Additional doctoral programs are being developed. Graduate certificates in adapting the curriculum frameworks, biotechnology, critical and creative thinking, database technology, dispute resolution, forensic services, instructional technology, family nurse practitioner studies (advanced certificate), gerontological nurse practitioner (advanced certificate), orientation and mobility, and women in politics and public policy are also offered.

Research Facilities

The University library holds a collection of more than 572,000 volumes and subscribes to 3,120 domestic and international journals and newspapers. The Joseph P. Healey Library is centrally located on the campus plaza, easily accessible from the bridge that connects all buildings on campus. UMass Boston is a member of the Boston Library Consortium, which includes the libraries of Boston College, Boston University, Brandeis University, Brown University, Massachusetts Institute of Technology, Northeastern University, Tufts University, all five University of Massachusetts campuses, Wellesley College, and Woods Hole Oceanographic Institute. Graduate students may use materials on site at any of these libraries and are eligible for cards that grant borrowing privileges at these institutions. UMass Boston's Computing Services provide a broad spectrum of computer-related services to students and staff on campus. Student and faculty researchers in Boston are provided with time-sharing, batch, and peer-to-peer access to a cluster of Digital VAX minicomputers over a local area Ethernet and twisted-pair network that includes VAX 8800, VAX 6000/410, and VAX 6000/510. Wide area access to worldwide computing and information resources is provided through Internet services. The John F. Kennedy Presidential Library, a public institution for education and research, stands on the coastal edge of the campus. Designed by I. M. Pei, the facility was established to preserve and make available the documents and memorabilia of President Kennedy and his contemporaries in politics and government. Its archival collection contains approximately 28 million pages of documents, 6.5 million feet of film, and more than 100,000 still photographs. The JFK Library is linked to the University by a series of educational programs enabling students and their instructors to share its rich resources. The Archives of the Commonwealth of Massachusetts are also adjacent to the campus. Members of the University community benefit greatly from this rich repository of research materials that cover 3½ centuries.

Financial Aid

Assistantships carrying stipends and tuition waivers are available to qualified full-time graduate students in all programs. The Office of Financial Aid Services assists students through the Federal Work-Study, Federal Perkins Loan, and Federal Stafford Student Loans programs. UMass Boston uses the FAFSA. A limited number of tuition waivers are available for international students who have completed at least one semester.

Cost of Study

In 2000–01, full-time graduate tuition was $2590 per year for state residents and $9758 per year for nonresidents. Part-time tuition was charged at a rate of $108 per credit hour for residents and $406 per credit hour for nonresidents. General fees for health and other services were approximately $2490 per year.

Living and Housing Costs

While the University of Massachusetts Boston does not have on-campus housing facilities, graduate students can find housing off campus by using the University's Housing Referral Service.

Student Group

In fall 2000, approximately 2,800 graduate students were enrolled. They represented more than 350 different colleges and universities. About 69 percent were women and 31 percent men. Most students pursue degrees part-time and take courses after 4 p.m. Undergraduate enrollment is approximately 10,600.

Location

Boston's urban setting offers a broad array of educational, professional, and cultural resources. These resources, in conjunction with the University's active concern for the student's individual development, enable the student to acquire an excellent education.

The University

The University of Massachusetts Boston was founded in 1964 to provide superior education for the people of the commonwealth and particularly of the greater Boston area. Since its founding, the University has demonstrated a deep commitment to serving students and the community. Situated on a peninsula reaching out into picturesque Dorchester Bay and Old Harbor, the campus is easily accessible by public and private transportation. The campus consists of seven buildings on about 100 acres of land surrounded on three sides by ever-changing seascapes. Life at the University is as rich and varied as the city of Boston itself. Students on campus can attend plays, musical recitals, and films; use outstanding specimen collections and facilities for research; navigate one of the University's sailboats; or conduct research on the islands of the harbor and at the University's Nantucket field station.

Applying

Deadlines for domestic applications along with the application fee ($40 for state residents and $50 for nonresidents) range from January 1 to June 1 for September enrollment and from October 1 to November 1 for January enrollment. The GRE is required by certain programs. The M.B.A. program requires the GMAT. Other programs, particularly in education, require the Miller Analogies Test (MAT). The Test of English as a Foreign Language (TOEFL) is required of all applicants from countries whose language is not English. Unless an earlier date is specified, completed applications from international students must be received by May 1 for September enrollment and by October 1 for January enrollment.

Correspondence and Information

For information about programs and admissions:

Admissions Information Service
University of Massachusetts Boston
100 Morrissey Boulevard
Boston, Massachusetts 02125-3393

Telephone: 617-287-6000
617-287-6010 (TTY/TDD)
Fax: 617-287-6264
E-mail: enrollment.info@umb.edu
World Wide Web: http://www.umb.edu

For information about research and service activities:

The Office of Public Information
University of Massachusetts Boston
100 Morrissey Boulevard
Boston, Massachusetts 02125-3393

Telephone: 617-287-5380
Fax: 617-287-5393
E-mail: news@umb.edu

PROGRAM DIRECTORS

College of Arts and Sciences
American Studies: Judith Smith, Ph.D.
Biology: Gregory Beck, Ph.D.
Biotechnology and Biomedical Science: Gregory Beck, Ph.D.
Biotechnology (certificate): Gregory Beck, Ph.D.
Chemistry: Jean-Pierre Anselme, Ph.D.
Clinical Psychology: Joan Liem, Ph.D.
Computer Science: Daniel Simovici, Ph.D.
Database Technology (certificate): Daniel Simovici, Ph.D.
English: Elizabeth Fay, Ph.D.
Environmental Sciences: Curtis Olsen, Ph.D.
Environmental Sciences/Environmental Biology: Gregory Beck, Ph.D.
Environmental Science/Green Chemistry: John Warner, Ph.D.
Environmental Science/Molecular, Cellular, and Organismal Biology: Gregory Beck, Ph.D.
Forensic Services (certificate): Stephanie Hartwell, Ph.D.
History: Marshall Shatz, Ph.D.
History/Historical Archaeology: Stephen Mrozowski, Ph.D.
History/Teaching: Marshall Shatz, Ph.D.
Linguistics (applied): Donaldo Macedo, Ed.D., Ph.D.
Physics (applied): Gopal Rao, D.Sc.
Sociology (applied): Siamak Movahedi, Ph.D.
Sociology (applied) B.A./M.A.: Siamak Movahedi, Ph.D.
Women in Politics and Public Policy (certificate): Catherine Lynde, Ph.D.

College of Management
M.B.A.: Daniel Robb, M.B.A.
B.A./M.B.A.: Daniel Robb, M.B.A.

College of Nursing
Family Nurse Practitioner Studies (advanced certificate): Jane Clouterbuck, Ph.D.
Gerontological Nurse Practitioner Studies (advanced certificate): Joan Garity, Ed.D.
Nursing M.S.: Amy Rex-Smith, D.N.Sc.
Nursing M.S./M.B.A.: Jane Clouterbuck, Ph.D.
Nursing R.N./M.S.: Jane Clouterbuck, Ph.D.
Nursing Ph.D.: Gail Russell, Ed.D.

College of Public and Community Service
Dispute Resolution: Eben Weitzman, Ph.D.
Dispute Resolution (certificate): Eben Weitzman, Ph.D.
Gerontology: Jeffrey Burr, Ph.D.
Human Services: Reebee Garafolo, Ph.D.

Graduate College of Education
Counseling: Rick Houser, Ph.D.
Critical and Creative Thinking: Peter Taylor, Ph.D.
Critical and Creative Thinking (certificate): Peter Taylor, Ph.D.
Education/Higher Education Administration: Linda Eisenmann, Ed.D.
Education/Urban School Leadership: Joseph Check, Ph.D.
Educational Administration: Lee Teitel, Ed.D.
Instructional Design: Canice McGarry, M.Ed.
Instructional Technology (certificate): Canice McGarry, M.Ed.
Orientation and Mobility (certificate): Robert McCulley, M.Ed.
School Psychology: Rick Houser, Ph.D.
Special Education: Mary Ann Byrnes, Ed.D.
Teacher Education: Mary Koerna, Ph.D.

McCormack Institute
Public Affairs: Carol Hardy-Fanta, Ph.D.

Center for Social Development and Education
Adapting the Curriculum Frameworks (certificate): Gary Siperstein, Ph.D.

Free-Standing Program
Public Policy: Carol Upshur, Ed.D.

Enviro-Lab III serves as a floating laboratory for the study of harbor ecology.

The Biology Department's modern facilities support a broad spectrum of research interests within the biological and environmental sciences.

At the University of Massachusetts Boston, diversity is an integral part of graduate education.

UNIVERSITY OF MASSACHUSETTS DARTMOUTH

Graduate School

Programs of Study

The University of Massachusetts Dartmouth (UMass Dartmouth) offers programs of study leading to a Doctor of Philosophy in electrical engineering. UMass Dartmouth is a home campus for the joint Master of Science/Doctor of Philosophy (M.S./Ph.D.) in marine sciences and technology, along with the UMass campuses of Amherst, Boston, and Lowell. UMass Dartmouth is also a home campus for a proposed joint M.S./Ph.D. in biomedical engineering/biotechnology, along with the UMass campuses of Boston, Lowell, and Worcester (approval anticipated for students entering in 2002). A joint program with UMass Lowell offers students the opportunity to study at UMass Dartmouth for a Ph.D. in chemistry.

The University awards the Master of Arts in professional writing and psychology; the Master of Science in biology/marine biology, chemistry, computer engineering (separate M.S. from electrical engineering with approval anticipated for students entering in fall 2002), computer science, electrical engineering, marine science and technology (joint UMass program), mechanical engineering, nursing, physics, textile chemistry, and textile technology; the Master of Art Education; the Master of Arts in teaching, elementary education or middle and secondary school, with emphasis in business, English, foreign literature and languages (French, Portuguese, Spanish), history, mathematics, and social studies; the Master of Fine Arts in artisanry (with emphasis on studios in ceramics, jewelry/metals, textile design/fiber arts, and wood and furniture design), fine arts (with emphasis on studios in drawing, painting, printmaking, and sculpture), and visual design (with emphasis on studios in graphic design, electronic imaging, illustration, multimedia, photography, and typography); and the Master of Business Administration (AACSB accredited).

In addition, some programs offer certificates, including a post-M.S. Adult Nurse Practitioner Certificate in nursing. UMass Dartmouth also cooperates with the nearby Southern New England School of Law in offering a joint J.D./M.B.A.

Research Facilities

Modern laboratories and studios provide space for graduate research and artwork. The University operates the School for Marine Science and Technology (SMAST), a full research facility directed by noted marine scientist Dr. Brian Rothschild. The library houses 400,000 volumes, 2,000 periodicals, and selected U.S. Government documents; the online catalog is available through the campus network to all University residences and in the library. Students use a large interlibrary loan system, including the Boston Library Consortium of major college and research libraries in Massachusetts. The campus DEC Alpha cluster has software including Basic, Fortran, Pascal, C++, Cobol, and SPSS. The University supports two types of computers: Apple Macintosh and PC Compatibles running Windows. Ten computer laboratories on campus offer MS Excel, Netscape Communicator, Statview, and Filemaker Pro as well as word processing software. The visual and performing arts facilities and equipment on the Dartmouth and New Bedford campuses are among the finest in New England. In addition to excellent studio facilities, students have access to microcomputing facilities with software oriented to the arts and design. The University also has fine video, electronic music, and computer animation equipment. In all, the University had $9.7 million in grants and contracts awarded in 2000–01.

Financial Aid

The departments offer graduate teaching assistantships, research assistantships, and tuition waivers. Stipends for full graduate teaching and research assistantships vary from approximately $5000 plus tuition waiver to approximately $16,000 plus tuition waiver, depending on academic field and level of study. The Financial Aid Office awards work-study stipends and assists students in obtaining loans.

Cost of Study

Tuition in 2001–02 for a full-time (9 credits per semester) Massachusetts resident graduate day student was $1553 for the academic year; tuition for a full-time (9 credits per semester) nonresident graduate day student was $6074 per academic year. Mandatory fees for the academic year (not including college fees) were $2316 for Massachusetts residents and $3138 for out-of-state residents.

Living and Housing Costs

The University has a town-house complex, and a number of these residences are available for graduate students. Each town house consists of six private bedrooms. The cost for academic year 2000–01 was $3391 per bedroom. In addition, the University's Housing Office maintains listings of off-campus accommodations in the area; these vary widely in price.

Student Group

During the 2001 fall semester, 822 graduate students were enrolled in graduate studies. The student body includes a significant proportion of out-of-state and international students and both part-time and full-time students.

Location

On 710 acres of former farmland, the main campus of the University is located in North Dartmouth, Massachusetts, between New Bedford and Fall River, the fourth- and fifth-largest cities in the commonwealth. Major highways provide easy access to Providence (35 minutes), Boston (1 hour), and Cape Cod (35 minutes), and the beach is just minutes away. The southeastern Massachusetts region, with a population of about 2 million, is noted for its scenic values, historical interest, and cultural variety.

The University

The University of Massachusetts Dartmouth is a fully accredited university, one of five university campuses in the University of Massachusetts system of public higher education that also includes the universities of Amherst, Boston, Lowell, and Worcester (the medical school). The University has 7,460 undergraduate and graduate students enrolled in five colleges and a graduate school, and its faculty is composed of more than 300 members.

The University of Massachusetts Dartmouth's campus master plan and architecture have been cited in national publications. The University has renovated a large department store building in downtown New Bedford to be a modern, rich facility for arts programs. UMass Dartmouth is actively developing its Advanced Technology and Manufacturing Center, which provides high-technology research opportunities for faculty members and students in partnership with industry, located in Fall River.

Applying

The requirements for admission to graduate study are successful completion of a baccalaureate degree in an appropriate field, evidence of the ability to pursue graduate study in the field, and the submission of test scores and recommendations. A completed application, which must include three letters of recommendation, official transcripts, test scores, and the application fee, must be filed with the Graduate School before a candidate can be considered. Several fields require scores on both the General Test and a Subject Test of the Graduate Record Examinations. Scores on the GMAT are required for the business administration program, and MAT scores are required for the program in professional writing. Portfolios are required in art education, artisanry, and visual design. Scores on the TOEFL are required of international students from non-English-speaking countries. Recommended application deadlines are February 20 (for international students) and April 20 (for U.S. students) for September admission and September 15 (international students) and November 15 (U.S. students) for January admission. The application fee is $25 for Massachusetts residents and $45 for out-of-state and international students.

Correspondence and Information

Office of Graduate Studies
University of Massachusetts Dartmouth
285 Old Wesport Road
North Dartmouth, Massachusetts 02747-2300

Telephone: 508-999-8604
Fax: 508-999-8183
E-mail: graduate@umassd.edu
World Wide Web: http://www.umassd.edu

FACULTY PROGRAM COORDINATORS AND FACULTY RESEARCH INTERESTS

Art Education: Arlene Mollo. Art education.
Artisanry/Fine Arts/Visual Design: Severin Haines. See list of program specializations under Programs of Study.
Biology/Marine Biology: Nancy O'Connor. Parasitology, marine mammal biology, marine microbiology, fish ecology and morphology, biological anthropology, biological oceanography.
Business Administration: Omar Khalil. Accounting, business law, social research methods, ethics, human resources management, artificial intelligence, computer technology.
Chemistry: Timothy Su. Marine and environmental chemistry, computer graphics in chemistry, ethnomedicinal chemistry, inorganic chemistry, polymer chemistry.
Computer Science: Jan Bergandy. Object-oriented programming, computer algebra, computer architecture, computer security, programming languages, mathematical applications, social implications.
Electrical Engineering and Computer Engineering: Paul Fortier. Underwater acoustics, image processing and machine vision, rehabilitation engineering, signal processing, electrooptics, ocean systems, computer performance evaluation, operating system, renewable energy, modern control and estimation theory, speech acoustics.
Marine Science and Technology: Wendell S. Brown. Basic and applied marine science and technology; economic development and policy issues; watersheds, embayments, and estuaries of coastal Massachusetts, New England, and the adjacent U.S. as well as remote regions of the global ocean.
Mechanical Engineering: Alex Fowler. Geothermal energy, computer-aided manufacturing, bioengineering, solid mechanics, facility planning and design, laser Doppler anemometry, robotics fire research.
Nursing: Nancy Dluhy. Adult health, family health, violence, gerontology, community health, school health, interpersonal relationships.
Physics: Jay Wang. Experimental high-energy physics, environmental physics, physical oceanography, astrophysics, computational physics, liquid crystals, atomic and optical processes.
Professional Writing: Catherine Houser. Business and technical communications, literary nonfiction, rhetorical theory, desktop and Web publishing, grants writing, environmental writing, communication theory.
Psychology: Paul Donnelly (Clinical Option); Judith Sims-Knight (General/Research Option). Behavioral medicine, experiential learning, eating disorders, hemispheric specialization, human–computer interaction.
Teaching: Gerard Koot. English education, foreign language education, bilingual education, school reform, social studies education.
Textile Chemistry/Technology: Yong Kim. Fiber physics, organic synthesis, dyeing, polymer materials science, textile valuation, microscopy, design, flocking.

A student strolls past one of the campus buildings, designed by architect Paul Rudolph, at University of Massachusetts Dartmouth.

UNIVERSITY OF MASSACHUSETTS LOWELL

Graduate School

Programs of Study

The University's thirty-one master's degrees, thirteen doctoral degrees, and thirty-one graduate certificate programs are regionally and nationally accredited. Through its internationally renowned research faculty, the University of Massachusetts (UMass) Lowell qualifies for the Carnegie Foundation ranking of Doctoral/Research University–Intensive status. The Doctor of Philosophy (Ph.D.) is offered in biomedical engineering and biotechnology [planned](intercampus), chemistry (environmental studies and biochemistry), marine sciences and technology (intercampus), nursing (health promotion), physics (applied mechanics, atmospheric physics, energy engineering, and radiological sciences), and polymer science (polymer science/plastics engineering). The Doctor of Science (Sc.D.) is offered in computer science (computational math) and work environment (industrial hygiene, occupational ergonomics, epidemiology, work environment policy, and cleaner production and pollution prevention). The Doctor of Education (Ed.D.) is available in language arts and literacy, leadership in schooling, and mathematics and science education. The Doctor of Engineering (D.Eng.) is available in electrical engineering, mechanical engineering (chemical and civil engineering options and design/manufacturing, dynamics/systems/controls, energy/environmental, solid mechanics/materials/structures, thermal/fluid/transport processes concentrations), and plastics engineering. A Doctor of Physical Therapy (D.P.T.) is planned. The Certificate of Advanced Graduate Study (C.A.G.S.) is offered in administration, planning and policy, curriculum and instruction, and reading and language. The Master of Arts (M.A.) is offered in community and social psychology, criminal justice, and economic and social development of regions. The Master of Science (M.S.) is available in biological sciences (biotechnology), chemistry, clinical laboratory sciences, computer science, environmental studies (atmospheric sciences), health services administration, marine sciences and technology (intercampus), mathematics (applied mathematics, mathematics for teachers, scientific computing, and statistics and operations research), nursing (gerontological, family health, and adult psychiatric/mental health), physical therapy, physical therapy advanced practice option, physics (optics), radiological sciences and protection, and work environment (industrial hygiene, occupational ergonomics, epidemiology, work environment policy, and cleaner production and pollution prevention). The Master of Science in Engineering (M.S.Eng.) is offered in chemical engineering, civil engineering (geotechnical, structural, transportation, environmental, and geoenvironmental), computer engineering, electrical engineering (optoelectronics), energy engineering (solar and nuclear), mechanical engineering, and plastics engineering (coatings and adhesives). The Master of Education (M.Ed.) is offered in educational administration, curriculum and instruction (English as a second language and teacher certification), and reading and language. The Master of Music (M.M.) is available in music education and performance (applied performance and conducting). Also available are the Master of Business Administration (M.B.A.) and Master of Management Science in Manufacturing (M.M.S.). Thirty-one 4-course graduate certificates are offered in four area clusters: biomedical, health, and social sciences; computers, communications, and information systems; environmental; and engineering, manufacturing, and management. Selected graduate courses have been offered off campus at sites in the region, including GTE/Verizon, Polaroid, Cadence Design Systems, NYPRO, Lahey Clinic, Raytheon, Gillette, Hewlett-Packard/Agilent, May Institute, Freudenberg-NOK, and the Department of Environmental Protection, BAE Systems, among others. Selected programs are also offered online.

Research Facilities

All graduate departments are equipped to support scholarly research through collaboration with thirty-two campus research centers and institutes. More than $32 million in sponsored research was realized in 2001. Computer and e-mail accounts are issued to all students. The University has numerous workstations, PCs, and terminals connected to multiple servers via a state-of-the-art network infrastructure composed of ATM and 10/100 megabit Ethernet switching technology. Multimedia labs, distance learning classrooms, and online programs are available. The library system, including 350 databases and some 9,000 full-text journals, is fully computerized, accessible on and off campus, and is linked to other major libraries. Industrial-community relations are nurtured and enhanced through research collaborations, technology exchange, student internships, and advisory boards. Faculty members routinely interact with industry, business, community groups, and government agencies.

Financial Aid

More than 300 teaching and research assistantships (TAs/RAs) were awarded in 2001–02; interested students should contact the graduate coordinator/chairperson of the department to which they are applying. Low-interest student loans are also available for citizens of Massachusetts and Canada through the Massachusetts Educational Financing Authority (MEFA). Federal Direct, Stafford, Perkins, and supplemental loans are available.

Cost of Study

In 2001–02, approximate tuition and fees for 9 credits per semester were $2297 for Massachusetts residents, and $4812 for out-of-state students. New England Regional Tuition is available for some programs of study in which qualified out-of-state students pay 150 percent of the Massachusetts resident tuition charges.

Living and Housing Costs

Costs for on-campus graduate housing were $3020 per year for single students in 2001–02 (meal plan was extra and ranged from $1740 to $2075). Married student housing ranged from $575 to $625 per month (unfurnished). Furnished efficiencies were $470 per month with utilities. Furnished and unfurnished rooms/apartments are available within walking distance of campus.

Student Group

The fall 2001 total enrollment was 13,500, of whom 2,700 were graduate students, 7,800 were undergraduate students, 3,000 were continuing education students, and nearly 700 were international students.

Student Outcomes

UMass Lowell awards one of the highest percentages of degrees (32 percent) at the graduate level of any New England university. Response from both graduate student alumni and industry-employers reveals high satisfaction with education received and level of preparedness and professional perspective. Graduate students are highly sought by major corporations, both as interns during the course of their studies and as full-time employees upon graduation.

Location

In the heart of the birthplace of America's Industrial Revolution, Lowell, Massachusetts, is 25 miles from Boston and home to the first urban National Park in the U.S. The Merrimack River runs through this city of 103,000, which hosts professional baseball and hockey adjacent to the campus. Access to Boston is easy via car or commuter train. New Hampshire, Vermont, and Maine, as well as the shores and beaches of the Atlantic and Cape Cod, are short driving distances away.

The University

The University of Massachusetts Lowell is one member of the five-campus University of Massachusetts system. Graduate students have access to selected courses at other UMass campuses.

Applying

Applications (except for computer science) can be submitted at any time; however, early applications ensure that all materials are processed on time and that due consideration is given to those seeking TAs. GRE General Test, GMAT (for the M.B.A.), and TOEFL (for international students) scores, official transcripts, statement of purpose, application fee ($20 for Massachusetts residents, $25 for all others), and three letters of reference are required. Some departments have deadlines and additional requirements. Complete application packages with step-by-step instructions and course catalogs are available upon request. Online applications are recommended and are available at the Web site listed below.

Correspondence and Information

Dr. Jerome Hojnacki, Dean, Graduate School,
Patricia Duff, Director, Graduate Academic Services,
Linda Southworth, Director, Graduate Admissions Office, or
James Magarian, Director, Corporate and Community Graduate Programs and Relations

The Graduate School
University of Massachusetts Lowell
One University Avenue
Lowell, Massachusetts 01854
Telephone: 978-934-2380
800-656-GRAD (toll-free)
Fax: 978-934-3010
E-mail: graduate_school@uml.edu
World Wide Web: http://www.uml.edu/grad

THE FACULTY

Students may e-mail any of the faculty members listed below (firstname_lastname@uml.edu).

COLLEGE DEANS

Arts and Sciences: Dr. Robert Tamarin (Dean, Sciences Division), Olney 524, telephone: 978-934-3847.
Dr. Nancy Kleniewski (Dean, Humanities, Fine Arts, and Social Sciences), Durgin 112, telephone: 978-934-3850.
Continuing Studies and Corporate Education: Dr. Jacqueline Fidler Moloney, Southwick 308A, telephone: 978-934-2260.
Education: Dr. Donald Pierson, Upham 101, telephone: 978-934-4601.
Engineering: Dr. Krishna Vedula, Kitson 311, telephone: 978-934-2577.
Health Professions: Dr. Janice Stecchi, Weed 104, telephone: 978-934-4461.
Management: Dr. Kathryn Verreault, Pasteur 305, telephone: 978-934-2741.

DEPARTMENT GRADUATE COORDINATORS AND CHAIRS

Biological Science: Dr. Susan Braunhut, Olsen 512F, telephone: 978-934-2876.
Dr. Robert Lynch, Chair, Olsen 603, telephone: 978-934-2891.
Chemical Engineering: Dr. Thomas Vasilos, Eng. 306, telephone: 978-934-3162.
Chemical and Energy: Dr. Alfred Donatelli, Chair, Eng. 104, telephone: 978-934-3171
Chemistry/Polymer Science: Dr. Eugene Barry, Chair, Olney 313, telephone: 978-934-3669.
Dr. Melisenda McDonald, Olney 413, telephone: 978-934-3683.
Civil Engineering: Dr. Chronis Stamatiadis, Pasteur 113, telephone: 978-934-2283.
Dr. John Ting, Chair, Falmouth 108, telephone: 978-934-2275.
Clinical Laboratory Science: Dr. Eugene Rogers, Coordinator, Weed 309A, telephone: 978-934-4478.
Dr. Beverly Volicer, Chair, Weed 320, telephone: 978-934-4479.
Computer Science: Dr. Giampiero Pecelli, Olsen 225, telephone: 978-934-3639.
Dr. Thomas Costello, Chair, Olsen 313, telephone: 978-934-2654.
Criminal Justice: Dr. David Hirschel, Mahoney 214, telephone: 978-934-4279.
Dr. Eve Buzawa, Chair, Mahoney 214, telephone: 978-934-4262.
Economic and Social Development of Regions: Dr. Chris Tilly, O'Leary 500-O, telephone: 978-934-2796.
Dr. John Wooding, Chair, O'Leary 500-B, telephone: 978-934-4257.
Education: Dr. William Harp (C.A.G.S./Ed.D.), Gould 201, telephone: 978-934-4617.
Dr. Vera Ossen, (M.Ed.), Upham 102, telephone: 978-934-4604.
Dr. William Phelan, Chair, Read, telephone: 978-934-4601.
Electrical and Computer Engineering: Dr. Tenneti Rao (M.S.), Ball 307, telephone: 978-934-3323. Dr. Ziad Salameh, Department Head, Ball 415, telephone: 978-934-3332.
Dr. Dikshitulu Kalluri (D.Eng.), Ball 419, telephone: 978-934-3318.
Energy Engineering (M.E.): Dr. John Duffy (solar), Eng. 330A, telephone: 978-934-2968.
Dr. Gilbert Brown (nuclear), Eng. 220, telephone: 978-934-3166.
Environmental Studies: Dr. Clifford Bruell, Eng. 105, telephone: 978-934-2284.
Health Services Administration: Dr. Vincent Pivnicny, Weed 300, telephone: 978-934-4482.
Dr. Beverly Volicer, Chair, Weed 320, telephone: 978-934-4479.
Management (M.B.A. and M.M.S.): Dr. Duncan LaBay, Pasteur 303, telephone: 978-934-2853.
Marine Science and Technology: Dr. Frank Colby, Olney 302C, telephone: 978-934-3906.
Mathematics: Dr. James Graham-Eagle, Olsen 215, telephone: 978-934-2712.
Dr. Charles Byrne, Olsen 221, telephone: 978-934-2447.
Mechanical Engineering (Manufacturing Engineering): Dr. John McKelliget, Chair, Eng. 331, telephone: 978-934-2974.
Dr. Majid Charmchi, Ball 224, telephone: 978-934-2969.
Music: Dr. William Moylan, Chair, Durgin 107, telephone: 978-934-3869.
Dr. Stuart Smith, Durgin 422, telephone: 978-934-3616.
Nursing: Dr. May Futrell, Chair and Coordinator, Weed 200-J, telephone: 978-934-4467.
Physical Therapy: Dr. Joseph Dorsey, Chair, Weed 220, telephone: 978-934-4517.
Physical Therapy (Advanced): Barbara Cocanour, Weed 208, telephone: 978-934-4413.
Physics: Dr. Lloyd Kannenberg, Olney 133, telephone: 978-934-3783.
Dr. James Egan, Chair, Olney 136, telephone: 978-934-3780.
Plastics: Dr. Rudolph Deanin, Ball 107, telephone: 978-934-3426.
Dr. Ross Stacer, Ball 205C, telephone: 978-934-3339.
Dr. Nick Schott, Chair, Ball 204, telephone: 978-934-3404.
Psychology: Dr. Richard Siegel, Mahoney 104B, telephone: 978-934-3961.
Dr. Charlotte Mandell, Chair, Mahoney 110, telephone: 978-934-3954.
Radiation Science (Physics): Dr. Clayton French, Pinanski 207, telephone: 978-934-3286.
Work Environment: Dr. Michael Ellenbecker, Pinanski 303, telephone: 978-934-3272.
Dr. Bryan Buchholz, Kitson 200L, telephone: 978-934-3241.
Dr. David Wegman, Chair, Kitson 200V, telephone: 978-934-3265.

The University of Massachusetts Lowell is an Affirmative Action/Equal Opportunity university and does not discriminate on the basis of sex or handicap status in its educational programs, activities, or employment policies as required by Title IX of the Education Amendments of 1972 and Section 504 of the Rehabilitation Act of 1973, as amended.
The University's Annual Campus Crime and Safety Report, which includes campus crime statistics and information about campus alcohol, drug, and sexual assault policies as well as other important matters, is available on the Web site and by request.

Sailing on the Merrimack River.

Riverside walk adjacent to the two campuses.

THE UNIVERSITY OF MEMPHIS

Graduate School

Programs of Study

The Doctor of Philosophy degree is awarded in audiology and speech pathology, biology, business administration, chemistry, communication arts, counseling psychology, earth sciences, educational psychology and research, engineering, English, history, mathematics, music, philosophy, and psychology. The degrees of Doctor of Audiology, Doctor of Education, and Doctor of Musical Arts are awarded by the School of Audiology and Speech-Language Pathology, the College of Education, and the College of Communication and Fine Arts, respectively. The College of Education also offers the degree of Education Specialist. Master's degrees are offered in forty-five major areas through six colleges and one school. The degrees are Master of Science, Master of Arts, Master of Fine Arts, Master of Arts in Teaching, Master of Business Administration, Master of Liberal Arts, Master of Music, Master of City and Regional Planning, Master of Health Administration, and Master of Public Administration. Master's degree majors are accounting, anthropology, ancient Egyptian history, art, art history, audiology and speech-language pathology, biology, biomedical engineering, business administration, chemistry, city and regional planning, civil engineering, clinical nutrition, communication, consumer science and education, counseling and personnel services, creative writing, criminal justice, economics, educational psychology and research, electrical engineering, engineering technology, English, geography, geological sciences, health administration, history, human movement science, industrial and systems engineering, instruction and curriculum leadership, journalism, leadership and policy studies, mathematics, mechanical engineering, music, philosophy, physics, political science, public administration, psychology, romance languages, school psychology, sociology, and theater.

Research Facilities

The University of Memphis Libraries contain more than 1 million bound volumes and 3.2 million microformat items in the Ned R. McWherter Library and five branch libraries (Audiology/Speech-Language Pathology, Chemistry, Earth Sciences, Mathematics, and Music. The Libraries' Web site (http://www.lib.Memphis.edu) offers access to the holdings of the libraries and more than 90 electronic databases (some full-text) from all on-campus workstations and via proxy-server from all off-campus sites. Reciprocal-use agreements with other academic libraries within the region allow University of Memphis students and faculty members to access additional library collections with the appropriate University of Memphis ID card. The University of Memphis is a full partner and early adopter of Internet-2 Technology for research and instruction. A network of computer labs provides U of M students with opportunities to tap numerous computing resources: software, utilities, the Internet, PC's, Macintoshes, and laser printers. Consulting, training, and help desk services are available as well.

Specialized research units include the Bureau of Business and Economic Research, Center for Earthquake Research and Information, Center for Humanities, Center for the Study of Higher Education, Institute for Intelligent Systems, Regional Economic Development Center, Center for Research on Women and, at off-campus sites, the Edward J. Meeman Biological Station (a biological research center), the Chucalissa Indian Village and Museum, and the Center for Community Health. Various service units maintained by the University, such as the Psychological Services Center, the Speech and Hearing Center, and the Integrated Microscopy Center, offer additional facilities. The University is affiliated with the Gulf Coast Research Laboratory, Oak Ridge Associated Universities, the National Center for Toxicological Research, and the St. Jude Children's Research Hospital, and it maintains joint programs with the University of Tennessee, Memphis. The University receives special funding from the state to support Centers of Excellence in the following areas: audiology and speech pathology, earthquake research, educational policy, Egyptology, and psychology.

Financial Aid

A limited number of fellowships, assistantships, and scholarships are available. Stipends for graduate assistants vary among departments and include tuition and fees. Inquiries regarding assistantships and fellowships should be addressed to the department chair or director of graduate studies of the appropriate college. Financial aid is also available through the Federal Perkins Loan, Federal Stafford Student Loan, and Federal Work-Study programs. Information about student loans and work-study programs should be requested through the Office of Student Aid.

Cost of Study

The 2001–02 tuition and fees for full-time study were $2108 per semester for Tennessee residents and $5435 per semester for nonresidents. Tuition for part-time students in 2001–02 was $234 per credit hour for Tennessee residents and $512 per credit hour for nonresidents.

Living and Housing Costs

The 2001–02 rates for residence halls on campus ranged from $955 to $1950 per semester. Single student apartments and town houses ranged from $1790 to $1850 per semester. The University has 150 apartments on the South Campus for student families, with some units specifically built for students with disabilities; the 2001–02 rates ranged from $405 to $570 per month. Utilities are paid by the tenant. Numerous housing facilities also exist off campus in the Memphis community.

Student Group

In the fall of 2001, the University of Memphis has an enrollment of 20,332 students, including 4,720 graduate students. Of the total graduate student population, 2,705 (54 percent) are women, and 25 percent are members of minority groups. The majority of students are from Tennessee, but the University attracts students from other states and countries as well.

Location

The Memphis metropolitan area has a population of 1 million and is one of the South's largest and most attractive cities. As a primary medical, educational, communication, and transportation center, Memphis offers a full range of research opportunities and cultural experiences. The city, known worldwide for its musical heritage, has many fine restaurants, museums, and theaters, as well as one of the nation's largest urban park systems. The Memphis Medical Center is the South's largest and one of the nation's foremost centers of medical research. A public transportation system serves the University and other parts of the city.

The University

The University's modern and beautifully landscaped campus is centrally located in an attractive residential area of Memphis, with shopping, recreation, and entertainment centers nearby. In addition to the facilities on the Main Campus, the University has research and athletic training facilities and housing for student families on the South Campus and research and clinical facilities in the medical center.

Applying

Electronic applications for graduate admission are available at http://www.embark.com. Hard copy applications are available from the individual graduate programs. Completed forms must be returned with a $25 nonrefundable application fee three to six weeks prior to the beginning of the semester. Individual programs may have earlier deadlines. Consideration for admission requires satisfactory scores on the General Test of the Graduate Record Examinations (GRE) or the Graduate Management Admission Test (GMAT) and an acceptable grade point average. Individual programs may have additional requirements. Students who do not hold degrees from colleges or universities in which English is the classroom language or for whom English is not the native language are also required to provide a satisfactory score on the TOEFL. Applicants whose highest degree is from an international university must have their credentials evaluated by World Education Services (P.O. Box 745, Old Chelsea Station, New York, New York 10113-0745; World Wide Web: http://wes.org). In most cases, the document-to-document report is sufficient.

Correspondence and Information

The Graduate School
The University of Memphis
Administration Building 308
Memphis, Tennessee 38152-3370

Telephone: 901-678-2531
World Wide Web: http://www.memphis.edu/gradschool/

FACULTY HEADS

GRADUATE SCHOOL

Dianne Horgan, Ph.D., Interim Dean of the Graduate School.

College of Arts and Sciences
Henry Kurtz, Ph.D., Interim Dean.
Linda Bennett, Ph.D., Associate Dean and Director of Graduate Studies.

Anthropology (M.A.): David H. Dye, Ph.D., Chair (901-678-2080).
Biology (M.S., Ph.D.): Jerry O. Wolff, Ph.D., Chair (901-678-2955).
Chemistry (M.S., Ph.D.): Peter Bridson and Theodore Burkey, Ph.D., Co-Chairs (901-678-2622).
City and Regional Planning (M.C.R.P.): Gene Pearson, M.U.R.P., Director (901-678-2057).
Criminal Justice (M.A.): Richard Janikowski, J.D., Chair (901-678-2737).
English (M.A., M.F.A., Ph.D.): Stephen Tabachnik, Ph.D., Chair (901-678-2651).
Foreign Languages and Literatures (M.A.): Ralph Albanese, Ph.D., Chair (901-678-2506).
Geography (M.A., M.S.): Roy Van Arsdale, Ph.D., Interim Chair (901-678-2386)
Geological Sciences (M.S.): Roy Van Arsdale, Ph.D., Interim Chair (901-678-2177).
Health Administration (M.H.A.): Paul E. Fitzgerald, Ph.D., Director (901-678-2794).
History (M.A., Ph.D.): F. Jack Hurley, Ph.D., Chair (901-678-2515).
Mathematics (M.S., Ph.D.): James Jamison, Ph.D., Chair (901-678-2482).
Microbiology and Molecular Cell Sciences (M.S., Ph.D.): Steven D. Schwartzbach, Ph.D., Chair (901-678-2594).
Philosophy (M.A., Ph.D.): Nancy Simco, Ph.D., Chair (901-678-2535).
Physics (M.S.): M. Shah Jahan, Ph.D., Chair (901-678-2410).
Political Science (M.A.): T. David Mason, Ph.D., Chair (901-678-2395).
Psychology (M.S., Ph.D.): Andrew Meyers, Ph.D., Chair (901-678-2145).
Public Administration (M.P.A.): Dorothy Norris-Tirrell, Ph.D., Director (901-678-3368).
Sociology (M.A.): York Bradshaw, Ph.D., Chair (901-678-2611).

Fogelman College of Business and Economics
John J. Pepin, Ph.D., Dean.
Coy A. Jones, Ph.D., Interim Associate Dean for Academic Programs (901-678-5402).
Carol Danehower, D.B.A., Director of Master's Programs (901-678-3721).

College of Communication and Fine Arts
Richard Ranta, Ph.D., Dean.
Moira Logan, M.F.A., Director of Graduate Studies.

Art (M.A., M.F.A.): Jed Jackson, M.F.A., Chair (901-678-2216).
Communication (M.A., Ph.D.): Lawrence Frey, Ph.D., Chair (901-678-2565).
Journalism (M.A.): James Redmond, Ph.D., Chair (901-678-2401).
Rudi E. Scheidt School of Music (M.Mu., D.M.A., Ph.D.): John W. Baut, D.M.A., Interim Director (901-678-3764).
Theater and Dance (M.F.A.): Robert A. Hetherington, M.A., Chair (901-678-2565).

College of Education
John Schifani, Ed.D., Interim Dean.
Karen Weddle-West, Ph.D., Assistant Dean for Graduate Studies.

Consumer Science and Education (M.S.): Dixie Crase, Ph.D., Chair (901-678-2301).
Counseling, Educational Psychology and Research (M.S., Ed.D., Ph.D.): Ronnie Priest, Ph.D., Chair (901-678-2841).
Human Movement Sciences and Education (M.S.): Ralph Wilcox, Ph.D., Chair (901-678-2324).
Instruction and Curriculum Leadership (M.S., M.A.T., Ed.D.): Dennie Smith, Ed.D., Chair (901-678-2365).
Leadership (M.S., Ed.D.): Linda Wesson, Ph.D., Chair (901-678-2368).

Herff College of Engineering
Richard C. Warder, Ph.D., Dean.
William S. Janna, Ph.D., Associate Dean and Director of Graduate Studies.

Biomedical Engineering (M.S., Ph.D.): Eugene Eckstein, Ph.D, Chair (901-678-3733).
Civil Engineering (M.S., Ph.D.): Martin Lipinski, Ph.D., Chair, (901-678-2746).
Electrical Engineering (M.S., Ph.D.): Babajide Familoni, Ph.D., Chair (901-678-2175).
Engineering Technology (M.S.): Ron Day, M.A., Chair (901-678-2238).
Mechanical Engineering (M.S., Ph.D.): John Hochstein, Ph.D., Chair (901-678-2173).
Industrial and Systems Engineering (M.S.): Michael Racer, Ph.D., Coordinator of Graduate Studies (901-678-3285).

School of Audiology and Speech-Language Pathology
Maurice I. Mendel, Ph.D., Dean.
David Wark, Ph.D., Director of Graduate Studies (901-678-5800).
Audiology and Speech Pathology (M.A., Ph.D., Au.D.).

University College
Susanne B. Darnell, Ph.D., Interim Dean.
Graves E. Enck, Ph.D., Coordinator of M.A.L.S. Program.
Interdisciplinary (M.A.L.S.).

UNIVERSITY OF MIAMI

Graduate School

Programs of Study

The Graduate School of the University of Miami offers programs of study leading to the Doctor of Philosophy (Ph.D.) degree in biology, business administration, chemistry, communications, economics, education (counseling psychology, educational research, educational research/exercise physiology, elementary education, TESOL, special education, and reading), engineering (biomedical, civil, electrical and computer, industrial, and mechanical), English, ergonomics, history, international studies, marine and atmospheric sciences (applied marine physics, marine and atmospheric chemistry, marine biology and fisheries, marine geology and geophysics, and meteorology and physical oceanography), mathematics, medicine (biochemistry and molecular biology, epidemiology, microbiology and immunology, molecular cell and developmental biology, molecular and cellular pharmacology, neuroscience, and physiology and biophysics), music education, nursing, philosophy, physical therapy, physics, psychology, Romance languages (French and Spanish), and sociology. Interdepartmental doctoral programs, tailored to the needs of the individual student, are available to qualified applicants. The Master of Architecture, Master of Arts, Master of Arts in Liberal Studies, Master of Business Administration, Master of Fine Arts, Master of Music, Specialist in Music Education, Master of Professional Accounting, Master of Public Administration, Master of Public Health, Master of Science, Master of Science in Education, Specialist in Education (Ed.S.), Master of Science in Engineering (architectural, biomedical, civil, electrical and computer, industrial, and mechanical), Master of Science in Music Engineering, Master of Science in Nursing, Master of Science in Physical Therapy, and Master of Science in Taxation are offered in the areas cited for doctoral study and through other programs. The Doctor of Musical Arts (D.M.A.) is offered with concentrations in applied music, composition, conducting, and accompanying and chamber music. The Doctor of Arts (D.A.) degree, an interdisciplinary degree designed for community college and four-year college teachers, is offered in the Departments of Civil Engineering, Mathematics, Mechanical Engineering, and Physics.

The basic requirements for the completion of the Ph.D. include a minimum of 60 credits beyond the bachelor's degree, including 12–24 credits of dissertation research; a minimum residence of two consecutive academic semesters at the University of Miami beyond the first year of graduate work, wherever taken; qualifying examinations; and the presentation and defense of a dissertation. Individual programs have their own requirements. The academic year consists of two semesters (fall and spring) and two 5-week summer sessions.

Research Facilities

In addition to providing a range of regular and specialized laboratories and libraries, the University has developed advanced facilities for study and research in tropical and subtropical ecology, marine and atmospheric sciences, and studies relating to the Caribbean and Latin America. The University operates or cooperates in teaching and research stations in the Caribbean, the Florida Keys, the Everglades, and Central and South America. Extensive research facilities exist at the University's Ungar Computing Center. Several major research centers—the North-South Center, the Center for Social Research in Aging, the Behavioral Medicine Division of Psychology, the Mailman Center for Child Development, the Miami Project to Cure Paralysis, the South Campus for Applied Research, the Rosenstiel School of Marine and Atmospheric Science, the Parkinson Research Foundation, and the Comprehensive Cancer Center—are available to qualified doctoral and postdoctoral students.

Financial Aid

Financial assistance is available to qualified graduate students. In 2002–03, this includes fellowships, with stipends ranging from $9000 to $19,000 plus tuition; teaching and research assistantships, with stipends ranging from $7000 to $15,000 plus tuition; graduate assistantships, with stipends ranging from $5000 to $12,000 plus tuition; and a variety of additional financial aids in the form of endowed fellowships and service assistantships. Various loan programs, work-study, and part-time employment opportunities are also available. Those interested should direct inquiries to the Office of Financial Assistance Services for loans and employment information and to the appropriate graduate department for assistantships and fellowships.

Cost of Study

Graduate tuition is $1010 per credit hour in 2002–03. The University fee is $62, and the student activity fee is $35.

Living and Housing Costs

A limited number of University rooms are available for single graduate students. Inquiries should be addressed to the director of housing. Generally, graduate students arrange for their own housing in the community. The cost of living varies with the accommodations desired and the needs and resources of the individual.

Student Group

During 2001–02, approximately 3,240 graduate students were enrolled for studies and programs leading to various degrees. This number includes students from all the states and from more than 100 other countries.

Location

The suburb of Coral Gables is one of the municipalities that make up the southeastern Florida metropolitan region. This subtropical area, which stretches from the Palm Beaches to the Florida Keys, is an exciting cosmopolitan community offering substantial cultural and recreational attractions. The University supports a full calendar of social, cultural, and academic events throughout the year. For those interested in outdoor recreation, the Atlantic Ocean, the Florida Keys, and Everglades National Parks are nearby.

The University

The University is an independent, nonprofit, nonsectarian, international institution open to all qualified individuals. Founded in Coral Gables in 1925, its schools, colleges, centers, and institutes now occupy four campuses: the Main Campus in Coral Gables, the Medical Campus in Miami, the Marine and Atmospheric Sciences Campus on Virginia Key, and the South Campus for medical research in Dade County.

Applying

Applicants for admission to the Graduate School must file application forms provided by the University. For the 2002–03 academic year, the application fee is $50, but is subject to change. Applicants are required to furnish transcripts of all postsecondary education, official Graduate Record Examinations scores, three letters of recommendation, and any other requirements of the program in which they seek admittance. The deadline for receiving applications for admission for the fall semester varies by department, but is generally no later than June 15; for fellowship and assistantship consideration, February 1; and for other financial aid, March 1. Some departments may require an earlier deadline. For the Graduate School *Bulletin,* students may visit the Web site (listed below) or write to the Graduate School at the address below.

Correspondence and Information

For specific admission information:
Graduate Admissions
Department of (specify)
University of Miami
Coral Gables, Florida 33124

For general information:
Graduate School
University of Miami
P.O. Box 248125
Coral Gables, Florida 33124-3220
Telephone: 305-284-4154
Fax: 305-284-5441
E-mail: graduateschool@miami.edu
World Wide Web: http://www.miami.edu/grad

DEGREE PROGRAMS AND GRADUATE PROGRAM DIRECTORS

Accounting (M.P.Acc.; M.S.Tax.): Paul Munter, Ph.D. Auditing and financial reporting, federal tax, accounting, information systems, financial information in the health-care industry, managerial accounting, internal control structure.
Architecture (M.Arch.): Teofilo Victoria, M.Arch. Town and suburb design, urban design and development, computer-aided urban and suburban design.
Art and Art History (M.A.; M.F.A.): Marion Jefferson, Ph.D., Graduate Adviser. Studio art-painting, sculpture, graphic design/illustration, printmaking, photography/digital imaging, and ceramics; art history.
Biochemistry and Molecular Biology (Ph.D.): Rudolf Werner, Ph.D. Macromolecular structure, gene expression and regulation, developmental biology, protein engineering, reproductive endocrinology, protein interactions and function, tumor biology, growth factors, hormones and signal transduction, extracellular matrix, macromolecular synthesis, cytoskeleton, neurobiology, oncogenes, retroviruses.
Biology (M.S.; Ph.D.): Carol Horvitz, Ph.D. Environmental biology, organismic biology, developmental biology, genetics, animal behavior, ecology, subtropical and tropical studies, cellular and molecular biology.
Business Administration (Exec. M.B.A.; M.B.A.; M.S.; Ph.D.): Harold Berkman, Ph.D.; Ania Nozewnik-Green, Director. Accounting, computer information systems, economics, finance, international business, legal implications, management, management science, marketing, political science.
Chemistry (M.S.; Ph.D.): Cecil Criss, Ph.D. Inorganic chemistry, organic chemistry, physical chemistry.
Communication (M.A.; M.F.A.; Ph.D.): John Soliday, Ph.D. Communication studies, public relations, communications, motion pictures, journalism.
Computer Information Systems (M.S.): Joel Stutz, Ph.D. Database, information systems analysis and design, microcomputer applications, artificial intelligence, expert systems, telecommunications.
Computer Science (M.S.): Dilip Sarkar, Ph.D.
Creative Writing (M.F.A.): Fred D'Aguiar, B.A.
Economics (M.A.; Ph.D.): David Kelly, Ph.D. International and developmental economics, microeconomic and macroeconomic theory, law and economics, human resources and health economics, public-sector economics, industrial organization.
Education (M.S.Ed.; Ed.S.; Ph.D.): Liz Rothlein, Ph.D. Special education and reading, teaching and learning, counseling and counseling psychology, educational leadership, higher education, educational research, exercise and sport sciences.
Engineering (M.S.; D.A.; Ph.D.): Thomas Waite, Ph.D. Biomedical, civil and architectural, electrical and computer, industrial, and mechanical engineering.
English (M.A.; Ph.D.): John Paul Russo, Ph.D. Renaissance, neoclassical, Romantic, Victorian, American, Anglo-Irish, and modern British literatures; feminist literary theory.
Epidemiology and Public Health (M.P.H.; Ph.D.): Jay Wilkinson, Ph.D. Epidemiology and biostatistics, public health administration, environmental health, health education, international health.
Ergonomics (M.S.; Ph.D.): Shihab Asfour, Ph.D.
Foreign Languages (Ph.D.): Michelle Warren, Ph.D. Spanish, French, Romance languages, comparative literature, critical theory.
History (M.A.; Ph.D.): Janet Martin, Ph.D. American, Asian, and European history (M.A. degree only); Latin American history (M.A. and Ph.D. degrees).
International Studies (M.A.; Ph.D.): Felipe Aguero, Ph.D. International affairs, comparative development, international security and conflict, international economics, international business, inter-American studies, European studies (including former Soviet states), Middle East studies.
Liberal Studies (M.A.L.S.): Eugene Clasby, Ph.D. Interdisciplinary studies in the arts and sciences.
Management Science (M.S.): Ronny Aboudi, Ph.D. Applied statistics, computer applications, logistics, operations research, systems analysis and man-machine systems, mathematical programming simulation.
Marine and Atmospheric Sciences (M.A.; M.S.; Ph.D.): Frank Millero, Ph.D. Physical oceanography, chemical oceanography, atmospheric science, marine affairs, marine geology and geophysics, marine biological science-including fisheries science.
Mathematics (M.S.; M.A.; D.A.; Ph.D.): Marvin Mielke, Ph.D. Pure mathematics-algebra, analysis, and topology; applied mathematics; statistics.
Microbiology and Immunology (Ph.D.): Robert B. Levy, Ph.D. Microbial genetics, microbial chemistry and physiology, molecular and cellular immunology, virology and tissue culture, mycology, pathogenic bacteriology, applied and industrial microbiology, environmental microbiology, marine microbiology.
Molecular and Cellular Pharmacology (Ph.D.): Kerry Burnstein, Ph.D. Mechanism of drug action at the molecular and cellular level, receptor pharmacology, signal transduction, cardiovascular biology, neuropharmacology, molecular neurobiology.
Molecular Cell and Developmental Biology (Ph.D): Nevis Fregien, Ph.D.
Music (M.M.; Spec.M.; D.M.A.; Ph.D.): Edward Asmus, Ph.D. Theory and composition; music education and music therapy; musicology; applied music-conducting, voice, piano, organ, harp, woodwind, brass, percussion, and stringed instruments; studio music and jazz; accompanying; music media and industry.
Neuroscience (Ph.D.): John L. Bixby, Ph.D. Study of brain and nervous systems from diverse vantage points-including cell and molecular biology, physiology, pharmacology, anatomy, and immunology. Includes 55 faculty members from throughout the University.
Nursing (M.S.N.; Ph.D.): Carolyn Lindgren, Ph.D. Nursing; primary health care, including adult nurse practitioner, family nurse practitioner, nurse midwifery; psychiatric/mental-health nursing; women's health.
Philosophy (M.A.; Ph.D.): Risto Hilpinen, Ph.D. History of philosophy, epistemology, metaphysics, logic, philosophy of language, ethics, political philosophy, aesthetics.
Physical Therapy (M.S.P.T.; Ph.D.): Sherrill Hayes, Ph.D. Orthopedics, sports, physical therapy, geriatrics. Entry-level master's degree, postprofessional master's degree.
Physics (M.S.; D.A.; Ph.D.): Rafael Nepomechie, Ph.D. Plasma physics, optics, solid-state physics, nonlinear phenomena and chaos, optical oceanography, environmental optics.
Physiology and Biophysics (Ph.D.): Ian Dickerson, Ph.D. Cell physiology; membrane biophysics; muscle cell physiology; neurobiology-including molecular biology, developmental biology, and neuroimmunology.
Political Science (M.P.A.): Jonathan West, Ph.D. Public administration, public-sector manpower management, budgetary and fiscal management, nonprofit management, environmental policy, international politics.
Psychology (M.S./Ph.D.): A. Rodney Wellens, Ph.D. Clinical psychology-adult, child, and health; experimental psychology-applied developmental, behavioral medicine, and behavioral neuroscience.
Sociology (M.A.; Ph.D.): Marvin Dawkins, Ph.D. Medical sociology, criminology, race and ethnic studies, sociology of education, sociological theory, sociology of science.

UNIVERSITY OF MICHIGAN–DEARBORN

Graduate Studies

Programs of Study

The University of Michigan–Dearborn (UM–Dearborn) is the campus of choice for more than 8,300 students in southeastern Michigan, including over 1,800 graduate students who value accessibility, flexibility, affordability, and preeminence in education. The University is distinguished by its commitment to the provision of exceptional educational opportunities in an interactive, student-centered environment. All of the programs reflect the traditions of excellence, innovation, and leadership that distinguish a University of Michigan degree.

The University of Michigan–Dearborn offers more than twenty graduate degrees oriented toward working professionals who seek further educational opportunities for career advancement and/or intellectual enrichment. Classes are offered in the late afternoon and evening or on Saturdays for the convenience of those wishing to pursue graduate studies while working full-time.

The College of Arts, Sciences, and Letters offers a Master of Arts in liberal studies, a Master of Science in applied and computational mathematics, and a Master of Science in environmental studies. The College of Engineering and Computer Science offers Master of Science in Engineering degrees in automotive systems engineering, computer engineering, electrical engineering, industrial and systems engineering, manufacturing systems engineering, and mechanical engineering. Master of Science degrees are offered in computer and information science, engineering management, information systems and technology, and software engineering. The Doctor of Engineering in Manufacturing degree is offered in collaboration with the Program in Manufacturing, College of Engineering, University of Michigan at Ann Arbor. The School of Education offers Master of Arts degrees in education, performance improvement and instructional design, and teaching as well as Master of Education degrees in special education and a Master of Public Administration degree program. The School of Management, accredited by AACSB International–The Association to Advance Collegiate Schools of Business, offers a Master of Business Administration (M.B.A.) degree and a Web-based M.B.A. as well as a Master of Science in accounting and a Master of Science in finance. The College of Engineering and Computer Science and the School of Management offer a dual degree M.B.A./M.S.E. in industrial and systems engineering.

Research Facilities

The University of Michigan–Dearborn's excellent facilities encourage a high level of student-faculty interaction both in the classroom and the laboratory. The Mardigian Library houses a collection of more than 300,000 bound volumes and approximately 1,200 current periodicals. In addition, students have access to the library collections of the University of Michigan–Ann Arbor, and both on-campus and off-campus access to many online resources, including full-text periodicals, reference sources, and abstracting and indexing services. The campus maintains two general purpose computer laboratories with the latest PC workstations. Each school also has dedicated computer laboratories equipped with PCs, Macs, and Sun Workstations, all networked and accessible from remote locations. The College of Engineering and Computer Science operates numerous laboratories, including specialized ones dedicated to manufacturing, machine vision, materials, engines, vehicle electronics, and networks.

Financial Aid

Graduate students may apply for scholarships, loans, internships, and employment. The College of Engineering and Computer Science has a limited number of assistantships available. Many current students obtain support for their graduate education through their employer's educational assistance programs.

Cost of Study

Graduate tuition for 2001–02 was $300.45 per credit hour for Michigan residents and $756.20 per credit hour for nonresidents. Michigan residents who were enrolled in either the Master of Public Administration or the Master of Arts in performance improvement and instructional design programs were assessed $218.80 per credit hour. Web M.B.A. assessments were $1599 per credit hour for Michigan residents and $1800 per credit hour for nonresidents. A $90.15 nonrefundable registration fee was assessed for all registrants. There are various additional fees assessed depending upon the course.

Living and Housing Costs

No on-campus housing is available. A Housing Referral Office is available for locating housing in the area.

Student Group

In fall 2001, the University had an approximate enrollment of 8,300, of whom 1,800 were graduate students. Of these graduate students, 38.9 percent were women, 6.5 percent were international, and 16.5 percent were members of minority groups.

Student Outcomes

Graduate students at UM–Dearborn come from all professions. Most have worked for several years and have gained valuable experience in their particular occupations. The graduate experience enhances their productivity and effectiveness in the workplace. Many report successful promotions within their organizations or higher-paying job offers after graduating. The automotive industry in southeastern Michigan provides worldwide employment opportunities for graduates.

Location

Located in the heart of one of the world's premier manufacturing regions, the University of Michigan–Dearborn campus is approximately 15 miles from downtown Detroit and 15 miles from the Detroit Metropolitan International Airport and is easily accessible from major area freeways. The Henry Ford Estate-Fair Lane, former home of the automotive pioneer, is a National Historic Landmark and is located on campus.

The University

The Dearborn campus is part of the University of Michigan system. It was established in 1956 through a gift from the Ford Motor Company consisting of 196 acres of land, which includes 70 acres of the Henry Ford Estate-Fair Lane and the funds for the construction of four buildings. The campus opened its doors in 1959 as a senior college serving the local engineering and business community. In 1971, UM–Dearborn began admitting freshmen and expanded its programs to focus on master's-level education. The campus recently completed a significant infrastructure growth with new buildings for the engineering and management schools and renovations in the School of Education building.

Applying

Criteria and deadline dates are included in the University's informational materials. Applications for admission and supporting documents should be sent directly to the program(s) of interest.

Correspondence and Information

Graduate Studies Office
University of Michigan–Dearborn
4901 Evergreen Road, 1080 AB
Dearborn, Michigan 48128-1491

Telephone: 313-593-1494
Fax: 313-436-9156
E-mail: umdgrad@umd.umich.edu
World Wide Web: http://www.umd.umich.edu/prospective/graduateadmissions.html

THE FACULTY AND ADMINISTRATORS

GRADUATE STUDIES OFFICE

Robert L. Simpson, Ph.D., Provost and Director, Graduate Studies.
Charlotte Otto, Ph.D., Chair of the Graduate Board.
Deborah Parker, Senior Executive Secretary.

COLLEGE OF ARTS, SCIENCES, AND LETTERS

Paul Wong, Ph.D., Dean.

Applied and Computational Mathematics (M.S.): Frank J. Massey, Ph.D., Director.
Environmental Science (M.S.): John Thomas, Ph.D., Director.
Liberal Studies (M.A.): Richard Roehl, Ph.D., Director.

COLLEGE OF ENGINEERING AND COMPUTER SCIENCE

Subrata Sengupta, Ph.D., Dean.

Automotive Systems Engineering (M.S.E.): Pankaj Mallick, Ph.D., Director.
Computer and Information Science (M.S.): William Grosky, Ph.D., Chair.
Computer Engineering (M.S.E.): Malayappan Shridhar, Ph.D., Chair.
Electrical Engineering (M.S.E.): Malayappan Shridhar, Ph.D., Chair.
Engineering Management (M.S.): Swatantra K. Kachhal, Ph.D., Chair.
Industrial and Systems Engineering (M.S.E.): Swatantra K. Kachhal, Ph.D., Chair.
Industrial and Systems Engineering (M.B.A./M.S.E.): S. Kachhal, Ph.D., and Tim Landon, Ph.D., Chairs.
Manufacturing Systems Engineering (M.S.E.): Pankaj Mallick, Ph.D., Director.
Mechanical Engineering (M.S.E.): Chi L. Chow, Ph.D., Chair.
Software Engineering (M.S.): W. Grosky, Ph.D., and M. Shridhar, Ph.D., Chairs.

SCHOOL OF EDUCATION

John B. Poster, Ph.D., Dean.

Education (M.A.): Claudia R. Collin, Ph.D., Director.
Performance Improvement and Instructional Design (M.A.): Darlene vanTiem, Ph.D., Director.
Public Administration (M.P.A.): Joseph Cepuran, Ph.D., Director.
Special Education (M.Ed.): Belinda Davis Lazarus, Ph.D., Director.

SCHOOL OF MANAGEMENT

Gary R. Waissi, Ph.D., Dean.

Accounting (M.S.): Timothy E. Landon, Ph.D., Director.
Business Administration (M.B.A.): Timothy E. Landon, Ph.D., Director.
Finance (M.S.): Timothy E. Landon, Ph.D., Director.
Industrial and Systems Engineering (M.B.A./M.S.E.): Timothy E. Landon, Ph.D., Director.

UNIVERSITY OF MISSOURI-KANSAS CITY

Graduate Studies

Programs of Study

The University of Missouri-Kansas City (UMKC) offers programs of study leading to master's degrees in accounting; art history; biology; business administration; cellular and molecular biology; chemistry; civil, mechanical, and electrical engineering; communication studies; computer science; conducting (music); counseling and guidance; criminal justice and criminology; curriculum and instruction; dental hygiene education; economics; educational administration; educational research; and psychology; English; history; law; liberal studies; mathematics; music; music composition; music education; music history and literature; music theory; nursing; oral biology; performance (music); pharmaceutical science; physics; political science; psychology; public administration; reading education; Romance languages and literature; social work; sociology; special education; studio art; taxation; theater; urban affairs; and urban environmental geology.

Fields of interdisciplinary doctoral (Ph.D.) studies include art history, cell biology and biophysics, chemistry, computer networking, education, engineering, English, geosciences, health psychology, history, mathematics, molecular biology and biochemistry, music education, oral biology, pharmaceutical sciences, pharmacology, physics, political science, psychology, public affairs and administration, religious studies, sociology, social sciences consortium (including economics, political science, and sociology) and software architecture, and telecommunications networking. Other doctoral fields include conducting, counseling psychology, education, music composition, nursing, performance and psychology.

Research Facilities

The UMKC library system holds more than 1.6 million volumes, more than 6,800 current serial subscriptions, and substantial collections of government documents, microforms, sound recordings, and musical scores. In addition, besides participating in a variety of local, state, and national library organizations, UMKC has close ties with the Linda Hall Library of Science and Technology. This independent research library is immediately adjacent to UMKC and contains one of the nation's largest research collections.

Extensive academic computing services include VMS mainframe systems, student labs, numerous microcomputers, workstations, and a comprehensive array of software.

Other research support services within the University available to UMKC graduate students include a research reactor facility, an environmental trace substances research center, a center for underground space studies, a hormone research laboratory, a biopharmacokinetics laboratory, a drug information center, an institute for human development, and a center for the study of metropolitan problems in education.

Financial Aid

Graduate research and teaching assistantships are available in many fields. The University offers one hundred Chancellor nonresident recruitment awards each year to the top out-of-state residents. These awards are based on academic merit as determined by the academic departments.

Cost of Study

In fall 2002, the cost per credit hour for graduate course work is $248.43 for Missouri residents and $638.33 for nonresidents. These costs do not apply to the Schools of Medicine, Dentistry, and Pharmacy. Full-time enrollment is considered to be 9 credits per term. Estimated annual expenses for international students is $15,000 for the academic year.

Living and Housing Costs

Room and board costs average $2433 per semester. Personal expenses vary widely according to individual lifestyles but are estimated to be in the range of $950 to $1500 per semester.

Student Group

In fall 2002, UMKC's enrollment was nearly 13,000, including 4,500 graduate and professional program students. Students come from all fifty states and 90 countries. Women represent 58 percent of the enrollment, and some 25 percent of the students who report their ethnic origin are nonwhite.

Location

UMKC is located in the educational and cultural center of Kansas City. Its 180-acre Volker Campus is unlike most urban university campuses because of its extensive array of trees and other greenery. Because UMKC is surrounded by residential areas, students are able to obtain housing easily either on or off campus.

The University

UMKC was established in 1929. A comprehensive state university, it offers fifty-seven undergraduate, fifty master's, four educational specialist's, four professional doctorates, eight graduate certificates in dentistry, three doctor of musical arts programs, and two academic doctorates in psychology and counseling psychology, as well as a large multi-interdisciplinary doctoral studies program and cooperative nursing–doctoral degrees.

Applying

Applicants for graduate study should apply by February 1. Preferred deadlines for interdisciplinary doctoral programs are February 1 for summer and fall terms and September 1 for the winter term; applicants for these programs are advised that some departments will only consider applications for the fall term. The date for application consideration for professional schools is generally February 1. The School of Pharmacy application deadline is March 1. The application deadline for advance standing in the School of Medicine is November 15; students are accepted for fall term admission only. If graduate assistantships are desired, application by February 1 is recommended. Scores on the TOEFL generally are required of all international applicants whose first language is not English. Scores on the GMAT are required of all applicants for M.S. in accounting and M.B.A. study. Scores on the GRE General Test are required for admission to M.P.A., M.S. in computer science, and interdisciplinary Ph.D. programs.

Correspondence and Information

General admissions:
Admissions Office
120 Administrative Center
University of Missouri-Kansas City
5100 Rockhill Road
Kansas City, Missouri 64110-2499
Telephone: 816-235-1111
Fax: 816-235-5544
E-mail: admit@umkc.edu
World Wide Web:
http://www.umkc.edu/admit

International admissions:
International Student Affairs Office
University of Missouri-Kansas City
5235 Rockhill Road
Kansas City, Missouri 64110-2499
Telephone: 816-235-1113
Fax: 816-235-6502
E-mail: isao@umkc.edu
World Wide Web: http://www.umkc.edu/isa

English as a second language admissions:
The Applied Language Institute
University of Missouri-Kansas City
5100 Rockhill Road
Kansas City, Missouri 64110-2499
Telephone: 816-235-1233
Fax: 816-235-5437
E-mail: umkc-ali@umkc.edu
World Wide Web:
http://www.umkc.edu/ali

DEGREE PROGRAMS AND AREAS OF EMPHASIS

For further information concerning the academic department prospectus, students should contact the appropriate unit chair at the University of Missouri-Kansas City, 5100 Rockhill Road, Kansas City, Missouri 64110-2499.

College of Arts and Sciences: Bruce Bubacz, Ph.D., Interim Dean.
Art history, chemistry (analytical, inorganic, organic, physical, and polymer), communication studies, criminal justice and criminology, economics (applied urban), English (professional writing), history, liberal studies, mathematics, physics, political science, psychology, Romance languages and literature, social work, sociology, studio art, theater, and urban environmental geology.

Interdisciplinary Doctoral Program: Ronald A. MacQuarrie, Ph.D., Dean, School of Graduate Studies.
Art history, cell biology and biophysics, chemistry, computer networking, economics, education, engineering, English, geosciences, health psychology, history, mathematics, molecular biology and biochemistry, music education, oral biology, pharmaceutical sciences, pharmacology, physics, political science, psychology, public affairs and administration, religious studies, sociology, telecommunications networking, and urban leadership and policy studies in education.

School of Biological Sciences: William T. Morgan, Ph.D., Interim Dean.
Biology and cellular and molecular biology (biochemistry, general).

School of Medicine: Betty Drees, M.D., Interim Dean.
Six-year program leading to B.A./M.D. or B.S./M.D. degrees.

Bloch School of Business and Public Administration: Lanny Solomon, Ph.D., Interim Dean.
Accounting, business administration (entrepreneurship, finance, health services administration, international business, management, management of information systems, marketing, and operations management), and public administration (general, gerontology administration, health services administration, human resources management, nonprofit management, organizational behavior, and urban administration).

Conservatory of Music: Terry L. Applebaum, D.M.A., Dean.
Conducting, music (music therapy), music composition, music education (choral and instrumental), music history and literature, music theory, and performance (accordion, bassoon, cello, clarinet, flute, general, guitar, harpsichord, horn, oboe, organ, percussion, piano, saxophone, string bass, trombone, trumpet, tuba, viola, violin, voice, and woodwinds).

School of Dentistry: Michael J. Reed, B.D.S., Ph.D., Dean.
Dental surgery (D.D.S.), dental hygiene education (general, research), oral biology, and certificates in advanced education in diagnostic sciences, endodontics, general dentistry, oral and maxillofacial surgery, orthodontics and dentofacial orthopedics, pediatric dentistry, periodontics, and prosthodontics.

School of Education: John E. Cleek, Ph.D., Interim Dean.
Counseling and guidance (elementary school, general, marriage and family, mental health, secondary school, and substance abuse), counseling psychology, curriculum and instruction (curriculum theory and leadership, early childhood education, elementary education, elementary or middle school specialty, English as a second language, subject matter specialty, and urban teaching), educational administration (elementary school, general, higher education, secondary school, and special education), educational research and psychology (general and research), reading education, and special education (behavior disorders, general, and learning disabilities).

School of Interdisciplinary Computing and Engineering: William P. Osborn, Ph.D., Dean.
Computer science (computer networking, software architecture, and telecommunications networking) and engineering (civil, mechanical, and electrical).

School of Law: Burnele V. Powell, LL.M., Dean.
Law, taxation, and urban affairs.

School of Nursing: Nancy M. Mills, Ph.D., Dean; RN.
Nursing (health care of adults, health care of children, health care of women) and cooperative programs.

School of Pharmacy: Robert W. Piepho, Ph.D., Dean.
Pharmacy and pharmaceutical sciences (pharmaceutical chemistry, pharmaceutics, pharmacology, and toxicology).

UNIVERSITY OF MISSOURI–ST. LOUIS

Graduate School

Programs of Study

The University of Missouri–St. Louis (UM–St. Louis) offers eleven programs of study leading to the Ph.D.: applied mathematics, biology, business administration (information systems), chemistry, criminology and criminal justice, education, nursing, physics, physiological optics, political science, and psychology. The Ed.D. in education and the M.F.A. are also administered by the Graduate School. The O.D. in optometry is administered by the School of Optometry.

Master's degrees are offered in thirty areas: accounting, biology, business administration, chemistry, communications, computer science, counseling, criminology and criminal justice, economics, educational administration, elementary education, English, gerontology, health sciences, history, management information systems, mathematics, museum studies, music education, nursing, philosophy, physics, physiological optics, political science, psychology, public policy administration, secondary education, social work, sociology, and special education.

Research Facilities

The three libraries at the University of Missouri–St. Louis (Thomas Jefferson, Ward E. Barnes, and Mercantile) hold more than 1 million volumes, 2,700 periodical subscriptions, and 1 million government documents and provide access to approximately 3,000 full-text, online journals. The Mercantile Library, with collection strengths in Western Americana, holds two distinguished transportation collections; the Barringer Collection focuses on American railroad history; and the Pott Waterways Collection focuses on United States river and inland waterways history. The Center for Molecular Electronics conducts research to understand and control actions at the atomic and molecular levels that are essential for state-of-the-art materials and devices. The International Center for Tropical Ecology promotes research in biodiversity, conservation, and sustainable use of tropical ecosystems. The Center for Neurodynamics conducts research on the effects of stochastic noise on information transfer in natural and artificial neurological systems. The Center for Trauma Recovery conducts research on the assessment and treatment of posttraumatic stress disorder. The Center for Business and Industrial Studies investigates managerial problems and performs applied research. The Center for International Studies supports academic programs, seminars, and conferences designed to promote and improve research in international studies and the methods of teaching international studies in schools and colleges. The Public Policy Research Center conducts research in the areas of employment, education, housing, and law, and offers training experiences for students in urban research.

Financial Aid

Financial assistance is available to graduate students primarily through assistantships. Departments determine the stipend level for teaching and research assistants. Appointments range from $5000 to $12,800 for master's students and from $7500 to $18,000 for doctoral students.

Cost of Study

Tuition and fees per semester (full-time, 9 credit hours) for 2002–03 are expected to be $1919 for residents and $5155 for nonresidents. Estimated annual expenses for international students are $19,015 for the academic year.

Living and Housing Costs

Single students living in University housing pay up to $5000 for room and board for a nine-month academic year. Married students living in University apartments pay between $5500 and 6360 for a one-year lease. Complete information is available at the Web site http://www.umsl.edu/html/housing.html.

Student Group

Enrollment in fall 2001 was 12,242 students, of whom 2,478 were graduate students. Sixty-six percent of the students are women, and 10 percent are African American.

Location

The University occupies a 250-acre suburban campus northwest of St. Louis, the major metropolitan area in the state. The campus has easy access to the airport and the downtown area via the MetroLink, which has stops on both the north and south campuses. St. Louis has an abundance of cultural, sports, and entertainment opportunities.

The University

UM–St. Louis is one of four campuses of the University of Missouri System. It was established in 1963 and is the third-largest university in the state. In addition to its role in advancing knowledge as part of a comprehensive research university, UM–St. Louis has a special mission determined by its urban location and its shared land-grant tradition. It works in partnership with other key community institutions to help the St. Louis region progress and prosper.

Applying

Doctoral applications have deadlines as early as January 15 and no later than July 15. Master's degree student applications are generally due July 1 for the fall semester, December 1 for the winter semester, and May 1 for the summer session. Applicants requesting financial aid should submit their applications by March 15. A Graduate Admissions form is available online at the Web address listed below.

Correspondence and Information

Graduate Admissions
351 Millenium Student Center
University of Missouri–St. Louis
8001 Natural Bridge Road
St. Louis, Missouri 63121-4499
Telephone: 314-516-5458
Fax: 314-516-5310
E-mail: gradadm@umsl.edu
World Wide Web: http://www.umsl.edu/divisions/graduate

FACULTY RESEARCH

Biology. Animal behavior, biochemistry, biogeography, community ecology, conservation biology, developmental biology, ecophysiology, evolutionary ecology, evolution of sociality in Hymenoptera, historical biogeography, molecular biology, molecular systematics, microbial genetics, neuroethology of freshwater and marine organisms, plant-animal/insect interactions, plant molecular biology, plant population genetics, population biology and systematics, RNA processing and metabolism, studies in tropical and temperate ecosystems.

Business. Accounting, accounting regulation, auditor judgment and decision making, taxation, commercial banking, corporate finance, investments and portfolio management, government regulations, telecommunications, client/server, IS sourcing, decision support systems, international information systems, management of information systems, production and operations management, mathematical programming, transportation routing and scheduling, logistic systems, freight consolidation, simulation, supply chain management, human resources, international management, strategic management, marketing strategy, new product development, advertising, consumer behavior.

Chemistry and Biochemistry. Organometallic chemistry of the platinum metals, metallaborane chemistry, supramolecular chemistry, transition metal–catalyzed reactions of silanes, redox enzymes based on cyclodextrin, serum transferrin chemistry, high-resolution intracavity laser spectroscopy, surface and interfacial chemistry, nonlinear optical effects, computational chemistry, effects of electrical fields on flames, natural products chemistry, carbohydrate chemistry, organic synthesis, physical organic chemistry, structure-function studies of enzymes, biophysical chemistry, structural studies using NMR spectroscopy and X-ray diffraction.

Computer Science. Computer graphics, scientific computation, CAGD, image processing, knowledge-based information retrieval and classification, artificial intelligence, evolutionary computation, genetic algorithms and genetic programming, fuzzy reasoning, software engineering, computer vision.

Criminology and Criminal Justice. Criminal careers, criminological theory, delinquency, drug trafficking, substance abuse, vice, violence, gangs, female crime, race and crime, deterrence, crime prevention, social control, crime and social institutions, offender decision making, community-oriented policing, court organizations, police policy and history, criminal justice policy analysis, juvenile justice, crime control, evaluation research, quantitative methods, qualitative methods, statistics.

Economics. Applied econometrics; microeconomics; macroeconomics; monetary theory; international trade and comparative systems; urban, state, and local finance; public sector; labor; public policy; law and economics; forensic economics; property rights; industrial organization; telecommunications; health economics; economics of aging; gender; poverty; science and technology.

Education. Instructional strategies; professional development school initiatives; inclusion; ethics and character education; motivation in learning; evaluation of educational programs; counseling (school, community, and marriage/family); remedial, corrective reading; literacy; action research on teacher development; technology and learning; mathematics education (manipulatives); constructivism; autism; behavioral disorder; performance-based assessment; motor development; postmodern thought and deconstruction; higher, adult, and vocational education. Research is sponsored in the Regional Insitute for Science Education, the Center for Human Origins and Cultural Diversity, and the Regional Center for Education and Work.

English. Chaucer, Milton, Shakespeare, medieval, early modern, eighteenth-century, Victorian, American, modern British, and Jewish literature; literary theory; feminist theory; composition theory; creative writing in fiction and poetry; linguistics.

Gerontology. Health-care policy, reform, and financing; social security and other pension policies; caregiving and other informal support of the elderly; mental health assessment and treatment; ethnic differences, particularly in health-care behavior; assessment and treatment of vision problems; cross-cultural comparisons of retirement patterns and policies.

History. United States social, political, and Colonial history; American Revolution; nineteenth-century; twentieth-century; African-American; women; slavery and emancipation; urban; environmental; military; St. Louis, Missouri; Native American; German-American ethnic; Roman Empire; European—French, German, Spanish, English; economic; Renaissance and Reformation; medieval; African; East Asian—Japan, China, Asian-Pacific Rim; Latin American colonial; nineteenth- and twentieth-century sports; museum studies.

Mathematics. Approximation theory, computational mathematics, wavelets, inverse problems, metric geometry, lattice theory, Boolean algebra, representation theory, combinatorics and algebraic structures, algebraic geometry, number theory, differential geometry, Markov processes, interacting particle systems, mathematical physics, hypergroups, orthogonal polynomials, transformation groups.

Music Education. Psychology of music, application of technology in music education, tests and measurements in music, conducting, choral and instrumental performance, music education curriculum design, affective response to music, music supervision and administration, music software design, urban music education, arts education.

Nursing. Adherence to health treatment, AIDS/HIV, catastrophic stress, exercise and hypertension, informatics and telemetry in health care, psychosocial nursing interventions, quantitative methods in nursing research, violence as a health problem, women's health.

Philosophy. Ethics (especially comtemporary ethical theory and bioethics), philosophy of science (especially philosophy of biology and philosophy of medicine), philosophy of mind (especially simulation theory), philosophy of social science (especially philosophy of history).

Physics. Astrophysics, observational astronomy, experimental atomic physics, biophysics, theoretical elementary particle physics, experimental and theoretical solid-state physics, physics of plasmas, nanoscale microscopy.

Physiological Optics (vision science). Aging and Alzheimer's disease, anatomy of the retina and visual pathways, binocular vision in children and adults, control of eye movements, electrophysiology in healthy and diseased visual systems, low vision, neurophysiology of visual and oculomotor pathways, public health, theoretical and applied visual optics, theoretical and applied visual psychophysics.

Political Science. American government and politics; political economy; public administration; urban politics and urban economic development; program evaluation; public law and judicial politics; public opinion and elections; methodology; labor relations; political thought, including normative and utopian political philosophy; international law and organization; civil liberties; comparative politics; comparative health policy; environmental politics; interpersonal politics; minority politics; policy implementation; political communication; African politics; Chinese and Japanese politics; Latin American politics; U.S. relations with East Asia; Western and Eastern European politics.

Psychology-Clinical. Bereavement and complicated loss, assessment and treatment of posttraumatic stress disorder, personal and professional relationships, interventions for victims of abuse linked to sexual orientation, psychology of women, treatment of family caregivers and depression in older adults, racial identification, multicultural issues, play, curiosity and children's development; mental illness and homelessness.

Psychology-Experimental. Behavioral neuroscience, with emphases on neuroendocrinology and neuropharmacology; cognitive processes.

Psychology-Industrial/Organizational. Employee recruitment; interviewing; performance appraisal; staffing; compensation and benefits; substance abuse; time management; job satisfaction; work motivation; decision making, conflict, and negotiation; group processes; leadership; psychometrics; statistics; personality measurement; research methodology; social psychology; nonverbal communication.

Public Policy Administration. Managing human resources and organization, local government management, health policy, nonprofit organization management and leadership, metropolitan governance, urban and regional planning, welfare policy, social security policy, organization theory, government contracting services, performance measurement, program evaluation, conflict resolution, defense conversion, labor economics, public-sector microeconomics.

Social Work. Urban-related research issues, family violence, social welfare, gerontology, child abuse and neglect, immigration, substance abuse and minorities, community economic development, international social welfare, addiction.

Sociology. Minority groups, stratification, deviance, comparative social organization, ethnomusicology, health, social psychology, conflict intervention, demography, aging, race and ethnic relations.

UNIVERSITY OF MONTANA–MISSOULA

Graduate Programs

Programs of Study

The University of Montana (UM) offers a wide array of graduate programs that are involved in research, scholarship, and professional activities. Nine programs lead to the degrees of Doctor of Philosophy (Ph.D.) and Doctor of Education (Ed.D.). Programs leading to the master's degree are offered by most departments and schools at UM. UM's Missoula campus is comprised of the College of Arts and Sciences, the Graduate School, the College of Technology, and seven professional schools: business administration, education, fine arts, forestry, journalism, law, and pharmacy and allied health sciences.

Research Facilities

In 1999–2000, the University of Montana received $35.5 million dollars in research grants. Broad-based research programs and excellent research faculty members combine with unique research facilities to create an environment that fosters excellence in research activities. Numerous institutes and programs support academic research programs, particularly in the natural science areas. Many faculty members at UM are national or international leaders in their fields. Details about the research interests and programs of individual faculty are available on UM's Web site at http://www.umt.edu. UM is classified as a Doctoral II university under the nationally recognized Carnegie Classification.

Financial Aid

There are two broad categories of financial assistance. The first category is given on the basis of academic merit or the ability to perform specific services. The second category is loans. Student loans are administered through the Financial Aid Office. Teaching assistantships are available in most graduate programs. Teaching assistantships provide a wage, a tuition fee waiver, and a waiver of the registration fee. Students in certain disciplines may be awarded appointments as graduate research assistants, which sometimes include remission of the tuition fee and the registration fee. Individual graduate programs award research and teaching assistantships. Scholarships and fellowships are available in some programs.

Cost of Study

The graduation tuition rates for master's students are $192 per credit for state residents and $467 for nonresidents. The rates for doctoral students are $208 per credit for state residents and $483 for nonresidents. In addition to tuition, all students must pay program and facilities fees based on their total credits hours of enrollment. These fees amount to approximately $950 per semester, with half of that total for use of the Student Health Service and health insurance.

Living and Housing Costs

UM has residence halls and family housing available. Dorm rooms run from $1121 to $1724 per semester. University Villages (family housing) is primarily for married students, married students with dependent children, and single parents with dependent children. Single graduate students may be assigned studio apartments, if available. Family housing units run from $363 for studios to $580 for four-bedroom apartments. Meal plans run from $888 to $1270 per year.

Student Group

Approximately 12,000 students are enrolled at the University of Montana. There are 1,600 graduate students, which includes the law school. UM enrolls approximately 500 international students from ninety countries.

Location

UM is located in Missoula, Montana (with a population of approximately 50,000). Situated in the hub of five valleys, it is the "Garden City" of Montana and is known for its natural beauty. Missoula offers the luxuries of metropolitan life, including museums, unique art galleries, and outstanding performing arts. Missoula was named "The 1999 Great American Place" by *American Heritage* magazine.

The University

UM has provided a high-quality, well-rounded education to students and a wide range of services to Montana residents since it was chartered in 1893. UM is the center of liberal arts education in Montana, balancing that core commitment with intensive programs of professional preparation. The University is a major source of research, continuing education, economic development, fine arts, and entertainment as well as a driving force in strengthening Montana's ties with countries throughout the world.

Applying

Complete instructions for applying and a downloadable application are available at the Graduate School's Web site at the address listed below. Applicants should contact individual departments early in the process for additional application information that may be required. Hard copies of the *Graduate Catalog* may be ordered by sending $4.30 to the Bookstore, The University of Montana, Missoula, Montana 59812.

Correspondence and Information

Graduate School
The University of Montana
32 Campus Drive #2592
Missoula, Montana 59812-2592
Telephone: 406-243-2572
Fax: 406-243-4593
E-mail: gradschl@mso.umt.edu
World Wide Web: http://www.umt.edu/grad

For program information:
Department Chair (see next page)
Department of (specify)
The University of Montana
Missoula, Montana 59812

DEPARTMENT CHAIRS AND RESEARCH TOPICS

Anthropology, M.A.: Gregory R. Campbell (406-243-4245) Research: social and cultural anthropology, archaeology, anthropological linguistics, and physical anthropology. **Art,** M.A., M.F.A.: James Bailey (406-243-4184). **Division of Biological Sciences,** M.S., Ph.D.: Janean Clark (406-243-5122) Research: avian biology, biochemistry, conservation biology, ecology and behavior, evolutionary and population genetics, microbiology (including medical and environmental microbiology), microbial ecology, and molecular biology. **Business,** M.B.A., M.Acct.: Teresa Beed (406-243-4983). **Chemistry,** M.S., Ph.D.: Michael DeGrandpre (406-243-4022) Research: wood and carbohydrate, organic and organometallic, physical, environmental, analytical, and chemical education. **Communication Studies,** M.A.: George Cheney (406-243-4293) Research: Chinese-American business negotiation, communication and emotion, mutual knowledge in conversation, feminist theorizing and feminine rhetorical style, organizational identity and power, participation and democracy at work, organizational socialization, mentoring, mediation and organizational intervention, misunderstanding in couples and families, communication and social support, Native American communication and educational practices, relationship functions of language. **Computer Science,** M.S.: Alden Wright (406-243-2830) Research: machine learning, scientific computing, genetic algorithms, and distributed applications and systems. **Drama/Dance,** M.A., M.F.A.: Randy Bolton (406-243-4481). **Economics,** M.A.: Douglas Dalenberg (406-243-2925) Research: environmental and natural resource economics, regional economics. **Education,** M.Ed., M.A., Ed.S., Ed.D.: Jodi Moreau (406-243-5586) Research: family structure and dynamics, acculturation and psychosocial adaptation, school leadership and decision making, standardized testing, images and roles of high school principals in school restructuring, international education, organizational behavior, leadership style, organizational change, policy formation, politics in education. **English,** M.A., M.F.A.: John Hunt (406-243-4062). **Environmental Studies,** M.S.: Tom Roy (406-243-6273). **Fish and Wildlife Biology,** Ph.D.: L. Scott Mills (406-243-5272) Research: impacts of a highway corridor on populations of painted turtles; genetic variability of core versus peripheral populations of rare carnivores; new monitoring techniques for American marten populations; effects of a recovering wolf population of deer, elk, and moose populations; predictors of nest success in ground nesting birds. **Foreign Languages and Literatures,** M.A.: Elizabeth Ametsbichler (406-243-5001). **Forestry,** M.S., M.E.M., Ph.D.: Donald F. Potts (406-243-5521) Research: biodiversity, landscape ecology, community ecology, forest planning and GIS, forest policy, ecosystem management, plant ecophysiology, restoration ecology, agroforestry, habitat management, international rangeland development, forest recreation management, perceived notion of wilderness, recreation behavior, resource planning, resource policy, forest community relationships, social assessment, forest products technology, growth-quality relationships of wood, soil biochemistry, nutrient cycling, mine reclamation, soil ecology, stand management, old-growth stand dynamics, uneven-aged silviculture, ecologicala restoration, visualization techniques, communication of natural resource issues, social carrying capacity and protected area planning, silviculture, stand dynamics, forest ecology, riparian ecology, forest economics, timber policy, wildfire management, forest health, ecosystem management, population ecology, waterfowl ecology, wildlife habitat, selection and habitat management, natural resource planning, forest management, dynamics of small populations, conservation ecology, site quality, ecological modeling, grass-brush-tree interactions, ecosystem modeling. **Geography,** M.A.: Paul B. Wilson (406-243-4302) Research: land-use geography, economic geography, GIS, global change, field methods, cultural ecology, cartography, water resources, meteorology, quantitative methods, urban geography. **Geology,** M.S., Ph.D.: Johnnie Moore (406-243-6807) Research: sedimentology and sedimentary basin analysis; applications of sedimentary epositional systems analysis to environmental and petroleum geology; geochemical processes in ancient and modern thermal springs; chemistry and chemical modeling of ground water; metal and metalloid transport, deposition, and remobilization in contaminated fluvial and lacustrine systems; geotectonics; structural geology and metamorphic petrology; paleomagnetism; living and fossil coral reefs; clay mineralogy; shale petrology; clay diagensis; sedimentology; carbonate petrology; stratigraphy. **Health and Human Performance,** M.S.: Annie Sondag (406-243-4211) Research: exercise and performance psychology, legal/ethical issues, exercise physiology, pedagogy, athletic training, health education and promotion, nutrition, health and fitness. **History,** M.A.: Michael Mayer (406-243-2231) Research: constitutional theories and issues, contemporary Italian political history and modern European intellectual history, Irish in the West, western regionalism, reservation Blackfeet in the early twentieth century, Native American interaction with the bison, revolutionary France and the International Order, the Lewis and Clark Expedition, women coming of age in the nineteenth-century South. **Interdisciplinary Programs,** M.I.S., Ph.D.: David Strobel (406-243-2572). **Journalism,** M.A.: Clem Work (406-243-4001). **Linguistics,** M.A.: (406-243-4751) Research: American Indian linguistics, second language acquisition. **Mathematical Sciences,** M.A., Ph.D.: Karel Stroethoff (406-243-5311) Research: noncummutative rings and invariant theory, division algebra, combinatorics and its applications, noncommutative algebra, complex and functional analysis, operator theory, functional and complex analysis, uniform algebras, functional analysis, approximation theory, linear algebra, harmonic and functional analysis, applied mathematics, asymptotic methods, mathematics and computer education, categorical algebra. **Media Arts,** M.F.A.: Michael Murphy (406-243-4504). **Music,** M.M., M.A.; Thomas A. Cook (406-243-6880). **Pharmaceutical Sciences,** M.S., Ph.D.: Beverly Owens (406-243-4765). **Philosophy,** M.A.: Deni Elliott (406-243-2171) Research: environmental philosophy, promoting excellence in end-of-life care, philosophy of science, ethics, moral theory, philosophy of education, existentialism, religious ethics, political philosophy, social theory, German idealism, political philosophy, feminist philosophy, ecofeminism. **Physical Therapy,** M.S.: Sheila Heffernan (406-243-4753) Research: pediatrics, electrotherapeutics, skeletal muscle strength, extensibility and stiffness, muscle mutability and adaptations, aging, exercise physiology, disabled athletes, neuroscience, motor control, clinical performance and learning, spinal cord injury, neurological disorders, neuropharmacology, geriatrics, psychosocial aspects of disability, health policy. **Political Science,** M.A., M.P.A.: Forest Grieves and Jon Tompkins (406-243-5202) Research: public administration, American and state and local government, political theory, international relations and comparative government, comparative politics, American government and public law. **Psychology,** M.A., Ph.D., Ed.S.: Nabil Haddad (406-243-4521) Research: psychopathology and addictive behaviors, detection of malingering, psychological effects of head injuries, vulnerability to depression and anxiety, psychological factors in chronic pain, infant-parent relationship, deafness within families, parent training, intuitive parenting, aging, pain and pain management in the elderly, animal cognition. **Sociology,** M.A.: Fred W. Reed (406-243-2855) Research: collective behavior, delinquency, sociology of development, rural sociology, environmental sociology, sex and gender, Native Americans, complex organizations, sociology of education, race and ethnic relations, cross-cultural criminology, juvenile delinquency, juvenile justice, criminology, criminal justice, sociology of law, research methods, adult socialization, stratification, population, rural and urban communities. **Technical Communications,** M.S.: Joanne Cortese (406-496-4460). **Wildlife Biology,** M.S.: L. Scott Mills (406-243-5272) Research: impacts of cowbirds on songbird reproductive success, vulnerability of elk to hunters, wintering ecology of rough-legged hawks, use of GIS to relate wildlife diversity to an existing reserve network, identification of potential linkage zones for grizzly bears, environmental factors affecting largemouth bass in western Montana.

UNIVERSITY OF NEBRASKA–LINCOLN

Graduate College

Programs of Study

The University of Nebraska–Lincoln (UNL) provides outstanding facilities for study and research. Thirty-eight programs lead to the degrees of Doctor of Philosophy (Ph.D.), Doctor of Education (Ed.D.), and Doctor of Musical Arts (D.M.A.). Programs leading to the master's degree are offered by most departments and schools at UNL. There are currently seventy-nine master's programs with sixteen separate degree titles.

Research Facilities

Research plays an integral role in the mission of the University of Nebraska–Lincoln, which is recognized as a Carnegie Doctoral Research Institution. By encouraging the discovery of new knowledge and supporting scholarly initiative in all fields of study, the University constantly brings innovative ideas, techniques, and perspectives into its classrooms. In addition, research done by University scientists and scholars directly supports UNL's extensive public service programs. A number of separately organized University research centers or units provide a focal point for faculty members with a common research interest. These centers or units may offer administration services, special facilities, or a means of financial support for the research and creative activities of the faculty and students.

Financial Aid

Because the University's academic mission is composed of teaching, research, and service, the importance of teaching and research in the professional development of graduate students is emphasized. More than 1,600 teaching and research assistantships are available to qualified graduate students during the academic year, and approximately 500 graduate assistantships are available during the summer. Most assistantships include tuition remission during the semester of the appointment, and, when the appointment is for the entire academic year, it may include tuition remission for the summer. Fellowships are available for graduate students admitted to a department or area with a specific graduate degree objective but without restrictions as to field of study. Minority graduate fellowships are available to qualified graduate students who are members of U.S. racial/ethnic groups. Fellowship recipients must be full-time students during the time of their appointment.

Cost of Study

The graduate tuition rates for 2001–02 were $134 per credit hour for state residents and $345.75 per credit hour for nonresidents. In addition to tuition, all students must pay program and facilities fees based on their total credit hours of enrollment. The 2001–02 rates were $140 for 1 to 6 credit hours and $286 for 7 or more credit hours. Program and facility fees for summer courses vary according to the number of credit hours and sessions taken. Rates for 2002–03 are available after July 2002.

Living and Housing Costs

UNL has fourteen residence halls and a limited number of apartments for married students. The residence hall room and board rates for 2001–02 were $4565 for a double-occupancy room and $5365 for a single room (availability of single rooms is not guaranteed). A limited number of married student apartments are available, and there is a waiting list of six to twelve months. Rates for 2001–02 ranged from $355 per month for a one-bedroom unfurnished apartment to $530 per month for a three-bedroom unfurnished apartment (rents are subject to change). The Student Information Center assists students in finding off-campus housing. The total net expenses (room and board and living expenses) for a student on a nine-month, half-time assistantship are estimated to be $11,180.

Student Group

Students from every state in the United States and ninety-two other countries have chosen to attend the University. Currently, UNL has an enrollment of 22,700 students, including 4,300 graduate students and 1,400 international students.

Location

The University is located in the capital city of Lincoln (population approximately 225,000), which is situated in the southeastern part of Nebraska. Lincoln has a cosmopolitan atmosphere yet maintains the friendliness of a small community. With outstanding educational, cultural, and recreational facilities, including several parks, bike trails, and lakes, Lincoln has received national awards as an All-America City and Most Livable City. Lincoln offers a calendar of social, cultural, and athletic activities surpassing that of many metropolitan areas. It is praised as clean, safe, and progressive. The city is the center of state government activity and headquarters for several major national businesses.

The University

The University of Nebraska was established by an act of the state legislature in 1869, two years after the state was admitted to the Union. The institution awarded its first undergraduate degrees in 1873 and its first graduate degrees in 1886. In 1896, the University of Nebraska became the first state university west of the Mississippi to formally establish a graduate school. UNL has two campuses: City Campus, near downtown Lincoln, and East Campus, approximately a mile from City Campus.

Applying

An online graduate application is available by visiting the UNL Web site listed below. Applicants are encouraged to use this method to submit their graduate school application. Credit card payment of the $40 application fee can also be made using the online system. Deadlines vary by major and are listed on the UNL Web site. Applicants should submit all required documents at least one month prior to the published deadline date to ensure adequate processing time.

Correspondence and Information

For general application information:

Graduate Admissions
Office of Graduate Studies
1100 Seaton Hall
University of Nebraska–Lincoln
P.O. Box 880619
Lincoln, Nebraska 68588-0619

Telephone: 402-472-2878
800-742-8800 Ext. 2878 (toll-free in the United States and Canada)
E-mail: grad_admissions@unl.edu
World Wide Web: http://www.unl.edu/gradstudies

For program information:

Graduate Committee Chair (see Faculty information)
Department of (specify)
Building Address (see Faculty information)
University of Nebraska–Lincoln
Lincoln, Nebraska 68588

GRADUATE COMMITTEE CHAIRS

Some degrees are available in given areas but are awarded under a different name of major. The M.S. is awarded in electrical engineering, but the Ph.D. is awarded in engineering; therefore, Electrical Engineering, M.S. (Ph.D. in engineering). The area code is 402 for each phone number given below.

Accountancy, M.P.A. (Ph.D. in business): Dr. Kung H. Chen, 386 College of Business Administration (472-3360). **Actuarial Science,** M.S.: Dr. Colin Ramsay, 210A College of Business Administration (472-5823). **Administration, Curriculum, and Instruction,** Ed.D. and Ph.D. (and Ed.D. in joint program with Nebraska–Omaha): Dr. Miles Bryant, 133 Teachers College Hall (472-0960). **Agricultural and Biological Systems Engineering,** M.S. (Ph.D. in engineering): Dr. Derrel Martin, 223 L. W. Chase Hall (472-1586). **Agricultural Economics,** M.S. and Ph.D.: Dr. E. Wesley Peterson, 314C Filley Hall (472-7871). **Agricultural Meteorology,** M.S. (Ph.D. in agronomy, M.S. in natural resource sciences): Dr. Albert Weiss, 245 L. W. Chase Hall (472-6761). **Agriculture,** M.Ag.: Interim Assistant Dean George Pfeiffer, 103 Ag Hall (472-7912). **Agronomy,** M.S. and Ph.D.: Dr. Rhae Drijber, 254 Keim Hall (472-0770). **Animal Science,** M.S. and Ph.D.: Dr. Merlyn Nielsen, A218 Animal Science (472-6406). **Anthropology,** M.A.: Dr. Raymond Hames, 228 Bessey Hall (472-6240). **Architecture,** M.Arch. and M.S.: Dr. Rumiko Handa, 237 Architecture Hall (472-0240). **Art and Art History,** M.F.A.: Professor Gail Kendall, 200B Richards Hall (472-5548). **Biochemistry,** M.S. and Ph.D.: Dr. Stephen Ragsdale, N114 Beadle Center (472-2943). **Biological Sciences,** M.S. and Ph.D.: Dr. Lawrence Harshman, 348 Manter Hall (472-0680). **Biometry,** M.S. (Ph.D. in agronomy and mathematics and statistics): Dr. Kent Eskridge, 103 Miller Hall (472-2903). **Business,** M.A., M.B.A., and Ph.D.: Dr. Gordon Karels, 256 College of Business Administration (472-2600). **Chemical Engineering,** M.S. (Ph.D. in engineering): Dr. Michael Meagher, 355 FIC (472-2342). **Chemistry,** M.S. and Ph.D.: Dr. Marjorie Langell, 629 Hamilton Hall (472-2702). **Civil Engineering,** M.S. (Ph.D. in engineering): Dr. Mohamed F. Dahab, W348 Nebraska Hall (472-2371). **Classics and Religious Studies,** M.A.: Dr. Valdis Leinieks, 234 Andrews Hall (472-4481). **Communication Studies,** M.A. and Ph.D.: Dr. Dawn Braithwaite, 424 Oldfather Hall (472-2239). **Community and Human Resources,** Ed.D. and Ph.D.: Dr. David Wilson, 44B Henzlik (472-3386). **Community and Regional Planning,** M.C.R.P.: Professor Gordon Scholz, 302 Architecture Hall (472-9279). **Computer Science,** M.S. and Ph.D. (Ph.D. in engineering): Dr. Sharad Sethl, 209 Ferguson (472-5003). **Curriculum and Instruction,** M.A., M.Ed., M.S.T., and Ed.S. (Ed.D. and Ph.D. in administion, curriculum, and instruction): Dr. David Wilson, 44B Henzlik Hall (472-3386). **Economics,** M.A. and Ph.D.: Dr. John. E. Anderson, 348 College of Business Administration (472-1190). **Educational Administration,** M.A. and M.Ed., UNL-UNO joint Ed.D. (Ed.D. and Ph.D. in administion, curriculum, and instruction): Dr. Donald Uerling, 141 Teachers College Hall (472-0970). **Educational Psychology,** M.A. and Ed.S. (Ph.D. in psychological and cultural studies): Dr. John Creswell, 241 Teachers College Hall (472-2248). **Electrical Engineering,** M.S. (Ph.D. in engineering): Dr. Robert Palmer, 216N Walter Scott Engineering Center (472-6849). **Engineering,** M.Eng.: Dr. Michael Riley, E175 Nebraska Hall (472-3495). **Engineering,** Ph.D.: Dr. Paul Snyder, 221N Walter Scott Engineering Center (472-5171). **Engineering Mechanics,** M.S. (Ph.D. in engineering): Dr. Mehrdad Negahban, W311 Nebraska Hall (472-2397). **English,** M.A. and Ph.D.: Dr. Barbara DiBernard, 201C Andrews Hall (472-1828). **Entomology,** M.S. and Ph.D.: Dr. John Foster, 312F Plant Industry (472-8686). **Environmental Engineering,** M.S.: Dr. Mohamed F. Dahab, W348 Nebraska Hall (472-2371). **Family and Consumer Sciences,** M.S. (Ph.D. in human resources and family sciences): Dr. Sheran Cramer, 105A Arts and Sciencs, UNO (554-2450). **Finance,** (M.A. and Ph.D. in business): Dr. Manferd Peterson, 210B College of Business Administration (472-2330). **Food Science and Technology,** M.S. and Ph.D.: Dr. Lloyd Bullerman, 349 FIC (472-2801). **Geography,** M.A. and Ph.D.: Dr. Stephen Lavin, 303 Avery Hall (472-3580 or 2865). **Geosciences,** M.S and Ph.D.: Dr. Richard Kettler, 321 Bessey Hall (472-0882). **Health and Human Performance,** M.Ed. and M.P.E. (Ph.D. in psychological and cultural studies): Dr. Richard Schmidt, 130 Mabel Lee Hall (472-1158). **History,** M.A. and Ph.D.: Dr. Parks Coble, 612 Oldfather Hall (472-3244). **Horticulture,** M.S. (Ph.D. in horticulture and forestry): Dr. Ellen T. Paparozzi, 377 Plant Sciences Hall (472-1129). **Human Resources and Family Sciences,** M.S. and Ph.D.: Dr. Lisa Crockett, 319 Burn (472-0584). **Industrial and Management Systems Engineering,** M.S. (Ph.D. in engineering): Dr. Robert E. Williams, E175 Nebraska Hall (472-4755). **Journalism and Mass Communications,** M.A.: Dr. Will Norton Jr., 139 Andersen Hall (472-8269). **Leadership Education,** M.S. (Ph.D. and Ed.D. in community and human resources): Dr. Jay Barbuto, 300 Agricultural Hall (472-8737). **Legal Studies,** M.L.S.: Craig Lawson, J.D., 238 Law College (472-1247). **Management,** (M.A. and Ph.D. in business): Dr. Sang Lee, 209 College of Business Administration (472-3915). **Manufacturing Systems Engineering,** M.S. (Ph.D. in engineering): Dr. Robert E. Williams, E175 Nebraska Hall (472-4755). **Marketing,** (M.A. and Ph.D. in business): Dr. Sanford Grossbart, 310B College of Business Administration (472-2316). **Mathematics and Statistics,** M.A., M.S., M.A.T., M.Sc.T., and Ph.D.: Dr. Roger Wiegand, 934 Oldfather Hall (472-7251). **Mechanical Engineering,** M.S. (Ph.D. in engineering): Dr. John Reid, N104 Walter Scott Engineering Center (472-3084). **Mechanized Systems Management,** M.S.: Dr. Derrel Martin, 223 L. W. Chase Hall (472-1586). **Modern Languages and Literatures,** M.A. and Ph.D.: Dr. Dieter Karch, 1104 Oldfather Hall (472-3757). **Museum Studies,** M.A. and M.S.: Dr. Hugh Genoways, W436 Nebraska Hall (472-2012). **Music,** M.M. and D.M.A.: Dr. Glenn Nierman, 361 Westbrook Music Building (472-2040). **Natural Resource Sciences,** M.S. and Ph.D.: Dr. F. Edwin Harvey, 113 Nebraska Hall (472-8237). **Nutrition,** M.S. and Ph.D.: Dr. Nancy Lewis, 316E Ruth Leverton Hall (472-4633). **Nutritional Science and Dietetics,** M.S. (Ph.D. in nutrition or human resources and family sciences): Dr. Timothy Carr, 316 Ruth Leverton Hall (472-7940). **Philosophy,** M.A. and Ph.D.: Dr. Joseph Mendola, 1009 Oldfather Hall (472-0528). **Physics and Astronomy,** M.S. and Ph.D.: Dr. Sitaram Jaswal, 266 Behlen Physics Lab (472-2787). **Plant Pathology,** (M.S. and Ph.D. in biological sciences): Dr. James Steadman, 406H Plant Sciences Hall (472-3163). **Political Science,** M.A. and Ph.D.: Dr. Kevin Smith, 529 Oldfather Hall (472-0779). **Psychological and Cultural Studies,** Ed.D. and Ph.D.: Dr. E. Charles Healey, 107H Barkley Center (472-5459). **Psychology,** M.A. and Ph.D.: Dr. Gustavo Carlo, 320 Burnett Hall (472-6931). **Sociology,** M.A. and Ph.D.: Dr. Miguel Carranza, 705 Oldfather Hall (472-3080). **Special Education and Communication Disorders,** M.A. and M.Ed. in special education; M.S. in speech-language pathology and audiology, Ed.S. in special education (Ed.D. and Ph.D. in psychological and cultural studies): Dr. Stanley Vasa, 318B Barkley Center (472-5494). **Survey Research and Methodology,** M.S. and Ph.D.: Dr. Allan McCutcheon, 200 N. 11th Street (458-2035). **Telecommunications Engineering,** M.S.: Dr. Hamid Sharif, Peter Kiewit Institute 200C, Omaha, Nebraska 68182-0116 (554-3628). **Textiles, Clothing, and Design,** M.A. and M.S. (Ph.D. in human resources and family sciences): Dr. Nancy Miller, 234 Home Economics (472-2911). **Theatre Arts,** M.F.A.: Dr. Tice Miller, 208 Temple Building (472-1617). **Toxicology,** M.S. and Ph.D. (in joint program with Nebraska Medical Center): Dr. David Hage, 738 Hamilton Hall (472-2744). **Veterinary Sciences,** M.S. (Ph.D. in medical sciences interdepartmental area): Dr. Fernando Osorio, 141 Vet Basic Sciences Building (472-7809).

The Lied Center for Performing Arts is the premiere stage in Lincoln, attracting regional, national, and international touring companies.

The Barkley Center on UNL's East campus is home to the Department of Special Education and Communication Disorders.

The Mueller Carillon Tower is a campus landmark, chiming various melodies as students walk to class.

UNLV
UNIVERSITY OF NEVADA LAS VEGAS

UNIVERSITY OF NEVADA, LAS VEGAS

Graduate College

Programs of Study

The University of Nevada, Las Vegas (UNLV), is committed to offering strong graduate programs in areas of regional and national need. The College of Business offers the Master of Arts in economics, the Master of Business Administration, the Executive Master of Business Administration, the dual Master of Business Administration/Master of Science in hotel administration, and the Master of Science. The College of Education offers the Master of Science in curriculum and instruction, special education, and educational psychology; the Master of Education in curriculum and instruction, special education, educational psychology, health and physical education, and educational leadership; the Doctor of Education in curriculum and instruction, special education, and educational leadership; the Doctor of Philosophy in curriculum and instruction, educational leadership, learning and technology, and special education; and the Executive Doctor of Education in educational leadership. The College of Engineering offers the Master of Science in civil and environmental engineering, computer science, electrical engineering, and mechanical engineering and the Doctor of Philosophy in engineering. The College of Fine Arts offers the Master of Architecture; the Master of Arts in theater; the Master of Fine Arts in art, theater, and screenwriting; the Master of Music; and the Doctor of Musical Arts. The College of Health Sciences offers the Master of Science in health physics, kinesiology, and physical therapy and the Master of Science in Nursing. The College of Hotel Administration offers the Master of Hospitality Administration, the Master of Science in hotel administration and in leisure studies, the dual Master of Business Administration/Master of Science in hotel administration, and the Doctor of Philosophy in hotel administration. The College of Liberal Arts offers the Master of Arts in anthropology, English, ethics and policy studies, foreign languages, history, political science, psychology, and sociology; the Master of Fine Arts in English; and the Doctor of Philosophy in anthropology, English, history, psychology, and sociology. The College of Sciences offers the Master of Arts in science; the Master of Science in biological sciences, biochemistry, chemistry, geoscience, mathematical sciences, physics, and water resource management; and the Doctor of Philosophy in biological science, geoscience, and physics. The College of Urban Affairs offers the Master of Arts in communication studies and in criminal justice, the Master of Science in counseling and environmental studies, the Master of Social Work, the Master of Public Administration, and the Doctor of Philosophy in environmental studies.

Research Facilities

The new Lied Library has the capacity to store more than 1.8 million volumes and occupies 300,000 square feet in five stories. UNLV's many research facilities include the Museum of Natural History, Fish Research Facility, Desert Biology Research Center, Center for Survey Research, Center for Business and Economic Research, Reading Center and Clinic, Center for Economic Education, Lake Mead Limnological Research Center, Center for Applied Computer Science, Center for Computer Applications in the Humanities, Environmental Monitoring Systems Laboratory, Exercise Physiology Laboratory, Nevada Small Business Development Center, and Work and Leisure Research Center.

The computer facility located on the campus is part of the University of Nevada System Computing Network. Computers are linked to UNS computers at the University of Nevada–Reno and at Clark County Community College. Time-sharing terminals, remote batch terminals, and local batch terminals give students and faculty members access to the computer network.

UNLV houses the National Supercomputer Center for Energy Research, funded through the Department of Energy. The $10-million center includes a CRAY Y-MP 2/216 supercomputer, a Sun-4/490 computer, a Silicon Graphics workstation, and graphics workstations for use by University faculty members and students.

Financial Aid

Financial assistance for graduate students is available in a variety of forms, including graduate teaching and research assistantships, fellowships, scholarships, fee waivers, Federal Work-Study, Federal Perkins Loans, Federal Stafford Student Loans, Federal Supplemental Loans, and Nevada Incentive Grants.

Cost of Study

Tuition was $103.50 per graduate credit per semester in 2001–02. Nonresidents paid $103.50 per graduate credit plus $160.50 for 1 to 6 graduate credits. For 7 or more credits, nonresidents paid $103.50 per graduate credit plus an additional $7215 per semester. There were special fees for some courses.

Living and Housing Costs

Eight dorms are available; on-campus housing costs include room and board. The Gym Road Residence Hall is available specifically for graduate and nontraditional students. Off-campus housing can be found close to the University. Rents average $550 to $650 per month.

Student Group

UNLV's 24,000 students come from all fifty states and many other countries. Approximately 2,000 of the students are fully admitted to graduate programs, and another 2,000 are enrolled in graduate courses. UNLV has designed programs for both the traditional student and the more mature student with a full-time job and a family.

Location

The beautiful, modern 335-acre Las Vegas campus is surrounded by apartments, restaurants, shopping centers, parks, libraries, hospitals, and other facilities of a dynamic city of more than 850,000 residents. Each year, the University offers a number of stage plays, film series, lectures, dances, and concerts. Excellent sports facilities are available, and the mild desert temperatures of the Southwest make outdoor recreation possible throughout the year.

The University

UNLV has grown dramatically since its founding in 1957. All programs are fully accredited by the Northwest Association of Schools and Colleges. The University is a member of the American Association of State Colleges and Universities, the Council of Graduate Schools, the Western Association of Graduate Schools, the American Council on Education, and the Western College Association. UNLV's 600 full-time professors bring degrees and teaching experience from leading universities around the world. Faculty members are involved in important research for government and public service agencies and for scholarly books and journals. Many faculty members have won major awards.

Applying

Minimum requirements for admission include official transcripts from all institutions attended, a bachelor's degree from an accredited four-year college or university, a GPA of 2.75 for the bachelor's degree or 3.0 for the last two years of work, two letters of recommendation, and adequate undergraduate prerequisite courses. Many programs require acceptable scores on standardized tests, such as the Graduate Record Examinations, Graduate Management Admissions Test, and Miller Analogies Test. International students must achieve a minimum score of 550 on the Test of English as a Foreign Language.

Correspondence and Information

Graduate College
4505 Maryland Parkway
University of Nevada
Las Vegas, Nevada 89154-1017
Telephone: 702-895-4391
E-mail: gradcollege@ccmail.nevada.edu
World Wide Web: http://www.unlv.edu/Colleges/Graduate

FACULTY HEADS

GRADUATE COLLEGE
Paul W. Ferguson, Ph.D., Dean.

COLLEGE OF BUSINESS
Richard Flaherty, Ph.D., Dean.
Accounting: Thomas McCaslin, Ph.D., Chair.
Business Administration: Nasser Daneshvary, Ph.D., Associate Dean.
Economics: Paul Thistle, Ph.D., Chair.

COLLEGE OF EDUCATION
Gene Hall, Ph.D., Dean.
Curriculum and Instruction: Gregory Levitt, Ph.D., Chair.
Educational Psychology: Ralph Reynolds, Ph.D., Chair.
Educational Leadership: Teresa Jordan, Ph.D., Chair.
Special Education: Thomas Pierce, Ph.D., Chair.

COLLEGE OF ENGINEERING
Ronald Sack, Ph.D., Dean.
Civil and Environmental Engineering: David James, Ph.D., Chair.
Computer Science: Hal Berghel, Ph.D., Chair.
Electrical and Computer Engineering: Rama Venkat, Ph.D., Chair.
Mechanical Engineering: Darrell Pepper, Ph.D., Chair.

COLLEGE OF FINE ARTS
Jeff Koep, Ph.D., Dean.
Architecture: Michael Alcorn, M.F.A., Chair.
Art: Mark Burns, M.F.A., Chair.
Music: Isabelle Emerson, Ph.D., Chair.
Theatre: Thomas Cooke, M.F.A., Chair.

COLLEGE OF HEALTH SCIENCES
Carolyn Sabo, Ed.D., Dean.
Health Physics: Mark Rudin, Ph.D., Chair.
Kinesiology: Mark Guadagnoli, Ph.D., Chair.
Nursing: Rosemary Witt, Ph.D., Chair.
Physical Therapy: Harvey Wallmann, Ph.D., Director.

COLLEGE OF HOTEL ADMINISTRATION
Stuart H. Mann, Ph.D., Dean.
Leisure Studies: Jim Busser, Ph.D., Chair.

COLLEGE OF LIBERAL ARTS
James H. Frey, Ph.D., Dean.
Anthropology: Malvin Miranda, Ph.D., Chair.
English: John Irsfeld, Ph.D., Chair.
Ethics and Policy Studies: Ted Jelen, Ph.D., Director.
Foreign Languages: Dick Gerdes, Ph.D., Chair.
History: Andy Fry, Ph.D., Chair.
Political Science: Ted Jelen, Ph.D., Chair.
Psychology: Charles Rasmussen, Ph.D., Chair.
Sociology: Ronald Smith, Ph.D., Chair.

COLLEGE OF SCIENCE
Frederick Bachhuber, PhD., Interim Dean.
Biological Sciences: Dawn Neuman, Ph.D., Chair.
Chemistry: Kathleen Robbins, Ph.D., Chair.
Geoscience: Rodney Metcalf, Ph.D., Chair.
Mathematical Sciences: Douglas Burke, Ph.D., Chair.
Physics: James Selser, Ph.D., Chair.

COLLEGE OF URBAN AFFAIRS
Martha Watson, Ph.D., Dean.
Communication Studies: David Henry, Ph.D., Director.
Counseling: Gerald Weeks, Ph.D., Chair.
Criminal Justice: Richard McCorkle, Ph.D., Chair.
Environmental Studies: Helen Neill, Ph.D., Chair.
Public Administration: E. Lee Bernick, Ph.D., Chair.
School of Social Work: Esther Langston, Ph.D., Director.

The central corridor of the campus contains (from left to right) Grant Hall, Dungan Humanities Building, Dickinson Library, Carlson Education Building, and Ham Hall.

UNIVERSITY OF NEW HAMPSHIRE

Graduate School

Programs of Study

The Graduate School at the University of New Hampshire offers programs leading to the degree of Doctor of Philosophy in animal and nutritional sciences, biochemistry, chemistry, computer science, earth and environmental sciences (geology, oceanography), economics, education, engineering (chemical, civil, electrical, materials, mechanical, ocean systems design), English, genetics, history, literacy and schooling, mathematics, mathematics education, microbiology, natural resources and environmental studies, physics, plant biology, psychology, sociology, and zoology.

Programs are available leading to the following master's degrees: Master of Arts in counseling, economics, English (literature, language and linguistics, writing), environmental education, history (museum studies), music (music history, music education), political science, sociology, and Spanish; Master of Arts in Liberal Studies; Master of Science in accounting, animal sciences, biochemistry, chemical engineering, chemistry, civil engineering, communication science and disorders, computer science, earth sciences (geology, ocean mapping, oceanography), electrical engineering, family studies (marriage and family therapy), genetics, hydrology, kinesiology, materials science, mathematics (applied mathematics, statistics), mechanical engineering, microbiology, natural resources (environmental conservation, forestry, soil science, water resources, wildlife), nursing, nutritional sciences, occupational therapy, ocean engineering (ocean mapping), physics, plant biology, resource administration and management, resource economics, and zoology; Master of Education in administration and supervision, counseling, early childhood education (special needs), elementary education, reading, secondary education, special education, and teacher leadership; Master of Arts in Teaching in elementary education and secondary education; Master of Science for Teachers in chemistry, college teaching, English, and mathematics (summer only); Master of Business Administration (day, evening, and executive programs with a health management option); Master of Adult and Occupational Education; Master of Fine Arts in painting; Master of Public Administration; and Master of Social Work.

The Certificate of Advanced Graduate Study is offered in educational administration and supervision.

Research Facilities

Modern facilities for both basic and applied research are available throughout the University. The University houses more than 100 research groups, and extensive additional research is conducted by individuals. Some of the research organizations included within the University are the Institute for the Study of Earth, Oceans and Space; the Marine Program; the Agricultural Experiment Station; the Family Research Laboratory; the Writing Process Laboratory; the Water Resources Research Center; the Center for Humanities; the Institute for Policy and Social Science Research; the Institute on Disability; the Environmental Research Group; the Center for Business and Economics Research; the Center for Venture Research; the New Hampshire Small Business Development Center; and the Teaching Excellence Program.

University Computing operates several large public-access computers in support of the instructional and research needs of the University; three public microcomputer centers are also available. Most departments are equipped with microcomputers. The Dimond Library houses more than 1 million volumes, more than 6,500 periodicals, and substantial microfilm collections. Specialized collections are housed in the chemistry, engineering and mathematics, biological sciences, and physics departments.

Financial Aid

Financial assistance is available on a competitive basis. Graduate assistantships pay a base stipend of $12,000 for the 2002–03 academic year. Students on assistantships receive a tuition waiver. Tuition scholarships are available to both full- and part-time students.

Cost of Study

Tuition for the 2002–03 academic year is $6640 for New Hampshire residents and $16,340 for nonresidents. Engineering and computer science students pay an additional $208 for the academic year. Business and economics students pay an additional $340 for the academic year. Mandatory fees are $1131 per year. Tuition and fees for part-time students are prorated.

Living and Housing Costs

Babcock House, the graduate residence hall, provides single rooms at a cost of $3854 for the academic year. Meal contracts are available, and students may remain in the house during the summer at special reduced rates. Limited on-campus housing for married students is provided at Forest Park. Prices for efficiency and one- or two-bedroom apartments range from $458 to $607 per month. Off-campus residence facilities are available at a wide range of prices.

Student Group

The University enrolls approximately 10,500 undergraduate students and 2,100 graduate students.

Location

The University is located in Durham, one of the oldest towns in northern New England. Its easy accessibility to Boston's cultural opportunities (65 miles south); to the unsurpassed skiing, hiking, and scenery in the White Mountains (60 miles northwest); and to the sandy beaches and rocky coast of New Hampshire and Maine (10 miles east) makes it an ideal location.

The University

The University was founded in 1866 as a land-grant college. In 1980, it was designated jointly with the University of Maine as a sea-grant college. In 1991, it was designated as a space grant college together with Dartmouth. The University occupies a picturesque 200-acre campus, with seventy-four buildings devoted to teaching, research, and service; it serves as the cultural and scientific center for southeastern New Hampshire. The development of graduate education has been carefully planned by the graduate faculty to provide programs of moderate size and high quality. The Graduate School is nationally recognized for its Preparing Future Faculty program.

Applying

Applications should be submitted before December 1 for spring admission and before April 1 for summer or fall admission. Applications from international students are considered for admission for the fall session only and must be completed by April 1. The application for admission also serves as the application for assistantships and scholarships. Prospective graduate students applying for financial assistance should file an application before February 15 to ensure consideration for the following year. Individual programs may require the GRE or GMAT. Scores on the TOEFL are required of all applicants whose native language is not English. Students should apply early since many programs fill before the published deadlines.

Correspondence and Information

Graduate School
University of New Hampshire
105 Main Street
Durham, New Hampshire 03824-3547
Telephone: 603-862-3000
E-mail: grad.school@unh.edu
World Wide Web: http://www.gradschool.unh.edu

DEANS AND PROGRAM COORDINATORS

Bruce L. Mallory, Dean; Ph.D., George Peabody.
Harry J. Richards, Associate Dean; Ph.D., Florida State.

The following individuals should be contacted for specific information on admissions and financial assistance in their respective program.
Accounting: George T. Abraham, Director of Graduate and Executive Programs; M.Ed., New Hampshire.
Adult and Occupational Education: David L. Howell, Professor; Ph.D., Ohio State.
Animal Science: Dennis J. Bobilya, Associate Professor; Ph.D., Missouri.
Biochemistry: Stacia A. Sower, Professor; Ph.D., Oregon State.
Business Administration: George T. Abraham, Director of Graduate and Executive Programs; M.Ed., New Hampshire.
Chemical Engineering: Stephen S. T. Fan, Professor; Ph.D., Stanford.
Chemistry: Richard P. Johnson, Professor; Ph.D., Syracuse.
Civil Engineering: Thomas P. Ballestero, Associate Professor; Ph.D., Colorado State.
Communication Sciences and Disorders: Frederick C. Lewis, Associate Professor; Ph.D., Ohio.
Computer Science: James L. Weiner, Associate Professor; Ph.D., UCLA.
Earth Sciences (Geology, Hydrology, Ocean Mapping, Oceanography): Theodore C. Loder, Professor; Ph.D., Alaska Fairbanks.
Economics: Karen Smith Conway, Associate Professor; Ph.D., North Carolina at Chapel Hill.
Education: E. Scott Fletcher, Associate Professor; Ph.D., Colorado.
Electrical Engineering: Kondagunta Sivaprasad, Professor; Ph.D., Harvard.
English: Brigitte G. Bailey, Associate Professor; Ph.D., Harvard.
Environmental Education: Eleanor D. Abrams, Associate Professor; Ph.D., LSU.
Family Studies (Marriage and Family Therapy): Larry J. Hansen, Associate Professor; Ph.D., Florida State.
Genetics: Thomas D. Kocher, Professor; Ph.D., Colorado.
History: Eliga H. Gould, Associate Professor; Ph.D., John Hopkins.
Kinesiology: Ronald Croce, Professor; Ph.D., New Mexico.
Liberal Studies: David Andrew, Professor; Ph.D., Washington (St. Louis).
Materials Science: James E. Krzanowski, Associate Professor; Ph.D., MIT.
Mathematics: Edward K. Hinson, Associate Professor; Ph.D., Northwestern.
Mathematics Education: Karen Graham, Associate Professor; Ph.D., New Hampshire.
Mechanical Engineering: James E. Krzanowski, Associate Professor; Ph.D., MIT.
Microbiology: Richard P. Blakemore, Professor; Ph.D., Massachusetts Amherst.
Music: Robert Stibler, Professor; D.M.A., Catholic University.
Natural Resources (Environmental Conservation, Forestry, Soil Science, Water Resources, Wildlife): Russell Congalton, Professor; Ph.D., Virginia Tech.
Natural Resources and Earth Systems Science: John D. Aber, Professor; Ph.D., Yale.
Nursing: Gene Harkless, Associate Professor; D.N.Sc., Boston University.
Nutritional Sciences: Dennis J. Bobilya, Associate Professor; Ph.D., Missouri.
Occupational Therapy: Judith D. Ward, Associate Professor; Ph.D., Fielding Institute.
Ocean Engineering (Ocean Mapping): Kenneth C. Baldwin, Professor; Ph.D., Rhode Island.
Painting: Langdon C. Quin, Associate Professor; M.F.A., Yale.
Physics: Richard L. Kaufmann, Professor; Ph.D., Yale.
Plant Biology: James E. Pollard, Associate Professor; Ph.D., Florida.
Political Science: John R. Kayser, Associate Professor; Ph.D., Claremont.
Psychology: Robert G. Mair, Professor; Ph.D., Brown.
Public Administration: John R. Kayser, Associate Professor; Ph.D., Claremont.
Resource Administration and Management: John M. Halstead, Professor; Ph.D., Virginia Tech.
Resource Economics: Douglas E. Morris, Associate Professor; Ph.D., Oklahoma State.
Social Work: Sharyn J. Zunz, Associate Professor; D.S.W., Fordham.
Sociology: James Tucker, Associate Professor; Ph.D., Virginia.
Spanish: Marco Dorfsman, Assistant Professor; Ph.D., Wisconsin–Madison.
Zoology: Michelle P. Scott, Professor; Ph.D., Harvard.

UNIVERSITY OF NEW HAVEN

Graduate Studies

Programs of Study

The University of New Haven (UNH) offers Master of Arts degree programs in community psychology and industrial/organizational psychology. The Master of Business Administration program has ten available areas of concentration, including options in accounting, finance, international business, technology management, marketing, health care administration, human resources, public relations, and sports management. Dual-degree programs allow students to earn both the M.B.A. and the Master of Science in Industrial Engineering and both the M.B.A. and the Master of Public Administration. An Executive M.B.A. degree program is also offered by the University. This program is restricted to experienced, upper-level executives and managers.

The Master of Science degree is offered in the areas of aviation science, cellular and molecular biology, computer and information science, criminal justice, education, electrical engineering, environmental engineering, environmental science, executive engineering management, fire science, forensic science, health-care administration, human nutrition, industrial engineering, industrial hygiene, industrial relations, management of sports industries, mechanical engineering, occupational safety and health management, operations research, and tourism and hospitality management. The Master of Public Administration degree is also offered.

All master's degree candidates must complete a minimum of 30 credit hours in residence at the University of New Haven. Degree requirements differ from program to program. Prospective students should consult with the chairperson of the department in which they are interested to ascertain specific requirements.

Research Facilities

The holdings of the Marvin K. Peterson Library include more than 300,000 volumes and documents, numerous corporate annual reports, pamphlet files, and microfilm as well as current and extensive back-issue files of periodicals on the main campus, plus collections at off-campus centers. Interlibrary loan search and other resources are available through OCLC, First Search, LEXIS-NEXIS, Dialog, Dow Jones News/Retrieval, and CD-ROM systems.

The UNH Center for Computing Services provides both administrative and academic computing support. Administrators, faculty members, and students have access to the latest in computer technology. Personal computers for student use are spread throughout the campus, with the largest concentration located at the Center for Computing Services. Personal computers are also available to students at the UNH-Southeastern location in Groton, Connecticut. In addition, the Computer-Aided Engineering Center laboratory in the School of Engineering houses DEC stations plus micros connected by an Ethernet LAN. Graphics, printing and plotting devices, laser printing, and a wide variety of data files, software, and simulation packages are also available.

Financial Aid

Financial aid is available for graduate students through a wide variety of sources, including assistantships, fellowships, and loans. The University participates in the Federal Stafford Loan programs.

Cost of Study

Tuition for master's degree students for the 2001–02 academic year was $445 per graduate credit or $1335 per course for most graduate courses. Engineering courses were subject to a $75-per-credit tuition differential. The Graduate Student Council fee was $10 per term. All charges and fees are subject to change.

Living and Housing Costs

Campus housing for graduate students is extremely limited, but the Residential Services Office maintains a listing of apartments in the local area at a variety of costs.

Student Group

Most students are from Connecticut, but each year an increasing number come from other states and many other countries. The graduate student body of about 1,900 ranges from recent college graduates to professionals with several years of experience in their fields. About 50 percent of the graduate students are women, about 12 percent receive some sort of financial aid, approximately 12 percent are international students, and about 12 percent are members of minority groups. Graduates are employed in government service, college and university teaching, private agencies, and business.

Location

The University of New Haven maintains a close relationship with the surrounding community. Although the campus is located in West Haven, it is less than 3 miles from downtown New Haven and students can easily take advantage of the cultural offerings of the city. New Haven has rail, bus, and air service, and its location at the junction of two major interstate highways places the school within easy driving distance of New York, Boston, and Providence.

The University

The University of New Haven was founded in 1920 and is accredited as a general-purpose institution by the New England Association of Schools and Colleges. A number of graduate classes are held at several off-campus locations across the state. Most graduate classes are held in the early evening to accommodate both part-time and full-time students.

Applying

Applicants must hold a baccalaureate degree from an accredited college or university. An applicant for admission to the Graduate School must submit the following before the initial registration: a formal application; a nonrefundable $50 application fee; two letters of recommendation; final official transcripts, in English, of all previous college work; a TOEFL score (except for students whose native language is English) and certified financial support forms for all international students. A GMAT score report is required for applicants to the M.B.A. program. A GRE General Test score report is required for all applicants to the M.S. in forensic science criminalistics program and is suggested for applicants to the M.A. in industrial/organizational psychology program. Late applicants may register as nonmatriculated students. All correspondence and requests for materials should be directed to the Graduate School. Descriptions of programs and procedures are available in the *Graduate Catalog*. Information about the University of New Haven is available on the Internet via the World Wide Web at the address listed below.

Correspondence and Information

Dr. Pamela Sommers
Director of Graduate Admissions
University of New Haven
300 Orange Avenue
West Haven, Connecticut 06516
Telephone: 203-932-7133 (option 5)
800-DIAL-UNH (toll-free)
Fax: 203-932-7137
E-mail: gradinfo@charger.newhaven.edu
World Wide Web: http://www.newhaven.edu

FACULTY HEADS

The faculty consists of 400 full-time and part-time professors. The coordinators for the various graduate programs and the Dean of Graduate Studies are listed below.

Graduate School: Ira Kleinfeld, Associate Provost and Dean of Graduate Studies; Eng.Sc.D., Columbia.
Aviation Science: Thomas A. Johnson, D.Crim., Berkeley.
Business Administration/Industrial Engineering (dual degree): Ronald N. Wentworth, Ph.D., Rensselaer.
Business Administration/Public Administration (dual degree): Charles N. Coleman, M.P.A., West Virginia.
Cellular and Molecular Biology: Michael J. Rossi, Ph.D., Kentucky.
Community Psychology: Robert J. Hoffnung, Ph.D., Cincinnati.
Computer and Information Science: Tahany Fergany, Ph.D., Connecticut.
Criminal Justice: William Norton, Ph.D., Florida State.
Education: Shirley Wakin, Ph.D., Massachusetts.
Electrical Engineering: Bijan Karimi, Ph.D., Oklahoma.
Environmental Engineering: Agamemnon D. Koutsospyros, Ph.D., Polytechnic.
Environmental Science: Roman N. Zajac, Ph.D., Connecticut.
Executive Master of Business Administration: Zeljan Schuster, Ph.D., Belgrade.
Executive Master of Science in Engineering Management: Zulma Toro-Ramos, Ph.D., Georgia Tech.
Fire Science: Robert E. Massicotte Jr., M.S., New Haven.
Forensic Science: Howard A. Harris, Ph.D., Yale.
Health-Care Administration: Charles N. Coleman, M.P.A., West Virginia.
Human Nutrition: Robert W. FitzGerald, Ph.D., Arizona State.
Industrial Engineering: Ronald N. Wentworth, Ph.D., Purdue.
Industrial Hygiene: Brad T. Garber, Ph.D., Berkeley.
Industrial/Organizational Psychology: Tara L'Heureux-Barratt, Ph.D., Connecticut.
Labor Relations: Charles N. Coleman, M.P.A., West Virginia.
Management of Sports Industries: Gil B. Fried, J.D., Ohio State.
M.B.A./Business Administration: Charles N. Coleman, Coordinator; M.P.A., West Virginia. Richard Laria, Director; M.B.A., Adelphi.
Mechanical Engineering: Konstantine C. Lambrakis, Ph.D., Rensselaer.
Occupational Safety and Health Management: Brad T. Garber, Ph.D., Berkeley.
Operations Research: Ronald N. Wentworth, Ph.D., Purdue.
Public Administration: Charles N. Coleman, M.P.A., West Virginia.
Taxation: Robert E. Wnek, J.D., Widener; LL.M., Boston University.
Tourism and Hospitality Management: Constantine E. Vlisides, Ph.D., North Texas.

Students enjoy easy access to laboratory facilities furnished with modern equipment, data acquisition systems, and software.

UNH engineering students have access to the latest technology in several fully equipped, state-of-the-art learning environments.

The Forensic Science Program, one of the finest in the world, supports extensive well-equipped labs for hands-on work with modern equipment and instruments used in this profession.

UNIVERSITY OF NEW MEXICO

Graduate Studies

Programs of Study

The University of New Mexico offers programs of study leading to the Ph.D. in American studies, anthropology, art history, biology, biomedical sciences, business and administrative services, chemistry, communication, computer science, counseling, earth and planetary sciences, economics, educational leadership, educational linguistics, educational psychology, educational thought and sociocultural studies, engineering, English, family studies, French studies, health physical education and recreation, history, Latin American studies, linguistics, mathematics, multicultural teacher and childhood education, optical sciences, organizational learning and instructional technologies, pharmaceutical sciences, pharmacy administration, philosophy, physics, political science, psychology, sociology, Spanish and Portuguese, special education, statistics, and toxicology. The Doctor of Education and Master of Fine Arts degrees are also offered, including concentrations in dramatic writing and art studio. Master's degrees are offered in all of the above areas (except optical sciences) and in architecture, art education, community and regional planning, comparative literature, elementary education, foundations of education, French, geography, German studies, hazardous waste engineering, health education, manufacturing engineering, music, nursing, nutrition, occupational therapy, physical education, physical therapy, Portuguese, public administration, public health, radiopharmacy, recreation, secondary education, Spanish, speech and hearing sciences, theater and dance, and water resources. Formalized as well as individualized dual degree programs are also offered. The University operates on an academic year of two semesters and two summer sessions.

Research Facilities

The General Library system is comprised of the Zimmerman Library, the Center for Academic Program Support, the Center for Southwest Research, the Centennial Science and Engineering Library, the Fine Arts Library, and the William J. Parish Business and Economics Library. The General Library collections contain 1.6 million cataloged volumes, 17,000 currently received journals, 5 million microform items, and vast quantities of archival material of all types. These resources provide study and research facilities for graduate students in specialized fields in which graduate work is offered. General Library faculty members teach graduate courses. In addition, the Law Library, Health Sciences Center Library, and the Tireman Learning Materials Library provide excellent reference sources. Specialized research facilities include the Centers for Alcohol and Substance Abuse, Learning and Research in Integrative Studies, Health Sciences, High Performance Computing and Education and Research, High Technology Materials, Microelectronics Research, Micro-Engineering Ceramics, and Radioactive Waste Management. Other research units include the Institute for Applied Research Services, the Institute for Astrophysics, the Institute for Environmental Education, the Latin American Institute, the New Mexico Engineering Research Institute, the Institute of Meteoritics, the Institute for Organizational Communication, the Training and Research Institute for Plastics, the Institute for Public Policy, the Institute for Social Research, the Institute for Space and Nuclear Power Studies, the Southwest Hispanic Research Institute, and the UNM Business Link. Special research opportunities exist with the Sandia and Los Alamos National Laboratories, which are located in Albuquerque and Los Alamos, respectively.

Financial Aid

Pre-master's stipends for teaching and graduate assistantships range from $10,000 to $11,000; post-master's stipends, from $11,000 to $16,500. These assistantships also include a tuition waiver. In addition, research and project assistantships are available, with stipends based upon departmental guidelines. Interested students should contact the appropriate department concerning assistantships. A limited number of fellowships are also available.

Cost of Study

For 2001–02, state residents paid $139.20 per credit hour. Nonresidents paid $139.20 per credit hour for 6 hours or less and $476 per credit hour for 7 hours or more. Tuition for dissertation students was $345 for residents; nonresident dissertation students paid $374 for 6 hours or less. All graduate, law, and medical students paid a fee of $20 to the Graduate and Professional Student Association (GPSA) per semester.

Living and Housing Costs

A limited number of residence hall accommodations are available for graduate students. The University also has 200 apartments for student families. Eligibility is limited to students enrolled for at least 6 hours. Annual housing cost averages $5000. Additional information may be obtained by contacting the Housing Reservations Office (505-277-2606).

Student Group

In spring 2001, the total University student population on the main and branch campuses was approximately 25,000, with close to 5,000 graduate students drawn from fifty states and seventy-five other countries. The average age of graduate students is 35. Numerous graduate courses are offered in the late afternoon and evening to accommodate the working student population. The University encourages and welcomes applications from members of U.S. groups that are underrepresented in higher education and from other countries.

Location

The University is situated in Albuquerque, a metropolitan area of more than 600,000 people and the center of much of the scientific development contributed by New Mexico to the atomic age. In a setting rich with the traditions of Indian, Spanish, Anglo, and African-American cultures, the University of New Mexico continues to strive for new levels of excellence in its teaching, research, and service.

The University

Created by an act of the territorial legislature in 1889, the University of New Mexico began full-term instruction in 1892. In 1916, a Committee on Graduate Study was formed at the University to structure postgraduate programs that would allow students an opportunity to continue beyond their undergraduate educations. The University is committed to providing its graduate students with a dedicated and distinguished faculty, up-to-date laboratories and libraries, and leading facilities that are equal to any in the region. The University has strong academic connections in the sciences and engineering with some of the world's best research laboratories, which are in proximity; these connections build on the state's historical association with advanced science and technology. The University and its programs are accredited by twenty-three separate accrediting bodies, and it is a charter member of both the Council of Graduate Schools in the United States and the Western Association of Graduate Schools.

Applying

Applicants for admission must submit a completed Self-Managed Application Packet (SMA), which may be obtained from the graduate unit the student is interested in or may be completed online at the Web address listed below. A $40 application fee must be sent to the Office of Graduate Studies or included with the online application, allowing sufficient time to conform to departmental application deadlines. These deadlines vary, and early application is encouraged.

Correspondence and Information

Information on graduate programs and assistantships may be obtained from the department of interest.

Office of Graduate Studies
Humanities 107
University of New Mexico
Albuquerque, New Mexico 87131-1041
Telephone: 505-277-2711
World Wide Web: http://www.unm.edu/~ogshmpg/

FACULTY HEADS

Provost: Brian L. Foster, Ph.D., Michigan, 1972.
Interim Dean of Graduate Studies: Kenneth D. Frandsen, Ph.D., Ohio, 1962.

Listed below are the chairpersons of the graduate departments, directors of divisions and programs, and deans of nondepartmentalized colleges.

Architecture and Planning
Dean Roger Schluntz, M.Arch., Berkeley, 1968.

Arts and Sciences
Dean Reed Dasenbrock, Ph.D., Johns Hopkins, 1982.
American Studies: Associate Professor Gabriel Melendez, Ph.D., New Mexico, 1984.
Anthropology: Professor Marta Weigle, Ph.D., Pennsylvania, 1971.
Biology: Professor Kathryn Vogel, Ph.D., UCLA, 1968.
Chemistry: Professor Thomas M. Niemczyk, Ph.D., Michigan State, 1972.
Communication: Associate Professor Bradford Hall, Ph.D., Washington (Seattle), 1989.
Comparative Literature: Professor Diana Robin, Director; Ph.D., Iowa, 1979.
Earth and Planetary Sciences: Professor Leslie M. McFadden, Ph.D., Arizona, 1982.
Economics: Associate Professor Richard Santos, Ph.D., Michigan State, 1977.
English: Professor Scott Sanders, Ph.D., Colorado at Boulder, 1980.
Foreign Languages and Literatures: Associate Professor Monica Cyrino, Ph.D., Yale, 1992.
Geography: Professor Olen Paul Matthews, Ph.D., Washington (Seattle), 1980.
History: Professor Jane Slaughter, Ph.D., New Mexico, 1972.
Latin American Studies: Associate Professor William B. Stanley, Ph.D., MIT, 1991.
Linguistics: Professor Joan L. Bybee, Ph.D., UCLA, 1973.
Mathematics and Statistics: Associate Professor Ronald Schrader, Ph.D., Penn State, 1976.
Philosophy: Professor Russell Goodman, Ph.D., Johns Hopkins, 1971.
Physics: Professor Marcus Price, Ph.D., Australian National, 1966.
Political Science: Associate Professor Kenneth Roberts, Ph.D., Stanford, 1992.
Psychology: Professor Michael Dougher, Ph.D., Illinois at Chicago, 1980.
Sociology: Professor Susan Tiano, Ph.D., Brown, 1979.
Spanish and Portuguese: Professor Anthony Cardenas, Ph.D., Wisconsin, 1974.
Speech and Hearing Sciences: Professor Amy Wohlert, Ph.D., Northwestern, 1989.

Biomedical Sciences
Biomedical Sciences: Professor William R. Galey, Ph.D., Oregon, 1969.
Public Health: Associate Professor Nina Wallerstein, Dr.P.H., Berkeley, 1988.

Education
Dean Viola Florez, Ed.D., Texas A&M, 1980.
Art Education: Associate Professor Carolyn Wix, M.Ed., Lesley, 1980.
Counseling: Associate Professor David Scherer, Ph.D., Virginia, 1989.
Educational Leadership: Lecturer John Mondragon, Ed.D., New Mexico, 1974.
Educational Linguistics: Associate Professor Melissa Axelrod, Ph.D., Colorado, 1990.
Educational Psychology: Associate Professor Jan Gamradt, Ph.D., Minnesota, 1987.
Education Thought Sociocultural Studies Program: Associate Professor Ann Nihlen, Ph.D., New Mexico, 1976.
Elementary Education—Early Childhood Multicultural Education: Professor Guillermina Engelbrecht, Ph.D., Arizona State, 1973.
Elementary/Secondary—Bilingual/TESOL Education: Associate Professor Rebecca Blum-Martinez, Ph.D., Berkeley, 1993.
Elementary/Secondary—Language and Literacy Education: Associate Professor Donald Zancanella, Ph.D., Missouri, 1981.
Elementary/Secondary—Mathematics, Science, and Educational Technology: Associate Professor Anne Madsen, Ph.D., Michigan State, 1988.
Family Studies: Professor Pauline Turner, Ph.D., Texas at Austin, 1974.
Health Education: Professor William Kane, Ph.D., Oregon, 1977.
Nutrition: Associate Professor Karen Heller, Ph.D., Colorado State, 1986; RD.
Organizational Learning and Instructional Technologies: Associate Professor Patricia Boverie, Ph.D., Texas at Austin, 1988.
Physical Education—Curriculum and Instruction, Exercise Science, Physical Education, and Sport Administration: Associate Professor Mary Jo Campbell, Ph.D., Ohio State, 1973.
Recreation, Recreation/Environmental Education, and Elementary/Secondary—Environmental Education: Professor Craig Kelsey, Ph.D., New Mexico, 1977.
Special Education: Professor Ginger Blalock, Ph.D., Texas at Austin, 1984, and Professor Ruth Luckasson, J.D., New Mexico, 1980.

Engineering
Dean Joseph L. Cecchi, Ph.D., Harvard, 1972.
Chemical and Nuclear Engineering: Professor Norman F. Roderick, Ph.D., Michigan, 1971.
Civil Engineering: Professor Timothy J. Ward, Ph.D., Colorado State, 1976.
Computer Science: Professor Deepak Kapur, Ph.D., MIT, 1980.
Electrical and Computer Engineering: Professor Christos Christadoulou, Ph.D., North Carolina State, 1985.
Mechanical Engineering: Professor Marc Ingber, Ph.D., Michigan, 1984.

Fine Arts
Interim Dean Christopher Mead, Ph.D., Pennsylvania, 1986.
Art and Art History: Associate Professor Joyce Szabo, Ph.D., New Mexico, 1983.
Music: Associate Professor Steven Block, Ph.D., Pittsburgh, 1981.
Theater and Dance: Associate Professor Denise Schulz, M.F.A., Texas at Austin, 1979.

Robert O. Anderson Graduate School of Management
Dean Howard L. Smith, Ph.D., Washington (Seattle), 1976.

Nursing
Dean Sandra Ferketich, Ph.D., Arizona, 1982.

Pharmacy
Dean William M. Hadley, Ph.D., Purdue, 1972.

Public Administration
Professor T. Zane Reeves, Director; Ph.D., USC, 1974.

University College
Interim Dean Peter L. White, Ph.D., Penn State, 1976.
Water Resources: Professor Michael E. Campana, Director; Ph.D., Arizona, 1975.

UNIVERSITY OF NORTH CAROLINA AT CHAPEL HILL

Graduate School

Programs of Study

The University of North Carolina at Chapel Hill (UNC-CH) offers programs of study leading to the Doctor of Philosophy (Ph.D.) degree in anthropology, art history, biochemistry and biophysics, biology, biomedical engineering, biostatistics, business administration, cell and molecular physiology, cell biology and anatomy, chemistry, city and regional planning, classics, communication studies, comparative literature, computer science, ecology, economics, education, English, environmental sciences and engineering, epidemiology, genetics and molecular biology, geography, geology, Germanic languages, health behavior and health education, health policy and administration, history, human movement science, information and library science, journalism and mass communication, linguistics, marine sciences, materials sciences, maternal and child health, mathematics, microbiology and immunology, music, neurobiology, nursing, nutrition, operations research, oral biology, pathology, pharmacology, pharmacy, philosophy, physics and astronomy, political science, psychology, public policy analysis, religious studies, Romance languages, Slavic languages and literatures, social work, sociology, statistics, and toxicology. The Doctor of Audiology (Au.D.), the Doctor of Education (Ed.D.), and the Doctor of Public Health (Dr.P.H.) degrees are also offered.

The Master of Arts (M.A.) or Master of Science (M.S.) degrees are also offered in most of the fields listed above. In addition, numerous professional masters' degrees in the liberal arts and health sciences are available, including communication studies, a number of dental specialties (including dental hygiene education, endodontics, operative dentistry, oral biology, oral and maxillofacial surgery, oral radiology, orthodontics, pediatric dentistry, periodontics, and prosthodontics), dramatic art, various fields in education, folklore, maternal and child health, nursing, nutrition, occupational sciences, physical education exercise and sports science, physical therapy, public administration, public health, recreation and leisure studies, rehabilitation psychology and counseling, Russian/East European studies, speech and hearing sciences, and studio art.

A number of dual-degree programs also are offered within the Graduate School at Chapel Hill and with North Carolina State University and Duke University.

Research Facilities

Nearly three dozen libraries, located in more than twenty sites, support the University's academic and professional programs. Their combined collections exceed 4 million print volumes, 3 million government publications, and 14 million manuscripts, as well as thousands of audiovisuals and electronic titles, and maps and photographs. Their subject range covers most areas of the fine arts, biomedical and physical sciences, humanities, law, and social sciences. In addition, the libraries offer a wide range of campuswide reference and referral services, some of which are now available remotely through the Internet or campus computer networks. Through cooperative agreements, users also have access to additional collections and services available from nearby libraries.

Financial Aid

A variety of support mechanisms are available for graduate students at UNC-CH, including teaching assistantships, research assistantships, fellowships, and traineeships. Most of these awards provide full tuition support. All teaching and research assistantships, as well as most fellowships and traineeships, provide health insurance.

Cost of Study

Tuition and fees vary somewhat by field. In 2001–02, yearly tuition and fees in Arts and Sciences were $3450 for North Carolina residents and $13,760 for nonresidents.

Living and Housing Costs

The University has 306 furnished family housing units; students are encouraged to apply for housing as early as possible since the waiting period is quite long. In 2000–01, rent ranged from $350 to $400 a month. Residence hall room costs for unmarried students ranged from $1255 to $1825 per semester. Meals may be purchased on a declining basis; students pay a minimum of $100, and the cost of each meal is deducted from this figure.

Student Group

The total enrollment of the University is about 24,000. Every state and many nations are represented. There are approximately 6,500 students pursuing graduate degrees.

Location

Chapel Hill offers the appeal of a small town and the cosmopolitan benefits of a larger city. Its rich blend of history, natural beauty, and culture is enjoyed by residents, students, and visitors. Its central location places the University within a few hours of North Carolina's mountains and seashore. The state capital, Raleigh, is 28 miles away. Durham and Research Triangle Park are 10 miles away.

The University

The University of North Carolina at Chapel Hill was the first state university to admit students. It was chartered in 1789 and formally opened in 1975. It announced programs for the Master of Arts and Doctor of Philosophy degrees in 1877, and these degrees were first awarded in 1883.

Applying

The UNC Graduate School relies solely on electronic media for the distribution and receipt of application materials. Prospective applicants are encouraged to visit the Web site listed below for complete information, a listing of all programs offered, and the online admission application. Fall applicants who wish to be considered for Graduate School funding should submit an online application, required transcripts, and all supporting materials by December 1. Some programs may elect to continue receiving applications past this date. If so, they will establish a later application deadline, and their applicants will be eligible for program-based funding. Students seeking spring admission should apply by October 15. A nonrefundable $60 application fee is required.

Correspondence and Information

Graduate School
CB#4010 Bynum Hall
University of North Carolina at Chapel Hill
Chapel Hill, North Carolina 27599-4010
Telephone: 919-966-2611
World Wide Web: http://gradschool.unc.edu

GRADUATE DEANS

Dean of the Graduate School: Linda A. Dykstra, Ph.D.
Dean of the School of Business: Robert Sullivan, Ph.D.
Dean of the School of Dentistry: John W. Stamm, Ph.D., D.D.P.H.
Dean of the School of Education: Madeleine Grumet, Ed.D.
Dean of the School of Information and Library Science: Joanne Gard Marshall, Ph.D.
Dean of the School of Journalism: Richard R. Cole, Ph.D.
Dean of the School of Medicine: Jeffrey L. Houpt, M.D.
Dean of the School of Nursing: Linda Cronenwett, Ph.D.
Dean of the School of Pharmacy: William H. Campbell, Ph.D.
Dean of the School of Public Health: William L. Roper, M.D., M.P.H.
Interim Dean of the School of Social Work: Jack Richman, Ph.D.

Bynum Hall, home of the Graduate School.

View of Dey Hall from the steps of the Wilson Library.

Aerial view of the South Building and the "Old Well".

UNIVERSITY OF NORTH CAROLINA AT GREENSBORO

Graduate School

Programs of Study

The University of North Carolina at Greensboro (UNCG) offers programs of study leading to the Ph.D., Ed.D., and D.M.A. degrees. The Ph.D. is offered in counseling and counselor education; curriculum and teaching; educational research, measurement, and evaluation; English; exercise and sport science; human development and family studies; music education; nutrition; psychology; and textile products design and marketing. Programs leading to the Ed.D. degree are offered in counseling and development, educational leadership, and exercise and sport science.

Sixth-year programs are available in counseling and development, educational leadership, and higher education, leading to the Ed.S. degree. Post-master's certificates are offered in adult nurse practitioner/gerontological nurse practitioner, gerontological counseling, information technology, international studies in business administration, management, marriage and family counseling, nurse anesthesia, and school counseling. Post-baccalaureate certificates are offered in business administration, geographic information science, gerontological nursing, gerontology, historic preservation, museum studies, nonprofit management, nursing administration, nursing case management, nursing education, technical writing, and women's studies.

Master's degrees (M.A., M.A.L.S., M.B.A., M.Ed., M.F.A., M.L.I.S., M.M., M.P.A., M.P.H., M.S., M.S.A., M.S.N., M.S.B.E., M.S.W., or an M.S.N./M.B.A. combined degree, according to the student's major and professional aims) are offered in more than sixty specializations. These include accounting; biology; business administration; business education; chemistry; communication studies; computer science; creative writing; curriculum and instruction (chemistry, elementary education, English as a second language (ESL), French, mathematics, middle grades education, reading, science, social studies, Spanish); dance; drama; economics; education research, measurement, and evaluation; educational supervision; English; exercise and sport science; genetic counseling; geography; gerontology; higher education; history; human development and family studies; information technology and management; interior architecture; Latin; liberal studies; library and information studies; mathematics; music; nursing; nutrition and food service systems; parks and recreation management; political science; psychology; public affairs; public health; romance languages (French and Spanish literature); school administration; social work; sociology; special education; speech pathology and audiology; studio arts; textile products design and marketing; and theater. (Details are contained in the *Graduate School Bulletin*, which is available on line at the Web site listed below.)

Research Facilities

The University's research facilities are substantial and constantly growing. Library holdings total more than 2 million, with approximately 5,300 serials. The University also draws upon the large libraries of nearby Duke University, North Carolina State University at Raleigh, and the University of North Carolina at Chapel Hill. UNCG supports computer systems ranging from a large DEC VAXcluster to a variety of personal computers; a campus network is linked to other major networks, including the Internet.

Financial Aid

More than half of the University's full-time graduate students hold assistantships of one kind or another. In 2001–02, these ranged upward from approximately $4000 a year and required such duties of the student as grading or assisting with teaching or research. Those interested in such appointments should apply as early as possible to the head of their prospective department (listed on the reverse of this page). A very limited number of Excellence Fellowships, which are worth about $14,000 (plus any nonresident tuition differential) and require no services in return, are also available to new doctoral students of outstanding ability. Other fellowships designated for specific disciplines are also available. It is not necessary to apply separately for these fellowships, since all doctoral applicants are routinely considered for them.

The Minority Presence Grant Program for Doctoral Study provides stipends of $4000 for the academic year, with an option of $500 in additional support for study in the summer session for African-American residents of North Carolina. Recipients must be full-time students pursuing doctoral degrees at the University of North Carolina at Greensboro. However, students admitted to a master's degree program in a department with a doctoral program, and who intend and will be eligible to pursue doctoral studies after completion of the master's degree, may also be eligible for a Minority Presence Grant.

Cost of Study

In 2001–02, a North Carolina resident's tuition and academic fees totaled $1117 per semester for a full course load; for a nonresident, the total was $5808. Nonresident students who have been recruited for their special talents and who perform substantial academic duties for their department or school as teaching or research assistants may, in some cases, be eligible for the resident tuition rate. A health service fee of $89 per semester may be required, depending upon the course load and whether the student lives on or off campus. General and technical fees ranged from $90 to $415 per semester, depending upon the course load. All charges are subject to change.

Living and Housing Costs

Housing is available on campus for unmarried students. The cost in 2001–02 for a standard (non–air-conditioned) double room was $1181 per semester. Air-conditioned and single rooms are available at a higher cost. A variety of meal plans are also available; graduate students most often opt for the $800 declining balance option, which is accepted at all dining facilities on campus. There are no University accommodations for married students, but apartments and houses may be rented in Greensboro at reasonable rates. All charges are subject to change. Students should contact the Office of Housing and Residence Life for additional information (telephone: 336-334-5636).

Student Group

The total enrollment of the University is approximately 13,000 students, of whom 2,800 are graduate students. Many areas and nationalities are represented, but the majority of students are from North Carolina.

Location

Greensboro is an attractive city of approximately 200,000, with a mild climate and a variety of cultural advantages. It has an active musical and theatrical life, and the University's Weatherspoon Gallery has an impressive collection of modern art. The Great Smoky Mountains to the west and the Atlantic beaches to the east are within a few hours' drive.

The University

Third in seniority among the sixteen institutions of the University of North Carolina System, the University of North Carolina at Greensboro was established in 1891. It has offered graduate work since 1920.

Applying

Early application is encouraged. Many programs have specific deadlines for fall admission only. Required are a completed application form, three recommendations, transcripts of earlier work, and, in most cases, appropriate test scores. There is a nonrefundable application fee of $35.

Correspondence and Information

The Graduate School
The University of North Carolina at Greensboro
241 Mossman Building
P.O. Box 26176
Greensboro, North Carolina 27402-6176
Telephone: 336-334-5596
E-mail: inquiries@uncg.edu
World Wide Web: http://www.uncg.edu/grs

FACULTY HEADS

Maureen Grasso, Ph.D., Interim Dean of the Graduate School
Rebecca Saunders, Ph.D., Interim Associate Dean of the Graduate School.

COLLEGE OF ARTS AND SCIENCES

Walter Beale, Ph.D., Dean.

Art: Patricia Wasserboehr, M.F.A.
Biology: Anne Hershey, Ph.D.
Broadcasting and Cinema: John Jellicorse, Ph.D.
Chemistry: Terence Nile, Ph.D.
Classical Studies: Susan Shelmerdine, Ph.D.
Communication: Harold Goodall, Ph.D.
English: Denise Baker, Ph.D.
Geography: Gordon Bennett, Ph.D.
History: William Link, Ph.D.
Liberal Studies: John Young, Ph.D.
Mathematical Sciences: Robert Miller, Ph.D.
Political Science: Charles Prysby, Ph.D.
Psychology: Timothy Johnston, Ph.D.
Romance Languages: Theresa Sears, Ph.D.
Sociology: Julie Brown, Ph.D.
Theater: Thomas Humphrey.

BRYAN SCHOOL OF BUSINESS AND ECONOMICS

James K. Weeks, Ph.D., Dean.

Accounting: C. Edward Arnington, D.B.A.
Business and Marketing Education: Stephen Lucas, Ph.D.
Economics: Stuart Allen, Ph.D.
Information Systems and Operations Management: Prashaut C. Palvia, Ph.D.
M.B.A. Program: Sheldon Balbirer, Ph.D.

SCHOOL OF EDUCATION

Dale Schunk, Ph.D., Dean.

Counseling and Educational Development: DiAnne Borders, Ph.D.
Curriculum and Instruction: Barbara Levin, Ph.D.
Educational Leadership and Cultural Foundations: Rick Reitzug, Ed.D.
Educational Research Methodology: Rick Luecht, Ph.D.
Library Science and Information Studies: Orvin Shiflett, Ph.D.
Specialized Education Services: Marilyn Friend, Ph.D.

SCHOOL OF HEALTH AND HUMAN PERFORMANCE

David Perrin, Ph.D., Dean.

Communication Science and Disorders: Jacqueline Cimorelli, Ph.D.
Dance: Susan Stinson, Ed.D.
Exercise and Sports Science: Kathleen Williams, Ph.D.
Public Health Education: Dan Bibeau, Ph.D.
Recreation, Parks, and Tourism: Stuart Schleien, Ph.D.

SCHOOL OF HUMAN ENVIRONMENTAL SCIENCES

Laura Sims, Ph.D., Dean.

Interior Architecture: Tom Lambeth, M.L.A.
Human Development and Family Studies: David Demo, Ph.D.
Nutrition and Food Service Systems: Rosemary C. Wander, Ph.D.
Social Work: John Rife, Ph.D.
Textile Products Design and Marketing: Martha McEnally, Ph.D.

SCHOOL OF MUSIC

Arthur R. Tollefson, D.M.A., Dean.

SCHOOL OF NURSING

Lynne G. Pearcey, Ph.D., Dean.

UNIVERSITY OF NORTHERN COLORADO

Graduate School

Programs of Study

The University of Northern Colorado (UNC) Graduate School offers programs of study leading to master's, specialist, and doctoral degrees. There are twenty-eight Master of Arts programs (several of which have optional fields of emphasis), as well as Master of Music, Master of Public Health, and Master of Science degree programs. The post-master's Specialist in Education (Ed.S) degree is offered in educational leadership and school psychology. At the doctoral level, the Doctor of Arts (D.A.) in music is offered. The Doctor of Education (Ed.D.) is offered in educational leadership, elementary education, physical education (emphases in kinesiology, pedagogy, sports administration), and special education. The Doctor of Philosophy (Ph.D.) is offered in applied statistics and research methods, biological education, chemical education, counselor education and supervision, educational mathematics, educational psychology, educational technology, higher education and student affairs leadership, human rehabilitation, and school psychology. The Doctor of Psychology (Psy.D.) is offered in counseling psychology. Individually designed graduate interdisciplinary programs may be approved for the M.A., and M.S. degrees. Master's degrees require a minimum of 30 semester hours. The specialist degree requires a minimum of 30 hours past the master's degree, and the doctoral programs all require a minimum of 64 hours past the master's. All degrees require the passing of a comprehensive examination or an approved equivalent capstone project. Many of the research oriented master's programs require a thesis, while practice-oriented programs usually require internships or practicums. Doctoral programs all require the completion of a dissertation.

Research Facilities

The University libraries contain more than 1.5 million catalogued pieces, including hardbound volumes, periodicals, monographs, government documents, archival materials, filmstrips, slides, maps, software programs, videos, and microforms. A new integrated library system, The Source, provides users with access to library collections worldwide. Other research facilities include the herbarium and greenhouses available for biological research and laboratories for chemistry, biology, and neuropsychology research in the College of Arts and Sciences, the Center for Educational Leadership, the Bresnahan-Halstead Center of Mental Retardation and Developmental Disabilities, the Kephart Memorial Child Study Center, and the Research Consulting Lab in the College of Education; multidisciplinary health clinics and human performance laboratories and the Rocky Mountain Cancer Rehabilitation Institute in the College of Health and Human Sciences; and the Music Technology Center in the College of Performing and Visual Arts.

Financial Aid

Financial support includes graduate assistantships, fellowships, and scholarships, as well as need-based grants and loans. The University uses the Free Application for Federal Student Aid (FAFSA) for need-based awards and loans. The deadline for priority consideration for all financial awards is March 1. Some programs have earlier deadlines. Full assistantships (appointments of .40 FTE or greater) usually include full tuition waivers and have stipends that vary by nature of assignment, discipline, and relevant expertise. Most assistantships are available through academic departments and some administrative units. Inquiries should be directed to the appropriate unit for assistantships. Application for graduate scholarships or fellowships should be submitted to the appropriate office upon admission.

Cost of Study

In 2001–02, the graduate student tuition for a full load (9 hours) per semester was estimated to be $1274 for Colorado residents and $5229 for nonresidents. In addition, student fees were estimated at $273 per semester and student health insurance at $368 per semester.

Living and Housing Costs

UNC has some on-campus housing for graduate students, offered on a space-available basis. Applications for on-campus housing are sent to admitted graduate students only on request. Apartment-style units range in rent from $1293 and up per semester. Family student apartments rent for $550 per month. Most graduate students live in off-campus apartments or houses near campus, at rents of approximately $400 and up per month.

Student Group

In fall 2001, UNC enrolled nearly 1,465 graduate students, constituting 13 percent of the total student body. Seventy percent of the graduate students were women, 8 percent were members of ethnic minority groups, and 6 percent were international students. Forty-eight percent of the graduate students were enrolled part-time and 83 percent were Colorado residents (it takes one full year to establish residency). An active Graduate Student Association participates in student government and the Graduate Council and supports graduate student initiatives.

Student Outcomes

Graduates of the UNC master's, specialist, and doctoral programs find leadership positions in public schools; in nonprofit and for-profit health, service, or arts agencies; and in universities and colleges. Others work in private practice or in professional roles in their chosen fields. Many master's graduates go on to doctoral programs in their disciplines.

Location

A pleasant city of 76,000 people, Greeley offers many cultural and recreational amenities. The climate is sunny and dry, facilitating a wide range of recreational pursuits such as biking, golf, hiking, backpacking, fishing, mountain-climbing, and skiing. Other cultural, shopping, and recreational opportunities can be found all along the Front Range (from Cheyenne, Wyoming, to Pueblo, Colorado). Nearby are Rocky Mountain National Park and the Pawnee National Grasslands.

The University

The University of Northern Colorado, founded in 1889 as a State Normal School, granted its first master's degree in 1913 and its first doctoral degree in 1929. Currently, the University offers graduate degree and post-baccalaureate professional educator licensure programs through four of its five colleges (Arts and Sciences, Education, Health and Human Sciences, and Performing and Visual Arts). UNC offers the personal attention and high quality instruction of a small private college with the focused research and public service of a university. It is located on a 240-acre campus just south of the Greeley city center.

Applying

The Graduate School Office is responsible for coordinating graduate admissions at UNC. Applications may be submitted at any time. Under UNC's student-administered application process the student is responsible for collecting and submitting all materials required for admission at one time, with the application fee ($35 for domestic and $50 for international students) to the Graduate School. Students may also apply online at the Web site listed below. Most programs have established application and financial aid deadlines. Applicants should contact the specific department of interest to them for information about such deadlines and admission requirements. Program specifics are available at the University of Northern Colorado Web site (http://www.unco.edu).

Correspondence and Information

For applications or general information:
Graduate School/International Admissions
Campus Box 135
University of Northern Colorado
Greeley, Colorado 80639
Telephone: 970-351-2831
800-776-GRAD (toll-free)
Fax: 970-351-2371
E-mail: gradsch@unco.edu
World Wide Web: http://www.unco.edu/grad/

SCHOOLS, PROGRAMS, AND FACULTY

COLLEGE OF ARTS AND SCIENCES

Sandra Flake, Dean.

Biological Sciences: Curt Peterson, Chair.
- **Biological Sciences (M.A.):** Catherine Gardiner, Coordinator
- **Biological Education (Ph.D.):** Catherine Gardiner, Coordinator.

Chemistry/Biochemistry: Richard Hyslop, Chair.
- **Chemistry (M.A., Chemical Education, Ph.D.):** Richard Hyslop, Coordinator.

Earth Sciences (M.A.): William Hoyt, Chair; William Neese, Coordinator.
English (M.A.): Jane Hinds, Chair/Coordinator.
Hispanic Studies: José Suarez, Chair.
- **Spanish Teaching (M.A.):** José Suarez, Chair.

History (M.A.): Barry Rothaus, Chair; Michael Welsh, Coordinator.
Mathematics–Teaching (M.A.): Richard Grassl, Chair; Jeff Farmer, Coordinator.
Mathematics–Liberal Arts (M.A.): Richard Grassl, Chair; Jeff Farmer, Coordinator.
Mathematics (M.A.); Educational Mathematics (Ph.D.): Richard Grassl, Chair; Jeff Farmer, Coordinator.
Psychology (M.A.): Mark Alcorn, Chair; David Gilliam, Coordinator.
Sociology: John Vonk, Chair.
- **Social Sciences–Clinical Sociology (M.A):** Karen Jennison, Coordinator.

Speech Communication (M.A.): Sherilyn Marrow, Coordinator.

COLLEGE OF EDUCATION

Eugene Sheehan, Dean.

Educational Leadership and Policy Studies Division: Richard King, Director.
- **Educational Leadership (M.A., Ed.S., Ed.D):** Bruce Barnett, Coordinator.
- **Higher Education and Student Affairs Leadership:** Michael Gimmestad, Coordinator.

Applied Statistics and Research Methods (M.S., Ph.D.): Daniel Mundfrom, Chair/Coordinator.

Educational Psychology (M.A., Ph.D.): Randy Lennon, Chair/Coordinator.

Educational Technology (M.A., Ph.D.): Randy Lennon, Chair/Coordinator.

School for the Study of Teaching and Teacher Education: Cliff Brookhart, Director.
- **Elementary Education (M.A., Ed.D.):** Carol Picard, Coordinator.
- **Elementary Education–Early Childhood Education (M.A.):** Phillip Wishon, Coordinator.
- **Elementary Education–Middle School (M.A.):** Barbara Whinery, Coordinator.
- **Reading (M.A.):** Roger Eldredge, Coordinator.

Professional Psychology Division: David Gonzalez, Director.
- **School Counseling (M.A.):** Lia Softas-Nall, Coordinator.
- **Community Counseling (M.A.):** Lia Softas-Nall, Coordinator.
- **Counseling Psychology (Psy.D.):** Brian Johnson, Coordinator.
- **School Psychology (Ed.S., Ph.D.):** Ellis Copeland, Coordinator.

Special Education Division: Barbara Rhine, Director.
- **Early Childhood Special Education (M.A.):** April Block, Coordinator.
- **Teaching Gifted and Talented (M.A.):** George Betts and Stuart Omdal, Coordinators.
- **Moderate Needs (M.A.):** Barbara Rhine, Coordinator.
- **Profound Needs (M.A.):** Lewis Jackson, Coordinator.
- **Severe Needs–Affective (M.A.):** Francie Murry, Coordinator.
- **Severe Needs–Cognitive (M.A.):** Mel Lane, Coordinator.
- **Severe Needs–Hearing (M.A.):** John Luckner, Coordinator.
- **Severe Needs–Vision (M.A.):** Kay Ferrell, Coordinator.
- **Special Education (Ed.D.):** Harvey Rude, Coordinator.

COLLEGE OF HEALTH AND HUMAN SCIENCES

Vincent Scalia, Dean.

Communication Disorders (M.A.): Kathryn Bright, Chair.
- **Audiology (M.A.):** Ellen Gregg, Coordinator.
- **Speech Language Pathology (M.A.):** Ellen Gregg, Coordinator.

Community Health and Nutrition: Larry Harrison, Chair.
- **Community Health Education (M.P.H.):** Bryan Cooke, Coordinator.

Human Services: Juliet Fried, Chair.
- **Gerontology (M.A.):** Marcia Carter, Coordinator.
- **Human Rehabilitation (Ph.D.) and Rehabilitation Counseling (M.A.):** Juliet Fried, Coordinator.

School of Kinesiology and Physical Education: James Stiehl, Director.
- **Physical Education (M.A., Ed.D.):** Gary Heise, Coordinator.

School of Nursing: Sandra Baird, Director.
- **Family Nurse Practitioner (M.S.):** Kathryn Blair, Coordinator.
- **Nursing (M.S.):** Judith Richter, Coordinator.

COLLEGE OF PERFORMING AND VISUAL ARTS

Kathleen Rountree, Dean.

School of Music: Rob Hallquist, Director.
- **Music (M.M., M.M.E., D.A.):** Robert Ehle, Coordinator.

Visual Arts: Virginia Jenkins, Chair.
- **Visual Arts (M.A.):** Dennis Morimoto, Coordinator.

GRADUATE SCHOOL

Allen Huang, Associate Vice President for Research and Graduate Studies and Dean of the Graduate School and University Research.

UNIVERSITY OF NORTH TEXAS

Toulouse School of Graduate Studies

Programs of Study

The University of North Texas offers graduate study leading to master's degrees and doctorates in more than ninety program areas. An interdisciplinary master's program is also available.

Doctoral degrees are offered in accounting, art (including art education), biochemistry, biological sciences, business computer information systems, chemistry, computer science, counseling, education (administration; applied technology, training, and development; curriculum and instruction; early childhood; educational computing; educational research; higher education; reading; and special education), English, environmental science, finance, history, information science, management, marketing, materials science, mathematics, molecular biology, music (composition, education, musicology, performance, and theory), physics, political science, psychology (including clinical, counseling, experimental, and health psychology/behavioral medicine and industrial/organizational psychology), and sociology.

Master's degrees are offered in most of the above areas plus the following: applied anthropology, applied economics, applied geography, applied gerontology, art (including ceramics, communication design, drawing and painting, fashion design, history, interior design, metalsmithing and jewelry, photography, printmaking, and sculpture), behavior analysis, communication and public address, communication disorders, computer education and cognitive systems, criminal justice, economics, education (including elementary human development and family studies, secondary education, and supervision), engineering technology, English (creative writing and technical writing), foreign languages and literatures, health promotion, hotel and restaurant management, industrial-technical merchandising and fabric analytics, journalism, kinesiology, labor and industrial relations, library science, linguistics, music (including jazz studies), philosophy, psychology (industrial and school), public administration, radio/television/film, recreation, rehabilitation studies, and theater arts.

Master's and doctoral degree programs in several areas are offered in cooperation with the Federation of North Texas Area Universities.

Research Facilities

The University libraries contain more than 2 million cataloged holdings and provide diverse, rapidly growing electronic resources. The libraries provide all of the services traditionally associated with academic research libraries, plus services provided by membership in national consortia and electronic access/searching of academic and commercial information resources.

The University's information resources infrastructure includes both central and distributed computing, combining personal computers and several major host computer systems. The campus backbone system combines high-speed fiber optics linking more than 3,000 personal computers in approximately thirty-five buildings and a broadband cable network linking video capabilities at more than 2,000 locations in approximately sixty buildings. The campus network is linked to a variety of external networks, including the Internet and World Wide Web, and students and faculty members have access to computer resources both on and off campus through dial-in procedures.

In addition to departmental facilities, specialized or interdisciplinary research facilities are housed in a variety of centers, institutes, and laboratories. Science and technology centers focus on the applied sciences, environmental archaeology, forensic anthropology, ion-beam modification and analysis, nanostructural materials research, network neuroscience, organometallic chemistry, parallel and distributed computing, remote sensing and geographic information systems, and water research. Business research includes centers for information systems research, quality and productivity, and small business. The fine arts include centers for experimental music and intermedia and visual arts education. Humanities, social sciences, and educational research centers focus on inter-American studies, diplomatic and military history, local history, aging, economic development, environmental economic studies, peace studies, public and international affairs, self-managed work teams, labor and industrial relations, addiction, minority aging, survey research, developmental studies, play therapy, public support of nonprofit agencies, educational reform, educational research, and the school-to-work transition.

Financial Aid

More than 1,000 assistantships are available. The stipends vary according to the amount and level of work required and the background of the student. Half-time appointments and University-awarded scholarships and fellowships of $1000 or more qualify graduate students for in-state tuition rates. The graduate school annually awards a growing number of fellowships to new doctoral and master's students who are departmental nominees. Doctoral awards are $16,000; master's awards are $8000. Many departments also award scholarships and fellowships.

Loans, including Federal Perkins Loans and Federal Stafford Student Loans, are also available to graduate students.

Cost of Study

For 2001–02, tuition and fees for out-of-state graduate students were estimated at $1108 per 3-credit course, and tuition and fees for in-state graduate students were estimated at $469 per 3-credit course (subject to change).

Living and Housing Costs

Graduate students attending the Toulouse School of Graduate Studies may live in University-owned residence halls for approximately $3200 for two semesters. Nearby off-campus housing is also available at reasonable rates.

Student Group

More than 6,100 of the University's approximately 28,000 students are in the graduate school. UNT serves students from every state in the nation and almost 100 other countries.

Location

The University of North Texas is located in Denton, Texas, about 35 miles north of Dallas–Fort Worth. With a population of more than 4 million, the metropolitan area is the largest in Texas and the ninth largest in the United States. There is a wide range of employment, cultural, and sports opportunities.

The University

Founded in 1890, the University of North Texas is one of Texas's five major research and graduate institutions and the only comprehensive graduate and research university in the region. The University began offering graduate work at the master's level in 1935 and at the doctoral level in 1950. Approximately 1,200 master's degrees and 200 doctoral degrees are awarded annually. UNT has awarded more than 147,000 degrees at the undergraduate and graduate levels. The University campus is composed of 139 buildings on 456 acres.

Applying

Applications for admission and supporting documents should be received at least six weeks before entrance. For many departments an earlier deadline must be met. Since deadlines vary, students should correspond with a specific department prior to the date of desired enrollment. If a student is also applying for a graduate teaching or research assistantship, fellowship, or scholarship, application materials should be received several months earlier and at least by the deadline established by the award committee.

Correspondence and Information

Toulouse School of Graduate Studies
354 Eagle Student Services Building
University of North Texas
Box 305459, NT Station
Denton, Texas 76203-5459

Telephone: 940-565-2383
Fax: 940-565-2141
E-mail: gradsch@abn.unt.edu
World Wide Web: http://www.unt.edu

FACULTY HEADS

Graduate School
Neal Tate, Dean.
Sandra Terrell, Associate Dean.
Donna Hughes, Coordinator of Graduate Services and Admissions.

College of Arts and Sciences
Warren Burggren, Dean
William Kamman, Associate Dean.
Jean Schaake, Associate Dean.

Biochemistry: Art Goven and Phyllis Brinkley, Advisers.
Biological Sciences: Earl Zimmerman, Chair; Don Smith and Tom Beitinger, Advisers.
Chemistry: Ruthanne Thomas, Chair; Martin Schwartz, Adviser.
Communication Studies: John Gossett, Chair; John Allison, Adviser.
Computer Science: Roy T. Jacob, Chair; Steven Tate, Adviser.
Dance and Theater Arts: Sandra Combest, Chair; Shelley Cushman, Adviser for Dance; Barbara Cox, Adviser for Drama.
Economics: Steven Cobb, Chair; Michael McPherson and Margie Tieslau, Advisers.
Engineering Technology: Albert Grubbs, Chair; Michael Kozak, Adviser.
English: James Tanner, Chair; Brenda Sims, Adviser.
Foreign Languages: Jerry Nash, Chair and Adviser.
Geography: Andrew Schoolmaster, Chair; Donald Lyons, Adviser.
History: Richard Golden, Chair; Richard Lowe, Adviser.
Journalism: Richard Wells, Chair; Mitch Land, Adviser.
Labor/Industrial Relations: Michael McPherson, Adviser.
Materials Science: Bruce Gnade, Chair; Witold Brostow, Adviser.
Mathematics: Neal Brand, Chair and Adviser.
Molecular Biology: Art Goven, Unit Head; Phyllis Brinkley, Adviser.
Philosophy: Eugene Hargrove, Chair and Adviser.
Physics: Sam Matteson, Chair; Duncan Weathers, Adviser.
Political Science: Harold Clarke, Chair; James Meernik, Adviser.
Psychology: Ernest Harrell, Chair; Joseph Critelli, Adviser.
Radio/TV/Film: Steve Craig, Chair, Melinda Nevin, Adviser.
Speech and Hearing: Pat Summers, Interim Chair; Fang-Ling Lu, Adviser.

College of Business Administration
Jared Hazelton, Dean.
Mary Thibodeaux, Associate Dean.
Richard White, Associate Dean.

Accounting: John Price, Chair.
Business (General): Denise Galubenski, Adviser.
Business Computer Information Systems: John Windsor, Chair; Robert Pavur and Richard Vedder, Advisers.
Finance: Imre Karafiath, Chair; Foster Roden and Niranjan Tripathy, Advisers.
Management: Lynn Johnson, Interim Chair.
Marketing: Jhinuk Chowdhury, Chair; G. Ganesh and Kenneth Thompson, Advisers.

School of Community Service
David Hartman, Dean.

Anthropology: Tyson Gibbs, Chair; Larry Naylor, Adviser.
Applied Economics: Bernard Weinstein, Director; Terry Clower, Adviser.
Applied Gerontology: Richard Lusky, Chair; Phyllis Eccleston, Adviser.
Behavioral Studies: Sigrid Glenn, Chair; Janet Ellis, Adviser.
Criminal Justice: Robert Taylor, Chair; Eric Fritsch, Adviser.
Public Administration: Bob Bland, Chair and Adviser.
Rehabilitation: Thomas Evenson, Chair; Paul Leung, Adviser.
Sociology: Dale Yeatts, Interim Chair; Rudy Seward, Adviser.

College of Education
Jean Keller, Dean.
Judith Adkison, Associate Dean.
Bertina Hildreth, Associate Dean.
Diane Allen, Associate Dean.

Counseling, Development and Higher Education: Michael Altekruse, Chair.
Counselor Education: Jan Holden, Adviser.
Kinesiology, Health Promotion and Recreation: James Morrow, Chair.
Teacher Education and Administration: John Stansell, Chair.
Technology and Cognition: Jon Young, Chair.

School of Merchandising and Hospitality Management
Judith Forney, Dean.
Johnny Sue Reynolds, Associate Dean; Youn-Yung Kim, Adviser.

School of Library and Information Sciences
Philip Turner, Dean; Donald Cleveland, Adviser for Information Science.
Herman Totten, Associate Dean and Adviser for Library Science.

College of Music
James Scott, Dean.
Thomas S. Clark and Jon C. Nelson, Associate Deans.

School of Visual Arts
D. Jack Davis, Dean.
Don Schol, Associate Dean.
Art History and Art Education: Jacqueline Chanda and Heather Close, Advisers.
Fashion Design: Marian O'Rourke-Kaplan, Adviser.
Studio Program: Kate Hunt, Adviser.

UNIVERSITY OF NOTRE DAME

The Graduate School

Programs of Study

Programs leading to the master's and Ph.D. degrees are offered in the University's four graduate divisions and the School of Architecture.

In the Humanities Division, the Ph.D. degree is offered in English, history, history and philosophy of science, philosophy, and theology. In addition, there an interdiscplinary Ph.D. degree in literature. The Medieval Institute offers the degrees of Master of Medieval Studies (M.M.S.) and Ph.D. Terminal M.A. degrees are offered in art history, early Christian studies, German language and literature, music, and Romance languages and literatures. Special master's degree programs lead to the Master of Divinity (M.Div.); Master of Fine Arts (M.F.A.) in creative writing, studio art, and design; Master of Music (M.M.); and Master of Theological Studies (M.T.S.).

In the Social Sciences Division, the Ph.D. degree is offered in economics, political science, psychology, and sociology. A terminal M.A. degree is offered in peace studies, and a Master of Education (M.Ed.) degree is offered to participants in the Alliance for Catholic Education (ACE) program.

In the Science Division, M.S. and Ph.D. degrees are offered in biological sciences and in chemistry and biochemistry. The Ph.D. degree is offered in mathematics and physics and the M.S.A.M. is offered in applied mathematics. An M.D./Ph.D. joint degree is offered.

In the Engineering Division, M.S. and Ph.D. degrees are offered in aerospace and mechanical, chemical, and electrical engineering; in civil engineering and geological sciences; and in computer science and engineering. Other degrees offered include M.S. degrees in bioengineering and environmental engineering, a Master of Engineering in Mechanical Engineering (M.E.M.E.) degree, and a dual engineering and law degree (M.Eng./J.D.).

A Master of Architecture (M.Arch.) is offered through the School of Architecture.

Research Facilities

The Theodore M. Hesburgh Library serves as the main University library. In addition, nine specialized libraries cover architecture, business, chemistry/physics, engineering, international studies, law, life sciences, mathematics, and radiation chemistry. Extensive campus computing resources include a high performance computing cluster to provide a parallel computing environment for computationally intensive work and research. The fiber-based Notre Dame Network provides access to many campus resources as well as the Internet. The University sponsors numerous interdisciplinary and specialized research institutes, including the Center for Applied Mathematics; the Center for Astrophysics; the Center for Biocomplexity; the Center for Environmental Science and Technology; the Center for Flow and Physics and Control; the Center for Molecularly Engineered Materials; the Center for Nanoscience and Technology; the Center for Philosophy of Religion; the Center for Tropical Disease Research and Training; the Center for Zebrafish Research; the Cushwa Center for the Study of American Catholicism; the Environmental Research Center; the Erasmus Institute; the Hessert Center for Aerospace Research; the Institute for Educational Initiatives; the Institute for Latino Studies; the Keck Center for Transgene Research; the Keck Foundation Initiative for Molecular Information Processing; the Kellogg Institute for International Studies; the Keough Institute for Irish Studies; the Kroc Institute for International Peace Studies; the Laboratory for Social Research; the Medieval Institute; the Radiation Laboratory; the Nanovic Institute for European Studies; the Reilly Center for Science, Technology and Values; and the Walther Cancer Research Center.

Financial Aid

More than 90 percent of the graduate students receive financial assistance. Aid is available from a number of sources, including fellowships, assistantships, scholarships, part-time employment, and loans. Funding is provided by the University, federal and state governments, industry, and foundations.

Cost of Study

Tuition for 2002–03 is $25,410 per year, or $1412 per credit hour.

Living and Housing Costs

University apartments for single students both on and near campus range from $3248 to $3920, including utilities, for nine months. University apartments for married students located near the campus range from $339 to $446 per month. Private rental houses and apartments are located within walking distance. The cost of on-campus meal plans ranges from approximately $209 to $1870 per semester. An on-campus child-care center bases the weekly cost of its programs on family income.

Student Group

The University of Notre Dame had an enrollment of 10,868 degree-seeking students in 2001–02: 8,204 undergraduates, 1,551 graduate students, and 1,113 professional (law and M.B.A.) students. The student body is drawn from every state and nearly ninety countries.

Student Outcomes

A total of 122 students received doctoral degrees in 2001. Upon graduation, 26 percent had secured tenure-track faculty positions; 40 percent had temporary academic positions, including postdoctoral fellowships and adjunct or visiting professorships; 28 percent had degree-related industrial, governmental, and professional positions; 3 percent were unemployed; and the remaining 2 percent did not report. About 82 percent of science and engineering Ph.D.'s went to postdoctoral or industrial and governmental positions. More than 76 percent of humanities and social sciences Ph.D.'s took either tenure-track or temporary academic positions.

Location

Notre Dame is located adjacent to South Bend, Indiana (metropolitan area population, 175,000), on a 1,250-acre wooded campus that encompasses two lakes. The physical plant includes 100 academic, residential, and activities buildings. The metropolitan area offers a wide variety of cultural and recreational opportunities. Lake Michigan beaches and Michigan ski slopes are nearby. Chicago is approximately 2 hours away by car, bus, or rail.

The University

The University of Notre Dame is a Catholic university, founded in 1842 by Edward F. Sorin of the Congregation of Holy Cross. The Graduate School was established in 1918 and currently awards advanced degrees in thirty-five academic and professional programs.

Applying

Applications for admission and financial aid are due by February 1 for the fall semester and by November 1 for the spring semester. Some departments have an earlier application deadline. Later applications may be considered for admission without aid. All applicants are required to supply transcripts of their undergraduate work and of any graduate work, letters of recommendation, and GRE General Test scores. Some departments also require GRE Subject Test scores. International applicants whose native language is not English are expected to provide TOEFL scores. Applicants are encouraged to use the electronic application for admission online at http://www.nd.edu/~gradsch/applying/appintro.html.

Correspondence and Information

Office of Graduate Admissions
University of Notre Dame
502 Main Building
Notre Dame, Indiana 46556-5602

Telephone: 574-631-7706
E-mail: gradad@nd.edu
World Wide Web: http://www.nd.edu/~gradsch

FACULTY HEADS

Vice President for Graduate Studies and Research and Dean of the Graduate School: Jeffrey C. Kantor, Ph.D., Princeton.
Associate Dean of the Graduate School and Director of Graduate Admissions: Terrence J. Akai, Ph.D., Illinois.

Humanities Division

Art, Art History, and Design: Austin Collins, C.S.C., M.F.A., Claremont. M.A. program in art history. M.F.A. programs in studio art: ceramics, painting, photography, printmaking, sculpture; graphic and industrial design.
Early Christian Studies: Martin Bloomer, Ph.D., Yale. M.A. program in early Christian studies.
English: Chris R. Vanden Bossche, Ph.D., California, Santa Cruz. M.A. and Ph.D. programs in Old and Middle English, Renaissance, Restoration and eighteenth-century, and Romantic and Victorian literature; African-American literature; American literature to 1900; modern British literature; modern American literature; drama; Irish studies; literary theory; novel; poetry; prose fiction. M.F.A. program in creative writing.
German Language and Literature: Robert E. Norton, Ph.D., Princeton. M.A. programs in German: the medieval period, Reformation and humanism, Goethe and his age, German classical literature, nineteenth-century drama and prose, modern lyric poetry, contemporary German prose, aethetics and ethics, philosophy and literature, drama and the theory of drama, intellectual history.
History: Thomas A. Kselman, Ph.D., Michigan. M.A. and Ph.D. programs in medieval history, United States history, modern European history.
History and Philosophy of Science: Don A. Howard, Ph.D., Boston University. Ph.D. programs in analytic philosophy of science and epistemology; history of the philosophy of science; philosophy of contemporary physics; history and philosophy of biology, 1700–1980; history of astronomy and physics; medieval natural philosophy and medicine; history and philosophy of economics; philosophy of mind and neuroscience; social history of medicine and technology; history and philosophy of mathematics; intellectual history of science 1600–1950; scientific revolution studies; science and literature.
Literature: Margaret Anne Doody, D.Phil., Oxford. Interdisciplinary Ph.D. program in literature.
Medieval Studies: Thomas F. X. Noble, Ph.D., Michigan State. M.M.S. and Ph.D. programs in medieval history, art, comparative literature, medieval literatures, music, philosophy, theology.
Music: Alexander Blachly, Ph.D., Columbia. M.A. programs in musicology, music theory. M.M. program in performance and literature.
Philosophy: Paul Weithman, Ph.D., Harvard. Ph.D. programs in ancient philosophy, medieval philosophy, modern philosophy, contemporary European philosophy, epistemology, ethics, logic, metaphysics, philosophy of language, philosophy of mathematics, philosophy of mind, philosophy of religion, philosophy of science, political philosophy.
Romance Languages and Literatures: Dayle Seidenspinner-Núñez, Ph.D., Stanford. M.A. programs in comparative literatures, French and Francophone studies, Italian studies, Iberian and Latin American studies.
Theology: John C. Cavadini, Ph.D., Yale. Ph.D. programs in Christianity and Judaism in antiquity: Hebrew Bible and Judaica, New Testament and Early Church; history of Christianity; liturgical studies; moral theology/Christian ethics; systematic theology. M.T.S. programs in biblical studies, history of Christianity, systematic theology, moral theology, liturgical studies. M.A. programs in biblical studies, early Christian studies, liturgical studies, theological studies. M.Div. programs in pastoral theology, professional ministry.

Social Sciences Division

Economics: Richard A. Jensen, Ph.D., Northwestern. Ph.D. programs in development and international economics; economic theory, thought, and methodology; institutions: labor, financial, industrial, public.
Education: G. Michael Pressley, Ph.D., Minnesota. M.Ed. program, restricted to participants in the Alliance for Catholic Education (ACE) program.
Peace Studies: R. Scott Appleby, Ph.D., Chicago. M.A. programs in the role of international norms and institutions in peacemaking; impact of religious, philosophical, and cultural influences on peace; dynamics of intergroup conflict and conflict transformation; promotion of social, economic, and environmental justice.
Political Science: Michael Zuckert, Ph.D., Chicago. Ph.D. programs in American government and politics (including public law), comparative politics, international relations, political theory.
Psychology: Jeanne D. Day, Ph.D., Illinois. Ph.D. programs in cognitive psychology: problem solving, memory, educational applications; counseling psychology; developmental psychology: cognitive development, socioemotional development, developmental psychopathology; quantitative psychology.
Sociology: Michael R. Welch, Ph.D., North Carolina. Ph.D. programs in social theory, research methods and statistics, family, organizations, social psychology, sociology of culture, sociology of education, sociology of religion, comparative historical sociology, political sociology, race and ethnicity.

Science Division

Biological Sciences: John G. Duman, Ph.D., California, San Diego. M.S. and Ph.D. programs in animal behavior, aquatic biology, biotechnology, cell and molecular biology, developmental biology, ecology, environmental biology, evolutionary and systematic biology, genetics, medical entomology, microbial physiology, neural biology, parasitology, physiology, vector biology.
Chemistry and Biochemistry: A. Graham Lappin, Ph.D., Glasgow. M.S. and Ph.D. programs in biochemistry; bioinorganic chemistry; bioorganic chemistry; inorganic chemistry; materials chemistry; molecular biology; organic chemistry; organometallic chemistry; physical chemistry and radiation chemistry; theoretical and computational chemistry.
Mathematics: Steven A. Buechler, Ph.D., Maryland. Ph.D. programs in algebra, algebraic geometry, applied mathematics, complex analysis, differential geometry, logic, partial differential equations, topology. M.S.A.M. program in applied mathematics.
M.D./Ph.D. Joint-Degree Program: John F. O'Malley, Ph.D., Creighton.
Physics: Bruce A. Bunker, Ph.D., Washington (Seattle). M.S. and Ph.D. programs in astrophysics, atomic physics, condensed-matter physics, elementary particle physics, nuclear physics, pattern formation/biophysics, theoretical physics.

Engineering Division

Aerospace and Mechanical Engineering: Robert C. Nelson, Ph.D., Penn State. M.S. and Ph.D. programs in aerospace sciences, mechanical systems and design, solid mechanics, thermal and fluid sciences.
Chemical Engineering: Mark J. McCready, Ph.D., Illinois. M.S. and Ph.D. programs in applied mathematics, bioseparations, catalysis and surface science, ceramics, chemical reaction engineering, combustion synthesis of materials, ecological modeling, environmentally conscious design, fluid mechanics, gas-liquid flows, materials science, molecular modeling and simulation, molecular theory of transport, nonlinear dynamics, parallel computing, phase equilibria, physiological dynamics, pollution prevention, polymer rheology, process dynamics and control, process optimization and design, process simulation, statistical mechanics, superconducting materials, supercritical fluids, suspension rheology, transport in porous media, waste minimization.
Civil Engineering and Geological Sciences: Ahsan Kareem, Ph.D., Colorado State. M.S. and Ph.D. programs in aquatic chemistry, bioengineering, biological treatment of hazardous waste, dynamics of offshore structures, earthquake engineering, environmental engineering, environmental mineralogy, finite-element modeling, groundwater hydrology, high- and low-temperature geochemistry, mantle petrology, multiphase flows, natural and man-made hazard reduction, paleontology, structural mechanics and design, structural reliability, wind engineering.
Computer Science and Engineering: Kevin Bowyer, Ph.D., Duke. M.S. and Ph.D. programs in algorithms and theory of computations, computationally intensive applications, parallel computer architecture, computer systems design, logic and VLSI design, programming and systems software, systems and networks.
Electrical Engineering: Yih-Fang Huang, Ph.D., Princeton. M.S. and Ph.D. programs in communication systems, control systems, nanoelectronics, optoelectronics, semiconductor materials and devices, signal and image processing, solid-state integrated circuits.
Engineering and Law Dual-Degree Program: M.Eng./J.D.

School of Architecture

Carroll William Westfall, Ph.D., Columbia. M.Arch. programs in architectural design, classical theory in architecture and urbanism, history and theory, urban theory and design.

UNIVERSITY OF OKLAHOMA

Graduate College

Programs of Study

The University of Oklahoma (OU) combines a mixture of academic excellence, varied social cultures, and a blend of scholarly and creative activities that offer exceptional opportunities for graduate study. Graduate education is offered in ninety-four master's programs and fifty-two doctoral programs on the Norman campus. At the OU Health Sciences Center (OU-HSC), located 19 miles away in Oklahoma City, graduate degrees are offered in twenty-nine master's programs and sixteen doctoral programs. In addition to the Doctor of Philosophy, the University confers the Doctor of Education, Doctor of Engineering, Doctor of Musical Arts, and Doctor of Public Health. The University of Oklahoma also offers graduate programs at the Tulsa Graduate Research and Education Center located approximately 120 miles northeast of the main campus in the city of Tulsa, Oklahoma. On the Tulsa campus, OU offers graduate programs in architecture, urban studies, economics, environmental science, human relations, library and information studies, public administration, social work, and telecomputing. Interdisciplinary degree programs are available at both the master's and doctoral levels on all three campuses. Master's degree programs require a minimum of 30 semester hours of course work. Doctoral programs require a minimum of 90 semester hours of course work and are awarded for excellence in research scholarship. Doctoral students are also required to complete general written and oral examinations and defend the results of their dissertation research.

Research Facilities

Expenditures in research and related activities by the University during the 1999 fiscal year exceeded $147 million. Research and scholarly activity take place on the well-landscaped 567-acre main campus in Norman, which houses most of the University's academic colleges and research buildings. The University of Oklahoma provides an exceptional networking and computational environment for students and faculty and staff members. All graduate students at the University of Oklahoma have access to electronic mail service, digital libraries, the Internet, a central help desk, campus software and licensing, and many other benefits to enhance their graduate experiences. The academic areas of campus are part of the University intranet system that provides computer access in residence halls, classrooms, student computer labs, and University offices. The University maintains an OC-3 high-speed connectivity to the commercial Internet, allowing seamless access to graduate resources elsewhere in the world. The University is a charter member of the Internet2 and vBNS initiatives and continues to expand the technological possibilities for research. The $50-million Sarkeys Energy Center has 207 teaching and research laboratories, as well as classrooms and offices and the Youngblood Energy Library. There are central advanced analytical services, including the Electron Microprobe Library and Samuel Robert Noble Electron Microscopy Laboratory.

The Norman campus houses Bizzell Memorial Library, the largest in the state, with more than 2.5 million volumes, 16,000 serial subscriptions, 1.6 million documents, 3 million microforms, and 160,000 photographs. Special collections include the internationally known History of Science Collections, the Western History Collections, and the Political Commercial Archives. There are also six specialized branch libraries. The new Sam Noble Museum of Natural History opened its doors in the spring of 2000. The 195,000-square-foot facility is the largest University-based museum in the country. The museum is home to 6 million artifacts including the longest Apatosauras, and priceless Native American objects. The Fred Jones Jr. Art Center, the Catlett Music Center, and the Rupel L. Jones Theatre provide excellent facilities for graduate studies in the College of Fine Arts. The University of Oklahoma Press and *World Literature Today* are two internationally recognized agencies for research and scholarship. The University's 622-acre south campus includes the Oklahoma Center for Continuing Education (OCCE) and the research programs of the Institute for Community and Economic Development. The White Forum Building at OCCE supports research symposia and teleconferencing. The OCCE is fully equipped with AV equipment and satellite communications capability. The University also has a north campus of 1,675 acres, which includes the University Research Park, incubator firms, NOAA's National Severe Storms Laboratory, and the National Weather Service's advanced weather forecasting office. OU's Health Sciences Center includes a 200-acre complex of educational, research, and health-care facilities operated by nineteen public and private entities along with an 11-acre College of Medicine campus in Tulsa. The OU-HSC is the recipient of an $8.7-million grant, which established the Oklahoma Center for Molecular Medicine.

Financial Aid

Nearly one third of all graduate students attending the University are employed by their departments as either teaching or research assistants. Salaries for these positions vary from unit to unit, but the University average for 1999 was $9939 for graduate teaching assistants and $10,436 for graduate research assistants. Out-of-state tuition is waived for all students holding a half-time teaching or research assistantship.

Cost of Study

Tuition for Oklahoma residents was $109.12 per graduate credit hour in 2001–02; nonresident tuition was $314.57 (nonresidents appointed as at least half-time graduate assistants pay the in-state rate). In addition, a $54 health fee and a $50 student facilities fee were charged each semester.

Living and Housing Costs

The monthly rent for University-owned apartments ranged from $388 to $632. There are a large number of privately owned apartments, duplexes, and houses available in Norman, many of which are served by the University's Campus Area Rapid Transit (CART) system.

Student Group

Enrollment was 28,000 students on the Norman campus and 2,862 at the Health Sciences Center during the 2001–02 academic year. More than 3,200 of these students were enrolled in the Graduate College in Norman and nearly 1,000 in the Graduate College at the Health Sciences Center. Approximately one third of the graduate students at the University of Oklahoma are enrolled in doctoral programs. Approximately one fifth of the student body comes from out of state, with students from every state. In addition, international students from seventy-two nations compose nearly 20 percent of the graduate student body.

Location

As part of the dynamic Southwest, Oklahoma benefits from both its rich historic heritage and the vital and modern growth of its metropolitan areas. Although by location a suburb of Oklahoma City, Norman is an independent community with a permanent population of more than 88,000. Norman residents enjoy extensive parks and recreation programs and a 10,000-acre lake and park area.

The College

The Graduate College is the center of advanced study, research, and creative activity for the University. Faculty members and students share an obligation to achieve greater knowledge in their chosen fields and to present their achievements to the scholarly community. Students were first accepted at the University of Oklahoma in 1892. Graduate instruction was offered as early as 1899, and the first master's degree was conferred in 1900. The Graduate School was formally organized in 1909, and the first doctorate was awarded in 1929.

Applying

Application procedures vary depending on the student's academic background. There is a $25 application fee for U.S. citizens and permanent residents and a $50 application fee for international students. Applications for assistantships, fellowships, and other forms of financial aid should be directed to the academic units. Deadlines vary from department to department, but applications should generally be filed no later than January for students desiring admission in the fall term.

Correspondence and Information

Graduate College
University of Oklahoma
Norman, Oklahoma 73019
Telephone: 800-522-0772 (toll-free)
E-mail: gradinfo@ou.edu
World Wide Web: http://gradweb.ou.edu/

AREAS OF INSTRUCTION

The graduate faculty consists of more than 600 active scholars in residence on the Norman campus and another 270 at the Health Sciences Center. In addition, the graduate faculty is supplemented by visiting scholars from other institutions and by specialists from government and industry. The names of the programs and the degrees offered are listed along with the telephone number. The area code for all numbers is 405.

Norman Campus

Accounting (M.Ac.): telephone: 325-4221; e-mail: fayres@ou.edu
Accounting (Ph.D.): telephone: 325-5696; e-mail: gwemery@ou.edu
Aerospace and Mechanical Engineering (M.S., Ph.D.): telephone: 325-1730; e-mail: striz@ou.edu
Anthropology (M.A., Ph.D.): telephone: 325-2490; e-mail: pgilman@ou.edu
Architecture (M.Arch., M.L.A., M.R.C.P., M.S.C.A.): telephone: 325-2444; e-mail: tpatterson@ou.edu
Art (M.A., M.F.A.): telephone: 325-2691; e-mail: alphelan@ou.edu
Botany and Microbiology (M.S., Ph.D.): telephone: 325-6281; e-mail: guno@ou.edu
Business Administration (M.B.A., Ph.D.): telephone: 325-5696; e-mail: gwemery@cbafac.cba.ou.edu
Chemical Engineering (M.S., Ph.D.): telephone: 325-4366; e-mail: nollert@ou.edu
Chemistry and Biochemistry (M.S., Ph.D.): telephone: 325-2967; e-mail: lblank@chemdept.ou.edu
Civil Engineering and Environmental Science (M.S., Ph.D.): telephone: 325-4256; e-mail: gamiller@ou.edu.
Communication (M.A., Ph.D.): telephone: 325-3112; e-mail: mpfau@ou.edu
Computer Science (M.S., Ph.D.): telephone: 325-4042; e-mail: sdhall@cs.ou.edu
Dance (M.F.A.): telephone: 325-4051; e-mail: marymholt@ou.edu
Drama (M.A., M.F.A.): telephone: 325-4021; e-mail: akoger@ou.edu
Economics (M.A., Ph.D.): telephone: 325-2861; e-mail: dsutter@ou.edu
Education (M.Ed., Ph.D., Ed.D.): telephone: 325-3257; e-mail: bdelong@ou.edu
Electrical and Computer Engineering (M.S., Ph.D.): telephone: 325-4721; e-mail: zelby@ou.edu
Engineering (M.S., Ph.D.): telephone: 325-2621; e-mail: hkumin@ou.edu
Engineering Physics (M.S., Ph.D.): telephone: 325-3961; e-mail: msantos@ou.edu
English (M.A., Ph.D.): telephone: 325-4661; e-mail: dmair@ou.edu
Geography (M.A., Ph.D.): telephone: 325-5325; e-mail: sgros@ou.edu
Geology and Geophysics (M.S., Ph.D.): telephone: 325-3253; e-mail: mengel@ou.edu
Health and Sports Sciences (M.S.): telephone: 325-5211; e-mail: eltaylor@ou.edu
History (M.A., Ph.D.): telephone: 325-6002; e-mail: pgilje@ou.edu
History of Science (M.A., Ph.D.): telephone: 325-2213; e-mail: ktaylor@ou.edu
Human Relations (M.H.R.): telephone: 325-1756; e-mail: smmendoza@ou.edu
Industrial Engineering (M.S., Ph.D.): telephone: 325-3721; e-mail: pulat@ou.edu
International Relations (M.A.): telephone: 325-1584; e-mail: rhcox@ou.edu
Journalism and Mass Communication (M.A.): telephone: 325-5206; e-mail: dcraig@ou.edu
Landscape Architecture (M.L.A.): telephone: 325-2444; e-mail: dalton@ou.edu
Liberal Studies (M.L.S.): telephone: 325-1061; e-mail: tgabert@ou.edu
Library and Information Studies (M.L.I.S.): telephone: 325-3921; e-mail:dwallace@ou.edu
Mathematics (M.A., M.S., M.S./M.B.A., Ph.D.): telephone: 325-6711; e-mail: pgoodey@math.ou.edu
Meteorology (M.S., Ph.D.): telephone: 325-6561; e-mail: wbeasley@ou.edu
Modern Languages (French, German, Spanish for M.A., Ph.D.): telephone: 325-6181; e-mail:hmadland@ou.edu
Music (M.Mus., D.M.A.): telephone: 325-2081; e-mail: memantione@ou.edu
Music Education (M.Mus.Educ., Ph.D.): telephone: 325-2081; e-mail: memantione@ou.edu
Natural Science (M.Nat.Sci.): telephone: 325-1498; e-mail: eamarek@ou.edu
Petroleum and Geological Engineering (M.S., Ph.D.): telephone: 325-6777; e-mail: dtiab@ou.edu
Philosophy (M.A., Ph.D.): telephone: 325-6324; e-mail: relugardo@ou.edu
Physics and Astronomy (M.S., Ph.D.): telephone: 325-3961; e-mail: kmilton@ou.edu
Political Science (M.A., Ph.D.): telephone: 325-2061; e-mail: rprters@ou.edu
Psychology (M.S., Ph.D.): telephone: 325-4511; e-mail: kirby@ou.edu
Public Administration (M.P.A.): telephone: 325-5517; e-mail: grussell@ou.edu
Regional and City Planning (M.R.C.P.): telephone: 325-2399; e-mail: rmarshment@ou.edu
Social Work (M.S.W.): telephone: 325-2821; e-mail: kwedel@ou.edu
Sociology (M.A., Ph.D.): telephone: 325-1571; e-mail: estjohn@ou.edu
Zoology (M.S., Ph.D.): telephone: 325-4821; e-mail: jthompson@ou.edu

Health Sciences Campus (e-mail: grad-college@ouhsc.edu)

Biochemistry and Molecular Biology (Ph.D.): telephone: 271-2227.
Biological Psychology (M.S., Ph.D.): telephone: 271-2011.
Biostatistics and Epidemiology (M.S., M.P.H., Ph.D., Dr.P.H.): telephone: 271-2229.
Cell Biology (M.S., Ph.D.): telephone: 271-2377.
Communication Sciences and Disorders (M.S., Ph.D.): telephone: 271-4124.
Health Administration and Policy (M.H.A., M.P.H., M.P.A./M.P.H., M.P.H./M.B.A., M.P.H./J.D., M.P.H./M.D., Dr.P.H.): telephone: 271-2114.
Health Promotion Sciences (M.S., M.P.H., Dr.P.H.): telephone: 271-2017.
Microbiology and Immunology (M.S., Ph.D.): telephone: 271-2133.
Neuroscience (M.S., Ph.D.): telephone: 271-6267.
Nursing (M.S., M.S./M.B.A.): telephone: 271-2125.
Nutritional Sciences (M.S.): telephone: 271-2113.
Occupational and Environmental Health (M.S., M.P.H., M.S./J.D., Ph.D., Dr.P.H.): telephone: 271-2070.
Orthodontics (M.S.): telephone: 271-4271.
Pathology (Ph.D.): telephone: 271-2693.
Periodontics (M.S.): telephone: 271-4544.
Pharmaceutical Sciences (M.S., M.S./M.B.A., Ph.D.): telephone: 271-6484.
Physiology (M.S., Ph.D.): telephone: 271-2226.
Radiological Sciences (M.S., Ph.D.): telephone: 271-5132.
Rehabilitation Sciences (M.S.): telephone: 271-2131.

The University of Oklahoma maintains its preeminence in energy-related education, research, and service through nationally and internationally recognized programs that offer many opportunities for students.

Culture embodies the very purpose of higher education: enlightenment, refinement, and advancement of knowledge.

UNIVERSITY OF PENNSYLVANIA

Graduate Studies

Programs of Study

The University of Pennsylvania offers Master of Arts (A.M.), Master of Science (M.S.), and Doctor of Philosophy (Ph.D.) degree programs in more than sixty areas of study. While Penn offers its graduate students outstanding faculty and facilities, what truly distinguishes graduate programs at Penn is the way that these resources are combined to encourage interdisciplinary pursuits. Penn's distinct success in interdisciplinary pursuits is sustained through the location of its twelve schools on one self-contained, 260-acre campus.

Research Facilities

Penn's interdisciplinary character is reflected in the more than 100 on-campus research institutes and centers. The Penn library provides access to one of the premier digital libraries in North America, and its open-stack collection contains more than 4.4 million volumes and 33,500 periodicals. As the birthplace of modern computing, the campus is home to a vast array of scientific workstations and computer-controlled instruments, thousands of desktop computers, many departmental computer labs, and thirty public computer labs. The computers, as well as all on-campus student residences, are connected by a high-speed network.

Financial Aid

Applicants who indicate on the application form that they wish to be considered for financial assistance are automatically considered for all awards for which they are eligible, including University fellowships and teaching and research assistantships. More than 90 percent of incoming doctoral students are awarded full support, including tuition, fees, and a maintenance stipend.

Cost of Study

Tuition and fees for 2001–02 totaled $27,362.

Living and Housing Costs

The projected nine-month budget for a single graduate student (excluding tuition and fees) is $14,000.

Student Group

The Penn campus is home to 20,400 students—among them approximately 9,900 undergraduate, 4,200 graduate, and 6,300 professional students—and 2,050 faculty members. More than one third of the graduate students come to Penn from other countries, 20 percent are members of U.S. minority groups, and women account for almost half of all graduate students. While there is no typical Penn graduate student in terms of experience or demographics, these students do share an exceptional academic ability and the recognized potential to conduct significant research.

Location

Penn's campus is situated adjacent to Center City Philadelphia, near the heart of the Boston–Washington, D.C., corridor, affording nearly unlimited possibilities for linkages with industry, government, and other centers of research. Philadelphia is ranked among the five most livable cities in the nation. Area cultural resources include the Philadelphia Museum of Art, the Rodin Museum, the Barnes Foundation, the Academy of Natural Sciences, and the Athenaeum.

The University

Founded in 1740 by Benjamin Franklin, the University of Pennsylvania is a private research university composed of twelve schools. There are more than 2,000 full-time faculty members, including Nobel laureates; winners of Guggenheim, McArthur, and Sloan fellowships; and members of the National Academy of Sciences, the National Academy of Engineers, and the Institute of Medicine. The University of Pennsylvania is an Equal Opportunity/Affirmative Action educator and employer.

Applying

To be ensured of receiving full consideration for fellowships and scholarships, completed applications, including the results of the Graduate Record Examinations (GRE), should be received no later than January 2. Most doctoral programs admit students for September only. Applicants may apply to most programs on line using Penn ExpressApp at the World Wide Web address below.

Correspondence and Information

Interested students should write to the address below and specify the program(s) of interest or browse the Web site listed below.

Office of Graduate Education
120 College Hall
University of Pennsylvania
Philadelphia, Pennsylvania 19104-6381
E-mail: graded@pobox.upenn.edu
World Wide Web: http://www.upenn.edu/grad

SCHOOLS, AREAS OF STUDY, AND CONTACTS

The School of Arts and Sciences: Dr. Joseph Farrell, Associate Dean for Graduate Studies, 3401 Walnut Street, 322A, Philadelphia, Pennsylvania 19104-6228; telephone: 215-898-7577; e-mail: patrea@sas.upenn.edu; World Wide Web: http://www.sas.upenn.edu.

Ancient history, anthropology, art and archaeology of the Mediterranean world, Asian and Middle Eastern studies, bioethics, biology, chemistry, classical studies, comparative literature and literary theory, criminology, earth and environmental science, economics, English, environmental studies, folklore and folklife, Germanic languages and literatures, government, history, history and sociology of science, history of art, international studies (M.B.A./A.M.), linguistics, mathematics, music, philosophy, physics and astronomy, political science, psychology, religious studies, Romance languages, sociology, and South Asia regional studies.

Biomedical Graduate Studies: Dr. Michael Selzer, Director, 240 John Morgan Building, University of Pennsylvania, Philadelphia, Pennsylvania 19104-6064; telephone: 215-898-1030; e-mail: bgs@mail.med.upenn.edu; World Wide Web: http://www.med.upenn.edu/biomgrad/

Biochemistry and molecular biophysics, cell and molecular biology, epidemiology and biostatistics, genomics and computational biology, immunology, neuroscience, parasitology, and pharmacological sciences.

School of Engineering and Applied Science: Dr. Norman Badler, Associate Dean, Graduate Education and Research, 113 Towne Building, University of Pennsylvania, Philadelphia, Pennsylvania 19104-6391; telephone: 215-898-4542; e-mail: engadmis@seas.upenn.edu; World Wide Web: http://www.seas.upenn.edu.

Bioengineering, chemical engineering, computer and information science, electrical engineering, materials science and engineering, mechanical engineering and applied mechanics, and systems engineering. Master's programs are available in biotechnology, computer and information technology, technology management, and telecommunications and networking.

The Wharton School: Ms. Mallory Hiatt, Associate Director, Wharton Doctoral Programs, 1150 SH-DH, University of Pennsylvania, Philadelphia, Pennsylvania 19104-6302; telephone: 215-898-4877; e-mail hiattm@wharton.upenn.edu; World Wide Web: http://www.wharton.upenn.edu.

Accounting, finance, health-care systems, insurance and risk management, management, marketing, operations and information management, public policy and management, real estate, and statistics.

The Graduate School of Education: Helen Albertson-Ploucha, Manager of Admissions, The Graduate School of Education, University of Pennsylvania, Philadelphia, Pennsylvania 19104-6216; telephone: 877-PENNGSE (toll-free); e-mail: admissions@gse.upenn.edu; World Wide Web: http://www.gse.upenn.edu.

Education.

The Graduate School of Fine Arts: Dr. Gary Hack, Dean, The Graduate School of Fine Arts, 102 Meyerson, University of Pennsylvania, Philadelphia, Pennsylvania 19104-6321; telephone: 215-898-6213; e-mail: gsfaadms@pobox.upenn.edu; World Wide Web: http://www.upenn.edu/gsfa.

Architecture, city and regional planning, fine arts, historic preservation, landscape architecture, and urban design.

The Annenberg School for Communication: Dr. Joseph Cappella, Associate Dean of Graduate Studies, The Annenberg School for Communication, 3620 Walnut Street–Room 315, University of Pennsylvania, Philadelphia, Pennsylvania 19104-6220; telephone: 215-898-7041; e-mail: apr@asc.upenn.edu; World Wide Web: http://www.asc.upenn.edu.

Communication.

The School of Nursing: Kari Szentesy, Associate Director of Graduate Enrollment Management, The School of Nursing, 420 Guardian Drive, University of Pennsylvania, Philadelphia, Pennsylvania 19104-6096; telephone: 866-867-6877 (toll-free); e-mail: nursing-phd-admissions@upenn.edu; World Wide Web: http://www.nursing.upenn.edu.

Nursing.

The School of Social Work: Mary Mazzolla, Director of Recruitment and Admissions, The School of Social Work, 3701 Locust Walk, University of Pennsylvania, Philadelphia, Pennsylvania 19104-6214; telephone: 215-898-5550; e-mail: admit@ssw.upenn.edu; World Wide Web: http://www.ssw.upenn.edu.

Social welfare and social work.

UNIVERSITY OF PITTSBURGH

Graduate Programs

Programs of Study

The several schools and faculties of the University of Pittsburgh offer programs of study leading to doctoral degrees (Ph.D., Psy.D., Ed.D., and Dr.P.H.) in the following fields: anthropology, astronomy, biological sciences, business administration, chemistry, classics, communication science and disorders, computer science, economics, education, engineering, English, French, geology and planetary science, Germanic languages and literatures, Hispanic languages and literatures, history, history and philosophy of science, history of art and architecture, intelligent systems, information science, library and information science, linguistics, mathematics, medicine, music, neuroscience, nursing, pharmacy, philosophy, physics, political science, psychology, public and international affairs, public health, rehabilitation science, religion, rhetoric and communication, Slavic languages and literatures, social work, sociology, statistics, and theatre arts.

Master's degree programs are available in most of the above fields, as well as in applied mathematics, applied statistics, Asian studies, bioethics, child development and child care, dental medicine specialities, health and rehabilitation sciences, health promotion and education, international business, Italian, law, management of information systems, occupational therapy, physical therapy, religious studies, and telecommunications.

First professional degree programs are offered in law (J.D., L.L.M.), dental medicine (D.M.D.), pharmacy (Pharm.D.), and medicine (M.D.). Certificate programs, dual-degree programs within schools, joint-degree programs between schools, and cooperative-degree programs with other institutions are also available.

Appointments for postdoctoral study and research are available in many of the University's departments.

The University calendar consists of three 15-week terms, which begin in August, January, and April. A number of summer sessions, varying in length, are offered in the summer.

Research Facilities

There are twenty-four University library collections on the Pittsburgh campus, of which the Hillman Library is the central facility. The libraries' collections contain more than 8.2 million items (volumes and microforms), 31,000 print subscriptions, and more than 5,400 electronic journals. Electronically, the University's libraries provide access to many remote resources. The government documents section in the Hillman facility alone contains nearly 403,000 items (volumes, microforms, and subscriptions). Cooperative arrangements have been developed with neighboring academic institutions, thus promoting a high level of information availability.

Computing Services and Systems Development operates personal and centralized computing hardware to support academic, instructional, and research programs.

Other resources for research include the Cleft Palate–Craniofacial Center, Learning Research and Development Center, Center for Philosophy of Science, Pymatuning Laboratory of Ecology, University Center for Social and Urban Research, University Center for International Studies, University of Pittsburgh Cancer Institute, Center for Biotechnology and Bioengineering, Surface Science Center, Center for Neuroscience, and Allegheny Observatory.

Financial Aid

Fellowships, traineeships, scholarships, teaching assistantships, and research assistantships are offered in the various fields of advanced study. The principal nonservice awards are the Andrew Mellon Fellowships for predoctoral study in arts and sciences. For the 2001–02 academic year, departmental support (teaching assistantships, teaching fellowships, and graduate student assistantships) paid salaries of $9780 to $12,465 for full-time, two-term appointments; full tuition scholarships based on merit were also awarded. Fractional appointments are available.

Cost of Study

Tuition for Pennsylvania residents for the 2001–02 academic year ranged from $4705 to $6256 per term for graduate degree programs and from $5853 to $12,050 per term for first professional degree programs. Tuition for out-of-state residents is usually double that for Pennsylvania residents.

Living and Housing Costs

Most graduate students live off campus since there are limited on-campus housing accommodations for these students. The University's Off-Campus Housing Service maintains lists of available rooms, apartments, and houses near the campus.

Student Group

The University's total enrollment at the Pittsburgh campus in fall 2001 was 26,710, including 12,546 men and 14,164 women. Enrollment in graduate and first professional programs was 8,912.

Location

Pittsburgh is the commercial, industrial, and cultural center of western Pennsylvania. It offers all of the advantages of a metropolitan setting—theaters, concert halls, museums, art galleries, a science center, a major symphony orchestra, parks, golf courses, playgrounds, major-league spectator sports, and an excellent public school system.

The University

The Faculty and College of Arts and Sciences offers undergraduate and graduate programs in the various fields of the arts and sciences. In addition, the University includes the following academic units: the University Honors College; the College of General Studies; the Schools of Education, Engineering, Law, Dental Medicine, Medicine, Nursing, Pharmacy, Health and Rehabilitation Sciences, Information Sciences, and Social Work; the Graduate Schools of Public and International Affairs and Public Health; and the Joseph M. Katz Graduate School of Business, including its undergraduate College of Business Administration. Certificate programs in international studies are offered through the University Center for International Studies. The University also operates four regional campuses in western Pennsylvania: Johnstown, Greensburg, and Bradford offer four-year baccalaureate programs, and Titusville offers primarily a lower-division curriculum, including two-year associate degree programs.

Applying

Admission to graduate programs is based on an overall evaluation of credentials, including the applicant's undergraduate record, which should show approximately a B average or better in the major field. Additional requirements as well as deadlines for admission, fellowships, scholarships, traineeships, and assistantships vary by school and department.

Correspondence and Information

School (or Department) of (specify)
University of Pittsburgh
Pittsburgh, Pennsylvania 15260
World Wide Web: http://www.pitt.edu/~graduate/

DEANS AND DEPARTMENT CHAIRS

Faculty and College of Arts and Sciences (e-mail: fasgrad@pitt.edu)
Dr. N. John Cooper, Dean, 917 Cathedral of Learning.
Anthropology: Dr. Robert Drennan, Chair, 3H01 Posvar Hall.
Biological Sciences: Dr. James M. Pipas, Chair, A234 Langley Hall.
Chemistry: Dr. Craig S. Wilcox, Chair, 234 Chevron Science Center.
Classics: Dr. Edwin D. Floyd, Chair, 1518 Cathedral of Learning.
Communication: Dr. John Lyne, Chair, 1117 Cathedral of Learning.
Computer Science: Dr. Rami Melhem, Chair, 322 Eberly Hall.
East Asian Languages and Literatures: Dr. J. Thomas Rimer, Chair, 1501 Cathedral of Learning.
Economics: Dr. Jean-Francois Richard, Chair, 4S01 Posvar Hall.
English: Dr. David Bartholomae, Chair, 526 Cathedral of Learning.
French and Italian Languages and Literatures: Dr. Dennis Looney, Chair, 1328-H Cathedral of Learning.
Geology and Planetary Science: Dr. Harold Rollins, Chair, 200 SRCC.
Germanic Languages and Literatures: Dr. Sabine von Dirke, Chair, 1409 Cathedral of Learning.
Hispanic Languages and Literatures: Dr. Mabel E. Moraña, Chair, 1309 Cathedral of Learning.
History: Dr. Van Beck Hall, Acting Chair, 3P01 Posvar Hall.
History and Philosophy of Science: Dr. John Norton, Chair, 1017 Cathedral of Learning.
History of Art and Architecture: Dr. David G. Wilkins, Chair, 105 Frick Fine Arts.
Linguistics: Dr. Alan Juffs, Chair, 2816 Cathedral of Learning.
Mathematics: Dr. John M. Chadam, Chair, 301 Thackeray Hall.
Music: Dr. David Brodbeck, Chair, 110 Music Building.
Neuroscience: Dr. Edward M. Stricker, Chair, 479 Crawford Hall.
Philosophy: Dr. Stephen Engstrom, Chair, 1001 Cathedral of Learning.
Physics and Astronomy: Dr. David Jasnow, Chair, 100 Allen Hall.
Political Science: Dr. Barry Ames, Chair, 4L01 Posvar Hall.
Psychology: Dr. Anthony R. Caggiula, Chair, 455 Langley Hall.
Religious Studies: Dr. S. Anthony Edwards, Chair, 2604 Cathedral of Learning.
Slavic Languages and Literatures: Dr. David Birnbaum, Chair, 1417 Cathedral of Learning.
Sociology: Dr. Patrick D. Dorein, Chair, 2G03 Posvar Hall.
Statistics: Dr. Satish Lyengar, Chair, 2700 Cathedral of Learning.
Theatre Arts: Dr. Attilio Favorini, Chair, 1617 Cathedral of Learning.

The Joseph M. Katz Graduate School of Business (e-mail: mba@katz.pitt.edu)
Dr. Frederick W. Winter, Dean, 372 Mervis Hall.

School of Dental Medicine (e-mail: pittdent@pitt.edu)
Dr. Thomas W. Braun, Dean, 440 Salk Hall.

School of Education (e-mail: jharden@pitt.edu)
Dr. Alan Lesgold, Dean, 5T01 Posvar Hall.
Administrative and Policy Studies: Dr. R. Tony Eichelberger, Acting Chair, 5SA03 Posvar Hall.
Health, Physical and Recreation Education: Dr. Jere D. Gallagher, Chair, 160 Trees Hall.
Instruction and Learning: Dr. George Zimmerman, Chair, 4H32 Posvar Hall.
Psychology in Education: Dr. Louis Chandler, Chair, 5C32 Posvar Hall.

School of Engineering (e-mail: admin@engrng.pitt.edu)
Dr. Gerald D. Holder, Dean, 240 Benedum Hall.
Bioengineering: Dr. Jerome S. Schultz, Chair, 407 Center for Biotechnology and Bioengineering.
Chemical and Petroleum Engineering: Eric J. Beckman, Interim Chair, 323 Benedum Hall.
Civil Engineering: Dr. Rafael G. Quimpo, Chair, 949 Benedum Hall.
Electrical Engineering: Dr. Joel Falk, Chair, 348 Benedum Hall.
Industrial Engineering: Dr. Bopaya Bidanda, Chair, 1048 Benedum Hall.
Materials Science and Engineering: Dr. Gerald H. Meier, Interim Chair, 848 Benedum Hall.
Mechanical Engineering: Dr. Minking Chyu, Chair, 648 Benedum Hall.

School of Health and Rehabilitation Sciences (e-mail: shrsadmi@pitt.edu)
Dr. Clifford E. Brubaker, Dean, 4029 Forbes Tower.

School of Information Sciences (e-mail: inquiry@mail.sis.pitt.edu)
Dr. Toni Carbo, Dean, 505 Information Sciences Building.
Information Science and Telecommunications: Dr. Martin B. H. Weiss, Chair, 737 Information Sciences Building.
Library and Information Science: Dr. Christinger Tomer, Chair, 640 Information Sciences Building.

School of Law (e-mail: admissions@law.pitt.edu)
Mr. David Herring, Dean, 219 Law School Building.

School of Medicine (e-mail: biomed_phd@fs1.dean-med.pitt.edu)
Dr. Arthur S. Levine, Dean, M240 Scaife Hall. Dr. Steve Phillips, Dean of Graduate Studies, 524 Scaife Hall.
Biochemistry and Molecular Genetics: Dr. Joseph C. Glorioso III, Chair, E1240 Biomedical Science Tower.
Cell Biology and Molecular Physiology: Dr. Raymond A. Frizzell, Chair, S368 Biomedical Science Tower.
Cellular and Molecular Pathology: Dr. George K. Michalopoulos, S410 Biomedical Science Tower.
Medicine: Dr. Mark Zeidel, Chair, 1218 Scaife Hall.
Neurobiology: Dr. Peter Strick, Interim Chair, W1640 Biomedical Science Tower.
Molecular Pharmacology: Dr. John S. Lazo, Chair, E134 Biomedical Science Tower.

School of Nursing (e-mail: nursing@pitt.edu)
Dr. Jacqueline Dunbar-Jacob, Dean, 350 Victoria Building.

School of Pharmacy (e-mail: rxschool@pitt.edu)
Dr. Randy P. Juhl, Dean, 1104 Salk Hall.

Graduate School of Public Health (e-mail: stuaff@gsphdean.gsph.pitt.edu)
Dr. Bernard Goldstein, Dean, 111 Public Health.
Biostatistics: Dr. Howard E. Rockette, Chair, 318B Public Health.
Environmental and Occupational Health: Dr. Bruce Pitt, Chair, A108 Public Health.
Epidemiology: Dr. Lewis H. Kuller, Chair, A527 Public Health.
Health Services Administration: Dr. Edmund M. Ricci, Chair, A620 Public Health.
Human Genetics: Dr. Robert E. Ferrell, Interim Chair, A304 Public Health.
Infectious Diseases and Microbiology: Dr. Charles R. Rinaldo, Chair, A427 Public Health.

Graduate School of Public and International Affairs (e-mail: gspia@pitt.edu)
Dr. Carolyn Ban, Dean, 3G07 Posvar Hall.

School of Social Work (e-mail: bpssw@pitt.edu)
Dr. Larry E. Davis, Dean, 2117 Cathedral of Learning.

UNIVERSITY OF RICHMOND

Arts and Sciences Graduate School

Programs of Study

The Arts and Sciences Graduate School offers programs of study leading to the degrees of Master of Arts (M.A.), Master of Science (M.S.), and Master of Liberal Arts (M.L.A.).

The M.A. degree is offered in English, history, and psychology. Course work requirements range from 27 to 36 semester hours. The programs in history and psychology require a thesis based on original research; students in English may choose between thesis and nonthesis tracks.

The M.S. degree is offered in biology. Degree requirements include 28 semester hours of course work and a thesis. The program has a strong research orientation.

The M.L.A. program is cross disciplinary in nature, consisting of courses taught by faculty members from a variety of disciplines, such as art, history, literature, music, philosophy, politics, and religion. Thirty semester hours are required.

Students may enroll on either a full-time or part-time basis in all programs except those in biology and psychology, which accept only full-time students.

Research Facilities

The libraries of the University contain more than 800,000 volumes and microforms. Collections in various Richmond-area libraries are also available for research and consultation, including those in the Richmond Public Library, Virginia State Library and Archives, Virginia Historical Society, and Virginia Baptist Historical Society Library (located on the campus). The Gottwald Science Center houses well-equipped laboratories and a science library. Computing support for research and instruction is provided by the University Computing Center.

Financial Aid

The Graduate School offers assistantships and a limited number of service-free scholarships to full-time graduate students who qualify on the basis of academic background and promise. Full-time students from Virginia may apply for a Virginia Tuition Assistance Grant. Various work-study and loan programs are also available to eligible graduate students. A special tuition remission, which results in substantially reduced fees, is provided for part-time students who enroll in one course per semester. Funds to support graduate student research are available through the Graduate Research Program.

Cost of Study

Tuition for full-time students for the two-semester academic year was $21,270 in 2001–02. Part-time students were charged at the reduced rate of $365 per credit hour for the first course taken each semester and at the full rate of $1060 per credit hour for additional courses.

Living and Housing Costs

The University has no on-campus housing for graduate students; however, accommodations for both single and married students are available within the Richmond community at various costs. Graduate students are welcome to eat in the University dining hall.

Student Group

The total University enrollment is approximately 4,700, of whom one fifth are graduate and professional students. About 100 students are enrolled in arts and sciences graduate programs each semester. Graduate students vary widely in age and background. Although the majority are from the states along the Atlantic seaboard, other parts of the nation and various other countries are represented. More than 80 percent of the full-time students receive financial aid.

Location

The University is located at the western edge of Richmond, Virginia, about 15 minutes by automobile from the city's center. Richmond is the state's capital and a major financial, business, and industrial center. The Richmond metropolitan area offers a full range of social, religious, cultural, and educational opportunities. Among cultural highlights are the Virginia Museum of Fine Arts, Richmond Symphony Orchestra, Virginia Opera, and Science Museum of Virginia. Eight other institutions of higher education are located within the metropolitan area. Richmond is only 2 hours' drive from Washington, D.C., and an hour from the Blue Ridge Mountains and Williamsburg.

The University

Founded in 1830, the University of Richmond has developed into the second-largest private university in the state. Currently among the fifty most heavily endowed universities in the nation, the University possesses the financial resources to further enhance its tradition of academic quality and humane values. The Arts and Sciences Graduate School is one of several schools and colleges that constitute the University. Other divisions include the T. C. Williams School of Law; the E. Claiborne Robins School of Business; University College for summer and continuing education programs; and the Jepson School of Leadership Studies.

Applying

Applicants are required to submit a completed application form, a $30 nonrefundable processing fee, official transcripts of all previous college work, three letters of recommendation, GRE scores (for most programs), and a statement of purpose. For most programs, applications must be received by March 15. Those wishing an assistantship or scholarship in any program should have their applications and supporting documents on file by March 15.

Correspondence and Information

Arts and Sciences Graduate School
University of Richmond
Richmond, Virginia 23173
Telephone: 804-289-8417
E-mail: asgrad@richmond.edu

THE FACULTY AND THEIR RESEARCH

Dona J. Hickey, Director; Ph.D., Wisconsin–Milwaukee. Rhetoric and composition, twentieth-century American and British poetry.

Biology
W. John Hayden, Chair; Ph.D., Maryland. Plant anatomy, plant systematics.
Rafael de Sá, Graduate Coordinator; Ph.D., Texas. Amphibian systematics.
John W. Bishop, Ph.D., Cornell. Aquatic ecology.
Krista Fischer-Stenger, Ph.D., Virginia Commonwealth. Immunology.
Roni J. Kingsley, Ph.D., South Carolina. Invertebrate mineralization.
Valerie M. Kish, Ph.D., Michigan. Cell biology.
Gary P. Radice, Ph.D., Yale. Developmental anatomy.
Penny Reynolds, Ph.D., Wisconsin. Animal physiology.
Peter Smallwood, Ph.D., Arizona. Ecology, evolutionary biology.
Debra L. Wohl, Ph.D., Georgia. Microbial ecology.

English
Raymond F. Hilliard, Chair; Ph.D., Rochester. British novel, eighteenth-century English literature, modern novel.
Anthony P. Russell, Graduate Coordinator; Ph.D., Yale. Shakespeare, English Renaissance.
Thomas M. Allen, Ph.D., Wisconsin. Nineteenth-century American literature.
Daryl Cumber Dance, Ph.D., Virginia. African-American literature and folklore, Caribbean literature and folklore.
Terry L. Givens, Ph.D., North Carolina. Romanticism, literary theory.
Elisabeth R. Gruner, Ph.D., UCLA. The novel, nineteenth- and twentieth-century British literature, women's literature.
Kathleen Hewett-Smith, Ph.D., California, Irvine. Medieval English literature, Piers Plowman, allegorical theory.
Dona J. Hickey, Ph.D., Wisconsin–Milwaulkee. Rhetoric and composition, twentieth-century American and British poetry.
Suzanne W. Jones, Ph.D., Virginia. Southern fiction, women writers, feminist theory, narrative theory, the novel.
Edward J. Larkin, Ph.D., Stanford. Early American literature, history of the book, political writing and rhetoric.
Alan S. Loxterman, Ph.D., Ohio State. Literary criticism, seventeenth-century poetry.
Joyce B. MacAllister, Ph.D., Texas. Rhetoric and composition
John B. Marx, Ph.D., Brown. British modernist and post- colonial fiction.
Josephine B. McMurtry, Ph.D., Rice. Shakespeare.
Robert M. Nelson, Ph.D., Stanford. Post-WWII literature, Native American literature.
Louis Schwartz, Ph.D., Brandeis. Sixteenth- and early seventeenth-century British nondramatic literature, John Milton.
Welford D. Taylor, Ph.D., Maryland. American literature, American novel, humor.
Louis B. Tremaine, Ph.D., Indiana. African literature, cultural studies.

History
Hugh A. West, Chair; Ph.D., Stanford. Modern European intellectual.
John D. Treadway, Graduate Coordinator; Ph.D., Virginia. European diplomatic, Eastern Europe.
Joan L. Bak, Ph.D., Yale. Latin America, modern Brazil.
Ernest C. Bolt Jr., Ph.D., Georgia. U.S. diplomatic, American social.
Joanna H. Drell, Ph.D., Brown. Medieval Europe.
John L. Gordon Jr., Ph.D., Vanderbilt. Modern Britain and empire, Canada.
Woody Holton, Ph.D., Duke. Colonial/Revolutionary America
Robert C. Kenzer, Ph.D., Harvard. Civil War and Reconstruction, nineteenth-century America, American South.
L. Carol Summers, Ph.D., Johns Hopkins. Africa.
Sydney Watts, Ph.D., Early modern Europe, eighteenth-century France.

Liberal Arts
Frank E. Eakin Jr., Graduate Coordinator; Ph.D., Duke.

Psychology
Craig H. Kinsley, Graduate Coordinator; Ph.D., SUNY at Albany. Behavioral neuroscience.
Scott T. Allison, Ph.D., California, Santa Barbara. Social, decision making, social inference.
Catherine Bagwell, Ph.D., Duke. Psychopathology, aggression, and antisocial behavior.
Jane M. Berry, Ph.D., Washington (St. Louis). Adult development, aging and memory.
Mary Churchill, Ph.D., Cincinnati. Clinical; ethics.
Elizabeth Crawford, Ph.D., Chicago. Spatial cognition, categorization, memory, emotion.
Warren Hopkins, Ph.D., Tennessee. Clinical, family studies, student development.
Frederick J. Kozub, Ph.D., Virginia. Biopsychology, history and systems.
Ping Li, Ph.D., Leiden. Psycholinguistics, cognitive science.
Andrew F. Newcomb, Ph.D., Minnesota. Child clinical, developmental.
Barbara K. Sholley, Ph.D., Ohio. Social, psychology of women.
Elizabeth Stott, Ph.D., Virginia Commonwealth. Clinical, eating disorders.

UNIVERSITY OF ST. AUGUSTINE FOR HEALTH SCIENCES

Programs of Study

The University of St. Augustine is a leading global institution in rehabilitation health sciences that offers entry-level and postprofessional graduate education in physical therapy (PT) and occupational therapy (OT). Practicing clinicians are able to pursue a postgraduate education in physical therapy and occupational therapy through advanced distance learning graduate degree programs. In addition, the University sponsors a wide range of continuing professional education seminars throughout the United States and internationally.

The entry-level Master of Occupational Therapy (M.O.T.), Doctor of Occupational Therapy (O.T.D.), and Doctor of Physical Therapy (D.P.T.) degrees are full-time semester programs that combine campus-based classroom instruction at St. Augustine and required clinical fieldwork and internships that are appropriate to the major. These clinical affiliations are conducted throughout the United States at more than 1,200 sites. Upon completion of the curriculum, the M.O.T., O.T.D., or D.P.T. graduate is able to sit for licensure in all fifty states.

Through the Advanced Studies Division, licensed therapists are able to complete degrees at the master's and doctoral levels through distance education delivery systems. Degrees offered are the transitional Doctor of Physical Therapy (D.P.T.), transitional Doctor of Occupational Therapy (O.T.D.), Master of Health Science (M.H.Sc.), and Doctor of Health Science (D.H.Sc.).

Clinical certifications in manual therapy, primary care, and sports physical therapy are offered through the Continuing Professional Education Division.

Research Facilities

Students in the M.O.T., O.T.D., and D.P.T. programs have daily access to the Learning Resource Center. Workstations in the computer lab have access to the Internet through the University's dedicated frame-relay connection. Membership in the Library Resource Network provides access to databases that are provided by Proquest, Infotrac, and Electric Library. The library's collections include journal subscriptions, monographs, and electronic media that encompass both disciplines.

The St. Augustine campus has well equipped classrooms and laboratories. Self-contained laboratories exist for assisted daily living, assistive technology, physical modalities, and Cybex, which provide students with access to equipment that will become the basis of clinical practice. A self-contained gross anatomy lab allows all students the opportunity to participate in cadaver dissection.

Financial Aid

The Outstanding Academic Achievement and Leadership Scholarship program provides six scholarships per semester to new campus-based students. The Financial Need Scholarship program provides two scholarships per semester to new students demonstrating financial need. A number of private loan agencies work with the University to assist students who are seeking financial assistance. In addition, the University extends loans to qualified students.

Cost of Study

Tuition for the campus-based D.P.T. and O.T.D. programs is $5334 per semester for seven semesters. Tuition for the M.O.T. program is $16,000 for three semesters per academic year, six semesters total. Tuition for the distance education D.P.T. is approximately $8800 for the 22-credit-hour program and approximately $16,095 for the 60-credit-hour program. The distance education D.H.Sc. is approximately $10,150 for the 26-credit-hour program.

Living and Housing Costs

Living and housing expenses are estimated at $9600 per year. Fees for advanced degrees vary depending on course work and length of the program.

Student Group

The campus-based student population is a diverse blend of individuals that ranges from those who have just completed undergraduate degrees to those who are seeking major career changes later in life. Out-of-state students represent approximately 65 percent of the student population. Through the admissions process, a diverse student population, in both prior educational and work experiences as well as ethnic and cultural differences, is encouraged. As an example, these programs have enrolled a former professional jockey, a concert pianist, a professional ballerina, and a licensed architect.

Location

The campus is located on a 28-acre site that is adjacent to the Intercoastal Waterway in St. Augustine, Florida. St. Augustine is the nation's oldest city and is known for its historic sites, unspoiled beaches, attractions, and moderate climate.

The University

Founded by Dr. Stanley V. Paris in 1966, the University has been teaching continuing professional education courses to physical therapists ever since. In 1979, the State of Georgia granted the University the authority to award the advanced Master of Science in Physical Therapy (M.S.P.T.) degree. After relocating to St. Augustine in 1991, the University added the Doctor of Physical Therapy (D.P.T.) degree, which was replaced by the Doctor of Health Science (D.H.Sc.) degree in January 2000. The M.P.T. program was established in 1994, and the M.O.T. program in 1997. Both programs received initial accreditations with no deficiencies cited. In October 2001, the University's state licensing board approved the entry-level O.T.D. and D.P.T. options.

Applying

The M.O.T., O.T.D., and D.P.T. programs admit new students for each semester. All applicants must have completed a bachelor's degree. Recommended prerequisites specific to the major should be completed prior to matriculation. GPAs in recent course work and in specific prerequisites and scores from the GRE are reviewed. Applicants are strongly encouraged to provide supporting documentation of potential success as a clinician. Applicants are invited to participate in personal interviews that provide additional information upon which admission decisions are based.

Application information for degree programs or Continuing Professional Education can be obtained at the sources below.

Correspondence and Information

Julie Cook or Kelly Payton
Enrollment Services Office
University of St. Augustine for Health Sciences
One University Boulevard
St. Augustine, Florida 32084

Telephone: 904-826-0084
800-241-1027 (toll-free)

Fax: 904-826-0085
E-mail: admissions@usa.edu
World Wide Web: http://www.usa.edu

THE FACULTY

The University of St. Augustine's faculty members are carefully chosen educators and practitioners with proven ability to provide students with a meaningful and exciting educational experience that is relevant to clinical practice. All faculty members possess a mastery of their field and a practical hands-on approach to their specialty. The University is proud of its faculty members and their strengths and diversity, as well as their commitment to the mission of the University.

Ronald D. Carson, Assistant Professor; M.H.S., Medical University of South Carolina. (OTR)
Mitzi Cavin, Instructor and Academic Coordinator of Clinical Education; B.S., Florida. (PT)
Lisa A. Chase, Associate Professor; Ph.D., Arizona State. (PT)
Karen S. Clayton, Professor and Director, Entry-Level Occupational Therapy Program; Ph.D., South Carolina. (OTR)
Jane A. Day, Associate Professor; Ph.D., Florida. (PT)
Bonnie R. Decker, Associate Professor and Academic Fieldwork Coordinator; M.H.S., Florida; BCD. (OTR)
Sharon E. Fair, Associate Professor; Psy.D., Southern California University for Professional Studies. (PT)
Emily Fox, Assistant Professor; M.H.Sc., Florida; NCS. (PT)
Gerard C. Gorniak, Professor and Director of Doctor of Physical Therapy Program; Ph.D., SUNY at Buffalo. (PT)
Kiren Jaswal, Assistant Professor; M.S., Western Ontario. (PT)
Richard H. Jensen, Professor and Dean, Division of Advanced Studies; Ph.D., Iowa; PT. (PT)
David A. Lehman, Assistant Professor; M.S., Miami. (PT)
Tammy LeSage, Assistant Professor; M.O.T., Texas Woman's; CHT.(OTR)
Dan R. Lofald, Associate Professor and Director of Instructional Technology; Ph.D., Florida.
Jodi Lowe, Associate Professor; D.H.Sc., University of St. Augustine for Health Sciences; NCS. (PT)
Patricia E. Marvin, Assistant Professor; M.A., Indiana of Pennsylvania. (OTR)
Cynthia Mathena, Assistant Professor and Director, On-Line Education; M.S., Old Dominion. (OTR)
Wanda B. Nitsch, Assistant Professor; M.S., M.T.C., University of St. Augustine for Health Sciences. (PT)
Jude C. Nwoga, Associate Professor; Ph.D., Wisconsin.
Stanley V. Paris, Professor and President; Ph.D., Union (Ohio). (PT)
Cathy Smith Paterson, Associate Professor; Ph.D., Florida.
Catherine E. Patla, Associate Professor and Clinical Residency Coordinator; D.H.Sc., University of St. Augustine for Health Sciences; PT. (PT)
Jeffrey A. Rot, Instructor; M.P.T., Shenandoah; OCS. (PT)
Ginger Tripp, Assistant Professor; M.S., Akron. (PT)
James A. Viti, Assistant Professor; M.Sc.P.T., University of St. Augustine for Health Sciences; OCS. (PT)

UNIVERSITY OF ST. THOMAS

Graduate and Professional Programs

Program of Study

As the largest private university in Minnesota, the University of St. Thomas features strong academic programs leading to advanced degrees enhancing both professional and personal growth. St. Thomas offers nearly fifty graduate-level degree programs in ten academic divisions.

The College of Arts and Sciences offers four degrees, including the Master of Arts degree in art history, English, Catholic studies, and music education.

The College of Business offers nine degree programs, including the Master of Business Administration (M.B.A.) in either a full-time day format or part-time evening format, the Accounting M.B.A., the Executive M.B.A., the M.B.A. in human resource management, and the M.B.A. in medical group management. The Master of International Management (M.I.M.), the Master of Business Communication, and the Master of Science in real estate appraisal are also offered.

Degrees offered in engineering and technology management include the Master of Manufacturing Systems Engineering, the Master of Science in manufacturing systems, the Master of Business Administration with a manufacturing concentration, and the Master of Science in technology management.

Graduate programs in software engineering include the Master of Software Design and Development, the Master of Science in software engineering, and the Master of Software Systems.

The St. Paul Seminary School of Divinity offers Master of Arts degrees in pastoral studies, theology, and religious education; the Master of Divinity (M.Div); and the Doctor of Ministry (D.Min.).

The School of Education provides graduate study leading to master's, education specialist, and education doctorate degrees. Graduate degree specialty areas in the School of Education include athletic administration; community education administration; critical pedagogy; curriculum and instruction; educational leadership; gifted, creative, and talented education; human resource development; learning technology; organization development; police leadership; reading; special education; student affairs leadership; and teacher education. Graduate programs can be designed to provide licensure for teaching, administrative, and other education positions.

The School of Law is a three-year, full-time law program leading to a Juris Doctor degree.

The Graduate School of Professional Psychology is accredited by the American Psychological Association and offers the Master of Arts in counseling psychology and the Doctor of Psychology in theory and clinical practice.

The School of Social Work offers the Master of Social Work (M.S.W.) degree, which prepares practitioners for clinical social work practice and leadership. The degree is offered collaboratively with the College of St. Catherine, also in St. Paul, Minnesota. An innovative dual-degree program that combines an M.S.W. degree with a master's degree in several areas, including theology, divinity, or pastoral studies, is also available.

Research Facilities

The St. Paul campus is home to the O'Shaughnessey-Frey Library Center, which serves the undergraduate college and selected graduate programs, and the Archbishop Ireland Memorial Library, which serves the School of Divinity. The Minneapolis campus is home to the Charles J. Keffer Library, which serves the Graduate Schools of Business, Professional Psychology, and Education, and the UST Law Library, which serves mainly St. Thomas law students.

Financial Aid

Federal, state, and private loans are available to qualified students through the Office of Student Financial Services at http://www.financialaid@stthomas.edu. A number of scholarships, grants, and assistantships are awarded by the individual graduate colleges or schools.

Cost of Study

Graduate school tuition varies depending on the program. Current tuition ranges from $428 to $776 per credit, except for law.

Living and Housing Costs

Most of St. Thomas graduate programs are intended for students who live and work within commuting distance of either campus. A shuttle service runs between the St. Paul and Minneapolis campus approximately every 20 minutes during the academic day and evening. Limited graduate-student on-campus housing is intended for selected international graduate students.

Student Group

Enrollment at St. Thomas includes more than 11,000 students. Of those, the largest group is graduate and professional students, who number more than 6,000. Approximately 51 percent of graduate students are women, and 17 percent of all graduate students are students of color. Geographic representation includes students from Minnesota, surrounding states, national locations, and many countries.

Location

Conveniently located in the metropolitan twin cities of St. Paul and Minneapolis, St. Thomas has a 78-acre campus that anchors the western end of St. Paul's historic Summit Avenue. In 1992, St. Thomas opened its Minneapolis campus in downtown Minneapolis. To date, two buildings housing several graduate programs have been built. In February 2002, St. Thomas broke ground on a new $33 million School of Law building. The Minneapolis campus of St. Thomas is connected to the skyway system, which allows people to make their way in the downtown area without walking outside.

The University

St. Thomas is a comprehensive, Catholic university founded in 1885 by Archbishop John Ireland. St. Thomas seeks to develop morally responsible individuals who combine career competency with cultural awareness and intellectual curiosity. Graduate programs emphasize the integration of theory with practice, enhance the professional competence and ethical judgment of students, and foster personal growth and an appreciation of lifelong learning.

Applying

Each program has an established application process. Interested students should contact specific programs for application guidelines. Some programs may require standardized tests; some have specific work experience requirements.

Correspondence and Information

Elizabeth A. Schmitt
Marketing Director
University of St. Thomas
Loras Hall 508
2115 Summit Avenue
St. Paul, Minnesota 55105-1096

Telephone: 651-962-6483
800-328-6319, Ext. 2-6483
Fax: 651-962-6410
E-mail: easchmitt@stthomas.edu
World Wide Web: http://www.stthomas.edu

GRADUATE AND PROFESSIONAL SCHOOL DEANS AND DIRECTORS

College of Arts and Sciences: Dr. Tom Connery, Dean.
Graduate Program in Art History: Dr. Mark Stansbury-O'Donnell, Director.
Graduate Program in English: Dr. Michael O. Bellamy, Director.
Graduate Program in Music Education: Dr. Jill Trinka, Director.

College of Business: Dr. William Raffield, Interim Associate Dean.
Master of Business Administration Program: Dr. Russell (Stan) Nyquist, Director.
Day Master of Business Administration Program: William Davidson and Dr. Russell (Stan) Nyquist, Co-Directors.
Accounting Master of Business Administration Program: William Davidson, Director.
Executive Master of Business Administration Program: William Monson and Nicholas Lauer, Co-Directors.
Master of Business Administration in Human Resource Management Program: Philip Schechter, Director.
Master of Business Administration in Medical Group Management Program: Thomas Gilliam, Director.
Master of Business Communication Program: Dr. Nona Mason, Director.
Master of International Management Program: Dr. Karen Gulliver, Director.
Master of Science in Real Estate Appraisal Program: Dr. Thomas Musil, Director.

Graduate School of Divinity (St. Paul Seminary School of Divinity of the University of St. Thomas): Dr. Jeanne P. McLean, Dean.

Programs in Engineering and Technology Management: Dr. Ronald J. Bennett, Director.

School of Education (Graduate): Dr. Miriam Williams, Dean.
Curriculum and Instruction Department: Dr. Eleni Roulis, Chair.
Educational Leadership Department: Dr. Tom Fish, Chair.
Organization Learning and Development Department: Dr. John Conbere, Chair.
Special Education Department: Dr. Michael Brown, Chair.
Teacher Education Department: Dr. Trudi Taylor, Chair.

School of Law: Thomas Mengler, Dean.

School of Social Work: Dr. Barbara W. Shank, Dean.

UNIVERSITY OF SAN DIEGO

Graduate Programs

Programs of Study

The University of San Diego (USD) offers programs leading to both doctoral and master's degrees. The College of Arts and Sciences offers the M.A. in history, international relations, pastoral care and counseling, peace and justice studies, and practical theology. A Certificate of Advanced Studies in pastoral counseling is offered for licensed health and mental health care givers. There is an advanced-certificate program offered in international relations. A joint-degree program leading to the J.D./M.A. in international relations is also offered in conjunction with the USD School of Law. The Globe Theatre/University of San Diego Professional Actor Training Program offers an M.F.A. in dramatic arts. The M.S. is offered in marine science, a research-based thesis program, with opportunities for research in biological, physical, chemical, and geological oceanography, for students with a bachelor's degree in natural science. The School of Business offers the M.B.A. degree, with areas of emphasis in management, marketing, finance, venture management, project management, electronic commerce, and supply management, as well as a comprehensive option. The International Master of Business Administration (I.M.B.A.) degree is also offered as a separate program. The M.S. in electronic commerce provides students skills to assume leadership positions with Internet-based businesses. A dual-degree program is available in conjunction with the Instituto Tecnológico y de Estudios Superiores de Monterrey (ITESM), Mexico. Joint-degree programs leading to the J.D./M.B.A., M.S.N./M.B.A., J.D./I.M.B.A., and M.B.A./M.S. in electronic commerce are offered in conjunction with the USD School of Law or School of Nursing and Health Science. Other degree programs include the M.S. in executive leadership and the M.S. in global leadership. The business administration programs are fully accredited by AACSB International–The Association to Advance Collegiate Schools of Business. The School of Education offers the Doctor of Education (Ed.D.) in leadership studies and has a joint doctoral program (Ed.D.) with San Diego State University with specializations in educational technology and teaching and learning (literacy). The school awards the M.A. in marital and family therapy, leadership studies, and counseling. The M.A. program in marital and family therapy is accredited by the Commission on Accreditation for Marriage and Family Therapy Education (COAMFTE). The Master of Arts in Teaching is also available. The Master of Education is awarded in learning and teaching and educational leadership/administration. The University is authorized by the California Commission on Teacher Credentialing (CCTC) to recommend candidates for credentials at USD in multiple subject, multiple subject (bilingual emphasis), CLAD and BCLAD certificates, preliminary administrative services, single subject, pupil personnel services in school counseling, special education (mild/moderate, moderate/severe), and the early childhood special education certificate. The Hahn School of Nursing and Health Science offers the Accelerated Bachelor of Science in Nursing/Master of Science in Nursing (B.S.N./M.S.N.) for registered nurses, a Master's Entry Program in Nursing (MEPN) for non-RNs, the Master of Science in Nursing (M.S.N.), a joint-degree program combining the Master of Business Administration/ Master of Science in Nursing (M.B.A./M.S.N.), and the Doctor of Philosophy (Ph.D.) in nursing. The School Nurse Health Services Credential, Post-Master's Health Care Systems Certificate, and Post-M.S.N. Nurse Practitioner Certificate are also offered. The M.S.N. program prepares family, pediatric, and adult nurse practitioners and nurse administrators for a variety of health-care settings and prepares nurse case managers for specific client groups in acute, long-term community, and home-health settings. The School of Law offers the Juris Doctor (J.D.); Master of Law (LL.M.) in international law, comparative law, business and corporate law, and taxation; and Master of Laws (LL.M.) general as well as the joint-degree programs mentioned above. The law school offers both day and evening programs.

Research Facilities

Copley Library features more than 360,000 books and 2,200 current journal subscriptions as well as newspapers, government documents, reference books, rare books, and access to many databases. The Media Center has an extensive audiovisual collection. The Legal Research Center in the School of Law maintains a collection in excess of 450,000 volumes.

Financial Aid

For application materials, students should contact the Office of Financial Aid Services, University of San Diego, Hughes Administration Center, 5998 Alcalá Park, San Diego, California 92110-2492; Telephone: 619-260-4514 or 800-248-4873 (toll-free); Web site: http://www.sandiego.edu/financial_aid. Students interested in applying for graduate fellowships should contact the graduate schools to which they are applying. For graduate assistantships, students should contact the Human Resources Office (619-260-4594).

Cost of Study

For the 2002–03 academic year, master's and credential tuition costs are $775 per semester unit. Doctoral tuition costs are $790 per semester unit.

Living and Housing Costs

Information on graduate housing can be obtained by contacting the Department of Housing and Residence Life, University of San Diego, Mission Crossroads, 5998 Alcalá Park, San Diego, California 92110; Telephone: 619-260-4777; Web site: http://www.housing.sandiego.edu.

Student Group

The student population in 2001–02 was 7,042, including 1,124 graduate and 1,129 law students. Students come from all over the U.S., and international students represent about 8 percent of the graduate enrollment.

Student Outcomes

Graduate degree recipients report employment in areas related to their fields of study. For example, in the College of Arts and Sciences, students with international relations degrees secured employment in international business, teaching, and corporate relations; practical theology degrees led to teaching, campus, and catechetical ministries. School of Business graduates were hired in areas such as e-commerce, finance development, project management, and supply chain management. School of Education graduates are employed in teaching at all levels and in counseling, administrative, nonprofit management, and consulting careers. School of Nursing graduates entered clinical, educational, and research settings as well as advanced degree programs.

Location

San Diego, a city of more than 1 million people, is the second-largest city in California and sixth largest in the country. Just 30 minutes north of the border with Mexico, it offers spectacular views of the Pacific Ocean and surrounding mountains. USD's 180-acre campus provides access to business, cultural, residential, and recreational areas by its proximity to air and rail terminals, city bus stops, and freeways.

The University

USD is an independent, Roman Catholic university that was founded in 1949. The University comprises five academic schools: the College of Arts and Sciences, the School of Business, School of Education, School of Law, and School of Nursing and Health Science. Class size averages 18 students, facilitating close rapport with faculty members.

Applying

Application for admission is made to the Office of Graduate Admissions. All applicants must submit the application form, application fee, one official copy (two for credential applicants) of all postsecondary transcripts, three letters of recommendation, and applicable standardized test scores. Application deadlines vary. Students should contact Graduate Admissions for program deadlines. The deadline for admission to the M.F.A. program is January 20. The priority deadline for admission to the M.S.N. program is May 1 for the fall semester and November 1 for the spring semester. The deadline for admission to the on-campus Ed.D. program is April 1. The deadline for the Ph.D. program is February 15 for the fall semester and the summer term. Applications for financial aid should be received by May 1 for the fall semester; however, applications are accepted during the year for any portion of the year remaining.

Correspondence and Information

Office of Graduate Admissions
University of San Diego
5998 Alcalá Park
San Diego, California 92110-2492
Telephone: 619-260-4524; 800-248-4873 (toll-free)
Fax: 619-260-4158
E-mail: grads@sandiego.edu
World Wide Web: http://www.sandiego.edu/gradmiss/

Office of Admissions and Financial Aid
School of Law
University of San Diego
Warren Hall, Room 203
5998 Alcalá Park
San Diego, California 92110-2492
Telephone: 619-260-4528; 800-248-4873 (toll-free)
E-mail: jdinfo@sandiego.edu
World Wide Web: http://www.sandiego.edu/~usdlaw/

FACULTY HEADS

DEANS

College of Arts and Sciences: Patrick F. Drinan, Ph.D.
School of Business: Curtis Cook, D.B.A.
School of Education: Paula A. Cordeiro, Ed.D.
School of Law: Daniel B. Rodriguez, J.D.
School of Nursing and Health Science: Janet A. Rodgers, Ph.D.

GRADUATE PROGRAM COORDINATORS

College of Arts and Sciences
Dramatic Arts: Richard Seer, M.F.A.
History: Michael Gonzalez, Ph.D.
International Relations: Vidya Nadkarni, Ph.D.
Marine Science: Hugh I. Ellis, Ph.D.
Pastoral Care and Counseling: Ellen Colangelo, Ph.D.
Practical Theology: Helen deLaurentis, Ph.D.

School of Business
Business Administration: Stephani Richards-Wilson, Ed.D. candidate.
Ahler's Center for International Business: Denise Dimon, Ph.D.

School of Education
American Humanics: Theresa Van Horn, M.A.
Counseling: Philip O. Hwang, Ph.D.
Learning and Teaching: Steven Gelb, Ph.D.
Leadership Studies: Edward F. DeRoche, Ph.D.
Marital and Family Therapy: Lee Williams, Ph.D.
Master of Arts in Teaching: Steven Gelb, Ph.D.
Multiple Subjects Credentials: Steven Gelb, Ph.D.
Single Subject Credentials: Steven Gelb, Ph.D.

School of Nursing
Accelerated B.S.N/M.S.N.: Mary Jo Clark, Ph.D.
Adult Nurse Practitioner: Louise Rauckhorst, Ed.D.
Case Management for Vulnerable Populations: Mary Ann Thurkettle, Ph.D.
Doctor of Philosophy (Ph.D.) in Nursing: Patricia Roth, Ed.D.
Family Nurse Practitioner: Louise Rauckhorst, Ed.D.
Health Care Systems Administration: Mary Ann Thurkettle, Ph.D.
Joint M.B.A./M.S.N.: Mary Ann Thurkettle, Ph.D.
Pediatric Nurse Practitioner: Susan Instone, D.N.Sc.
Post–FNP Urgent/Emergent Care Certificate: Louise Rauckhorst, Ed.D.
Post–M.S.N. Adult, Family, and Pediatric Nurse Practitioner Certificates: Louise Rauckhorst, Ed.D.
School Nurse Health Services Credentials: Louise Rauckhorst, Ed.D.
Web-Enhanced Family Nurse Practitioner: Louise Rauckhorst, Ed.D.

USF UNIVERSITY of SAN FRANCISCO

UNIVERSITY OF SAN FRANCISCO

Graduate Programs

Programs of Study The University Graduate Program consists of six colleges and professional schools. The College of Arts and Sciences offers three M.A. programs in cohort model in Asian-Pacific studies, with a joint degree program offered in conjunction with the McLaren School of Business; sport management; and an M.F.A. in writing. Master's programs are also offered in economics, international and development economics, and theology. Three research-focused M.S. programs are offered in biology, chemistry, and computer science. In addition, the M.S. degree is offered in environmental management. Environmental management and sport management are also offered at the Los Angeles/Orange Regional Campus.

The McLaren School of Business offers an M.B.A. degree, with areas of emphasis in finance, international business, management, marketing, and telecommunications. Two joint-degree programs are offered—the M.B.A./J.D. with the School of Law and an M.B.A./M.S.N. with the School of Nursing. Two cohort-based programs, the Executive M.B.A. program and the Professional M.B.A. for Executives (EPMBA) program, are also available. All business administration programs are fully accredited by AACSB International–The Association to Advance Collegiate Schools of Business.

The School of Education offers the Doctor of Education (Ed.D.) in learning and instruction, international and multicultural education, organization and leadership, and Catholic school leadership. The School awards the M.A. in counseling psychology with emphases in marriage and family therapy and educational counseling with a pupil personnel services credential; the M.A. in education with emphases in elementary education, secondary education, Catholic school leadership, and educational technology; the M.A. in learning and instruction, special education, international and multicultural education, teaching English as a second language, and organization and leadership with or without an emphasis in Pacific leadership international studies; The School's credential programs are accredited by the State of California Commission on Teacher Credentialing, and the School may recommend successful candidates for the following credentials: multiple subjects with the CLAD/BCLAD, single-subject CLAD/BCLAD, special education, pupil personnel services, and the preliminary and professional administrative services credentials.

The School of Nursing offers an M.S.N. degree in nursing administration, family nurse practitioner, and clinical nurse specialist as well as a master's entry option for those without a nursing background. In addition, the School of Nursing offers two joint degrees—an M.S.N./M.B.A. and an M.S.N./M.P.A. A family nurse practitioner certificate and a nursing informatics certificate are also available. All programs are certified by the National League for Nursing.

The College of Professional Studies offers the Master of Human Resources and Organization Development, Master of Science in Information Systems, Master of Nonprofit Organization, Master of Public Administration, and Master of Public Administration with a concentration in health services administration.

The School of Law offers the Juris Doctor (J.D.) and joint-degree programs leading to the J.D./M.B.A. offered in conjunction with the McLaren School of Business. The School is fully accredited by the American Bar Association and the American Association of Law Schools.

Research Facilities The Gleeson Library/Geschke Resource Center provides a welcoming environment for quiet and group study. Computers and network access are provided throughout the building. The collection of about 1.7 million items includes 650,000 books and bound journals, 2,800 current journal subscriptions, 240,000 government documents, and 255,000 audiovisual titles. Numerous information resources, databases, full-text journals, and e-books can be found through the library's Web page, which also offers online request forms for document delivery, interlibrary loan, Link+ quick borrowing, and research help. Reference and research assistance is available on the main campus, at the regional campuses, and to all distance learning students. Librarians are available to meet with students individually and to collaborate with faculty members to teach classes in graduate research skills using a dedicated electronic classroom. Each of the five professionally staffed regional libraries houses computer workstations, books, journals, and videos to support the curriculum. The state-of-the-art Zief Law Library, available to the USF community and practicing attorneys, includes holdings of more than 300,000 volume equivalents. The Ricci Institute Library specializes in more than 80,000 Chinese and other East Asian volumes. State-of-the-art campus facilities include major research equipment, high-quality laboratories, and science labs that support research and scholarly needs.

Financial Aid The University provides grants, loans, and employment opportunities to eligible graduate applicants. To apply, students must complete the Free Application for Federal Student Aid (FAFSA). For information, students should contact the Office of Financial Aid at 415-422-6303. Graduate merit scholarships and research and teaching assistantships are available in some programs. Students should contact the individual graduate program for information.

Cost of Study Tuition for the 2002–03 school year is $855 per unit, with the following exceptions—the College of Professional Studies programs ($710 per unit), the School of Education credential ($570 per unit), and doctoral programs ($880 per unit). The Law School tuition is $13,141 per semester for full-time study and $941 per unit for part-time study.

Living and Housing Costs Graduate housing is available for single students. A single room costs $3675 per semester, and a double room is $2860 per semester. Meal plans range from $1440 to $1890 per semester. The central location of the University makes it easily accessible to students who choose to live in one of the many unique neighborhoods of San Francisco. More information on housing is available from the Office of Residence Life at 415-422-6824.

Student Group Of the 8,000 students attending the University of San Francisco, half are graduate students. The graduate programs are uniquely designed to meet the needs of the University's diverse student population. Classes are small and most are scheduled in the late afternoon, evening, or on weekends to meet the demands of students continuing their careers.

Student Outcomes Graduates from the six colleges and professional schools at the University of San Francisco go on to a wide variety of positions as prominent educators, administrators, writers, researchers, jurists, health professionals, and business people. Graduates join a worldwide network of more than 70,000 alumni working around the globe. Individual programs can provide specific details of graduate student placement.

Location The University of San Francisco is situated in the heart of the city of San Francisco. The location itself is one of the great educational assets of the institution. This industrial metropolis, with its tradition of promoting the arts and its cosmopolitan population, provides an environment for culture and for business contacts that is unobtainable in a small community. The climate is world renowned, and every conceivable type of recreation can be found in or near the Bay Area.

The University USF is a private, Jesuit university. Founded in 1855 as San Francisco's first institution of higher education, the 55-acre hilltop campus overlooks Golden Gate Park, the Pacific Ocean, and downtown San Francisco. Students from more than seventy different countries are represented at the University, symbolic of the cultural diversity of San Francisco itself.

Applying Admission requirements vary according to the graduate program. Application dates, admissions procedures, entry dates, and options for full- or part-time study are described in individual program brochures. Information may be obtained by contacting the Office of Graduate Admission. Law School applicants should apply directly to the School of Law.

Correspondence and Information

Office of Graduate Admission
University of San Francisco
2130 Fulton Street
San Francisco, California 94117
Telephone: 415-422-GRAD
800-CALL-USF (toll-free outside California)
Fax: 415-422-2066
E-mail: graduate@usfca.edu
World Wide Web: http://www.usfca.edu

Office of Admission
School of Law
University of San Francisco
2130 Fulton Street
San Francisco, California 94117
Telephone: 415-422-6586
Fax: 415-422-6433
World Wide Web: http://www.law.usfca.edu

THE FACULTY

There are 290 full-time faculty members at the University of San Francisco. Of these, 92 percent hold doctorates or other terminal degrees. Specializations and research of faculty members can be obtained by contacting the individual graduate program.

Rev. Stephen A. Privett, S.J., President; D.Phil., Catholic University.

Deans
Academic Services: B. J. Johnson, Ed.D., San Francisco.
College of Arts and Sciences: Stanley D. Nel, Ph.D., Cape Town.
College of Professional Studies: Larry G. Brewster, Ph.D., USC.
McLaren School of Business: Gary G. Williams, Ph.D., Stanford.
School of Education: Paul B. Warren, Ph.D., NYU.
School of Nursing: John Lantz, Ph.D., Texas A&M.
School of Law: Jeffrey S. Brand, J.D., Berkeley.

Students find a perfect place for study at the Lone Mountain Library.

Located in the heart of San Francisco, the University's 55-acre hilltop campus overlooks Golden Gate Park, the Pacific Ocean, and downtown San Francisco.

Professor Anita DeFrantz interacts with students in the University's International and Multicultural Education Program.

UNIVERSITY OF SCRANTON

The Graduate School

Programs of Study

The Graduate School offers programs of study leading to the degrees of Master of Arts (M.A.), Master of Science (M.S.), Master of Business Administration (M.B.A.), Master of Health Administration (M.H.A.), and Master of Physical Therapy (M.P.T.). In English, history, and theology, the M.A. only is offered. The M.A. or M.S. may be obtained in biochemistry, chemistry, clinical chemistry, and secondary education. The M.S. only is offered in community counseling, early childhood education, elementary education, elementary school administration, human resources administration (concentrations available in human resource development, human resources, and organizational leadership), nursing (concentrations available in adult health, family nurse practitioner, and nurse anesthesia), occupational therapy, reading education, rehabilitation counseling, school counseling, secondary school administration, and software engineering. The M.H.A. only is offered in health administration. The M.B.A. is offered with concentrations in accounting, enterprise management technology, finance, international business, management information systems, marketing, and operations management. A post-master's Certificate of Advanced Graduate Study in Professional Counseling is available. There is also an executive certificate program in health administration.

The University has certification programs approved by the Pennsylvania Department of Education in the areas listed below. Some of these may be pursued in connection with an undergraduate degree, some in connection with a graduate degree, and some may be pursued independent of any degree program. Certification areas are: biology, chemistry, communications, elementary education, elementary principal studies, elementary school counseling, English, French, general science, German, Latin, mathematics, physics, reading specialist studies, secondary school principal studies, secondary school counseling, social studies, and Spanish. Supervisor certificates are available in communication (English), foreign languages, mathematics, reading, school guidance services, science, and social studies.

Research Facilities

The Weinberg Memorial Library collection has approximately 400,000 volumes as well as extensive holdings in periodical subscriptions, microforms, and nonprint items, including videocassettes, records, films, and filmstrips. Databases and major libraries throughout the world can be accessed through the library's Internet gateway.

The University provides an excellent array of computing facilities, and its status as one of "America's Most Wired Colleges" (*Yahoo! Internet Life* magazine) is evident throughout the campus. There are more than 700 computers for laboratory and student use.

The Institute of Molecular Biology and Medicine is housed in a newly built facility that includes a dedicated PCR laboratory complex with clean rooms, antechambers, and traffic flow; an automated DNA sequencing laboratory for high-throughput sequencing; a bioinformatics facility; a mutation detection laboratory containing DNA amplification systems for rapid mutation analyses in specific genes; a cancer biology laboratory dedicated to understanding the molecular biology of cancer; and a fully functional BSL 3 laboratory complex.

Financial Aid

Approximately sixty-five graduate assistantships are available each year that carry a stipend and a tuition scholarship. Information and application forms may be obtained from the Graduate School Office. The application deadline is March 1. Residence Life Coordinator positions are offered to single male and female graduate students, whereby room and board in the University's dormitories are provided. Applications may be obtained from the Student Affairs Office (telephone: 570-941-7680). A limited number of other campus jobs are also available. Inquiries regarding these should be directed to the Financial Aid Office (telephone: 570-941-7700).

ROTC scholarships, administered by the military science department (telephone: 570-941-4597), are also available.

Cost of Study

Graduate tuition for the 2001–02 academic year was $539 per credit for all programs except theology, which was $270 per credit. The cost of living and studying at the University of Scranton was estimated to be $22,486 per calendar year. Most graduate programs take 1½ to 2 years to complete.

Living and Housing Costs

Most graduate students live in private apartments near the campus. A two-bedroom apartment in Scranton near the campus typically rents for about $450 per month.

A limited number of University apartments are available. They are fully furnished, with heat and utilities included, at rents ranging from $225 to $275 per month per person. Questions about University housing should be directed to the Office of Residence Life (570-941-6226).

Student Group

The Graduate School enrolls approximately 700 students, of whom 64 percent are women. There are 113 international students from thirty-seven different countries. The University's graduate students range in age from 20 to over 50. Sixty-six percent of the students are employed full-time and are pursuing their studies on a part-time basis; 34 percent of the students are full-time students. Students finance their studies with their own personal earnings, student loans, and employer reimbursement.

Student Outcomes

The most recent Career Services Office study on the postgraduation activities of the class of 2000 indicated that 97 percent of the graduates are employed full-time or pursuing additional education. Eighty-eight percent of the graduates employed full-time are working in Pennsylvania, New York, or New Jersey. The average salary reported was just under $40,000. There was considerable variability by graduate program and geographic area.

Location

The University is located in the heart of the city of Scranton, 120 miles (190 kilometers) west of New York City and the same distance north of Philadelphia. It is easily accessible by car, bus, or air. Scranton's location provides plenty of opportunities for exciting holidays. The campus is close to shopping, restaurants, entertainment, and recreational areas.

The University

The University of Scranton is an urban Jesuit school for men and women. It was founded in 1888 and is accredited by the Commission on Higher Education of the Middle States Association of Colleges and Schools, AACSB International–The Association to Advance Collegiate Schools of Business, the Pennsylvania Department of Education, the National Council for Accreditation of Teacher Education, the National League for Nursing Accrediting Commission, the Council on Rehabilitation Education, the American Physical Therapy Association, and the Council for Accreditation of Counseling and Related Educational Programs.

Applying

A completed application for admission is required, as well as official transcripts, three letters of reference, and a statement of intentions. There is a $50 application fee that is not waived under any circumstances. Applicants to the M.B.A. program must also submit the GMAT test score. Software engineering applicants may submit either the GMAT or GRE General Test score. In addition to the requirements listed above, international students are required to submit an acceptable TOEFL score and a completed Certification of Finances form.

Correspondence and Information

James L. Goonan
Director, Graduate Admissions
The Estate, Room 210
University of Scranton
Scranton, Pennsylvania 18510-4631
Telephone: 570-941-7600
800-366-4723 (toll-free)
Fax: 570-941-5995
E-mail: graduateschool@scranton.edu
World Wide Web: http://www.scranton.edu/graduateschool
http://academic.scranton.edu/department/gradsch/gradadmis.html
(for a downloadable application)

GRADUATE PROGRAM DIRECTORS

Business Administration: Wayne H. J. Cunningham, Ph.D., Penn State. (telephone: 570-941-4387; e-mail: cunninghamw1@scranton.edu)
Chemistry: Christopher Baumann, Ph.D., Florida. (telephone: 570-941-6389; e-mail: cab302@scranton.edu)
Community Counseling: Thomas M. Collins, Ph.D., SUNY at Albany. (telephone: 570-941-4129; e-mail: collinst1@scranton.edu)
Education: Joseph A. Fusaro; Ed.D., SUNY at Albany. (telephone: 570-941-6123; e-mail: fusaroj1@scranton.edu)
English: John M. McInerney, Ph.D., Loyola Chicago. (telephone: 570-941-7659; e-mail: mcinerneyj1@scranton.edu)
Health Administration: Peter C. Olden, Ph.D., Virginia Commonwealth. (telephone: 570-941-4350; e-mail: oldenp1@scranton.edu)
History: Ray Champagne, Ph.D., Loyola Chicago. (telephone: 570-941-7428; e-mail: champagner1@scranton.edu)
Human Resources Administration: William G. Wallick, Ph.D., Penn State. (telephone: 570-941-4128; e-mail: wgw2@scranton.edu)
Nursing: Mary Jane Hanson, Ph.D., Pennsylvania. (telephone: 570-941-4060; e-mail: hansonm2@scranton.edu)
Occupational Therapy: Rhonda Waskiewicz; Ed.D. candidate, Temple. (telephone: 570-941-4125; e-mail: waskiewiczr1@scranton.edu)
Physical Therapy: Edmund M. Kosmahl; Ed.D., Nova. (telephone: 570-941-7499; e-mail: kosmahle1@scranton.edu)
Rehabilitation Counseling: Lori A. Bruch; Ed.D., George Washington. (telephone: 570-941-4308; e-mail: bruchl1@scranton.edu)
School Counseling: Lee Ann M. Eschbach, Ph.D., Washington State. (telephone: 570-941-6299; e-mail: eschbach@scranton.edu)
Software Engineering: Yaodong Bi, Ph.D., Illinois. (telephone: 570-941-6108; e-mail: biy1@scranton.edu)
Theology: Charles R. Pinches, Ph.D., Notre Dame. (telephone: 570-941-4302; e-mail: pinchesc1@scranton.edu

UNIVERSITY OF SOUTH ALABAMA

Graduate School

Programs of Study

The Graduate School offers a wide range of graduate degrees, including the M.S. in occupational therapy and in speech and hearing sciences, an M.H.S. in physician assistant studies, and a Master of Physical Therapy (College of Allied Health Professions); the M.A. in communication, English, history, and sociology; the M.S. in biological sciences, mathematics, marine sciences, and psychology; and the Master of Public Administration in the Department of Political Science (College of Arts and Sciences); the Master of Business Administration and the Master of Accounting (College of Business); the M.S. in computer and information sciences (School of Computer and Information Sciences); the Master of Education, with concentrations in alternative education, alternative secondary education, early childhood education, educational leadership, educational media, elementary education, health education, physical education, school counseling, school psychometry, and secondary education as well as a collaborative program; the M.S. in community counseling, exercise technology, instructional design and development, recreation administration, rehabilitation counseling, and therapeutic recreation; the Educational Specialist degree in counselor education, early childhood education, educational leadership, educational media, elementary education, health education, physical education, secondary education, and special education as well as a collaborative program (College of Education); the M.S. in electrical engineering, chemical engineering, and mechanical engineering (College of Engineering); and the Master of Science in Nursing, with concentrations in adult health nursing, community–mental health nursing, woman and child health nursing, nursing education, clinical nurse specialist, and executive and midlevel nursing administration (College of Nursing). The Ph.D. is offered in communication sciences and disorders, in instructional design and development, in marine sciences, and in the basic medical sciences with specializations available in biochemistry, microbiology/immunology, pharmacology, physiology, and structural and cellular biology.

Research Facilities

The graduate program in the basic medical sciences is housed in the College of Medicine, which has the Primate Center, Laboratory of Molecular Biology, Electron Microscopy Center, Mass Spectroscopy Center, Flow Cytometry Center, DNA-Protein Sequencing and Synthesis Center, Sickle-Cell Center, and Cancer Center. The graduate program in nursing has access to the clinical facilities of the three University of South Alabama (USA) hospitals and numerous outpatient clinics. The graduate program in marine sciences is housed in the College of Arts and Sciences, which has the Mineralization Laboratory and the Big Creek Biological Station available during the entire year for field research on reservoirs and streams. The University is a member of the Alabama Consortium for Marine and Environmental Sciences and has full access to the consortium's extensive research facilities, which are located on the Gulf of Mexico on Dauphin Island, Alabama. The University is also a member of the Mississippi-Alabama Sea Grant Consortium and the Oak Ridge Associated Universities Consortium. The University library houses 335,623 bound periodicals and volumes and 723,245 units of microform. As an official U.S. government depository, it houses 970,168 government documents (physical units) and a growing collection of other materials. It subscribes to more than 2,800 serial titles and contains an archive of approximately 600,000 historical photographic images. The University also operates a Biomedical Library with two branches, one on the main campus and one at the USA Medical Center, with a total of 78,128 bound volumes, 1,403 periodicals, and 8,594 units of microform. The Psychological Teaching Clinic is operated in support of the master's degree program in psychology, and the Business Resources Center is available to students in the M.B.A. program. A modern, fully equipped Speech and Hearing Clinic provides research facilities for graduate students in that program.

Financial Aid

The major University awards are assistantships in master's programs in all fields, with stipends of $4000 to $10,000 for the academic year plus remission of course fees. Assistants are expected to pay other specific fees. Stipends of $8000 to $13,000 per year, plus tuition remission, are awarded to students in the Ph.D. programs.

Cost of Study

The basic fees for fall 2001 amounted to $160 per semester plus course fees of $127 per semester hour (physician assistant studies—$127 per semester hour); thus, a student carrying a 9-semester-hour load paid a total of $1303 per semester or a total of $2606 for the academic year. Out-of-state rates were $254 per semester hour (physician assistant studies—$254 per semester hour); thus, a student carrying a 9-semester-hour load paid a total of $2446 per semester or a total of $4892 for the academic year. There is no tuition fee for Ph.D. students in basic medical sciences.

Living and Housing Costs

The University has extensive housing near the campus for single and married students; rent is about $215 to $265 per month. Single students may live in dorms; the cost is about $871 per semester for a suite to about $1485 per semester for a one-person efficiency apartment. A board plan is available, with options from $859 to $1049 per semester. The cost of living in Mobile is slightly below the national average.

Student Group

The University of South Alabama enrolled approximately 12,000 students in its most recent academic year; 1,800 of them were graduate students. Seventy-one percent of the students are from Alabama, 23 percent come from other states, and 6 percent come from other countries.

Student Outcomes

The University of South Alabama awards approximately 520 master's degrees each academic year. Graduates are currently enrolled in Ph.D. programs at Rutgers, Yale, Texas A&M, Emory, Missouri–Columbia, Arizona State, Michigan, Wisconsin, Washington University in St. Louis, and a number of other institutions. Education graduates have found teaching and administrative positions in all fifty states and in Australia, Bahrain, Canada, Germany, Hong Kong, Mexico, Nigeria, Russia, Venezuela, and the Virgin Islands. Others find employment in business and industry, government agencies, and in hospitals and clinics throughout the country.

Location

The University is in Mobile, Alabama, a port city and metropolitan area with a population of 476,000. While summers are warm, the overall climate is pleasantly mild. The nearby Gulf of Mexico beaches and extensive water resources of Mobile Bay and its tributaries provide outstanding recreational opportunities.

The University

Founded in 1964, the University comprises the Graduate School; the Colleges of Allied Health Professions, Arts and Sciences, Business, Education, Engineering, Medicine, and Nursing; the School of Continuing Education and Special Programs; and the School of Computer and Information Sciences. There are three specialized departments: Cooperative Education, Military Science, and Aerospace Studies. The University has three major teaching hospitals in Mobile. All facilities are entirely modern.

Applying

The deadlines for applications and all supporting documents are August 1 for fall, December 15 for spring, and May 20 for summer. The admission decision is based on the applicant's previous academic record and on evidence of the ability to pursue work on the graduate level.

Correspondence and Information

For admission information:
Director of Admissions
Administration Building 182
University of South Alabama
Mobile, Alabama 36688-0002
Telephone: 800-872-5247 (toll-free)

For the basic medical sciences program:
Graduate Director
Graduate Program in Basic Medical Sciences
College of Medicine (CSAB 251)
University of South Alabama
Mobile, Alabama 36688-0002
Telephone: 251-460-6153

For other graduate programs:
Dean of the Graduate School
Mobile Townhouse 222
University of South Alabama
Mobile, Alabama 36688-0002
Telephone: 251-460-6310
E-mail: dpatters@usouthal.edu
WWW: http://www.usouthal.edu

DEANS AND DIRECTORS

Graduate School: James L. Wolfe, Dean; Ph.D., Cornell.

College of Allied Health Professions: Daniel E. Sellers, Dean; Ph.D., Florida State. Julio Turrens, Director of Graduate Studies; Ph.D., Buenos Aires (Argentina).

College of Arts and Sciences: John W. Friedl, Dean; Ph.D., Berkeley. G. David Johnson, Director of Graduate Studies; Ph.D., Southern Illinois at Carbondale.

College of Business: Carl Moore, Dean; Ph.D., Alabama. W. Randolph Flynn, Director of Graduate Studies; D.B.A., Northern Colorado.

School of Computer and Information Sciences: David Feinstein, Dean; Ph.D., Stanford. Roy Daigle, Director of Graduate Studies; Ph.D., Georgia.

College of Education: George E. Uhlig, Dean; Ed.D., Nebraska. William Gilley, Director of Graduate Studies; Ph.D., Tennessee.

College of Engineering: David Hayhurst, Dean; Ph.D., Worcester Polytechnic. B. Keith Harrison, Director of Graduate Studies; Ph.D., Missouri.

College of Medicine: Robert A. Kreisberg, Dean; M.D., Northwestern. Mary I. Townsley, Director of Graduate Studies; Ph.D., California, Davis.

College of Nursing: Debra C. Davis, Dean; D.S.N., Alabama at Birmingham. Rosemary Rhodes, Director of Graduate Studies; D.N.S., LSU.

A lecture at sea for marine science students at the University of South Alabama.

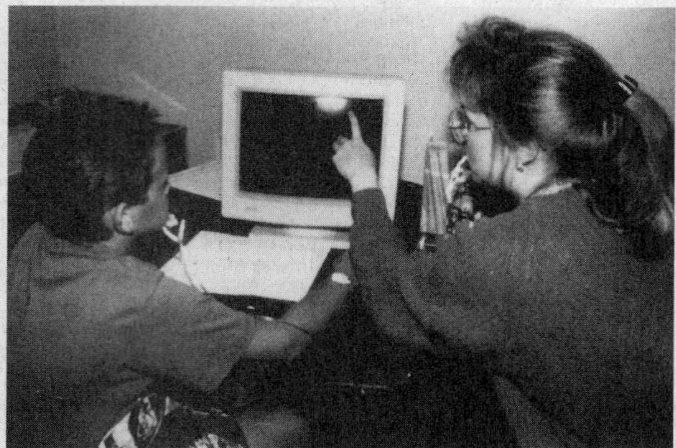

Research opportunities are available in the Master of Science and Doctor of Philosophy programs in the Department of Speech Pathology and Audiology (College of Allied Health Professions). Here a graduate student investigates the efficacy of computer-based instrumentation for remediation of speech sound production deficits.

Graduate students in the School of Computer and Information Sciences work in the project laboratory investigating methods for the development of new systems and application software.

UNIVERSITY OF SOUTH CAROLINA

The Graduate School

Programs of Study

The University of South Carolina offers the doctorate, with specializations in biology, biomedical science, business administration, chemistry, comparative literature, computer science, economics, education, engineering, English, geography, geology, history, international studies, journalism, linguistics, marine science, mathematics, music, nursing, pharmacy, philosophy, physical education, physical therapy, physics, political science, psychology, public health, social work, sociology, speech-language pathology, and statistics. Master's degrees are offered in all the above fields except biomedical science. Students can also earn master's degrees in accountancy; anthropology; creative writing; criminal justice; earth resources management; fine arts; French; genetic counseling; German; hotel, restaurant, and tourism administration; human resources; international business; library and information science; media arts; nurse anesthesia; public administration; religious studies; Spanish; taxation; teaching; and theater.

Research Facilities

The University's Thomas Cooper Library provides access to more than 7.5 million volumes, periodicals, microfilm entries, and manuscripts in the University system through the USCAN integrated information system. Outstanding research facilities are maintained in the sciences, humanities, and professional disciplines. Computer facilities include an Intel Paragon high-performance parallel computer system and an IBM 3090-400E mainframe computer. An extensive fiber-optic network connects local area networks to the Internet's global resources. A number of areas of particular research excellence are supported by research centers and institutes, including the Baruch Institute for Marine Biology and Coastal Research, the Institute for Biological Research and Technology, the Center for Family in Society, the Southeast Manufacturing Technology Center, the Research Division of the College of Business Administration, the Institute for International Studies, and the Institute for Southern Studies.

Financial Aid

Fellowships are available in many departments. Graduate assistantships are available in most departments and provide competitive stipends and special rates as low as $828 per semester for tuition and academic fees. Information about fellowships and assistantships should be obtained from the department of interest.

Cost of Study

Academic fees for full-time study in 2002–03 are $2838 per semester for South Carolina residents and $5719 per semester for nonresidents. Part-time resident students' academic fees are $280 per hour; part-time nonresident students' academic fees are $562 per hour. Academic fees for students in the health professions differ from the above-stated charges. Health services fees are included for students taking 9 or more hours and for students who have assistantships. Optional activity, athletic, and health services fees are based upon the student's full-time or part-time status. The University reserves the right to alter its charges without notice.

Living and Housing Costs

Graduate students normally live in off-campus housing. For 2002–03, a room in a private home averages $350 per month. An unfurnished apartment without utilities averages $450 per month (one bedroom) to $550 per month (two bedrooms). The Off-Campus Student Services Office assists students in locating off-campus housing. Total costs per academic year for a single resident student are estimated at $15,000 for tuition, room, board, and general expenses.

Student Group

During the 2001–02 academic year, graduate enrollment averaged about 6,600. Approximately 32 percent of the graduate students were from out of state, representing every state and ninety other countries.

Student Outcomes

Doctoral and master's program graduates are nationally competitive for academic, research, and leadership positions in national and multinational corporations, public and private institutions, and government agencies and are actively recruited on campus. Graduates seeking placement in the Southeast find positions in the rapidly expanding technology and manufacturing industries, major tourism and service industries, and educational and research institutions.

Location

Columbia, the capital of the state, has a population of approximately 500,000 residents within the metropolitan area. The University is located near the main downtown shopping areas and the state government complex of buildings. Greater Columbia offers a wide range of cultural attractions and entertainment, including the Koger Center for the Arts, the South Carolina Orchestra Association, the Columbia City Ballet, the Columbia Art Museum, several excellent community and children's theaters, and the nationally known Riverbanks Zoo. The city is located in the center of the state, and an excellent network of roads makes it easy to drive to the ocean and the mountains. Lake Murray, one of the largest lakes in the state and the setting for a range of aquatic activities, is only 15 miles from Columbia. Golf and tennis may be enjoyed the year round.

The University

The University was founded in 1801, the first state college to be supported by annual public appropriations. Having expanded through the years around the original horseshoe-shaped campus, the University today is the state's largest public institution of higher learning. Expansion in the last twenty years has been particularly rapid, and some of the most striking architecture of the region can be found on the campus.

Applying

Application must be made on Graduate School forms, which must be accompanied by a nonrefundable fee of $40. Applications should be submitted by July 1 for the fall semester, November 15 for the spring semester, May 1 for the first summer session, and June 1 for the second summer session. Some programs have earlier application deadlines; therefore, students should contact the academic unit to which they intend to apply. Earlier submission is necessary if financial aid is requested. An application cannot receive final consideration until all required credentials reach the Graduate School, including official transcripts, letters of recommendation, and test scores. Detailed admission requirements are given in the *Graduate Studies Bulletin.*

Correspondence and Information

The Graduate School
University of South Carolina
Columbia, South Carolina 29208
Telephone: 803-777-4243
Fax: 803-777-2972
E-mail: werner@sc.edu
World Wide Web: http://www.gradschool.sc.edu/

DEANS OF COLLEGES AND HEADS OF DEPARTMENTS

Graduate School: Gordon B. Smith, Dean.
Dale Moore, Director of Graduate Admissions.

Moore School of Business: Joel A. Smith, Dean.
Department of Economics: Ronald P. Wilder, Chair.

College of Criminal Justice: C. Blease Graham, Dean.

College of Education: Les Sternberg, Dean.
Department of Educational Leadership and Policies: Ken Stevenson, Chair.
Department of Educational Psychology: Michael Seaman, Chair.
Department of Instruction and Teacher Education: Therese Kuhs, Chair.
Department of Physical Education: Karen French, Chair.

College of Engineering and Information Technology: Ralph E. White, Dean.
Department of Chemical Engineering: Michael A. Matthews, Interim Chair.
Department of Civil Engineering: M. Hanif Chaudhry, Chair.
Department of Computer Science and Engineering: Duncan Buell, Chair.
Department of Electrical Engineering: Jerry Hudgins, Interim Chair.
Department of Mechanical Engineering: Abdel Bayoumi, Chair.

School of the Environment: Bruce C. Coull, Dean.
Program in Earth Resources Management: Jerome Eyer, Director.

College of Hospitality, Retail, and Sport Management: Patricia Moody, Dean.
School of Hospitality: Sandra K. Strick, Chair.
Department of Retail: Richard Clodfelter, Chair.
Department of Sport Management: Guy Lewis, Chair.

College of Liberal Arts: Joan Hinde Stewart, Dean.
Department of Anthropology: Thomas Leatherman, Chair.
Department of Art: Robert Lyon, Chair.
Program in Comparative Literature: Celso DeOliveira, Director.
Department of English: Steve Lynn, Chair.
Department of French and Classics: William Edmiston, Chair.
Department of Geography: David J. Cowen, Chair.
Department of German, Slavic, and Oriental Languages: Margit Resch, Chair.
Department of Government and International Studies: Harvey Starr, Interim Chair.
Department of History: Patrick Maney, Chair.
Program in Linguistics: Carol Myers-Scotton, Director.
Department of Philosophy: Davis W. Baird, Chair.
Department of Psychology: Jean Ann Linney, Chair.
Department of Religious Studies: Carl D. Evans, Chair.
Department of Sociology: Barry Markovsky, Chair.
Department of Spanish, Italian, and Portuguese: Edward Aylward, Interim Chair.
Department of Theatre, Speech, and Dance: Jim O'Connor, Chair.

College of Journalism: Henry T. Price, Interim Dean.

Law School: John Montgomery, Dean.

College of Library and Information Science: Fred W. Roper, Dean.

School of Medicine: Larry R. Faulkner, Dean.

School of Music: Jamal J. Rossi, Dean.

College of Nursing: Mary Ann Parsons, Dean.

College of Pharmacy: Farid Sadik, Dean.

School of Public Health: Harris Pastides, Dean.
Department of Environmental Health Science: G. Thomas Chandler, Chair.
Department of Epidemiology and Biostatistics: Cheryl Addy, Interim Chair.
Department of Exercise Science: Russell Pate, Chair.
Department of Health Administration: Carleen Stoskoph, Interim Chair.
Department of Health Promotion, Education, and Behavior: Donna L. Richter, Chair.
Department of Speech-Language Pathology: William A. Cooper, Chair.

College of Science and Mathematics: Gerard Crawley, Dean.
Department of Biology: Franklin Berger, Chair.
Department of Chemistry and Biochemistry: Daniel L. Reger, Chair.
Department of Geological Sciences: James N. Kellogg, Chair.
Program in Marine Science: Madilyn Fletcher, Director.
Department of Mathematics: Manfred Stoll, Chair.
Department of Physics and Astronomy: Fred Myrer, Chair.
Department of Statistics: James D. Lynch, Chair.

College of Social Work: Frank Raymond, Dean.

THE UNIVERSITY OF SOUTH DAKOTA

Graduate School

Programs of Study

The Graduate School of the University of South Dakota offers programs leading to the degrees of Master of Arts, Master of Business Administration, Master of Fine Arts, Master of Music, Master of Natural Science, Master of Professional Accountancy, Master of Public Administration, and Master of Science as well as to the degrees of Specialist in Education, Doctor of Education, Doctor of Philosophy, Juris Doctor, and Doctor of Medicine.

Majors leading to the degree of Master of Arts are offered in biology; chemistry; communication disorders; computer science; contemporary media and journalism; counseling and psychology in education; educational administration; elementary education; English; health, physical education and recreation; history; interdisciplinary studies; mathematics; political science; psychology; secondary education; sociology; special education; speech communication; and theater.

Majors leading to the degree of Master of Science are offered in administrative studies, basic biomedical sciences, biology, occupational therapy, physical therapy, and technology for training and development.

Majors leading to the Specialist in Education are counseling and psychology in education, curriculum and instruction, educational administration, and technology for training and development.

Majors leading to the degree of Doctor of Education include curriculum and instruction and educational administration.

Majors leading to the degree of Doctor of Philosophy are offered in basic biomedical science, biological science, counseling and psychology in education, English, and psychology.

Variations exist in the requirements of the graduate degree programs offered by respective departments. It is important for students to become acquainted with the specific requirements of their departments, because these, as well as certain University requirements, must be satisfied.

The University's academic year is divided into two semesters of approximately sixteen weeks each and a summer session of twelve weeks. By regular attendance during the summer sessions only, a student may earn a master's degree in four summers in some areas of the Graduate School.

Research Facilities

The University of South Dakota places great emphasis on the integration of research and teaching; consequently, graduate students have access to essentially all of the University's research facilities. There are a number of specialized research institutes, such as the Human Factors Laboratory, the Archaeology Laboratory, the Oral History Center, and the Business Research Bureau. Scientific instrumentation includes state-of-the-art equipment in the biological, physical, and computational sciences. Supporting on-campus organizations include the Shrine to Music Museum, which houses one of the world's largest collections of historic musical instruments; the W. H. Over Museum; the South Dakota State Geological Survey; and the Allen H. Neuharth Center for Excellence in Journalism.

Financial Aid

Financial assistance is available through a variety of graduate assistantships, grants, loans, scholarships, and work-study programs. Graduate assistantships range from $4000 to $17,000 for the nine-month academic year and qualify the student for a two-thirds tuition reduction. Summer assistantships are available in a variety of areas. To be eligible for an assistantship, a student must be fully admitted to a graduate degree program, have a minimum GPA of 3.0, and maintain full-time status with 9 or more credit hours per semester.

Cost of Study

Graduate tuition in 2001–02 was $94.75 per credit hour for state residents and $279.30 for nonresidents. Graduate assistants pay one third the graduate resident rate if registered for 9 credit hours or more. Other fees are added accordingly.

Living and Housing Costs

Assistance in finding off-campus rooms and apartments is available from the Director of Housing. Dormitory rooms are also available. Single-occupant rooms cost $987.50 per semester. Double-occupant rooms cost $760.45 per semester. Graduate students who reside in the dorms are not required to carry a meal plan; however, COYOTE CA$H is recommended. Married student housing is also available.

Student Group

There were approximately 5,300 undergraduate students and 2,400 graduate students enrolled during the 2001–02 academic year. Fifty-six percent of all enrolled students are women; approximately 22 percent of students are either nonresident or international.

Location

The University of South Dakota, authorized by the first territorial legislature in 1862, is located in Vermillion, a community of 10,000 people that is situated in the southeastern corner of the state. Vermillion overlooks the scenic and historic Missouri River Valley and is home to a special blend of agriculture, retail business, and light industry.

The University and The School

The University is accredited by the North Central Association of Colleges and Secondary Schools to offer master's, specialist's, and doctoral programs. The individual graduate programs are accredited by the appropriate agencies.

Applying

All students who wish to take graduate-level courses must register through the Graduate School of the University of South Dakota. A completed application packet must be sent to the Graduate School Office. The packet should include an application form, a $35 nonrefundable fee, three recommendation forms, two official transcripts, and official test score results.

Correspondence and Information

Office of Research and Graduate Education
Slagle Hall, Room 107
The University of South Dakota
414 East Clark Street
Vermillion, South Dakota 57069
Telephone: 605-677-6287
877-COYOTES (toll-free)
E-mail: gradsch@usd.edu
World Wide Web: http://www.usd.edu/gradsch

GRADUATE PROGRAMS AND DIRECTORS

Direct telephone contacts may be made by dialing area code 605 and the number listed for each program.

MASTER OF ARTS

Basic Biomedical Sciences: Steven Waller (677-5157).
Biology: Paula Mabee (677-5211).
Chemistry: Miles Koppang (677-5487).
Communication Disorders: Dean Lockwood (677-5474).
Computer Science: Richard McBride (677-5388).
Contemporary Media and Journalism: George Whitehouse (1677-5477).
Counseling and Psychology in Education: Frank Main (677-5250).
Educational Administration: Mark Baron (677-5260).
Elementary Education: Garreth Zalud (677-5451).
English: LeeAnn Roripaugh (677-5229).
Health, Physical Education and Recreation: Gale Wiedow (677-5336).
History: Robert Hilderbrand (677-5218).
Interdisciplinary Studies: John Day (677-5481).
Mathematics: Curt Olson (677-5262).
Political Science: Steve Feimer (677-5242).
Psychology: Barbara Yutrzenka (677-5351).
- Clinical Psychology: Barbara Yutrzenka (e-mail: byutrzyen@usd.edu).
- Human Factors: Jan Berkhout (e-mail: berkhout@usd.edu).

Secondary Education: Garreth Zalud (677-5451).
Sociology: Jon Flanagin (677-5401).
Special Education: Garreth Zalud (677-5451).
Speech Communication: Diane Kay Sloan (677-5476).
Theater: Ron Moyer (677-5418).

MASTER OF BUSINESS ADMINISTRATION: Diane Duin (677-5232).

MASTER OF FINE ARTS

Art: John Day (677-5636).
Theater: Ron Moyer (677-5418).

MASTER OF MUSIC: Gary Reeves (677-5274).

MASTER OF NATURAL SCIENCE: Miles Koppang (677-5211 or 5487).

MASTER OF PUBLIC ADMINISTRATION: Steve Feimer (677-5242).

MASTER OF SCIENCE

Administrative Studies: Diane Duin (677-5232).
Biology: Paula Mabee (677-5211).
Occupational Therapy: Barbara Brockevelt (677-5600).
Physical Therapy: Roy Osborn (677-5915).
Technology for Training and Development: Michael Hoadley (677-5839).

SPECIALIST IN EDUCATION

Counseling and Psychology in Education: Frank Main (677-5250).
Curriculum and Instruction: Garreth Zalud (677-5210).
Educational Administration: Mark Baron (677-5260).
Technology for Training and Development: Michael Hoadley (677-5839).

DOCTOR OF EDUCATION

Curriculum and Instruction: Garreth Zalud (677-5210).
Educational Administration: Mark Baron (677-5260).

DOCTOR OF PHILOSOPHY

Basic Biomedical Sciences: Steven Waller (677-5170).
English: LeeAnn Roripaugh (677-5229).
Counseling and Psychology in Education: Frank Main (677-5250).
Psychology: Barbara Yutrzenka (677-5351).
- Clinical Psychology: Barbara Yutrzenka (e-mail: byutrzyen@usd.edu).
- Human Factors: Jan Berkhout (e-mail: berkhout@usd.edu).

JURIS DOCTOR: Barry Vickrey (677-5443).

DOCTOR OF MEDICINE: Paul Bunger (677-6886).

UNIVERSITY OF SOUTHERN CALIFORNIA

Graduate Studies

Programs of Study

The University of Southern California (USC) offers programs of study leading to graduate degrees in the following major fields: accounting (including business taxation), American studies and ethnicity, anthropology, architecture (including building science and landscape), art history (including museum studies), biochemistry and molecular biology, biokinesiology (including physical therapy), biological sciences (including marine biology and molecular biology), biostatistics, business administration (including information and operations management, international business, and medical management), cell biology and neurobiology, chemistry (including chemical physics), cinema-television (including film, video, and computer animation; critical studies; interactive media; motion picture producing; production; and writing for screen and television), classics, communication (including global communication) communication management, comparative literature, computational linguistics, computational molecular biology, computer science (including computer networks, creative and multimedia technology, robotics, and software engineering), craniofacial biology, dentistry, earth sciences, East Asian languages and cultures (including area studies), economics (including economic developmental programming), education (including counseling psychology), engineering (aerospace, biomedical, chemical, civil, computer, electrical—including systems and electrophysics, environmental, industrial and systems, materials science, mechanical, and petroleum), English, epidemiology, environmental studies, fine arts (including public art studies), French, geography, German, gerontology, history, international relations, journalism (broadcast, international, print, and strategic public relations), kinesiology, law, linguistics, mathematical finance, mathematics (including applied mathematics and statistics), medicine, molecular epidemiology, molecular microbiology and immunology, molecular pharmacology and toxicology, music (early music performance, education, history and literature, musicology, performance, and theory), neuroscience, nursing, occupational therapy (including occupational science), pathobiology, pharmaceutical economics and policy, pharmaceutical sciences, pharmacy, philosophy, physician assistant practice, physics, physiology and biophysics, planning (including planning and development studies and real estate development), political economy and public policy, political science, preventive medicine (health behavior), professional writing, psychology, public administration (including health administration and public policy), public health, Slavic languages and literatures, social work, sociology, and theater (theatrical design and playwriting). The degrees offered in each area of study are shown on the reverse side of this page.

Research Facilities

The University Library, comprising the central library, high-technology library, specialized research libraries, and three independent libraries, houses 3 million volumes, 500,000 government documents, 3.6 million microforms, 3 million photographs, and 20,000 journals. The research centers at USC include the Annenberg Center for Communication, the Integrated Media Systems Center, the Loker Hydrocarbon Research Institute, Information Sciences Institute, Social Science Research Institute, Southern California Earthquake Center, and Wrigley Institute for Environmental Studies.

To support research, classroom learning, and independent study, USC provides students on the main campus, access to the latest computers, including Macintoshes with DVD, Windows PCs, UNIX workstations, scanners, Zip drives, and laser printers. Internet and Web tools and programs for word processing, spreadsheets, databases, graphics, and mathematics/statistics are available. USC's network connects the University community to the Internet. University housing complexes have Ethernet connections to the Internet.

Financial Aid

Graduate teaching and research assistantships are offered by most departments. The approximate value of these awards for the academic year range from $20,000 to $35,000, including full or partial tuition remission, the stipend, and a paid health care package. Other sources of financial aid are Graduate School Diversity Fellowships of up to $16,000 plus tuition and mandatory fees, Provost Graduate Fellowships of up to $17,000 plus tuition and mandatory fees, and federal assistance programs (Federal Work-Study, Federal Perkins Loan, and Federal Stafford Loan).

Cost of Study

In 2002–03, tuition is estimated at $891 per unit. Selected programs have higher rates.

Living and Housing Costs

University apartments for graduate students and their families are available on a limited and first-come, first-served basis. Housing facilities for Health Sciences Campus students is also available. All units are fully furnished, with estimated monthly rates ranging from $400 to $625 for a one-bedroom/2-person unit and $275 to $510 for a two-bedroom/4-person unit. Bachelor units for one person range from approximately $495 to $540 per month. Family housing is estimated to range from $680 to $845 per month.

Student Group

The University enrolls approximately 29,000 full- and part-time students, including more than 13,700 graduate students. Diversity is the hallmark of the USC student community with students from across the United States and more than 100 countries.

Location

Situated just 3 miles south of the Civic Center, the 155-acre University Park campus is adjacent to museums and recreational facilities of the Exposition Park complex. It is served by a network of freeways providing access to most cultural, business, and residential areas of southern California. The Health Sciences Campus is located 3 miles northeast of the Los Angeles Civic Center. Other teaching facilities include the Orange County Center; the Washington, D.C. Public Affairs Center; the Sacramento Center; and the Wrigley Marine Science Center at Catalina.

The University

Founded in 1880, the University of Southern California is a private research university of international distinction and the oldest such in the western United States. It ranks among the nation's top ten private research universities in terms of receiving federal funds for research and development support. USC is one of sixty-one U.S. research universities elected to the Association of American Universities.

Applying

Basic requirements for admission are an earned bachelor's degree or U.S. bachelor's equivalent from an accredited college or university, satisfactory scores on the GRE General Test or other required test, intellectual promise as demonstrated by a record of good performance in previous formal academic programs, and strong personal qualifications. Students should contact specific academic departments for additional requirements. An online application is available at http://www.usc.edu/dept/admissions/grad/.

Correspondence and Information

Office of Admission and Financial Aid
University of Southern California
Los Angeles, California 90089-0911
Telephone: 213-740-1111
E-mail: gradadm@usc.edu
World Wide Web: http://www.usc.edu

Chair
Department of (specify)
University of Southern California
Los Angeles, California 90089

FACULTY HEADS

Vice Provost for Academic Programs: Joseph B. Hellige, Ph.D.
Director of Graduate and Professional Studies: Jonathan Kotler, J.D.

Accounting (M.Acc.) and Business Taxation (M.B.T.): Randolph P. Beatty, Ph.D.
Aerospace (E.A.E., M.S., Ph.D.) and Mechanical Engineering (E.M.E., M.S., Ph.D.) and Computer-Aided Engineering (M.Eng.): E. Phillip Muntz, Ph.D.
Anthropology (M.A. in visual anthropology, Ph.D. in social anthropology): Craig Stanford, Ph.D.
Architecture (M.Arch., M.Arch./M.Pl.), Building Science (M.B.S.), and Landscape Architecture (M.L.Arch., M.L.Arch./M.Pl.): Robert Timme, M.Arch.; F.A.I.A.
Art History (Ph.D.), and Museum Studies (M.A.): Nancy Troy, Ph.D.
Biochemistry and Molecular Biology (M.S., Ph.D.): Laurence Kedes, M.D.
Biokinesiology (M.S., Ph.D.) and Physical Therapy (D.P.T.): James Gordon, Ed.D.; PT.
Biological Sciences (M.S., Ph.D.): Sarah Bottjer, Ph.D.; Marine Biology (Ph.D.): David Caron, Ph.D.; Molecular Biology (Ph.D.): Myron F. Goodman, Ph.D.
Biomedical Engineering (M.S., Ph.D.): David D'Argenio, Ph.D.
Biostatistics (M.S., Ph.D.); Applied Biometry and Epidemiology (M.S.), and Epidemiology (Ph.D.): Stanley Azen, Ph.D.
Business Administration (M.B.A., J.D./M.B.A., M.S., Ph.D.) and Information and Operations Management (M.S.): Randolph W. Westerfield, Ph.D.
Cell and Neurobiology (M.S., Ph.D.): Cheryl Craft, Ph.D.
Chemical Engineering (E.Ch.E., M.S., Ph.D.): Muhammad Sahimi, Ph.D.; Petroleum Engineering (E.Pt.E., M.S., Ph.D.): Iraj Ershaghi, Ph.D.
Chemistry (M.A., M.S., Ph.D.) and Chemical Physics (Ph.D.): Curt Wittig, Ph.D.
Cinema-Television (M.A., M.F.A., Ph.D.): Elizabeth M. Daley, Ph.D.
Civil Engineering (E.C.E., M.S., Ph.D.), Applied Mechanics (M.S.), Computer-Aided Engineering (M.Eng.), and Construction Management (M.C.M.): L. Carter Wellford, Ph.D.; Environmental Engineering (M.S., Ph.D.): Massoud Pirbazari, Ph.D.
Classics (M.A., Ph.D.): Amy Richlin, Ph.D.
Communication (M.A., Ph.D.) and Communication Management (M.A., J.D./M.A.): Patricia Riley, Ph.D.
Comparative Literature (M.A., Ph.D.): William Thalmann, Ph.D.
Computational Linguistics (M.S.): Eduard Hovey, Ph.D., and Jean Roger Vergnaud, Ph.D.
Computer Science (M.S., Ph.D.): Gerald Medioni, Ph.D.
Craniofacial Biology (M.S., Ph.D.): Charles Shuler, D.M.D., Ph.D.
Dentistry (D.D.S., M.B.A./D.D.S.): Harold C. Slavkin, D.D.S.
Earth Sciences (M.S., Ph.D. in geological sciences): J. Lawford Anderson, Ph.D.
East Asian Languages and Cultures (M.A., Ph.D.): Audrey Li, Ph.D.
East Asian Studies (M.A., M.B.A./M.A.): Gordon Berger, Ph.D.
Economics (M.A., J.D./M.A., M.Pl./M.A., Ph.D.): Quang Vuong, Ph.D.; Economic Developmental Programming (M.A.): Jeffrey Nugent, Ph.D.
Education (Ed.D., M.S., M.E., M.M.Ed., M.M.F.C.C., Ph.D.): Karen S. Gallagher, Ph.D.
Electrical Engineering (E.E.E., M.S., Ph.D.): Melvin Breuer, Ph.D. (systems), and Martin Gundersen, Ph.D. (electrophysics).
English (M.A., Ph.D.): Percival Everett.
Environmental Studies (M.A.): Linda E. Duguay, Ph.D.
Fine Arts (M.F.A., M.P.A.S.): Ruth Weisberg, M.A.
French (M.A., Ph.D.): Karen Pinkus, Ph.D.
Geography (M.A., M.S., Ph.D.): Bernard O. Bauer, Ph.D.
German (M.A., Ph.D.): Gerhard Clausing, Ph.D.
Gerontology (M.S., M.B.A./M.S., J.D./M.S., M.Pl./M.S., M.H.A./M.S., M.S.W./M.S., M.P.A./M.S., Ph.D.): Elizabeth M. Zelinski, Ph.D.
History (M.A., Ph.D.): Carole Shammas, Ph.D.
Industrial and Systems Engineering (E.I.S.E., M.S., M.B.A./M.S., Ph.D.), Manufacturing Engineering/Entrepreneurship (M.S.), Engineering Management (M.S.), and Operations Research Engineering (M.S.): Randolph Hall, Ph.D.
International Relations (M.A., J.D./M.A., Ph.D.): Steven Lamy, Ph.D.
Journalism (M.A.): Michael Parks
Kinesiology (Ph.D.): Casey Donovan, Ph.D.
Law (J.D.): Matthew L. Spitzer, J.D., Ph.D.
Linguistics (Ph.D.): John Dreher, Ph.D.
Materials Science (E.M.S., M.S., Ph.D.): Florian Mansfeld, Ph.D.
Mathematical Finance (M.S.): Jaksa Cvitanic, Ph.D.
Mathematics (M.A., Ph.D.): Wayne Raskin, Ph.D.; Graduate Studies (M.A., M.S., Ph.D. in applied mathematics and M.S. in statistics): Gary Rosen, Ph.D.
Medicine (M.D.): Stephen J. Ryan, M.D.
Molecular Epidemiology (M.S.): Stanley Azen, Ph.D., and Zoltan Tokes, Ph.D.
Molecular Microbiology and Immunology (M.S., Ph.D.): Gunther Dennert, Ph.D.
Molecular Pharmacology and Toxicology (M.S., Ph.D.): Enrique Cadenas, M.D., Ph.D.
Music (D.M.A., M.A., M.M., Ph.D., M.M.Ed.): Larry J. Livingston, M.M.
Neuroscience (Ph.D.): Richard F. Thompson, Ph.D.
Nursing (M.S., M.B.A./M.S.): Wynne R. Waugaman, Ph.D., C.R.N.A., F.A.A.N.
Occupational Therapy (M.A.) and Occupational Science (Ph.D.): Florence Clark, Ph.D.; OTR, FAOTA.
Pathology (M.S. in experimental and molecular pathology) and Pathobiology (Ph.D.): Clive Taylor, M.D., Ph.D.
Pharmaceutical Economics and Policy (M.S., Ph.D.): Michael B. Nichol, Ph.D.
Pharmaceutical Sciences (M.S., Ph.D.): Vincent H. L. Lee, Ph.D.
Pharmacy (Pharm.D., M.B.A./Pharm.D.): Fred Weissman, Ph.D.
Philosophy (M.A., J.D./M.A., Ph.D.): James Higginbotham, Ph.D.
Physics (M.A., M.S., Ph.D.): Tu-nan Chang, Ph.D.
Physiology and Biophysics (M.S., Ph.D.): Richard N. Bergman, Ph.D.
Policy, Planning, and Development (M.P.A., M.P.P., M.P.P.M., M.H.A., D.P.A., Ph.D., M.Pl., M.P.D.S., D.P.D.S., J.D./M.P.A., J.D./M.P.P., M.B.A./M.Pl.), Real Estate Development (M.R.E.D., M.B.A./M.R.E.D., J.D./M.R.E.D.), and Construction Management (M.C.M.): Daniel A. Mazmanian, Ph.D.
Political Economy and Public Policy (Ph.D.): John E. Elliott, Ph.D.
Political Science (M.A., Ph.D.): Mark Kann, Ph.D.
Preventive Medicine (Ph.D. in health behavior) and Public Health (M.P.H.): C. Anderson Johnson, Ph.D.
Professional Writing (M.P.W.): James Ragan, Ph.D.
Psychology (Ph.D.): Gerald Davison, Ph.D.
Religion and Social Ethics (M.A., J.D./M.A., Ph.D.): John Crossley, Th.D.
Slavic Languages and Literatures (M.A., Ph.D.): Marcus Levitt, Ph.D.
Social Work (M.S.W., J.D./M.S.W., M.Pl./M.S.W., M.P.A./M.S.W., M.S./M.S.W., Ph.D.): Marilyn S. Flynn, Ph.D.
Sociology (M.A., M.S., Ph.D.): Michael Messner, Ph.D.
Spanish (M.A., Ph.D.): Carmen Silva-Corvalan, Ph.D.
Theater (M.F.A.): Robert R. Scales, Ph.D.

University of South Florida
USF

UNIVERSITY OF SOUTH FLORIDA

Graduate Studies

Programs of Study

University of South Florida (USF) graduate programs address significant national, regional, and local issues. For example, USF hosts the only interdisciplinary program in aging studies in the nation and a new interdisciplinary Ph.D. cancer biology with the H. Lee Moffitt Cancer Center. USF offers ninety-four master's degrees and thirty-three separate doctoral degrees. More than fifty gtraduate certificates are also available. Some of USF's nationally recognized doctoral programs are applied anthropology, biology, chemistry, communication, computer science, education, electrical engineering, marine science, medical sciences, nursing, psychology, and public health. USF is home to the only college of public health in Florida.

Research Facilities

Outstanding among USF's more than seventy interdisciplinary research and education centers, bureaus, and institutes are the H. Lee Moffitt Cancer Center, the Florida Mental Health Institute, the Center for Urban Transportation and Research, the the Institute on Black Life, and the Florida Institute of Oceanography.

Financial Aid

Qualified graduate students may be eligible for a number of presidential and foundational fellowships, assistantships, and other awards. Interested students should contact the program director for information and applications. Additional information is available from the Web site listed below. USF also has a substantial number of fellowships targeted specifically toward underrepresented minority students; minority applicants can contact the Graduate Studies Office at 813-974-2846 for details. Tuition waivers are available to eligible graduate students who hold assistantships or certain fellowships.

Cost of Study

Tuition, including activity fees, for in-state residents for 2001–02 was $166.25 per credit hour or $1496 per semester, based on 9 hours of graduate enrollment. The comparable amount for out-of-state graduate students was $564.54 per credit hour or $5080 per semester.

Living and Housing Costs

USF's new nontraditional Magnolia Apartments are designed for both single and married graduate students. The $15.7 million structure includes two-bedroom family apartments as well as three- and four- bedroom apartments for single students. The cost per academic year is $5007 for single occupancy and $7207 per family. Dining plans are available. On-campus dining locations offer complete selection of entrees, beverages, and snacks. Additional information and floor plans may be found on the Web at http://reserv.usf.edu.

Student Group

The 37,535 University of South Florida students in fall 2001 came from 116 countries (of 1,724 international students, about 41 percent are graduate students), all fifty states and the District of Columbia, and nearly all of the sixty-seven counties in Florida. The ratio of men to women is 2:3. Approximately 63 percent of the students are undergraduates, 17 percent are graduate students, and 20 percent are in the professional programs or unclassified. About 3,400 African-American students, 3,500 Hispanic-American students, and 1,900 Asian-American students attend USF.

Location

Strategically located in the Tampa Bay metro area, this multicultural metropolis offers a wealth of arts and leisure activities—a professional orchestra, Broadway theatrical productions, world-class concert halls, art museums, big-city nightlife, bountiful ethnic restaurants and professional sports teams. In job opportunities, cost of living, education, climate, health care, and arts and recreation, this area ranks among the top five best places to live in the country, according to *Places Rated Almanac.*

The University

Established in 1956, the University of South Florida is a rising star in American education. The first of a new breed of universities created to meet America's urban higher education needs, this young, dynamic institution has experienced explosive growth. Today, it is the largest metropolitan university in the Southeast, serving students at four regional campuses in Tampa, St. Petersburg, Sarasota, and Lakeland. USF also has an outstanding intercollegiate sports program with a football team to be classified as Division I-A in 2001.

Applying

Admissions requirements vary among USF's graduate programs; applicants should contact the program of interest for specific admission requirements. For a complete list of colleges and graduate programs available at the University of South Florida, prospective students should visit the Web site at http://admissions.grad.usf.edu/programs.html or contact the Graduate Admissions Office listed below.

Correspondence and Information

For general information:
Graduate Admissions Office
4202 East Fowler Avenue, FAO174
University of South Florida
Tampa, Florida 33620-7910
Telephone: 813-974-8800
866-974-8800 (toll-free)
Fax: 813-974-7343
E-mail: admissions@grad.usf.edu
World Wide Web: http://www.grad.usf.edu

For program information:
Graduate Coordinator
(specify department or program)
University of South Florida
Tampa, Florida 33620

COLLEGES, DEANS, AND PROGRAMS

Graduate Studies (http://www.grad.usf.edu). Dale E. Johnson, Dean. Applied behavior analysis; School of Architecture and Community Design.

College of Arts and Sciences (http://www.cas.usf.edu). Renu Khator, Interim Dean. Aging studies, American studies, anthropology, applied anthropology, applied physics, audiology, aural rehabilitation, biology, chemistry, classics and classical language, communication, communication sciences and disorders, criminology, English, English as a second language, environmental science and policy, French, geography, geology, gerontology, history, Latin American and Caribbean studies, liberal arts, library and information science, linguistics, mass communication, mathematics, microbiology, philosophy, physics, political science, psychology, public administration, rehabilitation and mental health counseling, religious studies, social work, sociology, Spanish, speech-language pathology, women's studies.

College of Business (http://www.coba.usf.edu). Robert Anderson, Dean. Accountancy, business administration, business economics, Executive M.B.A., Executive M.B.A. for physicians, management, management information systems, Saturday M.B.A. program.

College of Education (http://www.coedu.usf.edu). Ed Steiner, Interim Dean. Adult education, business and office education, career and technical education, college student affairs, counselor education, early childhood education, educational leadership (K–12), educational leadership (college leadership), elementary education, English education, foreign language education, gifted education, guidance/counselor education, higher education, industrial arts/technology education, instructional technology, interdisciplinary education, interdisciplinary technology, junior college teaching, mathematics education, measurement and evaluation, physical education, reading education, reading/language arts education, school psychology, science education, second language acquisition/instructional technology, social science education, special education (specializations in behavior disorders, gifted, mental retardation, motor disabilities, and specific learning disabilities), and vocational education.

College of Engineering (http://www.eng.usf.edu). Louis Martin Vega, Dean. Biomedical engineering, chemical engineering, civil engineering, computer engineering, computer science, computer science and engineering, electrical engineering, engineering (postbaccalaureate), engineering management, engineering science, environmental engineering (five-year program), industrial engineering, information systems, mechanical engineering.

College of Marine Sciences (http://www.marine.usf.edu). Peter Betzer, Dean. Marine sciences: biological oceanography, chemical oceanography, geological oceanography, physical oceanography.

College of Medicine (http://www.med.usf.edu). Robert Daugherty, Dean. Medical sciences: anatomy, biochemistry and molecular biology, microbiology and immunology, pathology and lab medicine, pharmacology and therapeutics, physical therapy, physiology and biophysics.

College of Nursing (http://www.hsc.usf.edu). Patricia Burns, Dean. Nursing: adult health, child health, critical care, family health, gerontological, occupational health, oncology, psychiatric–mental health.

College of Public Health (http://www.hsc.usf.edu/publichealth). Charles Mahan, Dean. Adult/occupational health, applied anthropology (dual M.P.H./M.A), biostatistics, community and family health, environmental and occupational health, environmental health, epidemiology, Executive M.P.H. for health professionals, health administration, health education, health-care organizations and management, health policies and programs, industrial hygiene, international health management, maternal and child health/clinical social work, managed care, nurse practitioner and public health, occupational health for health professionals, occupational medicine residency, public health, public health by distance learning, safety management, social and behavioral sciences applied to public health, toxicology, tropical/communicable diseases.

College of Visual and Performing Arts (http://www.usf.edu/fa.html). Ronald Jones Jr., Dean. Art, art education, art history, dramatic writing, music, music education.

A typical scene at USF.

THE UNIVERSITY OF TENNESSEE

College of Arts and Sciences

Programs of Study

The College of Arts and Sciences at the University of Tennessee (UT), a Carnegie I Research Institution, provides graduate study in the natural sciences, social sciences, arts, and humanities. The degrees of Doctor of Philosophy and Master of Science or Master of Arts are offered in anthropology, biochemistry and cellular and molecular biology, botany, chemistry, computer science, ecology and evolutionary biology, English, geography, geological sciences, history, life sciences, mathematics, microbiology, philosophy, physics, political science, psychology, and sociology. Only the Master of Arts degree is offered in audiology, French, German, religious studies, Spanish, and speech pathology. The Master of Fine Arts is offered in art and in theater, and the Master of Music is available in music. The Master of Science in planning and the Master of Public Administration degrees are available. Only the Doctor of Philosophy is offered in modern foreign languages, in speech and hearing science, and in genome science and technology.

Research Facilities

UT's Hodges Library houses more than 2 million volumes and 11,000 periodical titles. Other University libraries include the Preston Medical Library at the UT Hospital, the DeVine Music Library, and the University Law Library. Through the fiber-optic network that links the campus, all students have access to campus mainframe resources, such as the online library catalogs and links to University of Kentucky and Vanderbilt online catalogs.

On-campus scientific research facilities are concentrated in a cluster of buildings referred to as The Hill, which is dominated by the Science and Engineering Research Facility. This new $28-million, 200,000-square-foot building contains sophisticated, state-of-the-art research equipment, such as an Electron Microscope Facility, an NMR Facility, an X-ray Diffraction Facility, and a DNA Sequencing Facility. Research Centers of Excellence have been established in environmental biotechnology, advanced materials, structural biology, and information technology.

These facilities are complemented by the facilities of the nearby Oak Ridge National Laboratory (ORNL). The Science Alliance promotes collaborative research ties between ORNL and UT scientists through the establishment of shared research centers. The Joint Institute for Neutron Science is poised to maximize the benefits of the $1.36-billion Spallation Neutron Source that is to be built at ORNL.

Financial Aid

Teaching and research assistantships are available through each department, as are some scholarships and fellowships. The University's financial aid office administers work-study and loan programs and may assist with on-campus part-time employment. The University, in conjunction with the Tennessee Higher Education Commission, also offers fellowships for underrepresented minorities.

Cost of Study

In 2001–02, in-state students paid a programs and services fee of $150, a technology fee of $100, a facilities fee of $25, and a maintenance fee of $1617 per semester. Out-of-state students paid fees of $5785 per semester. All fees, except the programs and services fee and the technology fee, are waived for graduate teaching assistants and fellows.

Living and Housing Costs

The University offers affordable, comfortable, and convenient housing both on and off campus. Off-campus University apartments are linked to campus by bus service at regular intervals throughout the day. Among other amenities, University residences provide fast, free in-room Internet access. In addition to University housing, suitable private housing is also available in the area.

Student Group

Approximately 25,000 students are enrolled on the Knoxville campus. Of these, approximately 6,000 are graduate students.

Location

Knoxville, Tennessee, is located at the foothills of the Great Smoky Mountains. The metropolitan area of Knoxville has a population of more than 400,000. The city and the University offer a wide variety of cultural attractions. The Great Smoky Mountains National Park and Tennessee Valley Authority lakes offer a wide variety of recreational opportunities, most of which are free. The University and the Great Smoky Mountains National Park jointly operate the Great Smoky Mountains Field School, which offers classes on plants, wildlife, and history.

The University

The University of Tennessee is a large state university with an extensive graduate program. The Graduate School maintains a high standard of training in the numerous departments that offer advanced degrees. The University has campuses in several cities across the state, with the main campus in Knoxville and the Medical Units in Memphis. Other major campuses are at Martin and Chattanooga. The University also has a Space Institute at Tullahoma and a Graduate Program in Genome Science and Technology at Oak Ridge. Oak Ridge National Laboratory is approximately 25 miles from the main campus, providing easy liaison with the staff of outstanding scientists there, through cooperative research and teaching programs with various science departments on the Knoxville campus.

Applying

Applications and credentials should be submitted as soon as possible. Individual departments should be consulted about their admission deadlines.

Correspondence and Information

Departmental information can be obtained by contacting the head of each department; these are listed on the reverse of this page. In addition, information can be obtained through the College's Web page by going to http://www.artsci.utk.edu/.

DEPARTMENTS AND PROGRAMS

Department of Anthropology: Dr. Andrew Kramer, Head.
School of Art: Dr. Jan Simek, Acting Director.
Department of Audiology and Speech Pathology: Dr. Ilsa Schwarz, Head.
Department of Biochemistry, and Cellular and Molecular Biology: Dr. Bruce McKee, Head.
Department of Botany: Dr. Edward E. Schilling, Head.
Department of Chemistry: Dr. Michael Sepaniak, Head.
Department of Computer Science: Dr. Robert C. Ward, Head.
Department of Ecology and Evolutionary Biology: Dr. Thomas G. Hallam, Head.
Department of English: Dr. D. Allen Carroll, Head.
UT-Oak Ridge Graduate Program in Genome Science and Technology: Dr. Jeffrey Becker, Director.
Department of Geography: Dr. Bruce Ralston, Head.
Department of Geological Sciences: Dr. William M. Dunne, Head.
Department of History: Dr. Todd Diacon, Acting Head.
Graduate Programs in Life Sciences: Dr. Robert N. Moore, Chair.
Department of Mathematics: Dr. John B. Conway, Head.
Department of Microbiology: Dr. Robert M. Moore, Head.
Department of Modern Foreign Languages and Literatures: Dr. Carolyn R. Hodges, Head.
School of Music: Dr. Roger Stephens, Director.
Department of Philosophy: Dr. John Hardwig, Head.
Department of Physics and Astronomy: Dr. Soren Sorenson, Head.
Department of Political Science: Dr. Patricia Freeland, Head.
Department of Psychology: Dr. James E. Lawler, Head.
Department of Religious Studies: Dr. James Fitzgerald, Acting Head.
Department of Sociology: Dr. Suzanne B. Kurth, Head.
Department of Theatre: Mr. Blake Robison, M.F.A., Head.
Department of Urban and Regional Planning: Dr. C. W. Minkel, Head.

Research Centers

Advanced Materials Center: Dr. Ward Plummer, Director.
Center for Applied and Professional Ethics: Dr. John Hardwig, Director.
Center for Biomarker Analysis: Dr. David White, Director.
Center for Environmental Biotechnology: Dr. Gary Sayler, Director.
Center for Quaternary Studies of the Southeastern U.S.: Dr. Paul Delcourt, Director.
Center for the Study of War and Society: Dr. Kurt Piehler, Director.
Environmental Biotechnology Center: Dr. Gary Sayler, Director.
Forensic Anthropology Center: Dr. Murray Marks, Director.
Hearing and Speech Center: Deborah King, Director.
Information Technology Research Center: Dr. Jack Dongarra, Director.
Institute for Resonance Ionization Spectroscopy: Dr. James Parks, Director.
Joint Institute for Heavy Ion Research: Dr. Carroll Bingham, Director.
Psychological Clinic: Dr. Lance Laurence, Director.
Science Alliance: Dr. Jesse Poore, Director.
Social Science Research Institute: Dr. Michael Gant, Director.
Structural Biology Center: Dr. Engin Serpersu, Director.

UNIVERSITY OF TEXAS AT ARLINGTON

Graduate School

Programs of Study

The University of Texas at Arlington (UTA) offers the Doctor of Philosophy degree in aerospace engineering, applied chemistry, biomedical engineering, business administration, civil engineering, computer science, computer science and engineering, education administration curriculum and instruction, education in teaching, electrical engineering, English (literature and rhetoric), environmental science and engineering, health-care administration, industrial engineering, linguistics, materials science and engineering, mathematical sciences, mechanical engineering, physics and applied physics, psychology, quantitative biology, social work, transatlantic history, and urban and public administration.

Master's degrees are offered in accounting, aerospace engineering, anthropology, biology, biomedical engineering, chemistry, civil engineering, computer science, computer science and engineering, criminology and criminal justice, economics, education, electrical engineering, English, environmental science and engineering, French, geology, German, health-care administration, history, human resource management, humanities, industrial engineering, information systems, interdisciplinary studies, linguistics, management of technology, marketing research, materials science and engineering, mathematics, mathematics teaching, mechanical engineering, music education, nursing, physics, political science, psychology, real estate, science teaching, sociology, software engineering, Spanish, taxation, and urban and regional affairs.

The University offers the M.Engr. in aerospace engineering, civil engineering, computer science and engineering, electrical engineering, industrial engineering, materials science and engineering, and mechanical engineering; the M.P.A. in accounting; the M.B.A. in business administration; the M.Ed. in teaching, administration, and curriculum and instruction; the M.P.A. in public administration; and the M.S.S.W. in social work. The M.Arch., M.C.R.P., and M.L.A. are offered in architecture, city and regional planning, and environmental design; the M.S.N. is offered with preparation as a nurse practitioner in acute care, adult, family, gerontology, pediatric, and psychiatric-mental health. An M.S.N. in nursing administration is also available.

Certificates are available in the Colleges of Business Administration, Education, Engineering, Liberal Arts, and Science; the Schools of Education, Nursing, Science, Social Work, Urban and Public Affairs; and the UTA Fort Worth campus (through the Public Broadcasting Station–National Technology University (PBS–NTU)).

The University of Texas at Arlington is recognized in the United States and abroad as a leader in the field of Internet-based education. From the award-winning, nationally advertised master's in curriculum and instruction (including course work for an English as a second language endorsement) to the internationally heralded classes that feature digital media, the University of Texas at Arlington is leading the way to the electronic future of higher education.

Research Facilities

The University of Texas at Arlington's libraries house a collection of more than 1 million books and provide access to more than 20,000 periodicals and newspapers, in print and electronic formats. This includes several special collections, most notably on Texas labor unions, the Texas Republic period, the Mexican War, and the history of cartography.

The Office of Information Technology (OIT) provides computer resources and facilities to support UTA's academic and research needs. OIT maintains a campuswide high-speed network that provides reliable access to UTA's computing resources and the Internet. OIT supports UTA's high-performance supercomputer, a cluster of Intel Pentium-based and Compaq Alpha-based servers dedicated to UTA researchers. OIT also maintains several systems for more general use, including a Compaq Alphaserver 4000 with two Alpha processors, an Alphaserver 4100 with four Alpha processors, a SUN Ultra Enterprise 3000 with two UltraSPARC processors, and forty-one SUN Ultra 1 Creators with UltraSPARC processors. OIT also provides more than forty Windows NT/2000 servers to support its six general-purpose computer labs. The Ransom Hall computing facility, open 24 hours a day, seven days a week, provides well-equipped classrooms and state-of-the-art networked computers and printers for students to use at any time of the day.

Other resources include research centers, divisions, and special facilities. The centers offer graduate students opportunities for advanced research and study in architecture, biology, biomedical engineering, business, chemistry, economics, energy systems, engineering, geology, linguistics, materials science, mathematics, physics, political science, social work, sociology, and urban planning. The University also publishes several journals and hosts the Walter Prescott Webb Memorial Theory Lectures and the Rudolf Hermann Memorial Colloquia.

The NanoFAB Center is an organization of engineers and scientists working on the frontiers of advanced microelectronic applications. The $8.5-million lab allows students to prepare for the technological revolution—the superminiaturization of electronic and mechanical devices. Other related activities include the development of tools designed to open pathways into nanoscale technologies. For more information, students should visit http://www.nanofab.uta.edu.

The Automation and Robotics Research Institute, on the 18.5-acre engineering research campus in Fort Worth, teams industry fellows, faculty members, professional staff members, and students in applied automation and robotics projects.

Financial Aid

Research assistantships, scholarships, and fellowships are available in most departments. Information about loans, grants, and work-study arrangements is available from the Financial Aid Office or the Web site (http://www.2uta.edu/fao).

Cost of Study

For the 2001–02 regular fall and spring sessions and eleven-week summer session, minimum tuition and fees for full-time students (based on 12 semester hours) are $2038.20 for Texas residents and $4752.20 for nonresidents, including international students. Tuition includes student activity and health-service fees. Additional expenses include the cost of books and supplies, parking fees, and special course fees. Tuition and fees are subject to change without notice.

Living and Housing Costs

A variety of housing options exist, including residence halls, apartments, and houses. An application and floor plans are available online at http://www.uta.edu/housing.

Student Group

There are 15,000 undergraduate and almost 5,000 graduate students enrolled, representing forty-seven states and territories and more than 100 countries. The average age of these students is 26; more than half are women.

Location

UTA offers classes on two campuses. The University of Texas at Arlington is centrally located between Dallas and Fort Worth and has a population of 320,000. The area offers a wide variety of cultural and recreational opportunities. The second campus, Riverbend, is located in Fort Worth at 7300 Jack Newell Boulevard South, near East Loop 820 and Randol Mill Road, just north of I-30.

The University

The University of Texas at Arlington, established as a private liberal arts college in 1895, is the second-largest of the fifteen institutions in the University of Texas system. The University has emerged as a comprehensive teaching, research, and public-service university. The University is a student-centered academic community that is dedicated to lifelong learning in an environment characterized by unity of purpose, diversity of opinion, and mutual respect.

Applying

General information about requirements and procedures for admission is in the current graduate catalog. Applications must be completed sixty days before registration (120 days for international students). Information about specific programs is available from graduate advisers, who are listed below under Faculty Heads. General information and application forms can be obtained from the address listed below under Correspondence and Information.

Correspondence and Information

Graduate School
University of Texas at Arlington
UTA Station, Box 19167
Arlington, Texas 76019

Telephone: 817-272-2688
E-mail: graduate.school@uta.edu
World Wide Web: http://orgs.uta.edu/

FACULTY HEADS

DEPARTMENTAL PROGRAMS

Accounting: Tom Hall, Associate Professor and Chair; Ph.D., Oklahoma State, 1981. Patsy Lee, Adjunct Assistant Professor and Graduate Adviser; Ph.D., North Texas, 1983.
Aerospace Engineering: Donald R. Wilson, Professor and Chair; Ph.D., Texas at Arlington, 1973. Thomas S. Lund, Professor and Graduate Adviser; Ph.D., Stanford, 1987.
Anthropology: Robert Young, Associate Professor and Chair; Ph.D., Michigan, 1982. Shelley L. Smith, Associate Professor and Graduate Adviser; Ph.D., Michigan, 1990.
Architecture: Martha LaGess, Associate Professor and Dean; B.Arch., Rice, 1984.
Architectural Association, History, and Theory, 1988: Craig Kuhner, Professor and Graduate Adviser. M.Arch., Pennsylvania, 1970.
Biology: John Bacon, Professor and Chair; Ph.D., Texas at Austin, 1975. Dan Formanowicz, Associate Professor and Graduate Adviser; Ph.D., SUNY at Albany, 1982.
Chemistry: Ronald Elsenbaumer, Professor and Chair; Ph.D., Stanford, 1978. Rasika Dias, Associate Professor and Graduate Adviser; Ph.D., California, Davis, 1988.
Civil Engineering: Siamak A. Ardekani, Professor and Chair; Ph.D., Texas at Austin, 1984. Ernest Crosby, Associate Professor and Graduate Adviser; Ph.D., Tennessee, 1979.
Computer Science, Computer Science and Engineering, Software Engineering: Behrooz A. Shirazi, Professor and Chair; Ph.D., Oklahoma, 1985. Ramesh Yerraballi, Assistant Professor and Graduate Adviser, Ph.D., Old Dominion, 1996.
Economics: Daniel D. Himarios, Professor and Chair; Ph.D., Virginia Tech, 1983. Paul Hayashi, Professor and Graduate Adviser; Ph.D., SMU, 1965.
Education: Jeannie Gerlach, Professor and Dean; Ph.D., North Texas State, 1992. Lou Schulze, Assistant Dean for Student Affairs; Ed.D., North Texas, 1992. Sarah Burkhalter, Assistant Dean for Teacher Education; Ph.D., Texas at Austin, 1996.
Electrical Engineering: Raymond R. Shoults, Professor and Chair, Texas at Arlington, 1974. Adrian K. Fung, Jenkins Garrett Professor and Graduate Adviser; Ph.D., Kansas, 1965.
English: Timothy Morris, Associate Professor and Interim Chair; Ph.D., Princeton, 1983. Stacy Alaimo, Assistant Professor, Illinois, 1994.
Foreign Languages: Elizabeth Ordonez, Chair; Ph.D., California, Irvine, 1976. Lana Rings, Associate Professor and Graduate Adviser; Ph.D., USC, 1985.
Geology: John Wickham, Professor and Chair; Ph.D., Johns Hopkins, 1969. William Balsam, Professor and Graduate Adviser; Ph.D., Brown, 1973.
Health-Care Administration: Darren Grant, Senior Lecturer and Graduate Adviser; Ph.D., Florida State, 1995.
History: Donald Kyle, Professor and Chair; Ph.D., McMaster, 1981. Stanley Palmer, Professor and Graduate Adviser; Ph.D., Harvard, 1973.
Industrial Engineering: Don Liles, Professor and Chair; Ph.D., Texas at Arlington, 1978. H. W. Corley, Professor and Graduate Adviser; Ph.D., Florida, 1971.
Information Systems and Management Science: R. C. Baker, Professor and Chair; Ph.D., Texas A&M, 1971. Carolyn Davis, Senior Lecturer and Graduate Adviser; Ph.D., Texas A&M, 1988.
Landscape Architecture: Pat D. Taylor, Director, Associate Professor, and Graduate Adviser; Ph.D., Texas at Austin, 1983.
Linguistics: David J. Silva, Director and Associate Professor; Ph.D., Cornell, 1992. Jerold A. Edmondson, Professor and Ph.D. Adviser; Ph.D., Technical (Berlin), 1979. Irwin Feigenbaum, Associate Professor and M.A. Adviser; Ph.D., Wisconsin–Milwaukee, 1978.
Management: Jeff McGee, Associate Professor and Chair; Ph.D., Georgia, 1992. Myrtle Bell, Associate Professor and Graduate Adviser; Ph.D., Texas at Arlington, 1996.
Marketing Research: Carl McDaniel, Professor and Chair; D.B.A., Arizona State, 1970. John Bassler, Senior Lecturer and Graduate Adviser; Ph.D., Carnegie-Mellon, 1972.
Mathematics: Danny Dyer, Professor and Chair; Ph.D., SMU, 1970. Tie Lou, Associate Professor and Graduate Adviser; Ph.D., Brandeis, 1987.
Mechanical Engineering: Donald R. Wilson, Professor and Chair; Ph.D., Texas at Arlington, 1973. B. P. Wang, Professor and Graduate Adviser; Ph.D., Virginia, 1974.
Modern Languages: Audley R. Elliott, Acting Chair; Indiana, 1992. Lana Rings, Associate Professor and Graduate Adviser; Ph.D., USC, 1985.
Music: Larry Wiley, Associate Professor and Chair; D.M.A., Louisiana, 1985. Elizabeth Morrow, Associate Professor and Graduate Adviser; Ph.D., USC, 1993.
Nursing: Elizabeth C. Poster, Professor and Dean; Ph.D., Boston College, 1981. Susan K. Grove, Professor, Assistant Dean, and Graduate Adviser; Ph.D., Texas Woman's, 1981.
Physics: John Fry, Professor and Chair; Ph.D., California, Riverside, 1966. Asok K. Ray, Professor and M.S. Adviser; Ph.D., Texas Tech, 1982. Ali R. Koymen, Associate Professor and Ph.D. Adviser; Ph.D., Michigan, 1984.
Political Science: Dale Story, Professor and Chair; Ph.D., Indiana, 1978. Jill Clark, Associate Professor and Graduate Adviser; Ph.D., Wisconsin–Milwaukee, 1974. Victoria Farrar-Myers, Assistant Professor and Associate Graduate Adviser; Ph.D., SUNY at Albany, 1997.
Psychology: Paul Paulus, Professor and Chair; Ph.D., Iowa, 1971. David S. Gorfein, Adjunct Professor and Graduate Adviser for Psychology; Ph.D., Columbia, 1962. William Ickes, Professor and Graduate Adviser; Ph.D., Texas at Austin, 1973.
Real Estate: Vince Apilado, Professor and Chair; Ph.D., Michigan, 1970. Richard Buttimer, Associate Professor and Graduate Adviser; Ph.D., Georgia, 1993.
Social Work: Fernando Galan, Associate Dean and Associate Professor; Ph.D., Massachusetts, 1978. Larry Watson, Assistant Dean; M.S.W., Texas at Arlington, 1980. Yvette Gonzalez, Director of Admissions; M.S.W., Texas at Arlington, 1988.
Sociology: Robert Young, Associate Professor and Chair; Ph.D., Michigan, 1982. Shelley L. Smith, Associate Professor and Graduate Adviser; Ph.D., Michigan, 1990.
Urban and Regional Affairs: Richard L. Cole, Professor and Dean; Ph.D., Purdue, 1972. Edith J. Barrett, Associate Professor and M.A. Adviser; Ph.D. Northwestern, 1987. Rod Hissong, Assistant Professor and Ph.D. Adviser; Ph.D., Rice, 1989. Guisette M. Salazar, Assistant Professor and M.P.A. Adviser; Ph.D., Florida State, 1992.

INTERDEPARTMENTAL AND INTERCAMPUS PROGRAMS

Biomedical Engineering: Khosrow Behbehani, Professor and Chair; Ph.D., Toledo, 1979. C. Chuong, Professor and Graduate Adviser; Ph.D., California, San Diego, 1981. **Business Administration:** James C. Quick, Professor and Doctoral Program Director; Ph.D., Houston, 1977. Greg Frazier, Associate Professor and Director of M.B.A. Programs; Ph.D., Texas A&M, 1989. **City and Regional Planning:** Richard L. Cole, Professor and Dean; Ph.D., Purdue, 1972. Elise Bright, Associate Professor and Graduate Adviser; Ph.D., Texas A&M, 1980. **Criminology and Criminal Justice:** Robert L. Bing III, Associate Professor and Director; Ph.D., Florida, 1987. Alejandro del Carmen, Assistant Professor and Graduate Adviser, Florida State, 1997. **Environmental Science and Engineering:** Robert McMahon, Professor and Director; Ph.D., Syracuse, 1972. Andrew P. Kruzic, Associate Professor and Graduate Adviser; Ph.D., California, Davis, 1984. **Health-Care Administration:** Darren Grant, Senior Lecturer and Graduate Adviser; Ph.D., Florida State, 1995. **Humanities:** Susan Hekman, Professor and Graduate Adviser; Ph.D., Washington (Seattle), 1976. **Interdisciplinary Studies:** Dale Anderson, Professor and Vice President for Research and Graduate Studies; Ph.D., Iowa State, 1964. **Logistics:** Katherine J. Rogers, Associate Professor and Graduate Adviser; Ph.D., Texas at Arlington, 1985. **Management of Technology:** G. T. Stevens, Professor and Graduate Adviser; Ph.D., Oklahoma State, 1966. **Materials Science and Engineering:** Ronald Elsenbaumer, Professor and Director; Ph.D., Stanford, 1978. Pranesh Aswath, Associate Professor and Graduate Adviser; Ph.D., Brown, 1990. **Mathematical Sciences:** Daniel Formanowicz, Associate Professor and Graduate Adviser for Biology; Ph.D., SUNY at Albany, 1982. Z. A. Schelly, Associate Professor and Graduate Adviser for Chemistry; D.Sc., Vienna Technical, 1967. Merlynd K. Nestell, Professor and Graduate Adviser for Geology; Ph.D., Oregon State, 1966. R. C. Baker, Professor and Graduate Adviser for Information Systems and Management Sciences; D.B.A., Texas A&M, 1971. Arthur Gillespie, Associate Professor and Graduate Adviser for Mathematics; M.A., North Texas State, 1960. Ali R. Koymen, Associate Professor and Ph.D. Adviser for Physics; Ph.D., Michigan, 1984. David S. Gorfein, Adjunct Professor and Graduate Adviser for Psychology; Ph.D., Columbia, 1962.

THE UNIVERSITY OF TEXAS AT EL PASO

Graduate School

Programs of Study

Doctoral degrees are offered in the following disciplines: biological sciences (Ph.D.), borderland history (Ph.D.), computer engineering (Ph.D.), educational leadership and administration (Ed.D.), environmental science and engineering (Ph.D.), geological sciences (Ph.D.), history (Ph.D.), materials science and engineering (Ph.D.), and psychology (Ph.D.). Master's degrees are offered in accounting (M.Acc.), adult health (M.S.N.), art education (M.A.), biological sciences (M.S.), border history (M.A.), business administration (M.B.A.), chemistry (M.S.), civil engineering (M.S.), clinical psychology (M.A.), communication (M.A.), computer engineering (M.S.), computer science (M.S.), creative writing—English or Spanish (M.F.A.), economics (M.S.), education (M.A.), educational administration (M.Ed.), educational diagnostician studies (M.Ed.), educational psychology and special services (M.A.), educational supervision (M.Ed.), electrical engineering (M.S.), engineering (M.S.), English and American literature (M.A.), environmental engineering (M.S. with thesis, M.Engr. without thesis), general experimental psychology (M.A.), geology (M.S.), geophysics (M.S.), guidance and counseling (M.Ed.), health and physical education (M.S.), history (M.A.), industrial engineering (M.S.), information technology (M.I.T.), instructional specialist studies (M.Ed.), interdisciplinary studies/liberal arts (M.A.I.S.), interdisciplinary studies/sciences (M.S.I.S.), kinesiology (M.S.), linguistics (M.A.), manufacturing engineering (M.S.), mathematical sciences (M.S.), mathematics teaching (M.A.T.), mechanical engineering (M.S.), metallurgical and materials engineering (M.S.), music education (M.M.), music performance (M.M.), nurse midwifery (M.S.N.), nursing administration (M.S.N.), parent/child nursing (M.S.N.), physical therapy (M.P.T.), physics (M.S.), political science (M.A.), psychiatric/mental health nursing (M.S.N.), public administration (M.P.A.), reading education (M.Ed.), sociology (M.A.), Spanish (M.A.), special education (M.Ed.), speech-language pathology (M.S.), statistics (M.S.), studio art (M.A.), teacher education (M.A.), theater arts (M.A.), and women's health care/nurse practitioner studies (M.S.N.).

Teaching certification is available in the areas of initial elementary, art, bilingual education, early childrood, English, French, German, health education, history, kinesiology, life/earth science, mathematics, physical science, reading, social science, Spanish, special education, theater arts, initial secondary, biology, business, chemistry, earth science, English, English language arts, French, history, journalism, life earth sciene, math, physical science, physics, political science, psychology, science composite, social studies composite, sociology, Spanish, speech, theater arts, all-level arts, all-levels music, all-levels kinesiology, and alternative certification. The following certification programs require a completed master's degree or concurrent enrollment in the M.Ed. program in educational administration: professional, midmanagement, and supervision.

Joint-degree programs include the M.A. in library science, the Doctor of Pharmacy, and the Doctor of Philosophy in border studies with the University of Texas at Austin and a master's degree in public health and doctorate in nursing with the University of Texas–Health Science Center in Houston.

Research Facilities

The University of Texas at El Paso (UTEP) library houses more than 850,000 volumes, 1.6 million microforms, and 2,499 current periodical subscriptions. Throughout the campus, there are PCs and Macs, including high-performance graphics workstations, available for academic and research purposes. Special research facilities include the El Paso Centennial Museum; the Oral History Institute; the NSF Materials Science Center; the El Paso Solar Pond Research Station; the Institute for Manufacturing and Materials Management; the Center for Environmental Resource Management; the Material Research Institute; the Inter-American and Border Studies Center; the Center for Entrepreneurial Development, Advancement, Research and Support; the Hemispheric Trade Center; and the Center for Public Policy. UTEP maintains research affiliations with the Southwest Center for Environmental Research and Policy, the Environmental Technology and Waste Management Consortium, the National Association of Research Centers of Excellence, Sandia National Laboratories (engineering, science, and materials), and the Jet Propulsion Laboratory (electrical engineering and information systems). Major research projects include the Minority Research Center of Excellence in Materials Science (NSF), with funding of $5 million; the Pan American Center for Earth and Environmental Studies, with funding of $6 million; the Border Biomedical Research Center (NIH), with funding of more than $4.6 million; and the Lithospheric Structure and Evolution of the Rocky Mountain Transect of the Western United States, with funding of $540,000.

Financial Aid

Scholarships, research assistantships, teaching assistantships, partial tuition waivers, Federal Work-Study, institutionally sponsored loans, and career-related internships or fieldwork are available. Aid is also available to part-time students. Applicants are required to submit GAPSFAS or FAFSA forms.

Cost of Study

For Texas residents in science, liberal arts, and education programs, tuition is $2118 per year for full-time study and $339 per semester (minimum) for part-time study. For nonresidents, tuition in these programs is $7230 per year for full-time study and $978 per semester (minimum) for part-time study. For business, nursing, engineering, materials science and engineering, and environmental science and engineering programs, tuition for Texas residents is $2790 per year for full-time study and $423 per semester (minimum) for part-time study. For nonresidents in these programs, tuition is $7710 per year for full-time study and $1038 per semester (minimum) for part-time study.

Living and Housing Costs

Rooms and/or apartments are available to single students (thirty-six units) at $425 per student per month, double occupancy (fifteen units) at $280 per student per month, two bedrooms (150 units) at $398 per student per month, and four bedrooms (eighteen units) at $375 per student per month. For more information, students should contact Karen Knight (telephone: 915-747-5352).

Student Group

The student body consists of 12,955 undergraduate students and 2,269 graduate students. Women comprise 79.46 percent of the student body. The average age is 34.

Location

El Paso is located in west Texas. It borders New Mexico and Mexico and has a population of more than 600,000 people. The area provides a variety of cultural and recreational opportunities.

The University

The University of Texas at El Paso is the second-oldest academic component of the University of Texas System. It was founded by the Texas Legislature in 1914 as the State School of Mines and Metallurgy, a name that reflected the scope of education that was offered at that time. UTEP's present 366-acre site features distinctive Bhutanese-style architecture. The campus's buildings resemble exotic oriental monasteries that are found in the small kingdom of Bhutan, which is nestled in the Himalayas. With its pivotal setting on the U.S.-Mexico border and as the largest Hispanic-majority university in the United States, UTEP is a nationally recognized leader in the meeting the challenges of providing higher education to the country's increasing minority populations.

Applying

General information about admission requirements and procedures can be found in the current UTEP *Graduate Catalog* http://www.utep.edu/catalogs/grad/. Application deadlines for the fall are May 1 for international students and July 31 for U.S. citizens; spring deadlines are October 1 for international students and December 31 for U.S. citizens; summer deadlines are March 1 for international students and May 31 for U.S. citizens. The financial aid deadline is March 15.

Correspondence and Information

Graduate School
200 Administration Building
500 West University Avenue
The University of Texas at El Paso
El Paso, Texas 79968-0587
Telephone: 915-747-5491
Fax: 915-747-5788
E-mail: gradschool@utep.edu
World Wide Web: http://www.utep.edu

FACULTY HEADS

Accounting: Gary J. Mann, Professor and Chair; Ph.D., Texas Tech, 1986.
Art Education: Albert Y. Wong, Associate Professor and Chair; M.F.A., Kent State, 1974.
Biology: Rael D. Eppie, Director and Chair; Ph.D., Arizona, 1975.
Business Administration: Frank Hoy, Professor and Dean; Ph.D., Texas A&M, 1979.
Chemistry: Russell R. Chianelli, Professor and Chair; Ph.D., Polytechnic of New York, 1974.
Civil Engineering: Carlos M. Ferregut, Professor and Chair; Ph.D., Waterloo, 1990.
Communication: Patricia D. Witherspoon, Professor; Ph.D., Texas at Austin.
Computer Science: David G. Novick, Professor; Ph.D., Oregon, 1999.
Creative Writing: Leslie Ulmann, Professor and Director; M.F.A., Iowa, 1972.
Economics: Timothy P. Roth, Professor and Chair; Ph.D., Texas A&M, 1970.
Educational Leadership: Susan Rippberger, Assistant Vice President of Academic Affairs; Ph.D., Pittsburgh, 1995.
Educational Psychology: Thomas A. Wood, Professor; Ph.D., Vanderbilt (Peabody), 1991.
Electrical and Computer Engineering: Mehdi Shadaram, Professor; Ph.D., Oklahoma, 1984.
English: Tony J. Stafford, Professor and Interim Chair; Ph.D., LSU, 1966.
Environmental Sciences and Engineering: Jorge Gardea-Torresdey, Professor and Director; Ph.D., New Mexico State, 1994.
Geology: Kate C. Miller, Associate Professor; Ph.D., Stanford, 1991.
History: Emma Perez, Associate Professor and Chair; Ph.D., UCLA, 1989.
Interdisciplinary Studies (Liberal Arts): Robert T. Bledsoe, Professor; Ph.D., Princeton, 1971.
Interdisciplinary Studies (Sciences): William C. Cornell, Professor and Director; Ph.D., UCLA, 1971.
Linguistics: Sandra S. Beyer, Associate Professor; Ph.D., Kansas, 1972.
Materials Science and Engineering: Lawrence E. Murr, Professor and Chair; Ph.D., Penn State, 1967.
Mathematics: Rolondo Quintana, Associate Professor; Ph.D., New Mexico State, 1992.
Mechanical and Industrial Engineering: William L. Craver, Professor and Chair; Ph.D., Oklahoma, 1970.
Metallurgical and Materials Engineering: Lawrence Murr, Professor, Chair, and Graduate Advisor; Ph.D., Penn State, 1967.
Music: Ronald A. Hufstader, Professor and Chair; Ph.D., Iowa, 1968.
Nursing: Audree J. Reynolds, Interim Associate Dean, College of Health Science and Interim Director, School of Nursing; Ph.D., New Mexico State, 1980.
Physical Therapy: J. A. Ryberg, Lecturer and Interim Program Coordinator; M.A., Iowa; PT.
Physics: Ramon E. Lopez, Professor; Ph.D., Rice, 1999.
Political Science: Roberto Villareal, Professor; Ph.D., Oklahoma, 1975.
Psychology: Judith P. Goggin, Professor and Chair; Ph.D., Berkeley, 1964.
Public Administration: Dennis Soden, Professor and Director, Ph.D., Washington State, 1985.
Sociology: S. Fernando Rodriguez, Associate Professor and Chair; Ph.D., Texas at Austin, 1990.
Spanish: Sandra S. Beyer, Associate Professor and Chair; Ph.D., Kansas, 1972.
Teacher Education: Milagros Seda, Associate Professor; Ed.D., Houston, 1987.
Theatre Arts: Charles Fensch, Professor and Chair; M.A., Michigan, 1976.

UNIVERSITY OF THE INCARNATE WORD

Programs of Study

The University of the Incarnate Word offers twelve master's degree programs, some with various concentrations, and one Ph.D. program in education with concentrations in organizational leadership, mathematics education, and international education and entrepreneurship. Most class meetings are held in the evening once a week. Some courses are offered off-campus, in classrooms made available to the University at Randolph Air Force Base and the United Services Automobile Association headquarters. In addition, some programs are offered online.

Approximately 800 students are enrolled in the graduate programs, and about 125 are in the doctoral program. The master's programs are in the following fields: administration (M.A. with concentrations available in sports management, international administration, and organizational development), biology (M.S.), business administration (M.B.A. with concentrations available in international business and sports management), communication arts (M.A.), education (M.A./M.Ed.), English (M.A.), mathematics (M.S./M.A.), mathematics teaching (M.A.), multidisciplinary sciences (M.A.), multidisciplinary studies (M.A.), nursing (M.S.N.), nursing and business administration combined degree (M.S.N./M.B.A.) nutrition (M.S.), and religious studies (M.A.).

The programs in education include both Master of Arts and Master of Education, with concentrations available in adult education (M.A./M.Ed.), deaf education (M.Ed.), early childhood education (M.Ed.), instructional technology (M.Ed.), international education (M.A./M.Ed.), organizational learning (M.A.), physical education (M.Ed.), professional education diagnostician (M.Ed.), reading (M.Ed.), special education (M.Ed.), and teaching (M.A./M.Ed.). For information on teacher certification, applicants should call Elizabeth Wiechmann at 210-829-3132 or e-mail wiechman@universe.uiwtx.edu.

Research Facilities

The J. E. and L. E. Mabee Library was doubled in size, remodeled, and rededicated in 1997 to incorporate the latest in library technology, climate control, handicap access, student and faculty conference rooms, reserve reading, photocopy rooms, and research areas. Other facilities include an electronic classroom, the Information Literacy Room, AV preview rooms, and an auditorium seating 125. These areas provide cable TV and satellite feed in addition to Internet access. Voice and data lines throughout the structure allow students to connect to the campus fiber-optic network. The library offers full Internet access and connects students to its local area network with more than 40 subscription databases, and to its integrated online webpac through its homepage. Wireless technology allows students to gain access anywhere in the structure. Technology permits student access to the library from any location. Computers running special applications software assist students with word processing, statistics packages, and other production needs.

In its 72,000 square feet, the library houses nearly 200,000 bound volumes and an extensive audiovisual collection. Print and electronic access provides 3,048 unique periodical subscriptions. The rare books room showcases the library's rare and first-edition books in a beautiful suite. Student seating is provided at carrels, tables, and informal arrangements on all three floors. The ground floor houses the Audiovisual Collection, Instructional Technology, and Media Services with production facilities and AV equipment delivery services.

Financial Aid

The Office of Financial Aid assists graduate students with obtaining loans to meet their tuition and other obligations.

Cost of Study

For the 2002–03 academic year, the cost of graduate tuition is $470 per credit hour in the master's programs and $505 per credit hour in the doctoral program. Fees (University, Student Center, and parking) amount to an additional $20 per credit hour.

Living and Housing Costs

On-campus housing and cafeteria services are available for graduate students. Room rates vary and there are various cafeteria plans. Housing applications can be obtained by calling the Campus Life Office at 210-829-6034.

Student Outcomes

As stated in its mission, the University is committed to the development and enrichment of the whole person. Accordingly, students at Incarnate Word can avail themselves of the various wellness and health, disability, counseling, and spiritual services that are provided on campus. Students also have access to the computer labs on campus and to career services. Student associations and a Student Government Association provide opportunities for leadership.

Location

San Antonio offers a rich mixture of cultural heritages derived from it historical settlement by Native Americans and people from Germany, France, Ireland, Mexico, and Spain. The city contains several historical landmarks from the 1700s, including vestiges of missionary-led Indian towns, the churches of the Alamo and San Fernando de Béxar, and several important buildings from the 1800s. The Paseo del Rio, or River Walk, with its restaurants, hotels, shops, and cultural attractions, has helped develop the city into a prime location for conventions and tourism. In its metropolitan area, San Antonio has more than 1 million residents.

As one of the largest cities in the nation, San Antonio has a flourishing arts community with active theater groups, dance companies, music and art associations, and art galleries and museums. The campus is located on the headwaters of the San Antonio River, a wooded area that is part of the estate of George W. Brackenridge, minutes from downtown San Antonio.

The University

Incarnate Word is a Catholic, coeducational institution that welcomes to its community people of diverse backgrounds in the belief that their interaction advances the discovery of truth, mutual understanding, self-realization, and the common good. The Sisters of Charity of the Incarnate Word founded Incarnate Word College more than 100 years ago. It was chartered by the state of Texas in 1881. In 1925, the College earned full accreditation by what was then the Association of Colleges and Secondary Schools of the Southern States. A 1996 amendment to its charter, reflecting in part the significant development of the College's graduate programs, recognized Incarnate Word as a university.

Applying

Applicants for master's degrees must have a bachelor's degree from an accredited college or university. They should submit a completed application, along with the appropriate fee, transcripts from all degree-granting institutions the candidate has attended, and official scores on the MAT, GRE, or GMAT as required by the specific program. Candidates for master's degrees and the Ph.D. should consult with program coordinators regarding specific requirements set by their program of interest.

Correspondence and Information

Dr. Gilberto M. Hinojosa
Dean, School of Graduate Studies and Research
University of the Incarnate Word
4301 Broadway
San Antonio, Texas 78209

Telephone: 210-829-3157
Fax: 210-805-3559
E-mail: hinojosa@universe.uiwtx.edu
World Wide Web: http:/www.uiw.edu/gradstudies.html

THE FACULTY AND THEIR RESEARCH

Graduate students have the opportunity to participate in various funded research projects in the sciences and in the research interests of scholars on the faculty. Information on science research endeavors is available by calling Dr. Sara Kerr at 210-829-3155 or e-mailing kerr@universe.uiwtx.edu. Research areas in mathematics education include the integration of mathematics with other disciplines, the participation of women and minorities in the mathematical sciences, and the oral histories of R. L. Moore and others. Information on mathematics research endeavors is available by calling Dr. Judy Beauford at 210-829-3171 or e-mailing beauford@universe.uiwtx.edu.

PROGRAM COORDINATORS

BUSINESS AND BUSINESS-RELATED PROGRAMS

Administration (M.A.)
Business Administration (M.B.A.)
Dr. John Seffel, 210-829-3182, seffel@universe.uiwtx.edu.

HUMANITIES

Communication Arts (M.A.)
Dr. Mary Beth Swofford, 210-829-3151, swofford@universe.uiwtx.edu.

English (M.A.)
Dr. Patricia Lonchar, 210-829-3880, fite@universe.uiwtx.edu.

Multidisciplinary Studies (M.A.)
Dr. Gilberto Hinojosa, 210-829-3157, hinojosa@universe.uiwtx.edu.

Religious Studies/Pastoral Instruction (M.A.)
Sr. Eilish Ryan, 210-829-3871, eryan@universe.uiwtx.edu.

MATHEMATICS, SCIENCES, AND HEALTH PROFESSIONS

Biology (M.A.)
Dr. Sara Kerr, 210-829-3155, kerr@universe.uiwtx.edu.

Mathematics (M.S.)
Mathematics Teaching (M.A.)
Dr. Judy Beauford, 210-829-3171, beauford@universe.uiwtx.edu.

Nursing (M.S.N.), Aggregate Focused Nursing Practice
Nursing/Business Administration (M.S.N./M.B.A.)
Dr. Sandra Strickland, 210-829-3988, strickla@universe.uiwtx.edu.
Dr. John Seffel, 210-829-3182, seffel@universe.uiwtx.edu.

Nutrition (M.S.)
Dr. Beth Senne-Duff, 210-829-3165, beths@universe.uiwtx.edu.

Multidisciplinary Sciences (M.A.)
Dr. Christy MacKinnon, 210-829-3147, mackinno@universe.uiwtx.edu.

EDUCATION

Education (Ph.D.)
Dr. Gilberto Hinojosa, 210-829-3157, hinojosa@universe.uiwtx.edu.

Education (M.A., M.Ed)
Dr. Jessica Kimmel, 210-829-3144, jessicak@universe.uiwtx.edu.

Teacher Certification
Dr. Denise Staudt, 210-283-5028, staudt@universe.uiwtx.edu.

UNIVERSITY OF TOLEDO

Graduate School

Programs of Study

The Graduate School at the University of Toledo (UT) offers programs from six colleges, including the College of Arts and Sciences, College of Business, College of Education, College of Engineering, College of Health and Human Services, and College of Pharmacy.

The following degrees are offered: the Master of Arts in economics, English, foreign language (French, German, Spanish), geography, history, mathematics, philosophy, political science, psychology, and sociology; the Master of Science in accounting, biology, chemistry, exercise science, geology, mathematics, medicinal chemistry, physics, bioengineering, chemical engineering, civil engineering, electrical engineering, engineering, industrial engineering, mechanical engineering, and pharmaceutical science; the Master of Manufacturing Management; the Master of Business Administration; the Master of Education; the Master of Arts and Liberal Studies; the Master of Public Administration; the Master of Public Health; and the Master of Music in music education and music performance. Doctoral programs are offered in biology, chemistry, education (Ph.D. and Ed.D.), engineering, health sciences, history, manufacturing management and engineering, mathematics, medicinal chemistry, physics, psychology, and pharmacy (Pharm.D.).

Research Facilities

The University of Toledo has state-of-the-art laboratories for each discipline. The $33-million Wolfe Hall offers one of the most advanced science facilities of its kind in the nation for pharmacy, chemistry, and life sciences. The Lake Erie Research and Education Center is a state-of-the-art environmental research and teaching facility located on the shore of Lake Erie. Carlson Library's holdings exceed 1.6 million volumes, 1.4 million microforms, 150,000 maps, and 5,000 periodicals. The library is a federal depository for government documents and is a charter member of the statewide cooperative program OhioLINK. The University has been named one of "America's Most Wired Colleges" by *Yahoo! Internet Life* magazine for three consecutive years.

Financial Aid

During the 2001–02 academic year, University Fellowships carried stipends of up to $14,000 for doctoral students on a competitive basis. Assistantships, available in all areas of graduate work, carried tuition remission plus a stipend ranging from $7200 to $14,000. Tuition scholarships, for up to 16 credit hours, provided tuition remission only. An additional fifty different awards and scholarships were available. Applicants may view this listing via the financial aid section of the University's Web site.

Cost of Study

In 2001–02, full-time instructional fees for residents of Ohio were $3167.52 per semester. The tuition surcharge for out-of-state students was an additional $3679.68 per semester. The general fee was $464.76 per semester.

Living and Housing Costs

Apartments and rooms for graduate students are available in privately owned houses near the University. Assistance in locating housing is provided via online listings or through the Center for Commuter and Off-Campus Services. Housing costs range from $225 and up for apartments and rooms, depending upon the number of occupants. Dining facilities are available on campus.

Student Group

Enrollment is approximately 21,000 students, including 4,400 graduate students representing a rich mixture of diverse backgrounds from almost every county in Ohio, all fifty states, and ninety-eight countries. Full- and part-time students are people of all races, cultures, and backgrounds.

Location

The community provides a broad range of cultural resources that complement academic life. The Toledo Museum of Art is one of the world's leading museums and is widely known for its antiquities and collections of paintings, sculpture, glass, and decorative arts. Music and theater abound through the Toledo Symphony Orchestra, the Toledo Choral Society, the Valentine Theater, and the Toledo Ballet Association. The Toledo Zoological Park boasts an extensive zoological collection, a museum of science and natural history, an amphitheater, a botanical center, and a large freshwater aquarium. The Center of Science and Industry (COSI) is a dynamic center of hands-on science. Recreational activities include two professional minor-league teams, the Toledo Storm (hockey), and the Toledo Mud Hens (baseball). More than twenty-five professional sports teams are within a 4-hour drive.

The University

Founded in 1872, the University is located in Toledo, Ohio, on a suburban campus 6 miles west of the downtown area. The fourth-largest state university in Ohio, UT offers graduate programs for master's and doctoral degrees through six colleges. Students benefit from cooperative educational (COOP) experiences, internships, and a diverse job market, as well as from the activities and excitement of the city of Toledo.

UT boasts nearly twenty student service-related offices and programs, more than 200 student organizations, more than forty intramural/sport programs, a $17.3-million Student Recreation Center, an honors-academic center residence hall, a housing village for members of fraternities and sororities, a visual arts building on the grounds of the world-renowned Toledo Museum of Art, the $25-million College of Engineering complex, and a $33-million pharmacy, chemistry, and life sciences complex.

University faculty include more than 1,400 graduate assistants, as well as full-time and part-time faculty members. More than 80 percent of the full-time faculty members hold doctorates. Faculty members are active within the University, as well as in community programs, research projects, and publication of professional articles and textbooks. University faculty members take an interest in students and commit to providing the best possible learning experience and environment.

The Graduate School is accredited by the North Central Association of Colleges and Schools. The University is a member of the Council of Graduate Schools in the United States, the Midwest Association of Graduate Schools, and the National Association of State Universities and Land Grant Colleges. The College of Education is approved by the National Council for Accreditation of Teacher Education. The Master of Business Administration program is approved by the American Assembly of Collegiate Schools of Business. The Accreditation Board for Engineering and Technology has approved all engineering programs. The University is a member of the American Society for Engineering Education and its Engineering College Council and Engineering Research Council.

Applying

To be admitted as a graduate student at the University of Toledo, an applicant must have received a bachelor's degree from an accredited college or university and must have compiled a minimum undergraduate grade point average of between 2.7 and 3.0 on a 4.0 scale, depending on the college to which he or she seeks admission. Some departments require scores on the Graduate Record Examinations (General Test and/or Subject Tests), or the Graduate Management Admission Test. All requirements for admission must be met at least two weeks prior to registration.

Correspondence and Information

Graduate School
University of Toledo
2801 West Bancroft Street
Toledo, Ohio 43606-3390

Telephone: 419-530-4723
Fax: 419-530-4724
E-mail: grdsch@utnet.utoledo.edu
World Wide Web: http://www.utoledo.edu/grad-school/

FACULTY HEADS

Richard A. Hudson, Ph.D.; Interim Vice Provost for Graduate Education and Dean of the Graduate School.

Arts and Sciences

David Stern, Ph.D.; Interim Dean, College of Arts and Sciences.
David Guip, Ph.D.; Chair, Department of Art Education.
Patricia Komuniecki, Ph.D.; Chair, Department of Biology.
Alan Pinkerton, Ph.D.; Chair, Department of Chemistry.
Richard Knecht, Ph.D.; Chair, Department of Communication.
Michael Phillips, Ph.D.; Chair, Department of Earth, Ecological, and Environmental Sciences.
Michael Dowd, Ph.D.; Interim Chair, Department of Economics.
Samir Abu-Absi, Ph.D.; Chair, Department of English.
Antonio Varela, Ph.D.; Chair, Department of Foreign Languages.
Samuel Aryeetey-Attoh, Ph.D.; Chair, Department of Geography.
William Longton, Ph.D.; Chair, Department of History.
En-Bing Lin, Ph.D.; Chair, Department of Mathematics.
Lois Schleuter, Ph.D.; Interim Chair, Department of Music.
Charles Blatz, Ph.D.; Chair, Department of Philosophy.
Phillip B. James, Ph.D.; Chair, Department of Physics and Astronomy.
Lynn Bachelor, Ph.D.; Chair, Department of Political Science.
Robert A. Haaf, Ph.D.; Chair, Department of Psychology.
Barbara Chesney, Ph.D.; Chair, Department of Sociology and Anthropology.
James Hill, Ph.D.; Chair, Department of Theatre and Film.
Jamie Barlowe, Ph.D.; Chair, Department of Women's and Gender Studies.

Business Administration

Diana Franz, Ph.D.; Interim Chair, Department of Accounting.
Andrew Solocha, Ph.D.; Interim Chair, Department of Finance and Business Economics.
Anand Kunathur, Ph.D.; Interim Chair, Department of Information Systems, Marketing, E-Commerce, and Sales.
Anthony Koh, Ph.D.; Interim Chair, Department of International Business, Entrepreneurship, and Strategy.
Deborah Dwyer, Ph.D.; Interim Chair, Department of Management.

Education

Linda Murphy, Ph.D.; Interim Dean, College of Education.
William Weber, Ph.D.; Interim Chair, Curriculum and Instruction.
John R. Cryan, Ph.D.; Interim Chair, Early Childhood, Physical, and Special Education.
Thomas Dunn, Ph.D.; Interim Chair, Foundations of Education.
Richard Perry, Ph.D.; Acting Chairperson, Department of Educational Leadership.

Engineering

Naganathan Ganapathy, Ph.D.; Interim Dean, College of Engineering.
Vijay A. Goel, Ph.D.; Chair, Department of Bioengineering.
Steven LeBlanc, Ph.D.; Chair, Department of Chemical Engineering.
Brian Randolph, Ph.D.; Chair, Department of Civil and Industrial Engineering.
Demetrios Kazakos, Ph.D.; Chair, Department of Electrical Engineering.
Abdollah Afjeh, Ph.D.; Interim Chair, Department of Mechanical, Industrial, and Manufacturing Engineering.
Martin Abraham, Ph.D.; Associate Dean, Research and Graduate Studies.

Health and Human Services

Jerome M. Sullivan, Ph.D.; Dean, College of Health and Human Services.

Pharmacy

Johnnie L. Early II, R.Ph., Ph.D.; Dean, College of Pharmacy.
Kenneth A. Bachmann, R.Ph., Ph.D.; Chair, Pharmaceutical Science Program.
Curtis D. Black, R.Ph., Ph.D.; Chair, Department of Pharmacy Practice.
Marcia McInerney, Ph.D.; Chair, Department of Medicinal Chemistry.
William Messer, Ph.D.; Chair, Department of Pharmacology.

UNIVERSITY OF TULSA

Graduate School

Programs of Study

The Graduate School offers graduate study leading to master's degrees in twenty-eight programs and to Ph.D.'s in nine programs. Interdisciplinary degree programs are also available.

Doctoral degrees conferred are the Doctor of Philosophy with specialization in biological science, chemical engineering, clinical psychology, computer science, English language and literature, geosciences, industrial/organizational psychology, mechanical engineering, and petroleum engineering.

Master's degrees conferred are the Master of Accounting and Information Systems, Master of Arts, Master of Business Administration, Master of Engineering, Master of Engineering and Technology Management, Master of Fine Arts, Master of Science, Master of Science in Engineering, Master of Science in Finance, Master of Science in Math/Science Education, Master of Taxation, and Master of Teaching Arts.

The master's degree is offered in accounting, anthropology, art, biological science, business administration (traditional and Internet-mediated programs), chemical engineering, chemistry, clinical psychology, computer science, education (with certification in elementary education, school counseling, and secondary education), electrical engineering, engineering and technology management, English language and literature, finance, fine art, geosciences (geochemistry, geology, and geophysics), history, industrial/organizational psychology, information systems, mathematics, math/science education, mechanical engineering, petroleum engineering, speech-language pathology, and taxation. Joint master's/Juris Doctor degree programs leading to J.D./M.A. degrees with specialization in anthropology, clinical psychology, English language and literature, history, and industrial/organizational psychology are offered in conjunction with the College of Law; the J.D./M.S. degree in biological science and geosciences, the J.D./Master of Accounting and Information Systems degree, the J.D./Master of Taxation degree, and the J.D./M.B.A. degree are also offered.

Research Facilities

The University libraries house more than 3 million books, bound periodical volumes, microforms, state and federal depository government documents, sound and video recordings, CD-ROM abstracts and indexes, and maps. McFarlin Library, the central facility, orders and catalogs 10,000 new titles each year, subscribes to 2,200 periodicals in paper and fiche formats, and, by way of an online service, provides full-text access to 2,000 more (as well as indexing for a further 10,000). A computerized catalog maintains both bibliographic and circulation records (which currently number more than 650,000). It can be accessed through more than eighty-five terminals in the libraries or remotely by way of campus networks and modem-equipped personal computers. It also acts as a gateway to other databases and, via the Internet, to several hundred library catalogs in this country and abroad. The libraries are also linked electronically to two national utilities (OCLC and RLIN) to facilitate an active interlibrary loan program that borrows about 10,000 items each year from other libraries and loans a slightly smaller number to them.

The College of Law library contains 280,000 volumes, with extensive holdings in natural resources and energy law. Special collections in three areas are recognized internationally for their quality and distinctiveness: twentieth-century American, British, and Irish literature (with holdings that include comprehensive collections for Faulkner, Graves, Joyce, Lawrence, Whitman, and many other writers and 3,500 feet of manuscripts, among them the papers of Richard Ellmann, Richard Murphy, 2001 Nobel laureate V. S. Naipaul, Jean Rhys, and Rebecca West); Native American history and law, with exceptional strength for the Cherokee, Creek, and Osage; holdings related to petroleum exploration and production in all parts of the world, among them the source documents abstracted for *Petroleum Abstracts,* published at the University since 1960.

The University maintains a robust fiber-optic network that interconnects computing and information resources in all of the University's buildings. Centralized and decentralized computing services are provided by numerous UNIX and NT servers networked to a full complement of peripheral devices. The servers are used for a variety of instructional and research activities, which include accessing the University's library database and other worldwide information resources available on the Internet. McFarlin Library reflects the convergence of traditional print and electronic media and provides a cyber-cafe, an open-computing student laboratory, an information/research laboratory, a training laboratory, and a faculty development center. Modern student computing laboratories and high-technology classrooms are located in the College of Arts and Sciences, the College of Business Administration, the College of Engineering and Natural Sciences, and the College of Law. The College of Engineering and Natural Sciences has numerous UNIX and NT engineering workstations to support the computer-intensive applications required by scientists and engineers.

Financial Aid

A number of assistantships and fellowships are available for full-time graduate students. The stipends vary according to the amount of work required and the experience of the student. Most appointments provide 9 credit hours of tuition scholarship per semester in addition to the monthly stipend. Other scholarships are available through the sponsorship of corporations, businesses, and individuals. Recipients of these scholarships are often chosen only from applicants interested in fields prescribed by the donors. Government-directed student aid is available through the Office of Financial Services.

Cost of Study

All graduate students at the University of Tulsa graduate school paid tuition at a rate of $530 per semester hour in 2001–02.

Living and Housing Costs

Full-time undergraduates are given priority in the allocation of residence hall housing; graduate students are welcome, however, when space is available. Room and board for two semesters (with a double-occupancy room) averaged $5200 in 2001–02. University apartments are also available for graduate and law students (including married students) at competitive rates.

Student Group

Approximately 770 of the University's 4,200 students are in the Graduate School; women make up more than 40 percent of that population. More than 10 percent of graduate students are members of minority groups. International students from dozens of nations constitute more than 30 percent of the graduate population.

Location

The University of Tulsa is located in a residential neighborhood just 2 miles from a renovated downtown area. Tulsa has a population of 700,000. Symphonies, theater, art galleries, opera, ballet, museums, and outdoor sports are all accessible to students. Guest performers and lecturers regularly visit the campus and the city.

The University

The University was founded in 1894 as Henry Kendall College in Muskogee, Indian Territory. Moving to Tulsa in 1907, the University of Tulsa was chartered in 1921. The oldest and largest private university in Oklahoma, the University of Tulsa began offering graduate course work in 1933 and was fully accredited through the doctoral level by 1972.

Applying

Applicants for admission to the graduate school must complete a Graduate School Application and provide official transcripts, three letters of recommendation, and all appropriate test scores. Admitted students may apply for financial aid by contacting the Financial Services Office. Full-time admitted students who wish to apply for a graduate assistantship must complete a graduate assistantship application.

Correspondence and Information

Dean, Graduate School
University of Tulsa
600 South College Avenue
Tulsa, Oklahoma 74104

Telephone: 918-631-2336
800-882-4723 (toll-free)
E-mail: grad@utulsa.edu
World Wide Web: http://www.utulsa.edu/graduate

FACULTY HEADS

GRADUATE SCHOOL
Janet Haggerty, Dean.
Richard Redner, Associate Dean.

College of Arts and Sciences
Thomas Horne, Dean.
Anthropology: George Odell, Chairperson; Michael Whalen, Adviser.
Art: Ronald Predl, Chairperson; Whitney Forsyth, Adviser.
Clinical Psychology: Allan Harkness, Chairperson; Thomas Brian, Adviser.
Education: Dale M. Johnson, Chairperson and Adviser.
English Language and Literature: Holly Laird, Chairperson; Hermione de Almeida, Adviser.
History: Joseph Bradley, Chairperson; Christine Ruane, Adviser.
Industrial/Organizational Psychology: Allan Harkness, Chairperson; Deidra Schleicher, Adviser.
Speech-Language Pathology: Paula Cadogan, Chairperson; Mary Moody, Adviser.

College of Business Administration
Gale Sullenberger, Dean.
Rebecca Holland, Director of Graduate Business Program and Adviser.
Accounting: Anita Hollander, Director.
Finance: Roger P. Bey, Chairperson.
Management: Ralph Jackson, Chairperson.
Management Information Systems: Anita Hollander, Chairperson.
Marketing: Ralph Jackson, Chairperson.
Operations Management: Roger P. Bey, Chairperson.
Nursing: Susan Gaston, Director.

College of Engineering and Applied Sciences
Steven Bellovich, Dean.
Biological Science: Glen Collier, Chairperson; Kenton Miller, Adviser.
Chemical Engineering: Geoffrey Price, Chairperson; Charles Sheppard, Adviser.
Chemistry and Biochemistry: Dale Teeters, Chairperson and Adviser.
Computer Science: William Coberly, Chairperson; Roger Wainwright, Adviser.
Electrical Engineering: Gerald Kane, Chairperson; Heng-Ming Tai, Adviser.
Engineering and Technology Management: Rebecca Holland, Adviser, Business Administration.
Geosciences: Colin Barker, Chairperson; Chris Liner, Adviser (Geophysics); Peter Michael, Adviser (Geology).
Mathematics: William Coberly, Chairperson; Kevin O'Neil, Adviser.
Mathematics and Science Education: Robert Howard and Dale M. Johnson, Program Coordinators.
Mechanical Engineering: Edmund Rybicki, Chairperson; Siamack Shirazi, Adviser.
Petroleum Engineering: Dean Oliver, Chairperson; Albert C. Reynolds, Adviser.
Physics and Engineering Physics: Kenneth Kuenhold, Chairperson.

Research Opportunities

Anthropological research projects range from archaeological research underway in Jordan, at Casas Grandes Pueblo in Chihuahua, Mexico, and Oklahoma. Students may also participate in ethnohistoric and linguistic research among Native American communities and in the South Pacific.

Research in **biological science** includes projects in molecular, cell, environmental, and comparative biology. Projects in molecular and cell biology include studies of lymphocyte development, glycobiology, development of the mammalian nervous system, molecular and developmental genetics, and structure-function relationships of microbial light harvesting proteins. Projects in environmental biology include behavioral ecology of colonial birds, population and pollination biology of bees, and microbial population biology. Projects in comparative biology include the evolutionary biology of reptilian viviparity, molecular systematics of algae and fish, aerobiology, and mammalian and invertebrate reproductive biology. The Mervin Bovaird Center for Molecular Biology and Biotechnology augments and promotes graduate training in molecular techniques.

Research in **chemical engineering** is largely experimentally based, involving laboratory and pilot scale programs. A major focus of activities is in the environmental field. Areas of current research include reaction kinetics and catalysis, supercritical fluids, multiphase chemical reactors and multiphase flows, capillary hydrodynamics, combustion, biological treatment of hazardous wastes and bioremediation of petroleum hydrocarbons, petroleum and natural gas processing, thermodynamics and phase equilibria, and particulate science.

Computer science faculty members are involved in research related to genetic algorithms, medical imaging, parallel and scientific computation, database security, fuzzy control, artificial intelligence, distributed artificial intelligence, software engineering and networking.

Research opportunities are available in **English language and literature.** The *James Joyce Quarterly, Tulsa Studies in Women's Literature,* and *Nimrod* are published at the University.

The Center for Environmental Research and Technology (CERT) is involved in a large number of **environmental** research projects related to the energy industry.

Geological research largely centers on "soft-rock" geology and includes funded research projects in carbonate, petrology and diagenesis, sand stone diagenesis, structural geology, and petroleum geology and geochemistry. The "hard-rock" geology projects are concerned with mid-ocean ridge basalts.

Geophysical research is primarily seismic and is processing oriented.

Mechanical engineering research is being conducted in thermal fluid sciences, solid mechanics, erosion/corrosion, composite materials, fatigue, manufacturing, thermal spray coatings, and residual stress analysis.

Research in **mathematics** is currently focused on Bayesian statistics, dynamical systems, computer graphics, numerical analysis, reservoir characterization, and mathematics education.

Petroleum engineering research opportunities derive from nine continuing, cooperative industry/University energy-related projects, including artificial lift, drilling, fluid flow, erosion/corrosion in the oil and gas industry, reservoir wettability, power application of submersible cables, reservoir exploration (well testing and reservoir engineering), separation technology, and wax deposition. Other petroleum-related projects include the impact of earthquakes on pipelines and phase behavior of CO_2 and heavy oils.

Research in **psychology** involves issues in theory and measurement of personality as applied to problems in clinical and organizational psychology. Current projects involve assessing personality disorders, evaluating competency to stand trial, leadership, and interpersonal skills. More basic research projects involve identifying qualified candidates for stressful jobs (e.g., police and firefighters), personality and career success, factors associated with managerial derailment, and self-perpetuating mechanisms in the development of dysfunctional, unconscious cognitive processes.

UNIVERSITY OF VERMONT

Graduate College

Programs of Study

The Graduate College offers programs of study leading to the Ph.D. in the following areas: anatomy and neurobiology, animal sciences, biochemistry, biology, botany, cell and molecular biology, chemistry, civil and environmental engineering, electrical engineering, materials science, mathematical sciences, mechanical engineering, microbiology and molecular genetics, molecular physiology and biophysics, natural resources, pharmacology, plant and soil science, and psychology. The Doctor of Education (Ed.D.) degree is offered in educational leadership and policy studies.

The M.S. degree is granted in all of the above fields except anatomy and neurobiology, education, molecular physiology and biophysics, and psychology. It is also offered in biomedical engineering, biomedical technology, biostatistics, communication sciences, community development and applied economics, computer science, counseling, field naturalist studies (botany), forestry, geology, historic preservation, natural resource planning, nursing, nutrition and food sciences, pathology, physics, statistics, water resources, and wildlife and fisheries biology. Opportunities for a combined M.D./M.S. or M.D./Ph.D. are available in cooperation with the College of Medicine.

The M.A. degree may be earned in English, French, geography, German, Greek and Latin, history, and psychology. The Graduate College offers Master of Business Administration (M.B.A.), Master of Physical Therapy (M.P.T.), Master of Public Administration (M.P.A.), and Master of Social Work (M.S.W.) degrees. Programs of study leading to the degrees of Master of Arts in Teaching (M.A.T.) and Master of Science for Teachers (M.S.T.) in several academic disciplines are also offered. The Master of Education (M.Ed.) degree may be pursued through programs in various areas, including curriculum and instruction, educational leadership, educational studies, higher education and student affairs, interdisciplinary, reading and language arts, and special education.

In general, the requirements for master's degree programs include the successful completion of a minimum of 30 semester hours of graduate credit, a comprehensive examination, and, depending upon the program, defense of an acceptable thesis. Many programs offer a nonthesis option. Doctoral degree programs require successful completion of a minimum of 75 credit hours, a comprehensive examination, and a dissertation.

Research Facilities

The University libraries consist of the Bailey/Howe, Physics/Chemistry, and Dana Medical libraries, with collections that total more than a million volumes. The Division of Computing and Information Technologies supports a variety of host systems on campus and provides Macintosh and DOS/Windows systems, software equipped, in public microcomputer labs. Workshops, tutorials, and publications support are available. All systems are connected directly to a campuswide network. Stand-alone and minicomputer systems are available in most laboratories. Specialized equipment is available in individual departments. State-of-the-art research equipment and instrumentation are supported by a University-wide engineering and fabrication facility.

Financial Aid

Financial support in the form of fellowships, assistantships, and traineeships is awarded on a competitive basis. The base fellowship stipend for 2002–03 is $12,100 for a nine-month appointment. Twelve-month and summer funding options are available in many programs. The stipend is accompanied by a tuition scholarship. Some other forms of financial support carry higher stipends; students receiving these awards are normally charged tuition at the in-state rate. Financial aid in the form of loans is available. Students may contact the department or program for information on fellowships and assistantships and the Office of Financial Aid for information on loans.

Cost of Study

For 2002–03, in-state tuition rates are $347 per credit hour, and nonresident rates are $867 per credit hour. Students who have completed all credit but not all degree requirements must pay a $100 continuous registration fee. University fees vary from none to $277 per semester, depending upon the number of credit hours taken.

Living and Housing Costs

For 2002–03, the average twelve-month budget (including food and housing, books and supplies, personal expenses, and transportation, but not tuition) is $10,000 for single students and $14,500 for married students with no children. Graduate student and married student housing is available.

Student Group

There are approximately 1,200 enrolled graduate students, with about 650 on campus as full-time students. The University encourages and welcomes applications from people with diverse backgrounds.

Location

The University of Vermont is located in Burlington, on the eastern shore of Lake Champlain, between the Adirondack and Green mountains. Numerous musical, artistic, and social opportunities are available through the University as well as the Burlington community, and the rural environment provides a splendid setting for outdoor activities, including seasonal swimming, boating, hiking, and skiing. Burlington is 300 miles north of New York City, 200 miles northwest of Boston, and 100 miles south of Montreal.

The University

The University of Vermont, or UVM (from the Latin "Universitas Virdis Montis," meaning University of the Green Mountains), was founded in 1791 as the fifth institution of higher education in New England and the twentieth in the nation. Today, UVM is a modern, comprehensive university with a teaching environment emphasizing close and sustained contacts between faculty members and students.

Applying

The deadline for receipt of completed applications and supporting materials for fall semester admission is April 1, except for programs in anatomy and neurobiology (February 15), botany (February 15), cell and molecular biology (January 15), civil and environmental engineering (February 1), communication sciences (February 1), counseling (February 1), curriculum and instruction (August 1), educational leadership (August 1), educational leadership and policy studies (May 1), educational studies (August 1), field naturalist studies (February 15), forestry (March 1), French (August 1), geography (March 1), geology (February 15), higher education and student affairs (January 1), historic preservation (March 1), interdisciplinary (August 1), microbiology and molecular genetics (February 1), natural resource planning (March 1), pharmacology (January 15), physical therapy (January 15), psychology (January 15), public administration (February 1), reading and language arts (August 1), social work (February 1), special education (August 1), water resources (March 1), and wildlife and fisheries biology (March 1). Applicants requesting financial support in the form of a fellowship, assistantship, or traineeship must have completed applications, including GRE General Test scores, on file by the earlier of March 1 or the program deadline.

Correspondence and Information

Graduate College Admissions Office
333 Waterman Building
University of Vermont
Burlington, Vermont 05405-0160

Telephone: 802-656-2699
Fax: 802-656-0519
E-mail: graduate.admissions@uvm.edu
World Wide Web: http://www.uvm.edu

THE FACULTY

Anne E. Huot, Interim Dean; Ph.D., Vermont.

DEPARTMENT AND PROGRAM CHAIRPERSONS

Biological and Physical Sciences
Anatomy and Neurobiology: Rodney L. Parsons, Ph.D., Stanford.
Animal Sciences: Karen I. Plaut, Ph.D., Cornell.
Biochemistry: Kenneth G. Mann, Ph.D., Iowa.
Biology: Judith VanHouten, Ph.D., California, Santa Barbara.
Biomedical Technologies: Paul Vichi, Ph.D., Vermont.
Botany: Thomas C. Vogelmann, Ph.D., Syracuse.
Cell and Molecular Biology: Ralph Budd, Ph.D., Cornell.
Chemistry: Willem R. Leenstra, Ph.D., Washington (Seattle).
Forestry: Carlton M. Newton, Ph.D., SUNY College of Forestry.
Geology: Barry L. Doolan, Ph.D., SUNY at Binghamton.
Microbiology and Molecular Genetics: Susan S. Wallace, Ph.D., Cornell.
Molecular Physiology and Biophysics: David M. Warshaw, Ph.D., Vermont.
Natural Resources: Patricia Stokowski, Ph.D., York.
Nutrition and Food Sciences: Robert S. Tyzbir, Ph.D., Rhode Island.
Pathology: Edwin G. Bovill, M.D., California.
Pharmacology: Mark T. Nelson, Ph.D., Washington.
Physical Therapy: Jean M. Held, Ed.D., Columbia.
Physics: Jun-Ru Wu, Ph.D., UCLA.
Plant and Soil Science: Alan R. Gotlieb, Ph.D., Wisconsin.
Water Resources: Alan W. McIntosh, Ph.D., Michigan State.
Wildlife and Fisheries Biology: David H. Hirth, Ph.D., Michigan.

Business Administration
James M. Sinkula, Ph.D., Arkansas.

Education
Education: James H. Mosenthal, Ph.D., Illinois.
Integrated Professional Studies: James R. Barbour, Ed.D., Fairleigh Dickinson.
Social Work: Gale Burford, Ph.D., Stirling (Scotland).

Engineering and Mathematics
Biomedical Engineering: Tony S. Keller, Ph.D., Vanderbilt.
Biostatistics: Larry D. Haugh, Ph.D., Wisconsin.
Civil and Environmental Engineering: James P. Olson, Ph.D., North Carolina State.
Computer Science: Xindong Xu, Ph.D., Edinburgh.
Electrical Engineering: Richard G. Absher, Ph.D., Duke.
Materials Science: Walter J. Varhue, Ph.D., Virginia.
Mathematics: Jeffrey H. Dinitz, Ph.D., Ohio State.
Mechanical Engineering: Tony S. Keller, Ph.D., Vanderbilt.
Statistics: Larry D. Haugh, Ph.D., Wisconsin.

Nursing
Gail DeLuca Havens, Ph.D., Maryland.

Social Sciences and Humanities
Classics: Z. Philip Ambrose, Ph.D., Princeton.
Communication Science and Disorders: Barry Guitar, Ph.D., Wisconsin.
Community Development and Applied Economics: Jane M. Kolodinsky, Ph.D., Cornell.
English: Robyn R. Warhol, Ph.D., Stanford.
French: Grant Crichfield, Ph.D., Wisconsin.
Geography: Joni K. Seager, Ph.D., Clark.
German: Wolfgang Mieder, Ph.D., Michigan State.
Historic Preservation: Thomas D. Visser, M.S., Vermont.
History: Denise J. Youngblood, Ph.D., Stanford.
Natural Resource Planning: Patricia Stokowski, Ph.D., York.
Psychology: Robert B. Lawson, Ph.D., Delaware.
Public Administration: Jane M. Kolodinsky, Ph.D., Cornell.

The statue of Ira Allen, in front of the Old Mill building, on the UVM green.

UNIVERSITY OF WISCONSIN–EAU CLAIRE

Graduate Studies

Programs of Study

Graduate programs at the University of Wisconsin–Eau Claire are intended to foster the intellectual development of postbaccalaureate students, enhancing both their personal and professional lives. Programs are offered in each of the three colleges that comprise the University: the College of Arts and Sciences, the College of Business, and the College of Professional Studies. The College of Arts and Sciences offers a Master of Arts in English and history, a Master of Science in biology, a Master of Science in Education, and a Specialist in Education in school psychology, including certification in school psychology. The College of Business offers a Master of Business Administration. The College of Professional Studies offers a Master of Science in Nursing; a Master of Arts in Teaching in the fields of biology, English, history, and mathematics; a Master of Science in Teaching in the fields of biology, elementary education, English, history, history/social science, mathematics, and reading; a Master of Science in communication disorders and in environmental and public health; a Master of Education in professional development; and a Master of Science in Education in special education.

Graduate studies at UW–Eau Claire emphasize personal working relationships between faculty members and students in a variety of learning situations. Seminars, colloquiums, and informal classes encourage active exchange of ideas, information, and experience. Independent studies, individual research projects, and joint faculty-student research efforts encourage individual investigation with helpful faculty supervision, and practicums and field experiences provide for direct application of academic learning to a wide variety of situations.

Each College is responsible for promoting high standards of scholarship, for offering professional preparation appropriate to societal needs, for maintaining an appropriate balance between the academic and professional components of graduate programs, and for coordinating all administrative aspects of graduate programming.

Research Facilities

Biology students have access to the electron microscopy lab, state-of-the-art TEM, physiological equipment for circadian rhythm studies, extensive field biology equipment, and molecular/cell biology labs with up-to-date equipment. The English department offers the Kate Gill Library, which includes special materials related to the faculty's specialties. Graduate students in history have access to all the libraries and archives affiliated with the University of Wisconsin system. This includes a two-day courier service of all the archival collections of the State Historical Society of Wisconsin and thirteen area research centers.

M.B.A. students have access to the Cargil Center, a computerized lab to conduct studies of decision making processes and other kinds of research. A new Business Telecommunications lab is also available for research studies, and a Business Communications writing lab provides a place to do educational research in writing. The Human Development Center (HDC) serves the purposes of educating graduate students in an interdisciplinary setting providing clinical services to clients in the community and surrounding region. It is also a center for interdisciplinary research on the UW–Eau Claire's campus. The HDC emphasizes student-faculty collaborative research for both graduate and undergraduate students and makes its human subjects laboratory available to all students.

Financial Aid

Merit-based financial aid is offered in the form of graduate assistantships, fellowships, and nonresident tuition waivers. Additional fellowships are available for qualified U.S. citizens who represent ethnic minority groups. Assistantship and fellowship application materials may be obtained from the Admissions Office. Information on need-based financial aid, such as the Ford and Perkins Loan programs, Federal Work-Study, grants, and partial tuition grants, may be obtained from the Office of Financial Aid, 115 Schofield Hall (telephone: 715-836-3373; e-mail: ausmansk@uwec.edu).

Cost of Study

Full-time in-state tuition and fees for 2001–02 (applicable to both Wisconsin and Minnesota residents, with reciprocity) were $4481 per academic year (for up to 15 credits per semester). Out-of-state tuition and fees were $14,305 (for up to 15 credits a semester). A limited number of full or partial nonresident tuition waivers are available to out-of-state and international graduate students with superior academic credentials. Certain programs may have different tuition and fees.

Living and Housing Costs

Most graduate students live in private apartments and homes near campus. Limited University-owned housing is available for single graduate students. No University-owned housing is available for married students. Further information about housing can be obtained from the Office of Residence Life, 112 Towers Hall (telephone: 715-836-3674). The cost of living in Eau Claire is moderate and slightly below the national average.

Student Group

The University annually enrolls about 10,500 students. Of these, approximately 450 are graduate students; about 25 percent of the students are men. Faculty and academic staff members who hold doctoral or appropriate terminal degrees and possess a broad array of special qualifications and backgrounds in their academic specialties teach graduate courses.

Location

Located in Eau Claire, Wisconsin, UW–Eau Claire also offers an attractive learning environment. Eau Claire (population 56,000) is located on Interstate 94, and it is 95 miles east of Minneapolis and 240 miles northwest of Milwaukee. Eau Claire and its surrounding countryside abound in beautiful rivers, lakes, and wooded areas, where students enjoy seasonal sports, camping, and other recreational activities throughout the year.

The University

The University of Wisconsin–Eau Claire, which celebrated its seventy-fifth anniversary during 1991–92, is a public institution governed by the Board of Regents of the University of Wisconsin system. With a faculty and staff of nearly 600 members, UWEC serves more than 10,500 students. The UW–Eau Claire campus includes twenty-six major buildings situated on a bilevel, 333-acre site. The major portion of the campus embraces Putnam Park on the south bank of the Chippewa River and connects by footbridge to the Fine Arts Center and the Human Sciences and Services Building, which are located on the north bank.

Applying

Admissions materials are available from the Office of Admissions, 112 Schofield Hall (telephone: 715-836-4733). Admission to a degree program is based upon evaluation of the student's academic record and previous experience by the graduate faculty of the department offering the program. Applicants for admission to graduate study must have a baccalaureate degree from a regionally accredited college or university. Admission of a student not fully qualified for a particular program may be made dependent upon completion of prerequisite requirements or examinations. Admission to particular degree programs may include additional requirements such as minimum undergraduate grade point average (GPA), entrance examinations, or prerequisite courses.

For general information about any of the graduate programs at UW–Eau Claire, students should contact the University at the address below. For more specific information about graduate admissions and financial aid or degrees and programs, students may contact specific departments through the University's Web site (listed below).

Correspondence and Information

Graduate Studies
Human Sciences and Services 158
University of Wisconsin–Eau Claire
Eau Claire, Wisconsin 54702-4004
Telephone: 715-836-2721
Fax: 715-836-4892
E-mail: graduate@uwec.edu
World Wide Web: http://www.uwec.edu/Admin/Grad/graduate.htm

FACULTY HEADS

Biology (M.A., M.S.T., and M.A.T.): Dr. Michael Weil
Business Administration (M.B.A.): Dr. Robert Erffmeyer
Communication Disorders (M.S.): Dr. Larry Solberg
Elementary Education (M.S.T.), Professional Development (M.E.), Reading (M.S.T.), and Education Component of all M.A.T. Programs: Dr. Susan McIntyre
English (M.A., M.S.T., and M.A.T.): Dr. Anne Utschig
Environmental and Public Health (M.S.): Dr. Robert Nelson
History (M.A., M.S.T., and M.A.T.), History/Social Science (M.S.T.): Dr. Jane Pederson
Mathematics (M.S.T. and M.A.T.): Dr. Thomas Wineinger
Nursing (M.S.N): Dr. Rita Kisting Sparks
Professional Development (M.E.) with Emphasis in Library Science: Ms. Gyneth Slygh
School Psychology (Ed.S. and M.S.E.): Dr. William Frankenberger
Special Education (M.S.E.) (BD, LD, EC, and CD): Dr. Vicki Snider

UNIVERSITY OF WISCONSIN–LA CROSSE

Graduate Studies

Programs of Study

Graduate programs at the University of Wisconsin–La Crosse (UW–L) are offered in each of the four colleges that comprise the University: the College of Business Administration; the College of Health, Physical Education, Recreation, and Teacher Education (HPERTE); the College of Liberal Studies; and the College of Science and Allied Health. The College of Business Administration offers a Master of Business Administration degree that is fully accredited by AACSB International–The Association to Advance Collegiate Schools of Business. The College of Health, Physical Education, Recreation, and Teacher Education offers the Master of Science degree in adult fitness/cardiac rehabilitation, exercise and sport science (with options in human performance, sport administration, physical education teaching, and special physical education and concentrations in adventure education and athletic training), therapeutic recreation, recreation management, community health education, and school health education. In addition, the College of HPERTE offers Wisconsin's only nationally accredited Master of Public Health in community health education. The School of Education, a unit within the College of HPERTE, offers the Master of Science in Education degree in reading, special education, and college student development and administration. In addition, the School of Education offers a Master of Education–Professional Development degree. The College of Liberal Studies offers an Education Specialist degree in school psychology. The College of Science and Allied Health offers both the Master of Science in biology (with concentrations in aquatic science, cellular and molecular biology, clinical microbiology, microbiology, nurse anesthesia, and physiology) and the Master of Science in physical therapy.

Research Facilities

UW–L is home to a number of research facilities that are accessible to graduate student researchers. Murphy Library has recently undergone an extensive expansion and modernization and contains more than 550,000 volumes; the online catalog allows users to search local and other University of Wisconsin catalogs. Modern microcomputer laboratories are available campuswide. The River Studies Center conducts research in aquatic ecology, watershed ecology, fisheries, aquatic parasitology, aquatic microbiology, aquatic toxicology, and water quality. The College of Science and Allied Health, the administrative home of the La Crosse Medical Health Science Consortium, Inc., in a public/private partnership with regional health-care providers and local colleges, has constructed the 168,000-square-foot La Crosse Medical Health Science Education and Research Center. The Center, completed in fall 2000, focuses on applied clinical research activities in microbiology, immunology, molecular diagnostics, virology, and human physiology. The Human Performance Laboratory, the La Crosse Exercise and Health Program, and the Special Populations Exercise Program of the College of HPERTE provide extensive opportunities for clinical work and basic and applied research in exercise and sport science. The Leisure Lifestyle Center provides research opportunities for therapeutic recreation students. The Small Business Development Center is affiliated with the College of Business Administration (CBA) and is part of a statewide organization that provides counseling to small business managers related to business start-up and management. The Bureau of Business and Economic Research is a University contract research facility for area businesses. The CBA also serves as a US-AID training site for large numbers of managers and public administrators from Central Europe.

Financial Aid

Merit-based financial aid is offered in the form of graduate assistantships and nonresident tuition waivers. Additional assistantships are available for qualified U.S. citizens who represent members of minority groups. Interested students should contact the appropriate graduate program director for assistantship application procedures. Information on need-based financial aid such as the Stafford and Perkins loan programs, College Work-Study, Advanced Opportunity Program grants, and partial tuition grants may be obtained from the Office of Financial Aid, 215 Graff Main Hall, (telephone: 608-785-8604, e-mail: stadthau.alfr@uwlax.edu).

Cost of Study

Tuition for 2001–02 (applicable to both Wisconsin and Minnesota residents, with reciprocity) was $231 per credit hour. Out-of-state tuition was $728 per credit hour. A limited number of full or partial nonresident tuition waivers are available to out-of-state and international graduate students with superior academic credentials. Certain programs may have different tuition and fees.

Living and Housing Costs

Most graduate students live in private apartments and homes near the campus. Limited University-owned housing is available for single graduate students and no University-owned housing is available for married students. Further information about housing can be obtained from the Office of Residence Life, 213 Wilder Hall (telephone: 608-785-8075). The cost of living in La Crosse is moderate and slightly below the national average.

Student Group

The University annually enrolls 700 graduate students; 40 percent of the students are male and 60 percent are female. The Office of Career Services serves graduate students from all schools and colleges in seeking professional employment upon degree completion. Ninety-six percent of the UW–L master's degree recipients in 1998–99 who were looking for employment found positions within approximately six months of graduation.

Location

La Crosse is famous for its exceptional natural beauty. The city (population 51,000) is located on the east bank of the Mississippi River below towering bluffs. The metro area population is 121,800. Abundant water and woodlands provide year-round recreation sites for skiing, hunting, bicycling, hiking, camping, and other outdoor activities. La Crosse is also home to two other colleges, a symphony orchestra, excellent theatrical and cultural events, superb health-care facilities, and first-class elementary and secondary schools.

The University

The University of Wisconsin–La Crosse, founded in 1909, is a public institution governed by the Board of Regents of the University of Wisconsin System. With a faculty and academic staff of more than 450, UW–L serves more than 9,000 students from Wisconsin, Minnesota, Iowa, Illinois, and forty other states and forty-two other countries. The 119-acre campus is located within easy walking distance of downtown La Crosse in a residential section of the city.

Applying

Applicants from the U.S. may request admissions materials from the Office of Admissions, 115 Graff Main Hall (telephone: 608-785-8939). International applicants may request complete application packets from the Office of International Education, 116 Graff Main Hall (telephone: 608-785-8016, fax: 608-785-8923, e-mail: uwlworld@uwlax.edu). All applicants must submit a completed application form, transcripts of all undergraduate course work, and a $45 application fee. M.B.A. students are required to submit a GMAT score. Applicants should check with specific graduate program directors regarding other required admission tests and application deadline dates.

Correspondence and Information

Dr. Dan Duquette
Director of University Graduate Studies
206 Mitchell Hall
University of Wisconsin–La Crosse
La Crosse, Wisconsin 54601

Telephone: 608-785-8939 (Admissions Office)
Fax: 608-785-8940 (Admissions Office)
E-mail: admissions@uwlax.edu
uwlworld@uwlax.edu (international student graduate admissions)
World Wide Web: http://www.uwlax.edu

THE FACULTY

Director of University Graduate Studies: Dr R. Daniel Duquette, 206 Mitchell Hall. Telephone: 608-785-8161 (duquette.rode@uwlax.edu).

ASSOCIATE DEANS OF THE COLLEGES

College of Business Administration: (Interim) Dr. James E. Finch, 316B Wimberly Hall. Telephone: 608-785-8120 (finch.jame@uwlax.edu); (Interim) Kenneth M. Winter, 405 Wimberly Hall. Telephone: 608-785-8120 (winter.kenn@uwlax.edu).

College of Health, Physical Education, Recreation, and Teacher Education: (Interim) Dr. Mandi Anderson, 124 Mitchell Hall. Telephone: 608-785-8155 (anderson.mary@uwlax); (Interim) Dr. Ronald S. Rochon, 205 Morris Hall. Telephone: 608-785-8142 (rochon.rona@uwlax.edu).

College of Liberal Studies: Dr. Ruth Ann Benson, 227E Graff Main Hall. Telephone: 608-785-8113 (benson.ruth@uwlax.edu).

College of Science and Allied Health: Dr. Martin R. Venneman, 105 Graff Main Hall. Telephone: 608-785-8218 (venneman.mart@uwlax.edu); (Interim) Dr. Mark Sandheinrich, 4030 Cowley Hall. Telephone: 608-785-8261 (sandhein.mark@uwlax.edu); (Interim) Dr. Karen Palmer McLean, 2025 Cowley Hall. Telephone: 608-785-8459 (mclean.kare@uwlax.edu).

GRADUATE PROGRAM DIRECTORS

MASTER OF SCIENCE

Adult Fitness-Cardiac Rehabilitation: Dr. John P. Porcari, 141 Mitchell Hall. Telephone: 608-785-8684 (porcari.john@uwlax.edu).
Biology (all concentrations): Dr. Steve Callister (Gundersen-Lutheran), 1836 South Avenue. Telephone: 608-782-7300 (scallist.gundluth.org); Dr. Thomas J. Volk, 3024 Cowley Hall. Telephone: 608-785-6972 (volk.thom@uwlax.edu).

Health Education and Health Promotion
Community Health Education: Dr. Gary Gilmore, 201 Mitchell Hall. Telephone: 608-785-8163 (gilmore.gary@uwlax.edu).
School Health Education: Dr. Mark Kelley, 209 Mitchell Hall. Telephone: 608-785-6791. (kelley.roy@uwlax.edu)

Exercise and Sport Science
Physical Education Teaching: Dr. Jeffrey P. Steffen, 217 Mitchell Hall. Telephone: 608-785-6536 (steffen.jeff@uwlax.edu).
Sport Administration: Dr. Paul M. Plinske, 126 Mitchell Hall. Telephone: 608-785-8616 (plinske.paul@uwlax.edu).
Human Performance: Dr. Richard Mikat, 129 Mitchell Hall. Telephone: 608-785-8182 (mikat.rich@uwlax.edu).
Special (Adapted) Physical Education: Dr. Patrick DiRocco, 137 Mithcell Hall. Telephone: 608-785-8173 (dirocco.patr@uwlax.edu).
Athletic Training Concentration: Mr. Mark H. Gibson, 135 Mitchell Hall. Telephone: 608-785-8190 (gibson.mark@uwlax.edu)

Recreation Management: Dr. Steve Simpson, 136 Wittich Hall. Telephone: 608-785-8126 (simpson.stev@uwlax.edu).

Therapeutic Recreation: Dr. Steve Simpson, 136 Wittich Hall. Telephone: 608-785-8126 (simpson.stev@uwlax.edu).

MASTER OF SCIENCE IN PHYSICAL THERAPY

Physical Therapy: Dr. Dennis C. Fater, 4031 HSC. Telephone: 608-785-8471 (fater.denn@uwlax.edu).

MASTER OF PUBLIC HEALTH

Community Health Education: Dr. Gary Gilmore, 201 Mitchell Hall. Telephone: 608-785-8163 (gilmore.gary@uwlax.edu).

MASTER OF SCIENCE IN EDUCATION

College Student Development and Administration: Dr. Larry Ringgenberg, 212 Cartwright. Telephone: 608-785-8888 (ringgenb.larr@uwlax.edu).
Reading: Dr. Carol Kirk, 300C Morris Hall. Telephone: 608-785-8136 (kirk.caro@uwlax.edu).

Special Education: Dr. Carroll Jones, 240C Morris Hall. Telephone: 608-785-6896 (jones.carr@uwlax.edu).

MASTER OF BUSINESS ADMINISTRATION (M.B.A.)

College of Business Administration: Ms. Amelia Dittman, 223C Wimberly Hall. Telephone: 608-785-8092 (dittman.amel@uwlax.edu).

MASTER OF EDUCATION–PROFESSIONAL DEVELOPMENT

Master of Education–Professional Development: Dr. Hal Hiebert, 205 Morris Hall. Telephone: 608-785-6500 (hiebert.haro@uwlax.edu).

EDUCATION SPECIALIST

School Psychology: Dr. Milton J. Dehn, 341A Graff Main Hall. Telephone: 608-785-8445 (dehn.milt@uwlax.edu).

Graduate students have clinical experiences in a variety of settings, including schools, hospitals, community agencies, and health-care organizations.

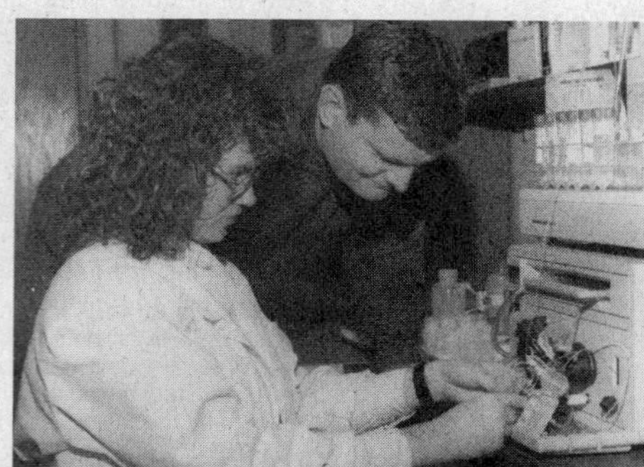

Graduate students at UW–L are guided in research by dedicated faculty members.

M.B.A. students bring real-world work experiences to their graduate courses and seminars.

UNIVERSITY OF WYOMING

Graduate School

Programs of Study

The Graduate School of the University of Wyoming (UW) awards the Doctor of Philosophy (Ph.D.) in twenty-five disciplines. The of Doctor of Education (Ed.D.) and Educational Specialist (Ed.S.) are also offered. The Master's degree is offered in sixty-four areas and include the following degree categories: Master of Arts (M.A.), Master of Science (M.S.), Master of Business Administration (M.B.A.), Master of Music (M.M.), Master of Planning (M.P.), Master of Public Administration (M.P.A.), Master of Social Work (M.S.W.), Master of Arts in Teaching (M.A.T.), and Master of Science in Teaching (M.S.T.). An interdisciplinary Master of Science and an interdisciplinary Master of Arts are available, in which students may combine up to three areas of study. For further information, students interested in a particular program should see the reverse of this page for a listing of degrees by discipline. The University of Wyoming is a Carnegie Research Extensive institution.

Research Facilities

Library holdings total more than 1 million volumes. The American Heritage Center has valuable collections dealing with American history. The Geology Museum, University Art Museum, Wilhelm G. Solheim Mycological Herbarium, Rocky Mountain Herbarium, Anthropology Museum, and Rocky Mountain Systematic Entomology Laboratory are located on the campus. The Survey Research Center, Wyoming Veterinary Diagnostic Laboratory, Institute of Business and Management Services, Wyoming Agricultural Experiment Station (including the Research and Extention Centers throughout the state) and Williams Botany Conservatory, among others, provide research opportunities. The Elk Mountain and Jelm Mountain observatories (facilities for the study of weather phenomena and infrared astrophysics, respectively), the Department of Atmospheric Science flight facility, and the only University-owned balloon launch facility in the world are located near Laramie. Eight miles south of Laramie, the Red Buttes Environmental Biology Laboratory has excellent facilities for the study of wild animals and for aquatic toxicology. The Mineral Research and Reclamation Center, which houses the Department of Geology and Geophysics, is the newest addition to the University's facilities. The Computer Center is equipped with modern, sophisticated computers. The University computer system is connected to the Internet, linking UW with other universities, national laboratories, and supercomputers. Personal computers are available for student use. In addition to University facilities, the Wyoming Geological Survey, Wyoming Cooperative Fishery and Wildlife Research Unit, Wyoming Research Corporation, and USDA Arthropod-Borne Animal Disease Research Laboratory are located on campus and provide opportunities for graduate research. The University of Wyoming/National Park Research Center in Grand Teton National Park offers a variety of possibilities for graduate research.

Financial Aid

Graduate assistantships are available. For each academic year, compensation starts at $8667 (for 18 to 20 hours of work per week) with no upper limit to stipends, depending on available resources. Graduate assistants also receive tuition and fee reductions. Graduate fellowships, scholarships, work-study opportunities, part-time work, and other forms of financial aid are also available.

Cost of Study

Full-time students who are Wyoming residents pay $1693.10 per semester, and out-of-state students pay $4429.10. Part-time registration is $170.35 per credit hour for residents and $474.35 per credit hour for nonresidents.

Living and Housing Costs

For single students living in campus dorms, a single room costs approximately $3018 for the academic year. The monthly cost of married student housing (one-, two-, or three-bedroom apartments) ranges from $358 to $626 (gas, electricity, basic phone, and basic cable included). Graduate students over 21 years old may elect a dorm reserved for those over 21. The board plan is flexible and optional. Many apartments and houses are available for rent in the town of Laramie.

Student Group

The University enrolls about 11,000 students. Of these, there are approximately 1,665 graduate students and 210 law students. About 75 percent of the students are residents of Wyoming, and 52 percent are women. The student-faculty ratio at the University of Wyoming is about 15:1.

Location

Laramie (population 29,187) is in southeastern Wyoming at a high elevation in a mountain valley. Denver, Colorado, is located 120 miles to the south. Several recreational areas are within a 15-minute drive. Some of the best ski areas in the United States are within 2½ hours from Laramie. The University of Wyoming draws many cultural events. The average summer temperature is 70 degrees; there may be some cold days in the winter, but the sun shines an average of 310 days per year.

The University

The University of Wyoming was established as a land-grant college in 1886. As the state's only institution of higher learning offering four-year and graduate programs, the University has developed broad undergraduate and graduate curricula. New facilities have enhanced scholarship and graduate degree programs in all Colleges.

Applying

Graduates of accredited institutions who have earned a B average or higher are eligible to apply. Applicants are expected to have a combined verbal and quantitative GRE General Test score of at least 900 for master's and specialist's programs and 1000 for doctoral programs. (For those students applying to graduate business programs, the University substitutes GMAT scores.) International applicants whose native language is not English must submit both GRE General Test scores and TOEFL scores. (The University requires a minimum TOEFL score of 525 (197 on the computerized test), but some programs require higher scores.) International students must provide a statement of financial independence; these students need approximately $17,200 in American dollars plus transportation expenses for the academic year. An additional $4840 is needed for the summer term. An application must be submitted along with an official copy of all transcripts, a $40 application fee, and three letters of recommendation.

Correspondence and Information

Applicants who seek general information should contact the Graduate School using the addresses or telephone number provided below. Complete information and applications are also available on the World Wide Web. For information concerning specific programs, students may write to the particular department at the address given on the back of this page or may access specific department Web pages through the University's Web site at (http://www.uwyo.edu). Department telephone numbers are also listed on the back of this page.

Graduate School Admissions
P.O. Box 3108
University of Wyoming
Laramie, Wyoming 82071-3108

Telephone: 307-766-2287
Fax: 307-766-2374
E-mail: UWGRAD@uwyo.edu
World Wide Web: http://grad.uwyo.edu

FACULTY HEADS

College of Agriculture
Dean: Frank Galey, P.O. Box 3354 (telephone: 307-766-4133; web: http://uwyo.edu/agcollege/).
Agricultural and Applied Economics (M.S.): Edward Bradley, P.O. Box 3354 (telephone: 307-766-2386).
Animal Science (Ph.D., M.S.): Douglas Hixon, P.O. Box 3684 (telephone: 307-766-2224).
Family and Consumer Sciences (M.S.): Bernita Quoss, P.O. Box 3354 (telphone: 307-766-4145).
Molecular Biology (Ph.D., M.S.): Jerry Johnson, P.O. Box 3944 (telephone: 307-766-3300).
Plant Sciences (Ph.D. and M.S. in agronomy): Ron Delaney, P.O. Box 3354 (telephone: 307-766-3103).
Renewable Resources (Ph.D. and M.S. in entomology, in rangeland ecology and watershed management, and in soil science): Tom Thurow, P.O. Box 3354 (telephone: 307-766-2263).
Veterinary Sciences (M.S. in pathobiology): Ken Mills, 1174 Snowy Range Road, Laramie, Wyoming 82070 (telephone: 307-742-6638).

College of Arts and Sciences
Dean: Oliver Walter, P.O. Box 3254 (telephone: 307-766-4106; web: uwadmnweb.uwyo.edu/a&s/index.htm).
Anthropology (M.A.): Audrey Shalinsky, P.O. Box 3431 (telephone: 307-766-5136).
Botany (Ph.D., M.S.): Gregory Brown. P.O. Box 3165 (telephone: 307-766-2380).
Chemistry (Ph.D., M.S., M.S.T.): Daniel Buttrey. P.O. Box 3838 (telephone: 307-766-4363).
Communication and Mass Media (M.A.): Conrad Smith, P.O. Box 3904 (telephone: 307-766-6277).
English (M.A.): Janice Harris, P.O. Box 3353 (telephone: 307-766-6452).
Geography and Recreation (M.A. and M.S.T. in geography, M.S. in recreation and park administration, M.P.): John Allen, P.O. Box 3371 (telephone: 307-766-3311).
Geology and Geophysics (Ph.D., M.S.): James Steidtmann, P.O. Box 3006 (telephone: 307-766-3386).
History (M.A., M.A.T.): Brian Hosmer, P.O. Box 3198 (telephone: 307-766-5101).
Mathematics (Ph.D., M.S., M.A., M.S.T., M.A.T.): Eric Moorehouse, P.O. Box 3036 (telephone: 307-766-4221).
Modern and Classical Languages (M.A. in French, in German, and in Spanish): Klaus Hanson, P.O. Box 3603 (telephone: 307-766-4177).
Music (M.A., M.M.): Julia Combs, P.O. Box 3037 (telephone: 307-766-5242).
Philosophy (M.A.): James Forrester, P.O. Box 3392 (telephone: 307-766-3204).
Physics and Astronomy (Ph.D., M.S., M.S.T.): Paul Johnson, P.O. Box 3905 (telephone: 307-766-6150).
Political Science (M.A., M.P.A.): R. McGreggor Cawley, P.O. Box 3197 (telephone: 307-766-6484).
Psychology (Ph.D., M.S., M.A.): Narina Nunez, P.O. Box 3415 (telephone: 307-766-6303).
Sociology (M.A.): Audie Blevins, P.O. Box 3293 (telephone: 307-766-3342).
Statistics (Ph.D., M.S.): Stephen Bieber, P.O. Box 3332 (telephone: 307-766-4229).
Zoology and Physiology (Ph.D., M.S.): Nancy Stanton, P.O. Box 3166 (telephone: 307-766-4207).

College of Business
Dean: Kenyon Griffin, P.O. Box 3275 (telephone: 307-766-4194; web: business.uwyo.edu).
Accounting (M.S.): Stuart Webster, P.O. Box 3275 (telephone: 307-766-3136).
E-Business (M.S.): Kenton Walker, P.O. Box 3275 (telephone: 307-766-6902).
Economics and Finance (Ph.D., M.S.): Owen Phillips, P.O. Box 3985 (telephone: 307-766-2178).
Graduate Business Programs (M.B.A.): Patricia Pattison, P.O. Box 3275 (telephone: 307-766-2449).

College of Education
Dean: Patricia McClurg, P.O. Box 3374 (telephone: 307-766-145; Web: edweb.uwyo.edu).
Adult Learning and Technology (M.A., Ed.S., Ed.D. in adult and postsecondary education option; M.S., Ed.D. in instructional technology option): Michael J. Day, P.O. Box 3374 (telephone: 307-766-3247).
Counselor Education (M.S. in community counseling, school counseling, and student affairs program options; Ph.D. in counselor education and supervision option): Mary Alice Bruce, P.O. Box 3374 (telephone: 307-766-2366).
Educational Leadership (M.A., Ed.S., Ed.D., Ph.D.): Alan D. Moore, P.O. Box 3374 (telephone: 307-766-5649).
Educational Studies (M.A., Ed.D., Ph.D. in curriculum and instruction option): Francisco Rios, P.O. Box 3374 (telephone: 307-766-3130).
Elementary and Early Childhood Education (M.A., Ed.D., Ph.D. in curriculum and instruction option): Margaret Cooney, P.O. Box 3374 (telephone: 307-766-6366).
Natural Science Program (M.S., M.S.T.): Patricia McClurg, P.O. Box 3992 (telephone: 307-766-6381).
Secondary Education (M.A., Ed.D., Ph.D. in curriculum and instruction option): Norman Peterson, P.O. Box 3374 (telephone: 307-766-3275).

College of Engineering
Dean: Gus Plumb, P.O. Box 3295 (telephone: 307-766-4253; web: http://www.eng.uwyo.edu).
Atmospheric Science (Ph.D., M.S.): Alfred Rodi, P.O. Box 3038 (telephone: 307-766-3246).
Chemical and Petroleum Engineering (Ph.D., M.S. in chemical engineering and in petroleum engineering): Maciej Radosz, P.O. Box 3295 (telephone: 307-766-2500).
Civil and Architectural Engineering (Ph.D., M.S.): Charles Dolan. P.O. Box 3295 (telephone: 307-766-5255).
Electrical and Computer Engineering (Ph.D., M.S.): John Steadman, P.O. Box 3295 (telephone: 307-766-2279).
Environmental Engineering (M.S.): M. P. Sharma, P.O. Box 3295 (telephone: 307-766-5255).
Mechanical Engineering (Ph.D., M.S.): William Lindberg, P.O. Box 3295 (telephone: 307-766-2122).

College of Health Sciences
Dean: Robert Kelley, P.O. Box 3432 (telephone: 307-766-6556; web: uwadmnweb.uwyo.edu/hs.defaulthtm).
Communication Disorders (M.S.): Mary Hardin-Jones, P.O. Box 3311 (telephone: 307-766-6427).
Kinesiology and Health Education (M.S.): Mark Byra, P.O. Box 3196 (telephone: 307-766-5285).
Nursing (M.S.): Marcia Dale, P.O. Box 3065 (telephone: 307-766-6569).
Social Work (M.S.W.): Deborah Valentine, P.O. Box 3632 (telephone: 307-766-6112).

Interdisciplinary Programs
American Studies (M.A.): Eric Sandeen, P.O. Box 4036 (telephone: 307-766-3898).
Environment and Natural Resources: Harold Bergman, P.O. Box 3985 (telephone: 307-766-2068).
Food Science and Human Nutrition (M.S.): Mike Liebman, P.O. Box 3354 (telephone: 307-766-4145).
Interdisciplinary Studies (M.A., M.S.): Stephen Williams, P.O. Box 3108 (telephone: 307-766-2287).
International Studies (M.A.): Garth Massey, P.O. Box 3293 (telephone: 307-766-3423).
Natural Science (M.S., M.S.T.): Patricia McClurg, P.O. Box 3992 (telephone: 307-766-6381).
Neuroscience: Francis Flynn, P.O. Box 3415 (telephone: 307-766-6303).
Reproductive Biology (Ph.D., M.S.): William J. Murdoch, P.O. Box 3684 (telephone: 307-766-2224).
Women's Studies: Catherine Connolly, P.O. Box 4297 (telephone: 307-766-3376).

College of Law
Dean: Jerry Parkinson, P.O. Box 3035 (telephone: 307-766-6416; web: http://www.wwyo.edu/law/law.htm).
Admissions: Debra J. Madsen, P.O. Box 3035 (telephone: 307-766-6416).

VILLANOVA UNIVERSITY

Graduate Studies—Liberal Arts and Sciences

Programs of Study

Master's degrees are offered in the following areas: Applied Statistics, Biology, Chemistry, Classical and Modern Languages and Literatures (Spanish), Counseling and Human Relations (Community, Elementary, and Secondary), Computer Science, Education (Elementary, Secondary, and School Leadership), Criminal Justice, English, History, Human Resource Development, Liberal Studies, Mathematics, Political Science, Psychology, Public Administration, Theater, and Theology. Doctoral degrees are offered in the area of Philosophy only.

The academic year consists of two semesters. The first semester begins in the last week of August and ends before Christmas. The second semester begins in the second week in January and ends in the second week of May. In addition, there are three summer sessions—two successive ones of five weeks each and a third (evenings) of ten weeks.

Research Facilities

The University library contains more than 780,000 volumes and 5,600 current periodicals. Special library holdings include the collection of the Augustinian Historical Institute and an extensive collection of works in contemporary continental philosophy.

The University Computer Center houses two VAX 4500-500 computers, a SUN Ultra Enterprise One computer, and five Data General machines. All facilities are available to University students and faculty. Standard and specialized research facilities and equipment are available in all departments engaged in graduate research.

Financial Aid

Graduate assistantships are awarded on a competitive basis. The assistantship stipend begins at approximately $10,635 in 2002–03 and carries with it a waiver of all tuition and academic fees. A few research fellowships are also awarded each year. A number of tuition scholarships are available; they provide a waiver of all tuition and academic fees.

In addition, the office of the director of financial aid administers the Federal Stafford Student Loan, the unsubsidized Federal Stafford Loan, and the Federal Supplemental Loans for Students.

Cost of Study

Graduate tuition ranges from $460 to $520 per credit hour in 2002–03. In addition, there is a University fee of $30 each semester.

Living and Housing Costs

The University does not maintain accommodations for graduate students, but second-year students are eligible for positions as resident counselors in the dormitories. The area has a wide selection of living quarters convenient to the campus.

Student Group

Approximately 1,900 graduate students were enrolled for the fall 2001 term, 1,000 of these in liberal arts and sciences programs. Total University enrollment is approximately 11,000, including 6,100 full-time undergraduates, 1,500 part-time evening (undergraduate) students, and 900 students in the School of Law. There are about equal numbers of men and women graduate students.

Location

Located in the heart of the Delaware Valley's "Main Line," the University occupies more than 200 handsomely landscaped acres in the town of Villanova, 12 miles west of Philadelphia. The location combines the advantages of a tranquil suburban setting with proximity to a large metropolitan city known for its outstanding contributions in the areas of culture, education, history, recreation, religion, and sport.

The University

Villanova University is a private institution founded in 1842 by the Augustinian Fathers. Graduate programs were first administered separately in 1931. Currently, there are six academic units in addition to Graduate Studies—the Colleges of Arts and Sciences, Commerce and Finance, Engineering, and Nursing; the Division of Part-Time Studies; and the School of Law.

Applying

Application forms and the *Graduate Studies Viewbook* may be obtained from the Graduate Studies Office. Due dates for submission of credentials vary by program. In addition to forwarding the completed application form and official college transcripts, applicants must also arrange to have three letters of recommendation submitted on their behalf. There is an application fee of $40. Graduate Record Examination scores are required by some departments. Descriptions of programs and procedures are found in the *Graduate Studies Viewbook* and on the University's Web site.

Correspondence and Information

Dean, Graduate Studies
Liberal Arts and Sciences
Villanova University
800 Lancaster Avenue
Villanova, Pennsylvania 19085-1688
Telephone: 610-519-7090
E-mail: gradinformation@email.villanova.edu
World Wide Web: http://www.gradartsci.villanova.edu/

THE FACULTY

Gerald M. Long, Ph.D., Stanford; Dean.

Listed below are the chairpersons, directors, or coordinators for the University's graduate programs.

Master's Programs
Applied Statistics: Thomas H. Short, Ph.D., Carnegie Mellon.
Biology: Russell M. Gardner, Ph.D., Indiana.
Chemistry: Barry S. Selinsky, Ph.D., SUNY at Buffalo.
Classical and Modern Languages and Literatures (Spanish): To be announced.
Community Counseling: Kenneth M. Davis, Ed.D., Northern Illinois.
Computer Science: Don Goelman, Ph.D., Pennsylvania.
Criminal Justice Administration: Stanley Jacobs, Acting Director; Ph.D., Maryland.
Elementary and Secondary Graduate Teacher Education: Gerald J. Flood, Ph.D., Johns Hopkins.
Elementary and Secondary School Counseling: Henry O. Nichols, Ed.D., Duke.
English: Charles L. Cherry, Ph.D., North Carolina.
History: Adele Lindenmeyr, Ph.D., Princeton.
Human Resource Development: David F. Bush, Ph.D., Purdue.
Liberal Studies: Joseph Betz, Ph.D., Chicago.
Mathematics: Robert Styer, Ph.D., MIT.
Philosophy: James J. McCartney, O.S.A., Ph.D., Georgetown.
Political Science: Lowell S. Gustafson, Ph.D., Virginia.
Psychology: Douglas M. Klieger, Ph.D., Iowa State.
Public Administration: Craig M. Wheeland, Ph.D., Penn State.
School Leadership: Catherine M. Hill, Ed.D., Harvard.
Theatre: Peter M. Donahue, O.S.A., Ph.D., Illinois.
Theology: Arthur B. Chappell, O.S.A., S.T.L., S.T.D., Pontifical University of St. Thomas.

Ph.D. Program
Philosophy: To be announced.

VIRGINIA COMMONWEALTH UNIVERSITY

School of Graduate Studies

Programs of Study

Virginia Commonwealth University (VCU) offers master's and doctoral degrees in anatomy, art history, biochemistry/molecular biophysics, biomedical engineering, biostatistics, business, chemistry, human genetics, microbiology/immunology, nursing, pathology, pharmaceutical studies, pharmacology/toxicology, physiology, psychology, and public policy and administration; doctoral degrees in education, health-related sciences, health services organization/research, and social work; and master's degrees in accountancy; administration of justice; administration/supervision; adult education; art education; art history; biology; business administration; clinical laboratory sciences; computer science; counselor education; crafts; creative writing; curriculum/instruction; dentistry; design; economics; English; genetic counseling; gerontology; health administration; history; interdisciplinary studies (including environmental studies); mathematical sciences; music; nurse anesthesia; occupational therapy (postprofessional, professional); painting/printmaking; physical education; physical therapy (advanced master's); physics; public health; reading; recreation, parks, and tourism; rehabilitation counseling; sculpture; social work; sociology; special education; taxation; teaching; theater; and urban and regional planning. The University also offers first professional degrees in medicine, dentistry, and pharmacy.

Research Facilities

VCU libraries provide a combined capacity of more than 1.5 million volumes and almost 10,000 periodical titles and an online bibliographic search service accessing hundreds of databases. In addition, the Virginia State and Richmond Public libraries are within walking distance of both VCU campuses. Academic Computing provides a variety of microcomputer, minicomputer, and mainframe computing services to support the research and instructional endeavors of its faculty and students, including consultation, instruction, and computer acquisition. Other research facilities operated by VCU include the Anderson Art Gallery Conservation Laboratory, Burn Trauma Clinic, Virginia Institute for Developmental Disabilities, Massey Cancer Center, Pharmacokinetics Laboratory, School of the Arts Library and Slide Collections, Sickle Cell Anemia Clinic, Survey Research Laboratory, Virginia Center on Aging, Virginia Biotechnology Research Park, and the Virginia Real Estate Research Center. VCU is a member of the Oak Ridge Associated Universities and is fully accredited by the Southern Association of Colleges and Schools.

Financial Aid

A number of departmental and University stipends and tuition awards are available. Students also may apply for need-based assistance with the University's Financial Aid Office. Part-time employment is often available.

Cost of Study

For full-time study in 2001–02, Virginia residents paid tuition and fees of $2627 per semester; nonresidents, $6663.50 per semester. For part-time study, Virginia residents paid tuition and fees of $270.65 per hour; nonresidents, $719.65 per hour. Some programs require additional fees.

Living and Housing Costs

Limited graduate student housing is available on campus. Off-campus housing is readily available in nearby residential areas.

Student Group

VCU enrolls 25,000 students, 6,300 of whom are graduate students. More than 175 student clubs and organizations reflect the diverse social, recreational, educational, political, and religious interests of the student body.

Location

Richmond is Virginia's capital and a major East Coast financial and manufacturing center that offers students a wide range of cultural, educational, and recreational activities. Richmond is only a 2-hour drive from the Atlantic seashore to the east, the Appalachian Mountains recreational sites to the west, and Washington, D.C., to the north.

The University

VCU is a state-supported coeducational university with a graduate school, a major teaching hospital, and ten academic and professional units that offer fifty undergraduate, twelve postbaccalaureate certificate, fifty-nine master's, six post-master's certificate, and twenty-three Ph.D. programs. VCU also offers M.D., D.D.S., and Pharm.D. programs as well as cooperative degree programs with other major Virginia colleges and universities. VCU has one of the largest evening colleges in the United States. The academic campus is located in Richmond's historic Fan District. The health sciences campus and hospital are located 2 miles east in the downtown business district. A University bus service provides intercampus transportation for faculty members and students.

VCU's level of funded research places it among the top 100 colleges and universities in the country in attracting research grants, receiving in fiscal 2000 more than $124 million in sponsored support from a variety of federal agencies, industries, and private organizations. VCU's faculty, representing the finest American and international graduate institutions, enhances the University's position among the important institutions of higher learning in the United States via work in the classroom, the laboratories, and the hospital and research published in scholarly journals.

Applying

Admission procedures and program requirements are detailed in the *Graduate Bulletin* and the *Graduate Application Prospectus,* which are available online at the Web site listed below. A paper copy of the *Bulletin* may be ordered by calling 877-574-0529 (toll-free). The *Graduate Application Prospectus* also may be obtained from the graduate school at the address below. Virginia Commonwealth University is an equal opportunity/affirmative action institution providing access to education and employment without regard to age, race, color, national origin, gender, religion, sexual orientation, veteran's status, political affiliation, or disability.

Correspondence and Information

School of Graduate Studies
Virginia Commonwealth University
P.O. Box 843051
Richmond, Virginia 23284-3051
Telephone: 804-828-6916
Fax: 804-828-6949
E-mail: vcu-grad@vcu.edu
World Wide Web: http://www.vcu.edu/gradweb

FACULTY HEADS

Dr. Albert T. Sneden, Interim Graduate Dean.
Dr. Sherry T. Sandkam, Associate Dean, Graduate Studies.

DEANS

Center for Environmental Studies: Dr. Gregory C. Garman.
Center for Public Policy: Dr. Robert D. Holsworth.
College of Humanities and Sciences: Dr. Stephen D. Gottfredson.
School of Allied Health Professions: Dr. Cecil B. Drain.
School of the Arts: Dr. Richard Toscan.
School of Business: Dr. Michael Sesnowicz.
School of Dentistry: Dr. Ronald J. Hunt.
School of Education: Dr. Richard J. Rezba.
School of Engineering: Dr. Robert J. Mattauch.
School of Medicine: Dr. Herber H. Newsome Jr.
School of Nursing: Dr. Nancy F. Langston.
School of Pharmacy: Dr. Victor A. Yanchick.
School of Social Work: Dr. Frank R. Baskind.

GRADUATE PROGRAM DIRECTORS

For the telephone numbers listed below, the area code is 804.

Center for Environmental Studies
Environmental Sciences: Dr. Gregory C. Garman, 828-7202.

Center for Public Policy
Public Policy and Administration, Ph.D.: Dr. Melvin I. Urofsky, 828-6837.

College of Humanities and Sciences
Adcenter: Patricia Alvey, 800-311-3341 (toll-free).
Biology: Dr. Donald R. Young, 828-1562.
Chemistry: Dr. Suzanne M. Ruder, 828-7519.
Creative Writing: Dr. Greg Donovan, 828-1329.
Criminal Justice: Dr. James L. Hague, 828-1050.
English: Dr. Catherine Ingrassia, 828-1331.
History: Dr. Joseph W. Bendersky, 828-1635.
Mass Communications: Dr. Clarence W. Thomas, 828-2660.
Mathematical Sciences: Dr. James A. Wood, 828-1301.
Physics: Dr. Alison A. Baski, 828-1818.
Psychology, Biopsychology: Dr. Joseph H. Porter, 828-1193.
Psychology, Clinical: Dr. Donald J. Kiesler, 828-1158.
Psychology, Counseling: Dr. Everett L. Worthington, 828-2975.
Psychology, Developmental: Dr. Barbara J. Myers, 828-1193.
Psychology, Social: Dr. Donelson R. Forsyth, 828-1193.
Public Administration, Master's: Dr. Janet R. Hutchinson, 828-8041.
Sociology: Dr. Nita L. Bryant, 828-6973.
Urban Studies and Planning: Dr. John J. Accordino, 828-2489.

School of Allied Health Professions
Clinical Laboratory Sciences: Ms. Barbara J. Lindsey, 828-9469.
Gerontology: Dr. Iris A. Parham, 828-1565.
Health Administration: Dr. Kenneth R. White, 828-9466.
Health Related Sciences: Ms. Monica White, 828-7247.
Health Services Organization and Research: Dr. Michael McCue, 828-1893.
Nurse Anesthesia: Dr. Michael D. Fallacaro, 828-9808.
Occupational Therapy: Dr. Janet Watts, 828-2219.
Patient Counseling: Dr. Alexander F. Tartaglia, 828-0540.
Physical Therapy: Dr. Robert L. Lamb, 828-0234.
Rehabilitation Counseling: Dr. Christine A. Reid, 828-1132.

School of the Arts
Art History, Crafts, Interior Environments, Music, Painting and Printmaking, Photography and Film, Sculpture, Theater and Visual Communication: Mr. Joseph H. Seipel, 828-2787.

School of Business
Accountancy, Business Administration (Master's), Decision Sciences, Economics, Finance, Financial Economics, Human Resources Management, Information Systems, Marketing, Real Estate Valuation, Risk Management, Taxation: Ms. Tracy S. Green, 828-1741.
Fast Track M.B.A.: Dr. William J. Miller, 828-3939.

School of Education
Administration/Supervision; Curriculum/Instruction; Physical Education; Recreation, Parks, and Tourism; Special Education; Teaching; Urban Services: Dr. Michael D. Davis, 828-6530.

School of Engineering
Biomedical Engineering: Dr. Gerald E. Miller, 828-7956.
Cooperative Engineering: Dr. Gerald E. Miller, 828-7956.
Computer Science: Dr. David Primeaux, 828-3068.
Engineering, M.S., Ph.D.: Dr. L. Thomas Overby, 828-3925.

School of Graduate Studies
Interdisciplinary Studies: Dr. Sherry T. Sandkam, 828-6916.

School of Medicine
Anatomy: Dr. George R. Leichnetz, 828-9512.
Biochemistry and Molecular Biophysics: Dr. Keith Shelton, 828-9762.
Biostatistics: Dr. Ronald K. Elswick, 828-9824.
Human Genetics: Dr. Linda A. Corey, 828-9632.
Microbiology and Immunology: Dr. Guy Cabral, 828-9728.
Microbiology, Molecular Biology, and Genetics: Dr. Gail E. Christie, 828-9093.
Medicine, M.D./Ph.D.: Dr. Earl Ellis, 828-7600.
Neuroscience: Dr. Les Satin, 828-7823.
Pathology: Dr. Alphonse Poklis, 828-0272.
Pharmacology and Toxicology: Dr. John J. Woodward, 828-8400.
Physiology and Biophysics: Dr. George D. Ford, 828-9501.
Public Health: Dr. Tilahun Adera, 828-9785.

School of Nursing
Nursing (Certificate, Master's, and Ph.D.): Dr. Inez Tuck, 828-5171.

School of Pharmacy
Medicinal Chemistry: Dr. Unesh R. Desai, 828-8486.
Pharmaceutics: Dr. Mohamadi Sarkar, 828-6321.
Pharmacy Administration: Dr. Ronald E. Polk, 828-8317.

School of Social Work
Social Work (Certificate, M.S.W., and Ph.D.): Dr. Ann Nichols-Casebolt, 828-0703.
Social Work (Ph.D.): Dr. Kia J. Bentley, 828-0453.

WAKE FOREST UNIVERSITY

Graduate School of Arts and Sciences

Programs of Study

The Graduate School of Arts and Sciences offers courses of study leading to the M.A., M.A.Ed., M.A.L.S., M.S., M.S.A., and Ph.D. degrees. Master's degrees may be earned in accountancy, biology, chemistry, clinical epidemiology and health services research, communication, comparative medicine, computer science, education, English, health and exercise science, liberal studies, mathematics, molecular medicine, physics, psychology, and religion. The Department of Education offers master's programs in teacher education and counselor education. Secondary teacher education programs are available for experienced teachers and for students whose non-education Bachelor's degree is in the content areas of English, French, math, science, social studies, or Spanish. In conjunction with the School of Pastoral Care of North Carolina Baptist Hospital, the Department of Religion offers the pastoral counseling program.

There are Ph.D. programs in biochemistry, biology, cancer biology, chemistry, medical engineering, microbiology and immunology, molecular and cellular pathobiology, molecular genetics, molecular medicine, neurobiology and anatomy, neuroscience, pharmacology, physics, and physiology. Combined M.D./Ph.D. and Ph.D./M.B.A. programs are also offered.

Residence requirements vary, but a master's program can generally be completed in two years and a Ph.D. program in approximately five years. Foreign language and special skill requirements vary with each program. Departmental programs are tailored to the individual. The Graduate School's educational philosophy encourages students to pursue an area of specialization in depth and to broaden their training while filling in any gaps in their earlier education. A Ph.D. scholar should be able to carry out teaching and research independently and competently. Various special programs of an interdisciplinary or tutorial nature enhance students' opportunities to develop their full potential.

Research Facilities

The Graduate School of Arts and Sciences conducts its programs on two campuses, the Reynolda Campus and the Bowman Gray Campus. Both campuses have excellent library resources open to all students. Each department has the facilities and equipment needed for its research programs.

Financial Aid

Financial support is available to qualified students. On the Bowman Gray campus, scholarships ($22,500 in 2002–03) and fellowships ($41,000) are awarded annually in the biomedical sciences. On the Reynolda Campus, scholarships ($22,200), fellowships ($26,200), and assistantships ($28,200–$39,700) are awarded annually in the arts and sciences. In addition, a number of miscellaneous grants are available each year to students on both campuses.

Cost of Study

In 2002–03, tuition is $22,200 (Reynolda Campus) or $22,500 (Bowman Gray Campus) per year for full-time students. Part-time students on both campuses register at $775 per semester hour. There is also a graduation fee.

Living and Housing Costs

Room and board costs depend upon the choice of accommodations. Apartments for married students and private off-campus housing units are available.

Student Group

Wake Forest University attracts superior students, largely from states east of the Mississippi. In 2001–02, undergraduate enrollment was 3,987, and graduate and professional enrollment was 2,373. International students and members of minority groups constitute a portion of the student body and teaching staff.

Location

Wake Forest University is located in the city of Winston-Salem, in the Piedmont section of North Carolina, about 75 miles from the Blue Ridge Mountains and 225 miles from the beaches of the Atlantic Ocean. The city's early Moravian heritage is reflected in its many cultural programs and community activities. Tanglewood Park, with its championship golf courses and recreational facilities, is nearby. Technology, health services, tobacco, textiles, transportation, and banking are the main business activities of Winston-Salem. Within 100 miles are the universities and research institutions associated with the Research Triangle.

The University

Wake Forest University is coeducational and has a strong academic orientation. It was founded in 1834 in Wake County, North Carolina. The School of Law was established in 1894, the School of Medicine in 1902, the Graduate School of Arts and Sciences in 1961, the Babcock Graduate School of Management in 1969, the School of Business and Accountancy in 1980 (in 1995, the name was changed to the Wayne Calloway School of Business and Accountancy), and the School of Divinity in 1999. In 1941, the School of Medicine moved to Winston-Salem, where it became affiliated with North Carolina Baptist Hospital and was renamed the Bowman Gray School of Medicine of Wake Forest College. In 1997, the name was changed to Wake Forest University School of Medicine. The remaining divisions of the institution moved to Winston-Salem in 1956, following acceptance of a Z. Smith Reynolds Foundation proposal to build a new campus under substantial continuing endowment. In 1967, the college's augmented character was recognized by the change in name to Wake Forest University. The University prides itself on its strong arts and sciences and basic medical sciences programs, all of which emphasize close student-professor interaction.

Applying

Applications for admission should be directed to the dean of the Graduate School at the Reynolda Campus or to the dean of the Graduate School at the Bowman Gray Campus. There is a $25 application fee. Completed applications should be in by February 1. The Master Teacher Fellows Program begins with the first summer session. Scores on the Graduate Record Examinations are required. Scores on the Graduate Management Admission Test are required for the accountancy program. International applicants whose native language is not English must submit their scores on the Test of English as a Foreign Language. Further details are available in the Graduate School bulletin and on the Web site.

Correspondence and Information

Dean of the Graduate School
Wake Forest University
P.O. Box 7487 Reynolda Station
Winston-Salem, North Carolina 27109-7487
Telephone: 336-758-5301
800-257-3166 (toll-free)
Fax: 336-758-4230
E-mail: gradschl@wfu.edu
World Wide Web: http://www.wfu.edu/graduate

Dean of the Graduate School
Biomedical Sciences
Bowman Gray Campus
Wake Forest University
Medical Center Boulevard
Winston-Salem, North Carolina 27157-1001
Telephone: 336-716-4303
800-438-4723 (toll-free)
Fax: 336-716-0185
E-mail: bggrad@wfubmc.edu
World Wide Web: http://www.wfu.edu/graduate

DEPARTMENTAL CHAIRS AND PROGRAM DIRECTORS

The graduate faculty of Wake Forest University consists of 448 members, all of whom hold earned academic or medical doctorates. Departmental chairs and program directors, who may be addressed concerning graduate study, are listed below. The administrative officials of the Graduate School are Thomas K. Hearn Jr., President; William B. Applegate, Senior Vice President for Health Affairs; William C. Gordon, Provost; Gordon A. Melson, Dean of the Graduate School; and Cecilia H. Solano, Associate Dean of the Graduate School.

Accountancy: Terry Baker, Ph.D., Kentucky.
Biochemistry (Bowman Gray Campus): William H. Gmeiner, Ph.D., Utah.
Biology: Herman E. Eure, Ph.D., Wake Forest.
Cancer Biology (Bowman Gray Campus): Frank Torti, M.D., Harvard.
Chemistry: Bradley T. Jones, Ph.D., Florida.
Clinical Epidemiology and Health Services Research (Bowman Gray Campus): Michelle J. Naughton, Ph.D., Iowa; Ronny A. Bell, Ph.D., North Carolina at Chapel Hill.
Communication: Randall G. Rogan, Ph.D., Michigan State.
Comparative Medicine (Bowman Gray Campus): Richard W. St. Clair, Ph.D., Colorado State.
Computer Science: Jennifer J. Burg, Ph.D., Central Florida.
Education: Joseph O. Milner, Ph.D., North Carolina.
English: Gale Sigal, Ph.D., CUNY Graduate Center.
Health and Exercise Science: Paul M. Ribisl, Ph.D., Illinois.
Liberal Studies: Cecilia H. Solano, Ph.D., Johns Hopkins.
Mathematics: Richard D. Carmichael, Ph.D., Duke.
M.D./Ph.D.: David A. Bass, Ph.D., Oxford, M.D., Johns Hopkins.
Medical Engineering: Peter Santago II, Ph.D., North Carolina State.
Microbiology and Immunology (Bowman Gray Campus): Steven Mizel, Ph.D., Stanford.
Molecular and Cellular Pathobiology (Bowman Gray Campus): John S. Parks, Ph.D., Wake Forest.
Molecular Genetics (Bowman Gray Campus): Mark Lively, Ph.D., Georgia Tech.
Molecular Medicine (Bowman Gray Campus): R. Mark Payne, M.D., Texas (Houston).
Neurobiology and Anatomy (Bowman Gray Campus): Barry E. Stein, Ph.D., CUNY Graduate Center.
Neuroscience (Bowman Gray Campus): Ronald W. Oppenheim, Ph.D., Washington (St. Louis).
Ph.D./M.B.A.: Dr. Dwayne Godwin, Ph.D., West Florida.
Physics: G. Eric Matthews, Ph.D., North Carolina at Chapel Hill.
Physiology and Pharmacology (Bowman Gray Campus): James E. Smith, Ph.D., Minnesota.
Psychology: Deborah L. Best, Ph.D., North Carolina.
Religion: Charles A. Kimball, Th.D., Harvard.

WALDEN UNIVERSITY

Graduate Studies

Programs of Study

Walden University offers graduate degrees for the busy professional through leading-edge distance delivery. Walden students pursue advanced education that helps them attain their professional goals while maintaining important careers. Walden University offers doctoral degrees in education, psychology, health services, human services, management, and public policy. Master's degrees include a Master of Science in Education (M.S.Ed.), a Master of Science in Public Health (M.S.P.H.), a Master of Science (M.S.) in professional psychology, a Master of Business Administration (M.B.A.), and a Master of Public Administration (M.P.A.). Walden University is accredited by the North Central Association of Colleges and Schools.

The time required to complete graduate study depends upon the personal circumstances and capabilities of each learner. Walden requires continued enrollment, but the great flexibility of distance education is the hallmark of Walden programs. Students access courses and academic materials and interact with faculty members and fellow students at their convenience via the Internet. Residencies are held throughout the academic year in various areas around the country, as required by each program. Doctoral students usually complete their degree in three years; a master's degree can be earned in eighteen to twenty-four months.

Walden's graduate students demonstrate competency by completing either traditional course-based curricula or individualized curricula developed under the mentorship of faculty members. As a companion to Walden's distance education under faculty advisement, students partake in residencies, workshops, seminars, and study groups as required by the individual program. Doctoral students prepare and defend a dissertation.

Research Facilities

Besides helping students access library resources at their home sites, Walden University maintains a collaborative relationship with the Indiana University Bloomington (IUB) Graduate Library. Through full year-round access and borrowing privileges at the IUB library and its seventy satellite libraries and through Walden's own resources, Walden students have access to 4 million books, manuscripts, electronic databases, and other publications. Interlibrary loan privileges allow materials to be forwarded directly to Walden students. They have direct access via telephone, fax, and the Internet to the Walden library staff members on-site at the IUB library. During the Summer Session, the library staff members assist Walden students through orientation, workshops, and training in developing research techniques and locating library resources.

Financial Aid

Walden University offers financial assistance in the form of low-interest federally guaranteed and private sector loans and extended payment plans. The financial aid office assists students in securing tuition benefits from employers and other agencies. Several competitive fellowships providing partial tuition are available.

The U.S. Department of Education has certified Walden University as being eligible to participate in the Federal Family Educational Loan Programs (formerly Guaranteed Student Loan Programs) under the Higher Education Act of 1965, as amended. Eligible students may apply for the Federal Stafford Loan, the Federal Unsubsidized Loan, and Veterans Administration Benefits.

Cost of Study

For the current academic year, the tuition for Walden programs is as follows: Ph.D. in education, health and human services, human services, management, and public policy and administration is $3355 per quarter; Ph.D. in psychology is $320 per credit hour; Master of Business Administration is $380 per credit hour; M.S. in education is $240 per credit hour or $250 per semester credit hour; M.S. in psychology is $320 per credit hour; Master of Public Administration is $310 per credit hour; and M.S. in public health is $310 per credit hour. For additional residency, materials, and other fees that apply to each program, students should visit the Web site (listed below).

Living and Housing Costs

Walden doctoral students should anticipate travel and room and board expenses for the dispersed academic residencies and the Summer Session.

Student Group

Walden students are generally midcareer professionals; average age is 44. Women and minorities together comprise more than half of Walden's student population of 2,082.

Location

Walden's academic administrative offices are located in Minneapolis, Minnesota, and its administrative and finance office is in Bonita Springs, Florida. Walden's students are primarily from the United States and Canada. Residency requirements for doctoral students at Walden are met by attendance at Regional Sessions held in professional conference and instructional centers throughout the country, an annual Summer Session in Bloomington, Indiana, or other specifically tailored residency opportunities.

The University

Founded in 1970, Walden University was conceived as and remains an institution dedicated to providing the established professional the opportunity to complete a challenging, accredited degree without sacrificing family and career commitments. Social betterment is important to Walden's philosophy, as is helping the mature student in understanding change within his or her chosen field. Program formats emphasize self-paced learning and program flexibility, which allow learners to create professionally relevant approaches to their graduate studies.

Applying

Walden University accepts students on a rolling admissions basis, depending on the program. Education (M.S.) and all professional psychology students matriculate quarterly. Applicants submit an application form and a nonrefundable fee ($50), official transcripts from previous degree programs, a resume, a goal statement (at least four pages), and two letters of recommendation.

Correspondence and Information

For further information:
Office of Academic Affairs
Walden University
155 Fifth Avenue South
Minneapolis, Minnesota 55401
Telephone: 612-338-7224
800-WALDENU (toll-free)
Fax: 612-338-5092
World Wide Web: http://www.waldenu.edu

For inquiries regarding admissions:
Office of Admissions
Walden University
24311 Walden Center Drive
Bonita Springs, Florida 34134
Telephone: 941-498-4700
800-444-6795 (toll-free)
Fax: 941-498-4266
E-mail: info@waldenu.edu

THE ADMINISTRATION AND FACULTY

Robert Scales, CEO/President; Ph.D., Duke.
Paula Peinovich, Vice President and Provost; Ph.D., Pennsylvania.

Management
Aqueil Ahmad, Ph.D., Aligarh (India). Michael S. Alexander, Ph.D., Minnesota. Constantine O. Alfred-Ockiya, Ph.D., Colorado School of Mines. Jonathan Anderson, Ph.D., Indiana Bloomington. Marion Angelica, Ph.D., Union (Ohio). Robert T. Aubey, Ph.D., UCLA. Joseph E. Barbeau, Ed.D., Boston University. Susan Baxter, M.S., Mankato State, M.R.P., Cornell. Larry Beebe, Ph.D., Nova Southeastern. Vicky K. Black, Ph.D., Ohio State. James Bowman, Ph.D., Nebraska–Lincoln. William H. Brent, D.B.A., Nova. James T. Brown, Ph.D., Union (Ohio). Harry S. Coblentz, M.R.P., North Carolina. Delroy Cornick, M.P.A., USC, M.A., American. Mary Lou Egan, Ph.D., George Washington. David Ford, Ph.D., Wisconsin–Madison. Gary Gemmill, Ph.D., Michigan State. James B. Goes, Ph.D., Oregon. Reza Hamzaee, Ph.D., Arizona State. Elizabeth Hirst, Ed.D., Tennessee. Arlene Hiss, Ph.D., US International. Lilburn P. Hoehn, Ph.D., Michigan State. Roger R. Israel, D.P.A., USC. David L. Johnson, M.M.J.L., Northwestern. Earl C. Joseph, B.A., Minnesota. Christopher J. Kalangi, Ph.D., Ohio State. Robert A. Kilmer, Ph.D., Pittsburgh. Marvel Lang, Ph.D., Michigan State. Lee W. Lee, Ph.D., SUNY at Buffalo. George Lermer, Ph.D., McGill. Barbara Libby, Ph.D., SUNY at Buffalo. Ruth Maurer, Ph.D., Colorado School of Mines. Abraham Meilich, Ph.D., Walden. Joseph Mitchell, J.D., Woodrow Wilson College of Law, Ph.D., George Washington. Charles Nichols, Ph.D., Union (Ohio). Robert O'Reilly, Ed.D., Kansas. John Parnell, Ed.D., Campbell, Ph.D., Memphis. George Priovolos, Ph.D., CUNY, Baruch. Robin Schaller, Ph.D., Minnesota. Thomas Spencer, Ph.D., Stevens. James Stahley, Ph.D., Walden. Claire Starry, Ph.D., Washington (Seattle). William D. Steeves Jr., Ed.D., George Washington. Marcia B. Steinhauer, Ph.D., Florida. Duane Tway, Ph.D., Texas. John C. Vinton, Ph.D., Case Western Reserve. Gwendoline A. Williams, Ph.D., Warwick (England). Ron Wood, M.A., SUNY Empire State College. Lyle Wray, Ph.D., Manitoba.

Education
Caroline L. Bassett, Ph.D., Iowa. William Bender, Ed.D., East Carolina, Ph.D., North Carolina. James E. Boddie, Ed.D., Kansas. Rosemary Bolig, Ph.D., Ohio State. Richard Brown, Ph.D., Florida State. Darragh Callahan, Ed.D., Boston University. Carolyn Calloway-Thomas, Ph.D., Indiana. Anthony Chan, Ph.D., York (England). Jesse Chou, Ed.D., Columbia. Philip Corkill, Ed.D., Northern Illinois. Linda M. Crawford, Ph.D., Minnesota. Xu Di, Ed.D., Harvard. Frank DiSilvestro, Ed.D., Indiana. Angela Wei Djao, Ph.D., Toronto. Bernice Folz, Ph.D., Minnesota. Peggy E. Gaskill, Ph.D., Michigan. Dale Good, Ed.D., Illinois at Urbana-Champaign. John R. Goss III, Ph.D., American. Carol G. Harding, Ph.D., Delaware. Sunil Hazari, Ed.D., West Virginia. Gwen Hillesheim, Ed.D., St. Thomas. Claire E. Hughes, Ph.D., William and Mary. Estelle Jorgensen, Ph.D., Calgary. Robert Kefferstan, Ed.D., West Virginia. Catherine Marienau, Ph.D., Minnesota. Elisamuel Martinez-Antonetty, Ed.D., Penn State. James McGettigan, Ph.D., Columbia. Henry S. Merrill, Ed.D., Ball State. Sigrin Newell, Ph.D., SUNY at Albany. Brian Noonan, Ph.D., Ottawa. Barry Persky, Ph.D., NYU. Marianne R. Phelps, Ph.D., George Washington. Brent Poppenhagen, Ph.D., Wisconsin–Madison. Stephen V. Powers, Ph.D., Arizona. José A. Quiles, Ph.D., NYU. Dennis Rislove, Ph.D., Wisconsin–Madison. Art Safer, Ph.D., Northwestern. Larry R. Selin, Ph.D., Minnesota. Rex Shahriari, Ed.D., Ball State. Marilyn K. Simon, Ph.D., Walden. David S. Stein, Ph.D., Michigan. Kathleen Taylor, Ph.D., Union (Ohio). Charmaine Villet, Ph.D., Ohio. David Whitfield, Ed.D., San Francisco. Iris M. Yob, Ed.D., Harvard.

Health
Marion Anema, Ph.D., Iowa. Carol Bauer, Ed.D., Rutgers. Anna Brock, Ph.D., Maryland. Carolyn Chambers Clark, Ed.D., Columbia. Jeanne L. Connors, Ph.D., Wisconsin–Madison. Sybil Delevan, Ph.D., SUNY at Binghamton. Daniel Girdano, Ph.D., Toledo. James B. Goes, Ph.D., Oregon. Talmage M. Holmes, Ph.D., Texas. Robert E. Hoye, Ph.D., Wisconsin–Madison. Ronald P. Hudak, J.D., Ph.D., George Washington. Samuel C. Morris, Sc.D., Pittsburgh. Evelyn Ortiz-Cruz, Ed.D., Puerto Rico. Clarence J. Schumaker Jr., Ph.D., Catholic University. Manoj Sharma, Ph.D., Ohio State. David S. Stein, Ph.D., Michigan. Raymond W. Thron, Ph.D., Minnesota. Morton Wagenfeld, Ph.D., Syracuse. William H. Wiist, D.H.Sc., Loma Linda.

Human Services
George Ayers, D.S.W., Tulane. William M. Barkley, Ph.D., Purdue. Raphael Becvar, Ph.D., Minnesota. Keith Bryett, Ph.D., Aberdeen (Scotland). Marie A. Caputi, Ph.D., Saint Louis. Donald Fausel, D.S.W., Columbia. A. Lina Giusti, Ph.D., Florida State. Monica Gordon, Ph.D., CUNY Graduate Center. Michael Graham, Ph.D., Ohio State. James L. Greenstone, Ed.D., North Texas. Sylvia Y. Kaneko, Ph.D., Smith. Barbara Knudson, Ph.D., Minnesota. Bruce Lackie, Ph.D., Rutgers. Harold Pepinsky, J.D., Harvard, Ph.D., Pennsylvania. Richard Percy, Ed.D., Virginia. Michael Reiter, Ph.D., Nova Southeastern. Elaine C. Spaulding, Ph.D., Smith. Joel H. Straussner, Ph.D., Yeshiva. Morton I. Teicher, Ph.D., Toronto. Charles Webel, Ph.D., Berkeley.

Psychology
Augustine Barón, Psy.D., Illinois at Urbana-Champaign. David Harold Bauer, Ph.D., Penn State. Eugene I. Bender, Ed.D., Jewish Theological Seminary. Scott Edward Borrelli, Ed.D., Boston University. Wayne Briner, Ph.D., Northern Illinois. Gary Burkholder, Ph.D., Rhode Island. James L. Carroll, Ed.D., Rutgers. Noor M. Damavandi, Ph.D., California School of Professional Psychology–Los Angeles. Denise M. DeZolt, Ph.D., Kent State. Loren Faibisch, Ed.D., Harvard. Patricia A. Farrell, Ph.D., NYU. John T. Flynn, Ed.D., Indiana. Frank Fox, Ph.D., Wisconsin–Madison. Gerald B. Fuller, Ph.D., Ottawa. Martin Gerstein, Ed.D., USC. Hilda Ruth Glazer, Ed.D., Rutgers. Marsha Hammond, Ph.D., North Texas. Garvey House, Ph.D., East Texas State. Robert D. Hunter, Ph.D., Saybrook Institute. Catherine E. James, Ph.D., Walden. Clarence Johnson, Ph.D., US International. Elizabeth Kincade, Ph.D., Penn State. Raymond Klein, Ed.D., SUNY at Buffalo. V. Wayne Leaver, D.Min., Wesley Theological Seminary, Ph.D., Union (Ohio). Maureen J. Levine, Ph.D., Michigan State. Stephen T. Lifrak, Ph.D., Rhode Island. Barry Linden, Ph.D., Wyoming. Robert J. Lovinger, Ph.D., NYU. Sophie L. Lovinger, Ph.D., NYU. Mindy Machanic, Ph.D., Union (Ohio). Brent L. Maguire, Ph.D., Saybrook Institute. Sandra D. Mahoney, Ph.D., Texas Tech. Marcia Moody, Ph.D., Wisconsin–Madison. Nina Nabors, Ph.D., Florida. Rita Posner, Ph.D., Seton Hall. Michael Raphael, Ph.D., Akron. Sandra Rasmussen, Ph.D., Harvard. John Schmidt, Ph.D., Houston. Scott W. Sumerall, Ph.D., North Dakota. Margaret Bly Turner, Ph.D., Oklahoma State. Richard W. Waite, Ph.D., Michigan. William L. Wilson, Ph.D., Rhode Island. Susan M. Zgliczynski, Ph.D., Texas A&M.

WASHINGTON STATE UNIVERSITY SPOKANE

Graduate Studies

Programs of Study

Graduate programs at Washington State University (WSU) Spokane take advantage of the campus's urban setting and land-grant mission to offer students opportunities for hands-on outcome-oriented research and engagement with the community through service, applying scholarly theory to solve real-world problems. Interdisciplinary approaches are emphasized, and students work with faculty members who are highly productive in generating grants and contracts to support research. Health sciences programs are the Master of Health Policy and Administration (accredited by ACEHSA; admitted to WICHE WRGP, which enables residents in fourteen western states, excluding California, to attend at Washington-resident tuition rates; innovative focus on community health), the M.A. in speech and hearing sciences (ASHA/CAA accredited, highly ranked by *U.S. News & World Report*), the M.S. in human nutrition, the Doctor of Pharmacy (completion of WSU Pullman program or external Doctor of Pharmacy for practicing pharmacists; ranked twenty-seventh in nation), a Graduate Certificate in aging, Registered Dietitian studies, and an M.S. in kinesiology (exercise science; focus on clinical and experimental exercise physiology). Design disciplines programs are an M.S. in architecture (including executive track and design-build management executive track), an M.A. in interior design, an M.S. in landscape architecture, and a doctoral program in interdisciplinary design, which is under development. Design is taught in the context of the Interdisciplinary Design Institute, where students and faculty members collaborate and learn together to reinforce individual disciplinary knowledge and skills, while developing additional interdisciplinary depth of understanding. Business programs are the Master of Technology Management (general business degree with special focus on the integration of strategy and technology for continuous innovation in organizations). Engineering programs are the Master of Engineering Management (designed to make practicing engineers more effective in and ultimately able to manage the business environment in technical organizations), the M.S. in electrical engineering, and the M.S. in computer science course work. Education programs are field-based principal's and superintendent's certification (course work may be applied toward the WSU Ed.D.), school psychology certification, and Master in Teaching course work (K–8 Washington certification). In criminal justice, an M.A. in criminal justice is offered (WSU Spokane is home to nationally recognized institutes focused on community-oriented public safety).

Research Facilities

WSU Spokane is a campus of Washington State University, one of the top fifty research universities nationwide as determined by the Carnegie Foundation. Its faculty members are among the most productive in the WSU system, with more than $45 million in grants and contracts generated during the campus's first twelve years to support outcome-oriented research and service. Research/service units include the Health Research and Education Center, Washington Institute for Mental Illness Research and Training, Area Health Education Center, Drug Information Center, WSU/EWU Speech and Hearing Clinic, Western Regional Institute for Community Oriented Public Safety, Washington State Institute for Community Oriented Policing, Interdisciplinary Design Institute, state office of the Small Business Development Center, and faculty members affiliated with WSU's Center for Reproductive Biology, Cancer Prevention and Research Center, and Center for Design of Analog-Digital Integrated Circuits. The Cooperative Academic Library Systems gives students access not only to the campus library, but to library holdings from throughout the WSU system, hospital libraries, and others through online catalogs as well as full-text databases that allow downloading and printing of articles.

Financial Aid

Merit-based financial aid is offered in the form of graduate assistantships and nonresident tuition waivers. Some scholarships are also available. Interested students should contact the appropriate graduate program coordinator for assistantship and scholarship application procedures. Students wishing to apply for financial aid must complete the Free Application for Federal Student Aid (FAFSA) to determine eligibility; processing can take up to six weeks, so students are encouraged to apply early. Information on financial aid and some scholarships is available from Student Services, 509-358-7534, enroll@wsu.edu, or at http://faoservr.finaid.wsu.edu/index.html.

Cost of Study

Estimated full-time in-state tuition and fees for 2002–03 are $5854. Estimated out-of-state tuition and fees are $14,344. A limited number of full or partial nonresident tuition waivers are available to out-of-state and international graduate students with superior academic credentials, and residential tuition rates are available to HPA students from fourteen western states enrolling under WICHE WRGP. Interested students should contact the academic program.

Living and Housing Costs

No University-owned housing is available. The campus is near the heart of downtown Spokane, accessible by public transit, and private apartments and homes are available for rent in the vicinity. More information about housing can be obtained from Student Services, 509-358-7534, enroll@wsu.edu. The cost of living in Spokane is moderate and slightly below the national average.

Student Group

The campus currently enrolls approximately 700 students, which includes transfer students completing baccalaureate programs. In 1999–2000, 58 percent of the students were women. WSU Spokane is committed to recruiting and retaining a student body that reflects the diversity of the state, the nation, and the world.

Location

Spokane enjoys four-season recreation and exceptional natural beauty, with skiing, camping, and dozens of lakes within an easy drive. The Spokane River and the Centennial Trail, a walking/biking path, run past campus and through downtown. The second-largest city in Washington, Spokane is served by an international airport and is home to a symphony orchestra, a wide array of theatrical and cultural offerings, high-quality health care, a strong school system, and diverse community events.

The University

Washington State University, a land-grant institution founded in 1890, serves more than 21,000 students statewide at its four campuses and dozens of learning centers. Six faculty members have been elected to the National Academy of Sciences, and the institution is ranked as a Doctoral/Research University–Extensive by the Carnegie Foundation. WSU Spokane, established in 1989, brings the best of WSU's scholarship to Spokane's "urban laboratory," giving students hands-on opportunities for professional growth and academic excellence. Caring, professional faculty and staff members work with students to make graduate school work for them.

Applying

Applicants may request admissions materials from Student Services, 509-358-7978, enroll@wsu.edu, or apply online at http://gradweb.gradsch.wsu.edu/ (specify Spokane campus). All applicants must submit a completed application form, official transcripts of all undergraduate course work, and a $35 application fee. Applicants should check with specific graduate program coordinators regarding required admission tests and application deadlines.

Correspondence and Information

Joan Menzies
Director of Student Services
Washington State University Spokane
310 North Riverpoint Boulevard
Spokane, Washington 99202

Telephone: 509-358-7978
Fax: 509-358-7505
E-mail: enroll@wsu.edu
World Wide Web: http://www.spokane.wsu.edu

GRADUATE PROGRAM CONTACTS

HEALTH SCIENCES

Graduate Certificate in Aging: Angie Freerksen, 509-358-7616; aging@wsu.edu; http://www.aging.spokane.wsu.edu
Master of Health Policy and Administration: Winsor Schmidt, J.D., LL.M., 509-358-7981, or Kiley Schenk, M.B.A., 509-358-7987; hpa@wsu.edu; http://www.hpa.spokane.wsu.edu
M.S. Human Nutrition: Linda Massey, Ph.D., 509-358-7621; nutrition@wsu.edu; http://www.nutrition.spokane.wsu.edu
Registered Dietitian: Janet Beary, Ph.D., RD, CHES, 509-358-7562; dietitian@wsu.edu; http://www.dietitian.spokane.wsu.edu
M.A. Speech and Hearing Sciences: Charles Madison, Ph.D., 509-358-7588; speech@wsu.edu; http://www.speech-hrg.spokane.wsu.edu
Doctor of Pharmacy: Dana Lohrey, WSU Pullman, 509-335-1402; lohrey@mail.wsu.edu; http://www.phar.wsu.edu/sserv/. For external Pharm.D.: Ginger Vietzke, 509-358-7659; vietzke@wsu.edu; http://depts.washington.edu/expharmd/
Health Research and Education Center: C. Harold Mielke, M.D., Director, 509-358-7632; hrec@wsu.edu; http://www.hrec.spokane.wsu.edu
Washington Institute for Mental Illness Research and Training: Dennis Dyck, Ph.D., Director, 509-358-7618; wimirt@wsu.edu; http://www.wimirt.spokane.wsu.edu

DESIGN DISCIPLINES

Interdisciplinary Design Institute: Forster Ndubisi, Ph.D., MSLA, Director, 509-358-7920; design@wsu.edu; http://www.idi.spokane.wsu.edu
M.S. Architecture, Full-Time and Executive Track Programs: David Wang, Ph.D., AIA, 509-358-7908; msarch@wsu.edu; http://www.msarch.spokane.wsu.edu or http://www.msarchexec.spokane.wsu.edu
M.S. Architecture, Design-Build Executive Track: Darlene Septelka, M.S., 509-358-7910; designbuild@wsu.edu; www.designbuild.spokane.wsu.edu
M.A. Interior Design: Catherine Bicknell, M.S.Des., Des RCA, Hons, 509-358-7944; interior@wsu.edu; http://www.interiordesign.spokane.wsu.edu
M.S. Landscape Architecture: Robert Scarfo, Ph.D., 509-358-7913; landscape@wsu.edu; http://www.msla.spokane.wsu.edu

BUSINESS

Master of Technology Management: Martin Hoegl, Ph.D., 509-358-7769; mtm@wsu.edu; http://www.mtm.spokane.wsu.edu

ENGINEERING

M.S. Computer Science: Margaret Mortz, Ph.D., 509-358-7935; eecs@wsu.edu; http://www.cptrsci.spokane.wsu.edu
M.S. Electrical Engineering: Margaret Mortz, Ph.D., 509-358-7935; eecs@wsu.edu; http://www.msee.spokane.wsu.edu
Master of Engineering Management: Hal Rumsey, Ph.D., PE, 509-358-7936; emgt@wsu.edu; http://www.engmgt.spokane.wsu.edu

CRIMINAL JUSTICE AND PUBLIC SAFETY

M.A. Criminal Justice: David Brody, J.D., Ph.D., 509-358-7952; crimj@wsu.edu; http://www.crimj.spokane.wsu.edu
Western Regional Institute for Community Oriented Public Safety: John Turner, Executive Director, 206-835-7322; wricops@wsu.edu; http://www.wricops.spokane.wsu.edu
Washington State Institute for Community Oriented Policing: Mike Erp, M.A., Director, 509-358-7951; wsicop@wsu.edu; http://www.wsicop.wsu.edu

EDUCATION

Master in Teaching: Lenore Schmidt, Ph.D., 509-358-7546; masterteach@wsu.edu; http://www.mit.spokane.wsu.edu
Field-Based Superintendent's Certification: Dennis Ray, Ed.D., 509-358-7941; edadmin@wsu.edu; http://www.supercert.spokane.wsu.edu
Field-Based Principal's Certification: James Howard, Ed.D., 509-358-7948; edadmin@wsu.edu; http://www.principalcert.spokane.wsu.edu
School Psychology Certification: Student Services, 509-358-7978; schoolpsych@wsu.edu; http://www.schoolpsych.spokane.wsu.edu

The new Health Sciences Building opened in January 2002 and has 144,000 gross square feet of laboratories, clinics, classrooms, and offices.

The Master of Health Policy and Administration ranks as one of the top four health services administration programs in the West.

The Interdisciplinary Design Institute prepares students for real-world professional interaction and hones problem-solving abilities. Here students work on the renovation of office space in a historic building in downtown Spokane that won Best of Show from the International Design Educators Council.

WASHINGTON UNIVERSITY IN ST. LOUIS

Graduate School of Arts and Sciences

Programs of Study

The Graduate School of Arts and Sciences offers thirty-three programs leading to the doctorate (Ph.D.) and thirty leading to the Master of Arts (A.M.). In addition, programs are offered leading to the Master of Arts in Education (M.A.Ed.), Master of Arts in Teaching (M.A.T.), Master of Fine Arts in Writing (M.F.A.W.), Master in Music (M.M.), Master of Liberal Arts (M.L.A.), and Master of Science in Speech and Hearing (M.S.S.H.).

Opportunities for combining a degree available through the Graduate School of Arts and Sciences with a degree from one of the University's professional schools (business, engineering, law, medicine) are also available.

Research Facilities

The Washington University community is served by a network of libraries designed to meet the instructional and research needs of faculty members, students, and staff. Washington University libraries contain the largest collection of any private academic library system between the Mississippi River and California. John M. Olin Library, the central University library, and twelve school and departmental libraries house many important and unique collections and provide state-of-the-art computerized information retrieval. The combined holdings include more than 3 million books and bound periodicals, 18,000 current serial subscriptions, and access to thousands of electronic journals and databases. For more information, students can visit http://library.wustl.edu

More than thirty centers and institutes provide a spectrum of research opportunities. They include Center for Air Pollution Impact and Trend Analysis; Center for the Study of American Business; Center for American Indian Studies; Business, Law, and Economics Center; Arts and Sciences Computing Center; Institutes for Biomedical Computing; McDonnell Center for Cellular and Molecular Neurobiology; Construction Management Center; Carolyne Roehm Electronic Media Center; Center for Engineering Computing; Center for Genetics in Medicine; McDonnell Center for Studies of Higher Brain Function; Center for the History of Freedom; Office of International Studies; International Writers Center; Center for the Study of Islamic Societies and Civilizations; Management Center; Fred Gasche Laboratory for Microstructured Materials Technologies; Markey Center for Research in Molecular Biology of Human Disease; Center for Optimization and Semantic Control; Center for Plant Science and Biotechnology; Center for Political Economy; Center for the Study of Public Affairs; Center for Robotics and Automation; Social Work Research Development Center; McDonnell Center for Space Sciences; Center for the Application of Information Technology; and Urban Research and Design Center.

Financial Aid

The majority of full-time students receive financial support. Financial assistance in the form of scholarships, fellowships, and traineeships is offered annually on a competitive basis through the Graduate School from government, private, or endowed sources. Also available are scholarships, teaching assistantships, research assistantships, and clinical internships in applied social sciences; grants and fellowships in national competition; and loans. Specific information may be obtained from the departmental or administrative unit to which the student intends to apply.

Cost of Study

Tuition for the 2001–02 academic year for the Graduate School was $25,700. The cost per credit unit was $1070.

Living and Housing Costs

Many graduate students live in University-owned apartments, some with data connections and shuttle bus service. Listing information for these units as well as non-University housing is available through the University's Apartment Referral Service (http://rescomp.wustl.edu/~och/). Rent ranges from $450 to $950 per month for one- to three-bedroom units, respectively.

Student Group

Of the 12,088 people attending Washington University, 5,579 are graduate students; 1,383 of those are enrolled in the Graduate School of Arts and Sciences. Students come to Washington University from all fifty states and more than eighty international locations.

Location

Washington University has two campuses that lie at opposite ends of Forest Park (one of the largest municipal parks in the nation). The campuses are approximately 5 miles west of downtown St. Louis. The main, or "hilltop," campus is the location of the Graduate School of Arts and Sciences and all other schools of the University except Medicine. The latter is located on the east, or medical, campus. The Division of Biology and Biomedical Sciences is also located on the medical campus. Free shuttle buses run between the campuses on a regular schedule.

The St. Louis area has nearly 2.4 million residents. The cost of living is affordable. The University's central location provides easy access to the zoo, museums, Science Center, Missouri Botanical Gardens, St. Louis Symphony, Opera Theatre, St. Louis Repertory Theatre, Black Repertory Theatre, Blues hockey, Rams football, and Cardinals baseball. Outdoor adventure beyond the city can be found in the Ozark Mountains and on the rivers of Missouri. Camping, hiking, floating, rock climbing, and spelunking are among the many possibilities within a few hours' drive of St. Louis.

The Graduate School

The Graduate School of Arts and Sciences is a charter member of both the Association of Graduate Schools and the Council of Graduate Schools. The School provides a physical and academic environment in which inquiry, intellectual growth, and discovery can thrive and flourish.

Applying

Prospective students may apply online at the Web address listed below. Application forms for admission and financial aid can also be obtained from either the Graduate School office or individual departments and are due by January 15 (December 15 for the Division of Biology and Biomedical Sciences, February 15 for Speech and Hearing) for entry into the next fall semester. For international students whose native language is not English, most programs require an official copy of a TOEFL or TSE score. Most programs require GRE scores.

Correspondence and Information

Graduate School of Arts and Sciences
Campus Box 1187
Washington University in St. Louis
One Brookings Drive
St. Louis, Missouri 63130-4899
Telephone: 314-935-6880
Fax: 314-935-4887
E-mail: graduateschool@artsci.wustl.edu
World Wide Web: http://www.artsci.wustl.edu/GSAS/

FACULTY HEADS, DEGREES OFFERED, AND DEPARTMENTAL INTERESTS

Anthropology (A.M., Ph.D.): Richard J. Smith (314-935-5252). Archaeology, medical anthropology, physical anthropology, primate studies, sociocultural anthropology, culture and political economy.
Art History and Archaeology (A.M., Ph.D.): William E. Wallace (314-935-5270). Classical archaeology; ancient, Renaissance, Baroque, nineteenth- and twentieth-century European and American, and Asian and Japanese art history.
Asian and Near Eastern Languages and Literatures (A.M., Ph.D.): Beata Grant (314-935-5156). Chinese literature; Japanese literature; Chinese, Japanese, and comparative literature.
Division of Biology and Biomedical Sciences (Ph.D.): Rosemary Garagnani (800-852-9074, toll-free; e-mail: admissions@dbbs.wustl.edu).
Biochemistry: David Cistola. Macromolecular interactions, molecular recognition, cell growth and regulation, signal transduction, protein structure-function, gene expression, enzymology, protein engineering and drug design.
Bioorganic Chemistry: George Gokel. Application of organic synthesis to biological problems in model systems, drug development and imaging.
Computational Biology: Gary Stomo. Computational techniques to address biological and biomedical questions, including bioinformatics, sequence analysis, structural biology, and modeling of complex systems.
Developmental Biology: Ross Cagan. Cell differentiation, developmental gene expression, early embryogenesis, morphogenesis, developmental neurobiology, plant development.
Evolutionary and Population Biology: Jonathan Losos. Population genetics, phylogenetics, ecology, molecular genetics, floristic taxonomy, phytogeography, the structure of tropical forests, molecular evolution.
Immunology: Robert Schreiber. Immune system development; antigen presentation, tolerance, autoimmunity, and immunopathology; cell-cell communication/signaling in immune system; molecular/cellular mechanisms of host defense.
Molecular Biophysics: Kathleen Hall. Structural biology and spectroscopy, macromolecular interactions and molecular recognition, computational biology and drug design: cell regulation and signal transduction.
Molecular Cell Biology: Robert Mercer. Application of biochemical, biophysical, and genetic techniques to the understanding of cellular structure and function at the cellular, tissue, and organismal levels.
Molecular Genetics: Mark Johnston. Human genetics and genomic analysis, developmental genetics, regulation of gene expression, DNA metabolism and molecular evolution, pathogenesis and bacterial and viral genetics.
Molecular Microbiology and Microbial Pathogenesis: William Goldman. Molecular microbiology, microbial physiology and genetics, microbial pathogenesis and host defense, molecular virology.
Neurosciences: Jeanne Nerbonne and Joshua Sanes. Molecular/cellular systems and integrative neuroscience, neuroanatomy; neurophysiology; behavior and perception; computational neuroscience.
Plant Biology: Craig Pikaard. Systematic botany, ethnobotany, genetics, phycology, mycology, ecology, plant physiology, cell biology, developmental biochemistry and virology, molecular biology.
Business Administration (M.S.B.A., Ph.D.): Nicholas Dopuch (314-935-6340). Accounting, business economics, finance, marketing, organizational behavior, operations and manufacturing management, strategy.
Chemistry (A.M., Ph.D.): Joseph Ackerman (800-223-0913). Organic chemistry, bioorganic chemistry, polymer chemistry, physical chemistry, biophysical chemistry, inorganic chemistry, organometallic chemistry, bioinorganic chemistry, nuclear chemistry and radiochemistry, environmental chemistry, materials chemistry.
Classics (A.M.): Robert Lamberton (314-935-5123). Greek and Latin languages and literatures.
Comparative Literature (A.M., Ph.D.): Robert E. Hegel (314-935-5170). Literary theory; comparative study involving two or more literatures in Arabic, Chinese, English, French, German, Greek, Hebrew, Italian, Japanese, Latin, Persian, Russian, and Spanish; comparative study of drama, music, visual arts, and literature.
Earth and Planetary Sciences (A.M., Ph.D.): Raymond E. Arvidson (314-935-5610). Planetary sciences, geodynamics, geochemistry, environmental dynamics, fluid-rock interactions, evolution of the continental crust, seismology, remote sensing.
East Asian Studies (A.M., A.M./J.D., A.M./M.B.A., A.M./M.Arch.): Rebecca Copeland (314-935-4448). East Asian languages, literature, history, religion, and culture; East Asian art history and archaeology; East Asian law, economic development, and political and intellectual history.
Economics (Ph.D.): Steven Fazzari (314-935-5646). Economic history, economic theory, econometrics, industrial organization, monetary economics, political economy, public economics, public finance, labor economics, advanced macroeconomics.
Education (M.A.Ed., M.A.T., Ph.D.): James Wertsch (314-935-6776). Teacher education, preservice and inservice, certification-only programs, literacy, language development, history of education, sociocultural research, cognitive bases of peak performance, action research in educational settings, discourse analysis, critical race theory, gender and education.
English and American Literature (A.M., Ph.D.): David Lawton (314-935-5190). Medieval literature and culture, Renaissance literature, early modern literature, the English novel, modern poetry and fiction, Irish poetry, literature and history, African-American studies, American literature to 1900, gender and cultural studies.
Germanic Languages and Literatures (A.M., Ph.D.): Lynne Tatlock (314-935-5160). Contemporary German literature, German literature prior to 1700, Austrian literature, literature and history, German-European literary relations, gender, literature and culture, literary theory.
History (Ph.D.): Derek Hirst (314-935-5450). British, American, Jewish, modern European intellectual, Latin-American, medical history, and world empire.
Islamic and Near Eastern Studies (A.M.): Fatemeh Keshavarz (314-935-5166). Near Eastern languages and literatures; literary criticism; women in the Muslim world; mysticism; Islamic civilization, cultures, and societies.
Jewish Studies (A.M.): Hillel Kieval (314-935-5461). Jewish history, literature, and religion.
Literature and History (A.M.): Gerald Izenberg (314-935-5445); Steven Zwicker (314-935-4405).
Mathematics (A.M., Ph.D.): Steven Krantz (314-935-8122). Analysis, geometry, topology, algebra, statistics.
Movement Science (Ph.D.): Shirley Sahrmann (314-286-1411). Biocontrol, bioenergetics, and biomechanics of normal and abnormal movement.
Music (M.M., A.M., Ph.D.): Craig Monson (314-935-5553). Musicology (medieval, Renaissance, seventeenth to nineteenth century), jazz studies, theory, composition, vocal studies, fortepiano, piano.
Drama (A.M.): Henry Schvey/Robert Henke (314-935-5858). Dramatic literature, criticism, and theory; modern drama; Renaissance drama; directing; theories of acting and directing; theater and other arts.
Philosophy (A.M., Ph.D.): William Bechtel/J. Claude Evans (314-935-5119). Ethics, social and political philosophy, philosophy of law, history of philosophy, philosophy of science, philosophy of language, philosophy of mind, philosophy of social science, philosophy/neuroscience/psychology.
Philosophy/Neuroscience/Psychology: William Bechtel (314-935-4297). Philosophy of mind and philosophy of science, with a special emphasis on philosophical issues raised by neuroscience, psychology, and computational models.
Physics (A.M., Ph.D.): Clifford M. Will (314-935-6250). Theoretical physics, computational physics, condensed matter/materials physics and ultrasonics, astrophysics, space physics, biophysics.
Political Economy (A.M.): Norman Schofield (314-935-5686). Social choice, international political economy, public policy, game theory.
Political Science (A.M., Ph.D.): Jack Knight/William Lowry (314-935-5810). American politics, comparative politics, formal theory, international political economy, policy, political methodology.
Psychology (Ph.D.): Randy Larson (314-935-8560). Experimental psychology, cognitive psychology, cognitive neuroscience, social and personality psychology, development and aging. Richard Kurtz (314-935-6520). Clinical psychology.
Romance Languages and Literatures (A.M., Ph.D.): Nina Cox Davis (314-935-5175). French literary studies, Spanish literary and cultural studies, optional graduate certificate in second language acquisition.
Social Work (M.S.W., Ph.D.): M.S.W. program: Brian Legate (314-935-6676); Ph.D. program: Lucinda Cobb (314-935-6605). Social welfare policy, community and family issues, health and mental health services, child welfare and youth development, gerontology, race relations, human service organizations, social and economic development.
Speech and Hearing (M.A., M.S., Ph.D.): William Clark (314-977-0240). Education of the hearing impaired, audiology, speech and hearing sciences.
Statistics (A.M.): Edward Wilson (314-935-6760). Mathematical statistics, biostatistics.
The Writing Program (M.F.A.): Carolyn Smith (314-935-7133). Fiction writing, poetry writing.

WEST CHESTER UNIVERSITY OF PENNSYLVANIA

Graduate Studies

Programs of Study

West Chester University of Pennsylvania offers graduate study leading to the M.A., M.B.A., M.Ed., M.M., M.S., M.S.W., M.S.N., and M.S.A. degrees. The Master of Arts is offered in biology, communication studies, communicative disorders, English, French, geography, history, Holocaust and genocide studies, mathematics, music history, philosophy, physical sciences (earth science and chemistry), psychology (general, clinical, and industrial/organizational psychology and group psychotherapy), Spanish, and teaching English as a second language. The Master of Business Administration is awarded in four concentrations: economics/finance, general business administration, management, and technology and electronic commerce. The Master of Education and/or certification is available in elementary and secondary school counseling, elementary education, French, German, history, Latin, reading, school health, secondary education, Spanish, and special education. The Master of Music is offered in music education, music theory or composition, and performance. The Master of Science is offered in chemistry (clinical and general), computer science, criminal justice, educational research, environmental health, higher education counseling, physical education, and public health. The Master of Science in Administration is awarded in eight concentrations: health services, human resource management, leadership for women, long-term care, public administration, sport and athletic administration, training and development, and urban and regional planning. West Chester University also offers the Master of Social Work and the Master of Science in Nursing degrees. Certificate programs are offered in administration, gerontology, computer science, teaching English as a second language, integrated health, Holocaust and genocide studies, leadership for women, and teaching and learning with technology.

Research Facilities

The Francis Harvey Green Library houses more than 500,000 volumes and a micromedia collection of more than 350,000 titles and subscribes to more than 2,800 periodicals. Its services include interlibrary loans, reference advice, computerized online literature searches, and an instructional materials center. The University's state-of-the-art computer facilities include an Ethernet Local Area Network, which connects all 1,400 computer workstations on campus. The LAN provides access to mainframe data, the library's online catalog, the Internet, and e-mail. Each student has an e-mail account and access to the Academic Computing Center 24 hours a day. The University makes Braille printers, translators, and speech synthesizers available to its visually impaired students. The Schmucker Science Center houses a fully equipped observatory and planetarium and extensive, well-equipped laboratories. Boucher Hall has state-of-the-art science labs for electronics, mineral spectroscopy, optics, and liquid crystal studies as well as an animal facility and greenhouse.

Financial Aid

A limited number of graduate assistantships are available on a competitive basis. In 2001–02, each carried an annual stipend of $5000 plus remission of tuition. In addition, some summer assistantships are available. Frederick Douglass Graduate Assistantships are also available. Scholarships and awards are offered by individual departments as well. West Chester University also participates in the Federal Perkins Loan and the Federal Stafford Student Loan programs.

Cost of Study

The basic per-semester tuition for full-time in-state residents taking 9 through 15 credits in 2001–02 was $2300 plus a $384 general fee; part-time and overload students were billed at a per-credit rate of $256 for tuition and a $44 general fee for fewer than 9 credits or for credits beyond 15. Out-of-state students paid $3777 for 9 through 15 credits and the general fee; part-time students were billed at the per-credit rate of $389.

Living and Housing Costs

West Chester University offers limited on-campus housing for single graduate students. Choices include designated quiet and honors dormitories, as well as apartment living in a 4- or 5-person fully furnished unit, with each bedroom having either single or double occupancy. Current costs (subject to change) are $2738 (single) in the residence hall and $1610 (double) or $2042 (single) in the apartments.

A variety of meal plans are available to students and range in cost from $513 to $885 per semester.

The Office of Off Campus and Commuter Services can provide assistance in identifying available off-campus housing. The Office maintains listings and evaluations of apartments and rooms, many within walking distance of the campus.

Student Group

The student body at West Chester University numbers 12,244, of whom 2,024 are graduate students. Graduate students are represented by the Graduate Student Association. The School of Education sponsors an active chapter of Phi Delta Kappa, the international graduate honor society. African-American and Hispanic student unions are active at West Chester. In addition, graduate students are invited to participate in the activities of undergraduate honor societies in which they hold membership. These include Alpha Lambda Delta, Alpha Mu Gamma, Alpha Psi Omega, Gamma Theta Upsilon, Kappa Delta Pi, Pi Gamma Mu, Pi Kappa Delta, Pi Mu Epsilon, Sigma Alpha Iota, Psi Chi, Phi Alpha Theta, Phi Delta Kappa, Phi Epsilon Kappa, Phi Eta Sigma, Phi Kappa Delta, Phi Mu Alpha Sinfonia, and Sigma Delta Pi.

Location

The University is located in West Chester, a community in southeastern Pennsylvania strategically located at the center of the mid-Atlantic corridor. The seat of Chester County government for almost two centuries, West Chester retains much of its historical charm in its buildings and unspoiled countryside, while offering the twentieth-century advantages of a town in the heart of an expanding economic area. West Chester is just 25 miles west of Philadelphia and 17 miles north of Wilmington, Delaware.

The interstate highway system and rail connections make the town accessible from many directions. Philadelphia is just an hour away, and travel to New York or Washington is possible in less than 3 hours.

The University

West Chester University is the second-largest of the fourteen institutions in the Pennsylvania State System of Higher Education and the fourth-largest in the Philadelphia metropolitan area. Officially founded in 1871, the University traces its heritage to the West Chester Academy, which existed from 1812 to 1869. The University's quadrangle buildings, part of the original campus, are on the National Register of Historic Places, and its 385-acre campus features well-maintained facilities, including eight modern residence halls.

In 1999–2000, the University awarded approximately 425 advanced degrees in more than sixty-one graduate programs.

Applying

Application forms are available from the Office of Graduate Studies and Extended Education. Students should apply by April 15 or October 15 prior to the desired semester of entry. Earlier deadlines exist for some programs and for eligibility for assistantships and financial aid. Students are required to submit two official transcripts from all postsecondary institutions they have attended. Letters of recommendation; scores on the General Test and any applicable Subject Test of the Graduate Record Examinations, Graduate Management Admission Test, or Miller Analogies Test; and/or an interview are required for most programs.

Correspondence and Information

Gopal Sankaran, Interim Dean of Graduate Studies and Extended Education
Office of Graduate Studies and Extended Education
McKelvie Hall, 102 Rosedale Avenue
West Chester University
West Chester, Pennsylvania 19383

Telephone: 610-436-2943
E-mail: gradstudy@wcupa.edu
World Wide Web: http://www.wcupa.edu/

GRADUATE PROGRAM INFORMATION AND COORDINATORS

Listed below are West Chester University's graduate degree programs and the program coordinators. For information concerning a specific degree program, students should contact the graduate coordinator listed; for applications and general information, they should contact the Office of Graduate Studies. All telephone numbers are in area code 610.

Administration (M.S.A. with concentrations in health services administration, leadership for women, long-term care administration, human resource management, training and development, public administration, sport and athletic administration, and regional planning; certificate in administration): Dr. Duane Milne (436-2438).
Biology (M.S.): Dr. Giovanni Casotti (436-2856).
Business (M.B.A. with concentrations in economics/finance, general studies, management, and technology and electronic commerce): Dr. Randall La Salle (436-2608).
Chemistry (M.S. in clinical chemistry, M.S. and M.Ed. in chemistry, and M.A. in physical science): Dr. Naseer Ahmad (436-2631).
Communication Studies (M.A. with emphasis on organizational studies, cross-cultural interaction, interpersonal relationships, communication education, language, group decision making, forensics, rhetorical theory and criticism, mass communication, and nonverbal communication): Dr. C. Jack Orr (436-2560).
Communicative Disorders (M.A.): Dr. Michael Weiss (436-3403).
Computer Science (M.S., certificate): Dr. Elaine Milito (436-2690).
Counselor Education (M.Ed. in elementary and secondary school counseling, M.S. in higher education/postsecondary studies, Specialist I certificate): Dr. Patricia Broderick (436-6963).
Criminal Justice (M.S.): Dr. Mary Brewster (436-2630).
Early Childhood and Special Education (M.Ed. and certificate programs): Dr. Vicki McGinley (436-1060).
Elementary Education (M.Ed. and certification; concentrations in general elementary education, creative teaching-learning, human development, and language arts; Certificate of Advanced Graduate Study): Frances Slostad (436-3512).
English (M.A.): Dr. Michael Brooks (436-2745).
Foreign Languages (M.Ed. or M.A. in French or Spanish): Dr. Rebecca Pauly (436-2700).
Geography (M.A.): Dr. Arlene Rengert (436-2746).
Geology (M.A. in physical science with a concentration in earth science) and Astronomy: Dr. Steve Good (436-2570).
Health (M.Ed. in school health, M.S. in public health and school health): Dr. Lynn Carson (436-2138).
History (M.A. in history, M.Ed. in social science): Dr. Charles Hardy (436-2168).
History (M.A. in Holocaust and Genocide Studies): Dr. Edward Pollack (436-2345)
Mathematics (M.A.): Dr. John Kerrigan (436-2351).
Music (M.A. in music history and M.M. in music education, instrumental performance, keyboard performance, music theory and composition, and vocal/choral performance): Dr. Bryan Burton (436-2739).
Nursing (M.S.N. in community health nursing with options in nursing education and nursing administration): Dr. Jan Hickman (436-2258).
Philosophy (M.A.): Dr. Thomas Platt (436-2857).
Physical Education (M.S. in physical education with concentrations in general physical education, exercise, and sport physiology): Dr. W. Craig Stevens (436-2386).
Psychology (M.A. in clinical, industrial/organizational, and general psychology): Dr. Deanne Bonifazi (436-3143).
Reading (M.Ed. and reading specialist certification): Dr. Sharon Kletzien (436-2944).
Secondary Education (M.Ed. and M.S. in educational research): Dr. Cynthia Haggard (436-6934); postbaccalaureate certification (in biology, chemistry, earth and space science, English, French, German, Latin, math, physics, social studies, and Spanish): Dr. James Pugh (436-3063).
Social Work (M.S.W.): Dr. D. Ann Abbott (738-0345).
TESL (M.A. in teaching English as a second language): Dr. Cheri Micheau (436-2822).

Students walking across the campus of West Chester University of Pennsylvania.

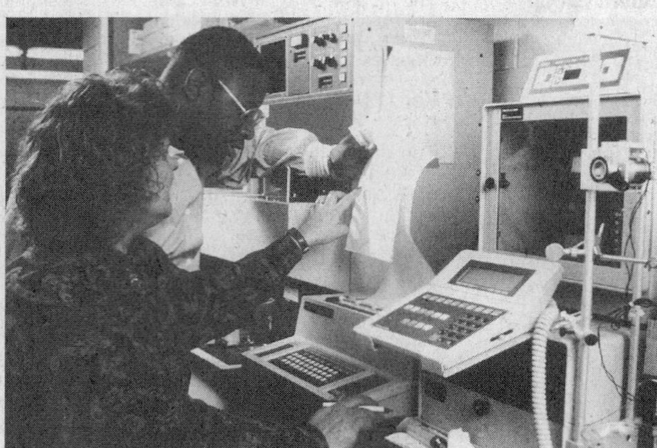

Research is an integral part of the graduate school experience at West Chester University.

WESTERN KENTUCKY UNIVERSITY

Graduate Studies

Programs of Study

Western Kentucky University (WKU) offers programs of study leading to the Master of Arts in communication, English, folk studies, history, interdisciplinary administration, psychology, and sociology; the Master of Arts in Education in counseling (with options in mental health counseling, school counseling, and student affairs in higher education), early childhood education, educational administration, elementary education, exceptional education, general education, and secondary education; the Master of Science in agriculture, biology, chemistry (including the coal chemistry option), communication disorders, computer science, geoscience, library media, mathematics, nursing, physical education, and recreation; the Master of Business Administration; the Master of Public Administration; the Master of Health Administration; and the Master of Public Health.

The Specialist in Education degree is available in counseling, elementary education, school administration, school psychology, and secondary education.

Western Kentucky University participates in cooperative doctoral programs in education with the University of Louisville and in the Master of Science in Criminal Justice program with Eastern Kentucky University.

The University is accredited by the Southern Association of Colleges and Schools. The academic year consists of two semesters and multiple summer terms.

Research Facilities

The main library complex serves the academic community at Western Kentucky University. The WKU libraries house 600,000 books, 100,000 volumes of periodicals, 1.1 million microforms, and 450,000 government documents. The libraries add 10,000 volumes a year and subscribe to 5,000 serials. Special collections, comprised of about 3.5 million manuscript pages, are resources for studies of Kentuckiana, the Shakers, Green River Valley, Mammoth Cave, and the Folk Life Archives. WKU is an associate member of the Center for Research Libraries. All holdings are available on TOPCAT, the libraries' online integrated catalog. Interlibrary loan service is free, and online searching is available for a fee. Graduate study carrels are available in the main library. Computer services may be used by graduate students without charge. University IBM, DEC VAX, and microcomputer systems are accessed through networked clusters at seven user facilities scattered across campus. Student research is facilitated by network access to systems at other universities and membership in major research data archiving organizations.

Financial Aid

Graduate assistantships are available in various departments. Stipends vary, depending upon the student's qualifications and duties assigned. In addition, the out-of-state portion of the graduate assistant's fees is awarded in the form of a scholarship. Other financial aid options include the Federal Perkins Loan Program, Federal Stafford Student Loan Program, and Federal Work-Study Program. To apply, students must file a CSS Financial Aid Form or Kentucky Financial Aid Form. Graduate students are also invited to submit proposals for University research grants.

Cost of Study

In 2002–03, tuition and fees for a full program of study are $1719 per semester for residents of Kentucky and $1890 per semester for nonresidents. Graduate assistants and other qualified students are exempted from the nonresident portion of the tuition. Tuition and fees are subject to change.

Living and Housing Costs

Graduate students usually make arrangements for their own housing; however, the University's Director of Housing will, upon request, provide information about both on- and off-campus housing.

Student Group

Current graduate enrollment is approximately 2,400. This enrollment figure represents students from many areas of the United States as well as a sizable number of international students.

Location

Located in south-central Kentucky, Bowling Green has a population of approximately 50,000. Interstate 65 and the Cumberland and Green River parkways provide easy access to surrounding areas, including Louisville (110 miles north) and Nashville, Tennessee (65 miles south); many fine state parks and recreation areas; and a number of historic sites of cultural interest.

The University

The University first offered the Master of Arts degree in 1931. The academic structure includes the College of Arts, Humanities, and Social Sciences; the College of Business Administration; the Community College; the College of Education and Behavioral Sciences; the College of Science and Engineering; and the School of Health and Human Services. Through the combined efforts of these academic divisions, Western Kentucky University offers a wide range of program areas for graduate study.

Applying

Admission to graduate study is based on the applicant's undergraduate work, scores on the Graduate Record Examinations and Graduate Management Admission Test, and specific departmental requirements. For maximum consideration, applicants should submit all required information at least two months prior to the planned enrollment date. Graduate assistantships are usually awarded in the spring preceding fall enrollment. In addition to academic records, international students are required to submit TOEFL scores and verification of financial resources. The application fee is $30.

Correspondence and Information

Office of Graduate Studies
Western Kentucky University
1 Big Red Way
Bowling Green, Kentucky 42101-3576
Telephone: 270-745-2446
800-896-6960 (toll-free)
Fax: 270-745-6950
E-mail: graduate.studies@wku.edu
World Wide Web: http://www.wku.edu/Dept/Academic/Graduate/

FACULTY HEADS

Elmer Gray, Ph.D., Dean of Graduate Studies and Research.

College of Arts, Humanities, and Social Sciences. David Lee, Ph.D., Dean.
Department of Art: James Chalmers, M.F.A., Head.
Department of Communication and Broadcasting: Sally Ray, Ph.D., Head.
Department of English: Linda Calendrillo, Ph.D., Head.
Department of Government: Saundra Ardrey, Ph.D., Head.
Department of History: Richard Weigel, Ph.D., Head.
Department of Modern Languages and Intercultural Studies: Linda Pickle, Ph.D., Head.
Department of Music: Mitzi Groom, Ph.D., Head
Department of Philosophy and Religion: John Long, Ph.D., Head.
Department of Sociology: Paul Wozniak, Ph.D., Head.
Department of Theatre and Dance: Scott Stroot, M.F.A., Head.

College of Business Administration. Robert W. Jefferson, Ph.D., Dean.
M.B.A. Director: Jipaum Askew-Gibson, M.B.A.

College of Education and Behavioral Sciences. Karen Adams, Ed.D., Dean.
Department of Consumer and Family Sciences: Lou Fong, Ph.D., Head.
Department of Counseling and Student Affairs: Donald Nims, Ed.D., Interim Head.
Department of Educational Leadership: Gayl Ecton Ed.D., Interim Head.
Department of Elementary and Interdisciplinary Early Childhood Education: Stanley Cooke, Ed.D., Interim Head.
Department of Middle Grades and Secondary Education: John Moore, Ed.D., Interim Head.
Department of Physical Education and Recreation: Thaddeus Crews, Ph.D., Head.
Department of Psychology: Steven Haggbloom, Ph.D., Head.
Department of Special Instructional Programs: Stanley Cooke, Ed.D., Head.
School of Teacher Education: Stanley Cooke, Ed.D., Head.

College of Science, Technology, and Health. Martin R. Houston, Ph.D., Dean.
Department of Agriculture: Jenks Britt, D.M.V., Head.
Department of Biology: Gary Dillard, Ph.D., Interim Head.
Department of Chemistry: Lowell W. Shank, Ph.D., Head.
Department of Computer Science: Arthur Shindhelm, Ph.D., Head.
Department of Geography and Geology: David Keeling, Ph.D., Head.
Department of Industrial Technology: Terry Leeper, Ed.D., Head.
Department of Mathematics: James Porter, Ph.D., Head.
Department of Physics and Astronomy: Charles McGruder, Ph.D., Head.

School of Health and Human Services. David Dunn, D.Sc., Director.
Department of Nursing: Donna Blackburn, Ph.D., Head.
Department of Public Health: Wayne Higgins, Ph.D., Head.

WESTERN MICHIGAN UNIVERSITY

The Graduate College

Programs of Study

Western Michigan University (WMU) offers more than ninety graduate degree programs at the doctoral, specialist, and master's level in a large number of disciplines. Doctoral degrees are available in applied economics, biological sciences, chemistry (environmental), comparative religion, computer science, counseling psychology, counselor education, educational leadership, electrical and computer engineering, English, geology, history, industrial engineering, interdisciplinary health studies, mathematics, mathematics education, mechanical engineering, paper and imaging science and engineering, physics, political science, psychology, public administration, science education, sociology, special education, and statistics. Specialist degrees are offered in educational leadership and school psychology. Master's degrees are available in accountancy, anthropology, applied mathematics, art, biological sciences, biostatistics, business administration, career and technical education, chemistry, communication, comparative religion, computational mathematics, computer engineering, computer science, construction management, counseling psychology, counselor education, creative writing, development administration, earth science, economics, education and professional development, educational leadership, educational technology, electrical engineering, engineering management, English, family and consumer sciences, geography, geology, history, industrial engineering, manufacturing engineering, materials science and engineering, mathematics, mathematics education, mechanical engineering, medieval studies, molecular biotechnology, music, occupational therapy, operations research, orientation and mobility, paper and imaging science and engineering, performing arts administration, philosophy, physical education, physician assistant studies, physics, political science, psychology, public administration, rehabilitation teaching, science education, social work, sociology, Spanish, special education, speech pathology and audiology, statistics, teaching of geography, and teaching of music. Dual master's degrees are offered in counselor education and rehabilitation teaching and in special education and orientation and mobility. Master's programs require a minimum of 30 semester hours. Part-time study is allowed in most programs. Graduate certificate programs are offered in alcohol and drug abuse, clinical trials administration, educational technology, electron microscopy, gerontology, health-care administration, hippotherapy, holistic health care, human performance technology, and nonprofit leadership and administration.

Research Facilities

The University's library system is the state's fourth largest, with 3.9 million items. Waldo Library, WMU's main library, seats 1,900, has multiple outlets for computer access, uses the Voyager Web-based library system for automated information retrieval, and contains special collections of old, expensive, beautiful, and/or rare books. Major special collections include the Cistercian Manuscript and Rare Book Collection, the LeFevre Miniature Book Collection, the Historical Children's Book Collection, the Dwight B. Waldo Lincoln Collection, and the Carol Ann Haenicke American Women's Poetry Collection. The Education Library, Music and Dance Library, Archives and Regional History Collections, and Visual Resources Library, housed in various campus buildings, together contain nearly 1 million of the library system's print and nonprint items.

Computing facilities are available in classrooms, laboratories, and residence halls. All residence hall rooms allow Ethernet connections to the Internet; all campus apartments allow direct connection to the WMU mainframe computer. Michigan students living outside the Kalamazoo area can access WMU through a local dial-up number for e-mail, library searches, and Web browsing. All branch campuses have full computer labs and compressed video interactive television hookups.

Financial Aid

The following types of fellowships and assistantships are available: Graduate College Fellowships for entering master's degree students; Doctoral Associateships for outstanding doctoral students; and King/Chavez/Parks Future Faculty Program, Thurgood Marshall Assistantships, and Professional Tuition Grants for qualified U.S. students from historically underrepresented groups. In addition, graduate departments have their own assistantship appointments. Federal and state work-study, Ford Federal Direct Loans, the WMU Non-Traditional Student Scholarship, and the University Dames Endowed Scholarship are also available.

Cost of Study

Tuition for 2001–02 was $185.62 per semester hour for Michigan residents and $441.83 per semester hour for nonresidents. An enrollment fee of $602 was required of all students.

Living and Housing Costs

A wide choice of graduate living accommodations is available, including on-campus family and single student apartments. For 2001–02, the cost of family housing ranged from $467 per month for one bedroom, unfurnished, to $717 per month for two bedrooms, furnished. The University also offers four residence halls specifically for students 21 years of age or older, at prices that ranged from $2607 (room only) to $5517 (room and meals) per academic year. The Office of Off-Campus Life assists students in locating off-campus housing and maintains lists of more than 2,500 rental units, area landlords, and students looking for roommates.

Student Group

Total enrollment for fall 2001 was 28,931. Twenty percent of the total enrollment, 5,775 students, were graduate students. Within the graduate enrollment, 60 percent were women. Members of U.S. ethnic minority groups comprise 9 percent and international students 15 percent of the graduate enrollment.

Location

Kalamazoo, located midway between Detroit and Chicago, just off I-94 and U.S. 131, is the home of the University's main campus. The city's resources, which include four institutions of higher learning and several Fortune 500 companies, offer an excellent environment for graduate study.

The University

Western Michigan University was founded in 1903. Ranked for three consecutive years among *U.S. News and World Report* magazine's top 100 national public universities and listed in *America's 100 Best College Buys* and *America's Best College Scholarships,* WMU is a nationally recognized, student-centered research institution. In August 2000, the Carnegie Foundation for the Advancement of Teaching gave WMU its highest ranking: Doctoral/Research University-Extensive. Only 148 institutions in the nation were given this ranking. WMU joins three other Michigan universities—the University of Michigan, Michigan State University, and Wayne State University—at this prestigious level of classification.

Total grant awards have increased each year of the past decade, topping $50 million in 2000–01. Graduate students have opportunities to conduct research under the direction of principal investigators who have been awarded grants and contracts from business, industry, and government agencies.

Applying

Applications are available from the Office of Admissions and Orientation. A nonrefundable $25 fee is required. The completed application, fee, and transcripts from all prior institutions attended must be received by the following dates: July 1 for fall; November 1 for winter; March 1 for spring; and May 1 for summer. Some programs have earlier application dates and not all departments admit students for all semesters or sessions. Applicants should consult with the department for specific information. The assistantship and fellowship application deadline is February 15.

Correspondence and Information

Paula J. Boodt, Director
Graduate Recruitment and Retention
The Graduate College
Western Michigan University
Kalamazoo, Michigan 49008-5242
Telephone: 616-387-8212
Fax: 616-387-8232
E-mail: ask-wmu@wmich.edu
WWW: http://www.wmich.edu

Jolene V. Jackson, Director
International Student Services
Western Michigan University
Kalamazoo, Michigan 49008
Telephone: 616-387-5865
Fax: 616-387-5899
E-mail: oiss.info@wmich.edu
WWW: http://www.wmich.edu/oiss

Chair
Department of (specify)
Western Michigan University
Kalamazoo, Michigan 49008

FACULTY HEADS

The administrative officers of the Graduate College and of the departments responsible for programs leading to graduate degrees are listed below.

Donald E. Thompson, Ed.D., Dean of the Graduate College and Vice President for Research.
William R. Wiener, Ph.D., Senior Associate Dean, Graduate College.
Michael S. Pritchard, Ph.D., Associate Dean, Graduate College.
Eileen B. Evans, Ph.D., Associate Dean, Graduate College.
Griselda Daniel, Assistant to the Dean and Director of Diversity Programs.

Graduate Departments
Accountancy: Jack Ruhl, Ph.D., Chair.
Anthropology: Robert Ulin, Ph.D., Chair.
Art: Phillip Vander Weg, M.F.A., Chair.
Biological Sciences: Alexander Enyedi, Ph.D., Interim Chair.
Blind Rehabilitation: Paul Ponchillia, Ph.D., Interim Chair.
Business Information Systems: Earl Halvas, Ph.D., Chair.
Chemistry: Jay Means, Ph.D., Chair.
Communication: Steven Rhodes, Ph.D., Chair.
Community Health Services: James Leja, Ph.D., Acting Director.
Comparative Religion: Brian Wilson, Ph.D., Chair.
Computer Science: Ajay Gupta, Ph.D., Chair.
Construction Engineering, Materials Engineering, and Industrial Design: Roman J. Rabiej, D.T.Sc., Chair.
Counselor Education and Counseling Psychology: Joseph Morris, Ph.D., Chair.
Economics: Bassam Harik, Ph.D., Chair.
Educational Studies: Elizabeth Whitten, Ph.D., Chair.
Electrical and Computer Engineering: S. Hossein Mousavinezhad, Ph.D., Chair.
English: Arnold Johnston, Ph.D., Chair.
Family and Consumer Sciences: Linda Dannison, Ph.D., Chair.
Finance and Commercial Law: Adrian Edwards, Ph.D., Chair.
Foreign Languages and Literatures: John Benson, Ph.D., Acting Chair.
Geography: David Dickason, Ph.D., Chair.
Geosciences: Alan Kehew, Ph.D., Chair.
Health, Physical Education and Recreation: Debra Berkey, Ed.D., Chair.
History: Marion Gray, Ph.D., Chair.
Industrial and Manufacturing Engineering: Michael Atkins, Ed.D., Chair.
Management: Thomas A. Carey, Ed.D., Chair.
Marketing: Andrew A. Brogowicz, Ph.D., Chair.
Mathematics: Jay Wood, Ph.D., Chair.
Mechanical and Aeronautical Engineering: Parviz Merati, Ph.D., Chair.
Medieval Studies: Paul Szarmach, Ph.D., Director.
Music: Richard O'Hearn, Ph.D., Director.
Occupational Therapy: Cindee Peterson, Ph.D., Chair.
Paper and Printing Science and Engineering: Said Avu Bakr, Ph.D., Chair.
Philosophy: Kent Baldner, Ph.D., Chair.
Physician Assistant Studies: James Van Rhee, M.S., Chair.
Physics: John Tanis, Ph.D., Chair.
Political Science: David G. Houghton, Ph.D., Chair.
Psychology: R. Wayne Fuqua, Ph.D., Chair.
Public Affairs and Administration: Robert Peters, Ph.D., Director.
Science Education: Leonard Ginsberg, Ph.D., Interim Director.
Social Work: Earlie Washington, Ph.D., Director.
Sociology: Thomas Van Valey, Ph.D., Chair.
Speech Pathology and Audiology: John M. Hanley, Ph.D., Chair.
Statistics: Daniel Mihalko, Ph.D., Chair.
Teaching, Learning and Leadership: Van Cooley, Ed.D., Chair.

Professor Judith Stone interacts with graduate students during a history seminar.

Students collaborate on a project in one of the University's computer labs.

Diether H. Haenicke Hall, WMU's state-of-the-art science building.

WEST TEXAS A&M UNIVERSITY

Graduate School

Programs of Study

West Texas A&M University offers graduate programs and concentrations leading to a master's degree in numerous areas at four separate colleges. The College of Agriculture, Nursing and Natural Sciences offers degrees in agriculture (M.S.), biology (M.S.), chemistry (M.S.), engineering technology (M.S.), environmental science (M.S.), family nursing (M.S.N.), and mathematics (M.S.). The College of Business offers degrees in accounting (B.B.A./M.P.A., M.P.Acc.), business (M.B.A.), and finance and economics (M.S.). The College of Education and Social Sciences has programs in education-administration (M.Ed.); counseling (M.Ed.); curriculum and instruction (M.Ed.); educational diagnostician studies (M.Ed.); elementary education (M.A., M.Ed.); instructional technology (M.Ed.); professional counseling (M.A.); reading specialist studies (M.Ed.); secondary education: art, biology, chemistry, economics, English, history, mathematics, music, political science, social studies, and speech education (M.Ed.); sports and exercise science (M.S.); criminal justice (M.A.); history (M.A.); political science (M.A.); and psychology (M.A.). The College of Fine Arts and Humanities offers degrees in art (M.A.), communication (M.A.), communication disorders (M.S.), English (M.A.), music (M.A., M.M.), and studio art (M.F.A.) and a University-wide program in interdisciplinary studies (M.A., M.S.).

West Texas A&M University's distance education program offers two degrees and other courses through the Internet. The degrees are the Master of Business Administration (M.B.A.) and the Master of Education (M.Ed.) in instructional technology. Graduate programs with online courses include the M.Ed. core, the M.Ed. in diagnostician studies, and the M.S. in agriculture (primarily for county extension agents). Information on admission and registration, a list of courses, and sample units from courses are available at http://wtonline.wtamu.edu.

Research Facilities

Students have access to the Alternative Energy Institute (AEI), which contains a wind energy test center. Other facilities available include the Hastings Electronic Learning Center (HELC), the Cornette Library, the Equine Center, the Killgore Research Center, the Dryland Agriculture Institute, and the Texas Engineering Experiment Station (TEES) Regional Division. Students also frequently work at facilities operated by the USDA Agricultural Research Service at Etter and Bushland, Texas Agricultural Experiment Station (TAES), and Texas Veterinary Medical Diagnostic Laboratory.

Financial Aid

The University provides a limited number of teaching and research assistantships for qualified graduate students as part of the educational and professional preparation programs. Stipends vary according to the assignment and qualifications of applicants. Applications for assistantships may be obtained from the head of the academic unit in which the applicant intends to study. Student loans, campus employment, and a number of graduate scholarships are also available.

Cost of Study

In 2001–02, graduate tuition was $52 per semester credit hour for residents and $285 per semester credit hour for nonresidents. Depending upon the area of study and number of hours, fees may vary from $102 to $400, and books are estimated at $200 per semester.

Living and Housing Costs

Double and private rooms ranging in cost from $787 to $1357 per long semester and a variety of meal plans are available on campus through the Office of Residential Living. Off-campus accommodations are available in a number of private apartment complexes located within a few minutes of the campus.

Student Group

West Texas A&M University has a growing population of approximately 5,400 undergraduates and 1,360 graduate students. WTAMU students, although primarily from Texas, represent more than thirty-five states and thirty-five other countries.

Location

West Texas A&M University is located in the heart of the Texas Panhandle in the rural community of Canyon, population 13,000. Amarillo, the region's metropolitan center, is just 17 miles north, and the state borders of New Mexico, Colorado, Kansas, and Oklahoma are within a 2-hour drive.

The University

West Texas A&M University was founded in 1909 and accepted its first class in 1910. Although traditionally recognized as a high-quality regional university, WTAMU is a member of the Texas A&M University System and supports a number of internationally respected and attended programs, such as the Alternative Energy and the Dryland Agriculture Institutes.

Applying

Applications for admission to the Graduate School are available from the dean of the Graduate School at and the Wed address listed below. General information about requirements and procedures for admission is in the current University catalog. Some admission requirements may vary among departments. Additional information concerning admission requirements may be obtained by contacting the Graduate School at the address given below.

Correspondence and Information

Dr. Vaughn Nelson
Dean of the Graduate School, Research and Information Technology
WTAMU Box 60215
West Texas A&M University
Canyon, Texas 79016-0001
Telephone: 806-651-2730
Fax: 806-651-2733
E-mail: graduateschool@mail.wtamu.edu
World Wide Web: http://www.wtamu.edu

ADMINISTRATIVE GRADUATE FACULTY

Graduate School
James R. Hallmark, Dean; Ph.D., Oklahoma.

Agriculture, Nursing and Natural Sciences
James Clark, Dean; Ph.D., Wisconsin.
Agriculture: Donald Topliff, Division Head; Ph.D., Texas A&M.
Biology and Geosciences: Douglas P. Bingham, Department Head; Ph.D., Brigham Young.
Mathematics, Physical Sciences and Engineering Technology: Kenneth Van Doren, Department Head; Ph.D., Auburn.
Nursing: Heidi Taylor, Division Head; Ph.D., Texas Woman's.

Business
John Cooley, Dean; Ph.D., Oklahoma State.
Accounting, Economics and Finance: Barry L. Duman, Department Head; Ph.D., USC.
Computer Information Systems: Amjad A. Abdullat, Department Head; Ed.D., Pepperdine.
Management, Marketing and General Business: Syed Anwar, Interim Department Head; D.B.A., US International.

Education and Social Sciences
Theodore Guffy, Dean; Ed.D., Oklahoma State.
Behavioral Sciences: Gary R. Byrd, Department Head; Ph.D., Texas Tech.
Education: Eddie. Henderson, Department Head; J.D., Texas Tech.
History and Political Science: Wade Shaffer, Department Head; Ph.D., William and Mary.
Sports and Exercise Sciences: William E. Johnson, Department Head; Ph.D., New Mexico.

Fine Arts and Humanities
Sue Simpson Park, Dean; Ph.D., Texas Tech.
Art, Communication and Theatre: Royal Rugel Brantley, Department Head; M.F.A., Trinity (San Antonio).
English and Modern Languages: Shearle Furnish, Department Head; Ph.D., Kentucky.
Music and Dance: Ted Dubois, Department Head; Ph.D., USC.

WHEATON COLLEGE

Graduate School

Programs of Study

Wheaton College offers a Doctor of Philosophy in biblical studies, a Doctor of Clinical Psychology (Psy.D.), and the Master of Arts (M.A.) degree in eight areas of study: biblical archaeology, biblical and theological studies, clinical psychology, educational ministries, evangelism and spiritual formation, missions/intercultural studies, secondary education (M.A.T.), and interdisciplinary studies. All of the graduate programs have core curriculum requirements, but elective options give students flexibility in arranging a program that suits their individual interests and goals.

In addition, nondegree certificates are available in teaching English as a second language, leadership and camp ministry, and advanced biblical studies.

Research Facilities

The Buswell Memorial and Billy Graham Center libraries contain more than 1 million items, including books, records, scores, audiovisuals, microforms, and curriculum materials. The libraries belong to LIBRAS, a consortium of sixteen metropolitan area college libraries; the Association of Chicago Theological Schools, a consortium of Chicago area seminaries; ILLINET; and OCLC.

The Billy Graham Center is a research and study center, with a museum featuring educational exhibits on the evangelical message and the history of evangelism. The archives of the Billy Graham Center contain a rich collection of documents on North American Protestant nondenominational missions and the history of evangelism. They include the files of organizations such as National Religious Broadcasters, the Billy Graham Evangelistic Association, and Youth for Christ as well as the private papers of evangelical leaders, including Billy Sunday, Donald McGavran, and Charles Colson.

Special collections, housed in the Wade Center, consist of the books and papers of C. S. Lewis, G. K. Chesterton, George MacDonald, Dorothy Sayers, J. R. R. Tolkien, Charles Williams, and Owen Barfield.

Financial Aid

There is more than $500,000 in grant money available to full-time, degree-seeking graduate students. Nearly two thirds of that sum is directed toward American and international applicants involved in missionary work. Financial aid is awarded on the basis of need as demonstrated on the Free Application for Federal Student Aid (FAFSA) and the Wheaton College Institutional Form. Assistantships are available in the various academic departments and are paid on a per-hour basis.

The Federal Stafford Student Loan Program is available to full- and part-time graduate students. Information and application forms may be acquired through the College Financial Aid Office, a local bank, savings and loan association, or credit union.

Cost of Study

Tuition for the 2002–03 school year is $435 per semester hour for the master's degree. The M.A. full-time academic load is 12 hours per semester; the Psy.D. full-time academic load is 10 hours per semester. The tuition is $560 per semester hour for the Psy.D. degree.

Living and Housing Costs

For 2002–03, a single graduate student should budget $11,369 for room, board, books, and personal expenses. Married students should plan on a budget of $14,917 plus $4516 for each dependent. These figures should be viewed as estimates.

Student Group

Total enrollment at Wheaton College is about 2,500. The graduate student body of 450 represents approximately twenty-eight states, twelve countries, 110 colleges, and more than twenty-five denominations. About 50 percent of the graduate students are women, and 10 percent are international students.

Location

Wheaton's 80-acre campus is located in Wheaton, Illinois, a residential suburb 25 miles west of Chicago with a population of 50,000. The educational and cultural resources of the Chicago metropolitan area are easily accessible. The Wheaton area is the home of approximately twenty Christian organizations.

The Graduate School

The Graduate School is an integral part of Wheaton College's distinguished history. It was founded in 1937 as the result of a generous gift. The emphasis of the Graduate School throughout its history has been on practical scholarship—scholarship that is totally rooted in the final authority of Scripture but is also practical, so that educated and trained Christian leaders are equipped to relate to the needs of modern man.

Applying

Application materials may be obtained by sending a request to the address below. In addition to the application for admission and a $30 nonrefundable application fee for the master's degree program and $50 for the Psy.D. program, the following materials are required: official transcripts of all academic work since high school graduation, three recommendations (one each from the applicant's pastor, an employer, and a college professor or academic adviser), employment resume, and scores from the General Test of the Graduate Record Examinations (GRE) or Miller Analogies Test (MAT). Applicants for the Psy.D. degree must also submit a recommendation from a mental health professional.

Application deadlines for the fall semester are January 1 (Ph.D. and international applicants), January 15 (Psy.D.), March 1 (clinical psychology, M.A. applicants), March 1 (priority deadline for all other degree programs), May 1 (final deadline). Psychology, Ph.D., and international students are admitted only in the fall semester.

Correspondence and Information

Graduate Admissions Office
Wheaton College
Wheaton, Illinois 60187
Telephone: 630-752-5195
800-888-0141 (toll-free)
E-mail: gradadm@wheaton.edu
World Wide Web: http://www.wheaton.edu

THE FACULTY AND THEIR RESEARCH

Biblical and Theological Studies/Biblical Archaeology

Vincent Bacote, Assistant Professor of Theology; M.Div., Trinity Evangelical Divinity School.
Gregory Beale, Kenneth T. Wessner Professor of Biblical Studies; Ph.D. Cambridge.
C. Hassell Bullock, Professor; Ph.D., Hebrew Union. Old Testament theology, Old Testament criticism.
Gary Burge, Professor of New Testament; Ph.D., Aberdeen.
Lynn Cohick, Assistant Professor of New Testament; Ph.D., Pennsylvania.
Walter A. Elwell, Professor; Ph.D., Edinburgh. Life and teachings of Jesus, New Testament Greek and interpretation, contemporary theology.
Gene Green, Professor; Ph.D., Aberdeen (Scotland). Macedonian and Anatolian Christianity.
Scott J. Hafeman, Gerald F. Hawthorne Professor of NT Greek and Exegesis.
Andrew Hill, Professor; Ph.D., Michigan. Hebrew and Old Testament.
Paul House, Professor of Old Testament; Ph.D., Southern Baptist Theological Seminary.
Mark Husbands, Assistant Professor of Theology; Ph.D., Toronto.
David Lauber, Visiting Assistant Professor of Theology; Ph.D., Princeton Theological Seminary.
Kathryn Long, Associate Professor; Ph.D., Duke. History of Christianity in North America, nineteenth-century Protestantism, women in religion.
Daniel Master, Assistant Professor of Archaeology; Ph.D., Harvard.
Laura Miguelez, Assistant Professor of Theology; M.Div., Gordon-Conwell Theological Seminary.
John Monson, Assistant Professor; Ph.D. candidate, Harvard. Archaeology and Old Testament.
Douglas Moo, Blanchard Professor of New Testament; Ph.D., St. Andrews.
Esther Ng, Visiting Assistant Professor of New Testament; Ph.D., Aberdeen (Scotland).
Mark A. Noll, Professor; Ph.D., Vanderbilt. American church history in the Revolutionary and national periods, American intellectual history, Evangelicalism, cultural history of the Bible.
Dennis L. Okholm, Professor; Ph.D., Princeton Theological Seminary. Reformation and medieval theory.
Arthur A. Rupprecht, Professor of Classical Languages; Ph.D., Pennsylvania.
Richard Schultz, Armerding Professor of Biblical Studies and Chair; Ph.D., Yale.
Stephen Spencer, Professor of Theology; Ph.D., Michigan State.
Sam Storms, Visiting Associate Professor of Theology; Ph.D., Texas at Dallas.
Daniel Treier, Assistant Professor of Theology; Ph.D.
John Walton, Professor of Old Testament; Ph.D., Hebrew Union–Jewish Institute of Religion.
Herbert M. Wolf, Professor; Ph.D., Brandeis. Old Testament Hebrew, Near Eastern culture, Pentateuch, prophetic books.

Christian Formation & Ministry

Lon Allison, Associate Professor of Evangelism and Spiritual Formation and Director of Billy Graham Center; D.Min., Gordon–Conwell.
Lyle Dorsett, Professor of Educational Ministries and Evangelism and Spiritual Formation; Ph.D., Missouri. History, evangelism, Christian ministry.
Nancy Grisham, Adjunct Instructor of Evangelism and Spiritual Formation; M.A., Wheaton. Evangelism and discipleship ministries, women's ministries.
Steven Kang, Assistant Professor of Christian Education; Ph.D., Northwestern. Foundational issues in Christian education and processes, cultural studies, educational research.
Scottie May, Assistant Professor of Educational Ministries; Ph.D., Trinity Evangelical Divinity School. Children's ministries, family studies, curriculum development.
Barrett McRay, Assistant Professor of Educational Ministries; Psy.D., Wheaton. Youth ministry, pastoral care, community mental health.
Jerry Root, Assistant Professor of Educational Ministries; Ph.D. candidate, Oxford Centre for Mission Studies. Sport ministry, youth evangelism/discipleship, C. S. Lewis writings.
David Setran, Assistant Professor of Educational Ministries; Ph.D., Indiana. History and philosophy of education, college ministry, small group discipleship.
James C. Wilhoit, Price-Lebar Professor of Educational Ministries and Chair; Ph.D., Northwestern. Religious education, history, Bible instruction, prayer/spirituality, author and editor of several books on Christian education.

Clinical Psychology

Trey Buchanan, Associate Professor of Psychology; Ph.D., New Hampshire.
Richard E. Butman, Professor; Ph.D., Fuller Theological Seminary. Psychological assessment.
Sally Canning, Associate Professor; Ph.D., Pennsylvania. Child and adolescent psychology, community psychology, and research.
Helen DeVries, Associate Professor; Ph.D., Virginia Commonwealth. Geropsychology, neuropsychology, marital and family functioning.
Robert Gregory, Professor and Director of Psy.D.; Ph.D., Minnesota. Neuropsychological assessment, psychodiagnosis.
Cynthia J. Neal Kimball, Associate Professor and Department Chair; Ph.D., New Mexico. High-risk families.
Michael W. Mangis, Associate Professor and Coordinator of M.A. Program; Ph.D., Wyoming. Psychodynamic psychology, assessment and treatment of adolescents.
Mark McMinn, Professor; Ph.D., Vanderbilt. Cognitive theory with adults. Author of *Cognitive Therapy Techniques in Christian Counseling.*
J. Derek McNeil, Assistant Professor and Coordinator of Diversity; Ph.D., Northwestern. Identity development of African-American males.
Carlos F. Pozzi, Assistant Professor and Director of Clinical Training; Psy.D., Illinois School of Professional Psychology. Health and psychological services to minorities.
Donald W. Preussler, Assistant Professor; Ph.D., North Dakota. Physiological psychology, psychopharmacology.
Robert Watson, Assistant Professor; Psy.D., Illinois School of Professional Psychology. Psychodynamic and psychoanalytic psychology.
Terri Watson, Assistant Professor; Psy.D., Illinois School of Professional Psychology. Child and adolescent therapy and child play therapy.

Education

Andrew Brulle, Professor and Department Chair; Ed.D., Northern Illinois. Special education and teacher preparation.
Sally Morrison, Assistant Professor; Ed.D., Northern Illinois. Reading and writing.

Missions/Intercultural Studies

Evvy Hay Campbell, Associate Professor and Chair; Ph.D., Michigan State. Specialist in community development.
Rob Gallagher, Associate Professor; Ph.D., Fuller Theological Seminary. Leadership development and contemporary evangelism and mission.
James Lewis, Associate Professor; Ph.D., Iowa. World religions; Asian art, culture, and religion.
A. Scott Moreau, Associate Professor; D.Miss., Trinity Evangelical Divinity School. Served as a missionary in Africa; served for seven years as a professor at the Nairobi International School of Theology (NIST); author of *The World of the Spirits: A Biblical Study in the African Context.*
Cheri Pierson, Visiting Assistant Professor; Ed.D. candidate, Northern Illinois. English for biblical and theological purposes.
Alan Seaman, Associate Professor; Ph.D., Virginia. Teaching English as a second language (TESL).

WICHITA STATE UNIVERSITY

Graduate School

Programs of Study

The Wichita State University Graduate School offers advanced professional training in fifty-four master's programs, one educational specialist program, and nine doctoral programs (see listing on reverse side of this page). The diversified programs are led by accomplished graduate faculty members.

The Master of Arts is awarded in anthropology, art education, communication, communicative disorders and sciences, criminal justice, economics, English, gerontology, history, liberal studies, Spanish, and sociology. The Master of Education is offered in counseling, curriculum and instruction, educational administration and supervision, educational psychology, physical education, special education, and sport administration. The Master of Science is awarded in aerospace engineering, biology, chemistry, computer science, electrical engineering, environmental science, geology, industrial engineering, mathematics, mechanical engineering, and physics. The Master of Fine Arts is awarded in studio art (ceramics, painting, printmaking, and sculpture) and in creative writing. The Master of Music is awarded in history/literature, instrumental conducting, opera performance, performance, piano pedagogy, and theory/composition. The Master of Music Education is awarded in choral music, elementary music, instrumental music, special education, and vocal music. The Master of Business Administration, Master of Physical Therapy, Master of Accountancy, Master of Public Administration, Master of Public Health, Master of Science in Nursing, Master of Engineering Management, and Master of Social Work are also offered.

The Specialist in Education degree is awarded in school psychology. Doctoral programs are offered in applied mathematics; chemistry; communicative disorders and sciences; educational administration and supervision; aerospace, electrical, industrial, and mechanical engineering; and psychology.

Research Facilities

The University library contains more than 2 million items, with additional specialized holdings in the various departments and colleges. On-campus research and learning facilities include a digital computing center, wind tunnels, a television station, the National Institute for Aviation Research, the Center for Entrepreneurship, the Hugo Wall School of Urban and Public Affairs, the Rehabilitation Engineering Center, the Center for Economic Development and Business Research, the Social Science Research Laboratory, the Center for Energy Studies, and the Interdisciplinary Communication Research Institute. In addition, the University has an outstanding cooperative relationship with numerous educational, social, health, business, and government organizations. Included among these are the Wichita public and private schools; Boeing, Cessna, Learjet, and Raytheon aircraft companies; L.S.I. Logic; the Wichita Symphony Orchestra; four medical centers; the Wichita city government; the Federal Aviation Administration; the National Institutes of Health; and the U.S. Department of the Army.

Financial Aid

Fellowships, traineeships, teaching assistantships, and research assistantships are available on a competitive basis. The awards range from $5000 to $12,000 per academic year, with some opportunity for remuneration during summer terms. Teaching assistants are eligible for waivers of up to 100 percent of tuition at in-state rates. Applications for this type of aid should be submitted to the major department involved. Educational Opportunity Fund scholarships are awarded each semester to eligible part-time graduate students. The WSU Office of Student Aid is an additional source for grants and loans. Opportunities exist for part-time student employment and cooperative education training positions.

Cost of Study

In 2002–03, tuition and fees per semester for in-state students are $135.87 per credit hour. For out-of-state students, tuition and fees per semester are $375.87 per credit hour. Students awarded assistantships are eligible for in-state tuition and fees. All fees are subject to change by the Kansas State Board of Regents.

Living and Housing Costs

In 2001–02, costs for University-owned residence hall rooms or apartments, including options for married couples and students with children, range from $1785 to $11,000 per year, depending on the hall and meal plan. Wichita offers a wide variety of affordable housing suitable for families near the University. Moderately priced child-care facilities and recreational areas are convenient.

Student Group

The total University enrollment is approximately 15,000, including more than 3,400 graduate students. About 1,025 pursue graduate degrees full-time; others work full-time and attend classes in the evening. Multicultural and ethnic diversity abounds and includes Native American, Hispanic, Asian, and Middle Eastern groups; there are approximately 500 international graduate students.

Student Outcomes

Engineering and business graduates are easily employed by one of the four major aircraft manufacturers located in Wichita. The large oil-based, banking, and agricultural industries offer job opportunities for all graduates. Four major medical centers offer job opportunities for health professionals, and the large school districts offer jobs for teachers. The music department is one of the best and supports the local symphony.

Location

Wichita, the largest city in Kansas, is part of a metropolitan area of 500,000. Home to Boeing, Cessna, Learjet, and Raytheon, Wichita is known as the "air capital of the world" and also is a major center for energy and agricultural industries. A regional medical center, Wichita has four major hospitals, and health-care positions are plentiful. Public and private schools offer diverse learning opportunities, and numerous cultural events provide entertainment for the whole family the year round.

The University

The Wichita State University began as Fairmount College in 1895 and became the Municipal University of Wichita in 1926. In 1964, the University entered the state system of higher education; it is now one of six state institutions of higher education governed by the Kansas Board of Regents. Since 1964, the University has more than doubled in enrollment, with a parallel growth in the size and scope of its academic and physical environment. The 330-acre campus borders an eighteen-hole University golf course and is adorned by more than sixty pieces of sculpture by internationally known artists. Wiedemann Hall houses a world-famous Marcussen organ, the first to be installed in North America. An expansion to Ablah Library includes a 24-hour study room that provides Internet-connected computers and study facilities. There are almost 200 active student groups and a continuous series of athletic and cultural events on campus, including baseball and basketball games, track and field meets, concerts, plays, recitals, art exhibits, and lectures.

Applying

Students may begin most programs in the fall or spring. Summer admission is limited. The application, $35 application fee (U.S. residents), and official transcripts of all previous work should be sent to the Graduate School at least thirty days prior to the semester for which the student is applying. Applications for financial aid should be received by February 15 for the following fall. International applicants must submit a $50 (U.S.) application fee, a TOEFL score, a TSE score (if applying for a graduate teaching assistantship), a financial support statement, and official transcripts of all academic work by April 1 for fall admission and August 1 for spring admission. Some departments have earlier application dates. Some departments require GRE scores; the GMAT is required for business programs.

Correspondence and Information

Assistant to the Dean, Graduate School
Wichita State University
Wichita, Kansas 67260
Telephone: 316-978-3095
Fax: 316-978-3253
E-mail: gradinqu@wichita.edu
World Wide Web: http://www.webs.wichita.edu/gradsch

Chairperson or Graduate Coordinator
Department of (specify)
Wichita State University
Wichita, Kansas 67260

DEANS AND PROGRAM COORDINATORS

Susan K. Kovar, Interim Dean.

FAIRMOUNT COLLEGE OF LIBERAL ARTS AND SCIENCES: William Bischoff, Interim Dean, Ph.D.
Anthropology (M.A.): C. A. Robarchek, Ph.D.
Biology (M.S.): William Hendry, Ph.D.
Chemistry (M.S., Ph.D.): K. Wimslasena, Ph.D. Research is conducted in bioorganic, bioanalytical, medicinal, polymer, and materials chemistry.
Communication (M.A.): Katherine Hawkins, Ph.D.
Computer Science (M.S.): Rodney Bates, Ph.D.
Creative Writing (M.F.A.): Diane Quantic, Ph.D.
English (M.A.): Sarah Daugherty, Ph.D.
Geology (M.S.): Sal Mazzullo, Ph.D.
History (M.A.): John Dreifort, Ph.D.
Hugo Wall Center of Public Administration (M.P.A.): Sam Yeager, Ph.D.
Liberal Studies (M.A.): R. Liera-Schwichtenberg, Ph.D.
Mathematics (M.S., Ph.D. in Applied Mathematics): Kenneth G. Miller, Ph.D. Research is conducted in numerical analysis, partial differential equations, mathematical physics, statistics, probability, stochastic processes, and computational mathematics.
Physics (M.S.): Seyed Taher, Ph.D.
Psychology (Ph.D. in Psychology–Human Factors and Psychology–Community/Clinical): Gary Greenberg, Ph.D. Research is conducted in memory and cognition, artificial intelligence, and aerospace psychology.
School of Community Affairs: Paul Cromwell, Ph.D., Director.
Criminal Justice (M.A.): Andra Bannister, Ph.D.
Gerontology (M.A.): William Hays, Ph.D.
School of Social Work (M.S.W.): Cathleen Lewandowski, Ph.D.
Sociology (M.A.): David Wright, Ph.D.
Spanish (M.A.): Eunice Myers, Ph.D.

W. FRANK BARTON SCHOOL OF BUSINESS: Dean John Beehler, Ph.D.
Accounting (M.P.A.): Michael Flores, M.P.A.
Economics (M.A.): Philip Hersch, Ph.D.
Graduate Studies in Business (M.B.A., M.S., E.M.B.A.): Dottie Harpool, M.B.A.

COLLEGE OF EDUCATION: Dean Jon Engelhardt, Ph.D.
Communicative Disorders and Sciences (M.A., Ph.D.): Barbara Hodson, Ph.D. Rosalind Scudder, M.A. Research is conducted in speech-language pathology and audiology.
Counseling (M.Ed.): Ruth A. Hitchcock, Ph.D.
Curriculum and Instruction (M.Ed.): T. Huber, Ph.D.
Educational Administration and Supervision (M.Ed., Ed.D.): Chuck Romig, Ph.D.
Educational Psychology (M.Ed.): Chuck Romig, Ph.D.
Physical Education (M.Ed.): Mike Rogers, Ph.D.
School Psychology (Ed.S.): Chuck Romig, Ph.D.
Special Education (M.Ed.): Robin Cook, Ph.D.
Sport Administration : Clay Stoldt, Ed.D.

COLLEGE OF ENGINEERING: Dean Dennis Siginer, Ph.D.
Aerospace Engineering (M.S., Ph.D.): Kamran Rokhsaz, Ph.D. (M.S. program); Klaus Hoffmann, Ph.D. (Ph.D. program). Research is conducted in experimental and computational aerodynamics/fluid mechanics/propulsion, structures/solid mechanics/composites, and dynamics and control.
Electrical Engineering (M.S., Ph.D.): M. Edward Sawan, Ph.D. Research is conducted in avionics, communication systems, computers, electromagnetic field theory, signal processing, control systems, circuit/system theory, digital systems, electronic systems, and power/energy systems.
Industrial Engineering (M.S., Ph.D. in Industrial and Manufacturing Engineering, M.E.M. in Engineering Management): Abu Masud, Ph.D. (M.S., M.E.M., Ph.D. programs). Research is conducted in applied statistical methods, manufacturing, production processes, human factors, computer integrated manufacturing, decision processes, knowledge base systems, neural networks, operations research, simulation, and multiple criteria programming.
Mechanical Engineering (M.S., Ph.D.): B. Bahr, Ph.D. Research is conducted in computational fluid mechanics, materials science, heat transfer, machine design, propulsion, thermodynamics, robotics and manufacturing automation, impact dynamics and multibody dynamic simulation, and internal combustion engines and fuels.

COLLEGE OF FINE ARTS: Dean Walter Myers, Ph.D.
Art Education (M.A.): Ronald Christ, M.F.A.
Music (M.M.): Tom Fowler, M.M.E.
Music Education (M.M.E.): Tom Fowler, M.M.E.
Performing Arts (M.A.): Bela Kiralyfalvi, Ph.D.
Studio Arts (M.F.A.): Ronald Christ, M.F.A.

COLLEGE OF HEALTH PROFESSIONS: Dean Peter A. Cohen, Ph.D.
Nursing (M.S.N.): Alicia Huckstadt, Ph.D.
Physical Therapy (M.P.T.): Kathleen Lewis, Ph.D.
Public Health (M.P.H.): Janet Wetta, M.A.

Wichita State University's 330-acre main campus is complemented by more than sixty works of art by world-renowned artists.

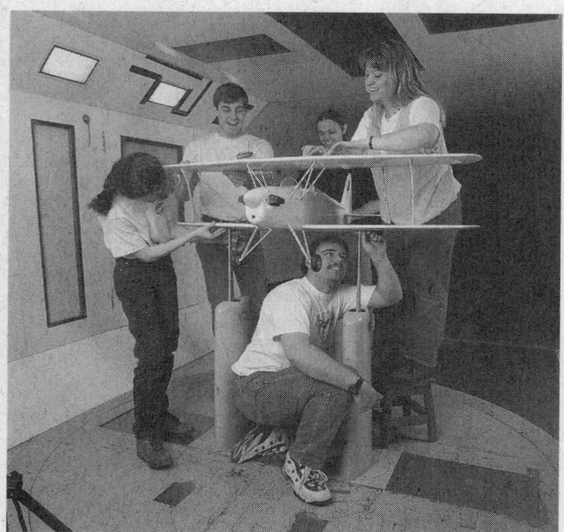

Research in the Beech wind tunnel exemplifies Wichita State's cooperative efforts with the aviation industry, including Boeing, Cessna, Learjet, and Raytheon.

WIDENER UNIVERSITY

Graduate Studies

Programs of Study

Widener University awards the degrees of Doctor of Education (Ed.D.), Doctor of Nursing Science (D.N.Sc.), Doctor of Physical Therapy (D.P.T.), Doctor of Psychology (Psy.D.), Juris Doctor (J.D.), Master of Arts (M.A.) in criminal justice, Master of Arts in Liberal Studies (M.L.S.), Master of Business Administration (M.B.A.), Master of Business Administration in health and medical services administration (M.B.A.–HMSA), Master of Education (M.Ed.), Master of Engineering (M.Eng.), Master of Health Administration (M.H.A.), Master of Science in Hospitality Management (M.S.H.M.), Master of Public Administration (M.P.A.), Master of Science in Nursing (M.S.N.), and Master of Social Work (M.S.W.). Master of Science degrees are also offered in the following business disciplines: accounting information systems (M.S.A.I.S.), human resource management (M.S.H.R.), information systems (M.S.I.S.), management and technology (M.S.M.T.), and taxation (M.S.T.). The M.Ed. program offers over twenty majors, including counselor education, educational leadership, elementary education, human sexuality education, reading, special education, and supervision. The M.S.N. program offers concentrations in the advanced practice roles of adult health nursing, community-based nursing, emergency/critical care, family nurse practitioner, nurse educator, and psychiatric/mental health. Post-master's degrees are available in all clinical specialty areas, as well as nursing education. The M.Eng. program offers specializations in engineering management, and chemical, civil, computer and software, electrical/telecommunications, and mechanical engineering. An environmental engineering option is also available.

Dual-degree programs include the M.Eng./M.B.A., J.D./M.B.A., J.D./Psy.D., Psy.D./M.B.A., Psy.D./M.B.A.–HMSA, Psy.D./M.H.A., Psy.D./M.S.H.R., Psy.D./M.A. in criminal justice, and the Psy.D./M.P.A.

Research Facilities

The Wolfgram Memorial Library has a fine collection that numbers close to 250,000 printed volumes, 165,000 microforms, and 2,100 periodical titles. Services include online access to bibliographic information, full-text electronic journals, Web-based databases, audiovisual-media collections and facilities, and access to other libraries' resources through interlibrary loans. Computing facilities are available to meet students' needs.

The Center for Education runs a full-time laboratory preschool and early childhood center. It also has an extensive collection of curriculum materials, a reading laboratory, and a personal computer laboratory for computer-assisted instruction and interactive video.

The School of Law library maintains a collection of more than 600,000 volumes. Contained in the collection are legal publications and journals, treatises, reports, and statutes. Access to a wide range of supporting materials is available through LEXIS and WESTLAW online legal research services.

Financial Aid

More than 80 percent of the law students receive some form of financial aid. Applicants should complete the Free Application for Federal Student Aid (FAFSA) form at the time of application.

Students in graduate programs other than law can apply for financial aid programs through the Financial Aid Office on the Main Campus. A limited number of graduate assistantships are available to full-time students in graduate programs other than law, and a number of loan programs are available to all eligible students.

Cost of Study

Tuition for Widener's graduate programs is as follows: $545 per credit for Ed.D. courses, $560 per credit for D.N.Sc. courses, $20,800 per year for the D.P.T. program, $17,325 per year for the Psy.D. program, $23,260 per year for first-year Regular Division J.D. students, $450 per credit for graduate criminal justice and M.P.A. courses, $420 per credit for M.L.S. courses, $570 per credit for graduate business courses (with the exception of foundation courses, which are $505 per credit), $420 per credit for M.Ed. courses, $625 per credit for M.Eng. courses, $450 per credit for M.S.H.M. courses, $550 per credit for M.S.N. courses, and $510 per credit for M.S.W. courses.

Living and Housing Costs

Affordable rental apartments are available within a 3-mile radius of all three campuses.

Student Group

Approximately 3,500 students are pursuing graduate or professional degrees at the University. About 55 percent are women. The student population is largely drawn from the mid-Atlantic region; about 5 percent of the graduate and professional students are from other countries. Students enter with a variety of undergraduate majors, including liberal arts, engineering, business, and nursing.

Location

Widener's Main Campus, occupying more than 100 acres in Chester, Pennsylvania, is easily accessible from Interstate 95. Located in Delaware County, one of the oldest counties in Pennsylvania, the campus is near historic and commercial areas; Philadelphia is just 15 miles north.

The 40-acre Delaware Campus (15 miles southwest of the Main Campus) is located on Route 202 (Concord Pike), north of Wilmington, and is only a short distance from Interstate 95. It houses the School of Law, and is also a course site for the School of Business Administration. A branch of the School of Law is located on the 21-acre Harrisburg Campus in central Pennsylvania. Graduate social work, nursing, and education courses are also offered on this campus.

The University

A private, accredited university founded in 1821, Widener offers doctoral, master's, baccalaureate, and associate degrees through its eight schools and colleges. Situated in both Pennsylvania and Delaware, the University has three campuses, which are located in Chester and Harrisburg, Pennsylvania, and Wilmington, Delaware. The total University enrollment is approximately 6,700.

Applying

Applicants for admission must file forms provided by the University, submit official transcripts of records covering all academic work beyond high school, and submit the standardized test scores (e.g., scores on the GMAT, GRE, or LSAT) appropriate to the program they wish to enter. An application fee is required. Final selection is based on the quality of the total application, as determined by the student's record of achievement and his or her personal qualification for graduate study and professional practice.

Correspondence and Information

For the Juris Doctor program:
Office of Admissions
Widener University School of Law
4601 Concord Pike
Wilmington, Delaware 19803
Telephone: 302-477-2160
E-mail: law.admissions@law.widener.edu
World Wide Web: http://www.law.widener.edu

For other graduate programs:
Office of Graduate Studies
Widener University
One University Place
Chester, Pennsylvania 19013
Telephone: 610-499-4372
E-mail: grad.programs@widener.edu
World Wide Web: http://www.widener.edu

FACULTY HEADS

Assistant Provost for Graduate Studies: Stephen C. Wilhite, D.Phil.

Deans
College of Arts and Sciences: Lawrence W. Panek, Ph.D.
School of Business Administration: Eric Brucker, Ph.D.
School of Engineering: Fred A. Akl, Ph.D.
School of Human Service Professions: Stephen C. Wilhite, D.Phil.
School of Law: Douglas E. Ray, J.D.
School of Nursing: Marguerite M. Barbiere, M.S.N., Ed.D.

Computer labs feature access to the Internet, e-mail, and a wide variety of course-specific software programs.

The School of Law campus in Wilmington, Delaware.

Old Main, Chester, Pennsylvania, houses the School of Nursing and administrative offices.

WILLIAM PATERSON UNIVERSITY OF NEW JERSEY

Graduate Programs

Programs of Study

William Paterson University offers nineteen degree programs in the University's five colleges. Eight degrees are awarded: Master of Arts, Master of Fine Arts, Master of Science, Master of Education, Master of Business Administration, Master of Arts in Teaching, Master of Music, and Master of Science in Nursing. Degree requirements vary. The M.A. is offered in communication and media studies, English (with concentrations in literature and writing), history, public policy, and sociology (with concentrations in diversity studies and crime and justice). The M.F.A. in art offers concentrations in fine arts, media arts, and design arts, with studio courses in computer arts and animation, ceramics, furniture design, painting, photography, printmaking, sculpture, fibers, foundry, and graphic design. The M.S. is offered in applied clinical psychology, biology, biotechnology and communication disorders (speech-language pathology). The M.Ed. is offered in counseling services (with concentrations in school counseling and agency counseling), education (with concentrations in bilingual/English as a second language, early childhood, educational media, language arts, learning technologies, and teaching children mathematics), educational leadership, reading, and special education (with specializations in developmental disability and learning disability). The M.M. is offered in music education, jazz studies, and music management. The M.B.A. is offered in marketing, finance, management, and general business. The M.S.N. is offered in community-based nursing with tracks in educational, administrative, and advanced practice. The M.A.T. is offered in elementary education. Teacher certification programs are offered for college graduates who wish to obtain initial teaching certification in New Jersey. Endorsement programs are offered for certified teachers who wish to obtain additional teaching certification.

Research Facilities

The biological science facilities include scanning and transmission electron microscopes; fully equipped biochemistry, molecular biology, and neurobiology laboratories; computer, animal care, and instrument rooms; NMR, IR, UV-visible, and AA spectrometers; GC and HPLC equipment; an amino acid analyzer; an ecology laboratory; and a greenhouse. Biotechnology facilities include an automated DNA sequencer, a DNA synthesizer, a DNA thermal coupler, gel electrophoresis equipment, and high-speed and ultracentrifuges; a modern tissue culture laboratory; a radioisotope laboratory; and a computer-assisted image processing system. Hobart Hall houses two broadcast-quality TV studios, a multipurpose computer lab, a film studio, an FCC-licensed FM radio station, an uplink and four downlink satellite dishes, a cable system, and a computerized telephone system for voice and data transmission. The Atrium is a new state-of-the-art technology center on campus that holds 128 Pentium multimedia computers arranged in classrooms with video projection capacity. The media center, which supports multimedia and Internet development, includes scanners, CD-ROM writers, digitizers, and related software tools. A multiphasic on-site clinic provides practical experience for special education, reading, and communication disorders program participants. William Paterson University is a member of the New Jersey Intercampus Network (NJIN), a nonprofit organization of forty-five colleges and universities fostering the growth of video, voice, and data networking in the state. NJIN has offices at Rutgers University, Stevens Institute of Technology, and William Paterson University. University administrative computer facilities consist of a Digital Equipment Corporation alpha cluster and interactive time-sharing terminals running VMS. The campus has a fiber-optic ATM backbone interconnecting all faculty offices, classrooms, and laboratories. There are currently more than 1,500 nodes on WPUNJnet. The David and Lorraine Cheng Library is open seven days a week when classes are in session and includes more than 350,000 volumes, more than 1,700 periodical titles, and an extensive collection of nonprint media. Services include professional reference assistance, online bibliographic searching, an interlibrary loan program, viewing facilities, and the latest in end-use searching. Nonprint resource materials include a microcomputer software collection and an audiovisual collection of film and videocassettes. The newly renovated library has added an electronic resource center and a graduate research center equipped with RJ-45 Ethernet data jacks so that laptops can be plugged into the William Paterson network and has doubled its seating capacity.

Financial Aid

The University is participating in the Federal Direct Student Loan Program. This program consists of Federal Direct Stafford Loans (subsidized and unsubsidized) and Federal Direct Plus Loans. Students must file the Free Application for Federal Student Aid (FAFSA) to determine their eligibility. The University makes a limited number of graduate assistantships available each year. Assistantships normally carry a stipend of $6000 and a waiver of tuition and fees. Graduate assistants must carry a minimum of 9 credits in each of the fall and spring semesters and work 20 hours a week in an assigned area. Graduate assistantships require a minimum grade point average of 3.0 and are awarded on the basis of availability and applicants' qualifications. Application forms are available in the Office of Graduate Studies.

Cost of Study

In 2001–02, full-time graduate tuition and fees were $267 per credit for New Jersey residents and $413 per credit for out-of-state students. Other fees apply for books, parking, the Student Center, information technology, and general services. Tuition and fees are subject to change in accordance with policies established by the Board of Trustees.

...ng and ...sing Costs

On-campus housing is available for single graduate students. Housing options include suite-style, single, and double accommodations or apartment-style living offered in a grouping of 4 students to an apartment. Currently, on-campus housing costs range from $2150 to $2310 per semester, with meal plans available at an additional cost of $1380 to $2370. The University does not offer family student housing; however, the Office of Residence Life provides an off-campus living listing service. These dwellings are not preapproved by the University and may include listings for shared homes or apartments as well as private rooms. A graduate student selecting such off-campus housing may expect room and board costs of $6950 for the combined fall and spring semesters. Students are also advised to include $1100 in their budgets for travel as well as an additional $1500 for miscellaneous and personal expenses.

...oup

The University has 10,466 students, of whom more than 18 percent are graduate students. Eighty-four percent of the students enrolled in graduate programs pursue their studies on a part-time basis. The traditional service area of the University consists of New Jersey's northernmost counties.

Set on a 370-acre wooded hilltop, the University commands a breathtaking view of the surrounding communities. Located 20 miles west of New York City, the campus is easily accessible from major highways that provide access to the cultural and educational resources available within the metropolitan area.

Founded in the city of Paterson in 1855, William Paterson is one of nine institutions in the New Jersey State Higher Education system. The University moved to the Wayne campus in 1951. In 1966, the University became a comprehensive institution offering undergraduate, graduate, and professional degrees. In 1997, William Paterson was awarded university status by the New Jersey Commission on Higher Education. Governed by a local board of trustees, William Paterson is accredited by the Middle States Association of Colleges and Schools. An on-campus state-certified center provides child care for eligible dependents of full- and part-time students. The Career Development Center helps matriculated students and alumni who seek professional advancement or career changes.

...o receive application information and materials, students should contact the Office of Graduate Studies.

...ice of Graduate Studies
...am Paterson University of New Jersey
... Pompton Road, R139
...e, New Jersey 07470-2103
...one: 973-720-2237
...graduate@wpunj.edu
...de Web: http://www.wpunj.edu

GRADUATE PROGRAMS AND DIRECTORS

Applied Clinical Psychology: Dr. Behnaz Pakizegi (973-720-2643).
Art: William Whiteley (973-720-3284). The M.F.A. program is designed as the professional degree for the fine artist, craftsperson, designer, media artist, or for those wishing to teach at the college or university level. Concentrations are in fine arts, design arts, or media arts.
Biological Science: Dr. Robert Chesney (973-720-3455). Neuroscience, image processing, transmission electron microscopy, protozoology, neuroendocrinology, teratogenic agents and development, animal behavior, behavior genetics, scanning electron microscopy, palynology, muscle physiology, invertebrate zoology, aquatic ecology, ecology and entomology, wetland ecology, and endocrinology.
Biotechnology: Dr. Robert Chesney (973-720-3455). Microbial genetics, molecular biology, protein biochemistry, neurochemistry, algal biochemistry, plant genetic engineering, parasitology, immunochemistry, mycology, molecular biology development, marine biochemistry, and gene activation.
Business Administration: Dr. Virginia Taylor (973-720-3679). The M.B.A. program is designed to provide students with both the background and perspective necessary for success in today's and tomorrow's business environments. Emphasis is placed on preparing students for the competitive global marketplace. Computer courses are designed to enhance the students' skills by providing up-to-date software packages. The major areas of concentration are marketing, management, finance, and general business.
Certification Programs: College of Education (973-720-2138). Certification programs are intended for graduates who wish to obtain initial certification or endorsement in the state of New Jersey.
Communication Disorders: Dr. Jennifer Hsu (973-720-3352). This ASHA-accredited program provides students the training required to work as speech/language pathologists. The program is affiliated with ASHA-accredited William Paterson University Speech and Hearing Clinic, which offers clinical services in the diagnosis or treatment of speech, language, and hearing disorders. Students have the opportunity to work with state-of-the-art equipment in audiometric testing, auditory brainstem-evoked responses, and speech and hearing science.
* **Counseling Services (Personnel or Agency):** Dr. Mathilda Catarina (973-720-2279).
Education: Dr. Rochelle Kaplan (973-720-2598). The M.Ed. program offers concentrations in bilingual/English as a second language, early childhood, educational leadership, educational media, language arts, learning technologies, and mathematics.
Education Leadership: Dr. Michael Chirichello (973-720-2130).
* **Elementary Education:** Dr. Roger Tesi (973-720-3088). The Master of Arts in Teaching degree also enables graduates to obtain elementary (N–8) teacher certification.
English: Dr. Linda Hamalian (973-720-3056). Literature concentration: modern English and its background, major authors, early drama, and the novel; seventeenth- and eighteenth-century, romantic, Victorian, and modern British literature; nineteenth- and twentieth-century American literature; and related literature, including women's studies and film. Writing concentration: creative writing, advanced critical writing, writing for the magazine market, fiction writing, poetry writing, book and magazine editing, teaching writing as process, journalism, and script writing for the media.
History: Dr. Sara Nalle (973-720-3049).
Media Studies: Dr. Sharmilla Ferris (973-720-3338). The program encompasses theory, philosophy, and applications in the various areas of communication, including interpersonal communication, mass communication, and telecommunication. Research areas are cable access policy, intercultural communication, legal communication, and film and broadcast theory.
Music: Jazz Studies, Dr. David Demsey (973-720-2268); Music Education, Dr. Diane Falk (973-720-3197); Music Management, Dr. Stephen Marcone (973-720-2314).
Nursing: Dr. Connie Bareford (973-720-3495). The M.S.N. program is designed to provide students the training to work as advanced practice nurses, educators, or administrators in community-based care. The program combines course work and clinical practice in a variety of community-based settings and includes courses in advanced nursing, health-care systems, health assessment, legislation and social policy, financial management, and labor law.
* **Reading:** Dr. Dorothy Feola (973-720-2577).
Sociology: Dr. Peter Stein (973-720-3429). The program consists of two interrelated tracks: diversity studies and crime and justice.
* **Special Education:** Dr. John Gangale (973-720-3087).

* *Teacher education programs are fully approved by the National Council of Accreditation of Teacher Education and meet the standards of the National Association of State Directors of Teacher Education and Certification.*

Applications are being accepted for the master's degree program in community-based nursing.

The suburban campus of William Paterson University in Wayne is situa 370-acre wooded hilltop.

WORCESTER POLYTECHNIC INSTITUTE

Graduate Programs

Programs of Study

Worcester Polytechnic Institute (WPI) offers M.S. and Ph.D. programs in the following applied sciences: computer science, mathematics, and physics. Programs are also offered in the following areas of engineering: biomedical, chemical, civil and environmental, electrical and computer, fire protection, manufacturing, materials science, and mechanical.

The programs for the M.S. degree require a minimum of 30 credit hours. Although the specific requirements vary, most departments require a thesis of at least 6 semester hours. Arrangements may be made with local industries for thesis research.

A biomedical science Ph.D. program is sponsored by WPI with the cooperation of the Worcester Foundation for Experimental Biology and the University of Massachusetts Medical School. A biomedical engineering/medical physics joint Ph.D. program is sponsored by WPI and the University of Massachusetts Medical School.

The Ph.D. degree requires a minimum of 90 credit hours beyond the bachelor's degree, with a minimum of one year of full-time residence at the Institute.

Research Facilities

In addition to the extensive facilities for research available in all departments, graduate students have the opportunity to conduct research in a number of research centers. These centers include the Accelerated Pavement Testing Facility; the Aerodynamics Laboratory; the Alternative Fuel Economics Laboratory; the Analog Research Laboratory; the Assistive Technology Resource Center; the Atomic Force Microscopy Laboratory; the Bioengineering Institute; the Biomaterials Laboratory; the Bioprocess Technology Laboratory; the Center for Holographic Studies and Laser micro-mechaTronics; the Center for Industrial Mathematics and Statistics; the Center for Inorganic Membrane Studies; the Center for Nuclear Technology and Society at WPI; the Center for Research in Electronic Commerce Technology; the Center for RF Electronics and Imaging; the Center for Sensory and Physiologic Signal Processing; the Center for Wireless Information Network Studies; the Ceramic/Powder Processing Laboratory; the Computer-Aided Manufacturing Laboratory; the Controls Library; the Convergent Technologies Center; the Cryptography and Information Security Research Laboratory; the Dynamics, Vibrations, and Control Laboratory; the Electrochemistry, Tribology, and Corrosion Laboratories; the Environmental Biotechnology Laboratory, the Fire Modeling Laboratory, the Fire Science Laboratory, the Heat Transfer Laboratory, the Hydrodynamics Laboratory, the IPG Photonics Laboratory, the In Vivo Magnetic Resonance Imaging and Spectroscopy, the Manufacturing Assistance Center, the Materials Characterization Laboratories, the Mechanical Testing Laboratory, the Metal Processing Institute, the Nondestructive Evaluation and Electromagnetics Research Laboratory, The New England Center for Analog and Mixed Signal Design at WPI, the Optical and Electron Metallography Laboratories, the Polymer Engineering Laboratory, the Robotics Laboratory, the Scanning Electron Laboratory, the Transmission Electron Microscope Laboratory, the Ultrasound Research Laboratory, and the X-ray Diffraction Laboratory.

Central and departmental computation facilities include parallel processing mainframes and UNIX-based engineering workstations/minicomputers connected by a campuswide fiber-optic-linked Ethernet network. There are approximately 1,000 Windows-based personal computers on campus, many in open-access laboratories.

Financial Aid

Graduate assistantships are available for teaching or research. These generally carry a stipend of $12,750 and remission of tuition for up to 20 credits for the academic year of 2000–01, although some assistantships have a higher basic stipend. Additional assistance may be available for the summer. A few fellowships are available from private industries. Goddard Institute Fellowships of $15,000 for a calendar year plus free tuition are also available.

Cost of Study

Graduate tuition for the 2001–02 academic year was $752 per credit hour. There are nominal extra charges for the thesis, health insurance, and other fees.

Living and Housing Costs

On-campus graduate student housing is limited to a space-available basis. There is no on-campus housing for married students. Apartments and rooms in private homes near the campus are available at varying costs.

Student Group

Worcester Polytechnic Institute has a student body of about 3,650, of whom 1,052 are full- or part-time graduate students. Most states and nearly fifty countries are represented.

Location

The university is located on an 80-acre campus in a residential section of Worcester. The city, the second-largest in New England, has many colleges and an unusual variety of cultural opportunities. Located three blocks from the campus, the nationally famous Worcester Art Museum contains one of the finest permanent collections in the country and offers many special activities of interest to students. The community also provides outstanding programs in music and theater. The Worcester Centrum offers rock concerts and semiprofessional athletic events. Easily reached for recreation are Boston and Cape Cod to the east and the Berkshires to the west, and good skiing is nearby to the north. Complete athletic and recreational facilities and a program of concerts and special events are available on campus to graduate students.

The Institute

Worcester Polytechnic Institute, founded in 1865, is the third-oldest private college of engineering and science in the United States. Graduate study has been a part of the Institute's activity for more than 100 years. Classes are small and provide for close student-faculty relationships. Graduate students frequently interact in research with undergraduates participating in WPI's unusual project-based program of education.

Applying

Application for admission and financial assistance should be made by February 1 but will be considered at any time. Inquiries should be directed to the head of the degree program of interest or to the address below.

Correspondence and Information

Graduate Admissions Office
Worcester Polytechnic Institute
100 Institute Road
Worcester, Massachusetts 01609
Telephone: 508-831-5301
Fax: 508-831-5717
E-mail: gao@wpi.edu
World Wide Web: http://www.wpi.edu/

FACULTY HEADS AND RESEARCH AREAS

Biology and Biotechnology: Associate Professor Jill Rulfs, Head. The M.S. and Ph.D. programs include formal course work along with an original research project. Graduate degrees in biotechnology require course work outside the department in an area relevant to the biotechnology industry. Research interests of the faculty include cell and molecular biology, applied microbiology, genetic engineering, developmental biology, environmental biology, neurophysiology, plant physiology, and bioprocess technology.

Biomedical Engineering: Professor Christopher H. Sotak, Head. Major research areas include cardiovascular electrophysiology, cardiac imaging, peripheral vascular instrumentation, nuclear magnetic resonance imaging and spectroscopy, optical imaging, invasive and noninvasive blood gas and biochemistry analysis, biomedical sensors, biological signal processing, patient monitoring, biomedical microprocessor applications, biomechanics, biofluids, biomedical materials, and tissue engineering. Internships in biomedical and clinical engineering are available at several hospitals and research institutions. A Nuclear Magnetic Resonance Imaging facility has been established as part of a joint research program between the Biomedical Engineering Department and the Department of Radiology at the University of Massachusetts Medical Center; the facility is equipped with a General Electric 2.0 Tesla instrument and two GE 1.5 T clinical imaging instruments.

Chemical Engineering: Professor Ravindra Datta, Head. Major research areas include zeolite synthesis and applications, inorganic membrane synthesis and applications, bioreactor analysis using whole cells, biological product recovery and purification, bioreactor design for plant tissue culture, inorganic materials, heterogeneous and homogeneous catalytic mechanisms and synthesis, surface science and chemical kinetics, nucleation and ultrafine aerosols, transport in heterogeneous reactors, environmental and nanostructured materials synthesis, and diamond thin-film synthesis.

Chemistry and Biochemistry: Professor James P. Dittami, Head. Research areas include laser photochemistry, medicinal chemistry, organic synthesis, natural products, molecular-scale devices, biochemistry, plant biochemistry, ion channels, and synthetic photochemistry.

Civil and Environmental Engineering: Professor Frederick L. Hart, Head. Research areas include impact analysis; vehicle crashworthiness; transportation safety and roadside safety; asphalt technology; materials, biological, chemical, and physical aspects of water and wastewater treatment; water quality and distribution; integration of design and construction; groundwater flow; and contaminant distribution and hazardous waste. Environmental graduate courses are offered on campus and via distance learning.

Computer Science: Professor Micha Hofri, Head. Departmental research includes analysis of algorithms, artificial intelligence, data mining, computer graphics, computer networks, computer vision, database systems, distributed systems, formal methods, image processing, knowledge-based systems, language translation, object-oriented methods, operating systems, performance evaluation, software engineering, user interfaces, verification, and visualization. The department is housed in Fuller Laboratories, in a building designed and wired for high-rate connections and multimedia education. The department has numerous general-purpose and specialized computing laboratories, including special graphics devices and printers, a Linux-running cluster, and scores of high-end personal computers and workstations.

Electrical and Computer Engineering: Professor John A. Orr, Head. M.S. and Ph.D. Research areas include wireless networking, cryptography and network security, multimedia networks, the global positioning system, image processing, computational methods for electromagnetics and ultrasonics, analog microelectronics, medical imaging, power quality, and power system state estimation. Approximately $1 million in external research support is received annually. Major facilities include an extensive network of UNIX workstations and PCs, a wireless networks lab, VLSI design and test facilities, RF/microwave laboratories, and power electronics and power systems laboratories.

Fire Protection Engineering: Professor David A. Lucht, Director, Center for Firesafety Studies. This is the first graduate studies program of its kind in the United States. Research areas include structural fire behavior, computer fire modeling, regulation reform, protective clothing, composite materials, building firesafety, and fire detection and explosion protection. WPI offers both the master's and doctoral degrees in fire protection engineering as well as a five-year dual-degree program for high school graduates. Graduate courses are offered on campus and via distance learning.

Management: Professor McRae C. Banks, Head. Offers applications-oriented programs designed for managers in technology-based organizations. Concentration areas include management information systems, management of technology, operations management, technological innovation, technology marketing, e-commerce, and entrepreneurship. Graduate degree programs include the Master of Business Administration, the Master of Science in marketing and technological innovation, and the Master of Science in operations and information technology.

Manufacturing Engineering: Christopher Brown, Saint-Gobain Professor and Director. Research areas include fixturing, computer-integrated manufacturing, machining dynamics, tool wear, grinding, and surface metrology. Resources include the Haas Technical Center for computer-controlled machining, with eight CNC tool and UNIX workstations. The program also has a dedicated surface metrology laboratory with conventional profiling, a scanning laser microscope, and software for area-scale fractal analysis. The M.S. program includes thesis and nonthesis options. There are no required courses for the Ph.D.; however, residency, a comprehensive exam, and a dissertation are required.

Materials Science and Engineering: Professor Richard D. Sisson Jr., Program Director. Graduate study ranges over various engineering and science disciplines after focusing on fundamental work in materials science and materials engineering. Close ties with mechanical engineering, manufacturing, and other engineering and science programs are maintained. Facilities include optical microscopy, X-ray diffraction, casting, welding, mechanical testing and fracture mechanics, and corrosion laboratories and scanning and transmission electron microscopes. There is the nation's only dedicated Surface Metrology Laboratory, with conventional profiling, scanning laser microscope, and fractal analysis software supporting surface engineering. The Metals Processing Institute, a major university-industry consortium with more than 100 industrial members, is also an integrated part of the program. The Metals Processing Institute is made up of three research centers: the Advanced Casting Research Center, the Powder Metallurgy Research Center, and the newly formed Center for Heat Treating Excellence.

Mathematical Sciences: Professor Homer Walker, Head. The department offers an M.S. in applied mathematics, which emphasizes numerical methods, mathematical modeling, and discrete mathematics; an M.S. in applied statistics, which emphasizes industrial and scientific applications; professional M.S. degrees in industrial mathematics and financial mathematics; a Master of Mathematics for Educators; and a Ph.D. in mathematical sciences, which emphasizes mathematical modeling, scientific computing, and industrial, scientific, and engineering applications. Research interests of the 25 full-time faculty members include Bayesian methods, bifurcation theory, biomathematics, composite materials and optimal design, computational fluid dynamics, computational mathematics, cryptography, discrete mathematics, graph theory, mathematical physics, matroid theory, numerical analysis, operations research, optimization, parallel computing, statistical computing, stochastic control, and time-series analysis.

Mechanical Engineering: Professor Gretar Tryggvason, Head. Departmental research includes theoretical, numerical, and experimental work in fluid mechanics, propulsion, multiphase flows, structural analysis, nonlinear dynamics and control, random vibrations, computational mechanics, assistive technology, biomechanics, biomedical imaging, microgravity combustions, economy of fuel cells, manufacturing, robotics, materials processing, mechanics of granular materials, holography, MEMS, and mechanical design. Facilities include the Aerospace Laboratory, Biomechanics/Biofluids Laboratory, the Center for Holographic Studies and Laser micro-mechaTronics, the Heat Transfer Laboratory, the Vibration/Dynamics and Control Laboratory, the Fluid Dynamics Laboratory, the Metal Processing Institute, the Advanced Casting Research Center, the Center for Heat Treating Excellence, the Powder Metallurgy Research Center, the Haas Technical Center, and the Robotics Laboratory.

Physics: Professor Thomas H. Keil, Head. Current research interests include theoretical and experimental work in optics, solid-state physics, chemical physics, statistical mechanics, and nuclear physics. Specializations include optical properties of semiconductor superlattices, as measured by inelastic light scattering, luminescence, and excitation spectroscopies; laser spectroscopy of impurity ions in fiber-optic glasses; nonlinear and quantum optics; coherent and squeezed states; light-scattering spectroscopy of transport phenomena in complex fluids, such as polymer and biomacromolecular solutions; magnetic systems and tunneling states; low-temperature behavior of glassy and amorphous materials; electronic properties of diluted magnetic semiconductors; lattice dynamics of dielectric crystals; and proton microbeam development.

Appendixes

This section contains two appendixes. The first, Institutional Changes Since the 2002 Edition, lists institutions that have closed, moved, merged, or changed their name or status since the last edition of the guides. The second, Abbreviations Used in the Guides, gives abbreviations of degree names, along with what those abbreviations stand for. These appendixes are identical in all six volumes of the Graduate Guides.

Institutional Changes Since the 2002 Edition

Following is an alphabetical listing of institutions that have recently closed, merged with other institutions, or changed their names or status. In the case of a name change, the former name appears first, followed by the new name.

Alliant International University–Mexico (Mexico City, Mexico): name changed to Alliant International University–Mexico City.

Argosy University–Los Angeles (Orange, CA): name changed to Argosy University–Orange County.

Avila College (Kansas City, MO): name changed to Avila University.

Barat College (Lake Forest, IL): merged into DePaul University (Chicago, IL).

Cleary College (Ann Arbor, MI): name changed to Cleary University.

Cleveland Chiropractic College of Kansas City (Kansas City, MO): name changed to Cleveland Chiropractic College–Kansas City Campus.

Cleveland Chiropractic College of Los Angeles (Los Angeles, CA): name changed to Cleveland Chiropractic College–Los Angeles Campus.

Cleveland College of Jewish Studies (Beachwood, OH): name changed to Laura and Alvin Siegal College of Judaic Studies.

Colgate Rochester Divinity School/Bexley Hall/Crozer Theological Seminary (Rochester, NY): name changed to Colgate Rochester Crozer Divinity School.

The College of Insurance (New York, NY): merged into St. John's University (Jamaica, NY).

College of Our Lady of the Elms (Chicopee, MA): name changed to Elms College.

Dr. William M. Scholl College of Podiatric Medicine (North Chicago, IL): name changed to The Scholl College of Podiatric Medicine at Finch University of Health Sciences/The Chicago Medical School.

Eastern College (St. Davids, PA): name changed to Eastern University.

Fairleigh Dickinson University, Florham-Madison Campus (Madison, NJ): name changed to Fairleigh Dickinson University, College at Florham.

Fairleigh Dickinson University, Teaneck-Hackensack Campus (Teaneck, NJ): name changed to Fairleigh Dickinson University, Metropolitan Campus.

Fontbonne College (St. Louis, MO): name changed to Fontbonne University.

Georgia College and State University (Milledgeville, GA): name changed to Georgia College & State University.

Grand Rapids Baptist Seminary (Grand Rapids, MI): name changed to Grand Rapids Baptist Seminary of Cornerstone University.

The Harid Conservatory (Boca Raton, FL): merged into Lynn University (Boca Raton, FL).

Hawaii Pacific University (Honolulu, HI): name changed to Hawai'i Pacific University.

Huron University (Huron, SD): name changed to Si Tanka Huron University.

Illinois School of Professional Psychology, Chicago Campus (Chicago, IL): name changed to Argosy University–Chicago.

Illinois School of Professional Psychology, Chicago Northwest Campus (Rolling Meadows, IL): name changed to Argosy University–Chicago Northwest.

Keller Graduate School of Management (Oakbrook Terrace, IL): name changed to DeVry University–Keller Graduate School of Management.

The Lake Forest Graduate School of Management (Lake Forest, IL): name changed to Lake Forest Graduate School of Management.

Marycrest International University (Davenport, IA): closed .

Mayo School of Health-Related Sciences (Rochester, MN): name changed to Mayo School of Health Sciences.

MCP Hahnemann University (Philadelphia, PA): merged into Drexel University (Philadelphia, PA).

Mount Vernon Nazarene College (Mount Vernon, OH): name changed to Mount Vernon Nazarene University.

The New York College for Wholistic Health Education & Research (Syosset, NY): name changed to The New York College of Health Professions.

North American Baptist College and Edmonton Baptist Seminary (Edmonton, AB Canada): name changed to Taylor University College and Seminary.

Notre Dame College of Ohio (South Euclid, OH): name changed to Notre Dame College.

Oklahoma State University College of Osteopathic Medicine (Tulsa, OK): name changed to Oklahoma State University Center for Health Sciences.

Pace University, New York City Campus (New York, NY): name changed to Pace University.

Palm Beach Atlantic College (West Palm Beach, FL): name changed to Palm Beach Atlantic University.

Polytechnic University, Farmingdale Campus (Melville, NY): name changed to Polytechnic University, Long Island Graduate Center.

Pope John XXIII National Seminary (Weston, MA): name changed to Blessed John XXIII National Seminary.

Queens College (Charlotte, NC): name changed to Queens University of Charlotte.

Robert Morris College (Moon Township, PA): name changed to Robert Morris University.

Saint Bernard's Institute (Rochester, NY): name changed to Saint Bernard's School of Theology and Ministry.

Salisbury State University (Salisbury, MD): name changed to Salisbury University.

Seton Hill College (Greensburg, PA): name changed to Seton Hill University.

Southwestern College of Christian Ministries (Bethany, OK): name changed to Southwestern Christian University.

Technical University of British Columbia (Surrey, BC Canada): merged into Simon Fraser University (Burnaby, BC Canada).

The Union Institute (Cincinnati, OH): name changed to Union Institute and University.

United States International University–Africa (Nairobi, Kenya): name changed to United States International University.

University of Advancing Computer Technology (Tempe, AZ): name changed to University of Advancing Technology.

University of New Brunswick (Fredericton, NB Canada): name changed to University of New Brunswick Fredericton.

University of New Brunswick (Saint John, NB Canada): name changed to University of New Brunswick Saint John.

University of Phoenix–Dallas/Ft. Worth Campus (Dallas, TX): name changed to University of Phoenix–Dallas Campus.

University of Phoenix–Grand Rapids Campus (Grand Rapids, MI): name changed to University of Phoenix–West Michigan Campus.

University of South Dakota (Vermillion, SD): name changed to The University of South Dakota.

The University of Texas Medical Branch at Galveston (Galveston, TX): name changed to The University of Texas Medical Branch.

Utica College of Syracuse University (Utica, NY): name changed to Utica College.

Western Maryland College (Westminster, MD): name changed to McDaniel College.

Abbreviations Used in the Guides

The following list includes abbreviations of degree names used in the profiles in the 2003 edition of the guides. Because some degrees (e.g., Doctor of Education) can be abbreviated in more than one way (e.g., D.Ed. or Ed.D.), and because the abbreviations used in the guides reflect the preferences of the individual colleges and universities, the list may include two or more abbreviations for a single degree.

Degrees

A Mus D	Doctor of Musical Arts
AC	Advanced Certificate
AD	Artist's Diploma
ADP	Artist's Diploma
Adv C	Advanced Certificate
Adv M	Advanced Master
Aerospace E	Aerospace Engineer
AGSC	Advanced Graduate Specialist Certificate
ALM	Master of Liberal Arts
AM	Master of Arts
AMRS	Master of Arts in Religious Studies
APC	Advanced Professional Certificate
App ME	Applied Mechanics
App Sc	Applied Scientist
Au D	Doctor of Audiology
B Th	Bachelor of Theology
C Phil	Certificate in Philosophy
CAES	Certificate of Advanced Educational Specialization
CAGS	Certificate of Advanced Graduate Studies
CAL	Certificate in Applied Linguistics
CALS	Certificate of Advanced Liberal Studies
CAMS	Certificate of Advanced Management Studies
CAPS	Certificate of Advanced Professional Studies
CAS	Certificate of Advanced Studies
CASPA	Certificate of Advanced Study in Public Administration
CASR	Certificate in Advanced Social Research
CATS	Certificate of Achievement in Theological Studies
CBHS	Certificate in Basic Health Sciences
CCJA	Certificate in Criminal Justice Administration
CCMBA	Cross-Continent Master of Business Administration
CCSA	Certificate in Catholic School Administration
CE	Civil Engineer
CEM	Certificate of Environmental Management
CG	Certificate in Gerontology
CGS	Certificate of Graduate Studies
Ch E	Chemical Engineer
CHSS	Counseling and Human Services Specialist
CIF	Certificate in International Finance
CITS	Certificate of Individual Theological Studies
CMH	Certificate in Medical Humanities
CMS	Certificate in Ministerial Studies Certificate in Museum Studies
CNM	Certificate in Nonprofit Management
CP	Certificate in Performance
CPC	Certificate in Professional Counseling Certificate in Publication and Communication
CPH	Certificate in Public Health
CPM	Certificate in Public Management
CPS	Certificate of Professional Studies
CSD	Certificate in Spiritual Direction
CSE	Computer Systems Engineer
CSS	Certificate of Special Studies
CTE	Certificate of Technologies of Education
CTS	Certificate of Theological Studies
CURP	Certificate in Urban and Regional Planning
D Arch	Doctor of Architecture
D Chem	Doctor of Chemistry
D Ed	Doctor of Education
D Eng	Doctor of Engineering
D Engr	Doctor of Engineering
D Env	Doctor of Environment
D Jur	Doctor of Jurisprudence
D Law	Doctor of Law
D Litt	Doctor of Letters
D Med Sc	Doctor of Medical Science
D Min	Doctor of Ministry
D Min PCC	Doctor of Ministry, Pastoral Care, and Counseling
D Miss	Doctor of Missiology
D Mus	Doctor of Music
D Mus A	Doctor of Musical Arts
D Mus Ed	Doctor of Music Education
D Phil	Doctor of Philosophy
D Ps	Doctor of Psychology
D Sc	Doctor of Science
D Sc D	Doctor of Science in Dentistry
D Th	Doctor of Theology
D Th P	Doctor of Practical Theology
DA	Doctor of Arts
DA Ed	Doctor of Arts in Education
DAST	Diploma of Advanced Studies in Teaching
DBA	Doctor of Business Administration
DBS	Doctor of Buddhist Studies
DC	Doctor of Chiropractic
DCC	Doctor of Computer Science
DCD	Doctor of Communications Design
DCL	Doctor of Comparative Law
DCM	Doctor of Church Music
DCS	Doctor of Computer Science
DDN	Diplôme du Droit Notarial
DDS	Doctor of Dental Surgery
DE	Doctor of Education Doctor of Engineering
DEIT	Doctor of Educational Innovation and Technology
DEM	Doctor of Educational Ministry
DEPD	Diplôme Études Spécialisées
DES	Doctor of Engineering Science
DESS	Diplôme Études Supérieures Spécialisées

DFA	Doctor of Fine Arts
DFES	Doctor of Forestry and Environmental Studies
DGP	Diploma in Graduate and Professional Studies
DH Sc	Doctor of Health Sciences
DHA	Doctor of Health Administration
DHCE	Doctor of Health Care Ethics
DHL	Doctor of Hebrew Letters Doctor of Hebrew Literature
DHS	Doctor of Human Services
DIBA	Doctor of International Business Administration
Dip CS	Diploma in Christian Studies
DIT	Doctor of Industrial Technology
DJ Ed	Doctor of Jewish Education
DJS	Doctor of Jewish Studies
DM	Doctor of Management Doctor of Music
DMA	Doctor of Musical Arts
DMD	Doctor of Dental Medicine
DME	Doctor of Music Education
DMFT	Doctor of Marital and Family Therapy
DMH	Doctor of Medical Humanities
DML	Doctor of Modern Languages
DMM	Doctor of Music Ministry
DN Sc	Doctor of Nursing Science
DNS	Doctor of Nursing Science
DO	Doctor of Osteopathy
DPA	Doctor of Public Administration
DPC	Doctor of Pastoral Counseling
DPDS	Doctor of Planning and Development Studies
DPE	Doctor of Physical Education
DPH	Doctor of Public Health
DPM	Doctor of Plant Medicine Doctor of Podiatric Medicine
DPS	Doctor of Professional Studies
DPT	Doctor of Physical Therapy
Dr DES	Doctor of Design
Dr OT	Doctor of Occupational Therapy
Dr PH	Doctor of Public Health
Dr Sc PT	Doctor of Science in Physical Therapy
DS	Doctor of Science
DS Sc	Doctor of Social Science
DSJS	Doctor of Science in Jewish Studies
DSL	Doctor of Strategic Leadership
DSM	Doctor of Sacred Music Doctor of Sport Management
DSN	Doctor of Science in Nursing
DSW	Doctor of Social Work
DTL	Doctor of Talmudic Law
DV Sc	Doctor of Veterinary Science
DVM	Doctor of Veterinary Medicine
EAA	Engineer in Aeronautics and Astronautics
EAS	Education Administration Specialist
Ed D	Doctor of Education
Ed DCT	Doctor of Education in College Teaching
Ed M	Master of Education
Ed S	Specialist in Education
Ed Sp	Specialist in Education
Ed Sp PTE	Specialist in Education in Professional Technical Education
EDM	Executive Doctorate in Management
EE	Electrical Engineer Environmental Engineer
EM	Mining Engineer
EMBA	Executive Master of Business Administration
EMCIS	Executive Master of Computer Information Systems
EMHA	Executive Master of Health Administration
EMIB	Executive Master of International Business
EMPA	Executive Master of Public Affairs
EMS	Executive Master of Science
EMSF	Executive Master of Science in Finance
EMTM	Executive Master of Technology Management
Eng	Engineer
Eng Sc D	Doctor of Engineering Science
Engr	Engineer
Exec Ed D	Executive Doctor of Education
Exec MBA	Executive Master of Business Administration
Exec MIM	Executive Master of International Management
Exec MPA	Executive Master of Public Administration
Exec MPH	Executive Master of Public Health
Exec MS	Executive Master of Science
GDPA	Graduate Diploma in Public Administration
GDRE	Graduate Diploma in Religious Education
GEMBA	Global Executive Master of Business Administration
Geol E	Geological Engineer
GMBA	Global Master of Business Administration
GPD	Graduate Performance Diploma
HS Dir	Director of Health and Safety
HSD	Doctor of Health and Safety
IAMBA	Information Age Master of Business Administration
IMA	Interdisciplinary Master of Arts
IMBA	International Master of Business Administration
IOE	Industrial and Operations Engineer
JCD	Doctor of Canon Law
JCL	Licentiate in Canon Law
JD	Juris Doctor
JSD	Doctor of Juridical Science Doctor of Jurisprudence Doctor of the Science of Law
JSM	Master of Science of Law
L Th	Licenciate in Theology
LL B	Bachelor of Laws
LL CM	Master of Laws in Comparative Law
LL D	Doctor of Laws
LL M	Master of Laws
LL M CL	Master of Laws in Comparative Law
LL M T	Master of Laws in Taxation
M Ac	Master of Accountancy Master of Accounting Master of Acupuncture
M Ac OM	Master of Acupuncture and Oriental Medicine
M Acc	Master of Accountancy Master of Accounting

M Acct	Master of Accountancy Master of Accounting
M Accy	Master of Accountancy
M Actg	Master of Accounting
M Acy	Master of Accountancy
M Ad	Master of Administration
M Ad Ed	Master of Adult Education
M Adm	Master of Administration
M Adm Mgt	Master of Administrative Management
M Aero E	Master of Aerospace Engineering
M Ag	Master of Agriculture
M Ag Ed	Master of Agricultural Education
M Agr	Master of Agriculture
M Anesth Ed	Master of Anesthesiology Education
M App Comp Sc	Master of Applied Computer Science
M App St	Master of Applied Statistics
M Appl Stat	Master of Applied Statistics
M Aq	Master of Aquaculture
M Arch	Master of Architecture
M Arch E	Master of Architectural Engineering
M Arch H	Master of Architectural History
M Arch UD	Master of Architecture in Urban Design
M Bio E	Master of Bioengineering
M Biomath	Master of Biomathematics
M Bus Ed	Master of Business Education
M Ch E	Master of Chemical Engineering
M Chem	Master of Chemistry
M Cl D	Master of Clinical Dentistry
M Cl Sc	Master of Clinical Science
M Co E	Master of Computer Engineering
M Comp E	Master of Computer Engineering
M Coun	Master of Counseling
M Cp E	Master of Computer Engineering
M Dec S	Master of Decision Sciences
M Dent	Master of Dentistry
M Dent Sc	Master of Dental Sciences
M Des	Master of Design
M Des S	Master of Design Studies
M Div	Master of Divinity
M Div CM	Master of Divinity in Church Music
M E Com	Master of Electronic Commerce
M Ec	Master of Economics
M Econ	Master of Economics
M Ed	Master of Education
M Ed T	Master of Education in Teaching
M En	Master of Engineering
M En S	Master of Environmental Sciences
M Eng	Master of Engineering
M Eng Mgt	Master of Engineering Management
M Eng Tel	Master of Engineering in Telecommunications
M Engr	Master of Engineering
M Env	Master of Environment
M Env Des	Master of Environmental Design
M Env E	Master of Environmental Engineering
M Env Sc	Master of Environmental Science
M Ext Ed	Master of Extension Education
M Fin	Master of Finance
M Fr	Master of French
M Gen E	Master of General Engineering
M Geo E	Master of Geological Engineering
M Geoenv E	Master of Geoenvironmental Engineering
M Hum	Master of Humanities
M Hum Svcs	Master of Human Services
M Kin	Master of Kinesiology
M Land Arch	Master of Landscape Architecture
M Lit M	Master of Liturgical Music
M Litt	Master of Letters
M Man	Master of Management
M Mat SE	Master of Material Science and Engineering
M Math	Master of Mathematics
M Med Sc	Master of Medical Science
M Mgmt	Master of Management
M Mgt	Master of Management
M Min	Master of Ministries
M Mtl E	Master of Materials Engineering
M Mu	Master of Music
M Mu Ed	Master of Music Education
M Mus	Master of Music
M Mus Ed	Master of Music Education
M Nat Sci	Master of Natural Science
M Nurs	Master of Nursing
M Oc E	Master of Oceanographic Engineering
M Ph M	Master of Science in Philanthropy and Media
M Pharm	Master of Pharmacy
M Phil	Master of Philosophy
M Phil F	Master of Philosophical Foundations
M Pl	Master of Planning
M Pol	Master of Political Science
M Pr A	Master of Professional Accountancy
M Pr Met	Master of Professional Meteorology
M Prob S	Master of Probability and Statistics
M Prof Past	Master of Professional Pastoral
M Ps	Master of Psychology
M Psych	Master of Psychology
M Pub	Master of Publishing
M Rel	Master of Religion
M Rel Ed	Master of Religious Education
M Sc	Master of Science
M Sc A	Master of Science (Applied)
M Sc AHN	Master of Science in Applied Human Nutrition
M Sc BMC	Master of Science in Biomedical Communications
M Sc CS	Master of Science in Computer Science
M Sc E	Master of Science in Engineering
M Sc Eng	Master of Science in Engineering
M Sc Engr	Master of Science in Engineering
M Sc F	Master of Science in Forestry
M Sc FE	Master of Science in Forest Engineering
M Sc Geogr	Master of Science in Geography
M Sc N	Master of Science in Nursing
M Sc P	Master of Science in Planning
M Sc Pl	Master of Science in Planning
M Sc T	Master of Science in Teaching

M Soc	Master of Sociology
M Sp Ed	Master of Special Education
M Stat	Master of Statistics
M Sw E	Master of Software Engineering
M Sw En	Master of Software Engineering
M Sys Sc	Master of Systems Science
M Tax	Master of Taxation
M Tech	Master of Technology
M Th	Master of Theology
M Th Past	Master of Pastoral Theology
M Tox	Master of Toxicology
M Trans E	Master of Transportation Engineering
M Vet Sc	Master of Veterinary Science
MA	Master of Administration Master of Arts
MA Comm	Master of Arts in Communication
MA Ed	Master of Arts in Education
MA Ed Ad	Master of Arts in Educational Administration
MA Ext	Master of Agricultural Extension
MA Min	Master of Arts in Ministry
MA Missions	Master of Arts in Missions
MA Past St	Master of Arts in Pastoral Studies
MA Ph	Master of Arts in Philosophy
MA Ps	Master of Arts in Psychology
MA Psych	Master of Arts in Psychology
MA Sc	Master of Applied Science
MA Th	Master of Arts in Theology
MA(R)	Master of Arts (Research)
MA(T)	Master of Arts in Teaching
MAA	Master of Administrative Arts Master of Applied Anthropology Master of Arts in Administration
MAAA	Master of Arts in Arts Administration
MAABS	Master of Arts in Applied Behavioral Sciences
MAAE	Master of Arts in Applied Economics Master of Arts in Art Education
MAAT	Master of Arts in Applied Theology Master of Arts in Art Therapy
MAB	Master of Agribusiness
MABC	Master of Arts in Biblical Counseling
MABM	Master of Agribusiness Management
MABS	Master of Arts in Biblical Studies
MAC	Master of Accounting Master of Addictions Counseling Master of Analytical Chemistry Master of Art Conservation Master of Arts in Communication Master of Arts in Counseling
MACAT	Master of Arts in Counseling Psychology: Art Therapy
MACCM	Master of Arts in Church and Community Ministry
MACCS	Master of Arts in Cross-Cultural Studies
MACCT	Master of Accounting
MACE	Master of Arts in Christian Education
MACFM	Master of Arts in Children's and Family Ministry
MACH	Master of Arts in Church History
MACL	Master of Arts in Classroom Psychology
MACM	Master of Arts in Christian Ministries Master of Arts in Church Music Master of Arts in Counseling Ministries
MACN	Master of Arts in Counseling
MACO	Master of Arts in Counseling
MACP	Master of Arts in Counseling Psychology
MACS	Master of Arts in Christian Service
MACSE	Master of Arts in Christian School Education
MACT	Master of Arts in Christian Thought
MACTM	Master of Applied Communication Theory and Methodology
MACY	Master of Arts in Accountancy
MAD	Master in Educational Institution Administration Master of Agricultural Development Master of Applied Development
MADH	Master of Applied Development and Health
MADR	Master of Arts in Dispute Resolution
MADT	Master of Arts in Digital Technology
MAE	Master of Aerospace Engineering Master of Agricultural Economics Master of Architectural Engineering Master of Art Education Master of Arts in Economics Master of Arts in Education Master of Arts in English Master of Automotive Engineering
MAEE	Master of Agricultural and Extension Education
MAEN	Master of Arts in English
MAEP	Master of Arts in Economic Policy
MAES	Master of Arts in Environmental Sciences
MAESL	Master of Arts in English as a Second Language
MAEV	Master of Arts in Evangelism
MAF	Master of Arts in Finance
MAFLL	Master of Arts in Foreign Language and Literature
MAFM	Master of Accounting and Financial Management
MAG	Master of Applied Geography
MAGP	Master of Arts in Gerontological Psychology
MAGU	Master of Urban Analysis and Management
MAH	Master of Arts in Humanities
MAHA	Master of Arts in Humanitarian Studies
MAHCM	Master of Arts in Health Care Mission
MAHL	Master of Arts in Hebrew Letters
MAHN	Master of Applied Human Nutrition
MAHRM	Master of Arts in Human Resources Management
MAHS	Master of Arts in Human Services
MAIB	Master of Arts in International Business
MAICS	Master of Arts in Intercultural Studies
MAIDM	Master of Arts in Interior Design and Merchandising
MAIM	Master of Arts in Intercultural Ministry
MAIPCR	Master of Arts in International Peace and Conflict Management
MAIPE	Master of Arts in International Political Economy
MAIR	Master of Arts in Industrial Relations
MAIS	Master of Accounting and Information Systems Master of Arts in Intercultural Studies Master of Arts in Interdisciplinary Studies Master of Arts in International Studies
MAIT	Master of Administration in Information Technology

MAJ	Master of Arts in Journalism
MAJ Ed	Master of Arts in Jewish Education
MAJCS	Master of Arts in Jewish Communal Service
MAJCS/MAJS	Master of Arts in Jewish Communal Service/ Master of Arts in Jewish Studies
MAJE	Master of Arts in Jewish Education
MAJS	Master of Arts in Jewish Studies
MALA	Master of Arts in Liberal Arts
MALD	Master of Arts in Law and Diplomacy
MALED	Master of Arts in Leadership for Evangelism/ Discipleship
MALER	Master of Arts in Labor and Employment Relations
MALL	Master of Arts in Liberal Learning
MALS	Master of Arts in Landscape Studies Master of Arts in Liberal Studies
MAM	Master of Acquisition Management Master of Agriculture and Management Master of Applied Mathematics Master of Applied Mechanics Master of Arts in Management Master of Arts in Ministry Master of Arts Management Master of Avian Medicine
MAMB	Master of Applied Molecular Biology
MAMC	Master of Arts in Mass Communication Master of Arts in Ministry and Culture
MAME	Master of Arts in Missions/Evangelism
MAMFC	Master of Arts in Marriage and Family Counseling
MAMFCC	Master of Arts in Marriage, Family, and Child Counseling
MAMFT	Master of Arts in Marriage and Family Therapy
MAMIS	Master of Arts in Missions
MAMM	Master of Arts in Ministry Management
MAMS	Master of Applied Mathematical Sciences Master of Arts in Ministerial Studies Master of Arts in Ministry and Spirituality Master of Associated Medical Sciences
MAMT	Master of Arts in Mathematics Teaching
MAN	Master of Applied Nutrition
MANM	Master of Arts in Nonprofit Management
MANT	Master of Arts in New Testament
MAO	Master of Arts in Organizational Psychology
MAOE	Master of Adult and Occupational Education
MAOL	Master of Arts in Organizational Leadership
MAOM	Master of Acupuncture and Oriental Medicine Master of Arts in Organizational Management
MAOT	Master of Arts in Old Testament
MAP	Master of Applied Psychology Master of Arts in Planning Master of Arts in Politics Master of Public Administration
MAP Min	Master of Arts in Pastoral Ministry
MAPA	Master of Arts in Public Administration
MAPC	Master of Arts in Pastoral Counseling
MAPCP	Master of Arts in Pastoral Counseling and Psychology
MAPE	Master of Arts in Political Economy
MAPEB	Master of Arts in Politics, Economics, and Business
MAPM	Master of Arts in Pastoral Ministry
MAPP	Master of Arts in Public Policy
MAPPS	Master of Arts in Asia Pacific Policy Studies
MAPS	Master of Arts in Pastoral Studies Master of Arts in Professional Studies
MAPW	Master of Arts in Professional Writing
MAR	Master of Arts in Religion
Mar Eng	Marine Engineer
MARC	Master of Arts in Rehabilitation Counseling Master of Arts in Religious Communication
MARE	Master of Arts in Religious Education
MARL	Master of Arts in Religious Leadership
MARS	Master of Arts in Religious Studies
MAS	Master of Accounting Science Master of Actuarial Science Master of Administrative Science Master of Aeronautical Science Master of American Studies Master of Applied Science Master of Applied Statistics Master of Archival Studies
MASA	Master of Advanced Studies in Architecture
MASAC	Master of Arts in Substance Abuse Counseling
MASD	Master of Arts in Spiritual Direction
MASF	Master of Arts in Spiritual Formation
MASL	Master of Arts in School Leadership
MASLA	Master of Advanced Studies in Landscape Architecture
MASM	Master of Arts in Special Ministries Master of Arts in Specialized Ministries
MASMED	Master of Arts in Science and Mathematics Education
MASP	Master of Applied Social Psychology Master of Arts in School Psychology
MASPAA	Master of Arts in Sports and Athletic Administration
MASS	Master of Applied Social Science Master of Arts in Social Science
MAT	Master of Arts in Teaching Master of Arts in Theology Master of Athletic Training Masters in Administration of Telecommunications
Mat E	Materials Engineer
MATCM	Master of Acupuncture and Traditional Chinese Medicine
MATDE	Master of Arts in Theology, Development, and Evangelism
MATE	Master of Arts for the Teaching of English
MATEFL	Master of Arts in Teaching English as a Foreign Language
MATESL	Master of Arts in Teaching English as a Second Language
MATESOL	Master of Arts in Teaching English to Speakers of Other Languages
MATFL	Master of Arts in Teaching Foreign Language
MATH	Master of Arts in Therapy
MATI	Master of Administration of Information Technology
MATL	Master of Arts in Teaching of Languages Master of Arts in Transformational Leadership
MATM	Master of Arts in Teaching of Mathematics
MATS	Master of Arts in Theological Studies Master of Arts in Transforming Spirituality

MATSL	Master of Arts in Teaching a Second Language
MAUA	Master of Arts in Urban Affairs
MAUD	Master of Arts in Urban Design
MAUM	Master of Arts in Urban Ministry
MAURP	Master of Arts in Urban and Regional Planning
MAW	Master of Arts in Writing
MAWB	Master of Arts in Wildlife Biology
MAWS	Master of Arts in Worship/Spirituality
MAYM	Master of Arts in Youth Ministry
MB	Master of Bioinformatics
MBA	Master of Business Administration
MBA-EB	Master of Business Administration-eBusiness
MBA-EP	Master of Business Administration–Experienced Professionals
MBA-PE	Master of Business Administration–Physician's Executive
MBAA	Master of Business Administration in Aviation
MBAE	Master of Biological and Agricultural Engineering Master of Biosystems and Agricultural Engineering
MBAH	Master of Business Administration in Health
MBAi	Master of Business Administration–International
MBAIM	Master of Business Administration in International Management
MBAPA	Master of Business Administration–Physician Assistant
MBATM	Master of Business in Telecommunication Management
MBC	Master of Building Construction
MBE	Master of Bilingual Education Master of Biomedical Engineering Master of Business Education
MBIOT	Master of Biotechnology
MBIT	Master of Business Information Technology
MBMSE	Master of Business Management and Software Engineering
MBOL	Master of Business and Organizational Leadership
MBS	Master of Basic Science Master of Behavioral Science Master of Biblical Studies Master of Biological Science Master of Biomedical Sciences Master of Bioscience Master of Building Science Master of Business Studies
MBSI	Master of Business Information Science
MBT	Master of Biomedical Technology Master of Business Taxation
MC	Master of Communication Master of Counseling
MC Ed	Master of Continuing Education
MC Sc	Master of Computer Science
MCA	Master of Arts in Applied Criminology Master of Commercial Aviation
MCALL	Master of Computer-Assisted Language Learning
MCAM	Master of Computational and Applied Mathematics
MCC	Master of Computer Science
MCCS	Master of Crop and Soil Sciences
MCD	Master of Communications Disorders Master of Community Development
MCE	Master in Electronic Commerce Master of Civil Engineering Master of Civil Engineering Master of Computer Engineering Master of Construction Engineering Master of Continuing Education Master of Control Engineering
MCEM	Master of Construction Engineering Management
MCG	Master of Clinical Gerontology
MCH	Master of Community Health
MCHS	Master of Clinical Health Sciences
MCIS	Master of Communication and Information Studies Master of Computer and Information Science Master of Computer Information Systems
MCIT	Master's of Computer and Information Technology
MCJ	Master of Criminal Justice
MCJA	Master of Criminal Justice Administration
MCL	Master of Canon Law Master of Civil Law Master of Comparative Law
MCM	Master of Christian Ministry Master of Church Management Master of Church Ministry Master of Church Music Master of City Management Master of Community Medicine Master of Construction Management
MCMS	Master of Clinical Medical Science
MCP	Master in Science Master of City Planning Master of Community Planning Master of Counseling Psychology
MCPD	Master of Community Planning and Development
MCRP	Master of City and Regional Planning
MCRS	Master of City and Regional Studies
MCS	Master of Christian Studies Master of Combined Sciences Master of Communication Studies Master of Computer Science
MCSE	Master of Computer Science and Engineering
MCSL	Master of Catholic School Leadership
MCTE	Master of Career and Technology Education
MCVS	Master of Cardiovascular Science
MD	Doctor of Medicine
MDA	Master of Development Administration Master of Dietetic Administration
MDE	Master of Developmental Economics Master of Distance Education
MDR	Master of Dispute Resolution
MDS	Master of Defense Studies Master of Dental Surgery
ME	Master of Education Master of Engineering
ME Sc	Master of Engineering Science
MEA	Master of Educational Administration Master of Engineering Administration
MEAP	Master of Environmental Administration and Planning
MEC	Master of Electronic Commerce
MECE	Master of Electrical and Computer Engineering
Mech E	Mechanical Engineer

MED	Master of Education of the Deaf
MEDS	Master of Environmental Design Studies
MEE	Master in Education Master of Electrical Engineering Master of Environmental Engineering
MEEM	Master of Environmental Engineering and Management
MEENE	Master of Engineering in Environmental Engineering
MEERM	Master of Earth and Environmental Resource Management
MEH	Master in Humanistics Studies
MEHS	Master of Environmental Health and Safety
MEHWE	Master of Engineering in Hazardous Waste Engineering
MEL	Master of Educational Leadership
MEM	Master of Ecosystem Management Master of Engineering Management Master of Environmental Management Master of Marketing
MEME	Master of Engineering in Manufacturing Engineering Master of Engineering in Mechanical Engineering
MEMS	Master of Engineering in Manufacturing Systems
MEP	Master of Engineering Physics Master of Environmental Planning
MEPC	Master of Environmental Pollution Control
MEPD	Master of Education–Professional Development
MEPM	Master of Environmental Policy and Management Master of Environmental Protection Management
MES	Master of Education and Science Master of Engineering Science Master of Environmental Science Master of Environmental Studies Master of Environmental Systems Master of Special Education
MESM	Master of Environmental Science and Management
MESS	Master of Exercise and Sport Sciences
MET	Master of Education in Teaching Master of Educational Technology Master of Engineering Technology Master of Entertainment Technology Master of Environmental Toxicology
Met E	Metallurgical Engineer
METM	Master of Engineering and Technology Management
MF	Master of Finance Master of Forestry
MFA	Master of Financial Administration Master of Fine Arts
MFAC	Master of Fine Arts in Computing
MFAS	Master of Fisheries and Aquatic Science
MFAW	Master of Fine Arts in Writing
MFC	Master of Forest Conservation
MFCC	Marriage and Family Counseling Certificate Marriage, Family, and Child Counseling
MFCS	Master of Family and Consumer Sciences
MFE	Master of Financial Engineering Master of Forest Engineering
MFG	Master of Functional Genomics
MFHD	Master of Family and Human Development
MFMS	Masters in Food Microbiology and Safety
MFR	Master of Forest Resources
MFRC	Master of Forest Resources and Conservation
MFS	Master of Family Studies Master of Food Science Master of Forensic Sciences Master of Forest Science Master of Forest Studies Master of French Studies
MFT	Master of Family Therapy Master of Food Technology
MGA	Master of Government Administration
MGD	Master of Graphic Design
MGE	Master of Geotechnical Engineering
MGH	Master of Geriatric Health
MGIS	Master of Geographic Information Science
MGP	Master of Gestion de Projet
MGS	Master of General Studies Master of Geosciences Master of Gerontological Studies
MH	Master of Humanities
MH Sc	Master of Health Sciences
MHA	Master of Health Administration Master of Healthcare Administration Master of Hospitality Administration
MHAMS	Master of Historical Administration and Museum Studies
MHCA	Master of Health Care Administration
MHCI	Master of Human-Computer Interaction
MHD	Master of Human Development
MHE	Master of Health Education
MHE Ed	Master of Home Economics Education
MHHS	Master of Health and Human Services
MHIS	Master of Health Information Systems
MHK	Master of Human Kinetics
MHL	Master of Health Law Master of Hebrew Literature
MHM	Master of Hospitality Management
MHMS	Master of Health Management Systems
MHP	Master of Health Physics Master of Heritage Preservation Master of Historic Preservation
MHPA	Master of Heath Policy and Administration
MHPE	Master of Health Professions Education Master of Health Promotion and Education
MHR	Master of Human Resources
MHRD	Master in Human Resource Development
MHRDL	Master of Human Resource Development Leadership
MHRDOD	Master of Human Resource Development/ Organizational Development
MHRIM	Master of Hotel, Restaurant, and Institutional Management
MHRIR	Master of Human Resources and Industrial Relations
MHRLR	Master of Human Resources and Labor Relations
MHRM	Master of Human Resources Management
MHROD	Master of Human Resources and Organization Development
MHRTA	Master in Hotel, Restaurant, Tourism, and Administration

MHS	Master of Health Sciences Master of Health Studies Master of Healthcare Systems Master of Hispanic Studies Master of Humanistic Studies
MHSA	Master of Health Services Administration Master of Human Services Administration
MHSE	Master of Health Science Education
MHSM	Master of Human Services Management
MI	Master of Instruction
MI Arch	Master of Interior Architecture
MI St	Master of Information Studies
MIA	Master of Interior Architecture Master of International Affairs
MIAA	Master of International Affairs and Administration
MIB	Master of International Business
MIBA	Master of International Business Administration
MIBS	Master of International Business Studies
MICM	Master of International Construction Management
MID	Master of Industrial Design Master of Industrial Engineering Master of Interior Design Master of International Development
MIE	Master of Industrial Engineering
MIE Mgmt	Master of Industrial Engineering Management
MIJ	Master of International Journalism
MILR	Master of Industrial and Labor Relations
MIM	Master of Information Management Master of International Management
MIMLA	Master of International Management for Latin America
MIMLAE	Master of International Management for Latin American Executives
MIMS	Master of Information Management and Systems Master of Integrated Manufacturing Systems
MIP	Master of Infrastructure Planning Master of Intellectual Property
MIPP	Master of International Public Policy
MIR	Master of Industrial Relations Master of International Relations
MIS	Master of Industrial Statistics Master of Information Science Master of Information Systems Master of Interdisciplinary Studies Master of International Studies
MISM	Master of Information Systems Management
MIT	Master in Teaching Master of Industrial Technology Master of Information Technology Master of Initial Teaching Master of International Taxation Master of International Trade Master of Internet Technology
MITA	Master of Information Technology Administration
MITE	Master of Information Technolgy Education
MJ	Master of Journalism Master of Jurisprudence
MJ Ed	Master of Jewish Education
MJA	Master of Justice Administration
MJPM	Master of Justice Policy and Management
MJS	Master of Judicial Studies Master of Juridical Science
ML Arch	Master of Landscape Architecture
MLA	Master of Landscape Architecture Master of Liberal Arts
MLAS	Master of Laboratory Animal Science
MLAUD	Master of Landscape Architecture in Urban Development
MLBLST	Master of Liberal Studies
MLD	Master of Leadership Studies
MLE	Master of Applied Linguistics and Exegesis
MLER	Master of Labor and Employment Relations
MLERE	Master of Land Economics and Real Estate
MLHR	Master of Labor and Human Resources
MLI	Master of Legal Institutions
MLI Sc	Master of Library and Information Science
MLIS	Master of Library and Information Science Master of Library and Information Services Master of Library and Information Studies
MLM	Master of Library Media
MLRHR	Master of Labor Relations and Human Resources
MLS	Master of Legal Studies Master of Liberal Studies Master of Library Science Master of Life Sciences Master of Medical Laboratory Sciences
MLSP	Master of Law and Social Policy
MLT	Master of Language Technologies
MM	Master of Management Master of Ministry Master of Music
MM Ed	Master of Music Education
MM Sc	Master of Medical Science
MM St	Master of Museum Studies
MMA	Master of Marine Affairs Master of Media Arts Master of Musical Arts
MMAE	Master of Mechanical and Aerospace Engineering
MMAS	Master of Military Art and Science
MMBA	Managerial Master of Business Administration
MMC	Master of Competitive Manufacturing Master of Mass Communications
MMCM	Master of Music in Church Music
MME	Master of Manufacturing Engineering Master of Mathematics for Educators Master of Mechanical Engineering Master of Medical Engineering Master of Mining Engineering Master of Music Education
MMF	Master of Mathematical Finance
MMFT	Master of Marriage and Family Therapy
MMH	Master of Management in Hospitality Master of Medical History Master of Medical Humanities
MMIS	Master of Management Information Systems
MMM	Master of Manufacturing Management Master of Marine Management Master of Medical Management
MMME	Master of Metallurgical and Materials Engineering
MMP	Master of Marine Policy
MMPA	Master of Management and Professional Accounting
MMQM	Master of Manufacuring Quality Management

MMR	Master of Marketing Research
MMS	Master of Management Science Master of Manufacturing Systems Master of Marine Science Master of Marine Studies Master of Materials Science Master of Medical Science Master of Medieval Studies
MMSE	Master of Manufacturing Systems Engineering
MMT	Master in Marketing Master of Music Teaching Master of Music Therapy Masters in Marketing Technology
MMus	Master of Music
MN	Master of Nursing
MN Sc	Master of Nursing Science
MNA	Master of Nonprofit Administration Master of Nurse Anesthesia
MNAS	Master of Natural and Applied Science
MNE	Master of Nuclear Engineering
MNL	Master in International Business for Latin America
MNM	Master of Nonprofit Management
MNO	Master of Nonprofit Organization
MNPL	Master of Not-for-Profit Leadership
MNR	Master of Natural Resources
MNRES	Master of Natural Resources and Environmental Studies
MNRM	Master of Natural Resource Management
MNS	Master of Natural Science
MOA	Maître d'Orthophonie et d'Audiologie
MOB	Master of Organizational Behavior
MOD	Master of Organizational Development
MOH	Master of Occupational Health
MOL	Master of Organizational Leadership
MOM	Master of Manufacturing Master of Oriental Medicine
MOR	Master of Operations Research
MOT	Master of Occupational Therapy
MoTM	Master of Technology Management
MP	Master of Planning
MP Ac	Master of Professional Accountancy
MP Acc	Master of Professional Accountancy Master of Professional Accounting Master's of Public Accounting
MP Acct	Master of Professional Accounting
MP Aff	Master of Public Affairs
MP Th	Master of Pastoral Theology
MPA	Master of Physician Assistant Master of Professional Accountancy Master of Professional Accounting Master of Public Administration Master of Public Affairs
MPA-URP	Master of Public Affairs and Urban and Regional Planning
MPAC	Masters in Professional Accounting
MPAD	Master of Public Administration
MPAID	Master of Public Administration and International Development
MPAP	Master of Public Affairs and Politics
MPAS	Master of Physician Assistant Science Master of Physician Assistant Studies Master of Public Art Studies
MPC	Master of Pastoral Counseling Master of Professional Communication
MPDS	Master of Planning and Development Studies
MPE	Master of Physical Education
MPEM	Master of Project Engineering and Management
MPH	Master of Public Health
MPHE	Master of Public Health Education
MPHTM	Master of Public Health and Tropical Medicine
MPIA	Master of Public and International Affairs
MPL	Master of Pastoral Leadership
MPM	Master of Pastoral Ministry Master of Pest Management Master of Practical Ministries Master of Project Management Master of Public Management
MPNA	Master of Public and Nonprofit Administration
MPP	Master of Public Policy
MPPA	Master of Public Policy Administration Master of Public Policy and Administration
MPPM	Master of Public and Private Management Master of Public Policy and Management
MPPPM	Master of Plant Protection and Pest Management
MPPUP	Master of Public Policy and Urban Planning
MPRTM	Master of Parks, Recreation, and Tourism Management
MPS	Master of Pastoral Studies Master of Policy Sciences Master of Political Science Master of Preservation Studies Master of Professional Studies Master of Public Service
MPSA	Master of Public Service Administration
MPSH	Master of Professional Studies in Horticulture
MPSL	Master of Public Safety Leadership
MPSRE	Master of Professional Studies in Real Estate
MPT	Master of Physical Therapy
MPVM	Master of Preventive Veterinary Medicine
MPW	Master of Public Works
MQF	Master of Quantitative Finance
MQM	Master of Quality Management
MQS	Master of Quality Systems
MRC	Master of Rehabilitation Counseling
MRCP	Master of Regional and City Planning Master of Regional and Community Planning
MRD	Master of Rural Development
MRE	Master of Religious Education
MRECM	Master of Real Estate and Construction Management
MRED	Master of Real Estate Development
MRLS	Master of Resources Law Studies
MRM	Master of Rehabilitation Medicine Master of Resources Management
MRP	Master of Regional Planning
MRRA	Master of Recreation Resources Administration
MRS	Master of Religious Studies
MRTP	Master of Rural and Town Planning
MS	Master of Science

MS Acct Master of Science in Accounting
MS Accy Master of Science in Accountancy
MS Admin Master of Science in Administration
MS Ag Master of Science in Agriculture
MS Arch Master of Science in Architecture
MS Arch St Master of Science in Architectural Studies
MS Bio E Master of Science in Biomedical Engineering
MS Biol Master of Science in Biology
MS Bm E Master of Science in Biomedical Engineering
MS Ch E Master of Science in Chemical Engineering
MS Chem Master of Science in Chemistry
MS Coun Master of Science in Counseling
MS Cp E Master of Science in Computer Engineering
MS Eco Master of Science in Economics
MS Econ Master of Science in Economics
MS Ed Master of Science in Education
MS El Master of Science in Educational Leadership and Administration
MS En E Master of Science in Environmental Engineering
MS Eng Master of Science in Engineering
MS Engr Master of Science in Engineering
MS Env E Master of Science in Environmental Engineering
MS Int A Master of Science in International Affairs
MS Mat E Master of Science in Materials Engineering
MS Mat SE Master of Science in Material Science and Engineering
MS Math Master of Science in Mathematics
MS Met E Master of Science in Metallurgical Engineering
MS Metr Master of Science in Meteorology
MS Mgt Master of Science in Management
MS Min Master of Science in Mining
MS Min E Master of Science in Mining Engineering
MS Mt E Master of Science in Materials Engineering
MS Nsg Master of Science in Nursing
MS Pet E Master of Science in Petroleum Engineering
MS Phr Master of Science in Pharmacy
MS Phys Master of Science in Physics
MS Phys Op Master of Science in Physiological Optics
MS Poly Master of Science in Polymers
MS Psy Master of Science in Psychology
MS Pub P Master of Science in Public Policy
MS Sc Master of Science in Social Science
MS Sp Ed Master of Science in Special Education
MS Stat Master of Science in Statistics
MS Tax Master of Science in Taxation
MS Tc E Master of Science in Telecommunications Engineering
MS Text Master of Science in Textiles
MS(R) Master of Science (Research)
MS-ASE Master of Science in Applied Science Education
MSA Master of School Administration
Master of Science Administration
Master of Science in Accountancy
Master of Science in Accounting
Master of Science in Administration
Master of Science in Agriculture
Master of Science in Anesthesia
Master of Science in Architecture
Master of Science in Aviation
Master of Sports Administration
MSA Phy Master of Science in Applied Physics
MSAA Master of Science in Astronautics and Aeronautics
MSAAE Master of Science in Aeronautical and Astronautical Engineering
MSABE Master of Science in Agricultural and Biological Engineering
MSACC Master of Science in Accounting
MSAE Master of Science in Aeronautical Engineering
Master of Science in Aerospace Engineering
Master of Science in Agricultural Engineering
Master of Science in Applied Economics
Master of Science in Architectural Engineering
Master of Science in Art Education
MSAH Master of Science in Allied Health
MSAIS Master of Science in Accounting Information Systems
MSAM Master of Science in Advanced Management
Master of Science in Applied Mathematics
MSAOM Master of Science in Agricultural Operations Management
MSAS Master of Science in Administrative Studies
Master of Science in Architectural Studies
MSAT Master of Science in Advanced Technology
MSB Master of Science in Bible
Master of Science in Business
MSBA Master of Science in Business Administration
MSBAE Master of Science in Biological and Agricultural Engineering
Master of Science in Biosystems and Agricultural Engineering
MSBC Master of Science in Building Construction
MSBE Master of Science in Biomedical Engineering
MSBENG Master of Science in Bioengineering
MSBIS Master of Science in Business Information Systems
MSBIT Master of Science in Business Information Technology
MSBME Master of Science in Biomedical Engineering
MSBMS Master of Science in Basic Medical Science
MSBS Master of Science in Biomedical Sciences
MSC Master of Science in Commerce
Master of Science in Communication
Master of Science in Computers
Master of Science in Counseling
Master of Science in Criminology
MSCC Master of Science in Christian Counseling
MSCD Master of Science in Communication Disorders
Master of Science in Community Development

MSCE	Master of Science in Civil Engineering Master of Science in Clinical Epidemiology Master of Science in Computer Engineering Master of Science in Continuing Education
MSCEE	Master of Science in Civil and Environmental Engineering
MSCET	Master of Science in Computer Education and Technology
MSCF	Master of Science in Computational Finance
MSCI	Master of Science in Clinical Investigation Master of Science in Curriculum and Instruction
MSCIS	Master of Science in Computer and Information Systems Master of Science in Computer Information Systems
MSCIT	Master of Science in Computer Information Technology
MSCJ	Master of Science in Criminal Justice
MSCJA	Master of Science in Criminal Justice Administration
MSCLS	Master of Science in Clinical Laboratory Science
MSCM	Master of Science in Conflict Management Master of Science in Construction Management
MScM	Master of Science in Management
MSCP	Master of Science in Clinical Psychology Master of Science in Counseling Psychology
MSCPharm	Master of Science in Pharmacy
MSCRP	Master of Science in City and Regional Planning Master of Science in Community and Regional Planning
MSCS	Master of Science in Computational Science Master of Science in Computer Science Master of Science in Construction Science
MSCSD	Master of Science in Communication Sciences and Disorders
MSCSE	Master of Science in Computer Science and Engineering Master of Science in Computer Systems Engineering
MSCTE	Master of Science in Career and Technical Education
MSD	Master of Science in Dentistry Master of Science in Design
MSDD	Master of Software Design and Development
MSE	Master of Science Education Master of Science in Education Master of Science in Engineering Master of Software Engineering Master of Structural Engineering
MSE Mgt	Master of Science in Engineering Management
MSEAS	Master of Science in Earth and Atmospheric Sciences
MSEBM	Master of Science in Electronic Business Management
MSEC	Master of Science in Electronic Commerce
MSECE	Master of Science in Electrical and Computer Engineering
MSED	Master of Sustainable Economic Development
MSEE	Master of Science in Electrical Engineering Master of Science in Environmental Engineering
MSEH	Master of Science in Environmental Health
MSEL	Master of Science in Executive Leadership Master of Studies in Environmental Law
MSEM	Master of Science in Engineering Management Master of Science in Engineering Mechanics Master of Science in Engineering of Mines Master of Science in Environmental Management
MSENE	Master of Science in Environmental Engineering
MSEO	Master of Science in Electro-Optics
MSEP	Master of Science in Economic Policy
MSES	Master of Science in Engineering Science Master of Science in Environmental Science Master of Science in Environmental Studies
MSESM	Master of Science in Engineering Science and Mechanics
MSESS	Master of Science in Exercise and Sport Studies
MSET	Master of Science in Engineering Technology
MSETA	Master of Science in Educational Technology Administration
MSETM	Master of Science in Environmental Technology Management
MSEVH	Master of Science in Enviromental Health and Safety
MSF	Master of Science in Finance Master of Science in Forestry Master of Social Foundations
MSFA	Master of Science in Financial Analysis
MSFAM	Master of Science in Family Studies
MSFCS	Master of Science in Family and Consumer Science
MSFE	Master of Science in Financial Engineering
MSFM	Master of Financial Management
MSFOR	Master of Science in Forestry
MSFP	Master of Science in Financial Planning
MSFS	Master of Science in Financial Sciences Master of Science in Forensic Science
MSFT	Master of Science in Family Therapy
MSG	Master of Science in Gerontology
MSGC	Master of Science in Genetic Counseling
MSGFA	Master of Science in Global Financial Analysis
MSGL	Master of Science in Global Leadership
MSH	Master of Science in Health Master of Science in Hospice
MSHA	Master of Science in Health Administration
MSHCA	Master of Science in Health Care Administration
MSHCI	Master of Science in Human Computer Interaction
MSHCPM	Master of Science in Health Care Policy and Management
MSHCS	Master of Science in Human and Consumer Science
MSHE	Master of Science in Health Education
MSHES	Master of Science in Human Environmental Sciences
MSHFID	Master of Science in Human Factors in Information Design
MSHFS	Master of Science in Human Factors and Systems
MSHP	Master of Science in Health Professions
MSHR	Master of Science in Human Resources
MSHRM	Master of Science in Human Resource Management
MSHROD	Master of Science in Human Resources and Organizational Development

MSHS	Master of Science in Health Science Master of Science in Health Services Master of Science in Health Systems
MSHSA	Master of Science in Human Service Administration
MSHSE	Master of Science in Health Science Education
MSHT	Master of Science in History of Technology
MSI	Master of Science in Instruction
MSIA	Master of Science in Industrial Administration
MSIAM	Master of Science in Information Age Marketing
MSIB	Master of Science in International Business
MSIDM	Master of Science in Interior Design and Merchandising
MSIDT	Master of Science in Information Design and Technology
MSIE	Master of Science in Industrial Engineering Master of Science in International Economics
MSIL	Master of Science in International Logistics
MSIM	Master of Science in Information Management Master of Science in Investment Management
MSIMC	Master of Science in Integrated Marketing Communications
MSIPC	Master of Science in Information Processing and Communications
MSIR	Master of Science in Industrial Relations
MSIS	Master of Science in Information Science Master of Science in Information Systems Master of Science in Interdisciplinary Studies
MSISE	Master of Science in Infrastructure Systems Engineering
MSISM	Master of Science in Information Systems Management
MSIST	Master of Science in Information Systems Technology
MSIT	Master of Science in Industrial Technology Master of Science in Information Technology Master of Science in Instructional Technology
MSITM	Master of Science in Information Technology Management
MSJ	Master of Science in Journalism Master of Science in Jurisprudence
MSJE	Master of Science in Jewish Education
MSJFP	Master of Science in Juvenile Forensic Psychology
MSJJ	Master of Science in Juvenile Justice
MSJPS	Master of Science in Justice and Public Safety
MSJS	Master of Science in Jewish Studies
MSK	Master of Science in Kinesiology
MSL	Master of School Leadership Master of Science in Limnology Master of Studies in Law
MSLA	Master of Science in Legal Administration
MSLD	Master of Science in Land Developement
MSLP	Master of Speech-Language Pathology
MSLS	Master of Science in Legal Studies Master of Science in Library Science Master of Science in Logistics Systems
MSLT	Master of Second Language Teaching
MSM	Master of Sacred Music Master of School Mathematics Master of Science in Management Master of Science in Mathematics Master of Service Management
MSMA	Master of Science in Marketing Analysis
MSMAE	Master of Science in Materials Engineering
MSMC	Master of Science in Management and Communications Master of Science in Mass Communications
MSMCS	Master of Science in Management and Computer Science
MSME	Master of Science in Mechanical Engineering
MSMFE	Master of Science in Manufacturing Engineering
MSMfSE	Master of Science in Manufacturing Systems Engineering
MSMGEN	Master of Science in Management and General Engineering
MSMI	Master of Science in Medical Illustration
MSMIS	Master of Science in Management Information Systems
MSMM	Master of Science in Manufacturing Management
MSMO	Master of Science in Manufacturing Operations
MSMOT	Master of Science in Management of Technology
MSMP	Master of Science in Molecular Pathology
MSMS	Master of Science in Management Science
MSMSA	Master of Science in Management Systems Analysis
MSMSE	Master of Science in Manufacturing Systems Engineering Master of Science in Material Science and Engineering Master of Science in Mathematics and Science Education
MSMT	Master of Science in Medical Technology
MSN	Master of Science in Nursing
MSN(R)	Master of Science in Nursing (Research)
MSN-OB	Master of Science in Nursing-Organizational Behavior
MSNA	Master of Science in Nurse Anesthesia
MSNE	Master of Science in Nuclear Engineering
MSNPS	Master of Science in New Professional Studies
MSNS	Master of Science in Natural Science
MSOD	Master of Science in Organizational Development
MSOES	Master of Science in Occupational Ergonomics and Safety
MSOL	Master of Science in Organizational Leadership
MSOM	Master of Science in Organization and Management Master of Science in Oriental Medicine
MSOR	Master of Science in Operations Research
MSOT	Master of Science in Occupational Technology Master of Science in Occupational Therapy
MSP	Master of Science in Pharmacy Master of Science in Planning Master of Speech Pathology
MSP Ex	Master of Science in Exercise Physiology
MSPA	Master of Science in Physician Assistant Master of Science in Professional Accountancy
MSPAS	Master of Science in Physician Assistant Studies

MSPC Master of Science in Professional Communications
MSPE Master of Science in Petroleum Engineering
Master of Science in Physical Education
MSPFP Master of Science in Personal Financial Planning
MSPG Master of Science in Psychology
MSPH Master of Science in Public Health
MSPHN Master of Science in Public Health Nursing
MSPHR Master of Science in Pharmacy
MSPNGE Master of Science in Petroleum and Natural Gas Engineering
MSPS Master of Science in Pharmaceutical Science
Master of Science in Psychological Services
MSPT Master of Science in Physical Therapy
MSR Master of Science in Radiology
Master of Science in Rehabilitation Sciences
MSRA Master of Science in Recreation Administration
MSRC Master of Science in Resource Conservation
MSRE Master of Science in Religious Education
MSRED Master of Science in Real Estate Development
MSRLS Master of Science in Recreation and Leisure Studies
MSRMP Master of Science in Radiological Medical Physics
MSRS Master of Science in Recreational Studies
MSRTM Master of Science in Resort and Tourism Management
MSS Master of Science in Sociology
Master of Science in Software
Master of Social Science
Master of Social Services
Master of Special Studies
Master of Sports Science
Master of Strategic Studies
MSSA Master of Science in Social Administration
MSSE Master of Science in Software Engineering
MSSEM Master of Science in Systems and Engineering Management
MSSI Master of Science in Strategic Intelligence
MSSL Master of Science in Strategic Leadership
MSSM Master of Science in Systems Management
MSSPA Master of Science in Student Personnel Administration
MSSR Master of Science in Social Research
MSSS Master of Science in Safety Science
Master of Science in Systems Science
MSSW Master of Science in Social Work
MST Master of Science in Taxation
Master of Science in Teaching
Master of Science in Technology
Master of Science in Telecommunications
Master of Science in Transportation
Master of Science Teaching
Master of Science Technology
Master of Systems Technology
MST Ch Master of Science in Textile Chemistry
MSTC Master of Science in Telecommunications
MSTD Master of Science in Training and Development
MSTE Master of Science in Telecommunications Engineering
Master of Science in Textile Engineering
Master of Science in Transportation Engineering
MSTIM Master of Science in Technology and Innovation Management
MSTM Master of Science in Technical Management
Master of Science in Technology Management
MSTOM Master of Science in Traditional Oriental Medicine
MSUD Master of Science in Urban Design
MSUESM Master of Science in Urban Environmental Systems Management
MSVE Master of Science in Vocational Education
MSW Master of Social Work
MSWE Master of Software Engineering
MSWREE Master of Science in Water Resources and Environmental Engineering
MT Master of Taxation
Master of Teaching
Master of Technology
Master of Textiles
MTA Master of Arts in Teaching
Master of Tax Accounting
Master of Teaching Arts
Master of Tourism Administration
MTCM Master of Traditional Chinese Medicine
MTD Master of Training and Development
MTE Master in Educational Technology
Master of Teacher Education
MTEL Master of Telecommunications
MTESL Master in Teaching English as a Second Language
MTESOL Master's in Teaching English to Speakers of Other Languages
MTHM Master of Tourism and Hospitality Management
MTI Master of Information Technology
MTIM Masters of Trust and Investment Management
MTL Master of Talmudic Law
MTLM Master of Transportation and Logistics Management
MTM Master of Technology Management
Master of Telecommunications Management
Master of the Teaching of Mathematics
MTMH Master of Tropical Medicine and Hygiene
MTOM Master of Traditional Oriental Medicine
MTP Master of Transpersonal Psychology
MTPW Master of Technical and Professional Writing
MTS Master of Teaching Science
Master of Theological Studies
MTSC Master of Technical and Scientific Communication
MTSE Master of Telecommunications and Software Engineering
MTT Master in Technology Management
MTX Master of Taxation
MUA Master of Urban Affairs
MUD Master of Urban Design
MUP Master of Urban Planning
MUPDD Master of Urban Planning, Design, and Development
MUPP Master of Urban Planning and Policy
MUPRED Masters of Urban Planning and Real Estate Development
MURP Master of Urban and Regional Planning
Master of Urban and Rural Planning
MUS Master of Urban Studies

Mus Doc	Doctor of Music
Mus M	Master of Music
MVE	Master of Vocational Education
MVR	Master of Vocational Rehabilitation
MVT Ed	Master of Vocational and Technical Education
MVTE	Master of Vocational-Technical Education
MWC	Master of Wildlife Conservation
MWPS	Master of Wood and Paper Science
MWR	Master of Water Resources
MWS	Master of Women's Studies
Nav Arch	Naval Architecture
Naval E	Naval Engineer
ND	Doctor of Naturopathic Medicine Doctor of Nursing
NE	Nuclear Engineer
NPMC	Nonprofit Management Certificate
Nuc E	Nuclear Engineer
Ocean E	Ocean Engineer
OD	Doctor of Optometry
OTD	Doctor of Occupational Therapy
PD	Professional Diploma
PDD	Professional Development Degree
PE Dir	Director of Physical Education
PED	Doctor of Physical Education
PGC	Post-Graduate Certificate
Ph L	Licentiate of Philosophy
Pharm D	Doctor of Pharmacy
PhD	Doctor of Philosophy
PM Sc	Professional Master of Science
PMBA	Professional Master of Business Administration
PMC	Post Master's Certificate
PMS	Professional Master of Science
PPDPT	Postprofessional Doctor of Physical Therapy
Pro MS	Professional Master of Computer Science
Psy D	Doctor of Psychology
Psy M	Master of Psychology
Psy S	Specialist in Psychology
Psya D	Doctor of Psychoanalysis
Re D	Doctor of Recreation
Re Dir	Director of Recreation
Rh D	Doctor of Rehabilitation
S Psy S	Specialist in Psychological Services
SAS	School Administrator and Supervisor
Sc D	Doctor of Science
Sc M	Master of Science
SCCT	Specialist in Community College Teaching
SD	Doctor of Science
SJD	Doctor of Juridical Science
SLPD	Doctor of Speech-Language Pathology
SLS	Specialist in Library Science
SM	Master of Science
SM Arch S	Master of Science in Architectural Studies
SM Vis S	Master of Science in Visual Studies
SMBT	Master of Science in Building Technology
SP	Specialist Degree
Sp C	Specialist in Counseling
Sp Ed	Specialist in Education
Sp Ed S	Special Education Specialist
SPA	Specialist in Public Administration
Spec	Specialist's Certificate
Spec M	Specialist in Music
SPS	School Psychology Specialist
Spt	Specialist Degree
SSP	Specialist in School Psychology
STB	Bachelor of Sacred Theology
STD	Doctor of Sacred Theology
STL	Licentiate of Sacred Theology
STM	Master of Sacred Theology
TDPT	Transitional Doctor of Physical Therapy
Th D	Doctor of Theology
Th M	Master of Theology
VMD	Doctor of Veterinary Medicine
WEMBA	Weekend Executive Master of Business Administration
WMBA	Web-based Master of Business Administration
XMBA	Executive Master of Business Administration

Indexes

There are two indexes in this section. The first, Index of Profiles, Announcements, and In-Depth Descriptions, gives page references for all information on all graduate and professional schools in this volume. The second, Index of Directories and Subject Areas in Books 2–6, gives references to the directories in other volumes of this set and also includes cross-references for subject area names not used in the directory structure, for example, "Arabic (*see* Near and Middle Eastern Languages)."

Index of Profiles, Announcements, and In-Depth Descriptions

Index of Directories and Subject Areas in Books 2–6

Following is an alphabetical listing of directories and subject areas in Books 2–6. Also listed are cross-references for subject area names not used in the directory structure of the guides, for example, "Arabic (*see* Near and Middle Eastern Languages)."